5th Edition
Goldmine

# Record Album PRICE GUIDE

Tim Neely

Published by

**700 East State Street • Iola, WI 54990-0001**
**715-445-2214 • 888-457-2873**
**www.krausebooks.com**

Our toll-free number to place an order or obtain
a free catalog is (800) 258-0929.



Library of Congress Control Number: 2007922995

ISBN-13: 978-0-89689-532-4
ISBN-10: 0-89689-532-7

Designed by Sally Olson
Edited by Dan Brownell

Printed in the United States of America

# Contents

# Acknowledgments

First, thank you to all those who have written, called, or e-mailed me since the last edition. Many of your suggestions and corrections have made it into this edition of the book. Others did not, but still could appear in future editions. I appreciate the input, without it, the price guide would not continue to evolve and improve.

Here are a few of those whose contributions are reflected in this edition:

| | | | |
|---|---|---|---|
| Burr Brockway | Russell Jenkins | Ernie Mabrey | Steve Schroeder |
| Joe Hill | Greg Loescher | Kent McCombs | Jeff Smith |

I also want to thank those people at Krause Publications, past and present, who helped make this fifth edition a reality: Paul Kennedy, Dan Brownell, Sandi Morrison, Brian Earnest, Peter Lindblad and Cathy Bernardy.

Finally, the two years since the 4th Edition came out have seen both incredible highs and staggering lows in my life. Through it all, the person who has been there the most for me, and I've thanked her before in this space, is my mom, Judy Neely. I cannot thank her enough.

**Tim Neely**

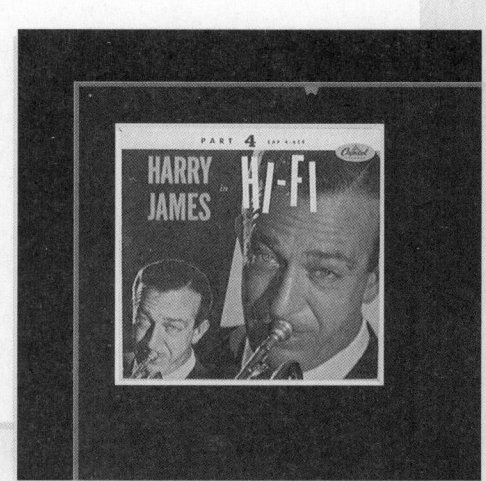

# Introduction

Welcome to the fifth edition of the *Goldmine® Record Album Price Guide*. We thank you for your support of the first four editions as we strive to create the world's most accurate guide to valuing your vinyl.

Record collecting continues to grow as a new generation of buyers discovers vinyl. In the two years since the publication of the fourth edition, we've seen countless articles about the resurgence in vinyl, both used and new. Indeed, it is almost impossible to keep up with all the vinyl releases in a given year, whether new or reissues. But we try; we already have some LPs from 2007 listed in here. So if this is the first time you've picked up this book, welcome and dig in!

Before we get into the areas where there has been the most action since the last edition, we first must mention this, because a certain percentage of readers of past editions have missed it:

-- In order to be listed in the *Goldmine® Record Album Price Guide*, **a performer must have at least one LP with a near-mint value of $20**. Thus, many popular artists of the 1970s and 1980s, an era where used vinyl albums remain plentiful and cheap, are not listed.

-- Unless a performer is in the jazz or classical realms, once we find that one of their albums is worth that much, we strive to list *all* of their albums, whether the others are worth that much or not.

## Market Trends, 2007

In general, the album market as a whole is flat. Many parts of the market have stabilized or even fallen off. Common LPs seem to be more common than ever. Albums with even the slightest flaws can be found at low prices once thought unimaginable.

But some areas are still seeing a lot of activity:

– **Near-mint, mint and sealed LPs.** One thing that the growth of eBay has shown is that albums in truly near-mint condition, especially original editions from the 1950s through the 1970s, are extremely hard to find.

Condition has always meant a lot when it came to records. Today, it means more than ever. Perhaps a new generation of record buyers has been spoiled by the quiet sound coming from a compact disc and won't tolerate the pops and ticks that sometimes are audible on even the best-pressed records. You'll find that some of the prices in this year's book, though still reflecting an average of many sources, may be low on certain items.

Along those lines, some of the prices I've seen for sealed vintage LPs border on the obscene.

There are sound reasons to be wary of sealed albums, especially older ones. But that hasn't stopped prices from going sky-high on some of them: As I type this, a sealed original mono copy of *Pet Sounds* by the Beach Boys has traded for over $1,500 and a sealed stereo copy of *The Beatles* (The White Album) has sold for over $1,400. The only thing extraordinary about them is that they were, presumably, never opened.

– **"Audiophile" LPs.** Albums that appeal to the audience that appreciates good sound quality are hotter than ever.

This does not only apply to the records of the 1980s and 1990s that were specially licensed and marketed to appeal to this small subset of collectors. True, albums on the DCC Compact Classics label from the 1990s are almost uniformly collectible, with near-mint copies of many titles trading for three figures routinely. And many albums on the Mobile Fidelity, Nautilus and Direct Disc labels are in that range.

Today, many audiophiles are paying closer attention to more mainstream albums. Indeed, the work of certain cutting engineers – the people who "translate" the sound of a master tape to the record – are becoming sought-after by this group. Often the only way these desirable pressings can be identified is by checking the trail-off wax of the albums. So far, this trend hasn't crossed over to the vast majority of record collectors, who still value a general first pressing over a specific one. But it's something we are watching closely.

– **Albums from the 1990s and early 2000s.** We noted in the 4th Edition that some albums from the "dark ages" of vinyl were becoming very collectible and very expensive. Not only has this not changed, but it's affected even more albums – some of which were still common in retail stores as recently as two years ago.

Among those not previously in the *Goldmine® Record Album Price Guide* that have been added are such popular performers as Christina Aguilera, No Doubt, Third Eye Blind, Tool and Rob Zombie. We've also raised many values of LPs by such icons as Neil Young and Johnny Cash, whose 1990s vinyl output has become scarce.

We have seen no letup in demand for vinyl LPs released from about 1991 to 2001. Indeed, many of the values listed for these records – some of which almost never show up for sale anywhere – are conservative, even for those with three-figure values attached.

## The eBay Effect

In general, eBay has not been kind to "old-line" album collecting. Albums once believed to be rare are found to be more common than expected, thus their values have stayed the same or, in some cases, even declined since the first edition of this book in 1999.

At the same time, eBay has had a positive effect on the values in some areas, especially modern jazz and vinyl albums of the 1991-2001 years. Demand in these areas is much greater than once believed.

You could theoretically use eBay as one's sole determinant of market value, and indeed, some people do. But you'd miss a large part of the market that still happens elsewhere. It would be like determining the price of everything by going to only one place. We look at as many sources as possible, thus the *Goldmine® Record Album Price Guide* remains vital to your enjoyment of collecting vinyl albums.

## The Real Deal

Record collectors are frequently fooled by certain albums. Following are articles on two such albums, one by The Who and the other by Elvis. Each explains how these albums came about and why they innocently, but convincingly, mislead collectors about their true rarity and value. Gimmicks intended simply as sales and marketing tools have inadvertently duped many into thinking they have valuable vinyl when, in reality, they don't.

## The Who's mis-Leeds-ing Packaging

Over the years, I've come across people telling me that they have an intriguing collection of papers, letters, and other odds and ends relating to The Who. Each thought he had a one-of-a-kind find, and each was wondering what they could be worth.

Those of us who know what this stuff is had to tell the disappointed inquirers that the items are not worth much. Although these papers look like authentic original "documents" to novices, there are actually hundreds of thousands of copies in existence.

In 1970, The Who released their first legitimate live album, *Live at Leeds*. Even by the standards of the day, it had quite elaborate packaging. The album cover itself was about as simple as it gets: The Decca originals were packaged like an advance press kit, with the album cover opening up into a 12 inch x 12 inch folder. The record, in a brown generic sleeve with a faux handwritten label, was in one of the two flaps inside the package. And in the other flap was an asortment of extremely well reproduced items from all the phases of The Whos' history. Among them:

• A contract for the band's appearance at Woodstock

• A rejection letter from EMI records to the The High Numbers' manager, Kit Lambert, dated "22nd October 1964" (The High Numbers were the early Who)

• A lyric sheet for "My Generation"

• A letter informing the band of the cancellation of a ballroom gig in 1965

• Notes of the payments for certain gigs

The album also has a poster and photos, 12 items in all. Also, some of the copies have a rectangular sticker at the upper left corner of the front cover stating, "It Is The Best Live Rock Album Ever Made ... —*The New York Times*."

It is not difficult to find Decca pressings of *Live at Leeds*. Finding one with all the missing pieces, however, is an entirely different matter. The item most likely to be missing is the poster, as many consumers took it out of the package to hang it on a wall. All in all, a near-mint copy of the entire package on Decca can go for $40 or so.

When MCA reissued the album in 1973, after consolidating all its labels (with Decca, Kapp, and Uni most prominent among them) into one, it deleted all the goodies and packaged the album in a more normal LP cover. So for more than 20 years, the *Live at Leeds* package was incomplete. In 1995, the original release was expanded to twice its prior length on a CD reissue. Early pressings came in a 12 inch x 12 inch box that reproduced all the goodies that had been in the original LP, at full size no less, not postage-stamp CD size.

So no, these contracts and things are not a rare find. Presumably, the true originals reside wherever The Who keeps such things.

## Elvis' Moody Blue: Black Is Beautiful

Thumb through this book and you'll notice many rare and valuable albums listed that were released on colored vinyl. Most of the time, colored vinyl issues are scarcer and thus more valuable than their black-vinyl counterparts. But there are exceptions, and the major exception is the colored vinyl album everyone seems to have —Elvis Presley's *Moody Blue* on blue vinyl.

Even before Elvis died August 16, 1977, *Moody Blue* was poised to be his most successful album of new material in some years. The title song, released months in advance of the album, had become Elvis' first No. 1 country song in almost 20 years. The second single, "Way Down," would become his second consecutive No. 1 country hit; it peaked there the week ending August 20, 1977, the *Billboard* issue that was on the stands the week he died.

To help spur sales of the new album, RCA decided to press the first run on blue vinyl. On the shrink wrap, these were called "The Blue Album." The original plan was then to start making *Moody Blue* albums on black vinyl once the blue ones ran out. The gimmick seemed to work: Even before the posthumous sales kicked in, the new album had reached No. 21 on the *Billboard* album charts, his highest peaking album since *Aloha From Hawaii Via Satellite* in 1973.Then Elvis keeled over that fateful Tuesday.

Not long before Presley's death, the first black vinyl versions began to appear on the market. Then RCA made a fateful decision. It chose to resume printing *Moody Blue* on blue vinyl. All the rest of the copies with the number AFL1-2428 were pressed in blue. Thus, what could have been a legitimate collector's item became the most common colored vinyl album in recorded music history.

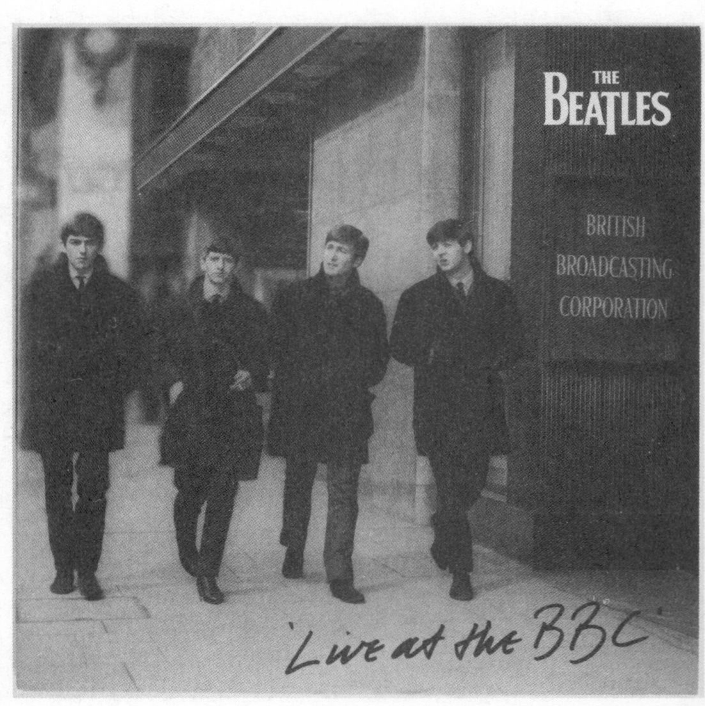

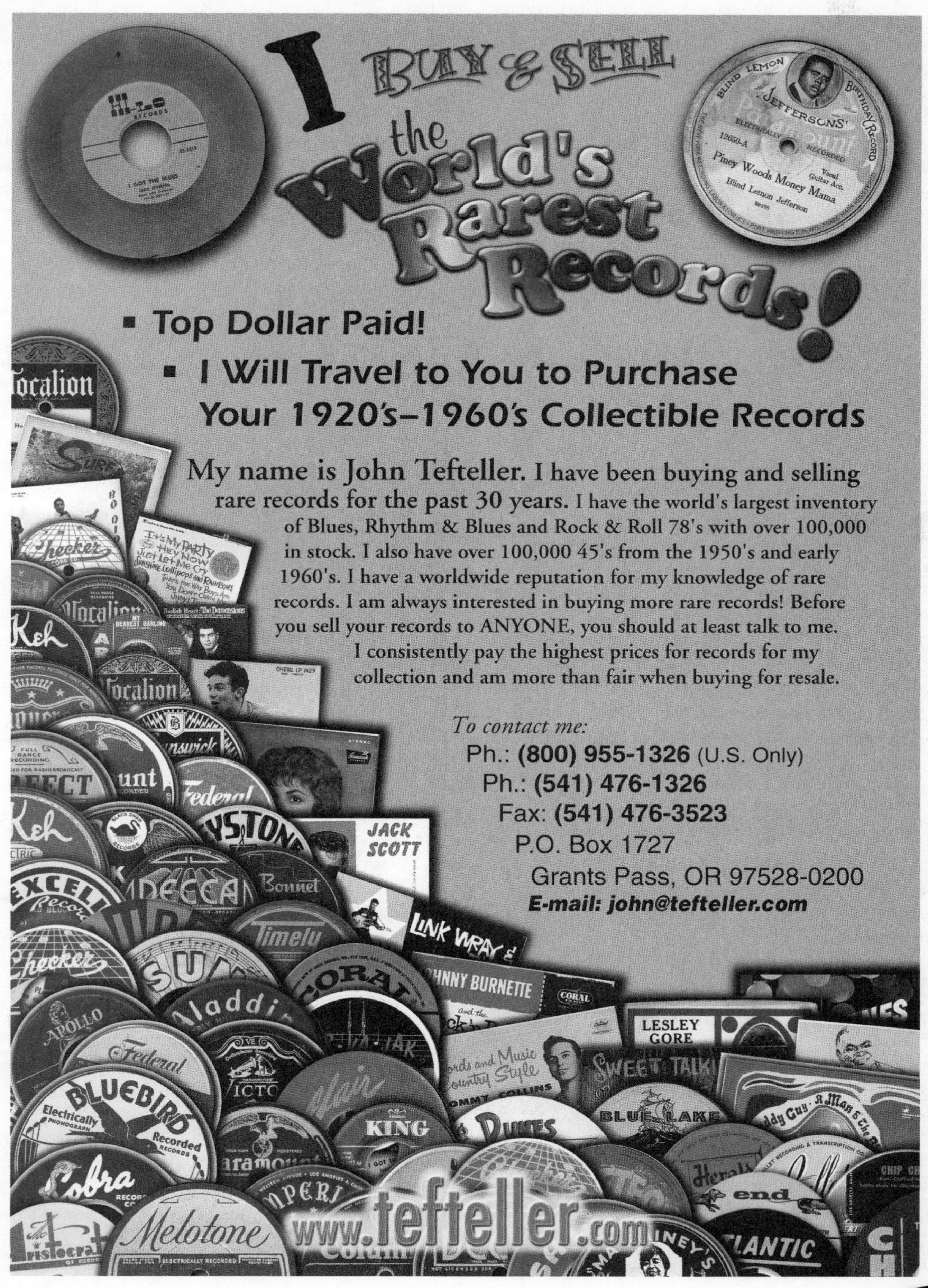
I Buy & Sell the World's Rarest Records!
▪ Top Dollar Paid!
▪ I Will Travel to You to Purchase Your 1920's–1960's Collectible Records
My name is John Tefteller. I have been buying and selling rare records for the past 30 years. I have the world's largest inventory of Blues, Rhythm & Blues and Rock & Roll 78's with over 100,000 in stock. I also have over 100,000 45's from the 1950's and early 1960's. I have a worldwide reputation for my knowledge of rare records. I am always interested in buying more rare records! Before you sell your records to ANYONE, you should at least talk to me. I consistently pay the highest prices for records for my collection and am more than fair when buying for resale.
To contact me:
Ph.: (800) 955-1326 (U.S. Only)
Ph.: (541) 476-1326
Fax: (541) 476-3523
P.O. Box 1727
Grants Pass, OR 97528-0200
E-mail: john@tefteller.com
www.tefteller.com

*Moody Blue* was eventually certified double platinum by the Recording Association of America, for the sales of two million copies although it probably sold even more than that. Nearly all the vinyl copies are on translucent blue vinyl. The real collector's item when it comes to *Moody Blue*, not including some custom-made test pressings in vinyl colors other than blue, is the commercial black vinyl version. In near-mint condition, it can go for $200. The blue vinyl? At *most* $10, and that's for a still-sealed copy.

## How to Use This Book

To quote my late father, who was often asked by his children who found a task difficult, "How do you do this?" He often replied, "Very carefully."

That is the same advice we give to you.

The prices in this book are taken from many sources, both online and off, and from the advice of many correspondents. ***It is only a guide; it is not holy writ.*** When using the prices in this book, to use another famous disclaimer, "Your mileage may vary."

That said, we at least can tell you what is in each listing and what it means. We have decided to emphasize some areas that seem to confuse the most readers, so those who do understand how to use the listings based on a casual glance of this listings, please bear with us.

**Records in this book, except for the sections after the letter Z, are listed alphabetically by artist.** The artist's name is in **BOLD CAPITAL LETTERS.** They are mostly alphabetized the way our computer did, so blame anything that seems out of order on that.

In some cases, we know that the artist name was used by several different performers. When we don't know for sure which are which, we have left them together. When we do know with some certainty, we have separated them.

In most but not all cases, the most collectible is listed first, usually with the number (1) in parentheses following it. The exceptions are those artists whose fame or number of records overshadows any other performer with the same name, or those who rarely used "The" in front of their name, such as Eagles, Outlaws and Pretenders. The rest of the performers with the same name will be arranged alphabetically by record label and will be followed by the appropriate parenthetical number – (2), (3), (4), and so on. If a number is skipped, it's because it's by an artist for whom we have only singles, but no albums, in our database. Finally, those for which we don't know where they go are listed with a (U) for Unknown after the name.

Underneath some artists are cross-references or other information we feel is helpful. Cross-references to other artists are in CAPITAL LETTERS.

Then we have grouped the record listings by label. Under each record label are the individual listings in **numerical, not necessarily chronological,** order.

Each line starts with a check box, which you can use to keep track of what you have. Then comes the record number. Then comes, in some cases, a couple letters enclosed in [brackets]. These designate something special about the record as follows:

[B]: the album is listed as stereo, but some of the tracks are in mono (the "B" means "both" stereo and mono);

[DJ]: some sort of promotional copy, usually for radio stations, and not meant for public sale;

[EP]: a 12-inch extended play album, usually with only four to six tracks. It is normally no more than half the length of a regular album. Rarely used to describe 12-inch records before the 1980s; before that, it refers to similar 7-inch records;

[M}: mono record (all 12-inch records released in either mono only or in both mono and stereo before 1968);

[P]: the album is listed as stereo, but only part of it is "true" two-channel stereo;

[PD]: picture disc (graphics actually appear as part of the record and not merely on the label area; these also are usually identified as such below the listing);

[Q]: quadraphonic record (mostly from the years 1972-1976, these were usually remixed, sometimes radically, to play on systems with four separate speakers);

[R]: the album is listed as stereo, but actually is all, or almost all, rechanneled or "fake" stereo (called "Duophonic" by Capitol or "Enhanced for Stereo" or "Simulated Stereo" by Decca); these almost always are less sought-after than the same material in "true mono";

[S}: stereo record (again, for those discs pressed in both mono and stereo). If we're not sure of an album's "true" stereo content, or if we know an album is all, or almost all, true stereo, we use "S";

[10]: a 10-inch album, most of which are from the early years of LPs, 1948-1954, and are quite difficult to find in top condition;

[(x)] where x is a number: the number of records in a set.

You'll next find the title of the album listed as best as we can determine. Sometimes, discerning the actual title of an LP isn't as straightforward as you might think; titles can be listed differently on the front cover, back cover, label, and spine.

After that information is the year of release of the record, based on record label information or chart data. **Sometimes, this differs from a year listed on a record itself. When in doubt, believe in the years WE list and NOT those on the record, unless you have an additional source OTHER THAN a year on the record label or jacket that proves us incorrect.**

Finally, each line ends with an approximate value in Near Mint condition.

Some records have an additional line of type *underneath the listing, in italics.* That denotes something about the item listed above it, such as who also is on the record, or color of label or color of vinyl.

In the back section, after the letter Z, records are sorted differently.

We have broken these sections into "Original Cast Recordings," "Soundtracks," "Television Albums" and "Various Artists Collections."

Within each of these categories, these are arranged alphabetically by the **title** of the release, ignoring "A," "An" and "The.". Albums that begin with a number are sorted as if the number was spelled out.

Underneath each title are the applicable releases, arranged alphabetically and numerically by label. (Thus the original version is not necessarily listed first!) Those lines start with a check box, then are followed by the label and number listed together. Any applicable abbreviations – the same as used in the A-Z section – follow; then the year of release; then the pricing information. Finally, some items have more information below the listing in *italics.*

## Selling Records

By far the most often asked question over the years has been some variation of the following:

How do I sell my records and get the most for them?

First, here's the Reader's Digest version of the answer to the question.

You will get more for your records if you can sell them directly to someone who wants what you have (a collector), rather than selling to someone who is going to turn around and re-sell them (a dealer).

A corollary to the first line of advice above: The prices in this book are RETAIL prices – what collectors might pay for these from a seller. They are NOT dealer's buying prices!

If you want to sell all your records at once to the same person, whether that person is a dealer or collector, expect to get almost nothing for them, no matter what condition or genre they are.

The more time you spend on the project, the more you'll likely get for each record.

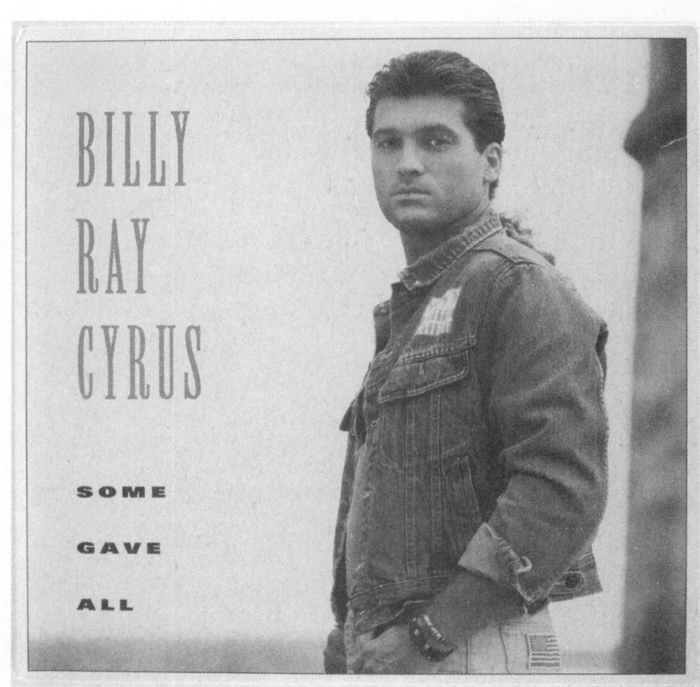

Now, some more details.

First, buy this book and use it. You are better off working from a position of knowing what you have rather than guessing,

Look through it and see if you have anything that is more valuable than the average. If not, or if your records and sleeves are "well loved" (say, VG condition or worse), it probably isn't worth your time to work hard to sell them. Be kind to a friend: Give them to someone who collects records. Or sell them at your next garage/rummage sale for 10 cents or a quarter each. Or donate them to Goodwill, the Salvation Army, the St. Vincent de Paul Society, or some other charity with a thrift shop, and get a tax receipt. But don't throw them away! We never recommend that unless your records are in truly poor condition.

Maybe your stash has some records of above-average value, or maybe you actually took good care of your records and they are still in VG+ condition or better. You can do either of two things:

-- sell them to a dealer;

-- sell them yourself, directly to collectors.

**What to expect when selling to a dealer.** As we already mentioned, the prices in this book are NOT dealer's prices; they are collector's prices. Also, please note that the prices in this book are a guide and not sent down from on high. You are in for a rude awakening if you expect to get these prices from a dealer.

For something genuinely rare, you might get 40 to 60 percent of the "book value." For many of these, all a dealer has to do is pick up the phone and call the right customer, and the record is sold. For less expensive records, though, don't expect to get more than 10 to 25 percent of the "book value." The less valuable a record is, the lower the percentage of the retail price a dealer will give you for it. Sellers, even those who only sell online, have overhead costs they have to recover, such as inventory, rent, utilities, postage and packing fees, employees, insurance, taxes, listing fees, bandwidth, and many more things that a dealer had to recoup in order to stay in business. Some dealers won't even try to get records from people who say they consulted a price guide, because these sellers sometimes get delusions about what they "deserve" for their records. If this happens to you, don't say we didn't warn you.

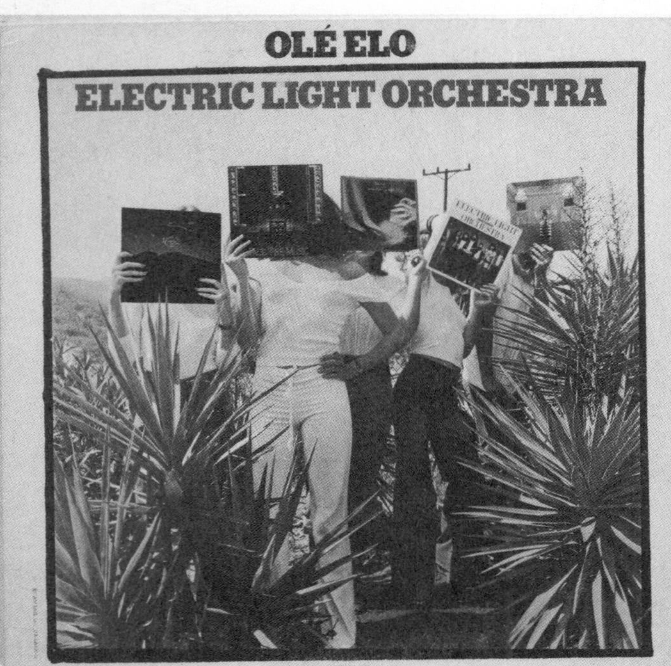


Sometimes, the hardest part of selling to a dealer is finding one. Most large cities, and many smaller ones, have used record stores. The best way to find them in your area is to look in your local Yellow Pages, Depending on who published the phone book, used record stores are found either under the heading "Records, Tapes and Compact Discs – Retail" or "Compact Discs, Tapes and Records – Retail."

Just because you've found that store (or stores) doesn't mean they will buy your records. From a dealer's standpoint, common records are almost literally a dime a dozen. You might get only a token amount for a pile of records if all of them are fairly common, regardless what this price guide says. But if the alternative was between getting something for them or getting nothing for them, you'll probably be happy with the result. And you no longer have the records in your way.

**What to expect when selling to a collector.** In the era of online auctions, this is a more appealing alternative than it used to be. Regardless what method you use, it will take longer and require more patience than selling to a dealer. Plus, if you will be selling through the mail, you have some additional costs, most notably for good packaging and postage. But it can be worth the effort.

It takes work to sell your records directly to someone who wants them for a collection. **We do not have lists of record collectors that you can contact, so don't bother to ask. Finding collectors is up to you.**

Before the Internet, you basically had two options for doing it yourself to reach the collector's market: Setting up at record shows/fairs, or advertising in record collecting magazine. And both still have their place.

For a seller, the record show is a great place to meet other collectors and dealers, get ideas and advice, and see some records you might not see anywhere else. Also, some high-value deals still take place at shows. If you like the direct interaction and the wheeling and dealing – and can resist the temptation to add to your own inventory or collection with the proceeds – then selling at a record show may be for you.

Record collecting magazines have shrunk in recent years, but they remain a viable outlet for certain kinds of collectibles. Indeed, only one significant record collecting magazine remains in the United States, and that is *Goldmine*®. It is best for selling middle- to higher-priced items that allow you to make up for the cost of the ad and still make money. And, as most serious collectors read *Goldmine*® at least occasionally, an ad letting them know of your existence can pay dividends. Its serves a smaller, but more targeted, audience than an online auction.

*Goldmine*® is published by F+W Publications; if you've never seen it, you can find it at many major bookstores and independent record shops, or a sample copy can be obtained by calling 800-258-0929.

For most people with an accumulation of records who want to "eliminate the middleman," online has been the way to go since the late 1990s. And the most popular site for this action is eBay (www.ebay.com).

Online selling seems to draw two widely different audiences. One is much the same as a stand-alone record store, except on a global scale rather than a regional one. Browsers who know next to nothing about record collecting and the relative scarcity of the listed pieces are common. These are people who can sometimes be fooled into paying too much for a common record if they get caught up in "auction fever," where the thrill of the hunt can override their rational knowledge that the item can be had cheaper somewhere else or with a bit more patience at eBay.

The other audience drawn to online sales is the hyper-specialist, and this is often where items can justifiably go for much more than in a retail store. Thanks to search engines, a fan of, say, Elvis Costello can type in the words "Elvis Costello" and find nothing but the Elvis Costello-related material. People who specialize in one artist will usually pay more – sometimes a *lot* more – than someone who collects a more broad range of artists.

Because they are specialists, though, they also know which items are common, so they don't get taken on the easy stuff.

As a seller, you are reaching a larger audience than you would in a record collecting magazine, but a much less targeted one. The Internet seems to be a good place to sell lower-priced items that might take up valuable space in an expensive print ad. But many more valuable items fetch less online than they do through more traditional means.

To do the best at selling online:

– Use the *Goldmine*® Grading Guide, which is elsewhere in this book. Don't say that your records are in "good condition," because "good" is a low grade… unless, of course, they really *are* in only "good" condition.

– Grade your records conservatively, and mention any flaws with them in your description.

– Always mention the record label and number of any record you sell. I am amazed at how many auctions lack this basic, and vital, information.

– Take a picture of, or scan, everything you sell, and post those images with your auctions. If possible, use multiple images. Photos can tell the potential buyer more than your words will.

– That said, don't alter your images in any way or steal someone else's better images! Your buyers probably won't deal with you again when they find out that your "pristine" record or sleeve has serious flaws.

– Answer all of your customers' questions, no matter how arcane or trivial they may seem. It could be the difference between a sale and no sale.

– Make your minimum bid the lowest amount you'll be willing to take for the item. Many items sell for only the minimum.

– However, if you really want to sell, don't set that minimum too high. It is better to start an auction low and watch the action send an item to new heights than to put a high minimum on an item. If you feel queasy, use a hidden reserve price, below which you won't sell the item.

– Charge a reasonable amount for shipping. It is expected that buyers will pay for shipping. But don't try to make a profit at it, either. If you charge more than what the Postal Service or your private shipper of choice charges to send an item, explain why.

– Once you sell the items, pack them well. Some customers will have specific requests on how they want an item sent. Listen to them!

Remember, too, that with tens of thousands of records for sale at any given time, approximately half of all records on eBay receive no bids at all. In addition to not following the advice for sellers listed above, it's possible that no one wanted to buy your record during the time your record was posted. Maybe at another time, you'll get bidders.

## Grading Your Records

Nothing is more important in determining the value of your records than their condition! Yes, their relative rarity and demand is important, but a collector or dealer will pay much more for a record in Near Mint condition than one in Very Good Minus condition.

However, I've found that most people with collections or accumulations have an inflated sense of the condition of their discs. I don't know how many times I've heard people who think they know what they are talking about tell me, "My records are all Mint!" Sure, and I've got some ocean front property in Arizona to sell you.

The truth is that most records, especially from before the 1970s, are *not* in anything close to Mint or Near Mint condition. That is why a collector will pay a premium for such a disc if he or she has to have it.

**This book lists values for records in Near Mint condition**. Records in lesser condition are worth a fraction of the Near Mint prices.

For most collectors, Very Good is the lowest grade for which they will pay more than bargain-bin prices. And some won't even do that. Lower-grade

records are only good as place holders, until a better copy comes along, or as examples of truly rare records that are difficult to find in any condition.

Most of the time, LPs are sold with two grades, one for the record and one for the cover. In this book, we list only one grade, however, because **with some exceptions, albums without covers are worthless, and covers without the accompanying record are worthless.** If an album is graded VG for the cover and VG+ for the record, add the two values together and divide by 2 to get a rough estimate of the value of a "mixed grade" LP.

Most records are graded visually. This is because most record dealers have lots of records – hundreds of thousands in some cases – and they don't have the time to play their entire stock. That said, some defects are easy to see, such as scratches and warps. Others are subtle, such as groove wear from using a cheap or poorly aligned tone arm. It has been our experience that older LPs (1950s to about 1971) tend to play better than they look, and newer LPs (at least until 1989) tend to play worse than they look.

When grading your records, do so under a strong light. Look at everything carefully, and then assign a grade based on your overall observations.

Some records will be worthy of a higher grade except for defects such as writing, tape or minor seam splits. Always mention these when selling a record! For some collectors, they will be irrelevant, but for others, they will be a deal-breaker. For all, they are important to know.

Also, some LPs were made for promotional purposes only. Again, always mention if a record is a promo copy when advertising it for sale!

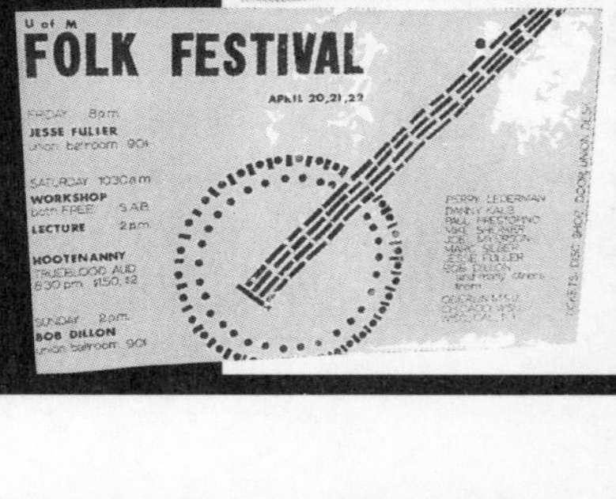

One of the obstacles to the further growth of record collecting is poor grading and a lack of consensus as to what constitutes a "Very Good Plus" or "Near Mint" record or cover. Over the years, the *Goldmine*® Grading Guide has tried to standardize this. It is now the most widely used guide for the buying and selling of vinyl albums; many eBay auctions and stand-alone Web sites swear by it. But we recognize that there are many variables to grading a record. As a seller, you are better off grading conservatively and

surprising the buyer with a better record than was expected, than by grading based on wishful thinking g and losing a customer.

That said, here are the standard grades for record albums, from best to worst.

## Mint (M)

These are absolutely perfect in every way. Often rumored but rarely seen, Mint should never be used as a grade unless more than one person agrees that the record or sleeve truly is in this condition. There is no set percentage of the Near Mint value these can bring; it is best negotiated between buyer and seller.

## Near Mint (NM or M-)

A good description of a NM record is "it looks like it just came from a retail store and it was opened for the first time." In other words, it's nearly perfect. Many dealers won't use a grade higher than this, implying (perhaps correctly) that no record or sleeve is ever truly perfect.

**NM records** are shiny, with no visible defects. Writing, stickers or other markings cannot appear on the label, nor can any "spindle marks" from someone trying to blindly put the record on the turntable. Major factory defects also must not be present; a record and label obviously pressed off center is not Near Mint. If played, it will do so with no surface noise. (NM records don't have to be "never played"; a record used on an excellent turntable can remain NM after many plays if the disc is properly cared for.)

**NM covers** have no creases, ring wear or seam splits of any kind.

These are high standards, and they are *not* on a sliding scale. A record or sleeve from the 1950s must meet the same standards as one from the 1990s or 2000s to be Near Mint! It's estimated that no more than 2 to 4 percent of all records remaining from the 1950s and 1960s are truly Near Mint. This is why they fetch such high prices, even for more common items. Do not assume your records are Near Mint. They *must* meet these standards to qualify!

## Very Good Plus (VG+) or Excellent (E)

A good description of a VG+ record is "except for a couple minor things, this would be Near Mint." Most collectors, especially those who want to play their records, will be happy with a VG+ record, especially if it toward the high end of the grade (sometimes called VG++ or E+).

**VG+ records** may show some slight signs of wear, including light scuffs or very light scratches that do not affect the listening experience. Slight warps that do not affect the sound are OK. Minor signs of handling are OK, too, such as telltale marks around the center hole, but repeated playing has not misshapen the hole. There may be some very light ring wear or discoloration, but it should be barely noticeable.

**VG+ covers** should have only minor wear. A VG+ cover might have some very minor seam wear or a split (less than one inch long) at the bottom, the most vulnerable location. Also, a VG+ cover may have some defacing, such as a cut-out marking. **Covers with cut-out markings can never be considered Near Mint.**

## Very Good (VG)

Many of the imperfections found on a VG+ record are more obvious on a VG record. That said, VG records – which usually sell for no more than 25 percent of a NM record – are among the biggest bargains in record collecting, because most of the "big money" goes for more perfect copies. For many listeners, a VG record or sleeve will be worth the money.

**VG records** have more obvious flaws than their counterparts in better shape. They lack most of the original gloss found on factory-fresh records. Groove wear is evident on sight, as are light scratches deep enough to feel with a fingernail. When played, a VG record has surface noise, and some scratches may be audible, especially in soft

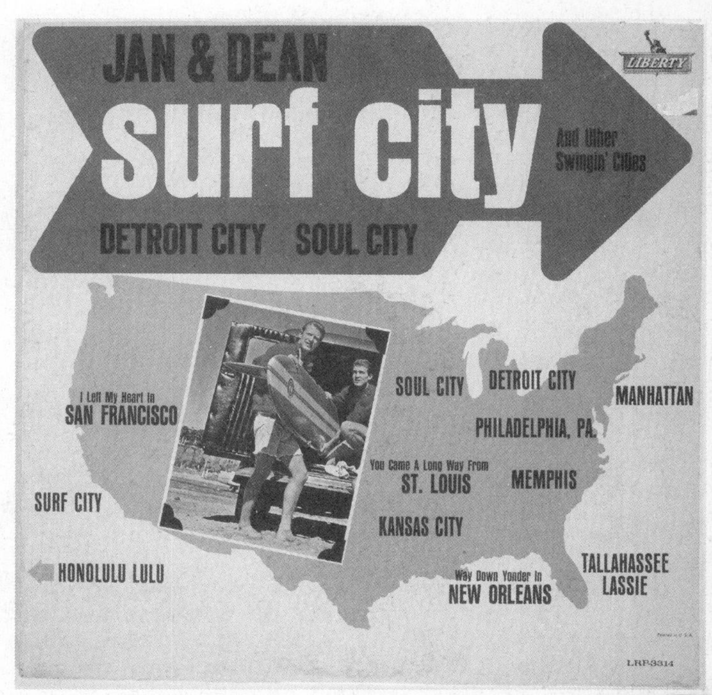

passages and during a song's intro and ending. But the noise will not overpower the music otherwise. Minor writing, tape or a sticker can detract from the label. Many collectors who have jukeboxes will use VG records in them and not think twice. They remain a fine listening experience, just not the same as if it were in better shape.

**VG covers** will have many signs of human handling. Ring wear in the middle or along the edges of the cover where the edge of a record would reside, is obvious, though not overwhelming. Some more creases might be visible. Seam splitting will be more obvious; it may appear on all three sides, though it won't be obvious upon looking. Someone might have written or it or stamped a price tag on it, too.

## Lower Grades

**Good (G), Good Plus (G+) or Very Good Minus (VG–)** records go for 10 to 15 percent of the Near Mint value, if you are lucky.

Good does not mean bad! The record still plays through without skipping, so it can serve as filler until something better comes along. But it has significant surface noise and groove wear, and the label is worn, with significant ring wear, heavy writing, or obvious damage caused by someone trying to remove tape or stickers and failing miserably. A Good to VG– cover has ring wear to the point of distraction, has seam splits obvious on sight and may have even heavier writing, such as, for example, huge radio station letters written across the front to deter theft.

If the item is common, it's probably better to pass it up. But if you've been seeking it for a long time, get it cheap and look to upgrade.

**Poor (P) and Fair (F)** records go for 0 to 5 percent of the Near Mint value, if they go at all. More likely, they end up going in the trash. Records are cracked, impossibly warped, or skip and/or repeat when an attempt is made to play them. Covers are so heavily damaged that you almost want to cry. Only the most outrageously rare items ever sell for more than a few cents in this condition – again, if they sell at all.

## Sealed Albums

Still-sealed albums can – and do – bring even higher prices than listed in the book.

However, one must be careful when paying a premium for sealed LPs of any kind for several reasons:

1. They may have been re-sealed;
2. The records might not be in Near Mint condition;
3. The record inside might not be the original pressing or the most desirable pressing;
4. Most bizarre of all, the wrong record might be inside. I've had this happen to me; I opened a sealed album by one MCA artist only to find a record by a different MCA artist inside! Fortunately, I didn't pay a lot for that sealed LP. I would have been quite upset if I had!

## Records Not in the Book

Obviously – or at least I *hope* it's obvious to you – no book of 712 pages could possibly list every album ever made.

From the first time we compiled this book in 1999, we've had to make decisions about what we could include and what we couldn't, based upon the apace available. The two biggest areas where we chose to limit our listings the most fit into the categories of **imports** and **promotional copies.**

## Imports

The *Goldmine® Record Album Price Guide* lists only those vinyl LPs manufactured in the United States or, in a few instances, manufactured in other countries, but specifically for release in the United States. Any record that fits the following criteria is an import, and you won't find it in the book:

– LPs on the Parlophone label by any artist, at least before 2000. Parlophone, best known as the Beatles' British label, was not used as a label in the United States until very recently.

– LPs that have the letters "BIEM," "GEMA" or "MAPL" on them.

– LPs that say anywhere on the label or cover, "Made in Canada," "Made in the UK," "Made in Germany," etc.

We have chosen not to list records from Great Britain, Canada, Japan, or any other nation for logistical reasons: Where do you start, and where do you stop?

Unfortunately, we realize that there is a lack of reliable information on the value of non-U.S. records, especially published in the United States. **Please don't contact us seeking information on non-U.S. records; we cannot help.**

Also unfortunately, there are few general rules about the value of an import as compared to an American edition. Some import albums, especially well-made Japanese imports that still have their "obi strip," can go for more than the U.S. counterpart. Others seem to attract little interest in the States.

One rule that is just as true of imports as it is with U.S. records: Those discs that are originals in the best condition will sell for more than reissues and those in less than top-notch shape.

## Promotional Copies

Basically, a promotional record is any copy of a record not meant for retail sale. Different labels identify these in different ways: The most common method on LPs is to use a white label instead of the regular-color label and/or to add words such as the following:

"Demonstration – Not for Sale"

"Audition Record"

"For Radio-TV Use Only"

"Promotional Copy"

Some labels, of course, used colors other than white; still others used the same labels as their stock copies, but added a promotional disclaimer to the label.

Most promotional albums have the same catalog number as the regular release, except for those differences.

Sometimes, regular stock copies have a "Demonstration – Not for Sale" or "Promo" rubber stamped on the cover; these are known as "designate promos" and are not of the same cachet as true promotional records. Treat these as stock copies that have been defaced. Exceptions are noted in the listings.

All of this is mentioned as a means of identification. **As a rule, we do not list promotional records separately in this book, nor are we interested in doing so.** There are exceptions, which we will list below. But we feel that the precious space in this book is better used for unique commercially available records rather than for thousands upon thousands of promotional copies.

**Most promotional LPs sell for approximately the same as a stock copy of the same catalog number.** That has been our experience.

However, there are certain exceptions. Those are the kinds of promos that you'll find documented in this book, and which we plan to continue to document. These include:

-- Colored vinyl promos.

-- Promos in special numbering series, such as Columbia albums with an "AS" or "CAS" prefix; Warner Bros, albums with a "PRO" or "PRO-A-" prefix; Capitol albums with a "PRO" or "SPRO" prefix; Mercury albums with an "MK" prefix; and other similar series on other labels.

-- Promos that are somehow different than the released versions, either because of changes in the cover or changes in the music between the promo LP and the regular stock LP.

-- Promos pressed on special high-quality vinyl; these were popular in the 1980s and can bring a premium above stock copies of the same titles.

## Other Records Not Listed

Over the years, we've received questions from readers asking why certain popular performers were left out of the *Goldmine® Record Album Price Guide* and what the criteria for inclusion are.

Most of the "missing" artists are missing for a good reason: **None of their American LPs have a near-mint value of at least $20.** This disclaimer has been in every edition of the book since the first, and yet we are amazed at how many people wonder where certain popular artists of the 1970s and 1980s are.

That said, did we miss some performers who have albums worth at least $20? Of course we did. And we'd like to know about those we missed.

Our first suggestion to finding out about some of the missing artists is to get the *Goldmine® Standard Catalog of American Records 1950-1975.* That book contains both singles and albums by quite a few performers who are not listed in this book

Our second suggestion is to get the *Goldmine® Standard Catalog of American Records 1976-Present.* It's not quite to the "present" any more, as it was released in 2001, but it's the best available source for popular vinyl of the 1970s and 1980s. That book, too, contains both singles and albums by performers who are not listed in this book

Unfortunately, it's impossible to assume that because a record isn't listed in a price guide that it has no value. There remain a lot of undocumented records out there that are collectible for different reasons, or would be collectible if they were more widely known. We are always interested in learning about records that ought to be listed because they have significant value, and not simply because they are missing from the book.

Some areas of records that are under-represented in this book deserve special mention.

-- **Children's records.** Most records that were marketed to children have some collectibility, especially if they have a legitimate tie-in to either a popular television show or to the Walt Disney empire. Some are listed in this book, but others are difficult to list because it's hard to define the "artist" under whom some of the ensemble pieces should be listed.

The challenge in collecting children's records is finding them in near-mint condition. Kids generally trashed anything they owned, and that included the records they played.

-- **Jazz LPs.** Only those jazz LPs worth at least $20, unless the artist had significant crossover success, are listed. To find more complete listings for these same performers, we recommend the *Goldmine® Jazz Album Price Guide, 2nd Edition,* which came out in 2004.

-- **Classical LPs.** About 98 percent of all classical albums are worth less than their original list price. Some of the other 2 percent are in this book. We have no interest in continuing a classical artist's discography beyond the bounds we've already set – basically RCA Victor Living Stereo "shaded dogs" and Mercury Living Presence stereo LPs. Mono versions of the same albums (with an LM- prefix on RCA Victor, for example) are generally not listed because they have a mere fraction of the value of the stereo counterpart.

-- **Spoken-word LPs.** Few have significant collector value. They are usually quite rare, but there is relatively little demand for them.

## Label Identification Guide

For the most part, the most collectible records are original pressings. Those are the ones that presumably were available when the album was first pressed.

Of course, not every copy of *Elvis' Golden Records* is created equal, no matter how similar the covers may look from pressing to pressing. Copyright dates on liner notes are meaningless when determining when the record was actually manufactured. A 1958 date on the cover can be attached to a pressing from the 1980s!

To tell for sure, you have to know the labels.

As opposed to 45s, which often were deleted quickly and replaced by "golden oldies" reissues, albums could stay in print for years, even decades, with a cover that, at least superficially, resembled that on an original edition. With only some slight differences, the same album cover could contain a copy of *Meet the Beatles!* that was pressed in 1964, 1974 or 1984. The same is true of an album such as *Johnny's Greatest Hits* by Johnny Mathis; it was in print from 1958 until vinyl was phased out as a mass-market item. In that time, Columbia went through several different label designs. It's only the originals that are the most sought after.

Reissues, with a few exceptions, are worth a fraction of the original issues.

Thus this guide to many of the most common and collectible labels.

**Warning:** Sometimes there is overlap between label designs.

This happened for one of two reasons. First, on major labels, the order of release may not exactly coincide with the order the numbers were assigned. Sometimes, a release was delayed or accelerated, which means that some albums with earlier numbers may be "original" on a later label variation than later ones. Second, most independent labels farmed out their production to independent pressing plants. If a record was in high demand, a plant sometimes used whatever label was available, even if it was the wrong color or an older design. This rarely happened on the major labels.

Two final disclaimers before we begin:

– This guide only covers regular U.S. LP issues. Records on Canadian or other countries' versions of the same label are not listed.

– The guide does not attempt to delve into promotional labels. The most common variant is a white label version of the design in use at the time. Promos, however, can also be pink, blue, lime green or cream (just to name a few shades of the rainbow); some used the same labels as stock copies and added promotional wording to the label typesetting; and still others didn't do promos at all.

### A&M

1963 (101 only?): Tan label, brown print, A&M trumpet logo unboxed in brown print at top.v

1963-1964 (102?-at least 106): Brown ("ochre") label, A&M trumpet logo in white box at top.

1965-1973 (starting at 107?): Brown ("ochre") label, A&M trumpet logo in white box at left.

Late 1973-1986: Silvery gray label with fading A&M logo.

Early 1981-mid 1986: Red label, black ring along outer edge (used on only a handful of albums in this period; most still used the fading logo).

Late 1986-end: Black label with five gold, black and white rounded squares across the center and A&M logo at right.

## ABC; ABC-Paramount

1955-1961: Black label, "ABC-Paramount" along top of black label with rainbow design underneath, "A Product of Am-Par Record Corp." in white at bottom.

1962-1966: Black label, "ABC-Paramount" along top of black label with rainbow design underneath, "A Product of ABC-Paramount Records Inc." in white at bottom.

1966-1967: Possible transition label with "abc" in a white circle at top of label, but not in a multicolored box.

1967-1972: Black label, "abc" in white circle at top with multi-color box around it.

1973: Short-lived label; black with white triangle at top and "ABC" in children's blocks inside. This label was gone by mid-1973 and replaced by the 1967-72 design until a new label could be created.

Mid 1974-1977: Multi-colored (yellow, orange, purple) "target" label with "abc Records" at top between two lines.

1977-1979: Multi-colored (yellow, orange, purple) "target" label with "abc" in an eighth note at top.

In 1979, the label was bought by MCA, which quickly replaced current ABC albums with tan-label MCA singles using the same number.

## ABC Dunhill – See Dunhill.

## ABC Impulse! – See Impulse!

## ABKCO

Allan Klein's reissue label, albums have light blue labels with a darker blue logo above the center hole. Some labels have blue print, some have black print; this seems to be merely a pressing plant difference.

## Abner

Only three albums came out on Abner, and all three exist on three different labels. One label is black with a logo of a falcon on a glove; another is maroon with the same logo of a falcon on a glove. Finally, Abner records were also released on Vee Jay with the same catalog number in Abner jackets.

## Ace

1958-1962: Black label, silver print.

1962: Dark blue label, white at top, "ACE" in blue oval.

1971 (2020-21): Yellow label, black print.

1975 (2022): Red label, black print.

Custom labels were used on 1007 and 1008.

## Aladdin

1952-1954 (10-inch albums, 701-709): Blue label.

1956-end (12-inch albums, 710 and 800 series): Red label. Records pressed on red vinyl have blue labels.

## Apple

1968-1974: Green Granny Smith apple on one side, sliced apple on the other. Some, though not all, albums from 1968-70 had a line of small white print on the sliced side with "A Subsidiary of Capitol Industries, Inc." along the bottom and a tiny Capitol logo. The small print was only used at one pressing plant, so two LPs could both be originals, yet one will have the "Capitol logo" and the other one won't.

1975: "All rights reserved" disclaimer added to the label print.

Apple 34001 was originally issued with a red apple label. Custom labele exist on many numbers.

## Argo

Early mono editions had a greenish label, some with gold print, some with silver print, with "ULTRA HIGH FIDELITY" adjacent to the vertical "ARGO." Later mono editions are known to have a silver label with black print or a black label with silver print, also with "ULTRA HIGH FIDELITY."

Early stereo editions have dark blue labels with silver print.

The next label was silver with black print, but without the words "ULTRA HIGH FIDELITY."

The final Argo label (to the end of 1965) was a brown label with a pink and white "ARGO" in an oval at left.

The Argo label was replaced by Cadet in 1966.

## Arista

1975-mid 1976 (AL 4001-4105?): Light blue label, white logo at top with "Arista Records" underneath.

Late 1976-early 1977: Light blue label, white logo at top with "Arista" underneath.

Early 1977-1979: Black label, blue logo at top, "Arista" underneath.

1979-1984: Fading blue label, three-dimensional Arista logo at top, "Arista" at left side of logo slanting upward.

1984-1990: Black label, "ARISTA" above multicolor mountain skyline.

1991-1997: Black label, "ARISTA" above white mountain skyline.

Custom labels were used on some releases.

## Asylum

1972-1973 (SD 5051 to SD 5066?): White label, "door-in-a-circle" logo at top.

1974-1984: "Clouds" label. Around 1975, a small "W" (Warner Communications logo) was added to the label print.

1976: Some 45s were issued with a solid blue label with a small stylized "a" at the top. All of these also exist on the clouds label. It's unknown if any LPs exist with this label

1985-end: Split black and gold label.

## Atco

1958-1961 (33-101 to 33-138): Yellow label with a harp at the upper left.

1961-1968 mono: Gold and gray (dark blue) label , "AT" to left of center hole, "CO" to right of center hole in white background.

1961-1968 stereo: Purple and brown label, "AT" to left of center hole, "CO" to right of center hole in white background.

1969-1977: Yellow label, "Atco" logo at left. Earlier labels have an "1841 Broadway" address, later ones have a "75 Rockefeller Plaza" address and add a small "W" (Warner Communications) logo in the small print.

1978-1984: Gray label, logo at top.

1985-1989: White label, "ATCO" in multi-colored letters at top.

1990-end: Mostly gray label, Atco logo at top surrounded by white.

## Atlantic

1950-1960 mono: Black label, silver print.

1959-1960 stereo: Green label, silver print.

1960: So-called "bullseye" label. Monos have orange, purple and black fan around the center hole and "Atlantic" in orange and purple band at top; stereos have blue and green fan around the center hole and "Atlantic" in blue and green band at top.

1960-1961: "White fan logo" issues. Monos were orange and purple, stereos were green and blue. Through the center hole is a white strip; on the right side of the center hole, a white "fan" in a black background can be found.

1961-1968: "Black fan logo" issues. Monos were orange and purple, stereos were green and blue. Through the center hole is a white strip; on the right side of the center hole, a black "fan" in a white background can be found.

Early 1969: Whether by accident or design, some Atlantic LPs are known to exist with the Atco purple and brown label.

1969-1990s: Red and green label with Atlantic logo at top. Early Earlier labels have an "1841 Broadway" address, later ones have a "75 Rockefeller Plaza" address and add a small "W" (Warner Communications) logo in the small print.

Some LPs were issued with custom labels.

## Audio Lab

A budget label created by Syd Nathan of King Records, all LPs have blue labels with silver print.

## B.T. Puppy

Black label, silver print, "B.T. Puppy Records" in red at top with cocker spaniel head underneath.

## Bang

1966-1973 (211-227): Mostly red label, white at top, with "BANG records" gun logo centered in a yellow background.

1974-1978 (400-410): Sky blue label with clouds and stylized "BANG" curving around the top.

1979-1982 (Columbia distribution): Light brown label, red logo at top.

## Barnaby

1970-1973 (CBS distribution): Light blue label, treble clef logo at left.

1973 (MGM distribution): White label with line drawing.

1974-1979 (4000, 5000, 6000 series, GRT/Janus distribution): Multicolor label, yellow rim, vinyl record hanging limply from tree.

## Bearsville

The label had the same basic design throughout its history; only the distribution changed.

1971: "Distributed by Ampex" at the bottom

1972-1976: "Distributed by Warner Bros. Records" at the bottom.

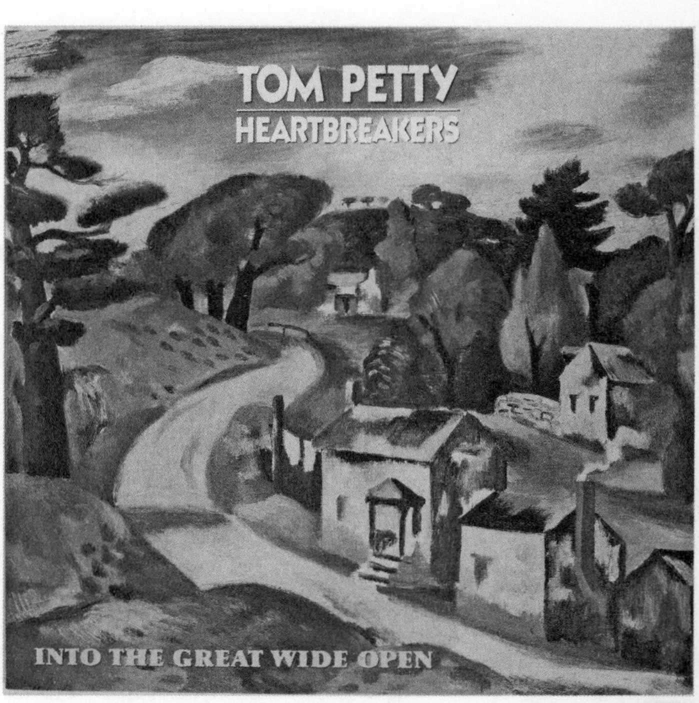

1976-1981: No distribution notice at bottom of label.

1981-1982: "3300 Warner Blvd." address added to bottom of label.

## Bell

1965-1969: Blue label, silver print.

1970-1974: Silver label, black print.

## Beltone

Only one album was released on the label, and it is mostly orange with black printing.

## Big Top

All releases have a black label with silver print.

## Big Tree

1970-1971 (distributed by Ampex): Red and yellow label.

1971-1974 (distributed by Bell): Red and white label

1974-1976 (distributed by Atco): Light blue and red label.

1976-1980: Multicolor label.

## Blue Thumb

1969 (first four LPs): Black label.

1969-1974 (Gulf + Western distribution): Off-white, almost gray label, with blue thumb print at upper left. Some labels in this period are orange.

1974-1978: Multi-colored (yellow, orange, purple) "target" label with "abc Blue Thumb" at top between two lines and a blue thumb print at upper right.

## Bluesville

1960-1963: Bright blue label with silver print.

1964-end: Lighter blue label with Prestige trident logo at right side.

## Bluesway

1967-1968: Blue label.

1968-1974: Black label, blue rim around outside.

## Brother

1967 (9001 only): Brown label with large horseman and "Brother records" at top.

1970-1975: Light yellow label, yellow rim around outside, "A Licensee of Warner Bros. Inc." at bottom.

1976-1978: Same basic design as 1970-1975, but print changes to "A Division of Warner Bros. Records Inc."

## Brunswick

1950-1963: Black label, silver print,

1963-1972: Black label, arrow-shaped color bars through center, "A Division of Decca Records" in fine print.

1972-end: Black label, arrow-shaped color bars through center, "Manufactured by Brunswick Record Corp." along rim.

## Buddah

1967-1972: Multi-color kaleidoscopic label with black drawing of Buddha at bottom and "BUDDAH RECORDS" on either side of drawing.

1972-1977: Maroon label with smiling Buddha figure, "BUDDAH RECORDS" in white at top.

1978-end: Black label, new logo at top, Arista logo added at bottom.

## Buena Vista

Best known as the label of Annette, the label pre-dates her hits by about a year.

The first series was BV-1300; these have turquoise labels with silver print.

The BV-3300 series, where Annette's LPs are, were first issued with a black label, silver print. Later ones were issued with a half black, half mostly yellow label with a slight rainbow effect, "Buena Vista" in black over the yellow section.

The BV-4000 series was a continuation of the Disneyland WDL-4000 series (see Disneyland listing for more detail). 4022-4025 were first issued on black label, silver print; 4026-4048 were first issued on the half black, half yellow label as described in the 3300 series.

The 1980s issues in the 62000 series have a blue and red label with a white strip just above the center hole that goes through the middle of the center hole. The "Buena Vista" logo is in red at the upper left.

## Cadence

1954-1961 (1000 series, 3000-3051?, 4000s, 5000s, 25000 series to 25051?): Maroon lower two-thirds of label, upper third is silver with "cadence" in lowercase and a metronome logo.

1961-1964 (3052?-3068, 25052?-25068): Red label, black rim with "CADENCE RECORDS" inside in white.

## Cadet

Cadet replaced the Argo label in 1965. Many Argo titles were reissued in Argo cover with Cadet labels.

The first label was an all light blue label with "CADET" across the top in black.

The second label was a fading blue label with "CADET" across the top in fading red, white and blue letters.

1971-end (50000 and 60000 series, GRT distribution): Yellow label, red rim, horizontal red stripe through center hole, "CADET" at left.

## Cadet Concept

All issues have a gray label with black print, "CADET" in pink, "CONCEPT" in orange (red).

## Camden—See RCA Camden.

## Cameo

1957 (1000): Orange label, black print, cameo at top.

1958-1959 (1001-1005): Black label, silver print. 1004 and 1005 were issued in stereo; these have a black label with gold print.

1959-1960 (1006-1009): Reverts to 1000 label – orange label, black print, cameo at top

1960-1967: Red and black label, white cameo in yellow border at left.

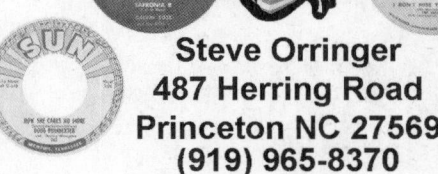

1967-1968: Red and tan label, new logo at top with interlocking "C-P" and the "C" filled in. All Cameo LPs known to exist with this label also exist on the 1960-1967 label.

1968: Pink label, large white area at top, "Cameo" across top in an arc with a cameo figure inside the "O."

## Canadian-American

1959-1961 (1001-1005?): Black label, silver print.

1961-1965 (1006?-1018): Black label, five color bars across top of label.

## Capitol

Capitol can be, at times, a very confusing label. The below sticks to the regular pop series; budget series starting in the 1970s (M or SM prefixes) and continuing into the 1980s (N or SN prefixes) often had different color schemes than the below.

1949-1954 (10-inch albums, most with an "H" prefix): Purple label with silver print. Some labels have a silver ring near the outer rim, some do not. Also, some exist with a red label and gold print and/or an "L" prefix.

1954-1958 (12-inch mono albums): On albums with a "T" prefix, turquoise label, with or without silver ring near outer rim. Some albums, those with a "W" prefix, were issued with a gray label.

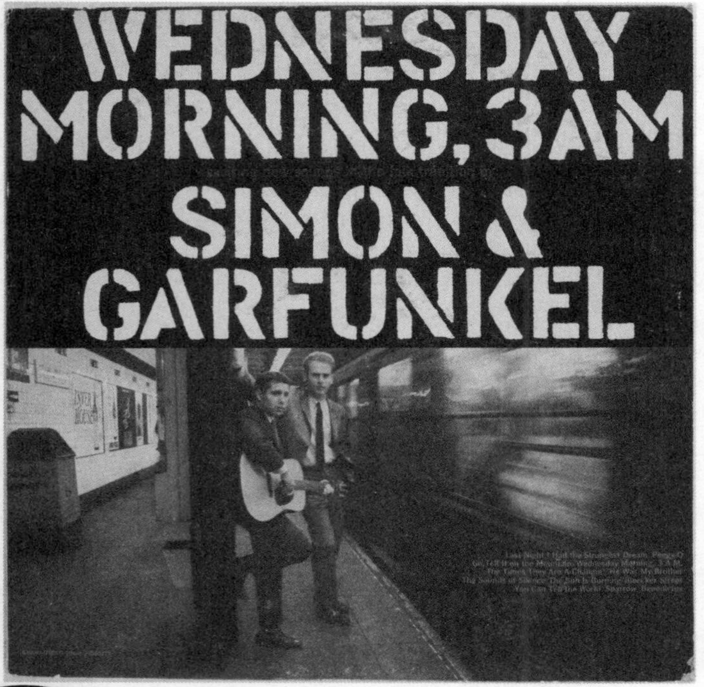


1958-1959 (mono and stereo, approximately 1021-1225): Black label, rainbow ring around outside rim (usually called the "black colorband label") with white Capitol logo and "Long Playing High Fidelity" at the left of the label.

1959-1962 (approximately 1226-1660): Same as 1958-1959, except a vertical white line replaces "Long Playing High Fidelity."

1962-1968 (approximately 1660-2999): Black colorband label, Capitol logo moved to top of label.

1968-1969 (approximately 101-200s in new numbering system): Black colorband label, Capitol logo at top, with extra print along the edge of the colorband "A Subsidiary of Capitol Industries, Inc." added to "Mfd. By Capitol Records Inc."

1969-1971 (200s into the 700s): Lime green label, "Capitol" at upper left and new "target" logo at top.

1971-1972 (700s into early 11000s): Red label, "Capitol" at upper left, purple Capitol "target" logo at top. Sometimes assumed to be a country label only, it was on all Capitol releases during this short period (two non-country examples include the debut albums by Rick Springfield and the Raspberries).

Late 1972-mid 1978 (early 11000s into 11800s): Orange label, olive green "Capitol" at bottom of label. Records by R&B-oriented performers have a red label with a black "Capitol" at bottom.

Mid 1978-mid 1983: Matte-finish purple label. Huge white Capitol logo dominates the upper third of the label; perimeter print is above the logo and at the bottom of the label.

Mid 1983-mid 1988: The black colorband label, logo at top, returns, except that there is black print inside the color ring, instead of outside it in white.

Mid 1988-present: Glossy purple label, much smaller Capitol logo at top than earlier purple label; perimeter print starts with the word "Manufactured" and is in an unbroken string along the edge.

Some Capitol LPs from the 1970s onward have custom labels or "retro" labels.

## Capricorn

1970: Yellow Atco label with "Capricorn Series" at bottom.

1970-1971: Pink label.

1972-1974: Plain tan label, 'CAPRICORN RECORDS" across the top.

1975-1978: Light brown label, large goat facing right.

1978-end (Polygram distribution): Light brown label, large goat facing left.

## Carlton

There are two basic varieties of this label. The first one is a tan label with a black "C" around the center hole and a white strip to the right with a black "Carlton" in it. The second one is the same, except that the "C" around the center hole is all-white.

## Casablanca

1974 (9000 series): Dark blue label, mug shot of Bogart at left, "Manufactured and Distributed by Warner Bros. Records Inc." in white along bottom.

1974-1976 (7000-7020s): Dark blue label, mug shot of Bogart at left, "Manufactured and Distributed by Casablanca Records, Inc." in white along bottom.

1976-1977 (7020s-7050?): Tan label, desert scene at top, "Casablanca" at top.

1977-1981 (7050?-7100s): Tan label, desert scene at top, "Casablanca Record and FilmWorks" at top.

1981-end (7100s into six-digit numbers): "Manufactured and Distributed by Polygram" at bottom.

## Challenge

1958-1963 mono (600-617): Blue label, silver print, "Challenge" logo in oval at top.

1960-1965 stereo (2500-2521): Black label, silver print, "Challenge" logo in oval at top.

1963-1965 mono (618-621): Blue-green label, "Challenge" logo in oval at top.

1966-1967 (622-624, 2522-2524): Black label, silver print, "CHALLENGE" in silver block letters across the top.

1969-end (2000 series): Black label, white coat of arms logo at top, "Challenge" in red.

## Chancellor

1958-1959: (5001-5003): Pink label, black print.

1959-1963 (5004-5032): Black label, silver print, "Chancellor" in red across top of label.

## Checker

1957-1965 (1400s and 2971-2995): Black label, silver print, "CHECKER" at left of center hole in vertical block letters. Some issues have a maroon label with silver print; otherwise, they are identical to the above.

1965-1966 (2996-3001): Light blue label with alternating black and red checkers at top.

1966-1971 (3002-3017): Fading blue label with "CHECKER" across the top in fading red, white and blue letters.

1971-end (reissues): Blue label, purple rim, purple stripe through center hole, "CHECKER" at left.

## Chess

1956-1963 (1425-1482): Black label, silver print, "CHESS" at left of center hole in vertical block letters. Some issues have blue labels with silver print that are otherwise identical to the black label versions. Those few stereo releases in this series had gold labels with black print.

1963-1965 (1483?-1500?): Black label, "CHESS" across the top in gold with a four-color knight chess piece in back. This basic label also exists on a blue label with all-silver print and no four-color graphics.

1965 (1490s): Fading blue label, "CHESS" across the top in all white labels.

1966-1971 (1500-1553 and 400 series): Fading blue label with "CHESS" across the top in fading red, white and blue letters.

1971-1976 (50000 and 6000 series, later 200, 400 and 700 series): Orange label, light blue rim, light blue stripe through center hole, "CHESS" at left.

1982-1989 (8200, 8300, 8400, 8500, 9000 series): Dark blue label, silver print, "CHESS RECORDS" in arc at top, checkerboard motif along lower edge.

## Chrysalis

1972-1977: Green label, red butterfly at lower left, "Chrysalis" in red along bottom.

1977-1987: White label fading to blue at bottom, white butterfly at lower left, "Chrysalis" in white along bottom. During this time, distribution changed from independent to the CBS family of labels; reissues of 1300-series albums have a new prefix, usually "PV," and the number "4" before the four digits.

1987-1989: White label, colored butterfly at left.

1989-end: Off-white label, different butterfly logo.

## Class

1957-1958 (5001-5002): Black label, silver print.

1959 (5003-5004): Maroon label, silver print.

## CO & CE

Three albums came out on this label, two by the Vogues and one by Lou Christie, all in mono only. The labels are yellow with a white hourglass at left.

## COED

1960 (901): Yellow label, black print.

1960 (902): Black label, silver print.

1961-1963 (903-906): Red label, black and white print.

## Colgems

1966-1967: Red label, white area at top in which "COLGEMS" appears in red, "TM of Colgems Records" appears underneath the top logo.

1967-1970: Same as above, but without "TM of Colgems Records."

## Colpix

1958-1962?: Gold label, "COLPIX" in red curving around top of label with line drawing of Statue of Liberty underneath.

1962?-1964?: Gold label, strip of movie film with "COLPIX RECORDS" in white background within.

1964?-1966?: Light blue label, strip of movie film with "COLPIX RECORDS" in white background within.

1966 (4001, stereo only): Dark blue label, silver print, no strip of movie film.

## Columbia (pop)

Another long and storied label, its history is less confusing if you break it into its pop and "Masterworks" divisions. The below apply only to pop (GL, CL, CS series before 1970, prefixes ending in C after 1970) releases.

10-Inch LPs

1948-1954 (6000 series): Maroon label, gold print, "Long Playing" at bottom.

1955-1956 (2500 House Party Series): Red and black label with six white "eye" logos, three at left, three at right.

12-Inch Mono LPs

1951-1953 (501-525): Black label, silver print, "Long Playing" at bottom. Originals have a "GL" prefix.

1953-1955 (525-600s): Maroon label, gold print, "Long Playing" at bottom.

1955-1962 (600s-no earlier than 1779): Red and black label with six white "eye" logos, three at left, three at right.

1962-1965 (1780?-2300s): Red label; "COLUMBIA" in white along the top; two white "eye" logos, one at 9 o'clock, the other at 3 o'clock; "GUARANTEED HIGH FIDELITY" in black at bottom.

1965-1968 (2300s-2800s): Red label; "COLUMBIA" in white along the top; two white "eye" logos, one at 9 o'clock, the other at 3 o'clock; "360 SOUND MONO 360 SOUND" in white at bottom. Later issues only say "MONO" at bottom.

12-Inch Stereo LPs

1958-1962 (8000-no earlier than 8579): Red and black label with six white "eye" logos, three at left, three at right, "STEREO FIDELITY" in white along bottom.

1962-1963 (8560?-unknown): Red label; "COLUMBIA" in white along the top; two white "eye" logos, one at 9 o'clock, the other at 3 o'clock; "360 SOUND STEREO 360 SOUND" in black along bottom, no arrows.

1963-1965 (range unknown): Red label; "COLUMBIA" in white along the top; two white "eye" logos, one at 9 o'clock, the other at 3 o'clock; "360 SOUND STEREO 360 SOUND" in black along bottom, arrows added to left of first "360" and right of second "SOUND."

1965-1970 (9100s-9999, CS 1000 series, 30000-30050?): Red label; "COLUMBIA" in white along the top; two white "eye" logos, one at 9 o'clock, the other at 3 o'clock; "360 SOUND STEREO 360 SOUND" in white along bottom.

1970-1990: Orange label, gold "COLUMBIA" six times in ring along outer edge, each one separated by an "eye" logo.

1990-present: Red label, "COLUMBIA" in white in an arc along top, all other label print in black.

Custom labels were used for some releases.

## Columbia Masterworks (classical and shows)

Before 1970, classical releases had "ML" or "MS" prefixes; movie and stage play releases used "OL" or "OS" prefixes, sometimes with a "K" before the first two letters.

*10-Inch LPs*

Two different labels exist. Some have green labels, gold print, "Long Playing" at bottom; others have a dark blue label, gold print, "Long Playing" at bottom

*12-Inch Mono LPs*

1948-1954 (4001-?): Dark blue label, gold print, "Long Playing" at bottom. Some also have green labels with gold print and "Long Playing" at bottom.

1955-1962: Gray and black label with six white "eye" logos, three at left, three at right.

1962-1965: Gray label; "COLUMBIA" in white along the top; two white "eye" logos, one at 9 o'clock, the other at 3 o'clock; "GUARANTEED HIGH FIDELITY" in black at bottom.

1965-1968: Gray label; "COLUMBIA" in white along the top; two white "eye" logos, one at 9 o'clock, the other at 3 o'clock; "360 SOUND MONO 360 SOUND" in white at bottom. Later issues only say "MONO" at bottom.

*12-Inch Stereo LPs*

1958-1962: Gray and black label with six white "eye" logos, three at left, three at right, "STEREO FIDELITY" in white along bottom.

1962-1963: Gray label; "COLUMBIA" in white along the top; two white "eye" logos, one at 9 o'clock, the other at 3 o'clock; "360 SOUND STEREO 360 SOUND" in black along bottom, no arrows.

1963-1965: Gray label; "COLUMBIA" in white along the top; two white "eye" logos, one at 9 o'clock, the other at 3 o'clock; "360 SOUND STEREO 360 SOUND" in black along bottom, arrows added to left of first "360" and right of second "SOUND."

1965-1970: Gray label; "COLUMBIA" in white along the top; two white "eye" logos, one at 9 o'clock, the other at 3 o'clock; "360 SOUND STEREO 360 SOUND" in white along bottom.

1970-early 1980: Olive label, gold "COLUMBIA" six times in ring along outer edge, each one separated by an "eye" logo.

Later variations include the "COLUMBIA" being replaced by "CBS," a large "FM" on labels, a special label for digital recordings, and a green label with "CBS" around the outer rim in white. By the end of the 1980s, no more vinyl was coming out in this series. Today this label is known as Sony Classical.

## Columbia Special Products (CSP)

Late 1950s-1970: Red label, black strip curving along the top of the label, "COLUMBIA SPECIAL PRODUCTS" in white over the black.

1971-1982?: Orange label, "CSP" in yellow at top of label, "COLUMBIA SPECIAL PRODUCTS" in smaller print beneath.

1982?-early 1990s: Orange label, "CBS SPECIAL PRODUCTS" in three lines to the left of the center hole.

Early 1990s: Orange label, "Sony Music Special Products" in two lines to the left of the center hole.

## Coral

1950-1963: Maroon label, silver print.

1963-1968: Black label, rainbow ring near center, "A Subsidiary of Decca Records" in fine print.

1968-1970: Black label, rainbow wing near center, "A Division of MCA Records" in fine print.

## Cotillion

1969-1972: Grayish label, "Cotillion" in box at top.

1976-1980s: Reactivated label; purple with a round "C" logo at top.

## Crown

This was a budget label. It began by putting some rare R&B and blues sides on LP, but eventually its issues became cheesier and cheesier.

1957-1960: Black label, gold or silver print. Some of the early Crown titles exist on red vinyl.

1960-mid 1960s: Black label, each letter of "CROWN" is a different color.

Mid 1960s-late 1960s: Gray label, black print.

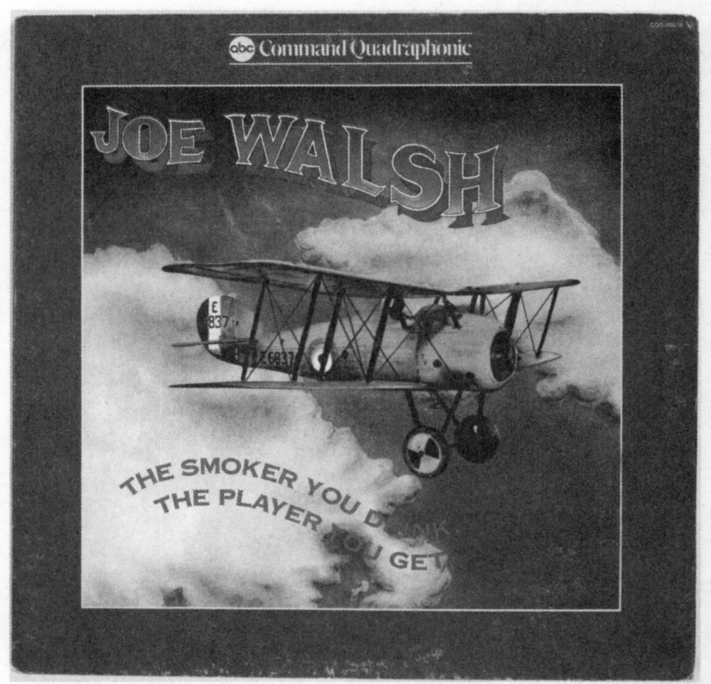

## Dakar

1969-1970 (9000s): Black label with rainbow colorband along the edge.

1972-1976 (76900s): White label, black print.

## Decca

1949-1954 (10-inch LPs in the 5000 series, 12-inch LPs in the 8000 series): Black label, gold print. Earliest pressings have a "DLP" prefix, which was quickly replaced on the labels (but not always on the covers) by "DL."

1954-1960 (later 10-inch LPs and 12-inch LPs from around 8100 to 8981): Black label, silver print. Stereo pressings, which added a "7" to the mono number, had maroon labels with silver print.

1960-1966 (4000-4830s, 74000-74830s): Black label with rainbow stripe through center hole and "Mfrd. by Decca Records" in the fine print.

1967-1971 (4830s to end of mono, 74830 into some 75000s and 79000s): Black label with rainbow stripe through center hole and "A Division of MCA" in the fine print.

1972-1973: Black label with rainbow stripe through center hole and "Mfrd. by MCA" in the fine print.

In addition to the regular series, Decca had a "Gold Label Series" of classical music; these have gold labels with black print.

MCA merged Decca, Uni and Kapp in January 1973 and closed down all three.

## Del-Fi

1959 (1201): Light blue, black printing, blue circles on a black background around the outside of the label.

1959 (1202-1204): Light blue label, gold and black diamonds around the outside of the label.

1959-1964 (1205-1249): Black label, blue and gold diamonds around the outside of the label.

## Deram

There are two different labels. The original label is believed to be a mostly white label with brown and black print with "DERAM" in a box at the top and the word "LONDON" in the same box below it. But the most predominant label is white at the bottom, brown at the top, with "DERAM" in white letters over the brown background.

## Dionn

The only album on this label has an orange label with black print.

## Disneyland

One of the most confusing labels, its albums were issued in several numerical series, sometimes simultaneously.

The first LPs on the label were in the WDL-4000 series. Early pressings have yellow labels and black print with "A Disneyland Record" underneath the center hole. Later editions have red labels with silver print and "Disneyland" in an arc above the center hole.

The WDL-3000 series came next. 3001 was issued with the above yellow label; it was reissued, and all others had their original issue, with a purple label, silver print, and "Disneyland" along the upper edge of the label.

Next were the ST-3900 series. Original editions were issued with purple labels, silver print. Some were reissued in the 1970s with a yellow label, a rainbow band curving around the top edge and "Disneyland" in white on the rainbow.

The next series was in the ST-1900 range. Original editions of these have light blue labels with black print; some later originals and first reissues have a darker blue label; the final reissues have green labels.

The next, and most common, series was the DQ-1200 and 1300 series. Original issues have yellow labels with black print, "Disneyland" curving along the top. Reissues from the 1970s and 1980s have the yellow rainbow label and usually omit the "DQ."

A 1970s and 1980s line was the 2500 series; all of these come with the yellow rainbow label.

## Dolton

1959-1962: Light blue label, dark blue print with fish logos at left of center hole.

1965-1965: Darker blue label, multicolor fish logo to the left of the center hole.

1966-1968: Mostly black label, blue section to left of center hole with stylized red-and-black "D" in white background.

## Dore

1960s: Light blue label, feather at top.
1970s: Dark blue label, larger feather on top.
1970s: Black label, multicolor logo.

## Dot

1954-1956: Maroon label, silver print, "Gallatin, Tenn." address on label. A possible transition label, maroon with "Hollywood, Calif." address on label, may exist. (45s exist with that label.)

1956-1968: Black label, script "Dot" in multi-color letters at top.

1968-1970: Black label, both "DOT" and Paramount logos appear at top of label.

1971-1974: Purple and orange label, "DOT" in box at top of label.

Mid 1974-1975: Multi-color (yellow, orange, purple) "target" label with "abc Dot Records" at top of label between two lines.

1976-1977: Multi-color (yellow, orange, purple) "target" label with "abc Dot" at top of label between two lines.

## Duke

1955 (70): Yellow and purple label, "DUKE" in yellow on purple background.

1957-1962 (71-75): Yellow and purple label, "DUKE" in yellow on purple background, purple stripe around the outside of the yellow part of the label.

1963-1970 (76-92): Orange label, fading to yellow toward the center hole.

1970s (reissues): Green label.

## Dunhill

1965-1968 (50000=50030s): Black label, "DUNHILL" in white at top with gold border around it.

1968-1972 (50030s-50170s): Black label, 'DUNHILL" and "abc" in multi-color boxes at top.

Early 1973: "DUNHILL" in a white rectangle at top of black label, spelled out in children's blocks; a very short-lived label. This was quickly replaced by the 1968-72 label until a new design could be created.

1974-1975: Multi-color (yellow, orange, purple) "target" label with "abc Dunhill" at top of label between two lines.

## Elektra

1950s: White label with "electron" logo.

Late 1950s-1961?: Gray label, small guitar player on top.

1961?-1966?: Gold label, large guitar player on top.

1966-1969: Gold (tan) label with large stylized "E" at top.

1969-1970: Red label with large stylized "E" on top.

1971-1974: Dark greenish label with butterfly holding stylized "E" logo at left, "13 Columbus Circle" address on label.

1975-1979: Lighter greenish label with butterfly holding stylized "E" logo at left, "W" (Warner Communications) logo added to the fine print.

1980-1983: Red label, small white stylized "E" at top.

1984-1989: Red and black label, "ELEKTRA" across top.

1989-1991: Gray label.

1991-2000s: Tan label.

Custom labels were used for some releases.

## Ember

1958 (100, 200, 300, 400): Red label, black print.

1959 (401, reissues of earlier titles): White label, black print, eight circles around the outside of the label. The word "EMBER" is depicted in burning logs.

1960s (reissues): Black label, silver print.

1960s (800 series): Black label, "EMBER" logo at left with red flames emanating from it.

## EMI America/EMI Manhattan/EMI

1978-1980: Green label.

1980-1987: Gray label.

1987-1988 (EMI Manhattan): White label, yellow and black design elements.

1989-end (EMI): Bluish label.

## End

All End LPs (301-316) were issued with a gray label, a front end of a dog at left, the back end of a dog at right and "end" in red letters. The words "A Product of End Music Inc., New York, N.Y." are at the bottom.

Reissues have the same basic design, but "A Division of Roulette Records, Inc." is the new fine print.

Still later reissues have a light blue label with an orange band through the center hole and the word "END" in blue on either end of the band.

## Enjoy

The only album released on this label has a gold label with blue print.

## Enterprise

1967-1968 (13-100 series): Blue label, rainbow at top with "ENTERPRISE" over the rainbow in black. These were distributed by Atlantic.

1968-1972 (1001-1024, 5000-5002): Black label, "ENTERPRISE" in yellow at top.

1972-1974 (1025-1038; 5003-5007; 7501-7510): Black label, "ENTERPRISE" in white directly above the center hole, colorful stylized "E" logo at top.

## Epic

1955-1962: Yellow label, black lines around outside of label and "EPIC" on top. Some early labels also are gold with a similar design. Stereo issues (1959-1962) have the same label but with a "Stereorama" above the word "Epic" on the top of the label.

1962-1963: Yellow label with "Epic" appearing eight times around the perimeter (mono); yellow label with "Epic Stereo" appearing three times around the perimeter (stereo).

1965-1965 (24040s-24160s mono, 26040s-26160s stereo): Yellow label, "A Product of CBS" as part of the fine print.

1965-1973 (all later monos, stereos into the 31000s): Yellow label, no "A Product of CBS" at bottom.

1973-1979: Orange label with white concentric circles and small white "e" and "Epic" at top.

1979-present: Dark blue label (not black), script "Epic" logo at top.

Some Epic LPs have custom labels.

## Excello

1960-mid 1960s (8000-8005?): Orange label, blue print.

Mid 1960s-early 1970s: White label, black print, pink and green arrows at top of label.

Early 1970s-1976: Light blue label, "excello" in white background in box.

## Famous

A reissue label for Keen material, the label was blue with silver print.

## Fantasy

*10-Inch LPs*

All of these have maroon labels with gold print. All were pressed on various shades of vinyl as well as black vinyl. Versions exist on red, blue, green, purple and even combinations of more than one color.

*12-Inch LPs (mono)*

Mono albums were originally numbered with a 3- prefix and starting at 200. Eventually, the dash was dropped and these became the 3200 series. All of these should have red labels with gold print, though some near the end of the mono series may have red labels with silver print. The below dates are approximate; we don't know at what numbers the changes occurred.

1955-1957: Records are deep red vinyl, almost maroon

1957-1958: Original pressings are on black vinyl. It is unknown how many records first issued on red vinyl between 1955 and 1957 were reissued at this time.

1958-1963: Original pressings are on bright red vinyl.

1963-1967: Original pressings are on black vinyl.

*12-Inch LPs (stereo)*

Stereo albums were numbered in the 8000s originally. With a change in the list price of LPs in the early 1970s, the "8" became a '9" on new issues.

Early 1960s-1963: Original pressings have a blue label with gold print, and the records are on bright blue vinyl.

1963-1972: Original pressings have a blue label with gold print and are on black vinyl. Some of the later issues have blue labels with silver print. Also, as one gets closer to 1972, the vinyl tends to get flimsier.

1972-1974: Brown label with circular stylized "F" logo at top. Lighter brown horizontal and vertical bars form the same "F" logo on the entire label.

1974-1978: Brown label with circular stylized "F" logo at top, with no lighter brown bars.

1978-early 1980s: Blue fading to white label with lightning bolts around the circular stylized "F" at the top.

Early 1980s on: Blue label with purple stylized "F" at top.

Some reissues in the "OJC" series use the label that was contemporary for the time when it was first released. The prefix and new number give away their reissue status.

Colored vinyl note

When Fantasy was doing red vinyl mono LPs and blue vinyl stereo LPs at the same time, sometimes the signals got crossed. We know of examples with blue labels and red vinyl; and we also know of records with red labels and blue vinyl. We do not yet know if the sound of the record matches the label or the vinyl color. These are uncommon, and unlike most "error pressings," these are quite collectible.

## Federal

Early 10-inch albums have all-green labels, "Federal" in silver across the top.

Albums in the 500 series have black labels with silver print and the word "Federal" straight across the top of the label. These are among the rarest and most valuable albums in all of record collecting. Federal 12-inch LPs with green labels and silver tops appear to be bootlegs.

## Felsted

All Felsted albums have orange labels with black print.

## Fire

1959-1960 (100-101): White label, red print.

1960-1962 (102-105): Red label, black print.

## Flip

Two albums, both of which were various-artists sets, were released on Flip. They have blue labels with silver print.

## Forum/Forum Circle

This budget label reissued material that first appeared on the Roulette label.

1960 (16000 series): Black label, gold print.

1961-1963 (9000 series): Mono issues have maroon labels; stereo issues have red labels.

1964 (Forum Circle series): Mono issues have light blue labels; stereo issues have yellow labels.

## Fraternity

1950s (1001-1012?): Light blue label.

Early 1960s (1013?-1018?): Red label, black print

Mid to late 1960s and beyond (1019?-1028): Maroon label, silver print.

## Fury

Two albums were issued on this label. Both have yellow labels with black print and a horse-in-a-tornado logo.

## Gee

1956-1959 (701-704): Red label, black print, "GEE" in large red letters in a black background on top.

1961-1962 (705-707): Gray label, "GEE RECORDS" across the bottom.

## Geffen

1980-1985: White label with horizontal pinstripes.

1985-1990s: Black label.

## Golden World

One album was issued on this label; it has a yellow label with black print.

## Goldwax

Only two albums are known to have been released on this label in the United States. Both are yellow with black print.

## Gone

All LPs on this label, which had LP releases from 1958 to 1961, have pink and tan labels.

## Gordy

1962-1967 (901-927?): Purple label, "Gordy" in cursive yellow at top superimposed over an oval with the slogan "IT'S WHAT'S IN THE GROOVES THAT COUNT."

1968-1980s (928? and forward): Purple label, "GORDY" in purple to left of center hole, yellow wedge going through center hole from left to right.

## Guaranteed

The only album issued on this label has a white label with black print and "GUARANTEED" in red, arc-shaped, at the top of the label.

## Guyden

Three albums were released on this label. All of them a purple label with a silver strip at the top, in which "Guyden Records" appears in purple print next to a torch.

## Harmony

This was Columbia's budget LP label from the mid-1950s to the early 1970s.

1957-early 1960s: Maroon label, silver print.

Early 1960s-late 1960s: Black label, silver print.

Late 1960s-early 1970s: Brown label.

Early 1970s: Gold label, Harmony logo in red.

## Herald

1955-1958 (0100-0111): "Spokes label": Multi-colored spokes emanate from the center hole to the outside. Above the center hole is a yellow trumpet with a yellow banner and "HERALD" in black print.

1960 (1012): Black label, silver print.

1960-1962 (1013-1015): Yellow label, silver print.

## Hickory

1960-1962 (100-110?): Black label, silver print, "Hickory" slants upward at top of label.

1963-1973 (111?-168): Black label, rainbow at upper left.

1973-1975 (4501-4524): Brown label, rainbow at upper left, "MGM Records" lion at right of center hole.

1976-1977 (44001-44009?): Multi-color (yellow, orange, purple) "target" label with "abc Records" at top of label between two lines and the "Hickory" logo at left of center hole.

1977-1979 (44010?-44017): Multi-color (yellow, orange, purple) "target" label with "abc" in an eighth note at top of label and the "Hickory" logo to the right of the note.

## HiFi

Standard issues have silver labels with "HIFIRECORD" three times around the perimeter. The word "HIFI" is in silver, "RECORD" is in red. Also see LIFE.

## Hip

Four albums came out on this label from 1969-1972. The label is red and pink with "Hip" in blue print bordered in black.

## Horizon

The folk music label of 1961-1964, distributed by Vee Jay for part of that time, issued its mono albums on black labels with silver print (sometimes white print) and its stereo albums on dark blue labels with silver print.

## Hull

Three albums came out on this label, each of them highly desirable. Each one had a different label:

1000: Dark red label, black print.

1001: Light blue label, black print.

1002: Red label, black print, "Hull Records Inc." in gold above the center hole.

## Impact

One label was issued on Impact; it has a red label with black print.

## Imperial

1950-1956 (10-inch LPs, 12-inch LPs in the 100 series): Blue label, script "IMPERIAL" at top.

1956-1957 (9001-9041?): Red label, block "IMPERIAL" in silver letters at top.

1957-1964 (9042?-9267? mono): Black label with colored rays emanating from white "IMPERIAL" logo at top.

1959-1964 (12001-12267? stereo): Black label, silver print, with "IMPERIAL STEREO" directly above the center hole. Some of the later 12250-12267 labels have the mono "colored rays" label with the word "Stereo" added.

1964-1966 (9268?-9320s mono, 12268?-12320s stereo): Black label, "IR/Imperial" to left of center hole, white area above logo, pink area below logo.

1966-1970 (9320s to end of monos, 12320s-12457): Black label, "IR/Imperial" logo to left of center hole in white with red background, green areas above and below logo, which has been enlarged.

## Impulse!

1961-1968 (1-100 and 9101-at least 9124): Orange label, wide black ring around outside, eith the word "impulse!" appearing four times in the black area.

1968-1972: Black label, red border, "impulse!" and "abc" in multicolored boxes at top.

1973-1974: Black label, no red border, "impulse" in multicolored letters, "impulse" and "abc" in boxes at top.

1974-1977: Multicolored (green, blue, purple) "target" label with "abc Impulse" at top of label between two lines.

1978-1979: Multicolored (yellow, red, purple) "target" label with "abc" musical note standing along and "Impulse" at top of label between two lines.

1980s reissues I: Records in the MCA-29000 series had MCA blue labels with a rainbow, with a small "impulse!" logo above "MCA RECORDS."

1980s reissues II: Some reissues have a black and red label with "MCA impulse!" in white just under the 9 o'clock position.

1990s reissues: Orange label, narrow black ring around outside, "impulse!" in black at 3 o'clock.

## Interphon

One album came out on the label. It is light blue with a red logo to the left of the center hole.

## Indigo

Black label, silver print, the word "Indigo" in indigo (purple) letters and "Records" next to it in blue.

## Infinity (pop)

In business for just over a year (late 1978 to late 1979), it lasted long enough to have two label variations. The earliest LPs have a primarily white label with "optical illusion" logo at the top. Later LPs have a primarily brown label with a slightly different rendering of the "optical illusion" logo.

## Island

Since the label was first set up as a U.S. entity in 1972, it's been distributed by Capitol, independently, by Warner Bros. and Atco (at the same time for different artists!), PolyGram and Universal Music Group. The labels have changed even more often than the distribution, and it's possible this list is incomplete.

1972-1974: Sunray label, "ISLAND" along bottom of label in stylized letters.

1974-1975: Yellow background on label, "water skier" offshore, "island" along top.

1975-1977: Black label with "i" logo at bottom and "Island Records" underneath.

1977-1980: Orange and blue label.

1981-1982: Light blue label with a darker blue ring around the outside.

1982-1983: Dark purple label with skyscraper at left and "Island" sloping upward.

1983-1984: Light blue label, "Island" in red across top.

1985-1990: Black label, logo at bottom.

1990s-2000s: Most have black labels with Island logo at top.

## Jamie

1958: Yellow label.

1959-1967: White and yellow label, "jamie" vertically at left.

1970 (3034): Orange and black label.

## Janus

1970-1977 (3000s, early 7000s): Brownish-gold label.

1977-1978 (later 7000s): Reddish orange label.

## Josie

The first label was cream colored with blue print and "josie" at the top of the label in a blue oval.

The second label was tan with black print with the "josie" logo in a black oval. The logo sits atop a group of multicolored stripes emanating vertically from a horizontal white line that goes through the center hole.

The third label was tan with black print, "JOSIE" spelled in five different colors vertically to the left of the center hole.

## Jubilee

1950s (10-inch LPs from 1-25, 12-inch LPs from 1000-1014?): Pink label, black print.

1956-1959 (1015?-1104?): Blue label, silver print.

1959-1961 (1105?-1121?): Flat black label, silver print, "jubilee" in silver spiked oval at top.

1961-1964 (5001-5055): Glossy black label, silver print, "jubilee" in large colored spike oval at top.

1965-1969 (8001-8031): Glossy black label, silver print, smaller colored spiked oval at top.

## Judd

The one LP on this label has a purple label with silver print.

## Kama Sutra

1965-1969: Yellow label.

1970-1971: Pink label.

1972-1974: Light blue label, Garden of Eden scene at top.

## Kapp

1955-1959: Maroon label, silver print. Some issues have a blue label, silver print.

1959-1962: Black and blue label with red "K" at top of label and "KAPP" underneath.

1962-1964: Black and blue label with white major's hat and "KAPP" underneath.

1964-1971: All-black label with white major's hat and "KAPP" underneath.

1971-1973: Orange and purple label.

MCA merged Decca, Kapp and Uni in January 1973 and closed down all three.

Custom labels were used on some issues. For example, there are some early Christmas releases with silver labels and red and green holly leaves adorning the outside of the label.

## Keen

1958-1959 (2000 series): Colored vertical stripes with letters of "KEEN" in individual gray circles.

1959-1960 (86100 series): Black label, "KEEN" to left of center hole, five-color vertical stripe next to it.

## King

At first glance, this label looks confusing. Even more interesting is the wide disparity in asking prices between what appear to be trivial differences in the size and style of logo.

Early to mid 1950s (10-inch LPs): Maroon label, silver print, "KING" in a straight line at the top of the label.

1955-early 1960s (500-late 600s): Black label, silver print; the word "KING" curves along the outside top of the label and is about two inches wide.

Early 1960s-mid 1960s (late 600s-unknown): Black label, silver print; the word "KING" curves along the outside top of the label and is about three inches wide (the letters are thicker and more stretched out than the earlier version).

Late 1950s-mid 1960s (stereo editions): Blue label, silver print; the word "KING" curves along the outside top of the label and is about three inches wide.

Mid 1960s-early 1970s: Blue label, silver print, "KING" straight across the top with a crown centered above the "I" and "N."

Late 1960s: James Brown LPs have a custom brown and orange label with his face on it.

Early 1970s (1146-1154): Yellow label with sitting king right of the center hole.

Mid 1970s (16000 series): Yellow label with "KING" vertically at top of label and two protrusions to form a stylized letter "K" coming from it.

Late 1970s (5000 series): Restores blue crowned King label of the mid- to late-1960s.

## Kirshner

Successor to Calendar Records.

1969-mid 1970s: Orange label, 'KIRSHNER" in individual boxes across the top.

Mid 1970s-early 1980s (CBS distribution): White label with multi-color top.

Custom labels were used on some CBS albums.

## KoKo

Mostly a custom label for Luther Ingram, these albums have white labels with the word "KOKO" on both sides of the center hole in alternating yellow, red, purple and blue labels.

## Laurie

1959 (1000-1002): Gold label, black print.

1960-1980s (1003-1010; 2002-2052; 4000 series): Gold "pentagram" in center of label with black background surrounding it. Early pressings tend to be quite firm and substantial, and some seem to be almost brittle; later pressings tend to have glossier labels and flimsier wax.

## Legrand

Original issues have red and gold labels with no crown on top. Legrand reissued most of its LPs in the 1980s, and these are easily distinguished by the white band through the center hole and the crown on the label.

## Liberty

1956-1960 (3001-3140? mono): Turquoise label, silver print, "LIBERTY" at top of label with drawing of Statue of Liberty above.

1958-1960 (early 7000s stereo to 7140?): Black label, silver print, "LIBERTY" at top of label with Statue of Liberty drawing above, huge word "STEREO" just below the logo.

1960-1966 (3141?-3420? mono, 7141?-7420? stereo): Black label, rainbow colored area left of center hole, "LIBERTY" in white over a gold crest left of center hole.

1960-1969 (12000 mono and 14000 stereo "Premier Series"): Gold label, black print, design similar to above except that black lines replace the rainbow area.

1966-1969 (3421?-end of mono, 7421?-7620? stereo): Black label, rainbow colored area left of center hole, white vertical line abutting rainbow area, "LIBERTY" in black inside a rounded white box with a Statue of Liberty graphic.

1970-1971 (7620?-end of original series): Black label, rainbow colored area left of center hole, white vertical line abutting rainbow area, "LIBERTY" in black inside a squared-off white box with a Statue of Liberty graphic, "Liberty/UA Inc." at bottom of label.

1980-1986 (reactivated label; 1000-51100 series and 10000 reissue series): Gray label, multicolored "Liberty" across top.

Custom labels were used for some issues, most notably 1960s issues by the Chipmunks, which have black labels with cartoon renditions of Alvin, Theodore, Simon and David Seville. For albums originally released in 1962 and earlier, these are reissues.

## Life (HiFi)

Actually the "Hifi Life Series," but because of the prominence of the word "Life" on the label, most collectors call this the Life label.

Original issues have a red label with the word "Life" in cursive white letters. Later issues have either a yellow or gold label with a smaller "Life" in black letters.

## London (pop)

London releases can be confusing. At times, its records for release in the United States were pressed in both the U.S. and England, and different labels were used in each country. The following applies to pop releases only – classical releases are a different ballgame. By the 1980s, most, if not all, London classical releases were being pressed in Europe, even those meant for sale in the United States.

*10-Inch Albums*

Early to mid-1950s: Some have deep blue labels with gold print; some have red labels with gold print.

*12-Inch Mono Albums*

Mid 1950s-1964 ("LL" prefix until about 3380): Deep red label, silver print, "LONDON" in cursive capital letters across the top with an "ffrr" ear above the "LONDON." Two horizontal silver lines go through the center hole; between these lines are the words "Full Frequency Range Recording."

1964-1965 (about 3380-3430): Deep red label, silver print, "LONDON" in a rounded parallelogram (box) with the "ffrr" ear to the right of this, All of these have print that says "Made in England by the Decca Record Co. Ltd." and have upside-down matrix numbers on the label.

1964-1965 (about 3380-3460): Deep red label, silver print, "LONDON" stands alone, unboxed, above the center hole. These labels have print that says "Made in U.S.A." Both the above two labels ran at the same time, thus neither is more "original" than the other, but the "ffrr" pressings are much more rare.

1966-1968 (about 3460 to end): Varying shades of red labels (1966s tend to be bright red, 1967s almost maroon) with "LONDON" in a box at the top.

*Stereo Albums*

1959-1964 ("PS" series to about 379): Deep blue label, silver print, "LONDON" in cursive capital letters across the top with an "ffss" ear above the "LONDON." Underneath this, in a silver box with blue type, are the words "Full Frequency Stereophonic Sound." The earliest stereos have blue shaded back cover slicks; these are known among audiophiles as "blue backs" and command a premium.

1964-1965 (about 380-430): Deep blue label, silver print, "LONDON" in a rounded parallelogram (box) with the "ffss" ear to the right of this, All of these have print that says "Made in England by the Decca Record Co. Ltd." and have upside-down matrix numbers on the label.

1964-1965 (about 380-460): Deep blue label, silver print, "LONDON" stands alone, unboxed, above the center hole. These labels have print that says "Made in U.S.A." Both the above two labels ran at the same time, thus neither is more "original" than the other, but the "ffss" pressings are much more rare.

1966-1978 (about 460-early 700s): Varying shades of blue labels (earlier ones are much richer blue than later ones) with "LONDON" in a box at top.

Some later London LPs until the early 1980s have a "sunrise" label. Later London pop labels (1980s) are white with red trim and "LONDON" in white inside a black upside-down triangle.

## Lucky Eleven

One album was issued on this label. It has a yellowish label with a greenish horseshoe in the background.

## Luniverse

One album was issued on this label. It has a yellow label with black print.

## Mainstream

1960s: Silvery-blue label.

1970s: Red and black label, "Red Lion Productions" at upper right, "Mainstream" at upper left.

## MCA

1972 (2100): All-black label, white print; appears to have been used only on this number.

1973-1977: Black label, silver print, rainbow at upper left.

1977-1979: Tan label, darker tan circle around outside.

1980-later 1990s: Light blue label, rainbow at upper left.

Late 1990s: White label, new "MCA/Music Corporation of America" logo left of center hole.

A few MCA albums have custom labels.

## Mercury (pop)

1949-1955 (25000 series, all 10-inch LPs): Black label, silver print, "MERCURY" curving around outside of top of label.

1955-early 1960s (12-inch mono, 20000-20700s, also stereo from 60000 to 60700s): Black label, silver print, "MERCURY" stands alone at top, no print along lower edge of label.

Early 1960s-1965 (20700s-20900s mono, 60700s-60900s stereo): Black label, silver print, "Mercury" in an oval. Some of these issues add "Vendor: Mercury Record Corporation" along the lower edge.

1965-1968 (20900s to end of mono, 60900s-61200? stereo): Red label, "MERCURY" is all capital letters across top with Mercury head at upper left.

1968-1972 (61200?-61300s? and early SRM-1 series to about 670): Bright red label, twelve "Mercury" logos along the outer rim of label.

1973-1974 (SRM-1-670 to 999?): Bright red label, seven "Mercury" logos along the outer rim of label.

Mid 1974-early 1983: Chicago skyline label.

Early 1983-1996: Black label, "Mercury" in neon-effect red letters across top.

1996-present: Black label, "Mercury" in white inside a red diamond at top.

Some Mercury LPs have custom labels or "retro" labels.

## Mercury (Classical Living Presence)

1950s-early 1960s: Flat maroon label, "MERCURY" stands alone, no print along lower rim.

Early 1960s-mid 1960s: Flat maroon label, "MERCURY" stands alone, "Vendor: Mercury Recordi Corporation" added to label print.

Mid 1960s-early 1970s: Glossy maroon label, "Mercury" in oval logo at top.

## MGM

1949-1959 (10-inch LPs and 12-inch LPs to approximately 3770): Yellow label, black trim and print.

1960-1968 (3771?-4515?): Black label, multicolor letters across top.

1968-1976 (4516? into 5000s): Blue and gold swirl label.

Except for a very few releases, MGM ceased to exist as a record label in 1976; its material became part of the growing PolyGram empire.

## Minit

1961-1963 (0001-0004): Orange label, black print.

1964-1968 (24005-24023? mono, 40005-40023? stereo): Black label, silver print, "MINIT" logo to left of center hole, "A Product of Liberty Records" along bottom.

1968-1969 (40024?-40028): Same as above, but "Liberty/UA Records" is the new perimeter print.

## Monument

1959 (4000 mono and 14000 stereo only): White label, gray to black vertical stripes, "MONUMENT" above center hole in black with gold trim.

1960-1962 (4001-4009 mono, 14001-14009 stereo): White label with copper swirl, "Monument" at top, Washington Monument right of center hole.

1963 (8000-8004? mono, 18000-18004? stereo): White label with multi-color swirl, "Monument" at top, Washington Monument right of center hole.

1963-1971 (8005?-end of mono, 18005?-18147? stereo): Light green label, gold band around rim, stylized blue, pink and yellow Washington Monument above "monument" at top of label.

1971-1976 (30000 series, CBS distribution): Dark orange, almost brown, label.

1977-1981 (6600, 7600, 8600 series): Black label with "MONUMENT" spelled out in simulated stone-carved letters across the top.

1982-1983 (38000 series): Silver label.

## Motown

1961 (1000): White label, blue print, large blue "M" at top center that serves to turn the two O's in "MOTOWN" on their sides.

1961-1962 (1001-1006): Blue label with map on upper half of the label. The original map stretches from western Kansas to the Atlantic coast with a red star over Detroit.

1962-1980s (1007 on): Blue label with map on upper half of label. This map stretches only from mid-Indiana to mid-Pennsylvania. This design remained basically unchanged into the 1980s, with only changes in perimeter print. There is also more yellow in the word "MOTOWN" in 1970s and 1980s pressings than in 1960s pressings, where the letters fade from red to yellow to blue. Later pressings never make it all the way to the same rich blue as earlier versions.

## Mowest

A short-lived Motown label of the early 1970s, all of its LPs have a beach-at-sunset label with the top and bottom parts in orange and the middle in light blue.

## Muse

Not the 1970s and 1980s jazz label, this came from the Ember-Herald family and was black with silver print.

## Musicor

1962: Brown label.
1962-1969: Black label.
1970-1975?: Tan label.
1976?-end: Green and yellow label.

## Mustang

Red label, black print. Two albums were issued on Mustang, both by the Bobby Fuller Four.

## Nasco

This label apparently didn't issue LPs until the later 1960s; several of these are sought-after by psychedelic music collectors. The label is black with silver print.

## Ode

1967-1970: Yellow label, "Ode" logo in black print left of the center hole.

1970-1971: White and silver label, "Ode 70" at upper right.

1971-1975: White and silver label, "Ode Records" at upper right.

1975-1978: Tan label with both Ode and Epic logos.

## Okeh

Though the label was around for a long time, Okeh albums were issued only from 1962 through 1969. All labels are purple with the familiar cursive "Okeh" logo in gold above the center hole.

## Paramount

Not to be confused with ABC-Paramount, this was an entirely unrelated label established around 1969.

Most, if not all, original issues have a gray label with Paramount logo to the left of the center hole in black. Some 1970s reissues, after ABC bought the rights to the label, have a blue label with a white "Paramount" logo at the top.

## Parkway

1960-1961 (7001-7005?): Orange label, "PARKWAY" in uneven black letters across top.

1961-1967 (7006?-7057): Orange and yellow label, "PARKWAY" in white letters straight across the top. Some of these have lyre figures on either side of "PARKWAY" and others don't.

1967 (50,000): Gold label, black "P" at top with a white line in the middle of the "P."

## Parrot

Except for some subtle perimeter print changes, this label was the same from 1964-1976: Black with a colored bird left of the center hole and the word "parrot" in yellow at the upper right.

## Peacock

Almost entirely a gospel label, it had three distinct label designs.

The first label was black with silver print, "PEACOCK" in silver above the center hole, with a drawing of a peacock in black over the logo.

The second label, after ABC picked up distribution, was also black with silver print, but "PEACOCK" was now in white and the peacock drawing was in color.

The third label, starting in 1974, had a multi-colored "target" label with "abc Peacock" at top between two lines.

## Phil-L.A. of Soul

Two albums were issued, both with light yellow labels and black print.

## Philips (pop)

The below does not apply to classical LPs issued on the Philips label in the 1980s. Most of those were pressed overseas, usually in The Netherlands, then exported to the U.S. for sale.

The basic label stayed the same from 1962 through the early 1970s. It was black with the "PHILIPS" shield above the center hole. The changes all had to do with the perimeter print, as follows:

1962-1963: "Chicago 1, Illinois" at bottom.

1963-1966: "Vendor: Mercury Record Corporation" at bottom.

1966-1970: No perimeter print at bottom.

1970-1974: "Manufactured and Distributed by Mercury" at bottom.

## Philles

1962-1963 (4001-4005): Light blue label with black print.

1964-1966 (4006-4011): Yellow and red label.

## Phillips International

All the LPs issued on this label have a blue world map with a red, white and blue banner across the top. Over the banner it says "Sam C. Phillips International Corp."

## Pickwick

A budget label, most of the albums on this label are common and rarely fetch more than single digits – even the Elvis ones! A couple exceptions are a 1967 Simon and Garfunkel compilation and a 1980 Doobie Brothers collection of demos.

From the mid-1960s to about 1976, the label was silver with black print. Starting around 1976 into the early 1980s, the label was black with a multicolored Pickwick logo.

## Polydor

Labels are red from 1969 into the 1990s, with the only changes taking place in the perimeter print. Orange label Polydor LPs are imports.

## Portrait

1976-early 1980s: Gray label.

1980s: Black label.

Custom labels were used on some releases.

## Rama

Labels are dark blue with silver print.

## Rare Earth

1969 (505-509): The lower half of the label is white. The upper half has an orange background, a drawing of a tree and the words "RARE EARTH" in white. This label was later used as the promo label, but for the first editions of these LPs, it was also the stock label.

1970-1976 (511-550): All-orange label with a drawing of a tree and the words "RARE EARTH" in white.

## RCA Camden

This was RCA Victor's budget label.

1954-1957: Pink label.

1957-1964: Blue label, purple perimeter.

1964-1968: Light blue label, dark blue perimeter.

1969-1975: All-blue label with "RCA" turned on its side at left and "Camden" right of the center hole.

Most Camden titles still in print in 1975 were reissues with the same number on Pickwick.

## RCA Special Products

Before 1973, there was no label with this official name. Special-products issues on RCA were easily identifiable by the prefix "PR," "PRM" or "PRS" before a three-digit number.

The earliest of these (early 1960s-1968) have a flat black label and silver print, "RCA Victor" in silver and an outline of the Nipper logo in silver underneath.

The next series of these (1968-1973) have a tan, almost maize, label, with "RCA" on its side left of the center hole, "Victor" to the right of the center hole, and no dog.

When the entire RCA catalog began using alphanumeric prefixes in 1973, RCA Special Products got its own series. These begin, for the most part, with "DPL1." Early label colors vary; some are green, some are light blue. By 1977 the label was black with the full Nipper logo at 1 o'clock, "RCA Special Products" on two lines in white to the left of the dog.

## RCA/RCA Victor (pop)

Another long and involved label with sometimes overlapping label designs. We welcome any corrections or clarifications. The below only apply to pop albums; Red Seal records are treated elsewhere.

*10-Inch Albums*

1950-1955: Most pop albums have black labels with silver print. A silver ring goes all the way around the label. The words "RCA VICTOR" are along the upper edge above the silver ring. An outline of Nipper is under the silver ring at top. Some albums of this period also have green labels with silver print; reissues of older material had silver-gray labels with red print.

*Mono 12-Inch Albums*

Before 1955 (early 1000s): Black labels with silver print; silver ring goes all the way around the label; the words "RCA VICTOR" are along the upper edge above the silver ring; an outline of Nipper is under the silver ring at top.

1955-1963 (mid 1000s-2700s): Shiny black label, "RCA VICTOR" in silver with full-bodied Nipper underneath. The bottom of the label says "LONG 33 1/3 PLAY."

1963-1964 (2700s-2999): Shiny black label, "RCA VICTOR" in white with full Nipper logo. The bottom of the label says "MONO" in some cases; others have an extra-bold "DYNAGROOVE" across the bottom with the word "MONO" in much smaller print on either side.

1965-1968 (3300s-early 4000s): Shiny black label, "RCA VICTOR" is much larger in white along top of label, the Nipper logo is slightly smaller underneath. Along the bottom is either "MONAURAL" or "MONO DYNAGROOVE."

*Stereo 12-Inch Albums*

1958-1963 (2000s-2700s): Shiny black label, "RCA VICTOR" in silver with full-bodied Nipper underneath. The bottom of the label says "LIVING STEREO."

1963-1964 (2700s-2999): Shiny black label, "RCA VICTOR" in white with full Nipper logo. The bottom of the label says "STEREO" in some cases; others have an extra-bold "DYNAGROOVE" across the bottom with the word "STEREO" in much smaller print on either side. This series also had the first rechanneled stereo releases, all of which had numbers before 2000; they have the extra-bold word "STEREO" at the bottom with "Electronically Reprocessed" underneath.

1965-1968 (3300s-early 4000s): Shiny black label, "RCA VICTOR" is much larger in white along top of label, the Nipper logo is slightly smaller underneath. Along the bottom is either "STEREO," "STEREO DYNAGROOVE" or "STEREO Electronically Reprocessed."

1969-1971 (early 4000s-about 4460): Orange label on rigid, non-flexible vinyl, "RCA" on its side to left of center hole, "Victor" to right of center hole, no dog logo.

1971-1976 (4460?-APL1-1000 or so): Orange label on so-called "Dynaflex" vinyl, "RCA" on its side to left of center hole, "Victor" to right of center hole, no dog logo.

1974-1976 (early APL1 series): Tan label, released simultaneously with above orange label. Tan labels were used in Indianapolis, which explains why most of these are found in the East, and the orange labels were used in Hollywood, which explains why these are more often found in the West.

1976-late 1980s: Black label, Nipper logo is restored and appears at 1 o'clock. "RCA" is now above the center hole to the left of Nipper, "Victor" is on its side to the left of the center hole.

Late 1980s-1990s and beyond: Mostly red label with circular "RCA" logo in black background at top. There are other variations as well. It was not until this label that the word "Victor" was dropped from pop LPs.

Custom labels were used on some releases.

## RCA/RCA Victor (Red Seal Classical)

*10-Inch Albums*

1950-1955: Red labels with silver print. A silver ring goes all the way around the label. The words "RCA VICTOR" are along the upper edge above the silver ring. Just under the silver ring are the words "RED SEAL RECORD." Under this is an outline of Nipper.

*Mono 12-Inch Albums*

Before 1955: Red labels with silver print; silver ring goes all the way around the label; the words "RCA VICTOR" are along the upper edge above the silver ring; "RED SEAL RECORD" just under the ring; outline of Nipper is under those words.

1955-1958: Maroon label, "RCA VICTOR" in silver with full-bodied Nipper logo underneath. The bottom of the label says "LONG 33 1/3 PLAY."

1958-1963: Deep red label, "RCA VICTOR" in white with full-bodied Nipper underneath. Behind the Nipper logo is a darker red area, thus leading to the nickname "shaded dog" for these pressings. The bottom of the label says "LONG 33 1/3 PLAY." These, usually with an "LM" prefix, are worth a fraction of their stereo "LSC" counterparts!

1963-1964: Deep red label, "RCA VICTOR" in white with full Nipper logo. The bottom of the label says "MONO" in some cases; others have an extra-bold "DYNAGROOVE" across the bottom with the word "MONO" in much smaller print on either side.

1965-1968: Red label, "RCA VICTOR" is much larger in white along top of label, the Nipper logo is slightly smaller underneath. Along the bottom is either "MONAURAL" or "MONO DYNAGROOVE." Collectors call these editions "white dogs."

*Stereo 12-Inch Albums*

1958-1963: Deep red label, "RCA VICTOR" in silver with full-bodied Nipper underneath. Behind the Nipper logo is a darker red area, thus leading to the nickname "shaded dog" for these pressings. The bottom of the label says "LIVING STEREO." Some of these stereo pressings, most of which start with "LSC," are among the most collectible stereo albums in the world.

1963-1964: Deep red label, "RCA VICTOR" in white with full Nipper logo. The bottom of the label says "STEREO" in some cases; others have an extra-bold "DYNAGROOVE" across the bottom with the word "STEREO" in much smaller print on either side. This series also had the first rechanneled stereo releases, all of which had numbers before 2000; they have the extra-bold word "STEREO" at the bottom with "Electronically Reprocessed" underneath. Although these still have the "shaded dog" motif, they are not as collectible as the "LIVING STEREO" originals.

1965-1968: Red label, "RCA VICTOR" is much larger in white along top of label, the Nipper logo is slightly smaller underneath. Along the bottom is either "STEREO," "STEREO DYNAGROOVE" or "STEREO Electronically Reprocessed." Collectors call these editions "white dogs."

1969-1971: Red label on rigid, non-flexible vinyl, "RCA" on its side to left of center hole, "Red Seal" to right of center hole, no dog logo. This and the next variation are known as "no dog" pressings.

1971-1976: Red label on so-called "Dynaflex" vinyl, "RCA" on its side to left of center hole, "Red Seal" to right of center hole, no dog logo.

1976-late 1980s: Red label, Nipper logo is restored and appears at 1 o'clock. "RCA" is now above the center hole to the left of Nipper, "Red Seal" is on its side to the left of the center hole.

## RCA Dating System

On all albums pressed by any of the RCA pressing plants from the early 1950s through 1972, there is an eight-digit master number, four of which are left of a hyphen, four of which are to the right

For albums first released before 1955, you can tell what year the record was mastered by looking at the first two digits. For albums mastered from 1955-1972, you can tell by looking at the first digit, which will always be a letter.

This won't tell you what year the record was actually pressed, however. For that, you still need to check the label guide, as the same masters were used over and over again once one was deemed OK.

The following works for all RCA family albums, including Red Seal, Camden, Bluebird and Victrola. It also works on non-RCA albums that were pressed at the RCA plants, including custom pressings. So you might want to check some albums on such labels as 20th Fox, Cadence and Motown, just to name three, to see if they have RCA-style master numbers.

Here is the RCA code.

1950-1954: The first two digits of the master number correspond to the following years.

E0: 1950
E1: 1951
E2: 1952
E3: 1953
E4: 1954

1955-1972: RCA altered the code so that only the first digit corresponded to the year.

F: 1955
G: 1956
H: 1957
J: 1958
K: 1959
L: 1960
M: 1961
N: 1962
P: 1963
R: 1964
S: 1965
T: 1966
U: 1967
W: 1968
X: 1969
Z: 1970
A: 1971
B: 1972

After 1972: RCA changed its published master number to the same number as the record number, with an added "A" for side 1 and a "B" for side 2. You can no longer tell the year based on the master number.

## Red Bird

A short-lived label, Red Bird released albums from 1964 to 1966. All have yellow labels with black print. A red bird is above the center hole, and the words "Red" and "Bird" are on either side of it in black.

## Rendezvous

1958-1960 (1301-1310?): Brown label, silver print.

1960-end (1311?-1314): Black label, silver print, "rendezvous records" in white above center hole.

## Reprise

1961-1967 (6001-6280?, 1000-1022?, 2000-2015?): Pink, gold and green label with a large steamboat at the upper left corner and the word "reprise:" on the label at upper right. Albums in the 1000 series, which were Frank Sinatra issues, had his photo on the label instead of the steamboat.

1968-1970 (6281?-6400s, 1024-1029, 2016?-2025?): Two-tone orange label – rich orange at top, duller orange at bottom – with a smaller steamboat, an "r:" logo in a red circle with a "W7" logo overlapping it at its left.

1970-early 1980s (6400s on, 2026?-2200s): All-tan (dull orange) label with steamboat; the "W7" logo is gone, but the "r:" logo remains, this time in a box rather than a circle.

Mid 1980s: Black and red label.

Late 1980s-present: Light blue and maize label.

## Ric-Tic

One album was released on this Detroit label. It has a red label with black print.

## Rising Sons

A short-lived subsidiary of Monument, this label was black with silver print and four colored arrows at upper left.

## Rolling Stones

1971 (59100): Earliest stock copies of this number have white labels.

1971-1984 (all others): Yellow label with red "lips and tongue" logo left of the center hole.

Custom labels exist for some releases.

## Roulette

1957 (25001-25003): Black label, silver print, "ROULETTE" in silver along top, silver roulette wheel under label name.

1957-1959 (25004-25045?): Black label, silver print, "ROULETTE" in white along top, red roulette wheel underneath label name.

1959-1962 (24046?-25180s?): White label, black print, "ROULETTE" in black along top, red, yellow and green "spokes" through center hole.

1962-1963 (25180s?-25230s?): Left side of label is orange, right side is pink; black print, "ROULETTE" in white to left of center hold between two white lines.

1963-1970s (25230s-25361; 42000 and 3000 series): Alternating orange and yellow label in the pattern of a roulette wheel, "ROULETTE" in black near the top of the label.

1980s (59000 series): Alternating orange and yellow label in the pattern of a roulette wheel, "ROULETTE" in green near the top of the label.

Roulette had several other numbering series, most notably the 52000 jazz series. The yearly breakdown holds, but we're not sure where the number breaks are.

## RSO

1973-1975: Peach label, distributed by Atco.

1976-1978: Tan label, distributed by Polydor (has Polydor logo in fine print at bottom).

1978-1981: Tan label, distributed by PolyGram (no Polydor logo in fine print).

1981-1983: Silver label.

## Savoy

1950s-1960s: Maroon label.

1970s reissues: Brown label, "Distributed by Arista."

## Scepter

1961 (501): Red label, "Scepter" in black script and a silver outline.

1962-1971: Red label, black wedge through center hole, "SCEPTER RECORDS" in white in two lines at the left of the center hole.

Early 1970s-1974: Kaleidoscopic label, "SCEPTER RECORDS" in black inside white oval at top of label. As with singles, there might be some overlap between this label and the one before it.

1974-1976: Dark blue label, "SCEPTER" in white.

## Score

A reissue label for Aladdin material, many of these are quite rare, though not nearly as rare as the Aladdin originals. All of these have maroon labels with "SCORE" above the center hole in an oval.

## Shelter

1971-1972: Red label with upside-down Superman logo at left.

1972-1973: Red label with blacked-out upside-down Superman logo at left.

1974-1976 (MCA distribution): Yellow label.

1977-1978 (ABC distribution): Orange label with crescent moon at left.

## Sire

1968-1970 (97000 series): White label, both Sire and London logos at top of label.

1970-1971: Yellow label, blue stylized "S" at top, "Distributed by Polydor Records" in fine print.

1972-1974: Yellow label, blue stylized "S" at top, "Distributed by Famous Music, a G+W Company" in fine print.

1974-1976: Yellow label, blue stylized "S" at top, "Distributed by ABC Records Inc." in fine print.

1977-1980s: Yellow label, blue stylized "S" at top, makes reference to distribution by Warner Bros.

## Smash

1961-1968: Flat red label, "SMASH" at top.

1968-1971: Red label, both "SMASH" and Mercury logos at top.

## Soul

1965-1966 (701-702): White label, black print, "SOUL" printed vertically in purple to the left of the center hole in a light purple background.

1966-1978 (703-751): Label has three circles with three shades of purple. The "SOUL" logo is in white, centered at the top of the label.

## Sound Stage 7

1963-1966 (5000-5003? mono, 15000-15003? stereo): Red label, black print, "SOUND 7 STAGE" above center hole.

1968-1970 (15004?-15009): Black label, "SOUND STAGE" in two rows in white print over a blue "7."

1972-1975 (30000 series): Gold label.

## Specialty

1957 (100): White label with wide black ring around the outside and a narrow yellow ring between the white and black areas. "Specialty" is in yellow cursive letters over the black ring at the top of the label.

1957-1970 (2100-2140s?): Gold label, black print, "Specialty" in gold letters across the top over a black background.

1971-1989 (2140s?-end): Black and white label, "Specialty" in large yellow letters over the black part of the label. This is similar in spirit to the design of the 1950s 45 rpm labels.

## Stax

1962-mid 1968 (701-726): Mono releases have light blue labels with black "STAX" logo at top and pile of records over it. Stereo records have yellow labels with the same logo.

Mid 1968-1972 (2000-2045, 3001): Yellow label with "finger snapping" logo at left; "stax" is in red and logo is in two shades of blue.

1972-1975 (2046-2047, 3002-3024, 5500 series): Yellow label with "finger snapping" logo at left; "stax" is in red and logo is in two shades of brown.

Late 1970s-early 1980s: Purple at top, white at bottom, "finger snapping" logo at left.

Early to late 1980s: Red label, "finger snapping" logo at left.

## Strand

Mostly a budget label, its labels were orange with black print.

## Sue

Early 1960s: Orange label, black print, "Sue RECORDS" in white print left of center hole.

Mid 1960s: Orange label, black print, "Sue RECORDS" in black print left of center hole.

1969 (8801): Red label, black print.

## Sun

1953-1965 (1220-1275): Yellow label, brown print. Musical notes ring the outer edge of the label. Alternating brown and yellow rays emanate from the center hole area. The letters "SUN" are in yellow over the rays. At the bottom of the label, in yellow print with brown background, are the words "Memphis, Tennessee."

Mid to late 1960s (90000 series): Labels are basically identical to the above, but these editions, made for the Capitol Record Club, have black print for the titles and artist.

1968-1986 (100-148, 1000-1035): Yellow label, brown print. Four "targets" are visible in the lower half of the label. The music notes only go around half the label instead of nearly all of it, and at the bottom is "Sun International Corp., A Division of the Shelby Singleton Corp., Nashville, U.S.A."

## Sunset

This was Liberty Records' budget label It has a black label with a light blue area to the left of the label; the "SUNSET" logo is to the left of the center hole.

## Swan

1959-1963 (501-512?): White label, red print.
1963-end (513?-517): Black label, silver print.

## Tamla

1961-1962 (220-231?): White label, black print. Above the center hole is an overlapping globe-record logo with "TAMLA" in an arc above the globe. The oceans of the world and center hole of the record are colored purple.

1962 (229?-233?): Yellow label, black print, otherwise same as above except that the oceans and record hole are colored brown.

1963-1967 (236?-280?): Yellow label, black print, side-by-side record and globe at top of label, "TAMLA" in yellow over the globe.

1968-1980s (281?-end): Yellow label, black print, brown areas at upper left and upper right of label, "TAMLA" logo, with flattened globe above, in box centered at top.

## Teem

Ace imprint; purple label with silver print.

## Three Brothers

A short-lived label, its only release was a 1973 Lou Christie album. It was mostly blue with white and yellow circles that share the same border.

## Threshold

1970-1973 (1-10?): White label, purple logo.
1974-1983 (11?-end): Dark blue label.

## Top Rank

On mono labels, the upper left quadrant of the label is white with a drawing in gold of a man hitting a gong; the other three quadrants of the label are red.

On stereo labels, the upper left quadrant of the label is white with a drawing in red of a man hitting a gong; the other three quadrants of the label are gold.

## Tower

1964-1968: Orange label.
1968-1969: Multi-color striped label.

## Track

1970-1971: Black label, distributed by Atlantic.

1972: Silver label with Decca logo.
1973-1975: Brown label, distributed by MCA.

## 20TH Century/20th Century Fox/ 20th Fox

1958-early 1960s: Light blue "clouds" label, "20th Fox" logo in red at top of label.

Mid 1960s-early 1970s: Black label with gold border, "20th Century Fox Records" logo at top of label. Most of these issues were distributed by ABC.

1972-1977: Light blue label, "20th Century" logo in white at top of label.

1978-early 1980s: Light brown label with added spotlights, logo again changes to "20th Century Fox."

## UNI

This label had two distinct incarnations.

From 1967-1972 it was a quasi-independent division of the MCA family of labels. Labels are yellow with several colored stripes and "uni" at the right. Uni, Kapp and Decca were folded at the end of 1972 into the all-encompassing MCA label.

In the mid-1980s, MCA briefly reactivated Uni. These labels were blue with "uni RECORDS" in two lines in black above the center hole.

## United Artists

1958-1959: Red and black label, "UNITED" at left of center hole, "ARTISTS" at right.

1959: Mono albums had an all-red label; stereo albums had blue labels.

1960: Black label, large "UA" logo on top.

1960-1968: Black label; blue, gold, white and red circles along upper edge of label, "UNITED" in gold, "ARTISTS" in white, both words in a rounded-off rectangle.

1968-1970: Pink and orange label.

1970-1971: Black label, orange area at left of label of center hole, "UA United Artists" logo in box directly left of center hole.

1971-1977: Tan label with "UA" in brown at top.

1977-1980: Multicolored "sunrise" label.

## Universal

A country label that lasted for exactly one year (1989), the earliest labels were black and pale yellow; later labels were black and red.

## V.I.P.

This Motown label had a brown, tan, orange, yellow and white label. The "V.I.P." logo is printed vertically to the left of the center hole, inside an oval with a white background.

## Valiant

Early 1960s: Purple label.

Mid 1960s: Red and black label.

## Vanguard

Early years through 1963: Mono issues were maroon with silver print.

Late 1950s-mid 1960s: Stereo issues were black with silver print.

Mid 1960s-early 1970s: Silvery-gray to bronze label with white horseman logo at bottom.

Other labels also existed, but we can't place them with certainty.

## Vee Jay

*Pre-bankruptcy issues (1957-1965)*

1957-1960 (1001-1016; 1022; 5001-5005?): Maroon label, silver print, with a squiggly line under the words "Vee-Jay RECORDS." A silver band is around the outside of the label. In this number range, stereo issues were gray with black print with otherwise identical graphics.

1960-1964 (1019-1021; 1023-1070s?; 5006?-5053?; 3004-3037): Black label, silver print, "Vee Jay" logo in white with a treble clef between the two words, surrounded by a red oval. The outer rim of the label has a rainbow band.

1964-1965 (1070s-1154; 5054?-5083; 2501-2509): Black label, silver print, "VJ" in white in large letters, "VEE-JAY RECORDS" in white, two lines, in smaller print below, all three lines surrounded by two large white brackets. The outer rim of the label has a rainbow band.

1964-1965 (various, as needed): Black label, silver print, no rainbow band. The letters "VJ" stand alone with "VEE JAY RECORDS" underneath on one line, all in silver print, no brackets.

*Post-bankruptcy issues (1966-1977)*

Late 1960s-early 1970s: Black label, silver print. Most have the "VJ" and "VEE-JAY RECORDS" on three lines, enclosed by silver brackets. Some have "VJ" on one line and "RECORDS" underneath with no brackets, still all in silver print. Although these records were issued in stereo jackets, all of them play in mono.

(Most of the fake copies of Vee Jay SR 1062, Introducing the Beatles, match this label description. Other records for which Vee Jay maintained the rights, such as The Duke of Earl by Gene Chandler, are considered legitimate product, though nowhere near as valuable as originals.)

1972-1974 (1001-1010 and 2-1000 to 2-1008): Red label, silver print, similar to original maroon Vee-Jay label. At least one of these (1002) was issued on a pink label with black print.

1977 (VJ International): Orange label, black "VJ International" logo in white circle.

## Verve

1956-1960 (4000 and 8000 series mono, 6000 and 60000 series stereo): Black label, silver print, "Verve Records, Inc." at bottom, "MG V" prefix. Early copies have the famous "trumpet player" logo at the left; these command a premium over those with the large "T" logo.

1961-early 1970s (8000 series): Black label, silver print, "MGM Records" at bottom, "V" prefix for mono, "V6" for stereo.

1966-early 1970s (5000 series): Dark blue label, silver print, "V" prefix for mono, "V6" for stereo.

Early 1970s-1975: White label with both "Verve" and "MGM" logos at top of label.

Various labels were used after Verve was re-activated in the 1980s.

## Vik

A 1950s RCA subsidiary, its issues were black with a multi-color "Vik" logo across the top.

## Virgin

Virgin's American history is spotty at times; for some years there was no Virgin Records in America, but material that came out on Virgin U.K. was leased to other labels.

1973-1975: White label, "two virgins" painting at top of label, distributed by Atlantic.

1976-1978: White label, "two virgins" painting at top of label, distributed by CBS.

1978-1979: Tan label, light red "Virgin" in cursive letters at the top with the word "INTERNATIONAL" below that; titles and artist are in black letters.

1979-1980: White label, "Virgin" in blue letters at bottom right, again distributed by Atlantic.

1983-1986: Black label, "Virgin" and "Epic" logos on label. (All of these were Culture Club albums.)

1987-1989: Black label, blue upside-down triangle logo at top of label.

1989-1990: Orange label.

1990-1992: Purple label.

Later issues usually have custom labels.

## Volt

1965-mid 1968 (411-419): Yellow label, black print, "VOLT RECORDS" above center hole, yellow lightning bolt in black background under that.

Mid 1968-late 1971 (6001-6017): Dark blue label, black print.

Late 1971-mid 1970s: Orange label, black print.

## Wand

1960s: White with black top.

1970s: Kaleidoscope label, "Wand" in black across top of label.

## Warner Bros.

*Mono Albums*

1958-1962 (1200-1470?): Gray label, black "WB" shield at top, "WB" letters in shield are in gold.

1962-1966 (1470?-1620?): Gray label, black "WB" shield at top, "WB" letters in shield are in white.

1966-1967 (1620?-1700s): Gold label.

*Stereo Albums*

1958-1967 (1200-1730?): Gold label.

1968-1970 (1730?-1840?): Olive green label with "W7" in a box at the top and "Warner Bros.-Seven Arts Records" along the top outer edge.

1970-mid 1973 (1840?-1890?, 2500-2700?): Olive green label with "WB" in a shield at the top and "Warner Bros. Records" along the top outer edge.

Mid 1973-late 1978: So-called "Burbank" label; color palm-tree street scene with "Burbank, Home of Warner Bros. Records" along top edge.

Late 1978-early 1980s: Gray or white label with horizontal pinstripes.

Early 1980s-present: White label.

Some Warner Bros. albums have custom labels.

## Warwick

Original mono labels were white with a green filled-in circle in the middle of the label. Four yellow circles are on the left of the label; four blue circles tend toward the right of the label. At the top is a Warwick crest logo with a green shield. Original stereo labels were also white, but instead of the green filled-in circle, a blue dot is to the right of the center hole and a yellow dot to the left of the center hole. Concentric like-colored circles surround each dot.

The second version of the mono label was plain white with black print and the Warwick logo in black. Stereo labels were purple with silver print and the Warwick logo in silver.

## Weed

Exactly one album came out on this short-lived Motown imprint. The label is black with silver print, with "WEED" in yellow and two fingers giving the peace sign above that. The label's slogan, which, alas, is not on the record, was "Your Favorite Artists Are On Weed."

## White Whale

1965-1967 (100-120?, 7100-7120?): Dark blue label.

1967-1970 (7120?-end): Lighter blue label with concentric white circles.

## "X"

This subsidiary of RCA Victor released albums from 1954 through 1956, then was replaced by the Vik label. The label is white with red print and a big red "X" at the top of the label. Some labels (3012 at least) are yellow with black print.

# Subscribe Today

GET ONE FULL YEAR AT A GREAT LOW RATE! 1 YEAR (52 HUGE ISSUES) $38.00

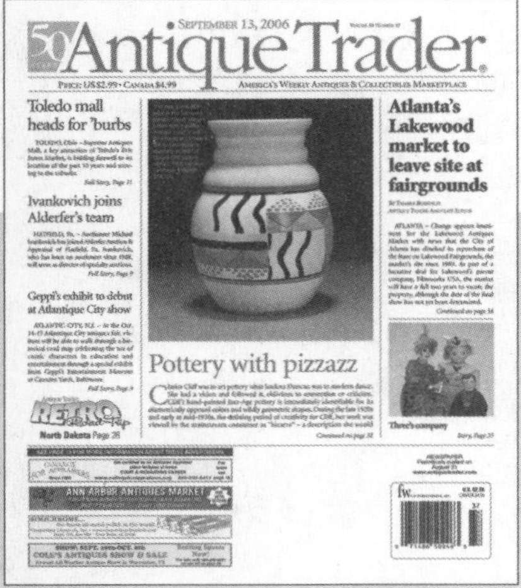

September 13, 2006

Antique Trader

Toledo mall heads for 'burbs

Ivankovich joins Alderfer's team

Geppi's exhibit to debut at Atlantique City show

Atlanta's Lakewood market to leave site at fairgrounds

Pottery with pizzazz

October 4, 2006

Antique Trader

Stevens sets post-fire sale

Hindman auction aids college debt

New law includes IRS appraisal language

NAA seeks support of new auction license law

Up to snuff

That's right. Try *Antique Trader* today and discover the most authoritative voice in the antiques world. Each issue's filled to the brim with valuable information for your pursuit of antiques.

You'll find…

- Current prices and values
- Dolls, toys, furniture, clocks, glass and all special interests
- Exclusive antique market trends
- Auctions tips, techniques and strategies
- Expert appraisals
- And much, much more!

Don't pay $155.48 at the newsstand.

Subscribe Today & Save 76%!

# DON'T WAIT–

## Log on to www.antiquetrader.com and subscribe today.

Call 877-300-0247; outside the U.S. & Canada, call 386-246-3434. Offer code: J7AHAD

Or write us at: P.O. Box 420235, Palm Coast, FL 32142-0235

# More Goldmine Record References to Rely On

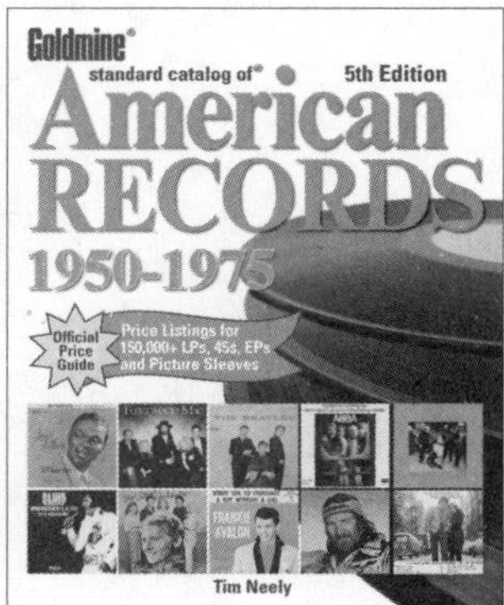


### Goldmine® Standard Catalog of® American Records

*1950-1975*
*5th Edition*
by Tim Neely

More information than any similar record price and identification guide, this mammoth book provides 150,000+ listings, in an easy-to-use format you can turn to with confidence.

Softcover • 8-1/4 x 10-7/8
1,376 pages • 400 b&w photos
16-page color section
**Item# REC5 • $34.99**

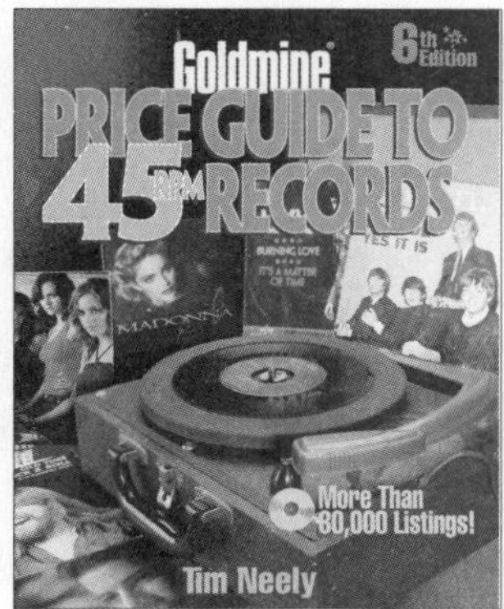


### Goldmine® Price Guide to 45 RPM Records

*6th Edition*
by Tim Neely

Asseses the worth of ur turntable treasures using 80,000 listings for American records, issued between 1949 and the present, in this must-have records price guide.

Softcover • 8-1/2 x 11 • 760 pages
400+ b&w photos • 96 color photos
**Item# Z0728 • $27.99**

### Goldmine® Records & Prices

*3rd Edition*
by John Koenig

Gain exclusive expert insight on what's hot and new, valuable market forecasts, up-to-date values and listings for 1,000+ artists from ABBA to ZZ Top. Plus, more than 1,000 photos.

Softcover • 6 x 9 • 624 pages
1,000 b&w photos • 50 color photos
**Item# Z0107 • $19.99**

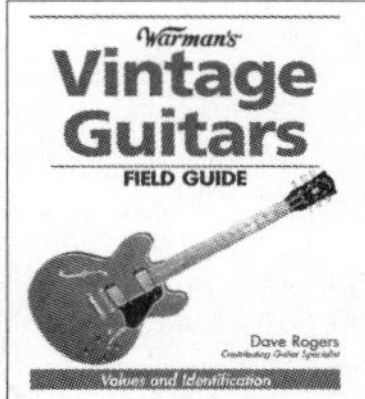


### Warman's® Vintage Guitars Field Guide

by Dave Rogers, Contributing Guitar Specialist

Warman's® Vintage Guitars Field Guide pulls together history, tips for collectors, lessons in guitar lingo, contact information and 350 photos of the leading guitars of the last 100 years including Gibson, Fender and Stratocaster

Softcover • 4-3/16 x 5-3/16 • 512 pages
350 color photos
**Item# GTRFG • $12.99**

Order directly from the publisher by calling
**800-258-0929** M-F 8 am - 5 pm,
Online at
**www.krausebooks.com**
or from booksellers and other retailers nationwide.

**Krause Publications**
700 E. State Street
Iola, WI 54990
**www.krausebooks.com**

Please reference offer **REB7** with all direct-to-publisher orders.

## A.F.O. EXECUTIVES WITH TAMI LYNN

| Number | Title (A Side/B Side) | Yr | NM |
|---|---|---|---|
| **A.F.O.** | | | |
| ❑ 5002 [M] | A Compendium | 1962 | 150.00 |

## ABBA

| Number | Title (A Side/B Side) | Yr | NM |
|---|---|---|---|
| **ATLANTIC** | | | |
| ❑ PR 300 [DJ] | Abba | 1978 | 30.00 |
| ❑ PR 432 [DJ] | A Collection of Hits | 1982 | 30.00 |
| ❑ PR 436 [(2)DJ] | The Abba Special | 1983 | 50.00 |
| ❑ SD 16000 | Voulez-Vous | 1979 | 10.00 |
| ❑ SD 16009 | Greatest Hits, Vol. 2 | 1979 | 12.00 |
| ❑ SD 16023 | Super Trouper | 1980 | 10.00 |
| ❑ SD 18101 | Waterloo | 1974 | 12.00 |
| ❑ SD 18146 | Abba | 1975 | 12.00 |
| ❑ SD 18189 | Greatest Hits | 1976 | 12.00 |
| ❑ SD 18207 | Arrival | 1977 | 12.00 |
| ❑ SD 19114 | Greatest Hits | 1977 | 10.00 |
| ❑ SD 19115 | Arrival | 1977 | 10.00 |
| ❑ SD 19164 | The Album | 1978 | 10.00 |
| ❑ SD 19332 | The Visitors | 1981 | 10.00 |
| ❑ 80036 [(2)] | The Singles — The First Ten Years | 1982 | 15.00 |
| ❑ 80142 | I Love Abba | 1984 | 10.00 |
| ❑ 81675 | Abba Live | 1986 | 12.00 |
| **CBS INTERNATIONAL** | | | |
| ❑ DAL 40301 | Gracias Por La Musica | 1980 | 40.00 |
| *—Spanish-language versions of some of their hits, this LP was pressed in the U.S.* | | | |
| **K-TEL** | | | |
| ❑ NU 9510 | The Magic of Abba | 1978 | 15.00 |
| **NAUTILUS** | | | |
| ❑ NR-20 | Arrival | 1981 | 30.00 |
| *—Audiophile vinyl* | | | |

## ABBEY TAVERN SINGERS, THE

| Number | Title (A Side/B Side) | Yr | NM |
|---|---|---|---|
| **V.I.P.** | | | |
| ❑ 402 [M] | We're Off to Dublin in the Green | 1966 | 40.00 |
| ❑ S-402 [S] | We're Off to Dublin in the Green | 1966 | 50.00 |

## ABDUL, PAULA

| Number | Title (A Side/B Side) | Yr | NM |
|---|---|---|---|
| **VIRGIN** | | | |
| ❑ IP-8128 | Spellbound | 1991 | 25.00 |
| *—Columbia House edition; the only U.S. vinyl of this LP* | | | |
| ❑ 90943 | Forever Your Girl | 1988 | 10.00 |
| ❑ 91362 | Shut Up and Dance | 1990 | 12.00 |
| *—Blue print on cover* | | | |
| ❑ 91362 | Shut Up and Dance | 1990 | 12.00 |
| *—Purple print on cover* | | | |
| ❑ 91362 | Shut Up and Dance | 1990 | 12.00 |
| *—Red print on cover* | | | |
| ❑ 91362 | Shut Up and Dance | 1990 | 12.00 |
| *—Yellow print on cover* | | | |

## ABDUL-MALIK, AHMED

| Number | Title (A Side/B Side) | Yr | NM |
|---|---|---|---|
| **NEW JAZZ** | | | |
| ❑ NJLP-8266 [M] | The Music of Ahmed Abdul-Malik | 1961 | 40.00 |
| *—Purple label* | | | |
| ❑ NJLP-8266 [M] | The Music of Ahmed Abdul-Malik | 1965 | 25.00 |
| *—Blue label, trident logo at right* | | | |
| ❑ NJLP-8282 [M] | Sounds of Africa | 1962 | 40.00 |
| *—Purple label* | | | |
| ❑ NJLP-8282 [M] | Sounds of Africa | 1965 | 25.00 |
| *—Blue label, trident logo at right* | | | |
| **PRESTIGE** | | | |
| ❑ PRLP-16003 [M] | Eastern Moods | 1963 | 30.00 |
| **RCA VICTOR** | | | |
| ❑ LPM-2015 [M] | East Meets West | 1959 | 30.00 |
| ❑ LSP-2015 [S] | East Meets West | 1959 | 40.00 |
| **RIVERSIDE** | | | |
| ❑ RLP 12-287 [M] | Jazz Sahara | 1958 | 50.00 |
| ❑ RLP-1121 [S] | Jazz Sahara | 1959 | 40.00 |
| **STATUS** | | | |
| ❑ ST-8303 [M] | Spellbound | 1965 | 30.00 |

## ABRAMS, MUHAL RICHARD

| Number | Title (A Side/B Side) | Yr | NM |
|---|---|---|---|
| **DELMARK** | | | |
| ❑ DS-413 | Levels and Degrees of Light | 1968 | 20.00 |
| ❑ DS-423 | Young at Heart, Wise in Time | 1970 | 20.00 |

## ABSTRACTS, THE

| Number | Title (A Side/B Side) | Yr | NM |
|---|---|---|---|
| **POMPEII** | | | |
| ❑ 6002 [M] | The Abstracts | 1968 | 80.00 |
| *—Stereo cover with "DJ Copy Monaural" sticker; white label promo record* | | | |
| ❑ SD 6002 [S] | The Abstracts | 1968 | 40.00 |

## AC/DC

| Number | Title (A Side/B Side) | Yr | NM |
|---|---|---|---|
| **ATCO** | | | |
| ❑ SD 36-142 | High Voltage | 1976 | 10.00 |
| ❑ SD 36-151 | Let There Be Rock | 1977 | 10.00 |

Abba, *The Singles: The First Ten Years,* Atlantic 80036, 1982, $15.

| Number | Title (A Side/B Side) | Yr | NM |
|---|---|---|---|
| ❑ 91413 | The Razors Edge | 1990 | 15.00 |
| **ATLANTIC** | | | |
| ❑ LAAS-001 [DJ] | Live at the Atlantic Studios | 1977 | 60.00 |
| *—This album has been counterfeited* | | | |
| ❑ PR 562 [DJ] | Flick of the Switch Interview Album | 1983 | 40.00 |
| ❑ SD 11111 | For Those About to Rock We Salute You | 1981 | 10.00 |
| ❑ SD 16018 | Back in Black | 1980 | 10.00 |
| ❑ SD 16033 | Dirty Deeds Done Dirt Cheap | 1981 | 10.00 |
| ❑ SD 19180 | Powerage | 1978 | 10.00 |
| ❑ SD 19212 | If You Want Blood You've Got It | 1978 | 10.00 |
| ❑ SD 19244 | Highway to Hell | 1979 | 10.00 |
| ❑ 80100 | Flick of the Switch | 1983 | 10.00 |
| ❑ 80178 [EP] | 74 Jailbreak | 1984 | 6.00 |
| ❑ 81263 | Fly on the Wall | 1985 | 10.00 |
| ❑ 81650 | Who Made Who | 1986 | 10.00 |
| ❑ 81828 | Blow Up Your Video | 1988 | 10.00 |
| **EASTWEST** | | | |
| ❑ 61780 | Ballbreaker | 1995 | 15.00 |
| **EPIC** | | | |
| ❑ E 80200 [EP] | 74 Jailbreak | 2003 | 10.00 |
| ❑ E 80201 | High Voltage | 2003 | 12.00 |
| ❑ E 80202 | Dirty Deeds Done Dirt Cheap | 2003 | 12.00 |
| ❑ E 80203 | Let There Be Rock | 2003 | 12.00 |
| ❑ E 80204 | Powerage | 2003 | 12.00 |
| ❑ E 80205 | If You Want Blood You've Got It | 2003 | 12.00 |
| ❑ E 80206 | Highway to Hell | 2003 | 12.00 |
| ❑ E 80207 | Back in Black | 2003 | 12.00 |
| ❑ E 80208 | For Those About to Rock We Salute You | 2003 | 12.00 |
| ❑ E 80209 | Flick of the Switch | 2003 | 12.00 |
| ❑ E 80210 | Fly on the Wall | 2003 | 12.00 |
| ❑ E 80211 | Who Made Who | 2003 | 12.00 |
| ❑ E 80212 | Blow Up Your Video | 2003 | 12.00 |
| ❑ E 80213 | The Razors Edge | 2003 | 12.00 |
| ❑ E2 90553 [(2)] | AC/DC Live | 2003 | 15.00 |
| ❑ 90643 [(16)] | AC/DC | 2003 | 200.00 |
| *—Box set with 15 albums on 16 LPs in black slipcase* | | | |

## ACE, JOHNNY

| Number | Title (A Side/B Side) | Yr | NM |
|---|---|---|---|
| **ABC DUKE** | | | |
| ❑ DLPX-71 | Memorial Album | 1974 | 20.00 |
| **DUKE** | | | |
| ❑ DLP-70 [10] | Memorial Album for Johnny Ace | 1955 | 1200. |
| *—VG value 400; VG+ value 800* | | | |
| ❑ DLP-71 [M] | Memorial Album for Johnny Ace | 1956 | 500.00 |
| *—With no playing card on front cover* | | | |
| ❑ DLP-71 [M] | Memorial Album for Johnny Ace | 1961 | 200.00 |
| *—With playing card on front cover* | | | |
| ❑ DLP-71 [M] | Memorial Album for Johnny Ace | 1961 | 4000. |
| *—Playing card cover; red vinyl; VG value 2000; VG+ value 3000* | | | |
| ❑ LP-71 [R] | Memorial Album for Johnny Ace | 196? | 50.00 |
| *—Orange label; trail-off number is "LRS-71"* | | | |
| **MCA** | | | |
| ❑ 27014 | Memorial Album | 1983 | 8.00 |

## ACKLIN, BARBARA

| Number | Title (A Side/B Side) | Yr | NM |
|---|---|---|---|
| **BRUNSWICK** | | | |
| ❑ BL 754129 | Great Soul Hits | 1967 | 25.00 |
| ❑ BL 754137 | Love Makes a Woman | 1968 | 20.00 |
| ❑ BL 754148 | Seven Days of Night | 1969 | 20.00 |
| ❑ BL 754156 | Someone Else's Arms | 1970 | 20.00 |
| ❑ BL 754166 | I Did It | 1971 | 20.00 |
| ❑ BL 754187 | I Call It Trouble | 1972 | 20.00 |
| **CAPITOL** | | | |
| ❑ ST-11377 | A Place in the Sun | 1975 | 12.00 |

## ACUFF, ROY

| Number | Title (A Side/B Side) | Yr | NM |
|---|---|---|---|
| **CAPITOL** | | | |
| ❑ T 617 [M] | Songs of the Smoky Mountains | 1955 | 60.00 |
| ❑ DT 1870 [R] | The Best of Roy Acuff | 1963 | 20.00 |
| ❑ T 1870 [M] | The Best of Roy Acuff | 1963 | 30.00 |
| ❑ DT 2103 [R] | The Great Roy Acuff | 1964 | 15.00 |
| ❑ T 2103 [M] | The Great Roy Acuff | 1964 | 25.00 |
| ❑ ST 2276 [S] | The Voice of Country Music | 1965 | 40.00 |
| ❑ T 2276 [M] | The Voice of Country Music | 1965 | 30.00 |
| **COLUMBIA** | | | |
| ❑ CL 9004 [10] | Songs of the Smoky Mountains | 1949 | 200.00 |
| ❑ CL 9010 [10] | Old Time Barn Dance | 1949 | 150.00 |
| ❑ CL 9013 [10] | Songs of the Saddle | 1950 | 150.00 |
| ❑ FC 39998 | Columbia Historic Edition | 1985 | 10.00 |
| **ELEKTRA** | | | |
| ❑ E-C 10-1-78 [DJ] | An Interview with Roy Acuff | 1978 | 25.00 |
| **HARMONY** | | | |
| ❑ HL 7082 [M] | Great Speckled Bird | 1958 | 25.00 |
| ❑ HL 7294 [M] | That Glory Bound Train | 1961 | 20.00 |
| ❑ HL 7342 [M] | The Great Roy Acuff | 196? | 15.00 |
| ❑ HL 7376 [M] | Waiting for My Call to Glory | 196? | 15.00 |

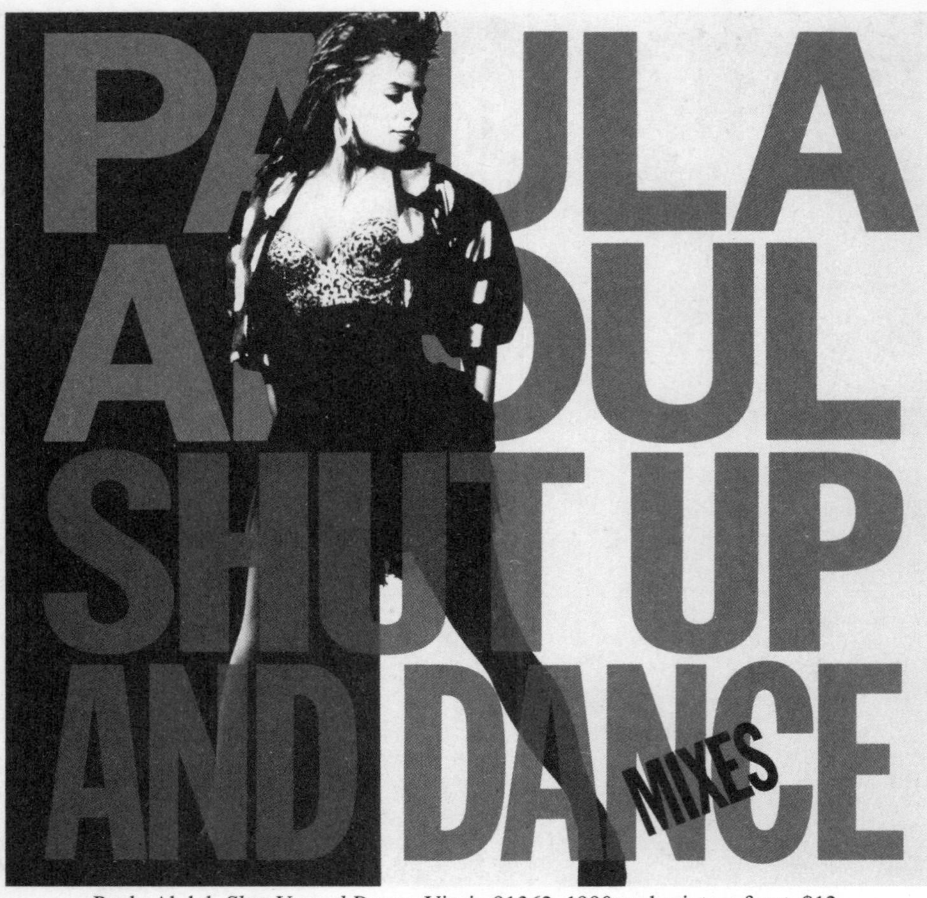


Paula Abdul, *Shut Up and Dance*, Virgin 91362, 1990, red print on front, $12.

| Number | Title (A Side/B Side) | Yr | NM |
|---|---|---|---|
| HICKORYA | | | |
| ❑ LPM-H-101 [M] | Once More It's Roy Acuff | 1961 | 30.00 |
| ❑ LPM-109 [M] | King of Country Music — All-Time Greatest Hits | 1962 | 25.00 |
| ❑ LPM-113 [M] | Roy Acuff — Star of the Grand Ole Opry | 1963 | 25.00 |
| ❑ LPM-114 [M] | The World Is His Stage | 1963 | 25.00 |
| ❑ LPM-115 [M] | Roy Acuff Sings American Folk Songs | 1963 | 25.00 |
| ❑ LPM-117 [M] | Hand-Clapping Gospel Songs | 1963 | 25.00 |
| ❑ LPM-119 [M] | Country Music Hall of Fame | 1964 | 20.00 |
| ❑ LPM-125 [M] | Great Train Songs | 1965 | 20.00 |
| ❑ LPM-134 [M] | Roy Acuff Sings Hank Williams | 1966 | 40.00 |
| ❑ LPS-134 [S] | Roy Acuff Sings Hank Williams | 1966 | 40.00 |
| ❑ LPS-139 | Famous Opry Favorites | 1967 | 20.00 |
| ❑ LPS-145 | Living Legend | 1968 | 20.00 |
| ❑ LPS-147 | Treasury of Country Hits | 1969 | 20.00 |
| ❑ LPS-156 | Roy Acuff Time | 1970 | 20.00 |
| ❑ DT-90698 [R] | Great Train Songs | 1965 | 25.00 |
| *—Capitol Record Club edition* | | | |
| ❑ T-90704 [M] | King of Country Music — All-Time Greatest Hits | 1966 | 25.00 |
| *—Capitol Record Club edition* | | | |
| ❑ ST-91297 | Famous Opry Favorites | 1967 | 25.00 |
| *—Capitol Record Club edition* | | | |
| METRO | | | |
| ❑ M 508 [M] | Roy Acuff | 1965 | 15.00 |
| ❑ MS 508 [R] | Roy Acuff | 1965 | 10.00 |
| MGM | | | |
| ❑ E-3707 [M] | Favorite Hymns | 1958 | 50.00 |
| ❑ E-4044 [M] | Hymn Time | 1962 | 25.00 |
| ❑ SE-4044 [R] | Hymn Time | 196? | 20.00 |
| ROUNDER | | | |
| ❑ SS-23 | 1936-1939: Steamboat Whistle Blues | 1985 | 10.00 |
| ❑ SS-24 | 1939-1941: Fly Birdie Fly | 1985 | 10.00 |
| **ADAMS, BRYAN** | | | |
| A&M | | | |
| ❑ SP-3100 | Bryan Adams | 198? | 8.00 |
| *—Budget-line reissue of 4800* | | | |
| ❑ SP-3154 | You Want It, You Got It | 198? | 8.00 |
| *—Budget-line reissue of 4864* | | | |
| ❑ SP-3288 | Cuts Like a Knife | 198? | 8.00 |
| *—Busget-line reissue of 4919* | | | |
| ❑ SP-3907 | Into the Fire | 1987 | 8.00 |

| Number | Title (A Side/B Side) | Yr | NM |
|---|---|---|---|
| ❑ SP-4800 | Bryan Adams | 1980 | 12.00 |
| ❑ SP-4864 | You Want It, You Got It | 1981 | 12.00 |
| ❑ SP-4919 | Cuts Like a Knife | 1984 | 8.00 |
| *—Reissue withouth the "6" in the catalog number* | | | |
| ❑ SP-6-4919 | Cuts Like a Knife | 1983 | 10.00 |
| *—Original with "6" as part of the catalog number* | | | |
| ❑ SP-5013 | Reckless | 1984 | 8.00 |
| ❑ SP-5327 [(2)] | Waking Up the Neighbours | 1991 | 20.00 |
| *—Columbia House edition; the only U.S. vinyl of this LP* | | | |
| ❑ SP-17231 [EP] | Cuts | 1983 | 25.00 |
| *—Promo-only four-song sampler from "Cuts Like a Knife" LP* | | | |
| ❑ SP-17321 [DJ] | Retail Sampler | 1985 | 30.00 |
| *—10-song collection, a sort of "greatest hits" compilation to that time; promo only* | | | |
| ❑ R 151540 | Reckless | 1984 | 10.00 |
| *—RCA Music Service edition* | | | |
| ❑ R 153919 | Into the Fire | 1987 | 10.00 |
| *—BMG Direct Marketing edition* | | | |
| **ADAMS, EDIE** | | | |
| DECCA | | | |
| ❑ DL 4488 [M] | Behind Those Swingin' Doors | 1964 | 20.00 |
| ❑ DL 74488 [S] | Behind Those Swingin' Doors | 1964 | 25.00 |
| MGM | | | |
| ❑ E-3751 [M] | Music to Listen to Records To | 1959 | 40.00 |
| ❑ SE-3751 [S] | Music to Listen to Records To | 1959 | 60.00 |
| **ADAMS, FAYE** | | | |
| COLLECTABLES | | | |
| ❑ COL-5122 | Golden Classics | 1988 | 10.00 |
| WARWICK | | | |
| ❑ W 2031 [M] | Shake a Hand | 1961 | 600.00 |
| **ADAMS, JERRI** | | | |
| COLUMBIA | | | |
| ❑ CL 916 [M] | It's Cool Inside | 1956 | 40.00 |
| ❑ CL 1258 [M] | Play for Keeps | 1958 | 40.00 |
| **ADAMS, JOHNNY** | | | |
| ANALOGUE PRODUCTIONS | | | |
| ❑ APP 028 | Johnny Adams Sings Doc Pomus — The Real Me | 199? | 20.00 |
| ARIOLA AMERICA | | | |
| ❑ SW 50038 | After All the Good Is Gone | 1978 | 15.00 |
| CHELSEA | | | |
| ❑ CHL 525 | Stand By Me | 1977 | 25.00 |

| Number | Title (A Side/B Side) | Yr | NM |
|---|---|---|---|
| HEP ME | | | |
| ❑ 159 | Christmas in New Orleans | 197? | 15.00 |
| ROUNDER | | | |
| ❑ 2044 | From the Heart | 1984 | 12.00 |
| SSS INTERNATIONAL | | | |
| ❑ 5 | Heart and Soul | 1969 | 20.00 |
| **ADAMS, KAY** | | | |
| TOWER | | | |
| ❑ ST 5033 [S] | Wheels & Tears | 1966 | 30.00 |
| ❑ T 5033 [M] | Wheels & Tears | 1966 | 25.00 |
| ❑ ST 5069 | Make Mine Country | 1967 | 20.00 |
| ❑ T 5069 [M] | Make Mine Country | 1967 | 25.00 |
| ❑ ST 5087 | Alcohol & Tears | 1968 | 20.00 |
| **ADAMS, MIKE, AND THE RED JACKETS** | | | |
| CROWN | | | |
| ❑ CST-255 [S] | Twist Contest | 1962 | 30.00 |
| ❑ CST-312 [S] | Surfer's Beat | 1963 | 30.00 |
| *—Black vinyl* | | | |
| ❑ CST-312 [S] | Surfer's Beat | 1963 | 100.00 |
| *—Red vinyl* | | | |
| ❑ CLP-5255 [M] | Twist Contest | 1962 | 25.00 |
| ❑ CLP-5312 [M] | Surfer's Beat | 1963 | 25.00 |
| **ADAMS, PEPPER** | | | |
| INTERLUDE | | | |
| ❑ MO-502 [M] | Pepper Adams 5 | 1959 | 80.00 |
| *—Reissue of Mode 112* | | | |
| ❑ ST-1002 [S] | Pepper Adams 5 | 1959 | 60.00 |
| *—Reissue of Mode 112; remixed into stereo; black vinyl* | | | |
| ❑ ST-1002 [S] | Pepper Adams 5 | 1959 | 100.00 |
| *—Orange vinyl* | | | |
| MODE | | | |
| ❑ LP-112 [M] | Pepper Adams 5 | 1957 | 150.00 |
| *—With Mel Lewis* | | | |
| PRESTIGE | | | |
| ❑ PRST-7677 | Encounter | 1969 | 20.00 |
| *—With Zoot Sims* | | | |
| REGENT | | | |
| ❑ MG-6066 [M] | The Cool Sound of Pepper Adams | 1958 | 180.00 |
| RIVERSIDE | | | |
| ❑ RLP 12-265 [M] | 10 to 4 at the 5 Spot | 1958 | 100.00 |
| ❑ RLP-1104 [S] | 10 to 4 at the 5 Spot | 1959 | 70.00 |
| SAVOY | | | |
| ❑ MG-12211 [M] | The Cool Sound of Pepper Adams | 196? | 40.00 |
| *—Reissue of Regent 6066* | | | |
| WARWICK | | | |
| ❑ W-2041 [M] | Out of This World | 1961 | 100.00 |
| *—With Donald Byrd* | | | |
| WORKSHOP JAZZ | | | |
| ❑ WSJ-219 [M] | Pepper Adams Plays the Compositions of Charles Mingus | 1964 | 150.00 |
| ❑ WSJS-219 [S] | Pepper Adams Plays the Compositions of Charles Mingus | 1964 | 140.00 |
| WORLD PACIFIC | | | |
| ❑ PJM-407 [M] | Critic's Choice | 1957 | 120.00 |
| *—With Mel Lewis* | | | |
| ❑ WPM-407 [M] | Critic's Choice | 1958 | 100.00 |
| *—With Mel Lewis; reissue with new prefix* | | | |
| **ADAMS, PEPPER, AND JIMMY KNEPPER** | | | |
| METROJAZZ | | | |
| ❑ E-1004 [M] | The Pepper-Knepper Quartet | 1958 | 200.00 |
| ❑ SE-1004 [S] | The Pepper-Knepper Quartet | 1959 | 150.00 |
| **ADAMS, RYAN** | | | |
| LOST HIGHWAY | | | |
| ❑ B0001376-01 | Rock N Roll | 2003 | 25.00 |
| ❑ B0001702-01 [(2)10] | Love Is Hell Pts. 1 & 2 | 2003 | 80.00 |
| *—Combination of two EPs on two 10-inch records in gatefold sleeve* | | | |
| ❑ B0004343-01 [(2)] | Cold Roses | 2005 | 30.00 |
| *—As "Ryan Adams and the Cardinals"* | | | |
| ❑ B0004707-01 [(2)] | Jacksonville City Nights | 2005 | 25.00 |
| *—As "Ryan Adams and the Cardinals"* | | | |
| ❑ B0005872-01 | 29 | 2005 | 20.00 |
| ❑ 088 170235-1 [(2)] | Gold | 2002 | 150.00 |
| ❑ 088 170333-1 | Demolition | 2002 | 30.00 |
| **ADDEO, LEO** | | | |
| RCA CAMDEN | | | |
| ❑ CAL-510 [M] | Hawaii in Hi-Fi | 1960 | 15.00 |
| ❑ CAS-510 [S] | Hawaii in Stereo | 1960 | 20.00 |
| ❑ CAL-594 [M] | More Hawaii in Hi-Fi | 1961 | 15.00 |
| ❑ CAS-594 [S] | More Hawaii in Hi-Fi | 1961 | 20.00 |
| ❑ CAL-672 [M] | Great Standards with a Hawaiian Touch | 1962 | 12.00 |
| ❑ CAS-672 [S] | Great Standards with a Hawaiian Touch | 1962 | 15.00 |
| ❑ CAL-726 [M] | Organ and Chimes Play Christmas Carols | 1962 | 12.00 |

| Number | Title (A Side/B Side) | Yr | NM |
|---|---|---|---|
| ❑ CAS-726 [S] | Organ and Chimes Play Christmas Carols | 1962 | 15.00 |
| ❑ CAL-759 [M] | Songs of Hawaii | 1963 | 12.00 |
| ❑ CAS-759 [S] | Songs of Hawaii | 1963 | 15.00 |
| ❑ CAL-807 [M] | Calypso and Other Island Favorites | 1963 | 12.00 |
| ❑ CAS-807 [S] | Calypso and Other Island Favorites | 1963 | 15.00 |
| ❑ CAL-828 [M] | "Hello Dolly" and Other Favorites | 1964 | 12.00 |
| ❑ CAS-828 [S] | "Hello Dolly" and Other Favorites | 1964 | 15.00 |
| ❑ CAL-853 [M] | Hawaiian Paradise | 1964 | 12.00 |
| ❑ CAS-853 [S] | Hawaiian Paradise | 1964 | 15.00 |
| ❑ CAL-901 [M] | Far Away Places | 1965 | 12.00 |
| ❑ CAS-901 [S] | Far Away Places | 1965 | 15.00 |
| ❑ CAL-977 [M] | Musical Orchids from Hawaii | 1966 | 12.00 |
| ❑ CAS-977 [S] | Musical Orchids from Hawaii | 1966 | 15.00 |
| ❑ CAL-2134 [M] | "Love Is a Hurtin' Thing" and Other Favorites | 1966 | 12.00 |
| ❑ CAS-2134 [S] | "Love Is a Hurtin' Thing" and Other Favorites | 1966 | 15.00 |
| ❑ CAL-2211 [M] | The Magic of Hawaii | 1967 | 12.00 |
| ❑ CAS-2211 [S] | The Magic of Hawaii | 1967 | 15.00 |
| RCA VICTOR | | | |
| ❑ LPM-2414 [M] | Paradise Regained | 1961 | 15.00 |
| ❑ LSA-2414 [S] | Paradise Regained | 1961 | 30.00 |

**ADDERLEY, CANNONBALL**

| Number | Title (A Side/B Side) | Yr | NM |
|---|---|---|---|
| BLUE NOTE | | | |
| ❑ BLP-1595 [M] | Somethin' Else | 1958 | 120.00 |
| *—Regular version; W. 63rd St. address on label* | | | |
| ❑ BLP-1595 [M] | Somethin' Else | 1958 | 250.00 |
| *—"Deep groove" version; W. 63rd St. address on label* | | | |
| ❑ BLP-1595 [M] | Somethin' Else | 1963 | 30.00 |
| *—"New York, USA" address on label* | | | |
| ❑ BLP-1595 [M] | Somethin' Else | 2002 | 30.00 |
| *—Classic Records reissue on 200-gram vinyl* | | | |
| ❑ BLP-1595C [(2)] | Somethin' Else | 2002 | 50.00 |
| *—"Comparison Pack"; contains both the mono and stereo versions of the LP; Classic Records issue on 200-gram vinyl* | | | |
| ❑ BST-1595 [S] | Somethin' Else | 1959 | 100.00 |
| *—Regular version; W. 63rd St. address on label* | | | |
| ❑ BST-1595 [S] | Somethin' Else | 1959 | 150.00 |
| *—"Deep groove" version; W. 63rd St. address on label* | | | |
| ❑ BST-1595 [S] | Somethin' Else | 2002 | 30.00 |
| *—Classic Records reissue on 200-gram vinyl* | | | |
| ❑ ST-46338 | Somethin' Else | 1997 | 20.00 |
| *—Audiophile reissue* | | | |
| ❑ BST-81595 | Somethin' Else | 199? | 30.00 |
| *—Classic Records reissue on 180-gram vinyl* | | | |
| ❑ BST-81595 [S] | Somethin' Else | 1963 | 25.00 |
| *—"New York, USA" address on label* | | | |
| CAPITOL | | | |
| ❑ ST 2203 [S] | Domination | 1964 | 25.00 |
| ❑ ST 2216 [S] | Fiddler on the Roof | 1965 | 25.00 |
| ❑ ST 2284 [S] | Live Session | 1965 | 25.00 |
| ❑ ST 2399 [S] | Cannonball Adderley — Live! | 1965 | 25.00 |
| ❑ ST 2531 [S] | Great Love Themes | 1966 | 25.00 |
| ❑ ST 2617 [S] | Why Am I Treated So Bad? | 1966 | 20.00 |
| ❑ ST-8-2663 [S] | Mercy, Mercy, Mercy! | 1969 | 20.00 |
| *—Capitol Record Club edition* | | | |
| ❑ T 2663 [M] | Mercy, Mercy, Mercy! | 1967 | 20.00 |
| ❑ T 2822 [M] | 74 Miles Away — Walk Tall | 1967 | 40.00 |
| EMARCY | | | |
| ❑ MG-36043 [M] | Julian "Cannonball" Adderley | 1955 | 80.00 |
| ❑ MG-36063 [M] | Julian "Cannonball" Adderley and Strings | 1956 | 80.00 |
| ❑ MG-36077 [M] | In the Land of Hi-Fi | 1956 | 100.00 |
| ❑ MG-36110 [M] | Sophisticated Swing | 1957 | 70.00 |
| ❑ MG-36135 [M] | Cannonball's Sharpshooters | 1958 | 60.00 |
| ❑ MG-36146 [M] | Jump for Joy | 1958 | 80.00 |
| ❑ SR-80017 [S] | Jump for Joy | 1958 | 60.00 |
| FANTASY | | | |
| ❑ FSP 2 [DJ] | Musical Highliights from Big Man | 1975 | 30.00 |
| LIMELIGHT | | | |
| ❑ LM 82009 [M] | Cannonball and Coltrane | 1964 | 25.00 |
| *—Reissue of Mercury 20449* | | | |
| ❑ LS 86009 [S] | Cannonball and Coltrane | 1964 | 20.00 |
| *—Reissue of Mercury 60134* | | | |
| MERCURY | | | |
| ❑ MG-20449 [M] | Cannonball Adderley Quintet in Chicago | 1959 | 50.00 |
| ❑ MG-20530 [M] | Jump for Joy | 1960 | 40.00 |
| *—Reissue of EmArcy 36146* | | | |
| ❑ MG-20531 [M] | Cannonball's Sharpshooters | 1960 | 40.00 |
| *—Reissue of EmArcy 36135* | | | |
| ❑ MG-20616 [M] | Cannonball En Route | 1961 | 50.00 |
| ❑ MG-20652 [M] | The Lush Side of Cannonball Adderley | 1961 | 40.00 |
| *—Reissue of EmArcy 36063* | | | |
| ❑ SR-60134 [S] | Cannonball Adderley Quintet in Chicago | 1960 | 40.00 |
| ❑ SR-60530 [S] | Jump for Joy | 1960 | 30.00 |
| ❑ SR-60531 [S] | Cannonball's Sharpshooters | 1960 | 30.00 |
| ❑ SR-60616 [S] | Cannonball En Route | 1961 | 40.00 |
| ❑ SR-60652 [R] | The Lush Side of Cannonball Adderley | 1961 | 25.00 |

AC/DC, *If You Want Blood You've Got It*, Atlantic SD 19212, 1978, $10.

| Number | Title (A Side/B Side) | Yr | NM |
|---|---|---|---|
| RIVERSIDE | | | |
| ❑ RLP 12-269 [M] | Portrait of Cannonball | 1958 | 100.00 |
| ❑ RLP 12-286 [M] | Things Are Getting Better | 1959 | 100.00 |
| ❑ RLP 12-303 [M] | Cannonball Takes Charge | 1959 | 100.00 |
| ❑ RLP 12-311 [M] | Cannonball Adderley Quintet in San Francisco | 1959 | 80.00 |
| ❑ RLP 12-322 [M] | Them Dirty Blues | 1960 | 80.00 |
| ❑ RLP 344 [M] | Cannonball Adderley Quintet at the Lighthouse | 1960 | 50.00 |
| ❑ RLP 355 [M] | Cannonball Adderley and the Poll-Winners | 1960 | 50.00 |
| ❑ RLP 377 [M] | African Waltz | 1961 | 50.00 |
| ❑ RLP 388 [M] | Cannonball Adderley Quintet Plus | 1961 | 50.00 |
| ❑ RLP 404 [M] | Cannonball Adderley Sextet In New York | 1962 | 50.00 |
| ❑ RLP 416 [M] | Cannonball's Greatest Hits | 1962 | 50.00 |
| ❑ RLP 433 [M] | Know What I Mean? | 1962 | 40.00 |
| ❑ RLP 444 [M] | Jazz Workshop Revisited | 1963 | 40.00 |
| ❑ RLP 455 [M] | Cannonball's Bossa Nova | 1963 | 40.00 |
| ❑ RLP 477 [M] | Nippon Soul — Recorded in Concert in Tokyo | 1964 | 40.00 |
| ❑ RM 499 [M] | Cannonball in Europe | 1964 | 40.00 |
| ❑ RLP 1128 [S] | Things Are Getting Better | 1959 | 80.00 |
| ❑ RLP 1148 [S] | Cannonball Takes Charge | 1959 | 80.00 |
| ❑ RLP 1157 [S] | Cannonball Adderley Quintet in San Francisco | 1959 | 60.00 |
| ❑ RLP 1170 [S] | Them Dirty Blues | 1960 | 60.00 |
| ❑ RS 9344 [S] | Cannonball Adderley Quintet at the Lighthouse | 1960 | 40.00 |
| ❑ RS 9355 [S] | Cannonball Adderley and the Poll-Winners | 1960 | 40.00 |
| ❑ RS 9377 [S] | African Waltz | 1961 | 40.00 |
| ❑ RS 9388 [S] | Cannonball Adderley Quintet Plus | 1961 | 40.00 |
| ❑ RS 9404 [S] | Cannonball Adderley Sextet In New York | 1962 | 40.00 |
| ❑ RS 9416 [S] | Cannonball's Greatest Hits | 1962 | 40.00 |
| ❑ RS 9433 [S] | Know What I Mean? | 1962 | 40.00 |
| ❑ RS 9444 [S] | Jazz Workshop Revisited | 1963 | 40.00 |
| ❑ RS 9455 [S] | Cannonball's Bossa Nova | 1963 | 40.00 |
| ❑ RS 9477 [S] | Nippon Soul — Recorded in Concert in Tokyo | 1964 | 40.00 |
| SAVOY | | | |
| ❑ MG-12018 [M] | Presenting Cannonball | 1955 | 150.00 |
| *—Band pictured on cover* | | | |

| Number | Title (A Side/B Side) | Yr | NM |
|---|---|---|---|
| ❑ MG-12018 [M] | Presenting Cannonball | 196? | 80.00 |
| *—Cannonballs pictured on cover with band members merely listed* | | | |
| TRIP | | | |
| ❑ TLP-5573 [M] | In the Land of Hi-Fi | 197? | 15.00 |
| WING | | | |
| ❑ SRW-16362 [S] | Cannonball Adderley Quintet | 196? | 20.00 |
| WONDERLAND/RIVERSIDE | | | |
| ❑ RLP 1435 [M] | A Child's Introduction to Jazz | 196? | 50.00 |
| *—Adderley narrates an album introducing the works of such artists as Armstrong, Monk, Waller, etc.* | | | |

**ADDERLEY, CANNONBALL AND NAT**

| Number | Title (A Side/B Side) | Yr | NM |
|---|---|---|---|
| LIMELIGHT | | | |
| ❑ LM 82032 [M] | Them Adderleys | 1966 | 50.00 |
| ❑ LS 86032 [S] | Them Adderleys | 1966 | 50.00 |

**ADDERLEY, NAT**

| Number | Title (A Side/B Side) | Yr | NM |
|---|---|---|---|
| A&M | | | |
| ❑ LP-2005 [M] | You, Baby | 1968 | 25.00 |
| *—Mono is promo only* | | | |
| ATLANTIC | | | |
| ❑ SD 1439 [S] | Autobiography | 1965 | 20.00 |
| ❑ SD 1460 [S] | Sayin' Something | 1966 | 20.00 |
| ❑ 1475 [M] | Live at Memory Lane | 1967 | 20.00 |
| CAPITOL | | | |
| ❑ SVBB-11025 [(2)] | Cannonball Adderley Presents Soul Zodiac | 1972 | 100.00 |
| EMARCY | | | |
| ❑ MG-36091 [M] | Introducing Nat Adderley | 1955 | 80.00 |
| ❑ MG-36100 [M] | To the Ivy League from Nat | 1956 | 80.00 |
| JAZZLAND | | | |
| ❑ JLP-47 [M] | Naturally! | 1961 | 30.00 |
| ❑ JLP-75 [M] | In the Bag | 1962 | 30.00 |
| ❑ JLP-947 [S] | Naturally! | 1961 | 40.00 |
| ❑ JLP-975 [S] | In the Bag | 1962 | 40.00 |
| RIVERSIDE | | | |
| ❑ RLP 12-285 [M] | Branching Out | 1958 | 50.00 |
| ❑ RLP 12-301 [M] | Much Brass | 1959 | 50.00 |
| ❑ RLP 12-318 [M] | The Work Song | 1960 | 40.00 |
| ❑ RLP-330 [M] | That's Right! | 1960 | 30.00 |
| ❑ RM-474 [M] | Little Big Horn! | 1964 | 30.00 |
| ❑ RLP-1143 [S] | Much Brass | 1959 | 50.00 |

Aerosmith, *Get Your Wings,* Columbia KC 32847, 1974, $12.

| Number | Title (A Side/B Side) | Yr | NM |
|---|---|---|---|
| ❑ RLP-1167 [S] | The Work Song | 1960 | 50.00 |
| ❑ RS-9330 [S] | That's Right! | 1960 | 40.00 |
| ❑ RS-9474 [S] | Little Big Horn! | 1964 | 40.00 |

SAVOY

| Number | Title (A Side/B Side) | Yr | NM |
|---|---|---|---|
| ❑ MG-12021 [M] | That's Nat | 1955 | 80.00 |

WING

| Number | Title (A Side/B Side) | Yr | NM |
|---|---|---|---|
| ❑ MGW-60000 [M] | Introducing Nat Adderley | 1956 | 50.00 |

**ADRIAN AND THE SUNSETS**

SUNSET

| Number | Title (A Side/B Side) | Yr | NM |
|---|---|---|---|
| ❑ 63-601 [M] | Breakthrough | 1963 | 80.00 |
| *—Black vinyl* | | | |
| ❑ 63-601 [M] | Breakthrough | 1963 | 150.00 |
| *—Multi-color vinyl* | | | |
| ❑ SD 63-601 [S] | Breakthrough | 1963 | 150.00 |
| *—Black vinyl* | | | |
| ❑ SD 63-601 [S] | Breakthrough | 1963 | 300.00 |
| *—Multi-color vinyl* | | | |

**ADVANCEMENT, THE**

PHILIPS

| Number | Title (A Side/B Side) | Yr | NM |
|---|---|---|---|
| ❑ PHS 600328 | The Advancement | 1969 | 40.00 |

**ADVENTURERS, THE (1)**

COLUMBIA

| Number | Title (A Side/B Side) | Yr | NM |
|---|---|---|---|
| ❑ CL 1747 [M] | Can't Stop Twistin' | 1961 | 60.00 |
| ❑ CS 8547 [S] | Can't Stop Twistin' | 1961 | 80.00 |

**AEROSMITH**

COLUMBIA

| Number | Title (A Side/B Side) | Yr | NM |
|---|---|---|---|
| ❑ A3S 187 [DJ] | Pure Gold from Rock 'n' Roll's Golden Boys | 1976 | 50.00 |
| *—Promo-only compilation of the first three albums* | | | |
| ❑ JC 32005 | Aerosmith | 1977 | 8.00 |
| ❑ KC 32005 | Aerosmith | 1973 | 12.00 |
| *—Light blue cover, most (if not all) of which say "Featuring 'Dream On' " on front* | | | |
| ❑ KC 32005 | Aerosmith | 1973 | 15.00 |
| *—Orange cover with correct title "Walking The Dog"* | | | |
| ❑ KC 32005 | Aerosmith | 1973 | 20.00 |
| *—Orange cover with back cover typo "Walking The Dig"* | | | |
| ❑ PC 32005 | Aerosmith | 1976 | 10.00 |
| *—Without bar code* | | | |
| ❑ PC 32005 | Aerosmith | 1984 | 8.00 |
| *—With bar code* | | | |
| ❑ JC 32847 | Get Your Wings | 1977 | 8.00 |
| ❑ KC 32847 | Get Your Wings | 1974 | 12.00 |
| ❑ KCQ 32847 [Q] | Get Your Wings | 1974 | 25.00 |
| ❑ PC 32847 | Get Your Wings | 1976 | 10.00 |
| *—Without bar code* | | | |
| ❑ PC 32847 | Get Your Wings | 1984 | 8.00 |
| *—With bar code* | | | |
| ❑ JC 33479 | Toys in the Attic | 1977 | 10.00 |
| ❑ PC 33479 | Toys in the Attic | 1975 | 12.00 |
| *—Without bar code* | | | |
| ❑ PC 33479 | Toys in the Attic | 1984 | 8.00 |
| *—With bar code* | | | |
| ❑ PCQ 33479 [Q] | Toys in the Attic | 1975 | 25.00 |
| ❑ JC 34165 | Rocks | 1976 | 10.00 |
| *—Some copies have "Rocks" in quotes on the cover, others don't; no difference in value* | | | |
| ❑ PC 34165 | Rocks | 1976 | 12.00 |
| *—Without bar code. Some copies have "Rocks" in quotes on the cover, others don't; no difference in value* | | | |
| ❑ PC 34165 | Rocks | 1984 | 8.00 |
| *—With bar code* | | | |
| ❑ PCQ 34165 [Q] | Rocks | 1976 | 25.00 |
| ❑ JC 34856 | Draw the Line | 1977 | 12.00 |
| ❑ PC 34856 | Draw the Line | 198? | 8.00 |
| ❑ PC2 35564 [(2)] | Live! Bootleg | 1978 | 15.00 |
| ❑ FC 36050 | Night in the Ruts | 1979 | 10.00 |
| ❑ PC 36050 | Night in the Ruts | 1984 | 8.00 |
| ❑ FC 36865 | Aerosmith's Greatest Hits | 1980 | 10.00 |
| ❑ PC 36865 | Aerosmith's Greatest Hits | 1984 | 8.00 |
| ❑ FC 38061 | Rock in a Hard Place | 1982 | 10.00 |
| ❑ PC 38061 | Rock in a Hard Place | 1984 | 8.00 |
| ❑ FC 40329 | Classics Live | 1986 | 10.00 |
| ❑ FC 40855 | Classics Live, Vol. 2 | 1987 | 10.00 |
| ❑ FC 44487 | Gems (1973-1982) | 1989 | 10.00 |
| ❑ C 62088 | Just Push Play | 2001 | 15.00 |
| ❑ C 87025 | Honkin' on Bobo | 2004 | 15.00 |

GEFFEN

| Number | Title (A Side/B Side) | Yr | NM |
|---|---|---|---|
| ❑ GHS 24091 | Done with Mirrors | 1985 | 10.00 |
| ❑ GHS 24162 | Permanent Vacation | 1987 | 10.00 |
| ❑ GHS 24254 | Pump | 1989 | 10.00 |

**AESOP'S FABLES**

CADET CONCEPT

| Number | Title (A Side/B Side) | Yr | NM |
|---|---|---|---|
| ❑ LPS-323 | In Due Time | 1969 | 20.00 |

**AFDEM, JEFF, AND THE SPRINGFIELD FLUTE**

BURDETTE

| Number | Title (A Side/B Side) | Yr | NM |
|---|---|---|---|
| ❑ 5162 | Something | 1969 | 40.00 |

**AFFECTION COLLECTION, THE**

EVOLUTION

| Number | Title (A Side/B Side) | Yr | NM |
|---|---|---|---|
| ❑ 2007 | The Affection Collection | 1969 | 20.00 |

**AFFINITY**

PARAMOUNT

| Number | Title (A Side/B Side) | Yr | NM |
|---|---|---|---|
| ❑ PAS-5027 | Affinity | 1970 | 25.00 |

**AFGHAN WHIGS**

COLUMBIA

| Number | Title (A Side/B Side) | Yr | NM |
|---|---|---|---|
| ❑ C 69450 | 1969 | 1998 | 12.00 |

SUB POP

| Number | Title (A Side/B Side) | Yr | NM |
|---|---|---|---|
| ❑ 60 | Up In It | 1990 | 12.00 |
| ❑ 60 | Up In It | 1990 | 25.00 |
| *—First pressings have orange vinyl and a different sleeve than the black vinyl version* | | | |
| ❑ 130 | Congregation | 1992 | 20.00 |
| *—Import only; made in Germany (no U.S. vinyl)* | | | |
| ❑ 238 | Gentlemen | 1993 | 12.00 |
| ❑ 353 | Black Love | 1996 | 12.00 |

ULTRASUEDE

| Number | Title (A Side/B Side) | Yr | NM |
|---|---|---|---|
| ❑ 001 | Big Top Halloween | 1988 | 50.00 |
| *—Approximately 2,000 copies were made* | | | |

**AFI**

ADELINE

| Number | Title (A Side/B Side) | Yr | NM |
|---|---|---|---|
| ❑ 026 [(2)] | Sing the Sorrow | 2003 | 20.00 |
| *—All copies on red vinyl* | | | |
| ❑ ADN 30035-1 [(2)] | Decemberunderground | 2006 | 15.00 |

NITRO

| Number | Title (A Side/B Side) | Yr | NM |
|---|---|---|---|
| ❑ 15805 | Very Proud of Ya | 1996 | 10.00 |
| *—Any other color vinyl ("Special Colored Vinyl" sticker on cover or shinkwrap)* | | | |
| ❑ 15805 | Very Proud of Ya | 1996 | 12.00 |
| *—Black or blue vinyl* | | | |
| ❑ 15811 | Answer That and Stay Fashionable | 1997 | 12.00 |
| *—Reissue; available on black, white, red, tan or gray vinyl* | | | |
| ❑ 15815 | Shut Your Mouth and Open Your Eyes | 1997 | 12.00 |
| *—Available on black, green, yellow, tan, white or gray vinyl* | | | |
| ❑ 15824 | Black Sails in the Sunset | 1999 | 12.00 |
| *—Available on black, lilac or gray vinyl* | | | |
| ❑ 15835 | The Art of Drowning | 2000 | 12.00 |
| *—Available on black, gray, green and purplish vinyl* | | | |

WINGNUT

| Number | Title (A Side/B Side) | Yr | NM |
|---|---|---|---|
| ❑ WLRP-1370 | Answer That and Stay Fashionable | 1995 | 25.00 |
| *—Second edition: Black vinyl; title on one line on front cover; address next to Wingnut logo on back* | | | |
| ❑ WLRP-1370 | Answer That and Stay Fashionable | 1995 | 30.00 |
| *—First edition: Black vinyl; title on two lines on front cover; no address next to Wingnut logo on back* | | | |
| ❑ WLRP-1370 | Answer That and Stay Fashionable | 1995 | 50.00 |
| *—Third edition: Same as second edition, except on red vinyl* | | | |

**AFRIKA CORPS**

IRON CROSS/DACOIT

| Number | Title (A Side/B Side) | Yr | NM |
|---|---|---|---|
| ❑ (# unknown) | Music to Kill By | 1977 | 60.00 |

KLEEN KUT/LIMP

| Number | Title (A Side/B Side) | Yr | NM |
|---|---|---|---|
| ❑ (# unknown) | Hello World! | 1978 | 20.00 |
| *—As "The Korps"; blue vinyl* | | | |

**AGAPE**

MARK

| Number | Title (A Side/B Side) | Yr | NM |
|---|---|---|---|
| ❑ MRS-2170 | Gospel Hard Rock | 1971 | 120.00 |

RENRUT

| Number | Title (A Side/B Side) | Yr | NM |
|---|---|---|---|
| ❑ 101 | Victims of Tradition | 1972 | 120.00 |

**AGE OF REASON, THE**

GEORGETOWNE

| Number | Title (A Side/B Side) | Yr | NM |
|---|---|---|---|
| ❑ (no #) | The Age of Reason | 1969 | 150.00 |

**AGGREGATION, THE**

LHI

| Number | Title (A Side/B Side) | Yr | NM |
|---|---|---|---|
| ❑ 12008 | Mind Odyssey | 1967 | 400.00 |

**AGUILERA, CHRISTINA**

RCA

| Number | Title (A Side/B Side) | Yr | NM |
|---|---|---|---|
| ❑ 07863-68037-1 [(2)] | Stripped | 2002 | 15.00 |
| ❑ 82876-82639-1 [(3)] | Back to Basics | 2006 | 50.00 |
| *—In oversize "album-style" packaging with fold-open cover* | | | |

**AHBEZ, EDEN**

DEL-FI

| Number | Title (A Side/B Side) | Yr | NM |
|---|---|---|---|
| ❑ DFLP-1211 [M] | Eden's Island | 1960 | 150.00 |
| ❑ DFST-1211 [S] | Eden's Island | 1960 | 200.00 |

**AIR SUPPLY**

ARISTA

| Number | Title (A Side/B Side) | Yr | NM |
|---|---|---|---|
| ❑ AL-4268 | Lost in Love | 1980 | 8.00 |
| ❑ AL-8024 | Greatest Hits | 1983 | 8.00 |
| ❑ AL-8283 | Air Supply | 1985 | 8.00 |

| Number | Title (A Side/B Side) | Yr | NM |
|---|---|---|---|
| ❑ AL-8292 | Now and Forever | 1985 | 6.00 |
| *—Budget-line reissue of 9587* | | | |
| ❑ AL-8311 | Lost in Love | 1985 | 6.00 |
| *—Budget-line reissue of 4268* | | | |
| ❑ AL-8312 | The One That You Love | 1985 | 6.00 |
| *—Budget-line reissue of 9551* | | | |
| ❑ AL-8426 | Hearts in Motion | 1986 | 8.00 |
| ❑ AL-8528 | The Christmas Album | 1987 | 10.00 |
| ❑ AL-9551 | The One That You Love | 1981 | 8.00 |
| ❑ AL-9587 | Now and Forever | 1982 | 8.00 |
| COLUMBIA | | | |
| ❑ JC 35047 | Love and Other Bruises | 1977 | 15.00 |
| ❑ PC 35047 | Love and Other Bruises | 1981 | 8.00 |
| *—Budget-line reissue; much more common than the original "JC" version* | | | |
| MOBILE FIDELITY | | | |
| ❑ 1-113 | The One That You Love | 1983 | 20.00 |
| *—Audiophile vinyl* | | | |
| NAUTILUS | | | |
| ❑ NR-31 | Lost in Love | 1982 | 20.00 |
| *—Audiophile vinyl* | | | |
| **AIRTO** | | | |
| CTI | | | |
| ❑ CTSQ-6028 [Q] | Fingers | 1974 | 20.00 |
| **AKENS, JEWEL** | | | |
| ERA | | | |
| ❑ EL-110 [M] | The Birds and the Bees | 1965 | 30.00 |
| ❑ ES-110 [S] | The Birds and the Bees | 1965 | 100.00 |
| **AKIYOSHI, TOSHIKO** | | | |
| CANDID | | | |
| ❑ CD-8012 [M] | Toshiko Mariano Quartet | 1960 | 40.00 |
| ❑ CD-8015 [M] | Toshiko Mariano | 1960 | 40.00 |
| ❑ CS-9012 [S] | Toshiko Mariano Quartet | 1960 | 50.00 |
| ❑ CS-9015 [S] | Toshiko Mariano | 1960 | 50.00 |
| DAUNTLESS | | | |
| ❑ DM-4308 [M] | The Country and Western Sounds of Jazz | 1963 | 40.00 |
| ❑ DS-6308 [S] | The Country and Western Sounds of Jazz | 1963 | 50.00 |
| METROJAZZ | | | |
| ❑ E-1001 [M] | United Notions | 1958 | 50.00 |
| ❑ SE-1001 [S] | United Notions | 1959 | 40.00 |
| NORGRAN | | | |
| ❑ MGN-22 [10] | Toshiko's Piano | 1954 | 150.00 |
| STORYVILLE | | | |
| ❑ STLP-912 [M] | The Toshiko Trio | 1956 | 60.00 |
| ❑ STLP-918 [M] | Toshiko Akiyoshi, Her Trio, Her Quartet | 1957 | 60.00 |
| VEE JAY | | | |
| ❑ LP-2505 [M] | Jazz in Japan | 1964 | 30.00 |
| *—As "Toshiko Mariano and Her Big Band"* | | | |
| VERVE | | | |
| ❑ MGV-8273 [M] | The Many Sides of Toshiko | 1958 | 60.00 |
| ❑ V-8273 [M] | The Many Sides of Toshiko | 1961 | 25.00 |
| **AKIYOSHI, TOSHIKO, AND LEON SASH** | | | |
| VERVE | | | |
| ❑ MGV-8236 [M] | Toshiko and Leon Sash at Newport | 1958 | 60.00 |
| ❑ V-8236 [M] | Toshiko and Leon Sash at Newport | 1961 | 25.00 |
| **AKIYOSHI, TOSHIKO-LEW TABACKIN BIG BAND** | | | |
| RCA VICTOR | | | |
| ❑ CPL2-2242 [(2)] | Road Time | 1977 | 20.00 |
| **ALABAMA** | | | |
| ACCORD | | | |
| ❑ SN-7132 | Pride of Dixie | 1981 | 10.00 |
| ALABAMA | | | |
| ❑ ALA-78-9-01 | The Alabama Band | 1978 | 400.00 |
| HEARTLAND | | | |
| ❑ HL 1186/7 [(2)] | The Very Best of Alabama | 1992 | 15.00 |
| LSI | | | |
| ❑ 0177 | Deuces Wild | 1977 | 1200. |
| *—As "Wild Country"* | | | |
| ❑ 0275 | Wild Country | 1975 | 1500. |
| *—As "Wild Country"; VG value 750; VG+ value 1125* | | | |
| PLANTATION | | | |
| ❑ 44 | Wild Country | 1981 | 60.00 |
| RCA | | | |
| ❑ 5649-1-R | The Touch | 1986 | 8.00 |
| ❑ 6495-1-R | Just Us | 1987 | 8.00 |
| ❑ 6825-1-R | Alabama Live | 1988 | 8.00 |
| ❑ 8587-1-R | Southern Star | 1989 | 8.00 |
| ❑ 9574-1-RDJ [DJ] | Open-Ended Interview | 1988 | 30.00 |
| RCA VICTOR | | | |
| ❑ AHL1-3644 | My Home's in Alabama | 1980 | 15.00 |

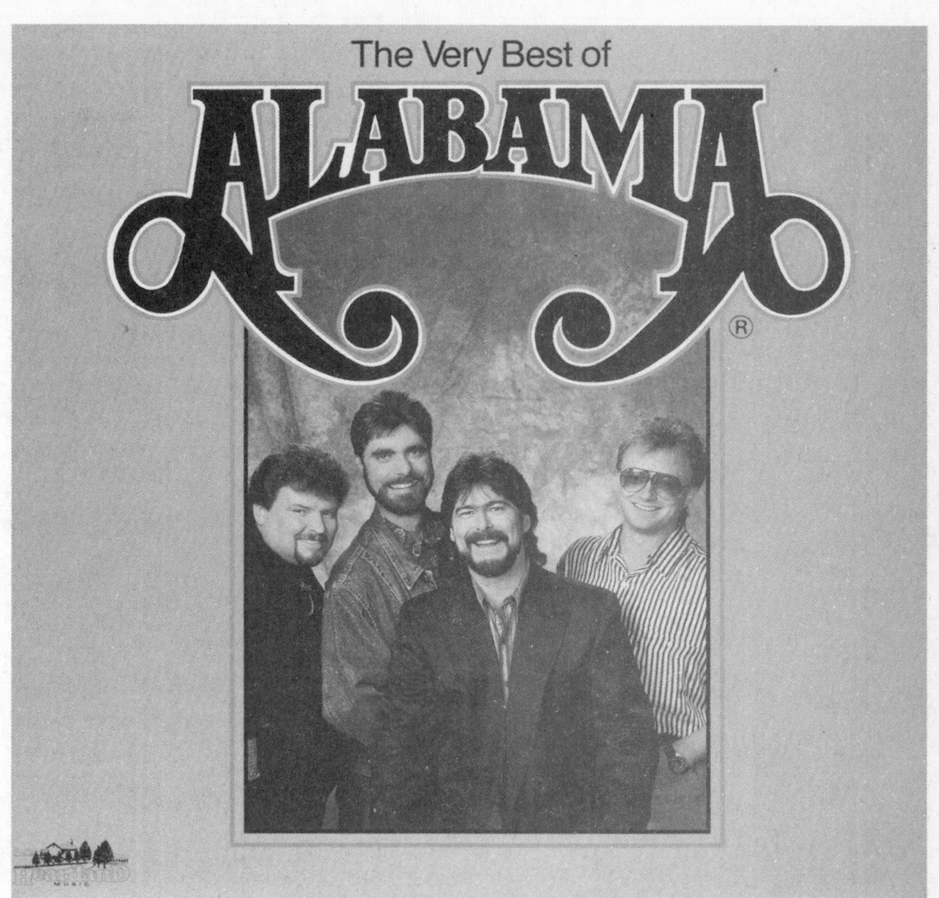


Alabama, *The Very Best of Alabama,* Heartland HL 1186/7, 1992, $15.

| Number | Title (A Side/B Side) | Yr | NM |
|---|---|---|---|
| ❑ AYL1-3644 | My Home's in Alabama | 1986 | 8.00 |
| *—"Best Buy Series" reissue* | | | |
| ❑ AHL1-3930 | Feels So Right | 1981 | 8.00 |
| ❑ AHL1-4229 | Mountain Music | 1982 | 8.00 |
| ❑ AHL1-4663 | The Closer You Get | 1983 | 8.00 |
| ❑ AHL1-4939 | Roll On | 1984 | 8.00 |
| ❑ AHL1-5339 | 40 Hour Week | 1985 | 8.00 |
| ❑ ASL1-7014 | Christmas | 1985 | 12.00 |
| *—Original copies have gold embossed letters on cover* | | | |
| ❑ ASL1-7014 | Christmas | 1986 | 10.00 |
| *—Later copies have white non-embossed letters on cover* | | | |
| ❑ AHL1-7170 | Greatest Hits | 1986 | 8.00 |
| SOUTHWAYS | | | |
| ❑ 101 | Pride of Dixie | 1981 | 10.00 |
| *—Same album as on Accord* | | | |
| **ALAIMO, STEVE** | | | |
| ABC-PARAMOUNT | | | |
| ❑ 501 [M] | Starring Steve Alaimo | 1965 | 40.00 |
| ❑ S-501 [S] | Starring Steve Alaimo | 1965 | 50.00 |
| ❑ 531 [M] | Where the Action Is | 1965 | 40.00 |
| ❑ S-531 [S] | Where the Action Is | 1965 | 50.00 |
| ❑ 551 [M] | Steve Alaimo Sings and Swings | 1966 | 40.00 |
| ❑ S-551 [S] | Steve Alaimo Sings and Swings | 1966 | 50.00 |
| CHECKER | | | |
| ❑ LP-2981 [M] | Twist with Steve Alaimo | 1962 | 150.00 |
| ❑ LP-2983 [M] | Mashed Potatoes | 1962 | 150.00 |
| ❑ LP-2986 [M] | Every Day I Have to Cry | 1963 | 150.00 |
| CROWN | | | |
| ❑ CST-382 [R] | Steve Alaimo | 1963 | 15.00 |
| ❑ CLP-5382 [M] | Steve Alaimo | 1963 | 25.00 |
| **ALAN, BUDDY** | | | |
| CAPITOL | | | |
| ❑ ST-592 | Whole Lot of Somethin' | 1970 | 20.00 |
| **ALAN, BUDDY, AND DON RICH** | | | |
| CAPITOL | | | |
| ❑ ST-769 | We're Real Good Friends | 1971 | 20.00 |
| **ALBAM, MANNY** | | | |
| CORAL | | | |
| ❑ CRL 57142 [M] | The Jazz Greats of Our Time | 1957 | 40.00 |
| ❑ CRL 57173 [M] | The Jazz Greats of Our Time, Volume 2 | 1957 | 40.00 |

| Number | Title (A Side/B Side) | Yr | NM |
|---|---|---|---|
| ❑ CRL 57207 [M] | West Side Story | 1958 | 40.00 |
| ❑ CRL 57231 [M] | Sophisticated Lady — The Songs of Duke Ellington | 1958 | 40.00 |
| ❑ CRL 59101 [M] | The Blues Is Everybody's Business | 195? | 40.00 |
| ❑ CRL 59102 [M] | A Gallery of Gershwin | 1958 | 40.00 |
| DECCA | | | |
| ❑ DL 74517 [S] | Music from West Side Story | 1964 | 20.00 |
| DOT | | | |
| ❑ DLP-9004 [M] | Jazz New York | 1958 | 40.00 |
| ❑ DLP-9008 [M] | Steve's Song | 1958 | 40.00 |
| IMPULSE! | | | |
| ❑ A-19 [M] | Jazz Goes to the Movies | 1962 | 25.00 |
| ❑ AS-19 [S] | Jazz Goes to the Movies | 1962 | 30.00 |
| MERCURY | | | |
| ❑ MG-20325 [M] | With All My Love | 1958 | 40.00 |
| RCA VICTOR | | | |
| ❑ LPM-1211 [M] | The RCA Victor Jazz Workshop | 1956 | 50.00 |
| ❑ LPM-1279 [M] | The Drum Suite | 1956 | 50.00 |
| ❑ LPM-2432 [M] | More Double Exposure | 1961 | 20.00 |
| ❑ LSA-2432 [S] | More Double Exposure | 1961 | 30.00 |
| ❑ LPM-2508 [M] | I Had the Craziest Dream | 1962 | 20.00 |
| ❑ LSA-2508 [S] | I Had the Craziest Dream | 1962 | 25.00 |
| SOLID STATE | | | |
| ❑ SM-17009 [M] | The Soul of the City | 1966 | 20.00 |
| ❑ SS-18000 [S] | Brass on Fire | 1966 | 20.00 |
| TOP RANK | | | |
| ❑ RM-313 [M] | Double Exposure | 1960 | 40.00 |
| UNITED ARTISTS | | | |
| ❑ UAL-3079 [M] | Drum Feast | 1959 | 30.00 |
| ❑ UAS-6079 [S] | Drum Feast | 1959 | 40.00 |
| **ALBANY, JOE, AND WARNE MARSH** | | | |
| RIVERSIDE | | | |
| ❑ RLP 12-270 [M] | The Right Combination | 1958 | 120.00 |
| **ALBERGHETTI, ANNA MARIA** | | | |
| CAPITOL | | | |
| ❑ T 887 [M] | I Can't Resist You | 1957 | 30.00 |
| ❑ ST 1379 [S] | Warm and Willing | 1960 | 30.00 |
| ❑ T 1379 [M] | Warm and Willing | 1960 | 20.00 |

| Number | Title (A Side/B Side) | Yr | NM |
|---|---|---|---|
| CELEBRITY HOUSE | | | |
| ❑ TW 2001 | Christmas with Anna Maria Alberghetti | 1984 | 12.00 |
| *—B-side by Reino Moisio* | | | |
| MERCURY | | | |
| ❑ MG-20056 [M] | Songs by Anna Maria Alberghetti | 1955 | 30.00 |
| MGM | | | |
| ❑ E-4001 [M] | Love Makes the World Go 'Round | 1962 | 20.00 |
| ❑ SE-4001 [S] | Love Makes the World Go 'Round | 1962 | 25.00 |
| **ALBERT, EDDIE** | | | |
| COLUMBIA | | | |
| ❑ CL 2599 [M] | The Eddie Albert Album | 1967 | 20.00 |
| ❑ CS 9399 [S] | The Eddie Albert Album | 1967 | 20.00 |
| DOT | | | |
| ❑ DLP-3109 [M] | High Upon a Mountain | 1958 | 20.00 |
| ❑ DLP-25109 [S] | High Upon a Mountain | 1958 | 25.00 |
| HAMILTON | | | |
| ❑ HLP-103 [(2)DJ] | Oh, What a Beautiful Mornin' | 1959 | 12.00 |
| ❑ HLP-12103 [S] | Oh, What a Beautiful Mornin' | 1959 | 15.00 |
| KAPP | | | |
| ❑ KL-1000 [M] | One God | 1954 | 30.00 |
| ❑ KL-1017 [M] | Eddie Albert and Margo | 1956 | 30.00 |
| ❑ KL-1083 [M] | September Song | 1958 | 25.00 |
| PICCADILLY | | | |
| ❑ PIC-3374 | Take Me Home | 1980 | 15.00 |
| WONDERLAND | | | |
| ❑ WLP-5000 | Eddie Albert Sings and Narrates Americana | 1975 | 15.00 |
| **ALBERT, THE** | | | |
| PERCEPTION | | | |
| ❑ 9 | The Albert | 1971 | 20.00 |
| **ALBERTS, AL** | | | |
| CORAL | | | |
| ❑ CRL 57259 [M] | A Man Has Got to Sing | 1959 | 25.00 |
| ❑ CRL 757259 [S] | A Man Has Got to Sing | 1959 | 30.00 |
| **ALBRIGHT, LOLA** | | | |
| COLUMBIA | | | |
| ❑ CL 1327 [M] | Dreamsville | 1959 | 40.00 |
| ❑ CS 8133 [S] | Dreamsville | 1959 | 50.00 |
| **ALBRIGHT, MAX** | | | |
| MOTIF | | | |
| ❑ 502 [M] | Mood for Max | 1956 | 60.00 |
| **ALCATRAZZ** | | | |
| CAPITOL | | | |
| ❑ ST-12385 | Disturbing the Peace | 1985 | 20.00 |
| ❑ ST-12477 | Dangerous Games | 1986 | 20.00 |
| ROCSHIRE | | | |
| ❑ 22016 | No Parole from Rock 'n' Roll | 1983 | 25.00 |
| ❑ 22020 | Live Sentence | 1984 | 20.00 |
| **ALDA, ROBERT** | | | |
| ROULETTE | | | |
| ❑ R-25006 [M] | Robert Alda | 1959 | 25.00 |
| ❑ SR-25006 [S] | Robert Alda | 1959 | 30.00 |
| **ALEONG, ALI, AND THE NOBLES** | | | |
| REPRISE | | | |
| ❑ R-6011 [M] | Twistin' the Hits | 1962 | 25.00 |
| ❑ R9-6011 [S] | Twistin' the Hits | 1962 | 30.00 |
| ❑ R-6020 [M] | C'mon Baby, Let's Dance | 1962 | 25.00 |
| ❑ R9-6020 [S] | C'mon Baby, Let's Dance | 1962 | 30.00 |
| VEE JAY | | | |
| ❑ LP-1060 [M] | Come Surf with Me | 1963 | 30.00 |
| ❑ SR-1060 [S] | Come Surf with Me | 1963 | 50.00 |
| **ALESS, TONY** | | | |
| ROOST | | | |
| ❑ RST-2202 [M] | Tony Aless and His Long Island Suite | 1955 | 80.00 |
| **ALEXANDER, ARTHUR** | | | |
| DOT | | | |
| ❑ DLP 3434 [M] | You Better Move On | 1962 | 100.00 |
| ❑ DLP 25434 [S] | You Better Move On | 1962 | 160.00 |
| WARNER BROS. | | | |
| ❑ BS 2592 | Arthur Alexander | 1972 | 25.00 |
| **ALEXANDER, BOB** See AL KLINK AND BOB ALEXANDER. | | | |
| **ALEXANDER, JOE, AND TIMMONS, BOBBY** | | | |
| JAZZLAND | | | |
| ❑ JLP-23 [M] | Blue Jubilee | 1960 | 30.00 |
| ❑ JLP-923 [S] | Blue Jubilee | 1960 | 40.00 |
| **ALEXANDER, MONTY** | | | |
| PACIFIC JAZZ | | | |
| ❑ PJ-86 [M] | Alexander the Great | 1966 | 20.00 |
| ❑ ST-86 [S] | Alexander the Great | 1966 | 25.00 |
| ❑ PJ-10094 [M] | Spooky | 1966 | 20.00 |
| ❑ ST-20094 [S] | Spooky | 1966 | 25.00 |
| RCA VICTOR | | | |
| ❑ LPM-3930 [M] | Zing | 1968 | 25.00 |
| **ALEXANDER, ROLAND** | | | |
| NEW JAZZ | | | |
| ❑ NJLP-8267 [M] | Pleasure Bent | 1962 | 50.00 |
| *—Purple label* | | | |
| ❑ NJLP-8267 [M] | Pleasure Bent | 1965 | 25.00 |
| *—Blue label, trident at right* | | | |
| **ALEXANDER'S TIMELESS BLOOZBAND** | | | |
| SMASK | | | |
| ❑ 1001 [M] | Alexander's Timeless Bloozband | 1967 | 200.00 |
| UNI | | | |
| ❑ 73021 | For Sale | 1968 | 25.00 |
| **ALEXANDRIA, LOREZ** | | | |
| ABC IMPULSE! | | | |
| ❑ AS-62 | Alexandria the Great | 1968 | 20.00 |
| *—Reissue of Impulse! AS-62* | | | |
| ❑ AS-76 | More of the Great Lorez Alexandria | 1968 | 20.00 |
| *—Reissue of Impulse! AS-76* | | | |
| ARGO | | | |
| ❑ LP-663 [M] | Early in the Morning | 1960 | 70.00 |
| ❑ LPS-663 [S] | Early in the Morning | 1960 | 100.00 |
| *—With the Ramsey Lewis Trio* | | | |
| ❑ LP-682 [M] | Sing No Sad Songs for Me | 1961 | 70.00 |
| ❑ LPS-682 [S] | Sing No Sad Songs for Me | 1961 | 100.00 |
| ❑ LP-694 [M] | Deep Roots | 1962 | 70.00 |
| ❑ LPS-694 [S] | Deep Roots | 1962 | 100.00 |
| ❑ LP-720 [M] | For Swingers Only | 1963 | 70.00 |
| ❑ LPS-720 [S] | For Swingers Only | 1963 | 100.00 |
| CADET | | | |
| ❑ LPS-682 | Sing No Sad Songs for Me | 1966 | 25.00 |
| *—Reissue of Argo 682* | | | |
| DISCOVERY | | | |
| ❑ DS-782 | How Will I Remember You? | 1978 | 60.00 |
| ❑ DS-800 | A Woman Knows | 1979 | 50.00 |
| ❑ DS-826 | Lorez Alexandria Sings Johnny Mercer | 1981 | 25.00 |
| ❑ DS-905 | Harlem Butterfly (Sings the Songs of Johnny Mercer Vol. 2) | 1984 | 20.00 |
| IMPULSE! | | | |
| ❑ A-62 [M] | Alexandria the Great | 1964 | 40.00 |
| ❑ AS-62 [S] | Alexandria the Great | 1964 | 50.00 |
| ❑ A-76 [M] | More of the Great Lorez Alexandria | 1965 | 40.00 |
| ❑ AS-76 [S] | More of the Great Lorez Alexandria | 1965 | 50.00 |
| KING | | | |
| ❑ 542 [M] | This Is Lorez | 1956 | 200.00 |
| *—Black label, crownless "King"* | | | |
| ❑ 565 [M] | Lorez Sings Prez | 1956 | 200.00 |
| *—Black label, crownless "King"* | | | |
| ❑ 657 [M] | The Band Swings, Lorez Sings | 1959 | 200.00 |
| *—Black label, crownless "King"* | | | |
| ❑ S-657 [S] | The Band Swings, Lorez Sings | 1959 | 300.00 |
| *—Dark blue label, crownless "King"* | | | |
| ❑ 676 [M] | Singing Songs Everyone Knows | 1959 | 200.00 |
| *—Black label, crownless "King"* | | | |
| PZAZZ | | | |
| ❑ LP-320 | Didn't We | 1968 | 50.00 |
| ❑ LP-324 | In a Different Bag | 1969 | 30.00 |
| TREND | | | |
| ❑ TR-538 | Tangerine (Sings the Songs of Johnny Mercer Vol. 3) | 1986 | 15.00 |
| ❑ TR-547 | Dear to My Heart | 1988 | 15.00 |
| **ALFRED, CHUZ** | | | |
| SAVOY | | | |
| ❑ MG-12030 [M] | Jazz Young Blood | 1955 | 60.00 |
| *—With Ola Hanson and Chuck Lee* | | | |
| **ALICE IN CHAINS** | | | |
| COLUMBIA | | | |
| ❑ CAS 2192 [EP] | We Die Young | 1990 | 50.00 |
| *—Five-song promo-only issue predating their first LP* | | | |
| ❑ C2 57804 [(2)] | Jar of Flies/Sap | 1994 | 20.00 |
| *—Two cassette/CD EP releases in one vinyl package* | | | |
| ❑ C2 67248 [(2)] | Alice in Chains | 1995 | 20.00 |
| **ALIOTTA-HAYNES-JEREMIAH** | | | |
| AMPEX | | | |
| ❑ A-10108 | Aliotta-Haynes Music | 1970 | 20.00 |
| *—As "Aliota-Haynes"* | | | |
| ❑ A-10119 | Aliotta-Haynes-Jeremiah | 1970 | 20.00 |
| BIG FOOT | | | |
| ❑ 714 | Lake Shore Drive | 1978 | 25.00 |
| LITTLE FOOT | | | |
| ❑ 711 | Slippin' Away | 1977 | 20.00 |
| **ALIVE AND KICKING** | | | |
| ROULETTE | | | |
| ❑ SR 42052 | Alive and Kicking | 1970 | 20.00 |
| **ALL AMERICAN RUMBLERS, THE** | | | |
| GONE | | | |
| ❑ LP-5006 [M] | Destination Dixie | 1959 | 50.00 |
| **ALL STARS, THE** | | | |
| GRAMOPHONE | | | |
| ❑ 20192 | Boogie Woogie | 196? | 50.00 |
| **ALLAN, DAVIE, AND THE ARROWS** | | | |
| TOWER | | | |
| ❑ DT 5002 [R] | Apache '65 | 1965 | 30.00 |
| ❑ T 5002 [M] | Apache '65 | 1965 | 40.00 |
| ❑ DT 5043 [R] | The Wild Angels | 1966 | 20.00 |
| ❑ T 5043 [M] | The Wild Angels | 1966 | 30.00 |
| ❑ DT 5056 [R] | The Wild Angels, Vol. II | 1967 | 20.00 |
| ❑ T 5056 [M] | The Wild Angels, Vol. II | 1967 | 30.00 |
| ❑ DT 5074 [R] | Devil's Angel | 1967 | 20.00 |
| ❑ T 5074 [M] | Devil's Angel | 1967 | 30.00 |
| ❑ DT 5078 [R] | Blues Theme | 1967 | 40.00 |
| ❑ T 5078 [M] | Blues Theme | 1967 | 50.00 |
| ❑ DT 5083 [R] | Mondo Hollywood | 1968 | 20.00 |
| ❑ T 5083 [M] | Mondo Hollywood | 1968 | 30.00 |
| ❑ DT 5094 [R] | Cycle-Delic Sounds | 1968 | 50.00 |
| ❑ T 5094 [M] | Cycle-Delic Sounds | 1968 | 100.00 |
| **ALLEN, BYRON, TRIO** | | | |
| ESP-DISK' | | | |
| ❑ 1005 [M] | The Byron Allen Trio | 1965 | 20.00 |
| ❑ S-1005 [S] | The Byron Allen Trio | 1965 | 25.00 |
| **ALLEN, DAVE** | | | |
| INTERNATIONAL ARTISTS | | | |
| ❑ 11 | Color Blind | 1969 | 60.00 |
| *—Original pressing* | | | |
| ❑ 11 | Color Blind | 1979 | 20.00 |
| *—Repressing with "RE2" and "Masterfonics" in dead wax* | | | |
| **ALLEN, DAVID** | | | |
| EVEREST | | | |
| ❑ SD-1224 [S] | David Allen | 1964 | 20.00 |
| PACIFIC JAZZ | | | |
| ❑ PJM-408 [M] | A Sure Thing | 1957 | 60.00 |
| ❑ ST-1006 [S] | A Sure Thing | 1959 | 60.00 |
| WORLD PACIFIC | | | |
| ❑ WP-1250 [M] | Let's Face the Music and Dance | 1958 | 40.00 |
| ❑ ST-1295 [S] | David Allen Sings the Jerome Kern Songbook | 1960 | 30.00 |
| ❑ WP-1295 [M] | David Allen Sings the Jerome Kern Songbook | 1960 | 30.00 |
| **ALLEN, DAYTON** | | | |
| GRAND AWARD | | | |
| ❑ GA 33-424 [M] | Why Not? | 1960 | 25.00 |
| **ALLEN, HENRY "RED"** | | | |
| AMERICAN RECORDING SOCIETY | | | |
| ❑ G-436 [M] | Traditional Jazz | 195? | 40.00 |
| COLUMBIA | | | |
| ❑ CS 9247 [S] | Feelin' Good | 1966 | 20.00 |
| RCA VICTOR | | | |
| ❑ LPM-1509 [M] | Ride, Red, Ride in Hi-Fi | 1957 | 50.00 |
| SWINGVILLE | | | |
| ❑ SWLP-2034 [M] | Mr. Allen | 1962 | 40.00 |
| *—Purple label* | | | |
| ❑ SWLP-2034 [M] | Mr. Allen | 1965 | 20.00 |
| *—Blue label, trident logo at right* | | | |
| ❑ SWST-2034 [S] | Mr. Allen | 1962 | 50.00 |
| *—Red label* | | | |
| ❑ SWST-2034 [S] | Mr. Allen | 1965 | 25.00 |
| *—Blue label, trident logo at right* | | | |
| VERVE | | | |
| ❑ MGV-1025 [M] | Red Allen Plays King Oliver | 1959 | 50.00 |
| ❑ V-1025 [M] | Red Allen Plays King Oliver | 1961 | 20.00 |
| ❑ V6-1025 [S] | Red Allen Plays King Oliver | 1961 | 25.00 |
| "X" | | | |
| ❑ LVA-3033 [M] | Ridin' with Red | 1955 | 50.00 |
| **ALLEN, HENRY "RED", AND RED NORVO** | | | |
| BRUNSWICK | | | |
| ❑ BL 58044 [10] | Battle of Jazz, Vol. 6 | 1953 | 60.00 |
| **ALLEN, HENRY "RED", AND KID ORY** | | | |
| VERVE | | | |
| ❑ MGV-1018 [M] | Henry "Red" Allen Meets Kid Ory | 1957 | 50.00 |
| ❑ V-1018 [M] | Henry "Red" Allen Meets Kid Ory | 1961 | 20.00 |

| Number | Title (A Side/B Side) | Yr | NM |
|---|---|---|---|
| ❑ V6-1018 [S] | Henry "Red" Allen Meets Kid Ory | 1961 | 20.00 |
| ❑ MGV-1020 [M] | We've Got Rhythm | 1958 | 50.00 |
| ❑ V-1020 [M] | We've Got Rhythm | 1961 | 20.00 |
| ❑ V6-1020 [S] | We've Got Rhythm | 1961 | 20.00 |
| ❑ MGVS-6076 [S] | Henry "Red" Allen Meets Kid Ory | 1959 | 40.00 |
| ❑ MGVS-6121 [S] | We've Got Rhythm | 1959 | 40.00 |

## ALLEN, HENRY "RED"; JACK TEAGARDEN; KID ORY

### VERVE

| Number | Title (A Side/B Side) | Yr | NM |
|---|---|---|---|
| ❑ MGV-8233 [M] | Red Allen, Jack Teagarden & Kid Ory at Newport | 1958 | 50.00 |
| ❑ V-8233 [M] | Red Allen, Jack Teagarden & Kid Ory at Newport | 1961 | 20.00 |

## ALLEN, LEE

### EMBER

| Number | Title (A Side/B Side) | Yr | NM |
|---|---|---|---|
| ❑ ELP-200 [M] | Walkin' with Mr. Lee | 1958 | 500.00 |
| *—Red label* | | | |
| ❑ ELP-200 [M] | Walkin' with Mr. Lee | 1959 | 200.00 |
| *—White "logs" label* | | | |
| ❑ ELP-200 [M] | Walkin' with Mr. Lee | 1961 | 100.00 |
| *—Red and black label* | | | |

## ALLEN, PHYLICIA

### CASABLANCA

| Number | Title (A Side/B Side) | Yr | NM |
|---|---|---|---|
| ❑ NBLP-7108 | Josephine Superstar | 1978 | 25.00 |

## ALLEN, RAY, AND THE UPBEATS

### BLAST

| Number | Title (A Side/B Side) | Yr | NM |
|---|---|---|---|
| ❑ BLP-6804 [M] | A Tribute to Six | 1962 | 120.00 |

## ALLEN, REX

### BUENA VISTA

| Number | Title (A Side/B Side) | Yr | NM |
|---|---|---|---|
| ❑ BV-3307 [M] | Rex Allen Sings 16 Golden Hits | 1961 | 40.00 |

### DECCA

| Number | Title (A Side/B Side) | Yr | NM |
|---|---|---|---|
| ❑ DL 8402 [M] | Under Western Skies | 1956 | 50.00 |
| ❑ DL 8776 [M] | Mister Cowboy | 1959 | 40.00 |
| ❑ DL 75011 [S] | The Smooth Country Sound of Rex Allen | 1968 | 20.00 |
| ❑ DL 75205 | The Touch of God's Hand | 1970 | 20.00 |
| ❑ DL 78776 [S] | Mister Cowboy | 1959 | 60.00 |

### HACIENDA

| Number | Title (A Side/B Side) | Yr | NM |
|---|---|---|---|
| ❑ WWLP-101 [M] | Rex Allen Sings | 1960 | 200.00 |

### MERCURY

| Number | Title (A Side/B Side) | Yr | NM |
|---|---|---|---|
| ❑ MG-20719 [M] | Faith of a Man | 1962 | 25.00 |
| ❑ MG-20752 [M] | Rex Allen Sings and Tells Tales | 1963 | 25.00 |
| ❑ SR-60719 [S] | Faith of a Man | 1962 | 30.00 |
| ❑ SR-60752 [S] | Rex Allen Sings and Tells Tales | 1963 | 30.00 |

## ALLEN, RICHIE

### IMPERIAL

| Number | Title (A Side/B Side) | Yr | NM |
|---|---|---|---|
| ❑ LP-9212 [M] | Stranger from Durango | 1962 | 40.00 |
| ❑ LP-9229 [M] | The Rising Surf | 1963 | 80.00 |
| ❑ LP-9243 [M] | Surfer's Slide | 1963 | 80.00 |
| ❑ LP-12212 [S] | Stranger from Durango | 1962 | 50.00 |
| ❑ LP-12229 [S] | The Rising Surf | 1963 | 150.00 |
| ❑ LP-12243 [S] | Surfer's Slide | 1963 | 150.00 |

## ALLEN, ROSALIE

### GRAND AWARD

| Number | Title (A Side/B Side) | Yr | NM |
|---|---|---|---|
| ❑ GA-33-330 [M] | Songs of the Golden West | 1957 | 40.00 |

### RCA VICTOR

| Number | Title (A Side/B Side) | Yr | NM |
|---|---|---|---|
| ❑ LPM-2313 [M] | Rosalie Allen | 1961 | 20.00 |
| ❑ LSP-2313 [S] | Rosalie Allen | 1961 | 25.00 |

### WALDORF

| Number | Title (A Side/B Side) | Yr | NM |
|---|---|---|---|
| ❑ 150 [10] | Rosalie Allen Sings Country and Western | 1955 | 80.00 |

## ALLEN, STEVE

### CASABLANCA

| Number | Title (A Side/B Side) | Yr | NM |
|---|---|---|---|
| ❑ 811366-1 | Funny Fone Calls | 1983 | 8.00 |
| *—Reissue of Dot 3472* | | | |
| ❑ 811367-1 | More Funny Fone Calls | 1983 | 8.00 |
| *—Reissue of Dot 3517* | | | |

### CORAL

| Number | Title (A Side/B Side) | Yr | NM |
|---|---|---|---|
| ❑ CRL 57004 [M] | Music for Tonight | 1955 | 25.00 |
| ❑ CRL 57015 [M] | Tonight at Midnight | 1956 | 25.00 |
| ❑ CRL 57018 [M] | Jazz for Tonight | 1956 | 25.00 |
| ❑ CRL 57019 [M] | Steve Sings | 1956 | 25.00 |
| ❑ CRL 57028 [M] | Let's Dance | 1956 | 25.00 |
| ❑ CRL 57048 [M] | Allen Plays Allen | 1956 | 25.00 |
| ❑ CRL 57070 [M] | The Steve Allen Show | 1957 | 25.00 |
| ❑ CRL 57138 [M] | Romantic Rendezvous | 1957 | 20.00 |
| ❑ CRL 57442 [M] | Songs Everybody Knows | 1964 | 15.00 |
| ❑ CRL 757442 [R] | Songs Everybody Knows | 1964 | 12.00 |

### DECCA

| Number | Title (A Side/B Side) | Yr | NM |
|---|---|---|---|
| ❑ DL 8151 [M] | Steve Allen's All Star Jazz Concert, Vol. 1 | 1955 | 30.00 |
| ❑ DL 8152 [M] | Steve Allen's All Star Jazz Concert, Vol. 2 | 1955 | 30.00 |

### DOT

| Number | Title (A Side/B Side) | Yr | NM |
|---|---|---|---|
| ❑ DLP 3472 [M] | Funny Fone Calls | 1963 | 20.00 |
| ❑ DLP 3473 [M] | 12 Greatest Hits | 1963 | 20.00 |
| ❑ DLP 3480 [M] | Bossa Nova Jazz | 1963 | 15.00 |
| ❑ DLP 3515 [M] | Gravy Waltz and 11 Current Hits! | 1963 | 15.00 |
| ❑ DLP 3517 [M] | More Funny Fone Calls | 1963 | 20.00 |
| ❑ DLP 3519 [M] | Steve Allen Plays the Piano Greats | 1963 | 15.00 |
| ❑ DLP 3530 [M] | Steve Allen Sings | 1963 | 15.00 |
| ❑ DLP 3538 [M] | Cuano Caliente El Sol and More | 1963 | 15.00 |
| ❑ DLP 3560 [M] | Great Ragtime Hits | 1963 | 15.00 |
| ❑ DLP 3587 [M] | Songs from the Steve Allen TV Show | 1964 | 12.00 |
| ❑ DLP 3597 [M] | Steve Allen, His Piano and Orchestra | 1964 | 12.00 |
| ❑ DLP 3624 [M] | I Play for You | 1965 | 12.00 |
| ❑ DLP 3683 [M] | Rhythm and Blues | 1966 | 12.00 |
| ❑ DLP 25380 [S] | Bossa Nova Jazz | 1963 | 20.00 |
| ❑ DLP 25515 [S] | Gravy Waltz and 11 Current Hits! | 1963 | 20.00 |
| ❑ DLP 25519 [S] | Steve Allen Plays the Piano Greats | 1963 | 20.00 |
| ❑ DLP 25530 [S] | Steve Allen Sings | 1963 | 20.00 |
| ❑ DLP 25538 [S] | Cuano Caliente El Sol and More | 1963 | 20.00 |
| ❑ DLP 25560 [S] | Great Ragtime Hits | 1963 | 20.00 |
| ❑ DLP 25587 [S] | Songs from the Steve Allen TV Show | 1964 | 15.00 |
| ❑ DLP 25597 [S] | Steve Allen, His Piano and Orchestra | 1964 | 15.00 |
| ❑ DLP 25624 [S] | I Play for You | 1965 | 15.00 |
| ❑ DLP 25683 [S] | Rhythm and Blues | 1966 | 15.00 |

### FORUM

| Number | Title (A Side/B Side) | Yr | NM |
|---|---|---|---|
| ❑ F-9014 [M] | Steve Allen at the Round Table | 196? | 20.00 |
| ❑ FS-9014 [S] | Steve Allen at the Round Table | 196? | 15.00 |

### HAMILTON

| Number | Title (A Side/B Side) | Yr | NM |
|---|---|---|---|
| ❑ HLP 132 [M] | Some of My Favorites | 196? | 12.00 |
| ❑ HLP 12132 [S] | Some of My Favorites | 196? | 15.00 |

### ROULETTE

| Number | Title (A Side/B Side) | Yr | NM |
|---|---|---|---|
| ❑ R-25053 [M] | Steve Allen at the Round Table | 1959 | 25.00 |
| ❑ SR-25053 [S] | Steve Allen at the Round Table | 1959 | 20.00 |

### SIGNATURE

| Number | Title (A Side/B Side) | Yr | NM |
|---|---|---|---|
| ❑ SM 1004 [M] | Man in the Street | 1959 | 30.00 |
| ❑ SM 1021 [M] | Monday Nights | 1960 | 30.00 |

## ALLEN, STEVE, AND MANNY ALBAM

### DOT

| Number | Title (A Side/B Side) | Yr | NM |
|---|---|---|---|
| ❑ DLP 3194 [M] | ...And All That Jazz | 1959 | 25.00 |
| ❑ DLP 25194 [S] | ...And All That Jazz | 1959 | 20.00 |

## ALLEN, TONY

### CROWN

| Number | Title (A Side/B Side) | Yr | NM |
|---|---|---|---|
| ❑ CST-240 [S] | Rock and Roll with Tony Allen | 1961 | 100.00 |
| ❑ CLP-5231 [M] | Rock and Roll with Tony Allen | 1960 | 100.00 |
| *—Black label* | | | |
| ❑ CLP-5231 [M] | Rock and Roll with Tony Allen | 1961 | 60.00 |
| *—Gray label* | | | |

## ALLEN, WOODY

### BELL

| Number | Title (A Side/B Side) | Yr | NM |
|---|---|---|---|
| ❑ 6008 | The Wonderful Wacky World of Woody Allen | 1967 | 20.00 |

### CAPITOL

| Number | Title (A Side/B Side) | Yr | NM |
|---|---|---|---|
| ❑ ST 2986 | The Third Woody Allen Album | 1968 | 25.00 |

### CASABLANCA

| Number | Title (A Side/B Side) | Yr | NM |
|---|---|---|---|
| ❑ NBLP2-7145 [(2)] | Woody Allen: Stand-Up Comic 1964-1968 | 1979 | 15.00 |
| *—Compilation of material from Colpix and Capitol LPs (different from either UA collection)* | | | |

### COLPIX

| Number | Title (A Side/B Side) | Yr | NM |
|---|---|---|---|
| ❑ CP 488 [M] | Woody Allen 2 | 1965 | 30.00 |
| ❑ SCP 488 [R] | Woody Allen 2 | 1965 | 25.00 |
| ❑ CP 518 [M] | Woody Allen | 1964 | 30.00 |

### UNITED ARTISTS

| Number | Title (A Side/B Side) | Yr | NM |
|---|---|---|---|
| ❑ UA-LA849-J2 [(2)] | Woody Allen: Stand-Up Comic 1964-1968 | 1977 | 20.00 |
| *—Compilation of material from Colpix and Capitol LPs (different from UA 9968)* | | | |
| ❑ UAS 9968 [(2)] | Woody Allen: The Nightclub Years | 1972 | 20.00 |
| *—Compilation of material from Colpix and Capitol LPs* | | | |

## ALLEN AND ROSSI

### ABC-PARAMOUNT

| Number | Title (A Side/B Side) | Yr | NM |
|---|---|---|---|
| ❑ ABC-270 [M] | Hello Dere | 1962 | 20.00 |
| ❑ ABC-445 [M] | One More Time Hello Dere | 1963 | 20.00 |

### MERCURY

| Number | Title (A Side/B Side) | Yr | NM |
|---|---|---|---|
| ❑ MG-21077 [M] | The Adventures of Batman and Rubin | 1966 | 40.00 |
| ❑ SR-61077 [S] | The Adventures of Batman and Rubin | 1966 | 50.00 |
| *—The above LP was written by "Batman" creator Bob Kane as a parody of his own comic book* | | | |

### REPRISE

| Number | Title (A Side/B Side) | Yr | NM |
|---|---|---|---|
| ❑ R-6104 [M] | Too Funny for Words | 1964 | 20.00 |

### ROULETTE

| Number | Title (A Side/B Side) | Yr | NM |
|---|---|---|---|
| ❑ R-507 [M] | The Truth About the Green Hornet | 1966 | 20.00 |
| ❑ R-508 [M] | Dedicated to Our Armed Forces | 1967 | 20.00 |

## ALLIN, GG

### ALIVE

| Number | Title (A Side/B Side) | Yr | NM |
|---|---|---|---|
| ❑ 0001 | Brutality and Bloodshed for All | 199? | 10.00 |
| ❑ 0012 | Terror in America | 199? | 10.00 |

### BLACK & BLUE

| Number | Title (A Side/B Side) | Yr | NM |
|---|---|---|---|
| ❑ (# unknown) | Eat My Fuc | 1988 | 12.00 |
| *—Reissue of Blood LP of the same name* | | | |
| ❑ (# unknown) | Banned in Boston | 1989 | 12.00 |
| ❑ 006053-X | Always Was, Is and Always Shall Be | 1985 | 50.00 |
| *—Reissue of Orange original* | | | |

### BLOOD

| Number | Title (A Side/B Side) | Yr | NM |
|---|---|---|---|
| ❑ (# unknown) | Eat My Fuc | 198? | 50.00 |
| *—Hand-decorated plain cover* | | | |

### HOMESTEAD

| Number | Title (A Side/B Side) | Yr | NM |
|---|---|---|---|
| ❑ HMS-069 | You Give Love a Bad Name | 1987 | 12.00 |

### ORANGE

| Number | Title (A Side/B Side) | Yr | NM |
|---|---|---|---|
| ❑ (# unknown) | Always Was, Is and Always Shall Be | 1980 | 100.00 |

## ALLISON, GENE

### VEE JAY

| Number | Title (A Side/B Side) | Yr | NM |
|---|---|---|---|
| ❑ LP-1009 [M] | Gene Allison | 1959 | 300.00 |
| *—Maroon label* | | | |
| ❑ LP-1009 [M] | Gene Allison | 196? | 100.00 |
| *—Black label, oval or brackets logo* | | | |

## ALLISON, KEITH

### COLUMBIA

| Number | Title (A Side/B Side) | Yr | NM |
|---|---|---|---|
| ❑ CL 2641 [M] | Keith Allison In Action | 1967 | 25.00 |
| ❑ CS 9441 [S] | Keith Allison In Action | 1967 | 25.00 |

## ALLISON, LUTHER

### DELMARK

| Number | Title (A Side/B Side) | Yr | NM |
|---|---|---|---|
| ❑ DS-625 | Love Me, Mama | 1969 | 25.00 |

### GORDY

| Number | Title (A Side/B Side) | Yr | NM |
|---|---|---|---|
| ❑ G-964 | Bad News Is Coming | 1973 | 10.00 |
| ❑ G-967 | Luther's Blues | 1974 | 10.00 |
| ❑ G-974 | Night Life | 1976 | 10.00 |

## ALLISON, MOSE

### ATLANTIC

| Number | Title (A Side/B Side) | Yr | NM |
|---|---|---|---|
| ❑ SD 1389 [S] | I Don't Worry About a Thing | 1962 | 30.00 |
| ❑ SD 1398 [S] | Swingin' Machine | 1963 | 25.00 |

### COLUMBIA

| Number | Title (A Side/B Side) | Yr | NM |
|---|---|---|---|
| ❑ CL 1444 [M] | The Transfiguration of Hiram Brown | 1960 | 25.00 |
| ❑ CL 1565 [M] | I Love the Life I Live | 1960 | 25.00 |
| *—Red and black label with six "eye" logos* | | | |
| ❑ CS 8240 [S] | The Transfiguration of Hiram Brown | 1960 | 30.00 |
| ❑ CS 8365 [S] | I Love the Life I Live | 1960 | 30.00 |
| *—Red and black label with six "eye" logos* | | | |

### EPIC

| Number | Title (A Side/B Side) | Yr | NM |
|---|---|---|---|
| ❑ BA 17031 [S] | Take to the Hills | 1962 | 40.00 |

### PRESTIGE

| Number | Title (A Side/B Side) | Yr | NM |
|---|---|---|---|
| ❑ PRLP-7091 [M] | Back Country Suite | 1957 | 100.00 |
| *—With "W. 50th St., NYC" address on label* | | | |
| ❑ PRLP-7121 [M] | Local Color | 1958 | 100.00 |
| *—With "W. 50th St., NYC" address on label* | | | |
| ❑ PRLP-7137 [M] | Young Man Blues | 1958 | 100.00 |
| *—With "W. 50th St., NYC" address on label* | | | |
| ❑ PRLP-7152 [M] | Creek Bank | 1959 | 80.00 |
| *—Yellow label with Bergenfield, NJ address on label* | | | |
| ❑ PRLP-7152 [M] | Creek Bank | 196? | 30.00 |
| *—Blue label, trident logo* | | | |
| ❑ PRLP-7189 [M] | Autumn Song | 196? | 20.00 |
| *—Blue label, trident logo* | | | |
| ❑ PRLP-7189 [M] | Autumn Song | 1960 | 50.00 |
| *—Yellow label with Bergenfield, NJ address on label* | | | |
| ❑ PRLP-7215 [M] | Ramblin' with Mose | 196? | 25.00 |
| *—Blue label, trident logo* | | | |
| ❑ PRLP-7215 [M] | Ramblin' with Mose | 1961 | 60.00 |
| *—Yellow label with Bergenfield, NJ address on label* | | | |
| ❑ PRLP-7279 [M] | Mose Allison Sings (The Seventh Son) | 1963 | 40.00 |
| *—Yellow label with Bergenfield, NJ address on label* | | | |
| ❑ PRST-7279 [S] | Mose Allison Sings (The Seventh Son) | 196? | 25.00 |
| *—Blue label, trident logo at right* | | | |
| ❑ PRST-7279 [S] | Mose Allison Sings (The Seventh Son) | 1963 | 50.00 |
| *—Silver label* | | | |
| ❑ PRLP-7423 [M] | Down Home Piano | 1966 | 20.00 |
| *—Blue label, trident logo at right* | | | |
| ❑ PRST-7423 [S] | Down Home Piano | 1966 | 25.00 |
| *—Blue label, trident logo at right* | | | |
| ❑ PRLP-7446 [M] | Mose Allison Plays for Lovers | 1967 | 25.00 |
| ❑ PRST-7446 [S] | Mose Allison Plays for Lovers | 1967 | 20.00 |

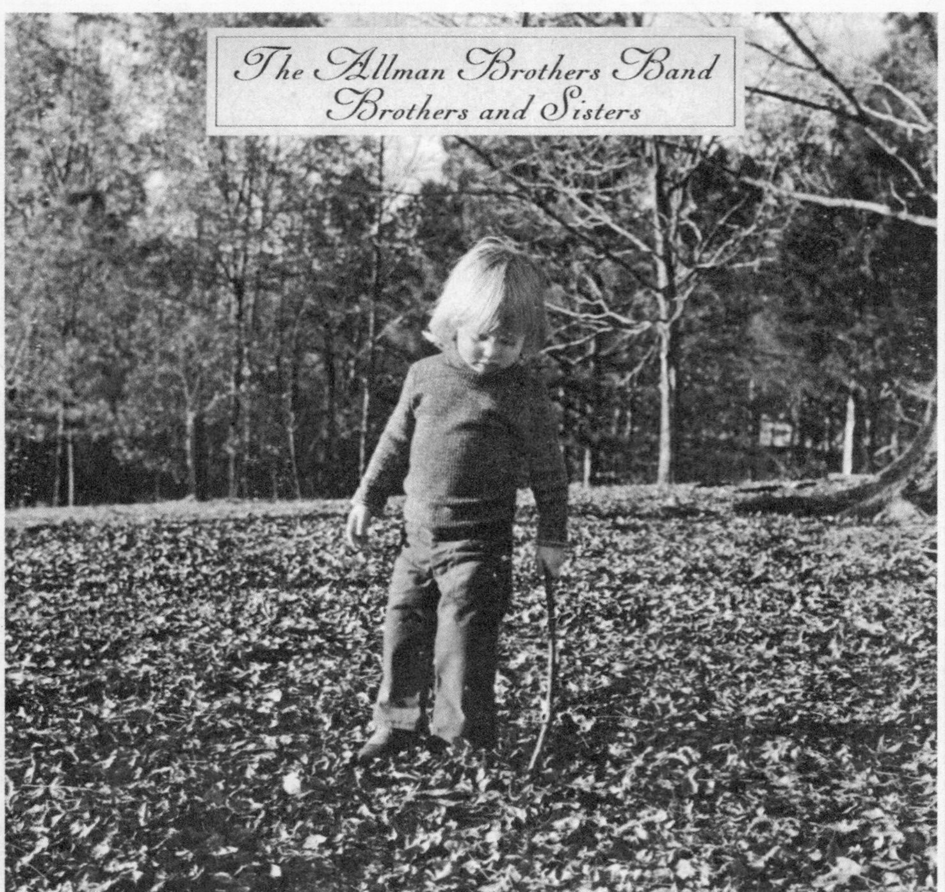


The Allman Brothers Band, *Brothers and Sisters,* Capricorn CP 0111, 1973, $12.

| Number | Title (A Side/B Side) | Yr | NM |
|---|---|---|---|
| **ALLMAN, DUANE** | | | |
| CAPRICORN | | | |
| ❑ 2CP 0108 [(2)] | An Anthology | 1972 | 20.00 |
| ❑ 2CP 0139 [(2)] | An Anthology, Vol. II | 1974 | 20.00 |
| POLYDOR | | | |
| ❑ PD-1-6338 | The Best of Duane Allman | 1981 | 12.00 |
| ❑ 827563-1 | The Best of Duane Allman | 1984 | 8.00 |
| **ALLMAN, DUANE AND GREGG** | | | |
| BOLD | | | |
| ❑ 33-301 | Duane and Gregg Allman | 197? | 12.00 |
| *—Non-gatefold cover* | | | |
| ❑ 33-301 | Duane and Gregg Allman | 1972 | 25.00 |
| *—Gatefold cover* | | | |
| **ALLMAN, SHELDON** | | | |
| DEL-FI | | | |
| ❑ DFLP-1213 [M] | Sing Along with Drac | 1961 | 40.00 |
| HIFI | | | |
| ❑ R-415 [M] | Folk Songs for the 21st Century | 1960 | 40.00 |
| **ALLMAN BROTHERS BAND, THE** | | | |
| ARISTA | | | |
| ❑ AL 9535 | Reach for the Sky | 1980 | 10.00 |
| ❑ AL 9564 | Brothers of the Road | 1981 | 10.00 |
| ATCO | | | |
| ❑ SD 33-308 | The Allman Brothers Band | 1969 | 15.00 |
| ❑ SD 33-342 | Idlewild South | 1970 | 15.00 |
| ❑ SD 2-805 [(2)] | Beginnings | 1973 | 20.00 |
| CAPRICORN | | | |
| ❑ 2CP 0102 [(2)] | Eat a Peach | 1972 | 15.00 |
| ❑ CPN2 0102 [(2)] | Eat a Peach | 198? | 12.00 |
| ❑ CX4 0102 [(2)Q] | Eat a Peach | 1974 | 30.00 |
| ❑ CP 0111 | Brothers and Sisters | 1973 | 12.00 |
| ❑ CPN 0111 | Brothers and Sisters | 198? | 8.00 |
| ❑ 2CP 0131 [(2)] | The Allman Brothers Band at Fillmore East | 1974 | 15.00 |
| ❑ CPN2 0131 [(2)] | The Allman Brothers Band at Fillmore East | 198? | 12.00 |
| ❑ CX4 0131 [(2)Q] | The Allman Brothers Band at Fillmore East | 1974 | 30.00 |
| ❑ 2CX 0132 [(2)] | Beginnings | 1974 | 15.00 |
| ❑ CPN2 0132 [(2)] | Beginnings | 198? | 12.00 |

| Number | Title (A Side/B Side) | Yr | NM |
|---|---|---|---|
| ❑ CP 0156 | Win, Lose or Draw | 1975 | 10.00 |
| ❑ CPN 0156 | Win, Lose or Draw | 198? | 8.00 |
| ❑ 2CX 0164 [(2)] | The Road Goes On Forever | 1975 | 12.00 |
| ❑ 2CX 0177 [(2)] | Wipe the Windows, Check the Oil, Dollar Gas | 1976 | 12.00 |
| ❑ CPN 0196 | The Allman Brothers Band | 1978 | 10.00 |
| ❑ CPN 0197 | Idlewild South | 1978 | 10.00 |
| ❑ CPN 0218 | Enlightened Rogues | 1979 | 10.00 |
| ❑ 2-802 [(2)M] | The Allman Brothers Band at Fillmore East | 1971 | 80.00 |
| *—Promo only; sticker on front cover says "Promotional DJ Copy Monaural Not for Sale"* | | | |
| ❑ SD 2-802 [(2)S] | The Allman Brothers Band at Fillmore East | 1971 | 20.00 |
| EPIC | | | |
| ❑ E 46144 | Seven Turns | 1990 | 15.00 |
| MOBILE FIDELITY | | | |
| ❑ 1-157 [(2)] | Eat a Peach | 1984 | 200.00 |
| *—Audiophile vinyl* | | | |
| ❑ 1-213 | Brothers and Sisters | 1994 | 30.00 |
| *—Audiophile vinyl* | | | |
| NAUTILUS | | | |
| ❑ NR-30 [(2)] | The Allman Brothers Band at Fillmore East | 1982 | 100.00 |
| *—Audiophile vinyl* | | | |
| POLYDOR | | | |
| ❑ PD-1-6339 | The Best of the Allman Brothers Band | 1981 | 10.00 |
| ❑ 823273-1 [(2)] | The Allman Brothers Band at Fillmore East | 1984 | 10.00 |
| ❑ 823653-1 | The Allman Brothers Band | 1984 | 8.00 |
| ❑ 823654-1 [(2)] | Eat a Peach | 1984 | 10.00 |
| ❑ 823708-1 | The Best of the Allman Brothers Band | 1984 | 8.00 |
| *—Reissue of PD-1-6339* | | | |
| ❑ 825092-1 | Brothers and Sisters | 1985 | 8.00 |
| ❑ 839417-1 [(6)] | Dreams | 1989 | 40.00 |
| **ALLSUP, TOMMY** | | | |
| GRT | | | |
| ❑ 20004 | Tommy Allsup and the Tennessee Saxes Play the Hits of Tammy Wynette | 1970 | 20.00 |

| Number | Title (A Side/B Side) | Yr | NM |
|---|---|---|---|
| METROMEDIA | | | |
| ❑ MM 1004 | Tommy Allsup and the Nashville Survey Play the Hits of Charley Pride | 1969 | 25.00 |
| REPRISE | | | |
| ❑ R 6182 [M] | Tommy Allsup Plays the Buddy Holly Songbook | 1965 | 40.00 |
| ❑ RS 6182 [S] | Tommy Allsup Plays the Buddy Holly Songbook | 1965 | 50.00 |
| **ALMEIDA, LAURINDO** | | | |
| CAPITOL | | | |
| ❑ H-193 [10] | Concert Creations for Guitar | 1950 | 80.00 |
| ❑ ST 1759 [S] | Viva Bossa Nova! | 1962 | 20.00 |
| ❑ ST 1872 [S] | Ole! Bossa Nova | 1963 | 20.00 |
| ❑ ST 1946 [S] | It's a Bossa Nova World | 1963 | 20.00 |
| ❑ SP 8482 [S] | Songs of Enchantment | 196? | 20.00 |
| CORAL | | | |
| ❑ CRL 56049 [10] | A Guitar Recital of Famous Serenades | 1952 | 80.00 |
| ❑ CRL 56086 [10] | Latin Melodies | 1952 | 80.00 |
| ❑ CRL 57056 [M] | A Guitar Recital of Famous Serenades | 1956 | 50.00 |
| *—Maroon label original* | | | |
| ❑ CRL 57056 [M] | A Guitar Recital of Famous Serenades | 196? | 25.00 |
| *—Black label with color bars* | | | |
| CRYSTAL CLEAR | | | |
| ❑ CCS-8001 | Virtuoso Guitar | 1978 | 25.00 |
| *—Direct-to-disc recording; plays at 45 rpm; black vinyl* | | | |
| ❑ CCS-8001 | Virtuoso Guitar | 1978 | 40.00 |
| *—Direct-to-disc recording; plays at 45 rpm; white vinyl* | | | |
| ❑ CCS-8007 | New Directions | 1979 | 40.00 |
| *—Direct-to-disc recording* | | | |
| PACIFIC JAZZ | | | |
| ❑ PJLP-7 [10] | Laurindo Almeida Quartet | 1953 | 200.00 |
| ❑ PJLP-13 [10] | Laurindo Almeida Quartet, Vol. 2 | 1954 | 200.00 |
| ❑ PJ-1204 [M] | Laurindo Almeida Quartet Featuring Bud Shank | 1955 | 80.00 |
| *—Reissue of 10-inch Pacific Jazz LPs; black vinyl* | | | |
| ❑ PJ-1204 [M] | Laurindo Almeida Quartet Featuring Bud Shank | 1955 | 120.00 |
| *—Reissue of 10-inch Pacific Jazz LPs; red vinyl* | | | |
| WORLD PACIFIC | | | |
| ❑ PJ-1204 [M] | Laurindo Almeida Quartet Featuring Bud Shank | 1958 | 50.00 |
| *—Reissue of Pacific Jazz 1204* | | | |
| ❑ WP-1412 [M] | Brazilliance, Vol. 1 | 1962 | 30.00 |
| *—Reissue of World Pacific 1204* | | | |
| ❑ ST-1419 [S] | Brazilliance, Vol. 2 | 1962 | 25.00 |
| ❑ WP-1419 [M] | Brazilliance, Vol. 2 | 1962 | 30.00 |
| ❑ ST-1425 [S] | Brazilliance, Vol. 3 | 1962 | 25.00 |
| ❑ WP-1425 [M] | Brazilliance, Vol. 3 | 1962 | 30.00 |
| ❑ WPS-21412 [S] | Brazilliance, Vol. 1 | 196? | 25.00 |
| ❑ T 90078 [M] | Brazilliance, Vol. 1 | 196? | 30.00 |
| *—Capitol Record Club edition* | | | |
| **ALMERICO, TONY** | | | |
| IMPERIAL | | | |
| ❑ LP-9151 [M] | French Quarter Jazz | 1961 | 20.00 |
| ❑ LP-12072 [S] | French Quarter Jazz | 1961 | 25.00 |
| **ALPERT, HERB** | | | |
| A&M | | | |
| ❑ SP-3714 | Rise | 1980 | 8.00 |
| *—Reissue of 4790* | | | |
| ❑ SP-3717 | Beyond | 1980 | 8.00 |
| ❑ SP-3728 | Magic Man | 1981 | 8.00 |
| ❑ SP-3731 | Fandango | 1982 | 8.00 |
| ❑ SP-4591 | Just You and Me | 1976 | 10.00 |
| ❑ SP-4790 | Rise | 1979 | 10.00 |
| ❑ SP-4949 | Blow Your Own Horn | 1983 | 8.00 |
| ❑ SP-5082 | Wild Romance | 1985 | 8.00 |
| ❑ SP-5125 | Keep Your Eye on Me | 1987 | 8.00 |
| ❑ SP-5209 | Under a Spanish Moon | 1988 | 8.00 |
| ❑ SP-5273 | My Abstract Heart | 1989 | 8.00 |
| ❑ 75021 5345 1 | North on South Street | 1991 | 12.00 |
| MOBILE FIDELITY | | | |
| ❑ 1-053 | Rise | 1981 | 25.00 |
| *—Audiophile vinyl* | | | |
| **ALPERT, HERB, AND THE TIJUANA BRASS** | | | |
| A&M | | | |
| ❑ LP-101 [M] | The Lonely Bull | 1962 | 20.00 |
| *—Originals on yellowish label with brown print* | | | |
| ❑ LP-101 [M] | The Lonely Bull | 1963 | 15.00 |
| *—Second pressings with brown label and A&M logo at top* | | | |
| ❑ LP-101 [M] | The Lonely Bull | 1964 | 12.00 |
| *—Third pressing with brown label and A&M logo at left* | | | |
| ❑ SP-101 [S] | The Lonely Bull | 1962 | 25.00 |
| *—Original editions had this number* | | | |
| ❑ LP-103 [M] | Herb Alpert's Tijuana Brass, Volume 2 | 1963 | 15.00 |
| *—Brown label with A&M logo at top* | | | |
| ❑ LP-103 [M] | Herb Alpert's Tijuana Brass, Volume 2 | 1964 | 12.00 |
| *—Brown label with A&M logo at left* | | | |

| Number | Title (A Side/B Side) | Yr | NM |
|---|---|---|---|
| ❑ SP-103 [S] | Herb Alpert's Tijuana Brass, Volume 2 | 1963 | 20.00 |
| *—Original issues had this number* | | | |
| ❑ LP-108 [M] | South of the Border | 1964 | 12.00 |
| ❑ SP-108 [S] | South of the Border | 1964 | 20.00 |
| *—Original issues had this number* | | | |
| ❑ LP-110 [M] | Whipped Cream & Other Delights | 1965 | 10.00 |
| ❑ LP-112 [M] | Going Places | 1965 | 10.00 |
| ❑ LP-114 [M] | What Now My Love | 1966 | 10.00 |
| ❑ LP-119 [M] | S.R.O. | 1966 | 10.00 |
| ❑ LP-124 [M] | Sounds Like | 1967 | 10.00 |
| ❑ LP166 [M] | Christmas Album | 1968 | 25.00 |
| *—Mono is white label promo only* | | | |
| ❑ SP-3101 | The Lonely Bull | 198? | 8.00 |
| *—Reissue* | | | |
| ❑ SP-3113 | Christmas Album | 198? | 8.00 |
| *—Reissue of SP-4166* | | | |
| ❑ SP-3157 | Whipped Cream & Other Delights | 198? | 8.00 |
| *—Reissue* | | | |
| ❑ SP-3263 | South of the Border | 1984 | 8.00 |
| ❑ SP-3264 | Going Places | 1984 | 8.00 |
| *—Reissue* | | | |
| ❑ SP-3265 | What Now My Love | 1984 | 8.00 |
| ❑ SP-3266 | The Beat of the Brass | 1984 | 8.00 |
| *—Reissue* | | | |
| ❑ SP-3267 | Greatest Hits | 1984 | 8.00 |
| *—Reissue* | | | |
| ❑ SP-3268 | Solid Brass | 1984 | 8.00 |
| ❑ SP-3269 | Greatest Hits, Vol. 2 | 1984 | 8.00 |
| ❑ SP-3521 [(2)] | Foursider | 1973 | 12.00 |
| ❑ SP-3620 | You Smile — The Song Begins | 1974 | 10.00 |
| ❑ SP-4101 [S] | The Lonely Bull | 1962 | 15.00 |
| ❑ SP-4103 [S] | Herb Alpert's Tijuana Brass, Volume 2 | 1963 | 15.00 |
| ❑ SP-4108 [S] | South of the Border | 1964 | 15.00 |
| ❑ SP-4110 [S] | Whipped Cream & Other Delights | 1965 | 12.00 |
| ❑ SP-4112 [S] | Going Places | 1965 | 12.00 |
| ❑ SP-4114 [S] | What Now My Love | 1966 | 12.00 |
| ❑ SP-4119 [S] | S.R.O. | 1966 | 12.00 |
| ❑ SP-4124 [S] | Sounds Like | 1967 | 12.00 |
| ❑ SP-4134 | Herb Alpert's Ninth | 1967 | 10.00 |
| ❑ SP-4146 | The Beat of the Brass | 1968 | 10.00 |
| ❑ SP-4166 [S] | Christmas Album | 1968 | 12.00 |
| ❑ SP-4190 | Warm | 1969 | 10.00 |
| ❑ SP-4228 | The Brass Are Comin' | 1969 | 10.00 |
| ❑ SP-4245 | Greatest Hits | 1970 | 10.00 |
| ❑ SP-4314 | Summertime | 1971 | 10.00 |
| ❑ SP-4341 | Solid Brass | 1972 | 10.00 |
| ❑ SP-4521 | Coney Island | 1975 | 10.00 |
| ❑ SP-4627 | Greatest Hits, Vol. 2 | 1976 | 10.00 |
| ❑ SP-5022 | Bullish | 1984 | 8.00 |
| ❑ SP-6011 [(2)] | Foursider | 197? | 10.00 |
| *—Reissue* | | | |
| ❑ LP-9004 [DJ] | The Best from Herb Alpert & The Tijuana Brass | 196? | 15.00 |
| *—Promo-only compilation* | | | |
| ❑ ST-90073 [S] | South of the Border | 1964 | 20.00 |
| *—Capitol Record Club edition* | | | |
| ❑ T-90074 [M] | Herb Alpert's Tijuana Brass, Volume 2 | 1964 | 20.00 |
| *—Capitol Record Club edition* | | | |
| ❑ ST-90387 [S] | Whipped Cream & Other Delights | 1965 | 15.00 |
| *—Capitol Record Club edition* | | | |
| ❑ ST-90507 [S] | Going Places | 1965 | 20.00 |
| *—Capitol Record Club edition* | | | |
| ❑ T-90507 [M] | Going Places | 1965 | 15.00 |
| *—Capitol Record Club edition* | | | |
| ❑ T-90655 [M] | What Now My Love | 1966 | 12.00 |
| *—Capitol Record Club edition* | | | |
| ❑ SW-93870 | Summertime | 197? | 12.00 |
| *—Capitol Record Club edition* | | | |
| LONGINES SYMPHONETTE | | | |
| ❑ LWS-500 [(5)] | Treasury of Herb Alpert and the Tijuana Brass | 196? | 25.00 |
| *—Also contains music by the Baja Marimba Band; records are individually numbered from 500 through 504* | | | |
| **ALVIN, DANNY** | | | |
| JAZZOLOGY | | | |
| ❑ 8 [M] | Danny Alvin and the Kings of Dixieland | 1964 | 20.00 |
| ❑ S-8 [S] | Danny Alvin and the Kings of Dixieland | 1964 | 20.00 |
| STEPHENY | | | |
| ❑ MF-4002 [M] | Club Basin Street | 1957 | 50.00 |
| **AMAZING RHYTHM ACES** | | | |
| ABC | | | |
| ❑ D-913 | Stacked Deck | 1975 | 20.00 |
| ❑ D-940 | Too Stuffed to Jump | 1976 | 15.00 |
| ❑ AB-1005 | Toucan Do It Too | 1977 | 15.00 |
| ❑ AA-1063 | Burning the Ballroom Down | 1978 | 15.00 |
| ❑ AA-1123 | The Amazing Rhythm Aces | 1979 | 20.00 |
| COLUMBIA | | | |
| ❑ JC 36083 | The Amazing Rhythm Aces | 1979 | 12.00 |
| *—Reissue of ABC 1123* | | | |

Herb Alpert and the Tijuana Brass, *What Now My Love,* A&M SP-4114, stereo, $12.

| Number | Title (A Side/B Side) | Yr | NM |
|---|---|---|---|
| WARNER BROS. | | | |
| ❑ BSK 3476 | How the Hell Do You Spell Rythum? | 1980 | 12.00 |
| **AMBASSADORS, THE (1)** | | | |
| ARCTIC | | | |
| ❑ ALPS-1005 | Soul Summit | 1969 | 25.00 |
| **AMBER** | | | |
| TOMMY BOY | | | |
| ❑ 1424 [(3)] | The Hits Remixed | 2000 | 20.00 |
| **AMBOY DUKES, THE** | | | |
| DISCREET | | | |
| ❑ DS 2181 | Call of the Wild | 1974 | 15.00 |
| *—As "Ted Nugent and the Amboy Dukes"* | | | |
| ❑ DS 2203 | Tooth, Fang and Claw | 1974 | 15.00 |
| *—As "Ted Nugent and the Amboy Dukes"* | | | |
| MAINSTREAM | | | |
| ❑ S-414 | Dr. Slingshot | 1975 | 15.00 |
| ❑ S-421 | Ted Nugent and the Amboy Dukes | 1976 | 30.00 |
| *—Reissue of early material* | | | |
| ❑ S-2-801 [(2)] | Journeys and Migrations | 1974 | 30.00 |
| *—Reissue of 6112 and 6118* | | | |
| ❑ S-6104 [S] | The Amboy Dukes | 1967 | 40.00 |
| ❑ S-6112 | Journey to the Center of the Mind | 1968 | 40.00 |
| ❑ S-6118 | Migration | 1968 | 40.00 |
| ❑ S-6125 | The Best of the Original Amboy Dukes | 1969 | 30.00 |
| ❑ 56104 [M] | The Amboy Dukes | 1967 | 80.00 |
| POLYDOR | | | |
| ❑ 24-4012 | Marriage on the Rocks/Rock Bottom | 1970 | 25.00 |
| ❑ 24-4035 | Survival of the Fittest/Live | 1971 | 25.00 |
| *—As "Ted Nugent and the Amboy Dukes"* | | | |
| **AMBROSE, AMANDA** | | | |
| DUNWICH | | | |
| ❑ 668 [M] | Amanda | 1966 | 15.00 |
| ❑ S-668 [S] | Amanda | 1966 | 20.00 |
| **AMBROSE SLADE** See SLADE. | | | |

| Number | Title (A Side/B Side) | Yr | NM |
|---|---|---|---|
| **AMBROSIA** | | | |
| NAUTILUS | | | |
| ❑ NR-23 | Life Beyond L.A. | 1981 | 30.00 |
| *—Audiophile vinyl* | | | |
| 20TH CENTURY | | | |
| ❑ T-434 | Ambrosia | 1975 | 10.00 |
| *—New cover without black border* | | | |
| ❑ T-434 | Ambrosia | 1975 | 12.00 |
| *—Original cover with black border* | | | |
| ❑ T-510 | Somewhere I've Never Traveled | 1976 | 10.00 |
| *—Standard cover* | | | |
| ❑ T-510 | Somewhere I've Never Traveled | 1976 | 12.00 |
| *—Fold-open cover in the shape of a pyramid* | | | |
| WARNER BROS. | | | |
| ❑ BSK 3135 | Life Beyond L.A. | 1978 | 10.00 |
| ❑ BSK 3181 | Ambrosia | 1978 | 8.00 |
| *—Reissue of 20th Century 434* | | | |
| ❑ BSK 3368 | One Eighty | 1980 | 10.00 |
| ❑ BSK 3638 | Road Island | 1982 | 10.00 |
| **AMECHE, DON, AND FRANCES LANGFORD** | | | |
| COLUMBIA | | | |
| ❑ CL 1692 | The Bickersons | 1962 | 20.00 |
| *—Live-in-the-studio recordings from 1961* | | | |
| ❑ CL 1883 | The Bickersons Fight Back | 1962 | 20.00 |
| *—More live-in-the-studio recordings from 1961* | | | |
| ❑ G 30523 [(2)] | The Bickersons Rematch | 1970 | 15.00 |
| *—Compilation of the earlier Columbia LPs* | | | |
| RADIOLA | | | |
| ❑ MR 1115 | The Bickersons | 198? | 12.00 |
| *—Compilation of radio shows* | | | |
| RADIOLA/MURRAY HILL | | | |
| ❑ 3MH 36721 [(3)] | Return of the Bickersons | 1987 | 20.00 |
| *—Compilation of radio shows* | | | |
| **AMERICA** | | | |
| CAPITOL | | | |
| ❑ SO-11950 | Silent Letter | 1979 | 10.00 |
| ❑ SOO-12098 | Alibi | 1980 | 10.00 |
| ❑ ST-12209 | View from the Ground | 1982 | 10.00 |
| ❑ ST-12277 | Your Move | 1983 | 10.00 |
| ❑ ST-12370 | Perspective | 1984 | 10.00 |
| ❑ ST-12422 | In Concert | 1985 | 10.00 |

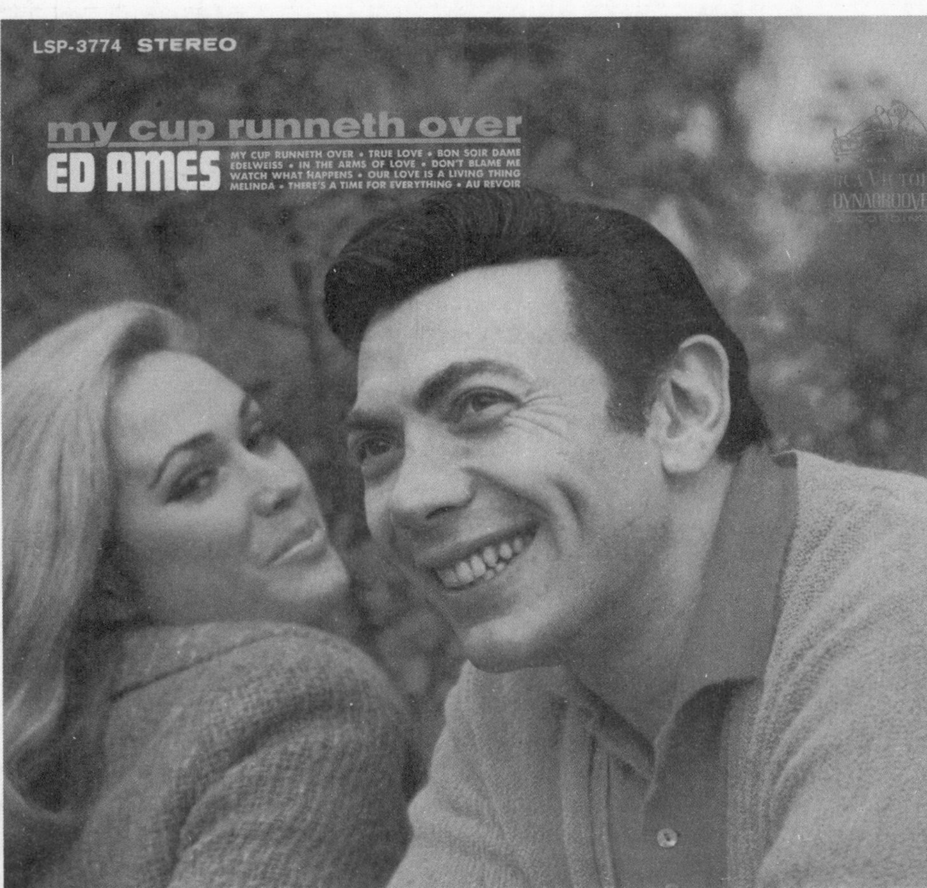


Ed Ames, *My Cup Runneth Over,* RCA Victor LSP-3774, stereo, $12.

| Number | Title (A Side/B Side) | Yr | NM |
|---|---|---|---|
| ❑ SN-16275 | Alibi | 1982 | 8.00 |
| ❑ SN-16350 | View from the Ground | 1985 | 8.00 |
| ❑ SN-16361 | Your Move | 1985 | 8.00 |

WARNER BROS.

| Number | Title (A Side/B Side) | Yr | NM |
|---|---|---|---|
| ❑ BS 2576 | America | 1971 | 25.00 |

*—First pressings omit "A Horse with No Name"*

| Number | Title (A Side/B Side) | Yr | NM |
|---|---|---|---|
| ❑ BS 2576 | America | 1972 | 12.00 |

*—With "A Horse with No Name" mentioned on front cover; green label*

| Number | Title (A Side/B Side) | Yr | NM |
|---|---|---|---|
| ❑ BS 2576 | America | 1972 | 15.00 |

*—Transitional edition includes "A Horse with No Name" but doesn't mention it on the front cover*

| Number | Title (A Side/B Side) | Yr | NM |
|---|---|---|---|
| ❑ BS 2655 | Homecoming | 1972 | 12.00 |
| ❑ BS 2728 | Hat Trick | 1973 | 12.00 |
| ❑ BS 2808 | Holiday | 1974 | 12.00 |
| ❑ BS4 2808 [Q] | Holiday | 1974 | 20.00 |
| ❑ BS 2852 | Hearts | 1975 | 12.00 |
| ❑ BS4 2852 [Q] | Hearts | 1975 | 20.00 |
| ❑ BS 2894 | History/America's Greatest Hits | 1975 | 12.00 |
| ❑ BS 2932 | Hideaway | 1976 | 12.00 |
| ❑ BSK 3017 | Harbor | 1977 | 12.00 |
| ❑ BSK 3110 | History/America's Greatest Hits | 1977 | 10.00 |

*—Reissue of BS 2894 with "Burbank" palm trees label (later white labels are $8 NM)*

| Number | Title (A Side/B Side) | Yr | NM |
|---|---|---|---|
| ❑ BSK 3136 | America/Live | 1977 | 12.00 |

## AMERICAN BLUES, THE Early incarnation of ZZ TOP.

KARMA

| Number | Title (A Side/B Side) | Yr | NM |
|---|---|---|---|
| ❑ 1001 | The American Blues Is Here | 1967 | 400.00 |

UNI

| Number | Title (A Side/B Side) | Yr | NM |
|---|---|---|---|
| ❑ 73044 | The American Blues Do Their Thing | 1968 | 60.00 |

## AMERICAN BLUES EXCHANGE, THE

TAYL

| Number | Title (A Side/B Side) | Yr | NM |
|---|---|---|---|
| ❑ TLS-1 | Blueprint | 1969 | 400.00 |

## AMERICAN BREED, THE

ACTA

| Number | Title (A Side/B Side) | Yr | NM |
|---|---|---|---|
| ❑ 8002 [M] | The American Breed | 1967 | 20.00 |
| ❑ 8003 [M] | Bend Me, Shape Me | 1968 | 20.00 |
| ❑ 8006 [M] | Pumpkin, Powder, Scarlet & Green | 1968 | 50.00 |

*—Stock label; the cover is the same as stereo but with a "Monaural" sticker attached*

| Number | Title (A Side/B Side) | Yr | NM |
|---|---|---|---|
| ❑ 8008 [M] | Lonely Side of the City | 1969 | 50.00 |

*—In stereo cover with "Monaural" sticker; record is regular yellow label*

| Number | Title (A Side/B Side) | Yr | NM |
|---|---|---|---|
| ❑ 38002 [S] | The American Breed | 1967 | 25.00 |
| ❑ 38003 [S] | Bend Me, Shape Me | 1968 | 25.00 |
| ❑ 38006 [S] | Pumpkin, Powder, Scarlet & Green | 1968 | 20.00 |
| ❑ 38008 [S] | Lonely Side of the City | 1969 | 20.00 |

## AMERICAN DREAM, THE

AMPEX

| Number | Title (A Side/B Side) | Yr | NM |
|---|---|---|---|
| ❑ A-10101 | The American Dream | 1970 | 20.00 |

*—Produced by Todd Rundgren*

## AMERICAN EAGLE

DECCA

| Number | Title (A Side/B Side) | Yr | NM |
|---|---|---|---|
| ❑ DL 75258 | American Eagle | 1971 | 20.00 |

## AMERICAN JAZZ ENSEMBLE, THE

EPIC

| Number | Title (A Side/B Side) | Yr | NM |
|---|---|---|---|
| ❑ LA 16040 [M] | New Dimensions | 1962 | 20.00 |
| ❑ BA 17040 [S] | New Dimensions | 1962 | 25.00 |

RCA VICTOR

| Number | Title (A Side/B Side) | Yr | NM |
|---|---|---|---|
| ❑ LPM-2557 [M] | The American Jazz Ensemble in Rome | 1962 | 20.00 |
| ❑ LSP-2557 [S] | The American Jazz Ensemble in Rome | 1962 | 25.00 |

## AMERICAN REVOLUTION, THE

FLICK DISC

| Number | Title (A Side/B Side) | Yr | NM |
|---|---|---|---|
| ❑ FL-45,002 [M] | The American Revolution | 1968 | 50.00 |

*—White label promo in stereo cover with "Not for Sale DJ Monaural" sticker on front*

| Number | Title (A Side/B Side) | Yr | NM |
|---|---|---|---|
| ❑ FLS-45,002 [S] | The American Revolution | 1968 | 25.00 |

## AMES, ED

RCA CAMDEN

| Number | Title (A Side/B Side) | Yr | NM |
|---|---|---|---|
| ❑ ACL1-0244 | Do You Hear What I Hear? | 1973 | 12.00 |
| ❑ CAS-2536 | Ed Ames | 1972 | 12.00 |
| ❑ CAS-2598 | Somewhere, My Love | 1972 | 12.00 |

RCA VICTOR

| Number | Title (A Side/B Side) | Yr | NM |
|---|---|---|---|
| ❑ ANL1-1780 | Pure Gold | 1976 | 10.00 |
| ❑ LPM-2781 [M] | Opening Night | 1963 | 12.00 |
| ❑ LSP-2781 [S] | Opening Night | 1963 | 15.00 |
| ❑ ANL1-2891 | The Impossible Dream | 1978 | 10.00 |
| ❑ LPM-2944 [M] | The Ed Ames Album | 1964 | 12.00 |
| ❑ LSP-2944 [S] | The Ed Ames Album | 1964 | 15.00 |
| ❑ LPM-3390 [M] | My Kind of Songs | 1965 | 12.00 |
| ❑ LSP-3390 [S] | My Kind of Songs | 1965 | 15.00 |
| ❑ LPM-3460 [M] | It's a Man's World | 1965 | 12.00 |
| ❑ LSP-3460 [S] | It's a Man's World | 1965 | 15.00 |
| ❑ LPM-3636 [M] | More I Cannot Wish You | 1966 | 10.00 |
| ❑ LSP-3636 [S] | More I Cannot Wish You | 1966 | 12.00 |
| ❑ LPM-3774 [M] | My Cup Runneth Over | 1967 | 10.00 |
| ❑ LSP-3774 [S] | My Cup Runneth Over | 1967 | 12.00 |
| ❑ LPM-3834 [M] | Time, Time | 1967 | 12.00 |
| ❑ LSP-3834 [S] | Time, Time | 1967 | 10.00 |
| ❑ LPM-3838 [M] | Christmas with Ed Ames | 1967 | 15.00 |
| ❑ LSP-3838 [S] | Christmas with Ed Ames | 1967 | 12.00 |
| ❑ LPM-3913 [M] | When the Snow Is On the Roses | 1967 | 12.00 |
| ❑ LSP-3913 [S] | When the Snow Is On the Roses | 1967 | 10.00 |
| ❑ LPM-3961 [M] | Who Will Answer? And Other Songs of Our Time | 1968 | 15.00 |
| ❑ LSP-3961 [S] | Who Will Answer? And Other Songs of Our Time | 1968 | 10.00 |
| ❑ LPM-4028 [M] | Apologize | 1968 | 20.00 |
| ❑ LSP-4028 [S] | Apologize | 1968 | 10.00 |
| ❑ LSP-4079 | The Hits of Broadway and Hollywood | 1968 | 10.00 |
| ❑ LSP-4128 | A Time for Living, A Time for Hope | 1969 | 10.00 |
| ❑ LSP-4172 | The Windmills of Your Mind | 1969 | 10.00 |
| ❑ LSP-4184 | The Best of Ed Ames | 1969 | 10.00 |
| ❑ LSP-4249 | Love of the Common People | 1969 | 10.00 |
| ❑ LSP-4381 | Sing Away the World | 1970 | 10.00 |
| ❑ LSP-4385 | Christmas Is the Warmest Time of the Year | 1970 | 20.00 |
| ❑ LSP-4453 | The Songs of Bacharach and David | 1971 | 10.00 |
| ❑ LSP-4634 | Ed Ames | 1972 | 15.00 |
| ❑ LSP-4683 | Ed Ames Remembers Jim Reeves | 1972 | 15.00 |
| ❑ LSP-4808 | Songs from "Lost Horizon" | 1973 | 15.00 |
| ❑ VPS-6023 [(2)] | This Is Ed Ames | 1970 | 20.00 |

## AMES, NANCY

EPIC

| Number | Title (A Side/B Side) | Yr | NM |
|---|---|---|---|
| ❑ LN 24189 [M] | Latin Pulse | 1966 | 12.00 |
| ❑ LN 24197 [M] | As Time Goes By | 1967 | 12.00 |
| ❑ LN 24238 [M] | Spiced with Brazil | 1967 | 12.00 |
| ❑ BN 26189 [S] | Latin Pulse | 1966 | 15.00 |
| ❑ BN 26197 [S] | As Time Goes By | 1967 | 15.00 |
| ❑ BN 26238 [S] | Spiced with Brazil | 1967 | 15.00 |
| ❑ BN 26378 | Nancy Ames at the Americana | 1968 | 12.00 |

LIBERTY

| Number | Title (A Side/B Side) | Yr | NM |
|---|---|---|---|
| ❑ LRP-3276 [M] | The Incredible Nancy Ames | 1963 | 15.00 |
| ❑ LRP-3299 [M] | Portrait of Nancy | 1963 | 15.00 |
| ❑ LRP-3329 [M] | I Never Will Marry | 1964 | 15.00 |
| ❑ LRP-3369 [M] | This Is the Girl That Is | 1964 | 15.00 |
| ❑ LRP-3400 [M] | Let It Be Me | 1965 | 15.00 |
| ❑ LST-7276 [S] | The Incredible Nancy Ames | 1963 | 20.00 |
| ❑ LST-7299 [S] | Portrait of Nancy | 1963 | 20.00 |
| ❑ LST-7329 [S] | I Never Will Marry | 1964 | 20.00 |
| ❑ LST-7369 [S] | This Is the Girl That Is | 1964 | 20.00 |
| ❑ LST-7400 [S] | Let It Be Me | 1965 | 20.00 |

SUNSET

| Number | Title (A Side/B Side) | Yr | NM |
|---|---|---|---|
| ❑ SUM-1109 [M] | The Versatile Nancy Ames | 196? | 12.00 |
| ❑ SUS-5109 [S] | The Versatile Nancy Ames | 196? | 15.00 |

## AMES BROTHERS, THE

CORAL

| Number | Title (A Side/B Side) | Yr | NM |
|---|---|---|---|
| ❑ CRL 56014 [10] | Sing a Song of Christmas | 1950 | 50.00 |
| ❑ CRL 56017 [10] | In the Evening by the Moonlight | 1951 | 50.00 |
| ❑ CRL 56024 [10] | Sentimental Me | 1951 | 50.00 |
| ❑ CRL 56025 [10] | Hoop-De-Hoo | 1951 | 50.00 |
| ❑ CRL 56042 [10] | Sweet Leilani | 1951 | 50.00 |
| ❑ CRL 56050 [10] | Favorite Spirituals | 1952 | 50.00 |
| ❑ CRL 56079 [10] | Home on the Range | 1952 | 50.00 |
| ❑ CRL 56080 [10] | Merry Christmas | 1952 | 50.00 |
| ❑ CRL 56097 [10] | Favorite Songs | 1954 | 50.00 |
| ❑ CRL 57031 [M] | Ames Brothers Concert | 1956 | 30.00 |
| ❑ CRL 57054 [M] | Love's Old Sweet Song | 1956 | 30.00 |
| ❑ CRL 57166 | Sounds of Christmas Harmony | 1957 | 30.00 |
| ❑ CRL 57176 [M] | Love Serenade | 1958 | 30.00 |
| ❑ CRL 57338 [M] | Our Golden Favorites | 1960 | 30.00 |

EPIC

| Number | Title (A Side/B Side) | Yr | NM |
|---|---|---|---|
| ❑ LN 24036 [M] | Hello Italy | 1962 | 15.00 |
| ❑ LN 24069 [M] | Knees Up Mother Brown | 1963 | 15.00 |
| ❑ BN 26036 [S] | Hello Italy | 1962 | 20.00 |
| ❑ BN 26069 [S] | Knees Up Mother Brown | 1963 | 20.00 |

MCA

| Number | Title (A Side/B Side) | Yr | NM |
|---|---|---|---|
| ❑ 1510 [R] | The Ames Brothers | 197? | 10.00 |

RCA CAMDEN

| Number | Title (A Side/B Side) | Yr | NM |
|---|---|---|---|
| ❑ CAL-571 [M] | The Ames Brothers — Sweet and Swing | 1958 | 15.00 |

RCA SPECIAL PRODUCTS

| Number | Title (A Side/B Side) | Yr | NM |
|---|---|---|---|
| ❑ DVL2-0207 [(2)] | All Their Greatest Hits | 1976 | 15.00 |

RCA VICTOR

| Number | Title (A Side/B Side) | Yr | NM |
|---|---|---|---|
| ❑ ANL1-1095e | The Best of the Ames Brothers | 1975 | 10.00 |
| ❑ LPM-1142 [M] | Exactly Like You | 1955 | 30.00 |
| ❑ LPM-1157 [M] | Four Brothers | 1955 | 30.00 |



**Except when noted otherwise, VG = 25% of NM, and VG+ = 50% of NM. (Example: VG = $2.00, VG+ = $4.00 and NM = $8.00.)**

Number | Title (A Side/B Side) | Yr | NM

❑ LPM-1228 [M] The Ames Brothers with Hugo Winterhalter 1956 30.00
❑ LPM-1487 [M] Sweet Seventeen 1957 30.00
❑ LPM-1541 [M] There'll Always Be a Christmas 1957 30.00
❑ LPM-1680 [M] Destination Moon 1958 25.00
❑ LSP-1680 [S] Destination Moon 1958 30.00
❑ LPM-1855 [M] Smoochin' Time 1958 25.00
❑ LSP-1855 [S] Smoochin' Time 1958 30.00
❑ LPM-1859 [M] The Best of the Ames Brothers 1958 25.00
❑ LSP-1859(e) [R] The Best of the Ames Brothers 196? 20.00
❑ LPM-1954 [M] Famous Hits of Famous Quartets 1959 20.00
❑ LSP-1954 [S] Famous Hits of Famous Quartets 1959 25.00
❑ LPM-1998 [M] The Ames Brothers Sing the Best in the Country 1959 20.00
❑ LSP-1998 [S] The Ames Brothers Sing the Best in the Country 1959 25.00
❑ LPM-2009 [M] Words and Music 1959 20.00
❑ LSP-2009 [S] Words and Music 1959 25.00
❑ LPM-2100 [M] Hello, Amigos 1960 20.00
❑ LSP-2100 [S] Hello, Amigos 1960 25.00
❑ LPM-2182 [M] The Blend and the Beat 1960 20.00
❑ LSP-2182 [S] The Blend and the Beat 1960 25.00
❑ LPM-2273 [M] The Best of the Bands 1960 20.00
❑ LSP-2273 [S] The Best of the Bands 1960 25.00
❑ LPM-2876 [M] For Sentimental Reasons 1964 12.00
❑ LSP-2876 [S] For Sentimental Reasons 1964 15.00
❑ LPM-2981 [M] Down Memory Lane with the Ames Brothers 1964 12.00
❑ LSP-2981 [S] Down Memory Lane with the Ames Brothers 1964 15.00
❑ LPM-3186 [10] It Must Be True 1954 50.00
❑ VPS-6068 [(2)] This Is the Ames Brothers 1972 15.00

READER'S DIGEST
❑ RDA-160 [(6)] Sentimentally Yours 1981 25.00

VOCALION
❑ VL 3617 [M] The Ames Brothers 196? 15.00
❑ VL 73788 [R] Christmas Harmony 196? 12.00
*—Reissue of some Coral tracks*
❑ VL 73818 The Ames Brothers Featuring Ed Ames 196? 10.00

**AMISH, THE**

SUSSEX
❑ SUX-7016 The Amish 1972 25.00

**AMMONS, ALBERT**

BLUE NOTE
❑ BLP-7017 [10] Boogie Woogie Classics 1951 300.00

MERCURY
❑ MG-25012 [10] Boogie Woogie Piano 1950 150.00

**AMMONS, ALBERT, AND PETE JOHNSON**

RCA VICTOR
❑ LPT-9 [10] 8 to the Bar 1952 100.00

**AMMONS, ALBERT / MEADE LUX LEWIS**

MOSAIC
❑ MR3-103 [(3)] The Complete Blue Note Recordings of Albert Ammons and Meade Lux Lewis 198? 50.00
*—Limited edition of 5,000*

**AMMONS, GENE**

ANALOGUE PRODUCTIONS
❑ AP 038 [M] The Soulful Moods of Gene Ammons 199? 30.00
*—180-gram reissue of Moodsville 28*

ARGO
❑ 697 [M] Dig Him 1962 60.00
❑ S-697 [S] Dig Him 1962 50.00
❑ 698 [M] Just Jug 1962 50.00
❑ S-698 [S] Just Jug 1962 40.00

CADET
❑ LP-783 [M] Makes It Happen 1967 40.00

CHESS
❑ LP 1442 [DJ] Soulful Saxophone 1959 150.00
*—White label promo; multicolor swirl vinyl*
❑ LP 1442 [M] Soulful Saxophone 1959 70.00
*—Black vinyl*

EMARCY
❑ MG-26031 [10] With or Without 1954 150.00

MOODSVILLE
❑ MVLP-18 [M] Nice and Cool 1961 80.00
*—Originals have green label*
❑ MVLP-18 [M] Nice and Cool 1965 40.00
*—Second editions have blue label with trident at right*
❑ MVLP-28 [M] The Soulful Moods of Gene Ammons 1963 80.00
*—Originals have green label*
❑ MVLP-28 [M] The Soulful Moods of Gene Ammons 1965 40.00
*—Second editions have blue label with trident at right*

Number | Title (A Side/B Side) | Yr | NM

❑ MVST-28 [S] The Soulful Moods of Gene Ammons 1963 80.00

PRESTIGE
❑ PRLP-107 [10] Gene Ammons 1951 300.00
❑ PRLP-112 [10] Tenor Sax Favorites, Volume 1 1951 300.00
❑ PRLP-127 [10] Gene Ammons Favorites, Volume 2 1952 300.00
❑ PRLP-149 [10] Gene Ammons Favorites, Volume 3 1953 300.00
❑ PRLP-211 [10] Gene Ammons Jazz Session 1955 300.00
❑ PRLP-7039 [M] Hi Fidelity Jam Session 1956 150.00
❑ PRLP-7039 [M] The Happy Blues 1960 80.00
*—Retitled version of "Hi Fidelity Jam Session"*
❑ PRLP-7050 [M] Gene Ammons All Star Session 1956 150.00
*—Compilation of Prestige 107 and 127*
❑ PRLP-7050 [M] Woofin' and Tweetin' 1960 80.00
*—Retitled version of "Gene Ammons All Star Session"*
❑ PRLP-7060 [M] Jammin' with Gene 1956 150.00
❑ PRLP-7060 [M] Not Really the Blues 1960 80.00
*—Retitled version of "Jammin' with Gene"*
❑ PRLP-7083 [M] Funky 1957 150.00
*—Originals have yellow label, "W. 50th St., NYC" address*
❑ PRLP-7110 [M] Jammin' in Hi-Fi with Gene Ammons 1957 150.00
*—Originals have yellow label, "W. 50th St., NYC" address*
❑ PRLP-7132 [M] The Big Sound 1958 150.00
*—Originals have yellow label, "W. 50th St., NYC" address*
❑ PRLP-7146 [M] Blue Gene 1958 80.00
*—Originals have yellow label, Bergenfield, N.J. address*
❑ PRLP-7176 [M] The Twister 1960 100.00
*—Originals have yellow label, Bergenfield, N.J. address; reissue of 7110*
❑ PRLP-7180 [M] Boss Tenor 1960 80.00
*—Originals have yellow label, Bergenfield, N.J. address*
❑ PRST-7180 [S] Boss Tenor 1960 60.00
*—Originals have silver label*
❑ PRLP-7192 [M] Jug 1960 100.00
*—Originals have yellow label, Bergenfield, N.J. address*
❑ PRST-7192 [S] Jug 1960 80.00
*—Originals have silver label*
❑ PRST-7192 [S] Jug 1972 30.00
*—Reissue; trident logo at top*
❑ PRLP-7201 [M] Groove Blues 1961 80.00
*—Originals have yellow label, Bergenfield, N.J. address*
❑ PRLP-7208 [M] Up Tight! 1961 80.00
*—Originals have yellow label, Bergenfield, N.J. address*
❑ PRST-7208 [S] Up Tight! 1961 60.00
*—Originals have silver label*
❑ PRLP-7238 [M] Twistin' the Jug 1962 80.00
*—Originals have yellow label, Bergenfield, N.J. address*
❑ PRST-7238 [S] Twistin' the Jug 1962 60.00
*—Originals have silver label*
❑ PRLP-7257 [M] Bad! Bossa Nova 1962 60.00
*—Originals have yellow label, Bergenfield, N.J. address; some copies have a cover calling this "Jungle Soul! (ca' purange)"*
❑ PRST-7257 [S] Bad! Bossa Nova 1962 50.00
*—Originals have silver label*
❑ PRLP-7270 [M] Preachin' 1963 60.00
*—Originals have yellow label, Bergenfield, N.J. address*
❑ PRST-7270 [S] Preachin' 1963 70.00
*—Originals have silver label*
❑ PRLP-7275 [M] Soul Summit, Volume 2 1963 60.00
*—Originals have yellow label, Bergenfield, N.J. address*
❑ PRST-7275 [S] Soul Summit, Volume 2 1963 70.00
*—Originals have silver label*
❑ PRLP-7287 [M] Late Hour Special 1964 40.00
*—Originals have yellow label, Bergenfield, N.J. address*
❑ PRST-7287 [S] Late Hour Special 1964 50.00
*—Originals have silver label*
❑ PRLP-7320 [M] Velvet Soul 1964 60.00
*—Originals have yellow label, Bergenfield, N.J. address*
❑ PRLP-7320 [M] Velvet Soul 1965 40.00
*—Blue label with tridenr at right*
❑ PRST-7320 [S] Velvet Soul 1964 80.00
*—Originals have silver label*
❑ PRST-7320 [S] Velvet Soul 1965 50.00
*—Blue label with tridenr at right*
❑ PRLP-7369 [M] Angel Eyes 1965 50.00
*—Originals have blue label with trident at right*
❑ PRST-7369 [S] Angel Eyes 1965 60.00
*—Originals have blue label with trident at right*
❑ PRLP-7400 [M] Sock! 1966 50.00
*—Originals have blue label with trident at right*
❑ PRST-7400 [S] Sock! 1966 60.00
*—Originals have blue label with trident at right*
❑ PRLP-7445 [M] Boss Soul! 1967 50.00
*—Originals have blue label with trident at right*
❑ PRST-7445 [S] Boss Soul! 1967 50.00
*—Originals have blue label with trident at right*
❑ PRLP-7495 [M] Gene Ammons Live in Chicago 1967 50.00
*—Originals have blue label with trident at right*
❑ PRST-7495 [S] Gene Ammons Live in Chicago 1967 40.00
*—Originals have blue label with trident at right*
❑ PRLP-7534 [M] Boss Tenor 1967 50.00
*—Reissue of 7180; originals have blue label with trident at right*
❑ PRST-7534 [S] Boss Tenor 1967 30.00
*—Reissue of 7180; originals have blue label with trident at right*
❑ PRST-7552 Jungle Soul 1968 40.00
*—Reissue of 7257*
❑ PRST-7774 The Best of Gene Ammons 1970 20.00

SAVOY
❑ MG-14033 [M] Golden Saxophone 1961 50.00

Number | Title (A Side/B Side) | Yr | NM

VEE JAY
❑ LP-3024 [M] Juggin' Around 1961 80.00
❑ LPS-3024 [S] Juggin' Around 1961 80.00

**AMMONS, GENE, AND RICHARD "GROOVE" HOLMES**

PACIFIC JAZZ
❑ PJ-32 [M] Groovin' with Jug 1961 80.00
❑ ST-32 [S] Groovin' with Jug 1961 60.00

**AMMONS, GENE, AND SONNY STITT**

CADET
❑ LP-785 [M] Jug and Sonny 1967 40.00

CHESS
❑ LP 1445 [M] Jug and Sonny 1960 80.00

PRESTIGE
❑ PRLP-107 [10] Gene Ammons vs. Sonny Stitt: Battle of the Saxes 1951 250.00
❑ PRLP-7234 [M] Soul Summit 1962 50.00
❑ PRST-7234 [S] Soul Summit 1962 40.00
❑ PRLP-7454 [M] Soul Summit 1967 20.00

VERVE
❑ V-8426 [M] Boss Tenors 1962 30.00
❑ V6-8426 [S] Boss Tenors 1962 25.00
❑ V-8468 [M] Boss Tenors in Orbit 1962 30.00
❑ V6-8468 [S] Boss Tenors in Orbit 1962 25.00
❑ 2V6S-8812 [(2)S] Prime Cuts 1972 20.00

**AMON DUUL**

PROPHESY
❑ PHS-1003 Amon Duul 1969 25.00

**AMOS, TORI** Also see Y KANT TORI READ. Also, any picture disc of any of her albums is a bootleg, no matter what they purport to be.

ATLANTIC
❑ 82567 Under the Pink 1995 25.00
*—Limited edition on pink vinyl*
❑ 82862 [(2)] Boys for Pele 1996 20.00
*—Clear vinyl*
❑ 83095 [(2)] From the Choirgirl Hotel 1998 25.00

**AMRAM-BARROW QUARTET, THE**

DECCA
❑ DL 8558 [M] Jazz Studio No. 6 1957 50.00

**AMY, CURTIS**

PACIFIC JAZZ
❑ PJ-62 [M] Tippin' On Through — Recorded "Live" at the Lighthouse 1962 25.00
❑ ST-62 [S] Tippin' On Through — Recorded "Live" at the Lighthouse 1962 30.00

PALOMAR
❑ GS-34003 [S] Sounds of Hollywood and Broadway 1965 20.00

VERVE
❑ V6-8684 [S] Mustang 1966 20.00

**AMY, CURTIS, AND DUPREE BOLTON**

PACIFIC JAZZ
❑ PJ-70 [M] Katanga! 1963 25.00
❑ ST-70 [S] Katanga! 1963 30.00
*—Black vinyl*
❑ ST-70 [S] Katanga! 1963 60.00
*—Red vinyl*

**AMY, CURTIS, AND PAUL BRYANT**

KIMBERLY
❑ 2020 [M] This Is the Blues 1963 20.00
❑ 11020 [S] This Is the Blues 1963 25.00

PACIFIC JAZZ
❑ PJ-9 [M] The Blues Message 1960 30.00
❑ ST-9 [S] The Blues Message 1960 40.00
❑ PJ-26 [M] Meetin' Here 1961 30.00
❑ ST-26 [S] Meetin' Here 1961 40.00

**AMY, CURTIS, AND FRANK BUTLER**

PACIFIC JAZZ
❑ PJ-19 [M] Groovin' Blue 1961 30.00
❑ ST-19 [S] Groovin' Blue 1961 40.00

**AMY, CURTIS, AND VICTOR FELDMAN**

PACIFIC JAZZ
❑ PJ-46 [M] Way Down 1962 25.00
❑ ST-46 [S] Way Down 1962 30.00

**ANCIENT GREASE**

MERCURY
❑ SR-61305 Women and Children First 1970 30.00

**ANDERS & PONCIA**

WARNER BROS.
❑ WS 1778 The Anders & Poncia Album 1969 30.00

### ANDERSEN, ERIC

**ARISTA**

| Number | Title (A Side/B Side) | Yr | NM |
|---|---|---|---|
| AL 4033 | Be True to You | 1975 | 10.00 |
| AL 4075 | Sweet Surprise | 1976 | 10.00 |
| AL 4128 | The Best Songs | 1977 | 10.00 |

**COLUMBIA**

| Number | Title (A Side/B Side) | Yr | NM |
|---|---|---|---|
| KC 31062 | Blue River | 1972 | 10.00 |
| PC 31062 | Blue River | 197? | 8.00 |
| *—Reissue* | | | |

**VANGUARD**

| Number | Title (A Side/B Side) | Yr | NM |
|---|---|---|---|
| VSD 7/8 [(2)] | The Best of Eric Andersen | 1971 | 15.00 |
| VSD 6540 | A Country Dream | 1969 | 15.00 |
| VRS 9157 [M] | Today Is the Highway | 1965 | 15.00 |
| VRS 9206 [M] | 'Bout Changes and Things | 1966 | 15.00 |
| VSD 79157 [S] | Today Is the Highway | 1965 | 20.00 |
| VSD 79206 [S] | 'Bout Changes and Things | 1966 | 20.00 |
| VSD 79236 | 'Bout Changes and Things, Take 2 | 1968 | 15.00 |
| VSD 79271 | More Hits from Tin Can Alley | 1969 | 15.00 |

**WARNER BROS.**

| Number | Title (A Side/B Side) | Yr | NM |
|---|---|---|---|
| WS 1748 | Avalanche | 1968 | 15.00 |
| WS 1806 | Eric Andersen | 1969 | 15.00 |

### ANDERSON, AL Also see NRBQ; THE WILDWEEDS.

**TWIN/TONE**

| Number | Title (A Side/B Side) | Yr | NM |
|---|---|---|---|
| TTR 88110 | Party Favors | 1989 | 12.00 |

**VANGUARD**

| Number | Title (A Side/B Side) | Yr | NM |
|---|---|---|---|
| VSD-79324 | Al Anderson | 1973 | 20.00 |

### ANDERSON, BILL

**DECCA**

| Number | Title (A Side/B Side) | Yr | NM |
|---|---|---|---|
| DL 4192 [M] | Bill Anderson Sings Country Songs | 1962 | 20.00 |
| DL 4427 [M] | Still | 1963 | 20.00 |
| DL 4499 [M] | Bill Anderson Sings | 1964 | 15.00 |
| DL 4600 [M] | Bill Anderson Showcase | 1964 | 15.00 |
| DL 4646 [M] | From This Pen | 1965 | 15.00 |
| DL 4686 [M] | Bright Lights and Country Music | 1965 | 15.00 |
| DL 4771 [M] | I Love You Drops | 1966 | 15.00 |
| DL 4855 [M] | Get While the Gettin's Good | 1967 | 15.00 |
| DL 4859 [M] | Bill Anderson's Greatest Hits | 1967 | 20.00 |
| DL 4886 [M] | I Can Do Nothing Alone | 1967 | 25.00 |
| DXSA 7198 [(2)] | The Bill Anderson Story | 1969 | 15.00 |
| DL 74192 [S] | Bill Anderson Sings Country Songs | 1962 | 25.00 |
| DL 74427 [S] | Still | 1963 | 25.00 |
| DL 74499 [S] | Bill Anderson Sings | 1964 | 20.00 |
| DL 74600 [S] | Bill Anderson Showcase | 1964 | 20.00 |
| DL 74646 [S] | From This Pen | 1965 | 20.00 |
| DL 74686 [S] | Bright Lights and Country Music | 1965 | 20.00 |
| DL 74771 [S] | I Love You Drops | 1966 | 20.00 |
| DL 74855 [S] | Get While the Gettin's Good | 1967 | 20.00 |
| DL 74859 [S] | Bill Anderson's Greatest Hits | 1967 | 20.00 |
| DL 74886 [S] | I Can Do Nothing Alone | 1967 | 20.00 |
| DL 74998 | Wild Weekend | 1968 | 15.00 |
| DL 75056 | Happy State of Mind | 1968 | 15.00 |
| DL 75142 | My Life/But You Know I Love You | 1969 | 15.00 |
| DL 75161 | Bill Anderson's Christmas | 1969 | 15.00 |
| DL 75206 | Love Is a Sometimes Thing | 1970 | 12.00 |
| DL 75254 | Where Have All Our Heroes Gone? | 1971 | 12.00 |
| DL 75275 | Always Remember | 1971 | 12.00 |
| DL 75315 | Bill Anderson's Greatest Hits, Vol. 2 | 1971 | 12.00 |
| DL 75339 | Singing His Praise | 1972 | 12.00 |
| DL 75344 | Bill Anderson Sings For "All the Lonely Women in the World" | 1972 | 12.00 |
| DL 75383 | Don't She Look Good | 1972 | 12.00 |

**MCA**

| Number | Title (A Side/B Side) | Yr | NM |
|---|---|---|---|
| 13 | Bill Anderson's Greatest Hits | 1973 | 10.00 |
| *—Reissue of Decca 74859* | | | |
| 320 | Bill | 1973 | 12.00 |
| 416 | "Whispering" Bill Anderson | 1974 | 12.00 |
| 454 | Every Time I Turn the Radio On/Talk to Me Ohio | 1974 | 10.00 |
| 693 | Love and Other Sad Stories | 198? | 8.00 |
| *—Reissue* | | | |
| 694 | Ladies' Choice | 198? | 8.00 |
| *—Reissue* | | | |
| 766 | Nashville Mirrors | 198? | 8.00 |
| *—Reissue* | | | |
| 2222 | Peanuts & Diamonds & Other Jewels | 1975 | 10.00 |
| 2264 | Scorpio | 1976 | 10.00 |
| 2371 | Love and Other Sad Stories | 1977 | 10.00 |
| 3075 | Ladies' Choice | 1979 | 10.00 |
| 3214 | Nashville Mirrors | 1980 | 10.00 |
| 4001 [(2)] | The Bill Anderson Story | 1973 | 12.00 |
| *—Reissue of Decca 7198* | | | |
| 35032 | Whispering | 197? | 10.00 |

**MCA CORAL**

| Number | Title (A Side/B Side) | Yr | NM |
|---|---|---|---|
| 20002 | I Can Do Nothing | 1973 | 10.00 |

**VOCALION**

| Number | Title (A Side/B Side) | Yr | NM |
|---|---|---|---|
| VL 3835 [M] | Bill Anderson's Country Style | 196? | 12.00 |
| VL 73835 [S] | Bill Anderson's Country Style | 196? | 15.00 |
| VL 73927 | Just Plain Bill | 197? | 10.00 |

### ANDERSON, BILL, AND JAN HOWARD

**DECCA**

| Number | Title (A Side/B Side) | Yr | NM |
|---|---|---|---|
| DL 4959 [M] | For Loving You | 1967 | 25.00 |
| DL 74959 [S] | For Loving You | 1967 | 20.00 |
| DL 75184 | If It's All the Same to You | 1970 | 20.00 |
| DL 75293 | Bill & Jan (Or Jan & Bill) | 1972 | 20.00 |

### ANDERSON, CASEY

**ATCO**

| Number | Title (A Side/B Side) | Yr | NM |
|---|---|---|---|
| 33-149 [M] | The Bag I'm In | 1962 | 20.00 |
| SD 33-149 [S] | The Bag I'm In | 1962 | 25.00 |
| 33-166 [M] | More Pretty Girls Than One | 1964 | 20.00 |
| SD 33-166 [S] | More Pretty Girls Than One | 1964 | 25.00 |
| 33-172 [M] | Live at the Ice House | 1965 | 20.00 |
| SD 33-172 [S] | Live at the Ice House | 1965 | 25.00 |
| 33-176 [M] | Blues Is a Woman Gone | 1965 | 20.00 |
| SD 33-176 [S] | Blues Is a Woman Gone | 1965 | 25.00 |

**ELEKTRA**

| Number | Title (A Side/B Side) | Yr | NM |
|---|---|---|---|
| EKL-192 [M] | Goin' Places | 1960 | 20.00 |
| EKS-7192 [S] | Goin' Places | 1960 | 25.00 |

### ANDERSON, CAT

**EMARCY**

| Number | Title (A Side/B Side) | Yr | NM |
|---|---|---|---|
| MG-36142 [M] | Cat on a Hot Tin Roof | 1958 | 50.00 |

**MERCURY**

| Number | Title (A Side/B Side) | Yr | NM |
|---|---|---|---|
| MG-20522 [M] | Cat on a Hot Tin Roof | 1959 | 40.00 |
| SR-60199 [S] | Cat on a Hot Tin Roof | 1959 | 40.00 |

### ANDERSON, CHRIS

**JAZZLAND**

| Number | Title (A Side/B Side) | Yr | NM |
|---|---|---|---|
| JLP-57 [M] | Inverted Images | 1961 | 30.00 |
| JLP-957 [S] | Inverted Images | 1961 | 40.00 |

### ANDERSON, ERNESTINE

**MERCURY**

| Number | Title (A Side/B Side) | Yr | NM |
|---|---|---|---|
| MG-20354 [M] | Hot Cargo | 1958 | 60.00 |
| MG-20400 [M] | Ernestine Anderson | 1959 | 40.00 |
| MG-20492 [M] | Fascinating Ernestine | 1959 | 50.00 |
| MG-20496 [M] | My Kinda Swing | 1959 | 60.00 |
| MG-20582 [M] | Moanin' | 1960 | 40.00 |
| SR-60074 [S] | Ernestine Anderson | 1959 | 100.00 |
| SR-60171 [S] | Fascinating Ernestine | 1959 | 80.00 |
| SR-60175 [S] | My Kinda Swing | 1959 | 80.00 |
| SR-60242 [S] | Moanin' | 1960 | 50.00 |

**SUE**

| Number | Title (A Side/B Side) | Yr | NM |
|---|---|---|---|
| LP 1015 [M] | The New Sound of Ernestine Anderson | 1963 | 20.00 |

### ANDERSON, HERB OSCAR

**VERVE**

| Number | Title (A Side/B Side) | Yr | NM |
|---|---|---|---|
| V-5021 [M] | What Would I Be | 1967 | 20.00 |
| V6-5021 [S] | What Would I Be | 1967 | 25.00 |

### ANDERSON, IVIE, AND LENA HORNE

**JAZZTONE**

| Number | Title (A Side/B Side) | Yr | NM |
|---|---|---|---|
| J-1262 [M] | Lena and Ivie | 1956 | 40.00 |

### ANDERSON, LAURIE

**WARNER BROS.**

| Number | Title (A Side/B Side) | Yr | NM |
|---|---|---|---|
| WBMS-134-2 [(2)DJ] | Home of the Brave Interview | 1986 | 30.00 |
| *—Part of the Warner Bros. Music Show series* | | | |
| PRO-A-2123 [EP] | Selections from Mister Heartbreak | 1984 | 8.00 |
| *—Promo-only sampler with three songs (Excellent Birds/Sharkey's Day/Sharkey's Night)* | | | |
| PRO-A-2229 [DJ] | Selections from United States Live | 1984 | 12.00 |
| *—Promo-only sampler with eight tracks* | | | |
| BSK 3674 | Big Science | 1982 | 10.00 |
| 25077 | Mister Heartbreak | 1984 | 10.00 |
| 25077 [DJ] | Mister Heartbreak | 1984 | 15.00 |
| *—"Quiex II" audiophile pressing* | | | |
| 25192 [(5)] | United States Live | 1984 | 40.00 |
| *—Boxed set* | | | |
| 25400 | Home of the Brave (Soundtrack) | 1986 | 10.00 |
| 25900 | Strange Angels | 1989 | 12.00 |

### ANDERSON, LEROY

**DECCA**

| Number | Title (A Side/B Side) | Yr | NM |
|---|---|---|---|
| DL 4335 [M] | New Music of Leroy Anderson | 1962 | 15.00 |
| DL 7509 [10] | Leroy Anderson Conducts His Own Compositions, Volume 1 | 195? | 30.00 |
| DL 7519 [10] | Leroy Anderson Conducts His Own Compositions, Volume 2 | 195? | 30.00 |
| DL 8121 [M] | Blue Tango and Other Favorites | 1955 | 20.00 |
| DL 8193 [M] | Christmas Carols | 1955 | 20.00 |
| DL 8865 [M] | Leroy Anderson Conducts Leroy Anderson | 1958 | 15.00 |
| DL 8925 [M] | Christmas Festival | 1959 | 12.00 |
| DL 8954 [M] | Leroy Anderson Conducts His Music | 1959 | 20.00 |
| DL 9749 [M] | Leroy Anderson "Pops" Concert | 195? | 20.00 |
| DL 74335 [S] | New Music of Leroy Anderson | 1962 | 20.00 |
| DL 78865 [S] | Leroy Anderson Conducts Leroy Anderson | 1958 | 20.00 |
| DL 78925 [S] | Christmas Festival | 1959 | 15.00 |
| DL 78954 [S] | Leroy Anderson Conducts His Music | 1959 | 25.00 |

**MCA**

| Number | Title (A Side/B Side) | Yr | NM |
|---|---|---|---|
| 531 | Leroy Anderson Conducts His Music | 197? | 12.00 |
| *—Reissue of Decca 78954; black label with rainbow* | | | |
| 555 | Leroy Anderson Conducts Leroy Anderson | 197? | 12.00 |
| *—Reissue of Decca 78665; black label with rainbow* | | | |

**PICKWICK**

| Number | Title (A Side/B Side) | Yr | NM |
|---|---|---|---|
| SPC-1036 | Christmas Festival | 197? | 15.00 |

### ANDERSON, LIZ

**RCA VICTOR**

| Number | Title (A Side/B Side) | Yr | NM |
|---|---|---|---|
| LPM-3769 [M] | Liz Anderson Sings | 1967 | 30.00 |
| LSP-3769 [S] | Liz Anderson Sings | 1967 | 20.00 |
| LPM-3852 [M] | Cookin' Up Hits | 1967 | 30.00 |
| LSP-3852 [S] | Cookin' Up Hits | 1967 | 20.00 |
| LPM-3908 [M] | Liz Anderson Sings Her Favorites | 1968 | 40.00 |
| LSP-3908 [S] | Liz Anderson Sings Her Favorites | 1968 | 20.00 |
| LSP-4014 | Like a Merry-Go-Round | 1968 | 20.00 |
| LSP-4222 | If the Creek Don't Rise | 1969 | 20.00 |
| LSP-4346 | Husband Hunting | 1970 | 20.00 |

### ANDERSON, LYNN

**CHART**

| Number | Title (A Side/B Side) | Yr | NM |
|---|---|---|---|
| CHM-1001 [M] | Ride, Ride, Ride | 1967 | 20.00 |
| CHS-1001 [S] | Ride, Ride, Ride | 1967 | 15.00 |
| CHM-1004 [M] | Promises, Promises | 1968 | 20.00 |
| CHS-1004 [S] | Promises, Promises | 1968 | 15.00 |
| CHS-1008 | Big Girls Don't Cry | 1969 | 15.00 |
| CHS-1009 | The Best of Lynn Anderson | 1969 | 15.00 |
| CHS-1013 | With Love, From Lynn | 1969 | 15.00 |
| CHS-1017 | At Home with Lynn | 1969 | 15.00 |
| CHS-1022 | Songs That Made Country Girls Famous | 1970 | 12.00 |
| CHS-1028 | Uptown Country Girl | 1970 | 12.00 |
| CHS-1032 | Songs My Mother Wrote | 1970 | 12.00 |
| CHS-1037 | I'm Alright | 1970 | 12.00 |
| CHS-1040 | Lynn Anderson's Greatest Hits | 1971 | 12.00 |
| CHS-1043 | Lynn Anderson with Strings | 1971 | 12.00 |
| CHS-1050 [(2)] | Lynn Anderson | 1972 | 15.00 |

**COLUMBIA**

| Number | Title (A Side/B Side) | Yr | NM |
|---|---|---|---|
| CS 1025 | Stay There 'Til I Get There | 1970 | 12.00 |
| C 30099 | No Love at All | 1970 | 12.00 |
| C 30411 | Rose Garden | 1970 | 10.00 |
| PC 30411 | Rose Garden | 197? | 8.00 |
| *—Reissue* | | | |
| C 30793 | You're My Man | 1971 | 10.00 |
| CG 30902 [(2)] | The World of Lynn Anderson | 1971 | 12.00 |
| C 30925 | How Can I Unlove You | 1971 | 10.00 |
| 3C 30957 | Christmas Album | 198? | 8.00 |
| *—Reissue of KC 30957* | | | |
| KC 30957 | Christmas Album | 1971 | 12.00 |
| KC 31316 | Cry | 1972 | 10.00 |
| KC 31641 | Lynn Anderson's Greatest Hits | 1972 | 10.00 |
| PC 31641 | Lynn Anderson's Greatest Hits | 197? | 8.00 |
| *—Reissue* | | | |
| KC 31647 | Listen to a Country Song | 1972 | 10.00 |
| KC 32078 | Keep Me in Mind | 1973 | 10.00 |
| KC 32429 | Top of the World | 1973 | 10.00 |
| KC 32719 | Queens of Country | 1974 | 10.00 |
| KC 32941 | Smile for Me | 1974 | 10.00 |
| KC 33293 | What a Man, My Man Is | 1974 | 10.00 |
| KC 33691 | I've Never Loved Anyone More | 1975 | 10.00 |
| PC 34089 | All the King's Horses | 1976 | 10.00 |
| PC 34308 | Lynn Anderson's Greatest Hits Volume II | 1976 | 10.00 |
| PC 34439 | Wrap Your Love All Around Your Man | 1977 | 10.00 |
| JC 34871 | I Love What Love Is Doing to Me/He Ain't You | 1977 | 10.00 |
| KC 35445 | From the Inside | 1978 | 10.00 |
| JC 35776 | Outlaw Is Just a State of Mind | 1979 | 10.00 |
| JC 36568 | Even Cowgirls Get the Blues | 1980 | 10.00 |
| FC 37354 | Encore | 1981 | 10.00 |
| PC 37354 | Encore | 1983 | 8.00 |
| *—Budget-line reissue* | | | |

**COLUMBIA LIMITED EDITION**

| Number | Title (A Side/B Side) | Yr | NM |
|---|---|---|---|
| LE 10053 | Stay Here 'Til I Get There | 197? | 10.00 |

**HARMONY**

| Number | Title (A Side/B Side) | Yr | NM |
|---|---|---|---|
| KH 32433 | Singing My Song | 1973 | 8.00 |

**MERCURY**

| Number | Title (A Side/B Side) | Yr | NM |
|---|---|---|---|
| 834625-1 | What She Does Best | 1988 | 8.00 |

**MOUNTAIN DEW**

| Number | Title (A Side/B Side) | Yr | NM |
|---|---|---|---|
| 7047 | Lynn Anderson | 197? | 10.00 |

**PERMIAN**

| Number | Title (A Side/B Side) | Yr | NM |
|---|---|---|---|
| ❑ 8205 | Back | 1983 | 10.00 |

**PICKWICK**

| Number | Title (A Side/B Side) | Yr | NM |
|---|---|---|---|
| ❑ PTP-2049 [(2)] | Lynn Anderson | 1973 | 12.00 |
| ❑ SPC-3267 | Flower of Love | 197? | 8.00 |
| ❑ SPC-3296 | It Makes You Happy | 197? | 8.00 |

**TIME-LIFE**

| Number | Title (A Side/B Side) | Yr | NM |
|---|---|---|---|
| ❑ STW-112 | Country Music | 1981 | 10.00 |

### ANDERSON, MARIAN

**RCA VICTOR RED SEAL**

| Number | Title (A Side/B Side) | Yr | NM |
|---|---|---|---|
| ❑ LM-110 [10] | Spirituals | 195? | 50.00 |
| ❑ LM-2032 [M] | Spirituals | 195? | 40.00 |
| ❑ LSC-2592 [S] | He's Got the Whole World in His Hands | 1962 | 20.00 |
| *—Originals with "shaded dog" label* | | | |
| ❑ LSC-2613 [S] | Marian Anderson Sings Christmas Carols | 1961 | 20.00 |
| *—Originals with "shaded dog" label* | | | |
| ❑ LSC-2613 [S] | Marian Anderson Sings Christmas Carols | 1965 | 25.00 |
| *—Second pressings with "white dog" label* | | | |
| ❑ LRM-7006 [10] | Eleven Great Spirituals | 1951 | 50.00 |
| ❑ LM 7008 [10] | Marian Anderson Sings Christmas Carols | 1954 | 50.00 |

### ANDERSON, MILDRED

**BLUESVILLE**

| Number | Title (A Side/B Side) | Yr | NM |
|---|---|---|---|
| ❑ BVLP-1004 [M] | Person to Person | 1960 | 50.00 |
| *—Blue and silver label* | | | |
| ❑ BVLP-1004 [M] | Person to Person | 1964 | 25.00 |
| *—Blue label with trident logo* | | | |
| ❑ BVLP-1017 [M] | No More in Life | 1961 | 50.00 |
| *—Blue and silver label* | | | |
| ❑ BVLP-1017 [M] | No More in Life | 1964 | 25.00 |
| *—Blue label with trident logo* | | | |

### ANDERSON, PINK

**BLUESVILLE**

| Number | Title (A Side/B Side) | Yr | NM |
|---|---|---|---|
| ❑ BVLP-1038 [M] | Carolina Blues Man | 1961 | 120.00 |
| *—Blue label, silver print* | | | |
| ❑ BVLP-1038 [M] | Carolina Blues Man | 1964 | 30.00 |
| *—Blue label with trident logo* | | | |
| ❑ BVLP-1051 [M] | Medicine Show Man | 1962 | 100.00 |
| *—Blue label, silver print* | | | |
| ❑ BVLP-1051 [M] | Medicine Show Man | 1964 | 30.00 |
| *—Blue label with trident logo* | | | |
| ❑ BVLP-1071 [M] | Ballad and Folk Singer | 1963 | 100.00 |
| *—Blue label, silver print* | | | |
| ❑ BVLP-1071 [M] | Ballad and Folk Singer | 1964 | 30.00 |
| *—Blue label with trident logo* | | | |

### ANDERSON, PINK, AND REV. GARY DAVIS

**RIVERSIDE**

| Number | Title (A Side/B Side) | Yr | NM |
|---|---|---|---|
| ❑ RLP 12-611 [M] | Carolina Street Ballads/Harlem Street Spirituals | 196? | 60.00 |

### ANDERZA, EARL

**PACIFIC JAZZ**

| Number | Title (A Side/B Side) | Yr | NM |
|---|---|---|---|
| ❑ PJ-65 [M] | Outa Sight | 1963 | 25.00 |
| ❑ ST-65 [S] | Outa Sight | 1963 | 30.00 |

### ANDRE'S CUBAN ALL-STARS

**CLEF**

| Number | Title (A Side/B Side) | Yr | NM |
|---|---|---|---|
| ❑ MGC-515 [10] | Cubano | 1954 | 100.00 |
| *—This was reissued on 12-inch as part of a JACK COSTANZO album.* | | | |

### ANDREWS, ERNIE

**GENE NORMAN PRESENTS**

| Number | Title (A Side/B Side) | Yr | NM |
|---|---|---|---|
| ❑ GNP-28 [M] | In the Dark | 1957 | 40.00 |
| ❑ GNP-42 [M] | Ernie Andrews | 1959 | 40.00 |
| ❑ GNP-43 [M] | Travelin' Light | 1959 | 40.00 |
| ❑ GNPS-10008 [S] | Travelin' Light | 1959 | 40.00 |

### ANDREWS, GAYLE

**HI-LIFE**

| Number | Title (A Side/B Side) | Yr | NM |
|---|---|---|---|
| ❑ HL-54 [M] | Love's a Snap | 195? | 30.00 |

### ANDREWS, JULIE

**COLUMBIA**

| Number | Title (A Side/B Side) | Yr | NM |
|---|---|---|---|
| ❑ CL 1712 [M] | Broadway's Fair Julie | 1962 | 20.00 |
| *—Red and black label with six "eye" logos* | | | |
| ❑ CL 1886 [M] | Don't Go In the Lion's Cage Tonight | 1963 | 20.00 |
| ❑ CS 8512 [S] | Broadway's Fair Julie | 1962 | 25.00 |
| *—Red and black label with six "eye" logos* | | | |
| ❑ CS 8686 [S] | Don't Go In the Lion's Cage Tonight | 1963 | 25.00 |

**RCA VICTOR**

| Number | Title (A Side/B Side) | Yr | NM |
|---|---|---|---|
| ❑ LPM-1403 [M] | The Lass with the Delicate Air | 1957 | 40.00 |
| *—With pale blue jacket and the words "Julie Andrews" in a picture frame* | | | |
| ❑ LPM-1403 [M] | The Lass with the Delicate Air | 1958 | 30.00 |
| *—With altered cover; "RE" on jacket* | | | |
| ❑ LSP-1403 [S] | The Lass with the Delicate Air | 1958 | 60.00 |
| ❑ LPM-1681 [M] | Julie Andrews Sings | 1958 | 30.00 |
| ❑ LSP-1681 [S] | Julie Andrews Sings | 1958 | 50.00 |
| ❑ LPM-3829 [M] | A Christmas Treasure | 1967 | 15.00 |
| ❑ LSP-3829 [S] | A Christmas Treasure | 1967 | 15.00 |

### ANDREWS, LEE, AND THE HEARTS

**COLLECTABLES**

| Number | Title (A Side/B Side) | Yr | NM |
|---|---|---|---|
| ❑ COL-5003 | Gotham Recording Sessions | 1982 | 12.00 |
| ❑ COL-5028 | Biggest Hits | 198? | 12.00 |

**LOST-NITE**

| Number | Title (A Side/B Side) | Yr | NM |
|---|---|---|---|
| ❑ LLP-1 [10] | The Best of Lee Andrews and the Hearts, Volume 1 | 1981 | 12.00 |
| *—Red vinyl; in die-cut cover with sticker* | | | |
| ❑ LLP-2 [10] | The Best of Lee Andrews and the Hearts, Volume 2 | 1981 | 12.00 |
| *—Red vinyl; in die-cut cover with sticker* | | | |
| ❑ LP-101 [M] | Biggest Hits | 1964 | 50.00 |
| *—Black vinyl* | | | |
| ❑ LP-101 [M] | Biggest Hits | 1964 | 100.00 |
| *—Yellow vinyl* | | | |
| ❑ LP-113 [M] | Lee Andrews and the Hearts Live | 1965 | 50.00 |

### ANDREWS, RUBY

**ABC**

| Number | Title (A Side/B Side) | Yr | NM |
|---|---|---|---|
| ❑ AB-1002 | Genuine Ruby | 1977 | 15.00 |

**ICHIBAN**

| Number | Title (A Side/B Side) | Yr | NM |
|---|---|---|---|
| ❑ 1104 | Kiss This | 1991 | 15.00 |

**ZODIAC**

| Number | Title (A Side/B Side) | Yr | NM |
|---|---|---|---|
| ❑ ZS 1001 | Everybody Saw You | 1970 | 80.00 |

### ANDREWS SISTERS, THE Also see BING CROSBY.

**ABC**

| Number | Title (A Side/B Side) | Yr | NM |
|---|---|---|---|
| ❑ 4003 | Sixteen Great Performances | 1975 | 12.00 |

**CAPITOL**

| Number | Title (A Side/B Side) | Yr | NM |
|---|---|---|---|
| ❑ T 790 [M] | The Andrews Sisters in Hi-Fi | 1957 | 30.00 |
| ❑ T 860 [M] | Fresh and Fancy Free | 1957 | 30.00 |
| ❑ T 973 [M] | The Dancing Twenties | 1957 | 30.00 |
| ❑ DT 1924 [R] | The Hits of the Andrews Sisters | 1963 | 12.00 |
| ❑ T 1924 [M] | The Hits of the Andrews Sisters | 1963 | 20.00 |

**DECCA**

| Number | Title (A Side/B Side) | Yr | NM |
|---|---|---|---|
| ❑ DL 4019 [M] | Curtain Call | 1956 | 30.00 |
| ❑ DL 5065 [10] | Tropical Songs | 1950 | 40.00 |
| ❑ DL 5120 [10] | The Andrews Sisters | 1951 | 40.00 |
| ❑ DL 5155 [10] | Club 15 | 1951 | 40.00 |
| ❑ DL 5264 [10] | Berlin Songs | 1951 | 40.00 |
| ❑ DL 5282 [10] | Christmas Cheer | 1950 | 40.00 |
| *—Also see "Crosby, Bing"* | | | |
| ❑ DL 5306 [10] | I Love to Tell the Story | 1952 | 40.00 |
| ❑ DL 5423 [10] | My Isle of Golden Dreams | 1953 | 40.00 |
| ❑ DL 5438 [10] | Sing, Sing, Sing | 1953 | 40.00 |
| ❑ DL 8354 [M] | Jingle Bells | 1956 | 30.00 |
| ❑ DL 8360 [M] | The Andrews Sisters — By Popular Demand | 1957 | 30.00 |

**DOT**

| Number | Title (A Side/B Side) | Yr | NM |
|---|---|---|---|
| ❑ DLP 3406 [M] | The Andrews Sisters' Greatest Hits | 1962 | 15.00 |
| ❑ DLP 3452 [M] | Great Golden Hits | 1962 | 15.00 |
| ❑ DLP 3529 [M] | Present | 1963 | 12.00 |
| ❑ DLP 3567 [M] | Great Country Hits | 1963 | 12.00 |
| ❑ DLP 3632 [M] | The Andrews Sisters Go Hawaiian | 1964 | 12.00 |
| ❑ DLP 25406 [S] | The Andrews Sisters' Greatest Hits | 1962 | 20.00 |
| ❑ DLP 25452 [S] | Great Golden Hits | 1962 | 20.00 |
| ❑ DLP 25529 [S] | Present | 1963 | 15.00 |
| ❑ DLP 25567 [S] | Great Country Hits | 1963 | 15.00 |
| ❑ DLP 25632 [S] | The Andrews Sisters Go Hawaiian | 1964 | 15.00 |

**HAMILTON**

| Number | Title (A Side/B Side) | Yr | NM |
|---|---|---|---|
| ❑ HLP 124 [M] | Pennsylvania Polka | 196? | 12.00 |
| ❑ HLP 12124 [S] | Pennsylvania Polka | 196? | 15.00 |

**MCA**

| Number | Title (A Side/B Side) | Yr | NM |
|---|---|---|---|
| ❑ 739 | Near You | 198? | 8.00 |
| *—Reissue of Vocalion album* | | | |
| ❑ 908 | Rarities | 198? | 8.00 |
| ❑ 2-4024 | The Best of the Andrews Sisters | 1973 | 15.00 |
| ❑ 2-4093 [(2)] | The Best of the Andrews Sisters, Vol. 2 | 197? | 15.00 |
| ❑ 24015 | Christmas | 1987 | 8.00 |
| *—Reissue* | | | |
| ❑ 27081 | Sixteen Great Performances | 1980 | 8.00 |
| *—Reissue of ABC 4003* | | | |
| ❑ 27082 | Boogie Woogie Bugle Girls | 1980 | 8.00 |
| *—Reissue of Paramount 6075* | | | |

**PARAMOUNT**

| Number | Title (A Side/B Side) | Yr | NM |
|---|---|---|---|
| ❑ PAS-1023 | In the Mood | 1974 | 15.00 |
| ❑ PAS-6075 | Boogie Woogie Bugle Girls | 1973 | 12.00 |

**PICKWICK**

| Number | Title (A Side/B Side) | Yr | NM |
|---|---|---|---|
| ❑ PC-3094 [M] | Don't Sit Under the Apple Tree | 196? | 15.00 |
| ❑ SPC-3094 [S] | Don't Sit Under the Apple Tree | 196? | 12.00 |
| ❑ SPC-3382 | Sing! Sing! Sing! | 197? | 10.00 |

**VOCALION**

| Number | Title (A Side/B Side) | Yr | NM |
|---|---|---|---|
| ❑ VL 3611 [M] | Near You | 196? | 12.00 |

### ANDY AND THE BEY SISTERS

**PRESTIGE**

| Number | Title (A Side/B Side) | Yr | NM |
|---|---|---|---|
| ❑ PRLP-7346 [M] | Now! Hear! | 1964 | 40.00 |
| ❑ PRST-7346 [S] | Now! Hear! | 1964 | 50.00 |
| ❑ PRLP-7411 [M] | 'Round About Midnight | 1965 | 40.00 |
| ❑ PRST-7411 [S] | 'Round About Midnight | 1965 | 50.00 |

### ANGELI, PIER

**ROULETTE**

| Number | Title (A Side/B Side) | Yr | NM |
|---|---|---|---|
| ❑ R-25051 [M] | Italia Con Pier Angeli | 1959 | 25.00 |
| ❑ SR-25051 [S] | Italia Con Pier Angeli | 1959 | 30.00 |

### ANGELOU, MAYA

**LIBERTY**

| Number | Title (A Side/B Side) | Yr | NM |
|---|---|---|---|
| ❑ LRP-3028 [M] | Miss Calypso | 1958 | 50.00 |

### ANGELS, THE (1)

**ASCOT**

| Number | Title (A Side/B Side) | Yr | NM |
|---|---|---|---|
| ❑ AM 13009 [M] | The Angels Sing — Twelve of Their Greatest Hits | 1964 | 25.00 |
| ❑ ALS 16009 [S] | The Angels Sing — Twelve of Their Greatest Hits | 1964 | 30.00 |

**CAPRICE**

| Number | Title (A Side/B Side) | Yr | NM |
|---|---|---|---|
| ❑ LP 1001 [M] | ...And the Angels Sing | 1962 | 120.00 |
| ❑ SLP 1001 [S] | ...And the Angels Sing | 1962 | 200.00 |

**COLLECTABLES**

| Number | Title (A Side/B Side) | Yr | NM |
|---|---|---|---|
| ❑ COL-5085 | My Boyfriend's Back: Golden Classics | 198? | 10.00 |

**SMASH**

| Number | Title (A Side/B Side) | Yr | NM |
|---|---|---|---|
| ❑ MGS-27039 [M] | My Boyfriend's Back | 1963 | 40.00 |
| ❑ MGS-27048 [M] | A Halo to You | 1964 | 40.00 |
| ❑ SRS-67039 [S] | My Boyfriend's Back | 1963 | 60.00 |
| ❑ SRS-67048 [S] | A Halo to You | 1964 | 60.00 |

### ANGRY SAMOANS

**BAD TRIP**

| Number | Title (A Side/B Side) | Yr | NM |
|---|---|---|---|
| ❑ (# unknown) | Back from Samoa | 1982 | 30.00 |
| ❑ 001 [EP] | Different World/Unhinged + 4 | 1986 | 50.00 |
| ❑ 002 | The Mistaken | 1987 | 50.00 |
| *—As "The Mistaken"; 1,000 copies made* | | | |
| ❑ 201 [EP] | Inside My Brain | 1981 | 25.00 |
| ❑ 201 [EP] | Inside My Brain | 1981 | 50.00 |
| *—Original with heavy gray cardboard cover* | | | |

**PVC**

| Number | Title (A Side/B Side) | Yr | NM |
|---|---|---|---|
| ❑ 6915 | Yesterday Started Tomorrow | 1987 | 15.00 |
| ❑ 8955 | Inside My Brain | 1987 | 15.00 |
| *—Reissue* | | | |
| ❑ 8965 | STP Not LSD | 1988 | 12.00 |

### ANIMALS, THE Includes "Eric Burdon and the Animals." Also see ERIC BURDON; ERIC BURDON AND WAR; ALAN PRICE.

**ABKCO**

| Number | Title (A Side/B Side) | Yr | NM |
|---|---|---|---|
| ❑ AB-4226 [(2)] | The Best of the Animals | 1973 | 12.00 |
| ❑ AB-4324 [M] | The Best of the Animals | 1987 | 10.00 |
| *—With alternate version of "We Gotta Get Out of This Place"* | | | |

**ACCORD**

| Number | Title (A Side/B Side) | Yr | NM |
|---|---|---|---|
| ❑ SN-7193 | Looking Back | 1981 | 8.00 |
| ❑ SN-7235 | The Animals with Eric Burdon | 1982 | 8.00 |

**I.R.S.**

| Number | Title (A Side/B Side) | Yr | NM |
|---|---|---|---|
| ❑ SP 70037 | The Ark | 1983 | 10.00 |
| ❑ SP 70043 | Rip It to Shreds: Their Greatest Hits Live | 1984 | 10.00 |

**JET/UA**

| Number | Title (A Side/B Side) | Yr | NM |
|---|---|---|---|
| ❑ JT-LA790-H | Before We Were So Rudely Interrupted | 1977 | 10.00 |
| *—As "The Original Animals"* | | | |

**MGM**

| Number | Title (A Side/B Side) | Yr | NM |
|---|---|---|---|
| ❑ E-4264 [M] | The Animals | 1964 | 30.00 |
| *—"The House of the Rising Sun" is the edited 45 version* | | | |
| ❑ E-4264 [M] | The Animals | 1964 | 100.00 |
| *—Yellow label promo* | | | |
| ❑ SE-4264 [R] | The Animals | 1964 | 25.00 |
| *—"The House of the Rising Sun" is the edited 45 version (rechanneled, like the rest of the LP)* | | | |
| ❑ E-4281 [M] | The Animals On Tour | 1965 | 30.00 |
| ❑ E-4281 [M] | The Animals On Tour | 1965 | 100.00 |
| *—Yellow label promo* | | | |
| ❑ SE-4281 [R] | The Animals On Tour | 1965 | 25.00 |
| ❑ E-4305 [M] | Animal Tracks | 1965 | 40.00 |
| ❑ E-4305 [M] | Animal Tracks | 1965 | 150.00 |
| *—Yellow label promo* | | | |
| ❑ SE-4305 [R] | Animal Tracks | 1965 | 30.00 |
| ❑ E-4324 [M] | The Best of the Animals | 1966 | 20.00 |
| *—This album was the first to contain the full-length version of "House of the Rising Sun."* | | | |
| ❑ E-4324 [M] | The Best of the Animals | 1966 | 80.00 |
| *—Yellow label promo* | | | |
| ❑ SE-4324 [R] | The Best of the Animals | 1966 | 25.00 |
| ❑ E-4384 [M] | Animalization | 1966 | 25.00 |
| ❑ E-4384 [M] | Animalization | 1966 | 100.00 |
| *—Yellow label promo* | | | |
| ❑ SE-4384 [P] | Animalization | 1966 | 30.00 |
| *—All stereo except "Inside Looking Out," which is rechanneled.* | | | |
| ❑ E-4414 [M] | Animalism | 1966 | 25.00 |

| Number | Title (A Side/B Side) | Yr | NM |
|---|---|---|---|
| ❑ E-4414 [M] | Animalism | 1966 | 100.00 |
| *—Yellow label promo* | | | |
| ❑ SE-4414 [S] | Animalism | 1966 | 30.00 |
| ❑ E-4433 [M] | Eric Is Here | 1967 | 15.00 |
| ❑ SE-4433 [S] | Eric Is Here | 1967 | 20.00 |
| ❑ E-4454 [M] | The Best of Eric Burdon and the Animals, Vol. 2 | 1967 | 20.00 |
| ❑ SE-4454 [P] | The Best of Eric Burdon and the Animals, Vol. 2 | 1967 | 20.00 |
| ❑ E-4484 [M] | Winds of Change | 1967 | 20.00 |
| ❑ SE-4484 [S] | Winds of Change | 1967 | 25.00 |
| ❑ E-4537 [M] | The Twain Shall Meet | 1968 | 20.00 |
| ❑ SE-4537 [S] | The Twain Shall Meet | 1968 | 25.00 |
| ❑ E-4553 [M] | Every One of Us | 1968 | 50.00 |
| *—Mono is promo only (yellow label)* | | | |
| ❑ SE-4553 [S] | Every One of Us | 1968 | 25.00 |
| ❑ SE-4591 [(2)] | Love Is | 1968 | 50.00 |
| ❑ SE-4602 | Greatest Hits of Eric Burdon and the Animals | 1969 | 15.00 |
| ❑ ST 90414 [R] | The Animals On Tour | 1965 | 40.00 |
| *—Capitol Record Club edition* | | | |
| ❑ T 90414 [M] | The Animals On Tour | 1965 | 50.00 |
| *—Capitol Record Club edition* | | | |
| ❑ T 90571 [M] | Animal Tracks | 1965 | 50.00 |
| *—Capitol Record Club edition* | | | |
| ❑ KAO 90622 [M] | The Best of the Animals | 1966 | 40.00 |
| *—Capitol Record Club edition* | | | |
| ❑ SKAO 90622 [R] | The Best of the Animals | 1966 | 40.00 |
| *—Capitol Record Club edition; black label* | | | |
| ❑ SKAO 90622 [R] | The Best of the Animals | 1969 | 30.00 |
| *—Capitol Record Club edition; blue and gold label* | | | |
| ❑ T 90687 [M] | The Animals | 1966 | 50.00 |
| *—Capitol Record Club edition* | | | |
| ❑ ST 90923 [P] | Animalization | 1966 | 50.00 |
| *—Capitol Record Club edition* | | | |
| ❑ T 90923 [M] | Animalization | 1966 | 50.00 |
| *—Capitol Record Club edition* | | | |
| ❑ T-91156 [M] | The Best of Eric Burdon and the Animals, Vol. 2 | 1967 | 30.00 |
| *—Capitol Record Club edition* | | | |
| ❑ ST-91550 [S] | Every One of Us | 1968 | 40.00 |
| *—Capitol Record Club edition; black label* | | | |

PICKWICK

| Number | Title (A Side/B Side) | Yr | NM |
|---|---|---|---|
| ❑ SPC-3330 | The Early Animals with Eric Burdon | 1971 | 8.00 |

POLYDOR

| Number | Title (A Side/B Side) | Yr | NM |
|---|---|---|---|
| ❑ 829091-1 [M] | Animalization | 1986 | 8.00 |

SCEPTER CITATION

| Number | Title (A Side/B Side) | Yr | NM |
|---|---|---|---|
| ❑ CTN-18026 | The Best of the Animals | 1972 | 8.00 |

SPRINGBOARD

| Number | Title (A Side/B Side) | Yr | NM |
|---|---|---|---|
| ❑ SPB-4025 | The Best of the Animals | 1972 | 8.00 |
| ❑ SPB-4065 | The Night Time Is the Right Time | 1973 | 8.00 |

WAND

| Number | Title (A Side/B Side) | Yr | NM |
|---|---|---|---|
| ❑ WDS-690 | In the Beginning | 1970 | 10.00 |

### ANIMATED EGG, THE

ALSHIRE

| Number | Title (A Side/B Side) | Yr | NM |
|---|---|---|---|
| ❑ SF-32700 | The Animated Egg | 1967 | 50.00 |

### ANKA, PAUL

ABC-PARAMOUNT

| Number | Title (A Side/B Side) | Yr | NM |
|---|---|---|---|
| ❑ 240 [M] | Paul Anka | 1958 | 50.00 |
| ❑ 296 [M] | My Heart Sings | 1959 | 30.00 |
| ❑ S-296 [S] | My Heart Sings | 1959 | 50.00 |
| ❑ 323 [M] | Paul Anka Sings His Big 15 | 1960 | 50.00 |
| ❑ S-323 [R] | Paul Anka Sings His Big 15 | 196? | 30.00 |
| ❑ 347 [M] | Paul Anka Swings for Young Lovers | 1960 | 30.00 |
| ❑ S-347 [S] | Paul Anka Swings for Young Lovers | 1960 | 40.00 |
| ❑ 353 [M] | Anka at the Copa | 1960 | 30.00 |
| ❑ S-353 [S] | Anka at the Copa | 1960 | 40.00 |
| ❑ ABC 360 [M] | It's Christmas Everywhere | 1960 | 30.00 |
| ❑ ABCS 360 [S] | It's Christmas Everywhere | 1960 | 40.00 |
| ❑ 371 [M] | Strictly Instrumental | 1961 | 30.00 |
| ❑ S-371 [S] | Strictly Instrumental | 1961 | 40.00 |
| ❑ 390 [M] | Paul Anka Sings His Big 15, Vol. 2 | 1961 | 30.00 |
| ❑ S-390 [S] | Paul Anka Sings His Big 15, Vol. 2 | 1961 | 40.00 |
| ❑ 409 [M] | Paul Anka Sings His Big, Big 15, Volume III | 1962 | 25.00 |
| ❑ S-409 [S] | Paul Anka Sings His Big, Big 15, Volume III | 1962 | 30.00 |
| ❑ 420 [M] | Diana | 1962 | 25.00 |
| ❑ S-420 [S] | Diana | 1962 | 30.00 |

ACCORD

| Number | Title (A Side/B Side) | Yr | NM |
|---|---|---|---|
| ❑ SN-7117 | She's a Lady | 1981 | 8.00 |

BUDDAH

| Number | Title (A Side/B Side) | Yr | NM |
|---|---|---|---|
| ❑ BDS 5093 | Paul Anka | 1971 | 12.00 |
| ❑ BDS 5114 | Jubilation | 1972 | 12.00 |
| ❑ BDS 5622 [(2)] | This Is Anka | 1974 | 15.00 |
| ❑ BDS 5667 [(2)] | The Essential Paul Anka | 1974 | 15.00 |

COLUMBIA

| Number | Title (A Side/B Side) | Yr | NM |
|---|---|---|---|
| ❑ FC 38442 | Walk a Fine Line | 1983 | 8.00 |
| ❑ FC 39323 | Paul Anka Live | 1984 | 8.00 |

LIBERTY

| Number | Title (A Side/B Side) | Yr | NM |
|---|---|---|---|
| ❑ LN-10000 | Paul Anka: His Best | 1980 | 8.00 |
| *—Budget-line reissue* | | | |
| ❑ LN-10001 | The Times of Your Life | 1980 | 8.00 |
| *—Budget-line reissue* | | | |
| ❑ LN-10149 | Feelings | 1982 | 8.00 |
| *—Budget-line reissue* | | | |
| ❑ LN-10220 | The Painter | 1983 | 8.00 |
| *—Budget-line reissue* | | | |

PAIR

| Number | Title (A Side/B Side) | Yr | NM |
|---|---|---|---|
| ❑ PDL2-1129 [(2)] | Songs I Write and Sing | 1986 | 12.00 |

PICKWICK

| Number | Title (A Side/B Side) | Yr | NM |
|---|---|---|---|
| ❑ PTP-2087 [(2)] | Paul Anka Way | 197? | 10.00 |
| ❑ SPC-3508 | Puppy Love | 1975 | 8.00 |
| ❑ SPC-3523 | She's a Lady | 1975 | 8.00 |

RANWOOD

| Number | Title (A Side/B Side) | Yr | NM |
|---|---|---|---|
| ❑ 8203 | The Very Best of Paul Anka | 1981 | 8.00 |

RCA CAMDEN

| Number | Title (A Side/B Side) | Yr | NM |
|---|---|---|---|
| ❑ ACL1-0616 | My Way | 1974 | 8.00 |

RCA VICTOR

| Number | Title (A Side/B Side) | Yr | NM |
|---|---|---|---|
| ❑ ANL1-0896 | Remember Diana | 1975 | 10.00 |
| ❑ ANL1-1054 | She's a Lady | 1975 | 10.00 |
| ❑ ANL1-1584 | Paul Anka Sings His Favorites | 1976 | 10.00 |
| ❑ ANL1-2482 | Songs I Wish I'd Written | 1977 | 10.00 |
| ❑ LPM-2502 [M] | Young, Alive and In Love! | 1962 | 15.00 |
| *—With portrait of Paul Anka on back cover* | | | |
| ❑ LPM-2502 [M] | Young, Alive and In Love! | 1962 | 25.00 |
| *—With portrait of Paul Anka on front cover* | | | |
| ❑ LSP-2502 [S] | Young, Alive and In Love! | 1962 | 20.00 |
| *—With portrait of Paul Anka on back cover* | | | |
| ❑ LSP-2502 [S] | Young, Alive and In Love! | 1962 | 30.00 |
| *—With portrait of Paul Anka on front cover* | | | |
| ❑ LPM-2575 [M] | Let's Sit This One Out | 1962 | 20.00 |
| ❑ LSP-2575 [S] | Let's Sit This One Out | 1962 | 25.00 |
| ❑ LPM-2614 [M] | Our Man Around the World | 1963 | 20.00 |
| ❑ LSP-2614 [S] | Our Man Around the World | 1963 | 25.00 |
| ❑ LPM-2691 [M] | Paul Anka's 21 Golden Hits | 1963 | 20.00 |
| ❑ LSP-2691 [S] | Paul Anka's 21 Golden Hits | 1963 | 25.00 |
| *—LPM/LSP-2691 has re-recorded versions of ABC-Paramount hits* | | | |
| ❑ LPM-2744 [M] | Songs I Wish I'd Written | 1963 | 15.00 |
| ❑ LSP-2744 [S] | Songs I Wish I'd Written | 1963 | 20.00 |
| ❑ AFL1-2892 | Listen to Your Heart | 1978 | 10.00 |
| ❑ LPM-2996 [M] | Excitement on Park Avenue | 1964 | 15.00 |
| ❑ LSP-2996 [S] | Excitement on Park Avenue | 1964 | 20.00 |
| ❑ AFL1-3382 | Headlines | 1979 | 10.00 |
| ❑ LPM-3580 [M] | Strictly Nashville | 1966 | 15.00 |
| ❑ LSP-3580 [S] | Strictly Nashville | 1966 | 20.00 |
| ❑ AYL1-3808 | Paul Anka's 21 Golden Hits | 1980 | 8.00 |
| *—"Best Buy Series" reissue* | | | |
| ❑ LPM-3875 [M] | Paul Anka Live | 1967 | 15.00 |
| ❑ LSP-3875 [S] | Paul Anka Live | 1967 | 20.00 |
| ❑ AFL1-3926 | Both Sides of Love | 1981 | 10.00 |
| ❑ LSP-4142 | Goodnight My Love | 1969 | 15.00 |
| ❑ LSP-4203 | Sincerely | 1969 | 15.00 |
| ❑ LSP-4250 | Life Goes On | 1969 | 15.00 |
| ❑ LSP-4300 | Paul Anka 70s | 1970 | 15.00 |

RHINO

| Number | Title (A Side/B Side) | Yr | NM |
|---|---|---|---|
| ❑ RNLP-70220 | The Best of Paul Anka (14 Original Hits, 1957-1961) | 1986 | 10.00 |

RIVIERA

| Number | Title (A Side/B Side) | Yr | NM |
|---|---|---|---|
| ❑ 0047 [M] | Paul Anka and Others | 1959 | 150.00 |
| *—With Paul Anka's RPM recordings plus tracks by other artists* | | | |

SIRE

| Number | Title (A Side/B Side) | Yr | NM |
|---|---|---|---|
| ❑ SASH-3704 [(2)] | Paul Anka Gold | 1974 | 15.00 |
| ❑ SBK 6043 [(2)] | The Vintage Years 1957-1961 | 1978 | 12.00 |

UNITED ARTISTS

| Number | Title (A Side/B Side) | Yr | NM |
|---|---|---|---|
| ❑ UA-LA314-G | Anka | 1974 | 10.00 |
| ❑ UA-LA367-G | Feelings | 1975 | 10.00 |
| ❑ UA-LA569-G | Times of Your Life | 1975 | 10.00 |
| ❑ UA-LA653-G [Q] | The Painter | 1976 | 12.00 |
| *—All copies are quadraphonic* | | | |
| ❑ UA-LA746-H | The Music Man | 1977 | 10.00 |
| ❑ UA-LA922-H | Paul Anka: His Best | 1978 | 10.00 |

### ANN-MARGRET
Also see AL HIRT.

LHI

| Number | Title (A Side/B Side) | Yr | NM |
|---|---|---|---|
| ❑ S-12007 | The Cowboy and the Lady | 1969 | 40.00 |
| *—With Lee Hazlewood* | | | |

MCA

| Number | Title (A Side/B Side) | Yr | NM |
|---|---|---|---|
| ❑ 3226 | Ann-Margret | 1980 | 12.00 |

RCA VICTOR

| Number | Title (A Side/B Side) | Yr | NM |
|---|---|---|---|
| ❑ LPM-2399 [M] | And Here She Is… | 1961 | 30.00 |
| ❑ LSP-2399 [S] | And Here She Is… | 1961 | 40.00 |
| ❑ LPM-2453 [M] | On the Way Up | 1961 | 30.00 |
| ❑ LSP-2453 [S] | On the Way Up | 1961 | 40.00 |
| ❑ LPM-2551 [M] | The Vivacious One | 1962 | 30.00 |
| ❑ LSP-2551 [S] | The Vivacious One | 1962 | 40.00 |
| ❑ LPM-2659 [M] | Bachelor's Paradise | 1963 | 30.00 |
| ❑ LSP-2659 [S] | Bachelor's Paradise | 1963 | 40.00 |
| ❑ LPM-3710 [M] | Songs from The Swinger and Others | 1966 | 60.00 |
| ❑ LSP-3710 [S] | Songs from The Swinger and Others | 1966 | 80.00 |

### ANNA MARIE
Possibly Anna Marie Wooldridge, who later recorded as ABBEY LINCOLN.

VESTA

| Number | Title (A Side/B Side) | Yr | NM |
|---|---|---|---|
| ❑ LP-101 [10] | Anna Marie | 1955 | 80.00 |

### ANNETTE

BUENA VISTA

| Number | Title (A Side/B Side) | Yr | NM |
|---|---|---|---|
| ❑ BV-3301 [M] | Annette | 1959 | 120.00 |
| ❑ BV-3302 [M] | Annette Sings Anka | 1960 | 100.00 |
| ❑ BV-3303 [M] | Hawaiiannette | 1960 | 75.00 |
| ❑ BV-3304 [M] | Italiannette | 1960 | 75.00 |
| ❑ BV-3305 [M] | Dance Annette | 1961 | 75.00 |
| ❑ BV-3312 [M] | The Story of My Teens | 1962 | 75.00 |
| ❑ BV-3313 [M] | Teen Street | 1962 | 75.00 |
| ❑ BV-3314 [M] | Muscle Beach Party | 1963 | 75.00 |
| ❑ STER-3314 [S] | Muscle Beach Party | 1963 | 150.00 |
| ❑ BV-3316 [M] | Beach Party | 1963 | 60.00 |
| ❑ STER-3316 [S] | Beach Party | 1963 | 100.00 |
| ❑ BV-3320 [M] | Annette on Campus | 1964 | 50.00 |
| ❑ STER-3320 [S] | Annette on Campus | 1964 | 100.00 |
| ❑ BV-3324 [M] | Annette at Bikini Beach | 1964 | 50.00 |
| ❑ STER-3324 [S] | Annette at Bikini Beach | 1964 | 100.00 |
| ❑ BV-3325 [M] | Annette's Pajama Party | 1964 | 40.00 |
| ❑ STER-3325 [S] | Annette's Pajama Party | 1964 | 100.00 |
| ❑ BV-3327 [M] | Annette Sings Golden Surfin' Hits | 1964 | 100.00 |
| ❑ STER-3327 [S] | Annette Sings Golden Surfin' Hits | 1964 | 150.00 |
| ❑ BV-3328 [M] | Something Borrowed, Something Blue | 1964 | 60.00 |
| ❑ STER-3328 [P] | Something Borrowed, Something Blue | 1964 | 100.00 |
| ❑ BV-4037 | Annette Funicello | 1972 | 50.00 |

RHINO

| Number | Title (A Side/B Side) | Yr | NM |
|---|---|---|---|
| ❑ RNDF-206 | The Best of Annette | 1984 | 12.00 |
| ❑ RNLP-702 [PD] | The Best of Annette | 1984 | 25.00 |

### ANNETTE / HAYLEY MILLS
Also see each artist's individual listings.

DISNEYLAND

| Number | Title (A Side/B Side) | Yr | NM |
|---|---|---|---|
| ❑ DL-3508 [M] | Annette and Hayley Mills (Singing 10 of Their Greatest All-Time Hits) | 1964 | 1000. |
| *—TV offer; issued with paper jacket. Though the cover says "Buena Vista Records Presents," the label is the yellow Disneyland label* | | | |

### ANONYMOUS

A-MAJOR

| Number | Title (A Side/B Side) | Yr | NM |
|---|---|---|---|
| ❑ AMLS-1002 | Inside the Shadow | 1976 | 250.00 |

### ANT TRIP CEREMONY

C.R.C.

| Number | Title (A Side/B Side) | Yr | NM |
|---|---|---|---|
| ❑ 2129 | 24 Hours | 1970 | 600.00 |

### ANTHEM

BUDDAH

| Number | Title (A Side/B Side) | Yr | NM |
|---|---|---|---|
| ❑ BDS-5071 | Anthem | 1971 | 20.00 |

### ANTHONY, RAY

CAPITOL

| Number | Title (A Side/B Side) | Yr | NM |
|---|---|---|---|
| ❑ H 258 [10] | Fox Trots | 195? | 40.00 |
| ❑ H 292 [10] | Houseparty Hop | 195? | 40.00 |
| *—Reissue of L 292; purple label; "This Album Contains 8 Selections" on upper right back cover* | | | |
| ❑ L 292 [10] | Houseparty Hop | 195? | 50.00 |
| *—Original issue; maroon label; "In addition to the selections listed, this long playing record contains: PERDIDO - WAGON WHEELS" under the title on back cover* | | | |
| ❑ H 362 [10] | Campus Rumpus | 195? | 50.00 |
| ❑ H 476 [10] | I Remember Glenn Miller | 1954 | 40.00 |
| ❑ T 749 [M] | Jam Session at the Tower | 1956 | 40.00 |

### AORTA

COLUMBIA

| Number | Title (A Side/B Side) | Yr | NM |
|---|---|---|---|
| ❑ CS 9785 | Aorta | 1969 | 30.00 |

HAPPY TIGER

| Number | Title (A Side/B Side) | Yr | NM |
|---|---|---|---|
| ❑ HT-1010 | Aorta 2 | 1970 | 40.00 |

### APHRODITE'S CHILD

VERTIGO

| Number | Title (A Side/B Side) | Yr | NM |
|---|---|---|---|
| ❑ VEL-2-500 [(2)] | 666 (The Apocalypse of John) | 1972 | 20.00 |

### APPLE PIE MOTHERHOOD BAND, THE

ATLANTIC

| Number | Title (A Side/B Side) | Yr | NM |
|---|---|---|---|
| ❑ SD 8189 | The Apple Pie Motherhood Band | 1968 | 25.00 |
| ❑ SD 8233 | Apple Pie | 1969 | 25.00 |

### APPLEJACKS, THE (1)

CAMEO

| Number | Title (A Side/B Side) | Yr | NM |
|---|---|---|---|
| ❑ C-1004 [M] | Alone Together | 1958 | 50.00 |
| *—As "Dave Appell"* | | | |

### APPLETREE THEATRE CO.

VERVE FORECAST

| Number | Title (A Side/B Side) | Yr | NM |
|---|---|---|---|
| ❑ FTS-3042 | Playback | 1968 | 30.00 |
| *—RICK NELSON appears on this album* | | | |

**APPLEYARD, PETER**

AUDIO FIDELITY

❑ AFLP-1901 [M] The Vibe Sound of Peter Appleyard 1958 40.00
❑ AFSD-5901 [S] The Vibe Sound of Peter Appleyard 1958 40.00

**APRIL WINE**

AQUARIUS

❑ AQR 504 Electric Jewels 1973 15.00
❑ AQR 505 Live 1974 15.00

ATLANTIC

❑ SD 19303 Stand Back 1981 10.00
*—Reissue of Big Tree 89506*

BIG TREE

❑ BTS 2012 April Wine 1972 20.00
❑ 89506 Stand Back 1975 15.00

CAPITOL

❑ SPRO-9632/3 [DJ]Summer Tour 1981 1981 20.00
*—Promo-only sampler*
❑ ST-11852 First Glance 1979 12.00
❑ ST-12013 Harder...Faster 1979 10.00
❑ SOO-12125 The Nature of the Beast 1981 10.00
❑ ST-12218 Power Play 1982 10.00
❑ ST-12311 Animal Grace 1984 10.00
❑ SN-16245 First Glance 1982 8.00
*—Budget-line reissue*
❑ SN-16322 Harder...Faster 1984 8.00
*—Budget-line reissue*
❑ SN-16344 Power Play 1984 8.00
*—Budget-line reissue*
❑ SN-16379 The Nature of the Beast 1986 8.00
*—Budget-line reissue*
❑ C1-48418 Walking Through Fire 1988 12.00

LONDON

❑ PS 675 The Whole World's Goin' Crazy 1976 15.00
❑ PS 699 Live at the El Mocambo 1977 15.00

**AQUATONES, THE**

FARGO

❑ 3001 [M] The Aquatones Sing 1964 500.00

RELIC/FARGO

❑ 5033 [M] The Aquatones Sing 198? 8.00

**ARBORS, THE**

DATE

❑ TEM 3003 [M] A Symphony for Susan 1967 15.00
❑ TEM 3011 [M] Valley of the Dolls 1967 20.00
❑ TES 4003 [S] A Symphony for Susan 1967 15.00
❑ TES 4011 [S] Valley of the Dolls 1967 15.00
❑ TES 4017 The Arbors Featuring I Can't Quit Her and The Letter 1969 15.00

**ARCHER, FRANCES, AND BEVERLY GILE**

DISNEYLAND

❑ WDL-1008 [M] A Child's Garden of Verses 1959 20.00
*—Reissue of 3004*
❑ DQ-1226 [M] Songs from All Around the World 1962 20.00
*—Black and white back cover (original)*
❑ DQ-1241 [M] A Child's Garden of Verses 1964 20.00
*—Reissue of 1008*
❑ EB-1347/8 [10] A Child's Garden of Verses 1955 150.00
*—The very first LP released on Disneyland Records*
❑ WDL-3004 [M] A Child's Garden of Verses 1956 25.00
*—Reissue of 1347/8*
❑ WDL-3006 [M] Folk Songs from the Far Corners 1957 25.00
❑ WDL-3023 [M] Community Concert 1958 30.00
❑ ST-3802 [M] A Child's Garden of Verses 1971 25.00
*—Reissue of 1241*

**ARCHIES, THE**

ACCORD

❑ SN-7149 Straight A's 1981 10.00

CALENDAR

❑ KES-101 The Archies 1968 25.00
❑ KES-103 Everything's Archie 1969 25.00

51 WEST

❑ 16002 The Archies 1979 10.00

KIRSHNER

❑ KES-103 [DJ] Everything's Archie Box 1969 100.00
*—Box with LP, photos, press kit and buttons*
❑ KES-105 Jingle Jangle 1969 25.00
❑ KES-107 Sunshine 1970 25.00
❑ KES-109 The Archies Greatest Hits 1970 25.00
❑ KES-110 This Is Love 1971 30.00

**ARDEN, TONI**

DECCA

❑ DL 4375 [M] Italian Gold 196? 12.00
❑ DL 8651 [M] Miss Toni Arden 1957 30.00
*—Black label, silver print*
❑ DL 8765 [M] Sing a Song of Italy 1958 25.00
*—Black label, silver print*

The Archies, *Everything's Archie,* Calendar KES-103, 1969, $25.

Number Title (A Side/B Side) Yr NM

❑ DL 8875 [M] Besame 1959 20.00
*—Black label, silver print*
❑ DL 74375 [S] Italian Gold 196? 15.00
❑ DL 78765 [S] Sing a Song of Italy 1959 30.00
*—Maroon label, silver print*
❑ DL 78875 [S] Besame 1959 30.00
*—Maroon label, silver print*

HARMONY

❑ HL 7212 [M] Exciting Toni Arden 196? 20.00

**AREA CODE 615**

POLYDOR

❑ 24-4002 Area Code 615 1969 20.00
❑ 24-4025 A Trip in the Country 1970 20.00

**ARGENT**

EPIC

❑ BN 26525 Argent 1970 20.00
*—Yellow label*
❑ BN 26525 Argent 1973 12.00
*—Orange label*
❑ E 30128 A Ring of Hands 1971 20.00
*—Yellow label*
❑ KE 30128 A Ring of Hands 1973 12.00
*—Orange label*
❑ KE 31556 All Together Now 1972 20.00
*—Yellow label*
❑ KE 31556 All Together Now 1973 12.00
*—Orange label*
❑ KE 32195 In Deep 1973 20.00
*—Orange label*
❑ KE 32195 In Deep 1973 25.00
*—Yellow label*
❑ PEQ 32195 [Q]In Deep 1974 30.00
❑ PE 32573 Nexus 1974 20.00
*—Orange label*
❑ PEG 33079 [(2)]Encore — Live in Concert 1975 20.00
*—Orange labels*
❑ PE 33422 Circus 1975 20.00
*—Orange label*
❑ PE 33955 Anthology 1976 15.00
*—Orange label*
❑ PE 33955 Anthology 1979 10.00
*—Dark blue label*

UNITED ARTISTS

❑ UA-LA560-G Counterpoint 1975 12.00

Number Title (A Side/B Side) Yr NM

**ARGO, TONY**

SAVOY

❑ MG-12157 [M] Jazz Argosy 1960 40.00

**ARISTOCATS, THE**

HIFI

❑ J-610 [M] Boogie and Blues 1959 30.00
❑ JS-610 [S] Boogie and Blues 1959 40.00

**ARLEN, HAROLD, AND "FRIEND"** The "Friend" is BARBRA STREISAND.

COLUMBIA MASTERWORKS

❑ OS 2920 [S] Harold Sings Arlen 1966 40.00
*—Gray label with "360 Sound" in white*
❑ OL 6520 [M] Harold Sings Arlen 1966 30.00

**ARMAGEDDON (1)**

AMOS

❑ 73075 Armageddon 1970 25.00

**ARMAGEDDON (2)** With KEITH RELF, ex-member of THE YARDBIRDS; his last material before his death.

A&M

❑ SP-4513 Armageddon 1975 20.00

**ARMEN, KAY**

DECCA

❑ DL 78835 [S] Golden Songs of Tin Pan Alley 1959 30.00

MGM

❑ E-277 [10] Kay Armen Sings "For No One But You" 1955 40.00
❑ E-3276 [M] If You Believe 1955 30.00

**ARMORED SAINT**

CHRYSALIS

❑ FV 41476 March of the Saint 1984 8.00
❑ BFV 41516 Delirious Nomad 1985 8.00
❑ BFV 41601 Raising Fear 1987 8.00

ENIGMA/METAL BLADE

❑ 72301 [EP] Live: Saints Will Conquer 1988 8.00

METAL BLADE

❑ MBR 1009 [EP]Armored Saint 1983 50.00

## ARMS, RUSSELL

### ERA

| Number | Title (A Side/B Side) | Yr | NM |
|---|---|---|---|
| ❑ EL-20013 [M] | Where Can a Wanderer Go | 1957 | 25.00 |

## ARMSTRONG, LIL HARDIN

### RIVERSIDE

| Number | Title (A Side/B Side) | Yr | NM |
|---|---|---|---|
| ❑ RLP 12-120 [M] | Satchmo and Me | 195? | 40.00 |
| *—Blue label with microphone logo at top* | | | |
| ❑ RLP 12-120 [M] | Satchmo and Me | 1956 | 60.00 |
| *—White label, blue print* | | | |
| ❑ RLP-401 [M] | Lil Armstrong and Her Orchestra | 1962 | 30.00 |

## ARMSTRONG, LOUIS

### ABC

| Number | Title (A Side/B Side) | Yr | NM |
|---|---|---|---|
| ❑ S-650 | What a Wonderful World | 1968 | 30.00 |

### ACCORD

| Number | Title (A Side/B Side) | Yr | NM |
|---|---|---|---|
| ❑ SN-7161 | Mr. Music | 1982 | 10.00 |

### AMSTERDAM

| Number | Title (A Side/B Side) | Yr | NM |
|---|---|---|---|
| ❑ AMS 12009 | Louis Armstrong and His Friends | 1970 | 15.00 |

### AUDIO FIDELITY

| Number | Title (A Side/B Side) | Yr | NM |
|---|---|---|---|
| ❑ AFLP-1924 [M] | Louie and the Dukes of Dixieland | 1960 | 30.00 |
| ❑ AFLP-1930 [M] | Louis Armstrong Plays King Oliver | 1960 | 30.00 |
| ❑ AFLP-2128 [M] | Ain't Gonna Give Nobody None of My Jelly Roll | 1964 | 15.00 |
| ❑ AFLP-2132 [M] | The Best of Louis Armstrong | 1964 | 15.00 |
| ❑ AFSD-5924 [S] | Louie and the Dukes of Dixieland | 1960 | 40.00 |
| ❑ AFSD-5930 [S] | Louis Armstrong Plays King Oliver | 1960 | 40.00 |
| ❑ AFSD-6128 [S] | Ain't Gonna Give Nobody None of My Jelly Roll | 1964 | 20.00 |
| ❑ AFSD-6132 [S] | The Best of Louis Armstrong | 1964 | 20.00 |
| ❑ AFSD-6241 | Louis Armstrong | 196? | 15.00 |

### BIOGRAPH

| Number | Title (A Side/B Side) | Yr | NM |
|---|---|---|---|
| ❑ C-5 | Great Soloists | 1973 | 12.00 |
| ❑ C-6 | Louis Armstrong Plays the Blues | 1973 | 12.00 |

### BLUEBIRD

| Number | Title (A Side/B Side) | Yr | NM |
|---|---|---|---|
| ❑ AXM2-5519 [(2)] | Young Louis (1932-1933) | 1984 | 12.00 |
| ❑ 5920-1-RB [(2)] | Pops: The 1940s Small Band Sides | 1987 | 15.00 |
| ❑ 8310-1-RB | What a Wonderful World | 1988 | 10.00 |
| ❑ 9759-1-RB | Louis Armstrong & His Orchestra 1932-33: Laughin' Louie | 1989 | 12.00 |

### BRUNSWICK

| Number | Title (A Side/B Side) | Yr | NM |
|---|---|---|---|
| ❑ BL 58004 [10] | Armstrong Classics | 1950 | 100.00 |
| ❑ BL 754136 | I Will Wait for You | 1968 | 15.00 |

### BUENA VISTA

| Number | Title (A Side/B Side) | Yr | NM |
|---|---|---|---|
| ❑ BV-4044 | Disney Swings the Satchmo Way | 1968 | 40.00 |

### CHIAROSCURO

| Number | Title (A Side/B Side) | Yr | NM |
|---|---|---|---|
| ❑ 2002 | Snake Rag | 1977 | 12.00 |
| ❑ 2003 | Great Alternatives | 1977 | 12.00 |
| ❑ 2006 | Sweetheart | 1977 | 12.00 |

### COLUMBIA

| Number | Title (A Side/B Side) | Yr | NM |
|---|---|---|---|
| ❑ CL 591 [M] | Louis Armstrong Plays W.C. Handy | 1954 | 60.00 |
| *—Maroon label, gold print (original)* | | | |
| ❑ CL 591 [M] | Louis Armstrong Plays W.C. Handy | 1955 | 40.00 |
| *—Red and black label with six "eye" logos* | | | |
| ❑ CL 708 [M] | Satch Plays Fats | 1955 | 40.00 |
| *—Red and black label with six "eye" logos* | | | |
| ❑ CL 840 [M] | Ambassador Satch | 1956 | 40.00 |
| ❑ CL 851 [M] | The Louis Armstrong Story, Volume 1: Louis Armstrong and His Hot Five | 1956 | 30.00 |
| *—Red and black label with six "eye" logos; reissue of 4383* | | | |
| ❑ CL 851 [M] | The Louis Armstrong Story, Volume 1: Louis Armstrong and His Hot Five | 197? | 12.00 |
| *—Orange label* | | | |
| ❑ CL 852 [M] | The Louis Armstrong Story, Volume 2: Louis Armstrong and His Hot Seven | 1956 | 30.00 |
| *—Red and black label with six "eye" logos; reissue of 5484* | | | |
| ❑ CL 853 [M] | The Louis Armstrong Story, Volume 3: Louis Armstrong and Earl Hines | 1956 | 30.00 |
| *—Red and black label with six "eye" logos; reissue of 4385* | | | |
| ❑ CL 853 [M] | The Louis Armstrong Story, Volume 3: Louis Armstrong and Earl Hines | 197? | 12.00 |
| *—Orange label reissue* | | | |
| ❑ CL 854 [M] | The Louis Armstrong Story, Volume 4: Louis Armstrong Favorites | 1956 | 30.00 |
| *—Red and black label with six "eye" logos; reissue of 4386* | | | |
| ❑ CL 1077 [M] | Satchmo the Great | 1957 | 30.00 |
| ❑ CL 2638 [M] | Louis Armstrong's Greatest Hits | 1967 | 20.00 |
| ❑ ML 4383 [M] | The Louis Armstrong Story, Volume 1: Louis Armstrong and His Hot Five | 1951 | 50.00 |
| *—Green label, gold or silver print* | | | |
| ❑ ML 4384 [M] | The Louis Armstrong Story, Volume 2: Louis Armstrong and His Hot Seven | 1951 | 50.00 |
| *—Green label, gold or silver print* | | | |
| ❑ ML 4385 [M] | The Louis Armstrong Story, Volume 3: Louis Armstrong and Earl Hines | 1951 | 50.00 |
| *—Green label, gold or silver print* | | | |
| ❑ ML 4386 [M] | The Louis Armstrong Story, Volume 4: Louis Armstrong Favorites | 1951 | 50.00 |
| *—Green label, gold or silver print* | | | |
| ❑ CL 6335 [10] | Louis Armstrong Plays W.C. Handy, Volume 2 | 1955 | 40.00 |
| ❑ CS 9438 [R] | Louis Armstrong's Greatest Hits | 1967 | 12.00 |
| ❑ PC 9438 [R] | Louis Armstrong's Greatest Hits | 198? | 8.00 |
| *—Budget-line reissue* | | | |
| ❑ G 30416 [(2)] | The Genius of Louis Armstrong, Vol. 1 | 1971 | 15.00 |

### COLUMBIA JAZZ MASTERPIECES

| Number | Title (A Side/B Side) | Yr | NM |
|---|---|---|---|
| ❑ CJ 40242 | Louis Armstrong Plays W.C. Handy | 1986 | 10.00 |
| ❑ CJ 40378 | Satch Plays Fats | 1986 | 10.00 |

### COLUMBIA MUSICAL TREASURIES

| Number | Title (A Side/B Side) | Yr | NM |
|---|---|---|---|
| ❑ P4M 5676 [(4)] | 40 Greatest Hits | 197? | 20.00 |

### COLUMBIA SPECIAL PRODUCTS

| Number | Title (A Side/B Side) | Yr | NM |
|---|---|---|---|
| ❑ JCL 708 [M] | Satch Plays Fats | 196? | 12.00 |
| *—"Special Collector's Series" reissue* | | | |

### DECCA

| Number | Title (A Side/B Side) | Yr | NM |
|---|---|---|---|
| ❑ DX 108 [(2)M] | Satchmo at Symphony Hall | 1954 | 75.00 |
| *—Black labels, silver print* | | | |
| ❑ DX 155 [(4)M] | Satchmo, A Musical Autobiography | 1956 | 100.00 |
| *—Black labels, silver print* | | | |
| ❑ DXM 155 [(4)M] | Satchmo, A Musical Autobiography | 1960 | 40.00 |
| *—Black labels with color bars* | | | |
| ❑ DXB 183 [(2)M] | The Best of Louis Armstrong | 196? | 30.00 |
| ❑ DL 4137 [M] | Satchmo's Golden Favorites | 1961 | 20.00 |
| ❑ DL 4227 [M] | I Love Jazz | 1962 | 20.00 |
| ❑ DL 4230 [M] | Satchmo, A Musical Autobiography, 1926-1927 | 1962 | 25.00 |
| ❑ DL 4245 [M] | King Louis | 1962 | 20.00 |
| ❑ DL 4330 [M] | Satchmo, A Musical Autobiography, 1928-1930 | 1962 | 25.00 |
| ❑ DL 4331 [M] | Satchmo, A Musical Autobiography, 1930-1934 | 1962 | 25.00 |
| ❑ DL 5225 [10] | New Orleans to New York | 1950 | 75.00 |
| ❑ DL 5279 [10] | New Orleans Days | 1950 | 75.00 |
| ❑ DL 5280 [10] | Jazz Concert | 1950 | 75.00 |
| ❑ DL 5401 [10] | Satchmo Serenades | 1952 | 75.00 |
| ❑ DL 5532 [10] | Latter-Day Louis | 1954 | 75.00 |
| ❑ DL 5536 [10] | Louis Armstrong-Gordon Jenkins | 1954 | 75.00 |
| ❑ DXSB 7183 [(2)R] | The Best of Louis Armstrong | 196? | 15.00 |
| ❑ DL 8037 [M] | Satchmo at Symphony Hall, Volume 1 | 1954 | 40.00 |
| *—Black label, silver print* | | | |
| ❑ DL 8037 [M] | Satchmo at Symphony Hall, Volume 1 | 1960 | 15.00 |
| *—Black label with color bars* | | | |
| ❑ DL 8038 [M] | Satchmo at Symphony Hall, Volume 2 | 1954 | 40.00 |
| *—Black label, silver print* | | | |
| ❑ DL 8038 [M] | Satchmo at Symphony Hall, Volume 2 | 1960 | 15.00 |
| *—Black label with color bars* | | | |
| ❑ DL 8041 [M] | Satchmo at Pasadena | 1954 | 40.00 |
| *—Black label, silver print* | | | |
| ❑ DL 8041 [M] | Satchmo at Pasadena | 1960 | 15.00 |
| *—Black label with color bars* | | | |
| ❑ DL 8126 [M] | Satchmo Sings | 1955 | 40.00 |
| *—Black label, silver print* | | | |
| ❑ DL 8126 [M] | Satchmo Sings | 1960 | 15.00 |
| *—Black label with color bars* | | | |
| ❑ DL 8168 [M] | Louis Armstrong at the Crescendo, Volume 1 | 1955 | 40.00 |
| *—Black label, silver print* | | | |
| ❑ DL 8169 [M] | Louis Armstrong at the Crescendo, Volume 2 | 1955 | 40.00 |
| *—Black label, silver print* | | | |
| ❑ DL 8211 [M] | Satchmo Serenades | 1956 | 40.00 |
| *—Black label, silver print* | | | |
| ❑ DL 8211 [M] | Satchmo Serenades | 1960 | 15.00 |
| *—Black label with color bars* | | | |
| ❑ DL 8283 [M] | New Orleans Jazz | 1956 | 40.00 |
| *—Black label, silver print* | | | |
| ❑ DL 8283 [M] | New Orleans Jazz | 1960 | 15.00 |
| *—Black label with color bars* | | | |
| ❑ DL 8284 [M] | Jazz Classics | 1956 | 40.00 |
| *—Black label, silver print* | | | |
| ❑ DL 8284 [M] | Jazz Classics | 1960 | 15.00 |
| *—Black label with color bars* | | | |
| ❑ DL 8327 [M] | Satchmo's Collector's Items | 1957 | 40.00 |
| *—Black label, silver print* | | | |
| ❑ DL 8327 [M] | Satchmo's Collector's Items | 1960 | 15.00 |
| *—Black label with color bars* | | | |
| ❑ DL 8329 [M] | New Orleans Nights | 1957 | 40.00 |
| *—Black label, silver print* | | | |
| ❑ DL 8329 [M] | New Orleans Nights | 1960 | 15.00 |
| *—Black label with color bars* | | | |
| ❑ DL 8330 [M] | Satchmo on Stage | 1957 | 40.00 |
| *—Black label, silver print* | | | |
| ❑ DL 8330 [M] | Satchmo on Stage | 1960 | 15.00 |
| *—Black label with color bars* | | | |
| ❑ DL 8488 [M] | Louis and the Angels | 1957 | 40.00 |
| *—Black label, silver print* | | | |
| ❑ DL 8488 [M] | Louis and the Angels | 1960 | 15.00 |
| *—Black label with color bars* | | | |
| ❑ DL 8741 [M] | Louis and the Good Book | 1960 | 15.00 |
| *—Black label with color bars* | | | |
| ❑ DL 8781 [M] | Louis and the Good Book | 1958 | 40.00 |
| *—Black label, silver print* | | | |
| ❑ DL 8840 [M] | Satchmo in Style | 1958 | 40.00 |
| *—Black label, silver print* | | | |
| ❑ DL 8840 [M] | Satchmo in Style | 1960 | 15.00 |
| *—Black label with color bars* | | | |
| ❑ DL 8963 [M] | Satchmo, A Musical Autobiography, 1923-1925 | 1960 | 25.00 |
| ❑ DL 9225 [M] | Rare Items (1935-1944) | 196? | 20.00 |
| ❑ DL 9233 [M] | Young Louis the Sideman (1924-1927) | 196? | 20.00 |
| ❑ DL 74137 [R] | Satchmo's Golden Favorites | 1961 | 12.00 |
| ❑ DL 74227 [R] | I Love Jazz | 1962 | 12.00 |
| ❑ DL 74245 [R] | King Louis | 1962 | 12.00 |
| ❑ DL 74330 [R] | A Musical Autobiography, 1928-1930 | 1962 | 12.00 |
| ❑ DL 78963 [R] | Satchmo, A Musical Autobiography, 1923-1925 | 196? | 12.00 |
| ❑ DL 79225 [R] | Rare Items (1935-1944) | 196? | 12.00 |
| ❑ DL 79233 [R] | Young Louis the Sideman (1924-1927) | 196? | 12.00 |

### DISNEYLAND

| Number | Title (A Side/B Side) | Yr | NM |
|---|---|---|---|
| ❑ STER-1341 | The Wonderful World of Walt Disney | 1971 | 20.00 |
| *—Reissue of Buena Vista 4044* | | | |

### EVEREST

| Number | Title (A Side/B Side) | Yr | NM |
|---|---|---|---|
| ❑ 3312 [R] | In Memoriam | 1971 | 10.00 |

### EVEREST ARCHIVE OF FOLK & JAZZ

| Number | Title (A Side/B Side) | Yr | NM |
|---|---|---|---|
| ❑ 258 | Louis "Satchmo" Armstrong | 197? | 12.00 |
| ❑ 312 | Louis Armstrong, Vol. 2 | 197? | 10.00 |

### GNP CRESCENDO

| Number | Title (A Side/B Side) | Yr | NM |
|---|---|---|---|
| ❑ 9050 | Pasadena Concert, Vol. II | 1987 | 10.00 |
| ❑ 11001 [(2)] | An Evening with Louis Armstrong | 1977 | 15.00 |

### HARMONY

| Number | Title (A Side/B Side) | Yr | NM |
|---|---|---|---|
| ❑ HS 11316 | Louis Armstrong | 197? | 12.00 |
| ❑ KH 31236 | The Louis Armstrong Saga | 1971 | 12.00 |

### IAJRC

| Number | Title (A Side/B Side) | Yr | NM |
|---|---|---|---|
| ❑ LP-29 | Oregon State Fair, 1960 | 198? | 10.00 |

### JOLLY ROGER

| Number | Title (A Side/B Side) | Yr | NM |
|---|---|---|---|
| ❑ 5009 [10] | Louis Armstrong | 1954 | 50.00 |

### KAPP

| Number | Title (A Side/B Side) | Yr | NM |
|---|---|---|---|
| ❑ KL-1364 [M] | Hello, Dolly! | 1964 | 12.00 |
| ❑ KS-3364 [S] | Hello, Dolly! | 1964 | 15.00 |

### MCA

| Number | Title (A Side/B Side) | Yr | NM |
|---|---|---|---|
| ❑ 538 | Hello, Dolly! | 197? | 10.00 |
| *—Reissue of Kapp LP* | | | |
| ❑ 1300 | Louis and the Good Book | 197? | 10.00 |
| *—Reissue of Decca 8741* | | | |
| ❑ 1301 | Young Louis the Sideman | 197? | 10.00 |
| *—Reissue of Decca 9233* | | | |
| ❑ 1304 | Back in New York | 197? | 10.00 |
| ❑ 1306 | Louis with Guest Stars | 197? | 10.00 |
| ❑ 1312 | Swing That Music! | 197? | 10.00 |
| ❑ 1316 | Satchmo Serenades | 197? | 10.00 |
| *—Reissue of Decca 8211* | | | |
| ❑ 1322 | Satchmo's Collector's Items | 197? | 10.00 |
| *—Reissue of Decca 8327* | | | |
| ❑ 1334 | Satchmo For Ever! | 197? | 10.00 |
| ❑ 1335 | Old Favorites | 197? | 10.00 |
| ❑ 2-4013 [(2)] | Louis Armstrong at the Crescendo | 197? | 12.00 |
| *—Reissue of Decca 8168/8169 in one sleeve* | | | |
| ❑ 2-4035 [(2)] | The Best of Louis Armstrong | 197? | 12.00 |
| *—Reissue of Decca 7183* | | | |
| ❑ 2-4057 [(2)] | Satchmo at Symphony Hall | 197? | 12.00 |
| *—Reissue of Decca 108* | | | |
| ❑ 10006 [(4)] | Satchmo, A Musical Autobiography | 197? | 25.00 |
| *—Reissue of Decca 155* | | | |
| ❑ 25204 | What a Wonderful World | 1988 | 10.00 |
| *—Reissue of ABC 650* | | | |
| ❑ 42328 | Louis Armstrong of New Orleans | 1990 | 12.00 |

### MERCURY

| Number | Title (A Side/B Side) | Yr | NM |
|---|---|---|---|
| ❑ MG-21081 [M] | Louis Armstrong Sings Louis Armstrong | 1965 | 12.00 |
| ❑ SR-61081 [S] | Louis Armstrong Sings Louis Armstrong | 1965 | 15.00 |



**Except when noted otherwise, VG = 25% of NM, and VG+ = 50% of NM. (Example: VG = $2.00, VG+ = $4.00 and NM = $8.00.)**

| Number | Title (A Side/B Side) | Yr | NM |
|---|---|---|---|
| **METRO** | | | |
| ❑ M-510 [M] | Hello, Louis | 1965 | 12.00 |
| ❑ MS-510 [S] | Hello, Louis | 1965 | 15.00 |
| **MILESTONE** | | | |
| ❑ 2010 | Early Portrait | 1969 | 10.00 |
| ❑ 47017 [(2)] | Louis Armstrong and King Oliver | 197? | 12.00 |
| **MOSAIC** | | | |
| ❑ MQ8-146 [(8)] | The Complete Decca Studio Recordings of Louis Armstrong and the All-Stars | 199? | 150.00 |
| **PABLO** | | | |
| ❑ 2310941 | Mack the Knife | 1990 | 12.00 |
| **PAIR** | | | |
| ❑ PDL2-1042 [(2)] | The Jazz Legend | 1986 | 12.00 |
| **PAUSA** | | | |
| ❑ 9018 | The Greatest of Louis Armstrong | 1983 | 10.00 |
| **RCA VICTOR** | | | |
| ❑ LPT 7 [10] | Louis Armstrong Town Hall Concert | 1951 | 80.00 |
| ❑ LJM-1005 [M] | Louis Armstrong Sings the Blues | 1954 | 50.00 |
| ❑ LPM-1443 [M] | Town Hall Concert Plus | 1957 | 50.00 |
| ❑ LPM-2322 [M] | A Rare Batch of Satch | 1961 | 25.00 |
| ❑ LPM-2971 [M] | Louis Armstrong in the '30s/in the '40s | 1964 | 20.00 |
| ❑ LSP-2971(e) [R] | Louis Armstrong in the '30s/in the '40s | 1964 | 12.00 |
| ❑ VPM-6044 [(2)] | July 4, 1900/July 6, 1971 | 1971 | 20.00 |
| **RIVERSIDE** | | | |
| ❑ RLP 12-101 [M] | The Young Louis Armstrong | 195? | 40.00 |
| *—Blue label* | | | |
| ❑ RLP 12-101 [M] | The Young Louis Armstrong | 1956 | 80.00 |
| *—White label, blue print* | | | |
| ❑ RLP 12-122 [M] | Louis Armstrong 1923 | 195? | 40.00 |
| *—Blue label* | | | |
| ❑ RLP 12-122 [M] | Louis Armstrong 1923 | 1956 | 80.00 |
| *—White label, blue print* | | | |
| ❑ RLP-1001 [10] | Louis Armstrong Plays the Blues | 1953 | 100.00 |
| ❑ RLP-1029 [10] | Louis Armstrong with King Oliver's Creole Jazz Band 1923 | 1953 | 100.00 |
| **SEAGULL** | | | |
| ❑ LG-8206 | Greatest Hits: Live in Concert | 198? | 12.00 |
| **STORYVILLE** | | | |
| ❑ 4012 | Louis Armstrong and His All-Stars | 1980 | 10.00 |
| **SWING** | | | |
| ❑ SW-8450 | Louis and the Big Bands | 1984 | 10.00 |
| **TIME-LIFE** | | | |
| ❑ STL-J-01 [(3)] | Giants of Jazz | 1978 | 20.00 |
| ❑ STBB-22 [(2)] | Big Bands: Louis Armstrong | 1985 | 15.00 |
| **VANGUARD** | | | |
| ❑ VSD 91/92 [(2)] | Essential Louis Armstrong | 1977 | 15.00 |
| ❑ VMS 73129 | Essential Louis Armstrong, Vol. 1 | 1986 | 8.00 |
| **VERVE** | | | |
| ❑ MGV-4012 [M] | Louis Under the Stars | 1957 | 50.00 |
| ❑ MGV-4012 [S] | Louis Under the Stars | 199? | 25.00 |
| *—180-gram reissue; distributed by Classic Records* | | | |
| ❑ V-4012 [M] | Louis Under the Stars | 1961 | 20.00 |
| ❑ V6-4012 [S] | Louis Under the Stars | 1961 | 15.00 |
| ❑ MGV-4035 [M] | I've Got the World on a String | 1959 | 50.00 |
| ❑ MGVS-4035 | I've Got the World on a String | 199? | 25.00 |
| *—Classic Records reissue* | | | |
| ❑ V-4035 [M] | I've Got the World on a String | 1961 | 20.00 |
| ❑ V6-4035 [S] | I've Got the World on a String | 1961 | 15.00 |
| ❑ MGVS-6044 [S] | Louis Under the Stars | 1960 | 40.00 |
| ❑ MGVS-6101 [S] | I've Got the World on a String | 1960 | 40.00 |
| ❑ V-8569 [M] | The Essential Louis A. | 1963 | 12.00 |
| ❑ V6-8569 [S] | The Essential Louis A. | 1963 | 15.00 |
| ❑ V-8595 [M] | The Best of Louis Armstrong | 1964 | 15.00 |
| ❑ V6-8595 [S] | The Best of Louis Armstrong | 1964 | 15.00 |
| ❑ SW-90658 [S] | The Best of Louis Armstrong | 1964 | 20.00 |
| *—Capitol Record Club edition* | | | |
| **VOCALION** | | | |
| ❑ VL 3851 [M] | Here's Louis Armstrong | 196? | 15.00 |
| ❑ VL 73851 [R] | Here's Louis Armstrong | 196? | 10.00 |
| ❑ VL 73871 [R] | The One and Only Louis Armstrong | 1968 | 10.00 |
| **WING** | | | |
| ❑ SR-16381 | Great Louis | 196? | 10.00 |

## ARMSTRONG, LOUIS, AND SIDNEY BECHET

| Number | Title (A Side/B Side) | Yr | NM |
|---|---|---|---|
| **JOLLY ROGER** | | | |
| ❑ 5029 [M] | Louis Armstrong and Sidney Bechet | 195? | 40.00 |

## ARMSTRONG, LOUIS, AND DUKE ELLINGTON

| Number | Title (A Side/B Side) | Yr | NM |
|---|---|---|---|
| **MOBILE FIDELITY** | | | |
| ❑ 2-155 [(2)] | The Great Reunion | 1984 | 80.00 |
| *—Audiophile vinyl* | | | |

Eddy Arnold, *I Want to Go with You,* RCA Victor LPM-3507, 1966, mono, $12.

| Number | Title (A Side/B Side) | Yr | NM |
|---|---|---|---|
| **ROULETTE** | | | |
| ❑ R 52074 [M] | Together for the First Time | 1961 | 25.00 |
| ❑ SR 52074 [S] | Together for the First Time | 1961 | 20.00 |
| ❑ R 52103 [M] | The Great Reunion | 1963 | 20.00 |
| ❑ SR 52103 [S] | The Great Reunion | 1963 | 25.00 |

## ARMSTRONG, LOUIS/AL HIRT

| Number | Title (A Side/B Side) | Yr | NM |
|---|---|---|---|
| **MURRAY HILL** | | | |
| ❑ 930633 [(4)] | Louis Armstrong and Al Hirt Play Dixieland Trumpet | 197? | 20.00 |

## ARMSTRONG, LOUIS, AND THE MILLS BROTHERS

| Number | Title (A Side/B Side) | Yr | NM |
|---|---|---|---|
| **DECCA** | | | |
| ❑ DL 5509 [10] | Louis Armstrong and the Mills Brothers | 1954 | 60.00 |

## ARMSTRONG, LOUIS, AND OSCAR PETERSON

| Number | Title (A Side/B Side) | Yr | NM |
|---|---|---|---|
| **VERVE** | | | |
| ❑ MGVS-6062 [S] | Louis Armstrong Meets Oscar Peterson | 1960 | 40.00 |
| ❑ MGV-8322 [M] | Louis Armstrong Meets Oscar Peterson | 1959 | 50.00 |
| ❑ V-8322 [M] | Louis Armstrong Meets Oscar Peterson | 1961 | 20.00 |

## ARNAZ, DESI

| Number | Title (A Side/B Side) | Yr | NM |
|---|---|---|---|
| **RCA VICTOR** | | | |
| ❑ LPM-3096 [10] | Babalu! | 1954 | 120.00 |

## ARNOLD, BILLY BOY See BILLY BOY.

## ARNOLD, BUDDY

| Number | Title (A Side/B Side) | Yr | NM |
|---|---|---|---|
| **ABC-PARAMOUNT** | | | |
| ❑ ABC-114 [M] | Wailing | 1956 | 60.00 |

## ARNOLD, EDDY

| Number | Title (A Side/B Side) | Yr | NM |
|---|---|---|---|
| **K-TEL** | | | |
| ❑ WC 307 | The Living Legend of Eddy Arnold | 1974 | 10.00 |
| **MGM** | | | |
| ❑ SE-4878 | So Many Ways/If the Whole World Stopped Lovin' | 1973 | 12.00 |
| ❑ SE-4912 | She's Got Everything I Need | 1974 | 12.00 |
| ❑ SE-4916 | I Wish I Had Loved You Better | 1974 | 12.00 |
| ❑ MG-1-4992 | The Wonderful World of Eddy Arnold | 1975 | 12.00 |
| ❑ MJB-5107 [(2)] | World of Hits | 1976 | 12.00 |
| **PAIR** | | | |
| ❑ PDL2-1000 [(2)] | The Mellow Side of Eddy Arnold | 1986 | 12.00 |
| **RCA** | | | |
| ❑ 9963-1-R | Hand-Holdin' Songs | 1990 | 15.00 |
| **RCA CAMDEN** | | | |
| ❑ CAL-471 [M] | Eddy Arnold (That's How Much I Love You) | 1959 | 20.00 |
| ❑ CAS-471(e) [R] | Eddy Arnold (That's How Much I Love You) | 1966 | 10.00 |
| ❑ CAL-563 [M] | More Eddy Arnold | 1960 | 20.00 |
| ❑ CAS-563(e) [R] | More Eddy Arnold | 1966 | 10.00 |
| ❑ CAL-741 [M] | Country Songs I Love to Sing | 1963 | 15.00 |
| ❑ CAS-741(e) [R] | Country Songs I Love to Sing | 1966 | 10.00 |
| ❑ CAL-799 [M] | Eddy's Songs | 1964 | 15.00 |
| ❑ CAS-799(e) [R] | Eddy's Songs | 1966 | 10.00 |
| ❑ CAL-897 [M] | I'm Throwing Rice (At the Girl That I Love) And Other Favorites | 1966 | 15.00 |
| ❑ CAS-897(e) [R] | I'm Throwing Rice (At the Girl That I Love) And Other Favorites | 1966 | 10.00 |
| ❑ CAS-2501 | Then You Can Tell Me Goodbye | 197? | 10.00 |
| **RCA VICTOR** | | | |
| ❑ DPL2-0051 [(2)] | The Greatest of Eddy Arnold | 1973 | 15.00 |
| *—Special products issue; "Tele House Inc. Presents" on labels* | | | |
| ❑ APL1-0239 | The World of Eddy Arnold | 1973 | 12.00 |
| ❑ PRS-346 | Christmas with Eddy Arnold | 1971 | 15.00 |
| *—Special-products issue* | | | |
| ❑ ANL1-1078 | Pure Gold | 1975 | 10.00 |
| ❑ LPM-1111 [M] | Wanderin' with Eddy Arnold | 1955 | 50.00 |
| ❑ LPM-1223 [M] | All-Time Favorites | 1955 | 50.00 |
| *—New version of LPM 3117* | | | |
| ❑ LSP-1223(e) [R] | All-Time Favorites | 1967 | 12.00 |
| *—Black label, dog on top* | | | |
| ❑ LSP-1223(e) [R] | All-Time Favorites | 1975 | 10.00 |
| *—Tan label; thin vinyl* | | | |
| ❑ LPM-1224 [M] | Anytime | 1955 | 50.00 |
| *—New version of LPM 3027* | | | |
| ❑ LPM-1225 [M] | The Chapel on the Hill | 1955 | 50.00 |
| *—New version of LPM 3031* | | | |
| ❑ LPM-1293 [M] | A Dozen Hits | 1956 | 50.00 |
| ❑ LPM-1377 [M] | A Little on the Lonely Side | 1956 | 50.00 |
| ❑ LPM-1484 [M] | When They Were Young | 1956 | 50.00 |
| ❑ LPM-1575 [M] | My Darling, My Darling | 1957 | 40.00 |

| Number | Title (A Side/B Side) | Yr | NM |
|---|---|---|---|
| ❑ LPM-1733 [M] | Praise Him, Praise Him | 1958 | 40.00 |
| ❑ APL1-1817 | Eddy | 1976 | 12.00 |
| ❑ ANL1-1926 | Christmas with Eddy Arnold | 1976 | 10.00 |
| *—Reissue of LSP-2554 with similar cover to the second edition* | | | |
| ❑ LPM-1928 [M] | Have Guitar, Will Travel | 1959 | 25.00 |
| ❑ LSP-1928 [S] | Have Guitar, Will Travel | 1959 | 30.00 |
| ❑ LPM-2036 [M] | Threrby Hangs a Tale | 1959 | 25.00 |
| ❑ LSP-2036 [S] | Threrby Hangs a Tale | 1959 | 30.00 |
| ❑ LPM-2185 [M] | Eddy Arnold Sings Them Again | 1960 | 25.00 |
| ❑ LSP-2185 [S] | Eddy Arnold Sings Them Again | 1960 | 30.00 |
| ❑ LPM-2268 [M] | You Gotta Have Love | 1960 | 25.00 |
| ❑ LSP-2268 [S] | You Gotta Have Love | 1960 | 30.00 |
| ❑ APL1-2277 | I Need You All the Time | 1977 | 12.00 |
| ❑ LPM-2337 [M] | Let's Make Memories Tonight | 1961 | 20.00 |
| ❑ LSP-2337 [S] | Let's Make Memories Tonight | 1961 | 25.00 |
| ❑ LPM-2471 [M] | One More Time | 1961 | 20.00 |
| ❑ LSP-2471 [S] | One More Time | 1961 | 25.00 |
| ❑ LSP-2471 [S] | One More Time | 1967 | 15.00 |
| *—Reissue with "Country Music Hall of Fame" on front cover and "RE" on back cover* | | | |
| ❑ LPM-2554 [M] | Christmas with Eddy Arnold | 1962 | 20.00 |
| ❑ LSP-2554 [S] | Christmas with Eddy Arnold | 1962 | 25.00 |
| *—Original cover; "Living Stereo" on label* | | | |
| ❑ LSP-2554 [S] | Christmas with Eddy Arnold | 1967 | 15.00 |
| *—Second cover with Eddy standing in front of a Christmas tree; "Country Music Hall of Fame" on front cover and "RE" on back cover* | | | |
| ❑ LPM-2578 [M] | Cattle Call | 1962 | 25.00 |
| ❑ LSP-2578 [S] | Cattle Call | 1962 | 30.00 |
| ❑ LSP-2578 [S] | Cattle Call | 1967 | 15.00 |
| *—Reissue with "Country Music Hall of Fame" on front cover and "RE" on back cover; black label* | | | |
| ❑ LSP-2578 [S] | Cattle Call | 1969 | 12.00 |
| *—Reissue with "Country Music Hall of Fame" on front cover and "RE" on back cover; orange label* | | | |
| ❑ LPM-2596 [M] | Our Man Down South | 1962 | 25.00 |
| ❑ LSP-2596 [S] | Our Man Down South | 1962 | 30.00 |
| ❑ LPM-2629 [M] | Faithfully Yours | 1963 | 25.00 |
| ❑ LSP-2629 [S] | Faithfully Yours | 1963 | 30.00 |
| ❑ LPM-2811 [M] | Folk Song Book | 1964 | 20.00 |
| ❑ LSP-2811 [S] | Folk Song Book | 1964 | 25.00 |
| *—Black label, dog on top* | | | |
| ❑ LSP-2811 [S] | Folk Song Book | 1971 | 10.00 |
| *—Orange label, thin vinyl* | | | |
| ❑ LPM-2909 [M] | Sometimes I'm Happy, Sometimes I'm Blue | 1964 | 20.00 |
| ❑ LSP-2909 [S] | Sometimes I'm Happy, Sometimes I'm Blue | 1964 | 25.00 |
| ❑ LPM-2951 [M] | Pop Hits from the Country Side | 1964 | 20.00 |
| ❑ LSP-2951 [S] | Pop Hits from the Country Side | 1964 | 25.00 |
| ❑ LSP-2951 [S] | Pop Hits from the Country Side | 1967 | 15.00 |
| *—Reissue with "Country Music Hall of Fame" on front cover and "RE" on back cover* | | | |
| ❑ LPM-3027 [10] | Anytime | 1952 | 120.00 |
| *—Label calls this "Country Classics"* | | | |
| ❑ LPM-3031 [10] | All-Time Hits from the Hills | 1952 | 100.00 |
| ❑ LPM-3117 [10] | All-Time Favorites | 1953 | 100.00 |
| ❑ LPM-3219 [10] | When It's Roundup Time in Heaven | 1954 | 100.00 |
| ❑ LPM-3230 | An American Institution Booklet | 1954 | 50.00 |
| ❑ LPM-3230 [10] | An American Institution | 1954 | 100.00 |
| ❑ AHL1-3358 | Somebody | 1979 | 10.00 |
| ❑ LPM-3361 [M] | The Easy Way | 1965 | 15.00 |
| ❑ LSP-3361 [S] | The Easy Way | 1965 | 20.00 |
| ❑ LPM-3466 [M] | My World | 1965 | 12.00 |
| ❑ LSP-3466 [S] | My World | 1965 | 15.00 |
| ❑ LPM-3507 [M] | I Want to Go with You | 1966 | 12.00 |
| ❑ LSP-3507 [S] | I Want to Go with You | 1966 | 15.00 |
| *—Black label, dog on top* | | | |
| ❑ LSP-3507 [S] | I Want to Go with You | 1971 | 10.00 |
| *—Orange label, thin vinyl* | | | |
| ❑ LPM-3565 [M] | The Best of Eddy Arnold | 1967 | 20.00 |
| ❑ LSP-3565 [S] | The Best of Eddy Arnold | 1967 | 15.00 |
| ❑ AHL1-3606 | A Legend and His Lady | 1980 | 10.00 |
| ❑ LPM-3622 [M] | The Last Word in Lonesome | 1966 | 12.00 |
| ❑ LSP-3622 [S] | The Last Word in Lonesome | 1966 | 15.00 |
| ❑ AYL1-3675 | The Best of Eddy Arnold | 1980 | 8.00 |
| *—"Best Buy Series" reissue* | | | |
| ❑ LPM-3715 [M] | Somebody Like Me | 1966 | 12.00 |
| ❑ LSP-3715 [S] | Somebody Like Me | 1966 | 15.00 |
| ❑ LSP-3715 [S] | Somebody Like Me | 1967 | 12.00 |
| *—Reissue with "Country Music Hall of Fame" on front cover and "RE" on back cover* | | | |
| ❑ LPM-3753 [M] | Lonely Again | 1967 | 20.00 |
| ❑ LSP-3753 [S] | Lonely Again | 1967 | 15.00 |
| *—Black label, dog on top* | | | |
| ❑ LSP-3753 [S] | Lonely Again | 1971 | 10.00 |
| *—Orange label, thin vinyl* | | | |
| ❑ LPM-3869 [M] | Turn the World Around | 1967 | 20.00 |
| ❑ LSP-3869 [S] | Turn the World Around | 1967 | 15.00 |
| ❑ AHL1-3914 | A Man for All Seasons | 1980 | 10.00 |
| ❑ LPM-3931 [M] | The Everlovin' World of Eddy Arnold | 1968 | 40.00 |
| ❑ LSP-3931 [S] | The Everlovin' World of Eddy Arnold | 1968 | 15.00 |
| ❑ AYL1-3937 | The Best of Eddy Arnold, Volume II | 1981 | 8.00 |
| *—"Best Buy Series" reissue* | | | |
| ❑ LPM-4009 [M] | The Romantic World of Eddy Arnold | 1968 | 150.00 |
| ❑ LSP-4009 [S] | The Romantic World of Eddy Arnold | 1968 | 15.00 |
| ❑ LSP-4089 | Walkin' in Love Land | 1968 | 15.00 |
| ❑ LSP-4110 | Songs of the Young World | 1969 | 15.00 |
| ❑ LSP-4179 | The Glory of Love | 1969 | 15.00 |
| ❑ LSP-4231 | The Warmth of Eddy | 1969 | 15.00 |
| ❑ AHL1-4263 | Don't Give Up on Me | 1981 | 10.00 |
| ❑ LSP-4304 | Love & Guitars | 1970 | 12.00 |
| *—Orange label, rigid vinyl* | | | |
| ❑ LSP-4304 | Love & Guitars | 1971 | 10.00 |
| *—Orange label, thin vinyl* | | | |
| ❑ LSP-4320 | The Best of Eddy Arnold, Volume II | 1970 | 12.00 |
| ❑ LSP-4471 | Portrait of My Woman | 1971 | 12.00 |
| ❑ LSP-4625 | Loving Her Was Easier | 1971 | 12.00 |
| ❑ AHL1-4661 | Close Enough to Love | 1983 | 10.00 |
| ❑ LSP-4738 | Eddy Arnold Sings for Housewives and Other Ladies | 1972 | 12.00 |
| ❑ CPL2-4885 [(2)] | The Legendary Performances (1945-1971) | 1983 | 12.00 |
| ❑ AHL1-5467 | Collector's Series | 1985 | 10.00 |
| ❑ VPS-6032 [(2)] | This Is Eddy Arnold | 1972 | 15.00 |
| **TIME-LIFE** | | | |
| ❑ STW-120 | Country Music | 1981 | 10.00 |

## ARNOLD, HARRY

| Number | Title (A Side/B Side) | Yr | NM |
|---|---|---|---|
| **ATCO** | | | |
| ❑ 33-120 [M] | I Love Harry Arnold (And All That Jazz) | 1960 | 40.00 |
| **EMARCY** | | | |
| ❑ MG-36139 [M] | Harry Arnold and His Orchestra | 1958 | 50.00 |
| ❑ SR-80006 [S] | Harry Arnold and His Orchestra | 1958 | 40.00 |
| **JAZZLAND** | | | |
| ❑ JLP-65 [M] | Harry Arnold's Great Big Band and Friends | 1962 | 25.00 |
| ❑ JLP-965 [S] | Harry Arnold's Great Big Band and Friends | 1962 | 30.00 |
| **JAZZTONE** | | | |
| ❑ J-1270 [M] | The Jazztone Mystery Band | 1957 | 40.00 |
| **RIVERSIDE** | | | |
| ❑ RM-7526 [M] | Let's Dance on Broadway | 196? | 20.00 |
| ❑ RM-7536 [M] | Dancing on Broadway to the Music of Cole Porter | 196? | 20.00 |
| ❑ RS-97526 [S] | Let's Dance on Broadway | 196? | 25.00 |
| ❑ RS-97536 [S] | Dancing on Broadway to the Music of Cole Porter | 196? | 25.00 |

## ARRESTED DEVELOPMENT

| Number | Title (A Side/B Side) | Yr | NM |
|---|---|---|---|
| **CHRYSALIS** | | | |
| ❑ F1-21929 | 3 Years, 5 Months, & 2 Days in the Life of... | 1992 | 30.00 |
| ❑ F1-29274 [(2)] | Zingalamaduni | 1994 | 20.00 |

## ART BEARS

| Number | Title (A Side/B Side) | Yr | NM |
|---|---|---|---|
| **RALPH** | | | |
| ❑ RR 7905 | Winter Songs | 1979 | 20.00 |

## ART ENSEMBLE OF CHICAGO

Also see LESTER BOWIE; ROSCOE MITCHELL.

| Number | Title (A Side/B Side) | Yr | NM |
|---|---|---|---|
| **NESSA** | | | |
| ❑ N-3 | People in Sorrow | 1969 | 25.00 |
| ❑ N-4 | Les Stances a Sophie | 1970 | 25.00 |
| *—With Fontella Bass* | | | |
| ❑ N-5 | Old/Quartet | 1975 | 20.00 |

## ART OF LOVIN'

| Number | Title (A Side/B Side) | Yr | NM |
|---|---|---|---|
| **MAINSTREAM** | | | |
| ❑ S-6113 | Art of Lovin' | 1968 | 200.00 |

## ARTHUR

| Number | Title (A Side/B Side) | Yr | NM |
|---|---|---|---|
| **LHI** | | | |
| ❑ 12000 | Dreams and Images | 1968 | 40.00 |

## ARTISTICS, THE

| Number | Title (A Side/B Side) | Yr | NM |
|---|---|---|---|
| **BRUNSWICK** | | | |
| ❑ BL 54123 [M] | I'm Gonna Miss You | 1967 | 25.00 |
| ❑ BL 754123 [S] | I'm Gonna Miss You | 1967 | 25.00 |
| ❑ BL 754139 | The Articulate Artistics | 1968 | 25.00 |
| ❑ BL 754153 | What Happened | 1969 | 25.00 |
| ❑ BL 754168 | I Want You to Make My Life Over | 1970 | 25.00 |
| ❑ BL 754195 | Look Out | 1973 | 20.00 |
| **OKEH** | | | |
| ❑ OKM-12119 [M] | Get My Hands on Some Lovin' | 1967 | 80.00 |
| ❑ OKS-14119 [S] | Get My Hands on Some Lovin' | 1967 | 80.00 |

## ARTISTS UNITED AGAINST APARTHEID

| Number | Title (A Side/B Side) | Yr | NM |
|---|---|---|---|
| **MANHATTAN** | | | |
| ❑ SPRO-9538 [DJ] | Voices of Sun City | 1985 | 25.00 |
| *—Promo album of interviews with participants in the benefit LP* | | | |
| ❑ ST-53019 | Sun City | 1985 | 12.00 |

## ARZACHEL

| Number | Title (A Side/B Side) | Yr | NM |
|---|---|---|---|
| **ROULETTE** | | | |
| ❑ SR 42036 | Arzachel | 1969 | 150.00 |

## ASGAERD

| Number | Title (A Side/B Side) | Yr | NM |
|---|---|---|---|
| **THRESHOLD** | | | |
| ❑ THS 6 | In the Realm of Asgaerd | 1972 | 20.00 |

## ASH, MARVIN

| Number | Title (A Side/B Side) | Yr | NM |
|---|---|---|---|
| **CAPITOL** | | | |
| ❑ H 188 [10] | Honky Tonk Piano | 1950 | 60.00 |
| **DECCA** | | | |
| ❑ DL 8346 [M] | New Orleans at Midnight | 1957 | 40.00 |
| **JAZZ MAN** | | | |
| ❑ LPJM-335 [10] | Marvin Ash | 1954 | 50.00 |
| **JUMP** | | | |
| ❑ JL-4 [10] | Marvin Ash | 1954 | 50.00 |

## ASHANTI

| Number | Title (A Side/B Side) | Yr | NM |
|---|---|---|---|
| **MURDER, INC.** | | | |
| ❑ B0000143-01 [(2)] | Chapter II | 2003 | 15.00 |
| ❑ B0003409-01 [(2)] | Concrete Rose | 2004 | 15.00 |
| ❑ 314586830-1 [(2)] | Ashanti | 2002 | 20.00 |

## ASHBY, DOROTHY

| Number | Title (A Side/B Side) | Yr | NM |
|---|---|---|---|
| **ARGO** | | | |
| ❑ LP-690 [M] | Dorothy Ashby | 1962 | 25.00 |
| ❑ LPS-690 [S] | Dorothy Ashby | 1962 | 30.00 |
| **ATLANTIC** | | | |
| ❑ SD 1447 [S] | The Fantastic Jazz Harp of Dorothy Ashby | 1966 | 20.00 |
| **JAZZLAND** | | | |
| ❑ JLP-61 [M] | Soft Winds | 1961 | 25.00 |
| ❑ JLP-961 [S] | Soft Winds | 1961 | 30.00 |
| **NEW JAZZ** | | | |
| ❑ NJLP-8209 [M] | In a Minor Groove | 1958 | 60.00 |
| *—Purple label* | | | |
| ❑ NJLP-8209 [M] | In a Minor Groove | 1965 | 25.00 |
| *—Blue label, trident logo at right* | | | |
| **PRESTIGE** | | | |
| ❑ PRLP-7140 [M] | Hip Harp | 1958 | 60.00 |
| **REGENT** | | | |
| ❑ MG-6039 [M] | Dorothy Ashby — Jazz Harpist | 1957 | 60.00 |

## ASHES

| Number | Title (A Side/B Side) | Yr | NM |
|---|---|---|---|
| **VAULT** | | | |
| ❑ 125 | Ashes | 1968 | 50.00 |

## ASHKAN

| Number | Title (A Side/B Side) | Yr | NM |
|---|---|---|---|
| **SIRE** | | | |
| ❑ SES-97107 | In from the Cold | 1970 | 25.00 |

## ASHLEY, LEON

| Number | Title (A Side/B Side) | Yr | NM |
|---|---|---|---|
| **ASHLEY** | | | |
| ❑ 54001 | The Best of Leon Ashley | 197? | 15.00 |
| **HILLTOP** | | | |
| ❑ JS-6069 | Flower of Love | 1968 | 15.00 |
| **RCA VICTOR** | | | |
| ❑ LPM-3900 [M] | Laura (What's He Got That I Ain't Got) | 1967 | 30.00 |
| ❑ LSP-3900 [S] | Laura (What's He Got That I Ain't Got) | 1967 | 20.00 |

## ASHWORTH, ERNEST

| Number | Title (A Side/B Side) | Yr | NM |
|---|---|---|---|
| **HICKORY** | | | |
| ❑ LPM-118 [M] | Hits of Today and Tomorrow | 1964 | 25.00 |

## ASIA

Includes members of KING CRIMSON and YES.

| Number | Title (A Side/B Side) | Yr | NM |
|---|---|---|---|
| **GEFFEN** | | | |
| ❑ GHS 2008 | Asia | 1982 | 8.00 |
| *—White label with pinstripes* | | | |
| ❑ GHS 2008 [DJ] | Asia | 1982 | 20.00 |
| *—Promo on "Quiex II" vinyl* | | | |
| ❑ GHS 4008 | Alpha | 1983 | 8.00 |
| *—White label with pinstripes* | | | |
| ❑ GHS 4008 [DJ] | Alpha | 1983 | 20.00 |
| *—Promo on "Quiex II" vinyl* | | | |
| ❑ GHS 24072 | Astra | 1985 | 8.00 |
| ❑ GHS 24298 | Then and Now | 1990 | 12.00 |

## ASLEEP AT THE WHEEL

| Number | Title (A Side/B Side) | Yr | NM |
|---|---|---|---|
| **ARISTA** | | | |
| ❑ AL-8550 | Keepin' Me Up Nights | 1990 | 12.00 |
| **CAPITOL** | | | |
| ❑ ST-11441 | Texas Gold | 1975 | 12.00 |
| ❑ ST-11548 | Wheelin' and Dealin' | 1976 | 12.00 |
| ❑ ST-11620 | The Wheel | 1977 | 12.00 |
| ❑ SW-11726 | Collision Course | 1978 | 12.00 |
| ❑ ST-11945 | Served Live | 1979 | 12.00 |
| ❑ SN-16306 | Served Live | 1984 | 8.00 |
| *—Budget-line reissue* | | | |
| **CAPITOL SPECIAL MARKETS** | | | |
| ❑ SL-8138 | Drivin' | 1980 | 12.00 |
| **DOT/MCA** | | | |
| ❑ 39036 | Asleep at the Wheel | 1985 | 10.00 |
| **EPIC** | | | |
| ❑ KE 33097 | Asleep at the Wheel | 1974 | 15.00 |
| ❑ PE 33097 | Asleep at the Wheel | 197? | 8.00 |
| *—Reissue* | | | |

| Number | Title (A Side/B Side) | Yr | NM |
|---|---|---|---|
| ❑ BG 33782 [(2)] | Fathers and Sons | 1974 | 25.00 |
| *—With Bob Wills* | | | |
| ❑ EG 33782 [(2)] | Fathers and Sons | 197? | 12.00 |
| *—Reissue* | | | |
| ❑ BFE 40681 | 10 | 1987 | 8.00 |
| ❑ FE 44213 | Western Standard Time | 1988 | 8.00 |
| LIBERTY | | | |
| ❑ LN-10296 | Comin' Right At Ya! | 1986 | 8.00 |
| *—Budget-line reissue* | | | |
| MCA | | | |
| ❑ 742 | Framed | 1982 | 8.00 |
| *—Reissue of 5131* | | | |
| ❑ 5131 | Framed | 1980 | 10.00 |
| UNITED ARTISTS | | | |
| ❑ UA-LA038-F | Comin' Right At Ya! | 1973 | 20.00 |
| **ASMUSSEN, SVEND** | | | |
| ANGEL | | | |
| ❑ ANG.60000 [10] | Svend Asmussen and His Unmelancholy Danes | 1955 | 60.00 |
| ❑ ANG.60010 [10] | Rhythm Is Our Business | 1955 | 60.00 |
| BRUNSWICK | | | |
| ❑ BL 58051 [10] | Hot Fiddle | 1953 | 80.00 |
| EPIC | | | |
| ❑ LN 3210 [M] | Skol! | 1955 | 50.00 |
| **ASSOCIATION, THE** | | | |
| COLUMBIA | | | |
| ❑ KC 31348 | Waterbeds in Trinidad | 1972 | 10.00 |
| HITBOUND/REALISTIC | | | |
| ❑ 51-3022 | New Memories | 1983 | 12.00 |
| PAIR | | | |
| ❑ PDL2-1061 [(2)] | Songs That Made Them Famous | 1986 | 12.00 |
| VALIANT | | | |
| ❑ VLM-5002 [M] | And Then...Along Comes The Association | 1966 | 20.00 |
| ❑ VLM-5004 [M] | Renaissance | 1966 | 20.00 |
| *—With no blurb for "No Fair at All" on cover* | | | |
| ❑ VLM-5004 [M] | Renaissance | 1967 | 15.00 |
| *—With blurb for "No Fair at All" on cover* | | | |
| ❑ VLS-25002 [S] | And Then...Along Comes The Association | 1966 | 25.00 |
| ❑ VLS-25004 [S] | Renaissance | 1966 | 25.00 |
| *—With no blurb for "No Fair at All" on cover* | | | |
| ❑ VLS-25004 [S] | Renaissance | 1967 | 20.00 |
| *—With blurb for "No Fair at All" on cover* | | | |
| WARNER BROS. | | | |
| ❑ W 1696 [M] | Insight Out | 1967 | 15.00 |
| ❑ WS 1696 [S] | Insight Out | 1967 | 20.00 |
| *—Gold label* | | | |
| ❑ WS 1696 [S] | Insight Out | 1968 | 12.00 |
| *—With "W7" logo on green label* | | | |
| ❑ W 1702 [M] | And Then...Along Comes The Association | 1967 | 20.00 |
| ❑ WS 1702 [S] | And Then...Along Comes The Association | 1967 | 12.00 |
| *—With "W7" logo on green label* | | | |
| ❑ WS 1702 [S] | And Then...Along Comes The Association | 1967 | 20.00 |
| *—Gold label* | | | |
| ❑ WS 1704 | Renaissance | 1967 | 12.00 |
| ❑ WS 1733 | Birthday | 1968 | 12.00 |
| *—With "W7" logo on green label* | | | |
| ❑ WS 1767 | Greatest Hits | 1968 | 12.00 |
| *—With "W7" logo on green label* | | | |
| ❑ WS 1767 | Greatest Hits | 197? | 8.00 |
| *—Any later pressing (LP in print until the late 1980s)* | | | |
| ❑ WS 1786 | Goodbye Columbus | 1969 | 12.00 |
| *—With "W7" logo on green label* | | | |
| ❑ WS 1800 | The Association | 1969 | 12.00 |
| *—With "W7" logo on green label* | | | |
| ❑ 2WS 1868 [(2)] | The Association "Live" | 1970 | 15.00 |
| ❑ WS 1927 | Stop Your Motor | 1971 | 12.00 |
| ❑ ST-91317 [S] | Insight Out | 1967 | 25.00 |
| *—Capitol Record Club edition* | | | |
| ❑ ST-91586 | Greatest Hits | 1968 | 20.00 |
| *—Capitol Record Club edition* | | | |
| ❑ STBO-93249 [(2)] | The Association "Live" | 1970 | 20.00 |
| *—Capitol Record Club edition* | | | |
| **ASTRONAUTS, THE (1)** | | | |
| RCA VICTOR | | | |
| ❑ PRM-183 [M] | Rockin' with the Astronauts | 1965 | 30.00 |
| ❑ LPM-2760 [M] | Surfin' with the Astronauts | 1963 | 60.00 |
| ❑ LSP-2760 [S] | Surfin' with the Astronauts | 1963 | 80.00 |
| ❑ LSP-2782 [S] | Everything Is A-OK! | 1964 | 60.00 |
| ❑ LPM-2858 [M] | Competition Coupe | 1964 | 60.00 |
| ❑ LSP-2858 [S] | Competition Coupe | 1964 | 80.00 |
| ❑ LPM-2903 [M] | The Astronauts Orbit Kampus | 1964 | 40.00 |
| ❑ LSP-2903 [S] | The Astronauts Orbit Kampus | 1964 | 50.00 |
| ❑ LPM-3307 [M] | The Astronauts Go, Go, Go | 1965 | 30.00 |
| ❑ LSP-3307 [S] | The Astronauts Go, Go, Go | 1965 | 40.00 |
| ❑ LPM-3359 [M] | Favorites for You from Us | 1965 | 30.00 |
| ❑ LSP-3359 [S] | Favorites for You from Us | 1965 | 40.00 |
| ❑ LPM-3454 [M] | Down the Line | 1966 | 30.00 |

The Association, *Renaissance,* Valiant VLS-25004, stereo, $25.

| Number | Title (A Side/B Side) | Yr | NM |
|---|---|---|---|
| ❑ LSP-3454 [S] | Down the Line | 1966 | 40.00 |
| ❑ LPM-3733 [M] | Travelin' Men | 1967 | 50.00 |
| ❑ LSP-3733 [S] | Travelin' Men | 1967 | 30.00 |
| **ASTRONAUTS, THE (1) / THE LIVERPOOL FIVE** | | | |
| RCA VICTOR | | | |
| ❑ PRS-251 [S] | Stereo Festival | 1967 | 100.00 |
| *—Special-prodcuts edition* | | | |
| **ASYLUM CHOIR** LEON RUSSELL and MARC BENNO. | | | |
| MCA | | | |
| ❑ 684 | Asylum Choir II | 1979 | 8.00 |
| *—Reissue of Shelter 52010* | | | |
| SHELTER | | | |
| ❑ SR 2120 | Asylum Choir II | 1974 | 12.00 |
| *—Reissue of 8910* | | | |
| ❑ SW-8910 | Asylum Choir II | 1971 | 15.00 |
| ❑ 52010 | Asylum Choir II | 1977 | 10.00 |
| *—Reissue of 2120* | | | |
| SMASH | | | |
| ❑ SRS-67107 | Look Inside the Asylum Choir | 1968 | 30.00 |
| *—Front cover has a roll of toilet paper* | | | |
| ❑ SRS-67107 | Look Inside the Asylum Choir | 197? | 15.00 |
| *—Front cover has a photo of Leon and Marc* | | | |
| **ATCHER, BOB** | | | |
| COLUMBIA | | | |
| ❑ CL 2232 [M] | The Dean of Cowboy Singers | 1964 | 25.00 |
| ❑ HL 9006 [10] | Early American Folk Songs | 1949 | 80.00 |
| ❑ HL 9013 [10] | Songs of the Saddle | 1949 | 80.00 |
| ❑ CS 9032 [R] | The Dean of Cowboy Singers | 1964 | 15.00 |
| HARMONY | | | |
| ❑ HL 7313 [M] | Bob Atcher's Best | 1964 | 20.00 |
| **ATKINS, CHET** | | | |
| COLUMBIA | | | |
| ❑ FC 38536 | Work It Out with Chet Atkins C.G.P. | 1983 | 10.00 |
| ❑ PC 38536 | Work It Out with Chet Atkins C.G.P. | 1985 | 8.00 |
| *—Budget-line reissue* | | | |
| ❑ PC 39003 | East Tennessee Christmas | 1983 | 10.00 |
| ❑ FC 39591 | Stay Tuned | 1985 | 10.00 |
| ❑ FC 40256 | Street Dreams | 1986 | 8.00 |
| ❑ FC 40593 | Sails | 1987 | 8.00 |
| ❑ FC 44323 | Chet Atkins, C.G.P. | 1989 | 8.00 |

| Number | Title (A Side/B Side) | Yr | NM |
|---|---|---|---|
| DOLTON | | | |
| ❑ BLP-16506 [M] | Play Guitar with Chet Atkins | 1967 | 25.00 |
| ❑ BST-17506 [S] | Play Guitar with Chet Atkins | 1967 | 30.00 |
| PAIR | | | |
| ❑ PDL2-1047 [(2)] | Tennessee Guitar Man | 1985 | 12.00 |
| ❑ PDL2-1115 [(2)] | Guitar for All Seasons | 1986 | 12.00 |
| RCA CAMDEN | | | |
| ❑ CAL-659 [M] | Chet Atkins and His Guitar | 196? | 15.00 |
| ❑ CAS-659(e) [R] | Chet Atkins and His Guitar | 1964 | 12.00 |
| ❑ CAL-753 [M] | Guitar Genius | 196? | 15.00 |
| ❑ CAS-753(e) [R] | Guitar Genius | 196? | 12.00 |
| ❑ CAL-981 [M] | Music from Nashville, My Home Town | 1966 | 12.00 |
| ❑ CAS-981 [S] | Music from Nashville, My Home Town | 1966 | 15.00 |
| ❑ CAL-2182 [M] | Chet | 1967 | 12.00 |
| ❑ CAS-2182 [S] | Chet | 1967 | 15.00 |
| ❑ CAS-2296 | Relaxin' with Chet | 1969 | 12.00 |
| ❑ CAS-2523 | Chet 'n Boots | 1972 | 12.00 |
| ❑ CAS-2555 | Nashville Gold | 1972 | 12.00 |
| ❑ CAS-2600 | Finger Pickin' Good | 1973 | 10.00 |
| ❑ ACL1-7042 | Love Letters | 197? | 10.00 |
| RCA RED SEAL | | | |
| ❑ LM-2870 [M] | The "Pops" Goes Country | 1966 | 15.00 |
| ❑ LSC-2870 [S] | The "Pops" Goes Country | 1966 | 20.00 |
| *—Above two with the Boston Pops Orchestra, Arthur Fiedler, conductor* | | | |
| ❑ LSC-3104 | Chet Picks On the Pops | 1969 | 15.00 |
| *—With the Boston Pops Orchestra, Arthur Fiedler, conductor* | | | |
| RCA VICTOR | | | |
| ❑ APL1-0159 | Alone | 1973 | 12.00 |
| ❑ APD1-0329 [Q] | Superpickers | 1974 | 20.00 |
| ❑ APL1-0329 | Superpickers | 1974 | 12.00 |
| ❑ APL1-0545 | Chet Atkins Picks On Jerry Reed | 1974 | 12.00 |
| ❑ APL1-0645 | Chat Atkins Goes to the Movies | 1973 | 12.00 |
| ❑ ANL1-0981 | Chet Atkins Picks the Best | 1975 | 10.00 |
| ❑ LPM-1090 [M] | A Session with Chet Atkins | 1954 | 60.00 |
| *—Red cover* | | | |
| ❑ LPM-1090 [M] | A Session with Chet Atkins | 1961 | 20.00 |
| *—Woman and guitars cover* | | | |
| ❑ LSP-1090(e) [R] | A Session with Chet Atkins | 1967 | 10.00 |
| ❑ LPM-1197 [M] | Chet Atkins in Three Dimensions | 1956 | 50.00 |
| *—Black-and-white guitar cover* | | | |

| Number | Title (A Side/B Side) | Yr | NM |
|---|---|---|---|
| ❑ LPM-1197 [M] | Chet Atkins in Three Dimensions | 1961 | 20.00 |
| *—Red guitar cover* | | | |
| ❑ LSP-1197(e) [R] | Chet Atkins in Three Dimensions | 1967 | 10.00 |
| ❑ APL1-1233 | The Night Atlanta Burned | 1975 | 12.00 |
| ❑ LPM-1236 [M] | Stringin' Along with Chet Atkins | 1956 | 50.00 |
| *—Orange cover* | | | |
| ❑ LPM-1236 [M] | Stringin' Along with Chet Atkins | 1961 | 20.00 |
| *—Full-color cover* | | | |
| ❑ LSP-1236(e) [R] | Stringin' Along with Chet Atkins | 1967 | 10.00 |
| ❑ LPM-1383 [M] | Finger Style Guitar | 1956 | 50.00 |
| *—Chet's face not visible on cover* | | | |
| ❑ LPM-1383 [M] | Finger Style Guitar | 1961 | 20.00 |
| *—Chet's face visible on cover* | | | |
| ❑ LSP-1383(e) [R] | Finger Style Guitar | 1962 | 12.00 |
| ❑ LPM-1544 [M] | Chet Atkins at Home | 1957 | 50.00 |
| *—Title in block letters on cover* | | | |
| ❑ LPM-1544 [M] | Chet Atkins at Home | 1961 | 20.00 |
| *—Title in script on cover* | | | |
| ❑ LSP-1544(e) [R] | Chet Atkins at Home | 1967 | 10.00 |
| ❑ LPM-1577 [M] | Hi-Fi in Focus | 1957 | 20.00 |
| *—Guitar on cover* | | | |
| ❑ LPM-1577 [M] | Hi-Fi in Focus | 1957 | 50.00 |
| *—No guitars on cover* | | | |
| ❑ LSP-1577(e) [R] | Hi-Fi in Focus | 196? | 10.00 |
| ❑ ANL1-1935 | Christmas with Chet Atkins | 1976 | 8.00 |
| *—Reissue of LSP-2423* | | | |
| ❑ APL1-1985 | The Best of Chet Atkins | 1975 | 12.00 |
| ❑ LPM-1993 [M] | Chet Atkins in Hollywood | 1959 | 30.00 |
| *—Night-time cover* | | | |
| ❑ LPM-1993 [M] | Chet Atkins in Hollywood | 1961 | 20.00 |
| *—Daylight "blonde" cover* | | | |
| ❑ LSP-1993 [S] | Chet Atkins in Hollywood | 1959 | 50.00 |
| *—Night-time cover* | | | |
| ❑ LSP-1993 [S] | Chet Atkins in Hollywood | 1961 | 30.00 |
| *—Daylight "blonde" cover* | | | |
| ❑ LPM-2025 [M] | Hum & Strum Along | 1959 | 25.00 |
| *—Add $10 NM if instruction book is included* | | | |
| ❑ LSP-2025 [S] | Hum & Strum Along | 1959 | 40.00 |
| *—Add $10 NM if instruction book is included* | | | |
| ❑ LPM-2103 [M] | Mister Guitar | 1959 | 30.00 |
| *—Lone guitar on cover* | | | |
| ❑ LPM-2103 [M] | Mister Guitar | 1961 | 20.00 |
| *—Guitar and woman on cover* | | | |
| ❑ LSP-2103 [S] | Mister Guitar | 1959 | 50.00 |
| *—Lone guitar on cover* | | | |
| ❑ LSP-2103 [S] | Mister Guitar | 1961 | 30.00 |
| *—Guitar and woman on cover* | | | |
| ❑ LPM-2161 [M] | Teensville | 1960 | 30.00 |
| *—Title overlaps cover photo* | | | |
| ❑ LPM-2161 [M] | Teensville | 1961 | 20.00 |
| *—Title in black strip at top of cover photo* | | | |
| ❑ LSP-2161 [S] | Teensville | 1960 | 50.00 |
| *—Title overlaps cover photo* | | | |
| ❑ LSP-2161 [S] | Teensville | 1961 | 30.00 |
| *—Title in black strip at top of cover photo* | | | |
| ❑ LPM-2175 [M] | The Other Chet Atkins | 1960 | 20.00 |
| ❑ LSP-2175 [S] | The Other Chet Atkins | 1960 | 30.00 |
| ❑ LPM-2232 [M] | Chet Atkins' Workshop | 1961 | 20.00 |
| ❑ LSP-2232 [S] | Chet Atkins' Workshop | 1961 | 30.00 |
| ❑ LPM-2346 [M] | The Most Popular Guitar | 1961 | 20.00 |
| ❑ LSP-2346 [S] | The Most Popular Guitar | 1961 | 30.00 |
| ❑ AHL1-2405 | My Guitar | 1977 | 12.00 |
| ❑ LPM-2423 [M] | Christmas with Chet Atkins | 1961 | 20.00 |
| ❑ LSP-2423 [S] | Christmas with Chet Atkins | 1961 | 30.00 |
| ❑ LPM-2450 [M] | Down Home | 1962 | 20.00 |
| ❑ LSP-2450 [S] | Down Home | 1962 | 25.00 |
| ❑ CPL1-2503 | A Legendary Performer | 1977 | 12.00 |
| ❑ LPM-2549 [M] | Caribbean Guitar | 1962 | 20.00 |
| ❑ LSP-2549 [S] | Caribbean Guitar | 1962 | 25.00 |
| ❑ LPM-2601 [M] | Back Home Hymns | 1962 | 20.00 |
| ❑ LSP-2601 [S] | Back Home Hymns | 1962 | 25.00 |
| ❑ LPM-2616 [M] | Our Man in Nashville | 1963 | 20.00 |
| ❑ LSP-2616 [S] | Our Man in Nashville | 1963 | 25.00 |
| ❑ LPM-2678 [M] | Travelin' | 1963 | 20.00 |
| ❑ LSP-2678 [S] | Travelin' | 1963 | 25.00 |
| ❑ LPM-2719 [M] | Teen Scene | 1963 | 20.00 |
| ❑ LSP-2719 [S] | Teen Scene | 1963 | 25.00 |
| ❑ LPM-2783 [M] | Guitar Country | 1964 | 15.00 |
| ❑ LSP-2783 [S] | Guitar Country | 1964 | 20.00 |
| ❑ LPM-2887 [M] | The Best of Chet Atkins | 1964 | 15.00 |
| ❑ LSP-2887 [S] | The Best of Chet Atkins | 1964 | 20.00 |
| ❑ LPM-2908 [M] | Progressive Pickin' | 1964 | 15.00 |
| ❑ LSP-2908 [S] | Progressive Pickin' | 1964 | 20.00 |
| ❑ LPM-3079 [10] | Chet Atkins' Gallopin' Guitar | 1952 | 150.00 |
| ❑ LPM-3169 [10] | Stringin' Along with Chet Atkins | 1953 | 100.00 |
| ❑ AHL1-3302 | The First Nashville Guitar Quartet | 1979 | 12.00 |
| ❑ LPM-3316 [M] | My Favorite Guitars | 1965 | 15.00 |
| ❑ LSP-3316 [S] | My Favorite Guitars | 1965 | 20.00 |
| ❑ LPM-3429 [M] | More of That "Guitar Country" | 1965 | 15.00 |
| ❑ LSP-3429 [S] | More of That "Guitar Country" | 1965 | 20.00 |
| ❑ AHL1-3505 | The Best of Chet On The Road...Live | 1980 | 12.00 |
| ❑ LPM-3531 [M] | Chet Atkins Picks On the Beatles | 1966 | 25.00 |
| ❑ LSP-3531 [S] | Chet Atkins Picks On the Beatles | 1966 | 30.00 |
| ❑ LPM-3558 [M] | The Best of Chet Atkins, Volume 2 | 1966 | 12.00 |
| ❑ LSP-3558 [S] | The Best of Chet Atkins, Volume 2 | 1966 | 15.00 |
| ❑ LPM-3647 [M] | From Nashville with Love | 1966 | 12.00 |
| ❑ LSP-3647 [S] | From Nashville with Love | 1966 | 15.00 |
| ❑ LPM-3728 [M] | It's a Guitar World | 1967 | 30.00 |
| ❑ LSP-3728 [S] | It's a Guitar World | 1967 | 12.00 |
| ❑ AYL1-3741 | The First Nashville Guitar Quartet | 1981 | 8.00 |
| *—"Best Buy Series" reissue* | | | |
| ❑ LPM-3818 [M] | Chet Atkins Picks the Best | 1967 | 30.00 |
| ❑ LSP-3818 [S] | Chet Atkins Picks the Best | 1967 | 12.00 |
| ❑ LPM-3885 [M] | Class Guitar | 1967 | 30.00 |
| ❑ LSP-3885 [S] | Class Guitar | 1967 | 12.00 |
| ❑ LPM-3992 [M] | Solo Flights | 1968 | 50.00 |
| ❑ LSP-3992 [S] | Solo Flights | 1968 | 12.00 |
| ❑ LPM-4017 [M] | Hometown Guitar | 1968 | 80.00 |
| ❑ LSP-4017 [S] | Hometown Guitar | 1968 | 15.00 |
| ❑ AHL1-4044 | Still Country — After All These Years | 1981 | 10.00 |
| ❑ LSP-4061 | Solid Gold '68 | 1968 | 15.00 |
| ❑ LSP-4135 | Lover's Guitar | 1968 | 15.00 |
| ❑ LSP-4244 | Solid Gold '69 | 1969 | 12.00 |
| ❑ LSP-4331 | Yestergroovin' | 1970 | 12.00 |
| ❑ LSP-4396 | Me & Jerry | 1971 | 15.00 |
| *—With Jerry Reed* | | | |
| ❑ LSP-4464 | For the Good Times | 1971 | 15.00 |
| ❑ AHL1-4724 | Great Hits of the Past | 1983 | 10.00 |
| ❑ LSP-4754 | Chet Atkins Picks the Hits | 1973 | 15.00 |
| ❑ AHL1-5495 | Collector's Series | 1985 | 10.00 |
| ❑ VPS-6030 [(2)] | This Is Chet Atkins | 1972 | 15.00 |
| ❑ VPXS-6079 [(2)] | Now & Then | 1972 | 15.00 |

TIME-LIFE

| Number | Title (A Side/B Side) | Yr | NM |
|---|---|---|---|
| ❑ STW-117 | Country Music | 1981 | 12.00 |

## ATLANTA RHYTHM SECTION

COLUMBIA

| Number | Title (A Side/B Side) | Yr | NM |
|---|---|---|---|
| ❑ FC 37550 | Quinella | 1981 | 10.00 |
| ❑ PC 37550 | Quinella | 1982 | 8.00 |
| *—Budget-line reissue* | | | |

DECCA

| Number | Title (A Side/B Side) | Yr | NM |
|---|---|---|---|
| ❑ DL 75265 | Atlanta Rhythm Section | 1972 | 25.00 |
| ❑ DL 75390 | Back Up Against the Wall | 1973 | 25.00 |

MCA

| Number | Title (A Side/B Side) | Yr | NM |
|---|---|---|---|
| ❑ 2-4114 [(2)] | Atlanta Rhythm Section | 1977 | 12.00 |
| *—Combines the two Decca LPs into one package* | | | |

MOBILE FIDELITY

| Number | Title (A Side/B Side) | Yr | NM |
|---|---|---|---|
| ❑ 1-038 | Champagne Jam | 1981 | 40.00 |
| *—Audiophile vinyl* | | | |

POLYDOR

| Number | Title (A Side/B Side) | Yr | NM |
|---|---|---|---|
| ❑ PD 6027 | Third Annual Pipe Dream | 1974 | 10.00 |
| ❑ PD 6041 | Dog Days | 1975 | 10.00 |
| ❑ PD-1-6060 | Red Tape | 1976 | 10.00 |
| ❑ PD-1-6080 | A Rock and Roll Alternative | 1977 | 10.00 |
| ❑ PD-1-6134 | Champagne Jam | 1978 | 10.00 |
| ❑ PD-1-6200 | Underdog | 1979 | 10.00 |
| ❑ PD-2-6236 [(2)] | Are You Ready! | 1979 | 12.00 |
| ❑ PD-1-6285 | The Boys from Doraville | 1980 | 10.00 |

## ATOMIC ROOSTER

ELEKTRA

| Number | Title (A Side/B Side) | Yr | NM |
|---|---|---|---|
| ❑ EKS-74094 | Death Walks Behind You | 1971 | 20.00 |
| ❑ EKS-74109 | In Hearing Of Atomic Rooster | 1971 | 20.00 |
| ❑ EKS-75039 | Made in England | 1972 | 20.00 |
| ❑ EKS-75074 | Atomic Rooster IV | 1973 | 15.00 |

## ATTILA

BACK-TRAC

| Number | Title (A Side/B Side) | Yr | NM |
|---|---|---|---|
| ❑ P 18808 | Attila | 1985 | 10.00 |

EPIC

| Number | Title (A Side/B Side) | Yr | NM |
|---|---|---|---|
| ❑ E 30030 | Attila | 1970 | 30.00 |

## AU GO-GO SINGERS, THE

With Stephen Stills and Richie Furay, later of BUFFALO SPRINGFIELD.

ROULETTE

| Number | Title (A Side/B Side) | Yr | NM |
|---|---|---|---|
| ❑ R 25280 [M] | They Call Us the Au Go-Go Singers | 1964 | 50.00 |
| ❑ SR 25280 [S] | They Call Us the Au Go-Go Singers | 1964 | 70.00 |

## AUDIO TWO

FIRST PRIORITY

| Number | Title (A Side/B Side) | Yr | NM |
|---|---|---|---|
| ❑ 90907 | What More Can I Say? | 1988 | 80.00 |
| ❑ 91358 | I Don't Care — The Album | 1990 | 80.00 |

## AUGER, BRIAN, TRINITY

ATCO

| Number | Title (A Side/B Side) | Yr | NM |
|---|---|---|---|
| ❑ 33-258 [M] | Open | 1968 | 20.00 |
| *—White label promo; no stock copies were issued in mono* | | | |
| ❑ SD 33-258 [S] | Open | 1968 | 12.00 |
| ❑ SD 33-273 | Definitely What! | 1969 | 12.00 |
| ❑ SD 2-701 [(2)] | Streetnoise | 1969 | 20.00 |

CAPITOL

| Number | Title (A Side/B Side) | Yr | NM |
|---|---|---|---|
| ❑ DT-136 [R] | Jools & Brian | 1969 | 12.00 |
| *—American issue of pre-Atco material* | | | |

HEADFIRST

| Number | Title (A Side/B Side) | Yr | NM |
|---|---|---|---|
| ❑ 9702 | Search Party | 1981 | 15.00 |

POLYDOR

| Number | Title (A Side/B Side) | Yr | NM |
|---|---|---|---|
| ❑ PD-1-6505 | Genesis | 1975 | 12.00 |

RCA VICTOR

| Number | Title (A Side/B Side) | Yr | NM |
|---|---|---|---|
| ❑ AFL1-0140 | Closer To It | 197? | 8.00 |
| *—Reissue* | | | |
| ❑ APL1-0140 | Closer To It | 1973 | 10.00 |
| ❑ AFL1-0454 | Straight Ahead | 197? | 8.00 |
| *—Reissue* | | | |
| ❑ CPL1-0454 | Straight Ahead | 1974 | 10.00 |
| ❑ CPL1-0645 | Live Oblivion | 1974 | 10.00 |
| ❑ APL1-1210 | Reinforcements | 1975 | 10.00 |
| ❑ CPL2-1230 [(2)] | Live Oblivion, Vol. 2 | 1976 | 15.00 |
| ❑ AFL1-2249 | The Best of Brian Auger | 1977 | 10.00 |
| ❑ ANL1-2481 | Live Oblivion | 1977 | 8.00 |
| *—Reissue* | | | |
| ❑ LSP-4372 | Befour | 1970 | 10.00 |
| ❑ AFL1-4462 | Brian Auger's Oblivion Express | 197? | 8.00 |
| *—Reissue* | | | |
| ❑ LSP-4462 | Brian Auger's Oblivion Express | 1971 | 10.00 |
| *—Starting here, group is "Oblivion Express"* | | | |
| ❑ LSP-4540 | A Better Land | 1971 | 10.00 |
| ❑ AFL1-4703 | Second Wind | 197? | 8.00 |
| *—Reissue* | | | |
| ❑ LSP-4703 | Second Wind | 1972 | 10.00 |

SPRINGBOARD

| Number | Title (A Side/B Side) | Yr | NM |
|---|---|---|---|
| ❑ SPB-4044 | Brian Auger | 1973 | 8.00 |
| *—Reissue of early material* | | | |

WARNER BROS.

| Number | Title (A Side/B Side) | Yr | NM |
|---|---|---|---|
| ❑ BS 2981 | Happiness Heartaches | 1977 | 10.00 |
| ❑ BSK 3153 | Encore | 1978 | 10.00 |

## AUGUST, JAN

MERCURY

| Number | Title (A Side/B Side) | Yr | NM |
|---|---|---|---|
| ❑ MG 20072 [M] | Jan August Plays Songs to Remember | 1955 | 25.00 |
| ❑ MG 20078 [M] | Music for the Quiet Hour | 1955 | 25.00 |
| ❑ MG 20147 [M] | Piano Roll Blues | 1955 | 25.00 |
| ❑ MG 20160 [M] | Christmas Favorites | 1955 | 25.00 |
| ❑ MG 20272 [M] | Cocktails and Conversation | 195? | 20.00 |
| ❑ MG 20273 [M] | Keyboard Waltzes | 195? | 20.00 |
| ❑ MG 20274 [M] | Latin Rhythms | 195? | 20.00 |
| ❑ MG 20408 [M] | Cha Cha Charm | 1959 | 15.00 |
| ❑ MG 20513 [M] | Jan August Plays Great Piano Hits | 195? | 15.00 |
| ❑ MG 20618 [M] | Accent! | 1961 | 15.00 |
| ❑ MG 20659 [M] | Jan August Styles the Great Pop Piano Classics | 196? | 15.00 |
| ❑ MG 20667 [M] | Jan August Styles the Great International Hits | 196? | 15.00 |
| ❑ MG 20744 [M] | Jan August Plays a Collection of 27 Popular Classical Melodies | 196? | 15.00 |
| ❑ MG 25087 [10] | Piano Favorites | 195? | 30.00 |
| ❑ MG 25136 [10] | Piano Poetry | 195? | 30.00 |
| ❑ SR 60082 [S] | Cha Cha Charm | 1959 | 20.00 |
| ❑ SR 60189 [S] | Jan August Plays Great Piano Hits | 195? | 20.00 |
| ❑ SR 60618 [S] | Accent! | 1961 | 20.00 |
| ❑ SR 60659 [S] | Jan August Styles the Great Pop Piano Classics | 196? | 20.00 |
| ❑ SR 60667 [S] | Jan August Styles the Great International Hits | 196? | 20.00 |
| ❑ SR 60744 [S] | Jan August Plays a Collection of 27 Popular Classical Melodies | 196? | 20.00 |

WING

| Number | Title (A Side/B Side) | Yr | NM |
|---|---|---|---|
| ❑ MGW 12129 [M] | Music for the Quiet Hour | 196? | 12.00 |
| ❑ MGW 12175 [M] | Christmas Favorites | 196? | 12.00 |
| ❑ MGW 12254 [M] | The Piano Wizardry of Jan August | 196? | 12.00 |
| ❑ SRW 16129 [R] | Music for the Quiet Hour | 196? | 10.00 |
| ❑ SRW 16254 [R] | The Piano Wizardry of Jan August | 196? | 10.00 |

## AUGUST SONS

EYES IN THE WOODS

| Number | Title (A Side/B Side) | Yr | NM |
|---|---|---|---|
| ❑ (# unknown) [EP] | I Am Not a Vampire | 1989 | 40.00 |

## AULD, GEORGIE

ABC-PARAMOUNT

| Number | Title (A Side/B Side) | Yr | NM |
|---|---|---|---|
| ❑ ABC-287 [M] | Georgie Auld Plays for Melancholy Babies | 1958 | 40.00 |
| ❑ ABCS-287 [S] | Georgie Auld Plays for Melancholy Babies | 1959 | 30.00 |

ALLEGRO

| Number | Title (A Side/B Side) | Yr | NM |
|---|---|---|---|
| ❑ 3102 [M] | Jazz Concert | 1953 | 40.00 |

APOLLO

| Number | Title (A Side/B Side) | Yr | NM |
|---|---|---|---|
| ❑ LAP-102 [10] | Concert in Jazz | 1951 | 80.00 |

CORAL

| Number | Title (A Side/B Side) | Yr | NM |
|---|---|---|---|
| ❑ CRL 56060 [10] | Tenderly | 1952 | 80.00 |
| ❑ CRL 56085 [10] | Manhattan | 1953 | 80.00 |
| ❑ CRL 57029 [M] | Lullaby of Broadway | 1956 | 40.00 |
| ❑ CRL 57032 [M] | Misty | 1956 | 40.00 |

DISCOVERY

| Number | Title (A Side/B Side) | Yr | NM |
|---|---|---|---|
| ❑ DL 3007 [10] | That's Auld | 1950 | 80.00 |



**Except when noted otherwise, VG = 25% of NM, and VG+ = 50% of NM. (Example: VG = $2.00, VG+ = $4.00 and NM = $8.00.)**

| Number | Title (A Side/B Side) | Yr | NM |
|---|---|---|---|
| **EMARCY** | | | |
| ❑ MG-36060 [M] | In the Land of Hi-Fi | 1955 | 40.00 |
| ❑ MG-36090 [M] | Dancing in the Land of Hi-Fi | 1956 | 40.00 |
| **JARO** | | | |
| ❑ JAM-5003 [M] | Hawaii on the Rocks | 1959 | 30.00 |
| **PHILIPS** | | | |
| ❑ PHS 600096 [S] | Georgie Auld Plays to the Winners | 1963 | 20.00 |
| ❑ PHS 600116 [S] | Here's to the Losers | 1963 | 20.00 |
| **ROOST** | | | |
| ❑ RST-403 [10] | Georgie Auld Quintet | 1951 | 80.00 |
| **TOP RANK** | | | |
| ❑ RM-306 [M] | The Melody Lingers On | 1959 | 40.00 |
| ❑ RM-333 [M] | Good Enough to Keep | 1960 | 40.00 |
| **UNITED ARTISTS** | | | |
| ❑ UAL-3068 [M] | Manhattan with Strings | 1959 | 40.00 |
| ❑ UAS-6068 [S] | Manhattan with Strings | 1959 | 30.00 |

### AUM

| Number | Title (A Side/B Side) | Yr | NM |
|---|---|---|---|
| **FILLMORE** | | | |
| ❑ Z 30002 | Resurrection | 1970 | 30.00 |
| **SIRE** | | | |
| ❑ SES-97007 | Bluesvibes | 1969 | 40.00 |

### AUSTIN, BOBBY

| Number | Title (A Side/B Side) | Yr | NM |
|---|---|---|---|
| **CAPITOL** | | | |
| ❑ ST 2773 [S] | Apartment No. 9 | 1967 | 20.00 |
| ❑ T 2773 [M] | Apartment No. 9 | 1967 | 25.00 |
| ❑ ST 2915 | Old Love Never Dies | 1968 | 20.00 |

### AUSTIN, CLAIRE

| Number | Title (A Side/B Side) | Yr | NM |
|---|---|---|---|
| **CONTEMPORARY** | | | |
| ❑ C-5002 [M] | When Your Lover Has Gone | 1956 | 50.00 |
| **GOOD TIME JAZZ** | | | |
| ❑ L-24 [10] | Claire Austin Sings the Blues | 1954 | 120.00 |

### AUSTIN, DONALD

| Number | Title (A Side/B Side) | Yr | NM |
|---|---|---|---|
| **EASTBOUND** | | | |
| ❑ EB-9005 | Crazy Legs | 1973 | 30.00 |

### AUSTIN, GENE

| Number | Title (A Side/B Side) | Yr | NM |
|---|---|---|---|
| **DECCA** | | | |
| ❑ DL 8433 [M] | My Blue Heaven | 1957 | 40.00 |
| **DOT** | | | |
| ❑ DLP 3300 [M] | Great Hits | 1960 | 20.00 |
| ❑ DLP 25300 [S] | Great Hits | 1960 | 25.00 |
| **FRATERNITY** | | | |
| ❑ F-1006 [M] | Gene Austin and His Lonesome Road | 1957 | 20.00 |
| **RCA VICTOR** | | | |
| ❑ LPM-1549 [M] | Restless Heart | 1957 | 40.00 |
| ❑ LPM-2490 [M] | My Blue Heaven | 1961 | 25.00 |
| ❑ LPM-3200 [10] | My Blue Heaven | 1953 | 60.00 |
| ❑ VPM-6065 [(2)] | This Is Gene Austin | 1972 | 20.00 |
| **"X"** | | | |
| ❑ LVA-1007 [M] | Gene Austin Sings All-Time Favorites | 1954 | 40.00 |

### AUSTIN, SIL

| Number | Title (A Side/B Side) | Yr | NM |
|---|---|---|---|
| **MERCURY** | | | |
| ❑ MG-20237 [M] | Slow Walk Rock | 1957 | 70.00 |
| ❑ MG-20320 [M] | Everything's Shakin' | 1958 | 70.00 |
| ❑ MG-20424 [M] | Sil Austin Plays Pretty for the People | 1959 | 40.00 |
| ❑ MG-20576 [M] | Soft, Plaintive and Moody | 1960 | 40.00 |
| ❑ MG-20663 [M] | Golden Saxophone Hits | 1961 | 25.00 |
| ❑ MG-20755 [M] | Folk Songs | 1963 | 15.00 |
| ❑ MG-20925 [M] | Sil Austin Plays Pretty Melodies of the World | 1964 | 20.00 |
| ❑ MG-21126 [M] | Sil Austin Plays Pretty for the People Again | 1967 | 20.00 |
| ❑ SR-60096 [S] | Sil Austin Plays Pretty for the People | 1959 | 60.00 |
| *—Black label* | | | |
| ❑ SR-60096 [S] | Sil Austin Plays Pretty for the People | 1965 | 20.00 |
| *—Red label, white "MERCURY" at top* | | | |
| ❑ SR-60096 [S] | Sil Austin Plays Pretty for the People | 1974 | 10.00 |
| *—"Chicago styline" label* | | | |
| ❑ SR-60236 [S] | Soft, Plaintive and Moody | 1960 | 60.00 |
| ❑ SR-60663 [S] | Golden Saxophone Hits | 1961 | 30.00 |
| ❑ SR-60755 [S] | Folk Songs | 1963 | 20.00 |
| ❑ SR-60925 [S] | Sil Austin Plays Pretty Melodies of the World | 1964 | 25.00 |
| ❑ SR-61126 [S] | Sil Austin Plays Pretty for the People Again | 1967 | 20.00 |
| **SSS INTERNATIONAL** | | | |
| ❑ 4 | Honey Sax | 1969 | 15.00 |
| ❑ 8 | Soft Soul with Strings | 1970 | 15.00 |
| ❑ 14 | Sil and Silver Screen | 1971 | 15.00 |
| ❑ 23 | Songs of Gold | 1971 | 15.00 |
| **WING** | | | |
| ❑ SRW-16227 [S] | Everything's Shakin' | 196? | 15.00 |
| ❑ SRW-16369 [S] | Sil Austin Again Plays Pretty for the People | 196? | 15.00 |

### AUSTRALIAN ALL STARS, THE

| Number | Title (A Side/B Side) | Yr | NM |
|---|---|---|---|
| **BETHLEHEM** | | | |
| ❑ BCP-6070 [M] | Jazz for Beach-Niks | 1963 | 40.00 |
| ❑ BCP-6073 [M] | Jazz for Surf-Niks | 1963 | 40.00 |

### AUSTRALIAN JAZZ QUARTET, THE

| Number | Title (A Side/B Side) | Yr | NM |
|---|---|---|---|
| **BETHLEHEM** | | | |
| ❑ BCP-1031 [10] | The Australian Jazz Quartet | 195? | 60.00 |
| ❑ BCP-6002 [M] | The Australian Jazz Quartet/ Quintet | 1955 | 40.00 |
| ❑ BCP-6012 [M] | The Australian Jazz Quartet at the Varsity Drag | 1956 | 40.00 |
| ❑ BCP-6015 [M] | The Australian Jazz Quartet Plus One | 1957 | 40.00 |
| ❑ BCP-6022 [M] | The Australian Jazz Quartet Plays the Best of Broadway Musical Hits | 1957 | 40.00 |
| ❑ BCP-6029 [M] | The Australian Jazz Quartet In Free Style | 1959 | 40.00 |
| ❑ BCP-6030 [M] | Three Penny Opera | 1959 | 40.00 |

### AUTOSALVAGE

| Number | Title (A Side/B Side) | Yr | NM |
|---|---|---|---|
| **RCA VICTOR** | | | |
| ❑ LPM-3940 [M] | Autosalvage | 1968 | 40.00 |
| ❑ LSP-3940 [S] | Autosalvage | 1968 | 40.00 |

### AUTRY, GENE

| Number | Title (A Side/B Side) | Yr | NM |
|---|---|---|---|
| **CBS SPECIAL PRODUCTS** | | | |
| ❑ P 18737 | Golden Hits | 1985 | 10.00 |
| ❑ P 18963 | His Golden Hits | 1985 | 10.00 |
| ❑ P 18964 | Famous Favorites | 1985 | 10.00 |
| **CHALLENGE** | | | |
| ❑ CHL-600 [M] | Christmas with Gene Autry | 1958 | 50.00 |
| **COLUMBIA** | | | |
| ❑ CL (# unk) [10] | Easter Favorites | 1949 | 150.00 |
| ❑ CL 677 [M] | Gene Autry and Champion — Western Adventures | 1955 | 120.00 |
| ❑ CS 1035 | Gene Autry's Country Music Hall of Fame Album | 1970 | 15.00 |
| ❑ CL 1575 [M] | Gene Autry's Greatest Hits | 1961 | 30.00 |
| *—Red and black label with six "eye" logos* | | | |
| ❑ CL 2547 [10] | Merry Christmas with Gene Autry | 1954 | 120.00 |
| *—"House Party Series" release* | | | |
| ❑ CL 2568 [10] | Easter Favorites | 1955 | 120.00 |
| *—"House Party Series" issue* | | | |
| ❑ CL 6020 [10] | Gene Autry's Western Classics | 1949 | 150.00 |
| ❑ CL 6137 [10] | Merry Christmas | 1950 | 150.00 |
| ❑ JL 8001 [10] | Gene Autry at the Rodeo | 1949 | 150.00 |
| ❑ JL 8009 [10] | Stampede | 1949 | 150.00 |
| ❑ JL 8012 [10] | Champion | 1950 | 150.00 |
| ❑ HL 9001 [10] | Gene Autry's Western Classics, Volume 1 | 1949 | 150.00 |
| ❑ HL 9002 [10] | Gene Autry's Western Classics, Volume 2 | 1949 | 150.00 |
| **COLUMBIA SPECIAL PRODUCTS** | | | |
| ❑ P 15766 | Christmas Favorites | 1981 | 12.00 |
| ❑ P 15767 | Everyone's a Child at Christmas | 1981 | 12.00 |
| **GRAND PRIX** | | | |
| ❑ KS-X11 [S] | The Original Gene Autry Sings Rudolph the Red-Nosed Reindeer and Other Christmas Favorites | 1961 | 20.00 |
| ❑ KX-11 [M] | The Original Gene Autry Sings Rudolph the Red-Nosed Reindeer and Other Christmas Favorites | 1961 | 15.00 |
| **GUSTO** | | | |
| ❑ 1038 | Christmas Classics | 1978 | 10.00 |
| **HARMONY** | | | |
| ❑ HL 7332 [M] | Gene Autry's Great Western Hits | 1965 | 30.00 |
| ❑ HL 7376 [M] | Back in the Saddle Again | 1966 | 20.00 |
| ❑ HL 7399 [M] | Gene Autry Sings | 1966 | 20.00 |
| ❑ HL 9505 [M] | Gene Autry and Champion — Western Adventures | 1959 | 30.00 |
| ❑ HL 9550 [M] | The Original Rudolph the Red-Nosed Reindeer and Other Children's Christmas Favorites | 1964 | 25.00 |
| ❑ HS 11199 [R] | Gene Autry Sings | 1966 | 15.00 |
| ❑ HS 11276 [R] | Back in the Saddle Again | 1966 | 15.00 |
| ❑ HS 14450 [R] | The Original Rudolph the Red-Nosed Reindeer and Other Children's Christmas Favorites | 1964 | 12.00 |
| **MELODY RANCH** | | | |
| ❑ 101 [M] | Melody Ranch | 1965 | 40.00 |
| **MURRAY HILL** | | | |
| ❑ 897296 [(4)] | Melody Ranch Radio Show | 197? | 60.00 |
| *—Compilation of some of Gene's radio shows in a box set* | | | |
| **RCA VICTOR** | | | |
| ❑ LPM-2623 [M] | Gene Autry's Golden Hits | 1962 | 30.00 |
| ❑ LSP-2623 [S] | Gene Autry's Golden Hits | 1962 | 40.00 |
| **REPUBLIC** | | | |
| ❑ 6011 | South of the Border, All American Cowboy | 1976 | 20.00 |
| ❑ 6012 | Cowboy Hall of Fame | 1976 | 20.00 |
| ❑ RLP 6018 [M] | Christmas with Gene Autry | 1976 | 12.00 |

### AVALANCHES, THE

| Number | Title (A Side/B Side) | Yr | NM |
|---|---|---|---|
| **WARNER BROS.** | | | |
| ❑ W 1525 [M] | Ski Surfin' | 1963 | 40.00 |
| ❑ WS 1525 [S] | Ski Surfin' | 1963 | 60.00 |

### AVALON, FRANKIE

| Number | Title (A Side/B Side) | Yr | NM |
|---|---|---|---|
| **ABC** | | | |
| ❑ ABCX-805 [R] | 16 Greatest Hits | 1974 | 12.00 |
| **CHANCELLOR** | | | |
| ❑ CHL 5001 [M] | Frankie Avalon | 1958 | 50.00 |
| *—Pink label* | | | |
| ❑ CHL 5001 [M] | Frankie Avalon | 1959 | 40.00 |
| *—Black label* | | | |
| ❑ CHL 5002 [M] | The Young Frankie Avalon | 1959 | 40.00 |
| *—Black label* | | | |
| ❑ CHL 5002 [M] | The Young Frankie Avalon | 1959 | 50.00 |
| *—Pink label* | | | |
| ❑ CHLS 5002 [S] | The Young Frankie Avalon | 1959 | 50.00 |
| *—Black label* | | | |
| ❑ CHLS 5002 [S] | The Young Frankie Avalon | 1959 | 60.00 |
| *—Pink label* | | | |
| ❑ CHLX 5004 [M] | Swingin' on a Rainbow | 1959 | 40.00 |
| ❑ CHLXS 5004 [S] | Swingin' on a Rainbow | 1959 | 50.00 |
| ❑ CHL 5011 [M] | Summer Scene | 1960 | 30.00 |
| ❑ CHLS 5011 [S] | Summer Scene | 1960 | 40.00 |
| ❑ CHL 5018 [M] | A Whole Lotta Frankie | 1961 | 30.00 |
| ❑ CHL 5022 [M] | And Now About Mr. Avalon | 1961 | 30.00 |
| ❑ CHLS 5022 [S] | And Now About Mr. Avalon | 1961 | 40.00 |
| ❑ CHL 5025 [M] | Italiano | 1962 | 30.00 |
| ❑ CHLS 5025 [S] | Italiano | 1962 | 40.00 |
| ❑ CHL 5027 [M] | You're Mine | 1962 | 30.00 |
| ❑ CHLS 5027 [S] | You're Mine | 1962 | 40.00 |
| ❑ CHL 5031 [M] | Frankie Avalon's Christmas Album | 1962 | 30.00 |
| ❑ CHLS 5031 [S] | Frankie Avalon's Christmas Album | 1962 | 40.00 |
| ❑ CHL 5032 [M] | Cleopatra Plus 13 Other Great Hits | 1963 | 30.00 |
| ❑ CHLS 5032 [S] | Cleopatra Plus 13 Other Great Hits | 1963 | 40.00 |
| ❑ 69801 [M] | Young and In Love | 1960 | 40.00 |
| *—LP without the box* | | | |
| ❑ 69801 [M] | Young and In Love | 1960 | 80.00 |
| *—LP in felt cover and 3-D portrait, all in box* | | | |
| **DE-LITE** | | | |
| ❑ 2020 | Venus | 1976 | 15.00 |
| ❑ 9504 | You're My Life | 1977 | 15.00 |
| **EVEREST** | | | |
| ❑ 4187 | Greatest Hits | 1982 | 10.00 |
| **LIBERTY** | | | |
| ❑ LN-10193 | Songs from Muscle Beach Party | 1981 | 8.00 |
| *—Budget-line reissue* | | | |
| **MCA** | | | |
| ❑ 27096 | The Best of Frankie Avalon | 1985 | 8.00 |
| **METROMEDIA** | | | |
| ❑ MD-1034 | I Want You Near Me | 1970 | 15.00 |
| **SUNSET** | | | |
| ❑ SUS-5244 | Frankie Avalon | 1969 | 15.00 |
| **TRIP** | | | |
| ❑ 1621 | 16 Greatest Hits of Frankie Avalon | 1977 | 10.00 |
| **UNITED ARTISTS** | | | |
| ❑ UA-LA450-F | The Very Best of Frankie Avalon | 1975 | 12.00 |
| ❑ UAL-3371 [M] | Songs from Muscle Beach Party | 1964 | 25.00 |
| ❑ UAL-3382 [M] | Frankie Avalon's 15 Greatest Hits | 1964 | 20.00 |
| ❑ UAS-6371 [S] | Songs from Muscle Beach Party | 1964 | 30.00 |
| ❑ UAS-6382 [S] | Frankie Avalon's 15 Greatest Hits | 1964 | 25.00 |

### AVENGERS

| Number | Title (A Side/B Side) | Yr | NM |
|---|---|---|---|
| **CD PRESENTS** | | | |
| ❑ 007 | Avengers | 1983 | 20.00 |
| *—Black vinyl* | | | |
| ❑ 007 | Avengers | 1983 | 30.00 |
| *—Red vinyl* | | | |
| **GO** | | | |
| ❑ 005 | Avengers | 1983 | 120.00 |

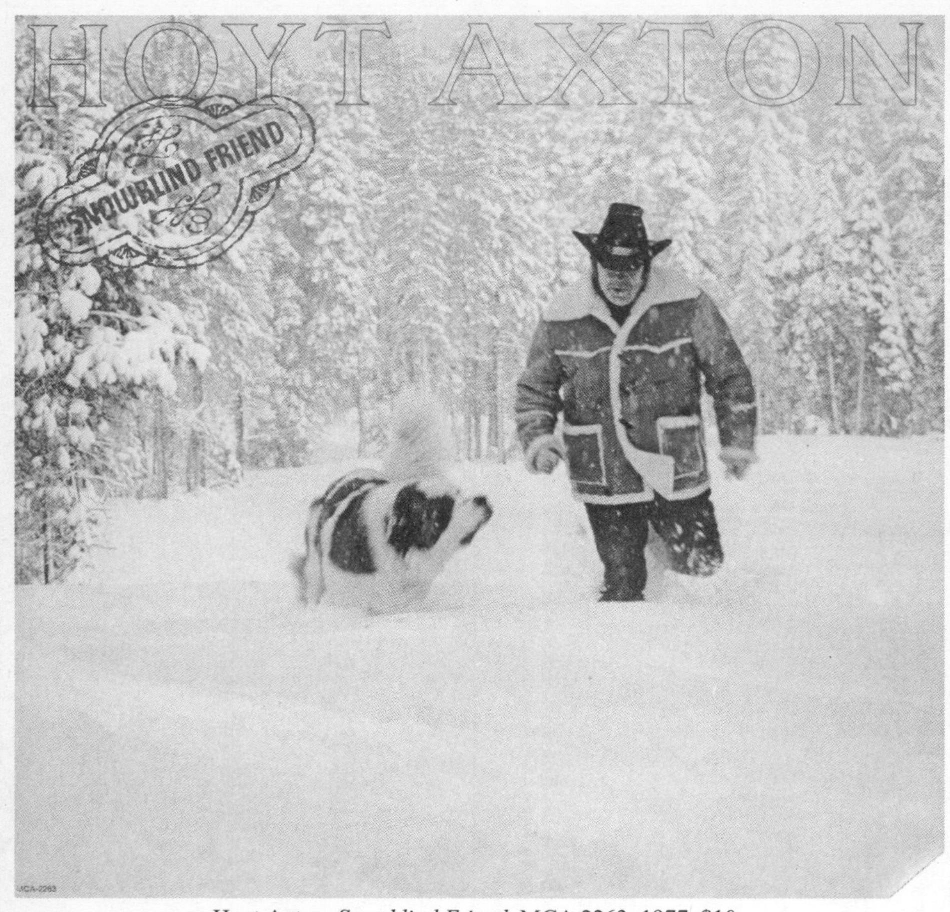


Hoyt Axton, *Snowblind Friend,* MCA 2263, 1977, $10.

| Number | Title (A Side/B Side) | Yr | NM |
|---|---|---|---|
| **LOOKOUT!** | | | |
| ❑ 217 | The Avengers Died for Your Sins | 1999 | 10.00 |
| **WHITE NOISE** | | | |
| ❑ 002 [EP] | Avengers | 1978 | 50.00 |

### AVENGERS VI, THE

| Number | Title (A Side/B Side) | Yr | NM |
|---|---|---|---|
| **MARK 56** | | | |
| ❑ 536 | Good Humor Presents Real Cool Hits | 1966 | 250.00 |
| *—Custom pressing for the Good Humor ice cream company* | | | |

### AVERAGE WHITE BAND

| Number | Title (A Side/B Side) | Yr | NM |
|---|---|---|---|
| **ARISTA** | | | |
| ❑ AB 9523 | Shine | 1980 | 10.00 |
| ❑ AB 9594 | Cupid's in Fashion | 1981 | 10.00 |
| **ATLANTIC** | | | |
| ❑ SD 2-1002 [(2)] | Person to Person | 1977 | 12.00 |
| ❑ QD 7308 [Q] | Average White Band | 1975 | 20.00 |
| ❑ SD 7308 | Average White Band | 1974 | 10.00 |
| ❑ SD 18140 | Cut the Cake | 1975 | 10.00 |
| ❑ SD 18179 | Soul Searching | 1976 | 10.00 |
| ❑ SD 19105 | Benny and Us | 1977 | 10.00 |
| *—With Ben E. King* | | | |
| ❑ SD 19116 | Average White Band | 1977 | 8.00 |
| *—Reissue* | | | |
| ❑ SD 19162 | Warmer Communications | 1978 | 10.00 |
| ❑ SD 19207 | Feel No Fret | 1979 | 10.00 |
| ❑ SD 19266 | Volume VIII | 1980 | 10.00 |
| **MCA** | | | |
| ❑ 345 | Show Your Hands | 1973 | 25.00 |
| ❑ 475 | Put It Where You Want It | 1975 | 10.00 |
| *—Reissue of MCA 345* | | | |
| **MOBILE FIDELITY** | | | |
| ❑ 1-245 | Average White Band | 1996 | 20.00 |
| *—Audiophile vinyl* | | | |
| **TRACK** | | | |
| ❑ 58830 | Aftershock | 1988 | 10.00 |

### AVONS, THE (1)

| Number | Title (A Side/B Side) | Yr | NM |
|---|---|---|---|
| **HULL** | | | |
| ❑ HLP-1000 [M] | The Avons | 1960 | 700.00 |

### AWESOME DRE AND THE HARDCORE COMMITTEE

| Number | Title (A Side/B Side) | Yr | NM |
|---|---|---|---|
| **BENTLEY** | | | |
| ❑ 12001 | You Can't Hold Me Back | 1989 | 20.00 |

### AXTON, HOYT

| Number | Title (A Side/B Side) | Yr | NM |
|---|---|---|---|
| **A&M** | | | |
| ❑ SP-3155 | Life Machine | 198? | 8.00 |
| *—Budget-line reissue* | | | |
| ❑ SP-3182 | Road Songs | 198? | 8.00 |
| *—Budget-line reissue* | | | |
| ❑ SP-4376 | Less Than a Song | 1973 | 10.00 |
| ❑ SP-4402 | Life Machine | 1974 | 10.00 |
| ❑ SP-4510 | Southbound | 1975 | 10.00 |
| ❑ SP-4571 | Fearless | 1976 | 10.00 |
| ❑ SP-4669 | Road Songs | 1977 | 10.00 |
| **ACCORD** | | | |
| ❑ SN-7197 | Heartbreak Hotel | 1982 | 10.00 |
| **ALLEGIANCE** | | | |
| ❑ AV-5023 | Down and Out | 1984 | 10.00 |
| **BRYLEN** | | | |
| ❑ BN 4400 | Double Dare | 1982 | 12.00 |
| **CAPITOL** | | | |
| ❑ ST-788 | Joy to the World | 1971 | 12.00 |
| ❑ SMAS-850 | Country Anthem | 1971 | 12.00 |
| **COLUMBIA** | | | |
| ❑ CS 9766 | My Griffin Is Gone | 1969 | 15.00 |
| ❑ KC 33103 | My Griffin Is Gone | 1975 | 10.00 |
| ❑ PC 33103 | My Griffin Is Gone | 1979 | 8.00 |
| *—Budget-line reissue* | | | |
| **EXODUS** | | | |
| ❑ EX-301 [M] | Hoyt Axton Sings Bessie Smith | 1966 | 20.00 |
| ❑ EXS-321 [M] | Saturday's Child | 1966 | 20.00 |
| *—Cover says stereo, record plays mono* | | | |
| **HORIZON** | | | |
| ❑ WP-1601 [M] | The Balladeer | 1962 | 25.00 |
| *—Black label* | | | |
| ❑ WP-1601 [M] | Greenback Dollar | 1963 | 20.00 |
| *—Black label; two fewer songs than "The Balladeer"* | | | |
| ❑ WP-1601 [S] | The Balladeer | 1962 | 30.00 |
| *—Same number as mono, but with blue label* | | | |
| ❑ WP-1601 [S] | Greenback Dollar | 1963 | 25.00 |
| *—Blue label; two fewer songs than "The Balladeer"* | | | |
| ❑ SWP-1613 [S] | Thunder 'N Lightnin' | 1963 | 30.00 |
| ❑ WP-1613 [M] | Thunder 'N Lightnin' | 1963 | 25.00 |
| ❑ SWP-1621 [S] | Saturday's Child | 1963 | 30.00 |
| ❑ WP-1621 [M] | Saturday's Child | 1963 | 25.00 |
| **JEREMIAH** | | | |
| ❑ JH-5000 | A Rusty Old Halo | 1979 | 12.00 |
| ❑ JH-5001 | Where Did the Money Go? | 1980 | 12.00 |
| **MCA** | | | |
| ❑ 647 | Snow Blind Friend | 198? | 8.00 |
| *—Budget-line reissue* | | | |
| ❑ 648 | Free Sailin' | 198? | 8.00 |
| *—Budget-line reissue* | | | |
| ❑ 2263 | Snow Blind Friend | 1977 | 10.00 |
| ❑ 2319 | Free Sailin' | 1978 | 10.00 |
| **SURREY** | | | |
| ❑ S-1005 [M] | Mr. Greenback Dollar Man | 1965 | 20.00 |
| ❑ SS-1005 [S] | Mr. Greenback Dollar Man | 1965 | 25.00 |
| **VEE JAY** | | | |
| ❑ LP-1098 [M] | Hoyt Axton Explodes! | 1964 | 25.00 |
| ❑ LPS-1098 [R] | Hoyt Axton Explodes! | 1964 | 20.00 |
| ❑ LP-1118 [M] | The Best of Hoyt Axton | 1965 | 20.00 |
| ❑ LPS-1118 [S] | The Best of Hoyt Axton | 1965 | 25.00 |
| ❑ LP-1126 [M] | Greenback Dollar | 1965 | 20.00 |
| ❑ LPS-1126 [S] | Greenback Dollar | 1965 | 25.00 |
| ❑ LP-1127 [M] | Saturday's Child | 1965 | 20.00 |
| ❑ LPS-1127 [S] | Saturday's Child | 1965 | 25.00 |
| *—Reissue of Horizon 1621* | | | |
| ❑ LP-1128 [M] | Thunder 'N Lightnin' | 1965 | 20.00 |
| ❑ LPS-1128 [S] | Thunder 'N Lightnin' | 1965 | 25.00 |
| *—Reissue of Horizon 1613* | | | |
| **VEE JAY INTERNATIONAL** | | | |
| ❑ VJS-2-1005 [(2)] | Gold | 1974 | 20.00 |
| *—Compilation of older Vee Jay material* | | | |
| ❑ LP-6001 | Long Old Road | 1977 | 15.00 |
| **VEE JAY/DYNASTY** | | | |
| ❑ VJS-7306 | Bessie Smith... My Way | 1974 | 15.00 |

### AYCOCK, EARL

| Number | Title (A Side/B Side) | Yr | NM |
|---|---|---|---|
| **MERCURY** | | | |
| ❑ MG-20282 [M] | Earl Aycock | 1958 | 25.00 |

### AYERS, ROY

| Number | Title (A Side/B Side) | Yr | NM |
|---|---|---|---|
| **ATLANTIC** | | | |
| ❑ 1488 [M] | Virgo Vibes | 1967 | 20.00 |
| ❑ SD 1514 | Stoned Soul Picnic | 1968 | 20.00 |
| ❑ SD 1538 | Daddy Bug | 1969 | 20.00 |
| ❑ SD 1692 | Daddy Bug & Friends | 1976 | 12.00 |
| **UNITED ARTISTS** | | | |
| ❑ UAL-3325 [M] | West Coast Vibes | 1964 | 20.00 |
| ❑ UAS-6325 [S] | West Coast Vibes | 1964 | 25.00 |

### AYLER, ALBERT

| Number | Title (A Side/B Side) | Yr | NM |
|---|---|---|---|
| **ABC IMPULSE!** | | | |
| ❑ AS-9165 | Love Cry | 1968 | 20.00 |
| ❑ AS-9175 | New Grass | 1969 | 20.00 |
| ❑ AS-9191 | Music Is the Healing Force of the Universe | 1969 | 20.00 |
| ❑ AS-9208 | The Last Album | 1971 | 20.00 |
| **ESP-DISK'** | | | |
| ❑ 1002 [M] | Spiritual Unity | 1965 | 25.00 |
| ❑ 1010 [M] | Bells | 1965 | 25.00 |
| *—Black vinyl* | | | |
| ❑ 1010 [M] | Bells | 1965 | 50.00 |
| *—Yellow vinyl* | | | |
| ❑ S-1010 [S] | Bells | 1965 | 20.00 |
| ❑ 1016 [M] | New York Eye and Ear Control | 1966 | 25.00 |
| ❑ S-1016 [S] | New York Eye and Ear Control | 1966 | 20.00 |
| ❑ 1020 [M] | Spirits Rejoice | 1966 | 25.00 |
| ❑ S-1020 [S] | Spirits Rejoice | 1966 | 20.00 |
| **FANTASY** | | | |
| ❑ 6016 [M] | My Name Is Albert Ayler | 196? | 20.00 |
| ❑ 86016 [S] | My Name Is Albert Ayler | 196? | 25.00 |
| **IMPULSE!** | | | |
| ❑ A-9155 [M] | Live at the Village Vanguard | 1967 | 30.00 |
| ❑ AS-9155 [S] | Live at the Village Vanguard | 1967 | 25.00 |

### AZAMA, ETHEL

| Number | Title (A Side/B Side) | Yr | NM |
|---|---|---|---|
| **LIBERTY** | | | |
| ❑ LRP-3104 [M] | Exotic Dreams | 1959 | 20.00 |
| ❑ LRP-3142 [M] | Cool Heat | 1960 | 40.00 |
| ❑ LST-7104 [S] | Exotic Dreams | 1959 | 30.00 |
| ❑ LST-7142 [S] | Cool Heat | 1960 | 50.00 |

### AZITIS

| Number | Title (A Side/B Side) | Yr | NM |
|---|---|---|---|
| **ELCO** | | | |
| ❑ SC-EC-5555 | Help! | 197? | 500.00 |

### AZTECA

| Number | Title (A Side/B Side) | Yr | NM |
|---|---|---|---|
| **COLUMBIA** | | | |
| ❑ CQ 31776 [Q] | Azteca | 1974 | 20.00 |
| ❑ KC 31776 | Azteca | 1972 | 12.00 |
| ❑ KC 32451 | Pyramid of the Sun | 1973 | 12.00 |

### AZTECS, THE

| Number | Title (A Side/B Side) | Yr | NM |
|---|---|---|---|
| **WORLD ARTISTS** | | | |
| ❑ WAM-2001 [M] | Live at the Ad Lib Club of London | 1964 | 60.00 |

# B

## BABASIN, HARRY

MODE
❑ LP-119 [M] Jazz Pickers 1957 100.00

NOCTURNE
❑ NLP-3 [10] Harry Babasin Quartet 1954 150.00

## BABE RUTH

CAPITOL
❑ ST-11515 Kids Stuff 1976 20.00

HARVEST
❑ SW-11151 First Base 1973 40.00
❑ ST-11275 Amar Caballero 1974 30.00
❑ ST-11367 Babe Ruth 1975 15.00
❑ ST-11451 Stealin' Home 1975 15.00

## BABY

LONE STARR
❑ 9782 Baby 1974 25.00

## BABY GRAND

ARISTA
❑ AL 4148 Baby Grand 1977 20.00

## BABY HUEY

CURTOM
❑ CRS-8007 The Living Legend 1970 40.00

## BABY RAY

IMPERIAL
❑ LP-9335 [M] Where Soul Lives 1967 25.00
❑ LP-12335 [S] Where Soul Lives 1967 30.00

## BACHAUER, GINA

MERCURY LIVING PRESENCE
❑ SR 90301 [S] Brahms: Piano Concerto No. 2 196? 30.00
*—With Stanislaw Skrowaczewski/London Symphony Orchestra; maroon label, no "Vendor: Mercury Record Corporation"*
❑ SR 90321 [S] Beethoven: Piano Concerto No. 5 "Emperor" 196? 60.00
*—With Stanislaw Skrowaczewski/London Symphony Orchestra; maroon label, no "Vendor: Mercury Record Corporation"*
❑ SR 90368 [S] Chopin: Piano Concerto No. 1; Nocturne; Three Etudes 196? 30.00
*—Maroon label, with "Vendor: Mercury Record Corporation"*
❑ SR 90368 [S] Chopin: Piano Concerto No. 1; Nocturne; Three Etudes 196? 40.00
*—Maroon label, no "Vendor: Mercury Record Corporation"*
❑ SR 90381 [S] Beethoven: Piano Concerto No. 4; Piano Sonata in E 196? 40.00
*—With Antal Dorati/London Symphony Orchestra; maroon label, no "Vendor: Mercury Record Corporation"*
❑ SR 90432 [S] Chopin: Piano Concerto No. 2 in F; Fantasy in F 1965 40.00
*—Maroon label, no "Vendor: Mercury Record Corporation"*

## BACHAUER, GINA, AND SIR JOHN GIELGUD

MERCURY LIVING PRESENCE
❑ SR 90391 [S] Collaboration in Poetry and Music 196? 30.00
*—Maroon label, no "Vendor: Mercury Record Corporation"*

## BACHELORS, THE (1)

LONDON
❑ PS 353 [S] Presenting the Bachelors 1964 20.00
❑ PS 393 [P] Back Again 1964 20.00
*—"I Wouldn't Trade You for the World" is rechanneled.*
❑ PS 418 [S] No Arms Can Ever Hold You 1965 20.00
❑ PS 435 [P] Marie 1965 20.00
*—"Marie" is rechanneled*
❑ PS 460 [S] Hits of the 60's 1966 20.00
❑ PS 491 [P] The Bachelors' Girls 1966 15.00
*—"Marie" is rechanneled*
❑ PS 518 [P] Golden All Time Hits 1967 15.00
❑ PS 528 [S] Bachelors '68 1968 12.00
❑ PS 611 Under and Over 1972 10.00
❑ LL 3353 [M] Presenting the Bachelors 1964 15.00
❑ LL 3393 [M] Back Again 1964 15.00
❑ LL 3418 [M] No Arms Can Ever Hold You 1965 15.00
❑ LL 3435 [M] Marie 1965 15.00
❑ LL 3460 [M] Hits of the 60's 1966 15.00
❑ LL 3491 [M] The Bachelors' Girls 1966 12.00
❑ LL 3518 [M] Golden All Time Hits 1967 15.00
❑ LL 3528 [M] Bachelors '68 1968 20.00

## BACHS, THE

ROTO
❑ PR-1044 Out of the Bachs 1967 4000.
*—VG value 2000, VG+ value 3000*

## BACK PORCH MAJORITY, THE

EPIC
❑ LN 24134 [M] Live from Ledbetter's 1965 15.00
❑ LN 24149 [M] Riverboat Days 1965 15.00
❑ LN 24184 [M] That's the Way It's Gonna Be 1966 15.00

The Bachelors, *Marie,* London LL 3435, 1965, mono, $15.

Number Title (A Side/B Side) Yr NM

❑ LN 24319 [M] Willy Nilly Wonder of Illusion 1967 20.00
❑ BN 26134 [S] Live from Ledbetter's 1965 20.00
❑ BN 26149 [S] Riverboat Days 1965 20.00
❑ BN 26184 [S] That's the Way It's Gonna Be 1966 20.00
❑ BN 26319 [S] Willy Nilly Wonder of Illusion 1967 15.00

## BACKUS, JIM

RCA VICTOR
❑ LPM-1362 [M] Mr. Magoo in Hi-Fi 1957 50.00

## BACON FAT

BLUE HORIZON
❑ BH-4807 Grease One for Me 1970 25.00

## BAD BRAINS

BAD BRAINS
❑ 003 [EP] I and I Survive/Destroy Babylon 1983 40.00

CAROLINE
❑ CAROL-1375 Quickness 1989 12.00
❑ CAROL-1613 Rock for Light 1990 12.00
*—Reissue of PVC 8917 with three bonus tracks*
❑ CAROL-1617 The Youth Are Getting Restless 1990 12.00

IMPORTANT
❑ 003 [EP] I and I Survive/Destroy Babylon 1983 20.00

MAVERICK
❑ 45882 God of Love 1995 10.00

PVC
❑ 8917 Rock for Light 1983 15.00

ROIR
❑ 8223 Bad Brains 1997 15.00
*—First issued in the early 1980s on cassette only, this is a limited vinyl reissue*

SST
❑ 065 I Against I 1986 15.00
*—No back cover bar code*
❑ 065 I Against I 199? 10.00
*—With back cover bar code*
❑ 160 Live 1988 12.00
❑ 228 [10] Spirit Electricity 1991 10.00

VICTORY
❑ VR 64 [10] The Omega Sessions 1997 10.00

Number Title (A Side/B Side) Yr NM

## BAD RELIGION

ATLANTIC
❑ 82658 Stranger Than Fiction 1994 25.00
*—Issued on red vinyl*
❑ 82870 The Gray Race 1996 20.00
*—Issued on gray vinyl*
❑ 83094 No Substance 1998 20.00
❑ 83303 The New America 2000 15.00

EPITAPH
❑ EPI-BRLP-1 How Could Hell Be Any Worse? 1982 100.00
*—Original edition with lyric sheet. Some copies have personal notes or autographs scribbled on the inner sleeves by the band members; these can bring significantly more than this.*
❑ EPI-BRLP-2 Into the Unknown 1983 200.00
❑ 86404 Suffer 1988 15.00
❑ 86406 No Control 1989 15.00
❑ 86407 How Could Hell Be Any Worse? 1989 25.00
*—Reissue of Epitaph BRLP-1*
❑ 86409 Against the Grain 1990 15.00
❑ 86416 Generator 1992 15.00
❑ 86420 Recipe for Hate 1993 15.00
❑ 86443 All Ages 1995 12.00
❑ 86635 The Process of Belief 2002 15.00
❑ 86694 The Empire Strikes First 2004 12.00

## BADFINGER

APPLE
❑ ST-3355 Maybe Tomorrow 1969 2000.
*—As "The Iveys"; album not released in US; price is for an LP slick, which does exist*
❑ ST 3364 Magic Christian Music 1970 20.00
❑ ST 3364 Magic Christian Music 1970 30.00
*—With Capitol logo on Side 2 bottom*
❑ SKAO 3367 No Dice 1970 30.00
❑ SW 3387 Straight Up 1971 60.00
❑ SW 3411 Ass 1973 20.00

ELEKTRA
❑ 6E-175 Airwaves 1979 12.00

RADIO
❑ RR 16030 Say No More 1981 10.00

RYKO ANALOGUE
❑ RALP 10189 Day After Day 1990 20.00
*—Limited edition on clear vinyl with obi*

Badfinger, *Ass,* Apple SW-3411, 1973, $20.

WARNER BROS.

| Number | Title (A Side/B Side) | Yr | NM |
|---|---|---|---|
| ❑ BS 2762 | Badfinger | 1974 | 15.00 |
| ❑ BS 2827 | Wish You Were Here | 1974 | 15.00 |

### BAEZ, JOAN

A&M

| Number | Title (A Side/B Side) | Yr | NM |
|---|---|---|---|
| ❑ SP-3103 | Come From the Shadows | 198? | 8.00 |
| *—Budget-line reissue* | | | |
| ❑ SP-3233 | Diamonds and Rust | 198? | 8.00 |
| *—Budget-line reissue* | | | |
| ❑ SP-3234 | The Best of Joan C. Baez | 198? | 8.00 |
| *—Budget-line reissue* | | | |
| ❑ SP-3614 | Gracias A La Vida | 1974 | 12.00 |
| ❑ SP-3704 [(2)] | From Every Stage | 1976 | 12.00 |
| ❑ SP-4339 | Come From the Shadows | 1972 | 10.00 |
| ❑ SP-4390 | Where Are You Now, My Son? | 1973 | 10.00 |
| ❑ SP-4527 | Diamonds and Rust | 1975 | 10.00 |
| ❑ SP-4603 | Gulf Winds | 1976 | 10.00 |
| ❑ SP-4668 | The Best of Joan C. Baez | 1977 | 10.00 |
| ❑ SP-6506 [(2)] | From Every Stage | 198? | 10.00 |
| *—Reissue* | | | |
| ❑ QU-54339 [Q] | Come From the Shadows | 1974 | 20.00 |
| ❑ QU-54527 [Q] | Diamonds and Rust | 1975 | 20.00 |

BOOK-OF-THE-MONTH

| Number | Title (A Side/B Side) | Yr | NM |
|---|---|---|---|
| ❑ 40-5711 [(4)] | Satisfied Mind | 1979 | 25.00 |
| *—With booklet* | | | |

GOLD CASTLE

| Number | Title (A Side/B Side) | Yr | NM |
|---|---|---|---|
| ❑ D1-71309 | Recently | 1989 | 12.00 |
| *—Reissue of 171 009* | | | |
| ❑ D1-71321 | Diamonds and Rust in the Castle | 1989 | 12.00 |
| ❑ D1-71324 | Speaking of Dreams | 1989 | 12.00 |
| ❑ 171009 | Recently | 1988 | 10.00 |

MOBILE FIDELITY

| Number | Title (A Side/B Side) | Yr | NM |
|---|---|---|---|
| ❑ 1-238 | Diamonds and Rust | 1996 | 60.00 |
| *—Audiophile vinyl* | | | |

NAUTILUS

| Number | Title (A Side/B Side) | Yr | NM |
|---|---|---|---|
| ❑ NR-12 | Diamonds and Rust | 1980 | 40.00 |
| *—Audiophile vinyl* | | | |

PORTRAIT

| Number | Title (A Side/B Side) | Yr | NM |
|---|---|---|---|
| ❑ PR 34697 | Blowin' Away | 1977 | 10.00 |
| ❑ JR 35766 | Honest Lullaby | 1979 | 10.00 |

SQUIRE

| Number | Title (A Side/B Side) | Yr | NM |
|---|---|---|---|
| ❑ SQ-33001 [M] | The Best of Joan Baez | 1963 | 20.00 |

VANGUARD

| Number | Title (A Side/B Side) | Yr | NM |
|---|---|---|---|
| ❑ VSD-41/42 [(2)] | The Joan Baez Ballad Book | 1972 | 12.00 |
| ❑ VSD-49/50 [(2)] | The Contemporary Ballad Book | 1974 | 12.00 |
| ❑ VSD-79/80 [(2)] | The Love Song Album | 197? | 12.00 |
| ❑ VSD-105/6 [(2)] | The Country Music Album | 1979 | 12.00 |
| ❑ VSD-2077 [S] | Joan Baez | 1960 | 25.00 |
| ❑ VSD-2097 [S] | Joan Baez, Vol. 2 | 1961 | 25.00 |
| ❑ VSD-2122 [S] | Joan Baez In Concert | 1962 | 25.00 |
| ❑ VSD-2123 [S] | Joan Baez In Concert, Part 2 | 1963 | 25.00 |
| ❑ VSD-6560/1 [(2)] | The First 10 Years | 1970 | 15.00 |
| ❑ VSD-6570/1 [(2)] | Blessed Are... | 1971 | 15.00 |
| *—Add 50 percent if bonus 7-inch single, "Maria Dolores"/"Plane Wreck at Los Gatos (Deportee)," and its special sleeve are still in the package* | | | |
| ❑ VRS-9078 [M] | Joan Baez | 1960 | 20.00 |
| ❑ VRS-9094 [M] | Joan Baez, Vol. 2 | 1961 | 20.00 |
| ❑ VRS-9112 [M] | Joan Baez In Concert | 1962 | 20.00 |
| ❑ VRS-9113 [M] | Joan Baez In Concert, Part 2 | 1963 | 20.00 |
| ❑ VRS-9160 [M] | Joan Baez/5 | 1964 | 15.00 |
| ❑ VRS-9200 [M] | Farewell, Angelina | 1965 | 15.00 |
| ❑ VRS-9230 [M] | Noel | 1966 | 15.00 |
| ❑ VRS-9240 [M] | Joan | 1967 | 15.00 |
| ❑ VSQ-40001/2 [(2)Q] | Blessed Are | 1973 | 25.00 |
| ❑ VSQ-40032 [Q] | Hits/Greatest & Others | 1973 | 20.00 |
| ❑ VMS-73107 | The Joan Baez Ballad Book, Vol. 1 | 1985 | 10.00 |
| ❑ VMS-73115 | The Joan Baez Ballad Book, Vol. 2 | 1985 | 10.00 |
| ❑ VMS-73119 | The Night They Drove Old Dixie Down | 198? | 10.00 |
| ❑ VSD-79160 [S] | Joan Baez/5 | 1964 | 20.00 |
| ❑ VSD-79200 [S] | Farewell, Angelina | 1965 | 20.00 |
| ❑ VSD-79230 [S] | Noel | 1966 | 20.00 |
| ❑ VSD-79240 [S] | Joan | 1967 | 20.00 |
| ❑ VSD-79275 | Baptism | 1968 | 20.00 |
| ❑ VSD-79306/7 [(2)] | Any Day Now | 1969 | 25.00 |
| ❑ VSD-79308 | David's Album | 1969 | 12.00 |
| ❑ VSD-79310 | One Day at a Time | 1970 | 12.00 |
| ❑ VSD-79313 | Carry It On | 1971 | 25.00 |
| *—Soundtrack album* | | | |
| ❑ VSD-79332 | Hits/Greatest & Others | 1973 | 10.00 |
| ❑ VSD-79446/7 | Very Early Joan | 1981 | 12.00 |

### BAGDASARIAN, ROSS

LIBERTY

| Number | Title (A Side/B Side) | Yr | NM |
|---|---|---|---|
| ❑ LRP-3451 [M] | The Crazy, Mixed-Up World of Ross Bagdasarian | 1966 | 40.00 |
| ❑ LST-7451 [S] | The Crazy, Mixed-Up World of Ross Bagdasarian | 1966 | 50.00 |

### BAGLEY, DON

DOT

| Number | Title (A Side/B Side) | Yr | NM |
|---|---|---|---|
| ❑ DLP-3070 [M] | Basically Bagley | 1957 | 50.00 |
| ❑ DLP-9007 [M] | The Soft Sell | 1959 | 50.00 |
| ❑ DLP-25070 [S] | Basically Bagley | 1959 | 40.00 |
| ❑ DLP-29007 [S] | The Soft Sell | 1959 | 40.00 |

REGENT

| Number | Title (A Side/B Side) | Yr | NM |
|---|---|---|---|
| ❑ MG-6061 [M] | Jazz on the Rocks | 1957 | 60.00 |

SAVOY

| Number | Title (A Side/B Side) | Yr | NM |
|---|---|---|---|
| ❑ MG-12210 [M] | Jazz on the Rocks | 196? | 20.00 |

### BAILES BROTHERS, THE

AUDIO LAB

| Number | Title (A Side/B Side) | Yr | NM |
|---|---|---|---|
| ❑ AL-1511 [M] | Avenues of Prayer | 1959 | 200.00 |

### BAILEY, BENNY

ARGO

| Number | Title (A Side/B Side) | Yr | NM |
|---|---|---|---|
| ❑ LP-668 [M] | The Music of Quincy Jones | 1961 | 25.00 |
| ❑ LPS-668 [S] | The Music of Quincy Jones | 1961 | 30.00 |

CANDID

| Number | Title (A Side/B Side) | Yr | NM |
|---|---|---|---|
| ❑ CD-8011 [M] | Big Brass | 1960 | 30.00 |
| ❑ CS-9011 [S] | Big Brass | 1960 | 40.00 |

### BAILEY, BUSTER

FELSTED

| Number | Title (A Side/B Side) | Yr | NM |
|---|---|---|---|
| ❑ SJA-2003 [S] | All About Memphis | 1959 | 40.00 |
| ❑ FAJ-7003 [M] | All About Memphis | 1959 | 40.00 |

### BAILEY, DAVE

EPIC

| Number | Title (A Side/B Side) | Yr | NM |
|---|---|---|---|
| ❑ LA 16008 [M] | One Foot in the Gutter | 1960 | 30.00 |
| ❑ LA 16011 [M] | Gettin' Into Something | 1960 | 30.00 |
| ❑ LA 16021 [M] | Two Feet in the Gutter | 1961 | 30.00 |
| ❑ BA 17008 [S] | One Foot in the Gutter | 1960 | 50.00 |
| ❑ BA 17008 [S] | One Foot in the Gutter | 199? | 25.00 |
| *—Classic Records reissue* | | | |
| ❑ BA 17011 [S] | Gettin' Into Something | 1960 | 40.00 |
| ❑ BA 17021 [S] | Two Feet in the Gutter | 1961 | 40.00 |

JAZZ LINE

| Number | Title (A Side/B Side) | Yr | NM |
|---|---|---|---|
| ❑ 33-01 [M] | Bash! | 1961 | 40.00 |

JAZZTIME

| Number | Title (A Side/B Side) | Yr | NM |
|---|---|---|---|
| ❑ JS-003 [S] | Reaching Out | 1961 | 40.00 |
| *—Reissued under GRANT GREEN's name* | | | |
| ❑ JT-003 [M] | Reaching Out | 1961 | 30.00 |

### BAILEY, MILDRED

ALLEGRO

| Number | Title (A Side/B Side) | Yr | NM |
|---|---|---|---|
| ❑ 3119 [M] | Mildred Bailey Sings | 1955 | 60.00 |
| ❑ 4009 [10] | Mildred Bailey Songs | 1952 | 80.00 |
| ❑ 4040 [10] | Mildred Bailey Songs | 1954 | 80.00 |

COLUMBIA

| Number | Title (A Side/B Side) | Yr | NM |
|---|---|---|---|
| ❑ C3L 22 [(3)] | Her Greatest Performances | 1962 | 50.00 |
| *—With booklet; originals have red labels with "Guaranteed High Fidelity" at bottom* | | | |
| ❑ CL 6094 [10] | Serenade | 1950 | 60.00 |

DECCA

| Number | Title (A Side/B Side) | Yr | NM |
|---|---|---|---|
| ❑ DL 5133 [10] | Mildred Bailey Memorial Album | 1950 | 60.00 |
| ❑ DL 5387 [10] | The Rockin' Chair Lady | 195? | 60.00 |

REGENT

| Number | Title (A Side/B Side) | Yr | NM |
|---|---|---|---|
| ❑ MG-6032 [M] | Me and the Blues | 1957 | 50.00 |

ROYALE

| Number | Title (A Side/B Side) | Yr | NM |
|---|---|---|---|
| ❑ VLP 6078 [10] | Mildred Bailey Sings | 195? | 80.00 |

SAVOY

| Number | Title (A Side/B Side) | Yr | NM |
|---|---|---|---|
| ❑ MG-12219 [M] | Me and the Blues | 196? | 20.00 |

### BAILEY, PEARL

COLUMBIA

| Number | Title (A Side/B Side) | Yr | NM |
|---|---|---|---|
| ❑ CL 985 [M] | The Definitive Pearl Bailey | 1957 | 25.00 |
| ❑ CL 6099 [10] | Pearl Bailey Entertains | 1950 | 50.00 |

CORAL

| Number | Title (A Side/B Side) | Yr | NM |
|---|---|---|---|
| ❑ CRL 56068 [10] | Say Si Si | 1953 | 50.00 |
| ❑ CRL 56078 [10] | I'm with You | 1954 | 50.00 |
| ❑ CRL 57037 [M] | Pearl Bailey | 1957 | 40.00 |
| ❑ CRL 57162 [M] | Cultured Pearl | 1958 | 40.00 |

MERCURY

| Number | Title (A Side/B Side) | Yr | NM |
|---|---|---|---|
| ❑ MG-20187 [M] | The One and Only Pearl Bailey Sings | 1956 | 40.00 |
| ❑ MG-20277 [M] | The Intoxicating Pearl Bailey | 1957 | 40.00 |

ROULETTE

| Number | Title (A Side/B Side) | Yr | NM |
|---|---|---|---|
| ❑ R-25012 [M] | Pearl Bailey A Broad | 1957 | 30.00 |
| *—Black label original* | | | |
| ❑ R-25016 [M] | Pearl Bailey Sings for Adults Only | 1959 | 20.00 |
| *—Originals have a white label with colored spokes* | | | |
| ❑ SR-25016 [S] | Pearl Bailey Sings for Adults Only | 1959 | 25.00 |
| *—Originals have a white label with colored spokes* | | | |
| ❑ R-25037 [M] | St. Louis Blues | 1958 | 30.00 |
| *—Black label original* | | | |

| Number | Title (A Side/B Side) | Yr | NM |
|---|---|---|---|
| ❑ SR-25037 [S] | St. Louis Blues | 1959 | 30.00 |
| *—Originals have a white label with colored spokes* | | | |
| ❑ R-25063 [M] | Pearl Bailey Sings Porgy and Bess and Other Gershwin Melodies | 1959 | 20.00 |
| *—Originals have a white label with colored spokes* | | | |
| ❑ SR-25063 [S] | Pearl Bailey Sings Porgy and Bess and Other Gershwin Melodies | 1959 | 25.00 |
| *—Originals have a white label with colored spokes* | | | |
| ❑ R-25101 [M] | More Songs for Adults Only | 1960 | 20.00 |
| *—Originals have a white label with colored spokes* | | | |
| ❑ SR-25101 [S] | More Songs for Adults Only | 1960 | 25.00 |
| *—Originals have a white label with colored spokes* | | | |
| ❑ R-25116 [M] | Songs of the Bad Old Days | 1960 | 20.00 |
| *—Originals have a white label with colored spokes* | | | |
| ❑ SR-25116 [S] | Songs of the Bad Old Days | 1960 | 25.00 |
| *—Originals have a white label with colored spokes* | | | |
| ❑ R-25125 [M] | Naughty But Nice | 1960 | 20.00 |
| *—Originals have a white label with colored spokes* | | | |
| ❑ SR-25125 [S] | Naughty But Nice | 1960 | 25.00 |
| *—Originals have a white label with colored spokes* | | | |
| ❑ R-25144 [M] | The Best of Pearl Bailey | 1961 | 20.00 |
| *—Originals have a white label with colored spokes* | | | |
| ❑ SR-25144 [S] | The Best of Pearl Bailey | 1961 | 25.00 |
| *—Originals have a white label with colored spokes* | | | |
| ❑ R-25155 [M] | Pearl Bailey Sings Songs of Harold Arlen | 1961 | 20.00 |
| *—Originals have a white label with colored spokes* | | | |
| ❑ SR-25155 [S] | Pearl Bailey Sings Songs of Harold Arlen | 1961 | 25.00 |
| *—Originals have a white label with colored spokes* | | | |
| ❑ R-25167 [M] | Happy Sounds | 1962 | 20.00 |
| *—Originals have a white label with colored spokes* | | | |
| ❑ SR-25167 [S] | Happy Sounds | 1962 | 25.00 |
| *—Originals have a white label with colored spokes* | | | |
| ❑ R-25181 [M] | Come On, Let's Play with Pearlie Mae | 1962 | 20.00 |
| *—Originals have a white label with colored spokes* | | | |
| ❑ SR-25181 [S] | Come On, Let's Play with Pearlie Mae | 1962 | 25.00 |
| *—Originals have a white label with colored spokes* | | | |
| ❑ R-25195 [M] | All About Good Little Girls and Bad Little Boys | 1963 | 20.00 |
| *—Originals have a pink and orange label* | | | |
| ❑ SR-25195 [S] | All About Good Little Girls and Bad Little Boys | 1963 | 25.00 |
| *—Originals have a pink and orange label* | | | |
| ❑ R-25222 [M] | C'est La Vie | 1963 | 20.00 |
| *—Originals have a pink and orange label* | | | |
| ❑ SR-25222 [S] | C'est La Vie | 1963 | 25.00 |
| *—Originals have a pink and orange label* | | | |
| ❑ SR-25259 [S] | The Risque World of Pearl Bailey | 1964 | 20.00 |
| ❑ SR-25271 [S] | Songs by James Van Heusen | 1964 | 20.00 |
| ❑ SR-25300 [S] | For Women Only | 1965 | 20.00 |
| **VOCALION** | | | |
| ❑ VL 3621 [M] | Gems by Pearl Bailey | 1958 | 25.00 |

### BAILLARGEON, HELENE

| Number | Title (A Side/B Side) | Yr | NM |
|---|---|---|---|
| **FOLKWAYS** | | | |
| ❑ FW 829 [10] | Christmas Songs of French Canada | 195? | 50.00 |
| ❑ FC 7229 | Christmas Songs of French Canada | 195? | 50.00 |

### BAIN, BOB

| Number | Title (A Side/B Side) | Yr | NM |
|---|---|---|---|
| **CAPITOL** | | | |
| ❑ T 965 [M] | Rockin', Rollin' and Strollin' | 1958 | 80.00 |
| ❑ ST 1201 [S] | Latin Love | 1959 | 40.00 |
| ❑ T 1201 [M] | Latin Love | 1959 | 30.00 |
| ❑ ST 1500 [S] | Guitar De Amor | 1961 | 40.00 |
| ❑ T 1500 [M] | Guitar De Amor | 1961 | 30.00 |

### BAKER, BUDDY

| Number | Title (A Side/B Side) | Yr | NM |
|---|---|---|---|
| **VERVE** | | | |
| ❑ MGV-2006 [M] | Two in Love | 1956 | 50.00 |
| ❑ V-2006 [M] | Two in Love | 1961 | 20.00 |

### BAKER, CHET

| Number | Title (A Side/B Side) | Yr | NM |
|---|---|---|---|
| **ANALOGUE PRODUCTIONS** | | | |
| ❑ AAPJ-016 | Chet | 199? | 25.00 |
| *—Audiophile reissue* | | | |
| **COLPIX** | | | |
| ❑ CP-476 [M] | Chet Baker Sings and Plays | 1964 | 40.00 |
| ❑ SCP-476 [S] | Chet Baker Sings and Plays | 1964 | 50.00 |
| **COLUMBIA** | | | |
| ❑ CL 549 [M] | Chet Baker and Strings | 1954 | 80.00 |
| *—Maroon label, gold print* | | | |
| ❑ CL 549 [M] | Chet Baker and Strings | 1955 | 50.00 |
| *—Red and black label with six "eye" logos* | | | |
| **CROWN** | | | |
| ❑ CLP-5317 [M] | Chet Baker Quintette | 196? | 20.00 |
| **HARMONY** | | | |
| ❑ HL 7320 [M] | Love Walked In | 1962 | 20.00 |
| **JAZZLAND** | | | |
| ❑ JLP-11 [M] | Chet Baker and Orchestra | 1960 | 40.00 |
| ❑ JLP-18 [M] | Chet Baker in Milan | 1960 | 40.00 |

Joan Baez, *Joan Baez,* Vanguard VSD-2077, stereo, $25.

| Number | Title (A Side/B Side) | Yr | NM |
|---|---|---|---|
| ❑ JLP-21 [M] | Chet Baker with Fifty Italian Strings | 1960 | 40.00 |
| ❑ JLP-911 [S] | Chet Baker and Orchestra | 1960 | 40.00 |
| ❑ JLP-918 [S] | Chet Baker in Milan | 1960 | 40.00 |
| ❑ JLP-921 [S] | Chet Baker with Fifty Italian Strings | 1960 | 40.00 |
| **LIMELIGHT** | | | |
| ❑ LM-82003 [M] | Baby Breeze | 1964 | 25.00 |
| ❑ LM-82019 [M] | Baker's Holiday | 1965 | 25.00 |
| ❑ LS-86003 [S] | Baby Breeze | 1964 | 30.00 |
| ❑ LS-86019 [S] | Baker's Holiday | 1965 | 30.00 |
| **MOSAIC** | | | |
| ❑ MR4-113 [(4)] | The Complete Pacific Jazz Live Recordings of the Chet Baker Quartet with Russ Freeman | 199? | 80.00 |
| ❑ MR4-122 [(4)] | The Complete Pacific Jazz Studio Recordings of the Chet Baker Quartet with Russ Freeman | 199? | 120.00 |
| **PACIFIC JAZZ** | | | |
| ❑ PJLP-3 [10] | Chet Baker Quartet | 1953 | 200.00 |
| ❑ PJLP-6 [10] | Chet Baker Quartet Featuring Russ Freeman | 1953 | 200.00 |
| ❑ PJLP-9 [10] | Chet Baker Ensemble | 1954 | 200.00 |
| ❑ PJLP-11 [10] | Chet Baker Sings | 1954 | 200.00 |
| ❑ PJLP-15 [10] | Chet Baker Sextet | 1954 | 200.00 |
| ❑ PJ-1202 [M] | Chet Baker Sings and Plays with Bud Shank, Russ Freeman and Strings | 1955 | 120.00 |
| ❑ PJ-1203 [M] | Jazz at Ann Arbor | 1955 | 120.00 |
| ❑ PJ-1206 [M] | The Trumpet Artistry of Chet Baker | 1955 | 120.00 |
| ❑ PJ-1218 [M] | Chet Baker in Europe | 1956 | 120.00 |
| ❑ PJ-1222 [M] | Chet Baker Sings | 1956 | 120.00 |
| ❑ PJ-1224 [M] | Chet Baker and Crew | 1956 | 120.00 |
| ❑ PJ-1229 [M] | Chet Baker Big Band | 1957 | 120.00 |
| **PRESTIGE** | | | |
| ❑ PRLP-7449 [M] | Smokin' with the Chet Baker Quintet | 1966 | 20.00 |
| ❑ PRST-7449 [S] | Smokin' with the Chet Baker Quintet | 1966 | 25.00 |
| ❑ PRLP-7460 [M] | Groovin' with the Chet Baker Quintet | 1966 | 20.00 |
| ❑ PRST-7460 [S] | Groovin' with the Chet Baker Quintet | 1966 | 25.00 |

| Number | Title (A Side/B Side) | Yr | NM |
|---|---|---|---|
| ❑ PRLP-7478 [M] | Comin' On with the Chet Baker Quintet | 1967 | 25.00 |
| ❑ PRST-7478 [S] | Comin' On with the Chet Baker Quintet | 1967 | 20.00 |
| ❑ PRLP-7496 [M] | Cool Burnin' with the Chet Baker Quintet | 1967 | 30.00 |
| ❑ PRST-7496 [S] | Cool Burnin' with the Chet Baker Quintet | 1967 | 20.00 |
| ❑ PRLP-7512 [M] | Boppin' with the Chet Baker Quintet | 1967 | 30.00 |
| ❑ PRST-7512 [S] | Boppin' with the Chet Baker Quintet | 1967 | 20.00 |
| **RIVERSIDE** | | | |
| ❑ RLP 12-278 [M] | It Could Happen to You — Chet Baker Sings | 1958 | 50.00 |
| ❑ RLP 12-281 [M] | Chet Baker in New York | 1958 | 50.00 |
| ❑ RLP 12-299 [M] | Chet | 1959 | 50.00 |
| ❑ RLP 12-307 [M] | Chet Baker Plays Lerner and Loewe | 1959 | 50.00 |
| ❑ RLP-1119 [S] | Chet Baker in New York | 1959 | 40.00 |
| ❑ RLP-1120 [S] | It Could Happen to You — Chet Baker Sings | 1959 | 40.00 |
| ❑ RLP-1135 [S] | Chet | 1959 | 40.00 |
| ❑ RLP-1152 [S] | Chet Baker Plays Lerner and Loewe | 1959 | 40.00 |
| **SCEPTER** | | | |
| ❑ 540 [M] | Angel Eyes | 1966 | 20.00 |
| ❑ S-540 [S] | Angel Eyes | 1966 | 25.00 |
| **WORLD PACIFIC** | | | |
| ❑ ST-1004 [S] | Chet Baker and Crew | 1959 | 60.00 |
| ❑ WP-1202 [M] | Chet Baker Sings and Plays with Bud Shank, Russ Freeman and Strings | 1958 | 80.00 |
| *—Reissue of Pacific Jazz 1202* | | | |
| ❑ WP-1203 [M] | Jazz at Ann Arbor | 1958 | 80.00 |
| *—Reissue of Pacific Jazz 1203* | | | |
| ❑ WP-1206 [M] | The Trumpet Artistry of Chet Baker | 1958 | 80.00 |
| *—Reissue of Pacific Jazz 1206* | | | |
| ❑ WP-1218 [M] | Chet Baker in Europe | 1958 | 80.00 |
| *—Reissue of Pacific Jazz 1218* | | | |
| ❑ WP-1222 [M] | Chet Baker Sings | 1958 | 80.00 |
| *—Reissue of Pacific Jazz 1222* | | | |
| ❑ WP-1224 [M] | Chet Baker and Crew | 1958 | 80.00 |
| *—Reissue of Pacific Jazz 1224* | | | |

Ginger Baker's Air Force, *Ginger Baker's Air Force 2,* Atco SD 33-343, $12.

| Number | Title (A Side/B Side) | Yr | NM |
|---|---|---|---|
| ❑ WP-1229 [M] | Chet Baker Big Band | 1958 | 80.00 |
| *—Reissue of Pacific Jazz 1229* | | | |
| ❑ WP-1249 [M] | Pretty/Groovy | 1958 | 100.00 |
| ❑ ST-1826 [R] | Chet Baker Sings | 1964 | 20.00 |
| ❑ WP-1826 [M] | Chet Baker Sings | 1964 | 30.00 |
| *—Reissue of World Pacific 1222* | | | |
| ❑ WP-1842 [M] | Hat's Off | 1966 | 20.00 |
| ❑ WP-1847 [M] | Quietly, There | 1966 | 20.00 |
| ❑ WP-1852 [M] | Double Shot | 1967 | 20.00 |
| ❑ WP-1858 [M] | Into My Life | 1967 | 25.00 |
| ❑ WPS-21842 [S] | Hat's Off | 1966 | 25.00 |
| ❑ WPS-21847 [S] | Quietly, There | 1966 | 25.00 |
| ❑ WPS-21852 [S] | Double Shot | 1967 | 25.00 |
| ❑ WPS-21858 [S] | Into My Life | 1967 | 20.00 |
| ❑ WPS-21859 [S] | In the Mood | 1968 | 20.00 |
| **WORLD PACIFIC JAZZ** | | | |
| ❑ ST-20138 [R] | Chet Baker Plays and Sings | 1968 | 12.00 |
| *—Compilation of 1950s Pacific Jazz material* | | | |

**BAKER, CHET, AND ART PEPPER**

| Number | Title (A Side/B Side) | Yr | NM |
|---|---|---|---|
| **PACIFIC JAZZ** | | | |
| ❑ PJ-18 [M] | Picture of Health | 1961 | 50.00 |
| ❑ PJ-1234 [M] | Playboys | 1957 | 150.00 |
| *—Pacific Jazz records come in World Pacific covers* | | | |
| **WORLD PACIFIC** | | | |
| ❑ PJ-1234 [M] | Playboys | 1958 | 120.00 |
| ❑ WP-1234 [M] | Playboys | 1958 | 80.00 |

**BAKER, GEORGE, SELECTION**

| Number | Title (A Side/B Side) | Yr | NM |
|---|---|---|---|
| **COLOSSUS** | | | |
| ❑ CS-1002 | Little Green Bag | 1970 | 20.00 |
| **WARNER BROS.** | | | |
| ❑ BS 2905 | Paloma Blanca | 1975 | 15.00 |

**BAKER, GINGER, 'S AIR FORCE**

| Number | Title (A Side/B Side) | Yr | NM |
|---|---|---|---|
| **ATCO** | | | |
| ❑ SD 33-343 | Ginger Baker's Air Force 2 | 1971 | 12.00 |
| ❑ SD 2-703 [(2)] | Ginger Baker's Air Force | 1970 | 20.00 |
| ❑ SD 7012 | Stratavarious | 1972 | 12.00 |
| **AXIOM** | | | |
| ❑ 539864-1 | Middle Passage | 1990 | 15.00 |
| **CELLULOID** | | | |
| ❑ CEL-6126 | Horses and Trees | 1986 | 10.00 |
| **POLYDOR** | | | |
| ❑ 3504 [(2)] | Ginger Baker At His Best | 1973 | 15.00 |
| **SIRE** | | | |
| ❑ SASD-7532 | Eleven Sides of Baker | 1977 | 10.00 |

**BAKER, JOSEPHINE**

| Number | Title (A Side/B Side) | Yr | NM |
|---|---|---|---|
| **COLUMBIA** | | | |
| ❑ FL 9532 [10] | Josephine Baker | 1951 | 100.00 |
| ❑ FL 9533 [10] | Chansons Americaines | 1951 | 100.00 |
| **COLUMBIA MASTERWORKS** | | | |
| ❑ ML 2608 [10] | Josephine Baker Sings | 1952 | 80.00 |
| ❑ ML 2609 [10] | Chansons Americaines | 1952 | 80.00 |
| ❑ ML 2613 [10] | Encores Americaines | 1952 | 80.00 |
| **JOLLY ROGER** | | | |
| ❑ 5015 [10] | Josephine Baker | 1951 | 50.00 |
| **MERCURY** | | | |
| ❑ MG-25105 [10] | The Inimitable Josephine Baker | 1952 | 80.00 |
| ❑ MG-25151 [10] | Avec Josephine Baker | 1952 | 80.00 |
| **RCA VICTOR RED SEAL** | | | |
| ❑ LM-2427 [M] | The Fabulous Josephine Baker | 1960 | 15.00 |
| *—Original with "shaded dog" label* | | | |
| ❑ LSC-2427 [S] | The Fabulous Josephine Baker | 1960 | 50.00 |
| *—Original with "shaded dog" label* | | | |

**BAKER, LAVERN**

| Number | Title (A Side/B Side) | Yr | NM |
|---|---|---|---|
| **ATCO** | | | |
| ❑ SD 33-372 | Her Greatest Recordings | 1971 | 12.00 |
| **ATLANTIC** | | | |
| ❑ 1281 [M] | LaVern Baker Sings Bessie Smith | 1958 | 120.00 |
| *—Black label* | | | |
| ❑ 1281 [M] | LaVern Baker Sings Bessie Smith | 1960 | 30.00 |
| *—Red and purple label, "fan" logo in white* | | | |
| ❑ 1281 [M] | LaVern Baker Sings Bessie Smith | 1963 | 20.00 |
| *—Red and purple label, "fan" logo in black* | | | |
| ❑ SD 1281 [S] | LaVern Baker Sings Bessie Smith | 1959 | 150.00 |
| *—Green label* | | | |
| ❑ SD 1281 [S] | LaVern Baker Sings Bessie Smith | 1960 | 40.00 |
| *—Green and blue label, "fan" logo in white* | | | |
| ❑ SD 1281 [S] | LaVern Baker Sings Bessie Smith | 1963 | 25.00 |
| *—Green and blue label, "fan" logo in black* | | | |
| ❑ 8002 [M] | LaVern | 1956 | 250.00 |
| *—Black label* | | | |
| ❑ 8002 [M] | LaVern | 1960 | 30.00 |
| *—Red and purple label, "fan" logo in white* | | | |
| ❑ 8002 [M] | LaVern | 1963 | 20.00 |
| *—Red and purple label, "fan" logo in black* | | | |
| ❑ 8007 [M] | LaVern Baker | 1957 | 250.00 |
| *—Black label* | | | |
| ❑ 8007 [M] | LaVern Baker | 1960 | 30.00 |
| *—Red and purple label, "fan" logo in white* | | | |
| ❑ 8007 [M] | LaVern Baker | 1963 | 20.00 |
| *—Red and purple label, "fan" logo in black* | | | |
| ❑ 8030 [M] | Blues Ballads | 1959 | 200.00 |
| *—Black label* | | | |
| ❑ 8030 [M] | Blues Ballads | 1960 | 30.00 |
| *—Red and purple label, "fan" logo in white* | | | |
| ❑ 8030 [M] | Blues Ballads | 1960 | 150.00 |
| *—White "bullseye" label* | | | |
| ❑ 8030 [M] | Blues Ballads | 1963 | 20.00 |
| *—Red and purple label, "fan" logo in black* | | | |
| ❑ 8036 [M] | Precious Memories | 1959 | 200.00 |
| *—Black label* | | | |
| ❑ 8036 [M] | Precious Memories | 1960 | 30.00 |
| *—Red and purple label, "fan" logo in white* | | | |
| ❑ 8036 [M] | Precious Memories | 1960 | 150.00 |
| *—White "bullseye" label* | | | |
| ❑ 8036 [M] | Precious Memories | 1963 | 20.00 |
| *—Red and purple label, "fan" logo in black* | | | |
| ❑ SD 8036 [S] | Precious Memories | 1959 | 300.00 |
| *—Green label* | | | |
| ❑ SD 8036 [S] | Precious Memories | 1960 | 40.00 |
| *—Green and blue label, "fan" logo in white* | | | |
| ❑ SD 8036 [S] | Precious Memories | 1960 | 200.00 |
| *—White "bullseye" label* | | | |
| ❑ SD 8036 [S] | Precious Memories | 1963 | 25.00 |
| *—Green and blue label, "fan" logo in black* | | | |
| ❑ 8050 [M] | Saved | 1961 | 100.00 |
| *—Red and purple label, "fan" logo in white* | | | |
| ❑ 8050 [M] | Saved | 1963 | 20.00 |
| *—Red and purple label, "fan" logo in black* | | | |
| ❑ SD 8050 [S] | Saved | 1961 | 150.00 |
| *—Green and blue label, "fan" logo in white* | | | |
| ❑ SD 8050 [S] | Saved | 1963 | 25.00 |
| *—Green and blue label, "fan" logo in black* | | | |
| ❑ 8071 [M] | See See Rider | 1962 | 100.00 |
| *—Red and purple label, "fan" logo in white* | | | |
| ❑ 8071 [M] | See See Rider | 1963 | 20.00 |
| *—Red and purple label, "fan" logo in black* | | | |
| ❑ SD 8071 [S] | See See Rider | 1962 | 150.00 |
| *—Green and blue label, "fan" logo in white* | | | |
| ❑ SD 8071 [S] | See See Rider | 1963 | 25.00 |
| *—Green and blue label, "fan" logo in black* | | | |
| ❑ 8078 [M] | The Best of LaVern Baker | 1963 | 150.00 |
| *—Red and purple label, "fan" logo in black* | | | |
| ❑ 90980 | LaVern Baker Sings Bessie Smith | 1989 | 12.00 |
| *—Reissue of SD 1281* | | | |
| **BRUNSWICK** | | | |
| ❑ BL 754160 | Let Me Belong to You | 1970 | 20.00 |

**BAKER, MICKEY "GUITAR"** Also see MICKEY AND SYLVIA.

| Number | Title (A Side/B Side) | Yr | NM |
|---|---|---|---|
| **ATLANTIC** | | | |
| ❑ 8035 [M] | The Wildest Guitar | 1959 | 150.00 |
| *—Black label* | | | |
| ❑ 8035 [M] | The Wildest Guitar | 1960 | 50.00 |
| *—Red and purple label, "fan" logo in white* | | | |
| ❑ SD 8035 [S] | The Wildest Guitar | 1959 | 250.00 |
| *—Green label* | | | |
| ❑ SD 8035 [S] | The Wildest Guitar | 1960 | 80.00 |
| *—Green and blue label, "fan" logo in white* | | | |
| **KICKING MULE** | | | |
| ❑ 140 | The Jazz Rock Guitar of Mickey Baker | 1978 | 12.00 |
| ❑ 142 | The Blues and Jazz Guitar of Mickey Baker | 1978 | 12.00 |
| **KING** | | | |
| ❑ 839 [M] | But Wild | 196? | 80.00 |
| *—Blue label with crown* | | | |
| ❑ 839 [M] | But Wild | 1963 | 400.00 |
| *—Black label, no crown* | | | |
| ❑ S-839 [R] | But Wild | 196? | 40.00 |

**BAKER, RONNIE**

| Number | Title (A Side/B Side) | Yr | NM |
|---|---|---|---|
| **WARNER BROS.** | | | |
| ❑ W 1212 [M] | Oh, Johnny! | 1958 | 30.00 |
| ❑ WS 1212 [S] | Oh, Johnny! | 1959 | 50.00 |

**BAKER, SHORTY**

| Number | Title (A Side/B Side) | Yr | NM |
|---|---|---|---|
| **KING** | | | |
| ❑ 608 [M] | Broadway Beat | 1958 | 80.00 |

**BAKER, SHORTY, AND DOC CHEATHAM**

| Number | Title (A Side/B Side) | Yr | NM |
|---|---|---|---|
| **SWINGVILLE** | | | |
| ❑ SVLP-2021 [M] | Shorty & Doc | 1961 | 50.00 |
| *—Purple label* | | | |
| ❑ SVLP-2021 [M] | Shorty & Doc | 1965 | 25.00 |
| *—Blue label with trident logo at right* | | | |

| Number | Title (A Side/B Side) | Yr | NM |
|---|---|---|---|
| **BALDRY, LONG JOHN** | | | |
| ASCOT | | | |
| ❑ AM-13022 [M] | Long John's Blues | 1965 | 50.00 |
| ❑ AS-16022 [R] | Long John's Blues | 1965 | 40.00 |
| CASABLANCA | | | |
| ❑ NBLP 7012 | Good to Be Alive | 1975 | 12.00 |
| ❑ NBLP 7035 | Welcome to the Club | 1976 | 12.00 |
| EMI AMERICA | | | |
| ❑ SW-17015 | Baldry's Out | 1979 | 10.00 |
| ❑ SW-17038 | Long John Baldry | 1980 | 10.00 |
| UNITED ARTISTS | | | |
| ❑ UAS-5543 [M] | Long John's Blues | 1971 | 12.00 |
| *—Reissue of Ascot 13022* | | | |
| WARNER BROS. | | | |
| ❑ WS 1921 | It Ain't Easy | 1971 | 15.00 |
| ❑ BS 2614 | Everything Stops for Tea | 1973 | 12.00 |
| **BALES, BURT** | | | |
| ABC-PARAMOUNT | | | |
| ❑ ABC-181 [M] | Jazz from the San Francisco Waterfront | 1957 | 40.00 |
| CAVALIER | | | |
| ❑ 5007 [10] | On the Waterfront | 195? | 60.00 |
| EUPHONIC | | | |
| ❑ ESR-1210 [M] | New Orleans Ragtime | 196? | 30.00 |
| GOOD TIME JAZZ | | | |
| ❑ L-19 [10] | New Orleans Joys | 1954 | 50.00 |
| **BALES & LINGLE** | | | |
| GOOD TIME JAZZ | | | |
| ❑ L-12025 [M] | They Tore My Playhouse Down | 1955 | 40.00 |
| **BALIN, MARTY** | | | |
| EMI AMERICA | | | |
| ❑ SPRO-9673 [DJ] | Balin | 1981 | 20.00 |
| *—Red vinyl* | | | |
| ❑ ST-17054 | Balin | 1981 | 10.00 |
| ❑ ST-17088 | Lucky | 1983 | 10.00 |
| **BALL, KENNY** | | | |
| KAPP | | | |
| ❑ KL-1276 [M] | Midnight in Moscow | 1962 | 20.00 |
| ❑ KL-1285 [M] | It's Trad | 1962 | 20.00 |
| ❑ KL-1294 [M] | Recorded Live | 1962 | 20.00 |
| ❑ KS-3276 [S] | Midnight in Moscow | 1962 | 20.00 |
| ❑ KS-3285 [S] | It's Trad | 1962 | 20.00 |
| ❑ KS-3294 [S] | Recorded Live | 1962 | 20.00 |
| ❑ KS-3314 [S] | More | 1963 | 20.00 |
| ❑ KS-3340 [S] | Big Ones | 1963 | 20.00 |
| ❑ KS-3348 [S] | Washington Square and the Best of Kenny Ball | 1964 | 20.00 |
| ❑ KS-3392 [S] | For the Jet Set | 1964 | 20.00 |
| **BALL, RONNIE** | | | |
| SAVOY | | | |
| ❑ MG-12075 [M] | All About Ronnie | 1956 | 40.00 |
| **BALLADEERS, THE** | | | |
| DEL-FI | | | |
| ❑ DFLP-1204 [M] | Alive-O! | 1959 | 40.00 |
| ❑ DFST-1204 [S] | Alive-O! | 1959 | 60.00 |
| **BALLARD, FRANK** | | | |
| PHILLIPS INTERNATIONAL | | | |
| ❑ 1985 [M] | Rhythm-Blues Party | 1962 | 5000. |
| *—VG value 2500; VG+ value 3750* | | | |
| **BALLARD, HANK, AND THE MIDNIGHTERS** | | | |
| KING | | | |
| ❑ 618 [M] | Singin' and Swingin' | 1959 | 250.00 |
| ❑ 674 [M] | The One and Only Hank Ballard | 1959 | 250.00 |
| *—Brown cover* | | | |
| ❑ 674 [M] | The One and Only Hank Ballard | 1960 | 150.00 |
| *—Green cover* | | | |
| ❑ 700 [M] | Mr. Rhythm and Blues | 1960 | 150.00 |
| ❑ 740 [M] | Spotlight on Hank Ballard | 1961 | 150.00 |
| ❑ KS-740 [S] | Spotlight on Hank Ballard | 1961 | 300.00 |
| ❑ 748 [M] | Let's Go Again | 1961 | 120.00 |
| ❑ 759 [M] | Dance Along | 1961 | 120.00 |
| ❑ 781 [M] | The Twistin' Fools | 1962 | 100.00 |
| ❑ 793 [M] | Jumpin' Hank Ballard | 1962 | 100.00 |
| ❑ 815 [M] | The 1963 Sound of Hank Ballard | 1963 | 100.00 |
| ❑ 867 [M] | Biggest Hits | 1963 | 100.00 |
| ❑ 896 [M] | A Star in Your Eyes | 1964 | 100.00 |
| ❑ 913 [M] | Those Lazy, Lazy Days | 1965 | 70.00 |
| ❑ 927 [M] | Glad Songs, Sad Songs | 1965 | 70.00 |
| ❑ 950 [M] | 24 Hit Tunes | 1966 | 60.00 |
| ❑ 981 [M] | 24 Great Songs | 1968 | 40.00 |
| ❑ KSD-1052 | You Can't Keep a Good Man Down | 1969 | 50.00 |
| **BALLARD, KAYE** | | | |
| UNITED ARTISTS | | | |
| ❑ UAL-3043 [M] | Kaye Ballard Swings | 1959 | 20.00 |

The Band, *Cahoots,* Capitol SMAS-651, $15.

| Number | Title (A Side/B Side) | Yr | NM |
|---|---|---|---|
| ❑ UAL-3155 [M] | Kaye Ballard Live? | 1960 | 20.00 |
| ❑ UAL-3165 [M] | Ha-Ha Boo-Hoo | 1960 | 20.00 |
| ❑ UAS-6043 [S] | Kaye Ballard Swings | 1959 | 25.00 |
| ❑ UAS-6155 [S] | Kaye Ballard Live? | 1960 | 25.00 |
| ❑ UAS-6165 [S] | Ha-Ha Boo-Hoo | 1960 | 25.00 |
| **BANANA SPLITS, THE** | | | |
| DECCA | | | |
| ❑ DL 75075 | We're the Banana Splits | 1969 | 200.00 |
| **BANCHEE** | | | |
| ATLANTIC | | | |
| ❑ SD 8240 | Banchee | 1969 | 20.00 |
| POLYDOR | | | |
| ❑ 24-4066 | Thinkin' | 1971 | 50.00 |
| **BAND, THE** | | | |
| CAPITOL | | | |
| ❑ STAO-132 | The Band | 1969 | 15.00 |
| *—Lime green label* | | | |
| ❑ STAO-8-0132 | The Band | 1969 | 100.00 |
| *—Capitol Record Club edition with black rainbow label; we don't know if any standard versions of this album exist with this label* | | | |
| ❑ SW-425 | Stage Fright | 1970 | 10.00 |
| *—Without tear-off wraparound cover* | | | |
| ❑ SW-425 | Stage Fright | 1970 | 15.00 |
| *—Includes tear-off wraparound cover* | | | |
| ❑ SMAS-651 | Cahoots | 1971 | 15.00 |
| ❑ SKAO 2955 | Music from Big Pink | 1968 | 25.00 |
| *—Black label with colorband* | | | |
| ❑ SKAO 2955 | Music from Big Pink | 1969 | 15.00 |
| *—Lime green label* | | | |
| ❑ SKAO 2955 | Music from Big Pink | 1971 | 15.00 |
| *—Red label, purple "C" logo at top* | | | |
| ❑ SABB-11045 [(2)] | Rock of Ages | 1972 | 20.00 |
| ❑ SW-11214 | Moondog Matinee | 1973 | 10.00 |
| *—Without tear-off wraparound cover* | | | |
| ❑ SW-11214 | Moondog Matinee | 1973 | 15.00 |
| *—Includes tear-off wraparound cover* | | | |
| ❑ ST-11440 | Northern Lights-Southern Cross | 1975 | 12.00 |
| ❑ ST-11553 | The Best of the Band | 1976 | 12.00 |
| ❑ SO-11602 | Islands | 1977 | 12.00 |
| ❑ SKBO-11856 [(2)] | Anthology | 1978 | 15.00 |
| ❑ SN-16003 | Cahoots | 1980 | 8.00 |
| *—Budget-line reissue* | | | |
| ❑ SN-16004 | Moondog Matinee | 1980 | 8.00 |
| *—Budget-line reissue* | | | |
| ❑ SN-16005 | Northern Lights-Southern Cross | 1980 | 8.00 |
| *—Budget-line reissue* | | | |
| ❑ SN-16006 | Stage Fright | 1980 | 8.00 |
| *—Budget-line reissue* | | | |
| ❑ SN-16007 | Islands | 1980 | 8.00 |
| *—Budget-line reissue* | | | |
| ❑ SN-16008 | Rock of Ages, Volume 1 | 1980 | 8.00 |
| *—Budget-line reissue* | | | |
| ❑ SN-16009 | Rock of Ages, Volume 2 | 1980 | 8.00 |
| *—Budget-line reissue* | | | |
| ❑ SN-16010 | Anthology, Volume 1 | 1980 | 8.00 |
| *—Budget-line reissue* | | | |
| ❑ SN-16011 | Anthology, Volume 2 | 1980 | 8.00 |
| *—Budget-line reissue* | | | |
| ❑ SN-16296 | The Band | 198? | 8.00 |
| *—Budget-line reissue* | | | |
| ❑ SN-16331 | The Best of the Band | 198? | 8.00 |
| *—Budget-line reissue* | | | |
| MOBILE FIDELITY | | | |
| ❑ 1-039 | Music from Big Pink | 1981 | 50.00 |
| *—Audiophile vinyl* | | | |
| RHINO HANDMADE | | | |
| ❑ RHM1-7801 [(3)] | The Last Waltz | 2003 | 60.00 |
| *—Box set with remixed version of the album, booklet, facsimiles of tickets, posters and other ephemera, many bonus photos, and a reproduction of the cover signed by Robbie Robertson* | | | |
| WARNER BROS. | | | |
| ❑ PRO-A-737 [DJ] | The Last Waltz Sampler | 1978 | 20.00 |
| ❑ 3WS 3146 [(3)] | The Last Waltz | 1978 | 20.00 |
| **BANDITS, THE** | | | |
| WORLD PACIFIC | | | |
| ❑ ST-1833 [S] | The Electric 12 String | 1964 | 25.00 |
| ❑ T-1833 [M] | The Electric 12 String | 1964 | 20.00 |
| **BANDWAGON, THE** | | | |
| EPIC | | | |
| ❑ BN 26426 | Johnny Johnson and the Bandwagon | 1969 | 20.00 |
| **BANG** | | | |
| CAPITOL | | | |
| ❑ ST-11015 | Bang | 1972 | 15.00 |
| ❑ SMAS-11110 | Mother/Bow to the Music | 1972 | 15.00 |
| ❑ ST-11190 | Music | 1973 | 20.00 |

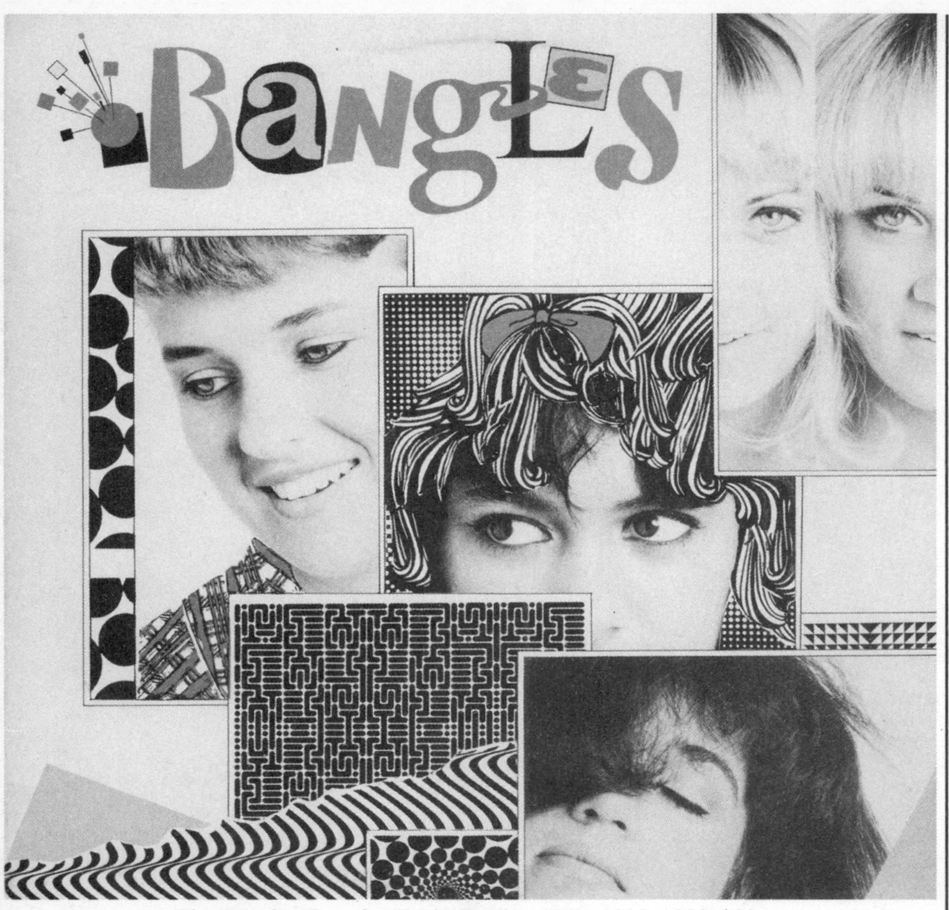


The Bangles, *Bangles,* Faulty Products FEP 1302, 1982, $20.

| Number | Title (A Side/B Side) | Yr | NM |
|---|---|---|---|
| **BANGLES** | | | |
| COLUMBIA | | | |
| ❑ CAS 2270 [DJ] | Interchords | 1986 | 25.00 |
| *—Promo-only interview album* | | | |
| ❑ BFC 39220 | All Over the Place | 1984 | 12.00 |
| ❑ PC 39220 | All Over the Place | 1986 | 8.00 |
| *—Reissue with new prefix and longer bar code* | | | |
| ❑ BFC 40039 | Different Light | 1986 | 12.00 |
| ❑ FC 40039 | Different Light | 1986 | 8.00 |
| *—Reissue with new prefix; "02" added to bar code on back cover* | | | |
| ❑ OC 44056 | Everything | 1988 | 10.00 |
| FAULTY PRODUCTS | | | |
| ❑ FEP 1302 [EP] | Bangles | 1982 | 20.00 |
| I.R.S. | | | |
| ❑ SP-70506 [EP] | Bangles | 1983 | 12.00 |
| *—Reissue of Faulty Products EP* | | | |
| **BANJO KINGS, THE** | | | |
| GOOD TIME JAZZ | | | |
| ❑ L-15 [10] | The Banjo Kings | 1953 | 50.00 |
| ❑ L-25 [10] | The Banjo Kings, Vol. 2 | 1954 | 50.00 |
| ❑ L-12015 [M] | The Banjo Kings | 1955 | 40.00 |
| ❑ L-12029 [M] | Nostalgia Revisited | 1956 | 40.00 |
| ❑ L-12036 [M] | The Banjo Kings Go West | 1957 | 40.00 |
| ❑ L-12047 [M] | The Banjo Kings Enjoy the Good Old Days | 1958 | 40.00 |
| ❑ S-12047 [S] | The Banjo Kings Enjoy the Good Old Days | 1959 | 30.00 |
| **BANKS, DARRELL** | | | |
| ATCO | | | |
| ❑ 33-216 [M] | Darrell Banks Is Here | 1967 | 25.00 |
| ❑ SD 33-216 [S] | Darrell Banks Is Here | 1967 | 30.00 |
| VOLT | | | |
| ❑ VOS-6002 | Here to Stay | 1969 | 25.00 |
| **BANTAMS, THE** | | | |
| WARNER BROS. | | | |
| ❑ W 1625 [M] | Beware the Bantams | 1966 | 20.00 |
| ❑ WS 1625 [S] | Beware the Bantams | 1966 | 25.00 |
| **BAR-KAYS, THE** | | | |
| ATCO | | | |
| ❑ SD 33-289 | Soul Finger | 1968 | 25.00 |

| Number | Title (A Side/B Side) | Yr | NM |
|---|---|---|---|
| MERCURY | | | |
| ❑ SRM-1-1099 | Too Hot to Stop | 1976 | 10.00 |
| ❑ SRM-1-1181 | Flying High on Your Love | 1977 | 10.00 |
| ❑ SRM-1-3732 | Light of Life | 1978 | 10.00 |
| ❑ SRM-1-3781 | Injoy | 1979 | 10.00 |
| ❑ SRM-1-3844 | As One | 1980 | 10.00 |
| ❑ SRM-1-4028 | Nightcruising | 1981 | 10.00 |
| ❑ SRM-1-4065 | Propositions | 1982 | 10.00 |
| ❑ 818478-1 | Dangerous | 1984 | 10.00 |
| ❑ 824727-1 | Banging the Wall | 1985 | 10.00 |
| ❑ 830305-1 | Contagious | 1987 | 10.00 |
| ❑ 836774-1 | Animal | 1989 | 10.00 |
| STAX | | | |
| ❑ 4106 | Money Talks | 1978 | 10.00 |
| ❑ 4130 | Gotta Groove | 1979 | 10.00 |
| ❑ MPS-8510 | Cold Blooded | 1981 | 10.00 |
| ❑ MPS-8542 | The Best of the Bar-Kays | 1988 | 10.00 |
| VOLT | | | |
| ❑ 417 [M] | Soul Finger | 1967 | 40.00 |
| ❑ S-417 [S] | Soul Finger | 1967 | 40.00 |
| ❑ 6004 | Gotta Groove | 1969 | 30.00 |
| ❑ 6011 | Black Rock | 1971 | 25.00 |
| ❑ VOS-8001 | Do You See What I See | 1972 | 25.00 |
| ❑ 9504 | Cold Blooded | 1974 | 25.00 |
| **BARBARIANS, THE** | | | |
| LAURIE | | | |
| ❑ LLP-2033 [M] | Are You a Boy or Are You a Girl? | 1966 | 150.00 |
| ❑ SLP-2033 [S] | Are You a Boy or Are You a Girl? | 1966 | 200.00 |
| RHINO | | | |
| ❑ RNLP 008 | The Barbarians | 1979 | 12.00 |
| **BARBARIN, PAUL** | | | |
| ATLANTIC | | | |
| ❑ 1215 [M] | New Orleans Jazz | 1955 | 50.00 |
| *—Black label* | | | |
| ❑ 1215 [M] | New Orleans Jazz | 1961 | 20.00 |
| *—Multi-color label, white "fan" logo at right* | | | |
| ❑ SD 1215 [S] | New Orleans Jazz | 1959 | 50.00 |
| *—Green label* | | | |
| ❑ SD 1215 [S] | New Orleans Jazz | 1961 | 20.00 |
| *—Multi-color label, white "fan" logo at right* | | | |
| CONCERT HALL JAZZ | | | |
| ❑ 1006 [10] | New Orleans Jamboree | 1954 | 50.00 |

| Number | Title (A Side/B Side) | Yr | NM |
|---|---|---|---|
| GHB | | | |
| ❑ GHB-2 [M] | Paul Barbarin and His New Orleans Jazz Band | 1962 | 20.00 |
| JAZZTONE | | | |
| ❑ J-1205 [M] | New Orleans Jamboree | 1955 | 40.00 |
| NOBILITY | | | |
| ❑ 708 | Last Journey of a Jazzman | 196? | 20.00 |
| SOUTHLAND | | | |
| ❑ SLP-237 [M] | Bourbon St. Beat | 195? | 40.00 |
| **BARBARIN, PAUL / SHARKEY BONANO** | | | |
| RIVERSIDE | | | |
| ❑ RLP 12-217 [M] | New Orleans Contrasts | 195? | 40.00 |
| *—Blue label with microphone logo* | | | |
| ❑ RLP 12-217 [M] | New Orleans Contrasts | 1955 | 60.00 |
| *—White label, blue print* | | | |
| **BARBARIN, PAUL, AND PUNCH MILLER** | | | |
| ATLANTIC | | | |
| ❑ 1410 [M] | Paul Barbarin and Punch Miller | 1963 | 20.00 |
| ❑ SD 1410 [S] | Paul Barbarin and Punch Miller | 1963 | 25.00 |
| **BARBARIN, PAUL / JOHNNY ST. CYR** | | | |
| SOUTHLAND | | | |
| ❑ SLP-212 [M] | Paul Barbarin and His Jazz Band/Johnny St. Cyr and His Hot Five | 1955 | 40.00 |
| **BARBARY, RICHARD** | | | |
| A&M | | | |
| ❑ SP-3010 | Soul Machine | 1969 | 20.00 |
| **BARBER, CHRIS** | | | |
| ATLANTIC | | | |
| ❑ 1292 [M] | Here Is Chris Barber | 1959 | 40.00 |
| COLPIX | | | |
| ❑ CP-404 [M] | Chris Barber Plays "Trad" | 1959 | 30.00 |
| LAURIE | | | |
| ❑ 1001 [M] | Petite Fleur | 1959 | 40.00 |
| ❑ LLP-1003 [M] | Trad Jazz Volume 1 | 1960 | 30.00 |
| ❑ LLP-1009 [M] | Chris Barber's "American" Jazz Band | 1962 | 30.00 |
| **BARBER, PATRICIA** | | | |
| PREMONITION | | | |
| ❑ PREM 737-1 | Café Blue | 199? | 30.00 |
| *—Audiophile vinyl* | | | |
| ❑ PREM 747-1 | Modern Cool | 1998 | 25.00 |
| *—Audiophile vinyl* | | | |
| ❑ 27290 | Nightclub | 2000 | 25.00 |
| *—Audiophile vinyl* | | | |
| ❑ 90747 | Companion | 1999 | 25.00 |
| *—Audiophile vinyl* | | | |
| **BARBIERI, GATO** | | | |
| ESP-DISK' | | | |
| ❑ 1049 | In Search of the Mystery | 1968 | 40.00 |
| FANIA | | | |
| ❑ JM 608 | Gato = Bahia | 1982 | 12.00 |
| **BARBOUR, KEITH** | | | |
| EPIC | | | |
| ❑ BN 26485 | Echo Park | 1969 | 20.00 |
| **BARCLAY JAMES HARVEST** | | | |
| HARVEST | | | |
| ❑ SW-11145 | Baby James Harvest | 1973 | 15.00 |
| MCA | | | |
| ❑ 2234 | Octoberon | 1976 | 10.00 |
| ❑ 2302 | Gone to Earth | 1977 | 10.00 |
| POLYDOR | | | |
| ❑ PD-1-6173 | XII | 1978 | 10.00 |
| ❑ PD-1-6267 | Eyes of the Universe | 1980 | 10.00 |
| ❑ PD-6508 | Everyone Is Everybody Else | 1974 | 12.00 |
| ❑ PD-6517 | Time Honoured Ghosts | 1975 | 12.00 |
| SIRE | | | |
| ❑ SI-4904 | Back Again | 1971 | 15.00 |
| ❑ SI-5904 | Other Short Stories | 1972 | 15.00 |
| ❑ SES-97026 | Barclay James Harvest | 1970 | 20.00 |
| **BARDOT, BRIGITTE** | | | |
| DOT | | | |
| ❑ DLP-3120 [M] | La Belle Bardot | 1958 | 100.00 |
| PHILIPS | | | |
| ❑ PCC 204 [M] | Brigitte Bardot Sings | 1963 | 30.00 |
| ❑ PCC 604 [S] | Brigitte Bardot Sings | 1963 | 40.00 |
| **BARE, BOBBY** | | | |
| COLUMBIA | | | |
| ❑ KC 35314 | Bare | 1977 | 10.00 |
| ❑ JC 36323 | Down & Dirty | 1978 | 10.00 |
| ❑ PC 36323 | Down & Dirty | 198? | 8.00 |
| *—Budget-line reissue* | | | |

| Number | Title (A Side/B Side) | Yr | NM |
|---|---|---|---|
| ❑ JC 36785 | Drunk & Crazy | 1980 | 10.00 |
| ❑ FC 37157 | As Is | 1981 | 10.00 |
| ❑ FC 37351 | Encore | 1981 | 10.00 |
| ❑ PC 37351 | Encore | 198? | 8.00 |
| *—Budget-line reissue* | | | |
| ❑ FC 37719 | Ain't Got Nothin' to Lose | 1982 | 10.00 |
| ❑ FC 38311 | Biggest Hits | 1982 | 10.00 |
| ❑ FC 38670 | Drinkin' from the Bottle, Singin' from the Heart | 1983 | 10.00 |
| HILLTOP | | | |
| ❑ 6026 | Tender Years | 196? | 12.00 |
| MERCURY | | | |
| ❑ SR-61290 | This Is Bare Country | 1970 | 20.00 |
| ❑ SR-61316 | Where Have All the Seasons Gone | 1971 | 20.00 |
| ❑ SR-61363 | What Am I Gonna Do? | 1972 | 20.00 |
| PICKWICK | | | |
| ❑ ACL-7003 | 500 Miles Away from Home | 1975 | 10.00 |
| RCA CAMDEN | | | |
| ❑ ACL1-0150 | Memphis, Tennessee | 1973 | 12.00 |
| ❑ CAS-2290 | Folsom Prison Blues | 1969 | 12.00 |
| ❑ CAS-2465 | I'm a Long Way from Home | 1971 | 12.00 |
| RCA VICTOR | | | |
| ❑ APL1-0040 | I Hate Goodbyes/Ride Me Down Easy | 1973 | 15.00 |
| ❑ CPL2-0290 [(2)] | Bobby Bare Sings Lullabys, Legends and Lies | 1973 | 20.00 |
| ❑ ANL1-0560 | Sunday Morning | 1974 | 10.00 |
| ❑ APL1-0700 | Singin' in the Kitchen | 1974 | 15.00 |
| ❑ APL1-0906 | Hard Time Hungrys | 1975 | 12.00 |
| ❑ APL1-1222 | Cowboys and Daddys | 1975 | 12.00 |
| ❑ APL1-1786 | The Winner and Other Losers | 1976 | 12.00 |
| ❑ APL1-2179 | Me and McDill | 1977 | 12.00 |
| ❑ LPM-2776 [M] | "Detroit City" and Other Hits | 1963 | 20.00 |
| ❑ LSP-2776 [S] | "Detroit City" and Other Hits | 1963 | 25.00 |
| ❑ LPM-2835 [M] | 500 Miles Away from Home | 1964 | 20.00 |
| ❑ LSP-2835 [S] | 500 Miles Away from Home | 1964 | 25.00 |
| ❑ LPM-2955 [M] | The Travelin' Bare | 1964 | 20.00 |
| ❑ LSP-2955 [S] | The Travelin' Bare | 1964 | 25.00 |
| ❑ LPM-3395 [M] | Constant Sorrow | 1965 | 20.00 |
| ❑ LSP-3395 [S] | Constant Sorrow | 1965 | 25.00 |
| ❑ LPM-3479 [M] | The Best of Bobby Bare | 1965 | 20.00 |
| ❑ LSP-3479 [S] | The Best of Bobby Bare | 1965 | 25.00 |
| ❑ LPM-3515 [M] | Talk Me Some Sense | 1966 | 20.00 |
| ❑ LSP-3515 [S] | Talk Me Some Sense | 1966 | 25.00 |
| ❑ LPM-3618 [M] | The Streets of Baltimore | 1966 | 20.00 |
| ❑ LSP-3618 [S] | The Streets of Baltimore | 1966 | 25.00 |
| ❑ LPM-3688 [M] | This I Believe | 1966 | 20.00 |
| ❑ LSP-3688 [S] | This I Believe | 1966 | 25.00 |
| ❑ LPM-3831 [M] | A Bird Named Yesterday | 1967 | 25.00 |
| ❑ LSP-3831 [S] | A Bird Named Yesterday | 1967 | 20.00 |
| ❑ LPM-3896 [M] | The English Country Side | 1967 | 40.00 |
| ❑ LSP-3896 [S] | The English Country Side | 1967 | 20.00 |
| ❑ LPM-3994 [M] | The Best of Bobby Bare — Volume 2 | 1968 | 40.00 |
| ❑ LSP-3994 [S] | The Best of Bobby Bare — Volume 2 | 1968 | 20.00 |
| ❑ AYL1-4118 | Greatest Hits | 1982 | 8.00 |
| ❑ LSP-4177 | (Margie's At) The Lincoln Park Inn (And Other Controversial Country Songs) | 1969 | 20.00 |
| ❑ LSP-4422 | Real Thing | 1970 | 15.00 |
| ❑ AHL1-5469 | Collector's Series | 1985 | 10.00 |
| ❑ VPS-6090 [(2)] | This Is Bobby Bare | 1972 | 20.00 |
| UNITED ARTISTS | | | |
| ❑ UA-LA621-G | Bare Country | 1977 | 12.00 |
| **BARE, BOBBY, AND SKEETER DAVIS** | | | |
| RCA VICTOR | | | |
| ❑ LPM-3336 [M] | Tunes for Two | 1965 | 20.00 |
| ❑ LSP-3336 [S] | Tunes for Two | 1965 | 25.00 |
| ❑ LSP-4335 | Your Husband, My Wife | 1970 | 15.00 |
| **BARE, BOBBY, NORMA JEAN, & LIZ ANDERSON** | | | |
| RCA VICTOR | | | |
| ❑ LPM-3764 [M] | The Game of Triangles | 1967 | 25.00 |
| ❑ LSP-3764 [S] | The Game of Triangles | 1967 | 20.00 |
| **BARGE, GENE** | | | |
| CHECKER | | | |
| ❑ LP-2994 [M] | Dance with Daddy G | 1965 | 50.00 |
| **BARKER, WARREN** | | | |
| WARNER BROS. | | | |
| ❑ W 1205 [M] | "The King and I" for Orchestra | 1958 | 20.00 |
| ❑ WS 1205 [S] | "The King and I" for Orchestra | 1958 | 25.00 |
| ❑ W 1290 [M] | TV Guide — Top TV Themes | 1959 | 30.00 |
| ❑ WS 1290 [S] | TV Guide — Top TV Themes | 1959 | 40.00 |
| ❑ B 1308 [M] | William Holden Presents a Musical Touch of Far Away Places | 1959 | 30.00 |
| ❑ BS 1308 [S] | William Holden Presents a Musical Touch of Far Away Places | 1959 | 40.00 |

| Number | Title (A Side/B Side) | Yr | NM |
|---|---|---|---|
| **BARNES, EMIL** | | | |
| AMERICAN MUSIC | | | |
| ❑ LP-641 [10] | New Orleans Trad Jazz | 1952 | 50.00 |
| **BARNES, GEORGE** | | | |
| DECCA | | | |
| ❑ DL 8658 [M] | Guitars — By George | 1957 | 40.00 |
| *—Black label, silver print* | | | |
| GRAND AWARD | | | |
| ❑ GA 33-358 [M] | Guitar in Velvet | 195? | 25.00 |
| MERCURY | | | |
| ❑ PPS-2011 [M] | Guitar Galaxies | 196? | 30.00 |
| ❑ PPS-6011 [S] | Guitar Galaxies | 196? | 40.00 |
| ❑ MG-20956 [M] | Guitar Galaxies | 1962 | 25.00 |
| ❑ SR-60956 [S] | Guitar Galaxies | 1962 | 30.00 |
| **BARNES, J.J.** | | | |
| VOLT | | | |
| ❑ VOS-6001 | Rare Stamps | 1969 | 30.00 |
| *—With Steve Mancha* | | | |
| **BARNES, MAE** | | | |
| ATLANTIC | | | |
| ❑ ALS-404 [10] | Fun with Mae Barnes | 1953 | 400.00 |
| VANGUARD | | | |
| ❑ VRS-9036 [M] | Meet Mae Barnes | 1958 | 50.00 |
| **BARNET, CHARLIE** | | | |
| AVA | | | |
| ❑ A-10 [M] | Charlie Barnet !?!?!?!?!?!?! | 1962 | 25.00 |
| ❑ AS-10 [S] | Charlie Barnet !?!?!?!?!?!?! | 1962 | 30.00 |
| CAPITOL | | | |
| ❑ H 235 [10] | Big Bands | 195? | 60.00 |
| ❑ H 325 [10] | The Modern Idiom | 1952 | 60.00 |
| ❑ T 624 [M] | Classics in Jazz | 1955 | 50.00 |
| ❑ ST 1403 [S] | Jazz Oasis | 1960 | 25.00 |
| ❑ T 1403 [M] | Jazz Oasis | 1960 | 20.00 |
| CHOREO | | | |
| ❑ A-10 [M] | Charlie Barnet !?!?!?!?!?!?! | 196? | 20.00 |
| ❑ AS-10 [S] | Charlie Barnet !?!?!?!?!?!?! | 196? | 25.00 |
| *—Some copies have Choreo logo on front cover, but Ava labels and back cover* | | | |
| CLEF | | | |
| ❑ MGC-114 [10] | Charlie Barnet Plays Charlie Barnet | 1953 | 100.00 |
| ❑ MGC-139 [10] | Dance with Charlie Barnet | 1953 | 100.00 |
| ❑ MGC-164 [10] | Charlie Barnet Dance Session, Vol. 1 | 1954 | 100.00 |
| ❑ MGC-165 [10] | Charlie Barnet Dance Session, Vol. 2 | 1954 | 100.00 |
| ❑ MGC-638 [M] | One Night Stand | 1955 | 80.00 |
| COLUMBIA | | | |
| ❑ CL 639 [M] | Town Hall Jazz Concert | 195? | 40.00 |
| *—Black and red label with six "eye" logos* | | | |
| ❑ CL 639 [M] | Town Hall Jazz Concert | 1955 | 50.00 |
| *—Maroon label, gold print* | | | |
| CROWN | | | |
| ❑ CLP-5114 [M] | A Tribute to Harry James | 195? | 20.00 |
| ❑ CLP-5127 [M] | Charlie Barnet Presents a Salute to Harry James | 195? | 20.00 |
| ❑ CLP-5134 [M] | On Stage with Charlie Barnet | 1959 | 20.00 |
| DECCA | | | |
| ❑ DL 8098 [M] | Hop on the Skyliner | 195? | 50.00 |
| EVEREST | | | |
| ❑ SDBR-1008 [S] | Cherokee | 1959 | 20.00 |
| ❑ LPBR-5008 [M] | Cherokee | 1958 | 25.00 |
| ❑ LPBR-5059 [M] | More Charlie Barnet | 196? | 20.00 |
| ❑ SDBR-5059 [S] | More Charlie Barnet | 196? | 25.00 |
| MERCURY | | | |
| ❑ MGC-114 [10] | Charlie Barnet Plays Charlie Barnet | 1952 | 150.00 |
| RCA VICTOR | | | |
| ❑ LPV-551 [M] | Charlie Barnet (Volume 1) | 1968 | 20.00 |
| ❑ LPV-567 [M] | Charlie Barnet (Volume 2) | 1969 | 20.00 |
| ❑ LPM-1091 [M] | Redskin Romp | 1955 | 50.00 |
| ❑ LPM-2081 [M] | The Great Dance Bands | 1960 | 20.00 |
| ❑ LPT-3062 [10] | Rockin' in Rhythm | 195? | 80.00 |
| SWING | | | |
| ❑ 103 [M] | Charlie Barnet and His Orchestra | 195? | 40.00 |
| VAULT | | | |
| ❑ LP-9004 [M] | Charlie Barnet Big Band 1967 | 1967 | 20.00 |
| VERVE | | | |
| ❑ MGV-2007 [M] | Dance Bash | 1956 | 50.00 |
| ❑ V-2007 [M] | Dance Bash | 1961 | 20.00 |
| ❑ MGV-2027 [M] | Dancing Party | 1956 | 50.00 |
| ❑ V-2027 [M] | Dancing Party | 1961 | 20.00 |
| ❑ MGV-2031 [M] | For Dancing Lovers | 1956 | 50.00 |
| ❑ V-2031 [M] | For Dancing Lovers | 1961 | 20.00 |
| ❑ MGV-2040 [M] | Lonely Street | 1957 | 50.00 |
| ❑ V-2040 [M] | Lonely Street | 1961 | 20.00 |

| Number | Title (A Side/B Side) | Yr | NM |
|---|---|---|---|
| **BARNETT, BOBBY** | | | |
| SIMS | | | |
| ❑ LP-198 [M] | Bobby Barnett at the World Famous Crystal Palace, Tombstone, Arizona | 1964 | 25.00 |
| **BARNUM, H.B.** | | | |
| CAPITOL | | | |
| ❑ ST 2278 [S] | Golden Boy | 1965 | 20.00 |
| ❑ T 2278 [M] | Golden Boy | 1965 | 15.00 |
| ❑ ST 2289 [S] | Big Hits of Detroit | 1965 | 20.00 |
| ❑ T 2289 [M] | Big Hits of Detroit | 1965 | 15.00 |
| ❑ ST 2583 [S] | Pop and Ice Cream Sodas | 1966 | 20.00 |
| ❑ T 2583 [M] | Pop and Ice Cream Sodas | 1966 | 15.00 |
| **BAROQUE ENSEMBLE OF THE MERSEYSIDE KAMMERMUSIKGESELLSCHAFT, THE** | | | |
| ELEKTRA | | | |
| ❑ EKL-306 [M] | The Baroque Beatles Book | 1966 | 25.00 |
| ❑ EKS-7306 [S] | The Baroque Beatles Book | 1966 | 30.00 |
| **BAROQUES, THE** | | | |
| CHESS | | | |
| ❑ LP-1516 [M] | The Baroques | 1967 | 80.00 |
| ❑ LPS-1516 [S] | The Baroques | 1967 | 100.00 |
| **BARRACUDAS, THE** | | | |
| JUSTICE | | | |
| ❑ JLP-143 | A Plane View | 1968 | 500.00 |
| **BARRETT, EMMA** | | | |
| NOBILITY | | | |
| ❑ 711 [M] | The Bell Gal and Her New Orleans Jazz | 196? | 20.00 |
| RIVERSIDE | | | |
| ❑ RLP-364 [M] | Sweet Emma | 1960 | 40.00 |
| ❑ RS-9364 [R] | Sweet Emma | 196? | 20.00 |
| SOUTHLAND | | | |
| ❑ 241 [M] | Sweet Emma Barrett and Her New Orleans Music | 1964 | 20.00 |
| ❑ 242 [M] | Emma Barrett at Disneyland | 1967 | 20.00 |
| **BARRETT, RONA** | | | |
| MISS RONA | | | |
| ❑ MRR 1001 | Miss Rona Sings Hollywood's Greatest Hits | 1974 | 40.00 |
| **BARRETT, SUSAN** | | | |
| CAPITOL | | | |
| ❑ T 1266 [M] | Mixed Emotions | 1959 | 50.00 |
| RCA VICTOR | | | |
| ❑ LPM-3738 [M] | Susan Barrett | 1967 | 40.00 |
| ❑ LSP-3738 [S] | Susan Barrett | 1967 | 30.00 |
| **BARRETT, SYD** | | | |
| CAPITOL | | | |
| ❑ C1-91206 | Opel | 1989 | 20.00 |
| HARVEST | | | |
| ❑ SABB-11314 [(2)] | The Madcap Laughs/Barrett | 1974 | 25.00 |
| **BARRETTO, RAY** | | | |
| FANIA | | | |
| ❑ SLP-346 | Acid | 196? | 20.00 |
| ❑ SLP-362 | Hard Hands | 1970 | 20.00 |
| ❑ SLP-378 | Together | 197? | 20.00 |
| ❑ SLP-388 | Barretto Head Sounds | 197? | 20.00 |
| ❑ SLP-391 | Power | 197? | 20.00 |
| ❑ SLP-403 | The Message | 197? | 20.00 |
| ❑ SLP-410 | From the Beginning | 197? | 20.00 |
| TICO | | | |
| ❑ LP-1087 [M] | Charanga Moderna | 1962 | 20.00 |
| ❑ SLP-1087 [S] | Charanga Moderna | 1962 | 25.00 |
| ❑ LP-1099 [M] | The Hit Latin Style of Ray Barretto | 1963 | 20.00 |
| ❑ SLP-1099 [S] | The Hit Latin Style of Ray Barretto | 1963 | 25.00 |
| ❑ LP-1102 [M] | La Moderna De Siempre | 1963 | 20.00 |
| ❑ SLP-1102 [S] | La Moderna De Siempre | 1963 | 25.00 |
| ❑ LP-1114 [M] | Guajira y Guaguanco | 1964 | 20.00 |
| ❑ SLP-1114 [S] | Guajira y Guaguanco | 1964 | 25.00 |
| **BARRON, BILL** | | | |
| AUDIO FIDELITY | | | |
| ❑ AFLP-2123 [M] | Now Hear This! | 1964 | 20.00 |
| ❑ AFSD-6123 [S] | Now Hear This! | 1964 | 25.00 |
| DAUNTLESS | | | |
| ❑ DM-4312 [M] | West Side Story Bossa Nova | 1963 | 25.00 |
| ❑ DS-6312 [S] | West Side Story Bossa Nova | 1963 | 30.00 |
| SAVOY | | | |
| ❑ MG-12160 [M] | The Tenor Stylings of Bill Barron | 1961 | 40.00 |
| ❑ MG-12163 [M] | Modern Windows | 1962 | 40.00 |
| ❑ MG-12183 [M] | Hot Line | 1965 | 25.00 |

**BARRY, GENE**

RCA VICTOR

| Number | Title (A Side/B Side) | Yr | NM |
|---|---|---|---|
| ❑ LPM-2975 [M] | The Star of "Burke's Law" Sings of Love and Things | 1964 | 25.00 |
| ❑ LSP-2975 [S] | The Star of "Burke's Law" Sings of Love and Things | 1964 | 30.00 |

**BARRY, JOHN**

BULLDOG

| Number | Title (A Side/B Side) | Yr | NM |
|---|---|---|---|
| ❑ BDL-1036 | Bond by Barry | 198? | 10.00 |

COLUMBIA

| Number | Title (A Side/B Side) | Yr | NM |
|---|---|---|---|
| ❑ C 1003 | Ready When You Are, Mr. J.B. | 1970 | 10.00 |
| ❑ CL 2493 [M] | Great Movie Sounds of John Barry | 1966 | 15.00 |
| ❑ CL 2708 [M] | You Only Live Twice | 1967 | 15.00 |
| ❑ CS 9293 [S] | Great Movie Sounds of John Barry | 1966 | 20.00 |
| ❑ CS 9508 [S] | You Only Live Twice | 1967 | 20.00 |

UNITED ARTISTS

| Number | Title (A Side/B Side) | Yr | NM |
|---|---|---|---|
| ❑ UAL 3424 [M] | Goldfinger and Other Favorites | 1965 | 12.00 |
| ❑ UAS 6424 [S] | Goldfinger and Other Favorites | 1965 | 15.00 |

**BARRY, LEN**

BUDDAH

| Number | Title (A Side/B Side) | Yr | NM |
|---|---|---|---|
| ❑ BDS-5105 | Ups & Downs | 1972 | 15.00 |

DECCA

| Number | Title (A Side/B Side) | Yr | NM |
|---|---|---|---|
| ❑ DL 4720 [M] | 1-2-3 | 1965 | 30.00 |
| ❑ DL 74720 [P] | 1-2-3 | 1965 | 40.00 |

*—"Lip Sync" is rechanneled*

RCA VICTOR

| Number | Title (A Side/B Side) | Yr | NM |
|---|---|---|---|
| ❑ LPM-3823 [M] | My Kind of Soul | 1967 | 25.00 |
| ❑ LSP-3823 [S] | My Kind of Soul | 1967 | 20.00 |

**BARRY AND BARRY** See BARRY McGUIRE AND BARRY KANE.

**BARRY AND THE TAMERLANES**

VALIANT

| Number | Title (A Side/B Side) | Yr | NM |
|---|---|---|---|
| ❑ LP-406 [M] | I Wonder What She's Doing Tonight | 1963 | 150.00 |
| ❑ LPS-406 [S] | I Wonder What She's Doing Tonight | 1963 | 300.00 |

**BARRYMORE, LIONEL, AS EBENEZER SCROOGE**

MGM

| Number | Title (A Side/B Side) | Yr | NM |
|---|---|---|---|
| ❑ CH 112 [10] | A Christmas Carol | 1952 | 40.00 |

**BARTEL, JON, THING**

CAPITOL

| Number | Title (A Side/B Side) | Yr | NM |
|---|---|---|---|
| ❑ ST-274 | The Jon Bartel Thing | 1969 | 25.00 |

**BARTHOLOMEW, DAVE**

BROADMOOR

| Number | Title (A Side/B Side) | Yr | NM |
|---|---|---|---|
| ❑ BR-1201 | Dave Bartholomew's New Orleans Jazz Band | 1981 | 15.00 |

IMPERIAL

| Number | Title (A Side/B Side) | Yr | NM |
|---|---|---|---|
| ❑ LP-9162 [M] | Fats Domino Presents Dave Bartholomew | 1961 | 100.00 |
| ❑ LP-9217 [M] | New Orleans House Party | 1963 | 100.00 |
| ❑ LP-12076 [S] | Fats Domino Presents Dave Bartholomew | 1961 | 150.00 |
| ❑ LP-12217 [S] | New Orleans House Party | 1963 | 150.00 |

**BARTLEY, CHARLENE**

RCA VICTOR

| Number | Title (A Side/B Side) | Yr | NM |
|---|---|---|---|
| ❑ LPM-1478 [M] | Weekend of a Private Secretary | 1957 | 50.00 |

**BARTLEY, CHRIS**

VANDO

| Number | Title (A Side/B Side) | Yr | NM |
|---|---|---|---|
| ❑ VA-60000 [M] | The Sweetest Thing This Side of Heaven | 1967 | 50.00 |
| ❑ VAS-60000 [S] | The Sweetest Thing This Side of Heaven | 1967 | 40.00 |

**BARTZ, GARY**

MILESTONE

| Number | Title (A Side/B Side) | Yr | NM |
|---|---|---|---|
| ❑ 9006 | Libra | 1968 | 20.00 |
| ❑ 9018 | Another Earth | 1969 | 20.00 |
| ❑ 9027 | Home! | 1970 | 20.00 |
| ❑ 9031 | Harlem Bush Music — Taifa | 1971 | 20.00 |
| ❑ 9032 | Harlem Bush Music — Uhuru | 1972 | 20.00 |

PRESTIGE

| Number | Title (A Side/B Side) | Yr | NM |
|---|---|---|---|
| ❑ 66001 [(2)] | I've Known Rivers | 197? | 20.00 |

**BASIE, COUNT**

ABC-PARAMOUNT

| Number | Title (A Side/B Side) | Yr | NM |
|---|---|---|---|
| ❑ ABC-570 [M] | Basie's Swingin' — Voices Singin' | 1966 | 20.00 |
| ❑ ABCS-570 [S] | Basie's Swingin' — Voices Singin' | 1966 | 25.00 |

AMERICAN RECORDING SOCIETY

| Number | Title (A Side/B Side) | Yr | NM |
|---|---|---|---|
| ❑ G-401 [M] | Count Basie | 1956 | 40.00 |
| ❑ G-402 [M] | The Band That Swings the Blues | 1956 | 40.00 |
| ❑ G-422 [M] | Basie's Best | 1957 | 40.00 |
| ❑ G-435 [M] | Mainstream Jazz Swing | 1957 | 40.00 |

BRIGHT ORANGE

| Number | Title (A Side/B Side) | Yr | NM |
|---|---|---|---|
| ❑ XBO-702 | Count Basie Featuring B.B. King | 196? | 20.00 |

BRUNSWICK

| Number | Title (A Side/B Side) | Yr | NM |
|---|---|---|---|
| ❑ BL 54012 [M] | Count Basie | 1957 | 40.00 |
| ❑ BL 58019 [10] | Basie's Best | 195? | 100.00 |

CLEF

| Number | Title (A Side/B Side) | Yr | NM |
|---|---|---|---|
| ❑ MCG-120 [10] | Count Basie and His Orchestra Collates | 1953 | 250.00 |
| ❑ MCG-146 [10] | Count Basie Sextet | 1954 | 250.00 |
| ❑ MGC-148 [10] | Count Basie Big Band | 1954 | 250.00 |
| ❑ MGC-626 [M] | Count Basie Dance Session #1 | 1954 | 100.00 |
| ❑ MGC-633 [M] | Basie Jazz | 1954 | 100.00 |
| ❑ MGC-647 [M] | Count Basie Jazz Session #2 | 1955 | 100.00 |
| ❑ MGC-666 [M] | Basie | 1955 | 100.00 |
| ❑ MGC-685 [M] | The Count | 1956 | 80.00 |
| ❑ MGC-706 [M] | The Swinging Count | 1956 | 60.00 |
| ❑ MGC-722 [M] | The Band of Distinction | 1956 | 60.00 |
| ❑ MGC-723 [M] | Basie Roars Again | 1956 | 60.00 |
| ❑ MGC-724 [M] | The King of Swing | 1956 | 60.00 |
| ❑ MGC-729 [M] | Basie Rides Again! | 1956 | 60.00 |

COLUMBIA

| Number | Title (A Side/B Side) | Yr | NM |
|---|---|---|---|
| ❑ CL 754 [M] | Classics | 1955 | 60.00 |
| ❑ CL 901 [M] | Blues By Basie | 1956 | 40.00 |
| ❑ CL 997 [M] | One O'Clock Jump | 1956 | 40.00 |
| ❑ CL 2560 [10] | Basie Bash | 1956 | 80.00 |
| ❑ CL 6079 [10] | Dance Parade | 1949 | 100.00 |

COMMAND

| Number | Title (A Side/B Side) | Yr | NM |
|---|---|---|---|
| ❑ CQ-40004 [Q] | Broadway Basie's…Way | 1972 | 20.00 |

DECCA

| Number | Title (A Side/B Side) | Yr | NM |
|---|---|---|---|
| ❑ DXB 170 [(2)M] | The Best of Count Basie | 196? | 25.00 |
| ❑ DL 5111 [10] | Count Basie at the Piano | 1950 | 120.00 |
| ❑ DL 8049 [M] | Count Basie and His Orchestra | 1954 | 50.00 |

EMARCY

| Number | Title (A Side/B Side) | Yr | NM |
|---|---|---|---|
| ❑ MG-26023 [10] | Jazz Royalty | 1954 | 70.00 |

EMUS

| Number | Title (A Side/B Side) | Yr | NM |
|---|---|---|---|
| ❑ ES12011 | Basie at Birdland | 197? | 10.00 |

EPIC

| Number | Title (A Side/B Side) | Yr | NM |
|---|---|---|---|
| ❑ LG 1021 [10] | The Old Count and the New Count — Basie | 1954 | 70.00 |
| ❑ LN 1117 [10] | Rock the Blues | 1955 | 70.00 |
| ❑ LN 3107 [M] | Lester Leaps In | 1955 | 50.00 |

*—With Lester Young*

| Number | Title (A Side/B Side) | Yr | NM |
|---|---|---|---|
| ❑ LN 3168 [M] | Let's Go to Prez | 1955 | 50.00 |

*—With Lester Young*

| Number | Title (A Side/B Side) | Yr | NM |
|---|---|---|---|
| ❑ LN 3169 [M] | Basie's Back in Town | 1955 | 50.00 |

HAPPY TIGER

| Number | Title (A Side/B Side) | Yr | NM |
|---|---|---|---|
| ❑ 1007 | Basie on the Beatles | 196? | 25.00 |

IMPULSE!

| Number | Title (A Side/B Side) | Yr | NM |
|---|---|---|---|
| ❑ A-15 [M] | Count Basie and the Kansas City Seven | 1962 | 30.00 |
| ❑ AS-15 [S] | Count Basie and the Kansas City Seven | 1962 | 40.00 |

JAZZ PANORAMA

| Number | Title (A Side/B Side) | Yr | NM |
|---|---|---|---|
| ❑ 1803 [10] | Count Basie and Lester Young | 1951 | 100.00 |

MERCURY

| Number | Title (A Side/B Side) | Yr | NM |
|---|---|---|---|
| ❑ MGC-120 [10] | Count Basie and His Orchestra Collates | 1952 | 220.00 |
| ❑ MG-25105 [10] | Count Basie and His Kansas City Seven | 1952 | 100.00 |

MOBILE FIDELITY

| Number | Title (A Side/B Side) | Yr | NM |
|---|---|---|---|
| ❑ 1-129 | Basie Plays Hefti | 1985 | 80.00 |

*—Audiophile vinyl*

| Number | Title (A Side/B Side) | Yr | NM |
|---|---|---|---|
| ❑ 1-237 | April in Paris | 1995 | 40.00 |

*—Audiophile vinyl*

MOSAIC

| Number | Title (A Side/B Side) | Yr | NM |
|---|---|---|---|
| ❑ MR12-135 [(12)] | The Complete Roulette Live Recordings of Count Basie and His Orchestra | 199? | 200.00 |
| ❑ MQ15-149 [(15)] | The Complete Roulette Studio Recordings of Count Basie and His Orchestra | 199? | 250.00 |

RCA CAMDEN

| Number | Title (A Side/B Side) | Yr | NM |
|---|---|---|---|
| ❑ CAL-395 [M] | The Count | 1958 | 25.00 |
| ❑ CAL-497 [M] | Basie's Basement | 1959 | 25.00 |
| ❑ CAL-514 [M] | Count Basie in Kansas City | 1959 | 25.00 |

RCA VICTOR

| Number | Title (A Side/B Side) | Yr | NM |
|---|---|---|---|
| ❑ LPM-1112 [M] | Count Basie | 1955 | 50.00 |

REPRISE

| Number | Title (A Side/B Side) | Yr | NM |
|---|---|---|---|
| ❑ R-6070 [M] | This Time by Basie! Hits of the 50's and 60's | 1963 | 20.00 |
| ❑ R9-6070 [S] | This Time by Basie! Hits of the 50's and 60's | 1963 | 25.00 |
| ❑ RS-6153 [S] | Pop Goes the Basie | 1965 | 20.00 |

ROULETTE

| Number | Title (A Side/B Side) | Yr | NM |
|---|---|---|---|
| ❑ RB-1 [(2)M] | The Count Basie Story | 1960 | 40.00 |
| ❑ SRB-1 [(2)S] | The Count Basie Story | 1960 | 50.00 |
| ❑ R 52003 [M] | Basie | 1958 | 50.00 |

*—White label with colored "spokes"*

| Number | Title (A Side/B Side) | Yr | NM |
|---|---|---|---|
| ❑ R 52003 [M] | Basie | 1964 | 30.00 |

*—Orange and yellow "roulette wheel" label*

| Number | Title (A Side/B Side) | Yr | NM |
|---|---|---|---|
| ❑ R 52003 [M] | Basie | 2003 | 30.00 |

*—200-gram vinyl reissue; distributed by Classic Records*

| Number | Title (A Side/B Side) | Yr | NM |
|---|---|---|---|
| ❑ SR 52003 [S] | Basie | 1958 | 60.00 |

*—Black vinyl; white label with colored "spokes"*

| Number | Title (A Side/B Side) | Yr | NM |
|---|---|---|---|
| ❑ SR 52003 [S] | Basie | 1958 | 150.00 |

*—Red vinyl; white label with colored "spokes"*

| Number | Title (A Side/B Side) | Yr | NM |
|---|---|---|---|
| ❑ SR 52003 [S] | Basie | 1964 | 40.00 |

*—Orange and yellow "roulette wheel" label*

| Number | Title (A Side/B Side) | Yr | NM |
|---|---|---|---|
| ❑ R 52011 [M] | Basie Plays Hefti | 1958 | 30.00 |
| ❑ SR 52011 [S] | Basie Plays Hefti | 1958 | 30.00 |
| ❑ R 52024 [M] | One More Time | 1959 | 30.00 |
| ❑ SR 52024 [S] | One More Time | 1959 | 30.00 |
| ❑ R 52028 [M] | Breakfast, Dance & Barbeque | 1959 | 30.00 |
| ❑ SR 52028 [S] | Breakfast, Dance & Barbeque | 1959 | 30.00 |
| ❑ R 52032 [M] | Chairman of the Board | 1959 | 30.00 |
| ❑ SR 52032 [S] | Chairman of the Board | 1959 | 30.00 |
| ❑ R 52036 [M] | Dance Along with Basie | 1959 | 30.00 |
| ❑ SR 52036 [S] | Dance Along with Basie | 1959 | 30.00 |
| ❑ R 52044 [M] | Not Now — I'll Tell You When | 1960 | 25.00 |
| ❑ SR 52044 [S] | Not Now — I'll Tell You When | 1960 | 30.00 |
| ❑ R 52051 [M] | String Along with Basie | 1960 | 25.00 |
| ❑ SR 52051 [S] | String Along with Basie | 1960 | 30.00 |
| ❑ R 52056 [M] | Benny Carter's Kansas City Suite | 1960 | 25.00 |
| ❑ SR 52056 [S] | Benny Carter's Kansas City Suite | 1960 | 30.00 |
| ❑ R 52065 [M] | Basie at Birdland | 1961 | 25.00 |
| ❑ SR 52065 [S] | Basie at Birdland | 1961 | 30.00 |
| ❑ SR 52081 [S] | The Best of Basie | 1962 | 20.00 |
| ❑ R 52086 [M] | The Legend | 1962 | 20.00 |
| ❑ SR 52086 [S] | The Legend | 1962 | 25.00 |
| ❑ SR 52089 [S] | The Best of Basie, Volume 2 | 1962 | 20.00 |
| ❑ R 52099 [M] | Count Basie in Sweden | 1963 | 20.00 |
| ❑ SR 52099 [S] | Count Basie in Sweden | 1963 | 25.00 |
| ❑ R 52106 [M] | Easin' It | 1963 | 20.00 |
| ❑ SR 52106 [S] | Easin' It | 1963 | 25.00 |
| ❑ R 52111/3 [(2)M] | The World of Count Basie | 1964 | 40.00 |
| ❑ SR 52111/3 [(2)S] | The World of Count Basie | 1964 | 50.00 |
| ❑ R 52113 [M] | Back with Basie | 1964 | 20.00 |
| ❑ SR 52113 [S] | Back with Basie | 1964 | 25.00 |

UNITED ARTISTS

| Number | Title (A Side/B Side) | Yr | NM |
|---|---|---|---|
| ❑ UAL-3480 [M] | Basie Meets Bond | 1966 | 25.00 |
| ❑ UAS-6480 [S] | Basie Meets Bond | 1966 | 30.00 |

VERVE

| Number | Title (A Side/B Side) | Yr | NM |
|---|---|---|---|
| ❑ VSPS-12 [S] | Inside Basie, Outside | 1966 | 20.00 |
| ❑ MGVS-6024 [S] | Count Basie at Newport | 1960 | 50.00 |
| ❑ MGV-8012 [M] | April in Paris | 1957 | 50.00 |
| ❑ V-8012 [M] | April in Paris | 1961 | 20.00 |
| ❑ MGV-8018 [M] | Basie Roars Again | 1957 | 50.00 |

*—Reissue of Clef 723*

| Number | Title (A Side/B Side) | Yr | NM |
|---|---|---|---|
| ❑ V-8018 [M] | Basie Roars Again | 1961 | 20.00 |
| ❑ MGV-8070 [M] | The Count | 1957 | 50.00 |

*—Reissue of Clef 120*

| Number | Title (A Side/B Side) | Yr | NM |
|---|---|---|---|
| ❑ V-8070 [M] | The Count | 1961 | 20.00 |
| ❑ MGV-8090 [M] | The Swinging Count! | 1957 | 50.00 |

*—Reissue of Clef 706*

| Number | Title (A Side/B Side) | Yr | NM |
|---|---|---|---|
| ❑ V-8090 [M] | The Swinging Count! | 1961 | 20.00 |
| ❑ MGV-8103 [M] | The Band of Distinction | 1957 | 50.00 |

*—Reissue of Clef 722*

| Number | Title (A Side/B Side) | Yr | NM |
|---|---|---|---|
| ❑ V-8103 [M] | The Band of Distinction | 1961 | 20.00 |
| ❑ MGV-8104 [M] | The King of Swing | 1957 | 50.00 |

*—Reissue of Clef 724*

| Number | Title (A Side/B Side) | Yr | NM |
|---|---|---|---|
| ❑ V-8104 [M] | The King of Swing | 1961 | 20.00 |
| ❑ MGV-8108 [M] | Basie Rides Again! | 1957 | 50.00 |

*—Reissue of Clef 729*

| Number | Title (A Side/B Side) | Yr | NM |
|---|---|---|---|
| ❑ V-8108 [M] | Basie Rides Again! | 1961 | 20.00 |
| ❑ MGV-8199 [M] | Basie in London | 1957 | 50.00 |
| ❑ V-8199 [M] | Basie in London | 1961 | 20.00 |
| ❑ MGV-8243 [M] | Count Basie at Newport | 1958 | 50.00 |
| ❑ V-8243 [M] | Count Basie at Newport | 1961 | 20.00 |
| ❑ V6-8243 [S] | Count Basie at Newport | 1961 | 20.00 |
| ❑ MGV-8291 [M] | Hall of Fame | 1958 | 50.00 |
| ❑ V-8291 [M] | Hall of Fame | 1961 | 20.00 |
| ❑ V6-8407 [S] | The Essential Count Basie | 1961 | 20.00 |
| ❑ V6-8511 [S] | On My Way and Shoutin' Again! | 1963 | 20.00 |
| ❑ V6-8549 [S] | Li'l Ol' Groovemaker…Basie! | 1963 | 25.00 |
| ❑ V6-8563 [S] | More Hits of the 50's and 60's | 1963 | 25.00 |
| ❑ V6-8596 [S] | Verve's Choice — Best of Count Basie | 1964 | 20.00 |
| ❑ V6-8597 [S] | Basie Land | 1964 | 20.00 |
| ❑ V6-8616 [S] | Basie Picks the Winners | 1965 | 20.00 |
| ❑ V-8659 [M] | Basie's Beatle Bag | 1966 | 30.00 |
| ❑ V6-8659 [S] | Basie's Beatle Bag | 1966 | 40.00 |
| ❑ V-8687 [M] | Basie's Beat | 1967 | 20.00 |

**BASIE, COUNT, AND SAMMY DAVIS, JR.**

VERVE

| Number | Title (A Side/B Side) | Yr | NM |
|---|---|---|---|
| ❑ V6-8605 [S] | Our Shining Hour | 1965 | 20.00 |

**BASIE, COUNT, AND BILLY ECKSTINE**

ROULETTE

| Number | Title (A Side/B Side) | Yr | NM |
|---|---|---|---|
| ❑ R 52029 [M] | Basie/Eckstine, Incorporated | 1959 | 30.00 |
| ❑ SR 52029 [S] | Basie/Eckstine, Incorporated | 1959 | 40.00 |

### BASIE, COUNT, AND MAYNARD FERGUSON

**ROULETTE**

| Number | Title (A Side/B Side) | Yr | NM |
|---|---|---|---|
| ❑ R 52117 [M] | Big Band Scene '65 | 1965 | 20.00 |
| ❑ SR 52117 [S] | Big Band Scene '65 | 1965 | 25.00 |

### BASIE, COUNT, AND DIZZY GILLESPIE

**VERVE**

| Number | Title (A Side/B Side) | Yr | NM |
|---|---|---|---|
| ❑ V-8560 [M] | The Count Basie Band and the Dizzy Gillespie Band at Newport | 1963 | 20.00 |
| ❑ V6-8560 [S] | The Count Basie Band and the Dizzy Gillespie Band at Newport | 1963 | 25.00 |

### BASIE, COUNT, AND JOE WILLIAMS

**CLEF**

| Number | Title (A Side/B Side) | Yr | NM |
|---|---|---|---|
| ❑ MGC-678 [M] | Count Basie Swings/Joe Williams Sings | 1955 | 50.00 |

**ROULETTE**

| Number | Title (A Side/B Side) | Yr | NM |
|---|---|---|---|
| ❑ R 52021 [M] | Memories Ad Lib | 1959 | 30.00 |
| ❑ SR 52021 [S] | Memories Ad Lib | 1959 | 40.00 |
| ❑ R 52033 [M] | Everyday I Have the Blues | 1959 | 30.00 |
| ❑ SR 52033 [S] | Everyday I Have the Blues | 1959 | 40.00 |
| ❑ R 52054 [M] | Just the Blues | 1960 | 30.00 |
| ❑ SR 52054 [S] | Just the Blues | 1960 | 40.00 |
| ❑ R 52093 [M] | Back to Basie and Blues | 1963 | 25.00 |
| ❑ SR 52093 [S] | Back to Basie and Blues | 1963 | 30.00 |

**VANGUARD**

| Number | Title (A Side/B Side) | Yr | NM |
|---|---|---|---|
| ❑ VRS-8508 [M] | A Night at Count Basie's | 1955 | 50.00 |

**VERVE**

| Number | Title (A Side/B Side) | Yr | NM |
|---|---|---|---|
| ❑ MGV-2016 [M] | The Greatest! Count Basie Swings/Joe Williams Sings Standards | 1956 | 50.00 |
| ❑ MGVS-6006 [S] | The Greatest! Count Basie Swings/Joe Williams Sings Standards | 1960 | 40.00 |
| ❑ MGV-8063 [M] | Count Basie Swings/Joe Williams Sings | 1957 | 40.00 |
| *—Reissue of Clef 678* | | | |
| ❑ V-8488 [M] | Count Basie Swings/Joe Williams Sings | 1962 | 25.00 |
| *—Reissue of 8063* | | | |

### BASIE, COUNT; JOE WILLIAMS; LAMBERT, HENDRICKS AND ROSS

**ROULETTE**

| Number | Title (A Side/B Side) | Yr | NM |
|---|---|---|---|
| ❑ R 52018 [M] | Sing Along with Basie | 1959 | 20.00 |
| ❑ SR 52018 [S] | Sing Along with Basie | 1959 | 25.00 |

### BASIN STREET SIX, THE

**CIRCLE**

| Number | Title (A Side/B Side) | Yr | NM |
|---|---|---|---|
| ❑ L-403 [10] | Dixieland from New Orleans | 1951 | 50.00 |

**EMARCY**

| Number | Title (A Side/B Side) | Yr | NM |
|---|---|---|---|
| ❑ MG-26012 [10] | The Basin Street Six | 1954 | 50.00 |

**MERCURY**

| Number | Title (A Side/B Side) | Yr | NM |
|---|---|---|---|
| ❑ MG-20151 [M] | Strictly Dixie | 195? | 40.00 |
| ❑ MG-25111 [10] | The Basin Street Six | 1951 | 50.00 |

### BASKERVILLE HOUNDS, THE

**DOT**

| Number | Title (A Side/B Side) | Yr | NM |
|---|---|---|---|
| ❑ DLP-3823 [M] | The Baskerville Hounds (Featuring Space Rock, Part 2) | 1967 | 150.00 |
| ❑ DLP-25823 [S] | The Baskerville Hounds (Featuring Space Rock, Part 2) | 1967 | 200.00 |

### BASS, FONTELLA

**CHECKER**

| Number | Title (A Side/B Side) | Yr | NM |
|---|---|---|---|
| ❑ LP-2997 [M] | The "New" Look | 1966 | 60.00 |
| *—Blue label with red and black checkers* | | | |
| ❑ LP-2997 [M] | The "New" Look | 1967 | 30.00 |
| *—Blue and white label* | | | |
| ❑ LPS-2997 [S] | The "New" Look | 1966 | 80.00 |
| *—Blue label with red and black checkers* | | | |
| ❑ LPS-2997 [S] | The "New" Look | 1967 | 40.00 |
| *—Blue and white label* | | | |

**PAULA**

| Number | Title (A Side/B Side) | Yr | NM |
|---|---|---|---|
| ❑ LPS-2203 | Free | 1971 | 12.00 |

### BASSEY, SHIRLEY

**APPLAUSE**

| Number | Title (A Side/B Side) | Yr | NM |
|---|---|---|---|
| ❑ APLP 1005 | Shirley Bassey | 1982 | 10.00 |

**EPIC**

| Number | Title (A Side/B Side) | Yr | NM |
|---|---|---|---|
| ❑ LN 3834 [M] | The Bewitching Shirley Bassey | 1962 | 20.00 |

**LIBERTY**

| Number | Title (A Side/B Side) | Yr | NM |
|---|---|---|---|
| ❑ LWB-111 [(2)] | Live at Carnegie Hall | 198? | 10.00 |
| ❑ LWB-715 [(2)] | Greatest Hits | 198? | 10.00 |
| ❑ LW-847 | Yesterdays | 198? | 8.00 |
| ❑ LM-1013 | Something Else | 198? | 8.00 |
| ❑ LN-10012 | The Magic Is You | 1980 | 8.00 |
| ❑ LN-10104 | The Best of Shirley Bassey | 1980 | 8.00 |
| ❑ LN-10180 | I, Capricorn | 198? | 8.00 |
| ❑ LN-10252 | Greatest Hits | 198? | 8.00 |
| ❑ LN-10262 | Shirley Means Bassey | 198? | 8.00 |

**MERCURY**

| Number | Title (A Side/B Side) | Yr | NM |
|---|---|---|---|
| ❑ 838033-1 | La Mujer | 1989 | 12.00 |

**MGM**

| Number | Title (A Side/B Side) | Yr | NM |
|---|---|---|---|
| ❑ E-3862 [M] | The Fabulous Shirley Bassey | 1960 | 20.00 |
| ❑ SE-3862 [S] | The Fabulous Shirley Bassey | 1960 | 25.00 |
| ❑ E-4301 [M] | Golden Sound | 1965 | 12.00 |
| ❑ SE-4301 [S] | Golden Sound | 1965 | 15.00 |

**PAIR**

| Number | Title (A Side/B Side) | Yr | NM |
|---|---|---|---|
| ❑ PDL2-1057 [(2)] | Sassy Bassey | 1986 | 12.00 |

**PHILIPS**

| Number | Title (A Side/B Side) | Yr | NM |
|---|---|---|---|
| ❑ PHM 200168 [M] | Spectacular Shirley Bassey | 1965 | 12.00 |
| ❑ PHS 600168 [S] | Spectacular Shirley Bassey | 1965 | 15.00 |

**PICKWICK**

| Number | Title (A Side/B Side) | Yr | NM |
|---|---|---|---|
| ❑ SPC-3303 | How About You | 197? | 10.00 |

**SPRINGBOARD**

| Number | Title (A Side/B Side) | Yr | NM |
|---|---|---|---|
| ❑ SPB-4045 | This Is My Life | 197? | 8.00 |

**UNITED ARTISTS**

| Number | Title (A Side/B Side) | Yr | NM |
|---|---|---|---|
| ❑ UA-LA055-F | Never, Never, Never | 1973 | 10.00 |
| ❑ UA-LA111-H2 [(2)] | Live at Carnegie Hall | 1973 | 15.00 |
| ❑ UA-LA214-G | Nobody Does It Like Me | 1974 | 10.00 |
| ❑ UA-LA542-G | Good, Bad But Beautiful | 1975 | 10.00 |
| ❑ UA-LA605-G | Love, Life and Feelings | 1976 | 10.00 |
| ❑ UA-LA715-H2 [(2)] | Greatest Hits | 1976 | 15.00 |
| ❑ UA-LA751-H | You Take My Heart Away | 1977 | 10.00 |
| ❑ UA-LA847-H | Yesterdays | 1977 | 10.00 |
| ❑ UA-LA926-H | The Magic Is You | 1978 | 10.00 |
| ❑ LM-1013 | Something Else | 1979 | 10.00 |
| ❑ UAL 3169 [M] | Shirley Bassey | 1962 | 15.00 |
| ❑ UAL 3237 [M] | Shirley Bassey Sings the Hits from "Oliver" | 1962 | 15.00 |
| ❑ UAL 3419 [M] | Shirley Bassey Belts the Best | 1965 | 12.00 |
| ❑ UAL 3463 [M] | In Person | 1965 | 12.00 |
| ❑ UAL 3545 [M] | Shirley Means Bassey | 1966 | 12.00 |
| ❑ UAL 3565 [M] | And We Were Lovers | 1967 | 12.00 |
| ❑ UAS 5565 | I, Capricorn | 1971 | 10.00 |
| ❑ UAS 5643 | And I Love You So | 1972 | 10.00 |
| ❑ UAS 6169 [S] | Shirley Bassey | 1962 | 20.00 |
| ❑ UAS 6237 [S] | Shirley Bassey Sings the Hits from "Oliver" | 1962 | 20.00 |
| ❑ UAS 6419 [S] | Shirley Bassey Belts the Best | 1965 | 15.00 |
| ❑ UAS 6463 [S] | In Person | 1965 | 15.00 |
| ❑ UAS 6545 [S] | Shirley Means Bassey | 1966 | 15.00 |
| ❑ UAS 6565 [S] | And We Were Lovers | 1967 | 15.00 |
| ❑ UAS 6675 | This Is My Life | 1969 | 12.00 |
| ❑ UAS 6713 | Does Anybody Miss Me? | 1969 | 12.00 |
| ❑ UAS 6765 | Shirley Bassey Is Really "Something" | 1970 | 10.00 |
| ❑ UAS 6797 | Something Else | 1971 | 10.00 |

### BASSO-VALDAMBRINI OCTET, THE

**VERVE**

| Number | Title (A Side/B Side) | Yr | NM |
|---|---|---|---|
| ❑ MGVS-6152 [S] | The New Sound from Italy | 1960 | 40.00 |
| ❑ MGV-20009 [M] | Jazz Festival, Milan | 1960 | 40.00 |
| ❑ V-20009 [M] | Jazz Festival, Milan | 1961 | 20.00 |
| ❑ MGV-20011 [M] | The New Sound from Italy | 1960 | 40.00 |
| ❑ V-20011 [M] | The New Sound from Italy | 1961 | 20.00 |
| ❑ V6-20011 [S] | The New Sound from Italy | 1961 | 20.00 |

### BASTARDS, THE

**TREEHOUSE**

| Number | Title (A Side/B Side) | Yr | NM |
|---|---|---|---|
| ❑ 016 | Monticallo | 1989 | 12.00 |

### BATTERED ORNAMENTS

**HARVEST**

| Number | Title (A Side/B Side) | Yr | NM |
|---|---|---|---|
| ❑ SKAO-422 | Mantle-Piece | 1970 | 40.00 |

### BAUDUC, RAY, AND NAPPY LAMARE

**CAPITOL**

| Number | Title (A Side/B Side) | Yr | NM |
|---|---|---|---|
| ❑ T 877 [M] | Riverboat Dandies | 1957 | 40.00 |

**MERCURY**

| Number | Title (A Side/B Side) | Yr | NM |
|---|---|---|---|
| ❑ MG-(# unknown) [M] | On a Swinging Date | 1960 | 30.00 |
| ❑ SR-60186 [S] | On a Swinging Date | 1960 | 25.00 |

### BAUER, BILLY

**AD LIB**

| Number | Title (A Side/B Side) | Yr | NM |
|---|---|---|---|
| ❑ AAL-5501 [10] | Let's Have a Session | 1955 | 200.00 |

**NORGRAN**

| Number | Title (A Side/B Side) | Yr | NM |
|---|---|---|---|
| ❑ MGN-1082 [M] | Billy Bauer Plectrist | 1956 | 80.00 |

**VERVE**

| Number | Title (A Side/B Side) | Yr | NM |
|---|---|---|---|
| ❑ MGV-8172 [M] | Billy Bauer Plectrist | 1957 | 50.00 |
| ❑ V-8172 [M] | Billy Bauer Plectrist | 1961 | 20.00 |

### BAUGH, PHIL

**ERA**

| Number | Title (A Side/B Side) | Yr | NM |
|---|---|---|---|
| ❑ ES-801 | California Guitar | 1969 | 25.00 |

**LONGHORN**

| Number | Title (A Side/B Side) | Yr | NM |
|---|---|---|---|
| ❑ LP-02 [M] | Country Guitar | 1965 | 50.00 |

**TORO**

| Number | Title (A Side/B Side) | Yr | NM |
|---|---|---|---|
| ❑ T-502 [M] | Country Guitar II | 1965 | 40.00 |

### BAUHAUS

**A&M**

| Number | Title (A Side/B Side) | Yr | NM |
|---|---|---|---|
| ❑ SP 4918 | The Sky's Gone Out | 1982 | 20.00 |
| ❑ SP-4953 | Burning from the Inside | 1983 | 20.00 |

**BEGGARS BANQUET**

| Number | Title (A Side/B Side) | Yr | NM |
|---|---|---|---|
| ❑ 9804-1-H [(2)] | Swing the Heartache/The BBC Sessions | 1989 | 20.00 |

### BAXTER

**PARAMOUNT**

| Number | Title (A Side/B Side) | Yr | NM |
|---|---|---|---|
| ❑ PAS-6050 | Baxter | 1973 | 20.00 |

### BAXTER, DUKE

**VMC**

| Number | Title (A Side/B Side) | Yr | NM |
|---|---|---|---|
| ❑ VS-138 | Everybody Knows Matilda | 1969 | 20.00 |

### BAXTER, LES

**CAPITOL**

| Number | Title (A Side/B Side) | Yr | NM |
|---|---|---|---|
| ❑ H (# unknown) [10] | Music for Peace of Mind | 1953 | 80.00 |
| ❑ DT 288 [R] | Ritual of the Savage (Le Sacre Du Sauvage) | 196? | 12.00 |
| ❑ H 288 [10] | Le Sacre Du Sauvage | 1952 | 80.00 |
| ❑ T 288 [M] | Le Sacre Du Sauvage | 1954 | 40.00 |
| ❑ T 390 [M] | Music Out of the Moon/Music for Peace of Mind | 1954 | 40.00 |
| ❑ H 474 [10] | Thinking of You | 1954 | 50.00 |
| ❑ T 474 [M] | Thinking of You | 1954 | 40.00 |
| ❑ LAL 486 [M] | The Passions | 1954 | 40.00 |
| ❑ T 594 [M] | Kaleidoscope | 1955 | 40.00 |
| ❑ T 655 [M] | Tamboo! | 1955 | 40.00 |
| ❑ T 733 [M] | Caribbean Moonlight | 1956 | 40.00 |
| ❑ T 774 [M] | Skins! | 1957 | 40.00 |
| ❑ T 780 [M] | 'Round the World | 1957 | 40.00 |
| ❑ T 843 [M] | Midnight on the Cliffs | 1957 | 40.00 |
| ❑ T 868 [M] | Ports of Pleasure | 1957 | 40.00 |
| ❑ T 968 [M] | Space Escapade | 1958 | 40.00 |
| ❑ T 1012 [M] | Selections from "South Pacific" | 1958 | 40.00 |
| ❑ T 1088 [M] | Love Is a Fabulous Thing | 1958 | 40.00 |
| ❑ T 1117 [M] | African Jazz | 1958 | 40.00 |
| ❑ DT 1388 [R] | Baxter's Best | 1960 | 15.00 |
| ❑ SM-1388 | Baxter's Best | 197? | 8.00 |
| ❑ T 1388 [M] | Baxter's Best | 1960 | 30.00 |
| ❑ ST 1537 [S] | Jewels of the Sea | 1961 | 30.00 |
| ❑ T 1537 [M] | Jewels of the Sea | 1961 | 25.00 |
| ❑ ST 1661 [S] | The Sensational Les Baxter | 1962 | 30.00 |
| ❑ T 1661 [M] | The Sensational Les Baxter | 1962 | 25.00 |
| ❑ ST 1846 [S] | The Original Quiet Village | 1963 | 25.00 |
| ❑ T 1846 [M] | The Original Quiet Village | 1963 | 20.00 |
| ❑ H 2000 [10] | Music Out of the Moon | 1953 | 80.00 |
| ❑ T 10015 [M] | La Femme | 1956 | 40.00 |
| ❑ M-11702 | Ritual of the Savage | 1977 | 10.00 |
| ❑ SQBO-90984 [(2)] | The Sounds of Adventure | 1967 | 30.00 |
| *—Capitol Record Club exclusive* | | | |

**GNP CRESCENDO**

| Number | Title (A Side/B Side) | Yr | NM |
|---|---|---|---|
| ❑ GNP-2036 [M] | Brazil Now | 1967 | 15.00 |
| ❑ GNPS-2036 [S] | Brazil Now | 1967 | 12.00 |
| ❑ GNPS-2042 | Love Is Blue | 1968 | 12.00 |
| ❑ GNPS-2047 | Aftrican Blue | 1969 | 12.00 |
| ❑ GNPS-2053 | Moon Rock | 1969 | 12.00 |

**PICKWICK**

| Number | Title (A Side/B Side) | Yr | NM |
|---|---|---|---|
| ❑ PC-3011 [M] | The Fabulous Sounds of Les Baxter | 196? | 15.00 |
| ❑ SPC-3011 [S] | The Fabulous Sounds of Les Baxter | 196? | 15.00 |
| ❑ PC-3048 [M] | I Could Have Danced All Night | 196? | 15.00 |
| ❑ SPC-3048 [S] | I Could Have Danced All Night | 196? | 12.00 |

**REPRISE**

| Number | Title (A Side/B Side) | Yr | NM |
|---|---|---|---|
| ❑ R-6036 [M] | Voices in Rhythm | 1961 | 15.00 |
| ❑ R9-6036 [S] | Voices in Rhythm | 1961 | 20.00 |
| ❑ R-6048 [M] | The Primitive and the Passionate | 1962 | 15.00 |
| ❑ R9-6049 [S] | The Primitive and the Passionate | 1962 | 20.00 |
| ❑ R-6079 [M] | Academy Award Winners '63 | 1963 | 15.00 |
| ❑ R9-6079 [S] | Academy Award Winners '63 | 1963 | 20.00 |
| ❑ R-6100 [M] | The Soul of the Drums | 1963 | 15.00 |
| ❑ R9-6100 [S] | The Soul of the Drums | 1963 | 20.00 |

### BAY CITY JAZZ BAND, THE

**GOOD TIME JAZZ**

| Number | Title (A Side/B Side) | Yr | NM |
|---|---|---|---|
| ❑ L-12017 [M] | The Bay City Jazz Band | 1955 | 30.00 |

### BAYETE

**PRESTIGE**

| Number | Title (A Side/B Side) | Yr | NM |
|---|---|---|---|
| ❑ 10045 | Worlds Around the Sun | 1972 | 30.00 |
| ❑ 10062 | Seeking Other Beauty | 1973 | 30.00 |

### BAYSIDERS, THE

**EVEREST**

| Number | Title (A Side/B Side) | Yr | NM |
|---|---|---|---|
| ❑ BRST-1124 [S] | Over the Rainbow | 1961 | 300.00 |
| ❑ LPBR-5124 [M] | Over the Rainbow | 1961 | 200.00 |

### BBC SYMPHONY ORCHESTRA (ANTAL DORATI, CONDUCTOR)

**MERCURY LIVING PRESENCE**

| Number | Title (A Side/B Side) | Yr | NM |
|---|---|---|---|
| ❑ SR 90416 [S] | Bartok: The Miraculous Mandarin | 196? | 25.00 |
| *—Maroon label, with "Vendor: Mercury Record Corporation"* | | | |
| ❑ SR 90416 [S] | Bartok: The Miraculous Mandarin | 196? | 50.00 |
| *—Maroon label, no "Vendor: Mercury Record Corporation"* | | | |

The Beach Boys, *15 Big Ones,* Brother/Reprise MS 2251, 1976, $12.

| Number | Title (A Side/B Side) | Yr | NM |
|---|---|---|---|

## BE-BOP DELUXE

### CAPITOL

❑ SPRO-8486 [DJ]Sunburst Finish 1975 25.00
*—Specially banded version for radio*
❑ SN-16022 Sunburst Finish 1980 8.00
*—Reissue of Harvest 11478*
❑ SN-16023 Drastic Plastic 1980 8.00
*—Reissue of Harvest 11750*
❑ SN-16024 Futurama 1980 8.00
*—Reissue of Harvest 11432*
❑ SN-16025 Axe Victim 1980 8.00
*—Reissue of Harvest 11689*
❑ SN-16026 Modern Music 1980 8.00
*—Reissue of Harvest 11575*

### HARVEST

❑ SPRO-8531 [DJ]Be-Bop's Biggest 1978 30.00
*—Promo-only compilation*
❑ ST-11432 Futurama 1975 10.00
❑ ST-11478 Sunburst Finish 1975 10.00
❑ ST-11575 Modern Music 1976 10.00
❑ SKBB-11666 [(2)]Live! In the Air Age 1977 12.00
❑ SM-11689 Axe Victim 1977 10.00
*—Their first UK album; first US issue has "SM" prefix*
❑ SW-11750 Drastic Plastic 1978 10.00
❑ SKBO-11870 [(2)]The Best Of & The Rest Of Be-Bop Deluxe 1979 12.00

## BEACH BOYS, THE

Also see GLEN CAMPBELL; BRUCE JOHNSTON; MIKE LOVE; BRIAN WILSON; CARL WILSON, DENNIS WILSON.

### ASYLUM

❑ R 113793 Surf's Up 1972 150.00
*—RCA Record Club edition, pressed with wrong labels*

### BROTHER

❑ ST 9001 [R] Smiley Smile 1967 15.00
*—"Title for this album by Barry Turnbull" on back cover*
❑ ST 9001 [R] Smiley Smile 1967 20.00
*—No mention of Barry Turnbull on cover*
❑ T 9001 [M] Smiley Smile 1967 30.00
*—"Title for this album by Barry Turnbull" on back cover*
❑ T 9001 [M] Smiley Smile 1967 40.00
*—No mention of Barry Turnbull on cover*

### BROTHER/REPRISE

❑ 2MS 2083 [(2)] Carl and the Passions "So Tough"/Pet Sounds 1972 30.00

| Number | Title (A Side/B Side) | Yr | NM |
|---|---|---|---|

❑ 2MS 2083 [(2)DJ]Carl and the Passions "So Tough"/Pet Sounds 1972 50.00
*—White label promo*
❑ MS 2118 Holland 1973 15.00
*—Includes bonus stock-copy EP, "Mount Vernon and Fairway," in picture sleeve, taped to back cover*
❑ MS 2118 [DJ] Holland 1973 40.00
*—White label promo; includes bonus white-label promo EP, "Mount Vernon and Fairway," in picture sleeve, taped to back cover*
❑ MS 2118 [DJ] Holland 1973 500.00
*—Test pressing with "We Got Love," deleted from promos and stock copies*
❑ 2MS 2166 [(2)] Wild Honey & 20/20 1974 15.00
❑ 2MS 2167 [(2)] Friends & Smiley Smile 1974 15.00
❑ MS 2197 [M] Pet Sounds 1974 20.00
❑ MS 2223 Good Vibrations — Best of the Beach Boys 1975 12.00
❑ MS 2251 15 Big Ones 1976 12.00
❑ MSK 2258 Love You 1977 12.00
❑ MSK 2268 M.I.U. Album 1978 12.00
❑ MSK 2280 Good Vibrations — Best of the Beach Boys 1978 10.00
❑ RS-6382 Sunflower 1970 25.00
❑ RS-6382 [DJ] Sunflower 1970 50.00
*—White label promo*
❑ RS 6453 Surf's Up 1971 20.00
❑ RS 6453 [DJ] Surf's Up 1971 40.00
*—White label promo*
❑ 2RS 6484 [(2)] The Beach Boys In Concert 1973 20.00
❑ 2RS 6484 [(2)DJ]The Beach Boys In Concert 1973 40.00
*—White label promo*
❑ SKAO-93352 Sunflower 1970 200.00
*—Capitol Record Club edition*
❑ R 113793 Surf's Up 1972 25.00
*—RCA Record Club edition*
❑ R 130223 15 Big Ones 1976 15.00
*—RCA Record Club edition*
❑ R 223569 [(2)] The Beach Boys In Concert 1973 25.00
*—RCA Record Club edition*

### CAPITOL

❑ SKAO-133 20/20 1969 15.00
*—"Starline" label*
❑ SKAO-133 20/20 1969 20.00
*—Black label with colorband*
❑ SKAO-8-0133 20/20 1969 30.00
*—Capitol Record Club edition; black label*

| Number | Title (A Side/B Side) | Yr | NM |
|---|---|---|---|

❑ SKAO-8-0133 20/20 1970 40.00
*—Capitol Record Club edition; lime label*
❑ SWBB-253 [(2)]Close-Up 1969 30.00
*—Reissue of "Surfin' U.S.A." and "All Summer Long" in one package; black labels with colorband*
❑ SWBB-253 [(2)]Close-Up 1970 40.00
*—Lime labels*
❑ ST-442 Good Vibrations 1970 20.00
*—Lime label (original)*
❑ ST-442 Good Vibrations 1972 25.00
*—Red or orange label*
❑ ST-8-0442 Good Vibrations 1970 30.00
*—Capitol Record Club edition*
❑ STBB-500 [(2)] All Summer Long/California Girls 1970 20.00
*—Lime labels; "Special Double Play" pack; two separate LPs (abridged versions of "All Summer Long" and "Summer Days [And Summer Nights!!]") bound together*
❑ STBB-500 [(2)] All Summer Long/California Girls 1971 25.00
*—Red labels; "Special Double Play" pack; two separate LPs (abridged versions of "All Summer Long" and "Summer Days [And Summer Nights!!]") bound together*
❑ SF-501 All Summer Long 1970 10.00
*—Individual record from above set*
❑ SF-8-0501 All Summer Long 1971 10.00
*—Capitol Record Club edition*
❑ SF-502 California Girls 1970 10.00
*—Individual record from above set*
❑ SF-8-0502 California Girls 1971 10.00
*—Capitol Record Club edition*
❑ STBB-701 [(2)] Fun, Fun, Fun/Dance, Dance, Dance 1970 20.00
*—Lime labels; "Special Double Play" pack; two separate LPs (abridged versions of "Shut Down, Volume 2" and "The Beach Boys Today!") bound together*
❑ STBB-701 [(2)] Fun, Fun, Fun/Dance, Dance, Dance 1971 25.00
*—Red labels; "Special Double Play" pack; two separate LPs (abridged versions of "Shut Down, Volume 2" and "The Beach Boys Today!") bound together*
❑ SF-702 Fun, Fun, Fun 1971 10.00
*—Individual record from above set*
❑ SF-8-0702 Fun, Fun, Fun 1971 10.00
*—Capitol Record Club edition*
❑ SF-703 Dance, Dance, Dance 1971 10.00
*—Individual record from above set*
❑ SF-8-0703 Dance, Dance, Dance 1971 10.00
*—Capitol Record Club edition*
❑ DT 1808 [R] Surfin' Safari 1962 25.00
*—With only the "Duophonic" banner at top*
❑ DT 1808 [R] Surfin' Safari 1962 80.00
*—With "Capitol Full Dimensional Stereo" banner under the "Duophonic" banner*
❑ SM-1808 [R] Surfin' Safari 197? 10.00
❑ T 1808 [M] Surfin' Safari 1962 40.00
❑ SM-1890 [S] Surfin' U.S.A. 197? 10.00
❑ ST 1890 [S] Surfin' U.S.A. 1963 50.00
❑ T 1890 [M] Surfin' U.S.A. 1963 40.00
❑ SM-1981 [S] Surfer Girl 197? 10.00
❑ ST 1981 [S] Surfer Girl 1963 50.00
*—With reference to "their other new single record, 'Little Deuce Coupe'" in liner notes*
❑ ST 1981 [S] Surfer Girl 1963 50.00
*—With reference to The Four Freshmen in liner notes*
❑ T 1981 [M] Surfer Girl 1963 40.00
*—With reference to "their other new single record, 'Little Deuce Coupe'" in liner notes*
❑ T 1981 [M] Surfer Girl 1963 40.00
*—With reference to The Four Freshmen in liner notes*
❑ SM-1998 [S] Little Deuce Coupe 197? 10.00
❑ ST 1998 [S] Little Deuce Coupe 1963 40.00
❑ T 1998 [M] Little Deuce Coupe 1963 40.00
❑ ST 2027 [P] Shut Down, Volume 2 1964 40.00
❑ T 2027 [M] Shut Down, Volume 2 1964 40.00
❑ ST 2110 [S] All Summer Long 1964 30.00
*—With "Don't Back Down" correctly listed on front cover*
❑ ST 2110 [S] All Summer Long 1964 50.00
*—With "Don't Break Down" erroneously listed on front cover*
❑ T 2110 [M] All Summer Long 1964 30.00
*—With "Don't Back Down" correctly listed on front cover*
❑ T 2110 [M] All Summer Long 1964 50.00
*—With "Don't Break Down" erroneously listed on front cover*
❑ SM-2164 The Beach Boys' Christmas Album 197? 10.00
❑ ST 2164 [S] The Beach Boys' Christmas Album 1964 50.00
❑ T 2164 [M] The Beach Boys' Christmas Album 1964 50.00
❑ SM-2198 Beach Boys Concert 197? 10.00
❑ STAO 2198 [S] Beach Boys Concert 1964 30.00
*—With bound-in booklet*
❑ STAO-8-2198 [S]Beach Boys Concert 196? 80.00
*—Capitol Record Club edition*
❑ TAO 2198 [M] Beach Boys Concert 1964 30.00
*—With bound-in booklet*
❑ DT 2269 [R] The Beach Boys Today! 1965 25.00
❑ DT-8-2269 [R] The Beach Boys Today! 1965 80.00
*—Capitol Record Club edition*
❑ T 2269 [M] The Beach Boys Today! 1965 30.00
❑ DT 2354 [R] Summer Days (And Summer Nights!!) 1965 25.00
*—With "Duophonic" banner*

**Except when noted otherwise, VG = 25% of NM, and VG+ = 50% of NM. (Example: VG = $2.00, VG+ = $4.00 and NM = $8.00.)**

| Number | Title (A Side/B Side) | Yr | NM |
|---|---|---|---|
| ❑ DT 2354 [R] | Summer Days (And Summer Nights!!) | 1965 | 50.00 |
| *—With "New Improved Full Dimensional Stereo" banner* | | | |
| ❑ T 2354 [M] | Summer Days (And Summer Nights!!) | 1965 | 30.00 |
| ❑ DMAS 2398 [R] | Beach Boys Party! | 1965 | 25.00 |
| *—Without sheet of photos* | | | |
| ❑ DMAS 2398 [R] | Beach Boys Party! | 1965 | 30.00 |
| *—With sheet of photos* | | | |
| ❑ MAS 2398 [M] | Beach Boys Party! | 1965 | 30.00 |
| *—Without sheet of photos* | | | |
| ❑ MAS 2398 [M] | Beach Boys Party! | 1965 | 40.00 |
| *—With sheet of photos* | | | |
| ❑ DT 2458 [R] | Pet Sounds | 1966 | 30.00 |
| ❑ T 2458 [M] | Pet Sounds | 1966 | 40.00 |
| ❑ DT 2545 [P] | Best of the Beach Boys | 1966 | 12.00 |
| *—Black "The Star Line" label* | | | |
| ❑ DT 2545 [P] | Best of the Beach Boys | 1966 | 15.00 |
| *—Black label with colorband* | | | |
| ❑ DT 2545 [P] | Best of the Beach Boys | 1967 | 15.00 |
| *—Red and white "Starline" label* | | | |
| ❑ DT 2545 [P] | Best of the Beach Boys | 1970 | 12.00 |
| *—Green "Starline" label* | | | |
| ❑ DT 2545 [P] | Best of the Beach Boys | 1973 | 10.00 |
| *—Orange label, "Capitol" on bottom* | | | |
| ❑ DT 2545 [P] | Best of the Beach Boys | 1978 | 10.00 |
| *—Purple label, large Capitol logo* | | | |
| ❑ DT 2545 [P] | Best of the Beach Boys | 1983 | 10.00 |
| *—Black label, print in colorband* | | | |
| ❑ T 2545 [M] | Best of the Beach Boys | 1966 | 15.00 |
| *—Black "The Star Line" label* | | | |
| ❑ T 2545 [M] | Best of the Beach Boys | 1966 | 20.00 |
| *—Black label with colorband* | | | |
| ❑ T 2545 [M] | Best of the Beach Boys | 1967 | 30.00 |
| *—Red and white "Starline" label* | | | |
| ❑ T/DT 2580 | Smile Booklet | 1966 | 300.00 |
| *—Printed for insertion into unreleased "Smile" LP; counterfeits exist* | | | |
| ❑ T/DT 2580 | Smile | 1966 | 1000. |
| *—Unreleased; price is for cover slick, which has been counterfeited* | | | |
| ❑ DT 2706 [P] | Best of the Beach Boys, Vol. 2 | 1967 | 15.00 |
| *—Red and while "Starline" label* | | | |
| ❑ DT 2706 [P] | Best of the Beach Boys, Vol. 2 | 1970 | 12.00 |
| *—Green "Starline" label* | | | |
| ❑ DT 2706 [P] | Best of the Beach Boys, Vol. 2 | 1973 | 10.00 |
| *—Orange label, "Capitol" on bottom* | | | |
| ❑ DT 2706 [P] | Best of the Beach Boys, Vol. 2 | 1978 | 10.00 |
| *—Purple label, large Capitol logo* | | | |
| ❑ T 2706 [M] | Best of the Beach Boys, Vol. 2 | 1967 | 25.00 |
| ❑ DTCL 2813 [(3)R] | The Beach Boys Deluxe Set | 1967 | 50.00 |
| *—Maroon border on box; custom pressings of LPs with "DTCL" prefixes* | | | |
| ❑ DTCL-8-2813 [(3)R] | The Beach Boys Deluxe Set | 1967 | 150.00 |
| *—Capitol Record Club edition; blue border on box; custom pressings of LPs with "DTCL" prefixes* | | | |
| ❑ TCL 2813 [(3)M] | The Beach Boys Deluxe Set | 1967 | 250.00 |
| *—Black border on box; albums have "T" prefixes* | | | |
| ❑ ST 2859 [S] | Wild Honey | 1967 | 20.00 |
| ❑ T 2859 [M] | Wild Honey | 1967 | 40.00 |
| ❑ ST-8-2891 [R] | Smiley Smile | 1968 | 300.00 |
| *—Capitol Record Club edition* | | | |
| ❑ DKAO 2893 | Stack-o-Tracks | 1968 | 50.00 |
| *—Without sheet music booklet* | | | |
| ❑ DKAO 2893 | Stack-o-Tracks | 1968 | 100.00 |
| *—With sheet music booklet* | | | |
| ❑ DKAO-8-2893 | Stack-o-Tracks | 1968 | 200.00 |
| *—Capitol Record Club edition* | | | |
| ❑ ST 2895 | Friends | 1968 | 25.00 |
| ❑ DKAO 2945 [P] | The Best of the Beach Boys, Vol. 3 | 1968 | 15.00 |
| *—Black label with colorband* | | | |
| ❑ DKAO 2945 [P] | The Best of the Beach Boys, Vol. 3 | 1969 | 20.00 |
| *—"Starline" label* | | | |
| ❑ PRO 3133 [DJ] | Silver Platter Service from Hollywood: The Beach Boys Christmas Special | 1964 | 200.00 |
| ❑ SY-4572 [R] | Surfin' Safari | 197? | 12.00 |
| *—Orange label, Capitol logo at bottom; reissue of DT-1808 with completely different back cover and the words "... A Collector's Item ... Special Collections of Classic Hit Recordings by the Brightest Stars ..."* | | | |
| ❑ SVBB-11307 [(2)] | Endless Summer | 1974 | 20.00 |
| *—Orange labels, "Capitol" on bottom; with poster* | | | |
| ❑ SVBB-11307 [(2)] | Endless Summer | 1978 | 15.00 |
| *—Purple labels, large Capitol logo* | | | |
| ❑ SVBB-11307 [(2)] | Endless Summer | 1983 | 12.00 |
| *—Black labels, print in colorband* | | | |
| ❑ SVBB-11307 [(2)] | Endless Summer | 1988 | 12.00 |
| *—Purple labels, small Capitol logo* | | | |
| ❑ SVBB-11384 [(2)] | Spirit of America | 1975 | 15.00 |
| *—Orange labels, "Capitol" on bottom* | | | |
| ❑ SVBB-11384 [(2)] | Spirit of America | 1978 | 12.00 |
| *—Purple labels, large Capitol logo* | | | |
| ❑ SVBB-11384 [(2)] | Spirit of America | 1983 | 10.00 |
| *—Black labels, print in colorband* | | | |
| ❑ SVBB-11384 [(2)] | Spirit of America | 1988 | 10.00 |
| *—Purple labels, small Capitol logo* | | | |
| ❑ ST-11584 | Beach Boys '69 (The Beach Boys Live in London) | 1976 | 12.00 |
| ❑ SN-12011 | Beach Boys '69 (The Beach Boys Live in London) | 1979 | 10.00 |
| ❑ SVBB-12220 [(2)] | Sunshine Dream | 1982 | 12.00 |
| ❑ ST-12293 | Rarities | 1983 | 15.00 |
| ❑ STBK-12396 [(2)] | Made in U.S.A. | 1986 | 12.00 |
| ❑ N-16012 [M] | Surfin' Safari | 1980 | 8.00 |
| ❑ SN-16013 [S] | Little Deuce Coupe | 1980 | 8.00 |
| ❑ SN-16014 [S] | Surfer Girl | 1980 | 8.00 |
| ❑ SN-16015 [S] | Surfin' U.S.A. | 1980 | 8.00 |
| ❑ SN-16016 [S] | All Summer Long | 1980 | 8.00 |
| ❑ DN-16017 [R] | California Girls | 1980 | 8.00 |
| ❑ SN-16018 [P] | Fun, Fun, Fun | 1980 | 8.00 |
| *—Reissue of "Shut Down, Vol. 2"* | | | |
| ❑ DN-16019 [R] | Dance, Dance, Dance | 1981 | 8.00 |
| ❑ SN-16134 | Beach Boys '69 (The Beach Boys Live in London) | 1981 | 8.00 |
| ❑ SN-16156 [M] | Pet Sounds | 1981 | 8.00 |
| ❑ SN-16157 | Friends | 1981 | 8.00 |
| ❑ SN-16158 [M] | Smiley Smile | 1981 | 8.00 |
| ❑ SN-16159 [S] | Wild Honey | 1981 | 8.00 |
| ❑ DN-16272 [R] | Beach Boys Party! | 1982 | 8.00 |
| ❑ N-16273 | Be True to Your School | 1983 | 8.00 |
| ❑ DN-16318 [R] | Best of the Beach Boys, Vol. 2 | 1984 | 8.00 |
| ❑ C1-21241 [S] | Pet Sounds | 1999 | 15.00 |
| *—True stereo version on heavyweight vinyl* | | | |
| ❑ C1-29628 [S] | Surfer Girl | 1994 | 15.00 |
| ❑ C1-29629 [M] | Shut Down, Volume 2 | 1994 | 15.00 |
| ❑ C1-29630 [S] | Little Deuce Coupe | 1994 | 15.00 |
| ❑ C1-29631 [S] | All Summer Long | 1994 | 15.00 |
| ❑ C1-29632 [M] | The Beach Boys Today! | 1994 | 15.00 |
| ❑ C1-29633 [M] | Summer Days (And Summer Nights!!) | 1994 | 15.00 |
| ❑ C1-29634 | Beach Boys '69 (The Beach Boys Live in London) | 1994 | 15.00 |
| ❑ C1-29635 [M] | Smiley Smile | 1994 | 15.00 |
| ❑ C1-29636 [S] | Wild Honey | 1994 | 15.00 |
| ❑ C1-29637 | Friends | 1994 | 15.00 |
| ❑ C1-29638 | 20/20 | 1994 | 15.00 |
| ❑ C1-29640 [M] | Beach Boys Party! | 1994 | 15.00 |
| ❑ C1-29641 | Stack-o-Tracks | 1994 | 15.00 |
| ❑ C1-29661 [M] | Surfin' Safari | 1994 | 15.00 |
| ❑ C1-48421 [M] | Pet Sounds | 1994 | 15.00 |
| ❑ C1-48422 [S] | Surfin' U.S.A. | 1994 | 15.00 |
| ❑ 09463-51370-1-9 [(2)] | Pet Sounds | 2006 | 30.00 |
| *—Limited two-record edition; one record is on yellow vinyl and contains the original mono mix; the other is on green vinyl and contains the 2003 stereo mix* | | | |
| ❑ C1-90427 | Beach Boys Concert | 1994 | 15.00 |
| ❑ C1-91318 [R] | Best of the Beach Boys | 1988 | 12.00 |
| *—Purple label, small Capitol logo* | | | |
| ❑ C1-92639 | Still Cruisin' | 1989 | 12.00 |
| ❑ R 123946 | Best of the Beach Boys | 197? | 15.00 |
| *—RCA Music Service edition* | | | |
| ❑ R 133854 | The Beach Boys' Christmas Album | 197? | 15.00 |
| *—RCA Music Service edition* | | | |
| ❑ R 223559 [(2)] | Endless Summer | 197? | 25.00 |
| *—RCA Music Service edition* | | | |
| ❑ R 233593 [(2)] | American Summer | 1975 | 25.00 |
| *—RCA Music Service exclusive* | | | |
| ❑ SF-500501 | All Summer Long | 1971 | 10.00 |
| *—Columbia Record Club edition* | | | |
| ❑ SF-500502 | California Girls | 1971 | 10.00 |
| *—Columbia Record Club edition* | | | |
| ❑ DT-502545 [P] | Best of the Beach Boys | 197? | 15.00 |
| *—Columbia Record Club edition* | | | |
| ❑ DT-502706 [P] | Best of the Beach Boys, Vol. 2 | 197? | 15.00 |
| *—Columbia Record Club edition* | | | |
| ❑ SVBB-511307 [(2)] | Endless Summer | 197? | 25.00 |
| *—Columbia Record Club edition* | | | |
| ❑ SVBB-511384 [(2)] | Spirit of America | 1975 | 20.00 |
| *—Columbia Record Club edition* | | | |

### CAPITOL SPECIAL MARKETS

| Number | Title (A Side/B Side) | Yr | NM |
|---|---|---|---|
| ❑ SLB-6994 [(2)] | Golden Years of the Beach Boys | 1975 | 20.00 |
| ❑ SL-8114 | Beach Boys Super Hits | 1978 | 10.00 |
| ❑ SLB-8134 [(2)] | The Beach Boys | 1980 | 20.00 |
| ❑ SL-9431 | Good Vibrations from the Beach Boys | 1986 | 15.00 |
| *—Special issue for Sunkist* | | | |

### CARIBOU

| Number | Title (A Side/B Side) | Yr | NM |
|---|---|---|---|
| ❑ JZ 35752 | L.A. (Light Album) | 1979 | 10.00 |
| ❑ JZ 35752 [DJ] | L.A. (Light Album) | 1979 | 15.00 |
| *—White label promo* | | | |
| ❑ PZ 35752 | L.A. (Light Album) | 1980 | 8.00 |
| *—Budget-line reissue* | | | |
| ❑ FZ 36283 | Keepin' the Summer Alive | 1980 | 10.00 |
| ❑ FZ 36283 [DJ] | Keepin' the Summer Alive | 1980 | 15.00 |
| *—White label promo* | | | |
| ❑ Z2X 37445 [(2)] | Ten Years of Harmony (1970-1980) | 1981 | 12.00 |
| ❑ BFZ 39946 | The Beach Boys | 1985 | 10.00 |
| ❑ PZ 39946 | The Beach Boys | 1988 | 8.00 |
| *—Budget-line reissue* | | | |

### DCC COMPACT CLASSICS

| Number | Title (A Side/B Side) | Yr | NM |
|---|---|---|---|
| ❑ LPZ-2006 [M] | Pet Sounds | 1995 | 120.00 |
| *—Audiophile vinyl* | | | |

### ERA

| Number | Title (A Side/B Side) | Yr | NM |
|---|---|---|---|
| ❑ HTE-805 [M] | The Beach Boys' Biggest Beach Hits | 1969 | 15.00 |
| *—Also contains non-Beach Boys filler* | | | |

### EVEREST

| Number | Title (A Side/B Side) | Yr | NM |
|---|---|---|---|
| ❑ 4108 [M] | Rare Early Recordings | 1981 | 8.00 |

### GATEWAY

| Number | Title (A Side/B Side) | Yr | NM |
|---|---|---|---|
| ❑ GSLP-10104 [M] | Surfing with the Beach Boys, the Marketts and the Frogmen | 1979 | 8.00 |

### MOBILE FIDELITY

| Number | Title (A Side/B Side) | Yr | NM |
|---|---|---|---|
| ❑ 1-116 | Surfer Girl | 1984 | 30.00 |
| *—Audiophile vinyl* | | | |

### ORBIT

| Number | Title (A Side/B Side) | Yr | NM |
|---|---|---|---|
| ❑ OR 688 [M] | The Beach Boys' Greatest Hits 1961-1963 | 1972 | 12.00 |
| *—Also contains non-Beach Boys filler* | | | |

### PAIR

| Number | Title (A Side/B Side) | Yr | NM |
|---|---|---|---|
| ❑ PDL2-1068 [(2)] | For All Seasons | 1986 | 15.00 |
| ❑ PDL2-1084 [(2)] | Golden Harmonies | 1986 | 15.00 |

### PICKWICK

| Number | Title (A Side/B Side) | Yr | NM |
|---|---|---|---|
| ❑ PTP-2059 [(2)] | High Water | 1973 | 12.00 |
| ❑ SPC-3221 | Summertime Blues | 1970 | 10.00 |
| ❑ SPC-3269 | Good Vibrations | 1971 | 10.00 |
| ❑ SPC-3309 | Wow! Great Concert! | 1972 | 10.00 |
| ❑ SPC-3351 | Surfer Girl | 1973 | 10.00 |
| ❑ SPC-3562 | Little Deuce Coupe | 1975 | 10.00 |

### READER'S DIGEST

| Number | Title (A Side/B Side) | Yr | NM |
|---|---|---|---|
| ❑ RBA-178 [(4)] | Their Greatest Hits and Finest Performances | 1989 | 50.00 |
| *—Box set* | | | |

### SCEPTER CITATION

| Number | Title (A Side/B Side) | Yr | NM |
|---|---|---|---|
| ❑ CTN-18004 [M] | The Best of the Beach Boys (1961-1963) | 1972 | 12.00 |
| *—Also contains non-Beach Boys filler* | | | |

### SEARS

| Number | Title (A Side/B Side) | Yr | NM |
|---|---|---|---|
| ❑ SPS-609 | Summertime Blues | 1970 | 50.00 |

### SPRINGBOARD

| Number | Title (A Side/B Side) | Yr | NM |
|---|---|---|---|
| ❑ SPB-4021 [M] | The Beach Boys 1961 | 1977 | 8.00 |
| *—Also contains non-Beach Boys filler* | | | |

### SUNDAZED

| Number | Title (A Side/B Side) | Yr | NM |
|---|---|---|---|
| ❑ LP 5005 [B] | Lost & Found! | 1991 | 12.00 |
| *—Colored vinyl (red, yellow and light blue are known); first LP issue of the 1961 sessions from the master tapes; three tracks are stereo* | | | |

### TIME-LIFE

| Number | Title (A Side/B Side) | Yr | NM |
|---|---|---|---|
| ❑ SRNR-03 [(2)] | The Beach Boys: 1963-1967 | 1986 | 15.00 |
| *—2 LPs in box with fold-open liner notes; second cover has a portrait of the Beach Boys* | | | |
| ❑ SRNR-03 [(2)] | The Beach Boys: 1963-1967 | 1986 | 25.00 |
| *—2 LPs in box with fold-open liner notes; original cover portrays the Beach Boys surfing* | | | |

### WAND

| Number | Title (A Side/B Side) | Yr | NM |
|---|---|---|---|
| ❑ WDS-688 [M] | The Beach Boys' Greatest Hits 1961-1963 | 1972 | 12.00 |
| *—Also contains non-Beach Boys filler* | | | |

## BEACON STREET UNION, THE

### MGM

| Number | Title (A Side/B Side) | Yr | NM |
|---|---|---|---|
| ❑ E-4517 [M] | The Eyes of the Beacon Street Union | 1967 | 30.00 |
| ❑ SE-4517 [S] | The Eyes of the Beacon Street Union | 1967 | 25.00 |
| ❑ E-4568 [M] | The Clown Died in Marvin Gardens | 1968 | 50.00 |
| *—May be promo only (yellow label)* | | | |
| ❑ SE-4568 [S] | The Clown Died in Marvin Gardens | 1968 | 25.00 |

## BEAN, BILLY

### RIVERSIDE

| Number | Title (A Side/B Side) | Yr | NM |
|---|---|---|---|
| ❑ RLP-380 [M] | The Trio | 1961 | 40.00 |
| ❑ RS-9380 [S] | The Trio | 1961 | 50.00 |

## BEANS

### AVALANCHE

| Number | Title (A Side/B Side) | Yr | NM |
|---|---|---|---|
| ❑ 9200 | Beans | 1971 | 20.00 |

## BEASLEY, JIMMY

### CROWN

| Number | Title (A Side/B Side) | Yr | NM |
|---|---|---|---|
| ❑ CLP-5014 [M] | The Fabulous Jimmy Beasley | 1957 | 150.00 |
| *—Black label* | | | |
| ❑ CLP-5247 [M] | Twist with Jimmy Beasley | 1962 | 40.00 |
| *—Gray label* | | | |

### MODERN

| Number | Title (A Side/B Side) | Yr | NM |
|---|---|---|---|
| ❑ MLP-1214 [M] | The Fabulous Jimmy Beasley | 1956 | 400.00 |

## BEASTIE BOYS Also see COUNTRY MIKE.

### CAPITOL

| Number | Title (A Side/B Side) | Yr | NM |
|---|---|---|---|
| ❑ C1-22940 [(4)] | The Sounds of Science | 2000 | 150.00 |
| *—Boxed set with hardbound booklet; released a year after a similar CD compilation* | | | |
| ❑ C1-28599 [(2)] | Ill Communications | 1994 | 20.00 |
| ❑ C1 37716 [(2)] | Hello Nasty | 1998 | 20.00 |
| ❑ SPRO 79461 [(2)DJ] | Hip Hop Sampler | 1994 | 50.00 |
| *—Promo-only compilation of remixes and rarities; 1,250 copies were pressed; only the Side 1 number is listed above (the other three sides are numbered SPRO-79463, SPRO-79472 and SPRO-79473); this album has been counterfeited; there are several differences; most notably that authentic copies have gatefold sleeves, and the counterfeits have single-pocket sleeves* | | | |

Beastie Boys, *Paul's Boutique,* Capitol C1-92844, 1989, multiple gatefold cover, $25.

**Number — Title (A Side/B Side) — Yr — NM**

❑ SPRO 79461 [(2)DJ]Hip Hop Sampler 1994 50.00
*—This album has been counterfeited; there are several differences, most notably that authentic copies have gatefold sleeves, and the counterfeits have single-pocket sleeves*
❑ C1-84571 [(2)] To the 5 Boroughs 2004 30.00
❑ C1-91743 Paul's Boutique 1989 15.00
*—Single gatefold edition*
❑ C1-92844 Paul's Boutique 1989 25.00
*—Multi-gatefold edition (number on record is 91743, the same as single gatefold edition)*
❑ C1-98938 [(2)] Check Your Head 1992 50.00

DEF JAM
❑ BFC 40238 Licensed to Ill 1986 20.00
❑ FC 40238 Licensed to Ill 1986 15.00
*—Second pressing, with "02" added to bar code on back cover*

GRAND ROYAL
❑ GR 003 Some Old Bullshit 1994 15.00
❑ GR 006 [(2)] Ill Communication 1994 25.00
❑ GR 013 The In Sound from Way Out! 1996 80.00
*—Original editions were limited to 5,000 and have a sticker indicating this on the back cover*
❑ GR 013 The In Sound from Way Out! 1999 25.00
*—Second editions were not limited and have no sticker on the back cover*
❑ GR 018 [EP] Root Down 1995 15.00
*—Black vinyl*
❑ GR 018 [EP] Root Down 1995 30.00
*—Blue vinyl*
❑ GR 026 [EP] Aglio E Olio 1995 15.00
❑ GR 061 [(2)] Hello Nasty 1998 25.00
*—Limited edition on yellow vinyl*
❑ GR 065 [(2)] Paul's Boutique 1999 20.00
*—Reissue of original multi-gatefold edition*
❑ GR 066 [(2)] Check Your Head 1998 25.00
*—Vinyl reissue of Capitol 98938*
❑ GR 071 [EP] Scientists of Sound 2000 12.00
*—Remix album*

RAT CAGE
❑ 026 [EP] Cookypuss 1983 40.00

**BEAT FARMERS**

MCA CURB
❑ 5759 Van Go 1986 12.00
❑ 5993 The Pursuit of Happiness 1987 12.00
❑ 6296 Poor and Famous 1989 12.00
❑ L33-17381 [EP]Home of Country Dick 1987 25.00
*—Promo-only compilation with four non-LP songs*

**Number — Title (A Side/B Side) — Yr — NM**

RHINO
❑ RNOR-021 [EP]Bigger Stones 1985 15.00
*—Promo-only four-song sampler from RNLP-853*
❑ RNLP-853 Tales of the New West 1985 12.00

**BEAT OF THE EARTH, THE**

ARDISH
❑ AS-001 The Beat of the Earth 1968 300.00
❑ AS-0001 The Beat of the Earth 1968 400.00

**BEATLE BUDDIES, THE**

DIPLOMAT
❑ D-2313 [M] The Beatle Buddies 1964 15.00
❑ DS-2313 [S] The Beatle Buddies 1964 20.00

**BEATLES, THE** Also see PETE BEST; GEORGE HARRISON; JOHN LENNON; PAUL McCARTNEY; RINGO STARR.

APPLE
❑ SBC-100 [M] The Beatles' Christmas Album 1970 400.00
*—Fan club issue of the seven Christmas messages; very good counterfeits exist*
❑ SWBO-101 [(2)]The Beatles 1968 200.00
*—Numbered copy; includes four individual photos and large poster (included in value); because the white cover shows ring wear so readily, this is an EXTREMELY difficult album to find in near-mint condition; second pressing labels have Side 1, Song 5 correctly listed as "The Continuing Story of Bungalow Bill"; VG value 37.50; VG+ value 75*
❑ SWBO-101 [(2)]The Beatles 1968 400.00
*—Numbered copy; includes four individual photos and large poster (included in value); because the white cover shows ring wear so readily, this is an EXTREMELY difficult album to find in near-mint condition; first pressing label has Side 1, Song 5 incorrectly listed as "Bungalow Bill"; VG value 60; VG+ value 120*
❑ SWBO-101 [(2)]The Beatles 197? 60.00
*—Un-numbered copy; includes four individual photos and large poster (included in value)*
❑ SWBO-101 [(2)]The Beatles 1975 70.00
*—With "All Rights Reserved" on labels; title in black on cover; photos and poster of thinner stock than originals*
❑ SW-153 [P] Yellow Submarine 1969 50.00
*—With Capitol logo on Side 2 bottom. "Only a Northern Song" is rechanneled.*
❑ SW-153 [P] Yellow Submarine 1971 20.00
*—With "Mfd. by Apple" on label*
❑ SW-153 [P] Yellow Submarine 1975 25.00
*—With "All Rights Reserved" on label*

**Number — Title (A Side/B Side) — Yr — NM**

❑ SO-383 Abbey Road 1969 20.00
*—With "Mfd. by Apple" on label; "Her Majesty" IS listed on the label*
❑ SO-383 Abbey Road 1969 20.00
*—With "Mfd. by Apple" on label; "Her Majesty" is NOT listed on the label*
❑ SO-383 Abbey Road 1969 40.00
*—With Capitol logo on Side 2 bottom; "Her Majesty" IS listed on both the jacket and the label*
❑ SO-383 Abbey Road 1969 75.00
*—With Capitol logo on Side 2 bottom; "Her Majesty" is NOT listed on either the jacket or the label*
❑ SO-383 Abbey Road 1975 25.00
*—With "All Rights Reserved" on label, either in black print or in light print along label edge (both versions exist)*
❑ SO-385 [DJ] The Beatles Again 1970 8000.
*—Prototype covers with "The Beatles Again" on cover; not released to the general public. This is NOT a standard issue! VG value 4000; VG+ value 6000*
❑ SW-385 Hey Jude 1970 20.00
*—With "Mfd. by Apple" on label; label calls the LP "Hey Jude"*
❑ SW-385 Hey Jude 1970 25.00
*—Label calls the LP "The Beatles Again"; record is "SW-385"*
❑ SW-385 Hey Jude 1970 40.00
*—Label calls the LP "The Beatles Again"; record is "SO-385" (this could be found in retail stores as late as 1973)*
❑ SW-385 Hey Jude 1970 75.00
*—With Capitol logo on Side 2 bottom; label calls the LP "Hey Jude"*
❑ SW-385 Hey Jude 1975 25.00
*—With "All Rights Reserved" on label; label calls the LP "Hey Jude"*
❑ SKBO-3403 [P]The Beatles 1962-1966 1973 30.00
*—Custom red Apple labels. "Love Me Do" and "I Want to Hold Your Hand" are rechanneled; "She Loves You," "A Hard Day's Night," "I Feel Fine" and "Ticket to Ride" are mono; "From Me to You," "Can't Buy Me Love" and everything else is stereo.*
❑ SKBO-3403 [P]The Beatles 1962-1966 1975 50.00
*—Custom red Apple labels with "All Rights Reserved" on labels*
❑ SKBO-3404 [B]The Beatles 1967-1970 1973 30.00
*—Custom blue Apple labels. "Hello Goodbye" and "Penny Lane" are mono, all others stereo.*
❑ SKBO-3404 [B]The Beatles 1967-1970 1975 50.00
*—Custom blue Apple labels with "All Rights Reserved" on labels*
❑ SPRO 11206/7 [EP]Anthology 2 Sampler 1996 150.00
*—Promo-only collection sent to college radio stations*
❑ C1-8-31796 [(2)]Live at the BBC 1994 50.00
❑ AR-34001 Let It Be 1970 25.00
*—Red Apple label; originals have "Bell Sound" stamped in trail-off area, counterfeits do not*
❑ C1-8-34445 [(3)]Anthology 1 1995 40.00
*—All copies distributed in the U.S. were manufactured in the U.K. with no distinguishing marks (some LPs imported directly from the U.K. have "Made in England" stickers, which can be removed easily)*
❑ C1-8-34448 [(3)]Anthology 2 1996 40.00
❑ C1-8-34451 [(3)]Anthology 3 1996 30.00
❑ C1-97036 [B] The Beatles 1962-1966 1993 25.00
*—Custom red Apple labels; red vinyl; all copies pressed in U.K; U.S. versions have a bar-code sticker over the international bar code on back cover. "Love Me Do," "Please Please Me," "From Me to You" and "She Loves You" are mono; all others are stereo.*
❑ C1-97039 The Beatles 1967-1970 1993 25.00
*—Custom blue Apple labels; blue vinyl; all copies pressed in U.K.; U.S. versions have a bar-code sticker over the international bar code on back cover*

APPLE FILMS
❑ KAL 004 [DJ] The Yellow Submarine (A United Artists Release) 1969 2000.
*—One-sided LP with radio spots for movie; VG value 1000; VG+ value 1500*

APPLE/CAPITOL
❑ (no #) [(10)] The Beatles Special Limited Edition 1974 1200.
❑ (no #) [(17)] The Beatles 10th Anniversary Box Set 1974 2000.
*—VG value 1000; VG+ value 1500*
❑ ST 2047 [P] Meet the Beatles! 1968 40.00
*—With Capitol logo on Side 2 bottom*
❑ ST 2047 [P] Meet the Beatles! 1971 20.00
*—With "Mfd. by Apple" on label*
❑ ST 2047 [P] Meet the Beatles! 1975 25.00
*—With "All Rights Reserved" on label*
❑ ST 2080 [P] The Beatles' Second Album 1968 40.00
*—With Capitol logo on Side 2 bottom*
❑ ST 2080 [P] The Beatles' Second Album 1971 20.00
*—With "Mfd. by Apple" on label*
❑ ST 2080 [P] The Beatles' Second Album 1975 25.00
*—With "All Rights Reserved" on label*
❑ ST 2108 [S] Something New 1968 40.00
*—With Capitol logo on Side 2 bottom*
❑ ST 2108 [S] Something New 1971 20.00
*—With "Mfd. by Apple" on label*
❑ ST 2108 [S] Something New 1975 25.00
*—With "All Rights Reserved" on label*
❑ STBO 2222 [(2)P]The Beatles' Story 1968 50.00
*—With Capitol logo on bottom of B-side of both records*
❑ STBO 2222 [(2)P]The Beatles' Story 1971 30.00
*—With "Mfd. by Apple" on labels*
❑ STBO 2222 [(2)P]The Beatles' Story 1975 40.00
*—With "All Rights Reserved" on labels*
❑ ST 2228 [P] Beatles '65 1968 40.00
*—With Capitol logo on Side 2 bottom*
❑ ST 2228 [P] Beatles '65 1971 20.00
*—With "Mfd. by Apple" on label*
❑ ST 2228 [P] Beatles '65 1975 25.00
*—With "All Rights Reserved" on label*



**Except when noted otherwise, VG = 25% of NM, and VG+ = 50% of NM. (Example: VG = $2.00, VG+ = $4.00 and NM = $8.00.)**

**Number Title (A Side/B Side) Yr NM**

❑ ST 2309 [P] The Early Beatles 1969 40.00
*—With Capitol logo on Side 2 bottom*
❑ ST 2309 [P] The Early Beatles 1971 20.00
*—With "Mfd. by Apple" on label*
❑ ST 2309 [P] The Early Beatles 1975 25.00
*—With "All Rights Reserved" on label*
❑ ST 2358 [P] Beatles VI 1969 40.00
*—With Capitol logo on Side 2 bottom*
❑ ST 2358 [P] Beatles VI 1971 20.00
*—With "Mfd. by Apple" on label*
❑ ST 2358 [P] Beatles VI 1975 25.00
*—With "All Rights Reserved" on label*
❑ SMAS 2386 [P]Help! 1969 40.00
*—With Capitol logo on Side 2 bottom*
❑ SMAS 2386 [P]Help! 1971 20.00
*—With "Mfd. by Apple" on label*
❑ SMAS 2386 [P]Help! 1975 25.00
*—With "All Rights Reserved" on label*
❑ ST 2442 [S] Rubber Soul 1969 40.00
*—With Capitol logo on Side 2 bottom*
❑ ST 2442 [S] Rubber Soul 1971 20.00
*—With "Mfd. by Apple" on label*
❑ ST 2442 [S] Rubber Soul 1975 25.00
*—With "All Rights Reserved" on label*
❑ ST 2553 [P] Yesterday and Today 1969 40.00
*—With Capitol logo on Side 2 bottom*
❑ ST 2553 [P] Yesterday and Today 1971 20.00
*—With "Mfd. by Apple" on label*
❑ ST 2553 [P] Yesterday and Today 1975 25.00
*—With "All Rights Reserved" on label*
❑ ST 2553 [S] Yesterday and Today 1971 25.00
*—With "Mfd. by Apple" on label; all 11 tracks are in true stereo. Check for a triangle in the record's trail-off area.*
❑ ST 2576 [S] Revolver 1969 40.00
*—With Capitol logo on Side 2 bottom*
❑ ST 2576 [S] Revolver 1971 20.00
*—With "Mfd. by Apple" on label*
❑ ST 2576 [S] Revolver 1975 25.00
*—With "All Rights Reserved" on label*
❑ SMAS 2653 [S]Sgt. Pepper's Lonely Hearts Club Band 1969 40.00
*—With Capitol logo on Side 2 bottom*
❑ SMAS 2653 [S]Sgt. Pepper's Lonely Hearts Club Band 1971 25.00
*—With "Mfd. by Apple" on label*
❑ SMAS 2653 [S]Sgt. Pepper's Lonely Hearts Club Band 1975 25.00
*—With "All Rights Reserved" on label*
❑ SMAL 2835 [P] Magical Mystery Tour 1969 40.00
*—With Capitol logo on Side 2 bottom; with 24-page booklet*
❑ SMAL 2835 [P] Magical Mystery Tour 1971 20.00
*—With "Mfd. by Apple" on label; with 24-page booklet*
❑ SMAL 2835 [P] Magical Mystery Tour 1975 25.00
*—With "All Rights Reserved" on label; with 24-page booklet*

### ATCO
❑ 33-169 [M] Ain't She Sweet 1964 200.00
❑ 33-169 [M] Ain't She Sweet 1964 1000.
*—White label promo*
❑ SD 33-169 [P] Ain't She Sweet 1964 400.00
*—Tan and purple label; all four Beatles tracks are rechanneled*
❑ SD 33-169 [P] Ain't She Sweet 1969 500.00
*—Yellow label*

### AUDIO RARITIES
❑ AR-2452 [M] The Complete Silver Beatles 1982 15.00
*—Contains 12 Decca audition tracks*

### AUDIOFIDELITY
❑ PD-339 [M] First Movement 1982 30.00
*—Contains eight Decca audition tracks; picture disc*
❑ PHX-339 [M] First Movement 1982 12.00
*—Contains eight Decca audition tracks*

### BACKSTAGE
❑ 2-201 [(2)M] Like Dreamers Do 1982 40.00
*—Gatefold package, individually numbered (numbers under 100 increase value significantly)*
❑ 2-201 [(2)M] Like Dreamers Do 1982 50.00
*—Non-gatefold package*
❑ BSR-1111 [DJ] Like Dreamers Do 1982 50.00
*—Gray vinyl promo in white sleeve*
❑ BSR-1111 [DJ] Like Dreamers Do 1982 50.00
*—White vinyl promo in white sleeve*
❑ BSR-1111 [(3)M]Like Dreamers Do 1982 60.00
*—Two picture discs (10 of 15 Decca audition tracks on one, interviews on the other) and one white-vinyl record (same contests as musical picture disc)*
❑ BSR-1111 [(3)M]Like Dreamers Do 1982 100.00
*—Same as above, except colored-vinyl LP is gray*
❑ BSR-1165 [PD]The Beatles Talk with Jerry G. 1982 25.00
*—Picture disc*
❑ BSR-1175 [PD]The Beatles Talk with Jerry G., Vol. 2 1983 25.00
*—Picture disc*

### CAPITOL
❑ (no #) [(18)] The Beatles Collection Platinum Series 1984 800.00
❑ BC-13 [(14)] The Beatles Collection 1978 250.00
*—American versions have "EMI" and "BC-13" on box spine; imports go for less*
❑ SWBO-101 [(2)]The Beatles 1976 30.00
*—Orange label; with photos and poster*
❑ SWBO-101 [(2)]The Beatles 1978 30.00
*—Purple label, large Capitol logo; with photos and poster (some copies have four photos as one perforated sheet)*

The Beatles, *The Beatles' Story,* Capitol TBO 2222, 1964, mono, $200.

**Number Title (A Side/B Side) Yr NM**

❑ SWBO-101 [(2)]The Beatles 1983 40.00
*—Black label, print in colorband; with photos and poster (some copies have four photos as one perforated sheet)*
❑ SW-153 [P] Yellow Submarine 1976 12.00
*—Orange label*
❑ SW-153 [P] Yellow Submarine 1978 10.00
*—Purple label, large Capitol logo*
❑ SW-153 [P] Yellow Submarine 1983 15.00
*—Black label, print in colorband*
❑ SJ-383 Abbey Road 1984 30.00
*—New prefix; black label, print in colorband*
❑ SO-383 Abbey Road 1976 12.00
*—Orange label*
❑ SO-383 Abbey Road 1978 10.00
*—Purple label, large Capitol logo*
❑ SO-383 Abbey Road 1983 15.00
*—Black label, print in colorband*
❑ SJ-385 Hey Jude 1984 30.00
*—New prefix; black label, print in colorband*
❑ SW-385 Hey Jude 1976 12.00
*—Orange label (all Capitol label versions call the LP "Hey Jude")*
❑ SW-385 Hey Jude 1978 10.00
*—Purple label, large Capitol logo*
❑ SW-385 Hey Jude 1983 50.00
*—Black label, print in colorband*
❑ ST 2047 [P] Meet the Beatles! 1964 120.00
*—Black label with colorband; "Beatles!" on cover in tan to brown print; some labels have "ASCAP" after every title except "I Want to Hold Your Hand"; other labels have "ASCAP" after every title except "I Want to Hold Your Hand," "I Saw Her Standing There" and "I Wanna Be Your Man"; still other labels have "ASCAP" after every title except "I Want to Hold Your Hand" and "I Wanna Be Your Man"; back cover adds "Produced by George Martin" to lower left*
❑ ST 2047 [P] Meet the Beatles! 1964 150.00
*—Black label with colorband; "Beatles!" on cover in tan to brown print; label has "ASCAP" after every title except "I Want to Hold Your Hand" (BMI); no producer credit on back cover (this is the second edition of this LP)*
❑ ST 2047 [P] Meet the Beatles! 1964 400.00
*—Black label with colorband; "Beatles!" on cover in tan to brown print; "ASCAP" and "BMI" credits are missing on the label; no producer credit on back cover (this is the first edition of the LP)*
❑ ST 2047 [P] Meet the Beatles! 1965 75.00
*—Black label with colorband; "Beatles!" on cover in green print; most of these have "Produced by George Martin" on lower left of back cover; many of these have a label giving "BMI" credit to every song except "Don't Bother Me" and "Till There Was You"*
❑ ST 2047 [P] Meet the Beatles! 1968 50.00
*—Black colorband label; border print adds "A Subsidiary of Capitol Industries Inc."*
❑ ST 2047 [P] Meet the Beatles! 1969 40.00
*—Lime green label*
❑ ST 2047 [P] Meet the Beatles! 1976 12.00
*—Orange label*
❑ ST 2047 [P] Meet the Beatles! 1978 10.00
*—Purple label, large Capitol logo*
❑ ST 2047 [P] Meet the Beatles! 1983 15.00
*—Black label, print in colorband*
❑ ST-8-2047 [P] Meet the Beatles! 1969 200.00
*—Capitol Record Club edition; lime green label*
❑ ST-8-2047 [P] Meet the Beatles! 1969 500.00
*—Capitol Record Club edition; black label with colorband*
❑ T 2047 [M] Meet the Beatles! 1964 150.00
*—Black label with colorband; "Beatles!" on cover in tan to brown print; some labels have "ASCAP" after every title except "I Want to Hold Your Hand"; other labels have "ASCAP" after every title except "I Want to Hold Your Hand," "I Saw Her Standing There" and "I Wanna Be Your Man"; still other labels have "ASCAP" after every title except "I Want to Hold Your Hand" and "I Wanna Be Your Man"; most of the back covers add "Produced by George Martin" to lower left*
❑ T 2047 [M] Meet the Beatles! 1964 200.00
*—Black label with colorband; "Beatles!" on cover in tan to brown print; label has "ASCAP" after every title except "I Want to Hold Your Hand" (BMI); no producer credit on back cover (this is the second edition of this LP)*
❑ T 2047 [M] Meet the Beatles! 1964 400.00
*—Black label with colorband; "Beatles!" on cover in tan to brown print; no producer credit on back cover; "ASCAP" and "BMI" credits are missing on the label (this is the first edition of the LP)*
❑ T 2047 [M] Meet the Beatles! 1965 100.00
*—Black label with colorband; "Beatles!" on cover in green print; most of these have "Produced by George Martin" on lower left of back cover; many of these have a label giving "BMI" credit to every song except "Don't Bother Me" and "Till There Was You"*
❑ ST 2080 [P] The Beatles' Second Album 1964 100.00
*—Black label with colorband. "She Loves You," "I'll Get You" and "You Can't Do That" are rechanneled*
❑ ST 2080 [P] The Beatles' Second Album 1968 50.00
*—Black colorband label; border print adds "A Subsidiary of Capitol Industries Inc."*
❑ ST 2080 [P] The Beatles' Second Album 1969 40.00
*—Lime green label*
❑ ST 2080 [P] The Beatles' Second Album 1976 12.00
*—Orange label*
❑ ST 2080 [P] The Beatles' Second Album 1978 10.00
*—Purple label, large Capitol logo*
❑ ST 2080 [P] The Beatles' Second Album 1983 15.00
*—Black label, print in colorband*

The Beatles, *Magical Mystery Tour,* Capitol MAL 2835, 1967, mono, $300.

| Number | Title (A Side/B Side) | Yr | NM |
|---|---|---|---|
| ❑ ST-8-2080 [P] | The Beatles' Second Album | 1964 | 500.00 |
| *—Capitol Record Club edition; black label with colorband* | | | |
| ❑ ST-8-2080 [P] | The Beatles' Second Album | 1969 | 300.00 |
| *—Capitol Record Club edition; lime green label* | | | |
| ❑ T 2080 [M] | The Beatles' Second Album | 1964 | 180.00 |
| ❑ ST 2108 [S] | Something New | 1964 | 80.00 |
| *—Black label with colorband* | | | |
| ❑ ST 2108 [S] | Something New | 1968 | 50.00 |
| *—Black colorband label; border print adds "A Subsidiary of Capitol Industries Inc."* | | | |
| ❑ ST 2108 [S] | Something New | 1969 | 40.00 |
| *—Lime green label* | | | |
| ❑ ST 2108 [S] | Something New | 1976 | 12.00 |
| *—Orange label* | | | |
| ❑ ST 2108 [S] | Something New | 1978 | 10.00 |
| *—Purple label, large Capitol logo* | | | |
| ❑ ST 2108 [S] | Something New | 1983 | 15.00 |
| *—Black label, print in colorband* | | | |
| ❑ ST-8-2108 [S] | Something New | 1964 | 300.00 |
| *—Capitol Record Club edition; black label with colorband* | | | |
| ❑ ST-8-2108 [S] | Something New | 1969 | 150.00 |
| *—Capitol Record Club edition; lime green label* | | | |
| ❑ ST-8-2108 [S] | Something New | 1969 | 300.00 |
| *—Longines Symphonette edition (will be stated on label); lime green label* | | | |
| ❑ T 2108 [M] | Something New | 1964 | 150.00 |
| ❑ STBO 2222 [(2)P] | The Beatles' Story | 1964 | 150.00 |
| *—Black label with colorband. Some of the musical snippets are rechanneled.* | | | |
| ❑ STBO 2222 [(2)P] | The Beatles' Story | 1968 | 80.00 |
| *—Black colorband label; border print adds "A Subsidiary of Capitol Industries Inc."* | | | |
| ❑ STBO 2222 [(2)P] | The Beatles' Story | 1969 | 50.00 |
| *—Lime green label* | | | |
| ❑ STBO 2222 [(2)P] | The Beatles' Story | 1976 | 20.00 |
| *—Orange label* | | | |
| ❑ STBO 2222 [(2)P] | The Beatles' Story | 1978 | 20.00 |
| *—Purple label, large Capitol logo* | | | |
| ❑ STBO 2222 [(2)P] | The Beatles' Story | 1983 | 40.00 |
| *—Black label, print in colorband* | | | |
| ❑ TBO 2222 [(2)M] | The Beatles' Story | 1964 | 200.00 |
| ❑ ST 2228 [P] | Beatles '65 | 1964 | 80.00 |
| *—Black label with colorband. "She's a Woman" and "I Feel Fine" are rechanneled.* | | | |
| ❑ ST 2228 [P] | Beatles '65 | 1968 | 50.00 |
| *—Black colorband label; border print adds "A Subsidiary of Capitol Industries Inc."* | | | |
| ❑ ST 2228 [P] | Beatles '65 | 1969 | 40.00 |
| *—Lime green label* | | | |
| ❑ ST 2228 [P] | Beatles '65 | 1976 | 12.00 |
| *—Orange label* | | | |
| ❑ ST 2228 [P] | Beatles '65 | 1978 | 10.00 |
| *—Purple label, large Capitol logo* | | | |
| ❑ ST 2228 [P] | Beatles '65 | 1983 | 15.00 |
| *—Black label, print in colorband* | | | |
| ❑ T 2228 [M] | Beatles '65 | 1964 | 120.00 |
| ❑ ST 2309 [P] | The Early Beatles | 1965 | 100.00 |
| *—Black label with colorband. "Love Me Do" and "P.S. I Love You" are rechanneled.* | | | |
| ❑ ST 2309 [P] | The Early Beatles | 1968 | 50.00 |
| *—Black colorband label; border print adds "A Subsidiary of Capitol Industries Inc."* | | | |
| ❑ ST 2309 [P] | The Early Beatles | 1969 | 40.00 |
| *—Lime green label* | | | |
| ❑ ST 2309 [P] | The Early Beatles | 1976 | 12.00 |
| *—Orange label* | | | |
| ❑ ST 2309 [P] | The Early Beatles | 1978 | 10.00 |
| *—Purple label, large Capitol logo* | | | |
| ❑ ST 2309 [P] | The Early Beatles | 1983 | 25.00 |
| *—Black label, print in colorband* | | | |
| ❑ T 2309 [M] | The Early Beatles | 1965 | 200.00 |
| ❑ ST 2358 [M] | Beatles VI | 1983 | 15.00 |
| *—Black label, print in colorband; plays in mono despite label designation* | | | |
| ❑ ST 2358 [M] | Beatles VI | 1988 | 80.00 |
| *—Purple label, small Capitol logo; plays in mono despite label designation* | | | |
| ❑ ST 2358 [P] | Beatles VI | 1965 | 75.00 |
| *—Black label with colorband; with song titles listed in correct order on back cover. "Yes It Is" is rechanneled.* | | | |
| ❑ ST 2358 [P] | Beatles VI | 1965 | 80.00 |
| *—Black label with colorband; with "See label for correct playing order" on back cover* | | | |
| ❑ ST 2358 [P] | Beatles VI | 1968 | 50.00 |
| *—Black colorband label; border print adds "A Subsidiary of Capitol Industries Inc."* | | | |
| ❑ ST 2358 [P] | Beatles VI | 1969 | 40.00 |
| *—Lime green label* | | | |
| ❑ ST 2358 [P] | Beatles VI | 1976 | 12.00 |
| *—Orange label* | | | |
| ❑ ST 2358 [P] | Beatles VI | 1978 | 10.00 |
| *—Purple label, large Capitol logo* | | | |
| ❑ ST-8-2358 [P] | Beatles VI | 1965 | 500.00 |
| *—Capitol Record Club edition; black label with colorband* | | | |
| ❑ ST-8-2358 [P] | Beatles VI | 1969 | 400.00 |
| *—Capitol Record Club edition; lime green label* | | | |
| ❑ T 2358 [M] | Beatles VI | 1965 | 100.00 |
| *—With song titles listed in correct order on back cover* | | | |
| ❑ T 2358 [M] | Beatles VI | 1965 | 120.00 |
| *—With "See label for correct playing order" on back cover* | | | |
| ❑ MAS 2386 [M] | Help! | 1965 | 150.00 |
| ❑ SMAS 2386 [P] | Help! | 1965 | 75.00 |
| *—Black label with colorband. Has incidental music by George Martin. "Ticket to Ride" is rechanneled.* | | | |
| ❑ SMAS 2386 [P] | Help! | 1968 | 50.00 |
| *—Black colorband label; border print adds "A Subsidiary of Capitol Industries Inc."* | | | |
| ❑ SMAS 2386 [P] | Help! | 1969 | 40.00 |
| *—Lime green label* | | | |
| ❑ SMAS 2386 [P] | Help! | 1976 | 12.00 |
| *—Orange label* | | | |
| ❑ SMAS 2386 [P] | Help! | 1978 | 10.00 |
| *—Purple label, large Capitol logo* | | | |
| ❑ SMAS 2386 [P] | Help! | 1983 | 15.00 |
| *—Black label, print in colorband* | | | |
| ❑ SMAS-8-2386 [P] | Help! | 1965 | 400.00 |
| *—Capitol Record Club edition; black label with colorband; no "8" on cover* | | | |
| ❑ SMAS-8-2386 [P] | Help! | 1965 | 600.00 |
| *—Capitol Record Club edition; black label with colorband; with "8" on cover* | | | |
| ❑ SMAS-8-2386 [P] | Help! | 1969 | 200.00 |
| *—Capitol Record Club edition; lime green label; no "8" on cover* | | | |
| ❑ SMAS-8-2386 [P] | Help! | 1969 | 400.00 |
| *—Capitol Record Club edition; lime green label; with "8" on cover* | | | |
| ❑ SMAS-8-2386 [P] | Help! | 197? | 700.00 |
| *—Longines Symphonette edition; with "Mfd. by Longines" and "8" on cover* | | | |
| ❑ ST 2442 [S] | Rubber Soul | 1965 | 60.00 |
| *—Black label with colorband* | | | |
| ❑ ST 2442 [S] | Rubber Soul | 1968 | 50.00 |
| *—Black colorband label; border print adds "A Subsidiary of Capitol Industries Inc."* | | | |
| ❑ ST 2442 [S] | Rubber Soul | 1969 | 40.00 |
| *—Lime green label* | | | |
| ❑ ST 2442 [S] | Rubber Soul | 1976 | 12.00 |
| *—Orange label* | | | |
| ❑ ST-8-2442 [S] | Rubber Soul | 1965 | 300.00 |
| *—Capitol Record Club edition; black label with colorband* | | | |
| ❑ ST-8-2442 [S] | Rubber Soul | 1969 | 200.00 |
| *—Capitol Record Club edition; lime green label* | | | |
| ❑ ST-8-2442 [S] | Rubber Soul | 1969 | 250.00 |
| *—Longines Symphonette edition (will be stated on label); lime green label* | | | |
| ❑ SW 2442 [S] | Rubber Soul | 1978 | 10.00 |
| *—Purple label, large Capitol logo* | | | |
| ❑ SW 2442 [S] | Rubber Soul | 1983 | 15.00 |
| *—Black label, print in colorband* | | | |
| ❑ T 2442 [M] | Rubber Soul | 1965 | 120.00 |
| ❑ ST 2553 [P] | Yesterday and Today | 1966 | 80.00 |
| *—Trunk cover; black label with colorband (all later variations have the trunk cover). "I'm Only Sleeping," "Dr. Robert" and "And Your Bird Can Sing" are rechanneled.* | | | |
| ❑ ST 2553 [P] | Yesterday and Today | 1966 | 1000. |
| *—"Second state" butcher cover (trunk cover pasted over original cover)* | | | |
| ❑ ST 2553 [P] | Yesterday and Today | 1966 | 1500. |
| *—"Third state" butcher cover (trunk cover removed, leaving butcher cover intact); cover will be about 3/16-inch narrower than other Capitol Beatles LPs; value is highly negotiable depending upon the success of removing the paste-over* | | | |
| ❑ ST 2553 [P] | Yesterday and Today | 1966 | 8000. |
| *—"First state" butcher cover (never had other cover on top); cover will be the same size as other Capitol Beatles LPs; VG value 4000; VG+ value 6000* | | | |
| ❑ ST 2553 [P] | Yesterday and Today | 1968 | 50.00 |
| *—Black colorband label; border print adds "A Subsidiary of Capitol Industries Inc."* | | | |
| ❑ ST 2553 [P] | Yesterday and Today | 1969 | 40.00 |
| *—Lime green label* | | | |
| ❑ ST 2553 [P] | Yesterday and Today | 1976 | 12.00 |
| *—Orange label; it's possible that this and all future pressings have all 11 tracks in true stereo, but we don't know.* | | | |
| ❑ ST 2553 [P] | Yesterday and Today | 1978 | 10.00 |
| *—Purple label, large Capitol logo* | | | |
| ❑ ST 2553 [P] | Yesterday and Today | 1983 | 15.00 |
| *—Black label, print in colorband* | | | |
| ❑ ST-8-2553 [P] | Yesterday and Today | 1966 | 300.00 |
| *—Capitol Record Club edition; black label with colorband* | | | |
| ❑ ST-8-2553 [S] | Yesterday and Today | 1969 | 150.00 |
| *—Capitol Record Club edition; lime green label; all 11 tracks are in true stereo! (We don't know if the same is true of the black label version.)* | | | |
| ❑ T 2553 [M] | Yesterday and Today | 1966 | 150.00 |
| *—Trunk cover* | | | |
| ❑ T 2553 [M] | Yesterday and Today | 1966 | 1000. |
| *—"Second state" butcher cover (trunk cover pasted over original cover)* | | | |
| ❑ T 2553 [M] | Yesterday and Today | 1966 | 1200. |
| *—"Third state" butcher cover (trunk cover removed, leaving butcher cover intact); cover will be about 3/16-inch narrower than other Capitol Beatles LPs; value is highly negotiable depending upon the success of removing the paste-over; VG value 400; VG+ value 800* | | | |
| ❑ T 2553 [M] | Yesterday and Today | 1966 | 4000. |
| *—"First state" butcher cover (never had other cover on top); cover will be the same size as other Capitol Beatles LPs; VG value 2000; VG+ value 3000* | | | |
| ❑ ST 2576 [S] | Revolver | 1966 | 100.00 |
| *—Black label with colorband* | | | |
| ❑ ST 2576 [S] | Revolver | 1968 | 50.00 |
| *—Black colorband label; border print adds "A Subsidiary of Capitol Industries Inc."* | | | |

| Number | Title (A Side/B Side) | Yr | NM |
|---|---|---|---|
| ❑ ST 2576 [S] | Revolver | 1969 | 40.00 |
| *—Lime green label* | | | |
| ❑ ST 2576 [S] | Revolver | 1970 | 300.00 |
| *—Red label with "target" Capitol at top (same design as lime green label)* | | | |
| ❑ ST 2576 [S] | Revolver | 1976 | 12.00 |
| *—Orange label* | | | |
| ❑ ST-8-2576 [S] | Revolver | 1966 | 400.00 |
| *—Capitol Record Club edition; black label with colorband* | | | |
| ❑ ST-8-2576 [S] | Revolver | 1969 | 120.00 |
| *—Capitol Record Club edition; lime green label* | | | |
| ❑ ST-8-2576 [S] | Revolver | 1973? | 200.00 |
| *—Longines Symphonette edition; orange label (a very late issue, as the club closed in 1974)* | | | |
| ❑ SW 2576 [S] | Revolver | 1978 | 10.00 |
| *—Purple label, large Capitol logo* | | | |
| ❑ SW 2576 [S] | Revolver | 1983 | 15.00 |
| *—Black label, print in colorband* | | | |
| ❑ T 2576 [M] | Revolver | 1966 | 200.00 |
| ❑ 2653 | Sgt. Pepper's Lonely Hearts Club Band Cut-Out Inserts | 1967 | 3.00 |
| ❑ 2653 | Sgt. Pepper's Lonely Hearts Club Band Special Inner Sleeve | 1967 | 15.00 |
| *—Red-pink psychedelic sleeve only issued with 1967 (mono and stereo) editions* | | | |
| ❑ MAS 2653 [M] | Sgt. Pepper's Lonely Hearts Club Band | 1967 | 300.00 |
| ❑ SMAS 2653 [S] | Sgt. Pepper's Lonely Hearts Club Band | 1967 | 100.00 |
| *—Black label with colorband* | | | |
| ❑ SMAS 2653 [S] | Sgt. Pepper's Lonely Hearts Club Band | 1968 | 60.00 |
| *—Black colorband label; border print adds "A Subsidiary of Capitol Industries Inc."* | | | |
| ❑ SMAS 2653 [S] | Sgt. Pepper's Lonely Hearts Club Band | 1969 | 50.00 |
| *—Lime green label* | | | |
| ❑ SMAS 2653 [S] | Sgt. Pepper's Lonely Hearts Club Band | 1976 | 12.00 |
| *—Orange label* | | | |
| ❑ SMAS 2653 [S] | Sgt. Pepper's Lonely Hearts Club Band | 1978 | 10.00 |
| *—Purple label, large Capitol logo. Many copies from 1978 had a "The Original Classic" sticker on shrink wrap; it was added at the time of the release of the bomb movie version of Sgt. Pepper. Double the value if the sticker is still there.* | | | |
| ❑ SMAS 2653 [S] | Sgt. Pepper's Lonely Hearts Club Band | 1983 | 15.00 |
| *—Black label, print in colorband; some of these had "The Original Classic" stickers, too. Add $10 to value if it is there.* | | | |
| ❑ MAL 2835 [M] | Magical Mystery Tour | 1967 | 300.00 |
| *—With 24-page book bound into center of gatefold* | | | |
| ❑ SMAL 2835 [P] | Magical Mystery Tour | 1967 | 100.00 |
| *—Black label with colorband; with 24-page booklet. "Penny Lane," "Baby You're a Rich Man" and "All You Need Is Love" is rechanneled, as is the second half of "I Am the Walrus" (every "stereo" version of "Walrus" is this way)* | | | |
| ❑ SMAL 2835 [P] | Magical Mystery Tour | 1968 | 60.00 |
| *—Black colorband label; border print adds "A Subsidiary of Capitol Industries Inc."; with 24-page booklet* | | | |
| ❑ SMAL 2835 [P] | Magical Mystery Tour | 1969 | 50.00 |
| *—Lime green label; with 24-page booklet* | | | |
| ❑ SMAL 2835 [P] | Magical Mystery Tour | 1976 | 12.00 |
| *—Orange label; with 24-page booklet* | | | |
| ❑ SMAL 2835 [P] | Magical Mystery Tour | 1978 | 10.00 |
| *—Purple label, large Capitol logo; this edition did not come with booklet* | | | |
| ❑ SMAL 2835 [P] | Magical Mystery Tour | 1983 | 15.00 |
| *—Black label, print in colorband; no booklet* | | | |
| ❑ SKBO-3403 [P] | The Beatles 1962-1966 | 1976 | 20.00 |
| *—Red labels* | | | |
| ❑ SKBO-3403 [P] | The Beatles 1962-1966 | 1976 | 30.00 |
| *—Blue labels (error pressing)* | | | |
| ❑ SKBO-3404 [B] | The Beatles 1967-1970 | 1976 | 20.00 |
| *—Blue labels* | | | |
| ❑ SPRO-8969 | Rarities | 1978 | 50.00 |
| *—Purple label, large Capitol logo; part of the U.S. box set The Beatles Collection (BC-13)* | | | |
| ❑ SKBO-11537 [(2)] | Rock 'n' Roll Music | 1976 | 25.00 |
| ❑ SMAS-11638 | The Beatles at the Hollywood Bowl | 1977 | 20.00 |
| *—Originals with embossed title and ticket on front cover* | | | |
| ❑ SMAS-11638 | The Beatles at the Hollywood Bowl | 1980 | 15.00 |
| *—Second pressing without embossed title and ticket* | | | |
| ❑ SMAS-11638 | The Beatles at the Hollywood Bowl | 1989 | 40.00 |
| *—With UPC code on back cover* | | | |
| ❑ SMAS-11638 [DJ] | The Beatles at the Hollywood Bowl | 1977 | 500.00 |
| *—Advance tan label promo in plain white jacket* | | | |
| ❑ SKBL-11711 [(2)P] | Love Songs | 1977 | 20.00 |
| *—With booklet and embossed, leather-like cover. "P.S. I Love You" and "Yes It Is" are rechanneled.* | | | |
| ❑ SKBL-11711 [(2)P] | Love Songs | 1988 | 30.00 |
| *—With booklet, but without embossed cover* | | | |
| ❑ SEAX-11840 [PD] | Sgt. Pepper's Lonely Hearts Club Band | 1978 | 20.00 |
| *—Picture disc; deduct 25% for cut-outs* | | | |
| ❑ SEBX-11841 [(2)] | The Beatles | 1978 | 50.00 |
| *—White vinyl; with photos and poster (with number "SEBX-11841" on each)* | | | |

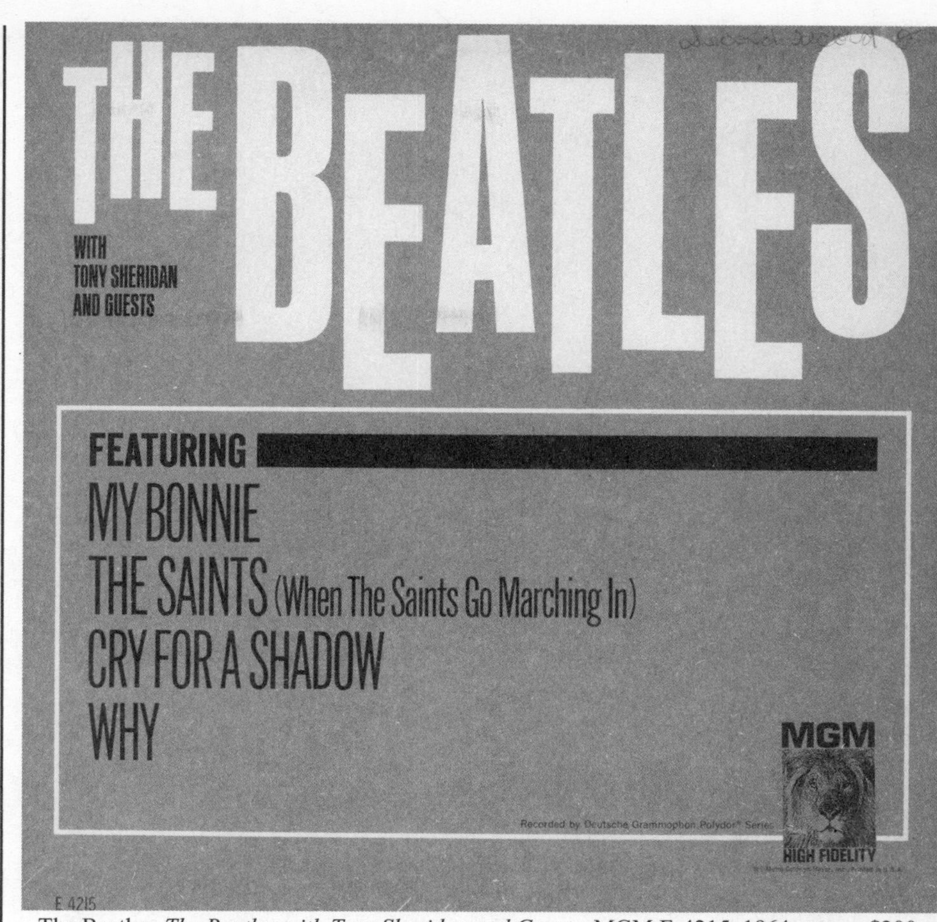


The Beatles, *The Beatles with Tony Sheridan and Guests,* MGM E-4215, 1964, mono, $200.

| Number | Title (A Side/B Side) | Yr | NM |
|---|---|---|---|
| ❑ SEBX-11842 [P] | The Beatles 1962-1966 | 1978 | 40.00 |
| *—Red vinyl* | | | |
| ❑ SEBX-11843 [B] | The Beatles 1967-1970 | 1978 | 40.00 |
| *—Blue vinyl* | | | |
| ❑ SEAX-11900 [PD] | Abbey Road | 1978 | 40.00 |
| *—Picture disc; deduct 25% for cut-outs* | | | |
| ❑ SW-11921 [P] | A Hard Day's Night | 1979 | 12.00 |
| *—Purple label, large Capitol logo* | | | |
| ❑ SW-11921 [P] | A Hard Day's Night | 1983 | 15.00 |
| *—Black label, print in colorband* | | | |
| ❑ SW-11921 [P] | A Hard Day's Night | 1988 | 25.00 |
| *—Purple label, small Capitol logo* | | | |
| ❑ SW-11922 | Let It Be | 1979 | 15.00 |
| *—Purple label, large Capitol logo; with poster and custom innersleeve* | | | |
| ❑ SW-11922 | Let It Be | 1983 | 15.00 |
| *—Black label, print in colorband; add 33% if poster is included* | | | |
| ❑ SW-11922 | Let It Be | 1988 | 25.00 |
| *—Purple label, small Capitol logo; add 20% if poster and custom innersleeve are included* | | | |
| ❑ SN-12009 [DJ] | Rarities | 1979 | 300.00 |
| *—Green label; withdrawn before official release; all known copies have a plain white sleeve* | | | |
| ❑ SHAL-12060 [B] | Rarities | 1980 | 15.00 |
| *—Same as above, with errors deleted and "Produced by George Martin" added to back cover* | | | |
| ❑ SHAL-12060 [B] | Rarities | 1980 | 20.00 |
| *—Black label with colorband. First pressing says that "There's a Place" debuts in stereo (false) and that the screaming at the end of "Helter Skelter" was a "classic Lennon statement" (it's actually Ringo).* | | | |
| ❑ SV-12199 | Reel Music | 1982 | 10.00 |
| *—Standard issue with 12-page booklet* | | | |
| ❑ SV-12199 [DJ] | Reel Music | 1982 | 20.00 |
| *—Yellow vinyl promo; plain white cover with 12-page booklet* | | | |
| ❑ SV-12199 [DJ] | Reel Music | 1982 | 40.00 |
| *—Yellow vinyl promo; numbered back cover with 12-page booklet* | | | |
| ❑ SV-12245 [P] | 20 Greatest Hits | 1982 | 20.00 |
| *—Purple label, large Capitol logo. "Love Me Do" and "She Loves You" are rechanneled, the other 18 tracks are stereo* | | | |
| ❑ SV-12245 [P] | 20 Greatest Hits | 1983 | 20.00 |
| *—Black label, print in colorband* | | | |
| ❑ SV-12245 [P] | 20 Greatest Hits | 1988 | 25.00 |
| *—Purple label, small Capitol logo* | | | |
| ❑ SN-16020 | Rock 'n' Roll Music, Volume 1 | 1980 | 10.00 |
| ❑ SN-16021 | Rock 'n' Roll Music, Volume 2 | 1980 | 10.00 |
| ❑ C1-46435 [M] | Please Please Me | 1995 | 12.00 |
| *—New prefix; Apple logo on back cover* | | | |

| Number | Title (A Side/B Side) | Yr | NM |
|---|---|---|---|
| ❑ CLJ-46435 [M] | Please Please Me | 1987 | 20.00 |
| *—Black label, print in colorband; first Capitol version of original British LP* | | | |
| ❑ CLJ-46435 [M] | Please Please Me | 1988 | 25.00 |
| *—Purple label, small Capitol logo* | | | |
| ❑ C1-46436 [M] | With the Beatles | 1995 | 12.00 |
| *—New prefix; Apple logo on back cover* | | | |
| ❑ CLJ-46436 [M] | With the Beatles | 1987 | 20.00 |
| *—Black label, print in colorband; first Capitol version of original British LP* | | | |
| ❑ CLJ-46436 [M] | With the Beatles | 1988 | 25.00 |
| *—Purple label, small Capitol logo* | | | |
| ❑ C1-46437 [M] | A Hard Day's Night | 1995 | 12.00 |
| *—New prefix; Apple logo on back cover* | | | |
| ❑ CLJ-46437 [M] | A Hard Day's Night | 1987 | 20.00 |
| *—Black label, print in colorband; first Capitol version of original British LP* | | | |
| ❑ CLJ-46437 [M] | A Hard Day's Night | 1988 | 25.00 |
| *—Purple label, small Capitol logo* | | | |
| ❑ C1-46438 [M] | Beatles for Sale | 1995 | 12.00 |
| *—New prefix; Apple logo on back cover* | | | |
| ❑ CLJ-46438 [M] | Beatles for Sale | 1987 | 20.00 |
| *—Black label, print in colorband; first Capitol version of original British LP* | | | |
| ❑ CLJ-46438 [M] | Beatles for Sale | 1988 | 25.00 |
| *—Purple label, small Capitol logo* | | | |
| ❑ C1-46439 [S] | Help! | 1995 | 12.00 |
| *—New prefix; Apple logo on back cover* | | | |
| ❑ CLJ-46439 [S] | Help! | 1987 | 20.00 |
| *—Black label, print in colorband; first Capitol version of original British LP* | | | |
| ❑ CLJ-46439 [S] | Help! | 1988 | 25.00 |
| *—Purple label, small Capitol logo* | | | |
| ❑ C1-46440 [S] | Rubber Soul | 1995 | 12.00 |
| *—New prefix; Apple logo on back cover* | | | |
| ❑ CLJ-46440 [S] | Rubber Soul | 1987 | 20.00 |
| *—Black label, print in colorband; first Capitol version of original British LP* | | | |
| ❑ CLJ-46440 [S] | Rubber Soul | 1988 | 25.00 |
| *—Purple label, small Capitol logo* | | | |
| ❑ C1-46441 [S] | Revolver | 1995 | 12.00 |
| *—New prefix; Apple logo on back cover* | | | |
| ❑ CLJ-46441 [S] | Revolver | 1987 | 20.00 |
| *—Black label, print in colorband; first Capitol version of original British LP* | | | |
| ❑ CLJ-46441 [S] | Revolver | 1988 | 25.00 |
| *—Purple label, small Capitol logo* | | | |
| ❑ C1-46442 [S] | Sgt. Pepper's Lonely Hearts Club Band | 1988 | 25.00 |
| *—New number; purple label, small Capitol logo* | | | |

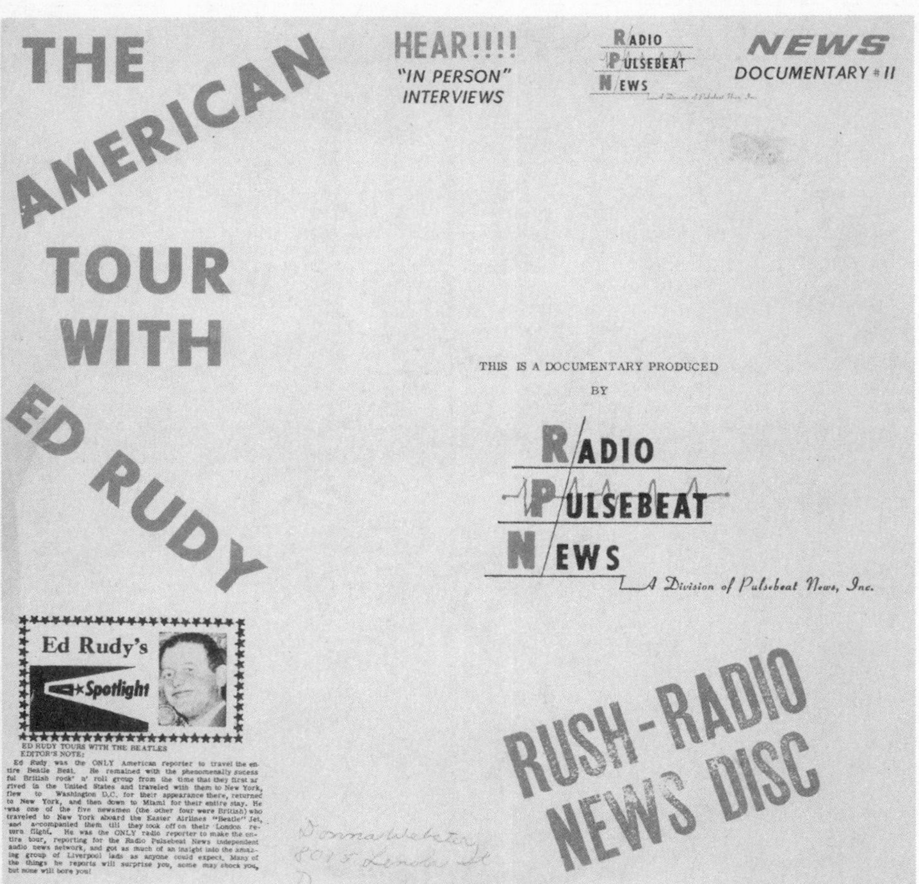

THE AMERICAN TOUR WITH ED RUDY
HEAR!!!!
"IN PERSON" INTERVIEWS
RADIO PULSEBEAT NEWS
NEWS
DOCUMENTARY #II
THIS IS A DOCUMENTARY PRODUCED BY
RADIO PULSEBEAT NEWS
A Division of Pulsebeat News, Inc.
Ed Rudy's
Spotlight
RUSH-RADIO NEWS DISC


The Beatles, *The American Tour with Ed Rudy,* Radio Pulsebeat News II, 1964, $100.

| Number | Title (A Side/B Side) | Yr | NM |
|---|---|---|---|
| ❑ C1-46442 [S] | Sgt. Pepper's Lonely Hearts Club Band | 1995 | 12.00 |
| *—With Apple logo on back cover* | | | |
| ❑ C1-46443 [(2)] | The Beatles | 1988 | 50.00 |
| *—New number; purple label, small Capitol logo; with photos and poster (some copies have four photos as one perforated sheet)* | | | |
| ❑ C1-46443 [(2)] | The Beatles | 1995 | 20.00 |
| *—With Apple logo on back cover* | | | |
| ❑ C1-46445 [P] | Yellow Submarine | 1988 | 25.00 |
| *—New number; purple label, small Capitol logo* | | | |
| ❑ C1-46445 [P] | Yellow Submarine | 1995 | 12.00 |
| *—Reissue has the British liner notes, which include a review of the White Album.* | | | |
| ❑ C1-46446 | Abbey Road | 1988 | 25.00 |
| *—New number; purple label, small Capitol logo* | | | |
| ❑ C1-46446 | Abbey Road | 1995 | 12.00 |
| *—Apple logo restored to back cover on reissue* | | | |
| ❑ C1-46447 | Let It Be | 1995 | 12.00 |
| *—New number (the only 1995 reissue with a completely new number)* | | | |
| ❑ C1-48062 [P] | Magical Mystery Tour | 1988 | 25.00 |
| *—New number; purple label, small Capitol logo; no booklet* | | | |
| ❑ C1-48062 [P] | Magical Mystery Tour | 1992 | 12.00 |
| *—With Apple logo on back cover; reissue restores booklet to package* | | | |
| ❑ C1-90435 [P] | The Beatles 1962-1966 | 1988 | 30.00 |
| *—New number; purple labels, small Capitol logo* | | | |
| ❑ C1-90438 [B] | The Beatles 1967-1970 | 1988 | 30.00 |
| *—New number; purple labels, small Capitol logo* | | | |
| ❑ C1-90441 [P] | Meet the Beatles! | 1988 | 25.00 |
| *—New number; purple label, small Capitol logo* | | | |
| ❑ C1-90442 | Hey Jude | 1988 | 25.00 |
| *—New number; purple label, small Capitol logo* | | | |
| ❑ C1-90443 [S] | Something New | 1988 | 25.00 |
| *—New number; purple label, small Capitol logo* | | | |
| ❑ C1-90444 [P] | The Beatles' Second Album | 1988 | 25.00 |
| *—New number; purple label, small Capitol logo* | | | |
| ❑ C1-90445 [M] | Beatles VI | 1988 | 25.00 |
| *—New number; purple label, small Capitol logo; plays in mono despite label designation* | | | |
| ❑ C1-90446 [P] | Beatles '65 | 1988 | 25.00 |
| *—New number; purple label, small Capitol logo* | | | |
| ❑ C1-90447 [P] | Yesterday and Today | 1988 | 25.00 |
| *—New number; purple label, small Capitol logo; stereo content uncertain* | | | |
| ❑ C1-90452 [S] | Revolver | 1988 | 25.00 |
| *—New number; purple label, small Capitol logo* | | | |
| ❑ C1-90453 [S] | Rubber Soul | 1988 | 25.00 |
| *—New number; purple label, small Capitol logo* | | | |

| Number | Title (A Side/B Side) | Yr | NM |
|---|---|---|---|
| ❑ C1-90454 [P] | Help! | 1988 | 25.00 |
| *—New number; purple label, small Capitol logo* | | | |
| ❑ C1-91135 [(2)B] | Past Masters Volume 1 and 2 | 1988 | 25.00 |
| *—Some early tracks are in mono, but "This Boy," "She's a Woman." "Yes It Is," and "The Inner Light" are in stereo.* | | | |
| ❑ BBX1-91302 [(14)] | The Beatles Deluxe Box Set | 1988 | 300.00 |
| **CICADELIC** | | | |
| ❑ 1960 | Moviemania | 1987 | 12.00 |
| ❑ 1961 | Not a Second Time | 1987 | 12.00 |
| ❑ 1962 | Things We Said Today | 1986 | 12.00 |
| ❑ 1963 | All Our Loving | 1986 | 12.00 |
| ❑ 1964 | East Coast Invasion | 1985 | 12.00 |
| ❑ 1965 | Round the World | 1986 | 12.00 |
| ❑ 1966 | West Coast Invasion | 1985 | 12.00 |
| ❑ 1967 | From Britain with Beat! | 1987 | 12.00 |
| ❑ 1968 | Here, There and Everywhere | 1988 | 12.00 |
| **CLARION** | | | |
| ❑ 601 [M] | The Amazing Beatles and Other Great English Group Sounds | 1966 | 100.00 |
| ❑ SD 601 [P] | The Amazing Beatles and Other Great English Group Sounds | 1966 | 200.00 |
| *—All four Beatles tracks are rechanneled* | | | |
| **GREAT NORTHWEST** | | | |
| ❑ GNW 4007 | Beatle Talk | 1978 | 10.00 |
| ❑ GNW 4007 | Beatle Talk | 1978 | 50.00 |
| *—Columbia Record Club edition; "CRC" on spine* | | | |
| **HALL OF MUSIC** | | | |
| ❑ HM-1-2200 [(2)M] | Live 1962, Hamburg, Germany | 1981 | 50.00 |
| *—Only American LP with the original Eurpoean contents -- "I Saw Her Standing There," "Twist and Shout," "Ask Me Why" and "Reminiscing" replace the four songs listed with the Lingasong issue* | | | |
| **I-N-S RADIO NEWS** | | | |
| ❑ DOC-1 [DJ] | Beatlemania Tour Coverage | 1964 | 1500. |
| *—Promo-only open-end interview with script in plain white jacket; VG value 750; VG+ value 1125* | | | |
| **LINGASONG** | | | |
| ❑ LS-2-7001 [(2)DJ] | Live at the Star Club in Hamburg, Germany, 1962 | 1977 | 40.00 |
| *—Promo on black vinyl; "D.J. Copy Not for Sale" on labels* | | | |
| ❑ LS-2-7001 [(2)DJ] | Live at the Star Club in Hamburg, Germany, 1962 | 1977 | 200.00 |
| *—Promo only on red vinyl* | | | |

| Number | Title (A Side/B Side) | Yr | NM |
|---|---|---|---|
| ❑ LS-2-7001 [(2)DJ] | Live at the Star Club in Hamburg, Germany, 1962 | 1977 | 300.00 |
| *—Promo only on blue vinyl* | | | |
| ❑ LS-2-7001 [(2)R] | Live at the Star Club in Hamburg, Germany, 1962 | 1977 | 20.00 |
| *—American version contains "I'm Gonna Sit Right Down and Cry," "Where Have You Been All My Life," "Till There Was You," and "Sheila," not on imports* | | | |
| **LLOYDS** | | | |
| ❑ ER-MC-LTD | The Great American Tour — 1965 Live Beatlemania Concert | 1965 | 600.00 |
| *—Another interview album from the Ed Rudy people, with a live Beatles show in the background and the songs poorly overdubbed by the Liverpool Lads* | | | |
| **METRO** | | | |
| ❑ M-563 [M] | This Is Where It Started | 1966 | 100.00 |
| *—Reissue of MGM album with two of the "others" tracks deleted* | | | |
| ❑ MS-563 [R] | This Is Where It Started | 1966 | 150.00 |
| *—In stereo cover* | | | |
| ❑ MS-563 [R] | This Is Where It Started | 1966 | 200.00 |
| *—In mono cover with "Stereo" sticker* | | | |
| **MGM** | | | |
| ❑ E-4215 [M] | The Beatles with Tony Sheridan and Their Guests | 1964 | 200.00 |
| *—Without "And Guests" on cover* | | | |
| ❑ E-4215 [M] | The Beatles with Tony Sheridan and Their Guests | 1964 | 250.00 |
| *—With "And Guests" on cover* | | | |
| ❑ SE-4215 [R] | The Beatles with Tony Sheridan and Their Guests | 1964 | 600.00 |
| *—With "And Guests" on cover* | | | |
| ❑ SE-4215 [R] | The Beatles with Tony Sheridan and Their Guests | 1964 | 800.00 |
| *—Without "And Guests" on cover* | | | |
| **MOBILE FIDELITY** | | | |
| ❑ BC-1 [(13)] | The Beatles Collection | 1982 | 500.00 |
| ❑ 1-023 | Abbey Road | 1979 | 50.00 |
| *—Audiophile vinyl* | | | |
| ❑ 1-047 [P] | Magical Mystery Tour | 1980 | 60.00 |
| *—Audiophile vinyl; yes, this contains the rechanneled stereo versions of "Penny Lane," "Baby You're a Rich Man" and "All You Need Is Love"* | | | |
| ❑ 2-072 [(2)] | The Beatles | 1982 | 50.00 |
| *—Audiophile vinyl; not issued with photos or poster* | | | |
| ❑ 1-100 [S] | Sgt. Pepper's Lonely Hearts Club Band | 1985 | 40.00 |
| *—Audiophile vinyl* | | | |
| ❑ UHQR 1-100 [S] | Sgt. Pepper's Lonely Hearts Club Band | 1982 | 300.00 |
| *—Ultra High Quality release with special cover; numbered edition of 5,000; numbers under 100 fetch even more* | | | |
| ❑ 1-101 [P] | Please Please Me | 1986 | 40.00 |
| *—Audiophile vinyl; British version of album. "Love Me Do" and "P.S. I Love You" are rechanneled.* | | | |
| ❑ 1-102 [S] | With the Beatles | 1986 | 150.00 |
| *—Audiophile vinyl; British version of album. Limited run because of a damaged stamper that was not replaced.* | | | |
| ❑ 1-103 [S] | A Hard Day's Night | 1987 | 40.00 |
| *—Audiophile vinyl; British version of album* | | | |
| ❑ 1-104 [S] | Beatles for Sale | 1986 | 40.00 |
| *—Audiophile vinyl; British version of album* | | | |
| ❑ 1-105 [S] | Help! | 1985 | 40.00 |
| *—Audiophile vinyl; British version of album* | | | |
| ❑ 1-106 [S] | Rubber Soul | 1985 | 40.00 |
| *—Audiophile vinyl; British version of album* | | | |
| ❑ 1-107 [S] | Revolver | 1986 | 40.00 |
| *—Audiophile vinyl; British version of album* | | | |
| ❑ 1-108 [P] | Yellow Submarine | 1987 | 60.00 |
| *—Audiophile vinyl* | | | |
| ❑ 1-109 | Let It Be | 1987 | 40.00 |
| *—Audiophile vinyl; gatefold cover* | | | |
| ❑ 1-109 | Let It Be | 1987 | 200.00 |
| *—Audiophile vinyl; regular cover* | | | |
| **ORANGE** | | | |
| ❑ ORC-12880 [DJ] | The Silver Beatles | 1985 | 300.00 |
| *—Test pressing; white cover with title sticker* | | | |
| ❑ ORC-12880 [DJ] | The Silver Beatles | 1985 | 400.00 |
| *—Test pressing; full cover cover slick folded around a white cover. Both contain all 15 Decca audition tracks* | | | |
| **PBR INTERNATIONAL** | | | |
| ❑ 7005/6 [(2)] | The David Wigg Interviews (The Beatles Tapes) | 1978 | 80.00 |
| *—Blue vinyl* | | | |
| ❑ 7005/6 [(2)] | The David Wigg Interviews (The Beatles Tapes) | 1980 | 60.00 |
| *—Black vinyl* | | | |
| **PHOENIX** | | | |
| ❑ PHX-352 [M] | Silver Beatles, Volume 1 | 1982 | 12.00 |
| *—Contains seven Decca audition tracks* | | | |
| ❑ PHX-353 [M] | Silver Beatles, Volume 2 | 1982 | 12.00 |
| *—Contains seven Decca audition tracks (different seven than Phoenix 352)* | | | |
| ❑ P20-623 | 20 Hits, Beatles | 1983 | 20.00 |
| *—With 12 Decca audition tracks, four Beatles/Tony Sheridan tracks, and four Tony Sheridan solo tracks* | | | |
| ❑ P20-629 | 20 Hits, Beatles | 1983 | 20.00 |
| *—With 20 live Hamburg tracks* | | | |
| **PICKWICK** | | | |
| ❑ PTP-2098 [(2)M] | The Historic First Live Recordings | 1980 | 18.00 |
| *—Same contents as Lingasong LP, plus "Hully Gully"* | | | |

| Number | Title (A Side/B Side) | Yr | NM |
|---|---|---|---|
| ❑ SPC-3661 [M] | The Beatles' First Live Recordings, Volume 1 | 1979 | 12.00 |
| ❑ SPC-3662 [M] | The Beatles' First Live Recordings, Volume 2 | 1979 | 12.00 |
| ❑ BAN-90051 [M] | Recorded Live in Hamburg, Vol. 1 | 1978 | 30.00 |
| ❑ BAN-90061 [M] | Recorded Live in Hamburg, Vol. 2 | 1978 | 30.00 |
| ❑ BAN-90071 [M] | Recorded Live in Hamburg, Vol. 3 | 1978 | 40.00 |

POLYDOR

❑ 24-4504 [P] The Beatles — Circa 1960 — In the Beginning Featuring Tony Sheridan 197? 40.00
*—Some copies of the record contain only the title "The Beatles - - In the Beginning"*
❑ 24-4504 [P] The Beatles — Circa 1960 — In the Beginning Featuring Tony Sheridan 1970 25.00
*—Originals have gatefold cover*
❑ PD-4504 [P] The Beatles — Circa 1960 — In the Beginning Featuring Tony Sheridan 1981 12.00
*—Reissue without gatefold cover*
❑ SKAO-93199 [P] The Beatles — Circa 1960 — In the Beginning Featuring Tony Sheridan 1970 40.00
*—Capitol Record Club edition*
❑ 825073-1 [P] The Beatles — Circa 1960 — In the Beginning Featuring Tony Sheridan 1988 20.00
*—Reissue with new number*

RADIO PULSEBEAT NEWS

❑ 2 The American Tour with Ed Rudy 1964 100.00
*—Yellow label; some copies came with a special edition of Teen Talk magazine (add 50%)*
❑ 2 The American Tour with Ed Rudy 1980 25.00
*—Blue label; authorized reissue with Beatles' photo on cover*
❑ 3 1965 Talk Album — Ed Rudy with New U.S. Tour 1965 150.00
*—"The Beatles" in black print under front cover photo (other versions appear to be bootlegs)*

RAVEN/PVC

❑ 8911 Talk Downunder 1981 10.00
❑ 8911 [DJ] Talk Downunder 1981 80.00
*—Promo only in white cover with title sticker. Label reads "For Radio Play Only"*

SAVAGE

❑ BM-69 [M] The Savage Young Beatles 1964 150.00
*—Orange label; no legitimate copy says "Stereo" on cover*
❑ BM-69 [M] The Savage Young Beatles 1964 1500.
*—Yellow label, glossy orange cover*

SILHOUETTE

❑ SM-10004 [PD] Timeless 1981 20.00
*—Picture disc with all interviews*
❑ SM-10004 [PD] Timeless 1981 25.00
*—Picture disc with interviews plus remakes of "Imagine" and "Let It Be" (by non-Beatles)*
❑ SM-10010 [PD] Timeless II 1982 20.00
*—Picture disc with mostly interviews*
❑ SM-10013 The British Are Coming 1984 15.00
*—Interview album with numbered sticker (very low numbers increase the value)*
❑ SM-10013 The British Are Coming 1984 80.00
*—Same as above, but on red vinyl*
❑ SM-10013 [DJ] The British Are Coming 1984 40.00
*—White label promo; no numbered sticker*
❑ SM-10015 Golden Beatles 1985 15.00
❑ SM-10015 Golden Beatles 1985 80.00
*—Gold vinyl*
❑ PD-83010 [PD] The British Are Coming 1985 30.00
*—Picture disc*

STERLING

❑ 8895-6481 I Apologize 1966 300.00
*—Same as above, but without photo*
❑ 8895-6481 I Apologize 1966 400.00
*—One-sided LP with John Lennon's "apology" for supposed anti-Christian remarks; includes photo*

UNITED ARTISTS

❑ UA-Help-A/B [DJ] United Artists Presents Help! 1965 1500.
*—Radio spots for movie; VG value 500; VG+ value 1000*
❑ UA-Help-INT [DJ] United Artists Presents Help! 1965 2000.
*—Open-end interview with script (red label); VG value 1000; VG+ value 1500*
❑ UA-Help-Show [DJ] United Artists Presents Help! 1965 3000.
*—One-sided interview with script (blue label); VG value 1500; VG+ value 2250*
❑ SP-2359/60 [DJ] United Artists Presents A Hard Day's Night 1964 2000.
*—Open-end interview with script; VG value 1000; VG+ value 1500*
❑ SP-2362/3 [DJ] United Artists Presents A Hard Day's Night 1964 1500.
*—Radio spots for movie*
❑ UAL 3366 [M] A Hard Day's Night 1964 200.00
*—With "I Cry Instead" listing*

Number Title (A Side/B Side) Yr NM

❑ UAL 3366 [M] A Hard Day's Night 1964 250.00
*—With "I'll Cry Instead" listing*
❑ UAL 3366 [M] A Hard Day's Night 1964 3000.
*—White label promo*
❑ UAS 6366 [P] A Hard Day's Night 1964 200.00
*—With "I Cry Instead" listing*
❑ UAS 6366 [P] A Hard Day's Night 1964 250.00
*—With "I'll Cry Instead" listing. Has incidental music by George Martin. All eight Beatles tracks are rechanneled; Martin's are in true stereo.*
❑ UAS 6366 [P] A Hard Day's Night 1964 12000.
*—Pink vinyl; only one copy known, probably privately (and secretly) done by a pressing-plant employee; VG value 6000; VG+ value 9000*
❑ UAS 6366 [P] A Hard Day's Night 1968 50.00
*—Pink and orange label*
❑ UAS 6366 [P] A Hard Day's Night 1970 50.00
*—Black and orange label*
❑ UAS 6366 [P] A Hard Day's Night 1971 20.00
*—Tan label*
❑ UAS 6366 [P] A Hard Day's Night 1975 20.00
*—Tan label with "All Rights Reserved" in perimeter print*
❑ UAS 6366 [P] A Hard Day's Night 1977 20.00
*—Sunrise label. Note: Any of the variations from 1968 on can have titles of songs incorrectly listed as "I Cry Instead" and "Tell Me Who," or only one can be wrong, or neither can be wrong. No difference in value at this time.*
❑ ST-90828 [P] A Hard Day's Night 1964 750.00
*—Capitol Record Club edition*
❑ T-90828 [M] A Hard Day's Night 1964 1500.
*—Capitol Record Club edition; VG value 750; VG+ value 1125*

UNITED DISTRIBUTORS

❑ UDL-2333 [M] Dawn of the Silver Beatles 1981 50.00
*—With numbered registration card (deduct 20% if missing)*
❑ UDL-2333 [M] Dawn of the Silver Beatles 1981 60.00
*—Hand-stamped numbers on back cover and label; contains 10 Decca audition tracks*
❑ UDL-2382 [M] Lightning Strikes Twice 1981 60.00
*—Side 1 has five Beatles' Decca audition tracks; Side 2 has live Elvis Presley performances from 1955*

VEE JAY

❑ DX(S)-30 The Beatles vs. The Four Seasons Poster 1964 300.00
❑ DX-30 [(2)M] The Beatles vs. The Four Seasons 1964 800.00
*—Combines "Introducing the Beatles" with "Golden Hits of the Four Seasons" (Vee Jay 1065)*
❑ DXS-30 [(2)S] The Beatles vs. The Four Seasons 1964 3000.
*—Combines "Introducing the Beatles" with "Golden Hits of the Four Seasons" (Vee Jay 1065); VG value 1500; VG+ value 2250*
❑ 202 [M] Hear the Beatles Tell All 1964 300.00
*—Without "PRO" prefix on label*
❑ PRO 202 [DJ] Hear the Beatles Tell All 1964 18000.
*—White label promo with blue print; VG value 6000; VG+ value 12000*
❑ PRO 202 [M] Hear the Beatles Tell All 1964 200.00
*—With "PRO" prefix on label*
❑ PRO 202 [M] Hear the Beatles Tell All 1979 10.00
*—Authorized reissue; every copy with the word "Stereo" on the front cover is this edition, though the record still plays in mono (no 1964 copies have "Stereo" on the cover)*
❑ PRO 202 [PD] Hear the Beatles Tell All 1987 20.00
*—Shaped picture disc with same recordings as the black vinyl versions*
❑ LP 1062 [M] Introducing the Beatles 1964 250.00
*—Song titles cover; with "Please Please Me" and "Ask Me Why"; plain Vee Jay logo on solid black label*
❑ LP 1062 [M] Introducing the Beatles 1964 250.00
*—Song titles cover; with "Please Please Me" and "Ask Me Why"; brackets Vee Jay logo with colorband (most common authentic version)*
❑ LP 1062 [M] Introducing the Beatles 1964 300.00
*—Song titles cover; with "Please Please Me" and "Ask Me Why"; oval Vee Jay logo on solid black label*
❑ LP 1062 [M] Introducing the Beatles 1964 300.00
*—Song titles cover; with "Please Please Me" and "Ask Me Why"; oval Vee Jay logo with colorband*
❑ LP 1062 [M] Introducing the Beatles 1964 800.00
*—Song titles cover; with "Love Me Do" and "P.S. I Love You"; oval Vee Jay logo with colorband only!*
❑ LP 1062 [M] Introducing the Beatles 1964 1000.
*—Blank back cover; with "Please Please Me" and "Ask Me Why"; oval Vee Jay logo with colorband only!*
❑ LP 1062 [M] Introducing the Beatles 1964 1000.
*—Song titles cover; with "Please Please Me" and "Ask Me Why"; brackets Vee Jay logo on solid black label*
❑ LP 1062 [M] Introducing the Beatles 1964 1200.
*—Blank back cover; with "Love Me Do" and "P.S. I Love You"; oval Vee Jay logo with colorband only!; VG value 400; VG+ value 800*
❑ LP 1062 [M] Introducing the Beatles 1964 4000.
*—"Ad back" cover; with "Love Me Do" and "P.S. I Love You"; oval Vee Jay logo with colorband only!; VG value 1500; VG+ value 2750*
❑ SR 1062 [B] Introducing the Beatles 1964 2500.
*—Blank back cover; with "Love Me Do" and "P.S. I Love You"; oval Vee Jay logo with colorband only!*
❑ SR 1062 [B] Introducing the Beatles 1964 8000.
*—Song titles cover; with "Love Me Do" and "P.S. I Love You"; oval Vee Jay logo with colorband only!; VG value 3000; VG+ value 5500; This album has been heavily counterfeited; please check the label of your copy before contacting the author. If the words "Introducing the Beatles" are above the center hole of the record, and the words "The Beatles" are below, it is automatically a counterfeit and almost worthless.*

Number Title (A Side/B Side) Yr NM

❑ SR 1062 [B] Introducing the Beatles 1964 12000.
*—"Ad back" cover; with "Love Me Do" and "P.S. I Love You" (both mono); oval Vee Jay logo with colorband only!; VG value 4000; VG+ value 8000*
❑ SR 1062 [S] Introducing the Beatles 1964 1500.
*—Song titles cover; with "Please Please Me" and "Ask Me Why"; brackets Vee Jay logo with colorband*
❑ SR 1062 [S] Introducing the Beatles 1964 1600.
*—Song titles cover; with "Please Please Me" and "Ask Me Why"; oval Vee Jay logo with colorband*
❑ SR 1062 [S] Introducing the Beatles 1964 1600.
*—Song titles cover; with "Please Please Me" and "Ask Me Why"; plain Vee Jay logo on solid black label*
❑ LP 1085 [M] Jolly What! The Beatles and Frank Ifield on Stage 1964 250.00
*—Man in Beatle wig cover; originals have printing on spine and a dark blue/purple background (counterfeits have a black background and no spine print)*
❑ LP 1085 [M] The Beatles and Frank Ifield on Stage 1964 5000.
*—Portrait of Beatles cover; counterfeits are poorly reproduced and have no spine print; VG value 2000; VG+ value 3500*
❑ SR 1085 [B] Jolly What! The Beatles and Frank Ifield on Stage 1964 500.00
*—Man in Beatle wig cover; "Stereo" on both cover and label. "From Me to You" is mono.*
❑ SR 1085 [B] The Beatles and Frank Ifield on Stage 1964 12000.
*—Portrait of Beatles cover; "Stereo" on both cover and label; VG value 4000; VG+ value 8000*
❑ LP 1092 [M] Songs, Pictures and Stories of the Fabulous Beatles 1964 500.00
*—See above; brackets Vee Jay logo with colorband*
❑ LP 1092 [M] Songs, Pictures and Stories of the Fabulous Beatles 1964 500.00
*—See above; oval Vee Jay logo on solid black label*
❑ LP 1092 [M] Songs, Pictures and Stories of the Fabulous Beatles 1964 500.00
*—See above; plain Vee Jay logo on solid black label*
❑ LP 1092 [M] Songs, Pictures and Stories of the Fabulous Beatles 1964 500.00
*—All copies have gatefold cover with 2/3 width on front; also, all copies have "Introducing the Beatles" records. Oval Vee Jay logo with colorband.*
❑ VJS 1092 [S] Songs, Pictures and Stories of the Fabulous Beatles 1964 2400.
*—See above; brackets Vee Jay logo with colorband; VG value 800; VG+ value 1600*
❑ VJS 1092 [S] Songs, Pictures and Stories of the Fabulous Beatles 1964 2400.
*—See above; plain Vee Jay logo on solid black label. NOTE: Any non-gatefold copy or any copy called "Songs and Pictures of the Fabulous Beatles" is a counterfeit; VG value 800; VG+ value 1600*
❑ VJS 1092 [S] Songs, Pictures and Stories of the Fabulous Beatles 1964 2400.
*—All copies have gatefold cover with 2/3 width on front; also, all copies have "Introducing the Beatles" records. Oval Vee Jay logo with colorband; VG value 800; VG+ value 1600*

## BEAU BRUMMELS, THE

ACCORD

❑ SN-7175 Just a Little 1982 10.00

AUTUMN

❑ LP 103 [M] Introducing the Beau Brummels 1965 50.00
❑ SLP 103 [S] Introducing the Beau Brummels 1965 60.00
❑ LP 104 [M] The Beau Brummels, Volume 2 1965 40.00
❑ SLP 104 [S] The Beau Brummels, Volume 2 1965 50.00

JAS

❑ 5000 Original Hits of the Beau Brummels 1976 15.00

POST

❑ 6000 The Beau Brummels Sing 196? 15.00

RHINO

❑ RNLP-101 The Best of the Beau Brummels 1981 10.00
❑ RNLP-102 Introducing the Beau Brummels 1981 10.00
❑ RNLP-104 From the Vaults 1981 12.00
❑ RNLP-70171 The Best of the Beau Brummels (Golden Archive Series) 1986 10.00

SUNDAZED

❑ LP 5088 North Beach Legends 2001 12.00
❑ LP 5089 Gentle Wanderin' Ways 2001 12.00

VAULT

❑ LP-114 [M] Best of the Beau Brummels 1967 25.00
❑ SLP-114 [S] Best of the Beau Brummels 1967 25.00
❑ SLP-121 Beau Brummels, Vol. 44 1968 25.00

WARNER BROS.

❑ W 1644 [M] Beau Brummels '66 1966 20.00
❑ WS 1644 [S] Beau Brummels '66 1966 25.00
❑ W 1692 [M] Triangle 1967 20.00
❑ WS 1692 [S] Triangle 1967 25.00
❑ WS 1760 Bradley's Barn 1968 25.00
❑ BS 2842 The Beau Brummels 1975 20.00

## BEAU COUP

AMHERST

❑ AMH 3316 Born and Raised on Rock-n-Roll 1987 15.00

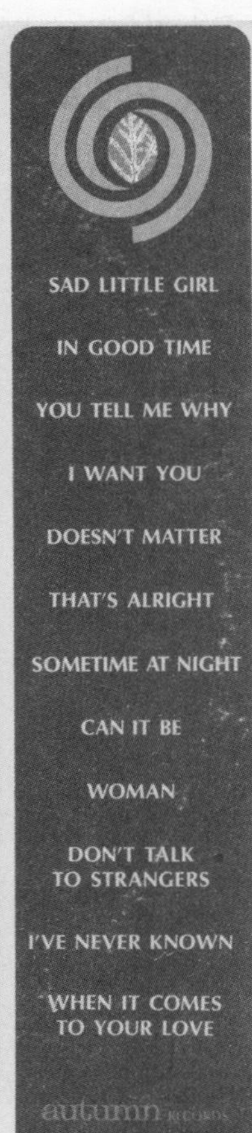


The Beau Brummels, *The Beau Brummels Volume 2,* Autumn 104, mono, $40.

**BEAUREGARDE**

| Number | Title (A Side/B Side) | Yr | NM |
|---|---|---|---|
| EMPIRE | | | |
| ❑ (no #) | Beauregarde | 1969 | 100.00 |
| SOUND | | | |
| ❑ 7104 | Beauregarde | 1969 | 80.00 |

**BEAVER, PAUL**

| Number | Title (A Side/B Side) | Yr | NM |
|---|---|---|---|
| RAPTURE | | | |
| ❑ 11111 | Perchance to Dream | 196? | 50.00 |

**BEAVER AND KRAUSE**

| Number | Title (A Side/B Side) | Yr | NM |
|---|---|---|---|
| LIMELIGHT | | | |
| ❑ 86069 | Ragnarok — Electronic Funk | 1969 | 30.00 |
| WARNER BROS. | | | |
| ❑ WS 1850 | In a Wild Sanctuary | 1969 | 15.00 |
| ❑ WS 1909 | Gandharva | 1970 | 15.00 |
| ❑ BS 2624 | All Good Men | 1972 | 15.00 |

**BECHET, SIDNEY**

| Number | Title (A Side/B Side) | Yr | NM |
|---|---|---|---|
| ATLANTIC | | | |
| ❑ ALS-118 [10] | Sidney Bechet Solos | 1952 | 250.00 |
| ❑ 1206 [M] | Sidney Bechet Duets | 1956 | 150.00 |
| *—With Muggsy Spanier* | | | |
| BLUE NOTE | | | |
| ❑ BLP-1201 [M] | Jazz Classics, Volume 1 | 1955 | 300.00 |
| *—"Deep groove" version; Lexington Ave. address on label* | | | |
| ❑ BLP-1201 [M] | Jazz Classics, Volume 1 | 1958 | 200.00 |
| *—"Deep groove" edition, W. 63rd St. address on label* | | | |
| ❑ BLP-1201 [M] | Jazz Classics, Volume 1 | 1963 | 80.00 |
| *—"New York, USA" on label* | | | |
| ❑ BLP-1202 [M] | Jazz Classics, Volume 2 | 1955 | 300.00 |
| *—"Deep groove" version; Lexington Ave. address on label* | | | |
| ❑ BLP-1202 [M] | Jazz Classics, Volume 2 | 1958 | 200.00 |
| *—"Deep groove" edition, W. 63rd St. address on label* | | | |
| ❑ BLP-1202 [M] | Jazz Classics, Volume 2 | 1963 | 80.00 |
| *—"New York, USA" on label* | | | |
| ❑ BLP-1203 [M] | Giant of Jazz, Volume 1 | 1955 | 200.00 |
| *—"Deep groove" edition, W. 63rd St. address on label* | | | |
| ❑ BLP-1203 [M] | Giant of Jazz, Volume 1 | 1955 | 300.00 |
| *—"Deep groove" version; Lexington Ave. address on label* | | | |
| ❑ BLP-1203 [M] | Giant of Jazz, Volume 1 | 1963 | 60.00 |
| *—"New York, USA" on label* | | | |
| ❑ BLP-1204 [M] | Giant of Jazz, Volume 2 | 1955 | 100.00 |
| *—Regular edition, Lexington Ave. address on label* | | | |
| ❑ BLP-1204 [M] | Giant of Jazz, Volume 2 | 1955 | 150.00 |
| *—"Deep groove" version (deep indentation under label on both sides)* | | | |
| ❑ BLP-1207 [M] | The Fabulous Sidney Bechet | 1956 | 200.00 |
| *—"Deep groove" edition, W. 63rd St. address on label* | | | |
| ❑ BLP-1207 [M] | The Fabulous Sidney Bechet | 1956 | 250.00 |
| *—"Deep groove" version; Lexington Ave. address on label* | | | |
| ❑ BLP-7001 [10] | Sidney Bechet's Blue Note Jazz Men | 1950 | 1000. |
| ❑ BLP-7002 [10] | Jazz Classics, Volume 1 | 1950 | 500.00 |
| ❑ BLP-7003 [10] | Jazz Classics, Volume 2 | 1950 | 500.00 |
| ❑ BLP-7008 [10] | Days Beyond Recall | 1951 | 500.00 |
| ❑ BLP-7009 [10] | Sidney Bechet with the Blue Note Jazz Men | 1951 | 500.00 |
| ❑ BLP-7014 [10] | Sidney Bechet's Blue Note Jazz Men, Volume 2 | 1951 | 500.00 |
| ❑ BLP-7020 [10] | The Fabulous Sidney Bechet and His Hot Six | 1952 | 500.00 |
| ❑ BLP-7022 [10] | The Port of Harlem Six | 1952 | 500.00 |
| ❑ BLP-7024 [10] | Jazz Festival Concert, Paris 1952 — Volume 1 | 1953 | 500.00 |
| ❑ BLP-7025 [10] | Jazz Festival Concert, Paris 1952 — Volume 2 | 1953 | 500.00 |
| ❑ BLP-7026 [10] | Dixie by the Fabulous Sidney Bechet | 1953 | 500.00 |
| ❑ BLP-7029 [10] | Olympia Concert, Paris 1954 — Volume 1 | 1954 | 500.00 |
| ❑ BLP-7030 [10] | Olympia Concert, Paris 1954 — Volume 2 | 1954 | 500.00 |
| BRUNSWICK | | | |
| ❑ BL 54037 [M] | Sidney Bechet in Paris | 1958 | 80.00 |
| ❑ BL 54048 [M] | The Sidney Bechet Story | 1959 | 60.00 |
| COLUMBIA | | | |
| ❑ CL 836 [M] | Grand Master of the Soprano Sax and Clarinet | 1956 | 60.00 |
| *—Red and black label with six "eye" logos* | | | |
| ❑ CL 1410 [M] | Sidney Bechet In Concert at the Brussels Fair | 1960 | 40.00 |
| *—Red and black label with six "eye" logos* | | | |
| COMMODORE | | | |
| ❑ FL-20020 [10] | New Orleans Style, Old and New | 1952 | 250.00 |
| DIAL | | | |
| ❑ LP-301 [10] | Black Stick | 195? | 600.00 |
| ❑ LP-302 [10] | Sidney Bechet with Wally Bishop's Orchestra | 195? | 600.00 |
| GOOD TIME JAZZ | | | |
| ❑ L-12013 [M] | King of the Soprano Saxophone | 1955 | 50.00 |
| JAZZ PANORAMA | | | |
| ❑ 1801 [10] | Sidney Bechet, Vol. 1 | 1951 | 200.00 |
| ❑ 1809 [10] | Sidney Bechet, Vol. 2 | 1951 | 200.00 |
| JOLLY ROGER | | | |
| ❑ 5028 [10] | Sidney Bechet | 1954 | 80.00 |
| LONDON | | | |
| ❑ WV 91050 [10] | La Nuit Est Une Sorciere | 1955 | 80.00 |
| MOSAIC | | | |
| ❑ MR6-110 [(6)] | The Complete Blue Note Recordings of Sidney Bechet | 198? | 250.00 |
| *—Limited edition of 7,500* | | | |
| RCA VICTOR | | | |
| ❑ LPT-22 [10] | Sidney Bechet | 1951 | 300.00 |
| ❑ LPT-31 [10] | Treasury of Immortal Performances | 1951 | 300.00 |
| ❑ LPV-510 [M] | Bechet of New Orleans | 1965 | 30.00 |
| *—Purple label original* | | | |
| ❑ LPV-510 [M] | Bechet of New Orleans | 1969 | 20.00 |
| *—Orange label reissue* | | | |
| ❑ LPV-535 [M] | Blue Bechet | 1966 | 30.00 |
| REPRISE | | | |
| ❑ R-6076 [M] | The Immortal Sidney Bechet | 1963 | 25.00 |
| ❑ R9-6076 [R] | The Immortal Sidney Bechet | 1963 | 20.00 |
| RIVERSIDE | | | |
| ❑ RLP-2516 [10] | Sidney Bechet and His Soprano Sax | 1955 | 250.00 |
| RONDO-LETTE | | | |
| ❑ A 24 [M] | Jam Session Vintage 1946 | 1953 | 30.00 |
| SAVOY | | | |
| ❑ MG-15013 [10] | Sidney Bechet | 1952 | 250.00 |
| STORYVILLE | | | |
| ❑ STLP-301 [10] | Sidney Bechet at Storyville, Vol. 1 | 1954 | 200.00 |
| ❑ STLP-306 [10] | Sidney Bechet at Storyville, Vol. 2 | 1954 | 200.00 |
| ❑ STLP-902 [M] | Sidney Bechet at Storyville | 1955 | 50.00 |
| "X" | | | |
| ❑ LVA-3024 [10] | Sidney Bechet and His New Orleans Feetwarmers | 1954 | 120.00 |

**BECHET, SIDNEY, AND EDDIE CONDON**

| Number | Title (A Side/B Side) | Yr | NM |
|---|---|---|---|
| SAVOY | | | |
| ❑ MG-12208 [M] | We Dig Dixieland | 196? | 20.00 |

**BECHET, SIDNEY / OMER SIMEON**

| Number | Title (A Side/B Side) | Yr | NM |
|---|---|---|---|
| JAZZTONE | | | |
| ❑ J-1213 [M] | Jazz A La Creole | 1955 | 40.00 |

**BECHET, SIDNEY, AND MARTIAL SOLAL**

| Number | Title (A Side/B Side) | Yr | NM |
|---|---|---|---|
| WORLD PACIFIC | | | |
| ❑ PJ-1236 [M] | Young Ideas | 1957 | 80.00 |
| ❑ WP-1236 [M] | Young Ideas | 1957 | 60.00 |
| *—Reissue with new prefix* | | | |

**BECHET, SIDNEY, AND MUGGSY SPANIER**

| Number | Title (A Side/B Side) | Yr | NM |
|---|---|---|---|
| ALLEGRO ELITE | | | |
| ❑ 4123 [10] | Bechet-Spanier Quartet | 1956 | 40.00 |

**BECK**

| Number | Title (A Side/B Side) | Yr | NM |
|---|---|---|---|
| BONG LOAD | | | |
| ❑ BL 12 | Mellow Gold | 1993 | 80.00 |
| ❑ BL 30 | Odelay | 1996 | 70.00 |
| ❑ BL 39 | Mutations | 1999 | 100.00 |
| *—Includes bonus 7-inch single with sleeve* | | | |
| ❑ BL 46 | Midnite Vultures | 2000 | 80.00 |
| DGC | | | |
| ❑ B0004372-01 [(2)] | Sea Change | 2006 | 15.00 |
| *—CD version issued in 2002* | | | |
| FINGERPAINT | | | |
| ❑ 02 [10] | A Western Harvest Field by Moonlight | 1992 | 120.00 |
| *—First 3,000 contain a unique insert fingerpainted by Beck and friends at the record release party* | | | |
| ❑ 02 [10] | A Western Harvest Field by Moonlight | 1995 | 80.00 |
| *—Later pressings do not contain a fingerpainted insert* | | | |
| FLIPSIDE | | | |
| ❑ 660 [(2)] | Stereopathetic Soulmanure | 2000 | 15.00 |
| *—Vinyl issue of 1994 CD compilation* | | | |
| INTERSCOPE | | | |
| ❑ B0003546-1 [(2)] | Guero | 2005 | 25.00 |
| ❑ B0005650-01 [(2)] | Guerolito | 2006 | 15.00 |
| K | | | |
| ❑ KLP 28 | One Foot in the Grave | 1994 | 50.00 |

**BECK, JEFF** Includes the Jeff Beck Group, of whom ROD STEWART was lead singer. Also see BECK, BOGERT AND APPICE; THE YARDBIRDS.

| Number | Title (A Side/B Side) | Yr | NM |
|---|---|---|---|
| ACCORD | | | |
| ❑ SN-7141 | Early Anthology | 1981 | 10.00 |

| Number | Title (A Side/B Side) | Yr | NM |
|---|---|---|---|
| **EPIC** | | | |
| ❑ AS 151 [DJ] | Everything You Always Wanted to Hear by Jeff Beck But Were Afraid to Ask For | 1977 | 20.00 |
| *—Promo-only sampler* | | | |
| ❑ A2S 850 [(2)DJ] | Then and Now | 1981 | 25.00 |
| *—Promo-only sampler* | | | |
| ❑ BN 26413 | Truth | 1973 | 10.00 |
| *—Orange label* | | | |
| ❑ BN 26413 [M] | Truth | 1968 | 40.00 |
| *—Mono is promo only with stereo number; cover has "Mono" sticker covering the word "Stereo"* | | | |
| ❑ BN 26413 [S] | Truth | 1968 | 15.00 |
| *—Yellow label* | | | |
| ❑ PE 26413 | Truth | 198? | 8.00 |
| *—Reissue with new prefix* | | | |
| ❑ BN 26478 | Beck-Ola | 1969 | 15.00 |
| *—Yellow label* | | | |
| ❑ BN 26478 | Beck-Ola | 1973 | 10.00 |
| *—Orange label* | | | |
| ❑ PE 26478 | Beck-Ola | 197? | 8.00 |
| *—Reissue with new prefix* | | | |
| ❑ PE 30973 | Rough and Ready | 198? | 8.00 |
| *—Budget-line reissue* | | | |
| ❑ EQ 30993 [Q] | Rough and Ready | 1972 | 20.00 |
| ❑ KE 30993 | Rough and Ready | 1971 | 15.00 |
| *—Yellow label* | | | |
| ❑ KE 30993 | Rough and Ready | 1973 | 10.00 |
| *—Orange label* | | | |
| ❑ EQ 31331 [Q] | Jeff Beck Group | 1972 | 20.00 |
| ❑ KE 31331 | Jeff Beck Group | 1972 | 15.00 |
| *—Yellow label* | | | |
| ❑ KE 31331 | Jeff Beck Group | 1973 | 10.00 |
| *—Orange label* | | | |
| ❑ PE 31331 | Jeff Beck Group | 198? | 8.00 |
| *—Budget-line reissue* | | | |
| ❑ PE 33409 | Blow by Blow | 1975 | 10.00 |
| *—Orange label, no bar code on cover* | | | |
| ❑ PE 33409 | Blow by Blow | 198? | 8.00 |
| *—Reissue with dark blue label and bar code on cover* | | | |
| ❑ PEQ 33409 [Q] | Blow by Blow | 1975 | 20.00 |
| ❑ BG 33779 [(2)] | Truth/Beck-Ola | 1975 | 12.00 |
| ❑ PE 33849 | Wired | 1976 | 10.00 |
| *—Orange label, no bar code on cover* | | | |
| ❑ PE 33849 | Wired | 1979 | 8.00 |
| *—Reissue with dark blue label; with or without bar code on cover* | | | |
| ❑ PEQ 33849 [Q] | Wired | 1976 | 20.00 |
| ❑ PE 34433 | Jeff Beck with the Jan Hammer Group Live | 1977 | 10.00 |
| *—Orange label, no bar code on cover* | | | |
| ❑ PE 34433 | Jeff Beck with the Jan Hammer Group Live | 198? | 8.00 |
| *—Reissue with dark blue label and bar code on cover* | | | |
| ❑ FE 35684 | There and Back | 1980 | 10.00 |
| ❑ PE 35684 | There and Back | 1985 | 8.00 |
| *—Budget-line reissue* | | | |
| ❑ FE 39483 | Flash | 1985 | 10.00 |
| ❑ HE 43409 | Blow by Blow | 1980 | 30.00 |
| *—Half-speed mastered edition* | | | |
| ❑ HE 43849 | Wired | 198? | 30.00 |
| *—Half-speed mastered edition* | | | |
| ❑ FE 44313 | Jeff Beck's Guitar Shop | 1989 | 15.00 |
| **BECK, PIA** | | | |
| **EPIC** | | | |
| ❑ LN 3269 [M] | Dutch Treat | 1956 | 40.00 |
| **BECK, BOGERT & APPICE** | | | |
| **EPIC** | | | |
| ❑ CQ 32140 [Q] | Beck, Bogert & Appice | 1973 | 20.00 |
| ❑ KE 32140 | Beck, Bogert & Appice | 1973 | 10.00 |
| *—Orange label* | | | |
| ❑ KE 32140 | Beck, Bogert & Appice | 1973 | 15.00 |
| *—Yellow label* | | | |
| ❑ PE 32140 | Beck, Bogert & Appice | 198? | 8.00 |
| *—Budget-line reissue* | | | |
| **BEDIENT, JACK** | | | |
| **EXECUTIVE PRODUCTIONS** | | | |
| ❑ (no #) [M] | Jack Bedient | 196? | 80.00 |
| **FANTASY** | | | |
| ❑ 3365 [M] | Live at Harvey's | 1965 | 60.00 |
| **SATORI** | | | |
| ❑ LP 1001 [M] | Where Did She Go? | 1966 | 60.00 |
| **TROPHY** | | | |
| ❑ 101 [M] | Two Sides of Jack Bedient | 1964 | 60.00 |
| **BEDLAM** | | | |
| **CHRYSALIS** | | | |
| ❑ CHR-1048 | Bedlam | 1973 | 25.00 |
| **BEE, DAVID** | | | |
| **BALLY** | | | |
| ❑ BAL-12005 [M] | Belgian Jazz | 1956 | 30.00 |
| **JUBILEE** | | | |
| ❑ JLP-1076 [M] | Dixieland at the World's Fair | 1958 | 25.00 |

Beck, *Mellow Gold,* Bong Load BL 12, $80.

| Number | Title (A Side/B Side) | Yr | NM |
|---|---|---|---|
| **BEE, MOLLY** | | | |
| **ACCORD** | | | |
| ❑ 7901 | Sounds Fine to Me | 1982 | 10.00 |
| **CAPITOL** | | | |
| ❑ T 1097 [M] | Young Romance | 1958 | 40.00 |
| **GRANITE** | | | |
| ❑ 1002 | Good Golly Ms. Molly | 1974 | 12.00 |
| **MGM** | | | |
| ❑ E-4303 [M] | It's Great, It's Molly Bee | 1965 | 20.00 |
| ❑ SE-4303 [S] | It's Great, It's Molly Bee | 1965 | 25.00 |
| ❑ E-4423 [M] | Swingin' Country | 1967 | 20.00 |
| ❑ SE-4423 [S] | Swingin' Country | 1967 | 25.00 |
| **BEE GEES** Also see ROBIN GIBB. | | | |
| **ATCO** | | | |
| ❑ 33-223 [M] | Bee Gees' 1st | 1967 | 30.00 |
| ❑ SD 33-223 | Bee Gees' 1st | 1969 | 10.00 |
| *—Yellow label reissue* | | | |
| ❑ SD 33-223 [S] | Bee Gees' 1st | 1967 | 20.00 |
| *—Brown and purple label original* | | | |
| ❑ 33-233 [M] | Horizontal | 1968 | 30.00 |
| ❑ SD 33-233 | Horizontal | 1969 | 10.00 |
| *—Yellow label reissue* | | | |
| ❑ SD 33-233 [S] | Horizontal | 1968 | 20.00 |
| *—Brown and purple label original* | | | |
| ❑ 33-253 [M] | Idea | 1968 | 50.00 |
| *—White label promo only* | | | |
| ❑ SD 33-253 | Idea | 1969 | 10.00 |
| *—Yellow label reissue* | | | |
| ❑ SD 33-253 [S] | Idea | 1968 | 20.00 |
| *—Brown and purple label original* | | | |
| ❑ 33-264 [M] | Rare, Precious & Beautiful | 1968 | 30.00 |
| *—White label promo only* | | | |
| ❑ SD 33-264 | Rare, Precious & Beautiful | 1969 | 10.00 |
| *—Yellow label reissue* | | | |
| ❑ SD 33-264 [R] | Rare, Precious & Beautiful | 1968 | 15.00 |
| *—Brown and purple label original* | | | |
| ❑ 33-292 [M] | Best of Bee Gees | 1969 | 30.00 |
| *—White label promo only* | | | |
| ❑ SD 33-292 [S] | Best of Bee Gees | 1969 | 12.00 |
| ❑ 33-321 [M] | Rare, Precious & Beautiful, Volume 2 | 1970 | 30.00 |
| *—White label promo only* | | | |
| ❑ SD 33-321 [R] | Rare, Precious & Beautiful, Volume 2 | 1970 | 12.00 |

| Number | Title (A Side/B Side) | Yr | NM |
|---|---|---|---|
| ❑ SD 33-327 | Cucumber Castle | 1970 | 12.00 |
| ❑ 33-353 [M] | 2 Years On | 1971 | 30.00 |
| *—White label promo only; "DJ Copy Monaural" sticker on cover* | | | |
| ❑ SD 33-353 [S] | 2 Years On | 1971 | 12.00 |
| ❑ SD 2-702 [(2)] | Odessa | 1969 | 40.00 |
| *—Red felt cover* | | | |
| ❑ SD 2-702 [(2)] | Odessa | 1969 | 80.00 |
| *—Record club editions with plain red cover* | | | |
| ❑ SD 7003 | Trafalgar | 1971 | 12.00 |
| ❑ SD 7012 | To Whom It May Concern | 1972 | 12.00 |
| **MOBILE FIDELITY** | | | |
| ❑ 1-263 | Trafalgar | 1996 | 40.00 |
| *—Audiophile vinyl* | | | |
| **NAUTILUS** | | | |
| ❑ NR-17 | Spirits Having Flown | 1981 | 30.00 |
| ❑ NR-42 | Living Eyes | 1982 | 100.00 |
| *—Record was never released; value is for test pressings* | | | |
| **PICKWICK** | | | |
| ❑ BAN-90011 [R] | Turn Around, Look at Me | 1978 | 8.00 |
| *—Reissue of Australian recordings* | | | |
| ❑ BAN-90021 [R] | Monday's Rain | 1978 | 8.00 |
| *—Reissue of Australian recordings* | | | |
| ❑ BAN-90031 [R] | Take Hold of That Star | 1978 | 8.00 |
| *—Reissue of Australian recordings* | | | |
| ❑ BAN-90041 [R] | Peace of Mind | 1978 | 8.00 |
| *—Reissue of Australian recordings; tracks on this LP were making their first appearance in the U.S.* | | | |
| **RSO** | | | |
| ❑ SMP-1 [DJ] | The Words and Music of Maurice, Barry and Robin Gibb | 1979 | 50.00 |
| *—Promo-only publisher's sampler* | | | |
| ❑ PRO 033 [DJ] | Saturday Night Fever Special Disco Versions | 1978 | 50.00 |
| *—Promo-only sampler; contains an otherwise unavailable extended version of "Stayin' Alive"* | | | |
| ❑ SO 870 [M] | Life in a Tin Can | 1973 | 60.00 |
| *—Mono is white label promo only; cover has red "d/j copy monaural" sticker on front; Side 1 master number is "SO-14153"; Side 2 master number is "SO-14154"* | | | |
| ❑ SO 870 [S] | Life in a Tin Can | 1973 | 10.00 |
| *—Side 1 master number is "ST-SO-722677"; Side 2 master number is "ST-SO-722678"* | | | |
| ❑ SO 874 | Best of Bee Gees | 1973 | 10.00 |
| *—Reissue of Atco SD 33-292* | | | |
| ❑ SO 875 | Best of Bee Gees, Vol. 2 | 1973 | 10.00 |

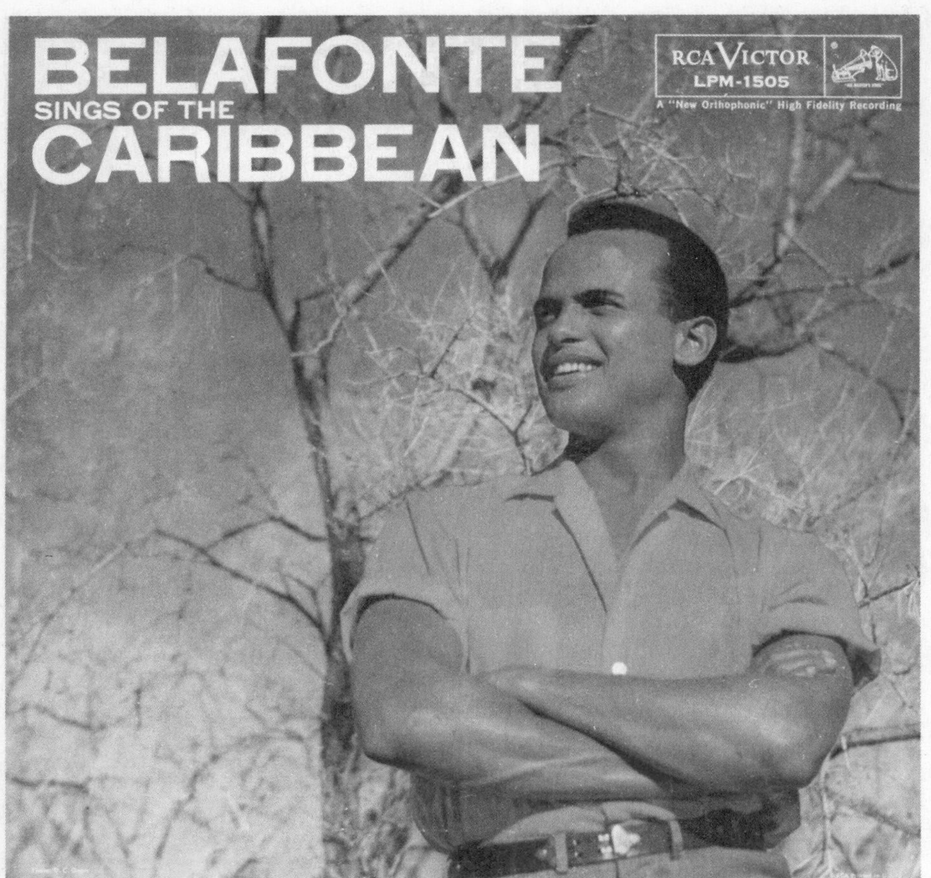


Harry Belafonte, *Belafonte Sings of the Caribbean,* RCA Victor LPM-1505, mono, $30.

| Number | Title (A Side/B Side) | Yr | NM |
|---|---|---|---|
| ❑ PUB-1000 [DJ] | Unichappell Publisher's Sampler | 1980 | 50.00 |
| ❑ RPO 1008 [DJ] | Select Disco Cuts from "Spirits Having Flown" | 1979 | 30.00 |
| ❑ RS-1-3003 | Children of the World | 1976 | 10.00 |
| ❑ RS-1-3006 | Bee Gees Gold, Volume One | 1976 | 10.00 |
| ❑ RS-1-3007 | Odessa | 1976 | 10.00 |
| *—Condensed version of Atco original* | | | |
| ❑ RS-1-3024 | Main Course | 1977 | 8.00 |
| ❑ RS-1-3041 | Spirits Having Flown | 1979 | 10.00 |
| *—Some pressings have a cardboard innersleeve, others a paper innersleeve. No difference in value.* | | | |
| ❑ RS-1-3042 [PD] | Spirits Having Flown | 1979 | 15.00 |
| ❑ RS-1-3098 | Living Eyes | 1981 | 10.00 |
| ❑ RS-2-3901 [(2)] | Here At Last...Bee Gees...Live | 1977 | 12.00 |
| ❑ RS-2-4200 [(2)] | Bee Gees' Greatest | 1979 | 12.00 |
| ❑ SO 4800 | Mr. Natural | 1974 | 10.00 |
| ❑ SO 4807 | Main Course | 1975 | 10.00 |
| ❑ 823274-1 [(2)] | Here At Last...Bee Gees...Live | 1984 | 10.00 |
| ❑ 823658-1 | Children of the World | 1984 | 8.00 |
| ❑ 823659-1 | Bee Gees Gold, Volume One | 1984 | 8.00 |
| ❑ 825390-1 [(2)] | Bee Gees' Greatest | 1984 | 10.00 |
| *—Gatefold replaced by single-pocket cover* | | | |

WARNER BROS.

| Number | Title (A Side/B Side) | Yr | NM |
|---|---|---|---|
| ❑ 25541 | E.S.P. | 1987 | 10.00 |
| ❑ 25887 | One | 1989 | 12.00 |

## BEETHOVEN SOUL

DOT

| Number | Title (A Side/B Side) | Yr | NM |
|---|---|---|---|
| ❑ DLP-3821 [M] | Beethoven Soul | 1967 | 25.00 |
| ❑ DLP-25821 [S] | Beethoven Soul | 1967 | 25.00 |

## BEGINNING OF THE END, THE

ALSTON

| Number | Title (A Side/B Side) | Yr | NM |
|---|---|---|---|
| ❑ SD 33-379 | Funky Nassau | 1971 | 20.00 |

## BEIDERBECKE, BIX

COLUMBIA

| Number | Title (A Side/B Side) | Yr | NM |
|---|---|---|---|
| ❑ CL 507 [M] | The Bix Beiderbecke Story, Volume 1: Bix and His Gang | 1953 | 40.00 |
| *—Maroon label, gold print* | | | |
| ❑ GL 507 [M] | The Bix Beiderbecke Story, Volume 1: Bix and His Gang | 1952 | 50.00 |
| *—Black label, silver print* | | | |
| ❑ CL 508 [M] | The Bix Beiderbecke Story, Volume 2: Bix and Tram | 1953 | 40.00 |
| *—Maroon label, gold print* | | | |
| ❑ GL 508 [M] | The Bix Beiderbecke Story, Volume 2: Bix and Tram | 1952 | 50.00 |
| *—Black label, silver print* | | | |
| ❑ CL 509 [M] | The Bix Beiderbecke Story, Volume 3: The Whiteman Years | 1953 | 40.00 |
| *—Maroon label, gold print* | | | |
| ❑ GL 509 [M] | The Bix Beiderbecke Story, Volume 3: The Whiteman Years | 1952 | 50.00 |
| *—Black label, silver print* | | | |
| ❑ CL 844 [M] | The Bix Beiderbecke Story, Volume 1: Bix and His Gang | 1956 | 30.00 |
| *—Red and black label with six "eye" logos* | | | |
| ❑ CL 844 [M] | The Bix Beiderbecke Story, Volume 1: Bix and His Gang | 1963 | 20.00 |
| *—"Guaranteed High Fidelity" label* | | | |
| ❑ CL 845 [M] | The Bix Beiderbecke Story, Volume 2: Bix and Tram | 1956 | 30.00 |
| *—Red and black label with six "eye" logos* | | | |
| ❑ CL 845 [M] | The Bix Beiderbecke Story, Volume 2: Bix and Tram | 1963 | 20.00 |
| *—"Guaranteed High Fidelity" label* | | | |
| ❑ CL 846 [M] | The Bix Beiderbecke Story, Volume 3: The Whiteman Years | 1956 | 30.00 |
| *—Red and black label with six "eye" logos* | | | |
| ❑ CL 846 [M] | The Bix Beiderbecke Story, Volume 3: The Whiteman Years | 1963 | 20.00 |
| *—"Guaranteed High Fidelity" label* | | | |

COLUMBIA MASTERWORKS

| Number | Title (A Side/B Side) | Yr | NM |
|---|---|---|---|
| ❑ ML 4811 [M] | The Bix Beiderbecke Story, Volume 1 | 1950 | 70.00 |
| ❑ ML 4812 [M] | The Bix Beiderbecke Story, Volume 2 | 1950 | 70.00 |
| ❑ ML 4813 [M] | The Bix Beiderbecke Story, Volume 3 | 1950 | 70.00 |

JOLLY ROGER

| Number | Title (A Side/B Side) | Yr | NM |
|---|---|---|---|
| ❑ 5010 [10] | Bix Beiderbecke | 1954 | 50.00 |

RCA VICTOR

| Number | Title (A Side/B Side) | Yr | NM |
|---|---|---|---|
| ❑ LPM-2323 [M] | The Bix Beiderbecke Legend | 1961 | 25.00 |
| *—"Long Play" on label* | | | |

RIVERSIDE

| Number | Title (A Side/B Side) | Yr | NM |
|---|---|---|---|
| ❑ RLP 12-123 [M] | Bix Beiderbecke and the Wolverines | 195? | 30.00 |
| *—Blue label with microphone logo* | | | |
| ❑ RLP 12-123 [M] | Bix Beiderbecke and the Wolverines | 1956 | 50.00 |
| *—White label, blue print* | | | |
| ❑ RLP-1023 [10] | Early Bix | 1954 | 80.00 |
| ❑ RLP-1050 [10] | Bix Beiderbecke and the Wolverines | 1954 | 80.00 |

## BEL-AIRE GIRLS, THE

EVEREST

| Number | Title (A Side/B Side) | Yr | NM |
|---|---|---|---|
| ❑ STBR-1081 [S] | The Bel-Aire Girls Sing Along with the Teen-Agers | 1960 | 80.00 |
| ❑ LPBR-5081 [M] | The Bel-Aire Girls Sing Along with the Teen-Agers | 1960 | 60.00 |

## BEL-AIRE POPS ORCHESTRA, THE

LIBERTY

| Number | Title (A Side/B Side) | Yr | NM |
|---|---|---|---|
| ❑ LRP-3414 [M] | Jan and Dean's Pop Symphony No. 1 | 1965 | 120.00 |
| ❑ LST-7414 [S] | Jan and Dean's Pop Symphony No. 1 | 1965 | 200.00 |

## BELAFONTE, HARRY

COLUMBIA

| Number | Title (A Side/B Side) | Yr | NM |
|---|---|---|---|
| ❑ FC 37489 | Loving You Is Where I Belong | 1981 | 10.00 |

DCC COMPACT CLASSICS

| Number | Title (A Side/B Side) | Yr | NM |
|---|---|---|---|
| ❑ LPZ-2039 | Jump Up Calypso | 1997 | 60.00 |
| *—Audiophile vinyl* | | | |

EMI

| Number | Title (A Side/B Side) | Yr | NM |
|---|---|---|---|
| ❑ E1-92247 | Belafonte '89 | 1989 | 12.00 |

EMI MANHATAN

| Number | Title (A Side/B Side) | Yr | NM |
|---|---|---|---|
| ❑ E1-46971 | Paradise in Gazankulu | 1988 | 12.00 |

PAIR

| Number | Title (A Side/B Side) | Yr | NM |
|---|---|---|---|
| ❑ PDL2-1060 [(2)] | The Belafonte Song Book | 1986 | 12.00 |

RCA CAMDEN

| Number | Title (A Side/B Side) | Yr | NM |
|---|---|---|---|
| ❑ ACL1-0502 | Abraham, Martin and John | 1974 | 10.00 |
| ❑ CAS-2599 | Harry | 1972 | 10.00 |

RCA CUSTOM EDITION

| Number | Title (A Side/B Side) | Yr | NM |
|---|---|---|---|
| ❑ DRL1-0068 | I Wish You a Merry Christmas | 1973 | 15.00 |
| *—Reissue of LSP-2424 with two tracks deleted* | | | |

RCA VICTOR

| Number | Title (A Side/B Side) | Yr | NM |
|---|---|---|---|
| ❑ APL1-0094 | Play Me | 1973 | 12.00 |
| ❑ ANL1-0979 | Pure Gold | 1975 | 10.00 |
| ❑ LOP-1006 [M] | Belafonte Sings the Blues | 1958 | 30.00 |
| *—Original issue* | | | |
| ❑ LPM-1022 [M] | "Mark Twain" and Other Folk Favorites | 1954 | 50.00 |
| ❑ LSP-1022(e) [R] | "Mark Twain" and Other Folk Favorites | 196? | 12.00 |
| ❑ LPM-1150 [M] | Belafonte | 1955 | 50.00 |
| ❑ LSP-1150(e) [R] | Belafonte | 196? | 12.00 |
| ❑ AFL1-1248 | Calypso | 1977 | 10.00 |
| *—Reissue with new prefix* | | | |
| ❑ LPM-1248 [M] | Calypso | 1956 | 30.00 |
| ❑ LSP-1248(e) [R] | Calypso | 196? | 12.00 |
| ❑ LPM-1402 [M] | An Evening with Belafonte | 1957 | 25.00 |
| ❑ LSP-1402(e) [R] | An Evening with Belafonte | 1960 | 12.00 |
| *—Dog on top* | | | |
| ❑ LSP-1402(e) [R] | An Evening with Belafonte | 1969 | 10.00 |
| *—Orange label* | | | |
| ❑ ANL1-1434 | An Evening with Belafonte | 1976 | 10.00 |
| *—Reissue of LSP-1402* | | | |
| ❑ LPM-1505 [M] | Belafonte Sings of the Caribbean | 1957 | 30.00 |
| ❑ LSP-1505(e) [R] | Belafonte Sings of the Caribbean | 196? | 12.00 |
| ❑ LOC-1507 [M] | Porgy and Bess | 1959 | 20.00 |
| ❑ LSO-1507 [S] | Porgy and Bess | 1959 | 25.00 |
| *—With Lena Horne* | | | |
| ❑ LPM-1887 [M] | To Wish You a Merry Christmas | 1958 | 25.00 |
| ❑ LSP-1887 [S] | To Wish You a Merry Christmas | 1958 | 40.00 |
| ❑ LPM-1927 [M] | Love Is a Gentle Thing | 1959 | 20.00 |
| ❑ LSP-1927 [S] | Love Is a Gentle Thing | 1959 | 25.00 |
| ❑ LPM-1972 [M] | Belafonte Sings the Blues | 1959 | 20.00 |
| *—Reissue of LOP-1006* | | | |
| ❑ LSP-1972 | Belafonte Sings the Blues | 199? | 25.00 |
| *—Classic Records reissue on audiophile vinyl* | | | |
| ❑ LSP-1972 [S] | Belafonte Sings the Blues | 1959 | 25.00 |
| ❑ LPM-2022 [M] | My Lord What a Mornin' | 1960 | 20.00 |
| ❑ LSP-2022 [S] | My Lord What a Mornin' | 1960 | 25.00 |
| ❑ LPM-2194 [M] | Swing Dat Hammer | 1961 | 20.00 |
| ❑ LSP-2194 [S] | Swing Dat Hammer | 1961 | 25.00 |
| ❑ LPM-2309 [M] | At Home and Abroad | 1961 | 20.00 |
| ❑ LSP-2309 [S] | At Home and Abroad | 1961 | 25.00 |
| ❑ ANL1-2324 | The Midnight Special | 1976 | 10.00 |
| *—Reissue of LSP-2449* | | | |
| ❑ LPM-2388 [M] | Jump Up Calypso | 1961 | 20.00 |
| ❑ LSP-2388 [S] | Jump Up Calypso | 1961 | 25.00 |
| ❑ LPM-2449 [M] | The Midnight Special | 1962 | 30.00 |
| ❑ LSP-2449 [S] | The Midnight Special | 1962 | 40.00 |
| *—The above LP features Bob Dylan on harmonica on the title track, his first appearance on record* | | | |
| ❑ CPL1-2469 | A Legendary Performer | 1977 | 10.00 |
| ❑ LPM-2574 [M] | The Many Moods of Belafonte | 1962 | 20.00 |



**Except when noted otherwise, VG = 25% of NM, and VG+ = 50% of NM. (Example: VG = $2.00, VG+ = $4.00 and NM = $8.00.)**

Number | Title (A Side/B Side) | Yr | NM

❑ LSP-2574 [S] The Many Moods of Belafonte 196? 20.00
*—"Stereo" on black label, "RCA Victor" in white*
❑ LSP-2574 [S] The Many Moods of Belafonte 1962 25.00
*—"Living Stereo" on label, "RCA Victor" in silver*
❑ LSP-2574 [S] The Many Moods of Belafonte 1969 12.00
*—Orange label*
❑ LPM-2626 [M] To Wish You a Merry Christmas 1962 20.00
*—Reissue of LPM-1887 with new cover and one additional track*
❑ LSP-2626 [S] To Wish You a Merry Christmas 1962 25.00
❑ LPM-2695 [M] Streets I Have Walked 1963 20.00
❑ LSP-2695 [S] Streets I Have Walked 1963 25.00
❑ LPM-2953 [M] Ballads, Blues and Boasters 1964 15.00
❑ LSP-2953 [S] Ballads, Blues and Boasters 1964 20.00
❑ LPM-3415 [M] An Evening with Belafonte/Mouskouri 1966 15.00
❑ LSP-3415 [S] An Evening with Belafonte/Mouskouri 1966 20.00
*—With Nana Mouskouri*
❑ LPM-3420 [M] An Evening with Belafonte/Makeba 1965 15.00
❑ LSP-3420 [S] An Evening with Belafonte/Makeba 1965 20.00
*—With Miriam Makeba*
❑ LPM-3571 [M] In My Quiet Room 1966 12.00
❑ LSP-3571 [S] In My Quiet Room 1966 15.00
❑ LPM-3658 [M] Calypso in Brass 1967 12.00
❑ LSP-3658 [S] Calypso in Brass 1967 15.00
❑ LPM-3779 [M] Belafonte on Campus 1967 12.00
❑ LSP-3779 [S] Belafonte on Campus 1967 15.00
❑ AYL1-3801(e) [R]Calypso 1980 8.00
❑ AYL1-3860(e) [R]Pure Gold 1980 8.00
❑ LPM-3938 [M] Belafonte Sings of Love 1968 15.00
❑ LSP-3938 [S] Belafonte Sings of Love 1968 15.00
❑ LSP-4255 Homeward Bound 1969 15.00
❑ LSP-4301 By Request 1970 12.00
❑ LSP-4481 Warm Touch 1971 12.00
❑ LSP-4521 Calypso Carnival 1971 12.00
❑ LOC-6006 [(2)M]Belafonte at Carnegie Hall 1959 25.00
❑ LSO-6006 [(2)S]Belafonte at Carnegie Hall 1959 100.00
❑ LSO-6006 [(2)S]Belafonte at Carnegie Hall 1996 40.00
*—Classic Records reissue on audiophile vinyl*
❑ LOC-6007 [(2)M]Belafonte Returns to Carnegie Hall 1960 20.00
❑ LSO-6007 [(2)] Belafonte Returns to Carnegie Hall 1996 40.00
*—Classic Records reissue on audiophile vinyl*
❑ LSO-6007 [(2)S]Belafonte Returns to Carnegie Hall 1960 50.00
*—The above LP also has tracks by Odetta, Miriam Makeba and The Chad Mitchell Trio (the latter for the first time on record)*
❑ LOC-6009 [(2)M]Belafonte at the Greek Theatre 1964 20.00
❑ LSO-6009 [(2)S]Belafonte at the Greek Theatre 1964 50.00
❑ VPS-6024 [(2)] This Is Harry Belafonte 1970 15.00
❑ VPSX-6077 [(2)]Belafonte Live 1972 15.00

TIME-LIFE
❑ SLGD-17 [(2)] Legendary Singers: Harry Belafonte 1986 15.00

**BELEW, CARL**

BUCKBOARD
❑ BBS 1014 Singing My Song 197? 10.00

DECCA
❑ DL 4074 [M] Carl Belew 1960 25.00
❑ DL 74074 [S] Carl Belew 1960 30.00

HILLTOP
❑ JM-6013 [M] Another Lonely Night 1965 20.00
❑ JS-6013 [S] Another Lonely Night 1965 20.00

PICCADILLY
❑ 3356 Big Time Gambling Man 198? 10.00

RCA VICTOR
❑ LPM-2848 [M] Hello Out There 1964 20.00
❑ LSP-2848 [S] Hello Out There 1964 25.00
❑ LPM-3381 [M] Am I That Easy to Forget? 1965 20.00
❑ LSP-3381 [S] Am I That Easy to Forget? 1965 25.00
❑ LPM-3919 [M] Twelve Shades of Belew 1968 50.00
❑ LSP-3919 [S] Twelve Shades of Belew 1968 20.00

VOCALION
❑ VL 3774 [M] Country Songs 196? 12.00
❑ VL 3791 [M] Lonely Street 1967 15.00
❑ VL 73774 [S] Country Songs 196? 12.00
❑ VL 73791 [S] Lonely Street 1967 12.00

WRANGLER
❑ WR 1007 [M] Carl Belew 1962 30.00
❑ WRS 31007 [S]Carl Belew 1962 40.00

**BELL, AARON**

HERALD
❑ HLP-0100 [M] Three Swinging Bells 1955 60.00

LION
❑ L-70111 [M] Music from "77 Sunset Strip" 1959 25.00
❑ L-70112 [M] Music from "Peter Gunn" 1959 25.00
❑ L-70113 [M] Music from "Victory at Sea" 1959 25.00

RCA VICTOR
❑ LPM-1876 [M] After the Party's Over 1958 50.00

**BELL, ARCHIE, AND THE DRELLS**

ATLANTIC
❑ 8181 [M] Tighten Up 1968 50.00
❑ SD 8181 [S] Tighten Up 1968 30.00
❑ SD 8204 I Can't Stop Dancing 1968 30.00
❑ SD 8226 There's Gonna Be a Showdown 1969 30.00

PHILADELPHIA INT'L.
❑ PZ 34323 Where Will You Go When the Party's Over 1976 10.00
❑ PZ 34855 Hard Not to Like It 1977 10.00
❑ JZ 36096 Strategy 1979 10.00

TSOP
❑ PZ 33844 Dance Your Troubles Away 1975 10.00

**BELL, CHARLES**

ATLANTIC
❑ SD 1400 [S] Another Dimension 1963 20.00

COLUMBIA
❑ CL 1582 [M] The Charles Bell Contemporary Jazz Quartet 1961 20.00
❑ CS 8382 [S] The Charles Bell Contemporary Jazz Quartet 1961 25.00

GATEWAY
❑ S-7012 [S] Charles Bell in Concert 1964 20.00

**BELL, FREDDIE, AND THE BELL BOYS**

MERCURY
❑ MG-20289 [M] Rock and Roll… All Flavors 1957 200.00

20TH FOX
❑ TF-4146 [M] Bells Are Swinging 1964 25.00
❑ TFS-4146 [S] Bells Are Swinging 1964 30.00

**BELL, GRAEME**

ANGEL
❑ ANG.60002 [10]Inside Jazz Down Under 1954 60.00

**BELL, MARTY**

RIVERSIDE
❑ RLP 12-206 [M]The Voice of Marty Bell 1956 60.00
*—White label, blue print*
❑ RLP 12-206 [M]The Voice of Marty Bell 1957 40.00
*—Blue label, microphone logo*

**BELL, VINCENT**

DECCA
❑ DL 4938 [M] Pop Goes the Electric Sitar 1967 20.00
❑ DL 74938 [S] Pop Goes the Electric Sitar 1967 15.00
❑ DL 75212 Airport Love Theme 1970 15.00

MUSICOR
❑ MM-3009 [M] 51 Motion Picture Favorites 1963 15.00
❑ MS-3009 [S] 51 Motion Picture Favorites 1963 20.00
❑ MM-3047 [M] Big 16 Guitar Favorites 1965 15.00
❑ MS-3047 [S] Big 16 Guitar Favorites 1965 20.00

VERVE
❑ V-8574 [M] Whistle Stop 1964 15.00
❑ V6-8574 [S] Whistle Stop 1964 20.00

**BELL, WILLIAM**

KAT FAMILY
❑ FZ 38643 Survivor 1983 10.00

MERCURY
❑ SRM-1-1146 Coming Back for More 1977 10.00
❑ SRM-1-1193 It's Time You Took Another Listen 1978 10.00

STAX
❑ 719 [M] Soul of a Bell 1967 40.00
❑ S-719 [S] Soul of a Bell 1967 50.00
❑ ST-2014 [M] Bound to Happen 1969 50.00
*—Mono is promo only*
❑ STS-2014 [S] Bound to Happen 1969 30.00
❑ STS-2037 Wow… 1971 30.00
❑ STS-3005 Phases of Reality 1973 20.00
❑ STS-5502 Relating 1974 20.00
❑ MPS-8541 The Best of William Bell 1988 10.00

WRC
❑ WL-3007 On a Roll 1986 12.00

**BELLETTO, AL**

CAPITOL
❑ T 751 [M] Half and Half 1956 50.00
❑ T 901 [M] Whisper Not 1957 50.00
❑ T 6506 [M] The Al Belletto Sextette 1955 60.00
❑ T 6514 [M] Sounds and Songs 1955 60.00

KING
❑ 716 [M] The Big Sound 1961 50.00

**BELLSON, LOUIS**

CAPITOL
❑ H 348 [10] Just Jazz All-Stars 1952 200.00

DISCWASHER
❑ 002 Note Smoking 1979 25.00
*—Direct-to-disc recording*

IMPULSE!
❑ A-9107 [M] Thunderbird 1966 25.00
❑ AS-9107 [S] Thunderbird 1966 30.00

NORGRAN
❑ MGN-7 [10] The Amazing Artistry of Louis Bellson 1954 200.00
❑ MGN-14 [10] The Exciting Mr. Bellson (And His Big Band) 1954 200.00
❑ MGN-1007 [M] Journey Into Love 1954 150.00
❑ MGN-1011 [M] Louis Bellson and His Drums 1954 150.00
❑ MGN-1020 [M] The Driving Louis Bellson 1955 100.00
❑ MGN-1046 [M] Skin Deep 1955 100.00
❑ MGN-1099 [M] The Hawk Talks 1956 80.00
*—Reissue of 1020*

ROULETTE
❑ R-52087 [M] Big Band Jazz from the Summit 1962 20.00
❑ SR-52087 [S] Big Band Jazz from the Summit 1962 25.00
❑ R-65002 [M] Around the World in Percussion 1962 20.00
❑ SR-65002 [S] Around the World in Percussion 1962 25.00

VERVE
❑ MGV-2123 [M] The Brilliant Bellson Sound 1960 50.00
❑ V-2123 [M] The Brilliant Bellson Sound 1960 20.00
❑ V6-2123 [S] The Brilliant Bellson Sound 1960 20.00
❑ MGV-2131 [M] Louis Bellson Swings Jules Styne 1960 50.00
❑ V-2131 [M] Louis Bellson Swings Jules Styne 1960 20.00
❑ V6-2131 [S] Louis Bellson Swings Jules Styne 1960 20.00
❑ MGVS-6093 [S]The Brilliant Bellson Sound 1960 40.00
❑ MGVS-6138 [S]Louis Bellson Swings Jules Styne 1960 40.00
❑ MGV-8016 [M] Concerto for Drums 1957 50.00
*—Reissue of Norgran 1011*
❑ V-8016 [M] Concerto for Drums 1961 20.00
❑ MGV-8137 [M] Skin Deep 1957 50.00
*—Reissue of Norgran 1046*
❑ V-8137 [M] Skin Deep 1957 20.00
❑ MGV-8186 [M] The Hawk Talks 1957 50.00
*—Reissue of Norgran 1099*
❑ V-8186 [M] The Hawk Talks 1957 20.00
❑ MGV-8193 [M] Drumorama! 1957 50.00
❑ V-8193 [M] Drumorama! 1957 20.00
❑ MGV-8256 [M] Louis Bellson at the Flamingo 1958 50.00
❑ V-8256 [M] Louis Bellson at the Flamingo 1958 20.00
❑ MGV-8258 [M] Let's Call It Swing 1958 50.00
❑ V-8258 [M] Let's Call It Swing 1958 20.00
❑ MGV-8280 [M] Music, Romance and Especially Love 1958 50.00
❑ V-8280 [M] Music, Romance and Especially Love 1958 20.00
❑ MGV-8354 [M] Drummer's Holiday 1959 50.00
❑ V-8354 [M] Drummer's Holiday 1959 20.00

**BELLSON, LOUIS, AND GENE KRUPA**

ROULETTE
❑ R-52098 [M] The Mighty Two 1962 20.00
❑ SR-52098 [S] The Mighty Two 1962 25.00

**BELLSON, LOUIS, AND LALO SCHIFRIN**

ROULETTE
❑ SR-52120 [S] Explorations 1964 20.00

**BELLUS, TONY**

NRC
❑ LPA-8 [M] Robbin' the Cradle 1960 100.00
*—Black label*
❑ LPA-8 [M] Robbin' the Cradle 1960 200.00
*—Blue label*

SHI-FI
❑ LP-11 [M] Gems of Tony Bellus 196? 60.00

**BELMONTS, THE**

BUDDAH
❑ BDS-5123 Cigars, Acapella, Candy 1972 50.00

DOT
❑ DLP-25949 Summer Love 1969 30.00

SABINA
❑ SALP-5001 [M]The Belmonts' Carnival of Hits 1962 150.00

STRAWBERRY
❑ 6001 Cheek to Cheek 1978 15.00

**BELVIN, JESSE**

CROWN
❑ CLP-5145 [M] The Casual Jesse Belvin 1959 70.00
*—Black label*
❑ CLP-5145 [M] The Casual Jesse Belvin 196? 15.00
*—Gray label*
❑ CLP-5187 [M] The Unforgettable Jesse Belvin 1959 70.00
*—Black label*
❑ CLP-5187 [M] The Unforgettable Jesse Belvin 196? 15.00
*—Gray label*

| Number | Title (A Side/B Side) | Yr | NM |
|---|---|---|---|
| **RCA CAMDEN** | | | |
| ❑ CAL-960 [M] | Jesse Belvin's Best | 1966 | 12.00 |
| ❑ CAS-960 [S] | Jesse Belvin's Best | 1966 | 15.00 |
| **RCA VICTOR** | | | |
| ❑ LPM-2089 [M] | Just Jesse Belvin | 1959 | 40.00 |
| ❑ LSP-2089 [S] | Just Jesse Belvin | 1959 | 60.00 |
| ❑ LPM-2105 [M] | Mr. Easy | 1960 | 30.00 |
| ❑ LSP-2105 [S] | Mr. Easy | 1960 | 40.00 |
| **SPECIALTY** | | | |
| ❑ SP-7003 | The Blues Balladeer | 1990 | 15.00 |

### BENATAR, PAT

| Number | Title (A Side/B Side) | Yr | NM |
|---|---|---|---|
| **CHRYSALIS** | | | |
| ❑ CHR 1236 | In the Heat of the Night | 1979 | 8.00 |
| ❑ CHE 1275 | Crimes of Passion | 1980 | 8.00 |
| ❑ CHE 1275 | Crimes of Passion | 1980 | 30.00 |
| *—Error pressing: White label (not a promo) with photo of Pat leaning on a barre, as on regular copies, but with no blue at all, and with no butterfly or "Chrysalis" on label* | | | |
| ❑ CHR 1346 | Precious Time | 1981 | 8.00 |
| ❑ CHR 1396 | Get Nervous | 1982 | 8.00 |
| ❑ F1-21715 | Best Shots | 1989 | 12.00 |
| ❑ FV 41236 | In the Heat of the Night | 1983 | 6.00 |
| *—Reissue of 1236* | | | |
| ❑ FV 41275 | Crimes of Passion | 1983 | 6.00 |
| *—Reissue of 1275* | | | |
| ❑ FV 41346 | Precious Time | 1983 | 6.00 |
| *—Reissue of 1346* | | | |
| ❑ FV 41396 | Get Nervous | 1983 | 6.00 |
| *—Reissue of 1396* | | | |
| ❑ FV 41444 | Live from Earth | 1983 | 8.00 |
| ❑ FV 41471 | Tropico | 1984 | 8.00 |
| ❑ FV 41507 | Seven the Hard Way | 1985 | 8.00 |
| ❑ FV 41628 | Wide Awake in Dreamland | 1988 | 8.00 |
| **MOBILE FIDELITY** | | | |
| ❑ 1-057 | In the Heat of the Night | 1981 | 25.00 |
| *—Audiophile vinyl* | | | |

### BENAY, BEN

| Number | Title (A Side/B Side) | Yr | NM |
|---|---|---|---|
| **CAPITOL** | | | |
| ❑ ST 2484 [S] | The Big Blues Harmonica of Ben Benay | 1966 | 25.00 |
| ❑ T 2484 [M] | The Big Blues Harmonica of Ben Benay | 1966 | 20.00 |

### BENDIX, WILLIAM

| Number | Title (A Side/B Side) | Yr | NM |
|---|---|---|---|
| **CRICKET** | | | |
| ❑ CR-30 [M] | William Bendix Sings and Tells Famous Pirate Stories | 1959 | 40.00 |

### BENET, VICKI

| Number | Title (A Side/B Side) | Yr | NM |
|---|---|---|---|
| **DECCA** | | | |
| ❑ DL 8233 [M] | Woman of Paris | 1956 | 40.00 |
| ❑ DL 8381 [M] | The French Touch | 1957 | 40.00 |
| ❑ DL 8987 [M] | Vicki Benet a Paris | 1959 | 30.00 |
| ❑ DL 78987 [S] | Vicki Benet a Paris | 1959 | 40.00 |
| **LIBERTY** | | | |
| ❑ LRP-3103 [M] | Sing to Me of Love | 1960 | 25.00 |
| ❑ LST-7103 [S] | Sing to Me of Love | 1960 | 30.00 |

### BENNETT, BETTY

| Number | Title (A Side/B Side) | Yr | NM |
|---|---|---|---|
| **ATLANTIC** | | | |
| ❑ 1226 [M] | Nobody Else But Me | 1956 | 100.00 |
| *—Black label* | | | |
| ❑ 1226 [M] | Nobody Else But Me | 1961 | 40.00 |
| *—Multicolor label, white "fan" logo* | | | |
| **KAPP** | | | |
| ❑ KL-1052 [M] | Blue Sunday | 1957 | 40.00 |
| **TREND** | | | |
| ❑ TL-1006 [10] | Betty Bennett Sings Previn Arrangements | 1954 | 120.00 |
| **UNITED ARTISTS** | | | |
| ❑ UAL-3070 [M] | I Love to Sing | 1959 | 40.00 |
| ❑ UAS-6070 [S] | I Love to Sing | 1959 | 50.00 |

### BENNETT, BOYD

| Number | Title (A Side/B Side) | Yr | NM |
|---|---|---|---|
| **KING** | | | |
| ❑ 395-594 [M] | Boyd Bennett | 1955 | 4000. |
| *—VG value 1500; VG+ value 2750* | | | |

### BENNETT, CONNIE, WITH BILL SMITH AND THE HARLEM-AIRES

| Number | Title (A Side/B Side) | Yr | NM |
|---|---|---|---|
| **HOLLYWOOD** | | | |
| ❑ LPH-30 [M] | Rhythm 'N Blues in the Night | 1957 | 500.00 |
| *—Photo of Julie "Catwoman" Newmar on front cover* | | | |

### BENNETT, MAX

| Number | Title (A Side/B Side) | Yr | NM |
|---|---|---|---|
| **BETHLEHEM** | | | |
| ❑ BCP-48 [M] | Johnny Jaguar | 1957 | 70.00 |
| ❑ BCP-50 [M] | Max Bennett Plays | 1957 | 70.00 |
| ❑ BCP-1028 [10] | Max Bennett Quintet | 1955 | 120.00 |

### BENNETT, TONY

| Number | Title (A Side/B Side) | Yr | NM |
|---|---|---|---|
| **COLUMBIA** | | | |
| ❑ GP 14 [(2)] | Love Songs | 1969 | 15.00 |
| ❑ C2L 23 [(2)M] | Tony Bennett at Carnegie Hall | 1962 | 20.00 |
| ❑ CL 621 [M] | Cloud Seven | 1955 | 40.00 |
| ❑ C2S 823 [(2)S] | Tony Bennett at Carnegie Hall | 1962 | 25.00 |
| ❑ CL 938 [M] | Tony | 1956 | 30.00 |
| ❑ CL 1079 [M] | The Beat of My Heart | 1957 | 30.00 |
| ❑ CL 1186 [M] | Long Ago and Far Away | 1958 | 30.00 |
| ❑ CL 1229 [M] | Tony's Greatest Hits | 1958 | 30.00 |
| ❑ CL 1292 [M] | Blue Velvet | 1958 | 30.00 |
| ❑ CL 1301 [M] | Hometown, My Hometown | 1959 | 25.00 |
| ❑ CL 1429 [M] | To My Wonderful One | 1960 | 25.00 |
| ❑ CL 1446 [M] | Tony Sings for Two | 1960 | 25.00 |
| ❑ CL 1471 [M] | Alone Together | 1960 | 25.00 |
| ❑ CL 1535 [M] | More Tony's Greatest Hits | 1961 | 20.00 |
| ❑ CL 1559 [M] | A String of Harold Arlen | 1961 | 20.00 |
| ❑ CL 1658 [M] | My Heart Sings | 1961 | 20.00 |
| ❑ CL 1763 [M] | Mr. Broadway | 1962 | 15.00 |
| ❑ CL 1869 [M] | I Left My Heart in San Francisco | 1962 | 15.00 |
| ❑ CL 1905 [M] | Tony Bennett at Carnegie Hall Vol. 1 | 1963 | 15.00 |
| ❑ CL 2000 [M] | I Wanna Be Around | 1963 | 15.00 |
| ❑ CL 2056 [M] | This Is All I Ask | 1963 | 15.00 |
| ❑ CL 2141 [M] | The Many Moods of Tony | 1964 | 15.00 |
| ❑ CL 2175 [M] | When Lights Are Low | 1964 | 15.00 |
| ❑ CL 2285 [M] | Who Can I Turn To | 1964 | 15.00 |
| ❑ CL 2343 [M] | If I Ruled the World — Songs for the Jet Set | 1965 | 12.00 |
| ❑ CL 2373 [M] | Tony's Greatest Hits, Volume III | 1965 | 12.00 |
| ❑ CL 2472 [M] | The Movie Song Album | 1966 | 12.00 |
| ❑ CL 2507 [10] | Alone at Last with Tony Bennett | 1955 | 60.00 |
| ❑ CL 2550 [10] | Because of You | 1956 | 60.00 |
| ❑ CL 2560 [M] | A Time for Love | 1966 | 12.00 |
| ❑ CL 2653 [M] | Tony Makes It Happen! | 1967 | 15.00 |
| ❑ CL 2773 [M] | For Once in My Life | 1967 | 30.00 |
| ❑ CL 6221 [10] | Because of You | 1952 | 80.00 |
| ❑ CS 8107 [S] | Hometown, My Hometown | 1959 | 40.00 |
| ❑ CS 8226 [S] | To My Wonderful One | 1960 | 40.00 |
| ❑ CS 8242 [S] | Tony Sings for Two | 1960 | 40.00 |
| ❑ CS 8262 [S] | Alone Together | 1960 | 40.00 |
| ❑ CS 8335 [S] | More Tony's Greatest Hits | 1961 | 25.00 |
| ❑ CS 8359 [S] | A String of Harold Arlen | 1961 | 25.00 |
| ❑ CS 8458 [S] | My Heart Sings | 1961 | 25.00 |
| ❑ CS 8563 [S] | Mr. Broadway | 1962 | 20.00 |
| ❑ CS 8652 [R] | Tony's Greatest Hits | 1962 | 15.00 |
| ❑ CS 8669 [S] | I Left My Heart in San Francisco | 1962 | 20.00 |
| ❑ PC 8669 | I Left My Heart in San Francisco | 198? | 8.00 |
| *—Reissue with new prefix* | | | |
| ❑ CS 8705 [S] | Tony Bennett at Carnegie Hall Vol. 1 | 1963 | 20.00 |
| ❑ CS 8800 [S] | I Wanna Be Around | 1963 | 25.00 |
| ❑ CS 8856 [S] | This Is All I Ask | 1963 | 20.00 |
| ❑ CS 8941 [S] | The Many Moods of Tony | 1964 | 20.00 |
| ❑ CS 8975 [S] | When Lights Are Low | 1964 | 20.00 |
| ❑ CS 9085 [S] | Who Can I Turn To | 1964 | 20.00 |
| ❑ CS 9143 [S] | If I Ruled the World — Songs for the Jet Set | 1965 | 15.00 |
| ❑ CS 9173 [S] | Tony's Greatest Hits, Volume III | 1965 | 15.00 |
| ❑ CS 9272 [S] | The Movie Song Album | 1966 | 15.00 |
| ❑ CS 9360 [S] | A Time for Love | 1966 | 15.00 |
| ❑ CS 9453 [S] | Tony Makes It Happen! | 1967 | 15.00 |
| ❑ CS 9573 [S] | For Once in My Life | 1967 | 15.00 |
| ❑ CS 9678 | Yesterday I Heard the Rain | 1968 | 15.00 |
| ❑ CS 9739 | Snowfall: The Tony Bennett Christmas Album | 1968 | 12.00 |
| ❑ CS 9814 | Tony Bennett's Greatest Hits, Volume IV | 1969 | 15.00 |
| ❑ CS 9882 | I've Gotta Be Me | 1969 | 15.00 |
| ❑ CS 9980 | Tony Sings the Great Hits of Today! | 1970 | 12.00 |
| ❑ C 30240 | All Time Hall of Fame Hits | 1971 | 12.00 |
| ❑ PC 30240 | All Time Hall of Fame Hits | 197? | 10.00 |
| *—Reissue with new prefix* | | | |
| ❑ C 30280 | Tony Bennett's "Something" | 1971 | 12.00 |
| ❑ C 30558 | Love Story | 1971 | 12.00 |
| ❑ C 31219 | Summer of '42 | 1972 | 12.00 |
| ❑ KC 31460 | With Love | 1972 | 12.00 |
| ❑ KG 31494 [(2)] | Tony Bennett's All-Time Greatest Hits | 1972 | 15.00 |
| ❑ CG 33612 [(2)] | I Left My Heart in San Francisco/Tony Sings the Great Hits of Today! | 1975 | 15.00 |
| ❑ FC 40344 | The Art of Excellence | 1986 | 10.00 |
| ❑ CG 40424 [(2)] | Tony Bennett Jazz | 1987 | 12.00 |
| ❑ FC 44029 | Bennett/Berlin | 1987 | 10.00 |
| ❑ C 63668 | Bennett Sings Ellington — Hot and Cool | 1999 | 12.00 |
| **COLUMBIA LIMITED EDITION** | | | |
| ❑ LE 10057 | For Once in My Life | 197? | 10.00 |
| **COLUMBIA SPECIAL PRODUCTS** | | | |
| ❑ CSM 552 [M] | Singer Presents Tony Bennett | 1966 | 15.00 |
| ❑ CSS 552 [S] | Singer Presents Tony Bennett | 1966 | 20.00 |
| ❑ CSR 8107 [S] | Hometown, My Town | 196? | 12.00 |
| ❑ C 11264 | This Is All I Ask | 1972 | 12.00 |
| *—"Distributed by Arc-Jay-Kay Distributing Co." on upper back cover* | | | |
| **DRG** | | | |
| ❑ MRS-910 | Make Magnificent Music | 1985 | 10.00 |
| ❑ DARC-2-2102 [(2)] | The Rodgers and Hart Songbook | 1986 | 15.00 |
| **HARMONY** | | | |
| ❑ HS 11340 | Just One of Those Things | 1969 | 10.00 |
| ❑ KH 30758 | The Very Thought of You | 1971 | 10.00 |
| ❑ KH 32171 | Tony | 1973 | 10.00 |
| **IMPROV** | | | |
| ❑ 7112 | Life Is Beautiful | 1975 | 12.00 |
| ❑ 7113 | Tony Bennett Sings Rodgers and Hart | 197? | 12.00 |
| ❑ 7120 | Tony Bennett Sings More Rodgers and Hart | 1978 | 12.00 |
| ❑ 7123 | Beautiful Music | 1979 | 12.00 |
| **MGM** | | | |
| ❑ SE-4929 | Greatest Hits, Vol. 7 | 1973 | 12.00 |
| **PAIR** | | | |
| ❑ PDL2-1102 [(2)] | All-Time Favorites | 1986 | 12.00 |
| **TIME-LIFE** | | | |
| ❑ SLGD-10 [(2)] | Legendary Singers: Tony Bennett | 1986 | 15.00 |
| **VERVE** | | | |
| ❑ MV-5088 | The Good Things in Life | 1972 | 12.00 |
| ❑ MV-5094 | Listen Easy | 1973 | 12.00 |

### BENNETT, TONY, AND COUNT BASIE

| Number | Title (A Side/B Side) | Yr | NM |
|---|---|---|---|
| **COLUMBIA** | | | |
| ❑ CL 1294 [M] | Tony Bennett In Person | 1959 | 25.00 |
| ❑ CS 8104 [S] | Tony Bennett In Person | 1959 | 40.00 |
| **COLUMBIA LIMITED EDITION** | | | |
| ❑ LE 10125 | Tony Bennett In Person | 197? | 12.00 |
| **ROULETTE** | | | |
| ❑ R 25072 [M] | Count Basie Swings/Tony Bennett Sings | 1961 | 25.00 |
| ❑ SR 25072 [S] | Count Basie Swings/Tony Bennett Sings | 1961 | 30.00 |
| ❑ R 25231 [M] | Bennett and Basie Strike Up the Band | 1963 | 20.00 |
| ❑ SR 25231 [S] | Bennett and Basie Strike Up the Band | 1963 | 25.00 |

### BENNETT, TONY, AND BILL EVANS

| Number | Title (A Side/B Side) | Yr | NM |
|---|---|---|---|
| **DRG** | | | |
| ❑ MRS-901 | Together Again | 1985 | 8.00 |
| **FANTASY** | | | |
| ❑ F-9489 | The Tony Bennett/Bill Evans Album | 1975 | 12.00 |
| **IMPROV** | | | |
| ❑ 7117 | Together Again | 1978 | 12.00 |
| **MOBILE FIDELITY** | | | |
| ❑ 1-117 | The Tony Bennett/Bill Evans Album | 1981 | 40.00 |
| *—Audiophile vinyl* | | | |

### BENSON, GEORGE

| Number | Title (A Side/B Side) | Yr | NM |
|---|---|---|---|
| **A&M** | | | |
| ❑ SP-3014 | Shape of Things to Come | 1969 | 20.00 |
| *—Brown label* | | | |
| ❑ SP-3020 | Tell It Like It Is | 1969 | 20.00 |
| *—Brown label* | | | |
| ❑ SP-3028 | The Other Side of Abbey Road | 1970 | 25.00 |
| *—Brown label* | | | |
| **COLUMBIA** | | | |
| ❑ CL 2525 [M] | The Most Exciting New Guitarist on the Jazz Scene Today — It's Uptown | 1966 | 20.00 |
| ❑ CL 2613 [M] | The George Benson Cook Book | 1967 | 20.00 |
| ❑ CS 9325 [S] | The Most Exciting New Guitarist on the Jazz Scene Today — It's Uptown | 1966 | 20.00 |
| *—Red "360 Sound" label* | | | |
| ❑ CS 9413 [S] | The George Benson Cook Book | 1967 | 20.00 |
| *—Red "360 Sound" label* | | | |
| **MOBILE FIDELITY** | | | |
| ❑ 1-011 | Breezin' | 1979 | 60.00 |
| *—Audiophile vinyl* | | | |
| **PRESTIGE** | | | |
| ❑ PRLP-7310 [M] | The New Boss Guitar of George Benson | 1964 | 30.00 |
| ❑ PRST-7310 [S] | The New Boss Guitar of George Benson | 1964 | 40.00 |
| **VERVE** | | | |
| ❑ V6-8749 | Giblet Gravy | 1968 | 20.00 |
| ❑ V6-8771 | Goodies | 1969 | 20.00 |

### BENTON, BROOK

| Number | Title (A Side/B Side) | Yr | NM |
|---|---|---|---|
| **ALL PLATINUM** | | | |
| ❑ 3015 | This Is Brook Benton | 1976 | 12.00 |
| **ALLEGIANCE** | | | |
| ❑ AV-5033 | Memories Are Made of This | 1986 | 10.00 |
| **COTILLION** | | | |
| ❑ SD 9002 | Do Your Own Thing | 1969 | 12.00 |

| Number | Title (A Side/B Side) | Yr | NM |
|---|---|---|---|
| ❑ SD 9018 | Brook Benton Today | 1970 | 12.00 |
| ❑ SD 9028 | Home Style | 1970 | 12.00 |
| ❑ SD 9050 | Story Teller | 1971 | 12.00 |
| ❑ SD 9058 | The Gospel Truth | 1972 | 12.00 |
| **EPIC** | | | |
| ❑ LN 3573 [M] | Brook Benton At His Best | 1959 | 50.00 |
| **HARMONY** | | | |
| ❑ HL 7346 [M] | The Soul of Brook Benton | 196? | 12.00 |
| ❑ HS †1146 [R] | The Soul of Brook Benton | 196? | 12.00 |
| **HMC** | | | |
| ❑ 830724 | Beautiful Memories of Christmas | 1983 | 12.00 |
| **MERCURY** | | | |
| ❑ MG-20421 [M] | It's Just a Matter of Time | 1959 | 40.00 |
| ❑ MG-20464 [M] | Endlessly | 1959 | 30.00 |
| ❑ MG-20565 [M] | So Many Ways I Love You | 1960 | 30.00 |
| ❑ MG-20602 [M] | Songs I Love to Sing | 1960 | 30.00 |
| ❑ MG-20607 [M] | Golden Hits | 1961 | 20.00 |
| ❑ MG-20619 [M] | If You Believe | 1961 | 20.00 |
| ❑ MG-20641 [M] | The Boll Weevil Song and 11 Other Great Hits | 1961 | 20.00 |
| ❑ MG-20673 [M] | There Goes That Song Again | 1962 | 20.00 |
| ❑ MG-20740 [M] | Singing the Blues — Lie to Me | 1962 | 20.00 |
| ❑ MG-20774 [M] | Golden Hits, Volume 2 | 1963 | 20.00 |
| ❑ MG-20830 [M] | Best Ballads of Broadway | 1963 | 20.00 |
| ❑ MG-20886 [M] | Born to Sing the Blues | 1964 | 20.00 |
| ❑ MG-20918 [M] | On the Country Side | 1964 | 15.00 |
| ❑ MG-20934 [M] | This Bitter Earth | 1964 | 15.00 |
| ❑ SR-60077 [S] | It's Just a Matter of Time | 1959 | 50.00 |
| ❑ SR-60146 [S] | Endlessly | 1959 | 40.00 |
| ❑ SR-60225 [S] | So Many Ways I Love You | 1960 | 40.00 |
| ❑ SR-60602 [S] | Songs I Love to Sing | 1960 | 40.00 |
| ❑ SR-60607 [S] | Golden Hits | 1961 | 30.00 |
| ❑ SR-60619 [S] | If You Believe | 1961 | 30.00 |
| ❑ SR-60641 [S] | The Boll Weevil Song and 11 Other Great Hits | 1961 | 30.00 |
| ❑ SR-60673 [S] | There Goes That Song Again | 1962 | 30.00 |
| ❑ SR-60740 [S] | Singing the Blues — Lie to Me | 1962 | 30.00 |
| ❑ SR-60774 [S] | Golden Hits, Volume 2 | 1963 | 30.00 |
| ❑ SR-60830 [S] | Best Ballads of Broadway | 1963 | 25.00 |
| ❑ SR-60886 [S] | Born to Sing the Blues | 1964 | 25.00 |
| ❑ SR-60918 [S] | On the Country Side | 1964 | 20.00 |
| ❑ SR-60934 [S] | This Bitter Earth | 1964 | 20.00 |
| ❑ 822321-1 | It's Just a Matter of Time: His Greatest Hits | 1984 | 10.00 |
| **MGM** | | | |
| ❑ SE-4874 | Something for Everyone | 1973 | 12.00 |
| **MUSICOR** | | | |
| ❑ 4603 [(2)] | The Best of Brook Benton | 1977 | 12.00 |
| **PAIR** | | | |
| ❑ PDL2-1100 [(2)] | Brook Benton's Best | 1986 | 12.00 |
| **RCA CAMDEN** | | | |
| ❑ CAL-564 [M] | Brook Benton | 1960 | 15.00 |
| ❑ CAS-2431 | I Wanna Be with You | 1970 | 12.00 |
| **RCA VICTOR** | | | |
| ❑ APL1-1044 | Book Benton Sings a Love Story | 1975 | 10.00 |
| ❑ LPM-3514 [M] | That Old Feeling | 1966 | 15.00 |
| ❑ LSP-3514 [S] | That Old Feeling | 1966 | 20.00 |
| ❑ LPM-3526 [M] | Mother Nature, Father Time | 1965 | 15.00 |
| ❑ LSP-3526 [S] | Mother Nature, Father Time | 1965 | 20.00 |
| ❑ LPM-3590 [M] | My Country | 1966 | 15.00 |
| ❑ LSP-3590 [S] | My Country | 1966 | 20.00 |
| **REPRISE** | | | |
| ❑ R-6268 [M] | Laura (What's He Got That I Ain't Got) | 1967 | 20.00 |
| ❑ RS-6268 [S] | Laura (What's He Got That I Ain't Got) | 1967 | 15.00 |
| **RHINO** | | | |
| ❑ RNFP 71497 [(2)] | The Brook Benton Anthology (1959-1970) | 1986 | 12.00 |
| **WING** | | | |
| ❑ MGW-12314 [M] | Brook Benton | 1966 | 12.00 |
| ❑ SRW-16314 [S] | Brook Benton | 1966 | 12.00 |

### BENTON, WALTER

| Number | Title (A Side/B Side) | Yr | NM |
|---|---|---|---|
| **JAZZLAND** | | | |
| ❑ JLP-28 [M] | Out of This World | 1960 | 40.00 |
| ❑ JLP-928 [S] | Out of This World | 1960 | 40.00 |

### BERBERIAN, JOHN, WITH THE ROCK EAST ENSEMBLE

| Number | Title (A Side/B Side) | Yr | NM |
|---|---|---|---|
| **MAINSTREAM** | | | |
| ❑ S-6123 | Impressions East | 1969 | 120.00 |
| **VERVE FORECAST** | | | |
| ❑ FTS-3073 | Middle Eastern Rock | 1969 | 50.00 |

### BERG, GERTRUDE

| Number | Title (A Side/B Side) | Yr | NM |
|---|---|---|---|
| **AMY** | | | |
| ❑ 8007 [M] | How to Be a Jewish Mother | 1965 | 25.00 |

### BERGEN, FRANCES

| Number | Title (A Side/B Side) | Yr | NM |
|---|---|---|---|
| **COLUMBIA** | | | |
| ❑ CL 873 [M] | The Beguiling Miss Bergen | 1956 | 30.00 |

### BERGEN, POLLY

| Number | Title (A Side/B Side) | Yr | NM |
|---|---|---|---|
| **COLUMBIA** | | | |
| ❑ CL 994 [M] | Bergen Sings Morgan | 1957 | 30.00 |
| ❑ CL 1031 [M] | The Party's Over | 1957 | 30.00 |
| ❑ CL 1138 [M] | Polly and Her Pop | 1958 | 25.00 |
| ❑ CL 1218 [M] | My Heart Sings | 1959 | 20.00 |
| ❑ CL 1300 [M] | All Alone by the Telephone | 1959 | 20.00 |
| ❑ CL 1451 [M] | Four Seasons of Love | 1960 | 20.00 |
| ❑ CL 1632 [M] | "Do Re Mi" and "Annie Get Your Gun" | 1961 | 20.00 |
| ❑ CS 8018 [S] | My Heart Sings | 1959 | 25.00 |
| ❑ CS 8100 [S] | All Alone by the Telephone | 1959 | 25.00 |
| ❑ CS 8246 [S] | Four Seasons of Love | 1960 | 25.00 |
| ❑ CS 8432 [S] | "Do Re Mi" and "Annie Get Your Gun" | 1961 | 25.00 |
| **JUBILEE** | | | |
| ❑ JGL-14 [10] | Polly Bergen | 1955 | 50.00 |
| **PHILIPS** | | | |
| ❑ PHM 200084 [M] | Act One — Sing, Too | 1963 | 15.00 |
| ❑ PHS 600084 [S] | Act One — Sing, Too | 1963 | 20.00 |

### BERGER, KARL

| Number | Title (A Side/B Side) | Yr | NM |
|---|---|---|---|
| **CMC** | | | |
| ❑ 00101 [(2)] | Peace Church | 197? | 20.00 |
| **ESP-DISK'** | | | |
| ❑ 1041 [M] | Karl Berger | 1967 | 30.00 |
| ❑ S-1041 [S] | Karl Berger | 1967 | 20.00 |

### BERIGAN, BUNNY

| Number | Title (A Side/B Side) | Yr | NM |
|---|---|---|---|
| **EPIC** | | | |
| ❑ LN 3109 [M] | Take It, Bunny! | 1955 | 50.00 |
| ❑ LA 16004 [M] | Bunny Berigan and His Boys | 196? | 20.00 |
| **RCA CAMDEN** | | | |
| ❑ CAL-550 [M] | Bunny | 195? | 20.00 |
| **RCA VICTOR** | | | |
| ❑ LPT-10 [10] | Bunny Berigan 1937-38 | 1951 | 80.00 |
| ❑ LPV-550 [M] | Bunny | 1966 | 20.00 |
| ❑ LPT-1003 [M] | Bunny Berigan Plays Again | 1952 | 50.00 |
| ❑ LPM-2078 [M] | Great Dance Bands of the 30s and 40s | 1959 | 40.00 |

### BERIGAN, BUNNY, AND WINGY MANONE

| Number | Title (A Side/B Side) | Yr | NM |
|---|---|---|---|
| **"X"** | | | |
| ❑ LVA-3034 [10] | Swing Session 1934 | 1954 | 80.00 |

### BERLE, MILTON

| Number | Title (A Side/B Side) | Yr | NM |
|---|---|---|---|
| **FORUM** | | | |
| ❑ F-9005 [M] | Songs My Mother Loved | 1963 | 20.00 |
| **ROULETTE** | | | |
| ❑ R-25018 [M] | Songs My Mother Loved | 1957 | 40.00 |

### BERLIN

| Number | Title (A Side/B Side) | Yr | NM |
|---|---|---|---|
| **ENIGMA** | | | |
| ❑ 3 [EP] | Pleasure Victim | 1982 | 25.00 |
| *—Original issue* | | | |
| **GEFFEN** | | | |
| ❑ GHS 2036 [EP] | Pleasure Victim | 1982 | 8.00 |
| ❑ GHS 4025 | Love Life | 1984 | 10.00 |
| ❑ GHS 24121 | Count Three and Pray | 1986 | 8.00 |
| ❑ GHS 24187 | Best of Berlin 1979-1988 | 1988 | 15.00 |
| ❑ R 100731 | Best of Berlin 1979-1988 | 1988 | 20.00 |
| *—BMG Direct Marketing edition* | | | |
| ❑ R 153624 | Count Three and Pray | 1986 | 10.00 |
| *—RCA Music Service edition* | | | |

### BERMAN, SHELLEY

| Number | Title (A Side/B Side) | Yr | NM |
|---|---|---|---|
| **METRO** | | | |
| ❑ M-546 [M] | Let Me Tell You a Funny Story | 1965 | 15.00 |
| ❑ MS-546 [R] | Let Me Tell You a Funny Story | 1965 | 12.00 |
| **VERVE** | | | |
| ❑ MGV-15003 [M] | Inside Shelley Berman | 1959 | 25.00 |
| ❑ V-15003 [M] | Inside Shelley Berman | 1962 | 15.00 |
| ❑ V6-15003 [R] | Inside Shelley Berman | 196? | 12.00 |
| ❑ MGV-15007 [M] | Outside Shelley Berman | 1959 | 25.00 |
| ❑ V-15007 [M] | Outside Shelley Berman | 1962 | 15.00 |
| ❑ V6-15007 [R] | Outside Shelley Berman | 196? | 12.00 |
| ❑ MGV-15008-2 [(2)M] | Inside and Outside Shelley Berman | 1959 | 30.00 |
| ❑ V-15008-2 [(2)M] | Inside and Outside Shelley Berman | 1962 | 20.00 |
| ❑ MGV-15013 [M] | The Edge of Shelley Berman | 1960 | 25.00 |
| ❑ V-15013 [M] | The Edge of Shelley Berman | 1962 | 15.00 |
| ❑ V6-15013 [R] | The Edge of Shelley Berman | 196? | 12.00 |
| ❑ MGV-15027 [M] | A Personal Appearance | 1961 | 20.00 |
| ❑ V-15027 [M] | A Personal Appearance | 1962 | 15.00 |
| ❑ V6-15027 [R] | A Personal Appearance | 196? | 12.00 |
| ❑ V-15036 [M] | New Sides | 1962 | 15.00 |
| ❑ V6-15036 [R] | New Sides | 196? | 12.00 |
| ❑ V-15043 [M] | The Sex Life of the Primate (And Other Bits of Gossip) | 1964 | 20.00 |
| ❑ V6-15043 [R] | The Sex Life of the Primate (And Other Bits of Gossip) | 1964 | 15.00 |
| ❑ V-15048 [M] | Great Moments in Comedy | 1965 | 20.00 |
| ❑ V6-15048 [R] | Great Moments in Comedy | 1965 | 15.00 |

### BERMAN, SONNY

| Number | Title (A Side/B Side) | Yr | NM |
|---|---|---|---|
| **ESOTERIC** | | | |
| ❑ ES-532 [M] | Sonny Berman 1946 | 1954 | 120.00 |

### BERNARDI, HERSCHEL

| Number | Title (A Side/B Side) | Yr | NM |
|---|---|---|---|
| **COLUMBIA** | | | |
| ❑ C 30004 | Show Stopper | 1970 | 20.00 |
| **COLUMBIA MASTERWORKS** | | | |
| ❑ OS 3010 [S] | Fiddler on the Roof | 1966 | 25.00 |
| ❑ OL 6610 [M] | Fiddler on the Roof | 1966 | 20.00 |

### BERNE, TIM

| Number | Title (A Side/B Side) | Yr | NM |
|---|---|---|---|
| **EMPIRE** | | | |
| ❑ EPC 24K | The Five Year Plan | 1979 | 20.00 |
| ❑ EPC 36K | 7X | 1980 | 20.00 |
| ❑ EPC 48K | Spectres | 1981 | 20.00 |
| ❑ EPC 60K-2 [(2)] | Songs and Rituals in Real Time | 1982 | 25.00 |

### BERNE, TIM, AND BILL FRISELL

| Number | Title (A Side/B Side) | Yr | NM |
|---|---|---|---|
| **EMPIRE** | | | |
| ❑ EPC 72K | ...Theoretically | 1984 | 20.00 |

### BERNHART, MILT

| Number | Title (A Side/B Side) | Yr | NM |
|---|---|---|---|
| **DECCA** | | | |
| ❑ DL 9214 [M] | The Sounds of Bernhart | 1959 | 30.00 |
| ❑ DL 79214 [S] | The Sounds of Bernhart | 1959 | 40.00 |
| **RCA VICTOR** | | | |
| ❑ LPM-1123 [M] | Modern Brass | 1955 | 50.00 |

### BERRY, BILL

| Number | Title (A Side/B Side) | Yr | NM |
|---|---|---|---|
| **DIRECTIONAL SOUND** | | | |
| ❑ 5002 [M] | Jazz and Swinging Percussion | 1963 | 20.00 |
| ❑ S-5002 [S] | Jazz and Swinging Percussion | 1963 | 25.00 |
| **PARADE** | | | |
| ❑ SP-353 [M] | Broadway Escapades | 196? | 20.00 |
| **REAL TIME** | | | |
| ❑ 101 | For Duke | 1980 | 25.00 |
| *—Direct-to-disc recording* | | | |

### BERRY, BROOKS, AND SCRAPPER BLACKWELL

| Number | Title (A Side/B Side) | Yr | NM |
|---|---|---|---|
| **BLUESVILLE** | | | |
| ❑ BVLP-1074 [M] | My Heart Struck Sorrow | 1963 | 80.00 |
| *—Blue label, silver print* | | | |
| ❑ BVLP-1074 [M] | My Heart Struck Sorrow | 1964 | 25.00 |
| *—Blue label with trident logo* | | | |

### BERRY, CHU

| Number | Title (A Side/B Side) | Yr | NM |
|---|---|---|---|
| **COMMODORE** | | | |
| ❑ FL-20024 [10] | Chu Berry Memorial | 1952 | 250.00 |
| ❑ DL-30017 [M] | Chu Berry | 1959 | 80.00 |
| **EPIC** | | | |
| ❑ LG 3124 [M] | Chu | 1955 | 80.00 |
| **MAINSTREAM** | | | |
| ❑ 56038 [M] | Sittin' In | 1965 | 30.00 |

### BERRY, CHUCK

| Number | Title (A Side/B Side) | Yr | NM |
|---|---|---|---|
| **ACCORD** | | | |
| ❑ SN-7171 | Toronto Rock 'N' Roll Revival, Vol. 2 | 1982 | 10.00 |
| ❑ SN-7172 | Toronto Rock 'N' Roll Revival, Vol. 3 | 1982 | 10.00 |
| **ATCO** | | | |
| ❑ SD 38-118 | Rockit | 1979 | 12.00 |
| **CHESS** | | | |
| ❑ LP-1426 [M] | After School Session | 1958 | 200.00 |
| ❑ LPS-1426 [R] | After School Session | 196? | 12.00 |
| ❑ LP-1432 [M] | One Dozen Berrys | 1958 | 200.00 |
| ❑ LPS-1432 [R] | One Dozen Berrys | 196? | 12.00 |
| ❑ LP-1435 [M] | Chuck Berry Is On Top | 1959 | 180.00 |
| ❑ LPS-1435 [R] | Chuck Berry Is On Top | 196? | 12.00 |
| ❑ LP-1448 [M] | Rockin' at the Hops | 1960 | 180.00 |
| ❑ LP-1456 [M] | New Juke Box Hits | 1961 | 180.00 |
| ❑ LP-1465 [M] | Chuck Berry Twist | 1962 | 100.00 |
| ❑ LP-1465 [M] | More Chuck Berry | 1963 | 120.00 |
| *—Retitled version of above* | | | |
| ❑ LPS-1465 [R] | More Chuck Berry | 196? | 12.00 |
| ❑ LP-1480 [M] | Chuck Berry On Stage | 1963 | 120.00 |
| ❑ LPS-1480 [R] | Chuck Berry On Stage | 196? | 12.00 |
| ❑ LP-1485 [M] | Chuck Berry's Greatest Hits | 1964 | 120.00 |
| ❑ LPS-1485 [R] | Chuck Berry's Greatest Hits | 196? | 12.00 |
| ❑ LP-1488 [M] | St. Louis to Liverpool | 1964 | 60.00 |
| ❑ LPS-1488 [S] | St. Louis to Liverpool | 1964 | 80.00 |
| ❑ LP-1495 [M] | Chuck Berry in London | 1965 | 30.00 |
| ❑ LPS-1495 [S] | Chuck Berry in London | 1965 | 40.00 |
| ❑ LP-1498 [M] | Fresh Berry's | 1965 | 30.00 |
| ❑ LPS-1498 [S] | Fresh Berry's | 1965 | 40.00 |

STEREO
S/6099
BIG BROTHER
&
THE
HOLDING
COMPANY
MAINSTREAM


Big Brother and the Holding Company,
*Big Brother and the Holding Company,* Mainstream S/6099, stereo, $50.

| Number | Title (A Side/B Side) | Yr | NM |
|---|---|---|---|
| ❑ 2CH-1514 [(2)R] | Chuck Berry's Golden Decade | 1972 | 15.00 |
| *—New cover has a pink radio* | | | |
| ❑ LP-1514 [(2)M] | Chuck Berry's Golden Decade | 1967 | 40.00 |
| ❑ LPS-1514 [(2)R] | Chuck Berry's Golden Decade | 1967 | 20.00 |
| *—Old cover does not have a pink radio* | | | |
| ❑ LPS-1550 | Back Home | 1970 | 20.00 |
| ❑ CH-9171 | New Juke Box Hits | 1986 | 10.00 |
| *—Reissue of 1456* | | | |
| ❑ CH-9186 | St. Louis to Liverpool | 1988 | 10.00 |
| *—Reissue of 1488* | | | |
| ❑ CH-9190 | More Rock 'n' Roll Rarities | 1986 | 10.00 |
| ❑ CH-9256 | Chuck Berry Is On Top | 1987 | 10.00 |
| *—Reissue of 1435* | | | |
| ❑ CH-9259 | Rockin' at the Hop | 1987 | 10.00 |
| *—Reissue of 1448* | | | |
| ❑ CH-9284 | After School Session | 1989 | 10.00 |
| *—Reissue of 1426* | | | |
| ❑ CH-9295 | The London Chuck Berry Sessions | 1989 | 10.00 |
| *—Reissue of 60020* | | | |
| ❑ CH-9318 | Missing Berries: Rarities, Volume 3 | 1990 | 10.00 |
| ❑ CH-50008 | San Fransisco Dues | 1971 | 20.00 |
| ❑ CH-50043 | Chuck Berry/Bio | 1973 | 20.00 |
| ❑ CH-60020 | The London Chuck Berry Sessions | 1972 | 20.00 |
| ❑ 2CH-60023 [(2)] | Chuck Berry's Golden Decade, Vol. 2 | 1973 | 25.00 |
| ❑ 2CH-60028 [(2)] | Chuck Berry's Golden Decade, Vol. 3 | 1974 | 25.00 |
| ❑ CH6-80001 [(6)] | The Chess Box | 1989 | 50.00 |
| ❑ CH2-92500 [(2)] | The Great Twenty-Eight | 1983 | 12.00 |
| ❑ CH2-92521 [(2)] | Rock 'n' Roll Rarities | 1986 | 15.00 |
| **EVEREST ARCHIVE OF FOLK & JAZZ** | | | |
| ❑ FS-321 | Chuck Berry's Greatest Hits | 1976 | 10.00 |
| **GUSTO** | | | |
| ❑ 0004 | The Best of the Best of Chuck Berry | 198? | 10.00 |
| **MERCURY** | | | |
| ❑ SRM-2-6501 [(2)] | St. Louis to Frisco to Memphis | 1972 | 20.00 |
| ❑ MG-21103 [M] | Chuck Berry's Golden Hits | 1967 | 15.00 |
| ❑ MG-21123 [M] | Chuck Berry in Memphis | 1967 | 15.00 |
| ❑ MG-21138 [M] | Love at the Fillmore Auditorium | 1967 | 20.00 |
| ❑ SR-61103 [S] | Chuck Berry's Golden Hits | 1967 | 15.00 |
| ❑ SR-61123 [S] | Chuck Berry in Memphis | 1967 | 15.00 |
| ❑ SR-61138 [S] | Love at the Fillmore Auditorium | 1967 | 20.00 |
| ❑ SR-61176 | From St. Louie to Frisco | 1968 | 20.00 |
| ❑ SR-61223 | Concerto in B Goode | 1969 | 20.00 |
| ❑ 826256-1 | Chuck Berry's Golden Hits | 1985 | 8.00 |
| *—Reissue* | | | |
| **PICKWICK** | | | |
| ❑ PTP-2061 [(2)] | Flashback | 1975 | 12.00 |
| ❑ SPC-3327 | Johnny B. Goode | 1973 | 10.00 |
| ❑ SPC-3345 | Sweet Little Rock and Roller | 1974 | 10.00 |
| ❑ SPC-3392 | Wild Berrys | 1974 | 10.00 |
| **QUICKSILVER** | | | |
| ❑ QS-1017 | Live Hits | 198? | 10.00 |
| **SSS INTERNATIONAL** | | | |
| ❑ 36 | Chuck Berry Live | 1981 | 10.00 |

### BERRY, KEN

| Number | Title (A Side/B Side) | Yr | NM |
|---|---|---|---|
| **BARNABY** | | | |
| ❑ Z 30014 | R.F.D. | 1970 | 25.00 |
| ❑ Z 30094 | Ken Berry, R.F.D. | 1970 | 30.00 |

### BERRY, RICHARD

| Number | Title (A Side/B Side) | Yr | NM |
|---|---|---|---|
| **CROWN** | | | |
| ❑ CST-371 [R] | Richard Berry and the Dreamers | 1963 | 30.00 |
| ❑ CLP-5371 [M] | Richard Berry and the Dreamers | 1963 | 60.00 |
| **PAM** | | | |
| ❑ 1001 | Live at the Century Restaurant | 1968 | 40.00 |
| ❑ 1002 | Wild Berry | 196? | 40.00 |

### BERT, EDDIE

| Number | Title (A Side/B Side) | Yr | NM |
|---|---|---|---|
| **DISCOVERY** | | | |
| ❑ DL-3020 [M] | Eddie Bert Quintet | 1953 | 100.00 |
| **JAZZTONE** | | | |
| ❑ J-1223 [M] | Modern Moods | 1956 | 40.00 |
| **SAVOY** | | | |
| ❑ MG-12015 [M] | Musician of the Year | 1955 | 60.00 |
| ❑ MG-12019 [M] | Encore | 1955 | 60.00 |
| **SOMERSET** | | | |
| ❑ SF-5200 [M] | Like Cool | 1958 | 40.00 |
| *—Reissue of Trans World LP* | | | |
| **TRANS WORLD** | | | |
| ❑ TWLP-208 [M] | Let's Dig Bert | 1955 | 100.00 |

### BEST, PETER (1)

| Number | Title (A Side/B Side) | Yr | NM |
|---|---|---|---|
| **PHOENIX** | | | |
| ❑ PHX-340 | The Beatle That Time Forgot | 1982 | 12.00 |
| **SAVAGE** | | | |
| ❑ BM-71 | Best of the Beatles | 1966 | 200.00 |
| *—Authentic copies have white circle around the word "Savage" and white circle around Pete Best's head on the album cover.* | | | |

### BETTERS, HAROLD

| Number | Title (A Side/B Side) | Yr | NM |
|---|---|---|---|
| **GATEWAY** | | | |
| ❑ GLP-7001 [M] | Harold Betters at the Encore | 1964 | 20.00 |
| ❑ GLP-7004 [M] | Take Off | 1964 | 20.00 |
| ❑ GLP-7008 [M] | Even Better | 1966 | 20.00 |
| ❑ GLP-7009 [M] | Harold Betters Meets Slide Hampton | 1966 | 20.00 |
| ❑ GLP-7014 [M] | Do Anything You Wanna | 1966 | 20.00 |
| ❑ GLP-7015 [M] | Swingin' on the Railroad | 1966 | 20.00 |
| **REPRISE** | | | |
| ❑ RS-6195 [S] | Ram-Bunk-Shush | 1965 | 20.00 |
| ❑ RS-6208 [S] | Out of Sight and Sound | 1966 | 20.00 |
| ❑ RS-6241 [S] | Funk City Express | 1966 | 20.00 |

### BEVERLY HILL BILLIES, THE

| Number | Title (A Side/B Side) | Yr | NM |
|---|---|---|---|
| **RAR-ARTS** | | | |
| ❑ 1000 [M] | Those Fabulous Beverly Hill Billies | 1961 | 100.00 |
| *—Gold vinyl* | | | |

### BIANCO

| Number | Title (A Side/B Side) | Yr | NM |
|---|---|---|---|
| **RCA/READER'S DIGEST** | | | |
| ❑ CSP-104 [S] | Joy to the World | 1962 | 20.00 |

### BIG BEATS, THE

| Number | Title (A Side/B Side) | Yr | NM |
|---|---|---|---|
| **LIBERTY** | | | |
| ❑ LRP-3407 [M] | The Big Beats Live | 1965 | 30.00 |
| ❑ LST-7407 [S] | The Big Beats Live | 1965 | 40.00 |

### BIG BOPPER

| Number | Title (A Side/B Side) | Yr | NM |
|---|---|---|---|
| **MERCURY** | | | |
| ❑ MG-20402 [M] | Chantilly Lace | 1959 | 500.00 |
| *—Black label* | | | |
| ❑ MG-20402 [M] | Chantilly Lace | 196? | 25.00 |
| *—Red label with twelve Mercury logos on label edge* | | | |
| ❑ MG-20402 [M] | Chantilly Lace | 1964 | 200.00 |
| *—Red label with black or black & white Mercury logo at top* | | | |
| ❑ MG-20402 [M] | Chantilly Lace | 1975 | 15.00 |
| *—Chicago skyline label* | | | |
| ❑ 832902-1 [M] | Chantilly Lace | 1988 | 15.00 |
| *—New number, black label* | | | |
| **PICKWICK** | | | |
| ❑ SPC-3365 | Chantilly Lace | 1973 | 15.00 |
| **RHINO** | | | |
| ❑ R1-70164 | Helloooo Baby! The Best of the Big Bopper 1954-1959 | 1989 | 12.00 |

### BIG BOYS

| Number | Title (A Side/B Side) | Yr | NM |
|---|---|---|---|
| **ENIGMA** | | | |
| ❑ E-1128 | Lullabies Help the Brain Grow | 1984 | 15.00 |
| *—Reissue of Moment 002* | | | |
| ❑ 72028 | No Matter How Long the Line Is at the Cafeteria, There's Always a Seat | 1984 | 30.00 |
| **MOMENT** | | | |
| ❑ 001 | Fun, Fun, Fun | 1982 | 80.00 |
| ❑ 002 | Lullabies Help the Brain Grow | 1983 | 50.00 |
| **RAT RACE** | | | |
| ❑ RRR 80351 | Recorded Live at Raul's | 1980 | 80.00 |
| *—One side features the Big Boys; the other side, the Dicks* | | | |
| **UNSEEN HAND** | | | |
| ❑ UHT 727-3 | Wreck Collection | 1988 | 15.00 |
| **WASTED TALENT** | | | |
| ❑ JWP 3405 | Where's My Towel/Industry Standard | 1981 | 60.00 |

### BIG BROTHER

| Number | Title (A Side/B Side) | Yr | NM |
|---|---|---|---|
| **ALL-AMERICAN** | | | |
| ❑ 5770 | Big Brother | 1970 | 150.00 |

### BIG BROTHER AND THE HOLDING COMPANY

| Number | Title (A Side/B Side) | Yr | NM |
|---|---|---|---|
| **COLUMBIA** | | | |
| ❑ KCL 2900 [M] | Cheap Thrills | 1968 | 300.00 |
| *—Red label stock copy has been confirmed* | | | |
| ❑ KCS 9700 | Cheap Thrills | 1970 | 12.00 |
| *—Orange label* | | | |
| ❑ KCS 9700 [M] | Cheap Thrills | 1968 | 100.00 |
| *—White label "Special Mono Radio Station Copy" with stereo number* | | | |
| ❑ KCS 9700 [S] | Cheap Thrills | 1968 | 25.00 |
| *—Red "360 Sound" label* | | | |
| ❑ PC 9700 | Cheap Thrills | 198? | 8.00 |
| *—Reissue with new prefix* | | | |
| ❑ C 30222 | Be a Brother | 1970 | 20.00 |



**Except when noted otherwise, VG = 25% of NM, and VG+ = 50% of NM. (Example: VG = $2.00, VG+ = $4.00 and NM = $8.00.)**

| Number | Title (A Side/B Side) | Yr | NM |
|---|---|---|---|
| C 30631 | Big Brother and the Holding Company | 1971 | 20.00 |
| | *—Reissue of Mainstream LP with two extra tracks* | | |
| C 30738 | How Hard It Is | 1971 | 20.00 |

**COLUMBIA SPECIAL PRODUCTS**

| Number | Title (A Side/B Side) | Yr | NM |
|---|---|---|---|
| P 13313 | Big Brother and the Holding Company | 197? | 15.00 |

**MAINSTREAM**

| Number | Title (A Side/B Side) | Yr | NM |
|---|---|---|---|
| S-6099 [S] | Big Brother and the Holding Company | 1967 | 50.00 |
| 56099 [M] | Big Brother and the Holding Company | 1967 | 100.00 |

### BIG DADDY

**REGENT**

| Number | Title (A Side/B Side) | Yr | NM |
|---|---|---|---|
| MG-6106 [M] | Twist Party | 1962 | 70.00 |

### BIG FOOT

**WINRO**

| Number | Title (A Side/B Side) | Yr | NM |
|---|---|---|---|
| 1004 | Big Foot | 1969 | 30.00 |

### BIG MAYBELLE

**BRUNSWICK**

| Number | Title (A Side/B Side) | Yr | NM |
|---|---|---|---|
| BL 54107 [M] | What More Can a Woman Do | 1962 | 50.00 |
| BL 754107 [S] | What More Can a Woman Do | 1962 | 70.00 |
| BL 754142 | The Gospel Soul of Big Maybelle | 1968 | 40.00 |

**EPIC**

| Number | Title (A Side/B Side) | Yr | NM |
|---|---|---|---|
| EE 22011 [M] | Gabbin' Blues | 196? | 30.00 |
| | *—Reissue of Okeh recordings* | | |

**PARAMOUNT**

| Number | Title (A Side/B Side) | Yr | NM |
|---|---|---|---|
| PAS-1011 [(2)] | The Last of Big Maybelle | 1973 | 25.00 |

**ROJAC**

| Number | Title (A Side/B Side) | Yr | NM |
|---|---|---|---|
| RS 123 | Saga of the Good Life and Hard Times | 196? | 40.00 |
| R 522 [M] | Got a Brand New Bag | 1967 | 40.00 |
| RS 522 [S] | Got a Brand New Bag | 1967 | 40.00 |

**SAVOY**

| Number | Title (A Side/B Side) | Yr | NM |
|---|---|---|---|
| MG-14005 [M] | Big Maybelle Sings | 1957 | 300.00 |
| MG-14011 [M] | Blues, Candy and Big Maybelle | 1958 | 300.00 |

**SAVOY JAZZ**

| Number | Title (A Side/B Side) | Yr | NM |
|---|---|---|---|
| SJL-1143 | Roots of Rock 'n' Roll Vol. 13: Blues & Early Soul | 1985 | 10.00 |
| SJL-1168 | Blues, Candy and Big Maybelle | 1986 | 10.00 |
| | *—Reissue of 14011* | | |

**SCEPTER**

| Number | Title (A Side/B Side) | Yr | NM |
|---|---|---|---|
| S-522 [M] | The Soul of Big Maybelle | 1964 | 40.00 |
| SS-522 [S] | The Soul of Big Maybelle | 1964 | 50.00 |

### BIG STAR

**ARDENT**

| Number | Title (A Side/B Side) | Yr | NM |
|---|---|---|---|
| ADS-1501 | Radio City | 1974 | 30.00 |
| ADS-2803 | #1 Record | 1972 | 25.00 |

**DBK WORKS**

| Number | Title (A Side/B Side) | Yr | NM |
|---|---|---|---|
| DBK 115 | In Space | 2005 | 15.00 |

**4 MEN WITH BEARDS**

| Number | Title (A Side/B Side) | Yr | NM |
|---|---|---|---|
| 4M-142 | 3rd | 2006 | 15.00 |
| | *—Reissue on 180-gram vinyl* | | |

**PVC**

| Number | Title (A Side/B Side) | Yr | NM |
|---|---|---|---|
| 7903 | Big Star's Third | 1978 | 25.00 |
| 8933 | Sister Lovers | 1985 | 15.00 |
| | *—Reissue of PVC 7903 with new title* | | |

### BIG THREE, THE

**FM**

| Number | Title (A Side/B Side) | Yr | NM |
|---|---|---|---|
| 307 [M] | The Big Three | 1963 | 30.00 |
| S-307 [S] | The Big Three | 1963 | 40.00 |
| 311 [M] | Live at the Recording Studio | 1964 | 30.00 |
| S-311 [S] | Live at the Recording Studio | 1964 | 40.00 |

**ROULETTE**

| Number | Title (A Side/B Side) | Yr | NM |
|---|---|---|---|
| R-42000 [M] | The Big Three Featuring Cass Elliot | 1967 | 20.00 |
| SR-42000 [S] | The Big Three Featuring Cass Elliot | 1967 | 25.00 |

### BIGARD, BARNEY

**LIBERTY**

| Number | Title (A Side/B Side) | Yr | NM |
|---|---|---|---|
| LRP-3072 [M] | Jazz Hall of Fame | 1957 | 40.00 |

### BIGARD, BARNEY/ALBERT NICHOLAS

**RCA VICTOR**

| Number | Title (A Side/B Side) | Yr | NM |
|---|---|---|---|
| LPV-566 [M] | Barney Bigard/Albert Nicholas | 1966 | 20.00 |

### BIGELOW, ARTHUR LYNDS

**COLUMBIA**

| Number | Title (A Side/B Side) | Yr | NM |
|---|---|---|---|
| CL 750 [M] | Christmas Carillon | 1955 | 25.00 |

### BIGGS, RICHARD KEYS

**CAPITOL**

| Number | Title (A Side/B Side) | Yr | NM |
|---|---|---|---|
| T 9013 [M] | Christmas Bells | 1954 | 20.00 |

**COLUMBIA**

| Number | Title (A Side/B Side) | Yr | NM |
|---|---|---|---|
| CL 6076 [10] | An Organ Concert of Carols | 1950 | 40.00 |

### BILK, ACKER

**ATCO**

| Number | Title (A Side/B Side) | Yr | NM |
|---|---|---|---|
| 33-129 [M] | Stranger on the Shore | 1961 | 15.00 |
| SD 33-129 [S] | Stranger on the Shore | 1961 | 20.00 |
| 33-144 [M] | Above the Stars | 1962 | 15.00 |
| SD 33-144 [S] | Above the Stars | 1962 | 20.00 |
| 33-150 [M] | Only You | 1963 | 15.00 |
| SD 33-150 [S] | Only You | 1963 | 20.00 |
| 33-158 [M] | Call Me Mister | 1963 | 15.00 |
| SD 33-158 [S] | Call Me Mister | 1963 | 20.00 |
| 33-168 [M] | A Touch of Latin | 1964 | 12.00 |
| SD 33-168 [S] | A Touch of Latin | 1964 | 15.00 |
| 33-170 [M] | Great Themes from Great Foreign Films | 1965 | 12.00 |
| SD 33-170 [S] | Great Themes from Great Foreign Films | 1965 | 15.00 |
| 33-181 [M] | Acker Bilk in Paris | 1966 | 12.00 |
| SD 33-181 [S] | Acker Bilk in Paris | 1966 | 15.00 |
| 33-197 [M] | Mood for Love | 1966 | 12.00 |
| SD 33-197 [S] | Mood for Love | 1966 | 15.00 |

**GNP CRESCENDO**

| Number | Title (A Side/B Side) | Yr | NM |
|---|---|---|---|
| GNPS-2116 | The Best of Acker Bilk: His Clarinet and Strings | 198? | 10.00 |
| GNPS-2171 | The Best of Acker Bilk: His Clarinet and Strings, Volume 2 | 198? | 10.00 |
| GNPS-2191 | Acker Bilk Plays Lennon and McCartney | 1988 | 12.00 |

**REPRISE**

| Number | Title (A Side/B Side) | Yr | NM |
|---|---|---|---|
| R-6031 [M] | A Stranger No More | 1962 | 20.00 |
| RS-6031 [R] | A Stranger No More | 1962 | 15.00 |

### BILLION DOLLAR BABIES

**POLYDOR**

| Number | Title (A Side/B Side) | Yr | NM |
|---|---|---|---|
| PRO 022 [DJ] | Battle Axe | 1977 | 20.00 |
| | *—Promo-only sampler* | | |
| PD-1-6100 | Battle Axe | 1977 | 15.00 |

### BILLY BOY

**PRESTIGE**

| Number | Title (A Side/B Side) | Yr | NM |
|---|---|---|---|
| PRLP-7389 [M] | Blues on the South Side | 1965 | 30.00 |
| | *—As "Billy Boy Arnold"* | | |
| PRST-7389 [S] | Blues on the South Side | 1965 | 40.00 |
| | *—As "Billy Boy Arnold"* | | |

### BIRKIN, JANE, AND SERGE GAINSBOURG

**FONTANA**

| Number | Title (A Side/B Side) | Yr | NM |
|---|---|---|---|
| SRF-67610 | Je T'aime | 1970 | 20.00 |

### BIRTH CONTROL

**PROPHESY**

| Number | Title (A Side/B Side) | Yr | NM |
|---|---|---|---|
| PRS-1002 | Birth Control: A New German Rock Group | 1970 | 30.00 |

### BISHOP, ELVIN

**ALLIGATOR**

| Number | Title (A Side/B Side) | Yr | NM |
|---|---|---|---|
| AL-4767 | Big Fun | 1987 | 10.00 |

**CAPRICORN**

| Number | Title (A Side/B Side) | Yr | NM |
|---|---|---|---|
| CP 0134 | Let It Flow | 1974 | 12.00 |
| CP 0151 | Juke Joint Jump | 1975 | 12.00 |
| CP 0165 | Struttin' My Stuff | 1975 | 12.00 |
| CPN-0165 | Struttin' My Stuff | 1980 | 10.00 |
| | *—Reissue with revised prefix and Polygram distribution* | | |
| CP 0176 | Hometown Boy Makes Good! | 1976 | 12.00 |
| 2CP 0185 [(2)] | Live! Raisin' Hell | 1977 | 15.00 |
| CPN-0215 | Hog Heaven | 1978 | 12.00 |

**EPIC**

| Number | Title (A Side/B Side) | Yr | NM |
|---|---|---|---|
| KE 31563 | Rock My Soul | 1972 | 15.00 |
| PE 33693 | The Best of Elvin Bishop | 1975 | 12.00 |

**FILLMORE**

| Number | Title (A Side/B Side) | Yr | NM |
|---|---|---|---|
| F 30001 | Elvin Bishop Group | 1969 | 20.00 |
| Z 30239 | Feel It | 1970 | 20.00 |

### BISHOP, JOEY

**ABC**

| Number | Title (A Side/B Side) | Yr | NM |
|---|---|---|---|
| ABCS-656 | Joey Bishop Sings Country and Western | 1968 | 30.00 |

### BISHOP, WALTER, JR.

**COTILLION**

| Number | Title (A Side/B Side) | Yr | NM |
|---|---|---|---|
| SD 236 | Walter Bishop | 1969 | 20.00 |

**JAZZTIME**

| Number | Title (A Side/B Side) | Yr | NM |
|---|---|---|---|
| JS-002 [S] | Speak Low | 1961 | 30.00 |
| JT-002 [M] | Speak Low | 1961 | 25.00 |

**PRESTIGE**

| Number | Title (A Side/B Side) | Yr | NM |
|---|---|---|---|
| PRST-7730 | The Walter Bishop Trio 1965 | 1969 | 20.00 |

### BIT 'A SWEET

**ABC**

| Number | Title (A Side/B Side) | Yr | NM |
|---|---|---|---|
| S-640 | Hypnotic 1 | 1968 | 40.00 |

### BIVONA, GUS

**MERCURY**

| Number | Title (A Side/B Side) | Yr | NM |
|---|---|---|---|
| MG-20157 [M] | Hey, Dig That Crazy Band | 195? | 30.00 |

### BJOERLING, JUSSI

**RCA VICTOR RED SEAL**

| Number | Title (A Side/B Side) | Yr | NM |
|---|---|---|---|
| LSC-2570 [S] | The Incomparable Jussi Bjoerling | 1962 | 20.00 |
| | *—Original with "shaded dog" label* | | |

### BLACK, BILL, 'S COMBO

**COLUMBIA**

| Number | Title (A Side/B Side) | Yr | NM |
|---|---|---|---|
| CS 1055 | Basic Black | 1970 | 12.00 |
| CS 9848 | Black with Sugar | 1969 | 12.00 |
| CS 9957 | Raindrops Keep Fallin' on My Head | 1970 | 12.00 |

**HI**

| Number | Title (A Side/B Side) | Yr | NM |
|---|---|---|---|
| 6005 | Award Winners | 1978 | 10.00 |
| 8004 | Memphis Tennessee | 1977 | 10.00 |
| HL-12001 [M] | Smokie | 1960 | 40.00 |
| | *—Orange and white label* | | |
| HL-12001 [M] | Smokie | 1960 | 60.00 |
| | *—Black label with red and silver logo* | | |
| HL-12002 [M] | Saxy Jazz | 1960 | 40.00 |
| HL-12003 [M] | Solid and Raunchy | 1960 | 40.00 |
| HL-12004 [M] | That Wonderful Feeling | 1961 | 20.00 |
| HL-12005 [M] | Movin' | 1961 | 20.00 |
| HL-12006 [M] | Let's Twist Her | 1961 | 15.00 |
| | *—Retitled version of above* | | |
| HL-12006 [M] | Bill Black's Record Hop | 1961 | 25.00 |
| HL-12009 [M] | The Untouchable Sound of Bill Black | 1962 | 15.00 |
| HL-12012 [M] | Bill Black's Greatest Hits | 1963 | 15.00 |
| HL-12013 [M] | Bill Black's Combo Goes West | 1963 | 15.00 |
| HL-12015 [M] | Bill Black Plays the Blues | 1964 | 15.00 |
| HL-12017 [M] | Bill Black Plays Tunes by Chuck Berry | 1964 | 15.00 |
| HL-12020 [M] | Bill Black's Combo Goes Big Band | 1964 | 15.00 |
| HL-12023 [M] | More Solid and Raunchy | 1965 | 15.00 |
| HL-12027 [M] | Mr. Beat | 1965 | 15.00 |
| HL-12032 [M] | All Timers | 1966 | 12.00 |
| HL-12033 [M] | Black Lace | 1966 | 12.00 |
| HL-12036 [M] | King of the Road | 1966 | 12.00 |
| HL-12041 [M] | The Beat Goes On | 1967 | 15.00 |
| HL-12044 [M] | Turn Your Lovelight On | 1967 | 15.00 |
| HL-12047 [M] | Soulin' the Blues | 1968 | 15.00 |
| SHL-32001 [R] | Smokie | 1964 | 20.00 |
| SHL-32002 [R] | Saxy Jazz | 1964 | 20.00 |
| SHL-32003 [R] | Solid and Raunchy | 1964 | 20.00 |
| SHL-32004 [S] | That Wonderful Feeling | 1961 | 25.00 |
| SHL-32005 [S] | Movin' | 1961 | 25.00 |
| SHL-32006 [S] | Let's Twist Her | 1961 | 20.00 |
| | *—Retitled version of above* | | |
| SHL-32006 [S] | Bill Black's Record Hop | 1961 | 30.00 |
| SHL-32009 [S] | The Untouchable Sound of Bill Black | 1962 | 20.00 |
| SHL-32012 [S] | Bill Black's Greatest Hits | 1963 | 20.00 |
| SHL-32013 [S] | Bill Black's Combo Goes West | 1963 | 20.00 |
| SHL-32015 [S] | Bill Black Plays the Blues | 1964 | 20.00 |
| SHL-32017 [S] | Bill Black Plays Tunes by Chuck Berry | 1964 | 20.00 |
| SHL-32020 [S] | Bill Black's Combo Goes Big Band | 1964 | 20.00 |
| SHL-32023 [S] | More Solid and Raunchy | 1965 | 20.00 |
| SHL-32027 [S] | Mr. Beat | 1965 | 20.00 |
| SHL-32032 [S] | All Timers | 1966 | 15.00 |
| SHL-32033 [S] | Black Lace | 1966 | 15.00 |
| SHL-32036 [S] | King of the Road | 1966 | 15.00 |
| SHL-32041 [S] | The Beat Goes On | 1967 | 15.00 |
| SHL-32044 [S] | Turn Your Lovelight On | 1967 | 15.00 |
| SHL-32047 [S] | Soulin' the Blues | 1968 | 15.00 |
| SHL-32052 | Solid and Raunchy The 3rd | 1969 | 15.00 |
| SHL-32061 | More Magic | 1971 | 12.00 |
| XSHL-32078 | Bill Black's Greatest Hits, Vol. 2 | 1973 | 12.00 |
| XSHL-32088 | Solid and Country | 1974 | 12.00 |
| SHL-32093 | The World's Greatest Honky Tonk Band | 1975 | 12.00 |
| SHL-32104 | It's Honky Tonk Time | 1976 | 12.00 |

**MEGA**

| Number | Title (A Side/B Side) | Yr | NM |
|---|---|---|---|
| MLPS-600 | Bill Black Is Back | 1973 | 12.00 |
| 31-1008 | The Memphis Scene | 1971 | 12.00 |
| 31-1014 | Juke Box Favorites | 1972 | 12.00 |
| 51-5008 | Rock 'n' Roll Forever | 1973 | 12.00 |

### BLACK, CILLA

**CAPITOL**

| Number | Title (A Side/B Side) | Yr | NM |
|---|---|---|---|
| ST 2308 [S] | Is It Love? | 1965 | 40.00 |
| T 2308 [M] | Is It Love? | 1965 | 25.00 |

### BLACK, CLINT

**RCA**

| Number | Title (A Side/B Side) | Yr | NM |
|---|---|---|---|
| 9668-1-R | Killin' Time | 1989 | 15.00 |
| R 124690 | Put Yourself in My Shoes | 1990 | 50.00 |
| | *—Released on vinyl only through BMG Direct Marketing* | | |

### BLACK, JEANNE

**CAPITOL**

| Number | Title (A Side/B Side) | Yr | NM |
|---|---|---|---|
| ST 1513 [S] | A Little Bit Lonely | 1961 | 25.00 |
| T 1513 [M] | A Little Bit Lonely | 1961 | 20.00 |

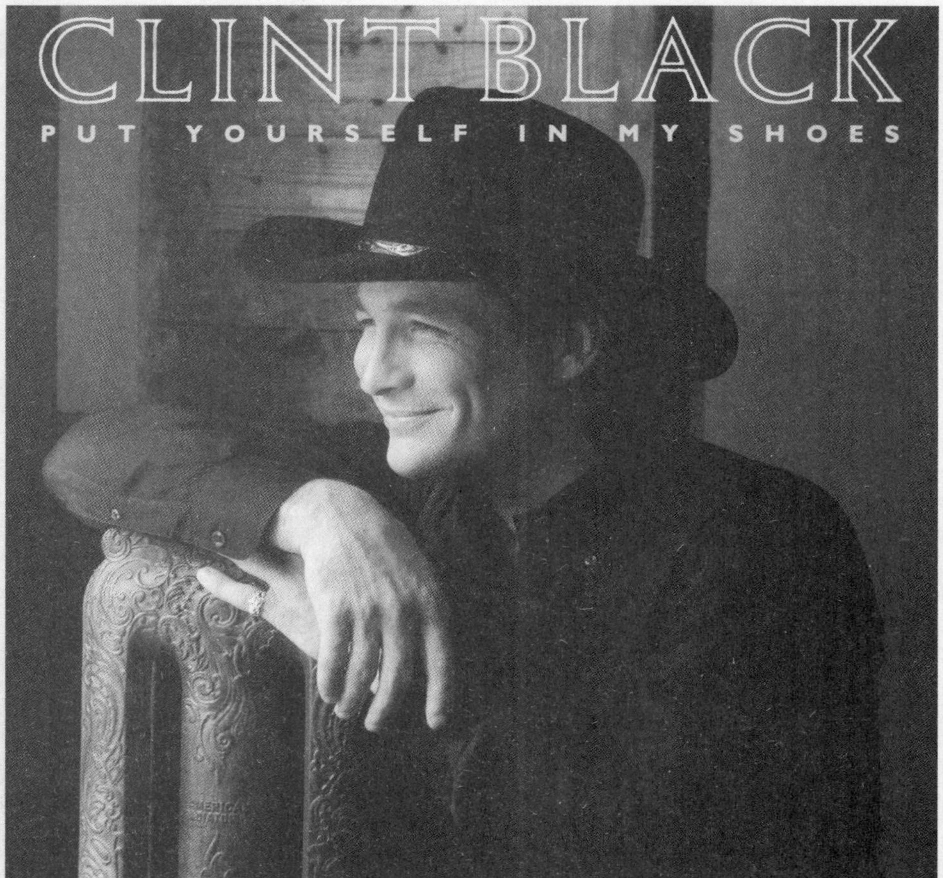


Clint Black, *Put Yourself in My Shoes,* RCA R124690, 1990, BMG Direct Marketing edition, $50.

## BLACK LIGHTNING

TOWER

| Number | Title (A Side/B Side) | Yr | NM |
|---|---|---|---|
| ❑ ST 5129 | Shades of Black Lightning | 1968 | 20.00 |

## BLACK MERDA

CHESS

| Number | Title (A Side/B Side) | Yr | NM |
|---|---|---|---|
| ❑ LP-1551 | Black Merda | 1970 | 50.00 |

## BLACK OAK ARKANSAS

ATCO

| Number | Title (A Side/B Side) | Yr | NM |
|---|---|---|---|
| ❑ SD 36-101 | Street Party | 1974 | 12.00 |
| ❑ SD 36-111 | Ain't Life Grand | 1975 | 12.00 |
| ❑ SD 36-128 | Live! Mutha | 1976 | 12.00 |
| ❑ SD 36-150 | The Best of Black Oak Arkansas | 1976 | 12.00 |
| ❑ SD 33-354 | Black Oak Arkansas | 1971 | 15.00 |
| ❑ 33-381 [M] | Keep the Faith | 1972 | 30.00 |
| *—White label promo, "DJ Copy Monaural" sticker on cover; no stock copies were issued in mono* | | | |
| ❑ SD 33-381 [S] | Keep the Faith | 1972 | 15.00 |
| ❑ SD 7008 | If An Angel Came to See You, Would You Make Her Feel at Home? | 1972 | 15.00 |
| ❑ QD 7019 [Q] | Raunch 'n' Roll/Live | 1974 | 20.00 |
| ❑ SD 7019 | Raunch 'n' Roll/Live | 1973 | 15.00 |
| ❑ SD 7035 | High on the Hog | 1973 | 15.00 |

CAPRICORN

| Number | Title (A Side/B Side) | Yr | NM |
|---|---|---|---|
| ❑ CP 0191 | Race with the Devil | 1977 | 12.00 |
| ❑ CP 0207 | I'd Rather Be Sailing | 1978 | 12.00 |

MCA

| Number | Title (A Side/B Side) | Yr | NM |
|---|---|---|---|
| ❑ 704 | X-Rated | 198? | 8.00 |
| *—Budget-line reissue* | | | |
| ❑ 2155 | X-Rated | 1975 | 12.00 |
| ❑ 2199 | Balls of Fire | 1976 | 12.00 |
| ❑ 2224 | 10 Year Overnight Success | 1977 | 12.00 |

STAX

| Number | Title (A Side/B Side) | Yr | NM |
|---|---|---|---|
| ❑ STS-5504 | Early Times | 1974 | 15.00 |

## BLACK PEARL

ATLANTIC

| Number | Title (A Side/B Side) | Yr | NM |
|---|---|---|---|
| ❑ SD 8220 | Black Pearl | 1969 | 25.00 |

PROPHESY

| Number | Title (A Side/B Side) | Yr | NM |
|---|---|---|---|
| ❑ PRS-1001 | Black Pearl — Live! | 1970 | 25.00 |

## BLACK RANDY AND THE METROSQUAD

DANGERHOUSE

| Number | Title (A Side/B Side) | Yr | NM |
|---|---|---|---|
| ❑ PCP 725 | "Pass the Dust, I Think I'm Bowie" | 1980 | 50.00 |

## BLACK SABBATH

I.R.S.

| Number | Title (A Side/B Side) | Yr | NM |
|---|---|---|---|
| ❑ 82002 | Headless Cross | 1989 | 10.00 |

WARNER BROS.

| Number | Title (A Side/B Side) | Yr | NM |
|---|---|---|---|
| ❑ WS 1871 | Black Sabbath | 1970 | 15.00 |
| *—Green label* | | | |
| ❑ WS 1871 | Black Sabbath | 1973 | 10.00 |
| *—"Burbank" palm trees label* | | | |
| ❑ WS 1871 | Black Sabbath | 1979 | 8.00 |
| *—White or tan label* | | | |
| ❑ WS 1887 | Paranoid | 1971 | 15.00 |
| *—Green label* | | | |
| ❑ WS 1887 | Paranoid | 1973 | 10.00 |
| *—"Burbank" palm trees label* | | | |
| ❑ WS4 1887 [Q] | Paranoid | 1974 | 30.00 |
| *—All quad copies have "Burbank" palm trees label* | | | |
| ❑ BS 2562 | Master of Reality | 1971 | 15.00 |
| *—Green label* | | | |
| ❑ BS 2562 | Master of Reality Poster | 1971 | 25.00 |
| ❑ BS 2562 | Master of Reality | 1973 | 10.00 |
| *—"Burbank" palm trees label* | | | |
| ❑ BS 2562 | Master of Reality | 1979 | 8.00 |
| *—White or tan label* | | | |
| ❑ BS 2602 | Black Sabbath, Vol. 4 | 1972 | 15.00 |
| *—Green label* | | | |
| ❑ BS 2602 | Black Sabbath, Vol. 4 | 1973 | 10.00 |
| *—"Burbank" palm trees label* | | | |
| ❑ BS 2602 | Black Sabbath, Vol. 4 | 1979 | 8.00 |
| *—White or tan label* | | | |
| ❑ BS 2695 | Sabbath Bloody Sabbath | 1974 | 15.00 |
| *—"Burbank" palm trees label* | | | |
| ❑ BS 2695 | Sabbath Bloody Sabbath | 1979 | 8.00 |
| *—White or tan label* | | | |
| ❑ BS 2822 | Sabotage | 1975 | 15.00 |
| *—"Burbank" palm trees label* | | | |
| ❑ BS 2822 | Sabotage | 1979 | 8.00 |
| *—White or tan label* | | | |
| ❑ 2BS 2923 [(2)] | We Sold Our Souls for Rock 'N' Roll | 1975 | 20.00 |
| *—"Burbank" palm trees label* | | | |
| ❑ 2BS 2923 [(2)] | We Sold Our Souls for Rock 'N' Roll | 1979 | 10.00 |
| *—White or tan label* | | | |
| ❑ BS 2969 | Technical Ecstasy | 1976 | 15.00 |
| *—"Burbank" palm trees label* | | | |
| ❑ BS 2969 | Technical Ecstasy | 1979 | 8.00 |
| *—White or tan label* | | | |
| ❑ BSK 3104 | Paranoid | 1978 | 10.00 |
| *—Reissue; "Burbank" palm trees label* | | | |
| ❑ BSK 3104 | Paranoid | 1979 | 8.00 |
| *—Reissue; white or tan label* | | | |
| ❑ BSK 3186 | Never Say Die! | 1978 | 12.00 |
| ❑ BSK 3372 | Heaven and Hell | 1980 | 12.00 |
| ❑ BSK 3605 | Mob Rules | 1981 | 12.00 |
| ❑ 23742 [(2)] | Live Evil | 1983 | 15.00 |
| ❑ 23978 | Born Again | 1983 | 10.00 |
| ❑ 25337 | Seventh Star | 1986 | 10.00 |
| ❑ 25548 | The Eternal Idol | 1987 | 10.00 |

## BLACK SHEEP

CAPITOL

| Number | Title (A Side/B Side) | Yr | NM |
|---|---|---|---|
| ❑ ST-11369 | Black Sheep | 1974 | 20.00 |
| ❑ ST-11447 | Encouraging Words | 1975 | 20.00 |

## BLACK VELVET

OKEH

| Number | Title (A Side/B Side) | Yr | NM |
|---|---|---|---|
| ❑ OKS 14130 | Love City | 1969 | 25.00 |

## BLACKBYRDS, THE

FANTASY

| Number | Title (A Side/B Side) | Yr | NM |
|---|---|---|---|
| ❑ FPM-4004 [Q] | Flying Start | 1975 | 25.00 |
| ❑ F-9444 | The Blackbyrds | 1974 | 15.00 |
| ❑ F-9472 | Flying Start | 1974 | 15.00 |
| ❑ F-9490 | City Life | 1975 | 15.00 |
| ❑ F-9518 | Unfinished Business | 1976 | 15.00 |
| ❑ F-9535 | Action | 1977 | 12.00 |
| ❑ F-9570 | Night Grooves | 1978 | 12.00 |
| ❑ F-9602 | Better Days | 1980 | 12.00 |

## BLACKFOOT, J.D.

FANTASY

| Number | Title (A Side/B Side) | Yr | NM |
|---|---|---|---|
| ❑ F-9468 | Song of Crazy Horse | 1974 | 20.00 |
| ❑ F-9487 | Southbound and Gone | 1975 | 20.00 |

MERCURY

| Number | Title (A Side/B Side) | Yr | NM |
|---|---|---|---|
| ❑ SR-61288 | The Ultimate Prophecy | 1970 | 60.00 |

## BLACKHORSE

DSDA

| Number | Title (A Side/B Side) | Yr | NM |
|---|---|---|---|
| ❑ 001 | Blackhorse | 1979 | 60.00 |

## BLACKMAN, HONOR

LONDON

| Number | Title (A Side/B Side) | Yr | NM |
|---|---|---|---|
| ❑ PS 408 [S] | Everything I've Got | 1964 | 40.00 |
| ❑ LL 3408 [M] | Everything I've Got | 1964 | 30.00 |

## BLACKSMOKE

CHOCOLATE CITY

| Number | Title (A Side/B Side) | Yr | NM |
|---|---|---|---|
| ❑ 2001 | Blacksmoke | 1976 | 20.00 |

## BLACKWELL, OTIS

DAVIS

| Number | Title (A Side/B Side) | Yr | NM |
|---|---|---|---|
| ❑ 109 [M] | Singin' the Blues | 1956 | 500.00 |

INNER CITY

| Number | Title (A Side/B Side) | Yr | NM |
|---|---|---|---|
| ❑ 1032 | These Are My Songs | 1977 | 20.00 |

## BLACKWELL, SCRAPPER

BLUESVILLE

| Number | Title (A Side/B Side) | Yr | NM |
|---|---|---|---|
| ❑ BVLP-1047 | Mr. Scrapper's Blues | 1962 | 180.00 |
| *—Blue label, silver print* | | | |
| ❑ BVLP-1047 | Mr. Scrapper's Blues | 1964 | 40.00 |
| *—Blue label with trident logo* | | | |

## BLADES, JIMMY, AND CHARLES SMART

LONDON

| Number | Title (A Side/B Side) | Yr | NM |
|---|---|---|---|
| ❑ LB 82 [10] | Christmas Chimes | 195? | 30.00 |
| *—Back cover with liner notes and other Christmas LPs mentioned* | | | |
| ❑ LB 82 [10] | Christmas Chimes | 195? | 40.00 |
| *—Back cover with liner notes and no reference to other LPs* | | | |

## BLAINE, HAL

ABC DUNHILL

| Number | Title (A Side/B Side) | Yr | NM |
|---|---|---|---|
| ❑ DS-50035 | Have Fun!!! Play Drums!!! | 1968 | 40.00 |
| *—Without instruction booklet* | | | |
| ❑ DS-50035 | Have Fun!!! Play Drums!!! | 1968 | 50.00 |
| *—With instruction booklet* | | | |

DUNHILL

| Number | Title (A Side/B Side) | Yr | NM |
|---|---|---|---|
| ❑ D-50002 [M] | Drums! Drums! A-Go-Go | 1966 | 30.00 |
| ❑ DS-50002 [S] | Drums! Drums! A-Go-Go | 1966 | 40.00 |
| ❑ D-50019 [M] | Psychedelic Percussion | 1967 | 40.00 |
| ❑ DS-50019 [S] | Psychedelic Percussion | 1967 | 60.00 |

RCA VICTOR

| Number | Title (A Side/B Side) | Yr | NM |
|---|---|---|---|
| ❑ LPM-2834 [M] | Deuces, "T's," Roadsters & Drums | 1963 | 100.00 |
| ❑ LSP-2834 [S] | Deuces, "T's," Roadsters & Drums | 1963 | 150.00 |

| Number | Title (A Side/B Side) | Yr | NM |
|---|---|---|---|

### BLAIR, SALLIE

**BETHLEHEM**

❑ BCP-6009 [M] Squeeze Me 1957 80.00

**MGM**

❑ E-3723 [M] Hello, Tiger! 1959 40.00
❑ SE-3723 [S] Hello, Tiger! 1959 50.00

### BLAKE, BETTY

**BETHLEHEM**

❑ BCP-6058 [M] Betty Blake Sings in a Tender Mood 1962 40.00
❑ BCPS-6058 [S] Betty Blake Sings in a Tender Mood 1962 50.00

### BLAKE, EUBIE

**COLUMBIA**

❑ C2S 847 [(2)] The Eighty-Six Years of Eubie Blake 1969 20.00
*—Red "360 Sound" labels*

### BLAKE, RAN

**ESP-DISK'**

❑ 1011 [M] Ran Blake Plays Solo Piano 1965 20.00
❑ S-1011 [S] Ran Blake Plays Solo Piano 1965 20.00

### BLAKE BABIES

**CHEWBUD**

❑ CBTW-001 [EP] Nicely, Nicely 1987 40.00
*—1,000 copies pressed*

**MAMMOTH**

❑ MR0016 Earwig 1989 12.00
❑ MR0022 Sunburn 1990 12.00
❑ MR0025 [EP] Rosy Jack World 1991 10.00
*—Red vinyl*

### BLAKEY, ART, AND THE JAZZ MESSENGERS

**BETHLEHEM**

❑ BCP-6023 [M] Hard Drive 1957 80.00
❑ BCP-6027 [M] Art Blakey's Big Band 1958 80.00
❑ BCPS-6027 [S] Art Blakey's Big Band 1959 50.00

**BLUE NOTE**

❑ BLP-1507 [M] At the Café Bohemia, Volume 1 1956 100.00
*—Regular version, Lexington Ave. address on label*
❑ BLP-1507 [M] At the Café Bohemia, Volume 1 1956 150.00
*—"Deep groove" version (deep indentation under label on both sides)*
❑ BLP-1507 [M] At the Café Bohemia, Volume 1 1957 50.00
*—With W. 63rd St. address on label*
❑ BLP-1507 [M] At the Café Bohemia, Volume 1 1963 25.00
*—With "New York, USA" address on label*
❑ BLP-1508 [M] At the Café Bohemia, Volume 2 1956 100.00
*—Regular version, Lexington Ave. address on label*
❑ BLP-1508 [M] At the Café Bohemia, Volume 2 1956 150.00
*—"Deep groove" version (deep indentation under label on both sides)*
❑ BLP-1508 [M] At the Café Bohemia, Volume 2 1957 50.00
*—With W. 63rd St. address on label*
❑ BLP-1508 [M] At the Café Bohemia, Volume 2 1963 25.00
*—With "New York, USA" address on label*
❑ BLP-1521 [M] A Night at Birdland, Volume 1 1956 100.00
*—Regular version, Lexington Ave. address on label*
❑ BLP-1521 [M] A Night at Birdland, Volume 1 1956 200.00
*—"Deep groove" version (deep indentation under label on both sides)*
❑ BLP-1521 [M] A Night at Birdland, Volume 1 1957 50.00
*—With W. 63rd St. address on label*
❑ BLP-1521 [M] A Night at Birdland, Volume 1 1963 25.00
*—With "New York, USA" address on label*
❑ BLP-1521 [M] A Night at Birdland, Volume 1 1967 20.00
*—"A Division of Liberty Records" on label*
❑ BLP-1522 [M] A Night at Birdland, Volume 2 1956 100.00
*—Regular version, Lexington Ave. address on label*
❑ BLP-1522 [M] A Night at Birdland, Volume 2 1956 200.00
*—"Deep groove" version (deep indentation under label on both sides)*
❑ BLP-1522 [M] A Night at Birdland, Volume 2 1957 50.00
*—With W. 63rd St. address on label*
❑ BLP-1522 [M] A Night at Birdland, Volume 2 1963 25.00
*—With "New York, USA" address on label*
❑ BLP-1554 [M] Orgy in Rhythm, Volume 1 1957 100.00
*—Regular version, with W. 63rd St. address on label*
❑ BLP-1554 [M] Orgy in Rhythm, Volume 1 1957 150.00
*—"Deep groove" version (deep indentation under label on both sides)*
❑ BLP-1554 [M] Orgy in Rhythm, Volume 1 1963 25.00
*—With "New York, USA" address on label*
❑ BLP-1555 [M] Orgy in Rhythm, Volume 2 1957 100.00
*—Regular version, with W. 63rd St. address on label*
❑ BLP-1555 [M] Orgy in Rhythm, Volume 2 1957 150.00
*—"Deep groove" version (deep indentation under label on both sides)*
❑ BLP-1555 [M] Orgy in Rhythm, Volume 2 1963 25.00
*—With "New York, USA" address on label*
❑ BLP-4003 [M] Art Blakey and the Jazz Messengers 1958 100.00
*—Regular version, with W. 63rd St. address on label*
❑ BLP-4003 [M] Art Blakey and the Jazz Messengers 1958 150.00
*—"Deep groove" version (deep indentation under label on both sides)*
❑ BLP-4003 [M] Art Blakey and the Jazz Messengers 1963 25.00
*—With "New York, USA" address on label*
❑ BST-4003 [S] Art Blakey and the Jazz Messengers 1959 100.00
*—"Deep groove" version (deep indentation under label on both sides)*
❑ BST-4003 [S] Art Blakey and the Jazz Messengers 1959 80.00
*—Regular version, with W. 63rd St. address on label*
❑ BST-4003 [S] Art Blakey and the Jazz Messengers 1963 20.00
*—With "New York, USA" address on label*
❑ BLP-4004 [M] Holiday for Skins, Volume 1 1958 150.00
*—Regular version, with W. 63rd St. address on label*
❑ BLP-4004 [M] Holiday for Skins, Volume 1 1958 200.00
*—"Deep groove" version (deep indentation under label on both sides)*
❑ BLP-4004 [M] Holiday for Skins, Volume 1 1963 25.00
*—With "New York, USA" address on label*
❑ BST-4004 [S] Holiday for Skins, Volume 1 1959 150.00
*—"Deep groove" version (deep indentation under label on both sides)*
❑ BST-4004 [S] Holiday for Skins, Volume 1 1959 120.00
*—Regular version, with W. 63rd St. address on label*
❑ BST-4004 [S] Holiday for Skins, Volume 1 1963 20.00
*—With "New York, USA" address on label*
❑ BLP-4005 [M] Holiday for Skins, Volume 2 1958 150.00
*—Regular version, with W. 63rd St. address on label*
❑ BLP-4005 [M] Holiday for Skins, Volume 2 1958 200.00
*—"Deep groove" version (deep indentation under label on both sides)*
❑ BLP-4005 [M] Holiday for Skins, Volume 2 1963 25.00
*—With "New York, USA" address on label*
❑ BST-4005 [S] Holiday for Skins, Volume 2 1959 150.00
*—"Deep groove" version (deep indentation under label on both sides)*
❑ BST-4005 [S] Holiday for Skins, Volume 2 1959 120.00
*—Regular version, with W. 63rd St. address on label*
❑ BST-4005 [S] Holiday for Skins, Volume 2 1963 20.00
*—With "New York, USA" address on label*
❑ BLP-4015 [M] At the Jazz Corner of the World, Volume 1 1958 80.00
*—Regular version, with W. 63rd St. address on label*
❑ BLP-4015 [M] At the Jazz Corner of the World, Volume 1 1958 120.00
*—"Deep groove" version (deep indentation under label on both sides)*
❑ BLP-4015 [M] At the Jazz Corner of the World, Volume 1 1963 25.00
*—With "New York, USA" address on label*
❑ BLP-4016 [M] At the Jazz Corner of the World, Volume 2 1958 80.00
*—Regular version, with W. 63rd St. address on label*
❑ BLP-4016 [M] At the Jazz Corner of the World, Volume 2 1958 120.00
*—"Deep groove" version (deep indentation under label on both sides)*
❑ BLP-4016 [M] At the Jazz Corner of the World, Volume 2 1963 25.00
*—With "New York, USA" address on label*
❑ BLP-4029 [M] The Big Beat 1960 80.00
*—Regular version, with W. 63rd St. address on label*
❑ BLP-4029 [M] The Big Beat 1960 100.00
*—"Deep groove" version (deep indentation under label on both sides)*
❑ BLP-4029 [M] The Big Beat 1963 25.00
*—With "New York, USA" address on label*
❑ BLP-4049 [M] A Night in Tunisia 1960 80.00
*—Regular version, with W. 63rd St. address on label*
❑ BLP-4049 [M] A Night in Tunisia 1960 100.00
*—"Deep groove" version (deep indentation under label on both sides)*
❑ BLP-4049 [M] A Night in Tunisia 1963 25.00
*—With "New York, USA" address on label*
❑ BLP-4054 [M] Meet You at the Jazz Corner of the World, Volume 1 1960 70.00
*—With W. 63rd St. address on label*
❑ BLP-4054 [M] Meet You at the Jazz Corner of the World, Volume 1 1963 25.00
*—With "New York, USA" address on label*
❑ BLP-4055 [M] Meet You at the Jazz Corner of the World, Volume 2 1960 70.00
*—With W. 63rd St. address on label*
❑ BLP-4055 [M] Meet You at the Jazz Corner of the World, Volume 2 1963 25.00
*—With "New York, USA" address on label*
❑ BLP-4090 [M] Mosaic 1961 80.00
*—With 61st St. address on label*
❑ BLP-4090 [M] Mosaic 1963 25.00
*—With "New York, USA" address on label*
❑ BLP-4097 [M] The African Beat 1961 80.00
*—With 61st St. address on label*
❑ BLP-4097 [M] The African Beat 1963 25.00
*—With "New York, USA" address on label*
❑ BLP-4104 [M] Buhaina's Delight 1962 30.00
*—With "New York, USA" on label*
❑ BLP-4156 [M] The Freedom Rider 1964 30.00
❑ BLP-4170 [M] Free for All 1965 30.00
❑ BLP-4193 [M] Indestructible 1966 30.00
❑ BLP-4245 [M] Like Someone in Love 1967 40.00
❑ BLP-5037 [10] A Night at Birdland, Volume 1 1954 300.00
❑ BLP-5038 [10] A Night at Birdland, Volume 2 1954 300.00
❑ BLP-5039 [10] A Night at Birdland, Volume 3 1954 300.00
❑ BST-84015 [S] At the Jazz Corner of the World, Volume 1 1959 60.00
*—Regular version, with W. 63rd St. address on label*
❑ BST-84015 [S] At the Jazz Corner of the World, Volume 1 1963 20.00
*—With "New York, USA" address on label*
❑ BST-84016 [S] At the Jazz Corner of the World, Volume 2 1959 80.00
*—"Deep groove" version (deep indentation under label on both sides)*
❑ BST-84016 [S] At the Jazz Corner of the World, Volume 2 1959 60.00
*—Regular version, with W. 63rd St. address on label*
❑ BST-84016 [S] At the Jazz Corner of the World, Volume 2 1963 20.00
*—With "New York, USA" address on label*
❑ BST-84029 [S] The Big Beat 1960 60.00
*—With W. 63rd St. address on label*
❑ BST-84029 [S] The Big Beat 1963 20.00
*—With "New York, USA" address on label*
❑ BST-84049 [S] A Night in Tunisia 1960 60.00
*—With W. 63rd St. address on label*
❑ BST-84049 [S] A Night in Tunisia 1963 20.00
*—With "New York, USA" address on label*
❑ BST-84054 [S] Meet You at the Jazz Corner of the World, Volume 1 1960 60.00
*—With W. 63rd St. address on label*
❑ BST-84054 [S] Meet You at the Jazz Corner of the World, Volume 1 1963 20.00
*—With "New York, USA" address on label*
❑ BST-84055 [S] Meet You at the Jazz Corner of the World, Volume 2 1960 60.00
*—With W. 63rd St. address on label*
❑ BST-84055 [S] Meet You at the Jazz Corner of the World, Volume 2 1963 20.00
*—With "New York, USA" address on label*
❑ BST-84090 [S] Mosaic 1963 20.00
*—With "New York, USA" address on label*
❑ BST-84097 [S] The African Beat 1961 60.00
*—With 61st St. address on label*
❑ BST-84097 [S] The African Beat 1963 25.00
*—With "New York, USA" address on label*
❑ BST-84104 [S] Buhaina's Delight 1962 40.00
*—With "New York, USA" address on label*
❑ BST-84156 [S] The Freedom Rider 1964 40.00
*—With "New York, USA" address on label*
❑ BST-84170 [S] Free for All 1965 40.00
*—With "New York, USA" address on label*
❑ BST-84193 [S] Indestructible 1966 40.00
*—With "New York, USA" address on label*
❑ BST-84245 [S] Like Someone in Love 1967 40.00
*—With "New York, USA" address on label*
❑ BST-84258 [S] The Witch Doctor 1969 20.00
*—With "A Division of Liberty Records" on label*

**CADET**

❑ LP-4049 [M] Tough! 1966 25.00
❑ LPS-4049 [S] Tough! 1966 30.00

**COLUMBIA**

❑ CL 897 [M] The Jazz Messengers 1956 80.00
*—Red and black label with six "eye" logos*
❑ CL 1002 [M] Drum Suite 1957 60.00
*—Red and black label with six "eye" logos*
❑ CL 1040 [M] Hard Bop 1957 60.00
*—Red and black label with six "eye" logos*

**ELEKTRA**

❑ EKL-120 [M] A Midnight Session with the Jazz Messengers 1957 80.00

**EMARCY**

❑ MG-26030 [10] Blakey 1954 500.00

**EPIC**

❑ LA 16009 [M] Paris Concert 1960 30.00
❑ LA 16017 [M] Art Blakey in Paris 1961 30.00
❑ BA 17009 [S] Paris Concert 1960 40.00
❑ BA 17017 [S] Art Blakey in Paris 1961 40.00

**IMPULSE!**

❑ A-7 [M] Art Blakey!!!! Jazz Messengers!!!! 1961 30.00
❑ AS-7 [S] Art Blakey!!!! Jazz Messengers!!!! 1961 40.00
❑ A-45 [M] A Jazz Message 1963 30.00
❑ AS-45 [S] A Jazz Message 1963 40.00

**JOSIE**

❑ JOZ-3501 [M] Cu-Bop 1962 40.00
*—Reissue of Jubilee LP*
❑ JS-3501 [S] Cu-Bop 1962 30.00

**JUBILEE**

❑ JLP-1049 [M] Cu-Bop 1958 80.00

**LIMELIGHT**

❑ LM-82001 [M] 'S Make It 1965 20.00
❑ LM-82019 [M] Soul Finger 1965 20.00
❑ LM-82034 [M] Buttercorn Lady 1966 20.00
❑ LM-82038 [M] Hold On, I'm Coming 1966 20.00
❑ LS-86001 [S] 'S Make It 1965 25.00
❑ LS-86019 [S] Soul Finger 1965 25.00
❑ LS-86034 [S] Buttercorn Lady 1966 25.00
❑ LS-86038 [S] Hold On, I'm Coming 1966 25.00

### MOSAIC

| Number | Title (A Side/B Side) | Yr | NM |
|---|---|---|---|
| ❑ MR10-141 [(10)] | The Complete Blue Note Recordings of Art Blakey's 1960 Jazz Messengers | 199? | 150.00 |

### PACIFIC JAZZ

| Number | Title (A Side/B Side) | Yr | NM |
|---|---|---|---|
| ❑ PJ-15 [M] | Ritual | 1961 | 40.00 |
| *—Reissue of 402* | | | |
| ❑ PJM-402 [M] | Ritual | 1957 | 80.00 |

### PRESTIGE

| Number | Title (A Side/B Side) | Yr | NM |
|---|---|---|---|
| ❑ 10047 | Child's Dance | 197? | 12.00 |

### RCA VICTOR

| Number | Title (A Side/B Side) | Yr | NM |
|---|---|---|---|
| ❑ LPM-2654 [M] | A Night in Tunisia | 1963 | 40.00 |
| *—Reissue of Vik 1115* | | | |
| ❑ LSP-2654 [R] | A Night in Tunisia | 1963 | 20.00 |

### RIVERSIDE

| Number | Title (A Side/B Side) | Yr | NM |
|---|---|---|---|
| ❑ RS-438 [M] | Caravan | 1962 | 25.00 |
| ❑ RS-464 [M] | Ugetsu | 1963 | 25.00 |
| ❑ RS-493 [M] | Kyoto | 1966 | 20.00 |
| ❑ RS-9438 [S] | Caravan | 1962 | 30.00 |
| ❑ RS-9464 [S] | Ugetsu | 1963 | 30.00 |
| ❑ RS-9493 [S] | Kyoto | 1966 | 25.00 |

### SAVOY

| Number | Title (A Side/B Side) | Yr | NM |
|---|---|---|---|
| ❑ MG-12171 [M] | Art Blakey and the Jazz Messengers | 1960 | 30.00 |

### UNITED ARTISTS

| Number | Title (A Side/B Side) | Yr | NM |
|---|---|---|---|
| ❑ UAJ-14002 [M] | Three Blind Mice | 1962 | 40.00 |
| ❑ UAJS-15002 [S] | Three Blind Mice | 1962 | 50.00 |

### VIK

| Number | Title (A Side/B Side) | Yr | NM |
|---|---|---|---|
| ❑ LX-1103 [M] | Art Blakey and the Jazz Messengers Play Selections from Lerner and Loewe | 1957 | 100.00 |
| ❑ LX-1115 [M] | A Night in Tunisia | 1958 | 100.00 |

## BLAKEY, ART, AND THE JAZZ MESSENGERS/ ELMO HOPE

### PACIFIC JAZZ

| Number | Title (A Side/B Side) | Yr | NM |
|---|---|---|---|
| ❑ PJ-33 [M] | The Jazz Messengers and Elmo Hope | 1962 | 40.00 |

## BLAKEY, ART, AND THE JAZZ MESSENGERS WITH THELONIOUS MONK

### ATLANTIC

| Number | Title (A Side/B Side) | Yr | NM |
|---|---|---|---|
| ❑ 1278 [M] | Art Blakey's Jazz Messengers with Thelonious Monk | 1958 | 50.00 |
| *—Black label* | | | |
| ❑ 1278 [M] | Art Blakey's Jazz Messengers with Thelonious Monk | 1960 | 20.00 |
| *—Multicolor label, white "fan" logo* | | | |
| ❑ SD 1278 [S] | Art Blakey's Jazz Messengers with Thelonious Monk | 1959 | 40.00 |
| *—Green label* | | | |

## BLANC, MEL

### CAPITOL

| Number | Title (A Side/B Side) | Yr | NM |
|---|---|---|---|
| ❑ H-436 [10] | Party Panic | 1953 | 100.00 |

## BLAND, BOBBY

### ABC

| Number | Title (A Side/B Side) | Yr | NM |
|---|---|---|---|
| ❑ D-895 | Get On Down with Bobby Bland | 1975 | 12.00 |
| ❑ AB-1018 | Reflections in Blue | 1977 | 10.00 |
| ❑ AA-1075 | Come Fly with Me | 1978 | 10.00 |

### ABC DUKE

| Number | Title (A Side/B Side) | Yr | NM |
|---|---|---|---|
| ❑ DLPS-74 | Two Steps from the Blues | 197? | 12.00 |
| ❑ DLP-75 | Here's the Man!!! | 1974 | 12.00 |
| ❑ DLP-77 | Call On Me/That's the Way Love Is | 1974 | 12.00 |
| ❑ DLP-78 | Ain't Nothing You Can Do | 1974 | 12.00 |
| ❑ DLP-79 | The Soul of the Man | 1974 | 12.00 |
| ❑ DLP-84 | The Best of Bobby Bland | 1974 | 12.00 |
| ❑ DLP-86 | The Best of Bobby Bland, Volume 2 | 1974 | 12.00 |
| ❑ DLP-88 | A Touch of the Blues | 1974 | 12.00 |
| ❑ DLP-89 | Spotlighting the Man | 1974 | 12.00 |
| ❑ DLP 92-2 [(2)] | Introspective of the Early Years | 1974 | 20.00 |

### ABC DUNHILL

| Number | Title (A Side/B Side) | Yr | NM |
|---|---|---|---|
| ❑ DSX-50163 | His California Album | 1973 | 15.00 |
| ❑ DSX-50169 | Dreamer | 1974 | 15.00 |

### BLUESWAY

| Number | Title (A Side/B Side) | Yr | NM |
|---|---|---|---|
| ❑ BLS-6065 | Call On Me | 197? | 15.00 |

### DUKE

| Number | Title (A Side/B Side) | Yr | NM |
|---|---|---|---|
| ❑ DLP-74 [M] | Two Steps from the Blues | 1961 | 250.00 |
| *—Purple and yellow label* | | | |
| ❑ DLP-74 [M] | Two Steps from the Blues | 1962 | 100.00 |
| *—Orange label, black vinyl* | | | |
| ❑ DLP-74 [M] | Two Steps from the Blues | 1962 | 250.00 |
| *—Orange label, red vinyl* | | | |
| ❑ DLPS-74 [R] | Two Steps from the Blues | 196? | 60.00 |
| ❑ DLP-75 [M] | Here's the Man!!! | 1962 | 100.00 |
| *—Orange label* | | | |
| ❑ DLP-75 [M] | Here's the Man!!! | 1962 | 200.00 |
| *—Purple and yellow label* | | | |
| ❑ DLPS-75 [S] | Here's the Man!!! | 196? | 100.00 |
| *—Without spoken intro to "36-22-36"* | | | |
| ❑ DLPS-75 [S] | Here's the Man!!! | 1962 | 200.00 |
| *—With spoken intro to "36-22-36"* | | | |
| ❑ DLP-77 [M] | Call On Me/That's the Way Love Is | 1963 | 100.00 |
| ❑ DLPS-77 [S] | Call On Me/That's the Way Love Is | 1963 | 150.00 |
| ❑ DLP-78 [M] | Ain't Nothing You Can Do | 1964 | 80.00 |
| ❑ DLPS-78 [S] | Ain't Nothing You Can Do | 1964 | 120.00 |
| ❑ DLP-79 [M] | The Soul of the Man | 1966 | 80.00 |
| ❑ DLPS-79 [S] | The Soul of the Man | 1966 | 120.00 |
| ❑ DLP-84 [M] | The Best of Bobby Bland | 1967 | 20.00 |
| ❑ DLPS-84 [P] | The Best of Bobby Bland | 1967 | 25.00 |
| ❑ DLP-86 [M] | The Best of Bobby Bland, Volume 2 | 1968 | 25.00 |
| ❑ DLPS-86 [P] | The Best of Bobby Bland, Volume 2 | 1968 | 20.00 |
| ❑ DLP-88 [M] | A Touch of the Blues | 1968 | 25.00 |
| ❑ DLPS-88 [S] | A Touch of the Blues | 1968 | 20.00 |
| ❑ DLPS-89 | Spotlighting the Man | 1969 | 20.00 |
| ❑ DLPS-90 | If Loving You Is Wrong | 1970 | 20.00 |

### MCA

| Number | Title (A Side/B Side) | Yr | NM |
|---|---|---|---|
| ❑ 3157 | I Feel Good, I Feel Fine | 1979 | 10.00 |
| ❑ 4172 [(2)] | Introspective of the Early Years | 198? | 10.00 |
| *—Reissue of Duke 92* | | | |
| ❑ 5145 | Sweet Vibrations | 1980 | 10.00 |
| ❑ 5233 | Try Me, I'm Real | 1981 | 10.00 |
| ❑ 5297 | Here We Go Again | 1982 | 10.00 |
| ❑ 5425 | Tell Mr. Bland | 1983 | 10.00 |
| ❑ 5503 | You've Got Me Loving You | 1984 | 10.00 |
| ❑ 27013 | The Best of Bobby Bland | 198? | 8.00 |
| *—Reissue of Duke 84* | | | |
| ❑ 27036 | Two Steps from the Blues | 198? | 8.00 |
| *—Reissue of Duke 74* | | | |
| ❑ 27038 | Here's the Man!!! | 198? | 8.00 |
| *—Reissue of Duke 75* | | | |
| ❑ 27040 | Ain't Nothing You Can Do | 198? | 8.00 |
| *—Reissue of Duke 78* | | | |
| ❑ 27041 | The Soul of the Man | 1984 | 8.00 |
| *—Reissue of Duke 79* | | | |
| ❑ 27042 | Call On Me/That's the Way Love Is | 1984 | 8.00 |
| *—Reissue of Duke 77* | | | |
| ❑ 27043 | Reflections in Blue | 1984 | 8.00 |
| *—Reissue of ABC 1018* | | | |
| ❑ 27044 | Come Fly with Me | 1984 | 8.00 |
| *—Reissue of ABC 1075* | | | |
| ❑ 27045 | The Best of Bobby Bland, Volume 2 | 1984 | 8.00 |
| *—Reissue of Duke 86* | | | |
| ❑ 27047 | A Touch of the Blues | 1984 | 8.00 |
| *—Reissue of Duke 88* | | | |
| ❑ 27048 | Spotlighting the Man | 1984 | 8.00 |
| *—Reissue of Duke 89* | | | |
| ❑ 27073 | I Feel Good, I Feel Fine | 1985 | 8.00 |
| *—Reissue of MCA 3157* | | | |
| ❑ 27076 | Sweet Vibrations | 198? | 8.00 |
| *—Reissue of 5145* | | | |

## BLAND, BOBBY, AND B.B. KING

### ABC DUNHILL

| Number | Title (A Side/B Side) | Yr | NM |
|---|---|---|---|
| ❑ DSY-50190 [(2)] | Together for the First Time...Live | 1974 | 15.00 |

### ABC IMPULSE!

| Number | Title (A Side/B Side) | Yr | NM |
|---|---|---|---|
| ❑ 9317 | Together Again...Live | 1976 | 12.00 |

### COMMAND

| Number | Title (A Side/B Side) | Yr | NM |
|---|---|---|---|
| ❑ CQDY-40012 [(2)Q] | Together for the First Time...Live | 1974 | 25.00 |

### MCA

| Number | Title (A Side/B Side) | Yr | NM |
|---|---|---|---|
| ❑ 4160 [(2)] | Together for the First Time...Live | 198? | 10.00 |
| *—Reissue of ABC Dunhill 50190* | | | |
| ❑ 27012 | Together Again...Live | 198? | 8.00 |
| *—Reissue of ABC Impulse! 9317* | | | |

## BLASSIE, FRED

### RHINO

| Number | Title (A Side/B Side) | Yr | NM |
|---|---|---|---|
| ❑ RNLP-813 [PD] | I Bite the Songs | 1985 | 20.00 |

## BLASTERS, THE

The group on Crown is not the same as the others.

### CROWN

| Number | Title (A Side/B Side) | Yr | NM |
|---|---|---|---|
| ❑ CST-392 [S] | Sounds of the Drags | 1963 | 25.00 |
| ❑ CLP-5392 [M] | Sounds of the Drags | 1963 | 20.00 |

### ROLLIN' ROCK

| Number | Title (A Side/B Side) | Yr | NM |
|---|---|---|---|
| ❑ 021 | American Music | 1980 | 50.00 |

### SLASH

| Number | Title (A Side/B Side) | Yr | NM |
|---|---|---|---|
| ❑ SR 109 | The Blasters | 1981 | 15.00 |
| ❑ BKS 3680 | The Blasters | 1982 | 10.00 |
| *—With blue labels; reissue of 109* | | | |
| ❑ 23735 [EP] | Over There: Live at the Venue, London | 1982 | 10.00 |
| ❑ 23818 | Non Fiction | 1983 | 10.00 |
| ❑ 25093 | Hard Line | 1985 | 10.00 |

### WARNER BROS.

| Number | Title (A Side/B Side) | Yr | NM |
|---|---|---|---|
| ❑ WBMS-130 [DJ] | Music and Interviews | 1985 | 40.00 |
| *—Part of "The Warner Bros. Music Show" series; one side is The Blasters; the other side is The Smiths, which accounts for this piece's value* | | | |

## BLAZING REDHEADS

### REFERENCE RECORDINGS

| Number | Title (A Side/B Side) | Yr | NM |
|---|---|---|---|
| ❑ RR-26 | Blazing Redheads | 1988 | 20.00 |
| ❑ RR-41 | Crazed Women | 1991 | 20.00 |

## BLESSED END

### TNS

| Number | Title (A Side/B Side) | Yr | NM |
|---|---|---|---|
| ❑ 248 | Movin' On | 1971 | 300.00 |

## BLEY, CARLA

### JCOA

| Number | Title (A Side/B Side) | Yr | NM |
|---|---|---|---|
| ❑ 3-LP-EOTH [(3)] | Escalator Over the Hill | 1971 | 25.00 |

## BLEY, PAUL

### DEBUT

| Number | Title (A Side/B Side) | Yr | NM |
|---|---|---|---|
| ❑ DLP-7 [10] | Introducing Paul Bley | 1954 | 600.00 |

### EMARCY

| Number | Title (A Side/B Side) | Yr | NM |
|---|---|---|---|
| ❑ MG-36092 [M] | Paul Bley | 1955 | 200.00 |

### ESP-DISK'

| Number | Title (A Side/B Side) | Yr | NM |
|---|---|---|---|
| ❑ S-1008 [S] | Barrage | 1965 | 40.00 |
| ❑ S-1021 [S] | Closer | 1966 | 50.00 |

### GENE NORMAN

| Number | Title (A Side/B Side) | Yr | NM |
|---|---|---|---|
| ❑ GNP-31 [M] | Solemn Meditation | 1957 | 80.00 |

### SAVOY

| Number | Title (A Side/B Side) | Yr | NM |
|---|---|---|---|
| ❑ MG-12182 [M] | Footloose! | 1964 | 80.00 |

### STEEPLECHASE

| Number | Title (A Side/B Side) | Yr | NM |
|---|---|---|---|
| ❑ SCS-1246 | The Nearness of You | 198? | 15.00 |

### WING

| Number | Title (A Side/B Side) | Yr | NM |
|---|---|---|---|
| ❑ MGW-60001 [M] | Paul Bley | 1956 | 120.00 |

## BLEYER, ARCHIE

### CADENCE

| Number | Title (A Side/B Side) | Yr | NM |
|---|---|---|---|
| ❑ CLP-3044 [M] | Moonlight Serenade | 1962 | 20.00 |
| ❑ CLP-25044 [S] | Moonlight Serenade | 1962 | 25.00 |

## BLIND FAITH

Also see GINGER BAKER'S AIR FORCE; ERIC CLAPTON; STEVE WINWOOD.

### ATCO

| Number | Title (A Side/B Side) | Yr | NM |
|---|---|---|---|
| ❑ 33-304A [M] | Blind Faith | 1969 | 200.00 |
| *—White label promo only* | | | |
| ❑ SD 33-304A [S] | Blind Faith | 1969 | 25.00 |
| *—Cover with naked girl on Side 1 and same scene without girl on Side 2* | | | |
| ❑ SD 33-304B [S] | Blind Faith | 1969 | 15.00 |
| *—Cover with band photo on Side 1 and song lyrics on Side 2* | | | |

### MOBILE FIDELITY

| Number | Title (A Side/B Side) | Yr | NM |
|---|---|---|---|
| ❑ 1-186 | Blind Faith | 1985 | 40.00 |
| *—Audiophile vinyl* | | | |

### RSO

| Number | Title (A Side/B Side) | Yr | NM |
|---|---|---|---|
| ❑ RS-1-3016 | Blind Faith | 1977 | 10.00 |
| *—Reissue with naked girl on one side and band photo on the other* | | | |
| ❑ 825094-1 | Blind Faith | 1986 | 8.00 |

## BLOCKER, DAN

### TREY

| Number | Title (A Side/B Side) | Yr | NM |
|---|---|---|---|
| ❑ TLP-903 [M] | Tales for Young 'Uns | 1961 | 50.00 |

## BLOCKER, DAN, AND JOHN MITCHUM

Also see LORNE GREENE, MICHAEL LANDON AND DAN BLOCKER.

### RCA VICTOR

| Number | Title (A Side/B Side) | Yr | NM |
|---|---|---|---|
| ❑ LPM-2896 [M] | Our Land — Our Heritage | 1964 | 30.00 |
| ❑ LSP-2896 [S] | Our Land — Our Heritage | 1964 | 40.00 |

## BLOND

### FONTANA

| Number | Title (A Side/B Side) | Yr | NM |
|---|---|---|---|
| ❑ SRF-67067 | Blond | 1969 | 20.00 |

## BLONDE ON BLONDE

### JANUS

| Number | Title (A Side/B Side) | Yr | NM |
|---|---|---|---|
| ❑ JLP-3003 | Contrasts | 1969 | 25.00 |

## BLONDIE

### CHRYSALIS

| Number | Title (A Side/B Side) | Yr | NM |
|---|---|---|---|
| ❑ CHS 24 PDJ [DJ] | At Home with Debbie Harry and Chris Stein | 1981 | 50.00 |
| *—Open-end interview with script* | | | |
| ❑ CHR 1165 | Blondie | 1977 | 12.00 |
| *—Reissue of Private Stock album* | | | |
| ❑ CHR 1166 | Plastic Letters | 1977 | 12.00 |
| *—Blue and white label* | | | |
| ❑ CHR 1166 | Plastic Letters | 1977 | 20.00 |
| *—Green label* | | | |
| ❑ CHR 1192 | Parallel Lines | 1978 | 15.00 |
| *—First pressing, with 3:54 version of "Heart of Glass"* | | | |
| ❑ CHR 1192 | Parallel Lines | 1979 | 10.00 |
| *—Second pressing, with 5:50 version of "Heart of Glass (Disco Version)"* | | | |
| ❑ CHE 1225 | Eat to the Beat | 1979 | 10.00 |
| ❑ CHE 1290 | Autoamerican | 1980 | 10.00 |
| ❑ CHS 1337 | The Best of Blondie | 1981 | 10.00 |
| ❑ CHR 1384 | The Hunter | 1982 | 8.00 |
| ❑ CHP 5001 [PD] | Parallel Lines | 1979 | 25.00 |
| *—Picture disc* | | | |

| Number | Title (A Side/B Side) | Yr | NM |
|---|---|---|---|
| ❑ F1 32748 [(2)] | The Remix Project: Remixed, Remade, Remodeled | 1995 | 15.00 |
| ❑ PV 41165 | Blondie | 1983 | 8.00 |
| *—Reissue* | | | |
| ❑ PV 41166 | Plastic Letters | 1983 | 8.00 |
| *—Reissue* | | | |
| ❑ FV 41192 | Parallel Lines | 1983 | 8.00 |
| *—Reissue* | | | |
| ❑ PV 41192 | Parallel Lines | 1986 | 8.00 |
| *—Reissue* | | | |
| ❑ PV 41225 | Eat to the Beat | 1983 | 8.00 |
| *—Reissue* | | | |
| ❑ PV 41290 | Autoamerican | 1983 | 8.00 |
| *—Reissue* | | | |
| ❑ FV 41337 | The Best of Blondie | 1983 | 8.00 |
| *—Reissue* | | | |
| ❑ PV 41337 | The Best of Blondie | 1986 | 8.00 |
| *—Reissue* | | | |
| ❑ PV 41384 | The Hunter | 1983 | 8.00 |
| *—Reissue* | | | |
| ❑ V2X 41658 [(2)] | Once More into the Bleach | 1988 | 15.00 |
| *—Remixes of Blondie and Debbie Harry tracks* | | | |
| ❑ R 200816 [(2)] | Once More into the Bleach | 1988 | 18.00 |
| *—BMG Music Service edition* | | | |
| **MOBILE FIDELITY** | | | |
| ❑ 1-050 | Parallel Lines | 1980 | 30.00 |
| *—Audiophile vinyl* | | | |
| **PRIVATE STOCK** | | | |
| ❑ PS-2023 | Blondie | 1976 | 25.00 |

### BLOOD, SWEAT AND TEARS

| Number | Title (A Side/B Side) | Yr | NM |
|---|---|---|---|
| **ABC** | | | |
| ❑ 1015 | Brand New Day | 1977 | 10.00 |
| **CBS SPECIAL PRODUCTS** | | | |
| ❑ P 16660 | Musically Speaking | 1982 | 10.00 |
| **COLUMBIA** | | | |
| ❑ CS 9616 | Child Is Father to the Man | 1970 | 10.00 |
| *—Orange label* | | | |
| ❑ CS 9616 [M] | Child Is Father to the Man | 1968 | 25.00 |
| *—White label promo only, "Special Mono Radio Station Copy" sticker on cover, with same number as stereo edition* | | | |
| ❑ CS 9616 [S] | Child Is Father to the Man | 1968 | 15.00 |
| *—Red "360 Sound" label* | | | |
| ❑ PC 9619 | Child Is Father to the Man | 1980 | 8.00 |
| ❑ CS 9720 | Blood, Sweat and Tears | 1969 | 15.00 |
| *—Red "360 Sound" label* | | | |
| ❑ CS 9720 | Blood, Sweat and Tears | 1970 | 10.00 |
| *—Orange label* | | | |
| ❑ PC 9720 | Blood, Sweat and Tears | 1980 | 8.00 |
| ❑ KC 30090 | Blood, Sweat and Tears 3 | 1970 | 10.00 |
| ❑ PC 30090 | Blood, Sweat and Tears 3 | 1986 | 8.00 |
| ❑ KC 30590 | BS&T: 4 | 1971 | 10.00 |
| ❑ CQ 30994 [Q] | Blood, Sweat and Tears | 1972 | 20.00 |
| ❑ CQ 31170 [Q] | Blood, Sweat and Tears' Greatest Hits | 1972 | 20.00 |
| ❑ KC 31170 | Blood, Sweat and Tears' Greatest Hits | 1972 | 10.00 |
| *—With the single versions of "You've Made Me So Very Happy," "Spinning Wheel," and "And When I Die" (all in mono)* | | | |
| ❑ PC 31170 | Blood, Sweat and Tears' Greatest Hits | 1980 | 8.00 |
| ❑ PCQ 31170 [Q] | Blood, Sweat and Tears' Greatest Hits | 1976 | 18.00 |
| *—Reissue with new prefix* | | | |
| ❑ KC 31780 | New Blood | 1972 | 10.00 |
| ❑ KC 32180 | No Sweat | 1973 | 10.00 |
| ❑ CQ 32929 [Q] | Mirror Image | 1974 | 20.00 |
| ❑ PC 32929 | Mirror Image | 1974 | 10.00 |
| ❑ PC 33484 | New City | 1975 | 10.00 |
| ❑ PCQ 33484 [Q] | New City | 1975 | 15.00 |
| ❑ PC 34233 | More Than Ever | 1976 | 10.00 |
| ❑ HC 49619 | Child Is Father to the Man | 1981 | 50.00 |
| *—Half-speed mastered edition* | | | |
| **DIRECT DISK** | | | |
| ❑ SD-16605 | Blood, Sweat and Tears | 1981 | 60.00 |
| **MCA** | | | |
| ❑ L33-1865 [DJ] | Nuclear Blues | 1980 | 15.00 |
| *—Promo only on gold vinyl* | | | |
| ❑ 3061 | Nuclear Blues | 1980 | 10.00 |
| ❑ 3227 | Blood, Sweat and Tears | 1981 | — |
| *—Canceled?* | | | |
| **MOBILE FIDELITY** | | | |
| ❑ 1-251 | Blood, Sweat and Tears | 1996 | 120.00 |
| *—Audiophile vinyl; fewer than 2,000 pressed* | | | |

### BLOODROCK

| Number | Title (A Side/B Side) | Yr | NM |
|---|---|---|---|
| **CAPITOL** | | | |
| ❑ ST-435 | Bloodrock | 1970 | 15.00 |
| ❑ ST-491 | Bloodrock 2 | 1970 | 15.00 |
| ❑ SM-645 | Bloodrock U.S.A. | 197? | 10.00 |
| *—Reissue with new prefix* | | | |
| ❑ SMAS-645 | Bloodrock U.S.A. | 1971 | 15.00 |
| ❑ SM-765 | Bloodrock 3 | 197? | 10.00 |
| *—Reissue with new prefix* | | | |
| ❑ ST-765 | Bloodrock 3 | 1971 | 15.00 |
| ❑ SVBB-11038 [(2)] | Bloodrock Live | 1972 | 20.00 |
| *—Original edition has a lime green label* | | | |
| ❑ SW-11109 | Bloodrock Passage | 1972 | 15.00 |
| ❑ SMAS-11259 | Whirlwind Tongues | 1973 | 15.00 |
| ❑ SM-11417 | Bloodrock 'N' Roll | 1975 | 12.00 |

Blood, Sweat and Tears, *Child Is Father to the Man,* Columbia CS 9619, 1968, stereo, "360 Sound" red label, $15.

### BLOODSTONE

| Number | Title (A Side/B Side) | Yr | NM |
|---|---|---|---|
| **LONDON** | | | |
| ❑ XPS 620 | Natural High | 1973 | 20.00 |
| ❑ XPS 634 | Unreal | 1973 | 20.00 |
| ❑ APS 647 | I Need Time | 1974 | 20.00 |
| ❑ PS 654 | Riddle of the Sphinx | 1975 | 15.00 |
| ❑ PS 671 | Do a Thing? | 1976 | 15.00 |
| **MOTOWN** | | | |
| ❑ M7-909 | Don't Stop! | 1978 | 12.00 |
| **T-NECK** | | | |
| ❑ FZ 38115 | We Go a Long Way Back | 1982 | 10.00 |
| ❑ FZ 39146 | Bloodstone's Party | 1984 | 10.00 |
| ❑ PZ 40016 | Greatest Hits | 1985 | 8.00 |
| ❑ PZ 40042 | Lullaby of Broadway | 1985 | 8.00 |

### BLOODY MARY

| Number | Title (A Side/B Side) | Yr | NM |
|---|---|---|---|
| **FAMILY PRODUCTIONS** | | | |
| ❑ FPS-2707 | Bloody Mary | 1972 | 25.00 |

### BLOOMFIELD, MIKE, AND AL KOOPER

| Number | Title (A Side/B Side) | Yr | NM |
|---|---|---|---|
| **COLUMBIA** | | | |
| ❑ KGP 6 [(2)] | The Live Adventures of Mike Bloomfield & Al Kooper | 1969 | 25.00 |
| *—Red "360 Sound" labels* | | | |
| ❑ PG 6 [(2)] | The Live Adventures of Mike Bloomfield & Al Kooper | 197? | 12.00 |
| *—Reissue with new prefix* | | | |

### BLOOMFIELD, MIKE/AL KOOPER/STEVE STILLS

| Number | Title (A Side/B Side) | Yr | NM |
|---|---|---|---|
| **COLUMBIA** | | | |
| ❑ CS 9701 | Super Session | 1968 | 20.00 |
| *—Red "360 Sound" label* | | | |
| ❑ CS 9701 | Super Session | 1970 | 10.00 |
| *—Orange label* | | | |
| ❑ PC 9701 | Super Session | 198? | 8.00 |
| *—Reissue with new prefix* | | | |
| ❑ CQ 30991 [Q] | Super Session | 1971 | 20.00 |
| **MOBILE FIDELITY** | | | |
| ❑ 1-178 | Super Session | 198? | 40.00 |
| *—Audiophile vinyl* | | | |

### BLUE, DAVID

| Number | Title (A Side/B Side) | Yr | NM |
|---|---|---|---|
| **ASYLUM** | | | |
| ❑ 7E-1043 | Com'n Back for More | 1975 | 10.00 |
| ❑ 7E-1077 | Cupid's Arrow | 1976 | 10.00 |
| ❑ SD 5052 | Stories | 1972 | 12.00 |
| ❑ SD 5066 | The Nice Baby and the Angel | 1973 | 12.00 |
| **ELEKTRA** | | | |
| ❑ EKM-4003 [M] | David Blue | 1966 | 20.00 |
| ❑ EKS-74003 [S] | David Blue | 1966 | 20.00 |
| **REPRISE** | | | |
| ❑ RS 6296 | These 23 Days in September | 1968 | 15.00 |

### BLUE ANGEL Features CYNDI LAUPER.

| Number | Title (A Side/B Side) | Yr | NM |
|---|---|---|---|
| **POLYDOR** | | | |
| ❑ PD-1-6300 | Blue Angel | 1980 | 20.00 |

### BLUE BARONS, THE

| Number | Title (A Side/B Side) | Yr | NM |
|---|---|---|---|
| **PHILIPS** | | | |
| ❑ PHM 200017 [M] | Twist to the Great Blues Hits | 1962 | 20.00 |
| ❑ PHS 600017 [S] | Twist to the Great Blues Hits | 1962 | 25.00 |

### BLUE BEATS, THE

| Number | Title (A Side/B Side) | Yr | NM |
|---|---|---|---|
| **A.A.** | | | |
| ❑ 133 [M] | The Beatle Beat | 1964 | 40.00 |

### BLUE BOYS, THE

| Number | Title (A Side/B Side) | Yr | NM |
|---|---|---|---|
| **RCA VICTOR** | | | |
| ❑ LPM-3331 [M] | We Remember Jim | 1965 | 25.00 |
| ❑ LSP-3331 [S] | We Remember Jim | 1965 | 30.00 |
| ❑ LPM-3529 [M] | Sounds of Jim Reeves | 1966 | 20.00 |
| ❑ LSP-3529 [S] | Sounds of Jim Reeves | 1966 | 25.00 |
| ❑ LPM-3696 [M] | The Blue Boys in Person | 1967 | 20.00 |
| ❑ LSP-3696 [S] | The Blue Boys in Person | 1967 | 25.00 |
| ❑ LPM-3794 [M] | Hit After Hit | 1967 | 25.00 |
| ❑ LSP-3794 [S] | Hit After Hit | 1967 | 20.00 |

### BLUE CHEER

| Number | Title (A Side/B Side) | Yr | NM |
|---|---|---|---|
| **MEGAFORCE** | | | |
| ❑ CAROL-1395-1 | The Beast Is Back | 198? | 12.00 |
| **PHILIPS** | | | |
| ❑ PHM 200264 [M] | Vincebus Eruptum | 1968 | 80.00 |
| ❑ PHS 600264 [S] | Vincebus Eruptum | 1968 | 40.00 |
| ❑ PHS 600278 | Outsideinside | 1968 | 40.00 |
| ❑ PHS 600305 | New! Improved! Blue Cheer | 1969 | 40.00 |
| ❑ PHS 600333 | Blue Cheer | 1970 | 40.00 |
| ❑ PHS 600347 | The Original Human Being | 1970 | 40.00 |
| ❑ PHS 600350 | Oh! Pleasant Hope | 1971 | 40.00 |

Bloodrock, *Bloodrock 2,* Capitol ST-491, 1970, $15.

| Number | Title (A Side/B Side) | Yr | NM |
|---|---|---|---|
| **RHINO** | | | |
| ❑ RNLP 70130 | Louder Than God (The Best of Blue Cheer, 1968-1969) | 1986 | 10.00 |

### BLUE DIAMONDS, THE

| Number | Title (A Side/B Side) | Yr | NM |
|---|---|---|---|
| **LONDON** | | | |
| ❑ LL 3235 [M] | Ramona1 | 1963 | 25.00 |

### BLUE JAYS, THE (1)

| Number | Title (A Side/B Side) | Yr | NM |
|---|---|---|---|
| **MILESTONE** | | | |
| ❑ 1001 [M] | The Blue Jays Meet Little Caesar and the Romans | 1962 | 100.00 |

### BLUE OYSTER CULT

| Number | Title (A Side/B Side) | Yr | NM |
|---|---|---|---|
| **COLUMBIA** | | | |
| ❑ KC 31063 | Blue Oyster Cult | 1972 | 12.00 |
| ❑ PC 31063 | Blue Oyster Cult | 197? | 8.00 |
| *—Reissue with new prefix* | | | |
| ❑ CQ 32017 [Q] | Tyranny and Mutation | 1973 | 30.00 |
| ❑ KC 32017 | Tyranny and Mutation | 1973 | 12.00 |
| ❑ PC 32017 | Tyranny and Mutation | 197? | 8.00 |
| *—Reissue with new prefix* | | | |
| ❑ CQ 32858 [Q] | Secret Treaties | 1974 | 30.00 |
| ❑ KC 32858 | Secret Treaties | 1974 | 12.00 |
| ❑ PC 32858 | Secret Treaties | 197? | 8.00 |
| *—Reissue with new prefix* | | | |
| ❑ KG 33371 [(2)] | On Your Feet or On Your Knees | 1975 | 15.00 |
| ❑ PC 34164 | Agents of Fortune | 1976 | 10.00 |
| *—Original gatefold with no bar code on cover* | | | |
| ❑ PC 34164 | Agents of Fortune | 198? | 8.00 |
| *—Budget-line reissue with bar code* | | | |
| ❑ JC 35019 | Spectres | 1977 | 10.00 |
| ❑ PC 35019 | Spectres | 198? | 8.00 |
| *—Budget-line reissue* | | | |
| ❑ JC 35563 | Some Enchanted Evening | 1978 | 10.00 |
| ❑ PC 35563 | Some Enchanted Evening | 198? | 8.00 |
| *—Budget-line reissue* | | | |
| ❑ JC 36009 | Mirrors | 1979 | 10.00 |
| ❑ PC 36009 | Mirrors | 198? | 8.00 |
| *—Budget-line reissue* | | | |
| ❑ JC 36550 | Cultosaurus Erectus | 1980 | 10.00 |
| ❑ PC 36550 | Cultosaurus Erectus | 198? | 8.00 |
| *—Budget-line reissue* | | | |
| ❑ FC 37389 | Fire of Unknown Origin | 1981 | 10.00 |
| ❑ PC 37389 | Fire of Unknown Origin | 1984 | 8.00 |
| *—Budget-line reissue* | | | |
| ❑ KG 37946 [(2)] | Extraterrestrial Live | 1982 | 12.00 |
| ❑ FC 38947 | The Revolution by Night | 1983 | 10.00 |
| ❑ PC 38947 | The Revolution by Night | 1985 | 8.00 |
| *—Budget-line reissue* | | | |
| ❑ FC 39979 | Club Ninja | 1986 | 10.00 |
| ❑ FC 40618 | Imaginos | 1988 | 10.00 |

### BLUE RIDGE MOUNTAIN BOYS, THE

| Number | Title (A Side/B Side) | Yr | NM |
|---|---|---|---|
| **TIME** | | | |
| ❑ ST-2083 [S] | Hootenanny and Bluegrass | 1963 | 20.00 |
| ❑ T-2083 [M] | Hootenanny and Bluegrass | 1963 | 15.00 |
| ❑ ST-2103 [S] | Bluegrass Down Home | 1963 | 20.00 |
| ❑ T-2103 [M] | Bluegrass Down Home | 1963 | 15.00 |

### BLUE SKY BOYS, THE

| Number | Title (A Side/B Side) | Yr | NM |
|---|---|---|---|
| **CAPITOL** | | | |
| ❑ ST 2483 [S] | Presenting the Blue Sky Boys | 1966 | 25.00 |
| ❑ T 2483 [M] | Presenting the Blue Sky Boys | 1966 | 20.00 |
| **PINE MOUNTAIN** | | | |
| ❑ PMR 257 | Together Again | 198? | 12.00 |
| **RCA CAMDEN** | | | |
| ❑ CAL-797 [M] | The Blue Sky Boys | 1963 | 20.00 |
| ❑ CAS-797(e) [R] | The Blue Sky Boys | 1963 | 15.00 |
| **ROUNDER** | | | |
| ❑ 0236 | 1964 | 198? | 15.00 |
| **STARDAY** | | | |
| ❑ SLP-205 [M] | Rare Treasury of Old Song Gems | 1962 | 40.00 |
| ❑ SLP-257 [M] | Together Again | 1963 | 40.00 |
| ❑ SLP-269 [M] | The Blue Sky Boys | 1964 | 40.00 |

### BLUE STARS

| Number | Title (A Side/B Side) | Yr | NM |
|---|---|---|---|
| **EMARCY** | | | |
| ❑ MG-36067 [M] | Lullaby of Birdland | 1956 | 40.00 |

### BLUE THINGS, THE

| Number | Title (A Side/B Side) | Yr | NM |
|---|---|---|---|
| **RCA VICTOR** | | | |
| ❑ LPM-3603 [M] | The Blue Things | 1966 | 120.00 |
| ❑ LSP-3603 [S] | The Blue Things | 1966 | 180.00 |

### BLUE VELVET BAND, THE

| Number | Title (A Side/B Side) | Yr | NM |
|---|---|---|---|
| **WARNER BROS.** | | | |
| ❑ WS 1802 | Sweet Moments | 1969 | 30.00 |

### BLUEGRASS HOPPERS, THE

| Number | Title (A Side/B Side) | Yr | NM |
|---|---|---|---|
| **CUCA** | | | |
| ❑ 1160 | The Country's Come to Town | 196? | 25.00 |

### BLUES CLIMAX

| Number | Title (A Side/B Side) | Yr | NM |
|---|---|---|---|
| **HORNE** | | | |
| ❑ JC-333 | Blues Climax | 1969 | 60.00 |

### BLUES IMAGE

| Number | Title (A Side/B Side) | Yr | NM |
|---|---|---|---|
| **ATCO** | | | |
| ❑ SD 33-300 | Blues Image | 1969 | 25.00 |
| ❑ SD 33-317 | Open | 1970 | 20.00 |
| ❑ SD 33-346 | Red, White and Blues Image | 1971 | 20.00 |

### BLUES MAGOOS

| Number | Title (A Side/B Side) | Yr | NM |
|---|---|---|---|
| **ABC** | | | |
| ❑ S-697 | Never Goin' Back to Georgia | 1969 | 20.00 |
| ❑ S-710 | Gulf Coast Bound | 1970 | 20.00 |
| **MERCURY** | | | |
| ❑ MG-21096 [M] | Psychedelic Lollipop | 1966 | 40.00 |
| *—With "21096" in trail-off; this record is mono* | | | |
| ❑ MG-21096 [S] | Psychedelic Lollipop | 1966 | 40.00 |
| *—With "2/61096" in trail-off; this record plays stereo, though labeled mono* | | | |
| ❑ 21104/61104 | Electric Comic Book Comic Book | 1967 | 15.00 |
| ❑ MG-21104 [M] | Electric Comic Book | 1967 | 30.00 |
| ❑ SR-61096 | Psychedelic Lollipop | 197? | 12.00 |
| *—Reissue on Chicago skyline label* | | | |
| ❑ SR-61096 [S] | Psychedelic Lollipop | 1966 | 50.00 |
| ❑ SR-61104 [S] | Electric Comic Book | 1967 | 40.00 |
| ❑ SR-61167 | Basic Blues Magoos | 1968 | 30.00 |

### BLUES PROJECT, THE

| Number | Title (A Side/B Side) | Yr | NM |
|---|---|---|---|
| **CAPITOL** | | | |
| ❑ ST-782 | Lazarus | 1971 | 12.00 |
| ❑ SMAS-11017 | The Blues Project | 1972 | 12.00 |
| **MCA** | | | |
| ❑ 8003 [(2)] | Reunion in Central Park | 1975 | 15.00 |
| *—Reissue of Sounds of the South LP; black rainbow labels* | | | |
| ❑ 25984 [(2)] | Reunion in Central Park | 1987 | 12.00 |
| *—Reissue of MCA 8003; blue rainbow labels* | | | |
| **MGM** | | | |
| ❑ GAS-118 | The Blues Project | 1970 | 12.00 |
| ❑ M3G-4953 | Archetypes | 1974 | 12.00 |
| **RHINO** | | | |
| ❑ R1-70165 | No Time Like the Right Time: The Best of the Blues Project | 1989 | 12.00 |
| **SOUNDS OF THE SOUTH** | | | |
| ❑ MCA2-8003 [(2)] | Reunion in Central Park | 1973 | 20.00 |
| *—Yellow labels* | | | |
| **VERVE** | | | |
| ❑ 827918-1 | Projections | 1986 | 8.00 |
| *—Reissue* | | | |
| **VERVE FOLKWAYS** | | | |
| ❑ FT-3000 [M] | Live at the Café a Go Go | 1966 | 20.00 |
| ❑ FTS-3000 [S] | Live at the Café a Go Go | 1966 | 25.00 |
| ❑ FT-3008 [M] | Projections | 1966 | 20.00 |
| ❑ FTS-3008 [S] | Projections | 1966 | 25.00 |
| **VERVE FORECAST** | | | |
| ❑ FT-3000 [M] | Live at the Café a Go Go | 1967 | 15.00 |
| *—Reissue of Verve Folkways 3000* | | | |
| ❑ FTS-3000 [S] | Live at the Café a Go Go | 1967 | 20.00 |
| *—Reissue of Verve Folkways 3000* | | | |
| ❑ FT-3008 [M] | Projections | 1967 | 15.00 |
| *—Reissue of Verve Folkways 3008* | | | |
| ❑ FTS-3008 [S] | Projections | 1967 | 20.00 |
| *—Reissue of Verve Folkways 3008* | | | |
| ❑ FT-3025 [M] | The Blues Project Live at Town Hall | 1967 | 20.00 |
| ❑ FTS-3025 [S] | The Blues Project Live at Town Hall | 1967 | 15.00 |
| ❑ FTS-3046 | Planned Obsolescence | 1968 | 15.00 |
| ❑ FTS-3069 | Flanders/Kalb/Katz, Etc. | 1969 | 15.00 |
| ❑ FTS-3077 | Best of the Blues Project | 1969 | 15.00 |

### BLUNT, JAMES

| Number | Title (A Side/B Side) | Yr | NM |
|---|---|---|---|
| **CUSTARD/ATLANTIC** | | | |
| ❑ R1-73396 | Back to Bedlam | 2006 | 20.00 |

### BLYTH, ANN

| Number | Title (A Side/B Side) | Yr | NM |
|---|---|---|---|
| **EVEREST** | | | |
| ❑ SDBR-1113 [S] | Hail Mary | 1960 | 40.00 |
| ❑ LPBR-5113 [M] | Hail Mary | 1960 | 30.00 |

### BLYTHE, JIMMY

| Number | Title (A Side/B Side) | Yr | NM |
|---|---|---|---|
| **RIVERSIDE** | | | |
| ❑ RLP-1031 [10] | Chicago Stomps and the Dixie Four | 1954 | 80.00 |
| ❑ RLP-1036 [10] | Jimmy Blythe's State Street Ramblers | 1954 | 80.00 |

### BLYTHE, STERLING

| Number | Title (A Side/B Side) | Yr | NM |
|---|---|---|---|
| **CROWN** | | | |
| ❑ CLP-5179 [M] | Sterling Blythe Sings | 1963 | 20.00 |
| **SAGE & SAND** | | | |
| ❑ C-14 [M] | A Night at the Showboat | 196? | 25.00 |
| *—Red vinyl; label print is multi-colored* | | | |
| ❑ C-14 [M] | A Night at the Showboat | 1962 | 40.00 |
| *—Red vinyl; label print is red and black* | | | |



Except when noted otherwise, VG = 25% of NM, and VG+ = 50% of NM. (Example: VG = $2.00, VG+ = $4.00 and NM = $8.00.)

| Number | Title (A Side/B Side) | Yr | NM |
|---|---|---|---|

**BO GRUMPUS**

ATCO

| | | | |
|---|---|---|---|
| ❑ 33-246 [M] | Bo Grumpus | 1968 | 30.00 |
| ❑ SD 33-246 [S] | Bo Grumpus | 1968 | 20.00 |

**BOA**

SNAKEFIELD

| | | | |
|---|---|---|---|
| ❑ SN-001 | Wrong Road | 1969 | 250.00 |

**BOB AND EARL**

CRESTVIEW

| | | | |
|---|---|---|---|
| ❑ CRS-3055 | Bob & Earl | 1969 | 25.00 |

TIP

| | | | |
|---|---|---|---|
| ❑ TLP-1011 [M] | Harlem Shuffle | 1964 | 30.00 |
| ❑ TLS-9011 [S] | Harlem Shuffle | 1964 | 50.00 |

**BOB AND RAY**

RCA VICTOR

| | | | |
|---|---|---|---|
| ❑ LPM-1773 [M] | Bob and Ray Throw a Stereo Spectacular | 1958 | 30.00 |
| ❑ LSP-1773 [S] | Bob and Ray Throw a Stereo Spectacular | 1958 | 80.00 |
| ❑ LSP-1773 [S] | Bob and Ray Throw a Stereo Spectacular | 199? | 30.00 |
| *—Classic Records reissue* | | | |
| ❑ LPM-2131 [M] | Bob and Ray on a Platter | 1960 | 30.00 |
| ❑ LSP-2131 [S] | Bob and Ray on a Platter | 1960 | 50.00 |

UNICORN

| | | | |
|---|---|---|---|
| ❑ UN 1001 [10] | Write If You Get Work | 1954 | 60.00 |

**BOB B. SOXX AND THE BLUE JEANS**

PHILLIES

| | | | |
|---|---|---|---|
| ❑ PHLP-4002 [M] | Zip-a-Dee Doo-Dah | 1963 | 500.00 |

**BOBO, WILLIE**

ROULETTE

| | | | |
|---|---|---|---|
| ❑ R-52097 [M] | Bobo's Beat | 1962 | 60.00 |
| ❑ SR-52097 [S] | Bobo's Beat | 1962 | 80.00 |

TICO

| | | | |
|---|---|---|---|
| ❑ ST-1108 [S] | Do That Thing | 1963 | 80.00 |
| *—Reproductions exist* | | | |
| ❑ T-1108 [M] | Do That Thing | 1963 | 60.00 |

VERVE

| | | | |
|---|---|---|---|
| ❑ V6-8631 [S] | Spanish Grease | 1965 | 40.00 |
| ❑ V6-8648 [S] | Uno, Dos, Tres | 1966 | 40.00 |
| ❑ V6-8669 [S] | Feelin' So Good | 1966 | 50.00 |
| ❑ V-8685 [M] | Juicy | 1967 | 40.00 |
| ❑ V6-8685 [S] | Juicy | 1967 | 40.00 |
| ❑ V-8699 [M] | Bobo Motion | 1967 | 40.00 |
| ❑ V6-8699 [S] | Bobo Motion | 1967 | 40.00 |
| ❑ V-8736 [M] | Spanish Blues Band | 1968 | 60.00 |
| *—May be promo only* | | | |
| ❑ V6-8736 [S] | Spanish Blues Band | 1968 | 40.00 |

**BOCAGE, PETER**

RIVERSIDE

| | | | |
|---|---|---|---|
| ❑ RLP-379 [M] | Peter Bocage with His Creole Serenaders | 1961 | 25.00 |
| ❑ RLP-9379 [S] | Peter Bocage with His Creole Serenaders | 1961 | 30.00 |

**BOETCHER, CURT**

ELEKTRA

| | | | |
|---|---|---|---|
| ❑ EKS-75037 | There's an Innocent Face | 1972 | 20.00 |

**BOFFALONGO**

UNITED ARTISTS

| | | | |
|---|---|---|---|
| ❑ UAS-6726 | Boffalongo | 1969 | 20.00 |
| ❑ UAS-6770 | Beyond Your Head | 1970 | 20.00 |

**BOGARDE, DIRK**

LONDON

| | | | |
|---|---|---|---|
| ❑ PS 210 [S] | Lyrics for Lovers | 1960 | 30.00 |
| ❑ LL 3187 [M] | Lyrics for Lovers | 1960 | 25.00 |

**BOHANNON, GEORGE**

WORKSHOP JAZZ

| | | | |
|---|---|---|---|
| ❑ WSJ-207 [M] | Boss Bossa Nova | 1963 | 80.00 |

**BOHEMIAN VENDETTA**

MAINSTREAM

| | | | |
|---|---|---|---|
| ❑ S-6106 [S] | Bohemian Vendetta | 1968 | 200.00 |
| ❑ 56106 [M] | Bohemian Vendetta | 1968 | 120.00 |

**BOLD**

ABC

| | | | |
|---|---|---|---|
| ❑ ABCS-705 | Bold | 1970 | 60.00 |

**BOLDER DAMN**

HIT

| | | | |
|---|---|---|---|
| ❑ HRI-5061 | Mourning | 1971 | 1000. |

**BOLGER, RAY**

DISNEYLAND

| | | | |
|---|---|---|---|
| ❑ ST-3930 [M] | The Story of the Scarecrow of Oz | 1965 | 30.00 |

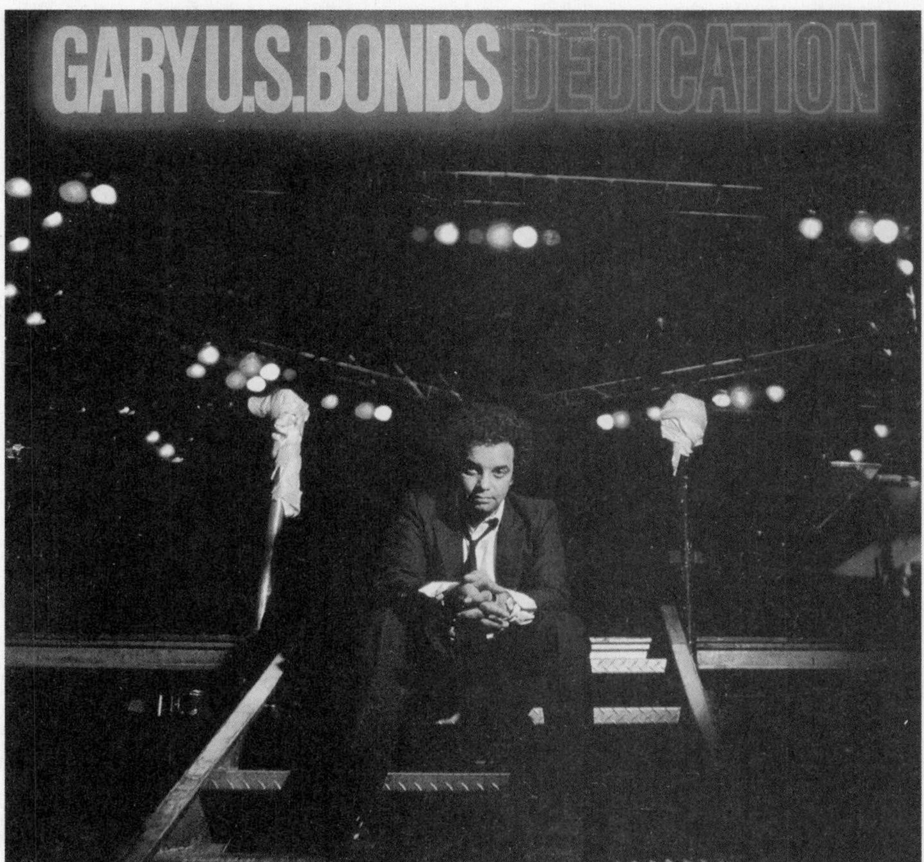


Gary U.S. Bonds, *Dedication,* EMI America SO-17051, 1981, $10.

| Number | Title (A Side/B Side) | Yr | NM |
|---|---|---|---|

**BOLIN, TOMMY**

COLUMBIA

| | | | |
|---|---|---|---|
| ❑ PC 34329 | Private Eyes | 1976 | 12.00 |
| *—Original with no bar code on cover* | | | |
| ❑ PC 34329 | Private Eyes | 198? | 8.00 |
| *—With bar code on cover* | | | |

GEFFEN

| | | | |
|---|---|---|---|
| ❑ 3GHS 24248 [(3)] | The Ultimate Tommy Bolin | 1989 | 30.00 |

NEMPEROR

| | | | |
|---|---|---|---|
| ❑ NE 436 | Teaser | 1975 | 12.00 |
| ❑ PZ 37534 | Teaser | 1982 | 8.00 |

**BOLLING, CLAUDE**

BALLY

| | | | |
|---|---|---|---|
| ❑ BAL-12003 [M] | French Jazz | 1956 | 40.00 |

CBS MASTERWORKS

| | | | |
|---|---|---|---|
| ❑ M3 36845 [(3)] | Bolling | 1981 | 25.00 |
| *—Combines 33233, 35128, and 35864 in one box* | | | |

OMEGA

| | | | |
|---|---|---|---|
| ❑ OKL-6 [M] | Rolling with Bolling | 1960 | 25.00 |
| ❑ OSL-6 [S] | Rolling with Bolling | 1960 | 30.00 |

PHILIPS

| | | | |
|---|---|---|---|
| ❑ PHS 600204 [S] | Two-Beat Mozart | 1966 | 20.00 |

**BOLTON, MICHAEL**

COLUMBIA

| | | | |
|---|---|---|---|
| ❑ BFC 38357 | Michael Bolton | 1983 | 10.00 |
| ❑ PC 38357 | Michael Bolton | 1985 | 6.00 |
| *—Reissue with new prefix* | | | |
| ❑ BFC 39328 | Everybody's Crazy | 1985 | 10.00 |
| ❑ FC 40473 | The Hunger | 1987 | 8.00 |
| ❑ OC 45012 | Soul Provider | 1989 | 10.00 |
| ❑ C 46771 | Time, Love and Tenderness | 1991 | 15.00 |

RCA VICTOR

| | | | |
|---|---|---|---|
| ❑ APL1-0992 | Michael Bolotin | 1975 | 20.00 |
| *—As "Michael Bolotin"* | | | |
| ❑ APL1-1551 | Every Day of My Life | 1976 | 20.00 |
| *—As "Michael Bolotin"* | | | |

**BONADUCE, DANNY**

LION

| | | | |
|---|---|---|---|
| ❑ LN-1015 | Danny Bonaduce | 1973 | 60.00 |

| Number | Title (A Side/B Side) | Yr | NM |
|---|---|---|---|

**BONANO, SHARKEY**

CAPITOL

| | | | |
|---|---|---|---|
| ❑ H 266 [10] | Sharkey's Southern Comfort | 1951 | 50.00 |
| ❑ T 266 [M] | Kings of Dixieland | 1954 | 40.00 |

CIRCLE

| | | | |
|---|---|---|---|
| ❑ LP-422 [10] | Sharkey Bonano | 1951 | 50.00 |

ROULETTE

| | | | |
|---|---|---|---|
| ❑ R-25112 [M] | Dixieland at the Roundtable | 1960 | 25.00 |

SOUTHLAND

| | | | |
|---|---|---|---|
| ❑ 205 [M] | New Orleans Jam Session | 1961 | 30.00 |
| ❑ SLP-205 [10] | New Orleans Dixieland Session | 1954 | 50.00 |
| ❑ 222 [M] | Kings of Dixieland | 1959 | 30.00 |

**BONANO, SHARKEY, AND LIZZIE MILES**

CAPITOL

| | | | |
|---|---|---|---|
| ❑ H 367 [10] | Midnight on Bourbon Street | 1952 | 50.00 |
| ❑ T 367 [M] | Midnight on Bourbon Street | 1954 | 40.00 |
| ❑ T 792 [M] | A Night in Old New Orleans | 1956 | 40.00 |

**BOND, EDDIE**

PHILLIPS INT'L.

| | | | |
|---|---|---|---|
| ❑ PLP-1980 [M] | The Greatest Country Gospel Hits | 1961 | 400.00 |

**BOND, GRAHAM**

MERCURY

| | | | |
|---|---|---|---|
| ❑ SRM-1-612 | We Put Our Magick on You | 1971 | 20.00 |
| ❑ SR-61327 | Holy Magick | 1970 | 20.00 |

PULSAR

| | | | |
|---|---|---|---|
| ❑ 10604 | Love Is the Law | 1969 | 25.00 |
| ❑ 10606 | Mighty Graham Bond | 1969 | 25.00 |

WARNER BROS.

| | | | |
|---|---|---|---|
| ❑ 2LS 2555 [(2)] | Solid Bond | 1971 | 20.00 |

**BOND, JAMES, SEXTETTE**

MIRWOOD

| | | | |
|---|---|---|---|
| ❑ M-7001 [M] | The James Bond Songbook | 1966 | 25.00 |
| ❑ S-7001 [S] | The James Bond Songbook | 1966 | 30.00 |

**BOND, JOHNNY**

CMH

| | | | |
|---|---|---|---|
| ❑ 6212 | The Singing Cowboy Again | 1981 | 10.00 |

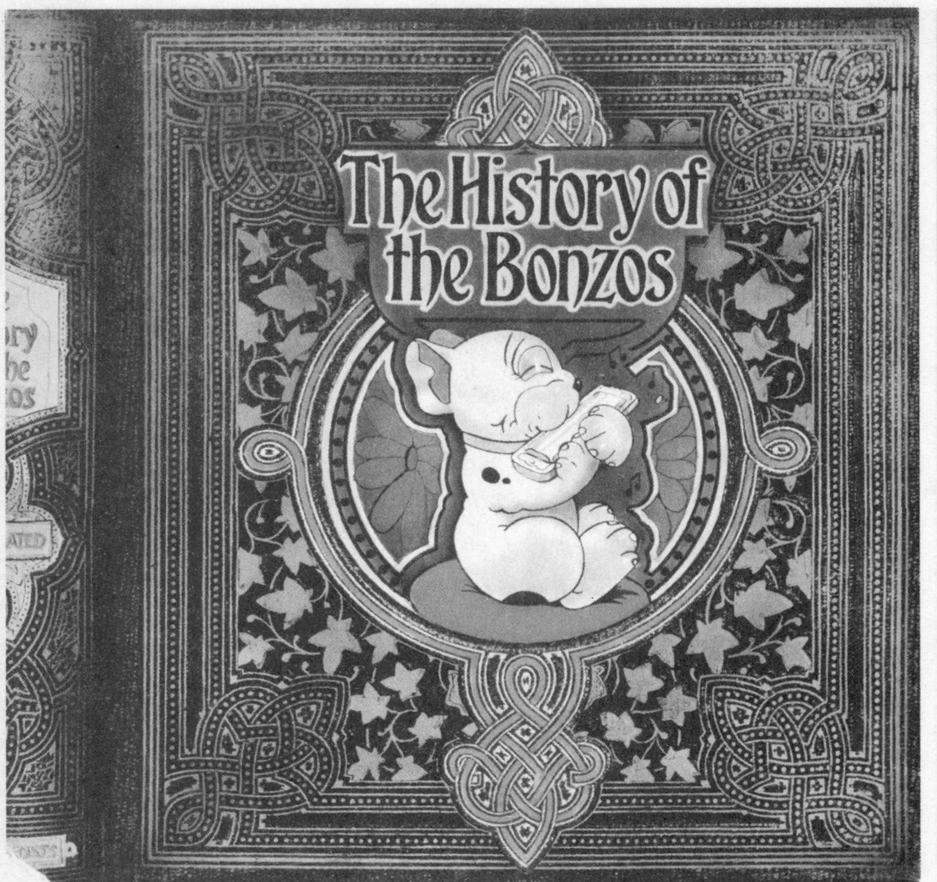


The Bonzo Dog Band, *The History of the Bonzos,* United Artists UA-LA321-H2, 1974, 2 records, $15.

| Number | Title (A Side/B Side) | Yr | NM |
|---|---|---|---|
| ❑ 6213 | The Return of the Singing Cowboy | 1981 | 10.00 |
| **HARMONY** | | | |
| ❑ HL 7308 [M] | Johnny Bond's Best | 1964 | 20.00 |
| ❑ HL 7353 [M] | Bottled in Bond | 1965 | 20.00 |
| **NASHVILLE** | | | |
| ❑ 2054 | Three Sheets to the Wind | 196? | 15.00 |
| **SHASTA** | | | |
| ❑ LP-516 | Johnny Bond Rides Again | 197? | 15.00 |
| **STARDAY** | | | |
| ❑ SLP-147 [M] | That Wild, Wicked But Wonderful Wesy | 1961 | 50.00 |
| ❑ SLP-227 [M] | Songs That Made Him Famous | 1963 | 40.00 |
| ❑ SLP-298 [M] | Hot Rod Lincoln | 1964 | 50.00 |
| ❑ SLP-333 [M] | Ten Little Bottles | 1965 | 30.00 |
| ❑ SLP-354 [M] | Famous Hot Rodders I Have Known | 1965 | 40.00 |
| ❑ SLP-368 [M] | The Man Who Comes Around | 1966 | 25.00 |
| ❑ SLP-378 [M] | Bottles Up | 1966 | 25.00 |
| ❑ SLP-388 [M] | The Branded Stock of Johnny Bond | 1966 | 20.00 |
| ❑ SLP-402 [M] | Ten Nights in a Barroom | 1967 | 20.00 |
| ❑ SLP-416 | Drink Up and Go Home | 1968 | 15.00 |
| ❑ SLP-444 | The Best of Johnny Bond | 1969 | 15.00 |
| ❑ SLP-456 | Old, New, Patriotic and Blue | 1970 | 15.00 |
| ❑ SLP-472 | Here Come the Elephants | 1971 | 15.00 |
| ❑ 954 | The Best of Johnny Bond | 1976 | 10.00 |

**BONDS, GARY U.S.**

| Number | Title (A Side/B Side) | Yr | NM |
|---|---|---|---|
| **EMI AMERICA** | | | |
| ❑ SPRO-9666 [EP] | Dedication Sampler | 1981 | 15.00 |
| *—Promo-only sampler with limited-edition number on pink sticker* | | | |
| ❑ SO-17051 | Dedication | 1981 | 10.00 |
| ❑ SO-17068 | On the Line | 1982 | 10.00 |
| **LEGRAND** | | | |
| ❑ LLP-3001 [M] | Dance 'Til Quarter to Three | 1961 | 100.00 |
| ❑ LLP-3002 [M] | Twist Up Calypso | 1962 | 70.00 |
| ❑ LLP-3003 [M] | Greatest Hits of Gary U.S. Bonds | 1962 | 70.00 |
| **MCA** | | | |
| ❑ 905 | The Best of Gary U.S. Bonds | 1984 | 10.00 |
| **PHOENIX** | | | |
| ❑ PRT 0072 | Standing in the Line of Fire | 1984 | 10.00 |

| Number | Title (A Side/B Side) | Yr | NM |
|---|---|---|---|
| **RHINO** | | | |
| ❑ RNLP-805 | Certified Soul | 1981 | 10.00 |

**BONFA, LUIZ**

| Number | Title (A Side/B Side) | Yr | NM |
|---|---|---|---|
| **ATLANTIC** | | | |
| ❑ 8028 [M] | The Fabulous Guitar of Luiz Bonfa/Amor! | 1959 | 40.00 |
| *—Black label* | | | |
| ❑ 8028 [M] | The Fabulous Guitar of Luiz Bonfa/Amor! | 1960 | 30.00 |
| *—White "bullseye" label* | | | |
| ❑ 8028 [M] | The Fabulous Guitar of Luiz Bonfa/Amor! | 1961 | 20.00 |
| *—Multicolor label, white "fan" logo at right* | | | |
| ❑ SD 8028 [S] | The Fabulous Guitar of Luiz Bonfa/Amor! | 1959 | 50.00 |
| *—Green label* | | | |
| ❑ SD 8028 [S] | The Fabulous Guitar of Luiz Bonfa/Amor! | 1960 | 40.00 |
| *—White "bullseye" label* | | | |
| ❑ SD 8028 [S] | The Fabulous Guitar of Luiz Bonfa/Amor! | 1961 | 25.00 |
| *—Multicolor label, white "fan" logo at right* | | | |
| ❑ SD 8028 [S] | The Fabulous Guitar of Luiz Bonfa/Amor! | 1963 | 20.00 |
| *—Multicolor label, black "fan" logo at right* | | | |
| **CAPITOL** | | | |
| ❑ T 10134 [M] | Brazilian Guitar | 1958 | 40.00 |
| *—Turquoise label* | | | |
| **DOT** | | | |
| ❑ DLP-3804 [M] | Luiz Bonfa | 1967 | 20.00 |
| ❑ DLP-25848 | Black Orpheus Impressions | 1969 | 15.00 |
| **EPIC** | | | |
| ❑ BN 26124 [S] | Softly | 1964 | 20.00 |
| **PHILIPS** | | | |
| ❑ PHS 600087 [S] | Brazil's King of the Bossa Nova and Guitar | 1963 | 20.00 |
| **RCA VICTOR** | | | |
| ❑ LSP-4376 | The New Face of Bonfa | 1970 | 15.00 |
| **VERVE** | | | |
| ❑ V6-8522 [S] | Luiz Bonfa Plays and Sings Bossa Nova | 1963 | 20.00 |

**BONFIRE, MARS**

| Number | Title (A Side/B Side) | Yr | NM |
|---|---|---|---|
| **COLUMBIA** | | | |
| ❑ CS 9834 | Faster Than the Speed of Life | 1969 | 15.00 |
| **UNI** | | | |
| ❑ 73027 | Mars Bonfire | 1968 | 20.00 |

**BONNEMERE, EDDIE**

| Number | Title (A Side/B Side) | Yr | NM |
|---|---|---|---|
| **PRESTIGE** | | | |
| ❑ PRLP-7354 [M] | Jazz Oriented | 1965 | 20.00 |
| ❑ PRST-7354 [S] | Jazz Oriented | 1965 | 25.00 |
| **ROOST** | | | |
| ❑ RST-419 [10] | Piano Mambo with Bonnemere | 1954 | 50.00 |
| ❑ RST-2236 [M] | Piano Bon Bons | 1959 | 30.00 |
| ❑ SLP-2236 [S] | Piano Bon Bons | 1959 | 40.00 |
| ❑ RST-2241 [M] | The Sound of Memory | 1960 | 30.00 |
| ❑ SLP-2241 [S] | The Sound of Memory | 1960 | 40.00 |

**BONNEVILLES, THE** More than one group.

| Number | Title (A Side/B Side) | Yr | NM |
|---|---|---|---|
| **DRUM BOY** | | | |
| ❑ DLM-1001 [M] | Meet the Bonnevilles | 1963 | 100.00 |
| ❑ DLS-1001 [S] | Meet the Bonnevilles | 1963 | 150.00 |
| **JUSTICE** | | | |
| ❑ JLP-146 | Bringing It Home | 196? | 500.00 |

**BONNIE LOU**

| Number | Title (A Side/B Side) | Yr | NM |
|---|---|---|---|
| **KING** | | | |
| ❑ 595 [M] | Bonnie Lou Sings | 1958 | 140.00 |

**BONNIWELL, T.S.**

| Number | Title (A Side/B Side) | Yr | NM |
|---|---|---|---|
| **CAPITOL** | | | |
| ❑ ST-377 | Close | 1969 | 50.00 |

**BONZO DOG BAND, THE**

| Number | Title (A Side/B Side) | Yr | NM |
|---|---|---|---|
| **IMPERIAL** | | | |
| ❑ LP 9370 [M] | Gorilla | 1968 | 20.00 |
| *—Without booklet* | | | |
| ❑ LP 9370 [M] | Gorilla | 1968 | 30.00 |
| *—With booklet* | | | |
| ❑ LP 12370 [S] | Gorilla | 1968 | 20.00 |
| *—Without booklet* | | | |
| ❑ LP 12370 [S] | Gorilla | 1968 | 30.00 |
| *—With booklet* | | | |
| ❑ LP 12432 | Urban Spaceman | 1968 | 20.00 |
| *—Without booklet* | | | |
| ❑ LP 12432 | Urban Spaceman | 1968 | 30.00 |
| *—With booklet* | | | |
| ❑ LP 12445 | Tadpoles | 1969 | 20.00 |
| ❑ LP 12457 | Keynsham | 1969 | 20.00 |
| **LIBERTY** | | | |
| ❑ LN-10206 | Some of the Best of the Bonzo Dog Band | 1983 | 8.00 |
| **UNITED ARTISTS** | | | |
| ❑ UA-LA321-H2 [(2)] | The History of the Bonzos | 1974 | 15.00 |
| ❑ UAS 5517 | The Beast of the Bonzos | 1971 | 15.00 |
| ❑ UAS 5584 | Let's Make Up and Be Friendly | 1972 | 15.00 |

**BOOGIE KINGS, THE**

| Number | Title (A Side/B Side) | Yr | NM |
|---|---|---|---|
| **MONTEL** | | | |
| ❑ LP-104 [M] | The Boogie Kings | 1966 | 25.00 |
| ❑ LP-109 [M] | Blue Eyed Soul | 1967 | 25.00 |

**BOOKER T. AND THE MG'S**

| Number | Title (A Side/B Side) | Yr | NM |
|---|---|---|---|
| **A&M** | | | |
| ❑ SP-4720 | Try and Love Again | 1978 | 10.00 |
| *—As "Booker T. Jones"* | | | |
| ❑ SP-4798 | The Best of You | 1979 | 10.00 |
| *—As "Booker T. Jones"* | | | |
| ❑ SP-4874 | I Want You | 1981 | 10.00 |
| *—As "Booker T. Jones"* | | | |
| **ASYLUM** | | | |
| ❑ 7E-1093 | Universal Language | 1977 | 10.00 |
| **ATLANTIC** | | | |
| ❑ 8202 [M] | The Best of Booker T. and the MG's | 1968 | 50.00 |
| *—Mono is white label promo only* | | | |
| ❑ SD 8202 [S] | The Best of Booker T. and the MG's | 1968 | 20.00 |
| ❑ 81285 | The Best of Booker T. and the MG's | 1985 | 8.00 |
| **EPIC** | | | |
| ❑ KE 33143 | Evergreen | 1974 | 12.00 |
| **MCA** | | | |
| ❑ 6282 | The Runaway | 1989 | 12.00 |
| *—As "Booker T. Jones"* | | | |
| **STAX** | | | |
| ❑ ST-701 [M] | Green Onions | 1962 | 70.00 |
| ❑ STS-701 [R] | Green Onions | 1966 | 50.00 |
| ❑ ST-705 [M] | Soul Dressing | 1965 | 70.00 |
| ❑ STS-705 [R] | Soul Dressing | 1966 | 50.00 |
| ❑ ST-711 [M] | And Now...Booker T. and the MG's | 1966 | 50.00 |
| ❑ STS-711 [S] | And Now...Booker T. and the MG's | 1966 | 80.00 |



**Except when noted otherwise, VG = 25% of NM, and VG+ = 50% of NM. (Example: VG = $2.00, VG+ = $4.00 and NM = $8.00.)**

| Number | Title (A Side/B Side) | Yr | NM |
|---|---|---|---|
| ❑ ST-713 [M] | In the Christmas Spirit | 1966 | 400.00 |
| *—Fingers and piano keys cover* | | | |
| ❑ ST-713 [M] | In the Christmas Spirit | 1967 | 200.00 |
| *—Same as above; Santa Claus cover* | | | |
| ❑ STS-713 [S] | In the Christmas Spirit | 1966 | 400.00 |
| *—Fingers and piano keys cover* | | | |
| ❑ STS-713 [S] | In the Christmas Spirit | 1967 | 200.00 |
| *—Santa Claus cover* | | | |
| ❑ ST-717 [M] | Hip Hug-Her | 1967 | 40.00 |
| ❑ STS-717 [S] | Hip Hug-Her | 1967 | 50.00 |
| ❑ ST-724 [M] | Doin' Our Thing | 1968 | 80.00 |
| ❑ STS-724 [S] | Doin' Our Thing | 1968 | 50.00 |
| ❑ STS-2001 | Soul Limbo | 1968 | 25.00 |
| ❑ STS-2006 | Uptight | 1969 | 25.00 |
| ❑ STS-2009 | The Booker T. Set | 1969 | 25.00 |
| ❑ STS-2027 | McLemore Avenue | 1970 | 25.00 |
| ❑ STS-2033 | Booker T. and the MG's Greatest Hits | 1970 | 15.00 |
| ❑ STM-2035 [M] | Melting Pot | 1971 | 40.00 |
| *—Mono is white label promo only* | | | |
| ❑ STS-2035 [S] | Melting Pot | 1971 | 15.00 |
| ❑ STX-4104 | Free Ride | 1978 | 10.00 |
| ❑ STX-4113 | Soul Limbo | 198? | 10.00 |
| *—Reissue of 2001* | | | |
| ❑ MPS-8505 | Booker T. and the MG's Greatest Hits | 1981 | 10.00 |
| ❑ MPS-8521 | Melting Pot | 198? | 10.00 |
| *—Reissue of 2035* | | | |
| ❑ MPS-8531 | The Booker T. Set | 1987 | 10.00 |
| *—Reissue of 2009* | | | |
| ❑ MPS-8552 | McLemore Avenue | 1990 | 12.00 |
| *—Reissue of 2027* | | | |

SUNDAZED

| Number | Title (A Side/B Side) | Yr | NM |
|---|---|---|---|
| ❑ LP 5042 | Soul Dressing | 2000 | 15.00 |
| *—Reissue on 180-gram vinyl* | | | |
| ❑ LP 5043 | And Now! Booker T. and the MG's | 2000 | 15.00 |
| *—Reissue on 180-gram vinyl* | | | |
| ❑ LP 5053 | In the Christmas Spirit | 2000 | 15.00 |
| *—Reissue on 180-gram vinyl* | | | |
| ❑ LP 5079 | Green Onions | 2002 | 12.00 |
| *—Reissue on 180-gram vinyl* | | | |
| ❑ LP 5080 | Hip Hug-Her | 2002 | 12.00 |
| *—Reissue on 180-gram vinyl* | | | |

**BOOMERANG**

RCA VICTOR

| Number | Title (A Side/B Side) | Yr | NM |
|---|---|---|---|
| ❑ LSP-4577 | Boomerang | 1971 | 20.00 |

**BOONE, PAT**

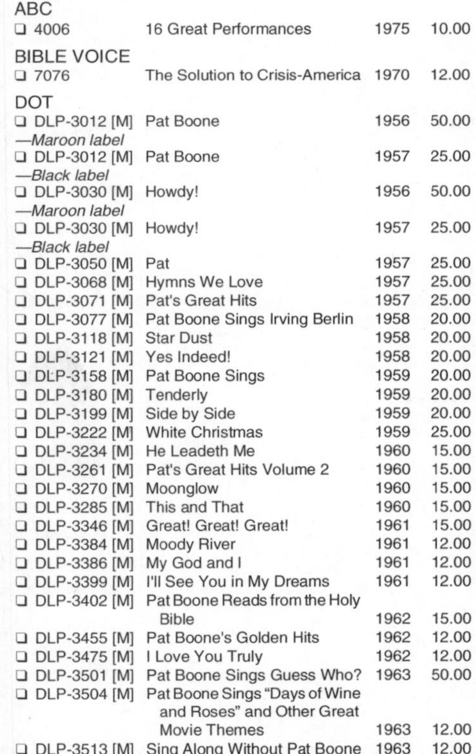

ABC

| Number | Title (A Side/B Side) | Yr | NM |
|---|---|---|---|
| ❑ 4006 | 16 Great Performances | 1975 | 10.00 |

BIBLE VOICE

| Number | Title (A Side/B Side) | Yr | NM |
|---|---|---|---|
| ❑ 7076 | The Solution to Crisis-America | 1970 | 12.00 |

DOT

| Number | Title (A Side/B Side) | Yr | NM |
|---|---|---|---|
| ❑ DLP-3012 [M] | Pat Boone | 1956 | 50.00 |
| *—Maroon label* | | | |
| ❑ DLP-3012 [M] | Pat Boone | 1957 | 25.00 |
| *—Black label* | | | |
| ❑ DLP-3030 [M] | Howdy! | 1956 | 50.00 |
| *—Maroon label* | | | |
| ❑ DLP-3030 [M] | Howdy! | 1957 | 25.00 |
| *—Black label* | | | |
| ❑ DLP-3050 [M] | Pat | 1957 | 25.00 |
| ❑ DLP-3068 [M] | Hymns We Love | 1957 | 25.00 |
| ❑ DLP-3071 [M] | Pat's Great Hits | 1957 | 25.00 |
| ❑ DLP-3077 [M] | Pat Boone Sings Irving Berlin | 1958 | 20.00 |
| ❑ DLP-3118 [M] | Star Dust | 1958 | 20.00 |
| ❑ DLP-3121 [M] | Yes Indeed! | 1958 | 20.00 |
| ❑ DLP-3158 [M] | Pat Boone Sings | 1959 | 20.00 |
| ❑ DLP-3180 [M] | Tenderly | 1959 | 20.00 |
| ❑ DLP-3199 [M] | Side by Side | 1959 | 20.00 |
| ❑ DLP-3222 [M] | White Christmas | 1959 | 25.00 |
| ❑ DLP-3234 [M] | He Leadeth Me | 1960 | 15.00 |
| ❑ DLP-3261 [M] | Pat's Great Hits Volume 2 | 1960 | 15.00 |
| ❑ DLP-3270 [M] | Moonglow | 1960 | 15.00 |
| ❑ DLP-3285 [M] | This and That | 1960 | 15.00 |
| ❑ DLP-3346 [M] | Great! Great! Great! | 1961 | 15.00 |
| ❑ DLP-3384 [M] | Moody River | 1961 | 12.00 |
| ❑ DLP-3386 [M] | My God and I | 1961 | 12.00 |
| ❑ DLP-3399 [M] | I'll See You in My Dreams | 1961 | 12.00 |
| ❑ DLP-3402 [M] | Pat Boone Reads from the Holy Bible | 1962 | 15.00 |
| ❑ DLP-3455 [M] | Pat Boone's Golden Hits | 1962 | 12.00 |
| ❑ DLP-3475 [M] | I Love You Truly | 1962 | 12.00 |
| ❑ DLP-3501 [M] | Pat Boone Sings Guess Who? | 1963 | 50.00 |
| ❑ DLP-3504 [M] | Pat Boone Sings "Days of Wine and Roses" and Other Great Movie Themes | 1963 | 12.00 |
| ❑ DLP-3513 [M] | Sing Along Without Pat Boone | 1963 | 12.00 |
| ❑ DLP-3520 [M] | The Star Spangled Banner | 1963 | 12.00 |
| ❑ DLP-3534 [M] | Tie Me Kangaroo Down, Sport | 1963 | 12.00 |
| ❑ DLP-3546 [M] | The Touch of Your Lips | 1963 | 12.00 |
| ❑ DLP-3582 [M] | The Lord's Prayer And Other Great Hymns | 1964 | 12.00 |
| ❑ DLP-3594 [M] | Boss Beat | 1964 | 12.00 |
| ❑ DLP-3601 [M] | Blest Be the Tie That Binds | 1965 | 12.00 |
| ❑ DLP-3606 [M] | Near You | 1965 | 12.00 |
| ❑ DLP-3626 [M] | The Golden Era of Country Hits | 1965 | 12.00 |

Pat Boone, *Pat Boone's Golden Hits,* Dot DLP 3455, 1962, mono, $12.

| Number | Title (A Side/B Side) | Yr | NM |
|---|---|---|---|
| ❑ DLP-3650 [M] | My 10th Anniversary with Dot Records | 1965 | 12.00 |
| ❑ DLP-3667 [M] | Winner of the Reader's Digest Poll | 1965 | 12.00 |
| ❑ DLP-3685 [M] | Great Hits of 1965 | 1965 | 12.00 |
| ❑ DLP-3748 [M] | Memories | 1966 | 12.00 |
| ❑ DLP-3764 [M] | Wish You Were Here, Buddy | 1966 | 12.00 |
| ❑ DLP-3770 [M] | Christmas Is a-Comin' | 1966 | 12.00 |
| ❑ DLP-3798 [M] | How Great Thou Art | 1967 | 15.00 |
| ❑ DLP-3805 [M] | I Was Kaiser Bill's Batman | 1967 | 15.00 |
| ❑ DLP-3814 [M] | 15 Hits of Pat Boone | 1967 | 15.00 |
| ❑ DLP-3876 [M] | Look Ahead | 1968 | 15.00 |
| ❑ DLP-25068 [S] | Hymns We Love | 1959 | 30.00 |
| ❑ DLP-25071 [P] | Pat's Great Hits | 1959 | 30.00 |
| ❑ DLP-25077 [S] | Pat Boone Sings Irving Berlin | 1959 | 25.00 |
| ❑ DLP-25118 [S] | Star Dust | 1959 | 25.00 |
| ❑ DLP-25121 [S] | Yes Indeed! | 1959 | 25.00 |
| ❑ DLP-25158 [S] | Pat Boone Sings | 1959 | 25.00 |
| ❑ DLP-25180 [S] | Tenderly | 1959 | 25.00 |
| ❑ DLP-25199 [S] | Side by Side | 1959 | 25.00 |
| ❑ DLP-25222 [S] | White Christmas | 1959 | 30.00 |
| ❑ DLP-25234 [S] | He Leadeth Me | 1960 | 20.00 |
| ❑ DLP-25261 [S] | Pat's Great Hits Volume 2 | 1960 | 20.00 |
| ❑ DLP-25270 [S] | Moonglow | 1960 | 20.00 |
| *—Black vinyl* | | | |
| ❑ DLP-25270 [S] | Moonglow | 1960 | 50.00 |
| *—Blue vinyl* | | | |
| ❑ DLP-25285 [S] | This and That | 1960 | 20.00 |
| ❑ DLP-25346 [S] | Great! Great! Great! | 1961 | 20.00 |
| ❑ DLP-25384 [S] | Moody River | 1961 | 15.00 |
| ❑ DLP-25386 [S] | My God and I | 1961 | 15.00 |
| ❑ DLP-25399 [S] | I'll See You in My Dreams | 1961 | 15.00 |
| ❑ DLP-25455 [S] | Pat Boone's Golden Hits | 1962 | 15.00 |
| ❑ DLP-25475 [S] | I Love You Truly | 1962 | 15.00 |
| ❑ DLP-25501 [S] | Pat Boone Sings Guess Who? | 1963 | 80.00 |
| ❑ DLP-25504 [S] | Pat Boone Sings "Days of Wine and Roses" and Other Great Movie Themes | 1963 | 15.00 |
| ❑ DLP-25513 [S] | Sing Along Without Pat Boone | 1963 | 15.00 |
| ❑ DLP-25520 [S] | The Star Spangled Banner | 1963 | 15.00 |
| ❑ DLP-25534 [S] | Tie Me Kangaroo Down, Sport | 1963 | 15.00 |
| ❑ DLP-25546 [S] | The Touch of Your Lips | 1963 | 15.00 |
| ❑ DLP-25573 [R] | Pat Boone | 1964 | 12.00 |
| ❑ DLP-25582 [S] | The Lord's Prayer And Other Great Hymns | 1964 | 15.00 |
| ❑ DLP-25594 [S] | Boss Beat | 1964 | 15.00 |
| ❑ DLP-25601 [S] | Blest Be the Tie That Binds | 1965 | 15.00 |

| Number | Title (A Side/B Side) | Yr | NM |
|---|---|---|---|
| ❑ DLP-25606 [S] | Near You | 1965 | 15.00 |
| ❑ DLP-25626 [S] | The Golden Era of Country Hits | 1965 | 15.00 |
| ❑ DLP-25650 [S] | My 10th Anniversary with Dot Records | 1965 | 15.00 |
| ❑ DLP-25667 [S] | Winner of the Reader's Digest Poll | 1965 | 15.00 |
| ❑ DLP-25685 [S] | Great Hits of 1965 | 1965 | 15.00 |
| ❑ DLP-25748 [S] | Memories | 1966 | 15.00 |
| ❑ DLP-25764 [S] | Wish You Were Here, Buddy | 1966 | 15.00 |
| ❑ DLP-25770 [S] | Christmas Is a-Comin' | 1966 | 15.00 |
| ❑ DLP-25798 [S] | How Great Thou Art | 1967 | 12.00 |
| ❑ DLP-25805 [S] | I Was Kaiser Bill's Batman | 1967 | 12.00 |
| ❑ DLP-25814 [S] | 15 Hits of Pat Boone | 1967 | 12.00 |
| ❑ DLP-25876 [S] | Look Ahead | 1968 | 12.00 |

HAMILTON

| Number | Title (A Side/B Side) | Yr | NM |
|---|---|---|---|
| ❑ HLP-118 [M] | 12 Great Hits | 196? | 12.00 |
| ❑ HLP-12118 [S] | 12 Great Hits | 196? | 12.00 |

HITSVILLE

| Number | Title (A Side/B Side) | Yr | NM |
|---|---|---|---|
| ❑ H6-405 | Texas Woman | 1976 | 12.00 |

LAMB & LION

| Number | Title (A Side/B Side) | Yr | NM |
|---|---|---|---|
| ❑ 1002 | New Songs of the Jesus People | 197? | 12.00 |
| ❑ 1004 | Pat Boone and the First Nashville Jesus Band | 197? | 12.00 |
| ❑ 1005 | Christian People, Vol. 1 | 197? | 10.00 |
| ❑ 1006 | The Family Who Prays | 197? | 10.00 |
| ❑ 1007 | Born Again | 197? | 10.00 |
| ❑ 1008 | All in the Boone Family | 1972 | 10.00 |
| ❑ 1013 | S-A-V-E-D | 197? | 10.00 |
| ❑ 1016 | Songs from the Inner Court | 197? | 10.00 |
| ❑ 5000 | The Pat Boone Family in the Holy Land | 197? | 10.00 |

MCA

| Number | Title (A Side/B Side) | Yr | NM |
|---|---|---|---|
| ❑ 658 | 16 Great Performances | 1980 | 8.00 |
| ❑ 6020 [(2)] | The Best of Pat Boone | 1980 | 12.00 |
| ❑ 15028 [S] | White Christmas | 198? | 10.00 |
| *—Reissue of Dot LP* | | | |

MELODYLAND

| Number | Title (A Side/B Side) | Yr | NM |
|---|---|---|---|
| ❑ 6-501 | The Country Side of Pat Boone | 1975 | 12.00 |

MGM

| Number | Title (A Side/B Side) | Yr | NM |
|---|---|---|---|
| ❑ SE-4899 | I Love You More and More Every Day | 1973 | 10.00 |

PARAMOUNT

| Number | Title (A Side/B Side) | Yr | NM |
|---|---|---|---|
| ❑ 1024 [(2)] | Pat Boone's Greatest Hymns | 1974 | 15.00 |
| ❑ 1043 [(2)] | Pat Boone's Greatest Hits | 1974 | 15.00 |

Boston, *Walk On,* MCA 10973, 1994, $25.

PICKWICK

| Number | Title (A Side/B Side) | Yr | NM |
|---|---|---|---|
| ❑ SPC-1024 | White Christmas | 1979 | 10.00 |
| ❑ SPC-3079 | True Love | 196? | 10.00 |
| ❑ SPC-3107 | Love Me Tender | 196? | 10.00 |
| ❑ SPC-3123 | Canadian Sunset | 196? | 10.00 |
| ❑ SPC-3145 | Favorite Hymns | 197? | 10.00 |
| ❑ SPC-3219 | You've Lost That Lovin' Feeling | 197? | 10.00 |
| ❑ SPC-3568 | The Old Rugged Cross | 1978 | 8.00 |
| ❑ SPC-3597 | Great Hits | 1978 | 8.00 |

SUPREME

| Number | Title (A Side/B Side) | Yr | NM |
|---|---|---|---|
| ❑ SS-2060 | Rapture | 1970 | 12.00 |

TETRAGRAMMATON

| Number | Title (A Side/B Side) | Yr | NM |
|---|---|---|---|
| ❑ T-118 | Departure | 1969 | 12.00 |

WORD

| Number | Title (A Side/B Side) | Yr | NM |
|---|---|---|---|
| ❑ WST-8536 | The Pat Boone Family | 1970 | 10.00 |
| ❑ WST-8664 | Hymns We Love | 197? | 10.00 |
| ❑ WST-8711 | He Leadeth Me | 197? | 10.00 |
| ❑ WST-8725 | The Star-Spangled Banner | 197? | 10.00 |
| ❑ WST-8738 | I Believe | 198? | 8.00 |

**BOONE, RANDY**

DECCA

| Number | Title (A Side/B Side) | Yr | NM |
|---|---|---|---|
| ❑ DL 4619 [M] | Singing Star of The Virginian | 1965 | 25.00 |
| ❑ DL 4663 [M] | Ramblin' Randy | 1965 | 20.00 |
| ❑ DL 74619 [S] | Singing Star of The Virginian | 1965 | 35.00 |
| ❑ DL 74663 [S] | Ramblin' Randy | 1965 | 30.00 |

**BOOT**

AGAPE

| Number | Title (A Side/B Side) | Yr | NM |
|---|---|---|---|
| ❑ 2601 | Boot | 1972 | 25.00 |

**BORDERSONG**

REAL GOOD

| Number | Title (A Side/B Side) | Yr | NM |
|---|---|---|---|
| ❑ 1001 | Morning | 1975 | 70.00 |

**BORODIN STRING QUARTET**

MERCURY LIVING PRESENCE

| Number | Title (A Side/B Side) | Yr | NM |
|---|---|---|---|
| ❑ SR 90309 [S] | Shostakovich: String Quartets No. 4 and 8 | 196? | 70.00 |
| *—Maroon label, no "Vendor: Mercury Record Corporation"* | | | |

**BOSTIC, EARL**

GRAND PRIX

| Number | Title (A Side/B Side) | Yr | NM |
|---|---|---|---|
| ❑ K-404 [M] | The Earl of Bostic | 196? | 15.00 |
| ❑ KS-404 [R] | The Earl of Bostic | 196? | 12.00 |
| ❑ K-416 [M] | Wild Man | 196? | 15.00 |
| ❑ KS-416 [R] | Wild Man | 196? | 12.00 |

KING

| Number | Title (A Side/B Side) | Yr | NM |
|---|---|---|---|
| ❑ 295-64 [10] | Earl Bostic and His Alto Sax | 1951 | 200.00 |
| *—Black vinyl* | | | |
| ❑ 295-64 [10] | Earl Bostic and His Alto Sax | 1951 | 400.00 |
| *—Red vinyl* | | | |
| ❑ 295-65 [10] | Earl Bostic and His Alto Sax | 1951 | 200.00 |
| *—Black vinyl* | | | |
| ❑ 295-65 [10] | Earl Bostic and His Alto Sax | 1951 | 400.00 |
| *—Red vinyl* | | | |
| ❑ 295-66 [10] | Earl Bostic and His Alto Sax | 1951 | 200.00 |
| *—Black vinyl* | | | |
| ❑ 295-66 [10] | Earl Bostic and His Alto Sax | 1951 | 400.00 |
| *—Red vinyl* | | | |
| ❑ 295-72 [10] | Earl Bostic and His Alto Sax | 1952 | 200.00 |
| ❑ 295-76 [10] | Earl Bostic and His Alto Sax | 1952 | 200.00 |
| ❑ 295-77 [10] | Earl Bostic and His Alto Sax | 1952 | 200.00 |
| ❑ 295-78 [10] | Earl Bostic and His Alto Sax | 1952 | 200.00 |
| ❑ 295-79 [10] | Earl Bostic and His Alto Sax | 1952 | 200.00 |
| ❑ 295-95 [10] | Earl Bostic Plays the Old Standards | 1954 | 200.00 |
| ❑ 295-103 [10] | Earl Bostic and His Alto Sax | 1954 | 200.00 |
| ❑ 395-500 [M] | Dance to the Best of Bostic | 195? | 80.00 |
| *—Second cover with girl in a swimsuit pictured* | | | |
| ❑ 395-500 [M] | Dance to the Best of Bostic | 1956 | 100.00 |
| *—Original cover with Earl Bostic pictured* | | | |
| ❑ 395-503 [M] | Bostic for You | 1956 | 100.00 |
| ❑ 395-515 [M] | Alto-Tude | 1956 | 100.00 |
| ❑ 395-525 [M] | Dance Time | 1956 | 80.00 |
| ❑ 395-529 [M] | Let's Dance with Earl Bostic | 1956 | 80.00 |
| ❑ 395-547 [M] | Invitation to Dance | 1956 | 80.00 |
| ❑ 558 [M] | C'mon and Dance with Earl Bostic | 1956 | 80.00 |
| ❑ KS-558 [S] | C'mon and Dance with Earl Bostic | 1959 | 150.00 |
| ❑ 571 [M] | Hits of the Swing Age | 1957 | 80.00 |
| ❑ 583 [M] | Showcase of Swinging Dance Hits | 1958 | 80.00 |
| ❑ 597 [M] | Alto Magic in Hi-Fi | 1958 | 80.00 |
| ❑ KS-597 [S] | Alto Magic in Hi-Fi | 1959 | 150.00 |
| ❑ 602 [M] | Sweet Tunes of the Fantastic Fifties | 1959 | 50.00 |
| ❑ KSD-602 [S] | Sweet Tunes of the Fantastic Fifties | 1959 | 100.00 |
| ❑ 613 [M] | Bostic Workshop | 1959 | 50.00 |
| ❑ KS-613 [S] | Bostic Workshop | 1959 | 100.00 |
| ❑ 620 [M] | Sweet Tunes from the Roaring Twenties | 1959 | 50.00 |
| ❑ KS-620 [S] | Sweet Tunes from the Roaring Twenties | 1959 | 100.00 |
| ❑ 632 [M] | Sweet Tunes of the Swinging Thirties | 1959 | 50.00 |
| ❑ KS-632 [S] | Sweet Tunes of the Swinging Thirties | 1959 | 100.00 |
| ❑ 640 [M] | Sweet Tunes of the Sentimental Forties | 1960 | 50.00 |
| ❑ KS-640 [S] | Sweet Tunes of the Sentimental Forties | 1960 | 80.00 |
| ❑ 662 [M] | Musical Pearls | 1960 | 50.00 |
| ❑ KS-662 [S] | Musical Pearls | 1960 | 80.00 |
| ❑ 705 [M] | Hit Tunes of Big Broadway Shows | 1960 | 50.00 |
| ❑ KS-705 [S] | Hit Tunes of Big Broadway Shows | 1960 | 80.00 |
| ❑ 786 [M] | By Popular Demand | 1961 | 50.00 |
| ❑ 827 [M] | Earl Bostic Plays Bossa Nova | 1963 | 50.00 |
| ❑ 838 [M] | Songs of the Fantastic Fifties, Volume 2 | 1963 | 50.00 |
| ❑ 846 [M] | Jazz As I Feel It | 1963 | 50.00 |
| ❑ 881 [M] | The Best of Earl Bostic, Volume 2 | 1964 | 50.00 |
| ❑ 900 [M] | The New Sound | 1964 | 50.00 |
| ❑ 921 [M] | The Great Hits of 1964 | 1964 | 50.00 |
| ❑ 947 [M] | 24 Songs That Earl Loved the Most | 1966 | 40.00 |
| ❑ KS-1048 [S] | Harlem Nocturne | 1969 | 25.00 |
| ❑ K-5010X | 14 Original Greatest Hits | 1977 | 12.00 |

PHILIPS

| Number | Title (A Side/B Side) | Yr | NM |
|---|---|---|---|
| ❑ PHM 200262 [M] | The Song Is Not Ended | 1967 | 25.00 |
| ❑ PHS 600262 [S] | The Song Is Not Ended | 1967 | 25.00 |

**BOSTIC, EARL/JIMMY LUNCEFORD**

ALLEGRO ELITE

| Number | Title (A Side/B Side) | Yr | NM |
|---|---|---|---|
| ❑ 4053 [10] | Earl Bostic/Jimmy Lunceford Orchestras | 195? | 40.00 |

**BOSTON**

EPIC

| Number | Title (A Side/B Side) | Yr | NM |
|---|---|---|---|
| ❑ E99 34188 | Boston | 1978 | 20.00 |
| *—Picture disc* | | | |
| ❑ HE 34188 | Boston | 1981 | 50.00 |
| *—First edition of the half-speed mastered edition* | | | |
| ❑ JE 34188 | Boston | 1977 | 8.00 |
| *—Second edition; orange label, different prefix* | | | |
| ❑ JE 34188 | Boston | 1979 | 6.00 |
| *—Third edition; dark blue label* | | | |
| ❑ PE 34188 | Boston | 1976 | 10.00 |
| *—Original edition; orange label* | | | |
| ❑ FE 35050 | Don't Look Back | 1978 | 10.00 |
| *—Original edition; orange label* | | | |
| ❑ FE 35050 | Don't Look Back | 1979 | 8.00 |
| *—Second edition; dark blue label* | | | |
| ❑ HE 44188 | Boston | 1982 | 40.00 |
| *—Second edition of the half-speed mastered edition* | | | |
| ❑ HE 45050 | Don't Look Back | 1982 | 50.00 |
| *—Half-speed mastered edition* | | | |

MCA

| Number | Title (A Side/B Side) | Yr | NM |
|---|---|---|---|
| ❑ 6188 | Third Stage | 1986 | 8.00 |
| ❑ 10973 | Walk On | 1994 | 25.00 |

MOBILE FIDELITY

| Number | Title (A Side/B Side) | Yr | NM |
|---|---|---|---|
| ❑ 1-249 | Boston | 1996 | 25.00 |
| *—Audiophile vinyl* | | | |

**BOSTON POPS ORCHESTRA (ARTHUR FIEDLER, CONDUCTOR)** Perhaps the most popular orchestra and conductor in American history, Fiedler and the Pops released literally hundreds of albums, of which the below are merely a sample. Most of these are from the "golden age of stereo" and also exist in monaural, but the mono versions are in much less demand than the stereo editions.

RCA VICTOR RED SEAL

| Number | Title (A Side/B Side) | Yr | NM |
|---|---|---|---|
| ❑ LSC-1817 [S] | Offenbach: Gaite Parisienne | 1958 | 400.00 |
| *—Original with "shaded dog" label* | | | |
| ❑ LSC-1817 [S] | Offenbach: Gaite Parisienne | 199? | 30.00 |
| *—Classic Records reissue* | | | |
| ❑ LSC-1990 [S] | Offenbach: In America | 1958 | 40.00 |
| *—Original with "shaded dog" label* | | | |
| ❑ LSC-1990 [S] | Offenbach: In America | 1964 | 50.00 |
| *—Second pressing with "white dog" label; a rare case where the second edition is more desirable than the first* | | | |
| ❑ LSC-2028 [S] | Waltzes by the Strauss Family | 1958 | 20.00 |
| *—Original with "shaded dog" label* | | | |
| ❑ LSC-2052 [S] | Tchaikovsky: The Nutcracker (selections) | 1958 | 20.00 |
| *—Original with "shaded dog" label* | | | |
| ❑ LSC-2084 [S] | Rossini-Respighi: La Boutique Fantasque | 1958 | 120.00 |
| *—Original with "shaded dog" label* | | | |
| ❑ LSC-2100 [S] | Hi-Fi Fiedler | 1958 | 25.00 |
| *—Original with "shaded dog" label* | | | |
| ❑ LSC-2125 [S] | Grieg: Music from Peer Gynt | 1958 | 20.00 |
| *—Original with "shaded dog" label* | | | |
| ❑ LSC-2130 [S] | Strauss, Johann: Orchestral Music from Gypsy Baron and Die Fledermaus | 1958 | 20.00 |
| *—Original with "shaded dog" label* | | | |



**Except when noted otherwise, VG = 25% of NM, and VG+ = 50% of NM. (Example: VG = $2.00, VG+ = $4.00 and NM = $8.00.)**

Number | Title (A Side/B Side) | Yr | NM

❑ LSC-2202 [S] Pops Caviar 1959 20.00
*—Original with "shaded dog" label*
❑ LSC-2213 [S] Boston Tea Party 1959 20.00
*—Original with "shaded dog" label*
❑ LSC-2229 [S] Marches in Hi-Fi 1959 20.00
*—Original with "shaded dog" label*
❑ LSC-2235 [S] Good Music to Have Fun With 1959 25.00
*—Original with "shaded dog" label*
❑ LSC-2240 [S] Kay, Hershey: Stars and Stripes 1959 40.00
*—Original with "shaded dog" label*
❑ LSC-2267 [S] Offenbach: Gaite Parisienne; Khachatourian: Gayne Suite 1959 20.00
*—Original with "shaded dog" label*
❑ LSC-2270 [S] Pops Stoppers 1959 20.00
*—Original with "shaded dog" label*
❑ LSC-2294 [S] Rodgers: Slaughter on Tenth Avenue 1959 20.00
*—Original with "shaded dog" label*
❑ LSC-2320 [S] Song of India 1959 20.00
*—Original with "shaded dog" label*
❑ LSC-2329 [S] Pops Christmas Party 1959 40.00
*—Original copies have "shaded dog" with small "RCA Victor" logo; large "Living Stereo" on front cover*
❑ LSC-2329 [S] Pops Christmas Party 1964 20.00
*—Second editions have "white dog" with large "RCA Victor" logo; small "Living Stereo" on front cover*
❑ LSC-2367 [S] Gershwin: Rhapsody in Blue; An American in Paris 1960 20.00
*—Earl Wild, piano; originals with "shaded dog" label*
❑ LSC-2380 [S] Music from Million Dollar Movies 1960 20.00
*—Original with "shaded dog" label*
❑ LSC-2439 [S] All-Time Favorites 1960 20.00
*—Original with "shaded dog" label*
❑ LSC-2442 [S] The Music of Franz Liszt 1960 20.00
*—Original with "shaded dog" label*
❑ LSC-2470 [S] More Classical Music for People Who Hate Classical Music 1961 40.00
*—Original with "shaded dog" label*
❑ LSC-2486 [S] Music of Frank Loesser 1961 40.00
*—Original with "shaded dog" label*
❑ LSC-2549 [S] Family Fun 1961 40.00
*—Original with "shaded dog" label*
❑ LSC-2586 [S] Gershwin: Piano Concerto 1962 20.00
*—Earl Wild, piano; originals with "shaded dog" label*
❑ LSC-2586 [S] Gershwin: Piano Concerto 199? 25.00
*—Earl Wild, piano; Classic Records reissue*
❑ LSC-2596 [S] Saint-Saens: Carnival of the Animals; Britten: Young Person's Guide to the Orchestra 1962 60.00
*—Original with "shaded dog" label*
❑ LSC-2621 [S] Chopin: Les Sylphides; Prokofiev: Love for Three Oranges 1962 30.00
*—Original with "shaded dog" label*
❑ LSC-2637 [S] Rodgers: No Strings; State Fair 1962 20.00
*—Original with "shaded dog" label*
❑ LSC-2702 [S] Milhaud: A Frenchman in New York; Gershwin: An American in Paris 1963 25.00
*—Original with "shaded dog" label*
❑ LSC-6082 [(2)S]Everything But the Beer 1959 100.00
*—Original with "shaded dog" label*

**BOSTON SYMPHONY ORCHESTRA (AARON COPLAND, CONDUCTOR)**

RCA VICTOR RED SEAL
❑ LSC-2401 [S] Copland: Appalachian Spring; The Tender Land Suite 1960 20.00
*—Original with "shaded dog" label*

**BOSTON SYMPHONY ORCHESTRA (ERICH LEINSDORF, CONDUCTOR)**

RCA VICTOR RED SEAL
❑ LSC-2707 [S] Prokofiev: Symphony No. 5 1963 20.00
*—Original with "shaded dog" label*

**BOSTON SYMPHONY ORCHESTRA (PIERRE MONTEUX, CONDUCTOR)**

RCA VICTOR RED SEAL
❑ LSC-1901 [S] Tchaikovsky: Symphony No. 6 "Pathetique" 1958 50.00
*—Original with "shaded dog" label*
❑ LSC-1901 [S] Tchaikovsky: Symphony No. 6 "Pathetique" 199? 30.00
*—Classic Records reissue*
❑ LSC-2239 [S] Tchaikovsky: Symphony No. 5 1959 25.00
*—Original with "shaded dog" label*
❑ LSC-2239 [S] Tchaikovsky: Symphony No. 5 1964 20.00
*—Second edition with "white dog" label*
❑ LSC-2369 [S] Tchaikovsky: Symphony No. 4 1959 50.00
*—Original with "shaded dog" label*
❑ LSC-2369 [S] Tchaikovsky: Symphony No. 4 199? 30.00
*—Classic Records reissue*
❑ LSC-2376 [S] Stravinsky: Petrouchka 1960 100.00
*—Original with "shaded dog" label*
❑ LSC-2376 [S] Stravinsky: Petrouchka 1964 50.00
*—Second edition with "white dog" label*

Number | Title (A Side/B Side) | Yr | NM

**BOSTON SYMPHONY ORCHESTRA (CHARLES MUNCH, CONDUCTOR)**

RCA VICTOR RED SEAL
❑ LSC-1893 [S] Ravel: Daphnis and Chloe 1958 400.00
*—Original with "shaded dog" label*
❑ LSC-1893 [S] Ravel: Daphnis and Chloe 199? 30.00
*—Classic Records reissue*
❑ LSC-1900 [S] Berlioz: Symphonie Fantastique 1958 —
*—No mention of Classic Records on cover. Unknown; "if a copy did exist it could fetch up to $25,000 or more," according to at least one audiophile source*
❑ LSC-1900 [S] Berlioz: Symphonie Fantastique 199? 30.00
*—Classic Records issue. This album is not known to have been issued in stereo before this.*
❑ LSC-1984 [S] Ravel: Bolero; La Valse; Rapsodie Espagnole; Debussy: Prelude 1958 80.00
*—Original with "shaded dog" label*
❑ LSC-2097 [S] Brahms: Symphony No. 1 1958 150.00
*—Original with "shaded dog" label*
❑ LSC-2105 [S] Tchaikovsky: Serenade for Strings 1958 40.00
*—Original with "shaded dog" label*
❑ LSC-2111 [S] Debussy: La Mer 1958 50.00
*—Original with "shaded dog" label*
❑ LSC-2131 [S] Franck: Symphony in D 1958 20.00
*—Original with "shaded dog" label*
❑ LSC-2221 [S] Mendelssohn: Symphony No. 4 and No. 5 1959 20.00
*—Original with "shaded dog" label*
❑ LSC-2228 [S] Berlioz: Harold in Italy 1959 20.00
*—Original with "shaded dog" label*
❑ LSC-2233 [S] Beethoven: Symphony No. 3 1959 50.00
*—Original with "shaded dog" label*
❑ LSC-2271 [S] Ravel: Concerto in G; d'Indy: Symphony on a French Mountain Air 1959 100.00
*—Original with "shaded dog" label*
❑ LSC-2271 [S] Ravel: Concerto in G; d'Indy: Symphony on a French Mountain Air 199? 30.00
*—Classic Records reissue*
❑ LM-2282 [M] Debussy: Images 1959 20.00
❑ LSC-2282 [S] Debussy: Images 1959 80.00
*—Original with "shaded dog" label*
❑ LSC-2292 [S] The French Touch 1959 200.00
*—Original with "shaded dog" label*
❑ LSC-2297 [S] Brahms: Symphony No. 4 1959 30.00
*—Original with "shaded dog" label*
❑ LSC-2341 [S] Saint-Saens: Symphony No. 3 1960 20.00
*—Original with "shaded dog" label*
❑ LSC-2344 [S] Schubert: Symphony No. 9 1960 40.00
*—Original with "shaded dog" label*
❑ LSC-2344 [S] Schubert: Symphony No. 9 1964 30.00
*—Second edition with "white dog" label*
❑ LM-2352 [M] Blackwood: Symphony No. 1; Haieff: Symphony No. 2 1960 20.00
❑ LSC-2352 [S] Blackwood: Symphony No. 1; Haieff: Symphony No. 2 1960 60.00
*—Original with "shaded dog" label*
❑ LSC-2371 [S] Mahler: Songs of a Wayfarer 1960 25.00
*—Original with "shaded dog" label*
❑ LSC-2438 [S] Berlioz: Overtures 1960 70.00
*—Original with "shaded dog" label*
❑ LSC-2474 [S] Schumann: Symphony No. 1 1961 20.00
*—Original with "shaded dog" label*
❑ LSC-2520 [S] Mendelssohn: Symphony No. 3 "Scotch"; Scherzo from Octet in E-flat 1961 20.00
*—Original with "shaded dog" label*
❑ LSC-2522 [S] Schubert: Symphony No. 2; Beethoven: Prometheus Ballet Excerpts 1961 20.00
*—Original with "shaded dog" label*
❑ LSC-2565 [S] Tchaikovsky: Romeo and Juliet; Strauss, Richard: Till Eulenspiegel 1961 40.00
*—Original with "shaded dog" label*
❑ LSC-2567 [S] Poulenc: Organ Concerto; Stravinsky: Jeu de Cartes 1961 40.00
*—Original with "shaded dog" label*
❑ LSC-2568 [S] Ravel: Daphnis et Chloe 1961 20.00
*—Original with "shaded dog" label*
❑ LSC-2608 [S] Berlioz: Symphonie Fantastique 1962 25.00
*—Original with "shaded dog" label*
❑ LDS-2625 [S] Milhaud: La Creation du Monde; Suite Provencale 1962 200.00
*—Original with "shaded dog" label*
❑ LSC-2625 [S] Milhaude: La Creation Du Monde 1962 200.00
*—With "shaded dog" or "white dog" label*
❑ LSC-2625 [S] Milhaude: La Creation Du Monde 199? 30.00
*—Classic Records reissue*
❑ LSC-2629 [S] Dvorak: Symphony No. 4 (8) in G 1962 50.00
*—Original with "shaded dog" label*

Number | Title (A Side/B Side) | Yr | NM

❑ LSC-2647 [S] Chausson: Symphony in B-flat; Franck: Le Chasseur Maudit 1962 40.00
*—Original with "shaded dog" label*
❑ LSC-2683 [S] Tchaikovsky: Symphony No. 6 1962 20.00
*—Original with "shaded dog" label*
❑ LSC-6140 [(3)S]Bach: Brandenburg Concertos No. 1-6 196? 150.00
*—Original with "shaded dog" label*

**BOSTON TEA PARTY, THE**

FLICK DISC
❑ 45000 The Boston Tea Party 1968 60.00

**BOSWELL, CONNEE**

DECCA
❑ DL 5390 [10] Connee Boswell 1951 80.00
❑ DL 5445 [10] Singing the Blues 1952 80.00
❑ DL 8356 [M] Connee 1956 50.00

RCA VICTOR
❑ LPM-1426 [M] Connee Boswell and the Original Memphis Five 1957 40.00

**BOTHWELL, JOHNNY**

BRUNSWICK
❑ BL 58033 [10] Presenting Johnny Bothwell 1953 100.00

**BOURBON STREET STOMPERS, THE**

TIME
❑ S-2118 [S] We Like Dixieland 196? 20.00

**BOW STREET RUNNERS, THE**

B.T. PUPPY
❑ BTPS-1026 The Bow Street Runners 1969 1000.

SUNDAZED
❑ LP 5029 The Bow Street Runners 199? 10.00
*—Reissue of B.T. Puppy LP*

**BOW WOW WOW**

HARVEST
❑ SK-12234 12 Original Recordings 1982 15.00

RCA VICTOR
❑ AFL1-4147 See Jungle, See Jungle! Go Join Your Gang, Yeah! City All Over, Go Ape Crazy 1981 12.00
❑ DJL1-4193 [DJ]RCA Special Radio Series 1981 30.00
❑ CPL1-4314 [EP]The Last of the Mohicans 1982 10.00
❑ AFL1-4375 I Want Candy 1982 12.00
❑ AFL1-4570 When the Going Gets Tough, the Tough Get Going 1983 10.00

**BOWEN, JIMMY**

DECCA
❑ DL 4816 [M] Margie Bowes Sings 1967 20.00

REPRISE
❑ R-6210 [M] Sunday Morning with the Comics 1966 30.00
❑ RS-6210 [S] Sunday Morning with the Comics 1966 40.00

ROULETTE
❑ R 25004 [M] Jimmy Bowen 1957 300.00
*—Black and silver label*
❑ R 25004 [M] Jimmy Bowen 1958 150.00
*—Red label*
❑ R 25004 [M] Jimmy Bowen 198? 12.00
*—Reissue for Publishers Central Bureau (it says so on the jacket)*

**BOWES, MARGIE**

DECCA
❑ DL 4816 [M] Margie Bowes Sings 1967 20.00
❑ DL 74816 [S] Margie Bowes Sings 1967 15.00
❑ DL 75023 Today's Country Sound 1968 15.00

**BOWIE, DAVID**

COLUMBIA
❑ C 86630 Heathen 2002 12.00

DERAM
❑ DE 16003 [M] David Bowie 1967 120.00
❑ DES 18003 [S] David Bowie 1967 150.00

EMI AMERICA
❑ SPRO 9960/1 [(2)DJ]Let's Talk 1983 25.00
*—Promo-only interview album*
❑ SO-17093 Let's Dance 1983 10.00
❑ SJ-17138 Tonight 1984 10.00
❑ PJ-17267 Never Let Me Down 1987 10.00
❑ SPRO-79112/3 [DJ]Never Let Me Down: The Interview 1987 25.00
❑ R 153730 Let's Dance 1983 12.00
*—RCA Music Service edition*
❑ R 174212 Never Let Me Down 1987 12.00
*—BMG Direct Marketing edition*

LONDON
❑ PS 628/9 [(2)] Images 1966-1967 1973 50.00
*—Original pressings have dark blue and silver labels. Later pressings, if any, are worth at least 50% less.*
❑ LC 50007 Starting Point 1977 12.00

David Bowie, *Changesbowie,* Ryko Analogue RALP 0171-2, 1990, 2 records, with obi strip, $20.

| Number | Title (A Side/B Side) | Yr | NM |
|---|---|---|---|
| **MERCURY** | | | |
| ❑ SR 61246 | Man of Words, Man of Music | 1969 | 150.00 |
| ❑ SR 61325 | The Man Who Sold the World | 1970 | 40.00 |
| *—An often-counterfeited album; originals have matrix numbers stamped in the trail-off area* | | | |
| **MOBILE FIDELITY** | | | |
| ❑ 1-064 | The Rise and Fall of Ziggy Stardust and the Spiders from Mars | 1983 | 50.00 |
| *—Audiophile vinyl* | | | |
| ❑ 1-083 | Let's Dance | 1984 | 30.00 |
| *—Audiophile vinyl* | | | |
| **RCA RED SEAL** | | | |
| ❑ ARL1-2743 | Peter and the Wolf | 1978 | 20.00 |
| *—With the Philadelphia Orchestra conducted by Eugene Ormandy; black vinyl* | | | |
| ❑ ARL1-2743 | Peter and the Wolf | 1978 | 20.00 |
| *—With the Philadelphia Orchestra conducted by Eugene Ormandy; green vinyl* | | | |
| **RCA VICTOR** | | | |
| ❑ AFL1-0291 | Pin Ups | 1978 | 10.00 |
| *—Reissue* | | | |
| ❑ APL1-0291 | Pin Ups | 1973 | 20.00 |
| ❑ CPL1-0576 | Diamond Dogs | 1974 | 20.00 |
| *—Standard issue, with dog's genitals airbrushed* | | | |
| ❑ CPL1-0576 | Diamond Dogs | 1974 | 4000. |
| *—Original copies have cover with dog's genitals clearly visible. Almost all were destroyed prior to release.* | | | |
| ❑ CPL2-0771 [(2)]David Live | | 1974 | 20.00 |
| *—At time of release, available with either orange or tan labels* | | | |
| ❑ CPL2-0771 [(2)]David Live | | 1976 | 12.00 |
| *—Reissue with black label, dog near top* | | | |
| ❑ APL1-0998 | Young Americans | 1975 | 12.00 |
| *—At time of release, available with either orange or tan label* | | | |
| ❑ APL1-0998 | Young Americans | 1976 | 10.00 |
| *—Black label* | | | |
| ❑ AQK1-0998 | Young Americans | 1984 | 10.00 |
| *—Reissue* | | | |
| ❑ APL1-1327 | Station to Station | 1976 | 10.00 |
| *—Black label* | | | |
| ❑ APL1-1327 | Station to Station | 1976 | 12.00 |
| *—Originals have a brown label* | | | |
| ❑ AQK1-1327 | Station to Station | 1984 | 10.00 |
| *—Reissue* | | | |
| ❑ AFL1-1732 | Changesonebowie | 1978 | 10.00 |
| *—Reissue* | | | |
| ❑ APL1-1732 | Changesonebowie | 1976 | 10.00 |

| Number | Title (A Side/B Side) | Yr | NM |
|---|---|---|---|
| ❑ AQL1-1732 | Changesonebowie | 1984 | 10.00 |
| *—Reissue* | | | |
| ❑ APL1-2030 | Low | 1977 | 10.00 |
| ❑ AFL1-2522 | "Heroes" | 1977 | 10.00 |
| ❑ DJL1-2697 [DJ]Bowie Now | | 1978 | 60.00 |
| ❑ CPL2-2913 [(2)]Stage | | 1978 | 20.00 |
| ❑ DJL1-3016 [DJ]An Evening with David Bowie | | 1978 | 50.00 |
| *—Music and interview for "Superstars Radio Network"* | | | |
| ❑ AQL1-3254 | Lodger | 1979 | 10.00 |
| ❑ DJL1-3545 [DJ]1980 All Clear | | 1980 | 25.00 |
| *—Promo-only compilation* | | | |
| ❑ AQL1-3647 | Scary Monsters | 1980 | 10.00 |
| ❑ DJL1-3829 [DJ]College Radio Series | | 1980 | 25.00 |
| ❑ DJL1-3829-A [DJ]Special Radio Series | | 1980 | 25.00 |
| *—Same material as DJL1-3829* | | | |
| ❑ DJL1-3840 [DJ]Scary Monsters Interview | | 1980 | 20.00 |
| ❑ AYL1-3843 | The Rise and Fall of Ziggy Stardust and the Spiders from Mars | 1980 | 8.00 |
| *—Reissue* | | | |
| ❑ AYL1-3844 | Hunky Dory | 1980 | 8.00 |
| *—Reissue* | | | |
| ❑ AYL1-3856 | Low | 1980 | 8.00 |
| *—Reissue* | | | |
| ❑ AYL1-3857 | "Heroes" | 1980 | 8.00 |
| *—Reissue* | | | |
| ❑ AYL1-3889 | Diamond Dogs | 1980 | 8.00 |
| *—Reissue* | | | |
| ❑ AYL1-3890 | Aladdin Sane | 1980 | 8.00 |
| *—Reissue* | | | |
| ❑ AFL1-4202 | Changestwobowie | 1981 | 10.00 |
| ❑ AYL1-4234 | Lodger | 1981 | 8.00 |
| *—Reissue* | | | |
| ❑ CPL1-4346 [EP]David Bowie in Berthold Brecht's Baal | | 1982 | 10.00 |
| ❑ LSP-4623 | Hunky Dory | 1972 | 20.00 |
| ❑ AYL1-4653 | Pin Ups | 1982 | 8.00 |
| *—Reissue* | | | |
| ❑ AFL1-4702 | The Rise and Fall of Ziggy Stardust and the Spiders from Mars | 1977 | 10.00 |
| *—Reissue* | | | |
| ❑ LSP-4702 | The Rise and Fall of Ziggy Stardust and the Spiders from Mars | 1972 | 20.00 |
| *—Orange label* | | | |

| Number | Title (A Side/B Side) | Yr | NM |
|---|---|---|---|
| ❑ LSP-4702 | The Rise and Fall of Ziggy Stardust and the Spiders from Mars | 1975 | 12.00 |
| *—Tan label* | | | |
| ❑ AFL1-4792 | Golden Years | 1983 | 10.00 |
| ❑ LSP-4813 | Space Oddity | 1973 | 20.00 |
| *—Reissue of Mercury SR-61246; add 1/3 if bonus poster is enclosed* | | | |
| ❑ LSP-4816 | The Man Who Sold the World | 1973 | 20.00 |
| *—Reissue of Mercury SR-61325; add 1/3 if bonus poster is enclosed* | | | |
| ❑ AFL1-4852 | Aladdin Sane | 1977 | 10.00 |
| *—Reissue* | | | |
| ❑ LSP-4852 | Aladdin Sane | 1973 | 20.00 |
| *—Orange label is original (deduct 50% for tan labels)* | | | |
| ❑ CPL2-4862 [(2)]Ziggy Stardust, The Motion Picture | | 1983 | 20.00 |
| ❑ CPL2-4862 [(2)DJ]Ziggy Stardust, The Motion Picture | | 1983 | 50.00 |
| *—Promo version on clear vinyl* | | | |
| ❑ AFL1-4919 | Fame and Fashion | 1984 | 10.00 |
| **RYKO ANALOGUE** | | | |
| ❑ RALP 0120/1/2 [(6)]Sound + Vision | | 1989 | 80.00 |
| *—Six-LP box set on clear vinyl with three gatefold cardboard inner sleeves* | | | |
| ❑ RALP 0131 [(2)]Space Oddity | | 1990 | 20.00 |
| *—Clear vinyl with "Limited Edition" obi* | | | |
| ❑ RALP 0132 [(2)]The Man Who Sold the World | | 1990 | 20.00 |
| *—Clear vinyl with "Limited Edition" obi* | | | |
| ❑ RALP 0133 [(2)]Hunky Dory | | 1990 | 20.00 |
| *—Clear vinyl with "Limited Edition" obi* | | | |
| ❑ RALP 0134 [(2)]The Rise and Fall of Ziggy Stardust and the Spiders from Mars | | 1990 | 20.00 |
| *—Clear vinyl with "Limited Edition" obi* | | | |
| ❑ RALP 0135 | Aladdin Sane | 1990 | 20.00 |
| *—Clear vinyl with "Limited Edition" obi* | | | |
| ❑ RALP 0136 | Pin Ups | 1990 | 20.00 |
| *—Clear vinyl with "Limited Edition" obi* | | | |
| ❑ RALP 0137 | Diamond Dogs | 1990 | 20.00 |
| *—Clear vinyl with "Limited Edition" obi; genitals on dog are restored* | | | |
| ❑ RALP 0138/9 [(2)]David Live | | 1990 | 20.00 |
| *—Clear vinyl with "Limited Edition" obi* | | | |
| ❑ RALP 0171 [(2)]Changesbowie | | 1990 | 20.00 |
| *—Clear vinyl with "Limited Edition" obi* | | | |
| ❑ LSD-4702 [DJ] The Rise and Fall of Ziggy Stardust and the Spiders from Mars | | 1990 | 100.00 |
| *—Special promo-only package with both the LP and CD versions* | | | |

## BOWIE, LESTER Also see ART ENSEMBLE OF CHICAGO.

| Number | Title (A Side/B Side) | Yr | NM |
|---|---|---|---|
| **NESSA** | | | |
| ❑ N-1 | Numbers 1 and 2 | 1968 | 25.00 |

## BOWIE, PAT

| Number | Title (A Side/B Side) | Yr | NM |
|---|---|---|---|
| **PRESTIGE** | | | |
| ❑ PRLP-7385 [M]Out of Sight | | 1965 | 30.00 |
| ❑ PRST-7385 [S]Out of Sight | | 1965 | 30.00 |
| ❑ PRLP-7437 [M]Feelin' Good | | 1967 | 30.00 |
| ❑ PRST-7437 [S]Feelin' Good | | 1967 | 25.00 |

## BOWMAN, DON

| Number | Title (A Side/B Side) | Yr | NM |
|---|---|---|---|
| **LONE STAR** | | | |
| ❑ 4605 | Still Fighting Mental Health | 1979 | 15.00 |
| **RCA VICTOR** | | | |
| ❑ LPM-2831 [M] | Our Man in Trouble | 1964 | 20.00 |
| ❑ LSP-2831 [S] | Our Man in Trouble | 1964 | 25.00 |
| ❑ LPM-3345 [M] | Fresh from the Funny Farm | 1965 | 20.00 |
| ❑ LSP-3345 [S] | Fresh from the Funny Farm | 1965 | 25.00 |
| ❑ LPM-3495 [M] | Funny Way to Make an Album | 1966 | 20.00 |
| ❑ LSP-3495 [S] | Funny Way to Make an Album | 1966 | 25.00 |
| ❑ LPM-3646 [M] | Don Bowman Recorded Almost Live | 1966 | 20.00 |
| ❑ LSP-3646 [S] | Don Bowman Recorded Almost Live | 1966 | 25.00 |
| ❑ LPM-3795 [M] | From Mexico with Laughs Featuring the Tijuana Drum and Bugle Corps | 1967 | 25.00 |
| ❑ LSP-3795 [S] | From Mexico with Laughs Featuring the Tijuana Drum and Bugle Corps | 1967 | 20.00 |
| ❑ LPM-3920 [M] | Funny Folk Flops | 1968 | 50.00 |
| ❑ LSP-3920 [S] | Funny Folk Flops | 1968 | 20.00 |

## BOWN, PATTI

| Number | Title (A Side/B Side) | Yr | NM |
|---|---|---|---|
| **COLUMBIA** | | | |
| ❑ CL 1379 [M] | Patti Bown Plays Big Piano | 1959 | 30.00 |

## BOX TOPS, THE

| Number | Title (A Side/B Side) | Yr | NM |
|---|---|---|---|
| **BELL** | | | |
| ❑ 6011 [M] | The Letter/Neon Rainbow | 1967 | 25.00 |
| ❑ S-6011 [S] | The Letter/Neon Rainbow | 1967 | 20.00 |
| ❑ 6017 | Cry Like a Baby | 1968 | 20.00 |
| ❑ 6023 | Non-Stop | 1968 | 20.00 |
| ❑ 6025 | The Box Tops Super Hits | 1968 | 20.00 |
| ❑ 6032 | Dimensions | 1969 | 20.00 |
| **RHINO** | | | |
| ❑ RNLP-161 | The Greatest Hits | 1982 | 12.00 |

**BOXCAR WILLIE**

AHMC
❑ AA 118 Marty Martin Sings Country Music 1976 50.00
*—As "Marty Martin"; he changed his name to "Boxcar Willie" after one of his early songs*

MAIN STREET
❑ 9309 ... Not the Man I Used to Be 1984 10.00
❑ 73000 King of the Road 1981 12.00
❑ 73001 Last Train to Heaven 1982 12.00
❑ 73002 Best of Boxcar, Vol. 1 1982 12.00

**BOYCE, TOMMY**

RCA CAMDEN
❑ CAL-2202 [M] Tommy Boyce 1967 20.00
❑ CAS-2202 [S] Tommy Boyce 1967 25.00

**BOYCE, TOMMY, AND BOBBY HART**

A&M
❑ LP-126 [M] Test Patterns 1967 20.00
❑ LP-143 [M] I Wonder What She's Doing Tonite? 1968 30.00
❑ SP-4126 [S] Test Patterns 1967 20.00
❑ SP-4143 [S] I Wonder What She's Doing Tonite? 1968 20.00
❑ SP-4162 It's All Happening on the Inside 1968 20.00

**BOYD, BILL, AND HIS COWBOY RAMBLERS**

BLUEBIRD
❑ AXM2-5503 [(2)]Bill Boyd and His Cowboy Ramblers 197? 20.00

**BOYD, BILLY**

CROWN
❑ CST-196 [R] Twangy Guitars 196? 12.00
*—Black vinyl*
❑ CST-196 [R] Twangy Guitars 196? 50.00
*—Red vinyl*
❑ CLP-5170 [M] Twangy Guitars 1960 60.00
*—Black label, silver print*
❑ CLP-5170 [M] Twangy Guitars 1961 20.00
*—Gray label*

**BOYD, EDDIE**

EPIC
❑ BN 26409 7936 South Rhodes 1968 30.00

LONDON
❑ PS 554 I'll Dust My Broom 1969 30.00

**BOYD, JIMMY**

COLUMBIA
❑ CL 2543 [10] I Saw Mommy Kissing Santa Claus 1955 40.00
*—"House Party Series" reissue*
❑ CL 6270 [10] Christmas with Jimmy Boyd 1953 100.00

**BOYD, ROCKY**

JAZZTIME
❑ JS-001 [S] Ease It 1961 30.00
❑ JT-001 [M] Ease It 1961 25.00

**BOYER, CHARLES**

VALIANT
❑ VLM-5001 [M] Where Does Love Go? 1966 25.00
❑ VLS-25001 [S] Where Does Love Go? 1966 30.00

**BOYZ II MEN**

MOTOWN
❑ 31453 0323-1 [DJ]II 1994 25.00
*—Vinyl is promo only; in Motown company cover*
❑ 31453 0819-1 [(2)]Evolution 1997 12.00

**BRACE, JANET**

ABC-PARAMOUNT
❑ ABC-116 [M] Special Delivery 1956 50.00

**BRADFORD, ALEX**

CHECKER
❑ LP-10041 [M] Alex Bradford 196? 25.00

SPECIALTY
❑ SP-2108 [M] Too Close to Heaven 1959 100.00

VEE JAY
❑ LP-5023 [M] One Step 1962 40.00
❑ LP-5056 [M] The Soul of Alex Bradford 1964 40.00

**BRADFORD, BOBBY** Also see JOHN CARTER AND BOBBY BRADFORD.

EMANEM
❑ 3302 Love's Dream 1976 20.00

**BRADFORD, CLEA**

MAINSTREAM
❑ S-6042 [S] Clea Bradford Now 1965 30.00
❑ 56042 [M] Clea Bradford Now 1965 25.00

STATUS
❑ ST-8320 [M] Clea Bradford with Clark Terry 1965 40.00

TRU-SOUND
❑ TRU-15005 [M]These Dues 1962 50.00

**BRADFORD, PERRY**

CRISPUS ATTUCKS
❑ 101 [M] The Perry Bradford Story 1957 60.00

**BRADFORD, SCOTT**

PROBE
❑ 4509 Rock Slides 1969 20.00

**BRADLEY, OWEN**

CORAL
❑ CRL 56012 [10]Christmas Time 1950 80.00
❑ CRL 56022 [10]Strauss Waltzes 195? 60.00
❑ CRL 56035 [10]Lazy River 195? 60.00
❑ CRL 56047 [10]Singin' in the Rain 195? 60.00
❑ CRL 56065 [10]Cherished Hymns 195? 60.00
❑ CRL 57071 [M] Organ and Chimes Played by Owen Bradley 1956 30.00

DECCA
❑ DL 4078 [M] Paradise Island 1960 20.00
❑ DL 8652 [M] Joyous Bells of Christmas 1957 30.00
❑ DL 8724 [M] Bandstand Hop 1958 30.00
❑ DL 8868 [M] Big Guitar 1958 30.00
❑ DL 74078 [S] Paradise Island 1960 25.00
❑ DL 78868 [S] Big Guitar 1958 40.00

**BRADLEY, WILL**

EPIC
❑ LG 1005 [10] Boogie Woogie 1954 120.00
❑ LN 1127 [10] The House of Bradley 1954 120.00
❑ LN 3115 [M] Boogie Woogie 1955 50.00
❑ LN 3199 [M] The House of Bradley 1955 50.00

RCA VICTOR
❑ LPM-2098 [M] Big Band Boogie 1960 40.00
❑ LSP-2098 [S] Big Band Boogie 1960 50.00

WALDORF MUSIC HALL
❑ MH 33-122 [10]Jazz Encounter 195? 40.00
❑ MH 33-132 [10]Jazz — Dixieland and Chicago Style 195? 40.00

**BRADSHAW, EVANS**

RIVERSIDE
❑ RLP 12-263 [M]Look Out for Evans Bradshaw 1958 40.00
❑ RLP 12-296 [M]Pieces of Eighty-Eight 1959 40.00
❑ RLP-1136 [S] Pieces of Eighty-Eight 1959 30.00

**BRADSHAW, TERRY**

BENSON
❑ R-3702 Until You 1980 15.00

HEART WARMING
❑ 3735 Here in My Heart 1983 15.00

MERCURY
❑ SRM-1-1073 I'm So Lonesome I Could Cry 1976 20.00

**BRADSHAW, TINY**

KING
❑ 295-74 [10] Off and On 1955 1000.
❑ 395-501 [M] Selections 1956 700.00
❑ 653 [M] Great Composer 1960 300.00
❑ 953 [M] 24 Great Songs 1966 40.00

**BRADY BUNCH, THE**

PARAMOUNT
❑ PAS-5026 Merry Christmas from the Brady Bunch 1971 80.00
❑ PAS-6032 Meet the Brady Bunch 1972 50.00
❑ PAS-6037 The Kids from the Brady Bunch 1972 40.00
❑ PAS-6058 The Brady Bunch Phonograph Record 1973 80.00

**BRAFF, RUBY**

ABC-PARAMOUNT
❑ ABC-141 [M] Ruby Braff Featuring Dave McKenna 1956 40.00

AMERICAN RECORDING SOCIETY
❑ G-445 [M] Hey, Ruby 1957 40.00

BETHLEHEM
❑ BCP-5 [M] Omnibus 1955 50.00
❑ BCP-82 [M] Handful of Cool Jazz 1958 40.00
❑ BCP-1005 [10] Ruby Braff Quartet 1954 120.00
❑ BCP-1032 [10] Holiday in Braff 1955 100.00
❑ BCP-1034 [10] Ball at Bethlehem 1955 100.00
❑ BCP-6043 [M] The Best of Braff 1960 30.00

CONCERT HALL JAZZ
❑ 1210 [M] Little Big Horn 1955 50.00

EPIC
❑ LN 3377 [M] Braff! 1957 50.00

JAZZTONE
❑ J-1210 [M] Little Big Horn 1955 40.00

RCA VICTOR
❑ LPM-1008 [M] To Fred Astaire with Love 1955 50.00
❑ LPM-1332 [M] The Magic Horn of Ruby Braff 1956 40.00
❑ LPM-1510 [M] Hi-Fi Salute to Bunny 1957 40.00
❑ LPM-1966 [M] Easy Now 1959 30.00
❑ LSP-1966 [S] Easy Now 1959 40.00

STEREO-CRAFT
❑ RTN-507 [M] You're Getting to Be a Habit with Me 1959 30.00
❑ RTS-507 [S] You're Getting to Be a Habit with Me 1959 40.00

STORYVILLE
❑ STLP-320 [10] Hustlin' and Bustlin' 1955 80.00
❑ STLP-908 [M] Hustlin' and Bustlin' 1956 50.00

UNITED ARTISTS
❑ UAL-3045 [M] Blowing Around the Around 1959 30.00
❑ UAL-4093 [M] Ruby Braff-Marshall Brown Sextet 1960 30.00
❑ UAS-5093 [S] Ruby Braff-Marshall Brown Sextet 1960 40.00
❑ UAS-6045 [S] Blowing Around the Around 1959 40.00

VANGUARD
❑ VRS-8504 [M] The Ruby Braff Special 1955 40.00

WARNER BROS.
❑ W 1273 [M] Ruby Braff Goes Girl Crazy 1959 30.00
❑ WS 1273 [S] Ruby Braff Goes Girl Crazy 1959 40.00

**BRAFF, RUBY, AND ELLIS LARKINS**

VANGUARD
❑ VRS-8019 [10] Inventions in Jazz — Volume 1 1955 80.00
❑ VRS-8020 [10] Inventions in Jazz — Volume 2 1955 80.00
❑ VRS-8507 [M] Two By Two 1956 40.00
❑ VRS-8516 [M] Pocketful of Dreams 1957 40.00

**BRAFF, RUBY; PEE WEE RUSSELL; BOBBY HENDERSON**

VERVE
❑ MGV-8241 [M] The Ruby Braff Octet with Pee Wee Russell and Bobby Henderson at Newport 1958 50.00
❑ V-8241 [M] The Ruby Braff Octet with Pee Wee Russell and Bobby Henderson at Newport 1961 25.00

**BRAITH, GEORGE**

BLUE NOTE
❑ BLP-4148 [M] Two Souls in One 1963 40.00
*—With "New York, USA" on label*
❑ BLP-4161 [M] Soul Dream 1964 40.00
*—With "New York, USA" on label*
❑ BLP-4171 [M] Extension 1964 40.00
*—With "New York, USA" on label*
❑ BST-84148 [S] Two Souls in One 1963 50.00
*—With "New York, USA" on label*
❑ BST-84148 [S] Two Souls in One 1966 20.00
*—With "A Division of Liberty Records" on label*
❑ BST-84161 [S] Soul Dream 1964 50.00
*—With "New York, USA" on label*
❑ BST-84161 [S] Soul Dream 1966 20.00
*—With "A Division of Liberty Records" on label*
❑ BST-84171 [S] Extension 1964 50.00
*—With "New York, USA" on label*
❑ BST-84171 [S] Extension 1966 20.00
*—With "A Division of Liberty Records" on label*

PRESTIGE
❑ PRLP-7474 [M]Laughing Soul 1967 25.00
❑ PRST-7474 [S]Laughing Soul 1967 20.00
❑ PRLP-7515 [M]Musart 1967 25.00
❑ PRST-7515 [S]Musart 1967 20.00

**BRAND, DOLLAR** See ABDULLAH IBRAHIM.

**BRAND, OSCAR**

ABC-PARAMOUNT
❑ ABC-388 [M] Oscar Brand Sings for Adults 1961 25.00
❑ ABCS-388 [S] Oscar Brand Sings for Adults 1961 30.00

AUDIO FIDELITY
❑ AFLP-1806 [M] Bawdy Songs and Backroom Ballads, Vol. II 195? 25.00
❑ AFLP-1824 [M] Bawdy Songs and Backroom Ballads, Vol. III 195? 25.00
❑ AFLP-1847 [M] Bawdy Songs and Backroom Ballads, Vol. IV 195? 25.00
❑ AFLP-1884 [M] Bawdy Sea Shanties (Vol. 5) 1959 25.00
❑ AFLP-1906 [M] Bawdy Songs and Backroom Ballads, Vol. I 195? 25.00
❑ AFLP-1920 [M] Bawdy Western Songs (Vol. VI) 1960 25.00
❑ AFLP-1952 [M] Bawdy Songs Goes to College 1961 25.00
❑ AFLP-1966 [M] Rollicking Sea Shanties 1962 25.00
❑ AFLP-1971 [M] Sing Along Bawdy Songs and Backroom Ballads 1962 25.00
❑ AFLP-2121 [M] Bawdy Hootenanny 1964 20.00
❑ AFSD-5824 [S] Bawdy Songs and Backroom Ballads, Vol. III 196? 25.00

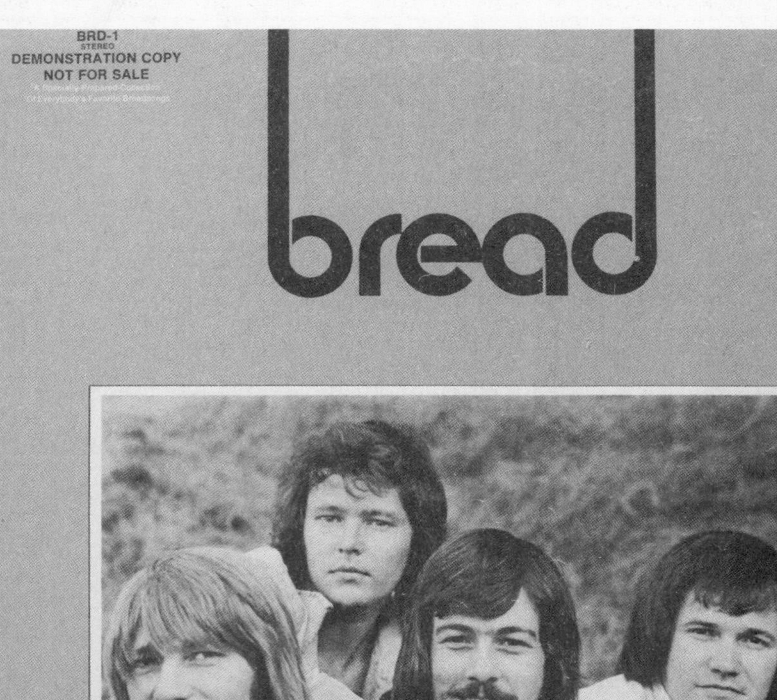


Bread, *Bread,* Elektra BRD-1, 1971, promo only, $20.

| Number | Title (A Side/B Side) | Yr | NM |
|---|---|---|---|
| ❑ AFSD-5847 [S] | Bawdy Songs and Backroom Ballads, Vol. IV | 195? | 25.00 |
| ❑ AFSD-5884 [S] | Bawdy Sea Shanties (Vol. 5) | 1959 | 30.00 |
| ❑ AFSD-5920 [S] | Bawdy Western Songs (Vol. VI) | 1960 | 30.00 |
| ❑ AFSD-5952 [S] | Bawdy Songs Goes to College | 1961 | 30.00 |
| ❑ AFSD-5966 [S] | Rollicking Sea Shanties | 1962 | 30.00 |
| ❑ AFSD-5971 [S] | Sing Along Bawdy Songs and Backroom Ballads | 1962 | 30.00 |
| ❑ AFSD-6121 [S] | Bawdy Hootenanny | 1964 | 25.00 |

CAEDMON

| Number | Title (A Side/B Side) | Yr | NM |
|---|---|---|---|
| ❑ TC 1658 | Singing Is Believing: Songs of the Advent Season | 1980 | 12.00 |

CHESTERFIELD

| Number | Title (A Side/B Side) | Yr | NM |
|---|---|---|---|
| ❑ CMS-101 [10] | Backroom Ballads | 195? | 50.00 |

DECCA

| Number | Title (A Side/B Side) | Yr | NM |
|---|---|---|---|
| ❑ DL 4275 [M] | Folk Songs for Fun | 1962 | 20.00 |
| ❑ DL 74275 [S] | Folk Songs for Fun | 1962 | 25.00 |

ELEKTRA

| Number | Title (A Side/B Side) | Yr | NM |
|---|---|---|---|
| ❑ EKL-168 [M] | The Wild Blue Yonder | 1959 | 20.00 |
| ❑ EKL-169 [M] | Every Inch a Sailor | 1960 | 20.00 |
| ❑ EKL-174 [M] | Tell It to the Marines | 1960 | 20.00 |
| ❑ EKL-178 [M] | Out of the Blue: Songs of a Fighting Airforce | 1960 | 20.00 |
| ❑ EKL-183 [M] | Boating Songs and All That Bilge | 1960 | 20.00 |
| ❑ EKL-188 [M] | Sports Car Songs for Big Wheels | 1960 | 25.00 |
| ❑ EKL-198 [M] | Up in the Air: Songs for the Madcap Airman | 1961 | 20.00 |
| ❑ EKL-204 [M] | For Doctors Only | 1961 | 20.00 |
| ❑ EKL-228 [M] | A Snow Job for Skiers | 1963 | 20.00 |
| ❑ EKL-237 [M] | Songs Fore Golfers | 1963 | 20.00 |
| ❑ EKL-242 [M] | Cough: Army Songs Out of the Barracks Bag | 1963 | 20.00 |
| ❑ EKS-7168 [S] | The Wild Blue Yonder | 1959 | 25.00 |
| ❑ EKS-7169 [S] | Every Inch a Sailor | 1960 | 25.00 |
| ❑ EKS-7174 [S] | Tell It to the Marines | 1960 | 25.00 |
| ❑ EKS-7178 [S] | Out of the Blue: Songs of a Fighting Airforce | 1960 | 25.00 |
| ❑ EKS-7183 [S] | Boating Songs and All That Bilge | 1960 | 25.00 |
| ❑ EKS-7188 [S] | Sports Car Songs for Big Wheels | 1960 | 30.00 |
| ❑ EKS-7198 [S] | Up in the Air: Songs for the Madcap Airman | 1961 | 25.00 |
| ❑ EKS-7204 [S] | For Doctors Only | 1961 | 25.00 |
| ❑ EKS-7228 [S] | A Snow Job for Skiers | 1963 | 25.00 |
| ❑ EKS-7237 [S] | Songs Fore Golfers | 1963 | 25.00 |
| ❑ EKS-7242 [S] | Cough: Army Songs Out of the Barracks Bag | 1963 | 25.00 |

FOLKWAYS

| Number | Title (A Side/B Side) | Yr | NM |
|---|---|---|---|
| ❑ FA 5280 [M] | Election Songs of the United States | 1960 | 25.00 |

KAPP

| Number | Title (A Side/B Side) | Yr | NM |
|---|---|---|---|
| ❑ KS-3629 | Oscar Brand "Live" On Campus | 1970 | 15.00 |

RIVERSIDE

| Number | Title (A Side/B Side) | Yr | NM |
|---|---|---|---|
| ❑ RLP 12-630 [M] | American Drinking Songs | 1956 | 30.00 |
| ❑ RLP 12-639 [M] | G.I. — American Army Songs | 195? | 30.00 |
| ❑ RLP 12-825 [M] | Absolute Nonsense | 195? | 30.00 |
| ❑ RLP 12-835 [M] | Songs Inane Only | 1959 | 30.00 |
| ❑ RLP 12-844 [M] | Songs of the U.S. Army | 1960 | 30.00 |
| ❑ RLP 1419 | Everybody Sing, Vol. 2 | 196? | 15.00 |
| ❑ RLP 1438 | Oscar Brand's Children's Concert | 196? | 15.00 |

ROULETTE

| Number | Title (A Side/B Side) | Yr | NM |
|---|---|---|---|
| ❑ SR-42060 | Brand X | 1971 | 15.00 |

TRADITION

| Number | Title (A Side/B Side) | Yr | NM |
|---|---|---|---|
| ❑ RLP 1014 [M] | Laughing America | 195? | 30.00 |
| ❑ TLP 1022 [M] | Pie in the Sky | 195? | 30.00 |
| ❑ TLP 2053 | The Best of Oscar Brand | 1967 | 20.00 |

**BRANDMEIER, JONATHON**

BRANDMEIER

| Number | Title (A Side/B Side) | Yr | NM |
|---|---|---|---|
| ❑ BPI 2004 | Almost Live | 1984 | 20.00 |

**BRASS ENSEMBLE OF THE JAZZ AND CLASSICAL MUSIC SOCIETY, THE**

COLUMBIA

| Number | Title (A Side/B Side) | Yr | NM |
|---|---|---|---|
| ❑ CL 941 [M] | Music for Brass | 1956 | 60.00 |

**BRASS RING, THE**

ABC DUNHILL

| Number | Title (A Side/B Side) | Yr | NM |
|---|---|---|---|
| ❑ DS-50034 | Gazpacho | 1968 | 12.00 |
| ❑ DS-50044 | Only Love | 1969 | 12.00 |
| ❑ DS-50051 | The Best of the Brass Ring | 1970 | 10.00 |

DUNHILL

| Number | Title (A Side/B Side) | Yr | NM |
|---|---|---|---|
| ❑ D 50008 [M] | Love Theme from The Flight of the Phoenix | 1966 | 12.00 |
| ❑ DS 50008 [S] | Love Theme from The Flight of the Phoenix | 1966 | 15.00 |
| ❑ D 50012 [M] | Lara's Theme | 1966 | 12.00 |
| ❑ DS 50012 [S] | Lara's Theme | 1966 | 15.00 |
| ❑ D 50015 [M] | Sunday Night at the Movies | 1967 | 12.00 |
| ❑ DS 50015 [S] | Sunday Night at the Movies | 1967 | 15.00 |
| ❑ D 50017 [M] | The Dis-Advantages of You | 1967 | 12.00 |
| ❑ DS 50017 [S] | The Dis-Advantages of You | 1967 | 15.00 |
| ❑ D 50023 [M] | The Now Sound | 1967 | 12.00 |
| ❑ DS 50023 [S] | The Now Sound | 1967 | 15.00 |
| ❑ ST-91039 [S] | Lara's Theme | 1966 | 20.00 |
| *—Capitol Record Club edition* | | | |

PROJECT 3

| Number | Title (A Side/B Side) | Yr | NM |
|---|---|---|---|
| ❑ 5067 | The Brass Ring | 1972 | 10.00 |

**BRASSELLE, KEEFE**

CORAL

| Number | Title (A Side/B Side) | Yr | NM |
|---|---|---|---|
| ❑ CRL 57295 [M] | Minstrel Man | 1959 | 20.00 |
| ❑ CRL 757295 [S] | Minstrel Man | 1959 | 25.00 |

**BRAUN, BOB**

DECCA

| Number | Title (A Side/B Side) | Yr | NM |
|---|---|---|---|
| ❑ DL 4339 [M] | Till Death Do Us Part | 1962 | 20.00 |
| ❑ DL 74339 [S] | Till Death Do Us Part | 1962 | 25.00 |

**BRAUTIGAN, RICHARD**

HARVEST

| Number | Title (A Side/B Side) | Yr | NM |
|---|---|---|---|
| ❑ ST-424 | Listening to Richard Brautigan | 1970 | 30.00 |

**BRAXTON, ANTHONY**

ARISTA

| Number | Title (A Side/B Side) | Yr | NM |
|---|---|---|---|
| ❑ AL 5002 [(2)] | The Montreux/Berlin Concerts | 1977 | 20.00 |

ARISTA FREEDOM

| Number | Title (A Side/B Side) | Yr | NM |
|---|---|---|---|
| ❑ AL 1902 [(2)] | The Complete Braxton 1971 | 1978 | 20.00 |

DELMARK

| Number | Title (A Side/B Side) | Yr | NM |
|---|---|---|---|
| ❑ DS-415 | Three Compositions of New Jazz | 1969 | 20.00 |
| ❑ DS-420/1 [(2)] | For Alto | 1971 | 25.00 |
| ❑ DS-428 | Together Alone | 1973 | 20.00 |
| *—With Joseph Jarman* | | | |

**BRAXTON, TONI**

LAFACE

| Number | Title (A Side/B Side) | Yr | NM |
|---|---|---|---|
| ❑ 26069 [(2)] | The Heat | 2000 | 20.00 |

**BRAZOS VALLEY BOYS, THE**

WARNER BROS.

| Number | Title (A Side/B Side) | Yr | NM |
|---|---|---|---|
| ❑ W 1664 [M] | Where Is the Circus | 1966 | 20.00 |
| ❑ WS 1664 [S] | Where Is the Circus | 1966 | 25.00 |
| ❑ W 1679 [M] | The Countrypolitan Sound | 1967 | 20.00 |
| ❑ WS 1679 [S] | The Countrypolitan Sound | 1967 | 25.00 |
| ❑ W 1686 [M] | The Gold Standard Collection | 1967 | 20.00 |
| ❑ WS 1686 [S] | The Gold Standard Collection | 1967 | 25.00 |

**BREAD**

ELEKTRA

| Number | Title (A Side/B Side) | Yr | NM |
|---|---|---|---|
| ❑ BRD-1 [DJ] | Bread | 1971 | 20.00 |
| *—In-store sampler; very similar to the future LP "The Best of Bread"* | | | |
| ❑ 6E-108 | The Best of Bread | 1977 | 8.00 |
| *—Reissue of 75056* | | | |
| ❑ 6E-110 | The Best of Bread, Volume 2 | 1977 | 8.00 |
| *—Reissue of 7E-1005* | | | |
| ❑ 7E-1005 | The Best of Bread, Volume 2 | 1974 | 12.00 |
| ❑ 7E-1094 | Lost Without Your Love | 1976 | 10.00 |
| ❑ EQ-5015 [Q] | Baby I'm-a Want You | 1974 | 20.00 |
| ❑ EQ-5056 [Q] | The Best of Bread | 1973 | 20.00 |
| ❑ 60414 | Anthology of Bread | 1985 | 10.00 |
| ❑ EKS-74044 | Bread | 1969 | 15.00 |
| *—Red label with large stylized "E"* | | | |
| ❑ EKS-74044 | Bread | 1971 | 10.00 |
| *—Butterfly label* | | | |
| ❑ EKS-74076 | On the Waters | 1970 | 15.00 |
| *—Red label with large stylized "E"* | | | |
| ❑ EKS-74076 | On the Waters | 1971 | 10.00 |
| *—Butterfly label* | | | |
| ❑ EKS-74086 | Manna | 1971 | 12.00 |
| ❑ EKS-75015 | Baby I'm-a Want You | 197? | 10.00 |
| *—Front photo is not raised* | | | |
| ❑ EKS-75015 | Baby I'm-a Want You | 1971 | 15.00 |
| *—Gatefold with raised photo on front* | | | |
| ❑ EKS-75047 | Guitar Man | 1972 | 12.00 |
| ❑ EKS-75056 | The Best of Bread | 1973 | 12.00 |

**BREAD, LOVE AND DREAMS**

LONDON

| Number | Title (A Side/B Side) | Yr | NM |
|---|---|---|---|
| ❑ PS 566 | Bread, Love and Dreams | 1969 | 30.00 |

**BREAM, JULIAN**

RCA VICTOR RED SEAL

| Number | Title (A Side/B Side) | Yr | NM |
|---|---|---|---|
| ❑ LSC-2448 [S] | The Art of Julian Bream | 1960 | 30.00 |
| *—Original with "shaded dog" label* | | | |
| ❑ LSC-2487 [S] | Giuliani: Guitar Concerto; Arnold: Guitar Concerto | 1961 | 30.00 |
| *—Original with "shaded dog" label* | | | |
| ❑ LDS-2560 [S] | The Golden Age of English Lute Music | 1961 | 25.00 |
| *—Original with "shaded dog" label* | | | |

| Number | Title (A Side/B Side) | Yr | NM |
|---|---|---|---|
| ❑ LSC-2606 [S] | Popular Classics for Spanish Guitar | 1962 | 25.00 |
| *—Original with "shaded dog" label* | | | |
| ❑ LDS-2656 [S] | An Evening of Elizabethan Music | 1962 | 40.00 |
| *—Original with "shaded dog" label* | | | |
| **BREEDLOVE, JIMMY** | | | |
| RCA CAMDEN | | | |
| ❑ CAL-430 [M] | Rock 'N' Roll Hits | 1958 | 40.00 |
| **BREEN, BOBBY** | | | |
| LONDON | | | |
| ❑ LB 270 [10] | Songs at Yuletide | 1953 | 50.00 |
| **BREGMAN, BUDDY** | | | |
| VERVE | | | |
| ❑ MGV-2042 [M] | Swingin' Kicks | 1957 | 50.00 |
| ❑ V-2042 [M] | Swingin' Kicks | 1961 | 20.00 |
| ❑ MGV-2064 [M] | Funny Face | 1958 | 50.00 |
| ❑ V-2064 [M] | Funny Face | 1961 | 20.00 |
| ❑ MGV-2093 [M] | The Gershwin Anniversary Album | 1959 | 50.00 |
| ❑ V-2093 [M] | The Gershwin Anniversary Album | 1961 | 20.00 |
| ❑ MGV-2094 [M] | Dig Buddy Bregman in Hi-Fi | 1959 | 50.00 |
| ❑ V-2094 [M] | Dig Buddy Bregman in Hi-Fi | 1961 | 20.00 |
| ❑ MGVS-6013 [S] | Swingin' Kicks | 1960 | 40.00 |
| WORLD PACIFIC | | | |
| ❑ ST-1024 [S] | Swingin' Standards | 1959 | 30.00 |
| ❑ WP-1263 [M] | Swingin' Standards | 1959 | 30.00 |
| **BRENDA AND THE TABULATIONS** | | | |
| CHOCOLATE CITY | | | |
| ❑ 2002 | I Keep Coming Back for More | 1977 | 10.00 |
| DIONN | | | |
| ❑ LPM-2000 [M] | Dry Your Eyes | 1967 | 40.00 |
| ❑ LPS-2000 [S] | Dry Your Eyes | 1967 | 50.00 |
| TOP & BOTTOM | | | |
| ❑ 100 | Brenda and the Tabulations | 1970 | 20.00 |
| **BRENNAN, WALTER** | | | |
| DOT | | | |
| ❑ DLP-3309 [M] | Dutchman's Gold | 1960 | 25.00 |
| ❑ DLP-25309 [S] | Dutchman's Gold | 1960 | 30.00 |
| EVEREST | | | |
| ❑ SDBR-1103 [S] | World of Miracles | 1960 | 30.00 |
| ❑ SDBR-1123 [S] | The President: A Musical Biography of Our Chief Executive | 1960 | 30.00 |
| ❑ LPBR-5103 [M] | World of Miracles | 1960 | 25.00 |
| ❑ LPBR-5123 [M] | The President: A Musical Biography of Our Chief Executive | 1960 | 25.00 |
| HAMILTON | | | |
| ❑ HLP-159 [M] | Dutchman's Gold | 1965 | 12.00 |
| ❑ HLP-12159 [S] | Dutchman's Gold | 1965 | 12.00 |
| LIBERTY | | | |
| ❑ LRP-3233 [M] | Old Rivers | 1962 | 20.00 |
| ❑ LRP-3241 [M] | The President: A Musical Biography of Our Chief Executive | 1962 | 15.00 |
| *—Reissue of Everest 5123* | | | |
| ❑ LRP-3244 [M] | World of Miracles | 1962 | 15.00 |
| *—Reissue of Everest 5103* | | | |
| ❑ LRP-3257 [M] | 'Twas the Night Before Christmas Back Home | 1962 | 20.00 |
| ❑ LRP-3266 [M] | Mama Sang a Song | 1963 | 20.00 |
| ❑ LRP-3317 [M] | Talkin' from the Heart | 1964 | 20.00 |
| ❑ LRP-3372 [M] | Gunfight at the O.K. Corral | 1964 | 20.00 |
| ❑ LST-7233 [S] | Old Rivers | 1962 | 25.00 |
| ❑ LST-7241 [S] | The President: A Musical Biography of Our Chief Executive | 1962 | 20.00 |
| *—Reissue of Everest 1123* | | | |
| ❑ LST-7244 [S] | World of Miracles | 1962 | 20.00 |
| *—Reissue of Everest 1103* | | | |
| ❑ LST-7257 [S] | 'Twas the Night Before Christmas Back Home | 1962 | 25.00 |
| ❑ LST-7266 [S] | Mama Sang a Song | 1963 | 25.00 |
| ❑ LST-7317 [S] | Talkin' from the Heart | 1964 | 25.00 |
| ❑ LST-7372 [S] | Gunfight at the O.K. Corral | 1964 | 25.00 |
| LONDON | | | |
| ❑ PS 577 | Yesterday, When I Was Young | 1970 | 15.00 |
| R.P.C. | | | |
| ❑ 108 [M] | By the Fireside | 1961 | 30.00 |
| ❑ 108S [S] | By the Fireside | 1961 | 40.00 |
| SUNSET | | | |
| ❑ SUM-1100 [M] | Country Heart | 1966 | 12.00 |
| ❑ SUS-5100 [S] | Country Heart | 1966 | 12.00 |
| ❑ SUS-5269 | God and Country | 1970 | 10.00 |
| UNITED ARTISTS | | | |
| ❑ UA-LA438-E | The Very Best of Walter Brennan | 1975 | 12.00 |

| Number | Title (A Side/B Side) | Yr | NM |
|---|---|---|---|
| **BREWER, TERESA** | | | |
| AMSTERDAM | | | |
| ❑ 12012 | The Doo Dah Song | 1973 | 10.00 |
| ❑ 12013 | Music, Music, Music | 1973 | 10.00 |
| ❑ 12015 | Teresa Brewer In London | 1974 | 10.00 |
| COLUMBIA | | | |
| ❑ FC 37363 | A Sophisticated Lady | 1981 | 10.00 |
| ❑ PC 37363 | A Sophisticated Lady | 198? | 8.00 |
| *—Budget-line reissue* | | | |
| CORAL | | | |
| ❑ CXB 7 [(2)M] | The Best of Teresa Brewer | 1965 | 20.00 |
| ❑ CXSB 7 [(2)P] | The Best of Teresa Brewer | 1965 | 20.00 |
| ❑ CRL 56072 [10] | A Bouquet of Hits | 1952 | 40.00 |
| ❑ CRL 56093 [10] | Till I Waltz Again with You | 1953 | 40.00 |
| ❑ CRL 57027 [M] | Music, Music, Music | 1955 | 30.00 |
| ❑ CRL 57053 [M] | Teresa | 1956 | 30.00 |
| ❑ CRL 57135 [M] | For Teenagers in Love | 1957 | 30.00 |
| ❑ CRL 57144 [M] | Teresa Brewer At Christmas Time | 1957 | 30.00 |
| ❑ CRL 57179 [M] | Miss Music | 1958 | 30.00 |
| ❑ CRL 57232 [M] | Time for Teresa | 1958 | 30.00 |
| ❑ CRL 57245 [M] | Teresa Brewer and the Dixieland Band | 1958 | 20.00 |
| ❑ 57297 [M] | Heavenly Lover | 1959 | 20.00 |
| ❑ CRL 57297 [M] | When Your Lover Has Gone | 1958 | 20.00 |
| ❑ CRL 57315 [M] | Ridin' High | 1960 | 20.00 |
| ❑ CRL 57329 [M] | Naughty, Naughty, Naughty | 1960 | 20.00 |
| ❑ CRL 57351 [M] | My Golden Favorites | 1960 | 20.00 |
| ❑ CRL 57361 [M] | Songs Everybody Knows | 1961 | 20.00 |
| ❑ CRL 57374 [M] | Aloha from Teresa | 1961 | 20.00 |
| ❑ CRL 57414 [M] | Don't Mess with Tess | 1962 | 20.00 |
| ❑ CRL 757245 [S] | Teresa Brewer and the Dixieland Band | 1958 | 30.00 |
| ❑ CRL 757297 [S] | When Your Lover Has Gone | 1959 | 30.00 |
| ❑ CRL 757315 [S] | Ridin' High | 1960 | 25.00 |
| ❑ CRL 757329 [S] | Naughty, Naughty, Naughty | 1960 | 25.00 |
| ❑ CRL 757351 [R] | My Golden Favorites | 1960 | 20.00 |
| ❑ CRL 757361 [S] | Songs Everybody Knows | 1961 | 25.00 |
| ❑ CRL 757374 [S] | Aloha from Teresa | 1961 | 25.00 |
| ❑ CRL 757414 [S] | Don't Mess with Tess | 1962 | 25.00 |
| DOCTOR JAZZ | | | |
| ❑ ASLP 804 | Good News | 198? | 10.00 |
| ❑ FW 38534 | I Dig Big Band Singers | 1983 | 10.00 |
| ❑ W2X 39521 [(2)] | Live at Carnegie Hall and Montreux, Switzerland | 1984 | 12.00 |
| ❑ FW 40232 | Midnight Café | 1986 | 10.00 |
| ❑ FW 40951 | Good News | 198? | 8.00 |
| FLYING DUTCHMAN | | | |
| ❑ BSL1-0577 | Good News | 1974 | 12.00 |
| LONDON | | | |
| ❑ APB-1006 [10] | Teresa Brewer | 1951 | 50.00 |
| PHILIPS | | | |
| ❑ PHM 200062 [M] | Teresa Brewer's Greatest Hits | 1962 | 15.00 |
| ❑ PHM 200099 [M] | Terrific Teresa | 1963 | 15.00 |
| ❑ PHM 200119 [M] | Moments to Remember | 1964 | 12.00 |
| ❑ PHM 200147 [M] | Golden Hits of 1964 | 1964 | 12.00 |
| ❑ PHM 200163 [M] | Dear Heart/Goldfinger | 1965 | 12.00 |
| ❑ PHM 200200 [M] | Songs for Our Fighting Men | 1966 | 12.00 |
| ❑ PHM 200216 [M] | Gold Country | 1966 | 12.00 |
| ❑ PHM 200230 [M] | Texas Leather and Mexican Lace | 1967 | 15.00 |
| ❑ PHS 600062 [S] | Teresa Brewer's Greatest Hits | 1962 | 20.00 |
| ❑ PHS 600099 [S] | Terrific Teresa | 1963 | 20.00 |
| ❑ PHS 600119 [S] | Moments to Remember | 1964 | 15.00 |
| ❑ PHS 600147 [S] | Golden Hits of 1964 | 1964 | 15.00 |
| ❑ PHS 600163 [S] | Dear Heart/Goldfinger | 1965 | 15.00 |
| ❑ PHS 600200 [S] | Songs for Our Fighting Men | 1966 | 15.00 |
| ❑ PHS 600216 [S] | Gold Country | 1966 | 15.00 |
| ❑ PHS 600230 [S] | Texas Leather and Mexican Lace | 1967 | 12.00 |
| PROJECT 3 | | | |
| ❑ 5108 | Come Follow the Band | 1982 | 10.00 |
| RCA VICTOR | | | |
| ❑ ANL1-1131 | The Best of Teresa Brewer | 1975 | 10.00 |
| SIGNATURE | | | |
| ❑ FW 39421 | Teresa Brewer In London | 1984 | 8.00 |
| *—Reissue of Amsterdam 12015* | | | |
| ❑ PW 40113 | Teresa Brewer At Christmas Time | 1985 | 10.00 |
| *—Reissue of Coral 57144* | | | |
| VOCALION | | | |
| ❑ VL 3693 [M] | Teresa Brewer | 1966 | 12.00 |
| ❑ VL 73847 [R] | Here's Teresa Brewer | 1969 | 10.00 |
| **BRIGADE, THE** | | | |
| BAND'N VOCAL | | | |
| ❑ 1066 | Last Laugh | 1970 | 2000. |
| *—VG value 1000; VG+ value 1500* | | | |
| **BRIGG** | | | |
| SUSQUEHANNA | | | |
| ❑ LP-301 | Brigg | 1973 | 180.00 |

| Number | Title (A Side/B Side) | Yr | NM |
|---|---|---|---|
| **BRIGGS, KAREN** | | | |
| VITAL | | | |
| ❑ VTL-009 | Karen | 1996 | 20.00 |
| **BRIGHT, RONNELL** | | | |
| REGENT | | | |
| ❑ MG-6041 [M] | Bright's Spot | 1957 | 100.00 |
| SAVOY | | | |
| ❑ MG-12206 [M] | Bright's Spot | 196? | 60.00 |
| *—Reissue of Regent LP* | | | |
| VANGUARD | | | |
| ❑ VRS-8512 [M] | Bright's Flight | 1957 | 100.00 |
| **BRIGHTER SIDE OF DARKNESS** | | | |
| 20TH CENTURY | | | |
| ❑ T-405 | Love Jones | 1973 | 30.00 |
| **BRIGMAN, GEORGE** | | | |
| SOLID | | | |
| ❑ SR-001 | Jungle Rot | 1975 | 120.00 |
| **BRILL, MARTY** | | | |
| MERCURY | | | |
| ❑ MG-20178 [M] | The Roving Balladeer | 1957 | 25.00 |
| **BRIMSTONE** | | | |
| BRIMSTONE | | | |
| ❑ (no #) | Paper Winged Dreams | 1968 | 200.00 |
| **BRINSLEY SCHWARZ** | | | |
| CAPITOL | | | |
| ❑ ST-589 | Brinsley Schwarz | 1970 | 20.00 |
| ❑ ST-744 | Despite It All | 1971 | 20.00 |
| ❑ SWBC-11869 [(2)] | Brinsley Schwarz | 1978 | 15.00 |
| LIBERTY | | | |
| ❑ LN 10145 | Silver Pistol | 1980 | 10.00 |
| *—10-track reissue* | | | |
| ❑ LN 10146 | Nervous on the Road | 1981 | 10.00 |
| *—10-track reissue* | | | |
| UNITED ARTISTS | | | |
| ❑ UAS-5566 | Silver Pistol | 1972 | 15.00 |
| ❑ UAS-5647 | Nervous on the Road | 1972 | 15.00 |
| **BRITT, ELTON** Also see THE BEVERLY HILL BILLIES. | | | |
| ABC-PARAMOUNT | | | |
| ❑ ABC-293 [M] | The Wandering Cowboy | 1959 | 25.00 |
| ❑ ABCS-293 [S] | The Wandering Cowboy | 1959 | 40.00 |
| ❑ ABC-322 [M] | Beyond the Sunset | 1960 | 25.00 |
| ❑ ABCS-322 [S] | Beyond the Sunset | 1960 | 40.00 |
| ❑ ABC-331 [M] | I Heard a Forest Praying | 1960 | 25.00 |
| ❑ ABCS-331 [S] | I Heard a Forest Praying | 1960 | 40.00 |
| ❑ ABC-521 [M] | The Singing Hills | 1965 | 25.00 |
| ❑ ABCS-521 [S] | The Singing Hills | 1965 | 40.00 |
| ❑ ABC-566 [M] | Somethin' for Everybody | 1966 | 25.00 |
| ❑ ABCS-566 [S] | Somethin' for Everybody | 1966 | 40.00 |
| RCA VICTOR | | | |
| ❑ LPM-1288 [M] | Yodel Songs | 1956 | 60.00 |
| ❑ LPM-2669 [M] | The Best of Elton Britt | 1963 | 25.00 |
| ❑ LPM-3222 [10] | Yodel Songs | 1954 | 120.00 |
| **BRITT, PAT** | | | |
| CRESTVIEW | | | |
| ❑ CR-3075 [M] | Jazz from San Francisco | 1967 | 20.00 |
| **BRITT, TINA** | | | |
| MINIT | | | |
| ❑ LP-24023 | Blue All the Way | 1968 | 20.00 |
| **BROCAS HELM** | | | |
| GARGOYLE | | | |
| ❑ 138801 | Black Death | 1988 | 50.00 |
| **BROCK, B., AND THE SULTANS** | | | |
| CROWN | | | |
| ❑ CST-399 [S] | Do the Beetle | 1964 | 50.00 |
| ❑ CLP-5399 [M] | Do the Beetle | 1964 | 40.00 |
| **BROCK, HERBIE** | | | |
| SAVOY | | | |
| ❑ MG-12066 [M] | Herbie Brock Solo | 1956 | 40.00 |
| ❑ MG-12069 [M] | Brock's Tops | 1956 | 40.00 |
| **BROKENSHA, JACK** | | | |
| SAVOY | | | |
| ❑ MG-12180 | And Then I Said | 1962 | 30.00 |
| **BROLIN, JAMES** | | | |
| ARTCO | | | |
| ❑ LPC-1099 | James Brolin Sings | 1974 | 25.00 |
| **BROOKLYN BRIDGE, THE** | | | |
| BUDDAH | | | |
| ❑ BDS-5034 | Brooklyn Bridge | 1969 | 20.00 |
| ❑ BDS-5042 | The Second Brooklyn Bridge | 1969 | 20.00 |

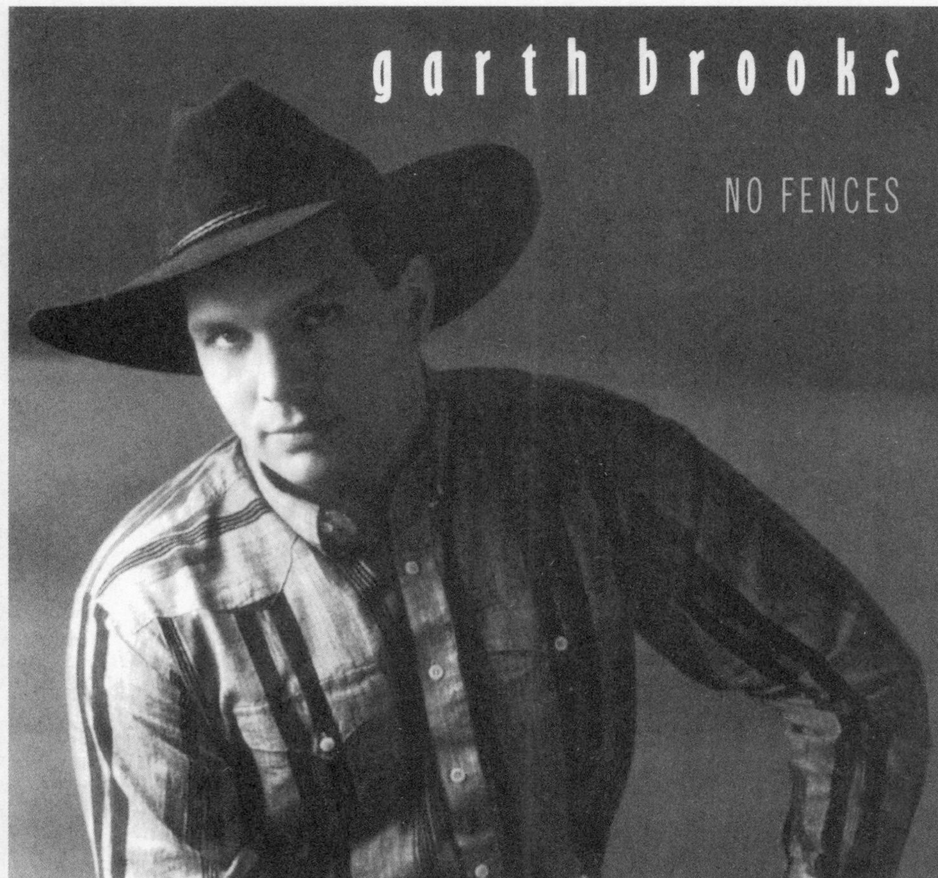


Garth Brooks, *No Fences,* Capitol Nashville R173266, 1991, BMG Direct Marketing edition, $60.

| Number | Title (A Side/B Side) | Yr | NM |
|---|---|---|---|
| ❑ BDS-5065 | The Brooklyn Bridge | 1970 | 20.00 |
| ❑ BDS-5107 | Bridge in Blue | 1972 | 20.00 |
| COLLECTABLES | | | |
| ❑ COL-5015 | The Greatest Hits | 198? | 12.00 |
| *—As "Johnny Maestro and the Brooklyn Bridge"* | | | |

**BROOKMEYER, BOB**

| Number | Title (A Side/B Side) | Yr | NM |
|---|---|---|---|
| ATLANTIC | | | |
| ❑ 1320 [M] | Portrait of the Artist | 1960 | 50.00 |
| *—Black label* | | | |
| ❑ 1320 [M] | Portrait of the Artist | 1961 | 25.00 |
| *—Multicolor label, white "fan" logo at right* | | | |
| ❑ SD 1320 [S] | Portrait of the Artist | 1960 | 50.00 |
| *—Green label* | | | |
| ❑ SD 1320 [S] | Portrait of the Artist | 1961 | 20.00 |
| *—Multicolor label, white "fan" logo at right* | | | |
| CLEF | | | |
| ❑ MGC-644 [M] | Bob Brookmeyer Plays Bob Brookmeyer and Some Others | 1955 | 100.00 |
| ❑ MGC-732 [M] | The Modernity of Bob Brookmeyer | 1956 | 70.00 |
| COLUMBIA | | | |
| ❑ CS 9037 [S] | Bob Brookmeyer and Friends | 1965 | 20.00 |
| MERCURY | | | |
| ❑ MG-20600 [M] | Jazz Is a Kick | 1960 | 25.00 |
| ❑ SR-60600 [S] | Jazz Is a Kick | 1960 | 30.00 |
| NEW JAZZ | | | |
| ❑ NJLP-8294 [M] | Revelation | 1963 | 50.00 |
| *—Purple label* | | | |
| ❑ NJLP-8294 [M] | Revelation | 1965 | 25.00 |
| *—Blue label, trident logo at right* | | | |
| PACIFIC JAZZ | | | |
| ❑ PJLP-16 [10] | Bob Brookmeyer Quartet | 1954 | 150.00 |
| PRESTIGE | | | |
| ❑ PRLP-214 [10] | Bob Brookmeyer with Jimmy Raney | 1955 | 150.00 |
| ❑ PRLP-7066 [M] | The Dual Role of Bob Brookmeyer | 1956 | 80.00 |
| STORYVILLE | | | |
| ❑ STLP-305 [10] | Bob Brookmeyer Featuring Al Cohn | 1954 | 300.00 |
| TODAY'S JAZZ | | | |
| ❑ J-1239 [M] | Bob Brookmeyer and Zoot Sims | 196? | 30.00 |
| UNITED ARTISTS | | | |
| ❑ UAL-4008 [M] | Kansas City Revisited | 1959 | 50.00 |
| ❑ UAS-5008 [S] | Kansas City Revisited | 1959 | 40.00 |
| VERVE | | | |
| ❑ MGV-8111 [M] | The Modernity of Bob Brookmeyer | 1957 | 50.00 |
| ❑ V-8111 [M] | The Modernity of Bob Brookmeyer | 1961 | 30.00 |
| ❑ MGV-8385 [M] | The Blues, Hot and Cold | 1960 | 50.00 |
| ❑ V-8385 [M] | The Blues, Hot and Cold | 1961 | 30.00 |
| ❑ V6-8385 [S] | The Blues, Hot and Cold | 1961 | 25.00 |
| ❑ V-8413 [M] | 7 X Wilder | 1961 | 50.00 |
| ❑ V6-8413 [S] | 7 X Wilder | 1961 | 50.00 |
| ❑ V-8455 [M] | Gloomy Sunday and Other Bright Moments | 1962 | 25.00 |
| ❑ V6-8455 [S] | Gloomy Sunday and Other Bright Moments | 1962 | 30.00 |
| ❑ V-8498 [M] | Trombone Jazz Samba | 1962 | 25.00 |
| ❑ V6-8498 [S] | Trombone Jazz Samba | 1962 | 30.00 |
| VIK | | | |
| ❑ LX-1071 [M] | Brookmeyer | 1957 | 50.00 |
| WORLD PACIFIC | | | |
| ❑ PJ-1233 [M] | Traditionalism Revisited | 1958 | 80.00 |

**BROOKMEYER, BOB, AND BILL EVANS**

| Number | Title (A Side/B Side) | Yr | NM |
|---|---|---|---|
| UNITED ARTISTS | | | |
| ❑ UAL-3044 [M] | The Ivory Hunters — Double Barreled Piano | 1959 | 50.00 |
| ❑ UAS-6044 [S] | The Ivory Hunters — Double Barreled Piano | 1959 | 40.00 |

**BROOKMEYER, BOB; JIM HALL; JIMMY RANEY**

| Number | Title (A Side/B Side) | Yr | NM |
|---|---|---|---|
| KIMBERLY | | | |
| ❑ 2021 [M] | Brookmeyer and Guitars | 1963 | 30.00 |
| ❑ 11021 [S] | Brookmeyer and Guitars | 1963 | 20.00 |
| WORLD PACIFIC | | | |
| ❑ PJ-1239 [M] | The Street Swingers | 1957 | 200.00 |
| ❑ WP-1239 [M] | The Street Swingers | 1958 | 120.00 |
| *—Reissue with new prefix* | | | |

**BROOKMEYER, BOB, AND ZOOT SIMS**

| Number | Title (A Side/B Side) | Yr | NM |
|---|---|---|---|
| JAZZTONE | | | |
| ❑ J-1239 [M] | Bob Brookmeyer and Zoot Sims | 1956 | 40.00 |
| STORYVILLE | | | |
| ❑ STLP-907 [M] | Tonight's Jazz Today | 1956 | 80.00 |
| ❑ STLP-914 [M] | Whoo-eeee! | 1956 | 80.00 |

**BROOKS, DONNA**

| Number | Title (A Side/B Side) | Yr | NM |
|---|---|---|---|
| DAWN | | | |
| ❑ DLP-1105 [M] | I'll Take Romance | 1956 | 120.00 |

**BROOKS, DONNIE**

| Number | Title (A Side/B Side) | Yr | NM |
|---|---|---|---|
| ERA | | | |
| ❑ EL-105 [M] | The Happiest | 1961 | 150.00 |

**BROOKS, GARTH**

| Number | Title (A Side/B Side) | Yr | NM |
|---|---|---|---|
| CAPITOL | | | |
| ❑ 1P-8042 | No Fences | 1990 | 40.00 |
| *—Columbia House version; cover photo is the size of CD cover* | | | |
| ❑ C1-90897 | Garth Brooks | 1989 | 25.00 |
| *—Non-record club edition* | | | |
| ❑ C1-590897 | Garth Brooks | 1989 | 20.00 |
| *—Columbia House edition* | | | |
| CAPITOL NASHVILLE | | | |
| ❑ R 173266 | No Fences | 1990 | 60.00 |
| *—BMG Direct Marketing version has a large cover photo* | | | |
| ❑ C1-596330 | Ropin' the Wind | 1991 | 50.00 |
| *—Only released on U.S. vinyl by Columbia House* | | | |

**BROOKS, HADDA**

| Number | Title (A Side/B Side) | Yr | NM |
|---|---|---|---|
| CROWN | | | |
| ❑ CLP-5010 [M] | Femme Fatale | 1957 | 60.00 |
| *—Black label; reissue of Modern LP* | | | |
| ❑ CLP-5374 [M] | Hadda Brooks Sings and Swings | 1963 | 25.00 |
| *—Gray label* | | | |
| MODERN | | | |
| ❑ MLP-1210 [M] | Femme Fatale | 1956 | 200.00 |

**BROOKS, HADDA / PETE JOHNSON**

| Number | Title (A Side/B Side) | Yr | NM |
|---|---|---|---|
| CROWN | | | |
| ❑ CLP-5058 [M] | Boogie | 1958 | 50.00 |

**BROOKS, JOHN BENSON**

| Number | Title (A Side/B Side) | Yr | NM |
|---|---|---|---|
| DECCA | | | |
| ❑ DL 5018 [M] | Avant Slant | 1968 | 40.00 |
| *—White label promo only; in stereo cover with "Monaural" sticker on front* | | | |
| ❑ DL 75018 [S] | Avant Slant | 1968 | 20.00 |
| RIVERSIDE | | | |
| ❑ RLP 12-276 [M] | The Alabama Concerto | 1958 | 50.00 |
| ❑ RLP-1123 [S] | The Alabama Concerto | 1959 | 40.00 |
| VIK | | | |
| ❑ LX-1083 [M] | Folk Jazz U.S.A. | 1957 | 40.00 |

**BROOKS, RANDY**

| Number | Title (A Side/B Side) | Yr | NM |
|---|---|---|---|
| DECCA | | | |
| ❑ DL 8201 [M] | Trumpet Moods | 195? | 30.00 |

**BROOKS, ROY**

| Number | Title (A Side/B Side) | Yr | NM |
|---|---|---|---|
| WORKSHOP JAZZ | | | |
| ❑ WSJ-220 [M] | Roy Brooks Beat | 1964 | 50.00 |
| ❑ WSJS-220 [S] | Roy Brooks Beat | 1964 | 60.00 |

**BROOKS, TINA**

| Number | Title (A Side/B Side) | Yr | NM |
|---|---|---|---|
| BLUE NOTE | | | |
| ❑ BLP-4041 [M] | True Blue | 1960 | 2000. |
| ❑ BLP-4052 [M] | Back to the Tracks | 1960 | — |
| *—Canceled* | | | |
| ❑ B1-28975 | True Blue | 1994 | 20.00 |
| ❑ BST-84041 [S] | True Blue | 1960 | — |
| *—Canceled* | | | |
| ❑ BST-84052 [S] | Back to the Tracks | 1960 | — |
| *—Canceled* | | | |
| ❑ BST-84052 [S] | Back to the Tracks | 199? | 40.00 |
| *—Classic Records reissue; first U.S. vinyl issue* | | | |
| MOSAIC | | | |
| ❑ MR4-106 [(4)] | The Complete Blue Note Recordings of the Tina Brooks Quintets | 1984 | 150.00 |

**BROONZY, BIG BILL**

| Number | Title (A Side/B Side) | Yr | NM |
|---|---|---|---|
| BIOGRAPH | | | |
| ❑ C-15 | Big Bill Broonzy 1932-1942 | 197? | 10.00 |
| CHESS | | | |
| ❑ LP-1468 [M] | Big Bill Broonzy and Washboard Sam | 1962 | 160.00 |
| COLUMBIA | | | |
| ❑ WL 111 [M] | Big Bill's Blues | 1958 | 100.00 |
| DIAL | | | |
| ❑ LP-306 [10] | Blues Concert | 1952 | 150.00 |

| Number | Title (A Side/B Side) | Yr | NM |
|---|---|---|---|
| **EMARCY** | | | |
| ❑ MG-26034 [10] | Folk Blues | 1954 | 120.00 |
| ❑ MG-36137 [M] | Blues by Broonzy | 1958 | 100.00 |
| **EPIC** | | | |
| ❑ EE 22017 [M] | Big Bill's Blues | 196? | 20.00 |
| **EVEREST ARCHIVE OF FOLK & JAZZ** | | | |
| ❑ 213 | Big Bill Broonzy | 1967 | 12.00 |
| **FOLKWAYS** | | | |
| ❑ FA-2315 [M] | Big Bill Broonzy | 1957 | 50.00 |
| ❑ FA-2326 [M] | Country Blues | 1957 | 50.00 |
| ❑ FG-3586 [M] | His Songs and Story | 195? | 50.00 |
| ❑ 31005 [R] | Big Bill Sings Country Blues | 196? | 15.00 |
| **GNP CRESCENDO** | | | |
| ❑ 10004 | Feeling Low Down | 1974 | 10.00 |
| ❑ 10009 | Lonesome Road Blues | 1975 | 10.00 |
| **MERCURY** | | | |
| ❑ MG-20822 [M] | Big Bill Broonzy — Memorial | 1963 | 30.00 |
| ❑ MG-20905 [M] | Remembering Big Bill Broonzy | 1964 | 30.00 |
| ❑ SR-60822 [R] | Big Bill Broonzy — Memorial | 1963 | 20.00 |
| ❑ SR-60905 [R] | Remembering Big Bill Broonzy | 1964 | 20.00 |
| **PERIOD** | | | |
| ❑ SLP-1114 [M] | Big Bill Broonzy Sings (Blues) | 1956 | 150.00 |
| ❑ SLP-1209 [M] | Big Bill Broonzy Sings and Josh White Comes a-Visiting | 1958 | 70.00 |
| **PORTRAIT MASTERS** | | | |
| ❑ RJ 44089 | Big Bill's Blues | 1988 | 15.00 |
| *—Reissue of Columbia 111* | | | |
| **SMITHSONIAN FOLKWAYS** | | | |
| ❑ SF-40023 | Big Bill Broonzy Sings Folk Songs | 1989 | 12.00 |
| **VERVE** | | | |
| ❑ MGV-3000-5 [(5)M] | The Big Bill Broonzy Story | 1959 | 200.00 |
| ❑ MGV-3001 [M] | Last Session, Vol. 1 | 1959 | 50.00 |
| ❑ MGV-3002 [M] | Last Session, Vol. 2 | 1959 | 50.00 |
| ❑ MGV-3003 [M] | Last Session, Vol. 3 | 1959 | 50.00 |
| **YAZOO** | | | |
| ❑ L-1011 | The Young Big Bill Broonzy | 1969 | 15.00 |
| ❑ L-1035 | Do That Guitar Rag | 197? | 15.00 |

### BROTH

| Number | Title (A Side/B Side) | Yr | NM |
|---|---|---|---|
| **MERCURY** | | | |
| ❑ SR-61298 | Broth | 1970 | 20.00 |

### BROTHER BONES

| Number | Title (A Side/B Side) | Yr | NM |
|---|---|---|---|
| **TEMPO** | | | |
| ❑ 7004 [M] | Bones on the Beat | 1958 | 150.00 |

### BROTHER FOX AND TAR BABY

| Number | Title (A Side/B Side) | Yr | NM |
|---|---|---|---|
| **CAPITOL** | | | |
| ❑ ST-544 | Brother Fox and Tar Baby | 1970 | 30.00 |
| **ORACLE** | | | |
| ❑ 1001 | Brother Fox and Tar Baby | 1969 | 30.00 |

### BROTHER MATTHEW

| Number | Title (A Side/B Side) | Yr | NM |
|---|---|---|---|
| **ABC-PARAMOUNT** | | | |
| ❑ ABC-121 | Brother Matthew | 1956 | 50.00 |

### BROTHERS FOUR, THE

| Number | Title (A Side/B Side) | Yr | NM |
|---|---|---|---|
| **COLUMBIA** | | | |
| ❑ CL 1402 [M] | The Brothers Four | 1960 | 12.00 |
| ❑ CL 1479 [M] | Rally 'Round the Brothers Four | 1960 | 12.00 |
| ❑ CL 1578 [M] | B.M.O.C. (Best Music On/Off Campus) | 1961 | 12.00 |
| ❑ CL 1625 [M] | Roamin' | 1961 | 12.00 |
| ❑ CL 1697 [M] | The Brothers Four Song Book | 1961 | 12.00 |
| ❑ CL 1803 [M] | The Brothers Four's Greatest Hits | 1962 | 12.00 |
| ❑ CL 1828 [M] | The Brothers Four: In Person | 1962 | 12.00 |
| ❑ CL 1946 [M] | Cross Country Concert | 1963 | 12.00 |
| ❑ CL 2033 [M] | The Big Folk Hits | 1963 | 12.00 |
| ❑ CL 2128 [M] | The Brothers Four Sing of Our Times | 1964 | 12.00 |
| ❑ CL 2213 [M] | More Big Folk Hits | 1964 | 12.00 |
| ❑ CL 2305 [M] | The Honey Wind Blows | 1965 | 12.00 |
| ❑ CL 2379 [M] | Try to Remember | 1965 | 12.00 |
| ❑ CL 2502 [M] | A Beatles' Songbook (The Brothers Four Sing Lennon/ McCartney) | 1966 | 15.00 |
| ❑ CL 2702 [M] | A New World's Record | 1967 | 15.00 |
| *—Corrected cover, with the guitarist using his right hand, as he does in real life* | | | |
| ❑ CL 2702 [M] | A New World's Record | 1967 | 25.00 |
| *—Original cover has a flopped image on the front cover, which makes it appear as if the guitarist is left-handed* | | | |
| ❑ CS 8197 [S] | The Brothers Four | 1960 | 15.00 |
| ❑ CS 8270 [S] | Rally 'Round the Brothers Four | 1960 | 15.00 |
| ❑ CS 8378 [S] | B.M.O.C. (Best Music On/Off Campus) | 1961 | 15.00 |
| ❑ CS 8425 [S] | Roamin' | 1961 | 15.00 |
| ❑ CS 8497 [S] | The Brothers Four Song Book | 1961 | 15.00 |
| ❑ CS 8603 | The Brothers Four's Greatest Hits | 1970 | 10.00 |
| *—Orange label* | | | |
| ❑ CS 8603 [S] | The Brothers Four's Greatest Hits | 1962 | 15.00 |
| *—Red "360 Sound" label* | | | |
| ❑ PC 8603 | The Brothers Four's Greatest Hits | 198? | 8.00 |
| *—Reissue with new prefix* | | | |
| ❑ CS 8628 [S] | The Brothers Four: In Person | 1962 | 15.00 |
| ❑ CS 8746 [S] | Cross Country Concert | 1963 | 15.00 |
| ❑ CS 8833 [S] | The Big Folk Hits | 1963 | 15.00 |
| ❑ CS 8928 [S] | The Brothers Four Sing of Our Times | 1964 | 15.00 |
| ❑ CS 9013 [S] | More Big Folk Hits | 1964 | 15.00 |
| ❑ CS 9105 [S] | The Honey Wind Blows | 1965 | 15.00 |
| ❑ CS 9179 [S] | Try to Remember | 1965 | 15.00 |
| ❑ CS 9302 [S] | A Beatles' Songbook (The Brothers Four Sing Lennon/ McCartney) | 1966 | 20.00 |
| ❑ CS 9502 [S] | A New World's Record | 1967 | 12.00 |
| *—Corrected cover, with the guitarist using his right hand, as he does in real life* | | | |
| ❑ CS 9502 [S] | A New World's Record | 1967 | 20.00 |
| *—Original cover has a flopped image on the front cover, which makes it appear as if the guitarist is left-handed* | | | |
| ❑ CS 9818 | Let's Get Together | 1969 | 12.00 |
| **FANTASY** | | | |
| ❑ 8400 | The Brothers Four 1970 | 1970 | 10.00 |
| **FIRST AMERICAN** | | | |
| ❑ 7705 | The Brothers Four Now | 1978 | 10.00 |
| ❑ 7722 [(2)] | Greenfields and Other Gold | 1980 | 12.00 |
| ❑ 7728 | New Gold | 1981 | 10.00 |
| **HARMONY** | | | |
| ❑ HS 11341 | Four Strong Winds | 1969 | 10.00 |
| ❑ H 31505 | Great Songs of Our Times | 1972 | 10.00 |

### BROWN, AL

| Number | Title (A Side/B Side) | Yr | NM |
|---|---|---|---|
| **AMY** | | | |
| ❑ A-1 [M] | Madison Dance Party | 1960 | 40.00 |
| ❑ AS-1 [S] | Madison Dance Party | 1960 | 50.00 |

### BROWN, ARTHUR, THE CRAZY WORLD OF

| Number | Title (A Side/B Side) | Yr | NM |
|---|---|---|---|
| **GULL** | | | |
| ❑ GU6-405 | Dance | 1975 | 12.00 |
| **PASSPORT** | | | |
| ❑ 98003 | Journey | 1974 | 12.00 |
| **TRACK** | | | |
| ❑ SD 8198 | The Crazy World of Arthur Brown | 1968 | 25.00 |

### BROWN, BOBBY

| Number | Title (A Side/B Side) | Yr | NM |
|---|---|---|---|
| **DESTINY** | | | |
| ❑ 4001 | Bobby Brown Live | 1972 | 100.00 |
| ❑ 4002 | The Enlightening Beam of Axonda | 1972 | 120.00 |

### BROWN, BOOTS / DAN DREW

| Number | Title (A Side/B Side) | Yr | NM |
|---|---|---|---|
| **GROOVE** | | | |
| ❑ LG-1000 [M] | Rock That Boat | 1955 | 300.00 |

### BROWN, BUSTER

| Number | Title (A Side/B Side) | Yr | NM |
|---|---|---|---|
| **COLLECTABLES** | | | |
| ❑ COL-5110 | Golden Classics: The New King of the Blues | 198? | 10.00 |
| **FIRE** | | | |
| ❑ FLP-102 [M] | The New King of the Blues | 1961 | 300.00 |
| *—Red and black label, white cover* | | | |
| ❑ FLP-102 [M] | The New King of the Blues | 1961 | 400.00 |
| *—Red and black label, purple cover* | | | |
| ❑ FLP-102 [M] | The New King of the Blues | 1961 | 700.00 |
| *—White and red label* | | | |
| **SOUFFLE** | | | |
| ❑ 2014 | Get Down | 1973 | 12.00 |

### BROWN, CHARLES

| Number | Title (A Side/B Side) | Yr | NM |
|---|---|---|---|
| **ALADDIN** | | | |
| ❑ LP-702 [10] | Mood Music | 1952 | 4000. |
| *—Black vinyl; VG value 1500; VG+ value 2750* | | | |
| ❑ LP-702 [10] | Mood Music | 1952 | 7500. |
| *—Red vinyl; VG value 3000; VG+ value 5250* | | | |
| ❑ LP-809 [M] | Mood Music | 1956 | — |
| *—Unreleased?* | | | |
| **ALLIGATOR** | | | |
| ❑ AL-4771 | One More for the Road | 1989 | 12.00 |
| **BIG TOWN** | | | |
| ❑ 1003 | Merry Christmas Baby | 1977 | 12.00 |
| ❑ 1005 | Music Maestro Please | 1978 | 10.00 |
| **BLUESWAY** | | | |
| ❑ BLS-6039 | Charles Brown — Legend | 1970 | 25.00 |
| **BULLSEYE BLUES** | | | |
| ❑ BB-9501 | All My Life | 1990 | 20.00 |
| **IMPERIAL** | | | |
| ❑ LP-9178 [M] | Charles Brown Sings Million Sellers | 1961 | 400.00 |
| **JEWEL** | | | |
| ❑ 5006 | Blues 'N' Brown | 1972 | 12.00 |
| **KING** | | | |
| ❑ 775 [M] | Charles Brown Sings Christmas Songs | 1961 | 150.00 |
| ❑ KS-775 [S] | Charles Brown Sings Christmas Songs | 1963 | 300.00 |
| *—Stereo copies (whether true stereo or rechanneled, we don't know) exist on blue labels with "King" in block letters (no crown)* | | | |
| ❑ 878 [M] | The Great Charles Brown | 1963 | 200.00 |
| **MAINSTREAM** | | | |
| ❑ S-6007 [S] | Boss of the Blues | 1965 | 30.00 |
| ❑ S-6035 [S] | Ballads My Way | 1965 | 30.00 |
| ❑ 56007 [M] | Boss of the Blues | 1965 | 20.00 |
| ❑ 56035 [M] | Ballads My Way | 1965 | 20.00 |
| **MOSAIC** | | | |
| ❑ MQ7-153 [(7)] | The Complete Aladdin Recordings of Charles Brown | 1994 | 150.00 |
| **SCORE** | | | |
| ❑ SLP-4011 [M] | Driftin' Blues | 1958 | 400.00 |
| ❑ SLP-4036 [M] | More Blues with Charles Brown | 1959 | — |
| *—Unreleased* | | | |

### BROWN, CHUCK AND THE SOUL SEARCHERS

Albums on Sussex are credited to "Soul Searchers."

| Number | Title (A Side/B Side) | Yr | NM |
|---|---|---|---|
| **SOURCE** | | | |
| ❑ SOR-3076 | Bustin' Loose | 1979 | 12.00 |
| ❑ SOR-3234 | Funk Express | 1980 | 15.00 |
| **SUSSEX** | | | |
| ❑ SXBS-7020 | We the People | 1972 | 100.00 |
| *—Reproductions exist* | | | |
| ❑ SRA-8030 | Salt of the Earth | 1974 | 100.00 |
| *—Reproductions exist* | | | |

### BROWN, CLIFFORD

| Number | Title (A Side/B Side) | Yr | NM |
|---|---|---|---|
| **BLUE NOTE** | | | |
| ❑ BLP-1526 [M] | Clifford Brown Memorial Album | 1956 | 150.00 |
| *—Regular edition, Lexington Ave. address on label* | | | |
| ❑ BLP-1526 [M] | Clifford Brown Memorial Album | 1956 | 200.00 |
| *—"Deep groove" version (deep indentation under label on both sides)* | | | |
| ❑ BLP-1526 [M] | Clifford Brown Memorial Album | 196? | 25.00 |
| *—With "New York, USA" address on label* | | | |
| ❑ BLP-1526 [M] | Clifford Brown Memorial Album | 196? | 50.00 |
| *—With W. 63rd St. address on label* | | | |
| ❑ BLP-5032 [10] | New Star on the Horizon | 1953 | 500.00 |
| ❑ BLP-5047 [10] | Clifford Brown Quartet | 1954 | 500.00 |
| **EMARCY** | | | |
| ❑ MG-36005 [M] | Clifford Brown with Strings | 1955 | 120.00 |
| ❑ MG-36102 [M] | Clifford Brown All Stars | 1956 | 120.00 |
| **JAZZTONE** | | | |
| ❑ J-1281 [M] | Jazz Messages | 195? | 40.00 |
| **LIMELIGHT** | | | |
| ❑ 2-8201 [(2)M] | The Immortal Clifford Brown | 1965 | 40.00 |
| ❑ 2-8601 [(2)R] | The Immortal Clifford Brown | 1965 | 25.00 |
| **MERCURY** | | | |
| ❑ MG-20827 [M] | Remember Clifford | 1963 | 40.00 |
| ❑ SR-60827 [R] | Remember Clifford | 1963 | 25.00 |
| **MOSAIC** | | | |
| ❑ MR5-104 [(5)] | The Complete Blue Note and Pacific Jazz Recordings of Clifford Brown | 198? | 80.00 |
| **PACIFIC JAZZ** | | | |
| ❑ PJ-3 [M] | Jazz Immortal | 1956 | 150.00 |
| ❑ PJLP-19 [10] | The Clifford Brown Ensemble | 1955 | 300.00 |
| **PRESTIGE** | | | |
| ❑ PRLP-7055 [M] | Clifford Brown Memorial | 1956 | 80.00 |
| ❑ PRLP-16008 [M] | Clifford Brown | 1964 | 40.00 |

### BROWN, CLIFFORD, AND ART FARMER

| Number | Title (A Side/B Side) | Yr | NM |
|---|---|---|---|
| **PRESTIGE** | | | |
| ❑ PRLP-167 [10] | Clifford Brown and Art Farmer with the Swedish All Stars | 1953 | 300.00 |

### BROWN, CLIFFORD, AND MAX ROACH

| Number | Title (A Side/B Side) | Yr | NM |
|---|---|---|---|
| **EMARCY** | | | |
| ❑ MG-26043 [10] | Clifford Brown and Max Roach | 1954 | 600.00 |
| ❑ MG-36008 [M] | Brown and Roach Incorporated | 1955 | 200.00 |
| ❑ MG-36036 [M] | Clifford Brown and Max Roach | 1955 | 200.00 |
| ❑ MG-36037 [M] | A Study in Brown | 1955 | 500.00 |
| ❑ MG-36070 [M] | Clifford Brown and Max Roach ar Basin Street | 1956 | 200.00 |
| **GENE NORMAN** | | | |
| ❑ GNP-5 [10] | Clifford Brown and Max Roach, Vol. 1 | 1954 | 300.00 |
| ❑ GNP-7 [10] | Clifford Brown and Max Roach, Vol. 2 | 1954 | 300.00 |
| ❑ GNP-18 [M] | The Best of Max Roach and Clifford Brown In Concert | 1955 | 250.00 |
| ❑ GNP-125 [10] | Gene Norman Presents Max Roach and Clifford Brown | 1954 | 400.00 |

| Number | Title (A Side/B Side) | Yr | NM |
|---|---|---|---|

## BROWN, HYLO

**CAPITOL**

| Number | Title (A Side/B Side) | Yr | NM |
|---|---|---|---|
| ❑ T 1168 [M] | Hylo Brown | 1959 | 80.00 |

**STARDAY**

| Number | Title (A Side/B Side) | Yr | NM |
|---|---|---|---|
| ❑ SLP-185 [M] | Bluegrass Balladeer | 1962 | 40.00 |
| ❑ SLP-204 [M] | Bluegrass Goes to College | 1962 | 40.00 |
| ❑ SLP-220 [M] | Hylo Brown Meets the Lonesome Pine Fiddlers | 1963 | 40.00 |
| ❑ SLP-249 [M] | Sing Me a Bluegrass Song | 1963 | 40.00 |

## BROWN, JAMES

**HRB**

| Number | Title (A Side/B Side) | Yr | NM |
|---|---|---|---|
| ❑ 1004 [(2)] | The Fabulous James Brown | 1974 | 25.00 |

**KING**

| Number | Title (A Side/B Side) | Yr | NM |
|---|---|---|---|
| ❑ 610 [M] | Please Please Please | 1958 | 1200. |
| *—"Woman's and man's legs" cover; "King" on label is two inches wide* | | | |
| ❑ 610 [M] | Please Please Please | 1961 | 1000. |
| *—"Woman's and man's legs" cover; "King" on label is three inches wide* | | | |
| ❑ 635 [M] | Try Me! | 1959 | 900.00 |
| *—"Woman with cigarette and gun" cover; "King" on label is two inches wide* | | | |
| ❑ 635 [M] | Try Me! | 1961 | 600.00 |
| *—"Woman with cigarette and gun" cover; "King" on label is three inches wide* | | | |
| ❑ 683 [M] | Think! | 1960 | 900.00 |
| *—"Baby" cover; "King" on label is two inches wide* | | | |
| ❑ 683 [M] | Think! | 1961 | 600.00 |
| *—"Baby" cover; "King" on label is three inches wide* | | | |
| ❑ 683 [M] | Think! | 1963 | 100.00 |
| *—James Brown photo cover; "crownless" King label* | | | |
| ❑ 683 [M] | Think! | 1966 | 50.00 |
| *—James Brown photo cover; "crown" King label* | | | |
| ❑ 743 [M] | The Amazing James Brown | 1961 | 500.00 |
| *—"James Brown in suit" cover* | | | |
| ❑ 743 [M] | The Amazing James Brown | 1963 | 150.00 |
| *—White title cover; "crownless" King label* | | | |
| ❑ 743 [M] | The Amazing James Brown | 1966 | 500.00 |
| *—White title cover with "James Brown" in huge letters; "crown" King label* | | | |
| ❑ 771 [M] | Night Train | 1961 | 300.00 |
| *—Original title* | | | |
| ❑ 771 [M] | Twist Around | 1962 | 250.00 |
| *—Second title* | | | |
| ❑ 771 [M] | Jump Around | 1963 | 200.00 |
| *—Third title* | | | |
| ❑ KS-771 [S] | Jump Around | 1963 | 300.00 |
| *—Stereo copies of King 771 only exist with this title* | | | |
| ❑ 780 [M] | Good Good Twistin' | 1962 | 200.00 |
| *—"Good Good Twistin' " on either label or cover, or both* | | | |
| ❑ 780 [M] | Shout and Shimmy | 1962 | 250.00 |
| *—"Shout and Shimmy" on both cover and label* | | | |
| ❑ 780 [M] | Excitement | 1963 | 150.00 |
| *—Third title; "crownless" King label* | | | |
| ❑ 780 [M] | Excitement | 1966 | 50.00 |
| *—Third title; "crown" King label* | | | |
| ❑ 804 [M] | James Brown & His Famous Flames Tour the U.S.A. | 1962 | 250.00 |
| *—"Crownless" King label* | | | |
| ❑ 804 [M] | James Brown & His Famous Flames Tour the U.S.A. | 1966 | 50.00 |
| *—"Crown" King label* | | | |
| ❑ 826 [M] | Live at the Apollo | 1963 | 150.00 |
| *—Other King albums on back cover; "crownless" King label* | | | |
| ❑ 826 [M] | Live at the Apollo | 1963 | 200.00 |
| *—Custom back cover; "crownless" King label* | | | |
| ❑ 826 [M] | Live at the Apollo | 1963 | 800.00 |
| *—White label promo, banded for airplay* | | | |
| ❑ 826 [M] | Live at the Apollo | 1966 | 50.00 |
| *—"Crown" King label* | | | |
| ❑ KS-826 [S] | Live at the Apollo | 1963 | 200.00 |
| *—Other King albums on back cover; "crownless" King label* | | | |
| ❑ KS-826 [S] | Live at the Apollo | 1963 | 300.00 |
| *—Custom back cover; "crownless" King label* | | | |
| ❑ KS-826 [S] | Live at the Apollo | 1966 | 70.00 |
| *—"Crown" King label* | | | |
| ❑ 851 [M] | Prisoner of Love | 1963 | 100.00 |
| *—Other King albums on back cover; "crownless" King label* | | | |
| ❑ 851 [M] | Prisoner of Love | 1963 | 200.00 |
| *—Custom back cover; "crownless" King label* | | | |
| ❑ 851 [M] | Prisoner of Love | 1966 | 50.00 |
| *—"Crown" King label* | | | |
| ❑ 883 [M] | Pure Dynamite! Live at the Royal | 1964 | 200.00 |
| *—"Crownless" King label* | | | |
| ❑ 883 [M] | Pure Dynamite! Live at the Royal | 1964 | 800.00 |
| *—White label promo; banded for airplay* | | | |
| ❑ 883 [M] | Pure Dynamite! Live at the Royal | 1966 | 50.00 |
| *—"Crown" King label* | | | |
| ❑ 909 [M] | Please Please Please | 1964 | 100.00 |
| *—Reissue of 610; "crownless" King label* | | | |
| ❑ 909 [M] | Please Please Please | 1966 | 50.00 |
| *—"Crown" King label* | | | |
| ❑ 919 [M] | The Unbeatable James Brown — 16 Hits | 1964 | 100.00 |
| *—Reissue of 635; "crownless" King label* | | | |
| ❑ 919 [M] | The Unbeatable James Brown — 16 Hits | 1966 | 50.00 |
| *—"Crown" King label* | | | |
| ❑ 938 [M] | Papa's Got a Brand New Bag | 1965 | 80.00 |
| *—Red cover; "crownless" King label* | | | |
| ❑ 938 [M] | Papa's Got a Brand New Bag | 1966 | 40.00 |
| *—"Crown" King label* | | | |
| ❑ 938 [M] | Papa's Got a Brand New Bag | 1966 | 50.00 |
| *—Green cover; "crownless" King label* | | | |
| ❑ LPS-938 [P] | Papa's Got a Brand New Bag | 1965 | 100.00 |
| *—Red cover; "crownless" King label* | | | |
| ❑ LPS-938 [P] | Papa's Got a Brand New Bag | 1966 | 50.00 |
| *—"Crown" King label* | | | |
| ❑ LPS-938 [P] | Papa's Got a Brand New Bag | 1966 | 60.00 |
| *—Green cover; "crownless" King label* | | | |
| ❑ 946 [M] | I Got You (I Feel Good) | 1966 | 40.00 |
| *—"Crown" King label* | | | |
| ❑ 946 [M] | I Got You (I Feel Good) | 1966 | 100.00 |
| *—"Crownless" King label* | | | |
| ❑ LPS-946 [S] | I Got You (I Feel Good) | 1966 | 50.00 |
| *—"Crown" King label* | | | |
| ❑ LPS-946 [S] | I Got You (I Feel Good) | 1966 | 150.00 |
| *—"Crownless" King label* | | | |
| ❑ 961 [M] | Mighty Instrumentals | 1966 | 100.00 |
| ❑ LPS-961 [S] | Mighty Instrumentals | 1966 | 150.00 |
| ❑ 985 [M] | It's a Man's Man's Man's World | 1966 | 50.00 |
| ❑ KS-985 [S] | It's a Man's Man's Man's World | 1966 | 70.00 |
| ❑ 1010 [M] | Christmas Songs | 1966 | 100.00 |
| *—Wreath on gray wall, no song titles on back* | | | |
| ❑ 1010 [M] | Christmas Songs | 1967 | 80.00 |
| *—Wreath on white wall, song titles are on back* | | | |
| ❑ KS-1010 [S] | Christmas Songs | 1966 | 150.00 |
| *—Wreath on gray wall, no song titles on back* | | | |
| ❑ KS-1010 [S] | Christmas Songs | 1967 | 100.00 |
| *—Wreath on white wall, song titles are on back* | | | |
| ❑ 1016 [M] | Raw Soul | 1967 | 50.00 |
| ❑ KS-1016 [P] | Raw Soul | 1967 | 70.00 |
| ❑ 1018 [M] | Live at the Garden | 1967 | 80.00 |
| ❑ 1018 [M] | Live at the Garden | 1967 | 400.00 |
| *—Black label promo; banded for airplay* | | | |
| ❑ KS-1018 [S] | Live at the Garden | 1967 | 100.00 |
| ❑ 1020 [M] | Cold Sweat | 1967 | 50.00 |
| ❑ KS-1020 [S] | Cold Sweat | 1967 | 70.00 |
| ❑ LPS-1022 [(2)] | Live at the Apollo, Volume II | 1968 | 70.00 |
| ❑ LPS-1024 | James Brown Presents His Show of Tomorrow | 1968 | 50.00 |
| *—Various-artists album* | | | |
| ❑ LPS-1030 | I Can't Stand Myself (When You Touch Me) | 1968 | 50.00 |
| ❑ LPS-1031 | I Got the Feelin' | 1968 | 50.00 |
| ❑ LPS-1034 | James Brown Plays Nothing But Soul | 1968 | 50.00 |
| ❑ LPS-1038 | Thinking About Little Willie John and a Few Nice Things | 1968 | 50.00 |
| ❑ KS-1040 | A Soulful Christmas | 1968 | 80.00 |
| ❑ KS-1047 | Say It Loud — I'm Black and I'm Proud | 1969 | 50.00 |
| ❑ KS-1051 | Gettin' Down To It | 1969 | 50.00 |
| ❑ KSD-1055 | James Brown Plays & Directs The Popcorn | 1969 | 40.00 |
| ❑ KSD-1063 | It's a Mother | 1969 | 40.00 |
| ❑ KSD-1092 | Ain't It Funky | 1970 | 40.00 |
| ❑ KSD-1095 | It's a New Day So Let a Man Come In | 1970 | 40.00 |
| ❑ KSD-1100 | Soul on Top | 1970 | 40.00 |
| ❑ KSD-1110 | Sho Is Funky Down Here | 1971 | 40.00 |
| ❑ KSD-1115 [(2)] | Sex Machine | 1970 | 50.00 |
| ❑ KSD-1124 | Hey America! | 1970 | 40.00 |
| ❑ KSD-1127 | Super Bad | 1971 | 40.00 |

**POLYDOR**

| Number | Title (A Side/B Side) | Yr | NM |
|---|---|---|---|
| ❑ 25-3003 [(2)] | Revolution of the Mind — Live at the Apollo, Volume III | 1971 | 60.00 |
| ❑ PD2-3004 [(2)] | Get On the Good Foot | 1972 | 60.00 |
| ❑ PD2-3007 [(2)] | The Payback | 1973 | 50.00 |
| ❑ 24-4054 | Hot Pants | 1971 | 40.00 |
| ❑ PD-5028 | There It Is | 1972 | 40.00 |
| ❑ SC-5401 | James Brown Soul Classics | 1972 | 25.00 |
| ❑ SC-5402 | Soul Classics, Volume 2 | 1973 | 25.00 |
| ❑ PD-6014 | Black Caesar | 1973 | 50.00 |
| ❑ PD-6015 | Slaughter's Big Rip-Off | 1973 | 50.00 |
| ❑ PD-1-6039 | Reality | 1975 | 40.00 |
| ❑ PD-1-6042 | Sex Machine Today | 1975 | 40.00 |
| ❑ PD-1-6054 | Everybody's Doin' the Hustle & Dead On the Double Bump | 1975 | 40.00 |
| ❑ PD-1-6059 | Hot | 1976 | 40.00 |
| ❑ PD-1-6071 | Get Up Offa That Thing | 1976 | 40.00 |
| ❑ PD-1-6093 | Bodyheat | 1976 | 40.00 |
| ❑ PD-1-6111 | Mutha's Nature | 1977 | 40.00 |
| ❑ PD-1-6140 | Jam/1980s | 1978 | 40.00 |
| ❑ PD-1-6181 | Take a Look at Those Cakes | 1978 | 30.00 |
| ❑ PD-1-6212 | The Original Disco Man | 1979 | 30.00 |
| ❑ PD-1-6258 | People | 1980 | 30.00 |
| ❑ PD-2-6290 [(2)] | James Brown...Live/Hot on the One | 1980 | 50.00 |
| ❑ PD-1-6318 | Nonstop! | 1981 | 30.00 |
| ❑ PD-1-6340 | The Best of James Brown | 1981 | 20.00 |
| ❑ PD-2-9001 [(2)] | Hell | 1974 | 80.00 |
| ❑ PD-2-9004 [(2)] | Sex Machine Live | 1976 | 50.00 |
| ❑ 821231-1 | Ain't That a Groove: The James Brown Story 1966-1969 | 1984 | 15.00 |
| ❑ 821232-1 | Doing It to Death: The James Brown Story 1970-1973 | 1984 | 15.00 |
| ❑ 823275-1 | The Best of James Brown | 1984 | 12.00 |
| *—Reissue of 6340* | | | |
| ❑ 827439-1 | Dead on the Heavy Funk: The James Brown Story 1974-1978 | 1985 | 15.00 |
| ❑ 829254-1 [(2)] | Solid Gold: 30 Golden Hits | 1985 | 20.00 |
| ❑ 829417-1 | James Brown's Funky People | 1986 | 15.00 |
| *—Various-artists LP* | | | |
| ❑ 829624-1 | In the Jungle Groove | 1986 | 15.00 |
| ❑ 835857-1 | James Brown's Funky People 2 | 1988 | 15.00 |
| *—Various-artists compilation* | | | |
| ❑ 837126-1 | Motherlode | 1988 | 15.00 |

**RHINO**

| Number | Title (A Side/B Side) | Yr | NM |
|---|---|---|---|
| ❑ RNLP-217 | Live at the Apollo, Volume 2, Part 1 | 1985 | 15.00 |
| ❑ RNLP-218 | Live at the Apollo, Volume 2, Part 2 | 1985 | 15.00 |
| ❑ RNLP-219 | Greatest Hits (1964-1968) | 1986 | 15.00 |
| ❑ R1 70194 | Santa's Got a Brand New Bag | 1986 | 10.00 |
| *—Reissue of King material* | | | |
| ❑ R1-70217 | Live at the Apollo, Volume 2, Part 1 | 1988 | 12.00 |
| *—Reissue of 217* | | | |
| ❑ R1-70218 | Live at the Apollo, Volume 2, Part 2 | 1988 | 12.00 |
| *—Reissue of 218* | | | |
| ❑ R1-70219 | Greatest Hits (1964-1968) | 1988 | 12.00 |
| *—Reissue of 219* | | | |

**SCOTTI BROTHERS**

| Number | Title (A Side/B Side) | Yr | NM |
|---|---|---|---|
| ❑ FZ 40380 | Gravity | 1986 | 12.00 |
| ❑ FZ 44241 | I'm Real | 1988 | 12.00 |
| ❑ FZ 45164 | Soul Session Live | 1989 | 15.00 |
| ❑ 75225-1 | Love Overdue | 1991 | 20.00 |

**SMASH**

| Number | Title (A Side/B Side) | Yr | NM |
|---|---|---|---|
| ❑ MGS-27054 [M] | Showtime | 1964 | 30.00 |
| ❑ MGS-27057 [M] | Grits & Soul | 1965 | 30.00 |
| ❑ MGS-27058 [M] | Out of Sight | 1965 | 100.00 |
| ❑ MGS-27072 [M] | James Brown Plays James Brown — Today & Yesterday | 1965 | 30.00 |
| ❑ MGS-27080 [M] | James Brown Plays New Breed | 1966 | 30.00 |
| ❑ MGS-27084 [M] | Handful of Soul | 1966 | 30.00 |
| ❑ MGS-27087 [M] | The James Brown Show | 1967 | 30.00 |
| *—Various-artists LP* | | | |
| ❑ MGS-27093 [M] | James Brown Plays the Real Thing | 1967 | 30.00 |
| ❑ SRS-67054 [S] | Showtime | 1964 | 40.00 |
| ❑ SRS-67057 [S] | Grits & Soul | 1965 | 40.00 |
| ❑ SRS-67058 [S] | Out of Sight | 1965 | 150.00 |
| ❑ SRS-67072 [S] | James Brown Plays James Brown — Today & Yesterday | 1965 | 40.00 |
| ❑ SRS-67080 [S] | James Brown Plays New Breed | 1966 | 40.00 |
| ❑ SRS-67084 [S] | Handful of Soul | 1966 | 40.00 |
| ❑ SRS-67087 [S] | The James Brown Show | 1967 | 40.00 |
| *—Various-artists LP* | | | |
| ❑ SRS-67093 [S] | James Brown Plays the Real Thing | 1967 | 40.00 |
| ❑ SRS-67109 | James Brown Sings Out of Sight | 1968 | 30.00 |
| *—Abridged reissue of 67058* | | | |

**SOLID SMOKE**

| Number | Title (A Side/B Side) | Yr | NM |
|---|---|---|---|
| ❑ SS-8006 | Live and Lowdown at the Apollo, Vol. 1 | 1980 | 12.00 |
| ❑ SS-8013 | Can Your Heart Stand It | 1981 | 12.00 |
| ❑ SS-8023 | The Federal Years, Part 1 | 198? | 12.00 |
| ❑ SS-8024 | The Federal Years, Part 2 | 198? | 12.00 |

**T.K.**

| Number | Title (A Side/B Side) | Yr | NM |
|---|---|---|---|
| ❑ 615 | Soul Syndrome | 1980 | 30.00 |

## BROWN, JIM ED

**RCA CAMDEN**

| Number | Title (A Side/B Side) | Yr | NM |
|---|---|---|---|
| ❑ ACL1-0197 | Hey Good Lookin' | 1973 | 10.00 |
| ❑ ACL1-0618 | The Three Bells | 1974 | 10.00 |
| ❑ CAS-2496 | Gentle on My Mind | 1971 | 10.00 |
| ❑ CAS-2549 | Country Cream | 1972 | 10.00 |

**RCA VICTOR**

| Number | Title (A Side/B Side) | Yr | NM |
|---|---|---|---|
| ❑ APL1-0172 | Bar-Rooms & Pop-A-Tops | 1973 | 15.00 |
| ❑ APL1-0324 | Best of Jim Ed Brown | 1973 | 15.00 |
| ❑ APL1-0572 | It's That Time of Night | 1974 | 15.00 |
| ❑ ANL1-1215 | It's That Time of Night | 1975 | 10.00 |
| *—Reissue of 0572* | | | |
| ❑ LPM-3569 [M] | Alone with You | 1966 | 20.00 |
| ❑ LSP-3569 [S] | Alone with You | 1966 | 25.00 |
| ❑ LPM-3744 [M] | Just Jim | 1967 | 25.00 |
| ❑ LSP-3744 [S] | Just Jim | 1967 | 20.00 |
| ❑ LPM-3853 [M] | Gems by Jim | 1967 | 25.00 |
| ❑ LSP-3853 [S] | Gems by Jim | 1967 | 20.00 |
| ❑ LPM-3942 [M] | Bottle, Bottle | 1968 | 40.00 |
| ❑ LSP-3942 [S] | Bottle, Bottle | 1968 | 20.00 |
| ❑ LSP-4011 | Country's Best on Record | 1968 | 20.00 |
| ❑ LSP-4130 | This Is My Best! | 1968 | 20.00 |
| ❑ LSP-4175 | Jim Ed Sings the Browns | 1969 | 20.00 |
| ❑ LSP-4262 | Going Up the Country | 1970 | 15.00 |
| ❑ LSP-4366 | Just for You | 1970 | 15.00 |
| ❑ LSP-4461 | Morning | 1971 | 15.00 |
| ❑ LSP-4525 | Angel's Sunday | 1971 | 15.00 |
| ❑ LSP-4614 | She's Leavin' | 1971 | 15.00 |
| ❑ LSP-4713 | Evening | 1972 | 15.00 |
| ❑ LSP-4755 | Brown Is Blue | 1972 | 15.00 |



**Except when noted otherwise, VG = 25% of NM, and VG+ = 50% of NM. (Example: VG = $2.00, VG+ = $4.00 and NM = $8.00.)**

| Number | Title (A Side/B Side) | Yr | NM |
|---|---|---|---|

### BROWN, LAWRENCE

CLEF

❑ MGC-682 [M] Slide Trombone 1955 120.00

IMPULSE!

❑ A-89 [M] Inspired Abandon 1965 25.00
❑ AS-89 [S] Inspired Abandon 1965 30.00

VERVE

❑ MGV-8067 [M] Slide Trombone 1957 50.00
❑ V-8067 [M] Slide Trombone 1961 20.00

### BROWN, LES

CAPITOL

❑ T 657 [M] College Classics 1955 30.00
*—Turquoise or gray label*
❑ T 659 [M] The Les Brown All Stars 1955 30.00
*—Turquoise or gray label*
❑ T 746 [M] Les Brown's in Town 1956 30.00
*—Turquoise or gray label*
❑ T 886 [M] Composer's Holiday 1957 30.00
*—Turquoise or gray label*
❑ T 959 [M] Concert Modern 1958 30.00
*—Turquoise or gray label*
❑ ST 1174 [S] The Les Brown Story 1959 25.00
*—Black colorband label, logo at left*
❑ T 1174 [M] The Les Brown Story 1959 25.00
*—Black colorband label, logo at left*

COLUMBIA

❑ CL 539 [M] Dance with Les Brown 1954 30.00
*—Maroon label, gold print*
❑ CL 649 [M] Sentimental Journey 1955 25.00
*—Red and black label with six "eye" logos*
❑ CL 649 [M] Sentimental Journey 1955 30.00
*—Maroon label, gold print*
❑ CL 2512 [10] I've Got My Love to Keep Me Warm 1955 40.00
❑ CL 2561 [10] The Cool Classics 1955 40.00
❑ CL 6060 [10] Dance Parade 1949 40.00
❑ CL 6123 [10] Your Dance Date with Les Brown 1950 40.00
❑ CL 6159 [10] Classics in Rhythm 195? 40.00
❑ CS 8288 [S] Bandland 1960 20.00
*—Red and black label with six "eye" logos*
❑ CS 8394 [S] The Lerner and Loewe Bandbook 1960 20.00
*—Red and black label with six "eye" logos*
❑ CS 8618 [S] Revolution in Sound 1962 20.00
*—Red and black label with six "eye" logos*
❑ CS 8830 [S] Explosive Sound 1964 20.00
*—"360 Sound Stereo" in black on label*
❑ CS 8919 [S] The Young Beat 1964 20.00
*—"360 Sound Stereo" in black on label*

CORAL

❑ CX-1 [(2)M] Les Brown Concert at the Palladium 1953 60.00
❑ CRL 56026 [10] Over the Rainbow 1951 50.00
❑ CRL 56030 [10] The Sound of Renown 1951 50.00
❑ CRL 56046 [10] You're My Everything 1952 50.00
❑ CRL 56077 [10] Musical Weather Vane 1953 50.00
❑ CRL 56094 [10] Les Dance 1953 50.00
❑ CRL 56108 [10] Invitation 1954 50.00
❑ CRL 56109 [10] Time to Dance 1954 50.00
❑ CRL 56116 [10] Les Dream 1954 50.00
❑ CRL 57000 [M] Les Brown Concert at the Palladium, Part 1 1954 30.00
❑ CRL 57001 [M] Les Brown Concert at the Palladium, Part 1 1954 30.00
❑ CRL 57030 [M] The Sound of Renown 1955 25.00
❑ CRL 57051 [M] Open House 1956 25.00
❑ CRL 57058 [M] More from Les 1956 25.00
❑ CRL 57165 [M] Love Letters in the Sand 1957 25.00
❑ CRL 57300 [M] Swing Song Book 1959 25.00
❑ CRL 57311 [M] Jazz Song Book 1959 25.00
❑ CRL 757300 [S] Swing Song Book 1959 30.00
❑ CRL 757311 [S] Jazz Song Book 1959 30.00

DECCA

❑ DL 4965 [M] The World of the Young 1968 20.00

GREAT AMERICAN

❑ 1010 Les Brown Goes Direct to Disc 1981 20.00

### BROWN, MARION

ESP-DISK'

❑ 1022 [M] Marion Brown Quartet 1966 20.00
❑ 1040 [M] Why Not? 1967 20.00

IMPULSE!

❑ A-9139 [M] Three for Shepp 1967 30.00
❑ AS-9139 [S] Three for Shepp 1967 20.00

### BROWN, MAXINE (1)

COLLECTABLES

❑ COL-5116 Golden Classics 198? 12.00

COMMONWEALTH UNITED

❑ CU-6001 We'll Cry Together 1969 20.00

GUEST STAR

❑ GS-1911 [M] Maxine Brown 1964 12.00

WAND

❑ LP-656 [M] The Fabulous Sound of Maxine Brown 1963 50.00
❑ WDS-656 [S] The Fabulous Sound of Maxine Brown 1963 60.00
❑ WD-663 [M] Spotlight on Maxine Brown 1965 30.00
❑ WDS-663 [S] Spotlight on Maxine Brown 1965 40.00
❑ WD-684 [M] Maxine Brown's Greatest Hits 1967 20.00
❑ WDS-684 [S] Maxine Brown's Greatest Hits 1967 25.00
❑ DT-91012 [R] The Fabulous Sound of Maxine Brown 196? 50.00
*—Capitol Record Club edition*

### BROWN, MAXINE (2)

One of THE BROWNS, she is no relation to the above.

CHART

❑ 1012 Sugar Cane Country 1969 20.00

### BROWN, MEL

ABC IMPULSE!

❑ A-9152 [M] Chicken Fat 1967 30.00
❑ AS-9152 [S] Chicken Fat 1967 20.00
❑ A-9169 [M] The Wizard 1968 40.00
❑ AS-9169 [S] The Wizard 1968 20.00
❑ A-9180 [M] Blues for We 1969 50.00
❑ AS-9180 [S] Blues for We 1969 20.00
❑ AS-9186 I'd Rather Suck My Thumb 1970 20.00
❑ AS-9209 Fifth 1971 20.00

### BROWN, NAPPY

BLACK TOP

❑ BT-1039 Something Gonna Jump Out the Bushes 1987 15.00

ICHIBAN

❑ ICH-1056 Apples and Lemons 1990 12.00

KING SNAKE/ICHIBAN

❑ ICH-9006 Aw! Shucks 1991 15.00

LANDSLIDE

❑ LD 1008 Tore Up 1984 15.00

MELTONE

❑ 1502 Deep Sea Diver 1989 15.00

SAVOY

❑ MG-14002 [M] Nappy Brown Sings 1958 400.00
❑ MG-14025 [M] The Right Time 1960 250.00
❑ 14427 Nappy Brown 1977 12.00

SAVOY JAZZ

❑ SJL-1149 Don't Be Angry 1984 10.00

### BROWN, ODELL

CADET

❑ LPS-775 [S] Raising the Roof 1966 20.00
❑ LP-788 [M] Mellow Yellow 1967 20.00
❑ LP-800 [M] Ducky 1967 20.00

### BROWN, OSCAR, JR.

COLUMBIA

❑ CL 1577 [M] Sin and Soul 1960 25.00
*—Red and black label with six "eye" logos*
❑ CL 1774 [M] Between Heaven and Hell 1962 25.00
*—Red and black label with six "eye" logos*
❑ CL 1873 [M] In a New Mood 1963 20.00
*—Red label, "Guaranteed High Fidelity" in black*
❑ CL 2025 [M] Oscar Brown Jr. Tells It Like It Is 1964 20.00
*—Red label, "Guaranteed High Fidelity" in black*
❑ CS 8377 [S] Sin and Soul 1960 30.00
*—Red and black label with six "eye" logos*
❑ CS 8574 [S] Between Heaven and Hell 1962 30.00
*—Red and black label with six "eye" logos*
❑ CS 8673 [S] In a New Mood 1963 25.00
*—Red label, "360 Sound Stereo" in black*
❑ CS 8825 [S] Oscar Brown Jr. Tells It Like It Is 1964 25.00
*—Red label, "360 Sound Stereo" in black*

FONTANA

❑ SRF-67540 [S] Mr. Oscar Brown Goes to Washington 1965 20.00
❑ SRF-67549 [S] Finding a New Friend 1966 20.00

### BROWN, PETE

BETHLEHEM

❑ BCP-1011 [10] Peter the Great 1954 120.00

VERVE

❑ MGVS-6133 [S] From the Heart 1960 40.00
❑ MGV-8365 [M] From the Heart 1958 50.00
❑ V-8365 [M] From the Heart 1962 20.00

### BROWN, PETE/JONAH JONES

BETHLEHEM

❑ BCP-4 [M] Jazz Kaleidoscope 1957 80.00

### BROWN, RAY

VERVE

❑ MGV-8022 [M] Bass Hit! 1957 50.00
❑ V-8022 [M] Bass Hit! 1961 20.00
❑ MGV-8290 [M] This Is Ray Brown 1958 50.00
❑ V-8290 [M] This Is Ray Brown 1961 20.00
❑ MGV-8390 [M] Jazz Cello 1960 50.00
❑ V-8390 [M] Jazz Cello 1961 20.00
❑ V-8444 [M] Ray Brown with the All Star Big Band Featuring Cannonball Adderley 1962 25.00
❑ V6-8444 [S] Ray Brown with the All Star Big Band Featuring Cannonball Adderley 1962 30.00
❑ V-8580 [M] Much in Common 1964 25.00
❑ V6-8580 [S] Much in Common 1964 30.00
*—With Milt Jackson*
❑ V-8615 [M] Ray Brown/Milt Jackson 1965 25.00
❑ V6-8615 [S] Ray Brown/Milt Jackson 1965 30.00

### BROWN, RONNIE

PHILIPS

❑ PHS 600130 [S] Jazz for Everyone 1964 20.00

### BROWN, ROY

BLUESWAY

❑ BLS-6019 The Blues Are Brown 1968 25.00
❑ BLS-6056 Hard Times 1973 25.00

EPIC

❑ E 30473 Live at Monterey 1971 25.00

INTERMEDIA

❑ QS-5027 Good Rockin' Tonight 198? 10.00

KING

❑ 956 [M] Roy Brown Sings 24 Hits 1966 50.00
❑ KS-956 [R] Roy Brown Sings 24 Hits 1966 50.00
❑ KS-1130 Hard Luck Blues 1971 25.00

### BROWN, ROY / WYNONIE HARRIS

KING

❑ 607 [M] Battle of the Blues 1958 600.00
❑ 627 [M] Battle of the Blues, Volume 2 1959 800.00

### BROWN, ROY / WYNONIE HARRIS / EDDIE VINSON

KING

❑ 668 [M] Battle of the Blues, Volume 4 1960 2500.

### BROWN, RUTH

ATLANTIC

❑ 1308 [M] Last Date with Ruth Brown 1959 200.00
*—Black label*
❑ 1308 [M] Last Date with Ruth Brown 1961 50.00
*—Red and purple label, "fan" logo in white*
❑ SD 1308 [S] Last Date with Ruth Brown 1959 300.00
*—Green label*
❑ SD 1308 [S] Last Date with Ruth Brown 1961 60.00
*—Blue and green label, "fan" logo in white*
❑ 8004 [M] Ruth Brown 1957 200.00
*—Black label*
❑ 8004 [M] Ruth Brown 1960 150.00
*—White "bullseye" label*
❑ 8004 [M] Ruth Brown 1961 50.00
*—Red and purple label, "fan" logo in white*
❑ 8026 [M] Miss Rhythm 1959 200.00
*—Black label*
❑ 8026 [M] Miss Rhythm 1960 150.00
*—White "bullseye" label*
❑ 8026 [M] Miss Rhythm 1961 50.00
*—Red and purple label, "fan" logo in white*
❑ 8080 [M] The Best of Ruth Brown 1963 40.00

DOBRE

❑ 1041 You Don't Know Me 1978 12.00

FANTASY

❑ F-9661 Have a Good Time 1988 12.00
❑ F-9662 Blues on Broadway 1989 12.00

ICHIBAN

❑ SPEG-4023 Brown, Black and Beautiful 198? 12.00

MAINSTREAM

❑ 369 Softly 1972 12.00
❑ S-6034 [S] Ruth Brown '65 1965 30.00
❑ 56034 [M] Ruth Brown '65 1965 25.00

PHILIPS

❑ PHM 200028 [M] Along Comes Ruth 1962 40.00
❑ PHM 200055 [M] Gospel Time 1962 30.00
❑ PHS 600028 [S] Along Comes Ruth 1962 50.00
❑ PHS 600055 [S] Gospel Time 1962 40.00

SKYE

❑ SK-13 Black Is Brown and Brown Is Beautiful 1970 15.00

### BROWN, TED

VANGUARD

❑ VRS-8515 [M] Free Wheeling 1956 500.00

### BROWN SUGAR

CHELSEA

❑ BCL1-0368 Brown Sugar Featuring Clydie King 1973 20.00

### BROWN'S FERRY FOUR, THE

KING

❑ 551 [M] Sacred Songs 1957 80.00
❑ 590 [M] Sacred Songs 1958 80.00
❑ 943 Wonderful Sacred Songs 1964 30.00

Jackson Browne, *The Pretender,* Mobile Fidelity 1-055, 1981, "Original Master Recording" at top, $25.

**BROWNE, JACKSON**

ASYLUM

| Number | Title (A Side/B Side) | Yr | NM |
|---|---|---|---|
| 6E-107 | The Pretender | 1977 | 10.00 |
| *—Reissue of 7E-1079* | | | |
| 6E-113 | Running on Empty | 1977 | 10.00 |
| 5E-511 | Hold Out | 1979 | 10.00 |
| 7E-1017 | Late for the Sky | 1974 | 12.00 |
| EQ-1017 [Q] | Late for the Sky | 1974 | 30.00 |
| 7E-1079 | The Pretender | 1976 | 12.00 |
| SD 5051 | Jackson Browne (Saturate Before Using) | 1972 | 8.00 |
| *—Standard cover* | | | |
| SD 5051 | Jackson Browne (Saturate Before Using) | 1972 | 12.00 |
| *—Burlap cover; "clouds" label* | | | |
| SD 5051 | Jackson Browne (Saturate Before Using) | 1972 | 16.00 |
| *—Burlap cover, opens at right side; white label with "Asylum Records" logo in a circle at top* | | | |
| SD 5051 | Jackson Browne (Saturate Before Using) | 1972 | 20.00 |
| *—Burlap cover, opens at top; white label with "Asylum Records" logo in a circle at top* | | | |
| SD 5067 | For Everyman | 1973 | 12.00 |
| 60268 | Lawyers in Love | 1983 | 10.00 |
| 60457 | Lives in the Balance | 1986 | 10.00 |

ELEKTRA

| Number | Title (A Side/B Side) | Yr | NM |
|---|---|---|---|
| 60830 | World in Motion | 1989 | 10.00 |

MOBILE FIDELITY

| Number | Title (A Side/B Side) | Yr | NM |
|---|---|---|---|
| 1-055 | The Pretender | 1981 | 25.00 |
| *—Audiophile vinyl* | | | |

NINA MUSIC PUBLISHING

| Number | Title (A Side/B Side) | Yr | NM |
|---|---|---|---|
| (no #) [(2)] | Songs by Jackson Browne | 1967 | 2000. |
| *—Publisher's demo in plain cardboard jacket; three sides performed by Jackson Browne, one side by Steve Noonan; VG value 1000; VG+ value 1500* | | | |

**BROWNS, THE**

RCA CAMDEN

| Number | Title (A Side/B Side) | Yr | NM |
|---|---|---|---|
| CAL-885 [M] | I Heard the Bluebirds Sing | 1965 | 12.00 |
| CAS-885 [S] | I Heard the Bluebirds Sing | 1965 | 12.00 |
| CAL-2142 [M] | Big Ones from the Country | 1967 | 12.00 |
| CAS-2142 [S] | Big Ones from the Country | 1967 | 10.00 |
| CAS-2262 | The Browns Sing a Harvest of Country Songs | 1968 | 10.00 |

RCA VICTOR

| Number | Title (A Side/B Side) | Yr | NM |
|---|---|---|---|
| ANL1-1083 | The Best of the Browns | 1975 | 10.00 |
| LPM-1438 [M] | Jim Edward, Maxine and Bonnie Brown | 1957 | 50.00 |
| LPM-2144 [M] | Sweet Sounds by the Browns | 1959 | 30.00 |
| LSP-2144 [S] | Sweet Sounds by the Browns | 1959 | 40.00 |
| LPM-2174 [M] | Town and Country | 1960 | 20.00 |
| LSP-2174 [S] | Town and Country | 1960 | 25.00 |
| LPM-2260 [M] | The Browns Sing Their Hits | 1960 | 20.00 |
| LSP-2260 [S] | The Browns Sing Their Hits | 1960 | 25.00 |
| LPM-2333 [M] | Our Favorite Folk Songs | 1961 | 20.00 |
| LSP-2333 [S] | Our Favorite Folk Songs | 1961 | 25.00 |
| LPM-2345 [M] | The Little Brown Church Hymnal | 1961 | 20.00 |
| LSP-2345 [S] | The Little Brown Church Hymnal | 1961 | 25.00 |
| LPM-2784 [M] | Grand Ole Opry Favorites | 1963 | 15.00 |
| LSP-2784 [S] | Grand Ole Opry Favorites | 1963 | 20.00 |
| LPM-2860 [M] | This Young Land | 1964 | 15.00 |
| LSP-2860 [S] | This Young Land | 1964 | 20.00 |
| LPM-2987 [M] | Three Shades of Brown | 1964 | 15.00 |
| LSP-2987 [S] | Three Shades of Brown | 1964 | 20.00 |
| LPM-3423 [M] | When Love Is Gone | 1965 | 15.00 |
| LSP-3423 [S] | When Love Is Gone | 1965 | 20.00 |
| LPM-3561 [M] | The Best of the Browns | 1966 | 15.00 |
| LSP-3561 [S] | The Best of the Browns | 1966 | 20.00 |
| LPM-3668 [M] | Our Kind of Country | 1966 | 15.00 |
| LSP-3668 [S] | Our Kind of Country | 1966 | 20.00 |
| LPM-3798 [M] | The Old Country Church | 1967 | 20.00 |
| LSP-3798 [S] | The Old Country Church | 1967 | 15.00 |

**BROWNSVILLE STATION**

BIG TREE

| Number | Title (A Side/B Side) | Yr | NM |
|---|---|---|---|
| BTS-2010 | A Night on the Town | 1972 | 12.00 |
| BTS-2102 | Yeah! | 1973 | 12.00 |
| BT 89500 | School Punks | 1974 | 12.00 |
| BT 89510 | Motor City Connection | 1975 | 12.00 |

EPIC

| Number | Title (A Side/B Side) | Yr | NM |
|---|---|---|---|
| JE 35606 | Air Special | 1978 | 10.00 |
| JE 35606 [DJ] | Air Special | 1978 | 20.00 |
| *—Orange vinyl promo* | | | |

PALLADIUM

| Number | Title (A Side/B Side) | Yr | NM |
|---|---|---|---|
| P-1004 | Brownsville Station | 1970 | 30.00 |

PRIVATE STOCK

| Number | Title (A Side/B Side) | Yr | NM |
|---|---|---|---|
| PS-2026 | Brownsville Station | 1977 | 10.00 |

WARNER BROS.

| Number | Title (A Side/B Side) | Yr | NM |
|---|---|---|---|
| WS 1888 | No B.S. | 1970 | 15.00 |

**BRUBECK, DAVE**

COLUMBIA

| Number | Title (A Side/B Side) | Yr | NM |
|---|---|---|---|
| C2L 26 [(2)M] | The Dave Brubeck Quartet at Carnegie Hall | 1963 | 25.00 |
| *—Red "Guaranteed High Fidelity" label* | | | |
| CL 566 [M] | Jazz Goes to College | 1954 | 80.00 |
| *—Dark red label, gold print; released at the same time as 6321 and 6322* | | | |
| CL 566 [M] | Jazz Goes to College | 1955 | 50.00 |
| *—Red/black label with six "eye" logos* | | | |
| CL 566 [M] | Jazz Goes to College | 1962 | 20.00 |
| *—Red "Guaranteed High Fidelity" label* | | | |
| CL 590 [M] | Dave Brubeck at Storyville: 1954 | 1954 | 80.00 |
| *—Dark red label, gold print; released at the same time as 6330 and 6331* | | | |
| CL 590 [M] | Dave Brubeck at Storyville: 1954 | 1955 | 50.00 |
| *—Red/black label with six "eye" logos* | | | |
| CL 590 [M] | Dave Brubeck at Storyville: 1954 | 1962 | 20.00 |
| *—Red "Guaranteed High Fidelity" label* | | | |
| CL 622 [M] | Brubeck Time | 1955 | 60.00 |
| *—Red/black label with six "eye" logos* | | | |
| CL 622 [M] | Brubeck Time | 1962 | 20.00 |
| *—Red "Guaranteed High Fidelity" label* | | | |
| CL 699 [M] | Jazz: Red Hot and Cool | 1955 | 60.00 |
| *—Red/black label with six "eye" logos* | | | |
| CL 699 [M] | Jazz: Red Hot and Cool | 1962 | 20.00 |
| *—Red "Guaranteed High Fidelity" label* | | | |
| C2S 826 [(2)S] | The Dave Brubeck Quartet at Carnegie Hall | 1963 | 30.00 |
| *—Red label, "360 Sound" in black* | | | |
| C2S 826 [(2)S] | The Dave Brubeck Quartet at Carnegie Hall | 1966 | 20.00 |
| *—Red label, "360 Sound" in white* | | | |
| CL 878 [M] | Brubeck Plays Brubeck | 1956 | 60.00 |
| *—Red/black label with six "eye" logos* | | | |
| CL 878 [M] | Brubeck Plays Brubeck | 1962 | 20.00 |
| *—Red "Guaranteed High Fidelity" label* | | | |
| CL 932 [M] | American Jazz Festival at Newport '56 | 1956 | 50.00 |
| *—Red/black label with six "eye" logos* | | | |
| CL 932 [M] | American Jazz Festival at Newport '56 | 1962 | 20.00 |
| *—Red "Guaranteed High Fidelity" label* | | | |
| CL 984 [M] | Jazz Impressions of the U.S.A. | 1957 | 50.00 |
| *—Red/black label with six "eye" logos* | | | |
| CL 984 [M] | Jazz Impressions of the U.S.A. | 1962 | 20.00 |
| *—Red "Guaranteed High Fidelity" label* | | | |
| CL 1034 [M] | Jazz Goes to Junior College | 1957 | 40.00 |
| *—Red/black label with six "eye" logos* | | | |
| CL 1034 [M] | Jazz Goes to Junior College | 1962 | 20.00 |
| *—Red "Guaranteed High Fidelity" label* | | | |
| CL 1059 [M] | Dave Digs Disney | 1957 | 40.00 |
| *—Red/black label with six "eye" logos* | | | |
| CL 1059 [M] | Dave Digs Disney | 1962 | 20.00 |
| *—Red "Guaranteed High Fidelity" label* | | | |
| CL 1168 [M] | The Dave Brubeck Quartet in Europe | 1958 | 40.00 |
| *—Red/black label with six "eye" logos* | | | |
| CL 1168 [M] | The Dave Brubeck Quartet in Europe | 1962 | 20.00 |
| *—Red "Guaranteed High Fidelity" label* | | | |
| CL 1249 [M] | Newport 1958 | 1958 | 40.00 |
| *—Red/black label with six "eye" logos* | | | |
| CL 1249 [M] | Newport 1958 | 1962 | 20.00 |
| *—Red "Guaranteed High Fidelity" label* | | | |
| CL 1251 [M] | Jazz Impressions of Eurasia | 1958 | 40.00 |
| *—Red/black label with six "eye" logos* | | | |
| CL 1251 [M] | Jazz Impressions of Eurasia | 1962 | 20.00 |
| *—Red "Guaranteed High Fidelity" label* | | | |
| CL 1347 [M] | Gone with the Wind | 1959 | 40.00 |
| *—Red/black label with six "eye" logos* | | | |
| CL 1347 [M] | Gone with the Wind | 1962 | 20.00 |
| *—Red "Guaranteed High Fidelity" label* | | | |
| CL 1397 [M] | Time Out | 1960 | 25.00 |
| *—Red/black label with six "eye" logos* | | | |
| CL 1439 [M] | Southern Scene | 1960 | 25.00 |
| *—Red/black label with six "eye" logos* | | | |
| CL 1454 [M] | The Riddle | 1960 | 25.00 |
| *—Red/black label with six "eye" logos* | | | |
| CL 1466 [M] | Bernstein Plays Brubeck Plays Bernstein | 1960 | 25.00 |
| *—Red/black label with six "eye" logos* | | | |
| CL 1553 [M] | Brubeck and Rushing | 1961 | 25.00 |
| *—Red/black label with six "eye" logos* | | | |
| CL 1609 [M] | Tonight Only! | 1961 | 25.00 |
| *—Red/black label with six "eye" logos* | | | |
| CL 1690 [M] | Time Further Out | 1961 | 25.00 |
| *—Red/black label with six "eye" logos* | | | |
| CL 1775 [M] | Countdown — Time in Outer Space | 1962 | 30.00 |
| *—Red/black label with six "eye" logos* | | | |
| CL 1963 [M] | Brandenburg Gate Revisited | 1963 | 20.00 |
| *—Red "Guaranteed High Fidelity" label* | | | |
| CL 1998 [M] | Bossa Nova U.S.A. | 1963 | 20.00 |
| *—Red "Guaranteed High Fidelity" label* | | | |
| CL 2127 [M] | Time Changes | 1964 | 20.00 |
| *—Red "Guaranteed High Fidelity" label* | | | |

| Number | Title (A Side/B Side) | Yr | NM |
|---|---|---|---|
| ❑ CL 2212 [M] | Jazz Impressions of Japan | 1964 | 20.00 |
| —Red "Guaranteed High Fidelity" label | | | |
| ❑ CL 2275 [M] | Jazz Impressions of New York | 1965 | 20.00 |
| —Red "Guaranteed High Fidelity" label | | | |
| ❑ CL 2316 [M] | Take Five | 1965 | 20.00 |
| —Red "Guaranteed High Fidelity" label | | | |
| ❑ CL 2348 [M] | Angel Eyes | 1965 | 20.00 |
| —Red "Guaranteed High Fidelity" label | | | |
| ❑ CL 2695 [M] | Bravo Brubeck! | 1967 | 20.00 |
| ❑ CL 2712 [M] | Jackpot | 1967 | 20.00 |
| ❑ CL 6321 [10] | Jazz Goes to College, Volume 1 | 1954 | 100.00 |
| ❑ CL 6322 [10] | Jazz Goes to College, Volume 2 | 1954 | 100.00 |
| ❑ CL 6330 [10] | Dave Brubeck at Storyville: 1954, Volume 1 | 1954 | 80.00 |
| ❑ CL 6331 [10] | Dave Brubeck at Storyville: 1954, Volume 2 | 1954 | 80.00 |
| ❑ CS 8058 [S] | Jazz Impressions of Eurasia | 1959 | 50.00 |
| —Red/black label with six "eye" logos | | | |
| ❑ CS 8058 [S] | Jazz Impressions of Eurasia | 1962 | 25.00 |
| —Red label, "360 Sound" in black | | | |
| ❑ CS 8082 [S] | Newport 1958 | 1959 | 50.00 |
| —Red/black label with six "eye" logos | | | |
| ❑ CS 8082 [S] | Newport 1958 | 1962 | 25.00 |
| —Red label, "360 Sound" in black | | | |
| ❑ CS 8090 [S] | Dave Digs Disney | 1959 | 50.00 |
| —Red/black label with six "eye" logos | | | |
| ❑ CS 8090 [S] | Dave Digs Disney | 1962 | 25.00 |
| —Red label, "360 Sound" in black | | | |
| ❑ CS 8156 [S] | Gone with the Wind | 1959 | 50.00 |
| —Red/black label with six "eye" logos | | | |
| ❑ CS 8156 [S] | Gone with the Wind | 1962 | 25.00 |
| —Red label, "360 Sound" in black | | | |
| ❑ CS 8192 | Time Out | 1995 | 30.00 |
| —Audiophile vinyl, distributed by Classic Records | | | |
| ❑ CS 8192 [S] | Time Out | 1960 | 30.00 |
| —Red/black label with six "eye" logos | | | |
| ❑ CS 8192 [S] | Time Out Featuring "Take Five" | 1962 | 20.00 |
| —Red label, "360 Sound" in black; beginning with this issue, the cover was altered to emphasize the hit | | | |
| ❑ CS 8235 [S] | Southern Scene | 1960 | 30.00 |
| —Red/black label with six "eye" logos | | | |
| ❑ CS 8235 [S] | Southern Scene | 1962 | 20.00 |
| —Red label, "360 Sound" in black | | | |
| ❑ CS 8248 [S] | The Riddle | 1960 | 30.00 |
| —Red/black label with six "eye" logos | | | |
| ❑ CS 8248 [S] | The Riddle | 1962 | 20.00 |
| —Red label, "360 Sound" in black | | | |
| ❑ CS 8257 [S] | Brubeck Plays Bernstein Plays Brubeck | 1960 | 30.00 |
| —Red/black label with six "eye" logos | | | |
| ❑ CS 8257 [S] | Brubeck Plays Bernstein Plays Brubeck | 1962 | 20.00 |
| —Red label, "360 Sound" in black | | | |
| ❑ CS 8353 [S] | Brubeck and Rushing | 1961 | 30.00 |
| —Red/black label with six "eye" logos | | | |
| ❑ CS 8353 [S] | Brubeck and Rushing | 1962 | 20.00 |
| —Red label, "360 Sound" in black | | | |
| ❑ CS 8409 [S] | Tonight Only! | 1961 | 30.00 |
| —Red/black label with six "eye" logos | | | |
| ❑ CS 8409 [S] | Tonight Only! | 1962 | 20.00 |
| —Red label, "360 Sound" in black | | | |
| ❑ CS 8490 [S] | Time Further Out | 1961 | 30.00 |
| —Red/black label with six "eye" logos | | | |
| ❑ CS 8490 [S] | Time Further Out | 1962 | 20.00 |
| —Red label, "360 Sound" in black | | | |
| ❑ CS 8575 [S] | Countdown — Time in Outer Space | 1962 | 20.00 |
| —Red label, "360 Sound" in black | | | |
| ❑ CS 8575 [S] | Countdown — Time in Outer Space | 1962 | 40.00 |
| —Red/black label with six "eye" logos | | | |
| ❑ CS 8763 [S] | Brandenburg Gate Revisited | 1963 | 25.00 |
| —Red label, "360 Sound" in black | | | |
| ❑ CS 8798 [S] | Bossa Nova U.S.A. | 1963 | 25.00 |
| —Red label, "360 Sound" in black | | | |
| ❑ CS 8927 [S] | Time Changes | 1964 | 25.00 |
| —Red label, "360 Sound" in black | | | |
| ❑ CS 9012 [S] | Jazz Impressions of Japan | 1964 | 25.00 |
| —Red label, "360 Sound" in black | | | |
| ❑ CS 9075 [S] | Jazz Impressions of New York | 1965 | 25.00 |
| —Red label, "360 Sound" in black | | | |
| ❑ CS 9116 [S] | Take Five | 1965 | 25.00 |
| —Red label, "360 Sound" in black | | | |
| ❑ CS 9148 [S] | Angel Eyes | 1965 | 25.00 |
| —Red label, "360 Sound" in black | | | |
| ❑ CS 9237 [S] | My Favorite Things | 1966 | 20.00 |
| —Red "360 Sound" label | | | |
| ❑ CS 9284 [S] | Dave Brubeck's Greatest Hits | 1966 | 20.00 |
| —Red "360 Sound" label | | | |
| ❑ CS 9312 [S] | Time In | 1966 | 20.00 |
| —Red "360 Sound" label | | | |
| ❑ CS 9402 [S] | Anything Goes! Dave Brubeck Quartet Plays Cole Porter | 1966 | 20.00 |
| —Red "360 Sound" label | | | |

COLUMBIA LIMITED EDITION

| Number | Title (A Side/B Side) | Yr | NM |
|---|---|---|---|
| ❑ LE 10013 | Gone with the Wind | 197? | 10.00 |

DIRECT DISK

| Number | Title (A Side/B Side) | Yr | NM |
|---|---|---|---|
| ❑ 106 [(2)] | A Cut Above | 1979 | 25.00 |

FANTASY

| Number | Title (A Side/B Side) | Yr | NM |
|---|---|---|---|
| ❑ 3-1 [10] | Dave Brubeck Trio | 1951 | 150.00 |
| ❑ 3-2 [10] | Dave Brubeck Trio | 1951 | 150.00 |
| ❑ 3-3 [10] | Dave Brubeck Octet | 1951 | 150.00 |
| ❑ 3-4 [10] | Dave Brubeck Trio | 1952 | 150.00 |
| ❑ 3-5 [10] | Dave Brubeck Quartet with Paul Desmond | 1952 | 150.00 |
| ❑ 3-7 [10] | Dave Brubeck Quartet with Paul Desmond | 1952 | 150.00 |
| ❑ 3-8 [10] | Jazz at Storyville | 1953 | 150.00 |
| ❑ 3-10 [10] | Jazz at the Blackhawk | 1953 | 150.00 |
| ❑ 3-11 [10] | Jazz at Oberlin | 1953 | 100.00 |
| —Black vinyl | | | |
| ❑ 3-11 [10] | Jazz at Oberlin | 1953 | 200.00 |
| —Red vinyl | | | |
| ❑ 3-13 [10] | Jazz at the College of the Pacific | 1954 | 150.00 |
| ❑ 3-16 [10] | Old Sounds from San Francisco | 1954 | 250.00 |
| —Red or purple vinyl | | | |
| ❑ 3-20 [10] | Paul and Dave's Jazz Interwoven | 1955 | 150.00 |
| ❑ 3204 [M] | Dave Brubeck Trio | 195? | 60.00 |
| —Black vinyl, red label, non-flexible vinyl | | | |
| ❑ 3204 [M] | Dave Brubeck Trio | 1956 | 100.00 |
| —Dark red vinyl; reissue of 3-1 | | | |
| ❑ 3204 [M] | Dave Brubeck Trio | 196? | 40.00 |
| —Black vinyl, red label, flexible vinyl | | | |
| ❑ 3205 [M] | Dave Brubeck Trio: Distinctive Rhythm Instrumentals | 195? | 60.00 |
| —Black vinyl, red label, non-flexible vinyl | | | |
| ❑ 3205 [M] | Dave Brubeck Trio: Distinctive Rhythm Instrumentals | 1956 | 100.00 |
| —Dark red vinyl; reissue of 3-2 | | | |
| ❑ 3205 [M] | Dave Brubeck Trio: Distinctive Rhythm Instrumentals | 196? | 40.00 |
| —Black vinyl, red label, flexible vinyl | | | |
| ❑ 3210 [M] | Jazz at the Blackhawk | 195? | 60.00 |
| —Black vinyl, red label, non-flexible vinyl | | | |
| ❑ 3210 [M] | Jazz at the Blackhawk | 1956 | 100.00 |
| —Dark red vinyl; reissue of 3-10 | | | |
| ❑ 3210 [M] | Jazz at the Blackhawk | 196? | 40.00 |
| —Black vinyl, red label, flexible vinyl | | | |
| ❑ 3223 [M] | Jazz at the College of the Pacific | 195? | 60.00 |
| —Black vinyl, red label, non-flexible vinyl | | | |
| ❑ 3223 [M] | Jazz at the College of the Pacific | 1956 | 100.00 |
| —Dark red vinyl; reissue of 3-13 | | | |
| ❑ 3223 [M] | Jazz at the College of the Pacific | 196? | 40.00 |
| —Black vinyl, red label, flexible vinyl | | | |
| ❑ 3229 [M] | Brubeck-Desmond | 195? | 60.00 |
| —Black vinyl, red label, non-flexible vinyl | | | |
| ❑ 3229 [M] | Brubeck-Desmond | 1956 | 100.00 |
| —Dark red vinyl; reissue of 3-5 | | | |
| ❑ 3229 [M] | Brubeck-Desmond | 196? | 40.00 |
| —Black vinyl, red label, flexible vinyl | | | |
| ❑ 3230 [M] | Dave Brubeck Quartet | 195? | 60.00 |
| —Black vinyl, red label, non-flexible vinyl | | | |
| ❑ 3230 [M] | Dave Brubeck Quartet | 1956 | 100.00 |
| —Dark red vinyl; reissue of 3-7 | | | |
| ❑ 3230 [M] | Dave Brubeck Quartet | 196? | 40.00 |
| —Black vinyl, red label, flexible vinyl | | | |
| ❑ 3239 [M] | Dave Brubeck Octet | 195? | 60.00 |
| —Black vinyl, red label, non-flexible vinyl | | | |
| ❑ 3239 [M] | Dave Brubeck Octet | 1956 | 100.00 |
| —Dark red vinyl; reissue of 3-3 | | | |
| ❑ 3239 [M] | Dave Brubeck Octet | 196? | 40.00 |
| —Black vinyl, red label, flexible vinyl | | | |
| ❑ 3240 [M] | Brubeck Desmond: Jazz at Storyville | 195? | 60.00 |
| —Black vinyl, red label, non-flexible vinyl | | | |
| ❑ 3240 [M] | Brubeck Desmond: Jazz at Storyville | 1957 | 100.00 |
| —Dark red vinyl; reissue of 3-8 | | | |
| ❑ 3240 [M] | Brubeck Desmond: Jazz at Storyville | 196? | 40.00 |
| —Black vinyl, red label, flexible vinyl | | | |
| ❑ 3245 [M] | Jazz at Oberlin | 195? | 60.00 |
| —Black vinyl, red label, non-flexible vinyl | | | |
| ❑ 3245 [M] | Jazz at Oberlin | 1957 | 100.00 |
| —Dark red vinyl; reissue of 3-11 | | | |
| ❑ 3245 [M] | Jazz at Oberlin | 196? | 40.00 |
| —Black vinyl, red label, flexible vinyl | | | |
| ❑ 3249 [M] | Brubeck & Desmond at Wilshire-Ebell | 195? | 60.00 |
| —Black vinyl, red label, non-flexible vinyl | | | |
| ❑ 3249 [M] | Brubeck & Desmond at Wilshire-Ebell | 1957 | 100.00 |
| —Dark red vinyl | | | |
| ❑ 3249 [M] | Brubeck & Desmond at Wilshire-Ebell | 196? | 40.00 |
| —Black vinyl, red label, flexible vinyl | | | |
| ❑ 3259 [M] | Dave Brubeck Plays and Plays and Plays and Plays and… | 195? | 40.00 |
| —Black vinyl, red label, non-flexible vinyl | | | |
| ❑ 3259 [M] | Dave Brubeck Plays and Plays and Plays and Plays and… | 196? | 30.00 |
| —Black vinyl, red label, flexible vinyl | | | |
| ❑ 3259 [M] | Dave Brubeck Plays and Plays and Plays and Plays and… | 1958 | 60.00 |
| —Red vinyl | | | |
| ❑ 3268 [M] | Re-Union | 195? | 40.00 |
| —Black vinyl, red label, non-flexible vinyl | | | |
| ❑ 3268 [M] | Re-Union | 1958 | 60.00 |
| —Red vinyl | | | |
| ❑ 3268 [M] | Re-Union | 196? | 30.00 |
| —Black vinyl, red label, flexible vinyl | | | |
| ❑ 3298 [M] | Two Knights at the Black Hawk | 1959 | 40.00 |
| —Black vinyl, red label, non-flexible vinyl | | | |
| ❑ 3298 [M] | Two Knights at the Black Hawk | 1959 | 60.00 |
| —Red vinyl | | | |
| ❑ 3298 [M] | Two Knights at the Black Hawk | 196? | 30.00 |
| —Black vinyl, red label, flexible vinyl | | | |
| ❑ 3301 [M] | Brubeck A La Mode | 196? | 30.00 |
| —Black vinyl, red label, flexible vinyl | | | |
| ❑ 3301 [M] | Brubeck A La Mode | 1960 | 40.00 |
| —Black vinyl, red label, non-flexible vinyl | | | |
| ❑ 3301 [M] | Brubeck A La Mode | 1960 | 60.00 |
| —Red vinyl | | | |
| ❑ 3319 [M] | Near-Myth | 196? | 30.00 |
| —Black vinyl, red label, flexible vinyl | | | |
| ❑ 3319 [M] | Near-Myth | 1961 | 40.00 |
| —Black vinyl, red label, non-flexible vinyl | | | |
| ❑ 3319 [M] | Near-Myth | 1961 | 60.00 |
| —Red vinyl | | | |
| ❑ 3331 [M] | Dave Brubeck Trio Featuring Cal Tjader | 196? | 30.00 |
| —Black vinyl, red label, flexible vinyl | | | |
| ❑ 3331 [M] | Dave Brubeck Trio Featuring Cal Tjader | 1962 | 40.00 |
| —Black vinyl, red label, non-flexible vinyl | | | |
| ❑ 3331 [M] | Dave Brubeck Trio Featuring Cal Tjader | 1962 | 60.00 |
| —Red vinyl | | | |
| ❑ 3332 [M] | Brubeck Tjader | 196? | 30.00 |
| —Black vinyl, red label, flexible vinyl | | | |
| ❑ 3332 [M] | Brubeck Tjader | 1962 | 40.00 |
| —Black vinyl, red label, non-flexible vinyl | | | |
| ❑ 3332 [M] | Brubeck Tjader | 1962 | 60.00 |
| —Red vinyl | | | |
| ❑ 8007 [S] | Re-Union | 196? | 20.00 |
| —Black vinyl, blue label, flexible vinyl | | | |
| ❑ 8007 [S] | Re-Union | 196? | 30.00 |
| —Black vinyl, blue label, non-flexible vinyl | | | |
| ❑ 8007 [S] | Re-Union | 1962 | 50.00 |
| —Blue vinyl | | | |
| ❑ 8047 [S] | Brubeck A La Mode | 196? | 20.00 |
| —Black vinyl, blue label, flexible vinyl | | | |
| ❑ 8047 [S] | Brubeck A La Mode | 196? | 30.00 |
| —Black vinyl, blue label, non-flexible vinyl | | | |
| ❑ 8047 [S] | Brubeck A La Mode | 1962 | 50.00 |
| —Blue vinyl | | | |
| ❑ 8063 [S] | Near-Myth | 196? | 20.00 |
| —Black vinyl, blue label, flexible vinyl | | | |
| ❑ 8063 [S] | Near-Myth | 196? | 30.00 |
| —Black vinyl, blue label, non-flexible vinyl | | | |
| ❑ 8063 [S] | Near-Myth | 1962 | 50.00 |
| —Blue vinyl | | | |
| ❑ 8069 [R] | Jazz at Oberlin | 196? | 20.00 |
| —Black vinyl, blue label, non-flexible vinyl | | | |
| ❑ 8069 [R] | Jazz at Oberlin | 1962 | 40.00 |
| —Blue vinyl | | | |
| ❑ 8073 [R] | Dave Brubeck Trio Featuring Cal Tjader | 1962 | 20.00 |
| —Black vinyl, blue label, non-flexible vinyl | | | |
| ❑ 8073 [R] | Dave Brubeck Trio Featuring Cal Tjader | 1962 | 40.00 |
| —Blue vinyl | | | |
| ❑ 8074 [R] | Brubeck Tjader | 1962 | 20.00 |
| —Black vinyl, blue label, non-flexible vinyl | | | |
| ❑ 8074 [R] | Brubeck Tjader | 1962 | 40.00 |
| —Blue vinyl | | | |
| ❑ 8078 [R] | Jazz at the College of the Pacific | 196? | 20.00 |
| —Black vinyl, blue label, non-flexible vinyl | | | |
| ❑ 8078 [R] | Jazz at the College of the Pacific | 1962 | 40.00 |
| —Blue vinyl | | | |
| ❑ 8080 [R] | Jazz at Storyville | 1962 | 20.00 |
| —Black vinyl, blue label, non-flexible vinyl | | | |
| ❑ 8080 [R] | Jazz at Storyville | 1962 | 40.00 |
| —Blue vinyl | | | |
| ❑ 8081 [R] | Two Knights at the Blackhawk | 1962 | 20.00 |
| —Black vinyl, blue label, non-flexible vinyl | | | |
| ❑ 8081 [R] | Two Knights at the Blackhawk | 1962 | 40.00 |
| —Blue vinyl | | | |
| ❑ 8092 [R] | Brubeck-Desmond | 1962 | 20.00 |
| —Black vinyl, blue label, non-flexible vinyl | | | |
| ❑ 8092 [R] | Brubeck-Desmond | 1962 | 40.00 |
| —Blue vinyl | | | |
| ❑ 8093 [R] | Dave Brubeck Quartet | 1962 | 20.00 |
| —Black vinyl, blue label, non-flexible vinyl | | | |
| ❑ 8093 [R] | Dave Brubeck Quartet | 1962 | 40.00 |
| —Blue vinyl | | | |
| ❑ 8094 [R] | Dave Brubeck Octet | 1962 | 20.00 |
| —Black vinyl, blue label, non-flexible vinyl | | | |
| ❑ 8094 [R] | Dave Brubeck Octet | 1962 | 40.00 |
| —Blue vinyl | | | |
| ❑ 8095 [S] | Brubeck and Desmond at Wilshire-Ebell | 196? | 20.00 |
| —Black vinyl, blue label, flexible vinyl | | | |
| ❑ 8095 [S] | Brubeck and Desmond at Wilshire-Ebell | 1962 | 30.00 |
| —Black vinyl, blue label, non-flexible vinyl | | | |
| ❑ 8095 [S] | Brubeck and Desmond at Wilshire-Ebell | 1962 | 50.00 |
| —Blue vinyl | | | |

Lenny Bruce, *The Essential Lenny Bruce Politics*, Douglas SD 788, 1968, $20.

| Number | Title (A Side/B Side) | Yr | NM |
|---|---|---|---|
| JAZZTONE | | | |
| ❑ J-1272 [M] | Best of Brubeck | 195? | 40.00 |
| MOBILE FIDELITY | | | |
| ❑ 1-216 | We're All Together Again for the First Time | 1994 | 60.00 |
| *—Audiophile vinyl* | | | |
| MOON | | | |
| ❑ 028 | St. Louis Blues | 1992 | 20.00 |

**BRUCE, ED**

| Number | Title (A Side/B Side) | Yr | NM |
|---|---|---|---|
| EPIC | | | |
| ❑ KE 35043 | Tennesseean | 1977 | 10.00 |
| ❑ KE 35541 | Cowboys and Dreamers | 1978 | 10.00 |
| MCA | | | |
| ❑ 3242 | Ed Bruce | 1980 | 10.00 |
| ❑ 5188 | One to One | 1981 | 10.00 |
| ❑ 5323 | I Write It Down | 1982 | 10.00 |
| ❑ 5416 | You're Not Leaving Here Tonight | 1983 | 10.00 |
| ❑ 5511 | Tell 'Em I've Gone Crazy | 1984 | 10.00 |
| ❑ 5577 | Greatest Hits | 1985 | 10.00 |
| ❑ 27068 | Ed Bruce | 198? | 8.00 |
| *—Reissue of 3242* | | | |
| MONUMENT | | | |
| ❑ SLP-18118 | Shades | 1969 | 20.00 |
| RCA VICTOR | | | |
| ❑ LPM-3948 [M] | If I Could Just Go Home | 1968 | 50.00 |
| ❑ LSP-3948 [S] | If I Could Just Go Home | 1968 | 25.00 |
| ❑ AHL1-5324 | Homecoming | 1985 | 10.00 |
| ❑ AHL1-5808 | Night Things | 1986 | 10.00 |
| UNITED ARTISTS | | | |
| ❑ UA-LA613-G | Ed Bruce | 1976 | 12.00 |

**BRUCE, LENNY**

| Number | Title (A Side/B Side) | Yr | NM |
|---|---|---|---|
| BIZARRE | | | |
| ❑ 2XS 6329 [(2)] | The Berkeley Concert | 1969 | 25.00 |
| DOUGLAS | | | |
| ❑ 2 | To Is a Preposition, Come Is a Verb | 196? | 20.00 |
| ❑ 788 | The Essential Lenny Bruce Politics | 1968 | 20.00 |
| ❑ Z 30872 | What I Was Arrested For | 1971 | 15.00 |
| *—Reissue of 2* | | | |
| FANTASY | | | |
| ❑ FP-1 [DJ] | The Promo Album | 196? | 200.00 |
| *—Promo-only compilation of material from albums 7001, 7003, 7007 and 7011* | | | |
| ❑ 7001 [M] | Interviews of Our Times | 1959 | 40.00 |
| *—Non-flexible black vinyl; cover changed to blue tint* | | | |
| ❑ 7001 [M] | Interviews of Our Times | 1959 | 100.00 |
| *—Opaque, non-flexible red vinyl; tan cover with Lenny Bruce's name blacked out throughout the back* | | | |
| ❑ 7001 [M] | Interviews of Our Times | 1962 | 20.00 |
| *—Flexible black vinyl* | | | |
| ❑ 7001 [M] | Interviews of Our Times | 1962 | 40.00 |
| *—Translucent, flexible red vinyl* | | | |
| ❑ 7003 [M] | The Sick Humor of Lenny Bruce | 1959 | 40.00 |
| *—Non-flexible black vinyl* | | | |
| ❑ 7003 [M] | The Sick Humor of Lenny Bruce | 1959 | 100.00 |
| *—Opaque, non-flexible red vinyl* | | | |
| ❑ 7003 [M] | The Sick Humor of Lenny Bruce | 1962 | 20.00 |
| *—Flexible black vinyl* | | | |
| ❑ 7003 [M] | The Sick Humor of Lenny Bruce | 1962 | 40.00 |
| *—Translucent, flexible red vinyl* | | | |
| ❑ 7007 [M] | I Am Not a Nut, Elect Me | 1960 | 40.00 |
| *—Non-flexible black vinyl* | | | |
| ❑ 7007 [M] | I Am Not a Nut, Elect Me | 1960 | 100.00 |
| *—Opaque, non-flexible red vinyl* | | | |
| ❑ 7007 [M] | I Am Not a Nut, Elect Me | 1962 | 20.00 |
| *—Flexible black vinyl* | | | |
| ❑ 7007 [M] | I Am Not a Nut, Elect Me | 1962 | 40.00 |
| *—Translucent, flexible red vinyl* | | | |
| ❑ 7011 [M] | Lenny Bruce, American | 1961 | 40.00 |
| *—Non-flexible black vinyl* | | | |
| ❑ 7011 [M] | Lenny Bruce, American | 1961 | 100.00 |
| *—Opaque, non-flexible red vinyl* | | | |
| ❑ 7011 [M] | Lenny Bruce, American | 1962 | 20.00 |
| *—Flexible black vinyl* | | | |
| ❑ 7011 [M] | Lenny Bruce, American | 1962 | 40.00 |
| *—Translucent, flexible red vinyl* | | | |
| ❑ 7012 [M] | The Best of Lenny Bruce | 1962 | 20.00 |
| *—Black vinyl* | | | |
| ❑ 7012 [M] | The Best of Lenny Bruce | 1962 | 50.00 |
| *—Red vinyl* | | | |
| ❑ 7017 | Thank You Masked Man | 1971 | 15.00 |
| ❑ 34201 [(3)] | Lenny Bruce at the Curran Theater | 1971 | 40.00 |
| ❑ 79003 [(2)] | The Real Lenny Bruce | 1975 | 20.00 |
| LENNY BRUCE | | | |
| ❑ LB-3001/2 [M] | Lenny Bruce Is Out Again | 196? | 300.00 |
| *—Privately pressed version with white labels and Lenny's address on cover* | | | |
| ❑ LB-9001/2 [10] | Warning: Sale of This Album... | 1962 | 500.00 |
| *—Privately pressed LP with routines used as evidence in Lenny's obscenity trial* | | | |
| PHILLIES | | | |
| ❑ PHLP-4010 [M] | Lenny Bruce Is Out Again | 1966 | 100.00 |
| *—Reissue of Lenny Bruce 3001/2* | | | |
| UNITED ARTISTS | | | |
| ❑ UAL 3580 [M] | The Midnight Concert | 1967 | 25.00 |
| ❑ UAS 6580 | The Midnight Concert | 1967 | 20.00 |
| ❑ UAS 6794 | The Midnight Concert | 1972 | 15.00 |
| *—Reissue of 6580* | | | |
| ❑ UAS 9800 [(3)] | Lenny Bruce/Carnegie Hall | 1972 | 25.00 |
| WARNER/SPECTOR | | | |
| ❑ SP 9101 | The Law, the Language and Lenny Bruce | 1975 | 15.00 |

**BRUEL, MAX**

| Number | Title (A Side/B Side) | Yr | NM |
|---|---|---|---|
| EMARCY | | | |
| ❑ MG-36062 [M] | Cool Bruel | 1955 | 60.00 |

**BRUNIS, GEORG**

| Number | Title (A Side/B Side) | Yr | NM |
|---|---|---|---|
| COMMODORE | | | |
| ❑ FL-20008 [10] | King of the Tailgate Trombone | 1950 | 80.00 |
| ❑ DL 30015 [M] | King of the Tailgate Trombone | 1959 | 40.00 |
| JOLLY ROGER | | | |
| ❑ 5024 [10] | Georg Brunis and the New Orleans Rhythm Kings | 1954 | 50.00 |
| RIVERSIDE | | | |
| ❑ RLP-1024 [10] | Georg Brunis and the Original New Orleans Rhythm Kings | 1954 | 80.00 |

**BRUNSON, FRANKIE**

| Number | Title (A Side/B Side) | Yr | NM |
|---|---|---|---|
| GEE | | | |
| ❑ GLP-704 [M] | Big Daddy's Blues | 1959 | 80.00 |
| ❑ SGLP-704 [S] | Big Daddy's Blues | 1959 | 120.00 |

**BRUTE FORCE**

| Number | Title (A Side/B Side) | Yr | NM |
|---|---|---|---|
| B.T. PUPPY | | | |
| ❑ BTPS-1015 | Extemporaneous | 1971 | 2000. |
| *—VG value 1000; VG+ value 1500* | | | |
| COLUMBIA | | | |
| ❑ CL 2615 [M] | I, Brute Force — Confections of Love | 1967 | 20.00 |
| ❑ CS 9415 [S] | I, Brute Force — Confections of Love | 1967 | 20.00 |
| EMBRYO | | | |
| ❑ 522 | Brute Force | 1970 | 20.00 |

**BRYAN, JOY**

| Number | Title (A Side/B Side) | Yr | NM |
|---|---|---|---|
| CONTEMPORARY | | | |
| ❑ M-3604 [M] | Make the Man Love Me | 1961 | 40.00 |
| ❑ S-7604 [S] | Make the Man Love Me | 1961 | 50.00 |
| MODE | | | |
| ❑ LP-108 [M] | Joy Bryan Sings | 1957 | 80.00 |

**BRYANT, ANITA**

| Number | Title (A Side/B Side) | Yr | NM |
|---|---|---|---|
| CARLTON | | | |
| ❑ LP-118 [M] | Anita Bryant | 1959 | 20.00 |
| ❑ STLP-118 [S] | Anita Bryant | 1959 | 30.00 |
| ❑ LP-127 [M] | Hear Anita Bryant in Your Home Tonight | 1960 | 20.00 |
| ❑ STLP-127 [S] | Hear Anita Bryant in Your Home Tonight | 1960 | 25.00 |
| ❑ LP-132 [M] | In My Little Corner of the World | 1961 | 20.00 |
| ❑ STLP-132 [S] | In My Little Corner of the World | 1961 | 25.00 |
| COLUMBIA | | | |
| ❑ CL 1719 [M] | Kisses Sweeter Than Wine | 1961 | 15.00 |
| ❑ CL 1767 [M] | Abiding Love | 1962 | 15.00 |
| ❑ CL 1885 [M] | In a Velvet Mood | 1962 | 12.00 |
| ❑ CL 1956 [M] | Anita Bryant's Greatest Hits | 1963 | 12.00 |
| ❑ CL 2035 [M] | As Long As He Needs Me | 1963 | 12.00 |
| ❑ CL 2069 [M] | Country's Best | 1964 | 12.00 |
| ❑ CL 2222 [M] | World of Lonely People | 1964 | 12.00 |
| ❑ CL 2573 [M] | Mine Eyes Have Seen the Glory | 1966 | 12.00 |
| ❑ CL 2706 [M] | I Believe | 1967 | 15.00 |
| ❑ CL 2720 [M] | Do You Hear What I Hear? | 1967 | 15.00 |
| ❑ CS 8519 [S] | Kisses Sweeter Than Wine | 1961 | 20.00 |
| ❑ CS 8567 [S] | Abiding Love | 1962 | 20.00 |
| ❑ CS 8685 [S] | In a Velvet Mood | 1962 | 15.00 |
| ❑ CS 8756 [S] | Anita Bryant's Greatest Hits | 1963 | 15.00 |
| ❑ CS 8835 [S] | As Long As He Needs Me | 1963 | 15.00 |
| ❑ CS 8869 [S] | Country's Best | 1964 | 15.00 |
| ❑ CS 9022 [S] | World of Lonely People | 1964 | 15.00 |
| ❑ CS 9373 [S] | Mine Eyes Have Seen the Glory | 1966 | 15.00 |
| ❑ CS 9506 [S] | I Believe | 1967 | 12.00 |
| ❑ CS 9520 [S] | Do You Hear What I Hear? | 1967 | 10.00 |
| ❑ CS 9607 | In Remembrance of You (The Story of a Love Affair) | 1968 | 12.00 |
| ❑ CS 9642 | How Great Thou Art | 1968 | 12.00 |



**Except when noted otherwise, VG = 25% of NM, and VG+ = 50% of NM. (Example: VG = $2.00, VG+ = $4.00 and NM = $8.00.)**

| Number | Title (A Side/B Side) | Yr | NM |
|---|---|---|---|
| COLUMBIA SPECIAL PRODUCTS | | | |
| ❑ CSS 900 | The Sunshine Tree | 1970 | 12.00 |
| HARMONY | | | |
| ❑ HL 9557 [M] | ABC Stories of Jesus | 196? | 12.00 |
| ❑ HS 11280 | Anita Bryant | 1968 | 10.00 |
| ❑ HS 11330 | Little Things Mean a Lot | 1969 | 10.00 |
| ❑ HS 11395 | A World Without Love | 1970 | 10.00 |
| ❑ H 31181 | You'll Never Walk Alone | 1972 | 10.00 |
| MYRRH | | | |
| ❑ MSB-6513 | Naturally | 197? | 12.00 |
| WORD | | | |
| ❑ WST-8532 | Abide with Me | 1970 | 12.00 |
| ❑ WST-8540 | Love Lifted Me | 1971 | 12.00 |
| ❑ WST-8558 | The Miracle of Christmas | 197? | 10.00 |
| ❑ WST-8571 | Battle Hymn of the Republic | 1972 | 12.00 |
| ❑ WST-8631 | This Is My Story | 1975 | 12.00 |
| ❑ WST-8652 | Hymns | 1976 | 12.00 |
| ❑ WST-8670 | Old Fashioned Prayin' | 1977 | 12.00 |
| ❑ 8785 | Singing a New Song | 198? | 10.00 |
| **BRYANT, BOBBY** | | | |
| CADET | | | |
| ❑ LP-795 [M] | Ain't Doing Too B-A-D, Bad | 1967 | 20.00 |
| VEE JAY | | | |
| ❑ VJS-3059 | Big Band Blues | 1974 | 20.00 |
| **BRYANT, BOUDLEAUX** | | | |
| MONUMENT | | | |
| ❑ MLP-8007 [M] | Boudleaux Bryant's Best Sellers | 1963 | 20.00 |
| ❑ SLP-18007 [S] | Boudleaux Bryant's Best Sellers | 1963 | 25.00 |
| **BRYANT, CLORA** | | | |
| MODE | | | |
| ❑ LP-106 [M] | Gal with a Horn | 1957 | 150.00 |
| **BRYANT, JIMMY** | | | |
| CAPITOL | | | |
| ❑ ST 1314 [S] | Country Cabin Jazz | 1960 | 100.00 |
| ❑ T 1314 [M] | Country Cabin Jazz | 1960 | 80.00 |
| DOLTON | | | |
| ❑ BLP-16505 [M] | Play Country Guitar with Jimmy Bryant | 196? | 25.00 |
| ❑ BST-17505 [S] | Play Country Guitar with Jimmy Bryant | 196? | 30.00 |
| IMPERIAL | | | |
| ❑ LP-9310 [M] | Bryant's Back in Town | 1966 | 20.00 |
| ❑ LP-9315 [M] | Laughing Guitar, Crying Guitar | 1966 | 20.00 |
| ❑ LP-9338 [M] | We Are Young | 1967 | 20.00 |
| ❑ LP-9360 [M] | That Fastest Guitar in the Country | 1967 | 25.00 |
| ❑ LP-12310 [S] | Bryant's Back in Town | 1966 | 25.00 |
| ❑ LP-12315 [S] | Laughing Guitar, Crying Guitar | 1966 | 25.00 |
| ❑ LP-12338 [S] | We Are Young | 1967 | 25.00 |
| ❑ LP-12360 [S] | That Fastest Guitar in the Country | 1967 | 20.00 |
| **BRYANT, PAUL** | | | |
| FANTASY | | | |
| ❑ 3357 [M] | Something's Happening | 1963 | 20.00 |
| ❑ 3363 [M] | Groove Time | 1964 | 20.00 |
| ❑ 8357 [S] | Something's Happening | 1963 | 25.00 |
| ❑ 8363 [S] | Groove Time | 1964 | 25.00 |
| PACIFIC JAZZ | | | |
| ❑ PJ-12 [M] | Burnin' | 1961 | 40.00 |
| **BRYANT, RAY** | | | |
| CADET | | | |
| ❑ LPS-767 [S] | Gotta Travel On | 1966 | 20.00 |
| ❑ LPS-778 [S] | Lonesome Traveler | 1966 | 20.00 |
| ❑ LPS-781 [S] | Slow Freight | 1967 | 20.00 |
| ❑ LP-793 [M] | The Ray Bryant Touch | 1967 | 20.00 |
| ❑ LP-801 [M] | Take a Bryant Step | 1967 | 20.00 |
| COLUMBIA | | | |
| ❑ CL 1449 [M] | Little Susie | 1960 | 20.00 |
| ❑ CL 1476 [M] | The Madison Time | 1960 | 25.00 |
| ❑ CL 1633 [M] | Con Alma | 1961 | 20.00 |
| ❑ CL 1746 [M] | Dancing the Big Twist | 1962 | 20.00 |
| ❑ CL 1867 [M] | Hollywood Jazz Beat | 1962 | 20.00 |
| ❑ CS 8244 [S] | Little Susie | 1960 | 25.00 |
| ❑ CS 8276 [S] | The Madison Time | 1960 | 30.00 |
| ❑ CS 8433 [S] | Con Alma | 1961 | 25.00 |
| ❑ CS 8546 [S] | Dancing the Big Twist | 1962 | 25.00 |
| ❑ CS 8667 [S] | Hollywood Jazz Beat | 1962 | 25.00 |
| EPIC | | | |
| ❑ LN 3279 [M] | Ray Bryant Trio | 1956 | 70.00 |
| NEW JAZZ | | | |
| ❑ NJLP-8213 [M] | Alone with the Blues | 1959 | 50.00 |
| *—Purple label* | | | |
| ❑ NJLP-8213 [M] | Alone with the Blues | 1965 | 25.00 |
| *—Blue label with trident logo* | | | |

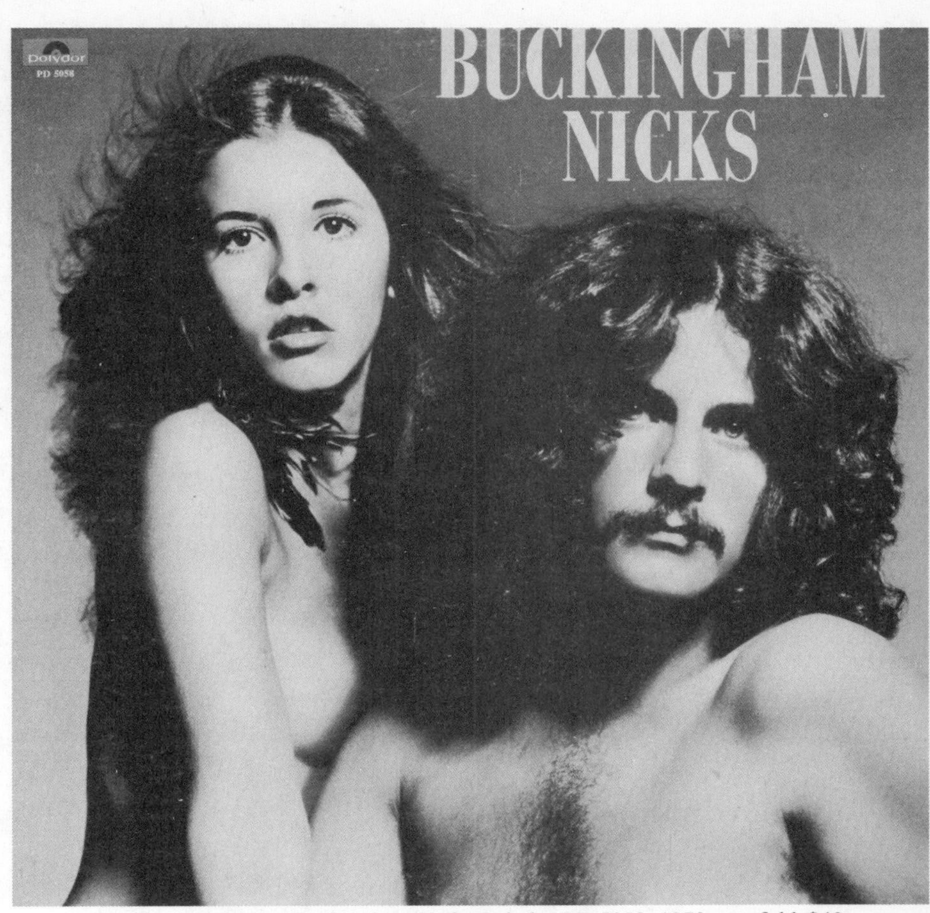


Buckingham Nicks, *Buckingham Nicks,* Polydor PD 5058, 1973, gatefold, $40.

| Number | Title (A Side/B Side) | Yr | NM |
|---|---|---|---|
| ❑ NJLP-8227 [M] | Ray Bryant Trio | 1959 | 50.00 |
| *—Purple label; reissue of Prestige 7098* | | | |
| ❑ NJLP-8227 [M] | Ray Bryant Trio | 1965 | 25.00 |
| *—Blue label with trident logo* | | | |
| PRESTIGE | | | |
| ❑ PRLP-7098 [M] | Ray Bryant Trio | 1957 | 70.00 |
| SIGNATURE | | | |
| ❑ SM-6008 [M] | Ray Bryant Plays | 1960 | 200.00 |
| ❑ SS-6008 [S] | Ray Bryant Plays | 1960 | 250.00 |
| SUE | | | |
| ❑ LP-1016 [M] | Groove House | 1963 | 40.00 |
| ❑ LPS-1016 [S] | Groove House | 1963 | 50.00 |
| ❑ LP-1019 [M] | Live at Basin Street | 1964 | 40.00 |
| ❑ LPS-1019 [S] | Live at Basin Street | 1964 | 50.00 |
| ❑ LP-1032 [M] | Cold Turkey | 1964 | 40.00 |
| ❑ LPS-1032 [S] | Cold Turkey | 1964 | 50.00 |
| ❑ STLP-1036 [M] | Ray Bryant Soul | 1965 | 40.00 |
| ❑ STLPS-1036 [S] | Ray Bryant Soul | 1965 | 50.00 |
| **BRYANT, RUSTY** | | | |
| DOT | | | |
| ❑ DLP-3006 [M] | All Night Long | 1956 | 40.00 |
| *—Maroon label* | | | |
| ❑ DLP-3079 [M] | Rusty Bryant Plays Jazz | 1957 | 40.00 |
| ❑ DLP-25353 [S] | America's Greatest Jazz | 1961 | 20.00 |
| **BRYNNER, YUL** | | | |
| VANGUARD | | | |
| ❑ VRS-9256 [M] | The Gypsy and I | 1967 | 30.00 |
| ❑ VSD-79256 [S] | The Gypsy and I | 1967 | 40.00 |
| **BUA, GENE** | | | |
| HERITAGE | | | |
| ❑ 35004 | Love of Life | 1973 | 20.00 |
| **BUBBLE GUM MACHINE, THE** | | | |
| SENATE | | | |
| ❑ 21002 [M] | The Bubble Gum Machine | 1968 | 25.00 |
| ❑ S-21002 [S] | The Bubble Gum Machine | 1968 | 30.00 |
| **BUBBLE PUPPY, THE** | | | |
| INTERNATIONAL ARTISTS | | | |
| ❑ 10 | A Gathering of Promises | 1969 | 100.00 |
| *—Original does not have "Masterfonics" in the dead wax* | | | |

| Number | Title (A Side/B Side) | Yr | NM |
|---|---|---|---|
| ❑ 10 | A Gathering of Promises | 1979 | 25.00 |
| *—Reissue has "Masterfonics" in the dead wax* | | | |
| **BUBBLES, JOHN W.** | | | |
| VEE JAY | | | |
| ❑ VJ-1109 [M] | Bubbles, John W., That Is | 1964 | 20.00 |
| **BUCCI, JOE** | | | |
| CAPITOL | | | |
| ❑ ST 1840 [S] | Wild About Basie | 1963 | 20.00 |
| **BUCHANAN, ROY** | | | |
| ALLIGATOR | | | |
| ❑ AL-4741 | When a Guitar Plays the Blues | 1985 | 10.00 |
| ❑ AL-4747 | Dancing on the Edge | 1986 | 10.00 |
| ❑ AL-4756 | Hot Wires | 1988 | 10.00 |
| ATLANTIC | | | |
| ❑ SD 18170 | A Street Called Straight | 1976 | 12.00 |
| ❑ SD 18219 | Loading Zone | 1977 | 12.00 |
| ❑ SD 19138 | Loading Zone | 1978 | 8.00 |
| *—Reissue of 18219* | | | |
| ❑ SD 19170 | You're Not Alone | 1978 | 12.00 |
| BIOYA | | | |
| ❑ MM-519 | Buch and the Snake Stretchers | 1971 | 200.00 |
| POLYDOR | | | |
| ❑ PD-5033 | Roy Buchanan | 1972 | 15.00 |
| ❑ PD-5046 | Second Album | 1973 | 15.00 |
| ❑ PD-6020 | That's What I Am Here For | 1974 | 15.00 |
| ❑ PD-6035 | In the Beginning | 1974 | 15.00 |
| ❑ PD-6048 | Live Stock | 1975 | 15.00 |
| WATERHOUSE | | | |
| ❑ 12 | My Babe | 1981 | 10.00 |
| **BUCHANAN BROTHERS** | | | |
| EVENT | | | |
| ❑ ES-101 | Medicine Man | 1969 | 25.00 |
| **BUCK, GARY** | | | |
| TOWER | | | |
| ❑ DT 5054 [R] | Country Scene | 1967 | 15.00 |
| ❑ T 5054 [M] | Country Scene | 1967 | 20.00 |

Buffalo Springfield, *Buffalo Springfield,* Atco SD 33-200-A, 1967, mono, revised version, purple and brown label, $25

### BUCKAROOS, THE

**CAPITOL**

| Number | Title (A Side/B Side) | Yr | NM |
|---|---|---|---|
| ❑ ST-194 | Anywhere U.S.A. | 1969 | 25.00 |
| ❑ ST-322 | Roll Your Own with Buck Owens' Buckaroos | 1969 | 25.00 |
| ❑ ST-440 | Rompin' and Stompin' | 1970 | 20.00 |
| ❑ ST-767 | The Buckaroos Play the Hits | 1971 | 20.00 |
| ❑ ST-860 | The Buckaroos Play the Songs of Merle Haggard | 1971 | 25.00 |
| ❑ ST 2436 [S] | The Buck Owens Song Book | 1966 | 25.00 |
| ❑ T 2436 [M] | The Buck Owens Song Book | 1966 | 20.00 |
| ❑ ST 2722 [S] | America's Most Wanted Band | 1967 | 25.00 |
| ❑ T 2722 [M] | America's Most Wanted Band | 1967 | 20.00 |
| ❑ ST 2828 [S] | The Buck Owens' Buckaroos Strike Again! | 1968 | 25.00 |
| ❑ T 2828 [M] | The Buck Owens' Buckaroos Strike Again! | 1968 | 40.00 |
| ❑ ST 2902 | A Night on the Town with Buck Owens' Buckaroos | 1968 | 25.00 |
| ❑ ST 2973 | Meanwhile Back at the Ranch | 1968 | 25.00 |

### BUCKINGHAM NICKS

**POLYDOR**

| Number | Title (A Side/B Side) | Yr | NM |
|---|---|---|---|
| ❑ PD-5058 | Buckingham Nicks | 1973 | 40.00 |
| *—Gatefold cover* | | | |
| ❑ PD-5058 | Buckingham Nicks | 1975 | 12.00 |
| *—Regular cover* | | | |

### BUCKINGHAMS, THE (1)

**COLUMBIA**

| Number | Title (A Side/B Side) | Yr | NM |
|---|---|---|---|
| ❑ CL 2669 [M] | Time & Charges | 1967 | 25.00 |
| ❑ CL 2798 [M] | Portraits | 1968 | 25.00 |
| ❑ CS 9469 [S] | Time & Charges | 1967 | 20.00 |
| ❑ CS 9598 [S] | Portraits | 1968 | 20.00 |
| ❑ CS 9703 | In One Ear and Gone Tomorrow | 1968 | 20.00 |
| ❑ CS 9812 | The Buckinghams Greatest Hits | 1969 | 20.00 |
| *—Red "360 Sound" label* | | | |
| ❑ CS 9812 | The Buckinghams Greatest Hits | 1970 | 12.00 |
| *—Orange label* | | | |
| ❑ PC 9812 | The Buckinghams Greatest Hits | 198? | 8.00 |
| *—Reissue with new prefix* | | | |
| ❑ KG 33333 [(2)] | Made in Chicago | 1975 | 20.00 |

**U.S.A.**

| Number | Title (A Side/B Side) | Yr | NM |
|---|---|---|---|
| ❑ 107 [M] | Kind of a Drag | 1967 | 30.00 |
| *—Without "I'm a Man"* | | | |
| ❑ 107 [M] | Kind of a Drag | 1967 | 600.00 |
| *—With "I'm a Man"* | | | |
| ❑ 107 [S] | Kind of a Drag | 1967 | 40.00 |
| *—No known stereo copy has "I'm a Man"* | | | |

### BUCKLEY, LORD

**CRESTVIEW**

| Number | Title (A Side/B Side) | Yr | NM |
|---|---|---|---|
| ❑ CRV-801 [M] | The Best of Lord Buckley | 1963 | 50.00 |
| ❑ CRV7-801 [S] | The Best of Lord Buckley | 1963 | 60.00 |

**ELEKTRA**

| Number | Title (A Side/B Side) | Yr | NM |
|---|---|---|---|
| ❑ EKS-74047 | The Best of Lord Buckley | 1969 | 25.00 |
| *—Reissue of Crestview 7-801* | | | |

**RCA VICTOR**

| Number | Title (A Side/B Side) | Yr | NM |
|---|---|---|---|
| ❑ LPM-3246 [10] | Hipsters, Flipsters and Finger Poppin' Daddies, Knock Me Your Lobes | 1955 | 600.00 |

**REPRISE**

| Number | Title (A Side/B Side) | Yr | NM |
|---|---|---|---|
| ❑ RS 6389 | A Most Immaculately Hip Aristocrat | 1970 | 50.00 |
| *—Reissue of Straight 1054* | | | |

**STRAIGHT**

| Number | Title (A Side/B Side) | Yr | NM |
|---|---|---|---|
| ❑ STS-1054 | A Most Immaculately Hip Aristocrat | 1970 | 80.00 |

**VAYA**

| Number | Title (A Side/B Side) | Yr | NM |
|---|---|---|---|
| ❑ 101/2 [M] | Euphoria, Volume 1 | 1955 | 300.00 |
| ❑ 107/8 [M] | Euphoria, Volume 2 | 1955 | 400.00 |
| ❑ 1715 [10] | Euphoria | 195? | 600.00 |
| *—Red vinyl* | | | |

**WORLD PACIFIC**

| Number | Title (A Side/B Side) | Yr | NM |
|---|---|---|---|
| ❑ WP-1279 [M] | The Way Out Humor of Lord Buckley | 1959 | 200.00 |
| *—With correct "Way Out Humor" on the back cover* | | | |
| ❑ WP-1279 [M] | The Way Out Humor of Lord Buckley | 1959 | 250.00 |
| *—With "Far Out Humor" on the back cover* | | | |
| ❑ WP-1815 [M] | Lord Buckley in Concert | 1964 | 50.00 |
| *—Reissue of 1279* | | | |
| ❑ WP-1849 [M] | Blowing His Mind (and Yours, Too) | 1966 | 80.00 |
| ❑ WPS-21879 | Buckley's Best | 1968 | 40.00 |
| ❑ WPS-21889 | Bad Rapping of the Marquis de Sade | 1969 | 80.00 |

### BUCKLEY, TIM

**DISCREET**

| Number | Title (A Side/B Side) | Yr | NM |
|---|---|---|---|
| ❑ MS 2157 | Sefronia | 1973 | 15.00 |
| ❑ DS 2201 | Look at the Fool | 1974 | 15.00 |

**ELEKTRA**

| Number | Title (A Side/B Side) | Yr | NM |
|---|---|---|---|
| ❑ EKL-318 [M] | Goodbye and Hello | 1967 | 25.00 |
| *—Original issue* | | | |
| ❑ EKL-4004 [M] | Tim Buckley | 1966 | 15.00 |
| ❑ EKL-4028 [M] | Goodbye and Hello | 1968 | — |
| *—Reissue of 318; may not exist with this number* | | | |
| ❑ EKS-7318 [S] | Goodbye and Hello | 1967 | 25.00 |
| *—Original issue; tan/brown/silvery label* | | | |
| ❑ EKS-74004 [S] | Tim Buckley | 1966 | 20.00 |
| ❑ EKS-74028 [S] | Goodbye and Hello | 1968 | 20.00 |
| *—Brown labels; reissue of 7318* | | | |
| ❑ EKS-74028 [S] | Goodbye and Hello | 1975 | 10.00 |
| *—Butterfly label with Warner Communications logo* | | | |
| ❑ EKS-74045 | Happy Sad | 1969 | 20.00 |
| ❑ EKS-74074 | Lorca | 1970 | 20.00 |

**RHINO**

| Number | Title (A Side/B Side) | Yr | NM |
|---|---|---|---|
| ❑ RNLP-112 | The Best of Tim Buckley | 1985 | 10.00 |

**STRAIGHT**

| Number | Title (A Side/B Side) | Yr | NM |
|---|---|---|---|
| ❑ STS-1060 | Blue Afternoon | 1969 | 30.00 |

**WARNER BROS.**

| Number | Title (A Side/B Side) | Yr | NM |
|---|---|---|---|
| ❑ WS 1842 | Blue Afternoon | 1970 | 15.00 |
| ❑ WS 1881 | Starsailor | 1970 | 15.00 |
| ❑ BS 2631 | Greetings from L.A. | 1972 | 15.00 |

### BUCKNER, MILT

**ARGO**

| Number | Title (A Side/B Side) | Yr | NM |
|---|---|---|---|
| ❑ LPS-660 [S] | Mighty High | 1960 | 20.00 |
| ❑ LPS-670 [S] | Please Mr. Organ Player | 1960 | 20.00 |
| ❑ LPS-702 [S] | Midnight Mood | 1962 | 20.00 |

**BETHLEHEM**

| Number | Title (A Side/B Side) | Yr | NM |
|---|---|---|---|
| ❑ BCP-6072 [M] | The New World of Milt Buckner | 1963 | 30.00 |

**CAPITOL**

| Number | Title (A Side/B Side) | Yr | NM |
|---|---|---|---|
| ❑ T 642 [M] | Rockin' with Milt | 1955 | 50.00 |
| *—Turquoise or gray label* | | | |
| ❑ T 722 [M] | Rockin' Hammond | 1956 | 50.00 |
| *—Turquoise or gray label* | | | |
| ❑ T 938 [M] | Send Me Softly | 1958 | 50.00 |
| *—Turquoise or gray label* | | | |

**REGENT**

| Number | Title (A Side/B Side) | Yr | NM |
|---|---|---|---|
| ❑ MG-6004 [M] | Organ — Sweet 'n' Swing | 195? | 30.00 |

**SAVOY**

| Number | Title (A Side/B Side) | Yr | NM |
|---|---|---|---|
| ❑ MG-15023 [10] | Milt Buckner Piano | 1953 | 120.00 |

### BUCKNER, TEDDY

**DIXIELAND JUBILEE**

| Number | Title (A Side/B Side) | Yr | NM |
|---|---|---|---|
| ❑ DJ-503 [M] | In Concert at the Dixieland Jubilee | 195? | 20.00 |
| ❑ DJ-504 [M] | Teddy Buckner and His Dixieland Band | 195? | 20.00 |
| ❑ DJ-505 [M] | A Salute to Louis Armstrong | 1959 | 20.00 |
| ❑ DJ-507 [M] | Teddy Buckner and the All Stars | 1959 | 20.00 |
| ❑ DJ-510 [M] | Teddy Buckner on the Sunset Strip | 1960 | 20.00 |

**GENE NORMAN**

| Number | Title (A Side/B Side) | Yr | NM |
|---|---|---|---|
| ❑ GNP-(# unk) [10] | Dixieland Jubilee | 195? | 50.00 |
| *—Red vinyl* | | | |
| ❑ GNP-11 [M] | Teddy Buckner | 1955 | 40.00 |

### BUD AND TRAVIS

**LIBERTY**

| Number | Title (A Side/B Side) | Yr | NM |
|---|---|---|---|
| ❑ LRP-3125 [M] | Bud and Travis | 1959 | 30.00 |
| ❑ LRP-3138 [M] | Spotlight On Bud and Travis | 1960 | 20.00 |
| ❑ LRP-3222 [M] | Bud and Travis In Concert at the Santa Monica Civic Auditorium, Vol. 2 | 1961 | 20.00 |
| ❑ LRP-3295 [M] | Naturally | 1963 | 20.00 |
| ❑ LRP-3341 [M] | Perspective on Bud and Travis | 1964 | 20.00 |
| ❑ LRP-3386 [M] | Bud and Travis In Person (At the Cellar Door) | 1964 | 20.00 |
| ❑ LRP-3398 [M] | The Latin Album | 1965 | 20.00 |
| ❑ LST-7125 [S] | Bud and Travis | 1959 | 40.00 |
| ❑ LST-7138 [S] | Spotlight On Bud and Travis | 1960 | 25.00 |
| ❑ LST-7222 [S] | Bud and Travis In Concert at the Santa Monica Civic Auditorium, Vol. 2 | 1961 | 25.00 |
| ❑ LST-7295 [S] | Naturally | 1963 | 25.00 |
| ❑ LST-7341 [S] | Perspective on Bud and Travis | 1964 | 25.00 |
| ❑ LST-7386 [S] | Bud and Travis In Person (At the Cellar Door) | 1964 | 25.00 |
| ❑ LST-7398 [S] | The Latin Album | 1965 | 25.00 |
| ❑ LDM-11001 [(2)M] | Bud and Travis...In Concert | 1960 | 25.00 |
| ❑ LDS-12001 [(2)S] | Bud and Travis...In Concert | 1960 | 30.00 |

**SUNSET**

| Number | Title (A Side/B Side) | Yr | NM |
|---|---|---|---|
| ❑ SUM-1154 [M] | Bud and Travis | 1967 | 12.00 |
| ❑ SUS-5154 [S] | Bud and Travis | 1967 | 12.00 |

### BUDDIES, THE

**WING**

| Number | Title (A Side/B Side) | Yr | NM |
|---|---|---|---|
| ❑ MGW-12293 [M] | The Buddies and the Compacts | 1965 | 50.00 |

| Number | Title (A Side/B Side) | Yr | NM |
|---|---|---|---|
| ❑ MGW-12306 [M] | Go Go with the Buddies | 1965 | 50.00 |
| ❑ SRW-16293 [S] | The Buddies and the Compacts | 1965 | 80.00 |
| ❑ SRW-16306 [S] | Go Go with the Buddies | 1965 | 80.00 |
| **BUDGIE** | | | |
| A&M | | | |
| ❑ SP-4593 | If I Were Brittania I'd Waive the Rules | 1976 | 15.00 |
| ❑ SP-4618 | Bandolier | 1977 | 15.00 |
| ❑ SP-4675 | Impeckable | 1978 | 15.00 |
| KAPP | | | |
| ❑ KS-3656 | Budgie | 1971 | 30.00 |
| ❑ KS-3669 | Squawk | 1972 | 30.00 |
| MCA | | | |
| ❑ 429 | In for the Kill | 1973 | 20.00 |
| **BUDIMIR, DENNIS** | | | |
| MAINSTREAM | | | |
| ❑ S-6059 [S] | Creeper | 1966 | 25.00 |
| ❑ 56059 [M] | Creeper | 1966 | 20.00 |
| REVELATION | | | |
| ❑ REV-1 [S] | Alone Together | 1967 | 20.00 |
| ❑ REV-M-1 [M] | Alone Together | 1967 | 25.00 |
| ❑ REV-4 | A Second Coming | 1968 | 20.00 |
| ❑ REV-8 | Sprung Free! | 1969 | 20.00 |
| ❑ REV-14 | Session with Albert | 1971 | 20.00 |
| **BUFFALO NICKEL JUGBAND, THE** | | | |
| HAPPY TIGER | | | |
| ❑ 1018 | The Buffalo Nickel Jugband | 1971 | 25.00 |
| **BUFFALO SPRINGFIELD** | | | |
| ATCO | | | |
| ❑ SD 38-105 [S] | Retrospective/The Best of Buffalo Springfield | 197? | 8.00 |
| *—Reissue of 33-283* | | | |
| ❑ 33-200 [M] | Buffalo Springfield | 1967 | 200.00 |
| *—With "Baby Don't Scold Me"* | | | |
| ❑ 33-200A [M] | Buffalo Springfield | 1967 | 25.00 |
| *—With "For What It's Worth" replacing "Baby Don't Scold Me"* | | | |
| ❑ SD 33-200 [S] | Buffalo Springfield | 1967 | 200.00 |
| *—With "Baby Don't Scold Me"* | | | |
| ❑ SD 33-200A [S] | Buffalo Springfield | 1967 | 25.00 |
| *—With "For What It's Worth" replacing "Baby Don't Scold Me"; purple and brown label* | | | |
| ❑ SD 33-200A [S] | Buffalo Springfield | 1969 | 15.00 |
| *—Reissue on yellow label* | | | |
| ❑ SD 33-200A [S] | Buffalo Springfield | 197? | 8.00 |
| *—Later white or gray label* | | | |
| ❑ 33-226 [M] | Buffalo Springfield Again | 1967 | 80.00 |
| ❑ SD 33-226 [S] | Buffalo Springfield Again | 1967 | 25.00 |
| *—Purple and brown label* | | | |
| ❑ SD 33-226 [S] | Buffalo Springfield Again | 1969 | 15.00 |
| *—Reissue on yellow label* | | | |
| ❑ SD 33-226 [S] | Buffalo Springfield Again | 197? | 8.00 |
| *—Later white or gray label* | | | |
| ❑ 33-256 [M] | Last Time Around | 1968 | 120.00 |
| *—White label promo only* | | | |
| ❑ SD 33-256 [S] | Last Time Around | 1968 | 30.00 |
| *—Purple and brown label* | | | |
| ❑ SD 33-256 [S] | Last Time Around | 1969 | 15.00 |
| *—Reissue on yellow label* | | | |
| ❑ SD 33-256 [S] | Last Time Around | 197? | 8.00 |
| *—Later white or gray label* | | | |
| ❑ 33-283 [M] | Retrospective/The Best of Buffalo Springfield | 1969 | 100.00 |
| *—White label promo only* | | | |
| ❑ SD 33-283 [S] | Retrospective/The Best of Buffalo Springfield | 1969 | 20.00 |
| *—Yellow label* | | | |
| ❑ SD 2-806 [(2)] | Buffalo Springfield | 197? | 12.00 |
| *—Later white or gray label* | | | |
| ❑ SD 2-806 [(2)] | Buffalo Springfield | 1973 | 20.00 |
| *—Yellow label* | | | |
| **BUFFETT, JIMMY** | | | |
| ABC | | | |
| ❑ SPDJ-43 [DJ] | Special Jimmy Buffett Sampler | 1978 | 20.00 |
| ❑ D-914 | Havana Daydreamin' | 1976 | 12.00 |
| ❑ AB-990 | Changes in Latitudes, Changes in Attitudes | 1977 | 12.00 |
| ❑ AK-1008 [(2)] | You Had to Be There | 1978 | 15.00 |
| ❑ AA-1046 | Son of a Son of a Sailor | 1978 | 12.00 |
| ABC DUNHILL | | | |
| ❑ DSD-50132 | Living and Dying in 3/4 Time | 1973 | 15.00 |
| ❑ DSX-50150 | A White Sport Coat and a Pink Crustaceon | 1974 | 15.00 |
| ❑ DSD-50183 | A1A | 1975 | 15.00 |
| BARNABY | | | |
| ❑ BR-6014 | High Cumberland Jubilee | 1975 | 40.00 |
| ❑ Z 30093 | Down to Earth | 1970 | 100.00 |
| MCA | | | |
| ❑ 5102 | Volcano | 1979 | 10.00 |
| ❑ 5169 | Coconut Telegraph | 1981 | 10.00 |
| ❑ 5285 | Somewhere Over China | 1982 | 10.00 |
| ❑ 5447 | One Particular Harbour | 1983 | 10.00 |
| ❑ 5512 | Riddles in the Sand | 1984 | 10.00 |

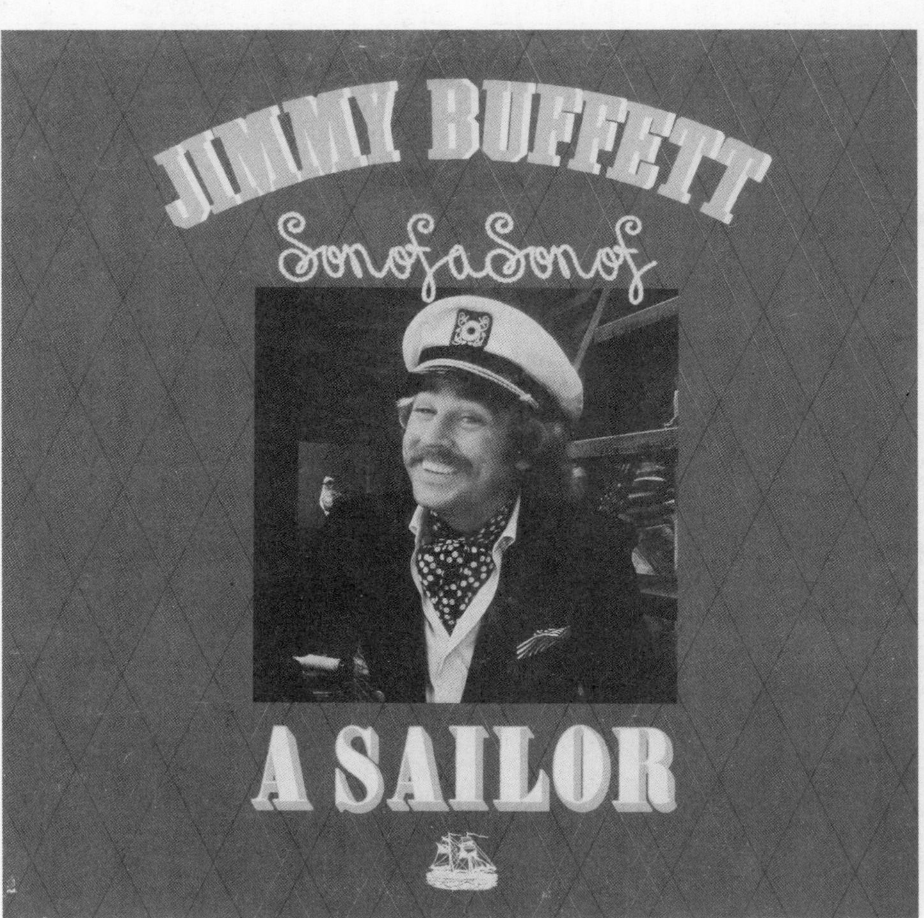

Jimmy Buffett, *Son of a Son of a Sailor,* ABC AA-1046, 1978, $12.

| Number | Title (A Side/B Side) | Yr | NM |
|---|---|---|---|
| ❑ 5600 | Last Mango in Paris | 1985 | 10.00 |
| ❑ 5633 | Songs You Know By Heart — Jimmy Buffett's Greatest Hit(s) | 1985 | 10.00 |
| ❑ 5730 | Floridays | 1986 | 10.00 |
| ❑ 2-6005 [(2)] | You Had to Be There | 1981 | 10.00 |
| ❑ 6314 | Off to See the Lizard | 1989 | 10.00 |
| ❑ 37023 | Havana Daydreamin' | 1981 | 8.00 |
| ❑ 37024 | Son of a Son of a Sailor | 1981 | 8.00 |
| ❑ 37025 | Living and Dying in 3/4 Time | 1981 | 8.00 |
| ❑ 37026 | A White Sport Coat and a Pink Crustaceon | 1981 | 8.00 |
| ❑ 37027 | A1A | 1981 | 8.00 |
| ❑ 37150 | Changes in Latitudes, Changes in Attitudes | 1982 | 8.00 |
| ❑ 37156 | Volcano | 1982 | 8.00 |
| ❑ 37246 | Somewhere Over China | 1984 | 8.00 |
| ❑ 42093 | Hot Water | 1988 | 10.00 |
| **BUGALOOS, THE** | | | |
| CAPITOL | | | |
| ❑ SW-621 | The Bugaloos | 1970 | 30.00 |
| **BUGGS, THE** | | | |
| CORONET | | | |
| ❑ CX-212 [M] | The Beatle Beat | 1964 | 20.00 |
| ❑ CXS-212 [R] | The Beatle Beat | 1964 | 12.00 |
| **BULLDOG** | | | |
| BUDDAH | | | |
| ❑ BDS-5600 | Smasher | 1974 | 15.00 |
| DECCA | | | |
| ❑ DL 75370 | Bulldog | 1972 | 20.00 |
| **BUNCH, THE** | | | |
| A&M | | | |
| ❑ SP-4354 | The Bunch | 1973 | 25.00 |
| **BUNKER, LARRY** | | | |
| VAULT | | | |
| ❑ LP-9005 [M] | Live at Shelly's Manne-Hole | 1966 | 20.00 |
| **BUNKERS, THE** | | | |
| RCA VICTOR | | | |
| ❑ APL1-0102 | Archie and Edith Side by Side | 1973 | 20.00 |

| Number | Title (A Side/B Side) | Yr | NM |
|---|---|---|---|
| **BUOYS, THE** | | | |
| SCEPTER | | | |
| ❑ SPS-593 | Timothy | 1971 | 25.00 |
| **BURDON, ERIC** | | | |
| CAPITOL | | | |
| ❑ ST-11359 | Sun Secrets | 1974 | 12.00 |
| ❑ S?A?11426 | Stop | 1975 | 20.00 |
| *—Cover shaped like a hexagon* | | | |
| ❑ ST-11426 | Stop | 1975 | 12.00 |
| *—Regular square cover* | | | |
| GNP CRESCENDO | | | |
| ❑ GNPS-2194 | Wicked Man | 1988 | 10.00 |
| LAX | | | |
| ❑ PW 37110 | Sun Secrets | 1981 | 10.00 |
| *—Reissue of Capitol 11359* | | | |
| STRIPED HORSE | | | |
| ❑ SHL 2006 | I Used to Be an Animal | 1988 | 10.00 |
| **BURDON, ERIC, AND WAR** | | | |
| ABC | | | |
| ❑ D-988 | Love Is All Around | 1976 | 12.00 |
| *—As "War Featuring Eric Burdon"* | | | |
| LAX | | | |
| ❑ PW 37109 | Spill the Wine | 1981 | 10.00 |
| *—Reissue of MGM 4663 with new title* | | | |
| MGM | | | |
| ❑ SE-4663 | Eric Burdon Declares "War" | 1970 | 15.00 |
| ❑ SE-4710-2 [(2)] | The Black Man's Burdon | 1970 | 20.00 |
| *—Add 50% if the package includes an "Official War Bond," entlitling the bearer to $1 off any Eric Burdon and War concert before December 31, 1973* | | | |
| **BURGER, JACK** | | | |
| HIFI | | | |
| ❑ R-803 [M] | Let's Play Bongos! | 1957 | 40.00 |
| ❑ R-804 [M] | The End on Bongos! | 1957 | 40.00 |
| ❑ R-809 [M] | Let's Play Congas | 1958 | 30.00 |
| ❑ RS-809 [S] | Let's Play Congas | 1959 | 40.00 |
| **BURGESS, WILMA** | | | |
| DECCA | | | |
| ❑ DL 4788 [M] | Don't Touch Me | 1966 | 15.00 |

| Number | Title (A Side/B Side) | Yr | NM |
|---|---|---|---|
| ❑ DL 4852 [M] | Wilma Burgess Sings Misty Blue | 1967 | 15.00 |
| ❑ DL 4935 [M] | Tear Time | 1967 | 25.00 |
| ❑ DL 74788 [S] | Don't Touch Me | 1966 | 20.00 |
| ❑ DL 74852 [S] | Wilma Burgess Sings Misty Blue | 1967 | 20.00 |
| ❑ DL 74935 [S] | Tear Time | 1967 | 20.00 |
| ❑ DL 75024 | The Tender Lovin' Country Sound | 1968 | 20.00 |
| ❑ DL 75090 | Parting Is Such Sweet Sorrow | 1968 | 20.00 |

## BURGHOFF, GARY

SHALOM

| Number | Title (A Side/B Side) | Yr | NM |
|---|---|---|---|
| ❑ 651 | Gary Burghoff and His Mardi Gras Celebration Band | 1983 | 40.00 |

## BURKE, RAY

SOUTHLAND

| Number | Title (A Side/B Side) | Yr | NM |
|---|---|---|---|
| ❑ SLP-209 [10] | Contemporary New Orleans Jazz | 1955 | 50.00 |

## BURKE, SOLOMON

| Number | Title (A Side/B Side) | Yr | NM |
|---|---|---|---|
| ABC DUNHILL | | | |
| ❑ DSX-50161 | I Have a Dream | 1974 | 12.00 |
| AMHERST | | | |
| ❑ AMH-1018 | Please Don't You Say Goodbye to Me | 1978 | 12.00 |
| APOLLO | | | |
| ❑ ALP-498 [M] | Solomon Burke | 1962 | 500.00 |
| ATLANTIC | | | |
| ❑ 8067 [M] | Solomon Burke's Greatest Hits | 1962 | 50.00 |
| ❑ SD 8067 [S] | Solomon Burke's Greatest Hits | 1962 | 80.00 |
| ❑ 8085 [M] | If You Need Me | 1963 | 50.00 |
| ❑ SD 8085 [S] | If You Need Me | 1963 | 80.00 |
| ❑ 8096 [M] | Rock N' Soul | 1964 | 50.00 |
| ❑ SD 8096 [S] | Rock N' Soul | 1964 | 80.00 |
| ❑ 8109 [M] | The Best of Solomon Burke | 1965 | 30.00 |
| ❑ SD 8109 [S] | The Best of Solomon Burke | 1965 | 40.00 |
| ❑ SD 8158 | King Solomon | 1968 | 25.00 |
| ❑ SD 8185 | I Wish I Knew | 1968 | 25.00 |
| BELL | | | |
| ❑ 6033 | Proud Mary | 1969 | 20.00 |
| CHESS | | | |
| ❑ CH-19002 | Back to My Roots | 1976 | 12.00 |
| ❑ CH-60042 | Music to Make Love By | 1975 | 12.00 |
| CLARION | | | |
| ❑ 607 [M] | I Almost Lost My Mind | 1966 | 20.00 |
| ❑ SD 607 [S] | I Almost Lost My Mind | 1966 | 25.00 |
| DBK WORKS | | | |
| ❑ 104 [(2)] | Don't Give Up on Me | 2003 | 20.00 |
| INFINITY | | | |
| ❑ INF-9024 | Sidewalks, Fences and Walls | 1979 | 12.00 |
| KENWOOD | | | |
| ❑ LP-498 [M] | Solomon Burke | 1964 | 200.00 |
| *—Reissue of Apollo 498* | | | |
| MGM | | | |
| ❑ SE-4767 | Electronic Magnetism | 1971 | 15.00 |
| ❑ SE-4830 | King Heavy | 1972 | 15.00 |
| PRIDE | | | |
| ❑ 0011 | The History of Solomon Burke | 1972 | 15.00 |
| ROUNDER | | | |
| ❑ 2042/3 [(2)] | Soul Alive! | 1984 | 12.00 |
| ❑ 2053 | A Change Is Gonna Come | 1986 | 10.00 |
| SAVOY | | | |
| ❑ 14660 | Solomon Burke | 1981 | 10.00 |
| ❑ 14679 | Into My Life | 1982 | 10.00 |
| ❑ 14717 | Take Me, Shake Me | 1983 | 10.00 |

## BURKE, VINNIE

| Number | Title (A Side/B Side) | Yr | NM |
|---|---|---|---|
| ABC-PARAMOUNT | | | |
| ❑ ABC-139 [M] | The Vinnie Burke All Stars | 1956 | 50.00 |
| ❑ ABC-170 [M] | The Vinnie Burke String Jazz Quartet | 1957 | 50.00 |
| BETHLEHEM | | | |
| ❑ BCP-1010 [10] | East Coast Jazz 2 | 1954 | 120.00 |

## BURNETT, CAROL

| Number | Title (A Side/B Side) | Yr | NM |
|---|---|---|---|
| DECCA | | | |
| ❑ DL 4049 [M] | Carol Burnett Remembers How They Stopped the Show | 1960 | 30.00 |
| ❑ DL 4437 [M] | Let Me Entertain You | 1964 | 20.00 |
| ❑ DL 74049 [S] | Carol Burnett Remembers How They Stopped the Show | 1960 | 40.00 |
| ❑ DL 74437 [S] | Let Me Entertain You | 1964 | 25.00 |
| RCA VICTOR | | | |
| ❑ LPM-3839 [M] | Carol Burnett Sings | 1967 | 20.00 |
| ❑ LSP-3839 [S] | Carol Burnett Sings | 1967 | 20.00 |

**BURNETT, J. HENRY** See T-BONE BURNETT.

## BURNETT, T-BONE

| Number | Title (A Side/B Side) | Yr | NM |
|---|---|---|---|
| UNI | | | |
| ❑ 73125 | The B-52 Band and the Fabulous Skyhawks | 1972 | 30.00 |
| *—As "J. Henry Burnett"* | | | |

## BURNETTE, BILLY

| Number | Title (A Side/B Side) | Yr | NM |
|---|---|---|---|
| COLUMBIA | | | |
| ❑ JC 36792 | Billy Burnette | 1980 | 10.00 |
| ❑ FC 37460 | Gimme You | 1981 | 10.00 |
| ENTRANCE | | | |
| ❑ Z 31228 | Billy Burnette | 1972 | 20.00 |
| MCA CURB | | | |
| ❑ 5604 | Try Me | 1985 | 10.00 |
| POLYDOR | | | |
| ❑ PD-1-6187 | Billy Burnette | 1979 | 10.00 |

## BURNETTE, DORSEY

| Number | Title (A Side/B Side) | Yr | NM |
|---|---|---|---|
| CALLIOPE | | | |
| ❑ CAL 7006 | Things I Treasure | 1977 | 12.00 |
| CAPITOL | | | |
| ❑ ST-11094 | Here and Now | 1972 | 15.00 |
| ❑ ST-11219 | Dorsey Burnette | 1973 | 15.00 |
| DOT | | | |
| ❑ DLP-3456 [M] | Dorsey Burnette Sings | 1963 | 40.00 |
| ❑ DLP-25456 [S] | Dorsey Burnette Sings | 1963 | 50.00 |
| ERA | | | |
| ❑ EL-102 [M] | Tall Oak Tree | 1960 | 150.00 |
| ❑ ES-102 [S] | Tall Oak Tree | 1960 | 300.00 |
| ❑ ES-800 [M] | Dorsey Burnette's Greatest Hits | 1969 | 25.00 |
| GUSTO | | | |
| ❑ 0050 | The Golden Hits of Dorsey Burnette | 197? | 12.00 |

## BURNETTE, DORSEY AND JOHNNY

| Number | Title (A Side/B Side) | Yr | NM |
|---|---|---|---|
| SOLID SMOKE | | | |
| ❑ SS-8005 | Together Again | 1978 | 15.00 |

## BURNETTE, JOHNNY

| Number | Title (A Side/B Side) | Yr | NM |
|---|---|---|---|
| CORAL | | | |
| ❑ CRL 57080 [M] | Johnny Burnette & the Rock 'N' Roll Trio | 1956 | 6000. |
| *—Originals have maroon labels, machine-stamped (not engraved) numbers in the dead wax, printing on jacket's spine and "Printed in U.S.A." in lower right of back cover; VG value 2000; VG+ value 4000* | | | |
| LIBERTY | | | |
| ❑ LRP-3179 [M] | Dreamin' | 1960 | 40.00 |
| ❑ LRP-3183 [M] | Johnny Burnette | 1961 | 40.00 |
| ❑ LRP-3190 [M] | Johnny Burnette Sings | 1961 | 40.00 |
| ❑ LRP-3206 [M] | Johnny Burnette's Hits and Other Favorites | 1962 | 40.00 |
| ❑ LRP-3255 [M] | Roses Are Red | 1962 | 40.00 |
| ❑ LRP-3389 [M] | The Johnny Burnette Story | 1964 | 40.00 |
| ❑ LST-7179 [S] | Dreamin' | 1960 | 60.00 |
| ❑ LST-7183 [S] | Johnny Burnette | 1961 | 60.00 |
| ❑ LST-7190 [S] | Johnny Burnette Sings | 1961 | 60.00 |
| ❑ LST-7206 [S] | Johnny Burnette's Hits and Other Favorites | 1962 | 50.00 |
| ❑ LST-7255 [S] | Roses Are Red | 1962 | 50.00 |
| ❑ LST-7389 [S] | The Johnny Burnette Story | 1964 | 50.00 |
| MCA | | | |
| ❑ 1513 | Listen to Johnny Burnette and the Rock 'N' Roll Trio | 1982 | 10.00 |
| SOLID SMOKE | | | |
| ❑ SS-8001 | Tear It Up | 1978 | 15.00 |
| *—Black viinyl* | | | |
| ❑ SS-8001 | Tear It Up | 1978 | 30.00 |
| *—Blue vinyl* | | | |
| SUNSET | | | |
| ❑ SUM-1179 [M] | Dreamin' | 1967 | 15.00 |
| ❑ SUS-5179 [S] | Dreamin' | 1967 | 20.00 |
| UNITED ARTISTS | | | |
| ❑ UA-LA432-G | The Very Best of Johnny Burnette | 1975 | 10.00 |

## BURNETTE, SMILEY

| Number | Title (A Side/B Side) | Yr | NM |
|---|---|---|---|
| CRICKET | | | |
| ❑ CR-11 [M] | Rodeo Songaree | 1959 | 30.00 |
| STARDAY | | | |
| ❑ SLP-191 [M] | Ole Frog | 1962 | 40.00 |

## BURNS, GEORGE

| Number | Title (A Side/B Side) | Yr | NM |
|---|---|---|---|
| BUDDAH | | | |
| ❑ BDS-5025 | George Burns Sings | 1969 | 15.00 |
| ❑ BDS-5127 | A Musical Trip with George Burns | 1972 | 12.00 |
| *—Reissue of 5027* | | | |
| MERCURY | | | |
| ❑ SRM-1-4061 | Young at Heart | 1982 | 10.00 |
| ❑ SRM-1-5025 | I Wish I Was Eighteen Again | 1980 | 10.00 |
| ❑ SRM-1-6001 | George Burns in Nashville | 1981 | 10.00 |
| PRIDE | | | |
| ❑ PRD-00 11 [(2)] | An Evening with George Burns | 1974 | 20.00 |

## BURNS, RALPH

| Number | Title (A Side/B Side) | Yr | NM |
|---|---|---|---|
| BETHLEHEM | | | |
| ❑ BCP-68 [M] | Bijou | 1957 | 80.00 |
| CLEF | | | |
| ❑ MGC-115 [10] | Free Forms | 1953 | 150.00 |
| DECCA | | | |
| ❑ DL 8235 [M] | Jazz Studio 5 | 1956 | 80.00 |
| ❑ DL 8555 [M] | The Masters Revisited | 1957 | 60.00 |
| ❑ DL 9068 [M] | New York's a Song | 1959 | 40.00 |
| ❑ DL 9207 [M] | Very Warm for Jazz | 1959 | 60.00 |
| ❑ DL 9215 [M] | Porgy and Bess | 1959 | 40.00 |
| ❑ DL 79068 [S] | New York's a Song | 1959 | 50.00 |
| ❑ DL 79207 [S] | Very Warm for Jazz | 1959 | 70.00 |
| ❑ DL 79215 [S] | Porgy and Bess | 1959 | 50.00 |
| EPIC | | | |
| ❑ LN 24015 [M] | Swingin' Down the Lane | 1962 | 30.00 |
| ❑ BN 26015 [S] | Swingin' Down the Lane | 1962 | 40.00 |
| JAZZTONE | | | |
| ❑ J-1228 [M] | Spring Sequence | 1956 | 50.00 |
| MERCURY | | | |
| ❑ MGC-115 [10] | Free Forms | 1952 | 200.00 |
| MGM | | | |
| ❑ E-3616 [M] | The Swinging Seasons | 1958 | 50.00 |
| ❑ SE-3616 [S] | The Swinging Seasons | 1959 | 40.00 |
| NORGRAN | | | |
| ❑ MGN-1028 [M] | Ralph Burns Among the JATP's | 1955 | 120.00 |
| PERIOD | | | |
| ❑ SPL-1105 [10] | Spring Sequence | 1955 | 120.00 |
| ❑ SPL-1109 [10] | Bijou | 1955 | 120.00 |
| VERVE | | | |
| ❑ MGV-8121 [M] | Ralph Burns Among the JATP's | 1957 | 50.00 |
| ❑ V-8121 [M] | Ralph Burns Among the JATP's | 1961 | 20.00 |
| WARWICK | | | |
| ❑ W-5001 [M] | Where There's Burns There's Fire | 1961 | 50.00 |
| ❑ W-5001 ST [S] | Where There's Burns There's Fire | 1961 | 70.00 |

## BURNS, RALPH/BILLIE HOLIDAY

| Number | Title (A Side/B Side) | Yr | NM |
|---|---|---|---|
| CLEF | | | |
| ❑ MGC-718 [M] | The Free Forms of Ralph Burns/The Songs of Billie Holiday | 1956 | 120.00 |
| VERVE | | | |
| ❑ MGV-8098 [M] | Jazz Recital | 1957 | 50.00 |
| ❑ V-8098 [M] | Jazz Recital | 1961 | 20.00 |

## BURNS, RANDY

| Number | Title (A Side/B Side) | Yr | NM |
|---|---|---|---|
| ESP-DISK' | | | |
| ❑ 1039 | Songs of Love and War | 1966 | 25.00 |
| ❑ 1089 | Evening of the Magician | 1968 | 25.00 |
| ❑ 2007 | Song for an Uncertain Lady | 1971 | 15.00 |
| MERCURY | | | |
| ❑ SR-61329 | Randy Burns and the Skydog Band | 1971 | 12.00 |
| POLYDOR | | | |
| ❑ PD-5030 | I'm a Lover, Not a Fool | 1972 | 12.00 |
| ❑ PD-5049 | Still On Our Feet | 1973 | 12.00 |

## BURNS, RON

| Number | Title (A Side/B Side) | Yr | NM |
|---|---|---|---|
| ROULETTE | | | |
| ❑ R-52095 [M] | Skin Burns | 1963 | 20.00 |
| ❑ SR-52095 [S] | Skin Burns | 1963 | 25.00 |

## BURNT SUITE

| Number | Title (A Side/B Side) | Yr | NM |
|---|---|---|---|
| B.J.W. | | | |
| ❑ 9 | Burnt Suite | 1967 | 200.00 |

## BURRELL, DAVE

| Number | Title (A Side/B Side) | Yr | NM |
|---|---|---|---|
| DOUGLAS | | | |
| ❑ SD 798 | High | 1969 | 20.00 |
| HAT HUT | | | |
| ❑ 05 [(2)] | Windward Passages | 1979 | 20.00 |

## BURRELL, KENNY

| Number | Title (A Side/B Side) | Yr | NM |
|---|---|---|---|
| ARGO | | | |
| ❑ LP-655 [M] | A Night at the Vanguard | 1959 | 30.00 |
| ❑ LPS-655 [S] | A Night at the Vanguard | 1959 | 40.00 |
| BLUE NOTE | | | |
| ❑ BLP-1523 [M] | Introducing Kenny Burrell | 1956 | 250.00 |
| *—Regular version, Lexington Ave. address on label* | | | |
| ❑ BLP-1523 [M] | Introducing Kenny Burrell | 1956 | 400.00 |
| *—"Deep groove" version (deep indentation under label on both sides)* | | | |

Number | Title (A Side/B Side) | Yr | NM

❑ BLP-1523 [M] Introducing Kenny Burrell 1957 80.00
*—W. 63rd St., NYC address on label*
❑ BLP-1523 [M] Introducing Kenny Burrell 1963 30.00
*—New York, USA address on label*
❑ BLP-1543 [M] Kenny Burrell, Volume 2 1957 50.00
*—W. 63rd St., NYC address on label*
❑ BLP-1543 [M] Kenny Burrell, Volume 2 1957 150.00
*—Regular version, Lexington Ave. address on label*
❑ BLP-1543 [M] Kenny Burrell, Volume 2 1957 200.00
*—"Deep groove" version (deep indentation under label on both sides)*
❑ BLP-1543 [M] Kenny Burrell, Volume 2 1963 25.00
*—New York, USA address on label*
❑ BLP-1596 [M] Blue Lights, Volume 1 1958 80.00
*—Regular version, W. 63rd St., NYC address on label*
❑ BLP-1596 [M] Blue Lights, Volume 1 1958 120.00
*—"Deep groove" version (deep indentation under label on both sides)*
❑ BLP-1596 [M] Blue Lights, Volume 1 1963 25.00
*—New York, USA address on label*
❑ BST-1596 [S] Blue Lights, Volume 1 1959 70.00
*—Regular version, W. 63rd St., NYC address on label*
❑ BST-1596 [S] Blue Lights, Volume 1 1959 100.00
*—"Deep groove" version (deep indentation under label on both sides)*
❑ BST-1596 [S] Blue Lights, Volume 1 1963 25.00
*—New York, USA address on label*
❑ BLP-1597 [M] Blue Lights, Volume 2 1958 70.00
*—Regular version, W. 63rd St., NYC address on label*
❑ BLP-1597 [M] Blue Lights, Volume 2 1958 100.00
*—"Deep groove" version (deep indentation under label on both sides)*
❑ BLP-1597 [M] Blue Lights, Volume 2 1963 25.00
*—New York, USA address on label*
❑ BST-1597 [S] Blue Lights, Volume 2 1959 70.00
*—Regular version, W. 63rd St., NYC address on label*
❑ BST-1597 [S] Blue Lights, Volume 2 1959 100.00
*—"Deep groove" version (deep indentation under label on both sides)*
❑ BST-1597 [S] Blue Lights, Volume 2 1963 25.00
*—New York, USA address on label*
❑ BLP-4021 [M] On View at the Five Spot Café 1960 70.00
*—Regular version, W. 63rd St., NYC address on label*
❑ BLP-4021 [M] On View at the Five Spot Café 1960 100.00
*—"Deep groove" version (deep indentation under label on both sides)*
❑ BLP-4021 [M] On View at the Five Spot Café 1963 25.00
*—New York, USA address on label*
❑ BLP-4123 [M] Midnight Blue 1963 30.00
*—New York, USA address on label*
❑ BST-84021 [S] On View at the Five Spot Café 1960 60.00
*—W. 63rd St., NYC address on label*
❑ BST-84021 [S] On View at the Five Spot Café 1963 25.00
*—New York, USA address on label*
❑ BST-84123 [S] Midnight Blue 1963 40.00
*—New York, USA address on label*

CADET
❑ LPS-769 [S] Men at Work 1965 20.00
*—Reissue of Argo 655*
❑ LPS-772 [S] The Tender Gender 1966 20.00
❑ LPS-779 [S] Have Yourself a Soulful Little Christmas 1966 20.00
❑ LP-798 [M] Ode to 52nd Street 1967 20.00

COLUMBIA
❑ CL 1703 [M] Weaver of Dreams 1961 20.00
❑ CS 8503 [S] Weaver of Dreams 1961 25.00

KAPP
❑ KL-1326 [M] Lotta Bossa Nova 1962 20.00
❑ KS-3326 [S] Lotta Bossa Nova 1962 25.00

MOODSVILLE
❑ MVLP-29 [M] Bluesy Burrell 1963 40.00
*—Green label*
❑ MVLP-29 [M] Bluesy Burrell 1965 20.00
*—Blue label with trident logo*
❑ MVST-29 [S] Bluesy Burrell 1963 40.00
*—Green label*
❑ MVST-29 [S] Bluesy Burrell 1965 25.00
*—Blue label with trident logo*

PRESTIGE
❑ PRLP-7073 [M] All Night Long 1957 100.00
*—Actually an all-star session; reissued as a Kenny Burrell album, thus it is listed here*
❑ PRLP-7081 [M] All Day Long 1957 100.00
*—Actually an all-star session; reissued as a Kenny Burrell album, thus it is listed here*
❑ PRLP-7088 [M] Kenny Burrell 1957 80.00
❑ PRLP-7277 [M] All Day Long 1963 50.00
*—Reissue of 7081*
❑ PRST-7277 [R] All Day Long 1963 20.00
❑ PRLP-7289 [M] All Night Long 1964 50.00
*—Reissue of 7073*
❑ PRST-7289 [R] All Night Long 1964 20.00
❑ PRLP-7308 [M] Blue Moods 1964 30.00
*—Reissue of 7088*
❑ PRST-7308 [R] Blue Moods 1964 20.00
❑ PRLP-7315 [M] Soul Call 1964 25.00
❑ PRST-7315 [S] Soul Call 1964 30.00
❑ PRLP-7347 [M] Crash 1964 25.00
❑ PRST-7347 [S] Crash 1964 30.00
❑ PRLP-7448 [M] The Best of Kenny Burrell 1967 30.00
❑ PRST-7448 [S] The Best of Kenny Burrell 1967 20.00

VERVE
❑ V-8553 [M] Blue Bash! 1963 20.00
❑ V6-8553 [S] Blue Bash! 1963 25.00
❑ V6-8612 [S] Guitar Forms 1965 20.00
❑ V6-8656 [S] A Generation Ago Today 1966 20.00
❑ V-8746 [M] Blues— The Common Ground 1968 20.00

## BURRELL, KENNY, AND JOHN COLTRANE

NEW JAZZ
❑ NJLP-8217 [M] The Cats 1959 80.00
*—Purple label*
❑ NJLP-8217 [M] The Cats 1965 25.00
*—Blue label with trident logo*
❑ NJLP-8276 [M] Kenny Burrell with John Coltrane 1962 60.00
*—Purple label*
❑ NJLP-8276 [M] Kenny Burrell with John Coltrane 1965 25.00
*—Blue label with trident logo*

PRESTIGE
❑ PRLP-7532 [M] Kenny Burrell Quintet with John Coltrane 1967 30.00
❑ PRST-7532 [S] Kenny Burrell Quintet with John Coltrane 1967 20.00

## BURRELL, KENNY; TINY GRIMES; BILL JENNINGS

STATUS
❑ ST-8318 [M] Guitar Soul 1965 40.00

## BURRELL, KENNY, AND JIMMY RANEY

PRESTIGE
❑ PRLP-7119 [M] Two Guitars 1957 80.00

## BURRITO BROTHERS, THE
See THE FLYING BURRITO BROTHERS.

## BURROUGHS, WILLIAM

ESP-DISK'
❑ 1050 [M] Call Me Burroughs 1967 100.00

## BURROWS, ABE

COLUMBIA
❑ CL 6128 [10] Abe Burrows Sings? 1950 40.00

DECCA
❑ DL 5288 [10] The Girl with the 3 Blue Eyes 1951 40.00

## BURTON, GARY

RCA VICTOR
❑ LPM-2420 [M] New Vibe Man in Town 1961 20.00
❑ LSP-2420 [S] New Vibe Man in Town 1961 25.00
❑ LPM-2665 [M] Who Is Gary Burton? 1963 20.00
❑ LSP-2665 [S] Who Is Gary Burton? 1963 25.00
❑ LPM-2880 [M] Something's Coming 1964 20.00
❑ LSP-2880 [S] Something's Coming 1964 25.00
❑ LSP-3360 [S] The Groovy Sound of Music 1965 20.00
❑ LSP-3642 [S] The Time Machine 1966 20.00
❑ LSP-3719 [S] Tennessee Firebird 1966 20.00
❑ LPM-3835 [M] Duster 1967 20.00
❑ LPM-3901 [M] Lofty Fake Anagram 1967 20.00
❑ LPM-3985 [M] Gary Burton Quartet In Concert 1968 30.00

## BURTON, GARY; SONNY ROLLINS; CLARK TERRY

RCA VICTOR
❑ LSP-2725 [S] Three in Jazz 1963 20.00

## BURTON, JAMES

A&M
❑ SP-4293 James Burton 1971 25.00

## BURTON, JOE

CORAL
❑ CRL 57098 [M] Joe Burton Session 1957 40.00
❑ CRL 57175 [M] Here I Am in Love Again 1958 40.00
❑ CRL 757175 [S] Here I Am in Love Again 1959 30.00

JODAY
❑ JS-1000 [S] The Subtle Sound of Joe Burton 1963 20.00

REGENT
❑ MG-6036 [M] Jazz Pretty 1957 50.00

## BUSH, JOHNNY

HILLTOP
❑ JS-6081 You Ought to Hear Me Cry 197? 15.00

MILLION
❑ 1001 The Best of Johnny Bush 1972 25.00

POWER PAK
❑ PO-217 Bush Country 197? 12.00

RCA VICTOR
❑ APL1-0216 Here Comes the World Again 1973 15.00
❑ APL1-0369 Texas Dance Hall Girl 1974 15.00
❑ LSP-10002 Whiskey River/There Stands the Glass 1973 15.00

STOP
❑ 1028 The Greatest Hits of Johnny Bush 1972 20.00
❑ 10002 Sound of a Heartache 1968 25.00
❑ 10005 Undo the Right 1968 20.00
❑ 10008 You Gave Me a Mountain 1969 20.00
❑ 10014 Johnny Bush 1970 20.00

WHISKEY RIVER
❑ 8024 [(2)] Live at Dance Town USA 1979 15.00

## BUSH, KATE

COLUMBIA
❑ OC 44164 The Sensual World 1989 12.00

EMI AMERICA
❑ SW-17003 The Kick Inside 1978 10.00
*—Reissue of Harvest release*
❑ SMAS-17008 Lionheart 1978 15.00
❑ ST-17084 The Dreaming 1982 10.00
❑ ST-17115 Never for Ever 1983 10.00
❑ ST-17171 Hounds of Love 1985 10.00
*—Black vinyl*
❑ ST-17171 Hounds of Love 1985 30.00
*—Marbled vinyl*
❑ PWAS-17242 The Whole Story 1986 15.00
❑ MLP-19004 [EP] Kate Bush 1983 15.00

HARVEST
❑ SW-11761 The Kick Inside 1978 25.00

## BUSHKIN, JOE

ATLANTIC
❑ ALR-108 [10] I Love a Piano 1950 50.00

CAPITOL
❑ T 711 [M] Midnight Rhapsody 1956 30.00
*—Turquoise or gray label*
❑ T 759 [M] Skylight Rhapsody 1956 30.00
*—Turquoise or gray label*
❑ T 832 [M] A Fellow Needs a Girl 1957 30.00
*—Turquoise or gray label*
❑ T 911 [M] Bushkin Spotlights Berlin 1958 30.00
*—Turquoise or gray label*
❑ ST 1094 [S] Blue Angels 1959 30.00
*—Black colorband label, logo at left*
❑ T 1094 [M] Blue Angels 1959 20.00
*—Black colorband label, logo at left*

COLUMBIA
❑ CL 6152 [10] Piano Moods 195? 50.00
❑ CL 6201 [10] After Hours 195? 50.00

EPIC
❑ LN 3345 [M] Piano After Midnight 1956 30.00

REPRISE
❑ RS-6119 [S] In Concert, Town Hall 1964 20.00

ROYALE
❑ 18118 [10] Joe Bushkin 195? 50.00

## BUSTA RHYMES

ELEKTRA
❑ ED 6052 [(2)DJ] When Disaster Strikes 1997 20.00
*—Promo-only version*
❑ 61742 [(2)] The Coming 1996 15.00
❑ 62064 [(2)] When Disaster Strikes 1997 15.00
❑ 62211 [(2)] E.L.E. (Extinction Level Event) 1998 15.00
❑ 62517 [(2)] Anarchy 2000 15.00

J
❑ 20009 [(2)] Genesis 2001 20.00

## BUTERA, SAM, AND THE WITNESSES

CAPITOL
❑ ST 1098 [S] The Big Horn 1959 40.00
❑ T 1098 [M] The Big Horn 1958 30.00
❑ ST 1521 [S] The Big Sax and the Big Voice 1960 30.00
❑ T 1521 [M] The Big Sax and the Big Voice 1960 25.00

DOT
❑ DLP-3272 [M] The Wildest Clan 1960 20.00
❑ DLP-3381 [M] Apache 1961 20.00
❑ DLP-25272 [S] The Wildest Clan 1960 25.00
❑ DLP-25381 [S] Apache 1961 25.00

## BUTLER, ARTIE

A&M
❑ SP-2007 [M] Have You Met Miss Jones? 1968 50.00
*—Mono appears to be promo only, in stereo cover with "Monaural" sticker*
❑ SP-3007 [S] Have You Met Miss Jones? 1968 30.00

## BUTLER, BILLY

PRESTIGE
❑ PRST-7622 This Is Billy Butler 1968 25.00
❑ PRST-7734 Guitar Soul 1969 25.00
❑ PRST-7797 Yesterday, Today and Tomorrow 1970 25.00
❑ PRST-7854 Night Life 1971 25.00

## BUTLER, CARL

COLUMBIA
❑ CL 2002 [M] Don't Let Me Cross Over 1963 20.00
❑ CS 8802 [S] Don't Let Me Cross Over 1963 25.00

HARMONY
❑ HL 7385 [M] The Great Carl Butler Sings 1966 12.00

Kate Bush, *The Dreaming,* EMI America ST-17084, 1982, $10.

| Number | Title (A Side/B Side) | Yr | NM |
|---|---|---|---|
| ❑ HS 11185 [S] | The Great Carl Butler Sings | 1966 | 15.00 |
| ❑ H 30674 | For the First Time | 1971 | 12.00 |
| **BUTLER, CARL, AND PEARL** | | | |
| CHART | | | |
| ❑ 1051 | Temptation Keeps Twistin' Her Arm | 1972 | 15.00 |
| COLUMBIA | | | |
| ❑ CS 1039 | Carl and Pearl Butler's Greatest Hits | 1970 | 15.00 |
| ❑ CL 2125 [M] | Loving Arms | 1964 | 20.00 |
| ❑ CL 2308 [M] | The Old and the New | 1965 | 15.00 |
| ❑ CL 2640 [M] | Avenue of Prayer | 1967 | 20.00 |
| ❑ CS 8925 [S] | Loving Arms | 1964 | 25.00 |
| ❑ CS 9108 [S] | The Old and the New | 1965 | 20.00 |
| ❑ CS 9440 [S] | Avenue of Prayer | 1967 | 15.00 |
| ❑ CS 9651 | Our Country World | 1968 | 15.00 |
| ❑ CS 9769 | Honky Tonkin' | 1969 | 15.00 |
| HARMONY | | | |
| ❑ H 31182 | Watch and Pray | 1972 | 12.00 |
| **BUTLER, FREDDIE** | | | |
| KAPP | | | |
| ❑ KS-3519 | With a Dab of Soul | 1968 | 30.00 |
| **BUTLER, JERRY** | | | |
| ABNER | | | |
| ❑ R-2001 [M] | Jerry Butler, Esq. | 1959 | 400.00 |
| BUDDAH | | | |
| ❑ BDS-4001 | The Very Best of Jerry Butler | 1969 | 15.00 |
| FOUNTAIN | | | |
| ❑ FR 2-82-1 | Ice 'n Hot | 1982 | 10.00 |
| MERCURY | | | |
| ❑ SRM-1-689 | The Power of Love | 1973 | 15.00 |
| ❑ SRM-1-1006 | Sweet Sixteen | 1974 | 15.00 |
| ❑ SRM-2-7502 [(2)] | The Spice of Life | 1972 | 20.00 |
| ❑ MG-21005 [M] | The Soul Artistry of Jerry Butler | 1967 | 20.00 |
| ❑ MG-21146 [M] | Mr. Dream Merchant | 1967 | 20.00 |
| ❑ SR-61005 [S] | The Soul Artistry of Jerry Butler | 1967 | 15.00 |
| ❑ SR-61146 [S] | Mr. Dream Merchant | 1967 | 15.00 |
| ❑ SR-61151 | Jerry Butler's Golden Hits Live | 1968 | 15.00 |
| ❑ SR-61171 | The Soul Goes On | 1968 | 15.00 |
| ❑ SR-61198 | The Ice Man Cometh | 1968 | 15.00 |
| ❑ SR-61234 | Ice On Ice | 1969 | 15.00 |

| Number | Title (A Side/B Side) | Yr | NM |
|---|---|---|---|
| ❑ SR-61269 | You & Me | 1970 | 15.00 |
| ❑ SR-61281 | The Best of Jerry Butler | 1970 | 15.00 |
| ❑ SR-61320 | Jerry Butler Sings Assorted Sounds | 1971 | 15.00 |
| ❑ SR-61347 | The Sagittarius Movement | 1971 | 15.00 |
| ❑ 810369-1 | The Best of Jerry Butler | 1983 | 10.00 |
| ❑ 822212-1 | Only the Strong Survive: The Great Philadelphia Hits | 1984 | 10.00 |
| MOTOWN | | | |
| ❑ M6-850 | Love's on the Menu | 1976 | 12.00 |
| ❑ M6-878 | Suite for the Single Girl | 1977 | 10.00 |
| ❑ M6-892 | It All Comes Out in My Songs | 1977 | 10.00 |
| PHILADELPHIA INT'L. | | | |
| ❑ JZ 35510 | Nothing Says I Love You Like I Love You | 1978 | 10.00 |
| ❑ JZ 36413 | The Best Love I Ever Had | 1979 | 10.00 |
| RHINO | | | |
| ❑ RNLP-216 | The Best of Jerry Butler (1958-1969) | 1984 | 10.00 |
| TRADITION | | | |
| ❑ TLP-2068 | Starring Jerry Butler | 1969 | 15.00 |
| TRIP | | | |
| ❑ 8011 [(2)] | All Time Hits | 1972 | 15.00 |
| UNITED ARTISTS | | | |
| ❑ UA-LA498-E | The Very Best of Jerry Butler | 1975 | 10.00 |
| VEE JAY | | | |
| ❑ VJLP2-1003 [(2)] | Jerry Butler Gold | 198? | 15.00 |
| ❑ LP-1027 [M] | Jerry Butler, Esquire | 1960 | 150.00 |
| *—Reissue of Abner 2001* | | | |
| ❑ LP-1029 [M] | He Will Break Your Heart | 1960 | 80.00 |
| ❑ LP-1034 [M] | Love Me | 1961 | 50.00 |
| *—Reissue of 1027* | | | |
| ❑ LP-1038 [M] | Aware of Love | 1961 | 40.00 |
| ❑ SR-1038 [S] | Aware of Love | 1961 | 50.00 |
| ❑ LP-1046 [M] | Moon River | 1962 | 40.00 |
| ❑ SR-1046 [S] | Moon River | 1962 | 50.00 |
| ❑ VJLP-1046 | Moon River | 1985 | 10.00 |
| *—Reissue of original 1046; has softer vinyl* | | | |
| ❑ LP-1048 [M] | The Best of Jerry Butler | 1962 | 25.00 |
| ❑ SR-1048 [P] | The Best of Jerry Butler | 1962 | 30.00 |
| ❑ VJLP-1048 | The Best of Jerry Butler | 1985 | 10.00 |
| *—Reissue of original 1048; has softer vinyl* | | | |
| ❑ LP-1057 [M] | Folk Songs | 1963 | 25.00 |

| Number | Title (A Side/B Side) | Yr | NM |
|---|---|---|---|
| ❑ SR-1057 [S] | Folk Songs | 1963 | 30.00 |
| ❑ LP-1075 [M] | For Your Precious Love | 1963 | 25.00 |
| ❑ SR-1075 [S] | For Your Precious Love | 1963 | 30.00 |
| ❑ LP-1076 [M] | Giving Up On Love/Need to Belong | 1963 | 25.00 |
| ❑ VJS-1076 [S] | Giving Up On Love/Need to Belong | 1963 | 30.00 |
| ❑ LP-1119 [M] | More of the Best of Jerry Butler | 1965 | 25.00 |
| ❑ VJS-1119 [S] | More of the Best of Jerry Butler | 1965 | 30.00 |
| ❑ D1-74807 | He Will Break Your Heart | 1989 | 12.00 |
| **BUTLER, LARRY** | | | |
| IMPERIAL | | | |
| ❑ LP-9354 [M] | Take Me | 1967 | 20.00 |
| ❑ LP-12354 [S] | Take Me | 1967 | 15.00 |
| ❑ LP-12410 | A Thing Called Love | 1968 | 15.00 |
| UNITED ARTISTS | | | |
| ❑ UA-LA739-G | Larry Butler and Friends | 1977 | 12.00 |
| **BUTTERFIELD, BILLY** | | | |
| CAPITOL | | | |
| ❑ H 201 [10] | Stardusting | 1950 | 50.00 |
| ❑ H 424 [10] | Classics in Jazz | 195? | 50.00 |
| COLUMBIA | | | |
| ❑ CL 1514 [M] | Billy Blows His Horn | 1960 | 20.00 |
| ❑ CL 1673 [M] | The Golden Horn | 1961 | 20.00 |
| *—Red and black label with six "eye" logos* | | | |
| ❑ CS 8314 [S] | Billy Blows His Horn | 1960 | 25.00 |
| ❑ CS 8473 [S] | The Golden Horn | 196? | 20.00 |
| *—"360 Sound Stereo" on label* | | | |
| ❑ CS 8473 [S] | The Golden Horn | 1961 | 25.00 |
| *—Red and black label with six "eye" logos* | | | |
| EPIC | | | |
| ❑ LA 16026 [M] | Billy Plays Bix | 1962 | 30.00 |
| ❑ BA 17026 [S] | Billy Plays Bix | 1962 | 40.00 |
| ESSEX | | | |
| ❑ ESLP-111 [10] | Far Away Places | 195? | 50.00 |
| ❑ 401 [M] | Billy Butterfield at Princeton | 1955 | 40.00 |
| ❑ 402 [M] | Billy Butterfield Goes to NYU | 1955 | 40.00 |
| ❑ 403 [M] | Billy Butterfield at Amherst | 1955 | 40.00 |
| ❑ 404 [M] | Billy Butterfield at Rutgers | 1955 | 40.00 |
| JOY | | | |
| ❑ JL-1003 [M] | The New Dance Sound of Billy Butterfield | 196? | 40.00 |
| RCA VICTOR | | | |
| ❑ LPM-1212 [M] | New York Land Dixie | 1956 | 40.00 |
| ❑ LPM-1441 [M] | They're Playing Our Song | 1957 | 40.00 |
| ❑ LPM-1566 [M] | A Touch of the Blues | 1958 | 40.00 |
| ❑ LPM-1590 [M] | Thank You for a Lovely Evening | 1958 | 30.00 |
| ❑ LPM-1699 [M] | A Lovely Way to Spend an Evening | 1958 | 30.00 |
| ❑ LSP-1699 [S] | A Lovely Way to Spend an Evening | 1958 | 40.00 |
| WESTMINSTER | | | |
| ❑ WL-3020 [10] | Billy Butterfield | 1954 | 50.00 |
| ❑ WL-6006 [M] | Dancing for Two in Love | 1955 | 40.00 |
| **BUTTERFIELD, ERSKINE** | | | |
| DAVIS | | | |
| ❑ JD-104 [M] | Piano Cocktail | 1951 | 40.00 |
| **BUTTERFIELD, PAUL** | | | |
| AMHERST | | | |
| ❑ AMH-3305 | The Legendary Paul Butterfield Rides Again | 1986 | 12.00 |
| BEARSVILLE | | | |
| ❑ BR 2119 | Paul Butterfield's Better Days | 1973 | 12.00 |
| ❑ BR 2170 | It All Comes Back | 1973 | 12.00 |
| ❑ BR 6960 | Put It In Your Ear | 1976 | 12.00 |
| ❑ BRK 6995 | North-South | 1978 | 12.00 |
| ELEKTRA | | | |
| ❑ EKL-294 [M] | The Paul Butterfield Blues Band | 1965 | 20.00 |
| *—Gold label with guitar player* | | | |
| ❑ EKL-294 [M] | The Paul Butterfield Blues Band | 1966 | 15.00 |
| *—Brown label* | | | |
| ❑ EKL-315 [M] | East-West | 1966 | 20.00 |
| *—Gold label with guitar player* | | | |
| ❑ EKL-315 [M] | East-West | 1967 | 15.00 |
| *—Brown label* | | | |
| ❑ 7E-2001 [(2)] | The Butterfield Blues Band/Live | 1970 | 25.00 |
| ❑ 7E-2005 [(2)] | Golden Butter/The Best of the Paul Butterfield Blues Band | 1972 | 25.00 |
| ❑ EKL-4015 [M] | The Resurrection of Pigboy Crabshaw | 1967 | 30.00 |
| ❑ EKS-7294 [S] | The Paul Butterfield Blues Band | 1965 | 25.00 |
| *—Gold label with guitar player* | | | |
| ❑ EKS-7294 [S] | The Paul Butterfield Blues Band | 1966 | 20.00 |
| *—Brown label* | | | |



**Except when noted otherwise, VG = 25% of NM, and VG+ = 50% of NM. (Example: VG = $2.00, VG+ = $4.00 and NM = $8.00.)**

| Number | Title (A Side/B Side) | Yr | NM |
|---|---|---|---|
| ❑ EKS-7294 [S] | The Paul Butterfield Blues Band | 1969 | 15.00 |
| *—Red label with large stylized "E"* | | | |
| ❑ EKS-7294 [S] | The Paul Butterfield Blues Band | 1971 | 12.00 |
| *—Butterfly label* | | | |
| ❑ EKS-7315 [S] | East-West | 1966 | 25.00 |
| *—Gold label with guitar player* | | | |
| ❑ EKS-7315 [S] | East-West | 1967 | 20.00 |
| *—Brown label* | | | |
| ❑ EKS-7315 [S] | East-West | 1969 | 15.00 |
| *—Red label with large stylized "E"* | | | |
| ❑ EKS-7315 [S] | East-West | 1971 | 12.00 |
| *—Butterfly label* | | | |
| ❑ EKS-74015 [S] | The Resurrection of Pigboy Crabshaw | 1967 | 20.00 |
| *—Brown label* | | | |
| ❑ EKS-74015 [S] | The Resurrection of Pigboy Crabshaw | 1969 | 15.00 |
| *—Red label with large stylized "E"* | | | |
| ❑ EKS-74015 [S] | The Resurrection of Pigboy Crabshaw | 1971 | 12.00 |
| *—Butterfly label* | | | |
| ❑ EKS-74025 | In My Own Dream | 1968 | 20.00 |
| *—Brown label* | | | |
| ❑ EKS-74025 | In My Own Dream | 1969 | 15.00 |
| *—Red label with large stylized "E"* | | | |
| ❑ EKS-74025 | In My Own Dream | 1971 | 12.00 |
| *—Butterfly label* | | | |
| ❑ EKS-74053 | Keep On Moving | 1969 | 20.00 |
| *—Red label with large stylized "E"* | | | |
| ❑ EKS-74053 | Keep On Moving | 1971 | 12.00 |
| *—Butterfly label* | | | |
| ❑ EKS-75013 | Sometimes I Just Feel Like Smilin' | 1971 | 20.00 |
| **RHINO** | | | |
| ❑ RNLP-70877 | Paul Butterfield's Better Days | 1987 | 8.00 |
| *—Reissue of Bearsville 2119* | | | |
| ❑ RNLP-70878 | It All Comes Back | 1987 | 8.00 |
| *—Reissue of Bearsville 2170* | | | |
| ❑ RNLP-70879 | Put It In Your Ear | 1987 | 8.00 |
| *—Reissue of Bearsville 6960* | | | |
| ❑ RNLP-70880 | North-South | 1987 | 8.00 |
| *—Reissue of Bearsville 6995* | | | |
| **SUNDAZED** | | | |
| ❑ LP 5095 [S] | The Paul Butterfield Blues Band | 2001 | 12.00 |
| *—Reissue on 180-gram vinyl* | | | |
| ❑ LP 5096 | East-West | 2001 | 12.00 |
| *—Reissue on 180-gram vinyl* | | | |

### BUTTHOLE SURFERS

| Number | Title (A Side/B Side) | Yr | NM |
|---|---|---|---|
| **ALTERNATIVE TENTACLES** | | | |
| ❑ VIRUS 32 [EP] | Brown Reason to Live | 198? | 8.00 |
| *—Black vinyl* | | | |
| ❑ VIRUS 32 [EP] | Brown Reason to Live | 1983 | 20.00 |
| *—Retitled version of debut EP with brown swirl vinyl* | | | |
| ❑ VIRUS 32 [EP] | Butthole Surfers | 1983 | 25.00 |
| *—Original pressing of debut EP with no title* | | | |
| ❑ VIRUS 39 [EP] | Live PCPPEP | 1984 | 8.00 |
| **CAPITOL** | | | |
| ❑ C1-29842 [(2)] | Electriclarryland | 1996 | 15.00 |
| ❑ C1-98798 | Independent Worm Saloon | 1993 | 15.00 |
| **HOLLYWOOD** | | | |
| ❑ 41447-1 | Weird Revolution | 2001 | 15.00 |
| *—Pressed in Germany for U.S. release* | | | |
| **LATINO BUGGERVEIL** | | | |
| ❑ LBV 07 [(2)] | Humpty Dumpty LSD | 2002 | 20.00 |
| **ROUGH TRADE** | | | |
| ❑ R260 | Pioughd | 1990 | 20.00 |
| **TOUCH & GO** | | | |
| ❑ 5 | Psychic...Powerless...Another Man's Sac | 1985 | 10.00 |
| *—Reissue on black vinyl* | | | |
| ❑ 5 | Psychic...Powerless...Another Man's Sac | 1985 | 20.00 |
| *—Original on clear vinyl* | | | |
| ❑ 8 | Rembrandt Pussyhorse | 1986 | 10.00 |
| *—Black vinyl* | | | |
| ❑ 8 | Rembrandt Pussyhorse | 1986 | 40.00 |
| *—Red vinyl; supposedly only 100 were pressed* | | | |
| ❑ 14 [EP] | Cream Corn from the Socket of Davis | 1985 | 10.00 |
| *—Black vinyl* | | | |
| ❑ 14 [EP] | Cream Corn from the Socket of Davis | 1985 | 20.00 |
| *—Red vinyl* | | | |
| ❑ 14 [EP] | Cream Corn from the Socket of Davis | 1985 | 25.00 |
| *—Yellow vinyl in green generic sleeve with sticker* | | | |
| ❑ 19 | Locust Abortion Technician | 1987 | 10.00 |
| ❑ 29 | Hairway to Steven | 1988 | 10.00 |
| ❑ 50 | Widowermaker! | 1989 | 10.00 |

### BYARD, JAKI

| Number | Title (A Side/B Side) | Yr | NM |
|---|---|---|---|
| **MUSE** | | | |
| ❑ 5007 | There'll Be Some Changes Made | 1974 | 20.00 |
| **NEW JAZZ** | | | |
| ❑ NJLP-8256 [M] | Here's Jaki | 1961 | 60.00 |
| *—Purple label* | | | |
| ❑ NJLP-8256 [M] | Here's Jaki | 1965 | 30.00 |
| *—Blue label with trident logo at right* | | | |
| ❑ NJLP-8273 [M] | Hi-Fly | 1962 | 60.00 |
| *—Purple label* | | | |
| ❑ NJLP-8273 [M] | Hi-Fly | 1965 | 30.00 |
| *—Blue label with trident logo at right* | | | |
| **PRESTIGE** | | | |
| ❑ PRLP-7397 [M] | Out Front | 1965 | 30.00 |
| *—Blue label with trident logo at right* | | | |
| ❑ PRST-7397 [S] | Out Front | 1965 | 40.00 |
| *—Blue label with trident logo at right* | | | |
| ❑ PRST-7397 [S] | Out Front | 1968 | 25.00 |
| *—Blue label with trident logo in circle at top* | | | |
| ❑ PRLP-7419 [M] | Live! | 1966 | 30.00 |
| *—Blue label with trident logo at right* | | | |
| ❑ PRST-7419 [S] | Live! | 1966 | 40.00 |
| *—Blue label with trident logo at right* | | | |
| ❑ PRST-7419 [S] | Live! | 1968 | 25.00 |
| *—Blue label with trident logo in circle at top* | | | |
| ❑ PRLP-7463 [M] | Freedom Together | 1967 | 40.00 |
| *—Blue label with trident logo at right* | | | |
| ❑ PRST-7463 [S] | Freedom Together | 1967 | 40.00 |
| *—Blue label with trident logo at right* | | | |
| ❑ PRST-7463 [S] | Freedom Together | 1968 | 25.00 |
| *—Blue label with trident logo in circle at top* | | | |
| ❑ PRLP-7477 [M] | Live! Volume 2 | 1967 | 40.00 |
| *—Blue label with trident logo at right* | | | |
| ❑ PRST-7477 [S] | Live! Volume 2 | 1967 | 40.00 |
| *—Blue label with trident logo at right* | | | |
| ❑ PRST-7477 [S] | Live! Volume 2 | 1968 | 25.00 |
| *—Blue label with trident logo in circle at top* | | | |
| ❑ PRLP-7524 [M] | On the Spot | 1967 | 50.00 |
| *—Blue label with trident logo at right* | | | |
| ❑ PRST-7524 [S] | On the Spot | 1967 | 40.00 |
| *—Blue label with trident logo at right* | | | |
| ❑ PRST-7524 [S] | On the Spot | 1968 | 25.00 |
| *—Blue label with trident logo in circle at top* | | | |
| ❑ PRST-7550 | The Sunshine of My Soul | 1968 | 25.00 |
| ❑ PRST-7573 | Jaki Byard with Strings! | 1968 | 25.00 |
| ❑ PRST-7615 | The Jaki Byard Experience | 1969 | 25.00 |
| ❑ PRST-7686 | Solo Piano | 1969 | 25.00 |
| ❑ 24086 [(2)] | Giant Steps | 197? | 20.00 |

### BYAS, DON

| Number | Title (A Side/B Side) | Yr | NM |
|---|---|---|---|
| **ATLANTIC** | | | |
| ❑ ALR-117 [10] | Don Byas Solos | 1952 | 250.00 |
| **BATTLE** | | | |
| ❑ B-6121 [M] | April in Paris | 1963 | 30.00 |
| ❑ BS-6121 [S] | April in Paris | 1963 | 40.00 |
| **DIAL** | | | |
| ❑ LP-216 [10] | Tenor Saxophone Concerto | 1951 | 300.00 |
| **DISCOVERY** | | | |
| ❑ 3022 [10] | Don Byas with Beryl Booker | 1954 | 150.00 |
| **EMARCY** | | | |
| ❑ MG-26026 [10] | Don Byas Sax | 1954 | 120.00 |
| **NORGRAN** | | | |
| ❑ MGN-12 [10] | In France "Don Byas Et Ses Rhythmes" | 1954 | 150.00 |
| **PRESTIGE** | | | |
| ❑ PRST-7598 | Don Byas In Paris | 1969 | 20.00 |
| ❑ PRST-7692 | Don Byas Meets Ben Webster | 1969 | 20.00 |
| **REGENT** | | | |
| ❑ MG-6044 [M] | Jazz Free and Easy | 1957 | 80.00 |
| **SAVOY** | | | |
| ❑ MG-9007 [10] | Don Byas Sax | 1952 | 150.00 |
| ❑ MG-15043 [10] | Tenor Sax Solos | 1955 | 120.00 |
| **SEECO** | | | |
| ❑ SLP-35 [10] | Don Byas Favorites | 1955 | 120.00 |

### BYAS, DON/ BERNARD PEIFFER

| Number | Title (A Side/B Side) | Yr | NM |
|---|---|---|---|
| **VERVE** | | | |
| ❑ MGV-8119 [M] | Jazz from Saint-Germain Des Pres | 1957 | 50.00 |
| ❑ V-8119 [M] | Jazz from Saint-Germain Des Pres | 1961 | 20.00 |

### BYAS, DON/BUDDY TATE

| Number | Title (A Side/B Side) | Yr | NM |
|---|---|---|---|
| **ALLEGRO** | | | |
| ❑ 1741 [M] | All Star Jazz | 1956 | 40.00 |

### BYERS, BILLY

| Number | Title (A Side/B Side) | Yr | NM |
|---|---|---|---|
| **CONCERT HALL JAZZ** | | | |
| ❑ 1217 [M] | Byers' Guide | 1955 | 80.00 |
| **MERCURY** | | | |
| ❑ PPM-2028 [M] | Impressions of Duke Ellington | 196? | 20.00 |
| ❑ PPS-6028 [S] | Impressions of Duke Ellington | 196? | 30.00 |
| **RCA VICTOR** | | | |
| ❑ LPM-1269 [M] | The Jazz Workshop | 1956 | 80.00 |
| **WING** | | | |
| ❑ SRW-16398 [S] | Impressions of Duke Ellington | 196? | 15.00 |

### BYERS, BILLY; JOE NEWMAN; EDDIE BERT

| Number | Title (A Side/B Side) | Yr | NM |
|---|---|---|---|
| **JAZZTONE** | | | |
| ❑ J-1276 [M] | East Coast Sounds | 1959 | 60.00 |

### BYERS, BRENDA

| Number | Title (A Side/B Side) | Yr | NM |
|---|---|---|---|
| **MTA** | | | |
| ❑ 5013 | The Auctioneer | 1968 | 20.00 |
| ❑ 5016 | Thank You for Loving Me | 1969 | 20.00 |

### BYRD, BILLY

| Number | Title (A Side/B Side) | Yr | NM |
|---|---|---|---|
| **REPRISE** | | | |
| ❑ R-6040 [M] | Lonesome Country Songs | 1962 | 20.00 |
| ❑ R9-6040 [S] | Lonesome Country Songs | 1962 | 25.00 |
| **WARNER BROS.** | | | |
| ❑ W 1327 [M] | I Love a Guitar | 1960 | 20.00 |
| ❑ WS 1327 [S] | I Love a Guitar | 1960 | 25.00 |
| ❑ W 1576 [M] | The Golden Guitar of Billy Byrd | 1964 | 20.00 |
| ❑ WS 1576 [S] | The Golden Guitar of Billy Byrd | 1964 | 25.00 |

### BYRD, BOBBY

| Number | Title (A Side/B Side) | Yr | NM |
|---|---|---|---|
| **KING** | | | |
| ❑ KS-1118 | I Need Help | 1970 | 200.00 |

### BYRD, CHARLIE

| Number | Title (A Side/B Side) | Yr | NM |
|---|---|---|---|
| **COLUMBIA** | | | |
| ❑ CL 2592 [M] | Byrdland | 1967 | 20.00 |
| ❑ CL 2652 [M] | Hollywood Byrd | 1967 | 20.00 |
| ❑ CL 2692 [M] | More Brazilian Byrd | 1967 | 20.00 |
| ❑ CS 9137 [S] | Brazilian Byrd | 1965 | 20.00 |
| *—Red label, "360 Sound" in black* | | | |
| ❑ CS 9355 [S] | Christmas Carols for Solo Guitar | 1966 | 20.00 |
| ❑ CS 9627 [M] | Hit Trip | 1968 | 25.00 |
| *—"Special Mono Radio Station Copy" with white label* | | | |
| **CRYSTAL CLEAR** | | | |
| ❑ 8002 | Charlie Byrd | 1979 | 30.00 |
| *—Direct-to-disc recording; plays at 45 rpm* | | | |
| **MOBILE FIDELITY** | | | |
| ❑ 1-515 | Byrd at the Gate | 1982 | 40.00 |
| *—Audiophile vinyl* | | | |
| **OFFBEAT** | | | |
| ❑ OJ-3001 [M] | Jazz at the Show Boat, Volume 1 | 1959 | 25.00 |
| ❑ OJ-3005 [M] | Jazz at the Show Boat, Volume 2 | 1959 | 25.00 |
| ❑ OJ-3006 [M] | Jazz at the Show Boat, Volume 3 | 1959 | 25.00 |
| ❑ OJ-3007 [M] | Charlie's Choice | 1960 | 25.00 |
| ❑ OLP-3009 [M] | Blues Sonata | 1960 | 25.00 |
| ❑ OS-93001 [S] | Jazz at the Show Boat, Volume 1 | 1959 | 30.00 |
| ❑ OS-93005 [S] | Jazz at the Show Boat, Volume 2 | 1959 | 30.00 |
| ❑ OS-93006 [S] | Jazz at the Show Boat, Volume 3 | 1959 | 30.00 |
| ❑ OS-93007 [S] | Charlie's Choice | 1960 | 30.00 |
| ❑ OS-93009 [S] | Blues Sonata | 1960 | 30.00 |
| **RIVERSIDE** | | | |
| ❑ RM-427 [M] | Latin Impressions | 1962 | 20.00 |
| ❑ RM-436 [M] | Bossa Nova Pelos Passaros | 1962 | 20.00 |
| ❑ RM-448 [M] | Byrd's Word | 1963 | 20.00 |
| ❑ RM-449 [M] | Byrd in the Wind | 1963 | 20.00 |
| ❑ RM-450 [M] | Mr. Guitar | 1963 | 20.00 |
| ❑ RM-451 [M] | The Guitar Artistry of Charlie Byrd | 1963 | 20.00 |
| ❑ RM-452 [M] | Charlie Byrd at the Village Vanguard | 1963 | 20.00 |
| ❑ RM-453 [M] | Blues Sonata | 1963 | 20.00 |
| ❑ RM-454 [M] | Once More! Bossa Nova | 1963 | 20.00 |
| ❑ RM-467 [M] | Byrd at the Gate | 1964 | 20.00 |
| ❑ RM-498 [M] | Solo Flight | 1967 | 20.00 |
| ❑ RS-9427 [S] | Latin Impressions | 1962 | 25.00 |
| ❑ RS-9436 [S] | Bossa Nova Pelos Passaros | 1962 | 25.00 |
| ❑ RS-9448 [S] | Byrd's Word | 1963 | 25.00 |
| ❑ RS-9449 [S] | Byrd in the Wind | 1963 | 25.00 |
| ❑ RS-9450 [S] | Mr. Guitar | 1963 | 25.00 |
| ❑ RS-9451 [S] | The Guitar Artistry of Charlie Byrd | 1963 | 25.00 |
| ❑ RS-9452 [S] | Charlie Byrd at the Village Vanguard | 1963 | 25.00 |
| ❑ RS-9453 [S] | Blues Sonata | 1963 | 25.00 |
| ❑ RS-9454 [S] | Once More! Bossa Nova | 1963 | 25.00 |
| ❑ RS-9467 [S] | Byrd at the Gate | 1964 | 25.00 |
| ❑ RS-9481 [S] | Byrd Song | 1966 | 20.00 |
| **SAVOY** | | | |
| ❑ MG-12099 [M] | Jazz Recital | 1957 | 40.00 |
| ❑ MG-12116 [M] | Blues for Night People | 1957 | 40.00 |

### BYRD, CHARLIE, AND FATHER MALCOLM BOYD

| Number | Title (A Side/B Side) | Yr | NM |
|---|---|---|---|
| **COLUMBIA** | | | |
| ❑ CS 9348 [S] | Are You Running With Me, Jesus? | 1966 | 20.00 |

### BYRD, CHARLIE, HERB ELLIS & BARNEY KESSEL

| Number | Title (A Side/B Side) | Yr | NM |
|---|---|---|---|
| **CONCORD JAZZ** | | | |
| ❑ CJD-1002 | Straight Tracks | 1986 | 20.00 |
| *—Direct-to-disc recording* | | | |

### BYRD, DONALD

| Number | Title (A Side/B Side) | Yr | NM |
|---|---|---|---|
| **AMERICAN RECORDING SOCIETY** | | | |
| ❑ G-437 [M] | Modern Jazz | 1957 | 40.00 |

| Number | Title (A Side/B Side) | Yr | NM |
|---|---|---|---|

**BLUE NOTE**

❑ BLP-4007 [M] Off to the Races 1959 80.00
*—W. 63rd St., NYC address on label*
❑ BLP-4007 [M] Off to the Races 1959 120.00
*—"Deep groove" version (deep indentation under label on both sides)*
❑ BLP-4007 [M] Off to the Races 1963 25.00
*—"New York, USA" address on label*
❑ BST-4007 [S] Off to the Races 1959 60.00
*—W. 63rd St., NYC address on label*
❑ BST-4007 [S] Off to the Races 1959 80.00
*—"Deep groove" version (deep indentation under label on both sides)*
❑ BST-4007 [S] Off to the Races 1963 25.00
*—"New York, USA" address on label*
❑ BLP-4019 [M] Byrd in Hand 1959 80.00
*—W. 63rd St., NYC address on label*
❑ BLP-4019 [M] Byrd in Hand 1959 120.00
*—"Deep groove" version (deep indentation under label on both sides)*
❑ BLP-4019 [M] Byrd in Hand 1963 25.00
*—"New York, USA" address on label*
❑ BLP-4026 [M] Fuego 1960 80.00
*—W. 63rd St., NYC address on label*
❑ BLP-4026 [M] Fuego 1960 120.00
*—"Deep groove" version (deep indentation under label on both sides)*
❑ BLP-4026 [M] Fuego 1963 25.00
*—"New York, USA" address on label*
❑ BLP-4048 [M] Byrd in Flight 1960 80.00
*—W. 63rd St., NYC address on label*
❑ BLP-4048 [M] Byrd in Flight 1960 120.00
*—"Deep groove" version (deep indentation under label on both sides)*
❑ BLP-4048 [M] Byrd in Flight 1963 25.00
*—"New York, USA" address on label*
❑ BLP-4060 [M] Donald Byrd at the Half Note Café, Volume 1 1961 80.00
*—W. 63rd St., NYC address on label*
❑ BLP-4060 [M] Donald Byrd at the Half Note Café, Volume 1 1963 25.00
*—"New York, USA" address on label*
❑ BLP-4061 [M] Donald Byrd at the Half Note Café, Volume 2 1961 80.00
*—W. 63rd St., NYC address on label*
❑ BLP-4061 [M] Donald Byrd at the Half Note Café, Volume 2 1963 25.00
*—"New York, USA" address on label*
❑ BLP-4075 [M] The Cat Walk 1961 80.00
*—61st St, New York address on label*
❑ BLP-4075 [M] The Cat Walk 1963 25.00
*—"New York, USA" address on label*
❑ BLP-4101 [M] Royal Flush 1962 20.00
❑ BLP-4118 [M] Free Form 1963 20.00
❑ BLP-4124 [M] A New Perspective 1964 20.00
❑ BLP-4188 [M] I'm Tryin' to Get Home 1965 20.00
❑ BLP-4238 [M] Mustang! 1966 20.00
❑ BLP-4259 [M] Blackjack 1967 25.00
❑ BST-84019 [S] Byrd in Hand 1959 60.00
*—W. 63rd St., NYC address on label*
❑ BST-84019 [S] Byrd in Hand 1963 25.00
*—"New York, USA" address on label*
❑ BST-84026 [S] Fuego 1959 60.00
*—W. 63rd St., NYC address on label*
❑ BST-84026 [S] Fuego 1963 25.00
*—"New York, USA" address on label*
❑ BST-84048 [S] Byrd in Flight 1960 60.00
*—W. 63rd St., NYC address on label*
❑ BST-84048 [S] Byrd in Flight 1963 25.00
*—"New York, USA" address on label*
❑ BST-84060 [S] Donald Byrd at the Half Note Café, Volume 1 1961 60.00
*—W. 63rd St., NYC address on label*
❑ BST-84060 [S] Donald Byrd at the Half Note Café, Volume 1 1963 25.00
*—"New York, USA" address on label*
❑ BST-84061 [S] Donald Byrd at the Half Note Café, Volume 2 1961 60.00
*—W. 63rd St., NYC address on label*
❑ BST-84061 [S] Donald Byrd at the Half Note Café, Volume 2 1963 25.00
*—"New York, USA" address on label*
❑ BST-84075 [S] The Cat Walk 1961 60.00
*—61st St, New York address on label*
❑ BST-84075 [S] The Cat Walk 1963 25.00
*—"New York, USA" address on label*
❑ BST-84101 [S] Royal Flush 1962 25.00
*—"New York, USA" address on label*
❑ BST-84118 [S] Free Form 1963 25.00
*—"New York, USA" address on label*
❑ BST-84124 [S] A New Perspective 1964 25.00
*—"New York, USA" address on label*
❑ BST-84188 [S] I'm Tryin' to Get Home 1965 25.00
*—"New York, USA" address on label*
❑ BST-84238 [S] Mustang! 1966 25.00
*—"New York, USA" address on label*
❑ BST-84259 [S] Blackjack 1967 20.00
❑ BST-84292 Slow Drag 1968 20.00
❑ BST-84319 Fancy Free 1969 20.00
❑ BST-84349 Electric 1970 20.00
❑ BST-84380 Ethiopian Nights 1972 20.00

**SAVOY**

❑ MG-12032 [M] Byrd's Word 1956 100.00
❑ MG-12064 [M] The Jazz Message of Donald Byrd 1956 120.00

**TRANSITION**

❑ TRLP-4 [M] Byrd's Eye View 1956 600.00
❑ TRLP-5 [M] Byrd Jazz 1956 600.00
❑ TRLP-17 [M] Byrd Blows on Beacon Hill 1956 600.00

**VERVE**

❑ V-8609 [M] Up with Donald Byrd 1965 20.00
❑ V6-8609 [S] Up with Donald Byrd 1965 25.00

## BYRD, DONALD; HANY MOBLEY; KENNY BURRELL

**STATUS**

❑ ST-8317 [M] Donald Byrd, Hank Mobley & Kenny Burrell 1965 40.00

## BYRD, JERRY

**DECCA**

❑ DL 4078 [M] Paradise Island 1961 20.00
❑ DL 8643 [M] Hi-Fi Guitar 1958 40.00
❑ DL 74078 [S] Paradise Island 1961 25.00

**MERCURY**

❑ MG-20230 [M] On the Shores of Waikiki 1960 30.00
❑ MG-20345 [M] Steel Guitar Favorites 1961 30.00
❑ MG-20693 [M] Hawaiian Golden Hits 1962 30.00
❑ MG-20856 [M] Blue Hawaiian Steel Guitar 1963 30.00
❑ MG-20932 [M] The Man of Steel 1964 20.00
❑ MG-25077 [10] Nani Hawaii 1953 80.00
❑ MG-25134 [10] Guitar Magic 1954 80.00
❑ MG-25169 [10] Byrd's Expedition 1954 80.00
❑ SR-60230 [S] On the Shores of Waikiki 1960 40.00
❑ SR-60345 [S] Steel Guitar Favorites 1961 40.00
❑ SR-60693 [S] Hawaiian Golden Hits 1962 40.00
❑ SR-60856 [S] Blue Hawaiian Steel Guitar 1963 40.00
❑ SR-60932 [S] The Man of Steel 1964 25.00

**MONUMENT**

❑ MLP-4008 [M] Memories of Maria 1962 20.00
❑ MLP-8009 [M] Byrd of Paradise 1962 20.00
❑ MLP-8014 [M] Admirable Byrd 1963 20.00
❑ SLP-14008 [S] Memories of Maria 1962 25.00
❑ SLP-18009 [S] Byrd of Paradise 1962 25.00
❑ SLP-18014 [S] Admirable Byrd 1963 25.00

## BYRD, JOE, AND THE FIELD HIPPIES

**COLUMBIA MASTERWORKS**

❑ MS 7317 The American Metaphysical Circus 1969 40.00

## BYRD, SENATOR ROBERT

**COUNTY**

❑ 769 Mountain Fiddler 1978 25.00

## BYRDS, THE

**ASYLUM**

❑ 5058 [M] Byrds 1973 40.00
*—Mono is white label promo only; "dj copy monaural" sticker on stereo cover*
❑ SD 5058 [S] Byrds 1973 12.00

**COLUMBIA**

❑ CL 2372 [M] Mr. Tambourine Man 1965 40.00
*—"Guaranteed High Fidelity" on label*
❑ CL 2372 [M] Mr. Tambourine Man 1966 30.00
*—"360 Sound Mono" on label*
❑ CL 2454 [M] Turn! Turn! Turn! 1965 30.00
❑ CL 2549 [M] Fifth Dimension (5D) 1966 30.00
❑ CL 2642 [M] Younger Than Yesterday 1967 30.00
❑ CL 2716 [M] The Byrds' Greatest Hits 1967 30.00
❑ CL 2775 [M] The Notorious Byrd Brothers 1968 50.00
❑ CS 9172 [S] Mr. Tambourine Man 1965 40.00
*—Red label, "360 Sound" in black*
❑ CS 9172 [S] Mr. Tambourine Man 1966 25.00
*—Red label, "360 Sound" in white*
❑ CS 9172 [S] Mr. Tambourine Man 1971 10.00
*—Orange label*
❑ PC 9172 [S] Mr. Tambourine Man 198? 8.00
*—Reissue with new prefix*
❑ CS 9254 [S] Turn! Turn! Turn! 1965 25.00
*—Red "360 Sound" label*
❑ CS 9254 [S] Turn! Turn! Turn! 1971 10.00
*—Orange label*
❑ PC 9254 [S] Turn! Turn! Turn! 198? 8.00
*—Reissue with new prefix*
❑ CS 9349 [S] Fifth Dimension (5D) 1966 25.00
*—Red "360 Sound" label*
❑ CS 9349 [S] Fifth Dimension (5D) 1971 10.00
*—Orange label*
❑ PC 9349 [S] Fifth Dimension (5D) 198? 8.00
*—Reissue with new prefix*
❑ CS 9442 [S] Younger Than Yesterday 1967 25.00
*—Red "360 Sound" label*
❑ CS 9442 [S] Younger Than Yesterday 1971 10.00
*—Orange label*
❑ PC 9442 [S] Younger Than Yesterday 198? 8.00
*—Reissue with new prefix*
❑ CS 9516 [S] The Byrds' Greatest Hits 1967 20.00
*—Red "360 Sound" label*
❑ KCS 9516 [S] The Byrds' Greatest Hits 1971 10.00
*—Orange label*
❑ PC 9516 [S] The Byrds' Greatest Hits 197? 8.00
*—Reissue with another new prefix*
❑ CS 9575 [S] The Notorious Byrd Brothers 1968 20.00
*—Red "360 Sound" label*
❑ CS 9575 [S] The Notorious Byrd Brothers 1971 10.00
*—Orange label*
❑ PC 9575 [S] The Notorious Byrd Brothers 198? 8.00
*—Reissue with new prefix*
❑ CS 9670 [M] Sweetheart of the Rodeo 1968 100.00
*—"Special Mono Radio Station Copy" with white label*
❑ CS 9670 [S] Sweetheart of the Rodeo 1968 20.00
*—Red "360 Sound" label*
❑ CS 9670 [S] Sweetheart of the Rodeo 1971 10.00
*—Orange label*
❑ PC 9670 [S] Sweetheart of the Rodeo 198? 8.00
*—Reissue with new prefix*
❑ CS 9755 [S] Dr. Byrds and Mr. Hyde 1969 20.00
*—Red "360 Sound" label*
❑ CS 9755 [S] Dr. Byrds and Mr. Hyde 1971 10.00
*—Orange label*
❑ PC 9755 [S] Dr. Byrds and Mr. Hyde 198? 8.00
*—Reissue with new prefix*
❑ CS 9942 [S] Ballad of Easy Rider 1969 20.00
*—Red "360 Sound" label*
❑ CS 9942 [S] Ballad of Easy Rider 1971 10.00
*—Orange label*
❑ PC 9942 Ballad of Easy Rider 1984 8.00
*—Reissue with new prefix*
❑ G 30127 [(2)] The Byrds (Untitled) 1970 15.00
*—Without "Kathleen" listed on back cover*
❑ G 30127 [(2)] The Byrds (Untitled) 1970 20.00
*—With "Kathleen" listed on back cover (it is not on the set)*
❑ KC 30640 Byrdmaniax 1971 12.00
❑ C 31050 Farther Along 1971 12.00
❑ C 31795 The Best of the Byrds (Greatest Hits, Volume II) 197? 10.00
*—Reissue with new prefix*
❑ KC 31795 The Best of the Byrds (Greatest Hits, Volume II) 1972 12.00
❑ PC 31795 The Best of the Byrds (Greatest Hits, Volume II) 198? 8.00
*—Reissue with another new prefix*
❑ C 32183 Preflyte 197? 10.00
*—Reissue with new prefix*
❑ KC 32183 Preflyte 1973 12.00
*—Reissue of Together LP*
❑ CG 33645 [(2)] Mr. Tambourine Man/Turn! Turn! Turn! 1976 15.00
❑ PC 36293 The Byrds Play Dylan 1980 10.00
❑ FC 37335 The Original Singles Volume 1 (1965-1967) 1981 10.00
❑ PC 37335 The Original Singles Volume 1 (1965-1967) 1985 8.00
*—Budget-line reissue*

**COLUMBIA LIMITED EDITION**

❑ LE 10215 Farther Along 197? 15.00
*—Reissue of 31050*

**PAIR**

❑ PDL2-1040 [(2)] The Very Best of the Byrds 1986 12.00

**RE-FLYTE**

❑ MH-70318 Never Before 1987 12.00
*—Released by Muuray Hill Records via mail order*

**RHINO**

❑ R1-70244 In the Beginning 1988 10.00

**SUNDAZED**

❑ LP 5057 Mr. Tambourine Man 1999 15.00
*—Reissue on 180-gram vinyl*
❑ LP 5058 Turn! Turn! Turn! 1999 15.00
*—Reissue on 180-gram vinyl*
❑ LP 5059 Fifth Dimension 1999 15.00
*—Reissue on 180-gram vinyl*
❑ LP 5060 Younger Than Yesterday 1999 15.00
*—Reissue on 180-gram vinyl*
❑ LP 5061 Sanctuary 2000 12.00
❑ LP 5065 Sanctuary II 2000 12.00
❑ LP 5066 Sanctuary III 2001 12.00
❑ LP 5090 Sanctuary IV 2002 12.00
❑ LP 5114 [(2)] The Preflyte Sessions 2001 15.00
❑ LP 5130 [(2)] The Columbia Singles '65-'67 2001 15.00
❑ LP 5197 [M] Mr. Tambourine Man 2006 15.00
*—Reissue on 180-gram vinyl*
❑ LP 5198 [M] Turn! Turn! Turn! 2006 15.00
*—Reissue on 180-gram vinyl*
❑ LP 5199 [M] Fifth Dimension 2006 15.00
*—Reissue on 180-gram vinyl*
❑ LP 5200 [M] Younger Than Yesterday 2006 15.00
*—Reissue on 180-gram vinyl*
❑ LP 5201 [M] The Notorious Byrd Brothers 2006 15.00
*—Reissue on 180-gram vinyl*

**TOGETHER**

❑ ST-T-1001 Preflyte 1969 25.00

## BYRNE, BOBBY

**COMMAND**

❑ RS 928 SD Sound in the 8th Dimension 1968 80.00

**GRAND AWARD**

❑ GA 206 SD [S] Great Song Hits of the Tommy and Jimmy Dorsey Orchestras 1958 40.00



Except when noted otherwise, VG = 25% of NM, and VG+ = 50% of NM. (Example: VG = $2.00, VG+ = $4.00 and NM = $8.00.)

| Number | Title (A Side/B Side) | Yr | NM |
|---|---|---|---|
| ❑ GA 207 SD [S] | Great Song Hits of the Glenn Miller Orchestra | 1958 | 40.00 |
| ❑ GA 225 SD [S] | Great Themes of America's Greatest Bands | 1959 | 40.00 |
| ❑ GA 248 SD [S] | The Jazzbone's Connected to the Trombone | 1959 | 50.00 |
| ❑ GA 33-381 [M] | Great Song Hits of the Glenn Miller Orchestra | 1958 | 30.00 |
| ❑ GA 33-382 [M] | Great Song Hits of the Tommy and Jimmy Dorsey Orchestras | 1958 | 30.00 |
| ❑ GA 33-392 [M] | Great Themes of America's Greatest Bands | 1958 | 30.00 |
| ❑ GA 33-416 [M] | The Jazzbone's Connected to the Trombone | 1959 | 40.00 |

WALDORF MUSIC HALL

| Number | Title (A Side/B Side) | Yr | NM |
|---|---|---|---|
| ❑ MH 33-121 [10] | Dixieland Jazz | 195? | 50.00 |

## BYRNE, BOBBY; WILL BRADLEY; BUD FREEMAN

GRAND AWARD

| Number | Title (A Side/B Side) | Yr | NM |
|---|---|---|---|
| ❑ GA 33-313 [M] | Jazz, Dixieland-Chicago | 1955 | 40.00 |

## BYRNE, DAVID

VIRGIN

| Number | Title (A Side/B Side) | Yr | NM |
|---|---|---|---|
| ❑ PR 2204 [DJ] | The Making of The Last Emperor: An Interview with David Byrne and Ryuichi Sakamoto | 1988 | 25.00 |

## BYRNES, EDD

WARNER BROS.

| Number | Title (A Side/B Side) | Yr | NM |
|---|---|---|---|
| ❑ W 1309 [M] | Kookie | 1959 | 100.00 |
| ❑ W/WS 1309 | Kookie Bonus Photo | 1959 | 50.00 |
| ❑ WS 1309 [S] | Kookie | 1959 | 120.00 |

## BYRON, GEORGE

ATLANTIC

| Number | Title (A Side/B Side) | Yr | NM |
|---|---|---|---|
| ❑ 1293 [M] | Premiere Performance | 1958 | 40.00 |
| *—Black label* | | | |
| ❑ SD 1293 [S] | Premiere Performance | 1958 | 50.00 |
| *—Green label* | | | |

# C

## C.A. QUINTET, THE

CANDY FLOSS

| Number | Title (A Side/B Side) | Yr | NM |
|---|---|---|---|
| ❑ 7764 | A Trip Through Hell | 1969 | 1500. |
| *—VG value 500; VG+ value 1000* | | | |

SUNDAZED

| Number | Title (A Side/B Side) | Yr | NM |
|---|---|---|---|
| ❑ LP-5037 [(2)] | Trip Thru Hell | 1997 | 15.00 |

## C.C.S.

RAK

| Number | Title (A Side/B Side) | Yr | NM |
|---|---|---|---|
| ❑ Z 30559 | Whole Lotta Love | 1971 | 20.00 |
| ❑ KZ 31569 | C.C.S. | 1972 | 20.00 |

## C.K. STRONG

EPIC

| Number | Title (A Side/B Side) | Yr | NM |
|---|---|---|---|
| ❑ BN 26473 | C.K. Strong | 1969 | 20.00 |

## CABARET VOLTAIRE

CAROLINE

| Number | Title (A Side/B Side) | Yr | NM |
|---|---|---|---|
| ❑ CAROL 1331 | The Covenant, the Sword, and the Arm of the Lord | 1985 | 10.00 |
| ❑ CAROL 2451 [(2)EP] | Drinking Gasoline | 1985 | 15.00 |

GIANT

| Number | Title (A Side/B Side) | Yr | NM |
|---|---|---|---|
| ❑ GR-16009 | Eight Crepuscule Tracks | 1988 | 15.00 |

MANHATTAN

| Number | Title (A Side/B Side) | Yr | NM |
|---|---|---|---|
| ❑ MLT-46999 | Code | 1987 | 15.00 |

RESTLESS

| Number | Title (A Side/B Side) | Yr | NM |
|---|---|---|---|
| ❑ 71475 | Listen Up with Cabaret Voltaire | 1990 | 10.00 |
| ❑ 71476 | The Living Legends | 1990 | 10.00 |

ROUGH TRADE

| Number | Title (A Side/B Side) | Yr | NM |
|---|---|---|---|
| ❑ ROUGH US-9 | The Voice of America | 1980 | 20.00 |
| ❑ TRADE US-12 [EP] | Three Crepuscule Tracks | 1981 | 12.00 |
| ❑ ROUGH US-15 | Red Mecca | 1981 | 20.00 |
| ❑ ROUGH US-24 | Hai! Live in Japan | 1982 | 20.00 |

## CABOT, SEBASTIAN

MGM

| Number | Title (A Side/B Side) | Yr | NM |
|---|---|---|---|
| ❑ E-4431 [M] | Sebastian Cabot, Actor; Bob Dylan, Poet: A Dramatic Reading with Music | 1967 | 30.00 |
| ❑ SE-4431 [S] | Sebastian Cabot, Actor; Bob Dylan, Poet: A Dramatic Reading with Music | 1967 | 40.00 |

## CACTUS

ATCO

| Number | Title (A Side/B Side) | Yr | NM |
|---|---|---|---|
| ❑ SD 33-340 | Cactus | 1970 | 20.00 |
| ❑ SD 33-356 | One Way...Or Another | 1971 | 20.00 |
| ❑ SD 33-377 | Restrictions | 1971 | 20.00 |
| ❑ SD 7011 | 'Ot 'N' Sweaty | 1972 | 20.00 |

## CADETS, THE

CROWN

| Number | Title (A Side/B Side) | Yr | NM |
|---|---|---|---|
| ❑ CST-370 [R] | The Cadets | 1963 | 100.00 |
| ❑ CLP-5015 [M] | Rockin' 'n' Reelin' | 1957 | 250.00 |
| *—Black label* | | | |
| ❑ CLP-5370 [M] | The Cadets | 1963 | 150.00 |

MODERN

| Number | Title (A Side/B Side) | Yr | NM |
|---|---|---|---|
| ❑ LPM-1215 [M] | Rockin' 'n' Reelin' | 1956 | — |
| *—Canceled* | | | |

RELIC

| Number | Title (A Side/B Side) | Yr | NM |
|---|---|---|---|
| ❑ 5025 | The Cadets' Greatest Hits | 197? | 12.00 |

## CADILLACS, THE

HARLEM HIT PARADE

| Number | Title (A Side/B Side) | Yr | NM |
|---|---|---|---|
| ❑ 5009 | Cruisin' with the Cadillacs | 197? | 10.00 |

JUBILEE

| Number | Title (A Side/B Side) | Yr | NM |
|---|---|---|---|
| ❑ JGM-1045 [M] | The Fabulous Cadillacs | 1957 | 400.00 |
| *—Blue label* | | | |
| ❑ JGM-1045 [M] | The Fabulous Cadillacs | 1959 | 250.00 |
| *—Flat black label* | | | |
| ❑ JGM-1045 [M] | The Fabulous Cadillacs | 1960 | 100.00 |
| *—Glossy black label* | | | |
| ❑ JGM-1089 [M] | The Crazy Cadillacs | 1959 | 300.00 |
| *—Flat black label* | | | |
| ❑ JGM-1089 [M] | The Crazy Cadillacs | 1960 | 100.00 |
| *—Glossy black label* | | | |
| ❑ JGM-5009 [M] | Twisting with the Cadillacs | 1962 | 200.00 |

MURRAY HILL

| Number | Title (A Side/B Side) | Yr | NM |
|---|---|---|---|
| ❑ 1195 | The Very Best of the Cadillacs | 198? | 15.00 |
| ❑ 1285 [(5)] | The Cadillacs | 198? | 40.00 |
| *—Box set* | | | |

## CADILLACS, THE/ THE ORIOLES

Also see each artist's individual listings.

JUBILEE

| Number | Title (A Side/B Side) | Yr | NM |
|---|---|---|---|
| ❑ JGM-1117 [M] | The Cadillacs Meet the Orioles | 1961 | 200.00 |

## CAGLE, BUDDY

IMPERIAL

| Number | Title (A Side/B Side) | Yr | NM |
|---|---|---|---|
| ❑ LP-9318 [M] | The Way You Like It | 1966 | 20.00 |
| ❑ LP-9348 [M] | Mi Casa, Tu Casa | 1967 | 20.00 |
| ❑ LP-9361 [M] | Longtime Traveling | 1967 | 30.00 |
| ❑ LP-12318 [S] | The Way You Like It | 1966 | 25.00 |
| ❑ LP-12348 [S] | Mi Casa, Tu Casa | 1967 | 25.00 |
| ❑ LP-12361 [S] | Longtime Traveling | 1967 | 25.00 |
| ❑ LP-12374 | Through a Crack in a Boxcar Door | 1968 | 25.00 |

## CAIN

A.S.I.

| Number | Title (A Side/B Side) | Yr | NM |
|---|---|---|---|
| ❑ 204 | A Pound of Flesh | 1974 | 60.00 |
| ❑ 214 | Stinger | 1975 | 40.00 |

## CAIN, JACKIE, AND ROY KRAL

ABC-PARAMOUNT

| Number | Title (A Side/B Side) | Yr | NM |
|---|---|---|---|
| ❑ ABC-120 [M] | The Glory of Love | 1956 | 50.00 |
| ❑ ABC-163 [M] | Bits and Pieces | 1957 | 50.00 |
| ❑ ABC-207 [M] | Free and Easy | 1958 | 50.00 |
| ❑ ABC-267 [M] | In the Spotlight | 1959 | 40.00 |
| ❑ ABCS-267 [S] | In the Spotlight | 1959 | 50.00 |

BRUNSWICK

| Number | Title (A Side/B Side) | Yr | NM |
|---|---|---|---|
| ❑ BL 54026 [M] | Jackie Cain and Roy Kral | 1957 | 50.00 |

COLUMBIA

| Number | Title (A Side/B Side) | Yr | NM |
|---|---|---|---|
| ❑ CL 1469 [M] | Sweet and Low Down | 1960 | 25.00 |
| ❑ CL 1704 [M] | Double Take | 1961 | 25.00 |
| ❑ CL 1934 [M] | Like Sing | 1963 | 20.00 |
| ❑ CS 8260 [S] | Sweet and Low Down | 1960 | 30.00 |
| ❑ CS 8504 [S] | Double Take | 1961 | 30.00 |
| ❑ CS 8734 [S] | Like Sing | 1963 | 25.00 |

REGENT

| Number | Title (A Side/B Side) | Yr | NM |
|---|---|---|---|
| ❑ MG-6057 [M] | Jackie & Roy | 1957 | 50.00 |

ROULETTE

| Number | Title (A Side/B Side) | Yr | NM |
|---|---|---|---|
| ❑ R-25278 [M] | By Jupiter & Girl Crazy | 1964 | 20.00 |
| ❑ SR-25278 [S] | By Jupiter & Girl Crazy | 1964 | 25.00 |

SAVOY

| Number | Title (A Side/B Side) | Yr | NM |
|---|---|---|---|
| ❑ MG-12198 [M] | Jackie and Roy | 196? | 20.00 |

STORYVILLE

| Number | Title (A Side/B Side) | Yr | NM |
|---|---|---|---|
| ❑ STLP-322 [10] | Jackie & Roy | 1955 | 120.00 |
| ❑ STLP-904 [M] | Storyville Presents Jackie & Roy | 1955 | 60.00 |
| ❑ STLP-915 [M] | Sing Baby, Sing! | 1956 | 60.00 |

VERVE

| Number | Title (A Side/B Side) | Yr | NM |
|---|---|---|---|
| ❑ V-8668 [M] | Changes | 1966 | 20.00 |
| ❑ V6-8668 [S] | Changes | 1966 | 25.00 |
| ❑ V-8688 [M] | Lovesick | 1967 | 25.00 |
| ❑ V6-8688 [S] | Lovesick | 1967 | 20.00 |

## CAIOLA, AL

ATCO

| Number | Title (A Side/B Side) | Yr | NM |
|---|---|---|---|
| ❑ 33-117 [M] | Music for Space Squirrels | 1960 | 25.00 |
| ❑ SD 33-117 [S] | Music for Space Squirrels | 1960 | 30.00 |

AVALANCHE

| Number | Title (A Side/B Side) | Yr | NM |
|---|---|---|---|
| ❑ AV-LA058-F | The Magnificent Seven Ride '73 | 1973 | 10.00 |
| ❑ 9201 | The Magnificent Seven | 1972 | 12.00 |

AVCO EMBASSY

| Number | Title (A Side/B Side) | Yr | NM |
|---|---|---|---|
| ❑ 33019 | Bonanza Guitars/50 Years of the Greatest Country Music | 1971 | 10.00 |

BAINBRIDGE

| Number | Title (A Side/B Side) | Yr | NM |
|---|---|---|---|
| ❑ 1010 | Soft Guitars | 198? | 8.00 |
| ❑ 1023 | Italian Guitars | 198? | 8.00 |
| ❑ 1030 | Guitar of Plenty | 1980 | 8.00 |

CHANCELLOR

| Number | Title (A Side/B Side) | Yr | NM |
|---|---|---|---|
| ❑ CHL-5008 [M] | Great Pickin' | 1960 | 25.00 |
| ❑ CHS-5008 [S] | Great Pickin' | 1960 | 30.00 |

PICKWICK

| Number | Title (A Side/B Side) | Yr | NM |
|---|---|---|---|
| ❑ SPC-3034 | Italian Style | 196? | 12.00 |

RCA CAMDEN

| Number | Title (A Side/B Side) | Yr | NM |
|---|---|---|---|
| ❑ CAL-710 [M] | The Guitar Style of Al Caiola | 1962 | 12.00 |
| ❑ CAS-710 [S] | The Guitar Style of Al Caiola | 1962 | 15.00 |
| ❑ CAS-2569 | Music from "The Godfather" | 1972 | 10.00 |

RCA VICTOR

| Number | Title (A Side/B Side) | Yr | NM |
|---|---|---|---|
| ❑ LPM-2031 [M] | High Strung | 1959 | 25.00 |
| ❑ LSP-2031 [S] | High Strung | 1959 | 30.00 |

ROULETTE

| Number | Title (A Side/B Side) | Yr | NM |
|---|---|---|---|
| ❑ R 25108 [M] | Salute Italia | 1960 | 20.00 |
| ❑ SR 25108 [S] | Salute Italia | 1960 | 25.00 |
| ❑ SR-42008 | Roman Guitar | 1968 | 10.00 |

SAVOY

| Number | Title (A Side/B Side) | Yr | NM |
|---|---|---|---|
| ❑ MG-12033 [M] | Deep in a Dream | 1955 | 40.00 |
| ❑ MG-12057 [M] | Serenade in Blue | 1956 | 40.00 |

SUNSET

| Number | Title (A Side/B Side) | Yr | NM |
|---|---|---|---|
| ❑ SUS-5292 | Guitar in Love | 1970 | 10.00 |

TIME

| Number | Title (A Side/B Side) | Yr | NM |
|---|---|---|---|
| ❑ S-2000 [S] | Percussion and Guitars | 1960 | 25.00 |
| ❑ S-2006 [S] | Percussion Espanol | 1960 | 25.00 |
| ❑ S-2026 [S] | Percussion Espanol, Vol. 2 | 1960 | 25.00 |
| ❑ S-2039 [S] | Spanish Guitars | 1960 | 25.00 |
| ❑ S-2101 [S] | Gershwin and Guitars | 1961 | 25.00 |
| ❑ 52000 [M] | Percussion and Guitars | 1960 | 20.00 |
| ❑ 52006 [M] | Percussion Espanol | 1960 | 20.00 |
| ❑ 52026 [M] | Percussion Espanol, Vol. 2 | 1960 | 20.00 |
| ❑ 52039 [M] | Spanish Guitars | 1960 | 20.00 |
| ❑ 52101 [M] | Gershwin and Guitars | 1961 | 20.00 |

UNITED ARTISTS

| Number | Title (A Side/B Side) | Yr | NM |
|---|---|---|---|
| ❑ UAL-3133 [M] | The Magnificent Seven | 1960 | 20.00 |
| ❑ UAL-3142 [M] | Golden Instrumental Hits | 1961 | 12.00 |
| ❑ UAL-3161 [M] | Hit Instrumentals from TV Westerns | 1961 | 15.00 |
| ❑ UAL-3180 [M] | Solid Gold Guitar | 1962 | 12.00 |
| ❑ UAL-3228 [M] | Midnight Dance Party | 1962 | 12.00 |
| ❑ UAL-3240 [M] | Golden Guitar | 1962 | 12.00 |
| ❑ UAL-3255 [M] | City Guy Goes Country | 1963 | 12.00 |
| ❑ UAL-3256 [M] | Acapulco 1922 and The Lonely Bull | 1963 | 12.00 |
| ❑ UAL-3263 [M] | Paradise Village | 1963 | 12.00 |
| ❑ UAL-3276 [M] | Ciao | 1963 | 12.00 |
| ❑ UAL-3280 [M] | Give Me the Simple Life | 1963 | 12.00 |
| ❑ UAL-3299 [M] | Cleopatra and All That Jazz | 1963 | 25.00 |
| ❑ UAL-3310 [M] | The Best of Al Caiola | 1964 | 12.00 |
| ❑ UAL-3330 [M] | 50 Fabulous Guitar Favorites | 1964 | 12.00 |
| ❑ UAL-3354 [M] | 50 Fabulous Italian Favorites | 1964 | 12.00 |
| ❑ UAL-3362 [M] | On the Trail | 1964 | 12.00 |
| ❑ UAL-3389 [M] | Tuff Guitar | 1965 | 12.00 |
| ❑ UAL-3403 [M] | Guitar for Lovers | 1965 | 12.00 |
| ❑ UAL-3405 [M] | Have Guitar Will Travel | 1965 | 12.00 |
| ❑ UAL-3418 [M] | Solid Gold Guitar Goes Hawaiian | 1965 | 12.00 |
| ❑ UAL-3435 [M] | Sounds for Spies and Private Eyes | 1965 | 15.00 |
| ❑ UAL-3454 [M] | Tuff Guitar English Style | 1966 | 12.00 |
| ❑ UAS-6133 [S] | The Magnificent Seven | 1960 | 25.00 |
| ❑ UAS-6142 [S] | Golden Instrumental Hits | 1961 | 15.00 |
| ❑ UAS-6161 [S] | Hit Instrumentals from TV Westerns | 1961 | 20.00 |
| ❑ UAS-6180 [S] | Solid Gold Guitar | 1962 | 15.00 |
| ❑ UAS-6228 [S] | Midnight Dance Party | 1962 | 15.00 |
| ❑ UAS-6240 [S] | Golden Guitar | 1962 | 15.00 |
| ❑ UAS-6255 [S] | City Guy Goes Country | 1963 | 15.00 |
| ❑ UAS-6256 [S] | Acapulco 1922 and The Lonely Bull | 1963 | 15.00 |
| ❑ UAS-6263 [S] | Paradise Village | 1963 | 15.00 |
| ❑ UAS-6276 [S] | Ciao | 1963 | 15.00 |
| ❑ UAS-6280 [S] | Give Me the Simple Life | 1963 | 15.00 |
| ❑ UAS-6299 [S] | Cleopatra and All That Jazz | 1963 | 30.00 |
| ❑ UAS-6310 [S] | The Best of Al Caiola | 1964 | 15.00 |
| ❑ UAS-6330 [S] | 50 Fabulous Guitar Favorites | 1964 | 15.00 |
| ❑ UAS-6354 [S] | 50 Fabulous Italian Favorites | 1964 | 15.00 |
| ❑ UAS-6362 [S] | On the Trail | 1964 | 15.00 |
| ❑ UAS-6389 [S] | Tuff Guitar | 1965 | 15.00 |
| ❑ UAS-6403 [S] | Guitar for Lovers | 1965 | 15.00 |
| ❑ UAS-6405 [S] | Have Guitar Will Travel | 1965 | 15.00 |
| ❑ UAS-6418 [S] | Solid Gold Guitar Goes Hawaiian | 1965 | 15.00 |
| ❑ UAS-6435 [S] | Sounds for Spies and Private Eyes | 1965 | 20.00 |
| ❑ UAS-6454 [S] | Tuff Guitar English Style | 1966 | 15.00 |
| ❑ UAS-6712 | Let the Sunshine In | 1969 | 10.00 |

| Number | Title (A Side/B Side) | Yr | NM |
|---|---|---|---|
| **CAJUN PETE** | | | |
| MERCURY | | | |
| ❑ MG-20633 [M] | Tales of the Bayou | 1961 | 20.00 |
| ❑ SR-60633 [S] | Tales of the Bayou | 1961 | 25.00 |
| **CAKE, THE** | | | |
| DECCA | | | |
| ❑ DL 4927 [M] | The Cake | 1967 | 20.00 |
| ❑ DL 5039 [M] | A Slice of the Cake | 1968 | 50.00 |
| *—Mono is white label promo only* | | | |
| ❑ DL 74927 [S] | The Cake | 1967 | 25.00 |
| ❑ DL 75039 [S] | A Slice of the Cake | 1968 | 25.00 |
| **CALDWELL, BOBBY** | | | |
| CLOUDS | | | |
| ❑ 8804 | Bobby Caldwell | 1978 | 12.00 |
| *—Black vinyl* | | | |
| ❑ 8804 | Bobby Caldwell | 1978 | 20.00 |
| *—Gold vinyl* | | | |
| ❑ 8810 | Cat in the Hat | 1980 | 15.00 |
| POLYDOR | | | |
| ❑ PD-1-6347 | Carry On | 1982 | 10.00 |
| **CALDWELL, LOUISE HARRISON** | | | |
| RECAR | | | |
| ❑ 2012 [M] | All About the Beatles | 1965 | 150.00 |
| *—Without insert* | | | |
| ❑ 2012 [M] | All About the Beatles | 1965 | 200.00 |
| *—With insert* | | | |
| **CALE, JOHN** Also see THE VELVET UNDERGROUND. | | | |
| A&M | | | |
| ❑ SP-4849 | Honi Soit | 1981 | 10.00 |
| ANTILLES | | | |
| ❑ AN-7063 | Guts | 198? | 12.00 |
| *—Reissue of Island 9459* | | | |
| COLUMBIA | | | |
| ❑ CS 1037 | Vintage Violence | 1970 | 25.00 |
| *—Red "360 Sound" label* | | | |
| ❑ CS 1037 | Vintage Violence | 1971 | 15.00 |
| *—Orange label* | | | |
| ❑ C 30131 | Church of Anthrax | 1971 | 15.00 |
| ISLAND | | | |
| ❑ IXP-2 [DJ] | Hear Fear | 1975 | 60.00 |
| *—Promo-only interview album* | | | |
| ❑ IT-8401 | Caribbean Sunset | 1984 | 10.00 |
| ❑ IT-8402 | John Cale Comes Alive | 1984 | 10.00 |
| ❑ ILPS 9301 | Fear | 1975 | 20.00 |
| ❑ ILPS 9317 | Slow Dazzle | 1975 | 15.00 |
| ❑ ILPS 9350 | Helen of Troy | 1975 | 20.00 |
| ❑ ILPS 9459 | Guts | 1977 | 20.00 |
| OPAL/WARNER BROS. | | | |
| ❑ 26024 | Words for the Dying | 1989 | 12.00 |
| PASSPORT | | | |
| ❑ PB 6019 | Music for a New Society | 1982 | 12.00 |
| PVC | | | |
| ❑ 8947 | Artificial Intelligence | 1985 | 15.00 |
| REPRISE | | | |
| ❑ MS 2079 | The Academy in Peril | 1972 | 25.00 |
| ❑ MS 2131 | Paris, 1919 | 1973 | 25.00 |
| SPY/I.R.S. | | | |
| ❑ SP-004 | Sabotage/Live | 1980 | 15.00 |
| **CALIFORNIA, RANDY** | | | |
| EPIC | | | |
| ❑ KE 31755 | Kapt. Kopter & the Fabulous Twirly Birds | 1972 | 25.00 |
| *—Yellow label* | | | |
| ❑ KE 31755 | Kapt. Kopter & the Fabulous Twirly Birds | 1973 | 12.00 |
| *—Orange label* | | | |
| **CALIFORNIA POPPY PICKERS, THE** | | | |
| ALSHIRE | | | |
| ❑ S-5153 | Hair-Aquarius | 1969 | 30.00 |
| ❑ S-5167 | Honky Tonk Women | 1970 | 40.00 |
| **CALIMAN, HADLEY** | | | |
| MAINSTREAM | | | |
| ❑ MRL-318 | Hadley Caliman | 1971 | 20.00 |
| ❑ MRL-342 | Iapetus | 1972 | 20.00 |
| **CALLENDER, BOBBY** | | | |
| MGM | | | |
| ❑ SE-4557 | Rainbow | 1968 | 150.00 |
| **CALLENDER, RED** | | | |
| CROWN | | | |
| ❑ CLP-5012 [M] | Callender Speaks Low | 1957 | 40.00 |
| ❑ CLP-5025 [M] | Swingin' Suite | 1957 | 40.00 |
| METROJAZZ | | | |
| ❑ E-1007 [M] | The Lowest | 1958 | 50.00 |
| ❑ SE-1007 [S] | The Lowest | 1959 | 40.00 |

| Number | Title (A Side/B Side) | Yr | NM |

| Number | Title (A Side/B Side) | Yr | NM |
|---|---|---|---|
| MODERN | | | |
| ❑ MLP-1201 [M] | Swingin' Suite | 1956 | 80.00 |
| **CALLIOPE** | | | |
| BUDDAH | | | |
| ❑ BDS-5023 | Steamed | 1968 | 20.00 |
| **CALLOWAY, CAB** | | | |
| BRUNSWICK | | | |
| ❑ BL 58101 [10] | Cab Calloway | 1954 | 100.00 |
| COLUMBIA | | | |
| ❑ CG 32593 [(2)] | The Hi De Ho Man | 1973 | 20.00 |
| CORAL | | | |
| ❑ CRL 57408 [M] | Blues Make Me Happy | 1962 | 25.00 |
| ❑ CRL 757408 [S] | Blues Make Me Happy | 1962 | 30.00 |
| EPIC | | | |
| ❑ LN 3265 [M] | Swing Showman | 1957 | 50.00 |
| GONE | | | |
| ❑ LP-101 [M] | Cotton Club Revue '58 | 1958 | 80.00 |
| RCA VICTOR | | | |
| ❑ LPM-2021 [M] | Hi De Hi De Ho | 1958 | 30.00 |
| ❑ LSP-2021 [S] | Hi De Hi De Ho | 1958 | 40.00 |
| **CAMARATA** | | | |
| BUENA VISTA | | | |
| ❑ BV-3319 [M] | 33 Great Walt Disney Motion Picture Melodies | 1963 | 25.00 |
| ❑ STER-3319 [S] | 33 Great Walt Disney Motion Picture Melodies | 1963 | 30.00 |
| ❑ BV-3321 [M] | The Changing Seasons | 1964 | 20.00 |
| ❑ STER-3321 [S] | The Changing Seasons | 1964 | 30.00 |
| ❑ BV-3322 [M] | In the Still of the Night | 1959 | 20.00 |
| ❑ STER-3322 [S] | In the Still of the Night | 1960 | 30.00 |
| ❑ BV-3330 [M] | Tinpanorama | 1965 | 20.00 |
| ❑ BV-4023 [M] | Camarata Conducts a Modern Interpretation of Snow White and the Seven Dwarfs | 1963 | 30.00 |
| *—Gatefold cover* | | | |
| ❑ BV-4023 [M] | Camarata Conducts a Modern Interpretation of Snow White and the Seven Dwarfs | 1967 | 20.00 |
| *—Regular cover* | | | |
| ❑ STER-4023 [S] | Camarata Conducts a Modern Interpretation of Snow White and the Seven Dwarfs | 1963 | 40.00 |
| *—Gatefold cover* | | | |
| ❑ STER-4023 [S] | Camarata Conducts a Modern Interpretation of Snow White and the Seven Dwarfs | 1967 | 25.00 |
| *—Regular cover* | | | |
| ❑ BV-4047 | Camarata Featuring Tutti's Trumpets | 1970 | 20.00 |
| *—Reissue of 3011* | | | |
| ❑ BV-4048 | Camarata Featuring Tutti's Trombones | 1970 | 20.00 |
| DISNEYLAND | | | |
| ❑ (# unknown) [(4)M] | Music of the Seasons | 1959 | 40.00 |
| *—Box set with mono versions of 3021, 3026, 3027 and 3032* | | | |
| ❑ (# unknown) [(4)S] | Music of the Seasons | 1959 | 80.00 |
| *—Box set with stereo versions of 3021, 3026, 3027 and 3032* | | | |
| ❑ DQ-1232 [M] | A Child's Introduction to Melody and Instruments of the Orchestra | 1963 | 20.00 |
| ❑ STER-3011 [S] | Tutti's Trumpets | 1959 | 30.00 |
| ❑ WDL-3011 [M] | Tutti's Trumpets | 1957 | 20.00 |
| ❑ STER-3021 [S] | Autumn | 1959 | 30.00 |
| ❑ WDL-3021 [M] | Autumn | 1958 | 20.00 |
| ❑ STER-3026 [S] | Winter | 1959 | 30.00 |
| ❑ WDL-3026 [M] | Winter | 1958 | 20.00 |
| ❑ STER-3027 [S] | Summer | 1959 | 25.00 |
| ❑ WDL-3027 [M] | Summer | 1958 | 20.00 |
| ❑ STER-3032 [S] | Spring | 1959 | 25.00 |
| ❑ WDL-3032 [M] | Spring | 1958 | 20.00 |
| ❑ WDL-4009 [M] | Camarata Interprets Music from Cinderella and Bambi | 1957 | 60.00 |
| **CAMBRIDGE, GODFREY** | | | |
| EPIC | | | |
| ❑ FLM 13101 [M] | Ready or Not...Here's Godfrey Cambridge | 1964 | 20.00 |
| ❑ FLM 13102 [M] | Them Cotton Pickin' Days Is Over | 1965 | 20.00 |
| ❑ FLM 13108 [M] | Godfrey Cambridge Toys with the World | 1966 | 20.00 |
| ❑ FLM 13115 [M] | The Godfrey Cambridge Show Live at the Aladdin | 1968 | 20.00 |
| ❑ FLS 15101 [S] | Ready or Not...Here's Godfrey Cambridge | 1964 | 20.00 |
| ❑ FLS 15102 [S] | Them Cotton Pickin' Days Is Over | 1965 | 20.00 |
| ❑ FLS 15108 [S] | Godfrey Cambridge Toys with the World | 1966 | 20.00 |
| ❑ FLS 15115 [S] | The Godfrey Cambridge Show Live at the Aladdin | 1968 | 20.00 |

| Number | Title (A Side/B Side) | Yr | NM |

| Number | Title (A Side/B Side) | Yr | NM |
|---|---|---|---|
| **CAMERON, JOHN** | | | |
| DERAM | | | |
| ❑ DES 18033 | Off Centre | 1969 | 20.00 |
| **CAMP, HAMILTON** | | | |
| ELEKTRA | | | |
| ❑ EKL-278 [M] | Paths of Victory | 1965 | 25.00 |
| ❑ EKS-7278 [S] | Paths of Victory | 1965 | 30.00 |
| **CAMP, RED** | | | |
| COOK | | | |
| ❑ LP-1087 [10] | Camp Inventions: Bold New Design for Jazz Piano | 1955 | 50.00 |
| ❑ LP-1089 [10] | Red Camp | 1955 | 50.00 |
| ❑ LP-5005 [M] | Camp Has a Ball | 1957 | 40.00 |
| **CAMPBELL, ALEX** | | | |
| STARDAY | | | |
| ❑ SLP-214 [M] | 16 Radio Favorites | 1963 | 25.00 |
| ❑ SLP-342 [M] | Travel On | 1965 | 25.00 |
| **CAMPBELL, ARCHIE** | | | |
| RCA VICTOR | | | |
| ❑ LPM-3504 [M] | Have a Laugh on Me | 1966 | 20.00 |
| ❑ LSP-3504 [S] | Have a Laugh on Me | 1966 | 25.00 |
| ❑ LPM-3699 [M] | The Cockfight and Other Tall Tales | 1967 | 20.00 |
| ❑ LSP-3699 [S] | The Cockfight and Other Tall Tales | 1967 | 25.00 |
| ❑ LPM-3780 [M] | Kids I Love 'Em | 1967 | 25.00 |
| ❑ LSP-3780 [S] | Kids I Love 'Em | 1967 | 20.00 |
| ❑ LPM-3892 [M] | The Golden Years | 1967 | 25.00 |
| ❑ LSP-3892 [S] | The Golden Years | 1967 | 20.00 |
| STARDAY | | | |
| ❑ SLP-162 [M] | Make Friends with Archie Campbell | 1962 | 30.00 |
| ❑ SLP-167 [M] | Bedtime Stories for Adults | 1962 | 30.00 |
| ❑ SLP-223 [M] | The Joker Is Wild | 1963 | 30.00 |
| ❑ SLP-377 [M] | The Grand Ole Opry's Good Humor Man | 1966 | 25.00 |
| **CAMPBELL, ARCHIE, AND LORENE MANN** | | | |
| RCA VICTOR | | | |
| ❑ LSP-4086 | Archie and Lorene Tell It Like It Is | 1968 | 20.00 |
| **CAMPBELL, CECIL** | | | |
| STARDAY | | | |
| ❑ SLP-254 [M] | Steel Guitar Jamboree | 1963 | 40.00 |
| **CAMPBELL, CHOKER** | | | |
| MOTOWN | | | |
| ❑ M-620 [M] | Hits of the Sixties | 1964 | 100.00 |
| ❑ MS-620 [S] | Hits of the Sixties | 1964 | 150.00 |
| **CAMPBELL, DICK** | | | |
| MERCURY | | | |
| ❑ MG-21060 [M] | Dick Campbell Sings Where It's At | 1966 | 30.00 |
| ❑ SR-61060 [S] | Dick Campbell Sings Where It's At | 1966 | 40.00 |
| **CAMPBELL, GLEN** | | | |
| ATLANTIC AMERICA | | | |
| ❑ 90016 | Old Home Town | 1983 | 8.00 |
| ❑ 90164 | Letter to Home | 1984 | 8.00 |
| ❑ 90483 | It's Just a Matter of Time | 1985 | 8.00 |
| CAPITOL | | | |
| ❑ SM-103 | Wichita Lineman | 1977 | 8.00 |
| *—Reissue with new prefix* | | | |
| ❑ ST-103 | Wichita Lineman | 1968 | 15.00 |
| ❑ ST-8-0103 | Wichita Lineman | 1968 | 20.00 |
| *—Capitol Record Club edition* | | | |
| ❑ ST-210 | Galveston | 1969 | 15.00 |
| ❑ STBO-268 | Glen Campbell — "Live" | 1969 | 20.00 |
| ❑ SM-389 | Try a Little Kindness | 1977 | 8.00 |
| *—Reissue with new prefix* | | | |
| ❑ SW-389 | Try a Little Kindness | 1970 | 12.00 |
| ❑ SW-443 | Oh Happy Day | 1970 | 12.00 |
| ❑ SW-493 | The Glen Campbell Goodtime Album | 1970 | 12.00 |
| ❑ SM-733 | The Last Time I Saw Her | 1977 | 8.00 |
| *—Reissue with new prefix* | | | |
| ❑ SW-733 | The Last Time I Saw Her | 1971 | 12.00 |
| ❑ SW-752 | Glen Campbell's Greatest Hits | 1971 | 12.00 |
| ❑ ST 1810 [S] | Big Bluegrass Special | 1962 | 100.00 |
| *—As "The Green River Boys Featuring Glen Campbell"* | | | |
| ❑ T 1810 [M] | Big Bluegrass Special | 1962 | 80.00 |
| *—As "The Green River Boys Featuring Glen Campbell"* | | | |
| ❑ ST 1881 [S] | Too Late to Worry, Too Blue to Cry | 1963 | 25.00 |
| ❑ T 1881 [M] | Too Late to Worry, Too Blue to Cry | 1963 | 20.00 |
| ❑ ST 2023 [S] | The Astounding 12-String Guitar of Glen Campbell | 1964 | 20.00 |
| ❑ T 2023 [M] | The Astounding 12-String Guitar of Glen Campbell | 1964 | 15.00 |



**Except when noted otherwise, VG = 25% of NM, and VG+ = 50% of NM. (Example: VG = $2.00, VG+ = $4.00 and NM = $8.00.)**

| Number | Title (A Side/B Side) | Yr | NM |
|---|---|---|---|
| ❑ ST 2392 [S] | The Big Bad Rock Guitar of Glen Campbell | 1965 | 20.00 |
| ❑ T 2392 [M] | The Big Bad Rock Guitar of Glen Campbell | 1965 | 15.00 |
| ❑ ST 2679 [S] | Burning Bridges | 1967 | 15.00 |
| ❑ T 2679 [M] | Burning Bridges | 1967 | 15.00 |
| ❑ ST 2809 [S] | Gentle on My Mind | 1967 | 15.00 |
| ❑ T 2809 [M] | Gentle on My Mind | 1967 | 15.00 |
| ❑ ST 2851 [S] | By the Time I Get to Phoenix | 1967 | 15.00 |
| ❑ T 2851 [M] | By the Time I Get to Phoenix | 1967 | 15.00 |
| ❑ ST 2878 [S] | Hey, Little One | 1968 | 15.00 |
| ❑ T 2878 [M] | Hey, Little One | 1968 | 25.00 |
| ❑ ST 2907 | A New Place in the Sun | 1968 | 15.00 |
| ❑ ST 2978 | That Christmas Feeling | 1968 | 15.00 |
| ❑ SW-11117 | Glen Travis Campbell | 1972 | 10.00 |
| ❑ SW-11185 | I Knew Jesus (Before He Was a Star) | 1973 | 10.00 |
| ❑ SW-11253 | I Remember Hank Williams | 1973 | 10.00 |
| ❑ SW-11293 | Hosuton (I'm Comin' to See You) | 1974 | 10.00 |
| ❑ SW-11336 | Reunion (The Songs of Jimmy Webb) | 1974 | 10.00 |
| ❑ SM-11407 | Arkansas | 1977 | 8.00 |
| *—Reissue with new prefix* | | | |
| ❑ SW-11407 | Arkansas | 1975 | 10.00 |
| ❑ SW-11430 | Rhinestone Cowboy | 1975 | 10.00 |
| ❑ SW-11516 | Bloodline | 1976 | 10.00 |
| ❑ ST-11577 | The Best of Glen Campbell | 1976 | 10.00 |
| ❑ SO-11601 | Southern Nights | 1977 | 10.00 |
| ❑ SWBC-11707 [(2)] | Live at the Royal Festival Hall | 1977 | 12.00 |
| ❑ SW-11722 | Basic | 1978 | 10.00 |
| ❑ SM-11960 | Gentle on My Mind | 1979 | 8.00 |
| *—Reissue of 2809* | | | |
| ❑ SOO-12008 | Highwayman | 1979 | 10.00 |
| ❑ SM-12040 | By the Time I Get to Phoenix | 1979 | 8.00 |
| *—Reissue of 2851* | | | |
| ❑ SOO-12075 | Somethin' 'Bout You Baby I Like | 1980 | 10.00 |
| ❑ SOO-12124 | It's the World Gone Crazy | 1981 | 10.00 |
| ❑ SN-16029 | Rhinestone Cowboy | 1980 | 6.00 |
| *—Budget-line reissue* | | | |
| ❑ SN-16030 | Southern Nights | 1980 | 6.00 |
| *—Budget-line reissue* | | | |
| ❑ SN-16031 | Glen Travis Campbell | 1980 | 6.00 |
| *—Budget-line reissue* | | | |
| ❑ SN-16160 | Wichita Lineman | 1981 | 6.00 |
| *—Budget-line reissue* | | | |
| ❑ SN-16258 | Hey Little Girl | 1982 | 6.00 |
| *—Budget-line reissue* | | | |
| ❑ SN-16259 | Galveston | 1982 | 6.00 |
| *—Budget-line reissue* | | | |
| ❑ SN-16297 | Glen Campbell's Greatest Hits | 1984 | 6.00 |
| *—Budget-line reissue* | | | |
| ❑ SN-16335 | The Best of Glen Campbell | 1984 | 6.00 |
| *—Budget-line reissue* | | | |
| ❑ SWAK-93157 | Limited Collector's Edition | 1970 | 20.00 |
| *—Capitol Record Club exclusive; includes tour program* | | | |
| **LONGINES SYMPHONETTE** | | | |
| ❑ LS-218 [(5)] | Glen Campbell's Golden Favorites | 1972 | 25.00 |
| **MCA** | | | |
| ❑ 42009 | Still Within the Sound of My Voice | 1987 | 8.00 |
| ❑ 42210 | Light Years | 1988 | 8.00 |
| **PAIR** | | | |
| ❑ PDL2-1089 [(2)] | All-Time Favorites | 1986 | 12.00 |
| **PICKWICK** | | | |
| ❑ PTP-2048 [(2)] | Only the Lonely | 197? | 10.00 |
| ❑ PC-3052 [M] | The 12 String Guitar of Glen Campbell | 196? | 12.00 |
| ❑ SPC-3052 [S] | The 12 String Guitar of Glen Campbell | 196? | 10.00 |
| ❑ SPC-3134 | A Satisfied Mind | 197? | 8.00 |
| ❑ SPC-3274 | The Glen Campbell Album | 197? | 8.00 |
| ❑ SPC-3346 | I'll Paint You a Song | 197? | 8.00 |
| **STARDAY** | | | |
| ❑ SLP-424 | Country Soul | 1968 | 15.00 |
| ❑ SLP-437 | Country Music Star #1 | 1969 | 15.00 |
| **SURREY** | | | |
| ❑ S 1007 [M] | Country Shindig | 196? | 12.00 |

### CAMPBELL, GLEN, AND BOBBIE GENTRY

| Number | Title (A Side/B Side) | Yr | NM |
|---|---|---|---|
| **CAPITOL** | | | |
| ❑ ST 2928 | Bobbie Gentry & Glen Campbell | 1968 | 15.00 |
| ❑ ST 8-2928 | Bobbie Gentry & Glen Campbell | 1968 | 20.00 |
| *—Capitol Record Club edition* | | | |

### CAMPBELL, JO ANN

| Number | Title (A Side/B Side) | Yr | NM |
|---|---|---|---|
| **ABC-PARAMOUNT** | | | |
| ❑ 393 [M] | Twistin' and Listenin' | 1962 | 80.00 |
| ❑ S-393 [S] | Twistin' and Listenin' | 1962 | 100.00 |
| **CAMEO** | | | |
| ❑ C-1026 [M] | All the Hits of Jo Ann Campbell | 1962 | 50.00 |
| ❑ SC-1026 [S] | All the Hits of Jo Ann Campbell | 1962 | 100.00 |
| **CORONET** | | | |
| ❑ CX-199 [M] | Starring Jo Ann Campbell | 196? | 20.00 |
| ❑ CXS-199 [R] | Starring Jo Ann Campbell | 196? | 12.00 |
| **END** | | | |
| ❑ LP-306 [M] | I'm Nobody's Baby | 1959 | 150.00 |

### CAMPER VAN BEETHOVEN

| Number | Title (A Side/B Side) | Yr | NM |
|---|---|---|---|
| **INDEPENDENT PROJECT** | | | |
| ❑ 016 | Telephone Free Landslide Victory | 1985 | 25.00 |
| *—"Manufactured and Distributed within the United States of America by Rough Trade" on back cover; non-letterpress edition; several color schemes exist, all of equal value* | | | |
| ❑ 016 | Telephone Free Landslide Victory | 1985 | 50.00 |
| *—Letterpress cover, "Second Edition: 1175 cp./September 1985" on back (un-numbered promo)* | | | |
| ❑ 016 | Telephone Free Landslide Victory | 1985 | 60.00 |
| *—Letterpress cover, "Second Edition: 1175 cp./September 1985" on back (numbered edition from 1251-2425)* | | | |
| ❑ 016 | Telephone Free Landslide Victory | 1985 | 70.00 |
| *—Letterpress cover, "First Edition: June 1985" on back (un-numbered promo); the basic color scheme is red, black and flourescent orange on brown chipboard* | | | |
| ❑ 016 | Telephone Free Landslide Victory | 1985 | 80.00 |
| *—Letterpress cover, "First Edition: June 1985" on back (numbered edition from 1-1,250); the basic color scheme is white, black and flourescent orange on brown chipboard* | | | |
| **PITCH A TENT** | | | |
| ❑ 01 | II & III | 1985 | 15.00 |
| ❑ 02 | Camper Van Beethoven | 1986 | 15.00 |
| ❑ 05 [EP] | Vampire Can Mating Oven | 1987 | 15.00 |
| **VIRGIN** | | | |
| ❑ 90918 | Our Beloved Revolutionary Sweetheart | 1988 | 10.00 |
| ❑ 91289 | Key Lime Pie | 1989 | 10.00 |

### CAMPUS SINGERS, THE

| Number | Title (A Side/B Side) | Yr | NM |
|---|---|---|---|
| **ARGO** | | | |
| ❑ LP-4023 [M] | The Campus Singers at the Fickle Pickle | 1963 | 20.00 |
| ❑ LPS-4023 [S] | The Campus Singers at the Fickle Pickle | 1963 | 25.00 |
| ❑ LP-4033 [M] | Road of Blue | 1964 | 20.00 |
| ❑ LPS-4033 [S] | Road of Blue | 1964 | 25.00 |

### CAN

| Number | Title (A Side/B Side) | Yr | NM |
|---|---|---|---|
| **MUTE** | | | |
| ❑ 9033-1 [(3)] | Sacrilege | 1997 | 25.00 |
| *—Album of remixes* | | | |

### CANADIAN BEADLES, THE

| Number | Title (A Side/B Side) | Yr | NM |
|---|---|---|---|
| **TIDE** | | | |
| ❑ 2005 [M] | Three Faces North | 1964 | 50.00 |

### CANADIAN SWEETHEARTS, THE

| Number | Title (A Side/B Side) | Yr | NM |
|---|---|---|---|
| **A&M** | | | |
| ❑ LP-106 [M] | Introducing the Canadian Sweethearts | 1964 | 40.00 |
| ❑ SP-4106 [S] | Introducing the Canadian Sweethearts | 1964 | 50.00 |

### CANARIES, THE

| Number | Title (A Side/B Side) | Yr | NM |
|---|---|---|---|
| **B.T. PUPPY** | | | |
| ❑ BTS-1007 | Flying High with the Canaries | 1970 | 100.00 |

### CANDIDO

| Number | Title (A Side/B Side) | Yr | NM |
|---|---|---|---|
| **ABC-PARAMOUNT** | | | |
| ❑ ABC-125 [M] | Candido Featuring Al Cohn | 1956 | 50.00 |
| ❑ ABC-180 [M] | The Volcanic Candido | 1957 | 50.00 |
| ❑ ABC-236 [M] | In Indigo | 1958 | 50.00 |
| ❑ ABCS-236 [S] | In Indigo | 1959 | 40.00 |
| ❑ ABC-286 [M] | Latin Fire | 1959 | 40.00 |
| ❑ ABCS-286 [S] | Latin Fire | 1959 | 50.00 |
| ❑ ABC-453 [M] | Candido's Comparsa | 1963 | 20.00 |
| ❑ ABCS-453 [S] | Candido's Comparsa | 1963 | 25.00 |
| **RCA VICTOR** | | | |
| ❑ LPM-2027 [M] | Beautiful | 1959 | 30.00 |
| ❑ LSP-2027 [S] | Beautiful | 1959 | 40.00 |
| **ROULETTE** | | | |
| ❑ R-52078 [M] | Conga Soul | 1962 | 20.00 |
| ❑ SR-52078 [S] | Conga Soul | 1962 | 25.00 |

### CANDOLI, CONTE

| Number | Title (A Side/B Side) | Yr | NM |
|---|---|---|---|
| **ANDEX** | | | |
| ❑ A-3002 [M] | Mucho Calor | 1958 | 50.00 |
| ❑ AS-3002 [S] | Mucho Calor | 1959 | 40.00 |
| **BETHLEHEM** | | | |
| ❑ BCP-30 [M] | Toots Sweet | 1956 | 80.00 |
| ❑ BCP-1016 [10] | Sincerely, Conte Candoli | 1954 | 150.00 |
| **CROWN** | | | |
| ❑ CST-190 [R] | Little Band, Big Jazz | 196? | 25.00 |
| *—Red vinyl* | | | |
| ❑ CLP-5162 [M] | Little Band, Big Jazz | 1960 | 20.00 |

### CANDOLI, CONTE, AND STAN LEVEY

| Number | Title (A Side/B Side) | Yr | NM |
|---|---|---|---|
| **BETHLEHEM** | | | |
| ❑ BCP-9 [M] | West Coasting | 1956 | 80.00 |

### CANDOLI, PETE

| Number | Title (A Side/B Side) | Yr | NM |
|---|---|---|---|
| **DECCA** | | | |
| ❑ DL 74761 [S] | Moscow Mule (And Many More Kicks) | 1966 | 20.00 |
| **KAPP** | | | |
| ❑ KL-1230 [M] | For Pete's Sake | 1960 | 20.00 |
| ❑ KS-3230 [S] | For Pete's Sake | 1960 | 25.00 |
| **SOMERSET** | | | |
| ❑ SF-17200 [M] | Blues, When Your Lover Has Gone | 1963 | 20.00 |
| ❑ SFS-17200 [S] | Blues, When Your Lover Has Gone | 1963 | 25.00 |

### CANDOLI BROTHERS, THE

| Number | Title (A Side/B Side) | Yr | NM |
|---|---|---|---|
| **DOT** | | | |
| ❑ DLP-3062 [M] | The Brothers Candoli | 1957 | 50.00 |
| ❑ DLP-3168 [M] | Bell, Book and Candoli | 1959 | 30.00 |
| ❑ DLP-25168 [S] | Bell, Book and Candoli | 1959 | 25.00 |
| **MERCURY** | | | |
| ❑ MG-20515 [M] | Two for the Money | 1959 | 30.00 |
| ❑ SR-60191 [S] | Two for the Money | 1959 | 25.00 |
| **WARNER BROS.** | | | |
| ❑ W 1462 [M] | The Brothers Candoli | 1962 | 20.00 |
| ❑ WS 1462 [S] | The Brothers Candoli | 1962 | 25.00 |

### CANDY STORE, THE

| Number | Title (A Side/B Side) | Yr | NM |
|---|---|---|---|
| **DECCA** | | | |
| ❑ DL 75147 | Turned-On Christmas | 1969 | 25.00 |

### CANDYMEN, THE

| Number | Title (A Side/B Side) | Yr | NM |
|---|---|---|---|
| **ABC** | | | |
| ❑ 616 [M] | The Candymen | 1967 | 25.00 |
| ❑ S-616 [S] | The Candymen | 1967 | 20.00 |
| ❑ S-633 | The Candymen Bring You Candypower | 1968 | 20.00 |

### CANNED HEAT

| Number | Title (A Side/B Side) | Yr | NM |
|---|---|---|---|
| **ACCORD** | | | |
| ❑ SN-7144 | Captured Live | 1981 | 10.00 |
| **ATLANTIC** | | | |
| ❑ SD 7289 | One More River to Cross | 1973 | 15.00 |
| **DALI** | | | |
| ❑ DCLP-89022 | Reheated | 1990 | 15.00 |
| **JANUS** | | | |
| ❑ JLS-3009 | Vintage — Canned Heat | 1969 | 15.00 |
| **LIBERTY** | | | |
| ❑ LRP-3526 [M] | Canned Heat | 1967 | 25.00 |
| ❑ LRP-3541 [M] | Boogie with Canned Heat | 1968 | 40.00 |
| *—Stock copy in stereo cover with "Audition Mono LP Not for Sale" sticker* | | | |
| ❑ LST-7526 [S] | Canned Heat | 1967 | 20.00 |
| ❑ LST-7541 [S] | Boogie with Canned Heat | 1968 | 20.00 |
| ❑ LST-7618 | Hallelujah | 1969 | 20.00 |
| ❑ LN-10105 | Boogie with Canned Heat | 1981 | 8.00 |
| *—Budget-line reissue* | | | |
| ❑ LN-10106 | Canned Heat Cook Book (The Best of Canned Heat) | 1981 | 8.00 |
| *—Budget-line reissue* | | | |
| ❑ LST-11000 | Canned Heat Cook Book (The Best of Canned Heat) | 1969 | 20.00 |
| ❑ LST-11002 | Future Blues | 1970 | 15.00 |
| ❑ LST-27200 [(2)] | Living the Blues | 1968 | 25.00 |
| **PICKWICK** | | | |
| ❑ SPC-3364 | Live at Topanga Canyon | 197? | 10.00 |
| ❑ SPC-3614 | Boogie | 1978 | 10.00 |
| **SCEPTER CITATION** | | | |
| ❑ CTN-18017 | The Best of Canned Heat | 1972 | 10.00 |
| **SUNSET** | | | |
| ❑ SUS-5298 | Collage | 1971 | 10.00 |
| **TAKOMA** | | | |
| ❑ 7066 | The Human Condition | 1980 | 12.00 |
| **UNITED ARTISTS** | | | |
| ❑ UA-LA049-F | The New Age | 1973 | 15.00 |
| ❑ LM-1015 | Boogie with Canned Heat | 1980 | 12.00 |
| *—Reissue of Liberty 7541* | | | |
| ❑ UAS-5509 | Canned Heat Concert (Recorded Live in Europe) | 1971 | 15.00 |
| ❑ UAS-5557 | Historical Figures and Ancient Heads | 1972 | 15.00 |
| ❑ UAS-9955 [(2)] | Living the Blues | 1971 | 20.00 |
| *—Reissue of Liberty 27200* | | | |
| **WAND** | | | |
| ❑ WDS-693 | Live at Topanga Canyon | 1970 | 25.00 |

**CANNED HEAT AND JOHN LEE HOOKER** See JOHN LEE HOOKER AND CANNED HEAT

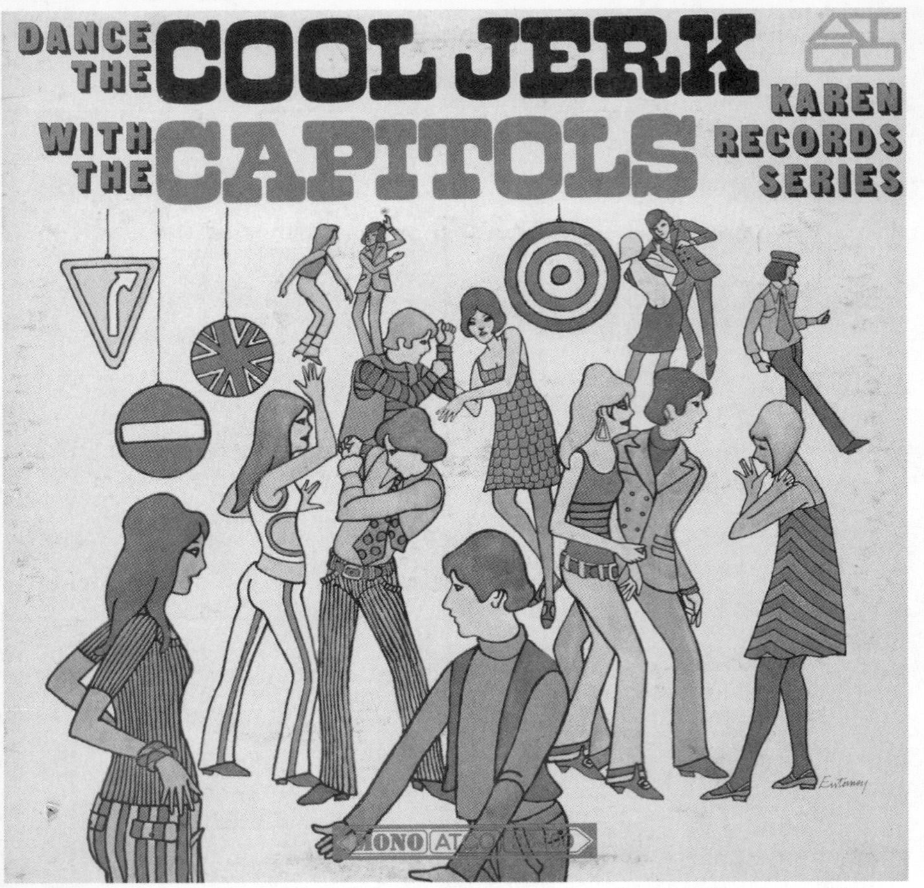


The Capitols, *Dance the Cool Jerk with the Capitols,* Atco 33-190, 1966, mono, $40.

### CANNIBAL AND THE HEADHUNTERS

DATE

| Number | Title (A Side/B Side) | Yr | NM |
|---|---|---|---|
| ❑ TEM 3001 [M] | Land of 1000 Dances | 1966 | 30.00 |
| ❑ TES 4001 [S] | Land of 1000 Dances | 1966 | 40.00 |

RAMPART

| Number | Title (A Side/B Side) | Yr | NM |
|---|---|---|---|
| ❑ RM-3302 [M] | Land of 1000 Dances | 1965 | 50.00 |
| ❑ RS-3302 [S] | Land of 1000 Dances | 1965 | 70.00 |

### CANNON, ACE

ALLEGIANCE

| Number | Title (A Side/B Side) | Yr | NM |
|---|---|---|---|
| ❑ AV-5024 | Ace in the Whole | 1986 | 8.00 |

HI

| Number | Title (A Side/B Side) | Yr | NM |
|---|---|---|---|
| ❑ 6006 | After Hours | 1978 | 10.00 |
| ❑ 8003 | Sax Man | 1977 | 10.00 |
| ❑ 8008 | Cannon Country | 1979 | 10.00 |
| ❑ HL-12007 [M] | Tuff Sax | 1962 | 25.00 |
| ❑ HL-12008 [M] | Looking Back | 1962 | 25.00 |
| ❑ HL-12014 [M] | The Moanin' Sax of Ace Cannon | 1963 | 25.00 |
| ❑ HL-12016 [M] | Aces Hi | 1964 | 20.00 |
| ❑ HL-12019 [M] | The Great Show Tunes | 1964 | 20.00 |
| ❑ HL-12022 [M] | Christmas Cheer | 1964 | 20.00 |
| ❑ HL-12025 [M] | Ace Cannon Live | 1965 | 15.00 |
| ❑ HL-12028 [M] | Nashville Hits | 1965 | 15.00 |
| ❑ HL-12030 [M] | Sweet and Tuff | 1966 | 15.00 |
| ❑ HL-12035 [M] | The Misty Sax of Ace Cannon | 1967 | 20.00 |
| ❑ HL-12040 [M] | Memphis Golden Hits | 1967 | 20.00 |
| ❑ SHL-32007 [S] | Tuff Sax | 1962 | 30.00 |
| ❑ SHL-32008 [S] | Looking Back | 1962 | 30.00 |
| ❑ SHL-32014 [S] | The Moanin' Sax of Ace Cannon | 1963 | 30.00 |
| ❑ SHL-32016 [S] | Aces Hi | 1964 | 25.00 |
| ❑ SHL-32019 [S] | The Great Show Tunes | 1964 | 25.00 |
| ❑ SHL-32022 [S] | Christmas Cheer | 1964 | 25.00 |
| ❑ SHL-32025 [S] | Ace Cannon Live | 1965 | 20.00 |
| ❑ SHL-32028 [S] | Nashville Hits | 1965 | 20.00 |
| ❑ SHL-32030 [S] | Sweet and Tuff | 1966 | 20.00 |
| ❑ SHL-32035 [S] | The Misty Sax of Ace Cannon | 1967 | 15.00 |
| ❑ SHL-32040 [S] | Memphis Golden Hits | 1967 | 15.00 |
| ❑ SHL-32043 | The Incomparable Sax of Ace Cannon | 1968 | 15.00 |
| ❑ SHL-32046 | In the Spotlight | 1968 | 15.00 |
| ❑ SHL-32051 | The Ace of Sax | 1969 | 15.00 |
| ❑ SHL-32057 | The Happy and Mellow Sax of Ace Cannon | 1970 | 12.00 |
| ❑ SHL-32060 | Cool 'n Saxy | 1971 | 12.00 |
| ❑ SHL-32067 | Blowing Wild | 1971 | 12.00 |
| ❑ SHL-32071 | Cannon Country | 1972 | 12.00 |
| ❑ SHL-32072/3 [(2)] | Aces Back to Back | 1972 | 15.00 |
| ❑ SHL-32076 | Baby Don't Get Hooked on Me | 1973 | 10.00 |
| ❑ SHL-32080 | Country Comfort | 1974 | 10.00 |
| ❑ SHL-32086 | That Music City Feeling | 1974 | 10.00 |
| ❑ SHL-32090 | Super Sax Country Style | 1975 | 10.00 |
| ❑ SHL-32101 | Peace in the Valley | 1976 | 10.00 |

### CANNON, FREDDY

RHINO

| Number | Title (A Side/B Side) | Yr | NM |
|---|---|---|---|
| ❑ RNLP-210 | 14 Booming Hits | 1982 | 10.00 |

SWAN

| Number | Title (A Side/B Side) | Yr | NM |
|---|---|---|---|
| ❑ LP-502 [M] | The Explosive! Freddy Cannon | 1960 | 120.00 |
| ❑ LPS-502 [S] | The Explosive! Freddy Cannon | 1960 | 300.00 |
| ❑ LP-504 [M] | Happy Shades of Blue | 1960 | 150.00 |
| ❑ LP-505 [M] | Solid Gold Hits | 1961 | 150.00 |
| ❑ LP-507 [M] | Freddy Cannon at Palisades Park | 1962 | 150.00 |
| ❑ LP-511 [M] | Freddy Cannon Steps Out | 1963 | 150.00 |

WARNER BROS.

| Number | Title (A Side/B Side) | Yr | NM |
|---|---|---|---|
| ❑ W 1544 [M] | Freddie Cannon | 1964 | 30.00 |
| ❑ WS 1544 [S] | Freddie Cannon | 1964 | 40.00 |
| ❑ W 1612 [M] | Action! | 1965 | 30.00 |
| ❑ WS 1612 [S] | Action! | 1965 | 40.00 |
| ❑ W 1628 [M] | Freddy Cannon's Greatest Hits | 1966 | 30.00 |
| ❑ WS 1628 [S] | Freddy Cannon's Greatest Hits | 1966 | 40.00 |

### CANNON, GUS

STAX

| Number | Title (A Side/B Side) | Yr | NM |
|---|---|---|---|
| ❑ ST-702 [M] | Walk Right In | 1962 | 600.00 |

### CANTELON, WILLARD

SUPREME

| Number | Title (A Side/B Side) | Yr | NM |
|---|---|---|---|
| ❑ M-113 [M] | L.S.D. Battle for the Mind | 1966 | 30.00 |
| ❑ S-113 [S] | L.S.D. Battle for the Mind | 1966 | 40.00 |

### CANTOR, EDDIE

VIK

| Number | Title (A Side/B Side) | Yr | NM |
|---|---|---|---|
| ❑ LXA-1119 [M] | The Best of Eddie Cantor | 1957 | 50.00 |

### CAPITAL CITY ROCKETS

ELEKTRA

| Number | Title (A Side/B Side) | Yr | NM |
|---|---|---|---|
| ❑ EKS-75079 | Capital City Rockets | 1973 | 20.00 |

### CAPITOLS, THE (1)

ATCO

| Number | Title (A Side/B Side) | Yr | NM |
|---|---|---|---|
| ❑ 33-190 [M] | Dance the Cool Jerk | 1966 | 40.00 |
| ❑ SD 33-190 [S] | Dance the Cool Jerk | 1966 | 50.00 |
| ❑ 33-201 [M] | We Got a Thing That's In the Groove | 1966 | 40.00 |
| ❑ SD 33-201 [S] | We Got a Thing That's In the Groove | 1966 | 50.00 |

COLLECTABLES

| Number | Title (A Side/B Side) | Yr | NM |
|---|---|---|---|
| ❑ COL-5105 | Golden Classics | 1988 | 10.00 |

SOLID SMOKE

| Number | Title (A Side/B Side) | Yr | NM |
|---|---|---|---|
| ❑ 8019 | The Capitols: Their Greatest Hits | 1983 | 12.00 |

### CAPRARO, JOE

SOUTHLAND

| Number | Title (A Side/B Side) | Yr | NM |
|---|---|---|---|
| ❑ 220 [M] | Dixieland | 1959 | 20.00 |

### CAPTAIN BEEFHEART

A&M

| Number | Title (A Side/B Side) | Yr | NM |
|---|---|---|---|
| ❑ SP-12510 [EP] | The Legendary A&M Sessions | 1984 | 10.00 |

BLUE THUMB

| Number | Title (A Side/B Side) | Yr | NM |
|---|---|---|---|
| ❑ BTS-1 | Strictly Personal | 1968 | 50.00 |
| *—Black label, unbanded sides* | | | |
| ❑ BTS-1 | Strictly Personal | 1969 | 30.00 |
| *—White label, unbanded sides* | | | |
| ❑ BTS-1 | Strictly Personal | 197? | 20.00 |
| *—White label, banded sides* | | | |

BUDDAH

| Number | Title (A Side/B Side) | Yr | NM |
|---|---|---|---|
| ❑ 1001/5001 | Safe As Milk "Baby Jesus" Bumper Sticker | 1967 | 25.00 |
| ❑ BDM-1001 [M] | Safe As Milk | 1967 | 100.00 |
| ❑ BDS-5001 [S] | Safe As Milk | 1967 | 60.00 |
| ❑ BDS-5063 | Safe As Milk | 1969 | 25.00 |
| ❑ BDS-5077 | Mirror Man | 197? | 25.00 |
| *—Regular cover* | | | |
| ❑ BDS-5077 | Mirror Man | 1971 | 50.00 |
| *—Die-cut gatefold cover* | | | |

MERCURY

| Number | Title (A Side/B Side) | Yr | NM |
|---|---|---|---|
| ❑ SRM-1-709 | Unconditionally Guaranteed | 1974 | 15.00 |
| ❑ SRM-1-1018 | Bluejeans and Moonbeams | 1975 | 20.00 |

REPRISE

| Number | Title (A Side/B Side) | Yr | NM |
|---|---|---|---|
| ❑ 2MS 2027 [(2)] | Trout Mask Replica | 1970 | 30.00 |
| *—Stock copy with 2027 labels and 2027 jacket* | | | |
| ❑ MS 2050 | The Spotlight Kid | 1971 | 20.00 |
| ❑ MS 2115 | Clear Spot | 1972 | 20.00 |
| ❑ RS 6420 | Lick My Decals Off, Baby | 1970 | 20.00 |

STRAIGHT

| Number | Title (A Side/B Side) | Yr | NM |
|---|---|---|---|
| ❑ 2 STS-1053 [(2)] | Trout Mask Replica | 1969 | 250.00 |
| *—Stock copy with 1053 labels (this has been confirmed to exist)* | | | |
| ❑ 2 STS-1053 [(2)DJ] | Trout Mask Replica | 1969 | 200.00 |
| *—White label promo with 1053 labels* | | | |
| ❑ 2MS 2027 [(2)] | Trout Mask Replica | 1969 | 60.00 |
| *—Stock copy with 2027 labels inside 1053 jacket* | | | |
| ❑ 2MS 2027 [(2)DJ] | Trout Mask Replica | 1969 | 150.00 |
| *—White label promo with 2027 labels inside 1053 jacket* | | | |
| ❑ RS 6420 | Lick My Decals Off, Baby | 1970 | 50.00 |

VERVE FORECAST

| Number | Title (A Side/B Side) | Yr | NM |
|---|---|---|---|
| ❑ FTS-3054 | Captain Beefheart and the Magic Band | 1968 | — |
| *—Canceled* | | | |

VIRGIN

| Number | Title (A Side/B Side) | Yr | NM |
|---|---|---|---|
| ❑ VA 13148 | Doc at the Radar Station | 1980 | 12.00 |

VIRGIN/EPIC

| Number | Title (A Side/B Side) | Yr | NM |
|---|---|---|---|
| ❑ ARE 38274 | Ice Cream for Crow | 1982 | 12.00 |

WARNER BROS.

| Number | Title (A Side/B Side) | Yr | NM |
|---|---|---|---|
| ❑ (no #) | Bat Chain Puller | 1978 | 400.00 |
| *—Test pressing with different selections than stock version* | | | |
| ❑ BSK 3256 | Shiny Beast (Bat Chain Puller) | 1978 | 12.00 |

### CAPTAIN BEYOND

CAPRICORN

| Number | Title (A Side/B Side) | Yr | NM |
|---|---|---|---|
| ❑ CP 0105 | Captain Beyond | 1972 | 15.00 |
| *—Later covers are normal* | | | |
| ❑ CP 0105 | Captain Beyond | 1972 | 30.00 |
| *—Original covers are 3-D* | | | |
| ❑ CP 0115 | Sufficiently Breathless | 1973 | 15.00 |

WARNER BROS.

| Number | Title (A Side/B Side) | Yr | NM |
|---|---|---|---|
| ❑ BS 3047 | Dawn Explosion | 1977 | 10.00 |

### CARAM, ANA

CHESKY

| Number | Title (A Side/B Side) | Yr | NM |
|---|---|---|---|
| ❑ JR-28 | Rio After Dark | 199? | 25.00 |
| *—Audiophile vinyl* | | | |

### CARAVAN

ARISTA

| Number | Title (A Side/B Side) | Yr | NM |
|---|---|---|---|
| ❑ AL 4088 | Blind Dog | 1976 | 10.00 |

BTM

| Number | Title (A Side/B Side) | Yr | NM |
|---|---|---|---|
| ❑ 5000 | Cunning Stunts | 1975 | 10.00 |

LONDON

| Number | Title (A Side/B Side) | Yr | NM |
|---|---|---|---|
| ❑ PS 582 | If I Could Do It All Over Again… | 1971 | 15.00 |
| ❑ PS 593 | In the Land of the Grey & Pink | 1971 | 15.00 |
| ❑ XPS 615 | Waterloo Lily | 1972 | 15.00 |
| ❑ XPS 637 | For Girls Who Grow Plump in the Night | 1973 | 15.00 |
| ❑ XPS 650 | Caravan and the New Symphonia | 1974 | 15.00 |
| ❑ LC 50011 | The Best of Caravan | 1978 | 10.00 |

VERVE FORECAST

| Number | Title (A Side/B Side) | Yr | NM |
|---|---|---|---|
| ❑ FTS-3066 | Caravan | 1969 | 40.00 |

**CARAVAN, JIMMY**

TOWER

| Number | Title (A Side/B Side) | Yr | NM |
|---|---|---|---|
| ❑ ST 5103 [S] | Look Into the Flower | 1968 | 20.00 |
| ❑ T 5103 [M] | Look Into the Flower | 1968 | 50.00 |

VAULT

| Number | Title (A Side/B Side) | Yr | NM |
|---|---|---|---|
| ❑ 9007 | Hey Jude | 1969 | 20.00 |

**CARAVELLES, THE (1)**

SMASH

| Number | Title (A Side/B Side) | Yr | NM |
|---|---|---|---|
| ❑ MGS-27044 [M] | You Don't Have to Be a Baby to Cry | 1963 | 60.00 |
| ❑ SRS-67044 [R] | You Don't Have to Be a Baby to Cry | 1963 | 60.00 |

**CARE PACKAGE**

LIBERTY

| Number | Title (A Side/B Side) | Yr | NM |
|---|---|---|---|
| ❑ LST-7647 | Keep On Keepin' On | 1970 | 25.00 |

**CAREFREES, THE**

LONDON

| Number | Title (A Side/B Side) | Yr | NM |
|---|---|---|---|
| ❑ PS 379 [S] | From England! The Carefrees | 1964 | 100.00 |
| ❑ LL 3379 [M] | From England! The Carefrees | 1964 | 80.00 |

**CAREY, DAVE**

LAURIE

| Number | Title (A Side/B Side) | Yr | NM |
|---|---|---|---|
| ❑ LLP-1004 [M] | Bandwagon Plus 2 | 1959 | 25.00 |

**CAREY, MARIAH**

COLUMBIA

| Number | Title (A Side/B Side) | Yr | NM |
|---|---|---|---|
| ❑ C 45202 | Mariah Carey | 1990 | 20.00 |
| ❑ C 47980 | Emotions | 1991 | 15.00 |
| ❑ C 53205 | Music Box | 1993 | 15.00 |
| ❑ C2 63800 [(2)] | Rainbow | 1999 | 15.00 |
| ❑ C2 69670 [(2)] | #1's | 1998 | 20.00 |

ISLAND

| Number | Title (A Side/B Side) | Yr | NM |
|---|---|---|---|
| ❑ B0003943-01 [(2)] | The Emancipation of Mimi | 2005 | 15.00 |
| ❑ 440 063467-1 [(2)] | Charmbracelet | 2002 | 15.00 |

VIRGIN

| Number | Title (A Side/B Side) | Yr | NM |
|---|---|---|---|
| ❑ 10797 [(2)] | Glitter | 2001 | 15.00 |
| ❑ SPRO-16452 [(2)DJ] | Glitter | 2001 | 20.00 |

*—Promo-only version*

**CAREY, MUTT**

RIVERSIDE

| Number | Title (A Side/B Side) | Yr | NM |
|---|---|---|---|
| ❑ RLP-1042 [10] | Mutt Carey Plays the Blues | 1954 | 100.00 |

**CAREY, MUTT, AND PUNCH MILLER**

SAVOY

| Number | Title (A Side/B Side) | Yr | NM |
|---|---|---|---|
| ❑ MG-12038 [M] | Jazz — New Orleans | 1955 | 50.00 |
| ❑ MG-12050 [M] | Jazz — New Orleans, Vol. 2 | 1955 | 50.00 |

**CARGILL, HENSON**

ATLANTIC

| Number | Title (A Side/B Side) | Yr | NM |
|---|---|---|---|
| ❑ SD 7279 | This Is Henson Cargill Country | 1973 | 12.00 |

HARMONY

| Number | Title (A Side/B Side) | Yr | NM |
|---|---|---|---|
| ❑ KH 31397 | Welcome to My World | 1972 | 10.00 |

MEGA

| Number | Title (A Side/B Side) | Yr | NM |
|---|---|---|---|
| ❑ 31-1016 | On the Road | 1972 | 15.00 |

MONUMENT

| Number | Title (A Side/B Side) | Yr | NM |
|---|---|---|---|
| ❑ SLP-18094 | Skip a Rope | 1968 | 20.00 |
| ❑ SLP-18103 | Coming On Strong | 1968 | 20.00 |
| ❑ SLP-18117 | None of My Business | 1969 | 20.00 |
| ❑ SLP-18137 | Uncomplicated | 1970 | 20.00 |

**CARISI, JOHN**

COLUMBIA

| Number | Title (A Side/B Side) | Yr | NM |
|---|---|---|---|
| ❑ CS (# unk) [S] | The New Jazz Sound of "Show Boat" | 1960 | 30.00 |
| ❑ CL 1419 [M] | The New Jazz Sound of "Show Boat" | 1960 | 25.00 |

**CARLIN, GEORGE**

ATLANTIC

| Number | Title (A Side/B Side) | Yr | NM |
|---|---|---|---|
| ❑ SD 19326 | A Place for My Stuff | 1981 | 10.00 |

EARDRUM

| Number | Title (A Side/B Side) | Yr | NM |
|---|---|---|---|
| ❑ 1001 | Carlin On Campus | 1984 | 10.00 |
| ❑ 90523 | Playin' with Your Head | 1986 | 10.00 |
| ❑ 90972 | What Am I Doing in New Jersey? | 1988 | 10.00 |

George Carlin, *Take-Offs and Put-Ons,* RCA Camden CAS-2566, 1972, $10.

ERA

| Number | Title (A Side/B Side) | Yr | NM |
|---|---|---|---|
| ❑ EL 103 [M] | George Carlin and Jack Burns At the Playboy Club Tonight | 1960 | 25.00 |
| ❑ E 600 | The Original George Carlin | 1972 | 12.00 |

LAFF

| Number | Title (A Side/B Side) | Yr | NM |
|---|---|---|---|
| ❑ A 219 | Killer Carlin | 1981 | 10.00 |

*—Reissue of Era material*

LITTLE DAVID

| Number | Title (A Side/B Side) | Yr | NM |
|---|---|---|---|
| ❑ LD 1004 | Class Clown | 1972 | 10.00 |
| ❑ LD 1005 | Occupation: Foole | 1973 | 10.00 |
| ● LD 1008 | An Evening with Wally Londo | 1975 | 10.00 |
| ❑ LD 1075 | On the Road | 1977 | 10.00 |
| ❑ LD 1076 | Indecent Exposure (Some of the Best of George Carlin) | 1978 | 10.00 |
| ● LD 3003 | Toledo Window Box | 1974 | 10.00 |
| ❑ LD 7214 | FM & AM | 1972 | 10.00 |
| ❑ 90129 | Toledo Window Box | 1983 | 8.00 |

*—Reissue of 3003*

| Number | Title (A Side/B Side) | Yr | NM |
|---|---|---|---|
| ❑ 90241 | The George Carlin Collection | 1984 | 8.00 |

RCA CAMDEN

| Number | Title (A Side/B Side) | Yr | NM |
|---|---|---|---|
| ❑ CAS-2566 | Take-Offs and Put-Ons | 1972 | 10.00 |

RCA VICTOR

| Number | Title (A Side/B Side) | Yr | NM |
|---|---|---|---|
| ❑ LPM-3772 [M] | Take-Offs and Put-Ons | 1967 | 20.00 |
| ❑ LSP-3772 [S] | Take-Offs and Put-Ons | 1967 | 15.00 |

**CARLISLE, BILL**

HICKORY

| Number | Title (A Side/B Side) | Yr | NM |
|---|---|---|---|
| ❑ LPM-129 [M] | The Best of Bill Carlisle | 1967 | 25.00 |
| ❑ LPS-129 [S] | The Best of Bill Carlisle | 1967 | 25.00 |

**CARLISLE BROTHERS, THE**

KING

| Number | Title (A Side/B Side) | Yr | NM |
|---|---|---|---|
| ❑ 643 [M] | Fresh from the Country | 1959 | 50.00 |

MERCURY

| Number | Title (A Side/B Side) | Yr | NM |
|---|---|---|---|
| ❑ MG-20359 [M] | On Stage with the Carlisles | 1958 | 50.00 |

**CARLOS, WALTER**

CBS MASTERWORKS

| Number | Title (A Side/B Side) | Yr | NM |
|---|---|---|---|
| ❑ M 39340 | Digital Moonscapes | 1984 | 10.00 |

*—As "Wendy Carlos"*

COLUMBIA

| Number | Title (A Side/B Side) | Yr | NM |
|---|---|---|---|
| ❑ KG 31236 [(2)] | Sonic Seasonings | 1972 | 15.00 |
| ❑ KC 31480 | Walter Carlos' Clockwork Orange | 1972 | 12.00 |

COLUMBIA MASTERWORKS

| Number | Title (A Side/B Side) | Yr | NM |
|---|---|---|---|
| ❑ MS 7194 | Switched-On Bach | 1968 | 15.00 |

*—"Standing Bach" cover; gray label with "360 Sound Stereo"*

| Number | Title (A Side/B Side) | Yr | NM |
|---|---|---|---|
| ❑ MS 7194 | Switched-On Bach | 1968 | 50.00 |

*—"Sitting Bach" (sometimes called "Constipated Bach") cover that was quickly replaced; gray label with "360 Sound Stereo"*

| Number | Title (A Side/B Side) | Yr | NM |
|---|---|---|---|
| ❑ MS 7194 | Switched-On Bach | 1970 | 12.00 |

*—Gray label with orange Columbia logos and no "360 Sound Stereo"*

| Number | Title (A Side/B Side) | Yr | NM |
|---|---|---|---|
| ❑ MS 7194 | Switched-On Bach | 198? | 15.00 |

*—Later reissue under the name "Wendy Carlos"; bar code on back cover*

| Number | Title (A Side/B Side) | Yr | NM |
|---|---|---|---|
| ❑ MS 7286 | The Well-Tempered Synthesizer | 1969 | 15.00 |

*—Gray label with "360 Sound Stereo"*

| Number | Title (A Side/B Side) | Yr | NM |
|---|---|---|---|
| ❑ MS 7286 | The Well-Tempered Synthesizer | 1970 | 12.00 |

*—Gray label with orange Columbia logos and no "360 Sound Stereo"*

| Number | Title (A Side/B Side) | Yr | NM |
|---|---|---|---|
| ❑ M 32088 | Walter Carlos By Request | 1973 | 12.00 |
| ❑ KM 32659 | More Switched-On Bach | 1974 | 12.00 |
| ❑ M2X 35895 [(2)] | Switched-On Brandenburgs | 1979 | 15.00 |
| ❑ HM 45950 | Switched-On Brandenburgs Vol. 1 | 1980 | 100.00 |

*—Half-speed mastered edition*

| Number | Title (A Side/B Side) | Yr | NM |
|---|---|---|---|
| ❑ HM 47194 | Switched-On Bach | 198? | 30.00 |

*—Half-speed mastered edition*

**CARLTON, LARRY**

UNI

| Number | Title (A Side/B Side) | Yr | NM |
|---|---|---|---|
| ❑ 73036 | With a Little Help from My Friends | 1968 | 20.00 |

**CARMEN**

EPIC

| Number | Title (A Side/B Side) | Yr | NM |
|---|---|---|---|
| ❑ BN 26479 | Carmen | 1969 | 20.00 |

**CARMICHAEL, HOAGY**

BOOK-OF-THE-MONTH

| Number | Title (A Side/B Side) | Yr | NM |
|---|---|---|---|
| ❑ 61-5450 [(3)] | Hoagy Carmichael | 1984 | 30.00 |

DECCA

| Number | Title (A Side/B Side) | Yr | NM |
|---|---|---|---|
| ❑ DL 5068 [10] | Stardust Road | 1950 | 80.00 |
| ❑ DL 8588 [M] | Stardust Road | 1958 | 30.00 |

GOLDEN

| Number | Title (A Side/B Side) | Yr | NM |
|---|---|---|---|
| ❑ LP-198-18 [M] | Havin' a Party | 1958 | 30.00 |

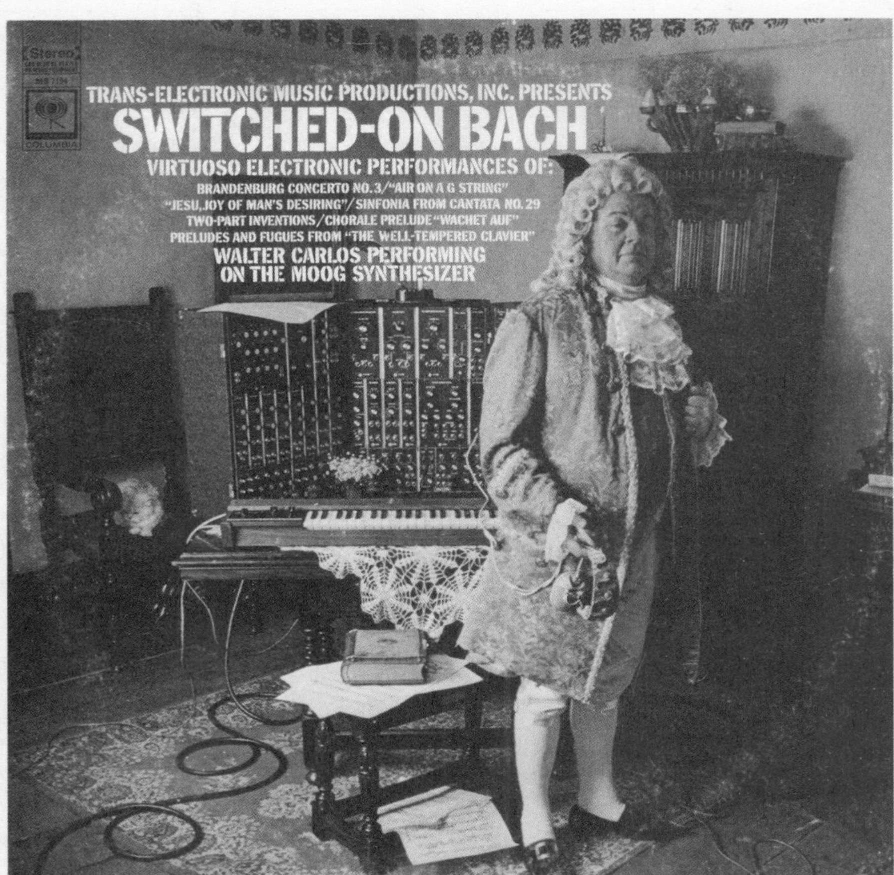


Walter Carlos, *Switched-On Bach,* Columbia Masterworks MS 7194, 1969, standing cover, gray "360 Sound" label, $15.

| Number | Title (A Side/B Side) | Yr | NM |
|---|---|---|---|
| JAZZTONE | | | |
| ❑ J-1266 [M] | Hoagy Sings Carmichael | 1957 | 30.00 |
| KIMBERLY | | | |
| ❑ 2023 [M] | The Legend of Hoagy Carmichael | 1962 | 25.00 |
| ❑ 11023 [R] | The Legend of Hoagy Carmichael | 196? | 20.00 |
| PACIFIC JAZZ | | | |
| ❑ PJ-1223 [M] | Hoagy Sings Carmichael | 1956 | 60.00 |
| RCA VICTOR | | | |
| ❑ LPT-3072 [10] | Old Rockin' Chair | 1953 | 80.00 |

**CARN, DOUG**

| Number | Title (A Side/B Side) | Yr | NM |
|---|---|---|---|
| SAVOY | | | |
| ❑ MG-12195 | The Doug Carn Trio | 1969 | 20.00 |

**CARNES, KIM**

| Number | Title (A Side/B Side) | Yr | NM |
|---|---|---|---|
| A&M | | | |
| ❑ SP-3114 | Sailin' | 198? | 8.00 |
| *—Budget-line reissue* | | | |
| ❑ SP-3204 | The Best of Kim Carnes | 1982 | 10.00 |
| ❑ SP-4548 | Kim Carnes | 1975 | 12.00 |
| ❑ SP-4606 | Sailin' | 1976 | 12.00 |
| AMOS | | | |
| ❑ AAS 7016 | Rest on Me | 1971 | 20.00 |
| EMI AMERICA | | | |
| ❑ SW-17004 | St. Vincent's Court | 1978 | 10.00 |
| ❑ SW-17030 | Romance Dance | 1980 | 10.00 |
| ❑ SO-17052 | Mistaken Identity | 1981 | 10.00 |
| ❑ SO-17078 | Voyeur | 1982 | 10.00 |
| ❑ SO-17107 | Café Racers | 1983 | 10.00 |
| ❑ SO-17159 | Barking at Airplanes | 1985 | 10.00 |
| ❑ ST-17198 | Light House | 1986 | 8.00 |
| MCA | | | |
| ❑ 914 | The Early Years | 1984 | 8.00 |
| ❑ 42200 | View from the House | 1988 | 8.00 |
| MOBILE FIDELITY | | | |
| ❑ 1-073 | Mistaken Identity | 1982 | 25.00 |
| *—Audiophile vinyl* | | | |

**CARNEY, ART**

| Number | Title (A Side/B Side) | Yr | NM |
|---|---|---|---|
| COLUMBIA | | | |
| ❑ CL 2595 [10] | Doodle-Li-Boops and Rhinocelopes | 1955 | 80.00 |

**CARNEY, HARRY**

| Number | Title (A Side/B Side) | Yr | NM |
|---|---|---|---|
| CLEF | | | |
| ❑ MGC-640 [M] | Harry Carney with Strings | 1955 | 80.00 |
| VERVE | | | |
| ❑ MGV-2028 [M] | Moods for Girl and Boy | 1957 | 50.00 |
| *—Reissue of Clef 640* | | | |
| ❑ V-2028 [M] | Moods for Girl and Boy | 1957 | 20.00 |

**CAROLEERS, THE**

| Number | Title (A Side/B Side) | Yr | NM |
|---|---|---|---|
| ALLEGRO ROYALE | | | |
| ❑ 1295 [M] | An Hour of Christmas Music | 195? | 20.00 |
| *—B-side by anonymous "Organ and Chimes"* | | | |

**CAROLINA SLIM**

| Number | Title (A Side/B Side) | Yr | NM |
|---|---|---|---|
| SHARP | | | |
| ❑ 2002 [M] | Blues from the Cotton Fields | 195? | 250.00 |

**CARP** Actor Gary Busey was in this group.

| Number | Title (A Side/B Side) | Yr | NM |
|---|---|---|---|
| EPIC | | | |
| ❑ E 30212 | Carp | 1970 | 25.00 |

**CARPENTER, IKE**

| Number | Title (A Side/B Side) | Yr | NM |
|---|---|---|---|
| ALADDIN | | | |
| ❑ LP-811 [M] | Lights Out | 1957 | — |
| *—Unreleased* | | | |
| DISCOVERY | | | |
| ❑ DL 3003 [10] | Dancers in Love | 1949 | 300.00 |
| INTRO | | | |
| ❑ 950 [10] | Lights Out | 1952 | 300.00 |
| SCORE | | | |
| ❑ SLP-4010 [M] | Lights Out | 1957 | 150.00 |

**CARPENTERS**

| Number | Title (A Side/B Side) | Yr | NM |
|---|---|---|---|
| A&M | | | |
| ❑ SP-3184 | Close to You | 1982 | 8.00 |
| *—Reissue of 4271* | | | |
| ❑ SP-3197 | A Kind of Hush | 1982 | 8.00 |
| *—Reissue of 4581* | | | |
| ❑ SP-3199 | Passage | 1982 | 8.00 |
| *—Reissue of 4703* | | | |
| ❑ SP-3210 | Christmas Portrait | 198? | 8.00 |
| *—Reissue of SP-4726* | | | |
| ❑ SP-3270 | An Old-Fashioned Christmas | 1984 | 10.00 |
| ❑ SP-3502 | Carpenters | 1971 | 12.00 |
| ❑ SP-3511 | A Song for You | 1972 | 12.00 |
| ❑ SP-3519 | Now & Then | 1973 | 12.00 |
| ❑ SP-3601 | The Singles 1969-1973 | 1973 | 12.00 |
| ❑ SP-3723 | Made in America | 1981 | 12.00 |
| ❑ SP-4205 | Offering | 1969 | 80.00 |
| ❑ SP-4205 | Ticket to Ride | 1970 | 12.00 |
| *—Reissue of "Offering" with new title and cover* | | | |
| ❑ SP-4271 | Close to You | 1970 | 12.00 |
| ❑ SP-4530 | Horizon | 1975 | 12.00 |
| ❑ SP-4581 | A Kind of Hush | 1976 | 12.00 |
| ❑ SP-4703 | Passage | 1977 | 12.00 |
| ❑ SP-4726 | Christmas Portrait | 1978 | 15.00 |
| ❑ SP-4954 | Voice of the Heart | 1983 | 12.00 |
| ❑ SP-5172 | An Old Fashioned Christmas | 1987 | 8.00 |
| *—Reissue of 3270 (record still says 3270 but cover is 5172)* | | | |
| ❑ SP-6601 [(2)] | Yesterday Once More | 1985 | 15.00 |
| ❑ QU-53502 [Q] | Carpenters | 1974 | — |
| *—Not released* | | | |
| ❑ QU-53511 [Q] | A Song for You | 1974 | — |
| *—Not released* | | | |
| ❑ QU-53519 [Q] | Now & Then | 1974 | 20.00 |
| ❑ QU-53601 [Q] | The Singles 1969-1973 | 1974 | 20.00 |
| ❑ QU-54271 [Q] | Close to You | 1974 | — |
| *—Not released* | | | |
| ❑ QU-54530 [Q] | Horizon | 1975 | 20.00 |
| ❑ SMAS-94398 | A Song for You | 1972 | 20.00 |
| *—Capitol Record Club edition; unlike the standard edition, the cover is smooth and not textured* | | | |

**CARR, CATHY**

| Number | Title (A Side/B Side) | Yr | NM |
|---|---|---|---|
| DOT | | | |
| ❑ DLP-3674 [M] | Ivory Tower | 1966 | 25.00 |
| ❑ DLP-25674 [S] | Ivory Tower | 1966 | 25.00 |
| FRATERNITY | | | |
| ❑ 1005 [M] | Ivory Tower | 1957 | 120.00 |
| ROULETTE | | | |
| ❑ R 25077 [M] | Shy | 1959 | 40.00 |
| ❑ SR 25077 [S] | Shy | 1959 | 50.00 |

**CARR, GEORGIA**

| Number | Title (A Side/B Side) | Yr | NM |
|---|---|---|---|
| TOPS | | | |
| ❑ L-1617 [M] | Songs by a Moody Miss | 195? | 30.00 |
| VEE JAY | | | |
| ❑ LP-1105 [M] | Rocks in My Bed | 1964 | 20.00 |
| ❑ VJS-1105 [S] | Rocks in My Bed | 1964 | 25.00 |

**CARR, HELEN**

| Number | Title (A Side/B Side) | Yr | NM |
|---|---|---|---|
| BETHLEHEM | | | |
| ❑ BCP-45 [M] | Why Do I Love You | 1956 | 60.00 |
| ❑ BCP-1027 [10] | Down in the Depths on the 90th Floor | 1955 | 120.00 |

**CARR, JAMES**

| Number | Title (A Side/B Side) | Yr | NM |
|---|---|---|---|
| GOLDWAX | | | |
| ❑ 3001S | You Got My Mind Messed Up | 1968 | 150.00 |
| ❑ 3002S | A Man Needs a Woman | 1968 | 150.00 |

**CARR, JOE "FINGERS"**

| Number | Title (A Side/B Side) | Yr | NM |
|---|---|---|---|
| CAPITOL | | | |
| ❑ T 280 [M] | Bar Room Piano | 1952 | 30.00 |
| ❑ T 345 [M] | Roughhouse Piano | 1953 | 30.00 |
| ❑ T 443 [M] | Joe "Fingers" Carr and His Ragtime Band | 1954 | 30.00 |
| ❑ T 527 [M] | Fireman's Ball | 1954 | 30.00 |
| ❑ ST 1151 [S] | "Fingers" and the Flapper | 1959 | 25.00 |
| ❑ T 1151 [M] | "Fingers" and the Flapper | 1959 | 20.00 |
| ❑ ST 1217 [S] | Joe "Fingers" Carr and His Swingin' String Band | 1959 | 25.00 |
| ❑ T 1217 [M] | Joe "Fingers" Carr and His Swingin' String Band | 1959 | 20.00 |
| WARNER BROS. | | | |
| ❑ W 1386 [M] | The World's Greatest Ragtime Piano Player | 1960 | 15.00 |
| ❑ WS 1386 [S] | The World's Greatest Ragtime Piano Player | 1960 | 20.00 |

**CARR, LEROY**

| Number | Title (A Side/B Side) | Yr | NM |
|---|---|---|---|
| COLUMBIA | | | |
| ❑ CL 1911 [M] | Blues Before Sunrise | 1962 | 30.00 |
| ❑ CS 8511 [R] | Blues Before Sunrise | 1962 | 20.00 |

**CARR, LODI**

| Number | Title (A Side/B Side) | Yr | NM |
|---|---|---|---|
| LAURIE | | | |
| ❑ LLP-1007 [M] | Lady Bird | 1960 | 25.00 |

**CARR, VIKKI**

| Number | Title (A Side/B Side) | Yr | NM |
|---|---|---|---|
| COLUMBIA | | | |
| ❑ C 30662 | Vikki Carr's Love Story | 1971 | 10.00 |
| ❑ C 31040 | Superstar | 1971 | 10.00 |
| ❑ KC 31453 | The First Time Ever (I Saw Your Face) | 1972 | 10.00 |

| Number | Title (A Side/B Side) | Yr | NM |
|---|---|---|---|
| ❑ KC 31470 | Canta En Espanol | 1972 | 10.00 |
| ❑ KC 32251 | Ms. America | 1973 | 10.00 |
| ❑ KG 32656 [(2)] | Live at the Greek Theatre | 1973 | 12.00 |
| ❑ KC 32860 | One Hell of a Woman | 1974 | 10.00 |
| ❑ PC 33340 | Hoy (Today) | 1975 | 10.00 |
| ❑ CG 33609 [(2)] | Love Story/The First Time Ever | 1976 | 12.00 |
| **LIBERTY** | | | |
| ❑ LRP-3314 [M] | Color Her Great | 1963 | 15.00 |
| ❑ LRP-3354 [M] | Discovery! | 1964 | 15.00 |
| ❑ LRP-3383 [M] | Discovery! Volume Two | 1964 | 15.00 |
| ❑ LRP-3420 [M] | The Anatomy of Love | 1965 | 15.00 |
| ❑ LRP-3456 [M] | The Way of Today | 1966 | 15.00 |
| ❑ LRP-3506 [M] | Intimate Excitement | 1967 | 20.00 |
| ❑ LRP-3533 [M] | It Must Be Him | 1967 | 20.00 |
| ❑ LRP-3548 [M] | Vikki | 1968 | 30.00 |
| *—Mono stock copy inside stereo cover with "Audition Mono LP Not for Sale" sticker* | | | |
| ❑ LST-7314 [S] | Color Her Great | 1963 | 20.00 |
| ❑ LST-7354 [S] | Discovery! | 1964 | 20.00 |
| ❑ LST-7383 [S] | Discovery! Volume Two | 1964 | 20.00 |
| ❑ LST-7420 [S] | The Anatomy of Love | 1965 | 20.00 |
| ❑ LST-7456 [S] | The Way of Today | 1966 | 20.00 |
| ❑ LST-7506 [S] | Intimate Excitement | 1967 | 15.00 |
| ❑ LST-7533 [S] | It Must Be Him | 1967 | 15.00 |
| ❑ LST-7548 [S] | Vikki | 1968 | 15.00 |
| ❑ LST-7565 | Don't Break My Pretty Balloon | 1969 | 15.00 |
| ❑ LST-7604 | For Once in My Life | 1969 | 15.00 |
| ❑ LN-10108 | The Best of Vikki Carr | 1981 | 8.00 |
| ❑ LST-11001 | Nashville by Carr | 1970 | 15.00 |
| **PAIR** | | | |
| ❑ PDL2-1082 [(2)] | From the Heart | 1986 | 12.00 |
| **PICKWICK** | | | |
| ❑ SPC-3587 | Intimate | 1978 | 8.00 |
| ❑ SPC-3613 | Unforgettable | 1978 | 8.00 |
| **SUNSET** | | | |
| ❑ SUS-5228 | That's All | 1969 | 10.00 |
| ❑ SUS-5293 | Unforgettable | 1971 | 10.00 |
| **UNITED ARTISTS** | | | |
| ❑ UA-LA089-G [(2)] | Vikki Carr's Golden Songbook/Superpak | 1973 | 12.00 |
| ❑ UA-LA244-G | The Very Best of Vikki Carr | 1974 | 10.00 |
| ❑ LM-1006 | It Must Be Him | 1980 | 10.00 |
| *—Abridged reissue of Liberty 7533* | | | |
| ❑ UAS-5581 [(2)] | The Best of Vikki Carr | 1972 | 12.00 |
| ❑ UAS-6813 | The Ways to Love a Man | 1972 | 10.00 |

### CARROLL, BAIKIDA

| Number | Title (A Side/B Side) | Yr | NM |
|---|---|---|---|
| **HAT HUT** | | | |
| ❑ M/N [(2)] | The Spoken Word | 197? | 20.00 |

### CARROLL, BARBARA

| Number | Title (A Side/B Side) | Yr | NM |
|---|---|---|---|
| **ATLANTIC** | | | |
| ❑ ALR-132 [10] | Piano Panorama | 195? | 80.00 |
| **KAPP** | | | |
| ❑ KS-(# unk) [S] | Flower Drum Song | 1958 | 25.00 |
| ❑ KL-1113 [M] | Flower Drum Song | 1958 | 25.00 |
| ❑ KL-1193 [M] | Satin Doll | 1959 | 25.00 |
| **LIVINGSTON** | | | |
| ❑ 1081 [10] | Barbara Carroll Trio | 1953 | 100.00 |
| **RCA VICTOR** | | | |
| ❑ LJM-1001 [M] | Barbara Carroll Trio | 1954 | 50.00 |
| ❑ LJM-1023 [M] | Lullabies in Rhythm | 1955 | 50.00 |
| ❑ LPM-1137 [M] | Have You Met Miss Carroll? | 1956 | 50.00 |
| ❑ LPM-1296 [M] | We Just Couldn't Say Goodbye | 1956 | 50.00 |
| ❑ LPM-1396 [M] | It's a Wonderful World | 1957 | 50.00 |
| **SESAC** | | | |
| ❑ N-3201 [M] | Why Not? | 1959 | 30.00 |
| ❑ SN-3201 [S] | Why Not? | 1959 | 40.00 |
| **UNITED ARTISTS** | | | |
| ❑ UA-LA778-H | From the Beginning | 1978 | 15.00 |
| **VERVE** | | | |
| ❑ MGV-2063 [M] | Funny Face | 1957 | 50.00 |
| *—Black label* | | | |
| ❑ MGV-2063 [M] | Funny Face | 1957 | 60.00 |
| *—Orange label* | | | |
| ❑ MGV-2092 [M] | The Best of George and Ira Gershwin | 1958 | 40.00 |
| ❑ V-2092 [M] | The Best of George and Ira Gershwin | 1961 | 20.00 |
| ❑ MGV-2095 [M] | Barbara | 1958 | 40.00 |
| ❑ V-2095 [M] | Barbara | 1961 | 20.00 |

### CARROLL, BARBARA/MARY LOU WILLIAMS

| Number | Title (A Side/B Side) | Yr | NM |
|---|---|---|---|
| **ATLANTIC** | | | |
| ❑ 1271 [M] | Ladies in Jazz | 1958 | 50.00 |
| *—Black label* | | | |
| ❑ 1271 [M] | Ladies in Jazz | 1961 | 20.00 |
| *—Multi-color label, white "fan" logo* | | | |

### CARROLL, CORKY

| Number | Title (A Side/B Side) | Yr | NM |
|---|---|---|---|
| **CASUAL TUNA** | | | |
| ❑ (# unknown) | A Surfer for President | 1979 | 40.00 |
| **RURAL** | | | |
| ❑ RR-001 | Corky Carroll and Friends | 1971 | 50.00 |

### CARROLL, DAVID

| Number | Title (A Side/B Side) | Yr | NM |
|---|---|---|---|
| **AMBASSADOR** | | | |
| ❑ S-98051 | All Time Great Hits | 196? | 10.00 |
| **MERCURY** | | | |
| ❑ PPS-2000 [M] | Latin Percussion | 196? | 15.00 |
| ❑ PPS-2008 [M] | Percussion Parisienne | 196? | 15.00 |
| ❑ PPS-2022 [M] | All the World Dances | 196? | 15.00 |
| ❑ PPS-6000 [S] | Latin Percussion | 196? | 20.00 |
| ❑ PPS-6008 [S] | Percussion Parisienne | 196? | 20.00 |
| ❑ PPS-6022 [S] | All the World Dances | 196? | 20.00 |
| ❑ MG-20064 [M] | Toe-Tappers | 195? | 20.00 |
| ❑ MG-20086 [M] | Waltzes, Wine and Candlelight | 195? | 20.00 |
| ❑ MG-20109 [M] | Dancer's Delight | 195? | 20.00 |
| ❑ MG-20154 [M] | Shimmering Strings | 195? | 20.00 |
| ❑ MG-20156 [M] | Serenade to a Princess | 195? | 20.00 |
| ❑ MG-20166 [M] | Percussion in Hi-Fi | 195? | 15.00 |
| ❑ MG-20281 [M] | Let's Dance | 195? | 15.00 |
| ❑ MG-20286 [M] | Feathery Feeling | 195? | 15.00 |
| ❑ MG-20301 [M] | Dreams | 195? | 20.00 |
| ❑ MG-20351 [M] | Dance and Stay Young | 195? | 15.00 |
| ❑ MG-20389 [M] | RePercussion | 195? | 15.00 |
| ❑ MG-20411 [M] | Show Stoppers from the Fabulous Fifties | 195? | 15.00 |
| ❑ MG-20470 [M] | Let's Dance Again | 195? | 15.00 |
| ❑ MG-20503 [M] | Solo Encores | 195? | 15.00 |
| ❑ MG-20649 [M] | Let's Dance Dance Dance | 196? | 15.00 |
| ❑ MG-20660 [M] | Mexico and 11 Other Great Hits | 196? | 15.00 |
| ❑ MG-20688 [M] | Let's Dance to the Movie Themes | 196? | 15.00 |
| ❑ MG-20690 [M] | David Carroll Galaxy | 196? | 15.00 |
| ❑ MG-20739 [M] | Let's Dance to America's Waltz Favorites | 196? | 15.00 |
| ❑ MG-20786 [M] | Today's Top Hits | 196? | 15.00 |
| ❑ MG-20846 [M] | Happy Feet | 196? | 15.00 |
| ❑ MG-20867 [M] | Percussion Orientale | 196? | 15.00 |
| ❑ MG-20873 [M] | All the World Dances | 196? | 15.00 |
| ❑ MG-20926 [M] | Music Makes Me Want to Dance! | 196? | 12.00 |
| ❑ MG-20935 [M] | Golden Oldies for Today's Teens | 196? | 12.00 |
| ❑ MG-20955 [M] | Percussion Parisienne | 196? | 12.00 |
| ❑ MG-20962 [M] | House Party Discotheque | 196? | 12.00 |
| ❑ SR-60001 [S] | Let's Dance | 1959 | 20.00 |
| ❑ SR-60003 [S] | Percussion in Hi-Fi | 1959 | 20.00 |
| ❑ SR-60026 [S] | Feathery Feeling | 1959 | 20.00 |
| ❑ SR-60027 [S] | Dance and Stay Young | 1959 | 20.00 |
| ❑ SR-60029 [S] | RePercussion | 1959 | 20.00 |
| ❑ SR-60060 [S] | Show Stoppers from the Fabulous Fifties | 1959 | 20.00 |
| ❑ SR-60152 [S] | Let's Dance Again | 1959 | 20.00 |
| ❑ SR-60180 [S] | Solo Encores | 195? | 20.00 |
| ❑ SR-60649 [S] | Let's Dance Dance Dance | 196? | 20.00 |
| ❑ SR-60660 [S] | Mexico and 11 Other Great Hits | 196? | 20.00 |
| ❑ MG-60688 [S] | Let's Dance to the Movie Themes | 196? | 20.00 |
| ❑ SR-60690 [S] | David Carroll Galaxy | 196? | 20.00 |
| ❑ SR-60739 [S] | Let's Dance to America's Waltz Favorites | 196? | 20.00 |
| ❑ SR-60786 [S] | Today's Top Hits | 196? | 20.00 |
| ❑ SR-60846 [S] | Happy Feet | 196? | 20.00 |
| ❑ SR-60867 [S] | Percussion Orientale | 196? | 20.00 |
| ❑ SR-60873 [S] | All the World Dances | 196? | 20.00 |
| ❑ SR-60926 [S] | Music Makes Me Want to Dance! | 196? | 15.00 |
| ❑ SR-60935 [S] | Golden Oldies for Today's Teens | 196? | 15.00 |
| ❑ SR-60955 [S] | Percussion Parisienne | 196? | 15.00 |
| ❑ SR-60962 [S] | House Party Discotheque | 196? | 15.00 |
| **WING** | | | |
| ❑ MGW-12106 [M] | Dance Date | 195? | 15.00 |
| ❑ MGW-12146 [M] | Contrasts | 195? | 15.00 |
| ❑ MGW-12256 [M] | Waltzes | 196? | 12.00 |
| ❑ SRW-12508 [S] | Contrasts | 195? | 15.00 |
| ❑ SRW-16106 [S] | Dance Date | 195? | 15.00 |
| ❑ SRW-16256 [S] | Waltzes | 196? | 12.00 |
| ❑ SRW-16367 | Let's Dance | 196? | 12.00 |

### CARROLL, DIAHANN

| Number | Title (A Side/B Side) | Yr | NM |
|---|---|---|---|
| **ATLANTIC** | | | |
| ❑ 8048 [M] | Fun Life | 1961 | 20.00 |
| ❑ SD 8048 [S] | Fun Life | 1961 | 25.00 |
| **RCA CAMDEN** | | | |
| ❑ CAL-695 [M] | Show-Stoppers (She's Diahann Carroll) | 1961 | 12.00 |
| **RCA VICTOR** | | | |
| ❑ LPM-1467 [M] | Diahann Carroll Sings Harold Arlen | 1957 | 40.00 |
| **UNITED ARTISTS** | | | |
| ❑ UAL 3080 [M] | Diahann Carroll at the Persian Room | 1960 | 20.00 |
| ❑ UAS 6080 [S] | Diahann Carroll at the Persian Room | 1960 | 25.00 |
| **VIK** | | | |
| ❑ LXA-1131 [M] | Best Beat Forward | 1958 | 30.00 |

### CARROLL, DIAHANN, AND ANDRE PREVIN

| Number | Title (A Side/B Side) | Yr | NM |
|---|---|---|---|
| **UNITED ARTISTS** | | | |
| ❑ UAL 3069 [M] | Diahann Carroll and Andre Previn | 1960 | 20.00 |
| ❑ UAL 4021 [M] | Porgy and Bess | 1959 | 20.00 |
| ❑ UAS 5021 [S] | Porgy and Bess | 1959 | 25.00 |
| ❑ UAS 6069 [S] | Diahann Carroll and Andre Previn | 1960 | 25.00 |

### CARROLL, JIM, BAND

| Number | Title (A Side/B Side) | Yr | NM |
|---|---|---|---|
| **ATCO** | | | |
| ❑ SD 38-132 | Catholic Boy | 1980 | 12.00 |
| ❑ SD 38-145 | Dry Dreams | 1982 | 10.00 |
| **ATLANTIC** | | | |
| ❑ 80123 | I Write Your Name | 1984 | 10.00 |

### CARROLL, JOE

| Number | Title (A Side/B Side) | Yr | NM |
|---|---|---|---|
| **CHARLIE PARKER** | | | |
| ❑ PLP-802 [M] | The Man with the Happy Sound | 1962 | 30.00 |
| ❑ PLP-802S [S] | The Man with the Happy Sound | 1962 | 30.00 |
| **EPIC** | | | |
| ❑ LN 3272 [M] | Joe Carroll | 1956 | 50.00 |

### CARROLL BROTHERS, THE

| Number | Title (A Side/B Side) | Yr | NM |
|---|---|---|---|
| **CAMEO** | | | |
| ❑ C-1015 [M] | College Twist Party | 1962 | 25.00 |
| ❑ SC-1015 [S] | College Twist Party | 1962 | 40.00 |

### CARS, THE

| Number | Title (A Side/B Side) | Yr | NM |
|---|---|---|---|
| **DCC COMPACT CLASSICS** | | | |
| ❑ LPZ-2056 | The Cars Greatest Hits | 1998 | 25.00 |
| *—Audiophile vinyl* | | | |
| **ELEKTRA** | | | |
| ❑ 6E-135 | The Cars | 1978 | 10.00 |
| ❑ 5E-507 | Candy-O | 1979 | 10.00 |
| *—No title and artist listed on front cover (information was on a sticker on the shrink wrap)* | | | |
| ❑ 5E-514 | Panorama | 1980 | 10.00 |
| ❑ 5E-567 | Shake It Up | 1981 | 10.00 |
| ❑ 5E-567 [PD] | Shake It Up | 1981 | 40.00 |
| *—Promo-only picture disc with blank back* | | | |
| ❑ 5E-567 [PD] | Shake It Up | 1981 | 50.00 |
| *—Promo-only picture disc with "KMET-FM" imprinted on back* | | | |
| ❑ 60296 | Heartbeat City | 1984 | 8.00 |
| ❑ 60296 [DJ] | Heartbeat City | 1984 | 15.00 |
| *—Promo-only audiophile pressing on Quiex II vinyl* | | | |
| ❑ 60464 | Greatest Hits | 1985 | 10.00 |
| ❑ 60747 | Door to Door | 1987 | 8.00 |
| ❑ R 123334 | Candy-O | 1979 | 12.00 |
| *—RCA Music Service edition has "The Cars Candy-O" printed on upper left front cover* | | | |
| ❑ R 143650 | Heartbeat City | 1984 | 10.00 |
| *—RCA Music Service edition* | | | |
| ❑ R 144033 | The Cars | 1978 | 12.00 |
| *—RCA Music Service edition* | | | |
| ❑ R 153702 | Greatest Hits | 1985 | 12.00 |
| *—RCA Music Service edition* | | | |
| ❑ R 161593 | Door to Door | 1987 | 10.00 |
| *—BMG Direct Marketing edition* | | | |
| **NAUTILUS** | | | |
| ❑ NR-14 | The Cars | 1981 | 30.00 |
| *—Audiophile "Super Disc"* | | | |
| ❑ NR-49 | Candy-O | 1982 | 30.00 |
| *—Audiophile "Super Disc"* | | | |

### CARSON, MARTHA

| Number | Title (A Side/B Side) | Yr | NM |
|---|---|---|---|
| **CAPITOL** | | | |
| ❑ ST 1507 [S] | Satisfied | 1960 | 30.00 |
| ❑ T 1507 [M] | Satisfied | 1960 | 25.00 |
| ❑ ST 1607 [S] | A Talk with the Lord | 1961 | 30.00 |
| ❑ T 1607 [M] | A Talk with the Lord | 1961 | 25.00 |
| **RCA VICTOR** | | | |
| ❑ LPM-1145 [M] | Journey to the Sky | 1955 | 40.00 |
| ❑ LPM-1490 [M] | Rock-a My Soul | 1957 | 50.00 |
| **SIMS** | | | |
| ❑ LP-100 [M] | Martha Carson | 196? | 25.00 |

### CARTER, ANITA

| Number | Title (A Side/B Side) | Yr | NM |
|---|---|---|---|
| **CAPITOL** | | | |
| ❑ ST-11085 | So Much Love | 1972 | 15.00 |
| **MERCURY** | | | |
| ❑ MG-20770 [M] | Folk Songs Old and New | 1963 | 25.00 |
| ❑ MG-20847 [M] | Anita of the Carter Family | 1964 | 25.00 |
| ❑ SR-60770 [S] | Folk Songs Old and New | 1963 | 30.00 |
| ❑ SR-60847 [S] | Anita of the Carter Family | 1964 | 30.00 |

### CARTER, BENNY

| Number | Title (A Side/B Side) | Yr | NM |
|---|---|---|---|
| **ANALOGUE PRODUCTIONS** | | | |
| ❑ AP-13 | Jazz Giant | 199? | 30.00 |
| *—Audiophile reissue* | | | |
| **AUDIO LAB** | | | |
| ❑ AL-1505 [M] | The Fabulous Benny Carter | 1959 | 150.00 |
| **CLEF** | | | |
| ❑ MGC-141 [10] | Cosmopolite | 1953 | 250.00 |

| Number | Title (A Side/B Side) | Yr | NM |
|---|---|---|---|
| **CONTEMPORARY** | | | |
| ❑ C-3555 [M] | Jazz Giant | 1958 | 50.00 |
| ❑ M-3561 [M] | Swingin' the Twenties | 1959 | 40.00 |
| ❑ S-7028 [S] | Jazz Giant | 1960 | 30.00 |
| *—Reissue of Stereo Records 7028* | | | |
| ❑ S-7561 [S] | Swingin' the Twenties | 1959 | 40.00 |
| **IMPULSE!** | | | |
| ❑ A-12 [M] | Further Definitions | 1962 | 25.00 |
| ❑ AS-12 [S] | Further Definitions | 1962 | 30.00 |
| ❑ A-9116 [M] | Additions to Further Definitions | 1966 | 30.00 |
| ❑ AS-9116 [S] | Additions to Further Definitions | 1966 | 40.00 |
| **MOVIETONE** | | | |
| ❑ 1020 [M] | Autumn Leaves | 1967 | 20.00 |
| **NORGRAN** | | | |
| ❑ MGN-10 [10] | The Urbane Mr. Carter | 1954 | 150.00 |
| ❑ MGN-21 [10] | The Formidable Benny Carter | 1954 | 150.00 |
| ❑ MGN-1015 [M] | Benny Carter Plays Pretty | 1955 | 200.00 |
| ❑ MGN-1025 [M] | Benny Carter | 1955 | — |
| *—Canceled* | | | |
| ❑ MGN-1044 [M] | New Jazz Sounds | 1955 | 120.00 |
| *—With Dizzy Gillespie, Bill Harris* | | | |
| ❑ MGN-1058 [M] | Alone Together | 1956 | 120.00 |
| *—With Oscar Peterson* | | | |
| ❑ MGN-1070 [M] | Cosmopolite | 1956 | 120.00 |
| **STEREO RECORDS** | | | |
| ❑ S-7028 [S] | Jazz Giant | 1959 | 40.00 |
| **20TH CENTURY-FOX** | | | |
| ❑ TFM-3134 [M] | Benny Carter in Paris | 1963 | 20.00 |
| ❑ TFS-4134 [S] | Benny Carter in Paris | 1963 | 25.00 |
| **UNITED ARTISTS** | | | |
| ❑ UAL-3055 [M] | "Can Can" and "Anything Goes" | 1959 | 30.00 |
| ❑ UAL-4017 [M] | Aspects | 1960 | 30.00 |
| ❑ UAL-4073 [M] | "Can Can" and "Anything Goes" | 1960 | 20.00 |
| ❑ UAL-4080 [M] | Jazz Calendar | 1960 | 20.00 |
| ❑ UAL-4094 [M] | Sax A La Carter | 1961 | 20.00 |
| ❑ UAS-5017 [S] | Aspects | 1960 | 40.00 |
| ❑ UAS-5073 [S] | "Can Can" and "Anything Goes" | 1960 | 25.00 |
| ❑ UAS-5080 [S] | Jazz Calendar | 1960 | 25.00 |
| ❑ UAS-5094 [S] | Sax A La Carter | 1961 | 25.00 |
| ❑ UAS-6055 [S] | "Can Can" and "Anything Goes" | 1959 | 40.00 |
| **VERVE** | | | |
| ❑ MGV-2025 [M] | Moonglow — Love Songs by Benny Carter | 1957 | 60.00 |
| *—Reissue of Norgran 1015* | | | |
| ❑ V-2025 [M] | Moonglow — Love Songs by Benny Carter | 1961 | 20.00 |
| ❑ MGV-8135 [M] | New Jazz Sounds | 1957 | 60.00 |
| *—Reissue of Norgran 1044* | | | |
| ❑ V-8135 [M] | New Jazz Sounds | 1961 | 20.00 |
| ❑ MGV-8148 [M] | Alone Together | 1957 | 60.00 |
| *—Reissue of Norgran 1058* | | | |
| ❑ V-8148 [M] | Alone Together | 1961 | 20.00 |
| ❑ MGV-8160 [M] | Cosmopolite | 1957 | 60.00 |
| *—Reissue of Norgran 1070* | | | |
| ❑ V-8160 [M] | Cosmopolite | 1961 | 20.00 |

## CARTER, BENNY; BEN WEBSTER; BARNEY BIGARD

| Number | Title (A Side/B Side) | Yr | NM |
|---|---|---|---|
| **SWINGVILLE** | | | |
| ❑ SVLP-2032 [M] | B.B.B. & Co. | 1962 | 40.00 |
| *—Purple label* | | | |
| ❑ SVLP-2032 [M] | B.B.B. & Co. | 1965 | 20.00 |
| *—Blue label, trident logo at right* | | | |
| ❑ SVST-2032 [S] | B.B.B. & Co. | 1962 | 50.00 |
| *—Red label* | | | |
| ❑ SVST-2032 [S] | B.B.B. & Co. | 1965 | 25.00 |
| *—Blue label, trident logo at right* | | | |

## CARTER, BETTY

| Number | Title (A Side/B Side) | Yr | NM |
|---|---|---|---|
| **ABC IMPULSE!** | | | |
| ❑ AS-9321 [(2)] | What a Little Moonlight | 197? | 20.00 |
| **ABC-PARAMOUNT** | | | |
| ❑ ABC-363 [M] | The Modern Sound of Betty Carter | 1960 | 60.00 |
| ❑ ABCS-363 [S] | The Modern Sound of Betty Carter | 1960 | 80.00 |
| **ATCO** | | | |
| ❑ 33-152 [M] | 'Round Midnight | 1963 | 50.00 |
| ❑ SD 33-152 [S] | 'Round Midnight | 1963 | 60.00 |
| **BET-CAR** | | | |
| ❑ 1001 | Betty Carter | 1970 | 30.00 |
| ❑ 1002 | The Betty Carter Album | 197? | 30.00 |
| ❑ MK 1003 [(2)] | The Audience with Betty Carter | 1980 | 20.00 |
| **PEACOCK** | | | |
| ❑ PLP-90 [M] | Out There with Betty Carter | 1958 | 120.00 |
| **ROULETTE** | | | |
| ❑ SR-5000 | Finally | 1969 | 25.00 |
| ❑ SR-5001 | 'Round Midnight | 1975 | 20.00 |
| ❑ SR-5005 | Now It's My Turn | 1976 | 20.00 |
| **UNITED ARTISTS** | | | |
| ❑ UAL 3379 [M] | Inside Betty Carter | 1964 | 50.00 |
| ❑ UAS-5639 | Inside Betty Carter | 1971 | 20.00 |
| *—Reissue of 6379* | | | |
| ❑ UAS 6379 [S] | Inside Betty Carter | 1964 | 60.00 |

## CARTER, CALVIN

| Number | Title (A Side/B Side) | Yr | NM |
|---|---|---|---|
| **VEE JAY** | | | |
| ❑ LP-1041 [M] | Twist with Calvin Carter | 1962 | 100.00 |
| ❑ SR-1041 [S] | Twist with Calvin Carter | 1962 | 150.00 |

## CARTER, CLARENCE

| Number | Title (A Side/B Side) | Yr | NM |
|---|---|---|---|
| **ABC** | | | |
| ❑ X-833 | Real | 1974 | 15.00 |
| ❑ X-896 | Loneliness & Temptation | 1975 | 15.00 |
| ❑ X-943 | A Heart Full of Song | 1976 | 15.00 |
| **ATLANTIC** | | | |
| ❑ SD 8192 | This Is Clarence Carter | 1968 | 30.00 |
| ❑ SD 8199 | The Dynamic Clarence Carter | 1969 | 30.00 |
| ❑ SD 8238 | Testifyin' | 1969 | 30.00 |
| ❑ 8267 [M] | Patches | 1970 | 60.00 |
| *—Mono is white label promo only; "d/j copy monaural" sticker on stereo cover* | | | |
| ❑ SD 8267 [S] | Patches | 1970 | 30.00 |
| ❑ SD 8282 | The Best of Clarence Carter | 1971 | 20.00 |
| **FAME** | | | |
| ❑ FM-LA186-F | Sixty Minutes | 1973 | 15.00 |
| **ICHIBAN** | | | |
| ❑ ICH-1001 | Messin' with My Mind | 1986 | 12.00 |
| ❑ ICH-1003 | Dr. C.C. | 1986 | 12.00 |
| ❑ ICH-1016 | Hooked on Love | 1987 | 12.00 |
| ❑ ICH-1032 | Touch of Blues | 1988 | 12.00 |
| ❑ ICH-1068 | Between a Rock and a Hard Place | 1989 | 12.00 |
| ❑ ICH-1116 | The Best of Clarence Carter: The Dr.'s Greatest Presciptions | 1991 | 12.00 |
| **VENTURE** | | | |
| ❑ VL 1005 | Let's Burn | 1980 | 10.00 |
| ❑ VL 1009 | Mr. Clarence Carter In Person | 1981 | 10.00 |

## CARTER, JACK

| Number | Title (A Side/B Side) | Yr | NM |
|---|---|---|---|
| **AAMCO** | | | |
| ❑ ALP-316 [M] | Broadway A La Carter | 1958 | 25.00 |

## CARTER, JOHN

| Number | Title (A Side/B Side) | Yr | NM |
|---|---|---|---|
| **FLYING DUTCHMAN** | | | |
| ❑ FDS-109 | John Carter | 1969 | 20.00 |

## CARTER, JOHN, AND BOBBY BRADFORD

| Number | Title (A Side/B Side) | Yr | NM |
|---|---|---|---|
| **FLYING DUTCHMAN** | | | |
| ❑ FDS-108 | Flight for Four | 1969 | 20.00 |
| ❑ FDS-128 | Self Determination Music | 1970 | 20.00 |

## CARTER, LYNDA

| Number | Title (A Side/B Side) | Yr | NM |
|---|---|---|---|
| **EPIC** | | | |
| ❑ 35308 [PD] | Portrait | 1978 | 60.00 |
| *—Picture disc version* | | | |
| ❑ JE 35308 | Portrait | 1978 | 15.00 |

## CARTER, MEL

| Number | Title (A Side/B Side) | Yr | NM |
|---|---|---|---|
| **AMOS** | | | |
| ❑ 7010 | This Is My Life | 1971 | 12.00 |
| **DERBY** | | | |
| ❑ LPM-702 [M] | When a Boy Falls in Love | 1963 | 300.00 |
| **IMPERIAL** | | | |
| ❑ LP-9289 [M] | Hold Me, Thrill Me, Kiss Me | 1965 | 15.00 |
| ❑ LP-9300 [M] | All of a Sudden My Heart Sings | 1966 | 15.00 |
| ❑ LP-9319 [M] | Easy Listening | 1966 | 15.00 |
| ❑ LP-12289 [S] | Hold Me, Thrill Me, Kiss Me | 1965 | 20.00 |
| ❑ LP-12300 [S] | All of a Sudden My Heart Sings | 1966 | 20.00 |
| ❑ LP-12319 [S] | Easy Listening | 1966 | 20.00 |
| **SUNSET** | | | |
| ❑ SUS-5227 | Mel Carter | 1968 | 10.00 |
| ❑ SUS-5295 | Easy Goin' | 1970 | 10.00 |

## CARTER, MOTHER MAYBELLE

| Number | Title (A Side/B Side) | Yr | NM |
|---|---|---|---|
| **AMBASSADOR** | | | |
| ❑ 98069 [M] | Mother Maybelle Carter | 195? | 150.00 |
| **COLUMBIA** | | | |
| ❑ CL 2475 [M] | A Living Legend | 1965 | 20.00 |
| ❑ CS 9275 [S] | A Living Legend | 1965 | 25.00 |
| ❑ KG 32436 [(2)] | Mother Maybelle Carter | 1973 | 25.00 |
| **KAPP** | | | |
| ❑ KL-1413 [M] | Queen of the Autoharp | 1964 | 20.00 |
| ❑ KS-3413 [S] | Queen of the Autoharp | 1964 | 25.00 |
| **SMASH** | | | |
| ❑ MGS-27025 [M] | Mother Maybelle Carter and Her Autoharp | 1963 | 20.00 |
| ❑ MGS-27041 [M] | Pickin' and Singin' | 1963 | 20.00 |
| ❑ SRS-67025 [S] | Mother Maybelle Carter and Her Autoharp | 1963 | 25.00 |
| ❑ SRS-67041 [S] | Pickin' and Singin' | 1963 | 25.00 |

## CARTER, RON

| Number | Title (A Side/B Side) | Yr | NM |
|---|---|---|---|
| **EMBRYO** | | | |
| ❑ SD 521 | Uptown Conversation | 1970 | 20.00 |
| **NEW JAZZ** | | | |
| ❑ NJLP-8265 [M] | Where? | 1961 | 80.00 |
| *—With Eric Dolphy and Mal Waldron; purple label* | | | |
| ❑ NJLP-8265 [M] | Where? | 1965 | 25.00 |
| *—With Eric Dolphy and Mal Waldron;; blue label, trident logo at right* | | | |

## CARTER, WILF See MONTANA SLIM.

## CARTER FAMILY, THE

| Number | Title (A Side/B Side) | Yr | NM |
|---|---|---|---|
| **ACME** | | | |
| ❑ LP-1 [M] | All Time Favorites | 1960 | 200.00 |
| ❑ LP-2 [M] | In Memory of A.P. Carter | 1960 | 200.00 |
| **COLUMBIA** | | | |
| ❑ CL 2319 [M] | The Best of the Carter Family | 1965 | 15.00 |
| ❑ CL 2617 [M] | Country Album | 1967 | 25.00 |
| ❑ CS 9119 [S] | The Best of the Carter Family | 1965 | 20.00 |
| ❑ CS 9417 [S] | Country Album | 1967 | 20.00 |
| ❑ KC 31454 | Travelin' Minstrel Band | 1972 | 20.00 |
| ❑ KC 33084 | Three Generations | 1974 | 20.00 |
| ❑ KC 34266 | Country's First Family | 1976 | 20.00 |
| **DECCA** | | | |
| ❑ DL 4404 [M] | A Collection of Favorites by the Carter Family | 1963 | 30.00 |
| ❑ DL 4557 [M] | More Favorites by the Carter Family | 1964 | 30.00 |
| **LIBERTY** | | | |
| ❑ LRP-3230 [M] | The Carter Family Album | 1962 | 30.00 |
| ❑ LST-7230 [S] | The Carter Family Album | 1962 | 40.00 |
| **RCA CAMDEN** | | | |
| ❑ ACL1-0047 [R] | My Old Cottage Home | 1973 | 10.00 |
| ❑ CAL-586 [M] | The Original and Great Carter Family | 1960 | 15.00 |
| *—Two-tone blue label with "RCA Camden" at top* | | | |
| ❑ CAL-586 [M] | The Original and Great Carter Family | 1969 | 10.00 |
| *—All-blue label with "RCA" on its side at left and "Camden" straight at right (reissue)* | | | |
| ❑ CAL-2473 [M] | Lonesome Pine Special | 1971 | 12.00 |
| ❑ CAS-2554(e) [R] | More Golden Gems from the Original Carter Family | 1972 | 10.00 |
| **RCA VICTOR** | | | |
| ❑ LPM-2772 [M] | 'Mid the Green Fields of Virginia | 1963 | 40.00 |
| ❑ LSP-2772 [R] | 'Mid the Green Fields of Virginia | 1963 | 20.00 |
| **STARDAY** | | | |
| ❑ SLP-248 [M] | Echoes of the Carter Family | 1963 | 40.00 |

## CARTOONE

| Number | Title (A Side/B Side) | Yr | NM |
|---|---|---|---|
| **ATLANTIC** | | | |
| ❑ SD 8219 | Cartoone | 1969 | 20.00 |

## CARTWRIGHT, ANGELA

| Number | Title (A Side/B Side) | Yr | NM |
|---|---|---|---|
| **STAR-BRIGHT** | | | |
| ❑ HLP-102 [M] | Angela Cartwright Sings | 1959 | 50.00 |

## CARVER, JOHNNY

| Number | Title (A Side/B Side) | Yr | NM |
|---|---|---|---|
| **ABC** | | | |
| ❑ ABCX-792 | Tie a Yellow Ribbon Around the Ole Oak Tree | 1973 | 12.00 |
| ❑ ABCX-812 | Double Exposure | 1974 | 12.00 |
| ❑ ABCD-843 | Please Don't Tell (That Sweet Ole Lady of Mine) | 1974 | 12.00 |
| ❑ ABCD-864 | Strings | 1975 | 12.00 |
| **ABC DOT** | | | |
| ❑ DO-2042 | Afternoon Delight | 1976 | 12.00 |
| ❑ DO-2083 | The Best of Johnny Carver | 1977 | 12.00 |
| **HARMONY** | | | |
| ❑ KH 32476 | I Start Thinking About You | 1973 | 12.00 |
| **IMPERIAL** | | | |
| ❑ LP-9347 [M] | Really Country | 1967 | 30.00 |
| ❑ LP-12347 [S] | Really Country | 1967 | 20.00 |
| ❑ LP-12380 | You're in Good Hands with Johnny Carver | 1968 | 20.00 |
| ❑ LP-12412 | Leaving Again | 1968 | 20.00 |

## CARY, DICK

| Number | Title (A Side/B Side) | Yr | NM |
|---|---|---|---|
| **BELL** | | | |
| ❑ BLP-44 [M] | Hot and Cool | 1961 | 30.00 |
| **GOLDEN CREST** | | | |
| ❑ GC-3024 [M] | Dixieland Goes Progressive | 1958 | 50.00 |
| **STEREOCRAFT** | | | |
| ❑ RTN-106 [S] | Hot and Cool | 196? | 25.00 |

## CASADESUS, JEAN

| Number | Title (A Side/B Side) | Yr | NM |
|---|---|---|---|
| **RCA VICTOR RED SEAL** | | | |
| ❑ LSC-2415 [S] | Debussy: Preludes, Book 1 | 1960 | 40.00 |
| *—Original with "shaded dog" label* | | | |

## CASCADES, THE

| Number | Title (A Side/B Side) | Yr | NM |
|---|---|---|---|
| **UNI** | | | |
| ❑ 73069 | Maybe the Rain Will Fall | 1969 | 25.00 |
| **VALIANT** | | | |
| ❑ W 405 [M] | Rhythm of the Rain | 1963 | 150.00 |
| ❑ WS 405 [S] | Rhythm of the Rain | 1963 | 300.00 |



Except when noted otherwise, VG = 25% of NM, and VG+ = 50% of NM. (Example: VG = $2.00, VG+ = $4.00 and NM = $8.00.)

| Number | Title (A Side/B Side) | Yr | NM |
|---|---|---|---|
| **CASE, ALLEN** | | | |
| COLUMBIA | | | |
| ❑ CL 1406 [M] | "The Deputy" Sings | 1960 | 20.00 |
| ❑ CS 8202 [S] | "The Deputy" Sings | 1960 | 30.00 |
| **CASEY, AL** | | | |
| STACY | | | |
| ❑ STM-100 [M] | Surfin' Hootenanny | 1963 | 300.00 |
| ❑ STS-100 [S] | Surfin' Hootenanny | 1963 | 400.00 |
| SUNDAZED | | | |
| ❑ LP-5026 | Surfin' Hootenanny | 1996 | 10.00 |
| **CASEY, AL (2)** | | | |
| MOODSVILLE | | | |
| ❑ MVLP-12 [M] | The Al Casey Quartet | 1960 | 50.00 |
| *—Green label* | | | |
| ❑ MVLP-12 [M] | The Al Casey Quartet | 1965 | 25.00 |
| *—Blue label, trident logo at right* | | | |
| SWINGVILLE | | | |
| ❑ SVLP-2007 [M] | Buck Jumpin' | 1960 | 50.00 |
| *—Purple label* | | | |
| ❑ SVLP-2007 [M] | Buck Jumpin' | 1965 | 25.00 |
| *—Blue label, trident logo at right* | | | |
| **CASH, ALVIN** | | | |
| MAR-V-LUS | | | |
| ❑ 1827 [M] | Twine Time | 1965 | 30.00 |
| **CASH, JOHNNY** | | | |
| ACCORD | | | |
| ❑ SN-7134 | I Walk the Line | 1983 | 10.00 |
| ❑ SN-7208 | Years Gone By | 1983 | 10.00 |
| ALLEGIANCE | | | |
| ❑ AV-5017 | The First Years | 1986 | 10.00 |
| AMERICAN | | | |
| ❑ B0002769-01 | American V: A Hundred Highways | 2006 | 12.00 |
| ❑ 43097 | Unchained | 1996 | 120.00 |
| ❑ 45520 | American Recordings | 1994 | 80.00 |
| ❑ 440-063336-1 [(2)] | American IV: The Man Comes Around | 2002 | 20.00 |
| ❑ C 69691 | American III: Solitary Man | 2000 | 50.00 |
| ARCHIVE OF FOLK MUSIC | | | |
| ❑ 278 | Johnny Cash | 198? | 12.00 |
| CACHET | | | |
| ❑ 9001 | A Believer Sings the Truth | 1979 | 15.00 |
| COLUMBIA | | | |
| ❑ GP 29 [(2)] | The World of Johnny Cash | 1970 | 15.00 |
| ❑ C2L 38 [(2)M] | Ballads of the True West | 1965 | 25.00 |
| ❑ C2S 838 [(2)S] | Ballads of the True West | 1965 | 25.00 |
| ❑ CL 1253 [M] | The Fabulous Johnny Cash | 1958 | 20.00 |
| ❑ CL 1284 [M] | Hymns by Johnny Cash | 1959 | 25.00 |
| ❑ CL 1339 [M] | Songs of Our Soil | 1959 | 25.00 |
| ❑ CL 1463 [M] | Now, There Was a Song! | 1960 | 25.00 |
| ❑ CL 1464 [M] | Ride This Train | 1960 | 25.00 |
| ❑ CL 1622 [M] | The Lure of the Grand Canyon | 1961 | 40.00 |
| *—Cash narrates; with Andre Kostelanetz and His Orchestra* | | | |
| ❑ CL 1722 [M] | Hymns from the Heart | 1962 | 20.00 |
| ❑ CL 1802 [M] | The Sound of Johnny Cash | 1962 | 20.00 |
| ❑ CL 1930 [M] | Blood, Sweat & Tears | 1963 | 20.00 |
| ❑ STS 2004 [(2)] | The Heart of Johnny Cash | 196? | 20.00 |
| *—"Columbia Star Series" release; has "360 Sound" labels* | | | |
| ❑ CL 2052 [M] | Ring of Fire (The Best of Johnny Cash) | 1963 | 20.00 |
| ❑ CL 2117 [M] | The Christmas Spirit | 1963 | 25.00 |
| ❑ CL 2190 [M] | I Walk the Line | 1964 | 15.00 |
| ❑ CL 2248 [M] | Bitter Tears (Ballads of the American Indian) | 1964 | 15.00 |
| ❑ CL 2309 [M] | Orange Blossom Special | 1965 | 15.00 |
| ❑ CL 2446 [M] | Mean as Hell | 1965 | 15.00 |
| ❑ CL 2492 [M] | Everybody Loves a Nut | 1966 | 15.00 |
| ❑ CL 2537 [M] | That's What You Get for Lovin' Me | 1966 | 15.00 |
| ❑ CL 2647 [M] | From Sea to Shining Sea | 1967 | 20.00 |
| ❑ CL 2678 [M] | Johnny Cash's Greatest Hits, Volume 1 | 1967 | 20.00 |
| ❑ CL 2839 [M] | Johnny Cash at Folsom Prison | 1968 | 150.00 |
| *—Red label with "Mono" at bottom; this is a stock copy* | | | |
| ❑ CS 8122 [S] | The Fabulous Johnny Cash | 1959 | 40.00 |
| ❑ CS 8125 [S] | Hymns by Johnny Cash | 1959 | 40.00 |
| ❑ CS 8148 [S] | Songs of Our Soil | 1959 | 40.00 |
| ❑ CS 8254 [S] | Now, There Was a Song! | 1960 | 40.00 |
| ❑ CS 8255 [S] | Ride This Train | 1960 | 40.00 |
| ❑ CS 8255 [S] | Ride This Train | 197? | 10.00 |
| *—Reissue on orange label* | | | |
| ❑ CS 8422 [S] | The Lure of the Grand Canyon | 1961 | 50.00 |
| *—Cash narrates; with Andre Kostelanetz and His Orchestra* | | | |
| ❑ CS 8522 [S] | Hymns from the Heart | 1962 | 30.00 |
| ❑ CS 8602 [S] | The Sound of Johnny Cash | 1962 | 30.00 |
| ❑ CS 8730 [S] | Blood, Sweat & Tears | 1963 | 25.00 |
| ❑ CS 8852 [S] | Ring of Fire (The Best of Johnny Cash) | 1963 | 25.00 |
| ❑ CS 8917 [S] | The Christmas Spirit | 1963 | 30.00 |
| ❑ CS 8990 [S] | I Walk the Line | 1964 | 20.00 |

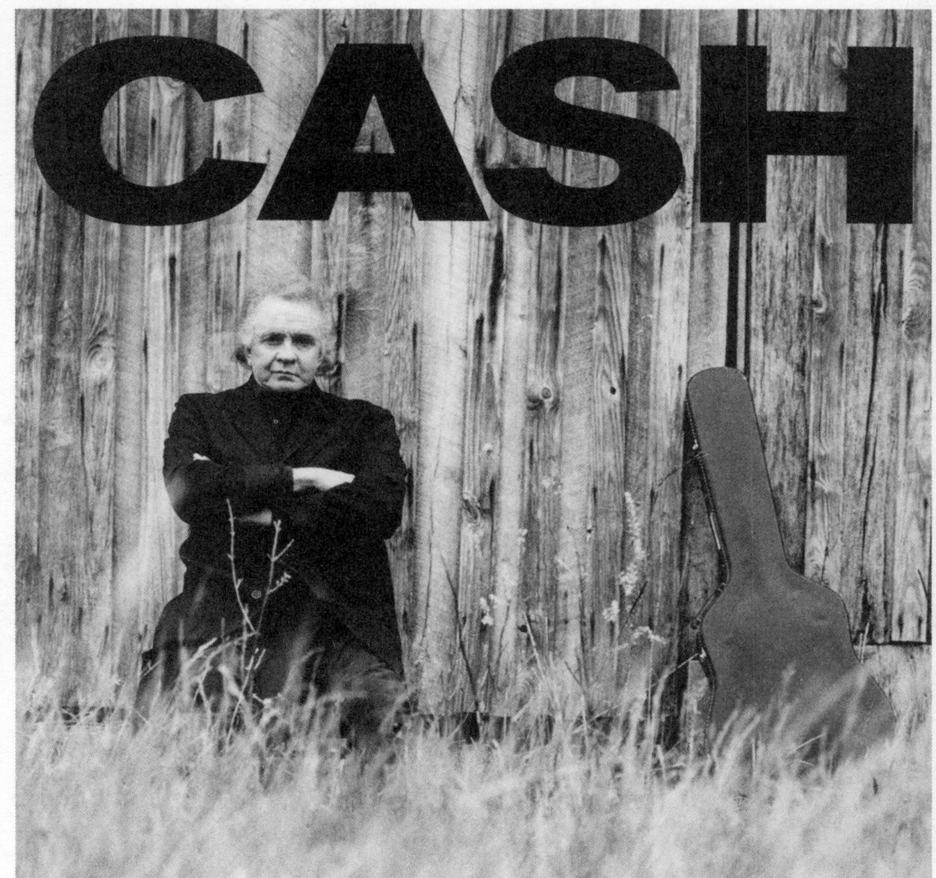


Johnny Cash, *Unchained,* American 43097-1, 1996, $120.

| Number | Title (A Side/B Side) | Yr | NM |
|---|---|---|---|
| ❑ CS 9048 [S] | Bitter Tears (Ballads of the American Indian) | 1964 | 20.00 |
| ❑ CS 9109 [S] | Orange Blossom Special | 1965 | 20.00 |
| ❑ CS 9246 [S] | Mean as Hell | 1965 | 20.00 |
| ❑ CS 9292 [S] | Everybody Loves a Nut | 1966 | 20.00 |
| ❑ CS 9337 [S] | That's What You Get for Lovin' Me | 1966 | 20.00 |
| ❑ CS 9447 [S] | From Sea to Shining Sea | 1967 | 20.00 |
| ❑ CS 9478 [S] | Johnny Cash's Greatest Hits, Volume 1 | 1967 | 20.00 |
| ❑ CS 9639 [M] | Johnny Cash at Folsom Prison | 1968 | 50.00 |
| *—White label promo with stereo number; "Special Mono Radio Station Copy" sticker on cover* | | | |
| ❑ CS 9639 [S] | Johnny Cash at Folsom Prison | 1968 | 20.00 |
| *—Red label with "360 Sound Stereo" at bottom* | | | |
| ❑ KCS 9726 | The Holy Land | 1969 | 15.00 |
| ❑ CS 9827 | Johnny Cash at San Quentin | 1969 | 12.00 |
| ❑ KCS 9943 | Hello, I'm Johnny Cash | 1970 | 12.00 |
| ❑ C 30100 | The Johnny Cash Show | 1970 | 12.00 |
| ❑ S 30397 | I Walk the Line | 1970 | 12.00 |
| *—Soundtrack from movie* | | | |
| ❑ KC 30550 | Man in Black | 1971 | 12.00 |
| ❑ KC 30887 | The Johnny Cash Collection (His Greatest Hits, Volume II) | 1971 | 12.00 |
| ❑ CQ 30961 [Q] | Johnny Cash at San Quentin | 1971 | 20.00 |
| ❑ KC 31256 | Give My Love to Rose | 1972 | 12.00 |
| ❑ KC 31332 | A Thing Called Love | 1972 | 12.00 |
| ❑ KC 31645 | Johnny Cash: America (A 200-Year Salute in Story and Song) | 1972 | 12.00 |
| ❑ KC 32091 | Any Old Wind That Blows | 1973 | 12.00 |
| ❑ C 32240 | Sunday Morning Coming Down | 1973 | 12.00 |
| ❑ C 32253 | The Gospel Road | 1973 | 12.00 |
| ❑ CG 32253 [(2)] | The Gospel Road | 1973 | 25.00 |
| ❑ KC 32898 | Children's Album | 1974 | 12.00 |
| ❑ C 32917 | The Ragged Old Flag | 1974 | 12.00 |
| ❑ C 32951 | Five Feet High and Rising | 1974 | 12.00 |
| ❑ KC 33086 | The Junkie and the Juicehead | 1974 | 12.00 |
| ❑ C 33087 | Johnny Cash Sings Precious Memories | 1974 | 12.00 |
| ❑ KC 33370 | John R. Cash | 1975 | 12.00 |
| ❑ CG 33639 [(2)] | Johnny Cash at Folsom Prison/ Johnny Cash at San Quentin | 1974 | 15.00 |
| ❑ KC 33814 | Look at Them Beans | 1975 | 12.00 |
| ❑ KC 34088 | Strawberry Cake | 1976 | 12.00 |
| ❑ KC 34193 | One Piece at a Time | 1976 | 12.00 |
| ❑ JC 34314 | The Last Gunfighter Ballad | 1977 | 12.00 |

| Number | Title (A Side/B Side) | Yr | NM |
|---|---|---|---|
| ❑ JC 34833 | The Rambler | 1977 | 12.00 |
| ❑ KC 35313 | I Would Like to See You Again | 1978 | 10.00 |
| ❑ JC 35637 | Johnny Cash's Greatest Hits, Volume 3 | 1978 | 12.00 |
| ❑ KC 35646 | Gone Girl | 1978 | 12.00 |
| ❑ JC 36086 | Silver | 1979 | 12.00 |
| ❑ JC 36779 | Rockabilly Blues | 1980 | 10.00 |
| ❑ JC 36866 | Classic Christmas | 1980 | 12.00 |
| ❑ FC 37179 | The Baron | 1981 | 10.00 |
| ❑ FC 37355 | Encore | 1981 | 10.00 |
| ❑ PC 38074 | A Believer Sings the Truth | 1985 | 8.00 |
| *—Reissue of Priority 38074* | | | |
| ❑ FC 38094 | The Adventures of Johnny Cash | 1982 | 10.00 |
| ❑ FC 38317 | Johnny Cash's Biggest Hits | 1982 | 10.00 |
| ❑ FC 38696 | Johnny 99 | 1983 | 10.00 |
| ❑ PC 38696 | Johnny 99 | 1986 | 8.00 |
| *—Budget-line reissue* | | | |
| ❑ FC 39951 | Rainbow | 1985 | 10.00 |
| COLUMBIA LIMITED EDITION | | | |
| ❑ LE 10063 [S] | The Fabulous Johnny Cash | 197? | 15.00 |
| *—Reissue of 8122* | | | |
| COLUMBIA SPECIAL PRODUCTS | | | |
| ❑ 363 | Legends and Love Songs | 196? | 20.00 |
| ❑ P 13043 | Destination Victoria Station | 1977 | 40.00 |
| *—Alternate number is "VS 150"* | | | |
| ❑ P 13832 | Hello, I'm Johnny Cash | 1977 | 12.00 |
| DORAL/CSP | | | |
| ❑ (# unknown) | Doral Presents Johnny Cash | 1972 | 40.00 |
| *—Mail-order offer from Doral cigarettes* | | | |
| EVEREST | | | |
| ❑ 276 | Johnny Cash | 19?? | 12.00 |
| HARMONY | | | |
| ❑ HS 11249 | Golden Sounds of Country Music | 1968 | 12.00 |
| ❑ HS 11342 | Johnny Cash | 1969 | 12.00 |
| ❑ KH 30138 | The Walls of a Prison | 1970 | 12.00 |
| ❑ KH 30916 | Understand Your Man | 1971 | 12.00 |
| ❑ KH 31602 | The Johnny Cash Songbook | 1972 | 12.00 |
| ❑ KH 32388 | Ballads of the American Indian | 1973 | 12.00 |
| MERCURY | | | |
| ❑ 832031-1 | Johnny Cash Is Coming to Town | 1987 | 10.00 |
| ❑ 834778-1 | Water from the Wells of Home | 1988 | 10.00 |

| Number | Title (A Side/B Side) | Yr | NM |
|---|---|---|---|
| **PAIR** | | | |
| ❑ PDL2-1107 [(2)] | Classic Cash | 1986 | 15.00 |
| **POWER PAK** | | | |
| ❑ 246 | Country Gold | 198? | 10.00 |
| **PRIORITY** | | | |
| ❑ UG 32253 [(2)] | The Gospel Road | 1981 | 15.00 |
| *—Reissue of Columbia album of the same name* | | | |
| ❑ PU 33087 | Johnny Cash Sings Precious Memories | 1982 | 12.00 |
| *—Reissue of Columbia album of the same name* | | | |
| ❑ PU 38074 | A Believer Sings the Truth | 1982 | 12.00 |
| *—Reissue of Cachet album* | | | |
| **RHINO** | | | |
| ❑ RNLP 70229 | The Vintage Years | 1987 | 12.00 |
| **SHARE** | | | |
| ❑ 5000 | I Walk the Line | 197? | 12.00 |
| ❑ 5001 | Folsom Prison Blues | 197? | 12.00 |
| ❑ 5002 | The Blue Train | 197? | 12.00 |
| ❑ 5003 | Johnny Cash Sings the Greatest Hits | 197? | 12.00 |
| **SUN** | | | |
| ❑ LP-100 | Original Golden Hits, Volume I | 1969 | 12.00 |
| ❑ LP-101 | Original Golden Hits, Volume II | 1969 | 12.00 |
| ❑ LP-104 | Story Songs of the Trains and Rivers | 1969 | 12.00 |
| ❑ LP-105 | Get Rhythm | 1969 | 12.00 |
| ❑ LP-106 | Showtime | 1969 | 12.00 |
| ❑ LP-115 | The Singing Story Teller | 1970 | 12.00 |
| ❑ LP-118 [(2)] | Johnny Cash — The Legend | 1970 | 20.00 |
| ❑ LP-122 | The Rough Cut King of Country Music | 1971 | 12.00 |
| ❑ LP-126 [(2)] | Johnny Cash: The Man, The World, His Music | 1971 | 20.00 |
| ❑ LP-127 | Original Golden Hits, Volume III | 1972 | 12.00 |
| ❑ LP-139 | I Walk the Line | 1979 | 10.00 |
| ❑ LP-140 | Folsom Prison Blues | 1979 | 10.00 |
| ❑ LP-141 | The Blue Train | 1979 | 10.00 |
| ❑ LP-142 | Johnny Cash Sings the Greatest Hits | 1979 | 10.00 |
| ❑ 1002 | Superbilly (1955-58) | 198? | 10.00 |
| ❑ 1006 | The Original Johnny Cash | 1980 | 10.00 |
| ❑ SLP-1220 [M] | Johnny Cash with His Hot and Blue Guitar | 1956 | 100.00 |
| ❑ SLP-1220 [R] | Johnny Cash with His Hot and Blue Guitar | 196? | 20.00 |
| *—Reissue in rechanneled stereo; front cover says "STEREO"* | | | |
| ❑ SLP-1235 [M] | The Songs That Made Him Famous | 1958 | 100.00 |
| ❑ SLP-1235 [R] | The Songs That Made Him Famous | 196? | 20.00 |
| *—Reissue in rechanneled stereo; front cover says "STEREO"* | | | |
| ❑ SLP-1240 [M] | Johnny Cash's Greatest! | 1959 | 50.00 |
| ❑ SLP-1245 [M] | Johnny Cash Sings Hank Williams | 1960 | 50.00 |
| ❑ SLP-1245 [R] | Johnny Cash Sings Hank Williams | 196? | 20.00 |
| *—Reissue in rechanneled stereo; front cover says "STEREO"* | | | |
| ❑ SLP-1255 [M] | Now Here's Johnny Cash | 1961 | 50.00 |
| ❑ SLP-1255 [R] | Now Here's Johnny Cash | 196? | 20.00 |
| *—Reissue in rechanneled stereo; front cover says "STEREO"* | | | |
| ❑ SLP-1270 [M] | All Aboard the Blue Train | 1963 | 50.00 |
| ❑ SLP-1275 [M] | The Original Sun Sound of Johnny Cash | 1965 | 50.00 |
| ❑ DT-90668 [R] | The Songs That Made Him Famous | 1966 | 25.00 |
| *—Capitol Record Club edition* | | | |
| ❑ T-90668 [M] | The Songs That Made Him Famous | 1966 | 40.00 |
| *—Capitol Record Club edition* | | | |
| ❑ DT-90678 [R] | Now Here's Johnny Cash | 1966 | 20.00 |
| *—Capitol Record Club edition* | | | |
| ❑ DT-91284 [R] | Johnny Cash Sings Hank Williams | 196? | 25.00 |
| *—Capitol Record Club edition* | | | |
| ❑ T-91284 [M] | Johnny Cash Sings Hank Williams | 196? | 40.00 |
| *—Capitol Record Club edition* | | | |
| ❑ DT-91458 [R] | All Aboard the Blue Train | 196? | 25.00 |
| *—Capitol Record Club edition* | | | |
| ❑ ST-92085 | Original Golden Hits, Volume I | 1969 | 20.00 |
| *—Capitol Record Club edition; uses older Sun label* | | | |
| ❑ ST-92086 | Original Golden Hits, Volume II | 1969 | 20.00 |
| *—Capitol Record Club edition; uses older Sun label* | | | |
| ❑ SQBO-93213 [(2)] | The Greatness of Johnny Cash | 197? | 20.00 |
| *—Capitol Record Club exclusive* | | | |
| **SUNDAZED** | | | |
| ❑ LP-5170 | Town Hall Party Live! 1958 | 2003 | 15.00 |
| *—Reissue on 180-gram vinyl* | | | |
| ❑ LP-5171 | Town Hall Party Live! 1959 | 2003 | 15.00 |
| *—Reissue on 180-gram vinyl* | | | |
| ❑ LP-5176 | Blood, Sweat & Tears | 2003 | 15.00 |
| *—Reissue on 180-gram vinyl* | | | |
| **TIME-LIFE** | | | |
| ❑ TLCS-3 [(3)] | Country & Western Classics | 1982 | 20.00 |
| ❑ STW-108 | Country Music | 1981 | 12.00 |
| **WORD** | | | |
| ❑ WR-8333 | Believe in Him | 1986 | 12.00 |

### CASH, JOHNNY, AND JUNE CARTER

| Number | Title (A Side/B Side) | Yr | NM |
|---|---|---|---|
| **COLUMBIA** | | | |
| ❑ CL 2728 [M] | Carryin' On with Johnny Cash and June Carter | 1967 | 20.00 |
| ❑ CS 9528 [S] | Carryin' On with Johnny Cash and June Carter | 1967 | 20.00 |
| ❑ KC 32443 | Johnny Cash and His Woman | 1973 | 15.00 |

### CASH, JOHNNY/TAMMY WYNETTE

| Number | Title (A Side/B Side) | Yr | NM |
|---|---|---|---|
| **COLUMBIA MUSICAL TREASURIES** | | | |
| ❑ DS 608 [(2)] | The King/The Queen | 1969 | 15.00 |
| *—One record by Johnny Cash, the other by Tammy Wynette* | | | |
| ❑ P4S 5376 [(4)] | The King/The Queen | 1969 | 25.00 |
| *—Box set; two records by Johnny Cash, two records by Tammy Wynette; records are individually numbered from DS 562 through DS 565* | | | |

### CASH, ROSEANNE

| Number | Title (A Side/B Side) | Yr | NM |
|---|---|---|---|
| **COLUMBIA** | | | |
| ❑ AS 1527 [DJ] | Interview with Martha Hume | 1982 | 30.00 |
| *—Generic cover with sticker* | | | |
| ❑ JC 36155 | Right or Wrong | 1980 | 10.00 |
| ❑ PC 36155 | Right or Wrong | 1984 | 8.00 |
| *—Budget-line reissue with new prefix and "02" added to bar code* | | | |
| ❑ JC 36965 | Seven Year Ache | 1981 | 10.00 |
| ❑ PC 36965 | Seven Year Ache | 1984 | 8.00 |
| *—Budget-line reissue with new prefix and "02" added to bar code* | | | |
| ❑ FC 37570 | Somewhere in the Stars | 1982 | 10.00 |
| ❑ PC 37570 | Somewhere in the Stars | 1984 | 8.00 |
| *—Budget-line reissue with new prefix and "02" added to bar code* | | | |
| ❑ FC 39463 | Rhythm and Romance | 1985 | 10.00 |
| ❑ FC 40777 | King's Record Shop | 1987 | 10.00 |
| ❑ OC 45054 | Hits 1979-1989 | 1989 | 12.00 |
| ❑ HC 46965 | Seven Year Ache | 1981 | 50.00 |
| *—Half-speed mastered edition* | | | |

### CASH, TOMMY

| Number | Title (A Side/B Side) | Yr | NM |
|---|---|---|---|
| **ELEKTRA** | | | |
| ❑ CM-5 | Only a Stone | 1975 | 15.00 |
| **EPIC** | | | |
| ❑ BN 26484 | Your Lovin' Takes the Leavin' Out of Me | 1969 | 20.00 |
| ❑ BN 26535 | Six White Horses | 1970 | 15.00 |
| ❑ E 30107 | Rise and Shine | 1970 | 15.00 |
| ❑ E 30556 | Cash Country | 1971 | 15.00 |
| ❑ E 30860 | American Way of Life | 1971 | 15.00 |
| ❑ KE 31747 | That Certain One | 1972 | 15.00 |
| ❑ KE 31995 | The Best of Tommy Cash, Volume I | 1972 | 15.00 |
| **MONUMENT** | | | |
| ❑ 7619 | The New Spirit | 1978 | 12.00 |
| **UNITED ARTISTS** | | | |
| ❑ UAS-6628 | Here Comes Tommy Cash | 1968 | 20.00 |

### CASHMAN, PISTILLI AND WEST

| Number | Title (A Side/B Side) | Yr | NM |
|---|---|---|---|
| **ABC** | | | |
| ❑ ABCS-629 | Bound to Happen | 1968 | 20.00 |
| **CAPITOL** | | | |
| ❑ ST-211 | Cashman, Pistilli, and West | 1969 | 15.00 |

### CASINOS, THE (1)

| Number | Title (A Side/B Side) | Yr | NM |
|---|---|---|---|
| **FRATERNITY** | | | |
| ❑ LP-1019 [M] | Then You Can Tell Me Goodbye | 1967 | 40.00 |
| ❑ LPS-1019 [S] | Then You Can Tell Me Goodbye | 1967 | 60.00 |

### CASSELL, PETE

| Number | Title (A Side/B Side) | Yr | NM |
|---|---|---|---|
| **HILLTOP** | | | |
| ❑ 6023 | The Legend of Pete Cassell | 1965 | 25.00 |

### CASSIDY, DAVID

| Number | Title (A Side/B Side) | Yr | NM |
|---|---|---|---|
| **BELL** | | | |
| ❑ 1109 | Rock Me Baby | 1972 | 20.00 |
| ❑ 1132 | Dreams Are Nothing More Than Wishes | 1973 | 20.00 |
| ❑ 1312 | Cassidy Live | 1974 | 25.00 |
| ❑ 1321 | David Cassidy's Greatest Hits | 1974 | 15.00 |
| ❑ 6070 | Cherish | 1972 | 20.00 |
| **RCA VICTOR** | | | |
| ❑ APL1-1066 | The Higher They Climb… | 1975 | 15.00 |
| *—Black vinyl* | | | |
| ❑ APL1-1066 | The Higher They Climb… | 1975 | 100.00 |
| *—Blue vinyl* | | | |
| ❑ APL1-1309 | Home Is Where the Heart Is | 1976 | 15.00 |
| ❑ APL1-1852 | Gettin' It in the Street | 1976 | 40.00 |

### CASSIDY, EVA

| Number | Title (A Side/B Side) | Yr | NM |
|---|---|---|---|
| **S&P** | | | |
| ❑ 501 | Songbird | 2004 | 30.00 |
| *—180-gram edition* | | | |

### CASTELLS, THE

| Number | Title (A Side/B Side) | Yr | NM |
|---|---|---|---|
| **ERA** | | | |
| ❑ EL-109 [M] | So This Is Love | 1962 | 120.00 |
| ❑ ES-109 [S] | So This Is Love | 1962 | 400.00 |

### CASTLE, LEE

| Number | Title (A Side/B Side) | Yr | NM |
|---|---|---|---|
| **CELEBRITY** | | | |
| ❑ CEL-203 [M] | World Famous Dixieland Favorites | 1952 | 40.00 |
| **DAVIS** | | | |
| ❑ JD-105 [M] | Dixieland Heaven | 1951 | 60.00 |

### CASTOR, JIMMY, BUNCH

| Number | Title (A Side/B Side) | Yr | NM |
|---|---|---|---|
| **ATLANTIC** | | | |
| ❑ SD 7305 | The Everything Man | 1974 | 10.00 |
| ❑ SD 18124 | Butt Of Course | 1975 | 10.00 |
| ❑ SD 18150 | Supersound | 1975 | 10.00 |
| ❑ SD 18186 | E-Man Groovin' | 1976 | 10.00 |
| ❑ SD 19111 | Maximum Stimulation | 1977 | 10.00 |
| **COTILLION** | | | |
| ❑ SD 5215 | The Jimmy Castor Bunch | 1979 | 12.00 |
| **DRIVE** | | | |
| ❑ 407 | Let It Out | 1978 | 12.00 |
| **LONG DISTANCE** | | | |
| ❑ 1201 | C | 1980 | 12.00 |
| **RCA VICTOR** | | | |
| ❑ APD1-0103 [Q] | Dimension III | 1973 | 20.00 |
| *—All copies are quadraphonic* | | | |
| ❑ APL1-0313 | The Everything Man | 1974 | 15.00 |
| ❑ LSP-4640 | It's Just Begun | 1972 | 15.00 |
| ❑ LSP-4783 | Phase Two | 1972 | 15.00 |
| **SMASH** | | | |
| ❑ MGS-27091 [M] | Hey Leroy! | 1967 | 40.00 |
| ❑ SRS-67091 [S] | Hey Leroy! | 1967 | 40.00 |

### CASTRO, JOE

| Number | Title (A Side/B Side) | Yr | NM |
|---|---|---|---|
| **ATLANTIC** | | | |
| ❑ 1264 [M] | Mood Jazz | 1957 | 50.00 |
| *—Black label* | | | |
| ❑ 1264 [M] | Mood Jazz | 1961 | 20.00 |
| *—Multicolor label with white "fan" logo* | | | |
| ❑ SD 1264 [S] | Mood Jazz | 1959 | 40.00 |
| *—Green label* | | | |
| ❑ 1324 [M] | Groove Funk Soul | 1960 | 40.00 |
| *—Black label* | | | |
| ❑ SD 1324 [S] | Groove Funk Soul | 1960 | 50.00 |
| *—Green label* | | | |

### CAT MOTHER AND THE ALL NIGHT NEWS BOYS

| Number | Title (A Side/B Side) | Yr | NM |
|---|---|---|---|
| **POLYDOR** | | | |
| ❑ 24-4001 | The Street Giveth…And the Street Taketh Away | 1969 | 25.00 |
| *—Produced by Jimi Hendrix* | | | |
| ❑ 24-4023 | Albion Doo-Wah | 1970 | 15.00 |
| ❑ PD-5017 | Cat Mother | 1972 | 15.00 |
| ❑ PD-5042 | Last Chance Dance | 1972 | 15.00 |

### CATALINAS, THE (1) Studio band of Los Angeles session pros.

| Number | Title (A Side/B Side) | Yr | NM |
|---|---|---|---|
| **RIC** | | | |
| ❑ M-1006 [M] | Fun, Fun, Fun | 1964 | 100.00 |
| ❑ S-1006 [S] | Fun, Fun, Fun | 1964 | 150.00 |

### CATALYST

| Number | Title (A Side/B Side) | Yr | NM |
|---|---|---|---|
| **COBBLESTONE** | | | |
| ❑ 9018 | Catalyst | 1972 | 20.00 |

### CATANOOGA CATS, THE

| Number | Title (A Side/B Side) | Yr | NM |
|---|---|---|---|
| **FORWARD** | | | |
| ❑ ST-F-1018 | The Catanooga Cats | 1969 | 40.00 |

### CATAPILLA

| Number | Title (A Side/B Side) | Yr | NM |
|---|---|---|---|
| **VERTIGO** | | | |
| ❑ 1006 | Catapilla | 1971 | 30.00 |

### CATES, GEORGE

| Number | Title (A Side/B Side) | Yr | NM |
|---|---|---|---|
| **CORAL** | | | |
| ❑ CRL 57126 [M] | Under European Skies | 1957 | 40.00 |
| ❑ CRL 57220 [M] | Exciting | 1958 | 30.00 |
| **DOT** | | | |
| ❑ DLP-3355 [M] | Polynesian Percussion | 1961 | 12.00 |
| ❑ DLP-3400 [M] | Take Five | 1961 | 12.00 |
| ❑ DLP-3422 [M] | Twistin' 12 Great Hits | 1962 | 15.00 |
| ❑ DLP-3464 [M] | Third Man Theme | 1962 | 12.00 |
| ❑ DLP-3564 [M] | Hit Songs — Hit Sounds | 1964 | 12.00 |
| ❑ DLP-25355 [S] | Polynesian Percussion | 1961 | 20.00 |
| ❑ DLP-25400 [S] | Take Five | 1961 | 20.00 |
| ❑ DLP-25422 [S] | Twistin' 12 Great Hits | 1962 | 20.00 |
| ❑ DLP-25464 [S] | Third Man Theme | 1962 | 15.00 |
| ❑ DLP-25564 [S] | Hit Songs — Hit Sounds | 1964 | 15.00 |
| **HAMILTON** | | | |
| ❑ HLP-127 [M] | The Great Hit Sounds of George Cates | 1964 | 10.00 |
| ❑ HLP-161 [M] | 1965's Great Hits | 1966 | 15.00 |
| ❑ HLP-12127 [S] | The Great Hit Sounds of George Cates | 1964 | 12.00 |
| ❑ HLP-12161 [S] | 1965's Great Hits | 1966 | 20.00 |
| **RANWOOD** | | | |
| ❑ 8039 | Hawaii | 1969 | 12.00 |



**Except when noted otherwise, VG = 25% of NM, and VG+ = 50% of NM. (Example: VG = $2.00, VG+ = $4.00 and NM = $8.00.)**

### CATES SISTERS, THE

| Number | Title (A Side/B Side) | Yr | NM |
|---|---|---|---|
| **OVATION** | | | |
| ❑ 1740 | Steppin' Out | 1979 | 12.00 |
| *—As "The Cates"* | | | |

### CATHCART, DICK

| Number | Title (A Side/B Side) | Yr | NM |
|---|---|---|---|
| **WARNER BROS.** | | | |
| ❑ W 1275 [M] | Bix/MCMLIX | 1959 | 25.00 |
| ❑ WS 1275 [S] | Bix/MCMLIX | 1959 | 30.00 |

### CATHY JEAN AND THE ROOMATES

| Number | Title (A Side/B Side) | Yr | NM |
|---|---|---|---|
| **VALMOR** | | | |
| ❑ 78 [M] | Great Oldies | 1962 | 800.00 |
| *—Reissue of 789 with titles on cover and no group shot* | | | |
| ❑ 789 [M] | At the Hop! | 1961 | 900.00 |

### CATINGUB, MATT

| Number | Title (A Side/B Side) | Yr | NM |
|---|---|---|---|
| **REFERENCE RECORDINGS** | | | |
| ❑ RR-14 | Your Friendly Neighborhood Big Band | 1985 | 20.00 |
| *—Plays at 45 rpm* | | | |

### CAUTHEN, STEVE

| Number | Title (A Side/B Side) | Yr | NM |
|---|---|---|---|
| **BAREBACK** | | | |
| ❑ BB 3334 | ...And Steve Cauthen Sings Too! | 1977 | 20.00 |

### CAVANAUGH, PAGE

| Number | Title (A Side/B Side) | Yr | NM |
|---|---|---|---|
| **CAPITOL** | | | |
| ❑ T 879 [M] | Fats Sent Me | 1957 | 40.00 |
| ❑ T 1001 [M] | Swingin' Down the Road from Paris to Rome | 1958 | 40.00 |
| **"X"** | | | |
| ❑ LX-3027 [10] | Page Cavanaugh Trio | 1954 | 50.00 |

### CAVE, NICK, AND THE BAD SEEDS

| Number | Title (A Side/B Side) | Yr | NM |
|---|---|---|---|
| **ANTI** | | | |
| ❑ 86668 | Nocturama | 2003 | 15.00 |
| *—Actually contains two records, but the second record is a single-sided disc with one song* | | | |
| **ENIGMA** | | | |
| ❑ 7 75401-1 | Tender Prey | 1988 | 30.00 |
| **HOMESTEAD** | | | |
| ❑ HMS 026 | The Firstborn is Dead | 1985 | 30.00 |
| ❑ HMS 065 | Kicking Against the Pricks | 1986 | 30.00 |
| ❑ HMS 073 | Your Funeral, My Trial | 1986 | 40.00 |

### CELESTIN, OSCAR

| Number | Title (A Side/B Side) | Yr | NM |
|---|---|---|---|
| **IMPERIAL** | | | |
| ❑ LP-9125 [M] | Dixieland King | 1961 | 20.00 |
| ❑ LP-9149 [M] | Birth of the Blues | 1961 | 20.00 |
| ❑ LP-9199 [M] | Oscar "Papa" Celestin's New Orleans Jazz Band | 1962 | 20.00 |

### CELL BLOCK SEVEN

| Number | Title (A Side/B Side) | Yr | NM |
|---|---|---|---|
| **DIXIELAND JUBILEE** | | | |
| ❑ DJ-506 [M] | A Dixieland Riot | 195? | 50.00 |

### CENTAURUS

| Number | Title (A Side/B Side) | Yr | NM |
|---|---|---|---|
| **AZRA** | | | |
| ❑ 61549 | Centaurus | 1978 | 50.00 |
| *—Issued on clear vinyl* | | | |

### CENTIPEDE

| Number | Title (A Side/B Side) | Yr | NM |
|---|---|---|---|
| **RCA VICTOR** | | | |
| ❑ CPL2-5042 [(2)] | Septober Energy | 1974 | 100.00 |

### CENTRAL NERVOUS SYSTEM

| Number | Title (A Side/B Side) | Yr | NM |
|---|---|---|---|
| **MUSIC FACTORY** | | | |
| ❑ MF-12003 [M] | I Could Have Danced All Night | 1968 | 30.00 |
| *—White label promo only (no stock copies were issued in mono)* | | | |
| ❑ MFS-12003 [S] | I Could Have Danced All Night | 1968 | 20.00 |

### CENTURIONS, THE

| Number | Title (A Side/B Side) | Yr | NM |
|---|---|---|---|
| **DEL-FI** | | | |
| ❑ DFLP-1228 [M] | Surfer's Pajama Party | 1963 | 100.00 |
| ❑ DFST-1228 [S] | Surfer's Pajama Party | 1963 | 200.00 |
| *—Above has the same title and number, and almost the same cover, as the album of the same name by Bruce Johnston, but the contents are different* | | | |

### CESANA

| Number | Title (A Side/B Side) | Yr | NM |
|---|---|---|---|
| **MODERN** | | | |
| ❑ M-100 [M] | Tender Emotions | 1964 | 20.00 |

### CEYLEIB PEOPLE, THE

| Number | Title (A Side/B Side) | Yr | NM |
|---|---|---|---|
| **VAULT** | | | |
| ❑ LP-117 | Tanyet | 1968 | 60.00 |

### CHAD AND JEREMY

| Number | Title (A Side/B Side) | Yr | NM |
|---|---|---|---|
| **CAPITOL** | | | |
| ❑ ST 2470 [P] | The Best of Chad and Jeremy | 1966 | 12.00 |
| *—Black label with colorband* | | | |
| ❑ ST 2470 [P] | The Best of Chad and Jeremy | 1967 | 10.00 |
| *—"Starline" label* | | | |

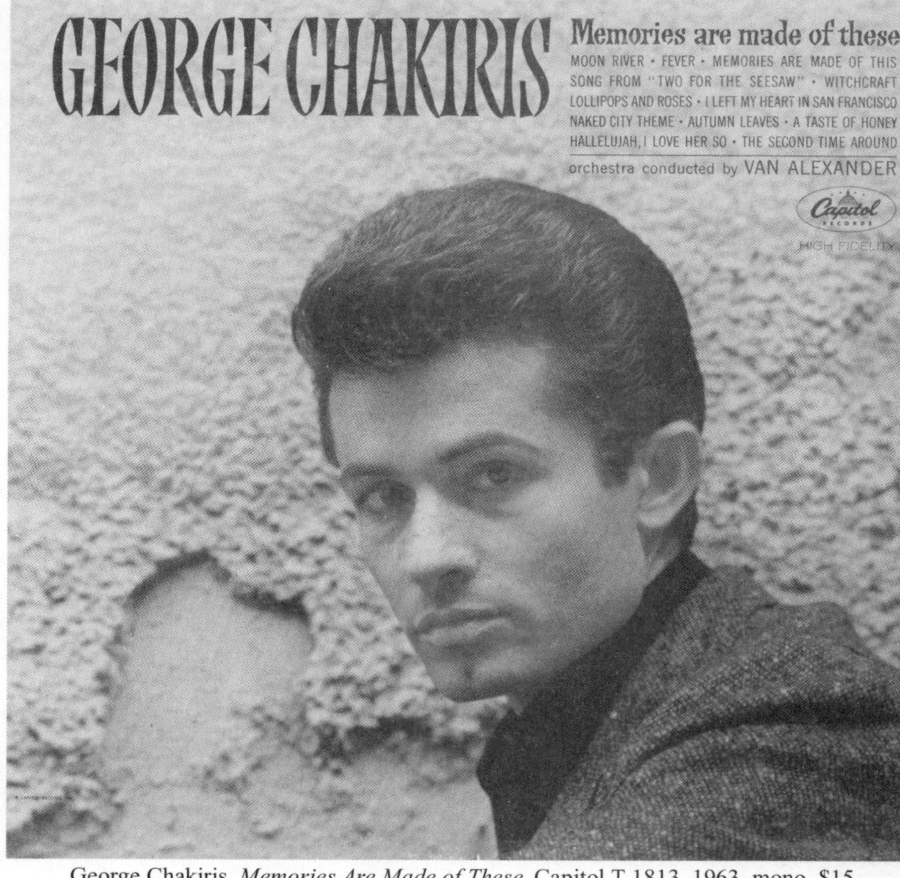


George Chakiris, *Memories Are Made of These,* Capitol T 1813, 1963, mono, $15.

| Number | Title (A Side/B Side) | Yr | NM |
|---|---|---|---|
| ❑ T 2470 [M] | The Best of Chad and Jeremy | 1966 | 10.00 |
| *—Black label with colorband* | | | |
| ❑ T 2470 [M] | The Best of Chad and Jeremy | 1967 | 8.00 |
| *—"Starline" label* | | | |
| ❑ STT 2546 [P] | More Chad and Jeremy | 1966 | 12.00 |
| ❑ TT 2546 [M] | More Chad and Jeremy | 1966 | 10.00 |
| ❑ SN-16135 [P] | The Best of Chad and Jeremy | 1980 | 8.00 |
| *—Budget-line reissue* | | | |
| **COLUMBIA** | | | |
| ❑ CL 2374 [M] | Before and After | 1965 | 20.00 |
| ❑ CL 2398 [M] | I Don't Want to Lose You Baby | 1966 | 25.00 |
| ❑ CL 2564 [M] | Distant Shores | 1966 | 20.00 |
| ❑ CL 2671 [M] | Of Cabbages and Kings | 1967 | 20.00 |
| ❑ CL 2899 [M] | The Ark | 1968 | 25.00 |
| ❑ CS 9174 [S] | Before and After | 1965 | 30.00 |
| ❑ CS 9198 [S] | I Don't Want to Lose You Baby | 1966 | 40.00 |
| ❑ CS 9364 [P] | Distant Shores | 1966 | 25.00 |
| *—"Distant Shores" is rechanneled* | | | |
| ❑ CS 9471 [S] | Of Cabbages and Kings | 1967 | 25.00 |
| ❑ CS 9699 [S] | The Arc | 1968 | 25.00 |
| *—Some copies spell the LP title this way on the cover* | | | |
| ❑ CS 9699 [S] | The Ark | 1968 | 25.00 |
| *—Correct spelling of LP title on cover* | | | |
| **FIDU** | | | |
| ❑ FM-101 [M] | 5 + 10 = 15 Fabulous Hits | 1966 | 10.00 |
| ❑ FS-101 [P] | 5 + 10 = 15 Fabulous Hits | 1966 | 12.00 |
| **HARMONY** | | | |
| ❑ HS 11357 [S] | Chad and Jeremy | 1973 | 8.00 |
| **ROCSHIRE** | | | |
| ❑ XR-22018 | Chad Stuart and Jeremy Clyde | 1983 | 10.00 |
| **WORLD ARTISTS** | | | |
| ❑ WAM-2002 [M] | Yesterday's Gone | 1964 | 12.00 |
| ❑ WAM-2005 [M] | Chad and Jeremy Sing for You | 1965 | 12.00 |
| ❑ WAS-3002 [P] | Yesterday's Gone | 1964 | 15.00 |
| *—"Yesterday's Gone" is rechanneled.* | | | |
| ❑ WAS-3005 [S] | Chad and Jeremy Sing for You | 1965 | 15.00 |

### CHAIRMEN OF THE BOARD

| Number | Title (A Side/B Side) | Yr | NM |
|---|---|---|---|
| **INVICTUS** | | | |
| ❑ ST-7300 | Chairmen of the Board (Featuring "Give Me Just a Little More Time") | 1970 | 40.00 |
| ❑ SKAO-7304 | In Session | 1970 | 40.00 |
| ❑ ST-9801 | Bittersweet | 1972 | 40.00 |
| ❑ KZ 32526 | The Skin I'm In | 1974 | 40.00 |

### CHAKIRIS, GEORGE

| Number | Title (A Side/B Side) | Yr | NM |
|---|---|---|---|
| **CAPITOL** | | | |
| ❑ ST 1750 [S] | George Chakiris | 1962 | 20.00 |
| ❑ T 1750 [M] | George Chakiris | 1962 | 15.00 |
| ❑ ST 1813 [S] | Memories Are Made of These | 1963 | 20.00 |
| ❑ T 1813 [M] | Memories Are Made of These | 1963 | 15.00 |
| ❑ ST 2391 [S] | It's Been a Swingin' Summer | 1965 | 15.00 |
| ❑ T 2391 [M] | It's Been a Swingin' Summer | 1965 | 12.00 |
| **HORIZON** | | | |
| ❑ ST-1610 [S] | The Gershwin Songbook | 1962 | 20.00 |
| ❑ WP-1610 [M] | The Gershwin Songbook | 1962 | 15.00 |

### CHALKER, CURLY

| Number | Title (A Side/B Side) | Yr | NM |
|---|---|---|---|
| **COLUMBIA** | | | |
| ❑ CL 2596 [M] | Big Hits on Big Steel | 1965 | 20.00 |
| ❑ CS 9396 [S] | Big Hits on Big Steel | 1965 | 30.00 |

### CHALLENGERS, THE (1)

| Number | Title (A Side/B Side) | Yr | NM |
|---|---|---|---|
| **FANTASY** | | | |
| ❑ F-9443 | Where Were You in the Summer of '62 | 1973 | 12.00 |
| **GNP CRESCENDO** | | | |
| ❑ GNP-609 [(2)M] | 25 Great Instrumental Hits | 1967 | 25.00 |
| ❑ GNPS-609 [(2)S] | 25 Great Instrumental Hits | 1967 | 20.00 |
| ❑ GNP-2010 [M] | The Challengers at the Teenage Fair | 1965 | 20.00 |
| ❑ GNPS-2010 [S] | The Challengers at the Teenage Fair | 1965 | 25.00 |
| ❑ GNP-2018 [M] | The Man from U.N.C.L.E. | 1965 | 20.00 |
| ❑ GNPS-2018 [S] | The Man from U.N.C.L.E. | 1965 | 25.00 |
| ❑ GNP-2025 [M] | California Kicks | 1966 | 20.00 |
| ❑ GNPS-2025 [S] | California Kicks | 1966 | 25.00 |
| ❑ GNP-2030 [M] | Billy Strange and the Challengers | 1966 | 20.00 |
| ❑ GNPS-2030 [S] | Billy Strange and the Challengers | 1966 | 25.00 |
| ❑ GNP-2031 [M] | Wipe Out | 1966 | 20.00 |
| ❑ GNPS-2031 [S] | Wipe Out | 1966 | 25.00 |
| ❑ GNPS-2045 | Light My Fire with Classical Gas | 1968 | 20.00 |
| ❑ GNPS-2056 | Vanilla Funk | 1970 | 20.00 |
| ❑ GNPS-2093 | Sidewalk Surfing | 1975 | 12.00 |
| **RHINO** | | | |
| ❑ RNLP-053 | Best of the Challengers | 1982 | 10.00 |

**TRIUMPH**
❑ TR-100 [M] The Challengers Go Sidewalk Surfing 1965 20.00
❑ TRS-100 [S] The Challengers Go Sidewalk Surfing 1965 25.00

**VAULT**
❑ LP-100 [M] Surfbeat 1963 50.00
❑ VS-100 [S] Surfbeat 1963 80.00
*—Black vinyl*
❑ VS-100 [S] Surfbeat 1963 250.00
*—Orange vinyl*
❑ VS-100 [S] Surfbeat 1963 250.00
*—Red vinyl*
❑ VS-100 [S] Surfbeat 1963 250.00
*—Yellow vinyl*
❑ LP-101 [M] Surfin' with the Challengers 1963 50.00
*—Altered title*
❑ LP-101 [M] Lloyd Thaxton Goes Surfin' with the Challengers 1963 60.00
*—Original title*
❑ VS-101 [S] Surfin' with the Challengers 1963 80.00
*—Altered title; black vinyl*
❑ VS-101 [S] Lloyd Thaxton Goes Surfin' with the Challengers 1963 100.00
*—Original title; black vinyl*
❑ VS-101 [S] (Lloyd Thaxton Goes) Surfin' with the Challengers 1963 250.00
*—Either title; blue vinyl*
❑ VS-101 [S] (Lloyd Thaxton Goes) Surfin' with the Challengers 1963 250.00
*—Either title; orange vinyl*
❑ VS-101 [S] (Lloyd Thaxton Goes) Surfin' with the Challengers 1963 250.00
*—Either title; red vinyl*
❑ VS-101 [S] (Lloyd Thaxton Goes) Surfin' with the Challengers 1963 250.00
*—Either title; yellow vinyl*
❑ LP-102 [M] The Challengers On The Move 1963 40.00
❑ VS-102 [S] The Challengers On The Move 1963 60.00
❑ LP-107 [M] K-39 1964 80.00
❑ LP-109 [M] The Surf's Up 1965 40.00
❑ VS-109 [S] The Surf's Up 1965 60.00
❑ LP-110 [M] The Challengers A-Go-Go 1966 30.00
❑ VS-110 [S] The Challengers A-Go-Go 1966 40.00
❑ LP-111 [M] The Challengers' Greatest Hits 1967 25.00
❑ VS-111 [S] The Challengers' Greatest Hits 1967 25.00

## CHALOFF, SERGE

**CAPITOL**
❑ T 742 [M] Blue Serge 1956 100.00
*—Turquoise label*
❑ T 742 [M] Blue Serge 1959 60.00
*—Black colorband label, logo at left*
❑ T 6510 [M] Boston Blow-Up 1955 150.00

**MOSAIC**
❑ MQ5-147 [(5)] The Complete Serge Chaloff Sessions 1993 120.00

**STORYVILLE**
❑ STLP-317 [10] The Fable of Mable 1954 300.00
❑ STLP-350 [10] Serge & Boots 1955 300.00

## CHALOFF, SERGE/OSCAR PETTIFORD

**MERCER**
❑ LP-1003 [10] New Stars, New Sounds, Volume 2 1951 300.00

## CHAMAELEON CHURCH
Chevy Chase was in this group.

**MGM**
❑ SE-4574 Chamaeleon Church 1968 20.00

## CHAMBERLAIN, RICHARD

**METRO**
❑ M-564 [M] Richard Chamberlain Sings 1966 12.00
❑ MS-564 [S] Richard Chamberlain Sings 1966 12.00

**MGM**
❑ E-4088 [M] Richard Chamberlain Sings 1962 15.00
❑ SE-4088 [S] Richard Chamberlain Sings 1962 20.00
❑ E-4185 [M] Twilight of Honor 1963 15.00
❑ SE-4185 [S] Twilight of Honor 1963 20.00
❑ E-4287 [M] Joy in the Morning 1965 15.00
❑ SE-4287 [S] Joy in the Morning 1965 20.00
❑ ST 90512 [S] Richard Chamberlain Sings 1965 30.00
*—Capitol Record Club edition*
❑ T 90512 [M] Richard Chamberlain Sings 1965 25.00
*—Capitol Record Club edition*

## CHAMBERS, PAUL

**BLUE NOTE**
❑ BLP-1534 [M] Whims of Chambers 1956 700.00
*—"Deep groove" version, Lexington Ave. address on label*
❑ BLP-1534 [M] Whims of Chambers 1958 250.00
*—"Deep groove" version, W. 63rd St. address on label*
❑ BLP-1534 [M] Whims of Chambers 1963 40.00
*—"New York, USA" address on label*
❑ BLP-1564 [M] Paul Chambers Quintet 1957 200.00
*—Regular version, W. 63rd St. address on label*
❑ BLP-1564 [M] Paul Chambers Quintet 1957 400.00
*—"Deep groove" version, W. 63rd St. address on label*
❑ BLP-1564 [M] Paul Chambers Quintet 1963 40.00
*—"New York, USA" address on label*
❑ BST-1564 [S] Paul Chambers Quintet 1959 150.00
*—Regular version, W. 63rd St. address on label*
❑ BST-1564 [S] Paul Chambers Quintet 1959 250.00
*—"Deep groove" version, W. 63rd St. address on label*
❑ BST-1564 [S] Paul Chambers Quintet 1963 30.00
*—"New York, USA" address on label*
❑ BLP-1569 [M] Bass on Top 1957 120.00
*—Regular version, W. 63rd St. address on label*
❑ BLP-1569 [M] Bass on Top 1957 300.00
*—"Deep groove" version; W. 63rd St. address on label*
❑ BLP-1569 [M] Bass on Top 1963 40.00
*—"New York, USA" address on label*
❑ BST-1569 [S] Bass on Top 1959 120.00
*—Regular version, W. 63rd St. address on label*
❑ BST-1569 [S] Bass on Top 1959 200.00
*—"Deep groove" version, W. 63rd St. address on label*
❑ BST-1569 [S] Bass on Top 1963 30.00
*—"New York, USA" address on label*

**IMPERIAL**
❑ LP-9182 [M] A Jazz Delegation from the East: Chambers' Music 1961 40.00
❑ LP-12182 [S] A Jazz Delegation from the East: Chambers' Music 1961 30.00

**JAZZ WEST**
❑ JWLP-7 [M] A Jazz Delegation from the East: Chambers' Music 1956 600.00

**SCORE**
❑ SLP-4033 [M] A Jazz Delegation from the East: Chambers' Music 1958 80.00

**VEE JAY**
❑ LP-1014 [M] Go 1959 60.00
❑ SR-1014 [S] Go 1959 100.00
❑ LP-3012 [M] First Bassman 1960 50.00
❑ SR-3012 [S] First Bassman 1960 80.00

## CHAMBERS BROTHERS, THE

**AVCO**
❑ 11013 Unbonded 1974 12.00
❑ 69003 Night Move 1975 20.00

**COLUMBIA**
❑ KGP 20 [(2)] Love, Peace and Happiness 1969 25.00
❑ CL 2722 [M] The Time Has Come 1967 30.00
❑ CS 9522 The Time Has Come 1971 12.00
*—Orange label*
❑ CS 9522 [S] The Time Has Come 1967 20.00
*—Red "360 Sound" label*
❑ PC 9522 The Time Has Come 198? 8.00
*—Reissue with new prefix*
❑ CS 9671 A New Time — A New Day 1968 20.00
❑ C 30032 New Generation 1970 15.00
❑ C 30871 The Chambers Brothers' Greatest Hits 1971 15.00
❑ PC 30871 The Chambers Brothers' Greatest Hits 198? 8.00
*—Reissue with new prefix*
❑ KC 31158 Oh My God 1972 —
*—Canceled*
❑ CG 33642 [(2)] The Time Has Come/A New Time — A New Day 1975 15.00

**FANTASY**
❑ 24718 [(2)] The Best of the Chambers Brothers 1973 15.00

**FOLKWAYS**
❑ 31008 Groovin' Time 1968 15.00

**ROXBURY**
❑ RLX-106 Live In Concert on Mars 1976 30.00

**VAULT**
❑ LP-115 [M] The Chambers Brothers Now 1967 15.00
❑ VS-115 [S] The Chambers Brothers Now 1967 15.00
❑ VS-120 The Chambers Brothers Shout 1968 15.00
❑ VS-128 Feelin' the Blues 1969 15.00
❑ VS-135 [(2)] The Chambers Brothers Greatest Hits 1970 20.00
❑ LP-9003 [M] People Get Ready 1966 20.00
❑ LPS-9003 [S] People Get Ready 1966 25.00

## CHAMBLEE, EDDIE

**EMARCY**
❑ MG-36124 [M] Chamblee Music 1958 50.00
❑ MG-36131 [M] Doodlin' 1958 50.00
❑ SR-80007 [S] Doodlin' 1959 40.00

**MERCURY**
❑ SR-60127 [S] Chamblee Music 1960 25.00

**PRESTIGE**
❑ PRLP-7321 [M] The Rocking Tenor Sax of Eddie Chamblee 1964 25.00
*—Yellow label*
❑ PRST-7321 [S] The Rocking Tenor Sax of Eddie Chamblee 1964 30.00
*—Silver label*

## CHAMPS, THE

**CHALLENGE**
❑ CHL-601 [M] Go Champs Go 1958 250.00
❑ CHL-601 [M] Go Champs Go 1958 2400.
*—Blue vinyl; VG value 800; VG+ value 1600*
❑ CHL-605 [M] Everybody's Rockin' with the Champs 1959 200.00
❑ CHL-613 [M] Great Dance Hits 1962 120.00
❑ CHL-614 [M] All American Music from the Champs 1962 120.00
❑ CHS-2500 [S] Everybody's Rockin' with the Champs 1959 300.00
❑ CHS-2513 [S] Great Dance Hits 1962 200.00
❑ CHS-2514 [S] All American Music from the Champs 1962 200.00

## CHANDLER, GENE

**BRUNSWICK**
❑ BL 54124 [M] The Girl Don't Care 1967 25.00
❑ BL 754124 [S] The Girl Don't Care 1967 20.00
❑ BL 754131 There Was a Time 1968 20.00
❑ BL 754149 The Two Sides of Gene Chandler 1969 20.00

**CHECKER**
❑ LP-3003 [M] The Duke of Soul 1967 50.00
❑ LPS-3003 [R] The Duke of Soul 1967 30.00

**CHI-SOUND**
❑ T-578 Get Down 1978 10.00

**CONSTELLATION**
❑ LP 1421 [M] Greatest Hits by Gene Chandler 1964 50.00
❑ LP 1423 [M] Just Be True 1964 50.00
❑ LP 1425 [M] Gene Chandler — Live On Stage in '65 1965 50.00

**MERCURY**
❑ SR-61304 The Gene Chandler Situation 1970 15.00

**SOLID SMOKE**
❑ SS-8027 Stroll On with the Duke 198? 10.00

**20TH CENTURY**
❑ T-598 When You're #1 1979 10.00
❑ T-605 Gene Chandler '80 1980 10.00
❑ T-625 Ear Candy 1980 10.00
❑ T-629 Here's to Love 1981 10.00

**VEE JAY**
❑ LP-1040 [M] The Duke of Earl 1962 120.00
❑ SR-1040 [R] The Duke of Earl 196? 50.00
*—"Stereophonic" on front; no "Important Notice..." on back; record plays mono. Most labels are all-black with "VJ" in brackets. This was a semi-authorized reissue after ex-Vee Jay executives bought the company's remnants in bankruptcy court in 1966.*
❑ SR-1040 [S] The Duke of Earl 1962 250.00
*—"Stereo" sticker on mono cover; "Stereo" on record labels*
❑ SR-1040 [S] The Duke of Earl 1962 800.00
*—"Stereophonic" on front cover; top back cover contains note that begins: "Important Notice...This Is a Stereophonic Record"; "Stereo" on record labels*
❑ VJLP-1040 The Duke of Earl 198? 10.00
*—Mid-1980s authorized reissue*

## CHANDLER, JEFF

**LIBERTY**
❑ LRP-3067 [M] Jeff Chandler Sings to You 1957 40.00
❑ LRP-3074 [M] Warm and Easy 1958 40.00

**SUNSET**
❑ SUS-5127 Sincerely Yours 1969 12.00

## CHANNEL, BRUCE

**SMASH**
❑ MGS-27008 [M] Hey! Baby (And 11 Other Songs About Your Baby) 1962 100.00
❑ SRS-67008 [R] Hey! Baby (And 11 Other Songs About Your Baby) 1962 60.00

## CHANNING, CAROL

**CAEDMON**
❑ TC 1303 The Year Without a Santa Claus and Other Stories for Christmas 1969 12.00
*—Spoken-word recordings*

**COMMAND**
❑ 880 SD [S] Carol Channing Entertains 1966 20.00
❑ 33-880 [M] Carol Channing Entertains 1966 15.00

**PLANTATION**
❑ PLP-527 Carol Channing With the Original Country Cast 1978 20.00

**VANGUARD**
❑ VSD-2041 [S] Carol Channing 1959 40.00
❑ VRS-9056 [M] Carol Channing 1959 30.00

## CHANTAY'S

**DOT**
❑ DLP 3516 [M] Pipeline 1963 50.00
❑ DLP 3771 [M] Two Sides of the Chantays 1966 50.00
❑ DLP 25516 [S] Pipeline 1963 80.00
❑ DLP 25771 [S] Two Sides of the Chantays 1966 80.00

**DOWNEY**
❑ DLP-1002 [M] Pipeline 1963 220.00
❑ DLPS-1002 [S] Pipeline 1963 350.00



**Except when noted otherwise, VG = 25% of NM, and VG+ = 50% of NM. (Example: VG = $2.00, VG+ = $4.00 and NM = $8.00.)**

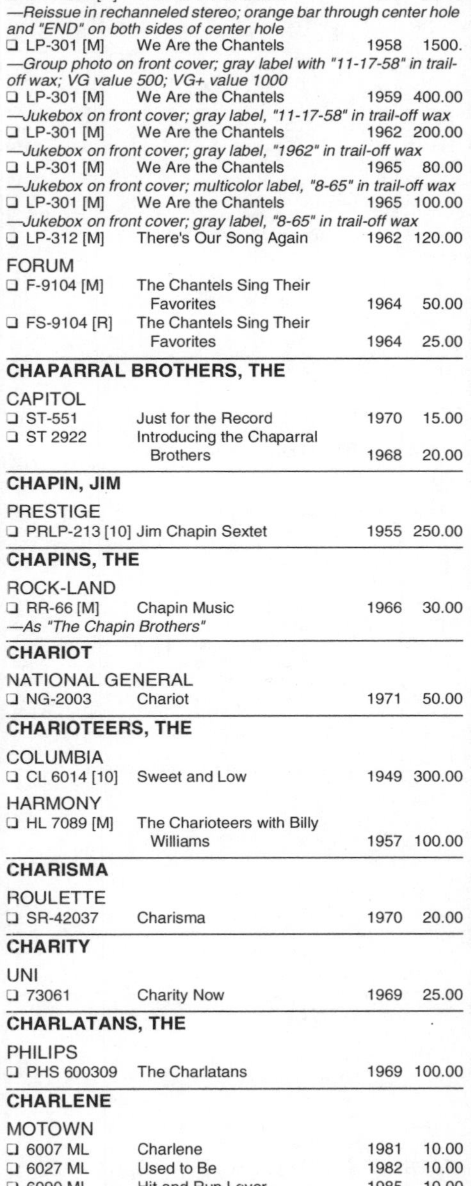

| Number | Title (A Side/B Side) | Yr | NM |
|---|---|---|---|
| **CHANTELS, THE** | | | |
| CARLTON | | | |
| ❑ LP-144 [M] | The Chantels On Tour/Look in My Eyes | 1962 | 200.00 |
| ❑ STLP-144 [P] | The Chantels On Tour/Look in My Eyes | 1962 | 400.00 |
| *—Eight tracks are true stereo, two are mono, two are rechanneled* | | | |
| END | | | |
| ❑ END-301 [R] | We Are the Chantels | 197? | 25.00 |
| *—Reissue in rechanneled stereo; orange bar through center hole and "END" on both sides of center hole* | | | |
| ❑ LP-301 [M] | We Are the Chantels | 1958 | 1500. |
| *—Group photo on front cover; gray label with "11-17-58" in trail-off wax; VG value 500; VG+ value 1000* | | | |
| ❑ LP-301 [M] | We Are the Chantels | 1959 | 400.00 |
| *—Jukebox on front cover; gray label, "11-17-58" in trail-off wax* | | | |
| ❑ LP-301 [M] | We Are the Chantels | 1962 | 200.00 |
| *—Jukebox on front cover; gray label, "1962" in trail-off wax* | | | |
| ❑ LP-301 [M] | We Are the Chantels | 1965 | 80.00 |
| *—Jukebox on front cover; multicolor label, "8-65" in trail-off wax* | | | |
| ❑ LP-301 [M] | We Are the Chantels | 1965 | 100.00 |
| *—Jukebox on front cover; gray label, "8-65" in trail-off wax* | | | |
| ❑ LP-312 [M] | There's Our Song Again | 1962 | 120.00 |
| FORUM | | | |
| ❑ F-9104 [M] | The Chantels Sing Their Favorites | 1964 | 50.00 |
| ❑ FS-9104 [R] | The Chantels Sing Their Favorites | 1964 | 25.00 |
| **CHAPARRAL BROTHERS, THE** | | | |
| CAPITOL | | | |
| ❑ ST-551 | Just for the Record | 1970 | 15.00 |
| ❑ ST 2922 | Introducing the Chaparral Brothers | 1968 | 20.00 |
| **CHAPIN, JIM** | | | |
| PRESTIGE | | | |
| ❑ PRLP-213 [10] | Jim Chapin Sextet | 1955 | 250.00 |
| **CHAPINS, THE** | | | |
| ROCK-LAND | | | |
| ❑ RR-66 [M] | Chapin Music | 1966 | 30.00 |
| *—As "The Chapin Brothers"* | | | |
| **CHARIOT** | | | |
| NATIONAL GENERAL | | | |
| ❑ NG-2003 | Chariot | 1971 | 50.00 |
| **CHARIOTEERS, THE** | | | |
| COLUMBIA | | | |
| ❑ CL 6014 [10] | Sweet and Low | 1949 | 300.00 |
| HARMONY | | | |
| ❑ HL 7089 [M] | The Charioteers with Billy Williams | 1957 | 100.00 |
| **CHARISMA** | | | |
| ROULETTE | | | |
| ❑ SR-42037 | Charisma | 1970 | 20.00 |
| **CHARITY** | | | |
| UNI | | | |
| ❑ 73061 | Charity Now | 1969 | 25.00 |
| **CHARLATANS, THE** | | | |
| PHILIPS | | | |
| ❑ PHS 600309 | The Charlatans | 1969 | 100.00 |
| **CHARLENE** | | | |
| MOTOWN | | | |
| ❑ 6007 ML | Charlene | 1981 | 10.00 |
| ❑ 6027 ML | Used to Be | 1982 | 10.00 |
| ❑ 6090 ML | Hit and Run Lover | 1985 | 10.00 |
| PRODIGAL | | | |
| ❑ P6-10015 | Charlene | 1976 | 20.00 |
| ❑ P6-10018 | Songs of Love | 1977 | 20.00 |
| **CHARLES, RAY** | | | |
| ABC | | | |
| ❑ S-335 [S] | The Genius Hits the Road | 1967 | 12.00 |
| ❑ S-355 [S] | Dedicated to You | 1967 | 12.00 |
| ❑ S-410 [S] | Modern Sounds in Country and Western Music | 1967 | 12.00 |
| ❑ S-415 [S] | Ray Charles' Greatest Hits | 1967 | 12.00 |
| ❑ S-435 [S] | Modern Sounds in Country and Western Music (Volume Two) | 1967 | 12.00 |
| ❑ S-465 [S] | Ingredients in a Recipe for Soul | 1967 | 12.00 |
| ❑ S-480 [S] | Sweet & Sour Tears | 1967 | 12.00 |
| ❑ S-495 [S] | Have a Smile with Me | 1967 | 12.00 |
| ❑ S-500 [S] | Ray Charles Live in Concert | 1967 | 12.00 |
| ❑ S-520 [S] | Together Again | 1967 | 12.00 |
| ❑ S-544 [S] | Crying Time | 1967 | 12.00 |
| ❑ S-550 [S] | Ray's Moods | 1967 | 12.00 |
| ❑ 590X [(2)M] | A Man and His Soul | 1967 | 15.00 |
| ❑ S-590X [(2)S] | A Man and His Soul | 1967 | 20.00 |

The Chapin Brothers, *Chapin Music!*, Rock-Land RR-66, 1966, mono, $30.

| Number | Title (A Side/B Side) | Yr | NM |
|---|---|---|---|
| ❑ 595 [M] | Ray Charles Invites You to Listen | 1967 | 20.00 |
| ❑ S-595 [S] | Ray Charles Invites You to Listen | 1967 | 15.00 |
| ❑ S-625 | A Portrait of Ray | 1968 | 12.00 |
| ❑ S-675 | I'm All Yours — Baby! | 1969 | 12.00 |
| ❑ S-695 | Doing His Thing | 1969 | 12.00 |
| ❑ S-707 | Love Country Style | 1971 | 12.00 |
| ❑ S-726 | Volcanic Action of My Soul | 1971 | 12.00 |
| ❑ H-731 [(2)] | A 25th Anniversary in Show Business Salute to Ray Charles | 1971 | 15.00 |
| ❑ X-755 | A Message from the People | 1972 | 12.00 |
| ❑ X-765 | Through the Eyes of Love | 1972 | 12.00 |
| ❑ X-781/2 [(2)] | All-Time Great Country & Western Hits | 1973 | 15.00 |
| ❑ QBO-91036 [(2)M] | The Ray Charles Story | 1967 | 30.00 |
| *—Capitol Record Club exclusive* | | | |
| ❑ SQBO-91036 [(2)S] | The Ray Charles Story | 1967 | 25.00 |
| *—Capitol Record Club exclusive* | | | |
| ❑ ST-91233 [S] | Ray Charles Invites You to Listen | 1967 | 15.00 |
| *—Capitol Record Club edition* | | | |
| ABC IMPULSE! | | | |
| ❑ AS-2 [S] | Genius + Soul = Jazz | 1968 | 12.00 |
| ABC-PARAMOUNT | | | |
| ❑ 335 [M] | The Genius Hits the Road | 1960 | 20.00 |
| ❑ S-335 [S] | The Genius Hits the Road | 1960 | 30.00 |
| ❑ 355 [M] | Dedicated to You | 1961 | 20.00 |
| ❑ S-355 [S] | Dedicated to You | 1961 | 30.00 |
| ❑ 410 [M] | Modern Sounds in Country and Western Music | 1962 | 25.00 |
| ❑ S-410 [S] | Modern Sounds in Country and Western Music | 1962 | 30.00 |
| ❑ 415 [M] | Ray Charles' Greatest Hits | 1962 | 20.00 |
| ❑ S-415 [S] | Ray Charles' Greatest Hits | 1962 | 25.00 |
| ❑ 435 [M] | Modern Sounds in Country and Western Music (Volume Two) | 1962 | 20.00 |
| ❑ S-435 [S] | Modern Sounds in Country and Western Music (Volume Two) | 1962 | 25.00 |
| ❑ 465 [M] | Ingredients in a Recipe for Soul | 1963 | 20.00 |
| ❑ S-465 [S] | Ingredients in a Recipe for Soul | 1963 | 25.00 |
| ❑ 480 [M] | Sweet & Sour Tears | 1964 | 20.00 |
| ❑ S-480 [S] | Sweet & Sour Tears | 1964 | 25.00 |
| ❑ 495 [M] | Have a Smile with Me | 1964 | 20.00 |
| ❑ S-495 [S] | Have a Smile with Me | 1964 | 25.00 |

| Number | Title (A Side/B Side) | Yr | NM |
|---|---|---|---|
| ❑ 500 [M] | Ray Charles Live in Concert | 1965 | 15.00 |
| ❑ S-500 [S] | Ray Charles Live in Concert | 1965 | 20.00 |
| ❑ 520 [M] | Together Again | 196? | 15.00 |
| *—Retitled version of "Country and Western Meets Rhythm and Blues"* | | | |
| ❑ 520 [M] | Country & Western Meets Rhythm & Blues | 1965 | 15.00 |
| ❑ S-520 [S] | Together Again | 196? | 20.00 |
| *—Retitled version of "Country and Western Meets Rhythm and Blues"* | | | |
| ❑ S-520 [S] | Country & Western Meets Rhythm & Blues | 1965 | 20.00 |
| ❑ 544 [M] | Crying Time | 1966 | 15.00 |
| ❑ S-544 [S] | Crying Time | 1966 | 20.00 |
| ❑ 550 [M] | Ray's Moods | 1966 | 15.00 |
| ❑ S-550 [S] | Ray's Moods | 1966 | 20.00 |
| ❑ ST-90144 [S] | Ray Charles Live in Concert | 1965 | 20.00 |
| *—Capitol Record Club edition* | | | |
| ❑ T-90144 [M] | Ray Charles Live in Concert | 1965 | 20.00 |
| *—Capitol Record Club edition* | | | |
| ❑ ST-90625 [S] | Crying Time | 1966 | 20.00 |
| *—Capitol Record Club edition* | | | |
| ❑ T-90625 [M] | Crying Time | 1966 | 20.00 |
| *—Capitol Record Club edition* | | | |
| ❑ ST-90847 [S] | Together Again | 1966 | 25.00 |
| *—Capitol Record Club edition* | | | |
| ❑ ST-90929 [S] | Ray's Moods | 1966 | 25.00 |
| *—Capitol Record Club edition* | | | |
| ATLANTIC | | | |
| ❑ SD 2-503 [(2)] | Ray Charles Live | 1973 | 15.00 |
| ❑ 2-900 [(2)M] | The Ray Charles Story | 1962 | 40.00 |
| ❑ 1259 [M] | The Great Ray Charles | 1957 | 50.00 |
| *—Black label* | | | |
| ❑ 1259 [M] | The Great Ray Charles | 1960 | 25.00 |
| *—Red and white label, white fan logo on right* | | | |
| ❑ 1259 [M] | The Great Ray Charles | 1962 | 20.00 |
| *—Red and white label, black fan logo on right* | | | |
| ❑ SD 1259 [S] | The Great Ray Charles | 1959 | 50.00 |
| *—Green label* | | | |
| ❑ SD 1259 [S] | The Great Ray Charles | 1960 | 25.00 |
| *—Blue and green label, white fan logo on right* | | | |
| ❑ SD 1259 [S] | The Great Ray Charles | 1962 | 20.00 |
| *—Blue and green label, black fan logo on right* | | | |
| ❑ 1289 [M] | Ray Charles at Newport | 1958 | 50.00 |
| *—Black label* | | | |
| ❑ 1289 [M] | Ray Charles at Newport | 1960 | 25.00 |
| *—Red and white label, white fan logo on right* | | | |

| Number | Title (A Side/B Side) | Yr | NM |
|---|---|---|---|
| ❑ 1289 [M] | Ray Charles at Newport | 1962 | 20.00 |
| *—Red and white label, black fan logo on right* | | | |
| ❑ SD 1289 [S] | Ray Charles at Newport | 1959 | 50.00 |
| *—Green label* | | | |
| ❑ SD 1289 [S] | Ray Charles at Newport | 1960 | 25.00 |
| *—Blue and green label, white fan logo on right* | | | |
| ❑ SD 1289 [S] | Ray Charles at Newport | 1962 | 20.00 |
| *—Blue and green label, black fan logo on right* | | | |
| ❑ 1312 [M] | The Genius of Ray Charles | 1960 | 25.00 |
| *—Red and white label, white fan logo on right* | | | |
| ❑ 1312 [M] | The Genius of Ray Charles | 1960 | 40.00 |
| *—Black label* | | | |
| ❑ 1312 [M] | The Genius of Ray Charles | 1960 | 40.00 |
| *—White "bullseye" label* | | | |
| ❑ 1312 [M] | The Genius of Ray Charles | 1962 | 20.00 |
| *—Red and white label, black fan logo on right* | | | |
| ❑ SD 1312 [S] | The Genius of Ray Charles | 1960 | 25.00 |
| *—Blue and green label, white fan logo on right* | | | |
| ❑ SD 1312 [S] | The Genius of Ray Charles | 1960 | 50.00 |
| *—Green label* | | | |
| ❑ SD 1312 [S] | The Genius of Ray Charles | 1960 | 50.00 |
| *—White "bullseye" label* | | | |
| ❑ SD 1312 [S] | The Genius of Ray Charles | 1962 | 20.00 |
| *—Blue and green label, black fan logo on right* | | | |
| ❑ SD 1312 [S] | The Genius of Ray Charles | 1968 | 20.00 |
| *—Brown and purple label* | | | |
| ❑ 1369 [M] | The Genius After Hours | 1961 | 25.00 |
| *—Red and white label, white fan logo on right* | | | |
| ❑ 1369 [M] | The Genius After Hours | 1962 | 20.00 |
| *—Red and white label, black fan logo on right* | | | |
| ❑ SD 1369 [S] | The Genius After Hours | 1961 | 30.00 |
| *—Blue and green label, white fan logo on right* | | | |
| ❑ SD 1369 [S] | The Genius After Hours | 1962 | 25.00 |
| *—Blue and green label, black fan logo on right* | | | |
| ❑ SD 1543 | The Best of Ray Charles | 1970 | 12.00 |
| ❑ 3700 [(6)] | Ray Charles: A Life in Music | 198? | 50.00 |
| ❑ SD 7101 [S] | The Great Hits of Ray Charles Recorded on 8-Track Stereo | 1966 | 25.00 |
| ❑ 8006 [M] | Ray Charles (Rock and Roll) | 1957 | 90.00 |
| *—Black label* | | | |
| ❑ 8006 [M] | Ray Charles (Rock and Roll) | 1960 | 25.00 |
| *—Red and white label, white fan logo on right* | | | |
| ❑ 8006 [M] | Hallelujah! I Love Her So | 1962 | 20.00 |
| *—Red and white label, black fan logo on right; retitled version* | | | |
| ❑ 8025 [M] | Yes, Indeed! | 1958 | 50.00 |
| *—Black label; cover has screaming girls* | | | |
| ❑ 8025 [M] | Yes, Indeed! | 1960 | 25.00 |
| *—Red and white label, white fan logo on right; cover has screaming girls* | | | |
| ❑ 8025 [M] | Yes, Indeed! | 1962 | 20.00 |
| *—Red and white label, black fan logo on right; cover has Ray on it* | | | |
| ❑ 8029 [M] | What'd I Say | 1959 | 50.00 |
| *—Black label* | | | |
| ❑ 8029 [M] | What'd I Say | 1960 | 25.00 |
| *—Red and white label, white fan logo on right* | | | |
| ❑ 8029 [M] | What'd I Say | 1960 | 40.00 |
| *—White "bullseye" label* | | | |
| ❑ 8029 [M] | What'd I Say | 1962 | 20.00 |
| *—Red and white label, black fan logo on right* | | | |
| ❑ 8039 [M] | Ray Charles In Person | 1960 | 25.00 |
| *—Red and white label, white fan logo on right* | | | |
| ❑ 8039 [M] | Ray Charles In Person | 1960 | 40.00 |
| *—Black label* | | | |
| ❑ 8039 [M] | Ray Charles In Person | 1962 | 20.00 |
| *—Red and white label, black fan logo on right* | | | |
| ❑ 8052 [M] | The Genius Sings the Blues | 1961 | 25.00 |
| *—Red and white label, white fan logo on right* | | | |
| ❑ 8052 [M] | The Genius Sings the Blues | 1962 | 20.00 |
| *—Red and white label, black fan logo on right* | | | |
| ❑ 8054 [M] | Do the Twist! | 1961 | 25.00 |
| *—Red and white label, white fan logo on right* | | | |
| ❑ 8054 [M] | Do the Twist! | 1962 | 20.00 |
| *—Red and white label, black fan logo on right* | | | |
| ❑ 8063 [M] | The Ray Charles Story, Volume 1 | 1962 | 20.00 |
| ❑ 8064 [M] | The Ray Charles Story, Volume 2 | 1962 | 20.00 |
| ❑ 8083 [M] | The Ray Charles Story, Volume 3 | 1963 | 20.00 |
| ❑ 8094 [M] | The Ray Charles Story, Volume 4 | 1964 | 20.00 |
| ❑ SD 8094 [S] | The Ray Charles Story, Volume 4 | 1964 | 25.00 |
| ❑ SD 19142 | True to Life | 1977 | 12.00 |
| ❑ SD 19199 | Love and Peace | 1978 | 12.00 |
| ❑ SD 19251 | Ain't It So | 1979 | 12.00 |
| ❑ SD 19281 | Brother Ray Is At It Again | 1980 | 12.00 |
| ❑ 90464 | The Genius After Hours | 1986 | 10.00 |
| *—Reissue* | | | |

BARONET

| Number | Title (A Side/B Side) | Yr | NM |
|---|---|---|---|
| ❑ B-111 [M] | The Artistry of Ray Charles | 196? | 12.00 |
| ❑ BS-111 [R] | The Artistry of Ray Charles | 196? | 10.00 |
| ❑ B-117 [M] | The Great Ray Charles | 196? | 12.00 |
| ❑ BS-117 [R] | The Great Ray Charles | 196? | 10.00 |

BLUESWAY

| Number | Title (A Side/B Side) | Yr | NM |
|---|---|---|---|
| ❑ 6053 | The Genius Live | 1973 | 12.00 |

COLUMBIA

| Number | Title (A Side/B Side) | Yr | NM |
|---|---|---|---|
| ❑ AS 1920 [DJ] | Friendship Radio Show | 1984 | 20.00 |
| ❑ FC 38293 | Wish You Were Here Tonight | 1983 | 10.00 |
| ❑ PC 38293 | Wish You Were Here Tonight | 1985 | 8.00 |
| *—Budget-line reissue* | | | |
| ❑ FC 38990 | Do I Ever Cross Your Mind | 1984 | 10.00 |
| ❑ FC 39415 | Friendship | 1985 | 10.00 |
| ❑ FC 40125 | The Spirit of Christmas | 1985 | 10.00 |
| ❑ FC 40338 | From the Pages of My Mind | 1986 | 10.00 |
| ❑ FC 45062 | Seven Spanish Angels and Other Hits (1982-1986) | 1989 | 12.00 |

CORONET

| Number | Title (A Side/B Side) | Yr | NM |
|---|---|---|---|
| ❑ CX-173 [M] | Ray Charles | 196? | 12.00 |
| ❑ CXS-173 [R] | Ray Charles | 196? | 10.00 |

CROSSOVER

| Number | Title (A Side/B Side) | Yr | NM |
|---|---|---|---|
| ❑ 9000 | Come Live with Me | 1974 | 12.00 |
| ❑ 9005 | Renaissance | 1975 | 12.00 |
| ❑ 9007 | My Kind of Jazz, Part 3 | 1976 | 12.00 |

DCC COMPACT CLASSICS

| Number | Title (A Side/B Side) | Yr | NM |
|---|---|---|---|
| ❑ LPZ-2012 | Greatest Country and Western Hits | 1995 | 100.00 |
| *—Audiophile vinyl* | | | |

DUNHILL COMPACT CLASSICS

| Number | Title (A Side/B Side) | Yr | NM |
|---|---|---|---|
| ❑ DZL-038 | Genius + Soul = Jazz | 1988 | 15.00 |
| *—Clear vinyl reissue* | | | |

EVEREST ARCHIVE OF FOLK & JAZZ

| Number | Title (A Side/B Side) | Yr | NM |
|---|---|---|---|
| ❑ 244 | Ray Charles | 1970 | 12.00 |
| ❑ 292 | Ray Charles, Vol. 2 | 197? | 10.00 |
| ❑ 358 | Rockin' with Ray | 1979 | 10.00 |

HOLLYWOOD

| Number | Title (A Side/B Side) | Yr | NM |
|---|---|---|---|
| ❑ 504 [M] | The Original Ray Charles | 1959 | 150.00 |
| ❑ 505 [M] | The Fabuolus Ray Charles | 1959 | 150.00 |

IMPULSE!

| Number | Title (A Side/B Side) | Yr | NM |
|---|---|---|---|
| ❑ A-2 [M] | Genius + Soul = Jazz | 1961 | 25.00 |
| ❑ AS-2 [S] | Genius + Soul = Jazz | 1961 | 30.00 |

INTERMEDIA

| Number | Title (A Side/B Side) | Yr | NM |
|---|---|---|---|
| ❑ QS-5013 | Goin' Down Slow | 198? | 10.00 |

LONGINES SYMPHONETTE

| Number | Title (A Side/B Side) | Yr | NM |
|---|---|---|---|
| ❑ 95647 [(5)] | The Greatest Hits of Ray Charles | 1974 | 40.00 |

PAIR

| Number | Title (A Side/B Side) | Yr | NM |
|---|---|---|---|
| ❑ PDL2-1139 [(2)] | The Real Ray Charles | 1986 | 12.00 |

PREMIER

| Number | Title (A Side/B Side) | Yr | NM |
|---|---|---|---|
| ❑ PM 2004 [M] | The Great Ray Charles | 196? | 12.00 |
| ❑ PS 2004 [R] | The Great Ray Charles | 196? | 10.00 |
| ❑ PS-6001 [R] | Fantastic Ray Charles | 196? | 10.00 |

RHINO

| Number | Title (A Side/B Side) | Yr | NM |
|---|---|---|---|
| ❑ R1-70097 | Greatest Hits, Volume 1 | 1988 | 10.00 |
| ❑ R1-70098 | Greatest Hits, Volume 2 | 1988 | 10.00 |
| ❑ R1-70099 | Modern Sounds in Country and Western Music | 1988 | 10.00 |

TANGERINE

| Number | Title (A Side/B Side) | Yr | NM |
|---|---|---|---|
| ❑ 1512 | My Kind of Jazz | 1970 | 12.00 |
| ❑ 1516 | My Kind of Jazz No. II | 1973 | 12.00 |

WARNER BROS.

| Number | Title (A Side/B Side) | Yr | NM |
|---|---|---|---|
| ❑ 26343 | Would You Believe? | 1990 | 15.00 |

## CHARLES, RAY / HARRY BELAFONTE

CORONET

| Number | Title (A Side/B Side) | Yr | NM |
|---|---|---|---|
| ❑ CX-203 [M] | The Greatest Ever | 196? | 12.00 |
| ❑ CXS-203 [R] | The Greatest Ever | 196? | 10.00 |

## CHARLES, RAY, AND BETTY CARTER

ABC

| Number | Title (A Side/B Side) | Yr | NM |
|---|---|---|---|
| ❑ S-385 [S] | Ray Charles and Betty Carter | 1967 | 20.00 |
| *—Reissue of ABC-Paramount ABCS-385* | | | |

ABC-PARAMOUNT

| Number | Title (A Side/B Side) | Yr | NM |
|---|---|---|---|
| ❑ ABC-385 [M] | Ray Charles and Betty Carter | 1961 | 60.00 |
| ❑ ABCS-385 [S] | Ray Charles and Betty Carter | 1961 | 80.00 |

DCC COMPACT CLASSICS

| Number | Title (A Side/B Side) | Yr | NM |
|---|---|---|---|
| ❑ LPZ-2005 | Ray Charles and Betty Carter | 1995 | 150.00 |
| *—Audiophile vinyl* | | | |

DUNHILL COMPACT CLASSICS

| Number | Title (A Side/B Side) | Yr | NM |
|---|---|---|---|
| ❑ DZL-039 | Ray Charles and Betty Carter | 1988 | 15.00 |
| *—Clear vinyl reissue* | | | |

## CHARLES, RAY/IVORY JOE HUNTER/JIMMY RUSHING

DESIGN

| Number | Title (A Side/B Side) | Yr | NM |
|---|---|---|---|
| ❑ DLP-909 [M] | Three of a Kind | 196? | 12.00 |
| ❑ DLS-909 [R] | Three of a Kind | 196? | 10.00 |

## CHARLES, RAY, AND MILT JACKSON

ATLANTIC

| Number | Title (A Side/B Side) | Yr | NM |
|---|---|---|---|
| ❑ 1279 [M] | Soul Brothers | 1958 | 50.00 |
| *—Black label* | | | |
| ❑ 1279 [M] | Soul Brothers | 1960 | 25.00 |
| *—Red and white label, white fan logo on right* | | | |
| ❑ 1279 [M] | Soul Brothers | 1962 | 20.00 |
| *—Red and white label, black fan logo on right* | | | |
| ❑ SD 1279 [S] | Soul Brothers | 1959 | 50.00 |
| *—Green label* | | | |
| ❑ SD 1279 [S] | Soul Brothers | 1960 | 25.00 |
| *—Blue and green label, white fan logo on right* | | | |
| ❑ SD 1279 [S] | Soul Brothers | 1962 | 20.00 |
| *—Blue and green label, black fan logo on right* | | | |
| ❑ 1360 [M] | Soul Meeting | 1961 | 25.00 |
| *—Red and white label, white fan logo on right* | | | |
| ❑ 1360 [M] | Soul Meeting | 1962 | 20.00 |
| *—Red and white label, black fan logo on right* | | | |
| ❑ SD 1360 [S] | Soul Meeting | 1961 | 30.00 |
| *—Blue and green label, white fan logo on right* | | | |
| ❑ SD 1360 [S] | Soul Meeting | 1962 | 25.00 |
| *—Blue and green label, black fan logo on right* | | | |

## CHARLES, RAY, AND CLEO LAINE

RCA VICTOR

| Number | Title (A Side/B Side) | Yr | NM |
|---|---|---|---|
| ❑ CPL2-1831 [(2)] | Porgy & Bess | 1976 | 15.00 |
| ❑ DJL1-2163 | Porgy & Bess | 1976 | 20.00 |
| *—Promo-only excerpts from 2-record set* | | | |

## CHARLES, TEDDY

ATLANTIC

| Number | Title (A Side/B Side) | Yr | NM |
|---|---|---|---|
| ❑ 1229 [M] | The Teddy Charles Tentet | 1956 | 80.00 |
| *—Black label* | | | |
| ❑ 1229 [M] | The Teddy Charles Tentet | 1961 | 30.00 |
| *—Multicolor label with white "fan" logo* | | | |
| ❑ 1274 [M] | Word from Bird | 1956 | 80.00 |
| *—Black label* | | | |
| ❑ 1274 [M] | Word from Bird | 1961 | 30.00 |
| *—Multicolor label with white "fan" logo* | | | |

BETHLEHEM

| Number | Title (A Side/B Side) | Yr | NM |
|---|---|---|---|
| ❑ BCP-6032 [M] | Salute to Hamp | 1959 | 50.00 |
| ❑ BCP-6044 [M] | On Campus — Ivy League Jazz Concert | 1960 | 50.00 |

ELEKTRA

| Number | Title (A Side/B Side) | Yr | NM |
|---|---|---|---|
| ❑ EKL-136 [M] | Vibe-Rant | 1957 | 60.00 |

JOSIE

| Number | Title (A Side/B Side) | Yr | NM |
|---|---|---|---|
| ❑ JJS-3505 [S] | Teddy Charles Trio Plays Duke Ellington | 1963 | 30.00 |
| ❑ JOZ-3505 [M] | Teddy Charles Trio Plays Duke Ellington | 1963 | 30.00 |

JUBILEE

| Number | Title (A Side/B Side) | Yr | NM |
|---|---|---|---|
| ❑ JGS-1047 [S] | Three for Duke | 1959 | 40.00 |
| ❑ JLP-1047 [M] | Three for Duke | 1957 | 50.00 |

NEW JAZZ

| Number | Title (A Side/B Side) | Yr | NM |
|---|---|---|---|
| ❑ NJLP-1106 [10] | Teddy Charles New Directions Quartet | 1955 | 600.00 |

PRESTIGE

| Number | Title (A Side/B Side) | Yr | NM |
|---|---|---|---|
| ❑ PRLP-132 [10] | Teddy Charles and His Trio | 1952 | 400.00 |
| ❑ PRLP-143 [10] | New Directions Vol. 1 | 1953 | 300.00 |
| ❑ PRLP-150 [10] | New Directions Vol. 2 | 1953 | 300.00 |
| ❑ PRLP-164 [10] | New Directions Vol. 3 | 1953 | 300.00 |
| ❑ PRLP-169 [10] | New Directions Vol. 4 | 1954 | 300.00 |
| ❑ PRLP-178 [10] | New Directions Vol. 5 | 1954 | 300.00 |
| *—With Bob Brookmeyer* | | | |
| ❑ PRLP-206 [10] | Teddy Charles New Directions Quartet | 1955 | 300.00 |
| *—Reissue of New Jazz 1106* | | | |
| ❑ PRLP-7028 [M] | Collaboration: West | 1956 | 100.00 |
| *—Yellow label with 446 W. 50th St. address* | | | |
| ❑ PRLP-7028 [M] | Collaboration: West | 196? | 30.00 |
| *—Blue label, trident logo on right* | | | |
| ❑ PRLP-7078 [M] | Evolution | 1957 | 100.00 |
| *—Yellow label* | | | |
| ❑ PRLP-7078 [M] | Evolution | 196? | 30.00 |
| *—Blue label, trident logo on right* | | | |

SAVOY

| Number | Title (A Side/B Side) | Yr | NM |
|---|---|---|---|
| ❑ MG-12174 [M] | The Vibe-Rant Quintet | 1961 | 30.00 |
| *—Reissue of Elektra LP* | | | |

UNITED ARTISTS

| Number | Title (A Side/B Side) | Yr | NM |
|---|---|---|---|
| ❑ UAL-3365 [M] | Russia Goes Jazz | 1964 | 25.00 |
| ❑ UAS-6365 [S] | Russia Goes Jazz | 1964 | 30.00 |

WARWICK

| Number | Title (A Side/B Side) | Yr | NM |
|---|---|---|---|
| ❑ W-2033 [M] | Jazz in the Garden of the Museum of Modern Art | 1960 | 50.00 |

## CHARLES RIVER VALLEY BOYS, THE

ELEKTRA

| Number | Title (A Side/B Side) | Yr | NM |
|---|---|---|---|
| ❑ EKL-4006 [M] | Beatle Country | 1967 | 20.00 |
| ❑ EKS-74006 [S] | Beatle Country | 1967 | 25.00 |

## CHARLESTON CITY ALL-STARS

GRAND AWARD

| Number | Title (A Side/B Side) | Yr | NM |
|---|---|---|---|
| ❑ GA 201 SD [S] | The Roaring 20's | 1958 | 20.00 |
| ❑ GA 211 SD [S] | The Roaring 20's, Volume 2 | 1958 | 20.00 |
| ❑ GA 229 SD [S] | The Roaring 20's, Volume 3 | 1958 | 20.00 |

## CHASE

EPIC

| Number | Title (A Side/B Side) | Yr | NM |
|---|---|---|---|
| ❑ E 30472 | Chase | 1971 | 12.00 |
| ❑ EQ 30472 [Q] | Chase | 1973 | 20.00 |
| ❑ KE 31097 | Ennea | 1972 | 12.00 |
| ❑ EQ 32572 [Q] | Pure Music | 1974 | 20.00 |
| ❑ KE 32572 | Pure Music | 1974 | 12.00 |
| ❑ EG 33737 [(2)] | Chase/Ennea | 1976 | 15.00 |

## CHASE, LINCOLN

LIBERTY

| Number | Title (A Side/B Side) | Yr | NM |
|---|---|---|---|
| ❑ LRP-3076 [M] | The Explosive Lincoln Chase | 1958 | 50.00 |

## CHEAP TRICK

**EPIC**

| Number | Title (A Side/B Side) | Yr | NM |
|---|---|---|---|
| ❑ AS 518 [DJ] | From Tokyo to You | 1979 | 30.00 |
| *—Promo-only sampler from Cheap Trick at Budokan* | | | |
| ❑ PE 34400 | Cheap Trick | 1976 | 12.00 |
| *—Originals have orange labels* | | | |
| ❑ PE 34400 | Cheap Trick | 1979 | 8.00 |
| *—Later editions have dark blue labels; may or may not have bar code on back* | | | |
| ❑ JE 34884 | In Color | 1977 | 12.00 |
| *—Originals have orange labels* | | | |
| ❑ PE 34884 | In Color | 1979 | 8.00 |
| *—Later editions have dark blue labels; may or may not have bar code on back* | | | |
| ❑ JE 35312 | Heaven Tonight | 1978 | 12.00 |
| *—Originals have orange labels* | | | |
| ❑ PE 35312 | Heaven Tonight | 1979 | 8.00 |
| *—Later editions have dark blue labels; may or may not have bar code* | | | |
| ❑ FE 35773 | Dream Police | 1979 | 10.00 |
| *—Despite lower number, this came out after Epic 35795* | | | |
| ❑ PE 35773 | Dream Police | 1984 | 8.00 |
| ❑ FE 35795 | Cheap Trick at Budokan | 1979 | 10.00 |
| *—Dark blue label; some copies came with gold-colored obi (add 100% if there) and all came with booklet (deduct 20% if missing)* | | | |
| ❑ FE 35795 | Cheap Trick at Budokan | 1979 | 12.00 |
| *—Orange label; came with gold-colored obi (add 5/6 if there) and booklet (deduct 1/6 if missing)* | | | |
| ❑ FE 35795 [DJ] | Cheap Trick at Budokan | 1979 | 20.00 |
| *—White label promo* | | | |
| ❑ PE 35795 | Cheap Trick at Budokan | 1984 | 8.00 |
| ❑ FE 36498 | All Shook Up | 1980 | 10.00 |
| ❑ PE 36498 | All Shook Up | 1984 | 8.00 |
| ❑ FE 38021 | One on One | 1982 | 10.00 |
| ❑ PE 38021 | One on One | 1984 | 8.00 |
| ❑ PE 38541 [EP] | Found All the Parts | 1983 | 8.00 |
| *—Six-song reissue of Epic/Nu-Disk release on 12-inch LP* | | | |
| ❑ FE 38794 | Next Position Please | 1983 | 10.00 |
| ❑ PE 38794 | Next Position Please | 1985 | 8.00 |
| ❑ FE 39592 | Standing on the Edge | 1985 | 10.00 |
| ❑ PE 39592 | Standing on the Edge | 1987 | 8.00 |
| ❑ FE 40405 | The Doctor | 1986 | 10.00 |
| ❑ PE 40405 | The Doctor | 1987 | 8.00 |
| *—Reissue with new prefix on cover* | | | |
| ❑ OE 40922 | Lap of Luxury | 1988 | 10.00 |
| ❑ E 46013 | Busted | 1990 | 12.00 |

**EPIC/NU-DISK**

| Number | Title (A Side/B Side) | Yr | NM |
|---|---|---|---|
| ❑ 4E 36453 [10] | Found All the Parts | 1980 | 15.00 |
| *—10-inch, four-track EP with bonus 45, "Everything Works If You Let It" (AE7 1206)* | | | |

## CHECKER, CHUBBY

**ABKCO**

| Number | Title (A Side/B Side) | Yr | NM |
|---|---|---|---|
| ❑ 4219 [(2)] | Chubby Checker's Greatest Hits | 1972 | 20.00 |

**EVEREST**

| Number | Title (A Side/B Side) | Yr | NM |
|---|---|---|---|
| ❑ 4111 | Chubby Checker's Greatest Hits | 1981 | 12.00 |

**MCA**

| Number | Title (A Side/B Side) | Yr | NM |
|---|---|---|---|
| ❑ 5291 | The Change Has Come | 1982 | 10.00 |

**PARKWAY**

| Number | Title (A Side/B Side) | Yr | NM |
|---|---|---|---|
| ❑ P 7001 [M] | Twist with Chubby Checker | 1960 | 40.00 |
| *—All-orange label* | | | |
| ❑ P 7001 [M] | Twist with Chubby Checker | 1962 | 30.00 |
| *—Orange and yellow label* | | | |
| ❑ P 7002 [M] | For Twisters Only | 1960 | 40.00 |
| *—All-orange label* | | | |
| ❑ P 7002 [M] | For Twisters Only | 1962 | 30.00 |
| *—Orange and yellow label* | | | |
| ❑ P 7003 [M] | It's Pony Time | 1961 | 40.00 |
| *—All-orange label* | | | |
| ❑ P 7003 [M] | It's Pony Time | 1962 | 30.00 |
| *—Orange and yellow label* | | | |
| ❑ P 7004 [M] | Let's Twist Again | 1961 | 40.00 |
| *—All-orange label* | | | |
| ❑ P 7004 [M] | Let's Twist Again | 1962 | 30.00 |
| *—Orange and yellow label* | | | |
| ❑ P 7007 [M] | Your Twist Party | 1961 | 40.00 |
| *—All-orange label* | | | |
| ❑ P 7007 [M] | Your Twist Party | 1962 | 30.00 |
| *—Orange and yellow label* | | | |
| ❑ P 7008 [M] | Twistin' Round the World | 1962 | 30.00 |
| ❑ SP 7008 [B] | Twistin' Round the World | 1962 | 40.00 |
| ❑ P 7009 [M] | For Teen Twisters Only | 1962 | 30.00 |
| ❑ SP 7009 [S] | For Teen Twisters Only | 1962 | 40.00 |
| ❑ P 7014 [M] | All the Hits (For Your Dancin' Party) | 1962 | 30.00 |
| ❑ P 7020 [M] | Limbo Party | 1962 | 30.00 |
| ❑ SP 7020 [S] | Limbo Party | 1962 | 40.00 |
| ❑ P 7022 [M] | Chubby Checker's Biggest Hits | 1962 | 30.00 |
| ❑ SP 7022 [R] | Chubby Checker's Biggest Hits | 1962 | 30.00 |
| ❑ P 7026 [M] | Chubby Checker In Person | 1963 | 30.00 |
| ❑ SP 7026 [S] | Chubby Checker In Person | 1963 | 40.00 |
| *—The above record is labeled "Twist It Up"* | | | |
| ❑ P 7027 [M] | Let's Limbo Some More | 1963 | 30.00 |
| ❑ SP 7027 [S] | Let's Limbo Some More | 1963 | 40.00 |
| ❑ P 7030 [M] | Beach Party | 1963 | 30.00 |
| ❑ SP 7030 [S] | Beach Party | 1963 | 40.00 |

Chubby Checker, *Let's Twist Again,* Parkway P 7004, 1961, mono, all-orange label $40, orange and yellow label $30.

| Number | Title (A Side/B Side) | Yr | NM |
|---|---|---|---|
| ❑ P 7036 [M] | Chubby Checker With Sy Oliver and His Orchestra | 1964 | 30.00 |
| ❑ SP 7036 [S] | Chubby Checker With Sy Oliver and His Orchestra | 1964 | 40.00 |
| ❑ P 7040 [M] | Folk Album | 1964 | 30.00 |
| ❑ SP 7040 [S] | Folk Album | 1964 | 40.00 |
| ❑ P 7045 [M] | Discotheque | 1965 | 30.00 |
| ❑ SP 7045 [S] | Discotheque | 1965 | 40.00 |
| ❑ P 7048 [M] | Chubby Checker's Eighteen Golden Hits | 1966 | 30.00 |
| ❑ SP 7048 [P] | Chubby Checker's Eighteen Golden Hits | 1966 | 40.00 |

## CHECKMATES, THE

**JUSTICE**

| Number | Title (A Side/B Side) | Yr | NM |
|---|---|---|---|
| ❑ JLP-149 | The Checkmates | 1966 | 400.00 |

## CHECKMATES LTD., THE

**A&M**

| Number | Title (A Side/B Side) | Yr | NM |
|---|---|---|---|
| ❑ SP-4183 | Love Is All I Have to Give | 1969 | 25.00 |

**CAPITOL**

| Number | Title (A Side/B Side) | Yr | NM |
|---|---|---|---|
| ❑ ST 2840 [S] | Live at Caesar's Palace | 1968 | 20.00 |
| ❑ T 2840 [M] | Live at Caesar's Palace | 1968 | 30.00 |

**FANTASY**

| Number | Title (A Side/B Side) | Yr | NM |
|---|---|---|---|
| ❑ 9541 | We Got the Moves | 1978 | 15.00 |

## CHELSEA

Future Kiss member Peter Criss (as "Peter Cris") played drums on this LP.

**DECCA**

| Number | Title (A Side/B Side) | Yr | NM |
|---|---|---|---|
| ❑ DL 75262 | The Chelsea Album | 1972 | 150.00 |

## CHER

**ATCO**

| Number | Title (A Side/B Side) | Yr | NM |
|---|---|---|---|
| ❑ 33-298 [M] | 3614 Jackson Highway | 1969 | 30.00 |
| *—White label promo only (no stock copies issued in mono)* | | | |
| ❑ SD 33-298 [S] | 3614 Jackson Highway | 1969 | 20.00 |

**CASABLANCA**

| Number | Title (A Side/B Side) | Yr | NM |
|---|---|---|---|
| ❑ NBLP-7133 | Take Me Home | 1979 | 10.00 |
| ❑ NBPIX-7133 [PD] | Take Me Home | 1979 | 50.00 |
| ❑ NBLP-7184 | Prisoner | 1980 | 10.00 |

**COLUMBIA**

| Number | Title (A Side/B Side) | Yr | NM |
|---|---|---|---|
| ❑ FC 38096 | I Paralyze | 1982 | 10.00 |

**GEFFEN**

| Number | Title (A Side/B Side) | Yr | NM |
|---|---|---|---|
| ❑ GHS 24164 | Cher | 1987 | 10.00 |
| ❑ GHS 24239 | Heart of Stone | 1989 | 10.00 |
| *—Later cover with larger picture of Cher and no rock* | | | |
| ❑ GHS 24239 | Heart of Stone | 1989 | 15.00 |
| *—Original cover with Cher in heart-shaped pose next to "skeleton rock"* | | | |

**IMPERIAL**

| Number | Title (A Side/B Side) | Yr | NM |
|---|---|---|---|
| ❑ LP-9292 [M] | All I Really Want to Do | 1965 | 20.00 |
| ❑ LP-9301 [M] | The Sonny Side of Cher | 1966 | 20.00 |
| ❑ LP-9320 [M] | Cher | 1966 | 15.00 |
| ❑ LP-9358 [M] | With Love — Cher | 1967 | 15.00 |
| ❑ LP-12292 [S] | All I Really Want to Do | 1965 | 25.00 |
| ❑ LP-12301 [S] | The Sonny Side of Cher | 1966 | 25.00 |
| ❑ LP-12320 [S] | Cher | 1966 | 20.00 |
| ❑ LP-12358 [S] | With Love — Cher | 1967 | 20.00 |
| ❑ LP-12373 [M] | Backstage | 1968 | 40.00 |
| *—Stereo cover with designate mono sticker attached; label is stock* | | | |
| ❑ LP-12373 [S] | Backstage | 1968 | 20.00 |
| ❑ LP-12406 | Cher's Golden Greats | 1968 | 20.00 |

**KAPP**

| Number | Title (A Side/B Side) | Yr | NM |
|---|---|---|---|
| ❑ KS-3649 | Gypsys, Tramps & Thieves | 1971 | 15.00 |
| *—Retitled version of above LP; red and orange swirl label* | | | |
| ❑ KS-3649 | Cher | 1971 | 20.00 |
| *—Original title of LP (without "Gypsys, Tramps & Thieves" title on front cover)* | | | |
| ❑ KRS-5514 | Foxy Lady | 1972 | 15.00 |
| ❑ KRS-5549 | Gypsys, Tramps & Thieves | 1972 | 15.00 |
| *—Reissue of 3649; black label* | | | |
| ❑ SW-94485 | Foxy Lady | 1972 | 20.00 |
| *—Capitol Record Club edition* | | | |

**LIBERTY**

| Number | Title (A Side/B Side) | Yr | NM |
|---|---|---|---|
| ❑ LN-10110 | The Very Best of Cher, Vol. 1 | 1981 | 8.00 |
| ❑ LN-10111 | The Very Best of Cher, Vol. 2 | 1981 | 8.00 |

**MCA**

| Number | Title (A Side/B Side) | Yr | NM |
|---|---|---|---|
| ❑ 624 | Cher | 197? | 10.00 |
| ❑ 2101 | Bittersweet White Light | 1973 | 12.00 |
| ❑ 2104 | Half-Breed | 1973 | 12.00 |
| ❑ 2113 | Dark Lady | 1974 | 12.00 |
| ❑ 2127 | Greatest Hits | 1974 | 12.00 |
| ❑ 37028 | Greatest Hits | 1981 | 8.00 |
| *—Reissue of MCA 2127* | | | |

**PICKWICK**

| Number | Title (A Side/B Side) | Yr | NM |
|---|---|---|---|
| ❑ SPC-3619 | This Is Cher | 1978 | 10.00 |

**SPRINGBOARD**

| Number | Title (A Side/B Side) | Yr | NM |
|---|---|---|---|
| ❑ SPB-4028 | Cher's Greatest Hits | 197? | 10.00 |

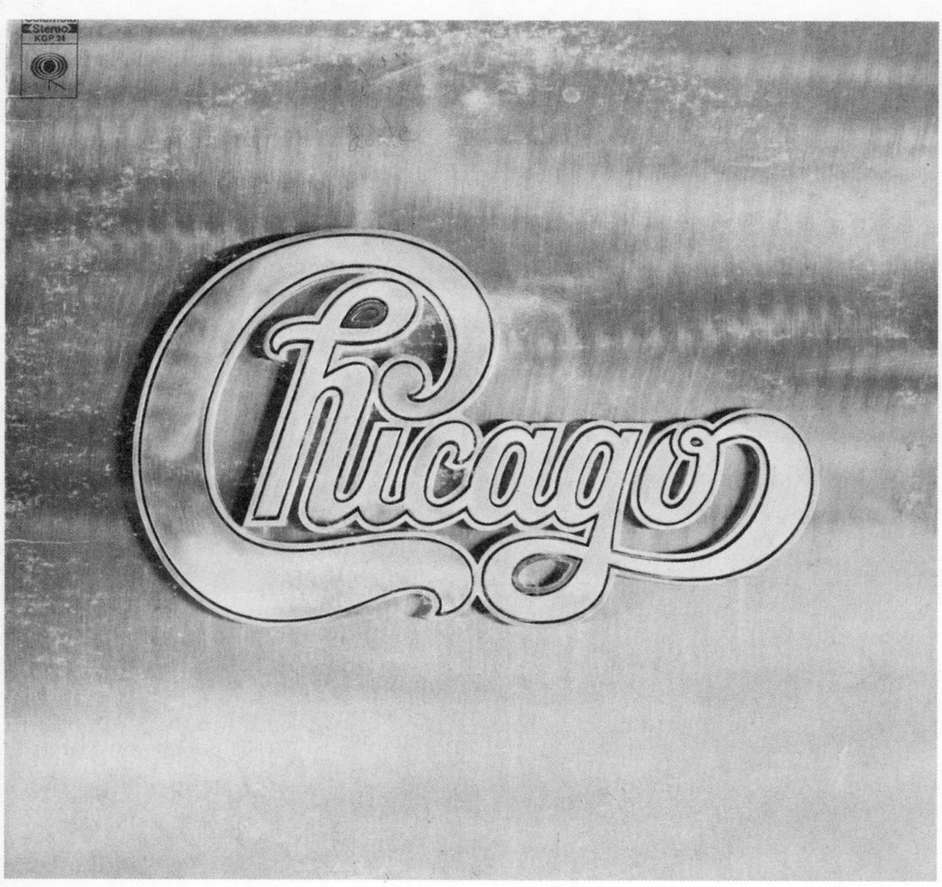


Chicago, *Chicago,* Columbia KGP 24, 1970, 2 records, red "360 Sound" labels, no "II" on records or spine, $40.

| Number | Title (A Side/B Side) | Yr | NM |
|---|---|---|---|
| ❑ SPB-4029 | Cher Sings the Hits | 197? | 10.00 |

**SUNSET**

| Number | Title (A Side/B Side) | Yr | NM |
|---|---|---|---|
| ❑ SUS-5276 | This Is Cher | 1970 | 15.00 |

**UNITED ARTISTS**

| Number | Title (A Side/B Side) | Yr | NM |
|---|---|---|---|
| ❑ UXS-88 [(2)] | Cher Superpak | 1971 | 20.00 |
| ❑ UXS-89 [(2)] | Cher Superpak, Vol. II | 1972 | 20.00 |

*—The above are reissues of Imperial recordings*

| Number | Title (A Side/B Side) | Yr | NM |
|---|---|---|---|
| ❑ UA-LA237-G | The Very Best of Cher | 1974 | 12.00 |
| ❑ UA-LA377-E | The Very Best of Cher | 1975 | 10.00 |
| ❑ UA-LA435-E | The Very Best of Cher, Vol. 2 | 1975 | 12.00 |

**WARNER BROS.**

| Number | Title (A Side/B Side) | Yr | NM |
|---|---|---|---|
| ❑ BS 2850 | Stars | 1975 | 12.00 |
| ❑ BS 2898 | I'd Rather Believe in You | 1976 | 12.00 |
| ❑ BS 3046 | Cherished | 1977 | 12.00 |

### CHEROKEE

**ABC**

| Number | Title (A Side/B Side) | Yr | NM |
|---|---|---|---|
| ❑ ABCS-719 | Cherokee | 1970 | 20.00 |

### CHERRY, DON

**COLUMBIA**

| Number | Title (A Side/B Side) | Yr | NM |
|---|---|---|---|
| ❑ CL 893 [M] | Swingin' for Two | 1956 | 25.00 |

**MONUMENT**

| Number | Title (A Side/B Side) | Yr | NM |
|---|---|---|---|
| ❑ MLP-8049 [M] | Don Cherry Smashes | 1966 | 12.00 |
| ❑ MLP-8075 [M] | There Goes My Everything | 1967 | 15.00 |
| ❑ 8601 [(2)] | The World of Don Cherry | 197? | 12.00 |

*—Reissue of 32334*

| Number | Title (A Side/B Side) | Yr | NM |
|---|---|---|---|
| ❑ SLP-18049 [S] | Don Cherry Smashes | 1966 | 15.00 |
| ❑ SLP-18075 [S] | There Goes My Everything | 1967 | 12.00 |
| ❑ SLP-18088 | Let It Be Me | 1968 | 12.00 |
| ❑ SLP-18109 | Take a Message to Mary | 1969 | 12.00 |
| ❑ SLP-18124 | Don Cherry | 1970 | 12.00 |
| ❑ KZG 32334 [(2)] | The World of Don Cherry | 1972 | 15.00 |

### CHERRY, DON (2)

Jazz trumpeter, also father of 1980s hitmaker Neneh Cherry and 1990s hitmaker Eagle-Eye Cherry.

**BASF**

| Number | Title (A Side/B Side) | Yr | NM |
|---|---|---|---|
| ❑ 20680 | Eternal Rhythm | 1972 | 30.00 |

**BLUE NOTE**

| Number | Title (A Side/B Side) | Yr | NM |
|---|---|---|---|
| ❑ BLP-4226 [M] | Complete Communion | 1966 | 50.00 |

*—"New York, USA" address on label*

| Number | Title (A Side/B Side) | Yr | NM |
|---|---|---|---|
| ❑ BLP-4247 [M] | Symphony for Improvisers | 1966 | 50.00 |

*—"New York, USA" address on label*

| Number | Title (A Side/B Side) | Yr | NM |
|---|---|---|---|
| ❑ BST-84226 [S] | Complete Communion | 1966 | 60.00 |

*—"New York, USA" address on label*

| Number | Title (A Side/B Side) | Yr | NM |
|---|---|---|---|
| ❑ BST-84247 [S] | Symphony for Improvisers | 1966 | 60.00 |

*—"New York, USA" address on label*

| Number | Title (A Side/B Side) | Yr | NM |
|---|---|---|---|
| ❑ BST-84311 | Where Is Brooklyn? | 1969 | 60.00 |

*—"A Division of Liberty Records" on label*

**INNER CITY**

| Number | Title (A Side/B Side) | Yr | NM |
|---|---|---|---|
| ❑ IC 1009 | Togetherness | 197? | 20.00 |

**JCOA**

| Number | Title (A Side/B Side) | Yr | NM |
|---|---|---|---|
| ❑ 1006 | Relativity Suite | 1974 | 50.00 |

**MOSAIC**

| Number | Title (A Side/B Side) | Yr | NM |
|---|---|---|---|
| ❑ MQ3-145 [(3)] | The Complete Blue Note Recordings of Don Cherry | 199? | 60.00 |

### CHERRY PEOPLE, THE

**HERITAGE**

| Number | Title (A Side/B Side) | Yr | NM |
|---|---|---|---|
| ❑ HT 35000 [M] | The Cherry People | 1968 | 40.00 |

*—Stereo cover with "Mono" and "DJ" stickers attached; all records appear to be white label promos*

| Number | Title (A Side/B Side) | Yr | NM |
|---|---|---|---|
| ❑ HTS 35000 [S] | The Cherry People | 1968 | 20.00 |

### CHESS, TUBBY, AND HIS CANDY STRIPE TWISTERS

**GRAND PRIX**

| Number | Title (A Side/B Side) | Yr | NM |
|---|---|---|---|
| ❑ K-187 [M] | Do the Twist | 1962 | 15.00 |
| ❑ KS-187 [S] | Do the Twist | 1962 | 20.00 |

### CHESTER, GARY

**DCP**

| Number | Title (A Side/B Side) | Yr | NM |
|---|---|---|---|
| ❑ DCL 3803 [M] | Yeah, Yeah, Yeah | 1964 | 20.00 |
| ❑ DCS 6803 [S] | Yeah, Yeah, Yeah | 1964 | 25.00 |

### CHEVALIER, MAURICE

**CAPITOL**

| Number | Title (A Side/B Side) | Yr | NM |
|---|---|---|---|
| ❑ T 10360 [M] | The Young Chevalier | 196? | 20.00 |

**EPIC**

| Number | Title (A Side/B Side) | Yr | NM |
|---|---|---|---|
| ❑ FXS 15117 | Maurice Chevalier at 80 | 1968 | 20.00 |

**LONDON**

| Number | Title (A Side/B Side) | Yr | NM |
|---|---|---|---|
| ❑ GH 46001/4 [(4)M] | 60 Years of Song | 1966 | 40.00 |
| ❑ GHS 56001/4 [(4)S] | 60 Years of Song | 1966 | 50.00 |

**MGM**

| Number | Title (A Side/B Side) | Yr | NM |
|---|---|---|---|
| ❑ 2E-5 [(2)M] | Yesterday…Today | 1958 | 40.00 |

*—Yellow label original; also released separately as 3702 and 3703*

| Number | Title (A Side/B Side) | Yr | NM |
|---|---|---|---|
| ❑ 2SE-5 [(2)S] | Yesterday…Today | 1958 | 60.00 |

*—Yellow label original; also released separately as 3702 and 3703*

| Number | Title (A Side/B Side) | Yr | NM |
|---|---|---|---|
| ❑ E-3702 [M] | Yesterday | 1958 | 25.00 |

*—Yellow label original*

| Number | Title (A Side/B Side) | Yr | NM |
|---|---|---|---|
| ❑ SE-3702 [S] | Yesterday | 1958 | 30.00 |

*—Yellow label original*

| Number | Title (A Side/B Side) | Yr | NM |
|---|---|---|---|
| ❑ E-3703 [M] | Today | 1958 | 25.00 |

*—Yellow label original*

| Number | Title (A Side/B Side) | Yr | NM |
|---|---|---|---|
| ❑ SE-3703 [S] | Today | 1958 | 30.00 |

*—Yellow label original*

| Number | Title (A Side/B Side) | Yr | NM |
|---|---|---|---|
| ❑ E-3738 [M] | Maurice Chevalier Sings Broadway | 1959 | 25.00 |

*—Yellow label original*

| Number | Title (A Side/B Side) | Yr | NM |
|---|---|---|---|
| ❑ SE-3738 [S] | Maurice Chevalier Sings Broadway | 1959 | 30.00 |

*—Yellow label original*

| Number | Title (A Side/B Side) | Yr | NM |
|---|---|---|---|
| ❑ E-3773 [M] | A Tribute to Al Jolson | 1959 | 25.00 |

*—Yellow label original*

| Number | Title (A Side/B Side) | Yr | NM |
|---|---|---|---|
| ❑ SE-3773 [S] | A Tribute to Al Jolson | 1959 | 30.00 |

*—Yellow label original*

| Number | Title (A Side/B Side) | Yr | NM |
|---|---|---|---|
| ❑ E-3801 [M] | Life Is Just a Bowl of Cherries | 1960 | 20.00 |
| ❑ SE-3801 [S] | Life Is Just a Bowl of Cherries | 1960 | 25.00 |
| ❑ E-3835 [M] | Thank Heaven for Little Girls | 1960 | 20.00 |
| ❑ SE-3835 [S] | Thank Heaven for Little Girls | 1960 | 25.00 |
| ❑ E-4015 [M] | Maurice Chevalier Sings Lerner, Loewe & Chevalier | 1962 | 20.00 |
| ❑ SE-4015 [S] | Maurice Chevalier Sings Lerner, Loewe & Chevalier | 1962 | 25.00 |
| ❑ E-4120 [M] | Paris to Broadway | 1963 | 20.00 |
| ❑ SE-4120 [S] | Paris to Broadway | 1963 | 25.00 |
| ❑ E-4205 [M] | The Very Best of Maurice Chevalier | 1964 | 15.00 |
| ❑ SE-4205 [S] | The Very Best of Maurice Chevalier | 1964 | 20.00 |

**RCA VICTOR**

| Number | Title (A Side/B Side) | Yr | NM |
|---|---|---|---|
| ❑ LPM-2076 [M] | Thank Heaven for Maurice Chevalier | 1960 | 25.00 |
| ❑ LSP-2076 [S] | Thank Heaven for Maurice Chevalier | 1960 | 30.00 |

**TIME**

| Number | Title (A Side/B Side) | Yr | NM |
|---|---|---|---|
| ❑ S-2072 [S] | Maurice Chevalier | 1963 | 25.00 |
| ❑ 52072 [M] | Maurice Chevalier | 1963 | 20.00 |

### CHEVRONS, THE

**TIME**

| Number | Title (A Side/B Side) | Yr | NM |
|---|---|---|---|
| ❑ T-10008 [M] | Sing-a-Long Rock & Roll | 1961 | 80.00 |

### CHI-LITES, THE

**BRUNSWICK**

| Number | Title (A Side/B Side) | Yr | NM |
|---|---|---|---|
| ❑ BL 754152 | Give It Away | 1969 | 25.00 |
| ❑ BL 754165 | I Like Your Lovin', Do You Like Mine? | 1970 | 25.00 |
| ❑ BL 754170 | (For God's Sake) Give More Power to the People | 1971 | 25.00 |
| ❑ BL 754179 | A Lonely Man | 1972 | 25.00 |
| ❑ BL 754184 | The Chi-Lites Greatest Hits | 1972 | 25.00 |
| ❑ BL 754188 | A Letter to Myself | 1973 | 25.00 |
| ❑ BL 754197 | Chi-Lites | 1973 | 25.00 |
| ❑ BL 754200 | Toby | 1974 | 25.00 |
| ❑ BL 754204 | Half a Love | 1975 | 25.00 |
| ❑ BL 754208 | The Chi-Lites Greatest Hits, Volume 2 | 1976 | 25.00 |

**CHI-SOUND**

| Number | Title (A Side/B Side) | Yr | NM |
|---|---|---|---|
| ❑ T-619 | Heavenly Body | 1980 | 15.00 |
| ❑ T-635 | Me and You | 1982 | 15.00 |

**EPIC**

| Number | Title (A Side/B Side) | Yr | NM |
|---|---|---|---|
| ❑ PE 38627 | Greatest Hits | 1983 | 10.00 |

**ICHIBAN**

| Number | Title (A Side/B Side) | Yr | NM |
|---|---|---|---|
| ❑ ICH-1057 | Just Say You Love Me | 198? | 10.00 |

**LARC**

| Number | Title (A Side/B Side) | Yr | NM |
|---|---|---|---|
| ❑ 8103 | Bottom's Up | 1983 | 12.00 |

**MERCURY**

| Number | Title (A Side/B Side) | Yr | NM |
|---|---|---|---|
| ❑ SRM-1-1118 | Happy Being Lonely | 1976 | 15.00 |
| ❑ SRM-1-1147 | Fantastic | 1977 | 15.00 |

**PRIVATE I**

| Number | Title (A Side/B Side) | Yr | NM |
|---|---|---|---|
| ❑ FZ 39316 | Steppin' Out | 1984 | 10.00 |
| ❑ PZ 39316 | Steppin' Out | 1985 | 8.00 |

*—Budget-line reissue*

### CHICAGO

**ACCORD**

| Number | Title (A Side/B Side) | Yr | NM |
|---|---|---|---|
| ❑ SN-7140 | Toronto Rock 'n Roll Revival, Part I | 1982 | 12.00 |

*—Reissue of Magnum LP*

**COLUMBIA**

| Number | Title (A Side/B Side) | Yr | NM |
|---|---|---|---|
| ❑ (no #) [(17)] | Chicago | 1976 | 250.00 |

*—Promo-only set: The first 10 Chicago LPs with gold stamps on covers, box, side panel and wraparound*

| Number | Title (A Side/B Side) | Yr | NM |
|---|---|---|---|
| ❑ GP 8 [(2)] | Chicago Transit Authority | 1969 | 25.00 |

*—Red labels with "360 Sound" at bottom*

| Number | Title (A Side/B Side) | Yr | NM |
|---|---|---|---|
| ❑ GP 8 [(2)] | Chicago Transit Authority | 1970 | 15.00 |

*—Orange labels; most copies add a Roman numeral "I" to the title on spine*

| Number | Title (A Side/B Side) | Yr | NM |
|---|---|---|---|
| ❑ KGP 24 [(2)] | Chicago II | 1970 | 15.00 |

*—Orange labels*

| Number | Title (A Side/B Side) | Yr | NM |
|---|---|---|---|
| ❑ KGP 24 [(2)] | Chicago II | 1970 | 25.00 |
| *—Red labels with "360 Sound" at bottom; label and spine call the album "Chicago II"* | | | |
| ❑ KGP 24 [(2)] | Chicago | 1970 | 40.00 |
| *—Red labels with "360 Sound" at bottom; label and spine call the album "Chicago"* | | | |
| ❑ C2 30110 [(2)] | Chicago III | 1971 | 15.00 |
| ❑ C2Q 30110 [(2)Q] | Chicago III | 1974 | 30.00 |
| ❑ KG 30863 [(2)] | Chicago at Carnegie Hall, Vol. 1 & 2 | 1971 | 15.00 |
| *—First half of the 4-LP box, possibly for Columbia Record Club only* | | | |
| ❑ KG 30864 [(2)] | Chicago at Carnegie Hall, Vol. 3 & 4 | 1971 | 15.00 |
| *—Second half of the 4-LP box, possibly for Columbia Record Club only* | | | |
| ❑ C4Q 30865 [(4)Q] | Chicago at Carnegie Hall | 1971 | — |
| *—Scheduled but never released* | | | |
| ❑ C4X 30865 [(4)] | Chicago at Carnegie Hall | 1971 | 30.00 |
| *—With box, 4 posters and program; deduct for missing items* | | | |
| ❑ CQ 31102 [Q] | Chicago V | 1974 | 25.00 |
| ❑ KC 31102 | Chicago V | 1972 | 15.00 |
| ❑ CQ 32400 [Q] | Chicago VI | 1974 | 25.00 |
| ❑ KC 32400 | Chicago VI | 1973 | 12.00 |
| ❑ C2 32810 [(2)] | Chicago VII | 1974 | 15.00 |
| ❑ C2Q 32810 [(2)Q] | Chicago VII | 1974 | 30.00 |
| ❑ PC 33100 | Chicago VIII | 1975 | 12.00 |
| ❑ PCQ 33100 [Q] | Chicago VIII | 1975 | 25.00 |
| ❑ GQ 33255 [(2)Q] | Chicago Transit Authority | 1975 | 25.00 |
| ❑ GQ 33258 [(2)Q] | Chicago II | 1975 | 25.00 |
| ❑ PC 33900 | Chicago IX — Chicago's Greatest Hits | 1975 | 10.00 |
| ❑ PCQ 33900 [Q] | Chicago IX — Chicago's Greatest Hits | 1975 | 25.00 |
| ❑ PC 34200 | Chicago X | 1976 | 10.00 |
| ❑ PCQ 34200 [Q] | Chicago X | 1976 | 25.00 |
| ❑ JC 34860 | Chicago XI | 1977 | 10.00 |
| ❑ FC 35512 | Hot Streets | 1978 | 10.00 |
| ❑ FC 36105 | Chicago 13 | 1979 | 12.00 |
| ❑ FC 36517 | Chicago XIV | 1980 | 12.00 |
| ❑ FC 37682 | Chicago — Greatest Hits, Volume II | 1981 | 12.00 |
| ❑ PC 38590 | If You Leave Me Now | 1982 | 12.00 |
| ❑ PC 39579 | Take Me Back to Chicago | 1983 | 12.00 |
| ❑ HC 43900 | Chicago IX — Chicago's Greatest Hits | 1982 | 30.00 |
| *—Half-speed mastered edition* | | | |
| ❑ HC 44200 | Chicago X | 1982 | 40.00 |
| *—Half-speed mastered edition* | | | |

FULL MOON

| Number | Title (A Side/B Side) | Yr | NM |
|---|---|---|---|
| ❑ 23689 | Chicago 16 | 1982 | 8.00 |

MAGNUM

| Number | Title (A Side/B Side) | Yr | NM |
|---|---|---|---|
| ❑ MR 604 | Chicago Transit Authority Live in Concert | 1978 | 20.00 |
| *—Taken from their 1969 Toronto Rock 'n Roll Revival performance* | | | |

MOBILE FIDELITY

| Number | Title (A Side/B Side) | Yr | NM |
|---|---|---|---|
| ❑ 2-128 [(2)] | Chicago Transit Authority | 1983 | 80.00 |
| *—Audiophile vinyl* | | | |

REPRISE

| Number | Title (A Side/B Side) | Yr | NM |
|---|---|---|---|
| ❑ 25714 | Chicago 19 | 1988 | 8.00 |
| ❑ 26080 | Greatest Hits 1982-1989 | 1989 | 10.00 |
| ❑ R 110533 | Twenty 1 | 1991 | 20.00 |
| *—BMG Direct Marketing version* | | | |

WARNER BROS.

| Number | Title (A Side/B Side) | Yr | NM |
|---|---|---|---|
| ❑ 25060 [DJ] | Chicago 17 | 1984 | 20.00 |
| *—Promo pressing on Quiex II vinyl* | | | |
| ❑ 25060 | Chicago 17 | 1984 | 8.00 |
| ❑ 25509 | Chicago 18 | 1986 | 8.00 |

## CHICAGO SYMPHONY ORCHESTRA (PIERRE MONTEUX, CONDUCTOR)

RCA VICTOR RED SEAL

| Number | Title (A Side/B Side) | Yr | NM |
|---|---|---|---|
| ❑ LSC-2514 [S] | Franck: Symphony in D | 1961 | 20.00 |
| *—Original with "shaded dog" label* | | | |

## CHICAGO SYMPHONY ORCHESTRA (FRITZ REINER, CONDUCTOR)

RCA VICTOR RED SEAL

| Number | Title (A Side/B Side) | Yr | NM |
|---|---|---|---|
| ❑ LSC-1806 [S] | Strauss: Also Sprach Zarathustra | 1958 | 300.00 |
| *—Original with "shaded dog" label* | | | |
| ❑ LSC-1806 [S] | Strauss: Also Sprach Zarathustra | 199? | 25.00 |
| *—Classic Records reissue* | | | |
| ❑ LSC-1934 [S] | Bartok: Concerto for Orchestra | 1958 | 40.00 |
| *—Original with "shaded dog" label* | | | |
| ❑ LSC-1934 [S] | Bartok: Concerto for Orchestra | 199? | 25.00 |
| *—Classic Records reissue* | | | |
| ❑ LSC-1991 [S] | Beethoven: Symphony No. 7 | 1958 | 40.00 |
| *—Original with "shaded dog" label* | | | |
| ❑ LSC-2112 [S] | Vienna | 1958 | 40.00 |
| *—Original with "shaded dog" label* | | | |
| ❑ LSC-2150 [S] | Prokofiev: Lieutenant Kije; Stravinsky: Song of the Nightingale | 1958 | 40.00 |
| *—Original with "shaded dog" label* | | | |

Chicago Symphony Orchestra, Fritz Reiner, conductor, *Moussorgsky/Ravel: Pictures at an Exhibition,* RCA Victor Red Seal LSC-2201, 1959, stereo "shaded dog" label, $50.

| Number | Title (A Side/B Side) | Yr | NM |
|---|---|---|---|
| ❑ LSC-2150 [S] | Prokofiev: Lieutenant Kije; Stravinsky: Song of the Nightingale | 1964 | 40.00 |
| *—Second edition with "white dog" label* | | | |
| ❑ LSC-2183 [S] | The Reiner Sound | 1958 | 100.00 |
| *—Original with "shaded dog" label* | | | |
| ❑ LSC-2183 [S] | The Reiner Sound | 199? | 25.00 |
| *—Classic Records reissue* | | | |
| ❑ LSC-2201 [S] | Mussorgsky-Ravel: Pictures at an Exhibition | 1959 | 50.00 |
| *—Original with "shaded dog" label* | | | |
| ❑ LSC-2201 [S] | Mussorgsky-Ravel: Pictures at an Exhibition | 1964 | 40.00 |
| *—Second edition with "white dog" label* | | | |
| ❑ LSC-2209 [S] | Brahms: Symphony No. 3 | 1959 | 40.00 |
| *—Original with "shaded dog" label* | | | |
| ❑ LSC-2209 [S] | Brahms: Symphony No. 3 | 1964 | 20.00 |
| *—Second edition with "white dog" label* | | | |
| ❑ LSC-2214 [S] | Dvorak: Symphony No. 9 "From the New World" | 1959 | 20.00 |
| *—Original with "shaded dog" label* | | | |
| ❑ LSC-2216 [S] | Tchaikovsky: Symphony No. 6 "Pathetique" | 1959 | 20.00 |
| *—Original with "shaded dog" label* | | | |
| ❑ LSC-2222 [S] | Debussy: Iberia | 1958 | 200.00 |
| *—Original with "shaded dog" label* | | | |
| ❑ LSC-2222 [S] | Debussy: Iberia | 199? | 25.00 |
| *—Classic Records reissue* | | | |
| ❑ LSC-2230 [S] | Spain | 1958 | 100.00 |
| *—Original with "shaded dog" label* | | | |
| ❑ LSC-2230 [S] | Spain | 1964 | 70.00 |
| *—Second issue with "white dog" label* | | | |
| ❑ LSC-2230 [S] | Spain | 199? | 25.00 |
| *—Classic Records reissue* | | | |
| ❑ LSC-2241 [S] | Tchaikovsky: 1812 Overture | 1958 | 500.00 |
| *—Original with "shaded dog" label* | | | |
| ❑ LSC-2241 [S] | Tchaikovsky: 1812 Overture | 199? | 25.00 |
| *—Classic Records reissue* | | | |
| ❑ LSC-2251 [S] | Hovhaness: Mysterious Mountain; Stravinsky: Divertimento | 1959 | 50.00 |
| *—Original with "shaded dog" label* | | | |
| ❑ LSC-2251 [S] | Hovhaness: Mysterious Mountain; Stravinsky: Divertimento | 1964 | 20.00 |
| *—Second edition with "white dog" label* | | | |
| ❑ LSC-2318 [S] | Rossini: Overtures | 1959 | 30.00 |
| *—Original with "shaded dog" label* | | | |

| Number | Title (A Side/B Side) | Yr | NM |
|---|---|---|---|
| ❑ LSC-2328 [S] | Tchaikovsky: The Nutcracker | 1959 | 50.00 |
| *—Original with "shaded dog" label* | | | |
| ❑ LSC-2343 [S] | Beethoven: Symphony No. 5 | 1960 | 20.00 |
| *—Original with "shaded dog" label* | | | |
| ❑ LSC-2364 [S] | Mahler: Symphony No. 4 | 1960 | 25.00 |
| *—Original with "shaded dog" label* | | | |
| ❑ LSC-2364 [S] | Mahler: Symphony No. 4 | 199? | 25.00 |
| *—Classic Records reissue* | | | |
| ❑ LSC-2374 [S] | Bartok: Music for Strings, Percussion and Celesta | 1959 | 40.00 |
| *—Original with "shaded dog" label* | | | |
| ❑ LSC-2374 [S] | Bartok: Music for Strings, Percussion and Celesta | 199? | 25.00 |
| *—Classic Records reissue* | | | |
| ❑ LDS-2384 [S] | Strauss, Richard: Don Quixote | 1960 | 70.00 |
| *—Original with "shaded dog" label* | | | |
| ❑ LSS-2384 [S] | Strauss, Richard: Don Quixote | 1960 | 120.00 |
| *—Original with "shaded dog" label; limited edition of 200 in box with booklet* | | | |
| ❑ LSC-2395 [S] | Prokofiev: Alexander Nevsky | 1960 | 60.00 |
| *—Original with "shaded dog" label* | | | |
| ❑ LSC-2395 [S] | Prokofiev: Alexander Nevsky | 1964 | 60.00 |
| *—Second edition with "white dog" label* | | | |
| ❑ LSC-2423 [S] | Festival | 1960 | 150.00 |
| *—Original with "shaded dog" label* | | | |
| ❑ LSC-2423 [S] | Festival | 199? | 25.00 |
| *—Classic Records reissue* | | | |
| ❑ LSC-2436 [S] | Respighi: Pines of Rome; Fountains of Rome | 1960 | 30.00 |
| *—Original with "shaded dog" label* | | | |
| ❑ LSC-2436 [S] | Respighi: Pines of Rome; Fountains of Rome | 199? | 25.00 |
| *—Classic Records reissue* | | | |
| ❑ LSC-2441 [S] | Reiner Conducts Wagner | 1960 | 40.00 |
| *—Original with "shaded dog" label* | | | |
| ❑ LSC-2441 [S] | Reiner Conducts Wagner | 1964 | 40.00 |
| *—Second edition with "white dog" label* | | | |
| ❑ LSC-2446 [S] | Rimsky-Korsakov: Scheherazade | 1960 | 100.00 |
| *—Original with "shaded dog" label* | | | |
| ❑ LSC-2446 [S] | Rimsky-Korsakov: Scheherazade | 1964 | 300.00 |
| *—Second edition with "white dog" label; a rare instance where a later edition is more desirable than the original* | | | |
| ❑ LSC-2446 [S] | Rimsky-Korsakov: Scheherazade | 199? | 25.00 |
| *—Classic Records reissue* | | | |

Number | Title (A Side/B Side) | Yr | NM

❑ LSC-2462 [S] Debussy: La Mer; Strauss, Richard: Don Juan 1961 50.00
*—Original with "shaded dog" label*
❑ LSC-2462 [S] Debussy: La Mer; Strauss, Richard: Don Juan 1964 40.00
*—Second edition with "white dog" label*
❑ LSC-2496 [S] The Heart of the Symphony 1961 40.00
*—Original with "shaded dog" label*
❑ LSC-2500 [S] Strauss: Waltzes 1960 40.00
*—Original with "shaded dog" label*
❑ LSC-2500 [S] Strauss: Waltzes 1964 40.00
*—Second edition with "white dog" label*
❑ LSC-2500 [S] Strauss: Waltzes 199? 25.00
*—Classic Records reissue*
❑ LSC-2516 [S] Schubert: Symphonies No. 5 and 8 1961 20.00
*—Original with "shaded dog" label*
❑ LSC-2609 [S] Strauss, Richard: Also Sprach Zarathustra 1962 40.00
*—Original with "shaded dog" label*
❑ LSC-2609 [S] Strauss, Richard: Also Sprach Zarathustra 1964 20.00
*—Second edition with "white dog" label*
❑ LMD-2614 [M] Beethoven: Symphony No. 6 "Pastorale" 1962 40.00
*—Gatefold with bound-in booklet*
❑ LSC-2614 [S] Beethoven: Symphony No. 6 "Pastorale" 1962 20.00
*—Original with "shaded dog" label; non-gatefold edition*
❑ LSCD-2614 [S] Beethoven: Symphony No. 6 "Pastorale" 1962 100.00
*—Gatefold with bound-in booklet*

## CHICKEN SHACK

BLUE HORIZON
❑ BH 4809 Accept Chicken Shack 1970 25.00
❑ BH 7705 O.K. Ken? 1969 25.00
❑ BH 7706 100-Ton Chicken 1969 25.00

DERAM
❑ DES 18063 Imagination Lady 1972 20.00

EPIC
❑ LN 24414 [M] Forty Blue Fingers, Freshly Packed and Ready to Serve 1968 100.00
❑ BN 26414 [S] Forty Blue Fingers, Freshly Packed and Ready to Serve 1968 30.00

LONDON
❑ XPS 632 Unlucky Boy 1973 20.00

## CHIFFONS, THE

B.T. PUPPY
❑ S-1011 My Secret Love 1970 400.00

COLLECTABLES
❑ COL-5042 Golden Classics 198? 12.00

LAURIE
❑ LLP-2018 [M] He's So Fine 1963 120.00
❑ LLP-2020 [M] One Fine Day 1963 200.00
❑ LLP-2036 [M] Sweet Talkin' Guy 1966 100.00
❑ SLP-2036 [S] Sweet Talkin' Guy 1966 150.00
❑ 4001 Everything You Always Wanted to Hear by the Chiffons 1975 20.00
❑ DT-90075 [R] He's So Fine 1965 200.00
*—Capitol Record Club edition*
❑ ST-90779 [S] Sweet Talkin' Guy 1966 200.00
*—Capitol Record Club edition*

## CHILDERS, BUDDY

LIBERTY
❑ LJH-6009 [M] Sam Songs 1956 100.00
❑ LJH-6013 [M] Buddy Childers Quartet 1957 100.00

## CHILDRE, LEW

STARDAY
❑ SLP-153 [M] Old Time Get Together 1961 25.00

## CHILDREN, THE

ATCO
❑ SD 33-271 Rebirth 1968 25.00

CINEMA
❑ CLP-1 Rebirth 1968 150.00

## CHILDS, SUE

STUDIO 4
❑ 200 [M] Sue Childs 195? 50.00

## CHILES AND PETTIFORD

ATLANTIC
❑ 8111 [M] Live at Jilly's 1965 40.00
❑ SD 8111 [S] Live at Jilly's 1965 50.00

## CHILLIWACK

A&M
❑ SP-3509 [(2)] Chilliwack 1971 25.00
❑ SP-4375 All Over You 1972 15.00

MILLENNIUM
❑ BXL1-7759 Wanna Be a Star 1981 10.00
❑ BXL1-7766 Opus X 1982 10.00

MUSHROOM
❑ MRS-5006 Dreams, Dreams, Dreams 1977 12.00
❑ MRS-5011 Lights from the Valley 1978 12.00
❑ MRS-5015 Breakdown in Paradise 1980 12.00

PARROT
❑ PAS 71040 Chilliwack 1970 20.00

SIRE
❑ SASD-7506 Chilliwack 1975 15.00
❑ SASD-7511 Rockerbox 1976 15.00

## CHIPMUNKS, THE, DAVID SEVILLE AND

LIBERTY
❑ LM-1070 Christmas with the Chipmunks 1980 8.00
*—Reissue with two tracks omitted*
❑ LRP-3132 [M] Let's All Sing with the Chipmunks 1959 30.00
*—Black vinyl; original cover features "realistic" chipmunks and no reference to "The Alvin Show"*
❑ LRP-3132 [M] Let's All Sing with the Chipmunks 1959 60.00
*—Red vinyl*
❑ LRP-3132 [M] Let's All Sing with the Chipmunks 1961 20.00
*—Second cover features the "cartoon" Chipmunks and a reference to "The Alvin Show"*
❑ LRP-3159 [M] Sing Again with the Chipmunks 1960 40.00
*—Original cover features "realistic" chipmunks*
❑ LRP-3159 [M] Sing Again with the Chipmunks 1961 20.00
*—Second cover features the "cartoon" Chipmunks*
❑ LRP-3170 [M] Around the World with the Chipmunks 1960 40.00
*—Original cover features "realistic" chipmunks on and near a plane*
❑ LRP-3170 [M] Around the World with the Chipmunks 1961 20.00
*—Second cover features the "cartoon" Chipmunks on and near a camel*
❑ LRP-3209 [M] The Alvin Show 1961 25.00
❑ LRP-3229 [M] The Chipmunks Songbook 1962 25.00
❑ LRP-3256 [M] Christmas with the Chipmunks 1962 25.00
❑ LRP-3334 [M] Christmas with the Chipmunks, Vol. 2 1963 25.00
❑ LRP-3388 [M] The Chipmunks Sing the Beatles Hits 1964 30.00
❑ LRP-3405 [M] The Chipmunks Sing with Children 1965 20.00
❑ LRP-3424 [M] The Chipmunks A-Go-Go 1965 20.00
❑ LST-7132 [S] Let's All Sing with the Chipmunks 1959 40.00
*—Black vinyl; original cover features "realistic" chipmunks and no reference to "The Alvin Show"*
❑ LST-7132 [S] Let's All Sing with the Chipmunks 1959 80.00
*—Red vinyl*
❑ LST-7132 [S] Let's All Sing with the Chipmunks 1961 25.00
*—Second cover features the "cartoon" Chipmunks and a reference to "The Alvin Show"*
❑ LST-7159 [S] Sing Again with the Chipmunks 1960 50.00
*—Original cover features "realistic" chipmunks*
❑ LST-7159 [S] Sing Again with the Chipmunks 1961 25.00
*—Second cover features the "cartoon" Chipmunks*
❑ LST-7170 [S] Around the World with the Chipmunks 1960 25.00
*—Second cover features the "cartoon" Chipmunks on and near a camel*
❑ LST-7170 [S] Around the World with the Chipmunks 1960 50.00
*—Original covers have "realistic" chipmunks on and near a plane.*
❑ LST-7209 [S] The Alvin Show 1961 30.00
❑ LST-7229 [S] The Chipmunks Songbook 1962 30.00
❑ LST-7256 [S] Christmas with the Chipmunks 1962 30.00
❑ LST-7334 [S] Christmas with the Chipmunks, Vol. 2 1963 30.00
❑ LST-7388 [S] The Chipmunks Sing the Beatles Hits 1964 40.00
❑ LST-7405 [S] The Chipmunks Sing with Children 1965 25.00
❑ LST-7424 [S] The Chipmunks A-Go-Go 1965 25.00

MISTLETOE
❑ MLP-1216 Christmas with the Chipmunks 197? 8.00
*—Reissue of Liberty LST-7256*
❑ MLP-1217 Christmas with the Chipmunks, Vol. 2 197? 8.00
*—Reissue of Liberty LST-7334*

PICKWICK
❑ SPC-1034 Christmas with the Chipmunks 1980 10.00
❑ SPC-1035 The Twelve Days of Christmas with The Chipmunks 1980 10.00
*—Reissue of "Christmas with the Chipmunks, Vol. 2"*

SUNSET
❑ LST-7334 [S] Christmas with the Chipmunks, Vol. 2 1968 20.00
*—Budget-line reissue of Liberty LST-7334*
❑ LST-7424 [S] The Chipmunks A-Go-Go 196? 15.00
*—Same cover as Liberty 7424, but with "SUNSET" sticker at upper right*

UNITED ARTISTS
❑ UA-LA352-E2 [(2)]Christmas with the Chipmunks 1974 20.00
*—Entire contents of both original Liberty LPs*

## CHITTISON, HERMAN

COLUMBIA
❑ CL 6134 [10] Herman Chittison 1950 50.00
❑ CL 6182 [10] Herman Chittison Trio 1951 50.00

ROYALE
❑ 1824 [10] Cocktail Time 195? 40.00

## CHOATES, HARRY

D
❑ 7000 [M] Jole Blon 196? 40.00

## CHOCO AND HIS MALIMBA DRUM RHYTHMS

AUDIO FIDELITY
❑ AFLP-2102 [M] African Latin Voodoo Drums 1962 20.00
❑ AFSD-6102 [S] African Latin Voodoo Drums 1962 30.00

## CHOCOLATE WATCH BAND, THE

RHINO
❑ RNLP-108 The Best of the Chocolate Watch Band 1983 12.00

TOWER
❑ ST 5096 [S] No Way Out 1967 400.00
❑ T 5096 [M] No Way Out 1967 300.00
❑ ST 5106 [S] The Inner Mystique 1968 300.00
❑ T 5106 [M] The Inner Mystique 1968 400.00
❑ ST 5153 One Step Beyond 1969 300.00

## CHORDETTES, THE

BARNABY
❑ BR-4003 All the Very Best of the Chordettes 1976 12.00

CADENCE
❑ CLP-1002 [10] Close Harmony 1955 50.00
❑ CLP-3001 [M] The Chordettes 1957 40.00
❑ CLP-3020 [M] Barbershop Harmony 1958 40.00
❑ CLP-3056 [M] Never on Sunday 1962 20.00
❑ CLP-25056 [S] Never on Sunday 1962 30.00

COLUMBIA
❑ CL 956 [M] Listen 1955 50.00
❑ CL 2519 [10] The Chordettes 1955 40.00
❑ CL 6111 [10] Harmony Time 1950 50.00
❑ CL 6170 [10] Harmony Time, Vol. 2 1951 50.00
❑ CL 6218 [10] Harmony Encores 1952 50.00
❑ CL 6285 [10] Your Requests 1953 50.00

HARMONY
❑ HL 7164 [M] The Chordettes 196? 15.00

RHINO
❑ R1-70849 The Best of the Chordettes 1989 12.00

## CHOSEN FEW, THE

MAPLE
❑ 6000 Takin' All the Love I Can 196? 20.00

RCA VICTOR
❑ LSP-4242 The Chosen Few 1969 20.00

## CHRISTIAN, CHARLIE

COLUMBIA
❑ G 30779 [(2)] Solo Flight — The Genius of Charlie Christian 1972 20.00

COUNTERPOINT
❑ 548 [M] The Harlem Jazz Scene 1941 195? 60.00

ESOTERIC
❑ ESJ-1 [10] Jazz Immortal 1951 200.00
*—Red vinyl*
❑ ES-548 [M] The Harlem Jazz Scene 1941 1956 80.00

## CHRISTIE, LOU

BUDDAH
❑ BDS-5052 I'm Gonna Make You Mine 1969 15.00
❑ BDS-5073 Paint America Love 1971 15.00

CO & CE
❑ LP-1231 [M] Lou Christie Strikes Back 1966 40.00
*—The front cover and spine use this title, but the back cover and label use "Lou Christie Strikes Again"*

COLPIX
❑ CP-4001 [M] Lou Christie Strikes Again 1966 30.00
❑ SCP-4001 [S] Lou Christie Strikes Again 1966 50.00

51 WEST
❑ P 18260 Lou Christie Does Detroit 1983 15.00

MGM
❑ E-4360 [M] Lightnin' Strikes 1966 15.00
❑ SE-4360 [S] Lightnin' Strikes 1966 20.00
❑ E-4394 [M] Painter of Hits 1966 15.00
❑ SE-4394 [S] Painter of Hits 1966 20.00

**Number | Title (A Side/B Side) | Yr | NM**

RHINO
❑ R1-70246 EnLightnin'Ment: The Best of Lou Christie 1988 12.00

ROULETTE
❑ R 25208 [M] Lou Christie 1963 40.00
*—White wall in background on front cover*
❑ R 25208 [M] Lou Christie 1963 50.00
*—Blue background on front cover*
❑ SR 25208 [S] Lou Christie 1963 60.00
*—White wall in background on front cover*
❑ SR 25208 [S] Lou Christie 1963 80.00
*—Blue background on front cover*
❑ R 25332 [M] Lou Christie Strikes Again 1966 25.00
❑ SR 25332 [S] Lou Christie Strikes Again 1966 30.00

SPIN-O-RAMA
❑ M-173 [M] Starring Lou Christie and the Classics 1966 20.00
❑ S-173 [R] Starring Lou Christie and the Classics 1966 12.00
*—The above LP also includes other artists*

THREE BROTHERS
❑ THB-2000 Lou Christie 1973 20.00

**CHRISTOPHER, JORDAN**

UNITED ARTISTS
❑ UAL 3479 [M] Jordan Christopher Has the Knack 1966 20.00
❑ UAS 6479 [S] Jordan Christopher Has the Knack 1966 25.00

**CHRISTOPHER (1)**

BELL
❑ 1203 R.P.M. 1970 20.00

**CHRISTOPHER (2)** Band from North Carolina.

CHRIS-TEE
❑ 12411 What'cha Gonna Do 1970 3000.
*—100 copies were pressed; VG value 1500; VG+ value 2250*

**CHRISTOPHER (3)** Band fron Texas.

METROMEDIA
❑ 1024 Christopher 1970 300.00

**CHRISTY, JUNE**

CAPITOL
❑ H 516 [10] Something Cool 1954 80.00
❑ ST 516 [S] Something Cool 1960 15.00
*—Re-recording of the original mono LP; issued with different cover than original mono LP, in color with June's eyes open; black label, Capitol logo at left*
❑ T 516 [M] Something Cool 1955 50.00
*—Turquoise label; blue-green cover with June's eyes closed*
❑ T 516 [M] Something Cool 1959 25.00
*—Black label with colorband, logo at left; with original blue-green cover with June's eyes closed*
❑ T 516 [M] Something Cool 1962 15.00
*—Black label with colorband, logo at top; issued with different cover than original mono LP, in color with June's eyes open*
❑ T 656 [M] Duets 1955 40.00
*—Turquoise label*
❑ T 725 [M] The Misty Miss Christy 1956 40.00
*—Turquoise label*
❑ T 833 [M] June — Fair and Warmer! 1957 40.00
*—Turquoise label*
❑ T 902 [M] Gone for the Day 1957 40.00
*—Turquoise label*
❑ T 1006 [M] This Is June Christy! 1958 40.00
*—Turquoise label*
❑ ST 1076 [S] June's Got Rhythm 1958 40.00
*—Black label with colorband, Capitol logo at left*
❑ T 1076 [M] June's Got Rhythm 1958 30.00
*—Black label with colorband, Capitol logo at left*
❑ ST 1114 [S] The Song Is June! 1959 40.00
*—Black label with colorband, Capitol logo at left*
❑ T 1114 [M] The Song Is June! 1959 30.00
*—Black label with colorband, Capitol logo at left*
❑ ST 1202 [S] June Christy Recalls Those Kenton Days 1959 40.00
*—Black label with colorband, Capitol logo at left*
❑ T 1202 [M] June Christy Recalls Those Kenton Days 1959 30.00
*—Black label with colorband, Capitol logo at left*
❑ ST 1308 [S] Ballads for Night People 1959 40.00
*—Black label with colorband, Capitol logo at left*
❑ T 1308 [M] Ballads for Night People 1959 30.00
*—Black label with colorband, Capitol logo at left*
❑ STBO 1327 [(2)S]Road Show 1960 40.00
*—Black label with colorband, Capitol logo at left*
❑ TBO 1327 [(2)M]Road Show 1960 30.00
*—Black label with colorband, Capitol logo at left*
❑ ST 1398 [S] The Cool School 1960 40.00
*—Black label with colorband, Capitol logo at left*
❑ T 1398 [M] The Cool School 1960 30.00
*—Black label with colorband, Capitol logo at left*
❑ ST 1498 [S] Off Beat 1961 50.00
*—Black label with colorband, Capitol logo at left*
❑ T 1498 [M] Off Beat 1961 40.00
*—Black label with colorband, Capitol logo at left*
❑ ST 1586 [S] Do-Re-Mi 1961 50.00
*—Black label with colorband, Capitol logo at left*

Circus Maximus, *Neverland Revisited,* Vanguard VSD-79274, 1968, $25.

**Number | Title (A Side/B Side) | Yr | NM**

❑ T 1586 [M] Do-Re-Mi 1961 40.00
*—Black label with colorband, Capitol logo at left*
❑ ST 1605 [S] That Time of Year 1961 50.00
*—Black label with colorband, Capitol logo at left*
❑ T 1605 [M] That Time of Year 1961 40.00
❑ ST 1693 [S] The Best of June Christy 1962 30.00
*—Black logo with colorband*
❑ T 1693 [M] The Best of June Christy 1962 25.00
*—Black label with colorband*
❑ ST 1845 [S] Big Band Specials 1962 25.00
❑ T 1845 [M] Big Band Specials 1962 20.00
❑ ST 1953 [S] The Intimate June Christy 1963 25.00
❑ T 1953 [M] The Intimate June Christy 1963 20.00
❑ ST 2410 [S] Something Broadway, Something Latin 1965 30.00
❑ T 2410 [M] Something Broadway, Something Latin 1965 25.00

**CHRYSALIS**

MGM
❑ SE-4547 Definition 1968 30.00

**CHURCH, THE**

ARISTA
❑ AL 8521 Starfish 1988 10.00
❑ AL 8563 Of Skins and Heart 1988 10.00
*—First U.S. issue of first Australian album*
❑ AL 8564 The Blurred Crusade 1988 10.00
*—First U.S. issue of second Australian album*
❑ AL 8565 Seance 1988 10.00
*—First U.S. issue of third Australian album*
❑ AL 8566 Remote Luxury 1988 10.00
*—Reissue of Warner Bros. 25152*
❑ AL 8567 Heyday 1988 10.00
*—Reissue of Warner Bros. 25370*
❑ AL 8579 Gold Afternoon Fix 1990 10.00
❑ ADP 9713 [DJ] Sum of the Parts 1988 40.00
*—Interviews and live acoustic tracks*
❑ 18727-1 [(2)] Sometime Anywhere 1994 15.00
❑ R 171667 Gold Afternoon Fix 1990 12.00
*—BMG Direct Marketing edition*
❑ R 173703 Starfish 1988 12.00
*—BMG Direct Marketing edition*

CAPITOL
❑ ST-12193 The Church 1982 15.00

WARNER BROS.
❑ 25152 Remote Luxury 1984 15.00

**Number | Title (A Side/B Side) | Yr | NM**

❑ 25370 Heyday 1985 15.00

**CIRCLE**

ECM
❑ 1018/19 ST [(2)]Paris Concert 197? 20.00
*—Original issue, made in Germany?*
❑ ECM2-1018 [(2)]Paris Concert 1972 15.00
*—Distributed by Polydor*

**CIRCUS**

METROMEDIA
❑ 7401 Circus 1973 30.00

**CIRCUS MAXIMUS** Group features JERRY JEFF WALKER.

VANGUARD
❑ VRS-9260 [M] Circus Maximus 1967 20.00
❑ VSD-79260 [S] Circus Maximus 1967 25.00
❑ VSD-79274 Neverland Revisited 1968 25.00

**CIRILLO, WALLY/BOBBY SCOTT**

SAVOY
❑ MG-15055 [10] Cirillo and Scott 1955 80.00

**CISSEL, CHUCK**

ARISTA
❑ AL 9581 If I Had the Chance 1982 30.00

**CITY, THE** CAROLE KING was a member.

ODE
❑ Z12 44012 Now That Everything's Been Said 1968 80.00
*—Color front cover*
❑ Z12 44012 Now That Everything's Been Said 1971 12.00
*—Black & white front cover*

**CLANTON, JIMMY**

ACE
❑ DLP-100 Jimmy's Happy/Jimmy's Blue Poster 1960 80.00
❑ DLP-100 [M] Jimmy's Happy/Jimmy's Blue 1960 150.00
*—Black vinyl; also released as two separate albums, 1007 and 1008*
❑ DLP-100 [M] Jimmy's Happy/Jimmy's Blue 1960 400.00
*—The "Happy" album is red vinyl, the "Blue" album is blue*
❑ 1001 [M] Just a Dream 1959 120.00
❑ 1007 [M] Jimmy's Happy 1960 40.00

Eric Clapton, *Eric Clapton,* Mobile Fidelity 1-220, 1995, "Original Master Recording" on front cover, $25.

| Number | Title (A Side/B Side) | Yr | NM |
|---|---|---|---|
| ❑ 1008 [M] | Jimmy's Blue | 1960 | 40.00 |
| ❑ 1011 [M] | My Best to You | 1960 | 100.00 |
| ❑ 1014 [M] | Teenage Millionaire | 1961 | 100.00 |
| ❑ 1026 [M] | Venus in Blue Jeans | 1962 | 100.00 |

PHILIPS

| Number | Title (A Side/B Side) | Yr | NM |
|---|---|---|---|
| ❑ PHM 200154 [M] | The Best of Jimmy Clanton | 1964 | 25.00 |
| ❑ PHS 600154 [S] | The Best of Jimmy Clanton | 1964 | 30.00 |

**CLAP**

NOVA SOL

| Number | Title (A Side/B Side) | Yr | NM |
|---|---|---|---|
| ❑ 1001 | Have You Reached Yet? | 1970 | 1000. |

**CLAPTON, ERIC**

ATCO

| Number | Title (A Side/B Side) | Yr | NM |
|---|---|---|---|
| ❑ 33-329 [DJ] | Eric Clapton | 1970 | 100.00 |
| *—Mono pressing is promo only* | | | |
| ❑ SD 33-329 | Eric Clapton | 1970 | 20.00 |
| ❑ SD 33-329 | Eric Clapton | 1970 | 200.00 |
| *—Odd pressing with alternate takes of "After Midnight" and "Blues Power" plus remixes of other tracks. Look for "CTH" in trail-off area.* | | | |
| ❑ SD 2-803 [(2)] | History of Eric Clapton | 1972 | 20.00 |
| *—Contains tracks from the Yardbirds, John Mayall's Bluesbreakers, Cream, Blind Faith, and solo records* | | | |

DUCK

| Number | Title (A Side/B Side) | Yr | NM |
|---|---|---|---|
| ❑ 23773 | Money and Cigarettes | 1983 | 10.00 |
| ❑ 25166 | Behind the Sun | 1985 | 10.00 |
| ❑ 25476 | August | 1986 | 10.00 |

MOBILE FIDELITY

| Number | Title (A Side/B Side) | Yr | NM |
|---|---|---|---|
| ❑ 1-030 | Slowhand | 1980 | 70.00 |
| *—Audiophile vinyl* | | | |
| ❑ 1-220 | Eric Clapton | 1995 | 25.00 |
| *—Audiophile vinyl* | | | |

NAUTILUS

| Number | Title (A Side/B Side) | Yr | NM |
|---|---|---|---|
| ❑ NR-32 [(2)] | Just One Night | 1981 | 150.00 |
| *—Audiophile vinyl* | | | |

POLYDOR

| Number | Title (A Side/B Side) | Yr | NM |
|---|---|---|---|
| ❑ PD 3503 [(2)] | Eric Clapton at His Best | 1972 | 20.00 |
| *—Compiles tracks from his first solo album plus Derek and the Dominos* | | | |
| ❑ 24-5526 | Clapton | 1973 | 15.00 |
| *—Compiles tracks from his first solo album plus Derek and the Dominos* | | | |
| ❑ SKBO-94837 [(2)] | Eric Clapton at His Best | 1972 | 30.00 |
| *—Capitol Record Club edition* | | | |
| ❑ 835261-1 [(6)] | Crossroads | 1988 | 50.00 |
| *—Box set; contains material from all phases of his career* | | | |

REPRISE

| Number | Title (A Side/B Side) | Yr | NM |
|---|---|---|---|
| ❑ 26074 | Journeyman | 1989 | 12.00 |
| ❑ W1-26420 [(2)] | 24 Nights | 1991 | 25.00 |
| *—Vinyl copies released only through Columbia House* | | | |
| ❑ 48423-1 | Me and Mr. Johnson | 2004 | 20.00 |
| *—Regular edition on 140-gram vinyl; distributed by Classic Records* | | | |
| ❑ 48423-1 SV | Me and Mr. Johnson | 2004 | 30.00 |
| *—200-gram vinyl edition, distributed by Classic Records* | | | |

RSO

| Number | Title (A Side/B Side) | Yr | NM |
|---|---|---|---|
| ❑ PRO 035 [DJ] | Slowhand | 1977 | 40.00 |
| *—White vinyl promo sampler* | | | |
| ❑ SO 877 | Eric Clapton's Rainbow Concert | 1973 | 15.00 |
| ❑ RPO-1009 [DJ] | Limited Backless | 1978 | 50.00 |
| *—White vinyl promo* | | | |
| ❑ RS-1-3004 | No Reason to Cry | 1976 | 12.00 |
| ❑ RS-1-3008 | Eric Clapton | 1977 | 12.00 |
| *—Reissue of Atco LP of the same name* | | | |
| ❑ RS-1-3023 | 461 Ocean Boulevard | 1977 | 12.00 |
| *—Reissue of RSO 4801* | | | |
| ❑ RS-1-3030 | Slowhand | 1977 | 12.00 |
| ❑ RS-1-3039 | Backless | 1978 | 12.00 |
| ❑ RX-1-3095 | Another Ticket | 1981 | 10.00 |
| ❑ RS-1-3099 | Time Pieces/The Best of Eric Clapton | 1982 | 10.00 |
| ❑ RS-2-4202 [(2)] | Just One Night | 1980 | 15.00 |
| ❑ QD 4801 [Q] | 461 Ocean Boulevard | 1974 | 25.00 |
| ❑ SO 4801 | 461 Ocean Boulevard | 1974 | 12.00 |
| *—With "Better Make It Through the Day"* | | | |
| ❑ SO 4801 | 461 Ocean Boulevard | 1974 | 15.00 |
| *—With "Give Me Strength"* | | | |
| ❑ QD 4806 [Q] | There's One in Every Crowd | 1975 | 25.00 |
| ❑ SO 4806 | There's One in Every Crowd | 1975 | 12.00 |
| ❑ SO 4809 | E.C. Was Here | 1975 | 12.00 |
| ❑ 811697-1 | 461 Ocean Boulevard | 198? | 8.00 |
| *—Reissue of RSO 3023* | | | |
| ❑ 823276-1 | Slowhand | 1983 | 8.00 |
| *—Reissue of RSO 3030* | | | |
| ❑ 825093-1 | Eric Clapton | 1984 | 8.00 |
| *—Reissue of RSO 3008* | | | |
| ❑ 825382-1 | Time Pieces/The Best of Eric Clapton | 1984 | 8.00 |
| *—Reissue of RSO 3099* | | | |
| ❑ 825391-1 [(2)] | Just One Night | 1984 | 10.00 |
| *—Reissue of RSO 4202* | | | |
| ❑ 827579-1 | Another Ticket | 1985 | 8.00 |
| *—Reissue of RSO 3095* | | | |

**CLARK, ALICE**

MAINSTREAM

| Number | Title (A Side/B Side) | Yr | NM |
|---|---|---|---|
| ❑ MRL-362 | Alice Clark | 1972 | 20.00 |

**CLARK, CHRIS**

MOTOWN

| Number | Title (A Side/B Side) | Yr | NM |
|---|---|---|---|
| ❑ M-664 [M] | Soul Sounds | 1967 | 50.00 |
| ❑ MS-664 [S] | Soul Sounds | 1967 | 60.00 |

WEED

| Number | Title (A Side/B Side) | Yr | NM |
|---|---|---|---|
| ❑ 801 | C.C. Rides Again | 1969 | 80.00 |

**CLARK, CLAUDINE**

CHANCELLOR

| Number | Title (A Side/B Side) | Yr | NM |
|---|---|---|---|
| ❑ CHL-5029 [M] | Party Lights | 1962 | 250.00 |

**CLARK, DAVE, FIVE**

CORTLEIGH

| Number | Title (A Side/B Side) | Yr | NM |
|---|---|---|---|
| ❑ C-1073 [M] | The Dave Clark Five with Ricky Astor | 1964 | 30.00 |
| *—With two early DC5 tracks and assorted other stuff by other artists* | | | |
| ❑ CS-1073 [R] | The Dave Clark Five with Ricky Astor | 1964 | 15.00 |
| *—With two early DC5 tracks and assorted other stuff by other artists* | | | |

CROWN

| Number | Title (A Side/B Side) | Yr | NM |
|---|---|---|---|
| ❑ CST-400 [R] | The Dave Clark Five with the Playbacks | 1964 | 15.00 |
| *—With two early DC5 tracks and assorted other stuff by other artists* | | | |
| ❑ CST-473 [R] | Chaquita/In Your Heart | 1964 | 15.00 |
| *—With two early DC5 tracks and assorted other stuff by other artists* | | | |
| ❑ CST-644 [R] | The Dave Clark Five with the Playbacks | 196? | 12.00 |
| *—Reissue* | | | |
| ❑ CLP-5400 [M] | The Dave Clark Five with the Playbacks | 1964 | 30.00 |
| *—With two early DC5 tracks and assorted other stuff by other artists* | | | |
| ❑ CLP-5473 [M] | Chaquita/In Your Heart | 1964 | 30.00 |
| *—With two early DC5 tracks and assorted other stuff by other artists* | | | |

CUSTOM

| Number | Title (A Side/B Side) | Yr | NM |
|---|---|---|---|
| ❑ CS 1098 [R] | The Dave Clark Five with the Playbacks | 196? | 12.00 |
| *—Reissue* | | | |

EPIC

| Number | Title (A Side/B Side) | Yr | NM |
|---|---|---|---|
| ❑ LN 24093 [M] | Glad All Over | 1964 | 40.00 |
| *—Group photo with instruments* | | | |
| ❑ LN 24093 [M] | Glad All Over | 1964 | 80.00 |
| *—Group photo, no instruments* | | | |
| ❑ LN 24104 [M] | The Dave Clark Five Return | 1964 | 40.00 |
| ❑ LN 24117 [M] | American Tour | 1964 | 40.00 |
| ❑ LN 24128 [M] | Coast to Coast | 1965 | 40.00 |
| ❑ LN 24139 [M] | Weekend in London | 1965 | 40.00 |
| ❑ LN 24162 [M] | Having a Wild Weekend | 1965 | 40.00 |
| ❑ LN 24178 [M] | I Like It Like That | 1965 | 40.00 |
| ❑ LN 24185 [M] | The Dave Clark Five's Greatest Hits | 1966 | 25.00 |
| ❑ LN 24198 [M] | Try Too Hard | 1966 | 30.00 |
| ❑ LN 24212 [M] | Satisfied with You | 1966 | 30.00 |
| ❑ LN 24221 [M] | More Greatest Hits | 1966 | 25.00 |
| ❑ LN 24236 [M] | 5 by 5 | 1967 | 30.00 |
| ❑ LN 24312 [M] | You Got What It Takes | 1967 | 30.00 |
| ❑ LN 24354 [M] | Everybody Knows | 1968 | 30.00 |
| ❑ BN 26093 [R] | Glad All Over | 1964 | 30.00 |
| *—Group photo with instruments* | | | |
| ❑ BN 26093 [R] | Glad All Over | 1964 | 50.00 |
| *—Group photo, no instruments* | | | |
| ❑ BN 26104 [R] | The Dave Clark Five Return | 1964 | 30.00 |
| ❑ BN 26117 [R] | American Tour | 1964 | 30.00 |
| ❑ BN 26128 [R] | Coast to Coast | 1965 | 30.00 |
| ❑ BN 26139 [R] | Weekend in London | 1965 | 30.00 |
| ❑ BN 26162 [R] | Having a Wild Weekend | 1965 | 30.00 |
| ❑ BN 26178 [R] | I Like It Like That | 1965 | 30.00 |
| ❑ BN 26185 [R] | The Dave Clark Five's Greatest Hits | 1966 | 20.00 |
| *—Yellow label* | | | |
| ❑ BN 26185 [R] | The Dave Clark Five's Greatest Hits | 1973 | 40.00 |
| *—Orange label* | | | |
| ❑ BN 26198 [R] | Try Too Hard | 1966 | 25.00 |
| ❑ BN 26212 [R] | Satisfied with You | 1966 | 25.00 |
| ❑ BN 26221 [R] | More Greatest Hits | 1966 | 20.00 |
| ❑ BN 26236 [S] | 5 by 5 | 1967 | 40.00 |
| ❑ BN 26312 [S] | You Got What It Takes | 1967 | 40.00 |
| ❑ BN 26354 [S] | Everybody Knows | 1968 | 40.00 |
| ❑ EG 30434 [(2)S] | The Dave Clark Five | 1971 | 100.00 |
| *—Twenty hits and near-hits, all in true stereo! Yellow label.* | | | |
| ❑ EG 30434 [(2)S] | The Dave Clark Five | 1973 | 80.00 |
| *—Twenty hits and near-hits, all in true stereo! Orange label.* | | | |
| ❑ KEG 33459 [(2)M] | Glad All Over Again | 1975 | 50.00 |
| ❑ XEM 77238/9 [DJ] | The Dave Clark Five Interview | 1964 | 600.00 |

**CLARK, DEE**

ABNER

| Number | Title (A Side/B Side) | Yr | NM |
|---|---|---|---|
| ❑ LP-2000 [M] | Dee Clark | 1959 | 120.00 |



Except when noted otherwise, VG = 25% of NM, and VG+ = 50% of NM. (Example: VG = $2.00, VG+ = $4.00 and NM = $8.00.)

| Number | Title (A Side/B Side) | Yr | NM |
|---|---|---|---|
| ❑ SR-2000 [S] | Dee Clark | 1959 | 350.00 |
| ❑ LP-2002 [M] | How About That | 1960 | 80.00 |
| ❑ SR-2002 [S] | How About That | 1960 | 120.00 |
| **SOLID SMOKE** | | | |
| ❑ 8026 | His Best Recordings | 1983 | 10.00 |
| **SUNSET** | | | |
| ❑ SUS-5217 | Wondering | 1968 | 12.00 |
| **VEE JAY** | | | |
| ❑ LP-1019 [M] | You're Looking Good | 1960 | 50.00 |
| ❑ LP-1037 [M] | Hold On, It's Dee Clark | 1961 | 50.00 |
| ❑ SR-1037 [S] | Hold On, It's Dee Clark | 1961 | 100.00 |
| ❑ LP-1047 [M] | The Best of Dee Clark | 1964 | 50.00 |
| ❑ SR-1047 [S] | The Best of Dee Clark | 1964 | 100.00 |
| ❑ VJLP-1047 | The Best of Dee Clark | 1986 | 12.00 |
| *—Authorized reissue* | | | |

### CLARK, DICK
See VARIOUS ARTISTS COLLECTIONS.

### CLARK, DOTTIE

| Number | Title (A Side/B Side) | Yr | NM |
|---|---|---|---|
| **MAINSTREAM** | | | |
| ❑ S-6006 [S] | I'm Lost | 1966 | 25.00 |
| ❑ 56006 [M] | I'm Lost | 1966 | 20.00 |

### CLARK, DOUG, AND THE HOT NUTS

| Number | Title (A Side/B Side) | Yr | NM |
|---|---|---|---|
| **GROSS** | | | |
| ❑ 101 | Nuts to You | 196? | 30.00 |
| ❑ 102 | On Campus | 196? | 30.00 |
| ❑ 103 | Homecoming | 196? | 30.00 |
| ❑ 104 | Rush Week | 1967 | 30.00 |
| ❑ 105 | Panty Raid | 196? | 30.00 |
| ❑ 106 | Summer Session | 196? | 30.00 |
| ❑ 107 | Hell Night | 196? | 30.00 |
| ❑ 108 | Freak Out | 196? | 30.00 |
| ❑ 109 | With a Hat On | 196? | 30.00 |

### CLARK, GENE

| Number | Title (A Side/B Side) | Yr | NM |
|---|---|---|---|
| **A&M** | | | |
| ❑ SP-4292 | White Light | 1971 | 15.00 |
| **ASYLUM** | | | |
| ❑ 7E-1016 | No Other | 1974 | 15.00 |
| **COLUMBIA** | | | |
| ❑ CL 2618 [M] | Gene Clark with the Gosdin Brothers | 1967 | 30.00 |
| ❑ CS 9418 [S] | Gene Clark with the Gosdin Brothers | 1967 | 50.00 |
| ❑ KC 31123 | Early L.A. Sessions | 1972 | 15.00 |
| **RSO** | | | |
| ❑ RS-1-3011 | Two Sides to Every Story | 1976 | 20.00 |
| **SUNDAZED** | | | |
| ❑ LP 5062 | Gene Clark with the Gosdin Brothers | 2000 | 15.00 |
| *—Reissue of Columbia LP* | | | |
| **TAKOMA** | | | |
| ❑ TAK-7112 | Firebyrd | 1984 | 10.00 |

### CLARK, GUY

| Number | Title (A Side/B Side) | Yr | NM |
|---|---|---|---|
| **RCA VICTOR** | | | |
| ❑ AHL1-1303 | Old No. 1 | 198? | 10.00 |
| *—Reissue with new prefix* | | | |
| ❑ APL1-1303 | Old No. 1 | 1976 | 20.00 |
| ❑ APL1-1944 | Texas Cookin' | 1976 | 20.00 |
| **SUGAR HILL** | | | |
| ❑ SH-1025 | Old Friends | 198? | 12.00 |
| **WARNER BROS.** | | | |
| ❑ WBMS-105 [DJ] | On the Road, Live! | 198? | 60.00 |
| *—Part of "The Warner Bros. Music Show" series; promo only* | | | |
| ❑ BSK 3241 | Guy Clark | 1978 | 15.00 |
| ❑ BSK 3381 | South Coast of Texas | 1981 | 15.00 |
| ❑ 23880 | Better Days | 1983 | 12.00 |

### CLARK, KEN, AND DON ANTHONY

| Number | Title (A Side/B Side) | Yr | NM |
|---|---|---|---|
| **STARDAY** | | | |
| ❑ SLP-114 [M] | Fiddlin' Country Style | 1959 | 40.00 |

### CLARK, PETULA

| Number | Title (A Side/B Side) | Yr | NM |
|---|---|---|---|
| **COCA-COLA** | | | |
| ❑ 103 [DJ] | Petula Clark Swings the Jingle | 1966 | 150.00 |
| **GNP CRESCENDO** | | | |
| ❑ 2069 | Live at the Royal Albert Hall | 1972 | 10.00 |
| ❑ 2170 | The Greatest Hits of Petula Clark | 1984 | 8.00 |
| **IMPERIAL** | | | |
| ❑ LP-9079 [M] | Pet Clark | 1959 | 50.00 |
| ❑ LP-9281 [M] | Uptown with Petula Clark | 1965 | 20.00 |
| *—Reissue of Imperial 9079* | | | |
| ❑ LP-12027 [S] | Pet Clark | 1959 | 80.00 |
| ❑ LP-12281 [S] | Uptown with Petula Clark | 1965 | 25.00 |
| *—Reissue of Imperial 12079* | | | |
| **JANGO** | | | |
| ❑ 779 | Give It a Try | 1986 | 10.00 |
| **LAURIE** | | | |
| ❑ LLP-2032 [M] | In Love! | 1965 | 15.00 |

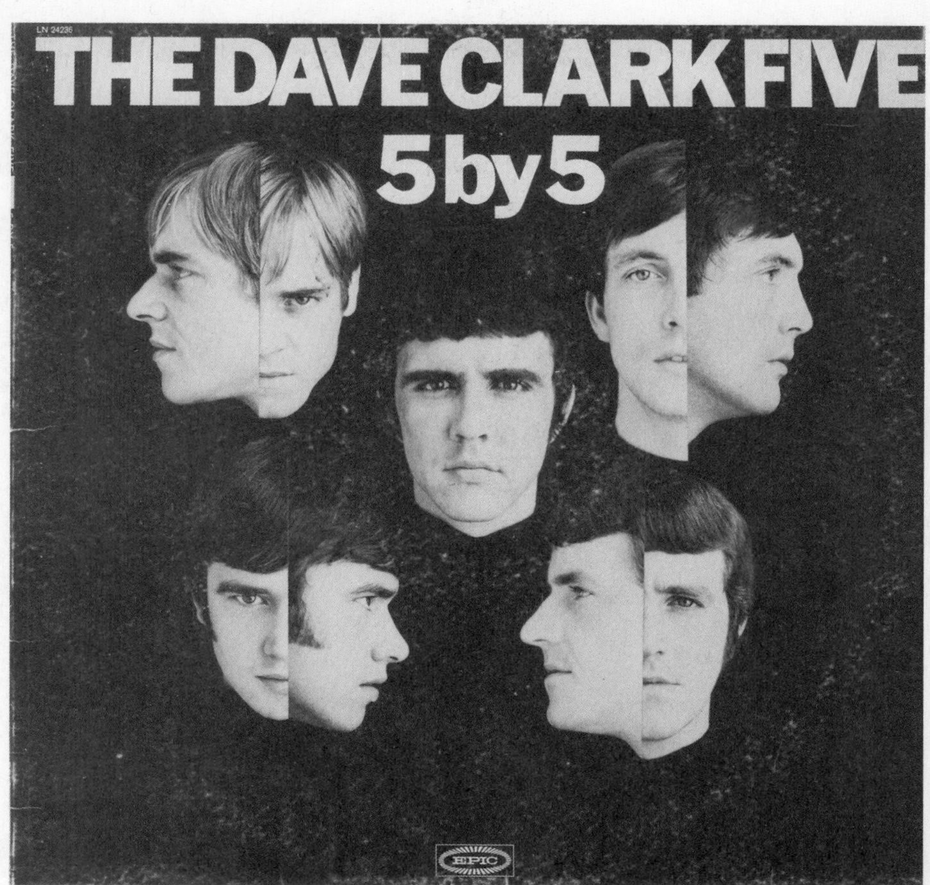


The Dave Clark Five, *5 by 5,* Epic BN 26236, 1967, stereo, $40.

| Number | Title (A Side/B Side) | Yr | NM |
|---|---|---|---|
| ❑ SLP-2032 [S] | In Love! | 1965 | 15.00 |
| ❑ ST-90497 [S] | In Love! | 1965 | 20.00 |
| *—Capitol Record Club edition* | | | |
| ❑ T-90497 [M] | In Love! | 1965 | 20.00 |
| *—Capitol Record Club edition* | | | |
| **MGM** | | | |
| ❑ SE-4859 | Pet Clark Now | 1972 | 10.00 |
| **PREMIER** | | | |
| ❑ PM-9016 [M] | The English Sound Starring Petula Clark | 1965 | 12.00 |
| ❑ PS-9016 [S] | The English Sound Starring Petula Clark | 1965 | 15.00 |
| **ROULETTE** | | | |
| ❑ 1 [(3)] | Petula | 1975 | 20.00 |
| **SUNSET** | | | |
| ❑ SUM-1101 [M] | This Is Petula Clark | 1965 | 12.00 |
| ❑ SUS-5101 [S] | This Is Petula Clark | 1965 | 15.00 |
| **WARNER BROS.** | | | |
| ❑ W 1590 [M] | Downtown | 1965 | 15.00 |
| *—Originals have gray labels* | | | |
| ❑ W 1590 [M] | Downtown | 1966 | 12.00 |
| *—Reissues have gold labels* | | | |
| ❑ WS 1590 [S] | Downtown | 1965 | 20.00 |
| *—Originals have gold labels* | | | |
| ❑ W 1598 [M] | I Know a Place | 1965 | 15.00 |
| *—Originals have gray labels* | | | |
| ❑ W 1598 [M] | I Know a Place | 1966 | 12.00 |
| *—Reissues have gold labels* | | | |
| ❑ WS 1598 [S] | I Know a Place | 1965 | 20.00 |
| *—Originals have gold labels* | | | |
| ❑ WS 1598 [S] | I Know a Place | 1968 | 12.00 |
| *—Green label with "W7" logo in box at top* | | | |
| ❑ W 1608 [M] | The World's Greatest International Hits | 1965 | 12.00 |
| *—Reissues have gold labels* | | | |
| ❑ W 1608 [M] | The World's Greatest International Hits | 1965 | 15.00 |
| *—Originals have gray labels* | | | |
| ❑ WS 1608 [S] | The World's Greatest International Hits | 1965 | 20.00 |
| *—Originals have gold labels* | | | |
| ❑ W 1630 [M] | My Love | 1966 | 10.00 |
| ❑ WS 1630 [S] | My Love | 1966 | 12.00 |
| ❑ W 1645 [M] | I Couldn't Live Without Your Love | 1966 | 10.00 |
| ❑ WS 1645 [S] | I Couldn't Live Without Your Love | 1966 | 12.00 |
| ❑ W 1673 [M] | Color My World/Who Am I | 1967 | 10.00 |
| ❑ WS 1673 [S] | Color My World/Who Am I | 1967 | 12.00 |
| ❑ W 1698 [M] | These Are My Songs | 1967 | 10.00 |
| ❑ WS 1698 [S] | These Are My Songs | 1967 | 12.00 |
| ❑ W 1719 [M] | The Other Man's Grass Is Always Greener | 1968 | 12.00 |
| ❑ WS 1719 [P] | The Other Man's Grass Is Always Greener | 1968 | 12.00 |
| *—"The Other Man's Grass Is Always Greener" is rechanneled.* | | | |
| ❑ W 1743 [M] | Petula | 1968 | 12.00 |
| ❑ WS 1743 [S] | Petula | 1968 | 12.00 |
| ❑ WS 1765 | Greatest Hits, Volume I | 1968 | 10.00 |
| ❑ WS 1789 | Portrait of Petula | 1969 | 10.00 |
| ❑ WS 1823 | Just Pet | 1969 | 10.00 |
| ❑ WS 1862 | Memphis | 1970 | 10.00 |
| ❑ WS 1865 | Warm and Tender (The Song of My Life) | 1971 | 10.00 |
| ❑ ST-91348 [S] | These Are My Songs | 1967 | 15.00 |
| *—Capitol Record Club edition* | | | |
| ❑ ST-91598 | Greatest Hits, Volume I | 1968 | 15.00 |
| *—Capitol Record Club edition* | | | |
| ❑ SQBO-93215 [(2)P] | Hits...My Way | 1969 | 25.00 |
| *—Capitol Record Club exclusive; "The Other Man's Grass Is Always Greener" is rechanneled.* | | | |

### CLARK, ROY

| Number | Title (A Side/B Side) | Yr | NM |
|---|---|---|---|
| **ABC** | | | |
| ❑ AB-1053 | Labor of Love | 1978 | 10.00 |
| **ABC DOT** | | | |
| ❑ DOSD-2001 | Roy Clark/The Entertainer | 1974 | 10.00 |
| ❑ DOSD-2005 | Roy Clark, Family & Friends | 1974 | 10.00 |
| ❑ DOSD-2010 | Classic Clark | 1974 | 10.00 |
| ❑ DOSD-2030 | Roy Clark's Greatest Hits — Volume 1 | 1975 | 10.00 |
| ❑ DOSD-2041 | Heart to Heart | 1975 | 10.00 |
| ❑ DOSD-2054 | Roy Clark In Concert | 1976 | 10.00 |
| ❑ DO-2072 [(2)] | My Music and Me/Vocal & Instrumental | 1977 | 12.00 |
| ❑ DO-2099 | Hookin' It | 1977 | 10.00 |
| *—Reissue of Record 2 of 2072* | | | |
| **CAPITOL** | | | |
| ❑ SKAO-369 | The Greatest! | 1969 | 12.00 |
| ❑ SM-369 | The Greatest! | 197? | 10.00 |
| *—Reissue with new prefix* | | | |

Doug Clark and the Hot Nuts, *Summer Session,* Gross 106, 1960s, mono, $30.

| Number | Title (A Side/B Side) | Yr | NM |
|---|---|---|---|
| ❑ ST 1780 [S] | The Lightning Fingers of Roy Clark | 1962 | 25.00 |
| ❑ T 1780 [M] | The Lightning Fingers of Roy Clark | 1962 | 20.00 |
| ❑ ST 1972 [S] | The Tip of My Fingers | 1963 | 25.00 |
| ❑ T 1972 [M] | The Tip of My Fingers | 1963 | 20.00 |
| ❑ ST 2031 [S] | Happy to Be Unhappy | 1964 | 25.00 |
| ❑ T 2031 [M] | Happy to Be Unhappy | 1964 | 20.00 |
| ❑ SM-2425 | The Roy Clark Guitar Spectacular | 197? | 10.00 |
| *—Reissue with new prefix* | | | |
| ❑ ST 2425 [S] | The Roy Clark Guitar Spectacular | 1965 | 25.00 |
| ❑ T 2425 [M] | The Roy Clark Guitar Spectacular | 1965 | 20.00 |
| ❑ ST 2452 [S] | Roy Clark Sings Lonesome Love Ballads | 1966 | 25.00 |
| ❑ T 2452 [M] | Roy Clark Sings Lonesome Love Ballads | 1966 | 20.00 |
| ❑ ST 2535 [S] | Stringing Along with the Blues | 1966 | 25.00 |
| ❑ T 2535 [M] | Stringing Along with the Blues | 1966 | 20.00 |
| ❑ SABB-11264 [(2)] | The Entertainer of the Year | 1974 | 15.00 |
| ❑ SM-11412 | So Much to Remember | 1975 | 10.00 |
| ❑ SM-12032 | The Tip of My Fingers | 1980 | 8.00 |
| ❑ SN-16161 | The Greatest! | 198? | 8.00 |
| ❑ SN-16227 | The Lightning Fingers of Roy Clark | 198? | 8.00 |

CHURCHILL

| Number | Title (A Side/B Side) | Yr | NM |
|---|---|---|---|
| ❑ 9421 | The Roy Clark Show Live from Austin City Limits | 1982 | 10.00 |
| ❑ 9425 | Turned Loose | 1982 | 10.00 |

DOT

| Number | Title (A Side/B Side) | Yr | NM |
|---|---|---|---|
| ❑ DOS-000112 | The Special Talents of Roy Clark | 1973 | 12.00 |
| ❑ DLP-25863 | Urban, Suburban | 1968 | 12.00 |
| ❑ DLP-25895 | Do You Believe This Roy Clark | 1968 | 12.00 |
| ❑ DLP-25953 | Yesterday, When I Was Young | 1969 | 12.00 |
| ❑ DLP-25972 | The Everlovin' Soul of Roy Clark | 1969 | 12.00 |
| ❑ DLP-25977 | The Other Side of Roy Clark | 1970 | 12.00 |
| ❑ DLP-25980 | I Never Picked Cotton | 1970 | 12.00 |
| ❑ DOS-25986 | The Best of Roy Clark | 1971 | 12.00 |
| ❑ DOS-25990 | The Incredible Roy Clark | 1971 | 12.00 |
| ❑ DOS-25993 | The Magnificent Sanctuary Band | 1971 | 12.00 |
| ❑ DOS-25997 | Roy Clark Country! | 1972 | 12.00 |
| ❑ DOS-26005 | Roy Clark Live! | 1972 | 12.00 |
| ❑ DOS-26008 | Roy Clark/Superpicker | 1973 | 12.00 |
| ❑ DOS-26010 | Come Live with Me | 1973 | 12.00 |
| ❑ DOS-26018 | Roy Clark's Family Album | 1973 | 12.00 |
| ❑ ST-93117 | The Everlovin' Soul of Roy Clark | 1969 | 15.00 |
| *—Capitol Record Club edition with old-style black Dot label with multi-color logo* | | | |
| ❑ ST-94463 | Roy Clark Country! | 1972 | 15.00 |
| *—Capitol Record Club edition* | | | |

HILLTOP

| Number | Title (A Side/B Side) | Yr | NM |
|---|---|---|---|
| ❑ 6046 | Roy Clartk | 196? | 15.00 |
| ❑ 6080 | Silver Threads and Golden Needles | 1970 | 10.00 |
| ❑ 6094 | He'll Have to Go | 1970 | 10.00 |
| ❑ 6135 | Take Me As I Am | 197? | 10.00 |
| ❑ 6154 | Honky Tonk | 197? | 10.00 |

MCA

| Number | Title (A Side/B Side) | Yr | NM |
|---|---|---|---|
| ❑ 675 | Labor of Love | 1980 | 8.00 |
| ❑ 676 | Heart to Heart | 1980 | 8.00 |
| ❑ 677 | Hookin' It | 1980 | 8.00 |
| ❑ 678 | Yesterday, When I Was Young | 198? | 8.00 |
| ❑ 679 | Roy Clark/Superpicker | 198? | 8.00 |
| ❑ 811 | Back to the Country | 198? | 8.00 |
| ❑ 3161 | Makin' Music | 1980 | 10.00 |
| *—With Gatemouth Brown* | | | |
| ❑ 3189 | My Music | 1980 | 10.00 |
| ❑ 27015 | The Best of Roy Clark | 198? | 8.00 |
| ❑ 27050 | Roy Clark's Greatest Hits — Volume 1 | 198? | 8.00 |
| ❑ 37130 | Banjo Bandits | 198? | 8.00 |
| *—With Buck Trent* | | | |
| ❑ 37131 | A Pair of Fives (Banjos, That Is) | 198? | 8.00 |
| ❑ 37132 | Roy Clark In Concert | 198? | 8.00 |
| ❑ 37134 | Roy Clark Live! | 198? | 8.00 |
| ❑ 37142 | My Music | 198? | 8.00 |

PAIR

| Number | Title (A Side/B Side) | Yr | NM |
|---|---|---|---|
| ❑ PDL2-1088 [(2)] | Country Standard Time | 1986 | 12.00 |

PICKWICK

| Number | Title (A Side/B Side) | Yr | NM |
|---|---|---|---|
| ❑ PTP-2043 [(2)] | Roy Clark | 1973 | 12.00 |
| ❑ PTP-2093 [(2)] | The Entertainer of the Year | 1978 | 12.00 |

SONGBIRD

| Number | Title (A Side/B Side) | Yr | NM |
|---|---|---|---|
| ❑ 5260 | The Last Word in Jesus Is Us | 1981 | 10.00 |

TOWER

| Number | Title (A Side/B Side) | Yr | NM |
|---|---|---|---|
| ❑ ST 5055 [S] | Roy Clark Live | 1967 | 20.00 |
| ❑ T 5055 [M] | Roy Clark Live | 1967 | 15.00 |
| ❑ DT 5118 [R] | In the Mood | 1968 | 15.00 |

WORD

| Number | Title (A Side/B Side) | Yr | NM |
|---|---|---|---|
| ❑ 8654 | Roy Clark Sings Gospel | 1975 | 12.00 |

## CLARK, ROY, AND BUCK TRENT

ABC

| Number | Title (A Side/B Side) | Yr | NM |
|---|---|---|---|
| ❑ AY-1084 | Banjo Bandits | 1978 | 10.00 |

ABC DOT

| Number | Title (A Side/B Side) | Yr | NM |
|---|---|---|---|
| ❑ 2015 | A Pair of Fives (Banjos, That Is) | 1975 | 10.00 |

## CLARK, SANFORD

LHI

| Number | Title (A Side/B Side) | Yr | NM |
|---|---|---|---|
| ❑ 12003 | Return of the Fool | 1968 | 60.00 |

## CLARK, SONNY

BLUE NOTE

| Number | Title (A Side/B Side) | Yr | NM |
|---|---|---|---|
| ❑ BLP-1570 [M] | Dial "S" for Sonny | 1957 | 200.00 |
| *—Regular version, W. 63rd St. address on label* | | | |
| ❑ BLP-1570 [M] | Dial "S" for Sonny | 1957 | 400.00 |
| *—"Deep groove" version; W. 63rd St. address on label* | | | |
| ❑ BLP-1570 [M] | Dial "S" for Sonny | 1963 | 50.00 |
| *—"New York, USA" address on label* | | | |
| ❑ BST-1570 [S] | Dial "S" for Sonny | 1959 | 120.00 |
| *—Regular version, W. 63rd St. address on label* | | | |
| ❑ BST-1570 [S] | Dial "S" for Sonny | 1959 | 300.00 |
| *—"Deep groove" version; W. 63rd St. address on label* | | | |
| ❑ BST-1570 [S] | Dial "S" for Sonny | 1963 | 40.00 |
| *—"New York, USA" address on label* | | | |
| ❑ BLP-1576 [M] | Sonny's Crib | 1957 | 200.00 |
| *—Regular version, W. 63rd St. address on label* | | | |
| ❑ BLP-1576 [M] | Sonny's Crib | 1957 | 400.00 |
| *—"Deep groove" version; W. 63rd St. address on label* | | | |
| ❑ BLP-1576 [M] | Sonny's Crib | 1963 | 50.00 |
| *—"New York, USA" address on label* | | | |
| ❑ BST-1576 [S] | Sonny's Crib | 1959 | 120.00 |
| *—Regular version, W. 63rd St. address on label* | | | |
| ❑ BST-1576 [S] | Sonny's Crib | 1959 | 250.00 |
| *—"Deep groove" version; W. 63rd St. address on label* | | | |
| ❑ BST-1576 [S] | Sonny's Crib | 1963 | 40.00 |
| *—"New York, USA" address on label* | | | |
| ❑ BLP-1579 [M] | Sonny Clark Trio | 1958 | 150.00 |
| *—Regular version, W. 63rd St. address on label* | | | |
| ❑ BLP-1579 [M] | Sonny Clark Trio | 1958 | 400.00 |
| *—"Deep groove" version; W. 63rd St. address on label* | | | |
| ❑ BLP-1579 [M] | Sonny Clark Trio | 1963 | 40.00 |
| *—"New York, USA" address on label* | | | |
| ❑ BST-1579 [S] | Sonny Clark Trio | 1959 | 120.00 |
| *—Regular version, W. 63rd St. address on label* | | | |
| ❑ BST-1579 [S] | Sonny Clark Trio | 1959 | 250.00 |
| *—"Deep groove" version; W. 63rd St. address on label* | | | |
| ❑ BST-1579 [S] | Sonny Clark Trio | 1963 | 30.00 |
| *—"New York, USA" address on label* | | | |
| ❑ BLP-1588 [M] | Cool Struttin' | 1958 | 80.00 |
| *—Regular version, W. 63rd St. address on label* | | | |
| ❑ BLP-1588 [M] | Cool Struttin' | 1958 | 150.00 |
| *—"Deep groove" version (deep indentation under label on both sides)* | | | |
| ❑ BLP-1588 [M] | Cool Struttin' | 1963 | 25.00 |
| *—"New York, USA" address on label* | | | |
| ❑ BST-1588 [S] | Cool Struttin' | 1959 | 60.00 |
| *—Regular version, W. 63rd St. address on label* | | | |
| ❑ BST-1588 [S] | Cool Struttin' | 1959 | 100.00 |
| *—"Deep groove" version (deep indentation under label on both sides)* | | | |
| ❑ BST-1588 [S] | Cool Struttin' | 1963 | 20.00 |
| *—"New York, USA" address on label* | | | |
| ❑ BST-1588 [S] | Cool Struttin' | 1997 | 30.00 |
| *—180-gram reissue; distributed by Classic Records* | | | |
| ❑ BST-1588-45 [(4)S] | Cool Struttin' | 200? | 150.00 |
| *—Classic Records box set of four 45 rpm 12-inch records* | | | |
| ❑ BLP-1592 [M] | Cool Struttin' — Volume 2 | 1959 | — |
| *—Canceled* | | | |
| ❑ BST-1592 [S] | Cool Struttin' — Volume 2 | 1959 | — |
| *—Canceled* | | | |
| ❑ BLP-4091 [M] | Leapin' and Lopin' | 1961 | 200.00 |
| *—W. 63rd St. address on label* | | | |
| ❑ BLP-4091 [M] | Leapin' and Lopin' | 1963 | 100.00 |
| *—"New York, USA" address on label* | | | |
| ❑ BST-84091 [S] | Leapin' and Lopin' | 1961 | 150.00 |
| *—W. 63rd St. address on label* | | | |
| ❑ BST-84091 [S] | Leapin' and Lopin' | 1963 | 50.00 |
| *—"New York, USA" address on label* | | | |

TIME

| Number | Title (A Side/B Side) | Yr | NM |
|---|---|---|---|
| ❑ S-2101 [S] | Sonny Clark Trio | 1962 | 30.00 |
| ❑ 52101 [M] | Sonny Clark Trio | 1962 | 25.00 |
| ❑ ST-70010 [S] | Sonny Clark Trio | 1960 | 50.00 |
| ❑ T-70010 [M] | Sonny Clark Trio | 1960 | 40.00 |

## CLARK, YODELING SLIM

CONTINENTAL

| Number | Title (A Side/B Side) | Yr | NM |
|---|---|---|---|
| ❑ C-1505 [M] | Cowboy and Yodel Songs | 1962 | 40.00 |

MASTERSEAL

| Number | Title (A Side/B Side) | Yr | NM |
|---|---|---|---|
| ❑ MS-57 [M] | Cowboy Songs | 1963 | 25.00 |
| ❑ MS-112 [M] | Songs by Yodeling Slim Clark | 1964 | 25.00 |
| ❑ MS-135 [M] | Cowboy Songs Vol. 2 | 1964 | 25.00 |

| Number | Title (A Side/B Side) | Yr | NM |
|---|---|---|---|
| PALOMINO | | | |
| ❑ 300 [M] | Yodeling Slim Clark Sings the Legendary Jimmie Rodgers Songs | 1966 | 60.00 |
| ❑ 301 [M] | Yodeling Slim Clark Sings and Yodels Favorite Montana Slim Songs of the Mountains and Plains, Vol. 1 | 1966 | 60.00 |
| ❑ 303 [M] | Yodeling Slim Clark Sings and Yodels Favorite Montana Slim Songs of the Mountains and Plains, Vol. 2 | 1966 | 40.00 |
| ❑ 306 [M] | I Feel a Trip Coming On | 1966 | 40.00 |
| ❑ 307 [M] | Old Chestnuts | 1967 | 40.00 |
| ❑ 310 [M] | Yodeling Slim Clark Happens Again | 1967 | 40.00 |
| ❑ 311 [M] | The Ballad of Billy Venero | 1968 | 40.00 |
| ❑ 314 [M] | Yodeling Slim Clark's 50th Anniversary Album | 1968 | 50.00 |
| *—Gold vinyl* | | | |
| PLAYHOUSE | | | |
| ❑ 2017 [10] | Western Songs and Dances | 1954 | 50.00 |
| **CLARK SISTERS, THE** | | | |
| CORAL | | | |
| ❑ CRL 57290 [M] | Beauty Shop Beat | 1960 | 20.00 |
| ❑ CRL 757290 [S] | Beauty Shop Beat | 1960 | 25.00 |
| DOT | | | |
| ❑ DLP-3104 [M] | Sing, Sing, Sing | 1957 | 30.00 |
| ❑ DLP-3137 [M] | The Clark Sisters Swing Again | 1958 | 25.00 |
| ❑ DLP-25137 [S] | The Clark Sisters Swing Again | 1958 | 30.00 |
| **CLARKE, BUCK** | | | |
| ARGO | | | |
| ❑ LP-4007 [M] | Drum Sum | 1961 | 25.00 |
| ❑ LPS-4007 [S] | Drum Sum | 1961 | 30.00 |
| ❑ LP-4021 [M] | The Buck Clarke Sound | 1963 | 25.00 |
| ❑ LPS-4021 [S] | The Buck Clarke Sound | 1963 | 30.00 |
| OFFBEAT | | | |
| ❑ OLP-3003 [M] | Cool Hands | 1960 | 30.00 |
| ❑ OS-93003 [S] | Cool Hands | 1960 | 40.00 |
| **CLARKE, KEN** | | | |
| MGM | | | |
| ❑ E-205 [10] | Jazz Piano | 1953 | 50.00 |
| **CLARKE, KENNY** | | | |
| EPIC | | | |
| ❑ LN 3376 [M] | Kenny Clarke Plays Andre Hodeir | 1957 | 40.00 |
| SAVOY | | | |
| ❑ MG-12006 [M] | Telefunken Blues | 1955 | 80.00 |
| ❑ MG-12017 [M] | Bohemia After Dark | 1955 | 80.00 |
| ❑ MG-12065 [M] | Klook's Clique | 1956 | 100.00 |
| ❑ MG-15051 [10] | Kenny Clarke, Vol. 1 | 195? | 200.00 |
| ❑ MG-15053 [10] | Kenny Clarke, Vol. 2 | 195? | 200.00 |
| **CLARKE, KENNY, AND ERNIE WILKINS** | | | |
| SAVOY | | | |
| ❑ MG-12007 [M] | Plenty for Kenny | 1955 | 80.00 |
| **CLARKE-BOLAND BIG BAND, THE** KENNY CLARKE and Francy Boland. | | | |
| ATLANTIC | | | |
| ❑ 1401 [M] | Jazz Is Universal | 1963 | 30.00 |
| ❑ SD 1401 [S] | Jazz Is Universal | 1963 | 40.00 |
| ❑ 1404 [M] | The Clarke-Boland Big Band | 1963 | 30.00 |
| ❑ SD 1404 [S] | The Clarke-Boland Big Band | 1963 | 40.00 |
| BASF | | | |
| ❑ 25102 [(2)] | The Big Band Sound | 1971 | 20.00 |
| BLUE NOTE | | | |
| ❑ BLP-4092 [M] | The Golden Eight | 1961 | 200.00 |
| *—As "Kenny Clarke-Francy Boland & Co."; W. 63rd St. address on label* | | | |
| ❑ BLP-4092 [M] | The Golden Eight | 1963 | 100.00 |
| *—As "Kenny Clarke-Francy Boland & Co."; "New York, USA" address on label* | | | |
| ❑ BST-84092 [S] | The Golden Eight | 1961 | 150.00 |
| *—As "Kenny Clarke-Francy Boland & Co."; W. 63rd St. address on label* | | | |
| ❑ BST-84092 [S] | The Golden Eight | 1963 | 80.00 |
| *—As "Kenny Clarke-Francy Boland & Co."; "New York, USA" address on label* | | | |
| COLUMBIA | | | |
| ❑ CS 9114 [S] | Now Hear Our Meanin' | 1965 | 20.00 |
| **CLARY, ROBERT** | | | |
| ATLANTIC | | | |
| ❑ 8053 [M] | Livin' It Up at the Playboy Club | 1961 | 30.00 |
| ❑ SD 8053 [S] | Livin' It Up at the Playboy Club | 1961 | 40.00 |
| EPIC | | | |
| ❑ LN 3171 [M] | Meet Robert Clary | 1955 | 25.00 |
| ❑ LN 3281 [M] | Hooray for Love | 1956 | 25.00 |

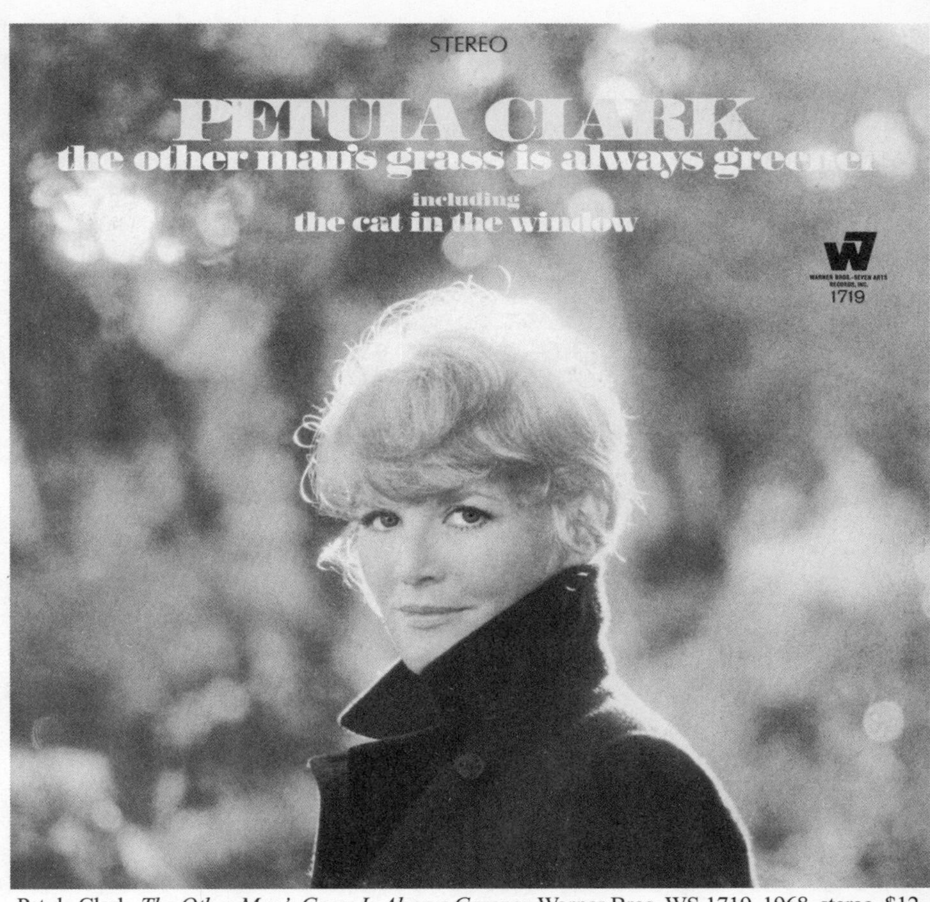


Petula Clark, *The Other Man's Grass Is Always Greener,* Warner Bros. WS 1719, 1968, stereo, $12.

| Number | Title (A Side/B Side) | Yr | NM |
|---|---|---|---|
| MERCURY | | | |
| ❑ MG-20367 [M] | Gigi Sung by Robert Clary | 1958 | 20.00 |
| ❑ SR-60042 [S] | Gigi Sung by Robert Clary | 1958 | 30.00 |
| **CLASH, THE** | | | |
| EPIC | | | |
| ❑ AS 913 [DJ] | Sandinista Now! | 1981 | 30.00 |
| *—Promo-only sampler* | | | |
| ❑ AS 952 [DJ] | If Music Could Talk (Interchords) | 1981 | 40.00 |
| *—Promo-only interview record* | | | |
| ❑ AS 99-1592 [PD] | Combat Rock | 1982 | 40.00 |
| *—Promo-only picture disc* | | | |
| ❑ AS 1594 [DJ] | The World According to the Clash | 1982 | 40.00 |
| *—Promo-only sampler* | | | |
| ❑ AS 99-1595 [DJ] | Combat Rock | 1982 | 30.00 |
| *—Camouflage green vinyl promo* | | | |
| ❑ JE 35543 | Give 'Em Enough Rope | 1978 | 15.00 |
| *—Block letters on cover; orange label* | | | |
| ❑ JE 35543 | Give 'Em Enough Rope | 1978 | 15.00 |
| *—Script cover; orange label* | | | |
| ❑ JE 35543 [DJ] | Give 'Em Enough Rope | 1978 | 30.00 |
| *—White label promo; timing strip; back cover has one incorrect song title* | | | |
| ❑ JE 36060 | The Clash | 1979 | 15.00 |
| ❑ PE 36060 | The Clash | 1979 | 8.00 |
| *—Budget-line reissue; no bonus single* | | | |
| ❑ E2 36238 [DJ] | London Calling | 1980 | 25.00 |
| *—White label promo* | | | |
| ❑ E2 36329 [(2)] | London Calling | 1979 | 15.00 |
| ❑ E3X 37037 [(3)] | Sandinista! | 1981 | 20.00 |
| ❑ FE 37689 | Combat Rock | 1982 | 10.00 |
| *—Second and later pressings (with standard dark blue labels) delete commercial during "Inoculated City"* | | | |
| ❑ FE 37689 | Combat Rock | 1982 | 15.00 |
| *—First pressings (with custom labels) contain a commercial in the middle of the song "Inoculated City"* | | | |
| ❑ PE 38540 | Black Market Clash | 1982 | 10.00 |
| *—12-inch version of 10-inch record* | | | |
| ❑ FE 40017 | Cut the Crap | 1985 | 10.00 |
| ❑ E2 44025 [(2)] | The Story of the Clash, Vol. 1 | 1988 | 15.00 |
| EPIC LEGACY | | | |
| ❑ E3 53191 [(3)10] | Super Black Market Clash | 1993 | 30.00 |
| EPIC NU-DISK | | | |
| ❑ 4E 36846 [10] | Black Market Clash | 1980 | 15.00 |

| Number | Title (A Side/B Side) | Yr | NM |
|---|---|---|---|
| **CLASS-AIRES, THE** | | | |
| HONEY BEE | | | |
| ❑ (# unknown) | Tears Start to Fall | 195? | 300.00 |
| **CLASSICS IV** | | | |
| ACCORD | | | |
| ❑ SN-7107 | Stormy | 1981 | 10.00 |
| IMPERIAL | | | |
| ❑ LP-9371 [M] | Spooky | 1968 | 40.00 |
| *—Mono has stock copy label inside stereo cover with white "Monaural" sticker* | | | |
| ❑ LP-12371 [S] | Spooky | 1968 | 20.00 |
| ❑ LP-12407 | Mamas and Papas/Soul Train | 1969 | 20.00 |
| ❑ LP-12429 | Traces | 1969 | 20.00 |
| ❑ LP-16000 | Dennis Yost & the Classics IV/ Golden Greats - Volume I | 1969 | 20.00 |
| LIBERTY | | | |
| ❑ LN-10109 | The Very Best of the Classics IV | 198? | 8.00 |
| ❑ LST-11003 | Song | 1970 | 15.00 |
| MGM SOUTH | | | |
| ❑ 702 | Dennis Yost and the Classics IV | 1973 | 15.00 |
| UNITED ARTISTS | | | |
| ❑ UA-LA446-E | The Very Best of the Classics IV | 1975 | 12.00 |
| **CLAUSON, WILLIAM** | | | |
| CAPITOL | | | |
| ❑ T 10158 [M] | Concert | 195? | 25.00 |
| ❑ T 10176 [M] | Scandinavia | 195? | 25.00 |
| RCA VICTOR | | | |
| ❑ LPM-1286 [M] | Folk Songs | 1956 | 30.00 |
| **CLAY, CASSIUS** | | | |
| COLUMBIA | | | |
| ❑ CL 2093 [M] | I Am the Greatest! | 1963 | 40.00 |
| ❑ CS 8893 [S] | I Am the Greatest! | 1963 | 50.00 |
| **CLAY, JAMES** | | | |
| RIVERSIDE | | | |
| ❑ RLP-349 [M] | A Double Dose of Soul | 1961 | 30.00 |
| *—Blue label* | | | |
| ❑ RS-9349 [S] | A Double Dose of Soul | 1961 | 40.00 |
| *—Black label* | | | |

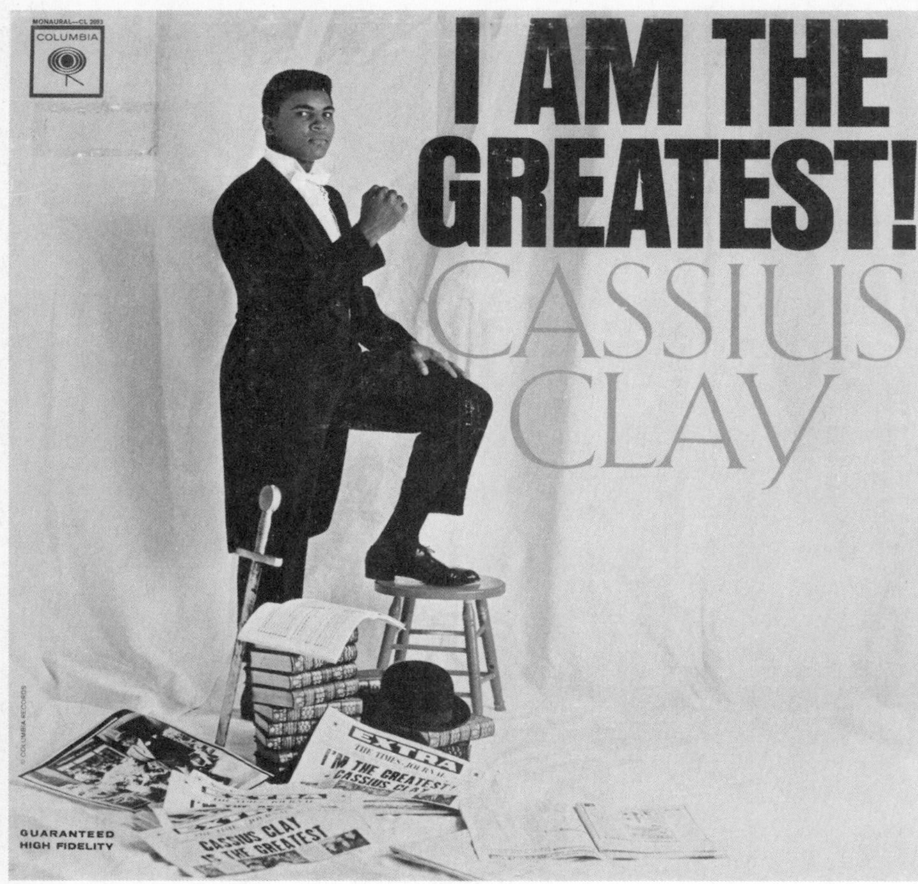


Cassius Clay, *I Am the Greatest!*, Columbia CL 2093, 1963, mono, $40.

## CLAY, JAMES, AND DAVID "FATHEAD" NEWMAN

RIVERSIDE

| Number | Title (A Side/B Side) | Yr | NM |
|---|---|---|---|
| ❑ RLP 12-327 [M] | The Sound of the Wide Open Spaces!!! | 1960 | 80.00 |
| *—Blue label* | | | |
| ❑ RLP-1178 [S] | The Sound of the Wide Open Spaces!!! | 1960 | 80.00 |
| *—Black label* | | | |

## CLAY, OTIS

HI

| Number | Title (A Side/B Side) | Yr | NM |
|---|---|---|---|
| ❑ HLP 6003 | I Can't Take It | 1977 | 15.00 |
| ❑ SHL 32075 | Trying to Live My Life Without You | 1972 | 20.00 |

ROOSTER BLUES

| Number | Title (A Side/B Side) | Yr | NM |
|---|---|---|---|
| ❑ R-7609 [(2)] | Soul Man: Live in Japan | 1985 | 15.00 |

## CLAYTON, BUCK

ALLEGRO ELITE

| Number | Title (A Side/B Side) | Yr | NM |
|---|---|---|---|
| ❑ 4121 [10] | Buck Clayton All Stars | 195? | 40.00 |

COLUMBIA

| Number | Title (A Side/B Side) | Yr | NM |
|---|---|---|---|
| ❑ CL 548 [M] | The Huckle-Buck and Robbins' Nest: A Jam Session | 1954 | 50.00 |
| *—Maroon label, gold print* | | | |
| ❑ CL 548 [M] | The Huckle-Buck and Robbins' Nest: A Jam Session | 1955 | 30.00 |
| *—Red and black label with six "eye" logos* | | | |
| ❑ CL 567 [M] | How Hi the Fi: A Jam Session | 1954 | 50.00 |
| *—Maroon label, gold print* | | | |
| ❑ CL 567 [M] | How Hi the Fi: A Jam Session | 1955 | 30.00 |
| *—Red and black label with six "eye" logos* | | | |
| ❑ CL 614 [M] | Buck Clayton Jams Benny Goodman | 1955 | 30.00 |
| *—Red and black label with six "eye" logos* | | | |
| ❑ CL 614 [M] | Buck Clayton Jams Benny Goodman | 1955 | 50.00 |
| *—Maroon label, gold print* | | | |
| ❑ CL 701 [M] | Jumpin' at the Woodside | 1955 | 40.00 |
| *—Red and black label with six "eye" logos* | | | |
| ❑ CL 808 [M] | Jazz Spectacular | 1956 | 40.00 |
| *—Red and black label with six "eye" logos* | | | |
| ❑ CL 882 [M] | All the Cats Join In | 1956 | 40.00 |
| *—Red and black label with six "eye" logos* | | | |
| ❑ CL 1320 [M] | Songs for Swingers | 1959 | 25.00 |
| *—Red and black label with six "eye" logos* | | | |
| ❑ CL 6325 [10] | Moten Swing — Sentimental Journey | 1954 | 60.00 |
| ❑ CL 6326 [10] | How Hi the Fi: A Jam Session | 1954 | 60.00 |
| ❑ CS 8123 [S] | Songs for Swingers | 1959 | 30.00 |
| *—Red and black label with six "eye" logos* | | | |

JAZZTONE

| Number | Title (A Side/B Side) | Yr | NM |
|---|---|---|---|
| ❑ J-1225 [M] | Meet Buck Clayton | 1956 | 40.00 |

## CLAYTON, BUCK; RUBY BRAFF; MEL POWELL

VANGUARD

| Number | Title (A Side/B Side) | Yr | NM |
|---|---|---|---|
| ❑ VRS-8514 [M] | Buckin' the Blues | 1957 | 40.00 |
| ❑ VRS-8517 [M] | Buck Meets Ruby and Mel | 1957 | 40.00 |

## CLAYTON, BUCK/WILD BILL DAVISON

JAZZTONE

| Number | Title (A Side/B Side) | Yr | NM |
|---|---|---|---|
| ❑ J-1267 [M] | Singing Trumpets | 1957 | 40.00 |

## CLAYTON, BUCK, AND BUDDY TATE

SWINGVILLE

| Number | Title (A Side/B Side) | Yr | NM |
|---|---|---|---|
| ❑ SVLP-2017 [M] | Buck and Buddy | 1961 | 50.00 |
| *—Purple label* | | | |
| ❑ SVLP-2017 [M] | Buck and Buddy | 1965 | 25.00 |
| *—Blue label, trident logo at right* | | | |
| ❑ SVLP-2030 [M] | Buck and Buddy Blow the Blues | 1962 | 40.00 |
| *—Purple label* | | | |
| ❑ SVLP-2030 [M] | Buck and Buddy Blow the Blues | 1965 | 20.00 |
| *—Blue label, trident logo at right* | | | |
| ❑ SVST-2030 [S] | Buck and Buddy Blow the Blues | 1962 | 50.00 |
| *—Red label* | | | |
| ❑ SVST-2030 [S] | Buck and Buddy Blow the Blues | 1965 | 25.00 |
| *—Blue label, trident logo at right* | | | |

## CLAYTON, PAUL

ELEKTRA

| Number | Title (A Side/B Side) | Yr | NM |
|---|---|---|---|
| ❑ EKL-147 [M] | Unholy Matrimony | 1958 | 30.00 |
| ❑ EKL-155 [M] | Bobby Burns' Merry Muses | 1958 | 30.00 |

FOLKWAYS

| Number | Title (A Side/B Side) | Yr | NM |
|---|---|---|---|
| ❑ FA-2007 [M] | Cumberland Mountain Folksongs | 1957 | 60.00 |
| ❑ FA-2106 [M] | Bay State Ballads | 1956 | 60.00 |
| ❑ FA-2110 [M] | Folksongs and Ballads of Virginia | 1956 | 60.00 |
| ❑ FA-2310 [M] | Folk Ballads of the English-Speaking World | 1956 | 60.00 |
| ❑ FA-2429 [M] | Foc'sle Songs and Shanties | 1959 | 30.00 |
| ❑ FW-8708 [M] | British Broadside Ballads in Popular Tradition | 1957 | 40.00 |

MONUMENT

| Number | Title (A Side/B Side) | Yr | NM |
|---|---|---|---|
| ❑ MLP-8017 [M] | Folk Singer | 1965 | 20.00 |
| ❑ SLP-18017 [S] | Folk Singer | 1965 | 25.00 |

RIVERSIDE

| Number | Title (A Side/B Side) | Yr | NM |
|---|---|---|---|
| ❑ RLP 12-615 [M] | Bloody Ballads | 1957 | 30.00 |
| ❑ RLP 12-640 [M] | Wanted for Murder — American Folksongs of Outlaws and Desperadoes | 1958 | 30.00 |
| ❑ RLP 12-648 [M] | Timber-r-r! — Folk Songs and Ballads of the Lumberjack | 1958 | 30.00 |

STINSON

| Number | Title (A Side/B Side) | Yr | NM |
|---|---|---|---|
| ❑ SLP-69 [10] | Whaling Songs and Ballads | 1958 | 40.00 |
| ❑ SLP-70 [10] | Waters of Tyme — English North Country Songs | 1958 | 40.00 |

TRADITION

| Number | Title (A Side/B Side) | Yr | NM |
|---|---|---|---|
| ❑ TLP-1005 [M] | Whaling and Sailing Songs from the Days of Moby Dick | 1956 | 30.00 |

## CLAYTON-THOMAS, DAVID

ABC

| Number | Title (A Side/B Side) | Yr | NM |
|---|---|---|---|
| ❑ AA-1104 | Clayton | 1978 | 10.00 |

COLUMBIA

| Number | Title (A Side/B Side) | Yr | NM |
|---|---|---|---|
| ❑ KC 31000 | David Clayton-Thomas | 1972 | 15.00 |
| ❑ KC 31700 | Tequila Sunrise | 1972 | 15.00 |

DECCA

| Number | Title (A Side/B Side) | Yr | NM |
|---|---|---|---|
| ❑ DL 75146 | David Clayton-Thomas! | 1969 | 20.00 |

RCA VICTOR

| Number | Title (A Side/B Side) | Yr | NM |
|---|---|---|---|
| ❑ APD1-0173 [Q] | David Clayton-Thomas | 1973 | 20.00 |
| ❑ APL1-0173 | David Clayton-Thomas | 1973 | 12.00 |

## CLEANLINESS AND GODLINESS SKIFFLE BAND, THE

VANGUARD

| Number | Title (A Side/B Side) | Yr | NM |
|---|---|---|---|
| ❑ VSD-79285 | Greatest Hits | 1968 | 25.00 |

## CLEAR LIGHT

ELEKTRA

| Number | Title (A Side/B Side) | Yr | NM |
|---|---|---|---|
| ❑ EKL-4011 [M] | Clear Light | 1967 | 25.00 |
| ❑ EKS-74011 [S] | Clear Light | 1967 | 25.00 |

SUNDAZED

| Number | Title (A Side/B Side) | Yr | NM |
|---|---|---|---|
| ❑ LP 5125 | Clear Light | 2002 | 12.00 |
| *—Reissue on 180-gram vinyl* | | | |

## CLEARY, DON

PALOMINO

| Number | Title (A Side/B Side) | Yr | NM |
|---|---|---|---|
| ❑ 302 [M] | Don Cleary Sings Traditional Cowboy Songs | 1966 | 50.00 |

## CLEAVER, ELDRIDGE

MORE

| Number | Title (A Side/B Side) | Yr | NM |
|---|---|---|---|
| ❑ 4000 [M] | Soul On Wax | 1968 | 25.00 |

## CLEFTONES, THE

GEE

| Number | Title (A Side/B Side) | Yr | NM |
|---|---|---|---|
| ❑ GLP-705 [M] | Heart and Soul | 1961 | 200.00 |
| ❑ SGLP-705 [S] | Heart and Soul | 1961 | 500.00 |
| ❑ GLP-707 [M] | For Sentimental Reasons | 1961 | 250.00 |
| ❑ SGLP-707 [S] | For Sentimental Reasons | 1961 | 1200. |

## CLEVELAND, JIMMY

EMARCY

| Number | Title (A Side/B Side) | Yr | NM |
|---|---|---|---|
| ❑ MG-26003 [M] | Rhythm Crazy | 1964 | 25.00 |
| ❑ MG-36066 [M] | Introducing Jimmy Cleveland and His All Stars | 1956 | 50.00 |
| ❑ MG-36126 [M] | Cleveland Style | 1958 | 50.00 |

MERCURY

| Number | Title (A Side/B Side) | Yr | NM |
|---|---|---|---|
| ❑ MG-20442 [M] | A Map of Jimmy Cleveland | 1959 | 40.00 |
| ❑ MG-20553 [M] | Cleveland Style | 1960 | 40.00 |
| ❑ SR-60117 [S] | A Map of Jimmy Cleveland | 1959 | 30.00 |
| ❑ SR-60121 [S] | Cleveland Style | 1959 | 30.00 |

## CLIBURN, VAN

RCA VICTOR RED SEAL

| Number | Title (A Side/B Side) | Yr | NM |
|---|---|---|---|
| ❑ LM-2252 [M] | Tchaikovsky: Piano Concerto No. 1 | 1958 | 20.00 |
| ❑ LSC-2252 [S] | Tchaikovsky: Piano Concerto No. 1 | 1958 | 25.00 |
| *—"Shaded dog" pressing ("Living Stereo" on label)* | | | |
| ❑ LSC-2252 [S] | Tchaikovsky: Piano Concerto No. 1 | 1965 | 15.00 |
| *—"White dog" pressing ("Stereo" on label)* | | | |
| ❑ LSC-2252 [S] | Tchaikovsky: Piano Concerto No. 1 | 1969 | 12.00 |
| *—"No dog" pressing ("RCA" sideways at left)* | | | |
| ❑ LSC-2252 [S] | Tchaikovsky: Piano Concerto No. 1 | 1976 | 8.00 |
| *—"Late dog" pressing (dog near top)* | | | |
| ❑ LM-2355 [M] | Rachmaninoff: Piano Concerto No. 3 | 1959 | 20.00 |
| ❑ LSC-2355 [S] | Rachmaninoff: Piano Concerto No. 3 | 1959 | 25.00 |
| *—"Shaded dog" pressing ("Living Stereo" on label)* | | | |

| Number | Title (A Side/B Side) | Yr | NM |
|---|---|---|---|
| ❑ LSC-2355 [S] | Rachmaninoff: Piano Concerto No. 3 | 1965 | 15.00 |
| *—"White dog" pressing ("Stereo" on label)* | | | |
| ❑ LSC-2355 [S] | Rachmaninoff: Piano Concerto No. 3 | 1969 | 12.00 |
| *—"No dog" pressing ("RCA" sideways at left)* | | | |
| ❑ LM-2455 [M] | Schumann: Piano Concerto in A Minor | 1960 | 15.00 |
| ❑ LSC-2455 [S] | Schumann: Piano Concerto in A Minor | 1960 | 20.00 |
| *—"Shaded dog" pressing ("Living Stereo" on label)* | | | |
| ❑ LSC-2455 [S] | Schumann: Piano Concerto in A Minor | 1965 | 15.00 |
| *—"White dog" pressing ("Stereo" on label)* | | | |
| ❑ LSC-2455 [S] | Schumann: Piano Concerto in A Minor | 1969 | 12.00 |
| *—"No dog" pressing ("RCA" sideways at left)* | | | |
| ❑ LM-2507 [M] | Prokofiev: Piano Concerto No. 3; MacDowell: Piano Concerto No. 2 | 1961 | 15.00 |
| ❑ LSC-2507 [S] | Prokofiev: Piano Concerto No. 3; MacDowell: Piano Concerto No. 2 | 1961 | 30.00 |
| *—"Shaded dog" pressing ("Living Stereo" on label)* | | | |
| ❑ LSC-2507 [S] | Prokofiev: Piano Concerto No. 3; MacDowell: Piano Concerto No. 2 | 1965 | 30.00 |
| *—"White dog" pressing ("Stereo" on label)* | | | |
| ❑ LSC-2507 [S] | Prokofiev: Piano Concerto No. 3; MacDowell: Piano Concerto No. 2 | 1969 | 12.00 |
| *—"No dog" pressing ("RCA" sideways at left)* | | | |
| ❑ LM-2562 [M] | Beethoven: Piano Concerto No. 5 (Emperor Concerto) | 1961 | 15.00 |
| ❑ LSC-2562 [S] | Beethoven: Piano Concerto No. 5 (Emperor Concerto) | 1961 | 20.00 |
| *—"Shaded dog" pressing ("Living Stereo" on label)* | | | |
| ❑ LSC-2562 [S] | Beethoven: Piano Concerto No. 5 (Emperor Concerto) | 1964 | 20.00 |
| *—"White dog" pressing ("Stereo" on label)* | | | |
| ❑ LSC-2562 [S] | Beethoven: Piano Concerto No. 5 (Emperor Concerto) | 1969 | 12.00 |
| *—"No dog" pressing ("RCA" sideways at left)* | | | |
| ❑ LM-2576 [M] | My Favorite Chopin | 1962 | 15.00 |
| ❑ LSC-2576 [S] | My Favorite Chopin | 1962 | 20.00 |
| *—"Shaded dog" pressing ("Living Stereo" on label)* | | | |
| ❑ LSC-2576 [S] | My Favorite Chopin | 1965 | 15.00 |
| *—"White dog" pressing ("Stereo" on label)* | | | |
| ❑ LSC-2576 [S] | My Favorite Chopin | 1969 | 12.00 |
| *—"No dog" pressing ("RCA" sideways at left)* | | | |
| ❑ LSC-2576 [S] | My Favorite Chopin | 1976 | 8.00 |
| *—"Late dog" pressing (dog near top)* | | | |
| ❑ LM-2581 [M] | Brahms: Piano Concerto No. 2 | 1962 | 15.00 |
| ❑ LSC-2581 [S] | Brahms: Piano Concerto No. 2 | 1962 | 20.00 |
| *—"Shaded dog" pressing ("Living Stereo" on label)* | | | |
| ❑ LSC-2581 [S] | Brahms: Piano Concerto No. 2 | 1965 | 15.00 |
| *—"White dog" pressing ("Stereo" on label)* | | | |
| ❑ LSC-2581 [S] | Brahms: Piano Concerto No. 2 | 1969 | 12.00 |
| *—"No dog" pressing ("RCA" sideways at left)* | | | |
| ❑ LSC-2581 [S] | Brahms: Piano Concerto No. 2 | 1976 | 8.00 |
| *—"Late dog" pressing (dog near top)* | | | |
| ❑ LM-2601 [M] | Rachmaninoff: Piano Concerto No. 2 | 1962 | 15.00 |
| ❑ LSC-2601 [S] | Rachmaninoff: Piano Concerto No. 2 | 1962 | 15.00 |
| *—"White dog" pressing ("Stereo" on label)* | | | |
| ❑ LSC-2601 [S] | Rachmaninoff: Piano Concerto No. 2 | 1962 | 20.00 |
| *—"Shaded dog" pressing ("Living Stereo" on label)* | | | |
| ❑ LSC-2601 [S] | Rachmaninoff: Piano Concerto No. 2 | 1969 | 12.00 |
| *—"No dog" pressing ("RCA" sideways at left)* | | | |
| ❑ LM-2680 [M] | Beethoven: Piano Concerto No. 4 | 1963 | 12.00 |
| ❑ LSC-2680 [S] | Beethoven: Piano Concerto No. 4 | 1963 | 15.00 |
| *—"Shaded dog" pressing ("Living Stereo" on label)* | | | |
| ❑ LSC-2680 [S] | Beethoven: Piano Concerto No. 4 | 1965 | 12.00 |
| *—"White dog" pressing ("Stereo" on label)* | | | |
| ❑ LSC-2680 [S] | Beethoven: Piano Concerto No. 4 | 1969 | 10.00 |
| *—"No dog" pressing ("RCA" sideways at left)* | | | |
| ❑ LSC-3323 | The World's Favorite Piano Music | 196? | 12.00 |
| ❑ ARP1-4441 | Tchaikovsky: Piano Concerto No. 1 | 198? | 10.00 |
| *—Half-speed mastered reissue* | | | |

## CLIFF, JIMMY

| Number | Title (A Side/B Side) | Yr | NM |
|---|---|---|---|
| **A&M** | | | |
| ❑ SP-3189 | Wonderful World, Beautiful People | 198? | 8.00 |
| *—Reissue of 4251* | | | |
| ❑ SP-4251 | Wonderful World, Beautiful People | 1970 | 25.00 |
| **COLUMBIA** | | | |
| ❑ FC 38099 | Special | 1982 | 10.00 |
| ❑ PC 38099 | Special | 198? | 8.00 |
| *—Budget-line reissue* | | | |
| ❑ FC 38986 | The Power and the Glory | 1983 | 10.00 |
| ❑ PC 38996 | The Power and the Glory | 1985 | 8.00 |
| *—Budget-line reissue* | | | |
| ❑ FC 40002 | Cliff Hanger | 1985 | 10.00 |
| ❑ FC 40845 | Hanging Fire | 1988 | 10.00 |
| **ISLAND** | | | |
| ❑ SW-9343 | Struggling Man | 1973 | 20.00 |
| **MANGO** | | | |
| ❑ ILPS 9235 | Struggling Man | 197? | 12.00 |
| *—Reissue of Island SW-9343* | | | |
| **MCA** | | | |
| ❑ 813 | I Am the Living | 198? | 8.00 |
| *—Reissue of 5153* | | | |
| ❑ 820 | Give the People What They Want | 198? | 8.00 |
| *—Reissue of 5217* | | | |
| ❑ 5153 | I Am the Living | 1980 | 12.00 |
| ❑ 5217 | Give the People What They Want | 1981 | 12.00 |
| **REPRISE** | | | |
| ❑ MS 2147 | Unlimited | 1973 | 15.00 |
| ❑ MS 2188 | Music Maker | 1974 | 15.00 |
| ❑ MS 2218 | Follow My Mind | 1975 | 15.00 |
| ❑ MS 2256 | In Concert: The Best of Jimmy Cliff | 1976 | 15.00 |
| **VEEP** | | | |
| ❑ VPS-16536 | Can't Get Enough of It | 1969 | 40.00 |
| **WARNER BROS.** | | | |
| ❑ BSK 3240 | Give Thankx | 1978 | 12.00 |

## CLIFFORD, BUZZ

| Number | Title (A Side/B Side) | Yr | NM |
|---|---|---|---|
| **COLUMBIA** | | | |
| ❑ CL 1616 [M] | Baby Sittin' with Buzz | 1961 | 100.00 |
| ❑ CS 8416 [S] | Baby Sittin' with Buzz | 1961 | 150.00 |
| **DOT** | | | |
| ❑ DLP-25965 | See Your Way Clear | 1969 | 30.00 |

## CLIFFORD, MIKE

| Number | Title (A Side/B Side) | Yr | NM |
|---|---|---|---|
| **UNITED ARTISTS** | | | |
| ❑ UAL-3409 [M] | For the Love of Mike | 1965 | 20.00 |
| ❑ UAS-6409 [S] | For the Love of Mike | 1965 | 25.00 |

## CLIFTON, BILL

| Number | Title (A Side/B Side) | Yr | NM |
|---|---|---|---|
| **COLUMBIA** | | | |
| ❑ CL 6166 [10] | Piano Moods | 1951 | 50.00 |

## CLIFTON, BILL, AND THE DIXIE MOUNTAIN BOYS

| Number | Title (A Side/B Side) | Yr | NM |
|---|---|---|---|
| **STARDAY** | | | |
| ❑ SLP-111 [M] | Mountain Folk Songs | 1959 | 40.00 |
| ❑ SLP-146 [M] | The Carter Family Memorial Album | 1961 | 30.00 |
| ❑ SLP-159 [M] | The Bluegrass Sound of Bill Clifton | 1961 | 30.00 |
| ❑ SLP-213 [M] | Soldier, Sing Me a Song | 1963 | 25.00 |
| ❑ SLP-271 [M] | Code of the Mountains | 1965 | 25.00 |

## CLINE, PATSY

| Number | Title (A Side/B Side) | Yr | NM |
|---|---|---|---|
| **ACCORD** | | | |
| ❑ SN-7153 | Let the Teardrops Fall | 1981 | 10.00 |
| **ALLEGIANCE** | | | |
| ❑ AV-5021 | Stop, Look and Listen | 198? | 10.00 |
| **DECCA** | | | |
| ❑ DXB 176 [(2)M] | The Patsy Cline Story | 1963 | 40.00 |
| ❑ DL 4202 [M] | Patsy Cline Showcase | 1961 | 40.00 |
| ❑ DL 4282 [M] | Sentimentally Yours | 1962 | 30.00 |
| ❑ DL 4508 [M] | A Portrait of Patsy Cline | 1964 | 30.00 |
| ❑ DL 4586 [M] | That's How a Heartache Begins | 1964 | 30.00 |
| ❑ DL 4854 [M] | Patsy Cline's Greatest Hits | 1967 | 20.00 |
| ❑ DXSB 7176 [(2)S] | The Patsy Cline Story | 1963 | 50.00 |
| ❑ DL 8611 [M] | Patsy Cline | 1957 | 100.00 |
| *—Black label with silver print* | | | |
| ❑ DL 8611 [M] | Patsy Cline | 1960 | 50.00 |
| *—Black label with color bars* | | | |
| ❑ DL 74202 [S] | Patsy Cline Showcase | 1961 | 50.00 |
| ❑ DL 74282 [S] | Sentimentally Yours | 1962 | 40.00 |
| ❑ DL 74508 [S] | A Portrait of Patsy Cline | 1964 | 40.00 |
| ❑ DL 74586 [S] | That's How a Heartache Begins | 1964 | 40.00 |
| ❑ DL 74854 [S] | Patsy Cline's Greatest Hits | 1967 | 25.00 |
| **EVEREST** | | | |
| ❑ 1200 [R] | Golden Hits | 1962 | 12.00 |
| ❑ 1204 [R] | Encores | 1962 | 12.00 |
| ❑ 1217 [R] | In Memoriam | 1963 | 12.00 |
| ❑ 1229 [R] | Reflections | 1964 | 12.00 |
| ❑ 5200 [M] | Golden Hits | 1962 | 20.00 |
| ❑ 5204 [M] | Encores | 1962 | 20.00 |
| ❑ 5217 [M] | In Memoriam | 1963 | 20.00 |
| ❑ 5223 [M] | Legend | 1963 | 20.00 |
| ❑ 5229 [M] | Reflections | 1964 | 20.00 |
| ❑ ST-90070 [R] | Golden Hits | 1962 | 15.00 |
| *—Capitol Record Club edition* | | | |
| **HILLTOP** | | | |
| ❑ 6001 [M] | Today, Tomorrow, Forever | 1965 | 12.00 |
| ❑ S-6001 [R] | Today, Tomorrow, Forever | 1965 | 10.00 |
| ❑ 6016 [M] | I Can't Forget You | 1966 | 12.00 |
| ❑ S-6016 [R] | I Can't Forget You | 1966 | 10.00 |
| ❑ S-6039 | Stop the World | 1968 | 10.00 |
| ❑ JS-6072 | In Care of the Blues | 1969 | 10.00 |
| ❑ 6148 | Country Music Hall of Fame | 197? | 10.00 |
| **MCA** | | | |
| ❑ 12 | Patsy Cline's Greatest Hits | 1973 | 12.00 |
| *—Reissue of Decca 74854; black label with rainbow* | | | |
| ❑ 12 | Patsy Cline's Greatest Hits | 1977 | 10.00 |
| *—Tan label* | | | |
| ❑ 12 | Patsy Cline's Greatest Hits | 1980 | 8.00 |
| *—Blue label with rainbow* | | | |
| ❑ 87 | Patsy Cline Showcase | 1973 | 12.00 |
| *—Reissue of Decca 74202; black label with rainbow* | | | |
| ❑ 90 | Sentimentally Yours | 1973 | 12.00 |
| *—Reissue of Decca 74282; black label with rainbow* | | | |
| ❑ 224 | A Portrait of Patsy Cline | 1973 | 12.00 |
| *—Reissue of Decca 74508; black label with rainbow* | | | |
| ❑ 736 | The Great Patsy Cline | 198? | 10.00 |
| *—Reissue of Vocalion 73872* | | | |
| ❑ 738 | Here's Patsy Cline | 198? | 10.00 |
| *—Reissue of Vocalion 73753* | | | |
| ❑ 1440 | Stop, Look and Listen | 198? | 8.00 |
| ❑ 1463 | Today, Tomorrow and Forever | 198? | 8.00 |
| ❑ 3263 | Always | 1980 | 15.00 |
| ❑ 4038 [(2)] | The Patsy Cline Story | 1974 | 15.00 |
| *—Reissue of Decca 7176;; black labels with rainbow* | | | |
| ❑ 6149 | Sweet Dreams — The Life and Times of Patsy Cline | 1985 | 10.00 |
| ❑ 27069 | Always | 198? | 8.00 |
| ❑ 42142 | Live at the Opry | 1988 | 10.00 |
| ❑ 42284 | Live Volume 2 | 1989 | 12.00 |
| **METRO** | | | |
| ❑ M-540 [M] | Gotta Lot of Rhythm in My Soul | 1965 | 12.00 |
| ❑ MS-540 [R] | Gotta Lot of Rhythm in My Soul | 1965 | 10.00 |
| **RHINO** | | | |
| ❑ R1-70048 | Her First Recordings, Vol. 1: Walkin' Dreams | 1989 | 12.00 |
| ❑ R1-70049 | Her First Recordings, Vol. 2: Hungry for Love | 1989 | 12.00 |
| ❑ R1-70050 | Her First Recordings, Vol. 3: The Rockin' Side | 1989 | 12.00 |
| **SEARS** | | | |
| ❑ SP-102 [M] | Walkin' After Midnight | 196? | 30.00 |
| ❑ SPS-102 [R] | Walkin' After Midnight | 196? | 20.00 |
| ❑ SPS-112 | I Can't Forget You | 1968 | 25.00 |
| ❑ SPS-127 | In Care of the Blues | 1968 | 25.00 |
| **VOCALION** | | | |
| ❑ VL 3753 [M] | Here's Patsy Cline | 1965 | 12.00 |
| ❑ VL 73753 [R] | Here's Patsy Cline | 1965 | 10.00 |
| ❑ VL 73872 | Country Great! | 1969 | 10.00 |

## CLINTON, GEORGE

| Number | Title (A Side/B Side) | Yr | NM |
|---|---|---|---|
| **ABC** | | | |
| ❑ D-831 | The George Clinton Band Arrives | 1974 | 15.00 |
| **CAPITOL** | | | |
| ❑ ST-12246 | Computer Games | 1982 | 10.00 |
| ❑ ST-12308 | You Shouldn't-Nuf Bit Fish | 1984 | 10.00 |
| ❑ ST-12417 | Some of My Best Jokes Are Friends | 1985 | 10.00 |
| ❑ ST-12481 | R&B Skeletons in the Closet | 1986 | 10.00 |
| ❑ MLP-15021 [EP] | The Mothership Connection Live from Houston, Texas | 1986 | 15.00 |
| ❑ C1-33911 [(2)] | Greatest Funkin' Hits | 1996 | 12.00 |
| *—Red vinyl* | | | |
| ❑ CJ-48424 | The Best of George Clinton | 1987 | 10.00 |
| **550 MUSIC** | | | |
| ❑ B2 67144 [(2)] | T.A.P.O.A.F.O.M. — The Awesome Power of a Fully Operational Mothership | 1996 | 15.00 |
| *—Red vinyl* | | | |
| **INVICTUS** | | | |
| ❑ ST-9815 | Black Vampire | 1973 | 20.00 |
| **PAISLEY PARK** | | | |
| ❑ PRO-A-6537 [(2)DJ] | Hey Man... Smell My Finger | 1993 | 25.00 |
| *—Promo-only vinyl issue* | | | |
| ❑ 25994 | The Cinderella Theory | 1989 | 12.00 |
| **WARNER BROS.** | | | |
| ❑ 25887 | George Clinton Presents Our Gang Funky | 1988 | 10.00 |
| ❑ 25991 | Under a Nouveau Groove | 1989 | 10.00 |

## CLINTON, LARRY

| Number | Title (A Side/B Side) | Yr | NM |
|---|---|---|---|
| **EVEREST** | | | |
| ❑ SDBR-1096 [S] | My Million Sellers | 196? | 25.00 |
| ❑ LPBR-5096 [M] | My Million Sellers | 196? | 20.00 |

## CLIQUE, THE (1)

| Number | Title (A Side/B Side) | Yr | NM |
|---|---|---|---|
| **WHITE WHALE** | | | |
| ❑ WWS-7126 | The Clique | 1969 | 20.00 |

## CLOONEY, ROSEMARY

| Number | Title (A Side/B Side) | Yr | NM |
|---|---|---|---|
| **COLUMBIA** | | | |
| ❑ CL 585 [M] | Hollywood's Best | 1955 | 50.00 |
| ❑ CL 872 [M] | Blue Rose | 1956 | 40.00 |

| Number | Title (A Side/B Side) | Yr | NM |
|---|---|---|---|
| ❑ CL 969 [M] | Clooney Tunes | 1957 | 80.00 |
| ❑ CL 1006 [M] | Ring Around the Rosie | 1957 | 40.00 |
| *—With the Hi-Lo's* | | | |
| ❑ CL 1230 [M] | Rosie's Greatest Hits | 1958 | 40.00 |
| *—Six "eye" logos on label* | | | |
| ❑ CL 1230 [M] | Rosie's Greatest Hits | 1962 | 25.00 |
| *—"Guaranteed High Fidelity" on label* | | | |
| ❑ CL 1230 [M] | Rosie's Greatest Hits | 1965 | 15.00 |
| *—"360 Sound Mono" on label* | | | |
| ❑ CL 2525 [10] | Tenderly | 1955 | 50.00 |
| ❑ CL 2569 [10] | Children's Favorites | 1955 | 50.00 |
| ❑ CL 2572 [10] | A Date with the King | 1956 | 50.00 |
| ❑ CL 2581 [10] | On Stage | 1956 | 50.00 |
| ❑ CL 2597 [10] | My Fair Lady | 1956 | 50.00 |
| ❑ CL 6224 [10] | Hollywood's Best | 1952 | 60.00 |
| ❑ CL 6297 [10] | Rosemary Clooney (While We're Young) | 1954 | 60.00 |
| ❑ CL 6338 [10] | White Christmas | 1954 | 60.00 |
| COLUMBIA SPECIAL PRODUCTS | | | |
| ❑ P 13083 | Hollywood's Best | 197? | 12.00 |
| ❑ P 13085 | Blue Rose | 197? | 12.00 |
| ❑ P 14382 | Come On-a My House | 197? | 12.00 |
| CONCORD JAZZ | | | |
| ❑ CJ-47 | Everything's Coming Up Rosie | 1978 | 12.00 |
| ❑ CJ-60 | Rosie Sings Bing | 1979 | 12.00 |
| ❑ CJ-81 | Here's to My Lady | 1979 | 12.00 |
| ❑ CJ-112 | Rosemary Clooney Sings Ira Gershwin | 1980 | 12.00 |
| ❑ CJ-144 | With Love | 1981 | 12.00 |
| ❑ CJ-185 | Rosemary Clooney Sings Cole Porter | 1982 | 12.00 |
| ❑ CJ-210 | Rosemary Clooney Sings Harold Arlen | 1983 | 12.00 |
| ❑ CJ-226 | My Buddy | 1984 | 12.00 |
| *—With Woody Herman* | | | |
| ❑ CJ-255 | Rosemary Clooney Sings the Music of Irving Berlin | 1985 | 12.00 |
| ❑ CJ-282 | Rosemary Clooney Sings Ballads | 1985 | 12.00 |
| ❑ CJ-308 | Rosemary Clooney Sings the Music of Jimmy Van Heusen | 1987 | 12.00 |
| ❑ CJ-333 | Rosemary Clooney Sings the Lyrics of Johnny Mercer | 1988 | 12.00 |
| ❑ CJ-364 | Show Tunes | 1989 | 12.00 |
| CORAL | | | |
| ❑ CRL 57266 [M] | Swing Around Rosie | 1959 | 30.00 |
| ❑ CRL 757266 [S] | Swing Around Rosie | 1959 | 40.00 |
| HARMONY | | | |
| ❑ HL 7123 [M] | Rosemary Clooney in High Fidelity | 195? | 25.00 |
| ❑ HL 7213 [M] | Hollywood Hits | 195? | 25.00 |
| ❑ HL 7454 [M] | Mixed Emotions | 1968 | 20.00 |
| ❑ HL 9501 [M] | Rosemary Clooney Sings for Children | 196? | 20.00 |
| ❑ HS 11254 [R] | Mixed Emotions | 1968 | 12.00 |
| HINDSIGHT | | | |
| ❑ HSR-234 | Rosemary Clooney 1951-1952 | 1988 | 10.00 |
| HOLIDAY | | | |
| ❑ 1946 | Christmas with Rosemary Clooney | 1981 | 10.00 |
| MGM | | | |
| ❑ E-3687 [M] | Oh, Captain! | 1958 | 40.00 |
| ❑ E-3782 [M] | Hymns from the Heart | 1959 | 30.00 |
| ❑ SE-3782 [S] | Hymns from the Heart | 1959 | 40.00 |
| ❑ E-3834 [M] | Rosie Clooney Swings Softly | 1960 | 30.00 |
| ❑ SE-3834 [S] | Rosie Clooney Swings Softly | 1960 | 40.00 |
| MISTLETOE | | | |
| ❑ MLP-1234 | Christmas with Rosemary Clooney | 1978 | 12.00 |
| RCA VICTOR | | | |
| ❑ LPM-2133 [M] | A Touch of Tabasco | 1960 | 20.00 |
| ❑ LSP-2133 [S] | A Touch of Tabasco | 1960 | 30.00 |
| ❑ LPM-2212 [M] | Clap Hands, Here Comes Rosie | 1960 | 20.00 |
| ❑ LSP-2212 [S] | Clap Hands, Here Comes Rosie | 1960 | 30.00 |
| ❑ LPM-2265 [M] | Rosie Solves the Swingin' Riddle | 1961 | 20.00 |
| ❑ LSP-2265 [S] | Rosie Solves the Swingin' Riddle | 1961 | 30.00 |
| ❑ LPM-2565 [M] | Country Hits from the Heart | 1963 | 20.00 |
| ❑ LSP-2565 [S] | Country Hits from the Heart | 1963 | 30.00 |
| REPRISE | | | |
| ❑ R-6088 [M] | Love | 1963 | 30.00 |
| ❑ R9-6088 [S] | Love | 1963 | 40.00 |
| ❑ R-6108 [M] | Thanks for Nothing | 1964 | 30.00 |
| ❑ RS-6108 [S] | Thanks for Nothing | 1964 | 40.00 |
| TIME-LIFE | | | |
| ❑ SLGD-16 [(2)] | Legendary Singers: Rosemary Clooney | 1986 | 15.00 |
| **CLOONEY, ROSEMARY, AND BING CROSBY** | | | |
| CAPITOL | | | |
| ❑ ST 2300 [S] | That Travelin' Two-Beat | 1965 | 30.00 |
| ❑ T 2300 [M] | That Travelin' Two-Beat | 1965 | 20.00 |
| RCA CAMDEN | | | |
| ❑ CAS-2330 | Rendezvous | 1968 | 15.00 |
| RCA VICTOR | | | |
| ❑ LPM-1854 [M] | Fancy Meeting You Here | 1958 | 20.00 |
| ❑ LSP-1854 [S] | Fancy Meeting You Here | 1958 | 30.00 |
| **CLOONEY SISTERS, THE** Also see ROSEMARY CLOONEY. | | | |
| EPIC | | | |
| ❑ LN 3160 [M] | The Clooney Sisters with Tony Pastor | 1956 | 60.00 |
| **CLOUD, BRUCE** | | | |
| CAPITOL | | | |
| ❑ ST-343 | California Soul | 1969 | 20.00 |
| **CLOVER** | | | |
| FANTASY | | | |
| ❑ 8395 | Clover | 1969 | 25.00 |
| ❑ 8405 | Forty-Niner | 1970 | 25.00 |
| **CLOVER, TIMOTHY** | | | |
| TOWER | | | |
| ❑ ST 5114 | A Harvard Square Affair | 1968 | 20.00 |
| **CLOVERS, THE** | | | |
| ATCO | | | |
| ❑ SD 33-374 | Their Greatest Recordings/The Early Years | 1971 | 12.00 |
| ATLANTIC | | | |
| ❑ 1248 [M] | The Clovers | 1956 | 600.00 |
| ❑ 8009 [M] | The Clovers | 1957 | 400.00 |
| *—Reissue of 1248 on the "pop" series; black label* | | | |
| ❑ 8009 [M] | The Clovers | 1960 | 300.00 |
| *—White "bullseye" label* | | | |
| ❑ 8009 [M] | The Clovers | 1961 | 200.00 |
| *—Red and white label* | | | |
| ❑ 8034 [M] | Dance Party | 1959 | 400.00 |
| *—Black label* | | | |
| ❑ 8034 [M] | Dance Party | 1960 | 300.00 |
| *—White "bullseye" label* | | | |
| ❑ 8034 [M] | Dance Party | 1961 | 200.00 |
| *—Red and white label* | | | |
| GRAND PRIX | | | |
| ❑ K-428 [M] | The Original Love Potion Number Nine | 1964 | 30.00 |
| ❑ KS-428 [R] | The Original Love Potion Number Nine | 1964 | 12.00 |
| POPLAR | | | |
| ❑ 1001 [M] | The Clovers In Clover | 1958 | 400.00 |
| UNITED ARTISTS | | | |
| ❑ UAL-3033 [M] | The Clovers In Clover | 1959 | 300.00 |
| ❑ UAL-3099 [M] | Love Potion Number Nine | 1959 | 250.00 |
| ❑ UAS-6033 [R] | The Clovers In Clover | 196? | 200.00 |
| ❑ UAS-6099 [S] | Love Potion Number Nine | 1959 | 500.00 |
| **COASTERS, THE** | | | |
| ATCO | | | |
| ❑ 33-101 [M] | The Coasters | 1958 | 300.00 |
| *—Yellow "harp" label* | | | |
| ❑ 33-101 [M] | The Coasters | 196? | 60.00 |
| *—Gold and dark blue label* | | | |
| ❑ 33-111 [M] | The Coasters' Greatest Hits | 1959 | 150.00 |
| *—Yellow "harp" label* | | | |
| ❑ 33-111 [M] | The Coasters' Greatest Hits | 196? | 60.00 |
| *—Gold and gray label* | | | |
| ❑ 33-123 [M] | One By One | 196? | 60.00 |
| *—Gold and gray label* | | | |
| ❑ 33-123 [M] | One By One | 1960 | 150.00 |
| *—Yellow "harp" label* | | | |
| ❑ SD 33-123 [S] | One By One | 196? | 150.00 |
| *—Purple and brown label* | | | |
| ❑ SD 33-123 [S] | One By One | 1960 | 400.00 |
| *—Yellow "harp" label* | | | |
| ❑ 33-135 [M] | Coast Along with the Coasters | 1962 | 100.00 |
| *—Gold and gray label* | | | |
| ❑ SD 33-135 [P] | Coast Along with the Coasters | 1962 | 150.00 |
| *—Purple and brown label; "Wait a Minute" is rechanneled* | | | |
| ❑ SD 33-371 | Their Greatest Recordings/The Early Years | 1971 | 20.00 |
| CLARION | | | |
| ❑ 605 [M] | That Is Rock and Roll | 1965 | 40.00 |
| ❑ SD 605 [S] | That Is Rock and Roll | 1965 | 50.00 |
| KING | | | |
| ❑ KS-1146 | The Coasters On Broadway | 1971 | 25.00 |
| POWER PAK | | | |
| ❑ 310 | Greatest Hits | 198? | 10.00 |
| TRIP | | | |
| ❑ 8028 | It Ain't Sanitary | 197? | 12.00 |
| **COATES, JOHN, JR.** | | | |
| SAVOY | | | |
| ❑ MG-12082 [M] | Portrait | 1956 | 40.00 |
| **COBB, ARNETT** | | | |
| APOLLO | | | |
| ❑ LAP-105 [10] | Swingin' with Arnett Cobb | 1952 | 250.00 |
| MOODSVILLE | | | |
| ❑ MVLP-14 [M] | Ballads by Cobb | 1961 | 50.00 |
| *—Green label* | | | |
| ❑ MVLP-14 [M] | Ballads by Cobb | 1965 | 25.00 |
| *—Blue label, trident logo at right* | | | |
| PRESTIGE | | | |
| ❑ PRLP-7151 [M] | Blow, Arnett, Blow | 1959 | 50.00 |
| *—Yellow label* | | | |
| ❑ PRLP-7151 [M] | Blow, Arnett, Blow | 1963 | 25.00 |
| *—Blue label, trident logo at right* | | | |
| ❑ PRLP-7165 [M] | Party Time | 1959 | 50.00 |
| *—Yellow label* | | | |
| ❑ PRLP-7165 [M] | Party Time | 1963 | 25.00 |
| *—Blue label, trident logo at right* | | | |
| ❑ PRLP-7175 [M] | More Party Time | 1960 | 50.00 |
| *—Yellow label* | | | |
| ❑ PRLP-7175 [M] | More Party Time | 1963 | 25.00 |
| *—Blue label, trident logo at right* | | | |
| ❑ PRLP-7184 [M] | Smooth Sailing | 1960 | 50.00 |
| *—Yellow label* | | | |
| ❑ PRLP-7184 [M] | Smooth Sailing | 1963 | 25.00 |
| *—Blue label, trident logo at right* | | | |
| ❑ PRLP-7216 [M] | Movin' Right Along | 1961 | 50.00 |
| *—Yellow label* | | | |
| ❑ PRLP-7216 [M] | Movin' Right Along | 1963 | 25.00 |
| *—Blue label, trident logo at right* | | | |
| ❑ PRLP-7227 [M] | Sizzlin' | 1962 | 40.00 |
| *—Yellow label* | | | |
| ❑ PRLP-7227 [M] | Sizzlin' | 1963 | 20.00 |
| *—Blue label, trident logo at right* | | | |
| ❑ PRST-7227 [S] | Sizzlin' | 1962 | 50.00 |
| *—Silver label* | | | |
| ❑ PRST-7227 [S] | Sizzlin' | 1963 | 25.00 |
| *—Blue label, trident logo at right* | | | |
| **COCHRAN, EDDIE** | | | |
| LIBERTY | | | |
| ❑ LRP-3061 [M] | Singin' to My Baby | 1957 | 800.00 |
| *—Green label* | | | |
| ❑ LRP-3061 [M] | Singin' to My Baby | 1960 | 300.00 |
| *—Black label* | | | |
| ❑ LRP-3172 [M] | Eddie Cochran (12 of His Biggest Hits) | 1960 | 120.00 |
| ❑ LRP-3220 [M] | Never to Be Forgotten | 1962 | 100.00 |
| ❑ LN-10137 | Singin' to My Baby | 198? | 12.00 |
| *—Budget-line reissue* | | | |
| ❑ LN-10204 | Great Hits | 198? | 8.00 |
| SUNSET | | | |
| ❑ SUM-1123 [M] | Summertime Blues | 1966 | 40.00 |
| ❑ SUS-5123 [R] | Summertime Blues | 1966 | 25.00 |
| UNITED ARTISTS | | | |
| ❑ UA-LA428-E | The Very Best of Eddie Cochran | 1975 | 12.00 |
| ❑ UAS-9959 [(2)] | Legendary Masters Series #4 | 1972 | 25.00 |
| **COCHRAN, HANK** | | | |
| CAPITOL | | | |
| ❑ ST-11807 | With a Little Help from His Friends | 1978 | 12.00 |
| ELEKTRA | | | |
| ❑ 6E-277 | Make the World Go Away | 1980 | 10.00 |
| MONUMENT | | | |
| ❑ SLP-18089 | The Heart of Hank | 1968 | 20.00 |
| RCA VICTOR | | | |
| ❑ LPM-3303 [M] | Hits from the Heart | 1965 | 20.00 |
| ❑ LSP-3303 [S] | Hits from the Heart | 1965 | 25.00 |
| ❑ LPM-3431 [M] | Going in Training | 1965 | 20.00 |
| ❑ LSP-3431 [S] | Going in Training | 1965 | 25.00 |
| **COCHRAN, TODD** | | | |
| VITAL | | | |
| ❑ VTL-001 [(2)] | Todd | 1991 | 20.00 |
| **COCHRAN, WAYNE** | | | |
| BETHLEHEM | | | |
| ❑ 10002 | High and Ridin' | 1970 | 15.00 |
| CHESS | | | |
| ❑ LPS-1519 | Wayne Cochran! | 1968 | 40.00 |
| EPIC | | | |
| ❑ KE 30889 | Cochran | 1972 | 15.00 |
| KING | | | |
| ❑ KS-1116 | Alive and Well | 1970 | 20.00 |
| **COCKBURN, BRUCE** | | | |
| EPIC | | | |
| ❑ E 30812 | True North | 1971 | 20.00 |
| ❑ KE 31768 | Sunwheel Dance | 1972 | 20.00 |
| GOLD CASTLE | | | |
| ❑ D1-71320 | Big Circumstance | 1988 | 8.00 |
| ❑ 171005-1 [(2)] | Waiting for a Miracle | 1987 | 12.00 |

**Number | Title (A Side/B Side) | Yr | NM**

❑ 171008-1 The Trouble with Normal 1987 8.00
*—Reissue of Gold Mountain GM-3283*
❑ 171009-1 Dancing in the Dragon's Jaws 1987 8.00
*—Reissue of Gold Mountain GM-3276*
❑ 171010-1 Stealing Fire 1987 8.00
*—Reissue of Gold Mountain GM-80012*

GOLD MOUNTAIN
❑ GM-3276 Dancing in the Dragon's Jaws 1985 8.00
*—Reissue of Millennium BXL1-7747*
❑ GM-3283 The Trouble with Normal 1985 8.00
❑ GM-80012 Stealing Fire 1984 8.00

ISLAND
❑ ILTN 9463 In the Falling Dark 1976 12.00
❑ ILTA 9475 [(2)] Circles in the Stream 1977 15.00
❑ ILSP 9528 Furhter Adventures of 1978 12.00

MCA
❑ 5772 World of Wonders 1986 8.00

MILLENNIUM
❑ DJL1-(# unknown) [DJ]Selected Cuts from 1980 U.S. Tour 1980 50.00
*—Promo-only four-song live EP*
❑ DJL1-3583 [DJ]RCA Special Radio Series 1980 20.00
*—Promo-only music and interview*
❑ DJL1-3830 [DJ]RCA College Radio Series, Vol. II 1980 20.00
*—Promo-only music and interview*
❑ BXL1-7747 Dancing in the Dragon's Jaws 1979 10.00
❑ BXL1-7752 Humans 1980 10.00
❑ BXL1-7757 Resume 1981 10.00
❑ BXL1-7761 Inner City Front 1981 10.00

**COCKER, JOE**

A&M
❑ SP-3106 With a Little Help from My Friends 1980 8.00
❑ SP-3175 I Can Stand a Little Rain 1980 8.00
❑ SP-3257 Joe Cocker's Greatest Hits 1982 8.00
❑ SP-3633 I Can Stand a Little Rain 1974 10.00
❑ SP-4182 With a Little Help from My Friends 1969 12.00
*—Brown label*
❑ SP-4182 With a Little Help from My Friends 1974 10.00
*—Silver label*
❑ SP-4224 Joe Cocker! 1969 12.00
*—Brown label*
❑ SP-4224 Joe Cocker! 1974 10.00
*—Silver label*
❑ SP-4368 Joe Cocker 1972 12.00
*—Brown label*
❑ SP-4368 Joe Cocker 1974 10.00
*—Silver label*
❑ SP-4529 Jamaica Say You Will 1975 10.00
❑ SP-4574 Stingray 1976 10.00
❑ SP-4670 Joe Cocker's Greatest Hits 1977 10.00
❑ SP-6002 [(2)] Mad Dogs and Englishmen 1970 15.00
*—Brown labels*
❑ SP-6002 [(2)] Mad Dogs and Englishmen 1974 12.00
*—Silver labels*
❑ QU-54182 [Q] With a Little Help from My Friends 1974 —
*—Not released*
❑ QU-54224 [Q] Joe Cocker! 1974 —
*—Not released*

ASYLUM
❑ 6E-145 Luxury You Can Afford 1978 10.00
❑ DP-400 [PD] Luxury You Can Afford 1978 15.00

CAPITOL
❑ ST-12335 Civilized Man 1984 10.00
❑ ST-12394 Cocker 1986 10.00
❑ CLT-48285 Unchain My Heart 1988 10.00
❑ C1-92861 One Night of Sin 1989 12.00

ISLAND
❑ IL 9750 Sheffield Steel 1982 10.00
❑ 90096 One More Time 1983 10.00

MOBILE FIDELITY
❑ 1-223 Sheffield Steel 1995 40.00
*—Audiophile vinyl*

**COCTEAU TWINS**

CAPITOL
❑ SPRO 79066/7 [DJ]Cocteau Twins 1991 50.00
*—Promo-only 10-song collection*
❑ C1-90892 Blue Bell Knoll 1988 12.00
❑ C1-93669 Heaven Or Las Vegas 1990 15.00

RELATIVITY/4AD
❑ EMC 8040 The Pink Opaque 1986 12.00
❑ 88561-8141-1 [EP]Love's Easy Tears 1986 12.00
❑ 88561-8143-1 The Moon and the Melodies 1987 12.00
*—With Harold Budd*

**COE, DAVID ALLAN**

COLUMBIA
❑ KC 32942 Mysterious Rhinestone Cowboy 1974 12.00
❑ PC 32942 Mysterious Rhinestone Cowboy 197? 10.00
*—Early reissue with new prefix and no bar code*
❑ KC 33085 Once Upon a Rhyme 1975 12.00
❑ PC 33085 Once Upon a Rhyme 197? 10.00
*—Early reissue with new prefix and no bar code*
❑ PC 33916 Longhaired Redneck 1976 10.00
❑ KC 34310 David Allan Coe Rides Again 1977 10.00
❑ PC 34780 Tattoo 1977 10.00
❑ KC 35306 Family Album 1978 10.00
❑ KC 35535 Human Emotions — Happy Side/Su-I-Side 1978 10.00
❑ KC 35627 Greatest Hits 1978 10.00
❑ PC 35627 Greatest Hits 198? 8.00
*—Budget-line reissue*
❑ KC 35789 Spectrum, VII 1979 10.00
❑ JC 36277 Compass Point 1980 10.00
❑ PC 36277 Compass Point 198? 8.00
*—Budget-line reissue with new prefix*
❑ JC 36489 I've Got Something to Say 1980 10.00
❑ PC 36489 I've Got Something to Say 198? 8.00
*—Budget-line reissue with new prefix*
❑ JC 36970 Invictus (Means) Unconquered 1981 10.00
❑ PC 36970 Invictus (Means) Unconquered 198? 8.00
*—Budget-line reissue with new prefix*
❑ FC 37352 Encore 1981 10.00
❑ PC 37352 Encore 198? 8.00
*—Budget-line reissue with new prefix*
❑ FC 37454 Tennessee Whiskey 1981 10.00
❑ PC 37454 Tennessee Whiskey 198? 8.00
*—Budget-line reissue with new prefix*
❑ FC 37736 Rough Rider 1982 10.00
❑ PC 37736 Rough Rider 198? 8.00
*—Budget-line reissue with new prefix*
❑ FC 38093 D.A.C. 1982 10.00
❑ FC 38318 Biggest Hits 1982 10.00
❑ FC 38535 Castles in the Sand 1983 10.00
❑ PC 38535 Castles in the Sand 1985 8.00
*—Budget-line reissue with new prefix*
❑ FC 38926 Hello In There 1983 10.00
❑ FC 39269 Just Divorced 1984 10.00
❑ PC 39269 Just Divorced 1986 8.00
*—Budget-line reissue with new prefix*
❑ KC2 39585 [(2)]For the Record — The First 10 Years 1984 12.00
❑ FC 39617 Darlin', Darlin' 1985 10.00
❑ FC 40195 Unchained 1985 10.00
❑ FC 40346 Son of the South 1986 10.00
❑ FC 40571 A Matter of Life... And Death 1987 10.00
❑ FC 45057 Crazy Daddy 1989 10.00

PAIR
❑ PDL2-1075 [(2)]Best of David Allan Coe 1986 12.00

PLANTATION
❑ 507 Texas Moon 197? 15.00

SSS INTERNATIONAL
❑ 9 Penitentiary Blues 1977 80.00

**COHEN, LEONARD**

COLUMBIA
❑ CL 2733 [M] Leonard Cohen 1967 25.00
❑ CS 9533 [S] Leonard Cohen 1967 12.00
*—Red "360 Sound" label*
❑ CS 9533 [S] Leonard Cohen 1970 10.00
*—Orange label*
❑ PC 9533 Leonard Cohen 198? 8.00
*—Reissue with new prefix*
❑ CS 9767 Songs From a Room 1969 12.00
*—Red "360 Sound" label*
❑ CS 9767 Songs From a Room 1970 10.00
*—Orange label*
❑ PC 9767 Songs From a Room 198? 8.00
*—Reissue with new prefix*
❑ C 30103 Songs of Love and Hate 1971 12.00
❑ PC 30103 Songs of Love and Hate 198? 8.00
*—Budget-line reissue*
❑ KC 31724 Leonard Cohen: Live Songs 1973 12.00
❑ KC 33167 New Skin for the Old Ceremony 1974 12.00
❑ PC 34077 The Best of Leonard Cohen 1975 10.00
*—No bar code*
❑ PC 34077 The Best of Leonard Cohen 198? 8.00
*—Reissue with bar code*
❑ JC 36264 Recent Songs 1979 10.00
❑ PC 36264 Recent Songs 198? 8.00
*—Budget-line reissue*
❑ FC 44191 I'm Your Man 1988 10.00
❑ C 85953 Ten New Songs 2001 20.00

PASSPORT
❑ PB-6045 Various Positions 1985 10.00

WARNER BROS.
❑ BSK 3125 Death of a Ladies' Man 1977 10.00

**COHEN, MYRON**

AUDIO FIDELITY
❑ 701 [M] Myron Cohen 196? 20.00

RCA VICTOR
❑ LPM-3534 [M] Everybody Gotta Be Someplace 1966 12.00
❑ LSP-3534 [S] Everybody Gotta Be Someplace 1966 15.00
❑ LPM-3791 [M] It's Not a Question 1967 12.00
❑ LSP-3791 [S] It's Not a Question 1967 15.00
❑ VPS-6052 [(2)] This Is Myron Cohen 1972 15.00

**COHN, AL**

CORAL
❑ CRL 57118 [M] Al Cohn Quintet 1957 50.00

DAWN
❑ DLP-1110 [M] Cohn on the Saxophone 1956 120.00

PROGRESSIVE
❑ PLP-3002 [10] Al Cohn Quartet 1953 300.00
❑ PLP-3004 [10] Al Cohn Quintet 1953 300.00

RCA VICTOR
❑ LJM-1024 [M] Mr. Music 1955 80.00
❑ LPM-1116 [M] The Natural Seven 1955 80.00
❑ LPM-1161 [M] Four Brass, One Tenor 1956 80.00
❑ LPM-1207 [M] That Old Feeling 1956 80.00
❑ LPM-2312 [M] Son of Drum Suite 1960 40.00
❑ LSP-2312 [S] Son of Drum Suite 1960 50.00

SAVOY
❑ MG-12048 [M] Cohn's Tones 1956 80.00

**COLDER, BEN** See SHEB WOOLEY.

**COLE, BUDDY**

COLUMBIA
❑ CL 1224 [M] Pipes & Chimes of Christmas 1958 20.00
*—Red label with six "eye" logos*
❑ CS 8032 [S] Pipes & Chimes of Christmas 1958 25.00
*—Red and black label with six "eye" logos*

**COLE, COZY**

AUDITION
❑ 33-5943 [M] Cozy Cole 1955 50.00

BETHLEHEM
❑ BCP-21 [M] Jazz at the Metropole Café 1955 50.00

CHARLIE PARKER
❑ PLP-403 [M] A Cozy Conaption of Carmen 1962 20.00
❑ PLP-403S [S] A Cozy Conaption of Carmen 1962 25.00

COLUMBIA
❑ CS 9353 [S] It's a Rockin' Thing 1965 20.00

CORAL
❑ CRL 757423 [S]Drum Beat Dancing Feet 1962 20.00
❑ CRL 757457 [S]It's a Cozy World 1964 20.00

FELSTED
❑ 2002 [S] Cozy's Caravan/Earl's Backroom 1958 40.00
❑ 7002 [M] Cozy's Caravan/Earl's Backroom 1958 50.00

GRAND AWARD
❑ GA 33-334 [M] After Hours 1956 40.00

KING
❑ 673 [M] Cozy Cole 1959 60.00
❑ KS-673 [S] Cozy Cole 1959 150.00

LOVE
❑ 500M [M] Topsy 1959 100.00
❑ 500S [S] Topsy 1959 200.00

PARIS
❑ 122 [M] Cozy Cole and His All-Stars 1958 50.00

PLYMOUTH
❑ P 12-155 [M] Cozy Cole and His All Stars 195? 30.00

SAVOY
❑ MG-12197 [M] Concerto for Cozy 196? 20.00

**COLE, COZY/JIMMY MCPARTLAND**

WALDORF MUSIC HALL
❑ MH 33-162 [10]After Hours 195? 50.00

**COLE, IKE**

DEE GEE
❑ LPM-4001 [M] Ike Cole's Tribute to His Brother Nat 1966 40.00
❑ ST-4001 [S] Ike Cole's Tribute to His Brother Nat 1966 50.00

DOT
❑ DLP-25943 Picture This! 1969 30.00

GUEST STAR
❑ G-1502 [M] Ike Cole — The Brother of Nat King Cole 196? 15.00
❑ GS-1502 [S] Ike Cole — The Brother of Nat King Cole 196? 15.00

PROMENADE
❑ 2099 [M] Ike Cole Sings 196? 15.00

UNITED ARTISTS
❑ UAL-3569 [M] Same Old You 1967 25.00
❑ UAS-6569 [S] Same Old You 1967 25.00

**COLE, JERRY**

BEAT ROCKET
❑ BR 117 Guitars A-Go-Go! 2000 12.00
❑ BR 118 Wild Strings! 2001 12.00

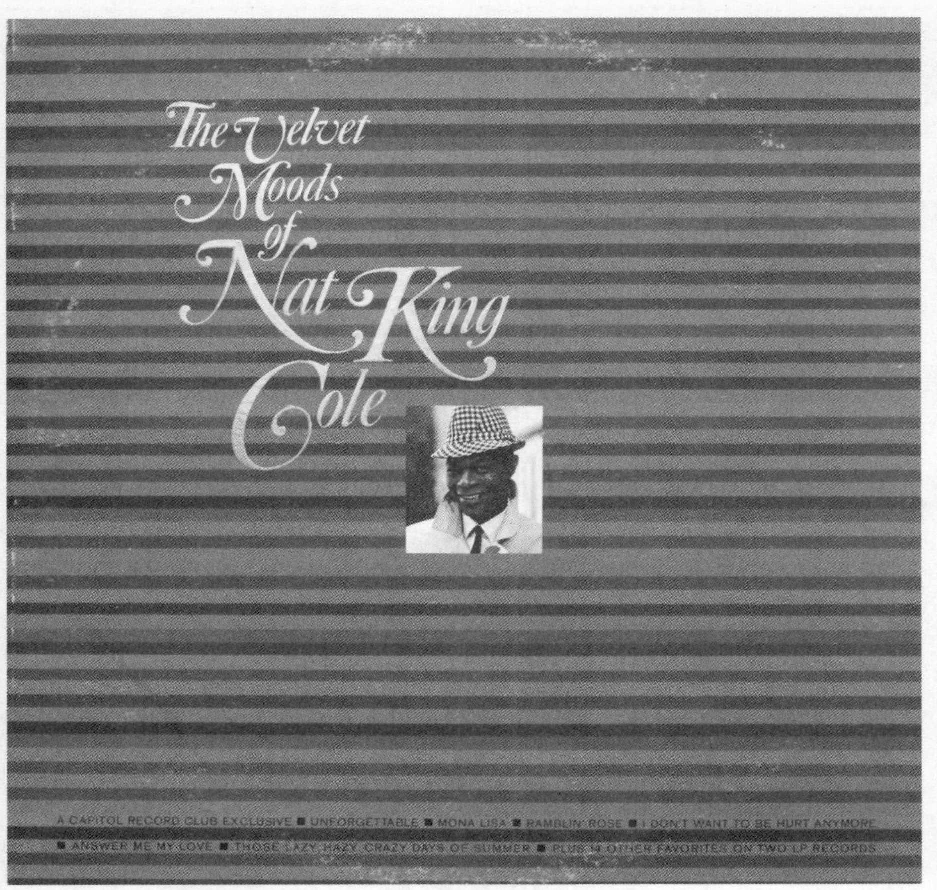


Nat King Cole, *The Velvet Moods of Nat King Cole,* Capitol SQBO 90938, 1967, 2 records, Capitol Record Club exclusive, $25.

**CAPITOL**

| Number | Title (A Side/B Side) | Yr | NM |
|---|---|---|---|
| ❑ ST 2044 [S] | Outer Limits | 1963 | 80.00 |
| ❑ T 2044 [M] | Outer Limits | 1963 | 50.00 |
| ❑ (S)T 2061 | Hot Rod Dance Party Bonus Photo | 1964 | 25.00 |
| ❑ ST 2061 [S] | Hot Rod Dance Party | 1964 | 100.00 |
| ❑ T 2061 [M] | Hot Rod Dance Party | 1964 | 80.00 |
| ❑ ST 2112 [S] | Surf Age | 1964 | 100.00 |
| *—With bonus single missing* | | | |
| ❑ ST 2112 [S] | Surf Age | 1964 | 120.00 |
| *—With bonus single by Dick Dale, "Thunder Wave"/"Spanish Kiss"* | | | |
| ❑ T 2112 [M] | Surf Age | 1964 | 80.00 |
| *—With bonus single missing* | | | |
| ❑ T 2112 [M] | Surf Age | 1964 | 100.00 |
| *—With bonus single by Dick Dale, "Thunder Wave"/"Spanish Kiss"* | | | |

**LIBERTY**

| Number | Title (A Side/B Side) | Yr | NM |
|---|---|---|---|
| ❑ LRP-3362 [M] | Sounds of the Big Irons | 1964 | 50.00 |
| ❑ LST-7362 [S] | Sounds of the Big Irons | 1964 | 60.00 |

## COLE, MARIA

**KAPP**

| Number | Title (A Side/B Side) | Yr | NM |
|---|---|---|---|
| ❑ 102 [10] | Maria Cole | 1954 | 50.00 |

## COLE, NAT KING

Includes reissues of material by the King Cole Trio.

**CAMAY**

| Number | Title (A Side/B Side) | Yr | NM |
|---|---|---|---|
| ❑ CA-3004 | Nat King Cole | 196? | 12.00 |

**CAPITOL**

| Number | Title (A Side/B Side) | Yr | NM |
|---|---|---|---|
| ❑ H 8 [10] | The King Cole Trio | 1950 | 100.00 |
| ❑ H 29 [10] | The King Cole Trio, Volume 2 | 1950 | 100.00 |
| ❑ H 59 [10] | The King Cole Trio, Volume 3 | 1950 | 100.00 |
| ❑ H 156 [10] | Nat King Cole at the Piano | 1950 | 100.00 |
| ❑ H 177 [10] | The King Cole Trio, Volume 4 | 1950 | 70.00 |
| ❑ H 213 [10] | Harvest of Hits | 1950 | 70.00 |
| *—Original; purple label* | | | |
| ❑ L 213 [10] | Harvest of Hits | 195? | 60.00 |
| *—Reissue; maroon label, "H" mechanically crossed out on back cover with "L" stamped next to it* | | | |
| ❑ H 220 [10] | The Nat King Cole Trio | 1950 | 60.00 |
| ❑ DWBB-252 [(2)] | Close-Up | 1969 | 15.00 |
| *—Reissue of 680 and 1891* | | | |
| ❑ ST-310 | There! I've Said It Again | 1969 | 12.00 |
| ❑ H 332 [10] | Penthouse Serenade | 1951 | 60.00 |
| *—Original; purple label* | | | |
| ❑ L 332 [10] | Penthouse Serenade | 195? | 50.00 |
| *—Reissue; maroon label, "H" mechanically crossed out on back cover with "L" stamped next to it* | | | |
| ❑ T 332 [M] | Penthouse Serenade | 1955 | 40.00 |
| ❑ DT 357 [R] | Unforgettable | 1965 | 12.00 |
| ❑ H 357 [10] | Unforgettable | 1952 | 60.00 |
| ❑ SM-357 | Unforgettable | 197? | 8.00 |
| *—Reissue with new prefix* | | | |
| ❑ T 357 [M] | Unforgettable | 1955 | 40.00 |
| *—Turquoise label* | | | |
| ❑ T 357 [M] | Unforgettable | 1958 | 30.00 |
| *—Black label with colorband, "Capitol" at left* | | | |
| ❑ T 357 [M] | Unforgettable | 1962 | 20.00 |
| *—Black label with colorband, "Capitol" at top* | | | |
| ❑ SKAO-373 | Nat King Cole's Greatest | 1969 | 12.00 |
| ❑ DT 420 [R] | Nat King Cole Sings for Two in Love | 1963 | 15.00 |
| ❑ H 420 [10] | Nat King Cole Sings for Two in Love | 1953 | 50.00 |
| *—Original; purple label* | | | |
| ❑ L 420 [10] | Nat King Cole Sings for Two in Love | 195? | 50.00 |
| *—Reissue; maroon label, back cover probably has "H" mechanically crossed out with "L" stamped next to it* | | | |
| ❑ T 420 [M] | Nat King Cole Sings for Two in Love | 1955 | 40.00 |
| *—Turquoise label* | | | |
| ❑ T 420 [M] | Nat King Cole Sings for Two in Love | 1958 | 30.00 |
| *—Black label with colorband, "Capitol" at left* | | | |
| ❑ T 420 [M] | Nat King Cole Sings for Two in Love | 1962 | 20.00 |
| *—Black label with colorband, "Capitol" at top* | | | |
| ❑ STBB-503 [(2)] | Walkin' My Baby Back Home/A Blossom Fell | 1970 | 15.00 |
| ❑ H 514 [10] | Tenth Anniversary Album | 1954 | 50.00 |
| ❑ W 514 [M] | Tenth Anniversary Album | 1955 | 40.00 |
| ❑ T 591 [M] | Vocal Classics | 1955 | 40.00 |
| ❑ T 592 [M] | Instrumental Classics | 1955 | 40.00 |
| ❑ DT 680 [R] | Ballads of the Day | 1963 | 15.00 |
| *—Black label with colorband* | | | |
| ❑ T 680 [M] | Ballads of the Day | 1956 | 40.00 |
| *—Turquoise label* | | | |
| ❑ T 680 [M] | Ballads of the Day | 1958 | 30.00 |
| *—Black label with colorband, "Capitol" at left* | | | |
| ❑ T 680 [M] | Ballads of the Day | 1962 | 20.00 |
| *—Black label with colorband, "Capitol" at top* | | | |
| ❑ W 689 [M] | The Piano Style of Nat King Cole | 1956 | 40.00 |
| *—Turquoise label* | | | |
| ❑ W 689 [M] | The Piano Style of Nat King Cole | 1958 | 30.00 |
| *—Black label with colorband, "Capitol" at left* | | | |
| ❑ W 689 [M] | The Piano Style of Nat King Cole | 1962 | 20.00 |
| *—Black label with colorband, "Capitol" at top* | | | |
| ❑ W 782 [M] | After Midnight | 1956 | 40.00 |
| *—Turquoise label* | | | |
| ❑ W 782 [M] | After Midnight | 1958 | 30.00 |
| *—Black label with colorband, "Capitol" at left* | | | |
| ❑ W 782 [M] | After Midnight | 1962 | 20.00 |
| *—Black label with colorband, "Capitol" at top* | | | |
| ❑ SM-824 | Love Is the Thing | 197? | 8.00 |
| *—Reissue with new prefix* | | | |
| ❑ SW 824 [S] | Love Is the Thing | 1959 | 30.00 |
| *—Black label with colorband, "Capitol" at left* | | | |
| ❑ SW 824 [S] | Love Is the Thing | 1962 | 20.00 |
| *—Black label with colorband, "Capitol" at top* | | | |
| ❑ SW 824 [S] | Love Is the Thing | 1969 | 12.00 |
| *—Lime green label* | | | |
| ❑ W 824 [M] | Love Is the Thing | 1957 | 40.00 |
| *—Turquoise or gray label* | | | |
| ❑ W 824 [M] | Love Is the Thing | 1958 | 30.00 |
| *—Black label with colorband, "Capitol" at left* | | | |
| ❑ W 824 [M] | Love Is the Thing | 1962 | 20.00 |
| *—Black label with colorband, "Capitol" at top* | | | |
| ❑ DT 870 [R] | This Is Nat "King" Cole | 1963 | 15.00 |
| *—Black label with colorband* | | | |
| ❑ T 870 [M] | This Is Nat "King" Cole | 1957 | 40.00 |
| *—Turquoise or gray label* | | | |
| ❑ T 870 [M] | This Is Nat "King" Cole | 1958 | 30.00 |
| *—Black label with colorband, "Capitol" at left* | | | |
| ❑ T 870 [M] | This Is Nat "King" Cole | 1962 | 20.00 |
| *—Black label with colorband, "Capitol" at top* | | | |
| ❑ SW 903 [S] | Just One of Those Things | 1959 | 30.00 |
| *—Black label with colorband, "Capitol" at left* | | | |
| ❑ SW 903 [S] | Just One of Those Things | 1962 | 20.00 |
| *—Black label with colorband, "Capitol" at top* | | | |
| ❑ W 903 [M] | Just One of Those Things | 1957 | 40.00 |
| *—Turquoise or gray label* | | | |
| ❑ W 903 [M] | Just One of Those Things | 1958 | 30.00 |
| *—Black label with colorband, "Capitol" at left* | | | |
| ❑ W 903 [M] | Just One of Those Things | 1962 | 20.00 |
| *—Black label with colorband, "Capitol" at top* | | | |
| ❑ SW 993 [S] | St. Louis Blues | 1959 | 50.00 |
| *—Black label with colorband, "Capitol" at left* | | | |
| ❑ W 993 [M] | St. Louis Blues | 1958 | 50.00 |
| *—Turquoise or gray label* | | | |
| ❑ W 993 [M] | St. Louis Blues | 1962 | 40.00 |
| *—Black label with colorband, "Capitol" at left* | | | |
| ❑ DW 1031 [R] | Cole Espanol | 196? | 15.00 |
| *—Black label with colorband* | | | |
| ❑ SM-1031 | Cole Espanol | 197? | 8.00 |
| *—Reissue with new prefix* | | | |
| ❑ W 1031 [M] | Cole Espanol | 1958 | 30.00 |
| *—Black label with colorband, "Capitol" at left* | | | |
| ❑ W 1031 [M] | Cole Espanol | 1962 | 20.00 |
| *—Black label with colorband, "Capitol" at top* | | | |
| ❑ SW 1084 [S] | The Very Thought of You | 1959 | 30.00 |
| *—Black label with colorband, "Capitol" at left* | | | |
| ❑ SW 1084 [S] | The Very Thought of You | 1962 | 20.00 |
| *—Black label with colorband, "Capitol" at top* | | | |
| ❑ W 1084 [M] | The Very Thought of You | 1958 | 30.00 |
| *—Black label with colorband, "Capitol" at left* | | | |
| ❑ W 1084 [M] | The Very Thought of You | 1962 | 20.00 |
| *—Black label with colorband, "Capitol" at top* | | | |
| ❑ SW 1120 [S] | Welcome to the Club | 1959 | 40.00 |
| *—Black label with colorband, "Capitol" at left* | | | |
| ❑ W 1120 [M] | Welcome to the Club | 1959 | 30.00 |
| *—Black label with colorband, "Capitol" at left* | | | |
| ❑ SW 1190 [S] | To Whom It May Concern | 1959 | 40.00 |
| *—Black label with colorband, "Capitol" at left* | | | |
| ❑ W 1190 [M] | To Whom It May Concern | 1959 | 30.00 |
| *—Black label with colorband, "Capitol" at left* | | | |
| ❑ SW 1220 [S] | A Mis Amigos | 1959 | 40.00 |
| *—Black label with colorband, "Capitol" at left* | | | |
| ❑ SW 1220 [S] | A Mis Amigos | 1962 | 25.00 |
| *—Black label with colorband, "Capitol" at top* | | | |
| ❑ W 1220 [M] | A Mis Amigos | 1959 | 30.00 |
| *—Black label with colorband, "Capitol" at left* | | | |
| ❑ W 1220 [M] | A Mis Amigos | 1962 | 20.00 |
| *—Black label with colorband, "Capitol" at top* | | | |
| ❑ SW 1249 [S] | Every Time I Feel the Spirit | 1960 | 30.00 |
| *—Black label with colorband, "Capitol" at left* | | | |
| ❑ W 1249 [M] | Every Time I Feel the Spirit | 1960 | 25.00 |
| *—Black label with colorband, "Capitol" at left* | | | |
| ❑ SW 1331 [S] | Tell Me About Yourself | 1960 | 30.00 |
| *—Black label with colorband, "Capitol" at left* | | | |
| ❑ W 1331 [M] | Tell Me About Yourself | 1960 | 25.00 |
| *—Black label with colorband, "Capitol" at left* | | | |
| ❑ SWAK 1392 [S] | Wild Is Love | 1960 | 30.00 |
| *—Black label with colorband, "Capitol" at left* | | | |
| ❑ WAK 1392 [M] | Wild Is Love | 1960 | 25.00 |
| *—Black label with colorband, "Capitol" at left* | | | |
| ❑ SW 1444 [S] | The Magic of Christmas | 1960 | 20.00 |
| ❑ W 1444 [M] | The Magic of Christmas | 1960 | 20.00 |
| ❑ SW 1574 [S] | The Touch of Your Lips | 1961 | 25.00 |
| *—Black label with colorband, "Capitol" at left* | | | |
| ❑ SW 1574 [S] | The Touch of Your Lips | 1962 | 20.00 |
| *—Black label with colorband, "Capitol" at top* | | | |
| ❑ W 1574 [M] | The Touch of Your Lips | 1961 | 20.00 |
| *—Black label with colorband, "Capitol" at left* | | | |



Except when noted otherwise, VG = 25% of NM, and VG+ = 50% of NM. (Example: VG = $2.00, VG+ = $4.00 and NM = $8.00.)

| Number | Title (A Side/B Side) | Yr | NM |
|---|---|---|---|
| ❑ W 1574 [M] | The Touch of Your Lips | 1962 | 15.00 |
| *—Black label with colorband, "Capitol" at top* | | | |
| ❑ SWCL 1613 [(3)S] | The Nat King Cole Story | 1961 | 30.00 |
| ❑ WCL 1613 [(3)M] | The Nat King Cole Story | 1961 | 25.00 |
| ❑ SM-1675 | Nat King Cole Sings/George Shearing Plays | 197? | 8.00 |
| *—Reissue with new prefix* | | | |
| ❑ SW 1675 [S] | Nat King Cole Sings/George Shearing Plays | 1962 | 30.00 |
| *—Black label with colorband, "Capitol" at left* | | | |
| ❑ SW 1675 [S] | Nat King Cole Sings/George Shearing Plays | 1963 | 20.00 |
| *—Black label with colorband, "Capitol" at top* | | | |
| ❑ W 1675 [M] | Nat King Cole Sings/George Shearing Plays | 1962 | 25.00 |
| *—Black label with colorband, "Capitol" at left* | | | |
| ❑ W 1675 [M] | Nat King Cole Sings/George Shearing Plays | 1963 | 15.00 |
| *—Black label with colorband, "Capitol" at top* | | | |
| ❑ SW 1713 [S] | Nat King Cole Sings the Blues | 1962 | 25.00 |
| *—Black label with colorband, "Capitol" at left* | | | |
| ❑ W 1713 [M] | Nat King Cole Sings the Blues | 1962 | 20.00 |
| *—Black label with colorband, "Capitol" at left* | | | |
| ❑ SM-1749 | More Cole Espanol | 197? | 8.00 |
| *—Reissue with new prefix* | | | |
| ❑ SW 1749 [S] | More Cole Espanol | 1962 | 30.00 |
| *—Black label with colorband, "Capitol" at left* | | | |
| ❑ SW 1749 [S] | More Cole Espanol | 1963 | 20.00 |
| *—Black label with colorband, "Capitol" at top* | | | |
| ❑ W 1749 [M] | More Cole Espanol | 1962 | 25.00 |
| *—Black label with colorband, "Capitol" at left* | | | |
| ❑ W 1749 [M] | More Cole Espanol | 1963 | 15.00 |
| *—Black label with colorband, "Capitol" at top* | | | |
| ❑ ST 1793 [S] | Ramblin' Rose | 1962 | 20.00 |
| ❑ T 1793 [M] | Ramblin' Rose | 1962 | 15.00 |
| ❑ ST 1838 [S] | Dear Lonely Hearts | 1962 | 20.00 |
| ❑ T 1838 [M] | Dear Lonely Hearts | 1962 | 15.00 |
| ❑ SW 1859 [S] | Where Did Everyone Go? | 1963 | 20.00 |
| ❑ W 1859 [M] | Where Did Everyone Go? | 1963 | 15.00 |
| ❑ DT 1891 [R] | Nat King Cole's Top Pops | 1963 | 12.00 |
| ❑ T 1891 [M] | Nat King Cole's Top Pops | 1963 | 15.00 |
| ❑ SW 1926 [S] | The Nat King Cole Story, Volume 1 | 1962 | 15.00 |
| ❑ W 1926 [M] | The Nat King Cole Story, Volume 1 | 1962 | 12.00 |
| ❑ SW 1927 [S] | The Nat King Cole Story, Volume 2 | 1963 | 15.00 |
| ❑ W 1927 [M] | The Nat King Cole Story, Volume 2 | 1963 | 12.00 |
| ❑ SW 1928 [S] | The Nat King Cole Story, Volume 3 | 1963 | 15.00 |
| ❑ W 1928 [M] | The Nat King Cole Story, Volume 3 | 1963 | 12.00 |
| ❑ SW 1929 [S] | Nat King Cole Sings the Blues, Volume 2 | 1963 | 20.00 |
| ❑ W 1929 [M] | Nat King Cole Sings the Blues, Volume 2 | 1963 | 15.00 |
| ❑ ST 1932 [S] | Those Lazy-Hazy-Crazy Days of Summer | 1963 | 20.00 |
| ❑ T 1932 [M] | Those Lazy-Hazy-Crazy Days of Summer | 1963 | 15.00 |
| ❑ SM-1967 [S] | The Christmas Song | 197? | 8.00 |
| *—Budget-line reissue* | | | |
| ❑ SW 1967 [S] | The Christmas Song | 1962 | 15.00 |
| *—Black label with colorband* | | | |
| ❑ SW 1967 [S] | The Christmas Song | 1969 | 12.00 |
| *—Lime-green label* | | | |
| ❑ SW 1967 [S] | The Christmas Song | 1971 | 12.00 |
| *—Red label* | | | |
| ❑ SW 1967 [S] | The Christmas Song | 1973 | 10.00 |
| *—Orange label, "Capitol" at bottom* | | | |
| ❑ W 1967 [M] | The Christmas Song | 1962 | 15.00 |
| *—Reissue of W 1444 with title song added and another deleted* | | | |
| ❑ SW 2008 [S] | Let's Face the Music | 1963 | 20.00 |
| ❑ W 2008 [M] | Let's Face the Music | 1963 | 15.00 |
| ❑ SM-2117 | My Fair Lady | 197? | 8.00 |
| *—Reissue with new prefix* | | | |
| ❑ SW 2117 [S] | My Fair Lady | 1964 | 20.00 |
| *—Black label with colorband* | | | |
| ❑ SW 2117 [S] | My Fair Lady | 1969 | 12.00 |
| *—Lime green label* | | | |
| ❑ W 2117 [M] | My Fair Lady | 1964 | 15.00 |
| ❑ ST 2118 [S] | I Don't Want to Be Hurt Anymore | 1964 | 20.00 |
| ❑ T 2118 [M] | I Don't Want to Be Hurt Anymore | 1964 | 15.00 |
| ❑ ST 2195 [S] | L-O-V-E | 1965 | 20.00 |
| ❑ T 2195 [M] | L-O-V-E | 1965 | 15.00 |
| ❑ T 2311 [M] | The Nat King Cole Trio | 1965 | 12.00 |
| ❑ ST 2340 [S] | Songs from "Cat Ballou" and Other Motion Pictures | 1965 | 15.00 |
| ❑ T 2340 [M] | Songs from "Cat Ballou" and Other Motion Pictures | 1965 | 12.00 |
| ❑ DT 2348 [R] | Nature Boy | 1965 | 12.00 |
| ❑ T 2348 [M] | Nature Boy | 1965 | 15.00 |
| ❑ ST 2361 [S] | Looking Back | 1965 | 15.00 |
| ❑ T 2361 [M] | Looking Back | 1965 | 12.00 |
| ❑ MAS 2434 [M] | Nat King Cole at the Sands | 1966 | 12.00 |
| ❑ SM-2434 | Nat King Cole at the Sands | 197? | 8.00 |
| *—Reissue with new prefix* | | | |
| ❑ SMAS 2434 [S] | Nat King Cole at the Sands | 1966 | 15.00 |
| ❑ ST 2454 [S] | Hymns and Spirituals | 1966 | 15.00 |
| ❑ T 2454 [M] | Hymns and Spirituals | 1966 | 12.00 |
| ❑ T 2529 [M] | The Vintage Years | 1966 | 12.00 |
| ❑ ST 2558 [S] | The Great Songs! | 1966 | 15.00 |
| ❑ T 2558 [M] | The Great Songs! | 1966 | 12.00 |
| ❑ ST 2680 [S] | Sincerely, Nat King Cole | 1967 | 12.00 |
| ❑ T 2680 [M] | Sincerely, Nat King Cole | 1967 | 15.00 |
| ❑ ST 2759 [S] | Thank You Pretty Baby | 1967 | 12.00 |
| ❑ T 2759 [M] | Thank You Pretty Baby | 1967 | 15.00 |
| ❑ ST 2820 [S] | Beautiful Ballads | 1967 | 12.00 |
| ❑ T 2820 [M] | Beautiful Ballads | 1967 | 15.00 |
| ❑ STCL 2873 [(3)P] | The Nat King Cole Deluxe Set | 1968 | 25.00 |
| ❑ TCL 2873 [(3)M] | The Nat King Cole Deluxe Set | 1968 | 30.00 |
| ❑ SKAO 2944 | The Best of Nat King Cole | 1968 | 12.00 |
| ❑ H 9110 [10] | Eight Top Pops | 1954 | 50.00 |
| ❑ M-11033 [M] | Trio Days | 1972 | 15.00 |
| ❑ SWAK-11355 | Love Is Here to Stay | 1974 | 12.00 |
| ❑ SM-11796 | After Midnight | 1978 | 10.00 |
| ❑ SM-11804 | Songs from "Cat Ballou" and Other Motion Pictures | 1978 | 10.00 |
| ❑ SM-11882 | Looking Back | 1979 | 10.00 |
| ❑ ST-12219 | 16 Grandes Exitos | 1982 | 10.00 |
| ❑ SN-16032 | Ramblin' Rose | 1980 | 8.00 |
| ❑ SN-16033 | The Nat King Cole Story, Volume 1 | 1980 | 8.00 |
| ❑ SN-16034 | The Nat King Cole Story, Volume 2 | 1980 | 8.00 |
| ❑ SN-16035 | The Nat King Cole Story, Volume 3 | 1980 | 8.00 |
| ❑ SN-16036 | The Best of Nat King Cole | 1980 | 8.00 |
| ❑ SN-16037 | Wild Is Love | 1980 | 8.00 |
| ❑ SN-16136 | A Mis Amigos | 1980 | 8.00 |
| ❑ SN-16137 | St. Louis Blues | 1980 | 8.00 |
| ❑ SN-16162 | Unforgettable | 1981 | 8.00 |
| ❑ SN-16163 | Love Is the Thing | 1981 | 8.00 |
| ❑ DN-16164 | Walkin' My Baby Back Home | 1981 | 8.00 |
| ❑ DN-16165 | A Blossom Fell | 1981 | 8.00 |
| ❑ N-16166 | Cole Espanol | 1981 | 8.00 |
| ❑ SN-16167 | More Cole Espanol | 1981 | 8.00 |
| ❑ N-16260 | The Best of the King Cole Trio — Volume 1 | 1982 | 8.00 |
| ❑ N-16281 | The Best of the King Cole Trio — Volume 2 | 1982 | 8.00 |
| ❑ SQBO 90938 [(2)] | The Velvet Moods of Nat King Cole | 1967 | 25.00 |
| *—Capitol Record Club exclusive* | | | |
| ❑ SQBO 91278 [(2)] | The Swingin' Moods of Nat King Cole | 1967 | 25.00 |
| *—Capitol Record Club exclusive* | | | |
| ❑ SQBO-93741 [(2)] | The Man and His Music | 197? | 20.00 |
| *—Capitol Record Club exclusive; with booklet* | | | |

**DCC COMPACT CLASSICS**

| Number | Title (A Side/B Side) | Yr | NM |
|---|---|---|---|
| ❑ LPZ-2029 | Love Is the Thing | 1997 | 120.00 |
| *—Audiophile vinyl* | | | |
| ❑ LPZ-2047 | The Very Thought of You | 1998 | 100.00 |
| *—Audiophile vinyl* | | | |
| ❑ LPZ-2061 [(2)] | The Greatest Hits | 1998 | 120.00 |
| *—Audiophile vinyl* | | | |

**DECCA**

| Number | Title (A Side/B Side) | Yr | NM |
|---|---|---|---|
| ❑ DL 8260 [M] | In the Beginning | 1956 | 40.00 |
| *—Black label, silver print* | | | |
| ❑ DL 8260 [M] | In the Beginning | 1960 | 25.00 |
| *—Black label with color bars* | | | |

**EVEREST ARCHIVE OF FOLK & JAZZ**

| Number | Title (A Side/B Side) | Yr | NM |
|---|---|---|---|
| ❑ 290 | Nature Boy | 197? | 10.00 |

**MARK 56**

| Number | Title (A Side/B Side) | Yr | NM |
|---|---|---|---|
| ❑ 739 [(2)] | Early 1940s | 197? | 15.00 |

**MCA**

| Number | Title (A Side/B Side) | Yr | NM |
|---|---|---|---|
| ❑ 4020 [(2)] | From the Very Beginning | 1973 | 12.00 |

**MOBILE FIDELITY**

| Number | Title (A Side/B Side) | Yr | NM |
|---|---|---|---|
| ❑ 1-081 | Nat King Cole Sings/George Shearing Plays | 1981 | 40.00 |
| *—Audiophile vinyl* | | | |

**MOSAIC**

| Number | Title (A Side/B Side) | Yr | NM |
|---|---|---|---|
| ❑ MR27-138 [(27)] | The Complete Capitol Recordings of the Nat King Cole Trio | 1991 | 800.00 |

**PAIR**

| Number | Title (A Side/B Side) | Yr | NM |
|---|---|---|---|
| ❑ PDL2-1025 [(2)] | Weaver of Dreams | 1986 | 12.00 |
| ❑ PDL2-1026 [(2)] | Love Moods | 1986 | 12.00 |
| ❑ PDL2-1128 [(2)] | Tenderly | 1986 | 12.00 |

**PICKWICK**

| Number | Title (A Side/B Side) | Yr | NM |
|---|---|---|---|
| ❑ PTP-2058 [(2)] | Nature Boy | 1973 | 12.00 |
| ❑ SPC-3046 | Love Is a Many Splendored Thing | 196? | 10.00 |
| ❑ SPC-3071 | When You're Smiling | 196? | 10.00 |
| ❑ SPC-3105 | Stay As Sweet As You Are | 196? | 10.00 |
| ❑ SPC-3154 | You're My Everything | 197? | 10.00 |
| ❑ SPC-3249 | Nature Boy | 197? | 10.00 |

**SAVOY JAZZ**

| Number | Title (A Side/B Side) | Yr | NM |
|---|---|---|---|
| ❑ SJL-1205 | Nat King Cole & The King Cole Trio | 1989 | 12.00 |

**SCORE**

| Number | Title (A Side/B Side) | Yr | NM |
|---|---|---|---|
| ❑ SLP-4019 [M] | The King Cole Trio and Lester Young | 1957 | 80.00 |

**TIME-LIFE**

| Number | Title (A Side/B Side) | Yr | NM |
|---|---|---|---|
| ❑ SLGD-01 [(2)] | Legendary Singers: Nat King Cole | 1985 | 15.00 |
| ❑ SLGD-15 [(2)] | Legendary Singers: Nat King Cole: Take Two | 1986 | 15.00 |

**TRIP**

| Number | Title (A Side/B Side) | Yr | NM |
|---|---|---|---|
| ❑ 7 | The Nat "King" Cole Trio | 197? | 12.00 |

**VERVE**

| Number | Title (A Side/B Side) | Yr | NM |
|---|---|---|---|
| ❑ VSP-14 [M] | Nat Cole at JATP | 1966 | 15.00 |
| ❑ VSPS-14 [R] | Nat Cole at JATP | 1966 | 12.00 |
| ❑ VSP-25 [M] | Nat Cole at JATP 2 | 1966 | 15.00 |
| ❑ VSPS-25 [R] | Nat Cole at JATP 2 | 1966 | 12.00 |

## COLE, NATALIE

**CAPITOL**

| Number | Title (A Side/B Side) | Yr | NM |
|---|---|---|---|
| ❑ ST-11429 | Inseparable | 1975 | 10.00 |
| ❑ ST-11517 | Natalie | 1976 | 10.00 |
| ❑ SO-11600 | Unpredictable | 1977 | 10.00 |
| ❑ SW-11708 | Thankful | 1978 | 10.00 |
| ❑ SKBL-11709 [(2)] | Natalie..Live! | 1978 | 12.00 |
| ❑ SO-11928 | I Love You So | 1979 | 10.00 |
| ❑ ST-12079 | Don't Look Back | 1980 | 10.00 |
| ❑ ST-12165 | Happy Love | 1981 | 10.00 |
| ❑ ST-12242 | A Collection | 1982 | 10.00 |
| ❑ SN-16038 | Inseparable | 198? | 8.00 |
| *—Budget-line reissue* | | | |
| ❑ SN-16310 | A Collection | 1985 | 8.00 |
| *—Budget-line reissue* | | | |

**ELEKTRA**

| Number | Title (A Side/B Side) | Yr | NM |
|---|---|---|---|
| ❑ 61049 [(2)] | Unforgettable | 1991 | 20.00 |

**EMI**

| Number | Title (A Side/B Side) | Yr | NM |
|---|---|---|---|
| ❑ E1-48902 | Good to Be Back | 1989 | 10.00 |

**EPIC**

| Number | Title (A Side/B Side) | Yr | NM |
|---|---|---|---|
| ❑ FE 38280 | I'm Ready | 1983 | 10.00 |

**MANHATTAN**

| Number | Title (A Side/B Side) | Yr | NM |
|---|---|---|---|
| ❑ 53051 | Everlasting | 1987 | 10.00 |

**MOBILE FIDELITY**

| Number | Title (A Side/B Side) | Yr | NM |
|---|---|---|---|
| ❑ 1-032 | Thankful | 1980 | 20.00 |
| *—Audiophile vinyl* | | | |

**MODERN**

| Number | Title (A Side/B Side) | Yr | NM |
|---|---|---|---|
| ❑ 90270 | Dangerous | 1985 | 10.00 |

## COLE, RICHIE

**ADELPHI**

| Number | Title (A Side/B Side) | Yr | NM |
|---|---|---|---|
| ❑ AD 5001 | Starburst | 1976 | 20.00 |

## COLEMAN, CY

**BENIDA**

| Number | Title (A Side/B Side) | Yr | NM |
|---|---|---|---|
| ❑ LP-1023A [10] | Cy Coleman | 1955 | 50.00 |

**CAPITOL**

| Number | Title (A Side/B Side) | Yr | NM |
|---|---|---|---|
| ❑ ST 1952 [S] | Piano Witchcraft | 1963 | 25.00 |
| ❑ T 1952 [M] | Piano Witchcraft | 1963 | 20.00 |
| ❑ ST 2355 [S] | The Art of Love | 1965 | 20.00 |

**EVEREST**

| Number | Title (A Side/B Side) | Yr | NM |
|---|---|---|---|
| ❑ SDBR-1092 [S] | Playboy's Penthouse | 196? | 30.00 |
| ❑ LPBR-5092 [M] | Playboy's Penthouse | 196? | 25.00 |

**MGM**

| Number | Title (A Side/B Side) | Yr | NM |
|---|---|---|---|
| ❑ SE-4501 | Ages of Rock | 1968 | 25.00 |

**WESTMINSTER**

| Number | Title (A Side/B Side) | Yr | NM |
|---|---|---|---|
| ❑ WLP-15001 [M] | Cool Coleman | 195? | 40.00 |

## COLEMAN, EARL

**PRESTIGE**

| Number | Title (A Side/B Side) | Yr | NM |
|---|---|---|---|
| ❑ PRLP-7045 [M] | Earl Coleman Returns | 1956 | 50.00 |
| *—Yellow label* | | | |
| ❑ PRLP-7045 [M] | Earl Coleman Returns | 196? | 25.00 |
| *—Blue label, trident logo at right* | | | |

## COLEMAN, GLORIA

**IMPULSE!**

| Number | Title (A Side/B Side) | Yr | NM |
|---|---|---|---|
| ❑ A-47 [M] | Soul Sisters | 1963 | 25.00 |
| ❑ AS-47 [S] | Soul Sisters | 1963 | 30.00 |

## COLEMAN, ORNETTE

**ABC IMPULSE!**

| Number | Title (A Side/B Side) | Yr | NM |
|---|---|---|---|
| ❑ AS-9178 | Ornette at 12 | 1968 | 25.00 |
| ❑ AS-9187 | Crisis | 1969 | 25.00 |

**ARISTA FREEDOM**

| Number | Title (A Side/B Side) | Yr | NM |
|---|---|---|---|
| ❑ AL 1900 [(2)] | The Great London Concert | 1978 | 20.00 |

**ARTISTS HOUSE**

| Number | Title (A Side/B Side) | Yr | NM |
|---|---|---|---|
| ❑ 1 | Body Meta | 1977 | 20.00 |
| ❑ 6 | Soapsuds | 1978 | 20.00 |

**ATLANTIC**

| Number | Title (A Side/B Side) | Yr | NM |
|---|---|---|---|
| ❑ 1317 [M] | The Shape of Jazz to Come | 1959 | 40.00 |
| *—"Bullseye" label* | | | |
| ❑ 1317 [M] | The Shape of Jazz to Come | 1960 | 25.00 |
| *—Multicolor label, white "fan" logo* | | | |
| ❑ SD 1317 [S] | The Shape of Jazz to Come | 1959 | 50.00 |
| *—"Bullseye" label* | | | |
| ❑ SD 1317 [S] | The Shape of Jazz to Come | 1960 | 30.00 |
| *—Multicolor label, white "fan" logo* | | | |

| Number | Title (A Side/B Side) | Yr | NM |
|---|---|---|---|
| ❑ SD 1317 [S] | The Shape of Jazz to Come | 1963 | 20.00 |
| *—Multicolor label, black "fan" logo* | | | |
| ❑ 1327 [M] | Change of the Century | 1960 | 30.00 |
| *—Multicolor label, white "fan" logo* | | | |
| ❑ 1327 [M] | Change of the Century | 1960 | 50.00 |
| *—Black label* | | | |
| ❑ SD 1327 [S] | Change of the Century | 1960 | 40.00 |
| *—Multicolor label, white "fan" logo* | | | |
| ❑ SD 1327 [S] | Change of the Century | 1960 | 60.00 |
| *—Green label* | | | |
| ❑ SD 1327 [S] | Change of the Century | 1963 | 20.00 |
| *—Multicolor label, black "fan" logo* | | | |
| ❑ SD 1327 [S] | Change of the Century | 1976 | 10.00 |
| ❑ 1353 [M] | This Is Our Music | 1960 | 30.00 |
| *—Multicolor label, white "fan" logo* | | | |
| ❑ SD 1353 [S] | This Is Our Music | 1960 | 40.00 |
| *—Multicolor label, white "fan" logo* | | | |
| ❑ SD 1353 [S] | This Is Our Music | 1963 | 20.00 |
| *—Multicolor label, black "fan" logo* | | | |
| ❑ 1364 [M] | Free Jazz | 1961 | 40.00 |
| *—Multicolor label, white "fan" logo* | | | |
| ❑ 1364 [M] | Free Jazz | 1963 | 20.00 |
| *—Multicolor label, black "fan" logo* | | | |
| ❑ SD 1364 [S] | Free Jazz | 1961 | 50.00 |
| *—Multicolor label, white "fan" logo* | | | |
| ❑ SD 1364 [S] | Free Jazz | 1963 | 25.00 |
| *—Multicolor label, black "fan" logo* | | | |
| ❑ 1378 [M] | Ornette | 1961 | 30.00 |
| *—Multicolor label, white "fan" logo* | | | |
| ❑ SD 1378 [S] | Ornette | 1961 | 40.00 |
| *—Multicolor label, white "fan" logo* | | | |
| ❑ SD 1378 [S] | Ornette | 1963 | 20.00 |
| *—Multicolor label, black "fan" logo* | | | |
| ❑ 1394 [M] | Ornette on Tenor | 1962 | 20.00 |
| *—Multicolor label, black "fan" logo* | | | |
| ❑ SD 1394 [S] | Ornette on Tenor | 1962 | 25.00 |
| *—Multicolor label, black "fan" logo* | | | |
| BLUE NOTE | | | |
| ❑ BLP-4224 [M] | Ornette Coleman at the Golden Circle, Stockholm, Volume 1 | 1965 | 30.00 |
| ❑ BLP-4225 [M] | Ornette Coleman at the Golden Circle, Stockholm, Volume 2 | 1965 | 30.00 |
| ❑ BLP-4246 [M] | The Empty Foxhole | 1966 | 30.00 |
| ❑ BST-84224 [S] | Ornette Coleman at the Golden Circle, Stockholm, Volume 1 | 1965 | 40.00 |
| *—"New York, USA" on label* | | | |
| ❑ BST-84225 [S] | Ornette Coleman at the Golden Circle, Stockholm, Volume 2 | 1965 | 40.00 |
| *—"New York, USA" on label* | | | |
| ❑ BST-84246 [S] | The Empty Foxhole | 1966 | 40.00 |
| *—"New York, USA" on label* | | | |
| ❑ BST-84246 [S] | The Empty Foxhole | 1967 | 30.00 |
| *—"A Division of Liberty Records" on label* | | | |
| ❑ BST-84287 | New York Is Now! | 1968 | 25.00 |
| ❑ BST-84356 | Love Call | 1970 | 20.00 |
| COLUMBIA | | | |
| ❑ KC 31061 | Science Fiction | 1972 | 20.00 |
| ❑ KC 31562 | Skies of America | 1972 | 20.00 |
| ❑ CG 33669 [(2)] | Science Fiction/Skies of America | 1976 | 20.00 |
| CONTEMPORARY | | | |
| ❑ C-3551 [M] | The Music of Ornette Coleman — Something Else! | 1958 | 120.00 |
| ❑ M-3569 [M] | Tomorrow Is the Question | 1959 | 80.00 |
| ❑ S-7551 [S] | The Music of Ornette Coleman — Something Else! | 1959 | 80.00 |
| ❑ S-7569 [S] | Tomorrow Is the Question | 1959 | 60.00 |
| ESP-DISK' | | | |
| ❑ 1006 [M] | Town Hall Concert, December 1962 | 1965 | 20.00 |
| ❑ S-1006 [S] | Town Hall Concert, December 1962 | 1965 | 25.00 |
| FLYING DUTCHMAN | | | |
| ❑ 123 | Friends and Neighbors | 1970 | 20.00 |
| IAI | | | |
| ❑ 373852 | Classics, Volume 1 | 197? | 20.00 |
| INNER CITY | | | |
| ❑ 1001 | Live at the Hillcrest Club 1958 | 197? | 20.00 |
| RCA VICTOR | | | |
| ❑ LPM-2982 [M] | The Music of Ornette Coleman | 1964 | 25.00 |
| ❑ LSP-2982 [S] | The Music of Ornette Coleman | 1964 | 30.00 |

**COLES, JOHNNY**

| Number | Title (A Side/B Side) | Yr | NM |
|---|---|---|---|
| BLUE NOTE | | | |
| ❑ BLP-4144 [M] | Little Johnny C | 1963 | 40.00 |
| *—"New York, USA" on label* | | | |
| ❑ BST-84144 [S] | Little Johnny C | 1963 | 50.00 |
| *—"New York, USA" on label* | | | |
| EPIC | | | |
| ❑ LA 16015 [M] | The Warm Sound | 1961 | 120.00 |
| ❑ BA 17015 [S] | The Warm Sound | 1961 | 150.00 |
| MAINSTREAM | | | |
| ❑ MRL-346 | Katumbo (Dance) | 1972 | 20.00 |

**COLLAGE, THE**

| Number | Title (A Side/B Side) | Yr | NM |
|---|---|---|---|
| SMASH | | | |
| ❑ SRS-67101 | The Collage | 1968 | 20.00 |

**COLLECTORS, THE**

| Number | Title (A Side/B Side) | Yr | NM |
|---|---|---|---|
| WARNER BROS. | | | |
| ❑ W 1746 [M] | The Collectors | 1968 | 50.00 |
| *—May be white label promo only* | | | |
| ❑ WS 1746 [S] | The Collectors | 1968 | 25.00 |
| ❑ WS 1774 | Grass and Wild Strawberries | 1969 | 25.00 |

**COLLEGIANS, THE (1)**

| Number | Title (A Side/B Side) | Yr | NM |
|---|---|---|---|
| LOST-NITE | | | |
| ❑ LLP-5 [10] | The Best of the Collegians | 1981 | 10.00 |
| *—Red vinyl* | | | |
| WINLEY | | | |
| ❑ LP-6004 [M] | Sing Along with the Collegians | 195? | 400.00 |

**COLLETTE, BUDDY**

| Number | Title (A Side/B Side) | Yr | NM |
|---|---|---|---|
| ABC-PARAMOUNT | | | |
| ❑ ABC-179 [M] | Calm, Cool and Collette | 1957 | 60.00 |
| CHALLENGE | | | |
| ❑ CHL-603 [M] | Everybody's Buddy | 1958 | 50.00 |
| CONTEMPORARY | | | |
| ❑ C-3522 [M] | Man of Many Parts | 1956 | 50.00 |
| ❑ C-3531 [M] | Nice Day with Buddy Collette | 1957 | 50.00 |
| ❑ S-7522 [S] | Man of Many Parts | 1959 | 40.00 |
| ❑ S-7531 [S] | Nice Day with Buddy Collette | 1959 | 40.00 |
| CROWN | | | |
| ❑ CLP-5019 [M] | Bongo Madness | 195? | 25.00 |
| DIG | | | |
| ❑ LP-101 [M] | Tanganyika | 1956 | 100.00 |
| DOOTO | | | |
| ❑ DTL-245 [M] | Buddy's Best | 1957 | 60.00 |
| *—Black vinyl* | | | |
| ❑ DTL-245 [M] | Buddy's Best | 1957 | 100.00 |
| *—Red vinyl* | | | |
| EMARCY | | | |
| ❑ MG-36133 [M] | Swingin' Shepherds | 1958 | 50.00 |
| ❑ SR-80005 [S] | Swingin' Shepherds | 1959 | 40.00 |
| INTERLUDE | | | |
| ❑ MO-505 [M] | Modern Interpretations of Porgy & Bess | 196? | 30.00 |
| ❑ ST-1005 [S] | Modern Interpretations of Porgy & Bess | 196? | 40.00 |
| MERCURY | | | |
| ❑ MG-20447 [M] | At the Cinema | 1959 | 40.00 |
| ❑ SR-60132 [S] | At the Cinema | 1959 | 40.00 |
| MUSIC & SOUND | | | |
| ❑ 1001 [M] | Polynesia | 196? | 30.00 |
| ❑ S-1001 [S] | Polynesia | 196? | 40.00 |
| SPECIALTY | | | |
| ❑ SP-5002 [M] | Jazz Loves Paris | 1960 | 50.00 |
| SURREY | | | |
| ❑ SS-1009 [S] | Buddy Collette on Broadway | 1965 | 20.00 |
| TAMPA | | | |
| ❑ TP-34 [M] | Star Studded Cast | 1959 | 80.00 |
| WORLD PACIFIC | | | |
| ❑ ST-1823 [S] | Warm Winds | 1964 | 25.00 |
| ❑ WP-1823 [M] | Warm Winds | 1964 | 20.00 |

**COLLIER, MITTY**

| Number | Title (A Side/B Side) | Yr | NM |
|---|---|---|---|
| CHESS | | | |
| ❑ LP-1492 [M] | Shades of a Genius | 1965 | 80.00 |
| ❑ LPS-1492 [S] | Shades of a Genius | 1965 | 120.00 |

**COLLINS, AARON**

| Number | Title (A Side/B Side) | Yr | NM |
|---|---|---|---|
| CROWN | | | |
| ❑ CLP-5028 [M] | Calypso U.S.A. | 1958 | 600.00 |

**COLLINS, AL "JAZZBO"**

| Number | Title (A Side/B Side) | Yr | NM |
|---|---|---|---|
| CORAL | | | |
| ❑ CRL 57035 [M] | East Coast Jazz Scene | 1956 | 80.00 |
| EVEREST | | | |
| ❑ SDBR-1097 [S] | Swingin' at the Opera | 1960 | 40.00 |
| ❑ LPBR-5097 [M] | Swingin' at the Opera | 1960 | 30.00 |
| IMPULSE! | | | |
| ❑ A-9150 [M] | A Lovely Bunch of Al "Jazzbo" Collins | 1967 | 40.00 |
| ❑ AS-9150 [S] | A Lovely Bunch of Al "Jazzbo" Collins | 1967 | 30.00 |
| OLD TOWN | | | |
| ❑ LP-2001 [M] | In the Purple Grotto | 1961 | 30.00 |

**COLLINS, ALBERT**

| Number | Title (A Side/B Side) | Yr | NM |
|---|---|---|---|
| ALLIGATOR | | | |
| ❑ AL-4713 | Ice Pickin' | 1978 | 10.00 |
| ❑ AL-4719 | Frostbite | 1980 | 10.00 |
| ❑ AL-4725 | Frozen Alive! | 1981 | 10.00 |
| ❑ AL-4730 | Don't Lose Your Cool | 1983 | 10.00 |
| ❑ AL-4733 | Live in Japan | 1984 | 10.00 |
| ❑ AL-4743 | Showdown! | 1985 | 10.00 |
| *—With Robert Cray and Johnny Copeland* | | | |
| ❑ AL-4752 | Cold Snap | 1986 | 10.00 |
| BLUE THUMB | | | |
| ❑ BTS 8 | Truckin' with Albert Collins | 1969 | 25.00 |
| *—Reissue of TCF Hall LP* | | | |
| IMPERIAL | | | |
| ❑ LP-12428 | Love Can Be Found Anywhere | 1968 | 30.00 |
| ❑ LP-12438 | Trash Talkin' | 1969 | 30.00 |
| ❑ LP-12449 | The Compleat Albert Collins | 1970 | 30.00 |
| MOBILE FIDELITY | | | |
| ❑ 1-217 | Showdown! | 1995 | 30.00 |
| *—With Robert Cray and Johnny Copeland; audiophile vinyl* | | | |
| ❑ 1-226 | Cold Snap | 1995 | 20.00 |
| *—Audiophile vinyl* | | | |
| TCF HALL | | | |
| ❑ 8002 [M] | The Cool Sound of Albert Collins | 1965 | 300.00 |
| TUMBLEWEED | | | |
| ❑ TWS-103 | There's Gotta Be a Change | 1971 | 15.00 |

**COLLINS, DAVE AND ANSIL**

| Number | Title (A Side/B Side) | Yr | NM |
|---|---|---|---|
| BIG TREE | | | |
| ❑ 2005 | Double Barrel | 1971 | 40.00 |

**COLLINS, DICK**

| Number | Title (A Side/B Side) | Yr | NM |
|---|---|---|---|
| RCA VICTOR | | | |
| ❑ LJM-1019 [M] | Horn of Plenty | 1955 | 100.00 |
| ❑ LJM-1027 [M] | King Richard the Swing Hearted | 1955 | 100.00 |

**COLLINS, DOROTHY**

| Number | Title (A Side/B Side) | Yr | NM |
|---|---|---|---|
| CORAL | | | |
| ❑ CRL 57105 [M] | Dorothy Collins at Home | 1957 | 25.00 |
| ❑ CRL 57106 [M] | Songs by Dorothy Collins | 1957 | 25.00 |
| ❑ CRL 57150 [M] | Picnic | 1958 | 25.00 |
| EVEREST | | | |
| ❑ SDBR-1026 [S] | Singing and Swinging | 196? | 25.00 |
| ❑ LPBR-5026 [M] | Singing and Swinging | 196? | 20.00 |
| TOP RANK | | | |
| ❑ TM-340 [M] | A New Way to Travel | 1959 | 25.00 |

**COLLINS, JOYCE**

| Number | Title (A Side/B Side) | Yr | NM |
|---|---|---|---|
| JAZZLAND | | | |
| ❑ JLP-24 [M] | The Girl Here Plays Mean Piano | 1960 | 25.00 |
| ❑ JLP-924 [S] | The Girl Here Plays Mean Piano | 1960 | 30.00 |

**COLLINS, JUDY**

| Number | Title (A Side/B Side) | Yr | NM |
|---|---|---|---|
| DCC COMPACT CLASSICS | | | |
| ❑ LPZ-2067 | Colors of the Day/The Best of Judy Collins | 1998 | 25.00 |
| *—Audiophile vinyl* | | | |
| DIRECT DISK | | | |
| ❑ SD-16607 | Judith | 1980 | 40.00 |
| *—Audiophile vinyl* | | | |
| ELEKTRA | | | |
| ❑ JC-1 [DJ] | Judy Collins | 1967 | 15.00 |
| *—Promo-only compilation of six songs, each in mono on one side, stereo on the other* | | | |
| ❑ 6E-111 | Judith | 1977 | 8.00 |
| *—Reissue of 7E-1032* | | | |
| ❑ 6E-171 | Hard Times for Lovers | 1979 | 10.00 |
| ❑ EKL-209 [M] | Maid of Constant Sorrow | 1961 | 40.00 |
| *—"Guitar player" label* | | | |
| ❑ EKL-209 [M] | Maid of Constant Sorrow | 1966 | 20.00 |
| *—Gold/tan label* | | | |
| ❑ EKL-222 [M] | Golden Apples of the Sun | 1962 | 30.00 |
| *—"Guitar player" label* | | | |
| ❑ EKL-222 [M] | Golden Apples of the Sun | 1966 | 20.00 |
| *—Gold/tan label* | | | |
| ❑ EKL-243 [M] | Judy Collins #3 | 1963 | 30.00 |
| *—"Guitar player" label* | | | |
| ❑ EKL-243 [M] | Judy Collins #3 | 1966 | 20.00 |
| *—Gold/tan label* | | | |
| ❑ 6E-253 | Running for My Life | 1980 | 10.00 |
| ❑ EKL-280 [M] | Judy Collins' Concert | 1964 | 30.00 |
| *—"Guitar player" label* | | | |
| ❑ EKL-280 [M] | Judy Collins' Concert | 1966 | 20.00 |
| *—Gold/tan label* | | | |
| ❑ EKL-300 [M] | Judy Collins' Fifth Album | 1965 | 30.00 |
| *—"Guitar player" label* | | | |
| ❑ EKL-300 [M] | Judy Collins' Fifth Album | 1966 | 20.00 |
| *—Gold/tan label* | | | |
| ❑ EKL-320 [M] | In My Life | 1966 | 20.00 |
| ❑ DS 500 | Judy | 1969 | 15.00 |
| *—Columbia Record Club exclusive; red label with large stylized "E"* | | | |
| ❑ 7E-1032 | Judith | 1975 | 12.00 |
| ❑ EQ-1032 [Q] | Judith | 1975 | 20.00 |
| ❑ 7E-1076 | Bread and Roses | 1976 | 10.00 |
| ❑ EKL-4012 [M] | Wildflowers | 1967 | 25.00 |
| ❑ EQ-5030 [Q] | Colors of the Day/The Best of Judy Collins | 1973 | 20.00 |
| ❑ 8E-6002 [(2)] | So Early in the Spring: The First 15 Years | 1977 | 12.00 |



**Except when noted otherwise, VG = 25% of NM, and VG+ = 50% of NM. (Example: VG = $2.00, VG+ = $4.00 and NM = $8.00.)**

Number | Title (A Side/B Side) | Yr | NM

❑ EKS-7209 [R] Maid of Constant Sorrow 1964 20.00
*—"Guitar player" label (first edition)*
❑ EKS-7209 [R] Maid of Constant Sorrow 1966 12.00
*—Gold/tan label or red label with large stylized "E"*
❑ EKS-7209 [R] Maid of Constant Sorrow 1971 10.00
*—Butterfly label, no Warner Communications logo*
❑ EKS-7209 [R] Maid of Constant Sorrow 1975 8.00
*—Any label with Warner Communications logo*
❑ EKS-7222 [R] Golden Apples of the Sun 196? 12.00
*—Gold/tan label or red label with large stylized "E"*
❑ EKS-7222 [R] Golden Apples of the Sun 1971 10.00
*—Butterfly label, no Warner Communications logo*
❑ EKS-7222 [R] Golden Apples of the Sun 1975 8.00
*—Any label with Warner Communications logo*
❑ EKS-7243 [S] Judy Collins #3 1963 40.00
*—"Guitar player" label*
❑ EKS-7243 [S] Judy Collins #3 1966 25.00
*—Gold/tan label*
❑ EKS-7243 [S] Judy Collins #3 1969 15.00
*—Red label with large stylized "E"*
❑ EKS-7243 [S] Judy Collins #3 1971 10.00
*—Butterfly label, no Warner Communications logo*
❑ EKS-7243 [S] Judy Collins #3 1975 8.00
*—Any label with Warner Communications logo*
❑ EKS-7280 [S] Judy Collins' Concert 1964 40.00
*—"Guitar player" label*
❑ EKS-7280 [S] Judy Collins' Concert 1966 25.00
*—Gold/tan label*
❑ EKS-7280 [S] Judy Collins' Concert 1969 15.00
*—Red label with large stylized "E"*
❑ EKS-7280 [S] Judy Collins' Concert 1971 12.00
*—Butterfly label, no Warner Communications logo*
❑ EKS-7280 [S] Judy Collins' Concert 1975 8.00
*—Any label with Warner Communications logo*
❑ EKS-7300 [S] Judy Collins' Fifth Album 1965 40.00
*—"Guitar player" label*
❑ EKS-7300 [S] Judy Collins' Fifth Album 1966 25.00
*—Gold/tan label*
❑ EKS-7300 [S] Judy Collins' Fifth Album 1969 15.00
*—Red label with large stylized "E"*
❑ EKS-7300 [S] Judy Collins' Fifth Album 1971 12.00
*—Butterfly label, no Warner Communications logo*
❑ EKS-7300 [S] Judy Collins' Fifth Album 1975 8.00
*—Any label with Warner Communications logo*
❑ EKS-7320 [S] In My Life 1966 25.00
❑ 60001 Times of Our Lives 1982 10.00
❑ 60304 Home Again 1985 10.00
❑ EKS-74012 [S] Wildflowers 1967 20.00
*—Gold/tan label*
❑ EKS-74012 [S] Wildflowers 1969 15.00
*—Red label with large stylized "E"*
❑ EKS-74012 [S] Wildflowers 1971 12.00
*—Butterfly label, no Warner Communications logo*
❑ EKS-74012 [S] Wildflowers 1975 8.00
*—Any label with Warner Communications logo*
❑ EKS-74027 In My Life 1968 20.00
*—Reissue of 7320; gold/tan label*
❑ EKS-74027 In My Life 1969 15.00
*—Red label with large stylized "E"*
❑ EKS-74027 In My Life 1971 12.00
*—Butterfly label, no Warner Communications logo*
❑ EKS-74027 In My Life 1975 8.00
*—Any label with Warner Communications logo*
❑ EKS-74033 Who Knows Where the Time Goes 1968 20.00
*—Gold/tan label*
❑ EKS-74033 Who Knows Where the Time Goes 1969 15.00
*—Red label with large stylized "E"*
❑ EKS-74033 Who Knows Where the Time Goes 1971 12.00
*—Butterfly label, no Warner Communications logo*
❑ EKS-74033 Who Knows Where the Time Goes 1975 8.00
*—Any label with Warner Communications logo*
❑ EKS-74055 Recollections 1969 15.00
*—Red label with large stylized "E"*
❑ EKS-74055 Recollections 1971 12.00
*—Butterfly label, no Warner Communications logo*
❑ EKS-74055 Recollections 1975 8.00
*—Any label with Warner Communications logo*
❑ EKS-75010 Whales & Nightingales 1970 12.00
*—Butterfly label, no Warner Communications logo*
❑ EKS-75010 Whales & Nightingales 1975 8.00
*—Any label with Warner Communications logo*
❑ EKS-75014 Living 1971 12.00
*—Butterfly label, no Warner Communications logo*
❑ EKS-75014 Living 1975 8.00
*—Any label with Warner Communications logo*
❑ EKS-75030 Colors of the Day/The Best of Judy Collins 1972 12.00
*—Butterfly label, no Warner Communications logo*
❑ EKS-75030 Colors of the Day/The Best of Judy Collins 1975 8.00
*—Any label with Warner Communications logo*
❑ EKS-75053 True Stories and Other Dreams 1973 12.00
*—Butterfly label*
❑ EKS-75053 True Stories and Other Dreams 1980 8.00
*—Red or red/black label*

GOLD CASTLE
❑ D1-71302 Trust Your Heart 1989 12.00
*—Reissue of 171002*
❑ D1-71318 Sanity and Grace 1989 12.00
❑ 171002 Trust Your Heart 1988 12.00

PAIR
❑ PDL2-1141 [(2)] Her Finest Hour 1986 12.00

WARNER SPECIAL PRODUCTS
❑ 61-6462 [(4)] Judy Collins 1981 80.00
*—Book-of-the-Month Club exclusive*

## COLLINS, LYN

PEOPLE
❑ PE-5602 Think (About It) 1972 150.00
*—This album has been "reissued"; be careful of sealed copies*
❑ PE-6605 Check Me Out 1975 100.00
*—This album has been "reissued"; be careful of sealed copies*

## COLLINS, SHIRLEY AND DOROTHY

HARVEST
❑ SKAO-370 Anthems in Eden 1969 50.00

## COLLINS, TOMMY

CAPITOL
❑ T 776 [M] Words and Music Country Style 1957 100.00
❑ T 1125 [M] Light of the Lord 1959 100.00
❑ T 1196 [M] This Is Tommy Collins 1959 60.00
❑ ST 1436 [S] Songs I Love to Sing 1961 60.00
❑ T 1436 [M] Songs I Love to Sing 1961 50.00

COLUMBIA
❑ CL 2510 [M] The Dynamic Tommy Collins 1966 30.00
❑ CL 2778 [M] Tommy Collins On Tour — His Most Requested Songs 1968 60.00
❑ CS 9310 [S] The Dynamic Tommy Collins 1966 40.00
❑ CS 9578 [S] Tommy Collins On Tour — His Most Requested Songs 1968 30.00

STARDAY
❑ SLP-474 Tommy Collins Callin' 1972 20.00

TOWER
❑ DT 5021 [R] Let's Live a Little 1966 20.00
❑ T 5021 [M] Let's Live a Little 1966 30.00
❑ DT 5107 [R] Shindig 1967 20.00
❑ T 5107 [M] Shindig 1967 40.00

## COLMAN, RONALD

DECCA
❑ DLP 8010 [M] A Christmas Carol/Mr. Pickwick's Christmas 1949 20.00
*—Side 2 read by Charles Laughton*

MCA
❑ 15010 A Christmas Carol/Mr. Pickwick's Christmas 1973 10.00
*—Side 2 read by Charles Laughton; reissue of Decca LP*

## COLONNA, JERRY

DECCA
❑ DL 5540 [10] Music? For Screaming!!! 1955 60.00

LIBERTY
❑ LRP-3046 [M] Let's All Sing with Jerry Colonna 1957 40.00
❑ SL-9004 [M] Along the Dixieland Hi-Fi Way 1957 40.00

## COLOSSEUM

ABC DUNHILL
❑ DS-50062 Those Who Are About to Die Salute You 1969 20.00
❑ DS-50079 The Grass Is Green 1970 20.00
❑ DSX-50101 Daughter of Time 1971 15.00

WARNER BROS.
❑ PRO 500 [DJ] Colosseum Live 1972 15.00
*—Highlights for radio*
❑ 2WS 1942 [(2)] Colosseum Live 1972 15.00

## COLOURS

DOT
❑ DLP-3854 [M] Colours 1968 50.00
*—Record has a black label, resembling a stock copy, but it is in a stereo cover with "Monaural" and "Promotional Copy Not for Sale" stickers on front*
❑ DLP-25854 [S] Colours 1968 25.00
❑ DLP-25935 Atmosphere 1969 25.00

## COLTER, JESSI

CAPITOL
❑ ST-11363 I'm Jessi Colter 1975 10.00
❑ ST-11477 Jessi 1976 10.00
❑ ST-11543 Diamond in the Rough 1976 10.00
❑ ST-11583 Mirriam 1977 10.00
❑ ST-11863 That's the Way a Cowboy Rocks and Rolls 1978 10.00
❑ ST-12185 Ridin' Shotgun 1981 10.00
❑ ST-511863 That's the Way a Cowboy Rocks and Rolls 1978 12.00
*—Columbia House edition*

RCA VICTOR
❑ LSP-4333 Country Star 1970 20.00

## COLTRANE, JOHN

ABC IMPULSE!
❑ AS-9148 Cosmic Music 1969 20.00
*—Credited to "Alice and John Coltrane"; reissue of Coltrane LP*
❑ AS-9161 Selflessness 1969 20.00
❑ AS-9195 Transition 1969 20.00
❑ AS-9200 [(2)] Greatest Years 1971 20.00
❑ AS-9202 [(2)] Live in Seattle 1971 20.00
❑ AS-9211 Sun Ship 1971 20.00

ATLANTIC
❑ 1311 [M] Giant Steps 1959 50.00
*—Black label*
❑ 1311 [M] Giant Steps 1960 25.00
*—Orange and purple label, white fan logo*
❑ SD 1311 [S] Giant Steps 1959 60.00
*—Green label*
❑ SD 1311 [S] Giant Steps 1959 70.00
*—"Bullseye" label*
❑ SD 1311 [S] Giant Steps 1960 25.00
*—Green and blue label, white fan logo*
❑ 1354 [M] Coltrane Jazz 1960 30.00
*—Orange and purple label, white fan logo*
❑ SD 1354 [S] Coltrane Jazz 1960 30.00
*—Green and blue label, white fan logo*
❑ 1361 [M] My Favorite Things 1961 30.00
*—Orange and purple label, white fan logo*
❑ SD 1361 [S] My Favorite Things 1961 30.00
*—Green and blue label, white fan logo*
❑ 1373 [M] Ole' Coltrane 1961 30.00
*—Orange and purple label, white fan logo*
❑ SD 1373 [S] Ole' Coltrane 1961 30.00
*—Green and blue label, white fan logo*
❑ 1382 [M] Coltrane Plays the Blues 1962 30.00
❑ SD 1382 [S] Coltrane Plays the Blues 1962 30.00
*—Green and blue label, black fan logo*
❑ 1419 [M] Coltrane's Sound 1964 25.00
❑ SD 1419 [S] Coltrane's Sound 1964 25.00
*—Green and blue label, black fan logo*
❑ 1451 [M] The Avant Garde 1966 25.00
❑ SD 1451 [S] The Avant Garde 1966 25.00
*—Green and blue label, black fan logo*

ATLANTIC/RHINO
❑ R1-71984 [(12)] The Heavyweight Champion: The Complete Atlantic Recordings 1995 250.00
*—Box set with liner notes; albums pressed on 150-gram vinyl*

ATLANTIC/RHINO HANDMADE
❑ RHM1-7784 [(12)] The Heavyweight Champion: The Complete Atlantic Recordings (Year 2000 Second Edition) 2000 200.00
*—"Year 2000 Second Edition" at lower right back cover; limited, numbered edition of 1,500 copies on 180-gram vinyl*
❑ RHM1-7784 [(12)] The Heavyweight Champion: The Complete Atlantic Recordings (Year 2000 Second Edition) 2000 200.00
*—"Year 2000 Second Edition" on lower left back cover; limited edition of 1,500, un-numbered, on 180-gram vinyl; pressed in the U.S. for export*

BLUE NOTE
❑ BLP-1577 [M] Blue Train 1957 250.00
*—Regular version, W. 63rd St., NYC address on label*
❑ BLP-1577 [M] Blue Train 1957 500.00
*—"Deep groove" version; W. 63rd St., NYC address on label*
❑ BLP-1577 [M] Blue Train 1965 60.00
*—"New York, USA" address on label*
❑ BST-1577 [S] Blue Train 1959 200.00
*—Regular version, W. 63rd St., NYC address on label*
❑ BST-1577 [S] Blue Train 1959 300.00
*—"Deep groove" version; W. 63rd St., NYC address on label*
❑ BST-1577 [S] Blue Train 1965 50.00
*—"New York, USA" address on label*

COLTRANE
❑ AU-4950 Cosmic Music 1966 300.00
❑ AU-5000 Cosmic Music 1966 200.00

DCC COMPACT CLASSICS
❑ LPZ-2032 Lush Life 1997 60.00
*—Audiophile vinyl*

IMPULSE!
❑ A-6 [M] Africa/Brass 1961 80.00
❑ AS-6 [S] Africa/Brass 1961 100.00
❑ A-10 [M] Live at the Village Vanguard 1962 60.00
❑ AS-10 [S] Live at the Village Vanguard 1962 80.00
❑ A-21 [M] Coltrane 1962 80.00
❑ AS-21 [S] Coltrane 1962 100.00
❑ A-30 [M] Duke Ellington and John Coltrane 1963 100.00
❑ AS-30 [S] Duke Ellington and John Coltrane 1963 150.00
❑ A-32 [M] Ballads 1963 80.00
❑ AS-32 [S] Ballads 1963 100.00
❑ A-40 [M] John Coltrane + Johnny Hartman 1963 100.00
❑ AS-40 [S] John Coltrane + Johnny Hartman 1963 120.00
❑ A-42 [M] Impressions 1963 60.00
❑ AS-42 [S] Impressions 1963 80.00
❑ A-50 [M] Coltrane Live at Birdland 1963 80.00
❑ AS-50 [S] Coltrane Live at Birdland 1963 100.00
❑ A-66 [M] Crescent 1964 80.00
❑ AS-66 [S] Crescent 1964 100.00

| Number | Title (A Side/B Side) | Yr | NM |
|---|---|---|---|
| ❑ A-77 [M] | A Love Supreme | 1965 | 120.00 |
| ❑ AS-77 [S] | A Love Supreme | 1965 | 150.00 |
| ❑ A-85 [M] | The John Coltrane Quartet Plays | 1965 | 60.00 |
| ❑ AS-85 [S] | The John Coltrane Quartet Plays | 1965 | 80.00 |
| ❑ A-94 [M] | New Thing at Newport | 1965 | 60.00 |
| ❑ AS-94 [S] | New Thing at Newport | 1965 | 80.00 |
| ❑ A-95 [M] | Ascension | 1965 | 150.00 |
| *—Without "Edition II" in dead wax* | | | |
| ❑ A-95 [M] | Ascension | 1966 | 100.00 |
| *—With "Edition II" in dead wax* | | | |
| ❑ AS-95 [S] | Ascension | 1965 | 180.00 |
| *—Without "Edition II" in dead wax* | | | |
| ❑ AS-95 [S] | Ascension | 1966 | 120.00 |
| *—With "Edition II" in dead wax* | | | |
| ❑ A-9106 [M] | Kulu Se Mama | 1966 | 100.00 |
| ❑ AS-9106 [S] | Kulu Se Mama | 1966 | 120.00 |
| ❑ A-9110 [M] | Meditations | 1966 | 80.00 |
| ❑ AS-9110 [S] | Meditations | 1966 | 100.00 |
| ❑ A-9120 [M] | Expression | 1967 | 100.00 |
| ❑ AS-9120 [S] | Expression | 1967 | 80.00 |
| ❑ A-9124 [M] | Live at the Village Vanguard Again! | 1967 | 100.00 |
| ❑ AS-9124 [S] | Live at the Village Vanguard Again! | 1967 | 80.00 |
| ❑ A-9140 [M] | Om | 1967 | 150.00 |
| ❑ AS-9140 [S] | Om | 1967 | 80.00 |
| ❑ SMAS-90232 [S] | Coltrane Live at Birdland | 1964 | 80.00 |
| *—Capitol Record Club edition* | | | |
| ❑ SMAS-91288 [S] | Expression | 1967 | 60.00 |
| *—Capitol Record Club edition* | | | |

PRESTIGE

| Number | Title (A Side/B Side) | Yr | NM |
|---|---|---|---|
| ❑ PRLP-7105 [M] | Coltrane | 1957 | 100.00 |
| *—Yellow label* | | | |
| ❑ PRLP-7105 [M] | Coltrane | 1964 | 30.00 |
| *—Blue label with trident logo* | | | |
| ❑ PRLP-7123 [M] | John Coltrane and the Red Garland Trio | 1957 | 100.00 |
| *—Yellow label* | | | |
| ❑ PRLP-7123 [M] | Traneing In | 1964 | 30.00 |
| *—Blue label with trident logo; reissue with new title* | | | |
| ❑ PRLP-7142 [M] | Soultrane | 1958 | 80.00 |
| *—Yellow label* | | | |
| ❑ PRLP-7142 [M] | Soultrane | 1964 | 25.00 |
| *—Blue label with trident logo* | | | |
| ❑ PRLP-7158 [M] | Cattin' with Coltrane and Quinichette | 1959 | 80.00 |
| *—Yellow label* | | | |
| ❑ PRLP-7158 [M] | Cattin' with Coltrane and Quinichette | 1964 | 25.00 |
| *—Blue label with trident logo* | | | |
| ❑ PRLP-7188 [M] | Lush Life | 1960 | 80.00 |
| *—Yellow label* | | | |
| ❑ PRLP-7188 [M] | Lush Life | 1964 | 25.00 |
| *—Blue label with trident logo* | | | |
| ❑ PRLP-7213 [M] | Settin' the Pace | 1961 | 80.00 |
| *—Yellow label* | | | |
| ❑ PRLP-7213 [M] | Settin' the Pace | 1964 | 25.00 |
| *—Blue label with trident logo* | | | |
| ❑ PRLP-7243 [M] | Standard Coltrane | 1962 | 40.00 |
| *—Yellow label* | | | |
| ❑ PRLP-7243 [M] | Standard Coltrane | 1964 | 25.00 |
| *—Blue label with trident logo* | | | |
| ❑ PRST-7243 [S] | Standard Coltrane | 1962 | 50.00 |
| *—Silver label* | | | |
| ❑ PRST-7243 [S] | Standard Coltrane | 1964 | 25.00 |
| *—Blue label with trident logo* | | | |
| ❑ PRLP-7247 [M] | Mating Call | 1962 | 40.00 |
| *—Yellow label* | | | |
| ❑ PRLP-7247 [M] | Mating Call | 1964 | 25.00 |
| *—Blue label with trident logo* | | | |
| ❑ PRST-7247 [R] | Mating Call | 196? | 25.00 |
| *—Silver label* | | | |
| ❑ PRST-7247 [R] | Mating Call | 1964 | 20.00 |
| *—Blue label with trident logo* | | | |
| ❑ PRLP-7249 [M] | Tenor Conclave | 1962 | 40.00 |
| *—Yellow label* | | | |
| ❑ PRLP-7249 [M] | Tenor Conclave | 1964 | 25.00 |
| *—Blue label with trident logo* | | | |
| ❑ PRST-7249 [R] | Tenor Conclave | 196? | 25.00 |
| *—Silver label* | | | |
| ❑ PRST-7249 [R] | Tenor Conclave | 1964 | 20.00 |
| *—Blue label with trident logo* | | | |
| ❑ PRLP-7268 [M] | Stardust | 1963 | 40.00 |
| *—Yellow label* | | | |
| ❑ PRLP-7268 [M] | Stardust | 1964 | 25.00 |
| *—Blue label with trident logo* | | | |
| ❑ PRST-7268 [S] | Stardust | 1963 | 40.00 |
| *—Silver label* | | | |
| ❑ PRST-7268 [S] | Stardust | 1964 | 25.00 |
| *—Blue label with trident logo* | | | |
| ❑ PRLP-7280 [M] | Dakar | 1963 | 40.00 |
| *—Yellow label* | | | |
| ❑ PRLP-7280 [M] | Dakar | 1964 | 25.00 |
| *—Blue label with trident logo* | | | |
| ❑ PRST-7280 [S] | Dakar | 1963 | 40.00 |
| *—Silver label* | | | |
| ❑ PRST-7280 [S] | Dakar | 1964 | 25.00 |
| *—Blue label with trident logo* | | | |
| ❑ PRLP-7292 [M] | The Believer | 1964 | 25.00 |
| *—Blue label with trident logo* | | | |
| ❑ PRLP-7292 [M] | The Believer | 1964 | 40.00 |
| *—Yellow label* | | | |
| ❑ PRST-7292 [S] | The Believer | 1964 | 25.00 |
| *—Blue label with trident logo* | | | |
| ❑ PRST-7292 [S] | The Believer | 1964 | 40.00 |
| *—Silver label* | | | |
| ❑ PRLP-7316 [M] | Black Pearls | 1964 | 25.00 |
| *—Blue label with trident logo* | | | |
| ❑ PRLP-7316 [M] | Black Pearls | 1964 | 40.00 |
| *—Yellow label* | | | |
| ❑ PRST-7316 [S] | Black Pearls | 1964 | 25.00 |
| *—Blue label with trident logo* | | | |
| ❑ PRST-7316 [S] | Black Pearls | 1964 | 40.00 |
| *—Silver label* | | | |
| ❑ PRLP-7353 [M] | Bahia | 1965 | 25.00 |
| ❑ PRST-7353 [S] | Bahia | 1965 | 25.00 |
| ❑ PRLP-7378 [M] | The Last Trane | 1965 | 30.00 |
| ❑ PRST-7378 [S] | The Last Trane | 1965 | 25.00 |
| ❑ PRLP-7426 [M] | John Coltrane Plays for Lovers | 1966 | 25.00 |
| ❑ PRST-7426 [S] | John Coltrane Plays for Lovers | 1966 | 25.00 |
| ❑ PRLP-7531 [M] | Soultrane | 1967 | 25.00 |

RHINO

| Number | Title (A Side/B Side) | Yr | NM |
|---|---|---|---|
| ❑ R1-75203 | Giant Steps | 2003 | 15.00 |
| *—Reissue on 180-gram vinyl* | | | |

SOLID STATE

| Number | Title (A Side/B Side) | Yr | NM |
|---|---|---|---|
| ❑ SM-17025 [M] | Coltrane Time | 1968 | 25.00 |

UNITED ARTISTS

| Number | Title (A Side/B Side) | Yr | NM |
|---|---|---|---|
| ❑ UAJ-14001 [M] | Coltrane Time | 1962 | 40.00 |
| ❑ UAJS-15001 [S] | Coltrane Time | 1962 | 50.00 |

## COLUMBIA CHOIR, THE

COLUMBIA

| Number | Title (A Side/B Side) | Yr | NM |
|---|---|---|---|
| ❑ CL (# unk) [10] | The Christmas Mood | 1954 | 50.00 |
| *—First appearance of the "Albert Burt Carols" on record* | | | |
| ❑ CL 1051 [M] | The Christmas Mood | 1957 | 30.00 |
| *—Expanded version of 10-inch LP with B-side instrumentals* | | | |
| ❑ CL 2546 [10] | The Christmas Mood | 1955 | 40.00 |
| *—"House Party Series" reissue* | | | |

## COLUMBO, CHRIS

STRAND

| Number | Title (A Side/B Side) | Yr | NM |
|---|---|---|---|
| ❑ SL-1044 [M] | Jazz Rediscovered | 1962 | 30.00 |
| ❑ SLS-1044 [S] | Jazz Rediscovered | 1962 | 40.00 |
| ❑ SL-1095 [M] | Summertime | 1963 | 30.00 |
| ❑ SLS-1095 [S] | Summertime | 1963 | 40.00 |

## COLWELL-WINFIELD BLUES BAND, THE

VERVE FORECAST

| Number | Title (A Side/B Side) | Yr | NM |
|---|---|---|---|
| ❑ FTS-3056 | Cold Wind Blues | 1968 | 20.00 |

ZA-ZOO

| Number | Title (A Side/B Side) | Yr | NM |
|---|---|---|---|
| ❑ 1 | Live Bust | 1971 | 30.00 |

## COLYER, KEN

LONDON

| Number | Title (A Side/B Side) | Yr | NM |
|---|---|---|---|
| ❑ PB 904 [10] | New Orleans to London | 1954 | 50.00 |
| ❑ LL 1340 [M] | Back to the Delta | 1956 | 40.00 |
| ❑ LL 1618 [M] | Club Session with Colyer | 1957 | 40.00 |

## COMFORTABLE CHAIR, THE

ODE

| Number | Title (A Side/B Side) | Yr | NM |
|---|---|---|---|
| ❑ Z12 44005 | The Comfortable Chair | 1968 | 20.00 |

## COMMANDERS, THE

DECCA

| Number | Title (A Side/B Side) | Yr | NM |
|---|---|---|---|
| ❑ DL 8117 [M] | Dance Party | 1955 | 40.00 |
| *—Led by Eddie Grady* | | | |

## COMMON PEOPLE, THE

CAPITOL

| Number | Title (A Side/B Side) | Yr | NM |
|---|---|---|---|
| ❑ ST-266 | Of the People/By the People/For the People/From the Common People | 1969 | 100.00 |

## COMO, PERRY

PAIR

| Number | Title (A Side/B Side) | Yr | NM |
|---|---|---|---|
| ❑ PDL2-1001 [(2)] | Easy Listening | 1986 | 12.00 |
| ❑ PDL2-1038 [(2)] | Love Moods | 1986 | 12.00 |
| ❑ PDL2-1112 [(2)] | Blue Skies | 1986 | 12.00 |

PICKWICK

| Number | Title (A Side/B Side) | Yr | NM |
|---|---|---|---|
| ❑ CAS-660 [R] | Perry Como Sings Merry Christmas Music | 1977 | 8.00 |
| *—Reissue of RCA Camden CAS-660 with another new cover* | | | |

RCA

| Number | Title (A Side/B Side) | Yr | NM |
|---|---|---|---|
| ❑ 6368-1-R | Perry Como Today | 1988 | 10.00 |

RCA CAMDEN

| Number | Title (A Side/B Side) | Yr | NM |
|---|---|---|---|
| ❑ CAL-403 [M] | Dream Along with Me | 1957 | 20.00 |
| ❑ CAS-403(e) [R] | Dream Along with Me | 1962 | 10.00 |
| ❑ CAL-440 [M] | Perry Como Sings Just for You | 1958 | 15.00 |
| ❑ CAS-440(e) [R] | Perry Como Sings Just for You | 1962 | 10.00 |
| ❑ CAL-511 [M] | Como's Wednesday Night Music Hall | 1959 | 20.00 |
| ❑ CAL-582 [M] | Dreamer's Holiday | 1960 | 15.00 |
| ❑ CAL-660 [M] | Perry Como Sings Merry Christmas Music | 1961 | 12.00 |
| *—Reissue of RCA Victor LPM-1243 with new cover* | | | |
| ❑ CAS-660(e) [R] | Perry Como Sings Merry Christmas Music | 1961 | 10.00 |
| ❑ CAL-694 [M] | Make Someone Happy | 1962 | 12.00 |
| ❑ CAL-742 [M] | An Evening with Perry Como | 196? | 15.00 |
| ❑ CAL-805 [M] | Love Makes the World Go 'Round | 1964 | 12.00 |
| ❑ CAS-805 [S] | Love Makes the World Go 'Round | 1964 | 10.00 |
| ❑ CAL-858 [M] | Somebody Loves Me | 1965 | 12.00 |
| ❑ CAS-858 [S] | Somebody Loves Me | 1965 | 10.00 |
| ❑ CAL-941 [M] | No Other Love | 1966 | 12.00 |
| ❑ CAS-941 [S] | No Other Love | 1966 | 10.00 |
| ❑ CAL-2122 [M] | Hello Young Lovers | 1967 | 15.00 |
| ❑ CAS-2122 [R] | Hello Young Lovers | 1967 | 10.00 |
| ❑ CAL-2201 [M] | You Are Never Far Away | 1968 | 15.00 |
| ❑ CAS-2201 [S] | You Are Never Far Away | 1968 | 10.00 |
| ❑ CAS-2299 | The Lord's Prayer | 1968 | 10.00 |
| ❑ CAS-2482 | Door of Dreams | 1971 | 10.00 |
| ❑ CAS-2547 | The Shadow of Your Smile | 1972 | 10.00 |
| ❑ CAS-2609 | Dream On Little Dreamer | 1972 | 10.00 |
| ❑ CXS-9002 [(2)] | Easy Listening | 1972 | 12.00 |

RCA CUSTOM EDITION

| Number | Title (A Side/B Side) | Yr | NM |
|---|---|---|---|
| ❑ DRL1-0010 | Seattle | 1973 | 12.00 |

RCA SPECIAL PRODUCTS

| Number | Title (A Side/B Side) | Yr | NM |
|---|---|---|---|
| ❑ DPL1-0193 | By Special Request | 1974 | 12.00 |
| *—Sold only at Sylvania dealers* | | | |

RCA VICTOR

| Number | Title (A Side/B Side) | Yr | NM |
|---|---|---|---|
| ❑ LPM-51 [10] | Merry Christmas | 1951 | 40.00 |
| ❑ APD1-0100 [Q] | And I Love You So | 1974 | 15.00 |
| ❑ APL1-0100 | And I Love You So | 1973 | 10.00 |
| ❑ ACL1-0444 | The Sweetest Sounds | 1974 | 10.00 |
| ❑ APD1-0585 [Q] | Perry | 1974 | 15.00 |
| ❑ CPL1-0585 | Perry | 1974 | 10.00 |
| ❑ APD1-0863 [Q] | Just Out of Reach | 1975 | 15.00 |
| ❑ APL1-0863 | Just Out of Reach | 1975 | 10.00 |
| ❑ ANL1-0972 | Pure Gold | 1975 | 10.00 |
| ❑ LSPX-1001 | Perry Como at the International Hotel, Las Vegas | 1970 | 15.00 |
| ❑ LOP-1004 [M] | Saturday Night with Mr. C. | 1958 | 25.00 |
| ❑ LOP-1007 [M] | Como's Golden Records | 1958 | 25.00 |
| ❑ LPM-1085 [M] | So Smooth | 1955 | 30.00 |
| ❑ LPM-1172 [M] | I Believe | 1956 | 30.00 |
| ❑ LSP-1172(e) [R] | I Believe | 1962 | 12.00 |
| ❑ LPM-1176 [M] | Relaxing with Perry Como | 1956 | 30.00 |
| ❑ LPM-1177 [M] | A Sentimental Date with Perry Como | 1956 | 30.00 |
| ❑ LPM-1191 [M] | Hits from Broadway Shows | 1956 | 30.00 |
| ❑ LPM-1243 [M] | Perry Como Sings Merry Christmas Music | 1956 | 30.00 |
| ❑ LPM-1463 [M] | We Get Letters | 1957 | 25.00 |
| ❑ CPL1-1752 | A Legendary Performer | 1976 | 10.00 |
| ❑ LPM-1885 [M] | When You Come to the End of the Day | 1958 | 20.00 |
| ❑ LSP-1885 [S] | When You Come to the End of the Day | 1958 | 30.00 |
| ❑ ANL1-1929 | The Perry Como Christmas Album | 1976 | 8.00 |
| *—Budget-line reissue of LSP-4016* | | | |
| ❑ LPM-1971 [M] | Saturday Night with Mr. C. | 1959 | 20.00 |
| *—Reissue of LOP-1004* | | | |
| ❑ LSP-1971 [S] | Saturday Night with Mr. C. | 1958 | 30.00 |
| ❑ AFL1-1981 | Como's Golden Records | 1977 | 10.00 |
| *—Reissue with new prefix* | | | |
| ❑ LPM-1981 [M] | Como's Golden Records | 1959 | 20.00 |
| *—Reissue of LOP-1007* | | | |
| ❑ LSP-1981(e) [R] | Como's Golden Records | 1962 | 12.00 |
| ❑ LPM-2010 [M] | Como Swings | 1959 | 20.00 |
| ❑ LSP-2010 [S] | Como Swings | 1959 | 25.00 |
| ❑ LPM-2066 [M] | Season's Greetings from Perry Como | 1959 | 20.00 |
| *—Later front covers have "LPM-2066" in upper right, inside RCA Victor box* | | | |
| ❑ LPM-2066 [M] | Season's Greetings from Perry Como | 1959 | 25.00 |
| *—Original front covers have "LPM-2066" in lower left corner* | | | |
| ❑ LSP-2066 [S] | Season's Greetings from Perry Como | 1959 | 25.00 |
| ❑ LPM-2343 [M] | For the Young at Heart | 1960 | 15.00 |
| ❑ LSP-2343 [S] | For the Young at Heart | 1960 | 20.00 |
| ❑ LPM-2390 [M] | Sing to Me, Mr. C. | 1961 | 15.00 |
| ❑ LSP-2390 [S] | Sing to Me, Mr. C. | 1961 | 20.00 |
| ❑ ANL1-2485 | Especially for You | 1977 | 10.00 |
| ❑ LPM-2567 [M] | By Request | 1962 | 15.00 |
| ❑ LSP-2567 [S] | By Request | 1962 | 20.00 |
| ❑ LPM-2630 [M] | The Best of Irving Berlin's Songs from "Mr. President" | 1962 | 15.00 |
| ❑ LSP-2630 [S] | The Best of Irving Berlin's Songs from "Mr. President" | 1962 | 20.00 |
| ❑ AFL1-2641 | Where You're Concerned | 1978 | 10.00 |
| ❑ LPM-2708 [M] | The Songs I Love | 1963 | 15.00 |
| ❑ LSP-2708 [S] | The Songs I Love | 1963 | 20.00 |
| ❑ ANL1-2969(e) | Over the Rainbow | 1976 | 10.00 |
| ❑ LPM-3013 [10] | TV Favorites | 1952 | 40.00 |
| ❑ LPM-3035 [10] | A Sentimental Date with Perry Como | 1952 | 40.00 |
| ❑ LPM-3044 [10] | Supper Club Favorites | 1952 | 40.00 |
| ❑ LPM-3124 [10] | Hits from Broadway Shows | 1953 | 40.00 |
| ❑ LPM-3133 [10] | Around the Christmas Tree | 1953 | 40.00 |
| ❑ LPM-3188 [10] | I Believe | 1954 | 40.00 |

| Number | Title (A Side/B Side) | Yr | NM |
|---|---|---|---|
| ❑ LPM-3224 [10] | Como's Golden Records | 1954 | 40.00 |
| ❑ LPM-3396 [M] | The Scene Changes | 1965 | 12.00 |
| ❑ LSP-3396 [S] | The Scene Changes | 1965 | 15.00 |
| ❑ LPM-3552 [M] | Lightly Latin | 1966 | 12.00 |
| ❑ LSP-3552 [S] | Lightly Latin | 1966 | 15.00 |
| ❑ LPM-3608 [M] | Perry Como in Italy | 1966 | 12.00 |
| ❑ LSP-3608 [S] | Perry Como in Italy | 1966 | 15.00 |
| ❑ AFL1-3629 | Perry Como | 1980 | 10.00 |
| ❑ AYL1-3672 | And I Love You So | 1980 | 8.00 |
| *—Reissue* | | | |
| ❑ AYL1-3802 | Como's Golden Records | 1981 | 8.00 |
| *—Reissue* | | | |
| ❑ AYL1-3803 | Where You're Concerned | 1981 | 8.00 |
| *—Reissue* | | | |
| ❑ AYL1-3804 | It's Impossible | 1981 | 8.00 |
| *—Reissue* | | | |
| ❑ LSP-4016 | The Perry Como Christmas Album | 1968 | 12.00 |
| ❑ LSP-4052 | Look to Your Heart | 1968 | 15.00 |
| ❑ LSP-4183 | Seattle | 1969 | 15.00 |
| ❑ AFL1-4272 | So It Goes | 1983 | 10.00 |
| ❑ AFL1-4473 | It's Impossible | 1977 | 10.00 |
| *—Reissue with new prefix* | | | |
| ❑ LSP-4473 | It's Impossible | 1970 | 15.00 |
| ❑ AYL1-4526 | I Wish It Could Be Christmas Forever | 1982 | 10.00 |
| ❑ AFL1-4539 | I Think of You | 1977 | 10.00 |
| *—Reissue with new prefix* | | | |
| ❑ LSP-4539 | I Think of You | 1971 | 15.00 |
| ❑ VPS-6026 [(2)] | This Is Perry Como | 1970 | 15.00 |
| ❑ VPS-6067 [(2)] | This Is Perry Como, Volume 2 | 1972 | 15.00 |

READER'S DIGEST

| Number | Title (A Side/B Side) | Yr | NM |
|---|---|---|---|
| ❑ RDA-144/D | Christmas with Perry Como | 1983 | 10.00 |

TIME-LIFE

| Number | Title (A Side/B Side) | Yr | NM |
|---|---|---|---|
| ❑ SLGD-04 [(2)] | Legendary Singers: Perry Como | 1985 | 15.00 |

**COMPETITORS, THE**

DOT

| Number | Title (A Side/B Side) | Yr | NM |
|---|---|---|---|
| ❑ DLP-3542 [M] | Hits of the Street and Strip | 1963 | 150.00 |
| ❑ DLP-25542 [S] | Hits of the Street and Strip | 1963 | 200.00 |

**COMPOSER'S WORKSHOP ENSEMBLE, THE**

STRATA-EAST

| Number | Title (A Side/B Side) | Yr | NM |
|---|---|---|---|
| ❑ 1972-3 | The Composer's Workshop Ensemble | 197? | 30.00 |
| ❑ 7422 | (We've Been) Around | 1974 | 30.00 |

**COMSTOCK, BOBBY**

ASCOT

| Number | Title (A Side/B Side) | Yr | NM |
|---|---|---|---|
| ❑ AM-13026 [M] | Out of Sight | 1966 | 25.00 |
| ❑ AS-16026 [S] | Out of Sight | 1966 | 30.00 |

**CONCRETE BLONDE**

I.R.S.

| Number | Title (A Side/B Side) | Yr | NM |
|---|---|---|---|
| ❑ 5835 | Concrete Blonde | 1987 | 12.00 |
| ❑ X1-13037 | Bloodletting | 1990 | 40.00 |
| *—Stock copy; red vinyl* | | | |
| ❑ 82001 | Free | 1989 | 12.00 |
| ❑ 82037 [DJ] | Bloodletting | 1990 | 30.00 |
| *—Promo only, sticker on generic cover, black vinyl* | | | |

**CONDELLO**

SCEPTER

| Number | Title (A Side/B Side) | Yr | NM |
|---|---|---|---|
| ❑ SPS-542 | Phase 1 | 1968 | 40.00 |

**CONDON, EDDIE**

COLUMBIA

| Number | Title (A Side/B Side) | Yr | NM |
|---|---|---|---|
| ❑ CL 616 [M] | Jammin' at Condon's | 1955 | 40.00 |
| *—Red and black label with six "eye" logos* | | | |
| ❑ CL 616 [M] | Jammin' at Condon's | 1955 | 50.00 |
| *—Maroon label, gold print* | | | |
| ❑ CL 632 [M] | Chicago Style Jazz | 1955 | 40.00 |
| *—Red and black label with six "eye" logos* | | | |
| ❑ CL 719 [M] | Bixieland | 1955 | 40.00 |
| *—Red and black label with six "eye" logos* | | | |
| ❑ CL 881 [M] | Eddie Condon's Treasury of Jazz | 1956 | 40.00 |
| *—Red and black label with six "eye" logos* | | | |
| ❑ CL 1089 [M] | The Roaring Twenties | 1958 | 40.00 |
| *—Red and black label with six "eye" logos* | | | |

COMMODORE

| Number | Title (A Side/B Side) | Yr | NM |
|---|---|---|---|
| ❑ FL 20022 [M] | Ballin' the Jack | 195? | 50.00 |
| ❑ FL 30010 [M] | Condon A La Carte | 195? | 60.00 |

DECCA

| Number | Title (A Side/B Side) | Yr | NM |
|---|---|---|---|
| ❑ DL 5137 [10] | George Gershwin Jazz Concert | 1950 | 50.00 |
| ❑ DL 5195 [10] | Jazz Band Ball (Volume 1) | 1951 | 50.00 |
| ❑ DL 5203 [10] | Jazz Concert at Eddie Condon's | 1951 | 50.00 |
| ❑ DL 5218 [10] | Jazz Concert at Eddie Condon's | 1950 | 50.00 |
| ❑ DL 5246 [10] | We Call It Music | 1951 | 50.00 |
| ❑ DL 8281 [M] | A Night at Eddie Condon's | 1956 | 40.00 |
| ❑ DL 8282 [M] | Ivy League Jazz | 195? | 40.00 |
| ❑ DL 9234 [M] | Gershwin Program (1941-1945) | 1968 | 25.00 |

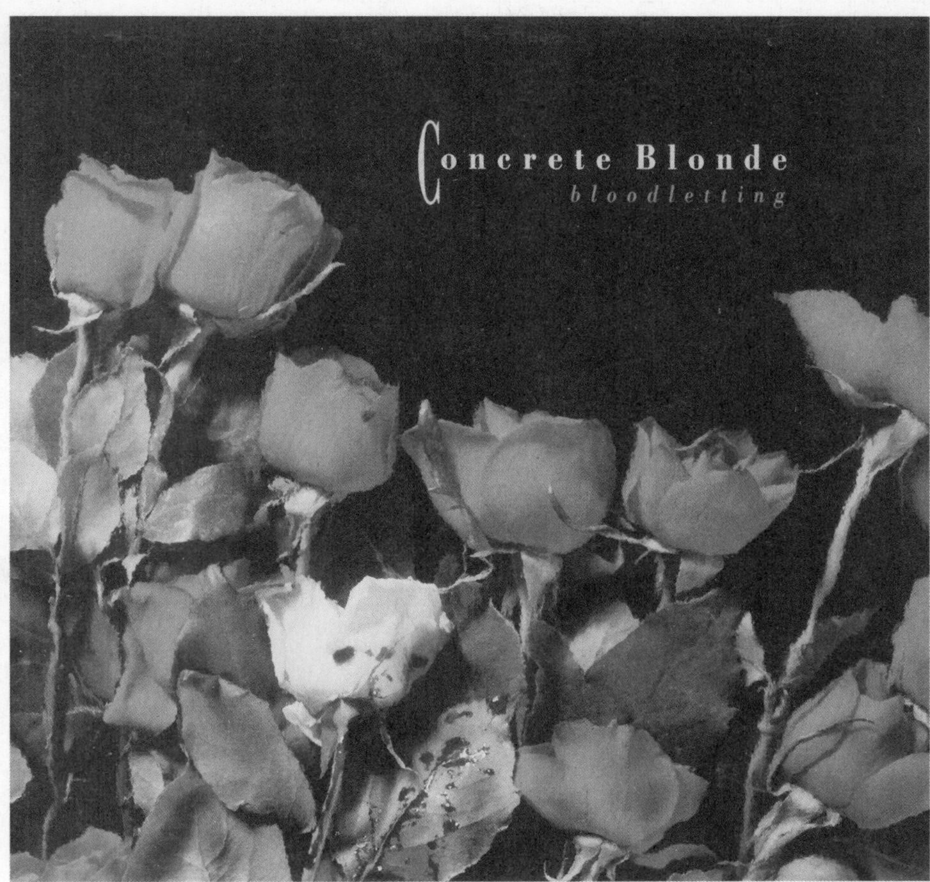


Concrete Blonde, *Bloodletting,* I.R.S. X1-13037, 1990, red vinyl, $40.

DOT

| Number | Title (A Side/B Side) | Yr | NM |
|---|---|---|---|
| ❑ DLP-3141 [M] | Dixieland Dance Party | 1958 | 40.00 |

EPIC

| Number | Title (A Side/B Side) | Yr | NM |
|---|---|---|---|
| ❑ BA 17024 [S] | Midnight in Moscow | 1962 | 20.00 |

JAZZ PANORAMA

| Number | Title (A Side/B Side) | Yr | NM |
|---|---|---|---|
| ❑ 1805 [10] | Eddie Condon | 1951 | 40.00 |

JOLLY ROGER

| Number | Title (A Side/B Side) | Yr | NM |
|---|---|---|---|
| ❑ 5018 [10] | Eddie Condon and His Orchestra Featuring Pee Wee Russell | 1954 | 40.00 |
| ❑ 5025 [10] | Eddie Condon | 1954 | 40.00 |

MAINSTREAM

| Number | Title (A Side/B Side) | Yr | NM |
|---|---|---|---|
| ❑ 56024 [M] | Eddie Condon: A Legend | 1965 | 25.00 |

MGM

| Number | Title (A Side/B Side) | Yr | NM |
|---|---|---|---|
| ❑ E-3651 [M] | Eddie Condon Is Uptown Now | 1960 | 25.00 |
| ❑ SE-3651 [S] | Eddie Condon Is Uptown Now | 1960 | 30.00 |

MOSAIC

| Number | Title (A Side/B Side) | Yr | NM |
|---|---|---|---|
| ❑ MQ7-152 [(7)] | The Complete CBS Recordings of Eddie Condon and His All-Stars | 199? | 120.00 |

SAVOY

| Number | Title (A Side/B Side) | Yr | NM |
|---|---|---|---|
| ❑ MG-12055 [M] | Ringside at Condon's | 1956 | 40.00 |

"X"

| Number | Title (A Side/B Side) | Yr | NM |
|---|---|---|---|
| ❑ LX-3005 [M] | Eddie Condon's Hot Shots | 1954 | 50.00 |

**CONLEY, ARTHUR**

ATCO

| Number | Title (A Side/B Side) | Yr | NM |
|---|---|---|---|
| ❑ 33-215 [M] | Sweet Soul Music | 1967 | 40.00 |
| ❑ SD 33-215 [S] | Sweet Soul Music | 1967 | 30.00 |
| ❑ 33-220 [M] | Shake, Rattle & Roll | 1967 | 40.00 |
| ❑ SD 33-220 [S] | Shake, Rattle & Roll | 1967 | 30.00 |
| ❑ 33-243 [M] | Soul Directions | 1968 | 60.00 |
| *—Mono is white label promo only; "Mono" sticker over the word "Stereo" on front cover* | | | |
| ❑ SD 33-243 [S] | Soul Directions | 1968 | 30.00 |
| ❑ 33-276 [M] | More Sweet Soul | 1969 | 70.00 |
| *—Mono is white label promo only; "d/j copy monaural" sticker on stereo cover* | | | |
| ❑ SD 33-276 [S] | More Sweet Soul | 1969 | 30.00 |

**CONNELLY, PEGGY**

BETHLEHEM

| Number | Title (A Side/B Side) | Yr | NM |
|---|---|---|---|
| ❑ BCP-53 [M] | That Old Black Magic | 1957 | 120.00 |

**CONNIFF, RAY**

COLUMBIA

| Number | Title (A Side/B Side) | Yr | NM |
|---|---|---|---|
| ❑ GP 3 [(2)] | Here We Come a-Caroling/Ray Conniff's World of Hits | 1968 | 15.00 |
| ❑ CL 925 [M] | 'S Wonderful! | 1956 | 20.00 |
| *—Red and black label with six "eye" logos* | | | |
| ❑ CL 1004 [M] | Dance the Bop | 1957 | 30.00 |
| *—Red and black label with six "eye" logos; includes instruction booklet* | | | |
| ❑ CS 1022 | Bridge Over Troubled Water | 1970 | 10.00 |
| ❑ CL 1074 [M] | 'S Marvelous | 1957 | 15.00 |
| ❑ CL 1137 [M] | 'S Awful Nice | 1958 | 15.00 |
| ❑ CL 1163 [M] | Concert in Rhythm | 1958 | 15.00 |
| ❑ CL 1252 [M] | Broadway in Rhythm | 1959 | 15.00 |
| ❑ CL 1310 [M] | Hollywood in Rhythm | 1959 | 15.00 |
| ❑ CL 1334 [M] | It's the Talk of the Town | 1959 | 12.00 |
| ❑ CL 1390 [M] | Christmas with Conniff | 1959 | 15.00 |
| ❑ CL 1415 [M] | Concert in Rhythm — Volume II | 1960 | 12.00 |
| ❑ CL 1489 [M] | Young at Heart | 1960 | 12.00 |
| ❑ CL 1490 [M] | Say It With Music (A Touch of Latin) | 1960 | 12.00 |
| ❑ CL 1574 [M] | Memories Are Made of This | 1961 | 12.00 |
| ❑ CL 1642 [M] | Somebody Loves Me | 1961 | 12.00 |
| ❑ CL 1720 [M] | So Much in Love | 1962 | 12.00 |
| ❑ CL 1776 [M] | 'S Continental | 1962 | 12.00 |
| ❑ CL 1878 [M] | Rhapsody in Rhythm | 1962 | 12.00 |
| ❑ CL 1892 [M] | We Wish You a Merry Christmas | 1962 | 15.00 |
| ❑ CL 1949 [M] | The Happy Beat | 1963 | 12.00 |
| ❑ CL 2022 [M] | Just Kiddin' Around | 1963 | 12.00 |
| ❑ CL 2118 [M] | You Make Me Feel So Young | 1964 | 12.00 |
| ❑ CL 2150 [M] | Speak to Me of Love | 1964 | 10.00 |
| ❑ CL 2210 [M] | Friendly Persuasion | 1964 | 10.00 |
| ❑ CL 2264 [M] | Invisible Tears | 1964 | 10.00 |
| ❑ CL 2352 [M] | Love Affair | 1965 | 10.00 |
| ❑ CL 2366 [M] | Music from Mary Poppins, The Sound of Music, My Fair Lady & Other Great Movie Themes | 1965 | 10.00 |
| ❑ CL 2406 [M] | Here We Come a-Caroling | 1965 | 12.00 |
| ❑ CL 2461 [M] | Happiness Is | 1966 | 10.00 |
| ❑ CL 2500 [M] | Ray Conniff's World of Hits | 1966 | 12.00 |
| ❑ CL 2519 [M] | Somewhere My Love | 1966 | 12.00 |
| ❑ CL 2608 [M] | En Espanol | 1967 | 12.00 |
| ❑ CL 2676 [M] | This Is My Song | 1967 | 12.00 |
| ❑ CL 2747 [M] | Hawaiian Album | 1967 | 12.00 |
| ❑ CL 2795 [M] | It Must Be Him | 1968 | 15.00 |

Chris Connor, *Chris Connor,* Atlantic 1228, 1956, mono, black label, $50.

| Number | Title (A Side/B Side) | Yr | NM |
|---|---|---|---|
| ❑ CS 8001 [S] | 'S Awful Nice | 1958 | 20.00 |
| *—Red and black label with six "eye" logos* | | | |
| ❑ CS 8022 [S] | Concert in Rhythm | 1958 | 20.00 |
| *—Red and black label with six "eye" logos* | | | |
| ❑ PC 8022 | Concert in Rhythm | 1988 | 6.00 |
| *—Reissue with new prefix* | | | |
| ❑ CS 8037 [S] | 'S Marvelous | 1958 | 20.00 |
| *—Red and black label with six "eye" logos* | | | |
| ❑ CS 8064 [S] | Broadway in Rhythm | 1959 | 20.00 |
| *—Red and black label with six "eye" logos* | | | |
| ❑ CS 8117 [S] | Hollywood in Rhythm | 1959 | 20.00 |
| *—Red and black label with six "eye" logos* | | | |
| ❑ CS 8143 [S] | It's the Talk of the Town | 1959 | 15.00 |
| ❑ CS 8155 [S] | Conniff Meets Butterfield | 1959 | 25.00 |
| *—Red and black label with six "eye" logos* | | | |
| ❑ CS 8185 [S] | Christmas with Conniff | 1959 | 12.00 |
| ❑ CS 8212 [S] | Concert in Rhythm — Volume II | 1960 | 15.00 |
| ❑ CS 8281 [S] | Young at Heart | 1960 | 15.00 |
| ❑ CS 8282 [S] | Say It With Music (A Touch of Latin) | 1960 | 15.00 |
| ❑ CS 8374 [S] | Memories Are Made of This | 1961 | 15.00 |
| ❑ CS 8442 [S] | Somebody Loves Me | 1961 | 15.00 |
| ❑ CS 8520 [S] | So Much in Love | 1962 | 15.00 |
| ❑ CS 8576 [S] | 'S Continental | 1962 | 15.00 |
| ❑ CS 8678 [S] | Rhapsody in Rhythm | 1962 | 15.00 |
| ❑ CS 8692 [S] | We Wish You a Merry Christmas | 1962 | 12.00 |
| ❑ CS 8749 [S] | The Happy Beat | 1963 | 15.00 |
| ❑ CS 8822 [S] | Just Kiddin' Around | 1963 | 15.00 |
| ❑ CS 8918 [S] | You Make Me Feel So Young | 1964 | 15.00 |
| ❑ CS 8950 [S] | Speak to Me of Love | 1964 | 12.00 |
| ❑ CS 9064 [S] | Invisible Tears | 1964 | 12.00 |
| ❑ CS 9110 [S] | Friendly Persuasion | 1964 | 12.00 |
| ❑ CS 9152 [S] | Love Affair | 1965 | 12.00 |
| ❑ CS 9166 [S] | Music from Mary Poppins, The Sound of Music, My Fair Lady & Other Great Movie Themes | 1965 | 12.00 |
| ❑ CS 9206 [S] | Here We Come a-Caroling | 1965 | 10.00 |
| ❑ CS 9261 [S] | Happiness Is | 1966 | 12.00 |
| ❑ CS 9300 [S] | Ray Conniff's World of Hits | 1966 | 10.00 |
| ❑ CS 9319 [S] | Somewhere My Love | 1966 | 10.00 |
| ❑ PC 9319 | Somewhere My Love | 198? | 6.00 |
| *—Reissue with new prefix* | | | |
| ❑ CS 9408 [S] | En Espanol | 1967 | 10.00 |
| ❑ CS 9476 [S] | This Is My Song | 1967 | 10.00 |
| ❑ CS 9547 [S] | Hawaiian Album | 1967 | 10.00 |
| ❑ PC 9547 | Hawaiian Album | 198? | 6.00 |
| *—Reissue with new prefix* | | | |
| ❑ CS 9595 [S] | It Must Be Him | 1968 | 10.00 |
| ❑ CS 9661 | Honey | 1968 | 10.00 |
| ❑ CS 9712 | Turn Around Look at Me | 1968 | 10.00 |
| ❑ CS 9777 | I Love How You Love Me | 1969 | 10.00 |
| ❑ CS 9839 | Ray Conniff's Greatest Hits | 1969 | 10.00 |
| ❑ PC 9839 | Ray Conniff's Greatest Hits | 198? | 6.00 |
| *—Reissue with new prefix* | | | |
| ❑ CS 9920 | Jean | 1969 | 10.00 |
| ❑ G 30122 [(2)] | Concert in Stereo/Live at the Sahara/Tahoe | 1970 | 15.00 |
| ❑ C 30410 | We've Only Just Begun | 1970 | 10.00 |
| ❑ C 30498 | Love Story | 1971 | 10.00 |
| ❑ CQ 30498 [Q] | Love Story | 1972 | 15.00 |
| ❑ C 30755 | Great Contemporary Instrumental Hits | 1971 | 10.00 |
| ❑ KC 31220 | I'd Like to Teach the World to Sing | 1972 | 10.00 |
| ❑ CQ 31473 [Q] | Love Theme from "The Godfather" | 1972 | 15.00 |
| ❑ KC 31473 | Love Theme from "The Godfather" | 1972 | 10.00 |
| ❑ CQ 31629 [Q] | Alone Again (Naturally) | 1972 | 15.00 |
| ❑ KC 31629 | Alone Again (Naturally) | 1972 | 10.00 |
| ❑ KC 32090 | I Can See Clearly Now | 1973 | 10.00 |
| ❑ KC 32376 | You Are the Sunshine of My Life | 1973 | 10.00 |
| ❑ C 32413 | Charlotte's Web | 1973 | 10.00 |
| ❑ CQ 32553 [Q] | Harmony | 1973 | 15.00 |
| ❑ KC 32553 | Harmony | 1973 | 10.00 |
| ❑ CQ 32802 [Q] | The Way We Were | 1974 | 15.00 |
| ❑ KC 32802 | The Way We Were | 1974 | 10.00 |
| ❑ CQ 33139 [Q] | The Happy Sound | 1974 | 15.00 |
| ❑ KC 33139 | The Happy Sound | 1974 | 10.00 |
| ❑ CQ 33332 [Q] | Laughter in the Rain | 1975 | 15.00 |
| ❑ CQ 33564 [Q] | Another Somebody Done Somebody Wrong Song | 1975 | 15.00 |
| ❑ KC 33564 | Another Somebody Done Somebody Wrong Song | 1975 | 10.00 |
| ❑ CG 33603 [(2)] | Somewhere My Love/Bridge Over Troubled Water | 1975 | 12.00 |
| ❑ CQ 33884 [Q] | Love Will Keep Us Together | 1975 | 15.00 |
| ❑ KC 33884 | Love Will Keep Us Together | 1975 | 10.00 |
| ❑ CQ 34040 [Q] | I Write the Songs | 1976 | 15.00 |
| ❑ KC 34040 | I Write the Songs | 1976 | 10.00 |
| ❑ CQ 34170 [Q] | Send In the Clowns | 1976 | 15.00 |
| ❑ KC 34170 | Send In the Clowns | 1976 | 10.00 |
| ❑ CQ 34312 [Q] | S.W.A.T. | 1976 | 15.00 |
| ❑ KC 34312 | S.W.A.T. | 1976 | 10.00 |
| ❑ PC 34477 | After the Lovin' | 1977 | 10.00 |
| ❑ JC 35659 | Ray Conniff Plays the Bee Gees and Other Hits | 1978 | 10.00 |
| ❑ PC 36255 | I Will Survive | 1979 | 10.00 |
| ❑ JC 36749 | Perfect "10" Classics | 1980 | 10.00 |
| ❑ FC 38072 | The Nashville Connection | 1981 | 10.00 |
| ❑ PC 38300 | Christmas Album | 1982 | 10.00 |
| ❑ PC 39470 | Christmas Caroling | 1984 | 10.00 |
| ❑ FC 40384 | Say You, Say Me | 1986 | 10.00 |
| ❑ FC 44152 | Always in My Heart | 1988 | 10.00 |

COLUMBIA RECORD CLUB

| Number | Title (A Side/B Side) | Yr | NM |
|---|---|---|---|
| ❑ D 267 [M] | Ray Conniff's World of Favorites | 196? | 12.00 |
| ❑ DS 267 [S] | Ray Conniff's World of Favorites | 196? | 15.00 |

HARMONY

| Number | Title (A Side/B Side) | Yr | NM |
|---|---|---|---|
| ❑ HS 11346 | Love Is a Many-Splendored Thing | 1969 | 10.00 |
| ❑ KH 30134 | The Impossible Dream | 1970 | 10.00 |

## CONNOR, CHRIS

ABC

| Number | Title (A Side/B Side) | Yr | NM |
|---|---|---|---|
| ❑ ABC-585 [M] | Chris Connor Now | 1966 | 20.00 |
| ❑ ABCS-585 [S] | Chris Connor Now | 1966 | 25.00 |

ABC-PARAMOUNT

| Number | Title (A Side/B Side) | Yr | NM |
|---|---|---|---|
| ❑ ABC-529 [M] | Gentle Bossa Nova | 1965 | 20.00 |
| ❑ ABCS-529 [S] | Gentle Bossa Nova | 1965 | 25.00 |

APPLAUSE

| Number | Title (A Side/B Side) | Yr | NM |
|---|---|---|---|
| ❑ APLP-1020 | Chris Connor Live | 1982 | 15.00 |

ATLANTIC

| Number | Title (A Side/B Side) | Yr | NM |
|---|---|---|---|
| ❑ 2-601 [(2)M] | Chris Connor Sings the George Gershwin Almanac of Song | 1957 | 100.00 |
| *—Black label* | | | |
| ❑ 2-601 [(2)M] | Chris Connor Sings the George Gershwin Almanac of Song | 196? | 20.00 |
| *—Multi-color label, black "fan" logo* | | | |
| ❑ 2-601 [(2)M] | Chris Connor Sings the George Gershwin Almanac of Song | 196? | 40.00 |
| *—Multi-color label, white "fan" logo* | | | |
| ❑ 1228 [M] | Chris Connor | 1956 | 50.00 |
| *—Black label* | | | |
| ❑ 1228 [M] | Chris Connor | 196? | 20.00 |
| *—Multi-color label, white "fan" logo* | | | |
| ❑ SD 1228 [S] | Chris Connor | 1958 | 60.00 |
| *—Green label* | | | |
| ❑ SD 1228 [S] | Chris Connor | 196? | 25.00 |
| *—Multi-color label, white "fan" logo* | | | |
| ❑ 1240 [M] | He Loves Me, He Loves Me Not | 1956 | 50.00 |
| *—Black label* | | | |
| ❑ 1240 [M] | He Loves Me, He Loves Me Not | 196? | 20.00 |
| *—Multi-color label, white "fan" logo* | | | |
| ❑ 1240 [M] | He Loves Me, He Loves Me Not | 1960 | 40.00 |
| *—White "bullseye" label* | | | |
| ❑ SD 1240 [S] | He Loves Me, He Loves Me Not | 1958 | 60.00 |
| *—Green label* | | | |
| ❑ SD 1240 [S] | He Loves Me, He Loves Me Not | 196? | 25.00 |
| *—Multi-color label, white "fan" logo* | | | |
| ❑ SD 1240 [S] | He Loves Me, He Loves Me Not | 1960 | 50.00 |
| *—White "bullseye" label* | | | |
| ❑ 1286 [M] | A Jazz Date with Chris Connor | 1958 | 50.00 |
| *—Black label* | | | |
| ❑ 1286 [M] | A Jazz Date with Chris Connor | 196? | 20.00 |
| *—Multi-color label, white "fan" logo* | | | |
| ❑ 1290 [M] | Chris Craft | 1958 | 50.00 |
| *—Black label* | | | |
| ❑ 1290 [M] | Chris Craft | 196? | 20.00 |
| *—Multi-color label, white "fan" logo* | | | |
| ❑ 1307 [M] | Ballads of the Sad Café | 1959 | 50.00 |
| *—Black label* | | | |
| ❑ 1307 [M] | Ballads of the Sad Café | 196? | 20.00 |
| *—Multi-color label, white "fan" logo* | | | |
| ❑ SD 1307 [S] | Ballads of the Sad Café | 1959 | 60.00 |
| *—Green label* | | | |
| ❑ SD 1307 [S] | Ballads of the Sad Café | 196? | 25.00 |
| *—Multi-color label, white "fan" logo* | | | |
| ❑ 1309 [M] | Chris Connor Sings the George Gershwin Almanac of Song, Vol. 1 | 1959 | 40.00 |
| *—Black label* | | | |
| ❑ 1309 [M] | Chris Connor Sings the George Gershwin Almanac of Song, Vol. 1 | 196? | 20.00 |
| *—Multi-color label, white "fan" logo* | | | |
| ❑ 1310 [M] | Chris Connor Sings the George Gershwin Almanac of Song, Vol. 2 | 1959 | 40.00 |
| *—Black label* | | | |
| ❑ 1310 [M] | Chris Connor Sings the George Gershwin Almanac of Song, Vol. 2 | 196? | 20.00 |
| *—Multi-color label, white "fan" logo* | | | |
| ❑ 8014 [M] | I Miss You So | 1957 | 50.00 |
| *—Black label* | | | |
| ❑ 8014 [M] | I Miss You So | 196? | 20.00 |
| *—Multi-color label, white "fan" logo* | | | |
| ❑ 8014 [M] | I Miss You So | 1960 | 40.00 |
| *—White "bullseye" label* | | | |
| ❑ 8032 [M] | Witchcraft | 1959 | 50.00 |
| *—Black label* | | | |

Number | Title (A Side/B Side) | Yr | NM

❑ 8032 [M] Witchcraft 196? 20.00
*—Multi-color label, white "fan" logo*
❑ 8032 [M] Witchcraft 1960 40.00
*—White "bullseye" label*
❑ SD 8032 [S] Witchcraft 1959 60.00
*—Green label*
❑ SD 8032 [S] Witchcraft 196? 25.00
*—Multi-color label, white "fan" logo*
❑ 8040 [M] Chris In Person 1959 50.00
*—Black label*
❑ 8040 [M] Chris In Person 196? 20.00
*—Multi-color label, white "fan" logo*
❑ SD 8040 [S] Chris In Person 1959 60.00
*—Green label*
❑ SD 8040 [S] Chris In Person 196? 25.00
*—Multi-color label, white "fan" logo*
❑ 8046 [M] A Portrait of Chris 1960 40.00
*—Multi-color label, white "fan" logo*
❑ SD 8046 [S] A Portrait of Chris 1960 50.00
*—Multi-color label, white "fan" logo*
❑ 8061 [M] Free Spirits 1962 30.00
*—Multi-color label, black "fan" logo*
❑ SD 8061 [S] Free Spirits 1962 40.00
*—Multi-color label, black "fan" logo*

BETHLEHEM
❑ BCP-20 [M] This Is Chris 1955 60.00
❑ BCP-56 [M] Chris 1957 60.00
❑ BCP-1001 [10] Chris Connor Sings Lullabys of Birdland 1954 80.00
❑ BCP-1002 [10] Chris Connor Sings Lullabys for Lovers 1954 80.00
❑ BCP-6004 [M] Chris Connor Sings Lullabys of Birdland 1955 50.00
❑ BCP-6004 [M] Chris Connor Sings Lullabys of Birdland 1984 12.00
*—Reissue*

CLARION
❑ 611 [M] Chris Connor Sings George Gershwin 1966 15.00
*—Abbreviated version of Atlantic 2-601*
❑ SD 611 [R] Chris Connor Sings George Gershwin 1966 10.00

FM
❑ 300 [M] Chris Connor at the Village Gate 1963 50.00
❑ S-300 [S] Chris Connor at the Village Gate 1963 60.00
❑ 312 [M] A Weekend in Paris 1964 50.00
❑ S-312 [S] A Weekend in Paris 1964 60.00

### CONNOR, CHRIS, AND MAYNARD FERGUSON

ATLANTIC
❑ 8049 [M] Double Exposure 1961 30.00
*—Multi-color label, white "fan" logo*
❑ SD 8049 [S] Double Exposure 1961 40.00
*—Multi-color label, white "fan" logo*

ROULETTE
❑ R 52068 [M] Two's Company 1961 30.00
*—White label with colored spokes*
❑ SR 52068 [S] Two's Company 1961 40.00
*—White label with colored spokes*

### CONNY

CAPITOL
❑ T 10253 [M] Germany's Greatest Record Star 1960 30.00

### CONSTANTINE, EDDIE

KAPP
❑ KL-1018 [M] La Grande Sensation de la Paris 1957 30.00

MERCURY
❑ MG-20339 [M] The Rage of Paris 1958 25.00

### CONTEMPORARY JAZZ ENSEMBLE, THE

PRESTIGE
❑ PRLP-163 [10] New Sounds from Rochester 1953 100.00

### CONTI, ROBERT

TREND
❑ TR-519 Solo Guitar 198? 20.00
*—Direct-to-disc recording*

### CONTINENTAL OCTETTE, THE

CROWN
❑ CLP-5220 [M] Modern Jazz Greats 196? 20.00

### CONTOURS, THE

GORDY
❑ G 901 [M] Do You Love Me? 1962 500.00

MOTOWN
❑ M5-188V1 Do You Love Me? 1981 10.00

### CONWAY, JULIE

HARMONY
❑ HL 7143 [M] Good Housekeeping's Plan for Reducing Off-the-Record 1960 20.00

### COODER, RY

MOBILE FIDELITY
❑ 1-085 Jazz 198? 400.00
*—Audiophile vinyl*

REPRISE
❑ PRO 588 [DJ] The Ry Cooder Radio Show 1976 100.00
❑ MS 2052 Into the Purple Valley 1972 12.00
❑ MS 2117 Boomer's Story 1973 12.00
❑ MS 2179 Paradise and Lunch 1974 12.00
❑ MS 2254 Chicken Skin Music 1976 12.00
❑ RS-6402 Ry Cooder 1969 15.00
*—Two-tone orange label with "r:" and "W7" logos*
❑ RS-6402 Ry Cooder 1970 12.00
*—No "W7" on label; one-tone orange (almost tan) label*

WARNER BROS.
❑ BS 3059 Show Time 1977 10.00
❑ BSK 3197 Jazz 1978 10.00
❑ BSK 3358 Bop Till You Drop 1979 10.00
❑ HS 3448 The Long Riders 1980 10.00
❑ BSK 3489 Borderline 1980 10.00
❑ BSK 3651 The Slide Area 1982 10.00
❑ 25270 Paris, Texas 1984 10.00
❑ 25399 Crossroads 1986 10.00
❑ 25639 Get Rhythm 1987 10.00
❑ 25996 Johnny Handsome 1989 10.00

### COOK, JUNIOR

JAZZLAND
❑ JLP-58 [M] Junior's Cookin' 1961 40.00
❑ JLP-958 [S] Junior's Cookin' 1961 50.00

### COOKE, ALISTAIR

COLUMBIA MASTERWORKS
❑ ML 4970 [M] An Evening with Alistair Cooke 1955 40.00

### COOKE, SAM

ABKCO
❑ 1124-1 Sam Cooke's Night Beat 1995 12.00
*—Reissue*
❑ 2970-1 Sam Cooke at the Copa 1988 12.00
*—Reissue*

FAMOUS
❑ 502 Sam's Songs 1969 40.00
❑ 505 Only Sixteen 1969 40.00
❑ 508 So Wonderful 1969 40.00
❑ 509 You Send Me 1969 40.00
❑ 512 Cha-Cha-Cha 1969 40.00

51 WEST
❑ Q 16032 My Foolish Heart 198? 12.00

KEEN
❑ A-2001 [M] Sam Cooke 1958 200.00
❑ A-2003 [M] Encore 1958 200.00
❑ A-2004 [M] Tribute to the Lady 1959 150.00
❑ AS-2004 [S] Tribute to the Lady 1959 200.00
❑ 86101 [M] Hit Kit 1959 250.00
❑ 86103 [M] I Thank God 1960 400.00
❑ 86106 [M] The Wonderful World of Sam Cooke 1960 350.00

PAIR
❑ PDL2-1006 [(2)] You Send Me 1986 15.00

RCA CAMDEN
❑ ACS1-0445 You Send Me 1974 12.00
❑ CAL-2264 [M] The One and Only Sam Cooke 1967 20.00
❑ CAS-2264 [R] The One and Only Sam Cooke 1967 12.00
❑ CAS-2433 Sam Cooke 1970 12.00
❑ CAS-2610 The Unforgettable Sam Cooke 1972 12.00

RCA VICTOR
❑ LPM-2221 [M] Cooke's Tour 1960 40.00
❑ LSP-2221 [S] Cooke's Tour 1960 50.00
❑ LPM-2236 [M] Hits of the 50's 1960 40.00
❑ LSP-2236 [S] Hits of the 50's 1960 50.00
❑ LPM-2293 [M] Swing Low 1960 40.00
❑ LSP-2293 [S] Swing Low 1960 50.00
❑ LPM-2392 [M] My Kind of Blues 1961 40.00
❑ LSP-2392 [S] My Kind of Blues 1961 50.00
❑ LPM-2555 [M] Twistin' the Night Away 1962 40.00
❑ LSP-2555 [S] Twistin' the Night Away 1962 50.00
❑ AFL1-2625 The Best of Sam Cooke 1977 12.00
*—Reissue with new prefix*
❑ LPM-2625 [M] The Best of Sam Cooke 1962 30.00
❑ LSP-2625 [R] The Best of Sam Cooke 1962 20.00
❑ ANL1-2658 Sam Cooke at the Copa 1977 12.00
*—Reissue of LSP-2970*
❑ LPM-2673 [M] Mr. Soul 1963 30.00
❑ LSP-2673 [S] Mr. Soul 1963 40.00
❑ LPM-2709 [M] Night Beat 1963 30.00
❑ LSP-2709 [S] Night Beat 1963 40.00
❑ LPM-2899 [M] Ain't That Good News 1964 30.00
❑ LSP-2899 [S] Ain't That Good News 1964 40.00
❑ LPM-2970 [M] Sam Cooke at the Copa 1964 30.00
❑ LSP-2970 [S] Sam Cooke at the Copa 1964 40.00
❑ LPM-3367 [M] Shake 1965 25.00
❑ LSP-3367 [S] Shake 1965 30.00
❑ LPM-3373 [M] The Best of Sam Cooke, Volume 2 1965 25.00
❑ LSP-3373 [S] The Best of Sam Cooke, Volume 2 1965 30.00
❑ LPM-3435 [M] Try a Little Love 1965 25.00
❑ LSP-3435 [S] Try a Little Love 1965 30.00
❑ LPM-3517 [M] The Unforgettable Sam Cooke 1966 20.00
❑ LSP-3517 [S] The Unforgettable Sam Cooke 1966 25.00
❑ AYL1-3863 The Best of Sam Cooke 1981 8.00
*—Budget-line reissue*
❑ LPM-3991 [M] The Man Who Invented Soul 1968 50.00
❑ LSP-3991 [S] The Man Who Invented Soul 1968 25.00
❑ AFL1-5181 Live at the Harlem Square Club, 1963 1985 12.00
❑ VPS-6027 [(2)] This Is Sam Cooke 1970 20.00
❑ CPL2-7127 [(2)] The Man and His Music 1986 15.00

SPECIALTY
❑ SPS-2106 Sam Cooke and the Soul Stirrers 1970 15.00
❑ SPS-2116 The Gospel Soul of Sam Cooke, Vol. 1 1970 15.00
❑ SPS-2119 Two Sides of Sam Cooke 1970 15.00
❑ SPS-2128 The Gospel Soul of Sam Cooke, Vol. 2 197? 15.00
❑ SPS-2146 That's Heaven to Me 197? 15.00

TRIP
❑ 8030 [(2)] The Golden Sound of Sam Cooke 1972 15.00

UPFRONT
❑ 160 The Billie Holiday Story 1973 15.00

### COOKIES, THE/LITTLE EVA/CAROLE KING

DIMENSION
❑ DLP-6001 [M] The Dimension Dolls, Vol. 1 1964 250.00

### COOL, CALVIN, AND THE SURF KNOBS

CHARTER
❑ CLP-103 [M] The Surfer's Beat 1963 40.00
❑ CLS-103 [S] The Surfer's Beat 1963 50.00

### COOL BRITONS, THE

BLUE NOTE
❑ BLP-5052 [10] New Sounds from Olde England 1954 300.00

### COOLEY, SPADE

COLUMBIA
❑ CL 9007 [10] Sagebrush Swing 1949 200.00

DECCA
❑ DL 5563 [10] Dance-O-Rama 1955 300.00

RAYNOTE
❑ R-5007 [M] Fidoolin' 1959 40.00
❑ RS-5007 [S] Fidoolin' 1959 50.00

ROULETTE
❑ R 25145 [M] Fidoolin' 1961 30.00
❑ SR 25145 [S] Fidoolin' 1961 40.00

### COOLIDGE, RITA

A&M
❑ SP-3107 Rita Coolidge 198? 8.00
*—Budget-line reissue*
❑ SP-3130 Nice Feelin' 198? 8.00
*—Budget-line reissue*
❑ SP-3163 Anytime...Anywhere 198? 8.00
*—Budget-line reissue*
❑ SP-3238 Greatest Hits 198? 8.00
*—Budget-line reissue*
❑ SP-3627 Fall Into Spring 1974 10.00
❑ SP-3727 Heartbreak Radio 1981 10.00
❑ SP-4291 Rita Coolidge 1971 10.00
❑ SP-4325 Nice Feelin' 1971 10.00
❑ SP-4370 The Lady's Not for Sale 1972 10.00
❑ SP-4531 It's Only Love 1975 10.00
❑ SP-4616 Anytime...Anywhere 1977 10.00
❑ SP-4669 Love Me Again 1978 10.00
❑ SP-4781 Satisfied 1979 10.00
❑ SP-4836 Greatest Hits 1981 10.00
❑ SP-4914 Never Let You Go 1983 10.00
❑ SP-5003 Inside the Fire 1984 10.00

NAUTILUS
❑ NR-16 Anytime...Anywhere 1981 25.00
*—Audiophile vinyl*

### COOPER, ALICE

ACCORD
❑ SN-7162 Toronto Rock 'n' Roll Revival 1969 1981 12.00

ATLANTIC
❑ SD 18130 Welcome to My Nightmare 1975 10.00
❑ SD 19157 Welcome to My Nightmare 1978 8.00
*—Reissue of 18130*

EPIC
❑ OE 45137 Trash 1989 12.00
❑ E 46786 Hey Stoopid 1991 15.00

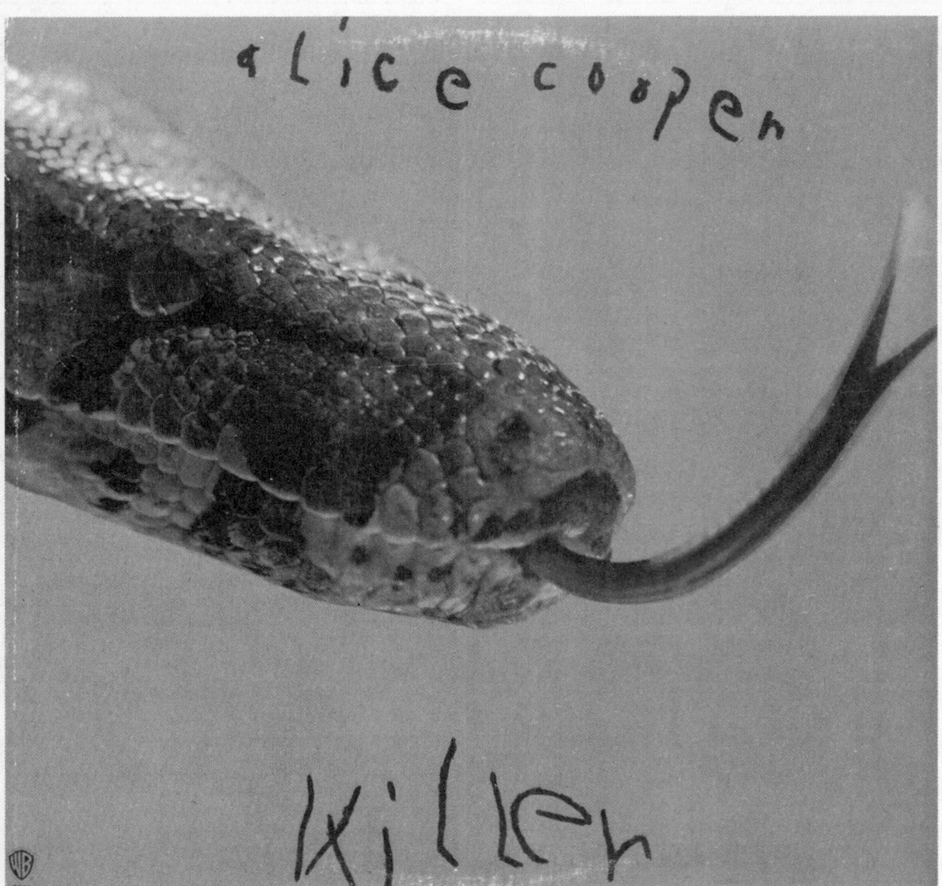


Alice Cooper, *Killer,* Warner Bros. BS 2567, 1971, green label, with 1972 calendar intact, $30.

| Number | Title (A Side/B Side) | Yr | NM |
|---|---|---|---|
| **MCA** | | | |
| ❑ 5761 | Constrictor | 1986 | 8.00 |
| ❑ 42091 | Raise Your Fist and Yell | 1987 | 8.00 |
| **MOBILE FIDELITY** | | | |
| ❑ 1-063 | Welcome to My Nightmare | 1980 | 50.00 |
| *—Audiophile vinyl* | | | |
| **PAIR** | | | |
| ❑ PDL2-1163 [(2)] | A Man Called Alice | 1987 | 15.00 |
| **STRAIGHT** | | | |
| ❑ STS-1051 | Pretties for You | 1969 | 150.00 |
| *—Yellow label stock copy* | | | |
| ❑ STS-1051 [DJ] | Pretties for You | 1969 | 200.00 |
| *—White label promo* | | | |
| ❑ WS 1840 | Pretties for You | 1970 | 60.00 |
| *—Pink label stock copy* | | | |
| ❑ WS 1845 | Easy Action | 1970 | 30.00 |
| *—Pink label stock copy; "Alice Cooper" in white on cover* | | | |
| ❑ WS 1845 | Easy Action | 1970 | 50.00 |
| *—Pink label stock copy; "Alice Cooper" in black on cover* | | | |
| ❑ WS 1845 [DJ] | Easy Action | 1970 | 100.00 |
| *—White label promo* | | | |
| ❑ WS 1883 | Love It to Death | 1971 | 50.00 |
| *—Pink label stock copy* | | | |
| ❑ WS 1883 [DJ] | Love It to Death | 1971 | 100.00 |
| *—White label promo* | | | |
| **WARNER BROS.** | | | |
| ❑ PRO 789 [DJ] | The Alice Cooper Radio Show | 1978 | 25.00 |
| ❑ WS 1840 | Pretties for You | 1971 | 25.00 |
| *—Green label; comes in "Straight" cover* | | | |
| ❑ WS 1840 | Pretties for You | 1973 | 20.00 |
| *—"Burbank" palm trees label; comes in Straight cover* | | | |
| ❑ WS 1883 | Love It to Death | 1971 | 12.00 |
| *—Version 4: Green "WB" label; with "I'm Eighteen" box and Alice's protruding thumb airbrushed off the cover* | | | |
| ❑ WS 1883 | Love It to Death | 1971 | 20.00 |
| *—Version 2: Green "WB" label; same as above, but has a white box reading "Contains the Hit 'I'm Eighteen' "* | | | |
| ❑ WS 1883 | Love It to Death | 1971 | 20.00 |
| *—Version 3: Green "WB" label; cover has large white areas at top and bottom with lower half of the photo cropped out* | | | |
| ❑ WS 1883 | Love It to Death | 1971 | 30.00 |
| *—Version 1: Green "WB" label; cover has Alice's thumb sticking out in such a way that it appears to be another part of the body* | | | |
| ❑ BS 2567 | Killer | 1971 | 30.00 |
| *—Early copies have an attached 1972 calendar/poster* | | | |
| ❑ BS 2567 | Killer | 1972 | 12.00 |
| *—Later copies no longer have the calendar/poster* | | | |
| ❑ BS 2623 | School's Out | 1972 | 12.00 |
| *—No panties, with song titles listed* | | | |
| ❑ BS 2623 | School's Out | 1972 | 20.00 |
| *—Back cover does not list song titles, but panties are missing* | | | |
| ❑ BS 2623 | School's Out | 1972 | 30.00 |
| *—With paper panties intact; back cover lists song titles* | | | |
| ❑ BS 2623 | School's Out | 1972 | 40.00 |
| *—With paper panties intact; back cover does not list song titles* | | | |
| ❑ BS 2685 | Billion Dollar Babies | 1973 | 12.00 |
| *—Green "WB" label* | | | |
| ❑ BS4 2685 [Q] | Billion Dollar Babies | 1974 | 25.00 |
| ❑ BS 2748 | Muscle of Love | 1973 | 10.00 |
| ❑ BS4 2748 [Q] | Muscle of Love | 1974 | 25.00 |
| ❑ BS4 2803 [Q] | Alice Cooper's Greatest Hits | 1974 | — |
| *—Not released* | | | |
| ❑ W 2803 | Alice Cooper's Greatest Hits | 1974 | 10.00 |
| ❑ BS 2896 | Alice Cooper Goes to Hell | 1976 | 10.00 |
| ❑ BSK 3027 | Lace and Whiskey | 1977 | 10.00 |
| ❑ BSK 3107 | Alice Cooper's Greatest Hits | 1977 | 8.00 |
| *—Reissue of BS 2803* | | | |
| ❑ BSK 3138 | The Alice Cooper Show | 1977 | 10.00 |
| ❑ BSK 3263 | From the Inside | 1978 | 10.00 |
| ❑ BSK 3436 | Flush the Fashion | 1980 | 10.00 |
| ❑ BSK 3581 | Special Forces | 1981 | 10.00 |
| ❑ 23719 | Zipper Catches Skin | 1982 | 10.00 |
| ❑ 23969 | Da Da | 1983 | 10.00 |

## COOPER, BOB

| Number | Title (A Side/B Side) | Yr | NM |
|---|---|---|---|
| **CAPITOL** | | | |
| ❑ ST 1586 [S] | Do Re Mi | 1961 | 30.00 |
| ❑ T 1586 [M] | Do Re Mi | 1961 | 25.00 |
| ❑ H 6501 [10] | Bob Cooper | 1954 | 80.00 |
| ❑ T 6501 [M] | Bob Cooper | 1955 | 50.00 |
| ❑ H 6513 [10] | Shifting Winds | 1955 | 60.00 |
| ❑ T 6513 [M] | Shifting Winds | 1955 | 50.00 |
| **CONTEMPORARY** | | | |
| ❑ C-3544 [M] | Coop! | 1958 | 50.00 |
| ❑ S-7012 [S] | Coop! | 1959 | 40.00 |
| *—Reissue of Stereo Records 7012* | | | |
| **STEREO RECORDS** | | | |
| ❑ S-7012 [S] | Coop! | 1958 | 50.00 |
| **TREND** | | | |
| ❑ TR-518 | Tenor Sax Impressions | 198? | 20.00 |
| *—Direct-to-disc recording* | | | |
| **WORLD PACIFIC** | | | |
| ❑ WPM-411 [M] | Bob Cooper Swings TV | 1958 | 50.00 |

## COOPER, JACKIE

| Number | Title (A Side/B Side) | Yr | NM |
|---|---|---|---|
| **DOT** | | | |
| ❑ DLP-3146 [M] | The Movies Swing! | 1958 | 30.00 |

## COOPER, LES, AND THE SOUL ROCKERS

| Number | Title (A Side/B Side) | Yr | NM |
|---|---|---|---|
| **EVERLAST** | | | |
| ❑ ELP-202 [M] | Wiggle Wobble | 1963 | 50.00 |

## COOPER, WILMA LEE AND STONEY

| Number | Title (A Side/B Side) | Yr | NM |
|---|---|---|---|
| **DECCA** | | | |
| ❑ DL 4784 [M] | Wilma Lee and Stoney Cooper Sing | 1966 | 20.00 |
| ❑ DL 74784 [S] | Wilma Lee and Stoney Cooper Sing | 1966 | 25.00 |
| **HARMONY** | | | |
| ❑ HL 7233 [M] | Sacred Songs | 1960 | 25.00 |
| **HICKORY** | | | |
| ❑ LP-100 [M] | There's a Big Wheel | 1960 | 50.00 |
| ❑ LP-106 [M] | Family Favorites | 1962 | 40.00 |
| ❑ LP-112 [M] | New Songs of Inspiration | 1962 | 40.00 |

## COPAS, COWBOY

| Number | Title (A Side/B Side) | Yr | NM |
|---|---|---|---|
| **KING** | | | |
| ❑ 553 [M] | Cowboy Copas Sings His All-Time Hits | 1957 | 100.00 |
| ❑ 556 [M] | Favorite Sacred Songs | 1957 | 80.00 |
| ❑ 619 [M] | Sacred Songs by Cowboy Copas | 1959 | 80.00 |
| ❑ 714 [M] | Tragic Tales of Love and Life | 1960 | 80.00 |
| ❑ 720 [M] | Broken Hearted Melodies | 1960 | 80.00 |
| ❑ 817 [M] | Country Gentleman of Song | 1963 | 40.00 |
| ❑ 824 [M] | As You Remember Cowboy Copas | 1963 | 40.00 |
| ❑ 894 [M] | Cowboy Copas Hymns | 1964 | 40.00 |
| **STARDAY** | | | |
| ❑ SLP-118 [M] | All Time Country Music Great | 1960 | 40.00 |
| ❑ SLP-133 [M] | Inspirational Songs | 1961 | 40.00 |
| ❑ SLP-144 [M] | Cowboy Copas | 1961 | 40.00 |
| ❑ SLP-157 [M] | Opry Star Spotlight on Cowboy Copas | 1962 | 40.00 |
| ❑ SLP-175 [M] | Mister Country Music | 1962 | 40.00 |
| ❑ SLP-184 [M] | Songs That Made Him Famous | 1962 | 40.00 |
| ❑ SLP-208 [M] | Country Music Entertainer #1 | 1963 | 40.00 |
| ❑ SLP-212 [M] | Beyond the Sunset | 1963 | 40.00 |
| ❑ SLP-234 [M] | The Unforgettable Cowboy Copas | 1963 | 40.00 |
| ❑ SLP-247 [M] | Star of the Grand Ole Opry | 1963 | 40.00 |
| ❑ SLP-268 [M] | Cowboy Copas and His Friends | 1964 | 40.00 |
| ❑ SLP-317 [M] | The Legend Lives On | 1965 | 30.00 |
| ❑ SLP (9)-347 [(2)R] | The Cowboy Copas Story | 1965 | 25.00 |
| ❑ SLP-347 [(2)M] | The Cowboy Copas Story | 1965 | 30.00 |
| ❑ SLP-458 | The Best of Cowboy Copas | 1970 | 15.00 |

## COPAS, COWBOY, AND HAWKSHAW HAWKINS

| Number | Title (A Side/B Side) | Yr | NM |
|---|---|---|---|
| **KING** | | | |
| ❑ 835 [M] | In Memory | 1963 | 40.00 |
| ❑ 850 [M] | The Legend of Cowboy Copas and Hawkshaw Hawkins | 1964 | 40.00 |
| ❑ 984 [M] | 24 Great Hits | 1968 | 25.00 |

## COPAS, COWBOY/HAWKSHAW HAWKINS/PATSY CLINE

| Number | Title (A Side/B Side) | Yr | NM |
|---|---|---|---|
| **STARDAY** | | | |
| ❑ SLP-346 [M] | Gone But Not Forgotten | 1965 | 30.00 |

## COPPER PLATED INTEGRATED CIRCUIT, THE

| Number | Title (A Side/B Side) | Yr | NM |
|---|---|---|---|
| **COMMAND** | | | |
| ❑ RS-945 SD | Plugged In Pop | 1969 | 25.00 |

## COPPERPENNY

| Number | Title (A Side/B Side) | Yr | NM |
|---|---|---|---|
| **RCA VICTOR** | | | |
| ❑ LSP-4291 | Copperpenny | 1970 | 20.00 |

## CORBIN, HAROLD

| Number | Title (A Side/B Side) | Yr | NM |
|---|---|---|---|
| **ROULETTE** | | | |
| ❑ R-52079 [M] | Soul Brother | 1961 | 25.00 |
| ❑ SR-52079 [S] | Soul Brother | 1961 | 30.00 |

## CORCORAN, CORKY

| Number | Title (A Side/B Side) | Yr | NM |
|---|---|---|---|
| **C.C. PRODUCTION** | | | |
| ❑ 4012 [M] | Corky Corcoran Plays Everywhere | 1974 | 12.00 |
| **CELESTIAL** | | | |
| ❑ Vol. 1 [M] | Sounds of Jazz | 1958 | 200.00 |
| *—Black vinyl* | | | |
| ❑ Vol. 1 [M] | Sounds of Jazz | 1958 | 300.00 |
| *—Red vinyl* | | | |
| **EPIC** | | | |
| ❑ LN 3319 [M] | The Sound of Love | 1956 | 80.00 |
| **RCS** | | | |
| ❑ 2555 [M] | Corky Corcoran Plays Something | 197? | 25.00 |

### CORDIALS, THE

| Number | Title (A Side/B Side) | Yr | NM |
|---|---|---|---|
| **CATAMOUNT** | | | |
| ❑ 902 | Blue Eyed Soul | 1967 | 25.00 |

### COREA, CHICK

| Number | Title (A Side/B Side) | Yr | NM |
|---|---|---|---|
| **BLUE NOTE** | | | |
| ❑ BST-84353 | Song of Singing | 1970 | 40.00 |
| *—"A Division of Liberty Records" on label* | | | |
| ❑ BST-84353 | Song of Singing | 1984 | 20.00 |
| *—Reissue, "The Finest in Jazz Since 1939" on label* | | | |
| **GROOVE MERCHANT** | | | |
| ❑ 2202 | Sundance | 1972 | 30.00 |
| **SOLID STATE** | | | |
| ❑ SS-18039 | Now He Sings, Now He Sobs | 1969 | 20.00 |
| ❑ SS-18055 | Chick Corea "Is" | 1969 | 20.00 |
| **VORTEX** | | | |
| ❑ 2004 | Tones for Joan's Bones | 1971 | 30.00 |

### COREY, JILL

| Number | Title (A Side/B Side) | Yr | NM |
|---|---|---|---|
| **COLUMBIA** | | | |
| ❑ CL 1095 [M] | Sometimes I'm Happy, Sometimes I'm Blue | 1957 | 30.00 |

### CORNELL, DON

| Number | Title (A Side/B Side) | Yr | NM |
|---|---|---|---|
| **ABC-PARAMOUNT** | | | |
| ❑ ABC-537 [M] | Incomparable | 1966 | 12.00 |
| ❑ ABCS-537 [S] | Incomparable | 1966 | 15.00 |
| **CORAL** | | | |
| ❑ CRL 57055 [M] | Don | 1955 | 30.00 |
| ❑ CRL 57133 [M] | For Teenagers Only | 1957 | 30.00 |
| **DOT** | | | |
| ❑ DLP-3160 [M] | Don Cornell's Great Hits | 1959 | 25.00 |
| ❑ DLP-25160 [S] | Don Cornell's Great Hits | 1959 | 30.00 |
| **MOVIETONE** | | | |
| ❑ 71013 [M] | I Wish You Love | 1966 | 12.00 |
| ❑ S-72013 [S] | I Wish You Love | 1966 | 15.00 |
| **SIGNATURE** | | | |
| ❑ SM-1001 [M] | Don Cornell Sings Love Songs | 1960 | 20.00 |
| ❑ SS-1001 [S] | Don Cornell Sings Love Songs | 1960 | 25.00 |
| **VOCALION** | | | |
| ❑ VL 3657 [M] | Don Cornell | 196? | 12.00 |

### CORNELLS, THE

| Number | Title (A Side/B Side) | Yr | NM |
|---|---|---|---|
| **GAREX** | | | |
| ❑ LPGA-100 [M] | Beach Bound | 1963 | 500.00 |
| **SUNDAZED** | | | |
| ❑ LP-5013 | Surf Fever! | 199? | 10.00 |

### CORPORATION, THE

| Number | Title (A Side/B Side) | Yr | NM |
|---|---|---|---|
| **AGE OF AQUARIUS** | | | |
| ❑ 4150 | Get On Our Swing | 1968 | 30.00 |
| ❑ 4250 | Hassles in My Mind | 1969 | 30.00 |
| **CAPITOL** | | | |
| ❑ ST-175 | The Corporation | 1969 | 50.00 |

### CORPUS

| Number | Title (A Side/B Side) | Yr | NM |
|---|---|---|---|
| **ACORN** | | | |
| ❑ 1001 | Creation: A Child | 1971 | 300.00 |

### CORTEZ, DAVE "BABY"

| Number | Title (A Side/B Side) | Yr | NM |
|---|---|---|---|
| **CHESS** | | | |
| ❑ LP-1473 [M] | Rinky Dink | 1962 | 50.00 |
| **CLOCK** | | | |
| ❑ C-331 [M] | Dave "Baby" Cortez | 1960 | 40.00 |
| ❑ CS-331 [S] | Dave "Baby" Cortez | 1960 | 50.00 |
| ❑ MGC-20647 [M] | Dave "Baby" Cortez | 1961 | 30.00 |
| ❑ SRC-60647 [S] | Dave "Baby" Cortez | 1961 | 40.00 |
| **CORONET** | | | |
| ❑ CX-201 [M] | The Whistling Organ | 196? | 15.00 |
| **DESIGN** | | | |
| ❑ DLP-163 [R] | The Happy Organ | 1962 | 12.00 |
| **METRO** | | | |
| ❑ M-550 [M] | The Fabulous Organ of Dave "Baby" Cortez | 1965 | 15.00 |
| ❑ MS-550 [R] | The Fabulous Organ of Dave "Baby" Cortez | 1965 | 12.00 |
| **RCA VICTOR** | | | |
| ❑ LPM-2099 [M] | The Happy Organ | 1959 | 80.00 |
| ❑ LSP-2099 [S] | The Happy Organ | 1959 | 100.00 |
| **ROULETTE** | | | |
| ❑ R-25298 [M] | Organ Shindig | 1965 | 20.00 |
| ❑ SR-25298 [S] | Organ Shindig | 1965 | 25.00 |
| ❑ R-25315 [M] | Tweety Pie | 1966 | 20.00 |
| ❑ SR-25315 [S] | Tweety Pie | 1966 | 25.00 |
| ❑ R-25328 [M] | In Orbit with Dave "Baby" Cortez | 1966 | 20.00 |
| ❑ SR-25328 [S] | In Orbit with Dave "Baby" Cortez | 1966 | 25.00 |
| **T-NECK** | | | |
| ❑ TNS-3005 | The Isley Brothers Way | 1970 | 20.00 |

### CORWIN, BOB

| Number | Title (A Side/B Side) | Yr | NM |
|---|---|---|---|
| **RIVERSIDE** | | | |
| ❑ RLP 12-220 [M] | Bob Corwin Quartet with Don Elliott | 1956 | 80.00 |
| *—White label, blue print* | | | |
| ❑ RLP 12-220 [M] | Bob Corwin Quartet with Don Elliott | 1957 | 40.00 |
| *—Blue label with microphone logo* | | | |

### CORYELL, LARRY

| Number | Title (A Side/B Side) | Yr | NM |
|---|---|---|---|
| **FLYING DUTCHMAN** | | | |
| ❑ 51-1000 | Fairyland | 1971 | 20.00 |
| **VANGUARD** | | | |
| ❑ VSQ-40006 [Q] | Larry Coryell at the Village Gate | 197? | 20.00 |
| ❑ VSQ-40013 [Q] | Offering | 197? | 20.00 |
| ❑ VSQ-40023 [Q] | The Real Great Escape | 197? | 20.00 |
| ❑ VSQ-40036 [Q] | Introducing the Eleventh House | 1974 | 20.00 |

### COSBY, BILL

| Number | Title (A Side/B Side) | Yr | NM |
|---|---|---|---|
| **CAPITOL** | | | |
| ❑ ST-11530 | Bill Cosby Is Not Himself These Days, Rat Own, Rat Own, Rat Own | 1976 | 10.00 |
| ❑ ST-11590 | My Father Confused Me...What Must I Do? What Must I Do? | 1977 | 10.00 |
| ❑ ST-11683 | Let's Boogie (Disco Bill) | 1977 | 10.00 |
| ❑ ST-11731 | Bill's Best Friend | 1978 | 10.00 |
| **GEFFEN** | | | |
| ❑ GHS 24104 | Those of You With or Without Children, You'll Understand | 1986 | 10.00 |
| **MCA** | | | |
| ❑ 169 | When I Was a Kid | 197? | 8.00 |
| *—Reissue of Uni 73100* | | | |
| ❑ 333 | Fat Albert | 1973 | 10.00 |
| ❑ 553 | For Adults Only | 197? | 8.00 |
| *—Reissue of Uni 73112* | | | |
| ❑ 554 | Inside the Mind of Bill Cosby | 197? | 8.00 |
| *—Reissue of Uni 73139* | | | |
| ❑ 8005 [(2)] | Bill | 197? | 12.00 |
| **MOTOWN** | | | |
| ❑ 5364 ML | Bill Cosby "Himself" | 198? | 10.00 |
| *—Reissue of 6026 with new cover* | | | |
| ❑ 6026 ML | Bill Cosby "Himself" | 1982 | 10.00 |
| **TETRAGRAMMATON** | | | |
| ❑ TD-5100 [(2)] | 8:15 12:15 | 1969 | 20.00 |
| **UNI** | | | |
| ❑ 73066 | Bill Cosby | 1969 | 10.00 |
| ❑ 73082 | "Live" Madison Square Garden Center | 1970 | 10.00 |
| ❑ 73100 | When I Was a Kid | 1971 | 10.00 |
| ❑ 73101 | Bill Cosby Talks to Kids About Drugs | 1971 | 15.00 |
| ❑ 73112 | For Adults Only | 1971 | 10.00 |
| ❑ 73139 | Inside the Mind of Bill Cosby | 1972 | 10.00 |
| **WARNER BROS.** | | | |
| ❑ PRO 249 [DJ] | Radio Sampler Album — The Best of Bill Cosby | 1969 | 20.00 |
| *—Promo LP with edits of 12 tracks for radio use* | | | |
| ❑ W 1518 [M] | Bill Cosby Is a Very Funny Fellow Right! | 1964 | 15.00 |
| ❑ W 1567 [M] | I Started Out as a Child | 1964 | 15.00 |
| ❑ WS 1567 [S] | I Started Out as a Child | 1964 | 20.00 |
| *—Gold label* | | | |
| ❑ W 1606 [M] | Why Is There Air? | 1965 | 15.00 |
| ❑ WS 1606 [S] | Why Is There Air? | 1965 | 20.00 |
| *—Gold label* | | | |
| ❑ W 1634 [M] | Wonderfulness | 1966 | 15.00 |
| ❑ WS 1634 [S] | Wonderfulness | 1966 | 15.00 |
| *—Gold label* | | | |
| ❑ W 1691 [M] | Revenge | 1967 | 15.00 |
| ❑ W 1709 [M] | Bill Cosby Sings/Silver Throat | 1967 | 15.00 |
| ❑ WS 1709 [S] | Bill Cosby Sings/Silver Throat | 1967 | 12.00 |
| ❑ W 1728 [M] | Bill Cosby Sings/Hooray for the Salvation Army Band | 1968 | 15.00 |
| ❑ WS 1728 [S] | Bill Cosby Sings/Hooray for the Salvation Army Band | 1968 | 12.00 |
| ❑ W 1734 [M] | To Russell, My Brother, Whom I Slept With | 1968 | 15.00 |
| ❑ WS 1734 [S] | To Russell, My Brother, Whom I Slept With | 1968 | 12.00 |
| ❑ WS 1757 | 200 M.P.H. | 1968 | 12.00 |
| ❑ WS 1770 | It's True! It's True! | 1969 | 12.00 |
| ❑ WS 1798 | The Best of Bill Cosby | 1969 | 12.00 |
| ❑ WS 1836 | More of the Best of Bill Cosby | 1970 | 12.00 |

### COSMIC TWINS, THE

| Number | Title (A Side/B Side) | Yr | NM |
|---|---|---|---|
| **STRATA-EAST** | | | |
| ❑ SES-7410 | The Waterbearers | 1974 | 30.00 |

### COSTA, DON

| Number | Title (A Side/B Side) | Yr | NM |
|---|---|---|---|
| **ABC-PARAMOUNT** | | | |
| ❑ ABC-107 [M] | Music to Break a Lease | 1956 | 25.00 |
| ❑ ABC-212 [M] | Music to Break a Sub-Lease | 1958 | 25.00 |
| ❑ ABC-362 [M] | Don Costa Conducts His 15 Hits | 1961 | 25.00 |
| **COLUMBIA** | | | |
| ❑ CL 1880 [M] | Hollywood Premiere | 1962 | 15.00 |
| ❑ CL 2041 [M] | Hits! Hits! Hits! | 1963 | 15.00 |
| ❑ CS 8680 [S] | Hollywood Premiere | 1962 | 25.00 |
| ❑ CS 8841 [S] | Hits! Hits! Hits! | 1963 | 25.00 |
| **DCP INTERNATIONAL** | | | |
| ❑ DCL 3802 [M] | The Golden Touch | 1964 | 12.00 |
| ❑ DCL 3806 [M] | Don Costa Plays Music from Umbrellas of Cherbourg and Other Film Music | 1965 | 12.00 |
| ❑ DCS 6802 [S] | The Golden Touch | 1964 | 15.00 |
| ❑ DCS 6806 [S] | Don Costa Plays Music from Umbrellas of Cherbourg and Other Film Music | 1965 | 15.00 |
| **HARMONY** | | | |
| ❑ HL 7347 [M] | Days of Wine and Roses and Other Great Hits | 1965 | 12.00 |
| ❑ HS 11147 [S] | Days of Wine and Roses and Other Great Hits | 1965 | 15.00 |
| **MERCURY** | | | |
| ❑ SR 61177 | Instrumental Versions of Simon and Garfunkel | 1968 | 20.00 |
| ❑ SR 61216 | The Don Costa Concept | 1969 | 20.00 |
| **UNITED ARTISTS** | | | |
| ❑ UAL 3119 [M] | The Unforgiven | 1960 | 20.00 |
| ❑ UAL 3134 [M] | Magnificent Motion Picture Music | 1960 | 15.00 |
| ❑ WW 3513 [M] | The Sound of the Million Sellers | 1960 | 15.00 |
| ❑ UAS 6134 [S] | Magnificent Motion Picture Music | 1960 | 20.00 |
| ❑ WW 7501 [M] | Echoing Voices and Trombones | 1960 | 20.00 |
| ❑ WWS 8501 [S] | Echoing Voices and Trombones | 1960 | 30.00 |
| ❑ WWS 8513 [S] | The Sound of the Million Sellers | 1960 | 25.00 |
| **VERVE** | | | |
| ❑ V-8702 [M] | Modern Delights | 1967 | 20.00 |
| ❑ V6-8702 [S] | Modern Delights | 1967 | 15.00 |

### COSTA, EDDIE

| Number | Title (A Side/B Side) | Yr | NM |
|---|---|---|---|
| **CORAL** | | | |
| ❑ CRL 57230 [M] | Guys and Dolls Like Vibes | 1958 | 200.00 |
| **DOT** | | | |
| ❑ DLP-3206 [M] | The House of Blue Lights | 1959 | 600.00 |
| ❑ DLP-25206 [S] | The House of Blue Lights | 1959 | 500.00 |
| **INTERLUDE** | | | |
| ❑ MO-508 [M] | Eddie Costa Quintet | 1959 | 100.00 |
| *—Reissue of Mode 118* | | | |
| ❑ ST-1008 [S] | Eddie Costa Quintet | 1959 | 60.00 |
| **JOSIE** | | | |
| ❑ JSS-2509 [S] | Eddie Costa with the Burke Trio | 1963 | 25.00 |
| ❑ JOZ-3509 [M] | Eddie Costa with the Burke Trio | 1963 | 20.00 |
| **JUBILEE** | | | |
| ❑ JLP-1025 [M] | Eddie Costa Quintet with the Vinnie Burke Trio | 1956 | 60.00 |
| **MODE** | | | |
| ❑ LP-118 [M] | Eddie Costa Quintet | 1957 | 250.00 |

### COSTA, EDDIE/MAT MATTHEWS AND DON ELLIOTT

| Number | Title (A Side/B Side) | Yr | NM |
|---|---|---|---|
| **VERVE** | | | |
| ❑ MGV-8237 [M] | Eddie Costa with Rolf Kuhn and Dick Johnson/Mat Matthews and Don Elliott at Newport | 1958 | 60.00 |
| ❑ V-8237 [M] | Eddie Costa with Rolf Kuhn and Dick Johnson/Mat Matthews and Don Elliott at Newport | 1961 | 30.00 |

### COSTA, JOHNNY

| Number | Title (A Side/B Side) | Yr | NM |
|---|---|---|---|
| **CORAL** | | | |
| ❑ CRL 57117 [M] | The Most Beautiful Girl in the World | 1957 | 30.00 |
| **SAVOY** | | | |
| ❑ MG-12052 [M] | The Amazing Johnny Costa | 1956 | 50.00 |
| ❑ MG-15056 [10] | Johnny Costa | 1955 | 80.00 |

### COSTANZO, JACK

| Number | Title (A Side/B Side) | Yr | NM |
|---|---|---|---|
| **GENE NORMAN** | | | |
| ❑ GNP-19 [M] | Mr. Bongo | 1955 | 50.00 |
| **LIBERTY** | | | |
| ❑ LRP-3093 [M] | Latin Fever | 1958 | 25.00 |
| ❑ LRP-3109 [M] | Bongo Fever | 1959 | 25.00 |
| ❑ LRP-3137 [M] | Afro Can-Can | 1960 | 25.00 |
| ❑ LRP-3177 [M] | Learn-Play Bongos | 1960 | 25.00 |
| ❑ LRP-3195 [M] | Naked City | 1961 | 25.00 |
| ❑ LST-7020 [S] | Latin Fever | 1958 | 30.00 |
| ❑ LST-7109 [S] | Bongo Fever | 1959 | 30.00 |
| ❑ LST-7137 [S] | Afro Can-Can | 1960 | 30.00 |
| ❑ LST-7195 [S] | Naked City | 1961 | 30.00 |
| **NORGRAN** | | | |
| ❑ MGN-32 [10] | Afro-Cubano | 1954 | 150.00 |

Elvis Costello, *This Year's Model,* Columbia JC 35331, 1978, "Costello" labels, $12.

### COSTANZO, JACK/ANDRE'S CUBAN ALL STARS

**NORGRAN**

| Number | Title (A Side/B Side) | Yr | NM |
|---|---|---|---|
| ❑ MGN-1067 [M] | Afro-Cubano | 1956 | 100.00 |
| *—Combined reissue of Norgran 32 (by the former) and Clef 515 (by the latter)* | | | |

**VERVE**

| Number | Title (A Side/B Side) | Yr | NM |
|---|---|---|---|
| ❑ MGV-8157 [M] | Afro-Cubano | 1957 | 50.00 |
| ❑ V-8157 [M] | Afro-Cubano | 1961 | 25.00 |

### COSTELLO, ELVIS

**COLUMBIA**

| Number | Title (A Side/B Side) | Yr | NM |
|---|---|---|---|
| ❑ (no #) [PD] | My Aim Is True/This Year's Model | 1978 | 80.00 |
| *—Promo-only picture disc; contains six songs from one album and six from the other* | | | |
| ❑ AS 529 [EP] | Live at Hollywood High | 1978 | 20.00 |
| *—Promo-only 12-inch version of 7-inch single* | | | |
| ❑ AS 958 [DJ] | The Elvis Costello Interview with Tom Snyder | 1981 | 20.00 |
| ❑ AS 1318 [DJ] | Almost Blue: Elvis Introduces His Favorite Country Songs | 1981 | 50.00 |
| *—Radio sampler with introductions by Elvis before each track* | | | |
| ❑ JC 35037 | My Aim Is True | 1977 | 15.00 |
| *—First pressings have yellow back covers* | | | |
| ❑ JC 35037 | My Aim Is True | 1978 | 10.00 |
| *—Second pressings have a white back cover and no bar code* | | | |
| ❑ PC 35037 | My Aim Is True | 1984 | 8.00 |
| *—Budget-line reissue with new prefix* | | | |
| ❑ JC 35331 | This Year's Model | 1978 | 10.00 |
| *—With standard Columbia label* | | | |
| ❑ JC 35331 | This Year's Model | 1978 | 12.00 |
| *—With "Costello" replacing "Columbia" on labels* | | | |
| ❑ PC 35331 | This Year's Model | 1984 | 8.00 |
| *—Budget-line reissue with new prefix* | | | |
| ❑ JC 35709 | Armed Forces | 1979 | 10.00 |
| *—Stock copy; add 30 percent if bonus 7-inch single is there; add another 50 percent if the 7-inch's picture sleeve is there* | | | |
| ❑ JC 35709 [DJ] | Armed Forces | 1979 | 15.00 |
| *—White label promo; add 20 percent if bonus 7-inch single is there; add another 33 percent if the 7-inch's picture sleeve is there* | | | |
| ❑ PC 35709 | Armed Forces | 1984 | 8.00 |
| *—Budget-line reissue with new prefix; not issued with bonus single* | | | |
| ❑ JC 36347 | Get Happy!! | 1980 | 10.00 |
| ❑ PC 36347 | Get Happy!! | 1984 | 8.00 |
| *—Budget-line reissue with new prefix* | | | |
| ❑ JC 36839 | Taking Liberties | 1980 | 8.00 |
| ❑ JC 36839 | Taking Liberties | 1980 | 10.00 |
| *—With custom old-style Columbia label* | | | |
| ❑ PC 36839 | Taking Liberties | 1984 | 8.00 |
| *—Budget-line reissue with new prefix* | | | |
| ❑ JC 37051 | Trust | 1981 | 10.00 |
| ❑ PC 37051 | Trust | 1984 | 8.00 |
| *—Budget-line reissue with new prefix* | | | |
| ❑ FC 37562 | Almost Blue | 1981 | 10.00 |
| ❑ PC 37562 | Almost Blue | 1984 | 8.00 |
| *—Budget-line reissue with new prefix* | | | |
| ❑ FC 38157 | Imperial Bedroom | 1982 | 10.00 |
| ❑ PC 38157 | Imperial Bedroom | 1984 | 8.00 |
| *—Budget-line reissue with new prefix* | | | |
| ❑ FC 38897 | Punch the Clock | 1983 | 10.00 |
| ❑ FC 39429 | Goodbye Cruel World | 1984 | 10.00 |
| ❑ PC 39429 | Goodbye Cruel World | 198? | 8.00 |
| *—Budget-line reissue with new prefix* | | | |
| ❑ FC 40101 | The Best of Elvis Costello | 1985 | 12.00 |
| ❑ FC 40173 | King of America | 1986 | 10.00 |
| *—By "The Costello Show Featuring Elvis Costello"* | | | |
| ❑ PC 40173 | King of America | 198? | 8.00 |
| *—By "The Costello Show Featuring Elvis Costello"; budget-line reissue with new prefix* | | | |
| ❑ FC 40518 | Blood & Chocolate | 1986 | 10.00 |
| ❑ HC 48157 | Imperial Bedroom | 1982 | 50.00 |
| *—Half-speed mastered edition* | | | |

**COSTELLO**

| Number | Title (A Side/B Side) | Yr | NM |
|---|---|---|---|
| ❑ AS 847 [EP] | Taking Liberties | 1980 | 15.00 |
| *—Promo-only four-song sampler' "Costello" is where "Columbia" would normally be on the 78-rpm-style label* | | | |

**LOST HIGHWAY**

| Number | Title (A Side/B Side) | Yr | NM |
|---|---|---|---|
| ❑ B0002593-01 [(2)] | The Delivery Man | 2004 | 20.00 |
| ❑ B0003905-01 [10] | Delta-Verite: The Clarksdale Sessions | 2005 | 10.00 |
| ❑ B0003905-01 [10] | Delta-Verite: The Clarksdale Sessions | 2005 | 10.00 |
| *—Black vinyl; this album has been counterfeited; originals have a white border around all four sides of the front cover and the words "The Round-Up Factor" at the bottom of the back cover, and counterfeits do not; also, counterfeits use the catalog number "CN-005" and have white labels* | | | |

**RHINO**

| Number | Title (A Side/B Side) | Yr | NM |
|---|---|---|---|
| ❑ R1-74285 | My Aim Is True | 2003 | 15.00 |
| *—180-gram vinyl; first U.S. issue of British track lineup* | | | |

**WARNER BROS.**

| Number | Title (A Side/B Side) | Yr | NM |
|---|---|---|---|
| ❑ PRO-A-3488 [(2)DJ] | The Elvis Costello Hour | 1989 | 40.00 |
| *—Music and interview; generic gatefold sleeve with sticker on cover* | | | |
| ❑ 25848 | Spike | 1989 | 10.00 |
| ❑ 46198 | All This Useless Beauty | 1996 | 100.00 |
| ❑ R 100841 | Spike | 1989 | 12.00 |
| *—BMG Direct Marketing edition* | | | |

### COTTON, JAMES

**ALLIGATOR**

| Number | Title (A Side/B Side) | Yr | NM |
|---|---|---|---|
| ❑ AL-4737 | High Compression | 1984 | 10.00 |
| ❑ AL-4746 | Live from Chicago | 1986 | 10.00 |

**ANTONE'S**

| Number | Title (A Side/B Side) | Yr | NM |
|---|---|---|---|
| ❑ ANT-0007 | James Cotton Live | 1988 | 12.00 |

**BLIND PIG**

| Number | Title (A Side/B Side) | Yr | NM |
|---|---|---|---|
| ❑ BP-2587 | Take Me Back | 1987 | 10.00 |

**BUDDAH**

| Number | Title (A Side/B Side) | Yr | NM |
|---|---|---|---|
| ❑ BDS-5620 | 100% Cotton | 1974 | 12.00 |
| ❑ BDS-5650 | High Energy | 1975 | 12.00 |
| ❑ BDS-5661 [(2)] | Live & On the Move! | 1976 | 15.00 |

**CAPITOL**

| Number | Title (A Side/B Side) | Yr | NM |
|---|---|---|---|
| ❑ SM-814 | Taking Care of Business | 197? | 10.00 |
| *—Reissue with new prefix* | | | |
| ❑ ST-814 | Taking Care of Business | 1971 | 15.00 |

**INTERMEDIA**

| Number | Title (A Side/B Side) | Yr | NM |
|---|---|---|---|
| ❑ QS-5006 | Dealing with the Devil | 198? | 10.00 |
| ❑ QS-5011 | Two Sides of the Blues | 198? | 10.00 |

**VANGUARD**

| Number | Title (A Side/B Side) | Yr | NM |
|---|---|---|---|
| ❑ VSD-79283 | Cut You Loose! | 1969 | 15.00 |

**VERVE FORECAST**

| Number | Title (A Side/B Side) | Yr | NM |
|---|---|---|---|
| ❑ FT-3023 [M] | The James Cotton Blues Band | 1967 | 25.00 |
| ❑ FTS-3023 [S] | The James Cotton Blues Band | 1967 | 20.00 |
| ❑ FTS-3038 | Pure Cotton | 1968 | 20.00 |

### COTTON PICKERS, THE

**PHILIPS**

| Number | Title (A Side/B Side) | Yr | NM |
|---|---|---|---|
| ❑ PHM 200025 [M] | Country Guitar | 1962 | 20.00 |
| ❑ PHS 600025 [S] | Country Guitar | 1962 | 25.00 |

### COTTRELL, LOUIS

**RIVERSIDE**

| Number | Title (A Side/B Side) | Yr | NM |
|---|---|---|---|
| ❑ RLP-385 [M] | Bourbon Street | 1961 | 20.00 |
| ❑ RS-9385 [S] | Bourbon Street | 1961 | 25.00 |

### COUCH, ORVILLE

**VEE JAY**

| Number | Title (A Side/B Side) | Yr | NM |
|---|---|---|---|
| ❑ VJLP-1087 [M] | Hello Trouble | 1964 | 20.00 |
| ❑ VJS-1087 [S] | Hello Trouble | 1964 | 40.00 |

### COULTER, CLIFF

**ABC IMPULSE!**

| Number | Title (A Side/B Side) | Yr | NM |
|---|---|---|---|
| ❑ AS-9197 | Eastside San Jose | 1971 | 20.00 |
| ❑ AS-9216 | Do It Now! | 1972 | 20.00 |

### COUNCE, CURTIS

**CONTEMPORARY**

| Number | Title (A Side/B Side) | Yr | NM |
|---|---|---|---|
| ❑ C-3526 [M] | Curtis Counce Group | 1957 | 80.00 |
| ❑ M-3539 [M] | You Get More Bounce with Curtis Counce | 1957 | 80.00 |
| ❑ M-3574 [M] | Carl's Blues | 1960 | 40.00 |
| ❑ S-7526 [S] | Curtis Counce Group | 1959 | 60.00 |
| ❑ S-7526 [S] | Landslide | 196? | 30.00 |
| *—Retitled version of "Curtis Counce Group"* | | | |
| ❑ C-7539 | Counceltation | 197? | 20.00 |
| *—Retitled version of "You Get More Bounce with Curtis Counce"* | | | |
| ❑ S-7539 [S] | You Get More Bounce with Curtis Counce | 1959 | 60.00 |
| ❑ S-7574 [S] | Carl's Blues | 1960 | 50.00 |
| ❑ C-7655 | Sonority | 198? | 20.00 |

**DOOTO**

| Number | Title (A Side/B Side) | Yr | NM |
|---|---|---|---|
| ❑ DTL-247 [M] | Exploring the Future | 1958 | 50.00 |

### COUNT FIVE, THE

**DOUBLE SHOT**

| Number | Title (A Side/B Side) | Yr | NM |
|---|---|---|---|
| ❑ DSM-1001 [M] | Psychotic Reaction | 1966 | 40.00 |
| ❑ DSS-5001 [R] | Psychotic Reaction | 1966 | 25.00 |

### COUNTING CROWS

**DGC**

| Number | Title (A Side/B Side) | Yr | NM |
|---|---|---|---|
| ❑ DGC2-24975 [(2)] | Recovering the Satellites | 1996 | 50.00 |
| ❑ 069 490415-1 [(2)] | This Desert Life | 1999 | 50.00 |
| *—Side 2 of the second record is blank* | | | |

### COUNTRY ALL-STARS, THE

**RCA VICTOR**

| Number | Title (A Side/B Side) | Yr | NM |
|---|---|---|---|
| ❑ LPM-3167 [10] | String Dustin' | 1953 | 150.00 |

### COUNTRY CUT-UPS, THE

**TOWN HOUSE**

| Number | Title (A Side/B Side) | Yr | NM |
|---|---|---|---|
| ❑ 1000 [M] | The Country Cut-Ups Go to College | 195? | 80.00 |

### COUNTRY GENTLEMEN, THE

**CIMARRON**

| Number | Title (A Side/B Side) | Yr | NM |
|---|---|---|---|
| ❑ 2001 [M] | Songs of the Pioneers | 1962 | 40.00 |



Except when noted otherwise, VG = 25% of NM, and VG+ = 50% of NM. (Example: VG = $2.00, VG+ = $4.00 and NM = $8.00.)

| Number | Title (A Side/B Side) | Yr | NM |
|---|---|---|---|
| **MERCURY** | | | |
| ❑ MG-20858 [M] | Folk Session Inside | 1963 | 20.00 |
| ❑ SR-60858 [S] | Folk Session Inside | 1963 | 25.00 |
| **STARDAY** | | | |
| ❑ SLP-109 [M] | Traveling Dobro Blues | 1959 | 50.00 |
| ❑ SLP-174 [M] | Bluegrass at Carnegie Hall | 1962 | 40.00 |
| ❑ SLP-311 [M] | Songs of the Pioneers | 1965 | 25.00 |

### COUNTRY GOSPELAIRES, THE

| Number | Title (A Side/B Side) | Yr | NM |
|---|---|---|---|
| **STARDAY** | | | |
| ❑ SLP-105 [M] | The Church Back Home | 1959 | 30.00 |

### COUNTRY JOE AND THE FISH

| Number | Title (A Side/B Side) | Yr | NM |
|---|---|---|---|
| **CUSTOM FIDELITY** | | | |
| ❑ CFS-2348 | Joe McDonald | 1968 | 1000. |
| *—Recorded in 1964, 200 copies were pressed for Joe McDonald; VG value 500; VG+ value 750* | | | |
| **FANTASY** | | | |
| ❑ 9495 | Paradise with an Ocean View | 1975 | 10.00 |
| ❑ 9511 | Love Is a Fire | 1976 | 10.00 |
| ❑ 9525 | Goodbye Blues | 1977 | 10.00 |
| ❑ 9530 | Reunion | 1977 | 12.00 |
| ❑ 9544 | Rock and Roll Music From the Planet Earth | 1978 | 10.00 |
| ❑ 9586 | Leisure Suite | 1980 | 10.00 |
| **FIRST AMERICAN** | | | |
| ❑ PIC-3309 | The Early Years | 1979 | 10.00 |
| **MOBLIE FIDELITY** | | | |
| ❑ 1-056 | Paradise with an Ocean View | 1981 | 30.00 |
| *—Audiophile vinyl* | | | |
| **VANGUARD** | | | |
| ❑ VSD-27/28 [(2)] | The Life and Times of Country Joe & the Fish From Haight-Ashbury to Woodstock | 1971 | 20.00 |
| ❑ VSD-85/86 [(2)] | The Essential Country Joe | 1977 | 12.00 |
| ❑ VSD-6545 | Country Joe & The Fish/ Greatest Hits | 1969 | 20.00 |
| ❑ VSD-6546 | Thinking of Woody | 1969 | 15.00 |
| ❑ VSD-6555 | C.J. Fish | 1970 | 20.00 |
| ❑ VSD-6557 | Tonight I'm Singing Just for You | 1970 | 15.00 |
| ❑ VRS-9244 [M] | Electric Music for the Mind and Body | 1967 | 20.00 |
| *—Gold label* | | | |
| ❑ VRS-9244 [M] | Electric Music for the Mind and Body | 1967 | 100.00 |
| *—Black label* | | | |
| ❑ 9266/79266 | I-Feel-Like-I'm-Fixin'-to-Die "Fish Game" Poster | 1967 | 10.00 |
| ❑ VRS-9266 [M] | I-Feel-Like-I'm-Fixin'-to-Die | 1967 | 20.00 |
| ❑ VSQ-40004/5 [(2)Q] | The Life and Times of Country Joe & the Fish From Haight-Ashbury to Woodstock | 197? | 40.00 |
| ❑ VSD-79244 [S] | Electric Music for the Mind and Body | 1967 | 20.00 |
| *—Gold label* | | | |
| ❑ VSD-79244 [S] | Electric Music for the Mind and Body | 1967 | 50.00 |
| *—Black label* | | | |
| ❑ VSD-79266 [S] | I-Feel-Like-I'm-Fixin'-to-Die | 1967 | 20.00 |
| ❑ VSD-79277 | Together | 1968 | 20.00 |
| ❑ VSD-79299 | Here We Are Again | 1969 | 20.00 |
| ❑ VSD-79304 | Hold On It's Coming | 1971 | 15.00 |
| ❑ VSD-79315 | War, War, War | 1971 | 15.00 |
| ❑ VSD-79316 | Incredible! Live! | 1972 | 12.00 |
| ❑ VSD-79328 | Paris Sessions | 1973 | 12.00 |
| ❑ VSD-79348 | Country Joe | 1974 | 12.00 |

### COUNTRY MIKE Actually Mike D of BEASTIE BOYS.

| Number | Title (A Side/B Side) | Yr | NM |
|---|---|---|---|
| **GRAND ROYAL** | | | |
| ❑ CM-1 | Country Mike's Greatest Hits | 2000 | 200.00 |
| *—Black vinyl; this album has been counterfeited; originals have a white border around all four sides of the front cover and the words "The Round-Up Factor" at the bottom of the back cover, and counterfeits do not; also, counterfeits use the catalog number "CN-005" and have white labels* | | | |
| ❑ CM-1 | Country Mike's Greatest Hits | 2000 | 300.00 |
| *—Red vinyl* | | | |

### COUNTS, THE (2) Detroit-based funk group.

| Number | Title (A Side/B Side) | Yr | NM |
|---|---|---|---|
| **AWARE** | | | |
| ❑ 2002 | Love Sign | 1973 | 25.00 |
| ❑ 2006 | Funk Pump | 1975 | 20.00 |
| **WESTBOUND** | | | |
| ❑ 2011 | What's Up Front That Counts | 1972 | 30.00 |

### COURTLAND, JEROME

| Number | Title (A Side/B Side) | Yr | NM |
|---|---|---|---|
| **JUBILEE** | | | |
| ❑ LP 22 [10] | Through a Long and Sleepless Night | 1955 | 40.00 |

### COURTNEY, LOU

| Number | Title (A Side/B Side) | Yr | NM |
|---|---|---|---|
| **EPIC** | | | |
| ❑ KE 33011 | I'm in Need of Love | 1974 | 12.00 |
| **RCA VICTOR** | | | |
| ❑ APL1-1969 | Buffalo Smoke | 1976 | 12.00 |

Country Joe & the Fish, *Greatest Hits,* Vanguard VSD-6545, 1969, $20.

| Number | Title (A Side/B Side) | Yr | NM |
|---|---|---|---|
| **RIVERSIDE** | | | |
| ❑ 92000 | Skate Now (Shing-a-Ling) | 1967 | 25.00 |

### COUSIN WILBUR

| Number | Title (A Side/B Side) | Yr | NM |
|---|---|---|---|
| **C.W.** | | | |
| ❑ 100 [M] | The Cousin Wilbur Show | 195? | 50.00 |

### COUSINS, THE (2)

| Number | Title (A Side/B Side) | Yr | NM |
|---|---|---|---|
| **PARKWAY** | | | |
| ❑ P-7005 [M] | Music of the Strip | 1961 | 20.00 |
| ❑ SP-7005 [S] | Music of the Strip | 1961 | 25.00 |

### COVAY, DON

| Number | Title (A Side/B Side) | Yr | NM |
|---|---|---|---|
| **ATLANTIC** | | | |
| ❑ 8104 [M] | Mercy | 1965 | 40.00 |
| ❑ SD 8104 [S] | Mercy | 1965 | 50.00 |
| ❑ 8120 [M] | See Saw | 1966 | 40.00 |
| ❑ SD 8120 [S] | See Saw | 1966 | 50.00 |
| ❑ SD 8237 | The House of Blue Lights | 1969 | 25.00 |
| **JANUS** | | | |
| ❑ 3038 | Different Strokes for Different Folks | 1972 | 15.00 |
| **MERCURY** | | | |
| ❑ SRM-1-653 | Super Dude I | 1973 | 12.00 |
| ❑ SRM-1-1020 | Hot Blood | 1974 | 12.00 |
| ❑ 835030-1 | Checkin' In with Don Covay | 1988 | 10.00 |
| **PHILADELPHIA INT'L.** | | | |
| ❑ PZ 33958 | Travelin' In Heavy Traffic | 1977 | 10.00 |

### COWARD, NOEL

| Number | Title (A Side/B Side) | Yr | NM |
|---|---|---|---|
| **COLUMBIA MASTERWORKS** | | | |
| ❑ ML 5063 [M] | Noel Coward at Las Vegas | 1955 | 30.00 |

### COWARD, NOEL, AND GERTRUDE LAWRENCE

| Number | Title (A Side/B Side) | Yr | NM |
|---|---|---|---|
| **RCA VICTOR** | | | |
| ❑ LPM-1156 [M] | Noel and Gertie | 1955 | 30.00 |

### COWBOY JUNKIES

| Number | Title (A Side/B Side) | Yr | NM |
|---|---|---|---|
| **LATENT RECORDINGS** | | | |
| ❑ LATEX 4 | Whites Off Earth Now!! | 1986 | 30.00 |
| *—Canada-only release* | | | |
| **RCA** | | | |
| ❑ 8568-1-R | The Trinity Session | 1988 | 15.00 |
| ❑ 8568-1-R | The Trinity Session | 1997 | 40.00 |
| *—Classic Records reissue on audiophile vinyl* | | | |

### COWELL, STANLEY

| Number | Title (A Side/B Side) | Yr | NM |
|---|---|---|---|
| **ECM** | | | |
| ❑ 1026 | Illusion Suite | 1973 | 25.00 |
| **STRATA-EAST** | | | |
| ❑ SES-19743 | Musa-Ancestral Streams | 1974 | 20.00 |
| ❑ SES-19765 | Regeneration | 1976 | 20.00 |

### COWSILLS, THE

| Number | Title (A Side/B Side) | Yr | NM |
|---|---|---|---|
| **LONDON** | | | |
| ❑ PS 587 | On My Side | 1971 | 30.00 |
| **MGM** | | | |
| ❑ GAS-103 | The Cowsills (Golden Archive Series) | 1970 | 15.00 |
| ❑ E-4498 [M] | The Cowsills | 1967 | 20.00 |
| ❑ SE-4498 [S] | The Cowsills | 1967 | 15.00 |
| ❑ E-4534 [M] | We Can Fly | 1968 | 30.00 |
| *—Appears to exist only as a yellow label promo* | | | |
| ❑ SE-4534 [S] | We Can Fly | 1968 | 15.00 |
| ❑ E-4554 [M] | Captain Sad and His Ship of Fools | 1968 | 40.00 |
| *—Mono appears to be yellow label promo only* | | | |
| ❑ SE-4554 [S] | Captain Sad and His Ship of Fools | 1968 | 15.00 |
| ❑ SE-4597 | The Best of the Cowsills | 1968 | 15.00 |
| ❑ SE-4619 | The Cowsills in Concert | 1969 | 15.00 |
| ❑ SE-4639 | II X II | 1969 | 20.00 |
| **WING** | | | |
| ❑ SRW-16354 | The Cowsills Plus the Lincoln Park Zoo | 1968 | 12.00 |

### COX, DANNY

| Number | Title (A Side/B Side) | Yr | NM |
|---|---|---|---|
| **PIONEER** | | | |
| ❑ 2125 | Sunny | 196? | 30.00 |
| **TOGETHER** | | | |
| ❑ 1011 | Birth Announcement | 1970 | 30.00 |

### COX, IDA

| Number | Title (A Side/B Side) | Yr | NM |
|---|---|---|---|
| **RIVERSIDE** | | | |
| ❑ RLP-374 [M] | Blues for Rampart Street | 1961 | 30.00 |
| ❑ RS-9374 [S] | Blues for Rampart Street | 1961 | 40.00 |

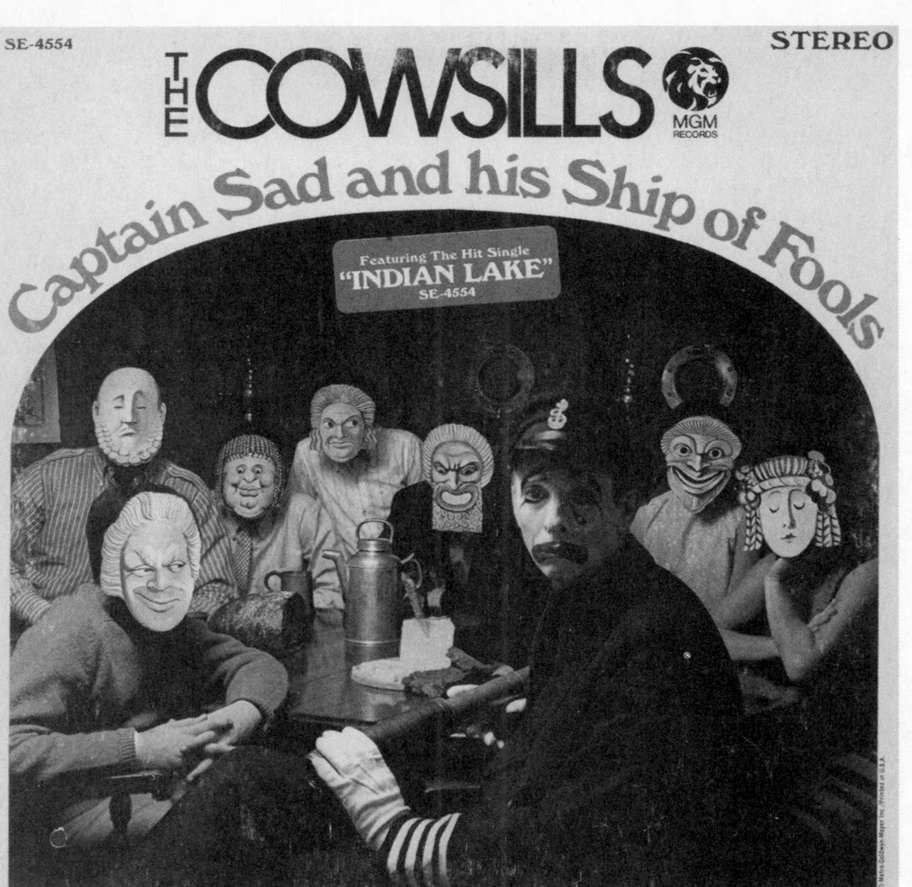

SE-4554
STEREO
THE COWSILLS
MGM RECORDS
Captain Sad and his Ship of Fools
Featuring The Hit Single
"INDIAN LAKE"
SE-4554


The Cowsills, *Captain Sad and His Ship of Fools,* MGM SE-4554, 1968, blue and gold label, stereo, $15.

## COX, KENNY, CONTEMPORARY JAZZ QUINTET

**BLUE NOTE**

| Number | Title (A Side/B Side) | Yr | NM |
|---|---|---|---|
| ❑ BST-84302 | Introducing Kenny Cox | 1969 | 20.00 |
| ❑ BST-84339 | Multidirection | 1970 | 20.00 |

## COX, SONNY

**CADET**

| Number | Title (A Side/B Side) | Yr | NM |
|---|---|---|---|
| ❑ LPS-765 [S] | The Wailer | 1966 | 20.00 |

## COXON'S ARMY Also see PAT BENATAR.

**TRACE**

| Number | Title (A Side/B Side) | Yr | NM |
|---|---|---|---|
| ❑ (# unknown) | Coxon's Army | 1975 | 400.00 |

## CRADDOCK, BILLY "CRASH"

**ABC**

| Number | Title (A Side/B Side) | Yr | NM |
|---|---|---|---|
| ❑ X-777 | Two Sides of "Crash" | 1973 | 15.00 |
| *—Retitled version of above* | | | |
| ❑ X-777 | Afraid I'll Want to Love Her One More Time | 1973 | 25.00 |
| ❑ X-788 | Mr. Country Rock | 1973 | 15.00 |
| ❑ X-817 | Rub It In | 1974 | 12.00 |
| *—Multicolor label* | | | |
| ❑ X-817 | Rub It In | 1974 | 15.00 |
| *—Black label* | | | |
| ❑ X-850 | Greatest Hits — Volume One | 1975 | 12.00 |
| ❑ ABCD-875 | Still Thinkin' Bout You | 1975 | 12.00 |
| ❑ AB-1078 | Billy "Crash" Craddock Sings His Greatest Hits | 1978 | 10.00 |

**ABC DOT**

| Number | Title (A Side/B Side) | Yr | NM |
|---|---|---|---|
| ❑ DOSD-2040 | Easy As Pie | 1976 | 12.00 |
| ❑ 2063 | Crash | 1976 | 12.00 |
| ❑ 2082 | Live! | 1977 | 12.00 |

**ATLANTIC**

| Number | Title (A Side/B Side) | Yr | NM |
|---|---|---|---|
| ❑ 82012 | Back on Track | 1989 | 12.00 |

**CAPITOL**

| Number | Title (A Side/B Side) | Yr | NM |
|---|---|---|---|
| ❑ ST-11758 | Billy "Crash" Craddock | 1978 | 10.00 |
| ❑ SW-11853 | Turning Up and Turning On | 1978 | 10.00 |
| ❑ ST-11946 | Laughing and Crying, Living and Dying | 1979 | 10.00 |
| ❑ ST-12054 | Changes | 1980 | 10.00 |
| ❑ ST-12249 | The New Will Never Wear Off | 1981 | 10.00 |
| ❑ ST-12304 | Greatest Hits | 1983 | 10.00 |

**CARTWHEEL**

| Number | Title (A Side/B Side) | Yr | NM |
|---|---|---|---|
| ❑ 193 | Knock Three Times | 1971 | 20.00 |
| ❑ 05001 | You Better Move On | 1972 | 20.00 |

**CHART**

| Number | Title (A Side/B Side) | Yr | NM |
|---|---|---|---|
| ❑ 1053 | The Best of Billy Crash Craddock | 1973 | 15.00 |

**HARMONY**

| Number | Title (A Side/B Side) | Yr | NM |
|---|---|---|---|
| ❑ KH 32186 | Billy "Crash" Craddock | 1973 | 12.00 |

**KING**

| Number | Title (A Side/B Side) | Yr | NM |
|---|---|---|---|
| ❑ 912 [M] | I'm Tore Up | 1964 | 100.00 |

**MCA**

| Number | Title (A Side/B Side) | Yr | NM |
|---|---|---|---|
| ❑ 662 | Greatest Hits — Volume One | 1981 | 8.00 |
| *—Reissue of ABC 850* | | | |
| ❑ 663 | Billy "Crash" Craddock Sings His Greatest Hits | 1981 | 8.00 |
| *—Reissue of ABC 1078* | | | |
| ❑ 664 | Easy As Pie | 1981 | 8.00 |
| *—Reissue of ABC Dot 2040* | | | |
| ❑ 665 | Live! | 1981 | 8.00 |
| *—Reissue of ABC Dot 2082* | | | |
| ❑ 666 | The First Time | 1981 | 8.00 |
| ❑ 4165 [(2)] | The Best of Billy "Crash" Craddock | 198? | 12.00 |

**MCA DOT**

| Number | Title (A Side/B Side) | Yr | NM |
|---|---|---|---|
| ❑ 39054 | Crash Craddock | 1986 | 10.00 |

**STARDAY**

| Number | Title (A Side/B Side) | Yr | NM |
|---|---|---|---|
| ❑ 3005 | 16 Favorite Hits | 1978 | 10.00 |

## CRAMER, FLOYD

**MGM**

| Number | Title (A Side/B Side) | Yr | NM |
|---|---|---|---|
| ❑ E-3502 [M] | That Honky-Tonk Piano | 1957 | 40.00 |
| ❑ E-4223 [M] | Floyd Cramer Goes Honky Tonkin' | 1964 | 15.00 |
| ❑ SE-4223 [R] | Floyd Cramer Goes Honky Tonkin' | 1964 | 12.00 |
| ❑ SE-4666 | Floyd Cramer Goes Honky Tonkin' | 1970 | 12.00 |
| *—Reissue of 4223* | | | |

**PAIR**

| Number | Title (A Side/B Side) | Yr | NM |
|---|---|---|---|
| ❑ PDL2-1049 [(2)] | Country Classics | 1986 | 12.00 |

**RCA**

| Number | Title (A Side/B Side) | Yr | NM |
|---|---|---|---|
| ❑ 5621-1-R | Our Class Reunion | 1987 | 10.00 |

**RCA CAMDEN**

| Number | Title (A Side/B Side) | Yr | NM |
|---|---|---|---|
| ❑ ACL2-0128 [(2)] | Floyd Cramer Plays the Big Hits | 1973 | 12.00 |
| ❑ ACL1-0563 | Spotlight On Floyd Cramer | 1974 | 10.00 |
| ❑ CAL-874 [M] | The Magic Touch | 1965 | 12.00 |
| ❑ CAS-874(e) [P] | The Magic Touch | 1965 | 12.00 |
| *—Even though this album is labeled "Stereo Electronically Reprocessed," nine of the 10 tracks are in true stereo* | | | |
| ❑ CAL-2104 [M] | Distinctive Piano Styling | 196? | 12.00 |
| ❑ CAS-2104 [S] | Distinctive Piano Styling | 196? | 12.00 |
| ❑ CAL-2152 [M] | Night Train | 1967 | 12.00 |
| ❑ CAS-2152 [S] | Night Train | 1967 | 12.00 |
| ❑ CAS-2508 | Almost Persuaded | 1971 | 12.00 |
| ❑ CXS-9016 [(2)] | A Date with Floyd Cramer | 1972 | 15.00 |

**RCA VICTOR**

| Number | Title (A Side/B Side) | Yr | NM |
|---|---|---|---|
| ❑ APD1-0155 [Q] | Super Country Hits | 1973 | 15.00 |
| *—All copies are in quadraphonic* | | | |
| ❑ APD1-0299 [Q] | Class of '73 | 1973 | 15.00 |
| ❑ APL1-0299 | Class of '73 | 1973 | 12.00 |
| ❑ APD1-0469 [Q] | The Young and the Restless | 1974 | 15.00 |
| ❑ APL1-0469 | The Young and the Restless | 1974 | 12.00 |
| ❑ APL1-0661 | Floyd Cramer In Concert | 1974 | 12.00 |
| ❑ APD1-0893 [Q] | Piano Masterpieces (1900-75) | 1975 | 15.00 |
| ❑ APL1-0893 | Piano Masterpieces (1900-75) | 1975 | 10.00 |
| ❑ APD1-1191 [Q] | Class of '74 and '75 | 1975 | 15.00 |
| ❑ APL1-1191 | Class of '74 and '75 | 1975 | 10.00 |
| ❑ APD1-1541 [Q] | Floyd Cramer Country | 1976 | 15.00 |
| ❑ APL1-1541 | Floyd Cramer Country | 1976 | 10.00 |
| ❑ LPM-2151 [M] | Hello Blues | 1960 | 15.00 |
| ❑ LSP-2151 [S] | Hello Blues | 1960 | 20.00 |
| ❑ APL1-2278 | Floyd Cramer & the Keyboard Kick Band | 1977 | 10.00 |
| ❑ ANL1-2344 | Hits from Country Hall | 1977 | 10.00 |
| ❑ LPM-2350 [M] | Last Date | 1961 | 20.00 |
| ❑ LSP-2350 [S] | Last Date | 1961 | 25.00 |
| ❑ LPM-2359 [M] | On the Rebound | 1961 | 15.00 |
| ❑ LSP-2359 [S] | On the Rebound | 1961 | 20.00 |
| ❑ LPM-2428 [M] | Floyd Cramer Gets Organ-ized | 1962 | 15.00 |
| ❑ LSP-2428 [S] | Floyd Cramer Gets Organ-ized | 1962 | 20.00 |
| ❑ LPM-2466 [M] | America's Biggest Selling Pianist | 1962 | 15.00 |
| ❑ LSP-2466 [S] | America's Biggest Selling Pianist | 1962 | 20.00 |
| ❑ LPM-2544 [M] | I Remember Hank Williams | 1962 | 15.00 |
| ❑ LSP-2544 [S] | I Remember Hank Williams | 1962 | 20.00 |
| ❑ LPM-2642 [M] | Swing Along | 1963 | 15.00 |
| ❑ LSP-2642 [S] | Swing Along | 1963 | 20.00 |
| ❑ AHL1-2644 | Looking for Mr. Goodbar | 1978 | 10.00 |
| ❑ LPM-2701 [M] | Comin' On | 1963 | 15.00 |
| ❑ LSP-2701 [S] | Comin' On | 1963 | 20.00 |
| ❑ LPM-2800 [M] | Country Piano — City Strings | 1964 | 15.00 |
| ❑ LSP-2800 [S] | Country Piano — City Strings | 1964 | 20.00 |
| ❑ LPM-2883 [M] | Cramer at the Console | 1964 | 15.00 |
| ❑ LSP-2883 [S] | Cramer at the Console | 1964 | 20.00 |
| ❑ LPM-2888 [M] | The Best of Floyd Cramer | 1964 | 12.00 |
| ❑ LSP-2888 [S] | The Best of Floyd Cramer | 1964 | 15.00 |
| ❑ AHL1-3209 | Super Hits | 1979 | 10.00 |
| ❑ LPM-3318 [M] | Hits from the Country Hall of Fame | 1965 | 15.00 |
| ❑ LSP-3318 [S] | Hits from the Country Hall of Fame | 1965 | 20.00 |
| ❑ LPM-3405 [M] | Class of '65 | 1965 | 12.00 |
| ❑ LSP-3405 [S] | Class of '65 | 1965 | 15.00 |
| ❑ ANL1-3469 | Floyd Cramer In Concert | 1979 | 8.00 |
| ❑ AHL1-3487 | Last Date | 1979 | 10.00 |
| ❑ LPM-3533 [M] | The Big Ones | 1966 | 12.00 |
| ❑ LSP-3533 [S] | The Big Ones | 1966 | 15.00 |
| ❑ AHL1-3613 | Dallas | 1980 | 10.00 |
| ❑ LPM-3650 [M] | Class of '66 | 1966 | 12.00 |
| ❑ LSP-3650 [S] | Class of '66 | 1966 | 15.00 |
| ❑ AYL1-3745 | Piano Masterpieces (1900-75) | 1980 | 8.00 |
| ❑ LPM-3746 [M] | Here's What's Happening! | 1967 | 15.00 |
| ❑ LSP-3746 [S] | Here's What's Happening! | 1967 | 15.00 |
| ❑ LPM-3811 [M] | Floyd Cramer Plays the Monkees | 1967 | 15.00 |
| ❑ LSP-3811 [S] | Floyd Cramer Plays the Monkees | 1967 | 15.00 |
| ❑ LPM-3827 [M] | Class of '67 | 1967 | 15.00 |
| ❑ LSP-3827 [S] | Class of '67 | 1967 | 15.00 |
| ❑ LPM-3828 [M] | We Wish You a Merry Christmas | 1967 | 30.00 |
| ❑ LSP-3828 [S] | We Wish You a Merry Christmas | 1967 | 12.00 |
| ❑ AYL1-3900 | The Best of Floyd Cramer | 1981 | 8.00 |
| ❑ LPM-3925 [M] | Floyd Cramer Plays Country Classics | 1968 | 20.00 |
| ❑ LSP-3925 [S] | Floyd Cramer Plays Country Classics | 1968 | 15.00 |
| ❑ AYL1-4008 | Great Country Hits | 1981 | 8.00 |
| ❑ LPM-4025 [M] | Class of '68 | 1968 | 50.00 |
| ❑ LSP-4025 [S] | Class of '68 | 1968 | 15.00 |
| ❑ LSP-4070 | MacArthur Park | 1968 | 15.00 |
| ❑ LSP-4091 | The Best of Floyd Cramer, Volume 2 | 1969 | 15.00 |
| ❑ AHL1-4119 | Best of the West | 1982 | 10.00 |
| ❑ LSP-4162 | Class of '69 | 1969 | 15.00 |
| ❑ LSP-4220 | Floyd Cramer Plays More Country Classics | 1969 | 15.00 |
| ❑ LSP-4312 | The Big Ones, Volume II | 1970 | 15.00 |

| Number | Title (A Side/B Side) | Yr | NM |
|---|---|---|---|
| ❑ LSP-4367 | Floyd Cramer with the Music City Pops | 1970 | 15.00 |
| ❑ LSP-4437 | Class of '70 | 1970 | 15.00 |
| ❑ LSP-4500 | Sounds of Sunday | 1971 | 15.00 |
| ❑ LSP-4590 | Class of '71 | 1971 | 15.00 |
| ❑ LSP-4676 | Detours | 1972 | 15.00 |
| ❑ LSP-4772 | Class of '72 | 1972 | 15.00 |
| ❑ LSP-4821 | Best of the Class of… | 1973 | 15.00 |
| ❑ AHL1-5452 | Collector's Series | 1985 | 10.00 |
| ❑ VPS-6031 [(2)] | This Is Floyd Cramer | 1970 | 20.00 |

### CRAMPS, THE

#### ENIGMA

| Number | Title (A Side/B Side) | Yr | NM |
|---|---|---|---|
| ❑ 21 | Smell of Female | 1983 | 15.00 |
| ❑ EPRO 268 [DJ] | Stay Sick! | 1990 | 25.00 |
| *—Promo-only version* | | | |
| ❑ 73543 | Stay Sick! | 1990 | 15.00 |

#### EPITAPH

| Number | Title (A Side/B Side) | Yr | NM |
|---|---|---|---|
| ❑ 86449 | Flamejob | 199? | 12.00 |
| *—Reissue of Medicine Label 24592* | | | |
| ❑ 86516 | Big Beat from Badsville | 1997 | 12.00 |

#### I.R.S.

| Number | Title (A Side/B Side) | Yr | NM |
|---|---|---|---|
| ❑ SP-007 | Songs the Lord Taught Us | 1980 | 20.00 |
| ❑ SP-501 [EP] | Gravest Hits | 1979 | 25.00 |
| ❑ SP-70007 | Songs the Lord Taught Us | 198? | 12.00 |
| *—Reissue of 007* | | | |
| ❑ SP-70016 | Psychedelic Jungle | 1981 | 20.00 |
| ❑ SP-70042 | Bad Music for Bad People | 1984 | 15.00 |
| ❑ SP-70501 [EP] | Gravest Hits | 198? | 10.00 |
| *—Reissue of 501* | | | |

#### MEDICINE LABEL

| Number | Title (A Side/B Side) | Yr | NM |
|---|---|---|---|
| ❑ 24592 | Flamejob | 1994 | 15.00 |

### CRANE, BOB

#### EPIC

| Number | Title (A Side/B Side) | Yr | NM |
|---|---|---|---|
| ❑ LN 24224 [M] | The Funny Side of TV | 1966 | 25.00 |
| ❑ BN 26224 [S] | The Funny Side of TV | 1966 | 30.00 |

### CRAWFORD, HANK

#### ATLANTIC

| Number | Title (A Side/B Side) | Yr | NM |
|---|---|---|---|
| ❑ 1356 [M] | More Soul | 1960 | 20.00 |
| *—Purple and red label, white fan logo* | | | |
| ❑ SD 1356 [S] | More Soul | 1960 | 25.00 |
| *—Green and blue label, white fan logo* | | | |
| ❑ 1372 [M] | The Soul Clinic | 1961 | 20.00 |
| *—Purple and red label, white fan logo* | | | |
| ❑ SD 1372 [S] | The Soul Clinic | 1961 | 25.00 |
| *—Green and blue label, white fan logo* | | | |
| ❑ SD 1387 [S] | From the Heart | 1962 | 20.00 |
| ❑ SD 1405 [S] | Soul of the Ballad | 1963 | 20.00 |
| ❑ SD 1423 [S] | True Blue | 1964 | 20.00 |
| ❑ SD 1436 [S] | Dig These Blues | 1965 | 20.00 |
| ❑ SD 1455 [S] | After Hours | 1966 | 20.00 |
| ❑ 1470 [M] | Mr. Blues | 1967 | 20.00 |

#### MOBILE FIDELITY

| Number | Title (A Side/B Side) | Yr | NM |
|---|---|---|---|
| ❑ 1-224 | Soul of the Ballad | 1995 | 25.00 |
| *—Audiophile vinyl* | | | |

### CRAWFORD, JOHNNY

#### DEL-FI

| Number | Title (A Side/B Side) | Yr | NM |
|---|---|---|---|
| ❑ DFLP-1220 [M] | The Captivating Johnny Crawford | 1962 | 40.00 |
| ❑ DFLP-1223 [M] | A Young Man's Fancy | 1962 | 30.00 |
| ❑ DFST-1223 [S] | A Young Man's Fancy | 1962 | 40.00 |
| ❑ DFLP-1224 [M] | Rumors | 1963 | 30.00 |
| ❑ DFST-1224 [S] | Rumors | 1963 | 40.00 |
| ❑ DFLP-1229 [M] | His Greatest Hits | 1963 | 30.00 |
| ❑ DFST-1229 [S] | His Greatest Hits | 1963 | 40.00 |
| ❑ DFLP-1248 [M] | Greatest Hits, Volume 2 | 1964 | 20.00 |
| ❑ DFST-1248 [S] | Greatest Hits, Volume 2 | 1964 | 25.00 |

#### GUEST STAR

| Number | Title (A Side/B Side) | Yr | NM |
|---|---|---|---|
| ❑ GS-1470 [M] | Johnny Crawford | 196? | 20.00 |
| ❑ GSS-1470 [S] | Johnny Crawford | 196? | 25.00 |

#### RHINO

| Number | Title (A Side/B Side) | Yr | NM |
|---|---|---|---|
| ❑ RNDF-202 | The Best of Johnny Crawford | 1982 | 12.00 |

#### SUPREME

| Number | Title (A Side/B Side) | Yr | NM |
|---|---|---|---|
| ❑ M-110 [M] | Songs from "The Restless Ones" | 1965 | 20.00 |
| ❑ MS-210 [S] | Songs from "The Restless Ones" | 1965 | 25.00 |

### CRAWFORD, RAY

#### CANDID

| Number | Title (A Side/B Side) | Yr | NM |
|---|---|---|---|
| ❑ CJM-8028 [M] | Smooth Groove | 1963 | 25.00 |
| ❑ CJS-9028 [S] | Smooth Groove | 1963 | 30.00 |

### CRAYTON, PEE WEE

#### CROWN

| Number | Title (A Side/B Side) | Yr | NM |
|---|---|---|---|
| ❑ CLP-5175 [M] | Pee Wee Crayton | 1959 | 100.00 |
| *—Black label* | | | |
| ❑ CLP-5175 [M] | Pee Wee Crayton | 196? | 20.00 |
| *—Gray label* | | | |

#### VANGUARD

| Number | Title (A Side/B Side) | Yr | NM |
|---|---|---|---|
| ❑ VSD-6566 | The Things I Used to Do | 1971 | 15.00 |

Creedence Clearwater Revival, *Pendulum,* Fantasy 8410, 1970, dark blue label, $15.

### CRAZY ELEPHANT

#### BELL

| Number | Title (A Side/B Side) | Yr | NM |
|---|---|---|---|
| ❑ 6034 | Crazy Elephant | 1969 | 20.00 |

### CRAZY OTTO

#### DECCA

| Number | Title (A Side/B Side) | Yr | NM |
|---|---|---|---|
| ❑ DL 4157 [M] | Have Piano, Will Travel | 1961 | 15.00 |
| ❑ DL 8113 [M] | Crazy Otto | 1955 | 20.00 |
| *—Black label, silver print* | | | |
| ❑ DL 8113 [M] | Crazy Otto | 1960 | 12.00 |
| *—Black label with color bars* | | | |
| ❑ DL 8163 [M] | Crazy Otto Rides Again | 1956 | 20.00 |
| ❑ DL 8367 [M] | Not So Crazy | 1956 | 20.00 |
| ❑ DL 8627 [M] | Crazy Otto's Back in Town | 1957 | 15.00 |
| ❑ DL 8737 [M] | Honky Tonk Piano | 1958 | 15.00 |
| ❑ DL 8919 [M] | Golden Award Songs | 1960 | 15.00 |
| ❑ DL 74157 [S] | Have Piano, Will Travel | 1961 | 20.00 |
| ❑ DL 78919 [S] | Golden Award Songs | 1960 | 20.00 |

#### MGM

| Number | Title (A Side/B Side) | Yr | NM |
|---|---|---|---|
| ❑ E-4150 [M] | Crazy Otto Plays Crazy Tunes | 1963 | 12.00 |
| ❑ SE-4150 [S] | Crazy Otto Plays Crazy Tunes | 1963 | 15.00 |

#### VOCALION

| Number | Title (A Side/B Side) | Yr | NM |
|---|---|---|---|
| ❑ VL 3663 [M] | Crazy Otto Goes Sentimental | 196? | 12.00 |

### CREAM

#### ATCO

| Number | Title (A Side/B Side) | Yr | NM |
|---|---|---|---|
| ❑ 33-206 [M] | Fresh Cream | 1967 | 50.00 |
| ❑ SD 33-206 [S] | Fresh Cream | 1967 | 30.00 |
| *—Purple and brown labels* | | | |
| ❑ SD 33-206 [S] | Fresh Cream | 1969 | 15.00 |
| *—Yellow labels* | | | |
| ❑ 33-232 [M] | Disraeli Gears | 1967 | 50.00 |
| ❑ SD 33-232 [S] | Disraeli Gears | 1967 | 30.00 |
| *—Purple and brown labels* | | | |
| ❑ SD 33-232 [S] | Disraeli Gears | 1969 | 15.00 |
| *—Yellow labels* | | | |
| ❑ SD 33-291 | Best of Cream | 1969 | 25.00 |
| ❑ SD 33-328 | Live Cream | 1970 | 25.00 |
| ❑ 2-700 [(2)M] | Wheels of Fire | 1968 | 200.00 |
| *—White label promo; no stock copies are mono* | | | |
| ❑ SD 2-700 [(2)S] | Wheels of Fire | 1968 | 50.00 |
| *—Purple and brown labels; foil-like cover* | | | |
| ❑ SD 2-700 [(2)S] | Wheels of Fire | 1969 | 20.00 |
| *—Yellow labels; dull gray cover* | | | |
| ❑ SD 7001 | Goodbye | 1969 | 15.00 |
| *—Yellow labels* | | | |
| ❑ SD 7001 | Goodbye | 1969 | 30.00 |
| *—Purple and brown labels; deduct 33% if poster is missing* | | | |
| ❑ SD 7005 | Live Cream — Volume II | 1972 | 25.00 |

#### DCC COMPACT CLASSICS

| Number | Title (A Side/B Side) | Yr | NM |
|---|---|---|---|
| ❑ LPZ-2015 | Fresh Cream | 1996 | 100.00 |
| *—Audiophile vinyl* | | | |

#### MOBILE FIDELITY

| Number | Title (A Side/B Side) | Yr | NM |
|---|---|---|---|
| ❑ 2-066 [(2)] | Wheels of Fire | 1980 | 90.00 |
| *—Audiophile vinyl* | | | |
| ❑ 1-264 | Goodbye | 1996 | — |
| *—Audiophile vinyl; canceled* | | | |

#### POLYDOR

| Number | Title (A Side/B Side) | Yr | NM |
|---|---|---|---|
| ❑ 24-3502 [(2)] | Heavy Cream | 1972 | 15.00 |
| ❑ 24-5529 | Off the Top | 1973 | 15.00 |

#### RSO

| Number | Title (A Side/B Side) | Yr | NM |
|---|---|---|---|
| ❑ 015 [(2)DJ] | Classic Cuts | 1978 | 40.00 |
| *—Promo-only compilation* | | | |
| ❑ RS-1-3009 | Fresh Cream | 1977 | 12.00 |
| ❑ RS-1-3010 | Disraeli Gears | 1977 | 12.00 |
| ❑ RS-1-3012 | Best of Cream | 1977 | 12.00 |
| ❑ RS-1-3013 | Goodbye | 1977 | 12.00 |
| ❑ RS-1-3014 | Live Cream | 1977 | 12.00 |
| ❑ RS-1-3015 | Live Cream — Volume 2 | 1977 | 12.00 |
| ❑ RS-2-3802 [(2)] | Wheels of Fire | 1977 | 15.00 |

#### SPRINGBOARD

| Number | Title (A Side/B Side) | Yr | NM |
|---|---|---|---|
| ❑ SPB 4037 | Early Cream | 1972 | 15.00 |

### CREATION OF SUNLIGHT

#### WINDI

| Number | Title (A Side/B Side) | Yr | NM |
|---|---|---|---|
| ❑ 1001 | Creation of Sunlight | 1968 | 600.00 |

### CREEDENCE CLEARWATER REVIVAL

#### ANALOGUE PRODUCTIONS

| Number | Title (A Side/B Side) | Yr | NM |
|---|---|---|---|
| ❑ AAPP-8382 | Creedence Clearwater Revival | 2002 | 25.00 |
| *—Audiophile edition on heavy vinyl* | | | |
| ❑ AAPP-8387 | Bayou Country | 2002 | 25.00 |
| *—Audiophile edition on heavy vinyl* | | | |
| ❑ AAPP-8393 | Green River | 2002 | 25.00 |
| *—Audiophile edition on heavy vinyl* | | | |
| ❑ AAPP-8397 | Willie and the Poor Boys | 2002 | 25.00 |
| *—Audiophile edition on heavy vinyl* | | | |
| ❑ AAPP-8402 | Cosmo's Factory | 2002 | 25.00 |
| *—Audiophile edition on heavy vinyl* | | | |

| Number | Title (A Side/B Side) | Yr | NM |
|---|---|---|---|
| ❑ AAPP-9404 | Mardi Gras | 2002 | 25.00 |
| *—Audiophile edition on heavy vinyl* | | | |

### DCC COMPACT CLASSICS

| Number | Title (A Side/B Side) | Yr | NM |
|---|---|---|---|
| ❑ LPZ-2019 | Willie and the Poor Boys | 1996 | 50.00 |
| *—Audiophile vinyl* | | | |

### FANTASY

| Number | Title (A Side/B Side) | Yr | NM |
|---|---|---|---|
| ❑ CCR-1 [(2)] | Live in Europe | 1973 | 12.00 |
| ❑ CCR-2 [(2)] | Chronicle (The 20 Greatest Hits) | 1976 | 15.00 |
| *—Brown labels* | | | |
| ❑ CCR-2 [(2)] | Chronicle (The 20 Greatest Hits) | 1979 | 12.00 |
| *—Whitish or light blue labels* | | | |
| ❑ CCR-3 [(2)] | Chronicle, Volume 2 | 1987 | 15.00 |
| ❑ CCR-68 [(2)] | Creedence Clearwater Revival 1968/69 | 1981 | 12.00 |
| *—Compilation of 8382 and 8387* | | | |
| ❑ CCR-69 [(2)] | Creedence Clearwater Revival 1969 | 1981 | 12.00 |
| *—Compilation of 8393 and 8397* | | | |
| ❑ CCR-70 [(2)] | Creedence Clearwater Revival 1970 | 1981 | 12.00 |
| *—Compilation of 8402 and 8410* | | | |
| ❑ FPM-4001 [Q] | Creedence Gold | 1975 | 50.00 |
| ❑ MPF-4501 | The Royal Albert Hall Concert | 1980 | 15.00 |
| *—Album withdrawn and changed when it was discovered this didn't come from the Royal Albert Hall* | | | |
| ❑ MPF-4501 | The Concert | 1981 | 10.00 |
| *—Retitled version* | | | |
| ❑ MPF-4509 | Creedence Country | 1981 | 10.00 |
| ❑ ORC-4512 | Creedence Clearwater Revival | 1981 | 8.00 |
| *—Reissue of 8382* | | | |
| ❑ ORC-4513 | Bayou Country | 1981 | 8.00 |
| *—Reissue of 8387* | | | |
| ❑ ORC-4514 | Green River | 1981 | 8.00 |
| *—Reissue of 8393* | | | |
| ❑ ORC-4515 | Willy and the Poor Boys | 1981 | 8.00 |
| *—Reissue of 8397* | | | |
| ❑ ORC-4516 | Cosmo's Factory | 1981 | 8.00 |
| *—Reissue of 8402* | | | |
| ❑ ORC-4517 | Pendulum | 1981 | 8.00 |
| *—Reissue of 8410* | | | |
| ❑ ORC-4518 | Mardi Gras | 1981 | 8.00 |
| *—Reissue of 9404* | | | |
| ❑ MPF-4522 | The Movie Album | 1985 | 8.00 |
| ❑ ORC-4526 [(2)] | Live in Europe | 1986 | 10.00 |
| ❑ F-8382 | Creedence Clearwater Revival | 1968 | 15.00 |
| *—With "Susie Q" mentioned on the front cover; dark blue label* | | | |
| ❑ F-8382 | Creedence Clearwater Revival | 1968 | 25.00 |
| *—With no reference to "Susie Q" on the front cover* | | | |
| ❑ F-8382 | Creedence Clearwater Revival | 1973 | 10.00 |
| *—Brown label* | | | |
| ❑ F-8382 [DJ] | Creedence Clearwater Revival | 1968 | 80.00 |
| *—White label promo* | | | |
| ❑ F-8387 | Bayou Country | 1969 | 15.00 |
| *—Dark blue label* | | | |
| ❑ F-8387 | Bayou Country | 1973 | 10.00 |
| *—Brown label* | | | |
| ❑ F-8387 [DJ] | Bayou Country | 1969 | 80.00 |
| *—White label promo* | | | |
| ❑ F-8393 | Green River | 1969 | 15.00 |
| *—Dark blue label* | | | |
| ❑ F-8393 | Green River | 1973 | 10.00 |
| *—Brown label* | | | |
| ❑ F-8393 [DJ] | Green River | 1969 | 80.00 |
| *—White label promo* | | | |
| ❑ F-8397 | Willy and the Poor Boys | 1969 | 15.00 |
| *—Dark blue label* | | | |
| ❑ F-8397 | Willy and the Poor Boys | 1973 | 10.00 |
| *—Brown label* | | | |
| ❑ F-8397 [DJ] | Willy and the Poor Boys | 1969 | 80.00 |
| *—White label promo* | | | |
| ❑ F-8402 | Cosmo's Factory | 1970 | 15.00 |
| *—Dark blue label* | | | |
| ❑ F-8402 | Cosmo's Factory | 1973 | 10.00 |
| *—Brown label* | | | |
| ❑ F-8402 [DJ] | Cosmo's Factory | 1970 | 80.00 |
| *—White label promo* | | | |
| ❑ F-8410 | Pendulum | 1970 | 15.00 |
| *—Dark blue label* | | | |
| ❑ F-8410 | Pendulum | 1973 | 10.00 |
| *—Brown label* | | | |
| ❑ F-9404 | Mardi Gras | 1972 | 15.00 |
| *—Dark blue label* | | | |
| ❑ F-9404 | Mardi Gras | 1973 | 10.00 |
| *—Brown label* | | | |
| ❑ F-9418 | Creedence Gold | 1972 | 10.00 |
| ❑ F-9430 | More Creedence Gold | 1973 | 10.00 |
| ❑ F-9621 | Chooglin' | 1982 | 8.00 |

### HEARTLAND

| Number | Title (A Side/B Side) | Yr | NM |
|---|---|---|---|
| ❑ HR 2039 [(3)] | Creedence Clearwater Revival | 1990 | 15.00 |

### K-TEL

| Number | Title (A Side/B Side) | Yr | NM |
|---|---|---|---|
| ❑ NU 9360 | The Best of Creedence Clearwater Revival — 20 Super Hits | 1978 | 15.00 |

### MOBILE FIDELITY

| Number | Title (A Side/B Side) | Yr | NM |
|---|---|---|---|
| ❑ 1-037 | Cosmo's Factory | 1979 | 70.00 |
| *—Audiophile vinyl* | | | |

### TIME-LIFE

| Number | Title (A Side/B Side) | Yr | NM |
|---|---|---|---|
| ❑ SCLR-18 [(2)] | Classic Rock: Creedence Clearwater Revival | 1989 | 15.00 |

## CREME SODA

### TRINITY

| Number | Title (A Side/B Side) | Yr | NM |
|---|---|---|---|
| ❑ CST-11 | Tricky Zingers | 197? | 100.00 |
| *—With photo of group on cover* | | | |
| ❑ CST-11 | Tricky Zingers | 197? | 40.00 |
| *—With white cover* | | | |

## CRESCENDOS, THE (1)

### GUEST STAR

| Number | Title (A Side/B Side) | Yr | NM |
|---|---|---|---|
| ❑ G-1453 [M] | Oh Julie | 1962 | 50.00 |
| ❑ GS-1453 [R] | Oh Julie | 1962 | 20.00 |

## CRESTS, THE

### COED

| Number | Title (A Side/B Side) | Yr | NM |
|---|---|---|---|
| ❑ LPC-901 [M] | The Crests Sing All Biggies | 1960 | 200.00 |
| *—Red label* | | | |
| ❑ LPC-901 [M] | The Crests Sing All Biggies | 1960 | 400.00 |
| *—Yellow label, black print* | | | |
| ❑ LPC-904 [M] | The Best of the Crests/16 Fabulous Hits | 1961 | 400.00 |
| *—Label simply calls this "16 Fabulous Hits"* | | | |

### COLLECTABLES

| Number | Title (A Side/B Side) | Yr | NM |
|---|---|---|---|
| ❑ COL-5009 | Greatest Hits | 1982 | 12.00 |

### POST

| Number | Title (A Side/B Side) | Yr | NM |
|---|---|---|---|
| ❑ 3000 | The Crests Sing | 196? | 40.00 |

### RHINO

| Number | Title (A Side/B Side) | Yr | NM |
|---|---|---|---|
| ❑ R1-70948 | The Best of the Crests | 1989 | 12.00 |

## CREVELING, CAROLE

### EUTERPE

| Number | Title (A Side/B Side) | Yr | NM |
|---|---|---|---|
| ❑ ETP-101 [M] | Carole Creveling | 1955 | 50.00 |

## CREW CUTS, THE

### CAMAY

| Number | Title (A Side/B Side) | Yr | NM |
|---|---|---|---|
| ❑ CA-1002 [M] | The Great New Sound of the Crew Cuts | 196? | 20.00 |
| ❑ CA-3002 [S] | The Great New Sound of the Crew Cuts | 196? | 25.00 |

### MERCURY

| Number | Title (A Side/B Side) | Yr | NM |
|---|---|---|---|
| ❑ MG-20067 [M] | The Crew Cuts Go Longhair | 1955 | 50.00 |
| ❑ MG-20140 [M] | The Crew Cuts On Campus | 1956 | 50.00 |
| ❑ MG-20143 [M] | Crew Cut Capers | 1956 | 50.00 |
| ❑ MG-20144 [M] | Rock and Roll Bash | 1956 | 80.00 |
| ❑ MG-20199 [M] | Music A La Carte | 1957 | 50.00 |
| ❑ MG-25200 [10] | The Crew Cuts On Campus | 1956 | 80.00 |

### PICADILLY

| Number | Title (A Side/B Side) | Yr | NM |
|---|---|---|---|
| ❑ PIC-3560 | The Wonderful Happy Crazy Innocent World | 1980 | 10.00 |

### RCA VICTOR

| Number | Title (A Side/B Side) | Yr | NM |
|---|---|---|---|
| ❑ PR-102 [M] | The Crew Cuts Sing Out! | 1960 | 25.00 |
| ❑ PR-129 [M] | The Crew Cuts Have a Ball | 1960 | 25.00 |
| *—Produced for Ebonite bowling balls; Side 2 has "Bowling Tips by Top Stars"* | | | |
| ❑ LPM-1933 [M] | Surprise Package | 1958 | 30.00 |
| ❑ LSP-1933 [S] | Surprise Package | 1959 | 40.00 |
| ❑ LPM-2037 [M] | The Crew Cuts Sing | 1959 | 30.00 |
| ❑ LSP-2037 [S] | The Crew Cuts Sing | 1959 | 40.00 |
| ❑ LPM-2067 [M] | You Must Have Been a Beautiful Baby | 1960 | 30.00 |
| ❑ LSP-2067 [S] | You Must Have Been a Beautiful Baby | 1960 | 40.00 |

### WING

| Number | Title (A Side/B Side) | Yr | NM |
|---|---|---|---|
| ❑ MGW-12125 [M] | Rock and Roll Bash | 196? | 25.00 |
| ❑ MGW-12145 [M] | The Crew Cuts On Campus | 196? | 20.00 |
| ❑ MGW-12177 [M] | The Crew Cuts | 196? | 20.00 |
| ❑ MGW-12180 [M] | High School Favorites | 196? | 20.00 |
| ❑ MGW-12195 [M] | The Crew Cuts Sing the Masters | 196? | 20.00 |

## CREWE, BOB

### CGC

| Number | Title (A Side/B Side) | Yr | NM |
|---|---|---|---|
| ❑ 1000 | Let Me Touch You | 1970 | 12.00 |

### DYNO VOICE

| Number | Title (A Side/B Side) | Yr | NM |
|---|---|---|---|
| ❑ DV-1902 [M] | Music to Watch Birds By | 1967 | 15.00 |
| ❑ DV-1906 [M] | The Bob Crewe Generation In Classic Form | 1968 | 15.00 |
| ❑ DV-9003 [M] | Music to Watch Girls By | 1967 | 15.00 |
| ❑ DVS-9003 [S] | Music to Watch Girls By | 1967 | 12.00 |
| ❑ DV-31902 [S] | Music to Watch Birds By | 1967 | 12.00 |
| ❑ DV-31906 [S] | The Bob Crewe Generation In Classic Form | 1968 | 12.00 |

### ELEKTRA

| Number | Title (A Side/B Side) | Yr | NM |
|---|---|---|---|
| ❑ 7E-1083 | Street Talk | 1976 | 12.00 |
| ❑ 7E-1103 | Motivation | 1977 | 12.00 |

### PHILIPS

| Number | Title (A Side/B Side) | Yr | NM |
|---|---|---|---|
| ❑ PHM 200150 [M] | All the Song Hits of the Four Seasons | 1964 | 25.00 |
| ❑ PHM 200238 [M] | Bob Crewe Plays the Four Seasons' Hits | 1967 | 20.00 |
| ❑ PHS 600150 [S] | All the Song Hits of the Four Seasons | 1964 | 30.00 |
| ❑ PHS 600238 [S] | Bob Crewe Plays the Four Seasons' Hits | 1967 | 15.00 |

### WARWICK

| Number | Title (A Side/B Side) | Yr | NM |
|---|---|---|---|
| ❑ W-2009 [M] | Kicks | 1960 | 25.00 |
| ❑ WST-2009 [S] | Kicks | 1960 | 50.00 |
| ❑ W-2034 [M] | Crazy in the Heart | 1961 | 25.00 |
| ❑ WST-2034 [S] | Crazy in the Heart | 1961 | 50.00 |

## CRICKETS, THE (1)

### BARNABY

| Number | Title (A Side/B Side) | Yr | NM |
|---|---|---|---|
| ❑ Z 30268 | Rockin' 50's Rock 'N' Roll | 1970 | 25.00 |

### BRUNSWICK

| Number | Title (A Side/B Side) | Yr | NM |
|---|---|---|---|
| ❑ BL 54038 [M] | The "Chirping" Crickets | 1957 | 800.00 |
| *—Textured cover* | | | |
| ❑ BL 54038 [M] | The "Chirping" Crickets | 1958 | 600.00 |
| *—Regular cover* | | | |

### CORAL

| Number | Title (A Side/B Side) | Yr | NM |
|---|---|---|---|
| ❑ CRL 57320 [M] | In Style with the Crickets | 1960 | 200.00 |
| ❑ CRL 757320 [S] | In Style with the Crickets | 1960 | 400.00 |

### EPIC

| Number | Title (A Side/B Side) | Yr | NM |
|---|---|---|---|
| ❑ FE 44446 | T-Shirt | 1988 | 15.00 |

### LIBERTY

| Number | Title (A Side/B Side) | Yr | NM |
|---|---|---|---|
| ❑ LRP-3272 [M] | Something Old, Something New, Something Blue, Somethin' Else | 1962 | 150.00 |
| ❑ LRP-3351 [M] | California Sun/She Loves You | 1964 | 100.00 |
| ❑ LST-7272 [S] | Something Old, Something New, Something Blue, Somethin' Else | 1962 | 200.00 |
| ❑ LST-7351 [S] | California Sun/She Loves You | 1964 | 150.00 |

### VERTIGO

| Number | Title (A Side/B Side) | Yr | NM |
|---|---|---|---|
| ❑ VEL-1020 | Remnants | 1973 | 20.00 |

## CRISS, PETER Also see CHELSEA; KISS.

### CASABLANCA

| Number | Title (A Side/B Side) | Yr | NM |
|---|---|---|---|
| ❑ NBLP-7122 | Peter Criss | 1978 | 20.00 |
| ❑ NBPIX-7122 [PD] | Peter Criss | 1978 | 50.00 |
| ❑ NBLP-7240 | Out of Control | 1980 | 25.00 |

## CRISS, SONNY

### CLEF

| Number | Title (A Side/B Side) | Yr | NM |
|---|---|---|---|
| ❑ MGC-122 [10] | Sonny Criss Collates | 1953 | 250.00 |

### IMPERIAL

| Number | Title (A Side/B Side) | Yr | NM |
|---|---|---|---|
| ❑ LP-9006 [M] | Jazz U.S.A. | 1956 | 200.00 |
| ❑ LP-9020 [M] | Go Man: It's Sonny Criss & Modern Jazz | 1956 | 200.00 |
| ❑ LP-9024 [M] | Sonny Criss Plays Cole Porter | 1956 | 200.00 |
| ❑ LP-9205 [M] | Criss Cross | 1963 | 80.00 |
| ❑ LP-12205 [R] | Criss Cross | 1963 | 20.00 |

### MERCURY

| Number | Title (A Side/B Side) | Yr | NM |
|---|---|---|---|
| ❑ MGC-122 [10] | Sonny Criss Collates | 1953 | — |
| *—Cover exists, but all known copies contain Clef labels* | | | |

### PEACOCK

| Number | Title (A Side/B Side) | Yr | NM |
|---|---|---|---|
| ❑ PLP-91 [M] | At the Crossroads | 1959 | 150.00 |

### PRESTIGE

| Number | Title (A Side/B Side) | Yr | NM |
|---|---|---|---|
| ❑ PRLP-7511 [M] | This Is Sonny Criss! | 1966 | 25.00 |
| ❑ PRST-7511 [S] | This Is Sonny Criss! | 1966 | 30.00 |
| ❑ PRLP-7526 [M] | Portrait of Sonny Criss | 1967 | 30.00 |
| ❑ PRST-7526 [S] | Portrait of Sonny Criss | 1967 | 25.00 |
| ❑ PRLP-7530 [M] | Up, Up and Away | 1967 | 40.00 |
| ❑ PRST-7530 [S] | Up, Up and Away | 1967 | 25.00 |
| ❑ PRST-7558 | The Beat Goes On | 1968 | 20.00 |
| ❑ PRST-7576 | Sonny's Dream | 1968 | 20.00 |
| ❑ PRST-7610 | Rockin' in Rhythm | 1969 | 20.00 |
| ❑ PRST-7628 | I'll Catch the Sun | 1969 | 20.00 |

## CRISS, SONNY, AND KENNY DORHAM

### ABC IMPULSE!

| Number | Title (A Side/B Side) | Yr | NM |
|---|---|---|---|
| ❑ IA-9337 [(2)] | Bopmasters | 197? | 20.00 |

## CRITTERS, THE

### KAPP

| Number | Title (A Side/B Side) | Yr | NM |
|---|---|---|---|
| ❑ KL-1485 [M] | Younger Girl | 1966 | 30.00 |
| ❑ KS-3485 [S] | Younger Girl | 1966 | 40.00 |

### PROJECT 3

| Number | Title (A Side/B Side) | Yr | NM |
|---|---|---|---|
| ❑ PR 4001SD | Touch 'n Go with the Critters | 1968 | 30.00 |
| ❑ PR 4002SD | The Critters | 1969 | 30.00 |

## CRITTERS, THE /THE YOUNG RASCALS/LOU CHRISTIE

### BOUTIQUE

| Number | Title (A Side/B Side) | Yr | NM |
|---|---|---|---|
| ❑ CA-1079 [M] | A Taste of the Critters & The Young Rascals & Lou Christie | 1966 | 40.00 |

## CROCE, JIM

### ABC

| Number | Title (A Side/B Side) | Yr | NM |
|---|---|---|---|
| ❑ ABCX-756 | You Don't Mess Around with Jim | 1972 | 20.00 |
| *—Original covers have no green box advertising "Time in a Bottle"* | | | |

| Number | Title (A Side/B Side) | Yr | NM |
|---|---|---|---|
| ❑ ABCX-756 | You Don't Mess Around with Jim | 1973 | 15.00 |

*—Posthumous covers have a green box advertising "Time in a Bottle"*

| Number | Title (A Side/B Side) | Yr | NM |
|---|---|---|---|
| ❑ ABCX-769 | Life and Times | 1973 | 15.00 |
| ❑ ABCX-797 | I Got a Name | 1973 | 15.00 |
| ❑ ABCD-835 | Photographs & Memories/His Greatest Hits | 1974 | 15.00 |

CAPITOL

| Number | Title (A Side/B Side) | Yr | NM |
|---|---|---|---|
| ❑ SMAS-315 | Jim and Ingrid Croce | 1970 | 30.00 |

COMMAND

| Number | Title (A Side/B Side) | Yr | NM |
|---|---|---|---|
| ❑ QD-40006 [Q] | You Don't Mess Around with Jim | 1974 | 30.00 |

*—With wide border around the outside of front cover*

| Number | Title (A Side/B Side) | Yr | NM |
|---|---|---|---|
| ❑ QD-40006 [Q] | You Don't Mess Around with Jim | 1974 | 25.00 |

*—Without border around outside of front cover*

| Number | Title (A Side/B Side) | Yr | NM |
|---|---|---|---|
| ❑ QD-40007 [Q] | Life and Times | 1974 | 25.00 |
| ❑ QD-40008 [Q] | I Got a Name | 1974 | 25.00 |
| ❑ QD-40020 [Q] | Photographs & Memories/His Greatest Hits | 1974 | 25.00 |

CROCE

| Number | Title (A Side/B Side) | Yr | NM |
|---|---|---|---|
| ❑ 101 | Facets | 1966 | 300.00 |

DCC COMPACT CLASSICS

| Number | Title (A Side/B Side) | Yr | NM |
|---|---|---|---|
| ❑ LPZ-2054 | His Greatest Recordings | 1998 | 40.00 |

*—Audiophile vinyl*

LIFESONG

| Number | Title (A Side/B Side) | Yr | NM |
|---|---|---|---|
| ❑ LS 900 [(2)] | The Faces I've Been | 1975 | 15.00 |
| ❑ LS 6007 | Time in a Bottle — Jim Croce's Greatest Love Songs | 1976 | 12.00 |
| ❑ JZ 34993 | You Don't Mess Around with Jim | 1978 | 10.00 |
| ❑ JZ 35000 | Time in a Bottle — Jim Croce's Greatest Love Songs | 1978 | 10.00 |
| ❑ JZ 35008 | Life and Times | 1978 | 10.00 |
| ❑ JZ 35009 | I Got a Name | 1978 | 10.00 |
| ❑ JZ 35010 | Photographs & Memories/His Greatest Hits | 1978 | 10.00 |
| ❑ JZ 35571 | Bad, Bad Leroy Brown: Jim Croce's Greatest Character Songs | 1978 | 10.00 |

MOBILE FIDELITY

| Number | Title (A Side/B Side) | Yr | NM |
|---|---|---|---|
| ❑ 1-079 | You Don't Mess Around with Jim | 1981 | 40.00 |

*—Audiophile vinyl*

PICKWICK

| Number | Title (A Side/B Side) | Yr | NM |
|---|---|---|---|
| ❑ SPC-3332 | Another Day, Another Town | 1973 | 10.00 |

*—Reissue of Capitol LP*

21 RECORDS

| Number | Title (A Side/B Side) | Yr | NM |
|---|---|---|---|
| ❑ 90467 | Photographs & Memories/His Greatest Hits | 1985 | 8.00 |
| ❑ 90468 | Time in a Bottle — Jim Croce's Greatest Love Songs | 1985 | 8.00 |
| ❑ 90469 | Down the Highway | 1985 | 10.00 |

**CROME SYRCUS, THE**

COMMAND

| Number | Title (A Side/B Side) | Yr | NM |
|---|---|---|---|
| ❑ RS 925 SD | The Love Cycle | 1968 | 40.00 |

**CROSBY, BING**

AMOS

| Number | Title (A Side/B Side) | Yr | NM |
|---|---|---|---|
| ❑ AAS-7001 | Hey Jude/Hey Bing! | 1969 | 12.00 |

BIOGRAPH

| Number | Title (A Side/B Side) | Yr | NM |
|---|---|---|---|
| ❑ M-1 | When the Blue of the Night Meets the Gold of the Day | 197? | 10.00 |
| ❑ C-13 | Bing Crosby 1929-33 | 1973 | 12.00 |

BRUNSWICK

| Number | Title (A Side/B Side) | Yr | NM |
|---|---|---|---|
| ❑ BL 54005 [M] | The Voice of Bing in the 1930s | 1957 | 25.00 |
| ❑ BL 58000 [10] | Bing Crosby, Volume 1 | 1950 | 50.00 |
| ❑ BL 58001 [10] | Bing Crosby, Volume 2 | 1950 | 50.00 |

CAPITOL

| Number | Title (A Side/B Side) | Yr | NM |
|---|---|---|---|
| ❑ ST 2300 [S] | That Travelin' Two-Beat | 1965 | 20.00 |
| ❑ T 2300 [M] | That Travelin' Two-Beat | 1965 | 15.00 |
| ❑ ST 2346 [S] | Great Country Hits | 1965 | 20.00 |
| ❑ T 2346 [M] | Great Country Hits | 1965 | 15.00 |
| ❑ SM-11732 | Bing Crosby's Christmas Classics | 1977 | 10.00 |

*—"A Capitol Re-Issue"; same recordings as on Warner Bros. 1484*

| Number | Title (A Side/B Side) | Yr | NM |
|---|---|---|---|
| ❑ SM-11736 | That Travelin' Two-Beat | 1977 | 10.00 |
| ❑ SM-11737 | Great Country Hits | 1977 | 10.00 |
| ❑ SM-11738 | Bing Crosby Classics, Vol. 1 | 1977 | 10.00 |
| ❑ SM-11739 | Bing Crosby Classics, Vol. 2 | 1977 | 10.00 |
| ❑ SM-11740 | Bing Crosby Classics, Vol. 3 | 1977 | 10.00 |

COLUMBIA

| Number | Title (A Side/B Side) | Yr | NM |
|---|---|---|---|
| ❑ C2L 43 [(2)] | Bing in Hollywood 1930-1934 | 196? | 15.00 |

*—Red "360 Sound" labels*

| Number | Title (A Side/B Side) | Yr | NM |
|---|---|---|---|
| ❑ C2L 43 [(2)] | Bing in Hollywood 1930-1934 | 1971 | 12.00 |

*—Orange labels*

| Number | Title (A Side/B Side) | Yr | NM |
|---|---|---|---|
| ❑ CL 2502 [10] | Der Bingle | 1955 | 40.00 |
| ❑ CL 6027 [10] | Crosby Classics | 1949 | 50.00 |
| ❑ CL 6105 [10] | Crosby Classics, Volume 2 | 1950 | 50.00 |
| ❑ C 35093 | Bing Crosby Collection, Vol. 1 | 1977 | 10.00 |
| ❑ C 35094 | Bing Crosby Collection, Vol. 2 | 1977 | 10.00 |

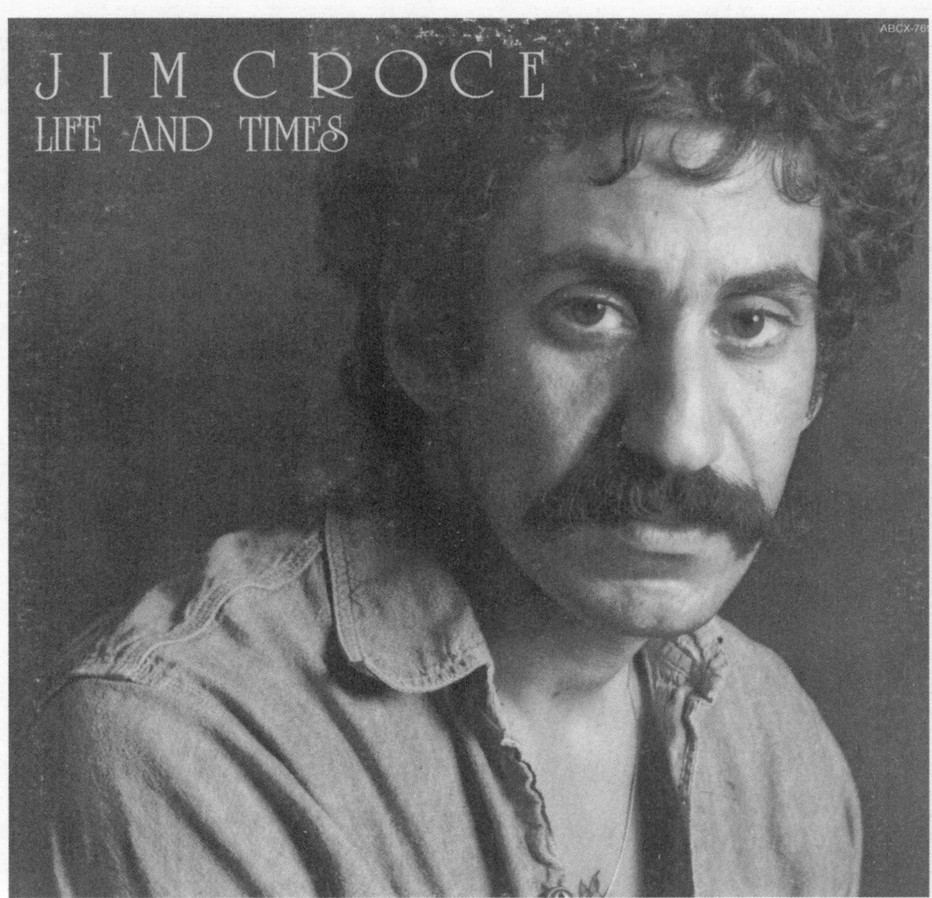


Jim Croce, *Life and Times,* ABC ABCX-769, 1973, $15.

| Number | Title (A Side/B Side) | Yr | NM |
|---|---|---|---|
| ❑ C4X 44229 [(4)] | The Crooner: The Columbia Years | 1988 | 40.00 |

COLUMBIA SPECIAL PRODUCTS

| Number | Title (A Side/B Side) | Yr | NM |
|---|---|---|---|
| ❑ CE2E-201 [(2)] | The Bing Crosby Story, Volume 1 | 1974 | 12.00 |

*—Reissue of Encore E2E-201*

| Number | Title (A Side/B Side) | Yr | NM |
|---|---|---|---|
| ❑ P 14369 | Bing | 197? | 10.00 |

DAYBREAK

| Number | Title (A Side/B Side) | Yr | NM |
|---|---|---|---|
| ❑ 2006 | A Time to Be Jolly | 1971 | 12.00 |
| ❑ 2014 | Bing and Basie | 1972 | 12.00 |

DECCA

| Number | Title (A Side/B Side) | Yr | NM |
|---|---|---|---|
| ❑ DX 151 [(5)M] | Bing: A Musical Autobiography | 195? | 150.00 |
| ❑ DX 152 [(3)M] | Old Masters | 195? | 150.00 |
| ❑ DXB 184 [(2)M] | The Best of Bing | 1965 | 25.00 |
| ❑ DL 4086 [M] | My Golden Favorites | 1961 | 25.00 |
| ❑ DL 4250 [M] | Bing's Hollywood: Easy to Remember | 1962 | 25.00 |
| ❑ DL 4251 [M] | Bing's Hollywood: Pennies from Heaven | 1962 | 25.00 |
| ❑ DL 4252 [M] | Bing's Hollywood: Pocket Full of Dreams | 1962 | 25.00 |
| ❑ DL 4253 [M] | Bing's Hollywood: East Side of Heaven | 1962 | 25.00 |
| ❑ DL 4254 [M] | Bing's Hollywood: The Road Begins | 1962 | 25.00 |
| ❑ DL 4255 [M] | Bing's Hollywood: Only Forever | 1962 | 25.00 |
| ❑ DL 4256 [M] | Bing's Hollywood: Holiday Inn | 1962 | 25.00 |
| ❑ DL 4257 [M] | Bing's Hollywood: Swinging on a Star | 1962 | 25.00 |
| ❑ DL 4258 [M] | Bing's Hollywood: Accentuate the Positive | 1962 | 25.00 |
| ❑ DL 4259 [M] | Bing's Hollywood: Blue Skies | 1962 | 25.00 |
| ❑ DL 4260 [M] | Bing's Hollywood: But Beautiful | 1962 | 25.00 |
| ❑ DL 4261 [M] | Bing's Hollywood: Sunshine Cake | 1962 | 25.00 |
| ❑ DL 4262 [M] | Bing's Hollywood: Cool of the Evening | 1962 | 25.00 |
| ❑ DL 4263 [M] | Bing's Hollywood: Zing a Little Zong | 1962 | 25.00 |
| ❑ DL 4264 [M] | Bing's Hollywood: Anything Goes | 1962 | 25.00 |
| ❑ DL 4281 [M] | Holiday in Europe | 1962 | 25.00 |
| ❑ DL 4283 | Two Favorite Stories by Bing Crosby | 1962 | 25.00 |
| ❑ DL 4415 [M] | Songs Everybody Knows | 1964 | 25.00 |

| Number | Title (A Side/B Side) | Yr | NM |
|---|---|---|---|
| ❑ DLP 5000 [10] | Hits from Musical Comedies | 1949 | 50.00 |
| ❑ DLP 5001 [10] | Jerome Kern Songs | 1949 | 50.00 |
| ❑ DLP 5010 [10] | Stephen Foster Songs | 1949 | 50.00 |
| ❑ DLP 5011 [10] | El Bingo | 1949 | 50.00 |
| ❑ DL 5019 [10] | Merry Christmas | 1950 | 50.00 |

*—Second editions have a blue-green cover, but a "DL" prefix on the record, though not necessarily on the cover*

| Number | Title (A Side/B Side) | Yr | NM |
|---|---|---|---|
| ❑ DL 5019 [10] | Merry Christmas | 1951 | 40.00 |

*—Third editions have a brand-new red and green cover*

| Number | Title (A Side/B Side) | Yr | NM |
|---|---|---|---|
| ❑ DLP 5019 [10] | Merry Christmas | 1949 | 60.00 |

*—Original editions have a light blue-green cover and "DLP" prefix*

| Number | Title (A Side/B Side) | Yr | NM |
|---|---|---|---|
| ❑ DLP 5020 [10] | Christmas Greetings | 1949 | 60.00 |
| ❑ DL 5028 [10] | Auld Lang Syne | 1950 | 50.00 |
| ❑ DL 5037 [10] | St. Patrick's Day | 1950 | 50.00 |
| ❑ DL 5039 [10] | St. Valentine's Day | 1950 | 50.00 |
| ❑ DL 5042 [10] | Blue Skies | 1950 | 50.00 |
| ❑ DL 5052 [10] | Going My Way/The Bells of St. Mary's | 1950 | 60.00 |
| ❑ DL 5063 [10] | Don't Fence Me In | 1950 | 50.00 |
| ❑ DL 5064 [10] | Cole Porter Songs | 1950 | 50.00 |
| ❑ DL 5081 [10] | Songs by Gershwin | 1950 | 50.00 |
| ❑ DL 5102 [10] | Blue of the Night | 1950 | 50.00 |
| ❑ DL 5107 [10] | Cowboy Songs | 1950 | 50.00 |
| ❑ DL 5119 [10] | Drifting and Dreaming | 1950 | 50.00 |
| ❑ DL 5122 [10] | Hawaiian Songs | 1950 | 50.00 |
| ❑ DL 5126 [10] | Stardust | 1950 | 50.00 |
| ❑ DL 5129 [10] | Cowboy Songs, Volume 2 | 1950 | 50.00 |
| ❑ DL 5220 [10] | Bing Sings Hits | 1950 | 50.00 |
| ❑ DL 5272 [10] | Top o' the Morning/The Emperor Waltz | 1950 | 50.00 |
| ❑ DL 5284 [10] | Mr. Music | 1950 | 50.00 |
| ❑ DL 5298 [10] | Hits from Broadway Shows | 1951 | 50.00 |
| ❑ DL 5299 [10] | Favorite Hawaiian Songs | 1951 | 50.00 |
| ❑ DL 5302 [10] | Go West, Young Man | 1951 | 50.00 |
| ❑ DL 5310 [10] | Way Back Home | 1951 | 50.00 |
| ❑ DL 5323 [10] | Bing and the Dixieland Bands | 1951 | 50.00 |
| ❑ DL 5326 [10] | Yours Is My Heart Alone | 1951 | 50.00 |
| ❑ DL 5331 [10] | Country Style | 1951 | 50.00 |
| ❑ DL 5340 [10] | Down Memory Lane | 1951 | 50.00 |
| ❑ DL 5343 [10] | Down Memory Lane, Volume 2 | 1951 | 50.00 |
| ❑ DL 5351 [10] | Beloved Hymns | 1951 | 50.00 |
| ❑ DL 5355 [10] | Bing Sings Victor Herbert | 1951 | 50.00 |
| ❑ DL 5390 [10] | Bing and Connee | 1953 | 50.00 |

*—With Connee Boswell*

| Number | Title (A Side/B Side) | Yr | NM |
|---|---|---|---|
| ❑ DL 5403 [10] | When Irish Eyes Are Smiling | 1952 | 50.00 |
| ❑ DL 5417 [10] | Just for You | 1952 | 50.00 |
| ❑ DL 5444 [10] | The Road to Bali | 1952 | 60.00 |

DL 78352
enhanced for
STEREO
SONGS I WISH I HAD SUNG
the
first
time
around...
DECCA
RECORDS
HIGH FIDELITY
APRIL SHOWERS
WHEN MY BABY SMILES AT ME
MY BLUE HEAVEN
AIN'T MISBEHAVIN'
A LITTLE KISS EACH MORNING
THIS LOVE OF MINE
PRISONER OF LOVE
THANKS FOR THE MEMORY
PAPER DOLL
MONA LISA
BLUES IN THE NIGHT
MEMORIES ARE MADE OF THIS
Orchestra Directed by Jack Pleis


Bing Crosby, *Songs I Wish I Had Sung... The First Time Around,* Decca DL 78352, 1960s, rechanneled stereo, $10.

| Number | Title (A Side/B Side) | Yr | NM |
|---|---|---|---|
| ❑ DL 5499 [10] | Song Hits of Paris/Le Bing | 1953 | 50.00 |
| ❑ DL 5508 [10] | Some Fine Old Chestnuts | 1953 | 50.00 |
| ❑ DL 5520 [10] | Bing Sings the Hits | 1954 | 50.00 |
| ❑ DL 5556 [10] | Country Girl/Little Boy Lost/ Anything Goes | 1954 | 50.00 |
| ❑ DL 6000 [10] | Two Favorite Stories by Bing Crosby | 1950 | 60.00 |
| ❑ DL 6001 [10] | Ichabod/Rip Van Winkle | 1950 | 50.00 |
| ❑ DL 6008 [10] | Collector's Classics: Mississippi/Here Is My Heart | 1951 | 60.00 |
| ❑ DL 6009 [10] | Collector's Classics: Anything Goes/Two for Tonight | 1951 | 60.00 |
| ❑ DL 6010 [10] | Collector's Classics: Rhythm on the Range/Pennies from Heaven | 1951 | 60.00 |
| ❑ DL 6011 [10] | Collector's Classics: Waikiki Wedding | 1951 | 60.00 |
| ❑ DL 6012 [10] | Collector's Classics: Paris Honeymoon | 1951 | 60.00 |
| ❑ DL 6013 [10] | Collector's Classics: The Star Maker/Doctor Rhythm | 1951 | 60.00 |
| ❑ DL 6014 [10] | Collector's Classics: Big Broadcast of 1936 | 1951 | 60.00 |
| ❑ DL 6015 [10] | Collector's Classics: The Road to Singapore/If I Had My Way | 1951 | 60.00 |
| ❑ DXSB 7184 [(2)R] | The Best of Bing | 1965 | 15.00 |
| ❑ DL 8020 [M] | The Man Without a Country/ What So Proudly We Hail | 1950 | 40.00 |
| ❑ DL 8110 [M] | Lullaby Time | 1955 | 40.00 |
| ❑ DL 8128 [M] | Merry Christmas | 1955 | 40.00 |
| *—Expanded version of 10-inch LP; all-black label* | | | |
| ❑ DL 8128 [M] | Merry Christmas | 1960 | 25.00 |
| *—Reissue on black label with color bars* | | | |
| ❑ DL 8178 [M] | Merry Christmas | 196? | 60.00 |
| *—Black label with color bars; at least one copy is known to exist on red vinyl* | | | |
| ❑ DL 8207 [M] | Shillelaghs and Shamrocks | 1956 | 40.00 |
| ❑ DL 8210 [M] | Home on the Range | 1956 | 40.00 |
| ❑ DL 8262 [M] | When Irish Eyes Are Smiling | 1956 | 40.00 |
| ❑ DL 8268 [M] | Drifting and Dreaming | 1956 | 40.00 |
| ❑ DL 8269 [M] | Blue Hawaii | 1956 | 40.00 |
| ❑ DL 8272 [M] | High Tor | 1956 | 400.00 |
| ❑ DL 8318 [M] | Anything Goes | 1956 | 50.00 |
| ❑ DL 8352 [M] | Song I Wish I Had Sung...The First Time Around | 1956 | 40.00 |
| ❑ DL 8365 [M] | Twilight on the Trail | 1957 | 40.00 |
| ❑ DL 8374 [M] | Some Fine Old Chestnuts | 1957 | 40.00 |

| Number | Title (A Side/B Side) | Yr | NM |
|---|---|---|---|
| ❑ DL 8419 [M] | A Christmas Sing with Bing Around the World | 1957 | 40.00 |
| ❑ DL 8493 [M] | Bing and the Dixieland Bands | 1957 | 40.00 |
| ❑ DL 8575 [M] | New Tricks | 1957 | 40.00 |
| ❑ DL 8687 [M] | Around the World | 1958 | 40.00 |
| ❑ DL 8780 [M] | Bing in Paris | 1958 | 40.00 |
| ❑ DL 8781 [M] | That Christmas Feeling | 1958 | 30.00 |
| *—Expanded version of DL 5020; all-black label, textured cover* | | | |
| ❑ DL 8781 [M] | That Christmas Feeling | 1960 | 20.00 |
| *—Reissue on black label with color bars, smooth cover* | | | |
| ❑ DL 8846 [M] | In a Little Spanish Town | 1959 | 30.00 |
| ❑ DL 9054 [M] | Bing: A Musical Autobiography 1927-1934 | 1961 | 40.00 |
| ❑ DL 9064 [M] | Bing: A Musical Autobiography 1934-1941 | 1961 | 40.00 |
| ❑ DL 9067 [M] | Bing: A Musical Autobiography 1941-44 | 1961 | 40.00 |
| ❑ DL 9077 [M] | Bing: A Musical Autobiography 1944-47 | 1961 | 40.00 |
| ❑ DL 9078 [M] | Bing: A Musical Autobiography 1947-1953 | 1961 | 40.00 |
| ❑ DL 9106 [M] | Ichabod/Rip Van Winkle | 1962 | 25.00 |
| ❑ DL 34522 | Favorite Songs of Christmas | 1968 | 15.00 |
| *—Decca Records Custom Division pressing* | | | |
| ❑ DL 74281 [R] | Holiday in Europe | 1962 | 15.00 |
| ❑ DL 74283 [R] | The Small One | 1962 | 10.00 |
| ❑ DL 74415 [R] | Songs Everybody Knows | 1964 | 15.00 |
| ❑ DL 78128 [R] | Merry Christmas | 196? | 10.00 |
| ❑ DL 78207 [R] | Shillelaghs and Shamrocks | 196? | 10.00 |
| ❑ DL 78262 [R] | When Irish Eyes Are Smiling | 196? | 10.00 |
| ❑ DL 78352 [R] | Songs I Wish I Had Sung...The First Time Around | 196? | 10.00 |
| ❑ DL 78419 [R] | A Christmas Sing with Bing Around the World | 196? | 10.00 |
| ❑ DL 78781 [R] | That Christmas Feeling | 196? | 10.00 |
| ❑ DL 79106 [R] | Ichabod/Rip Van Winkle | 1962 | 10.00 |
| **ENCORE** | | | |
| ❑ E2E-201 [(2)] | The Bing Crosby Story, Volume 1 | 1968 | 15.00 |
| ❑ E2E-202 [(2)] | The Bing Crosby Story, Volume 2 | 1968 | 15.00 |
| **FOX AMERICAN** | | | |
| ❑ SMF 210 | Bing Crosby Sings Christmas | 1978 | 10.00 |
| *—Side 1 from radio show Dec. 19, 1951; Side 2 from radio show Dec. 14, 1949* | | | |

| Number | Title (A Side/B Side) | Yr | NM |
|---|---|---|---|
| **GNP CRESCENDO** | | | |
| ❑ GNP-9044 | The Radio Years, Vol. 1 | 1985 | 8.00 |
| ❑ GNP-9046 | The Radio Years, Vol. 2 | 1986 | 8.00 |
| ❑ GNP-9047 | The Radio Years, Vol. 3 | 1986 | 8.00 |
| ❑ GNP-9048 | The Radio Years, Vol. 4 | 1986 | 8.00 |
| **GOLDEN** | | | |
| ❑ A298:20 [M] | Ali Baba and the 40 Thieves | 1957 | 25.00 |
| ❑ A298:21 [M] | How Lovely Is Christmas/A Christmas Story | 195? | 25.00 |
| **HARMONY** | | | |
| ❑ HL 7094 [M] | Crosby Classics | 1958 | 15.00 |
| ❑ HS 11313 [R] | Crosby Classics | 196? | 10.00 |
| **LONDON** | | | |
| ❑ PS 679 | Feels Good | 1977 | 12.00 |
| **MARK 56** | | | |
| ❑ 762 | Original Radio Broadcasts | 197? | 10.00 |
| **MCA** | | | |
| ❑ 177 | Shillelaghs and Shamrocks | 1973 | 10.00 |
| ❑ 519 | When Irish Eyes Are Smiling | 197? | 10.00 |
| ❑ 915 | Hey Bing! | 198? | 10.00 |
| ❑ 1502 | Rare 1930-31 Brunswick Recordings | 198? | 10.00 |
| ❑ 3031 | Bing Crosby's Greatest Hits | 1977 | 10.00 |
| ❑ 2-4045 [(2)] | The Best of Bing | 197? | 10.00 |
| *—Blue labels with rainbow; regular cover* | | | |
| ❑ 2-4045 [(2)] | The Best of Bing | 197? | 12.00 |
| *—Black labels with rainbow; gatefold cover* | | | |
| ❑ 15017 | Two Favorite Stories by Bing Crosby | 197? | 10.00 |
| *—Reissue of Decca DL 4283* | | | |
| ❑ 15018 [R] | A Christmas Sing with Bing Around the World | 197? | 8.00 |
| *—Reissue of Decca DL7-8419* | | | |
| ❑ 15019 [R] | That Christmas Feeling | 1973 | 8.00 |
| *—Reissue of Decca DL7-8781* | | | |
| ❑ 15024 [R] | Merry Christmas | 197? | 8.00 |
| *—Reissue of Decca DL7-8128* | | | |
| ❑ 37076 | Bing Crosby's Greatest Hits | 198? | 8.00 |
| **METRO** | | | |
| ❑ M-523 [M] | Bing Crosby | 1965 | 12.00 |
| ❑ MS-523 [S] | Bing Crosby | 1965 | 15.00 |
| **MGM** | | | |
| ❑ E-3890 [M] | Senor Bing | 1961 | 15.00 |
| ❑ SE-3890 [S] | Senor Bing | 1961 | 20.00 |
| ❑ E-4129 [M] | The Great Standards | 1963 | 15.00 |
| ❑ SE-4129 [S] | The Great Standards | 1963 | 20.00 |
| ❑ E-4203 [M] | The Very Best of Bing Crosby | 1964 | 15.00 |
| ❑ SE-4203 [S] | The Very Best of Bing Crosby | 1964 | 20.00 |
| **MOBILE FIDELITY** | | | |
| ❑ 1-260 | Bing Sings Whilst Bregman Swings | 1996 | 20.00 |
| *—Audiophile vinyl* | | | |
| **MURRAY HILL** | | | |
| ❑ 894637 [(4)] | Bing Crosby and His Friends | 197? | 25.00 |
| **P.I.P.** | | | |
| ❑ 6802 | Thoroughly Modern Bing | 1971 | 12.00 |
| **PHILCO** | | | |
| ❑ LP 436 [10] | Crosby Classics | 195? | 40.00 |
| *—Custom item for Philco (front cover has "Philco: Famous for Quality the World Over")* | | | |
| **PICKWICK** | | | |
| ❑ SPC-3583 | Thoroughly Modern Bing | 1978 | 8.00 |
| **POLYDOR** | | | |
| ❑ PD-1-6128 | Seasons: The Closing Chapter | 1978 | 12.00 |
| **RCA VICTOR** | | | |
| ❑ LPM-1473 [M] | Bing with a Beat | 1957 | 25.00 |
| ❑ AFL1-1854 | Fancy Meeting You Here | 1977 | 10.00 |
| ❑ LPM-1854 [M] | Fancy Meeting You Here | 1958 | 20.00 |
| ❑ LSP-1854 [S] | Fancy Meeting You Here | 1958 | 30.00 |
| ❑ LPM-2071 [M] | Young Bing Crosby | 1959 | 20.00 |
| ❑ CPL1-2086(e) | A Legendary Performer | 1976 | 10.00 |
| **READER'S DIGEST** | | | |
| ❑ RDA-175 | Christmas with Bing | 1980 | 10.00 |
| *—Repackage of Warner Bros.and Capitol recordings* | | | |
| **REPRISE** | | | |
| ❑ R-6106 [M] | Return to Paradise Islands | 1964 | 15.00 |
| ❑ R9-6106 [S] | Return to Paradise Islands | 1964 | 20.00 |
| **SPOKANE** | | | |
| ❑ 1 | Bing Crosby On the Air, 1934 and 1938 | 197? | 10.00 |
| ❑ 5 | Der Bingle, Vol. 1 | 197? | 10.00 |
| ❑ 10 | Der Bingle, Vol. 2 | 197? | 10.00 |
| ❑ 12 | Bing in the 30's | 197? | 10.00 |
| ❑ 14 | Bing in the 30s, Vol. 2 | 197? | 10.00 |
| ❑ 15 | Holiday Inn/The Bells of St. Mary's | 197? | 10.00 |
| ❑ 16 | Kraft Music Hall Highlights | 197? | 10.00 |
| ❑ 19 | Kraft Music Hall Highlights, Vol. 2 | 197? | 10.00 |
| ❑ 20 | Der Bingle, Vol. 3 | 197? | 10.00 |
| ❑ 21 | Bing Crosby & the Music Maids | 197? | 10.00 |

| Number | Title (A Side/B Side) | Yr | NM |
|---|---|---|---|
| ❑ 24 | Bing in the 30s, Vol. 3 | 1986 | 8.00 |
| ❑ 25 | Bing in the 30s, Vol. 4 | 1986 | 8.00 |
| ❑ 26 | Bing in the 30s, Vol. 5 | 1986 | 8.00 |
| ❑ 27 | Bing in the 30s, Vol. 6 | 1986 | 8.00 |
| SUNBEAM | | | |
| ❑ 502 | Distinctively Bing, Vol. 1 | 197? | 10.00 |
| ❑ 504 | Distinctively Bing, Vol. 2 | 197? | 10.00 |
| TIME-LIFE | | | |
| ❑ SLGD-06 [(2)] | Legendary Singers: Bing Crosby | 1985 | 15.00 |
| 20TH CENTURY | | | |
| ❑ T-551 | A Holiday Toast | 1977 | 12.00 |
| UNITED ARTISTS | | | |
| ❑ UA-LA554-G | That's What Life Is All About | 1976 | 12.00 |
| VERVE | | | |
| ❑ MGV 2020 [M] | Bing Sings Whilst Bregman Swings | 1956 | 50.00 |
| ❑ V-2020 [M] | Bing Sings Whilst Bregman Swings | 1961 | 25.00 |
| VOCALION | | | |
| ❑ VL 3603 [M] | Bing Crosby Sings | 195? | 15.00 |
| ❑ VL 73603 [R] | Bing Crosby Sings | 196? | 10.00 |
| WARNER BROS. | | | |
| ❑ W 1363 [M] | Join with Bing and Sing Along | 1960 | 15.00 |
| ❑ WS 1363 [S] | Join with Bing and Sing Along | 1960 | 20.00 |
| ❑ 2W 1401 [(2)M] | 101 Gang Songs | 1961 | 20.00 |
| ❑ 2WS 1401 [(2)S] | 101 Gang Songs | 1961 | 25.00 |
| ❑ W 1422 [M] | Join Bing in a Gang Song Sing-Along | 1961 | 15.00 |
| ❑ WS 1422 [S] | Join Bing in a Gang Song Sing-Along | 1961 | 20.00 |
| ❑ W 1435 [M] | Join Bing and Sing Along | 1962 | 15.00 |
| ❑ WS 1435 [S] | Join Bing and Sing Along | 1962 | 20.00 |
| ❑ W 1482 [M] | On the Happy Side | 1962 | 15.00 |
| ❑ WS 1482 [S] | On the Happy Side | 1962 | 20.00 |
| ❑ W 1484 [M] | I Wish You a Merry Christmas | 1962 | 15.00 |
| ❑ WS 1484 [S] | I Wish You a Merry Christmas | 1962 | 20.00 |
| "X" | | | |
| ❑ XLVA-4250 [M] | Young Bing Crosby | 1955 | 50.00 |

**CROSBY, BING, AND LOUIS ARMSTRONG**

| Number | Title (A Side/B Side) | Yr | NM |
|---|---|---|---|
| CAPITOL | | | |
| ❑ SM-11735 | Bing Crosby and Louis Armstrong | 1977 | 10.00 |
| MGM | | | |
| ❑ E-3882 [M] | Bing and Satchmo | 1960 | 15.00 |
| ❑ SE-3882 [S] | Bing and Satchmo | 1960 | 20.00 |

**CROSBY, BOB**

| Number | Title (A Side/B Side) | Yr | NM |
|---|---|---|---|
| CAPITOL | | | |
| ❑ H 293 [10] | Bob Crosby and His Bobcats | 1952 | 50.00 |
| ❑ T 293 [M] | Bob Crosby and His Bobcats | 1955 | 40.00 |
| ❑ T 1556 [M] | The Hits of Bob Crosby's Bobcats | 1961 | 20.00 |
| COLUMBIA | | | |
| ❑ CL 766 [M] | The Bob Crosby Show | 1956 | 30.00 |
| CORAL | | | |
| ❑ CRL 56000 [10] | Swinging at the Sugar Bowl | 1950 | 50.00 |
| ❑ CRL 56003 [10] | Dixieland Jazz 1 | 1950 | 50.00 |
| ❑ CRL 56018 [10] | Marches in Dixieland Style | 1950 | 50.00 |
| ❑ CRL 56039 [10] | St. Louis Blues | 1950 | 50.00 |
| ❑ CRL 57005 [M] | The Bobcats' Ball | 1955 | 40.00 |
| ❑ CRL 57060 [M] | Bobcats' Blues | 1956 | 40.00 |
| ❑ CRL 57061 [M] | Bobcats On Parade | 1956 | 40.00 |
| ❑ CRL 57062 [M] | Bob Crosby in Hi-Fi | 1956 | 40.00 |
| ❑ CRL 57089 [M] | Bob Crosby 1936-1956 | 1957 | 40.00 |
| ❑ CRL 57170 [M] | The Bobcats in Hi-Fi | 1958 | 40.00 |
| DECCA | | | |
| ❑ DL 4856 [M] | Bob Crosby's Bobcats — Their Greatest Hits | 1967 | 20.00 |
| ❑ DL 8042 [M] | Five Feet of Swing | 1954 | 40.00 |
| ❑ DL 8061 [M] | Bob Crosby's Bobcats | 1954 | 40.00 |
| DOT | | | |
| ❑ DLP-3136 [M] | South Pacific Blows Warm | 1958 | 20.00 |
| ❑ DLP-3170 [M] | Petite Fleur | 1959 | 20.00 |
| ❑ DLP-3278 [M] | Bob Crosby's Great Hits | 196? | 20.00 |
| ❑ DLP-3382 [M] | C'est Si Bon | 196? | 20.00 |
| ❑ DLP-25136 [S] | South Pacific Blows Warm | 1959 | 25.00 |
| ❑ DLP-25170 [S] | Petite Fleur | 1959 | 25.00 |
| ❑ DLP-25278 [S] | Bob Crosby's Great Hits | 196? | 25.00 |
| ❑ DLP-25382 [S] | C'est Si Bon | 196? | 25.00 |

**CROSBY, GARY**

| Number | Title (A Side/B Side) | Yr | NM |
|---|---|---|---|
| VERVE | | | |
| ❑ MGV-2112 [M] | Gary Crosby Belts the Blues | 1959 | 100.00 |

**CROSBY, STILLS AND NASH**

| Number | Title (A Side/B Side) | Yr | NM |
|---|---|---|---|
| ATLANTIC | | | |
| ❑ SD 8229 | Crosby, Stills & Nash | 1969 | 20.00 |
| ❑ SD 8229 | Crosby, Stills & Nash | 2000 | 25.00 |
| *—Classic Records reissue on 180-gram vinyl* | | | |
| ❑ SD 16026 | Replay | 1980 | 12.00 |
| *—Also has solo cuts by Stephen Stills* | | | |
| ❑ SD 19104 | CSN | 1977 | 12.00 |
| ❑ SD 19117 | Crosby, Stills & Nash | 1977 | 10.00 |
| *—Reissue of 8229* | | | |
| ❑ SD 19360 | Daylight Again | 1982 | 12.00 |
| ❑ 80075 | Allies | 1983 | 12.00 |
| ❑ 82107 | Live It Up | 1990 | 15.00 |
| NAUTILUS | | | |
| ❑ NR-48 | Crosby, Stills and Nash | 1982 | 150.00 |
| *—Audiophile vinyl* | | | |

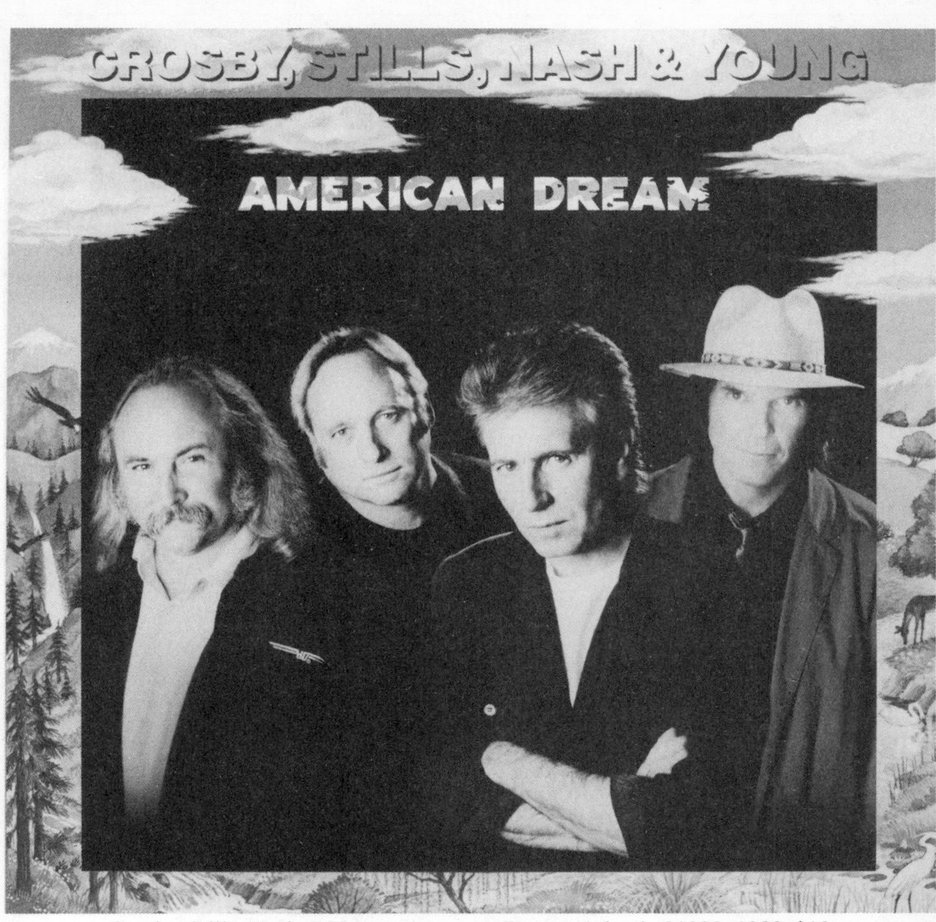


Crosby, Stills, Nash & Young, *American Dream,* Atlantic 81888, 1988, $10.

**CROSBY, STILLS, NASH & YOUNG**

| Number | Title (A Side/B Side) | Yr | NM |
|---|---|---|---|
| ATLANTIC | | | |
| ❑ PR 165 [M] | Celebration/CSNY Month | 1974 | 100.00 |
| *—Promo-only LP in mono* | | | |
| ❑ PR 165 [S] | Celebration/CSNY Month | 1974 | 50.00 |
| *—Promo-only LP in stereo* | | | |
| ❑ 2-902 [(2)M] | 4 Way Street | 1971 | 100.00 |
| *—White label promo; no stock copies are mono* | | | |
| ❑ SD 2-902 [(2)] | 4 Way Street | 1971 | 20.00 |
| ❑ SD 2-902 [(2)DJ] | 4 Way Street | 1971 | 50.00 |
| *—White label stereo promo* | | | |
| ❑ 7200 [M] | Deja Vu | 1970 | 150.00 |
| *—White label promo; no stock copies are mono* | | | |
| ❑ SD 7200 | Deja Vu | 1970 | 15.00 |
| *—Pasted-on front cover photo must still be intact* | | | |
| ❑ SD 7200 [DJ] | Deja Vu | 1970 | 60.00 |
| *—White label stereo promo* | | | |
| ❑ SD 18100 | So Far | 1974 | 12.00 |
| ❑ PR 18102 [DJ] | A Rap with C, S, N & Y | 1974 | 50.00 |
| *—Promo-only interview album* | | | |
| ❑ SD 19118 | Deja Vu | 1977 | 10.00 |
| *—Reissue of 7200, this time with photo as part of the cover rather than as a paste-on* | | | |
| ❑ SD 19119 | So Far | 1977 | 10.00 |
| *—Reissue of 18100* | | | |
| ❑ 81888 | American Dream | 1988 | 10.00 |
| MOBILE FIDELITY | | | |
| ❑ 1-088 | Deja Vu | 198? | 200.00 |
| *—Audiophile vinyl* | | | |

**CROSSFIRES, THE (3)**

| Number | Title (A Side/B Side) | Yr | NM |
|---|---|---|---|
| STRAND | | | |
| ❑ SL-1083 [M] | Limbo Rock | 1963 | 20.00 |
| ❑ SLS-1083 [S] | Limbo Rock | 1963 | 25.00 |

**CROSTON, JILL** See LACY J. DALTON.

**CROTHERS, SCATMAN**

| Number | Title (A Side/B Side) | Yr | NM |
|---|---|---|---|
| CRAFTSMAN | | | |
| ❑ 8036 [M] | Gone with the Scat Man | 1960 | 30.00 |
| DOOTO | | | |
| ❑ DTL 814 [M] | Comedy Sweepstakes | 1961 | 25.00 |
| MOTOWN | | | |
| ❑ M 777L | Big Ben Sings | 1973 | 20.00 |
| TOPS | | | |
| ❑ 1511 [M] | Rock and Roll with Scat Man | 1956 | 80.00 |

**CROW**

| Number | Title (A Side/B Side) | Yr | NM |
|---|---|---|---|
| AMARET | | | |
| ❑ ST-5002 | Crow Music | 1969 | 20.00 |
| ❑ ST-5006 | Crow By Crow | 1970 | 20.00 |
| ❑ ST-5009 | Mosaic | 1971 | 20.00 |
| ❑ AST-5012 | Best of Crow | 1972 | 15.00 |
| ❑ ST-5013 | David Crow d/b/a Crow | 1973 | 15.00 |

**CROWELL, RODNEY**

| Number | Title (A Side/B Side) | Yr | NM |
|---|---|---|---|
| COLUMBIA | | | |
| ❑ CAS 2001 [DJ] | Dialog with T-Bone Burnett | 1989 | 30.00 |
| *—Promo-only interview record* | | | |
| ❑ CAS 2456 [DJ] | Street Language Interchords | 1986 | 30.00 |
| *—Promo-only interview record* | | | |
| ❑ FC 40116 | Street Language | 1986 | 8.00 |
| ❑ FC 44076 | Diamonds and Dirt | 1988 | 10.00 |
| ❑ FC 45242 | Keys to the Highway | 1989 | 12.00 |
| WARNER BROS. | | | |
| ❑ BSK 3228 | Ain't Living Long Like This | 1978 | 15.00 |
| ❑ BSK 3407 | But What Will the Neighbors Think | 1980 | 10.00 |
| ❑ BSK 3587 | Rodney Crowell | 1981 | 10.00 |

**CROWS, THE / THE HARPTONES**

| Number | Title (A Side/B Side) | Yr | NM |
|---|---|---|---|
| ROULETTE | | | |
| ❑ RE-114 [(2)] | Echoes of a Rock Era: The Groups | 1973 | 20.00 |

**CRUCIFIX**

| Number | Title (A Side/B Side) | Yr | NM |
|---|---|---|---|
| UNIVERSAL | | | |
| ❑ RON 2 [EP] | Crucifix | 1982 | 40.00 |

| Number | Title (A Side/B Side) | Yr | NM |
|---|---|---|---|

## CRUDUP, ARTHUR

### COLLECTABLES
❑ COL-5130 Mean Ol' Frisco 1988 10.00

### DELMARK
❑ DS-614 Look on Yonder's Wall 1969 40.00
❑ DS-621 Crudup's Mood 1969 40.00

### FIRE
❑ 103 [M] Mean Ol' Frisco 1960 900.00

### RCA VICTOR
❑ LVP-573 Father of Rock and Roll 1971 20.00

### TRIP
❑ 7501 Mean Ol' Frisco 1975 15.00

## CRUM, SIMON See FERLIN HUSKY.

## CRUSADERS, THE (1)

### APPLAUSE
❑ APBL-2313 Powerhouse 197? 12.00
*—Reissue of Pacific Jazz 20136*

### CRUSADERS
❑ 16000 Street Life 1982 25.00
*—Audiophile vinyl*
❑ 16002 Ongaku-Kai: Live in Japan 1982 25.00
*—Audiophile vinyl*

### MOBILE FIDELITY
❑ 1-010 Chain Reaction 1979 20.00
*—Audiophile vinyl*

### PACIFIC JAZZ
❑ PJ-27 [M] Freedom Sound 1961 25.00
❑ ST-27 [S] Freedom Sound 1961 30.00
❑ PJ-43 [M] Lookin' Ahead 1962 25.00
❑ ST-43 [S] Lookin' Ahead 1962 30.00
*—Black vinyl*
❑ ST-43 [S] Lookin' Ahead 1962 60.00
*—Yellow vinyl*
❑ PJ-57 [M] The Jazz Crusaders at the Lighthouse 1962 25.00
❑ ST-57 [S] The Jazz Crusaders at the Lighthouse 1962 30.00
❑ PJ-68 [M] Tough Talk 1963 25.00
❑ ST-68 [S] Tough Talk 1963 30.00
❑ PJ-76 [M] Heat Wave 1963 25.00
❑ ST-76 [S] Heat Wave 1963 30.00
❑ PJ-83 [M] Stretchin' Out 1964 25.00
❑ ST-83 [S] Stretchin' Out 1964 30.00
❑ PJ-87 [M] The Thing 1964 25.00
❑ ST-87 [S] The Thing 1964 30.00
❑ PJ-10092 [M] Chili Con Soul 1965 20.00
❑ PJ-10098 [M] Live at the Lighthouse '66 1966 20.00
❑ PJ-10106 [M] Talk That Talk 1966 20.00
❑ PJ-10115 [M] The Festival Album 1967 25.00
❑ PJ-10124 Uh Huh 1967 25.00
❑ ST-20092 [S] Chili Con Soul 1965 25.00
❑ ST-20098 [S] Live at the Lighthouse '66 1966 25.00
❑ ST-20106 [S] Talk That Talk 1966 25.00
❑ ST-20115 [S] The Festival Album 1967 20.00
❑ ST-20124 Uh Huh 1967 20.00
❑ ST-20131 Lighthouse '68 1968 20.00
❑ ST-20136 Powerhouse 1968 20.00
❑ ST-20165 The Jazz Crusaders at the Lighthouse '69 1969 20.00
❑ ST-20175 The Best of the Jazz Crusaders 1969 20.00
❑ ST-90481 [S] The Jazz Crusaders at the Lighthouse 1965 30.00
*—Capitol Record Club edition*
❑ T-90598 [M] Chili Con Soul 1965 25.00
*—Capitol Record Club edition*

## CRYAN' SHAMES, THE

### COLUMBIA
❑ CL 2589 [M] Sugar & Spice 1967 20.00
❑ CL 2786 [M] A Scratch in the Sky 1967 25.00
❑ CS 9389 [S] Sugar & Spice 1967 25.00
❑ CS 9586 [S] A Scratch in the Sky 1967 20.00
❑ CS 9719 Synthesis 1969 20.00

## CRYSTAL MANSION, THE

### CAPITOL
❑ ST-227 The Crystal Mansion 1969 20.00

## CRYSTALS, THE (1)

### PHILLES
❑ PHLP-4000 [M] Twist Uptown 1962 600.00
❑ PHLP-4001 [M] He's a Rebel 1963 600.00
❑ PHLP-4003 [M] The Crystals Sing the Greatest Hits, Vol. 1 1963 600.00
❑ DT-90722 [R] Twist Uptown 1965 1200.
*—Capitol Record Club edition*
❑ T-90722 [M] Twist Uptown 1965 600.00
*—Capitol Record Club edition*

## CUBY AND THE BLIZZARDS

### PHILIPS
❑ PHS 600307 Cuby and the Blizzards Live 1969 20.00
❑ PHS 600331 King of the World 1970 20.00

## CUFF LINKS, THE (1)

### DECCA
❑ DL 75160 Tracy 1969 20.00
❑ DL 75235 The Cuff Links 1970 20.00

## CUGAT, XAVIER

### COLUMBIA
❑ CL 515 [M] Relaxing with Cugat (Quiet Music, Volume VI) 1953 40.00
*—Second editions have maroon label, gold print and a "CL" prefix*
❑ GL 515 [M] Relaxing with Cugat (Quiet Music, Volume VI) 1952 50.00
*—Original copies have black label, silver print and a "GL" prefix*
❑ CL 537 [M] Dance with Cugat 1953 40.00
*—Maroon label, gold print*
❑ CL 537 [M] Dance with Cugat 1955 25.00
*—Red and black label with six "eye" logos*
❑ CL 579 [M] Favorite Rhumbas 1954 40.00
*—Maroon label, gold print*
❑ CL 579 [M] Favorite Rhumbas 1955 25.00
*—Red and black label with six "eye" logos*
❑ CL 579 [M] Favorite Rhumbas 1962 15.00
*—Red "Guaranteed High Fidelity" label*
❑ CL 579 [M] Favorite Rhumbas 1965 12.00
*—Red "Mono 360 Sound" label*
❑ CL 610 [M] Ole 1955 25.00
*—Red and black label with six "eye" logos*
❑ CL 610 [M] Ole 1955 40.00
*—Maroon label, gold print*
❑ CL 626 [M] Mucho Mucho Mambo 1955 25.00
*—Red and black label with six "eye" logos*
❑ CL 626 [M] Mucho Mucho Mambo 1955 40.00
*—Maroon label, gold print*
❑ CL 718 [M] Cha Cha Cha 1956 30.00
*—Red and black label with six "eye" logos*
❑ CL 732 [M] Mambo at the Waldorf 1956 30.00
*—Red and black label with six "eye" logos*
❑ CL 733 [M] Merengue by Cugat 1956 30.00
*—Red and black label with six "eye" logos*
❑ CL 733 [M] Merengue by Cugat 1962 15.00
*—Red "Guaranteed High Fidelity" label*
❑ CL 733 [M] Merengue by Cugat 1965 12.00
*—Red "Mono 360 Sound" label*
❑ CL 1016 [M] Bread, Love and Cha Cha Cha 1957 12.00
❑ CL 1094 [M] Cugar Cavalcade 1958 25.00
*—Red and black label with six "eye" logos*
❑ CL 1143 [M] Waltzes! But By Cugat 1959 25.00
*—Red and black label with six "eye" logos*
❑ CL 2506 [10] Mambo! 1955 50.00
❑ CL 6005 [10] Cugat's Rhumba 1948 50.00
❑ CL 6021 [10] Cugat's Favoprite Rhumbas 1949 50.00
❑ CL 6036 [10] Rhumba with Cugat 1949 50.00
❑ CL 6077 [10] Conga with Cugat 1949 50.00
❑ CL 6086 [10] Tropical Bouquet 1950 50.00
❑ CL 6121 [10] Dance Date 1950 50.00
❑ CL 6213 [10] Mambo at the Waldorf 1951 50.00
❑ CL 6234 [10] Tango with Cugat 1951 50.00
❑ CL 6236 [10] Samba with Cugat 1951 50.00
❑ CS 8055 [S] Cugar Cavalcade 1959 30.00
*—Red and black label with six "eye" logos*
❑ CS 8059 [S] Waltzes! But By Cugat 1959 30.00
*—Red and black label with six "eye" logos*
❑ CS 8646 [R] Merengue by Cugat 1963 12.00

### DECCA
❑ DL 4672 [M] Feeling Good 1965 15.00
❑ DL 4740 [M] Dance Party 1966 15.00
❑ DL 4799 [M] Bang Bang 1966 15.00
❑ DL 4851 [M] Xavier Cugat Today 1967 15.00
❑ DL 74672 [S] Feeling Good 1965 20.00
❑ DL 74740 [S] Dance Party 1966 20.00
❑ DL 74799 [S] Bang Bang 1966 20.00
❑ DL 74851 [S] Xavier Cugat Today 1967 20.00

### MERCURY
❑ PPS-2003 [M] Viva Cugat! 1961 20.00
❑ PPS-2015 [M] The Best of Cugat 1961 20.00
❑ PPS-2021 [M] Cugat Plays Continental Favorites 1961 20.00
❑ PPS-6003 [S] Viva Cugat! 1961 25.00
❑ PPS-6015 [S] The Best of Cugat 1961 25.00
❑ PPS-6021 [S] Cugat Plays Continental Favorites 1961 25.00
❑ MG 20065 [M] Cugat's Favorites 1955 30.00
❑ MG 20108 [M] Mambo!/Music for Latin Lovers 1957 30.00
❑ MG-20705 [M] Twist with Cugat 1962 20.00
❑ MG-20745 [M] The Most Popular Movie Themes As Styled by Cugat 1961 20.00
❑ MG-20798 [M] Cugat's Golden Goodies 1963 20.00
❑ MG-20832 [M] Cugi's Cocktails 1963 20.00
❑ MG-20868 [M] Viva Cugat! 1964 15.00
*—Reissue of 2003*
❑ MG-20870 [M] The Best of Cugat 1964 15.00
*—Reissue of 2015*
❑ MG-20888 [M] Cugat Caricatures 1964 15.00
❑ MG 25120 [10] Here's Cugat 195? 40.00
❑ MG 25149 [10] Dance with Cugat/The Great Latin-American Rhythms of Xavier Cugat 195? 40.00
❑ MG 25168 [10] Mambos by Cugat 195? 40.00
❑ SR-60705 [S] Twist with Cugat 1962 25.00
❑ SR-60745 [S] The Most Popular Movie Themes As Styled by Cugat 1961 25.00
❑ SR-60798 [S] Cugat's Golden Goodies 1963 25.00
❑ SR-60832 [S] Cugi's Cocktails 1963 25.00
❑ SR-60868 [S] Viva Cugat! 1964 20.00
*—Reissue of 6003*
❑ SR-60870 [S] The Best of Cugat 1964 20.00
*—Reissue of 6015*
❑ SR-60888 [S] Cugat Caricatures 1964 20.00

### RCA VICTOR
❑ LPT-11 [10] Tangos 195? 40.00
❑ ANL1-1310 Pure Gold 1976 8.00
❑ LPM-1882 [M] The King Plays Some Aces 1958 20.00
❑ LSP-1882 [S] The King Plays Some Aces 1958 25.00
❑ LPM-1894 [M] Cugat in Spain 1959 20.00
❑ LSP-1894 [S] Cugat in Spain 1959 25.00
❑ LPM-1987 [M] Chili Con Cugie 1959 20.00
❑ LSP-1987 [S] Chili Con Cugie 1959 25.00
❑ LPM-2173 [M] Cugat in France, Spain and Italy 1960 20.00
❑ LSP-2173 [S] Cugat in France, Spain and Italy 1960 25.00

## CULLEY, FRANK "FLOORSHOW"

### BATON
❑ BL 1201 [M] Rock 'n Roll: Instrumentals for Dancing the Lindy Hop 1955 600.00
*—B-side tracks by Buddy Tate Orchestra*

## CULT, THE

### SIRE
❑ 25259 Love 1985 10.00
❑ 25555 Electric 1987 10.00
❑ 25871 Sonic Temple 1989 10.00
❑ R 101015 Sonic Temple 1989 12.00
*—BMG Direct Marketing edition*
❑ R 134608 Love 1985 12.00
*—RCA Music Service edition*
❑ R 184083 Electric 1987 12.00
*—RCA Music Service edition*

### WARNER BROS.
❑ WBMS-147 [DJ] Electric Interview 1987 50.00
*—Part of "The Warner Bros. Music Show" series*

## CULTURE CLUB

### VIRGIN/EPIC
❑ ARE 38398 Kissing to Be Clever 1982 12.00
*—First pressings have nine tracks and do not contain "Time (Clock of the Heart)"*
❑ FE 38398 Kissing to Be Clever 1983 10.00
*—This version has 10 tracks with the addition of "Time (Clock of the Heart)" as the first song on side 2*
❑ QE 39107 Colour by Numbers 1983 10.00
❑ 9E9-39237 [PD] Colour by Numbers 1983 25.00
*—Picture disc in plastic sleeve*
❑ OE 39881 Waking Up with the House on Fire 1984 10.00
❑ 9E9-40005 [PD] Waking Up with the House on Fire 1984 25.00
❑ OE 40345 From Luxury to Heartache 1986 10.00
❑ FE 40913 This Time: The First Four Years 1987 12.00

## CUMBERLAND THREE, THE

### ROULETTE
❑ R 25121 [M] Folk Scene U.S.A. 1960 20.00
❑ SR 25121 [S] Folk Scene U.S.A. 1960 25.00
❑ R 25132 [M] Civil War Almanac, Volume 1: The Yankees 1960 20.00
❑ SR 25132 [S] Civil War Almanac, Volume 1: The Yankees 1960 25.00
❑ R 25133 [M] Civil War Almanac, Volume 2: The Rebels 1960 20.00
❑ SR 25133 [S] Civil War Almanac, Volume 2: The Rebels 1960 25.00

## CUOZZO, MIKE

### JUBILEE
❑ JLP-1027 [M] Mike Cuozzo 1957 40.00

### SAVOY
❑ MG-12051 [M] Mighty Mike 1956 40.00

## CURE, THE

### A&M
❑ SP-4902 Pornography 1982 15.00
❑ SP-6020 [(2)] Happily Ever After 1981 30.00

### ELEKTRA
❑ 60435 The Head on the Door 1985 12.00
❑ 60477 Standing on a Beach — The Singles 1986 10.00
❑ 60737 [(2)] Kiss Me, Kiss Me, Kiss Me 1987 15.00
❑ 60737 [(2)DJ] Kiss Me, Kiss Me, Kiss Me 1987 30.00
*—Promo-only audiophile pressing*
❑ 60783 Faith 1988 10.00
*—Reissue of first U.K. album*
❑ 60784 Seventeen Seconds 1988 10.00
*—Reissue of second U.K. album*
❑ 60785 Pornography 1988 10.00
*—Reissue of A&M SP-4902*



Except when noted otherwise, VG = 25% of NM, and VG+ = 50% of NM. (Example: VG = $2.00, VG+ = $4.00 and NM = $8.00.)

| Number | Title (A Side/B Side) | Yr | NM |
|---|---|---|---|
| ❑ 60786 | Boys Don't Cry | 1988 | 10.00 |
| *—Reissue of PVC 7916* | | | |
| ❑ 60855 | Disintegration | 1989 | 10.00 |
| ❑ 60978 [(2)] | Mixed Up | 1990 | 40.00 |
| *—LP version has one extra track not on CD or cassette* | | | |
| ❑ 61744 [(2)] | Wild Mood Swings | 1996 | 30.00 |
| ❑ 62117 [(2)] | Galore: The Singles 1987-1997 | 1997 | 80.00 |
| ❑ 62236 [(2)] | Bloodflowers | 2000 | 40.00 |
| ❑ R 101109 | Disintegration | 1989 | 12.00 |
| *—BMG Direct Marketing edition* | | | |
| ❑ R 150024 | Standing on a Beach — The Singles | 1986 | 12.00 |
| *—BMG Direct Marketing edition* | | | |
| ❑ R 242404 | Kiss Me, Kiss Me, Kiss Me | 1987 | 18.00 |
| *—BMG Direct Marketing edition* | | | |
| ❑ R 274190 | Mixed Up | 1990 | 25.00 |
| *—BMG Direct Marketing edition* | | | |

GEFFEN

| Number | Title (A Side/B Side) | Yr | NM |
|---|---|---|---|
| ❑ B0002870-01 [(2)] | The Cure | 2004 | 15.00 |

PVC

| Number | Title (A Side/B Side) | Yr | NM |
|---|---|---|---|
| ❑ 7916 | Boys Don't Cry | 1980 | 15.00 |

SIRE

| Number | Title (A Side/B Side) | Yr | NM |
|---|---|---|---|
| ❑ 23928 [EP] | The Walk | 1983 | 12.00 |
| ❑ 25076 | Japanese Whispers | 1983 | 15.00 |
| ❑ 25086 | The Top | 1984 | 15.00 |

## CURLESS, DICK

CAPITOL

| Number | Title (A Side/B Side) | Yr | NM |
|---|---|---|---|
| ❑ ST-552 | Hard, Hard Travelin' Man | 1970 | 20.00 |
| ❑ ST-689 | Doggin' It | 1971 | 20.00 |
| ❑ ST-792 | Comin' On Country | 1971 | 20.00 |
| ❑ ST-11011 | Tombstone Every Mile | 1972 | 15.00 |
| *—Reissue of Tower DT 5005* | | | |
| ❑ ST-11087 | Stonin' Around | 1972 | 20.00 |
| ❑ ST-11119 | Live at the Wheeling Truck Driver's Jamboree | 1973 | 20.00 |
| ❑ ST-11211 | The Last Blues Song | 1973 | 20.00 |
| *—Second cover shows Dick Curless with no eye patch* | | | |
| ❑ ST-11211 | The Last Blues Song | 1973 | 30.00 |
| *—First cover shows Dick Curless with an eye patch* | | | |

TIFFANY

| Number | Title (A Side/B Side) | Yr | NM |
|---|---|---|---|
| ❑ 1016 [M] | Dick Curless Sings Songs of the Open Country | 1958 | 100.00 |
| ❑ 1028 [M] | Singing Just for Fun | 1959 | 100.00 |
| ❑ 1033 [M] | I Love to Tell a Story | 1960 | 100.00 |

TOWER

| Number | Title (A Side/B Side) | Yr | NM |
|---|---|---|---|
| ❑ DT 5005 [R] | Tombstone Every Mile | 1965 | 20.00 |
| ❑ T 5005 [M] | Tombstone Every Mile | 1965 | 30.00 |
| ❑ DT 5012 [R] | Hymns | 1965 | 20.00 |
| ❑ T 5012 [M] | Hymns | 1965 | 30.00 |
| ❑ DT 5013 [R] | The Soul of Dick Curless | 1966 | 20.00 |
| ❑ T 5013 [M] | The Soul of Dick Curless | 1966 | 30.00 |
| ❑ DT 5015 [R] | Travelin' Man | 1966 | 20.00 |
| ❑ T 5015 [M] | Travelin' Man | 1966 | 30.00 |
| ❑ DT 5016 [R] | At Home with Dick Curless | 1966 | 20.00 |
| ❑ T 5016 [M] | At Home with Dick Curless | 1966 | 30.00 |
| ❑ ST 5066 [S] | All of Me Belongs to You | 1967 | 30.00 |
| ❑ T 5066 [M] | All of Me Belongs to You | 1967 | 30.00 |
| ❑ ST 5089 [S] | Ramblin' Country | 1967 | 30.00 |
| ❑ T 5089 [M] | Ramblin' Country | 1967 | 30.00 |
| ❑ ST 5108 | The Long Lonesome Road | 1968 | 30.00 |
| ❑ ST 5139 | The Wild Side of Town | 1969 | 30.00 |

## CURLESS, DICK, AND KAY ADAMS

TOWER

| Number | Title (A Side/B Side) | Yr | NM |
|---|---|---|---|
| ❑ DT 5025 [R] | A Devil Like Me Needs an Angel Like You | 1966 | 20.00 |
| ❑ T 5025 [M] | A Devil Like Me Needs an Angel Like You | 1966 | 30.00 |

## CURRAN, ED

SAVOY

| Number | Title (A Side/B Side) | Yr | NM |
|---|---|---|---|
| ❑ MG-12191 [M] | Elysa | 1967 | 20.00 |

## CURRIE, CHERIE AND MARIE

CAPITOL

| Number | Title (A Side/B Side) | Yr | NM |
|---|---|---|---|
| ❑ ST-12022 | Messin' with the Boys | 1979 | 20.00 |

## CURSON, TED

ATLANTIC

| Number | Title (A Side/B Side) | Yr | NM |
|---|---|---|---|
| ❑ 1441 [M] | The New Thing and the Blue Thing | 1965 | 20.00 |
| ❑ SD 1441 [S] | The New Thing and the Blue Thing | 1965 | 25.00 |

AUDIO FIDELITY

| Number | Title (A Side/B Side) | Yr | NM |
|---|---|---|---|
| ❑ AFLP-2123 [M] | Now Hear This | 1964 | 20.00 |
| ❑ AFSD-6123 [S] | Now Hear This | 1964 | 25.00 |

OLD TOWN

| Number | Title (A Side/B Side) | Yr | NM |
|---|---|---|---|
| ❑ LP-2003 [M] | Plenty of Horn | 1961 | 200.00 |

PRESTIGE

| Number | Title (A Side/B Side) | Yr | NM |
|---|---|---|---|
| ❑ PRLP-7263 [M] | Fire Down Below | 1963 | 30.00 |
| *—Yellow label, Bergenfield, N.J. address* | | | |
| ❑ PRLP-7263 [M] | Fire Down Below | 1965 | 20.00 |
| *—Blue label with trident logo at right* | | | |
| ❑ PRST-7263 [S] | Fire Down Below | 1963 | 40.00 |
| *—Silver label, Bergenfield, N.J. address* | | | |
| ❑ PRST-7263 [S] | Fire Down Below | 1965 | 25.00 |
| *—Blue label with trident logo at right* | | | |

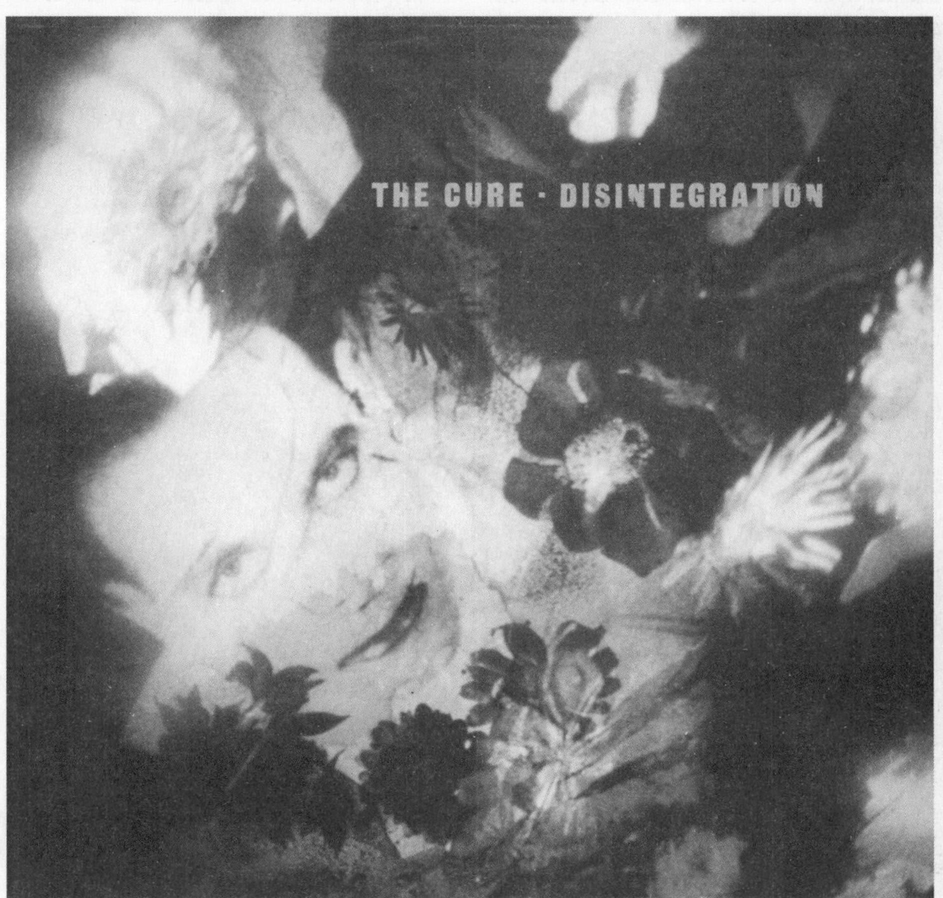


The Cure, *Disintegration,* Elektra 60855, 1989, $10.

## CURTIS, KEN

CAPITOL

| Number | Title (A Side/B Side) | Yr | NM |
|---|---|---|---|
| ❑ ST 2418 [S] | Gunsmoke's Festus | 1965 | 40.00 |
| ❑ T 2418 [M] | Gunsmoke's Festus | 1965 | 30.00 |

DOT

| Number | Title (A Side/B Side) | Yr | NM |
|---|---|---|---|
| ❑ DLP-25859 | Gunsmoke's Festus Calls Out Ken Curtis | 1968 | 30.00 |

## CURTIS, MAC

EPIC

| Number | Title (A Side/B Side) | Yr | NM |
|---|---|---|---|
| ❑ BN 26419 | The Sunshine Man | 1969 | 20.00 |

HMG/HIGHTONE

| Number | Title (A Side/B Side) | Yr | NM |
|---|---|---|---|
| ❑ HT 6601 | Rockabilly Uprising: The Best of Mac Curtis | 1997 | 10.00 |

ROLLIN' ROCK

| Number | Title (A Side/B Side) | Yr | NM |
|---|---|---|---|
| ❑ LP-002 | Ruffabilly | 197? | 10.00 |
| ❑ LP-007 | Good Rockin' Tomorrow | 197? | 10.00 |

## CURTIS, SONNY

ELEKTRA

| Number | Title (A Side/B Side) | Yr | NM |
|---|---|---|---|
| ❑ 6E-227 | Sonny Curtis | 1979 | 10.00 |
| ❑ 6E-283 | Love Is All Around | 1980 | 10.00 |
| ❑ 6E-349 | Rollin' | 1981 | 10.00 |

IMPERIAL

| Number | Title (A Side/B Side) | Yr | NM |
|---|---|---|---|
| ❑ LP-9276 [M] | Beatle Hits Flamenco Style | 1964 | 40.00 |
| ❑ LP-12276 [S] | Beatle Hits Flamenco Style | 1964 | 50.00 |

VIVA

| Number | Title (A Side/B Side) | Yr | NM |
|---|---|---|---|
| ❑ V-36012 | The First of Sonny Curtis | 1968 | 25.00 |
| ❑ V-36021 | The Sonny Curtis Style | 1969 | 25.00 |

## CYKLE, THE

LABEL

| Number | Title (A Side/B Side) | Yr | NM |
|---|---|---|---|
| ❑ 9-261 | The Cykle | 1969 | 500.00 |

## CYMBAL, JOHNNY

KAPP

| Number | Title (A Side/B Side) | Yr | NM |
|---|---|---|---|
| ❑ KL-1324 [M] | Mr. Bass Man | 1963 | 50.00 |
| ❑ KS-3324 [S] | Mr. Bass Man | 1963 | 70.00 |

## CYRILLE, ANDREW, AND MILFORD GRAVES

IPS

| Number | Title (A Side/B Side) | Yr | NM |
|---|---|---|---|
| ❑ 001 | Dialogue of the Drums | 1974 | 20.00 |

## CYRKLE, THE

COLUMBIA

| Number | Title (A Side/B Side) | Yr | NM |
|---|---|---|---|
| ❑ CL 2544 [M] | Red Rubber Ball | 1966 | 20.00 |
| ❑ CL 2632 [M] | Neon | 1967 | 15.00 |
| ❑ CS 9344 [S] | Red Rubber Ball | 1966 | 30.00 |
| ❑ CS 9432 [S] | Neon | 1967 | 20.00 |

## CYRUS, BILLY RAY

MERCURY

| Number | Title (A Side/B Side) | Yr | NM |
|---|---|---|---|
| ❑ 1P-8218 | Some Gave All | 1992 | 25.00 |
| *—Only released on vinyl through Columbia House* | | | |

# D

## D'AMICO, HANK

BETHLEHEM

| Number | Title (A Side/B Side) | Yr | NM |
|---|---|---|---|
| ❑ BCP-1006 [10] | Hank's Holiday | 1954 | 120.00 |

## D'RONE, FRANK

CADET

| Number | Title (A Side/B Side) | Yr | NM |
|---|---|---|---|
| ❑ LPS-806 | Brand New Morning | 1968 | 15.00 |

MERCURY

| Number | Title (A Side/B Side) | Yr | NM |
|---|---|---|---|
| ❑ MG-20418 [M] | Frank D'Rone Sings | 1959 | 30.00 |
| ❑ MG-20586 [M] | After the Ball | 1960 | 30.00 |
| ❑ MG-20721 [M] | Frank D'Rone In Person | 196? | 25.00 |
| ❑ SR-60246 [S] | After the Ball | 1960 | 40.00 |
| ❑ SR-60721 [S] | Frank D'Rone In Person | 196? | 30.00 |
| ❑ SR-90064 [S] | Frank D'Rone Sings | 1959 | 40.00 |

## DADDY COOL

REPRISE

| Number | Title (A Side/B Side) | Yr | NM |
|---|---|---|---|
| ❑ MS 2088 | Teenage Heaven | 1972 | 20.00 |
| ❑ RS 6471 | Daddy Who? Daddy Cool! | 1971 | 15.00 |

## DADDY DEWDROP

SUNFLOWER

| Number | Title (A Side/B Side) | Yr | NM |
|---|---|---|---|
| ❑ SNF-5006 | Daddy Dewdrop | 1971 | 20.00 |

## DAHLANDER, NILS-BERTIL "BERT"

### EVERYDAY

| Number | Title (A Side/B Side) | Yr | NM |
|---|---|---|---|
| ❑ EDLP 528 | Talkin' Jazz: Untitled #1 | 1990 | 15.00 |

*—As "Bert Dahlander"*

### VERVE

| Number | Title (A Side/B Side) | Yr | NM |
|---|---|---|---|
| ❑ MGV-8253 [M] | Skol | 1958 | 50.00 |
| ❑ V-8253 [M] | Skol | 1961 | 20.00 |

## DAILEY, DON

### CROWN

| Number | Title (A Side/B Side) | Yr | NM |
|---|---|---|---|
| ❑ CST-314 [R] | Surf Stompin' | 1963 | 15.00 |
| ❑ CLP-5314 [M] | Surf Stompin' | 1963 | 30.00 |

## DAILY, PETE

### CAPITOL

| Number | Title (A Side/B Side) | Yr | NM |
|---|---|---|---|
| ❑ H 183 [10] | Dixieland Band | 1950 | 50.00 |
| ❑ T 183 [M] | Dixieland Band | 1954 | 40.00 |
| ❑ H 385 [10] | Dixie by Daily | 1953 | 50.00 |
| ❑ T 385 [M] | Dixie by Daily | 1954 | 40.00 |

## DAILY, PETE/PHIL NAPOLEON

### DECCA

| Number | Title (A Side/B Side) | Yr | NM |
|---|---|---|---|
| ❑ DL 5261 [10] | Pete Daily/Phil Napoleon | 195? | 50.00 |

## DAKUS, WES

### KAPP

| Number | Title (A Side/B Side) | Yr | NM |
|---|---|---|---|
| ❑ KL-1536 [M] | Wes Dakus' Rebels | 1967 | 30.00 |
| ❑ KS-3536 [S] | Wes Dakus' Rebels | 1967 | 30.00 |

## DALE, DICK, AND THE DEL-TONES

### CAPITOL

| Number | Title (A Side/B Side) | Yr | NM |
|---|---|---|---|
| ❑ ST 1930 [S] | King of the Surf Guitar | 1963 | 100.00 |
| ❑ T 1930 [M] | King of the Surf Guitar | 1963 | 60.00 |
| ❑ ST 2002 [S] | Checkered Flag | 1963 | 80.00 |
| ❑ T 2002 [M] | Checkered Flag | 1963 | 50.00 |
| ❑ ST 2053 [S] | Mr. Eliminator | 1964 | 80.00 |
| ❑ T 2053 [M] | Mr. Eliminator | 1964 | 50.00 |
| ❑ ST 2111 [S] | Summer Surf | 1964 | 70.00 |

*—Without bonus single*

| Number | Title (A Side/B Side) | Yr | NM |
|---|---|---|---|
| ❑ ST 2111 [S] | Summer Surf | 1964 | 120.00 |

*—With bonus single by Jerry Cole, "Racing Waves"/"Movin' Surf," in front cover pocket*

| Number | Title (A Side/B Side) | Yr | NM |
|---|---|---|---|
| ❑ T 2111 [M] | Summer Surf | 1964 | 50.00 |

*—Without bonus single*

| Number | Title (A Side/B Side) | Yr | NM |
|---|---|---|---|
| ❑ T 2111 [M] | Summer Surf | 1964 | 100.00 |

*—With bonus single by Jerry Cole, "Racing Waves"/"Movin' Surf," in front cover pocket*

| Number | Title (A Side/B Side) | Yr | NM |
|---|---|---|---|
| ❑ ST 2293 [S] | Rock Out — Live at Ciro's | 1965 | 150.00 |
| ❑ T 2293 [M] | Rock Out — Live at Ciro's | 1965 | 100.00 |

### CLOISTER

| Number | Title (A Side/B Side) | Yr | NM |
|---|---|---|---|
| ❑ CLP-6301 [M] | Silver Sounds of the Surf | 1963 | 200.00 |

*—With tracks by the Stompers*

### DELTONE

| Number | Title (A Side/B Side) | Yr | NM |
|---|---|---|---|
| ❑ LPM-1001 [M] | Surfer's Choice | 1962 | 150.00 |
| ❑ DT 1886 [R] | Surfer's Choice | 1962 | 40.00 |
| ❑ T 1886 [M] | Surfer's Choice | 1962 | 60.00 |

### DUB TONE

| Number | Title (A Side/B Side) | Yr | NM |
|---|---|---|---|
| ❑ LP-1246 [M] | The Surf Family | 1964 | 30.00 |

*—With tracks by the Hollywood Surfers*

### GNP CRESCENDO

| Number | Title (A Side/B Side) | Yr | NM |
|---|---|---|---|
| ❑ GNPS-2095 | Greatest Hits | 1975 | 12.00 |

### RHINO

| Number | Title (A Side/B Side) | Yr | NM |
|---|---|---|---|
| ❑ RNLP-70074 | King of the Surf Guitar: The Best of Dick Dale and the Del-Tones, 1961-1964 | 1986 | 12.00 |

## DALE AND GRACE

### MICHELLE

| Number | Title (A Side/B Side) | Yr | NM |
|---|---|---|---|
| ❑ 100 [M] | I'm Leaving It Up to You | 1964 | 150.00 |

### MONTEL

| Number | Title (A Side/B Side) | Yr | NM |
|---|---|---|---|
| ❑ 100 [M] | I'm Leaving It Up to You | 1964 | 150.00 |

## DALEY, JOE

### RCA VICTOR

| Number | Title (A Side/B Side) | Yr | NM |
|---|---|---|---|
| ❑ LPM-2763 [M] | Joe Daley at Newport '63 | 1963 | 20.00 |
| ❑ LSP-2763 [S] | Joe Daley at Newport '63 | 1963 | 25.00 |

## DALLAS, DEAN, AND THE DOUGHBOYS

### CUMBERLAND

| Number | Title (A Side/B Side) | Yr | NM |
|---|---|---|---|
| ❑ MGC-29516 [M] | Golden Country Hits | 1965 | 20.00 |
| ❑ SRC-69516 [S] | Golden Country Hits | 1965 | 25.00 |

## DALLAS, MARIA

### RCA VICTOR

| Number | Title (A Side/B Side) | Yr | NM |
|---|---|---|---|
| ❑ LPM-3950 [M] | Tumblin' Down | 1968 | 40.00 |
| ❑ LSP-3950 [S] | Tumblin' Down | 1968 | 20.00 |

## DALTON, LACY J.

### COLUMBIA

| Number | Title (A Side/B Side) | Yr | NM |
|---|---|---|---|
| ❑ JC 36322 | Lacy J. Dalton | 1980 | 10.00 |
| ❑ PC 36322 | Lacy J. Dalton | 198? | 6.00 |

*—Budget-line reissue with new prefix*

| Number | Title (A Side/B Side) | Yr | NM |
|---|---|---|---|
| ❑ JC 36763 | Hard Times | 1980 | 10.00 |
| ❑ PC 36763 | Hard Times | 1985 | 6.00 |

*—Budget-line reissue with new prefix*

| Number | Title (A Side/B Side) | Yr | NM |
|---|---|---|---|
| ❑ FC 37327 | Takin' It Easy | 1981 | 8.00 |
| ❑ PC 37327 | Takin' It Easy | 1985 | 6.00 |

*—Budget-line reissue with new prefix*

| Number | Title (A Side/B Side) | Yr | NM |
|---|---|---|---|
| ❑ FC 37975 | 16th Avenue | 1982 | 8.00 |
| ❑ FC 38604 | Dream Baby | 1983 | 8.00 |
| ❑ FC 38883 | Greatest Hits | 1984 | 8.00 |
| ❑ FC 40028 | Can't Run Away from Your Heart | 1985 | 8.00 |
| ❑ FC 40393 | Highway Diner | 1986 | 8.00 |
| ❑ FC 40780 | Blue Eyed Blues | 1987 | 8.00 |

### HARBOR

| Number | Title (A Side/B Side) | Yr | NM |
|---|---|---|---|
| ❑ 001 | Jill Croston | 1978 | 25.00 |

*—As "Jill Croston"*

### UNIVERSAL

| Number | Title (A Side/B Side) | Yr | NM |
|---|---|---|---|
| ❑ 42294 | Survivor | 1989 | 10.00 |

## DAMERON, TADD

### JAZZLAND

| Number | Title (A Side/B Side) | Yr | NM |
|---|---|---|---|
| ❑ JLP-50 [M] | Fats Navarro Featured with the Tadd Dameron Quintet | 1962 | 150.00 |
| ❑ JLP-68 [M] | The Tadd Dameron Band | 1962 | 150.00 |

### PRESTIGE

| Number | Title (A Side/B Side) | Yr | NM |
|---|---|---|---|
| ❑ PRLP-159 [10] | A Study in Dameronia | 1953 | 600.00 |
| ❑ PRLP-7037 [M] | Fontainebleu | 1956 | 250.00 |
| ❑ PRLP-7070 [M] | Mating Call | 1956 | 200.00 |

*—Reissued as 7247 and 7725 as a John Coltrane LP; see his listings*

| Number | Title (A Side/B Side) | Yr | NM |
|---|---|---|---|
| ❑ PRLP-16007 [M] | Dameronia | 1964 | 100.00 |

### RIVERSIDE

| Number | Title (A Side/B Side) | Yr | NM |
|---|---|---|---|
| ❑ RLP-419 [M] | The Magic Touch of Tadd Dameron | 1962 | 80.00 |
| ❑ RS-3019 | Good Bait | 1968 | 30.00 |
| ❑ RS-9419 [S] | The Magic Touch of Tadd Dameron | 1962 | 80.00 |

## DAMIN EIH, A.L.K. AND BROTHER CLARK

### DEMELOT

| Number | Title (A Side/B Side) | Yr | NM |
|---|---|---|---|
| ❑ 7310 | Never Mind | 1973 | 150.00 |

## DAMITA JO

### ABC-PARAMOUNT

| Number | Title (A Side/B Side) | Yr | NM |
|---|---|---|---|
| ❑ 378 [M] | The Big Fifteen | 1961 | 80.00 |
| ❑ S-378 [S] | The Big Fifteen | 1961 | 100.00 |

### EPIC

| Number | Title (A Side/B Side) | Yr | NM |
|---|---|---|---|
| ❑ LN 24131 [M] | This Is Damita Jo | 1965 | 15.00 |
| ❑ LN 24164 [M] | One More Time with Feeling | 1965 | 15.00 |
| ❑ LN 24202 [M] | Midnight Session | 1966 | 15.00 |
| ❑ LN 24244 [M] | If You Go Away | 1967 | 20.00 |
| ❑ BN 26131 [S] | This Is Damita Jo | 1965 | 20.00 |
| ❑ BN 26164 [S] | One More Time with Feeling | 1965 | 20.00 |
| ❑ BN 26202 [S] | Midnight Session | 1966 | 20.00 |
| ❑ BN 26244 [S] | If You Go Away | 1967 | 15.00 |

### MERCURY

| Number | Title (A Side/B Side) | Yr | NM |
|---|---|---|---|
| ❑ MG-20642 [M] | I'll Save the Last Dance for You | 1961 | 30.00 |
| ❑ MG-20703 [M] | Damita Jo Live at the Diplomat | 1962 | 25.00 |
| ❑ MG-20734 [M] | Sing a Country Song | 1962 | 25.00 |
| ❑ MG-20818 [M] | This One's for Me | 1963 | 20.00 |
| ❑ SR-60642 [S] | I'll Save the Last Dance for You | 1961 | 40.00 |
| ❑ SR-60703 [S] | Damita Jo Live at the Diplomat | 1962 | 30.00 |
| ❑ SR-60734 [S] | Sing a Country Song | 1962 | 30.00 |
| ❑ SR-60818 [S] | This One's for Me | 1963 | 25.00 |

### RANWOOD

| Number | Title (A Side/B Side) | Yr | NM |
|---|---|---|---|
| ❑ RLP.8037 | Miss Damita Jo | 1968 | 15.00 |

### RCA CAMDEN

| Number | Title (A Side/B Side) | Yr | NM |
|---|---|---|---|
| ❑ CAL-900 [M] | Go Go with Damita Jo | 196? | 15.00 |
| ❑ CAS-900(e) [R] | Go Go with Damita Jo | 196? | 12.00 |

### SUNSET

| Number | Title (A Side/B Side) | Yr | NM |
|---|---|---|---|
| ❑ SUS-5198 | The Irresistible Damita Jo | 1968 | 12.00 |

### VEE JAY

| Number | Title (A Side/B Side) | Yr | NM |
|---|---|---|---|
| ❑ LP-1137 [M] | Damita Jo Sings | 1965 | 25.00 |
| ❑ LPS-1137 [S] | Damita Jo Sings | 1965 | 50.00 |

### WING

| Number | Title (A Side/B Side) | Yr | NM |
|---|---|---|---|
| ❑ WC-16333 | This One's for Me | 196? | 12.00 |

## DAMNATION OF ADAM BLESSING, THE

### UNITED ARTISTS

| Number | Title (A Side/B Side) | Yr | NM |
|---|---|---|---|
| ❑ UAS-5533 | Which Is the Justice, Which Is the Thief | 1971 | 20.00 |
| ❑ UAS-6738 | The Damnation of Adam Blessing | 1970 | 20.00 |
| ❑ UAS-6773 | The Second Damnation | 1970 | 20.00 |

## DAMON

### ANKH

| Number | Title (A Side/B Side) | Yr | NM |
|---|---|---|---|
| ❑ 968 | Song of a Gypsy | 1970 | 1500. |

*—Regular cover; VG value 500; VG+ value 1000*

| Number | Title (A Side/B Side) | Yr | NM |
|---|---|---|---|
| ❑ 968 | Song of a Gypsy | 1970 | 3000. |

*—Gatefold cover; VG value 1500; VG+ value 2250*

## DAMON, LIZ, 'S ORIENT EXPRESS

### MAKAHA

| Number | Title (A Side/B Side) | Yr | NM |
|---|---|---|---|
| ❑ MS-5003 | Liz Damon's Orient Express | 1970 | 20.00 |

## DAMONE, VIC

### APPLAUSE

| Number | Title (A Side/B Side) | Yr | NM |
|---|---|---|---|
| ❑ 1018 | Over the Rainbow | 197? | 10.00 |

### CAPITOL

| Number | Title (A Side/B Side) | Yr | NM |
|---|---|---|---|
| ❑ ST 1646 [S] | Linger Awhile with Vic Damone | 1962 | 15.00 |
| ❑ T 1646 [M] | Linger Awhile with Vic Damone | 1962 | 12.00 |
| ❑ ST 1691 [S] | Strange Enchantment | 1962 | 15.00 |
| ❑ T 1691 [M] | Strange Enchantment | 1962 | 12.00 |
| ❑ ST 1748 [S] | The Lively Ones | 1962 | 15.00 |
| ❑ T 1748 [M] | The Lively Ones | 1962 | 12.00 |
| ❑ ST 1811 [S] | My Baby Loves to Swing | 1963 | 15.00 |
| ❑ T 1811 [M] | My Baby Loves to Swing | 1963 | 12.00 |
| ❑ ST 1944 [S] | The Liveliest | 1963 | 15.00 |
| ❑ T 1944 [M] | The Liveliest | 1963 | 12.00 |
| ❑ ST 2123 [S] | On the Street Where You Live | 1964 | 15.00 |
| ❑ T 2123 [M] | On the Street Where You Live | 1964 | 12.00 |

### COLUMBIA

| Number | Title (A Side/B Side) | Yr | NM |
|---|---|---|---|
| ❑ CL 900 [M] | That Towering Feeling! | 1956 | 25.00 |
| ❑ CL 1088 [M] | Angela Mia | 1957 | 20.00 |
| ❑ CL 1174 [M] | Closer Than a Kiss | 195? | 20.00 |
| ❑ CL 1368 [M] | This Game of Love | 1960 | 15.00 |
| ❑ CL 1573 [M] | On the Swingin' Side | 1961 | 15.00 |
| ❑ CS 8019 [S] | Closer Than a Kiss | 1959 | 30.00 |
| ❑ CS 8046 [S] | Angela Mia | 1959 | 30.00 |
| ❑ CS 8169 [S] | This Game of Love | 1960 | 20.00 |
| ❑ CS 8373 [S] | On the Swingin' Side | 1961 | 20.00 |

### HARMONY

| Number | Title (A Side/B Side) | Yr | NM |
|---|---|---|---|
| ❑ HL 7328 [M] | The Best of Vic Damone | 196? | 12.00 |
| ❑ HL 7431 [M] | Vic Damone Sings | 196? | 12.00 |
| ❑ HS 11128 [S] | The Best of Vic Damone | 196? | 12.00 |
| ❑ HS 11231 [S] | Vic Damone Sings | 196? | 12.00 |

### HOLIDAY

| Number | Title (A Side/B Side) | Yr | NM |
|---|---|---|---|
| ❑ HDY 1936 | Christmas with Vic Damone | 1981 | 10.00 |

### MERCURY

| Number | Title (A Side/B Side) | Yr | NM |
|---|---|---|---|
| ❑ MG-20163 [M] | Yours for a Song | 1957 | 25.00 |
| ❑ MG-20193 [M] | My Favorites | 1957 | 25.00 |
| ❑ MG-25028 [10] | Vic Damone | 1950 | 40.00 |
| ❑ MG-25029 [10] | Vic Damone | 1950 | 40.00 |
| ❑ MG-25045 [10] | Vic Damone | 1950 | 40.00 |
| ❑ MG-25054 [10] | Song Hits | 1950 | 40.00 |
| ❑ MG-25092 [10] | Christmas Favorites | 1951 | 40.00 |
| ❑ MG-25100 [10] | Vic Damone and Others | 1952 | 40.00 |
| ❑ MG-25131 [10] | The Night Has a Thousand Eyes | 1952 | 40.00 |
| ❑ MG-25132 [10] | Vocals by Vic | 1952 | 40.00 |
| ❑ MG-25133 [10] | April in Paris | 1952 | 40.00 |
| ❑ MG-25156 [10] | Vic Damone | 1952 | 40.00 |

### RANWOOD

| Number | Title (A Side/B Side) | Yr | NM |
|---|---|---|---|
| ❑ 8204 | The Best of Vic Damone — Live | 198? | 10.00 |

### RCA VICTOR

| Number | Title (A Side/B Side) | Yr | NM |
|---|---|---|---|
| ❑ ANL1-2462 | The Best of Vic Damone | 1977 | 10.00 |
| ❑ LPM-3671 [M] | Stay with Me | 1966 | 12.00 |
| ❑ LSP-3671 [S] | Stay with Me | 1966 | 15.00 |
| ❑ LPM-3765 [M] | On the South Side of Chicago | 1967 | 12.00 |
| ❑ LSP-3765 [S] | On the South Side of Chicago | 1967 | 15.00 |
| ❑ LPM-3916 [M] | A Damone Type of Thing | 1968 | 15.00 |
| ❑ LSP-3916 [S] | A Damone Type of Thing | 1968 | 15.00 |
| ❑ LSP-3984 | Why Can't I Walk Away | 1968 | 15.00 |

### REBECCA

| Number | Title (A Side/B Side) | Yr | NM |
|---|---|---|---|
| ❑ 100 [(2)] | Let's Fall in Love Again | 1981 | 12.00 |
| ❑ 1212 | Feelings | 1976 | 10.00 |
| ❑ 1213 | Inspiration | 19?? | 10.00 |

### UNITED TALENT

| Number | Title (A Side/B Side) | Yr | NM |
|---|---|---|---|
| ❑ 4501 | Don't Let Me Go | 1969 | 12.00 |

### WARNER BROS.

| Number | Title (A Side/B Side) | Yr | NM |
|---|---|---|---|
| ❑ W 1602 [M] | You Were Only Fooling | 1965 | 12.00 |
| ❑ WS 1602 [S] | You Were Only Fooling | 1965 | 15.00 |
| ❑ W 1607 [M] | Country Love Songs | 1965 | 12.00 |
| ❑ WS 1607 [S] | Country Love Songs | 1965 | 15.00 |

### WING

| Number | Title (A Side/B Side) | Yr | NM |
|---|---|---|---|
| ❑ MGW 12113 [M] | I'll Sing for You | 196? | 12.00 |
| ❑ MGW 12157 [M] | Tenderly | 196? | 12.00 |
| ❑ MGW 12182 [M] | Yours for a Song | 196? | 12.00 |
| ❑ SRW 16113 [R] | I'll Sing for You | 196? | 12.00 |
| ❑ SRW 16157 [R] | Tenderly | 196? | 12.00 |
| ❑ SRW 16182 [R] | Yours for a Song | 196? | 12.00 |

## DAN AND DALE

### DIPLOMAT

| Number | Title (A Side/B Side) | Yr | NM |
|---|---|---|---|
| ❑ D-2340 [M] | Dear Heart, Willow Weep for Me and Other Love Songs | 196? | 10.00 |
| ❑ DS-2340 [S] | Dear Heart, Willow Weep for Me and Other Love Songs | 196? | 12.00 |
| ❑ D-2343 [M] | Themes from Goldfinger and Zorba the Greek | 196? | 10.00 |
| ❑ DS-2343 [S] | Themes from Goldfinger and Zorba the Greek | 196? | 12.00 |
| ❑ D-2361 [M] | Country and Western Waltzes | 196? | 10.00 |
| ❑ DS-2361 [S] | Country and Western Waltzes | 196? | 12.00 |
| ❑ D-2364 [M] | Country & Western Hits | 196? | 10.00 |
| ❑ DS-2364 [S] | Country & Western Hits | 196? | 12.00 |
| ❑ D-2390 [M] | The Nearness of You | 196? | 10.00 |
| ❑ DS-2390 [S] | The Nearness of You | 196? | 12.00 |



**Except when noted otherwise, VG = 25% of NM, and VG+ = 50% of NM. (Example: VG = $2.00, VG+ = $4.00 and NM = $8.00.)**

**TIFTON**

❑ M-8002 [M] Batman and Robin 1966 30.00
❑ S-78002 [S] Batman and Robin 1966 40.00

## DANA, BILL See JOSE JIMENEZ.

## ❑ DANA, VIC

**DOLTON**

❑ BLP-2013 [M] This Is Vic Dana 1961 20.00
❑ BLP-2015 [M] Warm and Wild 1962 15.00
❑ BLP-2026 [M] More 1963 15.00
❑ BLP-2028 [M] Shangri-La 1964 15.00
❑ BLP-2032 [M] Now 1964 15.00
❑ BLP-2034 [M] Red Roses for a Blue Lady 1965 15.00
❑ BLP-2036 [M] Moonlight and Roses 1965 15.00
❑ BLP-2041 [M] Crystal Chandelier 1966 15.00
❑ BLP-2046 [M] Town and Country 1966 15.00
❑ BLP-2048 [M] Golden Greats 1966 15.00
❑ BLP-2049 [M] Little Altar Boy and Other Christmas Songs 1966 15.00
❑ BST-8013 [S] This Is Vic Dana 1961 30.00
❑ BST-8015 [S] Warm and Wild 1962 20.00
❑ BST-8026 [S] More 1963 20.00
❑ BST-8028 [S] Shangri-La 1964 20.00
❑ BST-8032 [S] Now 1964 20.00
❑ BST-8034 [S] Red Roses for a Blue Lady 1965 20.00
❑ BST-8036 [S] Moonlight and Roses 1965 20.00
❑ BST-8041 [S] Crystal Chandelier 1966 20.00
❑ BST-8046 [S] Town and Country 1966 20.00
❑ BST-8048 [S] Golden Greats 1966 20.00
❑ BST-8049 [S] Little Altar Boy and Other Christmas Songs 1966 20.00

**LIBERTY**

❑ BST-8049 [S] Little Altar Boy and Other Christmas Songs 1967 12.00
*—Liberty record in Dolton cover*
❑ LST-8063 If I Never Knew Your Name 1969 12.00

**SUNSET**

❑ SUM-1130 [M] Warm and Wonderful 196? 10.00
❑ SUM-1182 [M] On the Country Side 1967 10.00
❑ SUS-5130 [S] Warm and Wonderful 196? 12.00
❑ SUS-5182 [S] On the Country Side 1967 12.00

## DANE, BARBARA

**BARBARY COAST**

❑ 33014 [M] Trouble in Mind 1959 40.00
*—Reissue of San Francisco LP*

**CAPITOL**

❑ ST 1758 [S] On My Way 1962 40.00
❑ T 1758 [M] On My Way 1962 30.00

**DOT**

❑ DLP-3177 [M] Living with the Blues 1959 30.00
❑ DLP-25177 [S] Living with the Blues 1959 40.00

**FOLKWAYS**

❑ FA-2468 Barbara Dane and the Chambers Brothers 1966 50.00
❑ FA-2471 Folk Songs 1966 30.00

**HORIZON**

❑ WP-1602 [M] When I Was a Young Girl 1962 30.00
❑ WPS-1602 [S] When I Was a Young Girl 1962 40.00
*—Black vinyl*
❑ WPS-1602 [S] When I Was a Young Girl 1962 60.00
*—Gold vinyl*

**SAN FRANCISCO**

❑ 33014 [M] Trouble in Mind 1957 60.00

## DANIELS, CHARLIE, BAND

**CAPITOL**

❑ ST-790 Charlie Daniels 1971 25.00
❑ ST-11414 Charlie Daniels 1975 12.00
*—Reissue of ST-790*
❑ SN-16039 Charlie Daniels 1979 8.00
*—Budget-line reissue*

**EPIC**

❑ AS 586 [DJ] Interchords 1979 15.00
*—Music and interviews; promo only*
❑ EAS 1780 [DJ] The Charlie Daniels Story 1990 15.00
*—Promo-only interview/radio show*
❑ PE 34150 Saddle Tramp 1976 10.00
*—Orange label, no bar code on cover*
❑ PE 34150 Saddle Tramp 198? 8.00
*—With bar code on cover*
❑ JE 34365 Fire on the Mountain 1976 10.00
*—Reissue of Kama Sutra 2603 without bonus EP; orange label, no bar code on cover*
❑ PE 34365 Fire on the Mountain 198? 8.00
*—Budget-line reissue*
❑ JE 34369 Uneasy Rider 1976 10.00
*—Reissue of Kama Sutra 2071 with new name; orange label, no bar code on cover*
❑ PE 34369 Uneasy Rider 198? 8.00
*—Budget-line reissue*
❑ JE 34377 High Lonesome 1976 10.00
*—Orange label, no bar code on cover*
❑ PE 34377 High Lonesome 198? 8.00
*—Budget-line reissue*
❑ JE 34402 Nightrider 1977 10.00
*—Reissue of Kama Sutra 2607; orange label, no bar code on cover*
❑ PE 34402 Nightrider 198? 8.00
*—Budget-line reissue*
❑ JE 34664 Whiskey 1977 10.00
*—Reissue of Kama Sutra 2076 with new name; orange label, no bar code on cover*
❑ PE 34664 Whiskey 198? 8.00
*—Budget-line reissue*
❑ JE 34665 Te John, Grease and Wolfman 1977 10.00
*—Reissue of Kama Sutra 2060; orange label, no bar code on cover*
❑ PE 34665 Te John, Grease and Wolfman 198? 8.00
*—Budget-line reissue*
❑ JE 34970 Midnight Wind 1977 10.00
*—Orange label, no bar code on cover*
❑ PE 34970 Midnight Wind 198? 8.00
*—Budget-line reissue*
❑ JE 35751 Million Mile Reflections 1979 10.00
❑ PE 35751 Million Mile Reflections 198? 8.00
*—Budget-line reissue*
❑ FE 36571 Full Moon 1980 10.00
❑ PE 36571 Full Moon 198? 8.00
*—Budget-line reissue*
❑ FE 37694 Windows 1982 10.00
❑ PE 37694 Windows 198? 8.00
*—Budget-line reissue*
❑ FE 38795 A Decade of Hits 1983 10.00
❑ FE 39878 Me and the Boys 1985 10.00
❑ PE 39878 Me and the Boys 198? 8.00
*—Budget-line reissue*
❑ FE 40760 Powder Keg 1987 8.00
❑ FE 44324 Homesick Man 1988 8.00
❑ HE 44365 Fire on the Mountain 1982 40.00
*—Half-speed mastered edition*
❑ FE 45316 Simple Man 1989 12.00
❑ HE 45751 Million Mile Reflections 1982 40.00
*—Half-speed mastered edition*

**KAMA SUTRA**

❑ KSBS 2060 Te John, Grease and Wolfman 1972 15.00
❑ KSBS 2071 Honey in the Rock 1973 15.00
❑ KSBS 2076 Way Down Yonder 1974 15.00
❑ KSBS 2603 Fire on the Mountain 1974 15.00
*—Includes bonus EP, "Volunteer Jam" (deduct 20% if missing)*
❑ KSBS 2607 Nightrider 1975 15.00

**MOBILE FIDELITY**

❑ 1-176 Million Mile Reflections 1984 30.00
*—Audiophile vinyl*

## DANIELS, EDDIE

**PRESTIGE**

❑ PRLP-7506 [M] First Prize 1967 40.00
❑ PRST-7506 [S] First Prize 1967 25.00

## DANIELS, HALL

**JUMP**

❑ JL-9 [10] Hall Daniels Septet 1955 80.00
*—Issued on blue vinyl*

## DANIELS, SLOPPY

**DOOTO**

❑ DTL-266 [M] Sloppy's House Party 1959 25.00

## DANKWORTH, JOHN

**FONTANA**

❑ SRF-67543 [S] Zodiac Variations 1966 20.00
❑ SRF-67603 The Sophisticated Johnnie Dankworth 1969 20.00

**ROULETTE**

❑ R-52040 [M] England's Ambassador of Jazz 1960 20.00
❑ SR-52040 [S] England's Ambassador of Jazz 1960 25.00
❑ R-52059 [M] Collaboration 1961 20.00
❑ SR-52059 [S] Collaboration 1961 25.00
❑ R-52096 [M] Jazz from Abroad 1963 20.00
❑ SR-52096 [S] Jazz from Abroad 1963 25.00

## DANTE

**MADISON**

❑ MA-LP 1002 [M] Dante and the Evergreens 1961 500.00

## DANTE, RON

**HANDSHAKE**

❑ JW 37341 Street Angel 1981 12.00

**KIRSHNER**

❑ KES-106 Ron Dante Brings You Up 1970 20.00

## DARCEL, DENISE

**CAMEO**

❑ C-1002 [M] Banned in Boston 1958 40.00

## DARCH, BOB

**UNITED ARTISTS**

❑ UAL-3120 [M] Ragtime Piano 1960 20.00
❑ UAS-6120 [S] Ragtime Piano 1960 25.00

## DARIN, BOBBY

**ATCO**

❑ 33-102 [M] Bobby Darin 1958 100.00
*—Yellow "harp" label*
❑ 33-102 [M] Bobby Darin 1962 30.00
*—Gold and dark blue label*
❑ 33-104 [M] That's All 1959 40.00
*—Yellow "harp" label*
❑ 33-104 [M] That's All 1962 20.00
*—Gold and dark blue label*
❑ SD 33-104 [S] That's All 1959 100.00
*—Yellow "harp" label*
❑ SD 33-104 [S] That's All 1962 25.00
*—Purple and brown label*
❑ 33-115 [M] This Is Darin 1960 40.00
*—Yellow "harp" label*
❑ 33-115 [M] This Is Darin 1962 20.00
*—Gold and dark blue label*
❑ SD 33-115 [S] This Is Darin 1960 25.00
*—Purple and brown label*
❑ SD 33-115 [S] This Is Darin 1960 80.00
*—Yellow "harp" label*
❑ 33-122 [M] Darin at the Copa 1960 40.00
*—Yellow "harp" label*
❑ 33-122 [M] Darin at the Copa 1962 20.00
*—Gold and dark blue label*
❑ SD 33-122 [S] Darin at the Copa 1960 80.00
*—Yellow "harp" label*
❑ SD 33-122 [S] Darin at the Copa 1962 25.00
*—Purple and brown label*
❑ 33-124 [M] It's You or No One 1960 40.00
*—Yellow "harp" label*
❑ 33-124 [M] It's You or No One 1962 20.00
*—Gold and dark blue label*
❑ SD 33-124 [S] It's You or No One 1960 80.00
*—Yellow "harp" label*
❑ SD 33-124 [S] It's You or No One 1962 25.00
*—Purple and brown label*
❑ 33-125 [M] The 25th Day of December 1960 50.00
*—Yellow "harp" label*
❑ 33-125 [M] The 25th Day of December 1962 20.00
*—Gold and dark blue label*
❑ SD 33-125 [S] The 25th Day of December 1960 60.00
*—Yellow "harp" label*
❑ SD 33-125 [S] The 25th Day of December 1962 25.00
*—Gold and dark blue label*
❑ 33-126 [M] Two of a Kind 1961 40.00
*—Yellow "harp" label*
❑ 33-126 [M] Two of a Kind 1962 20.00
*—Gold and dark blue label*
❑ SD 33-126 [S] Two of a Kind 1961 50.00
*—Yellow "harp" label*
❑ SD 33-126 [S] Two of a Kind 1962 25.00
*—Purple and brown label*
❑ 33-131 [M] The Bobby Darin Story 1961 40.00
*—Yellow "harp" label; white cover*
❑ 33-131 [M] The Bobby Darin Story 1962 20.00
*—Gold and dark blue label; black cover*
❑ SD 33-131 The Bobby Darin Story 1969 12.00
*—Yellow label, "Atco" on left*
❑ SD 33-131 The Bobby Darin Story 1978 8.00
*—Any later Atco label*
❑ SD 33-131 [S] The Bobby Darin Story 1961 50.00
*—Yellow "harp" label; white cover*
❑ SD 33-131 [S] The Bobby Darin Story 1962 25.00
*—Purple and brown label; black cover*
❑ 33-134 [M] Love Swings 1961 40.00
*—Yellow "harp" label*
❑ 33-134 [M] Love Swings 1962 20.00
*—Gold and dark blue label*
❑ SD 33-134 [S] Love Swings 1961 50.00
*—Yellow "harp" label*
❑ SD 33-134 [S] Love Swings 1962 25.00
*—Purple and brown label*
❑ 33-138 [M] Twist with Bobby Darin 1961 40.00
*—Yellow "harp" label*
❑ 33-138 [M] Twist with Bobby Darin 1962 20.00
*—Gold and dark blue label*
❑ SD 33-138 [S] Twist with Bobby Darin 1961 50.00
*—Yellow "harp" label*
❑ SD 33-138 [S] Twist with Bobby Darin 1962 25.00
*—Purple and brown label*
❑ 33-140 [M] Bobby Darin Sings Ray Charles 1962 25.00
❑ SD 33-140 [S] Bobby Darin Sings Ray Charles 1962 30.00
❑ 33-146 [M] Things & Other Things 1962 25.00
❑ SD 33-146 [S] Things & Other Things 1962 30.00
❑ 33-167 [M] Winners 1964 25.00
❑ SD 33-167 [S] Winners 1964 30.00
❑ SP 1001 [M] For Teenagers Only 1960 75.00
*—With extras missing*
❑ SP 1001 [M] For Teenagers Only 1960 150.00
*—Gatefold with fold-open poster and paper insert*
❑ 90484 Two of a Kind 1986 10.00

**ATLANTIC**

❑ 8121 [M] The Shadow of Your Smile 1966 15.00
❑ SD 8121 [S] The Shadow of Your Smile 1966 20.00
❑ 8126 [M] In a Broadway Bag 1966 15.00
❑ SD 8126 [S] In a Broadway Bag 1966 20.00
❑ 8135 [M] If I Were a Carpenter 1967 15.00
❑ SD 8135 [S] If I Were a Carpenter 1967 50.00
*—Inexplicably rare in stereo*
❑ 8142 [M] Inside Out 1967 15.00
❑ SD 8142 [S] Inside Out 1967 30.00
❑ 8154 [M] Bobby Darin Sings Doctor Dolittle 1967 15.00
❑ SD 8154 [S] Bobby Darin Sings Doctor Dolittle 1967 15.00

| Number | Title (A Side/B Side) | Yr | NM |
|---|---|---|---|
| **BAINBRIDGE** | | | |
| ❑ 6220 | Bobby Darin at the Copa | 1981 | 10.00 |
| **CAPITOL** | | | |
| ❑ ST 1791 [S] | Oh! Look at Me Now | 1962 | 20.00 |
| ❑ SW 1791 [S] | Oh! Look at Me Now | 1962 | 25.00 |
| ❑ T 1791 [M] | Oh! Look at Me Now | 1962 | 15.00 |
| ❑ W 1791 [M] | Oh! Look at Me Now | 1962 | 20.00 |
| ❑ ST 1826 [S] | Earthy | 1963 | 20.00 |
| ❑ T 1826 [M] | Earthy | 1963 | 15.00 |
| ❑ ST 1866 [S] | You're the Reason I'm Living | 1963 | 20.00 |
| ❑ T 1866 [M] | You're the Reason I'm Living | 1963 | 15.00 |
| ❑ ST 1942 [S] | 18 Yellow Roses | 1963 | 20.00 |
| ❑ T 1942 [M] | 18 Yellow Roses | 1963 | 15.00 |
| ❑ ST 2007 [S] | Golden Folk Hits | 1963 | 20.00 |
| ❑ T 2007 [M] | Golden Folk Hits | 1963 | 15.00 |
| ❑ ST 2084 [S] | As Long As I'm Singing | 1964 | 200.00 |
| *—Canceled; price is for an acetate, which is known to exist* | | | |
| ❑ T 2084 [M] | As Long As I'm Singing | 1964 | — |
| *—Canceled* | | | |
| ❑ ST 2194 [S] | From Hello Dolly to Goodbye Charlie | 1964 | 20.00 |
| ❑ T 2194 [M] | From Hello Dolly to Goodbye Charlie | 1964 | 15.00 |
| ❑ ST 2322 [S] | Venice Blue | 1965 | 20.00 |
| ❑ T 2322 [M] | Venice Blue | 1965 | 15.00 |
| ❑ ST 2571 [S] | The Best of Bobby Darin | 1966 | 15.00 |
| ❑ T 2571 [M] | The Best of Bobby Darin | 1966 | 15.00 |
| **CLARION** | | | |
| ❑ 603 [M] | Clementine | 1966 | 20.00 |
| ❑ SD 603 [S] | Clementine | 1966 | 25.00 |
| **DIRECTION** | | | |
| ❑ 1936 | Born Walden Robert Cassotto | 1968 | 25.00 |
| ❑ 1937 | Commitment | 1969 | 25.00 |
| **MOTOWN** | | | |
| ❑ M5-185V1 | Darin 1936-1973 | 1981 | 12.00 |
| *—Reissue* | | | |
| ❑ MS-739 | Finally | 1972 | 500.00 |
| *—Unreleased; value is for RCA test pressing* | | | |
| ❑ M 753L | Bobby Darin | 1972 | 20.00 |
| ❑ M6-813L | Darin 1936-1973 | 1974 | 15.00 |

### DARIUS

| Number | Title (A Side/B Side) | Yr | NM |
|---|---|---|---|
| **CHARTMAKER** | | | |
| ❑ 1102 | Darius | 1969 | 250.00 |

### DARNEL, BILL

| Number | Title (A Side/B Side) | Yr | NM |
|---|---|---|---|
| **"X"** | | | |
| ❑ LVA-(# unk) [10] | Bill Darnel Sings | 1955 | 40.00 |

### DARR, ALICE

| Number | Title (A Side/B Side) | Yr | NM |
|---|---|---|---|
| **CHARLIE PARKER** | | | |
| ❑ PLP-611 [M] | I Only Know How to Cry | 1962 | 30.00 |
| ❑ PLP-611S [S] | I Only Know How to Cry | 1962 | 40.00 |

### DARRELL, JOHNNY

| Number | Title (A Side/B Side) | Yr | NM |
|---|---|---|---|
| **CAPRICORN** | | | |
| ❑ CP 0154 | Water Glass Full of Whiskey | 1975 | 10.00 |
| **SUNSET** | | | |
| ❑ SUS-5232 | The Johnny Darrell Sound | 1969 | 10.00 |
| **UNITED ARTISTS** | | | |
| ❑ UAL 3594 [M] | Ruby, Don't Take Your Love to Town | 1967 | 25.00 |
| ❑ UAS 6594 [S] | Ruby, Don't Take Your Love to Town | 1967 | 20.00 |
| ❑ UAS 6634 | The Son of Hickory Holler's Tramp | 1968 | 20.00 |
| ❑ UAS 6660 | With Pen in Hand | 1968 | 20.00 |
| ❑ UAS 6707 | Why You Been Gone So Long | 1969 | 20.00 |
| ❑ UAS 6752 | California Stop-Over | 1970 | 20.00 |
| ❑ UAS 6759 | The Best of Johnny Darrell, Volume 1 | 1970 | 15.00 |

### DARREN, JAMES

| Number | Title (A Side/B Side) | Yr | NM |
|---|---|---|---|
| **COLPIX** | | | |
| ❑ CP-406 [M] | James Darren (Album No. 1) | 1960 | 40.00 |
| *—Black vinyl* | | | |
| ❑ CP-406 [M] | James Darren (Album No. 1) | 1960 | 150.00 |
| *—Green vinyl* | | | |
| ❑ CP-418 [M] | Gidget Goes Hawaiian (James Darren Sings the Movies) | 1961 | 30.00 |
| ❑ SCP-418 [S] | Gidget Goes Hawaiian (James Darren Sings the Movies) | 1961 | 40.00 |
| ❑ CP-424 [M] | James Darren Sings for All Sizes | 1962 | 30.00 |
| ❑ SCP-424 [S] | James Darren Sings for All Sizes | 1962 | 40.00 |
| ❑ CP-428 [M] | Love Among the Young | 1962 | 30.00 |
| ❑ SCP-428 [S] | Love Among the Young | 1962 | 40.00 |
| **KIRSHNER** | | | |
| ❑ KES-115 | Mammy Blue | 1971 | 15.00 |
| ❑ KES-116 | Love Songs from the Movies | 1972 | 15.00 |
| **WARNER BROS.** | | | |
| ❑ W 1668 [M] | James Darren/All | 1967 | 15.00 |
| ❑ WS 1668 [S] | James Darren/All | 1967 | 20.00 |

### DARREN, JAMES/ SHELLEY FABARES/PAUL PETERSEN

| Number | Title (A Side/B Side) | Yr | NM |
|---|---|---|---|
| **COLPIX** | | | |
| ❑ CP-444 [M] | Teenage Triangle | 1963 | 40.00 |
| ❑ SCP-444 [R] | Teenage Triangle | 1963 | 40.00 |
| ❑ CP-468 [M] | More Teenage Triangle | 1964 | 40.00 |
| ❑ SCP-468 [P] | More Teenage Triangle | 1964 | 60.00 |

### DARRIEU, DANIELLE

| Number | Title (A Side/B Side) | Yr | NM |
|---|---|---|---|
| **LONDON** | | | |
| ❑ LB-616 [10] | Le Voix de France | 1954 | 50.00 |

### DARRIEUX, DANIELLE

| Number | Title (A Side/B Side) | Yr | NM |
|---|---|---|---|
| **CAPITOL** | | | |
| ❑ ST 10319 [S] | Incomparable Danielle Darrieux | 1963 | 30.00 |
| ❑ T 10319 [M] | Incomparable Danielle Darrieux | 1963 | 20.00 |

### DARTELLS, THE

| Number | Title (A Side/B Side) | Yr | NM |
|---|---|---|---|
| **DOT** | | | |
| ❑ DLP-3522 [M] | Hot Pastrami | 1963 | 30.00 |
| ❑ DLP-25522 [S] | Hot Pastrami | 1963 | 40.00 |

### DARTMOUTH INDIAN CHIEFS

| Number | Title (A Side/B Side) | Yr | NM |
|---|---|---|---|
| **TRANSITION** | | | |
| ❑ TRLP-23 [M] | Chiefly Jazz | 1956 | 120.00 |

### DARTS, THE

| Number | Title (A Side/B Side) | Yr | NM |
|---|---|---|---|
| **DEL-FI** | | | |
| ❑ DFLP-1244 [M] | Hollywood Drag | 1963 | 40.00 |
| ❑ DFST-1244 [S] | Hollywood Drag | 1963 | 50.00 |

### DASH, JULIAN

| Number | Title (A Side/B Side) | Yr | NM |
|---|---|---|---|
| **MASTER JAZZ** | | | |
| ❑ 8106 | Portrait | 1970 | 20.00 |

### DASHIEL, BUD, AND THE KINSMEN

| Number | Title (A Side/B Side) | Yr | NM |
|---|---|---|---|
| **WARNER BROS.** | | | |
| ❑ W 1429 [M] | Folk Music in a Contemporary Manner | 1961 | 25.00 |
| ❑ WS 1429 [S] | Folk Music in a Contemporary Manner | 1961 | 30.00 |
| ❑ W 1432 [M] | Live Concert Extraordinaire — Bud Dashiel and the Kinsmen Sing Everybody's Hits | 1961 | 25.00 |
| ❑ WS 1432 [S] | Live Concert Extraordinaire — Bud Dashiel and the Kinsmen Sing Everybody's Hits | 1961 | 30.00 |

### DAUGHERTY, JACK

| Number | Title (A Side/B Side) | Yr | NM |
|---|---|---|---|
| **A&M** | | | |
| ❑ SP-3038 | Jack Daugherty and the Class of '71 | 1971 | 20.00 |

### DAUGHTERS OF ALBION, THE

| Number | Title (A Side/B Side) | Yr | NM |
|---|---|---|---|
| **FONTANA** | | | |
| ❑ SRF-67586 | The Daughters of Albion | 1968 | 20.00 |

### DAVE DEE, DOZY, BEAKY, MICK & TICH

| Number | Title (A Side/B Side) | Yr | NM |
|---|---|---|---|
| **FONTANA** | | | |
| ❑ MGF-27567 [M] | Greatest Hits | 1967 | 30.00 |
| ❑ SRF-67567 [P] | Greatest Hits | 1967 | 40.00 |
| *—"Bend It" and "Hold Tight" are rechanneled.* | | | |
| **IMPERIAL** | | | |
| ❑ LP-12402 [P] | Time to Take Off | 1968 | 40.00 |
| *—"Zabadak" is rechanneled.* | | | |

### DAVEY AND THE BADMEN

| Number | Title (A Side/B Side) | Yr | NM |
|---|---|---|---|
| **GOTHIC** | | | |
| ❑ KRW-054 | Wanted | 1963 | 200.00 |

### DAVID, THE

| Number | Title (A Side/B Side) | Yr | NM |
|---|---|---|---|
| **V.M.C.** | | | |
| ❑ 124 | Another Day, Another Lifetime | 1968 | 100.00 |

### DAVID AND JONATHAN

| Number | Title (A Side/B Side) | Yr | NM |
|---|---|---|---|
| **CAPITOL** | | | |
| ❑ ST 2473 [S] | Michelle | 1966 | 20.00 |
| ❑ T 2473 [M] | Michelle | 1966 | 15.00 |

### DAVIDSON, LOWELL

| Number | Title (A Side/B Side) | Yr | NM |
|---|---|---|---|
| **ESP-DISK'** | | | |
| ❑ S-1012 [S] | Lowell Davidson Trio | 1965 | 20.00 |

### DAVIE, HUTCH

| Number | Title (A Side/B Side) | Yr | NM |
|---|---|---|---|
| **ATCO** | | | |
| ❑ 33-105 [M] | Much Hutch | 1958 | 50.00 |

### DAVIS, BOB

| Number | Title (A Side/B Side) | Yr | NM |
|---|---|---|---|
| **STEPHENY** | | | |
| ❑ MF-4000 [M] | Jazz in Orbit | 1958 | 60.00 |
| ❑ MFS-8003 [S] | Jazz in Orbit | 1960 | 50.00 |
| **ZEPHYR** | | | |
| ❑ 12001 [M] | Jazz from the North Coast | 1959 | 50.00 |

### DAVIS, EDDIE "LOCKJAW"

| Number | Title (A Side/B Side) | Yr | NM |
|---|---|---|---|
| **BETHLEHEM** | | | |
| ❑ BCP-6069 [M] | The Best of Eddie "Lockjaw" Davis | 1963 | 40.00 |
| ❑ BCPS-6069 [R] | The Best of Eddie "Lockjaw" Davis | 196? | 20.00 |
| **JAZZLAND** | | | |
| ❑ JLP-97 [M] | Alma Alegre | 1962 | 25.00 |
| ❑ JLP-997 [S] | Alma Alegre | 1962 | 30.00 |
| **KING** | | | |
| ❑ 395-506 [M] | Modern Jazz Expression | 1956 | 100.00 |
| ❑ 395-526 [M] | Jazz with a Horn | 1957 | 100.00 |
| ❑ 566 [M] | Jazz with a Beat | 1957 | 100.00 |
| ❑ 599 [M] | Big Beat Jazz | 1958 | 100.00 |
| ❑ 606 [M] | Uptown | 1958 | 100.00 |
| ❑ 637 [M] | This and That | 1959 | 100.00 |
| **PRESTIGE** | | | |
| ❑ PRLP-7141 [M] | The Eddie "Lockjaw" Davis Cookbook | 1958 | 80.00 |
| *—Cover photo features Davis with no hat* | | | |
| ❑ PRLP-7141 [M] | The Eddie "Lockjaw" Davis Cookbook | 1959 | 50.00 |
| *—Cover photo features Davis with hat* | | | |
| ❑ PRLP-7161 [M] | The Eddie "Lockjaw" Davis Cookbook, Vol. 2 | 1959 | 50.00 |
| ❑ PRLP-7206 [M] | Trane Whistle | 1961 | 50.00 |
| ❑ PRLP-7219 [M] | The Eddie "Lockjaw" Davis Cookbook, Vol. 3 | 1961 | 50.00 |
| ❑ PRST-7219 [S] | The Eddie "Lockjaw" Davis Cookbook, Vol. 3 | 1961 | 40.00 |
| ❑ PRLP-7242 [M] | Goin' to the Meeting | 1962 | 40.00 |
| ❑ PRST-7242 [S] | Goin' to the Meeting | 1962 | 50.00 |
| ❑ PRLP-7261 [M] | I Only Have Eyes for You | 1963 | 40.00 |
| ❑ PRST-7261 [S] | I Only Have Eyes for You | 1963 | 50.00 |
| ❑ PRLP-7271 [M] | Trackin' | 1963 | 40.00 |
| ❑ PRST-7271 [S] | Trackin' | 1963 | 50.00 |
| **RCA VICTOR** | | | |
| ❑ LPM-3652 [M] | Lock the Fox | 1966 | 20.00 |
| ❑ LSP-3652 [S] | Lock the Fox | 1966 | 25.00 |
| ❑ LPM-3741 [M] | The Fox and the Hounds | 1967 | 25.00 |
| ❑ LSP-3741 [S] | The Fox and the Hounds | 1967 | 20.00 |
| ❑ LPM-3882 [M] | Love Calls | 1967 | 25.00 |
| ❑ LSP-3882 [S] | Love Calls | 1967 | 20.00 |
| **RIVERSIDE** | | | |
| ❑ RLP-373 [M] | Afro-Jaws | 1961 | 30.00 |
| ❑ RLP-430 [M] | Jawbreakers | 1962 | 30.00 |
| ❑ RS-9373 [S] | Afro-Jaws | 1961 | 40.00 |
| ❑ RS-9430 [S] | Jawbreakers | 1962 | 40.00 |
| **ROOST** | | | |
| ❑ LP-422 [10] | Goodies | 1954 | 150.00 |
| ❑ RST-2227 [M] | Eddie Davis Trio | 1957 | 100.00 |
| **ROULETTE** | | | |
| ❑ R-52007 [M] | Count Basie Presents Eddie Davis | 1958 | 60.00 |
| *—White label with color spokes* | | | |
| ❑ R-52007 [M] | Count Basie Presents Eddie Davis | 1963 | 25.00 |
| *—Orange and yellow "roulette wheel" label* | | | |
| ❑ SR-52007 [S] | Count Basie Presents Eddie Davis | 1959 | 50.00 |
| *—White label with color spokes* | | | |
| ❑ SR-52007 [S] | Count Basie Presents Eddie Davis | 1963 | 20.00 |
| *—Orange and yellow "roulette wheel" label* | | | |
| ❑ R-52019 [M] | Eddie Davis Trio | 1959 | 60.00 |
| *—White label with color spokes* | | | |
| ❑ R-52019 [M] | Eddie Davis Trio | 1963 | 25.00 |
| *—Orange and yellow "roulette wheel" label* | | | |
| ❑ SR-52019 [S] | Eddie Davis Trio | 1959 | 50.00 |
| *—White label with color spokes* | | | |
| ❑ SR-52019 [S] | Eddie Davis Trio | 1963 | 20.00 |
| *—Orange and yellow "roulette wheel" label* | | | |

### DAVIS, EDDIE "LOCKJAW", AND JOHNNY GRIFFIN

| Number | Title (A Side/B Side) | Yr | NM |
|---|---|---|---|
| **JAZZLAND** | | | |
| ❑ JLP-31 [M] | Tough Tenors | 1960 | 40.00 |
| ❑ JLP-39 [M] | Lookin' at Monk | 1961 | 40.00 |
| ❑ JLP-42 [M] | Griff & Lock | 1961 | 40.00 |
| ❑ JLP-60 [M] | Blues Up and Down | 1961 | 40.00 |
| ❑ JLP-76 [M] | Tough Tenor Favorites | 1962 | 40.00 |
| ❑ JLP-931 [S] | Tough Tenors | 1960 | 50.00 |
| ❑ JLP-939 [S] | Lookin' at Monk | 1961 | 50.00 |
| ❑ JLP-942 [S] | Griff & Lock | 1961 | 50.00 |
| ❑ JLP-960 [S] | Blues Up and Down | 1961 | 50.00 |
| ❑ JLP-976 [S] | Tough Tenor Favorites | 1962 | 50.00 |
| **PRESTIGE** | | | |
| ❑ PRLP-7191 [M] | The Tenor Scene | 1961 | 50.00 |
| ❑ PRLP-7282 [M] | Battle Stations | 1963 | 30.00 |
| ❑ PRST-7282 [S] | Battle Stations | 1963 | 40.00 |
| ❑ PRLP-7309 [M] | The First Set — Recorded Live at Minton's | 1964 | 30.00 |
| ❑ PRST-7309 [S] | The First Set — Recorded Live at Minton's | 1964 | 40.00 |
| ❑ PRLP-7330 [M] | The Midnight Show at Minton's Playhouse | 1964 | 25.00 |



**Except when noted otherwise, VG = 25% of NM, and VG+ = 50% of NM. (Example: VG = $2.00, VG+ = $4.00 and NM = $8.00.)**

Number | Title (A Side/B Side) | Yr | NM

❑ PRST-7330 [S] The Midnight Show at Minton's Playhouse 1964 30.00
❑ PRLP-7357 [M] The Late Show — Recorded Live! 1965 25.00
❑ PRST-7357 [S] The Late Show — Recorded Live! 1965 30.00
❑ PRLP-7407 [M] The Breakfast Show 1965 30.00
*—Reissue of 7191*
❑ PRST-7407 [S] The Breakfast Show 1965 25.00

## DAVIS, EDDIE "LOCKJAW", AND SHIRLEY SCOTT

### MOODSVILLE

❑ MVLP-4 [M] Eddie "Lockjaw" Davis with Shirley Scott 1960 50.00
*—Green label*
❑ MVLP-4 [M] Eddie "Lockjaw" Davis with Shirley Scott 1965 25.00
*—Blue label, trident logo on right*
❑ MVLP-30 [M] Misty 1963 50.00
*—Green label*
❑ MVLP-30 [M] Misty 1965 25.00
*—Blue label, trident logo on right*
❑ MVST-30 [S] Misty 1963 50.00
*—Green label*
❑ MVST-30 [S] Misty 1965 25.00
*—Blue label, trident logo on right*

### PRESTIGE

❑ PRLP-7154 [M] Jaws 1959 50.00
❑ PRLP-7171 [M] Jaws in Orbit 1959 50.00
❑ PRLP-7178 [M] Bacalao 1960 50.00
❑ PRLP-7301 [M] Smokin' 1964 40.00
❑ PRST-7301 [S] Smokin' 1964 30.00

## DAVIS, JACKIE

### CAPITOL

❑ T 815 [M] Chasing Shadows 1957 40.00
*—Turquoise or gray label*
❑ T 1180 [M] Jackie Davis Meets the Trombones 1959 30.00
*—Black colorband label, logo at left*

## DAVIS, JIMMIE

### DECCA

❑ DL 4587 [M] It's Christmas Time Again 1964 12.00
❑ DL 4868 [M] Going Home for Christmas 1967 12.00
❑ DL 8174 [M] Near the Cross 1955 25.00
❑ DL 8572 [M] Hymn Time 1957 25.00
❑ DL 8729 [M] The Door Is Always Open 1958 25.00
❑ DL 8786 [M] Hail Him with a Song 1958 25.00
❑ DL 8896 [M] You Are My Sunshine 1959 20.00
❑ DL 8953 [M] Suppertime 1960 20.00
❑ DL 74587 [S] It's Christmas Time Again 1964 15.00
❑ DL 74868 [S] Going Home for Christmas 1967 12.00
❑ DL 78896 [S] You Are My Sunshine 1959 25.00
❑ DL 78953 [S] Suppertime 1960 25.00

## DAVIS, JOHNNY "SCAT"

### KING

❑ 626 [M] Here's Lookin' Atcha 1959 80.00

## DAVIS, LINK

### MERCURY

❑ SR-61243 Cajun Crawdaddy 1969 20.00

## DAVIS, MARTHA Also see THE MOTELS.

### CAPITOL

❑ CLT-48054 Policy 1988 12.00
❑ CLT-79197/8 [DJ] Policy (Radio Cue Card) 1987 25.00

## DAVIS, MAXWELL

### ALADDIN

❑ LP-709 [10] Maxwell Davis 1955 400.00
❑ LP-804 [M] Maxwell Davis 1956 200.00

### SCORE

❑ SLP-4106 [M] Blue Tango 1957 200.00

## DAVIS, MEL

### EPIC

❑ LN 3268 [M] Trumpet with a Soul 1956 40.00

### TIME

❑ S-2087 [S] Shoot the Trumpet Player 1962 25.00
❑ S-2117 [S] We Like Broadway 1963 25.00
❑ 52087 [M] Shoot the Trumpet Player 1962 20.00
❑ 52117 [M] We Like Broadway 1963 20.00

## DAVIS, MILES

### BLUE NOTE

❑ BLP-1501 [M] Miles Davis, Volume 1 1955 500.00
*—"Deep groove" version; Lexington Ave. address on label*
❑ BLP-1501 [M] Miles Davis, Volume 1 1958 100.00
*—Regular version, W. 63rd St. address on label*
❑ BLP-1501 [M] Miles Davis, Volume 1 1958 250.00
*—"Deep groove" version, W. 63rd St. address on label*
❑ BLP-1501 [M] Miles Davis, Volume 1 1963 40.00
*—"New York, USA" address on label*
❑ BLP-1502 [M] Miles Davis, Volume 2 1955 250.00
*—"Deep groove" version; W. 63rd St. address on label*
❑ BLP-1502 [M] Miles Davis, Volume 2 1955 500.00
*—"Deep groove" version; Lexington Ave. address on label*
❑ BLP-1502 [M] Miles Davis, Volume 2 1958 100.00
*—Regular version, W. 63rd St. address on label*
❑ BLP-1502 [M] Miles Davis, Volume 2 1963 40.00
*—With New York, USA address on label*
❑ BLP-5013 [10] Miles Davis (Young Man with a Horn) 1952 1000.
❑ BLP-5022 [10] Miles Davis, Vol. 2 1953 1000.
❑ BLP-5040 [10] Miles Davis, Vol. 3 1954 1000.

### BOOK-OF-THE-MONTH CLUB

❑ 91-7725 [(3)] Master of Styles 198? 40.00

### CAPITOL

❑ H 459 [10] Classics in Jazz 1954 250.00
*—First 33 1/3 rpm issue of some of the "Birth of the Cool" sessions*
❑ T 762 [M] Birth of the Cool 1956 200.00
*—Turquoise label*
❑ T 762 [M] Birth of the Cool 1958 100.00
*—Black label wirh rainbow ring, Capitol logo at left*
❑ T 762 [M] Birth of the Cool 2003 40.00
*—Classic Records reissue on 200-gram vinyl*
❑ T 1974 [M] Birth of the Cool 1963 40.00
*—Reissue of 762; black label with rainbow ring, Capitol logo at top*

### COLUMBIA

❑ C2L 20 [(2)M] Miles Davis in Person (Friday & Saturday Nights at the Blackhawk, San Francisco) 1961 50.00
*—Six "eye" logos on label*
❑ C2L 20 [(2)M] Miles Davis in Person (Friday & Saturday Nights at the Blackhawk, San Francisco) 1963 30.00
*—"Guaranteed High Fidelity" on label*
❑ C2L 20 [(2)M] Miles Davis in Person (Friday & Saturday Nights at the Blackhawk, San Francisco) 1965 25.00
*—"Mono" on label*
❑ GP 26 [(2)] Bitches Brew 1970 60.00
*—"360 Sound Stereo" on red labels*
❑ C2S 820 [(2)S] Miles Davis in Person (Friday & Saturday Nights at the Blackhawk, San Francisco) 1961 60.00
*—Red and black label with six "eye" logos*
❑ C2S 820 [(2)S] Miles Davis in Person (Friday & Saturday Nights at the Blackhawk, San Francisco) 1963 30.00
*—"360 Sound Stereo" in black on label*
❑ C2S 820 [(2)S] Miles Davis in Person (Friday & Saturday Nights at the Blackhawk, San Francisco) 1965 25.00
*—"360 Sound Stereo" in white on label*
❑ CL 949 [M] 'Round About Midnight 1957 50.00
*—Six "eye" logos on label*
❑ CL 949 [M] 'Round About Midnight 1963 25.00
*—"Guaranteed High Fidelity" on label*
❑ CL 949 [M] 'Round About Midnight 1965 20.00
*—"Mono" on label*
❑ CL 1041 [M] Miles Ahead 1957 100.00
*—Red and black label with six "eye" logos; cover has Miles Davis blowing his trumpet*
❑ CL 1041 [M] Miles Ahead 1957 200.00
*—Red and black label with six "eye" logos; cover has a while woman and her child on a sailboat*
❑ CL 1041 [M] Miles Ahead 1963 40.00
*—"Guaranteed High Fidelity" on label*
❑ CL 1041 [M] Miles Ahead 1965 30.00
*—"360 Sound Mono" on label*
❑ CL 1193 [M] Milestones 1958 80.00
*—Red and black label with six "eye" logos*
❑ CL 1193 [M] Milestones 1963 40.00
*—"Guaranteed High Fidelity" on label*
❑ CL 1193 [M] Milestones 1965 25.00
*—"360 Sound Mono" on label*
❑ CL 1268 [M] Jazz Track 1958 70.00
*—Red and black label with six "eye" logos; with Miles and a woman on cover*
❑ CL 1268 [M] Jazz Track 1958 100.00
*—Red and black label with six "eye" logos; with abstract drawing on cover*
❑ CL 1274 [M] Porgy and Bess 1958 50.00
*—Six "eye" logos on label*
❑ CL 1274 [M] Porgy and Bess 1963 25.00
*—"Guaranteed High Fidelity" on label*
❑ CL 1274 [M] Porgy and Bess 1965 20.00
*—"Mono" on label*
❑ CL 1355 [M] Kind of Blue 1959 100.00
*—Red and black label with six "eye" logos*
❑ CL 1355 [M] Kind of Blue 1963 50.00
*—"Guaranteed High Fidelity" on label*
❑ CL 1355 [M] Kind of Blue 1965 30.00
*—"360 Sound Mono" on label*
❑ A2S 1374 [(2)DJ] Miles to Go 1982 40.00
*—Promo-only compilation*
❑ CL 1480 [M] Sketches of Spain 1960 50.00
*—Six "eye" logos on label*
❑ CL 1480 [M] Sketches of Spain 1963 25.00
*—"Guaranteed High Fidelity" on label*
❑ CL 1480 [M] Sketches of Spain 1965 20.00
*—"Mono" on label*
❑ CL 1656 [M] Someday My Prince Will Come 1961 40.00
*—Six "eye" logos on label*
❑ CL 1656 [M] Someday My Prince Will Come 1963 25.00
*—"Guaranteed High Fidelity" on label*
❑ CL 1656 [M] Someday My Prince Will Come 1965 20.00
*—"Mono" on label*
❑ CL 1669 [M] Miles Davis in Person, Vol. 1 (Friday Nights at the Blackhawk, San Francisco) 1961 30.00
*—Red and black label with six "eye" logos; later pressings may exist*
❑ CL 1670 [M] Miles Davis in Person, Vol. 2 (Saturday Nights at the Blackhawk, San Francisco) 1961 30.00
*—Six "eye" logos on label; later pressings may exist*
❑ CL 1812 [M] Miles Davis at Carnegie Hall 1962 50.00
*—Red and black label with six "eye" logos*
❑ CL 1812 [M] Miles Davis at Carnegie Hall 1963 25.00
*—"Guaranteed High Fidelity" on label*
❑ CL 1812 [M] Miles Davis at Carnegie Hall 1965 20.00
*—"Mono" on label*
❑ CL 2051 [M] Seven Steps to Heaven 1963 25.00
*—"Guaranteed High Fidelity" on label*
❑ CL 2051 [M] Seven Steps to Heaven 1965 20.00
*—"Mono" on label*
❑ CL 2106 [M] Quiet Nights 1964 25.00
*—"Guaranteed High Fidelity" on label*
❑ CL 2106 [M] Quiet Nights 1965 20.00
*—"Mono" on label*
❑ CL 2183 [M] Miles Davis in Europe 1964 40.00
*—"Guaranteed High Fidelity" on label*
❑ CL 2183 [M] Miles Davis in Europe 1965 25.00
*—"360 Sound Mono" on label*
❑ CL 2306 [M] My Funny Valentine 1965 20.00
*—"Mono" on label*
❑ CL 2306 [M] My Funny Valentine 1965 25.00
*—"Guaranteed High Fidelity" on label*
❑ CL 2350 [M] E.S.P. 1965 20.00
*—"360 Sound Mono" on label*
❑ CL 2350 [M] E.S.P. 1965 25.00
*—"Guaranteed High Fidelity" on label*
❑ CL 2453 [M] "Four" & More — Recorded Live in Concert 1966 30.00
❑ CL 2601 [M] Miles Smiles 1966 40.00
❑ CL 2628 [M] Milestones 1967 30.00
*—Reissue of 1193?*
❑ CL 2732 [M] Sorcerer 1967 30.00
❑ CL 2794 [M] Nefertiti 1968 50.00
❑ CL 2828 [M] Miles in the Sky 1968 150.00
❑ CS 8021 [S] Milestones 1959 200.00
*—Red and black label with six "eye" logos*
❑ CS 8021 [S] Milestones 1963 100.00
*—"360 Sound Stereo" in black on label*
❑ CS 8021 [S] Milestones 1965 60.00
*—"360 Sound Stereo" in white on label*
❑ CS 8085 [S] Porgy and Bess 1959 50.00
*—Six "eye" logos on label*
❑ CS 8085 [S] Porgy and Bess 1963 25.00
*—"360 Sound Stereo" in black on label*
❑ CS 8085 [S] Porgy and Bess 1965 20.00
*—"360 Sound Stereo" in white on label*
❑ CS 8163 [(2)] Kind of Blue 1997 150.00
*—Contains both the original Side 1, which was mastered slightly fast, and the "correct" Side 1 (as Side 3), with an alternate take of "Flamenco Sketches" on Side 4 (at 45 rpm); distributed by Classic Records*
❑ CS 8163 Kind of Blue 2001 30.00
*—200-gram pressing; distributed by Classic Records; contains Side 1 at its "correct" speed*
❑ CS 8163 Kind of Blue 2002 200.00
*—Blue vinyl; 180-gram edition; distributed by Classic Records; 500 copies were pressed*
❑ CS 8163 Kind of Blue 2002 300.00
*—Blue vinyl; 200-gram edition; distributed by Classic Records; approximately 100 copies were pressed*
❑ CS 8163 [S] Kind of Blue 1959 250.00
*—Black and red label with "Stereo Fidelity" at top and "Columbia" in white at bottom; six white "eye" logos on label*
❑ CS 8163 [S] Kind of Blue 1963 60.00
*—"360 Sound Stereo" in black on label*
❑ CS 8163 [S] Kind of Blue 1965 40.00
*—"360 Sound Stereo" in white on label*
❑ CS 8163-45 [(4)] Kind of Blue 1999 100.00
*—Distributed by Classic Records; pressed on four single-sided 12-inch 45 rpm records*
❑ CS 8271 [S] Sketches of Spain 1960 80.00
*—Red and black label with six "eye" logos*
❑ CS 8271 [S] Sketches of Spain 1963 25.00
*—"360 Sound Stereo" in black on label*
❑ CS 8271 [S] Sketches of Spain 1965 20.00
*—"360 Sound Stereo" in white on label*
❑ CS 8271 [S] Sketckes of Spain 1999 25.00
*—Audiophile reissue; distributed by Classic Records*
❑ CS 8456 [S] Someday My Prince Will Come 1961 40.00
*—Six "eye" logos on label*
❑ CS 8456 [S] Someday My Prince Will Come 1963 25.00
*—"360 Sound Stereo" in black on label*
❑ CS 8456 [S] Someday My Prince Will Come 1965 20.00
*—"360 Sound Stereo" in white on label*
❑ CS 8469 [S] Miles Davis in Person, Vol. 1 (Friday Nights at the Blackhawk, San Francisco) 1961 30.00
*—Red and black label with six "eye" logos; later pressings may exist*
❑ CS 8470 [S] Miles Davis in Person, Vol. 2 (Saturday Nights at the Blackhawk, San Francisco) 1961 30.00
*—Six "eye" logos on label; later pressings may exist*

| Number | Title (A Side/B Side) | Yr | NM |
|---|---|---|---|
| ❑ CS 8612 [S] | Miles Davis at Carnegie Hall | 1962 | 30.00 |
| *—"360 Sound Stereo" in black on label* | | | |
| ❑ CS 8612 [S] | Miles Davis at Carnegie Hall | 1962 | 60.00 |
| *—Red and black label with six "eye" logos* | | | |
| ❑ CS 8612 [S] | Miles Davis at Carnegie Hall | 1965 | 25.00 |
| *—"360 Sound Stereo" in white on label* | | | |
| ❑ CS 8851 [S] | Seven Steps to Heaven | 1963 | 25.00 |
| *—"360 Sound Stereo" in black on label* | | | |
| ❑ CS 8851 [S] | Seven Steps to Heaven | 1965 | 20.00 |
| *—"360 Sound Stereo" in white on label* | | | |
| ❑ CS 8906 [S] | Quiet Nights | 1964 | 25.00 |
| *—"360 Sound Stereo" in black on label* | | | |
| ❑ CS 8906 [S] | Quiet Nights | 1965 | 20.00 |
| *—"360 Sound Stereo" in white on label* | | | |
| ❑ CS 8983 [S] | Miles Davis in Europe | 1964 | 40.00 |
| *—"360 Sound Stereo" in black on label* | | | |
| ❑ CS 8983 [S] | Miles Davis in Europe | 1965 | 25.00 |
| *—"360 Sound Stereo" in white on label* | | | |
| ❑ CS 9106 [S] | My Funny Valentine | 1965 | 20.00 |
| *—"360 Sound Stereo" in white on label* | | | |
| ❑ CS 9106 [S] | My Funny Valentine | 1965 | 25.00 |
| *—"360 Sound Stereo" in black on label* | | | |
| ❑ CS 9150 [S] | E.S.P. | 1965 | 50.00 |
| *—"360 Sound Stereo" in white on label* | | | |
| ❑ CS 9150 [S] | E.S.P. | 1965 | 60.00 |
| *—"360 Sound Stereo" in black on label* | | | |
| ❑ CS 9253 [S] | "Four" & More — Recorded Live in Concert | 1966 | 30.00 |
| *—"360 Sound Stereo" on red label* | | | |
| ❑ CS 9401 [S] | Miles Smiles | 1966 | 30.00 |
| *—"360 Sound Stereo" on red label* | | | |
| ❑ CS 9428 [R] | Milestones | 1967 | 25.00 |
| *—"360 Sound Stereo" on red label; reissue of 8021* | | | |
| ❑ CS 9532 [S] | Sorcerer | 1967 | 20.00 |
| *—"360 Sound Stereo" on red label* | | | |
| ❑ CS 9594 [S] | Nefertiti | 1968 | 20.00 |
| *—"360 Sound Stereo" on red label* | | | |
| ❑ CS 9628 [S] | Miles in the Sky | 1968 | 25.00 |
| *—"360 Sound Stereo" on red label* | | | |
| ❑ CS 9750 | Filles de Kilimanjaro | 1969 | 20.00 |
| *—"360 Sound Stereo" on red label* | | | |
| ❑ CS 9808 | Miles Davis' Greatest Hits | 1969 | 20.00 |
| *—"360 Sound Stereo" on red label* | | | |
| ❑ CS 9875 | In a Silent Way | 1969 | 40.00 |
| *—"360 Sound Stereo" on red label* | | | |
| ❑ GQ 30954 [(2)Q] | Live-Evil | 1973 | 60.00 |
| ❑ GQ 30997 [(2)Q] | Bitches Brew | 1972 | 60.00 |
| ❑ C6X 36976 [(6)] | The Miles Davis Collection Vol. 1: 12 Sides of Miles | 1980 | 100.00 |
| ❑ C2 38266 [(2)] | Live at the Plugged Nickel | 1982 | 20.00 |
| ❑ C5X 45000 [(5)] | The Columbia Years 1955-1985 | 1988 | 60.00 |
| ❑ HC 46790 | The Man with the Horn | 1982 | 50.00 |
| *—"Half-Speed Mastered" on cover* | | | |

### COLUMBIA LIMITED EDITION

| Number | Title (A Side/B Side) | Yr | NM |
|---|---|---|---|
| ❑ LE 10018 | Miles Davis in Person, Vol. 1 (Friday Nights at the Blackhawk, San Francisco) | 197? | 15.00 |

### DEBUT

| Number | Title (A Side/B Side) | Yr | NM |
|---|---|---|---|
| ❑ DEB 120 [M] | Blue Moods | 1955 | 400.00 |

### FANTASY

| Number | Title (A Side/B Side) | Yr | NM |
|---|---|---|---|
| ❑ 6001 [M] | Blue Moods | 1962 | 150.00 |
| *—Reissue of Debut album; red vinyl* | | | |
| ❑ 6001 [M] | Blue Moods | 1963 | 70.00 |
| *—Black vinyl, red label* | | | |
| ❑ 86001 [R] | Blue Moods | 1962 | 60.00 |
| *—Blue vinyl* | | | |

### FONTANA

| Number | Title (A Side/B Side) | Yr | NM |
|---|---|---|---|
| ❑ MGF-27532 [M] | Jazz on the Screen | 1965 | 40.00 |
| *—With Art Blakey and the Jazz Messengers* | | | |

### JAZZ HERITAGE

| Number | Title (A Side/B Side) | Yr | NM |
|---|---|---|---|
| ❑ 913427F [M] | Dig Miles Davis/Sonny Rollins | 198? | 15.00 |
| *—Mail-order reissue* | | | |

### MOBILE FIDELITY

| Number | Title (A Side/B Side) | Yr | NM |
|---|---|---|---|
| ❑ 1-177 | Someday My Prince Will Come | 1985 | 80.00 |
| *—Audiophile vinyl* | | | |

### MOSAIC

| Number | Title (A Side/B Side) | Yr | NM |
|---|---|---|---|
| ❑ MQ10-158 [(10)] | The Complete Plugged Nickel Sessions | 1995 | 300.00 |
| ❑ MQ11-164 [(11)] | Miles Davis & Gil Evans: The Complete Columbia Studio Recordings | 1996 | 400.00 |
| ❑ MQ10-177 [(10)] | The Complete Studio Recordings of the Miles Davis Quintet 1965-June 1968 | 1998 | 150.00 |
| ❑ MQ6-183 [(6)] | The Complete Bitches Brew Sessions | 1999 | 100.00 |
| ❑ MQ9-191 [(9)] | The Complete Columbia Recordings of Miles Davis with John Coltrane | 2000 | 170.00 |
| ❑ MQ5-209 [(5)] | The Complete In a Silent Way Sessions (September 1968-February 1969) | 2002 | 80.00 |
| ❑ MQ6-220 [(6)] | The Complete Blackhawk Sessions | 2003 | 100.00 |

### PRESTIGE

| Number | Title (A Side/B Side) | Yr | NM |
|---|---|---|---|
| ❑ 16-3 [M] | Miles Davis and the Modern Jazz Giants | 1957 | 1000. |
| *—This album plays at 16 2/3 rpm and is marked as such; white label* | | | |
| ❑ P-12 [(12)] | Chronicle: The Complete Prestige Recordings | 1980 | 150.00 |
| ❑ PRLP-124 [10] | The New Sounds of Miles Davis | 1952 | 250.00 |
| ❑ PRLP-140 [10] | Blue Period | 1953 | 250.00 |
| ❑ PRLP-154 [10] | Miles Davis Plays Al Cohn Compositions | 1953 | 250.00 |
| ❑ PRLP-161 [10] | Miles Davis Featuring Sonny Rollins | 1953 | 250.00 |
| ❑ PRLP-182 [10] | Miles Davis Sextet | 1954 | 250.00 |
| ❑ PRLP-185 [10] | Miles Davis Quintet | 1954 | 250.00 |
| ❑ PRLP-187 [10] | Miles Davis Quintet Featuring Sonny Rollins | 1954 | 250.00 |
| ❑ PRLP-196 [10] | Miles Davis All Stars, Volume 1 | 1955 | 250.00 |
| ❑ PRLP-200 [10] | Miles Davis All Stars, Volume 2 | 1955 | 250.00 |
| ❑ PRLP-7007 [M] | The Musings of Miles | 1955 | 400.00 |
| *—Yellow label with W. 50th St. address* | | | |
| ❑ PRLP-7012 [M] | Dig Miles Davis/Sonny Rollins | 1956 | 250.00 |
| *—Gray cover* | | | |
| ❑ PRLP-7012 [M] | Dig Miles Davis/Sonny Rollins | 1957 | 200.00 |
| *—Color cover; yellow label with W. 50th St. address* | | | |
| ❑ PRLP-7014 [M] | Miles — The New Miles Davis Quintet | 1956 | 300.00 |
| *—Yellow label with W. 50th St. address* | | | |
| ❑ PRLP-7025 [M] | Miles Davis and Horns | 1956 | 400.00 |
| *—Yellow label with W. 50th St. address* | | | |
| ❑ PRLP-7025 [M] | Miles Davis and Horns | 1958 | 250.00 |
| *—Yellow label, Bergenfield, N.J. address* | | | |
| ❑ PRLP-7034 [M] | Miles Davis and the Milt Jackson Quintet/Sextet | 1956 | 400.00 |
| *—With W. 50th St. address on yellow label* | | | |
| ❑ PRLP-7034 [M] | Miles Davis and the Milt Jackson Quintet/Sextet | 1958 | 250.00 |
| *—Yellow label with Bergenfield, N.J. address* | | | |
| ❑ PRLP-7034 [M] | Miles Davis and the Milt Jackson Quintet/Sextet | 196? | 40.00 |
| *—With trident on blue label* | | | |
| ❑ PRLP-7044 [M] | Collectors' Item | 1956 | 200.00 |
| *—With W. 50th St. address on yellow label* | | | |
| ❑ PRLP-7044 [M] | Collectors' Item | 196? | 40.00 |
| *—With trident on blue label* | | | |
| ❑ PRLP-7054 [M] | Blue Haze | 1956 | 200.00 |
| *—With W. 50th St. address on yellow label* | | | |
| ❑ PRLP-7054 [M] | Blue Haze | 196? | 40.00 |
| *—With trident on blue label* | | | |
| ❑ PRLP-7076 [M] | All Stars | 1957 | 200.00 |
| *—With W. 50th St. address on yellow label* | | | |
| ❑ PRLP-7076 [M] | All Stars | 1958 | 100.00 |
| *—With Bergenfield, N.J. address on yellow label* | | | |
| ❑ PRLP-7076 [M] | All Stars | 196? | 40.00 |
| *—With trident on blue label* | | | |
| ❑ PRLP-7094 [M] | Cookin' with the Miles Davis Quintet | 1957 | 300.00 |
| *—With W. 50th St. address on yellow label* | | | |
| ❑ PRLP-7094 [M] | Cookin' with the Miles Davis Quintet | 1958 | 120.00 |
| *—With Bergenfield, N.J. address on yellow label* | | | |
| ❑ PRLP-7094 [M] | Cookin' with the Miles Davis Quintet | 196? | 40.00 |
| *—With trident on blue label* | | | |
| ❑ PRLP-7109 [M] | Bags Groove | 1957 | 200.00 |
| *—With W. 50th St. address on yellow label* | | | |
| ❑ PRLP-7109 [M] | Bags Groove | 1958 | 100.00 |
| *—With Bergenfield, N.J. address on yellow label* | | | |
| ❑ PRLP-7109 [M] | Bags Groove | 196? | 40.00 |
| *—With trident on blue label* | | | |
| ❑ PRLP-7129 [M] | Relaxin' with the Miles Davis Quintet | 1957 | 120.00 |
| *—With Bergenfield, NJ address on yellow label* | | | |
| ❑ PRLP-7129 [M] | Relaxin' with the Miles Davis Quintet | 1957 | 300.00 |
| *—With W. 50th St. address on yellow label* | | | |
| ❑ PRLP-7129 [M] | Relaxin' with the Miles Davis Quintet | 196? | 40.00 |
| *—With trident on blue label* | | | |
| ❑ PRLP-7150 [M] | Miles Davis and the Modern Jazz Giants | 1958 | 250.00 |
| *—With Bergenfield, NJ address on yellow label* | | | |
| ❑ PRLP-7150 [M] | Miles Davis and the Modern Jazz Giants | 196? | 40.00 |
| *—With trident on blue label* | | | |
| ❑ PRLP-7166 [M] | Workin' with the Miles Davis Quintet | 1959 | 80.00 |
| *—With Bergenfield, NJ address on yellow label* | | | |
| ❑ PRLP-7166 [M] | Workin' with the Miles Davis Quintet | 196? | 30.00 |
| *—With trident on blue label* | | | |
| ❑ PRLP-7168 [M] | Early Milès | 1959 | 150.00 |
| *—Reissue of 7025; with Bergenfield, NJ address on yellow label* | | | |
| ❑ PRLP-7168 [M] | Early Miles | 196? | 40.00 |
| *—With trident on blue label* | | | |
| ❑ PRLP-7200 [M] | Steamin' with the Miles Davis Quintet | 196? | 30.00 |
| *—With trident on blue label* | | | |
| ❑ PRLP-7200 [M] | Steamin' with the Miles Davis Quintet | 1961 | 80.00 |
| *—With Bergenfield, NJ address on yellow label* | | | |
| ❑ PRLP-7221 [M] | The Beginning | 196? | 30.00 |
| *—With trident on blue label* | | | |
| ❑ PRLP-7221 [M] | The Beginning | 1962 | 50.00 |
| *—Reissue of 7007; with Bergenfield, NJ address on yellow label* | | | |
| ❑ PRLP-7254 [M] | The Original Quintet | 196? | 30.00 |
| *—With trident on blue label* | | | |
| ❑ PRLP-7254 [M] | The Original Quintet | 1963 | 50.00 |
| *—Reissue of 7014; with Bergenfield, NJ address on yellow label* | | | |
| ❑ PRST-7254 [R] | The Original Quintet | 1963 | 20.00 |
| ❑ PRLP-7281 [M] | Diggin' | 196? | 40.00 |
| *—With trident on blue label* | | | |
| ❑ PRLP-7281 [M] | Diggin' | 1963 | 100.00 |
| *—Reissue of 7012; with Bergenfield, NJ address on yellow label* | | | |
| ❑ PRST-7281 [R] | Diggin' | 1963 | 25.00 |
| ❑ PRLP-7322 [M] | Miles Davis Plays Richard Rodgers | 1964 | 30.00 |
| ❑ PRST-7322 [R] | Miles Davis Plays Richard Rodgers | 1964 | 20.00 |
| ❑ PRLP-7352 [M] | Miles Davis Plays for Lovers | 1965 | 30.00 |
| ❑ PRST-7352 [R] | Miles Davis Plays for Lovers | 1965 | 20.00 |
| ❑ PRLP-7373 [M] | Jazz Classics | 1965 | 30.00 |
| ❑ PRST-7373 [R] | Jazz Classics | 1965 | 20.00 |
| ❑ PRLP-7457 [M] | Miles Davis' Greatest Hits | 1967 | 30.00 |

## DAVIS, MILES, AND JOHN COLTRANE

### MOODSVILLE

| Number | Title (A Side/B Side) | Yr | NM |
|---|---|---|---|
| ❑ MVLP-32 [M] | Miles Davis and John Coltrane Play Richard Rodgers | 1963 | 50.00 |
| *—Green label* | | | |
| ❑ MVLP-32 [M] | Miles Davis and John Coltrane Play Richard Rodgers | 1965 | 25.00 |
| *—Blue label, trident logo at right* | | | |

### PRESTIGE

| Number | Title (A Side/B Side) | Yr | NM |
|---|---|---|---|
| ❑ PRLP-7322 [M] | Miles Davis and John Coltrane Play Rodgers and Hart | 1964 | 40.00 |
| ❑ PRST-7322 [R] | Miles Davis and John Coltrane Play Rodgers and Hart | 1964 | 20.00 |

## DAVIS, MILES, AND THELONIOUS MONK

### COLUMBIA

| Number | Title (A Side/B Side) | Yr | NM |
|---|---|---|---|
| ❑ CL 2178 [M] | Miles and Monk at Newport | 1964 | 40.00 |
| *—"Guaranteed High Fidelity" on label* | | | |
| ❑ CL 2178 [M] | Miles and Monk at Newport | 1965 | 25.00 |
| *—"360 Sound Mono" on label* | | | |
| ❑ CS 8978 [S] | Miles and Monk at Newport | 1964 | 60.00 |
| *—"360 Sound Stereo" in black on label* | | | |
| ❑ CS 8978 [S] | Miles and Monk at Newport | 1965 | 30.00 |
| *—"360 Sound Stereo" in white on label* | | | |

## DAVIS, PAUL

### ARISTA

| Number | Title (A Side/B Side) | Yr | NM |
|---|---|---|---|
| ❑ AL 8376 | Cool Night | 198? | 8.00 |
| *—Reissue of 9578* | | | |
| ❑ AL 9578 | Cool Night | 1981 | 10.00 |

### BANG

| Number | Title (A Side/B Side) | Yr | NM |
|---|---|---|---|
| ❑ BLPS-223 | A Little Bit of Paul Davis | 1970 | 40.00 |
| ❑ 401 | Ride 'Em Cowboy | 1974 | 12.00 |
| ❑ 405 | Southern Tracks and Fantasies | 1976 | 12.00 |
| ❑ 410 | Singer of Songs — Teller of Tales | 1977 | 12.00 |
| ❑ JZ 36094 | Paul Davis | 1980 | 10.00 |
| ❑ PZ 37973 | The Best of Paul Davis | 1982 | 10.00 |

## DAVIS, REVEREND GARY

### BLUESVILLE

| Number | Title (A Side/B Side) | Yr | NM |
|---|---|---|---|
| ❑ BVLP-1015 [M] | Harlem Street Singer | 1961 | 100.00 |
| *—Blue label, silver print* | | | |
| ❑ BVLP-1015 [M] | Harlem Street Singer | 1964 | 30.00 |
| *—Blue label with trident logo* | | | |
| ❑ BVLP-1032 [M] | A Little More Faith | 1961 | 100.00 |
| *—Blue label, silver print* | | | |
| ❑ BVLP-1032 [M] | A Little More Faith | 1964 | 30.00 |
| *—Blue label with trident logo* | | | |
| ❑ BVLP-1049 [M] | Say No to the Devil | 1962 | 100.00 |
| *—Blue label, silver print* | | | |
| ❑ BVLP-1049 [M] | Say No to the Devil | 1964 | 30.00 |
| *—Blue label with trident logo* | | | |

### FOLKLORE

| Number | Title (A Side/B Side) | Yr | NM |
|---|---|---|---|
| ❑ F-14028 [M] | Pure Religion | 196? | 40.00 |
| ❑ F-14033 [M] | Guitar and Banjo | 196? | 40.00 |

### STINSON

| Number | Title (A Side/B Side) | Yr | NM |
|---|---|---|---|
| ❑ SLP-56 [10] | The Singing Reverend | 195? | 100.00 |

## DAVIS, SAMMY, JR.

### DECCA

| Number | Title (A Side/B Side) | Yr | NM |
|---|---|---|---|
| ❑ DXB 192 [(2)M] | The Best of Sammy Davis, Jr. | 1966 | 15.00 |
| ❑ DL 4153 [M] | Mr. Entertainment | 1961 | 15.00 |
| ❑ DL 4381 [M] | Forget-Me-Nots for First Nighters | 1963 | 15.00 |
| ❑ DL 4582 [M] | Try a Little Tenderness | 1965 | 12.00 |
| ❑ DXSB 7192 [(2)S] | The Best of Sammy Davis, Jr. | 1966 | 20.00 |
| ❑ DL 8118 [M] | Starring Sammy Davis, Jr. | 1955 | 30.00 |
| ❑ DL 8170 [M] | Just for Lovers | 1955 | 30.00 |
| ❑ DL 8351 [M] | Here's Looking at You | 1956 | 25.00 |
| ❑ DL 8486 [M] | Sammy Swings | 1957 | 25.00 |
| ❑ DL 8641 [M] | It's All Over But the Swingin' | 1957 | 25.00 |
| ❑ DL 8676 [M] | Mood to Be Wooed | 1958 | 25.00 |
| ❑ DL 8779 [M] | All the Way And Then Some | 1958 | 25.00 |
| ❑ DL 8841 [M] | Sammy Davis, Jr., at Town Hall | 1959 | 20.00 |
| ❑ DL 8854 [M] | Porgy and Bess | 1959 | 20.00 |
| ❑ DL 8921 [M] | The Sammy Awards | 1960 | 20.00 |
| ❑ DL 8981 [M] | I Got a Right to Swing | 1960 | 20.00 |
| ❑ DL 74153 [S] | Mr. Entertainment | 1961 | 20.00 |

| Number | Title (A Side/B Side) | Yr | NM |
|---|---|---|---|
| DL 74381 [S] | Forget-Me-Nots for First Nighters | 1963 | 20.00 |
| DL 74582 [S] | Try a Little Tenderness | 1965 | 15.00 |
| DL 78841 [S] | Sammy Davis, Jr., at Town Hall | 1959 | 25.00 |
| DL 78854 [S] | Porgy and Bess | 1959 | 25.00 |
| DL 78921 [S] | The Sammy Awards | 1960 | 25.00 |
| DL 78981 [S] | I Got a Right to Swing | 1960 | 25.00 |

**HARMONY**

| Number | Title (A Side/B Side) | Yr | NM |
|---|---|---|---|
| HS 11299 | The Great Sammy Davis, Jr. | 196? | 12.00 |
| HS 11365 | Let There Be Love | 1970 | 10.00 |
| H 30568 | What Kind of Fool Am I | 1971 | 10.00 |

**MCA**

| Number | Title (A Side/B Side) | Yr | NM |
|---|---|---|---|
| 4109 [(2)] | Sammy Davis Jr. At His Greatest | 1975 | 12.00 |

**MGM**

| Number | Title (A Side/B Side) | Yr | NM |
|---|---|---|---|
| SE-4832 | Sammy Davis Jr. Now | 1972 | 10.00 |
| SE-4852 | Portrait of Sammy Davis, Jr. | 1972 | 10.00 |
| M3G-4965 | That's Entertainment! | 1974 | 10.00 |

**MOTOWN**

| Number | Title (A Side/B Side) | Yr | NM |
|---|---|---|---|
| MS 710 | Something for Everyone | 1970 | 12.00 |
| 4519 ML | Hello Detroit! | 1984 | 10.00 |

**PICKWICK**

| Number | Title (A Side/B Side) | Yr | NM |
|---|---|---|---|
| SPC-3002 | The Many Faces of Sammy Davis, Jr. | 196? | 10.00 |

**REPRISE**

| Number | Title (A Side/B Side) | Yr | NM |
|---|---|---|---|
| R-2003 [M] | The Wham of Sam | 1961 | 15.00 |
| R9-2003 [S] | The Wham of Sam | 1961 | 20.00 |
| R-2010 [M] | Sammy Davis, Jr., Belts the Best of Broadway | 1962 | 15.00 |
| R9-2010 [S] | Sammy Davis, Jr., Belts the Best of Broadway | 1962 | 20.00 |
| R-6033 [M] | All Star Spectacular | 1962 | 15.00 |
| R9-6033 [S] | All Star Spectacular | 1962 | 20.00 |
| R-6051 [M] | What Kind of Fool Am I and Other Show-Stoppers | 1962 | 15.00 |
| R9-6051 [S] | What Kind of Fool Am I and Other Show-Stoppers | 1962 | 20.00 |
| R-6063 [(2)M] | Sammy Davis Jr. at the Cocoanut Grove | 1963 | 20.00 |
| R9-6063 [(2)S] | Sammy Davis Jr. at the Cocoanut Grove | 1963 | 25.00 |
| R-6082 [M] | As Long As She Needs Me | 1963 | 15.00 |
| R9-6082 [S] | As Long As She Needs Me | 1963 | 20.00 |
| R-6095 [M] | Sammy Davis Jr. Salutes the Stars of the London Palladium | 1964 | 15.00 |
| RS-6095 [S] | Sammy Davis Jr. Salutes the Stars of the London Palladium | 1964 | 20.00 |
| R-6096 [M] | Treasury of Golden Hits | 1964 | 15.00 |
| RS-6096 [S] | Treasury of Golden Hits | 1964 | 20.00 |
| R-6114 [M] | The Shelter of Your Arms | 1964 | 15.00 |
| RS-6114 [S] | The Shelter of Your Arms | 1964 | 20.00 |
| R-6126 [M] | California Suite | 1964 | 15.00 |
| RS-6126 [S] | California Suite | 1964 | 20.00 |
| R-6131 [M] | Sammy Davis Jr. Sings the Big Ones for Young Lovers | 1964 | 12.00 |
| RS-6131 [S] | Sammy Davis Jr. Sings the Big Ones for Young Lovers | 1964 | 15.00 |
| R-6144 [M] | When the Feeling Hits You | 1965 | 12.00 |
| RS-6144 [S] | When the Feeling Hits You | 1965 | 15.00 |
| R-6159 [M] | If I Ruled the World | 1965 | 12.00 |
| RS-6159 [S] | If I Ruled the World | 1965 | 15.00 |
| R-6164 [M] | The Nat Cole Song Book | 1965 | 12.00 |
| RS-6164 [S] | The Nat Cole Song Book | 1965 | 15.00 |
| R-6169 [M] | Sammy's Back on Broadway | 1965 | 12.00 |
| RS-6169 [S] | Sammy's Back on Broadway | 1965 | 15.00 |
| R-6188 [M] | The Sammy Davis, Jr., Show | 1965 | 12.00 |
| RS-6188 [S] | The Sammy Davis, Jr., Show | 1965 | 15.00 |
| R-6214 [M] | The Sounds of '66 | 1966 | 12.00 |
| RS-6214 [S] | The Sounds of '66 | 1966 | 15.00 |
| R-6236 [M] | Sammy Davis. Jr., Sings/ Laurindo Almeida Plays | 1966 | 12.00 |
| RS-6236 [S] | Sammy Davis. Jr., Sings/ Laurindo Almeida Plays | 1966 | 15.00 |
| R-6237 [(2)M] | That's All | 1967 | 15.00 |
| RS-6237 [(2)S] | That's All | 1967 | 20.00 |
| R-6264 [M] | Sammy Davis Jr. Sings the Complete Dr. Dolittle | 1967 | 20.00 |
| RS-6264 [S] | Sammy Davis Jr. Sings the Complete Dr. Dolittle | 1967 | 12.00 |
| RS-6291 | Sammy Davis, Jr.'s Greatest Hits | 1968 | 12.00 |
| RS-6308 | Lonely Is the Name | 1968 | 12.00 |
| RS-6324 | I've Gotta Be Me | 1969 | 12.00 |
| RS-6339 | The Goin's Great | 1969 | 12.00 |
| RS-6410 | Sammy Davis, Jr., Steps Out | 1970 | 12.00 |

**WARNER BROS.**

| Number | Title (A Side/B Side) | Yr | NM |
|---|---|---|---|
| BSK 3128 | Live Performance | 1977 | 10.00 |

**WARNER SPECIAL PRODUCTS**

| Number | Title (A Side/B Side) | Yr | NM |
|---|---|---|---|
| OP-1501 | The Sound of Sammy | 1978 | 10.00 |

*—Special item for Alka-Seltzer*

## DAVIS, SAMMY, JR., AND CARMEN MCRAE

**DECCA**

| Number | Title (A Side/B Side) | Yr | NM |
|---|---|---|---|
| DL 8490 [M] | Boy Meets Girl | 1957 | 30.00 |

## DAVIS, SKEETER

**GUSTO**

| Number | Title (A Side/B Side) | Yr | NM |
|---|---|---|---|
| 0014 | Best of the Best | 1978 | 10.00 |

**RCA CAMDEN**

| Number | Title (A Side/B Side) | Yr | NM |
|---|---|---|---|
| ACL1-0622 | He Wakes Me with a Kiss | 1974 | 10.00 |
| CAL-818 [M] | I Forgot More Than You'll Ever Know | 196? | 12.00 |
| CAS-818(e) [R] | I Forgot More Than You'll Ever Know | 196? | 15.00 |
| CAL-899 [M] | Blueberry Hill and Other Favorites | 1965 | 12.00 |
| CAS-899 [S] | Blueberry Hill and Other Favorites | 1965 | 15.00 |
| CAS-2367 | Easy to Love | 1970 | 12.00 |
| CAS-2517 | Foggy Mountain Top | 1971 | 12.00 |
| CAS-2607 | The End of the World | 1972 | 10.00 |

**RCA VICTOR**

| Number | Title (A Side/B Side) | Yr | NM |
|---|---|---|---|
| APL1-0190 | The Best of Skeeter Davis, Volume 2 | 1973 | 12.00 |
| APL1-0322 | I Can't Believe That It's All Over | 1974 | 12.00 |
| LPM-2197 [M] | I'll Sing You a Song and Harmonize, Too | 1960 | 25.00 |
| LSP-2197 [S] | I'll Sing You a Song and Harmonize, Too | 1960 | 30.00 |
| LPM-2327 [M] | Here's the Answer | 1961 | 25.00 |
| LSP-2327 [S] | Here's the Answer | 1961 | 30.00 |
| LPM-2699 [M] | The End of the World | 1963 | 25.00 |
| LSP-2699 [S] | The End of the World | 1963 | 30.00 |
| LPM-2736 [M] | Cloudy, With Occasional Tears | 1963 | 25.00 |
| LSP-2736 [S] | Cloudy, With Occasional Tears | 1963 | 30.00 |
| LPM-2980 [M] | Let Me Get Close to You | 1964 | 20.00 |
| LSP-2980 [S] | Let Me Get Close to You | 1964 | 25.00 |
| LPM-3374 [M] | The Best of Skeeter Davis | 1965 | 20.00 |
| LSP-3374 [S] | The Best of Skeeter Davis | 1965 | 25.00 |
| LPM-3382 [M] | Written by the Stars | 1965 | 20.00 |
| LSP-3382 [S] | Written by the Stars | 1965 | 25.00 |
| LPM-3463 [M] | Skeeter Sings Standards | 1965 | 20.00 |
| LSP-3463 [S] | Skeeter Sings Standards | 1965 | 25.00 |
| LPM-3567 [M] | Singin' in the Summer Sun | 1966 | 20.00 |
| LSP-3567 [S] | Singin' in the Summer Sun | 1966 | 25.00 |
| LPM-3667 [M] | My Heart's in the Country | 1966 | 20.00 |
| LSP-3667 [S] | My Heart's in the Country | 1966 | 25.00 |
| LPM-3763 [M] | Hand in Hand with Jesus | 1967 | 30.00 |
| LSP-3763 [S] | Hand in Hand with Jesus | 1967 | 20.00 |
| LPM-3790 [M] | Skeeter Davis Sings Buddy Holly | 1967 | 50.00 |
| LSP-3790 [S] | Skeeter Davis Sings Buddy Holly | 1967 | 40.00 |
| LPM-3876 [M] | What Does It Take (To Keep a Man Like You Satisfied) | 1967 | 30.00 |
| LSP-3876 [S] | What Does It Take (To Keep a Man Like You Satisfied) | 1967 | 20.00 |
| LPM-3960 [M] | Why So Lonely? | 1968 | 50.00 |
| LSP-3960 [S] | Why So Lonely? | 1968 | 20.00 |
| LSP-4055 | I Love Flatt & Scruggs | 1968 | 20.00 |
| LSP-4124 | The Closest Thing to Love | 1969 | 20.00 |
| LSP-4200 | Maryfrances | 1969 | 20.00 |
| LSP-4310 | A Place in the Country | 1970 | 15.00 |
| LSP-4382 | It's Hard to Be a Woman | 1970 | 15.00 |
| LSP-4486 | Skeeter | 1971 | 15.00 |
| LSP-4557 | Love Takes a Lot | 1971 | 15.00 |
| LSP-4642 | Bring It on Home | 1972 | 15.00 |
| LSP-4732 | Skeeter Sings Dolly | 1972 | 15.00 |
| LSP-4818 | Hillbilly Singer | 1972 | 15.00 |

## DAVIS, SPENCER, GROUP

**ALLEGIANCE**

| Number | Title (A Side/B Side) | Yr | NM |
|---|---|---|---|
| AV-442 | Crossfire | 1983 | 10.00 |

**DATE**

| Number | Title (A Side/B Side) | Yr | NM |
|---|---|---|---|
| TES-4021 | Funky | 1971 | 150.00 |

*—Deleted almost immediately upon release*

**MEDIARTS**

| Number | Title (A Side/B Side) | Yr | NM |
|---|---|---|---|
| 41-11 | It's Been So Long | 1971 | 12.00 |

**RHINO**

| Number | Title (A Side/B Side) | Yr | NM |
|---|---|---|---|
| RNLP 117 | The Best of the Spencer Davis Group | 1983 | 8.00 |
| RNLP 70172 | The Best of the Spencer Davis Group (Golden Archive Series) | 1987 | 12.00 |

**UNITED ARTISTS**

| Number | Title (A Side/B Side) | Yr | NM |
|---|---|---|---|
| UA-LA433-E | The Very Best of the Spencer Davis Group | 1975 | 10.00 |
| UAL 3578 [M] | Gimme Some Lovin' | 1967 | 50.00 |
| UAL 3589 [M] | I'm a Man | 1967 | 40.00 |
| UAS 6578 [R] | Gimme Some Lovin' | 1967 | 40.00 |
| UAS 6589 [P] | I'm a Man | 1967 | 50.00 |
| UAS 6641 [P] | The Spencer Davis Group's Greatest Hits | 1968 | 25.00 |
| UAS 6652 | With Their New Face On | 1968 | 20.00 |
| UAS 6691 | Heavies | 1969 | 20.00 |
| ST-91127 [R] | Gimme Some Lovin' | 1967 | 50.00 |

*—Capitol Record Club edition*

**VERTIGO**

| Number | Title (A Side/B Side) | Yr | NM |
|---|---|---|---|
| VEL-1015 | Gluggo | 1973 | 12.00 |
| VEL-1021 | Living in a Back Street | 1974 | 12.00 |

## DAVIS, TYRONE

**COLUMBIA**

| Number | Title (A Side/B Side) | Yr | NM |
|---|---|---|---|
| PC 34268 | Love and Touch | 1976 | 12.00 |
| PC 34654 | Let's Be Closer Together | 1977 | 12.00 |
| JC 35305 | I Can't Go On This Way | 1978 | 12.00 |
| JC 35723 | In the Mood with Tyrone Davis | 1979 | 12.00 |
| JC 36230 | Can't You Tell It's Me | 1979 | 12.00 |
| JC 36598 | I Just Can't Keep On Going | 1980 | 12.00 |
| FC 37366 | Everything in Place | 1981 | 12.00 |
| PC 37979 | The Best of Tyrone Davis | 1982 | 10.00 |

**DAKAR**

| Number | Title (A Side/B Side) | Yr | NM |
|---|---|---|---|
| DK-9005 | Can I Change My Mind | 1969 | 30.00 |
| DK-9027 | Turn Back the Hands of Time | 1970 | 30.00 |
| DK-76901 | I Had It All the Time | 1972 | 30.00 |
| DK-76902 | Tyrone Davis' Greatest Hits | 1972 | 25.00 |
| DK-76904 | Without You in My Life | 1973 | 25.00 |
| DK-76909 | It's All in the Game | 1974 | 20.00 |
| DK-76915 | Homewrecker | 1975 | 20.00 |
| DK-76918 | Turning Point | 1976 | 20.00 |

**EPIC**

| Number | Title (A Side/B Side) | Yr | NM |
|---|---|---|---|
| PE 38626 | Tyrone Davis' Greatest Hits | 1983 | 8.00 |

**HIGHRISE**

| Number | Title (A Side/B Side) | Yr | NM |
|---|---|---|---|
| 103 | Tyrone Davis | 1982 | 10.00 |

**ICHIBAN**

| Number | Title (A Side/B Side) | Yr | NM |
|---|---|---|---|
| ICH 1103 | I'll Always Love You | 1991 | 12.00 |

## DAVIS, WALTER, JR.

**BLUE NOTE**

| Number | Title (A Side/B Side) | Yr | NM |
|---|---|---|---|
| BLP-4018 [M] | Davis Cup | 1959 | 80.00 |

*—Regular version with W. 63rd St. address on label*

| Number | Title (A Side/B Side) | Yr | NM |
|---|---|---|---|
| BLP-4018 [M] | Davis Cup | 1959 | 150.00 |

*—"Deep groove" version (deep indentation under label on both sides)*

| Number | Title (A Side/B Side) | Yr | NM |
|---|---|---|---|
| BLP-4018 [M] | Davis Cup | 1964 | 25.00 |

*—With New York, USA address on label*

| Number | Title (A Side/B Side) | Yr | NM |
|---|---|---|---|
| BST-84018 [S] | Davis Cup | 1959 | 60.00 |

*—Regular version with W. 63rd St. address on label*

| Number | Title (A Side/B Side) | Yr | NM |
|---|---|---|---|
| BST-84018 [S] | Davis Cup | 1964 | 20.00 |

*—With New York, USA address on label*

## DAVIS, WILD BILL

**CORAL**

| Number | Title (A Side/B Side) | Yr | NM |
|---|---|---|---|
| CRL 57417 [M] | One More Time | 1962 | 20.00 |
| CRL 57427 [M] | Lover | 1962 | 20.00 |
| CRL 757417 [S] | One More Time | 1962 | 25.00 |
| CRL 757427 [S] | Lover | 1962 | 25.00 |

**EPIC**

| Number | Title (A Side/B Side) | Yr | NM |
|---|---|---|---|
| LN 1004 [10] | Here's Wild Bill Davis | 1954 | 100.00 |
| LN 1121 [M] | On the Loose | 1955 | 60.00 |
| LN 3118 [M] | Wild Bill Davis at Birdland | 1955 | 60.00 |
| LN 3308 [M] | Evening Concerto | 1956 | 60.00 |

**EVEREST**

| Number | Title (A Side/B Side) | Yr | NM |
|---|---|---|---|
| SDBR-1014 [S] | My Fair Lady | 1959 | 25.00 |
| SDBR-1052 [S] | Flying High | 1959 | 30.00 |
| SDBR-1094 [S] | Dance the Madison | 1960 | 30.00 |
| SDBR-1116 [S] | Organ Grinder's Swing | 1960 | 30.00 |
| SDBR-1125 [S] | Dis Heah | 1961 | 30.00 |
| SDBR-1133 [S] | The Music from "Milk and Honey" | 1961 | 30.00 |
| LPBR-5014 [M] | My Fair Lady | 1958 | 30.00 |
| LPBR-5052 [M] | Flying High | 1959 | 25.00 |
| LPBR-5094 [M] | Dance the Madison | 1960 | 25.00 |
| LPBR-5116 [M] | Organ Grinder's Swing | 1960 | 25.00 |
| LPBR-5125 [M] | Dis Heah | 1961 | 25.00 |
| LPBR-5133 [M] | The Music from "Milk and Honey" | 1961 | 25.00 |

**IMPERIAL**

| Number | Title (A Side/B Side) | Yr | NM |
|---|---|---|---|
| LP-9010 [M] | Wild Bill Davis on Broadway | 1956 | 50.00 |
| LP-9015 [M] | Wild Bill Davis in Hollywood | 1956 | 50.00 |
| LP-9201 [M] | Wild Wild Wild Wild Wild Wild Wild Wild Wild | 1963 | 40.00 |
| LP-12201 [R] | Wild Wild Wild Wild Wild Wild Wild Wild Wild | 1963 | 20.00 |

**RCA VICTOR**

| Number | Title (A Side/B Side) | Yr | NM |
|---|---|---|---|
| LSP-3314 [S] | Free, Frantic and Funky | 1965 | 20.00 |
| LSP-3578 [S] | Live at Count Basie's | 1966 | 20.00 |
| LPM-3799 [M] | Midnight to Dawn | 1967 | 20.00 |

## DAVISON, WILD BILL

**CIRCLE**

| Number | Title (A Side/B Side) | Yr | NM |
|---|---|---|---|
| LP-405 [10] | Showcase | 1951 | 80.00 |

**COLUMBIA**

| Number | Title (A Side/B Side) | Yr | NM |
|---|---|---|---|
| CL 871 [M] | Pretty Wild: Wild Bill Davison with Strings | 1956 | 40.00 |
| CL 983 [M] | Wild Bill Davison with Strings Attached | 1957 | 40.00 |

**COMMODORE**

| Number | Title (A Side/B Side) | Yr | NM |
|---|---|---|---|
| FL-20000 [10] | Dixieland Jazz Jamboree | 1950 | 100.00 |

| Number | Title (A Side/B Side) | Yr | NM |
|---|---|---|---|
| ❑ FL-30009 [M] | Mild and Wild | 1959 | 60.00 |

### DIXIELAND JUBILEE

| Number | Title (A Side/B Side) | Yr | NM |
|---|---|---|---|
| ❑ DJ-508 [M] | Greatest of the Greats | 1958 | 25.00 |
| ❑ DJS-508 [S] | Greatest of the Greats | 1958 | 20.00 |

### JAZZOLOGY

| Number | Title (A Side/B Side) | Yr | NM |
|---|---|---|---|
| ❑ J-2 [M] | Wild Bill Davison's Jazzologists | 1962 | 20.00 |
| ❑ J-14 [M] | Rompin' and Stompin' | 196? | 20.00 |

### REGENT

| Number | Title (A Side/B Side) | Yr | NM |
|---|---|---|---|
| ❑ MG-6026 [M] | When the Saints Go Marching In | 196? | 20.00 |

### RIVERSIDE

| Number | Title (A Side/B Side) | Yr | NM |
|---|---|---|---|
| ❑ RLP 12-211 [M] | Sweet and Hot | 195? | 30.00 |
| *—Blue label, microphone logo at top* | | | |
| ❑ RLP 12-211 [M] | Sweet and Hot | 1956 | 60.00 |
| *—White label, blue print* | | | |

### SAVOY

| Number | Title (A Side/B Side) | Yr | NM |
|---|---|---|---|
| ❑ MG-12035 [M] | Jazz at Storyville | 1955 | 60.00 |
| ❑ MG-12055 [M] | Ringside at Condon's | 1955 | 60.00 |
| *—Reissue of two 10-inch LPs (15029 and 15030) that are listed in the Various Artists Collection area* | | | |

## DAWE, TIM

### STRAIGHT

| Number | Title (A Side/B Side) | Yr | NM |
|---|---|---|---|
| ❑ STS-1058 | Penrod | 1969 | 30.00 |

### WARNER BROS.

| Number | Title (A Side/B Side) | Yr | NM |
|---|---|---|---|
| ❑ WS 1841 | Penrod | 1970 | 15.00 |

## DAWSON, SID

### DELMAR

| Number | Title (A Side/B Side) | Yr | NM |
|---|---|---|---|
| ❑ DL-109 [10] | Sid Dawson's Riverboat Gamblers | 195? | 60.00 |

## DAY, BOBBY

### CLASS

| Number | Title (A Side/B Side) | Yr | NM |
|---|---|---|---|
| ❑ LP-5002 [M] | Rockin' with Robin | 1959 | 400.00 |

### COLLECTABLES

| Number | Title (A Side/B Side) | Yr | NM |
|---|---|---|---|
| ❑ COL-5074 | Golden Classics | 198? | 10.00 |

### RENDEZVOUS

| Number | Title (A Side/B Side) | Yr | NM |
|---|---|---|---|
| ❑ M-1312 [M] | Rockin' with Robin | 196? | 80.00 |

### RHINO

| Number | Title (A Side/B Side) | Yr | NM |
|---|---|---|---|
| ❑ RNDF-208 | The Best of Bobby Day | 1984 | 12.00 |

## DAY, CORA LEE

### ROULETTE

| Number | Title (A Side/B Side) | Yr | NM |
|---|---|---|---|
| ❑ R-52048 [M] | My Crying Hour | 1960 | 30.00 |
| ❑ SR-52048 [S] | My Crying Hour | 1960 | 40.00 |

## DAY, DENNIS

### DESIGN

| Number | Title (A Side/B Side) | Yr | NM |
|---|---|---|---|
| ❑ DLPX-1 [M] | Dennis Day Sings "Christmas Is for the Family" | 195? | 20.00 |
| *—Cover features Jack Benny as Santa; he also appears briefly on the LP* | | | |

## DAY, DORIS

### COLUMBIA

| Number | Title (A Side/B Side) | Yr | NM |
|---|---|---|---|
| ❑ DD 1 [M] | Listen to Day | 1960 | 20.00 |
| ❑ DDS 1 [S] | Listen to Day | 1960 | 25.00 |
| ❑ C2L 5 [(2)M] | Hooray for Hollywood | 1959 | 40.00 |
| ❑ CL 582 [M] | Young Man with a Horn | 1954 | 40.00 |
| *—Reissue of 6106; red label, gold print* | | | |
| ❑ CL 624 [M] | Day Dreams | 1955 | 40.00 |
| *—Red label, gold print* | | | |
| ❑ CL 624 [M] | Day Dreams | 1956 | 25.00 |
| *—Six "eye" logos on label* | | | |
| ❑ CL 710 [M] | Love Me or Leave Me | 1955 | 50.00 |
| *—Red label, gold print* | | | |
| ❑ CL 710 [M] | Love Me or Leave Me | 1956 | 25.00 |
| *—Six "eye" logos on label* | | | |
| ❑ CL 710 [M] | Love Me or Leave Me | 1962 | 15.00 |
| *—"Guaranteed High Fidelity" or "Mono" on label* | | | |
| ❑ CL 749 [M] | Day in Hollywood | 1956 | 30.00 |
| ❑ C2S 805 [(2)S] | Hooray for Hollywood | 1959 | 50.00 |
| ❑ CL 942 [M] | Day By Day | 1957 | 30.00 |
| ❑ CL 1053 [M] | Day By Night | 1958 | 20.00 |
| ❑ CL 1210 [M] | Doris Day's Greatest Hits | 1958 | 30.00 |
| *—Six "eye" logos on label* | | | |
| ❑ CL 1210 [M] | Doris Day's Greatest Hits | 1962 | 12.00 |
| *—"Guaranteed High Fidelity" or "Mono" on label* | | | |
| ❑ CL 1232 [M] | Cuttin' Capers | 1959 | 20.00 |
| ❑ CL 1366 [M] | Hooray for Hollywood, Volume 1 | 1959 | 20.00 |
| ❑ CL 1367 [M] | Hooray for Hollywood, Volume 2 | 1959 | 20.00 |
| ❑ CL 1438 [M] | What Every Girl Should Know | 1960 | 20.00 |
| ❑ CL 1470 [M] | Show Time | 1960 | 20.00 |
| ❑ CL 1614 [M] | Bright and Shiny | 1960 | 20.00 |
| ❑ CL 1660 [M] | I Have Dreamed | 1961 | 20.00 |
| ❑ CL 1752 [M] | Duet | 1962 | 20.00 |
| *—With Andre Previn* | | | |
| ❑ CL 1904 [M] | You'll Never Walk Alone | 1962 | 15.00 |
| ❑ CL 2131 [M] | Love Him! | 1964 | 15.00 |
| ❑ CL 2226 [M] | The Doris Day Christmas Album | 1964 | 12.00 |
| ❑ CL 2266 [M] | With a Smile and a Song | 1965 | 12.00 |
| ❑ CL 2310 [M] | Latin for Lovers | 1965 | 12.00 |
| ❑ CL 2360 [M] | Sentimental Journey | 1965 | 12.00 |
| ❑ CL 2518 [10] | Lights, Camera, Action | 1955 | 50.00 |
| ❑ CL 6071 [10] | You're My Thrill | 1949 | 60.00 |
| ❑ CL 6106 [10] | Young Man with a Horn | 1950 | 100.00 |
| ❑ CL 6149 [10] | Tea for Two | 1950 | 60.00 |
| ❑ CL 6168 [10] | Lullaby of Broadway | 1951 | 60.00 |
| ❑ CL 6186 [10] | On Moonlight Bay | 1951 | 60.00 |
| ❑ CL 6198 [10] | I'll See You in My Dreams | 1951 | 60.00 |
| ❑ CL 6248 [10] | By the Light of the Silvery Moon | 1953 | 60.00 |
| ❑ CL 6273 [10] | Calamity Jane | 1953 | 60.00 |
| ❑ CL 6339 [10] | Young at Heart | 1954 | 60.00 |
| *—Six songs by Doris Day, two by Frank Sinatra* | | | |
| ❑ CS 8066 [S] | Hooray for Hollywood, Volume 1 | 1959 | 25.00 |
| ❑ CS 8067 [S] | Hooray for Hollywood, Volume 2 | 1959 | 25.00 |
| ❑ CS 8078 [S] | Cuttin' Capers | 1959 | 25.00 |
| ❑ CS 8089 [S] | Day By Night | 1959 | 25.00 |
| ❑ CS 8234 [S] | What Every Girl Should Know | 1960 | 25.00 |
| ❑ CS 8261 [S] | Show Time | 1960 | 20.00 |
| ❑ CS 8414 [S] | Bright and Shiny | 1960 | 25.00 |
| ❑ CS 8460 [S] | I Have Dreamed | 1961 | 25.00 |
| ❑ CS 8552 [S] | Duet | 1962 | 25.00 |
| *—With Andre Previn* | | | |
| ❑ CS 8635 [P] | Doris Day's Greatest Hits | 1962 | 15.00 |
| *—"360 Sound Stereo" in black at bottom* | | | |
| ❑ PC 8635 | Doris Day's Greatest Hits | 198? | 8.00 |
| *—Budget-line reissue* | | | |
| ❑ CS 8704 [S] | You'll Never Walk Alone | 1962 | 20.00 |
| ❑ CS 8773 [R] | Love Me or Leave Me | 1963 | 12.00 |
| ❑ CS 8931 [S] | Love Him! | 1964 | 20.00 |
| ❑ CS 9026 [S] | The Doris Day Christmas Album | 1964 | 15.00 |
| ❑ CS 9066 [S] | With a Smile and a Song | 1965 | 15.00 |
| ❑ CS 9110 [S] | Latin for Lovers | 1965 | 15.00 |
| ❑ CS 9160 [S] | Sentimental Journey | 1965 | 15.00 |

### COLUMBIA LIMITED EDITION

| Number | Title (A Side/B Side) | Yr | NM |
|---|---|---|---|
| ❑ LE 10197 | The Doris Day Christmas Album | 197? | 10.00 |

### COLUMBIA SPECIAL PRODUCTS

| Number | Title (A Side/B Side) | Yr | NM |
|---|---|---|---|
| ❑ C 10988 | The Doris Day Christmas Album | 197? | 10.00 |
| *—Reissue of CS 9026* | | | |
| ❑ P2 13231 [(2)] | The Magic of Doris Day | 1976 | 15.00 |
| ❑ P 13346 | The Doris Day Christmas Album | 197? | 10.00 |
| *—Reissue of CS 9026* | | | |
| ❑ XTV 82021/2 [M] | Wonderful Day | 1961 | 40.00 |

### HARMONY

| Number | Title (A Side/B Side) | Yr | NM |
|---|---|---|---|
| ❑ HL 7392 [M] | Great Movie Hits | 1966 | 12.00 |
| ❑ HL 9559 [M] | Do Re Mi (And Other Children's Favorites) | 196? | 12.00 |
| ❑ HS 11192 [R] | Great Movie Hits | 1966 | 12.00 |
| ❑ HS 11282 | Whatever Will Be, Will Be (Que Sera, Sera) | 1968 | 12.00 |
| ❑ HS 11382 | The Magic of Doris Day | 1970 | 12.00 |
| ❑ HS 14559 [S] | Do Re Mi (And Other Children's Favorites) | 196? | 12.00 |
| ❑ KH 31498 | Softly, As I Leave You | 1972 | 10.00 |

### HEARTLAND

| Number | Title (A Side/B Side) | Yr | NM |
|---|---|---|---|
| ❑ HL 1102/3 [(2)] | The Best of Doris Day | 1990 | 15.00 |
| *—Mail-order offer; alternate number is CBS Special Products P2 22031* | | | |

### HINDSIGHT

| Number | Title (A Side/B Side) | Yr | NM |
|---|---|---|---|
| ❑ HSR-200 | Doris Day with Van Alexander's Orchestra | 198? | 10.00 |

## DAY, JIMMY

### PHILIPS

| Number | Title (A Side/B Side) | Yr | NM |
|---|---|---|---|
| ❑ PHM 200016 [M] | Golden Steel Guitar Hits | 1962 | 25.00 |
| ❑ PHM 200075 [M] | Steel and Strings | 1963 | 25.00 |
| ❑ PHS 600016 [S] | Golden Steel Guitar Hits | 1962 | 30.00 |
| ❑ PHS 600075 [S] | Steel and Strings | 1963 | 30.00 |

## DAY BLINDNESS

### STUDIO 10

| Number | Title (A Side/B Side) | Yr | NM |
|---|---|---|---|
| ❑ DBX-101 | Day Blindness | 1969 | 60.00 |

## DE-FENDERS, THE

### DEL-FI

| Number | Title (A Side/B Side) | Yr | NM |
|---|---|---|---|
| ❑ DFLP-1242 [M] | Drag Beat | 1963 | 50.00 |
| ❑ DFST-1242 [S] | Drag Beat | 1963 | 60.00 |

### WORLD PACIFIC

| Number | Title (A Side/B Side) | Yr | NM |
|---|---|---|---|
| ❑ ST-1810 [S] | The De-Fenders Play the Big Ones | 1963 | 70.00 |
| *—Black vinyl* | | | |
| ❑ ST-1810 [S] | The De-Fenders Play the Big Ones | 1963 | 150.00 |
| *—Green vinyl* | | | |
| ❑ ST-1810 [S] | The De-Fenders Play the Big Ones | 1963 | 150.00 |
| *—Red vinyl* | | | |
| ❑ WP-1810 [M] | The De-Fenders Play the Big Ones | 1963 | 50.00 |

## DE LA SOUL

### TOMMY BOY

| Number | Title (A Side/B Side) | Yr | NM |
|---|---|---|---|
| ❑ TB 1019 | 3 Feet High and Rising | 1989 | 20.00 |
| *—Original edition* | | | |
| ❑ TB 1019 [(2)] | 3 Feet High and Rising | 2001 | 15.00 |
| *—Reissue, expanded to a two-disc set* | | | |
| ❑ TB 1029 | De La Soul Is Dead | 1991 | 20.00 |
| ❑ TB 1041 [(2)DJ] | De La Soul Is Dead | 1991 | 25.00 |
| *—Promo-only two-record set* | | | |
| ❑ TB 1063 [DJ] | Buhloone Mindstate | 1993 | 25.00 |
| *—Vinyl appears to be promo only* | | | |
| ❑ TB 1093 [DJ] | Clear Lake Auditorium | 1994 | 25.00 |
| *—Promo-only on clear vinyl (black vinyl editions are counterfeits)* | | | |
| ❑ TB 1149 [(2)] | Stakes Is High | 1996 | 15.00 |
| ❑ TB 1175 [DJ] | Stakes Is High Sampler | 1996 | 25.00 |
| *—Promo only; contains eight songs from the full-length edition* | | | |
| ❑ TB 1361 [(2)] | Art Official Intelligence: Mosaic Thump | 2000 | 15.00 |
| ❑ TB 1362 [(2)] | AOI: Bionix | 2001 | 15.00 |
| ❑ TB 1437 [(2)] | Art Official Intelligence: Mosaic Thump Instrumentals | 2000 | 15.00 |
| ❑ TB 1443 [(2)DJ] | AOI: Bionix//Edited | 2001 | 15.00 |
| *—Promo-only "clean" version* | | | |
| ❑ TB 1546 [(2)] | AOI: Bionix Instrumentals | 2002 | 15.00 |

## DEAD BOYS

### BOMP!

| Number | Title (A Side/B Side) | Yr | NM |
|---|---|---|---|
| ❑ 4017 | Night of the Living Dead Boys | 1981 | 15.00 |

### SIRE

| Number | Title (A Side/B Side) | Yr | NM |
|---|---|---|---|
| ❑ SR-6038 | Young, Loud & Snotty | 1977 | 25.00 |
| ❑ SRK-6054 | We Have Come for Your Children | 1978 | 25.00 |

## DEAD KENNEDYS

### ALTERNATIVE TENTACLES

| Number | Title (A Side/B Side) | Yr | NM |
|---|---|---|---|
| ❑ VIRUS 1 | Fresh Fruit for Rotting Vegetables | 1988 | 12.00 |
| *—Reissue of I.R.S. album* | | | |
| ❑ VIRUS 5 [EP] | In God We Trust, Inc. | 1981 | 12.00 |
| ❑ VIRUS 27 | Plastic Surgery Disasters | 1982 | 12.00 |
| ❑ VIRUS 45 | Frankenchrist | 1985 | 10.00 |
| *—Originals have a poster of H.R. Giger's painting Landscape #20, which was involved in an obscenity trial. The poster is still available, but only by mailing in a coupon inside the LP.* | | | |
| ❑ VIRUS 50 | Bedtime for Democracy | 1986 | 12.00 |
| *—Originals have a newspaper insert* | | | |
| ❑ VIRUS 57 | Give Me Convenience or Give Me Death | 1987 | 10.00 |

### FAULTY

| Number | Title (A Side/B Side) | Yr | NM |
|---|---|---|---|
| ❑ 70014 | Fresh Fruit for Rotting Vegetables | 1982 | 40.00 |
| *—With nursing home photo on back cover, no reference to I.R.S. on label or cover* | | | |

### I.R.S./FAULTY PRODUCTS

| Number | Title (A Side/B Side) | Yr | NM |
|---|---|---|---|
| ❑ SP-70014 | Fresh Fruit for Rotting Vegetables | 1980 | 15.00 |
| *—Reissues have a black front cover, same as imports; it was changed at the insistence of band member Jello Biafra* | | | |
| ❑ SP-70014 | Fresh Fruit for Rotting Vegetables | 1980 | 20.00 |
| *—Originals have an orange cover "to distinguish it from imports"* | | | |

## DEAD OR ALIVE

### EPIC

| Number | Title (A Side/B Side) | Yr | NM |
|---|---|---|---|
| ❑ EAS 2668 [DJ] | Radio Special with Pete Burns | 1986 | 70.00 |
| *—Promo-only music and interviews* | | | |
| ❑ BFE 39274 | Sophisticated Boom Boom | 1984 | 12.00 |
| ❑ FE 39274 | Sophisticated Boom Boom | 1985 | 8.00 |
| *—Reissue with new prefix* | | | |
| ❑ FE 40119 | Youthquake | 1985 | 8.00 |
| *—Reissue with new prefix* | | | |

## DEADLY ONES, THE

### VEE JAY

| Number | Title (A Side/B Side) | Yr | NM |
|---|---|---|---|
| ❑ LP-1090 [M] | It's Monster Surfing Time | 1964 | 100.00 |
| ❑ LPS-1090 [S] | It's Monster Surfing Time | 1964 | 120.00 |

## DEAL, BILL, AND THE RHONDELS

### HERITAGE

| Number | Title (A Side/B Side) | Yr | NM |
|---|---|---|---|
| ❑ HTS 35003 | Vintage Rock | 1969 | 30.00 |
| ❑ HTS 35006 | The Best of Bill Deal and the Rhondels | 1970 | 30.00 |

### RHINO

| Number | Title (A Side/B Side) | Yr | NM |
|---|---|---|---|
| ❑ RNLP-70129 | The Best of Bill Deal and the Rhondels (1969-1970) | 1986 | 10.00 |

## DEAN, EDDIE

### SAGE AND SAND

| Number | Title (A Side/B Side) | Yr | NM |
|---|---|---|---|
| ❑ C-1 [M] | Greatest Westerns | 1956 | 50.00 |
| ❑ C-5 [M] | Hi-Country | 1957 | 50.00 |
| ❑ C-16 [M] | Hillbilly Heaven | 1961 | 30.00 |

### SOUND

| Number | Title (A Side/B Side) | Yr | NM |
|---|---|---|---|
| ❑ LP-603 [M] | Greatest Westerns | 1957 | 30.00 |

## DEAN, JIMMY

### COLUMBIA

| Number | Title (A Side/B Side) | Yr | NM |
|---|---|---|---|
| ❑ CL 1025 [M] | Jimmy Dean's Hour of Prayer | 1957 | 40.00 |

| Number | Title (A Side/B Side) | Yr | NM |
|---|---|---|---|
| ❑ CL 1735 [M] | Big Bad John and Other Fabulous Songs and Tales | 1961 | 20.00 |
| *—With the version of "Big Bad John" containing the lyric "At the bottom of this mine lies a big, big man"; confirmed copies have trail-off numbers of "XLP-54925-1F" and "XLP-54925-1J"* | | | |
| ❑ CL 1735 [M] | Big Bad John and Other Fabulous Songs and Tales | 1961 | 30.00 |
| *—With the version of "Big Bad John" containing the lyric "At the bottom of this mine lies one hell of a man"; confirmed copies have a trail-off number of "XLP-54925-2A" and "XLP-54925-2B"* | | | |
| ❑ CL 1894 [M] | Portrait of Jimmy Dean | 1962 | 20.00 |
| ❑ CL 2027 [M] | Everybody's Favorite | 1963 | 15.00 |
| ❑ CL 2188 [M] | Songs We All Love Best | 1964 | 15.00 |
| ❑ CL 2401 [M] | The First Thing Every Morning | 1965 | 15.00 |
| ❑ CL 2404 [M] | Jimmy Dean's Christmas Card | 1965 | 15.00 |
| ❑ CL 2485 [M] | Jimmy Dean's Greatest Hits | 1966 | 15.00 |
| ❑ CL 2538 [M] | The Big Ones | 1966 | 15.00 |
| ❑ CS 8535 [S] | Big Bad John and Other Fabulous Songs and Tales | 1961 | 25.00 |
| *—It's possible that two different editions exist, one with the "hell of a man" lyrics of "Big Bad John" and the other with the "big, big man" lyrics, but this has not been confirmed.* | | | |
| ❑ CS 8694 [S] | Portrait of Jimmy Dean | 1962 | 25.00 |
| ❑ CS 8827 [S] | Everybody's Favorite | 1963 | 20.00 |
| ❑ CS 8988 [S] | Songs We All Love Best | 1964 | 20.00 |
| ❑ CS 9201 [S] | The First Thing Every Morning | 1965 | 20.00 |
| ❑ CS 9204 [S] | Jimmy Dean's Christmas Card | 1965 | 12.00 |
| ❑ CS 9285 [S] | Jimmy Dean's Greatest Hits | 1966 | 15.00 |
| ❑ PC 9285 | Jimmy Dean's Greatest Hits | 198? | 8.00 |
| *—Budget-line reissue* | | | |
| ❑ CS 9338 [S] | The Big Ones | 1966 | 15.00 |
| ❑ CS 9424 [R] | Jimmy Dean's Hour of Prayer | 1966 | 12.00 |
| ❑ CS 9677 [M] | Dean's List | 1968 | 30.00 |
| *—White label promo; "Special Mono Radio Station Copy" sticker on cover* | | | |
| ❑ CS 9677 [S] | Dean's List | 1968 | 15.00 |
| **CROWN** | | | |
| ❑ 291 | Jimmy Dean and the Western Gentlemen | 196? | 12.00 |
| **GRT** | | | |
| ❑ 8014 | I.O.U. | 1977 | 10.00 |
| **HARMONY** | | | |
| ❑ HL 7268 [M] | Hymns | 1960 | 15.00 |
| ❑ HL 7408 [M] | Mr. Country Music | 1967 | 12.00 |
| ❑ HS 11042 [R] | Hymns | 1960 | 12.00 |
| ❑ HS 11208 [S] | Mr. Country Music | 1967 | 12.00 |
| ❑ HS 11270 | The Country's Favorite Son | 1968 | 12.00 |
| **HILLTOP** | | | |
| ❑ 6004 | Golden Favorites | 196? | 12.00 |
| **KING** | | | |
| ❑ 686 [M] | Favorites of Jimmy Dean | 1961 | 60.00 |
| **MERCURY** | | | |
| ❑ MG-20319 [M] | Jimmy Dean Sings His Television Favorites | 1957 | 40.00 |
| **RCA VICTOR** | | | |
| ❑ LPM-3727 [M] | Jimmy Dean Is Here | 1967 | 15.00 |
| ❑ LSP-3727 [S] | Jimmy Dean Is Here | 1967 | 15.00 |
| ❑ LPM-3824 [M] | Most Richly Blesed | 1967 | 20.00 |
| ❑ LSP-3824 [S] | Most Richly Blesed | 1967 | 15.00 |
| ❑ LPM-3890 [M] | The Jimmy Dean Show | 1967 | 20.00 |
| ❑ LSP-3890 [S] | The Jimmy Dean Show | 1967 | 15.00 |
| ❑ LPM-3999 [M] | A Thing Called Love | 1968 | 30.00 |
| ❑ LSP-3999 [S] | A Thing Called Love | 1968 | 15.00 |
| ❑ LSP-4035 | Speaker of the House | 1968 | 15.00 |
| ❑ LSP-4323 | Dean of Country | 1970 | 15.00 |
| ❑ LSP-4434 | Country Boy and Country Girl | 1970 | 15.00 |
| ❑ LSP-4511 | Everybody Knows | 1971 | 15.00 |
| ❑ LSP-4618 | These Hands | 1972 | 15.00 |
| **SEARS** | | | |
| ❑ 105 | Jimmy Dean's Golden Favorites | 196? | 15.00 |
| **SPIN-O-RAMA** | | | |
| ❑ 108 | Featuring the Coutnry Singing of Jimmy Dean | 196? | 12.00 |
| ❑ 137 | Coutnry Round-Up Featuring Jimmy Dean | 196? | 12.00 |
| **WING** | | | |
| ❑ MGW-12292 [M] | Jimmy Dean Sings His Television Favorites | 196? | 15.00 |
| ❑ SRW-16292 [R] | Jimmy Dean Sings His Television Favorites | 196? | 12.00 |
| **WYNCOTE** | | | |
| ❑ 9032 | Country Favorites | 196? | 12.00 |

**DEAN, JIMMY / JOHNNY HORTON**

| Number | Title (A Side/B Side) | Yr | NM |
|---|---|---|---|
| **LA BREA** | | | |
| ❑ L 8014 [M] | Bummin' Around with Jimmy Dean and Johnny Horton | 1961 | 80.00 |
| **STARDAY** | | | |
| ❑ SLP-325 [M] | Bummin' Around with Jimmy Dean and Johnny Horton | 1965 | 30.00 |

**DEARANGO, BILL**

| Number | Title (A Side/B Side) | Yr | NM |
|---|---|---|---|
| **EMARCY** | | | |
| ❑ MG-26020 [10] | Bill DeArango | 1954 | 50.00 |

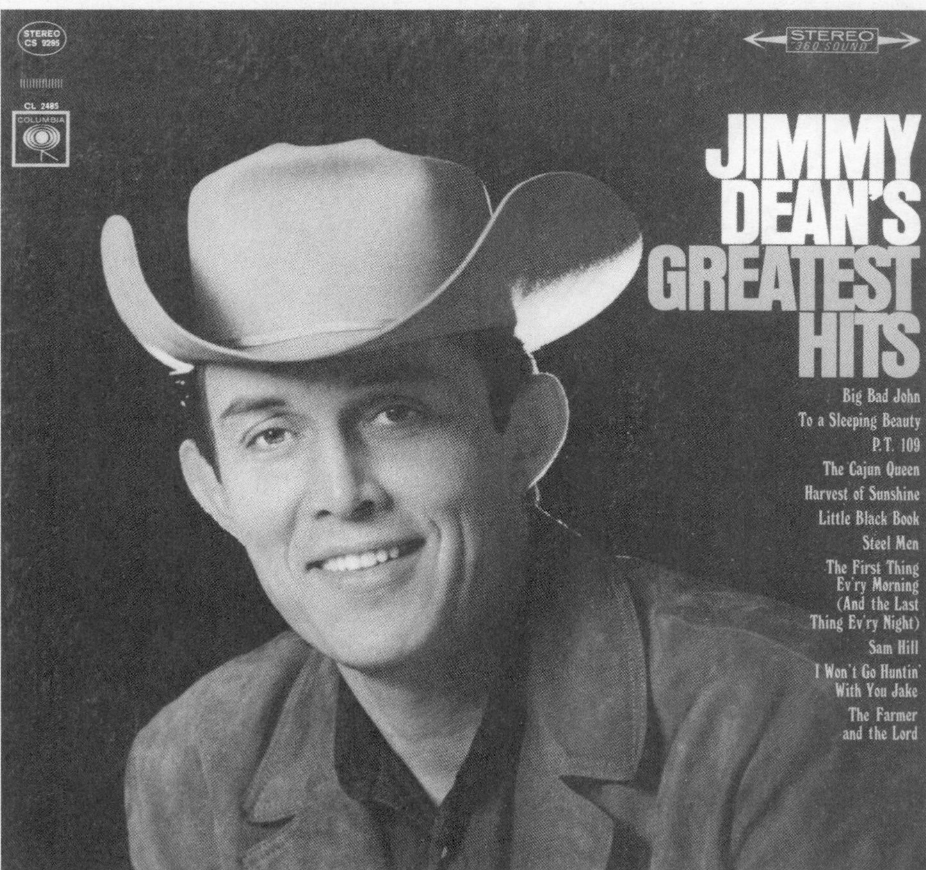


Jimmy Dean, *Jimmy Dean's Greatest Hits,* Columbia CS 9285, 1966, stereo, $15.

**DEARIE, BLOSSOM**

| Number | Title (A Side/B Side) | Yr | NM |
|---|---|---|---|
| **CAPITOL** | | | |
| ❑ ST 2086 [S] | May I Come In | 1964 | 20.00 |
| **DAFFODIL** | | | |
| ❑ BMD-103 [(2)] | My New Celebrity Is You | 197? | 20.00 |
| ❑ BMD-104 [(2)] | Winchester in Apple Blossom Time | 197? | 20.00 |
| **FONTANA** | | | |
| ❑ SRF-67562 [S] | Blossom Time | 1966 | 20.00 |
| **VERVE** | | | |
| ❑ MGV-2037 [M] | Blossom Dearie | 1957 | 60.00 |
| ❑ V-2037 [M] | Blossom Dearie | 1961 | 20.00 |
| ❑ MGV-2081 [M] | Give Him the Ooh-La-La | 1958 | 60.00 |
| ❑ V-2081 [M] | Give Him the Ooh-La-La | 1961 | 20.00 |
| ❑ MGV-2109 [M] | Blossom Dearie Sings Comden & Green | 1959 | 60.00 |
| ❑ V-2109 [M] | Blossom Dearie Sings Comden & Green | 1961 | 20.00 |
| ❑ V6-2109 [S] | Blossom Dearie Sings Comden & Green | 1961 | 25.00 |
| ❑ MGV-2111 [M] | Once Upon a Summertime | 1958 | 60.00 |
| ❑ V-2111 [M] | Once Upon a Summertime | 1961 | 20.00 |
| ❑ V6-2111 [S] | Once Upon a Summertime | 1961 | 25.00 |
| ❑ MGV-2125 [M] | My Gentleman Friend | 1959 | 60.00 |
| ❑ V-2125 [M] | My Gentleman Friend | 1961 | 20.00 |
| ❑ V6-2125 [S] | My Gentleman Friend | 1961 | 25.00 |
| ❑ MGV-2133 [M] | Broadway Song Hits | 1960 | 50.00 |
| ❑ V-2133 [M] | Broadway Song Hits | 1961 | 20.00 |
| ❑ V6-2133 [S] | Broadway Song Hits | 1961 | 25.00 |
| ❑ MGVS-6020 [S] | Once Upon a Summertime | 1960 | 50.00 |
| ❑ MGVS-6050 [S] | Blossom Dearie Sings Comden & Green | 1960 | 50.00 |
| ❑ MGVS-6112 [S] | My Gentleman Friend | 1960 | 50.00 |
| ❑ MGVS-6139 [S] | Broadway Song Hits | 1960 | 60.00 |

**DEATH CAB FOR CUTIE**

| Number | Title (A Side/B Side) | Yr | NM |
|---|---|---|---|
| **BARSUK** | | | |
| ❑ BARK 11 | We Have the Facts and We're Voting Yes | 2000 | 50.00 |
| ❑ BARK 21 [(2)] | The Photo Album | 2001 | 50.00 |
| ❑ BARK 47 [(2)] | Plans | 2005 | 25.00 |
| **SONIC BOOM** | | | |
| ❑ SBR 002 [(2)] | Something About Airplanes | 1998 | 50.00 |
| *—Blue marbled vinyl* | | | |
| ❑ SBR 012 [(2)] | Transatlanticism | 2004 | 20.00 |

**DEAUVILLE, RONNIE**

| Number | Title (A Side/B Side) | Yr | NM |
|---|---|---|---|
| **ERA** | | | |
| ❑ 20002 [M] | Smoke Dreams | 1957 | 40.00 |
| **IMPERIAL** | | | |
| ❑ LP-9060 [M] | Romance | 1959 | 25.00 |
| ❑ LP-12009 [S] | Romance | 1959 | 30.00 |

**DEBRIS**

| Number | Title (A Side/B Side) | Yr | NM |
|---|---|---|---|
| **STATIC DISPOSAL** | | | |
| ❑ 0000 | Debris | 1976 | 80.00 |

**DECARLO, YVONNE**

| Number | Title (A Side/B Side) | Yr | NM |
|---|---|---|---|
| **MASTERSEAL** | | | |
| ❑ MS33-1869/70 [M] | Yvonne DeCarlo Sings | 1957 | 80.00 |

**DECASTRO SISTERS, THE**

| Number | Title (A Side/B Side) | Yr | NM |
|---|---|---|---|
| **ABBOTT** | | | |
| ❑ 5002 [M] | The DeCastro Sisters | 1956 | 60.00 |
| **CAPITOL** | | | |
| ❑ ST 1402 [S] | The DeCastros Sing | 1960 | 30.00 |
| ❑ T 1402 [M] | The DeCastros Sing | 1960 | 25.00 |
| ❑ ST 1501 [S] | The Rockin' Beat | 1961 | 30.00 |
| ❑ T 1501 [M] | The Rockin' Beat | 1961 | 25.00 |

**DECEMBER'S CHILDREN**

| Number | Title (A Side/B Side) | Yr | NM |
|---|---|---|---|
| **MAINSTREAM** | | | |
| ❑ S-6128 | December's Children | 1970 | 50.00 |

**DEDRICK, RUSTY**

| Number | Title (A Side/B Side) | Yr | NM |
|---|---|---|---|
| **COUNTERPOINT** | | | |
| ❑ 552 [M] | Salute to Bunny | 1957 | 50.00 |
| **ESOTERIC** | | | |
| ❑ ESJ-9 [10] | Rhythm and Winds | 1955 | 100.00 |
| **4 CORNERS OF THE WORLD** | | | |
| ❑ FCS-4207 [S] | The Big Band Sound | 1964 | 20.00 |
| **KEYNOTE** | | | |
| ❑ 1103 [M] | Rusty Dedrick | 1955 | 60.00 |
| **MONUMENT** | | | |
| ❑ SLP-16502 [S] | A Jazz Journey | 1965 | 20.00 |

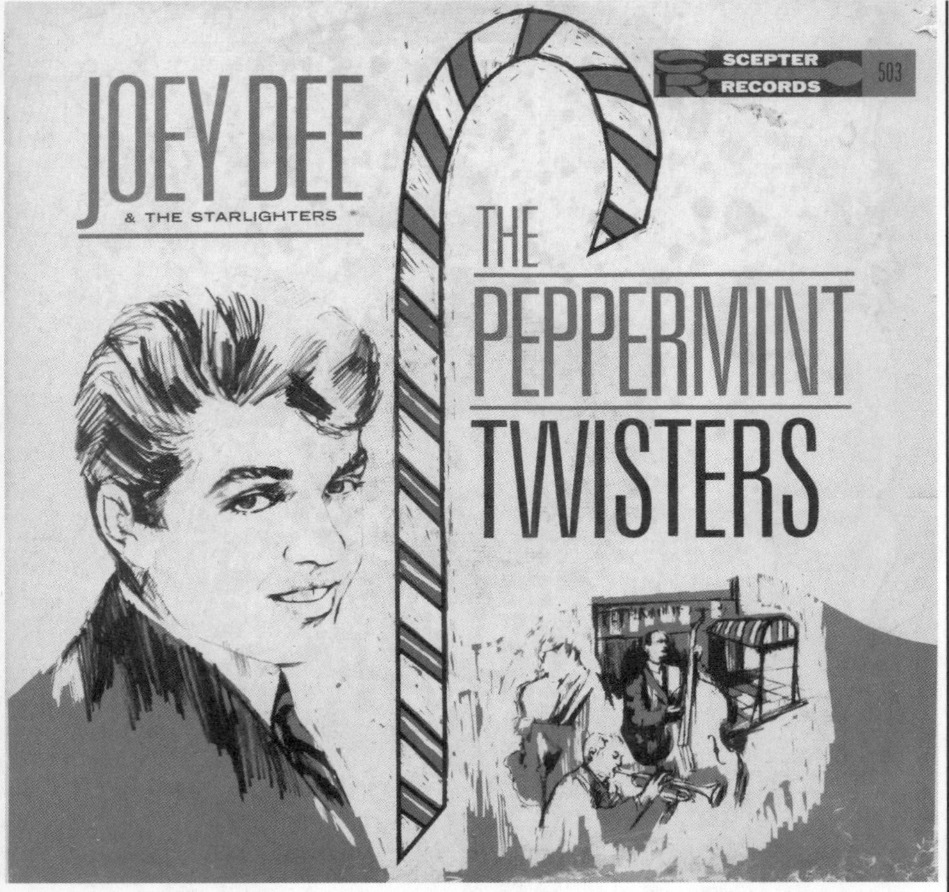


Joey Dee and the Starlighters (sic), *The Peppermint Twisters,* Scepter 503, 1962, mono, $25.

| Number | Title (A Side/B Side) | Yr | NM |
|---|---|---|---|
| **DEE, JOEY, AND THE STARLITERS** | | | |
| FORUM | | | |
| ❑ FC 9099 [M] | Joey Dee and the Starliters | 1963 | 12.00 |
| ❑ FCS 9099 [S] | Joey Dee and the Starliters | 1963 | 12.00 |
| JUBILEE | | | |
| ❑ JGM-8000 [M] | Hitsville | 1966 | 20.00 |
| ❑ JGS-8000 [S] | Hitsville | 1966 | 25.00 |
| ROULETTE | | | |
| ❑ R-25166 [M] | Doin' the Twist at the Peppermint Lounge | 1961 | 40.00 |
| ❑ SR-25166 [S] | Doin' the Twist at the Peppermint Lounge | 1961 | 50.00 |
| ❑ R-25171 [M] | All the World Is Twistin' | 1962 | 30.00 |
| ❑ SR-25171 [S] | All the World Is Twistin' | 1962 | 40.00 |
| ❑ R-25173 [M] | Back at the Peppermint Lounge — Twistin' | 1962 | 30.00 |
| ❑ SR-25173 [S] | Back at the Peppermint Lounge — Twistin' | 1962 | 40.00 |
| ❑ R-25197 [M] | Joey Dee | 1963 | 25.00 |
| ❑ SR-25197 [S] | Joey Dee | 1963 | 30.00 |
| ❑ R-25221 [M] | Dance, Dance, Dance | 1963 | 25.00 |
| ❑ SR-25221 [S] | Dance, Dance, Dance | 1963 | 30.00 |
| SCEPTER | | | |
| ❑ S 503 [M] | The Peppermint Twisters | 1962 | 25.00 |
| ❑ SS 503 [S] | The Peppermint Twisters | 1962 | 30.00 |
| **DEEP, THE** | | | |
| PARKWAY | | | |
| ❑ P 7051 [M] | Psychedelic Moods | 1966 | 250.00 |
| ❑ SP 7051 [S] | Psychedelic Moods | 1966 | 500.00 |
| **DEEP PURPLE** | | | |
| DCC COMPACT CLASSICS | | | |
| ❑ LPZ-2052 [(2)] | Made in Japan | 1998 | 40.00 |
| *—Audiophile vinyl* | | | |
| EAGLE ROCK | | | |
| ❑ ER 20083-1 [(2)] | Rapture of the Deep | 2005 | 20.00 |
| MERCURY | | | |
| ❑ 824003-1 | Perfect Strangers | 1984 | 10.00 |
| ❑ 831318-1 | The House of Blue Light | 1987 | 8.00 |
| ❑ 835897-1 | Nobody's Perfect | 1988 | 10.00 |

| Number | Title (A Side/B Side) | Yr | NM |
|---|---|---|---|
| RCA | | | |
| ❑ 2421-1-R | Slaves and Masters | 1990 | 15.00 |
| RHINO | | | |
| ❑ R1-75622 | Machine Head | 2003 | 15.00 |
| *—180-gram reissue* | | | |
| SCEPTER CITATION | | | |
| ❑ CTN-18010 | The Best of Deep Purple | 1972 | 10.00 |
| TETRAGRAMMATON | | | |
| ❑ T-102 | Shades of Deep Purple | 1968 | 30.00 |
| ❑ T-107 | The Book of Taliesyn | 1968 | 30.00 |
| ❑ T-119 | Deep Purple | 1969 | 30.00 |
| ❑ T-131 | Concerto for Group and Orchestra | 1970 | 200.00 |
| WARNER BROS. | | | |
| ❑ WS 1860 | Concerto for Group and Orchestra | 1970 | 12.00 |
| ❑ WS 1877 | Deep Purple in Rock | 1970 | 12.00 |
| ❑ BS 2564 | Fireball | 1971 | 12.00 |
| ❑ BS 2607 | Machine Head | 1972 | 12.00 |
| *—Original copies have green "WB" labels* | | | |
| ❑ BS 2607 | Machine Head | 1973 | 10.00 |
| *—"Burbank" labels* | | | |
| ❑ BS4 2607 [Q] | Machine Head | 1974 | 25.00 |
| ❑ 2LS 2644 [(2)] | (Purple Passages) | 1972 | 15.00 |
| ❑ BS 2678 | Who Do We Think We Are! | 1973 | 10.00 |
| *—"Burbank" labels* | | | |
| ❑ BS 2678 | Who Do We Think We Are! | 1973 | 12.00 |
| *—Original copies have green "WB" labels* | | | |
| ❑ 2WS 2701 [(2)] | Made in Japan | 1973 | 15.00 |
| ❑ 2WS 2701 [(2)] | Made in Japan | 1979 | 12.00 |
| *—White labels* | | | |
| ❑ W 2766 | Burn | 1974 | 10.00 |
| ❑ BSK 3100 | Machine Head | 1976 | 8.00 |
| WARNER BROS./PURPLE | | | |
| ❑ PR 2832 | Stormbringer | 1974 | 10.00 |
| ❑ PR4 2832 [Q] | Stormbringer | 1974 | 25.00 |
| ❑ PR 2895 | Come Taste the Band | 1975 | 10.00 |
| ❑ PR 2995 | Made in Europe | 1976 | 10.00 |
| ❑ PRK 3223 | When We Rock, We Rock, and When We Roll, We Roll | 1978 | 10.00 |
| ❑ PRK 3486 | Deepest Purple: The Best of Deep Purple | 1980 | 10.00 |

| Number | Title (A Side/B Side) | Yr | NM |
|---|---|---|---|
| **DEEP RIVER BOYS, THE** | | | |
| QUE | | | |
| ❑ FLS-104 [M] | Midnight Magic | 1957 | 150.00 |
| RCA CAMDEN | | | |
| ❑ CAL-303 [M] | Presenting the Deep River Boys | 1957 | 60.00 |
| *—Reissue of "X" album* | | | |
| WALDORF MUSIC HALL | | | |
| ❑ MH 33-108 [10] | The Deep River Boys Sing Songs of Jubilee | 195? | 150.00 |
| *—Cartoon on cover* | | | |
| ❑ MH 33-108 [10] | The Deep River Boys Sing Songs of Jubilee | 1954 | 300.00 |
| *—Photo of group on cover* | | | |
| "X" | | | |
| ❑ LXA-1019 [M] | Presenting the Deep River Boys | 1956 | 120.00 |
| **DEEP SIX, THE** | | | |
| LIBERTY | | | |
| ❑ LRP-3475 [M] | The Deep Six | 1966 | 15.00 |
| ❑ LST-7475 [S] | The Deep Six | 1966 | 20.00 |
| **DEERFIELD** | | | |
| FLAT ROCK | | | |
| ❑ FRS-1 | Nil Desperandum | 1971 | 120.00 |
| **DEES, RICK** | | | |
| ATLANTIC | | | |
| ❑ 81231 | Put It Where the Moon Don't Shine | 1984 | 12.00 |
| ❑ 81288 | I'm Not Crazy | 1985 | 12.00 |
| NO BUDGET | | | |
| ❑ NBR 102 | Hurt Me Baby — Make Me Write Bad Checks! | 1983 | 15.00 |
| RSO | | | |
| ❑ RS-1-3017 | The Original Disco Duck | 1976 | 30.00 |
| **DEES, SAM** | | | |
| ATLANTIC | | | |
| ❑ SD 18134 | The Show Must Go On | 1975 | 150.00 |
| **DEFRANCO, BUDDY** | | | |
| DECCA | | | |
| ❑ DL 4031 [M] | Pacific Standard Swingin' Time | 1961 | 20.00 |
| ❑ DL 74031 [S] | Pacific Standard Swingin' Time | 1961 | 25.00 |
| DOT | | | |
| ❑ DLP-9006 [M] | Cross-Country Suite | 1958 | 40.00 |
| GENE NORMAN | | | |
| ❑ GNP-2 [10] | Buddy DeFranco Takes You to the Stars | 1954 | 120.00 |
| HAMILTON | | | |
| ❑ HL-133 [M] | Cross-Country Suite | 1964 | 20.00 |
| MGM | | | |
| ❑ E-177 [10] | King of the Clarinet | 1952 | 120.00 |
| ❑ E-253 [10] | Buddy DeFranco with Strings | 1954 | 100.00 |
| ❑ E-3396 [M] | Buddy DeFranco | 1956 | 80.00 |
| MOSAIC | | | |
| ❑ MR5-117 [(5)] | The Complete Recordings of the Buddy DeFranco Quartet/Quintet with Sonny Clark | 199? | 100.00 |
| NORGRAN | | | |
| ❑ MGN-3 [10] | The Buddy DeFranco Quartet | 1954 | 150.00 |
| ❑ MGN-16 [10] | Pretty Moods by Buddy DeFranco | 1954 | 150.00 |
| ❑ MGN-1006 [M] | The Progressive Mr. DeFranco | 1954 | 120.00 |
| ❑ MGN-1012 [M] | Buddy DeFranco and His Clarinet | 1954 | 100.00 |
| ❑ MGN-1016 [M] | Buddy DeFranco and Oscar Peterson Play George Gershwin | 1955 | 100.00 |
| ❑ MGN-1026 [M] | Buddy DeFranco Quartet | 1955 | 100.00 |
| ❑ MGN-1068 [M] | Jazz Tones | 1956 | 80.00 |
| ❑ MGN-1069 [M] | Mr. Clarinet | 1956 | 80.00 |
| ❑ MGN-1079 [M] | In a Mellow Mood | 1956 | 80.00 |
| ❑ MGN-1085 [M] | The Buddy DeFranco Wailers | 1956 | 80.00 |
| ❑ MGN-1094 [M] | Odalisque | 1956 | 80.00 |
| ❑ MGN-1096 [M] | Autumn Leaves | 1956 | 80.00 |
| VERVE | | | |
| ❑ MGV-2022 [M] | The George Gershwin Songbook | 1956 | 50.00 |
| *—Reissue of Norgran 1016* | | | |
| ❑ MGV-2033 [M] | Broadway Showcase | 1957 | 50.00 |
| ❑ V-2033 [M] | Broadway Showcase | 1961 | 20.00 |
| ❑ MGV-2089 [M] | Buddy DeFranco Plays Benny Goodman | 1958 | 50.00 |
| ❑ V-2089 [M] | Buddy DeFranco Plays Benny Goodman | 1961 | 20.00 |
| ❑ MGV-2090 [M] | Buddy DeFranco Plays Artie Shaw | 1958 | 50.00 |
| ❑ V-2090 [M] | Buddy DeFranco Plays Artie Shaw | 1961 | 20.00 |

| Number | Title (A Side/B Side) | Yr | NM |
|---|---|---|---|
| ❑ MGV-2108 [M] | I Hear Benny Goodman and Artie Shaw | 1958 | 50.00 |
| ❑ V-2108 [M] | I Hear Benny Goodman and Artie Shaw | 1961 | 20.00 |
| ❑ V6-2108 [S] | I Hear Benny Goodman and Artie Shaw | 1961 | 20.00 |
| ❑ MGVS-6032 [S] | I Hear Benny Goodman and Artie Shaw | 1960 | 40.00 |
| ❑ MGVS-6051 [S] | Bravura | 1960 | 40.00 |
| ❑ MGVS-6132 [S] | Generalissimo | 1960 | 40.00 |
| ❑ MGVS-6150 [S] | Wholly Cats | 1960 | 40.00 |
| ❑ MGVS-6165 [S] | Closed Session | 1960 | 40.00 |
| ❑ MGVS-6166 [S] | Live Date! | 1960 | 40.00 |
| ❑ MGV-8158 [M] | Jazz Tones | 1957 | 50.00 |

*—Reissue of Norgran 1068*

| Number | Title (A Side/B Side) | Yr | NM |
|---|---|---|---|
| ❑ V-8158 [M] | Jazz Tones | 1961 | 20.00 |
| ❑ MGV-8159 [M] | Mr. Clarinet | 1957 | 50.00 |

*—Reissue of Norgran 1069*

| Number | Title (A Side/B Side) | Yr | NM |
|---|---|---|---|
| ❑ V-8159 [M] | Mr. Clarinet | 1961 | 20.00 |
| ❑ MGV-8169 [M] | In a Mellow Mood | 1957 | 50.00 |

*—Reissue of Norgran 1079*

| Number | Title (A Side/B Side) | Yr | NM |
|---|---|---|---|
| ❑ V-8169 [M] | In a Mellow Mood | 1961 | 20.00 |
| ❑ MGV-8175 [M] | The Buddy DeFranco Wailers | 1957 | 50.00 |

*—Reissue of Norgran 1085*

| Number | Title (A Side/B Side) | Yr | NM |
|---|---|---|---|
| ❑ V-8175 [M] | The Buddy DeFranco Wailers | 1961 | 20.00 |
| ❑ MGV-8182 [M] | Odalisque | 1957 | 50.00 |

*—Reissue of Norgran 1094*

| Number | Title (A Side/B Side) | Yr | NM |
|---|---|---|---|
| ❑ V-8182 [M] | Odalisque | 1961 | 20.00 |
| ❑ MGV-8183 [M] | Autumn Leaves | 1957 | 50.00 |

*—Reissue of Norgran 1096*

| Number | Title (A Side/B Side) | Yr | NM |
|---|---|---|---|
| ❑ V-8183 [M] | Autumn Leaves | 1961 | 20.00 |
| ❑ MGV-8210 [M] | Buddy DeFranco and the Oscar Peterson Quartet | 1958 | 50.00 |
| ❑ V-8210 [M] | Buddy DeFranco and the Oscar Peterson Quartet | 1961 | 20.00 |
| ❑ MGV-8221 [M] | Cooking the Blues | 1958 | 80.00 |
| ❑ V-8221 [M] | Cooking the Blues | 1961 | 20.00 |
| ❑ MGV-8224 [M] | Sweet and Lovely | 1958 | 50.00 |
| ❑ V-8224 [M] | Sweet and Lovely | 1961 | 20.00 |
| ❑ MGV-8315 [M] | Bravura | 1959 | 50.00 |
| ❑ V-8315 [M] | Bravura | 1961 | 20.00 |
| ❑ V6-8315 [S] | Bravura | 1961 | 20.00 |
| ❑ MGV-8363 [M] | Generalissimo | 1960 | 50.00 |
| ❑ V-8363 [M] | Generalissimo | 1961 | 20.00 |
| ❑ V6-8363 [S] | Generalissimo | 1961 | 20.00 |
| ❑ MGV-8375 [M] | Wholly Cats | 1960 | 40.00 |
| ❑ V-8375 [M] | Wholly Cats | 1961 | 20.00 |
| ❑ V6-8375 [S] | Wholly Cats | 1961 | 20.00 |
| ❑ MGV-8382 [M] | Closed Session | 1960 | 40.00 |
| ❑ V-8382 [M] | Closed Session | 1961 | 20.00 |
| ❑ V6-8382 [S] | Closed Session | 1961 | 20.00 |
| ❑ MGV-8383 [M] | Live Date! | 1960 | 40.00 |
| ❑ V-8383 [M] | Live Date! | 1961 | 20.00 |
| ❑ V6-8383 [S] | Live Date! | 1961 | 20.00 |

### DEFRANCO, BUDDY, AND TOMMY GUMINA

MERCURY

| Number | Title (A Side/B Side) | Yr | NM |
|---|---|---|---|
| ❑ MG-20685 [M] | Presenting the Buddy DeFranco-Tommy Gumina Quintet | 1962 | 20.00 |
| ❑ MG-20743 [M] | Kaleidoscope | 1962 | 20.00 |
| ❑ MG-20833 [M] | Polytones | 1963 | 20.00 |
| ❑ MG-20900 [M] | The Girl from Ipanema | 1964 | 20.00 |
| ❑ SR-60685 [S] | Presenting the Buddy DeFranco-Tommy Gumina Quintet | 1962 | 25.00 |
| ❑ SR-60743 [S] | Kaleidoscope | 1962 | 25.00 |
| ❑ SR-60833 [S] | Polytones | 1963 | 25.00 |
| ❑ SR-60900 [S] | The Girl from Ipanema | 1964 | 25.00 |

### DEHAVEN, DOC

CUCA

| Number | Title (A Side/B Side) | Yr | NM |
|---|---|---|---|
| ❑ K-3000 [M] | Dixieland Treasure | 1962 | 20.00 |
| ❑ K-3100 [M] | Doc DeHaven On Location | 1963 | 20.00 |
| ❑ K-3200 [M] | Doc Swings a Little | 1964 | 20.00 |
| ❑ K-3300 [M] | Just Off State Street | 1966 | 20.00 |
| ❑ KS-3300 [S] | Just Off State Street | 1966 | 25.00 |
| ❑ K-3400 [M] | Erle of Madison | 1967 | 20.00 |

### DEJOHN SISTERS, THE

EPIC

| Number | Title (A Side/B Side) | Yr | NM |
|---|---|---|---|
| ❑ LN 1116 [M] | The DeJohn Sisters | 195? | 30.00 |

UNITED ARTISTS

| Number | Title (A Side/B Side) | Yr | NM |
|---|---|---|---|
| ❑ UAL-3103 [M] | Yes Indeed | 1960 | 20.00 |
| ❑ UAS-6103 [S] | Yes Indeed | 1960 | 25.00 |

### DEJOHNETTE, JACK

COLUMBIA

| Number | Title (A Side/B Side) | Yr | NM |
|---|---|---|---|
| ❑ C 31176 | Compost (Take Off Your Body) | 1971 | 20.00 |

MILESTONE

| Number | Title (A Side/B Side) | Yr | NM |
|---|---|---|---|
| ❑ MSP-9022 | The DeJohnette Complex | 1969 | 20.00 |

### DEKKER, DESMOND, AND THE ACES

BULLDOG

| Number | Title (A Side/B Side) | Yr | NM |
|---|---|---|---|
| ❑ 1037 | The Israelites | 198? | 10.00 |

UNI

| Number | Title (A Side/B Side) | Yr | NM |
|---|---|---|---|
| ❑ 73059 | Israelites | 1969 | 30.00 |

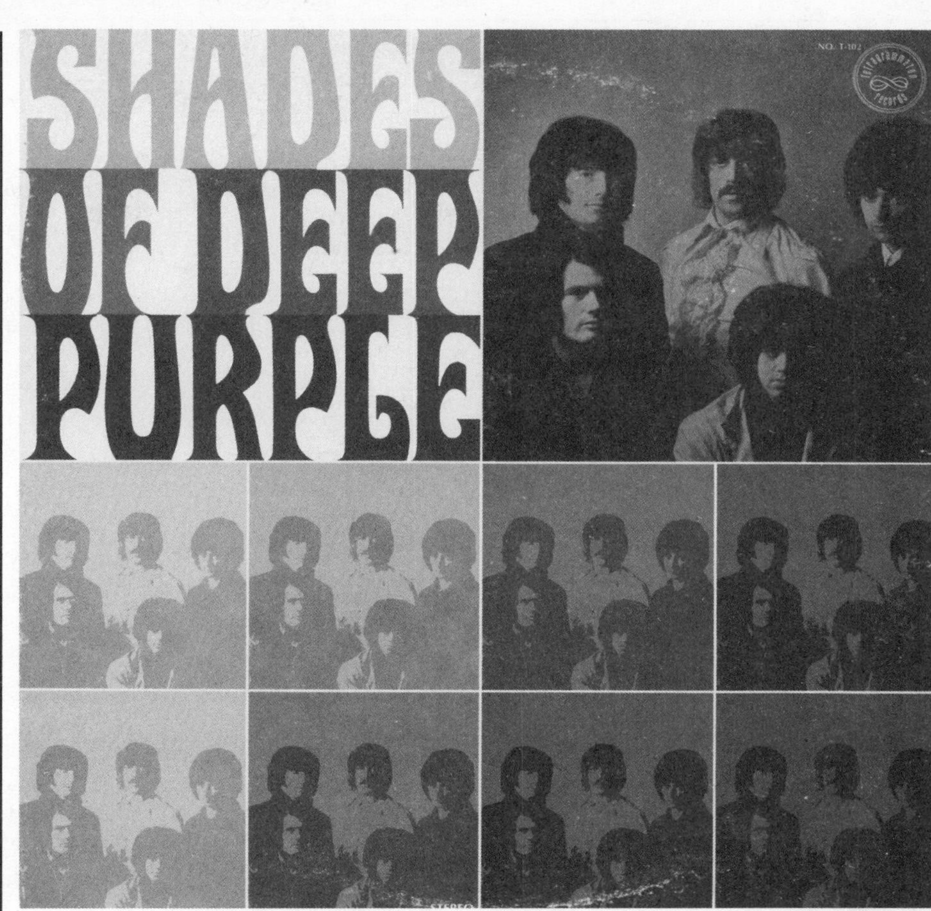


Deep Purple, *Shades of Deep Purple,* Tetragrammaton T-102, 1968, $30.

### DEL SATINS

B.T. PUPPY

| Number | Title (A Side/B Side) | Yr | NM |
|---|---|---|---|
| ❑ BTS-1019 | Out to Lunch | 1972 | 300.00 |

### DEL VIKINGS, THE

COLLECTABLES

| Number | Title (A Side/B Side) | Yr | NM |
|---|---|---|---|
| ❑ COL-5010 | The Best of the Dell-Vikings | 198? | 12.00 |

DOT

| Number | Title (A Side/B Side) | Yr | NM |
|---|---|---|---|
| ❑ DLP-3685 [M] | Come Go with Me | 1966 | 200.00 |
| ❑ DLP-25685 [R] | Come Go with Me | 1966 | 150.00 |

LUNIVERSE

| Number | Title (A Side/B Side) | Yr | NM |
|---|---|---|---|
| ❑ LP-1000 [M] | Come Go with the Del Vikings | 1957 | 500.00 |

*—Eight tracks, cover is composed of slicks. Counterfeits have more tracks and a preprinted cover (not slicks)*

MERCURY

| Number | Title (A Side/B Side) | Yr | NM |
|---|---|---|---|
| ❑ MG-20314 [M] | They Sing — They Swing | 1957 | 300.00 |
| ❑ MG-20353 [M] | A Swinging, Singing Record Session | 1958 | 200.00 |

### DEL VIKINGS, THE / THE SONNETS

CROWN

| Number | Title (A Side/B Side) | Yr | NM |
|---|---|---|---|
| ❑ CLP-5368 [M] | The Del Vikings and the Sonnets | 1963 | 40.00 |

### DELANEY, JACK

SOUTHLAND

| Number | Title (A Side/B Side) | Yr | NM |
|---|---|---|---|
| ❑ LP-201 [10] | Jack Delaney and George Girard in New Orleans | 1954 | 50.00 |
| ❑ LP-214 [10] | Jack Delaney with Lee Collins | 1954 | 50.00 |
| ❑ LP-214 [M] | Jack Delaney and the New Orleans Jazz Babies | 195? | 40.00 |

### DELANEY AND BONNIE

ATCO

| Number | Title (A Side/B Side) | Yr | NM |
|---|---|---|---|
| ❑ SD 33-326 | Delaney & Bonnie & Friends On Tour with Eric Clapton | 197? | 10.00 |

*—Later pressings on other labels*

| Number | Title (A Side/B Side) | Yr | NM |
|---|---|---|---|
| ❑ SD 33-326 | Delaney & Bonnie & Friends On Tour with Eric Clapton | 1970 | 25.00 |

*—Yellow label original*

| Number | Title (A Side/B Side) | Yr | NM |
|---|---|---|---|
| ❑ 33-341 [M] | To Bonnie from Delaney | 1970 | 40.00 |

*—White label promo; no stock copies were issued in mono*

| Number | Title (A Side/B Side) | Yr | NM |
|---|---|---|---|
| ❑ SD 33-341 [S] | To Bonnie from Delaney | 1970 | 25.00 |
| ❑ SD 33-358 | Motel Shot | 1971 | 25.00 |
| ❑ SD 33-383 | Country Life | 1972 | 20.00 |
| ❑ SD 7014 | The Best of Delaney and Bonnie | 1972 | 20.00 |

COLUMBIA

| Number | Title (A Side/B Side) | Yr | NM |
|---|---|---|---|
| ❑ KC 31377 | D&B Together | 1972 | 20.00 |

ELEKTRA

| Number | Title (A Side/B Side) | Yr | NM |
|---|---|---|---|
| ❑ EKS-74039 | Accept No Substitute — The Original Delaney & Bonnie & Friends | 1969 | 30.00 |

GNP CRESCENDO

| Number | Title (A Side/B Side) | Yr | NM |
|---|---|---|---|
| ❑ GNPS-2054 | Genesis | 1970 | 20.00 |

STAX

| Number | Title (A Side/B Side) | Yr | NM |
|---|---|---|---|
| ❑ STS-2026 | Home | 1969 | 30.00 |

### DELEGATES, THE (1)

MAINSTREAM

| Number | Title (A Side/B Side) | Yr | NM |
|---|---|---|---|
| ❑ 100 | The Delegates | 1973 | 20.00 |

### DELEGATES, THE (2) See BILLY LARKIN.

### DELFONICS, THE

ARISTA

| Number | Title (A Side/B Side) | Yr | NM |
|---|---|---|---|
| ❑ AL 8333 | The Best of the Delfonics | 198? | 10.00 |

COLLECTABLES

| Number | Title (A Side/B Side) | Yr | NM |
|---|---|---|---|
| ❑ COL-5109 | Golden Classics | 198? | 10.00 |

KORY

| Number | Title (A Side/B Side) | Yr | NM |
|---|---|---|---|
| ❑ 1002 | The Best of the Delfonics | 1977 | 12.00 |

PHILLY GROOVE

| Number | Title (A Side/B Side) | Yr | NM |
|---|---|---|---|
| ❑ 1150 | La La Means I Love You | 1968 | 80.00 |
| ❑ 1151 | The Sexy Sound of Soul | 1969 | 80.00 |
| ❑ 1152 | The Delfonics Super Hits | 1969 | 50.00 |
| ❑ 1153 | The Delfonics | 1970 | 50.00 |
| ❑ 1154 | Tell Me This Is a Dream | 1972 | 50.00 |
| ❑ 1501 | Alive & Kicking | 1974 | 50.00 |

POOGIE

| Number | Title (A Side/B Side) | Yr | NM |
|---|---|---|---|
| ❑ 121680 | The Delfonics Return | 1981 | 12.00 |

### DELLER, ALFRED

VANGUARD

| Number | Title (A Side/B Side) | Yr | NM |
|---|---|---|---|
| ❑ VRS-479 [M] | The Three Ravens | 195? | 40.00 |
| ❑ VRS-499 [M] | The Holly and the Ivy — Christmas Songs of Old England | 1956 | 40.00 |

Number | Title (A Side/B Side) | Yr | NM

## DELLS, THE

### ABC
❑ AA-1100 New Beginnings 1978 12.00
❑ AA-1113 Face to Face 1978 12.00

### BUDDAH
❑ BDS-5053 The Dells 1969 15.00

### CADET
❑ LPS-804 There Is 1968 50.00
❑ LPS-822 The Dells Musical Menu/ Always Together 1969 50.00
❑ LPS-824 The Dells Greatest Hits 1969 50.00
❑ LPS-829 Love Is Blue 1969 50.00
❑ LPS-837 Like It Is, Like It Was 1970 50.00
❑ 50004 Freedom Means 1971 25.00
❑ 50017 The Dells Sing Dionne Warwicke's Greatest Hits 1972 25.00
❑ 50021 Sweet As Funk Can Be 1972 25.00
❑ 50037 Give Your Baby a Standing Ovation 1973 25.00
❑ 50046 The Dells 1973 25.00
❑ 60030 The Mighty Mighty Dells 1974 25.00
❑ 60036 The Dells' Greatest Hits, Vol. 2 1975 20.00

### CHESS
❑ CH-9103 The Dells 198? 10.00
*—Reissue*
❑ CH-9288 There Is 1989 10.00
*—Reissue of Cadet 804*

### LOST-NITE
❑ LLP-21 [10] The Dells 1981 15.00
*—Red vinyl, generic red cover*

### MERCURY
❑ SRM-1-1059 We Got to Get Our Thing Together 1975 15.00
❑ SRM-1-1084 No Way Back 1976 15.00
❑ SRM-1-1145 They Said It Couldn't Be Done 1977 15.00
❑ SRM-1-3711 Love Connection 1977 15.00

### PRIVATE I
❑ BFZ 39309 One Step Closer 1984 10.00

### SOLID SMOKE
❑ 8029 Breezy Ballads and Tender Tunes: The Best of the Early Years (1955-65) 1984 10.00

### 20TH CENTURY
❑ T-618 I Touched a Dream 1980 12.00
❑ T-633 Whatever Turns You On 1981 12.00

### UPFRONT
❑ UPF-105 Stay In My Corner 1968 15.00

### URGENT
❑ URG-4108 The Second Time 1991 12.00

### VEE JAY
❑ LP 1010 [M] Oh What a Nite 1959 800.00
*—Maroon label*
❑ LP 1010 [M] Oh What a Nite 1961 300.00
*—Black label with colorband*
❑ VJLP-1010 Oh What a Nite 198? 10.00
*—Late-80s reissue on reactivated Vee Jay label. "Trade Mark Reg." on label.*
❑ LP 1141 [M] It's Not Unusual 1965 100.00
❑ LPS 1141 [S] It's Not Unusual 1965 150.00

### VJ INTERNATIONAL
❑ 7305 The Dells In Concert 197? 12.00

### ZOO
❑ 11023 I Salute You 1992 15.00

## DELLS, THE, AND THE DRAMATICS

### CADET
❑ 60027 The Dells Vs. the Dramatics 1974 25.00

## DELMORE BROTHERS, THE

### KING
❑ 589 [M] Songs by the Delmore Brothers 1958 150.00
❑ 785 [M] 30th Anniversary Album 1962 80.00
❑ 910 [M] In Memory 1964 40.00
❑ 920 [M] In Memory, Volume 2 1964 40.00
❑ 983 [M] 24 Great Country Songs 1966 30.00
❑ KS-983 [R] 24 Great Country Songs 1966 20.00

## DEMANO, HANK

### FREEWAY
❑ FLJP-1 [M] Hank DeMano Quartet 1955 50.00

## DEMENSIONS, THE

### CORAL
❑ CRL 57430 [M] My Foolish Heart 1963 150.00
❑ CRL 757430 [S] My Foolish Heart 1963 300.00

## DEMIAN

### ABC
❑ ABCS-718 Demian 1970 60.00

## DENNIS, JOHN

### DEBUT
❑ DEB-121 [M] New Piano Expressions 1955 120.00

## DENNY, DOTTY

### A440
❑ AJ-505 [M] Tribute to Edgar Sampson 1954 70.00
❑ AJ-506 [M] Dotty Digs Duke 1954 70.00

## DENNY, MARTIN

### FIRST AMERICAN
❑ 7743 From Hawaii With Love 1981 10.00

### LIBERTY
❑ LM-1009 Exotica Vol. 1 1982 8.00
*—Reissue of United Artists 1009*
❑ LRP-3034 [M] Exotica 1957 40.00
*—Turquoise label*
❑ LRP-3034 [M] Exotica 1960 25.00
*—Black rainbow label*
❑ LRP-3077 [M] Exotica, Volume II 1957 30.00
*—Turquoise label*
❑ LRP-3077 [M] Exotica, Volume II 1960 20.00
*—Black rainbow label*
❑ LRP-3081 [M] Forbidden Island 1958 30.00
*—Turquoise label; woman in jungle on cover*
❑ LRP-3081 [M] Forbidden Island 1960 20.00
*—Black rainbow label; white foil on cover*
❑ LRP-3087 [M] Primitiva 1958 30.00
*—Turquoise label*
❑ LRP-3087 [M] Primitiva 1960 20.00
*—Black rainbow label*
❑ LRP-3102 [M] Hypnotique 1958 30.00
*—Turquoise label*
❑ LRP-3102 [M] Hypnotique 1960 20.00
*—Black rainbow label*
❑ LRP-3111 [M] Afro-Desia 1959 30.00
*—Turquoise label*
❑ LRP-3111 [M] Afro-Desia 1960 20.00
*—Black rainbow label*
❑ LRP-3116 [M] Exotica, Vol. III 1959 30.00
*—Turquoise label*
❑ LRP-3116 [M] Exotica, Vol. III 1960 20.00
*—Black rainbow label*
❑ LRP-3122 [M] Quiet Village 1959 30.00
*—Turquoise label*
❑ LRP-3122 [M] Quiet Village 1960 20.00
*—Black rainbow label*
❑ LRP-3141 [M] The Enchanted Sea 1959 30.00
*—Turquoise label*
❑ LRP-3141 [M] The Enchanted Sea 1960 20.00
*—Black rainbow label*
❑ LRP-3158 [M] Exotic Sounds from the Silver Screen 1960 20.00
❑ LRP-3163 [M] Exotic Sounds Visit Broadway 1960 20.00
❑ LRP-3168 [M] Exotic Percussion 1961 20.00
❑ LRP-3224 [M] The Exotic Sounds of Martin Denny In Person 1962 15.00
❑ LRP-3237 [M] A Taste of Honey 1962 15.00
❑ LRP-3277 [M] Another Taste of Honey 1963 15.00
❑ LRP-3307 [M] The Versatile Martin Denny 1963 15.00
❑ LRP-3328 [M] A Taste of Hits 1964 12.00
❑ LRP-3378 [M] Latin Village 1964 12.00
❑ LRP-3394 [M] Hawaii Tattoo 1964 12.00
❑ LRP-3415 [M] 20 Golden Hawaiian Hits 1965 12.00
❑ LRP-3438 [M] Martin Denny 1965 12.00
❑ LRP-3445 [M] Hawaiian A-Go-Go 1966 12.00
❑ LRP-3467 [M] Golden Greats 1966 12.00
❑ LRP-3488 [M] Hawaii 1967 12.00
❑ LRP-3513 [M] Exotica Classica 1967 12.00
❑ L-5502 [M] The Best of Martin Denny 1962 15.00
❑ S-6602 [S] The Best of Martin Denny 1962 20.00
❑ LST-7001 [S] Forbidden Island 1958 40.00
*—All-black label; woman in jungle on cover*
❑ LST-7001 [S] Forbidden Island 1960 25.00
*—Black rainbow label; white foil on cover*
❑ LST-7006 [S] Exotica, Volume II 1958 40.00
*—All-black label*
❑ LST-7006 [S] Exotica, Volume II 1960 25.00
*—Black rainbow label*
❑ LST-7023 [S] Primitiva 1958 40.00
*—All-black label*
❑ LST-7023 [S] Primitiva 1960 25.00
*—Black rainbow label*
❑ LST-7034 [R] Exotica 1958 25.00
*—All-black label*
❑ LST-7034 [R] Exotica 1960 20.00
*—Black rainbow label*
❑ LST-7102 [S] Hypnotique 1958 40.00
*—All-black label*
❑ LST-7102 [S] Hypnotique 1960 25.00
*—Black rainbow label*
❑ LST-7111 [S] Afro-Desia 1959 40.00
*—All-black label*
❑ LST-7111 [S] Afro-Desia 1960 25.00
*—Black rainbow label*
❑ LST-7116 [S] Exotica, Vol. III 1959 40.00
*—All-black label*
❑ LST-7116 [S] Exotica, Vol. III 1960 25.00
*—Black rainbow label*
❑ LST-7122 [S] Quiet Village 1959 40.00
*—All-black label*
❑ LST-7122 [S] Quiet Village 1960 25.00
*—Black rainbow label*
❑ LST-7141 [S] The Enchanted Sea 1959 40.00
*—All-black label*
❑ LST-7141 [S] The Enchanted Sea 1960 25.00
*—Black rainbow label*
❑ LST-7158 [S] Exotic Sounds from the Silver Screen 1960 25.00
❑ LST-7163 [S] Exotic Sounds Visit Broadway 1960 25.00
❑ LST-7168 [S] Exotic Percussion 1961 25.00
❑ LST-7224 [S] The Exotic Sounds of Martin Denny In Person 1962 20.00
❑ LST-7237 [S] A Taste of Honey 1962 20.00
❑ LST-7277 [S] Another Taste of Honey 1963 20.00
❑ LST-7307 [S] The Versatile Martin Denny 1963 20.00
❑ LST-7328 [S] A Taste of Hits 1964 15.00
❑ LST-7378 [S] Latin Village 1964 15.00
❑ LST-7394 [S] Hawaii Tattoo 1964 15.00
❑ LST-7415 [S] 20 Golden Hawaiian Hits 1965 15.00
❑ LST-7438 [S] Martin Denny 1965 15.00
❑ LST-7445 [S] Hawaiian A-Go-Go 1966 15.00
❑ LST-7467 [S] Golden Greats 1966 15.00
❑ LST-7488 [S] Hawaii 1967 15.00
❑ LST-7513 [S] Exotica Classica 1967 15.00
❑ LST-7621 Exotic Moog 1969 40.00

### SUNSET
❑ SUM-1102 [M] Paradise Moods 196? 12.00
❑ SUM-1169 [M] Sayonara 1967 12.00
❑ SUS-5102 [S] Paradise Moods 196? 12.00
❑ SUS-5169 [S] Sayonara 1967 12.00
❑ SUS-5199 Exotic Night 1969 12.00

### UNITED ARTISTS
❑ UA-LA234-G The Very Best of Martin Denny 1974 10.00
❑ UA-LA383-E The Very Best of Martin Denny 1975 10.00
❑ LM-1009 Exotica Vol. 1 1980 10.00
*—Reissue of Liberty 7034*

## DENNY, SANDY

### A&M
❑ SP-4317 The Northstar Grassman and the Ravens 1971 15.00
❑ SP-4371 Sandy 1972 15.00

### CARTHAGE
❑ CGLP-4423 Rendezvous 1985 10.00
*—Reissue of Island 9433*
❑ CGLP-4425 Like an Old Fashioned Waltz 1985 10.00
*—Reissue of Island 9340*
❑ CGLP-4429 The Northstar Grassman and the Ravens 1985 10.00
*—Reissue of A&M 4317*

### HANNIBAL
❑ HNBX-5301 [(3)] Who Knows Where the Time Goes 198? 20.00

### ISLAND
❑ SW-9340 Like an Old Fashioned Waltz 1974 15.00
❑ ILPS 9433 Rendezvous 1977 15.00

## DENVER, JOHN

### HJD
❑ 66 John Denver Sings 1966 500.00
*—Private issue of 300 or so, made by JD as Christmas gifts to friends.*

### MERCURY
❑ SRM-1-704 Beginnings 1972 20.00
*—With illustration on cover*
❑ SRM-1-704 Beginnings 1974 12.00
*—With mountain scene on cover*

### RCA
❑ 7624-1-R Back Home Again 1988 10.00
*—Last vinyl reissue*
❑ 7631-1-R Poems, Prayers and Promises 1988 10.00
*—Last vinyl reissue*
❑ 7632-1-R Rocky Mountain High 1988 10.00
*—Last vinyl reissue*

### RCA VICTOR
❑ DJL1-0075 [DJ] The John Denver Radio Show 1973 30.00
❑ APL1-0101 Farewell Andromeda 1973 12.00
*—Orange label*
❑ APL1-0101 Farewell Andromeda 1975 10.00
*—Tan label or black label, dog near top*
❑ APL1-0374 John Denver's Greatest Hits 197? 8.00
*—Reissue*
❑ AQL1-0374 John Denver's Greatest Hits 197? 8.00
*—Later reissue*
❑ CPL1-0374 John Denver's Greatest Hits 1974 10.00
*—Orange label*
❑ CPL1-0374 John Denver's Greatest Hits 1975 8.00
*—Tan label or black label, dog near top*
❑ AFL1-0548 Back Home Again 197? 8.00
*—Reissue*
❑ AQL1-0548 Back Home Again 197? 8.00
*—Later reissue*
❑ CPL1-0548 Back Home Again 1974 10.00
*—Orange or tan label*
❑ CPL1-0548 Back Home Again 1976 8.00
*—Black label, dog near top*

| Number | Title (A Side/B Side) | Yr | NM |
|---|---|---|---|
| ❑ DJL1-0683 [DJ] | The Second John Denver Radio Show | 1974 | 30.00 |
| ❑ CPL2-0764 [(2)] | An Evening with John Denver | 1975 | 12.00 |
| —Orange or tan labels | | | |
| ❑ CPL2-0764 [(2)] | An Evening with John Denver | 1976 | 10.00 |
| —Black label, dog near top | | | |
| ❑ AFL1-1183 | Windsong | 197? | 8.00 |
| —Reissue | | | |
| ❑ APL1-1183 | Windsong | 1975 | 10.00 |
| —Tan label | | | |
| ❑ APL1-1183 | Windsong | 1976 | 8.00 |
| —Black label, dog near top | | | |
| ❑ AQL1-1183 | Windsong | 197? | 8.00 |
| —Later reissue | | | |
| ❑ AFL1-1201 | Rocky Mountain Christmas | 197? | 8.00 |
| —Reissue | | | |
| ❑ APL1-1201 | Rocky Mountain Christmas | 1975 | 10.00 |
| —Tan label | | | |
| ❑ APL1-1201 | Rocky Mountain Christmas | 1976 | 8.00 |
| —Black label, dog near top | | | |
| ❑ APL2-1263 [(2)] | The John Denver Gift Pak | 1974 | 30.00 |
| —Contains "Rocky Mountain Christmas" and "Windsong" in a special Christmas sleeve. | | | |
| ❑ AFL1-1694 | Spirit | 197? | 8.00 |
| —Reissue | | | |
| ❑ APL1-1694 | Spirit | 1976 | 10.00 |
| —Originals are black label, dog near top | | | |
| ❑ AQL1-2195 | John Denver's Greatest Hits, Volume 2 | 197? | 8.00 |
| —Reissue | | | |
| ❑ CPL1-2195 | John Denver's Greatest Hits, Volume 2 | 1977 | 10.00 |
| ❑ AFL1-2521 | I Want to Live | 1977 | 8.00 |
| ❑ AQL1-3075 | John Denver | 1979 | 8.00 |
| ❑ AQL1-3449 | Autograph | 1980 | 8.00 |
| ❑ AFL1-4055 | Some Days Are Diamonds | 1981 | 8.00 |
| ❑ LSP-4207 | Rhymes & Reasons | 1969 | 15.00 |
| —Orange label, non-flexible vinyl | | | |
| ❑ AFL1-4256 | Seasons of the Heart | 1982 | 8.00 |
| ❑ LSP-4278 | Take Me to Tomorrow | 1970 | 15.00 |
| —Orange label, non-flexible vinyl | | | |
| ❑ LSP-4414 | Whose Garden Was This? | 1970 | 15.00 |
| —Orange label, non-flexible vinyl | | | |
| ❑ AFL1-4499 | Poems, Prayers and Promises | 197? | 8.00 |
| —Reissue | | | |
| ❑ LSP-4499 | Poems, Prayers and Promises | 1971 | 12.00 |
| —Orange label | | | |
| ❑ LSP-4499 | Poems, Prayers and Promises | 1975 | 10.00 |
| —Tan label or black label, dog near top | | | |
| ❑ AFL1-4607 | Aerie | 197? | 8.00 |
| —Reissue | | | |
| ❑ LSP-4607 | Aerie | 1971 | 12.00 |
| —Orange label | | | |
| ❑ LSP-4607 | Aerie | 1975 | 10.00 |
| —Tan label or black label, dog near top | | | |
| ❑ AFL1-4683 | It's About Time | 1983 | 8.00 |
| ❑ AFL1-4731 | Rocky Mountain High | 197? | 8.00 |
| —Reissue | | | |
| ❑ AQL1-4731 | Rocky Mountain High | 197? | 8.00 |
| —Later reissue | | | |
| ❑ LSP-4731 | Rocky Mountain High | 1972 | 12.00 |
| —Orange label | | | |
| ❑ LSP-4731 | Rocky Mountain High | 1975 | 10.00 |
| —Tan label or black label, dog near top | | | |
| ❑ AYL1-5189 | Poems, Prayers and Promises | 198? | 6.00 |
| —"Best Buy Series" reissue | | | |
| ❑ AYL1-5190 | Rocky Mountain High | 198? | 6.00 |
| —"Best Buy Series" reissue | | | |
| ❑ AYL1-5191 | Windsong | 198? | 6.00 |
| —"Best Buy Series" reissue | | | |
| ❑ AYL1-5192 | I Want to Live | 198? | 6.00 |
| —"Best Buy Series" reissue | | | |
| ❑ AYL1-5193 | Back Home Again | 198? | 6.00 |
| —"Best Buy Series" reissue | | | |
| ❑ AYL1-5194 | Spirit | 198? | 6.00 |
| —"Best Buy Series" reissue | | | |
| ❑ AYL1-5195 | Farewell Andromeda | 198? | 6.00 |
| —"Best Buy Series" reissue | | | |
| ❑ AJL1-5313 | John Denver's Greatest Hits, Volume 3 | 1984 | 8.00 |
| ❑ DJL1-5398 [DJ] | The John Denver Holiday Radio Show | 1984 | 20.00 |
| ❑ AFL1-5458 | Dreamland Express | 1985 | 8.00 |
| ❑ AFL1-5811 | One World | 1986 | 8.00 |

## DEPARIS, SIDNEY

BLUE NOTE

| Number | Title (A Side/B Side) | Yr | NM |
|---|---|---|---|
| ❑ B-6501 | DeParis Dixie | 1969 | 20.00 |
| ❑ BLP-7016 [10] | Sidney DeParis' Blue Note Stompers | 1951 | 300.00 |

## DEPARIS, SIDNEY/JAMES P. JOHNSON

BLUE NOTE

| Number | Title (A Side/B Side) | Yr | NM |
|---|---|---|---|
| ❑ B-6506 | Original Blue Note Jazz, Volume 3 | 1969 | 20.00 |

## DEPARIS, WILBUR

A440

| Number | Title (A Side/B Side) | Yr | NM |
|---|---|---|---|
| ❑ AJ-503 [10] | New New Orleans Jazz | 1954 | 60.00 |

ATLANTIC

| Number | Title (A Side/B Side) | Yr | NM |
|---|---|---|---|
| ❑ ALS-141 [10] | Wilbur DeParis and His Rampart Street Ramblers | 1952 | 100.00 |
| ❑ ALS-143 [10] | Wilbur DeParis, Volume 2 | 1953 | 100.00 |
| ❑ 1219 [M] | New New Orleans Jazz | 1956 | 50.00 |
| —Black label | | | |
| ❑ 1219 [M] | New New Orleans Jazz | 1961 | 20.00 |
| —Multicolor label, white "fan" logo | | | |
| ❑ SD 1219 [S] | New New Orleans Jazz | 1958 | 40.00 |
| —Green label | | | |
| ❑ SD 1219 [S] | New New Orleans Jazz | 1961 | 20.00 |
| —Multicolor label, white "fan" logo | | | |
| ❑ 1233 [M] | Marchin' and Swingin' | 1956 | 50.00 |
| —Black label | | | |
| ❑ 1233 [M] | Marchin' and Swingin' | 1961 | 20.00 |
| —Multicolor label, white "fan" logo | | | |
| ❑ SD 1233 [S] | Marchin' and Swingin' | 1958 | 40.00 |
| —Green label | | | |
| ❑ SD 1233 [S] | Marchin' and Swingin' | 1961 | 20.00 |
| —Multicolor label, white "fan" logo | | | |
| ❑ 1253 [M] | Wilbur DeParis at Symphony Hall | 1957 | 50.00 |
| —Black label | | | |
| ❑ 1253 [M] | Wilbur DeParis at Symphony Hall | 1961 | 20.00 |
| —Multicolor label, white "fan" logo | | | |
| ❑ SD 1253 [S] | Wilbur DeParis at Symphony Hall | 1958 | 40.00 |
| —Green label | | | |
| ❑ SD 1253 [S] | Wilbur DeParis at Symphony Hall | 1961 | 20.00 |
| —Multicolor label, white "fan" logo | | | |
| ❑ 1288 [M] | Wilbur DeParis Plays Cole Porter | 1958 | 50.00 |
| —Black label | | | |
| ❑ 1288 [M] | Wilbur DeParis Plays Cole Porter | 1961 | 20.00 |
| —Multicolor label, white "fan" logo | | | |
| ❑ 1300 [M] | Something Old, New, Gay, Blue | 1958 | 50.00 |
| —Black label | | | |
| ❑ 1300 [M] | Something Old, New, Gay, Blue | 1961 | 20.00 |
| —Multicolor label, white "fan" logo | | | |
| ❑ SD 1300 [S] | Something Old, New, Gay, Blue | 1958 | 40.00 |
| —Green label | | | |
| ❑ SD 1300 [S] | Something Old, New, Gay, Blue | 1961 | 20.00 |
| —Multicolor label, white "fan" logo | | | |
| ❑ 1318 [M] | That's a-Plenty | 1959 | 50.00 |
| —Black label | | | |
| ❑ 1318 [M] | That's a-Plenty | 1961 | 20.00 |
| —Multicolor label, white "fan" logo | | | |
| ❑ SD 1318 [S] | That's a-Plenty | 1959 | 40.00 |
| —Green label | | | |
| ❑ SD 1318 [S] | That's a-Plenty | 1961 | 20.00 |
| —Multicolor label, white "fan" logo | | | |
| ❑ 1336 [M] | The Wild Jazz Age | 1960 | 25.00 |
| —Multicolor label, white "fan" logo | | | |
| ❑ SD 1336 [S] | The Wild Jazz Age | 1960 | 30.00 |
| —Multicolor label, white "fan" logo | | | |
| ❑ SD 1336 [S] | The Wild Jazz Age | 1964 | 20.00 |
| —Multicolor label, black "fan" logo | | | |
| ❑ 1363 [M] | Wilbur DeParis on the Riviera | 1961 | 25.00 |
| —Multicolor label, white "fan" logo | | | |
| ❑ SD 1363 [S] | Wilbur DeParis on the Riviera | 1961 | 30.00 |
| —Multicolor label, white "fan" logo | | | |
| ❑ SD 1363 [S] | Wilbur DeParis on the Riviera | 1964 | 20.00 |
| —Multicolor label, black "fan" logo | | | |

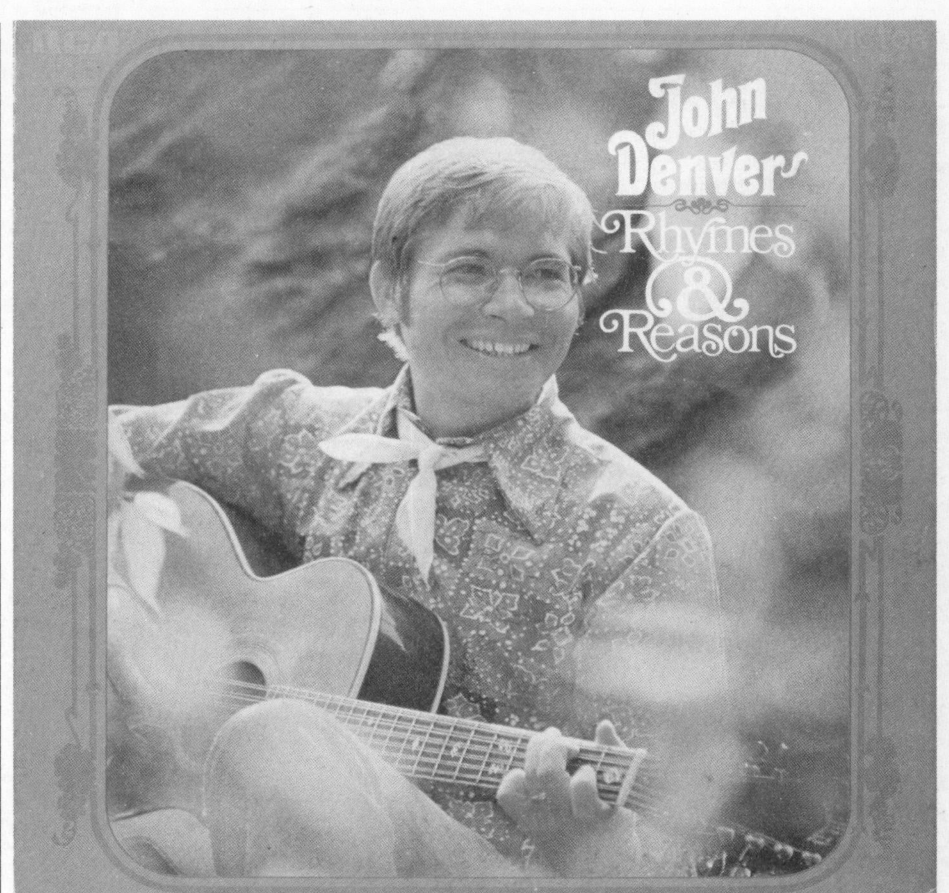


John Denver, *Rhymes & Reasons,* RCA Victor LSP-4207, 1969, orange label, rigid vinyl, $15.

HERITAGE

| Number | Title (A Side/B Side) | Yr | NM |
|---|---|---|---|
| ❑ SS-1207 [M] | Wilbur DeParis | 1956 | 50.00 |

## DEPARIS, WILBUR, AND JIMMY WITHERSPOON

ATLANTIC

| Number | Title (A Side/B Side) | Yr | NM |
|---|---|---|---|
| ❑ 1266 [M] | New Orleans Blues | 1957 | 70.00 |
| —Black label | | | |
| ❑ 1266 [M] | New Orleans Blues | 1961 | 30.00 |
| —Multicolor label, white "fan" logo | | | |
| ❑ 1266 [M] | New Orleans Blues | 1964 | 25.00 |
| —Multicolor label, black "fan" logo | | | |

## DEPAUR CHORUS, THE

COLUMBIA

| Number | Title (A Side/B Side) | Yr | NM |
|---|---|---|---|
| ❑ CL 725 [M] | The Spirit of Christmas/God Is With Us | 1955 | 30.00 |
| ❑ CL 923 [M] | Calypso Christmas | 1956 | 40.00 |

COLUMBIA MASTERWORKS

| Number | Title (A Side/B Side) | Yr | NM |
|---|---|---|---|
| ❑ AL 45 [10] | Swing Low | 1953 | 60.00 |
| ❑ ML 2119 [10] | Work Songs and Spirituals | 195? | 60.00 |

MERCURY LIVING PRESENCE

| Number | Title (A Side/B Side) | Yr | NM |
|---|---|---|---|
| ❑ SR 90382 [S] | Songs of New Nations | 196? | 40.00 |
| —Maroon label, with "Vendor: Mercury Record Corporation" | | | |
| ❑ SR 90382 [S] | Songs of New Nations | 196? | 60.00 |
| —Maroon label, no "Vendor: Mercury Record Corporation" | | | |
| ❑ SR 90418 [S] | Danse Calinda! Creole Songs, Work Songs and Spirituals | 196? | 30.00 |
| —Maroon label, with "Vendor: Mercury Record Corporation" | | | |
| ❑ SR 90418 [S] | Danse Calinda! Creole Songs, Work Songs and Spirituals | 196? | 50.00 |
| —Maroon label, no "Vendor: Mercury Record Corporation" | | | |

| Number | Title (A Side/B Side) | Yr | NM |
|---|---|---|---|
| **DEPECHE MODE** | | | |
| MUTE | | | |
| ❑ MUTEL 5 [(3)] | The Singles 86-98 | 1998 | 30.00 |
| *—Numbered, limited box set pressed in England with U.S. bar code sticker* | | | |
| SIRE | | | |
| ❑ SRK 3642 | Speak & Spell | 1981 | 15.00 |
| ❑ PRO-A-5192 [(2)DJ] | Selections from the Commercially Available Limited Edition Box Sets One and Two | 1991 | 40.00 |
| *—Promo-only sampler* | | | |
| ❑ PRO-A-5242 [(2)DJ] | Selections from the Commercially Available Limited Edition Box Set Three | 1991 | 40.00 |
| ❑ 23751 | A Broken Frame | 1982 | 12.00 |
| ❑ 23900 | Construction Time Again | 1983 | 12.00 |
| ❑ 25124 | People Are People | 1984 | 10.00 |
| ❑ 25194 | Some Great Reward | 1984 | 12.00 |
| ❑ 25346 | Catching Up with Depeche Mode | 1985 | 10.00 |
| ❑ 25429 | Black Celebration | 1986 | 10.00 |
| ❑ 25614 | Music for the Masses | 1987 | 10.00 |
| ❑ 25853 [(2)] | 101 | 1989 | 15.00 |
| ❑ 26081 | Violator | 1990 | 15.00 |
| ❑ R 100560 | Catching Up with Depeche Mode | 1990 | 12.00 |
| *—BMG Direct Marketing edition; reissue* | | | |
| ❑ R 100598 | Music for the Masses | 1988 | 12.00 |
| *—BMG Direct Marketing edition* | | | |
| ❑ R 143674 | Catching Up with Depeche Mode | 1985 | 12.00 |
| *—RCA Music Service edition* | | | |
| ❑ R 173408 | Violator | 1990 | 15.00 |
| *—BMG Direct Marketing edition* | | | |
| **DEPENDABLES, THE** | | | |
| UNITED ARTISTS | | | |
| ❑ UAS-6799 | Klaatu Berrada Niktu | 1971 | 20.00 |
| **DEPUTIES, THE** | | | |
| FARON YOUNG | | | |
| ❑ 002 [M] | Sounds of the Deputies | 1965 | 30.00 |
| **DEREK AND THE DOMINOS** Also see ERIC CLAPTON. | | | |
| ATCO | | | |
| ❑ 2-704 [(2)M] | Layla and Other Assorted Love Songs | 1970 | 300.00 |
| *—White label promo only* | | | |
| ❑ SD 2-704 [(2)DJ] | Layla and Other Assorted Love Songs | 1970 | 200.00 |
| *—White label promo* | | | |
| ❑ SD 2-704 [(2)S] | Layla and Other Assorted Love Songs | 1970 | 30.00 |
| DIRECT DISK | | | |
| ❑ SD-16629 [(2)] | Layla and Other Assorted Love Songs | 1981 | 150.00 |
| *—Audiophile vinyl* | | | |
| MOBILE FIDELITY | | | |
| ❑ 2-239 [(2)] | Derek and the Dominos in Concert | 1996 | 50.00 |
| *—Audiophile vinyl* | | | |
| POLYDOR | | | |
| ❑ PD2-3501 [(2)] | Layla and Other Assorted Love Songs | 1972 | 20.00 |
| RSO | | | |
| ❑ RS-2-3801 [(2)] | Layla and Other Assorted Love Songs | 1977 | 15.00 |
| ❑ SO 2-8800 [(2)] | Derek and the Dominos in Concert | 1973 | 20.00 |
| ❑ 823277-1 [(2)] | Layla and Other Assorted Love Songs | 1985 | 12.00 |
| **DERISE, JOE** | | | |
| BETHLEHEM | | | |
| ❑ BCP-51 [M] | Joe DeRise with the Australian Jazz Quintet | 1956 | 50.00 |
| ❑ BCP-1039 [10] | Joe DeRise Sings | 1955 | 100.00 |
| **DERRINGER, RICK** Also see THE McCOYS. | | | |
| BLUE SKY | | | |
| ❑ KZ 32481 | All American Boy | 1973 | 15.00 |
| ❑ PZ 32481 | All American Boy | 197? | 8.00 |
| *—Reissue with new prefix* | | | |
| ❑ ZQ 32481 [Q] | All American Boy | 1974 | 20.00 |
| ❑ PZ 33423 | Spring Fever | 1975 | 12.00 |
| ❑ PZQ 33423 [Q] | Spring Fever | 1975 | 20.00 |
| ❑ PZ 34181 | Derringer | 1976 | 12.00 |
| ❑ PZ 34470 | Sweet Evil | 1977 | 12.00 |
| ❑ PZ 34848 | Derringer Live | 1977 | 12.00 |
| *—Without bar code* | | | |
| ❑ PZ 34848 | Derringer Live | 198? | 8.00 |
| *—Reissue with bar code* | | | |
| ❑ JZ 35075 | If I Weren't So Romantic I'd Shoot You | 1978 | 10.00 |
| ❑ JZ 36092 | Guitars and Women | 1979 | 10.00 |
| ❑ JZ 36551 | Face to Face | 1980 | 10.00 |
| PASSPORT | | | |
| ❑ PB-6025 | Good Dirty Fun | 1983 | 10.00 |
| **DESANTO, SUGAR PIE** | | | |
| CHECKER | | | |
| ❑ LP-2979 [M] | Sugar Pie DeSanto | 1961 | 200.00 |
| **DESCENDANTS OF MIKE & PHOEBE, THE** | | | |
| STRATA-EAST | | | |
| ❑ SES-19744 | A Spirit Speaks | 1973 | 60.00 |
| **DESHANNON, JACKIE** | | | |
| AMHERST | | | |
| ❑ AMX 1010 | You're the Only Dancer | 1977 | 12.00 |
| ❑ AMH 1016 | Quick Touches | 1978 | 12.00 |
| ATLANTIC | | | |
| ❑ SD 7231 | Jackie | 1972 | 12.00 |
| ❑ SD 7303 | Your Baby Is a Lady | 1974 | 12.00 |
| CAPITOL | | | |
| ❑ ST-772 | Songs | 1971 | 12.00 |
| COLUMBIA | | | |
| ❑ PC 33500 | New Arrangement | 1975 | 12.00 |
| IMPERIAL | | | |
| ❑ LP-9286 [M] | This Is Jackie DeShannon | 1965 | 20.00 |
| *—Black and pink label* | | | |
| ❑ LP-9286 [M] | This Is Jackie DeShannon | 1966 | 15.00 |
| *—Black and green label* | | | |
| ❑ LP-9294 [M] | You Won't Forget Me | 1965 | 20.00 |
| *—Black and pink label* | | | |
| ❑ LP-9294 [M] | You Won't Forget Me | 1966 | 15.00 |
| *—Black and green label* | | | |
| ❑ LP-9296 [M] | In the Wind | 1965 | 20.00 |
| *—Black and pink label* | | | |
| ❑ LP-9296 [M] | In the Wind | 1966 | 15.00 |
| *—Black and green label* | | | |
| ❑ LP-9328 [M] | Are You Ready for This? | 1966 | 15.00 |
| ❑ LP-9344 [M] | New Image | 1967 | 15.00 |
| ❑ LP-9352 [M] | For You | 1967 | 15.00 |
| ❑ LP-12286 [S] | This Is Jackie DeShannon | 1965 | 25.00 |
| *—Black and pink label* | | | |
| ❑ LP-12286 [S] | This Is Jackie DeShannon | 1966 | 20.00 |
| *—Black and green label* | | | |
| ❑ LP-12294 [S] | You Won't Forget Me | 1965 | 25.00 |
| *—Black and pink label* | | | |
| ❑ LP-12294 [S] | You Won't Forget Me | 1966 | 20.00 |
| *—Black and green label* | | | |
| ❑ LP-12296 [S] | In the Wind | 1965 | 25.00 |
| *—Black and pink label* | | | |
| ❑ LP-12296 [S] | In the Wind | 1966 | 20.00 |
| *—Black and green label* | | | |
| ❑ LP-12328 [S] | Are You Ready for This? | 1966 | 20.00 |
| ❑ LP-12344 [S] | New Image | 1967 | 20.00 |
| ❑ LP-12352 [S] | For You | 1967 | 20.00 |
| ❑ LP-12386 | Me About You | 1968 | 15.00 |
| ❑ LP-12404 | What the World Needs Now Is Love | 1968 | 15.00 |
| ❑ LP-12415 | Laurel Canyon | 1969 | 15.00 |
| ❑ LP-12442 | Put a Little Love in Your Heart | 1969 | 15.00 |
| ❑ LP-12453 | To Be Free | 1970 | 15.00 |
| LIBERTY | | | |
| ❑ LRP-3320 [M] | Jackie DeShannon | 1963 | 40.00 |
| ❑ LRP-3390 [M] | Breakin' It Up on the Beatles Tour! | 1964 | 40.00 |
| ❑ LST-7320 [S] | Jackie DeShannon | 1963 | 50.00 |
| ❑ LST-7390 [S] | Breakin' It Up on the Beatles Tour! | 1964 | 50.00 |
| ❑ LN-10179 | The Very Best of Jackie DeShannon | 1983 | 8.00 |
| *—Reissue of United Artists 434* | | | |
| ❑ LN-10265 | Jackie DeShannon | 1985 | 8.00 |
| SUNSET | | | |
| ❑ SUS-5225 | Lonely Girl | 1968 | 12.00 |
| ❑ SUS-5322 | Jackie DeShannon | 1970 | 12.00 |
| UNITED ARTISTS | | | |
| ❑ UA-LA434-E | The Very Best of Jackie DeShannon | 1975 | 12.00 |
| **DESMOND, JOHNNY** | | | |
| COLUMBIA | | | |
| ❑ CL 1399 [M] | Once Upon a Time | 1959 | 20.00 |
| ❑ CL 1477 [M] | Blue Smoke | 1960 | 15.00 |
| ❑ CS 8194 [S] | Once Upon a Time | 1959 | 25.00 |
| ❑ CS 8268 [S] | Blue Smoke | 1960 | 20.00 |
| CORAL | | | |
| ❑ CRL 56124 [10] | Hearts and Flowers | 1955 | 60.00 |
| ❑ CRL 57073 [M] | Desmo Sings Desmond | 195? | 50.00 |
| ❑ CRL 57079 [M] | Souvenir d'Italie | 195? | 40.00 |
| ❑ CRL 57130 [M] | Easy Come Easy Go | 195? | 40.00 |
| CORONET | | | |
| ❑ CXS-236 [S] | Johnny Desmond In Las Vegas! | 196? | 10.00 |
| CRAFTSMEN | | | |
| ❑ C-8019 [M] | Hymns | 196? | 10.00 |
| ❑ C-8030 [M] | Johnny Desmond Sings for Dancing | 196? | 10.00 |
| EVON | | | |
| ❑ 343 [M] | Johnny Desmond Sings Hymns for You | 196? | 10.00 |
| GOLDEN TONE | | | |
| ❑ C-4031 [M] | Hymns | 196? | 10.00 |
| ❑ C-4045 [M] | Dance Party Featuring Johnny Desmond | 196? | 10.00 |
| ❑ 9628 S [S] | Hymns | 196? | 12.00 |
| ❑ 14045 [S] | Dance Party Featuring Johnny Desmond | 196? | 12.00 |
| LION | | | |
| ❑ L-70061 [M] | Dreams of Paris | 1958 | 15.00 |
| MAYFAIR | | | |
| ❑ 9628 S [S] | Hymns | 1958 | 15.00 |
| *—Yellow vinyl* | | | |
| ❑ 9635 S [S] | Johnny Desmond Swings | 1958 | 15.00 |
| *—Yellow vinyl* | | | |
| MGM | | | |
| ❑ E-186 [10] | Hands Across the Table | 1952 | 40.00 |
| ❑ E-3561 [M] | Hands Across the Table | 1957 | 25.00 |
| MOVIETONE | | | |
| ❑ 71011 [M] | Johnny Desmond On Location | 1966 | 12.00 |
| ❑ S-72011 [S] | Johnny Desmond On Location | 1966 | 15.00 |
| PICKWICK | | | |
| ❑ SPC-3558 | Hymns for the Family | 197? | 10.00 |
| RONDO | | | |
| ❑ 1762 [M] | Dance Party Featuring Johnny Desmond | 196? | 10.00 |
| ❑ 9762 [S] | Dance Party Featuring Johnny Desmond | 196? | 12.00 |
| TOPS | | | |
| ❑ L1628 [M] | Hymns | 1958 | 10.00 |
| ❑ L1635 [M] | Johnny Desmond Swings | 1958 | 12.00 |
| ❑ 1762 [M] | Dance Party Featuring Johnny Desmond | 196? | 10.00 |
| ❑ 9762 [S] | Dance Party Featuring Johnny Desmond | 196? | 12.00 |
| VENISE | | | |
| ❑ 7013 [M] | So Nice! | 196? | 10.00 |
| ❑ 10013 [S] | So Nice! | 196? | 15.00 |
| *—Yellow vinyl* | | | |
| VOCALION | | | |
| ❑ VL 3773 [M] | Johnny Desmond | 1966 | 12.00 |
| ❑ VL 73773 [R] | Johnny Desmond | 1966 | 10.00 |
| **DESMOND, PAUL** | | | |
| FANTASY | | | |
| ❑ 3-21 [10] | Paul Desmond | 1955 | 100.00 |
| ❑ 3235 [M] | Paul Desmond Quartet Featuring Don Elliott | 1956 | 80.00 |
| *—Red vinyl* | | | |
| ❑ 3235 [M] | Paul Desmond Quartet Featuring Don Elliott | 1957 | 40.00 |
| *—Black vinyl, red label, non-flexible vinyl* | | | |
| ❑ 3235 [M] | Paul Desmond Quartet Featuring Don Elliott | 1962 | 20.00 |
| *—Black vinyl, red label, flexible vinyl* | | | |
| MOSAIC | | | |
| ❑ MR6-120 [(6)] | The Complete Recordings of the Paul Desmond Quartet with Jim Hall | 199? | 300.00 |
| RCA VICTOR | | | |
| ❑ LPM-2438 [M] | Desmond Blue | 1961 | 30.00 |
| ❑ LSP-2438 [S] | Desmond Blue | 1961 | 30.00 |
| ❑ LPM-2569 [M] | Take Ten | 1962 | 25.00 |
| ❑ LSP-2569 [S] | Take Ten | 1962 | 30.00 |
| ❑ LPM-2654 [M] | Two of a Mind | 1963 | 25.00 |
| ❑ LSP-2654 [S] | Two of a Mind | 1963 | 30.00 |
| ❑ LPM-3320 [M] | Boss Antigua | 1965 | 20.00 |
| ❑ LSP-3320 [S] | Boss Antigua | 1965 | 25.00 |
| ❑ LPM-3407 [M] | Glad to Be Unhappy | 1965 | 20.00 |
| ❑ LSP-3407 [S] | Glad to Be Unhappy | 1965 | 25.00 |
| ❑ LPM-3480 [M] | Easy Living | 1965 | 20.00 |
| ❑ LSP-3480 [S] | Easy Living | 1965 | 25.00 |
| WARNER BROS. | | | |
| ❑ W 1356 [M] | First Place Again | 1960 | 30.00 |
| ❑ WS 1356 [S] | First Place Again | 1960 | 30.00 |
| **DETERGENTS, THE** | | | |
| ROULETTE | | | |
| ❑ R 25308 [M] | The Many Faces of the Detergents | 1965 | 120.00 |
| ❑ SR 25308 [R] | The Many Faces of the Detergents | 1965 | 100.00 |
| **DETROIT CITY LIMITS, THE** | | | |
| OKEH | | | |
| ❑ OKS 14127 | 98c + Tax | 1968 | 30.00 |



**Except when noted otherwise, VG = 25% of NM, and VG+ = 50% of NM. (Example: VG = $2.00, VG+ = $4.00 and NM = $8.00.)**

Number — Title (A Side/B Side) — Yr — NM

## DETROIT EMERALDS

### WESTBOUND
❑ 302 Feel the Need 1977 15.00
❑ 2006 Do Me Right 1971 40.00
❑ 2013 You Want It, You Got It 1972 40.00
❑ 2018 I'm in Love with You 1973 40.00
❑ 6101 Let's Get Together 1978 15.00

## DETROIT SYMPHONY ORCHESTRA (PAUL PARAY, CONDUCTOR)

### MERCURY LIVING PRESENCE
❑ SR 90001 [S] Bizet: Carmen Suite 1959 50.00
*—Maroon label, no "Vendor: Mercury Record Corporation"*
❑ SR 90005 [S] Ravel: Bolero; Ma Mere L'Oye; Chabrier: Bourree Fantasque 1959 30.00
*—Maroon label, no "Vendor: Mercury Record Corporation"*
❑ SR 90010 [S] Debussy: La Mer; Iberia 1959 80.00
*—Maroon label, no "Vendor: Mercury Record Corporation"*
❑ SR 90012 [S] Saint-Saens: Symphony No. 3 1959 75.00
*—Maroon label, no "Vendor: Mercury Record Corporation"*
❑ SR 90017 [S] Chausson: Symphony in B-flat 1959 40.00
*—Maroon label, no "Vendor: Mercury Record Corporation"*
❑ SR 90019 [S] Rachmaninoff: Symphony No. 2 1959 40.00
*—Maroon label, no "Vendor: Mercury Record Corporation"*
❑ SR 90102 [S] Schumann: Symphony No. 2 196? 25.00
*—Maroon label, with "Vendor: Mercury Record Corporation"*
❑ SR 90102 [S] Schumann: Symphony No. 2 1960 40.00
*—Maroon label, no "Vendor: Mercury Record Corporation"*
❑ SR 90107 [S] Wagner: Dawn & Sigfried's Rhine Journey, etc. 196? 20.00
*—Maroon label, no "Vendor: Mercury Record Corporation"*
❑ SR 90128 [S] Paray: Mass for Joan of Arc 1960 20.00
*—Maroon label, no "Vendor: Mercury Record Corporation"*
❑ SR 90129 [S] Haydn: Symphony No. 96; Mozart: Symphony No. 35 1960 40.00
*—Maroon label, no "Vendor: Mercury Record Corporation"*
❑ SR 90133 [S] Schumann: Symphony No. 3 "Rhenish" 1960 20.00
*—Maroon label, no "Vendor: Mercury Record Corporation"*
❑ SR 90174 [S] Mendelssohn: A Midsummer Night's Dream; Symphony No. 5 196? 25.00
*—Maroon label, with "Vendor: Mercury Record Corporation"*
❑ SR 90174 [S] Mendelssohn: A Midsummer Night's Dream; Symphony No. 5 196? 40.00
*—Maroon label, no "Vendor: Mercury Record Corporation"*
❑ SR 90177 [S] Schmitt: Tragedie de Salome; Strauss, Richard: Salome-Dance; Lalo: Namouna, Suite 1 196? 80.00
*—Maroon label, no "Vendor: Mercury Record Corporation"*
❑ SR 90191 [S] Ouvertures Francaises 196? 150.00
*—Maroon label, no "Vendor: Mercury Record Corporation"*
❑ SR 90198 [S] Schumann: Symphony No. 1; Manfred Overture 196? 25.00
*—Maroon label, no "Vendor: Mercury Record Corporation"*
❑ SR 90203 [S] Bouquet de Paray 196? 30.00
*—Maroon label, with "Vendor: Mercury Record Corporation"*
❑ SR 90203 [S] Bouquet de Paray 196? 60.00
*—Maroon label, no "Vendor: Mercury Record Corporation"*
❑ SR 90204 [S] Sibelius: Symphony No. 2 196? 20.00
*—Third edition: Dark red (not maroon) label*
❑ SR 90204 [S] Sibelius: Symphony No. 2 196? 50.00
*—Maroon label, with "Vendor: Mercury Record Corporation"*
❑ SR 90204 [S] Sibelius: Symphony No. 2 196? 100.00
*—Maroon label, no "Vendor: Mercury Record Corporation"*
❑ SR 90205 [S] Beethoven: Symphonies No. 1 and 2 196? 120.00
*—Maroon label, no "Vendor: Mercury Record Corporation"*
❑ SR 90211 [S] Vive La Marche! 196? 30.00
*—Maroon label, no "Vendor: Mercury Record Corporation"*
❑ SR 90212 [S] Chabrier: Espana; Suite Pastorale; Fete Polonaise; Overture to "Gwendoline"; Danse Slave 196? 120.00
*—Maroon label, no "Vendor: Mercury Record Corporation"*
❑ SR 90212 [S] Chabrier: Espana; Suite Pastorale; Fete Polonaise; Overture to "Gwendoline"; Danse Slave 199? 25.00
*—Classic Records reissue*
❑ SR 90213 [S] Ravel: La Tombeau de Couperin; Valses Nobles et Sentimentales; Debussy: Petite Suite; Prelude 196? 200.00
*—Maroon label, no "Vendor: Mercury Record Corporation"*
❑ SR 90215 [S] Overtures 196? 60.00
*—Maroon label, no "Vendor: Mercury Record Corporation"*
❑ SR 90232 [S] Wagner: Rienzi Overture; Magic Fire Music; Flying Dutchman Overture; Meistersinger Excerpts 196? 30.00
*—Maroon label, no "Vendor: Mercury Record Corporation"*
❑ SR 90247 [S] French Overtures 196? 80.00
*—Maroon label, no "Vendor: Mercury Record Corporation"*
❑ SR 90254 [S] Berlioz: Symphonie Fantastique 196? 20.00
*—Maroon label, with "Vendor: Mercury Record Corporation"*
❑ SR 90254 [S] Berlioz: Symphonie Fantastique 196? 120.00
*—Maroon label, no "Vendor: Mercury Record Corporation"*
❑ SR 90262 [S] Dvorak: Symphony No. 9 "From the New World" 196? 150.00
*—Maroon label, no "Vendor: Mercury Record Corporation"*
❑ SR 90269 [S] Suppe: Overtures 196? 20.00
*—Maroon label, with "Vendor: Mercury Record Corporation"*
❑ SR 90269 [S] Suppe: Overtures 196? 30.00
*—Maroon label, no "Vendor: Mercury Record Corporation"*
❑ SR 90281 [S] Debussy: Nocturnes; Ravel: Daphnis et Chloe Suite 2 196? 300.00
*—Maroon label, no "Vendor: Mercury Record Corporation"*
❑ SR 90285 [S] Franck: Symphony in D 196? 20.00
*—Maroon label, with "Vendor: Mercury Record Corporation"*
❑ SR 90285 [S] Franck: Symphony in D 196? 50.00
*—Maroon label, no "Vendor: Mercury Record Corporation"*
❑ SR 90313 [S] Ravel: Rapsodie Espagnole; La Valse; Pavane; Alborada; Ibert: Escales 196? 500.00
*—Maroon label, no "Vendor: Mercury Record Corporation"*
❑ SR 90318 [S] Ballet Highlights from French Opera 196? 100.00
*—Maroon label, with "Vendor: Mercury Record Corporation"*
❑ SR 90318 [S] Ballet Highlights from French Opera 196? 150.00
*—Maroon label, no "Vendor: Mercury Record Corporation"*
❑ SR 90330 [S] Schumann: Symphonies No. 1 and 3 196? 25.00
*—Maroon label, no "Vendor: Mercury Record Corporation"*
❑ SR 90330 [S] Schumann: Symphonies No. 1 and 3 196? 25.00
*—Maroon label, with "Vendor: Mercury Record Corporation"*
❑ SR 90331 [S] Saint-Saens: Symphony No. 3; Chausson: Symphony in B-flat 196? 30.00
*—Maroon label, no "Vendor: Mercury Record Corporation"*
❑ SR 90359 [S] Curtain Up! Heroic Overtures 196? 30.00
*—Maroon label, no "Vendor: Mercury Record Corporation"*
❑ SR 90372 [S] Debussy: La Mer; Petite Suite; Iberia; Prelude 196? 40.00
*—Maroon label, no "Vendor: Mercury Record Corporation"*
❑ SR 90373 [S] Ravel: Ma Mere L'Oye; Pavane; Tombeau de Couperin; Valses Nobles et Sentimentales 196? 30.00
*—Maroon label, no "Vendor: Mercury Record Corporation"*
❑ SR 90374 [S] Bizet: Carmen Suite; L'Arlesienne Suites No. 1 and 2; Chabrier: Espana; Bourree; Marche 196? 20.00
*—Maroon label, no "Vendor: Mercury Record Corporation"*
❑ SR 90375 [S] Berlioz: Symphonie Fantastique; Le Corsair Overture; Royal Hunt and Storm 196? 50.00
*—Maroon label, no "Vendor: Mercury Record Corporation"*
❑ SR 90377 [S] Overtures and Excerpts from French Opera 196? 40.00
*—Maroon label, no "Vendor: Mercury Record Corporation"*

## DEUCE COUPES, THE
May be two different groups.

### CROWN
❑ CST-393 [S] The Shut Downs 1963 25.00
❑ CLP-5393 [M] The Shut Downs 1963 20.00

### DEL-FI
❑ DFLP-1243 [M] Hotrodder's Choice 1963 50.00
❑ DFST-1243 [S] Hotrodder's Choice 1963 60.00

## DEUCHAR, JIMMY

### CONTEMPORARY
❑ C-3529 [M] Pub Crawling 1957 50.00

### DISCOVERY
❑ DL-2004 [10] New Sounds from England 1953 80.00

## DEVIANTS, THE

### SIRE
❑ SES-97001 Ptoof! 1968 60.00
❑ SES-97005 Disposable 1969 60.00
❑ SES-97016 No. 3 1969 60.00

## DEVIL'S ANVIL, THE

### COLUMBIA
❑ CL 2664 [M] Hard Rock from the Middle East 1967 25.00
❑ CS 9464 [S] Hard Rock from the Middle East 1967 30.00

## DEVILED HAM

### SUPER K
❑ SKS-6003 I Had Too Much to Dream Last Night 1968 25.00

## DEVO

### DUTCH EAST INDIA
❑ DE-112008-1 Smooth Noodle Maps 1991 15.00
*—Red vinyl, 1,000 copies pressed*

### ENIGMA
❑ EPRO 326 [DJ] Smooth Noodle Maps 1990 20.00
*—Promo only, no picture cover*
❑ 73303 Total Devo 1988 10.00
❑ 73514 Now It Can Be Told! 1989 10.00

### WARNER BROS.
❑ PRO-A-928 [EP] Freedom of Choice/Whip It/Be Still/Gates of Steel 1980 10.00
*—Promo version of "Dev-O Live"*
❑ BSK 3239 Q: Are We Not Men? A: We Are Devo! 1978 10.00
❑ BSK 3337 Duty Now for the Future 1979 10.00
❑ BSK 3435 Freedom of Choice 1980 10.00
❑ MINI 3548 [EP] Dev-O Live 1981 10.00
*—All copies came in plastic sleeve*
❑ BSK 3595 New Traditionalists 1981 15.00
*—First pressings include bonus 45 (EP 3595) and poster; deduct 1/3 if missing*
❑ 23741 Oh No! It's Devo 1982 10.00
❑ W1-23741 Oh No! It's Devo 1982 12.00
*—Columbia House version, no easel cutout on back cover*
❑ 25097 Shout 1984 10.00

## DEVOL, FRANK

### ABC-PARAMOUNT
❑ 513 [M] Theme from "Peyton Place" and 11 Other Great Themes 1965 12.00
❑ S-513 [S] Theme from "Peyton Place" and 11 Other Great Themes 1965 15.00
❑ 534 [M] Italian Romance American Style 1966 12.00
❑ S-534 [S] Italian Romance American Style 1966 15.00

### COLUMBIA
❑ CS (# unk) [S] Four Seasons of Love 1960 20.00
❑ C2L 12 [(2)M] The Columbia Album of Irving Berlin 1958 30.00
❑ C2S 812 [(2)S] The Columbia Album of Irving Berlin 1958 40.00
❑ CL 1108 [M] Portraits 1957 15.00
❑ CL 1260 [M] The Columbia Album of Irving Berlin, Volume 1 1958 15.00
❑ CL 1261 [M] The Columbia Album of Irving Berlin, Volume 2 1958 15.00
❑ CL 1371 [M] Fabulous Hollywood 1959 15.00
❑ CL 1413 [M] The Old Sweet Songs 1960 15.00
❑ CL 1451 [M] Four Seasons of Love 1960 15.00
❑ CL 1482 [M] More Old Sweet Songs 1960 15.00
❑ CL 1543 [M] The Old Sweet Songs of Christmas 1960 15.00
❑ CS 8044 [S] The Columbia Album of Irving Berlin, Volume 1 1958 20.00
❑ CS 8045 [S] The Columbia Album of Irving Berlin, Volume 2 1958 20.00
❑ CS 8172 [S] Fabulous Hollywood 1959 20.00
❑ CS 8209 [S] The Old Sweet Songs 1960 20.00
❑ CS 8273 [S] More Old Sweet Songs 1960 20.00
❑ CS 8343 [S] The Old Sweet Songs of Christmas 1960 15.00

### COLUMBIA SPECIAL PRODUCTS
❑ EN2 16437 [(2)] The Columbia Album of Irving Berlin 1983 12.00

### HARMONY
❑ HL 7356 [M] The Old Sweet Songs of Christmas 196? 12.00
❑ HS 11156 [S] The Old Sweet Songs of Christmas 196? 15.00

## DEVROE, BILLY, AND THE DEVILAIRES

### TAMPA
❑ TP-31 [M] Billy Devroe and the Devilaires, Vol. 1 1957 40.00
❑ TP-39 [M] Billy Devroe and the Devilaires, Vol. 2 1958 40.00

## DEWITT, GEORGE

### EPIC
❑ BN 531 [S] George DeWitt Sings That Tune 1959 30.00
❑ LN 3562 [M] George DeWitt Sings That Tune 1959 20.00

## DEXTER, AL

### CAPITOL
❑ ST 1701 [S] Al Dexter Sings and Plays His Greatest Hits 1962 40.00
❑ T 1701 [M] Al Dexter Sings and Plays His Greatest Hits 1962 30.00

### COLUMBIA
❑ CL 9005 [10] Songs of the Southwest 195? 50.00

### HARMONY
❑ HL 7293 [M] Pistol Packin' Mama 1961 20.00

## DIALOGUE

### COLD
❑ (no #) Dialogue 1968 100.00
*—Orange cover with insert*
❑ (no #) Dialogue 1968 300.00
*—White cover with insert*

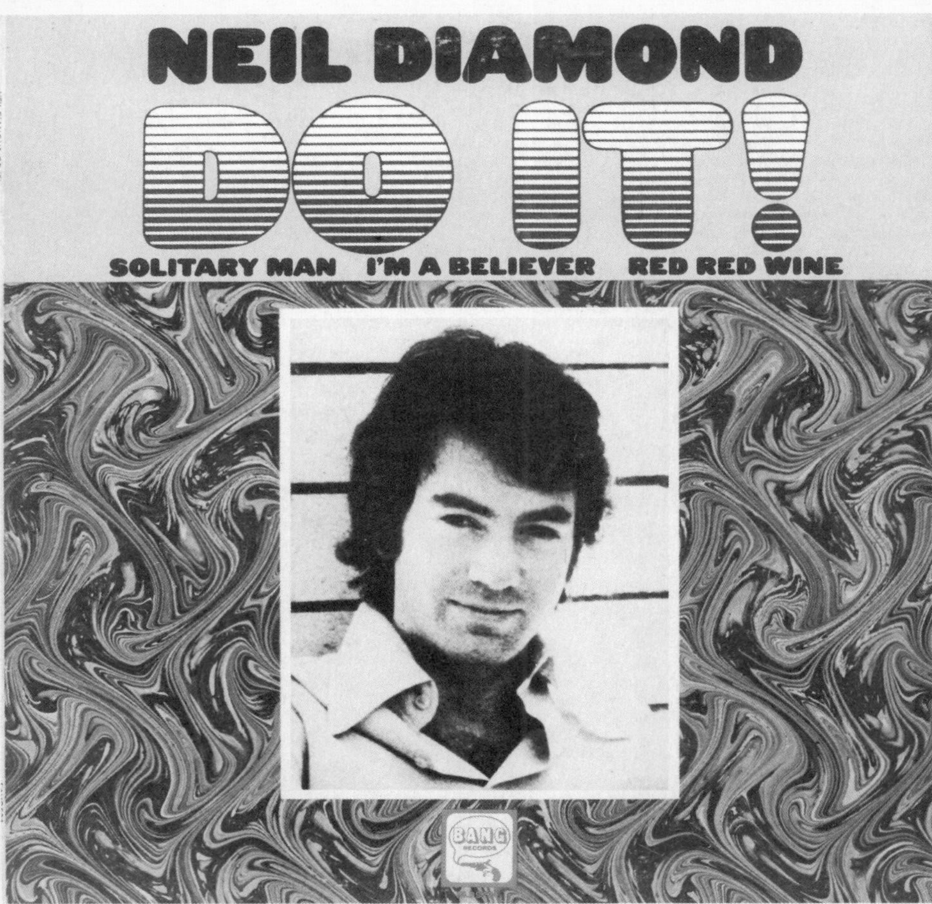

NEIL DIAMOND
DO IT!
SOLITARY MAN I'M A BELIEVER RED RED WINE
BANG


Neil Diamond, *Do It!*, Bang BLPS-224, 1971, yellow and red label, $30.

| Number | Title (A Side/B Side) | Yr | NM |
|---|---|---|---|
| **DIALS, THE** | | | |
| TIME | | | |
| ❑ S-2100 [S] | It's Monkey Time | 1964 | 30.00 |
| ❑ 52100 [M] | It's Monkey Time | 1964 | 25.00 |
| **DIAMOND, LEO** | | | |
| ABC-PARAMOUNT | | | |
| ❑ ABC-303 [M] | Subliminal Sounds | 1960 | 30.00 |
| ❑ ABCS-303 [S] | Subliminal Sounds | 1960 | 40.00 |
| RCA VICTOR | | | |
| ❑ LPM-1165 [M] | Skin Diver Suite and Other Selections | 1955 | 60.00 |
| REPRISE | | | |
| ❑ R-6002 [M] | Exciting Sounds of the South Seas | 1961 | 25.00 |
| ❑ R9-6002 [S] | Exciting Sounds of the South Seas | 1961 | 30.00 |
| ❑ R-6009 [M] | Themes from Great Foreign Films | 1961 | 25.00 |
| ❑ R9-6009 [S] | Themes from Great Foreign Films | 1961 | 30.00 |
| ❑ R-6024 [M] | Off Shore | 1962 | 25.00 |
| ❑ R9-6024 [S] | Off Shore | 1962 | 30.00 |
| **DIAMOND, NEIL** | | | |
| BANG | | | |
| ❑ BLP 214 [M] | The Feel of Neil Diamond | 1966 | 60.00 |
| *—All tracks play mono* | | | |
| ❑ BLP 214 [P] | The Feel of Neil Diamond | 1966 | 80.00 |
| *—Album is labeled mono, but plays in stereo* | | | |
| ❑ BLPS 214 | The Feel of Neil Diamond | 1974 | 12.00 |
| *—Later pressing on blue "clouds" label* | | | |
| ❑ BLPS 214 [P] | The Feel of Neil Diamond | 1966 | 100.00 |
| *—Album is labeled stereo and plays in stereo (except "Solitary Man," "Do It," "I'll Come Running" are rechanneled)* | | | |
| ❑ BLP 217 [M] | Just for You | 1967 | 40.00 |
| *—With blurb for "Thank the Lord for the Night Time" on cover* | | | |
| ❑ BLPS 217 | Just for You | 1974 | 12.00 |
| *—Later pressing on blue "clouds" label* | | | |
| ❑ BLPS 217 [P] | Just for You | 1967 | 50.00 |
| *—With blurb for "Thank the Lord for the Night Time" on cover* | | | |
| ❑ BLPS 217 [P] | Just for You | 1968 | 40.00 |
| *—With blurb for "Shilo" pasted over "Thank the Lord for the Night Time" blurb* | | | |
| ❑ BLPS 217 [P] | Just for You | 1970 | 20.00 |
| *—With blurb for "Shilo" imprinted on cover* | | | |
| ❑ BLPS 219 | Neil Diamond's Greatest Hits | 1974 | 12.00 |
| *—Later pressing on blue "clouds" label* | | | |
| ❑ BLPS 219 [P] | Neil Diamond's Greatest Hits | 196? | 20.00 |
| *—Later editions have an alternate take of "Solitary Man" in true stereo* | | | |
| ❑ BLPS 219 [P] | Neil Diamond's Greatest Hits | 1968 | 40.00 |
| *—First editions have the single version of "Solitary Man" in rechanneled stereo* | | | |
| ❑ BLPS 221 | Shilo | 1974 | 12.00 |
| *—Later pressing on blue "clouds" label* | | | |
| ❑ BLPS 221 [S] | Shilo | 1970 | 40.00 |
| ❑ BLPS 224 | Do It! | 1974 | 12.00 |
| *—Later pressing on blue "clouds" label* | | | |
| ❑ BLPS 224 [P] | Do It! | 1971 | 30.00 |
| ❑ BLPS 227 [(2)] | Double Gold | 1974 | 15.00 |
| *—Later pressing on blue "clouds" label* | | | |
| ❑ BLPS-227 [(2)S] | Double Gold | 1973 | 40.00 |
| CAPITOL | | | |
| SWAV-12120 | The Jazz Singer | 1980 | 10.00 |
| COLUMBIA | | | |
| ❑ AS 99-1586 [DJ] | Heartlight | 1982 | 25.00 |
| *—Promo-only picture disc* | | | |
| ❑ KS 32550 | Jonathan Livingston Seagull | 1973 | 12.00 |
| *—With booklet* | | | |
| ❑ PC 32919 | Serenade | 1974 | 12.00 |
| ❑ PCQ 32919 [Q] | Serenade | 1974 | 25.00 |
| ❑ PC 33965 | Beautiful Noise | 1976 | 12.00 |
| *—Originals have no bar code* | | | |
| ❑ KC2 34404 [(2)] | Love at the Greek | 1977 | 15.00 |
| ❑ JC 34990 | I'm Glad You're Here with Me Tonight | 1977 | 12.00 |
| ❑ FC 35625 | You Don't Bring Me Flowers | 1978 | 12.00 |
| ❑ FC 36121 | September Morn | 1979 | 12.00 |
| ❑ TC 37628 | On the Way to the Sky | 1981 | 10.00 |
| ❑ TC 38068 | 12 Greatest Hits, Vol. II | 1982 | 10.00 |
| ❑ TC 38359 | Heartlight | 1982 | 10.00 |
| ❑ PC 38792 | Classics — The Early Years | 1983 | 10.00 |
| *—Possibly a reissue of Frog King 1* | | | |
| ❑ QC 39199 | Primitive | 1984 | 10.00 |
| ❑ 9C9 39915 [PD] | Primitive | 1984 | 20.00 |
| ❑ OC 40368 | Headed for the Future | 1986 | 8.00 |
| ❑ CG2 40990 [(2)] | Hot August Night II | 1987 | 12.00 |
| ❑ HC 42550 | Jonathan Livingston Seagull | 1982 | 50.00 |
| *—Half-speed mastered edition* | | | |
| ❑ OC 45025 | The Best Years of Our Lives | 1988 | 8.00 |
| ❑ HC 45625 | You Don't Bring Me Flowers | 1982 | 40.00 |
| *—Half-speed mastered edition* | | | |
| ❑ HC 47628 | On the Way to the Sky | 1982 | 30.00 |
| *—Half-speed mastered edition* | | | |
| ❑ HC 48068 | 12 Greatest Hits, Vol. II | 1982 | 100.00 |
| *—Half-speed mastered edition* | | | |
| ❑ HC 48359 | Heartlight | 1982 | 40.00 |
| *—Half-speed mastered edition* | | | |
| ❑ C 48610 | Lovescape | 1991 | 25.00 |
| ❑ 8-2876-77507-1 [(2)] | 12 Songs | 2006 | 20.00 |
| DIRECT DISK | | | |
| ❑ SD 16612 | His 12 Greatest Hits | 1982 | 50.00 |
| *—Audiophile vinyl* | | | |
| FROG KING | | | |
| ❑ AAR-1 | Early Classics | 1972 | 40.00 |
| *—Compilation of Bang material for Columbia Record Club; includes songbook (deduct 25% if missing)* | | | |
| MCA | | | |
| ❑ 1489 | Neil Diamond/His 12 Greatest Hits | 1987 | 8.00 |
| *—Reissue of MCA 5219* | | | |
| ❑ 2005 | Moods | 1973 | 10.00 |
| ❑ 2006 | Touching You Touching Me | 1973 | 10.00 |
| ❑ 2007 | Neil Diamond/Gold | 1973 | 10.00 |
| ❑ 2008 | Stones | 1973 | 10.00 |
| ❑ 2011 | Sweet Caroline (Brother Love's Travelling Salvation Show) | 1973 | 10.00 |
| ❑ 2013 | Tap Root Manuscript | 1973 | 10.00 |
| ❑ 2103 | Rainbow | 1973 | 15.00 |
| *—Compilation of Uni tracks* | | | |
| ❑ 2106 | Neil Diamond/His 12 Greatest Hits | 1974 | 15.00 |
| ❑ 2227 | And the Singer Sings His Song | 1976 | 15.00 |
| ❑ 5219 | Neil Diamond/His 12 Greatest Hits | 1981 | 10.00 |
| *—Reissue of MCA 2106* | | | |
| ❑ 5239 | Love Songs | 1981 | 10.00 |
| ❑ 6896 [(2)] | Hot August Night | 1980 | 12.00 |
| *—Reissue of MCA 2-8000* | | | |
| ❑ 8000 [(2)] | Hot August Night | 1972 | 20.00 |
| ❑ 37056 | Velvet Gloves and Spit | 1980 | 8.00 |
| ❑ 37057 | Sweet Caroline/Brother Love's Travelling Salvation Show | 1980 | 8.00 |
| ❑ 37058 | Touching You Touching Me | 1980 | 8.00 |
| ❑ 37059 | Rainbow | 1980 | 8.00 |
| ❑ 37060 | And the Singer Sings His Song | 1980 | 8.00 |
| ❑ 37194 | Moods | 1981 | 8.00 |
| ❑ 37195 | Stones | 1981 | 8.00 |
| ❑ 37196 | Tap Root Manuscript | 1981 | 8.00 |
| ❑ 37209 | Gold | 1981 | 8.00 |
| ❑ 37252 | Neil Diamond/His 12 Greatest Hits | 198? | 8.00 |
| *—Reissue of MCA 5219* | | | |
| MOBILE FIDELITY | | | |
| ❑ 2-024 [(2)] | Hot August Night | 1979 | 40.00 |
| *—Audiophile vinyl* | | | |
| ❑ 1-071 | The Jazz Singer | 1981 | 30.00 |
| *—Audiophile vinyl* | | | |
| SILVER EAGLE | | | |
| ❑ MSM-35151 [(3)] | The Neil Diamond Collection | 1988 | 25.00 |
| *—Mail-order offer; contains material from his Uni period* | | | |
| UNI | | | |
| ❑ ND-11 [DJ] | Neil Diamond DJ Sampler | 1970 | 200.00 |
| ❑ 1913 [DJ] | Open-End Interview with Neil Diamond | 1971 | 300.00 |
| ❑ 73030 | Velvet Gloves and Spit | 1968 | 30.00 |
| *—First editions do not include "Shilo"* | | | |
| ❑ 73030-N | Velvet Gloves and Spit | 1970 | 20.00 |
| *—Later editions add a new recording of "Shilo"* | | | |
| ❑ 73047 | Brother Love's Travelling Salvation Show | 1969 | 20.00 |
| *—Later editions add "Sweet Caroline"* | | | |
| ❑ 73047 | Brother Love's Travelling Salvation Show | 1969 | 30.00 |
| *—First editions do not include "Sweet Caroline"* | | | |
| ❑ 73071 | Touching You Touching Me | 1969 | 20.00 |
| ❑ 73084 | Neil Diamond/Gold | 1970 | 20.00 |
| ❑ 73092 | Tap Root Manuscript | 1970 | 20.00 |
| ❑ 93030-N | Velvet Gloves and Spit | 1971 | 15.00 |
| *—Reissue of the version with "Shilo" added, with new number* | | | |
| ❑ 93047 | Brother Love's Travelling Salvation Show | 1971 | 15.00 |
| *—Reissue of the version with "Sweet Caroline," with new number* | | | |
| ❑ 93071 | Touching You Touching Me | 1971 | 15.00 |
| *—Reissue of 73071* | | | |
| ❑ 93106 | Stones | 1971 | 20.00 |
| ❑ 93136 | Moods | 1972 | 20.00 |
| ❑ ST-93501 | Tap Root Manuscript | 1970 | 25.00 |
| *—Capitol Record Club issue* | | | |
| **DIAMONDS, THE (1)** | | | |
| MERCURY | | | |
| ❑ MG-20213 [M] | Collection of Golden Hits | 1956 | 120.00 |
| ❑ MG-20309 [M] | The Diamonds | 1957 | 120.00 |
| ❑ MG-20368 [M] | The Diamonds Meet Pete Rugolo | 1958 | 80.00 |
| ❑ MG-20480 [M] | Songs from the Old West | 1959 | 80.00 |

| Number | Title (A Side/B Side) | Yr | NM |
|---|---|---|---|
| ❑ SR-60076 [S] | The Diamonds Meet Pete Rugolo | 1959 | 120.00 |
| ❑ SR-60159 [S] | Songs from the Old West | 1959 | 120.00 |
| **RHINO** | | | |
| ❑ RNDF-209 | The Best of the Diamonds | 1984 | 12.00 |
| **WING** | | | |
| ❑ MGW-12114 [M] | The Diamonds: America's Famous Song Stylists | 1959 | 30.00 |
| ❑ MGW-12178 [M] | Pop Hits by the Diamonds | 1962 | 30.00 |

### DIAZ MENA, ANTONIO

| Number | Title (A Side/B Side) | Yr | NM |
|---|---|---|---|
| **AUDIO FIDELITY** | | | |
| ❑ AFSD-6117 [S] | Eso Es En Latin Jazz Man | 1963 | 20.00 |

### DICK AND DEEDEE

| Number | Title (A Side/B Side) | Yr | NM |
|---|---|---|---|
| **LIBERTY** | | | |
| ❑ LRP-3236 [M] | Tell Me/The Mountain's High | 1962 | 50.00 |
| ❑ LST-7236 [R] | Tell Me/The Mountain's High | 1962 | 40.00 |
| **WARNER BROS.** | | | |
| ❑ W 1500 [M] | Young and In Love | 1963 | 25.00 |
| ❑ WS 1500 [S] | Young and In Love | 1963 | 30.00 |
| ❑ W 1538 [M] | Turn Around | 1964 | 25.00 |
| ❑ WS 1538 [S] | Turn Around | 1964 | 30.00 |
| ❑ W 1586 [M] | Thou Shalt Not Steal | 1965 | 25.00 |
| ❑ WS 1586 [S] | Thou Shalt Not Steal | 1965 | 30.00 |
| ❑ W 1623 [M] | Song We've Sung on "Shindig" | 1966 | 25.00 |
| ❑ WS 1623 [S] | Song We've Sung on "Shindig" | 1966 | 30.00 |

### DICKENS, JIMMY

| Number | Title (A Side/B Side) | Yr | NM |
|---|---|---|---|
| **COLUMBIA** | | | |
| ❑ CL 1047 [M] | Raisin' the Dickens | 1957 | 80.00 |
| ❑ CL 1545 [M] | Big Songs by Little Jimmy Dickens | 1960 | 30.00 |
| ❑ CL 1887 [M] | Little Jimmy Dickens Sings Out Behind the Barn | 1962 | 30.00 |
| ❑ CL 2288 [M] | Handle with Care | 1964 | 25.00 |
| ❑ CL 2442 [M] | May the Bird of Paradise Fly Up Your Nose | 1965 | 25.00 |
| ❑ CL 2551 [M] | Little Jimmy Dickens' Greatest Hits | 1966 | 25.00 |
| ❑ CS 8345 [S] | Big Songs by Little Jimmy Dickens | 1960 | 40.00 |
| ❑ CS 8687 [S] | Little Jimmy Dickens Sings Out Behind the Barn | 1962 | 40.00 |
| ❑ CL 9053 [10] | The Old Country Church | 1954 | 120.00 |
| ❑ CS 9088 [S] | Handle with Care | 1964 | 30.00 |
| ❑ CS 9242 [S] | May the Bird of Paradise Fly Up Your Nose | 1965 | 30.00 |
| ❑ CS 9351 [S] | Little Jimmy Dickens' Greatest Hits | 1966 | 30.00 |
| ❑ CS 9648 [M] | Big Man in Country Music | 1968 | 50.00 |
| *—White label promo with stereo number and "Mono" on label; "Special Mono Radio Station Copy" sticker and timing strip on front cover* | | | |
| ❑ CS 9648 [S] | Big Man in Country Music | 1968 | 25.00 |
| **DECCA** | | | |
| ❑ DL 4967 [M] | Jimmy Dickens Sings | 1967 | 30.00 |
| ❑ DL 74967 [S] | Jimmy Dickens Sings | 1967 | 20.00 |
| ❑ DL 75091 | Jimmy Dickens Comes Callin' | 1968 | 20.00 |
| ❑ DL 75133 | Jimmy Dickens' Greatest Hits | 1969 | 20.00 |

### DICKENSON, VIC

| Number | Title (A Side/B Side) | Yr | NM |
|---|---|---|---|
| **JAZZTONE** | | | |
| ❑ J-1259 [M] | Slidin' Swing | 1956 | 40.00 |
| **STORYVILLE** | | | |
| ❑ STLP-920 [M] | Vic's Boston Story | 1957 | 40.00 |
| **VANGUARD** | | | |
| ❑ VRS-8001 [10] | Vic Dickenson Septet, Volume 1 | 1953 | 50.00 |
| ❑ VRS-8002 [10] | Vic Dickenson Septet, Volume 2 | 1953 | 50.00 |
| ❑ VRS-8012 [10] | Vic Dickenson Septet, Volume 3 | 1954 | 50.00 |
| ❑ VRS-8013 [10] | Vic Dickenson Septet, Volume 4 | 1954 | 50.00 |
| ❑ VRS-8520 [M] | Vic Dickenson Showcase, Volume 1 | 1958 | 40.00 |
| ❑ VRS-8521 [M] | Vic Dickenson Showcase, Volume 2 | 1958 | 40.00 |

### DICKENSON, VIC, AND JOE THOMAS

| Number | Title (A Side/B Side) | Yr | NM |
|---|---|---|---|
| **ATLANTIC** | | | |
| ❑ 1303 [M] | Mainstream | 1958 | 50.00 |
| *—Black label* | | | |
| ❑ 1303 [M] | Mainstream | 1961 | 20.00 |
| *—Multicolor label, white "fan" logo* | | | |
| ❑ SD 1303 [S] | Mainstream | 1958 | 40.00 |
| *—Green label* | | | |
| ❑ SD 1303 [S] | Mainstream | 1961 | 20.00 |
| *—Multicolor label, white "fan" logo* | | | |

### DICKERSON, WALT

| Number | Title (A Side/B Side) | Yr | NM |
|---|---|---|---|
| **AUDIO FIDELITY** | | | |
| ❑ AFLP-2131 [M] | Unity | 1963 | 20.00 |
| ❑ AFLP-2217 [M] | Vibes in Motion | 1968 | 25.00 |
| *—Reissue of Dauntless 4313* | | | |
| ❑ AFSD-6131 [S] | Unity | 1963 | 25.00 |
| **DAUNTLESS** | | | |
| ❑ DM-4313 [M] | Jazz Impressions of "Lawrence of Arabia" | 1963 | 25.00 |
| ❑ DS-6313 [S] | Jazz Impressions of "Lawrence of Arabia" | 1963 | 30.00 |
| **MGM** | | | |
| ❑ E-4358 [M] | Impressions of "A Patch of Blue" | 1965 | 20.00 |
| ❑ SE-4358 [S] | Impressions of "A Patch of Blue" | 1965 | 25.00 |
| **NEW JAZZ** | | | |
| ❑ NJLP-8254 [M] | This Is Walt Dickerson | 1961 | 50.00 |
| *—Purple label* | | | |
| ❑ NJLP-8254 [M] | This Is Walt Dickerson | 1965 | 25.00 |
| *—Blue label, trident logo at right* | | | |
| ❑ NJLP-8268 [M] | A Sense of Direction | 1962 | 50.00 |
| *—Purple label* | | | |
| ❑ NJLP-8268 [M] | A Sense of Direction | 1965 | 25.00 |
| *—Blue label, trident logo at right* | | | |
| ❑ NJLP-8275 [M] | Relativity | 1962 | 50.00 |
| *—Purple label* | | | |
| ❑ NJLP-8275 [M] | Relativity | 1965 | 25.00 |
| *—Blue label, trident logo at right* | | | |
| ❑ NJLP-8283 [M] | To My Queen | 1962 | 50.00 |
| *—Purple label* | | | |
| ❑ NJLP-8283 [M] | To My Queen | 1965 | 25.00 |
| *—Blue label, trident logo at right* | | | |
| **STEEPLECHASE** | | | |
| ❑ SCD-17002 | Shades of Love | 198? | 25.00 |
| *—Direct-to-disc recording* | | | |

### DICKIES, THE

| Number | Title (A Side/B Side) | Yr | NM |
|---|---|---|---|
| **A&M** | | | |
| ❑ SP-4742 | The Incredible Shrinking Dickies | 1979 | 15.00 |
| ❑ SP-4742 | The Incredible Shrinking Dickies | 1979 | 20.00 |
| *—First pressing on yellow vinyl* | | | |
| ❑ SP-4796 | Dawn of the Dickies | 1979 | 15.00 |
| **ENIGMA** | | | |
| ❑ D1-73289 | Second Coming | 1989 | 8.00 |
| ❑ D1-73322 [EP] | Killer Klowns (From Outer Space) | 1988 | 8.00 |
| **PVC** | | | |
| ❑ 6903 | Stukas Over Disneyland | 1983 | 12.00 |
| **TAANG!** | | | |
| ❑ 56 | Locked and Loaded | 1991 | 12.00 |
| **TRIPLE X** | | | |
| ❑ 51168 | Idjit Savant | 1994 | 10.00 |

### DICKS, THE

| Number | Title (A Side/B Side) | Yr | NM |
|---|---|---|---|
| **ALTERNATIVE TENTACLES** | | | |
| ❑ VIRUS 43 | These People | 1985 | 15.00 |
| **RADICAL** | | | |
| ❑ RRR 80351 | Recorded Live at Raul's | 1980 | 60.00 |
| *—One side features the Big Boys; the other side, the Dicks* | | | |
| **SST** | | | |
| ❑ 017 | Kill from the Heart | 1983 | 25.00 |

### DICKY DOO AND THE DON'TS

| Number | Title (A Side/B Side) | Yr | NM |
|---|---|---|---|
| **UNITED ARTISTS** | | | |
| ❑ UAL-3094 [M] | The Madison and Other Dances | 1959 | 40.00 |
| ❑ UAL-3097 [M] | Teen Scene | 1959 | 40.00 |
| ❑ UAS-6094 [S] | The Madison and Other Dances | 1959 | 50.00 |
| ❑ UAS-6097 [S] | Teen Scene | 1959 | 50.00 |

### DIDDLEY, BO

| Number | Title (A Side/B Side) | Yr | NM |
|---|---|---|---|
| **ACCORD** | | | |
| ❑ SN-7182 | Toronto Rock and Roll Revival, Vol. 5 | 1982 | 20.00 |
| **CHECKER** | | | |
| ❑ LP 1431 [M] | Bo Diddley | 1958 | 150.00 |
| ❑ LP 1436 [M] | Go Bo Diddley | 1959 | 150.00 |
| ❑ LP 2974 [M] | Have Guitar, Will Travel | 1960 | 150.00 |
| ❑ LP 2976 [M] | Spotlight on Bo Diddley | 1960 | 150.00 |
| ❑ LP 2977 [M] | Bo Diddley Is a Gunslinger | 1961 | 150.00 |
| ❑ LP 2980 [M] | Bo Diddley Is a Lover | 1961 | 150.00 |
| ❑ LP 2982 [M] | Bo Diddley's a Twister | 1962 | 100.00 |
| ❑ LP 2982 [M] | Road Runner | 1967 | 80.00 |
| *—Reissue of "Bo Diddley's a Twister"* | | | |
| ❑ LPS- 2982 [R] | Road Runner | 1967 | 50.00 |
| ❑ LP 2984 [M] | Bo Diddley | 1962 | 100.00 |
| ❑ LP 2985 [M] | Bo Diddley and Company | 1963 | 120.00 |
| ❑ LP 2987 [M] | Surfin' with Bo Diddley | 1964 | 120.00 |
| ❑ LPS 2987 [R] | Surfin' with Bo Diddley | 1964 | 30.00 |
| ❑ LP 2988 [M] | Bo Diddley's Beach Party | 1963 | 100.00 |
| ❑ LP 2989 [M] | 16 All Time Greatest Hits | 1964 | 50.00 |
| ❑ LPS 2989 [R] | 16 All Time Greatest Hits | 1964 | 30.00 |
| ❑ LP 2992 [M] | Hey! Good Lookin' | 1965 | 60.00 |
| ❑ LPS 2992 [R] | Hey! Good Lookin' | 1965 | 30.00 |
| ❑ LP 2996 [M] | 500% More Man | 1965 | 60.00 |
| ❑ LPS 2996 [R] | 500% More Man | 1965 | 30.00 |
| ❑ LP 3001 [M] | The Originator | 1966 | 30.00 |
| ❑ LPS 3001 [S] | The Originator | 1966 | 40.00 |
| ❑ LP 3006 [M] | Go Bo Diddley | 1967 | 50.00 |
| *—Reissue of 1436* | | | |
| ❑ LPS 3006 [R] | Go Bo Diddley | 1967 | 40.00 |
| ❑ LP 3007 [M] | Boss Man | 1967 | 80.00 |
| *—Reissue of Chess 1431* | | | |
| ❑ LPS 3007 [R] | Boss Man | 1967 | 50.00 |
| ❑ LPS 3013 | The Black Gladiator | 1968 | 30.00 |
| **CHESS** | | | |
| ❑ LP 1431 [M] | Bo Diddley | 1958 | 200.00 |
| ❑ CH-9106 | His Greatest Sides, Vol. 1 | 1984 | 10.00 |
| ❑ CH-9187 | Have Guitar, Will Travel | 1985 | 10.00 |
| *—Reissue of Checker 2974* | | | |
| ❑ CH-9194 | Bo Diddley | 1986 | 10.00 |
| *—Reissue of 1431* | | | |
| ❑ CH-9196 | Go Bo Diddley | 1986 | 10.00 |
| *—Reissue of Checker 1436* | | | |
| ❑ CH-9264 | Spotlight on Bo Diddley | 1987 | 10.00 |
| *—Reissue of Checker 2976* | | | |
| ❑ CH-9285 | Bo Diddley Is a Gunslinger | 1989 | 10.00 |
| *—Reissue of Checker 2977* | | | |
| ❑ CH-9296 | The London Bo Diddley Sessions | 1989 | 10.00 |
| *—Reissue of 50029* | | | |
| ❑ CH3-19502 [(3)] | The Chess Box | 1990 | 40.00 |
| ❑ CH 50001 | Another Dimension | 1971 | 40.00 |
| ❑ CH 50016 | Where It All Began | 1972 | 40.00 |
| ❑ CH 50029 | The London Bo Diddley Sessions | 1973 | 25.00 |
| ❑ CH 50047 | Big Bad Bo | 1974 | 25.00 |
| ❑ 2CH 60005 [(2)] | Got My Own Bag of Tricks | 1972 | 25.00 |
| **RCA VICTOR** | | | |
| ❑ APL1-1229 | The 20th Anniversary of Rock and Roll | 1976 | 20.00 |

### DIDDLEY, BO/CHUCK BERRY

Also see each artist's individual listings.

| Number | Title (A Side/B Side) | Yr | NM |
|---|---|---|---|
| **CHECKER** | | | |
| ❑ LP 2991 [M] | Two Great Guitars | 1964 | 60.00 |
| ❑ LPS 2991 [R] | Two Great Guitars | 1964 | 40.00 |
| **CHESS** | | | |
| ❑ CH-9170 | Two Great Guitars | 1985 | 10.00 |
| *—Reissue of Checker 2991* | | | |

### DIDDLEY, BO/MUDDY WATERS/HOWLIN' WOLF

Also see each artist's individual listings.

| Number | Title (A Side/B Side) | Yr | NM |
|---|---|---|---|
| **CHECKER** | | | |
| ❑ LP 3010 [M] | Super, Super Blues Band | 1968 | 50.00 |
| ❑ LPS 3010 [S] | Super, Super Blues Band | 1968 | 40.00 |
| **CHESS** | | | |
| ❑ CH-9169 | Super, Super Blues Band | 1985 | 10.00 |
| *—Reissue of Checker 3010* | | | |

### DIDDLEY, BO/MUDDY WATERS/LITTLE WALTER

Also see each artist's individual listings.

| Number | Title (A Side/B Side) | Yr | NM |
|---|---|---|---|
| **CHECKER** | | | |
| ❑ LP 3008 [M] | Super Blues Band | 1968 | 50.00 |
| ❑ LPS 3008 [S] | Super Blues Band | 1968 | 40.00 |
| **CHESS** | | | |
| ❑ CH-9168 | Super Blues Band | 1985 | 10.00 |
| *—Reissue of Checker 3008* | | | |

### DIDO

| Number | Title (A Side/B Side) | Yr | NM |
|---|---|---|---|
| **ARISTA** | | | |
| ❑ RTH-2003 | No Angel | 2001 | 25.00 |
| *—Audiophile edition on 200-gram vinyl* | | | |
| ❑ RTH-2015 | Life for Rent | 2004 | 25.00 |
| *—Audiophile edition on 200-gram vinyl* | | | |

### DIETRICH, MARLENE

| Number | Title (A Side/B Side) | Yr | NM |
|---|---|---|---|
| **CAPITOL** | | | |
| ❑ STCR-300 [(3)] | The Magic of Marlene | 1969 | 40.00 |
| *—All three of her Capitol LPs in one box* | | | |
| ❑ ST 10282 [S] | Wiedersehn Mit Marlene | 1961 | 25.00 |
| ❑ T 10282 [M] | Wiedersehn Mit Marlene | 1961 | 20.00 |
| ❑ ST 10397 [S] | Marlene (Songs in German by the Inimitable Dietrich) | 1965 | 25.00 |
| ❑ T 10397 [M] | Marlene (Songs in German by the Inimitable Dietrich) | 1965 | 20.00 |
| ❑ ST 10443 [S] | Marlene Dietrich's Berlin | 1966 | 25.00 |
| ❑ T 10443 [M] | Marlene Dietrich's Berlin | 1966 | 20.00 |
| **COLUMBIA** | | | |
| ❑ CL 105 [10] | Overseas — Songs for the O.S.S. | 1953 | 100.00 |
| ❑ CL 1275 [M] | Lili Marlene | 1959 | 50.00 |
| ❑ C 32245 | The Best of Marlene Dietrich | 1973 | 12.00 |
| **COLUMBIA MASTERWORKS** | | | |
| ❑ WL 164 [M] | Dietrich in Rio | 195? | 40.00 |
| ❑ WS 316 [S] | Dietrich in Rio | 195? | 50.00 |
| ❑ OS 2830 [S] | Dietrich in London | 1966 | 30.00 |
| ❑ ML 4975 [M] | At the Café de Paris | 1955 | 50.00 |
| ❑ OL 6430 [M] | Dietrich in London | 1966 | 25.00 |
| **DECCA** | | | |
| ❑ DL 5100 [10] | Souvenir Album | 1950 | 80.00 |

Dino, Desi & Billy, *Our Time's Coming,* Reprise R 6194, 1966, mono, $20.

| Number | Title (A Side/B Side) | Yr | NM |
|---|---|---|---|
| ❑ DL 8465 [M] | Marlene Dietrich | 1957 | 40.00 |
| *—Black label, silver print* | | | |
| ❑ DL 8465 [M] | Marlene Dietrich | 196? | 25.00 |
| *—Black label with color bars* | | | |
| ❑ DL 78465 [R] | Marlene Dietrich | 196? | 20.00 |

MURRAY HILL/CSP

| Number | Title (A Side/B Side) | Yr | NM |
|---|---|---|---|
| ❑ P3 14689 [(3)] | The Legendary Marlene Dietrich | 1978 | 30.00 |

VOX

| Number | Title (A Side/B Side) | Yr | NM |
|---|---|---|---|
| ❑ VS-3040 [10] | Marlene Dietrich Sings | 1950 | 80.00 |

**DIGA RHYTHM BAND, THE** Also see THE GRATEFUL DEAD.

ROUND

| Number | Title (A Side/B Side) | Yr | NM |
|---|---|---|---|
| ❑ RX-110 | The Diga Rhythm Band | 1976 | 25.00 |

**DILCHER, CHERYL**

A&M

| Number | Title (A Side/B Side) | Yr | NM |
|---|---|---|---|
| ❑ SP-3640 | Magic | 1974 | 20.00 |
| ❑ SP-4394 | Butterfly | 1973 | 30.00 |

AMPEX

| Number | Title (A Side/B Side) | Yr | NM |
|---|---|---|---|
| ❑ A-10109 | Special Songs | 1970 | 50.00 |

BUTTERFLY

| Number | Title (A Side/B Side) | Yr | NM |
|---|---|---|---|
| ❑ FLY 003 | Blue Sailor | 1977 | 12.00 |
| *—Black vinyl* | | | |

**DILL, DANNY**

LIBERTY

| Number | Title (A Side/B Side) | Yr | NM |
|---|---|---|---|
| ❑ LRP-3301 [M] | Folk Songs from the Country | 1963 | 20.00 |
| ❑ LST-7301 [S] | Folk Songs from the Country | 1963 | 25.00 |

MGM

| Number | Title (A Side/B Side) | Yr | NM |
|---|---|---|---|
| ❑ E-3819 [M] | Folk Songs from the Wild West | 1960 | 20.00 |
| ❑ SE-3819 [S] | Folk Songs from the Wild West | 1960 | 25.00 |

**DILLARD, DOUG**

TOGETHER

| Number | Title (A Side/B Side) | Yr | NM |
|---|---|---|---|
| ❑ STT-1003 | The Banjo Album | 1970 | 80.00 |

**DILLARD AND CLARK**

A&M

| Number | Title (A Side/B Side) | Yr | NM |
|---|---|---|---|
| ❑ SP-4158 | The Fantastic Expedition of Dillard and Clark | 1968 | 20.00 |
| *—Brown label* | | | |

**DILLARDS, THE**

ANTHEM

| Number | Title (A Side/B Side) | Yr | NM |
|---|---|---|---|
| ❑ ANS-5901 | Roots and Branches | 1972 | 15.00 |

CRYSTAL CLEAR

| Number | Title (A Side/B Side) | Yr | NM |
|---|---|---|---|
| ❑ CCS-5007 | Mountain Rock | 1979 | 25.00 |
| *—Direct-to-disc recording* | | | |

ELEKTRA

| Number | Title (A Side/B Side) | Yr | NM |
|---|---|---|---|
| ❑ EKL-232 [M] | Back Porch Bluegrass | 1963 | 25.00 |
| ❑ EKL-265 [M] | The Dillards, Live!!! Almost!!! | 1964 | 20.00 |
| ❑ EKL-285 [M] | Pickin' and Fiddlin' | 1965 | 20.00 |
| ❑ EKS-7232 [S] | Back Porch Bluegrass | 1963 | 30.00 |
| *—Mandolin-player label* | | | |
| ❑ EKS-7265 [S] | The Dillards, Live!!! Almost!!! | 1964 | 25.00 |
| *—Mandolin-player label* | | | |
| ❑ EKS-7285 [S] | Pickin' and Fiddlin' | 1965 | 25.00 |
| *—Mandolin-player label* | | | |
| ❑ EKS-74035 | Wheatstraw Suite | 1968 | 20.00 |
| *—Tan label with large stylized "E" on top* | | | |
| ❑ EKS-74035 | Wheatstraw Suite | 1969 | 15.00 |
| *—Red label with large stylized "E" on top* | | | |
| ❑ EKS-74054 | Copperfields | 1969 | 20.00 |
| *—Red label with large stylized "E" on top* | | | |

FLYING FISH

| Number | Title (A Side/B Side) | Yr | NM |
|---|---|---|---|
| ❑ FF 040 | The Dillards Vs. the Incredible L.A. Time Machine | 1977 | 12.00 |
| ❑ FF 082 | Decade Waltz | 1979 | 12.00 |
| ❑ FF 215 | Homecoming and Family Reunion | 1979 | 12.00 |

POPPY

| Number | Title (A Side/B Side) | Yr | NM |
|---|---|---|---|
| ❑ PP-LA175-F | Tribute to the American Duck | 1973 | 15.00 |

**DILLER, PHYLLIS**

COLUMBIA

| Number | Title (A Side/B Side) | Yr | NM |
|---|---|---|---|
| ❑ CS 9623 | Born to Sing | 1969 | 20.00 |

**DIMENSIONS, THE**

SAHARA

| Number | Title (A Side/B Side) | Yr | NM |
|---|---|---|---|
| ❑ (# unknown) | From All Dimensions | 1966 | 800.00 |

**DIMEOLA, AL**

COLUMBIA

| Number | Title (A Side/B Side) | Yr | NM |
|---|---|---|---|
| ❑ HC 44461 | Elegant Gypsy | 198? | 40.00 |
| *—Half-speed mastered edition* | | | |
| ❑ HC 46454 | Electric Rendezvous | 198? | 50.00 |
| *—Half-speed mastered edition* | | | |
| ❑ HC 47152 | Friday Night in San Francisco | 198? | 50.00 |
| *—Half-speed mastered edition* | | | |

**DINNING, MARK**

MGM

| Number | Title (A Side/B Side) | Yr | NM |
|---|---|---|---|
| ❑ E-3828 [M] | Teen Angel | 1960 | 80.00 |
| ❑ SE-3828 [S] | Teen Angel | 1960 | 150.00 |
| ❑ E-3855 [M] | Wanderin' | 1960 | 80.00 |
| ❑ SE-3855 [S] | Wanderin' | 1960 | 120.00 |

**DINNING SISTERS, THE**

CAPITOL

| Number | Title (A Side/B Side) | Yr | NM |
|---|---|---|---|
| ❑ H 318 [10] | The Dinning Sisters | 195? | 50.00 |

**DINO, DESI AND BILLY**

REPRISE

| Number | Title (A Side/B Side) | Yr | NM |
|---|---|---|---|
| ❑ R 6176 [M] | I'm a Fool | 1965 | 20.00 |
| ❑ RS 6176 [S] | I'm a Fool | 1965 | 25.00 |
| ❑ R 6194 [M] | Our Time's Coming | 1966 | 20.00 |
| ❑ RS 6194 [S] | Our Time's Coming | 1966 | 25.00 |
| ❑ R 6198 [M] | Memories Are Made of This | 1966 | 20.00 |
| ❑ RS 6198 [S] | Memories Are Made of This | 1966 | 25.00 |
| ❑ R 6224 [M] | Souvenir | 1966 | 20.00 |
| ❑ R/RS 6224 | Souvenir Bonus Photo Sheet | 1966 | 5.00 |
| ❑ RS 6224 [S] | Souvenir | 1966 | 25.00 |

**DINOSAUR JR**

HOMESTEAD

| Number | Title (A Side/B Side) | Yr | NM |
|---|---|---|---|
| ❑ 015-2 | Dinosaur | 1985 | 50.00 |
| *—Released under the name "Dinosaur"* | | | |

RHINO VINYL

| Number | Title (A Side/B Side) | Yr | NM |
|---|---|---|---|
| ❑ 77630 | Green Mind | 2006 | 15.00 |
| *—Reissue on 180-gram vinyl* | | | |
| ❑ 77631 | Where You Been | 2006 | 15.00 |
| *—Reissue of Sire 45108 on 180-gram vinyl* | | | |

SIRE

| Number | Title (A Side/B Side) | Yr | NM |
|---|---|---|---|
| ❑ 26479 | Green Mind | 1991 | 40.00 |
| ❑ 45108 | Where You Been | 1993 | 15.00 |
| ❑ 45719 | Without a Sound | 1994 | 10.00 |

SST

| Number | Title (A Side/B Side) | Yr | NM |
|---|---|---|---|
| ❑ 130 | You're Living All Over Me | 1987 | 10.00 |
| *—As "Dinosaur Jr"; black vinyl* | | | |
| ❑ 130 | You're Living All Over Me | 1987 | 15.00 |
| *—As "Dinosaur Jr"; purple swirl vinyl* | | | |
| ❑ 130 | You're Living All Over Me | 1987 | 20.00 |
| *—First released under the name "Dinosaur"* | | | |
| ❑ 152 [EP] | Dinosaur Jr | 1987 | 12.00 |
| *—Originals on purple swirl vinyl* | | | |
| ❑ 216 | Bug | 1988 | 10.00 |
| ❑ 244 [EP] | Just Like Heaven | 1989 | 8.00 |
| ❑ 275 [EP] | Fossils | 1991 | 8.00 |
| ❑ 910 [10] | Dinosaur Jr | 1987 | 6.00 |
| ❑ 914 [10] | Just Like Heaven | 1989 | 6.00 |
| ❑ 925 [10] | Fossils | 1991 | 6.00 |

**DIO, RONNIE**

JOVE

| Number | Title (A Side/B Side) | Yr | NM |
|---|---|---|---|
| ❑ J-108 | Dio at Domino's | 1963 | 200.00 |

**DION**

ARISTA

| Number | Title (A Side/B Side) | Yr | NM |
|---|---|---|---|
| ❑ AL 8549 | Yo Frankie | 1989 | 10.00 |

COLLECTABLES

| Number | Title (A Side/B Side) | Yr | NM |
|---|---|---|---|
| ❑ 5027 | Runaround Sue | 198? | 10.00 |

COLUMBIA

| Number | Title (A Side/B Side) | Yr | NM |
|---|---|---|---|
| ❑ CL 2010 [M] | Ruby Baby | 1963 | 30.00 |
| ❑ CL 2107 [M] | Donna the Prima Donna | 1963 | 30.00 |
| ❑ CS 8810 [S] | Ruby Baby | 1963 | 40.00 |
| ❑ CS 8907 [S] | Donna the Prima Donna | 1963 | 40.00 |
| ❑ CS 9773 | Wonder Where I'm Bound | 1969 | 20.00 |
| ❑ KC 31942 | Dion's Greatest Hits | 1973 | 20.00 |
| ❑ PC 31942 | Dion's Greatest Hits | 198? | 8.00 |
| *—Budget-line reissue* | | | |

DAYSPRING

| Number | Title (A Side/B Side) | Yr | NM |
|---|---|---|---|
| ❑ DST-4022 | Inside Job | 1980 | 12.00 |
| ❑ DST-4027 | Only Jesus | 198? | 12.00 |
| ❑ WR-8111 | I Put Away My Idols | 198? | 12.00 |
| ❑ WR-8112 | Seasons (The Best of Dion) | 198? | 12.00 |
| ❑ 7-01-412901-5 | Seasons | 1984 | 12.00 |

LAURIE

| Number | Title (A Side/B Side) | Yr | NM |
|---|---|---|---|
| ❑ LLP 2004 [M] | Alone with Dion | 1960 | 200.00 |
| *—With three wallet-size photos on inside strip (deduct 50% if missing)* | | | |
| ❑ LLP 2009 [M] | Runaround Sue | 1961 | 100.00 |
| *—Black vinyl* | | | |
| ❑ LLP 2009 [M] | Runaround Sue | 1961 | 800.00 |
| *—Colored vinyl (gold, green or blue)* | | | |
| ❑ LLP 2009 [M] | Runaround Sue | 1962 | 80.00 |
| *—Black vinyl; with sticker on front cover: "Includes the Hit Singles 'The Majestic'/'The Wanderer'"* | | | |
| ❑ LLP 2012 [M] | Lovers Who Wander | 1962 | 70.00 |
| ❑ LLP 2013 [M] | Dion Sings His Greatest Hits | 1962 | 70.00 |
| ❑ SLP 2013 [R] | Dion Sings His Greatest Hits | 196? | 50.00 |
| ❑ LLP 2015 [M] | Love Came to Me | 1963 | 70.00 |

| Number | Title (A Side/B Side) | Yr | NM |
|---|---|---|---|
| ❑ LLP 2017 [M] | Dion Sings to Sandy (And All His Other Girls) | 1963 | 50.00 |
| ❑ LLP 2019 [M] | Dion Sings the 15 Million Sellers | 1963 | 50.00 |
| ❑ SLP 2019 [R] | Dion Sings the 15 Million Sellers | 196? | 30.00 |
| ❑ LLP 2022 [M] | More of Dion's Greatest Hits | 1964 | 50.00 |
| ❑ SLP 2022 [R] | More of Dion's Greatest Hits | 196? | 30.00 |
| ❑ SLP 2047 | Dion | 1968 | 20.00 |
| ❑ LES-4004 | Abraham, Martin and John | 197? | 12.00 |
| *—Reissue of SLP-2047* | | | |
| ❑ LES-4013 | Dion Sings the Hits of the 50's and 60's | 1978 | 12.00 |
| ❑ DT-90366 [R] | Dion Sings His Greatest Hits | 1965 | 120.00 |
| *—Capitol Record Club edition* | | | |
| ❑ T-90366 [M] | Dion Sings His Greatest Hits | 1965 | 120.00 |
| *—Capitol Record Club edition* | | | |
| ❑ DT-91027 [R] | Runaround Sue | 196? | 120.00 |
| *—Capitol Record Club edition* | | | |
| ❑ T-91027 [M] | Runaround Sue | 196? | 120.00 |
| *—Capitol Record Club edition* | | | |
| ❑ DT-91128 [R] | More of Dion's Greatest Hits | 196? | 120.00 |
| *—Capitol Record Club edition* | | | |
| ❑ T-91128 [M] | More of Dion's Greatest Hits | 196? | 120.00 |
| *—Capitol Record Club edition* | | | |
| ❑ ST-91577 | Dion | 1968 | 25.00 |
| *—Capitol Record Club edition* | | | |
| **LIFESONG** | | | |
| ❑ JZ 35356 | Return of the Wanderer | 1978 | 12.00 |
| **WARNER BROS.** | | | |
| ❑ WS 1826 | Sit Down, Old Friend | 1969 | 20.00 |
| ❑ WS 1872 | You're Not Alone | 1971 | 15.00 |
| ❑ WS 1945 | Sanctuary | 1971 | 15.00 |
| ❑ BS 2642 | Suite for Late Summer | 1972 | 15.00 |
| ❑ BS 2954 | Streetheart | 1976 | 15.00 |
| **WORD** | | | |
| ❑ WR-8285 | Kingdom in the Streets | 1985 | 12.00 |

### DION AND THE BELMONTS

| Number | Title (A Side/B Side) | Yr | NM |
|---|---|---|---|
| **ABC** | | | |
| ❑ 599 [M] | Together Again | 1967 | 30.00 |
| ❑ S-599 [S] | Together Again | 1967 | 40.00 |
| **ARISTA** | | | |
| ❑ A2L 8206 [(2)] | 24 Original Classics | 1984 | 12.00 |
| **COLLECTABLES** | | | |
| ❑ 5025 | Presenting Dion & The Belmonts | 198? | 10.00 |
| ❑ 5026 | Wish Upon a Star | 198? | 10.00 |
| ❑ 5041 | 20 Golden Classics | 198? | 10.00 |
| **LAURIE** | | | |
| ❑ LLP 1002 [M] | Presenting Dion & The Belmonts | 1959 | 250.00 |
| ❑ LLP 2002 [M] | Presenting Dion & The Belmonts | 1960 | 150.00 |
| ❑ SLP 2002 [R] | Presenting Dion & The Belmonts | 196? | 900.00 |
| *—Despite its rechanneled stereo sound, this record is collectible because of its utter rarity* | | | |
| ❑ LLP 2006 [M] | Wish Upon a Star | 1960 | 150.00 |
| ❑ LLP 2016 [M] | "Together" On Records — By Special Request | 1963 | 50.00 |
| ❑ LES 4002 | Everything You Always Wanted to Hear by Dion and the Belmonts | 197? | 15.00 |
| ❑ SLP 6000 [(3)] | 60 Greatest Hits | 197? | 20.00 |
| *—In regular cover* | | | |
| ❑ SLP 6000 [(3)] | 60 Greatest Hits | 197? | 30.00 |
| *—In box* | | | |
| **PAIR** | | | |
| ❑ PDL2-1142 [(2)] | The Best of Dion and the Belmonts | 1986 | 12.00 |
| **PICKWICK** | | | |
| ❑ SPC-3521 | Doo Wop | 1975 | 10.00 |
| *—Reissue of ABC tracks* | | | |
| **RHINO** | | | |
| ❑ RNLP 70228 | Reunion — Live at Madison Square Garden — 1972 | 1987 | 10.00 |
| *—Reissue of ABC tracks* | | | |
| **WARNER BROS.** | | | |
| ❑ BS 2664 | Reunion — Live at Madison Square Garden — 1972 | 1973 | 15.00 |

### DIRE STRAITS

| Number | Title (A Side/B Side) | Yr | NM |
|---|---|---|---|
| **WARNER BROS.** | | | |
| ❑ WBMS-109 [DJ] | Dire Straits Live | 1980 | 80.00 |
| *—"The Warner Bros. Music Show" promo* | | | |
| ❑ PRO-A-2149 [EP] | Selectins from Dire Straits Live — Alchemy | 1984 | 15.00 |
| *—Three-song promo-only sampler* | | | |
| ❑ BSK 3266 | Dire Straits | 1979 | 10.00 |
| ❑ HS 3330 | Communique | 1979 | 10.00 |
| ❑ BSK 3480 | Making Movies | 1980 | 10.00 |
| ❑ 23728 | Love Over Gold | 1982 | 10.00 |
| *—On U.S. stock copies, the times of the songs as listed on the labels are rounded to the nearest 0 or 5* | | | |
| ❑ 23728 [DJ] | Love Over Gold | 1982 | 50.00 |
| *—Promo on Quiex II vinyl; the times of the songs are listed differently than on stock copies, for they are not rounded to the nearest 0 or 5* | | | |
| ❑ 25085 [(2)] | Dire Straits Live — Alchemy | 1984 | 12.00 |
| ❑ 25085 [(2)DJ] | Dire Straits Live — Alchemy | 1984 | 60.00 |
| *—Promo on Quiex II vinyl* | | | |
| ❑ 25264 | Brothers in Arms | 1985 | 10.00 |
| ❑ 25264 [DJ] | Brothers in Arms | 1985 | 50.00 |
| *—Promo on Quiex II vinyl* | | | |
| ❑ 25794 | Money for Nothing | 1989 | 15.00 |
| ❑ 26680 | On Every Street | 1991 | 25.00 |
| ❑ 29800 [EP] | Twisting by the Pool | 1983 | 6.00 |
| *—Also known as "ExtendeDancEPlay"* | | | |
| ❑ 49377-1 [(2)] | Brothers in Arms | 2006 | 30.00 |
| *—Remastered reissue; contains the full-length version of the album as it appears on the CD version, with longer versions of five songs* | | | |

Dion, *Seasons*, DaySpring 7-01-412901-5, 1984, $12.

### DIRECT FLIGHT

| Number | Title (A Side/B Side) | Yr | NM |
|---|---|---|---|
| **DIRECT DISC** | | | |
| ❑ DD-104 | Spectrum | 1980 | 25.00 |
| *—Direct-to-disc recording* | | | |

### DIRKSEN, SENATOR EVERETT MCKINLEY

| Number | Title (A Side/B Side) | Yr | NM |
|---|---|---|---|
| **CAPITOL** | | | |
| ❑ ST 2643 [S] | Gallant Men | 1966 | 15.00 |
| ❑ T 2643 [M] | Gallant Men | 1966 | 15.00 |
| ❑ ST 2754 [S] | Man Is Not Alone | 1967 | 15.00 |
| ❑ T 2754 [M] | Man Is Not Alone | 1967 | 20.00 |
| ❑ ST 2792 [S] | Everett McKinley Dirksen at Christmas Time | 1967 | 20.00 |
| ❑ T 2792 [M] | Everett McKinley Dirksen at Christmas Time | 1967 | 30.00 |

### DIRT BAND, THE See NITTY GRITTY DIRT BAND.

### DIRTY BLUES BAND, THE

| Number | Title (A Side/B Side) | Yr | NM |
|---|---|---|---|
| **BLUESWAY** | | | |
| ❑ BLS-6010 | The Dirty Blues Band | 1968 | 20.00 |
| ❑ BLS-6020 | Stone Dirt | 1968 | 20.00 |

### DIVINYLS

| Number | Title (A Side/B Side) | Yr | NM |
|---|---|---|---|
| **CHRYSALIS** | | | |
| ❑ BFV 41404 | Desperate | 1983 | 10.00 |
| ❑ BFV 41511 | What a Life! | 1985 | 12.00 |
| ❑ BFV 41627 | Temperamental | 1989 | 12.00 |

### DIXIE CUPS, THE

| Number | Title (A Side/B Side) | Yr | NM |
|---|---|---|---|
| **ABC-PARAMOUNT** | | | |
| ❑ 525 [M] | Riding High | 1965 | 60.00 |
| ❑ S-525 [S] | Riding High | 1965 | 80.00 |
| **RED BIRD** | | | |
| ❑ RB 20-100 [M] | Chapel of Love | 1964 | 60.00 |
| ❑ RBS 20-100 [S] | Chapel of Love | 1964 | 80.00 |
| ❑ RB 20-103 [M] | Iko Iko | 1965 | 150.00 |

### DIXIE DREGS, THE

| Number | Title (A Side/B Side) | Yr | NM |
|---|---|---|---|
| **DIRECT DISK** | | | |
| ❑ SD-16620 | Dregs of the Earth | 1980 | 40.00 |
| *—Audiophile vinyl* | | | |

### DIXIE SMALL FRY, THE

| Number | Title (A Side/B Side) | Yr | NM |
|---|---|---|---|
| **LIBERTY** | | | |
| ❑ LRP-3057 [M] | The Dixie Small Fry in Hi-Fi | 1957 | 40.00 |
| ❑ LST-7010 [S] | The Dixie Small Fry in Hi-Fi | 1958 | 40.00 |

### DIXIE STOMPERS, THE

| Number | Title (A Side/B Side) | Yr | NM |
|---|---|---|---|
| **DELMAR** | | | |
| ❑ DL-112 [10] | The Dixie Stompers Play New Orleans Jazz | 195? | 80.00 |
| ❑ DL-113 [10] | Wake the Levee | 195? | 80.00 |
| ❑ DL-204 [M] | Jazz at Westminster College | 195? | 60.00 |
| *—Blue vinyl; label says "DL-201" though cover says "204"* | | | |
| **RCA VICTOR** | | | |
| ❑ LPM-1212 [M] | New York Land Dixie | 1956 | 80.00 |

### DIXIEBELLES, THE

| Number | Title (A Side/B Side) | Yr | NM |
|---|---|---|---|
| **SOUND STAGE 7** | | | |
| ❑ SSM-5000 [M] | Down at Papa Joe's | 1963 | 40.00 |
| ❑ SSS-15000 [R] | Down at Papa Joe's | 1963 | 30.00 |

### DIXIELAND RHYTHM KINGS, THE

| Number | Title (A Side/B Side) | Yr | NM |
|---|---|---|---|
| **EMPIRICAL** | | | |
| ❑ LP-102 [10] | The Dixieland Rhythm Kings | 1954 | 80.00 |
| **RIVERSIDE** | | | |
| ❑ RLP 12-210 [M] | Dixieland in Hi-Fi | 1956 | 60.00 |
| *—White label, blue print* | | | |
| ❑ RLP 12-210 [M] | Dixieland in Hi-Fi | 1957 | 50.00 |
| *—Blue label, microphone logo* | | | |
| ❑ RLP 12-259 [M] | The Dixieland Rhythm Kings at the Hi-Fi Jazz Band Ball | 1958 | 40.00 |

| Number | Title (A Side/B Side) | Yr | NM |
|---|---|---|---|
| ❑ RLP 12-289 [M] | Jazz in Retrospect | 1959 | 40.00 |
| ❑ RLP-2505 [10] | New Orleans Jazz Party | 1954 | 80.00 |
| **DIXON, BILL** | | | |
| CADENCE JAZZ | | | |
| ❑ CJ-1024/25 [(2)] | Collection | 1985 | 20.00 |
| RCA VICTOR | | | |
| ❑ LPM-3844 [M] | Intents and Purposes | 1967 | 30.00 |
| ❑ LSP-3844 [S] | Intents and Purposes | 1967 | 20.00 |
| SAVOY | | | |
| ❑ MG-12184 | The Bill Dixon 7-Tette | 1964 | 20.00 |
| **DIXON, WILLIE** | | | |
| BLUESVILLE | | | |
| ❑ BVLP-1003 [M] | Willie's Blues | 1960 | 150.00 |
| *—Blue and silver label* | | | |
| ❑ BVLP-1003 [M] | Willie's Blues | 1964 | 40.00 |
| *—Blue label, trident logo at right* | | | |
| CHESS | | | |
| ❑ CH3-16500 [(3)] | The Chess Box: Willie Dixon | 1988 | 30.00 |
| COLUMBIA | | | |
| ❑ CS 9987 | I Am the Blues | 1970 | 25.00 |
| *—Red label, "360 Sound"* | | | |
| **DIXON, WILLIE, AND MEMPHIS SLIM** | | | |
| BATTLE | | | |
| ❑ BV-6122 [M] | In Paris | 1963 | 30.00 |
| ❑ BVS-6122 [S] | In Paris | 1963 | 40.00 |
| VERVE | | | |
| ❑ MGV-3007 [M] | Blues Every Which Way | 1961 | 120.00 |
| **DOBKINS, CARL, JR.** | | | |
| DECCA | | | |
| ❑ DL 8938 [M] | Carl Dobkins, Jr. | 1959 | 100.00 |
| ❑ DL 78938 [S] | Carl Dobkins, Jr. | 1959 | 150.00 |
| **DOC HOLLIDAY** | | | |
| METROMEDIA | | | |
| ❑ 1017 | Doc Holliday | 1973 | 20.00 |
| **DR. FEELGOOD AND THE INTERNS** | | | |
| OKEH | | | |
| ❑ OKM 12101 [M] | Dr. Feelgood and the Interns | 1962 | 100.00 |
| ❑ OKS 14101 [S] | Dr. Feelgood and the Interns | 1962 | 200.00 |
| **DR. JOHN** | | | |
| ACCORD | | | |
| ❑ SN-7118 | Love Potion | 1982 | 10.00 |
| ALLIGATOR | | | |
| ❑ AL-3901 | Dr. John's Gumbo | 1986 | 10.00 |
| *—Reissue of Atco 7006* | | | |
| ❑ AL-3904 | Gris-Gris | 1987 | 10.00 |
| *—Reissue of Atco 33-234* | | | |
| ATCO | | | |
| ❑ SD 33-234 | Gris-Gris | 1968 | 15.00 |
| *—Yellow label* | | | |
| ❑ SD 33-234 | Gris-Gris | 1968 | 30.00 |
| *—Purple and brown label* | | | |
| ❑ SD 33-270 | Babylon | 1969 | 15.00 |
| ❑ SD 33-316 | Remedies | 1970 | 15.00 |
| ❑ SD 33-362 | Dr. John, The Night Tripper (The Sun, Moon & Herbs) | 1971 | 15.00 |
| ❑ SD 7006 | Dr. John's Gumbo | 1972 | 12.00 |
| ❑ SD 7018 | In the Right Place | 1973 | 12.00 |
| ❑ SD 7043 | Desitively Bonaroo | 1974 | 12.00 |
| CLEAN CUTS | | | |
| ❑ 705 | Dr. John Plays Mac Rebennack | 1982 | 10.00 |
| ❑ 707 | The Brightest Smile in Town | 1984 | 10.00 |
| HORIZON | | | |
| ❑ SP-732 | City Lights | 1978 | 10.00 |
| ❑ SP-740 | Tango Palace | 1979 | 10.00 |
| KARATE | | | |
| ❑ 5404 | One Night Late | 1978 | 10.00 |
| TRIP | | | |
| ❑ TLX-350 [(2)] | Superpak | 1975 | 12.00 |
| UNITED ARTISTS | | | |
| ❑ UA-LA552-G | Hollywood Be Thy Name | 1975 | 12.00 |
| WARNER BROS. | | | |
| ❑ 25889 | In a Sentimental Mood | 1989 | 12.00 |
| **DOCTOR ROSS** | | | |
| FORTUNE | | | |
| ❑ F-3011 [M] | Doctor Ross, The Harmonica Boss | 1962 | 50.00 |
| ❑ FS-3011 [S] | Doctor Ross, The Harmonica Boss | 1962 | 100.00 |
| TESTAMENT | | | |
| ❑ 2206 [M] | Doctor Ross | 196? | 20.00 |
| **DR. WEST'S MEDICINE SHOW AND JUG BAND** Also see NORMAN GREENBAUM. | | | |
| GO GO | | | |
| ❑ 22-17-001 [M] | The Eggplant That Ate Chicago | 1967 | 50.00 |

| Number | Title (A Side/B Side) | Yr | NM |
|---|---|---|---|
| ❑ 22-17-002 [S] | The Eggplant That Ate Chicago | 1967 | 25.00 |
| GREGAR | | | |
| ❑ GG-101 | Norman Greenbaum with Dr. West's Medicine Show and Jug Band | 1970 | 20.00 |
| **DODD, DICK** | | | |
| TOWER | | | |
| ❑ ST 5142 | The First Evolution of Dick Dodd | 1968 | 50.00 |
| **DODD, JIMMIE** | | | |
| DISNEYLAND | | | |
| ❑ WDL-1014 [M] | Jimmie Dodd Sings His Favorite Hymns | 1959 | 25.00 |
| *—Reissue of 3014 with new number* | | | |
| ❑ DQ-1235 [M] | Sing Along with Jimmie Dodd | 1963 | 30.00 |
| ❑ DQ-1302 [M] | Favorite Hymns for Family Singing | 1967 | 15.00 |
| *—Reissue of 1014* | | | |
| ❑ WDL-3014 [M] | Jimmie Dodd Sings His Favorite Hymns | 1958 | 25.00 |
| IMPERIAL | | | |
| ❑ LP-9089 [M] | Lonely Guitar | 1959 | 40.00 |
| ❑ LP-9121 [M] | Swing-A-Spell | 1960 | 40.00 |
| ❑ LP-12058 [S] | Swing-A-Spell | 1960 | 50.00 |
| **DODD, KEN** | | | |
| LIBERTY | | | |
| ❑ LRP-3442 [M] | Tears and The River | 1966 | 15.00 |
| ❑ LST-7442 [S] | Tears and The River | 1966 | 20.00 |
| **DODDS, BABY** | | | |
| AMERICAN MUSIC | | | |
| ❑ 1 [M] | Baby Dodds No. 1 | 1951 | 50.00 |
| ❑ 2 [M] | Baby Dodds No. 2 | 1951 | 50.00 |
| ❑ 3 [M] | Baby Dodds No. 3 | 1951 | 50.00 |
| FOLKWAYS | | | |
| ❑ FP-30 [10] | Footnotes to Jazz, Vol. 1 — Baby Dodds' Drum Solos | 1951 | 60.00 |
| **DODDS, JOHNNY** | | | |
| BRUNSWICK | | | |
| ❑ BL 58016 [10] | The King of New Orleans Clarinets | 1951 | 100.00 |
| JOLLY ROGER | | | |
| ❑ 5012 [10] | Johnny Dodds | 1954 | 50.00 |
| MILESTONE | | | |
| ❑ M-2002 [M] | The Immortal Johnny Dodds | 1967 | 20.00 |
| ❑ M-2011 | Chicago Mess Around | 1968 | 20.00 |
| RCA VICTOR | | | |
| ❑ LPV-558 [M] | Sixteen Rare Recordings | 1965 | 25.00 |
| RIVERSIDE | | | |
| ❑ RLP 12-104 [M] | Johnny Dodds' New Orleans Clarinet | 195? | 40.00 |
| *—Blue label with microphone logo* | | | |
| ❑ RLP 12-104 [M] | Johnny Dodds' New Orleans Clarinet | 1956 | 60.00 |
| *—White label, blue print* | | | |
| ❑ RLP 12-135 [M] | In the Alley: Johnny Dodds, Volume 2 | 1961 | 40.00 |
| ❑ RLP-1002 [10] | Johnny Dodds, Volume 1 | 1953 | 80.00 |
| ❑ RLP-1015 [10] | Johnny Dodds, Volume 2 | 1953 | 80.00 |
| TIME-LIFE | | | |
| ❑ STL-J-26 [(3)] | Giants of Jazz | 1982 | 20.00 |
| "X" | | | |
| ❑ LX-3006 [10] | Johnny Dodds' Washboard Band | 1954 | 60.00 |
| **DODSON, MARGE** | | | |
| COLUMBIA | | | |
| ❑ CL 1309 [M] | In the Still of the Night | 1959 | 30.00 |
| ❑ CL 1458 [M] | New Voice in Town | 1960 | 30.00 |
| ❑ CS 8258 [S] | New Voice in Town | 1960 | 40.00 |
| **DOGGETT, BILL** | | | |
| ABC-PARAMOUNT | | | |
| ❑ 507 [M] | Wow! | 1965 | 20.00 |
| ❑ S-507 [S] | Wow! | 1965 | 25.00 |
| AFTER HOURS | | | |
| ❑ AFT-4112 | The Right Choice | 1991 | 15.00 |
| COLUMBIA | | | |
| ❑ CL 1814 [M] | Oops! | 1962 | 20.00 |
| ❑ CL 1942 [M] | Prelude to the Blues | 1963 | 20.00 |
| ❑ CL 2082 [M] | Fingertips | 1963 | 20.00 |
| ❑ CS 8614 [S] | Oops! | 1962 | 25.00 |
| ❑ CS 8742 [S] | Prelude to the Blues | 1963 | 25.00 |
| ❑ CS 8882 [S] | Fingertips | 1963 | 25.00 |
| KING | | | |
| ❑ 295-82 [10] | Bill Doggett — His Organ and Combo | 1955 | 150.00 |
| ❑ 295-83 [10] | Bill Doggett — His Organ and Combo, Volume 2 | 1955 | 150.00 |

| Number | Title (A Side/B Side) | Yr | NM |
|---|---|---|---|
| ❑ 295-89 [10] | All-Time Christmas Favorites | 1955 | 200.00 |
| ❑ 295-102 [10] | Sentimentally Yours | 1956 | 150.00 |
| ❑ 395-502 [M] | Moondust | 1957 | 60.00 |
| ❑ 395-514 [M] | Hot Doggett | 1957 | 60.00 |
| ❑ 395-523 [M] | As You Desire | 1957 | 60.00 |
| ❑ KLP-523 [M] | As You Desire | 1987 | 10.00 |
| *—Reissue with "Highland Records" on label* | | | |
| ❑ 395-531 [M] | Everybody Dance to the Honky Tonk | 1958 | 60.00 |
| ❑ 395-532 [M] | Dame Dreaming | 1958 | 60.00 |
| ❑ KLP-532 [M] | Dame Dreaming | 1987 | 10.00 |
| *—Reissue with "Highland Records" on label* | | | |
| ❑ 395-533 [M] | A Salute to Ellington | 1958 | 60.00 |
| ❑ 395-557 [M] | The Doggett Beat for Dancing Feet | 1958 | 60.00 |
| ❑ KLP-557 [M] | The Doggett Beat for Dancing Feet | 1987 | 10.00 |
| *—Reissue with "Highland Records" on label* | | | |
| ❑ 395-563 [M] | Candle Glow | 1958 | 60.00 |
| ❑ 395-582 [M] | Swingin' Easy | 1959 | 60.00 |
| ❑ 395-585 [M] | Dance Awhile | 1959 | 60.00 |
| ❑ KLP-585 [M] | Dance Awhile | 1987 | 10.00 |
| *—Reissue with "Highland Records" on label* | | | |
| ❑ 395-600 [M] | A Bill Doggett Christmas | 1959 | 40.00 |
| ❑ 395-609 [M] | Hold It | 1959 | 60.00 |
| ❑ 633 [M] | High and Wide | 1959 | 50.00 |
| ❑ 641 [M] | Big City Dance Party | 1959 | 50.00 |
| ❑ 667 [M] | Bill Doggett On Tour | 1959 | 50.00 |
| ❑ 706 [M] | For Reminiscent Lovers, Romantic Songs | 1960 | 50.00 |
| ❑ 723 [M] | Back Again with More | 1960 | 50.00 |
| ❑ 759 [M] | Bonanza of 24 Songs | 1960 | 50.00 |
| ❑ 778 [M] | The Many Moods of Bill Doggett | 1960 | 50.00 |
| ❑ KLP-778 [M] | The Many Moods of Bill Doggett | 1987 | 10.00 |
| *—Reissue with "Highland Records" on label* | | | |
| ❑ 830 [M] | American Songs in the Bossa Nova Style | 1963 | 40.00 |
| ❑ 868 [M] | Impressions | 1964 | 40.00 |
| ❑ 908 [M] | The Best of Bill Doggett | 1964 | 40.00 |
| ❑ 959 [M] | Bonanza of 24 Hit Songs | 1966 | 30.00 |
| ❑ KS-1078 | Honky Tonk Popcorn | 1969 | 50.00 |
| ❑ KS-1097 | The Nearness of You | 1970 | 25.00 |
| ❑ KS-1101 | Ram-Bunk-Shush | 1970 | 25.00 |
| ❑ KS-1104 | Sentimental Journey | 1970 | 25.00 |
| ❑ KS-1108 | Soft | 1970 | 25.00 |
| ❑ K-5009 | 14 Original Greatest Hits | 1977 | 10.00 |
| POWER PAK | | | |
| ❑ 269 | Hold It! | 197? | 10.00 |
| ROULETTE | | | |
| ❑ R 25330 [M] | Honky Tonk A La Mod | 1966 | 20.00 |
| ❑ SR 25330 [S] | Honky Tonk A La Mod | 1966 | 25.00 |
| STARDAY | | | |
| ❑ 3023 | 16 Bandstand Favorites | 197? | 10.00 |
| WARNER BROS. | | | |
| ❑ W 1404 [M] | 3,046 People Danced 'Til 4 AM | 1960 | 20.00 |
| ❑ WS 1404 [S] | 3,046 People Danced 'Til 4 AM | 1960 | 25.00 |
| ❑ W 1421 [M] | The Band with the Beat | 1961 | 20.00 |
| ❑ WS 1421 [S] | The Band with the Beat | 1961 | 25.00 |
| ❑ W 1452 [M] | Bill Doggett Swings | 1962 | 20.00 |
| ❑ WS 1452 [S] | Bill Doggett Swings | 1962 | 25.00 |
| WHO'S WHO IN JAZZ | | | |
| ❑ 21002 | Lionel Hampton Presents Bill Doggett | 1977 | 12.00 |
| **DOHENY, NED** | | | |
| ASYLUM | | | |
| ❑ SD 5059 | Ned Doheny | 1973 | 20.00 |
| **DOJO** | | | |
| ECLIPSE | | | |
| ❑ ES-7309 | Down for the Last Time | 1971 | 25.00 |
| **DOLDINGER, KLAUS** | | | |
| PHILIPS | | | |
| ❑ PHM 200125 [M] | Dig Doldinger | 1966 | 20.00 |
| ❑ PHS 600125 [S] | Dig Doldinger | 1966 | 25.00 |
| WORLD PACIFIC | | | |
| ❑ WPS-20176 | Blues Happening | 1969 | 20.00 |
| **DOLLAR, JOHNNY** | | | |
| DATE | | | |
| ❑ TEM 3009 [M] | Johnny Dollar | 1967 | 25.00 |
| ❑ TES 4009 [S] | Johnny Dollar | 1967 | 20.00 |
| **DOLPHY, ERIC** | | | |
| BLUE NOTE | | | |
| ❑ BLP-4163 [M] | Out to Lunch! | 1964 | 80.00 |
| ❑ BST-84163 [S] | Out to Lunch! | 1964 | 80.00 |
| *—"New York, USA" on label* | | | |
| ❑ BT-85131 | Other Aspects | 1987 | 20.00 |
| DOUGLAS | | | |
| ❑ SD 785 | Iron Man | 1969 | 25.00 |
| ❑ KZ 30873 | Iron Man | 1971 | 20.00 |
| EXODUS | | | |
| ❑ EX-6005 [M] | The Memorial Album | 1966 | 20.00 |
| *—Reissue of Vee Jay LP-2503* | | | |

| Number | Title (A Side/B Side) | Yr | NM |
|---|---|---|---|
| ❑ EXS-6005 [S] | The Memorial Album | 1966 | 20.00 |
| *—Reissue of Vee Jay LPS-2503* | | | |
| FM | | | |
| ❑ 308 [M] | Conversations | 1963 | 40.00 |
| ❑ S-308 [S] | Conversations | 1963 | 50.00 |
| LIMELIGHT | | | |
| ❑ LM-82013 [M] | Last Date | 1964 | 30.00 |
| ❑ LS-86013 [S] | Last Date | 1964 | 40.00 |
| NEW JAZZ | | | |
| ❑ NJLP-8236 [M] | Outward Bound | 1960 | 250.00 |
| ❑ NJLP-8252 [M] | Out There | 1960 | 200.00 |
| *—Purple label* | | | |
| ❑ NJLP-8252 [M] | Out There | 1965 | 50.00 |
| *—Blue label, trident logo at right* | | | |
| ❑ NJLP-8260 [M] | Eric Dolphy at the Five Spot | 1961 | 200.00 |
| *—Purple label* | | | |
| ❑ NJLP-8260 [M] | Eric Dolphy at the Five Spot | 1965 | 60.00 |
| *—Blue label, trident logo at right* | | | |
| ❑ NJLP-8270 [M] | Far Cry | 1962 | 200.00 |
| *—Purple label* | | | |
| ❑ NJLP-8270 [M] | Far Cry | 1965 | 60.00 |
| *—Blue label, trident logo at right* | | | |
| PRESTIGE | | | |
| ❑ PRLP-7294 [M] | Eric Dolphy at the Five Spot, Volume 2 | 1964 | 40.00 |
| *—Yellow label* | | | |
| ❑ PRLP-7294 [M] | Eric Dolphy at the Five Spot, Volume 2 | 1965 | 20.00 |
| *—Blue label, trident logo at right* | | | |
| ❑ PRST-7294 [S] | Eric Dolphy at the Five Spot, Volume 2 | 1964 | 50.00 |
| *—Silver label* | | | |
| ❑ PRST-7294 [S] | Eric Dolphy at the Five Spot, Volume 2 | 1965 | 25.00 |
| *—Blue label, trident logo at right* | | | |
| ❑ PRLP-7304 [M] | Eric Dolphy in Europe, Volume 1 | 1964 | 40.00 |
| *—Yellow label* | | | |
| ❑ PRLP-7304 [M] | Eric Dolphy in Europe, Volume 1 | 1965 | 20.00 |
| *—Blue label, trident logo at right* | | | |
| ❑ PRST-7304 [S] | Eric Dolphy in Europe, Volume 1 | 1964 | 50.00 |
| *—Silver label* | | | |
| ❑ PRST-7304 [S] | Eric Dolphy in Europe, Volume 1 | 1965 | 25.00 |
| *—Blue label, trident logo at right* | | | |
| ❑ PRLP-7311 [M] | Outward Bound | 1964 | 50.00 |
| *—Yellow label* | | | |
| ❑ PRLP-7311 [M] | Outward Bound | 1965 | 25.00 |
| *—Blue label, trident logo at right* | | | |
| ❑ PRST-7311 [S] | Outward Bound | 1964 | 40.00 |
| *—Silver label* | | | |
| ❑ PRST-7311 [S] | Outward Bound | 1965 | 20.00 |
| *—Blue label, trident logo at right* | | | |
| ❑ PRLP-7334 [M] | Eric Dolphy Memorial Album | 1964 | 20.00 |
| ❑ PRST-7334 [S] | Eric Dolphy Memorial Album | 1964 | 25.00 |
| ❑ PRLP-7350 [M] | Eric Dolphy in Europe, Volume 2 | 1965 | 20.00 |
| ❑ PRST-7350 [S] | Eric Dolphy in Europe, Volume 2 | 1965 | 25.00 |
| ❑ PRLP-7366 [M] | Eric Dolphy in Europe, Volume 3 | 1965 | 20.00 |
| ❑ PRST-7366 [S] | Eric Dolphy in Europe, Volume 3 | 1965 | 25.00 |
| ❑ PRLP-7382 [M] | Here and There | 1965 | 20.00 |
| ❑ PRST-7382 [S] | Here and There | 1965 | 25.00 |
| ❑ 24008 [(2)] | Eric Dolphy | 197? | 20.00 |
| ❑ 24027 [(2)] | Copenhagen Concert | 197? | 20.00 |
| ❑ 34002 [(3)] | Great Concert | 1974 | 25.00 |
| VEE JAY | | | |
| ❑ LP-2503 [M] | The Memorial Album | 1964 | 30.00 |
| ❑ LPS-2503 [S] | The Memorial Album | 1964 | 40.00 |

## DOMINO, FATS

| Number | Title (A Side/B Side) | Yr | NM |
|---|---|---|---|
| ABC | | | |
| ❑ S-455 [S] | Here Comes... Fats Domino | 1967 | 15.00 |
| ❑ S-479 [S] | Fats on Fire | 1967 | 15.00 |
| ❑ S-510 [S] | Get Away with Fats Domino | 1967 | 15.00 |
| ❑ ST-90167 [S] | Get Away with Fats Domino | 1969 | 25.00 |
| *—Capitol Record Club edition; reissue* | | | |
| ABC-PARAMOUNT | | | |
| ❑ 455 [M] | Here Comes... Fats Domino | 1963 | 20.00 |
| ❑ S-455 [S] | Here Comes... Fats Domino | 1963 | 25.00 |
| ❑ 479 [M] | Fats on Fire | 1964 | 20.00 |
| ❑ S-479 [S] | Fats on Fire | 1964 | 25.00 |
| ❑ 510 [M] | Get Away with Fats Domino | 1965 | 20.00 |
| ❑ S-510 [S] | Get Away with Fats Domino | 1965 | 25.00 |
| ❑ ST-90167 [S] | Get Away with Fats Domino | 1965 | 30.00 |
| *—Capitol Record Club edition* | | | |
| ❑ T-90167 [M] | Get Away with Fats Domino | 1965 | 25.00 |
| *—Capitol Record Club edition* | | | |
| ATLANTIC | | | |
| ❑ 81751 | Live in Montreux | 1987 | 12.00 |
| COLUMBIA | | | |
| ❑ C 35996 | When I'm Walking | 1979 | 10.00 |
| *—Reissue of Harmony LP* | | | |

| Number | Title (A Side/B Side) | Yr | NM |
|---|---|---|---|
| ❑ PC 35996 | When I'm Walking | 1986 | 8.00 |
| *—Budget-line reissue* | | | |
| COLUMBIA SPECIAL PRODUCTS | | | |
| ❑ P2 13197 [(2)] | The Legendary Music Man | 1976 | 15.00 |
| *—Candelite Music TV offer* | | | |
| EVEREST ARCHIVE OF FOLK & JAZZ | | | |
| ❑ 280 | Fats Domino | 1974 | 10.00 |
| ❑ 330 | Fats Domino, Vol. II | 1975 | 10.00 |
| GRAND AWARD | | | |
| ❑ 267 [M] | Fats Domino | 196? | 20.00 |
| ❑ S-267 [R] | Fats Domino | 196? | 10.00 |
| HARLEM HIT PARADE | | | |
| ❑ 5005 | Fats' Hits | 197? | 10.00 |
| HARMONY | | | |
| ❑ HS 11343 | When I'm Walking | 1969 | 12.00 |
| IMPERIAL | | | |
| ❑ LP-9004 [M] | Rock and Rollin' with Fats Domino | 1956 | 150.00 |
| *—Maroon label* | | | |
| ❑ LP-9004 [M] | Rock and Rollin' with Fats Domino | 1958 | 80.00 |
| *—Black label with stars on top* | | | |
| ❑ LP-9004 [M] | Rock and Rollin' with Fats Domino | 1964 | 25.00 |
| *—Black and pink label* | | | |
| ❑ LP-9004 [M] | Rock and Rollin' with Fats Domino | 1967 | 20.00 |
| *—Black and green label* | | | |
| ❑ LP-9009 [M] | Fats Domino Rock and Rollin' | 1956 | 150.00 |
| *—Maroon label* | | | |
| ❑ LP-9009 [M] | Fats Domino Rock and Rollin' | 1958 | 80.00 |
| *—Black label with stars on top* | | | |
| ❑ LP-9009 [M] | Fats Domino Rock and Rollin' | 1964 | 25.00 |
| *—Black and pink label* | | | |
| ❑ LP-9009 [M] | Fats Domino Rock and Rollin' | 1967 | 20.00 |
| *—Black and green label* | | | |
| ❑ LP-9028 [M] | This Is Fats Domino! | 1957 | 150.00 |
| *—Maroon label* | | | |
| ❑ LP-9028 [M] | This Is Fats Domino! | 1958 | 80.00 |
| *—Black label with stars on top* | | | |
| ❑ LP-9028 [M] | This Is Fats Domino! | 1964 | 25.00 |
| *—Black and pink label* | | | |
| ❑ LP-9028 [M] | This Is Fats Domino! | 1967 | 20.00 |
| *—Black and green label* | | | |
| ❑ LP-9038 [M] | Here Stands Fats Domino | 1957 | 150.00 |
| *—Maroon label* | | | |
| ❑ LP-9038 [M] | Here Stands Fats Domino | 1958 | 80.00 |
| *—Black label with stars on top* | | | |
| ❑ LP-9038 [M] | Here Stands Fats Domino | 1964 | 25.00 |
| *—Black and pink label* | | | |
| ❑ LP-9038 [M] | Here Stands Fats Domino | 1967 | 20.00 |
| *—Black and green label* | | | |
| ❑ LP-9040 [M] | This Is Fats | 1957 | 150.00 |
| *—Maroon label* | | | |
| ❑ LP-9040 [M] | This Is Fats | 1958 | 80.00 |
| *—Black label with stars on top* | | | |
| ❑ LP-9040 [M] | This Is Fats | 1964 | 25.00 |
| *—Black and pink label* | | | |
| ❑ LP-9040 [M] | This Is Fats | 1967 | 20.00 |
| *—Black and green label* | | | |
| ❑ LP-9055 [M] | The Fabulous Mr. D. | 1958 | 100.00 |
| *—Black label with stars on top* | | | |
| ❑ LP-9055 [M] | The Fabulous Mr. D. | 1964 | 30.00 |
| *—Black and pink label* | | | |
| ❑ LP-9055 [M] | The Fabulous Mr. D. | 1967 | 20.00 |
| *—Black and green label* | | | |
| ❑ LP-9062 [M] | Fats Domino Swings | 1959 | 100.00 |
| *—Black label with stars on top* | | | |
| ❑ LP-9062 [M] | Fats Domino Swings | 1964 | 30.00 |
| *—Black and pink label* | | | |
| ❑ LP-9062 [M] | Fats Domino Swings | 1967 | 20.00 |
| *—Black and green label* | | | |
| ❑ LP-9065 [M] | Let's Play Fats Domino | 1959 | 100.00 |
| *—Black label with stars on top* | | | |
| ❑ LP-9065 [M] | Let's Play Fats Domino | 1964 | 30.00 |
| *—Black and pink label* | | | |
| ❑ LP-9065 [M] | Let's Play Fats Domino | 1967 | 20.00 |
| *—Black and green label* | | | |
| ❑ LP-9103 [M] | Million Record Hits | 1960 | 100.00 |
| *—Black label with stars on top* | | | |
| ❑ LP-9103 [M] | Million Record Hits | 1964 | 30.00 |
| *—Black and pink label* | | | |
| ❑ LP-9103 [M] | Million Record Hits | 1967 | 20.00 |
| *—Black and green label* | | | |
| ❑ LP-9127 [M] | A Lot of Dominos | 1960 | 100.00 |
| *—Black label with stars on top* | | | |
| ❑ LP-9127 [M] | A Lot of Dominos | 1964 | 30.00 |
| *—Black and pink label* | | | |
| ❑ LP-9127 [M] | A Lot of Dominos | 1967 | 20.00 |
| *—Black and green label* | | | |
| ❑ LP-9138 [M] | I Miss You So | 1961 | 100.00 |
| *—Black label with stars on top* | | | |
| ❑ LP-9138 [M] | I Miss You So | 1964 | 30.00 |
| *—Black and pink label* | | | |
| ❑ LP-9138 [M] | I Miss You So | 1967 | 20.00 |
| *—Black and green label* | | | |
| ❑ LP-9153 [M] | Let the Four Winds Blow | 1961 | 100.00 |
| *—Black label with stars on top* | | | |
| ❑ LP-9153 [M] | Let the Four Winds Blow | 1964 | 30.00 |
| *—Black and pink label* | | | |

| Number | Title (A Side/B Side) | Yr | NM |
|---|---|---|---|
| ❑ LP-9153 [M] | Let the Four Winds Blow | 1967 | 20.00 |
| *—Black and green label* | | | |
| ❑ LP-9164 [M] | What a Party | 1962 | 60.00 |
| *—Black label with stars on top* | | | |
| ❑ LP-9164 [M] | What a Party | 1964 | 30.00 |
| *—Black and pink label* | | | |
| ❑ LP-9164 [M] | What a Party | 1967 | 20.00 |
| *—Black and green label* | | | |
| ❑ LP-9170 [M] | Twistin' the Stomp | 1962 | 60.00 |
| *—Black label with stars on top* | | | |
| ❑ LP-9170 [M] | Twistin' the Stomp | 1964 | 30.00 |
| *—Black and pink label* | | | |
| ❑ LP-9170 [M] | Twistin' the Stomp | 1967 | 20.00 |
| *—Black and green label* | | | |
| ❑ LP-9195 [M] | Million Sellers by Fats | 1962 | 50.00 |
| *—Black label with stars on top* | | | |
| ❑ LP-9195 [M] | Million Sellers by Fats | 1964 | 30.00 |
| *—Black and pink label* | | | |
| ❑ LP-9195 [M] | Million Sellers by Fats | 1967 | 20.00 |
| *—Black and green label* | | | |
| ❑ LP-9208 [M] | Just Domino | 1962 | 50.00 |
| *—Black label with stars on top* | | | |
| ❑ LP-9208 [M] | Just Domino | 1964 | 30.00 |
| *—Black and pink label* | | | |
| ❑ LP-9208 [M] | Just Domino | 1967 | 20.00 |
| *—Black and green label* | | | |
| ❑ LP-9227 [M] | Walking to New Orleans | 1963 | 50.00 |
| *—Black label with stars on top* | | | |
| ❑ LP-9227 [M] | Walking to New Orleans | 1964 | 30.00 |
| *—Black and pink label* | | | |
| ❑ LP-9227 [M] | Walking to New Orleans | 1967 | 20.00 |
| *—Black and green label* | | | |
| ❑ LP-9239 [M] | Let's Dance with Domino | 1963 | 50.00 |
| *—Black label with stars on top* | | | |
| ❑ LP-9239 [M] | Let's Dance with Domino | 1964 | 30.00 |
| *—Black and pink label* | | | |
| ❑ LP-9239 [M] | Let's Dance with Domino | 1967 | 20.00 |
| *—Black and green label* | | | |
| ❑ LP-9248 [M] | Here He Comes Again | 1963 | 50.00 |
| *—Black label with stars on top* | | | |
| ❑ LP-9248 [M] | Here He Comes Again | 1964 | 30.00 |
| *—Black and pink label* | | | |
| ❑ LP-9248 [M] | Here He Comes Again | 1967 | 20.00 |
| *—Black and green label* | | | |
| ❑ LP-12066 [S] | A Lot of Dominos | 1961 | 150.00 |
| *—Black label with silver top* | | | |
| ❑ LP-12066 [S] | A Lot of Dominos | 1964 | 40.00 |
| *—Black and pink label* | | | |
| ❑ LP-12066 [S] | A Lot of Dominos | 1967 | 25.00 |
| *—Black and green label* | | | |
| ❑ LP-12073 [S] | Let the Four Winds Blow | 1961 | 150.00 |
| *—Black label with silver top* | | | |
| ❑ LP-12073 [S] | Let the Four Winds Blow | 1964 | 40.00 |
| *—Black and pink label* | | | |
| ❑ LP-12073 [S] | Let the Four Winds Blow | 1967 | 25.00 |
| *—Black and green label* | | | |
| ❑ LP-12091 [R] | Fats Domino Swings | 1964 | 20.00 |
| *—Black and pink label* | | | |
| ❑ LP-12091 [R] | Fats Domino Swings | 1967 | 15.00 |
| *—Black and green label* | | | |
| ❑ LP-12103 [R] | Million Record Hits | 1964 | 20.00 |
| *—Black and pink label* | | | |
| ❑ LP-12103 [R] | Million Record Hits | 1967 | 15.00 |
| *—Black and green label* | | | |
| ❑ LP-12195 [R] | Million Sellers by Fats | 1964 | 20.00 |
| *—Black and pink label* | | | |
| ❑ LP-12195 [R] | Million Sellers by Fats | 1967 | 15.00 |
| *—Black and green label* | | | |
| ❑ LP-12227 [R] | Walking to New Orleans | 1964 | 20.00 |
| *—Black and pink label* | | | |
| ❑ LP-12227 [R] | Walking to New Orleans | 1967 | 15.00 |
| *—Black and green label* | | | |
| ❑ LP-12248 [R] | Here He Comes Again | 1964 | 20.00 |
| *—Black and pink label* | | | |
| ❑ LP-12248 [R] | Here He Comes Again | 1967 | 15.00 |
| *—Black and green label* | | | |
| ❑ LP-12387 [R] | Rock and Rollin' with Fats Domino | 1968 | 12.00 |
| *—Rechanneled reissue of 9004* | | | |
| ❑ LP-12388 [R] | Fats Domino Rock and Rollin' | 1968 | 12.00 |
| *—Rechanneled reissue of 9009* | | | |
| ❑ LP-12389 [R] | This Is Fats Domino! | 1968 | 12.00 |
| *—Rechanneled reissue of 9028* | | | |
| ❑ LP-12390 [R] | Here Stands Fats Domino | 1968 | 12.00 |
| *—Rechanneled reissue of 9038* | | | |
| ❑ LP-12391 [R] | This Is Fats | 1968 | 12.00 |
| *—Rechanneled reissue of 9040* | | | |
| ❑ LP-12394 [R] | The Fabulous Mr. D. | 1968 | 12.00 |
| *—Rechanneled reissue of 9055* | | | |
| ❑ LP-12395 [R] | Let's Play Fats Domino | 1968 | 12.00 |
| *—Rechanneled reissue of 9065* | | | |
| ❑ LP-12398 [R] | I Miss You So | 1968 | 12.00 |
| *—Rechanneled reissue of 9138* | | | |
| LIBERTY | | | |
| ❑ LWB-122 [(2)] | Cookin' with Fats (Superpak) | 1981 | 12.00 |
| *—Budget-line reissue of UA 122* | | | |
| ❑ LM-1027 | Million Sellers by Fats | 1981 | 8.00 |
| *—Budget-line reissue of UA 1027* | | | |
| ❑ LWB-9958 [(2)] | Legendary Masters | 1981 | 10.00 |
| *—Budget-line reissue of UA 9958* | | | |
| ❑ LN-10135 | Let's Play Fats Domino | 1981 | 8.00 |
| *—Budget-line reissue* | | | |
| ❑ LN-10136 | The Fabulous Mr. D. | 1981 | 8.00 |
| *—Budget-line reissue* | | | |

Number | Title (A Side/B Side) | Yr | NM

MCA/SILVER EAGLE

❑ 6170 Greatest Hits 198? 10.00

MERCURY

❑ MG-21039 [M] Fats Domino '65 1965 25.00
❑ 21065/61065 Southland U.S.A. 1966 —
*—Canceled*
❑ SR-61039 [S] Fats Domino '65 1965 40.00

PICKWICK

❑ SPC-3111 Blueberry Hill 197? 10.00
❑ SPC-3165 When My Dreamboat Comes Home 197? 10.00
❑ SPC-3295 My Blue Heaven 1971 10.00

QUICKSILVER

❑ QS-1016 Live Hits 198? 10.00

REPRISE

❑ RS 6304 Fats Is Back 1968 30.00
❑ RS 6439 Fats 1970 500.00
*—Officially unreleased, test pressings and coverless stock copies are known to exist*

SEARS

❑ SPS-473 Blueberry Hill! 1970 25.00

SUNSET

❑ SUM-1103 [M] Fats Domino 1966 12.00
❑ SUM-1158 [M] Stompin' Fats Domino 1967 12.00
❑ SUS-5103 [R] Fats Domino 1966 12.00
❑ SUS-5158 [R] Stompin' Fats Domino 1967 12.00
❑ SUS-5200 [P] Trouble in Mind 1968 20.00
❑ SUS-5299 [R] Ain't That a Shame 1970 12.00

UNITED ARTISTS

❑ UAMG-104 [DJ]The Fats Domino Sound 1973 40.00
*—Promo compilation of 30 excerpts of Fats hits*
❑ UA-LA122-F2 [(2)]Cookin' with Fats (Superpak) 1974 30.00
❑ UA-LA122-F2 [(2)DJ]Cookin' with Fats (Superpak) 1974 300.00
*—Promo with one black vinyl record and one colored vinyl record*
❑ UA-LA233-G The Very Best of Fats Domino 1974 12.00
❑ LM-1027 Million Sellers by Fats 1980 10.00
❑ UAS-9958 [(2)] Legendary Masters 1972 15.00

**DOMINOES, THE** See BILLY WARD AND THE DOMINOES.

**DOMNERUS, ARNE**

PRESTIGE

❑ PRLP-134 [10] New Sounds from Sweden, Volume 4 1952 250.00

RCA VICTOR

❑ LPT-3032 [10] Around the World in Jazz 1953 250.00

**DOMNERUS, ARNE/LARS GULLIN**

PRESTIGE

❑ PRLP-133 [10] New Sounds from Sweden, Volume 3 1952 250.00

**DON AND DEWEY**

SPECIALTY

❑ SPS-2131 They're Rockin' Til Midnight, Rollin' Til Dawn 1970 30.00
*—Original labels are black and gold*

**DON AND EDDIE**

MODERN

❑ M 7014 [M] Rock and Roll Party 1963 40.00

**DON AND THE GOODTIMES**

BEAT ROCKET

❑ BR-130 The Original Northwest Sound of Don and the Goodtimes 2000 12.00

BURDETTE

❑ 300 [M] Don and the Goodtimes' Greatest Hits 1966 150.00
❑ 300S [R] Don and the Goodtimes' Greatest Hits 1966 100.00
*—LP plays rechanneled stereo*
❑ 300S [S] Don and the Goodtimes' Greatest Hits 1966 300.00
*—LP plays true stereo*

EPIC

❑ LN 24311 [M] So Good 1967 20.00
❑ BN 26311 [S] So Good 1967 20.00

PICCADILLY

❑ 3394 Goodtime Rock 'n' Roll 1980 25.00

WAND

❑ WDS-679 Where the Action Is 1969 30.00

**DON, DICK & JIMMY**

CROWN

❑ CLP-5005 [M] Spring Fever 1958 40.00

DOT

❑ DLP-3152 [M] Don, Dick & Jimmy 1959 30.00

MODERN

❑ MLP-1205 [M] Spring Fever 1957 120.00

VERVE

❑ MGV-2084 [M] Medium Rare 1958 40.00
❑ MGV-2107 [M] Songs for the Hearth 1959 40.00

**DONAHUE, SAM**

CAPITOL

❑ H 613 [10] For Young Moderns in Love 1955 60.00
❑ T 613 [M] For Young Moderns in Love 1956 40.00
❑ H 626 [10] Classics in Jazz 1955 50.00

**DONALDSON, BOBBY**

GOLDEN CREST

❑ GC-1003 Unlimited 196? 20.00

SAVOY

❑ MG-12128 [M] Dixieland Jazz Party 1958 40.00
❑ SST-13003 [S] Dixieland Jazz Party 1959 30.00

WORLD WIDE

❑ 20005 Bobby Donaldson and the 7th Avenue Stompers 196? 20.00

**DONALDSON, LOU**

ARGO

❑ LP-724 [M] Signifyin' 1963 25.00
❑ LPS-724 [S] Signifyin' 1963 25.00
❑ LP-734 [M] Possum Head 1964 25.00
❑ LPS-734 [S] Possum Head 1964 25.00
❑ LP-747 [M] Cole Slaw 1965 25.00
❑ LPS-747 [S] Cole Slaw 1965 25.00

BLUE NOTE

❑ BLP-1537 [M] Lou Donaldson Quartet/Quintet/Sextet 1958 100.00
*—Regular version with W. 63rd St. address on label*
❑ BLP-1537 [M] Lou Donaldson Quartet/Quintet/Sextet 1958 300.00
*—"Deep groove" version; W. 63rd St. address on label*
❑ BLP-1537 [M] Lou Donaldson Quartet/Quintet/Sextet 1963 40.00
*—With New York, USA address on label*
❑ BLP-1545 [M] Wailing with Lou 1957 150.00
*—Regular version with W. 63rd St. address on label*
❑ BLP-1545 [M] Wailing with Lou 1957 250.00
*—"Deep groove" version; W. 63rd St. address on label*
❑ BLP-1545 [M] Wailing with Lou 1963 40.00
*—With New York, USA address on label*
❑ BLP-1566 [M] Swing and Soul 1957 150.00
*—Regular version with W. 63rd St. address on label*
❑ BLP-1566 [M] Swing and Soul 1957 250.00
*—"Deep groove" version; W. 63rd St. address on label*
❑ BLP-1566 [M] Swing and Soul 1963 40.00
*—With New York, USA address on label*
❑ BST-1566 [S] Swing and Soul 1959 100.00
*—Regular version with W. 63rd St. address on label*
❑ BST-1566 [S] Swing and Soul 1959 150.00
*—"Deep groove" version; W. 63rd St. address on label*
❑ BST-1566 [S] Swing and Soul 1963 30.00
*—With New York, USA address on label*
❑ BLP-1591 [M] Lou Takes Off 1958 150.00
*—Regular version with W. 63rd St. address on label*
❑ BLP-1591 [M] Lou Takes Off 1958 250.00
*—"Deep groove" version; W. 63rd St. address on label*
❑ BLP-1591 [M] Lou Takes Off 1963 40.00
*—With New York, USA address on label*
❑ BST-1591 [S] Lou Takes Off 1959 100.00
*—Regular version with W. 63rd St. address on label*
❑ BST-1591 [S] Lou Takes Off 1959 150.00
*—"Deep groove" version; W. 63rd St. address on label*
❑ BST-1591 [S] Lou Takes Off 1963 30.00
*—With New York, USA address on label*
❑ BLP-1593 [M] Blues Walk 1958 150.00
*—Regular version with W. 63rd St. address on label*
❑ BLP-1593 [M] Blues Walk 1958 250.00
*—"Deep groove" version; W. 63rd St. address on label*
❑ BLP-1593 [M] Blues Walk 1963 40.00
*—With New York, USA address on label*
❑ BST-1593 [S] Blues Walk 1959 50.00
*—Regular version with W. 63rd St. address on label*
❑ BST-1593 [S] Blues Walk 1959 80.00
*—"Deep groove" version (deep indentation under label on both sides)*
❑ BST-1593 [S] Blues Walk 1963 20.00
*—With New York, USA address on label*
❑ BLP-4012 [M] LD + 3 1959 120.00
*—Regular version with W. 63rd St. address on label*
❑ BLP-4012 [M] LD + 3 1959 200.00
*—"Deep groove" version; W. 63rd St. address on label*
❑ BLP-4012 [M] LD + 3 1963 40.00
*—With New York, USA address on label*
❑ BST-4012 [S] LD + 3 1960 80.00
*—Regular version with W. 63rd St. address on label*
❑ BST-4012 [S] LD + 3 1960 150.00
*—"Deep groove" version; W. 63rd St. address on label*
❑ BST-4012 [S] LD + 3 1963 30.00
*—With New York, USA address on label*
❑ BLP-4025 [M] The Time Is Right 1960 80.00
*—Regular version with W. 63rd St. address on label*
❑ BLP-4025 [M] The Time Is Right 1960 120.00
*—"Deep groove" version (deep indentation under label on both sides)*
❑ BLP-4025 [M] The Time Is Right 1963 25.00
*—With New York, USA address on label*
❑ BLP-4036 [M] Sunny Side Up 1960 120.00
*—Regular version with W. 63rd St. address on label*
❑ BLP-4036 [M] Sunny Side Up 1960 200.00
*—"Deep groove" version; W. 63rd St. address on label*
❑ BLP-4036 [M] Sunny Side Up 1963 40.00
*—With New York, USA address on label*
❑ BLP-4053 [M] Light Foot 1960 120.00
*—With W. 63rd St. address on label*
❑ BLP-4053 [M] Light Foot 1963 50.00
*—With New York, USA address on label*
❑ BLP-4066 [M] Here 'Tis 1961 200.00
*—With W. 63rd St. address on label*
❑ BLP-4066 [M] Here 'Tis 1963 80.00
*—With New York, USA address on label*
❑ BLP-4079 [M] Gravy Train 1962 200.00
*—With W. 63rd St. address on label*
❑ BLP-4079 [M] Gravy Train 1963 100.00
*—With New York, USA address on label*
❑ BLP-4108 [M] The Natural Soul 1963 150.00
❑ BLP-4125 [M] Good Gracious 1963 80.00
❑ BLP-4263 [M] Alligator Boogaloo 1967 80.00
❑ BLP-4271 [M] Mr. Shing-a-Ling 1968 120.00
❑ BLP-5021 [10] Lou Donaldson Quintet/Quartet 1953 500.00
❑ BLP-5030 [10] Lou Donaldson-Clifford Brown 1954 500.00
❑ BLP-5055 [10] Lou Donaldson Sextet, Volume 2 1955 500.00
❑ BST-84025 [S] The Time Is Right 1960 100.00
*—With W. 63rd St. address on label*
❑ BST-84025 [S] The Time Is Right 1963 50.00
*—With New York, USA address on label*
❑ BST-84036 [S] Sunny Side Up 1960 100.00
*—With W. 63rd St. address on label*
❑ BST-84036 [S] Sunny Side Up 1963 50.00
*—With New York, USA address on label*
❑ BST-84053 [S] Light Foot 1960 100.00
*—With W. 63rd St. address on label*
❑ BST-84053 [S] Light Foot 1963 50.00
*—With New York, USA address on label*
❑ BST-84066 [S] Here 'Tis 1961 100.00
*—With W. 63rd St. address on label*
❑ BST-84066 [S] Here 'Tis 1963 50.00
*—With New York, USA address on label*
❑ BST-84079 [S] Gravy Train 1962 100.00
*—With W. 63rd St. address on label*
❑ BST-84079 [S] Gravy Train 1963 50.00
*—With New York, USA address on label*
❑ BST-84108 [S] The Natural Soul 1963 60.00
*—With "New York, USA" on label*
❑ BST-84125 [S] Good Gracious 1963 50.00
*—With "New York, USA" on label*
❑ BST-84263 [S] Alligator Boogaloo 1967 50.00
*—With "A Division of Liberty Records" on label*
❑ BST-84271 [S] Mr. Shing-a-Ling 1968 50.00
*—With "A Division of Liberty Records" on label*
❑ BST-84280 Midnight Creeper 1968 60.00
*—"A Division of Liberty Records" on label*
❑ BST-84299 Say It Loud! 1969 50.00
*—With "A Division of Liberty Records" on label*
❑ BST-84318 Hot Dog 1969 50.00
*—With "A Division of Liberty Records" on label*

CADET

❑ LP-724 [M] Signifyin' 1966 20.00
*—Reissue of Argo 724*
❑ LP-734 [M] Possum Head 1966 20.00
*—Reissue of Argo 734*
❑ LP-747 [M] Cole Slaw 1966 20.00
*—Reissue of Argo 747*
❑ LP-759 [M] Musty Rusty 1966 25.00
❑ LPS-759 [S] Musty Rusty 1966 25.00
❑ LP-768 [M] Rough House Blues 1966 25.00
❑ LPS-768 [S] Rough House Blues 1966 25.00
❑ LP-789 [M] Blowin' in the Wind 1967 25.00
❑ LPS-789 [S] Blowin' in the Wind 1967 20.00
❑ LPS-815 Lou Donaldson At His Best 1969 20.00
❑ LPS-842 Fried Buzzard — Lou Donaldson Live 1970 20.00

**DONATO, JOAO**

BLUE THUMB

❑ BT-8821 A Bad Donato 1970 20.00
*—Distributed by Capitol*

RCA VICTOR

❑ LSP-3473 [S] The New Sound of Brazil 1966 20.00

**DONEGAN, DOROTHY**

CAPITOL

❑ ST 1135 [S] Dorothy Donegan Live! 1959 40.00
❑ T 1135 [M] Dorothy Donegan Live! 1959 30.00
❑ ST 1226 [S] Donnybrook with Dorothy 1960 40.00
❑ T 1226 [M] Donnybrook with Dorothy 1960 30.00

JUBILEE

❑ LP-11 [10] Dorothy Donegan Trio 1955 80.00
❑ JLP-1013 [M] September Song 1956 60.00

MGM

❑ E-278 [10] Dorothy Donegan Piano 1954 80.00

ROULETTE

❑ R-25010 [M] Dorothy Donegan at the Embers 1957 50.00
❑ R-25154 [M] It Happened One Night 1961 30.00
❑ SR-25154 [S] It Happened One Night 1961 40.00

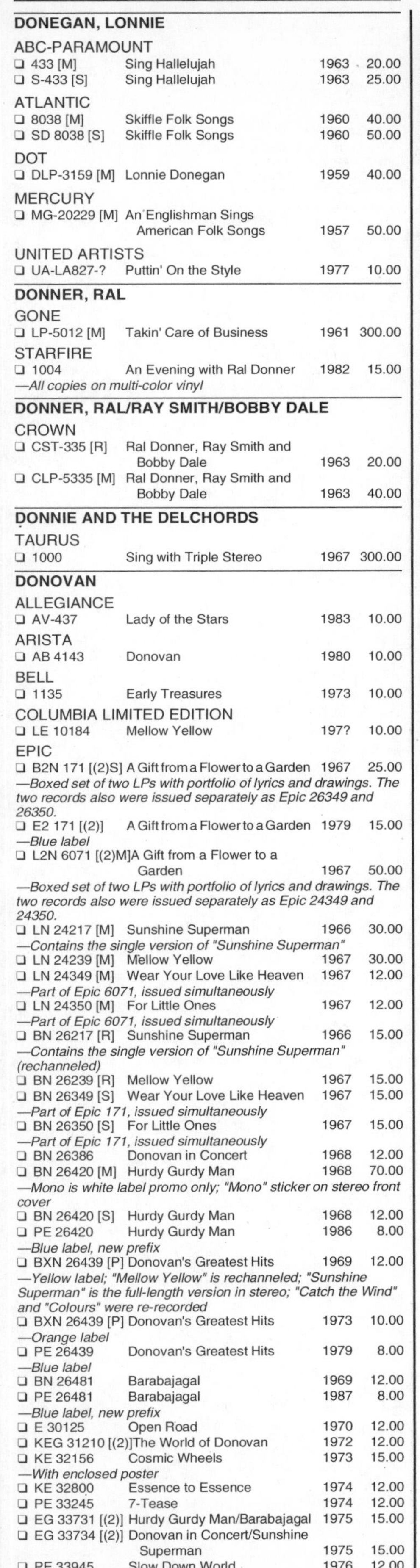

| Number | Title (A Side/B Side) | Yr | NM |
|---|---|---|---|
| **DONEGAN, LONNIE** | | | |
| ABC-PARAMOUNT | | | |
| 433 [M] | Sing Hallelujah | 1963 | 20.00 |
| S-433 [S] | Sing Hallelujah | 1963 | 25.00 |
| ATLANTIC | | | |
| 8038 [M] | Skiffle Folk Songs | 1960 | 40.00 |
| SD 8038 [S] | Skiffle Folk Songs | 1960 | 50.00 |
| DOT | | | |
| DLP-3159 [M] | Lonnie Donegan | 1959 | 40.00 |
| MERCURY | | | |
| MG-20229 [M] | An Englishman Sings American Folk Songs | 1957 | 50.00 |
| UNITED ARTISTS | | | |
| UA-LA827-? | Puttin' On the Style | 1977 | 10.00 |
| **DONNER, RAL** | | | |
| GONE | | | |
| LP-5012 [M] | Takin' Care of Business | 1961 | 300.00 |
| STARFIRE | | | |
| 1004 | An Evening with Ral Donner | 1982 | 15.00 |
| *—All copies on multi-color vinyl* | | | |
| **DONNER, RAL/RAY SMITH/BOBBY DALE** | | | |
| CROWN | | | |
| CST-335 [R] | Ral Donner, Ray Smith and Bobby Dale | 1963 | 20.00 |
| CLP-5335 [M] | Ral Donner, Ray Smith and Bobby Dale | 1963 | 40.00 |
| **DONNIE AND THE DELCHORDS** | | | |
| TAURUS | | | |
| 1000 | Sing with Triple Stereo | 1967 | 300.00 |
| **DONOVAN** | | | |
| ALLEGIANCE | | | |
| AV-437 | Lady of the Stars | 1983 | 10.00 |
| ARISTA | | | |
| AB 4143 | Donovan | 1980 | 10.00 |
| BELL | | | |
| 1135 | Early Treasures | 1973 | 10.00 |
| COLUMBIA LIMITED EDITION | | | |
| LE 10184 | Mellow Yellow | 197? | 10.00 |
| EPIC | | | |
| B2N 171 [(2)S] | A Gift from a Flower to a Garden | 1967 | 25.00 |
| *—Boxed set of two LPs with portfolio of lyrics and drawings. The two records also were issued separately as Epic 26349 and 26350.* | | | |
| E2 171 [(2)] | A Gift from a Flower to a Garden | 1979 | 15.00 |
| *—Blue label* | | | |
| L2N 6071 [(2)M] | A Gift from a Flower to a Garden | 1967 | 50.00 |
| *—Boxed set of two LPs with portfolio of lyrics and drawings. The two records also were issued separately as Epic 24349 and 24350.* | | | |
| LN 24217 [M] | Sunshine Superman | 1966 | 30.00 |
| *—Contains the single version of "Sunshine Superman"* | | | |
| LN 24239 [M] | Mellow Yellow | 1967 | 30.00 |
| LN 24349 [M] | Wear Your Love Like Heaven | 1967 | 12.00 |
| *—Part of Epic 6071, issued simultaneously* | | | |
| LN 24350 [M] | For Little Ones | 1967 | 12.00 |
| *—Part of Epic 6071, issued simultaneously* | | | |
| BN 26217 [R] | Sunshine Superman | 1966 | 15.00 |
| *—Contains the single version of "Sunshine Superman" (rechanneled)* | | | |
| BN 26239 [R] | Mellow Yellow | 1967 | 15.00 |
| BN 26349 [S] | Wear Your Love Like Heaven | 1967 | 15.00 |
| *—Part of Epic 171, issued simultaneously* | | | |
| BN 26350 [S] | For Little Ones | 1967 | 15.00 |
| *—Part of Epic 171, issued simultaneously* | | | |
| BN 26386 | Donovan in Concert | 1968 | 12.00 |
| BN 26420 [M] | Hurdy Gurdy Man | 1968 | 70.00 |
| *—Mono is white label promo only; "Mono" sticker on stereo front cover* | | | |
| BN 26420 [S] | Hurdy Gurdy Man | 1968 | 12.00 |
| PE 26420 | Hurdy Gurdy Man | 1986 | 8.00 |
| *—Blue label, new prefix* | | | |
| BXN 26439 [P] | Donovan's Greatest Hits | 1969 | 12.00 |
| *—Yellow label; "Mellow Yellow" is rechanneled; "Sunshine Superman" is the full-length version in stereo; "Catch the Wind" and "Colours" were re-recorded* | | | |
| BXN 26439 [P] | Donovan's Greatest Hits | 1973 | 10.00 |
| *—Orange label* | | | |
| PE 26439 | Donovan's Greatest Hits | 1979 | 8.00 |
| *—Blue label* | | | |
| BN 26481 | Barabajagal | 1969 | 12.00 |
| PE 26481 | Barabajagal | 1987 | 8.00 |
| *—Blue label, new prefix* | | | |
| E 30125 | Open Road | 1970 | 12.00 |
| KEG 31210 [(2)] | The World of Donovan | 1972 | 12.00 |
| KE 32156 | Cosmic Wheels | 1973 | 15.00 |
| *—With enclosed poster* | | | |
| KE 32800 | Essence to Essence | 1974 | 12.00 |
| PE 33245 | 7-Tease | 1974 | 12.00 |
| EG 33731 [(2)] | Hurdy Gurdy Man/Barabajagal | 1975 | 15.00 |
| EG 33734 [(2)] | Donovan in Concert/Sunshine Superman | 1975 | 15.00 |
| PE 33945 | Slow Down World | 1976 | 12.00 |

Donovan, *Fairy Tale,* Hickory LP 127, 1966, mono, $20.

| Number | Title (A Side/B Side) | Yr | NM |
|---|---|---|---|
| HICKORY | | | |
| LPM-123 [M] | Catch the Wind | 1965 | 25.00 |
| *—Most pressings have Donovan facing left, so he is correctly strumming his guitar with his right hand* | | | |
| LPM-123 [M] | Catch the Wind | 1965 | 40.00 |
| *—First pressings have Donovan facing right, so it appears as if he's strumming his guitar with his left hand* | | | |
| LPS-123 [R] | Catch the Wind | 1965 | 25.00 |
| LPM-127 [M] | Fairy Tale | 1965 | 20.00 |
| LPS-127 [P] | Fairy Tale | 1965 | 25.00 |
| *—"Colours" is rechanneled* | | | |
| LPM-135 [M] | The Real Donovan | 1966 | 20.00 |
| LPS-135 [P] | The Real Donovan | 1966 | 25.00 |
| *—Half stereo, including "Colours," the rest rechanneled.* | | | |
| LPS-143 [P] | Like It Is, Was and Evermore Shall Be | 1968 | 20.00 |
| LPS-149 [P] | The Best of Donovan | 1969 | 20.00 |
| JANUS | | | |
| 3022 | Donovan P. Leitch | 1970 | 10.00 |
| 3025 | Hear Me Now | 1971 | 10.00 |
| KORY | | | |
| 3012 | Early Treasures | 1977 | 8.00 |
| PYE | | | |
| 502 | Donovan | 1975 | 10.00 |
| **DOOBIE BROTHERS, THE** | | | |
| CAPITOL | | | |
| C1-90371 | Cycles | 1989 | 12.00 |
| C1-594623 | Brotherhood | 1991 | 20.00 |
| *—U.S. vinyl version available only through Columbia House* | | | |
| DCC COMPACT CLASSICS | | | |
| LPZ-2053 | Best of the Doobies | 1998 | 40.00 |
| *—Audiophile vinyl* | | | |
| MOBILE FIDELITY | | | |
| 1-122 | Takin' It to the Streets | 1983 | 40.00 |
| *—Audiophile vinyl* | | | |
| NAUTILUS | | | |
| NR-5 | The Captain and Me | 1980 | 40.00 |
| *—Audiophile vinyl* | | | |
| NR-18 | Minute by Minute | 1981 | 30.00 |
| *—Audiophile vinyl* | | | |
| PICKWICK | | | |
| SPC-3721 | Introducing the Doobie Brothers | 1980 | 40.00 |
| *—Pre-Warner Bros. recordings; withdrawn shortly after release* | | | |
| WARNER BROS. | | | |
| WS 1919 | The Doobie Brothers | 1971 | 15.00 |
| *—Green label original* | | | |
| WS 1919 | The Doobie Brothers | 1973 | 10.00 |
| *—"Burbank" label* | | | |
| BS 2634 | Toulouse Street | 1972 | 15.00 |
| *—Green label original* | | | |
| BS 2634 | Toulouse Street | 1973 | 10.00 |
| *—"Burbank" label* | | | |
| BS4 2634 [Q] | Toulouse Street | 1975 | 25.00 |
| BS 2694 | The Captain and Me | 1973 | 12.00 |
| *—"Burbank" label* | | | |
| BS 2694 | The Captain and Me | 1973 | 20.00 |
| *—Green label* | | | |
| BS 2694 | The Captain and Me | 1979 | 8.00 |
| *—Cream label* | | | |
| BS4 2694 [Q] | The Captain and Me | 1974 | 20.00 |
| W 2750 | What Were Once Vices Are Now Habits | 1974 | 10.00 |
| *—"Burbank" label* | | | |
| W 2750 | What Were Once Vices Are Now Habits | 1979 | 8.00 |
| *—Cream label* | | | |
| W4 2750 [Q] | What Were Once Vices Are Now Habits | 1974 | 20.00 |
| BS 2835 | Stampede | 1975 | 10.00 |
| *—"Burbank" label* | | | |
| BS 2835 | Stampede | 1979 | 8.00 |
| *—Cream label* | | | |
| BS4 2835 [Q] | Stampede | 1975 | 20.00 |
| BS 2899 | Takin' It to the Streets | 1976 | 10.00 |
| *—"Burbank" label* | | | |
| BS 2899 | Takin' It to the Streets | 1979 | 8.00 |
| *—Cream label* | | | |
| BS 2978 | Best of the Doobies | 1976 | 12.00 |
| BSK 3045 | Livin' on the Fault Line | 1977 | 8.00 |
| *—Cream label* | | | |
| BSK 3045 | Livin' on the Fault Line | 1977 | 10.00 |
| *—"Burbank" label* | | | |
| BSK 3112 | Best of the Doobies | 1978 | 10.00 |
| *—"Burbank" label* | | | |
| BSK 3112 | Best of the Doobies | 1979 | 8.00 |
| *—Cream label* | | | |
| BSK 3193 | Minute by Minute | 1978 | 10.00 |
| HS 3452 | One Step Closer | 1980 | 10.00 |
| BSK 3612 | Best of the Doobies, Volume 2 | 1981 | 10.00 |
| 23772 [(2)] | Farewell Tour | 1983 | 15.00 |

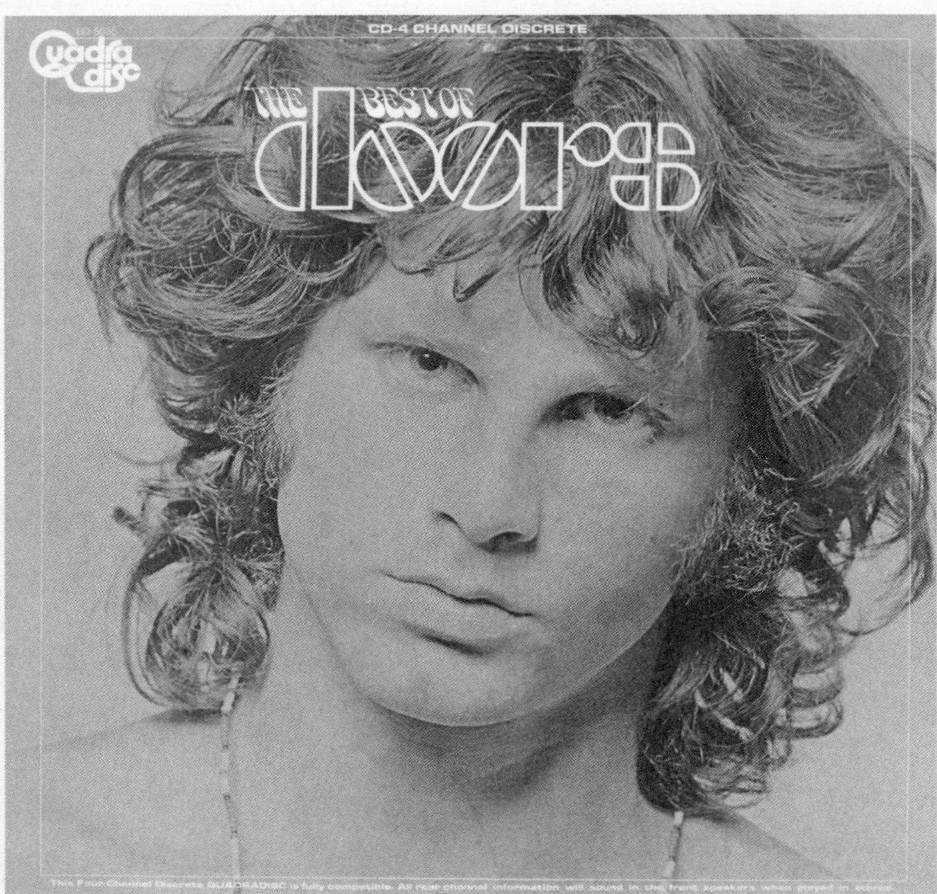


The Doors, *The Best of the Doors,* Elektra EQ-5035, 1973, butterfly label, $20.

**Number | Title (A Side/B Side) | Yr | NM**

## DOORS, THE

### DCC COMPACT CLASSICS
❑ LPZ-2045 Strange Days 1997 80.00
*—Audiophile vinyl*
❑ LPZ-2046 The Doors 1997 150.00
*—Audiophile vinyl*
❑ LPZ-2049 Waiting for the Sun 1998 120.00
*—Audiophile vinyl*
❑ LPZ-2050 L.A. Woman 1998 150.00
*—Audiophile vinyl*

### ELEKTRA
❑ 5E-502 An American Prayer 1978 12.00
*—Butterfly labels*
❑ 5E-502 An American Prayer 1980 10.00
*—Red labels with Warner Communications logo in lower right*
❑ 5E-502 An American Prayer 1983 8.00
*—Red and black labels*
❑ 5E-502 SP DJ [DJ]An American Prayer 1978 60.00
*—White label; with sticker on cover "This album has been edited for broadcast from..."; only six tracks are on Side One rather than the eight on stock copies*
❑ 5E-515 Greatest Hits 1980 10.00
*—Red labels with Warner Communications logo in lower right*
❑ 5E-515 Greatest Hits 1983 8.00
*—Red and black labels*
❑ EKL-4007 [M] The Doors 1967 200.00
❑ EKL-4014 [M] Strange Days 1967 600.00
*—Value assumes the record is mono. There are two different covers for this; some copies have mono numbers on the two covers and the stereo number on the spine, and others have the mono number on the spine and stereo number on front and back covers.*
❑ EKL-4024 [M] Waiting for the Sun 1968 1000.
❑ 6E-5035 [S] Best of the Doors 1977 20.00
*—Columbia Record Club edition in stereo with the quad markings blacked out on the cover; note different prefix*
❑ EQ-5035 [Q] Best of the Doors 1973 20.00
*—Butterfly labels*
❑ EQ-5035 [Q] Best of the Doors 1980 12.00
*—Red labels with Warner Communications logo in lower right*
❑ EQ-5035 [Q] Best of the Doors 1983 10.00
*—Red and black labels*
❑ 8E-6001 [(2)] Weird Scenes Inside the Gold Mine 1972 20.00
*—Butterfly labels*
❑ 8E-6001 [(2)] Weird Scenes Inside the Gold Mine 1980 12.00
*—Red labels with Warner Communications logo in lower right*

**Number | Title (A Side/B Side) | Yr | NM**

❑ 8E-6001 [(2)] Weird Scenes Inside the Gold Mine 1983 10.00
*—Red and black labels*
❑ EKS-9002 [(2)] Absolutely Live 1970 25.00
*—Butterfly labels*
❑ EKS-9002 [(2)] Absolutely Live 1980 15.00
*—Red labels with Warner Communications logo in lower right*
❑ EKS-9002 [(2)] Absolutely Live 1983 12.00
*—Red and black labels*
❑ EKS-9002 [(2)DJ]Absolutely Live 1970 80.00
*—White label promo*
❑ 60269 Alive, She Cried 1984 12.00
❑ 60345 [(2)] The Best of the Doors 1985 15.00
❑ 60345 [(2)] The Best of the Doors 1985 40.00
*—White label promo on audiophile vinyl*
❑ 60417 Classics 1986 12.00
❑ 60741 [EP] Live at the Hollywood Bowl 1988 12.00
❑ E1-61047 The Doors 1991 100.00
*—Soundtrack from the movie; only available on US vinyl from Columbia House*
❑ 61812 An American Prayer 1995 15.00
*—Remastered and lengthened version of 5E-502*
❑ EKS-74007 [S] The Doors 1967 50.00
*—Brown labels*
❑ EKS-74007 [S] The Doors 1969 15.00
*—Red labels with large stylized "E"*
❑ EKS-74007 [S] The Doors 1971 12.00
*—Butterfly labels*
❑ EKS-74007 [S] The Doors 1980 10.00
*—Red labels with Warner Communications logo in lower right*
❑ EKS-74007 [S] The Doors 1983 8.00
*—Red and black labels*
❑ EKS-74014 [S] Strange Days 1967 40.00
*—Brown labels*
❑ EKS-74014 [S] Strange Days 1969 15.00
*—Red labels with large stylized "E"*
❑ EKS-74014 [S] Strange Days 1971 12.00
*—Butterfly labels*
❑ EKS-74014 [S] Strange Days 1980 10.00
*—Red labels with Warner Communications logo in lower right*
❑ EKS-74014 [S] Strange Days 1983 8.00
*—Red and black labels*
❑ EKS-74024 [S] Waiting for the Sun 1968 30.00
*—Brown labels*
❑ EKS-74024 [S] Waiting for the Sun 1968 150.00
*—White label promo*
❑ EKS-74024 [S] Waiting for the Sun 1969 15.00
*—Red labels with large stylized "E"*

**Number | Title (A Side/B Side) | Yr | NM**

❑ EKS-74024 [S] Waiting for the Sun 1971 12.00
*—Butterfly labels*
❑ EKS-74024 [S] Waiting for the Sun 1980 10.00
*—Red labels with Warner Communications logo in lower right*
❑ EKS-74024 [S] Waiting for the Sun 1983 8.00
*—Red and black labels*
❑ EKS-74079 13 1970 15.00
*—Butterfly labels*
❑ EKS-74079 13 1980 10.00
*—Red labels with Warner Communications logo in lower right*
❑ EKS-74079 13 1983 8.00
*—Red and black labels*
❑ EKS-74079 [DJ]13 1970 40.00
*—White label promo*
❑ EKS-75005 The Soft Parade 1969 20.00
*—Red labels with large stylized "E"*
❑ EKS-75005 The Soft Parade 1969 50.00
*—Brown or tan labels*
❑ EKS-75005 The Soft Parade 1971 12.00
*—Butterfly labels*
❑ EKS-75005 The Soft Parade 1980 10.00
*—Red labels with Warner Communications logo in lower right*
❑ EKS-75005 The Soft Parade 1983 8.00
*—Red and black labels*
❑ EKS-75007 Morrison Hotel 1970 25.00
*—Red labels with large stylized "E"*
❑ EKS-75007 Morrison Hotel 1970 60.00
*—Brown or tan labels*
❑ EKS-75007 Morrison Hotel 1971 12.00
*—Butterfly labels*
❑ EKS-75007 Morrison Hotel 1980 10.00
*—Red labels with Warner Communications logo in lower right*
❑ EKS-75007 Morrison Hotel 1983 8.00
*—Red and black labels*
❑ EKS-75007 [DJ]Morrison Hotel 1970 100.00
*—White label promo*
❑ EKS-75011 L.A. Woman 197? 12.00
*—Butterfly label, standard cover*
❑ EKS-75011 L.A. Woman 1971 50.00
*—With see-through window on cover and yellow innersleeve with photo of Jim Morrison on a cross*
❑ EKS-75011 L.A. Woman 1980 10.00
*—Red labels with Warner Communications logo in lower right*
❑ EKS-75011 L.A. Woman 1983 8.00
*—Red and black labels*
❑ EKS-75011 [DJ]L.A. Woman 1971 100.00
*—White label promo*
❑ EKS-75017 Other Voices 1971 15.00
❑ EKS-75038 Full Circle 1972 15.00

### MOBILE FIDELITY
❑ 1-051 The Doors 1980 60.00
*—Audiophile vinyl*

## DORFMAN, ANIA

### RCA VICTOR RED SEAL
❑ LSC-2207 [S] Schumann: Carnaval 1959 25.00
*—Original with "shaded dog" label*

## DORHAM, KENNY

### ABC-PARAMOUNT
❑ ABC-122 [M] Kenny Dorham and the Jazz Prophets 1956 80.00

### BLUE NOTE
❑ BLP-1524 [M] 'Round About Midnight at the Café Bohemia 1956 150.00
*—Regular version with Lexington Ave. address on label*
❑ BLP-1524 [M] 'Round About Midnight at the Café Bohemia 1956 200.00
*—"Deep groove" version (deep indentation under label on both sides)*
❑ BLP-1524 [M] 'Round About Midnight at the Café Bohemia 1963 30.00
*—"New York, USA" address on label*
❑ BLP-1535 [M] Kenny Dorham Octet/Sextet 1956 150.00
*—Regular version with Lexington Ave. address on label*
❑ BLP-1535 [M] Kenny Dorham Octet/Sextet 1956 200.00
*—"Deep groove" version (deep indentation under label on both sides)*
❑ BLP-1535 [M] Kenny Dorham Octet/Sextet 1963 30.00
*—"New York, USA" address on label*
❑ BLP-4063 [M] Whistle Stop 1961 80.00
*—W. 63rd St. address on label*
❑ BLP-4063 [M] Whistle Stop 1963 30.00
*—"New York, USA" address on label*
❑ BLP-4127 [M] Una Mas 1963 30.00
*—"New York, USA" address on label*
❑ BLP-4181 [M] Trompeta Toccata 1964 30.00
*—"New York, USA" address on label*
❑ BLP-5055 [10] Afro-Cuban Holiday 1955 300.00
❑ BST-84063 [S] Whistle Stop 1961 60.00
*—W. 63rd St. address on label*
❑ BST-84063 [S] Whistle Stop 1963 25.00
*—"New York, USA" address on label*
❑ BST-84127 [S] Una Mas 1963 40.00
*—"New York, USA" address on label*
❑ BST-84181 [S] Trompeta Toccata 1964 40.00
*—"New York, USA" address on label*

### DEBUT
❑ DLP-9 [10] Kenny Dorham Quintet 1954 300.00

### JARO
❑ JAM-5007 [M] The Arrival of Kenny Dorham 1960 400.00

| Number | Title (A Side/B Side) | Yr | NM |
|---|---|---|---|
| ❑ JAS-8007 [S] | The Arrival of Kenny Dorham | 1960 | 400.00 |

### JAZZLAND

| Number | Title (A Side/B Side) | Yr | NM |
|---|---|---|---|
| ❑ JLP-3 [M] | The Swingers | 1960 | 40.00 |
| ❑ JLP-14 [M] | Kenny Dorham and Friends | 1960 | 40.00 |
| ❑ JLP-82 [M] | Kenny Dorham and Friends | 1962 | 20.00 |
| ❑ JLP-903 [S] | The Swingers | 1960 | 50.00 |
| ❑ JLP-914 [S] | Kenny Dorham and Friends | 1960 | 50.00 |
| ❑ JLP-982 [S] | Kenny Dorham and Friends | 1962 | 25.00 |

### NEW JAZZ

| Number | Title (A Side/B Side) | Yr | NM |
|---|---|---|---|
| ❑ NJLP-8225 [M] | Quiet Kenny | 1959 | 80.00 |
| *—Purple label* | | | |
| ❑ NJLP-8225 [M] | Quiet Kenny | 1965 | 25.00 |
| *—Blue label, trident logo at right* | | | |

### PACIFIC JAZZ

| Number | Title (A Side/B Side) | Yr | NM |
|---|---|---|---|
| ❑ PJ-41 [M] | Inta Somethin' — Recorded Live at the Jazz Workshop | 1962 | 30.00 |
| ❑ ST-41 [S] | Inta Somethin' — Recorded Live at the Jazz Workshop | 1962 | 40.00 |

### PRESTIGE

| Number | Title (A Side/B Side) | Yr | NM |
|---|---|---|---|
| ❑ PRST-7754 | Kenny Dorham 1959 | 1970 | 20.00 |

### RIVERSIDE

| Number | Title (A Side/B Side) | Yr | NM |
|---|---|---|---|
| ❑ RLP 12-239 [M] | Jazz Contrasts | 1957 | 80.00 |
| *—White label, blue print* | | | |
| ❑ RLP 12-239 [M] | Jazz Contrasts | 1959 | 40.00 |
| *—Blue label, microphone logo* | | | |
| ❑ RLP 12-255 [M] | 2 Horns 2 Rhythm | 1957 | 50.00 |
| ❑ RLP 12-275 [M] | This Is the Moment! | 1958 | 50.00 |
| ❑ RLP 12-297 [M] | Blue Spring | 1959 | 50.00 |
| ❑ RLP-1105 [S] | Jazz Contrasts | 1959 | 30.00 |
| *—Black label, microphone logo* | | | |
| ❑ RLP-1139 [S] | Blue Spring | 1959 | 40.00 |

### TIME

| Number | Title (A Side/B Side) | Yr | NM |
|---|---|---|---|
| ❑ S-2004 [S] | Jazz Contemporary | 1960 | 50.00 |
| ❑ S-2024 [S] | Show Boat | 1960 | 50.00 |
| ❑ 52004 [M] | Jazz Contemporary | 1960 | 40.00 |
| ❑ 52024 [M] | Show Boat | 1960 | 40.00 |

### UNITED ARTISTS

| Number | Title (A Side/B Side) | Yr | NM |
|---|---|---|---|
| ❑ UAS-5631 | Matador | 1971 | 20.00 |
| *—Reissue of 15007* | | | |
| ❑ UAJ-14007 [M] | Matador | 1962 | 30.00 |
| ❑ UAJS-15007 [S] | Matador | 1962 | 40.00 |

## DORHAM, KENNY/CLARK TERRY

### JAZZLAND

| Number | Title (A Side/B Side) | Yr | NM |
|---|---|---|---|
| ❑ JLP-10 [M] | Top Trumpets | 1960 | 40.00 |
| ❑ JLP-910 [S] | Top Trumpets | 1960 | 50.00 |

## DOROUGH, BOB

### BETHLEHEM

| Number | Title (A Side/B Side) | Yr | NM |
|---|---|---|---|
| ❑ BCP-11 [M] | Devil May Care | 1955 | 120.00 |
| ❑ BCP-6023 | Yardbird Suite | 197? | 20.00 |
| *—Reissue of 11, distributed by RCA Victor* | | | |

### FOCUS

| Number | Title (A Side/B Side) | Yr | NM |
|---|---|---|---|
| ❑ FL-336 [M] | Better Than Anything | 1967 | 25.00 |
| ❑ FS-336 [S] | Better Than Anything | 1967 | 20.00 |

### LAISSEZ-FAIRE

| Number | Title (A Side/B Side) | Yr | NM |
|---|---|---|---|
| ❑ 02 | Beginning to See the Light | 1976 | 20.00 |

### MUSIC MINUS ONE

| Number | Title (A Side/B Side) | Yr | NM |
|---|---|---|---|
| ❑ 225 [M] | Oliver | 1963 | 25.00 |

## DORS, DIANA

### COLUMBIA

| Number | Title (A Side/B Side) | Yr | NM |
|---|---|---|---|
| ❑ CL 1436 [M] | Swingin' Dors | 1960 | 80.00 |
| ❑ CS 8232 [S] | Swingin' Dors | 1960 | 100.00 |

## DORSEY, JIMMY

### COLUMBIA

| Number | Title (A Side/B Side) | Yr | NM |
|---|---|---|---|
| ❑ CL 608 [M] | Dixie by Dorsey | 1955 | 30.00 |
| *—Red and black label with six "eye" logos* | | | |
| ❑ CL 608 [M] | Dixie by Dorsey | 1955 | 40.00 |
| *—Maroon label with gold print* | | | |
| ❑ CL 6095 [10] | Dixie by Dorsey | 1950 | 50.00 |
| ❑ CL 6114 [10] | Dorseyland Band | 1950 | 50.00 |

### CORAL

| Number | Title (A Side/B Side) | Yr | NM |
|---|---|---|---|
| ❑ CRL 56004 [10] | Contrasting Music, Volume 1 | 1950 | 50.00 |
| ❑ CRL 56008 [10] | Contrasting Music, Volume 2 | 1950 | 50.00 |
| ❑ CRL 56033 [10] | Gershwin Music | 1950 | 50.00 |

### DECCA

| Number | Title (A Side/B Side) | Yr | NM |
|---|---|---|---|
| ❑ DL 4853 [M] | Jimmy Dorsey's Greatest Hits | 1967 | 20.00 |
| ❑ DL 5091 [10] | Latin American Favorites | 1950 | 50.00 |
| ❑ DL 8153 [M] | Latin American Favorites | 1955 | 30.00 |
| *—Black label, silver print* | | | |
| ❑ DL 8609 [M] | The Great Jimmy Dorsey | 1957 | 25.00 |
| *—Black label, silver print* | | | |

### DOT

| Number | Title (A Side/B Side) | Yr | NM |
|---|---|---|---|
| ❑ DLP-3437 [M] | So Rare | 1962 | 20.00 |
| *—Reissue of Fraternity LP* | | | |

### FRATERNITY

| Number | Title (A Side/B Side) | Yr | NM |
|---|---|---|---|
| ❑ F-1008 [M] | Fabulous Jimmy Dorsey | 1957 | 30.00 |

### LION

| Number | Title (A Side/B Side) | Yr | NM |
|---|---|---|---|
| ❑ L-70063 [M] | Jimmy Dorsey and His Orchestra | 1958 | 20.00 |

## DORSEY, LEE

### AMY

| Number | Title (A Side/B Side) | Yr | NM |
|---|---|---|---|
| ❑ 8010 [M] | Ride Your Pony | 1966 | 30.00 |
| ❑ 8010-S [S] | Ride Your Pony | 1966 | 40.00 |
| ❑ 8011 [M] | The New Lee Dorsey/Working in the Coal Mine-Holy Cow | 1966 | 25.00 |
| ❑ 8011-S [S] | The New Lee Dorsey/Working in the Coal Mine-Holy Cow | 1966 | 30.00 |

### ARISTA

| Number | Title (A Side/B Side) | Yr | NM |
|---|---|---|---|
| ❑ AL 8387 | Holy Cow! The Best of Lee Dorsey | 1985 | 10.00 |

### FURY

| Number | Title (A Side/B Side) | Yr | NM |
|---|---|---|---|
| ❑ 1002 [M] | Ya Ya | 1962 | 300.00 |

### POLYDOR

| Number | Title (A Side/B Side) | Yr | NM |
|---|---|---|---|
| ❑ 24-4024 | Yes We Can | 1970 | 12.00 |

### SPHERE SOUND

| Number | Title (A Side/B Side) | Yr | NM |
|---|---|---|---|
| ❑ SR-7003 [M] | Ya Ya | 196? | 100.00 |
| *—Reissue of Fury 1002* | | | |
| ❑ SSR-7003 [R] | Ya Ya | 196? | 50.00 |
| *—Rechanneled reissue of Fury 1002* | | | |

## DORSEY, TOMMY

On albums with asterisks (*) after them, some of the tracks feature FRANK SINATRA as lead vocalist.

### DECCA

| Number | Title (A Side/B Side) | Yr | NM |
|---|---|---|---|
| ❑ DL 5317 [10] | Tommy Dorsey Plays Howard Dietz | 1951 | 50.00 |
| ❑ DL 5448 [10] | In a Sentimental Mood | 1952 | 50.00 |
| ❑ DL 5449 [10] | Tenderly | 1952 | 50.00 |
| ❑ DL 5452 [10] | Your Invitation to Dance | 1952 | 50.00 |

### RCA VICTOR

| Number | Title (A Side/B Side) | Yr | NM |
|---|---|---|---|
| ❑ LPT-10 [M] | Getting Sentimental with Tommy Dorsey* | 1951 | 80.00 |
| ❑ ALPT-15 [M] | All Time Hits* | 1951 | 80.00 |
| ❑ LPM-22 [10] | Tommy Dorsey Plays Cole Porter for Dancing | 1951 | 50.00 |
| ❑ LPM-1229 [M] | Yes Indeed* | 1956 | 50.00 |
| ❑ LPM-1425 [M] | Tommy Dorsey Plays Cole Porter and Jerome Kern | 1956 | 25.00 |
| ❑ LPM-1432 [M] | Tribute to Dorsey, Volume 1* | 1956 | 40.00 |
| ❑ LPM-1433 [M] | Tribute to Dorsey, Volume 2* | 1956 | 40.00 |
| ❑ LPM-1643 [M] | Having a Wonderful Time* | 1958 | 40.00 |
| ❑ LPT-3005 [M] | This Is Tommy Dorsey* | 1952 | 80.00 |
| ❑ LPT-3018 [10] | This Is Tommy Dorsey | 1952 | 50.00 |
| ❑ LPM-3674 [M] | The Best of Tommy Dorsey* | 1966 | 20.00 |
| ❑ LPM-6003 [(2)M] | That Sentimental Gentleman* | 1957 | 80.00 |
| *—Box set* | | | |
| ❑ VPM-6038 [(2)] | This Is Tommy Dorsey* | 1971 | 25.00 |
| ❑ VPM-6064 [(2)] | This Is Tommy Dorsey, Volume 2* | 197? | 25.00 |
| ❑ VPM-6087 [(2)] | This Is Tommy Dorsey and His Clambake Seven | 1973 | 20.00 |
| *—Orange labels* | | | |
| ❑ VPM-6087 [(2)] | This Is Tommy Dorsey and His Clambake Seven | 1977 | 15.00 |
| *—Black labels, dog near top* | | | |

### TIME-LIFE

| Number | Title (A Side/B Side) | Yr | NM |
|---|---|---|---|
| ❑ STBB-02 [(2)] | Big Bands: Tommy Dorsey* | 1983 | 20.00 |
| ❑ STBB-19 [(2)] | Big Bands: Sentimental Genrtleman* | 1985 | 20.00 |

### 20TH CENTURY FOX

| Number | Title (A Side/B Side) | Yr | NM |
|---|---|---|---|
| ❑ TCF 101/102 [(2)M] | Tommy Dorsey's Greatest Band | 1959 | 30.00 |
| ❑ FOX 1005 [M] | Tommy Dorsey and His Orchestra: His Greatest Arrangements — His Greatest Band | 196? | 15.00 |
| *—"Million Seller Hits" reissue series* | | | |
| ❑ TFM-3157 [M] | This Is Tommy Dorsey and His Greatest Band, Vol. 1 | 196? | 20.00 |
| ❑ TFM-3158 [M] | This Is Tommy Dorsey and His Greatest Band, Vol. 2 | 196? | 20.00 |

## DORSEY, TOMMY, ORCHESTRA (WARREN COVINGTON, DIRECTOR)

### DECCA

| Number | Title (A Side/B Side) | Yr | NM |
|---|---|---|---|
| ❑ DL 74120 [S] | Dance to the Songs Everybody Knows | 1960 | 20.00 |
| ❑ DL 74130 [S] | Tricky Trombones | 1961 | 20.00 |
| ❑ DL 78802 [S] | The Fabulous Arrangements of Tommy Dorsey | 1958 | 20.00 |
| ❑ DL 78842 [S] | Tea for Two Cha Chas | 1958 | 20.00 |
| ❑ DL 78904 [S] | Dance and Romance | 1959 | 20.00 |
| ❑ DL 78943 [S] | More Tea for Two Cha Chas | 1959 | 20.00 |
| ❑ DL 78980 [S] | It Takes Two to Cha-Cha… | 1959 | 20.00 |
| ❑ DL 78996 [S] | It Takes Two to Bunny Hop.. | 1960 | 20.00 |

## DORSEY BROTHERS, THE

### COLUMBIA

| Number | Title (A Side/B Side) | Yr | NM |
|---|---|---|---|
| ❑ C2L 8 [(2)] | The Fabulous Dorseys in Hi-Fi | 1958 | 40.00 |
| *—Red and black labels with six "eye" logos* | | | |
| ❑ CL 1190 [M] | The Fabulous Dorseys in Hi Fi, Volume I | 1957 | 25.00 |
| *—Red and black labels with six "eye" logos* | | | |
| ❑ CL 1240 [M] | Sentimental and Swinging | 1958 | 25.00 |
| *—Red and black label with six "eye" logos* | | | |

### DECCA

| Number | Title (A Side/B Side) | Yr | NM |
|---|---|---|---|
| ❑ DL 8631 [M] | Dixieland Jazz | 1958 | 25.00 |
| *—Black label, silver print* | | | |
| ❑ DL 8654 [M] | The Swinging Dorseys | 1958 | 25.00 |
| *—Black label, silver print* | | | |

### RIVERSIDE

| Number | Title (A Side/B Side) | Yr | NM |
|---|---|---|---|
| ❑ RLP 12-811 [M] | A Backward Glance | 1958 | 60.00 |
| ❑ RLP-1008 [10] | Jazz of the Roaring Twenties | 1953 | 80.00 |
| ❑ RLP-1051 [10] | The Dorsey Brothers with the California Ramblers | 1955 | 80.00 |

## DOUBLE SIX OF PARIS, THE

### CAPITOL

| Number | Title (A Side/B Side) | Yr | NM |
|---|---|---|---|
| ❑ ST 10259 [S] | The Double Six of Paris | 1961 | 100.00 |
| ❑ T 10259 [M] | The Double Six of Paris | 1961 | 80.00 |

### PHILIPS

| Number | Title (A Side/B Side) | Yr | NM |
|---|---|---|---|
| ❑ PHM 200026 [M] | Swingin' Singin' | 1962 | 40.00 |
| ❑ PHM 200141 [M] | The Double Six of Paris Sings Ray Charles | 1964 | 100.00 |
| ❑ PHS 600026 [S] | Swingin' Singin' | 1962 | 60.00 |
| ❑ PHS 600141 [S] | The Double Six of Paris Sings Ray Charles | 1964 | 150.00 |

## DOUGLAS, GLENN

### DECCA

| Number | Title (A Side/B Side) | Yr | NM |
|---|---|---|---|
| ❑ DL 8748 [M] | Heartbreak Alley | 1958 | 50.00 |

## DOUGLAS, K.C.

### BLUESVILLE

| Number | Title (A Side/B Side) | Yr | NM |
|---|---|---|---|
| ❑ BVLP-1023 [M] | K.C.'s Blues | 1961 | 80.00 |
| *—Blue label, silver print* | | | |
| ❑ BVLP-1023 [M] | K.C.'s Blues | 1964 | 30.00 |
| *—Blue label, trident logo at right* | | | |
| ❑ BVLP-1050 [M] | Big Road Blues | 1962 | 80.00 |
| *—Blue label, silver print* | | | |
| ❑ BVLP-1050 [M] | Big Road Blues | 1964 | 30.00 |
| *—Blue label, trident logo at right* | | | |

### COOK ROAD

| Number | Title (A Side/B Side) | Yr | NM |
|---|---|---|---|
| ❑ 5002 [M] | A Dead Beat Guitar and the Mississippi Blues | 1956 | 500.00 |

## DOUGLAS, LEW

### CARLTON

| Number | Title (A Side/B Side) | Yr | NM |
|---|---|---|---|
| ❑ LP 12-126 [M] | Themes from Motion Pictures and TV | 1960 | 25.00 |

## DOUGLAS, STEVE

### CROWN

| Number | Title (A Side/B Side) | Yr | NM |
|---|---|---|---|
| ❑ CLP-5251 [M] | Twist with Steve Douglas and the Rebel Rousers | 1962 | 20.00 |

### MERCURY

| Number | Title (A Side/B Side) | Yr | NM |
|---|---|---|---|
| ❑ SR-61217 | Reflections in a Golden Horn | 1969 | 25.00 |

## DOUGLAS, TONY

### DOT

| Number | Title (A Side/B Side) | Yr | NM |
|---|---|---|---|
| ❑ DLP-26009 | Thank You for Touching My Life | 1973 | 15.00 |

### PAULA

| Number | Title (A Side/B Side) | Yr | NM |
|---|---|---|---|
| ❑ LP 2198 | Heart | 1967 | 20.00 |

## DOVAL, JIM, AND THE GAUCHOS

### ABC-PARAMOUNT

| Number | Title (A Side/B Side) | Yr | NM |
|---|---|---|---|
| ❑ ABC-506 [M] | The Gauchos Featuring Jim Doval | 1965 | 30.00 |
| ❑ ABCS-506 [S] | The Gauchos Featuring Jim Doval | 1965 | 40.00 |

## DOVE, RONNIE

### DIAMOND

| Number | Title (A Side/B Side) | Yr | NM |
|---|---|---|---|
| ❑ D 5002 [M] | Right or Wrong | 1964 | 20.00 |
| ❑ DS 5002 [S] | Right or Wrong | 1964 | 25.00 |
| ❑ D 5003 [M] | One Kiss for Old Times' Sake | 1965 | 20.00 |
| ❑ DS 5003 [S] | One Kiss for Old Times' Sake | 1965 | 25.00 |
| ❑ D 5004 [M] | I'll Make All Your Dreams Come True | 1965 | 20.00 |
| ❑ DS 5004 [S] | I'll Make All Your Dreams Come True | 1965 | 25.00 |
| ❑ D 5005 [M] | The Best of Ronnie Dove | 1966 | 15.00 |
| ❑ DS 5005 [S] | The Best of Ronnie Dove | 1966 | 20.00 |
| ❑ D 5006 [M] | Ronnie Dove Sings the Hits for You | 1966 | 15.00 |
| ❑ DS 5006 [S] | Ronnie Dove Sings the Hits for You | 1966 | 20.00 |
| ❑ D 5007 [M] | Cry | 1967 | 15.00 |
| ❑ DS 5007 [S] | Cry | 1967 | 20.00 |
| ❑ D-5008 [M] | The Best of Ronnie Dove — Vol. 2 | 1968 | 30.00 |
| ❑ SD-5008 [S] | The Best of Ronnie Dove — Vol. 2 | 1968 | 15.00 |

### POWER PAK

| Number | Title (A Side/B Side) | Yr | NM |
|---|---|---|---|
| ❑ 286 | Greatest Hits | 1975 | 12.00 |

## DOVELLS, THE

### CAMEO

| Number | Title (A Side/B Side) | Yr | NM |
|---|---|---|---|
| ❑ C-1082 [M] | Len Barry Sings with the Dovells | 1965 | 30.00 |

| Number | Title (A Side/B Side) | Yr | NM |
|---|---|---|---|
| ❑ SC-1082 [S] | Len Barry Sings with the Dovells | 1965 | 50.00 |

PARKWAY

| Number | Title (A Side/B Side) | Yr | NM |
|---|---|---|---|
| ❑ P 7006 [M] | The Bristol Stomp | 1961 | 80.00 |
| *—Light orange label* | | | |
| ❑ P 7006 [M] | The Bristol Stomp | 1962 | 50.00 |
| *—Dark orange and yellow label* | | | |
| ❑ P 7010 [M] | All the Hits of the Teen Groups | 1962 | 50.00 |
| ❑ P 7021 [M] | For Your Hully Gully Party | 1962 | 50.00 |
| ❑ P 7025 [M] | You Can't Sit Down | 1963 | 50.00 |

WYNCOTE

| Number | Title (A Side/B Side) | Yr | NM |
|---|---|---|---|
| ❑ SW 9052 [R] | Discotheque | 1965 | 15.00 |
| ❑ W 9052 [M] | Discotheque | 1965 | 20.00 |
| ❑ SW 9114 [R] | The Dovells' Biggest Hits | 1965 | 15.00 |
| ❑ W 9114 [M] | The Dovells' Biggest Hits | 1965 | 20.00 |

**DOWELL, JOE**

SMASH

| Number | Title (A Side/B Side) | Yr | NM |
|---|---|---|---|
| ❑ MGS-27000 [M] | Wooden Heart | 1961 | 40.00 |
| ❑ MGS-27011 [M] | German American Hits | 1962 | 25.00 |
| ❑ SRS-67000 [S] | Wooden Heart | 1961 | 50.00 |
| ❑ SRS-67011 [S] | German American Hits | 1962 | 30.00 |

WING

| Number | Title (A Side/B Side) | Yr | NM |
|---|---|---|---|
| ❑ MGW-12328 [M] | Wooden Heart | 196? | 20.00 |
| ❑ SRW-16328 [S] | Wooden Heart | 196? | 20.00 |

**DOWLING, CHET, AND BILL MINKIN**

COLUMBIA

| Number | Title (A Side/B Side) | Yr | NM |
|---|---|---|---|
| ❑ CL 2776 [M] | Senator Bobby's Christmas Party | 1967 | 20.00 |
| ❑ CS 9576 [S] | Senator Bobby's Christmas Party | 1967 | 20.00 |

**DOWNS, HUGH**

EPIC

| Number | Title (A Side/B Side) | Yr | NM |
|---|---|---|---|
| ❑ BN 541 [S] | An Evening with Hugh Downs | 1961 | 30.00 |
| ❑ LN 3597 [M] | An Evening with Hugh Downs | 1961 | 25.00 |

**DOYLE, BOBBY, THREE** KENNY ROGERS was in this group.

COLUMBIA

| Number | Title (A Side/B Side) | Yr | NM |
|---|---|---|---|
| ❑ CL 1858 [M] | In a Most Unusual Way | 1962 | 40.00 |
| ❑ CS 8658 [S] | In a Most Unusual Way | 1962 | 50.00 |

**DOYLE, MIKE**

FLEETWOOD

| Number | Title (A Side/B Side) | Yr | NM |
|---|---|---|---|
| ❑ FLP-3018 [M] | The Secrets of Surfing | 1963 | 120.00 |

**DOZIER, GENE, AND THE BROTHERHOOD**

MINIT

| Number | Title (A Side/B Side) | Yr | NM |
|---|---|---|---|
| ❑ 24010 [S] | Blues Power | 1967 | 25.00 |
| ❑ 40010 [M] | Blues Power | 1967 | 25.00 |

**DRAGONFLY**

MEGAPHONE

| Number | Title (A Side/B Side) | Yr | NM |
|---|---|---|---|
| ❑ MS-1202 | Dragonfly | 1968 | 300.00 |

**DRAGSTERS, THE**

WING

| Number | Title (A Side/B Side) | Yr | NM |
|---|---|---|---|
| ❑ MGW-12269 [M] | Hey Little Cobra/Drag City | 1964 | 80.00 |
| ❑ SRW-16269 [S] | Hey Little Cobra/Drag City | 1964 | 100.00 |

**DRAKE, DONNA**

LUXOR

| Number | Title (A Side/B Side) | Yr | NM |
|---|---|---|---|
| ❑ LP-1 [M] | The Wynton Kelly Trio Introduces Donna Drake — Donna Sings Dinah | 1968 | 30.00 |
| ❑ LPS-1 [S] | The Wynton Kelly Trio Introduces Donna Drake — Donna Sings Dinah | 1968 | 20.00 |

**DRAKE, GUY**

ROYAL AMERICAN

| Number | Title (A Side/B Side) | Yr | NM |
|---|---|---|---|
| ❑ 1001 | Welfare Cadillac | 1970 | 25.00 |

**DRAKE, NICK**

ANTILLES

| Number | Title (A Side/B Side) | Yr | NM |
|---|---|---|---|
| ❑ AN-7010 | Five Leaves Left | 1976 | 25.00 |
| *—Released in England in 1969* | | | |
| ❑ AN-7028 | Bryter Layter | 1977 | 25.00 |
| *—Released in England in 1970* | | | |

HANNIBAL

| Number | Title (A Side/B Side) | Yr | NM |
|---|---|---|---|
| ❑ HNBL-1318 | Time of No Reply | 1987 | 40.00 |
| ❑ HNBX-5302 [(4)] | Fruit Tree | 1986 | 150.00 |

ISLAND

| Number | Title (A Side/B Side) | Yr | NM |
|---|---|---|---|
| ❑ SMAS-9307 | Nick Drake | 1971 | 80.00 |
| *—U.S.-only compilation of selected songs from his first two British LPs* | | | |
| ❑ SMAS-9318 | Pink Moon | 1972 | 50.00 |

**DRAKE, PETE**

CANAAN

| Number | Title (A Side/B Side) | Yr | NM |
|---|---|---|---|
| ❑ 4640 [M] | Steel Away | 1967 | 15.00 |
| ❑ 9640 [S] | Steel Away | 1967 | 20.00 |

CUMBERLAND

| Number | Title (A Side/B Side) | Yr | NM |
|---|---|---|---|
| ❑ MGC-29053 [M] | Country Steel Guitar | 1963 | 20.00 |
| ❑ SRC-69053 [S] | Country Steel Guitar | 1963 | 25.00 |

HILLTOP

| Number | Title (A Side/B Side) | Yr | NM |
|---|---|---|---|
| ❑ 6052 [M] | Are You Sincere | 1967 | 12.00 |
| ❑ S-6052 [S] | Are You Sincere | 1967 | 12.00 |

SMASH

| Number | Title (A Side/B Side) | Yr | NM |
|---|---|---|---|
| ❑ MGS-27053 [M] | Forever | 1964 | 15.00 |
| ❑ MGS-27060 [M] | Talking Steel Guitar | 1965 | 15.00 |
| ❑ MGS-27064 [M] | Talking Steel and Singing Strings | 1965 | 15.00 |
| ❑ SRS-67053 [S] | Forever | 1964 | 20.00 |
| ❑ SRS-67060 [S] | Talking Steel Guitar | 1965 | 20.00 |
| ❑ SRS-67064 [S] | Talking Steel and Singing Strings | 1965 | 20.00 |

STARDAY

| Number | Title (A Side/B Side) | Yr | NM |
|---|---|---|---|
| ❑ SLP-180 [M] | The Fabulous Steel Guitar of Pete Drake | 1962 | 40.00 |
| ❑ SLP-319 [M] | The Amazing Incredible Pete Drake | 1964 | 30.00 |

STOP

| Number | Title (A Side/B Side) | Yr | NM |
|---|---|---|---|
| ❑ 1011 | The Pete Drake Show | 1970 | 12.00 |

**DRAMATICS, THE**

ABC

| Number | Title (A Side/B Side) | Yr | NM |
|---|---|---|---|
| ❑ D-867 | The Dramatic Jackpot | 1975 | 15.00 |
| ❑ D-916 | Drama V | 1975 | 15.00 |
| ❑ D-955 | Joy Ride | 1976 | 15.00 |
| ❑ AB-1010 | Shake It Well | 1977 | 15.00 |
| ❑ AA-1072 | Do What You Wanna Do | 1978 | 15.00 |
| ❑ AA-1125 | Anytime, Anyplace | 1979 | 15.00 |

CAPITOL

| Number | Title (A Side/B Side) | Yr | NM |
|---|---|---|---|
| ❑ ST-12205 | New Dimension | 1982 | 10.00 |

FANTASY

| Number | Title (A Side/B Side) | Yr | NM |
|---|---|---|---|
| ❑ 9642 | Somewhere in Time: A Dramatic Reunion | 1986 | 12.00 |

MCA

| Number | Title (A Side/B Side) | Yr | NM |
|---|---|---|---|
| ❑ 761 | Dramatic Way | 198? | 8.00 |
| *—Reissue of 5149* | | | |
| ❑ 762 | 10 1/2 | 198? | 8.00 |
| *—Reissue of 3196* | | | |
| ❑ AA-1125 | Anytime, Anyplace | 1979 | 12.00 |
| *—Reissue of ABC 1125* | | | |
| ❑ 3196 | 10 1/2 | 1980 | 10.00 |
| ❑ 5149 | Dramatic Way | 1981 | 10.00 |

STAX

| Number | Title (A Side/B Side) | Yr | NM |
|---|---|---|---|
| ❑ STX-4111 | Whatcha See Is Whatcha Get | 1978 | 12.00 |
| *—Reissue of Volt 6018* | | | |
| ❑ STX-4131 | A Dramatic Experience | 1979 | 12.00 |
| *—Reissue of Volt 6019* | | | |
| ❑ MPS-8523 | Dramatically Yours | 198? | 8.00 |
| *—Reissue of Volt 9501* | | | |
| ❑ MPS-8526 | The Best of the Dramatics | 198? | 10.00 |
| ❑ MPS-8545 | The Dramatics Live | 1988 | 10.00 |

VOLT

| Number | Title (A Side/B Side) | Yr | NM |
|---|---|---|---|
| ❑ V-3402 | Positive State of Mind | 1989 | 10.00 |
| ❑ V-3407 | Stone Cold | 1990 | 10.00 |
| ❑ VOS-6018 | Whatcha See Is Whatcha Get | 1972 | 25.00 |
| ❑ VOS-6019 | A Dramatic Experience | 1973 | 25.00 |
| ❑ VOS-9501 | Dramatically Yours | 1974 | 25.00 |

**DRAPER, RAY**

JOSIE

| Number | Title (A Side/B Side) | Yr | NM |
|---|---|---|---|
| ❑ JLPS-3004 [S] | Tuba Jazz | 1963 | 20.00 |
| ❑ JOZ-3004 [M] | Tuba Jazz | 1963 | 25.00 |

JUBILEE

| Number | Title (A Side/B Side) | Yr | NM |
|---|---|---|---|
| ❑ JLP-1090 [M] | Tuba Jazz | 1959 | 50.00 |

NEW JAZZ

| Number | Title (A Side/B Side) | Yr | NM |
|---|---|---|---|
| ❑ NJLP-8228 [M] | Ray Draper Quintet Featuring John Coltrane | 1958 | 60.00 |
| *—Purple label* | | | |
| ❑ NJLP-8228 [M] | Ray Draper Quintet Featuring John Coltrane | 1965 | 25.00 |
| *—Blue label, trident logo at right* | | | |

PRESTIGE

| Number | Title (A Side/B Side) | Yr | NM |
|---|---|---|---|
| ❑ PRLP-7096 [M] | Tuba Sounds | 1957 | 80.00 |

**DRAPER, RUSTY**

GOLDEN CREST

| Number | Title (A Side/B Side) | Yr | NM |
|---|---|---|---|
| ❑ 31029 | The Rusty Draper Show | 1973 | 12.00 |
| ❑ 31030 | Tour the USA | 1973 | 12.00 |

MERCURY

| Number | Title (A Side/B Side) | Yr | NM |
|---|---|---|---|
| ❑ MG-20068 [M] | Music for a Rainy Night | 1956 | 30.00 |
| ❑ MG-20117 [M] | Encores | 1957 | 30.00 |
| ❑ MG-20118 [M] | Rusty Draper Sings | 1957 | 30.00 |
| ❑ MG-20173 [M] | Rusty Meets Hoagy | 1957 | 30.00 |
| ❑ MG-20499 [M] | Hits That Sold a Million | 1960 | 30.00 |
| ❑ MG-20657 [M] | Country and Western Golden Greats | 1961 | 30.00 |
| ❑ SR-60176 [S] | Hits That Sold a Million | 1960 | 40.00 |
| ❑ SR-60657 [S] | Country and Western Golden Greats | 1961 | 40.00 |

MONUMENT

| Number | Title (A Side/B Side) | Yr | NM |
|---|---|---|---|
| ❑ 6638 | Greatest Hits | 1977 | 12.00 |
| ❑ MLP-8005 [M] | Greatest Hits | 1964 | 15.00 |
| ❑ MLP-8018 [M] | Night Life | 1964 | 15.00 |
| ❑ MLP-8026 [M] | Rusty Draper Plays Guitar | 1965 | 15.00 |
| ❑ SLP-18005 [S] | Greatest Hits | 1964 | 20.00 |
| ❑ SLP-18018 [S] | Night Life | 1964 | 20.00 |
| ❑ SLP-18026 [S] | Rusty Draper Plays Guitar | 1965 | 20.00 |
| ❑ SLP-18105 | Something Old, Something New | 1969 | 15.00 |
| ❑ ZG 33870 [(2)] | Swingin' Country/Something Old, Something New | 1976 | 15.00 |

WING

| Number | Title (A Side/B Side) | Yr | NM |
|---|---|---|---|
| ❑ MGW-12243 [M] | Hits That Sold a Million | 196? | 15.00 |
| ❑ MGW-12274 [M] | Country Classics | 196? | 15.00 |
| ❑ SRW-16243 [S] | Hits That Sold a Million | 196? | 15.00 |
| ❑ SRW-16274 [S] | Country Classics | 196? | 15.00 |

**DREAD ZEPPELIN**

I.R.S.

| Number | Title (A Side/B Side) | Yr | NM |
|---|---|---|---|
| ❑ X1-13048 | Un-Led-Ed | 1990 | 20.00 |
| *—All copies on gold vinyl* | | | |

**DREAM 6** With Johnette Napolitano, later of CONCRETE BLONDE.

HAPPY HERMIT

| Number | Title (A Side/B Side) | Yr | NM |
|---|---|---|---|
| ❑ 1983 [EP] | Dream 6 | 1983 | 40.00 |

**DREAM SYNDICATE, THE**

A&M

| Number | Title (A Side/B Side) | Yr | NM |
|---|---|---|---|
| ❑ SP-12511 | This Is Not the New Dream Syndicate Album...Live | 1984 | 12.00 |

BIG TIME

| Number | Title (A Side/B Side) | Yr | NM |
|---|---|---|---|
| ❑ 10022 | Out of the Grey | 1985 | 10.00 |

DOWN THERE

| Number | Title (A Side/B Side) | Yr | NM |
|---|---|---|---|
| ❑ 2 [EP] | Sure Thing + 3 | 1982 | 20.00 |

ENIGMA

| Number | Title (A Side/B Side) | Yr | NM |
|---|---|---|---|
| ❑ 73341 | Ghost Stories | 1988 | 8.00 |

RUBY

| Number | Title (A Side/B Side) | Yr | NM |
|---|---|---|---|
| ❑ 807 | The Days of Wine and Roses | 1982 | 20.00 |

SLASH

| Number | Title (A Side/B Side) | Yr | NM |
|---|---|---|---|
| ❑ 23844 | The Days of Wine and Roses | 1982 | 15.00 |

**DREAMLOVERS, THE**

COLLECTABLES

| Number | Title (A Side/B Side) | Yr | NM |
|---|---|---|---|
| ❑ COL-5004 | The Best of the Dreamlovers | 198? | 12.00 |
| ❑ COL-5005 | The Best of the Dreamlovers, Volume Two | 198? | 12.00 |

COLUMBIA

| Number | Title (A Side/B Side) | Yr | NM |
|---|---|---|---|
| ❑ CL 2020 [M] | The Bird and Other Golden Dancing Grooves | 1963 | 40.00 |
| ❑ CS 8820 [S] | The Bird and Other Golden Dancing Grooves | 1963 | 50.00 |

**DREAMS AND ILLUSIONS**

VERVE FORECAST

| Number | Title (A Side/B Side) | Yr | NM |
|---|---|---|---|
| ❑ FTS-3040 | Dreams and Illusions | 1968 | 20.00 |

**DREW, DAN** See BOOTS BROWN.

**DREW, DORIS**

MODE

| Number | Title (A Side/B Side) | Yr | NM |
|---|---|---|---|
| ❑ MOD-126 [M] | The Delightful Doris Drew | 1957 | 80.00 |

**DREW, KENNY**

BLUE NOTE

| Number | Title (A Side/B Side) | Yr | NM |
|---|---|---|---|
| ❑ BLP-4059 [M] | Undercurrent | 1961 | 80.00 |
| *—"W. 63rd St." address on label* | | | |
| ❑ BLP-4059 [M] | Undercurrent | 1964 | 25.00 |
| *—"New York, USA" address on label* | | | |
| ❑ BLP-5023 [10] | Introducing the Kenny Drew Trio | 1953 | 400.00 |
| ❑ BST-84059 [S] | Undercurrent | 1961 | 80.00 |
| *—"W. 63rd St." address on label* | | | |
| ❑ BST-84059 [S] | Undercurrent | 1964 | 25.00 |
| *—"New York, USA" address on label* | | | |

JAZZ WEST

| Number | Title (A Side/B Side) | Yr | NM |
|---|---|---|---|
| ❑ JWLP-4 [M] | Talkin' and Walkin' with the Kenny Drew Quartet | 1955 | 700.00 |

JUDSON

| Number | Title (A Side/B Side) | Yr | NM |
|---|---|---|---|
| ❑ L-3004 [M] | Harry Warren Showcase | 1957 | 50.00 |
| ❑ L-3005 [M] | Harold Arlen Showcase | 1957 | 50.00 |

NORGRAN

| Number | Title (A Side/B Side) | Yr | NM |
|---|---|---|---|
| ❑ MGN-29 [10] | The Ideation of Kenny Drew | 1954 | 250.00 |
| ❑ MGN-1002 [M] | Progressive Piano | 1954 | 200.00 |
| ❑ MGN-1066 [M] | The Modernity of Kenny Drew | 1956 | 150.00 |

RIVERSIDE

| Number | Title (A Side/B Side) | Yr | NM |
|---|---|---|---|
| ❑ RLP 12-224 [M] | Kenny Drew Trio | 195? | 50.00 |
| *—Blue labe, microphone logo at top* | | | |
| ❑ RLP 12-224 [M] | Kenny Drew Trio | 1956 | 150.00 |
| *—White label, blue print* | | | |
| ❑ RLP 12-236 [M] | This Is New | 195? | 50.00 |
| *—Blue labe, microphone logo at top* | | | |



**Except when noted otherwise, VG = 25% of NM, and VG+ = 50% of NM. (Example: VG = $2.00, VG+ = $4.00 and NM = $8.00.)**

| Number | Title (A Side/B Side) | Yr | NM |
|---|---|---|---|
| ❑ RLP 12-236 [M] | This Is New | 1957 | 150.00 |
| *—White label, blue print* | | | |
| ❑ RLP 12-249 [M] | Pal Joey | 1957 | 50.00 |
| ❑ RLP 12-811 [M] | I Love Jerome Kern | 1956 | 150.00 |
| ❑ RLP-1112 [S] | Pal Joey | 1959 | 40.00 |

### DREW, KENNY; DONALD BYRD; HANK MOBLEY

JAZZLAND

| Number | Title (A Side/B Side) | Yr | NM |
|---|---|---|---|
| ❑ JLP-6 [M] | Hard Bop | 1960 | 50.00 |
| *—Reissue of Riverside 236* | | | |
| ❑ JLP-906 [S] | Hard Bop | 1960 | 40.00 |

### DREW, KENNY; PAUL CHAMBERS; PHILLY JOE JONES

JAZZLAND

| Number | Title (A Side/B Side) | Yr | NM |
|---|---|---|---|
| ❑ JLP-9 [M] | The Tough Piano Trio | 1960 | 50.00 |
| *—Reissue of Riverside 224* | | | |
| ❑ JLP-909 [S] | The Tough Piano Trio | 1960 | 40.00 |

### DREW, PATTI

CAPITOL

| Number | Title (A Side/B Side) | Yr | NM |
|---|---|---|---|
| ❑ ST-156 | I've Been Here All the Time | 1969 | 20.00 |
| ❑ ST-408 | Wild Is Love | 1970 | 20.00 |
| ❑ ST 2804 [S] | Tell Him | 1968 | 30.00 |
| ❑ T 2804 [M] | Tell Him | 1968 | 30.00 |

### DRIFTERS, THE

ARISTA

| Number | Title (A Side/B Side) | Yr | NM |
|---|---|---|---|
| ❑ AB 4140 | Every Night Is Saturday Night | 1976 | 12.00 |

ATCO

| Number | Title (A Side/B Side) | Yr | NM |
|---|---|---|---|
| ❑ SD 33-375 [R] | Their Greatest Recordings — The Early Years | 1971 | 12.00 |

ATLANTIC

| Number | Title (A Side/B Side) | Yr | NM |
|---|---|---|---|
| ❑ 8003 [M] | Clyde McPhatter and the Drifters | 1956 | 500.00 |
| *—Black label* | | | |
| ❑ 8003 [M] | Clyde McPhatter and the Drifters | 1959 | 60.00 |
| *—Red and purple label, white "fan" logo at right* | | | |
| ❑ 8003 [M] | Clyde McPhatter and the Drifters | 1963 | 40.00 |
| *—Red and purple label, black "fan" logo at right* | | | |
| ❑ 8022 [M] | Rockin' and Driftin' | 1958 | 500.00 |
| *—White "bullseye" label* | | | |
| ❑ 8022 [M] | Rockin' and Driftin' | 1958 | 600.00 |
| *—Black label* | | | |
| ❑ 8022 [M] | Rockin' and Driftin' | 1959 | 60.00 |
| *—Red and purple label, white "fan" logo at right* | | | |
| ❑ 8022 [M] | Rockin' and Driftin' | 1963 | 40.00 |
| *—Red and purple label, black "fan" logo at right* | | | |
| ❑ 8041 [M] | The Drifters' Greatest Hits | 1960 | 100.00 |
| *—Red and purple label, white "fan" logo at right* | | | |
| ❑ 8041 [M] | The Drifters' Greatest Hits | 1960 | 600.00 |
| *—Black label* | | | |
| ❑ 8041 [M] | The Drifters' Greatest Hits | 1963 | 50.00 |
| *—Red and purple label, black "fan" logo at right* | | | |
| ❑ 8059 [M] | Save the Last Dance for Me | 1962 | 120.00 |
| *—Red and purple label, white "fan" logo at right* | | | |
| ❑ 8059 [M] | Save the Last Dance for Me | 1963 | 60.00 |
| *—Red and purple label, black "fan" logo at right* | | | |
| ❑ SD 8059 [S] | Save the Last Dance for Me | 1962 | 200.00 |
| *—Green and blue label, white "fan" logo at right* | | | |
| ❑ SD 8059 [S] | Save the Last Dance for Me | 1963 | 100.00 |
| *—Green and blue label, black "fan" logo at right* | | | |
| ❑ SD 8059 [S] | Save the Last Dance for Me | 1969 | 25.00 |
| *—Red and green label, white horizontal stripe through center hole* | | | |
| ❑ 8073 [M] | Up on the Roof — The Best of the Drifters | 1963 | 100.00 |
| *—Red and purple label, black "fan" logo at right* | | | |
| ❑ SD 8073 [S] | Up on the Roof — The Best of the Drifters | 1963 | 150.00 |
| *—Green and blue label, black "fan" logo at right* | | | |
| ❑ 8093 [M] | Our Biggest Hits | 1964 | 60.00 |
| *—Red and purple label, white "fan" logo at right* | | | |
| ❑ SD 8093 [S] | Our Biggest Hits | 1964 | 80.00 |
| *—Mostly red label, black "fan" logo* | | | |
| ❑ 8099 [M] | Under the Boardwalk | 1964 | 50.00 |
| *—Color photo of group on cover* | | | |
| ❑ 8099 [M] | Under the Boardwalk | 1964 | 80.00 |
| *—Black and white photo of group on cover* | | | |
| ❑ SD 8099 [S] | Under the Boardwalk | 1964 | 60.00 |
| *—Color photo of group on cover* | | | |
| ❑ SD 8099 [S] | Under the Boardwalk | 1964 | 120.00 |
| *—Black and white photo of group on cover* | | | |
| ❑ 8103 [M] | The Good Life with the Drifters | 1965 | 40.00 |
| ❑ SD 8103 [S] | The Good Life with the Drifters | 1965 | 50.00 |
| ❑ 8113 [M] | I'll Take You Where the Music's Playing | 1965 | 40.00 |
| ❑ SD 8113 [S] | I'll Take You Where the Music's Playing | 1965 | 50.00 |
| ❑ 8153 [M] | The Drifters' Golden Hits | 1968 | 30.00 |
| ❑ SD 8153 [P] | The Drifters' Golden Hits | 1968 | 30.00 |
| *—Green and blue label* | | | |
| ❑ SD 8153 [P] | The Drifters' Golden Hits | 1969 | 15.00 |
| *—Red and green label* | | | |
| ❑ 81927 [(2)] | Let the Boogie-Woogie Roll: Greatest Hits 1953-1958 | 1989 | 15.00 |
| ❑ 81931 [(2)] | All-Time Greatest Hits and More: 1959-1965 | 1989 | 15.00 |

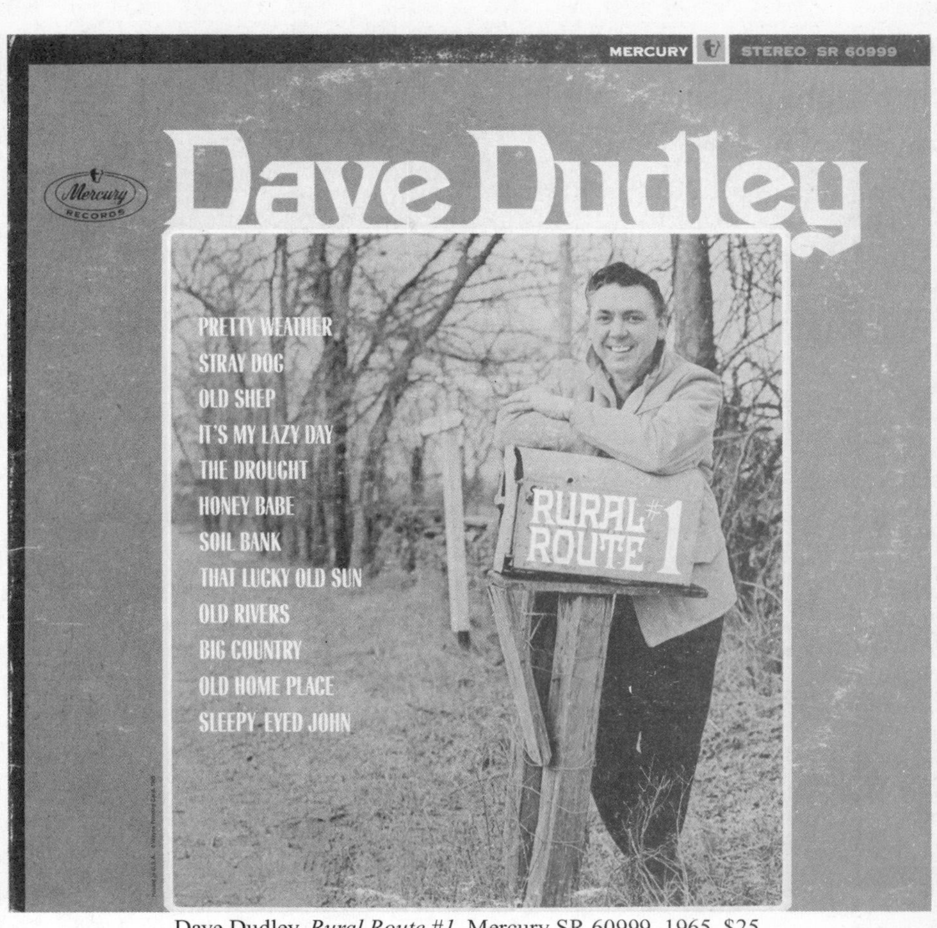


Dave Dudley, *Rural Route #1,* Mercury SR 60999, 1965, $25.

CLARION

| Number | Title (A Side/B Side) | Yr | NM |
|---|---|---|---|
| ❑ 608 [M] | The Drifters | 1964 | 20.00 |
| ❑ SD 608 [P] | The Drifters | 1964 | 30.00 |

GUSTO

| Number | Title (A Side/B Side) | Yr | NM |
|---|---|---|---|
| ❑ 0063 | Greatest Hits — The Drifters | 1980 | 10.00 |

TRIP

| Number | Title (A Side/B Side) | Yr | NM |
|---|---|---|---|
| ❑ TOP-16-6 | 16 Greatest Hits — The Drifters | 1976 | 10.00 |

### DRIFTIN' SLIM

MILESTONE

| Number | Title (A Side/B Side) | Yr | NM |
|---|---|---|---|
| ❑ MLS-93004 [(2)] | Driftin' Slim and His Blues Band | 1968 | 25.00 |

### DRIFTING COWBOYS, THE

MGM

| Number | Title (A Side/B Side) | Yr | NM |
|---|---|---|---|
| ❑ SE-4626 | We Remember Hank Williams | 1968 | 20.00 |

### DRIFTWOOD, JIMMIE

MONUMENT

| Number | Title (A Side/B Side) | Yr | NM |
|---|---|---|---|
| ❑ MLP-8006 [M] | Voice of the People | 1963 | 20.00 |
| ❑ MLP-8019 [M] | Down in the Arkansas | 1965 | 20.00 |
| ❑ SLP-18006 [S] | Voice of the People | 1963 | 25.00 |
| ❑ SLP-18019 [S] | Down in the Arkansas | 1965 | 25.00 |

RCA VICTOR

| Number | Title (A Side/B Side) | Yr | NM |
|---|---|---|---|
| ❑ LPM-1635 [M] | Newly Discovered Early American Folk Songs | 1958 | 50.00 |
| ❑ LPM-1994 [M] | Jimmie Driftwood and the Wilderness Road | 1959 | 30.00 |
| ❑ LSP-1994 [S] | Jimmie Driftwood and the Wilderness Road | 1959 | 40.00 |
| ❑ LPM-2171 [M] | The Westward Movement | 1960 | 30.00 |
| ❑ LSP-2171 [S] | The Westward Movement | 1960 | 40.00 |
| ❑ LPM-2228 [M] | Tall Tales in Song | 1960 | 30.00 |
| ❑ LSP-2228 [S] | Tall Tales in Song | 1960 | 40.00 |
| ❑ LPM-2316 [M] | Songs of Billy Yank and Johnny Reb | 1961 | 30.00 |
| ❑ LSP-2316 [S] | Songs of Billy Yank and Johnny Reb | 1961 | 40.00 |
| ❑ LPM-2443 [M] | Driftwood at Sea | 1962 | 30.00 |
| ❑ LSP-2443 [S] | Driftwood at Sea | 1962 | 40.00 |

### DRIVE-BY TRUCKERS

LOST HIGHWAY

| Number | Title (A Side/B Side) | Yr | NM |
|---|---|---|---|
| ❑ 088 170308-1 [(2)] | Southern Rock Opera | 2003 | 20.00 |

### DRUIDS OF STONEHENGE, THE

UNI

| Number | Title (A Side/B Side) | Yr | NM |
|---|---|---|---|
| ❑ 3004 [M] | Creation | 1967 | 60.00 |
| ❑ 73004 [S] | Creation | 1967 | 80.00 |

### DRUSKY, ROY

DECCA

| Number | Title (A Side/B Side) | Yr | NM |
|---|---|---|---|
| ❑ DL 4160 [M] | Anymore with Roy Drusky | 1961 | 25.00 |
| ❑ DL 4340 [M] | It's My Way | 1962 | 20.00 |
| ❑ DL 74160 [S] | Anymore with Roy Drusky | 1961 | 30.00 |
| ❑ DL 74340 [S] | It's My Way | 1962 | 25.00 |

MERCURY

| Number | Title (A Side/B Side) | Yr | NM |
|---|---|---|---|
| ❑ MG-20883 [M] | Songs of the Cities | 1963 | 20.00 |
| ❑ MG-20919 [M] | Yesterday's Gone | 1964 | 20.00 |
| ❑ MG-20973 [M] | The Pick of the Country | 1964 | 20.00 |
| ❑ MG-21006 [M] | Country Music All Around the World | 1965 | 20.00 |
| ❑ MG-21052 [M] | Roy Drusky's Greatest Hits | 1965 | 20.00 |
| ❑ MG-21083 [M] | In a New Dimension | 1966 | 20.00 |
| ❑ MG-21097 [M] | If the Whole World Stopped Lovin' | 1966 | 20.00 |
| ❑ MG-21118 [M] | Now Is a Lonely Time | 1967 | 25.00 |
| ❑ MG-21145 [M] | Roy Drusky's Greatest Hits Vol. 2 | 1968 | 40.00 |
| *—Mono is white label promo only* | | | |
| ❑ SR-60883 [S] | Songs of the Cities | 1963 | 25.00 |
| ❑ SR-60919 [S] | Yesterday's Gone | 1964 | 25.00 |
| ❑ SR-60973 [S] | The Pick of the Country | 1964 | 25.00 |
| ❑ SR-61006 [S] | Country Music All Around the World | 1965 | 25.00 |
| ❑ SR-61052 [S] | Roy Drusky's Greatest Hits | 1965 | 25.00 |
| ❑ SR-61083 [S] | In a New Dimension | 1966 | 25.00 |
| ❑ SR-61097 [S] | If the Whole World Stopped Lovin' | 1966 | 25.00 |
| ❑ SR-61118 [S] | Now Is a Lonely Time | 1967 | 20.00 |
| ❑ SR-61145 [S] | Roy Drusky's Greatest Hits Vol. 2 | 1968 | 20.00 |
| ❑ SR-61173 | Jody and the Kid | 1968 | 20.00 |
| ❑ SR-61206 | Portrait of Roy Drusky | 1969 | 20.00 |
| ❑ SR-61233 | My Grass Is Green | 1969 | 20.00 |
| ❑ SR-61260 | I'll Make Amends | 1970 | 20.00 |
| ❑ SR-61266 | The Best of Roy Drusky | 1970 | 20.00 |
| ❑ SR-61306 | All My Hard Times | 1970 | 20.00 |
| ❑ SR-61336 | I Love the Way That You've Been Lovin' Me | 1971 | 20.00 |

### DRUSKY, ROY, AND PRISCILLA MITCHELL

**MERCURY**

❑ MG-21078 [M] Together Again 1966 20.00
❑ SR-61078 [S] Together Again 1966 25.00

### DRY CITY SCAT BAND, THE

**ELEKTRA**

❑ EKL-292 [M] The Dry City Scat Band 1965 25.00
❑ EKS-7292 [S] The Dry City Scat Band 1965 30.00

### DUALS, THE

**SUE**

❑ LP-2002 [M] Stick Shift 1961 400.00
*—Cartoon cover*
❑ LP-2002 [M] Stick Shift 1964 200.00
*—Photo cover*

### DUBS, THE / THE SHELLS

Also see each artist's individual listings.

**JOSIE**

❑ JM-4001 [M] The Dubs Meet the Shells 1962 300.00
❑ JSS-4001 [S] The Dubs Meet the Shells 1962 600.00

### DUDLEY, DAVE

**GOLDEN RING**

❑ GR 110 [M] Dave Dudley Sings Six Days on the Road 1963 80.00

**MERCURY**

❑ SRM-1-669 Keep On Truckin' 1973 15.00
❑ MG-20899 [M] Songs About the Working Man 1964 20.00
❑ MG-20927 [M] Travelin' with Dave Dudley 1964 20.00
❑ MG-20970 [M] Talk of the Town 1964 20.00
❑ MG-20999 [M] Rural Route #1 1965 20.00
❑ MG-21028 [M] Truck Drivin' Son-of-a-Gun 1965 20.00
❑ MG-21046 [M] Dave Dudley's Greatest Hits 1965 20.00
❑ MG-21057 [M] There's a Star Spangled Banner Waving Somewhere 1966 20.00
❑ MG-21074 [M] Lonelyville 1966 20.00
❑ MG-21098 [M] Free and Easy 1966 20.00
❑ MG-21133 [M] Dave Dudley Country 1967 25.00
❑ MG-21144 [M] Greatest Hits Vol. 2 1968 30.00
❑ SR-60899 [S] Songs About the Working Man 1964 25.00
❑ SR-60927 [S] Travelin' with Dave Dudley 1964 25.00
❑ SR-60970 [S] Talk of the Town 1964 25.00
❑ SR-60999 [S] Rural Route #1 1965 25.00
❑ SR-61028 [S] Truck Drivin' Son-of-a-Gun 1965 25.00
❑ SR-61046 [S] Dave Dudley's Greatest Hits 1965 25.00
❑ SR-61057 [S] There's a Star Spangled Banner Waving Somewhere 1966 25.00
❑ SR-61074 [S] Lonelyville 1966 25.00
❑ SR-61098 [S] Free and Easy 1966 20.00
❑ SR-61133 [S] Dave Dudley Country 1967 20.00
❑ SR-61144 [S] Greatest Hits Vol. 2 1968 20.00
❑ SR-61172 Thanks for All the Miles 1968 20.00
❑ SR-61215 One More Mile 1969 20.00
❑ SR-61268 The Best of Dave Dudley 1970 15.00
❑ SR-61276 The Pool Shark 1970 15.00
❑ SR-61315 Dave Dudley Sings "Listen Betty, I'm Singing Your Song" 1971 15.00
❑ SR-61351 Will the Real Dave Dudley Please Sing 1971 15.00
❑ SR-61365 The Original Traveling Man 1972 15.00

**UNITED ARTISTS**

❑ UA-LA512-G Uncommonly Good Country 1975 12.00

### DUDZIAK, URSZULA

**COLUMBIA**

❑ KC 32902 Newborn Light 1972 20.00

### DUKE, DOUGLAS

**HERALD**

❑ HLP-0102 [M] Sounds Impossible 1956 50.00

**REGENT**

❑ MG-6013 [M] Jazz Organist 196? 30.00

### DUKE, KENO

**STRATA-EAST**

❑ SES-7416 Sense of Values 1974 25.00

**TRIDENT**

❑ 501 Crest of the Wave 197? 20.00

### DUKE, PATTY

**UNART**

❑ 20005 [M] TV's Teen Star 1967 12.00
❑ S 20005 [S] TV's Teen Star 1967 15.00

**UNITED ARTISTS**

❑ UAL-3452 [M] Don't Just Stand There 1965 20.00
❑ UAL-3492 [M] Patty 1966 20.00
❑ UAL-3535 [M] Patty Duke's Greatest Hits 1966 15.00
❑ UAS-6452 [S] Don't Just Stand There 1965 30.00
❑ UAS-6492 [S] Patty 1966 30.00
❑ UAS-6535 [S] Patty Duke's Greatest Hits 1966 25.00
❑ UAS-6623 Songs from the Valley of the Dolls 1968 25.00

### DUKE, PATTY, WITH NORMAN VINCENT PEALE

**GUIDEPOSTS**

❑ GP-101 [M] Guideposts for Christmas 1963 80.00

### DUKE, VERNON

**ATLANTIC**

❑ 407 [10] Vernon Duke Plays Vernon Duke 1954 100.00

### DUKE OF IRON, THE

**PRESTIGE**

❑ PRLP-13068 [M] Limbo, Limbo, Limbo 1963 30.00

### DUKE OF PADUCAH, THE

**STARDAY**

❑ SLP-148 [M] Button Shoes, Belly Laughs and Monkey Business 1961 40.00

### DUKE'S MEN, THE

**EPIC**

❑ LG 3108 [M] The Duke's Men 1955 50.00
❑ LN 3237 [M] Ellington's Sidekicks 1956 50.00

### DUKES, JOE, AND JACK MCDUFF

**PRESTIGE**

❑ PRLP-7324 [M] Soulful Drums 1964 25.00
❑ PRST-7324 [S] Soulful Drums 1964 30.00

### DUKES OF DIXIELAND, THE

**AUDIO FIDELITY**

❑ AFSD-5823 [S] You Have to Hear It to Believe It — The Dukes of Dixieland, Vol. 1 196? 20.00
❑ AFSD-5840 [S] You Have to Hear It to Believe It — The Dukes of Dixieland, Vol. 2 196? 20.00
❑ AFSD-5851 [S] Marching Along with the Dukes of Dixieland, Vol. 3 1958 20.00
❑ AFSD-5860 [S] The Dukes of Dixieland On Bourbon Street, Vol. 4 1958 20.00
❑ AFSD-5861 [S] Minstrel Time with the Phenomenal Dukes of Dixieland, Volume 5 1958 20.00
❑ AFSD-5862 [S] Mardi Gras Time 1958 20.00
❑ AFSD-5891 [S] The Dukes of Dixieland On Campus 1959 20.00
❑ AFSD-5892 [S] Up the Mississippi 1959 20.00

**VIK**

❑ LX-1025 [M] The Dukes of Dixieland at the Jazz Band Ball 1956 30.00

### DUNBAR, AYNSLEY

**BLUE THUMB**

❑ BTS-4 The Aynsley Dunbar Retaliation 1968 25.00
❑ BTS-6 Doctor Dunbar's Prescription 1969 25.00
❑ BTS-16 To Mum From Aynsley and the Boys 1970 25.00

### DUNCAN, BILL

**KING**

❑ 825 [M] A Scene Near My Country Home 1962 30.00

### DUNCAN, DANNY

**"X"**

❑ LVA-3040 [10] Ragtime Jamboree 1955 50.00

### DUNCAN, JOHNNY

**COLUMBIA**

❑ CS 9824 Johnny One Time 1969 20.00
❑ C 30618 There's Something About a Lady 1971 15.00
❑ KC 32440 Sweet Country Woman 1973 15.00
❑ KC 34243 The Best of Johnny Duncan 1976 12.00
❑ PC 34442 Johnny Duncan 1977 12.00
❑ KC 35039 Come a Little Bit Closer 1977 12.00
❑ KC 35451 The Best Is Yet to Come 1978 12.00
❑ KC 35628 Greatest Hits 1978 12.00
❑ KC 35775 See You When the Sun Goes Down 1979 12.00
❑ JC 36260 Straight from Texas 1980 10.00
❑ JC 36508 In My Dreams 1980 10.00
❑ JC 36829 You're On My Mind 1981 10.00

**HARMONY**

❑ KH 32477 You're Gonna Need a Man 1973 12.00

### DUNHAM, KATHERINE

**AUDIO FIDELITY**

❑ AFLP-1803 [M] The Singing Gods-Drum Rhythms of Cuba, Haiti, Brazil 1957 40.00

**DECCA**

❑ DL 5251 [10] Afro-Caribbean Songs and Rhythms 1951 60.00

### DUNN, HOLLY

**MTM**

❑ ST-71052 Holly Dunn 1986 12.00
❑ ST-71063 Cornerstone 1987 12.00
❑ ST-71070 Across the Rio Grande 1988 12.00

**WARNER BROS.**

❑ PRO-A-3692 [DJ] Blue Rose of Texas Radio Special 1989 30.00
*—Promo-only interview record*
❑ 25939 The Blue Rose of Texas 1989 10.00

### DUPRE, MARCEL

**MERCURY LIVING PRESENCE**

❑ SR 90168 [S] Franck: Piece Heroique; 3 Chorales 196? 20.00
*—Third edition: Dark red (not maroon) label*
❑ SR 90168 [S] Franck: Piece Heroique; 3 Chorales 196? 25.00
*—Maroon label, with "Vendor: Mercury Record Corporation"*
❑ SR 90168 [S] Franck: Piece Heroique; 3 Chorales 196? 50.00
*—Maroon label, no "Vendor: Mercury Record Corporation"*
❑ SR 90169 [S] Organ Recital 196? 200.00
*—Maroon label, no "Vendor: Mercury Record Corporation"*
❑ SR 90169 [S] Organ Recital 196? 200.00
*—Maroon label, with "Vendor: Mercury Record Corporation"*
❑ SR 90227 [S] Dupre at Saint-Sulpice, Vol. 1 196? 40.00
*—Maroon label, no "Vendor: Mercury Record Corporation"*
❑ SR 90228 [S] Dupre at Saint-Sulpice, Vol. 3 196? 20.00
*—Maroon label, with "Vendor: Mercury Record Corporation"*
❑ SR 90228 [S] Dupre at Saint-Sulpice, Vol. 3 196? 40.00
*—Maroon label, no "Vendor: Mercury Record Corporation"*
❑ SR 90229 [S] Dupre at Saint-Sulpice, Vol. 2 196? 50.00
*—Maroon label, with "Vendor: Mercury Record Corporation"*
❑ SR 90229 [S] Dupre at Saint-Sulpice, Vol. 2 196? 80.00
*—Maroon label, no "Vendor: Mercury Record Corporation"*
❑ SR 90230 [S] Dupre at Saint-Sulpice, Vol. 4 196? 20.00
*—Maroon label, with "Vendor: Mercury Record Corporation"*
❑ SR 90230 [S] Dupre at Saint-Sulpice, Vol. 4 196? 80.00
*—Maroon label, no "Vendor: Mercury Record Corporation"*
❑ SR 90231 [S] Dupre at Saint-Sulpice, Vol. 5 196? 30.00
*—Maroon label, with "Vendor: Mercury Record Corporation"*
❑ SR 90231 [S] Dupre at Saint-Sulpice, Vol. 5 196? 60.00
*—Maroon label, no "Vendor: Mercury Record Corporation"*

### DUPREE, CHAMPION JACK

**ATLANTIC**

❑ 8019 [M] Blues from the Gutter 1959 150.00
*—Black label*
❑ 8019 [M] Blues from the Gutter 1960 50.00
*—White "fan" logo at right of label*
❑ 8019 [M] Blues from the Gutter 1963 20.00
*—Black "fan" logo at right of label*
❑ SD 8019 [S] Blues from the Gutter 1959 200.00
*—Green label*
❑ SD 8019 [S] Blues from the Gutter 1960 60.00
*—Green and blue label, white "fan" logo at right of label*
❑ SD 8019 [S] Blues from the Gutter 1963 25.00
*—Green and blue label, black "fan" logo at right of label*
❑ 8045 [M] Natural and Soulful Blues 1961 50.00
*—White "fan" logo at right of label*
❑ 8045 [M] Natural and Soulful Blues 1963 20.00
*—Black "fan" logo at right of label*
❑ SD 8045 [S] Natural and Soulful Blues 1961 60.00
*—Green and blue label, white "fan" logo at right of label*
❑ SD 8045 [S] Natural and Soulful Blues 1963 25.00
*—Green and blue label, black "fan" logo at right of label*
❑ 8056 [M] Champion of the Blues 1961 50.00
*—White "fan" logo at right of label*
❑ 8056 [M] Champion of the Blues 1963 20.00
*—Black "fan" logo at right of label*
❑ SD 8056 [R] Champion of the Blues 196? 15.00
❑ SD 8255 Blues from the Gutter 1970 15.00

**BLUE HORIZON**

❑ 7702 When You Feel the Feeling 1969 25.00

**BULLSEYE**

❑ BB-9502 Back Home In New Orleans 1990 12.00

**CONTINENTAL**

❑ CLP-16002 [M] Low Down Blues 1961 250.00

**EVEREST ARCHIVE OF FOLK & JAZZ**

❑ 217 Champion Jack Dupree 197? 10.00

**FOLKWAYS**

❑ FS-3825 [M] Women Blues of Champion Jack Dupree 1961 25.00

**GNP CRESCENDO**

❑ GNPS-10001 Tricks 1974 12.00
❑ GNPS-10005 Happy to Be Free 1974 12.00
❑ GNPS-10013 Legacy of Blues 3 197? 12.00

**JAZZ MAN**

❑ BLZ-5501 Champion Jack Dupree 1982 10.00

**KING**

❑ 735 [M] Champion Jack Dupree Sings the Blues 1961 300.00
❑ KS-1084 Walking the Blues 1970 15.00

**LONDON**

❑ PS 553 From New Orleans to Chicago 1969 20.00



**Except when noted otherwise, VG = 25% of NM, and VG+ = 50% of NM. (Example: VG = $2.00, VG+ = $4.00 and NM = $8.00.)**

| Number | Title (A Side/B Side) | Yr | NM |
|---|---|---|---|

OKEH
❑ OKM 12103 [M]Cabbage Greens 1963 30.00

STORYVILLE
❑ 4010 Best of the Blues 1982 10.00
❑ 4040 I'm Growing Older Every Day 198? 10.00

**DUPREE, CHAMPION JACK, AND MICKEY BAKER**
Also see each artist's individual listings.

SIRE
❑ SES-97010 In Heavy Blues 1969 30.00

**DUPREE, CHAMPION JACK, AND JIMMY RUSHING**

AUDIO LAB
❑ AL-1512 [M] Two Shades of Blue 1958 200.00

**DUPREE, SIMON, AND THE BIG SOUND**

TOWER
❑ ST-5097 [S] Without Reservations 1968 40.00
❑ T-5097 [M] Without Reservations 1968 100.00

**DUPREES, THE**

COED
❑ LPC-905 [M] You Belong to Me 1962 300.00
❑ LPC-906 [M] Have You Heard 1963 200.00

COLLECTABLES
❑ COL-5008 The Best of the Duprees 198? 12.00

COLOSSUS
❑ 5000 Duprees Gold 1970 30.00
*—As "The Italian Asphalt & Pavement Co."*

HERITAGE
❑ HT-35002 [M] Total Recall 1968 80.00
*—Mono is promo only; in stereo cover with "DJ Monaural" sticker on front*
❑ HTS-35002 [S] Total Recall 1968 30.00

POST
❑ 1000 The Duprees Sing 196? 30.00

**DURAN, EDDIE**

FANTASY
❑ 3247 [M] Jazz Guitarist 195? 40.00
*—Black vinyl*
❑ 3247 [M] Jazz Guitarist 1957 80.00
*—Red vinyl*

**DURAN DURAN**

CAPITOL
❑ ST-12158 Duran Duran 1983 10.00
*—Reissue of Harvest 12158 with new cover and 9 tracks, adding "Is There Something I Should Know"*
❑ ST-12211 Rio 1983 8.00
*—Version 4: Capitol logo replaces Harvest logo on back cover, otherwise it's the same as Harvest Version 3, with the same trail-off markings*
❑ ST-12310 Seven and the Ragged Tiger 1983 8.00
❑ SWAV-12374 Arena 1984 10.00
*—With booklet (deduct 25% if cut out or if booklet is missing)*
❑ PJ-12540 Notorious 1986 8.00
❑ SPRO-79097/8 [EP]Duran Goes Dutch 1987 80.00
*—Promo-only five-song EP recorded live in Rotterdam*
❑ C1-90958 Big Thing 1988 10.00
*—Deduct 25% for cut-outs*
❑ C1-93178 Decade 1989 12.00
❑ C1-94292 Liberty 1990 15.00
❑ R 100682 Big Thing 1988 12.00
*—BMG Direct Marketing edition*
❑ R 114794 Notorious 1987 12.00
*—RCA Music Service edition*
❑ R 134452 Duran Duran 1983 12.00
*—RCA Music Service edition; with "Is There Something I Should Know?"*
❑ R 140395 Arena 1984 12.00
*—RCA Music Service edition*
❑ R 163452 Rio 1983 15.00
*—RCA Music Service edition; contains Harvest Version 1 of the album*
❑ R 163458 Liberty 1990 15.00
*—BMG Direct Marketing edition*
❑ R 173573 Decade 1989 12.00
*—BMG Direct Marketing edition*
❑ ST-512211 Rio 1983 10.00
*—Columbia House edition; otherwise the same as Version 4*

EPIC
❑ E2 92900 [(2)] Astronaut 2004 15.00

HARVEST
❑ ST-12158 Duran Duran 1981 15.00
*—Original US issue with yellow label and 8 songs*
❑ ST-12211 Rio 1982 12.00
*—Version 3: Harvest logo on lower back cover, with five songs remixed by David Kershenbaum, but with a different mix of "Hungry Like the Wolf" than Version 2; Side 1 trail-off wax number is "ST-1-12211-Z18"*
❑ ST-12211 Rio 1982 15.00
*—Version 2: Harvest logo on lower back cover, with five songs remixed by David Kershenbaum; Side 1 trail-off wax number is "ST-1-12211-Z13-RE1 #1"*

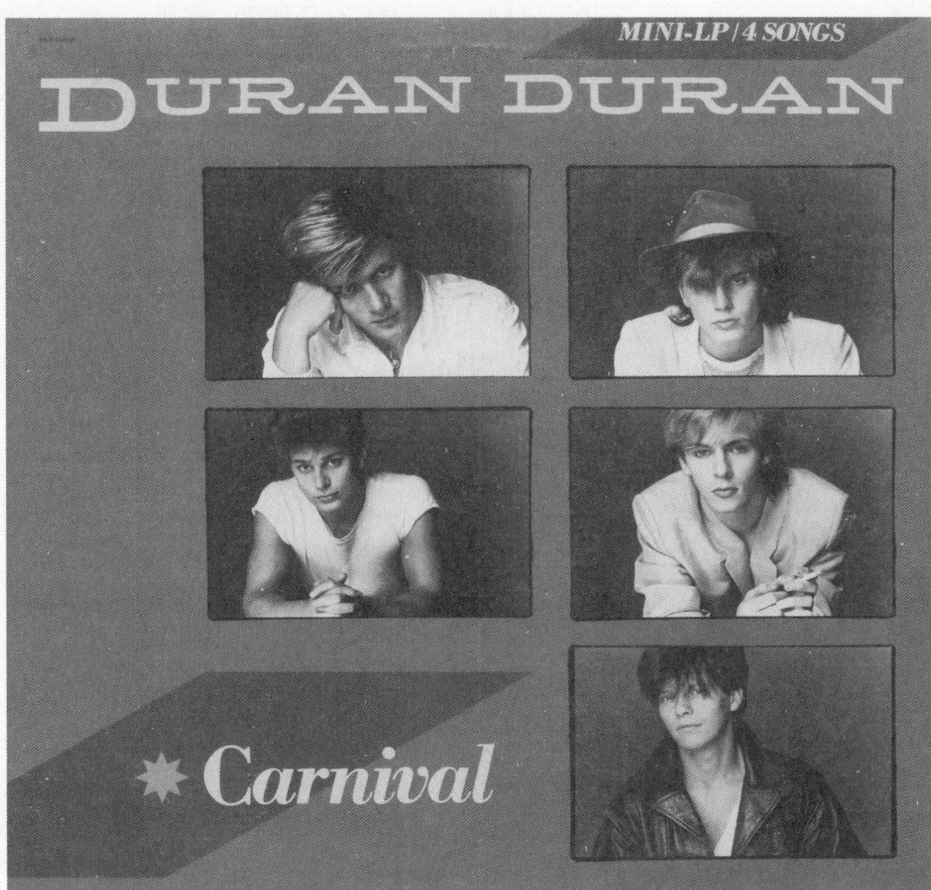


Duran Duran, *Carnival,* Harvest DLP-15006, 1982, $20.

| Number | Title (A Side/B Side) | Yr | NM |
|---|---|---|---|

❑ ST-12211 Rio 1982 20.00
*—Version 1: Harvest logo on lower back cover, contains the same versions of the songs as the original UK release; trail-off wax number on Side 1 is "ST-1-12211 Z1"*
❑ MLP-15006 [EP]Carnival 1982 20.00

MOBILE FIDELITY
❑ 1-182 Seven and the Ragged Tiger 1985 20.00
*—Audiophile vinyl*

**DURANTE, JIMMY**

DECCA
❑ DL 5116 [10] Jimmy Durante 195? 50.00
❑ DL 8884 [M] Jimmy Durante at the Piano 1959 15.00
❑ DL 9049 [M] Club Durant 195? 25.00
❑ DL 78884 [S] Jimmy Durante at the Piano 1959 20.00

LION
❑ L-70053 [M] Jimmy Durante in Person 195? 30.00

MGM
❑ E-3242 [M] Jimmy Durante in Person 1955 30.00
❑ E-4207 [M] The Very Best of Jimmy Durante 1964 12.00
❑ SE-4207 [S] The Very Best of Jimmy Durante 1964 15.00

ROULETTE
❑ R-25123 [M] Jimmy Durante at the Copacabana 1961 20.00
❑ SR-25123 [S] Jimmy Durante at the Copacabana 1961 25.00

WARNER BROS.
❑ W 1506 [M] September Song 1963 15.00
❑ WS 1506 [S] September Song 1963 20.00
❑ W 1531 [M] Hello Young Lovers 1964 15.00
❑ WS 1531 [S] Hello Young Lovers 1964 20.00
❑ W 1577 [M] Jimmy Durante's Way of Life 1965 15.00
❑ WS 1577 [S] Jimmy Durante's Way of Life 1965 20.00
❑ W 1655 [M] One of Those Songs 1966 15.00
❑ WS 1655 [S] One of Those Songs 1966 20.00
❑ W 1713 [M] Songs for Sunday 1967 15.00
❑ WS 1713 [S] Songs for Sunday 1967 20.00

**DURBIN, DEANNA**

DECCA
❑ DL 8785 [M] Deanna Durbin 1958 50.00

| Number | Title (A Side/B Side) | Yr | NM |
|---|---|---|---|

**DUSHON, JEAN**

ARGO
❑ LP-4039 [M] Make Way for Jean DuShon 1964 25.00
❑ LPS-4039 [S] Make Way for Jean DuShon 1964 30.00

**DUST**

KAMA SUTRA
❑ KSBS-2041 Dust 1971 25.00
*—Pink label*
❑ KSBS-2059 Hard Attack 1972 25.00
*—Pink label*

**DUTCH SWING COLLEGE BAND, THE**

EPIC
❑ LN 3211 [M] Dixieland Goes Dutch 1955 40.00

PHILIPS
❑ PHS 600010 [S]Dixie Goes Dutch 1962 20.00

**DUVAL, DENISE / GEORGES PRETRE**

RCA VICTOR RED SEAL
❑ LDS-2385 [S] Poulenc: La Voix Humana 1960 60.00
*—Original with "shaded dog" label; also includes booklet*

**DWARVES**

SUB POP
❑ 67 Blood, Guts and Pussy 1990 10.00
❑ 67 Blood, Guts and Pussy 1990 20.00
*—First 1,000 on red vinyl*
❑ 126 Thank Heaven for Little Girls 1991 10.00
❑ 197 Sugar Fix 1993 10.00

**DYANI, JOHNNY; OKAY TEMIZ; MONGEZI FEZA**

ANTILLES
❑ AN-7035 Music for Xaba 197? 30.00

**DYKE AND THE BLAZERS**

ORIGINAL SOUND
❑ LP 8876 [M] The Funky Broadway 1967 50.00
❑ LPS 8876 [S] The Funky Broadway 1967 75.00
❑ LPS 8877 Dyke's Greatest Hits 1968 75.00

**DYLAN, BOB**

ASYLUM
❑ AB-201 [(2)] Before the Flood 1974 20.00

Bob Dylan, *Highway61 Revisited,* Columbia CL 2389, 1965, mono, $80.

| Number | Title (A Side/B Side) | Yr | NM |
|---|---|---|---|
| ❑ AB-201 [(2)DJ] | Before the Flood | 1974 | 50.00 |
| *—White label promo* | | | |
| ❑ 7E-1003 | Planet Waves | 1974 | 15.00 |
| *—Without wraparound (olive green) second cover* | | | |
| ❑ 7E-1003 | Planet Waves | 1974 | 20.00 |
| *—With wraparound (olive green) second cover* | | | |
| ❑ 7E-1003 [DJ] | Planet Waves | 1974 | 50.00 |
| *—White label promo* | | | |
| ❑ 7E-1003 [DJ] | Ceremonies of the Horsemen | 1974 | 3000. |
| *—Original title of "Planet Waves"; no records were pressed with this title, but never-glued covers exist, of which 3 or 4 are known. Value is for one of these covers; VG value 1500; VG+ value 2250* | | | |
| ❑ EQ-1003 [Q] | Planet Waves | 1974 | 50.00 |
| COLUMBIA | | | |
| ❑ C2L 41 [(2)M] | Blonde on Blonde | 1966 | 100.00 |
| *—"Female photos" inner gatefold with two women pictured* | | | |
| ❑ C2L 41 [(2)M] | Blonde on Blonde | 1966 | 1000. |
| *—White label promo* | | | |
| ❑ C2L 41 [(2)M] | Blonde on Blonde | 1968 | 300.00 |
| *—No photos of women inside gatefold* | | | |
| ❑ AS 422 [DJ] | Renaldo and Clara | 1976 | 50.00 |
| *—Promo-only sampler from the movie. Authentic copies have a sticker on a white cover; counterfeits have the title printed on the cover* | | | |
| ❑ AS 798 [DJ] | Saved | 1980 | 25.00 |
| *—Promo sampler from LP* | | | |
| ❑ C2S 841 [(2)S] | Blonde on Blonde | 1966 | 60.00 |
| *—"Female photos" inner gatefold with two women pictured* | | | |
| ❑ C2S 841 [(2)S] | Blonde on Blonde | 1968 | 30.00 |
| *—No photos of women inside gatefold; "360 Sound Stereo" on label* | | | |
| ❑ C2S 841 [(2)S] | Blonde on Blonde | 1970 | 15.00 |
| *—Orange label* | | | |
| ❑ CG 841 [(2)S] | Blonde on Blonde | 198? | 12.00 |
| ❑ AS 1259 [DJ] | The Dylan London Interview, July 1981 | 1981 | 25.00 |
| ❑ AS 1471 [DJ] | Electric Lunch | 1982 | 25.00 |
| *—Promo-only sampler* | | | |
| ❑ AS 1770 [DJ] | Infidels | 1983 | 20.00 |
| *—Promo-only sampler* | | | |
| ❑ CL 1779 [M] | Bob Dylan | 1962 | 250.00 |
| *—Black and red (not orange) label with six white "eye" logos, three at 9 o'clock, three at 3 o'clock; stock copy* | | | |
| ❑ CL 1779 [M] | Bob Dylan | 1962 | 500.00 |
| *—Six "eye" logos on label; "A New Star on Columbia" sticker on cover and promo stamp on label* | | | |
| ❑ CL 1779 [M] | Bob Dylan | 1963 | 40.00 |
| *—"Guaranteed High Fidelity" on label* | | | |

| Number | Title (A Side/B Side) | Yr | NM |
|---|---|---|---|
| ❑ CL 1779 [M] | Bob Dylan | 1966 | 30.00 |
| *—"Mono" on label* | | | |
| ❑ CL 1986 [M] | The Freewheelin' Bob Dylan | 1963 | 40.00 |
| *—"Guaranteed High Fidelity" on label; corrected version (record plays what label says)* | | | |
| ❑ CL 1986 [M] | The Freewheelin' Bob Dylan | 1963 | 500.00 |
| *—White label promo; label AND timing strip list, and record plays, "correct" tracks* | | | |
| ❑ CL 1986 [M] | The Freewheelin' Bob Dylan | 1963 | 800.00 |
| *—White label promo; timing strip lists deleted tracks; label lists, and record plays, "correct" tracks* | | | |
| ❑ CL 1986 [M] | The Freewheelin' Bob Dylan | 1963 | 2000. |
| *—White label promo; label lists deleted tracks; timing strip lists, and record plays, "correct" tracks* | | | |
| ❑ CL 1986 [M] | The Freewheelin' Bob Dylan | 1963 | 3000. |
| *—White label promo; label and timing strip list the deleted tracks but record plays the "correct" tracks; VG value 1000; VG+ value 2000* | | | |
| ❑ CL 1986 [M] | The Freewheelin' Bob Dylan | 1963 | 12000. |
| *—"Guaranteed High Fidelity" on label; plays "Let Me Die in My Footsteps," "Rocks and Gravel," "Talkin' John Birch Blues" and "Gamblin' Willie's Dead Man's Hand." Label does NOT list these. In dead wax, matrix number ends in "--1" followed by a letter; VG value 4000; VG+ value 8000* | | | |
| ❑ CL 1986 [M] | The Freewheelin' Bob Dylan | 1966 | 30.00 |
| *—"Mono" on label* | | | |
| ❑ CL 2105 [M] | The Times They Are a-Changin' | 1964 | 40.00 |
| *—"Guaranteed High Fidelity" on label* | | | |
| ❑ CL 2105 [M] | The Times They Are a-Changin' | 1964 | 400.00 |
| *—White label promo* | | | |
| ❑ CL 2105 [M] | The Times They Are a-Changin' | 1965 | 30.00 |
| *—"Mono" on label* | | | |
| ❑ CL 2193 [M] | Another Side of Bob Dylan | 1964 | 40.00 |
| *—"Guaranteed High Fidelity" on label* | | | |
| ❑ CL 2193 [M] | Another Side of Bob Dylan | 1964 | 400.00 |
| *—White label promo* | | | |
| ❑ CL 2193 [M] | Another Side of Bob Dylan | 1965 | 30.00 |
| *—"Mono" on label* | | | |
| ❑ CAS 2222 [DJ] | Time Passes Slowly | 1985 | 25.00 |
| *—Promo-only sampler from Biograph box set* | | | |
| ❑ CL 2302/CS 9102 | Bob Dylan In Concert | 1965 | 4000. |
| *—Never pressed; value is for a cover slick, some of which were printed; VG value 2000; VG+ value 3000* | | | |
| ❑ CL 2328 [M] | Bringing It All Back Home | 1965 | 30.00 |
| *—"Mono" on label* | | | |
| ❑ CL 2328 [M] | Bringing It All Back Home | 1965 | 50.00 |
| *—"Guaranteed High Fidelity" on label* | | | |

| Number | Title (A Side/B Side) | Yr | NM |
|---|---|---|---|
| ❑ CL 2328 [M] | Bringing It All Back Home | 1965 | 300.00 |
| *—White label promo* | | | |
| ❑ CL 2389 [M] | Highway 61 Revisited | 1965 | 80.00 |
| ❑ CL 2389 [M] | Highway 61 Revisited | 1965 | 400.00 |
| *—White label promo* | | | |
| ❑ 2663/9463 | Bob Dylan's Greatest Hits Poster | 1967 | 4.00 |
| *—Almost every copy into the late 1970s came with a poster* | | | |
| ❑ KCL 2663 [M] | Bob Dylan's Greatest Hits | 1967 | 50.00 |
| ❑ CL 2804 [M] | John Wesley Harding | 1968 | 150.00 |
| ❑ CS 8579 [S] | Bob Dylan | 1962 | 400.00 |
| *—Red and black label with six white "eye" logos, three together at the left, three together at the right, with "Stereo Fidelity" at the top of the label and "Columbia" at the bottom; stock copy* | | | |
| ❑ CS 8579 [S] | Bob Dylan | 1962 | 600.00 |
| *—Six "eye" logos on label; "A New Star on Columbia" sticker on cover and promo stamp on label* | | | |
| ❑ CS 8579 [S] | Bob Dylan | 1963 | 40.00 |
| *—"360 Sound Stereo" in black on label* | | | |
| ❑ CS 8579 [S] | Bob Dylan | 1965 | 25.00 |
| *—"360 Sound Stereo" in white on label* | | | |
| ❑ CS 8579 [S] | Bob Dylan | 1970 | 12.00 |
| *—Orange label* | | | |
| ❑ JC 8579 [S] | Bob Dylan | 197? | 8.00 |
| *—Some copies of this pressing of the above album may have the song "You're No Good" listed on the label as "She's No Good." No extra premium has been attached to this error as yet.* | | | |
| ❑ KCS 8579 [S] | Bob Dylan | 197? | 10.00 |
| ❑ PC 8579 [S] | Bob Dylan | 198? | 8.00 |
| *—Budget-line reissue* | | | |
| ❑ PC 8579 [S] | Bob Dylan | 2001 | 12.00 |
| *—Reissue on 180-gram vinyl (sealed copies have a sticker indicating this)* | | | |
| ❑ CS 8786 [S] | The Freewheelin' Bob Dylan | 1963 | 50.00 |
| *—"360 Sound Stereo" in black on label (no arrows)* | | | |
| ❑ CS 8786 [S] | The Freewheelin' Bob Dylan | 1963 | 400.00 |
| *—Canadian pressing with the deleted tracks listed on the front cover. The label lists, and the record plays, the "correct" tracks.* | | | |
| ❑ CS 8786 [S] | The Freewheelin' Bob Dylan | 1963 | 30000. |
| *—"360 Sound Stereo" in black on label (no arrows); record plays, and label lists, "Let Me Die in My Footsteps," "Rocks and Gravel," "Talkin' John Birch Blues" and "Gamblin' Willie's Dead Man's Hand." No known stereo copies play these without listing them, but just in case, check the trail-off for the numbers "XSM-58719-1A" and "XSM-58720-1A." If the number after the dash is "2" or higher, it's the standard version; VG value 15000; VG+ value 22500* | | | |
| ❑ CS 8786 [S] | The Freewheelin' Bob Dylan | 1964 | 40.00 |
| *—"360 Sound Stereo" in black on label (with arrows)* | | | |
| ❑ CS 8786 [S] | The Freewheelin' Bob Dylan | 1965 | 25.00 |
| *—"360 Sound Stereo" in white on label* | | | |
| ❑ CS 8786 [S] | The Freewheelin' Bob Dylan | 197? | 1000. |
| *—Orange label; unauthorized red vinyl pressing* | | | |
| ❑ CS 8786 [S] | The Freewheelin' Bob Dylan | 1970 | 12.00 |
| *—Orange label* | | | |
| ❑ KCS 8786 [S] | The Freewheelin' Bob Dylan | 197? | 10.00 |
| ❑ PC 8786 [S] | The Freewheelin' Bob Dylan | 198? | 8.00 |
| *—Budget-line reissue* | | | |
| ❑ PC 8786 [S] | The Freewheelin' Bob Dylan | 2001 | 12.00 |
| *—Reissue on 180-gram vinyl (sealed copies have a sticker indicating this)* | | | |
| ❑ CS 8905 [S] | The Times They Are a-Changin' | 1964 | 40.00 |
| *—"360 Sound Stereo" in black on label* | | | |
| ❑ CS 8905 [S] | The Times They Are a-Changin' | 1965 | 25.00 |
| *—"360 Sound Stereo" in white on label* | | | |
| ❑ CS 8905 [S] | The Times They Are a-Changin' | 1970 | 12.00 |
| *—Orange label* | | | |
| ❑ KCS 8905 [S] | The Times They Are a-Changin' | 197? | 10.00 |
| ❑ PC 8905 [S] | The Times They Are a-Changin' | 198? | 8.00 |
| *—Budget-line reissue* | | | |
| ❑ PC 8905 [S] | The Times They Are a-Changin' | 2001 | 12.00 |
| *—Reissue on 180-gram vinyl (sealed copies have a sticker indicating this)* | | | |
| ❑ CS 8993 [S] | Another Side of Bob Dylan | 1964 | 40.00 |
| *—"360 Sound Stereo" in black on label* | | | |
| ❑ CS 8993 [S] | Another Side of Bob Dylan | 1965 | 25.00 |
| *—"360 Sound Stereo" in white on label* | | | |
| ❑ CS 8993 [S] | Another Side of Bob Dylan | 1970 | 12.00 |
| *—Orange label* | | | |
| ❑ KCS 8993 [S] | Another Side of Bob Dylan | 197? | 10.00 |
| ❑ PC 8993 [S] | Another Side of Bob Dylan | 198? | 8.00 |
| *—Budget-line reissue* | | | |
| ❑ PC 8993 [S] | Another Side of Bob Dylan | 2001 | 12.00 |
| *—Reissue on 180-gram vinyl (sealed copies have a sticker indicating this)* | | | |
| ❑ CS 9128 [S] | Bringing It All Back Home | 1965 | 25.00 |
| *—"360 Sound Stereo" in white on label* | | | |
| ❑ CS 9128 [S] | Bringing It All Back Home | 1965 | 40.00 |
| *—"360 Sound Stereo" in black on label* | | | |
| ❑ CS 9128 [S] | Bringing It All Back Home | 1970 | 12.00 |
| *—Orange label* | | | |
| ❑ JC 9128 [S] | Bringing It All Back Home | 197? | 10.00 |
| ❑ KCS 9128 [S] | Bringing It All Back Home | 197? | 10.00 |
| ❑ PC 9128 [S] | Bringing It All Back Home | 198? | 8.00 |
| *—Budget-line reissue* | | | |
| ❑ PC 9128 [S] | Bringing It All Back Home | 2001 | 12.00 |
| *—Reissue on 180-gram vinyl (sealed copies have a sticker indicating this)* | | | |



**Except when noted otherwise, VG = 25% of NM, and VG+ = 50% of NM. (Example: VG = $2.00, VG+ = $4.00 and NM = $8.00.)**

| Number | Title (A Side/B Side) | Yr | NM |
|---|---|---|---|
| ❑ CS 9189 [S] | Highway 61 Revisited | 1965 | 30.00 |
| *—With "regular" take of "From a Buick 6." Matrix number on Side 1 will end in "--2" or higher, plus a letter; "360 Sound Stereo" on label* | | | |
| ❑ CS 9189 [S] | Highway 61 Revisited | 1965 | 250.00 |
| *—With alterrnate take of "From a Buick 6." Matrix number on Side 1 will end in "--1" plus a letter* | | | |
| ❑ CS 9189 [S] | Highway 61 Revisited | 1970 | 12.00 |
| *—Orange label* | | | |
| ❑ JC 9189 [S] | Highway 61 Revisited | 197? | 10.00 |
| ❑ KCS 9189 [S] | Highway 61 Revisited | 197? | 10.00 |
| ❑ PC 9189 [S] | Highway 61 Revisited | 198? | 8.00 |
| *—Budget-line reissue* | | | |
| ❑ PC 9189 [S] | Highway 61 Revisited | 2001 | 12.00 |
| *—Reissue on 180-gram vinyl (sealed copies have a sticker indicating this)* | | | |
| ❑ JC 9463 [S] | Bob Dylan's Greatest Hits | 197? | 10.00 |
| ❑ JC 9463 [S] | Bob Dylan's Greatest Hits | 2001 | 12.00 |
| *—Reissue on 180-gram vinyl (sealed copies have a sticker indicating this)* | | | |
| ❑ KCS 9463 [S] | Bob Dylan's Greatest Hits | 1967 | 15.00 |
| *—"360 Sound Stereo" label* | | | |
| ❑ KCS 9463 [S] | Bob Dylan's Greatest Hits | 1970 | 12.00 |
| *—Orange label* | | | |
| ❑ CS 9604 [S] | John Wesley Harding | 1968 | 20.00 |
| *—"360 Sound Stereo" label* | | | |
| ❑ CS 9604 [S] | John Wesley Harding | 1970 | 12.00 |
| *—Orange label* | | | |
| ❑ JC 9604 [S] | John Wesley Harding | 197? | 10.00 |
| ❑ KCS 9604 [S] | John Wesley Harding | 197? | 10.00 |
| ❑ PC 9604 [S] | John Wesley Harding | 198? | 8.00 |
| *—Budget-line reissue* | | | |
| ❑ PC 9604 [S] | John Wesley Harding | 2001 | 12.00 |
| *—Reissue on 180-gram vinyl (sealed copies have a sticker indicating this)* | | | |
| ❑ JC 9825 | Nashville Skyline | 197? | 10.00 |
| ❑ KCS 9825 | Nashville Skyline | 1969 | 30.00 |
| *—"360 Sound Stereo" label* | | | |
| ❑ KCS 9825 | Nashville Skyline | 1970 | 12.00 |
| *—Orange label* | | | |
| ❑ PC 9825 | Nashville Skyline | 198? | 8.00 |
| *—Budget-line reissue* | | | |
| ❑ C2X 30050 [(2)] | Self Portrait | 1970 | 20.00 |
| *—Orange labels* | | | |
| ❑ C2X 30050 [(2)] | Self Portrait | 1970 | 150.00 |
| *—"360 Sound Stereo" labels* | | | |
| ❑ CG 30050 [(2)] | Self Portrait | 198? | 12.00 |
| ❑ P2X 30050 [(2)] | Self Portrait | 197? | 15.00 |
| ❑ KC 30290 | New Morning | 1970 | 15.00 |
| ❑ PC 30290 | New Morning | 197? | 8.00 |
| ❑ PC 30290 | New Morning | 2001 | 12.00 |
| *—Reissue on 180-gram vinyl (sealed copies have a sticker indicating this)* | | | |
| ❑ CG 31120 [(2)] | Bob Dylan's Greatest Hits, Vol. II | 198? | 10.00 |
| ❑ KG 31120 [(2)] | Bob Dylan's Greatest Hits, Vol. II | 1971 | 15.00 |
| ❑ PG 31120 [(2)] | Bob Dylan's Greatest Hits, Vol. II | 197? | 12.00 |
| ❑ KC 32460 | Pat Garrett and Billy the Kid | 1973 | 15.00 |
| ❑ PC 32460 | Pat Garrett and Billy the Kid | 197? | 8.00 |
| ❑ PC 32747 | Dylan | 1973 | 15.00 |
| *—No bar code on cover* | | | |
| ❑ PC 32747 | Dylan | 1979 | 8.00 |
| *—With bar code on back cover* | | | |
| ❑ KCQ 32825 [Q] | Nashville Skyline | 1973 | 30.00 |
| ❑ PC 33235 | Blood on the Tracks | 1975 | 10.00 |
| *—Third editions have liner notes restored (after they won a Grammy), but in white print* | | | |
| ❑ PC 33235 | Blood on the Tracks | 1975 | 12.00 |
| *—First editions have liner notes on the back cover in black print* | | | |
| ❑ PC 33235 | Blood on the Tracks | 1975 | 15.00 |
| *—With drawing on back cover and no liner notes. Actually a second pressing, but available only for a short time* | | | |
| ❑ PC 33235 | Blood on the Tracks | 1975 | 2000. |
| *—First edition cover; with the original rejected version of Side 2, though Side 1 is the standard version; the master number in the trail-off wax on Side 2 is "-1A"; one copy known, but others may exist* | | | |
| ❑ PC 33235 | Blood on the Tracks | 1979 | 8.00 |
| *—With bar code on back cover* | | | |
| ❑ PC 33235 | Blood on the Tracks | 2001 | 12.00 |
| *—Reissue on 180-gram vinyl (sealed copies have a sticker indicating this)* | | | |
| ❑ PC 33235 [DJ] | Blood on the Tracks | 1975 | 30.00 |
| *—Regular white label promo* | | | |
| ❑ PC 33235 [DJ] | Blood on the Tracks | 1975 | 5000. |
| *—Test pressing with radically different versions of five songs including "Idiot Wind" and "Tangled Up in Blue"; VG value 2500; VG+ value 3750* | | | |
| ❑ CG 33682 [(2)] | The Basement Tapes | 198? | 12.00 |
| ❑ PC2 33682 [(2)] | The Basement Tapes | 1975 | 20.00 |
| ❑ PC2 33682 [(2)DJ] | The Basement Tapes | 1975 | 40.00 |
| *—White label promo* | | | |
| ❑ JC 33893 | Desire | 1977 | 10.00 |
| *—No bar code on back cover* | | | |
| ❑ JC 33893 | Desire | 1979 | 8.00 |
| *—With bar code on back cover* | | | |
| ❑ PC 33893 | Desire | 1976 | 12.00 |
| ❑ PC 33893 [DJ] | Desire | 1976 | 30.00 |
| *—White label promo* | | | |
| ❑ PCQ 33893 [Q] | Desire | 1976 | 30.00 |
| ❑ JC 34349 | Hard Rain | 1977 | 10.00 |
| ❑ PC 34349 | Hard Rain | 1976 | 12.00 |
| *—No bar code on back cover* | | | |
| ❑ PC 34349 | Hard Rain | 198? | 8.00 |
| *—With bar code on back cover* | | | |

Bob Dylan, *Blood on the Tracks,* Columbia PC 33235, 1975, black print on back, $12.

| Number | Title (A Side/B Side) | Yr | NM |
|---|---|---|---|
| ❑ PC 34349 [DJ] | Hard Rain | 1976 | 30.00 |
| *—White label promo* | | | |
| ❑ JC 35453 | Street Legal | 1978 | 12.00 |
| ❑ JC 35453 [DJ] | Street Legal | 1978 | 25.00 |
| *—White label promo* | | | |
| ❑ PC 35453 | Street Legal | 198? | 8.00 |
| ❑ CG 36067 [(2)] | Bob Dylan at Budokan | 198? | 12.00 |
| ❑ PC2 36067 [(2)] | Bob Dylan at Budokan | 1979 | 15.00 |
| ❑ PC2 36067 [(2)DJ] | Bob Dylan at Budokan | 1979 | 30.00 |
| *—White label promo* | | | |
| ❑ FC 36120 | Slow Train Coming | 1979 | 10.00 |
| ❑ FC 36120 [DJ] | Slow Train Coming | 1979 | 25.00 |
| *—White label promo* | | | |
| ❑ PC 36120 | Slow Train Coming | 198? | 8.00 |
| *—Budget-line reissue* | | | |
| ❑ FC 36553 | Saved | 1980 | 10.00 |
| ❑ PC 36553 | Saved | 198? | 8.00 |
| *—Budget-line reissue with new cover* | | | |
| ❑ PC 37496 | Shot of Love | 198? | 8.00 |
| *—Budget-line reissue* | | | |
| ❑ TC 37496 | Shot of Love | 1981 | 10.00 |
| ❑ PC 37637 | Planet Waves | 1981 | 10.00 |
| *—Reissue of Asylum 7E-1003* | | | |
| ❑ CG 37661 [(2)] | Before the Flood | 1983 | 12.00 |
| *—Reissue of Asylum AB-201* | | | |
| ❑ PC 38819 | Infidels | 1986 | 8.00 |
| *—Budget-line reissue* | | | |
| ❑ QC 38819 | Infidels | 1983 | 10.00 |
| ❑ C5X 38830 [(5)] | Biograph | 1985 | 30.00 |
| ❑ FC 39944 | Real Live | 1984 | 10.00 |
| ❑ FC 40110 | Empire Burlesque | 1985 | 10.00 |
| ❑ OC 40439 | Knocked Out Loaded | 1986 | 10.00 |
| ❑ OC 40957 | Down in the Groove | 1988 | 10.00 |
| ❑ HC 43235 | Blood on the Tracks | 198? | 50.00 |
| *—Half-speed mastered edition* | | | |
| ❑ OC 45056 | Dylan and the Dead | 1989 | 12.00 |
| *—With backing by The Grateful Dead* | | | |
| ❑ OC 45281 | Oh Mercy | 1989 | 12.00 |
| ❑ C 46794 | Under the Red Sky | 1990 | 12.00 |
| ❑ HC 49825 | Nashville Skyline | 198? | 60.00 |
| *—Half-speed mastered edition* | | | |
| ❑ C 53200 | Good As I Been to You | 1992 | 60.00 |
| ❑ CK2-65759-1 [(2)] | The Bootleg Series Vol. 4: Bob Dylan Live 1966, The "Royal Albert Hall" Concert | 1999 | 100.00 |
| *—Classic Records box set with 12x12 booklet and two records individually packaged in cardboard jackets and sleeves* | | | |
| ❑ C2 67000 [(2)] | MTV Unplugged | 1995 | 15.00 |

| Number | Title (A Side/B Side) | Yr | NM |
|---|---|---|---|
| ❑ C2 68556 [(2)] | Time Out of Mind | 1998 | 15.00 |
| ❑ C2 85975 [(2)] | Love and Theft | 2001 | 15.00 |
| ❑ C2K-87047-1 [(3)] | The Bootleg Series Vol. 5: Rolling Thunder Revue Starring Bob Dylan | 2003 | 50.00 |
| *—Similar to the other package, but records are pressed on 140-gram vinyl and come in plain paper (rather than lined) sleeves* | | | |
| ❑ C2K-87047-1 [(3)] | The Bootleg Series Vol. 5: Rolling Thunder Revue Starring Bob Dylan | 2003 | 100.00 |
| *—Classic Records box set with 12x12 booklet, three 200-gram 12-inch records individually packaged in cardboard jackets and sleeves, a blue vinyl 7-inch single in a picture sleeve, a poster, a souvenir handbill and facsimile tickets to the show* | | | |
| ❑ 82876-87606-1 [(2)] | Modern Times | 2006 | 15.00 |
| ❑ 474000 [(3)] | Bob Dylan — The 30th Anniversary Concert Celebration | 1993 | 30.00 |
| *—Albums pressed in US for export to Europe; some stayed here* | | | |
| **ISLAND** | | | |
| ❑ AB-201 [(2)] | Before the Flood | 1974 | 40.00 |
| *—Error pressing with wrong labels (should be Asylum)* | | | |
| **MOBILE FIDELITY** | | | |
| ❑ 1-114 | The Times They Are a-Changin' | 1982 | 50.00 |
| *—Audiophile vinyl* | | | |
| **SUNDAZED** | | | |
| ❑ LP 5070 [M] | Bringing It All Back Home | 2001 | 15.00 |
| *—180-gram reissue of the original mono mix* | | | |
| ❑ LP 5071 [M] | Highway 61 Revisited | 2001 | 15.00 |
| *—180-gram reissue of the original mono mix* | | | |
| ❑ LP 5108 [M] | The Times They Are a-Changin' | 2001 | 15.00 |
| *—180-gram reissue of the original mono mix* | | | |
| ❑ LP 5110 [(2)M] | Blonde on Blonde | 2002 | 25.00 |
| *—180-gram reissue of the original mono mix* | | | |
| ❑ LP 5115 [M] | The Freewheelin' Bob Dylan | 2001 | 15.00 |
| *—180-gram reissue of the original mono mix* | | | |
| ❑ LP 5120 [M] | Bob Dylan | 2004 | 15.00 |
| *—180-gram reissue of the original mono mix* | | | |
| ❑ LP 5121 [M] | Another Side of Bob Dylan | 2002 | 15.00 |
| *—180-gram reissue of the original mono mix* | | | |
| ❑ LP 5123 [M] | John Wesley Harding | 2003 | 15.00 |
| *—180-gram reissue of the original mono mix* | | | |
| ❑ LP 5156 [M] | Bob Dylan's Greatest Hits | 2003 | 15.00 |
| *—180-gram reissue of the original mono mix* | | | |

Eagles, *Eagles,* Asylum SD 5054, 1972, gatefold cover, $15.

| Number | Title (A Side/B Side) | Yr | NM |
|---|---|---|---|
| **WARNER BROS./7 ARTS MUSIC** | | | |
| ❑ XTV 221567 [DJ] | Bob Dylan | 1969 | 1500. |
| *—One-sided publisher's demo with 8 Dylan performances of then-unreleased songs from the "Basement Tapes" era* | | | |

## DYLAN, BOB, AND ALAN J. WEBERMAN

| Number | Title (A Side/B Side) | Yr | NM |
|---|---|---|---|
| **FOLKWAYS** | | | |
| ❑ FB-5322 [M] | Bob Dylan Vs. A.J. Weberman | 1977 | 300.00 |
| *—A tape-recorded phone conversation; quickly withdrawn from the market* | | | |

## DYNAMICS, THE (2)

| Number | Title (A Side/B Side) | Yr | NM |
|---|---|---|---|
| **BOLO** | | | |
| ❑ BLP-8001 [M] | The Dynamics with Jimmy Hanna | 1964 | 50.00 |

## DYNATONES, THE (1)

| Number | Title (A Side/B Side) | Yr | NM |
|---|---|---|---|
| **HANNA-BARBERA** | | | |
| ❑ HLP-8509 [M] | The Fife Piper | 1966 | 20.00 |
| ❑ HST-8509 [S] | The Fife Piper | 1966 | 25.00 |

# E

## EAGER, ALLAN

| Number | Title (A Side/B Side) | Yr | NM |
|---|---|---|---|
| **SAVOY** | | | |
| ❑ MG-9015 [10] | New Trends in Modern Music, Volume 2 | 1952 | 250.00 |
| ❑ MG-15044 [10] | Tenor Sax | 1954 | 200.00 |

## EAGLE

| Number | Title (A Side/B Side) | Yr | NM |
|---|---|---|---|
| **JANUS** | | | |
| ❑ JLS-3011 | Come Under Nancy's Tent | 1970 | 20.00 |

## EAGLES

| Number | Title (A Side/B Side) | Yr | NM |
|---|---|---|---|
| **ASYLUM** | | | |
| ❑ 6E-103 | Hotel California | 1977 | 8.00 |
| ❑ 6E-105 | Eagles — Their Greatest Hits 1971-1975 | 1977 | 8.00 |
| ❑ 5E-508 | The Long Run | 1979 | 8.00 |
| ❑ BB-705 [(2)] | Eagles Live | 1980 | 12.00 |
| ❑ 7E-1004 | On the Border | 1974 | 12.00 |
| *—Clouds label* | | | |
| ❑ EQ 1004 [Q] | On the Border | 1974 | 20.00 |
| ❑ 7E-1039 | One of These Nights | 1975 | 10.00 |
| *—Clouds label* | | | |
| ❑ EQ 1039 [Q] | One of These Nights | 1975 | 20.00 |
| ❑ 7E-1052 | Eagles — Their Greatest Hits 1971-1975 | 1976 | 10.00 |
| ❑ 7E-1084 | Hotel California | 1976 | 10.00 |
| ❑ 5054 [M] | Eagles | 1972 | 40.00 |
| *—Promo only; white label with "d/j copy monaural" sticker on cover* | | | |
| ❑ SD 5054 | Eagles | 1972 | 15.00 |
| *—Gatefold cover; white label with door-in-a-circle logo at top* | | | |
| ❑ SD 5054 | Eagles | 1973 | 12.00 |
| *—Regular cover; clouds label* | | | |
| ❑ SD 5068 | Desperado | 1973 | 12.00 |
| *—Clouds label* | | | |
| ❑ 60205 | Eagles Greatest Hits, Volume 2 | 1982 | 10.00 |
| **DCC COMPACT CLASSICS** | | | |
| ❑ LPZ-2043 | Hotel California | 1997 | 120.00 |
| *—Audiophile vinyl* | | | |
| ❑ LPZ-2051 | Eagles — Their Greatest Hits 1971-1975 | 1998 | 100.00 |
| *—Audiophile vinyl* | | | |
| **ELEKTRA** | | | |
| ❑ 60422 | Anthology of the Eagles | 1985 | — |
| *—Canceled* | | | |
| **MOBILE FIDELITY** | | | |
| ❑ 1-126 | Hotel California | 1984 | 100.00 |
| *—Audiophile vinyl* | | | |

## EAGLIN, SNOOKS

| Number | Title (A Side/B Side) | Yr | NM |
|---|---|---|---|
| **ARHOOLIE** | | | |
| ❑ 2014 | Possum Up a Simmon Tree | 198? | 10.00 |
| **BLACK TOP** | | | |
| ❑ BT-1037 | Baby, You Can Get Your Gun | 1987 | 10.00 |
| ❑ BT-1046 | Out of Nowhere | 198? | 10.00 |
| **BLUESVILLE** | | | |
| ❑ BVLP-1046 [M] | That's All Right | 1962 | 60.00 |
| *—Blue label, silver print* | | | |
| ❑ BVLP-1046 [M] | That's All Right | 1964 | 25.00 |
| *—Blue label, trident logo at right* | | | |
| **FOLKWAYS** | | | |
| ❑ FA-2476 [M] | New Orleans Street Singer | 1959 | 40.00 |
| **GNP CRESCENDO** | | | |
| ❑ 10023 | Down Yonder | 1979 | 10.00 |

## EARDLEY, JON

| Number | Title (A Side/B Side) | Yr | NM |
|---|---|---|---|
| **NEW JAZZ** | | | |
| ❑ NJLP-1105 [10] | Jon Eardley in Hollywood | 1954 | 200.00 |
| **PRESTIGE** | | | |
| ❑ PRLP-205 [10] | Jon Eardley in Hollywood | 1955 | 150.00 |
| ❑ PRLP-207 [10] | Hey There | 1955 | 150.00 |
| ❑ PRLP-7033 [M] | Jon Eardley Seven | 1956 | 100.00 |

## EARLAND, CHARLES

| Number | Title (A Side/B Side) | Yr | NM |
|---|---|---|---|
| **PRESTIGE** | | | |
| ❑ PRST-7758 | Black Talk! | 1970 | 20.00 |

## EARLS, THE (1)

| Number | Title (A Side/B Side) | Yr | NM |
|---|---|---|---|
| **CHANCE** | | | |
| ❑ 1001 | The Earls Today | 1983 | 12.00 |
| **OLD TOWN** | | | |
| ❑ LP-104 [M] | Remember Me Baby | 1963 | 500.00 |
| *—Counterfeit identification: Counterfeits have more than 1-inch trailoffs or as little as 1/2 inch trailoffs; legitimate copies have 5/8- to 3/4-inch trailoff* | | | |
| **WOODBURY** | | | |
| ❑ 104 | Remember Me Baby | 1976 | 15.00 |

## EARTH ISLAND

| Number | Title (A Side/B Side) | Yr | NM |
|---|---|---|---|
| **PHILPS** | | | |
| ❑ PHS 600340 | We Must Survive | 1970 | 25.00 |

## EARTH OPERA

| Number | Title (A Side/B Side) | Yr | NM |
|---|---|---|---|
| **ELEKTRA** | | | |
| ❑ EKS-74016 | Earth Opera | 1968 | 20.00 |
| ❑ EKS-74038 | The Great American Eagle Tragedy | 1969 | 20.00 |

## EARTH, WIND, AND FIRE

| Number | Title (A Side/B Side) | Yr | NM |
|---|---|---|---|
| **ARC** | | | |
| ❑ FC 35647 | The Best of Earth, Wind & Fire, Vol. 1 | 1978 | 10.00 |
| ❑ FC 35730 | I Am | 1979 | 10.00 |
| ❑ PC 35730 | I Am | 1984 | 8.00 |
| *—Budget-line reissue* | | | |
| ❑ KC2 36795 [(2)] | Faces | 1980 | 12.00 |
| ❑ PC 37548 | Raise! | 1984 | 8.00 |
| *—Budget-line reissue* | | | |
| ❑ TC 37548 | Raise! | 1981 | 10.00 |
| ❑ HC 45647 | The Best of Earth, Wind & Fire, Vol. 1 | 1981 | 30.00 |
| *—Half-speed mastered edition* | | | |
| ❑ HC 45730 | I Am | 1981 | 30.00 |
| *—Half-speed mastered edition* | | | |
| ❑ HC 47548 | Raise! | 1982 | 30.00 |
| *—Half-speed mastered edition* | | | |
| **COLUMBIA** | | | |
| ❑ KC 31702 | Last Days and Time | 1972 | 15.00 |
| ❑ PC 31702 | Last Days and Time | 197? | 8.00 |
| *—Reissue* | | | |
| ❑ CQ 32194 [Q] | Head to the Sky | 1973 | 20.00 |
| ❑ KC 32194 | Head to the Sky | 1973 | 12.00 |
| ❑ PC 32194 | Head to the Sky | 197? | 8.00 |
| *—Reissue* | | | |
| ❑ CQ 32712 [Q] | Open Our Eyes | 1974 | 20.00 |
| ❑ KC 32712 | Open Our Eyes | 1974 | 12.00 |
| ❑ PC 32712 | Open Our Eyes | 197? | 8.00 |
| *—Reissue* | | | |
| ❑ PC 33280 | That's the Way of the World | 1975 | 12.00 |
| *—No bar code* | | | |
| ❑ PC 33280 | That's the Way of the World | 198? | 8.00 |
| *—Budget-line reissue with bar code* | | | |
| ❑ PCQ33280 [Q] | That's the Way of the World | 1975 | 20.00 |
| ❑ PG 33694 [(2)] | Gratitude | 1975 | 15.00 |
| *—No bar code* | | | |
| ❑ PG 33694 [(2)] | Gratitude | 198? | 10.00 |
| *—Budget-line reissue with bar code* | | | |
| ❑ PC 34241 | Spirit | 1976 | 12.00 |
| *—No bar code* | | | |
| ❑ PC 34241 | Spirit | 198? | 8.00 |
| *—Budget-line reissue with bar code* | | | |
| ❑ PCQ 34241 [Q] | Spirit | 1976 | 25.00 |
| ❑ JC 34905 | All 'N All | 1977 | 12.00 |
| ❑ PC 34905 | All 'N All | 198? | 8.00 |
| *—Budget-line reissue* | | | |
| ❑ PC 38367 | Powerlight | 1984 | 8.00 |
| *—Budget-line reissue* | | | |
| ❑ TC 38367 | Powerlight | 1983 | 10.00 |
| ❑ QC 38980 | Electric Universe | 1983 | 10.00 |
| ❑ FC 40596 | Touch the World | 1987 | 10.00 |
| ❑ OC 45013 | The Best of Earth, Wind & Fire, Vol. II | 1988 | 10.00 |
| ❑ C 45268 | Heritage | 1990 | 15.00 |
| ❑ HC 48367 | Powerlight | 1983 | 40.00 |
| *—Half-speed mastered edition* | | | |
| **MOBILE FIDELITY** | | | |
| ❑ 1-159 | That's the Way of the World | 198? | 30.00 |
| *—Audiophile vinyl* | | | |
| **PAIR** | | | |
| ❑ PDL2-1064 [(2)] | Beat It to Life | 1986 | 12.00 |

| Number | Title (A Side/B Side) | Yr | NM |
|---|---|---|---|
| **WARNER BROS.** | | | |
| ❑ WS 1905 | Earth, Wind, and Fire | 1971 | 20.00 |
| *—Green label* | | | |
| ❑ WS 1958 | The Need of Love | 1971 | 20.00 |
| *—Green label* | | | |
| ❑ 2WS 2798 [(2)] | Another Time | 1974 | 20.00 |
| *—"Burbank" palm trees labels* | | | |

### EAST

| Number | Title (A Side/B Side) | Yr | NM |
|---|---|---|---|
| **CAPITOL** | | | |
| ❑ ST-11083 | East | 1972 | 25.00 |

### EAST OF EDEN

| Number | Title (A Side/B Side) | Yr | NM |
|---|---|---|---|
| **DERAM** | | | |
| ❑ DES 18023 | Mercator Projected | 1969 | 20.00 |
| ❑ DES 18043 | Snafu | 1970 | 20.00 |
| **HARVEST** | | | |
| ❑ SW-806 | East of Eden | 1971 | 20.00 |

### EAST SIDE KIDS, THE

| Number | Title (A Side/B Side) | Yr | NM |
|---|---|---|---|
| **UNI** | | | |
| ❑ 73032 | The Tiger and the Lamb | 1968 | 25.00 |

### EASTMAN-ROCHESTER ORCHESTRA (HOWARD HANSON, CONDUCTOR)

| Number | Title (A Side/B Side) | Yr | NM |
|---|---|---|---|
| **MERCURY LIVING PRESENCE** | | | |
| ❑ SR 90018 [S] | Chadwick: Symphonic Sketches | 1959 | 30.00 |
| *—Maroon label, no "Vendor: Mercury Record Corporation"* | | | |
| ❑ SR 90049 [S] | Grofe: Grand Canyon Suite; Mississippi Suite | 1959 | 30.00 |
| *—Maroon label, no "Vendor: Mercury Record Corporation"* | | | |
| ❑ SR 90053 [S] | Music for Quiet Listening | 1959 | 60.00 |
| *—Maroon label, no "Vendor: Mercury Record Corporation"* | | | |
| ❑ SR 90053 [S] | Music for Quiet Listening | 196? | 50.00 |
| *—Maroon label, with "Vendor: Mercury Record Corporation"* | | | |
| ❑ SR 90103 [S] | McPhee: Tabuh-Tauhan; Sessions: The Black Maskers | 196? | 250.00 |
| *—Maroon label, no "Vendor: Mercury Record Corporation"* | | | |
| ❑ SR 90134 [S] | Fiesta in Hi-Fi | 1960 | 100.00 |
| *—Maroon label, no "Vendor: Mercury Record Corporation"* | | | |
| ❑ SR 90136 [S] | Carpenter: Adventures in a Perambulator; Phillips: Selections from McGuffey's Readers | 1960 | 100.00 |
| *—Maroon label, no "Vendor: Mercury Record Corporation"* | | | |
| ❑ SR 90147 [S] | Kennan: Three Pieces; Rogers: Once Upon a Time; Bergama: Gold and the Senor Commandante | 196? | 200.00 |
| *—Maroon label, no "Vendor: Mercury Record Corporation"* | | | |
| ❑ SR 90149 [S] | Ives: Three Places in New England; Symphony No. 3 | 196? | 20.00 |
| *—Maroon label, with "Vendor: Mercury Record Corporation"* | | | |
| ❑ SR 90149 [S] | Ives: Three Places in New England; Symphony No. 3 | 196? | 40.00 |
| *—Maroon label, no "Vendor: Mercury Record Corporation"* | | | |
| ❑ SR 90150 [S] | Hanson: Elegy in Memory of Koussevitzky; Song of Democracy; Lane: 4 Songs | 196? | 50.00 |
| *—Maroon label, with "Vendor: Mercury Record Corporation"* | | | |
| ❑ SR 90150 [S] | Hanson: Elegy in Memory of Koussevitzky; Song of Democracy; Lane: 4 Songs | 196? | 100.00 |
| *—Maroon label, no "Vendor: Mercury Record Corporation"* | | | |
| ❑ SR 90163 [S] | Herbert: Cello Concerto; Peter: Sinfonia in G | 196? | 40.00 |
| *—Maroon label, no "Vendor: Mercury Record Corporation"* | | | |
| ❑ SR 90165 [S] | Hanson: Symphony No. 1 "Nordic"; Fantasy Variations on a Theme of Youth | 196? | 20.00 |
| *—Maroon label, with "Vendor: Mercury Record Corporation"* | | | |
| ❑ SR 90165 [S] | Hanson: Symphony No. 1 "Nordic"; Fantasy Variations on a Theme of Youth | 196? | 40.00 |
| *—Maroon label, no "Vendor: Mercury Record Corporation"* | | | |
| ❑ SR 90175 [S] | The Composer and His Orchestra | 196? | 20.00 |
| *—Maroon label, with "Vendor: Mercury Record Corporation"* | | | |
| ❑ SR 90175 [S] | The Composer and His Orchestra | 196? | 25.00 |
| *—Maroon label, no "Vendor: Mercury Record Corporation"* | | | |
| ❑ SR 90192 [S] | Hanson: Symphony No. 2 "Romantic"; Lament for Beowulf | 196? | 20.00 |
| *—Maroon label, with "Vendor: Mercury Record Corporation"* | | | |
| ❑ SR 90192 [S] | Hanson: Symphony No. 2 "Romantic"; Lament for Beowulf | 196? | 30.00 |
| *—Maroon label, no "Vendor: Mercury Record Corporation"* | | | |
| ❑ SR 90206 [S] | Piston: The Incredible Flutist; Moore: Pageant of P.T. Barnum | 196? | 20.00 |
| *—Maroon label, with "Vendor: Mercury Record Corporation"* | | | |
| ❑ SR 90206 [S] | Piston: The Incredible Flutist; Moore: Pageant of P.T. Barnum | 196? | 40.00 |
| *—Maroon label, no "Vendor: Mercury Record Corporation"* | | | |
| ❑ SR 90223 [S] | Bloch: Concerti Grossi No. 1 and 2 | 196? | 20.00 |
| *—Third edition: Dark red (not maroon) label* | | | |

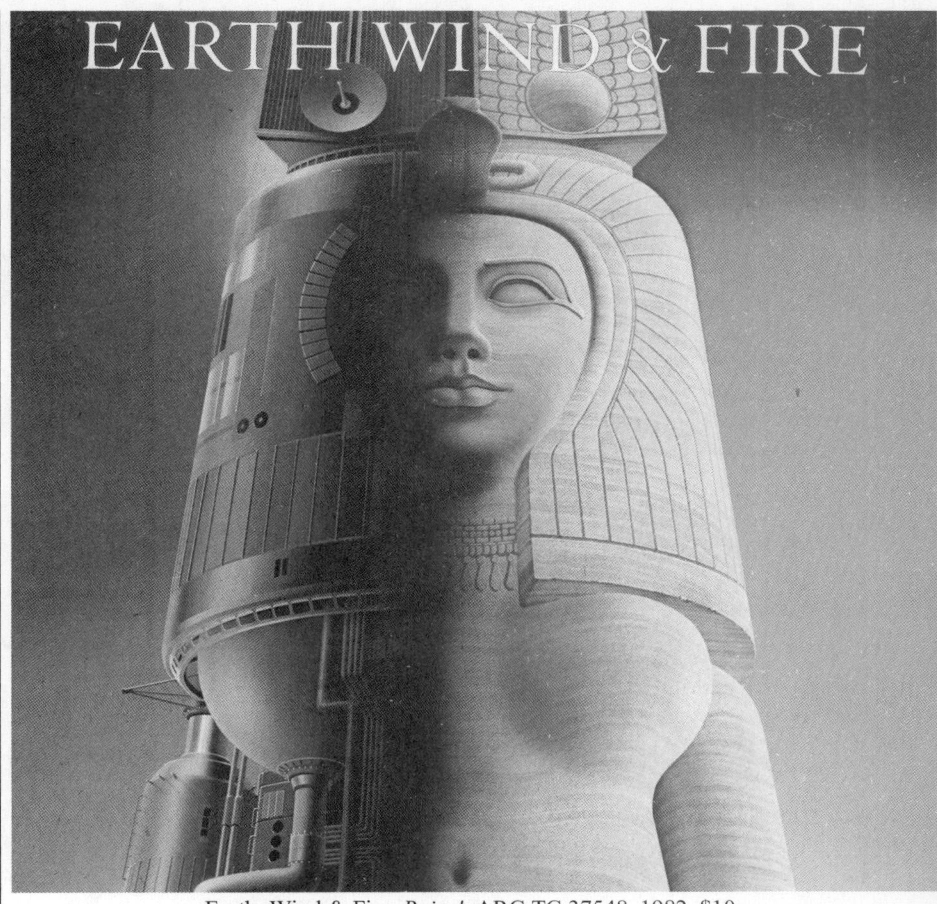


Earth, Wind & Fire, *Raise!*, ARC TC 37548, 1982, $10.

| Number | Title (A Side/B Side) | Yr | NM |
|---|---|---|---|
| ❑ SR 90223 [S] | Bloch: Concerti Grossi No. 1 and 2 | 196? | 30.00 |
| *—Maroon label, no "Vendor: Mercury Record Corporation"* | | | |
| ❑ SR 90223 [S] | Bloch: Concerti Grossi No. 1 and 2 | 196? | 40.00 |
| *—Maroon label, with "Vendor: Mercury Record Corporation"; a rare instance where the second edition is more sought-after than the first* | | | |
| ❑ SR 90224 [S] | Barber: Medea; Capricorn Concerto | 196? | 20.00 |
| *—Maroon label, no "Vendor: Mercury Record Corporation"* | | | |
| ❑ SR 90257 [S] | Ginastera: Overture to a Creole "Faust"; Guarnieri: Three Dances; Still: Sahdji Ballet | 196? | 200.00 |
| *—Maroon label, no "Vendor: Mercury Record Corporation"* | | | |
| ❑ SR 90263 [S] | Gould, Morton: Fall River Legend; Spirituals | 196? | 20.00 |
| *—Maroon label, with "Vendor: Mercury Record Corporation"* | | | |
| ❑ SR 90263 [S] | Gould, Morton: Fall River Legend; Spirituals | 196? | 40.00 |
| *—Maroon label, no "Vendor: Mercury Record Corporation"* | | | |
| ❑ SR 90267 [S] | The Composer and His Orchestra, Volume 2 | 196? | 20.00 |
| *—Maroon label, with "Vendor: Mercury Record Corporation"* | | | |
| ❑ SR 90267 [S] | The Composer and His Orchestra, Volume 2 | 196? | 25.00 |
| *—Maroon label, no "Vendor: Mercury Record Corporation"* | | | |
| ❑ SR 90277 [S] | Loeffler: Deux Rapsodies; Barlow: Night Song; McCauley: Five Miniatures | 196? | 200.00 |
| *—Maroon label, no "Vendor: Mercury Record Corporation"* | | | |
| ❑ SR 90286 [S] | Bloch: Schelomo; Herbert: Cello Concerto No. 2 | 196? | 50.00 |
| *—Maroon label, no "Vendor: Mercury Record Corporation"* | | | |
| ❑ SR 90379 [S] | Schuman: New England Tripytch; Mennin: Symphony No. 5; Griffes: Poem for Flute and Orchestra | 196? | 20.00 |
| *—Maroon label, with "Vendor: Mercury Record Corporation"* | | | |
| ❑ SR 90379 [S] | Schuman: New England Tripytch; Mennin: Symphony No. 5; Griffes: Poem for Flute and Orchestra | 196? | 50.00 |
| *—Maroon label, no "Vendor: Mercury Record Corporation"* | | | |
| ❑ SR 90429 [S] | Thomson: Symphony on a Hymn Tune; The Feast of Love; Hanson: Four Psalms | 196? | 20.00 |
| *—Maroon label, with "Vendor: Mercury Record Corporation"* | | | |
| ❑ SR 90429 [S] | Thomson: Symphony on a Hymn Tune; The Feast of Love; Hanson: Four Psalms | 196? | 20.00 |
| *—Third edition: Dark red (not maroon) label* | | | |
| ❑ SR 90429 [S] | Thomson: Symphony on a Hymn Tune; The Feast of Love; Hanson: Four Psalms | 196? | 40.00 |
| *—Maroon label, no "Vendor: Mercury Record Corporation"* | | | |
| ❑ SR 90430 [S] | Hanson: Piano Concerto; Mosaics; LaMontaine: Birds of Paradise | 196? | 20.00 |
| *—Maroon label, with "Vendor: Mercury Record Corporation"* | | | |
| ❑ SR 90430 [S] | Hanson: Piano Concerto; Mosaics; LaMontaine: Birds of Paradise | 1965 | 20.00 |
| *—Maroon label, no "Vendor: Mercury Record Corporation"* | | | |
| ❑ SR 90449 [S] | Hanson: Symphony No. 3; MacDowell: Symphony No. 1 | 1965 | 40.00 |
| *—Maroon label, with "Vendor: Mercury Record Corporation"* | | | |

### EASTMAN-ROCHESTER PHILHARMONIA (HOWARD HANSON, CONDUCTOR)

| Number | Title (A Side/B Side) | Yr | NM |
|---|---|---|---|
| **MERCURY LIVING PRESENCE** | | | |
| ❑ SR 90299 [S] | Musical Diplomats USA | 196? | 25.00 |
| *—Maroon label, no "Vendor: Mercury Record Corporation"* | | | |
| ❑ SR 90357 [S] | The Composer and His Orchestra, Volume 3 | 196? | 20.00 |
| *—Maroon label, no "Vendor: Mercury Record Corporation"* | | | |

### EASTMAN-ROCHESTER "POPS" ORCHESTRA (FREDERICK FENNELL, CONDUCTOR)

| Number | Title (A Side/B Side) | Yr | NM |
|---|---|---|---|
| **MERCURY LIVING PRESENCE** | | | |
| ❑ SR 90043 [S] | Music of Leroy Anderson, Vol. 2 | 1959 | 25.00 |
| *—Maroon label, no "Vendor: Mercury Record Corporation"* | | | |
| ❑ SR 90043 [S] | Music of Leroy Anderson, Vol. 2 | 196? | 20.00 |
| *—Maroon label, with "Vendor: Mercury Record Corporation"* | | | |
| ❑ SR 90144 [S] | Hi-Fi A La Espanola | 196? | 1000. |
| *—Maroon label, no "Vendor: Mercury Record Corporation"* | | | |
| ❑ SR 90144 [S] | Hi-Fi A La Espanola | 199? | 25.00 |
| *—Classic Records reissue* | | | |
| ❑ SR 90219 [S] | Grainger: Country Gardens | 196? | 50.00 |
| *—Maroon label, no "Vendor: Mercury Record Corporation"* | | | |
| ❑ SR 90222 [S] | Popovers | 196? | 20.00 |
| *—Maroon label, no "Vendor: Mercury Record Corporation"* | | | |
| ❑ SR 90271 [S] | Marches for Orchestra | 196? | 25.00 |
| *—Maroon label, with "Vendor: Mercury Record Corporation"* | | | |
| ❑ SR 90271 [S] | Marches for Orchestra | 196? | 40.00 |
| *—Maroon label, no "Vendor: Mercury Record Corporation"* | | | |

| Number | Title (A Side/B Side) | Yr | NM |
|---|---|---|---|
| ❑ SR 90400 [S] | Music of Leroy Anderson, Volume 3 | 196? | 50.00 |
| *—Maroon label, with "Vendor: Mercury Record Corporation"* | | | |
| ❑ SR 90400 [S] | Music of Leroy Anderson, Volume 3 | 196? | 80.00 |
| *—Maroon label, no "Vendor: Mercury Record Corporation"* | | | |

**EASTMAN-ROCHESTER WIND ENSEMBLE (FREDERICK FENNELL, CONDUCTOR)**

MERCURY LIVING PRESENCE

| Number | Title (A Side/B Side) | Yr | NM |
|---|---|---|---|
| ❑ SR 90105 [S] | Marching Along | 196? | 40.00 |
| *—Maroon label, with "Vendor: Mercury Record Corporation"; a rare instance where the second edition is more sought-after than the first* | | | |
| ❑ SR 90105 [S] | Marching Along | 1960 | 20.00 |
| *—Maroon label, no "Vendor: Mercury Record Corporation"* | | | |
| ❑ SR 90111 [S] | Spirit of '76: Music for Fifes and Drums | 1960 | 40.00 |
| *—Maroon label, no "Vendor: Mercury Record Corporation"* | | | |
| ❑ SR 90112 [S] | Ruffles and Flourishes | 1960 | 25.00 |
| *—Maroon label, no "Vendor: Mercury Record Corporation"* | | | |
| ❑ SR 90143 [S] | Hindemith: Symphony in B-flat; Schoenberg: Theme and Variations; Stravinsky: Symphony of Wind Instru | 196? | 30.00 |
| *—Maroon label, with "Vendor: Mercury Record Corporation"* | | | |
| ❑ SR 90143 [S] | Hindemith: Symphony in B-flat; Schoenberg: Theme and Variations; Stravinsky: Symphony of Wind Instru | 196? | 60.00 |
| *—Maroon label, no "Vendor: Mercury Record Corporation"* | | | |
| ❑ SR 90170 [S] | March Time | 196? | 20.00 |
| *—Maroon label, no "Vendor: Mercury Record Corporation"* | | | |
| ❑ SR 90173 [S] | Winds in Hi-Fi | 196? | 20.00 |
| *—Third edition: Dark red (not maroon) label* | | | |
| ❑ SR 90173 [S] | Winds in Hi-Fi | 196? | 50.00 |
| *—Maroon label, with "Vendor: Mercury Record Corporation"* | | | |
| ❑ SR 90173 [S] | Winds in Hi-Fi | 196? | 80.00 |
| *—Maroon label, no "Vendor: Mercury Record Corporation"* | | | |
| ❑ SR 90176 [S] | Mozart: Serenade No. 10 in E-flat | 196? | 25.00 |
| *—Maroon label, with "Vendor: Mercury Record Corporation"* | | | |
| ❑ SR 90176 [S] | Mozart: Serenade No. 10 in E-flat | 196? | 50.00 |
| *—Maroon label, no "Vendor: Mercury Record Corporation"* | | | |
| ❑ SR 90197 [S] | British Band Classics, Vol. 2 | 196? | 20.00 |
| *—Third edition: Dark red (not maroon) label* | | | |
| ❑ SR 90197 [S] | British Band Classics, Vol. 2 | 196? | 40.00 |
| *—Maroon label, with "Vendor: Mercury Record Corporation"* | | | |
| ❑ SR 90197 [S] | British Band Classics, Vol. 2 | 196? | 150.00 |
| *—Maroon label, no "Vendor: Mercury Record Corporation"* | | | |
| ❑ SR 90207 [S] | Hands Across the Sea | 196? | 50.00 |
| *—Maroon label, no "Vendor: Mercury Record Corporation"* | | | |
| ❑ SR 90220 [S] | Gould: West Point Symphony; Bennett: Songs; Williams: Fanfare and Allegro; Work: Autumn Walk | 196? | 50.00 |
| *—Maroon label, with "Vendor: Mercury Record Corporation"* | | | |
| ❑ SR 90220 [S] | Gould: West Point Symphony; Bennett: Songs; Williams: Fanfare and Allegro; Work: Autumn Walk | 196? | 70.00 |
| *—Maroon label, no "Vendor: Mercury Record Corporation"* | | | |
| ❑ SR 90221 [S] | Diverse Winds | 196? | 120.00 |
| *—Maroon label, no "Vendor: Mercury Record Corporation"* | | | |
| ❑ SR 90245 [S] | Gabrieli Music for Wind Instruments | 196? | 20.00 |
| *—Maroon label, no "Vendor: Mercury Record Corporation"* | | | |
| ❑ SR 90256 [S] | Ballet for Band | 196? | 80.00 |
| *—Maroon label, with "Vendor: Mercury Record Corporation"* | | | |
| ❑ SR 90256 [S] | Ballet for Band | 196? | 180.00 |
| *—Maroon label, no "Vendor: Mercury Record Corporation"* | | | |
| ❑ SR 90264 [S] | Sousa Sound Off | 196? | 25.00 |
| *—Maroon label, no "Vendor: Mercury Record Corporation"* | | | |
| ❑ SR 90276 [S] | Wagner for Band | 196? | 40.00 |
| *—Third edition: Dark red (not maroon) label* | | | |
| ❑ SR 90276 [S] | Wagner for Band | 196? | 50.00 |
| *—Maroon label, with "Vendor: Mercury Record Corporation" (second edition is more sought after than the first)* | | | |
| ❑ SR 90276 [S] | Wagner for Band | 196? | 70.00 |
| *—Maroon label, no "Vendor: Mercury Record Corporation"* | | | |
| ❑ SR 90284 [S] | Sousa on Review | 196? | 30.00 |
| *—Maroon label, no "Vendor: Mercury Record Corporation"* | | | |
| ❑ SR 90284 [S] | Sousa on Review | 196? | 80.00 |
| *—Maroon label, with "Vendor: Mercury Record Corporation"; a rare instance where the second edition is more sought-after than the first* | | | |
| ❑ SR 90314 [S] | Screamers (Circus Marches) | 196? | 25.00 |
| *—Maroon label, with "Vendor: Mercury Record Corporation"* | | | |
| ❑ SR 90314 [S] | Screamers (Circus Marches) | 196? | 40.00 |
| *—Maroon label, no "Vendor: Mercury Record Corporation"* | | | |
| ❑ SR 90390 [S] | Broadway Marches | 196? | 20.00 |
| *—Maroon label, no "Vendor: Mercury Record Corporation"* | | | |

**EASTMAN-ROCHESTER WIND ENSEMBLE (A. CLYDE ROLLER, CONDUCTOR)**

MERCURY LIVING PRESENCE

| Number | Title (A Side/B Side) | Yr | NM |
|---|---|---|---|
| ❑ SR 90366 [S] | Hovhaness: Symphony No. 4; Giannini: Symphony No. 3 | 196? | 20.00 |
| *—Third edition: Dark red (not maroon) label* | | | |
| ❑ SR 90366 [S] | Hovhaness: Symphony No. 4; Giannini: Symphony No. 3 | 196? | 40.00 |
| *—Maroon label, with "Vendor: Mercury Record Corporation"* | | | |
| ❑ SR 90366 [S] | Hovhaness: Symphony No. 4; Giannini: Symphony No. 3 | 196? | 80.00 |
| *—Maroon label, no "Vendor: Mercury Record Corporation"* | | | |

**EASTWOOD, CLINT**

CAMEO

| Number | Title (A Side/B Side) | Yr | NM |
|---|---|---|---|
| ❑ C-1056 [M] | Clint Eastwood Sings Cowboy Favorites | 1963 | 100.00 |
| ❑ SC-1056 [S] | Clint Eastwood Sings Cowboy Favorites | 1963 | 150.00 |

**EASY RIDERS, THE** See TERRY GILKYSON.

**EASY RIDERS JAZZ BAND, THE**

JAZZ CRUSADE

| Number | Title (A Side/B Side) | Yr | NM |
|---|---|---|---|
| ❑ 1002 | My Life Will Be Sweeter Someday | 1963 | 40.00 |

**EASYBEATS, THE**

RARE EARTH

| Number | Title (A Side/B Side) | Yr | NM |
|---|---|---|---|
| ❑ 517 | Easy Ridin' | 1970 | — |
| *—Canceled* | | | |

RHINO

| Number | Title (A Side/B Side) | Yr | NM |
|---|---|---|---|
| ❑ RNLP-124 | The Best of the Easybeats | 1985 | 8.00 |

UNITED ARTISTS

| Number | Title (A Side/B Side) | Yr | NM |
|---|---|---|---|
| ❑ UAL 3588 [M] | Friday on My Mind | 1967 | 40.00 |
| ❑ UAS 6588 [P] | Friday on My Mind | 1967 | 50.00 |
| *—"Make You Feel Alright" is rechanneled.* | | | |
| ❑ UAS 6667 [P] | Falling Off the Edge of the World | 1968 | 40.00 |
| *—"Women" is rechanneled.* | | | |

**EATON, CLEVELAND**

OVATION

| Number | Title (A Side/B Side) | Yr | NM |
|---|---|---|---|
| ❑ OV-1703 | Instant Hip | 1974 | 20.00 |

**EATON, JOHNNY**

COLUMBIA

| Number | Title (A Side/B Side) | Yr | NM |
|---|---|---|---|
| ❑ CL 737 [M] | College Jazz: Modern | 1956 | 40.00 |
| ❑ CL 996 [M] | Far Out, Far In | 1957 | 40.00 |

**EAVES, HUBERT**

INNER CITY

| Number | Title (A Side/B Side) | Yr | NM |
|---|---|---|---|
| ❑ IC-6012 | Esteric Funk | 1976 | 20.00 |

**EBON-KNIGHTS, THE**

STEPHENY

| Number | Title (A Side/B Side) | Yr | NM |
|---|---|---|---|
| ❑ 4001 [M] | First Date | 1959 | 1500. |

**EBONYS, THE**

BUDDAH

| Number | Title (A Side/B Side) | Yr | NM |
|---|---|---|---|
| ❑ BDS 5679 | Sing About Life | 1976 | 40.00 |

**EBSEN, BUDDY**

REPRISE

| Number | Title (A Side/B Side) | Yr | NM |
|---|---|---|---|
| ❑ R-6174 [M] | Buddy Ebsen Sings Howdy! | 1965 | 30.00 |
| ❑ RS-6174 [S] | Buddy Ebsen Sings Howdy! | 1965 | 40.00 |

**ECHOES OF HARLEM**

ROYALE

| Number | Title (A Side/B Side) | Yr | NM |
|---|---|---|---|
| ❑ LP-18128 [10] | Echoes of Harlem | 195? | 80.00 |

**ECKSTINE, BILLY**

AUDIO LAB

| Number | Title (A Side/B Side) | Yr | NM |
|---|---|---|---|
| ❑ AL-1549 [M] | Mr. B | 1960 | 120.00 |

DELUXE

| Number | Title (A Side/B Side) | Yr | NM |
|---|---|---|---|
| ❑ FA-2010 [M] | Billy Eckstine and His Orchestra | 195? | 80.00 |

EMARCY

| Number | Title (A Side/B Side) | Yr | NM |
|---|---|---|---|
| ❑ MG-26025 [10] | Blues for Sale | 1954 | 120.00 |
| ❑ MG-26027 [10] | The Love Songs of Mr. B | 1954 | 120.00 |
| ❑ MG-36010 [M] | I Surrender, Dear | 1955 | 80.00 |
| ❑ MG-36029 [M] | Blues for Sale | 1955 | 80.00 |
| ❑ MG-36030 [M] | The Love Songs of Mr. B | 1955 | 80.00 |
| ❑ MG-36129 [M] | Billy Eckstine's Imagination | 1958 | 60.00 |

KING

| Number | Title (A Side/B Side) | Yr | NM |
|---|---|---|---|
| ❑ 295-12 [10] | The Great Mr. B | 1953 | 300.00 |

LION

| Number | Title (A Side/B Side) | Yr | NM |
|---|---|---|---|
| ❑ L-70057 [M] | The Best of Billy Eckstine | 1958 | 25.00 |

MERCURY

| Number | Title (A Side/B Side) | Yr | NM |
|---|---|---|---|
| ❑ MG-20333 [M] | Billy's Best | 1958 | 40.00 |
| ❑ MG-20637 [M] | Broadway, Bongos and Mr. B | 1961 | 25.00 |
| ❑ MG-20674 [M] | Billy Eckstine and Quincy Jones at Basin St. East | 1962 | 25.00 |
| ❑ MG-20736 [M] | Don't Worry 'Bout Me | 1962 | 25.00 |
| ❑ SR-60086 [S] | Billy's Best | 1958 | 50.00 |
| ❑ SR-60637 [S] | Broadway, Bongos and Mr. B | 1961 | 30.00 |
| ❑ SR-60674 [S] | Billy Eckstine and Quincy Jones at Basin St. East | 1962 | 30.00 |
| ❑ SR-60736 [S] | Don't Worry 'Bout Me | 1962 | 30.00 |
| ❑ SR-60796 [S] | The Golden Hits of Billy Eckstine | 1963 | 20.00 |

MGM

| Number | Title (A Side/B Side) | Yr | NM |
|---|---|---|---|
| ❑ E-153 [10] | Billy Eckstine Sings Rodgers & Hammerstein | 1952 | 150.00 |
| ❑ E-219 [10] | Tenderly | 1953 | 150.00 |
| ❑ E-257 [10] | I Let a Song Go Out of My Heart | 1954 | 150.00 |
| ❑ E-523 [10] | Songs by Billy Eckstine | 1951 | 160.00 |
| ❑ E-548 [10] | Favorites | 1951 | 160.00 |
| ❑ E-3176 [M] | Mr. B with a Beat | 1955 | 50.00 |
| ❑ E-3209 [M] | Rendezvous | 1955 | 50.00 |
| ❑ E-3275 [M] | That Old Feeling | 1956 | 50.00 |

MOTOWN

| Number | Title (A Side/B Side) | Yr | NM |
|---|---|---|---|
| ❑ M 632 [M] | Prime of My Life | 1965 | 20.00 |
| ❑ MS 632 [S] | Prime of My Life | 1965 | 25.00 |
| ❑ M 646 [M] | My Way | 1966 | 20.00 |
| ❑ MS 646 [S] | My Way | 1966 | 25.00 |
| ❑ MS 677 | For Love of Ivy | 1969 | 25.00 |

NATIONAL

| Number | Title (A Side/B Side) | Yr | NM |
|---|---|---|---|
| ❑ NLP-2001 [10] | Billy Eckstine Sings | 1949 | 200.00 |

REGENT

| Number | Title (A Side/B Side) | Yr | NM |
|---|---|---|---|
| ❑ MG-6052 [M] | Prisoner of Love | 1957 | 50.00 |
| ❑ MG-6053 [M] | The Duke, the Blues and Me | 1957 | 50.00 |
| ❑ MG-6054 [M] | My Deep Blue Dream | 1957 | 50.00 |
| ❑ MG-6058 [M] | You Call It Madness | 1957 | 50.00 |

ROULETTE

| Number | Title (A Side/B Side) | Yr | NM |
|---|---|---|---|
| ❑ R-25052 [M] | No Cover, No Minimum | 1961 | 25.00 |
| ❑ SR-25052 [S] | No Cover, No Minimum | 1961 | 30.00 |
| ❑ R-25104 [M] | Once More with Feeling | 1962 | 25.00 |
| ❑ SR-25104 [S] | Once More with Feeling | 1962 | 30.00 |

**EDDIE AND BETTY**

WARNER BROS.

| Number | Title (A Side/B Side) | Yr | NM |
|---|---|---|---|
| ❑ W 1350 [M] | Nightlife for Daydreamers | 1959 | 25.00 |
| ❑ WS 1350 [S] | Nightlife for Daydreamers | 1959 | 30.00 |

**EDDIE AND THE SUBTITLES**

(NO LABEL)

| Number | Title (A Side/B Side) | Yr | NM |
|---|---|---|---|
| ❑ (no #) | Skeletons in the Closet | 1981 | 40.00 |

13TH STORY

| Number | Title (A Side/B Side) | Yr | NM |
|---|---|---|---|
| ❑ MR 3301 | Dead Drunks Don't Dance | 1983 | 25.00 |

**EDDY, DUANE**

CAPITOL

| Number | Title (A Side/B Side) | Yr | NM |
|---|---|---|---|
| ❑ ST-12567 | Duane Eddy | 1987 | 12.00 |

COLPIX

| Number | Title (A Side/B Side) | Yr | NM |
|---|---|---|---|
| ❑ CP-490 [M] | Duane A-Go-Go | 1965 | 30.00 |
| ❑ CPS-490 [S] | Duane A-Go-Go | 1965 | 40.00 |
| ❑ CPL-494 [M] | Duane Eddy Does Bob Dylan | 1965 | 30.00 |
| ❑ SCP-494 [S] | Duane Eddy Does Bob Dylan | 1965 | 40.00 |

JAMIE

| Number | Title (A Side/B Side) | Yr | NM |
|---|---|---|---|
| ❑ JLP-3000 [M] | Have "Twangy" Guitar — Will Travel | 1958 | 120.00 |
| *—Duane sitting with guitar case, title on cover in white (1st)* | | | |
| ❑ JLP-3000 [M] | Have "Twangy" Guitar — Will Travel | 1959 | 50.00 |
| *—Duane standing with guitar (3rd)* | | | |
| ❑ JLP-3000 [M] | Have "Twangy" Guitar — Will Travel | 1959 | 100.00 |
| *—Duane sitting with guitar case, title on cover in green and red (2nd)* | | | |
| ❑ JLPS-3000 [R] | Have "Twangy" Guitar — Will Travel | 196? | 50.00 |
| *—Duane standing with guitar (3rd), album plays fake stereo* | | | |
| ❑ JLPS-3000 [S] | Have "Twangy" Guitar — Will Travel | 1958 | 400.00 |
| *—Duane sitting with guitar case, title on cover in white (1st)* | | | |
| ❑ JLPS-3000 [S] | Have "Twangy" Guitar — Will Travel | 1959 | 100.00 |
| *—Duane standing with guitar (3rd), album plays true stereo* | | | |
| ❑ JLPS-3000 [S] | Have "Twangy" Guitar — Will Travel | 1959 | 300.00 |
| *—Duane sitting with guitar case, title on cover in green and red (2nd)* | | | |
| ❑ JLPM-3006 [M] | Especially for You… | 1959 | 40.00 |
| ❑ JLPS-3006 [S] | Especially for You… | 1959 | 60.00 |
| ❑ JLPM-3009 [M] | The "Twangs" The "Thang" | 1959 | 40.00 |
| ❑ JLPS-3009 [S] | The "Twangs" The "Thang" | 1959 | 60.00 |
| ❑ JLPM-3011 [M] | Songs of Our Heritage | 196? | 30.00 |
| *—Regular cover* | | | |
| ❑ JLPM-3011 [M] | Songs of Our Heritage | 1960 | 80.00 |
| *—Gatefold cover* | | | |
| ❑ JLPS-3011 [S] | Songs of Our Heritage | 196? | 40.00 |
| *—Regular cover* | | | |
| ❑ JLPS-3011 [S] | Songs of Our Heritage | 1960 | 100.00 |
| *—Gatefold cover* | | | |
| ❑ JLPS-3011 [S] | Songs of Our Heritage | 1960 | 500.00 |
| *—Gatefold cover, blue vinyl* | | | |
| ❑ JLPS-3011 [S] | Songs of Our Heritage | 1960 | 500.00 |
| *—Gatefold cover, red vinyl* | | | |
| ❑ JLPM-3014 [M] | $1,000,000.00 Worth of Twang | 1960 | 40.00 |
| ❑ JLPS-3014 [S] | $1,000,000.00 Worth of Twang | 1960 | 70.00 |
| *—All but one song -- "Up and Down" -- is in true stereo* | | | |
| ❑ JLPM-3019 [M] | Girls! Girls! Girls! | 1961 | 40.00 |
| ❑ JLPS-3019 [R] | Girls! Girls! Girls! | 1961 | 30.00 |
| ❑ JLPM-3021 [M] | $1,000,000.00 Worth of Twang, Volume 2 | 1962 | 40.00 |
| ❑ JLPS-3021 [R] | $1,000,000.00 Worth of Twang, Volume 2 | 1962 | 30.00 |
| ❑ JLPM-3022 [M] | Twistin' with Duane Eddy | 1962 | 40.00 |
| ❑ JLPS-3022 [P] | Twistin' with Duane Eddy | 1962 | 40.00 |
| ❑ JLPM-3024 [M] | Surfin' | 1963 | 50.00 |



Except when noted otherwise, VG = 25% of NM, and VG+ = 50% of NM. (Example: VG = $2.00, VG+ = $4.00 and NM = $8.00.)

| Number | Title (A Side/B Side) | Yr | NM |
|---|---|---|---|
| ❑ JLPS-3024 [S] | Surfin' | 1963 | 80.00 |
| ❑ JLPM-3025 [M] | Duane Eddy & The Rebels — In Person | 1963 | 30.00 |
| ❑ JLPS-3025 [S] | Duane Eddy & The Rebels — In Person | 1963 | 40.00 |
| ❑ JLPM-3026 [M] | 16 Greatest Hits | 1964 | 40.00 |
| ❑ JLPS-3026 [R] | 16 Greatest Hits | 1964 | 30.00 |
| ❑ ST-90663 [S] | Duane Eddy & The Rebels — In Person | 1965 | 50.00 |
| *—Capitol Record Club edition* | | | |
| ❑ T-90663 [M] | Duane Eddy & The Rebels — In Person | 1965 | 40.00 |
| *—Capitol Record Club edition* | | | |
| ❑ ST-90682 [S] | Have "Twangy" Guitar — Will Travel | 1965 | 80.00 |
| *—Capitol Record Club edition* | | | |
| ❑ T-90682 [M] | Have "Twangy" Guitar — Will Travel | 1965 | 60.00 |
| *—Capitol Record Club edition* | | | |
| ❑ ST-91301 [S] | The "Twangs" The "Thang" | 1966 | 60.00 |
| *—Capitol Record Club edition* | | | |
| ❑ T-91301 [M] | The "Twangs" The "Thang" | 1966 | 60.00 |
| *—Capitol Record Club edition* | | | |

RCA VICTOR

| Number | Title (A Side/B Side) | Yr | NM |
|---|---|---|---|
| ❑ LPM-2525 [M] | Twistin' 'N' Twangin' | 1962 | 25.00 |
| ❑ LSP-2525 [S] | Twistin' 'N' Twangin' | 1962 | 40.00 |
| ❑ LPM-2576 [M] | Twangy Guitar — Silky Strings | 1962 | 25.00 |
| ❑ LSP-2576 [S] | Twangy Guitar — Silky Strings | 1962 | 40.00 |
| ❑ LPM-2648 [M] | Dance with the Guitar Man | 1962 | 25.00 |
| ❑ LSP-2648 [S] | Dance with the Guitar Man | 1962 | 40.00 |
| ❑ ANL1-2671 | Pure Gold | 1978 | 10.00 |
| ❑ LPM-2681 [M] | Twang a Country Song | 1963 | 25.00 |
| ❑ LSP-2681 [S] | Twang a Country Song | 1963 | 40.00 |
| ❑ LPM-2700 [M] | "Twangin' " Up a Storm! | 1963 | 25.00 |
| ❑ LSP-2700 [S] | "Twangin' " Up a Storm! | 1963 | 40.00 |
| ❑ LPM-2798 [M] | Lonely Guitar | 1964 | 20.00 |
| ❑ LSP-2798 [S] | Lonely Guitar | 1964 | 30.00 |
| ❑ LPM-2918 [M] | Water Skiing | 1964 | 20.00 |
| ❑ LSP-2918 [S] | Water Skiing | 1964 | 30.00 |
| ❑ LPM-2993 [M] | Twangin' the Golden Hits | 1965 | 20.00 |
| ❑ LSP-2993 [S] | Twangin' the Golden Hits | 1965 | 30.00 |
| ❑ LPM-3432 [M] | Twangsville | 1965 | 20.00 |
| ❑ LSP-3432 [S] | Twangsville | 1965 | 30.00 |
| ❑ LPM-3477 [M] | The Best of Duane Eddy | 1965 | 20.00 |
| ❑ LSP-3477 [P] | The Best of Duane Eddy | 1965 | 25.00 |
| *—Black "Stereo" label* | | | |
| ❑ LSP-3477 [P] | The Best of Duane Eddy | 1969 | 15.00 |
| *—Orange label* | | | |

REPRISE

| Number | Title (A Side/B Side) | Yr | NM |
|---|---|---|---|
| ❑ R-6218 [M] | The Biggest Twang of Them All | 1966 | 30.00 |
| ❑ RS-6218 [S] | The Biggest Twang of Them All | 1966 | 40.00 |
| ❑ R-6240 [M] | The Roaring Twangies | 1967 | 30.00 |
| ❑ RS-6240 [S] | The Roaring Twangies | 1967 | 40.00 |

SIRE

| Number | Title (A Side/B Side) | Yr | NM |
|---|---|---|---|
| ❑ SASH-3707-2 [(2)] | The Vintage Years | 1975 | 25.00 |

**EDDY, NELSON**

COLUMBIA MASTERWORKS

| Number | Title (A Side/B Side) | Yr | NM |
|---|---|---|---|
| ❑ ML 4442 [M] | Songs for Christmas | 195? | 40.00 |

HARMONY

| Number | Title (A Side/B Side) | Yr | NM |
|---|---|---|---|
| ❑ HL 7201 [M] | Nelson Eddy Sings the Best Loved Carols of Christmas | 195? | 20.00 |

**EDEN, BARBARA**

DOT

| Number | Title (A Side/B Side) | Yr | NM |
|---|---|---|---|
| ❑ DLP-3795 [M] | Miss Barbara Eden | 1967 | 40.00 |
| ❑ DLP-25795 [S] | Miss Barbara Eden | 1967 | 50.00 |

**EDEN'S CHILDREN**

ABC

| Number | Title (A Side/B Side) | Yr | NM |
|---|---|---|---|
| ❑ 624 [M] | Eden's Children | 1968 | 40.00 |
| ❑ S-624 [S] | Eden's Children | 1968 | 25.00 |
| ❑ S-652 | Sure Looks Real | 1968 | 20.00 |

**EDGE, THE**

NOSE

| Number | Title (A Side/B Side) | Yr | NM |
|---|---|---|---|
| ❑ NRS-48003 | The Edge | 1970 | 40.00 |

**EDISON, HARRY "SWEETS"**

AMERICAN RECORDING SOCIETY

| Number | Title (A Side/B Side) | Yr | NM |
|---|---|---|---|
| ❑ G-430 [M] | Sweets | 1957 | 40.00 |

CLEF

| Number | Title (A Side/B Side) | Yr | NM |
|---|---|---|---|
| ❑ MGC-717 [M] | Sweets | 1956 | 80.00 |

LIBERTY

| Number | Title (A Side/B Side) | Yr | NM |
|---|---|---|---|
| ❑ LRP-3484 [M] | When Lights Are Low | 1966 | 20.00 |
| ❑ LST-7484 [S] | When Lights Are Low | 1966 | 25.00 |

PACIFIC JAZZ

| Number | Title (A Side/B Side) | Yr | NM |
|---|---|---|---|
| ❑ PJLP-4 [10] | Harry Edison Quartet | 1953 | 150.00 |
| ❑ PJ-11 [M] | The Inventive Harry Edison | 1960 | 50.00 |

ROULETTE

| Number | Title (A Side/B Side) | Yr | NM |
|---|---|---|---|
| ❑ R-52023 [M] | Sweetenings | 1960 | 40.00 |
| ❑ SR-52023 [S] | Sweetenings | 1960 | 40.00 |
| ❑ R-52041 [M] | Patented by Edison | 1960 | 30.00 |
| ❑ SR-52041 [S] | Patented by Edison | 1960 | 40.00 |

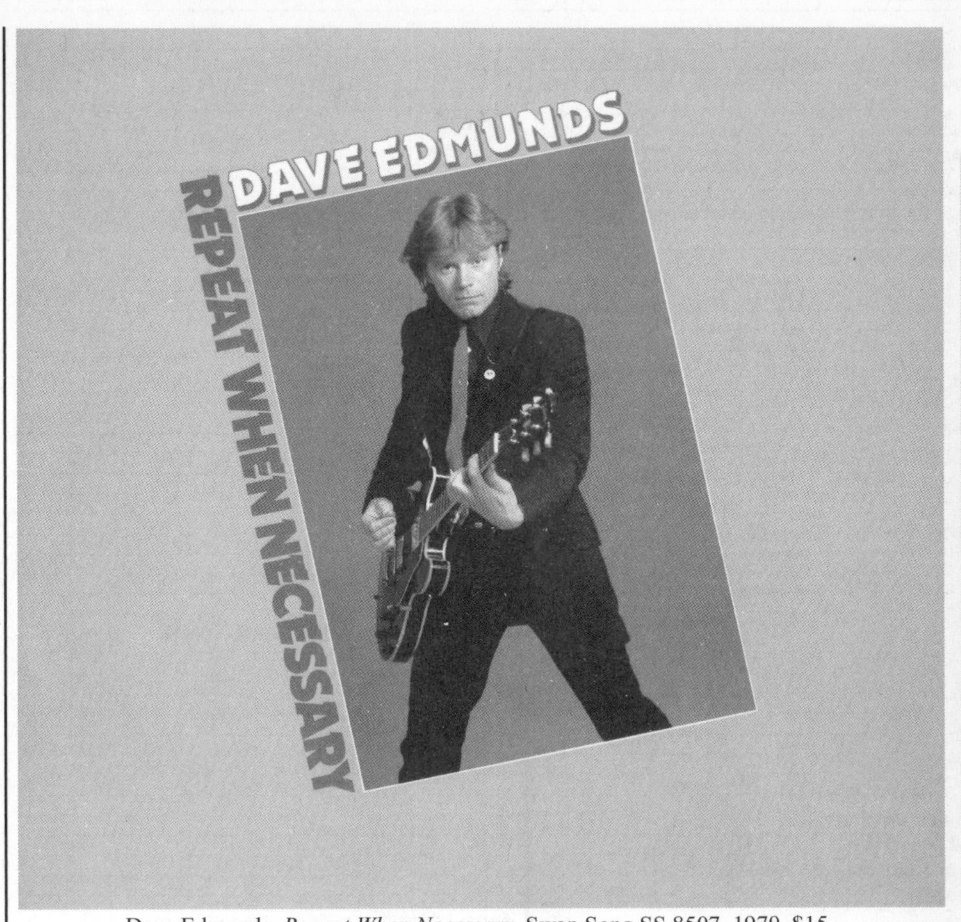


Dave Edmunds, *Repeat When Necessary,* Swan Song SS 8507, 1979, $15.

SUE

| Number | Title (A Side/B Side) | Yr | NM |
|---|---|---|---|
| ❑ LP-1030 [M] | Sweets for the Sweet | 1964 | 40.00 |
| ❑ STLP-1030 [S] | Sweets for the Sweet | 1964 | 50.00 |

VEE JAY

| Number | Title (A Side/B Side) | Yr | NM |
|---|---|---|---|
| ❑ LP-1104 [M] | For the Sweet Taste of Love | 1964 | 30.00 |
| ❑ LPS-1104 [S] | For the Sweet Taste of Love | 1964 | 40.00 |
| ❑ VJS-3065 | Home with Sweets | 1975 | 20.00 |

VERVE

| Number | Title (A Side/B Side) | Yr | NM |
|---|---|---|---|
| ❑ MGVS-6016 [S] | Harry Edison Swings Buck Clayton, And Vice Versa | 1959 | 40.00 |
| ❑ MGVS-6037 [S] | The Swinger | 1960 | 40.00 |
| ❑ MGVS-6118 [S] | Mr. Swing | 1960 | 40.00 |
| ❑ MGV-8097 [M] | Sweets | 1957 | 50.00 |
| ❑ V-8097 [M] | Sweets | 1961 | 20.00 |
| ❑ MGV-8211 [M] | Gee Baby, Ain't I Good to You? | 1958 | 50.00 |
| ❑ V-8211 [M] | Gee Baby, Ain't I Good to You? | 1961 | 20.00 |
| ❑ MGV-8293 [M] | Harry Edison Swings Buck Clayton, And Vice Versa | 1958 | 50.00 |
| ❑ V-8293 [M] | Harry Edison Swings Buck Clayton, And Vice Versa | 1961 | 20.00 |
| ❑ V6-8293 [S] | Harry Edison Swings Buck Clayton, And Vice Versa | 1961 | 20.00 |
| ❑ MGV-8295 [M] | The Swinger | 1959 | 50.00 |
| ❑ V-8295 [M] | The Swinger | 1961 | 20.00 |
| ❑ V6-8295 [S] | The Swinger | 1961 | 20.00 |
| ❑ MGV-8353 [M] | Mr. Swing | 1959 | 50.00 |
| ❑ V-8353 [M] | Mr. Swing | 1961 | 20.00 |
| ❑ V6-8358 [S] | Mr. Swing | 1961 | 20.00 |

**EDISON ELECTRIC BAND, THE**

COTILLION

| Number | Title (A Side/B Side) | Yr | NM |
|---|---|---|---|
| ❑ SD 9022 | Bless You, Dr. Woodward | 1970 | 20.00 |

**EDMONSON, TRAVIS** Also see BUD AND TRAVIS.

HORIZON

| Number | Title (A Side/B Side) | Yr | NM |
|---|---|---|---|
| ❑ WP-1606 [M] | Travis On Cue | 1962 | 20.00 |
| ❑ WPS-1606 [S] | Travis On Cue | 1962 | 25.00 |

REPRISE

| Number | Title (A Side/B Side) | Yr | NM |
|---|---|---|---|
| ❑ R-6035 [M] | Travis On His Own | 1962 | 25.00 |
| ❑ R9-6035 [S] | Travis On His Own | 1962 | 30.00 |

**EDMUNDS, DAVE**

ATLANTIC

| Number | Title (A Side/B Side) | Yr | NM |
|---|---|---|---|
| ❑ PR 320 [DJ] | College Network | 1978 | 50.00 |
| *—Promo-only interview album* | | | |

CAPITOL

| Number | Title (A Side/B Side) | Yr | NM |
|---|---|---|---|
| ❑ C1-90372 | Closer to the Flame | 1990 | 15.00 |

COLUMBIA

| Number | Title (A Side/B Side) | Yr | NM |
|---|---|---|---|
| ❑ FC 37930 | D.E. 7th | 1982 | 12.00 |
| ❑ PC 37930 | D.E. 7th | 198? | 8.00 |
| *—Budget-line reissue ("02" added to bar code on back cover)* | | | |
| ❑ FC 38651 | Information | 1983 | 12.00 |
| ❑ PC 38651 | Information | 198? | 8.00 |
| *—Budget-line reissue ("02" added to bar code on back cover)* | | | |
| ❑ FC 39273 | Riff Raff | 1984 | 10.00 |
| ❑ FC 40603 | I Hear You Rockin' | 1987 | 10.00 |
| ❑ PC 40603 | I Hear You Rockin' | 198? | 8.00 |
| *—Budget-line reissue ("02" added to bar code on back cover)* | | | |

MAM

| Number | Title (A Side/B Side) | Yr | NM |
|---|---|---|---|
| ❑ 3 | Rockpile | 1972 | 40.00 |

RCA VICTOR

| Number | Title (A Side/B Side) | Yr | NM |
|---|---|---|---|
| ❑ AYL1-4238 | Subtle as a Flying Mallet | 1982 | 10.00 |
| *—Reissue (black label, dog near top)* | | | |
| ❑ LPL1-5003 | Subtle as a Flying Mallet | 1975 | 12.00 |

SWAN SONG

| Number | Title (A Side/B Side) | Yr | NM |
|---|---|---|---|
| ❑ SS 8418 | Get It | 1977 | 15.00 |
| ❑ SS 8505 | Trax on Wax 4 | 1978 | 15.00 |
| ❑ SS 8507 | Repeat When Necessary | 1979 | 15.00 |
| ❑ SS 8510 | The Best of Dave Edmunds | 1981 | 12.00 |
| ❑ SD 16034 | Twangin' | 1981 | 12.00 |

**EDWARDS, EDDIE**

COMMODORE

| Number | Title (A Side/B Side) | Yr | NM |
|---|---|---|---|
| ❑ FL-20003 [10] | Eddie Edwards' Original Dixieland Jazz Band | 1950 | 60.00 |

**EDWARDS, JONATHAN AND DARLENE** Actually JO STAFFORD and PAUL WESTON as a comedy team.

COLUMBIA

| Number | Title (A Side/B Side) | Yr | NM |
|---|---|---|---|
| ❑ CL 1024 [M] | The Piano Artistry of Jonathan Edwards | 1955 | 50.00 |
| ❑ CL 1513 [M] | Jonathan and Darlene Edwards In Paris | 1960 | 25.00 |
| ❑ CS 8313 [S] | Jonathan and Darlene Edwards In Paris | 1960 | 30.00 |

CORINTHIAN

| Number | Title (A Side/B Side) | Yr | NM |
|---|---|---|---|
| ❑ 103 | Jonathan and Darlene Edwards In Paris | 198? | 10.00 |
| ❑ 104 | The Original Piano Artistry of Jonathan Edwards | 198? | 10.00 |

| Number | Title (A Side/B Side) | Yr | NM |
|---|---|---|---|
| ❑ 120 | Sing Along with Jonathan and Darlene | 198? | 10.00 |
| ❑ 122 | Songs for Sheiks and Flappers | 1986 | 10.00 |

DOT

| Number | Title (A Side/B Side) | Yr | NM |
|---|---|---|---|
| ❑ DLP-3792 [M] | Songs for Sheiks and Flappers | 1967 | 15.00 |
| ❑ DLP-25792 [S] | Songs for Sheiks and Flappers | 1967 | 20.00 |

RCA VICTOR

| Number | Title (A Side/B Side) | Yr | NM |
|---|---|---|---|
| ❑ LPM-2495 [M] | Sing Along with Jonathan and Darlene | 1962 | 20.00 |
| ❑ LSP-2495 [S] | Sing Along with Jonathan and Darlene | 1962 | 25.00 |

### EDWARDS, STONEY

CAPITOL

| Number | Title (A Side/B Side) | Yr | NM |
|---|---|---|---|
| ❑ ST-741 | Country Singer | 1970 | 25.00 |
| ❑ ST-834 | Down Home in the Country | 1971 | 20.00 |
| ❑ ST-11090 | Stoney Edwards | 1972 | 20.00 |
| ❑ ST-11173 | She's My Rock | 1973 | 20.00 |
| ❑ ST-11401 | Mississippi on My Mind | 1975 | 20.00 |
| ❑ ST-11499 | Blackbird | 1976 | 20.00 |

### EDWARDS, TEDDY

CONTEMPORARY

| Number | Title (A Side/B Side) | Yr | NM |
|---|---|---|---|
| ❑ M-3583 [M] | Teddy's Ready | 1960 | 25.00 |
| ❑ M-3588 [M] | Together Again | 1961 | 30.00 |
| ❑ M-3592 [M] | Good Gravy | 1961 | 25.00 |
| ❑ M-3606 [M] | Heart and Soul | 1962 | 25.00 |
| ❑ S-7583 [S] | Teddy's Ready | 1960 | 30.00 |
| ❑ S-7588 [S] | Together Again | 1961 | 40.00 |
| ❑ S-7592 [S] | Good Gravy | 1961 | 30.00 |
| ❑ S-7606 [S] | Heart and Soul | 1962 | 30.00 |

PACIFIC JAZZ

| Number | Title (A Side/B Side) | Yr | NM |
|---|---|---|---|
| ❑ PJ-6 [M] | It's About Time | 1960 | 40.00 |
| ❑ ST-6 [S] | It's About Time | 1960 | 40.00 |
| ❑ PJ-14 [M] | Sunset Eyes | 1961 | 40.00 |

PRESTIGE

| Number | Title (A Side/B Side) | Yr | NM |
|---|---|---|---|
| ❑ PRLP-7518 [M] | Nothin' But the Truth | 1967 | 30.00 |
| ❑ PRST-7518 [S] | Nothin' But the Truth | 1967 | 25.00 |
| ❑ PRLP-7522 [M] | It's Alright | 1967 | 30.00 |
| ❑ PRST-7522 [S] | It's Alright | 1967 | 25.00 |

### EDWARDS, TOMMY

LION

| Number | Title (A Side/B Side) | Yr | NM |
|---|---|---|---|
| ❑ L-70120 [M] | Tommy Edwards | 1959 | 30.00 |

METRO

| Number | Title (A Side/B Side) | Yr | NM |
|---|---|---|---|
| ❑ M-511 [M] | Tommy Edwards | 1965 | 12.00 |
| ❑ MS-511 [S] | Tommy Edwards | 1965 | 15.00 |

MGM

| Number | Title (A Side/B Side) | Yr | NM |
|---|---|---|---|
| ❑ GAS-123 | Tommy Edwards (Golden Archive Series) | 1970 | 15.00 |
| ❑ E-3732 [M] | It's All in the Game | 1958 | 30.00 |
| *—Yellow label* | | | |
| ❑ E-3732 [M] | It's All in the Game | 1960 | 20.00 |
| *—Black label* | | | |
| ❑ SE-3732 [S] | It's All in the Game | 1959 | 40.00 |
| *—Yellow label* | | | |
| ❑ SE-3732 [S] | It's All in the Game | 1960 | 25.00 |
| *—Black label* | | | |
| ❑ E-3760 [M] | For Young Lovers | 1959 | 30.00 |
| *—Yellow label* | | | |
| ❑ E-3760 [M] | For Young Lovers | 1960 | 20.00 |
| *—Black label* | | | |
| ❑ SE-3760 [S] | For Young Lovers | 1959 | 40.00 |
| *—Yellow label* | | | |
| ❑ SE-3760 [S] | For Young Lovers | 1960 | 25.00 |
| *—Black label* | | | |
| ❑ E-3805 [M] | You Started Me Dreaming | 1960 | 20.00 |
| ❑ SE-3805 [S] | You Started Me Dreaming | 1960 | 25.00 |
| ❑ E-3822 [M] | Step Out Singing | 1960 | 20.00 |
| ❑ SE-3822 [S] | Step Out Singing | 1960 | 25.00 |
| ❑ E-3838 [M] | Tommy Edwards in Hawaii | 1960 | 20.00 |
| ❑ SE-3838 [S] | Tommy Edwards in Hawaii | 1960 | 25.00 |
| ❑ E-3884 [M] | Tommy Edwards' Greatest Hits | 1961 | 20.00 |
| ❑ SE-3884 [S] | Tommy Edwards' Greatest Hits | 1961 | 25.00 |
| ❑ E-3959 [M] | Golden Coutnry Hits | 1961 | 20.00 |
| ❑ SE-3959 [S] | Golden Coutnry Hits | 1961 | 25.00 |
| ❑ E-4020 [M] | Stardust | 1962 | 20.00 |
| ❑ SE-4020 [S] | Stardust | 1962 | 25.00 |
| ❑ E-4060 [M] | Soft Strings and Two Guitars | 1962 | 20.00 |
| ❑ SE-4060 [S] | Soft Strings and Two Guitars | 1962 | 25.00 |
| ❑ E-4141 [M] | The Very Best of Tommy Edwards | 1963 | 15.00 |
| ❑ SE-4141 [S] | The Very Best of Tommy Edwards | 1963 | 20.00 |

REGENT

| Number | Title (A Side/B Side) | Yr | NM |
|---|---|---|---|
| ❑ MG-6096 [M] | Tommy Edwards Sings | 1958 | 60.00 |

### EDWARDS, VINCENT

DECCA

| Number | Title (A Side/B Side) | Yr | NM |
|---|---|---|---|
| ❑ DL 4311 [M] | Vincent Edwards Sings | 1962 | 20.00 |
| ❑ DL 4336 [M] | Sometimes I'm Happy...Sometimes I'm Blue | 1962 | 20.00 |
| ❑ DL 4399 [M] | In Person at the Riviera | 1963 | 20.00 |
| ❑ DL 74311 [S] | Vincent Edwards Sings | 1962 | 25.00 |
| ❑ DL 74336 [S] | Sometimes I'm Happy...Sometimes I'm Blue | 1962 | 25.00 |
| ❑ DL 74399 [S] | In Person at the Riviera | 1963 | 25.00 |

VOCALION

| Number | Title (A Side/B Side) | Yr | NM |
|---|---|---|---|
| ❑ VL 3852 [M] | Here's Vincent Edwards | 1967 | 12.00 |
| ❑ VL 73852 [S] | Here's Vincent Edwards | 1967 | 12.00 |

### EELS

BONG LOAD

| Number | Title (A Side/B Side) | Yr | NM |
|---|---|---|---|
| ❑ BL 47 | Daisies of the Galaxy | 2000 | 100.00 |

DREAMWORKS

| Number | Title (A Side/B Side) | Yr | NM |
|---|---|---|---|
| ❑ DRM2-50052 [(2)10] | Electro-shock Blues | 1998 | 50.00 |

SPINART

| Number | Title (A Side/B Side) | Yr | NM |
|---|---|---|---|
| ❑ 128 | Shootenanny! | 2003 | 25.00 |

### EIGHT MINUTES, THE

PERCEPTION

| Number | Title (A Side/B Side) | Yr | NM |
|---|---|---|---|
| ❑ 27 | An American Family | 1973 | 50.00 |

### EIRE APPARENT, THE

BUDDAH

| Number | Title (A Side/B Side) | Yr | NM |
|---|---|---|---|
| ❑ BDS-5031 | Sunrise | 1969 | 40.00 |

### EL CAMPO JADES, THE

GOLD EAGLE

| Number | Title (A Side/B Side) | Yr | NM |
|---|---|---|---|
| ❑ LP-101 [M] | The El Campo Jades | 1966 | 50.00 |

### EL DORADOS

LOST-NITE

| Number | Title (A Side/B Side) | Yr | NM |
|---|---|---|---|
| ❑ LLP-20 [10] | The El Dorados | 1981 | 12.00 |
| *—Red vinyl* | | | |

SOLID SMOKE

| Number | Title (A Side/B Side) | Yr | NM |
|---|---|---|---|
| ❑ 8025 | Low Mileage/High Octane | 1984 | 10.00 |

VEE JAY

| Number | Title (A Side/B Side) | Yr | NM |
|---|---|---|---|
| ❑ LP-1001 [M] | Crazy Little Mama | 1959 | 800.00 |
| *—Maroon label, thick silver band* | | | |
| ❑ LP-1001 [M] | Crazy Little Mama | 1960 | 400.00 |
| *—Maroon label, thin silver band* | | | |
| ❑ LP-1001 [M] | Crazy Little Mama | 1962 | 250.00 |
| *—Black label with colorband* | | | |
| ❑ VJLP-1001 [M] | Crazy Little Mama | 198? | 10.00 |
| *—Authorized reissue* | | | |

### ELBERT, DONNIE

ALL PLATINUM

| Number | Title (A Side/B Side) | Yr | NM |
|---|---|---|---|
| ❑ 3007 | Where Did Our Love Go | 1971 | 25.00 |
| ❑ 3019 | Dancin' the Night Away | 1977 | 25.00 |

DELUXE

| Number | Title (A Side/B Side) | Yr | NM |
|---|---|---|---|
| ❑ 12003 | Have I Sinned | 1971 | 25.00 |

KING

| Number | Title (A Side/B Side) | Yr | NM |
|---|---|---|---|
| ❑ 629 [M] | The Sensational Donnie Elbert Sings | 1959 | 400.00 |

SUGAR HILL

| Number | Title (A Side/B Side) | Yr | NM |
|---|---|---|---|
| ❑ 256 | From the Git Go | 1981 | 12.00 |

TRIP

| Number | Title (A Side/B Side) | Yr | NM |
|---|---|---|---|
| ❑ 9514 | Donnie Elbert Sings | 197? | 15.00 |
| ❑ 9524 | Stop in the Name of Love | 197? | 15.00 |

### ELDRIDGE, ROY

AMERICAN RECORDING SOCIETY

| Number | Title (A Side/B Side) | Yr | NM |
|---|---|---|---|
| ❑ G-420 [M] | Swing Goes Dixie | 1956 | 40.00 |

CLEF

| Number | Title (A Side/B Side) | Yr | NM |
|---|---|---|---|
| ❑ MGC-113 [10] | Roy Eldridge Collates | 1953 | 150.00 |
| ❑ MGC-150 [10] | The Roy Eldridge Quintet | 1954 | 150.00 |
| ❑ MGC-162 [10] | The Strolling Mr. Eldridge | 1954 | 150.00 |
| ❑ MGC-683 [M] | Little Jazz | 1956 | 100.00 |
| ❑ MGC-704 [M] | Rockin' Chair | 1956 | 100.00 |
| ❑ MGC-705 [M] | Dale's Wail | 1956 | 100.00 |

DIAL

| Number | Title (A Side/B Side) | Yr | NM |
|---|---|---|---|
| ❑ LP-304 [10] | Little Jazz Four: Trumpet Fantasy | 1953 | 400.00 |

DISCOVERY

| Number | Title (A Side/B Side) | Yr | NM |
|---|---|---|---|
| ❑ DL-2009 [10] | Roy Eldridge with Zoot Sims | 1954 | 120.00 |

EMARCY

| Number | Title (A Side/B Side) | Yr | NM |
|---|---|---|---|
| ❑ MG-36084 [M] | Roy's Got Rhythm | 1956 | 80.00 |

LONDON

| Number | Title (A Side/B Side) | Yr | NM |
|---|---|---|---|
| ❑ PB 375 [10] | Roy Eldridge Quartet | 1954 | 120.00 |

MASTER JAZZ

| Number | Title (A Side/B Side) | Yr | NM |
|---|---|---|---|
| ❑ 8110 | The Nifty Cat | 1970 | 20.00 |
| ❑ 8121 | The Nifty Cat Strikes West | 197? | 20.00 |

MERCURY

| Number | Title (A Side/B Side) | Yr | NM |
|---|---|---|---|
| ❑ MGC-113 [10] | Roy Eldridge Collates | 1952 | 200.00 |

PRESTIGE

| Number | Title (A Side/B Side) | Yr | NM |
|---|---|---|---|
| ❑ PRLP-114 [10] | Roy Eldridge in Sweden | 1951 | 250.00 |

VERVE

| Number | Title (A Side/B Side) | Yr | NM |
|---|---|---|---|
| ❑ MGV-1010 [M] | Swing Goes Dixie | 1957 | 50.00 |
| ❑ V-1010 [M] | Swing Goes Dixie | 1961 | 20.00 |
| ❑ MGV-8068 [M] | Little Jazz | 1957 | 50.00 |
| *—Reissue of Clef 683* | | | |
| ❑ V-8068 [M] | Little Jazz | 1961 | 20.00 |
| ❑ MGV-8088 [M] | Rockin' Chair | 1957 | 50.00 |
| *—Reissue of Clef 704* | | | |
| ❑ V-8088 [M] | Rockin' Chair | 1961 | 20.00 |
| ❑ MGV-8089 [M] | Dale's Wail | 1957 | 50.00 |
| *—Reissue of Clef 705* | | | |
| ❑ V-8089 [M] | Dale's Wail | 1961 | 20.00 |
| ❑ MGV-8389 [M] | Swingin' on the Town | 1960 | 50.00 |
| ❑ V-8389 [M] | Swingin' on the Town | 1961 | 20.00 |

### ELDRIDGE, ROY, AND BENNY CARTER

AMERICAN RECORDING SOCIETY

| Number | Title (A Side/B Side) | Yr | NM |
|---|---|---|---|
| ❑ G-413 [M] | The Urbane Jazz of Roy Eldridge and Benny Carter | 1957 | 40.00 |

VERVE

| Number | Title (A Side/B Side) | Yr | NM |
|---|---|---|---|
| ❑ MGV-8202 [M] | The Urbane Jazz of Roy Eldridge and Benny Carter | 1957 | 50.00 |
| ❑ V-8202 [M] | The Urbane Jazz of Roy Eldridge and Benny Carter | 1961 | 20.00 |

### ELDRIDGE, ROY, AND DIZZY GILLESPIE

CLEF

| Number | Title (A Side/B Side) | Yr | NM |
|---|---|---|---|
| ❑ MGC-641 [M] | Roy and Diz | 1955 | 150.00 |
| ❑ MGC-671 [M] | Roy and Diz, Volume 2 | 1955 | 150.00 |
| ❑ MGC-730 [M] | Trumpet Battle | 1956 | 100.00 |
| ❑ MGC-731 [M] | The Trumpet Kings | 1956 | 100.00 |

VERVE

| Number | Title (A Side/B Side) | Yr | NM |
|---|---|---|---|
| ❑ MGV-8109 [M] | Trumpet Battle | 1957 | 50.00 |
| ❑ V-8109 [M] | Trumpet Battle | 1961 | 20.00 |
| ❑ MGV-8110 [M] | The Trumpet Kings | 1957 | 50.00 |
| ❑ V-8110 [M] | The Trumpet Kings | 1961 | 20.00 |

### ELDRIDGE, ROY; DIZZY GILLESPIE; HARRY "SWEETS" EDISON

VERVE

| Number | Title (A Side/B Side) | Yr | NM |
|---|---|---|---|
| ❑ MGV-8212 [M] | Tour de Force | 1958 | 50.00 |
| ❑ V-8212 [M] | Tour de Force | 1961 | 20.00 |

### ELDRIDGE, ROY/SAMMY PRICE

BRUNSWICK

| Number | Title (A Side/B Side) | Yr | NM |
|---|---|---|---|
| ❑ BL 58045 [10] | Battle of Jazz, Volume 7 | 1953 | 60.00 |

### ELECTRAS, THE

John Kerry, senator from Massachusetts and presidential candidate, played bass on this album.

(NO LABEL)

| Number | Title (A Side/B Side) | Yr | NM |
|---|---|---|---|
| ❑ ELT-201 | The Electras | 1961 | 2000. |

### ELECTRIC LIGHT ORCHESTRA

CBS ASSOCIATED

| Number | Title (A Side/B Side) | Yr | NM |
|---|---|---|---|
| ❑ FZ 40048 | Balance of Power | 1986 | 10.00 |

JET

| Number | Title (A Side/B Side) | Yr | NM |
|---|---|---|---|
| ❑ JT-LA823-L2 [(2)] | Out of the Blue | 1977 | 15.00 |
| *—Originals include poster and die-cut cardboard "spaceship"* | | | |
| ❑ JT-LA823-L2 [(2)DJ] | Out of the Blue | 1977 | 25.00 |
| *—Promo only on blue vinyl* | | | |
| ❑ JZ 35524 | No Answer | 1978 | 10.00 |
| ❑ PZ 35524 | No Answer | 1981 | 8.00 |
| ❑ JZ 35525 | On the Third Day | 1978 | 10.00 |
| ❑ PZ 35525 | On the Third Day | 1981 | 8.00 |
| ❑ JZ 35526 | Eldorado | 1978 | 10.00 |
| ❑ PZ 35526 | Eldorado | 198? | 8.00 |
| ❑ JZ 35527 | Face the Music | 1978 | 10.00 |
| ❑ PZ 35527 | Face the Music | 1981 | 8.00 |
| ❑ JZ 35528 | Ole Elo | 1978 | 10.00 |
| ❑ PZ 35528 | Ole Elo | 1981 | 8.00 |
| ❑ JZ 35529 | A New World Record | 1978 | 10.00 |
| ❑ PZ 35529 | A New World Record | 1981 | 8.00 |
| ❑ KZ2 35530 [(2)] | Out of the Blue | 1978 | 12.00 |
| ❑ JZ 35533 | Electric Light Orchestra II | 1978 | 10.00 |
| ❑ PZ 35533 | Electric Light Orchestra II | 1981 | 8.00 |
| ❑ FZ 35769 | Discovery | 1979 | 10.00 |
| ❑ PZ 35769 | Discovery | 1987 | 8.00 |
| ❑ FZ 36310 | ELO's Greatest Hits | 1979 | 10.00 |
| ❑ HZ 36310 | ELO's Greatest Hits | 1981 | 40.00 |
| *—Half-speed mastered edition* | | | |
| ❑ PZ 36310 | ELO's Greatest Hits | 1987 | 8.00 |
| ❑ Z4X 36966 [(4)] | A Box of Their Best | 1980 | 25.00 |
| ❑ FZ 37371 | Time | 1981 | 10.00 |
| ❑ PZ 37371 | Time | 1987 | 8.00 |
| ❑ PZ 38490 | Secret Messages | 1987 | 8.00 |
| ❑ QZ 38490 | Secret Messages | 1983 | 10.00 |
| ❑ HZ 45789 | Discovery | 1980 | 25.00 |
| *—Half-speed mastered edition* | | | |
| ❑ HZ 47371 | Time | 1982 | 25.00 |
| *—Half-speed mastered edition* | | | |
| ❑ HZ 48490 | Secret Messages | 1983 | 30.00 |
| *—Half-speed mastered edition* | | | |

UNITED ARTISTS

| Number | Title (A Side/B Side) | Yr | NM |
|---|---|---|---|
| ❑ UA-LA040-F | Electric Light Orchestra II | 1973 | 15.00 |
| *—Tan label* | | | |
| ❑ UA-LA040-F | Electric Light Orchestra II | 1978 | 10.00 |
| *—Sunrise label* | | | |
| ❑ SP-123 [DJ] | Ole Elo | 1976 | 50.00 |
| *—Gold vinyl promo with generic cover* | | | |
| ❑ SP-123 [DJ] | Ole Elo | 1976 | 80.00 |
| *—Red, blue or white vinyl promos with generic cover* | | | |
| ❑ SP-123 [DJ] | Ole Elo | 1976 | 100.00 |
| *—Gold vinyl, cover similar to the released version except for the single line "Ole Elo" (no "Electric Light Orchestra" underneath) at the top of the front cover* | | | |

| Number | Title (A Side/B Side) | Yr | NM |
|---|---|---|---|
| ❑ UA-LA188-F | On the Third Day | 1973 | 15.00 |
| *—Tan label* | | | |
| ❑ UA-LA188-F | On the Third Day | 1978 | 10.00 |
| *—Sunrise label* | | | |
| ❑ UA-LA318-F | The Night the Light Went On in Long Beach | 1974 | — |
| *—Canceled* | | | |
| ❑ UA-LA339-G | Eldorado | 1974 | 12.00 |
| *—Tan label* | | | |
| ❑ UA-LA339-G | Eldorado | 1977 | 10.00 |
| *—Sunrise label* | | | |
| ❑ UA-LA546-DJ [DJ] | Face the Music | 1975 | 25.00 |
| *—Promo only, banded for airplay* | | | |
| ❑ UA-LA546-G | Face the Music | 1975 | 12.00 |
| *—Tan label* | | | |
| ❑ UA-LA546-G | Face the Music | 1978 | 10.00 |
| *—Sunrise label* | | | |
| ❑ UA-LA630-G | Ole Elo | 1976 | 12.00 |
| *—Tan label* | | | |
| ❑ UA-LA630-G | Ole Elo | 1978 | 10.00 |
| *—Sunrise label* | | | |
| ❑ UA-LA679-G | A New World Record | 1976 | 12.00 |
| *—All copies have custom labels* | | | |
| ❑ UAS-5573 | No Answer | 1972 | 15.00 |
| *—Tan label* | | | |
| ❑ UAS-5573 | No Answer | 1978 | 10.00 |
| *—Sunrise label* | | | |

### ELECTRIC PRUNES, THE

**REPRISE**

| Number | Title (A Side/B Side) | Yr | NM |
|---|---|---|---|
| ❑ R-6248 [M] | The Electric Prunes | 1967 | 50.00 |
| ❑ RS-6248 [S] | The Electric Prunes | 1967 | 40.00 |
| ❑ R-6262 [M] | Underground | 1967 | 50.00 |
| ❑ RS-6262 [S] | Underground | 1967 | 40.00 |
| ❑ R-6275 [M] | Mass in F Minor | 1967 | 40.00 |
| ❑ RS-6275 [S] | Mass in F Minor | 1967 | 30.00 |
| ❑ RS-6316 | Release of an Oath | 1968 | 30.00 |
| ❑ RS-6342 | Just Good Rock 'n Roll | 1969 | 30.00 |

### ELECTRIC TOILET, THE

**NASCO**

| Number | Title (A Side/B Side) | Yr | NM |
|---|---|---|---|
| ❑ 9004 | In the Hands of Karma | 1970 | 200.00 |

### ELECTRIC UNDERGROUND, THE

**PREMIER**

| Number | Title (A Side/B Side) | Yr | NM |
|---|---|---|---|
| ❑ P-9060 [M] | Guitar Explosion | 1967 | 50.00 |
| ❑ PS-9060 [S] | Guitar Explosion | 1967 | 50.00 |

### ELECTROSONICS, THE

**PHILIPS**

| Number | Title (A Side/B Side) | Yr | NM |
|---|---|---|---|
| ❑ PHM 200047 [M] | Electronic Music | 1962 | 70.00 |
| ❑ PHS 600047 [S] | Electronic Music | 1962 | 90.00 |

### ELEPHANTS MEMORY

**APPLE**

| Number | Title (A Side/B Side) | Yr | NM |
|---|---|---|---|
| ❑ SMAS-3389 | Elephants Memory | 1972 | 25.00 |

**BUDDAH**

| Number | Title (A Side/B Side) | Yr | NM |
|---|---|---|---|
| ❑ BDS-5033 | Elephants Memory | 1969 | 15.00 |
| ❑ BDS-5038 | Songs from Midnight Cowboy | 1970 | 15.00 |

**METROMEDIA**

| Number | Title (A Side/B Side) | Yr | NM |
|---|---|---|---|
| ❑ MD-1035 | Take It to the Streets | 1970 | 20.00 |

**RCA VICTOR**

| Number | Title (A Side/B Side) | Yr | NM |
|---|---|---|---|
| ❑ APL1-0569 | Angela Forever | 1974 | 15.00 |

### ELEVENTH HOUSE, THE See LARRY CORYELL.

### ELF

**EPIC**

| Number | Title (A Side/B Side) | Yr | NM |
|---|---|---|---|
| ❑ KE 31789 | Elf | 1972 | 30.00 |
| *—Yellow label* | | | |
| ❑ KE 31789 | Elf | 1973 | 20.00 |
| *—Orange label* | | | |

**MGM**

| Number | Title (A Side/B Side) | Yr | NM |
|---|---|---|---|
| ❑ M3G 4974 | L.A. 59 | 1974 | 20.00 |
| ❑ M3G 4994 | Trying to Burn the Sun | 1975 | 20.00 |

### ELGART, BILL

**MARK LEVINSON**

| Number | Title (A Side/B Side) | Yr | NM |
|---|---|---|---|
| ❑ 3 | A Life | 1980 | 25.00 |

### ELGART, LARRY

**BRUNSWICK**

| Number | Title (A Side/B Side) | Yr | NM |
|---|---|---|---|
| ❑ BL 58054 [10] | Impressions of Outer Space | 1954 | 60.00 |

**DECCA**

| Number | Title (A Side/B Side) | Yr | NM |
|---|---|---|---|
| ❑ DL 5526 [10] | The Larry Elgart Band with Strings | 1954 | 100.00 |
| ❑ DL 8034 [M] | Music for Barefoot Ballerinas | 1955 | 40.00 |

**MGM**

| Number | Title (A Side/B Side) | Yr | NM |
|---|---|---|---|
| ❑ SE-3891 [S] | Sophisticated Sixties | 1960 | 20.00 |
| ❑ SE-3896 [S] | The Shape of Sounds to Come | 1961 | 20.00 |
| ❑ SE-3961 [S] | Visions | 1961 | 20.00 |
| ❑ SE-4007 [S] | The City | 1961 | 20.00 |
| ❑ SE-4028 [S] | Music in Motion! | 1962 | 20.00 |
| ❑ SE-4080 [S] | More Music in Motion! | 1962 | 20.00 |

**RCA VICTOR**

| Number | Title (A Side/B Side) | Yr | NM |
|---|---|---|---|
| ❑ LSP-1961 [S] | Larry Elgart and His Orchestra | 1959 | 20.00 |
| ❑ LSP-2045 [S] | New Sounds at the Roosevelt | 1959 | 20.00 |
| ❑ LSP-2166 [S] | Saratoga | 1960 | 20.00 |

### ELGART, LES

**COLUMBIA**

| Number | Title (A Side/B Side) | Yr | NM |
|---|---|---|---|
| ❑ CL 536 [M] | Sophisticated Swing | 1953 | 30.00 |
| *—Maroon label, gold print* | | | |
| ❑ CL 594 [M] | Just One More Dance | 1954 | 30.00 |
| *—Maroon label, gold print* | | | |
| ❑ CL 594 [M] | Just One More Dance | 1955 | 20.00 |
| *—Red and black label with six "eye" logos* | | | |
| ❑ CL 619 [M] | The Band of the Year | 1955 | 40.00 |
| *—Maroon label, gold print; first LP appearance of "Bandstand Boogie"* | | | |
| ❑ CL 684 [M] | The Dancing Sound | 1955 | 30.00 |
| ❑ CL 803 [M] | For Dancers Only | 1956 | 30.00 |
| ❑ CL 875 [M] | The Elgart Touch | 1956 | 30.00 |
| *—Red and black label, six "eye" logos* | | | |
| ❑ CL 1008 [M] | For Dancers Also | 1957 | 25.00 |
| ❑ CL 1052 [M] | Les and Larry Elgart and Their Orchestra | 1957 | 20.00 |
| ❑ CL 1291 [M] | Les Elgart On Tour | 1959 | 20.00 |
| ❑ CL 1350 [M] | The Great Sound of Les Elgart | 1959 | 20.00 |
| ❑ CL 1450 [M] | The Band with That Sound | 1960 | 20.00 |
| ❑ CL 1500 [M] | Designs for Dancing | 1960 | 20.00 |
| ❑ CL 1567 [M] | Half Satin - Half Latin | 1961 | 20.00 |
| ❑ CL 1659 [M] | It's De-Lovely | 1961 | 20.00 |
| ❑ CL 1785 [M] | The Twist Goes to College | 1962 | 20.00 |
| ❑ CL 1890 [M] | Best Band on Campus | 1963 | 20.00 |
| ❑ CL 2503 [10] | Prom Date | 1954 | 40.00 |
| ❑ CL 2578 [10] | Campus Hop | 1955 | 40.00 |
| ❑ CL 2590 [10] | More of Les | 1955 | 40.00 |
| ❑ CL 6287 [10] | Just One More Dance | 195? | 40.00 |
| ❑ CS 8002 [S] | Sound Ideas | 1958 | 25.00 |
| ❑ CS 8092 [S] | Les and Larry Elgart and Their Orchestra | 1959 | 25.00 |
| ❑ CS 8103 [S] | Les Elgart On Tour | 1959 | 25.00 |
| ❑ CS 8159 [S] | The Great Sound of Les Elgart | 1959 | 25.00 |
| ❑ CS 8245 [S] | The Band with That Sound | 1960 | 25.00 |
| ❑ CS 8291 [S] | Designs for Dancing | 1960 | 25.00 |
| ❑ CS 8367 [S] | Half Satin - Half Latin | 1961 | 25.00 |
| ❑ CS 8459 [S] | It's De-Lovely | 1961 | 25.00 |
| ❑ CS 8585 [S] | The Twist Goes to College | 1962 | 25.00 |
| ❑ CS 8690 [S] | Best Band on Campus | 1963 | 25.00 |

### ELGART, LES AND LARRY

**COLUMBIA**

| Number | Title (A Side/B Side) | Yr | NM |
|---|---|---|---|
| ❑ CL 1123 [M] | Sound Ideas | 1958 | 20.00 |
| ❑ CL 2633 [M] | Girl Watchers | 1967 | 20.00 |
| ❑ CL 2780 [M] | The Wonderful World of Today's Hits | 1968 | 25.00 |
| ❑ CS 8912 [S] | Big Band Hootenanny | 1963 | 20.00 |
| ❑ CS 9021 [S] | Command Performance! Les & Larry Elgart Play the Great Dance Hits | 1964 | 20.00 |
| ❑ CS 9101 [S] | The New Elgart Touch | 1965 | 20.00 |
| ❑ CS 9155 [S] | Elgart Au-Go-Go | 1965 | 20.00 |
| ❑ CS 9311 [S] | Sound of the Times | 1966 | 20.00 |
| ❑ CS 9391 [S] | Warm and Sensuous | 1966 | 20.00 |

### ELGINS, THE (1)

**V.I.P.**

| Number | Title (A Side/B Side) | Yr | NM |
|---|---|---|---|
| ❑ 400 [M] | Darling Baby | 1966 | 70.00 |
| ❑ S-400 [S] | Darling Baby | 1966 | 100.00 |

### ELIAS, ROSALIND, AND GIORGIO TOZZI

**RCA VICTOR RED SEAL**

| Number | Title (A Side/B Side) | Yr | NM |
|---|---|---|---|
| ❑ LSC-2350 [S] | A Yuletide Song Fest | 1959 | 40.00 |
| *—Original with "shaded dog" label* | | | |

### ELIGIBLES, THE

**CAPITOL**

| Number | Title (A Side/B Side) | Yr | NM |
|---|---|---|---|
| ❑ ST 1310 [S] | Along the Trail | 1960 | 30.00 |
| ❑ T 1310 [M] | Along the Trail | 1960 | 25.00 |
| ❑ ST 1411 [S] | Love Is a Gamble | 1960 | 30.00 |
| ❑ T 1411 [M] | Love Is a Gamble | 1960 | 25.00 |

### ELIMINATORS, THE

**LIBERTY**

| Number | Title (A Side/B Side) | Yr | NM |
|---|---|---|---|
| ❑ LRP-3365 [M] | Liverpool! Dragsters! Cycles! Surfing! | 1964 | 80.00 |
| ❑ LST-7365 [S] | Liverpool! Dragsters! Cycles! Surfing! | 1964 | 100.00 |

### ELIZABETH

**VANGUARD**

| Number | Title (A Side/B Side) | Yr | NM |
|---|---|---|---|
| ❑ VSD-6501 | Elizabeth | 1968 | 60.00 |

### ELLIE POP

**MAINSTREAM**

| Number | Title (A Side/B Side) | Yr | NM |
|---|---|---|---|
| ❑ S-6115 | Ellie Pop | 1968 | 40.00 |

### ELLINGTON, DUKE

**AAMCO**

| Number | Title (A Side/B Side) | Yr | NM |
|---|---|---|---|
| ❑ ALP-301 [M] | The Royal Concert of Duke Ellington, Vol. 1 | 196? | 30.00 |
| *—Reissue of Bethlehem material* | | | |
| ❑ ALP-313 [M] | The Royal Concert of Duke Ellington, Vol. 2 | 196? | 30.00 |
| *—Reissue of Bethlehem material* | | | |

**ALLEGRO**

| Number | Title (A Side/B Side) | Yr | NM |
|---|---|---|---|
| ❑ 1591 [M] | Duke Ellington and His Orchestra Play | 1955 | 50.00 |
| ❑ 3082 [M] | Duke Ellington | 1953 | 50.00 |
| ❑ 4014 [10] | Duke Ellington and His Orchestra Play | 1954 | 100.00 |
| ❑ 4038 [10] | Duke Ellington and His Orchestra Play | 1954 | 100.00 |

**ATLANTIC**

| Number | Title (A Side/B Side) | Yr | NM |
|---|---|---|---|
| ❑ QD 1580 [Q] | New Orleans Suite | 1974 | 25.00 |

**BETHLEHEM**

| Number | Title (A Side/B Side) | Yr | NM |
|---|---|---|---|
| ❑ BCP-60 [M] | Historically Speaking, The Duke | 1956 | 60.00 |
| ❑ BCP-6005 [M] | Duke Ellington Presents | 1956 | 60.00 |

**BLUEBIRD**

| Number | Title (A Side/B Side) | Yr | NM |
|---|---|---|---|
| ❑ 5659-1-RB [(4)] | Duke Ellington: The Blanton-Webster Band | 1986 | 25.00 |
| ❑ 6641-1-RB [(4)] | Black, Brown and Beige | 1988 | 25.00 |

**BRUNSWICK**

| Number | Title (A Side/B Side) | Yr | NM |
|---|---|---|---|
| ❑ BL 54007 [M] | Early Ellington | 1954 | 50.00 |
| ❑ BL 58002 [10] | Ellingtonia, Volume 1 | 1950 | 100.00 |
| ❑ BL 58012 [10] | Ellingtonia, Volume 2 | 1950 | 100.00 |

**CAPITOL**

| Number | Title (A Side/B Side) | Yr | NM |
|---|---|---|---|
| ❑ H 440 [10] | Premiered by Ellington | 1953 | 100.00 |
| ❑ H 477 [10] | The Duke Plays Ellington | 1954 | 100.00 |
| ❑ T 477 [M] | The Duke Plays Ellington | 1954 | 40.00 |
| *—Turquoise label* | | | |
| ❑ T 477 [M] | The Duke Plays Ellington | 1958 | 20.00 |
| *—Black label with colorband, logo at left* | | | |
| ❑ T 521 [M] | Ellington '55 | 1955 | 40.00 |
| *—Turquoise label* | | | |
| ❑ T 521 [M] | Ellington '55 | 1958 | 20.00 |
| *—Black label with colorband, logo at left* | | | |
| ❑ T 637 [M] | Dance to the Duke | 1955 | 40.00 |
| *—Turquoise label* | | | |
| ❑ T 637 [M] | Dance to the Duke | 1958 | 20.00 |
| *—Black label with colorband, logo at left* | | | |
| ❑ T 679 [M] | Ellington Showcase | 1956 | 40.00 |
| *—Turquoise label* | | | |
| ❑ T 679 [M] | Ellington Showcase | 1958 | 20.00 |
| *—Black label with colorband, logo at left* | | | |
| ❑ T 1602 [M] | The Best of Duke Ellington | 1961 | 20.00 |

**COLUMBIA**

| Number | Title (A Side/B Side) | Yr | NM |
|---|---|---|---|
| ❑ C3L 27 [(3)M] | The Ellington Era, Vol. 1 | 1963 | 40.00 |
| ❑ C3L 39 [(3)M] | The Ellington Era, Vol. 2 | 1964 | 40.00 |
| ❑ CL 558 [M] | The Music of Duke Ellington | 1954 | 50.00 |
| *—Maroon label with gold print* | | | |
| ❑ CL 558 [M] | The Music of Duke Ellington | 1956 | 40.00 |
| *—Red and black label with six "eye" logos* | | | |
| ❑ CL 663 [M] | Blue Light | 1955 | 40.00 |
| ❑ CL 825 [M] | Masterpieces by Ellington | 1956 | 40.00 |
| *—Reissue of Columbia Masterworks 4418* | | | |
| ❑ CL 830 [M] | Hi-Fi Ellington Uptown | 1956 | 40.00 |
| ❑ CL 848 [M] | Liberian Suite | 1956 | 40.00 |
| *—Reissue of Columbia 6073* | | | |
| ❑ CL 934 [M] | Ellington at Newport '56 | 1957 | 40.00 |
| *—Red and black label with six "eye" logos* | | | |
| ❑ CL 951 [M] | A Drum Is a Woman | 1957 | 40.00 |
| ❑ CL 1033 [M] | Such Sweet Thunder | 1957 | 40.00 |
| ❑ CL 1085 [M] | Ellington Indigos | 1958 | 25.00 |
| ❑ CL 1162 [M] | Brown, Black and Beige | 1958 | 25.00 |
| ❑ CL 1198 [M] | The Cosmic Scene | 1959 | 80.00 |
| ❑ CL 1245 [M] | Newport 1958 | 1959 | 25.00 |
| ❑ CL 1282 [M] | Duke Ellington at the Bal Masque | 1959 | 25.00 |
| ❑ CL 1323 [M] | Duke Ellington Jazz Party | 1959 | 25.00 |
| ❑ CL 1400 [M] | Festival Session | 1960 | 25.00 |
| ❑ CL 1445 [M] | Blues in Orbit | 1960 | 25.00 |
| ❑ CL 1541 [M] | The Nutcracker Suite | 1960 | 30.00 |
| ❑ CL 1546 [M] | Piano in the Background | 1960 | 30.00 |
| ❑ CL 1597 [M] | Peer Gynt Suite/Suite Thursday | 1961 | 25.00 |
| ❑ CL 1715 [M] | First Time | 1962 | 25.00 |
| ❑ CL 1790 [M] | All American | 1962 | 20.00 |
| ❑ CL 1907 [M] | Midnight in Paris | 1963 | 20.00 |
| ❑ CL 2522 [10] | Duke's Mixture | 1955 | 80.00 |
| ❑ CL 2562 [10] | Here's the Duke | 1955 | 80.00 |
| ❑ CL 2593 [10] | Al Hibbler with the Duke | 1956 | 80.00 |
| ❑ CL 6024 [10] | Mood Ellington | 1949 | 100.00 |
| ❑ CL 6073 [10] | Liberian Suite | 1949 | 100.00 |
| ❑ CS 8015 [S] | Brown, Black and Beige | 1958 | 30.00 |
| ❑ CS 8053 [S] | Ellington Indigos | 1958 | 30.00 |
| *—Red and black label with six "eye" logos* | | | |
| ❑ CS 8072 [S] | Newport 1958 | 1959 | 30.00 |
| ❑ CS 8098 [S] | Duke Ellington at the Bal Masque | 1959 | 30.00 |
| ❑ CS 8127 [S] | Duke Ellington Jazz Party | 1959 | 30.00 |
| ❑ CS 8241 [S] | Blues in Orbit | 1960 | 30.00 |
| ❑ CS 8341 [S] | The Nutcracker Suite | 1960 | 40.00 |
| ❑ CS 8346 [S] | Piano in the Background | 1960 | 40.00 |
| ❑ CS 8397 [S] | Peer Gynt Suite/Suite Thursday | 1961 | 30.00 |
| ❑ CS 8515 [S] | First Time | 1962 | 30.00 |
| ❑ CS 8590 [S] | All American | 1962 | 25.00 |
| ❑ CS 8829 [S] | Midnight in Paris | 1963 | 25.00 |

| Number | Title (A Side/B Side) | Yr | NM |
|---|---|---|---|
| **COLUMBIA MASTERWORKS** | | | |
| ❑ ML 4418 [M] | Masterpieces by Ellington | 1951 | 100.00 |
| ❑ ML 4639 [M] | Ellington Uptown | 195? | 50.00 |
| *—Oddly, this exists as a reissue on the red and black "6 eye" label* | | | |
| ❑ ML 4639 [M] | Ellington Uptown | 1951 | 100.00 |
| *—Blue or green label, gold print* | | | |
| **DECCA** | | | |
| ❑ DL 9224 [M] | Duke Ellington, Volume 1 — In the Beginning | 1958 | 40.00 |
| *—Black label, silver print* | | | |
| ❑ DL 9241 [M] | Duke Ellington, Volume 2 — Hot in Harlem | 1959 | 40.00 |
| *—Black label, silver print* | | | |
| ❑ DL 9247 [M] | Duke Ellington, Volume 3 — Rockin' in Rhythm | 1959 | 40.00 |
| *—Black label, silver print* | | | |
| ❑ DL 79224 [R] | Duke Ellington, Volume 1 — In the Beginning | 1958 | 25.00 |
| *—Black label, silver print* | | | |
| ❑ DL 79241 [R] | Duke Ellington, Volume 2 — Hot in Harlem | 1959 | 25.00 |
| *—Black label, silver print* | | | |
| ❑ DL 79247 [R] | Duke Ellington, Volume 3 — Rockin' in Rhythm | 1959 | 25.00 |
| *—Black label, silver print* | | | |
| **HALL OF FAME** | | | |
| ❑ 625/6/7 [(3)] | The Immortal Duke Ellington | 197? | 20.00 |
| **JAZZ PANORAMA** | | | |
| ❑ 1802 [10] | Duke Ellington — Vol. 1 | 1951 | 100.00 |
| ❑ 1811 [10] | Duke Ellington — Vol. 2 | 1951 | 100.00 |
| ❑ 1816 [10] | Duke Ellington — Vol. 3 | 1951 | 100.00 |
| **LONDON** | | | |
| ❑ AL-3551 [10] | The Duke — 1926 | 195? | 100.00 |
| **MOBILE FIDELITY** | | | |
| ❑ 1-214 | Anatomy of a Murder | 1995 | 40.00 |
| *—Audiophile vinyl* | | | |
| **MOSAIC** | | | |
| ❑ MQ8-160 [(8)] | The Complete Capitol Recordings of Duke Ellington | 199? | 150.00 |
| **PRESTIGE** | | | |
| ❑ 34003 [(3)] | The Carnegie Hall Concerts: January 1943 | 197? | 20.00 |
| **RCA CAMDEN** | | | |
| ❑ CAL-394 [M] | Duke Ellington at Tanglewood | 1958 | 20.00 |
| ❑ CAL-459 [M] | Duke Ellington at the Cotton Club | 1959 | 20.00 |
| **RCA VICTOR** | | | |
| ❑ WPT-11 [10] | Duke Ellington | 1951 | 100.00 |
| ❑ SP-33-394 [M] | The Duke at Tanglewood | 1966 | 25.00 |
| *—"Special Interview Recording for Radio Station Programming"* | | | |
| ❑ LPV-506 [M] | Daybreak Express | 1964 | 20.00 |
| ❑ LPV-517 [M] | Jumpin' Punkins | 1965 | 20.00 |
| ❑ LPV-541 [M] | Johnny Come Lately | 1967 | 20.00 |
| ❑ LPV-553 [M] | Pretty Woman | 1968 | 20.00 |
| ❑ LPV-568 [M] | Flaming Youth | 1969 | 20.00 |
| ❑ LJM-1002 [M] | Seattle Concert | 1954 | 50.00 |
| ❑ LPT-1004 [M] | Ellington's Greatest | 1954 | 40.00 |
| ❑ LPM-1092 [M] | Duke and His Men | 1955 | 40.00 |
| ❑ LPM-1364 [M] | In a Mellotone | 1957 | 40.00 |
| *—Black label, dog at top, "Long Play" at bottom* | | | |
| ❑ LPM-1364 [M] | In a Mellotone | 196? | 25.00 |
| *—Black label, dog at top, "Mono" at bottom* | | | |
| ❑ LPM-1364 [M] | In a Mellotone | 1969 | 20.00 |
| *—Orange label* | | | |
| ❑ LPM-1715 [M] | Duke Ellington at His Very Best | 1958 | 40.00 |
| ❑ LPT-3017 [10] | This Is Duke Ellington and His Orchestra | 1952 | 100.00 |
| ❑ LPT-3067 [10] | Duke Ellington Plays the Blues | 1952 | 100.00 |
| ❑ LSP-3576 [S] | The Popular Duke Ellington | 1966 | 20.00 |
| ❑ LSP-3582 [S] | Concert of Sacred Music | 1966 | 20.00 |
| ❑ LPM-3782 [M] | Far East Suite | 1967 | 25.00 |
| ❑ LPM-3906 [M] | And His Mother Called Him Bill | 1968 | 50.00 |
| ❑ LPM-6009 [(2)M] | The Indispensible Duke Ellington | 1961 | 50.00 |
| **RCA VICTOR RED SEAL** | | | |
| ❑ LSC-2857 [S] | The Duke at Tanglewood | 1966 | 20.00 |
| **REPRISE** | | | |
| ❑ R-6069 [M] | Afro-Bossa | 1962 | 20.00 |
| ❑ R9-6069 [S] | Afro-Bossa | 1962 | 20.00 |
| ❑ R-6097 [M] | The Symphonic Ellington | 1963 | 20.00 |
| ❑ R9-6097 [S] | The Symphonic Ellington | 1963 | 20.00 |
| ❑ R-6122 [M] | Ellington '65: Hits of the '60s/This Time by Ellington | 1964 | 20.00 |
| ❑ RS-6122 [S] | Ellington '65: Hits of the '60s/This Time by Ellington | 1964 | 20.00 |
| ❑ R-6141 [M] | Mary Poppins | 1964 | 20.00 |
| ❑ RS-6141 [S] | Mary Poppins | 1964 | 20.00 |
| ❑ R-6154 [M] | Ellington '66 | 1965 | 20.00 |
| ❑ R-6168 [M] | Will Big Bands Ever Come Back? | 1965 | 20.00 |
| ❑ R-6185 [M] | Concert in the Virgin Islands | 1965 | 20.00 |
| ❑ R-6234 [M] | Duke Ellington's Greatest Hits | 1967 | 20.00 |
| **RIVERSIDE** | | | |
| ❑ RLP 12-129 [M] | Birth of Big Band Jazz | 195? | 30.00 |
| *—Blue label with mike logo* | | | |
| ❑ RLP 12-129 [M] | Birth of Big Band Jazz | 1956 | 60.00 |
| *—White label, blue print* | | | |
| ❑ RLP-475 [M] | Great Times! | 1963 | 25.00 |
| ❑ RS-9475 [S] | Great Times! | 1963 | 25.00 |
| **RONDO-LETTE** | | | |
| ❑ A-7 [M] | Duke Ellington and Orchestra | 1958 | 30.00 |
| **ROYALE** | | | |
| ❑ 18143 [10] | Duke Ellington and His Orchestra | 195? | 50.00 |
| ❑ 18152 [10] | Duke Ellington Plays Ellington | 195? | 50.00 |
| **SOLID STATE** | | | |
| ❑ SS-19000 [(2)] | 75th Birthday | 1970 | 20.00 |
| **TIME-LIFE** | | | |
| ❑ STL-J-02 [(3)] | Giants of Jazz | 1978 | 20.00 |
| ❑ STBB-05 [(2)] | Big Bands: Duke Ellington | 1983 | 15.00 |
| ❑ STBB-16 [(2)] | Big Bands: Cotton Club Nights | 1983 | 15.00 |
| **TREND** | | | |
| ❑ 529 | The Symphonic Ellington | 1982 | 20.00 |
| **UNITED ARTISTS** | | | |
| ❑ UAJ-14017 [M] | Money Jungle | 1962 | 40.00 |
| ❑ UAJS-15017 [S] | Money Jungle | 1962 | 40.00 |
| **"X"** | | | |
| ❑ LVA-3037 [10] | Duke Ellington Plays | 1955 | 100.00 |
| **ELLINGTON, HARVEY** | | | |
| **STEPHENY** | | | |
| ❑ MF-4010 [M] | I Can't Hide the Blues | 1959 | 80.00 |
| **ELLINGTON, MERCER** | | | |
| **CORAL** | | | |
| ❑ CRL (# unk) [M] | Black and Tan Fantasy | 1958 | 30.00 |
| ❑ CRL (# unk) [S] | Black and Tan Fantasy | 1958 | 40.00 |
| ❑ CRL 57225 [M] | Stepping Into Swing Society | 1958 | 30.00 |
| ❑ CRL 57293 [M] | Colors in Rhythm | 1959 | 30.00 |
| ❑ CRL 757225 [S] | Stepping Into Swing Society | 1958 | 40.00 |
| ❑ CRL 757293 [S] | Colors in Rhythm | 1959 | 40.00 |
| **ELLINGTONIANS, THE** | | | |
| **MERCER** | | | |
| ❑ LP-1004 [10] | The Ellingtonians with Al Hibbler | 1951 | 250.00 |
| **ELLIOT, CASS** Also see THE BIG THREE; THE MAMAS AND THE PAPAS; DAVE MASON; THE MUGWUMPS. | | | |
| **ABC DUNHILL** | | | |
| ❑ DS-50040 | Dream a Little Dream | 1968 | 20.00 |
| ❑ DS-50055 | Bubble Gum, Lemonade &...Something for Mama | 1969 | 20.00 |
| ❑ DS-50071 | Make Your Own Kind of Music | 1969 | 15.00 |
| *—Reissue of 50055 with new title and one added song* | | | |
| ❑ DS-50093 | Mama's Big Ones | 1970 | 15.00 |
| **MCA** | | | |
| ❑ 719 | Mama's Big Ones | 1980 | 8.00 |
| **RCA VICTOR** | | | |
| ❑ APL1-0303 | Don't Call Me Mama Anymore | 1973 | 15.00 |
| ❑ LSP-4619 | Cass Elliot | 1971 | 15.00 |
| ❑ LSP-4753 | The Road Is No Place for a Lady | 1972 | 15.00 |
| **ELLIOTT, DEAN** | | | |
| **CAPITOL** | | | |
| ❑ ST 1834 [S] | Zounds! What Sounds! | 1962 | 50.00 |
| ❑ T 1834 [M] | Zounds! What Sounds! | 1962 | 40.00 |
| ❑ ST 1864 [S] | Heartstrings | 1962 | 25.00 |
| ❑ T 1864 [M] | Heartstrings | 1962 | 20.00 |
| **ELLIOTT, DON** | | | |
| **ABC-PARAMOUNT** | | | |
| ❑ ABC-106 [M] | Musical Offering | 1956 | 40.00 |
| ❑ ABC-142 [M] | Don Elliott at the Modern Jazz Room | 1956 | 40.00 |
| ❑ ABC-190 [M] | The Voices of Don Elliott | 1957 | 50.00 |
| ❑ ABC-228 [M] | Jamaica Jazz | 1958 | 40.00 |
| ❑ ABCS-228 [S] | Jamaica Jazz | 1959 | 30.00 |
| **BETHLEHEM** | | | |
| ❑ BCP-12 [M] | Mellophone | 1955 | 50.00 |
| ❑ BCP-15 [M] | Don Elliott Sings | 1955 | 50.00 |
| **DECCA** | | | |
| ❑ DL 9208 [M] | The Mello Sound | 1958 | 40.00 |
| ❑ DL 79208 [S] | The Mello Sound | 1958 | 50.00 |
| **HALLMARK** | | | |
| ❑ 317 [M] | Pal Joey | 1957 | 50.00 |
| **JAZZLAND** | | | |
| ❑ JLP-15 [M] | Double Trumpet Doings | 1960 | 40.00 |
| ❑ JLP-915 [S] | Double Trumpet Doings | 1960 | 30.00 |
| **RCA VICTOR** | | | |
| ❑ LJM-1007 [M] | Don Elliott Quintet | 1954 | 60.00 |
| **RIVERSIDE** | | | |
| ❑ RLP 12-218 [M] | Counterpoint for Six Valves | 195? | 40.00 |
| *—Blue label, microphone logo* | | | |
| ❑ RLP 12-218 [M] | Counterpoint for Six Valves | 1956 | 100.00 |
| *—White label, blue print* | | | |
| ❑ RLP-2517 [10] | Six Valves | 1955 | 120.00 |
| **SAVOY** | | | |
| ❑ MG-9033 [10] | The Versatile Don Elliott | 1953 | 120.00 |
| **VANGUARD** | | | |
| ❑ VRS-8016 [10] | Doubles in Brass | 1954 | 100.00 |
| **ELLIOTT, DON/SAM MOST** | | | |
| **JAZZTONE** | | | |
| ❑ J-1256 [M] | Doubles in Jazz | 1957 | 40.00 |
| **VANGUARD** | | | |
| ❑ VRS-8522 [M] | Doubles in Jazz | 1957 | 60.00 |
| *—Partial reissue of 8016 and 8014* | | | |
| **ELLIOTT, RAMBLIN' JACK** | | | |
| **FOLKLORE** | | | |
| ❑ FL 14011 [M] | The Songs of Woody Guthrie | 1964 | 20.00 |
| ❑ FL 14014 [M] | Ramblin' | 1964 | 20.00 |
| ❑ FL 14019 [M] | Hootenanny with Jack Elliott | 1964 | 20.00 |
| ❑ FL 14029 [M] | Country Style | 1964 | 20.00 |
| **MONITOR** | | | |
| ❑ MF-379 [M] | Ramblin' Cowboy | 1962 | 25.00 |
| ❑ MF-380 [M] | Jack Elliott Sings Woody Guthrie and Jimmie Rodgers | 1962 | 25.00 |
| ❑ MS-380 [S] | Jack Elliott Sings Woody Guthrie and Jimmie Rodgers | 1962 | 30.00 |
| **PRESTIGE** | | | |
| ❑ PRLP-13016 [M] | The Songs of Woody Guthrie | 1961 | 30.00 |
| ❑ PRLP-13033 [M] | Ramblin' | 1961 | 30.00 |
| ❑ PRLP-13045 [M] | Country Style | 1962 | 30.00 |
| ❑ PRLP-13065 [M] | Jack Elliott at the Second Fret | 1962 | 30.00 |
| **TOPIC** | | | |
| ❑ T-15 [10] | Jack Takes the Floor | 195? | 40.00 |
| **VANGUARD** | | | |
| ❑ VRS-9151 [M] | Jack Elliott | 1964 | 20.00 |
| ❑ VSD-79151 [S] | Jack Elliott | 1964 | 25.00 |
| **ELLIOTT, WALTER & BENNETT** | | | |
| **JAM** | | | |
| ❑ (# unknown) | Save a Piece of the World | 1975 | 50.00 |
| *—As "Elliott and Walter"* | | | |
| ❑ 104/105 [(2)] | Elliott, Walter & Bennett | 197? | 20.00 |
| ❑ 106 | Zeti Reticuli | 197? | 80.00 |
| **ELLIS, ANITA** | | | |
| **ELEKTRA** | | | |
| ❑ EKL-179 [M] | The World in My Arms | 1959 | 40.00 |
| **EPIC** | | | |
| ❑ LN 3280 [M] | I Wonder What Became of Me | 1956 | 40.00 |
| ❑ LN 3419 [M] | Him | 1958 | 40.00 |
| **ELLIS, DON** | | | |
| **CANDID** | | | |
| ❑ CJM-8004 [M] | How Time Passes | 1961 | 50.00 |
| ❑ CJS-9004 [S] | How Time Passes | 1961 | 60.00 |
| **COLUMBIA** | | | |
| ❑ CL 2785 [M] | Electric Bath | 1968 | 30.00 |
| ❑ CS 9889 | The New Don Ellis Band Goes Underground | 1969 | 20.00 |
| ❑ G 30243 [(2)] | Don Ellis at the Fillmore | 1970 | 20.00 |
| ❑ G 30927 [(2)] | Tears of Joy | 1971 | 20.00 |
| **NEW JAZZ** | | | |
| ❑ NJLP-8257 [M] | New Ideas | 1961 | 50.00 |
| *—Purple label* | | | |
| ❑ NJLP-8257 [M] | New Ideas | 1965 | 25.00 |
| *—Blue label, trident logo at right* | | | |
| **PACIFIC JAZZ** | | | |
| ❑ PJ-55 [M] | Essence | 1962 | 30.00 |
| ❑ ST-55 [S] | Essence | 1962 | 40.00 |
| ❑ PJ-10112 [M] | Don Ellis "Live" At Monterey | 1967 | 20.00 |
| ❑ PJ-10123 [M] | Live in 3/2 3/4 Time | 1967 | 20.00 |
| **ELLIS, HERB** | | | |
| **COLUMBIA** | | | |
| ❑ CS 9130 [S] | Herb Ellis Guitar | 1965 | 20.00 |
| **DOT** | | | |
| ❑ DLP-25678 [S] | The Man with the Guitar | 1965 | 20.00 |
| **EPIC** | | | |
| ❑ LA 16034 [M] | The Midnight Roll | 1962 | 25.00 |
| ❑ LA 16036 [M] | Three Guitars in Bossa Nova Time | 1963 | 20.00 |
| ❑ LA 16039 [M] | Herb Ellis and "Stuff" Smith Together | 1963 | 20.00 |
| ❑ BA 17034 [S] | The Midnight Roll | 1962 | 30.00 |
| ❑ BA 17036 [S] | Three Guitars in Bossa Nova Time | 1963 | 25.00 |
| ❑ BA 17039 [S] | Herb Ellis and "Stuff" Smith Together | 1963 | 25.00 |
| **NORGRAN** | | | |
| ❑ MGN-1081 [M] | Ellis in Wonderland | 1956 | 100.00 |
| **VERVE** | | | |
| ❑ MGVS-6045 [S] | Herb Ellis Meets Jimmy Giuffre | 1960 | 40.00 |

| Number | Title (A Side/B Side) | Yr | NM |
|---|---|---|---|
| ❑ MGVS-6164 [S] | Thank You, Charlie Christian | 1960 | 40.00 |
| ❑ MGV-8171 [M] | Ellis in Wonderland | 1957 | 50.00 |
| *—Reissue of Norgran 1081* | | | |
| ❑ V-8171 [M] | Ellis in Wonderland | 1961 | 20.00 |
| ❑ MGV-8252 [M] | Nothing But the Blues | 1958 | 50.00 |
| ❑ V-8252 [M] | Nothing But the Blues | 1961 | 20.00 |
| ❑ MGV-8311 [M] | Herb Ellis Meets Jimmy Giuffre | 1959 | 50.00 |
| ❑ V-8311 [M] | Herb Ellis Meets Jimmy Giuffre | 1961 | 20.00 |
| ❑ V6-8311 [S] | Herb Ellis Meets Jimmy Giuffre | 1961 | 20.00 |
| ❑ MGV-8381 [M] | Thank You, Charlie Christian | 1960 | 50.00 |
| ❑ V-8381 [M] | Thank You, Charlie Christian | 1961 | 20.00 |
| ❑ V6-8381 [S] | Thank You, Charlie Christian | 1961 | 20.00 |
| ❑ V-8448 [M] | Softly...But With That Feeling | 1962 | 20.00 |
| ❑ V6-8448 [S] | Softly...But With That Feeling | 1962 | 25.00 |

**ELLIS, JIMMY**

BOBLO

| Number | Title (A Side/B Side) | Yr | NM |
|---|---|---|---|
| ❑ 78-829 | By Request Jimmy Sings Elvis | 1978 | 100.00 |

**ELLIS, LLOYD**

CARLTON

| Number | Title (A Side/B Side) | Yr | NM |
|---|---|---|---|
| ❑ LP 12-104 [M] | Fastest Guitar in the World | 1958 | 50.00 |

TREY

| Number | Title (A Side/B Side) | Yr | NM |
|---|---|---|---|
| ❑ TLP-902 [M] | So Tall, So Cool, So There! | 1960 | 30.00 |

**ELLIS, PEE WEE**

SAVOY

| Number | Title (A Side/B Side) | Yr | NM |
|---|---|---|---|
| ❑ SJL-3301 | Home in the Country | 1976 | 20.00 |

**ELLIS, RED**

STARDAY

| Number | Title (A Side/B Side) | Yr | NM |
|---|---|---|---|
| ❑ SLP-168 [M] | Holy Cry from the Cross | 1962 | 25.00 |
| ❑ SLP-203 [M] | The Sacred Sound of Bluegrass Music | 1962 | 25.00 |
| ❑ SLP-273 [M] | Old Time Religion Bluegrass Style | 1963 | 25.00 |

**ELLIS, SHIRLEY**

COLUMBIA

| Number | Title (A Side/B Side) | Yr | NM |
|---|---|---|---|
| ❑ CL 2679 [M] | Sugar, Let's Shing-a-Ling | 1967 | 20.00 |
| ❑ CS 9479 [S] | Sugar, Let's Shing-a-Ling | 1967 | 25.00 |

CONGRESS

| Number | Title (A Side/B Side) | Yr | NM |
|---|---|---|---|
| ❑ CGL-3002 [M] | Shirley Ellis In Action | 1964 | 25.00 |
| ❑ CGS-3002 [S] | Shirley Ellis In Action | 1964 | 30.00 |
| ❑ CGL-3003 [M] | The Name Game | 1965 | 25.00 |
| ❑ CGS-3003 [S] | The Name Game | 1965 | 30.00 |

**ELLIS, STEVE, AND THE STARFIRES**

I.G.L.

| Number | Title (A Side/B Side) | Yr | NM |
|---|---|---|---|
| ❑ 105 | The Steve Ellis Songbook | 1967 | 500.00 |

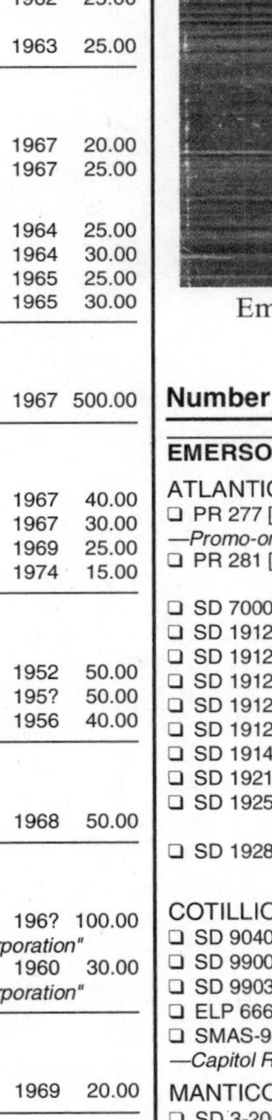

**ELLISON, LORRAINE**

WARNER BROS.

| Number | Title (A Side/B Side) | Yr | NM |
|---|---|---|---|
| ❑ W 1674 [M] | Heart and Soul | 1967 | 40.00 |
| ❑ WS 1674 [S] | Heart and Soul | 1967 | 30.00 |
| ❑ WS 1821 | Stay with Me | 1969 | 25.00 |
| ❑ BS 2780 [S] | Lorraine Ellison | 1974 | 15.00 |

**ELMAN, ZIGGY**

MGM

| Number | Title (A Side/B Side) | Yr | NM |
|---|---|---|---|
| ❑ E-163 [10] | Dancing with Zig | 1952 | 50.00 |
| ❑ E-535 [10] | Ziggy Elman and His Orchestra | 195? | 50.00 |
| ❑ E-3389 [M] | Sentimental Trumpet | 1956 | 40.00 |

**ELMER GANTRY'S VELVET OPERA**

EPIC

| Number | Title (A Side/B Side) | Yr | NM |
|---|---|---|---|
| ❑ BN 26415 | Elmer Gantry's Velvet Opera | 1968 | 50.00 |

**ELMORE, ROBERT**

MERCURY LIVING PRESENCE

| Number | Title (A Side/B Side) | Yr | NM |
|---|---|---|---|
| ❑ SR 90109 [S] | Boardwalk Pipes | 196? | 100.00 |
| *—Maroon label, no "Vendor: Mercury Record Corporation"* | | | |
| ❑ SR 90127 [S] | Bach on the Biggest | 1960 | 30.00 |
| *—Maroon label, no "Vendor: Mercury Record Corporation"* | | | |

**ELSTAK, NEDLEY**

ESP-DISK'

| Number | Title (A Side/B Side) | Yr | NM |
|---|---|---|---|
| ❑ 1076 | The Machine | 1969 | 20.00 |

**EMANUELE, VITTORIO**

RCA VICTOR RED SEAL

| Number | Title (A Side/B Side) | Yr | NM |
|---|---|---|---|
| ❑ LSC-2424 [S] | Vivaldi: The Four Seasons | 1960 | 20.00 |
| *—With the Societa Corelli; original with "shaded dog" label* | | | |

**EMBERS, THE**

JCP

| Number | Title (A Side/B Side) | Yr | NM |
|---|---|---|---|
| ❑ 2006 [M] | The Embers Roll Eleven | 1965 | 200.00 |
| ❑ 2009 [M] | Just for the Birds | 1966 | 150.00 |

**EMERSON, KEITH**

EMERSON

| Number | Title (A Side/B Side) | Yr | NM |
|---|---|---|---|
| ❑ KEITH LP-1 | The Christmas Album | 1993 | 20.00 |
| *—British import only* | | | |

Emerson, Lake & Palmer, *Pictures at an Exhibition,* Cotillion ELP 66666, 1971, $12.

**EMERSON, LAKE AND PALMER**

ATLANTIC

| Number | Title (A Side/B Side) | Yr | NM |
|---|---|---|---|
| ❑ PR 277 [DJ] | Works Volume 1 | 1977 | 15.00 |
| *—Promo-only sampler* | | | |
| ❑ PR 281 [DJ] | On Tour with Emerson, Lake and Palmer | 1977 | 40.00 |
| ❑ SD 7000 [(2)] | Works Volume 1 | 1977 | 15.00 |
| ❑ SD 19120 | Emerson, Lake and Palmer | 1977 | 8.00 |
| ❑ SD 19121 | Tarkus | 1977 | 8.00 |
| ❑ SD 19122 | Pictures at an Exhibition | 1977 | 8.00 |
| ❑ SD 19123 | Trilogy | 1977 | 8.00 |
| ❑ SD 19124 | Brain Salad Surgery | 1977 | 8.00 |
| ❑ SD 19147 | Works Volume 2 | 1977 | 10.00 |
| ❑ SD 19211 | Love Beach | 1978 | 10.00 |
| ❑ SD 19255 | Emerson, Lake and Palmer In Concert | 1979 | 10.00 |
| ❑ SD 19283 | The Best of Emerson, Lake and Palmer | 1980 | 10.00 |

COTILLION

| Number | Title (A Side/B Side) | Yr | NM |
|---|---|---|---|
| ❑ SD 9040 | Emerson, Lake and Palmer | 1971 | 12.00 |
| ❑ SD 9900 | Tarkus | .1971 | 12.00 |
| ❑ SD 9903 | Trilogy | 1972 | 12.00 |
| ❑ ELP 66666 | Pictures at an Exhibition | 1971 | 12.00 |
| ❑ SMAS-94773 | Trilogy | 1972 | 15.00 |
| *—Capitol Record Club edition* | | | |

MANTICORE

| Number | Title (A Side/B Side) | Yr | NM |
|---|---|---|---|
| ❑ SD 3-200 [(3)] | Welcome Back, My Friends, to the Show That Never Ends, Ladies and Gentlemen | 1974 | 20.00 |
| ❑ ELP 66669 | Brain Salad Surgery | 1973 | 12.00 |

MOBILE FIDELITY

| Number | Title (A Side/B Side) | Yr | NM |
|---|---|---|---|
| ❑ 1-031 | Pictures at an Exhibition | 1980 | 30.00 |
| *—Audiophile vinyl* | | | |
| ❑ 1-203 | Tarkus | 1994 | 25.00 |
| *—Audiophile vinyl* | | | |
| ❑ 1-218 | Trilogy | 1994 | 40.00 |
| *—Audiophile vinyl* | | | |

**EMERSON'S OLD-TIMEY CUSTARD-SUCKIN' BAND**

ESP-DISK'

| Number | Title (A Side/B Side) | Yr | NM |
|---|---|---|---|
| ❑ 2006 | Emerson's Old-Timey Custard-Suckin' Band | 1970 | 30.00 |

**EMF**

EMI

| Number | Title (A Side/B Side) | Yr | NM |
|---|---|---|---|
| ❑ E1-96238 | Schubert Dip | 1991 | 25.00 |

**EMMONS, BOBBY**

HI

| Number | Title (A Side/B Side) | Yr | NM |
|---|---|---|---|
| ❑ HL-32024 [M] | Blues with a Beat | 1965 | 25.00 |
| ❑ SHL-32024 [S] | Blues with a Beat | 1965 | 30.00 |

**EMMONS, BUDDY**

MERCURY

| Number | Title (A Side/B Side) | Yr | NM |
|---|---|---|---|
| ❑ MG-20843 [M] | Steel Guitar Jazz | 1963 | 80.00 |
| ❑ SR-60843 [S] | Steel Guitar Jazz | 1963 | 100.00 |

**EMMONS, BUDDY, AND SHOT JACKSON**

STARDAY

| Number | Title (A Side/B Side) | Yr | NM |
|---|---|---|---|
| ❑ SLP-230 [M] | Singing Strings of Steel and Dobro | 196? | 40.00 |

**EMOTIONS, THE (1)**

ARC

| Number | Title (A Side/B Side) | Yr | NM |
|---|---|---|---|
| ❑ JC 36149 | Come Into Our World | 1979 | 10.00 |
| ❑ FC 37456 | New Affair | 1981 | 10.00 |

COLUMBIA

| Number | Title (A Side/B Side) | Yr | NM |
|---|---|---|---|
| ❑ PC 34163 | Flowers | 1976 | 10.00 |
| *—No bar code on cover* | | | |
| ❑ PC 34163 | Flowers | 198? | 8.00 |
| *—With bar code on cover* | | | |
| ❑ PC 34762 | Rejoice | 1977 | 10.00 |
| *—No bar code on cover* | | | |
| ❑ PC 34762 | Rejoice | 198? | 8.00 |
| *—With bar code on cover* | | | |
| ❑ JC 35385 | Sunbeam | 1978 | 10.00 |

MOTOWN

| Number | Title (A Side/B Side) | Yr | NM |
|---|---|---|---|
| ❑ 6136 ML | If I Only Knew | 1985 | 8.00 |

RED LABEL

| Number | Title (A Side/B Side) | Yr | NM |
|---|---|---|---|
| ❑ 001 | Sincerely | 1984 | 10.00 |

STAX

| Number | Title (A Side/B Side) | Yr | NM |
|---|---|---|---|
| ❑ STX-4100 | Sunshine | 1977 | 10.00 |
| ❑ STX-4110 | So I Can Love You | 1978 | 10.00 |
| *—Reissue of Volt 6008* | | | |
| ❑ STX-4112 | Untouched | 1978 | 10.00 |
| *—Reissue of Volt 6015* | | | |
| ❑ STX-4121 | Chronicle | 1979 | 10.00 |

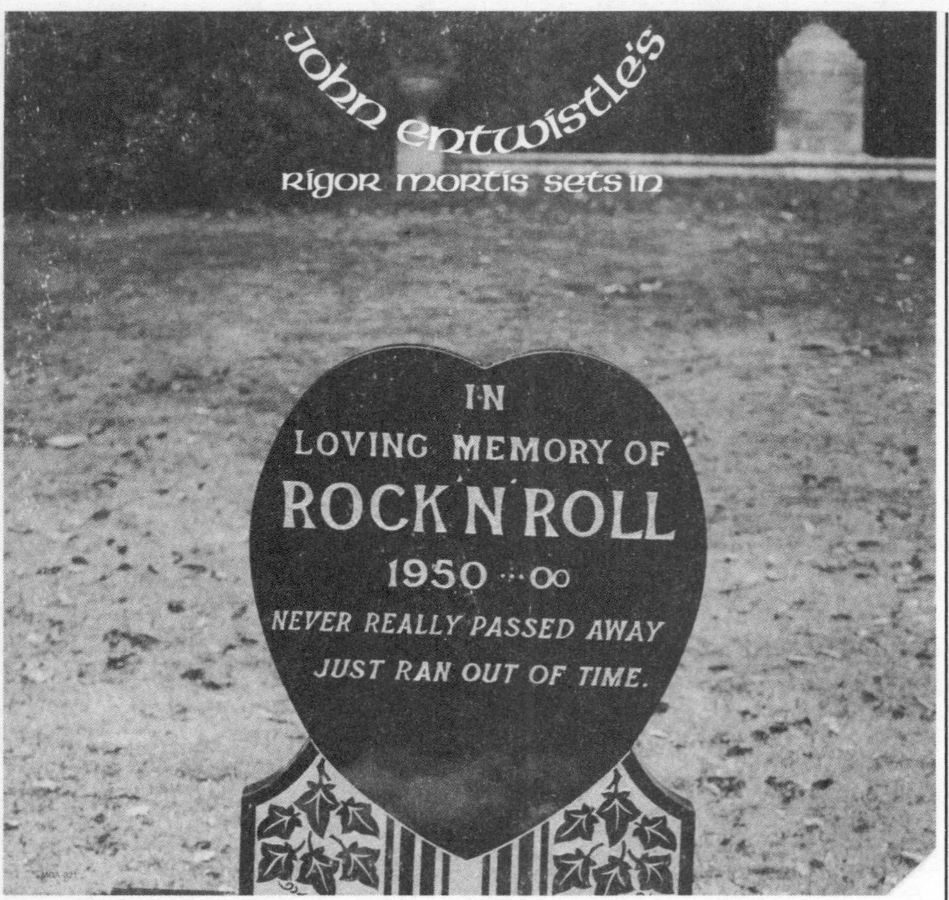


John Entwistle, *John Entwistle's Rigor Mortis Sets In*, Track MCA-321, 1973, $15.

| Number | Title (A Side/B Side) | Yr | NM |
|---|---|---|---|
| **VOLT** | | | |
| ❑ VOS-6008 | So I Can Love You | 1971 | 25.00 |
| ❑ VOS-6015 | Untouched | 1972 | 25.00 |

### END, THE

| Number | Title (A Side/B Side) | Yr | NM |
|---|---|---|---|
| **LONDON** | | | |
| ❑ PS 560 | Introspection | 1969 | 50.00 |

### ENESCU, GEORGE

| Number | Title (A Side/B Side) | Yr | NM |
|---|---|---|---|
| **CONTINENTAL** | | | |
| ❑ CLP 104 [(3)M] | Bach: Six Sonatas and Partitas for Unaccompanied Violin | 1949 | 10000. |
| *—In original box* | | | |
| ❑ CLP 106 [M] | Bach: Sonatas 5 and 6 | 1949 | 4000. |

### ENEVOLDSEN, BOB

| Number | Title (A Side/B Side) | Yr | NM |
|---|---|---|---|
| **LIBERTY** | | | |
| ❑ LJH-6008 [M] | Smorgasboard | 1956 | 50.00 |
| **NOCTURNE** | | | |
| ❑ NLP-6 [M] | Bob Enevoldsen Quintet | 1954 | 150.00 |
| **TAMPA** | | | |
| ❑ TP-14 [M] | Reflections in Jazz | 1957 | 100.00 |
| *—Colored vinyl* | | | |
| ❑ TP-14 [M] | Reflections in Jazz | 1958 | 50.00 |
| *—Black vinyl* | | | |

### ENGEL, SCOTT, AND JOHN STEWART See THE WALKER BROTHERS.

### ENNIS, ETHEL

| Number | Title (A Side/B Side) | Yr | NM |
|---|---|---|---|
| **CAPITOL** | | | |
| ❑ T 941 | Change of Scenery | 1957 | 40.00 |
| ❑ T 1078 [M] | Have You Forgotten? | 1959 | 40.00 |
| **JUBILEE** | | | |
| ❑ JLP-1021 [M] | Lullabies for Losers | 1956 | 50.00 |
| ❑ JLP-5024 [M] | Ethel Ennis Sings | 1963 | 20.00 |
| ❑ SJLP-5024 [S] | Ethel Ennis Sings | 1963 | 25.00 |
| **RCA VICTOR** | | | |
| ❑ LPM-2786 [M] | This Is Ethel Ennis | 1964 | 20.00 |
| ❑ LSP-2786 [S] | This Is Ethel Ennis | 1964 | 25.00 |
| ❑ LPM-2862 [M] | Once Again, Ethel Ennis | 1964 | 20.00 |
| ❑ LSP-2862 [S] | Once Again, Ethel Ennis | 1964 | 25.00 |
| ❑ LPM-2984 [M] | Eyes for You | 1964 | 20.00 |
| ❑ LSP-2984 [S] | Eyes for You | 1964 | 25.00 |

### ENO, BRIAN

| Number | Title (A Side/B Side) | Yr | NM |
|---|---|---|---|
| **ANTILLES** | | | |
| ❑ AN-7001 | No Pussyfooting | 1973 | 15.00 |
| *—By Robert Fripp and Eno* | | | |
| ❑ AN-7018 | Evening Star | 1975 | 12.00 |
| *—By Robert Fripp and Eno* | | | |
| ❑ AN-7030 | Discreet Music | 1975 | 12.00 |
| ❑ AN-7070 | Music for Films | 1978 | 15.00 |
| **EDITIONS EG** | | | |
| ❑ ENO-1 | Here Come the Warm Jets | 1982 | 10.00 |
| *—Reissue* | | | |
| ❑ EGBS-2 [(11)] | Working Backwards: 1983-1973 | 1984 | 60.00 |
| *—Boxed set of nine albums plus Music For Films II and Rarities 12"* | | | |
| ❑ ENO-2 | Taking Tiger Mountain (By Strategy) | 1982 | 10.00 |
| *—Reissue* | | | |
| ❑ ENO-3 | Another Green World | 1982 | 10.00 |
| *—Reissue* | | | |
| ❑ ENO-4 | Before and After Science | 1982 | 10.00 |
| *—Reissue* | | | |
| ❑ ENO-5 | Apollo: Atmospheres and Soundtracks | 1983 | 10.00 |
| ❑ EGED-20 | Ambient 4 — On Land | 1982 | 10.00 |
| ❑ EGED-37 | The Pearl | 1984 | 12.00 |
| *—By Harold Budd and Brian Eno* | | | |
| ❑ EGS-102 | No Pussyfooting | 1982 | 10.00 |
| *—By Robert Fripp and Eno; reissue* | | | |
| ❑ EGS-103 | Evening Star | 1982 | 10.00 |
| *—By Robert Fripp and Eno; reissue* | | | |
| ❑ EGS-105 | Music for Films | 1982 | 10.00 |
| *—Reissue* | | | |
| ❑ EGS-107 | Fourth World Volume 1: Possible Musics | 1980 | 12.00 |
| *—With Jon Hassell* | | | |
| ❑ EGS-201 | Ambient #1 — Music for Airports | 1982 | 12.00 |
| *—Reissue* | | | |
| ❑ EGS-202 | Ambient 2 — The Plateaux of Mirrors | 1982 | 12.00 |
| *—By Harold Budd and Brian Eno* | | | |
| ❑ EGS-301 | Pavilion of Dreams | 1982 | 12.00 |
| *—By Harold Budd and Brian Eno* | | | |
| ❑ EGS-303 | Discreet Music | 1983 | 12.00 |
| *—Reissue* | | | |
| **ISLAND** | | | |
| ❑ ILPS 9268 | Here Come the Warm Jets | 1973 | 12.00 |
| ❑ ILPS 9309 | Taking Tiger Mountain (By Strategy) | 1974 | 12.00 |
| ❑ ILPS 9351 | Another Green World | 1975 | 12.00 |
| ❑ ILPS 9478 | Before and After Science | 1977 | 12.00 |
| *—Double the value if four lithographs are included with the package.* | | | |
| **JEM** | | | |
| ❑ ENO DJ [DJ] | Music for Airplay | 1981 | 50.00 |
| *—Promo-only 10-track sampler* | | | |
| **OPAL/WARNER BROS.** | | | |
| ❑ 25769 | Music for Films, Vol. III | 1988 | 10.00 |
| ❑ 26421 | Wrong Way Up | 1990 | 10.00 |
| *—With John Cale* | | | |
| **PVC** | | | |
| ❑ 7908 | Ambient #1 — Music for Airports | 1979 | 12.00 |

### ENSEMBLE AL-SALAAM, THE

| Number | Title (A Side/B Side) | Yr | NM |
|---|---|---|---|
| **STRATA-EAST** | | | |
| ❑ SES-7418 | The Sojourner | 1974 | 40.00 |

### ENTWISTLE, JOHN

| Number | Title (A Side/B Side) | Yr | NM |
|---|---|---|---|
| **ATCO** | | | |
| ❑ SD 38-142 | Too Late the Hero | 1981 | 10.00 |
| **DECCA** | | | |
| ❑ DL 79183 | Smash Your Head Against the Wall | 1971 | 25.00 |
| **MCA** | | | |
| ❑ 2024 | Smash Your Head Against the Wall | 1973 | 12.00 |
| *—Reissue of Decca 79183* | | | |
| **TRACK** | | | |
| ❑ MCA-321 | Rigor Mortis Sets In | 1973 | 15.00 |
| ❑ L33-1926 [DJ] | Who's Ox | 1975 | 50.00 |
| *—Promo-only sampler* | | | |
| ❑ MCA-2129 | Mad Dog | 1975 | 15.00 |
| ❑ DL 79190 | Whistle Rymes | 1972 | 25.00 |

### EPIC CHOIR, THE

| Number | Title (A Side/B Side) | Yr | NM |
|---|---|---|---|
| **EPIC** | | | |
| ❑ LC 3144 [M] | The Story of Christmas | 1954 | 25.00 |
| *—Gatefold cover with bound-in booklet* | | | |

### EPPS, PRESTON

| Number | Title (A Side/B Side) | Yr | NM |
|---|---|---|---|
| **ORIGINAL SOUND** | | | |
| ❑ LPM-5002 [M] | Bongo, Bongo, Bongo | 1960 | 50.00 |
| ❑ LPM-5009 [M] | Surfin' Bongos | 1963 | 40.00 |
| ❑ LPS-8851 [S] | Bongo, Bongo, Bongo | 1960 | 80.00 |
| ❑ LPS-8872 [S] | Surfin' Bongos | 1963 | 50.00 |
| **TOP RANK** | | | |
| ❑ RM-349 [M] | Bongola | 1961 | 40.00 |
| ❑ RS-349 [S] | Bongola | 1961 | 50.00 |

### EQUALS, THE

| Number | Title (A Side/B Side) | Yr | NM |
|---|---|---|---|
| **LAURIE** | | | |
| ❑ LLP-2045 [M] | Unequalled | 1967 | 25.00 |
| ❑ SLP-2045 [S] | Unequalled | 1967 | 30.00 |
| **PRESIDENT** | | | |
| ❑ PTL-1015 | Equal Sensation | 1968 | 25.00 |
| ❑ PTL-1020 | The Sensational Equals | 1968 | 25.00 |
| ❑ PTL-1025 | Equals Supreme | 1968 | 25.00 |
| ❑ PTL-1030 | Strikeback | 1969 | 25.00 |
| **RCA VICTOR** | | | |
| ❑ LSP-4078 | Baby Come Back | 1968 | 25.00 |

### ERASURE

| Number | Title (A Side/B Side) | Yr | NM |
|---|---|---|---|
| **MUTE** | | | |
| ❑ 9198 | Other People's Songs | 2003 | 12.00 |
| **MUTE/ELEKTRA** | | | |
| ❑ ED 5621 [EP] | Abba-esque | 1992 | 25.00 |
| *—Promo-only vinyl; remixes of 4-song EP; no special jacket* | | | |
| **SIRE** | | | |
| ❑ 25354 | Wonderland | 1987 | 10.00 |
| ❑ 25554 | The Circus | 1987 | 10.00 |
| ❑ 25667 [(2)] | The Two Ring Circus | 1988 | 15.00 |
| ❑ 25730 | The Innocents | 1988 | 10.00 |
| ❑ 25904 [EP] | Crackers International | 1989 | 8.00 |
| ❑ 26026 | Wild! | 1989 | 12.00 |
| ❑ R 101009 | The Innocents | 1988 | 12.00 |
| *—BMG Music Service edition* | | | |

### ERICA

| Number | Title (A Side/B Side) | Yr | NM |
|---|---|---|---|
| **ESP-DISK'** | | | |
| ❑ 1099 | You Used to Think | 1968 | 60.00 |

### ERICSON, ROLF

| Number | Title (A Side/B Side) | Yr | NM |
|---|---|---|---|
| **EMARCY** | | | |
| ❑ MG-36106 [M] | Rolf Ericson and His All American Stars | 1957 | 50.00 |



**Except when noted otherwise, VG = 25% of NM, and VG+ = 50% of NM. (Example: VG = $2.00, VG+ = $4.00 and NM = $8.00.)**

### ERIK

**VANGUARD**

| Number | Title (A Side/B Side) | Yr | NM |
|---|---|---|---|
| ❑ VRS-9267 [M] | Look Where I Am | 1967 | 20.00 |
| ❑ VSD-79267 [S] | Look Where I Am | 1967 | 20.00 |

### ERIK AND THE VIKINGS

**KARATE**

| Number | Title (A Side/B Side) | Yr | NM |
|---|---|---|---|
| ❑ KLP-1401 [M] | Sing A-Long Rock 'n Roll | 1965 | 200.00 |

### ERVIN, BOOKER

**BETHLEHEM**

| Number | Title (A Side/B Side) | Yr | NM |
|---|---|---|---|
| ❑ BCP-6048 [M] | The Book Cooks | 1961 | 40.00 |

**BLUE NOTE**

| Number | Title (A Side/B Side) | Yr | NM |
|---|---|---|---|
| ❑ BN-LA488-H2 [(2)] | Back from the Gig | 1975 | 20.00 |
| ❑ BST-84283 | The In Between | 1969 | 30.00 |

**CANDID**

| Number | Title (A Side/B Side) | Yr | NM |
|---|---|---|---|
| ❑ CJM-8014 [M] | That's It! | 1961 | 40.00 |
| ❑ CJS-9014 [S] | That's It! | 1961 | 50.00 |

**PACIFIC JAZZ**

| Number | Title (A Side/B Side) | Yr | NM |
|---|---|---|---|
| ❑ PJ-10199 [M] | Structurally Sound | 1968 | 40.00 |
| ❑ ST-20199 [S] | Structurally Sound | 1968 | 20.00 |

**PRESTIGE**

| Number | Title (A Side/B Side) | Yr | NM |
|---|---|---|---|
| ❑ PRLP-7293 [M] | Exultation! | 1964 | 25.00 |
| ❑ PRST-7293 [S] | Exultation! | 1964 | 30.00 |
| ❑ PRLP-7295 [M] | The Freedom Book | 1964 | 25.00 |
| ❑ PRST-7295 [S] | The Freedom Book | 1964 | 30.00 |
| ❑ PRLP-7318 [M] | The Song Book | 1964 | 25.00 |
| ❑ PRST-7318 [S] | The Song Book | 1964 | 30.00 |
| ❑ PRLP-7340 [M] | The Blues Book | 1965 | 25.00 |
| ❑ PRST-7340 [S] | The Blues Book | 1965 | 30.00 |
| ❑ PRLP-7386 [M] | The Space Book | 1965 | 25.00 |
| ❑ PRST-7386 [S] | The Space Book | 1965 | 30.00 |
| ❑ PRLP-7417 [M] | Groovin' High | 1966 | 20.00 |
| ❑ PRST-7417 [S] | Groovin' High | 1966 | 25.00 |
| ❑ PRLP-7435 [M] | Settin' the Pace | 1967 | 25.00 |
| ❑ PRST-7435 [S] | Settin' the Pace | 1967 | 20.00 |
| ❑ PRLP-7462 [M] | The Trance | 1967 | 25.00 |
| ❑ PRST-7462 [S] | The Trance | 1967 | 20.00 |
| ❑ PRLP-7499 [M] | Heavy! | 1968 | 30.00 |
| ❑ PRST-7499 [S] | Heavy! | 1968 | 20.00 |

**SAVOY**

| Number | Title (A Side/B Side) | Yr | NM |
|---|---|---|---|
| ❑ MG-12154 [M] | Cookin' | 1960 | 50.00 |

### ERVIN, SENATOR SAM

**COLUMBIA**

| Number | Title (A Side/B Side) | Yr | NM |
|---|---|---|---|
| ❑ KC 32756 | Senator Sam at Home | 1973 | 25.00 |

### ERWIN, PEE WEE

**BRUNSWICK**

| Number | Title (A Side/B Side) | Yr | NM |
|---|---|---|---|
| ❑ BL 54011 [M] | The Land of Dixie | 1956 | 40.00 |

**CADENCE**

| Number | Title (A Side/B Side) | Yr | NM |
|---|---|---|---|
| ❑ CLP-1011 [M] | Dixieland at Grandview Inn | 1956 | 40.00 |

**STRAND**

| Number | Title (A Side/B Side) | Yr | NM |
|---|---|---|---|
| ❑ SL-1001 [M] | Peter Meets the Wolf in Dixieland | 1959 | 50.00 |
| ❑ SLS-1001 [S] | Peter Meets the Wolf in Dixieland | 1959 | 60.00 |

**URANIA**

| Number | Title (A Side/B Side) | Yr | NM |
|---|---|---|---|
| ❑ UJLP-1202 [M] | Accent on Dixieland | 1955 | 40.00 |

### ESCORTS, THE (4)

**TEO**

| Number | Title (A Side/B Side) | Yr | NM |
|---|---|---|---|
| ❑ LPM-5000 [M] | The Escorts Bring Down the House | 1966 | 120.00 |

### ESP

**DREAM**

| Number | Title (A Side/B Side) | Yr | NM |
|---|---|---|---|
| ❑ DRE 187301 | The Future Is Now | 1986 | 50.00 |

### ESQUERITA

**CAPITOL**

| Number | Title (A Side/B Side) | Yr | NM |
|---|---|---|---|
| ❑ T 1186 [M] | Esquerita | 1959 | 1000. |

### ESQUIRES, THE (1)

**BUNKY**

| Number | Title (A Side/B Side) | Yr | NM |
|---|---|---|---|
| ❑ 300 | Get On Up and Get Away | 1968 | 35.00 |

### ESQUIVEL

**BAR NONE**

| Number | Title (A Side/B Side) | Yr | NM |
|---|---|---|---|
| ❑ LP-043 | Space Age Bachelor Pad Music | 1994 | 12.00 |
| ❑ LP-056 | Music for a Sparkling Planet | 1995 | 12.00 |

**RCA VICTOR**

| Number | Title (A Side/B Side) | Yr | NM |
|---|---|---|---|
| ❑ LPM-1345 [M] | To Love Again | 1957 | 50.00 |
| ❑ LPM-1749 [M] | Four Corners of the World | 1958 | 25.00 |
| ❑ LSP-1749 [S] | Four Corners of the World | 1958 | 50.00 |
| ❑ LPM-1753 [M] | Other Worlds, Other Sounds | 1959 | 25.00 |
| ❑ LSP-1753 [S] | Other Worlds, Other Sounds | 1959 | 50.00 |
| ❑ LPM-1978 [M] | Exploring New Sounds in Hi-Fi | 1959 | 30.00 |
| ❑ LSP-1978 [S] | Exploring New Sounds in Hi-Fi | 1959 | 60.00 |
| ❑ LPM-1988 [M] | Strings Aflame | 1959 | 25.00 |
| ❑ LSP-1988 [S] | Strings Aflame | 1959 | 50.00 |
| ❑ LPM-2225 [M] | Infinity in Sound | 1960 | 30.00 |
| ❑ LSP-2225 [S] | Infinity in Sound | 1960 | 60.00 |
| ❑ LPM-2296 [M] | Infinity in Sound, Vol. 2 | 1961 | 30.00 |
| ❑ LSP-2296 [S] | Infinity in Sound, Vol. 2 | 1961 | 60.00 |
| ❑ LPM-2418 [M] | Latin-esque | 1962 | 20.00 |
| ❑ LSP-2418 [S] | Latin-esque<br>*—Standard cover* | 1962 | 40.00 |
| ❑ LSP-2418 [S] | Latin-esque<br>*—Die-cut cover that reveals inner sleeve* | 1962 | 60.00 |
| ❑ LPM-3502 [M] | The Best of Esquivel | 1966 | 20.00 |
| ❑ LSP-3502 [S] | The Best of Esquivel | 1966 | 30.00 |
| ❑ LPM-3697 [M] | The Genius of Esquivel | 1967 | 20.00 |
| ❑ LSP-3697 [S] | The Genius of Esquivel | 1967 | 30.00 |

**REPRISE**

| Number | Title (A Side/B Side) | Yr | NM |
|---|---|---|---|
| ❑ P9-6046 [S] | More of Other World, Other Sounds | 1962 | 30.00 |
| ❑ R-6046 [M] | More of Other World, Other Sounds | 1962 | 25.00 |

### ESSEX, DAVID

**COLUMBIA**

| Number | Title (A Side/B Side) | Yr | NM |
|---|---|---|---|
| ❑ CQ 32560 [Q] | Rock On | 1974 | 30.00 |
| ❑ KC 32560 | Rock On | 1974 | 20.00 |
| ❑ KC 33289 | David Essex | 1974 | 15.00 |
| ❑ PC 33813 | All the Fun of the Fair | 1975 | 15.00 |

**MERCURY**

| Number | Title (A Side/B Side) | Yr | NM |
|---|---|---|---|
| ❑ 812936-1 | David Essex | 1983 | 15.00 |

### ESSEX, THE

**ROULETTE**

| Number | Title (A Side/B Side) | Yr | NM |
|---|---|---|---|
| ❑ R-25234 [M] | Easier Said Than Done | 1963 | 40.00 |
| ❑ SR-25234 [S] | Easier Said Than Done | 1963 | 50.00 |
| ❑ R-25235 [M] | A Walkin' Miracle | 1963 | 40.00 |
| ❑ SR-25235 [S] | A Walkin' Miracle | 1963 | 50.00 |
| ❑ R-25246 [M] | Young and Lively | 1964 | 40.00 |
| ❑ SR-25246 [S] | Young and Lively | 1964 | 50.00 |

### ETC.

**WINDI**

| Number | Title (A Side/B Side) | Yr | NM |
|---|---|---|---|
| ❑ WLPS-1011 | Etc. Is the Name of the Band! | 1976 | 25.00 |

### ETERNITY'S CHILDREN

**TOWER**

| Number | Title (A Side/B Side) | Yr | NM |
|---|---|---|---|
| ❑ ST-5123 | Eternity's Children | 1968 | 25.00 |
| ❑ ST-5144 | Timeless | 1969 | 30.00 |

### EUBANKS, JACK

**MONUMENT**

| Number | Title (A Side/B Side) | Yr | NM |
|---|---|---|---|
| ❑ LP-8044 [M] | Guitar Sounds of the South | 1966 | 15.00 |
| ❑ SLP-18044 [S] | Guitar Sounds of the South | 1966 | 20.00 |

### EUPHONIOUS WAIL

**KAPP**

| Number | Title (A Side/B Side) | Yr | NM |
|---|---|---|---|
| ❑ KS-3668 | Euphonious Wail | 1973 | 40.00 |

### EUPHORIA (2)

**HERITAGE**

| Number | Title (A Side/B Side) | Yr | NM |
|---|---|---|---|
| ❑ HTS 35005 | Euphoria | 1971 | 30.00 |

### EUPHORIA (3)

**CAPITOL**

| Number | Title (A Side/B Side) | Yr | NM |
|---|---|---|---|
| ❑ SKAO-363 | A Gift from Euphoria | 1969 | 120.00 |

### EUPHORIA (4)

**RAINBOW**

| Number | Title (A Side/B Side) | Yr | NM |
|---|---|---|---|
| ❑ 1003 | Lost in a Trance | 1973 | 300.00 |

### EUREKA BRASS BAND, THE

**ATLANTIC**

| Number | Title (A Side/B Side) | Yr | NM |
|---|---|---|---|
| ❑ SD 1408 [S] | The Eureka Brass Band<br>*—Multicolor label with black "fan" logo at right* | 1963 | 20.00 |

**FOLKWAYS**

| Number | Title (A Side/B Side) | Yr | NM |
|---|---|---|---|
| ❑ FA-2642 [M] | Music of New Orleans | 195? | 50.00 |

**PAX**

| Number | Title (A Side/B Side) | Yr | NM |
|---|---|---|---|
| ❑ LP-9001 [10] | New Orleans Parade | 1954 | 60.00 |

### EUROPEAN JAZZ QUARTET, THE

**PULSE**

| Number | Title (A Side/B Side) | Yr | NM |
|---|---|---|---|
| ❑ 3001 [M] | New Jazz from the Old World | 1957 | 50.00 |

### EURYTHMICS

**ARISTA**

| Number | Title (A Side/B Side) | Yr | NM |
|---|---|---|---|
| ❑ AL 8606 | We Too Are One | 1989 | 12.00 |

**RCA**

| Number | Title (A Side/B Side) | Yr | NM |
|---|---|---|---|
| ❑ 5707-1-RDAA [EP] | Rough and Tough at the Roxy<br>*—Promo-only 4-song live album* | 1986 | 30.00 |
| ❑ 6794-1-R | Savage | 1987 | 12.00 |

**RCA VICTOR**

| Number | Title (A Side/B Side) | Yr | NM |
|---|---|---|---|
| ❑ AFL1-4681 | Sweet Dreams (Are Made of This) | 1983 | 10.00 |
| ❑ AFL1-4917 | Touch | 1984 | 12.00 |
| ❑ CPL1-5086 [EP] | Touch Dance | 1983 | 12.00 |
| ❑ ABL1-5371 | 1984 (For the Love of Big Brother) | 1984 | 12.00 |
| ❑ AJL1-5429 | Be Yourself Tonight | 1985 | 12.00 |
| ❑ AJL1-5847 | Revenge | 1986 | 12.00 |

### EVANS, BILL (1)

**MOSAIC**

| Number | Title (A Side/B Side) | Yr | NM |
|---|---|---|---|
| ❑ MQ10-171 [(10)] | The Final Village Vanguard Sessions — June 1980 | 1996 | 200.00 |

**RIVERSIDE**

| Number | Title (A Side/B Side) | Yr | NM |
|---|---|---|---|
| ❑ R-018 [(18)] | The Complete Riverside Recordings | 1985 | 200.00 |
| ❑ RLP 12-223 [M] | New Jazz Conceptions<br>*—Photo on cover, label is white with blue print* | 1956 | 500.00 |
| ❑ RLP 12-223 [M] | New Jazz Conceptions<br>*—New cover, label is blue with microphone logo at top* | 1958 | 30.00 |
| ❑ RLP 12-291 [M] | Everybody Digs Bill Evans | 1958 | 40.00 |
| ❑ RLP 12-315 [M] | Portrait in Jazz | 1959 | 40.00 |
| ❑ RLP-351 [M] | Explorations | 1960 | 30.00 |
| ❑ RLP-376 [M] | Sunday at the Village Vanguard | 1961 | 25.00 |
| ❑ RLP-399 [M] | Waltz for Debby | 1961 | 25.00 |
| ❑ RLP-428 [M] | Moonbeams | 1962 | 25.00 |
| ❑ RLP-445 [M] | Interplay | 1963 | 25.00 |
| ❑ RLP-473 [M] | How My Heart Sings! | 1964 | 25.00 |
| ❑ RLP-487 [M] | Bill Evans at Shelly's Manne-Hole, Hollywood, California | 1965 | 20.00 |
| ❑ RLP 1129 [S] | Everybody Digs Bill Evans | 1959 | 30.00 |
| ❑ RLP 1162 [S] | Portrait in Jazz | 1959 | 30.00 |
| ❑ RS-9351 [S] | Explorations | 1960 | 30.00 |
| ❑ RS-9376 [S] | Sunday at the Village Vanguard | 1961 | 30.00 |
| ❑ RS-9399 [S] | Waltz for Debby | 1961 | 30.00 |
| ❑ RS-9428 [S] | Moonbeams | 1962 | 30.00 |
| ❑ RS-9445 [S] | Interplay | 1963 | 30.00 |
| ❑ RS-9473 [S] | How My Heart Sings! | 1964 | 30.00 |
| ❑ RS-9487 [S] | Bill Evans at Shelly's Manne-Hole, Hollywood, California | 1965 | 25.00 |

**VERVE**

| Number | Title (A Side/B Side) | Yr | NM |
|---|---|---|---|
| ❑ V-8497 [M] | Empathy | 1962 | 25.00 |
| ❑ V6-8497 [S] | Empathy | 1962 | 30.00 |
| ❑ V-8526 [M] | Conversations with Myself | 1963 | 20.00 |
| ❑ V6-8526 [S] | Conversations with Myself | 1963 | 25.00 |
| ❑ V6-8578 [S] | Bill Evans Trio '64 | 1964 | 20.00 |
| ❑ V6-8613 [S] | Bill Evans Trio '65 | 1965 | 20.00 |
| ❑ V6-8640 [S] | Bill Evans Trio with Symphony Orchestra | 1965 | 20.00 |
| ❑ V6-8655 [S] | Intermodulation | 1966 | 20.00 |
| ❑ V6-8675 [S] | A Simple Matter of Conviction | 1966 | 20.00 |
| ❑ V6-8683 [S] | Bill Evans at Town Hall | 1966 | 20.00 |
| ❑ V-8727 [M] | Further Conversations with Myself | 1967 | 20.00 |
| ❑ V-8747 [M] | The Best of Bill Evans | 1967 | 20.00 |
| ❑ V6-8762 | Bill Evans at the Montreux Jazz Festival<br>*—Classic Records reissue on audiophile vinyl* | 199? | 25.00 |
| ❑ V3HB-8841 [(3)] | Return Engagement | 1973 | 20.00 |

### EVANS, BILL (1), AND JIM HALL

**SOLID STATE**

| Number | Title (A Side/B Side) | Yr | NM |
|---|---|---|---|
| ❑ SS-18018 | Undercurrent | 1968 | 20.00 |

**UNITED ARTISTS**

| Number | Title (A Side/B Side) | Yr | NM |
|---|---|---|---|
| ❑ UAJ-14003 [M] | Undercurrent | 1962 | 40.00 |
| ❑ UAJS-15003 [S] | Undercurrent | 1962 | 50.00 |

### EVANS, DALE

**ALLEGRO ELITE**

| Number | Title (A Side/B Side) | Yr | NM |
|---|---|---|---|
| ❑ 4116 [10] | Dale Evans Sings | 195? | 40.00 |

**CAPITOL**

| Number | Title (A Side/B Side) | Yr | NM |
|---|---|---|---|
| ❑ ST-399 | Get to Know the Lord | 1970 | 15.00 |
| ❑ ST 2772 [S] | It's Real | 1967 | 25.00 |
| ❑ T 2772 [M] | It's Real | 1967 | 25.00 |

**EVON**

| Number | Title (A Side/B Side) | Yr | NM |
|---|---|---|---|
| ❑ 336 [M] | Dale Evans Sings Western Favorites/Johnny 'O Calls Western Dances<br>*—Only Side 1 is by Dale Evans* | 195? | 30.00 |

**MANNA**

| Number | Title (A Side/B Side) | Yr | NM |
|---|---|---|---|
| ❑ MS-2075 | Reflections of Life | 1981 | 12.00 |

**SACRED**

| Number | Title (A Side/B Side) | Yr | NM |
|---|---|---|---|
| ❑ LPS-4507 | Favorite Gospel Songs<br>*—Reissue of Word WST-8546* | 197? | 12.00 |

**WORD**

| Number | Title (A Side/B Side) | Yr | NM |
|---|---|---|---|
| ❑ WST-8546 | It's Real | 1971 | 15.00 |
| ❑ WST-8566 | Faith, Hope and Charity | 1972 | 15.00 |
| ❑ WST-8658 | Heart of the Country | 1975 | 15.00 |
| ❑ WST-8661 | Country Dale | 1976 | 12.00 |
| ❑ WST-8803 | Totally Free | 1979 | 12.00 |

### EVANS, DOC

**AUDIOPHILE**

| Number | Title (A Side/B Side) | Yr | NM |
|---|---|---|---|
| ❑ AP-11 [M] | Doc Evans and His Band, Volume 1 | 195? | 40.00 |
| ❑ AP-12 [M] | Doc Evans and His Band, Volume 2 | 195? | 40.00 |
| ❑ AP-29 [M] | Dixieland Session | 195? | 40.00 |
| ❑ AP-31 [M] | The Cornet Artistry of Doc Evans | 195? | 40.00 |
| ❑ AP-33 [M] | Traditional Jazz<br>*—Red vinyl* | 195? | 40.00 |

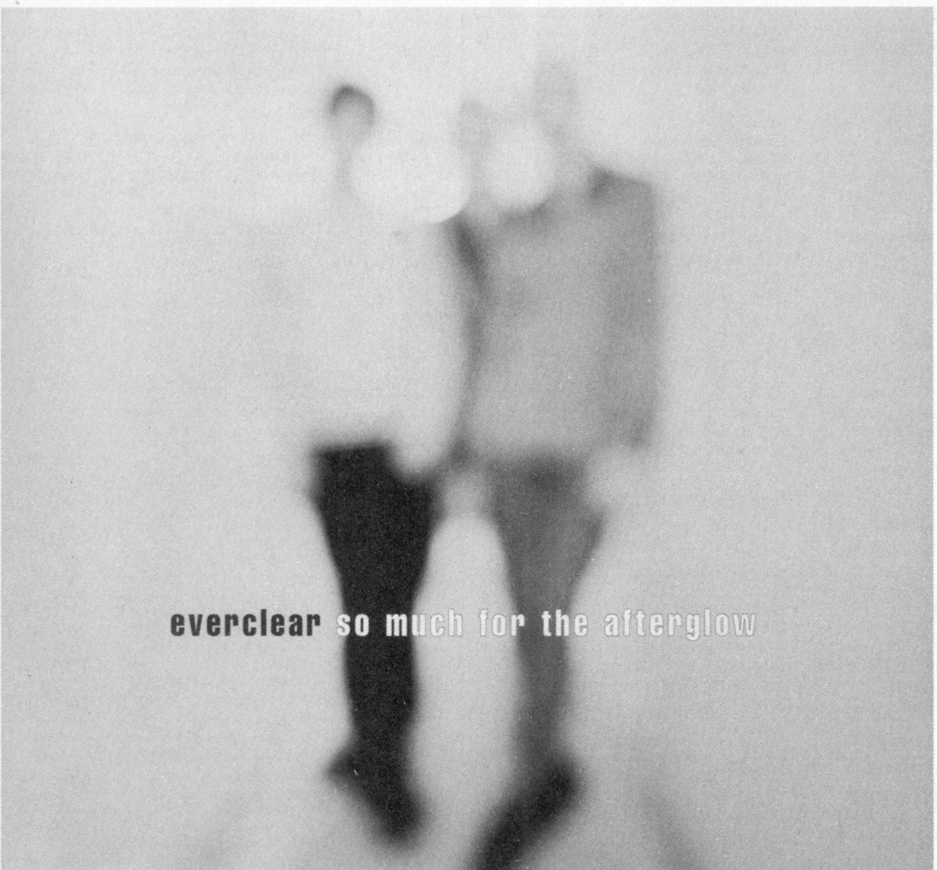


Everclear, *So Much for the Afterglow,* Capitol C1-36503, 1997, $20.

| Number | Title (A Side/B Side) | Yr | NM |
|---|---|---|---|
| ❑ AP-34 [M] | Traditional Jazz | 195? | 40.00 |
| *—Red vinyl* | | | |
| ❑ AP-44 [M] | Traditional Jazz | 195? | 40.00 |
| *—Red vinyl* | | | |
| ❑ AP-45 [M] | Traditional Jazz | 195? | 40.00 |
| *—Red vinyl* | | | |
| ❑ AP-50 [M] | Classics of the 20's | 195? | 40.00 |
| *—Red vinyl* | | | |
| ❑ AP-95 [M] | Doc Evans at the Gas Light | 196? | 20.00 |
| ❑ AS-95 [S] | Doc Evans at the Gas Light | 196? | 25.00 |
| ❑ XL-328 [M] | Traditional Jazz | 195? | 40.00 |
| ❑ XL-329 [M] | Traditional Jazz | 195? | 40.00 |
| ❑ APS-5968 | Reminiscing in Dixieland | 196? | 25.00 |
| *—Red vinyl* | | | |
| CONCERT DISC | | | |
| ❑ CS-47 | Doc Evans + 4 = Dixie | 1961 | 25.00 |
| ❑ CS-48 | Muskrat Ramble | 196? | 25.00 |
| FOLKWAYS | | | |
| ❑ FA-2855 | Doc Evans and His Dixieland Jazz Band | 195? | 20.00 |
| SOMA | | | |
| ❑ MG-100 [M] | Dixieland Concert | 1953 | 50.00 |
| ❑ MG-101 [10] | Dixieland Concert | 1953 | 50.00 |
| ❑ MG-1201 [M] | Classic Jazz at Carleton | 1954 | 40.00 |
| **EVANS, GIL** | | | |
| ATLANTIC | | | |
| ❑ QD 1643 [Q] | Svengali | 1973 | 20.00 |
| IMPULSE! | | | |
| ❑ A-4 [M] | Out of the Cool | 1961 | 25.00 |
| ❑ AS-4 [S] | Out of the Cool | 1961 | 30.00 |
| ❑ A-9 [M] | Into the Hot | 1962 | 25.00 |
| ❑ AS-9 [S] | Into the Hot | 1962 | 30.00 |
| NEW JAZZ | | | |
| ❑ NJLP-8215 [M] | Big Stuff | 1959 | 50.00 |
| *—Purple label* | | | |
| ❑ NJLP-8215 [M] | Big Stuff | 1965 | 25.00 |
| *—Blue label, trident logo at right* | | | |
| PACIFIC JAZZ | | | |
| ❑ PJ-28 [M] | America's #1 Arranger | 1961 | 30.00 |
| ❑ PJ-40 [M] | Cannonball Adderley/Gil Evans | 1962 | 25.00 |
| ❑ ST-40 [S] | Cannonball Adderley/Gil Evans | 1962 | 30.00 |
| PRESTIGE | | | |
| ❑ PRLP-7120 [M] | Gil Evans Plus Ten | 1957 | 80.00 |

| Number | Title (A Side/B Side) | Yr | NM |
|---|---|---|---|
| RCA VICTOR | | | |
| ❑ CPL1-0667 | Gil Evans Plays Jimi Hendrix | 1974 | 20.00 |
| ❑ LPM-1057 [M] | There Comes a Time | 1955 | 80.00 |
| VERVE | | | |
| ❑ V-8555 [M] | The Individualism of Gil Evans | 1963 | 20.00 |
| ❑ V6-8555 [S] | The Individualism of Gil Evans | 1963 | 25.00 |
| WORLD PACIFIC | | | |
| ❑ ST-1011 [S] | New Bottle, Old Wine | 1959 | 40.00 |
| ❑ ST-1027 [S] | Great Jazz Standards | 1959 | 40.00 |
| ❑ WP-1246 [M] | New Bottle, Old Wine | 1958 | 50.00 |
| ❑ WP-1270 [M] | Great Jazz Standards | 1959 | 50.00 |
| **EVANS, JOHN** | | | |
| OMEGA | | | |
| ❑ OL-49 [M] | Mainstream Jazz Piano | 1960 | 20.00 |
| ❑ OSL-49 [S] | Mainstream Jazz Piano | 1960 | 20.00 |
| **EVANS, LEE** | | | |
| CAPITOL | | | |
| ❑ ST 1625 [S] | Big Piano/Big Band/Big Sound | 1962 | 20.00 |
| ❑ ST 1847 [S] | The Lee Evans Trio | 1963 | 20.00 |
| **EVANS, PAUL** | | | |
| CARLTON | | | |
| ❑ STLP-129 [S] | Hear Paul Evans in Your Home Tonight | 1961 | 60.00 |
| ❑ TLP-129 [M] | Hear Paul Evans in Your Home Tonight | 1961 | 40.00 |
| ❑ STLP-130 [S] | Folk Songs of Many Lands | 1961 | 60.00 |
| ❑ TLP-130 [M] | Folk Songs of Many Lands | 1961 | 40.00 |
| GUARANTEED | | | |
| ❑ GUL-1000 [M] | Fabulous Teens | 1960 | 70.00 |
| ❑ GUS-1000 [S] | Fabulous Teens | 1960 | 80.00 |
| KAPP | | | |
| ❑ KL-1346 [M] | 21 Years in a Tennessee Jail | 1964 | 25.00 |
| ❑ KL-1475 [M] | Another Town, Another Jail | 1966 | 25.00 |
| ❑ KS-3346 [S] | 21 Years in a Tennessee Jail | 1964 | 40.00 |
| ❑ KS-3475 [S] | Another Town, Another Jail | 1966 | 30.00 |
| **EVANS, RICHARD** | | | |
| ARGO | | | |
| ❑ LP-658 [M] | Richard's Almanac | 1960 | 30.00 |
| ❑ LPS-658 [S] | Richard's Almanac | 1960 | 40.00 |
| ❑ LP-675 [M] | Home Cookin' | 1961 | 25.00 |
| ❑ LPS-675 [S] | Home Cookin' | 1961 | 30.00 |

| Number | Title (A Side/B Side) | Yr | NM |
|---|---|---|---|
| **EVEN DOZEN JUG BAND, THE** Among the members of the group were John Sebastian and Maria D'Amato (later Muldaur). | | | |
| ELEKTRA | | | |
| ❑ EKL-246 [M] | The Even Dozen Jug Band | 1964 | 30.00 |
| ❑ EKS-7246 [S] | The Even Dozen Jug Band | 1964 | 50.00 |
| **EVERCLEAR** | | | |
| CAPITOL | | | |
| ❑ C1-36503 | So Much for the Afterglow | 1997 | 20.00 |
| *—Blue vinyl* | | | |
| CAPITOL/TIMKERR | | | |
| ❑ C1 30929 | Sparkle and Fade | 1995 | 40.00 |
| *—Price includes bonus 45 "Live on the Radio"; deduct 25 percent if missing* | | | |
| **EVERETT, BETTY** | | | |
| FANTASY | | | |
| ❑ 9447 | Love Rhymes | 1974 | 12.00 |
| ❑ 9480 | Happy Endings | 1975 | 12.00 |
| SUNSET | | | |
| ❑ SUS-5220 | I Need You So | 1968 | 15.00 |
| UNI | | | |
| ❑ 73048 | There'll Come a Time | 1969 | 25.00 |
| VEE JAY | | | |
| ❑ LP 1077 [M] | It's In His Kiss | 1964 | 30.00 |
| ❑ LP 1077 [M] | You're No Good | 1964 | 40.00 |
| ❑ SR 1077 [S] | It's In His Kiss | 1964 | 50.00 |
| ❑ SR 1077 [S] | You're No Good | 1964 | 70.00 |
| ❑ LP 1122 [M] | The Very Best of Betty Everett | 1965 | 40.00 |
| ❑ VJLP 1122 | The Very Best of Betty Everett | 198? | 10.00 |
| *—Authorized reissue* | | | |
| ❑ VJS 1122 [S] | The Very Best of Betty Everett | 1965 | 50.00 |
| **EVERETT, BETTY, AND JERRY BUTLER** | | | |
| BUDDAH | | | |
| ❑ BDS-7505 | Together | 1969 | 15.00 |
| TRADITION | | | |
| ❑ 2073 | Starring Betty Everett with Jerry Butler | 197? | 12.00 |
| VEE JAY | | | |
| ❑ LP 1099 [M] | Delicious Together | 1964 | 20.00 |
| ❑ LP-1099 [M] | Delicious Together | 1964 | 20.00 |
| ❑ VJLP 1099 | Delicious Together | 198? | 12.00 |
| *—Authorized reissue* | | | |
| ❑ VJLP-1099 | Delicious Together | 198? | 10.00 |
| *—Reissue of original 1099; has softer vinyl* | | | |
| ❑ VJS 1099 [S] | Delicious Together | 1964 | 25.00 |
| ❑ VJS-1099 [S] | Delicious Together | 1964 | 25.00 |
| **EVERETTE, LEON** | | | |
| MERCURY | | | |
| ❑ 824309-1 | Where's the Fire | 1985 | 8.00 |
| ORLANDO | | | |
| ❑ 1101 | I Don't Want to Lose | 1980 | 12.00 |
| RCA VICTOR | | | |
| ❑ AHL1-3916 | If I Keep On Going Crazy | 1981 | 10.00 |
| ❑ AHL1-4152 | Hurricane | 1981 | 10.00 |
| ❑ MHL1-8513 [EP] | Doin' What I Feel | 1984 | 8.00 |
| ❑ MHL1-8600 [EP] | Leon Everette | 1983 | 8.00 |
| TRUE | | | |
| ❑ 1002 | Goodbye King of Rock and Roll | 1977 | 25.00 |
| *—Deduct 40% if poster of Elvis Presley is missing* | | | |
| **EVERGREEN BLUES, THE** | | | |
| ABC | | | |
| ❑ S-669 | Comin' On | 1969 | 15.00 |
| MERCURY | | | |
| ❑ MG-21157 [M] | 7 Do 11 | 1968 | 50.00 |
| *—Mono is white label promo only* | | | |
| ❑ SR-61157 [S] | 7 Do 11 | 1968 | 20.00 |
| **EVERLAST** Also see HOUSE OF PAIN. | | | |
| TOMMY BOY | | | |
| ❑ TBLP 1411 [(2)] | Eat at Whitey's | 2000 | 20.00 |
| WARNER BROS. | | | |
| ❑ 26007 | Forever Everlasting | 1990 | 20.00 |
| **EVERLY BROTHERS, THE** | | | |
| ARISTA | | | |
| ❑ AL9-8207 [(2)] | 24 Original Classics | 1985 | 15.00 |
| BARNABY | | | |
| ❑ BGP-350 [(2)] | The Everly Brothers' Original Golden Hits | 1970 | 20.00 |
| ❑ 4004 | Greatest Hits, Vol. 1 | 1977 | 10.00 |
| ❑ 4005 | Greatest Hits, Vol. 2 | 1977 | 10.00 |
| ❑ 4006 | Greatest Hits, Vol. 3 | 1977 | 10.00 |
| ❑ BR-6006 [(2)] | The Everly Brothers' Greatest Hits | 1974 | 15.00 |
| ❑ BR-15008 [(2)] | History of the Everly Brothers | 1973 | 15.00 |
| ❑ ZG 30260 [(2)] | End of an Era | 1971 | 15.00 |

| Number | Title (A Side/B Side) | Yr | NM |
|---|---|---|---|
| **CADENCE** | | | |
| ❑ CLP-3003 [M] | The Everly Brothers | 1958 | 100.00 |
| *—Maroon label with metronome logo* | | | |
| ❑ CLP-3003 [M] | The Everly Brothers | 1962 | 60.00 |
| *—Red label with black border* | | | |
| ❑ CLP-3016 [M] | Songs Our Daddy Taught Us | 1958 | 100.00 |
| *—Maroon label with metronome logo* | | | |
| ❑ CLP-3016 [M] | Songs Our Daddy Taught Us | 1962 | 60.00 |
| *—Red label with black border* | | | |
| ❑ CLP-3025 [M] | The Everly Brothers' Best | 1959 | 90.00 |
| *—Maroon label with metronome logo* | | | |
| ❑ CLP-3025 [M] | The Everly Brothers' Best | 1962 | 60.00 |
| *—Red label with black border* | | | |
| ❑ CLP-3040 [M] | The Fabulous Style of the Everly Brothers | 1960 | 80.00 |
| *—Maroon label with metronome logo* | | | |
| ❑ CLP-3040 [M] | The Fabulous Style of the Everly Brothers | 1962 | 50.00 |
| *—Red label with black border* | | | |
| ❑ CLP-3059 [M] | Folk Songs of the Everly Brothers | 1963 | 50.00 |
| *—Reissue of 3016* | | | |
| ❑ CLP-3062 [M] | 15 Everly Hits 15 | 1963 | 40.00 |
| ❑ CLP-25040 [P] | The Fabulous Style of the Everly Brothers | 1960 | 120.00 |
| *—Maroon label with metronome logo* | | | |
| ❑ CLP-25040 [P] | The Fabulous Style of the Everly Brothers | 1962 | 60.00 |
| *—Red label with black border* | | | |
| ❑ CLP-25059 [R] | Folk Songs of the Everly Brothers | 1963 | 40.00 |
| ❑ CLP-25062 [P] | 15 Everly Hits 15 | 1963 | 50.00 |
| **HARMONY** | | | |
| ❑ HS 11304 | Wake Up Little Susie | 1969 | 12.00 |
| ❑ HS 11350 | Christmas with the Everly Brothers and the Boys Town Choir | 1969 | 20.00 |
| ❑ KH 11388 | Chained to a Memory | 1970 | 12.00 |
| **MERCURY** | | | |
| ❑ 822431-1 | EB 84 | 1984 | 10.00 |
| ❑ 826142-1 | Born Yesterday | 1986 | 10.00 |
| ❑ 832520-1 | Some Hearts | 1989 | 12.00 |
| **PAIR** | | | |
| ❑ PDL1-1063 [(2)] | Living Legends | 1986 | 12.00 |
| **PASSPORT** | | | |
| ❑ 11001 [(2)] | The Everly Brothers Reunion Concert | 1984 | 15.00 |
| **RCA VICTOR** | | | |
| ❑ LSP-4620 | Stories We Could Tell | 1972 | 15.00 |
| ❑ LSP-4781 | Pass the Chicken and Listen | 1972 | 15.00 |
| ❑ AFL1-5401 | Home Again | 1985 | 10.00 |
| **RHINO** | | | |
| ❑ RNLP-211 | The Everly Brothers | 1985 | 10.00 |
| ❑ RNLP-212 | Songs Our Daddy Taught Us | 1985 | 10.00 |
| ❑ RNLP-213 | The Fabulous Style of the Everly Brothers | 1985 | 10.00 |
| ❑ RNLP-214 | All They Had to Do Was Dream | 1985 | 10.00 |
| ❑ RNDF-258 [PD] | Heartaches and Harmonies | 1985 | 20.00 |
| ❑ RNLP-70173 | The Best of the Everly Brothers (Golden Archive Series) | 1987 | 10.00 |
| **TIME-LIFE** | | | |
| ❑ SRNR-09 [(2)] | The Everly Brothers: 1957-1962 | 1986 | 20.00 |
| *—Part of "The Rock 'n' Roll Era" series; box set with insert* | | | |
| **WARNER BROS.** | | | |
| ❑ PRO 134 [10] | It's Everly Time! | 1960 | 600.00 |
| *—Promo "souvenir sampler" from their debut on WB* | | | |
| ❑ W 1381 [M] | It's Everly Time! | 1960 | 30.00 |
| ❑ WS 1381 [S] | It's Everly Time! | 1960 | 40.00 |
| ❑ W 1395 [M] | A Date with the Everly Brothers | 1960 | 40.00 |
| *—Gatefold edition without poster or photos* | | | |
| ❑ W 1395 [M] | A Date with the Everly Brothers | 1960 | 50.00 |
| *—Gatefold edition with poster and wallet-size photos* | | | |
| ❑ W 1395 [M] | A Date with the Everly Brothers | 1961 | 30.00 |
| *—Regular edition* | | | |
| ❑ WS 1395 [S] | A Date with the Everly Brothers | 1960 | 50.00 |
| *—Gatefold edition without poster or photos* | | | |
| ❑ WS 1395 [S] | A Date with the Everly Brothers | 1960 | 75.00 |
| *—Gatefold edition with poster and wallet-size photos* | | | |
| ❑ WS 1395 [S] | A Date with the Everly Brothers | 1961 | 40.00 |
| *—Regular edition* | | | |
| ❑ W 1418 [M] | Both Sides of an Evening | 1961 | 30.00 |
| ❑ WS 1418 [S] | Both Sides of an Evening | 1961 | 40.00 |
| ❑ W 1430 [M] | Instant Party! | 1962 | 30.00 |
| ❑ WS 1430 [S] | Instant Party! | 1962 | 40.00 |
| ❑ W 1471 [M] | The Golden Hits of the Everly Brothers | 1962 | 30.00 |
| ❑ WS 1471 | The Golden Hits of the Everly Brothers | 1967 | 20.00 |
| *—Green "W7" label* | | | |
| ❑ WS 1471 | The Golden Hits of the Everly Brothers | 1970 | 15.00 |
| *—Green "WB" label* | | | |
| ❑ WS 1471 | The Golden Hits of the Everly Brothers | 1973 | 12.00 |
| *—"Burbank" palm-tree label* | | | |
| ❑ WS 1471 | The Golden Hits of the Everly Brothers | 1979 | 10.00 |
| *—White or tan label* | | | |
| ❑ WS 1471 [S] | The Golden Hits of the Everly Brothers | 1962 | 40.00 |
| *—Gold label* | | | |
| ❑ W 1483 [M] | Christmas with the Everly Brothers and the Boys Town Choir | 1962 | 40.00 |
| ❑ WS 1483 [S] | Christmas with the Everly Brothers and the Boys Town Choir | 1962 | 50.00 |
| ❑ W 1513 [M] | Great Country Hits | 1963 | 40.00 |
| ❑ WS 1513 [S] | Great Country Hits | 1963 | 50.00 |
| ❑ W 1554 [M] | The Very Best of the Everly Brothers | 1964 | 30.00 |
| *—Originals have yellow covers* | | | |
| ❑ W 1554 [M] | The Very Best of the Everly Brothers | 1965 | 20.00 |
| *—Later pressings have white covers* | | | |
| ❑ WS 1554 | The Very Best of the Everly Brothers | 1967 | 20.00 |
| *—Green "W7" label* | | | |
| ❑ WS 1554 | The Very Best of the Everly Brothers | 1970 | 15.00 |
| *—Green "WB" label* | | | |
| ❑ WS 1554 | The Very Best of the Everly Brothers | 1973 | 12.00 |
| *—"Burbank" palm-tree label* | | | |
| ❑ WS 1554 | The Very Best of the Everly Brothers | 1979 | 10.00 |
| *—White or tan label* | | | |
| ❑ WS 1554 [S] | The Very Best of the Everly Brothers | 1964 | 40.00 |
| *—Originals have yellow covers* | | | |
| ❑ WS 1554 [S] | The Very Best of the Everly Brothers | 1965 | 25.00 |
| *—White cover; gold label* | | | |
| ❑ W 1578 [M] | Rock & Soul | 1964 | 40.00 |
| ❑ WS 1578 [S] | Rock & Soul | 1964 | 50.00 |
| ❑ W 1585 [M] | Gone, Gone, Gone | 1965 | 40.00 |
| ❑ WS 1585 [S] | Gone, Gone, Gone | 1965 | 50.00 |
| ❑ W 1605 [M] | Beat & Soul | 1965 | 40.00 |
| ❑ WS 1605 [S] | Beat & Soul | 1965 | 50.00 |
| ❑ W 1620 [M] | In Our Image | 1966 | 40.00 |
| ❑ WS 1620 [S] | In Our Image | 1966 | 50.00 |
| ❑ W 1646 [M] | Two Yanks in England | 1966 | 40.00 |
| ❑ WS 1646 [S] | Two Yanks in England | 1966 | 50.00 |
| ❑ W 1676 [M] | The Hit Sound of the Everly Brothers | 1967 | 50.00 |
| ❑ WS 1676 [S] | The Hit Sound of the Everly Brothers | 1967 | 40.00 |
| ❑ W 1708 [M] | The Everly Brothers Sing | 1967 | 50.00 |
| ❑ WS 1708 [S] | The Everly Brothers Sing | 1967 | 40.00 |
| ❑ WS 1752 | Roots | 1968 | 40.00 |
| ❑ WS 1858 | The Everly Brothers Show | 1970 | 30.00 |
| ❑ ST-91343 [S] | The Very Best of the Everly Brothers | 1967 | 40.00 |
| *—Capitol Record Club edition* | | | |
| ❑ ST-91601 | Roots | 1968 | 50.00 |
| *—Capitol Record Club edition* | | | |
| ❑ STAO-93286 | The Everly Brothers Show | 1970 | 40.00 |
| *—Capitol Record Club edition* | | | |

## EVERPRESENT FULLNESS, THE

| Number | Title (A Side/B Side) | Yr | NM |
|---|---|---|---|
| **WHITE WHALE** | | | |
| ❑ 7132 | The Everpresent Fullness | 1970 | 25.00 |

## EVERY MOTHERS' SON

| Number | Title (A Side/B Side) | Yr | NM |
|---|---|---|---|
| **MGM** | | | |
| ❑ E-4471 [M] | Every Mothers' Son | 1967 | 20.00 |
| ❑ SE-4471 [S] | Every Mothers' Son | 1967 | 20.00 |
| ❑ E-4504 [M] | Every Mothers' Son's Back | 1967 | 20.00 |
| ❑ SE-4504 [S] | Every Mothers' Son's Back | 1967 | 20.00 |

## EVERYTHING IS EVERYTHING

| Number | Title (A Side/B Side) | Yr | NM |
|---|---|---|---|
| **VANGUARD** | | | |
| ❑ VSD-6512 | Everything Is Everything | 1969 | 25.00 |

## EWELL, DON

| Number | Title (A Side/B Side) | Yr | NM |
|---|---|---|---|
| **ANALOGUE PRODUCTIONS** | | | |
| ❑ APJ-19 | Yellow Dog Blues | 199? | 25.00 |
| *—Audiophile reissue on red vinyl* | | | |
| **AUDIOPHILE** | | | |
| ❑ APS-5966 | Yellow Dog Blues | 196? | 20.00 |
| **GHB** | | | |
| ❑ 30 | Don Ewell in New Orleans | 196? | 20.00 |
| **GOOD TIME JAZZ** | | | |
| ❑ S-10043 [S] | The Man Here Plays Fine Piano | 1960 | 25.00 |
| ❑ S-10046 [S] | Free 'N Easy | 1960 | 25.00 |
| ❑ L-12021 [M] | Music to Listen to Don Ewell By | 1955 | 40.00 |
| ❑ L-12043 [M] | The Man Here Plays Fine Piano | 1956 | 40.00 |
| ❑ L-12046 [M] | Free 'N Easy | 1956 | 40.00 |
| **WINDIN' BALL** | | | |
| ❑ LP-101 [10] | Don Ewell | 1953 | 50.00 |
| ❑ LP-102 [10] | Don Ewell and Mama Yancey | 1953 | 50.00 |
| ❑ LP-103 [10] | Don Ewell Plays Tunes Played by the King Oliver Band | 1953 | 50.00 |
| ❑ LP-103 [M] | Don Ewell Plays Tunes Played by the King Oliver Band | 195? | 30.00 |

## EXCITERS, THE

| Number | Title (A Side/B Side) | Yr | NM |
|---|---|---|---|
| **RCA VICTOR** | | | |
| ❑ LSP-4211 | Caviar and Chitlins | 1969 | 30.00 |
| **ROULETTE** | | | |
| ❑ R 25326 [M] | The Exciters | 1966 | 30.00 |
| ❑ SR 25326 [S] | The Exciters | 1966 | 40.00 |
| **TODAY** | | | |
| ❑ 1001 | Black Beauty | 1971 | 20.00 |
| **UNITED ARTISTS** | | | |
| ❑ UAL-3264 [M] | Tell Him | 1963 | 70.00 |
| ❑ UAS-6264 [S] | Tell Him | 1963 | 150.00 |

## EYES OF BLUE

| Number | Title (A Side/B Side) | Yr | NM |
|---|---|---|---|
| **MERCURY** | | | |
| ❑ SR-61184 | Crossroads of Time | 1968 | 30.00 |
| ❑ SR-61220 | In Fields of Ardath | 1969 | 30.00 |

## EZELL, WILLIAM

| Number | Title (A Side/B Side) | Yr | NM |
|---|---|---|---|
| **RIVERSIDE** | | | |
| ❑ RLP-1043 [10] | Gin Mill Jazz | 1954 | 80.00 |

# F

## FABARES, SHELLEY

| Number | Title (A Side/B Side) | Yr | NM |
|---|---|---|---|
| **COLPIX** | | | |
| ❑ CP-426 [M] | Shelley! | 1962 | 150.00 |
| ❑ SCP-426 [S] | Shelley! | 1962 | 600.00 |
| ❑ CP-431 [M] | The Things We Did Last Summer | 1962 | 100.00 |
| ❑ SCP-431 [S] | The Things We Did Last Summer | 1962 | 400.00 |

## FABIAN

| Number | Title (A Side/B Side) | Yr | NM |
|---|---|---|---|
| **ABC** | | | |
| ❑ X-806 | 16 Greatest Hits | 1973 | 12.00 |
| **CHANCELLOR** | | | |
| ❑ CHL-5003 [M] | Hold That Tiger! | 1959 | 50.00 |
| *—Black label* | | | |
| ❑ CHL-5003 [M] | Hold That Tiger! | 1959 | 100.00 |
| *—Pink label* | | | |
| ❑ CHLS-5003 [S] | Hold That Tiger! | 1959 | 75.00 |
| *—Black label* | | | |
| ❑ CHLS-5003 [S] | Hold That Tiger! | 1959 | 150.00 |
| *—Pink label* | | | |
| ❑ CHL-5005 [M] | Fabulous Fabian | 1959 | 50.00 |
| ❑ CHLS-5005 [S] | Fabulous Fabian | 1959 | 75.00 |
| ❑ CHL-5012 [M] | The Good Old Summertime | 1960 | 50.00 |
| ❑ CHLS-5012 [S] | The Good Old Summertime | 1960 | 75.00 |
| ❑ CHL-5019 [M] | Rockin' Hot | 1961 | 75.00 |
| ❑ CHL-5024 [M] | Fabian's 16 Fabulous Hits | 1962 | 75.00 |
| ❑ CHL-69802 [M] | The Fabian Facade: Young and Wonderful | 1960 | 80.00 |
| *—Felt gatefold cover with die-cut window* | | | |
| **MCA** | | | |
| ❑ 27095 | The Best of Fabian | 1985 | 8.00 |
| **UNITED ARTISTS** | | | |
| ❑ UA-LA449-E | The Very Best of Fabian | 1975 | 12.00 |

## FABIAN / FRANKIE AVALON

| Number | Title (A Side/B Side) | Yr | NM |
|---|---|---|---|
| **CHANCELLOR** | | | |
| ❑ CHL-5009 [M] | The Hit Makers | 1960 | 100.00 |

## FABRIC, BENT

| Number | Title (A Side/B Side) | Yr | NM |
|---|---|---|---|
| **ATCO** | | | |
| ❑ SD 33-148 [S] | Alley Cat | 1962 | 20.00 |

## FABULOUS COUNTS, THE

| Number | Title (A Side/B Side) | Yr | NM |
|---|---|---|---|
| **COTILLION** | | | |
| ❑ SD 9011 | Jan Jan | 1969 | 100.00 |
| ❑ SD 9011 | Jan Jan | 199? | 12.00 |
| *—Reissue; superficially almost identical to original* | | | |

## FABULOUS FLIPPERS, THE

| Number | Title (A Side/B Side) | Yr | NM |
|---|---|---|---|
| **VERITAS** | | | |
| ❑ VS-2570 | Something Tangible | 1970 | 25.00 |

## FABULOUS JOKERS, THE

| Number | Title (A Side/B Side) | Yr | NM |
|---|---|---|---|
| **MONUMENT** | | | |
| ❑ MLP-8059 [M] | Guitars Extraordinaire | 1966 | 100.00 |
| ❑ SLP-18059 [S] | Guitars Extraordinaire | 1966 | 150.00 |

## FABULOUS POODLES

| Number | Title (A Side/B Side) | Yr | NM |
|---|---|---|---|
| **EPIC** | | | |
| ❑ JE 35666 [DJ] | Mirror Stars | 1978 | 20.00 |
| *—White label promo on pink vinyl* | | | |

## FACENDA, JOHN (NARRATOR)

| Number | Title (A Side/B Side) | Yr | NM |
|---|---|---|---|
| **MANUSCRIPT** | | | |
| ❑ MLP-571 [M] | The Nativity | 1957 | 40.00 |
| *—Original Philadelphia-area issue; gatefold with 12-page booklet* | | | |

| Number | Title (A Side/B Side) | Yr | NM |
|---|---|---|---|

RCA VICTOR

❑ LOP-1504 [M] The Nativity 1958 30.00
*—National reissue of Manuscript LP; very similar to original issue*

## FACES

Also see SMALL FACES; ROD STEWART; RONNIE WOOD.

WARNER BROS.

❑ WS 1851 First Step 197? 12.00
*—Later pressings have "faces." on front cover*
❑ WS 1851 First Step 1970 20.00
*—First pressings have "small faces." on front cover*
❑ WS 1892 Long Player 1971 15.00
❑ BS 2574 A Nod Is As Good As a Wink...To a Blind Horse 1971 15.00
*—Green label*
❑ BS 2574 A Nod Is As Good As a Wink...To a Blind Horse 1973 12.00
*—"Burbank" palm trees label*
❑ BS 2665 Ooh La La 1973 12.00
*—"Burbank" palm trees label*
❑ BS 2665 Ooh La La 1973 15.00
*—Green label*
❑ BS 2897 Snakes and Ladders: The Best of Faces 1976 12.00
❑ ST-93718 Long Player 1971 20.00
*—Capitol Record Club edition*

## FAGAN, SCOTT

ATCO

❑ SD 33-267 South Atlantic Blues 1968 20.00

RCA VICTOR

❑ APL1-1185 Many Sunny Places 1976 15.00

## FAGEN, DONALD

MOBILE FIDELITY

❑ 1-120 The Nightfly 1982 40.00
*—Audiophile vinyl*

WARNER BROS.

❑ 23696 The Nightfly 1982 8.00

## FAGERQUIST, DON

MODE

❑ LP-124 [M] Music to Fill a Void 1957 100.00

## FAHEY, JOHN

REPRISE

❑ MS 2089 Of Rivers and Religions 1972 20.00
❑ MS 2145 After the Ball 1973 20.00

RIVERBOAT

❑ RB-1 [M] The Transfiguration of Blind Joe Death 1965 200.00
*—Original issue of 50 copies with booklet, hand-written labels and no "Volume 5" anywhere on the cover*
❑ RB-1 [M] The Transfiguration of Blind Joe Death 1967 60.00
*—Green cover with booklet; "Volume 5" added to back cover*

SHANACHIE

❑ 97006 God, Time and Causality 1990 15.00

TABLE OF THE ELEMENTS

❑ 38 [(2)] Georgia Stomps, Atlanta Struts, and Other Contemporary Dance Favorites 1999 20.00

TAKOMA

❑ (# unknown) Blind Joe Death 1959 200.00
*—Original edition of 1,000 has a white cover with "Blind Joe Death" on one side and "John Fahey" on the other; possibly pressed by RCA Victor Custom Division; no Berkeley, California address on cover*
❑ C-1002 Blind Joe Death 1964 50.00
*—White cover, similar to first edition, except it has a Berkeley, California address on cover; six tracks were re-recorded for this edition*
❑ C-1002 Volume 1: Blind Joe Death 1967 40.00
*—Psychedelic gold and blue cover; the entire album was re-recorded for this edition, including the six songs re-recorded for the first Berkeley edition and one song not on the white-cover editions, "I'm Gonna Do All I Can For My Lord"*
❑ C-1002 Volume 1: Blind Joe Death 1968 15.00
*—Blue and white cover with "Stereo" added to upper left*
❑ C-1003 Death Chants, Break Downs & Military Waltzes 1964 60.00
*—First cover is white with block print with title on cover as above*
❑ C-1003 Death Chants, Breakdowns and Military Waltzes Vol. II 1965 50.00
*—Second cover is white with what looks like handwritten print; title is as listed above and "Vol. II" is added to the lower left corner*
❑ C-1003 Volume 2: Death Chants, Breakdowns & Military Waltzes 1967 40.00
*—Psychedelic gold and orange cover; most of the album was re-recorded for this edition*
❑ C-1003 Volume 2: Death Chants, Breakdowns & Military Waltzes 1968 15.00
*—Orange and white cover with orange lettering*
❑ C-1004 Dance of Death & Other Plantation Favorites/John Fahey Vol. 3 1964 60.00
*—White cover with block lettering*
❑ C-1004 Volume 3: The Dance of Death & Other Plantation Favorites 1967 40.00
*—Psychedelic gold and brown cover*
❑ C-1004 Volume 3: The Dance of Death & Other Plantation Favorites 1968 15.00
*—Brown and white cover*
❑ C-1008 Vol. 4: The Great San Bernardino Birthday Party 1966 30.00
*—First pressings have a discography on the back cover*
❑ C-1008 Vol. 4: The Great San Bernardino Birthday Party 1968 12.00
*—Without discography on back cover*
❑ C-1014 Days Have Gone By Volume 6 1967 30.00
*—With booklet*
❑ C-1014 Days Have Gone By Volume 6 1968 12.00
*—Without booklet*
❑ C-1019 The Voice of the Turtle 197? 15.00
*—Later pressings with no gatefold*
❑ C-1019 The Voice of the Turtle 1971 30.00
*—With gatefold jacket and booklet*
❑ C-1020 The New Possibility: John Fahey's Guitar Soli Christmas Album 1968 25.00
*—Originals with back cover liner notes*
❑ C-1020 The New Possibility: John Fahey's Guitar Soli Christmas Album 197? 15.00
*—Later pressings with no liner notes*
❑ C-1030 America 197? 15.00
*—Later pressings with no gatefold*
❑ C-1030 America 1972 25.00
*—With gatefold jacket and booklet*
❑ C-1035 Fare Forward Voyagers 1973 20.00
❑ C-1043 Old Fashioned Love 1975 15.00
❑ C-1045 Christmas with John Fahey, Vol. 2 1975 15.00
❑ C-1058 The Best of John Fahey 1959-1977 1977 15.00
❑ TAK-7002 Blind Joe Death 1979 12.00
*—Reissue of 1002*
❑ TAK-7003 Death Chants, Breakdowns and Military Waltzes 198? 12.00
*—Reissue of 1003*
❑ TAK-7004 Dance of Death and Other Plantation Favorites 198? 12.00
*—Reissue of 1004*
❑ TAK-7015 The Transfiguration of Blind Joe Death 198? 12.00
*—Reissue of 9015*
❑ TAK-7020 The New Possibility: John Fahey's Guitar Soli Christmas Album 198? 12.00
*—Reissue of 1020*
❑ TAK-7035 Fare Forward Voyagers 198? 12.00
*—Reissue of 1035*
❑ TAK-7043 Old Fashioned Love 198? 12.00
*—Reissue of 1043*
❑ TAK-7045 Christmas with John Fahey, Vol. 2 198? 12.00
*—Reissue of 1045*
❑ TAK-7058 The Best of John Fahey 1959-1977 198? 12.00
*—Reissue of 1058*
❑ TAK-7069 John Fahey Visits Washington, D.C. 1979 12.00
❑ TAK-7085 Yes! Jesus Loves Me 1980 12.00
❑ TAK-7089 Live in Tasmania 198? 12.00
❑ TAK-7102 Railroads I 1981 12.00
❑ R-9015 The Transfiguration of Blind Joe Death 1969 20.00
*—Reissue of Riverboat RB-1; logo added to lower right front cover, and the drawing in the center is much more green than on 1967 Riverboat covers*

TERRA

❑ T-2 Requia 1985 10.00
*—Reissue of Vanguard 79259*

VANGUARD

❑ VSD 55/56 [(2)] Essential John Fahey 1974 20.00
❑ VRS-9259 [M] Requia 1968 25.00
❑ VSD-79259 [S] Requia 1968 20.00
❑ VSD-79293 The Yellow Princess 1969 20.00

VARRICK

❑ VR-002 John Fahey Christmas Guitar, Volume 1 1982 15.00
❑ VR-008 Let Go 1983 15.00
❑ VR-012 Popular Songs of Christmas and New Year's 1983 15.00
❑ VR-019 Rain Forests, Oceans & Other Themes 1985 12.00
❑ VR-028 I Remember Blind Joe Death 1987 12.00

## FAIR, YVONNE

MOTOWN

❑ M6-832S1 The Bitch Is Black 1975 30.00

## FAIRPORT CONVENTION

A&M

❑ SP-3530 [(2)] The Fairport Chronicles 1976 15.00
❑ SP-3603 Fairport Nine 1974 12.00
*—Early reissue of 4407*
❑ SP-4185 Fairport Convention 1969 15.00
*—Not a reissue of Cotillion LP, but the US issue of the second UK LP "What We Did On Our Holidays"*
❑ SP-4206 Unhalfbricking 1969 15.00
❑ SP-4257 Liege and Lief 1970 15.00
❑ SP-4265 Full House 1970 15.00
❑ SP-4316 Angel Delight 1971 15.00
❑ SP-4333 "Babbacombe" Lee 1972 15.00
❑ SP-4383 Rosie 1973 15.00
❑ SP-4407 Fairport Nine 1973 15.00
❑ SP-6016 [(2)] The Fairport Chronicles 198? 12.00
*—Reissue of 3530*

ANTILLES

❑ 7054 Gottle O' Geer 1976 12.00

CARTHAGE

❑ CGLP-4417 Full House 198? 10.00
*—Reissue of A&M 4265*
❑ CGLP-4418 Unhalfbricking 198? 10.00
*—Reissue of A&M 4206*
❑ CGLP-4430 What We Did on Our Holidays 198? 10.00
*—Reissue of A&M 4185 with UK title restored*

COTILLION

❑ 9024 [M] Fairport Convention 1968 80.00
*—Mono is white label promo only; "DJ Copy Monaural" sticker on front cover*
❑ SD 9024 [S] Fairport Convention 1968 30.00

HANNIBAL

❑ HNBL-1319 House Full 1986 10.00
❑ HNBL-1329 Heyday 1987 10.00

ISLAND

❑ ILPS-9285 Fairport Live/A Movable Feast 1974 12.00
❑ ILPS-9313 Rising for the Moon 1975 12.00
❑ 90678 In Real Time — Live '87 1987 10.00

VARRICK

❑ VR-023 Gladys' Leap 1986 10.00
❑ VR-029 Expletive Delighted! 1987 10.00

## FAITH, ADAM

AMY

❑ 8005 [M] Adam Faith 1965 25.00
❑ S-8005 [S] Adam Faith 1965 30.00

MGM

❑ E-3951 [M] England's Top Singer 1961 40.00
❑ SE-3951 [S] England's Top Singer 1961 50.00

## FAITH, PERCY

COLUMBIA

❑ GP 1 [(2)] Forever Young 1968 15.00
❑ C2L 15 [(2)M] The Columbia Album of Christmas Music 1958 30.00
*—Combines CL 588 and CL 1187 into one gatefold package*
❑ CL 525 [M] Continental Music 1955 20.00
❑ CL 550 [M] Kismet 1955 20.00
❑ CL 577 [M] Music from Hollywood 1955 20.00
❑ CL 588 [M] Music of Christmas 1955 25.00
❑ CL 640 [M] House of Flowers 1956 20.00
❑ CL 681 [M] Delicado 1956 20.00
❑ CL 705 [M] Music for Her 1956 20.00
❑ CL 880 [M] Passport to Romance 1956 20.00
❑ CL 895 [M] My Fair Lady 1957 20.00
❑ CL 955 [M] L'il Abner 1957 20.00
❑ CL 1010 [M] Adventure in the Sun 1957 20.00
❑ CS 1019 Held Over! Today's Great Movie Themes 1970 12.00
❑ CL 1075 [M] Viva! 1957 20.00
❑ CL 1105 [M] South Pacific 1957 15.00
❑ CL 1182 [M] Touchdown! 1957 20.00
❑ CL 1187 [M] Hallelujah! 1957 20.00
❑ CL 1188 [M] Jubliation! 1957 20.00
❑ CL 1267 [M] Malaguena 1958 20.00
❑ CL 1298 [M] Porgy and Bess 1958 15.00
❑ CL 1302 [M] A Night with Sigmund Romberg 1959 15.00
❑ CL 1322 [M] Bouquet 1959 15.00
❑ CL 1381 [M] Music of Christmas 1959 20.00
*—Re-recorded version of CL 588 with same track order*
❑ CL 1386 [M] A Night with Jerome Kern 1959 15.00
❑ CL 1417 [M] Bon Voyage! 1960 15.00
❑ CL 1418 [M] The Sound of Music 1960 15.00
❑ CL 1493 [M] Percy Faith's Greatest Hits 1960 15.00
❑ CL 1501 [M] Jealousy 1960 12.00
❑ CL 1570 [M] Camelot 1960 12.00
❑ CL 1627 [M] Tara's Theme from "Gone with the Wind" and Other Themes 1961 12.00
❑ CL 1639 [M] Mucho Gusto! More Music of Brazil 1961 12.00
❑ CL 1681 [M] Bouquet of Love 1962 12.00
❑ CL 1783 [M] Hollywood's Great Themes 1962 12.00
❑ CL 1822 [M] The Music of Brazil! 1962 12.00
❑ CL 1902 [M] Exotic Strings 1963 12.00
❑ CL 1957 [M] American Serenade 1963 12.00
❑ CL 2023 [M] Themes for Young Lovers 1963 12.00
❑ CL 2024 [M] Shangri-La! 1963 12.00
❑ CL 2108 [M] Great Folk Themes 1964 12.00
❑ CL 2167 [M] More Themes for Young Lovers 1964 12.00
❑ CL 2209 [M] Love Goddess 1966 12.00
❑ CL 2279 [M] Latin Themes for Young Lovers 1966 12.00



Except when noted otherwise, VG = 25% of NM, and VG+ = 50% of NM. (Example: VG = $2.00, VG+ = $4.00 and NM = $8.00.)

| Number | Title (A Side/B Side) | Yr | NM |
|---|---|---|---|
| ❑ CL 2317 [M] | Do I Hear a Waltz | 1965 | 12.00 |
| ❑ CL 2356 [M] | Broadway Bouquet | 1965 | 12.00 |
| ❑ CL 2405 [M] | Music of Christmas, Volume 2 | 1965 | 12.00 |
| ❑ CL 2441 [M] | Themes for the "In" Crowd | 1966 | 12.00 |
| ❑ CL 2529 [M] | Bim Bam Boom | 1966 | 12.00 |
| ❑ CL 2577 [M] | Christmas Is... | 1966 | 12.00 |
| ❑ CL 2650 [M] | The Academy Award Winner and Other Great Movie Themes | 1967 | 15.00 |
| ❑ CL 2704 [M] | Today's Themes for Young Lovers | 1967 | 15.00 |
| ❑ CL 2810 [M] | For Those in Love | 1968 | 20.00 |
| ❑ CL 2906 [M] | Angel of the Morning (Hit Themes for Young Lovers) | 1968 | 20.00 |
| ❑ CL 6148 [10] | Football Songs | 1950 | 40.00 |
| ❑ CS 8005 [S] | South Pacific | 1958 | 25.00 |
| ❑ CS 8033 [S] | Hallelujah! | 1958 | 25.00 |
| ❑ CS 8038 [S] | Viva! | 1958 | 25.00 |
| ❑ CS 8081 [S] | Malaguena | 1958 | 25.00 |
| ❑ CS 8105 [S] | Porgy and Bess | 1959 | 20.00 |
| ❑ CS 8108 [S] | A Night with Sigmund Romberg | 1959 | 20.00 |
| ❑ CS 8124 [S] | Bouquet | 1959 | 15.00 |
| ❑ CS 8176 [S] | Music of Christmas | 1959 | 15.00 |
| ❑ CS 8181 [S] | A Night with Jerome Kern | 1959 | 20.00 |
| ❑ CS 8214 [S] | Bon Voyage! | 1960 | 15.00 |
| ❑ CS 8215 [S] | The Sound of Music | 1960 | 15.00 |
| ❑ CS 8292 [S] | Jealousy | 1960 | 15.00 |
| ❑ CS 8370 [S] | Camelot | 1960 | 15.00 |
| ❑ CS 8427 [S] | Tara's Theme from "Gone with the Wind" and Other Themes | 1961 | 15.00 |
| ❑ CS 8439 [S] | Mucho Gusto! More Music of Brazil | 1961 | 15.00 |
| ❑ CS 8481 [S] | Bouquet of Love | 1962 | 15.00 |
| ❑ CS 8583 [S] | Hollywood's Great Themes | 1962 | 15.00 |
| ❑ CS 8622 [S] | The Music of Brazil! | 1962 | 15.00 |
| ❑ CS 8637 [R] | Percy Faith's Greatest Hits | 1963 | 10.00 |
| ❑ PC 8637 [R] | Percy Faith's Greatest Hits | 198? | 8.00 |
| *—Budget-line reissue* | | | |
| ❑ CS 8642 [R] | Kismet | 1963 | 10.00 |
| ❑ CS 8702 [S] | Exotic Strings | 1963 | 12.00 |
| ❑ CS 8757 [S] | American Serenade | 1963 | 12.00 |
| ❑ CS 8823 [S] | Themes for Young Lovers | 1963 | 12.00 |
| ❑ CS 8824 [S] | Shangri-La! | 1963 | 12.00 |
| ❑ CS 8908 [S] | Great Folk Themes | 1964 | 12.00 |
| ❑ CS 8967 [S] | More Themes for Young Lovers | 1964 | 12.00 |
| ❑ CS 9004 [R] | My Fair Lady | 1964 | 12.00 |
| ❑ CS 9009 [S] | Love Goddess | 1964 | 12.00 |
| ❑ CS 9079 [S] | Latin Themes for Young Lovers | 1965 | 12.00 |
| ❑ CS 9117 [S] | Do I Hear a Waltz | 1965 | 12.00 |
| ❑ CS 9156 [S] | Broadway Bouquet | 1965 | 12.00 |
| ❑ CS 9205 [S] | Music of Christmas, Volume 2 | 1965 | 12.00 |
| ❑ CS 9241 [S] | Themes for the "In" Crowd | 1966 | 12.00 |
| ❑ CS 9329 [S] | Bim Bam Boom | 1966 | 12.00 |
| ❑ 3C 9377 | Christmas Is... | 198? | 8.00 |
| *—Budget-line reissue* | | | |
| ❑ CS 9377 [S] | Christmas Is... | 1966 | 12.00 |
| ❑ CS 9450 [S] | The Academy Award Winner and Other Great Movie Themes | 1967 | 12.00 |
| ❑ CS 9504 [S] | Today's Themes for Young Lovers | 1967 | 12.00 |
| ❑ CS 9610 [S] | For Those in Love | 1968 | 12.00 |
| ❑ CS 9706 [S] | Angel of the Morning (Hit Themes for Young Lovers) | 1968 | 12.00 |
| ❑ CS 9762 | Those Were the Days | 1969 | 12.00 |
| ❑ CS 9835 | Windmills of Your Mind | 1969 | 12.00 |
| ❑ CS 9906 | Love Theme from "Romeo & Juliet" | 1969 | 12.00 |
| ❑ CS 9983 | Leaving on a Jet Plane | 1970 | 12.00 |
| ❑ C 30097 | The Beatles Album | 1970 | 12.00 |
| ❑ G 30330 [(2)] | A Time for Love | 1971 | 15.00 |
| ❑ C 30502 | I Think I Love You | 1971 | 10.00 |
| ❑ CQ 30502 [Q] | I Think I Love You | 1971 | 15.00 |
| ❑ C 30800 | Black Magic Woman | 1971 | 10.00 |
| ❑ CQ 31004 [Q] | Love Theme from "Romeo & Juliet" | 1971 | 15.00 |
| ❑ C 31042 | Jesus Christ Superstar | 1971 | 10.00 |
| ❑ C 31301 | Joy | 1972 | 10.00 |
| ❑ CQ 31301 [Q] | Joy | 1972 | 15.00 |
| ❑ KG 31588 [(2)] | All-Time Greatest Hits | 1972 | 12.00 |
| ❑ PG 31588 [(2)] | All-Time Greatest Hits | 198? | 10.00 |
| *—Budget-line reissue* | | | |
| ❑ CQ 31627 [Q] | Day By Day | 1972 | 15.00 |
| ❑ KC 31627 | Day By Day | 1972 | 10.00 |
| ❑ CQ 32164 [Q] | Clair | 1973 | 15.00 |
| ❑ KC 32164 | Clair | 1973 | 10.00 |
| ❑ KC 32380 | My Love | 1973 | 10.00 |
| ❑ C 32585 | Remembering the Hits of the 60's | 1973 | 10.00 |
| ❑ KC 32714 | Corazon | 1974 | 10.00 |
| ❑ CQ 32803 [Q] | A New Thing | 1974 | 15.00 |
| ❑ KC 32803 | A New Thing | 1974 | 10.00 |
| ❑ PCQ 33006 [Q] | The Entertainer | 1974 | 15.00 |
| ❑ KC 33142 | Country Bouquet | 1975 | 10.00 |
| ❑ CQ 33244 [Q] | Chinatown (Featuring "The Entertainer") | 1974 | 15.00 |
| ❑ KC 33244 | Chinatown (Featuring "The Entertainer") | 1974 | 10.00 |
| ❑ KC 33549 | Disco Party | 1975 | 10.00 |
| ❑ CG 33606 [(2)] | Viva!/Mucho Gusto! | 1975 | 12.00 |
| ❑ CG 33895 [(2)] | Great Moments of Percy Faith | 1976 | 12.00 |
| ❑ KC 33915 | Summer of '76 | 1976 | 10.00 |
| ❑ PC 38302 | Music of Christmas | 1983 | 8.00 |
| ❑ PC 39471 | Christmas Melodies | 1984 | 8.00 |
| *—Repackage of previously released material* | | | |

**COLUMBIA LIMITED EDITION**

| Number | Title (A Side/B Side) | Yr | NM |
|---|---|---|---|
| ❑ LE 10004 | Tara's Theme from "Gone with the Wind" and Other Themes | 197? | 10.00 |
| ❑ LE 10015 | Windmills of Your Mind | 197? | 10.00 |
| ❑ LE 10041 | Themes for the "In" Crowd | 197? | 10.00 |
| ❑ LE 10042 | Bouquet | 197? | 10.00 |
| ❑ LE 10082 | Music of Christmas | 197? | 10.00 |
| *—Brown label "Limited Edition" series; same contents as CS 8176* | | | |
| ❑ LE 10088 | Music of Christmas, Volume 2 | 197? | 10.00 |
| ❑ LE 10095 | Great Folk Themes | 197? | 10.00 |
| ❑ LE 10131 | Jealousy | 197? | 10.00 |
| ❑ LE 10185 | Those Were the Days | 197? | 10.00 |
| ❑ LE 10350 | Hallelujah! | 197? | 10.00 |

**COLUMBIA SPECIAL PRODUCTS**

| Number | Title (A Side/B Side) | Yr | NM |
|---|---|---|---|
| ❑ P 13091 | Broadway Bouquet | 197? | 8.00 |
| ❑ P 13277 | Leaving on a Jet Plane | 197? | 8.00 |
| ❑ P2 13719 [(2)] | The Columbia Album of George Gershwin | 197? | 12.00 |
| ❑ P 13827 | American Serenade | 197? | 8.00 |

**HARMONY**

| Number | Title (A Side/B Side) | Yr | NM |
|---|---|---|---|
| ❑ HS 11348 | Sounds of Music | 1969 | 10.00 |
| ❑ H 30020 | Younger Than Springtime | 1970 | 10.00 |
| ❑ KH 30607 | A Summer Place | 1971 | 10.00 |
| ❑ KH 30977 | Raindrops Keep Fallin' | 1971 | 10.00 |
| ❑ KH 31777 | Every Night at the Movies | 1972 | 10.00 |

**VOCALION**

| Number | Title (A Side/B Side) | Yr | NM |
|---|---|---|---|
| ❑ VL 3600 [M] | North and South of the Border | 1958 | 15.00 |

## FAITH BAND

**MERCURY**

| Number | Title (A Side/B Side) | Yr | NM |
|---|---|---|---|
| ❑ SRM-1-3759 | Rock'n Romance | 1978 | 12.00 |
| ❑ SRM-1-3770 | Face to Face | 1979 | 12.00 |
| ❑ SRM-1-3807 | Vital Signs | 1979 | 10.00 |

**VILLAGE**

| Number | Title (A Side/B Side) | Yr | NM |
|---|---|---|---|
| ❑ VR 7703 | Excuse Me ... I Just Cut an Album | 1977 | 20.00 |
| ❑ VR 7805 | Rock'n Romance | 1978 | 20.00 |

## FAITH NO MORE

**MORDAM**

| Number | Title (A Side/B Side) | Yr | NM |
|---|---|---|---|
| ❑ FNM 1 | We Care a Lot | 1985 | 25.00 |

**SLASH**

| Number | Title (A Side/B Side) | Yr | NM |
|---|---|---|---|
| ❑ 25559 | Introduce Yourself | 1987 | 15.00 |
| ❑ 25878 | The Real Thing | 1989 | 20.00 |
| ❑ 45723 [(2)] | King for a Day/Fool for a Lifetime | 1995 | 25.00 |

## FAITHFULL, MARIANNE

**ABKCO**

| Number | Title (A Side/B Side) | Yr | NM |
|---|---|---|---|
| ❑ 75471 | Greatest Hits | 1988 | 10.00 |
| *—Reissue of London PS 547* | | | |

**ISLAND**

| Number | Title (A Side/B Side) | Yr | NM |
|---|---|---|---|
| ❑ PRO 794 [EP] | Blazing Away Sampler | 1990 | 20.00 |
| *—Promo-only sampler for radio* | | | |
| ❑ ILPS 9570 | Broken English | 1979 | 10.00 |
| ❑ ILPS 9648 | Dangerous Acquaintances | 1981 | 10.00 |
| ❑ 90039 | Broken English | 1983 | 8.00 |
| *—Reissue* | | | |
| ❑ 90066 | A Child's Adventure | 1983 | 10.00 |
| ❑ 90066 [DJ] | A Child's Adventure | 1983 | 15.00 |
| *—Promo-only Quiex II audiophile pressing* | | | |
| ❑ 90613 | Strange Weather | 1987 | 10.00 |

**LONDON**

| Number | Title (A Side/B Side) | Yr | NM |
|---|---|---|---|
| ❑ PS 423 [R] | Marianne Faithfull | 1965 | 15.00 |
| ❑ PS 452 [S] | Go Away from My World | 1965 | 20.00 |
| ❑ PS 482 [S] | Faithfull Forever | 1966 | 20.00 |
| ❑ PS 547 | Greatest Hits | 1969 | 15.00 |
| ❑ LL 3423 [M] | Marianne Faithfull | 1965 | 20.00 |
| ❑ LL 3452 [M] | Go Away from My World | 1965 | 15.00 |
| ❑ LL 3482 [M] | Faithfull Forever | 1966 | 15.00 |

**MOBILE FIDELITY**

| Number | Title (A Side/B Side) | Yr | NM |
|---|---|---|---|
| ❑ 1-235 | Broken English | 1995 | 25.00 |
| *—Audiophile vinyl* | | | |

## FALL, THE

**BEGGARS BANQUET**

| Number | Title (A Side/B Side) | Yr | NM |
|---|---|---|---|
| ❑ 2430-1-H | 458489 | 1990 | 10.00 |
| ❑ 6897-1-H | The Frenz Experiment | 1988 | 10.00 |
| ❑ 9582-1-H | I Am Kurious Oranj | 1988 | 10.00 |
| ❑ 9807-1-H | Seminal Live | 1989 | 10.00 |

**I.R.S.**

| Number | Title (A Side/B Side) | Yr | NM |
|---|---|---|---|
| ❑ SP-003 | Live at the Witch Trials | 1979 | 20.00 |

**I.R.S./FAULTY**

| Number | Title (A Side/B Side) | Yr | NM |
|---|---|---|---|
| ❑ COPE-2 | Early Years 77-79 | 1981 | 15.00 |

**MATADOR**

| Number | Title (A Side/B Side) | Yr | NM |
|---|---|---|---|
| ❑ OLE 55-1 | The Infotainment Scan | 1993 | 10.00 |
| ❑ OLE 95-1 | Middle Class Revolt | 1994 | 10.00 |

**PVC**

| Number | Title (A Side/B Side) | Yr | NM |
|---|---|---|---|
| ❑ 8932 | The Wonderful and Frightening World of The Fall | 1984 | 16.00 |
| ❑ 8940 | This Nation's Saving Grace | 1985 | 15.00 |

**ROUGH TRADE**

| Number | Title (A Side/B Side) | Yr | NM |
|---|---|---|---|
| ❑ TRADE 3/10 [10] | Slates | 1981 | 12.00 |
| *—10-inch EP* | | | |
| ❑ ROUGH US-8 | Grotesque (After the Gramme) | 1981 | 15.00 |

## FALLEN ANGELS, THE

**ROULETTE**

| Number | Title (A Side/B Side) | Yr | NM |
|---|---|---|---|
| ❑ R 25358 [M] | The Fallen Angels | 1967 | 30.00 |
| ❑ SR 25358 [S] | The Fallen Angels | 1967 | 40.00 |
| ❑ SR 42011 | It's a Long Way Down | 1968 | 100.00 |

## FAME, GEORGIE

**EPIC**

| Number | Title (A Side/B Side) | Yr | NM |
|---|---|---|---|
| ❑ BN 26368 | The Ballad of Bonnie and Clyde | 1968 | 25.00 |

**IMPERIAL**

| Number | Title (A Side/B Side) | Yr | NM |
|---|---|---|---|
| ❑ LP-9282 [M] | Yeh, Yeh | 1965 | 25.00 |
| ❑ LP-9331 [M] | Get Away | 1966 | 25.00 |
| ❑ LP-12282 [P] | Yeh, Yeh | 1965 | 30.00 |
| *—Entire album is stereo except "Yeh, Yeh" (rechanneled)* | | | |
| ❑ LP-12331 [R] | Get Away | 1966 | 20.00 |

**ISLAND**

| Number | Title (A Side/B Side) | Yr | NM |
|---|---|---|---|
| ❑ ILPS 9293 | Georgie Fame | 1975 | 10.00 |

## FAME GANG, THE

**FAME**

| Number | Title (A Side/B Side) | Yr | NM |
|---|---|---|---|
| ❑ SKAO-4200 | Solid Gold from Muscle Shoals | 1969 | 25.00 |

## FAMILY

**REPRISE**

| Number | Title (A Side/B Side) | Yr | NM |
|---|---|---|---|
| ❑ RS-6313 | Music in a Doll's House | 1968 | 20.00 |
| ❑ RS-6340 | Family Entertainment | 1969 | 15.00 |
| ❑ RS-6384 | A Song for Me | 1970 | 15.00 |

**UNITED ARTISTS**

| Number | Title (A Side/B Side) | Yr | NM |
|---|---|---|---|
| ❑ UA-LA181-F | It's Only a Movie | 1974 | 12.00 |
| ❑ UAS-5527 | Anyway | 1971 | 15.00 |
| ❑ UAS-5562 | Fearless | 1972 | 15.00 |
| ❑ UAS-5644 | Bandstand | 1972 | 15.00 |

## FAMILY DOGG

**BUDDAH**

| Number | Title (A Side/B Side) | Yr | NM |
|---|---|---|---|
| ❑ BDS-5100 | The View from Rowland's Head | 1972 | 25.00 |

## FAMOUS CASTLE JAZZ BAND, THE

**GOOD TIME JAZZ**

| Number | Title (A Side/B Side) | Yr | NM |
|---|---|---|---|
| ❑ S-7021 [S] | The Famous Castle Jazz Band in Stereo | 1959 | 30.00 |
| ❑ S-10037 [S] | The Famous Castle Jazz Band Plays the Five Pennies | 1959 | 30.00 |
| ❑ L-12030 [M] | The Famous Castle Jazz Band in Hi-Fi | 1957 | 40.00 |
| ❑ L-12037 [M] | The Famous Castle Jazz Band Plays the Five Pennies | 1959 | 40.00 |

**STEREO RECORDS**

| Number | Title (A Side/B Side) | Yr | NM |
|---|---|---|---|
| ❑ S-7021 [S] | The Famous Castle Jazz Band in Stereo | 1958 | 40.00 |

## FANKHAUSER, MERRILL Also see FAPARDOKLY.

**MAUI**

| Number | Title (A Side/B Side) | Yr | NM |
|---|---|---|---|
| ❑ 101 | Merrill Fankhauser | 1976 | 50.00 |

**SHAMLEY**

| Number | Title (A Side/B Side) | Yr | NM |
|---|---|---|---|
| ❑ SS-701 | Things Going Round in My Mind | 1968 | 80.00 |

## FANTASTIC BAGGYS, THE

**IMPERIAL**

| Number | Title (A Side/B Side) | Yr | NM |
|---|---|---|---|
| ❑ LP-9270 [M] | Tell 'Em I'm Surfin' | 1964 | 150.00 |
| ❑ LP-12270 [S] | Tell 'Em I'm Surfin' | 1964 | 300.00 |

**LIBERTY**

| Number | Title (A Side/B Side) | Yr | NM |
|---|---|---|---|
| ❑ LN-10192 | Tell 'Em I'm Surfin' | 1982 | 10.00 |

## FANTASTIC DEE JAYS, THE

**STONE**

| Number | Title (A Side/B Side) | Yr | NM |
|---|---|---|---|
| ❑ SLP-4003 | The Fantastic Dee Jays | 1966 | 1000. |

## FANTASTIC FOUR, THE

**SOUL**

| Number | Title (A Side/B Side) | Yr | NM |
|---|---|---|---|
| ❑ SS-717 | The Best of the Fantastic Four | 1969 | 40.00 |
| ❑ SS-722 | How Sweet He Is | 1970 | — |
| *—Canceled* | | | |

**WESTBOUND**

| Number | Title (A Side/B Side) | Yr | NM |
|---|---|---|---|
| ❑ W 201 | Alvin Stone (The Birth and Death of a Gangster) | 1975 | 15.00 |
| ❑ W 226 | Night People | 1976 | 15.00 |
| ❑ WT 306 | Got to Have Your Love | 1977 | 15.00 |
| ❑ WT 6108 | BYOF (Bring Your Own Funk) | 1978 | 15.00 |

## FANTASTIC JOHNNY C, THE

**PHIL-LA OF SOUL**

| Number | Title (A Side/B Side) | Yr | NM |
|---|---|---|---|
| ❑ 4000 | Boogaloo Down Broadway | 1968 | 80.00 |

Number | Title (A Side/B Side) | Yr | NM

## FANTASY

### LIBERTY
❏ LSP-7643 | Fantasy | 1970 | 20.00

## FAPARDOKLY
Also see MERRILL FANKHAUSER.

### U.I.P.
❏ 2250 | Fapardokly | 1967 | 1000.

## FAR CRY

### VANGUARD
❏ VSD-6510 | Far Cry | 1969 | 25.00

## FARDON, DON

### DECCA
❏ DL 75225 | I've Paid My Dues | 1970 | 15.00

### GNP CRESCENDO
❏ GNPS-2044 | Indian Reservation | 1968 | 20.00

## FARLOW, TAL

### AMERICAN RECORDING SOCIETY
❏ G-418 [M] | The Swinging Guitar of Tal Farlow | 1957 | 40.00

### BLUE NOTE
❏ BLP-5042 [10] | Tal Farlow Quartet | 1954 | 300.00

### NORGRAN
❏ MGN-19 [10] | The Tal Farlow Album | 1954 | 150.00
❏ MGN-1014 [M] | The Artistry of Tal Farlow | 1955 | 120.00
❏ MGN-1027 [M] | The Interpretations of Tal Farlow | 1955 | 120.00
❏ MGN-1030 [M] | A Recital by Tal Farlow | 1955 | 100.00
❏ MGN-1047 [M] | The Tal Farlow Album | 1955 | 100.00
❏ MGN-1097 [M] | Autumn in New York | 1956 | 100.00
❏ MGN-1101 [M] | Fascinating Rhythm | 1956 | 100.00
❏ MGN-1102 [M] | Tal | 1956 | 100.00

### PRESTIGE
❏ PRST-7732 | The Return of Tal Farlow/1969 | 1969 | 20.00
❏ 24042 [(2)] | Guitar Player | 197? | 20.00

### VERVE
❏ MGVS-6143 [S] | The Guitar Artistry of Tal Farlow | 1960 | 40.00
❏ MGV-8011 [M] | The Interpretations of Tal Farlow | 1957 | 50.00
*—Reissue of Norgran 1027*
❏ V-8011 [M] | The Interpretations of Tal Farlow | 1961 | 20.00
❏ MGV-8021 [M] | Tal | 1957 | 50.00
*—Reissue of Norgran 1102*
❏ V-8021 [M] | Tal | 1961 | 20.00
❏ MGV-8123 [M] | A Recital by Tal Farlow | 1957 | 50.00
*—Reissue of Norgran 1030*
❏ V-8123 [M] | A Recital by Tal Farlow | 1961 | 20.00
❏ MGV-8138 [M] | The Tal Farlow Album | 1957 | 50.00
*—Reissue of Norgran 1047*
❏ V-8138 [M] | The Tal Farlow Album | 1961 | 20.00
❏ MGV-8184 [M] | Autumn in New York | 1957 | 50.00
*—Reissue of Norgran 1097*
❏ V-8184 [M] | Autumn in New York | 1961 | 20.00
❏ MGV-8201 [M] | The Swinging Guitar of Tal Farlow | 1957 | 50.00
❏ V-8201 [M] | The Swinging Guitar of Tal Farlow | 1961 | 20.00
❏ MGV-8289 [M] | This Is Tal Farlow | 1958 | 50.00
❏ V-8289 [M] | This Is Tal Farlow | 1961 | 20.00
❏ MGV-8370 [M] | The Guitar Artistry of Tal Farlow | 1960 | 50.00
❏ V-8370 [M] | The Guitar Artistry of Tal Farlow | 1961 | 20.00
❏ MGV-8371 [M] | Tal Farlow Plays the Music of Harold Arlen | 1960 | 50.00
❏ V-8371 [M] | Tal Farlow Plays the Music of Harold Arlen | 1961 | 20.00

## FARLOWE, CHRIS

### COLUMBIA
❏ CL 2593 [M] | The Fabulous Chris Farlowe | 1966 | 40.00
❏ CS 9393 [R] | The Fabulous Chris Farlowe | 1966 | 25.00

### IMMEDIATE
❏ Z12 52010 | Paint It Farlowe | 1968 | 20.00

### POLYDOR
❏ 24-4041 | From Here to Mama Rosa with the Hill | 1970 | 12.00

## FARM BAND, THE

### MANTRA
❏ 777 [(2)] | The Farm Band | 1972 | 30.00
*—With poster*

## FARMER, ART

### ABC-PARAMOUNT
❏ ABC-200 [M] | Last Night When We Were Young | 1958 | 60.00

### ARGO
❏ LP-678 [M] | Art | 1961 | 25.00
❏ LPS-678 [S] | Art | 1961 | 30.00
❏ LP-738 [M] | Perception | 1964 | 25.00
❏ LPS-738 [S] | Perception | 1964 | 30.00

### ATLANTIC
❏ 1412 [M] | Interaction | 1963 | 25.00
❏ SD 1412 [S] | Interaction | 1963 | 30.00
❏ 1421 [M] | Live at the Half Note | 1964 | 25.00
❏ SD 1421 [S] | Live at the Half Note | 1964 | 30.00
❏ 1430 [M] | To Sweden with Love | 1964 | 20.00
❏ SD 1430 [S] | To Sweden with Love | 1964 | 25.00
❏ 1442 [M] | Sing Me Softly of the Blues | 1965 | 20.00
❏ SD 1442 [S] | Sing Me Softly of the Blues | 1965 | 25.00

### COLUMBIA
❏ CL 2588 [M] | Baroque Sketches | 1966 | 20.00
❏ CL 2649 [M] | The Time and the Place | 1967 | 25.00
❏ CL 2746 [M] | Art Farmer Plays the Great Jazz Hits | 1967 | 30.00
❏ CS 9388 [S] | Baroque Sketches | 1966 | 20.00
❏ CS 9449 [S] | The Time and the Place | 1967 | 20.00
❏ CS 9546 [S] | Art Farmer Plays the Great Jazz Hits | 1967 | 20.00

### CONTEMPORARY
❏ C-3554 [M] | Portrait of Art Farmer | 1958 | 50.00
❏ S-7027 [S] | Portrait of Art Farmer | 1959 | 30.00

### MAINSTREAM
❏ MRL-332 | Homecoming | 1971 | 20.00
❏ MRL-371 | Gentle Eyes | 1972 | 20.00

### MERCURY
❏ MG-20786 [M] | Listen to Art Farmer and the Orchestra | 1963 | 20.00
❏ SR-60786 [S] | Listen to Art Farmer and the Orchestra | 1963 | 25.00

### NEW JAZZ
❏ NJLP-8203 [M] | Farmer's Market | 1958 | 50.00
*—Purple label*
❏ NJLP-8203 [M] | Farmer's Market | 1958 | 100.00
*—Yellow label*
❏ NJLP-8203 [M] | Farmer's Market | 1965 | 25.00
*—Blue label, trident logo at right*
❏ NJLP-8258 [M] | Early Art | 1961 | 40.00
*—Purple label*
❏ NJLP-8258 [M] | Early Art | 1965 | 25.00
*—Blue label, trident logo at right*
❏ NJLP-8278 [M] | Work of Art | 1962 | 40.00
*—Purple label*
❏ NJLP-8278 [M] | Work of Art | 1965 | 25.00
*—Blue label, trident logo at right*
❏ NJLP-8289 [M] | Evening in Casablanca | 1962 | 40.00
*—Purple label*
❏ NJLP-8289 [M] | Evening in Casablanca | 1965 | 25.00
*—Blue label, trident logo at right*

### PRESTIGE
❏ PRLP-162 [10] | Art Farmer Septet | 1953 | 300.00
❏ PRLP-177 [10] | Art Farmer Quintet Featuring Sonny Rollins | 1954 | 400.00
❏ PRLP-181 [10] | Art Farmer Quintet | 1954 | 300.00
❏ PRLP-193 [10] | Art Farmer Quartet | 1954 | 300.00
❏ PRLP-209 [10] | Art Farmer Quintet | 1955 | 300.00
❏ PRLP-7017 [M] | Art Farmer Quintet Featuring Gigi Gryce | 1956 | 150.00
*—Yellow label with W. 50th St. address*
❏ PRLP-7031 [M] | Art Farmer Septet | 1956 | 150.00
*—Yellow label with W. 50th St. address*
❏ PRLP-7062 [M] | Two Trumpets | 1956 | 150.00
❏ PRLP-7085 [M] | When Farmer Met Gryce | 1957 | 150.00
❏ PRLP-7092 [M] | Three Trumpets | 1957 | 150.00
❏ PRLP-7344 [(2)M] | Trumpets All Out | 1964 | 50.00
❏ PRST-7344 [(2)R] | Trumpets All Out | 1964 | 30.00

### SCEPTER
❏ S-521 [M] | The Many Faces of Art Farmer | 1964 | 20.00
❏ SS-521 [S] | The Many Faces of Art Farmer | 1964 | 25.00

### STEREO RECORDS
❏ S-7027 [S] | Portrait of Art Farmer | 1958 | 40.00

### UNITED ARTISTS
❏ UAL-4007 [M] | Modern Art | 1958 | 50.00
❏ UAL-4047 [M] | Brass Shout | 1959 | 50.00
❏ UAL-4062 [M] | Aztec Suite | 1959 | 50.00
❏ UAS-5007 [S] | Modern Art | 1959 | 40.00
❏ UAS-5047 [S] | Brass Shout | 1959 | 40.00
❏ UAS-5062 [S] | Aztec Suite | 1959 | 40.00

## FARMER, ART/ART TAYLOR

### PRESTIGE
❏ PRLP-7342 [(2)M] | Hard Cookin' | 1964 | 50.00
❏ PRST-7342 [(2)R] | Hard Cookin' | 1964 | 30.00

## FARNER, MARK, AND DON BREWER

### QUADICO
❏ 7401 | Monumental Funk | 1977 | 10.00
❏ 7401 [PD] | Monumental Funk | 1977 | 20.00
*—Picture disc*

## FARRAH, SHAMEK

### STRATA-EAST
❏ SES-7412 | First Impressions | 1974 | 40.00

## FARRELL, JOE

### CTI
❏ 6003 | Joe Farrell Quartet | 1970 | 20.00
❏ 6014 | Outback | 1971 | 20.00
❏ 6023 | Moon Germs | 1972 | 20.00

## FARRELL, JOE; FLORA PURIM; AIRTO MOREIRA

### REFERENCE RECORDINGS
❏ RR-24 | Three-Way Mirror | 1989 | 20.00

## FARRELL, RICHARD

### MERCURY LIVING PRESENCE
❏ SR 90126 [S] | Lizst: Piano Concerto No. 1; Grieg: Piano Concerto in A | 1960 | 25.00
*—Maroon label, no "Vendor: Mercury Record Corporation"*

## FAT CITY

### ABC PROBE
❏ 4508 | Reincarnation | 1969 | 20.00

### PARAMOUNT
❏ PAS-6028 | Welcome to Fat City | 1972 | 15.00

## FAT MATTRESS

### ATCO
❏ 33-309 [M] | Fat Mattress | 1969 | 40.00
*—White label promo only; "DJ Copy Monaural" sticker on cover*
❏ SD 33-309 [S] | Fat Mattress | 1969 | 20.00
❏ 33-347 [M] | Fat Mattress II | 1970 | 40.00
*—White label promo only; "DJ Copy Monaural" sticker on cover*
❏ SD 33-347 [S] | Fat Mattress II | 1970 | 15.00

## FATHER M.C.

### UPTOWN
❏ 10061 | Father's Day | 1990 | 15.00
❏ 10542 | Close to You | 1992 | 20.00
❏ 10937 | Sex Is Law | 1993 | 20.00
*—As "Father"*

## FATHER YOD AND THE SPIRIT OF '76
See YA HO WA 13.

## FAUN

### GREGAR
❏ 7000 | Faun | 1969 | 50.00

## FAY, FRANK

### BALLY
❏ BAL-10215 [M] | Be Frank with Fay | 1957 | 40.00

## FAYE, FRANCES

### BETHLEHEM
❏ BCP-23 [M] | I'm Wild Again | 1955 | 50.00
❏ BCP-62 [M] | Relaxin' with Frances Faye | 1957 | 40.00
❏ BCP-6017 [M] | Frances Faye Sings Folk Songs | 1957 | 40.00

### CAPITOL
❏ H 512 [10] | No Reservations | 1954 | 80.00
❏ T 512 [M] | No Reservations | 1955 | 50.00
*—Turquoise or gray label*
❏ T 512 [M] | No Reservations | 1958 | 30.00
*—Black label with colorband, logo at left*

### GENE NORMAN
❏ GNP-41 [M] | Caught in the Act | 1958 | 40.00
❏ GNP-92 [M] | Caught in the Act, Volume 2 | 1959 | 40.00

### IMPERIAL
❏ LP-9059 [M] | Frances Faye Swings Fats Domino | 1958 | 40.00
❏ LP-9158 [M] | Frances Faye Sings the Blues | 1961 | 40.00
❏ LP-12007 [S] | Frances Faye Swings Fats Domino | 1959 | 50.00

### REGINA
❏ R-315 [M] | You Gotta Go! Go! Go! | 1964 | 25.00
❏ RS-315 [S] | You Gotta Go! Go! Go! | 1964 | 30.00

### VERVE
❏ MGV-2147 [M] | Frances Faye in Frenzy | 1961 | 40.00
❏ V-2147 [M] | Frances Faye in Frenzy | 1961 | 20.00
❏ V-8434 [M] | Swinging All the Way with Frances Faye | 1962 | 20.00
❏ V6-8434 [S] | Swinging All the Way with Frances Faye | 1962 | 25.00

## FAZOLA, IRVING

### MERCURY
❏ MG-25016 [10] | Irving Fazola and His Dixielanders | 1950 | 50.00

## FAZOLA, IRVING/GEORGE HARTMANN

### EMARCY
❏ MG-36022 [M] | New Orleans Express | 1954 | 40.00

## FEAR

### RESTLESS
❏ 72039 | More Beer | 1985 | 15.00

### SLASH
❏ SR 111 | The Record | 1982 | 20.00
❏ 23933 | The Record | 1982 | 10.00



**Except when noted otherwise, VG = 25% of NM, and VG+ = 50% of NM. (Example: VG = $2.00, VG+ = $4.00 and NM = $8.00.)**

| Number | Title (A Side/B Side) | Yr | NM |
|---|---|---|---|
| **FEAR ITSELF** | | | |
| DOT | | | |
| ❑ DLP-25942 | Fear Itself | 1969 | 20.00 |
| **FEATHER, LEONARD** | | | |
| ABC-PARAMOUNT | | | |
| ❑ ABC-110 [M] | Swingin' on the Vibories | 1956 | 60.00 |
| INTERLUDE | | | |
| ❑ MO-511 [M] | Leonard Feather Presents 52nd Street | 1959 | 40.00 |
| ❑ ST-1011 [S] | Leonard Feather Presents 52nd Street | 1959 | 30.00 |
| MAINSTREAM | | | |
| ❑ MRL-348 | Night Blooming Jazzmen | 1972 | 20.00 |
| ❑ MRL-388 | Freedom Jazz Dance | 1974 | 20.00 |
| MGM | | | |
| ❑ E-270 [10] | Winter Sequence | 1954 | 120.00 |
| ❑ E-3494 [M] | Hi-Fi Suite | 1957 | 50.00 |
| ❑ E-3650 [M] | Oh, Captain! | 1958 | 50.00 |
| MODE | | | |
| ❑ LP-127 [M] | Leonard Feather Presents Bop | 1957 | 60.00 |
| **FEDERAL DUCK** | | | |
| MUSICOR | | | |
| ❑ MS-3162 | Federal Duck | 1968 | 20.00 |
| **FEELIES, THE** | | | |
| A&M | | | |
| ❑ SP-5214 | Only Life | 1988 | 12.00 |
| ❑ 75021 5344-1 | Time for a Witness | 1991 | 12.00 |
| ❑ 75021 7403-1 [DJ] | Paint It Black + 5 | 1990 | 15.00 |
| *—Promo-only 6-song sampler* | | | |
| COYOTE/TWINTONE | | | |
| ❑ TTC 8673 | The Good Earth | 1986 | 12.00 |
| STIFF | | | |
| ❑ USE-4 | Crazy Rhythms | 1980 | 30.00 |
| *—Price is for an actual U.S. pressing. Most copies sold in U.S. were U.K. copies with stickers.* | | | |
| **FELDMAN, VICTOR** | | | |
| AVA | | | |
| ❑ A-19 [M] | Soviet Jazz Themes | 1963 | 25.00 |
| ❑ AS-19 [S] | Soviet Jazz Themes | 1963 | 25.00 |
| CONTEMPORARY | | | |
| ❑ C-3541 [M] | Suite Sixteen | 1957 | 40.00 |
| ❑ C-3549 [M] | The Arrival of Victor Feldman | 1958 | 40.00 |
| ❑ M-5005 [M] | Latinsville | 1960 | 150.00 |
| ❑ S-7541 [S] | Suite Sixteen | 1959 | 30.00 |
| ❑ S-7549 [S] | The Arrival of Victor Feldman | 1959 | 30.00 |
| ❑ S-9005 [S] | Latinsville | 1960 | 100.00 |
| INTERLUDE | | | |
| ❑ MO-510 [M] | With Mallets Aforethought | 1959 | 40.00 |
| *—Reissue of Mode LP* | | | |
| MODE | | | |
| ❑ LP-120 [M] | Victor Feldman on Vibes | 1957 | 60.00 |
| NAUTILUS | | | |
| ❑ NR-50 | The Secret of the Andes | 1982 | 20.00 |
| *—Audiophile vinyl* | | | |
| PACIFIC JAZZ | | | |
| ❑ PJ-10121 [M] | Victor Feldman Plays Everything in Sight | 196? | 20.00 |
| ❑ ST-20121 [S] | Victor Feldman Plays Everything in Sight | 196? | 25.00 |
| ❑ PJ-20128 [M] | Venezuela Joropo | 196? | 25.00 |
| ❑ ST-20128 [S] | Venezuela Joropo | 196? | 25.00 |
| RIVERSIDE | | | |
| ❑ RLP-366 [M] | Merry Ole Soul | 1961 | 25.00 |
| ❑ RS-9366 [S] | Merry Ole Soul | 1961 | 25.00 |
| VEE JAY | | | |
| ❑ LP-1096 [M] | Love Me with All Your Heart | 1964 | 30.00 |
| ❑ LP-2507 [M] | It's a Wonderful World | 1965 | 20.00 |
| WORLD PACIFIC | | | |
| ❑ ST-1807 [S] | Stop the World, I Want to Get Off | 1962 | 20.00 |
| *—Black vinyl* | | | |
| ❑ ST-1807 [S] | Stop the World, I Want to Get Off | 1962 | 50.00 |
| *—Yellow vinyl* | | | |
| ❑ WP-1807 [M] | Stop the World, I Want to Get Off | 1962 | 30.00 |
| **FELICE, DEE** | | | |
| BETHLEHEM | | | |
| ❑ B-10000 | In Heat | 1969 | 50.00 |
| *—Produced by JAMES BROWN.* | | | |
| **FELICE, ERNICE** | | | |
| CAPITOL | | | |
| ❑ H 192 [10] | Ernice Felice Quartet | 1950 | 60.00 |

LSP-3957 STEREO
Feliciano!
RCA VICTOR
DYNAGROOVE
RECORDING


Jose Feliciano, *Feliciano!*, RCA Victor LSP-3957, 1968, stereo, black label, dog at top, $15.

| Number | Title (A Side/B Side) | Yr | NM |
|---|---|---|---|
| **FELICIANO, JOSE** | | | |
| MOTOWN | | | |
| ❑ M8-953 | Jose Feliciano | 1981 | 10.00 |
| ❑ 6018 ML | Escenas de Amor | 1982 | 10.00 |
| ❑ 6035 ML | Romance in the Night | 1983 | 10.00 |
| PAIR | | | |
| ❑ PDL2-1091 [(2)] | His Hits and Other Classics | 1986 | 12.00 |
| PRIVATE STOCK | | | |
| ❑ PS-2010 | Angela | 1976 | 10.00 |
| ❑ PS-2022 | Sweet Soul | 1977 | 10.00 |
| RCA CAMDEN | | | |
| ❑ CAS-2563 | Jose Feliciano Sings | 1972 | 10.00 |
| RCA VICTOR | | | |
| ❑ APD1-0141 [Q] | Compartments | 1973 | 15.00 |
| *—All copies are quadraphonic* | | | |
| ❑ FSP-253 | Fantastico | 1970 | 18.00 |
| ❑ AFL1-0266 | For My Love...Mother Music | 1977 | 8.00 |
| *—Reissue with new prefix* | | | |
| ❑ APL1-0266 | For My Love...Mother Music | 1974 | 10.00 |
| ❑ FSP-277 | En Mi Soldead | 1971 | 18.00 |
| ❑ AFL1-0407 | And the Feeling's Good | 1977 | 8.00 |
| *—Reissue with new prefix* | | | |
| ❑ CPL1-0407 | And the Feeling's Good | 1974 | 10.00 |
| ❑ AFL1-1005 | Just Wanna Rock 'n' Roll | 1977 | 8.00 |
| *—Reissue with new prefix* | | | |
| ❑ APL1-1005 | Just Wanna Rock 'n' Roll | 1975 | 10.00 |
| ❑ LSPX-1005 | Encore! Jose Feliciano's Finest Performances | 1971 | 12.00 |
| ❑ AFL1-2824 | Encore! Jose Feliciano's Finest Performances | 1978 | 10.00 |
| *—Reissue of LSPX-1005* | | | |
| ❑ LPM-3358 [M] | The Voice and Guitar of Jose Feliciano | 1965 | 15.00 |
| ❑ LSP-3358 [S] | The Voice and Guitar of Jose Feliciano | 1965 | 20.00 |
| ❑ LPM-3503 [M] | Bag Full of Soul (Folk, Rock and Blues) | 1966 | 15.00 |
| ❑ LSP-3503 [S] | Bag Full of Soul (Folk, Rock and Blues) | 1966 | 20.00 |
| ❑ LPM-3581 [M] | Fantastic Feliciano | 1966 | 15.00 |
| ❑ LSP-3581 [S] | Fantastic Feliciano | 1966 | 20.00 |
| ❑ AFL1-3957 | Feliciano! | 1977 | 8.00 |
| *—Reissue with new prefix* | | | |
| ❑ LPM-3957 [M] | Feliciano! | 1968 | 25.00 |
| ❑ LSP-3957 [S] | Feliciano! | 1968 | 15.00 |
| ❑ LSP-4045 | Souled | 1968 | 15.00 |
| ❑ AFL1-4185 | Feliciano/10 to 23 | 1977 | 8.00 |
| *—Reissue with new prefix* | | | |
| ❑ LSP-4185 | Feliciano/10 to 23 | 1969 | 15.00 |
| ❑ AFL1-4370 | Fireworks | 1977 | 8.00 |
| *—Reissue with new prefix* | | | |
| ❑ LSP-4370 | Fireworks | 1970 | 12.00 |
| ❑ LSP-4421 | Jose Feliciano | 1970 | 15.00 |
| ❑ LSP-4573 | That the Spirit Needs | 1971 | 12.00 |
| ❑ LSP-4656 | Memphis Menu | 1972 | 12.00 |
| ❑ LSP-6021 [(2)] | Alive Alive-O! | 1969 | 15.00 |
| **FELT** | | | |
| NASCO | | | |
| ❑ 9006 | Felt | 1971 | 200.00 |
| **FEMININE COMPLEX, THE** | | | |
| ATHENA | | | |
| ❑ 600 | The Feminine Complex | 1969 | 30.00 |
| **FENDERMEN, THE** | | | |
| BEAT ROCKET | | | |
| ❑ BR 116 | Mule Skinner Blues | 199? | 12.00 |
| SOMA | | | |
| ❑ MG-1240 [M] | Mule Skinner Blues | 1960 | 1200. |
| *—Black vinyl* | | | |
| ❑ MG-1240 [M] | Mule Skinner Blues | 1960 | 4000. |
| *—Blue vinyl; VG value 2000; VG+ value 3000* | | | |
| **FERGUSON, ALLYN** | | | |
| AVA | | | |
| ❑ A-32 [M] | Pictures at an Exhibition Framed in Jazz | 1963 | 25.00 |
| ❑ AS-32 [S] | Pictures at an Exhibition Framed in Jazz | 1963 | 30.00 |
| **FERGUSON, MAYNARD** | | | |
| CAMEO | | | |
| ❑ C-1046 [M] | The New Sounds of Maynard Ferguson | 1963 | 20.00 |
| ❑ SC-1046 [S] | The New Sounds of Maynard Ferguson | 1963 | 25.00 |
| ❑ C-1066 [M] | Come Blow Your Horn | 1964 | 20.00 |
| ❑ SC-1066 [S] | Come Blow Your Horn | 1964 | 25.00 |

Maynard Ferguson, *A Message from Birdland,* Roulette SR-52027, 1959, stereo, $25.

| Number | Title (A Side/B Side) | Yr | NM |
|---|---|---|---|
| **COLUMBIA** | | | |
| ❑ PCQ 34457 [Q] | Conquistador | 1977 | 20.00 |
| ❑ HC 44457 | Conquistador | 1982 | 50.00 |
| *—Half-speed mastered edition* | | | |
| **EMARCY** | | | |
| ❑ MG-26017 [10] | Maynard Ferguson's Hollywood Party | 1954 | 100.00 |
| ❑ MG-26024 [10] | Dimensions | 1954 | 100.00 |
| ❑ MG-36009 [M] | Jam Session Featuring Maynard Ferguson | 1955 | 50.00 |
| ❑ MG-36021 [M] | Maynard Ferguson Octet | 1955 | 60.00 |
| ❑ MG-36044 [M] | Dimensions | 1956 | 50.00 |
| ❑ MG-36046 [M] | Maynard Ferguson's Hollywood Party | 1956 | 50.00 |
| ❑ MG-36076 [M] | Around the Horn with Maynard Ferguson | 1956 | 50.00 |
| ❑ MG-36114 [M] | Boy with Lots of Brass | 1957 | 50.00 |
| **EMUS** | | | |
| ❑ ES-12024 [S] | Maynard | 197? | 10.00 |
| *—Reissue of Roulette material* | | | |
| **MAINSTREAM** | | | |
| ❑ S-6031 [S] | Color Him Wild | 1965 | 20.00 |
| ❑ S-6045 [S] | The Blues Roar | 1965 | 20.00 |
| ❑ S-6060 [S] | Maynard Ferguson Sextet | 1966 | 20.00 |
| **MERCURY** | | | |
| ❑ MG-20556 [M] | Boy with Lots of Brass | 1960 | 30.00 |
| ❑ SR-60124 [S] | Boy with Lots of Brass | 1960 | 30.00 |
| **MOSAIC** | | | |
| ❑ MQ14-156 [(14)] | The Complete Roulette Recordings of the Maynard Ferguson Orchestra | 1994 | 250.00 |
| **NAUTILUS** | | | |
| ❑ NR-57 | Storm | 1983 | 40.00 |
| *—Audiophile vinyl* | | | |
| **ROULETTE** | | | |
| ❑ R 52012 [M] | A Message from Newport | 1958 | 25.00 |
| ❑ SR 52012 [S] | A Message from Newport | 1958 | 25.00 |
| ❑ R 52027 [M] | A Message from Birdland | 1959 | 25.00 |
| ❑ SR 52027 [S] | A Message from Birdland | 1959 | 25.00 |
| ❑ R 52038 [M] | Maynard Ferguson Plays Jazz for Dancing | 1959 | 25.00 |
| ❑ SR 52038 [S] | Maynard Ferguson Plays Jazz for Dancing | 1959 | 25.00 |
| ❑ R 52047 [M] | Newport Suite | 1960 | 25.00 |
| ❑ SR 52047 [S] | Newport Suite | 1960 | 25.00 |
| ❑ R 52055 [M] | Let's Face the Music and Dance | 1960 | 25.00 |
| ❑ SR 52055 [S] | Let's Face the Music and Dance | 1960 | 25.00 |
| ❑ R 52058 [M] | Swingin' My Way Through College | 1960 | 25.00 |
| ❑ SR 52058 [S] | Swingin' My Way Through College | 1960 | 25.00 |
| ❑ R 52064 [M] | Maynard '61 | 1961 | 25.00 |
| ❑ SR 52064 [S] | Maynard '61 | 1961 | 25.00 |
| ❑ SR 52083 [S] | Maynard '62 | 1962 | 20.00 |
| ❑ SR 52084 [S] | Si! Si! M.F. | 1962 | 20.00 |
| ❑ SR 52097 [S] | Maynard '63 | 1963 | 20.00 |
| ❑ SR 52107 [S] | Maynard '64 | 1964 | 20.00 |
| ❑ SR 52110 [S] | The World of Maynard Ferguson | 1964 | 20.00 |
| **VIK** | | | |
| ❑ LX-1070 [M] | Birdland Dream Band, Vol. 1 | 1957 | 40.00 |
| ❑ LX-1077 [M] | Birdland Dream Band, Vol. 2 | 1957 | 40.00 |

### FERKO STRING BAND

| Number | Title (A Side/B Side) | Yr | NM |
|---|---|---|---|
| **ABC-PARAMOUNT** | | | |
| ❑ ABC 440 [M] | The World Renowned Ferko String Band | 1963 | 12.00 |
| ❑ ABCS 440 [S] | The World Renowned Ferko String Band | 1963 | 15.00 |
| **ESSEX** | | | |
| ❑ ESLP-209 [M] | Happy Days Are Here Again! | 1956 | 20.00 |
| **FERKO** | | | |
| ❑ LP 3301 [10] | Favorites | 195? | 20.00 |
| **REGENT** | | | |
| ❑ MG-6007 [M] | Ferko String Band | 195? | 15.00 |
| ❑ MG-6008 [M] | Ferko String Band, Vol. 2 | 195? | 15.00 |
| **SOMERSET** | | | |
| ❑ P 3700 [M] | The Happiest Music in the World | 196? | 10.00 |
| ❑ P 12700 [M] | Happy Days Are Here Again! | 196? | 10.00 |
| **STEREO-FIDELITY** | | | |
| ❑ SF 12700 [S] | Happy Days Are Here Again! | 196? | 12.00 |
| **SURE** | | | |
| ❑ SM-7 [M] | The World Renowned Ferko String Band | 1963 | 15.00 |
| ❑ Vol. 8 | Ferko String Band On Broadway | 196? | 10.00 |
| ❑ Vol. 42 | Before the Parade Passes By | 197? | 10.00 |

### FERLINGHETTI, LAWRENCE

| Number | Title (A Side/B Side) | Yr | NM |
|---|---|---|---|
| **FANTASY** | | | |
| ❑ 7004 [M] | The Impeachment of Eisenhower | 1958 | 100.00 |
| *—Black vinyl* | | | |
| ❑ 7004 [M] | The Impeachment of Eisenhower | 1958 | 200.00 |
| *—Red vinyl* | | | |

### FERRANTE AND TEICHER

| Number | Title (A Side/B Side) | Yr | NM |
|---|---|---|---|
| **ABC** | | | |
| ❑ 553 [M] | World's Greatest Semi-Classical Favorites | 1966 | 10.00 |
| ❑ S-553 [S] | World's Greatest Semi-Classical Favorites | 1966 | 12.00 |
| ❑ 554 [M] | Memories | 1966 | 10.00 |
| ❑ S-554 [S] | Memories | 1966 | 12.00 |
| ❑ 555 [M] | Heaven Sounds | 1966 | 10.00 |
| ❑ S-555 [S] | Heaven Sounds | 1966 | 12.00 |
| ❑ 556 [M] | We've Got Rhythm | 1966 | 10.00 |
| ❑ S-556 [S] | We've Got Rhythm | 1966 | 12.00 |
| ❑ 557 [M] | Twin Piano Magic, Vol. 1 | 1966 | 10.00 |
| ❑ S-557 [S] | Twin Piano Magic, Vol. 1 | 1966 | 12.00 |
| ❑ 558 [M] | Autumn Leaves | 1966 | 10.00 |
| ❑ S-558 [S] | Autumn Leaves | 1966 | 12.00 |
| ❑ 559 [M] | Twin Piano Magic, Vol. 2 | 1966 | 10.00 |
| ❑ S-559 [S] | Twin Piano Magic, Vol. 2 | 1966 | 12.00 |
| ❑ 560 [M] | Bolero | 1966 | 10.00 |
| ❑ S-560 [S] | Bolero | 1966 | 12.00 |
| ❑ 561 [M] | Temptation | 1966 | 10.00 |
| ❑ S-561 [S] | Temptation | 1966 | 12.00 |
| **ABC-PARAMOUNT** | | | |
| ❑ 221 [M] | Heavenly Sounds in Hi-Fi | 1958 | 15.00 |
| ❑ S-221 [S] | Heavenly Sounds in Hi-Fi | 1958 | 20.00 |
| ❑ 248 [M] | Ferrante and Teicher with Percussion | 1958 | 15.00 |
| ❑ S-248 [S] | Ferrante and Teicher with Percussion | 1958 | 20.00 |
| ❑ 285 [M] | Ferrante and Teicher Blast Off | 1959 | 15.00 |
| ❑ S-285 [S] | Ferrante and Teicher Blast Off | 1959 | 20.00 |
| ❑ 313 [M] | Ferrante and Teicher Play Light Classics | 1960 | 15.00 |
| ❑ S-313 [S] | Ferrante and Teicher Play Light Classics | 1960 | 20.00 |
| ❑ 336 [M] | Themes from Broadway Shows | 1960 | 15.00 |
| ❑ S-336 [S] | Themes from Broadway Shows | 1960 | 20.00 |
| ❑ 430 [M] | Postcards from Paris | 1962 | 12.00 |
| ❑ S-430 [S] | Postcards from Paris | 1962 | 15.00 |
| ❑ 437 [M] | Popular Classics | 1962 | 12.00 |
| ❑ S-437 [S] | Popular Classics | 1962 | 15.00 |
| ❑ 454 [M] | The Artistry of Ferrante and Teicher | 1963 | 12.00 |
| ❑ S-454 [S] | The Artistry of Ferrante and Teicher | 1963 | 15.00 |
| ❑ ST-90467 [S] | Postcards from Paris | 196? | 15.00 |
| *—Capitol Record Club edition* | | | |
| **BAINBRIDGE** | | | |
| ❑ BT-6263 | A Few of Our Favorites on Stage | 1986 | 10.00 |
| ❑ BT-6266 | American Fantasy | 1987 | 10.00 |
| **COLUMBIA** | | | |
| ❑ CL 573 [M] | Hi-Fire Works | 1955 | 25.00 |
| **GRAND AWARD** | | | |
| ❑ GA-263 | Themes from Broadway Shows | 1962 | 12.00 |
| **HARMONY** | | | |
| ❑ HL 7325 [M] | Twin Piano Magic | 1965 | 12.00 |
| ❑ HL 7427 [M] | Fireworks | 1967 | 12.00 |
| ❑ HS 11125 [R] | Twin Piano Magic | 1965 | 10.00 |
| ❑ HS 11227 [R] | Fireworks | 1967 | 10.00 |
| ❑ HS 11411 | Encore | 1970 | 10.00 |
| **LIBERTY** | | | |
| ❑ LWB-70 [(2)] | 10th Anniversary — Golden Piano Hits | 198? | 10.00 |
| *—Reissue of United Artists 70* | | | |
| ❑ LWB-73 [(2)] | The Best of Ferrante and Teicher | 198? | 10.00 |
| *—Reissue of United Artists 73* | | | |
| ❑ LW-662 | Feelings | 198? | 8.00 |
| *—Reissue of United Artists 662* | | | |
| ❑ LT-782 | Rocky and Other Knockouts | 198? | 8.00 |
| *—Reissue of United Artists 782* | | | |
| ❑ LKDL-831 [(4)] | For You with Love | 198? | 18.00 |
| *—Reissue of United Artists 831* | | | |
| ❑ LT-908 | You Light Up My Life | 198? | 8.00 |
| *—Reissue of United Artists 908* | | | |
| ❑ LT-980 | Classical Disco | 198? | 8.00 |
| *—Reissue of United Artists 980* | | | |
| ❑ LM-1016 | Midnight Cowboy | 1981 | 8.00 |
| *—Reissue of United Artists 1016* | | | |
| ❑ LN-10112 | Supermen | 198? | 8.00 |
| *—Reissue of United Artists 941* | | | |
| ❑ LN-10113 | Star Wars | 198? | 8.00 |
| *—Reissue of United Artists 855* | | | |

| Number | Title (A Side/B Side) | Yr | NM |
|---|---|---|---|
| ❑ LN-10141 | The People's Choice | 1981 | 8.00 |
| *—Budget-line reissue of United Artists 6385* | | | |
| ❑ LN-10142 | Snowbound | 1981 | 8.00 |
| *—Budget-line reissue of United Artists 6233* | | | |
| ❑ LN-10158 | Concert for Lovers | 1981 | 8.00 |
| *—Budget-line reissue of United Artists 6315* | | | |
| ❑ LN-10175 | Showstoppers | 1983 | 8.00 |
| ❑ LN-10176 | The Movie Theme Team | 1983 | 8.00 |
| ❑ LN-10198 | Classic Lites | 1983 | 8.00 |
| ❑ LN-10210 | The Movie Theme Team II | 1984 | 8.00 |
| ❑ LN-10242 [(2)] | Ferrante and Teicher Superpak | 1984 | 10.00 |

PICKWICK

| Number | Title (A Side/B Side) | Yr | NM |
|---|---|---|---|
| ❑ PC-3003 [M] | Excitement | 196? | 10.00 |
| ❑ SPC-3003 [S] | Excitement | 196? | 10.00 |
| ❑ PC-3077 [M] | In Love | 196? | 10.00 |
| ❑ SPC-3077 [S] | In Love | 196? | 10.00 |
| ❑ SPC-3397 | How High the Moon | 197? | 8.00 |
| ❑ SPC-3586 | Getting Together | 1978 | 8.00 |
| ❑ SPC-3612 | Fabulous Favorites | 197? | 8.00 |

SUNSET

| Number | Title (A Side/B Side) | Yr | NM |
|---|---|---|---|
| ❑ SUS-5235 | Incomparable Piano | 1969 | 8.00 |
| ❑ SUS-5277 | Midnight Memories | 1970 | 8.00 |
| ❑ SUS-5313 | Love Is a Rainbow | 1971 | 8.00 |

UNITED ARTISTS

| Number | Title (A Side/B Side) | Yr | NM |
|---|---|---|---|
| ❑ UA-LA018-F | Hear & Now | 1972 | 10.00 |
| ❑ UXS-70 [(2)] | 10th Anniversary — Golden Piano Hits | 1969 | 12.00 |
| ❑ UA-LA072-G | The Roaring 20's | 1973 | 10.00 |
| ❑ UXS-73 [(2)] | The Best of Ferrante and Teicher | 1971 | 12.00 |
| ❑ UXS-77 [(2)] | Ferrante and Teicher Superpak | 1972 | 12.00 |
| ❑ UA-LA101-G2 [(2)] | Greatest Love Themes of the Twentieth Century | 1973 | 12.00 |
| ❑ UA-LA118-G | Killing Me Softly | 1973 | 10.00 |
| ❑ UA-LA195-G | Dial M for Music | 1974 | 10.00 |
| ❑ UA-LA227-G | In a Soulful Mood | 1974 | 10.00 |
| ❑ UA-LA236-G | The Very Best of Ferrante and Teicher | 1974 | 10.00 |
| ❑ UA-LA490-G | The Carpenters Songbook | 1975 | 10.00 |
| ❑ UA-LA573-G | Spirit of 1976 | 1975 | 10.00 |
| ❑ UA-LA585-G | Piano Portraits | 1976 | 10.00 |
| ❑ UA-LA662-G | Feelings | 1976 | 10.00 |
| ❑ UA-LA681-G | Around | 1977 | 10.00 |
| ❑ UA-LA782-G | Rocky and Other Knockouts | 1977 | 10.00 |
| ❑ UA-LA831-P [(4)] | For You with Love | 1978 | 20.00 |
| ❑ UA-LA855-G | Star Wars | 1978 | 12.00 |
| ❑ UA-LA908-H | You Light Up My Life | 1978 | 10.00 |
| ❑ UA-LA941-H | Supermen | 1979 | 10.00 |
| ❑ LT-980 | Classical Disco | 1979 | 10.00 |
| ❑ LM-1016 | Midnight Cowboy | 1980 | 8.00 |
| *—Reissue of 6725* | | | |
| ❑ UAL 3121 [M] | The World's Greatest Themes | 1960 | 12.00 |
| ❑ UAL 3135 [M] | Latin Pianos | 1960 | 12.00 |
| ❑ UAL 3166 [M] | West Side Story & Other Motion Picture & Broadway Hits | 1961 | 12.00 |
| ❑ UAL 3171 [M] | Tonight | 1962 | 12.00 |
| ❑ UAL 3210 [M] | Golden Themes from Motion Pictures | 1962 | 12.00 |
| ❑ UAL 3211 [M] | The Many Moods of Ferrante & Teicher | 1962 | 12.00 |
| ❑ UAL 3230 [M] | Pianos in Paradise | 1962 | 12.00 |
| ❑ UAL 3233 [M] | Snowbound | 1962 | 12.00 |
| ❑ UAL 3247 [M] | Keys to Her Apartment | 1963 | 12.00 |
| ❑ UAL 3269 [M] | Golden Piano Hits | 1963 | 10.00 |
| *—Reissue of 7505* | | | |
| ❑ UAL 3282 [M] | Love Themes | 1963 | 10.00 |
| *—Reissue of 7514* | | | |
| ❑ UAL 3284 [M] | Keyboard Kapers | 1963 | 10.00 |
| ❑ UAL 3290 [M] | Love Themes from Cleopatra | 1963 | 12.00 |
| ❑ UAL 3298 [M] | Holiday for Pianos | 1963 | 10.00 |
| ❑ UAL 3315 [M] | Concert for Lovers | 1964 | 12.00 |
| ❑ UAL 3340 [M] | Exotic Love Themes | 1964 | 12.00 |
| ❑ UAL 3343 [M] | 50 Fabulous Piano Favorites | 1964 | 12.00 |
| ❑ UAL 3361 [M] | My Fair Lady | 1964 | 10.00 |
| ❑ UAL 3375 [M] | The Enchanted World of Ferrante and Teicher | 1964 | 12.00 |
| ❑ UAL 3385 [M] | The People's Choice | 1964 | 10.00 |
| ❑ UAL 3406 [M] | Springtime | 1965 | 10.00 |
| ❑ UAL 3416 [M] | By Popular Demand | 1965 | 10.00 |
| ❑ UAL 3434 [M] | Only the Best | 1965 | 10.00 |
| ❑ UAL 3444 [M] | The Ferrante and Teicher Concert | 1965 | 10.00 |
| ❑ UAL 3475 [M] | The Ferrante and Teicher Concert, Part 2 | 1966 | 10.00 |
| ❑ UAL 3483 [M] | For Lovers of All Ages | 1966 | 10.00 |
| ❑ UAL 3526 [M] | You Asked For It! | 1966 | 10.00 |
| ❑ UAL 3536 [M] | We Wish You a Merry Christmas | 1966 | 15.00 |
| ❑ UAL 3556 [M] | Our Golden Favorites | 1967 | 12.00 |
| ❑ UAL 3572 [M] | A Man and a Woman & Other Motion Picture Themes | 1967 | 10.00 |
| ❑ UAS 5501 | Getting Together | 1970 | 10.00 |
| ❑ UAS 5531 | It's Too Late | 1971 | 10.00 |
| ❑ UAS 5552 | Fiddler on the Roof | 1971 | 10.00 |
| ❑ UAS 5588 | Ferrante and Teicher Play Hit Themes | 1972 | 10.00 |
| ❑ UAS 5645 | Ferrante and Teicher Salute Nashville | 1972 | 10.00 |
| ❑ UAS 6121 [S] | The World's Greatest Themes | 1960 | 15.00 |
| ❑ UAS 6135 [S] | Latin Pianos | 1960 | 15.00 |
| ❑ UAS 6166 [S] | West Side Story & Other Motion Picture & Broadway Hits | 1961 | 15.00 |
| ❑ UAS 6171 [S] | Tonight | 1962 | 15.00 |
| ❑ UAS 6210 [S] | Golden Themes from Motion Pictures | 1962 | 15.00 |
| ❑ UAS 6211 [S] | The Many Moods of Ferrante & Teicher | 1962 | 15.00 |
| ❑ UAS 6230 [S] | Pianos in Paradise | 1962 | 15.00 |
| ❑ UAS 6233 [S] | Snowbound | 1962 | 15.00 |
| ❑ UAS 6247 [S] | Keys to Her Apartment | 1963 | 15.00 |
| ❑ UAS 6269 [S] | Golden Piano Hits | 1963 | 12.00 |
| *—Reissue of 8505* | | | |
| ❑ UAS 6282 [S] | Love Themes | 1963 | 12.00 |
| *—Reissue of 8514* | | | |
| ❑ UAS 6284 [S] | Keyboard Kapers | 1963 | 12.00 |
| ❑ UAS 6290 [S] | Love Themes from Cleopatra | 1963 | 15.00 |
| ❑ UAS 6298 [S] | Holiday for Pianos | 1963 | 12.00 |
| ❑ UAS 6315 [S] | Concert for Lovers | 1964 | 15.00 |
| ❑ UAS 6340 [S] | Exotic Love Themes | 1964 | 15.00 |
| ❑ UAS 6343 [S] | 50 Fabulous Piano Favorites | 1964 | 15.00 |
| ❑ UAS 6361 [S] | My Fair Lady | 1964 | 12.00 |
| ❑ UAS 6375 [S] | The Enchanted World of Ferrante and Teicher | 1964 | 15.00 |
| ❑ UAS 6385 [S] | The People's Choice | 1964 | 12.00 |
| ❑ UAS 6406 [S] | Springtime | 1965 | 12.00 |
| ❑ UAS 6416 [S] | By Popular Demand | 1965 | 12.00 |
| ❑ UAS 6434 [S] | Only the Best | 1965 | 12.00 |
| ❑ UAS 6444 [S] | The Ferrante and Teicher Concert | 1965 | 12.00 |
| ❑ UAS 6475 [S] | The Ferrante and Teicher Concert, Part 2 | 1966 | 12.00 |
| ❑ UAS 6483 [S] | For Lovers of All Ages | 1966 | 12.00 |
| ❑ UAS 6526 [S] | You Asked For It! | 1966 | 12.00 |
| ❑ UAS 6536 [S] | We Wish You a Merry Christmas | 1966 | 12.00 |
| ❑ UAS 6536 [S] | We Wish You a Merry Christmas | 1972 | 8.00 |
| *—Tan label (may also exist on late-1960s UA labels)* | | | |
| ❑ UAS 6556 [S] | Our Golden Favorites | 1967 | 10.00 |
| ❑ UAS 6572 [S] | A Man and a Woman & Other Motion Picture Themes | 1967 | 12.00 |
| ❑ UAS 6659 | A Bouquet of Hits | 1968 | 10.00 |
| ❑ UAS 6701 | Listen to the Movies | 1969 | 10.00 |
| ❑ UAS 6725 | Midnight Cowboy | 1969 | 10.00 |
| ❑ UAS 6771 | Love Is a Soft Touch | 1970 | 10.00 |
| ❑ UAS 6792 | The Music Lovers | 1971 | 10.00 |
| ❑ WW 7504 [M] | Dynamic Twin Pianos | 1961 | 12.00 |
| ❑ WW 7505 [M] | Golden Piano Hits | 1961 | 12.00 |
| ❑ WW 7514 [M] | Love Themes | 1961 | 12.00 |
| ❑ WWS 8505 [S] | Golden Piano Hits | 1961 | 15.00 |
| ❑ WWS 8514 [S] | Love Themes | 1961 | 15.00 |
| ❑ ST-90931 [S] | You Asked For It! | 1966 | 15.00 |
| *—Capitol Record Club edition* | | | |

URANIA

| Number | Title (A Side/B Side) | Yr | NM |
|---|---|---|---|
| ❑ 8011 | Rhapsody | 196? | 12.00 |

WESTMINSTER

| Number | Title (A Side/B Side) | Yr | NM |
|---|---|---|---|
| ❑ SW 1045 [S] | Soundproof | 195? | 25.00 |
| ❑ SW 1048 [S] | Latin American Adventure | 195? | 25.00 |
| ❑ WL 3044 [M] | Christmas Hi-Fi Favorites | 195? | 20.00 |
| ❑ WP 6001 [M] | Postcards from Paris | 195? | 20.00 |
| ❑ WP 6021 [M] | Adventure in Carols | 195? | 20.00 |

### FERRE, BOULOU

4 CORNERS OF THE WORLD

| Number | Title (A Side/B Side) | Yr | NM |
|---|---|---|---|
| ❑ FCL-4211 [M] | Boulou with the Paris All Stars | 1966 | 20.00 |
| ❑ FCS-4211 [S] | Boulou with the Paris All Stars | 1966 | 25.00 |
| ❑ FCL-4234 [M] | Jazz/Left Bank | 1967 | 25.00 |
| ❑ FCS-4234 [S] | Jazz/Left Bank | 1967 | 20.00 |
| *—As "Boulou with the Paris All Stars"* | | | |

### FERRE, CLIFF

KEM

| Number | Title (A Side/B Side) | Yr | NM |
|---|---|---|---|
| ❑ LP-100 [M] | Looks Like Fun | 195? | 25.00 |

### FESTIVAL CHAMBER ORCHESTRA (ANTAL DORATI, CONDUCTOR)

MERCURY LIVING PRESENCE

| Number | Title (A Side/B Side) | Yr | NM |
|---|---|---|---|
| ❑ SR 90436 [S] | Haydn: Symphonies No. 59 and 81 | 1965 | 20.00 |
| *—Maroon label, with "Vendor: Mercury Record Corporation"* | | | |
| ❑ SR 90438 [S] | Mozart: Marches; Lucio Silva Overture; Menuet; German Dances | 1965 | 30.00 |
| *—Maroon label, with "Vendor: Mercury Record Corporation"* | | | |

### FESTIVAL QUARTET

RCA VICTOR RED SEAL

| Number | Title (A Side/B Side) | Yr | NM |
|---|---|---|---|
| ❑ LSC-2147 [S] | Schubert: Trout Quintet | 1958 | 180.00 |
| *—Original with "shaded dog" label* | | | |
| ❑ LSC-2147 [S] | Schubert: Trout Quintet | 1964 | 120.00 |
| *—Second edition with "white dog" label* | | | |
| ❑ LSC-2330 [S] | Brahms: Piano Quartet in C | 1959 | 200.00 |
| *—Original with "shaded dog" label* | | | |
| ❑ LM-2473 [M] | Brahms: Piano Quartet in G | 1961 | 20.00 |
| *—Originals with "shaded dog" label; a rare instance when even the mono version is sought after* | | | |
| ❑ LSC-2473 [S] | Brahms: Piano Quartet in G | 1961 | 120.00 |
| *—Originals with "shaded dog" label* | | | |
| ❑ LSC-2517 [S] | Brahms: Piano Quartet in A | 1961 | 200.00 |
| *—Originals with "shaded dog" label* | | | |
| ❑ LSC-2735 [S] | Faure: Piano Quartet in G | 1963 | 60.00 |
| *—Original with "shaded dog" label* | | | |

### FEVER TREE

AMPEX

| Number | Title (A Side/B Side) | Yr | NM |
|---|---|---|---|
| ❑ A-10113 | For Sale | 1970 | 25.00 |

MCA

| Number | Title (A Side/B Side) | Yr | NM |
|---|---|---|---|
| ❑ 551 | Fever Tree | 197? | 10.00 |

UNI

| Number | Title (A Side/B Side) | Yr | NM |
|---|---|---|---|
| ❑ 73024 | Fever Tree | 1968 | 25.00 |
| ❑ 73040 | Another Time, Another Place | 1968 | 25.00 |
| ❑ 73067 | Creation | 1970 | 25.00 |

### FIELD, SALLY

COLGEMS

| Number | Title (A Side/B Side) | Yr | NM |
|---|---|---|---|
| ❑ COM-106 [M] | The Flying Nun | 1967 | 30.00 |
| ❑ COS-106 [S] | The Flying Nun | 1967 | 25.00 |

### FIELDING, JANE

JAZZ WEST

| Number | Title (A Side/B Side) | Yr | NM |
|---|---|---|---|
| ❑ LP-3 [M] | Jazz Trio for Voice, Piano and Bass | 1955 | 300.00 |
| ❑ LP-5 [M] | Embers Glow | 1956 | 300.00 |

### FIELDING, JERRY

ABC-PARAMOUNT

| Number | Title (A Side/B Side) | Yr | NM |
|---|---|---|---|
| ❑ ABCS-542 [S] | Hollywood Brass | 1966 | 20.00 |

COMMAND

| Number | Title (A Side/B Side) | Yr | NM |
|---|---|---|---|
| ❑ RS 33-921 [M] | Near East Brass | 1967 | 30.00 |

DECCA

| Number | Title (A Side/B Side) | Yr | NM |
|---|---|---|---|
| ❑ DL 8100 [M] | Sweet with a Beat | 1955 | 30.00 |
| ❑ DL 8371 [M] | Swingin' in Hi-Fi | 1956 | 30.00 |
| ❑ DL 8450 [M] | Fielding's Formula | 1957 | 30.00 |
| ❑ DL 8669 [M] | Hollywood Wind Jazztet | 1958 | 30.00 |

KAPP

| Number | Title (A Side/B Side) | Yr | NM |
|---|---|---|---|
| ❑ KL-1026 [M] | Dance Concert | 1956 | 50.00 |

SIGNATURE

| Number | Title (A Side/B Side) | Yr | NM |
|---|---|---|---|
| ❑ SM-1028 [M] | Favorite Christmas Music | 1960 | 20.00 |
| ❑ SS-1028 [S] | Favorite Christmas Music | 1960 | 25.00 |

TIME

| Number | Title (A Side/B Side) | Yr | NM |
|---|---|---|---|
| ❑ S-2042 [S] | Magnificence in Brass | 196? | 20.00 |
| ❑ S-2059 [S] | A Bit of Ireland | 196? | 20.00 |
| ❑ S-2119 [S] | We Like Brass | 196? | 20.00 |

TREND

| Number | Title (A Side/B Side) | Yr | NM |
|---|---|---|---|
| ❑ TL-1000 [10] | Jerry Fielding and His Great New Orchestra | 1953 | 120.00 |
| ❑ TL-1004 [10] | Jerry Fielding Plays a Dance Concert | 1954 | 100.00 |

### FIELDS, ERNIE

RENDEZVOUS

| Number | Title (A Side/B Side) | Yr | NM |
|---|---|---|---|
| ❑ 1309 [M] | In the Mood | 1960 | 60.00 |

### FIELDS, GRACIE

LIBERTY

| Number | Title (A Side/B Side) | Yr | NM |
|---|---|---|---|
| ❑ LRP-3059 [M] | Our Gracie | 1957 | 40.00 |

### FIELDS, HERBIE

DECCA

| Number | Title (A Side/B Side) | Yr | NM |
|---|---|---|---|
| ❑ DL 8130 [M] | Blow Hot — Blow Cool | 1956 | 40.00 |

FRATERNITY

| Number | Title (A Side/B Side) | Yr | NM |
|---|---|---|---|
| ❑ F-1011 [M] | Fields in Clover | 1959 | 60.00 |

RKO UNIQUE

| Number | Title (A Side/B Side) | Yr | NM |
|---|---|---|---|
| ❑ ULP-146 [M] | A Night at Kitty's | 1957 | 50.00 |

### FIELDS, IRVING

ABC-PARAMOUNT

| Number | Title (A Side/B Side) | Yr | NM |
|---|---|---|---|
| ❑ ABC-187 [M] | Irving Fields at the St. Moritz | 1956 | 30.00 |

DECCA

| Number | Title (A Side/B Side) | Yr | NM |
|---|---|---|---|
| ❑ DL 4114 [M] | More Bagels and Bongos | 1961 | 20.00 |
| ❑ DL 4174 [M] | Pizzas and Bongos | 1961 | 20.00 |
| ❑ DL 4238 [M] | Champagne and Bongos | 1962 | 20.00 |
| ❑ DL 4323 [M] | Bikinis and Bongos | 1962 | 20.00 |
| ❑ DL 8856 [M] | Bagels and Bongos | 1959 | 20.00 |
| ❑ DL 8901 [M] | At the Emerald Room, Hotel Astor | 1959 | 20.00 |
| ❑ DL 74114 [S] | More Bagels and Bongos | 1961 | 25.00 |
| ❑ DL 74174 [S] | Pizzas and Bongos | 1961 | 25.00 |
| ❑ DL 74238 [S] | Champagne and Bongos | 1962 | 25.00 |
| ❑ DL 74323 [S] | Bikinis and Bongos | 1962 | 25.00 |
| ❑ DL 78856 [S] | Bagels and Bongos | 1959 | 30.00 |
| ❑ DL 78901 [S] | At the Emerald Room, Hotel Astor | 1959 | 30.00 |

EVEREST

| Number | Title (A Side/B Side) | Yr | NM |
|---|---|---|---|
| ❑ SDBR-1134 [S] | Twisting | 1962 | 25.00 |
| ❑ LPBR-5134 [M] | Twisting | 1962 | 20.00 |

FIESTA

| Number | Title (A Side/B Side) | Yr | NM |
|---|---|---|---|
| ❑ FLP-1228 [M] | Fabulous Fingers | 195? | 30.00 |

The Fifth Dimension, *Stoned Soul Picnic,* Soul City SCS-92002, 1968, $15.

| Number | Title (A Side/B Side) | Yr | NM |
|---|---|---|---|
| **GONE** | | | |
| ❑ LP-5003 [M] | Fabulous Touch | 1959 | 25.00 |
| **KING** | | | |
| ❑ 703 [M] | Irving Fields Favorites | 1960 | 30.00 |
| ❑ 709 [M] | Live It Up | 1960 | 30.00 |
| ❑ 724 [M] | Classics Go Latin | 1960 | 20.00 |
| ❑ 724-S [S] | Classics Go Latin | 1960 | 30.00 |
| ❑ 742 [M] | Lox, Latin and Bongos | 1960 | 20.00 |
| ❑ 742-S [S] | Lox, Latin and Bongos | 1960 | 30.00 |
| **RCA VICTOR** | | | |
| ❑ LPT-38 [10] | Fields Favorites | 195? | 50.00 |
| **TOPS** | | | |
| ❑ L-1562 [M] | Irving Fields Plays Irving Berlin | 1957 | 30.00 |

## FIELDS, SHEP

| Number | Title (A Side/B Side) | Yr | NM |
|---|---|---|---|
| **DOT** | | | |
| ❑ DLP-25348 [S] | The Rippling Rhythm of Shep Fields | 1960 | 20.00 |
| **GOLDEN CREST** | | | |
| ❑ 3037 [M] | Rippling Rhythms | 196? | 20.00 |
| ❑ 3061 [M] | Shep Fields at the Shamrock Hilton | 196? | 20.00 |
| **JUBILEE** | | | |
| ❑ JLP-1056 [M] | Cocktails, Dinner and Dancing | 1958 | 20.00 |

## FIFTH DIMENSION, THE

| Number | Title (A Side/B Side) | Yr | NM |
|---|---|---|---|
| **ABC** | | | |
| ❑ D-897 | Earthbound | 1975 | 10.00 |
| **ARISTA** | | | |
| ❑ ABM-1106 | Greatest Hits on Earth | 1975 | 8.00 |
| *—Reissue of Bell 1106* | | | |
| ❑ AL 8335 | Greatest Hits on Earth | 198? | 8.00 |
| *—Reissue of Arista 1106* | | | |
| **BELL** | | | |
| ❑ 1106 | Greatest Hits on Earth | 1972 | 10.00 |
| ❑ 1116 | Living Together, Growing Together | 1973 | 10.00 |
| ❑ 1315 | Soul and Inspiration | 1974 | 10.00 |
| ❑ 6045 | Portrait | 1970 | 12.00 |
| ❑ 6060 | Love's Lines, Angles and Rhymes | 1971 | 12.00 |
| ❑ 6065 | Reflections | 1971 | 10.00 |
| ❑ 6073 | Individually & Collectively | 1972 | 10.00 |
| ❑ 9000 [(2)] | The 5th Dimension/Live!! | 1971 | 12.00 |
| **MOTOWN** | | | |
| ❑ M7-896 | Star | 1978 | 10.00 |
| **PAIR** | | | |
| ❑ PDL2-1108 [(2)] | The Glory Days | 1986 | 12.00 |
| **RHINO** | | | |
| ❑ RNDA-71104 [(2)] | The 5th Dimension Anthology | 1986 | 12.00 |
| **SOUL CITY** | | | |
| ❑ SCS-33900 | The 5th Dimension/Greatest Hits | 1970 | 12.00 |
| ❑ SCS-33901 | The July 5th Album | 1970 | 12.00 |
| ❑ SCM-91000 [M] | Up, Up and Away | 1967 | 20.00 |
| ❑ SCM-91001 [M] | The Magic Garden | 1967 | 20.00 |
| ❑ SCS-92000 [S] | Up, Up and Away | 1967 | 15.00 |
| ❑ SCS-92001 [S] | The Magic Garden | 1967 | 15.00 |
| ❑ SCS-92002 | Stoned Soul Picnic | 1968 | 15.00 |
| ❑ SCS-92005 | The Age of Aquarius | 1969 | 15.00 |

## FIFTH ESTATE, THE

| Number | Title (A Side/B Side) | Yr | NM |
|---|---|---|---|
| **JUBILEE** | | | |
| ❑ JGM-8005 [M] | Ding Dong! The Witch Is Dead | 1967 | 25.00 |
| ❑ JGS-8005 [S] | Ding Dong! The Witch Is Dead | 1967 | 30.00 |

## FIFTY FOOT HOSE

| Number | Title (A Side/B Side) | Yr | NM |
|---|---|---|---|
| **LIMELIGHT** | | | |
| ❑ 86062 | Cauldron | 1968 | 100.00 |

## FILETS OF SOUL

| Number | Title (A Side/B Side) | Yr | NM |
|---|---|---|---|
| **SQUID** | | | |
| ❑ 4857 | Freedom | 1968 | 100.00 |

## FINCHLEY BOYS, THE

| Number | Title (A Side/B Side) | Yr | NM |
|---|---|---|---|
| **GOLDEN THROAT** | | | |
| ❑ 200-19 | Everlasting Tribute | 1971 | 200.00 |

## FINE, MILO

| Number | Title (A Side/B Side) | Yr | NM |
|---|---|---|---|
| **HAT HUT** | | | |
| ❑ S/T [(2)] | MFG in Minnesota | 1978 | 20.00 |

## FINNEY, ALBERT

| Number | Title (A Side/B Side) | Yr | NM |
|---|---|---|---|
| **MOTOWN** | | | |
| ❑ M6-889 | The Albert Finney Album | 1977 | 20.00 |

## FIRE

| Number | Title (A Side/B Side) | Yr | NM |
|---|---|---|---|
| **ABC** | | | |
| ❑ ABCS-661 | Fire | 1969 | 20.00 |

## FIRE & ICE LTD.

| Number | Title (A Side/B Side) | Yr | NM |
|---|---|---|---|
| **CAPITOL** | | | |
| ❑ ST 2577 [S] | The Happening | 1966 | 40.00 |
| ❑ T 2577 [M] | The Happening | 1966 | 30.00 |

## FIRE ESCAPE, THE

| Number | Title (A Side/B Side) | Yr | NM |
|---|---|---|---|
| **GNP CRESCENDO** | | | |
| ❑ GNP-2034 [M] | Psychotic Reaction | 1967 | 40.00 |
| ❑ GNPS-2034 [S] | Psychotic Reaction | 1967 | 30.00 |

## FIREBALLS, THE

| Number | Title (A Side/B Side) | Yr | NM |
|---|---|---|---|
| **ATCO** | | | |
| ❑ 33-239 [M] | Bottle of Wine | 1968 | 40.00 |
| ❑ SD 33-239 [S] | Bottle of Wine | 1968 | 25.00 |
| ❑ SD 33-275 | Come On, React! | 1969 | 25.00 |
| **CROWN** | | | |
| ❑ CST-376 [R] | Jimmy Gilmer and the Fireballs & The Sugar Shackers | 1963 | 25.00 |
| ❑ CST-387 [R] | The Sensational Jimmy Gilmer & The Fireballs | 1964 | 25.00 |
| ❑ CLP-5376 [M] | Jimmy Gilmer and the Fireballs & The Sugar Shackers | 1963 | 25.00 |
| ❑ CLP-5387 [M] | The Sensational Jimmy Gilmer & The Fireballs | 1964 | 25.00 |
| **DOT** | | | |
| ❑ DLP-3512 [M] | Torquay | 1963 | 50.00 |
| ❑ DLP-3545 [M] | Sugar Shack | 1963 | 40.00 |
| *—Jimmy Gilmer and the Fireballs* | | | |
| ❑ DLP-3577 [M] | Buddy's Buddy | 1964 | 50.00 |
| *—Jimmy Gilmer and the Fireballs* | | | |
| ❑ DLP-3643 [M] | Lucky 'Leven | 1965 | 30.00 |
| ❑ DLP-3668 [M] | Folkbeat | 1965 | 30.00 |
| ❑ DLP-3709 [M] | Campusology | 1966 | 30.00 |
| ❑ DLP-3856 [M] | Firewater | 1968 | 50.00 |
| *—Stereo cover with "Monaural" and "Promotional Copy Not for Sale" stickers, but the record is stock mono* | | | |
| ❑ DLP-25512 [S] | Torquay | 1963 | 80.00 |
| ❑ DLP-25545 [S] | Sugar Shack | 1963 | 60.00 |
| *—Jimmy Gilmer and the Fireballs* | | | |
| ❑ DLP-25577 [S] | Buddy's Buddy | 1964 | 80.00 |
| *—Jimmy Gilmer and the Fireballs* | | | |
| ❑ DLP-25643 [S] | Lucky 'Leven | 1965 | 40.00 |
| ❑ DLP-25668 [S] | Folkbeat | 1965 | 40.00 |
| ❑ DLP-25709 [S] | Campusology | 1966 | 40.00 |
| ❑ DLP-25856 [S] | Firewater | 1968 | 25.00 |
| **SUNDAZED** | | | |
| ❑ LP-5016 | The Fireballs | 1995 | 10.00 |
| ❑ LP-5017 | Torquay | 1995 | 10.00 |
| ❑ LP-5018 | Gunshot! | 1995 | 10.00 |
| **TOP RANK** | | | |
| ❑ RM-324 [M] | The Fireballs | 1960 | 150.00 |
| ❑ RM-343 [M] | Vaquero | 1960 | 150.00 |
| ❑ RS-643 [S] | Vaquero | 1960 | 200.00 |
| **WARWICK** | | | |
| ❑ W-2042 [M] | Here Are the Fireballs | 1961 | 150.00 |
| ❑ WST-2042 [S] | Here Are the Fireballs | 1961 | 250.00 |

## FIREBIRDS, THE

| Number | Title (A Side/B Side) | Yr | NM |
|---|---|---|---|
| **CROWN** | | | |
| ❑ CST-589 | Light My Fire | 1968 | 70.00 |

## FIREFLIES, THE

| Number | Title (A Side/B Side) | Yr | NM |
|---|---|---|---|
| **TAURUS** | | | |
| ❑ 1002 [M] | You Were Mine | 196? | 100.00 |
| ❑ S-1002 [S] | You Were Mine | 196? | 300.00 |

## FIREHOUSE FIVE PLUS TWO, THE

| Number | Title (A Side/B Side) | Yr | NM |
|---|---|---|---|
| **GOOD TIME JAZZ** | | | |
| ❑ L-1 [10] | The Firehouse Five Plus Two, Volume 1 | 1953 | 50.00 |
| ❑ L-2 [10] | The Firehouse Five Plus Two, Volume 2 | 1953 | 50.00 |
| ❑ L-6 [10] | The Firehouse Five Plus Two, Volume 3 | 1953 | 50.00 |
| ❑ L-16 [10] | The Firehouse Five Plus Two, Volume 4 | 1953 | 50.00 |
| ❑ L-23 [10] | The Firehouse Five Plus Two Goes South!, Volume 5 | 1954 | 60.00 |
| ❑ S-10028 [S] | The Firehouse Five Plus Two Goes to Sea | 1960 | 25.00 |
| ❑ S-10038 [S] | The Firehouse Five Plus Two Crashes a Party | 1960 | 25.00 |
| ❑ S-10040 [S] | Dixieland Favorites | 1960 | 25.00 |
| ❑ S-10044 [S] | Around the World | 1961 | 25.00 |
| ❑ S-10049 [S] | The Firehouse Five Plus Two at Disneyland | 1962 | 25.00 |
| ❑ S-10052 [S] | The Firehouse Five Plus Two Goes to a Fire | 1964 | 25.00 |
| ❑ S-10054 [S] | Twenty Years Later | 1969 | 25.00 |
| ❑ L-12010 [M] | The Firehouse Five Story, Volume 1 | 1955 | 30.00 |



**Except when noted otherwise, VG = 25% of NM, and VG+ = 50% of NM. (Example: VG = $2.00, VG+ = $4.00 and NM = $8.00.)**

| Number | Title (A Side/B Side) | Yr | NM |
|---|---|---|---|
| ❑ L-12011 [M] | The Firehouse Five Story, Volume 2 | 1955 | 30.00 |
| ❑ L-12012 [M] | The Firehouse Five Story, Volume 3 | 1955 | 30.00 |
| ❑ L-12014 [M] | The Firehouse Five Plus Two Plays for Lovers | 1955 | 30.00 |
| ❑ L-12018 [M] | The Firehouse Five Plus Two Goes South! | 1955 | 30.00 |
| ❑ L-12028 [M] | The Firehouse Five Plus Two Goes to Sea | 1957 | 30.00 |
| ❑ L-12038 [M] | The Firehouse Five Plus Two Crashes a Party | 1960 | 30.00 |
| ❑ L-12040 [M] | Dixieland Favorites | 1960 | 30.00 |
| ❑ L-12044 [M] | Around the World | 1961 | 30.00 |
| ❑ L-12049 [M] | The Firehouse Five Plus Two at Disneyland | 1962 | 30.00 |
| ❑ L-12052 [M] | The Firehouse Five Plus Two Goes to a Fire | 1964 | 25.00 |
| ❑ L-12054 [M] | Twenty Years Later | 196? | 25.00 |

### STEREO RECORDS

| Number | Title (A Side/B Side) | Yr | NM |
|---|---|---|---|
| ❑ S-7005 [S] | The Firehouse Five Plus Two Goes to Sea | 1959 | 40.00 |

## FIRESIGN THEATRE, THE

### BUTTERFLY

| Number | Title (A Side/B Side) | Yr | NM |
|---|---|---|---|
| ❑ 001 | Jost Folks...A Firesign Chat | 1977 | 10.00 |

### COLUMBIA

| Number | Title (A Side/B Side) | Yr | NM |
|---|---|---|---|
| ❑ CL 2718 [M] | Waiting for the Electrician or Someone Like Him | 1968 | 25.00 |
| ❑ CS 9518 [S] | Waiting for the Electrician or Someone Like Him | 1968 | 15.00 |
| *—"360 Sound" label* | | | |
| ❑ CS 9884 | How Can You Be in Two Places at Once When You're Not Anywhere at All | 1969 | 15.00 |
| *—"360 Sound" label* | | | |
| ❑ C 30102 | Don't Crush That Dwarf, Hand Me the Pliers | 1970 | 15.00 |
| ❑ C 30737 | I Think We're All Bozos on This Bus | 1971 | 15.00 |
| ❑ CQ 30737 [Q] | I Think We're All Bozos on This Bus | 1972 | 20.00 |
| ❑ KG 31099 [(2)] | Dear Friends | 1972 | 20.00 |
| ❑ KC 31585 | Not Insane or Anything You Want To | 1972 | 15.00 |
| ❑ KC 32411 | David Ossman's How Time Flys | 1973 | 12.00 |
| ❑ KC 32730 | The Tale of the Giant Rat of Sumatra | 1974 | 12.00 |
| ❑ CQ 33141 [Q] | Everything You Know Is Wrong | 1974 | 20.00 |
| ❑ KC 33141 | Everything You Know Is Wrong | 1974 | 12.00 |
| ❑ PC 33475 | In the Next World You're On Your Own | 1975 | 12.00 |
| ❑ PG 34391 [(2)] | Forward Into the Past (An Anthology) | 1977 | 15.00 |

### MERCURY

| Number | Title (A Side/B Side) | Yr | NM |
|---|---|---|---|
| ❑ 826452-1 | Eat or Be Eaten | 1985 | 10.00 |

### RHINO

| Number | Title (A Side/B Side) | Yr | NM |
|---|---|---|---|
| ❑ RNLP-018 | Fighting Clowns | 1979 | 12.00 |
| ❑ RNEP-506 [EP] | Nick Danger, Third Eye | 1983 | 10.00 |
| ❑ RNLP-806 | Lawyer's Hospital | 1981 | 12.00 |
| ❑ RNLP-807 | Shakespeare's Lost Comedie | 1982 | 12.00 |
| ❑ RNLP-812 | Nick Danger In: The Three Faces of Al | 1984 | 12.00 |
| ❑ RNLP-904 | Reagan/Carter | 1980 | 12.00 |

## FIRM, THE

### ATLANTIC

| Number | Title (A Side/B Side) | Yr | NM |
|---|---|---|---|
| ❑ PR 883 [DJ] | Talks Business | 1985 | 20.00 |
| *—Promo-only music and interview album* | | | |
| ❑ 81239 | The Firm | 1985 | 8.00 |
| ❑ 81628 | Mean Business | 1986 | 8.00 |

## FIRST EDITION, THE

### JOLLY ROGERS

| Number | Title (A Side/B Side) | Yr | NM |
|---|---|---|---|
| ❑ 5001 | Backroads | 1973 | 15.00 |
| ❑ 5003 | Rollin' | 1974 | 15.00 |
| ❑ 5004 | Monumental | 1974 | 15.00 |
| *—All the above as "Kenny Rogers and the First Edition"* | | | |

### MCA

| Number | Title (A Side/B Side) | Yr | NM |
|---|---|---|---|
| ❑ 912 | Love Songs | 1984 | 8.00 |
| ❑ 913 | Country Songs | 1984 | 8.00 |
| ❑ 942 | Hits and Pieces | 1985 | 8.00 |
| ❑ 943 | The 60's Revisited | 1985 | 8.00 |
| ❑ 944 | Pieces of Calico Silver | 1985 | 8.00 |
| ❑ 1460 | Greatest Hits | 1985 | 8.00 |
| *—Reissue of Reprise 6437* | | | |

### REPRISE

| Number | Title (A Side/B Side) | Yr | NM |
|---|---|---|---|
| ❑ MS 2039 | Transition | 1971 | 20.00 |
| *—As "Kenny Rogers and the First Edition"* | | | |
| ❑ R-6276 [M] | The First Edition | 1967 | 30.00 |
| ❑ RS-6276 [S] | The First Edition | 1967 | 25.00 |
| ❑ RS-6302 | The First Edition's Second | 1968 | 25.00 |
| ❑ RS-6328 | The First Edition '69 | 1969 | 25.00 |
| ❑ RS-6352 | Ruby, Don't Take Your Love to Town | 1969 | 20.00 |
| *—Starting above, as "Kenny Rogers and the First Edition"* | | | |
| ❑ RS-6385 | Something's Burning | 1970 | 20.00 |
| ❑ RS-6412 | Tell It All Brother | 1970 | 20.00 |
| ❑ RS-6437 | Greatest Hits | 1971 | 20.00 |
| ❑ 2XS 6476 [(2)] | The Ballad of Calico | 1972 | 25.00 |
| ❑ ST-92060 | Ruby, Don't Take Your Love to Town | 1969 | 25.00 |
| *—Capitol Record Club edition* | | | |

### WARNER SPECIAL PRODUCTS

| Number | Title (A Side/B Side) | Yr | NM |
|---|---|---|---|
| ❑ OP-2514 [(2)] | Kenny Rogers and the First Edition | 1979 | 15.00 |
| *—Manufactured for Lakeshore Music* | | | |

## FIRST JAZZ PIANO QUARTET, THE

### WARNER BROS.

| Number | Title (A Side/B Side) | Yr | NM |
|---|---|---|---|
| ❑ W 1274 [M] | The First Jazz Piano Quartet | 1959 | 25.00 |
| ❑ WS 1274 [S] | The First Jazz Piano Quartet | 1959 | 30.00 |

## FISCHER, CLARE

### COLUMBIA

| Number | Title (A Side/B Side) | Yr | NM |
|---|---|---|---|
| ❑ CL 2691 [M] | Songs for Rainy Day Lovers | 1967 | 25.00 |

### PACIFIC JAZZ

| Number | Title (A Side/B Side) | Yr | NM |
|---|---|---|---|
| ❑ PJ-52 [M] | First Time Out | 1962 | 25.00 |
| ❑ ST-52 [S] | First Time Out | 1962 | 30.00 |
| ❑ PJ-67 [M] | Surging Ahead | 1963 | 25.00 |
| ❑ ST-67 [S] | Surging Ahead | 1963 | 30.00 |
| ❑ PJ-77 [M] | Extension | 1963 | 25.00 |
| ❑ ST-77 [S] | Extension | 1963 | 30.00 |
| ❑ ST-20096 [S] | Manteca | 1966 | 20.00 |

### WORLD PACIFIC

| Number | Title (A Side/B Side) | Yr | NM |
|---|---|---|---|
| ❑ WP-1830 [M] | So Danco Samba | 1964 | 20.00 |
| ❑ ST-21830 [S] | So Danco Samba | 1964 | 25.00 |

## FISCHER, WILD MAN

### REPRISE

| Number | Title (A Side/B Side) | Yr | NM |
|---|---|---|---|
| ❑ 2XS 6332 [(2)] | An Evening with Wild Man Fischer | 1969 | 50.00 |

### RHINO

| Number | Title (A Side/B Side) | Yr | NM |
|---|---|---|---|
| ❑ RNLP-001 | Wildmania | 1978 | 15.00 |
| ❑ RNLP-021 | Pronounced Normal | 1981 | 10.00 |
| ❑ RNLP-022 | Nothing Scary | 1981 | 10.00 |

## FISCHOFF, GEORGE

### MMG

| Number | Title (A Side/B Side) | Yr | NM |
|---|---|---|---|
| ❑ 1140 | Pretty Kitty: The Piano Magic of George Fischoff | 1982 | 20.00 |

## FISELE, JERRY

### DELMAR

| Number | Title (A Side/B Side) | Yr | NM |
|---|---|---|---|
| ❑ DL-101 [10] | Jerry Fisele and the Fabulous Windy City Six | 1954 | 50.00 |

## FISHER, AL, AND LOU MARKS

### CAMEO

| Number | Title (A Side/B Side) | Yr | NM |
|---|---|---|---|
| ❑ C-1081 [M] | Rome on the Range | 1964 | 20.00 |

### SWAN

| Number | Title (A Side/B Side) | Yr | NM |
|---|---|---|---|
| ❑ SLP-514 [M] | It's a Beatle (Coo-Coo) World | 1964 | 40.00 |

## FISHER, CHIP

### RCA VICTOR

| Number | Title (A Side/B Side) | Yr | NM |
|---|---|---|---|
| ❑ LPM-1797 [M] | Chipper at the Sugar Bowl | 1958 | 40.00 |
| ❑ LSP-1797 [S] | Chipper at the Sugar Bowl | 1958 | 50.00 |

## FISHER, EDDIE

### DOT

| Number | Title (A Side/B Side) | Yr | NM |
|---|---|---|---|
| ❑ DLP-3631 [M] | Eddie Fisher Today! | 1965 | 12.00 |
| ❑ DLP-3648 [M] | When I Was Young | 1965 | 12.00 |
| ❑ DLP-3658 [M] | Mary Christmas | 1965 | 15.00 |
| ❑ DLP-3670 [M] | Young and Foolish | 1966 | 12.00 |
| ❑ DLP-3785 [M] | His Greatest Hits | 1967 | 12.00 |
| ❑ DLP-25361 [S] | Eddie Fisher Today! | 1965 | 15.00 |
| ❑ DLP-25648 [S] | When I Was Young | 1965 | 15.00 |
| ❑ DLP-25658 [S] | Mary Christmas | 1965 | 20.00 |
| ❑ DLP-25670 [S] | Young and Foolish | 1966 | 15.00 |
| ❑ DLP-25785 [S] | His Greatest Hits | 1967 | 15.00 |

### MCA

| Number | Title (A Side/B Side) | Yr | NM |
|---|---|---|---|
| ❑ 1549 | The Best of Eddie Fisher | 1983 | 8.00 |

### PICKWICK

| Number | Title (A Side/B Side) | Yr | NM |
|---|---|---|---|
| ❑ SPC-3141 | Oh My Papa | 196? | 12.00 |

### RAMROD

| Number | Title (A Side/B Side) | Yr | NM |
|---|---|---|---|
| ❑ RR-1 [(2)M] | Eddie Fisher at the Winter Garden | 1963 | 15.00 |
| ❑ RRS-1 [(2)S] | Eddie Fisher at the Winter Garden | 1963 | 20.00 |

### RCA CAMDEN

| Number | Title (A Side/B Side) | Yr | NM |
|---|---|---|---|
| ❑ CAL-789 [M] | Bring Back the Thrill | 196? | 12.00 |
| ❑ CAS-789 [R] | Bring Back the Thrill | 196? | 10.00 |

### RCA VICTOR

| Number | Title (A Side/B Side) | Yr | NM |
|---|---|---|---|
| ❑ LOC-1024 [M] | Academy Award Winners | 1955 | 40.00 |
| ❑ LPM-1097 [M] | I Love You | 1955 | 30.00 |
| ❑ ANL1-1138 | Eddie Fisher's Greatest Hits | 1975 | 8.00 |
| ❑ LPM-1180 [M] | I'm in the Mood for Love | 1955 | 30.00 |
| ❑ LPM-1181 [M] | May I Sing to You? | 1955 | 30.00 |
| ❑ LPM-1399 [M] | Bundle of Joy | 1957 | 30.00 |
| ❑ LPM-1548 [M] | Thinking of You | 1957 | 30.00 |
| ❑ LPM-1647 [M] | As Long As There's Music | 1958 | 30.00 |
| ❑ LSP-1647 [S] | As Long As There's Music | 1958 | 50.00 |
| ❑ LPM-2504 [M] | Eddie Fisher's Greatest Hits | 1962 | 15.00 |
| ❑ LSP-2504 [S] | Eddie Fisher's Greatest Hits | 1962 | 20.00 |
| ❑ LPM-3025 [10] | Fisher Sings | 1952 | 50.00 |
| ❑ LPM-3058 [10] | I'm in the Mood for Love | 1952 | 50.00 |
| ❑ LPM-3065 [10] | Christmas with Eddie Fisher | 1952 | 50.00 |
| ❑ LPM-3122 [10] | Irving Berlin Favorites | 1953 | 50.00 |
| ❑ LPM-3185 [10] | May I Sing to You? | 1953 | 50.00 |
| ❑ LPM-3375 [M] | The Best of Eddie Fisher | 1965 | 15.00 |
| ❑ LSP-3375 [R] | The Best of Eddie Fisher | 1965 | 12.00 |
| ❑ LPM-3726 [M] | Games That Lovers Play | 1966 | 15.00 |
| ❑ LSP-3726 [S] | Games That Lovers Play | 1966 | 15.00 |
| ❑ LPM-3820 [M] | People Like You | 1967 | 20.00 |
| ❑ LSP-3820 [S] | People Like You | 1967 | 12.00 |
| ❑ LSP-3914 | You Ain't Heard Nothin' Yet | 1968 | 12.00 |

## FISHER, TONI

### SIGNET

| Number | Title (A Side/B Side) | Yr | NM |
|---|---|---|---|
| ❑ WP-509 [S] | The Big Hurt | 1960 | 50.00 |
| *—Issued in "Stereomonic"* | | | |

## FITCH, MAL

### EMARCY

| Number | Title (A Side/B Side) | Yr | NM |
|---|---|---|---|
| ❑ MG-36041 [M] | Mal Fitch | 1956 | 50.00 |

## FITZGERALD, ELLA

### CAPITOL

| Number | Title (A Side/B Side) | Yr | NM |
|---|---|---|---|
| ❑ T 2685 [M] | Brighten the Corner | 1967 | 20.00 |
| ❑ T 2805 [M] | Ella Fitzgerald's Christmas | 1967 | 20.00 |

### DECCA

| Number | Title (A Side/B Side) | Yr | NM |
|---|---|---|---|
| ❑ DXB 156 [(2)M] | The Best of Ella | 1959 | 40.00 |
| *—Black labels, silver print* | | | |
| ❑ DXB 156 [(2)M] | The Best of Ella | 1961 | 25.00 |
| *—Black labels with color bars* | | | |
| ❑ DL 4129 [M] | Golden Favorites | 1961 | 20.00 |
| ❑ DL 5084 [10] | Souvenir Album | 1950 | 120.00 |
| ❑ DL 5300 [10] | Ella Fitzgerald Sings Gershwin Songs | 1951 | 120.00 |
| ❑ DXSB 7156 [(2)R] | The Best of Ella | 196? | 20.00 |
| ❑ DL 8068 [M] | Songs in a Mellow Mood | 1954 | 50.00 |
| ❑ DL 8149 [M] | Lullabies of Birdland | 1955 | 50.00 |
| ❑ DL 8155 [M] | Sweet and Hot | 1955 | 50.00 |
| ❑ DL 8378 [M] | Ella Sings Gershwin | 1957 | 40.00 |
| ❑ DL 8477 [M] | Ella and Her Fellas | 1957 | 40.00 |
| ❑ DL 8695 [M] | The First Lady of Song | 1958 | 40.00 |
| ❑ DL 8696 [M] | Miss Ella Fitzgerald and Mr. Nelson Riddle Invite You to Listen and Relax | 1958 | 40.00 |
| ❑ DL 8832 [M] | For Sentimental Reasons | 1958 | 40.00 |

### VERVE

| Number | Title (A Side/B Side) | Yr | NM |
|---|---|---|---|
| ❑ V-10-4 [(4)M] | Ella Fitzgerald Sings the Duke Ellington Song Book | 196? | 50.00 |
| ❑ V-29-5 [(5)M] | Ella Fitzgerald Sings the George and Ira Gershwin Song Book | 196? | 100.00 |
| *—Reissue of MGV-4029* | | | |
| ❑ V6-29-5 [(5)S] | Ella Fitzgerald Sings the George and Ira Gershwin Song Book | 196? | 100.00 |
| *—Reissue of MGVS-6082* | | | |
| ❑ MGV-4001-2 [(2)M] | Ella Fitzgerald Sings the Cole Porter Song Book | 1956 | 80.00 |
| ❑ V-4001-2 [(2)M] | Ella Fitzgerald Sings the Cole Porter Song Book | 1961 | 25.00 |
| ❑ MGV-4002-2 [(2)M] | Ella Fitzgerald Sings the Rodgers & Hart Song Book | 1956 | 80.00 |
| ❑ V-4002-2 [(2)M] | Ella Fitzgerald Sings the Rodgers and Hart Song Book | 1961 | 25.00 |
| ❑ MGV-4004 [M] | Like Someone in Love | 1957 | 50.00 |
| ❑ V-4004 [M] | Like Someone in Love | 1961 | 20.00 |
| ❑ V6-4004 [S] | Like Someone in Love | 1961 | 20.00 |
| ❑ MGV-4008-2 [(2)M] | Ella Fitzgerald Sings the Duke Ellington Song Book, Vol. 1 | 1957 | 80.00 |
| ❑ V-4008-2 [(2)M] | Ella Fitzgerald Sings the Duke Ellington Song Book, Vol. 1 | 1961 | 25.00 |
| ❑ MGV-4009-2 [(2)M] | Ella Fitzgerald Sings the Duke Ellington Song Book, Vol. 2 | 1957 | 80.00 |
| ❑ V-4009-2 [(2)M] | Ella Fitzgerald Sings the Duke Ellington Song Book, Vol. 2 | 1961 | 25.00 |
| ❑ MGV-4010-4 [(4)M] | Ella Fitzgerald Sings the Duke Ellington Song Book | 1957 | 150.00 |
| *—Combines 4008 and 4009 into one package* | | | |
| ❑ MGV-4013 [M] | Ella Fitzgerald Sings the Gershwin Song Book | 1957 | 50.00 |
| ❑ MGV-4019-2 [(2)M] | Ella Fitzgerald Sings the Irving Berlin Song Book | 1958 | 80.00 |
| ❑ V-4019-2 [(2)M] | Ella Fitzgerald Sings the Irving Berlin Song Book | 1961 | 25.00 |
| ❑ V6-4019-2 [(2)S] | Ella Fitzgerald Sings the Irving Berlin Song Book | 1961 | 25.00 |
| ❑ MGV-4021 [M] | Ella Swings Lightly | 1958 | 50.00 |
| ❑ V-4021 [M] | Ella Swings Lightly | 1961 | 20.00 |
| ❑ V6-4021 [S] | Ella Swings Lightly | 1961 | 20.00 |
| ❑ MGV-4022 [M] | Ella Fitzgerald Sings the Rodgers & Hart Song Book, Vol. 1 | 1959 | 50.00 |

| Number | Title (A Side/B Side) | Yr | NM |
|---|---|---|---|
| ❑ V-4022 [M] | Ella Fitzgerald Sings the Rodgers & Hart Song Book, Vol. 1 | 1961 | 20.00 |
| ❑ V6-4022 [S] | Ella Fitzgerald Sings the Rodgers & Hart Song Book, Vol. 1 | 1961 | 20.00 |
| ❑ MGV-4023 [M] | Ella Fitzgerald Sings the Rodgers & Hart Song Book, Vol. 2 | 1959 | 50.00 |
| ❑ V-4023 [M] | Ella Fitzgerald Sings the Rodgers & Hart Song Book, Vol. 2 | 1961 | 20.00 |
| ❑ V6-4023 [S] | Ella Fitzgerald Sings the Rodgers & Hart Song Book, Vol. 2 | 1961 | 20.00 |
| ❑ MGV-4024 [M] | Ella Fitzgerald Sings the George and Ira Gershwin Song Book, Vol. 1 | 1959 | 50.00 |
| ❑ V-4024 [M] | Ella Fitzgerald Sings the George and Ira Gershwin Song Book, Vol. 1 | 1961 | 20.00 |
| ❑ V6-4024 [S] | Ella Fitzgerald Sings the George and Ira Gershwin Song Book, Vol. 1 | 1961 | 20.00 |
| ❑ MGV-4025 [M] | Ella Fitzgerald Sings the George and Ira Gershwin Song Book, Vol. 2 | 1959 | 50.00 |
| ❑ V-4025 [M] | Ella Fitzgerald Sings the George and Ira Gershwin Song Book, Vol. 2 | 1961 | 20.00 |
| ❑ V6-4025 [S] | Ella Fitzgerald Sings the George and Ira Gershwin Song Book, Vol. 2 | 1961 | 20.00 |
| ❑ MGV-4026 [M] | Ella Fitzgerald Sings the George and Ira Gershwin Song Book, Vol. 3 | 1959 | 50.00 |
| ❑ V-4026 [M] | Ella Fitzgerald Sings the George and Ira Gershwin Song Book, Vol. 3 | 1961 | 20.00 |
| ❑ V6-4026 [S] | Ella Fitzgerald Sings the George and Ira Gershwin Song Book, Vol. 3 | 1961 | 20.00 |
| ❑ MGV-4027 [M] | Ella Fitzgerald Sings the George and Ira Gershwin Song Book, Vol. 4 | 1959 | 50.00 |
| ❑ V-4027 [M] | Ella Fitzgerald Sings the George and Ira Gershwin Song Book, Vol. 4 | 1961 | 20.00 |
| ❑ V6-4027 [S] | Ella Fitzgerald Sings the George and Ira Gershwin Song Book, Vol. 4 | 1961 | 20.00 |
| ❑ MGV-4028 [M] | Ella Fitzgerald Sings the George and Ira Gershwin Song Book, Vol. 5 | 1959 | 50.00 |
| ❑ V-4028 [M] | Ella Fitzgerald Sings the George and Ira Gershwin Song Book, Vol. 5 | 1961 | 20.00 |
| ❑ V6-4028 [S] | Ella Fitzgerald Sings the George and Ira Gershwin Song Book, Vol. 5 | 1961 | 20.00 |
| ❑ MGV-4029-5 [(5)M] | Ella Fitzgerald Sings the George and Ira Gershwin Song Book | 1959 | 250.00 |

*—Box set with 4024 through 4028 plus bonus 10-inch LP*

| Number | Title (A Side/B Side) | Yr | NM |
|---|---|---|---|
| ❑ MGV-4029-5 [(5)M] | Ella Fitzgerald Sings the George and Ira Gershwin Song Book | 1959 | 500.00 |

*—Box set with 4024 through 4028 plus bonus 10-inch LP, all in walnut box with leather pockets*

| Number | Title (A Side/B Side) | Yr | NM |
|---|---|---|---|
| ❑ MGV-4030 [M] | Ella Fitzgerald Sings the Irving Berlin Song Book, Vol. 1 | 1959 | 50.00 |
| ❑ V-4030 [M] | Ella Fitzgerald Sings the Irving Berlin Song Book, Vol. 1 | 1961 | 20.00 |
| ❑ V6-4030 [S] | Ella Fitzgerald Sings the Irving Berlin Song Book, Vol. 1 | 1961 | 20.00 |
| ❑ MGV-4031 [M] | Ella Fitzgerald Sings the Irving Berlin Song Book, Vol. 2 | 1959 | 50.00 |
| ❑ V-4031 [M] | Ella Fitzgerald Sings the Irving Berlin Song Book, Vol. 2 | 1961 | 20.00 |
| ❑ V6-4031 [S] | Ella Fitzgerald Sings the Irving Berlin Song Book, Vol. 2 | 1961 | 20.00 |
| ❑ MGV-4032 [M] | Sweet Songs for Swingers | 1959 | 50.00 |
| ❑ V-4032 [M] | Sweet Songs for Swingers | 1961 | 20.00 |
| ❑ V6-4032 [S] | Sweet Songs for Swingers | 1961 | 20.00 |
| ❑ MGV-4034 [M] | Hello, Love | 1959 | 50.00 |
| ❑ V-4034 [M] | Hello, Love | 1961 | 20.00 |
| ❑ V6-4034 [S] | Hello, Love | 1961 | 20.00 |
| ❑ MGV-4036 [M] | Get Happy! | 1960 | 40.00 |
| ❑ V-4036 [M] | Get Happy! | 1961 | 20.00 |
| ❑ V6-4036 [S] | Get Happy! | 1961 | 20.00 |
| ❑ MGV-4041 [M] | Mack the Knife — Ella in Berlin | 1960 | 40.00 |
| ❑ V-4041 [M] | Mack the Knife — Ella in Berlin | 1961 | 20.00 |
| ❑ V6-4041 [S] | Mack the Knife — Ella in Berlin | 1961 | 20.00 |
| ❑ MGV-4042 [M] | Ella Wishes You a Swinging Christmas | 1960 | 50.00 |
| ❑ V-4042 [M] | Ella Wishes You a Swinging Christmas | 1961 | 40.00 |
| ❑ V6-4042 [S] | Ella Wishes You a Swinging Christmas | 1961 | 50.00 |
| ❑ MGV-4043 [M] | Let No Man Write My Epitaph | 1961 | 40.00 |

| Number | Title (A Side/B Side) | Yr | NM |
|---|---|---|---|
| ❑ V-4043 [M] | Let No Man Write My Epitaph | 1961 | 20.00 |
| ❑ V6-4043 [S] | Let No Man Write My Epitaph | 1961 | 20.00 |
| ❑ MGV-4046-2 [(2)M] | Ella Fitzgerald Sings the Harold Arlen Song Book | 1961 | 60.00 |
| ❑ MGV-4049 [M] | Ella Fitzgerald Sings Cole Porter | 1961 | 40.00 |
| ❑ V-4049 [M] | Ella Fitzgerald Sings Cole Porter | 1961 | 20.00 |
| ❑ MGV-4050 [M] | Ella Fitzgerald Sings More Cole Porter | 1961 | 40.00 |
| ❑ V-4050 [M] | Ella Fitzgerald Sings More Cole Porter | 1961 | 20.00 |
| ❑ MGV-4052 [M] | Ella in Hollywood | 1961 | 40.00 |
| ❑ V-4052 [M] | Ella in Hollywood | 1961 | 20.00 |
| ❑ V-4053 [M] | Clap Hands, Here Comes Charley | 1962 | 40.00 |
| ❑ V6-4053 [S] | Clap Hands, Here Comes Charley | 1962 | 150.00 |
| ❑ V-4054 [M] | Ella Swings Brightly with Nelson | 1962 | 30.00 |
| ❑ V6-4054 [S] | Ella Swings Brightly with Nelson | 1962 | 30.00 |
| ❑ V-4055 [M] | Ella Swings Gently with Nelson | 1962 | 30.00 |
| ❑ V6-4055 [S] | Ella Swings Gently with Nelson | 1962 | 30.00 |
| ❑ V-4056 [M] | Rhythm Is My Business | 1962 | 30.00 |
| ❑ V6-4056 [S] | Rhythm Is My Business | 1962 | 30.00 |
| ❑ V-4057 [M] | Ella Fitzgerald Sings the Harold Arlen Song Book, Vol. 1 | 1962 | 30.00 |
| ❑ V6-4057 [S] | Ella Fitzgerald Sings the Harold Arlen Song Book, Vol. 1 | 1962 | 30.00 |
| ❑ V-4058 [M] | Ella Fitzgerald Sings the Harold Arlen Song Book, Vol. 2 | 1962 | 30.00 |
| ❑ V6-4058 [S] | Ella Fitzgerald Sings the Harold Arlen Song Book, Vol. 2 | 1962 | 30.00 |
| ❑ V-4059 [M] | Ella Sings Broadway | 1963 | 25.00 |
| ❑ V6-4059 [S] | Ella Sings Broadway | 1963 | 25.00 |
| ❑ V-4060 [M] | Ella Fitzgerald Sings the Jerome Kern Song Book | 1963 | 25.00 |
| ❑ V6-4060 [S] | Ella Fitzgerald Sings the Jerome Kern Song Book | 1963 | 25.00 |
| ❑ V-4062 [M] | These Are the Blues | 1963 | 25.00 |
| ❑ V6-4062 [S] | These Are the Blues | 1963 | 25.00 |
| ❑ V-4064 [M] | Hello, Dolly! | 1964 | 25.00 |
| ❑ V6-4064 [S] | Hello, Dolly! | 1964 | 25.00 |
| ❑ V-4065 [M] | Ella at Juan Les Pins | 1964 | 25.00 |
| ❑ V6-4065 [S] | Ella at Juan Les Pins | 1964 | 25.00 |
| ❑ V-4066 [M] | A Tribute to Cole Porter | 1964 | 25.00 |
| ❑ V6-4066 [S] | A Tribute to Cole Porter | 1964 | 25.00 |
| ❑ V-4067 [M] | Ella Fitzgerald Sings the Johnny Mercer Song Book | 1965 | 20.00 |
| ❑ V6-4067 [S] | Ella Fitzgerald Sings the Johnny Mercer Song Book | 1965 | 20.00 |
| ❑ V-4068 [M] | Porgy & Bess | 1965 | 20.00 |
| ❑ V6-4068 [S] | Porgy & Bess | 1965 | 20.00 |
| ❑ V-4069 [M] | Ella in Hamburg | 1966 | 20.00 |
| ❑ V6-4069 [S] | Ella in Hamburg | 1966 | 20.00 |
| ❑ V-4070 [M] | Ella at Duke's Place | 1966 | 20.00 |
| ❑ V6-4070 [S] | Ella at Duke's Place | 1966 | 20.00 |
| ❑ V-4071 [M] | Whisper Not | 1966 | 20.00 |
| ❑ V6-4071 [S] | Whisper Not | 1966 | 20.00 |
| ❑ V-4072 [(2)M] | Ella & Duke at Cote d'Azur | 1967 | 40.00 |
| ❑ MGVS-6000 [S] | Like Someone in Love | 1960 | 40.00 |
| ❑ MGVS-6005-2 [(2)S] | Ella Fitzgerald Sings the Irving Berlin Song Book | 1960 | 60.00 |
| ❑ MGVS-6009 [S] | Ella Fitzgerald Sings the Rodgers & Hart Song Book, Vol. 1 | 1960 | 40.00 |
| ❑ MGVS-6010 [S] | Ella Fitzgerald Sings the Rodgers & Hart Song Book, Vol. 2 | 1960 | 40.00 |
| ❑ MGVS-6019 [S] | Ella Swings Lightly | 1960 | 40.00 |
| ❑ MGVS-6026 [S] | Ella Fitzgerald at the Opera House | 1960 | 40.00 |
| ❑ MGVS-6052 [S] | Ella Fitzgerald Sings the Irving Berlin Song Book, Vol. 1 | 1960 | 40.00 |
| ❑ MGVS-6053 [S] | Ella Fitzgerald Sings the Irving Berlin Song Book, Vol. 2 | 1960 | 40.00 |
| ❑ MGVS-6072 [S] | Sweet Songs for Swingers | 1960 | 40.00 |
| ❑ MGVS-6077 [S] | Ella Fitzgerald Sings the George and Ira Gershwin Song Book, Vol. 1 | 1960 | 40.00 |
| ❑ MGVS-6078 [S] | Ella Fitzgerald Sings the George and Ira Gershwin Song Book, Vol. 2 | 1960 | 40.00 |
| ❑ MGVS-6079 [S] | Ella Fitzgerald Sings the George and Ira Gershwin Song Book, Vol. 3 | 1960 | 40.00 |
| ❑ MGVS-6080 [S] | Ella Fitzgerald Sings the George and Ira Gershwin Song Book, Vol. 4 | 1960 | 40.00 |
| ❑ MGVS-6081 [S] | Ella Fitzgerald Sings the George and Ira Gershwin Song Book, Vol. 5 | 1960 | 40.00 |
| ❑ MGVS-6082-5 [(5)S] | Ella Fitzgerald Sings the George and Ira Gershwin Song Book | 1960 | 200.00 |

*—Box set with 6077 through 6081 plus bonus 10-inch LP*

| Number | Title (A Side/B Side) | Yr | NM |
|---|---|---|---|
| ❑ MGVS-6100 [S] | Hello, Love | 1960 | 40.00 |
| ❑ MGVS-6102 [S] | Get Happy! | 1960 | 40.00 |

| Number | Title (A Side/B Side) | Yr | NM |
|---|---|---|---|
| ❑ MGVS-6163 [S] | Mack the Knife — Ella in Berlin | 1960 | 40.00 |
| ❑ MGVS-7000 [S] | Ella Fitzgerald Sings the Gershwin Song Book | 1959 | 50.00 |
| ❑ MGV-8264 [M] | Ella Fitzgerald at the Opera House | 1958 | 50.00 |
| ❑ V-8264 [M] | Ella Fitzgerald at the Opera House | 1961 | 20.00 |
| ❑ V6-8264 [S] | Ella Fitzgerald at the Opera House | 1961 | 20.00 |
| ❑ MGV-8288 [M] | One O'Clock Jump | 1958 | 50.00 |
| ❑ V-8288 [M] | One O'Clock Jump | 1961 | 20.00 |
| ❑ V-8745 [M] | Ella "Live" | 1968 | 30.00 |
| ❑ MGVS-64041 [S] | Mack the Knife — Ella in Berlin | 1960 | 50.00 |
| ❑ MGVS-64042 [S] | Ella Wishes You a Swinging Christmas | 1960 | 60.00 |
| ❑ SMAS-90644 [S] | Ella at Duke's Place | 1966 | 25.00 |

*—Capitol Record Club edition*

| Number | Title (A Side/B Side) | Yr | NM |
|---|---|---|---|
| ❑ 825024-1 [(5)] | The George and Ira Gershwin Songbook (Complete) | 198? | 25.00 |

**FITZGERALD, ELLA, AND LOUIS ARMSTRONG** Also see each artist's individual listings.

MOBILE FIDELITY

| Number | Title (A Side/B Side) | Yr | NM |
|---|---|---|---|
| ❑ 2-248 [(2)] | Ella and Louis Again | 1996 | 150.00 |

*—Audiophile vinyl*

VERVE

| Number | Title (A Side/B Side) | Yr | NM |
|---|---|---|---|
| ❑ MGV-4003 [M] | Ella and Louis | 1956 | 50.00 |
| ❑ V-4003 [M] | Ella and Louis | 1961 | 20.00 |
| ❑ MGV-4006-2 [(2)M] | Ella and Louis Again | 1956 | 80.00 |
| ❑ V-4006-2 [(2)M] | Ella and Louis Again | 1961 | 25.00 |
| ❑ MGV-4011-2 [(2)M] | Porgy and Bess | 1957 | 80.00 |
| ❑ V-4011-2 [(2)M] | Porgy and Bess | 1961 | 25.00 |
| ❑ V6-4011-2 [(2)S] | Porgy and Bess | 1961 | 25.00 |
| ❑ MGV-4017 [M] | Ella and Louis Again, Vol. 1 | 1958 | 50.00 |
| ❑ V-4017 [M] | Ella and Louis Again, Vol. 1 | 1961 | 20.00 |
| ❑ MGV-4018 [M] | Ella and Louis Again, Vol. 2 | 1958 | 50.00 |
| ❑ V-4018 [M] | Ella and Louis Again, Vol. 2 | 1961 | 20.00 |
| ❑ MGVS-6040-2 [(2)S] | Porgy and Bess | 1960 | 60.00 |

**FITZGERALD, ELLA, AND COUNT BASIE**

VERVE

| Number | Title (A Side/B Side) | Yr | NM |
|---|---|---|---|
| ❑ V-4061 [M] | Ella and Basie! | 1963 | 25.00 |
| ❑ V6-4061 [S] | Ella and Basie! | 1963 | 25.00 |
| ❑ ST-90028 [S] | Ella and Basie! | 1964 | 30.00 |

*—Capitol Record Club edition*

| Number | Title (A Side/B Side) | Yr | NM |
|---|---|---|---|
| ❑ T-90028 [M] | Ella and Basie! | 1964 | 30.00 |

*—Capitol Record Club edition*

**FITZGERALD, ELLA, AND BILLIE HOLIDAY** Also see each artist's individual listings.

AMERICAN RECORDING SOCIETY

| Number | Title (A Side/B Side) | Yr | NM |
|---|---|---|---|
| ❑ G-433 [M] | Ella Fitzgerald and Billie Holiday at Newport | 1957 | 40.00 |

VERVE

| Number | Title (A Side/B Side) | Yr | NM |
|---|---|---|---|
| ❑ MGVS-6022 [S] | Ella Fitzgerald and Billie Holiday at Newport | 1960 | 40.00 |
| ❑ MGV-8234 [M] | Ella Fitzgerald and Billie Holiday at Newport | 1958 | 50.00 |
| ❑ V-8234 [M] | Ella Fitzgerald and Billie Holiday at Newport | 1961 | 20.00 |
| ❑ V6-8234 [S] | Ella Fitzgerald and Billie Holiday at Newport | 1961 | 20.00 |

**FIVE, THE**

RCA VICTOR

| Number | Title (A Side/B Side) | Yr | NM |
|---|---|---|---|
| ❑ LPM-1121 [M] | The Five | 1955 | 80.00 |

**FIVE AMERICANS, THE**

ABNAK

| Number | Title (A Side/B Side) | Yr | NM |
|---|---|---|---|
| ❑ AB-1967 [M] | Western Union/Sound of Love | 1967 | 20.00 |
| ❑ AB-1969 [M] | Progressions | 1967 | 20.00 |
| ❑ ABST-2067 [S] | Western Union/Sound of Love | 1967 | 30.00 |
| ❑ ABST-2069 [S] | Progressions | 1967 | 30.00 |
| ❑ ABST-2071 [(2)] | Now and Then | 1968 | 25.00 |

HANNA-BARBERA

| Number | Title (A Side/B Side) | Yr | NM |
|---|---|---|---|
| ❑ HLP-8503 [M] | I See the Light | 1966 | 40.00 |
| ❑ HST-9503 [S] | I See the Light | 1966 | 60.00 |

**FIVE BROTHERS**

TAMPA

| Number | Title (A Side/B Side) | Yr | NM |
|---|---|---|---|
| ❑ TP-25 [M] | Five Brothers | 1957 | 150.00 |

*—Red vinyl*

| Number | Title (A Side/B Side) | Yr | NM |
|---|---|---|---|
| ❑ TP-25 [M] | Five Brothers | 1958 | 80.00 |

*—Black vinyl*

**FIVE BY FIVE**

PAULA

| Number | Title (A Side/B Side) | Yr | NM |
|---|---|---|---|
| ❑ LPS-2202 | Next Exit | 1969 | 25.00 |

**FIVE DISCS, THE**

CRYSTAL BALL

| Number | Title (A Side/B Side) | Yr | NM |
|---|---|---|---|
| ❑ 119 | Unchained | 1978 | 15.00 |

MAGIC CARPET

| Number | Title (A Side/B Side) | Yr | NM |
|---|---|---|---|
| ❑ 1002 | The Five Discs Sing Again | 1991 | 20.00 |

*—Dark blue cover*

Number | Title (A Side/B Side) | Yr | NM

### FIVE EMPREES, THE

FREEPORT
❑ 3001 [M] The Five Emprees 1965 50.00
❑ 3001 [M] Little Miss Sad 1966 30.00
*—Same LP, new title*
❑ 4001 [S] The Five Emprees 1965 60.00
❑ 4001 [S] Little Miss Sad 1966 40.00
*—Same LP, new title*

### FIVE KEYS, THE

ALADDIN
❑ LP-806 [M] The Best of the Five Keys 1956 2000.
*—Copies of Aladdin 806 entitled "On the Town" are bootlegs made in the 1970s; VG value 1000; VG+ value 1500*
CAPITOL
❑ T 828 [M] The Five Keys On Stage! 1957 300.00
*—On cover, the far left singer has his thumb sticking out (inadvertently?) in a phallic way*
❑ T 828 [M] The Five Keys On Stage! 1957 500.00
*—On cover, the far left singer's "offending" thumb is airbrushed out*
❑ M-1769 The Fantastic Five Keys 1977 20.00
*—Reissue with new prefix*
❑ T 1769 [M] The Fantastic Five Keys 1962 300.00
HARLEM HIT PARADE
❑ 5004 The Five Keys 1972 15.00
KING
❑ 688 [M] The Five Keys 1960 800.00
❑ 692 [M] Rhythm and Blues Hits, Past and Present 1960 600.00
❑ 5013 14 Hits 1978 12.00
SCORE
❑ LP-4003 [M] The Five Keys On the Town 1957 800.00
*—Reissue of Aladdin 806.*

### FIVE MAN ELECTRICAL BAND

CAPITOL
❑ ST-165 Five Man Electrical Band 1969 20.00
LION
❑ LN-1009 Sweet Paradise 1973 20.00
LIONEL
❑ LRS-1100 Good-Byes & Butterflies 1970 30.00
❑ LRS-1101 Coming of Age 1971 20.00
MGM
❑ SE-4725 Good-Byes & Butterflies 1970 50.00
PICKWICK
❑ SPC-3289 Five Man Electrical Band 1973 10.00
*—Reissue of Capitol material*

### FIVE ROYALES, THE

APOLLO
❑ LP-488 [M] The Rockin' 5 Royales 1956 1000.
*—Yellow label*
❑ LP-488 [M] The Rockin' 5 Royales 1956 2000.
*—Green label; VG value 1000; VG+ value 1500*
❑ LP-488 [M] The Rockin' 5 Royales 1956 4000.
*—Purple label; VG value 2000; VG+ value 3000*
KING
❑ 580 [M] Dedicated to You 1957 500.00
❑ 616 [M] The 5 Royales Sing for You 1959 400.00
❑ 678 [M] The Five Royales 1960 250.00
❑ 955 [M] 24 All Time Hits 1966 100.00
❑ 5014 17 Hits 197? 12.00

### FIVE SATINS, THE

BUDDAH
❑ BDS-5654 Black Satin 1976 15.00
*—As "Black Satin"*
CELEBRITY SHOWCASE
❑ JB-7671 The Best of the Five Satins 1970 20.00
COLLECTABLES
❑ COL-5017 The Five Satins Sing Their Greatest Hits 198? 10.00
ELEKTRA
❑ 60152 Fred Parris and the Satins 1982 20.00
EMBER
❑ ELP-100 [M] The Five Satins Sing 1957 600.00
*—Red label; group pictured on front cover; black vinyl*
❑ ELP-100 [M] The Five Satins Sing 1957 2000.
*—Red label; group pictured on front cover; blue vinyl; VG value 1000; VG+ value 1500*
❑ ELP-100 [M] The Five Satins Sing 1959 200.00
*—Mostly white "logs" label; no picture on cover*
❑ ELP-100 [M] The Five Satins Sing 1959 300.00
*—Mostly white "logs" label; group pictured on front cover*
❑ ELP-100 [M] The Five Satins Sing 1961 100.00
*—Black label; no picture on cover*
❑ ELP-401 [M] The Five Satins Encore 1960 200.00
*—Mostly white "logs" label*
❑ ELP-401 [M] The Five Satins Encore 1961 100.00
*—Black label*
LOST-NITE
❑ LLP-8 [10] The Five Satins 1981 10.00
*—Red vinyl*
❑ LLP-9 [10] The Five Satins 1981 10.00
*—Red vinyl*
MOUNT VERNON
❑ 108 The Five Satins Sing 196? 30.00
RELIC
❑ 5008 The Five Satins' Greatest Hits (1956-1959), Volume 1 198? 10.00
❑ 5013 The Five Satins' Greatest Hits (1956-1959), Volume 2 198? 10.00
❑ 5024 The Five Satins' Greatest Hits (1956-1959), Volume 3 198? 10.00

### FIVE SPECIAL

ELEKTRA
❑ 5E-553 Trak'n 1981 20.00

### FIVE STAIRSTEPS, THE

BUDDAH
❑ BDS-5008 Our Family Portrait 1967 20.00
❑ BDS-5061 Stairsteps 1970 15.00
*—As "Stairsteps"*
❑ BDS-5068 Step by Step by Step 1970 15.00
*—As "Stairsteps"*
COLLECTABLES
❑ COL-5023 Greatest Hits 1985 10.00
CURTOM
❑ 8002 Love's Happening 1969 20.00
WINDY C
❑ 6000 [M] The Five Stairsteps 1967 25.00
❑ S-6000 [S] The Five Stairsteps 1967 25.00

### FLACK, ROBERTA

ATLANTIC
❑ SD 1569 Chapter Two 1970 10.00
❑ SD 1594 Quiet Fire 1971 10.00
❑ QD 7271 [Q] Killing Me Softly 1973 15.00
❑ SD 7271 Killing Me Softly 1973 10.00
❑ SD 8230 First Take 1969 10.00
*—Red and green label (second edition)*
❑ SD 8230 First Take 1969 20.00
*—Brown and purple label (first edition)*
❑ SD 16013 Roberta Flack Featuring Donny Hathaway 1980 10.00
*—Only two tracks feature Mr. Hathaway*
❑ SD 18131 Feel Like Makin' Love 1974 10.00
❑ SD 19149 Blue Lights in the Basement 1977 10.00
❑ SD 19154 Killing Me Softly 1978 8.00
*—Reissue of 7271*
❑ SD 19186 Roberta Flack 1978 10.00
❑ SD 19317 The Best of Roberta Flack 1981 10.00
❑ SD 19354 I'm the One 1982 10.00
❑ 81916 Oasis 1988 10.00
❑ SW-94346 First Take 1972 15.00
*—Capitol Record Club edition*

### FLAGG, FANNIE

RCA VICTOR
❑ LPM-3856 [M] Rally 'Round the Flagg 1967 20.00
❑ LSP-3856 [S] Rally 'Round the Flagg 1967 15.00

### FLAIRS, THE (1)

CROWN
❑ CLP-5356 [M] The Flairs 1963 80.00

### FLAME, THE

BROTHER
❑ BR-2500 The Flame 1970 30.00
*—Deduct 1/3 if poster is missing*

### FLAMIN' GROOVIES, THE

BUDDAH
❑ BDS-5683 Shill Shakin' 1977 15.00
EPIC
❑ BN 26487 Supersnazz 1969 50.00
KAMA SUTRA
❑ KSBS-2021 Flamingo 1970 30.00
*—Pink label*
❑ KSBS-2021 Flamingo 1972 15.00
*—Blue label*
❑ KSBS-2031 Teenage Head 1971 30.00
*—Pink label*
❑ KSBS-2031 Teenage Head 1972 15.00
*—Blue label*
SIRE
❑ SRK 6059 The Flamin' Groovies Now 1978 12.00
*—Reissues have 14 tracks*
❑ SRK 6059 The Flamin' Groovies Now 1978 15.00
*—Originals have 12 tracks*
❑ SRK 6067 Jumpin' in the Night 1979 12.00
❑ SASD-7521 Shake Some Action 1976 15.00
SNAZZ
❑ R-2371 [10] Sneekers 1969 100.00
*—This album has been counterfeited*

### FLAMING LIPS, THE

ATAVISTIC
❑ ALP-04 [EP] Unconsciously Screamin' 1991 25.00
LOVELY SORTS OF DEATH
❑ (# unknown) [EP]The Flaming Lips (Bag Full of Thoughts) 1984 80.00
*—Red vinyl; black background on jacket*
❑ (# unknown) [EP]The Flaming Lips (Bag Full of Thoughts) 1984 120.00
*—Green vinyl; dark brown background on jacket*
PINK DUST
❑ 72173 Hear It Is 1986 40.00
*—Originals on white vinyl*
❑ 72188 [EP] The Flaming Lips 1985 40.00
*—Originals on lavender vinyl; reissue of Lovely Sorts of Death EP*
PLAIN
❑ 111 Hear It Is 2006 15.00
*—Reissue on white vinyl*
❑ 112 Oh My Gawd!!!... The Flaming Lips 2006 15.00
*—Reissue on clear vinyl*
❑ 113 [(2)] Telepathic Surgery 2006 15.00
*—Reissue on blue vinyl*
❑ 114 [(2)] In a Priest Driven Ambulance 2006 15.00
*—Reissue on pink vinyl*
RESTLESS
❑ 72207 Oh My Gawd, The Flaming Lips 1987 40.00
*—Clear vinyl*
❑ 72350 Telepathic Surgery 1989 25.00
❑ 72359 In a Priest Driven Ambulance 1990 25.00
*—Pink vinyl*
WARNER BROS.
❑ 1-44250 [(2)] At War with the Mystics 2006 30.00
*—180-gram edition on black vinyl*
❑ 45334 Transmissions from the Satellite Heart 1993 20.00
❑ 45911 Clouds Taste Metallic 1995 15.00
❑ 48141 Yoshimi Battles the Pink Robots 2002 20.00
❑ 1-49966 [(2)] At War with the Mystics 2006 25.00
*—150-gram edition; one record is on orange vinyl, the other is on turquoise vinyl*

### FLAMING YOUTH Phil Collins was in this group.

UNI
❑ 73075 Ark 2 1969 40.00

### FLAMINGO, JOHNNY

DIADON
❑ 201 [M] Johnny Flamingo Sings In the Wee Small Hours 1961 100.00

### FLAMINGOS, THE

CHECKER
❑ LP-1433 [M] The Flamingos 1959 400.00
*—Black label*
❑ LP-1433 [M] The Flamingos 196? 150.00
*—Blue label*
❑ LPS-3005 [R] The Flamingos 1966 25.00
*—Rechanneled reissue of 1433*
CONSTELLATION
❑ CS-3 [M] Collectors Showcase: The Flamingos 1964 50.00
*—With more restrained pink lettering on cover*
❑ CS-3 [M] Collectors Showcase: The Flamingos 1964 100.00
*—With hot pink lettering on cover*
END
❑ LP-304 [M] Flamingo Serenade 1959 200.00
*—Gray label with dog*
❑ LP-304 [M] Flamingo Serenade 1959 400.00
*—Black label with shadow print logo*
❑ LPS-304 [S] Flamingo Serenade 1959 500.00
*—Cover says "Stereo"*
❑ LPS-304 [S] Flamingo Serenade 196? 200.00
*—Cover says "Rechanneled Stereo" (only one track is)*
❑ LP-307 [M] Flamingo Favorites 1960 100.00
❑ LPS-307 [R] Flamingo Favorites 1960 70.00
❑ LP-308 [M] Requestfully Yours 1960 100.00
❑ LPS-308 [R] Requestfully Yours 1960 70.00
❑ LP-316 [M] The Sound of the Flamingos 1962 100.00
❑ LPS-316 [R] The Sound of the Flamingos 1962 70.00
❑ LPS-316 [S] The Sound of the Flamingos 1962 200.00
*—"Stereo" at upper right corner of front cover*
LOST-NITE
❑ LLP-7 [10] The Flamingos 1981 10.00
*—Red vinyl*
PHILIPS
❑ PHM 200206 [M]Their Hits — Then and Now 1966 25.00
❑ PHS 600206 [S]Their Hits — Then and Now 1966 30.00
RONZE
❑ RLP-1001 The Flamingos Today 1972 15.00
SOLID SMOKE
❑ 8018 Golden Teardrops 198? 10.00

### FLAMINGOS, THE, AND THE MOONGLOWS

VEE JAY
❑ LP-1052 [M] The Flamingos Meet the Moonglows on the Dusty Road of Hits 1962 150.00

Fleetwood Mac, *Behind the Mask,* Warner Bros. 26111, 1990, $15.

| Number | Title (A Side/B Side) | Yr | NM |
|---|---|---|---|
| ❑ VJLP-1052 [M] | The Flamingos Meet the Moonglows on the Dusty Road of Hits | 198? | 12.00 |

*—Authorized reissue*

## FLANAGAN, TOMMY

MOODSVILLE

| Number | Title (A Side/B Side) | Yr | NM |
|---|---|---|---|
| ❑ MVLP-9 [M] | The Tommy Flanagan Trio | 1960 | 50.00 |
| *—Green label* | | | |
| ❑ MVLP-9 [M] | The Tommy Flanagan Trio | 1965 | 25.00 |
| *—Blue label, trident logo at right* | | | |

PRESTIGE

| Number | Title (A Side/B Side) | Yr | NM |
|---|---|---|---|
| ❑ PRLP-7134 [M] | Overseas | 1958 | 150.00 |

REGENT

| Number | Title (A Side/B Side) | Yr | NM |
|---|---|---|---|
| ❑ MG-6055 [M] | Jazz... It's Magic | 1958 | 80.00 |

## FLANDERS, TOMMY

VERVE FORECAST

| Number | Title (A Side/B Side) | Yr | NM |
|---|---|---|---|
| ❑ FTS-3075 | Moonstone | 1969 | 20.00 |

## FLANDERS AND SWANN

ANGEL

| Number | Title (A Side/B Side) | Yr | NM |
|---|---|---|---|
| ❑ 35797 [M] | At the Drop of a Hat | 196? | 20.00 |
| ❑ S 35797 [S] | At the Drop of a Hat | 196? | 25.00 |
| ❑ 36112 [M] | The Bestiary of Flanders and Swann | 196? | 20.00 |
| ❑ S 36112 [S] | The Bestiary of Flanders and Swann | 196? | 25.00 |
| ❑ 36388 [M] | At the Drop of Another Hat | 1966 | 20.00 |
| ❑ S 36388 [S] | At the Drop of Another Hat | 1966 | 25.00 |
| ❑ 65042 [M] | At the Drop of a Hat | 1959 | 25.00 |
| *—Original issue* | | | |

## FLARES, THE

PRESS

| Number | Title (A Side/B Side) | Yr | NM |
|---|---|---|---|
| ❑ PR 73001 [M] | Encore of Foot Stompin' Hits | 196? | 80.00 |
| ❑ PRS 83001 [S] | Encore of Foot Stompin' Hits | 196? | 120.00 |

## FLAT EARTH SOCIETY, THE

FLEETWOOD

| Number | Title (A Side/B Side) | Yr | NM |
|---|---|---|---|
| ❑ 3027 | Waleeco | 1968 | 300.00 |

## FLATT, LESTER

COLUMBIA

| Number | Title (A Side/B Side) | Yr | NM |
|---|---|---|---|
| ❑ CS 1006 | Flatt Out | 1970 | 20.00 |

NUGGET

| Number | Title (A Side/B Side) | Yr | NM |
|---|---|---|---|
| ❑ 104 | The One and Only | 1971 | 20.00 |

RCA VICTOR

| Number | Title (A Side/B Side) | Yr | NM |
|---|---|---|---|
| ❑ APL1-0131 | Country Boy | 1973 | 15.00 |
| ❑ LSP-4495 | Lester Flatt on Victor | 1971 | 20.00 |
| ❑ LSP-4633 | Kentucky Ridgerunner | 1972 | 20.00 |
| ❑ LSP-4789 | Foggy Mountain Breakdown | 1972 | 20.00 |

## FLATT, LESTER, AND MAC WISEMAN

RCA VICTOR

| Number | Title (A Side/B Side) | Yr | NM |
|---|---|---|---|
| ❑ LSP-4547 | Lester 'n' Mac | 1971 | 20.00 |
| ❑ LSP-4688 | On the South Bound | 1972 | 20.00 |

## FLATT AND SCRUGGS

COLUMBIA

| Number | Title (A Side/B Side) | Yr | NM |
|---|---|---|---|
| ❑ GP 30 [(2)] | 20 All-Time Great Recordings | 1970 | 20.00 |
| ❑ CL 1019 [M] | Foggy Mountain Jamboree | 1957 | 50.00 |
| ❑ CL 1424 [M] | Songs of Glory | 1960 | 20.00 |
| ❑ CL 1564 [M] | Foggy Mountain Banjo | 1961 | 20.00 |
| ❑ CL 1664 [M] | Songs of the Famous Carter Family | 1961 | 20.00 |
| ❑ CL 1830 [M] | Folk Songs of Our Land | 1962 | 20.00 |
| ❑ CL 1951 [M] | Hard Travelin' Featuring The Ballad of Jed Clampett | 1963 | 20.00 |
| ❑ CL 2045 [M] | Flatt and Scruggs at Carnegie Hall | 1963 | 20.00 |
| ❑ CL 2134 [M] | Recorded Live at Vanderbilt University | 1964 | 20.00 |
| ❑ CL 2255 [M] | The Fabulous Sound of Flatt & Scruggs | 1964 | 20.00 |
| ❑ CL 2354 [M] | Pickin' Strummin' and Singin' | 1965 | 15.00 |
| ❑ CL 2443 [M] | Town and Country | 1966 | 15.00 |
| ❑ CL 2513 [M] | When the Saints Go Marching In | 1966 | 15.00 |
| ❑ CL 2570 [M] | Flatt and Scruggs' Greatest Hits | 1966 | 15.00 |
| ❑ CL 2643 [M] | Strictly Instrumental | 1967 | 20.00 |
| ❑ CL 2686 [M] | Hear the Whistle Blow | 1967 | 20.00 |
| ❑ CL 2796 [M] | Changin' Times Featuring Foggy Mountain Breakdown | 1968 | 40.00 |
| ❑ CS 8221 [S] | Songs of Glory | 1960 | 25.00 |
| ❑ CS 8364 [S] | Foggy Mountain Banjo | 1961 | 25.00 |
| ❑ CS 8464 [S] | Songs of the Famous Carter Family | 1961 | 25.00 |
| ❑ CS 8630 [S] | Folk Songs of Our Land | 1962 | 25.00 |
| ❑ CS 8751 [S] | Hard Travelin' Featuring The Ballad of Jed Clampett | 1963 | 25.00 |
| ❑ CS 8845 [S] | Flatt and Scruggs at Carnegie Hall | 1963 | 25.00 |
| ❑ PC 8845 | Flatt and Scruggs at Carnegie Hall | 198? | 8.00 |
| *—Budget-line reissue* | | | |
| ❑ CS 8934 [S] | Recorded Live at Vanderbilt University | 1964 | 25.00 |
| ❑ CS 9055 [S] | The Fabulous Sound of Flatt & Scruggs | 1964 | 25.00 |
| ❑ CS 9154 [S] | Pickin' Strummin' and Singin' | 1965 | 20.00 |
| ❑ CS 9243 [S] | Town and Country | 1966 | 20.00 |
| ❑ CS 9313 [S] | When the Saints Go Marching In | 1966 | 20.00 |
| ❑ CS 9370 [S] | Flatt and Scruggs' Greatest Hits | 1966 | 20.00 |
| ❑ PC 9370 | Flatt and Scruggs' Greatest Hits | 198? | 8.00 |
| *—Budget-line reissue* | | | |
| ❑ CS 9443 [S] | Strictly Instrumental | 1967 | 20.00 |
| ❑ CS 9486 [S] | Hear the Whistle Blow | 1967 | 20.00 |
| ❑ CS 9596 | Changin' Times Featuring Foggy Mountain Breakdown | 1970 | 12.00 |
| *—Orange label with six "Columbia"s along edge* | | | |
| ❑ CS 9596 [S] | Changin' Times Featuring Foggy Mountain Breakdown | 1968 | 20.00 |
| *—Red "360 Sound" label* | | | |
| ❑ CS 9649 [M] | The Story of Bonnie & Clyde | 1968 | 40.00 |
| *—White label promo with "Special Mono Radio Station Copy" sticker and timing strip on front cover* | | | |
| ❑ CS 9649 [S] | The Story of Bonnie & Clyde | 1968 | 20.00 |
| ❑ CS 9741 | Nashville Airplane | 1969 | 20.00 |
| ❑ CS 9945 | Final Fling | 1970 | 15.00 |
| ❑ C 30347 | Breaking Out | 1971 | 12.00 |
| ❑ CG 31964 [(2)] | The World of Flatt and Scruggs | 1972 | 15.00 |
| ❑ C 32244 | A Boy Named Sue | 1973 | 12.00 |
| ❑ FC 37469 | Lester Flatt & Earl Scruggs | 1981 | 10.00 |

COLUMBIA LIMITED EDITION

| Number | Title (A Side/B Side) | Yr | NM |
|---|---|---|---|
| ❑ LE 10149 | Breaking Out | 197? | 10.00 |

COLUMBIA MUSICAL TREASURY

| Number | Title (A Side/B Side) | Yr | NM |
|---|---|---|---|
| ❑ DS 493 | Detroit City | 1969 | 15.00 |

COUNTY

| Number | Title (A Side/B Side) | Yr | NM |
|---|---|---|---|
| ❑ CCS-111 | You Can Feel It in Your Soul | 1988 | 10.00 |

EVEREST ARCHIVE OF FOLK & JAZZ

| Number | Title (A Side/B Side) | Yr | NM |
|---|---|---|---|
| ❑ 259 | Lester Flatt & Earl Scruggs | 197? | 10.00 |

HARMONY

| Number | Title (A Side/B Side) | Yr | NM |
|---|---|---|---|
| ❑ HL 7250 [M] | Lester Flatt & Earl Scruggs | 1960 | 15.00 |
| ❑ HL 7340 [M] | Great Original Recordings | 1965 | 15.00 |
| ❑ HL 7402 [M] | Sacred Songs | 1967 | 15.00 |
| ❑ HL 7465 [M] | Songs to Cherish | 1968 | 15.00 |
| ❑ HS 11202 [S] | Sacred Songs | 1967 | 12.00 |
| ❑ HS 11265 [S] | Songs to Cherish | 1968 | 12.00 |
| ❑ HS 11401 | Foggy Mountain Chimes | 1970 | 12.00 |
| ❑ H 30932 | Wabash Cannonball | 197? | 10.00 |

MERCURY

| Number | Title (A Side/B Side) | Yr | NM |
|---|---|---|---|
| ❑ MG-20358 [M] | Country Music | 1958 | 40.00 |
| ❑ MG-20542 [M] | Lester Flatt & Earl Scruggs | 1959 | 40.00 |
| ❑ MG-20773 [M] | The Original Sound of Flatt & Scruggs | 1963 | 25.00 |
| ❑ SR-60773 [R] | The Original Sound of Flatt & Scruggs | 1963 | 15.00 |
| ❑ SR-61162 | Original Theme from Bonnie & Clyde | 1968 | 20.00 |

NASHVILLE

| Number | Title (A Side/B Side) | Yr | NM |
|---|---|---|---|
| ❑ 2087 | The Best of Flatt and Scruggs | 1970 | 12.00 |

PICKWICK

| Number | Title (A Side/B Side) | Yr | NM |
|---|---|---|---|
| ❑ 6093 | Foggy Mountain Breakdown | 197? | 12.00 |
| ❑ 6140 | Blue Grass Banjos | 197? | 10.00 |

POWER PAK

| Number | Title (A Side/B Side) | Yr | NM |
|---|---|---|---|
| ❑ 297 | Golden Hits | 197? | 10.00 |

ROUNDER

| Number | Title (A Side/B Side) | Yr | NM |
|---|---|---|---|
| ❑ SS-05 | The Golden Era | 198? | 10.00 |
| ❑ SS-08 | Don't Get Above Your Raisin' | 198? | 10.00 |
| ❑ SS-18 | The Mercury Sessions, Volume 1 | 1985 | 10.00 |
| ❑ SS-19 | The Mercury Sessions, Volume 2 | 1985 | 10.00 |

STARDAY

| Number | Title (A Side/B Side) | Yr | NM |
|---|---|---|---|
| ❑ SLP-365 [M] | Stars of the Grand Ol' Opry | 1966 | 25.00 |
| *—With Jim and Jesse* | | | |

WING

| Number | Title (A Side/B Side) | Yr | NM |
|---|---|---|---|
| ❑ SRW-16376 | The Original Foggy Mountain Breakdown | 1968 | 12.00 |

## FLAVOR

JU-PAR

| Number | Title (A Side/B Side) | Yr | NM |
|---|---|---|---|
| ❑ JP6-1002S1 | In Good Taste | 1976 | 20.00 |

## FLEETWOOD MAC

Also see BUCKINGHAM NICKS; PETER GREEN; STEVIE NICKS.

BLUE HORIZON

| Number | Title (A Side/B Side) | Yr | NM |
|---|---|---|---|
| ❑ BH-3801 [(2)] | Fleetwood Mac in Chicago | 1970 | 30.00 |
| ❑ BH-4802 | Blues Jam in Chicago, Vol. 1 | 1970 | 15.00 |
| ❑ BH-4803 | Blues Jam in Chicago, Vol. 2 | 1970 | 15.00 |

EPIC

| Number | Title (A Side/B Side) | Yr | NM |
|---|---|---|---|
| ❑ LN 24402 [M] | Fleetwood Mac | 1968 | 100.00 |
| *—White label promo only* | | | |
| ❑ LN 24446 [M] | English Rose | 1969 | 100.00 |
| *—White label promo only* | | | |
| ❑ BN 26402 [S] | Fleetwood Mac | 1968 | 30.00 |
| ❑ BN 26446 [S] | English Rose | 1969 | 30.00 |
| ❑ KE 30632 [(2)] | Black Magic Woman | 1971 | 20.00 |
| ❑ KE 33740 [(2)] | Fleetwood Mac/English Rose | 1974 | 15.00 |

Number | Title (A Side/B Side) | Yr | NM

MOBILE FIDELITY
❑ 1-012 Fleetwood Mac 1980 40.00
*—Audiophile vinyl*
❑ 1-119 Mirage 1984 40.00
*—Audiophile vinyl*

NAUTILUS
❑ NR-8 Rumours 1980 40.00
*—Audiophile vinyl*

REPRISE
❑ MS 2080 Bare Trees 197? 15.00
*—Without brown line on front cover; uncommon with the MS 2080 number*
❑ MS 2080 Bare Trees 1972 12.00
*—With brown line near all four edges of the front cover*
❑ MS 2138 Penguin 1973 15.00
❑ MS 2158 Mystery to Me 1973 12.00
*—With "For Your Love" listed correctly on the back cover*
❑ MS 2158 Mystery to Me 1973 20.00
*—With "Good Things (Come to Those Who Wait)" listed on the album cover; it was replaced at the last minute by "For Your Love"*
❑ MS 2196 Heroes Are Hard to Find 1974 12.00
❑ MS 2225 Fleetwood Mac 1975 10.00
❑ MSK 2278 Bare Trees 1977 8.00
*—Reissue; no brown line on the front cover*
❑ MSK 2279 Mystery to Me 1977 8.00
❑ MSK 2281 Fleetwood Mac 1977 8.00
❑ RS 6368 Then Play On 1969 25.00
*—First pressings include "When You Say" and "My Dream"*
❑ RS 6368 Then Play On 1970 15.00
*—Later pressings replace above two tracks with "Oh Well (Parts 1 and 2)."*
❑ RS 6408 Kiln House 1970 15.00
❑ RS 6465 Future Games 1971 25.00
*—Originals have a pale yellow cover*
❑ RS 6465 Future Games 1972 15.00
*—Later pressings have a pale green cover*

SIRE
❑ SASH-3706 [(2)]Vintage Years 1975 15.00
❑ SASH-3715 [(2)]Fleetwood Mac in Chicago 1975 15.00
*—Reissue of Blue Horizon 3801*
❑ 2XS-6006 [(2)] Vintage Years 1977 12.00
❑ 2XS-6009 [(2)] Fleetwood Mac in Chicago 1977 12.00
❑ 2XS-6045 [(2)] The Original Fleetwood Mac 1977 12.00

VARRICK
❑ VR-020 Jumping at Shadows 1985 12.00

WARNER BROS.
❑ PRO-A-866 [DJ]Tusk Remix 1979 20.00
*—Promo-only EP*
❑ BSK 3010 Rumours 1977 8.00
*—With long version (2:16) of "Never Going Back Again"; we do not yet know how to identify these without playing them*
❑ BSK 3010 Rumours 1977 10.00
*—With short version (2:02) of "Never Going Back Again"; we do not yet know how to identify these without playing them*
❑ 2HS 3350 [(2)] Tusk 1979 15.00
❑ 2WB 3500 [(2)] Fleetwood Mac Live 1980 12.00
❑ 23607 Mirage 1982 10.00
❑ 23607 [DJ] Mirage 1982 20.00
*—Promo on Quiex II vinyl*
❑ 25471 Tango in the Night 1987 10.00
❑ 25801 Greatest Hits 1989 10.00
❑ 26111 Behind the Mask 1990 15.00

## FLEETWOODS, THE

DOLTON
❑ BLP-2001 [M] Mr. Blue 1959 80.00
*—Pale blue label with dolphins on top*
❑ BLP-2001 [M] Mr. Blue 1963 20.00
*—Dark label, logo on left*
❑ BLP-2002 [M] The Fleetwoods 1960 50.00
*—Pale blue label with dolphins on top*
❑ BLP-2002 [M] The Fleetwoods 1963 20.00
*—Dark label, logo on left*
❑ BLP-2005 [M] Softly 1961 50.00
*—Pale blue label with dolphins on top*
❑ BLP-2005 [M] Softly 1963 20.00
*—Dark label, logo on left*
❑ BLP-2007 [M] Deep in a Dream 1961 40.00
*—Pale blue label with dolphins on top*
❑ BLP-2007 [M] Deep in a Dream 1963 20.00
*—Dark label, logo on left*
❑ BLP-2011 [M] The Best of the Oldies 1962 40.00
*—Pale blue label with dolphins on top*
❑ BLP-2011 [M] The Best of the Oldies 1963 20.00
*—Dark label, logo on left*
❑ BLP-2018 [M] The Fleetwoods' Greatest Hits 1962 25.00
❑ BLP-2020 [M] The Fleetwoods Sings for Lovers by Night 1963 30.00
❑ BLP-2025 [M] Goodnight My Love 1963 30.00
❑ BLP-2030 [M] Before and After 1965 30.00
❑ BLP-2039 [M] Folk Rock 1965 30.00
❑ BST-8001 [S] Mr. Blue 1959 100.00
*—Pale blue label with dolphins on top*
❑ BST-8001 [S] Mr. Blue 1963 25.00
*—Dark label, logo on left*
❑ BST-8002 [S] The Fleetwoods 1960 70.00
*—Pale blue label with dolphins on top*
❑ BST-8002 [S] The Fleetwoods 1963 25.00
*—Dark label, logo on left*
❑ BST-8005 [S] Softly 1961 70.00
*—Pale blue label with dolphins on top*
❑ BST-8005 [S] Softly 1963 25.00
*—Dark label, logo on left*
❑ BST-8007 [S] Deep in a Dream 1961 50.00
*—Pale blue label with dolphins on top*
❑ BST-8007 [S] Deep in a Dream 1963 25.00
*—Dark label, logo on left*
❑ BST-8011 [S] The Best of the Oldies 1962 50.00
*—Pale blue label with dolphins on top*
❑ BST-8011 [S] The Best of the Oldies 1963 25.00
*—Dark label, logo on left*
❑ BST-8018 [S] The Fleetwoods' Greatest Hits 1962 30.00
❑ BST-8020 [S] The Fleetwoods Sings for Lovers by Night 1963 40.00
❑ BST-8025 [S] Goodnight My Love 1963 40.00
❑ BST-8030 [S] Before and After 1965 40.00
❑ BST-8039 [S] Folk Rock 1965 40.00

LIBERTY
❑ LN-10159 The Fleetwoods' Greatest Hits 1982 8.00
❑ LN-10160 The Best Goodies of the Oldies 1982 8.00
❑ LN-10199 Buried Treasure 1983 8.00

SUNSET
❑ SUM-1131 [M] In a Mellow Mood 1966 12.00
❑ SUS-5131 [S] In a Mellow Mood 1966 15.00

UNITED ARTISTS
❑ UA-LA334-E The Very Best of the Fleetwoods 1975 12.00

## FLEMING, KING

ARGO
❑ LP-4004 [M] Misty Night 1961 25.00
❑ LPS-4004 [S] Misty Night 1961 30.00
❑ LP-4019 [M] Stand By! 1962 25.00
❑ LPS-4019 [S] Stand By! 1962 30.00

CADET
❑ LPS-4053 [S] Weary Traveler 1966 20.00

## FLEMING, RHONDA

COLUMBIA
❑ CL 1080 [M] Rhonda 1958 60.00

## FLEMONS, WADE

VEE JAY
❑ LP-1011 [M] Wade Flemons 1959 150.00
*—Maroon label*
❑ LP-1011 [M] Wade Flemons 196? 80.00
*—Black label*

## FLESH FOR LULU

CAPITOL
❑ CLT-48217 Long Live the New Flesh 1987 12.00
❑ SPRO 79992/3 [DJ]Final Vinyl (And Live Flesh) 1990 20.00
*—Red vinyl; sticker on generic cover*
❑ C1-90232 Plastic Fantastic 1989 12.00

## FLESHEATERS

HOMESTEAD
❑ (# unknown) Prehistoric Hits Vol. 1 198? 12.00
❑ 124-1 Live 1988 10.00

RUBY
❑ JRR-101 A Minute to Pray, a Second to Die 1981 20.00
❑ JRR 805 Forever Came Today 1982 20.00

SST
❑ 094 Greatest Hits 1986 12.00
❑ 094 Destroyed by Fire/Greatest Hits 1991 10.00
*—Reissue with new name*
❑ 264 Prehistoric Fits 1990 12.00
❑ 273 [(2)] Dragstrip Riot 1991 12.00

UPSETTER
❑ UPCJ-34 No Questions Asked 1980 40.00
❑ UP 56 A Hard Road to Follow 1983 30.00

## FLETCHER, SAM

VAULT
❑ LP-116 [M] The Look of Love, the Sound of Soul 1967 30.00
❑ VS-116 [S] The Look of Love, the Sound of Soul 1967 30.00

VEE JAY
❑ LP-1094 [M] Sam Fletcher Sings 1964 40.00

## FLINT, SHELBY

MAD SATYR
❑ MSR-101 You've Been On My Mind 1982 25.00

VALIANT
❑ LP-401 [M] Shelby Flint — The Quiet Girl 1961 40.00
❑ LP-403 [M] Shelby Flint Sings Folk 1962 40.00
❑ LPS-403 [S] Shelby Flint Sings Folk 1962 50.00
❑ VL-5003 [M] Cast Your Fate to the Wind 1966 25.00
❑ VLS-25003 [S] Cast Your Fate to the Wind 1966 30.00

## FLIRTATIONS, THE (1)

DERAM
❑ DES-18028 Nothing But a Heartache 1969 20.00

## FLO AND EDDIE

COLUMBIA
❑ PC 33554 Illegal, Immoral and Fattening 1975 12.00
❑ PC 34262 Moving Targets 1976 12.00

EPIPHANY
❑ ELP-4010 Rock Steady with Flo & Eddie 1981 10.00

REPRISE
❑ MS 2099 The Phlorescent Leech and Eddie 1972 20.00
❑ MS 2141 Flo and Eddie 1973 20.00

RHINO
❑ RNTA-1999 [(3)]History of Flo & Eddie 198? 20.00

## FLOATERS, THE

ABC
❑ AB-1030 Floaters 1977 10.00
❑ AA-1047 Magic 1978 10.00

FEE
❑ WW-711 Get Ready for the Floaters and Shu-Ga 1981 30.00

## FLOATING BRIDGE, THE

VAULT
❑ VS-124 The Floating Bridge 1969 30.00

## FLOCK, THE

COLUMBIA
❑ CS 9911 The Flock 1969 20.00
*—"360 Sound" label*
❑ CS 9911 The Flock 1970 15.00
*—Orange label*
❑ C 30007 Dinosaur Swamps 1970 15.00
*—Orange label*
❑ C 30007 Dinosaur Swamps 1970 20.00
*—"360 Sound" label*

MERCURY
❑ SRM-1-1035 Inside Out 1975 15.00

## FLORENCE, BOB

CARLTON
❑ LP 12-115 [M] Name Band: 1959 1959 40.00
❑ STLP 12-115 [S]Name Band: 1959 1959 60.00

ERA
❑ EL-20003 [M] Bob Florence and Trio 1956 100.00

WORLD PACIFIC
❑ WP-1860 [M] Pet Project: The Bob Florence Big Band Plays Petula Clark Hits 196? 20.00
❑ WPS-21860 [S]Pet Project: The Bob Florence Big Band Plays Petula Clark Hits 196? 25.00

## FLORY, MED

JOSIE
❑ JJS-3506 [S] Med Flory Big Band 1963 20.00
❑ JOZ-3506 [M] Med Flory Big Band 1963 25.00

JUBILEE
❑ JLP-1066 [M] Jazzwave 1958 50.00
❑ SDJLP-1066 [S]Jazzwave 1959 40.00

## FLOW

CTI
❑ 1003 Flow 1970 20.00

## FLOWERS, PHIL

GUEST STAR
❑ G-1456 [M] I Am the Greatest 1964 30.00
❑ GS-1456 [S] I Am the Greatest 1964 40.00
❑ G-1457 [M] Phil Flowers Sings a Tribute 1964 30.00
❑ GS-1457 [S] Phil Flowers Sings a Tribute 1964 40.00

MOUNT VERNON
❑ 154 [M] Rhythm and Blues 196? 25.00

## FLOYD, EDDIE

MALACO
❑ 6352 Experience 1977 12.00

STAX
❑ 714 [M] Knock on Wood 1967 70.00
❑ ST 714 [S] Knock on Wood 1967 70.00
❑ STS-2002 I've Never Found a Girl 1968 30.00
❑ STS-2011 Rare Stamps 1969 25.00
❑ STS-2017 You've Got to Have Eddie 1969 25.00
❑ STS-2029 California Girl 1970 25.00
❑ STS-2041 Down to Earth 1971 25.00
❑ STS-3016 Baby Lay Your Head Down 1973 25.00
❑ STX-4122 Chronicle 1979 12.00
❑ STS-5512 Soul Street 1974 25.00
❑ MPS-8527 Soul Street 198? 10.00

## FLOYD, KING

CHIMNEYVILLE
❑ SD 9047 King Floyd 1971 15.00

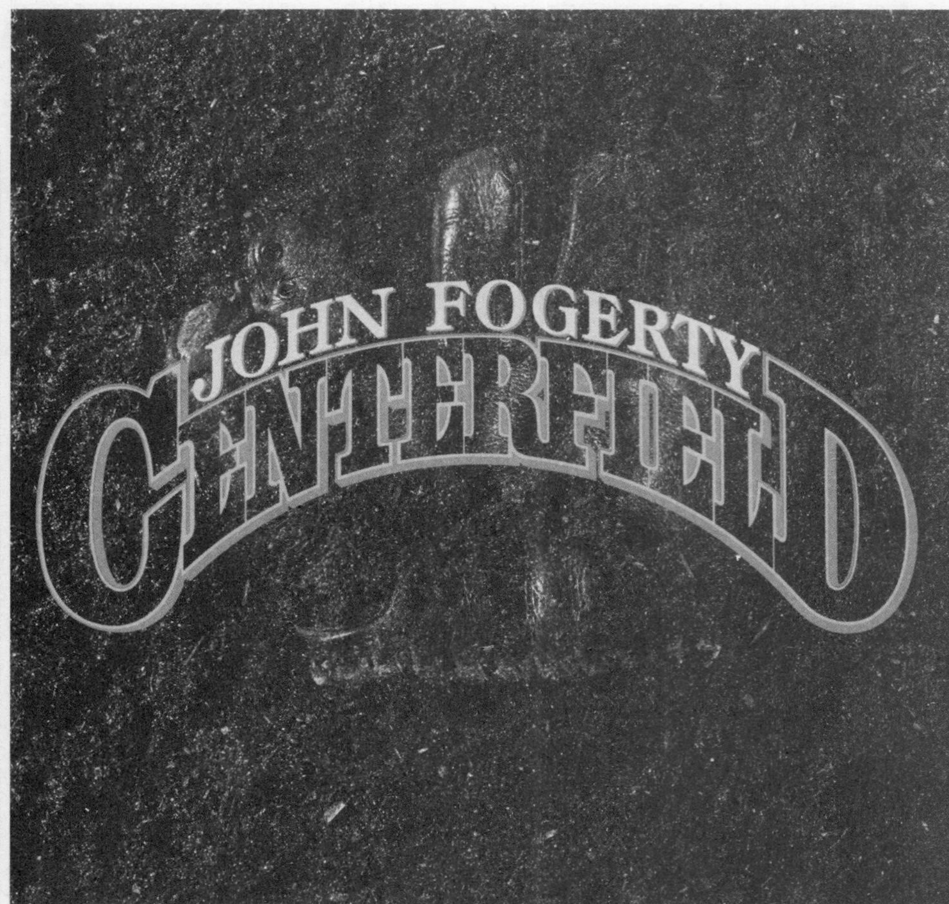


John Fogerty, *Centerfield,* Warner Bros. 25203, 1985, with "Zanz Kant Danz," $15.

PULSAR

| Number | Title (A Side/B Side) | Yr | NM |
|---|---|---|---|
| ❑ 10602 | A Man in Love | 1969 | 20.00 |

V.I.P.

| Number | Title (A Side/B Side) | Yr | NM |
|---|---|---|---|
| ❑ 407 | The Heart of the Matter | 1970 | 40.00 |

### FLYING BURRITO BROTHERS, THE

A&M

| Number | Title (A Side/B Side) | Yr | NM |
|---|---|---|---|
| ❑ SP-3122 | The Gilded Palace of Sin | 198? | 8.00 |
| *—Budget-line reissue* | | | |
| ❑ SP-3631 [(2)] | Close Up the Honky-Tonks | 1974 | 15.00 |
| ❑ SP-4175 | The Gilded Palace of Sin | 1969 | 20.00 |
| *—Brown label* | | | |
| ❑ SP-4175 | The Gilded Palace of Sin | 1974 | 12.00 |
| *—Silvery label* | | | |
| ❑ SP-4258 | Burrito Deluxe | 1970 | 15.00 |
| *—Brown label* | | | |
| ❑ SP-4258 | Burrito Deluxe | 1974 | 12.00 |
| *—Silvery label* | | | |
| ❑ SP-4295 | The Flying Burrito Bros. | 1971 | 15.00 |
| *—Brown label* | | | |
| ❑ SP-4295 | The Flying Burrito Bros. | 1974 | 12.00 |
| *—Silvery label* | | | |
| ❑ SP-4343 | Last of the Red Hot Burritos | 1972 | 15.00 |
| *—Brown label* | | | |
| ❑ SP-4343 | Last of the Red Hot Burritos | 1974 | 12.00 |
| *—Silvery label* | | | |
| ❑ SP-4578 | Sleepless Nights | 1976 | 12.00 |
| *—As "Gram Parsons/The Flying Burrito Bros."* | | | |
| ❑ SP-6510 [(2)] | Close Up the Honky-Tonks | 198? | 12.00 |
| *—Reissue of 3631* | | | |
| ❑ SP-8070 [DJ] | Hot Burrito | 1975 | 40.00 |
| *—Promo-only issue with poster* | | | |

COLUMBIA

| Number | Title (A Side/B Side) | Yr | NM |
|---|---|---|---|
| ❑ PC 33817 | Flying Again | 1975 | 12.00 |
| ❑ PC 34222 | Airborne | 1976 | 12.00 |

CURB

| Number | Title (A Side/B Side) | Yr | NM |
|---|---|---|---|
| ❑ JZ 37004 | Hearts on the Line | 1981 | 10.00 |
| *—As "Burrito Brothers"* | | | |
| ❑ FZ 37705 | Sunset Sundown | 1982 | 10.00 |
| *—As "Burrito Brothers"* | | | |

REGENCY

| Number | Title (A Side/B Side) | Yr | NM |
|---|---|---|---|
| ❑ REG-79001 | Live from Tokyo | 1980 | 10.00 |

### FOCUS

ATCO

| Number | Title (A Side/B Side) | Yr | NM |
|---|---|---|---|
| ❑ SD 36-100 | Hamburger Concerto | 1974 | 12.00 |
| ❑ SD 36-117 | Mother Focus | 1975 | 12.00 |

HARVEST

| Number | Title (A Side/B Side) | Yr | NM |
|---|---|---|---|
| ❑ ST-11721 | Focus Con Proby | 1978 | 12.00 |
| *—With P.J. Proby* | | | |

MERCURY

| Number | Title (A Side/B Side) | Yr | NM |
|---|---|---|---|
| ❑ 824524-1 | Focus: Jan Akkerman and Thijs Van Leer | 1986 | 12.00 |

SIRE

| Number | Title (A Side/B Side) | Yr | NM |
|---|---|---|---|
| ❑ SAS-3901 [(2)] | Focus 3 | 1973 | 15.00 |
| ❑ SAS-7401 | Moving Waves | 1972 | 12.00 |
| ❑ SAS-7404 | In and Out of Focus | 1973 | 12.00 |
| *—Reissue of 97027* | | | |
| ❑ SAS-7408 | Live at the Rainbow | 1973 | 12.00 |
| ❑ SASD-7505 | Dutch Masters — A Selection of Their Finest Recordings 1969-1973 | 1975 | 12.00 |
| ❑ SASD-7531 | Ship of Memories | 1977 | 12.00 |
| ❑ SES-97027 | In and Out of Focus | 1970 | 20.00 |
| *—Original issue* | | | |

### FOGELBERG, DAN

COLUMBIA

| Number | Title (A Side/B Side) | Yr | NM |
|---|---|---|---|
| ❑ KC 31751 | Home Free | 1972 | 12.00 |
| ❑ PC 31751 | Home Free | 197? | 8.00 |
| *—Reissue with new prefix* | | | |

FULL MOON/EPIC

| Number | Title (A Side/B Side) | Yr | NM |
|---|---|---|---|
| ❑ AS 1284 [DJ] | The Innocent Age Sampler | 1982 | 12.00 |
| *—Promo only; 6 songs* | | | |
| ❑ A2S 1335 [(2)DJ] | Interchords | 1982 | 25.00 |
| *—Promo-only release* | | | |
| ❑ KE 33137 | Souvenirs | 1974 | 12.00 |
| *—First pressings have orange Epic label with small Full Moon logo* | | | |
| ❑ KE 33137 | Souvenirs | 1975 | 10.00 |
| *—Second pressings have dark blue/black Full Moon label* | | | |
| ❑ PE 33137 | Souvenirs | 197? | 8.00 |
| *—Reissue with new prefix* | | | |
| ❑ PE 33499 | Captured Angel | 1975 | 10.00 |
| *—No bar code on cover* | | | |
| ❑ PE 33499 | Captured Angel | 198? | 8.00 |
| *—With bar code on cover* | | | |
| ❑ PEQ 33499 [Q] | Captured Angel | 1975 | 20.00 |
| ❑ PE 34185 | Nether Lands | 1977 | 10.00 |
| *—No bar code on cover* | | | |
| ❑ PE 34185 | Nether Lands | 198? | 8.00 |
| *—With bar code on cover* | | | |
| ❑ PE 35364 | Phoenix | 198? | 8.00 |
| *—Budget-line reissue* | | | |
| ❑ FE 35634 | Phoenix | 1979 | 10.00 |
| ❑ KE2 37393 [(2)] | The Innocent Age | 1981 | 12.00 |
| ❑ QE 38308 | Dan Fogelberg/Greatest Hits | 1982 | 10.00 |
| ❑ QE 39004 | Windows and Walls | 1984 | 10.00 |
| ❑ FE 39616 | High Country Snows | 1985 | 10.00 |
| ❑ OE 40271 | Exiles | 1987 | 10.00 |
| ❑ HE 45634 | Phoenix | 1981 | 30.00 |
| *—Half-speed mastered edition* | | | |
| ❑ HE 48308 | Dan Fogelberg/Greatest Hits | 1983 | 30.00 |
| *—Half-speed mastered edition* | | | |

### FOGELBERG, DAN, AND TIM WEISBERG

FULL MOON/EPIC

| Number | Title (A Side/B Side) | Yr | NM |
|---|---|---|---|
| ❑ JE 35339 | Twin Sons of Different Mothers | 1978 | 10.00 |
| ❑ PE 35339 | Twin Sons of Different Mothers | 198? | 8.00 |
| *—Budget-line reissue* | | | |
| ❑ HE 45339 | Twin Sons of Different Mothers | 198? | 30.00 |
| *—Half-speed mastered edition* | | | |

### FOGERTY, JOHN

Includes records as "The Blue Ridge Rangers." Also see CREEDENCE CLEARWATER REVIVAL; THE GOLLIWOGS.

ASYLUM

| Number | Title (A Side/B Side) | Yr | NM |
|---|---|---|---|
| ❑ 7E-1046 | John Fogerty | 1975 | 12.00 |
| ❑ 7E-1081 | Hoodoo | 1976 | — |
| *—Canceled; poor quality bootleg cassettes exist* | | | |

FANTASY

| Number | Title (A Side/B Side) | Yr | NM |
|---|---|---|---|
| ❑ MPF-4502 | John Fogerty: The Blue Ridge Rangers | 1981 | 10.00 |
| *—Reissues prominently place John Fogerty's name on the cover* | | | |
| ❑ F-9415 | The Blue Ridge Rangers | 1973 | 15.00 |
| *—As "The Blue Ridge Rangers"* | | | |

WARNER BROS.

| Number | Title (A Side/B Side) | Yr | NM |
|---|---|---|---|
| ❑ 25203 | Centerfield | 1985 | 15.00 |
| *—Originals have the last song on side 2 as "Zanz Kant Danz"* | | | |
| ❑ 25203 | Centerfield | 1986 | 10.00 |
| *—Later editions have the last song on side 2 re-recorded and listed as "Vanz Kant Danz"* | | | |
| ❑ 25203 [DJ] | Centerfield | 1985 | 30.00 |
| *—Promo versions on Quiex II audiophile vinyl* | | | |
| ❑ 25449 | Eye of the Zombie | 1986 | 10.00 |

### FOLDS, BEN, FIVE

Includes Ben Folds solo.

EPIC

| Number | Title (A Side/B Side) | Yr | NM |
|---|---|---|---|
| ❑ E2 61610 [(2)] | Rockin' the Suburbs | 2001 | 15.00 |

550 MUSIC

| Number | Title (A Side/B Side) | Yr | NM |
|---|---|---|---|
| ❑ B 67762 | Whatever and Ever, Amen | 1997 | 15.00 |
| ❑ B 68809 | Fear of Pop Volume 1 | 1998 | 15.00 |
| *—By Ben Folds with numerous guests* | | | |

SUNDAZED

| Number | Title (A Side/B Side) | Yr | NM |
|---|---|---|---|
| ❑ LP 5164 [(2)] | Ben Folds Live | 2003 | 20.00 |

### FOLEY, LORD ADRIAN

MGM

| Number | Title (A Side/B Side) | Yr | NM |
|---|---|---|---|
| ❑ E-3358 [M] | Lord Adrian Foley at the Piano | 1955 | 40.00 |

### FOLEY, RED

DECCA

| Number | Title (A Side/B Side) | Yr | NM |
|---|---|---|---|
| ❑ DXB 177 [(2)M] | The Red Foley Story | 1964 | 25.00 |
| ❑ DL 4107 [M] | Red Foley's Golden Favorites | 1961 | 20.00 |
| ❑ DL 4140 [M] | Company's Comin' | 1961 | 20.00 |
| ❑ DL 4198 [M] | Songs of Devotion | 1961 | 20.00 |
| ❑ DL 4290 [M] | Dear Hearts and Gentle People | 1962 | 20.00 |
| ❑ DL 4341 [M] | The Red Foley Show | 1963 | 20.00 |
| ❑ DL 4603 [M] | Songs Everybody Knows | 1965 | 20.00 |
| ❑ DL 4849 [M] | Songs for the Soul | 1967 | 25.00 |
| ❑ DL 5003 [M] | Red Foley's Greatest Hits | 1968 | 50.00 |
| *—White label promo; mono copies may only exist as promos* | | | |
| ❑ DL 5303 [10] | Red Foley Souvenir Album | 1951 | 80.00 |
| ❑ DL 5338 [10] | Lift Up Your Voice | 1952 | 80.00 |
| ❑ DXSB 7177 [(2)S] | The Red Foley Story | 1964 | 30.00 |
| ❑ DL 8294 [M] | Red Foley Souvenir Album | 1956 | 50.00 |
| ❑ DL 8296 [M] | Beyond the Sunset | 1956 | 50.00 |
| ❑ DL 8767 [M] | He Walks with Thee | 1958 | 50.00 |
| ❑ DL 8806 [M] | My Keepsake Album | 1958 | 50.00 |
| ❑ DL 8847 [M] | Let's All Sing with Red Foley | 1959 | 40.00 |
| ❑ DL 8903 [M] | Let's All Sing to Him | 1959 | 40.00 |
| ❑ DL 38068 [M] | Gratefully | 1958 | 100.00 |
| *—Special-products issue for Dickies clothing* | | | |
| ❑ DL 74107 [S] | Red Foley's Golden Favorites | 1961 | 25.00 |
| ❑ DL 74140 [S] | Company's Comin' | 1961 | 25.00 |
| ❑ DL 74198 [S] | Songs of Devotion | 1961 | 25.00 |
| ❑ DL 74290 [S] | Dear Hearts and Gentle People | 1962 | 25.00 |
| ❑ DL 74341 [S] | The Red Foley Show | 1963 | 25.00 |
| ❑ DL 74603 [S] | Songs Everybody Knows | 1965 | 25.00 |
| ❑ DL 74849 [S] | Songs for the Soul | 1967 | 20.00 |
| ❑ DL 75003 [S] | Red Foley's Greatest Hits | 1968 | 15.00 |
| ❑ DL 78847 [S] | Let's All Sing with Red Foley | 1959 | 50.00 |
| ❑ DL 78903 [S] | Let's All Sing to Him | 1959 | 50.00 |

### FOLK SINGERS, THE

ELEKTRA

| Number | Title (A Side/B Side) | Yr | NM |
|---|---|---|---|
| ❑ EKL-157 [M] | The Folk Singers | 1958 | 30.00 |

**FOLKNIKS, THE**

HIFI-LIFE SERIES

| Number | Title (A Side/B Side) | Yr | NM |
|---|---|---|---|
| ❑ L-1017 [M] | The Sound of Twelve-String Guitar and Banjo | 1964 | 20.00 |
| ❑ SL-1017 [S] | The Sound of Twelve-String Guitar and Banjo | 1964 | 25.00 |

**FOLKSWINGERS, THE**

WORLD PACIFIC

| Number | Title (A Side/B Side) | Yr | NM |
|---|---|---|---|
| ❑ ST-1812 [S] | 12 String Guitar! | 1963 | 30.00 |
| *—Black vinyl* | | | |
| ❑ ST-1812 [S] | 12 String Guitar! | 1963 | 60.00 |
| *—Red vinyl* | | | |
| ❑ WP-1812 [M] | 12 String Guitar! | 1963 | 25.00 |
| ❑ ST-1814 [S] | 12 String Guitar, Volume 2 | 1963 | 30.00 |
| ❑ WP-1814 [M] | 12 String Guitar, Volume 2 | 1963 | 25.00 |
| ❑ ST-1846 [S] | Raga Rock | 1966 | 30.00 |
| ❑ WP-1846 [M] | Raga Rock | 1966 | 25.00 |

**FONDA, HENRY**

CORAL

| Number | Title (A Side/B Side) | Yr | NM |
|---|---|---|---|
| ❑ CRL 57308 [M] | Voices of the 20th Century | 1958 | 60.00 |

**FONTAINE, FRANK**

ABC-PARAMOUNT

| Number | Title (A Side/B Side) | Yr | NM |
|---|---|---|---|
| ❑ 442 [M] | Songs I Sing on the Jackie Gleason Show | 1963 | 15.00 |
| ❑ S-442 [S] | Songs I Sing on the Jackie Gleason Show | 1963 | 20.00 |
| ❑ 460 [M] | Sings Like Crazy | 1963 | 15.00 |
| ❑ S-460 [S] | Sings Like Crazy | 1963 | 20.00 |
| ❑ 470 [M] | How Sweet It Is | 1964 | 15.00 |
| ❑ S-470 [S] | How Sweet It Is | 1964 | 20.00 |
| ❑ 490 [M] | More Songs I Sing on the Jackie Gleason Show | 1964 | 15.00 |
| ❑ S-490 [S] | More Songs I Sing on the Jackie Gleason Show | 1964 | 20.00 |
| ❑ 514 [M] | I'm Counting on You | 1965 | 15.00 |
| ❑ S-514 [S] | I'm Counting on You | 1965 | 20.00 |
| ❑ 541 [M] | All Time Great Hits | 1966 | 15.00 |
| ❑ S-541 [S] | All Time Great Hits | 1966 | 20.00 |
| ❑ T-90121 [M] | Songs I Sing on the Jackie Gleason Show | 1964 | 20.00 |
| *—Capitol Record Club edition* | | | |

MGM

| Number | Title (A Side/B Side) | Yr | NM |
|---|---|---|---|
| ❑ E-4470 [M] | Frank Fontaine's Ireland | 1967 | 12.00 |
| ❑ SE-4470 [S] | Frank Fontaine's Ireland | 1967 | 15.00 |

**FONTANA, WAYNE** Also see WAYNE FONTANA AND THE MINDBENDERS.

MGM

| Number | Title (A Side/B Side) | Yr | NM |
|---|---|---|---|
| ❑ E-4459 [M] | Wayne Fontana | 1967 | 20.00 |
| ❑ SE-4459 [S] | Wayne Fontana | 1967 | 25.00 |

**FONTANA, WAYNE, AND THE MINDBENDERS** Also see WAYNE FONTANA; THE MINDBENDERS.

FONTANA

| Number | Title (A Side/B Side) | Yr | NM |
|---|---|---|---|
| ❑ MGF-27542 [M] | The Game of Love | 1965 | 30.00 |
| ❑ SRF-67542 [R] | The Game of Love | 1965 | 25.00 |

**FONTANE SISTERS, THE**

DOT

| Number | Title (A Side/B Side) | Yr | NM |
|---|---|---|---|
| ❑ DLP-104 [10] | The Fontane Sisters | 1955 | 50.00 |
| ❑ DLP-3004 [M] | The Fontanes Sing | 1956 | 40.00 |
| *—Maroon label* | | | |
| ❑ DLP-3004 [M] | The Fontanes Sing | 1957 | 25.00 |
| *—Black label* | | | |
| ❑ DLP-3042 [M] | A Visit with the Fontane Sisters | 1957 | 30.00 |
| ❑ DLP-3531 [M] | The Tips of My Fingers | 1963 | 15.00 |
| ❑ DLP-25531 [S] | The Tips of My Fingers | 1963 | 20.00 |

**FOO FIGHTERS**

ROSWELL/CAPITOL

| Number | Title (A Side/B Side) | Yr | NM |
|---|---|---|---|
| ❑ C1-34027 | Foo Fighters | 1995 | 20.00 |
| ❑ 55832 [(2)] | The Colour and the Shape | 1997 | 100.00 |

ROSWELL/RCA

| Number | Title (A Side/B Side) | Yr | NM |
|---|---|---|---|
| ❑ 07863-67892-1 | There Is Nothing Left to Lose | 1999 | 15.00 |
| ❑ 07863-68008-1 [(2)10] | One By One | 2002 | 15.00 |
| ❑ 82876-68038-1 [(4)] | In Your Honor | 2005 | 40.00 |
| *—Box set; all four records play at 45 rpm* | | | |

**FOOD**

CAPITOL

| Number | Title (A Side/B Side) | Yr | NM |
|---|---|---|---|
| ❑ ST-304 | Forever Is a Dream | 1969 | 60.00 |

**FOOL, THE**

MERCURY

| Number | Title (A Side/B Side) | Yr | NM |
|---|---|---|---|
| ❑ SR-61178 | The Fool | 1968 | 30.00 |

**FOOLS, THE**

EMI AMERICA

| Number | Title (A Side/B Side) | Yr | NM |
|---|---|---|---|
| ❑ SPRO-9393/4 [DJ] | The First Annual Official Unofficial April Fools Day Live Bootleg... | 1980 | 20.00 |
| ❑ SW-17024 | Sold Out | 1980 | 12.00 |
| ❑ SW-17046 | Heavy Mental | 1981 | 12.00 |

PVC

| Number | Title (A Side/B Side) | Yr | NM |
|---|---|---|---|
| ❑ 8930 | World Dance Party | 1985 | 15.00 |

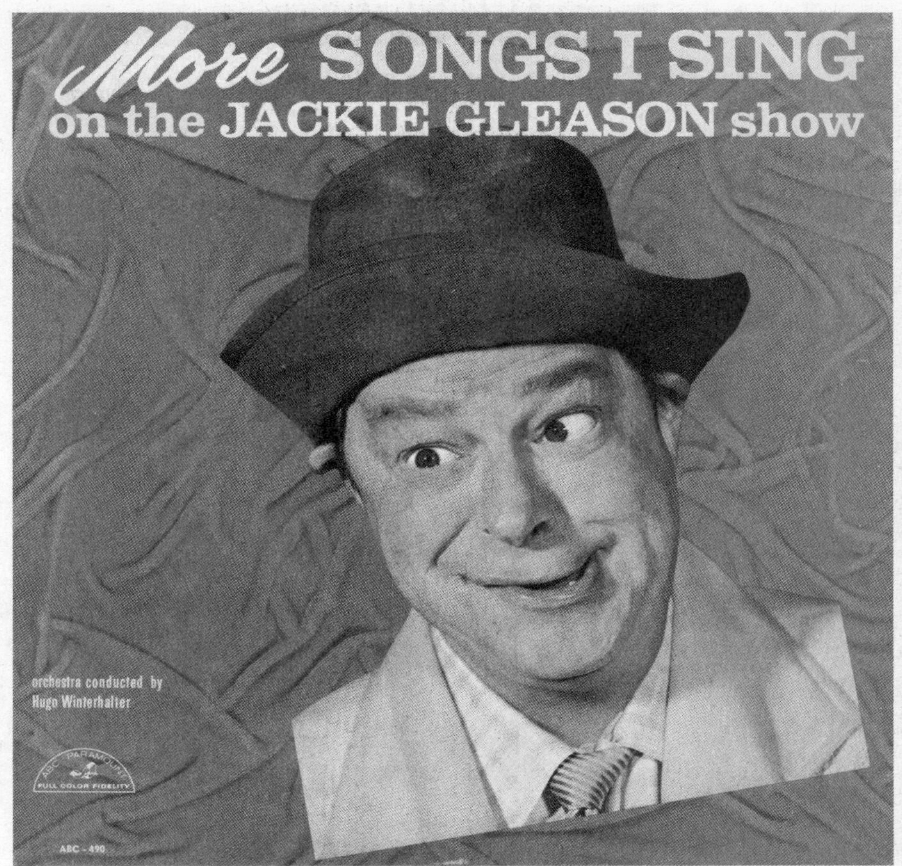


Frank Fontaine, *More Songs I Sing on the Jackie Gleason Show,* ABC-Paramount ABC-490, 1964, mono, $15.

**FORBES, GRAHAM**

PHILLIPS INTERNATIONAL

| Number | Title (A Side/B Side) | Yr | NM |
|---|---|---|---|
| ❑ PLP-1955 [M] | The Martini Set | 1959 | 800.00 |

**FORD, FRANKIE**

ACE

| Number | Title (A Side/B Side) | Yr | NM |
|---|---|---|---|
| ❑ LP 1005 [M] | Let's Take a Sea Cruise | 1959 | 300.00 |

BRIARMEADE

| Number | Title (A Side/B Side) | Yr | NM |
|---|---|---|---|
| ❑ BR-5002 | Frankie Ford | 1976 | 12.00 |

**FORD, LITA** Also see THE RUNAWAYS.

MERCURY

| Number | Title (A Side/B Side) | Yr | NM |
|---|---|---|---|
| ❑ 810331-1 | Out for Blood | 1984 | 8.00 |
| *—Reissue cover has a different photo of Lita holding a non-bloody guitar* | | | |
| ❑ 810331-1 | Out for Blood | 1984 | 25.00 |
| *—Original cover has Lita holding a bloody, gored guitar* | | | |
| ❑ 818864-1 | Dancin' on the Edge | 1984 | 10.00 |

RCA

| Number | Title (A Side/B Side) | Yr | NM |
|---|---|---|---|
| ❑ 2090-1-R | Stiletto | 1990 | 10.00 |
| ❑ 6397-1-R | Lita | 1988 | 8.00 |

**FORD, MARY** Also see LES PAUL AND MARY FORD.

CHALLENGE

| Number | Title (A Side/B Side) | Yr | NM |
|---|---|---|---|
| ❑ CHL-623 [M] | A Brand New Ford | 1966 | 25.00 |
| ❑ CHS-2623 [S] | A Brand New Ford | 1966 | 30.00 |

**FORD, NEAL, AND THE FANATICS**

HICKORY

| Number | Title (A Side/B Side) | Yr | NM |
|---|---|---|---|
| ❑ LPS-141 | Neal Ford and the Fanatics | 1968 | 25.00 |

**FORD, RITA**

COLUMBIA

| Number | Title (A Side/B Side) | Yr | NM |
|---|---|---|---|
| ❑ CL 1698 [M] | A Music Box Christmas | 1961 | 20.00 |
| *—Black and red label with six "eye" logos* | | | |

EPIC

| Number | Title (A Side/B Side) | Yr | NM |
|---|---|---|---|
| ❑ LN 24022 [M] | Music Box Wonderland Christmas with Rita Ford's Music Boxes | 1962 | 20.00 |

**FORD, ROCKY BILLY**

AUDIO LAB

| Number | Title (A Side/B Side) | Yr | NM |
|---|---|---|---|
| ❑ AL-1561 [M] | A New Singing Star | 1960 | 150.00 |

**FORD, TENNESSEE ERNIE**

CAPITOL

| Number | Title (A Side/B Side) | Yr | NM |
|---|---|---|---|
| ❑ ST-127 | Songs I Like to Sing | 1969 | 12.00 |
| ❑ ST-334 | Holy, Holy, Holy | 1969 | 12.00 |
| ❑ SM-412 | America the Beautiful | 197? | 8.00 |
| *—Reissue with new prefix* | | | |
| ❑ STAO-412 | America the Beautiful | 1970 | 12.00 |
| ❑ STBB-485 [(2)] | Christmas Special | 1970 | 15.00 |
| ❑ STBB-506 [(2)] | Sweet Hour of Prayer/Let Me Walk with Thee | 1971 | 15.00 |
| ❑ SF-8-0507 | Sweet Hour of Prayer | 1970 | 15.00 |
| *—Capitol Record Club edition* | | | |
| ❑ SF-8-0508 | Let Me Walk with Thee | 1970 | 15.00 |
| *—Capitol Record Club edition* | | | |
| ❑ ST-583 | Everything Is Beautiful | 1971 | 12.00 |
| ❑ DT 700 [R] | This Lusty Land! | 196? | 12.00 |
| ❑ T 700 [M] | This Lusty Land | 1956 | 25.00 |
| *—Turquoise label* | | | |
| ❑ T 700 [M] | This Lusty Land | 1959 | 20.00 |
| *—Black label with colorband, logo at left* | | | |
| ❑ T 700 [M] | This Lusty Land! | 1963 | 15.00 |
| *—Black label with colorband, logo at top* | | | |
| ❑ ST-730 | Abide with Me | 1971 | 12.00 |
| ❑ ST 756 [S] | Hymns | 1962 | 15.00 |
| *—Re-recording of the original mono LP* | | | |
| ❑ T 756 [M] | Hymns | 1956 | 25.00 |
| *—Turquoise label* | | | |
| ❑ T 756 [M] | Hymns | 1959 | 20.00 |
| *—Black label with colorband, logo at left* | | | |
| ❑ T 756 [M] | Hymns | 1962 | 15.00 |
| *—Black label with colorband, logo at top* | | | |
| ❑ ST 818 [S] | Spirituals | 1962 | 15.00 |
| *—Re-recording of the original mono LP* | | | |
| ❑ T 818 [M] | Spirituals | 1957 | 25.00 |
| *—Turquoise label* | | | |
| ❑ T 818 [M] | Spirituals | 1959 | 20.00 |
| *—Black label with colorband, logo at left* | | | |
| ❑ T 818 [M] | Spirituals | 1962 | 15.00 |
| *—Black label with colorband, logo at top* | | | |
| ❑ ST-831 [S] | C-H-R-I-S-T-M-A-S | 1971 | 12.00 |
| ❑ ST-833 | The Folk Album | 1971 | 12.00 |
| ❑ DT 841 [R] | Tennessee Ernie Ford Favorites | 196? | 12.00 |
| ❑ T 841 [M] | Tennessee Ernie Ford Favorites | 1957 | 30.00 |
| *—Turquoise label* | | | |

| Number | Title (A Side/B Side) | Yr | NM |
|---|---|---|---|
| ❑ T 841 [M] | Tennessee Ernie Ford Favorites | 1958 | 20.00 |
| *—Black label with colorband, logo at left* | | | |
| ❑ T 841 [M] | Tennessee Ernie Ford Favorites | 1962 | 15.00 |
| *—Black label with colorband, logo at top* | | | |
| ❑ T 888 [M] | Ol' Rockin' Ern | 1957 | 50.00 |
| *—Turquoise or gray label* | | | |
| ❑ ST 1005 [S] | Nearer the Cross | 1959 | 25.00 |
| *—Black label with colorband, logo at left* | | | |
| ❑ ST 1005 [S] | Nearer the Cross | 1962 | 20.00 |
| *—Black label with colorband, logo at top* | | | |
| ❑ T 1005 [M] | Nearer the Cross | 1958 | 20.00 |
| *—Black label with colorband, logo at left* | | | |
| ❑ T 1005 [M] | Nearer the Cross | 1962 | 15.00 |
| *—Black label with colorband, logo at top* | | | |
| ❑ ST 1071 [S] | The Star Carol | 1958 | 30.00 |
| *—Black labels with colorband, Capitol logo on left* | | | |
| ❑ T 1071 [S] | The Star Carol | 1962 | 20.00 |
| *—Black label with colorband, "Capitol" logo on top. This was also reissued on later Capitol labels into the 1970s with values no more than half the above.* | | | |
| ❑ T 1071 [M] | The Star Carol | 1958 | 25.00 |
| *—Black labels with colorband, "Capitol" logo on left* | | | |
| ❑ T 1071 [M] | The Star Carol | 1962 | 15.00 |
| *—Black label with colorband, logo on top* | | | |
| ❑ ST 1227 [S] | Gather 'Round | 1959 | 20.00 |
| ❑ T 1227 [M] | Gather 'Round | 1959 | 15.00 |
| ❑ ST 1272 [S] | A Friend We Have | 1959 | 20.00 |
| ❑ T 1272 [M] | A Friend We Have | 1959 | 15.00 |
| ❑ STAO 1332 [S] | Sing a Hymn with Me | 1960 | 25.00 |
| *—With hymnal* | | | |
| ❑ TAO 1332 [M] | Sing a Hymn with Me | 1960 | 20.00 |
| *—With hymnal* | | | |
| ❑ DT 1380 [R] | Sixteen Tons | 196? | 12.00 |
| ❑ T 1380 [M] | Sixteen Tons | 1960 | 15.00 |
| ❑ ST 1539 [S] | Civil War Songs of the North | 1961 | 20.00 |
| ❑ T 1539 [M] | Civil War Songs of the North | 1961 | 15.00 |
| ❑ ST 1540 [S] | Civil War Songs of the South | 1961 | 20.00 |
| ❑ T 1540 [M] | Civil War Songs of the South | 1961 | 15.00 |
| ❑ ST 1679 [S] | Sing a Hymn with Me | 1962 | 15.00 |
| *—Reissue of 1332 with standard cover?* | | | |
| ❑ T 1679 [M] | Sing a Hymn with Me | 1962 | 12.00 |
| *—Reissue of 1332 with standard cover?* | | | |
| ❑ ST 1680 [S] | Sing a Spiritual with Me | 1962 | 15.00 |
| ❑ T 1680 [M] | Sing a Spiritual with Me | 1962 | 12.00 |
| ❑ ST 1684 [S] | Here Comes the Mississippi Showboat | 1962 | 15.00 |
| ❑ T 1684 [M] | Here Comes the Mississippi Showboat | 1962 | 12.00 |
| ❑ ST 1694 [S] | Hymns at Home | 1962 | 15.00 |
| ❑ T 1694 [M] | Hymns at Home | 1962 | 12.00 |
| ❑ ST 1751 [S] | I Love to Tell the Story | 1962 | 15.00 |
| ❑ T 1751 [M] | I Love to Tell the Story | 1962 | 12.00 |
| ❑ ST 1794 [S] | Book of Favorite Hymns | 1962 | 20.00 |
| ❑ T 1794 [M] | Book of Favorite Hymns | 1962 | 15.00 |
| ❑ ST 1875 [S] | Long Long Ago | 1963 | 15.00 |
| ❑ T 1875 [M] | Long Long Ago | 1963 | 12.00 |
| ❑ ST 1937 [S] | We Gather Together | 1963 | 15.00 |
| ❑ T 1937 [M] | We Gather Together | 1963 | 12.00 |
| ❑ ST 1994 [S] | The Story of Christmas | 1963 | 20.00 |
| ❑ T 1994 [M] | The Story of Christmas | 1963 | 15.00 |
| *—With the Roger Wagner Chorale* | | | |
| ❑ SM-2026 | Great Gospel Songs | 197? | 8.00 |
| *—Reissue with new prefix* | | | |
| ❑ ST 2026 [S] | Great Gospel Songs | 1964 | 15.00 |
| ❑ T 2026 [M] | Great Gospel Songs | 1964 | 12.00 |
| ❑ SM-2097 | Country Hits...Feelin' Blue | 197? | 8.00 |
| *—Reissue with new prefix* | | | |
| ❑ ST 2097 [S] | Country Hits...Feelin' Blue | 1964 | 15.00 |
| ❑ T 2097 [M] | Country Hits...Feelin' Blue | 1964 | 12.00 |
| ❑ STBL 2183 [(2)S] | The World's Best Loved Hymns | 1964 | 25.00 |
| ❑ TBL 2183 [(2)M] | The World's Best Loved Hymns | 1964 | 20.00 |
| ❑ ST 2296 [S] | Let Me Walk with Thee | 1965 | 15.00 |
| ❑ T 2296 [M] | Let Me Walk with Thee | 1965 | 12.00 |
| ❑ ST 2394 [S] | Sing We Now of Christmas | 1965 | 15.00 |
| *—Same as above, but in stereo* | | | |
| ❑ T 2394 [M] | Sing We Now of Christmas | 1965 | 12.00 |
| ❑ ST 2444 [S] | My Favorite Things | 1966 | 15.00 |
| ❑ T 2444 [M] | My Favorite Things | 1966 | 12.00 |
| ❑ ST 2557 [S] | Wonderful Peace | 1966 | 15.00 |
| ❑ T 2557 [M] | Wonderful Peace | 1966 | 12.00 |
| ❑ ST 2618 [S] | God Lives | 1966 | 15.00 |
| ❑ T 2618 [M] | God Lives | 1966 | 12.00 |
| ❑ ST 2681 [S] | Aloha from Tennessee Ernie Ford | 1967 | 12.00 |
| ❑ T 2681 [M] | Aloha from Tennessee Ernie Ford | 1967 | 15.00 |
| ❑ SM-2761 | Faith of Our Fathers | 197? | 8.00 |
| *—Reissue with new prefix* | | | |
| ❑ ST 2761 [S] | Faith of Our Fathers | 1967 | 12.00 |
| ❑ T 2761 [M] | Faith of Our Fathers | 1967 | 15.00 |
| ❑ ST 2845 [S] | Our Garden of Hymns | 1968 | 12.00 |
| ❑ T 2845 [M] | Our Garden of Hymns | 1968 | 20.00 |
| ❑ ST 2896 | The World of Pop and Country Hits | 1968 | 12.00 |
| ❑ STCL 2942 [(3)] | The Tennessee Ernie Ford Deluxe Set | 1968 | 20.00 |
| ❑ SKAO 2949 | Best Hymns | 1968 | 12.00 |
| ❑ ST 2968 | O Come All Ye Faithful | 1968 | 12.00 |
| ❑ ST-11001 | Mr. Words and Music | 1972 | 10.00 |
| ❑ ST-11092 | It's Tennessee Ernie Ford | 1973 | 10.00 |
| ❑ ST-11232 | Tennessee Ernie Ford Sings About Jesus | 1973 | 10.00 |
| ❑ ST-11290 | Make a Joyful Noise | 1974 | 10.00 |
| ❑ SVBB-11325 [(2)] | 25th Anniversary/Yesterday and Today | 1974 | 12.00 |
| ❑ SVBB-11326 [(2)] | 25th Anniversary/Hymns & Gospel | 1974 | 12.00 |
| ❑ SVBB-11382 [(2)] | Precious Memories | 1975 | 12.00 |
| ❑ ST-11495 | Tennessee Ernie Ford Sings His Great Love Songs | 1975 | 10.00 |
| ❑ SM-12033 | Book of Favorite Hymns | 1980 | 10.00 |
| ❑ SN-16040 | Yesterday | 1981 | 8.00 |
| ❑ SN-16042 | Gospel | 1981 | 8.00 |
| ❑ SN-16043 | Hymns | 1981 | 8.00 |
| ❑ SN-16173 | Hymns | 1981 | 8.00 |
| ❑ SN-16174 | Spirituals | 1981 | 8.00 |
| ❑ SN-16289 | The Star Carol | 1982 | 8.00 |
| *—Budget-line reissue* | | | |

**EVEREST ARCHIVE OF FOLK & JAZZ**

| Number | Title (A Side/B Side) | Yr | NM |
|---|---|---|---|
| ❑ 279 | Tennessee Ernie Ford | 197? | 10.00 |

**PICKWICK**

| Number | Title (A Side/B Side) | Yr | NM |
|---|---|---|---|
| ❑ PTP-2016 [(2)] | Tennessee Ernie Ford | 197? | 12.00 |
| ❑ PTP-2050 [(2)] | Hymns | 197? | 12.00 |
| ❑ SPC-3047 | Bless Your Pea-Pickin' Heart | 196? | 12.00 |
| ❑ SPC-3066 | I Love You So Much | 196? | 12.00 |
| ❑ SPC-3222 | The Need for Prayer | 197? | 10.00 |
| ❑ SPC-3268 | Sixteen Tons | 197? | 10.00 |
| ❑ SPC-3273 | Jesus Loves Me | 197? | 10.00 |
| ❑ SPC-3308 | Amazing Grace | 197? | 10.00 |
| ❑ SPC-3353 | Rock of Ages | 197? | 10.00 |

**RANWOOD**

| Number | Title (A Side/B Side) | Yr | NM |
|---|---|---|---|
| ❑ RLP-7026 [(2)] | Tennessee Ernie Ford Sings 22 Favorite Hymns | 198? | 12.00 |

**WORD**

| Number | Title (A Side/B Side) | Yr | NM |
|---|---|---|---|
| ❑ 8764 | He Touched Me | 1978 | 10.00 |
| ❑ 8798 | Swing Wide Your Golden Gate | 198? | 10.00 |
| ❑ 8841 | Tell Me the Old Story | 1979 | 10.00 |
| ❑ 8841 | Tell Me the Old Story | 198? | 10.00 |
| ❑ 8858 | There's a Song in My Heart | 198? | 10.00 |

### FORD THEATRE, THE

**ABC**

| Number | Title (A Side/B Side) | Yr | NM |
|---|---|---|---|
| ❑ S-658 | Trilogy | 1968 | 25.00 |
| ❑ S-681 | Time Changes | 1969 | 20.00 |

### FOREFRONT, THE

**AFI**

| Number | Title (A Side/B Side) | Yr | NM |
|---|---|---|---|
| ❑ 21557 | Incantation | 197? | 20.00 |

### FOREIGNER

**ATLANTIC**

| Number | Title (A Side/B Side) | Yr | NM |
|---|---|---|---|
| ❑ SD 16999 | 4 | 1981 | 10.00 |
| *—First pressings have a hologram sticker on the upper back cover* | | | |
| ❑ SD 16999 | 4 | 1982 | 8.00 |
| *—No hologram sticker on back cover* | | | |
| ❑ SD 18215 | Foreigner | 1977 | 10.00 |
| ❑ SD 19109 | Foreigner | 1977 | 8.00 |
| *—Reissue of 18215* | | | |
| ❑ SD 19999 | Double Vision | 1978 | 10.00 |
| *—Second cover has a blue tint with the words "Double Vision" right under the band name* | | | |
| ❑ SD 19999 | Double Vision | 1978 | 12.00 |
| *—Original cover is mostly brown with the words "Double Vision" barely visible along the bottom edge of front cover* | | | |
| ❑ SD 19999 | Double Vision | 1979 | 8.00 |
| *—Third cover is the same as the second cover, but has a red tint* | | | |
| ❑ SD 29999 | Head Games | 1979 | 10.00 |
| ❑ 80999 | Records | 1982 | 10.00 |
| ❑ 81808 | Inside Information | 1988 | 10.00 |
| ❑ 81999 | Agent Provocateur | 1984 | 10.00 |
| ❑ A1-82299 | Unusual Heat | 1990 | 25.00 |
| *—U.S. vinyl available only through Columbia House* | | | |

**MOBILE FIDELITY**

| Number | Title (A Side/B Side) | Yr | NM |
|---|---|---|---|
| ❑ 1-052 | Double Vision | 1981 | 30.00 |
| *—Audiophile vinyl* | | | |

### FOREST

**HARVEST**

| Number | Title (A Side/B Side) | Yr | NM |
|---|---|---|---|
| ❑ SKAO-419 | Forest | 1970 | 50.00 |

### FORGOTTEN CHILD

**BLUE LAMPION**

| Number | Title (A Side/B Side) | Yr | NM |
|---|---|---|---|
| ❑ BLM 10001 | Forgotten Child | 1986 | 60.00 |

### FORMULA V

**BURLINGUEN**

| Number | Title (A Side/B Side) | Yr | NM |
|---|---|---|---|
| ❑ (# unknown) | Formula V | 197? | 25.00 |

**MIAMI**

| Number | Title (A Side/B Side) | Yr | NM |
|---|---|---|---|
| ❑ 6076 | Formula V | 197? | 25.00 |

### FORREST, EUGENE "FLIP"

**SAVOY**

| Number | Title (A Side/B Side) | Yr | NM |
|---|---|---|---|
| ❑ MG-14392 | I Heard It on the Radio | 197? | 20.00 |

### FORREST, HELEN

**AUDIOPHILE**

| Number | Title (A Side/B Side) | Yr | NM |
|---|---|---|---|
| ❑ AP-47 | On the Sunny Side of the Street | 1958 | 60.00 |

**CAPITOL**

| Number | Title (A Side/B Side) | Yr | NM |
|---|---|---|---|
| ❑ T 704 [M] | Voice of the Name Bands | 1956 | 50.00 |
| *—Turquoise label* | | | |

**JOYCE**

| Number | Title (A Side/B Side) | Yr | NM |
|---|---|---|---|
| ❑ 6008 | Big Bands' Greatest Vocalists, Vol. 2 | 197? | 15.00 |
| ❑ 6012 | Big Bands' Greatest Vocalists, Vol. 4 | 197? | 15.00 |
| ❑ 6019 | Big Bands' Greatest Vocalists, Vol. 7 | 197? | 15.00 |
| ❑ 6021 | Big Bands' Greatest Vocalists, Vol. 8 | 197? | 15.00 |

### FORREST, JIMMY

**NEW JAZZ**

| Number | Title (A Side/B Side) | Yr | NM |
|---|---|---|---|
| ❑ NJLP-8250 [M] | Forrest Fire | 1960 | 100.00 |
| *—Purple label* | | | |
| ❑ NJLP-8250 [M] | Forrest Fire | 1965 | 50.00 |
| *—Blue label with trident logo at right* | | | |
| ❑ NJLP-8293 [M] | Soul Street | 1962 | 100.00 |
| *—Purple label* | | | |
| ❑ NJLP-8293 [M] | Soul Street | 1965 | 50.00 |
| *—Blue label with trident logo at right* | | | |

**PRESTIGE**

| Number | Title (A Side/B Side) | Yr | NM |
|---|---|---|---|
| ❑ PRLP-7202 [M] | Out of the Forrest | 1961 | 80.00 |
| *—Yellow label* | | | |
| ❑ PRLP-7202 [M] | Out of the Forrest | 1965 | 40.00 |
| *—Blue label with trident logo at right* | | | |
| ❑ PRLP-7218 [M] | Most Much! | 1961 | 80.00 |
| *—Yellow label* | | | |
| ❑ PRLP-7218 [M] | Most Much! | 1965 | 40.00 |
| *—Blue label with trident logo at right* | | | |
| ❑ PRLP-7235 [M] | Sit Down and Relax with Jimmy Forrest | 1962 | 80.00 |
| *—Yellow label* | | | |
| ❑ PRLP-7235 [M] | Sit Down and Relax with Jimmy Forrest | 1965 | 40.00 |
| *—Blue label with trident logo at right* | | | |
| ❑ PRST-7235 [S] | Sit Down and Relax with Jimmy Forrest | 1962 | 100.00 |
| *—Silver label* | | | |
| ❑ PRST-7235 [S] | Sit Down and Relax with Jimmy Forrest | 1965 | 50.00 |
| *—Blue label with trident logo at right* | | | |
| ❑ PRST-7235 [S] | Sit Down and Relax with Jimmy Forrest | 1973 | 25.00 |
| *—Green label reissue* | | | |

**UNITED**

| Number | Title (A Side/B Side) | Yr | NM |
|---|---|---|---|
| ❑ 002 [10] | Night Train | 1955 | 120.00 |

### FORRESTER, HOWDY

**CUB**

| Number | Title (A Side/B Side) | Yr | NM |
|---|---|---|---|
| ❑ 8008 [M] | Fancy Fiddlin' Country Style | 1960 | 40.00 |

**MGM**

| Number | Title (A Side/B Side) | Yr | NM |
|---|---|---|---|
| ❑ E-4035 [M] | Fancy Fiddlin' Country Style | 1962 | 30.00 |
| *—Reissue of Cub LP* | | | |

**UNITED ARTISTS**

| Number | Title (A Side/B Side) | Yr | NM |
|---|---|---|---|
| ❑ UAL-3295 [M] | Fiddlin' Country Style | 1963 | 20.00 |
| ❑ UAS-6295 [S] | Fiddlin' Country Style | 1963 | 25.00 |

### FORRESTER, MAUREEN

**RCA VICTOR RED SEAL**

| Number | Title (A Side/B Side) | Yr | NM |
|---|---|---|---|
| ❑ LSC-2275 [S] | Brahms, Schumann: Lieder | 1959 | 20.00 |
| *—Original with "shaded dog" label* | | | |

### FORT MUDGE MEMORIAL DUMP, THE

**MERCURY**

| Number | Title (A Side/B Side) | Yr | NM |
|---|---|---|---|
| ❑ SR-61256 | The Fort Mudge Memorial Dump | 1970 | 30.00 |

### FORTUNE, JOHNNY

**PARK AVENUE**

| Number | Title (A Side/B Side) | Yr | NM |
|---|---|---|---|
| ❑ S-401 [S] | Soul Surfer | 1963 | 300.00 |
| ❑ P-1301 [M] | Soul Surfer | 1963 | 200.00 |

### FORTUNE, SONNY

**STRATA-EAST**

| Number | Title (A Side/B Side) | Yr | NM |
|---|---|---|---|
| ❑ SES-7423 | Long Before Our Mothers Cried | 1974 | 20.00 |

### FORTUNES, THE (1)

**CAPITOL**

| Number | Title (A Side/B Side) | Yr | NM |
|---|---|---|---|
| ❑ ST-647 | Freedom | 1971 | — |
| *—Canceled* | | | |
| ❑ ST-809 | Here Comes That Rainy Day Feeling Again | 1971 | 20.00 |
| ❑ ST-11041 | Storm in a Teacup | 1972 | 15.00 |
| *—Contains the canceled "Freedom" LP with one track deleted, plus the title song added* | | | |

**COCA-COLA**

| Number | Title (A Side/B Side) | Yr | NM |
|---|---|---|---|
| ❑ (no #) [DJ] | It's the Real Thing | 1969 | 60.00 |

**PRESS**

| Number | Title (A Side/B Side) | Yr | NM |
|---|---|---|---|
| ❑ PR 73002 [M] | The Fortunes | 1965 | 35.00 |
| ❑ PRS 83002 [S] | The Fortunes | 1965 | 50.00 |

WORLD PACIFIC

| Number | Title (A Side/B Side) | Yr | NM |
|---|---|---|---|
| ❑ WPS-21904 | That Same Old Feeling | 1970 | 15.00 |

### 49TH PARALLEL, THE

MAVERICK

| Number | Title (A Side/B Side) | Yr | NM |
|---|---|---|---|
| ❑ MAS-7001 | The 49th Parallel | 1969 | 250.00 |

### FORUM, THE

MIRA

| Number | Title (A Side/B Side) | Yr | NM |
|---|---|---|---|
| ❑ MLP-301 [M] | The River Is Wide | 1967 | 15.00 |
| ❑ MLPS-301 [S] | The River Is Wide | 1967 | 20.00 |

### FOSTER, CHUCK

PHILLIPS INTERNATIONAL

| Number | Title (A Side/B Side) | Yr | NM |
|---|---|---|---|
| ❑ PLP-1965 [M] | Chuck Foster at the Hotel Peabody | 1961 | 200.00 |

### FOSTER, DAVID

MOBILE FIDELITY

| Number | Title (A Side/B Side) | Yr | NM |
|---|---|---|---|
| ❑ 1-123 | The Best of Me | 1982 | 20.00 |
| *—Audiophile vinyl* | | | |

### FOSTER, FRANK

ARGO

| Number | Title (A Side/B Side) | Yr | NM |
|---|---|---|---|
| ❑ LP-717 [M] | Basie Is Our Boss | 1963 | 25.00 |
| ❑ LPS-717 [S] | Basie Is Our Boss | 1963 | 30.00 |

BLUE NOTE

| Number | Title (A Side/B Side) | Yr | NM |
|---|---|---|---|
| ❑ BLP-5043 [10] | Frank Foster Quintet | 1954 | 400.00 |
| ❑ BST-84278 | Manhattan Fever | 1968 | 25.00 |

MAINSTREAM

| Number | Title (A Side/B Side) | Yr | NM |
|---|---|---|---|
| ❑ MRL-349 | The Loud Minority | 1972 | 20.00 |

PRESTIGE

| Number | Title (A Side/B Side) | Yr | NM |
|---|---|---|---|
| ❑ PRLP-7461 [M] | Fearless | 1966 | 25.00 |
| ❑ PRST-7461 [S] | Fearless | 1966 | 30.00 |
| ❑ PRLP-7479 [M] | Soul Outing! | 1967 | 30.00 |
| ❑ PRST-7479 [S] | Soul Outing! | 1967 | 25.00 |

### FOSTER, GARY

REVELATION

| Number | Title (A Side/B Side) | Yr | NM |
|---|---|---|---|
| ❑ REV-5 | Subconsciously | 1968 | 20.00 |
| ❑ REV-19 | Grand Clu Classe | 197? | 20.00 |

### FOSTER, HERMAN

ARGO

| Number | Title (A Side/B Side) | Yr | NM |
|---|---|---|---|
| ❑ LP-727 [M] | Ready and Willing | 1964 | 20.00 |
| ❑ LPS-727 [S] | Ready and Willing | 1964 | 25.00 |

EPIC

| Number | Title (A Side/B Side) | Yr | NM |
|---|---|---|---|
| ❑ LA 16010 [M] | Have You Heard? | 1960 | 20.00 |
| ❑ LA 16016 [M] | The Explosive Piano of Herman Foster | 1961 | 20.00 |
| ❑ BA 17010 [S] | Have You Heard? | 1960 | 25.00 |
| ❑ BA 17016 [S] | The Explosive Piano of Herman Foster | 1961 | 25.00 |

### FOSTER, PAT

COUNTERPOINT

| Number | Title (A Side/B Side) | Yr | NM |
|---|---|---|---|
| ❑ CPT-560 [M] | Documentary Talking Blues | 195? | 40.00 |

RIVERSIDE

| Number | Title (A Side/B Side) | Yr | NM |
|---|---|---|---|
| ❑ RLP-12-654 [M] | Gold Rush Songs | 195? | 40.00 |

### FOSTER, RONNIE

BLUE NOTE

| Number | Title (A Side/B Side) | Yr | NM |
|---|---|---|---|
| ❑ BST-84382 | Two Headed Freap | 1972 | 20.00 |

### FOUL DOGS, THE

RHYTHM SOUND

| Number | Title (A Side/B Side) | Yr | NM |
|---|---|---|---|
| ❑ GA-481 | No. 1 | 1968 | 300.00 |

### FOUNDATIONS, THE

UNI

| Number | Title (A Side/B Side) | Yr | NM |
|---|---|---|---|
| ❑ 73016 | Baby Now That I've Found You | 1968 | 30.00 |
| ❑ 73043 | Build Me Up Buttercup | 1969 | 30.00 |
| ❑ 73058 | Digging the Foundations | 1969 | 30.00 |

### FOUNTAIN, PETE

CORAL

| Number | Title (A Side/B Side) | Yr | NM |
|---|---|---|---|
| ❑ CRL 57200 [M] | Lawrence Welk Presents Pete Fountain | 1958 | 20.00 |
| ❑ CRL 757282 [S] | Pete Fountain's New Orleans | 1959 | 20.00 |
| ❑ CRL 757284 [S] | The Blues | 1959 | 20.00 |
| ❑ CRL 757313 [S] | Pete Fountain Day | 1960 | 20.00 |
| ❑ CRL 757314 [S] | Pete Fountain at the Bateau Lounge | 1960 | 20.00 |
| ❑ CRL 757333 [S] | Pete Fountain Salutes the Great Clarinetists | 1960 | 20.00 |
| ❑ CRL 757357 [S] | Pete Fountain On Tour | 1961 | 20.00 |
| ❑ CRL 757359 [S] | Pete Fountain's French Quarter | 1961 | 20.00 |
| ❑ CRL 757378 [S] | I Love Paris | 1961 | 20.00 |
| ❑ CRL 757394 [S] | Swing Low Sweet Chariot | 1962 | 20.00 |
| ❑ CRL 757401 [S] | Pete Fountain's Music from Dixie | 1962 | 20.00 |
| ❑ CRL 757419 [S] | New Orleans Scene | 1963 | 20.00 |

RCA VICTOR

| Number | Title (A Side/B Side) | Yr | NM |
|---|---|---|---|
| ❑ LSP-2097 [S] | Pete Fountain at the Jazz Band Ball | 1960 | 20.00 |

### FOUNTAIN, PETE, AND AL HIRT

CORAL

| Number | Title (A Side/B Side) | Yr | NM |
|---|---|---|---|
| ❑ CRL 757389 [S] | Bourbon Street | 1962 | 20.00 |

### FOUNTAIN, PETE, AND "BIG" TINY LITTLE

CORAL

| Number | Title (A Side/B Side) | Yr | NM |
|---|---|---|---|
| ❑ CRL 757334 [S] | Mr. New Orleans Meets Mr. Honky Tonk | 1961 | 20.00 |

### FOUR ACES

DECCA

| Number | Title (A Side/B Side) | Yr | NM |
|---|---|---|---|
| ❑ DL 4013 [M] | The Golden Hits of the Four Aces | 1960 | 20.00 |
| ❑ DL 5429 [10] | The Four Aces | 1952 | 80.00 |
| ❑ DL 8122 [M] | The Mood for Love | 1955 | 50.00 |
| *—All-black label, silver print* | | | |
| ❑ DL 8122 [M] | The Mood for Love | 196? | 20.00 |
| *—Black label with color bars* | | | |
| ❑ DL 8191 [M] | Merry Christmas | 1956 | 50.00 |
| ❑ DL 8227 [M] | Sentimental Souvenirs | 1956 | 50.00 |
| *—All-black label, silver print* | | | |
| ❑ DL 8227 [M] | Sentimental Souvenirs | 196? | 20.00 |
| *—Black label with color bars* | | | |
| ❑ DL 8228 [M] | Heart and Soul | 1956 | 50.00 |
| *—All-black label, silver print* | | | |
| ❑ DL 8228 [M] | Heart and Soul | 196? | 20.00 |
| *—Black label with color bars* | | | |
| ❑ DL 8312 [M] | She Sees All the Hollywood Hits | 1957 | 50.00 |
| ❑ DL 8567 [M] | Shuffling Along | 1957 | 50.00 |
| *—All-black label, silver print* | | | |
| ❑ DL 8567 [M] | Shuffling Along | 196? | 20.00 |
| *—Black label with color bars* | | | |
| ❑ DL 8693 [M] | Hits from Hollywood | 1958 | 50.00 |
| *—All-black label, silver print* | | | |
| ❑ DL 8693 [M] | Hits from Hollywood | 196? | 20.00 |
| *—Black label with color bars* | | | |
| ❑ DL 8766 [M] | The Swingin' Aces | 1958 | 40.00 |
| *—All-black label, silver print* | | | |
| ❑ DL 8766 [M] | The Swingin' Aces | 196? | 20.00 |
| *—Black label with color bars* | | | |
| ❑ DL 8855 [M] | Hits from Broadway | 1959 | 40.00 |
| *—All-black label, silver print* | | | |
| ❑ DL 8855 [M] | Hits from Broadway | 196? | 20.00 |
| *—Black label with color bars* | | | |
| ❑ DL 8944 [M] | Beyond the Blue Horizon | 1959 | 40.00 |
| *—All-black label, silver print* | | | |
| ❑ DL 8944 [M] | Beyond the Blue Horizon | 196? | 20.00 |
| *—Black label with color bars* | | | |
| ❑ DL 74013 [S] | The Golden Hits of the Four Aces | 1960 | 25.00 |
| ❑ DL 78766 [S] | The Swingin' Aces | 1958 | 50.00 |
| *—All-black label, silver print* | | | |
| ❑ DL 78766 [S] | The Swingin' Aces | 196? | 25.00 |
| *—Black label with color bars* | | | |
| ❑ DL 78855 [S] | Hits from Broadway | 1959 | 50.00 |
| *—All-black label, silver print* | | | |
| ❑ DL 78855 [S] | Hits from Broadway | 196? | 25.00 |
| *—Black label with color bars* | | | |
| ❑ DL 78944 [S] | Beyond the Blue Horizon | 1959 | 50.00 |
| *—All-black label, silver print* | | | |
| ❑ DL 78944 [S] | Beyond the Blue Horizon | 196? | 25.00 |
| *—Black label with color bars* | | | |

MCA

| Number | Title (A Side/B Side) | Yr | NM |
|---|---|---|---|
| ❑ 4033 [(2)] | The Best of the Four Aces | 197? | 15.00 |

PICKWICK

| Number | Title (A Side/B Side) | Yr | NM |
|---|---|---|---|
| ❑ SPC-3527 | Love Is a Many-Splendored Thing | 197? | 10.00 |

UNITED ARTISTS

| Number | Title (A Side/B Side) | Yr | NM |
|---|---|---|---|
| ❑ UAL-3337 [M] | Record Oldies | 1963 | 20.00 |
| ❑ UAS-6337 [S] | Record Oldies | 1963 | 25.00 |

VOCALION

| Number | Title (A Side/B Side) | Yr | NM |
|---|---|---|---|
| ❑ VL 3604 [M] | The Four Aces Sing | 196? | 15.00 |
| ❑ VL 73881 | There Goes My Heart | 1969 | 12.00 |
| ❑ VL 73902 | Written on the Wind | 1970 | 12.00 |

### FOUR BROTHERS, THE

VIK

| Number | Title (A Side/B Side) | Yr | NM |
|---|---|---|---|
| ❑ LX-1096 [M] | The Four Brothers — Together Again | 1957 | 80.00 |

### FOUR COINS, THE

EPIC

| Number | Title (A Side/B Side) | Yr | NM |
|---|---|---|---|
| ❑ LN 1104 [M] | The Four Coins | 1955 | 50.00 |
| ❑ LN 3445 [M] | The Four Coins in Shangri-La | 1958 | 30.00 |

MGM

| Number | Title (A Side/B Side) | Yr | NM |
|---|---|---|---|
| ❑ E-3944 [M] | Greek Songs | 1961 | 15.00 |
| ❑ SE-3944 [S] | Greek Songs | 1961 | 20.00 |

ROULETTE

| Number | Title (A Side/B Side) | Yr | NM |
|---|---|---|---|
| ❑ R-25288 [M] | Greek Songs Mama Never Taught Me | 1965 | 15.00 |
| ❑ SR-25288 [S] | Greek Songs Mama Never Taught Me | 1965 | 20.00 |

### FOUR FRESHMEN, THE

CAPITOL

| Number | Title (A Side/B Side) | Yr | NM |
|---|---|---|---|
| ❑ H 522 [10] | Voices in Modern | 1955 | 50.00 |
| ❑ T 522 [M] | Voices in Modern | 1955 | 40.00 |
| ❑ T 683 [M] | Four Freshmen and Five Trombones | 1956 | 40.00 |
| ❑ DT 743 [R] | Freshmen Favorites | 196? | 12.00 |
| ❑ SM-743 | Freshmen Favorites | 197? | 10.00 |
| ❑ T 743 [M] | Freshmen Favorites | 1956 | 40.00 |
| ❑ T 763 [M] | 4 Freshmen and 5 Trumpets | 1957 | 40.00 |
| ❑ T 844 [M] | Four Freshmen and Five Saxes | 1957 | 40.00 |
| ❑ T 992 [M] | Voices in Latin | 1958 | 30.00 |
| ❑ ST 1008 [S] | The Four Freshmen In Person | 1958 | 40.00 |
| ❑ T 1008 [M] | The Four Freshmen In Person | 1958 | 30.00 |
| ❑ ST 1074 [S] | Voices in Love | 1958 | 30.00 |
| ❑ T 1074 [M] | Voices in Love | 1958 | 20.00 |
| ❑ ST 1103 [S] | Freshmen Favorites, Vol. 2 | 1959 | 30.00 |
| ❑ T 1103 [M] | Freshmen Favorites, Vol. 2 | 1959 | 20.00 |
| ❑ ST 1189 [S] | Love Lost | 1959 | 30.00 |
| ❑ T 1189 [M] | Love Lost | 1959 | 20.00 |
| ❑ ST 1255 [S] | The Four Freshmen and Five Guitars | 1959 | 30.00 |
| ❑ T 1255 [M] | The Four Freshmen and Five Guitars | 1959 | 20.00 |
| ❑ ST 1295 [S] | Voices and Brass | 1960 | 30.00 |
| ❑ T 1295 [M] | Voices and Brass | 1960 | 20.00 |
| ❑ ST 1378 [S] | First Affair | 1960 | 30.00 |
| ❑ T 1378 [M] | First Affair | 1960 | 20.00 |
| ❑ ST 1485 [S] | Freshmen Year | 1961 | 25.00 |
| ❑ T 1485 [M] | Freshmen Year | 1961 | 20.00 |
| ❑ ST 1543 [S] | Voices in Fun | 1961 | 25.00 |
| ❑ T 1543 [M] | Voices in Fun | 1961 | 20.00 |
| ❑ ST 1640 [S] | The Best of the Four Freshmen | 1962 | 25.00 |
| ❑ T 1640 [M] | The Best of the Four Freshmen | 1962 | 20.00 |
| ❑ ST 1682 [S] | Stars in Our Eyes | 1962 | 25.00 |
| ❑ T 1682 [M] | Stars in Our Eyes | 1962 | 20.00 |
| ❑ ST 1753 [S] | Swingers | 1963 | 20.00 |
| ❑ T 1753 [M] | Swingers | 1963 | 15.00 |
| ❑ ST 1860 [S] | The Four Freshmen In Person, Volume 2 | 1963 | 20.00 |
| ❑ T 1860 [M] | The Four Freshmen In Person, Volume 2 | 1963 | 15.00 |
| ❑ ST 1950 [S] | Got That Feelin' | 1963 | 20.00 |
| ❑ T 1950 [M] | Got That Feelin' | 1963 | 15.00 |
| ❑ ST 2067 [S] | Funny How Time Slips Away | 1964 | 20.00 |
| ❑ T 2067 [M] | Funny How Time Slips Away | 1964 | 15.00 |
| ❑ ST 2168 [S] | More Four Freshmen and Five Trombones | 1964 | 20.00 |
| ❑ T 2168 [M] | More Four Freshmen and Five Trombones | 1964 | 15.00 |
| ❑ SM-11639 | Four Freshmen and Five Trombones | 1977 | 10.00 |
| ❑ SM-11965 | Best of the Four Freshmen | 1978 | 10.00 |

CREATIVE WORLD

| Number | Title (A Side/B Side) | Yr | NM |
|---|---|---|---|
| ❑ ST-1059 [(2)] | Stan Kenton and the Four Freshmen at Butler University | 1972 | 20.00 |

LIBERTY

| Number | Title (A Side/B Side) | Yr | NM |
|---|---|---|---|
| ❑ LST-7563 | Today Is Tomorrow | 1968 | 15.00 |
| ❑ LST-7590 | In a Class By Themselves | 1969 | 15.00 |
| ❑ LST-7630 | Different Strokes | 1969 | 15.00 |
| ❑ LN-10181 | In a Class By Themselves | 198? | 8.00 |

PAUSA

| Number | Title (A Side/B Side) | Yr | NM |
|---|---|---|---|
| ❑ PR-7193 | Fresh! | 1986 | 10.00 |
| ❑ PR-9029 | The Four Freshmen and Five Guitars | 198? | 10.00 |
| ❑ PR-9040 | 4 Freshmen and 5 Trumpets | 1985 | 10.00 |

PICKWICK

| Number | Title (A Side/B Side) | Yr | NM |
|---|---|---|---|
| ❑ SPC-3080 | The Fabulous Four Freshmen | 196? | 12.00 |
| ❑ SPC-3563 | A Taste of Honey | 1977 | 10.00 |

SUNSET

| Number | Title (A Side/B Side) | Yr | NM |
|---|---|---|---|
| ❑ SUS-5289 | My Special Angel | 1970 | 12.00 |

### FOUR GIRLS, THE

CORAL

| Number | Title (A Side/B Side) | Yr | NM |
|---|---|---|---|
| ❑ CRL 57158 [M] | Make a Joyful Noise Unto the Lord | 1957 | 60.00 |

### FOUR JACKS AND A JILL (1)

RCA VICTOR

| Number | Title (A Side/B Side) | Yr | NM |
|---|---|---|---|
| ❑ LPM-4019 [M] | Master Jack | 1968 | 30.00 |
| ❑ LSP-4019 [S] | Master Jack | 1968 | 15.00 |
| ❑ LSP-4103 | Fables | 1968 | 15.00 |

### FOUR KNIGHTS, THE

CAPITOL

| Number | Title (A Side/B Side) | Yr | NM |
|---|---|---|---|
| ❑ H 346 [10] | Spotlight Songs | 1953 | 200.00 |
| ❑ T 346 [M] | Spotlight Songs | 1956 | 150.00 |

CORAL

| Number | Title (A Side/B Side) | Yr | NM |
|---|---|---|---|
| ❑ CRL 57221 [M] | The Four Knights | 1959 | 100.00 |
| ❑ CRL 57309 [M] | Million Dollar Baby | 1960 | 60.00 |
| ❑ CRL 757309 [S] | Million Dollar Baby | 1960 | 80.00 |

### FOUR LADS, THE

COLUMBIA

| Number | Title (A Side/B Side) | Yr | NM |
|---|---|---|---|
| ❑ CL 861 [M] | The Four Lads with Frankie Laine | 1956 | 40.00 |
| ❑ CL 912 [M] | On the Sunny Side | 1956 | 40.00 |
| ❑ CL 1045 [M] | The Four Lads Sing Frank Loesser | 1957 | 40.00 |

The 4 Seasons, *Edizione d'Oro,* Philips PHS 2-6501, 1968, 2 records, white "4" on cover, $30.

| Number | Title (A Side/B Side) | Yr | NM |
|---|---|---|---|
| ❑ CL 1111 [M] | Four on the Aisle | 1958 | 25.00 |
| ❑ CL 1223 [M] | Breezin' Along | 1958 | 25.00 |
| ❑ CL 1235 [M] | The Four Lads' Greatest Hits | 1958 | 25.00 |
| ❑ CL 1299 [M] | The Four Lads Swing Along | 1959 | 25.00 |
| ❑ CL 1407 [M] | High Spirits! | 1959 | 25.00 |
| ❑ CL 1502 [M] | Love Affair | 1960 | 15.00 |
| ❑ CL 1550 [M] | Everything Goes | 1960 | 15.00 |
| ❑ CL 2545 [10] | The Four Lads Sing Frank Loesser | 1956 | 50.00 |
| ❑ CL 2577 [10] | Stage Show | 1956 | 50.00 |
| ❑ CL 6329 [10] | Stage Show | 1954 | 50.00 |
| ❑ CS 8035 [S] | Breezin' Along | 1958 | 30.00 |
| ❑ CS 8047 [S] | Four on the Aisle | 1958 | 30.00 |
| ❑ CS 8106 [S] | The Four Lads Swing Along | 1959 | 30.00 |
| ❑ CS 8203 [S] | High Spirits! | 1959 | 30.00 |
| ❑ CS 8293 [S] | Love Affair | 1960 | 20.00 |
| ❑ CS 8350 [S] | Everything Goes | 1960 | 20.00 |

DOT

| Number | Title (A Side/B Side) | Yr | NM |
|---|---|---|---|
| ❑ DLP-3438 [M] | Hits of the 60's | 1962 | 15.00 |
| ❑ DLP-3533 [M] | Oh Happy Day | 1963 | 15.00 |
| ❑ DLP-25438 [S] | Hits of the 60's | 1962 | 20.00 |
| ❑ DLP-25533 [S] | Oh Happy Day | 1963 | 20.00 |

HARMONY

| Number | Title (A Side/B Side) | Yr | NM |
|---|---|---|---|
| ❑ HS 11369 | Moments to Remember | 1970 | 12.00 |

KAPP

| Number | Title (A Side/B Side) | Yr | NM |
|---|---|---|---|
| ❑ KL-1224 [M] | Twelve Hits | 1961 | 15.00 |
| ❑ KL-1254 [M] | Dixieland Doin's | 1961 | 15.00 |
| ❑ KS-3224 [S] | Twelve Hits | 1961 | 20.00 |
| ❑ KS-3254 [S] | Dixieland Doin's | 1961 | 20.00 |

UNITED ARTISTS

| Number | Title (A Side/B Side) | Yr | NM |
|---|---|---|---|
| ❑ UAL-3356 [M] | This Year's Top Movie Hits | 1964 | 15.00 |
| ❑ UAL-3399 [M] | Songs of World War I | 1964 | 15.00 |
| ❑ UAS-6356 [S] | This Year's Top Movie Hits | 1964 | 20.00 |
| ❑ UAS-6399 [S] | Songs of World War I | 1964 | 20.00 |

**FOUR LOVERS, THE**

RCA VICTOR

| Number | Title (A Side/B Side) | Yr | NM |
|---|---|---|---|
| ❑ LPM-1317 [M] | Joyride | 1956 | 700.00 |

**FOUR MOST, THE**

DAWN

| Number | Title (A Side/B Side) | Yr | NM |
|---|---|---|---|
| ❑ DLP-1111 [M] | The Four Most | 1956 | 80.00 |

**FOUR PREPS, THE**

CAPITOL

| Number | Title (A Side/B Side) | Yr | NM |
|---|---|---|---|
| ❑ T 994 [M] | The Four Preps | 1958 | 30.00 |
| ❑ T 1090 [M] | The Things We Did Last Summer | 1958 | 25.00 |
| ❑ ST 1216 [S] | Dancing and Dreaming | 1959 | 25.00 |
| ❑ T 1216 [M] | Dancing and Dreaming | 1959 | 20.00 |
| ❑ DT 1291 [R] | Early in the Morning | 1960 | 12.00 |
| ❑ T 1291 [M] | Early in the Morning | 1960 | 25.00 |
| ❑ ST 1566 [S] | The Four Preps on Campus | 1961 | 25.00 |
| ❑ T 1566 [M] | The Four Preps on Campus | 1961 | 20.00 |
| ❑ ST 1647 [S] | Campus Encore | 1962 | 25.00 |
| ❑ T 1647 [M] | Campus Encore | 1962 | 20.00 |
| ❑ ST 1814 [S] | Campus Confidential | 1963 | 20.00 |
| ❑ T 1814 [M] | Campus Confidential | 1963 | 15.00 |
| ❑ ST 1976 [S] | Songs for a Campus Party | 1963 | 20.00 |
| ❑ T 1976 [M] | Songs for a Campus Party | 1963 | 15.00 |
| ❑ ST 2169 [S] | How to Succeed in Love | 1964 | 20.00 |
| ❑ T 2169 [M] | How to Succeed in Love | 1964 | 15.00 |
| ❑ ST 2708 [S] | The Best of the Four Preps | 1967 | 12.00 |
| ❑ T 2708 [M] | The Best of the Four Preps | 1967 | 15.00 |

**FOUR SEASONS, THE**

MCA/CURB

| Number | Title (A Side/B Side) | Yr | NM |
|---|---|---|---|
| ❑ 5632 | Starfighter | 1985 | 10.00 |

MOTOWN

| Number | Title (A Side/B Side) | Yr | NM |
|---|---|---|---|
| ❑ 788 | Inside Out | 1973 | — |
| *—Canceled* | | | |

MOWEST

| Number | Title (A Side/B Side) | Yr | NM |
|---|---|---|---|
| ❑ MW 108L | Chameleon | 1972 | 12.00 |

PHILIPS

| Number | Title (A Side/B Side) | Yr | NM |
|---|---|---|---|
| ❑ PHS-2-6501 [(2)] | Edizione d'Oro | 1968 | 25.00 |
| *—Number "4" on cover is red on gold foil* | | | |
| ❑ PHS-2-6501 [(2)] | Edizione d'Oro | 1968 | 30.00 |
| *—Number "4" on cover is white on gold foil* | | | |
| ❑ PHS-2-6501 [(2)] | Edizione d'Oro | 1969 | 25.00 |
| *—Number "4" on cover is white on gold board* | | | |
| ❑ PHM 200124 [M] | Dawn (Go Away) and 11 Other Great Songs | 1964 | 20.00 |
| ❑ PHM 200129 [M] | Born to Wander | 1964 | 20.00 |
| ❑ PHM 200146 [M] | Rag Doll | 1964 | 20.00 |
| *—With yellow seal noting presence of "Save It For Me"* | | | |
| ❑ PHM 200146 [M] | Rag Doll | 1964 | 20.00 |
| *—Without yellow seal noting presence of "Save It For Me"* | | | |
| ❑ PHM 200150 [M] | All the Song Hits of the Four Seasons | 1964 | 20.00 |
| ❑ PHM 200164 [M] | The 4 Seasons Entertain You | 1965 | 15.00 |
| *—With blue seal noting presence of "Bye Bye Baby" and "Toy Soldier"* | | | |
| ❑ PHM 200164 [M] | The 4 Seasons Entertain You | 1965 | 20.00 |
| *—With orange seal noting presence of "Bye Bye Baby" and "Toy Soldier"* | | | |
| ❑ PHM 200164 [M] | The 4 Seasons Entertain You | 1965 | 20.00 |
| *—With orange seal noting presence of "Bye Bye Baby"* | | | |
| ❑ PHM 200193 [M] | Big Hits by Burt Bacharach...Hal David...Bob Dylan | 1965 | 20.00 |
| *—"Open book" cover* | | | |
| ❑ PHM 200193 [M] | Big Hits by Burt Bacharach...Hal David...Bob Dylan | 1966 | 30.00 |
| *—Group photos on cover* | | | |
| ❑ PHM 200196 [M] | The 4 Seasons' Gold Vault of Hits | 196? | 12.00 |
| *—Title in all-black print* | | | |
| ❑ PHM 200196 [M] | The 4 Seasons' Gold Vault of Hits | 1965 | 15.00 |
| *—Title in red print with black border* | | | |
| ❑ PHM 200196 [M] | The 4 Seasons' Gold Vault of Hits | 1965 | 20.00 |
| *—Title in red print with no border* | | | |
| ❑ PHM 200201 [M] | Working My Way Back to You | 1966 | 20.00 |
| ❑ PHM 200221 [M] | 2nd Vault of Golden Hits | 1966 | 15.00 |
| ❑ PHM 200222 [M] | Lookin' Back | 1966 | 20.00 |
| ❑ PHM 200223 [M] | The Four Seasons' Christmas Album | 1966 | 25.00 |
| *—Reissue of Vee Jay album (same contents and order) with new cover* | | | |
| ❑ PHM 200243 [M] | New Gold Hits | 1967 | 20.00 |
| ❑ PHS 600124 [S] | Dawn (Go Away) and 11 Other Great Songs | 1964 | 25.00 |
| ❑ PHS 600129 [S] | Born to Wander | 1964 | 25.00 |
| ❑ PHS 600146 [S] | Rag Doll | 1964 | 25.00 |
| *—With yellow seal noting presence of "Save It For Me"* | | | |
| ❑ PHS 600146 [S] | Rag Doll | 1964 | 25.00 |
| *—Without yellow seal noting presence of "Save It For Me"* | | | |
| ❑ PHS 600150 [S] | All the Song Hits of the Four Seasons | 1964 | 25.00 |
| ❑ PHS 600164 [S] | The 4 Seasons Entertain You | 1965 | 20.00 |
| *—With blue seal noting presence of "Bye Bye Baby" and "Toy Soldier"* | | | |
| ❑ PHS 600164 [S] | The 4 Seasons Entertain You | 1965 | 25.00 |
| *—With orange seal noting presence of "Bye Bye Baby" and "Toy Soldier"* | | | |
| ❑ PHS 600164 [S] | The 4 Seasons Entertain You | 1965 | 25.00 |
| *—With orange seal noting presence of "Bye Bye Baby"* | | | |
| ❑ PHS 600193 [S] | Big Hits by Burt Bacharach...Hal David...Bob Dylan | 1965 | 25.00 |
| *—"Open book" cover* | | | |
| ❑ PHS 600193 [S] | Big Hits by Burt Bacharach...Hal David...Bob Dylan | 1966 | 40.00 |
| *—Group photos on cover* | | | |
| ❑ PHS 600196 [S] | The 4 Seasons' Gold Vault of Hits | 196? | 15.00 |
| *—Title in all-black print* | | | |
| ❑ PHS 600196 [S] | The 4 Seasons' Gold Vault of Hits | 1965 | 20.00 |
| *—Title in red print with black border* | | | |
| ❑ PHS 600196 [S] | The 4 Seasons' Gold Vault of Hits | 1965 | 25.00 |
| *—Title in red print with no border* | | | |
| ❑ PHS 600201 [S] | Working My Way Back to You | 1966 | 25.00 |
| ❑ PHS 600221 [S] | 2nd Vault of Golden Hits | 1966 | 20.00 |
| ❑ PHS 600222 [S] | Lookin' Back | 1966 | 25.00 |
| ❑ PHS 600223 [S] | The Four Seasons' Christmas Album | 1966 | 30.00 |
| ❑ PHS 600243 [S] | New Gold Hits | 1967 | 25.00 |
| ❑ PHS 600290 | The Genuine Imitation Life Gazette | 1969 | 15.00 |
| *—White newspaper* | | | |
| ❑ PHS 600290 | The Genuine Imitation Life Gazette | 1969 | 25.00 |
| *—Yellow newspaper* | | | |
| ❑ PHS 600341 | Half & Half | 1970 | 20.00 |

PICKWICK

| Number | Title (A Side/B Side) | Yr | NM |
|---|---|---|---|
| ❑ SPC-3223 | Brotherhood of Man | 1970 | 12.00 |
| *—Mass-market version of Sears 609* | | | |

PRIVATE STOCK

| Number | Title (A Side/B Side) | Yr | NM |
|---|---|---|---|
| ❑ PS-7000 [(2)] | The Four Seasons Story | 1975 | 15.00 |

RHINO

| Number | Title (A Side/B Side) | Yr | NM |
|---|---|---|---|
| ❑ RNLP 70234 | The Four Seasons' Christmas Album | 1987 | 12.00 |
| *—Reissue of Philips album (same contents and order)* | | | |
| ❑ R1-70247 | Working My Way Back to You | 1988 | 10.00 |
| *—Reissue of Philips 600-201* | | | |
| ❑ R1-70249 | The Genuine Imitation Life Gazette | 1988 | 10.00 |
| *—Reissue of Philips 600-290* | | | |
| ❑ R1-71248 | Big Hits by Burt Bacharach...Hal David...Bob Dylan | 1988 | 10.00 |
| *—Reissue of Philips 600-193* | | | |
| ❑ R1-71490 [(2)] | Anthology | 1988 | 12.00 |
| ❑ RNRP-72998 [(4)] | 25th Anniversary Collection | 1987 | 25.00 |



Except when noted otherwise, VG = 25% of NM, and VG+ = 50% of NM. (Example: VG = $2.00, VG+ = $4.00 and NM = $8.00.)

| Number | Title (A Side/B Side) | Yr | NM |
|---|---|---|---|
| **SEARS** | | | |
| ❑ SPS-609 | Brotherhood of Man | 1970 | 25.00 |
| **VEE JAY** | | | |
| ❑ LP-1053 [M] | Sherry & 11 Others | 1962 | 40.00 |
| ❑ SR-1053 [S] | Sherry & 11 Others | 1962 | 60.00 |
| ❑ LP 1055 [M] | The Four Seasons Greetings | 1962 | 30.00 |
| ❑ SR 1055 [S] | The Four Seasons Greetings | 1962 | 40.00 |
| ❑ LP-1056 [M] | Big Girls Don't Cry and Twelve Others | 1963 | 30.00 |
| ❑ SR-1056 [S] | Big Girls Don't Cry and Twelve Others | 1963 | 40.00 |
| ❑ LP-1059 [M] | Ain't That a Shame and 11 Others | 1963 | 30.00 |
| ❑ SR-1059 [S] | Ain't That a Shame and 11 Others | 1963 | 40.00 |
| ❑ LP-1065 [M] | Golden Hits of the Four Seasons | 1963 | 30.00 |
| ❑ SR-1065 [S] | Golden Hits of the Four Seasons | 1963 | 40.00 |
| ❑ LP-1082 [M] | Stay & Other Great Hits | 1964 | 25.00 |
| *—Retitled version of Folk-Nanny* | | | |
| ❑ LP-1082 [M] | Folk-Nanny | 1964 | 30.00 |
| ❑ SR-1082 [S] | Stay & Other Great Hits | 1964 | 30.00 |
| *—Retitled version of Folk-Nanny* | | | |
| ❑ SR-1082 [S] | Folk-Nanny | 1964 | 40.00 |
| ❑ LP-1088 [M] | More Golden Hits by the Four Seasons | 1964 | 20.00 |
| *—With "Apple of My Eye" on record* | | | |
| ❑ LP-1088 [M] | More Golden Hits by the Four Seasons | 1964 | 30.00 |
| *—With "Long Lonely Nights" on record* | | | |
| ❑ SR-1088 [S] | More Golden Hits by the Four Seasons | 1964 | 25.00 |
| *—With "Apple of My Eye" on record* | | | |
| ❑ SR-1088 [S] | More Golden Hits by the Four Seasons | 1964 | 40.00 |
| *—With "Long Lonely Nights" on record* | | | |
| ❑ LP-1121 [M] | We Love Girls | 1965 | 30.00 |
| ❑ LPS-1121 [S] | We Love Girls | 1965 | 40.00 |
| ❑ LP-1154 [M] | Recorded Live on Stage | 1965 | 30.00 |
| ❑ LPS-1154 [S] | Recorded Live on Stage | 1965 | 40.00 |
| **WARNER BROS.** | | | |
| ❑ BS 2900 | Who Loves You | 1975 | 12.00 |
| ❑ BS 3016 | Helicon | 1977 | 12.00 |
| ❑ 2WB 3497 [(2)] | Reunited Live | 1980 | 15.00 |

## FOUR TOPS, THE

| Number | Title (A Side/B Side) | Yr | NM |
|---|---|---|---|
| **ABC** | | | |
| ❑ D-862 | Night Lights Harmony | 1975 | 12.00 |
| ❑ D-968 | Catfish | 1976 | 12.00 |
| ❑ D-1014 | The Show Must Go On | 1977 | 12.00 |
| ❑ AA-1092 | At the Top | 1978 | 12.00 |
| **ABC DUNHILL** | | | |
| ❑ DSX-50129 | Keeper of the Castle | 1972 | 12.00 |
| ❑ DSX-50144 | Main Street People | 1973 | 12.00 |
| ❑ DSX-50166 | Meeting of the Minds | 1974 | 12.00 |
| ❑ DSX-50188 | Live & In Concert | 1974 | 12.00 |
| **ARISTA** | | | |
| ❑ AL-8492 | Indestructible | 1988 | 8.00 |
| **CASABLANCA** | | | |
| ❑ NBLP 7258 | Tonight! | 1981 | 10.00 |
| ❑ NBLP 7266 | One More Mountain | 1982 | 10.00 |
| **COMMAND** | | | |
| ❑ CQD-40011 [Q] | Keeper of the Castle | 1974 | 20.00 |
| ❑ CQD-40012 [Q] | Main Street People | 1974 | 20.00 |
| **MCA** | | | |
| ❑ 27019 | Greatest Hits | 198? | 10.00 |
| **MOTOWN** | | | |
| ❑ M5-114V1 | Superstar Series, Vol. 14 | 1981 | 10.00 |
| ❑ M5-122V1 | Four Tops | 1981 | 8.00 |
| *—Reissue of 622* | | | |
| ❑ M5-149V1 | Four Tops Reach Out | 1981 | 8.00 |
| *—Reissue of 660* | | | |
| ❑ M5-209V1 | The Four Tops' Greatest Hits | 1981 | 8.00 |
| *—Reissue of 662* | | | |
| ❑ 622 [M] | Four Tops | 1964 | 30.00 |
| ❑ MS-622 [S] | Four Tops | 1964 | 40.00 |
| ❑ 634 [M] | Four Tops Second Album | 1965 | 25.00 |
| ❑ MS-634 [S] | Four Tops Second Album | 1965 | 30.00 |
| ❑ 647 [M] | 4 Tops On Top | 1966 | 25.00 |
| ❑ MS-647 [S] | 4 Tops On Top | 1966 | 30.00 |
| ❑ 654 [M] | Four Tops Live! | 1966 | 25.00 |
| ❑ MS-654 [S] | Four Tops Live! | 1966 | 30.00 |
| ❑ 657 [M] | 4 Tops on Broadway | 1967 | 25.00 |
| ❑ MS-657 [S] | 4 Tops on Broadway | 1967 | 30.00 |
| ❑ 660 [M] | Four Tops Reach Out | 1967 | 30.00 |
| ❑ MS-660 [S] | Four Tops Reach Out | 1967 | 25.00 |
| ❑ 662 [M] | The Four Tops Greatest Hits | 1967 | 30.00 |
| ❑ MS-662 [S] | The Four Tops Greatest Hits | 1967 | 20.00 |
| ❑ 669 [M] | Yesterday's Dreams | 1968 | 30.00 |
| ❑ MS-669 [S] | Yesterday's Dreams | 1968 | 20.00 |
| ❑ MS-675 | Four Tops Now! | 1969 | 20.00 |
| ❑ MS-695 | Soul Spin | 1969 | 20.00 |
| ❑ MS-704 | Still Waters Run Deep | 1970 | 20.00 |
| ❑ MS-721 | Changing Times | 1970 | 20.00 |
| ❑ M-740L | Four Tops Greatest Hits, Vol. 2 | 1971 | 20.00 |
| ❑ M-748L | Nature Planned It | 1972 | 20.00 |
| ❑ M-764D [(2)] | The Best of the 4 Tops | 1973 | 15.00 |
| ❑ M9-809A3 [(3)] | Anthology | 1974 | 20.00 |
| ❑ 5224 ML | Still Waters Run Deep | 1982 | 8.00 |
| *—Reissue of 704* | | | |
| ❑ 5258 ML | Four Tops Live! | 1983 | 8.00 |
| *—Reissue of 654* | | | |
| ❑ 5314 ML | Great Songs | 1983 | 10.00 |
| ❑ 6066 ML | Back Where I Belong | 1983 | 10.00 |
| ❑ 6130 ML | Magic | 1985 | 10.00 |
| **WORKSHOP JAZZ** | | | |
| ❑ 217 [M] | Breakin' Through | 1962 | — |
| *—This album is pictured on some early Motown inner sleeves, but is not known to exist* | | | |

## FOUR TUNES, THE

| Number | Title (A Side/B Side) | Yr | NM |
|---|---|---|---|
| **JUBILEE** | | | |
| ❑ LP-1039 [M] | 12 x 4 | 1957 | 250.00 |

## FOURTH CEKCION, THE

| Number | Title (A Side/B Side) | Yr | NM |
|---|---|---|---|
| **SOLAR** | | | |
| ❑ 110 | The Fourth Cekcion | 1970 | 60.00 |

## FOURTH WAY, THE

| Number | Title (A Side/B Side) | Yr | NM |
|---|---|---|---|
| **CAPITOL** | | | |
| ❑ ST-317 | The Fourth Way | 1969 | 25.00 |
| **HARVEST** | | | |
| ❑ SKAO-423 | The Sun and Moon Have Come Together | 1970 | 20.00 |
| ❑ ST-666 | Werewolf | 1971 | 20.00 |

## FOWLER, WALLY

| Number | Title (A Side/B Side) | Yr | NM |
|---|---|---|---|
| **DECCA** | | | |
| ❑ DL 8560 [M] | Call of the Cross | 1958 | 40.00 |
| **DOVE** | | | |
| ❑ 1000 | A Tribute to Elvis Presley | 1977 | 20.00 |
| **KING** | | | |
| ❑ 702 [M] | Gospel Song Festival | 1960 | 100.00 |
| **STARDAY** | | | |
| ❑ SLP-112 [M] | All Nite Singing Gospel Concert | 1960 | 40.00 |
| ❑ SLP-301 [M] | All Nite Singing Concert | 1964 | 30.00 |

## FOWLEY, KIM

| Number | Title (A Side/B Side) | Yr | NM |
|---|---|---|---|
| **ANTILLES** | | | |
| ❑ AN-7075 | Snake Document Masquerade | 1979 | 12.00 |
| **CAPITOL** | | | |
| ❑ ST-11075 | I'm Bad | 1972 | 20.00 |
| ❑ ST-11159 | International Heroes | 1973 | 20.00 |
| ❑ ST-11248 | Automatic | 1974 | 20.00 |
| **GNP CRESCENDO** | | | |
| ❑ GNPS-2132 | Hollywood Confidential | 197? | 12.00 |
| **IMPERIAL** | | | |
| ❑ LP-12413 | Born to Be Wild | 1968 | 40.00 |
| ❑ LP-12423 | Outrageous | 1969 | 40.00 |
| ❑ LP-12443 | Good Clean Fun | 1969 | 40.00 |
| **PVC** | | | |
| ❑ 7906 | Sunset Boulevard | 1978 | 12.00 |
| **TOWER** | | | |
| ❑ ST 5080 [S] | Love Is Alive and Well | 1967 | 40.00 |
| ❑ T 5080 [M] | Love Is Alive and Well | 1967 | 30.00 |

## FOX, CURLY

| Number | Title (A Side/B Side) | Yr | NM |
|---|---|---|---|
| **HARMONY** | | | |
| ❑ HL 7302 [M] | Traveling Blues | 1963 | 20.00 |
| **STARDAY** | | | |
| ❑ SLP-235 [M] | Curly Fox and Texas Ruby | 1963 | 30.00 |

## FOXX, INEZ (AND CHARLIE)

| Number | Title (A Side/B Side) | Yr | NM |
|---|---|---|---|
| **DYNAMO** | | | |
| ❑ DM-7000 [M] | Come By Here | 1967 | 30.00 |
| ❑ DM-7002 [M] | Inez and Charlie Foxx's Greatest Hits | 1967 | 30.00 |
| ❑ DS-8000 [S] | Come By Here | 1967 | 40.00 |
| ❑ DS-8002 [S] | Inez and Charlie Foxx's Greatest Hits | 1967 | 40.00 |
| ❑ DS-8003 | Swingin' Mockin' Band | 1968 | 30.00 |
| **SUE** | | | |
| ❑ LP-1027 [M] | Mockingbird | 1966 | 100.00 |
| **SYMBOL** | | | |
| ❑ SYM-4400 [M] | Mockingbird | 1963 | 150.00 |
| **VOLT** | | | |
| ❑ VOS-6022 | Inez Foxx at Memphis | 1973 | 15.00 |

## FRACTION

| Number | Title (A Side/B Side) | Yr | NM |
|---|---|---|---|
| **ANGELUS** | | | |
| ❑ 571 | Moon Blood | 1971 | 2000. |
| *—VG value 1000; VG+ value 1500* | | | |

## FRAGER, MALCOLM

| Number | Title (A Side/B Side) | Yr | NM |
|---|---|---|---|
| **RCA VICTOR RED SEAL** | | | |
| ❑ LSC-2465 [S] | Prokofiev: Piano Concerto No. 2 | 1961 | 100.00 |
| *—Originals with "shaded dog" label* | | | |

## FRAMPTON, PETER

| Number | Title (A Side/B Side) | Yr | NM |
|---|---|---|---|
| **A&M** | | | |
| ❑ SP-3133 | Wind of Change | 198? | 8.00 |
| *—Budget-line reissue* | | | |
| ❑ SP-3619 | Somethin's Happening | 1974 | 12.00 |
| ❑ PR-3703 | Frampton Comes Alive! | 1976 | 20.00 |
| *—Single-record picture disc of highlights* | | | |
| ❑ SP-3703 [(2)] | Frampton Comes Alive! | 1976 | 12.00 |
| ❑ SP-3710 | Where I Should Be | 1979 | 10.00 |
| ❑ SP-3722 | Breaking All the Rules | 1981 | 10.00 |
| ❑ SP-4348 | Wind of Change | 1972 | 12.00 |
| *—Brown label* | | | |
| ❑ SP-4348 | Wind of Change | 1974 | 10.00 |
| *—Silvery label* | | | |
| ❑ SP-4389 | Frampton's Camel | 1973 | 12.00 |
| *—Brown label* | | | |
| ❑ SP-4389 | Frampton's Camel | 1974 | 10.00 |
| *—Silvery label* | | | |
| ❑ SP-4512 | Frampton | 1975 | 10.00 |
| ❑ SP-4704 | I'm In You | 1977 | 10.00 |
| ❑ SP-4704 [DJ] | I'm In You | 1977 | 40.00 |
| *—Promo-only picture disc* | | | |
| ❑ SP-4905 | The Art of Control | 1982 | 10.00 |
| ❑ SP-6505 [(2)] | Frampton Comes Alive! | 198? | 10.00 |
| *—Budget-line reissue* | | | |
| ❑ SP-17100 [DJ] | Peter Frampton Radio Special | 1979 | 20.00 |
| *—Promo-only interview record* | | | |
| **ATLANTIC** | | | |
| ❑ PR 848 [DJ] | Frampton Is Alive! | 1986 | 20.00 |
| *—Promo-only interview record* | | | |
| ❑ PR 3093 [DJ] | Perfect Fit: A Candid Interview | 1989 | 20.00 |
| *—Promo-only album* | | | |
| ❑ 81290 | Premonition | 1986 | 8.00 |
| ❑ 82030 | Where All the Pieces Fit | 1989 | 8.00 |
| **MOBILE FIDELITY** | | | |
| ❑ 2-262 [(2)] | Frampton Comes Alive! | 1996 | 40.00 |
| *—Audiophile vinyl* | | | |
| **SWEET THUNDER** | | | |
| ❑ 6 [(2)] | Frampton Comes Alive! | 198? | 100.00 |
| *—Audiophile edition* | | | |

## FRANCIS, CONNIE

| Number | Title (A Side/B Side) | Yr | NM |
|---|---|---|---|
| **LEO** | | | |
| ❑ LE-903 [M] | Connie Francis and the Kids Next Door | 1967 | 50.00 |
| ❑ LES-903 [S] | Connie Francis and the Kids Next Door | 1967 | 60.00 |
| **MATI-MOR** | | | |
| ❑ 8002 [M] | Sing Along wth Connie Francis | 1961 | 40.00 |
| *—Made for Brylcreem* | | | |
| **METRO** | | | |
| ❑ M-519 [M] | Connie Francis | 1964 | 20.00 |
| ❑ MS-519 [S] | Connie Francis | 1964 | 25.00 |
| ❑ M-538 [M] | Folk Favorites | 1965 | 20.00 |
| ❑ MS-538 [S] | Folk Favorites | 1965 | 25.00 |
| ❑ M-571 [M] | Songs of Love | 1966 | 20.00 |
| ❑ MS-571 [S] | Songs of Love | 1966 | 25.00 |
| ❑ M-603 [M] | The Incomparable Connie Francis | 1967 | 20.00 |
| ❑ MS-603 [S] | The Incomparable Connie Francis | 1967 | 25.00 |
| **MGM** | | | |
| ❑ GAS-109 | Greatest Golden Groovie Goodies (Golden Archive Series) | 1970 | 25.00 |
| ❑ E-3686 [M] | Who's Sorry Now? | 1958 | 100.00 |
| *—Yellow label* | | | |
| ❑ E-3686 [M] | Who's Sorry Now? | 1960 | 40.00 |
| *—Black label* | | | |
| ❑ E-3761 [M] | The Exciting Connie Francis | 1959 | 30.00 |
| *—Black label* | | | |
| ❑ E-3761 [M] | The Exciting Connie Francis | 1959 | 80.00 |
| *—Yellow label* | | | |
| ❑ SE-3761 [S] | The Exciting Connie Francis | 1959 | 40.00 |
| *—Black label* | | | |
| ❑ SE-3761 [S] | The Exciting Connie Francis | 1959 | 100.00 |
| *—Yellow label* | | | |
| ❑ E-3776 [M] | My Thanks to You | 1959 | 30.00 |
| ❑ SE-3776 [S] | My Thanks to You | 1959 | 40.00 |
| ❑ E-3791 [M] | Italian Favorites | 1959 | 30.00 |
| ❑ SE-3791 [S] | Italian Favorites | 1959 | 40.00 |
| ❑ E-3792 [M] | Christmas in My Heart | 1959 | 30.00 |
| ❑ SE-3792 [S] | Christmas in My Heart | 1959 | 40.00 |
| *—Same as above, but in stereo* | | | |
| ❑ E-3793 [M] | Connie's Greatest Hits | 1960 | 30.00 |
| ❑ E-3794 [M] | Rock 'N' Roll Million Sellers | 1960 | 30.00 |
| ❑ SE-3794 [S] | Rock 'N' Roll Million Sellers | 1960 | 40.00 |
| ❑ E-3795 [M] | Country and Western Golden Hits | 1960 | 30.00 |
| ❑ SE-3795 [S] | Country and Western Golden Hits | 1960 | 40.00 |
| ❑ E-3853 [M] | Spanish and Latin American Favorites | 1960 | 30.00 |
| ❑ SE-3853 [S] | Spanish and Latin American Favorites | 1960 | 40.00 |
| ❑ E-3869 [M] | Jewish Favorites | 1961 | 30.00 |
| ❑ SE-3869 [S] | Jewish Favorites | 1961 | 40.00 |

Aretha Franklin, *Amazing Grace,* Atlantic SD 2-906, 1972, 2 records, $20.

| Number | Title (A Side/B Side) | Yr | NM |
|---|---|---|---|
| ❑ E-3871 [M] | More Italian Favorites | 1960 | 30.00 |
| ❑ SE-3871 [S] | More Italian Favorites | 1960 | 40.00 |
| ❑ E-3893 [M] | Songs to a Swinging Band | 1961 | 30.00 |
| ❑ SE-3893 [S] | Songs to a Swinging Band | 1961 | 40.00 |
| ❑ E-3913 [M] | Connie Francis at the Copa | 1961 | 30.00 |
| ❑ SE-3913 [S] | Connie Francis at the Copa | 1961 | 40.00 |
| ❑ E-3942 [M] | More Greatest Hits | 1961 | 30.00 |
| ❑ SE-3942 [S] | More Greatest Hits | 1961 | 40.00 |
| ❑ E-3965 [M] | Never on Sunday and Other Title Songs from Motion Pictures | 1961 | 30.00 |
| ❑ SE-3965 [S] | Never on Sunday and Other Title Songs from Motion Pictures | 1961 | 40.00 |
| ❑ E-3969 [M] | Folk Song Favorites | 1961 | 30.00 |
| ❑ SE-3969 [S] | Folk Song Favorites | 1961 | 40.00 |
| ❑ E-4013 [M] | Irish Favorites | 1962 | 30.00 |
| ❑ SE-4013 [S] | Irish Favorites | 1962 | 40.00 |
| ❑ E-4022 [M] | Dance Party | 196? | 25.00 |
| *—Retitled version of "Do the Twist"* | | | |
| ❑ E-4022 [M] | Do the Twist | 1962 | 30.00 |
| ❑ SE-4022 [S] | Dance Party | 196? | 30.00 |
| *—Retitled version of "Do the Twist"* | | | |
| ❑ SE-4022 [S] | Do the Twist | 1962 | 40.00 |
| ❑ E-4023 [M] | Fun Songs for Children | 1962 | 50.00 |
| ❑ E-4048 [M] | Award Winning Motion Picture Hits | 1963 | 25.00 |
| ❑ SE-4048 [S] | Award Winning Motion Picture Hits | 1963 | 30.00 |
| ❑ E-4049 [M] | Connie Francis Sings Second Hand Love and Other Hits | 1962 | 25.00 |
| ❑ SE-4049 [S] | Connie Francis Sings Second Hand Love and Other Hits | 1962 | 30.00 |
| ❑ E-4079 [M] | Country Music Connie Style | 1962 | 25.00 |
| ❑ SE-4079 [S] | Country Music Connie Style | 1962 | 30.00 |
| ❑ E-4102 [M] | Modern Italian Hits | 1963 | 25.00 |
| ❑ SE-4102 [S] | Modern Italian Hits | 1963 | 30.00 |
| ❑ E-4123 [M] | Follow the Boys | 1963 | 25.00 |
| ❑ SE-4123 [S] | Follow the Boys | 1963 | 30.00 |
| ❑ E-4124 [M] | German Favorites | 1963 | 25.00 |
| ❑ SE-4124 [S] | German Favorites | 1963 | 30.00 |
| ❑ E-4145 [M] | Greatest American Waltzes | 1963 | 25.00 |
| ❑ SE-4145 [S] | Greatest American Waltzes | 1963 | 30.00 |
| ❑ E-4161 [M] | Mala Femmena & Connie's Big Hits from Italy | 1963 | 25.00 |
| ❑ SE-4161 [S] | Mala Femmena & Connie's Big Hits from Italy | 1963 | 30.00 |
| ❑ E-4167 [M] | The Very Best of Connie Francis | 1963 | 25.00 |
| ❑ SE-4167 [S] | The Very Best of Connie Francis | 1963 | 30.00 |
| ❑ E-4210 [M] | In the Summer of His Years | 1964 | 25.00 |
| ❑ SE-4210 [S] | In the Summer of His Years | 1964 | 30.00 |
| ❑ E-4229 [M] | Looking for Love | 1964 | 25.00 |
| ❑ SE-4229 [S] | Looking for Love | 1964 | 30.00 |
| ❑ E-4253 [M] | A New Kind of Connie | 1964 | 25.00 |
| ❑ SE-4253 [S] | A New Kind of Connie | 1964 | 30.00 |
| ❑ E-4294 [M] | Connie Francis Sings For Mama | 1965 | 25.00 |
| ❑ SE-4294 [S] | Connie Francis Sings For Mama | 1965 | 30.00 |
| ❑ E-4298 [M] | All Time International Hits | 1965 | 25.00 |
| ❑ SE-4298 [S] | All Time International Hits | 1965 | 30.00 |
| ❑ E-4355 [M] | Jealous Heart | 1966 | 25.00 |
| ❑ SE-4355 [S] | Jealous Heart | 1966 | 30.00 |
| ❑ E-4382 [M] | Movie Greats of the 60's | 1966 | 25.00 |
| ❑ SE-4382 [S] | Movie Greats of the 60's | 1966 | 30.00 |
| ❑ E-4399 [M] | Connie's Christmas | 1966 | 25.00 |
| ❑ SE-4399 [S] | Connie's Christmas | 1966 | 30.00 |
| ❑ E-4411 [M] | Live at the Sahara in Las Vegas | 1967 | 25.00 |
| ❑ SE-4411 [S] | Live at the Sahara in Las Vegas | 1967 | 30.00 |
| ❑ E-4448 [M] | Love, Italian Style | 1967 | 25.00 |
| ❑ SE-4448 [S] | Love, Italian Style | 1967 | 30.00 |
| ❑ E-4472 [M] | Connie Francis On Broadway Today | 1967 | 25.00 |
| ❑ SE-4472 [S] | Connie Francis On Broadway Today | 1967 | 30.00 |
| ❑ E-4474 [M] | Grandes Exitos del Cine de los Anos 60 | 1967 | 25.00 |
| ❑ SE-4474 [S] | Grandes Exitos del Cine de los Anos 60 | 1967 | 30.00 |
| ❑ E-4487 [M] | My Heart Cries for You | 1967 | 30.00 |
| ❑ SE-4487 [S] | My Heart Cries for You | 1967 | 25.00 |
| ❑ E-4522 [M] | Hawaii: Connie | 1968 | 100.00 |
| ❑ SE-4522 [S] | Hawaii: Connie | 1968 | 25.00 |
| ❑ E-4573 [M] | Connie & Clyde | 1968 | 150.00 |
| *—Yellow label "Special Disc Jockey Record" in stereo cover with "Mono" sticker* | | | |
| ❑ SE-4573 [S] | Connie & Clyde | 1968 | 25.00 |
| ❑ SE-4585 | Connie Francis Sings Bacharach & David | 1968 | 25.00 |
| ❑ SE-4637 | The Wedding Cake | 1969 | 25.00 |
| ❑ SE-4655 | The Songs of Les Reed | 1969 | 25.00 |
| ❑ MG-1-5406 | I'm Me Again | 198? | 12.00 |
| ❑ MG-1-5410 | Greatest Hits | 198? | 12.00 |
| ❑ MG-1-5411 | Greatest Jewish Hits | 198? | 12.00 |
| ❑ ST-90027 [S] | Award Winning Motion Picture Hits | 196? | 30.00 |
| *—Capitol Record Club edition* | | | |
| ❑ T-90027 [M] | Award Winning Motion Picture Hits | 196? | 30.00 |
| *—Capitol Record Club edition* | | | |
| ❑ ST-90068 [S] | A New Kind of Connie | 1964 | 35.00 |
| *—Capitol Record Club issue* | | | |
| ❑ T-90068 [M] | A New Kind of Connie | 1964 | 30.00 |
| *—Capitol Record Club issue* | | | |
| ❑ ST 90510 [S] | The Very Best of Connie Francis | 1965 | 40.00 |
| *—Capitol Record Club edition* | | | |
| ❑ T 90510 [M] | The Very Best of Connie Francis | 1965 | 40.00 |
| *—Capitol Record Club edition* | | | |
| ❑ ST-90592 [S] | Never on Sunday and Other Title Songs from Motion Pictures | 1965 | 25.00 |
| *—Capitol Record Club edition* | | | |
| ❑ ST-91145 | My Best to You | 1968 | 30.00 |
| *—Capitol Record Club* | | | |

POLYDOR

| Number | Title (A Side/B Side) | Yr | NM |
|---|---|---|---|
| ❑ 827569-1 | The Very Best of Connie Francis | 1985 | 10.00 |
| ❑ 827582-1 | Greatest Hits | 1985 | 10.00 |
| ❑ 827584-1 | Greatest Jewish Hits | 1985 | 10.00 |
| ❑ 839922-1 | Lo Mejor De Su Repertorio | 198? | 10.00 |
| ❑ 839923-1 | 12 Exitos De Connie Francis | 198? | 10.00 |

## FRANCIS, CONNIE, AND HANK WILLIAMS, JR.

Also see each artist's individual listings.

MGM

| Number | Title (A Side/B Side) | Yr | NM |
|---|---|---|---|
| ❑ E-4251 [M] | Connie Francis & Hank Williams, Jr. Sing Great Country Favorites | 1964 | 30.00 |
| ❑ SE-4251 [S] | Connie Francis & Hank Williams, Jr. Sing Great Country Favorites | 1964 | 40.00 |

## FRANCIS, PANAMA

EPIC

| Number | Title (A Side/B Side) | Yr | NM |
|---|---|---|---|
| ❑ BN 629 [S] | Exploding Drums | 1959 | 30.00 |
| ❑ LN 3839 [M] | Exploding Drums | 1959 | 30.00 |

20TH CENTURY FOX

| Number | Title (A Side/B Side) | Yr | NM |
|---|---|---|---|
| ❑ TFM-6101 [M] | Tough Talk | 196? | 25.00 |
| ❑ TFS-6101 [S] | Tough Talk | 196? | 30.00 |

## FRANKE AND THE KNOCKOUTS

MCA

| Number | Title (A Side/B Side) | Yr | NM |
|---|---|---|---|
| ❑ 5473 | Makin' the Point | 1984 | 10.00 |

MILLENNIUM

| Number | Title (A Side/B Side) | Yr | NM |
|---|---|---|---|
| ❑ DJL1-4015 [DJ] | Special Radio Series Volume X | 1981 | 20.00 |
| *—Promo-only music and interview disc* | | | |
| ❑ BXL1-7755 | Franke and the Knockouts | 1981 | 8.00 |
| ❑ BXL1-7763 | Below the Belt | 1982 | 8.00 |
| ❑ DJL1-7764 [EP] | Below the Belt Sampler | 1982 | 20.00 |
| *—Promo-only three-song sampler; contains live version of "I Need Love (The Knockout Shuffle)" that was not issued on LP* | | | |

## FRANKIE AND JOHNNY

WARNER BROS.

| Number | Title (A Side/B Side) | Yr | NM |
|---|---|---|---|
| ❑ BS 2675 | The Sweetheart Sampler | 1973 | 20.00 |

## FRANKLIN, ALAN, EXPLOSION

ALADDIN

| Number | Title (A Side/B Side) | Yr | NM |
|---|---|---|---|
| ❑ 104049 | Come Home Baby | 1969 | 80.00 |

HORNE

| Number | Title (A Side/B Side) | Yr | NM |
|---|---|---|---|
| ❑ JC-888 | The Blues Climax | 1970 | 80.00 |

## FRANKLIN, ARETHA

ARISTA

| Number | Title (A Side/B Side) | Yr | NM |
|---|---|---|---|
| ❑ AL8-8019 | Get It Right | 1983 | 10.00 |
| ❑ AL8-8286 | Who's Zoomin' Who | 1985 | 10.00 |
| ❑ AL-8344 | Jump To It | 1985 | 8.00 |
| *—Budget-line reissue* | | | |
| ❑ AL-8368 | Love All the Hurt Away | 1985 | 8.00 |
| *—Budget-line reissue* | | | |
| ❑ AL-8442 | Aretha | 1986 | 10.00 |
| *—Different album than 9538* | | | |
| ❑ A2L-8497 [(2)] | One Lord, One Faith, One Baptism | 1987 | 20.00 |
| ❑ AL-8572 | Through the Storm | 1989 | 10.00 |
| ❑ AL-9538 | Aretha | 1980 | 10.00 |
| ❑ AL-9552 | Love All the Hurt Away | 1981 | 10.00 |
| ❑ AL-9602 | Jump To It | 1982 | 10.00 |

ATLANTIC

| Number | Title (A Side/B Side) | Yr | NM |
|---|---|---|---|
| ❑ SD 2-906 [(2)] | Amazing Grace | 1972 | 20.00 |
| ❑ 7205 [M] | Aretha Live at Fillmore West | 1971 | 40.00 |
| *—Mono is white label promo only with "d/j copy monaural" sticker on front cover* | | | |
| ❑ QD 7205 [Q] | Aretha Live at Fillmore West | 1973 | 25.00 |
| ❑ SD 7205 [S] | Aretha Live at Fillmore West | 1971 | 15.00 |
| ❑ 7213 [M] | Yoing, Gifted & Black | 1972 | 40.00 |
| *—Mono is promo only; "d/j copy monaural" sticker on front cover* | | | |
| ❑ SD 7213 [S] | Yoing, Gifted & Black | 1972 | 15.00 |



**Except when noted otherwise, VG = 25% of NM, and VG+ = 50% of NM. (Example: VG = $2.00, VG+ = $4.00 and NM = $8.00.)**

| Number | Title (A Side/B Side) | Yr | NM |
|---|---|---|---|
| ❑ SD 7265 | Hey Now Hey (The Other Side of the Sky) | 1973 | 12.00 |
| ❑ SD 7292 | Let Me in Your Life | 1974 | 12.00 |
| ❑ 8139 [M] | I Never Loved a Man the Way I Love You | 1967 | 25.00 |
| ❑ SD 8139 | I Never Loved a Man the Way I Love You | 1969 | 12.00 |
| *—Green and red label* | | | |
| ❑ SD 8139 [S] | I Never Loved a Man the Way I Love You | 1967 | 20.00 |
| *—Green and blue label* | | | |
| ❑ 8150 [M] | Aretha Arrives | 1967 | 25.00 |
| ❑ SD 8150 | Aretha Arrives | 1969 | 12.00 |
| *—Green and red label* | | | |
| ❑ SD 8150 [S] | Aretha Arrives | 1967 | 20.00 |
| *—Green and blue label* | | | |
| ❑ 8176 [M] | Aretha: Lady Soul | 1968 | 30.00 |
| ❑ SD 8176 | Aretha: Lady Soul | 1969 | 12.00 |
| *—Green and red label* | | | |
| ❑ SD 8176 [S] | Aretha: Lady Soul | 1968 | 20.00 |
| *—Green and blue label* | | | |
| ❑ SD 8186 | Aretha Now | 1968 | 20.00 |
| *—Green and blue label* | | | |
| ❑ SD 8186 | Aretha Now | 1969 | 12.00 |
| *—Green and red label* | | | |
| ❑ SD 8207 | Aretha in Paris | 1968 | 15.00 |
| ❑ 8212 [M] | Aretha Franklin: Soul '69 | 1969 | 50.00 |
| *—White label promo; no stock copies in mono* | | | |
| ❑ SD 8212 [S] | Aretha Franklin: Soul '69 | 1969 | 15.00 |
| ❑ SD 8227 | Aretha's Gold | 1969 | 15.00 |
| ❑ 8248 [M] | This Girl's in Love with You | 1970 | 40.00 |
| *—Mono is white label promo only; cover has "d/j copy monaural" sticker on front* | | | |
| ❑ SD 8248 [S] | This Girl's in Love with You | 1970 | 15.00 |
| ❑ 8265 [M] | Spirit in the Dark | 1970 | 40.00 |
| *—Mono is white label promo only in stereo cover with "d/j monaural" sticker* | | | |
| ❑ SD 8265 [S] | Spirit in the Dark | 1970 | 15.00 |
| ❑ 8295 [M] | Aretha's Greatest Hits | 1971 | 40.00 |
| *—Mono is white label promo only in stereo cover with "d/j monaural" sticker* | | | |
| ❑ SD 8295 [S] | Aretha's Greatest Hits | 1971 | 15.00 |
| ❑ QD 8305 [Q] | The Best of Aretha Franklin | 1974 | 20.00 |
| ❑ SD 18116 | With Everything I Feel in Me | 1974 | 12.00 |
| ❑ SD 18151 | You | 1975 | 12.00 |
| ❑ SD 18176 | Sparkle | 1976 | 12.00 |
| ❑ SD 18204 | Ten Years of Gold | 1976 | 12.00 |
| ❑ SD 19102 | Sweet Passion | 1977 | 12.00 |
| ❑ SD 19161 | Almighty Fire | 1978 | 12.00 |
| ❑ SD 19248 | La Diva | 1979 | 12.00 |
| ❑ 81230 | Aretha's Jazz | 1984 | 10.00 |
| ❑ 81280 | The Best of Aretha Franklin | 1985 | 10.00 |
| ❑ 81668 [(2)] | 30 Greatest Hits | 1986 | 15.00 |
| ❑ STAO-95151 | Hey Now Hey (The Other Side of the Sky) | 1973 | 15.00 |
| *—Capitol Record Club edition* | | | |

CHECKER

| Number | Title (A Side/B Side) | Yr | NM |
|---|---|---|---|
| ❑ 10009 [M] | Songs of Faith | 1965 | 500.00 |
| *—Original issue of this album; cover has Aretha sitting at a piano* | | | |
| ❑ 10009 [M] | Gospel Soul | 1967 | 20.00 |
| *—Reissue with new title and cover* | | | |

COLUMBIA

| Number | Title (A Side/B Side) | Yr | NM |
|---|---|---|---|
| ❑ GP 4 [(2)] | Two All-Time Great Albums in One Great Package | 196? | 25.00 |
| *—Contains CS 9081 and CS 9429* | | | |
| ❑ CL 1612 [M] | Aretha | 1961 | 50.00 |
| *—Red and black label with six "eye" logos* | | | |
| ❑ CL 1612 [M] | Aretha | 1963 | 20.00 |
| *—"Guaranteed High Fidelity" on label* | | | |
| ❑ CL 1612 [M] | Aretha | 1965 | 15.00 |
| *—"360 Sound Mono" on label* | | | |
| ❑ CL 1761 [M] | The Electrifying Aretha Franklin | 1962 | 40.00 |
| *—Red and black label with six "eye" logos* | | | |
| ❑ CL 1761 [M] | The Electrifying Aretha Franklin | 1963 | 20.00 |
| *—"Guaranteed High Fidelity" on label* | | | |
| ❑ CL 1761 [M] | The Electrifying Aretha Franklin | 1965 | 15.00 |
| *—"360 Sound Mono" on label* | | | |
| ❑ CL 1876 [M] | The Tender, The Moving, The Swinging Aretha Franklin | 1962 | 40.00 |
| *—Red and black label with six "eye" logos* | | | |
| ❑ CL 1876 [M] | The Tender, The Moving, The Swinging Aretha Franklin | 1963 | 20.00 |
| *—"Guaranteed High Fidelity" on label* | | | |
| ❑ CL 1876 [M] | The Tender, The Moving, The Swinging Aretha Franklin | 1965 | 15.00 |
| *—"360 Sound Mono" on label* | | | |
| ❑ CL 2079 [M] | Laughing on the Outside | 1963 | 20.00 |
| *—"Guaranteed High Fidelity" on label* | | | |
| ❑ CL 2079 [M] | Laughing on the Outside | 1965 | 15.00 |
| *—"360 Sound Mono" on label* | | | |
| ❑ CL 2163 [M] | Unforgettable | 1964 | 20.00 |
| *—"Guaranteed High Fidelity" on label* | | | |
| ❑ CL 2163 [M] | Unforgettable | 1965 | 15.00 |
| *—"360 Sound Mono" on label* | | | |
| ❑ CL 2281 [M] | Runnin' Out of Fools | 1964 | 20.00 |
| *—"Guaranteed High Fidelity" on label* | | | |
| ❑ CL 2281 [M] | Runnin' Out of Fools | 1965 | 15.00 |
| *—"360 Sound Mono" on label* | | | |
| ❑ CL 2351 [M] | Yeah!!! | 1965 | 20.00 |
| *—"Guaranteed High Fidelity" on label* | | | |
| ❑ CL 2351 [M] | Yeah!!! | 1966 | 15.00 |
| *—"360 Sound Mono" on label* | | | |
| ❑ CL 2521 [M] | Soul Sister | 1966 | 20.00 |
| ❑ CL 2629 [M] | Take It Like You Give It | 1967 | 25.00 |
| ❑ CL 2673 [M] | Aretha Franklin's Greatest Hits | 1967 | 25.00 |
| ❑ CL 2754 [M] | Take a Look | 1967 | 30.00 |
| ❑ CS 8412 [S] | Aretha | 1961 | 80.00 |
| *—Red and black label with six "eye" logos* | | | |
| ❑ CS 8412 [S] | Aretha | 1963 | 25.00 |
| *—"360 Sound Stereo" on label* | | | |
| ❑ CS 8561 [S] | The Electrifying Aretha Franklin | 1962 | 50.00 |
| *—Red and black label with six "eye" logos* | | | |
| ❑ CS 8561 [S] | The Electrifying Aretha Franklin | 1963 | 25.00 |
| *—"360 Sound Stereo" on label* | | | |
| ❑ CS 8676 [S] | The Tender, The Moving, The Swinging Aretha Franklin | 1962 | 50.00 |
| *—Red and black label with six "eye" logos* | | | |
| ❑ CS 8676 [S] | The Tender, The Moving, The Swinging Aretha Franklin | 1963 | 25.00 |
| *—"360 Sound Stereo" on label* | | | |
| ❑ CS 8879 [S] | Laughing on the Outside | 1963 | 25.00 |
| *—"360 Sound Stereo" on label* | | | |
| ❑ CS 8963 [S] | Unforgettable | 1964 | 25.00 |
| *—"360 Sound Stereo" on label* | | | |
| ❑ CS 9081 [S] | Runnin' Out of Fools | 1964 | 25.00 |
| *—"360 Sound Stereo" on label* | | | |
| ❑ CS 9151 [S] | Yeah!!! | 1965 | 25.00 |
| *—"360 Sound Stereo" on label* | | | |
| ❑ CS 9321 [S] | Soul Sister | 1966 | 25.00 |
| *—"360 Sound Stereo" on label* | | | |
| ❑ CS 9429 [S] | Take It Like You Give It | 1967 | 20.00 |
| *—"360 Sound Stereo" on label* | | | |
| ❑ CS 9473 [S] | Aretha Franklin's Greatest Hits | 1967 | 20.00 |
| *—"360 Sound Stereo" on label* | | | |
| ❑ CS 9554 [S] | Take a Look | 1967 | 20.00 |
| *—"360 Sound Stereo" on label* | | | |
| ❑ CS 9601 | Aretha Franklin's Greatest Hits, Volume 2 | 1968 | 20.00 |
| *—"360 Sound Stereo" on label* | | | |
| ❑ CS 9776 | Soft and Beautiful | 1969 | 20.00 |
| *—"360 Sound Stereo" on label* | | | |
| ❑ CS 9956 | Today I Sing the Blues | 1970 | 15.00 |
| *—"360 Sound Stereo" on label* | | | |
| ❑ KG 31355 [(2)] | In the Beginning/The World of Aretha Franklin 1960-1967 | 1972 | 20.00 |
| ❑ KC 31953 | The First 12 Sides | 1973 | 12.00 |
| ❑ C2 37377 [(2)] | The Legendary Queen of Soul | 1981 | 12.00 |
| ❑ PC 38042 | Sweet Bitter Love | 1982 | 10.00 |
| ❑ FC 40105 | Aretha Franklin Sings the Blues | 1985 | 10.00 |
| ❑ FC 40708 | Aretha After Hours | 1987 | 10.00 |

COLUMBIA SPECIAL PRODUCTS

| Number | Title (A Side/B Side) | Yr | NM |
|---|---|---|---|
| ❑ C 10589 | Take a Look | 1971 | 12.00 |
| ❑ C 11282 | Runnin' Out of Fools | 1972 | 12.00 |

4 MEN WITH BEARDS

| Number | Title (A Side/B Side) | Yr | NM |
|---|---|---|---|
| ❑ 4M 101 | I Never Loved a Man the Way I Love You | 2001 | 15.00 |
| *—Reissue on 180-gram vinyl* | | | |
| ❑ 4M 111 | Soul '69 | 2002 | 15.00 |
| *—Reissue on 180-gram vinyl* | | | |
| ❑ 4M 114 | Spirit in the Dark | 2003 | 15.00 |
| *—Reissue on 180-gram vinyl* | | | |
| ❑ 4M 115 | Aretha Live at Fillmore West | 2003 | 15.00 |
| *—Reissue on 180-gram vinyl* | | | |
| ❑ 4M 130 | Lady Soul | 2006 | 15.00 |
| *—Reissue on 180-gram vinyl* | | | |
| ❑ 4M 131 | Aretha Now | 2006 | 15.00 |
| *—Reissue on 180-gram vinyl* | | | |

HARMONY

| Number | Title (A Side/B Side) | Yr | NM |
|---|---|---|---|
| ❑ HS 11349 | Once in a Lifetime | 1969 | 12.00 |
| ❑ HS 11418 | Two Sides of Love | 1970 | 12.00 |
| ❑ KH 30606 | Greatest Hits 1960-1965 | 1971 | 12.00 |
| ❑ KH 30606 | Greatest Hits 1960-1966 | 1972 | 12.00 |

**FRANKLIN, CAROLYN**

RCA VICTOR

| Number | Title (A Side/B Side) | Yr | NM |
|---|---|---|---|
| ❑ LSP-4160 | Baby Dynamite | 1969 | 20.00 |
| ❑ LSP-4317 | Chain Reaction | 1970 | 20.00 |
| ❑ LSP-4411 | I'd Rather Be Lonely | 1973 | 20.00 |

**FRANKLIN, ERMA**

BRUNSWICK

| Number | Title (A Side/B Side) | Yr | NM |
|---|---|---|---|
| ❑ BL 754147 | Soul Sister | 1969 | 20.00 |

EPIC

| Number | Title (A Side/B Side) | Yr | NM |
|---|---|---|---|
| ❑ BN 619 [S] | Her Name Is Erma | 1962 | 40.00 |
| ❑ LN 3824 [M] | Her Name Is Erma | 1962 | 30.00 |

**FRANKLIN, HENRY**

BLACK JAZZ

| Number | Title (A Side/B Side) | Yr | NM |
|---|---|---|---|
| ❑ QD-7 | The Skipper | 1972 | 20.00 |
| ❑ QD-17 | The Skipper At Home | 1974 | 20.00 |

**FRANKS, MICHAEL**

BRUT

| Number | Title (A Side/B Side) | Yr | NM |
|---|---|---|---|
| ❑ 6005 | Michael Franks | 1973 | 20.00 |

DIRECT DISK

| Number | Title (A Side/B Side) | Yr | NM |
|---|---|---|---|
| ❑ SD-16611 | Tiger in the Rain | 1980 | 30.00 |
| *—Audiophile vinyl* | | | |

**FRANTIC**

LIZARD

| Number | Title (A Side/B Side) | Yr | NM |
|---|---|---|---|
| ❑ 20103 | Conception | 1971 | 25.00 |

**FRATERNITY OF MAN, THE**

ABC

| Number | Title (A Side/B Side) | Yr | NM |
|---|---|---|---|
| ❑ S-647 | The Fraternity of Man | 1968 | 30.00 |

DOT

| Number | Title (A Side/B Side) | Yr | NM |
|---|---|---|---|
| ❑ DLP-25955 | Get It On | 1969 | 25.00 |

**FRAWLEY, WILLIAM**

DOT

| Number | Title (A Side/B Side) | Yr | NM |
|---|---|---|---|
| ❑ DLP-3061 [M] | William Frawley Sings the Old Ones | 1958 | 40.00 |

**FRAZIER, CAESAR** Some of these may spell his first name "Ceasar."

EASTBOUND

| Number | Title (A Side/B Side) | Yr | NM |
|---|---|---|---|
| ❑ 9002 | Hail Caesar! | 1973 | 50.00 |
| ❑ 9009 | Caesar Frazier '74 | 1974 | 40.00 |

WESTBOUND

| Number | Title (A Side/B Side) | Yr | NM |
|---|---|---|---|
| ❑ 206 | Caesar Frazier '75 | 1975 | 30.00 |
| ❑ WT 6103 | Another Life | 1978 | 30.00 |

**FRAZIER, DALLAS**

CAPITOL

| Number | Title (A Side/B Side) | Yr | NM |
|---|---|---|---|
| ❑ ST 2552 [S] | Elvira | 1966 | 25.00 |
| ❑ T 2552 [M] | Elvira | 1966 | 20.00 |
| ❑ ST 2764 [S] | Tell It Like It Is | 1967 | 20.00 |
| ❑ T 2764 [M] | Tell It Like It Is | 1967 | 25.00 |

**FREAK SCENE, THE**

COLUMBIA

| Number | Title (A Side/B Side) | Yr | NM |
|---|---|---|---|
| ❑ CL 2656 [M] | Psychedelic Psoul | 1967 | 70.00 |
| ❑ CS 9456 [S] | Psychedelic Psoul | 1967 | 100.00 |

**FREBERG, STAN**

CAPITOL

| Number | Title (A Side/B Side) | Yr | NM |
|---|---|---|---|
| ❑ T 777 [M] | A Child's Garden of Freberg | 1957 | 50.00 |
| *—Turquoise label* | | | |
| ❑ WBO 1035 [(2)M] | The Best of the Stan Freberg Shows | 1958 | 60.00 |
| ❑ SM-1242 [R] | Stan Freberg with the Original Cast | 197? | 10.00 |
| ❑ T 1242 [M] | Stan Freberg with the Original Cast | 1959 | 30.00 |
| ❑ SW 1573 [S] | Stan Freberg Presents the United States of America | 1961 | 30.00 |
| ❑ W 1573 [M] | Stan Freberg Presents the United States of America | 1961 | 25.00 |
| ❑ T 1694 [M] | Face the Funnies | 1962 | 25.00 |
| ❑ T 1816 [M] | Madison Ave. Werewolf | 1962 | 25.00 |
| ❑ SM-2020 [R] | The Best of Stan Freberg | 197? | 10.00 |
| ❑ T 2020 [M] | The Best of Stan Freberg | 1964 | 25.00 |
| ❑ SM-2551 [S] | The Stan Freberg Underground Show #1 | 197? | 10.00 |
| ❑ ST 2551 [S] | The Stan Freberg Underground Show #1 | 1966 | 25.00 |
| ❑ T 2551 [M] | The Stan Freberg Underground Show #1 | 1966 | 20.00 |
| ❑ SM-11765 | The Best of the Stan Freberg Shows | 197? | 12.00 |

**FRED, JOHN, AND HIS PLAYBOY BAND**

JIN

| Number | Title (A Side/B Side) | Yr | NM |
|---|---|---|---|
| ❑ 9027 | The Best of John Fred and His Playboys | 198? | 10.00 |

PAULA

| Number | Title (A Side/B Side) | Yr | NM |
|---|---|---|---|
| ❑ LP-2191 [M] | John Fred and His Playboys | 1966 | 20.00 |
| ❑ LPS-2191 [S] | John Fred and His Playboys | 1966 | 25.00 |
| ❑ LP-2193 [M] | 34:40 of John Fred and His Playboys | 1967 | 20.00 |
| ❑ LPS-2193 [S] | 34:40 of John Fred and His Playboys | 1967 | 25.00 |
| ❑ LP-2197 [M] | Agnes English | 1967 | 25.00 |
| ❑ LPS-2197 [S] | Agnes English | 1967 | 20.00 |
| ❑ LPS-2197 [S] | Judy in Disguise with Glasses | 1968 | 20.00 |
| *—Retitled version of "Agnes English"* | | | |
| ❑ LPS-2201 | Permanently Stated | 1969 | 20.00 |

UNI

| Number | Title (A Side/B Side) | Yr | NM |
|---|---|---|---|
| ❑ 73077 | Love in My Soul | 1970 | 40.00 |

**FREDDIE AND THE DREAMERS**

CAPITOL

| Number | Title (A Side/B Side) | Yr | NM |
|---|---|---|---|
| ❑ SM-11896 [B] | The Best of Freddie and the Dreamers | 1976 | 10.00 |
| *—"I'm Telling You Now," "You Were Made for Me," "I Just Don't Understand," "A Little You" and "Over You" are in stereo, the rest are mono.* | | | |

MERCURY

| Number | Title (A Side/B Side) | Yr | NM |
|---|---|---|---|
| ❑ MG-21017 [M] | Freddie and the Dreamers | 1965 | 25.00 |
| ❑ MG-21026 [M] | Do the Freddie | 1965 | 20.00 |
| ❑ MG-21031 [M] | Seaside Swingers | 1965 | 20.00 |
| ❑ MG-21053 [M] | Frantic Freddie | 1965 | 15.00 |
| ❑ MG-21061 [M] | Fun Lovin' Freddie | 1966 | 15.00 |
| ❑ SR-61017 [R] | Freddie and the Dreamers | 1965 | 20.00 |
| ❑ SR-61026 [S] | Do the Freddie | 1965 | 25.00 |
| ❑ SR-61031 [S] | Seaside Swingers | 1965 | 25.00 |
| ❑ SR-61053 [S] | Frantic Freddie | 1965 | 20.00 |
| ❑ SR-61061 [S] | Fun Lovin' Freddie | 1966 | 20.00 |

**TOWER**

| Number | Title (A Side/B Side) | Yr | NM |
|---|---|---|---|
| ❑ DT 5003 [R] | I'm Telling You Now | 1965 | 20.00 |

*—Contains only two Freddie and the Dreamers songs, but the group's picture is on the cover. Also includes Four Just Men (2), Heinz (2), Linda Laine and the Sinners (2), Mike Rabin and the Demons (2) and The Toggery Five (2)*

| Number | Title (A Side/B Side) | Yr | NM |
|---|---|---|---|
| ❑ T 5003 [M] | I'm Telling You Now | 1965 | 25.00 |

*—Contains only two Freddie and the Dreamers songs, but the group's picture is on the cover. Also includes Four Just Men (2), Heinz (2), Linda Laine and the Sinners (2), Mike Rabin and the Demons (2) and The Toggery Five (2)*

### FREDRIC

**FORTE**

| Number | Title (A Side/B Side) | Yr | NM |
|---|---|---|---|
| ❑ 80461 | Phases and Faces | 1968 | 800.00 |

### FREE BAND, THE

**VANGUARD**

| Number | Title (A Side/B Side) | Yr | NM |
|---|---|---|---|
| ❑ VSD-6507 | The Free Band | 1969 | 20.00 |

### FREE DESIGN, THE

**AMBROTYPE**

| Number | Title (A Side/B Side) | Yr | NM |
|---|---|---|---|
| ❑ 1016 | There Is a Song | 1972 | 50.00 |

**PROJECT 3**

| Number | Title (A Side/B Side) | Yr | NM |
|---|---|---|---|
| ❑ PR 4006 SD | The Free Design Sing for Very Important People | 1970 | 25.00 |
| ❑ PR-5019 QD [Q] | Kites Are Fun | 197? | 40.00 |
| ❑ PR-5019 SD | Kites Are Fun | 1967 | 25.00 |
| ❑ PR-5031 SD | You Could Be Born Again | 1968 | 25.00 |
| ❑ PR-5037 SD | Heaven/Earth | 1969 | 25.00 |
| ❑ PR-5045 SD | Stars/Times/Bubbles/Love | 1971 | 25.00 |
| ❑ PR-5061 SD | One By One | 1971 | 25.00 |

### FREE MUSIC QUARTET, THE

**ESP-DISK'**

| Number | Title (A Side/B Side) | Yr | NM |
|---|---|---|---|
| ❑ 1083 | Free Music One and Two | 1969 | 20.00 |

### FREEBORNE

**MONITOR**

| Number | Title (A Side/B Side) | Yr | NM |
|---|---|---|---|
| ❑ MPS-607 | Peak Impressions | 1967 | 100.00 |

### FREED, ALAN

**BRUNSWICK**

| Number | Title (A Side/B Side) | Yr | NM |
|---|---|---|---|
| ❑ BL 54043 [M] | The Alan Freed Rock 'n' Roll Show | 1959 | 150.00 |

**CORAL**

| Number | Title (A Side/B Side) | Yr | NM |
|---|---|---|---|
| ❑ CRL 57063 [M] | Alan Freed's Rock 'n' Roll Dance Party, Vol. 1 | 1956 | 150.00 |
| ❑ CRL 57115 [M] | Alan Freed's Rock 'n' Roll Dance Party, Vol. 2 | 1957 | 150.00 |
| ❑ CRL 57177 [M] | Go Go Go — Alan Freed's TV Record Hop | 1957 | 150.00 |
| ❑ CRL 57213 [M] | Rock Around the Block | 1958 | 150.00 |
| ❑ CRL 57216 [M] | Alan Freed Presents the King's Henchmen | 1958 | 150.00 |

**MGM**

| Number | Title (A Side/B Side) | Yr | NM |
|---|---|---|---|
| ❑ E-293 [10] | The Big Beat | 195? | 200.00 |

### FREEDMAN, BOB

**COBBLESTONE**

| Number | Title (A Side/B Side) | Yr | NM |
|---|---|---|---|
| ❑ 9009 | Journeys of Odysseus | 1972 | 20.00 |

**SAVOY**

| Number | Title (A Side/B Side) | Yr | NM |
|---|---|---|---|
| ❑ MG-15040 [10] | Piano Moods | 1954 | 50.00 |

### FREEMAN, BOBBY

**AUTUMN**

| Number | Title (A Side/B Side) | Yr | NM |
|---|---|---|---|
| ❑ LP 102 [M] | C'mon and S-W-I-M | 1964 | 50.00 |

**JOSIE**

| Number | Title (A Side/B Side) | Yr | NM |
|---|---|---|---|
| ❑ JM-4007 [M] | Get In the Swim with Bobby Freeman | 1965 | 30.00 |
| ❑ JS-4007 [R] | Get In the Swim with Bobby Freeman | 1965 | 25.00 |

**JUBILEE**

| Number | Title (A Side/B Side) | Yr | NM |
|---|---|---|---|
| ❑ JLP-1086 [M] | Do You Wanna Dance? | 1959 | 140.00 |
| ❑ JLPS-1086 [S] | Do You Wanna Dance? | 1959 | 200.00 |
| ❑ JGM-5010 [M] | Twist with Bobby Freeman | 1962 | 100.00 |

**KING**

| Number | Title (A Side/B Side) | Yr | NM |
|---|---|---|---|
| ❑ 930 [M] | The Lovable Style of Bobby Freeman | 1965 | 250.00 |

### FREEMAN, BUD

**BETHLEHEM**

| Number | Title (A Side/B Side) | Yr | NM |
|---|---|---|---|
| ❑ BCP-29 [M] | Newport News | 1955 | 80.00 |

**CAPITOL**

| Number | Title (A Side/B Side) | Yr | NM |
|---|---|---|---|
| ❑ H 625 [10] | Classics in Jazz | 1955 | 80.00 |
| ❑ T 625 [M] | Classics in Jazz | 1955 | 50.00 |

**COLUMBIA**

| Number | Title (A Side/B Side) | Yr | NM |
|---|---|---|---|
| ❑ CL 2558 [10] | Jazz — Chicago Style | 1955 | 80.00 |
| ❑ CL 6107 [10] | Comes Jazz | 1950 | 100.00 |

**DECCA**

| Number | Title (A Side/B Side) | Yr | NM |
|---|---|---|---|
| ❑ DL 5213 [10] | Wolverine Jazz | 1950 | 100.00 |

**DOT**

| Number | Title (A Side/B Side) | Yr | NM |
|---|---|---|---|
| ❑ DLP-3166 [M] | Bud Freeman and His Summa Cum Laude Trio | 1959 | 40.00 |
| ❑ DLP-3254 [M] | Midnight Session | 1960 | 30.00 |
| ❑ DLP-25166 [S] | Bud Freeman and His Summa Cum Laude Trio | 1959 | 30.00 |
| ❑ DLP-25254 [S] | Midnight Session | 1960 | 40.00 |

**EMARCY**

| Number | Title (A Side/B Side) | Yr | NM |
|---|---|---|---|
| ❑ MG-36013 [M] | Midnight at Eddie Condon's | 1955 | 60.00 |

**HARMONY**

| Number | Title (A Side/B Side) | Yr | NM |
|---|---|---|---|
| ❑ HL 7046 [M] | Bud Freeman and His All-Star Jazz | 1957 | 25.00 |

**MONMOUTH-EVERGREEN**

| Number | Title (A Side/B Side) | Yr | NM |
|---|---|---|---|
| ❑ 7022 | The Compleat Bud Freeman | 1970 | 20.00 |

**PARAMOUNT**

| Number | Title (A Side/B Side) | Yr | NM |
|---|---|---|---|
| ❑ CJS-105 [10] | Bud Freeman and the Chicagoans | 195? | 80.00 |

**RCA VICTOR**

| Number | Title (A Side/B Side) | Yr | NM |
|---|---|---|---|
| ❑ LPM-1508 [M] | Chicago Austin High School Jazz in Hi-Fi | 1957 | 50.00 |

**SWINGVILLE**

| Number | Title (A Side/B Side) | Yr | NM |
|---|---|---|---|
| ❑ SVLP-2012 [M] | Bud Freeman All Stars | 1960 | 50.00 |

*—Purple label*

| Number | Title (A Side/B Side) | Yr | NM |
|---|---|---|---|
| ❑ SVLP-2012 [M] | Bud Freeman All Stars | 1965 | 25.00 |

*—Blue label with trident logo at right*

**UNITED ARTISTS**

| Number | Title (A Side/B Side) | Yr | NM |
|---|---|---|---|
| ❑ UAJ-14033 [M] | Something Tender — Bud Freeman and Two Guitars | 1963 | 40.00 |
| ❑ UAJS-15033 [S] | Something Tender — Bud Freeman and Two Guitars | 1963 | 50.00 |

### FREEMAN, ERNIE

**DUNHILL**

| Number | Title (A Side/B Side) | Yr | NM |
|---|---|---|---|
| ❑ D 50026 [M] | Hitmaker | 1967 | 12.00 |
| ❑ DS 50026 [S] | Hitmaker | 1967 | 15.00 |

**IMPERIAL**

| Number | Title (A Side/B Side) | Yr | NM |
|---|---|---|---|
| ❑ LP-9022 [M] | Ernie Freeman Plays Irving Berlin | 1957 | 50.00 |
| ❑ LP-9030 [M] | Jivin' Around | 1957 | 50.00 |
| ❑ LP-9057 [M] | Ernie Freeman | 1958 | 50.00 |
| ❑ LP-9133 [M] | Dark at the Top of the Stairs | 1959 | 30.00 |
| ❑ LP-9148 [M] | Raunchy | 1960 | 50.00 |
| ❑ LP-9157 [M] | Twistin' Time | 1961 | 30.00 |
| ❑ LP-9193 [M] | The Stripper | 1962 | 20.00 |
| ❑ LP-12067 [S] | Dark at the Top of the Stairs | 1959 | 40.00 |
| ❑ LP-12081 [S] | Twistin' Time | 1961 | 40.00 |
| ❑ LP-12193 [S] | The Stripper | 1962 | 25.00 |

**LIBERTY**

| Number | Title (A Side/B Side) | Yr | NM |
|---|---|---|---|
| ❑ LRP-3264 [M] | Ernie Freeman's Soulful Sounds of Country Classics | 1962 | 20.00 |
| ❑ LRP-3283 [M] | Limbo Dance Party | 1962 | 20.00 |
| ❑ LRP-3331 [M] | Comin' Home Baby | 1963 | 20.00 |
| ❑ LST-7264 [S] | Ernie Freeman's Soulful Sounds of Country Classics | 1962 | 25.00 |
| ❑ LST-7283 [S] | Limbo Dance Party | 1962 | 25.00 |
| ❑ LST-7331 [S] | Comin' Home Baby | 1963 | 25.00 |

### FREEMAN, EVELYN

**IMPERIAL**

| Number | Title (A Side/B Side) | Yr | NM |
|---|---|---|---|
| ❑ LP-9101 [M] | Sky High | 1960 | 20.00 |
| ❑ LP-12043 [S] | Sky High | 1960 | 30.00 |

**UNITED ARTISTS**

| Number | Title (A Side/B Side) | Yr | NM |
|---|---|---|---|
| ❑ UAL-3178 [M] | Didn't It Rain | 1962 | 20.00 |
| ❑ UAS-6178 [S] | Didn't It Rain | 1962 | 25.00 |

### FREEMAN, RUSS

**PACIFIC JAZZ**

| Number | Title (A Side/B Side) | Yr | NM |
|---|---|---|---|
| ❑ PJLP-8 [10] | The Russ Freeman Trio | 1953 | 120.00 |
| ❑ PJ-1212 [M] | Trio: Russ Freeman/Richard Twardzik | 1956 | 100.00 |
| ❑ PJ-1232 [M] | Quartet: Russ Freeman/Chet Baker | 1957 | 100.00 |

*—Label says Pacific Jazz, but cover is on World Pacific*

**WORLD PACIFIC**

| Number | Title (A Side/B Side) | Yr | NM |
|---|---|---|---|
| ❑ WP-1212 [M] | Trio: Russ Freeman/Richard Twardzik | 1958 | 50.00 |
| ❑ WP-1232 [M] | Quartet: Russ Freeman/Chet Baker | 1958 | 50.00 |

*—Both label and cover are on World Pacific*

### FREEMAN, STAN

**COLUMBIA**

| Number | Title (A Side/B Side) | Yr | NM |
|---|---|---|---|
| ❑ CL 1120 [M] | Stan Freeman Swings "The Music Man" | 1958 | 30.00 |
| ❑ CL 6158 [10] | Piano Moods | 1951 | 50.00 |
| ❑ CL 6193 [10] | Come On-a Stan's House | 1951 | 60.00 |

**HARMONY**

| Number | Title (A Side/B Side) | Yr | NM |
|---|---|---|---|
| ❑ HL 7067 [M] | Stan Freeman Plays 30 All-Time Hits | 195? | 20.00 |

### FREEPORT

**MAINSTREAM**

| Number | Title (A Side/B Side) | Yr | NM |
|---|---|---|---|
| ❑ S-6130 | Freeport | 1970 | 50.00 |

### FREES, PAUL

**MGM**

| Number | Title (A Side/B Side) | Yr | NM |
|---|---|---|---|
| ❑ SE-4735 | Paul Frees and the Poster People | 1969 | 25.00 |

### FREHLEY, ACE Also see KISS.

**CASABLANCA**

| Number | Title (A Side/B Side) | Yr | NM |
|---|---|---|---|
| ❑ NBLP-7121 | Ace Frehley | 1978 | 20.00 |
| ❑ NBPIX-7121 [PD] | Ace Frehley | 1978 | 50.00 |

**MEGAFORCE/ATLANTIC**

| Number | Title (A Side/B Side) | Yr | NM |
|---|---|---|---|
| ❑ 81749 | Frehley's Comet | 1987 | 8.00 |
| ❑ 81826 | Live + 1 | 1988 | 8.00 |
| ❑ 81862 | Second Sighting | 1988 | 8.00 |
| ❑ 82042 | Trouble Walkin' | 1989 | 10.00 |

### FRENCH, ALBERT "PAPA"

**NOBILITY**

| Number | Title (A Side/B Side) | Yr | NM |
|---|---|---|---|
| ❑ LP-702 [M] | A Night at Dixieland Hall | 195? | 40.00 |

### FRESH, DOUG E., AND THE GET FRESH CREW

**GEE STREET**

| Number | Title (A Side/B Side) | Yr | NM |
|---|---|---|---|
| ❑ 444069-1 | Play | 1993 | 15.00 |

**REALITY**

| Number | Title (A Side/B Side) | Yr | NM |
|---|---|---|---|
| ❑ 9649 | Oh, My God! | 1986 | 40.00 |
| ❑ 9658 | The World's Greatest Entertainer | 1988 | 30.00 |

### FRIAR TUCK

**MERCURY**

| Number | Title (A Side/B Side) | Yr | NM |
|---|---|---|---|
| ❑ MG-21111 [M] | Friar Tuck and His Psychedelic Guitar | 1967 | 40.00 |
| ❑ SR-61111 [S] | Friar Tuck and His Psychedelic Guitar | 1967 | 50.00 |

### FRICKE, JANIE

**COLUMBIA**

| Number | Title (A Side/B Side) | Yr | NM |
|---|---|---|---|
| ❑ AS99 1535 [DJ] | Janie Fricke On Tour | 1982 | 60.00 |

*—Promo-only picture disc*

| Number | Title (A Side/B Side) | Yr | NM |
|---|---|---|---|
| ❑ KC 35315 | Singer of Songs | 1978 | 12.00 |
| ❑ PC 35315 | Singer of Songs | 198? | 8.00 |

*—Budget-line reissue with new prefix*

| Number | Title (A Side/B Side) | Yr | NM |
|---|---|---|---|
| ❑ KC 35774 | Love Notes | 1979 | 12.00 |
| ❑ PC 35774 | Love Notes | 198? | 8.00 |

*—Budget-line reissue with new prefix*

| Number | Title (A Side/B Side) | Yr | NM |
|---|---|---|---|
| ❑ JC 36268 | From the Heart | 1980 | 12.00 |
| ❑ JC 36820 | I'll Need Someone to Hold Me When I Cry | 1980 | 10.00 |
| ❑ PC 36820 | I'll Need Someone to Hold Me When I Cry | 198? | 8.00 |

*—Budget-line reissue with new prefix*

| Number | Title (A Side/B Side) | Yr | NM |
|---|---|---|---|
| ❑ FC 37535 | Sleeping with Your Memory | 1981 | 10.00 |
| ❑ PC 37535 | Sleeping with Your Memory | 198? | 8.00 |

*—Budget-line reissue with new prefix*

| Number | Title (A Side/B Side) | Yr | NM |
|---|---|---|---|
| ❑ FC 38214 | It Ain't Easy | 1982 | 10.00 |
| ❑ FC 38310 | Greatest Hits | 1982 | 10.00 |
| ❑ FC 38730 | Love Lies | 1983 | 10.00 |
| ❑ PC 38730 | Love Lies | 1985 | 8.00 |

*—Budget-line reissue with new prefix*

| Number | Title (A Side/B Side) | Yr | NM |
|---|---|---|---|
| ❑ FC 39338 | The First Word in Memory | 1984 | 10.00 |
| ❑ FC 39975 | Somebody Else's Fire | 1985 | 10.00 |
| ❑ FC 40165 | The Very Best of Janie | 1985 | 10.00 |
| ❑ FC 40383 | Black & White | 1986 | 10.00 |
| ❑ FC 40666 | After Midnight | 1987 | 10.00 |
| ❑ C2 40684 [(2)] | Celebration | 1987 | 12.00 |
| ❑ FC 44143 | Saddle the Wind | 1988 | 10.00 |
| ❑ FC 45087 | Labor of Love | 1989 | 12.00 |

### FRIEDMAN, DON

**PRESTIGE**

| Number | Title (A Side/B Side) | Yr | NM |
|---|---|---|---|
| ❑ PRLP-7488 [M] | Metamorphosis | 1966 | 25.00 |
| ❑ PRST-7488 [S] | Metamorphosis | 1966 | 30.00 |

**RIVERSIDE**

| Number | Title (A Side/B Side) | Yr | NM |
|---|---|---|---|
| ❑ RLP-384 [M] | A Day in the City | 1961 | 40.00 |
| ❑ RLP-431 [M] | Circle Waltz | 1962 | 30.00 |
| ❑ RLP-463 [M] | Flashback | 1963 | 30.00 |
| ❑ RLP-485 [M] | Dreams and Explorations | 1965 | 20.00 |
| ❑ RS-9384 [S] | A Day in the City | 1961 | 50.00 |
| ❑ RS-9431 [S] | Circle Waltz | 1962 | 40.00 |
| ❑ RS-9463 [S] | Flashback | 1963 | 40.00 |
| ❑ RS-9485 [S] | Dreams and Explorations | 1965 | 25.00 |

### FRIEDMAN, ERICK

**RCA VICTOR RED SEAL**

| Number | Title (A Side/B Side) | Yr | NM |
|---|---|---|---|
| ❑ LSC-2610 [S] | Paganini: Violin Concerto No. 1; Saint-Saens: Intro and Rondo Capriccioso | 1962 | 40.00 |

*—Original with "shaded dog" label*

| Number | Title (A Side/B Side) | Yr | NM |
|---|---|---|---|
| ❑ LSC-2610 [S] | Paganini: Violin Concerto No. 1; Saint-Saens: Intro and Rondo Capriccioso | 1964 | 20.00 |

*—Second edition with "white dog" label*

### FRIEND AND LOVER

**VERVE FORECAST**

| Number | Title (A Side/B Side) | Yr | NM |
|---|---|---|---|
| ❑ FTS-3055 | Reach Out of the Darkness | 1968 | 20.00 |



Except when noted otherwise, VG = 25% of NM, and VG+ = 50% of NM. (Example: VG = $2.00, VG+ = $4.00 and NM = $8.00.)

| Number | Title (A Side/B Side) | Yr | NM |
|---|---|---|---|
| **FRIENDS** | | | |
| OBLIVION | | | |
| ❑ OD-3 | Friends | 1974 | 20.00 |
| *—Jazz-rock band with John Abercrombie and Marc Cohen* | | | |
| **FRIENDS OF DISTINCTION, THE** | | | |
| RCA VICTOR | | | |
| ❑ APD1-0276 [Q] | Greatest Hits | 1973 | 20.00 |
| ❑ LSP-4149 | Grazin' | 1969 | 15.00 |
| ❑ LSP-4212 | Highly Distinct | 1969 | 15.00 |
| ❑ LSP-4313 | Real Friends | 1970 | 15.00 |
| ❑ LSP-4408 | Whatever | 1970 | 15.00 |
| ❑ LSP-4492 | Friends & People | 1971 | 15.00 |
| ❑ LSP-4819 | Greatest Hits | 1972 | 12.00 |
| ❑ LSP-4829 | Love Can Make It Easier | 1973 | 12.00 |
| **FRIESEN, DAVID** | | | |
| GLOBAL PACIFIC | | | |
| ❑ OW 40718 | Inner Voices | 1987 | 10.00 |
| **FRIGO, JOHNNY** | | | |
| MERCURY | | | |
| ❑ MG-20285 [M] | I Love Johnny Frigo, He Swings | 1957 | 30.00 |
| **FRIJID PINK** | | | |
| FANTASY | | | |
| ❑ 9464 | All Pink Inside | 1974 | 15.00 |
| LION | | | |
| ❑ LN-1004 | Earth Omen | 1972 | 20.00 |
| PARROT | | | |
| ❑ PAS 71033 | Frijid Pink | 1970 | 25.00 |
| ❑ PAS 71041 | Defrosted | 1970 | 25.00 |
| **FRIZZELL, LEFTY** | | | |
| ABC | | | |
| ❑ ABCX-799 | The Legendary Lefty Frizzell | 1974 | 20.00 |
| *—Revised title* | | | |
| ❑ ABCX-799 | Lefty | 1974 | 30.00 |
| *—Original title* | | | |
| ❑ AC-30035 | The ABC Collection | 1976 | 20.00 |
| COLUMBIA | | | |
| ❑ CL 1342 [M] | The One and Only Lefty Frizzell | 1959 | 120.00 |
| ❑ CL 2169 [M] | Saginaw, Michigan | 1964 | 30.00 |
| ❑ CL 2386 [M] | The Sad Side of Love | 1965 | 30.00 |
| ❑ CL 2488 [M] | Lefty Frizzell's Greatest Hits | 1966 | 30.00 |
| ❑ CL 2772 [M] | Puttin' On | 1967 | 50.00 |
| ❑ CS 8969 [S] | Saginaw, Michigan | 1964 | 40.00 |
| ❑ CL 9019 [10] | Lefty Frizzell Sings the Songs of Jimmie Rodgers | 1951 | 250.00 |
| ❑ CL 9021 [10] | Listen to Lefty | 1952 | 250.00 |
| ❑ CS 9186 [S] | The Sad Side of Love | 1965 | 40.00 |
| ❑ CS 9288 [S] | Lefty Frizzell's Greatest Hits | 1966 | 40.00 |
| *—Red label, "360 Sound Stereo" at bottom* | | | |
| ❑ CS 9572 [S] | Puttin' On | 1967 | 40.00 |
| ❑ C 32249 | Lefty Frizzell Sings the Songs of Jimmie Rodgers | 1973 | 20.00 |
| ❑ PC 33882 | Remembering…The Greatest Hits of Lefty Frizzell | 1975 | 20.00 |
| COLUMBIA LIMITED EDITION | | | |
| ❑ LE 10027 | Saginaw, Michigan | 197? | 10.00 |
| HARMONY | | | |
| ❑ HL 7241 [M] | Lefty Frizzell Sings the Songs of Jimmie Rodgers | 1960 | 30.00 |
| ❑ HS 11186 [R] | The Great Sound of "Lefty" Frizzell | 196? | 20.00 |
| **FROEBA, FRANK** | | | |
| DECCA | | | |
| ❑ DL 5043 [10] | Back Room Piano | 1950 | 50.00 |
| ❑ DL 5048 [10] | Old Time Piano | 1950 | 50.00 |
| ROYALE | | | |
| ❑ 1818 [10] | Old Time Piano | 1954 | 40.00 |
| VARSITY | | | |
| ❑ 6031 [10] | Boys in the Backroom | 1950 | 50.00 |
| **FROGGIE BEAVER** | | | |
| FROGGIE BEAVER | | | |
| ❑ 7301 | From the Pond | 1973 | 50.00 |
| **FROLK HEAVEN** | | | |
| LRS | | | |
| ❑ RF-6023 | At the Apex of High | 197? | 400.00 |
| **FROMAN, JANE** | | | |
| CAPITOL | | | |
| ❑ H 354 [10] | Yours Alone | 1952 | 40.00 |
| ❑ T 726 [M] | Faith | 1956 | 25.00 |
| ❑ T 889 [M] | Songs at Sunset | 1957 | 25.00 |
| DECCA | | | |
| ❑ DL 6021 [10] | Souvenirs | 1952 | 40.00 |
| RCA VICTOR | | | |
| ❑ LPT-3055 [10] | Gems from Gershwin | 1952 | 40.00 |

Frijid Pink, *Frijid Pink,* Parrot PAS 71033, 1970, $25.

| Number | Title (A Side/B Side) | Yr | NM |
|---|---|---|---|
| **FRONTIERE, DOMINIC** | | | |
| COLUMBIA | | | |
| ❑ CL 1273 [M] | Pagan Festival | 1958 | 40.00 |
| ❑ CL 1427 [M] | Love Eyes: The Moods of Romance | 1960 | 30.00 |
| ❑ CS 8224 [S] | Love Eyes: The Moods of Romance | 1960 | 40.00 |
| LIBERTY | | | |
| ❑ LRP-3015 [M] | Fabulous! | 1956 | 40.00 |
| ❑ LRP-3032 [M] | Dom Frontiere Plays the Classics | 1957 | 40.00 |
| ❑ LJH-6002 [M] | The Dom Frontiere Sextet | 1956 | 50.00 |
| ❑ LST-7008 [S] | Mr. Accordion | 1958 | 40.00 |
| *—Evidently not issued in mono* | | | |
| **FROST, FRANK** | | | |
| EARWIG | | | |
| ❑ 4901 | Rockin' the Juke Joint Down | 1986 | 10.00 |
| ❑ 4914 | Midnight Prowler | 1990 | 10.00 |
| JEWEL | | | |
| ❑ LPS-5013 | Frank Frost | 1973 | 15.00 |
| PHILLIPS INTERNATIONAL | | | |
| ❑ PLP-1975 [M] | Hey Boss Man! | 1962 | 3000. |
| *—VG value 1500; VG+ value 2250* | | | |
| **FROST, MAX, AND THE TROOPERS** | | | |
| TOWER | | | |
| ❑ ST-5147 | Shape of Things to Come | 1968 | 50.00 |
| **FROST, THE** | | | |
| VANGUARD | | | |
| ❑ VSD-6520 | Frost Music | 1969 | 20.00 |
| ❑ VSD-6541 | Rock and Roll Music | 1969 | 20.00 |
| ❑ VSD-6556 | Through the Eyes of Love | 1970 | 20.00 |
| ❑ VSD-79392 | Early Frost | 1978 | 15.00 |
| **FRUSCELLA, TONY** | | | |
| ATLANTIC | | | |
| ❑ 1220 [M] | Tony Fruscella | 1955 | 80.00 |
| **FRUT** | | | |
| TRASH | | | |
| ❑ (# unknown) | Keep On Truckin' | 1971 | 80.00 |
| *—Originals on yellow vinyl* | | | |
| WESTBOUND | | | |
| ❑ WB-2005 | Keep On Truckin' | 1971 | 30.00 |
| *—Reissue of Trash LP* | | | |
| ❑ WB-2008 | Spoiled Rotten | 1972 | 30.00 |
| **FUGITIVES, THE** | | | |
| HIDEOUT | | | |
| ❑ 1001 [M] | The Fugitives at Dave's Hideout | 1965 | 1200. |
| JUSTICE | | | |
| ❑ JLP-141 | The Fugitives On the Run | 1967 | 300.00 |
| **FUGITIVES, THE, AND OTHERS** | | | |
| WESTCHESTER | | | |
| ❑ 1005 [M] | Friday at the Cage A-Go-Go | 1965 | 1500. |
| **FUGS, THE** | | | |
| BROADSIDE | | | |
| ❑ 304 [M] | The Village Fugs Sing Ballads of Contemporary Protest, Point of View, and General Dissatisfaction | 1965 | 400.00 |
| *—Without insert* | | | |
| ❑ 304 [M] | The Village Fugs Sing Ballads of Contemporary Protest, Point of View, and General Dissatisfaction | 1965 | 500.00 |
| *—With insert* | | | |
| ESP-DISK | | | |
| ❑ 1018 [M] | The Fugs First Album | 1966 | 40.00 |
| *—"Reissue of Broadside 304" on cover* | | | |
| ❑ 1018 [M] | The Fugs First Album | 1966 | 150.00 |
| *—Turquoise and black cover, different from all other versions* | | | |
| ❑ 1018 [M] | The Fugs First Album | 1967 | 30.00 |
| *—No reference to reissue on cover* | | | |
| ❑ 1028 [S] | The Fugs | 1966 | 30.00 |
| *—Black and white cover, back cover photos aligned* | | | |
| ❑ 1028 [S] | The Fugs | 1966 | 50.00 |
| *—Black and white cover, back cover photos staggered* | | | |
| ❑ 1028 [S] | The Fugs | 1966 | 80.00 |
| *—Psychedelic color shield on cover* | | | |
| ❑ 1038 [S] | Virgin Fugs | 1967 | 30.00 |
| *—"For Adult Minds" printed on cover* | | | |
| ❑ 1038 [S] | Virgin Fugs | 1967 | 50.00 |
| *—"For Adult Minds" stamped on cover* | | | |
| ❑ 1038 [S] | Virgin Fugs | 1967 | 50.00 |
| *—"For Adult Minds" sticker, no inserts* | | | |

| Number | Title (A Side/B Side) | Yr | NM |
|---|---|---|---|
| ❑ 1038 [S] | Virgin Fugs | 1967 | 100.00 |
| *—"For Adult Minds" sticker on cover; with poster, book and stickers* | | | |
| ❑ 2018 | Fugs 4, Rounders Score | 196? | 80.00 |
| **PVC** | | | |
| ❑ 8914 | Proto Punk: The Fugs Greatest Hits, Vol. 1 | 1982 | 15.00 |
| **REPRISE** | | | |
| ❑ R-6280 [M] | Tenderness Junction | 1968 | 40.00 |
| ❑ RS-6280 [S] | Tenderness Junction | 1968 | 30.00 |
| ❑ RS-6305 | It Crawled Into My Hand, Honest | 1968 | 25.00 |
| ❑ RS-6359 | Belle of Avenue A | 1969 | 25.00 |
| ❑ RS-6396 | Golden Fifth | 1970 | 25.00 |

### FULLER, BOBBY, FOUR

| Number | Title (A Side/B Side) | Yr | NM |
|---|---|---|---|
| **MUSTANG** | | | |
| ❑ M-900 [M] | KRLA King of the Wheels | 1965 | 150.00 |
| ❑ MS-900 [S] | KRLA King of the Wheels | 1965 | 200.00 |
| ❑ M-901 [M] | I Fought the Law | 1966 | 80.00 |
| ❑ MS-901 [S] | I Fought the Law | 1966 | 150.00 |
| **RHINO** | | | |
| ❑ RNLP-057 | The Bobby Fuller Tapes, Vol. 1 | 1983 | 10.00 |
| ❑ RNDF-201 | The Best of the Bobby Fuller Four | 1981 | 12.00 |
| ❑ RNLP 70174 | The Best of the Bobby Fuller Four (Golden Archive Series) | 1987 | 10.00 |
| **VOXX** | | | |
| ❑ VXS 200028 | The Bobby Fuller Tapes, Vol. 2 | 1984 | 10.00 |

### FULLER, CURTIS

| Number | Title (A Side/B Side) | Yr | NM |
|---|---|---|---|
| **BLUE NOTE** | | | |
| ❑ BLP-1567 [M] | The Opener | 1957 | 80.00 |
| *—Regular version with W. 63rd St. address on label* | | | |
| ❑ BLP-1567 [M] | The Opener | 1957 | 120.00 |
| *—"Deep groove" version (deep indentation under label on both sides)* | | | |
| ❑ BLP-1567 [M] | The Opener | 1963 | 25.00 |
| *—"New York, USA" address on label* | | | |
| ❑ BST-1567 [S] | The Opener | 1959 | 50.00 |
| *—Regular version with W. 63rd St. address on label* | | | |
| ❑ BST-1567 [S] | The Opener | 1959 | 80.00 |
| *—"Deep groove" version (deep indentation under label on both sides)* | | | |
| ❑ BST-1567 [S] | The Opener | 1963 | 20.00 |
| *—"New York, USA" address on label* | | | |
| ❑ BLP-1572 [M] | Bone and Bari | 1957 | 80.00 |
| *—Regular version with W. 63rd St. address on label* | | | |
| ❑ BLP-1572 [M] | Bone and Bari | 1957 | 120.00 |
| *—"Deep groove" version (deep indentation under label on both sides)* | | | |
| ❑ BLP-1572 [M] | Bone and Bari | 1963 | 25.00 |
| *—"New York, USA" address on label* | | | |
| ❑ BST-1572 [S] | Bone and Bari | 1959 | 50.00 |
| *—Regular version with W. 63rd St. address on label* | | | |
| ❑ BST-1572 [S] | Bone and Bari | 1959 | 80.00 |
| *—"Deep groove" version (deep indentation under label on both sides)* | | | |
| ❑ BST-1572 [S] | Bone and Bari | 1963 | 20.00 |
| *—"New York, USA" address on label* | | | |
| ❑ BLP-1583 [M] | Curtis Fuller, Volume 3 | 1958 | 80.00 |
| *—Regular version with W. 63rd St. address on label* | | | |
| ❑ BLP-1583 [M] | Curtis Fuller, Volume 3 | 1958 | 120.00 |
| *—"Deep groove" version (deep indentation under label on both sides)* | | | |
| ❑ BLP-1583 [M] | Curtis Fuller, Volume 3 | 1963 | 25.00 |
| *—"New York, USA" address on label* | | | |
| ❑ BST-1583 [S] | Curtis Fuller, Volume 3 | 1959 | 50.00 |
| *—Regular version with W. 63rd St. address on label* | | | |
| ❑ BST-1583 [S] | Curtis Fuller, Volume 3 | 1959 | 80.00 |
| *—"Deep groove" version (deep indentation under label on both sides)* | | | |
| ❑ BST-1583 [S] | Curtis Fuller, Volume 3 | 1963 | 20.00 |
| *—"New York, USA" address on label* | | | |
| **EPIC** | | | |
| ❑ LA 16013 [M] | The Magnificent Trombone | 1961 | 30.00 |
| ❑ LA 16020 [M] | South American Cookin' | 1961 | 40.00 |
| ❑ BA 17013 [S] | The Magnificent Trombone | 1961 | 40.00 |
| ❑ BA 17020 [S] | South American Cookin' | 1961 | 50.00 |
| **IMPULSE!** | | | |
| ❑ A-13 [M] | Soul Trombone | 1962 | 25.00 |
| ❑ AS-13 [S] | Soul Trombone | 1962 | 30.00 |
| ❑ A-22 [M] | Cabin in the Sky | 1962 | 25.00 |
| ❑ AS-22 [S] | Cabin in the Sky | 1962 | 30.00 |
| **MAINSTREAM** | | | |
| ❑ MRL-333 | Crankin' | 1971 | 20.00 |
| ❑ MRL-370 | Smokin' | 1972 | 20.00 |
| **NEW JAZZ** | | | |
| ❑ NJLP-8277 [M] | Curtis Fuller with Red Garland | 1962 | 50.00 |
| *—Purple label* | | | |
| ❑ NJLP-8277 [M] | Curtis Fuller with Red Garland | 1965 | 25.00 |
| *—Blue label, trident logo at right* | | | |
| **PRESTIGE** | | | |
| ❑ PRLP-7107 [M] | New Trombone | 1957 | 100.00 |
| **REGENT** | | | |
| ❑ MG-6055 [M] | Jazz...It's Magic | 1957 | 80.00 |
| **SAVOY** | | | |
| ❑ MG-12141 [M] | Blues-Ette | 1959 | 50.00 |
| ❑ MG-12143 [M] | The Curtis Fuller Jazztet with Benny Golson | 1959 | 40.00 |
| ❑ MG-12144 [M] | Imagination | 1959 | 40.00 |
| ❑ MG-12151 [M] | Curtis Fuller | 1960 | 40.00 |
| ❑ MG-12164 [M] | Images of Curts Fuller | 1960 | 40.00 |
| ❑ MG-12209 [M] | Jazz...It's Magic | 196? | 20.00 |
| ❑ ST-13006 [S] | Blues-Ette | 1959 | 40.00 |
| **SMASH** | | | |
| ❑ MGS-27034 [M] | Jazz Conference Abroad | 1962 | 25.00 |
| ❑ SRS-67034 [S] | Jazz Conference Abroad | 1962 | 30.00 |
| **STATUS** | | | |
| ❑ ST-8305 [M] | Curtis Fuller and Hampton Hawes with French Horns | 1965 | 40.00 |
| **UNITED ARTISTS** | | | |
| ❑ UAL-4051 [M] | Sliding Easy | 1959 | 50.00 |
| ❑ UAS-5051 [S] | Sliding Easy | 1959 | 40.00 |
| **WARWICK** | | | |
| ❑ W-2038 [M] | Boss of the Soul Stream Trombone | 1961 | 30.00 |
| ❑ W-2038ST [S] | Boss of the Soul Stream Trombone | 1961 | 50.00 |

### FULLER, GIL

| Number | Title (A Side/B Side) | Yr | NM |
|---|---|---|---|
| **PACIFIC JAZZ** | | | |
| ❑ PJ-93 [M] | Gil Fuller and the Monterey Jazz Orchestra with Dizzy Gillespie | 1965 | 25.00 |
| ❑ ST-93 [S] | Gil Fuller and the Monterey Jazz Orchestra with Dizzy Gillespie | 1965 | 30.00 |
| ❑ PJ-10101 [M] | Night Flight | 1966 | 20.00 |
| ❑ ST-20101 [S] | Night Flight | 1966 | 25.00 |

### FULLER, JERRY Country-pop singer.

| Number | Title (A Side/B Side) | Yr | NM |
|---|---|---|---|
| **LIN** | | | |
| ❑ 100 [M] | Teenage Love | 1960 | 250.00 |

### FULLER, JERRY (2) Jazz clarinetist.

| Number | Title (A Side/B Side) | Yr | NM |
|---|---|---|---|
| **ANDEX** | | | |
| ❑ A-3008 [M] | Clarinet Portrait | 1958 | 40.00 |
| ❑ AS-3008 [S] | Clarinet Portrait | 1959 | 30.00 |

### FULSON, LOWELL

| Number | Title (A Side/B Side) | Yr | NM |
|---|---|---|---|
| **ARHOOLIE** | | | |
| ❑ R-2003 | Early Recordings | 1962 | 30.00 |
| **BIG TOWN** | | | |
| ❑ 1008 | Lovemaker | 1978 | 12.00 |
| **CHESS** | | | |
| ❑ 408 | Hung Down Head | 197? | 15.00 |
| **GRANITE** | | | |
| ❑ 1006 | Ol' Blues Singer | 1976 | 15.00 |
| **JEWEL** | | | |
| ❑ LPS-5003 | In a Heavy Bag | 1970 | 15.00 |
| ❑ LPS-5009 | I've Got the Blues | 1973 | 15.00 |
| **KENT** | | | |
| ❑ KST-516 [S] | Lowell Fulsom | 1965 | 40.00 |
| ❑ KST-520 [S] | Tramp | 1967 | 40.00 |
| ❑ KST-531 | Lowell Fulsom Now | 1969 | 30.00 |
| ❑ KLP-5016 [M] | Lowell Fulsom | 1965 | 30.00 |
| ❑ KLP-5020 [M] | Tramp | 1967 | 30.00 |
| **ROUNDER** | | | |
| ❑ 2088 | It's a Good Day | 198? | 12.00 |

### FUN AND GAMES

| Number | Title (A Side/B Side) | Yr | NM |
|---|---|---|---|
| **UNI** | | | |
| ❑ 73042 | Elephant Candy | 1968 | 25.00 |

### FUNKADELIC Also see PARLIAMENT.

| Number | Title (A Side/B Side) | Yr | NM |
|---|---|---|---|
| **SCARFACE/PRIORITY** | | | |
| ❑ 53872 | One Nation Under a Groove | 1993 | 15.00 |
| *—Limited-edition reissue of Warner Bros. 3209* | | | |
| ❑ 53873 | Hardcore Jollies | 1993 | 15.00 |
| *—Limited-edition reissue of Warner Bros. 2973* | | | |
| ❑ 53874 | The Electric Spanking of War Babies | 1993 | 15.00 |
| *—Limited-edition reissue of Warner Bros. 3482* | | | |
| ❑ 53875 | Uncle Jam Wants You | 1993 | 15.00 |
| *—Limited-edition reissue of Warner Bros. 3371* | | | |
| **WARNER BROS.** | | | |
| ❑ BS 2973 | Hardcore Jollies | 1976 | 25.00 |
| ❑ BS 3209 | One Nation Under a Groove | 1978 | 25.00 |
| *—Includes bonus 7-inch single with small hole (deduct 20% if missing)* | | | |
| ❑ BSK 3371 | Uncle Jam Wants You | 1979 | 25.00 |
| ❑ BSK 3482 | The Electric Spanking of War Babies | 1981 | 25.00 |
| **WESTBOUND** | | | |
| ❑ 208 | Standing on the Verge of Getting It On | 1975 | 25.00 |
| *—Reissue of Westbound 1001* | | | |
| ❑ 215 | Let's Take It to the Stage | 1975 | 50.00 |
| ❑ 215 | Let's Take It to the Stage | 1992 | 15.00 |
| *—Reissue with bar code* | | | |
| ❑ 216 | Funkadelic | 1975 | 30.00 |
| *—Reissue of Westbound 2000* | | | |
| ❑ 217 | Free Your Mind...And Your Ass Will Follow | 1975 | 25.00 |
| *—Reissue of Westbound 2001* | | | |
| ❑ 218 | Maggot Brain | 1975 | 25.00 |
| *—Reissue of Westbound 2007* | | | |
| ❑ 221 [(2)] | America Eats Its Young | 1976 | 25.00 |
| *—Reissue of Westbound 2020* | | | |
| ❑ 223 | Cosmic Slop | 1976 | 25.00 |
| *—Reissue of Westbound 2022* | | | |
| ❑ 227 | Tales of Kidd Funkadelic | 1976 | 50.00 |
| ❑ 227 | Tales of Kidd Funkadelic | 1992 | 15.00 |
| *—Reissue with bar code* | | | |
| ❑ 303 | Best of the Early Years | 197? | 40.00 |
| ❑ 1001 | Standing on the Verge of Getting It On | 1974 | 50.00 |
| ❑ 1001 | Standing on the Verge of Getting It On | 1991 | 15.00 |
| *—Reissue with bar code* | | | |
| ❑ 1004 | Funkadelic's Greatest Hits | 1975 | 50.00 |
| ❑ 2000 | Funkadelic | 1970 | 50.00 |
| ❑ 2000 | Funkadelic | 1990 | 15.00 |
| *—Reissue with bar code* | | | |
| ❑ 2001 | Free Your Mind...And Your Ass Will Follow | 1970 | 50.00 |
| ❑ 2001 | Free Your Mind...And Your Ass Will Follow | 1990 | 15.00 |
| *—Reissue with bar code* | | | |
| ❑ 2007 | Maggot Brain | 1971 | 50.00 |
| ❑ 2007 | Maggot Brain | 1990 | 15.00 |
| *—Reissue with bar code* | | | |
| ❑ 2020 [(2)] | America Eats Its Young | 1972 | 60.00 |
| ❑ 2020 [(2)] | America Eats Its Young | 1991 | 20.00 |
| *—Reissue with bar code* | | | |
| ❑ 2022 | Cosmic Slop | 1973 | 50.00 |
| ❑ 2022 | Cosmic Slop | 1991 | 15.00 |
| *—Reissue with bar code* | | | |

### FUNT, ALLEN

| Number | Title (A Side/B Side) | Yr | NM |
|---|---|---|---|
| **BLOOPERS** | | | |
| ❑ CM 0001 [M] | The Best of Allen Funt's Candid Mike | 196? | 20.00 |
| **COLUMBIA MASTERWORKS** | | | |
| ❑ ML 4344 [M] | Allen Funt's Candid Microphone | 1950 | 40.00 |
| *—Green label* | | | |
| ❑ ML 4449 [M] | Allen Funt's Candid Microphone, Vol. 2 | 1951 | 40.00 |
| *—Green label* | | | |
| ❑ ML 4450 [M] | Allen Funt's Candid Microphone, Vol. 3 | 1951 | 40.00 |
| **HARMONY** | | | |
| ❑ HL 7243 [M] | Allen Funt's Candid Microphone | 195? | 20.00 |
| **JUBILEE** | | | |
| ❑ KS-2 [(2)M] | Candid Camera | 196? | 20.00 |
| **RCA VICTOR** | | | |
| ❑ LPM-3679 [M] | Allen Funt and Candid Kids | 1967 | 40.00 |
| ❑ LSP-3679 [S] | Allen Funt and Candid Kids | 1967 | 30.00 |

### FURAY, RICHIE

| Number | Title (A Side/B Side) | Yr | NM |
|---|---|---|---|
| **MYRRH** | | | |
| ❑ MSB-6672 | I've Got a Reason | 1981 | 20.00 |
| *—Christian-market reissue of Asylum 7E-1067* | | | |
| ❑ MSB-6695 | Seasons of Change | 1982 | 10.00 |

### FUSE

| Number | Title (A Side/B Side) | Yr | NM |
|---|---|---|---|
| **EPIC** | | | |
| ❑ BN 26502 | Fuse | 1970 | 80.00 |

### FUTURE, THE

| Number | Title (A Side/B Side) | Yr | NM |
|---|---|---|---|
| **SHAMLEY** | | | |
| ❑ 703 | Down the Country Road | 1969 | 20.00 |

### FUTURES, THE

| Number | Title (A Side/B Side) | Yr | NM |
|---|---|---|---|
| **BUDDAH** | | | |
| ❑ BDS-5630 | Castles in the Sky | 1975 | 100.00 |
| **PHILADELPHIA INT'L.** | | | |
| ❑ JZ 35458 | Past, Present and the Futures | 1979 | 50.00 |
| ❑ JZ 36414 | Greetings of Peace | 1980 | 60.00 |

# G

### G.T.O.'S, THE (2)

| Number | Title (A Side/B Side) | Yr | NM |
|---|---|---|---|
| **REPRISE** | | | |
| ❑ RS 6390 | Permanent Damage | 1970 | 50.00 |
| *—Without booklet* | | | |
| ❑ RS 6390 | Permanent Damage | 1970 | 70.00 |
| *—With booklet* | | | |
| **STRAIGHT** | | | |
| ❑ STS-1059 | Permanent Damage | 1969 | 80.00 |
| *—Without booklet* | | | |
| ❑ STS-1059 | Permanent Damage | 1969 | 100.00 |
| *—With booklet* | | | |

**GABRIEL, PETER** Also see GENESIS.

| Number | Title (A Side/B Side) | Yr | NM |
|---|---|---|---|
| **ATCO** | | | |
| ❑ SD 36-147 | Peter Gabriel | 1977 | 15.00 |
| *—(The "Solsbury Hill" album) -- Original pressing has yellow labels* | | | |
| ❑ SD 36-147 | Peter Gabriel | 1980 | 10.00 |
| *—(The "Solsbury Hill" album) -- Other than yellow labels* | | | |
| **ATLANTIC** | | | |
| ❑ SD-19181 | Peter Gabriel | 1978 | 15.00 |
| *—(The "D.I.Y." album)* | | | |
| **DIRECT DISK** | | | |
| ❑ SD-16615 | Peter Gabriel | 1980 | 80.00 |
| *—The "Solsbury Hill" album; contains a long version of "Slowburn" not available elsewhere* | | | |
| **GEFFEN** | | | |
| ❑ GHS 2011 | Peter Gabriel (Security) | 1982 | 10.00 |
| ❑ GHS 2011 [DJ] | Peter Gabriel (Security) | 1982 | 15.00 |
| *—Promo-only Quiex II audiophile pressing* | | | |
| ❑ GHSP 2035 | Peter Gabriel | 1983 | 10.00 |
| *—Reissue of Mercury album* | | | |
| ❑ 2GHS 4012 [(2)] | Plays Live | 1983 | 15.00 |
| ❑ GHS 24070 | Birdy (Soundtrack) | 1985 | 10.00 |
| ❑ GHS 24088 | So | 1986 | 10.00 |
| ❑ GHS 24206 | Passion: Music for "The Last Temptation of Christ" | 1989 | 15.00 |
| ❑ R 114764 | So | 1986 | 12.00 |
| *—BMG Direct Marketing edition* | | | |
| ❑ R 153801 | Peter Gabriel (Security) | 1982 | 12.00 |
| *—RCA Music Service edition* | | | |
| ❑ R 243372 [(2)] | Plays Live | 1983 | 18.00 |
| *—RCA Music Service edition* | | | |
| **MERCURY** | | | |
| ❑ SRM-1-3848 | Peter Gabriel | 1980 | 12.00 |
| *—(The "Games Without Frontiers" album)* | | | |
| **REAL WORLD** | | | |
| ❑ PGDLP-1 | Peter Gabriel | 2002 | 25.00 |
| *—(The "Solsbury Hill" album) -- Classic Records audiophile issue* | | | |
| ❑ PGDLP-2 | Peter Gabriel | 2002 | 25.00 |
| *—(The "D.I.Y." album) -- Classic Records audiophile issue* | | | |
| ❑ PGDLP-3 | Peter Gabriel | 2003 | 25.00 |
| *—(The "Games Without Frontiers" album) -- Classic Records audiophile issue* | | | |
| ❑ PGDLP-4 | Peter Gabriel (Security) | 2003 | 25.00 |
| *—Classic Records audiophile edition* | | | |
| ❑ PGDLP 5 [(2)] | Plays Live | 2004 | 40.00 |
| *—Classic Records audiophile issue* | | | |
| ❑ PGDLP-6 | Birdy (Soundtrack) | 2004 | 25.00 |
| *—Classic Records reissue on 200-gram vinyl* | | | |
| ❑ PGDLP-7 | So | 2003 | 25.00 |
| *—Classic Records audiophile edition* | | | |
| ❑ PGDLP-8 | Passion: Music for "The Last Temptation of Christ" | 2004 | 30.00 |
| *—Classic Records reissue on 200-gram vinyl* | | | |
| ❑ PGDLP-9 [(2)] | Us | 2004 | 40.00 |
| *—Classic Records edition on 200-gram vinyl* | | | |
| ❑ PGDLP 11 [(2)] | Up | 2002 | 40.00 |
| *—Classic Records audiophile issue; includes bonus 45 in picture sleeve* | | | |

**GABRIEL BONDAGE**

| Number | Title (A Side/B Side) | Yr | NM |
|---|---|---|---|
| **DHARMA** | | | |
| ❑ D-804 | Angel Dust | 1975 | 50.00 |
| ❑ D-808 | Another Trip to Earth | 1977 | 20.00 |
| *—Exists on white, red, or blue vinyl; each of similar value* | | | |

**GAILLARD, SLIM**

| Number | Title (A Side/B Side) | Yr | NM |
|---|---|---|---|
| **ALLEGRO ELITE** | | | |
| ❑ 4050 [10] | Slim Gaillard Plays | 195? | 30.00 |
| **CLEF** | | | |
| ❑ MGC-126 [10] | Mish Mash | 1953 | 100.00 |
| ❑ MGC-138 [10] | Slim Cavorts | 1953 | 100.00 |
| **DISC** | | | |
| ❑ DLP-505 [10] | Opera in Vout | 195? | 200.00 |
| **DOT** | | | |
| ❑ DLP-3190 [M] | Slim Gaillard Rides Again | 1959 | 30.00 |
| ❑ DLP-25190 [S] | Slim Gaillard Rides Again | 1959 | 40.00 |
| **KING** | | | |
| ❑ 295-80 [10] | Slim Gaillard/Boogie | 195? | 100.00 |
| **NORGRAN** | | | |
| ❑ MGN-13 [10] | Slim Gaillard and His Musical Aggregation Wherever They May Be | 1954 | 100.00 |
| **VERVE** | | | |
| ❑ MGV-2013 [M] | Smorgasbord, Help Yourself | 1956 | 50.00 |
| ❑ V-2013 [M] | Smorgasbord, Help Yourself | 1961 | 20.00 |

**GAILLARD, SLIM/DIZZY GILLESPIE**

| Number | Title (A Side/B Side) | Yr | NM |
|---|---|---|---|
| **ULTRAPHONIC** | | | |
| ❑ ULP-50273 [M] | Gaillard and Gillespie | 1958 | 40.00 |

**GAILLARD, SLIM/MEADE LUX LEWIS**

| Number | Title (A Side/B Side) | Yr | NM |
|---|---|---|---|
| **CLEF** | | | |
| ❑ MGC-506 [10] | Boogie Woogie at the Philharmonic | 1954 | 150.00 |
| **MERCURY** | | | |
| ❑ MGC-506 [10] | Boogie Woogie at the Philharmonic | 1951 | 250.00 |

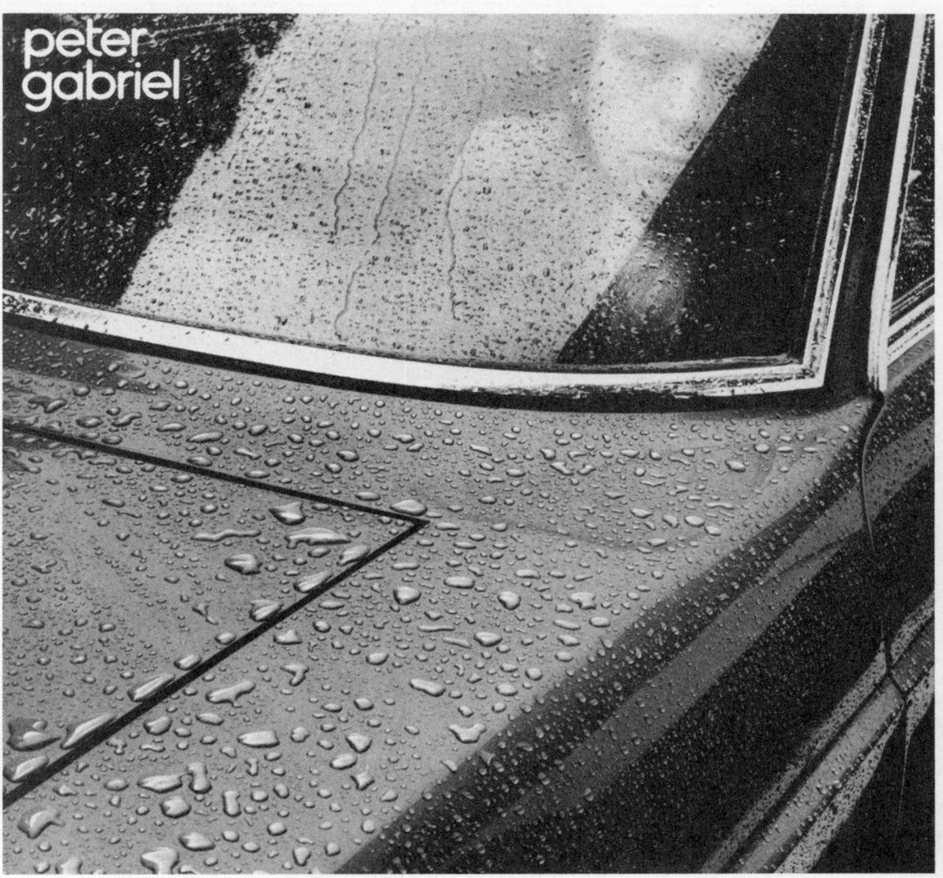


Peter Gabriel, *Peter Gabriel,* Atco SD 36-147, 1977, yellow label $15, gray label $10.

**GALAHADS, THE**

| Number | Title (A Side/B Side) | Yr | NM |
|---|---|---|---|
| **LIBERTY** | | | |
| ❑ LRP-3371 [M] | Hello, Galahads | 1964 | 20.00 |
| ❑ LST-7371 [S] | Hello, Galahads | 1964 | 25.00 |

**GALBRAITH, BARRY**

| Number | Title (A Side/B Side) | Yr | NM |
|---|---|---|---|
| **DECCA** | | | |
| ❑ DL 9200 [M] | Guitar and the Wind | 1958 | 50.00 |
| ❑ DL 79200 [S] | Guitar and the Wind | 1959 | 40.00 |

**GALBRAITH, ROB**

| Number | Title (A Side/B Side) | Yr | NM |
|---|---|---|---|
| **COLUMBIA** | | | |
| ❑ CS 1057 | Nashville Dirt | 1970 | 20.00 |

**GALE, EDDIE**

| Number | Title (A Side/B Side) | Yr | NM |
|---|---|---|---|
| **BLUE NOTE** | | | |
| ❑ BST-84294 | Eddie Gale's Ghetto Music | 1968 | 25.00 |
| ❑ BST-84320 | Black Rhythm Happening | 1969 | 25.00 |

**GALE, SUNNY**

| Number | Title (A Side/B Side) | Yr | NM |
|---|---|---|---|
| **CANADIAN AMERICAN** | | | |
| ❑ CALP-1015 [M] | Goldies by the Girls | 1964 | 25.00 |
| **RCA VICTOR** | | | |
| ❑ LPM-1277 [M] | Sunny and Blue | 1956 | 40.00 |
| **ROYALE** | | | |
| ❑ 18123 [10] | Sunny Gale and Jazz Orchestra | 1954 | 50.00 |
| **THIMBLE** | | | |
| ❑ TLP-10 | Sunny Sings Dixieland and Blues | 1974 | 20.00 |
| **WARWICK** | | | |
| ❑ W-2018 [M] | Sunny | 1960 | 30.00 |

**GALLODORO, AL**

| Number | Title (A Side/B Side) | Yr | NM |
|---|---|---|---|
| **ARCO** | | | |
| ❑ AL-3 [10] | Al Gallodoro Concert | 1950 | 50.00 |
| **COLUMBIA** | | | |
| ❑ CL 6188 [10] | Al Gallodoro | 1951 | 50.00 |

**GALLOP, FRANK**

| Number | Title (A Side/B Side) | Yr | NM |
|---|---|---|---|
| **MUSICOR** | | | |
| ❑ MM-2110 [M] | Frank Gallop Sings | 1966 | 15.00 |
| ❑ MS-3110 [S] | Frank Gallop Sings | 1966 | 20.00 |

**GALPER, HAL**

| Number | Title (A Side/B Side) | Yr | NM |
|---|---|---|---|
| **MAINSTREAM** | | | |
| ❑ MRL-337 | The Guerrilla Band | 1971 | 20.00 |
| ❑ MRL-354 | Wild Bird | 1972 | 20.00 |
| ❑ MRL-398 | Inner Journey | 1974 | 20.00 |

**GALS & PALS**

| Number | Title (A Side/B Side) | Yr | NM |
|---|---|---|---|
| **FONTANA** | | | |
| ❑ MGF-27538 [M] | Gals & Pals (The Exciting Vocal Sounds of Europe's Newest "In" Group) | 1965 | 15.00 |
| ❑ MGF-27557 [M] | Gals & Pals Sing Something for Everybody | 1966 | 15.00 |
| ❑ SRF-67538 [S] | Gals & Pals (The Exciting Vocal Sounds of Europe's Newest "In" Group) | 1965 | 20.00 |
| ❑ SRF-67557 [S] | Gals & Pals Sing Something for Everybody | 1966 | 20.00 |

**GAMBRELL, FREDDIE**

| Number | Title (A Side/B Side) | Yr | NM |
|---|---|---|---|
| **WORLD PACIFIC** | | | |
| ❑ WP-1256 [M] | Freddie Gambrell | 1959 | 50.00 |

**GAMBRELL, FREDDIE, AND PAUL HORN**

| Number | Title (A Side/B Side) | Yr | NM |
|---|---|---|---|
| **WORLD PACIFIC** | | | |
| ❑ ST-1023 [S] | Mikado | 1959 | 30.00 |
| ❑ WP-1262 [M] | Mikado | 1959 | 40.00 |

**GAME**

| Number | Title (A Side/B Side) | Yr | NM |
|---|---|---|---|
| **EVOLUTION** | | | |
| ❑ 2021 | Game | 1970 | 12.00 |
| ❑ 3008 | Long Hot Summer | 1971 | 12.00 |
| **FAITHFUL VIRTUE** | | | |
| ❑ 2003 | Game | 1969 | 20.00 |

**GANDALF**

| Number | Title (A Side/B Side) | Yr | NM |
|---|---|---|---|
| **CAPITOL** | | | |
| ❑ ST-121 | Gandalf | 1969 | 200.00 |

## GANDALF THE GREY

**G.W.R.**

| Number | Title (A Side/B Side) | Yr | NM |
|---|---|---|---|
| ❑ 7 | The Grey Wizard Am I | 1972 | 300.00 |

## GANG STARR

**VIRGIN**

| Number | Title (A Side/B Side) | Yr | NM |
|---|---|---|---|
| ❑ 47279 [(4)] | Full Clip — A Decade of Gang Starr | 1999 | 20.00 |

## GANT, CECIL

**KING**

| Number | Title (A Side/B Side) | Yr | NM |
|---|---|---|---|
| ❑ 671 [M] | Cecil Gant | 1960 | 80.00 |

**RED MILL**

| Number | Title (A Side/B Side) | Yr | NM |
|---|---|---|---|
| ❑ (no #) [M] | Cecil Gant | 1956 | 500.00 |
| *—Red vinyl* | | | |

**SOUND**

| Number | Title (A Side/B Side) | Yr | NM |
|---|---|---|---|
| ❑ 601 [M] | The Incomparable Cecil Gant | 1958 | 100.00 |

## GANTS, THE

**LIBERTY**

| Number | Title (A Side/B Side) | Yr | NM |
|---|---|---|---|
| ❑ LRP-3432 [M] | Road Runner | 1965 | 30.00 |
| ❑ LRP-3455 [M] | The Gants Galore | 1966 | 30.00 |
| ❑ LRP-3473 [M] | The Gants Again | 1966 | 30.00 |
| ❑ LST-7432 [S] | Road Runner | 1965 | 40.00 |
| ❑ LST-7455 [S] | The Gants Galore | 1966 | 40.00 |
| ❑ LST-7473 [S] | The Gants Again | 1966 | 40.00 |

## GARAGIOLA, JOE

**UNITED ARTISTS**

| Number | Title (A Side/B Side) | Yr | NM |
|---|---|---|---|
| ❑ UAL-3032 [M] | That Holler Guy! | 1959 | 40.00 |
| ❑ UAS-6032 [S] | That Holler Guy! | 1959 | 50.00 |

## GARBAREK, JAN

**FLYING DUTCHMAN**

| Number | Title (A Side/B Side) | Yr | NM |
|---|---|---|---|
| ❑ FD-10125 | The Esoteric Circle | 1971 | 20.00 |

## GARBER, JAN

**DECCA**

| Number | Title (A Side/B Side) | Yr | NM |
|---|---|---|---|
| ❑ DL 8482 [M] | Dance at Home | 195? | 20.00 |
| *—Black label, silver print* | | | |
| ❑ DL 8483 [M] | In a Dancing Mood | 195? | 20.00 |
| *—Black label, silver print* | | | |
| ❑ DL 8484 [M] | Designed for Dancing | 195? | 20.00 |
| *—Black label, silver print* | | | |
| ❑ DL 78793 [S] | Music from the Blue Room, Roosevelt Hotel, New Orleans | 195? | 20.00 |
| *—Black label, silver print* | | | |
| ❑ DL 78824 [S] | Waltzes | 195? | 20.00 |
| *—Black label, silver print* | | | |
| ❑ DL 78867 [S] | Jan Garber in Danceland | 195? | 20.00 |
| *—Black label, silver print* | | | |
| ❑ DL 78932 [S] | Christmas Dance Party | 1959 | 20.00 |
| *—Black label, silver print* | | | |

## GARBO, GRETA

**MGM**

| Number | Title (A Side/B Side) | Yr | NM |
|---|---|---|---|
| ❑ E-4201 [M] | Garbo | 1964 | 40.00 |

## GARCIA, DICK

**DAWN**

| Number | Title (A Side/B Side) | Yr | NM |
|---|---|---|---|
| ❑ DLP-1106 [M] | A Message from Dick Garcia | 1956 | 50.00 |

**SEECO**

| Number | Title (A Side/B Side) | Yr | NM |
|---|---|---|---|
| ❑ SLP-428 [M] | A Message from Dick Garcia | 1958 | 40.00 |

## GARCIA, JERRY

**ARISTA**

| Number | Title (A Side/B Side) | Yr | NM |
|---|---|---|---|
| ❑ AB 4160 | Cats Under the Stars | 1978 | 12.00 |
| ❑ AL 8364 | Run for the Roses | 198? | 8.00 |
| *—Reissue of 9603* | | | |
| ❑ AL 9603 | Run for the Roses | 1982 | 12.00 |

**ROUND**

| Number | Title (A Side/B Side) | Yr | NM |
|---|---|---|---|
| ❑ RX-102 | Garcia | 1974 | 25.00 |
| ❑ RX-107 | Reflections | 1975 | 30.00 |
| ❑ RN-LA565-G | Reflections | 1976 | 20.00 |
| *—Reissue of Round 107 with United Artists distribution* | | | |

**WARNER BROS.**

| Number | Title (A Side/B Side) | Yr | NM |
|---|---|---|---|
| ❑ BS 2582 | Garcia | 1972 | 40.00 |
| *—Green label with "WB" logo* | | | |

## GARCIA, RUSS

**ABC-PARAMOUNT**

| Number | Title (A Side/B Side) | Yr | NM |
|---|---|---|---|
| ❑ ABC-147 [M] | The Johnny Evergreens | 1956 | 50.00 |

**BETHLEHEM**

| Number | Title (A Side/B Side) | Yr | NM |
|---|---|---|---|
| ❑ BCP-46 [M] | Four Horns and a Lush Life | 1956 | 50.00 |
| ❑ BCP-1040 [10] | Wigville | 1955 | 200.00 |

**KAPP**

| Number | Title (A Side/B Side) | Yr | NM |
|---|---|---|---|
| ❑ KL-1050 [M] | Listen to the Music of Russell Garcia | 1957 | 50.00 |

**LIBERTY**

| Number | Title (A Side/B Side) | Yr | NM |
|---|---|---|---|
| ❑ LRP-3062 [M] | Enchantment (The Music of Joe Greene) | 1958 | 25.00 |
| ❑ LRP-3084 [M] | Fantastica | 1958 | 30.00 |
| ❑ LST-7005 [S] | Fantastica | 1958 | 40.00 |

**VERVE**

| Number | Title (A Side/B Side) | Yr | NM |
|---|---|---|---|
| ❑ MGV-2088 [M] | The Warm Feeling | 1957 | 50.00 |
| ❑ V-2088 [M] | The Warm Feeling | 1961 | 20.00 |

## GARCIA, RUSS, AND MARTY PAICH

**BETHLEHEM**

| Number | Title (A Side/B Side) | Yr | NM |
|---|---|---|---|
| ❑ BCP-6039 [M] | Jazz Music for Birds and Hep Cats | 1960 | 50.00 |
| ❑ SBCP-6039 [S] | Jazz Music for Birds and Hep Cats | 1960 | 50.00 |

## GARDNER, BROTHER DAVE

**CAPITOL**

| Number | Title (A Side/B Side) | Yr | NM |
|---|---|---|---|
| ❑ ST 1867 [S] | It Don't Make No Difference | 1963 | 25.00 |
| ❑ T 1867 [M] | It Don't Make No Difference | 1963 | 20.00 |
| ❑ ST 2055 [S] | It's All in How You Look at It | 1964 | 25.00 |
| ❑ T 2055 [M] | It's All in How You Look at It | 1964 | 20.00 |

**4 STAR**

| Number | Title (A Side/B Side) | Yr | NM |
|---|---|---|---|
| ❑ 4S 75003 | Brother Dave Gardner's New Comedy Album | 1976 | 20.00 |

**RCA VICTOR**

| Number | Title (A Side/B Side) | Yr | NM |
|---|---|---|---|
| ❑ LPM-2083 [M] | Rejoice, Dear Hearts! | 1960 | 20.00 |
| ❑ LSP-2083(e) [S] | Rejoice, Dear Hearts! | 196? | 25.00 |
| ❑ LPM-2239 [M] | Kick Thy Own Self | 1960 | 20.00 |
| ❑ LSP-2239(e) [S] | Kick Thy Own Self | 196? | 25.00 |
| ❑ LPM-2335 [M] | Ain't That Weird? | 1961 | 20.00 |
| ❑ LSP-2335 [S] | Ain't That Weird? | 1961 | 25.00 |
| ❑ LPM-2498 [M] | Did You Ever? | 1962 | 20.00 |
| ❑ LSP-2498 [S] | Did You Ever? | 1962 | 25.00 |
| ❑ LPM-2628 [M] | All Seriousness Aside | 1963 | 20.00 |
| ❑ LSP-2628 [S] | All Seriousness Aside | 1963 | 25.00 |
| ❑ LPM-2761 [M] | It's Bigger Than Both of Us | 1963 | 20.00 |
| ❑ LSP-2761 [S] | It's Bigger Than Both of Us | 1963 | 25.00 |
| ❑ LPM-2852 [M] | Best of Dave Gardner | 1964 | 20.00 |
| ❑ LSP-2852 [S] | Best of Dave Gardner | 1964 | 25.00 |

**TONKA**

| Number | Title (A Side/B Side) | Yr | NM |
|---|---|---|---|
| ❑ TLP 713 | Out Front | 1969 | 20.00 |

**TOWER**

| Number | Title (A Side/B Side) | Yr | NM |
|---|---|---|---|
| ❑ ST 5050 [S] | Hip-ocracy | 1966 | 20.00 |
| ❑ T 5050 [M] | Hip-ocracy | 1966 | 15.00 |
| ❑ ST 5075 [S] | It Don't Make No Difference | 1967 | 20.00 |
| ❑ T 5075 [M] | It Don't Make No Difference | 1967 | 15.00 |

## GARDNER, DON, AND DEE DEE FORD

**COLLECTABLES**

| Number | Title (A Side/B Side) | Yr | NM |
|---|---|---|---|
| ❑ COL-5155 | Golden Classics: Need Your Lovin' | 198? | 12.00 |

**FIRE**

| Number | Title (A Side/B Side) | Yr | NM |
|---|---|---|---|
| ❑ LP-105 [M] | Need Your Lovin' | 1962 | 400.00 |

**SUE**

| Number | Title (A Side/B Side) | Yr | NM |
|---|---|---|---|
| ❑ LP-1044 [M] | Don Gardner and Dee Dee Ford In Sweden | 1965 | 120.00 |

## GARDNER, FREDDY

**COLUMBIA**

| Number | Title (A Side/B Side) | Yr | NM |
|---|---|---|---|
| ❑ CL 6187 [10] | Freddy Gardner | 195? | 50.00 |

## GARDNER, FREDDY, AND AL GALLODORO

**COLUMBIA**

| Number | Title (A Side/B Side) | Yr | NM |
|---|---|---|---|
| ❑ CL 623 [M] | The Immortal Freddy Gardner and Al Gallodoro | 1954 | 40.00 |
| *—Maroon label, gold print* | | | |

## GARDNERS, THE

**PRESTIGE INT'L.**

| Number | Title (A Side/B Side) | Yr | NM |
|---|---|---|---|
| ❑ PRLP-13062 [M] | Folk Songs Far and Near | 1962 | 30.00 |

## GARFUNKEL, ART

**COLUMBIA**

| Number | Title (A Side/B Side) | Yr | NM |
|---|---|---|---|
| ❑ CQ 31474 [Q] | Angel Clare | 1973 | 20.00 |
| ❑ KC 31474 | Angel Clare | 1973 | 12.00 |
| ❑ PC 31474 | Angel Clare | 197? | 8.00 |
| *—Reissue* | | | |
| ❑ PC 33700 | Breakaway | 197? | 8.00 |
| *—With bar code on cover* | | | |
| ❑ PC 33700 | Breakaway | 1975 | 12.00 |
| *—Originals have no bar code* | | | |
| ❑ PCQ 33700 [Q] | Breakaway | 1975 | 20.00 |
| ❑ JC 34975 | Watermark | 1978 | 12.00 |
| *—Stock copy with "(What a) Wonderful World" on side 2* | | | |
| ❑ JC 34975 | Watermark | 1978 | 100.00 |
| *—Stock copy with "Fingerpaint" on side 2* | | | |
| ❑ JC 34975 [DJ] | Watermark | 1978 | 60.00 |
| *—Test pressing or white label promo with "Fingerpaint" on side 2* | | | |
| ❑ PC 34975 | Watermark | 198? | 8.00 |
| *—Reissue* | | | |
| ❑ JC 35780 | Fate for Breakfast | 1979 | 12.00 |
| *—With six different covers, each illustrating Art Garfunkel at a different stage of eating breakfast. No difference in value.* | | | |
| ❑ FC 37392 | Scissors Cut | 1981 | 10.00 |
| ❑ FC 40212 | The Animals' Christmas By Jimmy Webb | 1986 | 10.00 |
| *—With Amy Grant* | | | |
| ❑ FC 40942 | Lefty | 1988 | 8.00 |
| ❑ OC 45008 | Garfunkel | 1989 | 10.00 |

## GARI, RALPH

**EMARCY**

| Number | Title (A Side/B Side) | Yr | NM |
|---|---|---|---|
| ❑ MG-36019 [M] | Ralph Gari | 1955 | 50.00 |

## GARLAND, HANK

**COLUMBIA**

| Number | Title (A Side/B Side) | Yr | NM |
|---|---|---|---|
| ❑ CL 1572 [M] | Jazz Winds from a New Direction | 1961 | 30.00 |
| ❑ CL 1913 [M] | The Unforgettable Guitar of Hank Garland | 1962 | 30.00 |
| ❑ CS 8372 [S] | Jazz Winds from a New Direction | 1961 | 40.00 |
| ❑ CS 8713 [S] | The Unforgettable Guitar of Hank Garland | 1962 | 40.00 |

**HARMONY**

| Number | Title (A Side/B Side) | Yr | NM |
|---|---|---|---|
| ❑ HL 7231 [M] | Velvet Guitar | 196? | 20.00 |
| ❑ HS 11028 [S] | Velvet Guitar | 196? | 25.00 |

**SESAC**

| Number | Title (A Side/B Side) | Yr | NM |
|---|---|---|---|
| ❑ SN-2301/2 [M] | Subtle Swing | 196? | 100.00 |

## GARLAND, JUDY

**A.E.I.**

| Number | Title (A Side/B Side) | Yr | NM |
|---|---|---|---|
| ❑ 2108 | Judy Garland Vol. 1: Born in a Trunk | 198? | 10.00 |
| ❑ 2109 [M] | Judy Garland Vol. 2: Stardom 1940-45 | 1980 | 10.00 |
| ❑ 2110 | Judy Garland Vol. 3: Superstar 1945-50 | 198? | 10.00 |

**ABC**

| Number | Title (A Side/B Side) | Yr | NM |
|---|---|---|---|
| ❑ 620 [M] | Judy Garland At Home at the Palace — Opening Night | 1967 | 20.00 |
| ❑ S-620 [S] | Judy Garland At Home at the Palace — Opening Night | 1967 | 25.00 |
| ❑ AC-30007 | The ABC Collection | 1976 | 15.00 |

**CAPITOL**

| Number | Title (A Side/B Side) | Yr | NM |
|---|---|---|---|
| ❑ DW 676 [R] | Miss Show Business | 1963 | 12.00 |
| ❑ W 676 [M] | Miss Show Business | 1955 | 40.00 |
| ❑ DT 734 [R] | Judy | 1963 | 15.00 |
| ❑ T 734 [M] | Judy | 1956 | 40.00 |
| ❑ DT 835 [R] | Alone | 1963 | 15.00 |
| ❑ T 835 [M] | Alone | 1957 | 40.00 |
| ❑ ST 1036 [S] | Judy in Love | 1959 | 40.00 |
| ❑ T 1036 [M] | Judy in Love | 1958 | 25.00 |
| ❑ ST 1118 [S] | Garland at the Grove | 1959 | 40.00 |
| ❑ T 1118 [M] | Garland at the Grove | 1959 | 25.00 |
| ❑ ST 1188 [S] | The Letter | 1959 | 40.00 |
| *—Add 80% if letter is on cover* | | | |
| ❑ T 1188 [M] | The Letter | 1959 | 25.00 |
| *—Add 80% if letter is on cover* | | | |
| ❑ ST 1467 [S] | Judy — That's Entertainment | 196? | 20.00 |
| *—Black rainbow label, Capitol logo at top* | | | |
| ❑ ST 1467 [S] | Judy — That's Entertainment | 1960 | 40.00 |
| *—Black rainbow label, Capitol logo at left* | | | |
| ❑ T 1467 [M] | Judy — That's Entertainment | 196? | 15.00 |
| *—Black rainbow label, Capitol logo at top* | | | |
| ❑ T 1467 [M] | Judy — That's Entertainment | 1960 | 25.00 |
| *—Black rainbow label, Capitol logo at left* | | | |
| ❑ SWBO 1569 [(2)S] | Judy at Carnegie Hall | 1961 | 50.00 |
| ❑ WBO 1569 [(2)M] | Judy at Carnegie Hall | 1961 | 40.00 |
| ❑ SW 1710 [S] | The Garland Touch | 1962 | 30.00 |
| ❑ W 1710 [M] | The Garland Touch | 1962 | 20.00 |
| ❑ SW 1861 [P] | I Could Go On Singing | 1963 | 60.00 |
| *—"I Am the Monarch of the Sea" and "It Never Was You" are rechanneled* | | | |
| ❑ W 1861 [M] | I Could Go On Singing | 1963 | 40.00 |
| ❑ ST 1941 [S] | Our Love Letter | 1963 | 30.00 |
| *—Reissue of ST 1188* | | | |
| ❑ T 1941 [M] | Our Love Letter | 1963 | 20.00 |
| *—Reissue of T 1188* | | | |
| ❑ SM-1999 | The Hits of Judy Garland | 197? | 10.00 |
| *—Reissue* | | | |
| ❑ ST 1999 [P] | The Hits of Judy Garland | 1964 | 30.00 |
| *—"Over the Rainbow," "Come Rain or Come Shine" and "April Showers" are rechanneled* | | | |
| ❑ T 1999 [M] | The Hits of Judy Garland | 1964 | 20.00 |
| ❑ DW 2062 [R] | Just for Openers | 1964 | 15.00 |
| ❑ W 2062 [M] | Just for Openers | 1964 | 20.00 |
| ❑ STCL 2988 [(3)] | The Judy Garland Deluxe Set | 1968 | 40.00 |
| ❑ DNFR-7632 [(6)] | The Magic of Judy Garland | 196? | 40.00 |
| *—Box set with 4-page insert; 20 of the 60 tracks are rechanneled* | | | |
| ❑ SM-11763 | Alone | 1978 | 10.00 |
| *—Edited reissue of 835* | | | |
| ❑ SM-11876 | Judy — That's Entertainment | 1978 | 10.00 |
| *—Edited reissue* | | | |
| ❑ M-12034 | Just for Openers | 1979 | 10.00 |
| *—Edited reissue* | | | |
| ❑ SN-16175 | The Hits of Judy Garland | 198? | 8.00 |
| *—Budget-line reissue* | | | |

**DECCA**

| Number | Title (A Side/B Side) | Yr | NM |
|---|---|---|---|
| ❑ DXB 172 [(2)M] | The Best of Judy Garland | 1963 | 20.00 |
| ❑ DL 4199 [M] | The Magic of Judy Garland | 1961 | 30.00 |
| ❑ DL 6020 [10] | Judy at the Palace | 1952 | 100.00 |
| ❑ DXSB 7172 [(2)R] | The Best of Judy Garland | 1963 | 20.00 |
| ❑ DL 8190 [M] | Judy Garland's Greatest Performances | 1955 | 40.00 |
| *—Black label, silver print* | | | |

Number | Title (A Side/B Side) | Yr | NM

❑ DL 8190 [M] Judy Garland's Greatest Performances 196? 25.00
—Black label with color bars
❑ DL 75150 [R] Judy Garland's Greatest Hits 1969 12.00

DRG
❑ SL 5179 The Wit and the Wonder of Judy Garland 1977 15.00
❑ SL-5187 The Beginning 1979 15.00

LONGINES SYMPHONETTE
❑ SY 5217 [(5)] The Magic of Judy Garland 197? 30.00

MARK 56
❑ 632 [PD] In Concert: San Francisco 1978 60.00

MCA
❑ 907 From the Decca Vaults 1984 10.00
❑ 4003 [(2)] The Best of Judy Garland 1973 15.00
—Black label with rainbow
❑ 4003 [(2)] The Best of Judy Garland 1980 10.00
—Blue label with rainbow
❑ 4046 [(2)] Collector's Items (1936-45) 197? 12.00
❑ 25165 The Best of Judy Garland from MGM Classic Films 1988 12.00

METRO
❑ M-505 [M] Judy Garland 1965 15.00
❑ MS-505 [S] Judy Garland 1965 20.00
❑ M-581 [M] Judy Garland in Song 1966 15.00
❑ MS-581 [S] Judy Garland in Song 1966 20.00

MGM
❑ SDP-1 [(2)] Golden Years at MGM 1969 30.00
❑ E-82 [10] Judy Garland Sings 1951 100.00
❑ PX 102 Forever Judy 1969 25.00
—White label "Limited Edition" with poster
❑ E-3149 [M] If You Feel Like Singing, Sing 1955 60.00
❑ E-3989 [M] The Judy Garland Story Vol. 1: The Star Years 1961 30.00
❑ E-4005 [M] The Judy Garland Story Vol. 2: The Hollywood Years 1962 30.00
❑ E-4204 [M] The Very Best of Judy Garland 1964 30.00
❑ SE-4204 [R] The Very Best of Judy Garland 1964 10.00
—Blue and gold label
❑ SE-4204 [R] The Very Best of Judy Garland 1964 15.00
—Black label

MINERVA
❑ LP-6JG-FNJ Judy Garland and Friends 1982 10.00
❑ LP-6JG-FST The Judy Garland Show: Mutual Admiration Society 1982 10.00

PAIR
❑ PDL2-1030 [(2)]Golden Memories 1986 12.00
❑ PDL2-1127 [(2)]The Legendary Judy Garland 1986 12.00

PICKWICK
❑ PTP-2010 [(2)] Her Greatest Hits 197? 12.00
❑ SPC-3053 I Feel a Song Coming On 197? 12.00

SPRINGBOARD
❑ SPB-4054 Over the Rainbow 197? 8.00

STANYAN
❑ POW-3001 More Than a Memory 198? 10.00
—Reissue of 10095
❑ 10095 More Than a Memory 1974 10.00

TIME-LIFE
❑ SLGD-12 [(2)] Legendary Singers: Judy Garland 1986 20.00

TROPHY
❑ TR-7-2145 [(2)]Judy Garland Concert 1974 15.00

**GARLAND, JUDY, AND LIZA MINNELLI**

CAPITOL
❑ SWBO 2295 [(2)S]"Live" at the London Palladium 1965 30.00
❑ WBO 2295 [(2)M]"Live" at the London Palladium 1965 25.00
❑ ST-11191 "Live" at the London Palladium 1973 12.00
—Condensation of above 2-record set

MOBILE FIDELITY
❑ 1-048 "Live" at the London Palladium 1981 25.00
—Audiophile vinyl

**GARLAND, RED**

JAZZLAND
❑ JLP-48 [M] Bright and Breezy 1961 100.00
❑ JLP-62 [M] The Nearness of You — Ballads Played by Red Garland 1962 100.00
❑ JLP-73 [M] Solar 1962 100.00
❑ JLP-87 [M] Red's Good Groove! 1963 120.00
❑ JLP-948 [S] Bright and Breezy 1961 120.00
❑ JLP-962 [S] The Nearness of You — Ballads Played by Red Garland 1962 120.00
❑ JLP-973 [S] Solar 1962 120.00
❑ JLP-987 [S] Red's Good Groove! 1963 120.00

MOODSVILLE
❑ MVLP-1 [M] Red Garland & Eddie "Lockjaw" Davis 1960 100.00
—Green label
❑ MVLP-1 [M] Red Garland & Eddie "Lockjaw" Davis 1965 50.00
—Blue label, trident logo at right
❑ MVLP-3 [M] Red Alone — Vol. 3 1960 100.00
—Green label
❑ MVLP-3 [M] Red Alone — Vol. 3 1965 50.00
—Blue label, trident logo at right
❑ MVLP-6 [M] The Red Garland Trio 1960 100.00
—Green label
❑ MVLP-6 [M] The Red Garland Trio 1965 50.00
—Blue label, trident logo at right
❑ MVLP-10 [M] Alone with the Blues 1960 100.00
—Green label
❑ MVLP-10 [M] Alone with the Blues 1965 50.00
—Blue label, trident logo at right

PRESTIGE
❑ PRLP-7064 [M]A Garland of Red 1956 200.00
—Yellow label, W. 50th St., New York address on label
❑ PRLP-7064 [M]A Garland of Red 1958 120.00
—Yellow label with Bergenfield, N.J. address
❑ PRLP-7086 [M]Red Garland's Piano 1957 200.00
—Yellow label, W. 50th St., New York address on label
❑ PRLP-7086 [M]Red Garland's Piano 1958 120.00
—Yellow label with Bergenfield, N.J. address
❑ PRLP-7113 [M]Groovy 1957 200.00
—Yellow label, W. 50th St., New York address on label
❑ PRLP-7113 [M]Groovy 1958 120.00
—Yellow label with Bergenfield, N.J. address
❑ PRLP-7130 [M]All Morning Long 1958 120.00
—Yellow label with Bergenfield, N.J. address
❑ PRLP-7130 [M]All Morning Long 1958 200.00
—Yellow label, W. 50th St., New York address on label
❑ PRLP-7139 [M]Manteca 1958 120.00
—Yellow label with Bergenfield, N.J. address
❑ PRLP-7139 [M]Manteca 1958 200.00
—Yellow label, W. 50th St. NYC address on label
❑ PRLP-7148 [M]All Kinds of Weather 1958 100.00
—Yellow label with Bergenfield, N.J. address
❑ PRLP-7157 [M]Red in Bluesville 1959 100.00
—Yellow label with Bergenfield, N.J. address
❑ PRLP-7170 [M]Red Garland at the Prelude 1959 100.00
—Yellow label with Bergenfield, N.J. address
❑ PRLP-7181 [M]Soul Junction 1960 100.00
—Yellow label with Bergenfield, N.J. address
❑ PRLP-7193 [M]Rojo 1961 80.00
—Yellow label with Bergenfield, N.J. address
❑ PRLP-7209 [M]High Pressure 1961 100.00
—Yellow label with Bergenfield, N.J. address
❑ PRLP-7229 [M]Dig It! 1962 80.00
❑ PRST-7229 [S] Dig It! 1962 80.00
❑ PRLP-7258 [M]When There Are Grey Skies 1963 60.00
❑ PRST-7258 [S] When There Are Grey Skies 1963 60.00
❑ PRLP-7276 [M]Can't See for Lookin' 1963 60.00
❑ PRST-7276 [S] Can't See for Lookin' 1963 60.00
❑ PRLP-7288 [M]Halleloo-Y'all 1964 60.00
❑ PRST-7288 [S] Halleloo-Y'all 1964 80.00
❑ PRLP-7307 [M]Soul Burnin' 1964 50.00
❑ PRST-7307 [S] Soul Burnin' 1964 60.00

STATUS
❑ ST-8314 [M] Li'l Darlin' 1965 60.00
❑ ST-8325 [M] High Pressure 1965 60.00
❑ ST-8326 [M] Red Garland Live! 1965 60.00

**GARNER, ERROLL**

ABC-PARAMOUNT
❑ 365 [M] Dreamstreet 1961 20.00
❑ S-365 [S] Dreamstreet 1961 25.00
❑ 395 [M] Closeup in Swing 1961 20.00
❑ S-395 [S] Closeup in Swing 1961 25.00

ATLANTIC
❑ ALR-109 [10] Rhapsody 1950 200.00
❑ ALR-112 [10] Erroll Garner at the Piano 1951 200.00
❑ ALR-128 [10] Passport to Fame 1952 200.00
❑ ALR-135 [10] Piano Solos, Volume 2 1952 200.00
❑ 1227 [M] The Greatest Garner 1956 40.00
—Black label
❑ 1315 [M] Perpetual Motion 1959 40.00
—Black label

BLUE NOTE
❑ BLP-5007 [10] Overture to Dawn, Volume 1 1952 500.00
❑ BLP-5008 [10] Overture to Dawn, Volume 2 1952 500.00
❑ BLP-5014 [10] Overture to Dawn, Volume 3 1953 500.00
❑ BLP-5015 [10] Overture to Dawn, Volume 4 1953 500.00
❑ BLP-5016 [10] Overture to Dawn, Volume 5 1953 500.00

COLUMBIA
❑ C2L 9 [(2)M] Paris Impressions 1958 40.00
❑ CL 535 [M] Erroll Garner 1953 60.00
—Red label with gold print
❑ CL 535 [M] Erroll Garner 1956 30.00
—Red and black label with six "eye" logos
❑ CL 583 [M] Gems 1954 60.00
—Red label with gold print
❑ CL 583 [M] Gems 1956 30.00
—Red and black label with six "eye" logos
❑ CL 617 [M] Gone Garner Gonest 1955 60.00
—Red label with gold print
❑ CL 617 [M] Gone Garner Gonest 1956 30.00
—Red and black label with six "eye" logos
❑ CL 667 [M] Erroll Garner Plays for Dancing 1956 30.00
❑ CL 883 [M] Concert by the Sea 1956 30.00
❑ CL 939 [M] The Most Happy Piano 1957 30.00
❑ CL 1014 [M] Other Voices 1957 30.00
—Red and black label wirh six "eye" logos
❑ CL 1060 [M] Soliloquy 1957 30.00
❑ CL 1141 [M] Encores in Hi-Fi 1958 30.00
❑ CL 1216 [M] Paris Impressions, Volume 1 1958 20.00
❑ CL 1217 [M] Paris Impressions, Volume 2 1958 20.00
❑ CL 1452 [M] The One and Only Erroll Garner 1960 20.00
❑ CL 1512 [M] Swinging Solos 1960 20.00
❑ CL 1587 [M] The Provocative Erroll Garner 1961 20.00
❑ CL 2540 [10] Garnerland 1955 60.00
❑ CL 2606 [10] He's Here! He's Gone! He's Garner! 1956 60.00
❑ CL 6139 [10] Piano Moods 1950 80.00
❑ CL 6173 [10] Gems 1951 80.00
❑ CL 6209 [10] Solo Flight 1952 80.00
❑ CL 6259 [10] Erroll Garner Plays for Dancing 1953 80.00
❑ CS 8131 [S] Paris Impressions, Volume 1 1958 30.00
❑ CS 8252 [S] The One and Only Erroll Garner 1960 25.00
❑ CS 8312 [S] Swinging Solos 1960 25.00
❑ CS 8387 [S] The Provocative Erroll Garner 1961 25.00

DIAL
❑ LP-205 [10] Erroll Garner, Volume 1 1950 200.00
❑ LP-902 [M] Free Piano Improvisations Recorded by Baron Timme Rosenkranz at One of His Famous Gaslight Jazz Sessions 1949 300.00

EMARCY
❑ MG-26016 [10] Garnering 1954 80.00
❑ MG-26042 [10] Gone with Garner 1954 80.00
❑ MG-36001 [M] Contrasts 1955 30.00
❑ MG-36026 [M] Garnering 1955 30.00
❑ MG-36069 [M] Erroll! 1956 30.00

JAZZTONE
❑ J-1269 [M] Early Erroll 1957 40.00

KING
❑ 295-17 [10] Piano Stylist 1952 80.00
❑ 395-540 [M] Piano Variations 1958 150.00

MERCURY
❑ MG-20009 [M] Erroll Garner at the Piano 1953 50.00
❑ MG-20055 [M] Mambo Moves Garner 1954 50.00
❑ MG-20063 [M] Solitaire 1954 50.00
❑ MG-20090 [M] Afternoon of an Elf 1955 50.00
❑ MG-25117 [10] Erroll Garner at the Piano 1951 80.00
❑ MG-25157 [10] Gone with Garner 1951 80.00
❑ SR-60662 [S] Erroll Garner Plays Misty 1962 20.00
—Black label, all-silver print
❑ SR-60803 [S] The Best of Erroll Garner 1963 20.00
❑ SR-60859 [S] New Kind of Love 1963 20.00
❑ SR-61308 [S] Feeling Is Believing 1964 20.00
❑ SR-61308 [S] Feeling Is Believing 1970 12.00
—Newer Mercury logo on cover

REPRISE
❑ R 6080 [DJ] One World Concert 1963 40.00
—Six-song sampler -- three on each side -- on a 12-inch record that plays at 45 rpm. This comes in a different cover than the stock copy; this is clearly marked "Special 45 RPM Preview Record" on the top front.
❑ R 6080 [M] One World Concert 1963 20.00
❑ RS 6080 [S] One World Concert 1963 25.00

RONDO-LETTE
❑ A-15 [M] Erroll Garner 1958 25.00

SAVOY
❑ MG-12002 [M] Penthouse Serenade 1955 30.00
❑ MG-12003 [M] Serenade to "Laura" 1955 30.00
❑ MG-15000 [10] Erroll Garner Plays Piano Solos 1950 80.00
❑ MG-15001 [10] Erroll Garner Plays Piano Solos, Volume 2 1950 80.00
❑ MG-15002 [10] Erroll Garner Plays Piano Solos, Volume 3 1950 80.00
❑ MG-15003 [10] Erroll Garner Plays Piano Solos, Volume 4 1950 80.00
❑ MG-15026 [10] Erroll Garner at the Piano 1953 80.00

**GARNER, ERROLL/PETE JOHNSON**

GRAND AWARD
❑ GA 33-321 [M] Jazz Piano 1956 25.00
—Without removable cover
❑ GA 33-321 [M] Jazz Piano 1956 80.00
—With removable David Stone Martin cover still attached

**GARNER, ERROLL/BILLY TAYLOR**

SAVOY
❑ MG-12008 [M] Erroll Garner/Billy Taylor 1955 50.00

**GARNER, MORRIS**

THUNDERBIRD
❑ TH-1958 [M] The Worst of Morris Garner 196? 25.00

**GARNETT, CARLOS**

MUSE
❑ MR-5057 Journey to Enlightenment 1974 20.00
❑ MR-5079 Let the Melody Ring On 1975 30.00
❑ MR-5104 Cosmos Nucleus 1976 40.00
❑ MR-5133 New Love 1977 40.00

### GARNETT, GALE

#### COLUMBIA

| Number | Title (A Side/B Side) | Yr | NM |
|---|---|---|---|
| CL 2825 [M] | An Audience with the King of Wands | 1968 | 30.00 |
| CS 9625 [M] | An Audience with the King of Wands | 1968 | 30.00 |

*—White label promo with stereo number and "Mono" on label; "Special Mono Radio Station Copy" sticker and timing strip on front cover*

| Number | Title (A Side/B Side) | Yr | NM |
|---|---|---|---|
| CS 9625 [S] | An Audience with the King of Wands | 1968 | 15.00 |
| CS 9760 | Sausalito Heliport | 1969 | 15.00 |

#### RCA VICTOR

| Number | Title (A Side/B Side) | Yr | NM |
|---|---|---|---|
| LPM-2833 [M] | My Kind of Folk Songs | 1964 | 40.00 |
| *—Black and white/blueish cover* | | | |
| LPM-2833 [M] | My Kind of Folk Songs | 1965 | 15.00 |
| *—Color photo on cover* | | | |
| LSP-2833 [S] | My Kind of Folk Songs | 1964 | 50.00 |
| *—Black and white/blueish cover* | | | |
| LSP-2833 [S] | My Kind of Folk Songs | 1965 | 20.00 |
| *—Color photo on cover* | | | |
| LPM-3305 [M] | Lovin' Place | 1965 | 15.00 |
| LSP-3305 [S] | Lovin' Place | 1965 | 20.00 |
| LPM-3325 [M] | The Many Faces of Gale Garnett | 1965 | 15.00 |
| LSP-3325 [S] | The Many Faces of Gale Garnett | 1965 | 20.00 |
| LPM-3493 [M] | Variety Is the Spice of Gale Garnett | 1966 | 15.00 |
| LSP-3493 [S] | Variety Is the Spice of Gale Garnett | 1966 | 20.00 |
| LPM-3586 [M] | New Adventures | 1966 | 15.00 |
| LSP-3586 [S] | New Adventures | 1966 | 20.00 |
| LPM-3747 [M] | Gale Garnett Sings About Flying & Rainbows & Love & Other Groovy Things | 1967 | 25.00 |
| LSP-3747 [S] | Gale Garnett Sings About Flying & Rainbows & Love & Other Groovy Things | 1967 | 20.00 |

### GARROWAY, DAVE

#### CAMEO

| Number | Title (A Side/B Side) | Yr | NM |
|---|---|---|---|
| C-1001 [M] | An Adventure in Hi-Fi Music | 1958 | 40.00 |

*—Black label, brown print, cameo figure at top*

### GARSON, GREER

#### LION

| Number | Title (A Side/B Side) | Yr | NM |
|---|---|---|---|
| L-70102 [M] | Greer Garson Babysits with Stories and Songs | 1958 | 30.00 |

### GARSON, MIKE

#### REFERENCE RECORDINGS

| Number | Title (A Side/B Side) | Yr | NM |
|---|---|---|---|
| RR-37 | The Oxnard Sessions | 1991 | 20.00 |
| RR-53 [(2)] | The Oxnard Sessions, Volume Two | 1993 | 25.00 |

### GARVIN, REX, AND THE MIGHTY CRAVERS

#### TOWER

| Number | Title (A Side/B Side) | Yr | NM |
|---|---|---|---|
| ST 5130 | Raw Funky Earth | 1968 | 30.00 |

### GARY, JOHN

#### CHURCHILL

| Number | Title (A Side/B Side) | Yr | NM |
|---|---|---|---|
| 67236 | In a Class By Himself | 1977 | 10.00 |

#### LA BREA

| Number | Title (A Side/B Side) | Yr | NM |
|---|---|---|---|
| 8010 [M] | John Gary | 1961 | 25.00 |
| S-8010 [S] | John Gary | 1961 | 30.00 |

#### METRO

| Number | Title (A Side/B Side) | Yr | NM |
|---|---|---|---|
| M-522 [M] | John Gary | 1966 | 10.00 |
| MS-522 [S] | John Gary | 1966 | 12.00 |

#### PICKWICK

| Number | Title (A Side/B Side) | Yr | NM |
|---|---|---|---|
| SPC-3025 | John Gary | 197? | 10.00 |

#### RCA CAMDEN

| Number | Title (A Side/B Side) | Yr | NM |
|---|---|---|---|
| CAL-983 [M] | The One and Only John Gary | 1966 | 10.00 |
| CAS-983 [S] | The One and Only John Gary | 1966 | 12.00 |

#### RCA VICTOR

| Number | Title (A Side/B Side) | Yr | NM |
|---|---|---|---|
| LOC-1139 [M] | The John Gary Carnegie Hall Concert | 1967 | 20.00 |
| LSO-1139 [S] | The John Gary Carnegie Hall Concert | 1967 | 12.00 |
| ANL1-2342 | Pure Gold | 1977 | 10.00 |
| ANL1-2672 | A Little Bit of Heaven | 1978 | 10.00 |
| *—Reissue of LSP-2994* | | | |
| LPM-2745 [M] | Catch a Rising Star | 1963 | 15.00 |
| LSP-2745 [S] | Catch a Rising Star | 1963 | 20.00 |
| LPM-2804 [M] | Encore | 1964 | 15.00 |
| LSP-2804 [S] | Encore | 1964 | 20.00 |
| LPM-2922 [M] | So Tenderly | 1964 | 15.00 |
| LSP-2922 [S] | So Tenderly | 1964 | 20.00 |
| LPM-2940 [M] | The John Gary Christmas Album | 1964 | 15.00 |
| LSP-2940 [S] | The John Gary Christmas Album | 1964 | 20.00 |
| LPM-2994 [M] | A Little Bit of Heaven | 1965 | 12.00 |
| LSP-2994 [S] | A Little Bit of Heaven | 1965 | 15.00 |
| LPM-3349 [M] | The Nearness of You | 1965 | 12.00 |
| LSP-3349 [S] | The Nearness of You | 1965 | 15.00 |
| LPM-3411 [M] | Your All-Time Favorite Songs | 1965 | 12.00 |
| LSP-3411 [S] | Your All-Time Favorite Songs | 1965 | 15.00 |
| LPM-3501 [M] | Choice | 1966 | 12.00 |
| LSP-3501 [S] | Choice | 1966 | 15.00 |
| LPM-3570 [M] | Your All-Time Country Favorites | 1966 | 12.00 |
| LSP-3570 [S] | Your All-Time Country Favorites | 1966 | 15.00 |
| LPM-3666 [M] | A Heart Filled with Song | 1966 | 12.00 |
| LSP-3666 [S] | A Heart Filled with Song | 1966 | 15.00 |
| LPM-3695 [M] | Especially for You | 1967 | 15.00 |
| LSP-3695 [S] | Especially for You | 1967 | 12.00 |
| LPM-3730 [M] | The Best of John Gary | 1967 | 15.00 |
| LSP-3730 [S] | The Best of John Gary | 1967 | 12.00 |
| LPM-3785 [M] | Spanish Moonlight | 1967 | 15.00 |
| LSP-3785 [S] | Spanish Moonlight | 1967 | 12.00 |
| LPM-3928 [M] | John Gary On Broadway | 1968 | 20.00 |
| LSP-3928 [S] | John Gary On Broadway | 1968 | 12.00 |
| LPM-3992 [M] | John Gary Sings/John Gary Swings | 1968 | 20.00 |
| LSP-3992 [S] | John Gary Sings/John Gary Swings | 1968 | 12.00 |
| LSP-4075 | Holding Your Mind | 1969 | 12.00 |
| LSP-4134 | Love of a Gentle Woman | 1970 | 12.00 |
| LSP-4233 | That's the Way It Was | 1971 | 12.00 |
| VPS-6041 [(2)] | This Is John Gary | 1971 | 15.00 |

### GARY, SAM

#### TRANSITION

| Number | Title (A Side/B Side) | Yr | NM |
|---|---|---|---|
| TRLP-F-1 [M] | Spirituals and Work Songs | 1958 | 30.00 |

### GAS MASK

#### TONSIL

| Number | Title (A Side/B Side) | Yr | NM |
|---|---|---|---|
| 4001 | Gas Mask | 1970 | 20.00 |

### GASKIN, LEONARD

#### SWINGVILLE

| Number | Title (A Side/B Side) | Yr | NM |
|---|---|---|---|
| SVLP-2031 [M] | At the Jazz Band Ball | 1962 | 40.00 |
| *—Purple label* | | | |
| SVLP-2031 [M] | At the Jazz Band Ball | 1965 | 20.00 |
| *—Blue label, trident logo at right* | | | |
| SVST-2031 [S] | At the Jazz Band Ball | 1962 | 50.00 |
| *—Red label* | | | |
| SVST-2031 [S] | At the Jazz Band Ball | 1965 | 25.00 |
| *—Blue label, trident logo at right* | | | |
| SVLP-2033 [M] | At the Darktown Strutters' Ball | 1962 | 40.00 |
| *—Purple label* | | | |
| SVLP-2033 [M] | At the Darktown Strutters' Ball | 1965 | 20.00 |
| *—Blue label, trident logo at right* | | | |
| SVST-2033 [S] | At the Darktown Strutters' Ball | 1962 | 50.00 |
| *—Red label* | | | |
| SVST-2033 [S] | At the Darktown Strutters' Ball | 1965 | 25.00 |
| *—Blue label, trident logo at right* | | | |

### GATES, DAVID

#### ARISTA

| Number | Title (A Side/B Side) | Yr | NM |
|---|---|---|---|
| AL 9563 | Take Me Now | 1981 | 10.00 |

#### ELEKTRA

| Number | Title (A Side/B Side) | Yr | NM |
|---|---|---|---|
| 6E-148 | Goodbye Girl | 1978 | 12.00 |
| 6E-251 | Falling in Love Again | 1980 | 10.00 |
| 7E-1028 | Never Let Her Go | 1975 | 12.00 |
| EQ-1028 [Q] | Never Let Her Go | 1975 | 20.00 |
| EQ-5066 [Q] | First | 1973 | 20.00 |
| EKS-75066 | First | 1973 | 12.00 |

### GATES, HEN

#### MASTERSEAL

| Number | Title (A Side/B Side) | Yr | NM |
|---|---|---|---|
| MLP-700 [M] | Let's All Dance to Rock and Roll | 1956 | 100.00 |

#### PALACE

| Number | Title (A Side/B Side) | Yr | NM |
|---|---|---|---|
| P-700 [M] | Let's All Dance to Rock and Roll | 1958 | 60.00 |
| *—Reissue of Masterseal 700* | | | |
| PST-700 [S] | Let's All Dance to Rock and Roll | 1958 | 80.00 |
| *—Labeled stereo, but plays in mono* | | | |

#### PARIS

| Number | Title (A Side/B Side) | Yr | NM |
|---|---|---|---|
| 101 [M] | Rock and Roll Festival | 1957 | 60.00 |

#### PLYMOUTH

| Number | Title (A Side/B Side) | Yr | NM |
|---|---|---|---|
| R12-144 [M] | Rock and Roll | 1956 | 60.00 |
| R12-149 [M] | Rock and Roll, No. 2 | 1957 | 60.00 |

### GATEWAY SINGERS, THE

#### DECCA

| Number | Title (A Side/B Side) | Yr | NM |
|---|---|---|---|
| DL 8413 [M] | Puttin' On the Style | 1956 | 40.00 |
| DL 8671 [M] | The Gateway Singers at the Hungry I | 1958 | 30.00 |
| DL 8742 [M] | The Gateway Singers in Hi-Fi | 1958 | 30.00 |

#### MGM

| Number | Title (A Side/B Side) | Yr | NM |
|---|---|---|---|
| E-3905 [M] | Down in the Valley | 1961 | 20.00 |
| SE-3905 [S] | Down in the Valley | 1961 | 25.00 |
| E-4154 [M] | Hootenanny | 1963 | 20.00 |
| SE-4154 [S] | Hootenanny | 1963 | 25.00 |

#### WARNER BROS.

| Number | Title (A Side/B Side) | Yr | NM |
|---|---|---|---|
| W 1295 [M] | The Gateway Singers on the Lot | 1959 | 25.00 |
| WS 1295 [S] | The Gateway Singers on the Lot | 1959 | 30.00 |
| W 1334 [M] | Wagons West | 1960 | 25.00 |
| WS 1334 [S] | Wagons West | 1960 | 30.00 |

### GATEWAY TRIO, THE

#### CAPITOL

| Number | Title (A Side/B Side) | Yr | NM |
|---|---|---|---|
| ST 1868 [S] | The Mad, Mad, Mad Gateway Trio | 1963 | 20.00 |
| T 1868 [M] | The Mad, Mad, Mad Gateway Trio | 1963 | 15.00 |
| ST 2184 [S] | The Gateway Trio | 1964 | 20.00 |
| T 2184 [M] | The Gateway Trio | 1964 | 15.00 |

### GATLIN, LARRY, AND THE GATLIN BROTHERS BAND

#### COLUMBIA

| Number | Title (A Side/B Side) | Yr | NM |
|---|---|---|---|
| JC 36250 | Straight Ahead | 1979 | 10.00 |
| JC 36488 | Larry Gatlin's Greatest Hits, Volume 1 | 1980 | 8.00 |
| *—Reissue of Monument 7628* | | | |
| PC 36541 | The Pilgrim | 1980 | 8.00 |
| *—Reissue of Monument 6632* | | | |
| JC 36582 | Help Yourself | 1980 | 10.00 |
| PC 36582 | Help Yourself | 198? | 8.00 |
| *—Budget-line reissue* | | | |
| FC 37464 | Not Guilty | 1981 | 10.00 |
| PC 37464 | Not Guilty | 198? | 8.00 |
| *—Budget-line reissue* | | | |
| FC 38135 | Sure Feels Like Love | 1982 | 10.00 |
| PC 38135 | Sure Feels Like Love | 198? | 8.00 |
| *—Budget-line reissue* | | | |
| FC 38183 | A Gatlin Family Christmas | 1982 | 12.00 |
| PC 38183 | A Gatlin Family Christmas | 198? | 8.00 |
| *—Budget-line reissue* | | | |
| PC 38336 | Love Is Just a Game | 1982 | 8.00 |
| *—Reissue of Monument 7616* | | | |
| PC 38337 | Larry Gatlin with Family and Friends | 1982 | 8.00 |
| *—Reissue of Monument 6634* | | | |
| PC 38338 | High Time | 1982 | 8.00 |
| *—Reissue of Monument 6644* | | | |
| PC 38339 | Rain-Rainbow | 1982 | 8.00 |
| *—Reissue of Monument 6633* | | | |
| PC 38340 | Oh! Brother | 1982 | 8.00 |
| *—Reissue of Monumnet 7626* | | | |
| FC 38923 | Larry Gatlin's Greatest Hits, Volume 2 | 1983 | 10.00 |
| FC 39291 | Houston to Denver | 1984 | 10.00 |
| FC 40068 | Smile! | 1985 | 10.00 |
| FC 40431 | Partners | 1986 | 10.00 |
| FC 40905 | Alive and Well...Living in the Land of Dreams | 1988 | 10.00 |
| FC 44471 | The Gatlin Brothers' Biggest Hits (1984-88) | 1989 | 10.00 |
| HC 48135 | Sure Feels Like Love | 1982 | 250.00 |
| *—Half-speed mastered edition* | | | |

#### MONUMENT

| Number | Title (A Side/B Side) | Yr | NM |
|---|---|---|---|
| 6632 | The Pilgrim | 1976 | 12.00 |
| *—Reissue of KZ 32571* | | | |
| 6633 | Rain-Rainbow | 1976 | 12.00 |
| *—Reissue of KZ 33069* | | | |
| 6634 | Larry Gatlin with Family and Friends | 1976 | 12.00 |
| *—Reissue of KZ 34042* | | | |
| 6644 | High Time | 1977 | 12.00 |
| MG 7616 | Love Is Just a Game | 1978 | 12.00 |
| MG 7626 | Oh! Brother | 1978 | 12.00 |
| MG 7628 | Larry Gatlin's Greatest Hits | 1978 | 12.00 |
| KZ 32571 | The Pilgrim | 1974 | 15.00 |
| KZ 33069 | Rain-Rainbow | 1974 | 15.00 |
| KZ 34042 | Larry Gatlin with Family & Friends | 1975 | 15.00 |

#### SWORD & SHIELD

| Number | Title (A Side/B Side) | Yr | NM |
|---|---|---|---|
| 9009 [M] | The Old Country Church | 1961 | 100.00 |

*—As "The Gatlin Quartet" (with sister La Donna joining Larry, Rudy and Steve)*

### GAUCHOS, THE See JIM DOVAL AND THE GAUCHOS.

### GAULT, JONNA, AND HER SYMPHONOPOP SCENE

#### RCA VICTOR

| Number | Title (A Side/B Side) | Yr | NM |
|---|---|---|---|
| LSP-4081 | Watch Me | 1968 | 25.00 |

### GAVIN, KEVIN

#### CHARLIE PARKER

| Number | Title (A Side/B Side) | Yr | NM |
|---|---|---|---|
| PLP-810 [M] | Hey! This Is Kevin Gavin | 1962 | 30.00 |
| PLP-810S [S] | Hey! This Is Kevin Gavin | 1962 | 40.00 |

### GAYE, MARVIN

#### COLUMBIA

| Number | Title (A Side/B Side) | Yr | NM |
|---|---|---|---|
| FC 38197 | Midnight Love | 1982 | 10.00 |
| PC 38197 | Midnight Love | 1986 | 8.00 |
| *—Budget-line reissue* | | | |
| FC 39916 | Dream of a Lifetime | 1985 | 10.00 |
| 9C9 40133 [PD] | Dream of a Lifetime | 1985 | 20.00 |
| FC 40208 | Romantically Yours | 1986 | 10.00 |
| HC 48197 | Midnight Love | 1984 | 40.00 |
| *—Half-speed mastered edition* | | | |

#### MOTOWN

| Number | Title (A Side/B Side) | Yr | NM |
|---|---|---|---|
| M5-115V1 | Motown Superstar Series, Vol. 15 | 1981 | 10.00 |
| M5-125V1 | M.P.G. | 1981 | 10.00 |

*—Reissue of Tamla 292*

| Number | Title (A Side/B Side) | Yr | NM |
|---|---|---|---|
| ❑ M5-181V1 | Marvin Gaye Live! | 1981 | 10.00 |
| *—Reissue of Tamla 333* | | | |
| ❑ M5-191V1 | Marvin Gaye's Greatest Hits | 1981 | 10.00 |
| *—Reissue of Tamla 348* | | | |
| ❑ M5-192V1 | Let's Get It On | 1981 | 10.00 |
| *—Reissue of Tamla 329* | | | |
| ❑ M5-216V1 | A Tribute to the Great Nat King Cole | 1981 | 10.00 |
| *—Reissue of Tamla 261* | | | |
| ❑ M5-218V1 | That Stubborn Kinda' Fellow | 1981 | 10.00 |
| *—Reissue of Tamla 239* | | | |
| ❑ M9-791A3 [(3)] | Anthology | 1974 | 20.00 |
| ❑ 37463 1296-1 [DJ] | The Master 1961-1984 | 1995 | 20.00 |
| *—Vinyl is promo only; 8-song sampler from box set* | | | |
| ❑ 5259 ML [(2)] | Marvin Gaye Live at the London Palladium | 1983 | 12.00 |
| *—Reissue of Tamla 352* | | | |
| ❑ 5306 ML | Super Hits | 198? | 10.00 |
| ❑ 5339 ML | What's Going On | 198? | 10.00 |
| *—Reissue of Tamla 322* | | | |
| ❑ 6058 ML | Every Great Motown Hit of Marvin Gaye | 1983 | 10.00 |
| ❑ 6255 ML [(2)] | A Musical Testament 1964-1984 | 1988 | 12.00 |
| NATURAL RESOURCES | | | |
| ❑ NR 4007T1 | The Soulful Moods of Marvin Gaye | 1978 | 12.00 |
| *—Reissue of Tamla 221* | | | |
| TAMLA | | | |
| ❑ TM 221 [M] | The Soulful Moods of Marvin Gaye | 1961 | 1000. |
| ❑ T 239 [M] | That Stubborn Kinda' Fella | 1963 | 600.00 |
| ❑ T 242 [M] | Recorded Live — Marvin Gaye on Stage | 1963 | 300.00 |
| ❑ T 251 [M] | When I'm Alone I Cry | 1964 | 250.00 |
| ❑ T 252 [M] | Marvin Gaye/Greatest Hits | 1964 | 30.00 |
| ❑ TS 252 [S] | Marvin Gaye/Greatest Hits | 1964 | 40.00 |
| ❑ T 258 [M] | How Sweet It Is to Be Loved by You | 1965 | 40.00 |
| ❑ TS 258 [S] | How Sweet It Is to Be Loved by You | 1965 | 50.00 |
| ❑ T 259 [M] | Hello Broadway, This Is Marvin | 1965 | 40.00 |
| ❑ TS 259 [S] | Hello Broadway, This Is Marvin | 1965 | 50.00 |
| ❑ T 261 [M] | A Tribute to the Great Nat King Cole | 1965 | 40.00 |
| ❑ TS 261 [S] | A Tribute to the Great Nat King Cole | 1965 | 50.00 |
| ❑ T 266 [M] | Moods of Marvin Gaye | 1966 | 40.00 |
| ❑ TS 266 [S] | Moods of Marvin Gaye | 1966 | 50.00 |
| ❑ T 278 [M] | Marvin Gaye/Greatest Hits, Vol. 2 | 1967 | 25.00 |
| ❑ TS 278 [S] | Marvin Gaye/Greatest Hits, Vol. 2 | 1967 | 20.00 |
| ❑ T 285 [M] | In the Groove | 1968 | 50.00 |
| ❑ TS 285 [S] | In the Groove | 1968 | 25.00 |
| ❑ TS 285 [S] | I Heard It Through the Grapevine | 1969 | 20.00 |
| *—Retitled version of "In the Groove"* | | | |
| ❑ TS 292 | M.P.G. | 1969 | 20.00 |
| ❑ TS 293 | Marvin Gaye and His Girls | 1969 | 20.00 |
| *—Includes duets with Tammi Terrell, Mary Wells, Kim Weston* | | | |
| ❑ TS 299 | That's the Way Love Is | 1969 | 20.00 |
| ❑ TS 300 | Marvin Gaye Super Hits | 1970 | 20.00 |
| ❑ T5-310 | What's Going On | 1971 | 15.00 |
| ❑ T5-322 | Trouble Man | 1972 | 15.00 |
| ❑ T6-329 | Let's Get It On | 1973 | 15.00 |
| ❑ T6-333 | Marvin Gaye Live! | 1974 | 15.00 |
| ❑ T6-342 | I Want You | 1976 | 15.00 |
| ❑ T6-348 | Marvin Gaye's Greatest Hits | 1976 | 15.00 |
| ❑ T7-352 [(2)] | Marvin Gaye Live at the London Palladium | 1977 | 15.00 |
| ❑ T13-364 [(2)] | Here, My Dear | 1978 | 15.00 |
| ❑ T8-374 | In Our Lifetime | 1981 | 10.00 |
| ❑ 6172 TL | Motown Remembers Marvin Gaye | 1986 | 10.00 |

**GAYE, MARVIN, AND TAMMI TERRELL**

| Number | Title (A Side/B Side) | Yr | NM |
|---|---|---|---|
| MOTOWN | | | |
| ❑ M5-102V1 | Motown Superstar Series, Vol. 2 | 1981 | 10.00 |
| ❑ M5-142V1 | You're All I Need | 1981 | 10.00 |
| *—Reissue of Tamla 284* | | | |
| ❑ M5-200V1 | United | 1981 | 10.00 |
| *—Reissue of Tamla 277* | | | |
| TAMLA | | | |
| ❑ T 277 [M] | United | 1967 | 30.00 |
| ❑ TS 277 [S] | United | 1967 | 25.00 |
| ❑ T 284 [M] | You're All I Need | 1968 | 50.00 |
| ❑ TS 284 [S] | You're All I Need | 1968 | 20.00 |
| ❑ TS 294 | Easy | 1969 | 20.00 |
| ❑ TS 302 | Marvin Gaye & Tammi Terrell/Greatest Hits | 1970 | 20.00 |

**GAYE, MARVIN, AND MARY WELLS**

| Number | Title (A Side/B Side) | Yr | NM |
|---|---|---|---|
| MOTOWN | | | |
| ❑ M 613 [M] | Together | 1964 | 50.00 |
| ❑ 5260 ML | Together | 1982 | 10.00 |

The J. Geils Band, *Ladies Invited,* Atlantic SD 7286, 1973, $12.

**GAYE, MARVIN, AND KIM WESTON**

| Number | Title (A Side/B Side) | Yr | NM |
|---|---|---|---|
| TAMLA | | | |
| ❑ T/TS 260 | Side by Side | 1965 | — |
| *—Canceled* | | | |
| ❑ T 270 [M] | Take Two | 1966 | 30.00 |
| ❑ TS 270 [S] | Take Two | 1966 | 40.00 |

**GAYLE, CRYSTAL**

| Number | Title (A Side/B Side) | Yr | NM |
|---|---|---|---|
| COLUMBIA | | | |
| ❑ JC 36203 | Miss the Mississippi | 1979 | 10.00 |
| ❑ PC 36203 | Miss the Mississippi | 198? | 8.00 |
| *—Budget-line reissue* | | | |
| ❑ JC 36512 | These Days | 1980 | 10.00 |
| ❑ PC 36512 | These Days | 198? | 8.00 |
| *—Budget-line reissue* | | | |
| ❑ FC 37438 | Hollywood, Tennessee | 1981 | 10.00 |
| ❑ PC 37438 | Hollywood, Tennessee | 198? | 8.00 |
| *—Budget-line reissue* | | | |
| ❑ FC 38803 | Crystal Gayle's Greatest Hits | 1983 | 10.00 |
| ELEKTRA | | | |
| ❑ 60200 | True Love | 1982 | 10.00 |
| LIBERTY | | | |
| ❑ LMAS-858 | When I Dream | 1981 | 8.00 |
| *—Reissue of UA 858* | | | |
| ❑ LOO-1034 | Favorites | 1981 | 8.00 |
| *—Reissue of UA 1034* | | | |
| ❑ LOO-1080 | A Woman's Heart | 1981 | 10.00 |
| ❑ LN-10002 | Crystal Gayle | 1981 | 8.00 |
| ❑ LN-10003 | Somebody Loves You | 1981 | 8.00 |
| *—Budget-line reissue of UA 543* | | | |
| ❑ LN-10004 | Crystal | 1981 | 8.00 |
| *—Budget-line reissue of UA 614* | | | |
| ❑ LN-10005 | We Must Believe in Magic | 1981 | 8.00 |
| *—Budget-line reissue of UA 771* | | | |
| ❑ LN-10006 | We Should Be Together | 1980 | 8.00 |
| *—Budget-line reissue* | | | |
| ❑ LN-10150 | Classic Crystal | 1982 | 8.00 |
| *—Budget-line reissue of UA 982* | | | |
| ❑ LN-10227 | When I Dream | 1984 | 8.00 |
| *—Budget-line reissue* | | | |
| ❑ LN-10229 | Favorites | 1984 | 8.00 |
| *—Budget-line reissue* | | | |
| MCA | | | |
| ❑ 2334 | I've Cried the Blue Right Out of My Eyes | 1977 | 10.00 |
| *—Reissue of Decca material* | | | |
| ❑ 37077 | I've Cried the Blue Right Out of My Eyes | 198? | 8.00 |
| *—Budget-line reissue* | | | |
| MOBILE FIDELITY | | | |
| ❑ 1-043 | We Must Believe in Magic | 1981 | 20.00 |
| *—Audiophile vinyl* | | | |
| NAUTILUS | | | |
| ❑ NR-36 | When I Dream | 198? | 30.00 |
| *—Audiophile vinyl* | | | |
| PAIR | | | |
| ❑ PDL2-1083 [(2)] | Country Pure | 1986 | 12.00 |
| ❑ PDL2-1126 [(2)] | Musical Jewels | 1986 | 12.00 |
| UNITED ARTISTS | | | |
| ❑ UA-LA543-G | Somebody Loves You | 1975 | 12.00 |
| ❑ UA-LA614-G | Crystal | 1976 | 12.00 |
| ❑ UA-LA771-G | We Must Believe in Magic | 1977 | 10.00 |
| ❑ UA-LA858-H | When I Dream | 1978 | 10.00 |
| ❑ UA-LA969-H | We Should Be Together | 1979 | 10.00 |
| ❑ LOO-982 | Classic Crystal | 1979 | 10.00 |
| ❑ LOO-1034 | Favorites | 1980 | 10.00 |
| WARNER BROS. | | | |
| ❑ 23958 | Cage the Songbird | 1983 | 10.00 |
| ❑ 25154 | Nobody Wants to Be Alone | 1984 | 10.00 |
| ❑ 25405 | Straight to the Heart | 1986 | 10.00 |
| ❑ 25508 | A Crystal Christmas | 1986 | 15.00 |
| *—Original cover has decorated Christmas tree on front* | | | |
| ❑ 25508 | A Crystal Christmas | 1987 | 10.00 |
| *—Reissue cover has photo of Crystal Gayle on front* | | | |
| ❑ 25622 | The Best of Crystal Gayle | 1987 | 10.00 |
| ❑ 25706 | Nobody's Angel | 1988 | 10.00 |
| ❑ 60200 | True Love | 1983 | 8.00 |
| *—Reissue of Elektra 60200* | | | |

**GAYLE, ROZELLE**

| Number | Title (A Side/B Side) | Yr | NM |
|---|---|---|---|
| MERCURY | | | |
| ❑ MG-20374 [M] | Like, Be My Guest | 1958 | 40.00 |

**GAYLORDS, THE**

| Number | Title (A Side/B Side) | Yr | NM |
|---|---|---|---|
| MERCURY | | | |
| ❑ MG-20186 [M] | Italia | 1957 | 30.00 |
| ❑ MG-20213 [M] | Collection of Golden Hits | 1957 | 30.00 |
| ❑ MG-20356 [M] | Let's Have a Pizza Party | 1958 | 20.00 |
| ❑ MG-20430 [M] | That's Amore | 1959 | 20.00 |
| ❑ MG-20620 [M] | American Hits in Italian | 1961 | 20.00 |
| ❑ MG-20695 [M] | The Gaylords at the Shamrock | 1962 | 20.00 |

Genesis, *Foxtrot,* Charisma CAS-1058, 1972, $15.

| Number | Title (A Side/B Side) | Yr | NM |
|---|---|---|---|
| ❑ MG-20742 [M] | Party Style | 1963 | 20.00 |
| ❑ MG-25198 [10] | By Request | 1955 | 50.00 |
| ❑ SR-60075 [S] | Let's Have a Pizza Party | 1959 | 30.00 |
| ❑ SR-60102 [S] | That's Amore | 1959 | 30.00 |
| ❑ SR-60620 [S] | American Hits in Italian | 1961 | 30.00 |
| ❑ SR-60695 [S] | The Gaylords at the Shamrock | 1962 | 25.00 |
| ❑ SR-60742 [S] | Party Style | 1963 | 25.00 |

**TIME**

| Number | Title (A Side/B Side) | Yr | NM |
|---|---|---|---|
| ❑ S-2109 [S] | Live at Lake Tahoe | 196? | 20.00 |
| ❑ S-2127 [S] | Bella Italia | 196? | 20.00 |
| ❑ 52109 [M] | Live at Lake Tahoe | 196? | 15.00 |
| ❑ 52127 [M] | Bella Italia | 196? | 15.00 |

**WING**

| Number | Title (A Side/B Side) | Yr | NM |
|---|---|---|---|
| ❑ MGW-12139 [M] | Italiano Favorites | 196? | 12.00 |
| ❑ MGW-12278 [M] | Let's Have a Pizza Party | 196? | 12.00 |
| ❑ SRW-16139 [S] | Italiano Favorites | 196? | 12.00 |
| ❑ SRW-16278 [S] | Let's Have a Pizza Party | 196? | 12.00 |

### GAYNOR, MITZI

**VERVE**

| Number | Title (A Side/B Side) | Yr | NM |
|---|---|---|---|
| ❑ MGV-2110 [M] | Mitzi | 1959 | 30.00 |
| ❑ MGV-2115 [M] | Mitzi Gaynor Sings the Lyrics of Ira Gershwin | 1959 | 30.00 |
| ❑ MGVS-6014 [S] | Mitzi | 1959 | 40.00 |
| ❑ MGVS-6049 [S] | Mitzi Gaynor Sings the Lyrics of Ira Gershwin | 1959 | 40.00 |

### GEARS, THE

**PLAYGEMS**

| Number | Title (A Side/B Side) | Yr | NM |
|---|---|---|---|
| ❑ GS 6471 | Rockin' at Ground Zero | 1980 | 30.00 |

### GEE, MATTHEW

**RIVERSIDE**

| Number | Title (A Side/B Side) | Yr | NM |
|---|---|---|---|
| ❑ RLP 12-221 [M] | Jazz by Gee! | 1956 | 80.00 |
| *—White label, blue print* | | | |
| ❑ RLP 12-221 [M] | Jazz by Gee! | 1958 | 40.00 |
| *—Blue label, microphone logo at top* | | | |

### GEEZINSLAW BROTHERS, THE

**CAPITOL**

| Number | Title (A Side/B Side) | Yr | NM |
|---|---|---|---|
| ❑ ST-130 | The Geezinslaw Brothers Are Alive | 1969 | 20.00 |
| ❑ ST 2570 [S] | Can You Believe...The Geezinslaw Brothers! | 1966 | 25.00 |
| ❑ T 2570 [M] | Can You Believe...The Geezinslaw Brothers! | 1966 | 20.00 |
| ❑ ST 2771 [S] | My Dirty, Lowdown, Rotten, Cotton-Pickin' Little Darlin' | 1967 | 25.00 |
| ❑ T 2771 [M] | My Dirty, Lowdown, Rotten, Cotton-Pickin' Little Darlin' | 1967 | 20.00 |
| ❑ ST 2885 [S] | The Geezinslaw Brothers & "Chubby" | 1968 | 25.00 |
| ❑ T 2885 [M] | The Geezinslaw Brothers & "Chubby" | 1968 | 40.00 |

**COLUMBIA**

| Number | Title (A Side/B Side) | Yr | NM |
|---|---|---|---|
| ❑ CL 2100 [M] | The Kooky World of the Geezinslaw Brothers | 1963 | 25.00 |
| ❑ CS 8900 [S] | The Kooky World of the Geezinslaw Brothers | 1963 | 30.00 |

### GEILS, J., BAND

**ATLANTIC**

| Number | Title (A Side/B Side) | Yr | NM |
|---|---|---|---|
| ❑ SD 2-507 [(2)] | Live — Blow Your Face Out | 1976 | 15.00 |
| ❑ SD 7241 | "Live" — Full House | 1972 | 12.00 |
| ❑ QD 7260 [Q] | Bloodshot | 1973 | 20.00 |
| ❑ SD 7260 | Bloodshot | 1973 | 12.00 |
| *—Black vinyl* | | | |
| ❑ SD 7260 | Bloodshot | 1973 | 20.00 |
| *—Red vinyl* | | | |
| ❑ QD 7286 [Q] | Ladies Invited | 1973 | — |
| *—Not released* | | | |
| ❑ SD 7286 | Ladies Invited | 1973 | 12.00 |
| ❑ 8275 [M] | The J. Geils Band | 1970 | 40.00 |
| *—Mono is white label promo only; stereo cover with "dj copy monaural" sticker* | | | |
| ❑ SD 8275 [S] | The J. Geils Band | 1970 | 15.00 |
| ❑ 8297 [M] | The Morning After | 1971 | 40.00 |
| *—Mono version is white label promo only with "d/j copy monaural" stucker on front cover* | | | |
| ❑ SD 8297 [S] | The Morning After | 1971 | 12.00 |
| ❑ QD 18107 [Q] | Nightmares and Other Tales from the Vinyl Jungle | 1974 | 20.00 |
| ❑ SD 18107 | Nightmares and Other Tales from the Vinyl Jungle | 1974 | 12.00 |
| ❑ SD 18147 | Hotline | 1975 | 12.00 |
| ❑ SD 19103 | Monkey Island | 1977 | 12.00 |
| *—As "Geils"* | | | |
| ❑ SD 19234 | Best of the J. Geils Band | 1979 | 10.00 |
| ❑ SD 19284 | Best of the J. Geils Band — 2 | 1980 | 10.00 |

**EMI AMERICA**

| Number | Title (A Side/B Side) | Yr | NM |
|---|---|---|---|
| ❑ SN-16316 | Sanctuary | 1985 | 8.00 |
| *—Reissue* | | | |
| ❑ SN-16373 | Showtime! | 1986 | 8.00 |
| *—Reissue* | | | |
| ❑ SN-16374 | Freeze-Frame | 1986 | 8.00 |
| *—Reissue* | | | |
| ❑ SN-16375 | Love Stinks | 1986 | 8.00 |
| *—Reissue* | | | |
| ❑ SO-17006 | Sanctuary | 1978 | 10.00 |
| ❑ SOO-17016 | Love Stinks | 1980 | 10.00 |
| ❑ SOO-17062 | Freeze-Frame | 1981 | 10.00 |
| ❑ SO-17087 | Showtime! | 1982 | 10.00 |
| ❑ SJ-17137 | You're Gettin' Even While I'm Gettin' Odd | 1984 | 8.00 |
| ❑ ST-17174 | Flashback — The Best of the J. Geils Band | 1985 | 8.00 |

**NAUTILUS**

| Number | Title (A Side/B Side) | Yr | NM |
|---|---|---|---|
| ❑ NR-25 | Love Stinks | 1982 | 20.00 |
| *—Audiophile vinyl* | | | |

### GELLER, HERB

**ATCO**

| Number | Title (A Side/B Side) | Yr | NM |
|---|---|---|---|
| ❑ 33-109 [M] | Gypsy | 1959 | 40.00 |

**EMARCY**

| Number | Title (A Side/B Side) | Yr | NM |
|---|---|---|---|
| ❑ MG-26045 [10] | Herb Geller Plays | 1954 | 120.00 |
| ❑ MG-36024 [M] | The Gellers | 1955 | 100.00 |
| ❑ MG-36040 [M] | The Herb Geller Sextette | 1955 | 80.00 |
| ❑ MG-36045 [M] | Herb Geller Plays | 1955 | 80.00 |

**JOSIE**

| Number | Title (A Side/B Side) | Yr | NM |
|---|---|---|---|
| ❑ JLPS-3502 [S] | Alto Saxophone | 1962 | 20.00 |
| ❑ JOZ-3502 [M] | Alto Saxophone | 1962 | 25.00 |

**JUBILEE**

| Number | Title (A Side/B Side) | Yr | NM |
|---|---|---|---|
| ❑ JLP-1044 [M] | Fire in the West | 1957 | 50.00 |
| ❑ SDJLP-1044 [S] | Fire in the West | 1959 | 40.00 |
| ❑ JG-1094 [M] | Stax of Sax | 1959 | 50.00 |

### GELLER, LORRAINE

**DOT**

| Number | Title (A Side/B Side) | Yr | NM |
|---|---|---|---|
| ❑ DLP-3174 [M] | Lorraine Geller at the Piano | 1959 | 500.00 |

### GENE AND DEBBE

**TRX**

| Number | Title (A Side/B Side) | Yr | NM |
|---|---|---|---|
| ❑ 1001 | Here and Now | 1968 | 25.00 |

### GENE LOVES JEZEBEL

**GEFFEN**

| Number | Title (A Side/B Side) | Yr | NM |
|---|---|---|---|
| ❑ 4192 [EP] | Remix Sampler | 1990 | 20.00 |
| *—Promo-only collection* | | | |
| ❑ GHS 24118 | Discover | 1986 | 10.00 |
| ❑ GHS 24165 | Promise | 1988 | 10.00 |
| *—First American issue of 1983 U.K. debut* | | | |
| ❑ GHS 24171 | The House of Dolls | 1988 | 10.00 |
| ❑ GHS 24260 | Kiss of Life | 1990 | 12.00 |

**RELATIVITY**

| Number | Title (A Side/B Side) | Yr | NM |
|---|---|---|---|
| ❑ EMC 8036 | Immigrant | 1985 | 12.00 |
| ❑ EMC 8075 [EP] | Desire | 1985 | 8.00 |

**WARNER BROS.**

| Number | Title (A Side/B Side) | Yr | NM |
|---|---|---|---|
| ❑ WBMS-141 [DJ] | Discover Interview | 1986 | 20.00 |
| *—Part of "The Warner Bros. Music Show" series; in die-cut cover* | | | |

### GENERATION BAND, THE

**NAUTILUS**

| Number | Title (A Side/B Side) | Yr | NM |
|---|---|---|---|
| ❑ NR-62 | Soft Shoulder | 198? | 40.00 |
| *—Audiophile vinyl* | | | |

### GENERATION X

**CHRYSALIS**

| Number | Title (A Side/B Side) | Yr | NM |
|---|---|---|---|
| ❑ CHR 1169 | Generation X | 1978 | 25.00 |
| ❑ CHR 1193 | Valley of the Dolls | 1979 | 30.00 |
| ❑ CHR 1327 | Kiss Me Deadly | 1981 | 25.00 |
| ❑ PV 41169 | Generation X | 1984 | 15.00 |
| *—Reissue* | | | |
| ❑ PV 41193 | Valley of the Dolls | 1984 | 20.00 |
| *—Reissue* | | | |
| ❑ PV 41327 | Kiss Me Deadly | 1985 | 15.00 |
| *—Reissue* | | | |

### GENESIS Also see PHIL COLLINS; PETER GABRIEL.

**ABC**

| Number | Title (A Side/B Side) | Yr | NM |
|---|---|---|---|
| ❑ ABCX-816 | Trespass | 1971 | 15.00 |
| *—Reissue of Impulse album; black label* | | | |
| ❑ ABCX-816 | Trespass | 1974 | 12.00 |
| *—Reissue; concentric yellow/orange/purple "target" label* | | | |

**ABC IMPULSE!**

| Number | Title (A Side/B Side) | Yr | NM |
|---|---|---|---|
| ❑ ASD-9205 | Trespass | 1971 | 30.00 |

**ATCO**

| Number | Title (A Side/B Side) | Yr | NM |
|---|---|---|---|
| ❑ SD 38-100 | Wind & Wuthering | 1978 | 10.00 |
| *—Reissue of SD 36-144* | | | |
| ❑ SD 38-101 | A Trick of the Tail | 1978 | 10.00 |
| *—Reissue of SD 36-129* | | | |
| ❑ SD 36-129 | A Trick of the Tail | 1976 | 12.00 |
| ❑ SD 36-144 | Wind & Wuthering | 1977 | 12.00 |
| ❑ SD 2-401 [(2)] | The Lamb Lies Down on Broadway | 1974 | 15.00 |
| *—Originals have yellow labels (other labels worth less)* | | | |

**ATLANTIC**

| Number | Title (A Side/B Side) | Yr | NM |
|---|---|---|---|
| ❑ PR 965 [DJ] | Tonight, Tonight, Tonight — Exclusive Candid Interview | 1986 | 30.00 |
| *—Promo-only music and interviews; came with cover letter and cue sheet (deduct 1/3 if missing)* | | | |

Number | Title (A Side/B Side) | Yr | NM

❑ SD 2-2000 [(2)] Three Sides Live 1982 12.00
❑ SD 2-9002 [(2)] Seconds Out 1977 12.00
❑ SD 16014 Duke 1980 10.00
❑ SD 19173 ...And Then There Were Three 1978 10.00
❑ SD 19277 Selling England by the Pound 1981 8.00
*—Reissue of Charisma LP of same name*
❑ SD 19313 Abacab 1981 10.00
*—Released with four different covers, lettered "A" through "D" on the upper part of the spine; no difference in value*
❑ 80030 Nursery Cryme 1982 8.00
*—Reissue of Charisma LP of same name*
❑ 80116 Genesis 1983 8.00
❑ 81641 Invisible Touch 1986 8.00
❑ 81848 Foxtrot 1988 10.00
*—Reissue of Charisma LP of the same name*
❑ 81855 Genesis Live 1988 10.00
*—Reissue of Charisma LP of the same name*

BUDDAH
❑ BDS-5659 [(2)] The Best ... Genesis 1976 20.00
*—Reissue of "Nursery Cryme" and "Foxtrot" in one set*

CHARISMA
❑ CAS-1052 Nursery Cryme 1971 15.00
❑ CAS-1052 Nursery Cryme 2000 25.00
*—Classic Records reissue on 180-gram vinyl*
❑ CAS-1058 Foxtrot 1972 15.00
❑ CAS-1058 Foxtrot 2001 25.00
*—Classic Records reissue on 180-gram vinyl*
❑ CAS-1666 Genesis Live 1974 15.00
❑ CAS-1666 Genesis Live 2001 25.00
*—Classic Records reissue on 180-gram vinyl*
❑ CA2-2701 [(2)] Nursery Cryme/Foxtrot 1976 15.00
*—Repackage of the individual albums of these names*
❑ FC-6060 Selling England by the Pound 1973 15.00
❑ FC-6060 Selling England by the Pound 2001 25.00
*—Classic Records reissue on 180-gram vinyl*

LONDON
❑ PS 643 From Genesis to Revelation 1974 25.00
*—First US release of debut album*
❑ LC-50006 In the Beginning 1977 12.00
❑ 820322-1 In the Beginning 198? 10.00
*—Reissue of London 50006*

MCA
❑ ABCX-816 Trespass 1979 10.00
*—Reissue of ABC ABCX-816*
❑ 37151 Trespass 198? 8.00
*—Reissue of MCA 816*

MOBILE FIDELITY
❑ 1-062 A Trick of the Tail 1981 50.00
*—Audiophile vinyl*

## GENESIS (3)

MERCURY
❑ SR 61175 In the Beginning 1968 40.00

## GENTLE SOUL, THE

EPIC
❑ BN 26374 The Gentle Soul 1969 200.00
*—Reproductions exist*

## GENTRY, BOBBIE

CAPITOL
❑ ST-155 Touch 'Em with Love 1969 15.00
❑ SKAO-381 Bobbie Gentry's Greatest! 1969 15.00
❑ SM-381 Bobbie Gentry's Greatest! 197? 8.00
❑ ST-428 Fancy 1970 15.00
❑ ST-494 Patchwork 1970 15.00
❑ STBB-704 [(2)] Sittin' Pretty/Tobacco Road 1971 15.00
❑ SM-2830 Ode to Billie Joe 197? 8.00
❑ ST 2830 [S] Ode to Billie Joe 1967 15.00
❑ T 2830 [M] Ode to Billie Joe 1967 20.00
❑ ST 2842 [S] The Delta Sweete 1968 15.00
❑ T 2842 [M] The Delta Sweete 1968 25.00
❑ ST 2964 The Local Gentry 1968 15.00

## GENTRYS, THE

MGM
❑ GAS-127 The Gentrys (Golden Archive Series) 1970 20.00
❑ E-4336 [M] Keep On Dancing 1965 25.00
❑ SE-4336 [P] Keep On Dancing 1965 30.00
❑ E-4346 [M] Gentry Time 1966 20.00
❑ SE-4346 [S] Gentry Time 1966 25.00

SUN
❑ LP-117 The Gentrys 1970 30.00

## GEORDIE

MGM
❑ SE-4903 Hope You Like It 1973 30.00

## GEORGE, BARBARA

A.F.O.
❑ LP 5001 [M] I Know (You Don't Love Me No More) 1962 250.00

## GERHARD, RAMONA

SOMA
❑ MG 1202 Christmas in Hi-Fi with Ramona Gerhard 195? 20.00
*—Red vinyl*

## GERMS, THE

MOHAWK
❑ SCALP-001 Recorded Live at the Whiskey, June, 1977 1981 20.00
*—Second edition: Un-numbered edition, with sticker*
❑ SCALP-001 Recorded Live at the Whiskey, June, 1977 1981 50.00
*—First edition: Numbered edition, with sticker*

RHINO
❑ R1-78602 (GI) 2005 15.00
*—Reissue on 180-gram vinyl*

SLASH
❑ SR-103 (GI) 1981 15.00
❑ SREP 108 What We Do Is Secret 1981 15.00
❑ 23932 (GI) 1983 12.00
*—Reissue*

## GERONIMO BLACK

UNI
❑ 73132 Geronimo Black 1972 25.00

## GERRY AND THE PACEMAKERS

CAPITOL
❑ SM-11898 [B] The Best of Gerry and the Pacemakers 1979 8.00
*—All stereo except "I Like It," "Away from You" and "I'm the One," which are mono.*

LAURIE
❑ LLP-2024 [M] Don't Let the Sun Catch You Crying 1964 30.00
❑ SLP-2024 [R] Don't Let the Sun Catch You Crying 1964 25.00
❑ LLP-2027 [M] Gerry and the Pacemakers' Second Album 1964 30.00
❑ SLP-2027 [R] Gerry and the Pacemakers' Second Album 1964 25.00
❑ LLP-2030 [M] I'll Be There 1964 30.00
❑ SLP-2030 [R] I'll Be There 1964 25.00
❑ LLP-2031 [M] Greatest Hits 1965 25.00
❑ SLP-2031 [R] Greatest Hits 1965 15.00
❑ LLP-2037 [M] Girl on a Swing 1966 25.00
❑ SLP-2037 [S] Girl on a Swing 1966 20.00
❑ DT 90384 [R] Greatest Hits 1965 25.00
*—Capitol Record Club edition*
❑ T 90384 [M] Greatest Hits 1965 25.00
*—Capitol Record Club edition*
❑ DT 90555 [R] Don't Let the Sun Catch You Crying 1964 30.00
*—Capitol Record Club edition*
❑ T 90555 [M] Don't Let the Sun Catch You Crying 1964 40.00
*—Capitol Record Club edition*

UNITED ARTISTS
❑ UAL 3387 [M] Ferry Cross the Mersey 1965 25.00
*—Also contains incidental music by George Martin*
❑ UAS 6387 [S] Ferry Cross the Mersey 1965 40.00
❑ ST 90812 [S] Ferry Cross the Mersey 1965 50.00
*—Capitol Record Club edition*
❑ T 90812 [M] Ferry Cross the Mersey 1965 40.00
*—Capitol Record Club edition*

## GETZ, EDDIE

MGM
❑ E-3462 [M] The Eddie Getz Quintette 1957 50.00

## GETZ, STAN

AMERICAN RECORDING SOCIETY
❑ G-407 [M] Cool Jazz of Stan Getz 1956 40.00
❑ G-428 [M] Intimate Portrait 1957 40.00
❑ G-443 [M] Stan Getz '57 1957 40.00

BLUE RIBBON
❑ BR-8012 [M] Rhythms 1961 20.00

CLEF
❑ MGC-137 [10] Stan Getz Plays 1953 200.00
❑ MGC-143 [10] The Artistry of Stan Getz 1953 200.00

CROWN
❑ CLP-5002 [M] Groovin' High 1957 40.00
*—Reissue of Modern 1202*
❑ CLP-5284 [M] Groovin' High 196? 20.00
*—Reissue of 5002*

DALE
❑ 21 [10] In Retrospect 1951 300.00

JAZZTONE
❑ J-1230 [M] Stan Getz 1956 40.00
❑ J-1240 [M] Stan Getz '57 1957 40.00

METRONOME
❑ BLP-6 [M] The Sound 1956 50.00

MODERN
❑ MLP-1202 [M] Groovin' High 1956 150.00

MOSAIC
❑ MR4-131 [(4)] The Complete Recordings of the Stan Getz Quintet with Jimmy Raney 199? 60.00

NEW JAZZ
❑ NJLP-8214 [M] Long Island Sound 1959 60.00
*—Reissue of Prestige 7002; purple label*
❑ NJLP-8214 [M] Long Island Sound 1965 25.00
*—Blue label with trident logo on right*

NORGRAN
❑ MGN-1000 [M] Interpretations by the Stan Getz Quintet 1954 120.00
❑ MGN-1008 [M] Interpretations by the Stan Getz Quintet #2 1954 120.00
❑ MGN-1029 [M] Interpretations by the Stan Getz Quintet #3 1955 150.00
❑ MGN-1032 [M] West Coast Jazz 1955 150.00
❑ MGN-1042 [M] Stan Getz Plays 1955 100.00
*—Reissue of Clef 137 and 143 on one 12-inch LP*
❑ MGN-1087 [M] Stan Getz '56 1956 100.00
❑ MGN-1088 [M] More West Coast Jazz with Stan Getz 1956 100.00
❑ MGN-2000-2 [(2)M] Stan Getz at the Shrine 1955 200.00
*—Boxed set with booklet*

PRESTIGE
❑ PRLP-102 [10] Stan Getz and the Tenor Sax Stars 1951 200.00
❑ PRLP-104 [10] Stan Getz, Volume 2 1951 200.00
❑ PRLP-108 [10] Stan Getz-Lee Konitz 1951 200.00
❑ PRLP-7002 [M] Stan Getz Quartets 1955 100.00
❑ PRLP-7255 [M] Early Stan 1963 40.00
❑ PRST-7255 [R] Early Stan 1963 20.00
❑ PRLP-7256 [M] Stan Getz' Greatest Hits 1963 40.00
❑ PRST-7256 [R] Stan Getz' Greatest Hits 1963 20.00
❑ PRLP-7337 [M] Stan Getz' Greatest Hits 1967 25.00
*—Reissue of PRLP 7256*
❑ PRLP-7434 [M] Getz Plays Jazz Classics 1967 25.00
*—Reissue of PRLP 7255*
❑ PRLP-7516 [M] Preservation 1967 25.00

ROOST
❑ RK-103 [(2)M] The Stan Getz Years 1964 40.00
❑ SRK-103 [(2)R] The Stan Getz Years 1964 25.00
❑ R-402 [10] Stan Getz 1950 200.00
❑ R-404 [10] Stan Getz and the Swedish All Stars 1951 200.00
❑ R-407 [10] Jazz at Storyville 1952 150.00
❑ R-411 [10] Jazz at Storyville, Volume 2 1952 150.00
❑ R-417 [10] Chamber Music 1953 150.00
❑ R-420 [10] Jazz at Storyville, Volume 3 1954 150.00
❑ R-423 [10] Split Kick 1954 150.00
❑ LP-2207 [M] The Sounds of Stan Getz 1956 80.00
*—Reissue of R-402*
❑ LP-2209 [M] Storyville 1956 80.00
*—Reissue of R-407 and half of R-411*
❑ LP-2225 [M] Storyville, Volume 2 1957 80.00
*—Reissue of R-423 and the other half of R-411*
❑ LP-2249 [M] The Greatest of Stan Getz 1963 30.00
❑ LP-2251 [M] Moonlight in Vermont 1963 30.00
❑ LP-2255 [M] Modern World 1963 30.00
❑ LP-2258 [M] Getz Age 1963 30.00

SAVOY
❑ MG-9004 [10] New Sounds in Modern Music 1951 300.00

VERVE
❑ MGV-8028 [M] West Coast Jazz 1957 50.00
*—Reissue of Norgran 1032*
❑ V-8028 [M] West Coast Jazz 1961 20.00
*—Reissue of MGV-8028*
❑ MGV-8029 [M] Stan Getz '57 1957 50.00
*—Reissue of Norgran 1087 with revised title*
❑ V-8029 [M] Stan Getz '57 1961 20.00
*—Reissue of MGV-8029*
❑ MGV-8122 [M] Interpretations by the Stan Getz Quintet #3 1957 50.00
*—Reissue of Norgran 1029*
❑ V-8122 [M] Interpretations by the Stan Getz Quintet #3 1961 20.00
*—Reissue of MGV-8122*
❑ MGV-8133 [M] Stan Getz Plays 1957 50.00
*—Reissue of Norgran 1042*
❑ V-8133 [M] Stan Getz Plays 1961 20.00
*—Reissue of MGV-8133*
❑ MGV-8177 [M] More West Coast Jazz with Stan Getz 1957 50.00
*—Reissue of Norgran 1088*
❑ V-8177 [M] More West Coast Jazz with Stan Getz 1961 20.00
*—Reissue of MGV-8177*
❑ MGV-8188-2 [M] Stan Getz at the Shrine 1957 100.00
*—Reissue of Norgran 2000-2*
❑ V-8188-2 [(2)M] Stan Getz at the Shrine 1961 25.00
*—Reissue of MGV-8188-2*
❑ MGV-8200 [M] Stan Getz and the Cool Sounds 1957 50.00
*—Reissue of American Recording Society 407 with new name*
❑ V-8200 [M] Stan Getz and the Cool Sounds 1961 20.00
*—Reissue of MGV-8200*
❑ MGV-8213 [M] Stan Getz in Stockholm 1958 50.00
*—Reissue of American Recording Society 428 with new name*
❑ V-8213 [M] Stan Getz in Stockholm 1961 20.00
*—Reissue of MGV-8213*
❑ MGV-8263 [M] Stan Meets Chet 1958 60.00
*—With Chet Baker*
❑ V-8263 [M] Stan Meets Chet 1961 20.00
*—Reissue of MGV-8263*

| Number | Title (A Side/B Side) | Yr | NM |
|---|---|---|---|
| ❑ MGV-8294 [M] | The Steamer | 1959 | 50.00 |
| ❑ V-8294 [M] | The Steamer | 1961 | 20.00 |
| *—Reissue of MGV-8294* | | | |
| ❑ MGV-8296 [M] | Award Winner | 1959 | 50.00 |
| ❑ V-8296 [M] | Award Winner | 1961 | 20.00 |
| *—Reissue of MGV-8296* | | | |
| ❑ MGV-8321 [M] | The Soft Swing | 1959 | 50.00 |
| ❑ V-8321 [M] | The Soft Swing | 1961 | 20.00 |
| *—Reissue of MGV-8321* | | | |
| ❑ MGV-8331 [M] | Imported from Europe | 1959 | 50.00 |
| ❑ V-8331 [M] | Imported from Europe | 1961 | 20.00 |
| *—Reissue of MGV-8331* | | | |
| ❑ MGV-8379 [M] | Cool Velvet — Stan Getz and Strings | 1960 | 50.00 |
| ❑ V-8379 [M] | Cool Velvet — Stan Getz and Strings | 1961 | 20.00 |
| *—Reissue of MGV-8379* | | | |
| ❑ V6-8379 [S] | Cool Velvet — Stan Getz and Strings | 1961 | 20.00 |
| ❑ MGV-8393-2 [(2)M] | Stan Getz At Large | 1960 | 60.00 |
| ❑ V-8393-2 [(2)M] | Stan Getz At Large | 1961 | 25.00 |
| *—Reissue of MGV-8393-2* | | | |
| ❑ V-8412 [M] | Focus | 1961 | 25.00 |
| ❑ V6-8412 [S] | Focus | 1961 | 20.00 |
| ❑ V-8494 [M] | Big Band Bossa Nova | 1962 | 20.00 |
| ❑ V6-8494 [S] | Big Band Bossa Nova | 1962 | 25.00 |
| ❑ V-8523 [M] | Jazz Samba Encore! | 1963 | 20.00 |
| *—With Luiz Bonfa* | | | |
| ❑ V6-8523 [S] | Jazz Samba Encore! | 1963 | 25.00 |
| *—With Luiz Bonfa* | | | |
| ❑ V6-8554 [S] | Reflections | 1964 | 20.00 |
| ❑ V6-8600 [S] | Getz Au Go Go | 1964 | 20.00 |
| ❑ V-8693 [M] | Sweet Rain | 1967 | 25.00 |
| ❑ V-8707 [M] | Voices | 1967 | 25.00 |
| ❑ V-8719 [M] | The Best of Stan Getz | 1967 | 25.00 |
| ❑ V-8752 [M] | What the World Needs Now — Stan Getz Plays Bacharach and David | 1968 | 30.00 |
| ❑ V6-8802-2 [(2)] | Dynasty | 1971 | 20.00 |
| ❑ 823611-1 [(5)] | The Girl from Ipamena: The Bossa Nova Years | 1984 | 50.00 |

## GETZ, STAN, AND LAURINDO ALMEIDA

### VERVE

| Number | Title (A Side/B Side) | Yr | NM |
|---|---|---|---|
| ❑ V6-8665 [S] | Stan Getz with Guest Artist Laurindo Almeida | 1965 | 20.00 |

## GETZ, STAN, AND BOB BROOKMEYER

### VERVE

| Number | Title (A Side/B Side) | Yr | NM |
|---|---|---|---|
| ❑ V-8418 [M] | Stan Getz and Bob Brookmeyer (Recorded Fall 1961) | 1961 | 20.00 |
| ❑ V6-8418 [S] | Stan Getz and Bob Brookmeyer (Recorded Fall 1961) | 1961 | 20.00 |

## GETZ, STAN, AND CHARLIE BYRD

### DCC COMPACT CLASSICS

| Number | Title (A Side/B Side) | Yr | NM |
|---|---|---|---|
| ❑ LPZ-2011 | Jazz Samba | 1995 | 25.00 |
| *—Audiophile vinyl* | | | |

### VERVE

| Number | Title (A Side/B Side) | Yr | NM |
|---|---|---|---|
| ❑ V-8432 [M] | Jazz Samba | 1962 | 20.00 |
| ❑ V6-8432 [S] | Jazz Samba | 1962 | 25.00 |
| *—With "MGM Records" on label print* | | | |
| ❑ V6-8432 [S] | Jazz Samba | 1976 | 12.00 |
| *—"Manufactured and Marketed by Polydor Incorporated" on label* | | | |

## GETZ, STAN, AND JOAO GILBERTO

### MOBILE FIDELITY

| Number | Title (A Side/B Side) | Yr | NM |
|---|---|---|---|
| ❑ 1-208 | Getz/Gilberto | 1994 | 50.00 |
| *—Audiophile vinyl* | | | |

### VERVE

| Number | Title (A Side/B Side) | Yr | NM |
|---|---|---|---|
| ❑ V6-8545 [S] | Getz/Gilberto | 1964 | 20.00 |
| ❑ V6-8623 [S] | Getz/Gilberto #2 | 1965 | 20.00 |

## GETZ, STAN; DIZZY GILLESPIE; SONNY STITT

### VERVE

| Number | Title (A Side/B Side) | Yr | NM |
|---|---|---|---|
| ❑ MGV-8198 [M] | For Musicians Only | 1958 | 80.00 |
| ❑ V-8198 [M] | For Musicians Only | 1961 | 25.00 |

## GETZ, STAN, AND WARDELL GRAY

### DAWN

| Number | Title (A Side/B Side) | Yr | NM |
|---|---|---|---|
| ❑ DLP-1126 [M] | Tenors Anyone? | 1958 | 120.00 |

### SEECO

| Number | Title (A Side/B Side) | Yr | NM |
|---|---|---|---|
| ❑ SLP-7 [10] | Highlights in Modern Jazz | 1954 | 200.00 |

## GETZ, STAN, AND J.J. JOHNSON

### VERVE

| Number | Title (A Side/B Side) | Yr | NM |
|---|---|---|---|
| ❑ MGVS-6027 [S] | Stan Getz and J.J. Johnson at the Opera House | 1960 | 40.00 |
| ❑ MGV-8265 [M] | Stan Getz and J.J. Johnson at the Opera House | 1958 | 50.00 |
| ❑ V-8265 [M] | Stan Getz and J.J. Johnson at the Opera House | 1961 | 20.00 |
| ❑ V-8490 [M] | Stan Getz and J.J. Johnson at the Opera House | 1962 | 15.00 |

## GETZ, STAN, AND OSCAR PETERSON

### VERVE

| Number | Title (A Side/B Side) | Yr | NM |
|---|---|---|---|
| ❑ MGV-8251 [M] | Stan Getz and the Oscar Peterson Trio | 1958 | 50.00 |
| ❑ V-8251 [M] | Stan Getz and the Oscar Peterson Trio | 1961 | 20.00 |
| *—Reissue of MGV-8251* | | | |
| ❑ MGV-8348 [M] | Stan Getz with Gerry Mulligan and the Oscar Peterson Trio | 1959 | 50.00 |
| ❑ V-8348 [M] | Stan Getz with Gerry Mulligan and the Oscar Peterson Trio | 1961 | 20.00 |
| *—Reissue of MGV-8348* | | | |

## GETZ, STAN, AND ZOOT SIMS

### PRESTIGE

| Number | Title (A Side/B Side) | Yr | NM |
|---|---|---|---|
| ❑ PRLP-7022 [M] | The Brothers | 1956 | 400.00 |
| *—Yellow label with W. 50th St. address* | | | |
| ❑ PRLP-7252 [M] | The Brothers | 1963 | 100.00 |
| *—Yellow label with Bergenfield, N.J. address* | | | |

## GHOULS, THE

### CAPITOL

| Number | Title (A Side/B Side) | Yr | NM |
|---|---|---|---|
| ❑ ST 2215 [S] | Dracula's Deuce | 1965 | 150.00 |
| ❑ T 2215 [M] | Dracula's Deuce | 1965 | 120.00 |

## GIANT CRAB, THE

### UNI

| Number | Title (A Side/B Side) | Yr | NM |
|---|---|---|---|
| ❑ 73037 | A Giant Crab Comes Forth | 1968 | 25.00 |
| ❑ 73057 | Cool It, Helios | 1969 | 25.00 |

## GIBB, ROBIN

### ATCO

| Number | Title (A Side/B Side) | Yr | NM |
|---|---|---|---|
| ❑ SD 33-323 | Robin's Reign | 1969 | 40.00 |

### MIRAGE

| Number | Title (A Side/B Side) | Yr | NM |
|---|---|---|---|
| ❑ 90170 | Secret Agent | 1984 | 8.00 |

### POLYDOR

| Number | Title (A Side/B Side) | Yr | NM |
|---|---|---|---|
| ❑ 810896-1 | How Old Are You? | 1983 | 10.00 |

## GIBBS, GEORGIA

### BELL

| Number | Title (A Side/B Side) | Yr | NM |
|---|---|---|---|
| ❑ 6000 [M] | Call Me Georgia Gibbs | 1966 | 15.00 |
| ❑ 6000S [S] | Call Me Georgia Gibbs | 1966 | 20.00 |

### CORAL

| Number | Title (A Side/B Side) | Yr | NM |
|---|---|---|---|
| ❑ CRL 56037 [10] | Ballin' the Jack | 1951 | 50.00 |
| ❑ CRL 57183 [M] | Her Nibs | 1957 | 40.00 |

### EMARCY

| Number | Title (A Side/B Side) | Yr | NM |
|---|---|---|---|
| ❑ MG-36103 [M] | Swingin' with Gibbs | 1957 | 30.00 |

### EPIC

| Number | Title (A Side/B Side) | Yr | NM |
|---|---|---|---|
| ❑ LN 24059 [M] | Georgia Gibbs' Greatest Hits | 1963 | 15.00 |
| ❑ BN 26059 [S] | Georgia Gibbs' Greatest Hits | 1963 | 20.00 |

### GOLDEN TONE

| Number | Title (A Side/B Side) | Yr | NM |
|---|---|---|---|
| ❑ 4093 [M] | Her Nibs!! Miss Georgia Gibbs | 1962 | 12.00 |
| ❑ 14093 [R] | Her Nibs!! Miss Georgia Gibbs | 1962 | 10.00 |
| *—Cover misspells it "Nibbs"* | | | |

### IMPERIAL

| Number | Title (A Side/B Side) | Yr | NM |
|---|---|---|---|
| ❑ LP-9107 [M] | Something's Gotta Give | 1960 | 20.00 |
| ❑ LP-12064 [S] | Something's Gotta Give | 1960 | 25.00 |

### MERCURY

| Number | Title (A Side/B Side) | Yr | NM |
|---|---|---|---|
| ❑ MG-20071 [M] | Music and Memories | 1955 | 40.00 |
| ❑ MG-20114 [M] | Song Favorites | 1956 | 40.00 |
| ❑ MG-20170 [M] | Swingin' with Her Nibs | 1956 | 40.00 |
| ❑ MG-25175 [10] | Georgia Gibbs Sings Oldies | 1953 | 50.00 |
| ❑ MG-25199 [10] | The Man That Got Away | 1954 | 50.00 |

### ROYALE

| Number | Title (A Side/B Side) | Yr | NM |
|---|---|---|---|
| ❑ 18126 [10] | Georgia Gibbs and Orchestra | 195? | 40.00 |

### SUNSET

| Number | Title (A Side/B Side) | Yr | NM |
|---|---|---|---|
| ❑ SUM-1113 [M] | Her Nibs, Miss Georgia Gibbs | 196? | 15.00 |
| ❑ SUS-5113 [S] | Her Nibs, Miss Georgia Gibbs | 196? | 15.00 |

## GIBBS, MICHAEL

### DERAM

| Number | Title (A Side/B Side) | Yr | NM |
|---|---|---|---|
| ❑ DES 18048 | Michael Gibbs | 1970 | 20.00 |

## GIBBS, TERRY

### BRUNSWICK

| Number | Title (A Side/B Side) | Yr | NM |
|---|---|---|---|
| ❑ BL 54009 [M] | Terry | 1955 | 50.00 |
| ❑ BL 56055 [10] | Terry Gibbs Quartet | 1954 | 100.00 |

### DOT

| Number | Title (A Side/B Side) | Yr | NM |
|---|---|---|---|
| ❑ DLP-25726 [S] | Reza | 1966 | 20.00 |

### EMARCY

| Number | Title (A Side/B Side) | Yr | NM |
|---|---|---|---|
| ❑ MG-36047 [M] | Terry Gibbs | 1956 | 50.00 |
| ❑ MG-36064 [M] | Vibes on Velvet | 1956 | 50.00 |
| ❑ MG-36075 [M] | Mallets A-Plenty | 1956 | 50.00 |
| ❑ MG-36103 [M] | Swingin' Terry Gibbs | 1957 | 50.00 |
| ❑ MG-36128 [M] | Terry Plays the Duke | 1958 | 50.00 |
| ❑ MG-36138 [M] | Steve Allen's All Stars | 1958 | 50.00 |
| ❑ MG-36148 [M] | More Vibes on Velvet | 1959 | 50.00 |
| ❑ SR-80004 [S] | Steve Allen's All Stars | 1959 | 40.00 |

### IMPULSE!

| Number | Title (A Side/B Side) | Yr | NM |
|---|---|---|---|
| ❑ A-58 [M] | Take It from Me | 1964 | 25.00 |
| ❑ AS-58 [S] | Take It from Me | 1964 | 30.00 |

### INTERLUDE

| Number | Title (A Side/B Side) | Yr | NM |
|---|---|---|---|
| ❑ MO-506 [M] | Vibrations | 1959 | 40.00 |
| ❑ ST-1006 [S] | Vibrations | 1959 | 30.00 |

### LIMELIGHT

| Number | Title (A Side/B Side) | Yr | NM |
|---|---|---|---|
| ❑ LM-82005 [M] | El Nutto | 1964 | 20.00 |
| ❑ LS-86005 [S] | El Nutto | 1964 | 25.00 |

### MAINSTREAM

| Number | Title (A Side/B Side) | Yr | NM |
|---|---|---|---|
| ❑ S-6048 [S] | It's Time We Met | 1965 | 20.00 |

### MERCURY

| Number | Title (A Side/B Side) | Yr | NM |
|---|---|---|---|
| ❑ MG-20440 [M] | Launching a New Sound in Music | 1959 | 40.00 |
| ❑ MG-20518 [M] | Steve Allen's All Stars | 1960 | 30.00 |
| ❑ SR-60112 [S] | Launching a New Sound in Music | 1959 | 30.00 |
| ❑ SR-60195 [S] | Steve Allen's All Stars | 1960 | 25.00 |
| ❑ SR-60704 [S] | Explosion! | 1962 | 20.00 |
| ❑ SR-60812 [S] | Jewish Melodies in Jazztime | 1963 | 20.00 |

### MODE

| Number | Title (A Side/B Side) | Yr | NM |
|---|---|---|---|
| ❑ LP-123 [M] | A Jazz Band Ball | 1957 | 80.00 |

### ROOST

| Number | Title (A Side/B Side) | Yr | NM |
|---|---|---|---|
| ❑ RS-2260 [S] | Latino | 1965 | 20.00 |

### TIME

| Number | Title (A Side/B Side) | Yr | NM |
|---|---|---|---|
| ❑ S-2105 [S] | Hootenanny My Way | 1963 | 30.00 |
| ❑ S-2120 [S] | Terry Gibbs with Sal Nistico | 196? | 25.00 |
| ❑ 52105 [M] | Hootenanny My Way | 1963 | 25.00 |
| ❑ 52120 [M] | Terry Gibbs with Sal Nistico | 196? | 20.00 |

### VERVE

| Number | Title (A Side/B Side) | Yr | NM |
|---|---|---|---|
| ❑ MGV-2134 [M] | Swing Is Here! | 1960 | 40.00 |
| ❑ V-2134 [M] | Swing Is Here! | 1961 | 20.00 |
| ❑ V6-2134 [S] | Swing Is Here! | 1961 | 20.00 |
| ❑ MGV-2136 [M] | Music from Cole Porter's "Can-Can" | 1960 | 40.00 |
| ❑ V-2136 [M] | Music from Cole Porter's "Can-Can" | 1961 | 20.00 |
| ❑ V6-2136 [S] | Music from Cole Porter's "Can-Can" | 1961 | 20.00 |
| ❑ MGV-2151 [M] | The Exciting Terry Gibbs Big Band | 1960 | 40.00 |
| ❑ V-2151 [M] | The Exciting Terry Gibbs Big Band | 1961 | 20.00 |
| ❑ V6-2151 [S] | The Exciting Terry Gibbs Big Band | 1961 | 25.00 |
| ❑ MGVS-6140 [S] | Swing Is Here! | 1960 | 40.00 |
| ❑ MGVS-6145 [S] | Music from Cole Porter's "Can-Can" | 1960 | 40.00 |
| ❑ V-8447 [M] | That Swing Thing | 1962 | 20.00 |
| ❑ V6-8447 [S] | That Swing Thing | 1962 | 25.00 |
| ❑ V-8496 [M] | Straight Ahead | 1962 | 20.00 |
| ❑ V6-8496 [S] | Straight Ahead | 1962 | 25.00 |

## GIBBS, TERRY, AND BILL HARRIS

### MODE

| Number | Title (A Side/B Side) | Yr | NM |
|---|---|---|---|
| ❑ LP-129 [M] | The Ex-Hermanites | 1957 | 80.00 |

## GIBSON, ALTHEA

### DOT

| Number | Title (A Side/B Side) | Yr | NM |
|---|---|---|---|
| ❑ DLP-3105 [M] | Althea Gibson Sings | 1959 | 40.00 |
| ❑ DLP-25105 [S] | Althea Gibson Sings | 1959 | 50.00 |

## GIBSON, BOB

### ELEKTRA

| Number | Title (A Side/B Side) | Yr | NM |
|---|---|---|---|
| ❑ EKL-177 [M] | Ski Songs | 1959 | 25.00 |
| ❑ EKL-197 [M] | Yes I See | 1961 | 20.00 |
| ❑ EKL-239 [M] | Where I'm Bound | 1964 | 20.00 |
| ❑ EKS-7177 [S] | Ski Songs | 1959 | 30.00 |
| ❑ EKS-7197 [S] | Yes I See | 1961 | 25.00 |
| ❑ EKS-7239 [S] | Where I'm Bound | 1964 | 25.00 |

### RIVERSIDE

| Number | Title (A Side/B Side) | Yr | NM |
|---|---|---|---|
| ❑ RLP 12-802 [M] | Offbeat Folk Songs | 1956 | 40.00 |
| ❑ RLP 12-806 [M] | I Come For to Sing | 1957 | 40.00 |
| ❑ RLP 12-816 [M] | Carnegie Concert | 1958 | 40.00 |
| ❑ RLP 12-830 [M] | There's a Meetin' Here Tonight | 1958 | 40.00 |
| ❑ RLP-1111 [S] | There's a Meetin' Here Tonight | 1959 | 50.00 |
| ❑ RM 7542 [M] | Hootenanny at Carnegie | 1963 | 20.00 |
| *—Reissue of 12-816 with slightly altered lineup* | | | |

### STINSON

| Number | Title (A Side/B Side) | Yr | NM |
|---|---|---|---|
| ❑ SLP-76 [10] | Folksongs of Ohio | 1954 | 50.00 |

## GIBSON, BOB, AND BOB CAMP

### ELEKTRA

| Number | Title (A Side/B Side) | Yr | NM |
|---|---|---|---|
| ❑ EKL-207 [M] | Gibson and Camp at the Gate of Horn | 1961 | 20.00 |
| ❑ EKS-7207 [S] | Gibson and Camp at the Gate of Horn | 1961 | 25.00 |

## GIBSON, DON

### ABC HICKORY

| Number | Title (A Side/B Side) | Yr | NM |
|---|---|---|---|
| ❑ AH-44001 | I'm All Wrapped Up in You | 1976 | 12.00 |
| ❑ AH-44007 | If You Ever | 1977 | 12.00 |
| ❑ AH-44010 | Starting All Over | 1978 | 12.00 |
| ❑ AH-44014 | Look Who's Blue | 1978 | 12.00 |

### HARMONY

| Number | Title (A Side/B Side) | Yr | NM |
|---|---|---|---|
| ❑ HL 7358 [M] | The Fabulous Don Gibson Sings | 196? | 15.00 |
| ❑ HS 11158 [R] | The Fabulous Don Gibson Sings | 196? | 12.00 |
| ❑ KH 31765 | Sample Kisses | 1972 | 10.00 |

### HICKORY

| Number | Title (A Side/B Side) | Yr | NM |
|---|---|---|---|
| ❑ LPS-153 | Hits, The Don Gibson Way | 1970 | 15.00 |
| ❑ LPS-155 | Perfect Mountain | 1971 | 15.00 |

| Number | Title (A Side/B Side) | Yr | NM |
|---|---|---|---|
| ❑ LPS-157 | Don Gibson Sings Hank Williams | 1971 | 15.00 |
| ❑ LPS-160 | Country Green | 1971 | 15.00 |
| ❑ LPS-166 | Woman (Sensuous Woman) | 1972 | 15.00 |
| ❑ ST-94817 | Woman (Sensuous Woman) | 1972 | 20.00 |

*—Capitol Record Club edition*

HICKORY/MGM

| Number | Title (A Side/B Side) | Yr | NM |
|---|---|---|---|
| ❑ HR-4501 | Touch the Morning/That's What I'll Do | 1973 | 15.00 |
| ❑ H3G-4502 | The Very Best of Don Gibson | 1974 | 15.00 |
| ❑ H3F-4509 | Snap Your Fingers | 1974 | 15.00 |
| ❑ H3G-4516 | Bring Back Your Love to Me | 1974 | 12.00 |
| ❑ H3G-4519 | I'm the Loneliest Man | 1975 | 12.00 |

LION

| Number | Title (A Side/B Side) | Yr | NM |
|---|---|---|---|
| ❑ L-70069 [M] | Songs by Don Gibson | 1958 | 80.00 |

METRO

| Number | Title (A Side/B Side) | Yr | NM |
|---|---|---|---|
| ❑ M-529 [M] | Don Gibson | 1965 | 12.00 |
| ❑ MS-529 [R] | Don Gibson | 1965 | 10.00 |

MGM

| Number | Title (A Side/B Side) | Yr | NM |
|---|---|---|---|
| ❑ GAS-138 | Don Gibson (Golden Archive Series) | 1970 | 15.00 |

RCA CAMDEN

| Number | Title (A Side/B Side) | Yr | NM |
|---|---|---|---|
| ❑ ACL1-0328 | Just Call Me Lonesome | 1973 | 10.00 |
| ❑ ACL1-0758 | Just One Time | 1974 | 10.00 |
| ❑ CAL-852 [M] | A Blue Million Tears | 196? | 12.00 |
| ❑ CAS-852 [P] | A Blue Million Tears | 196? | 12.00 |

*—All tracks are rechanneled except "I Let Her Get Lonely" and "I May Never Get to Heaven," which are true stereo*

| Number | Title (A Side/B Side) | Yr | NM |
|---|---|---|---|
| ❑ CAL-2101 [M] | Hurtin' Inside | 1966 | 12.00 |
| ❑ CAS-2101 [S] | Hurtin' Inside | 1966 | 15.00 |
| ❑ CAS-2246 | I Love You So Much | 1968 | 12.00 |
| ❑ CAS-2317 | My God Is Real | 1969 | 12.00 |
| ❑ CAS-2392 | Lovin' Lies | 1970 | 12.00 |
| ❑ CAS-2502 | I Walk Alone | 1971 | 12.00 |
| ❑ CAS-2592 | Am I That Easy to Forget | 1972 | 12.00 |

RCA VICTOR

| Number | Title (A Side/B Side) | Yr | NM |
|---|---|---|---|
| ❑ LPM-1743 [M] | Oh Lonesome Me | 1958 | 50.00 |
| ❑ LPM-1918 [M] | No One Stands Alone | 1959 | 30.00 |
| ❑ LSP-1918 [S] | No One Stands Alone | 1959 | 40.00 |
| ❑ LPM-2038 [M] | That Gibson Boy | 1959 | 30.00 |
| ❑ LSP-2038 [S] | That Gibson Boy | 1959 | 40.00 |
| ❑ LPM-2184 [M] | Look Who's Blue | 1960 | 30.00 |
| ❑ LSP-2184 [S] | Look Who's Blue | 1960 | 40.00 |
| ❑ LPM-2269 [M] | Sweet Dreams | 1960 | 30.00 |
| ❑ LSP-2269 [S] | Sweet Dreams | 1960 | 40.00 |
| ❑ LPM-2361 [M] | Girls, Guitars and Gibson | 1961 | 30.00 |
| ❑ LSP-2361 [S] | Girls, Guitars and Gibson | 1961 | 40.00 |
| ❑ LPM-2448 [M] | Some Favorites of Mine | 1962 | 30.00 |
| ❑ LSP-2448 [S] | Some Favorites of Mine | 1962 | 40.00 |
| ❑ LPM-2702 [M] | I Wrote a Song | 1963 | 30.00 |
| ❑ LSP-2702 [S] | I Wrote a Song | 1963 | 40.00 |
| ❑ LPM-2878 [M] | God Walks These Hills | 1964 | 20.00 |
| ❑ LSP-2878 [S] | God Walks These Hills | 1964 | 25.00 |
| ❑ LPM-3376 [M] | The Best of Don Gibson | 1965 | 20.00 |
| ❑ LSP-3376 [S] | The Best of Don Gibson | 1965 | 25.00 |
| ❑ LPM-3470 [M] | Too Much Hurt | 1965 | 20.00 |
| ❑ LSP-3470 [S] | Too Much Hurt | 1965 | 25.00 |
| ❑ LPM-3594 [M] | Don Gibson with Spanish Guitars | 1966 | 20.00 |
| ❑ LSP-3594 [S] | Don Gibson with Spanish Guitars | 1966 | 25.00 |
| ❑ LPM-3680 [M] | Great Country Songs | 1966 | 20.00 |
| ❑ LSP-3680 [S] | Great Country Songs | 1966 | 25.00 |
| ❑ LPM-3843 [M] | All My Love | 1967 | 20.00 |
| ❑ LSP-3843 [S] | All My Love | 1967 | 25.00 |
| ❑ LPM-3974 [M] | The King of Country Soul | 1968 | 50.00 |
| ❑ LSP-3974 [S] | The King of Country Soul | 1968 | 20.00 |
| ❑ LSP-4053 | More Country Soul | 1968 | 20.00 |
| ❑ LSP-4169 | All-Time Country Gold | 1969 | 15.00 |
| ❑ LSP-4281 | The Best of Don Gibson, Vol. 2 | 1970 | 15.00 |
| ❑ CPL1-7052 | Collector's Series | 1985 | 10.00 |

**GIBSON, STEVE, AND THE RED CAPS**

MERCURY

| Number | Title (A Side/B Side) | Yr | NM |
|---|---|---|---|
| ❑ MG-25115 [10] | You're Driving Me Crazy (Harmony Time) | 1952 | 400.00 |
| ❑ MG-25116 [10] | Blueberry Hill (Singing & Swinging) | 1952 | 400.00 |

**GIFFORD, KATHIE LEE**

HEARTLAND

| Number | Title (A Side/B Side) | Yr | NM |
|---|---|---|---|
| ❑ HL-3046 [(2)] | Christmas with Kathie Lee Gifford | 1993 | 20.00 |

**GILBERT, ANN**

GROOVE

| Number | Title (A Side/B Side) | Yr | NM |
|---|---|---|---|
| ❑ LG-1004 [M] | The Many Moods of Ann | 1956 | 50.00 |

**GILBERT, RONNIE** Also see THE WEAVERS.

MERCURY

| Number | Title (A Side/B Side) | Yr | NM |
|---|---|---|---|
| ❑ MG-20917 [M] | Alone with Ronnie Gilbert | 1964 | 20.00 |
| ❑ SR-60917 [S] | Alone with Ronnie Gilbert | 1964 | 25.00 |

RCA VICTOR

| Number | Title (A Side/B Side) | Yr | NM |
|---|---|---|---|
| ❑ LPM-1591 [M] | In Hi-Fi, The Legend of Bessie Smith | 1958 | 40.00 |

**GILBERT & SULLIVAN JAZZ WORKSHOP, THE**

ANDEX

| Number | Title (A Side/B Side) | Yr | NM |
|---|---|---|---|
| ❑ A-27101 [M] | The Coolest Mikado | 1961 | 20.00 |
| ❑ AS-27101 [S] | The Coolest Mikado | 1961 | 25.00 |

**GILBERTO, JOAO**

ATLANTIC

| Number | Title (A Side/B Side) | Yr | NM |
|---|---|---|---|
| ❑ SD 8070 [S] | The Boss of the Bossa Nova | 1963 | 20.00 |
| ❑ SD 8076 [S] | The Warm World of Joao Gilberto | 1964 | 20.00 |

CAPITOL

| Number | Title (A Side/B Side) | Yr | NM |
|---|---|---|---|
| ❑ ST 2160 [S] | Joao Gilberto and Antonio Carlos Jobim | 1964 | 20.00 |
| ❑ ST 2160 [S] | Joao Gilberto and Antonio Carlos Jobim | 1978 | 10.00 |

*—Purple label, large Capitol logo*

| Number | Title (A Side/B Side) | Yr | NM |
|---|---|---|---|
| ❑ ST 10280 [S] | Pops in Portuguese | 196? | 25.00 |
| ❑ T 10280 [M] | Pops in Portuguese | 196? | 20.00 |

**GILELS, EMIL**

RCA VICTOR RED SEAL

| Number | Title (A Side/B Side) | Yr | NM |
|---|---|---|---|
| ❑ LSC-2219 [S] | Brahms: Piano Concerto No. 2 | 1959 | 80.00 |

*—With Fritz Reiner/Chicago Symphony Orchestra; original with "shaded dog" label*

| Number | Title (A Side/B Side) | Yr | NM |
|---|---|---|---|
| ❑ LSC-2493 [S] | Schubert: Piano Sonata, op. 53 | 1961 | 50.00 |

*—Original with "shaded dog" label*

**GILES, GILES & FRIPP**

DERAM

| Number | Title (A Side/B Side) | Yr | NM |
|---|---|---|---|
| ❑ DES 18019 | The Cheerful Insanity of Giles, Giles & Fripp | 1968 | 60.00 |

**GILKYSON, TERRY**

COLUMBIA

| Number | Title (A Side/B Side) | Yr | NM |
|---|---|---|---|
| ❑ CL 990 [M] | Marianne and Other Songs | 1957 | 50.00 |
| ❑ CL 1302 [M] | Wanderin' Folk Songs | 1959 | 30.00 |

DECCA

| Number | Title (A Side/B Side) | Yr | NM |
|---|---|---|---|
| ❑ DL 5263 [10] | Folk Songs | 1950 | 50.00 |
| ❑ DL 5457 [10] | Golden Minutes of Folk Music | 1952 | 50.00 |

KAPP

| Number | Title (A Side/B Side) | Yr | NM |
|---|---|---|---|
| ❑ KL 1196 [M] | Rollin' | 1960 | 15.00 |
| ❑ KL 1327 [M] | The Cry of the Wild Goose | 1963 | 15.00 |
| ❑ KS 3196 [S] | Rollin' | 1960 | 20.00 |
| ❑ KS 3327 [S] | The Cry of the Wild Goose | 1963 | 20.00 |

**GILL, VINCE**

MCA

| Number | Title (A Side/B Side) | Yr | NM |
|---|---|---|---|
| ❑ 42321 | When I Call Your Name | 1989 | 20.00 |
| ❑ R 173599 | Pocket Full of Gold | 1991 | 20.00 |

*—Only released on vinyl through BMG Direct Marketing*

RCA

| Number | Title (A Side/B Side) | Yr | NM |
|---|---|---|---|
| ❑ 5923-1-R | The Way Back Home | 1987 | 15.00 |

RCA VICTOR

| Number | Title (A Side/B Side) | Yr | NM |
|---|---|---|---|
| ❑ CPL1-5348 | The Things That Matter | 1985 | 15.00 |
| ❑ MHL1-8517 [EP] | Turn Me Loose | 1984 | 10.00 |

**GILLESPIE, DANA**

LONDON

| Number | Title (A Side/B Side) | Yr | NM |
|---|---|---|---|
| ❑ PS 540 | Foolish Seasons | 1968 | 20.00 |

**GILLESPIE, DARLENE**

DISNEYLAND

| Number | Title (A Side/B Side) | Yr | NM |
|---|---|---|---|
| ❑ WDL-1010 [M] | Top Tunes of the '50's — Darlene Gillespie Sings TV Favorites | 1959 | 40.00 |

*—Reissue of 3010*

| Number | Title (A Side/B Side) | Yr | NM |
|---|---|---|---|
| ❑ DQ-1228 [M] | Sleeping Beauty | 1962 | 20.00 |

*—Cover is black and white; later pressings, which go for less, are shaded blue on the back*

| Number | Title (A Side/B Side) | Yr | NM |
|---|---|---|---|
| ❑ WDL-3010 [M] | Darlene of the Teens | 1957 | 80.00 |
| ❑ WDL-3010 [M] | Top Tunes of the '50's — Darlene Gillespie Sings TV Favorites | 1958 | 50.00 |

*—Reissue with new title and cover*

MICKEY MOUSE CLUB

| Number | Title (A Side/B Side) | Yr | NM |
|---|---|---|---|
| ❑ MM-32 [M] | Sleeping Beauty | 1959 | 40.00 |

**GILLESPIE, DIZZY**

ALLEGRO

| Number | Title (A Side/B Side) | Yr | NM |
|---|---|---|---|
| ❑ 3017 [M] | Dizzy Gillespie Plays | 195? | 120.00 |
| ❑ 3083 [M] | Dizzy Gillespie | 195? | 120.00 |
| ❑ 4023 [10] | Dizzy Gillespie | 195? | 200.00 |
| ❑ 4108 [10] | Dizzy Gillespie Plays | 195? | 200.00 |

AMERICAN RECORDING SOCIETY

| Number | Title (A Side/B Side) | Yr | NM |
|---|---|---|---|
| ❑ G-405 [M] | Jazz Creations/Dizzy Gillespie | 1955 | 100.00 |
| ❑ G-423 [M] | Big Band Jazz | 1955 | 100.00 |

ATLANTIC

| Number | Title (A Side/B Side) | Yr | NM |
|---|---|---|---|
| ❑ ALR-138 [10] | Dizzy Gillespie | 1952 | 400.00 |
| ❑ ALR-142 [10] | Dizzy Gillespie, Vol. 2 | 1952 | 400.00 |
| ❑ 1257 [M] | Dizzy at Home and Abroad | 1957 | 100.00 |

*—Black label*

| Number | Title (A Side/B Side) | Yr | NM |
|---|---|---|---|
| ❑ 1257 [M] | Dizzy at Home and Abroad | 1961 | 30.00 |

*—Multi-color label with white "fan" logo*

BARONET

| Number | Title (A Side/B Side) | Yr | NM |
|---|---|---|---|
| ❑ 105 [M] | A Handful of Modern Jazz | 1961 | 40.00 |

BLUE NOTE

| Number | Title (A Side/B Side) | Yr | NM |
|---|---|---|---|
| ❑ BLP-5017 [10] | Horn of Plenty | 1953 | 300.00 |

CLEF

| Number | Title (A Side/B Side) | Yr | NM |
|---|---|---|---|
| ❑ MGC-136 [10] | Dizzy Gillespie with Strings | 1953 | 200.00 |

CONTEMPORARY

| Number | Title (A Side/B Side) | Yr | NM |
|---|---|---|---|
| ❑ C-2504 [10] | Dizzy in Paris | 1953 | 200.00 |

DEE GEE

| Number | Title (A Side/B Side) | Yr | NM |
|---|---|---|---|
| ❑ LP-1000 [10] | Dizzy Gillespie | 1950 | 300.00 |

DIAL

| Number | Title (A Side/B Side) | Yr | NM |
|---|---|---|---|
| ❑ 212 [10] | Modern Trumpets | 1952 | 400.00 |

DISCOVERY

| Number | Title (A Side/B Side) | Yr | NM |
|---|---|---|---|
| ❑ DL-3013 [10] | Dizzy Gillespie Plays, Johnny Richards Conducts | 1950 | 300.00 |

EVEREST ARCHIVE OF FOLK & JAZZ

| Number | Title (A Side/B Side) | Yr | NM |
|---|---|---|---|
| ❑ 301 | Dizzy Gillespie, Volume 3 | 197? | 10.00 |

GENE NORMAN

| Number | Title (A Side/B Side) | Yr | NM |
|---|---|---|---|
| ❑ GNP-4 [10] | Dizzy Gillespie with His Original Big Band | 195? | 200.00 |
| ❑ GNP-23 [M] | Dizzy Gillespie and His Big Band | 1957 | 80.00 |

GNP CRESCENDO

| Number | Title (A Side/B Side) | Yr | NM |
|---|---|---|---|
| ❑ GNP-23 [M] | Dizzy Gillespie and His Big Band | 196? | 20.00 |

IMPULSE!

| Number | Title (A Side/B Side) | Yr | NM |
|---|---|---|---|
| ❑ AS-9149 | Swing Low, Sweet Cadillac! | 1967 | 20.00 |

LIMELIGHT

| Number | Title (A Side/B Side) | Yr | NM |
|---|---|---|---|
| ❑ LM-82007 [M] | Jambo Caribe | 1964 | 20.00 |
| ❑ LM-82022 [M] | The New Continent | 1965 | 20.00 |
| ❑ LM-82042 [M] | The Melody Lingers On | 1967 | 20.00 |
| ❑ LS-86007 [S] | Jambo Caribe | 1964 | 25.00 |
| ❑ LS-86022 [S] | The New Continent | 1965 | 25.00 |
| ❑ LS-86042 [S] | The Melody Lingers On | 1967 | 25.00 |

NORGRAN

| Number | Title (A Side/B Side) | Yr | NM |
|---|---|---|---|
| ❑ MGN-1003 [M] | Afro Dizzy | 1954 | 120.00 |
| ❑ MGN-1023 [M] | Dizzy and Strings | 1955 | 120.00 |
| ❑ MGN-1083 [M] | Jazz Recital | 1956 | 120.00 |
| ❑ MGN-1084 [M] | World Statesman | 1956 | 120.00 |
| ❑ MGN-1090 [M] | Diz Big Band | 1956 | 120.00 |

PHILIPS

| Number | Title (A Side/B Side) | Yr | NM |
|---|---|---|---|
| ❑ PHM 200048 [M] | Dizzy at the French Riviera | 1962 | 20.00 |
| ❑ PHM 200070 [M] | New Wave! | 1962 | 20.00 |
| ❑ PHM 200091 [M] | Something Old, Something New | 1963 | 20.00 |
| ❑ PHM 200106 [M] | Dizzy Gillespie and the Double Six of Paris | 1963 | 100.00 |
| ❑ PHM 200123 [M] | Dizzy Gillespie Goes Hollywood | 1964 | 20.00 |
| ❑ PHM 200138 [M] | The Cool World | 1964 | 50.00 |
| ❑ PHS 600048 [S] | Dizzy at the French Riviera | 1962 | 25.00 |
| ❑ PHS 600070 [S] | New Wave! | 1962 | 25.00 |
| ❑ PHS 600091 [S] | Something Old, Something New | 1963 | 25.00 |
| ❑ PHS 600106 [S] | Dizzy Gillespie and the Double Six of Paris | 1963 | 150.00 |
| ❑ PHS 600123 [S] | Dizzy Gillespie Goes Hollywood | 1964 | 25.00 |
| ❑ PHS 600138 [S] | The Cool World | 1964 | 80.00 |

RCA VICTOR

| Number | Title (A Side/B Side) | Yr | NM |
|---|---|---|---|
| ❑ LPV-530 [M] | Dizzy Gillespie | 1966 | 25.00 |
| ❑ LJM-1009 [M] | Dizzier and Dizzier | 1954 | 120.00 |
| ❑ LPM-2398 [M] | The Greatest of Dizzy Gillespie | 1961 | 50.00 |

*—"Long Play" on label*

REGENT

| Number | Title (A Side/B Side) | Yr | NM |
|---|---|---|---|
| ❑ MG-6043 [M] | School Days | 1957 | 100.00 |

REPRISE

| Number | Title (A Side/B Side) | Yr | NM |
|---|---|---|---|
| ❑ R-6072 [M] | Dateline: Europe | 1963 | 20.00 |
| ❑ R9-6072 [S] | Dateline: Europe | 1963 | 25.00 |

RONDO-LETTE

| Number | Title (A Side/B Side) | Yr | NM |
|---|---|---|---|
| ❑ A-11 [M] | Dizzy Gillespie | 195? | 30.00 |

ROOST

| Number | Title (A Side/B Side) | Yr | NM |
|---|---|---|---|
| ❑ R-414 [10] | Dizzy Over Paris | 1953 | 250.00 |
| ❑ LP-2214 [M] | Concert in Paris | 1957 | 120.00 |

SAVOY

| Number | Title (A Side/B Side) | Yr | NM |
|---|---|---|---|
| ❑ MG-12020 [M] | Groovin' High | 1955 | 60.00 |
| ❑ MG-12047 [M] | The Champ | 1956 | 60.00 |
| ❑ MG-12110 [M] | The Dizzy Gillespie Story | 1957 | 60.00 |

SOLID STATE

| Number | Title (A Side/B Side) | Yr | NM |
|---|---|---|---|
| ❑ SS-18034 | Live at the Village Vanguard | 1968 | 20.00 |
| ❑ SS-18054 | My Way | 1969 | 20.00 |
| ❑ SS-18061 | Cornucopia | 1969 | 20.00 |

SUTTON

| Number | Title (A Side/B Side) | Yr | NM |
|---|---|---|---|
| ❑ SSU-287 [S] | Featuring Dizzy Gillespie | 196? | 12.00 |
| ❑ SU-287 [M] | Featuring Dizzy Gillespie | 196? | 15.00 |

VERVE

| Number | Title (A Side/B Side) | Yr | NM |
|---|---|---|---|
| ❑ MGVS-6023 [S] | Dizzy Gillespie at Newport | 1960 | 60.00 |
| ❑ MGVS-6047 [S] | Have Trumpet, Will Excite | 1960 | 60.00 |

| Number | Title (A Side/B Side) | Yr | NM |
|---|---|---|---|
| MGVS-6068 [S] | The Ebullient Mr. Gillespie | 1960 | 60.00 |
| MGVS-6117 [S] | Greatest Trumpet of Them All | 1960 | 60.00 |
| MGV-8017 [M] | Dizzy in Greece | 1957 | 60.00 |
| V-8017 [M] | Dizzy in Greece | 1961 | 25.00 |
| MGV-8173 [M] | Jazz Recital | 1957 | 60.00 |
| V-8173 [M] | Jazz Recital | 1961 | 25.00 |
| MGV-8174 [M] | World Statesman | 1957 | 60.00 |
| V-8174 [M] | World Statesman | 1961 | 25.00 |
| MGV-8178 [M] | Diz Big Band | 1957 | 70.00 |
| V-8178 [M] | Diz Big Band | 1961 | 25.00 |
| MGV-8191 [M] | Afro Dizzy | 1957 | 60.00 |
| MGV-8208 [M] | Manteca | 1958 | 60.00 |
| V-8208 [M] | Manteca | 1961 | 25.00 |
| MGV-8214 [M] | Dizzy Gillespie and Stuff Smith | 1958 | 60.00 |
| V-8214 [M] | Dizzy Gillespie and Stuff Smith | 1961 | 25.00 |
| MGV-8242 [M] | Dizzy Gillespie at Newport | 1958 | 60.00 |
| V-8242 [M] | Dizzy Gillespie at Newport | 1961 | 25.00 |
| V6-8242 [S] | Dizzy Gillespie at Newport | 1961 | 25.00 |
| MGV-8260 [M] | Duets | 1958 | 60.00 |
| *—With Sonny Rollins and Sonny Stitt* | | | |
| MGV-8313 [M] | Have Trumpet, Will Excite | 1959 | 60.00 |
| V-8313 [M] | Have Trumpet, Will Excite | 1961 | 25.00 |
| V6-8313 [S] | Have Trumpet, Will Excite | 1961 | 25.00 |
| MGV-8328 [M] | The Ebullient Mr. Gillespie | 1959 | 60.00 |
| V-8328 [M] | The Ebullient Mr. Gillespie | 1961 | 25.00 |
| V6-8328 [S] | The Ebullient Mr. Gillespie | 1961 | 25.00 |
| MGV-8352 [M] | Greatest Trumpet of Them All | 1959 | 60.00 |
| V-8352 [M] | Greatest Trumpet of Them All | 1961 | 25.00 |
| V6-8352 [S] | Greatest Trumpet of Them All | 1961 | 25.00 |
| MGV-8386 [M] | Portrait of Duke | 1960 | 60.00 |
| V-8386 [M] | Portrait of Duke | 1961 | 25.00 |
| MGV-8394 [M] | Gillespiana | 1960 | 60.00 |
| V-8394 [M] | Gillespiana | 1961 | 25.00 |
| V6-8394 [S] | Gillespiana | 1961 | 25.00 |
| V-8401 [M] | An Electrifying Evening with the Dizzy Gillespie Quintet | 1961 | 20.00 |
| V6-8401 [S] | An Electrifying Evening with the Dizzy Gillespie Quintet | 1961 | 25.00 |
| V-8411 [M] | Perceptions | 1961 | 20.00 |
| V6-8411 [S] | Perceptions | 1961 | 25.00 |
| V-8423 [M] | Carnegie Hall Concert | 1962 | 20.00 |
| V6-8423 [S] | Carnegie Hall Concert | 1962 | 25.00 |
| V-8477 [M] | Dizzy, Rollins & Stitt | 1962 | 20.00 |
| *—Reissue of MGV-8260* | | | |
| V6-8477 [S] | Dizzy, Rollins & Stitt | 1962 | 25.00 |
| V-8560 [M] | Dizzy at Newport | 1964 | 20.00 |
| V6-8560 [S] | Dizzy at Newport | 1964 | 25.00 |
| V-8566 [M] | The Essential Dizzy Gillespie | 1964 | 20.00 |
| V6-8566 [S] | The Essential Dizzy Gillespie | 1964 | 25.00 |

### GILLESPIE, DIZZY, AND STAN GETZ

**NORGRAN**

| Number | Title (A Side/B Side) | Yr | NM |
|---|---|---|---|
| MGN-2 [10] | The Dizzy Gillespie-Stan Getz Sextet #1 | 1954 | 300.00 |
| MGN-18 [10] | The Dizzy Gillespie-Stan Getz Sextet #2 | 1954 | 300.00 |
| MGN-1050 [M] | Diz and Getz | 1956 | 120.00 |

**VERVE**

| Number | Title (A Side/B Side) | Yr | NM |
|---|---|---|---|
| MGV-8141 [M] | Diz and Getz | 1957 | 80.00 |
| *—Reissue of Norgran 1050* | | | |

### GILLESPIE, DIZZY/JIMMY MCPARTLAND

**MGM**

| Number | Title (A Side/B Side) | Yr | NM |
|---|---|---|---|
| E-3286 [M] | Hot vs. Cool | 1955 | 80.00 |

### GILLESPIE, DIZZY, AND CHARLIE PARKER

**ROOST**

| Number | Title (A Side/B Side) | Yr | NM |
|---|---|---|---|
| SK-106 [(2)M] | The Beginning: Diz and Bird | 1960 | 100.00 |
| LP-2234 [M] | Diz 'n' Bird In Concert | 1959 | 80.00 |

### GILLESPIE, DIZZY, AND DJANGO REINHARDT

**VERVE**

| Number | Title (A Side/B Side) | Yr | NM |
|---|---|---|---|
| MGV-8015 [M] | Jazz from Paris | 1957 | 60.00 |
| V-8015 [M] | Jazz from Paris | 1961 | 25.00 |

### GILLEY, MICKEY

**ACCORD**

| Number | Title (A Side/B Side) | Yr | NM |
|---|---|---|---|
| SN-7151 | Suburban Cowboy | 1981 | 10.00 |

**ASTRO**

| Number | Title (A Side/B Side) | Yr | NM |
|---|---|---|---|
| 101 [M] | Lonely Wine | 1964 | 300.00 |

**COLUMBIA SPECIAL PRODUCTS**

| Number | Title (A Side/B Side) | Yr | NM |
|---|---|---|---|
| P 16198 | All My Best | 1982 | 10.00 |

**EPIC**

| Number | Title (A Side/B Side) | Yr | NM |
|---|---|---|---|
| PE 34736 | Room Full of Roses | 198? | 8.00 |
| *—Budget-line reissue* | | | |
| PE 34749 | Smokin' | 198? | 8.00 |
| *—Budget-line reissue* | | | |
| PE 34776 | First Class | 198? | 8.00 |
| *—Budget-line reissue* | | | |
| KE 35174 | Songs We Made Love To | 1979 | 10.00 |
| JE 36201 | Mickey Gilley | 1980 | 10.00 |
| JE 36492 | That's All That Matters to Me | 1980 | 10.00 |
| PE 36492 | That's All That Matters to Me | 198? | 8.00 |
| *—Budget-line reissue* | | | |
| JE 36851 | Encore | 1981 | 10.00 |
| FE 37416 | You Don't Know Me | 1981 | 10.00 |
| PE 37416 | You Don't Know Me | 198? | 8.00 |
| *—Budget-line reissue* | | | |
| PE 37595 | Christmas at Gilley's | 1981 | 10.00 |
| *—Some labels have "FE" prefix* | | | |
| FE 38082 | Put Your Dreams Away | 1982 | 10.00 |
| PE 38082 | Put Your Dreams Away | 198? | 8.00 |
| *—Budget-line reissue* | | | |
| FE 38320 | Mickey Gilley's Biggest Hits | 1982 | 10.00 |
| FE 38583 | Fool for Your Love | 1983 | 10.00 |
| PE 38583 | Fool for Your Love | 1985 | 8.00 |
| *—Budget-line reissue* | | | |
| FE 39000 | You've Really Got a Hold on Me | 1983 | 10.00 |
| FE 39324 | Too Good to Stop Now | 1983 | 10.00 |
| KE2 39867 [(2)] | Ten Years of Hits | 1984 | 12.00 |
| FE 39900 | Live at Gilley's | 1984 | 10.00 |
| FE 40115 | I Feel Good (About Lovin' You) | 1985 | 10.00 |
| FE 40353 | The One and Only | 1986 | 10.00 |

**INTERMEDIA**

| Number | Title (A Side/B Side) | Yr | NM |
|---|---|---|---|
| QS-5024 | With Love from Pasadena, Texas | 198? | 10.00 |

**J.M.**

| Number | Title (A Side/B Side) | Yr | NM |
|---|---|---|---|
| 8127 | Norwegian Wood | 1981 | 12.00 |

**PAIR**

| Number | Title (A Side/B Side) | Yr | NM |
|---|---|---|---|
| PDL2-1072 [(2)] | The Best of Mickey Gilley | 1986 | 12.00 |

**PAULA**

| Number | Title (A Side/B Side) | Yr | NM |
|---|---|---|---|
| LP-2195 [M] | Down the Line | 1967 | 40.00 |
| LPS-2195 [S] | Down the Line | 1967 | 40.00 |
| LPS-2224 | Mickey Gilley at His Best | 1974 | 15.00 |
| LPS-2234 | Mickey Gilley | 1978 | 12.00 |

**PICKWICK**

| Number | Title (A Side/B Side) | Yr | NM |
|---|---|---|---|
| SPC-6180 | Wild Side of Life | 1975 | 10.00 |

**PLAYBOY**

| Number | Title (A Side/B Side) | Yr | NM |
|---|---|---|---|
| PB-128 | Room Full of Roses | 1974 | 20.00 |
| PB-403 | City Lights | 1974 | 20.00 |
| PB-405 | Mickey's Movin' On | 1975 | 15.00 |
| PB-408 | Overnight Sensation | 1976 | 15.00 |
| PB-409 | Gilley's Greatest Hits Vol. 1 | 1976 | 15.00 |
| PB-415 | Gilley's Smokin' | 1976 | 15.00 |
| PZ 34736 | Room Full of Roses | 1977 | 10.00 |
| *—Reissue of 128* | | | |
| PZ 34742 | Overnight Sensation | 1977 | 10.00 |
| *—Reissue of 408* | | | |
| PZ 34743 | Gilley's Greatest Hits Vol. 1 | 1977 | 10.00 |
| *—Reissue of 409* | | | |
| PZ 34749 | Gilley's Smokin' | 1977 | 12.00 |
| *—Reissue of 415* | | | |
| PZ 34776 | First Class | 1977 | 12.00 |
| KZ 34881 | Gilley's Greatest Hits, Vol. 2 | 1977 | 12.00 |
| KZ 35099 | Flyin' High | 1978 | 12.00 |

### GILMER, JIMMY, AND THE FIREBALLS

See THE FIREBALLS.

### GILMER, JULIA ANN

**ABC-PARAMOUNT**

| Number | Title (A Side/B Side) | Yr | NM |
|---|---|---|---|
| ABC-168 [M] | Cads, Blackguards and False True-Loves | 1956 | 30.00 |

### GIN BLOSSOMS

**A&M**

| Number | Title (A Side/B Side) | Yr | NM |
|---|---|---|---|
| 75021 5369 1 [EP] | Up and Crumbling | 1991 | 15.00 |

**SAN JACINTO**

| Number | Title (A Side/B Side) | Yr | NM |
|---|---|---|---|
| DRAM 019 | Dusted | 1989 | 20.00 |
| *—With picture insert and biographical material* | | | |

### GINNY AND THE GALLIONS

**DOWNEY**

| Number | Title (A Side/B Side) | Yr | NM |
|---|---|---|---|
| D-1003 [M] | Two Sides of Ginny and the Gallions | 1964 | 30.00 |
| DS-1003 [S] | Two Sides of Ginny and the Gallions | 1964 | 40.00 |

### GINSBERG, ALLEN

**ATLANTIC**

| Number | Title (A Side/B Side) | Yr | NM |
|---|---|---|---|
| 4001 [M] | Allen Ginsburg Reads Kaddish | 1966 | 30.00 |

**FANTASY**

| Number | Title (A Side/B Side) | Yr | NM |
|---|---|---|---|
| F-7006 [M] | Howl and Other Poems | 1959 | 200.00 |
| *—Black non-flexible vinyl* | | | |
| F-7006 [M] | Howl and Other Poems | 1959 | 400.00 |
| *—Red vinyl* | | | |

### GIRARD, GEORGE

**VIK**

| Number | Title (A Side/B Side) | Yr | NM |
|---|---|---|---|
| LX-1058 [M] | Jam Session on Bourbon Street | 1957 | 40.00 |
| LX-1063 [M] | Stompin' at the Famous Door | 1957 | 40.00 |

### GITS, THE

**BROKEN REKIDS**

| Number | Title (A Side/B Side) | Yr | NM |
|---|---|---|---|
| SKIP 44 | Kings & Queens | 1995 | 12.00 |
| SKIP 87 | Seafish Louisville | 2000 | 12.00 |

**C/Z**

| Number | Title (A Side/B Side) | Yr | NM |
|---|---|---|---|
| 051 | Frenching the Bully | 1992 | 25.00 |
| *—Originals on red vinyl* | | | |

### GIUFFRE, JIMMY

**ATLANTIC**

| Number | Title (A Side/B Side) | Yr | NM |
|---|---|---|---|
| 1238 [M] | The Jimmy Giuffre Clarinet | 1956 | 50.00 |
| *—Black label* | | | |
| 1238 [M] | The Jimmy Giuffre Clarinet | 1960 | 20.00 |
| *—Multicolor label, white "fan" logo at right* | | | |
| 1254 [M] | The Jimmy Giuffre Three | 1957 | 50.00 |
| *—Black label* | | | |
| 1254 [M] | The Jimmy Giuffre Three | 1960 | 20.00 |
| *—Multicolor label, white "fan" logo at right* | | | |
| 1276 [M] | Music Man | 1958 | 50.00 |
| *—Black label* | | | |
| 1276 [M] | Music Man | 1960 | 20.00 |
| *—Multicolor label, white "fan" logo at right* | | | |
| SD 1276 [S] | Music Man | 1959 | 50.00 |
| *—Green label* | | | |
| SD 1276 [S] | Music Man | 1960 | 20.00 |
| *—Multicolor label, white "fan" logo at right* | | | |
| 1282 [M] | Trav'lin' Light | 1958 | 50.00 |
| *—Black label* | | | |
| 1282 [M] | Trav'lin' Light | 1960 | 20.00 |
| *—Multicolor label, white "fan" logo at right* | | | |
| SD 1282 [S] | Trav'lin' Light | 1959 | 50.00 |
| *—Green label* | | | |
| SD 1282 [S] | Trav'lin' Light | 1960 | 20.00 |
| *—Multicolor label, white "fan" logo at right* | | | |
| 1295 [M] | Four Brothers Sound | 1959 | 50.00 |
| *—Black label* | | | |
| 1295 [M] | Four Brothers Sound | 1960 | 20.00 |
| *—Multicolor label, white "fan" logo at right* | | | |
| SD 1295 [S] | Four Brothers Sound | 1959 | 50.00 |
| *—Green label* | | | |
| SD 1295 [S] | Four Brothers Sound | 1960 | 20.00 |
| *—Multicolor label, white "fan" logo at right* | | | |
| 1330 [M] | Western Suite | 1960 | 25.00 |
| *—Multicolor label, white "fan" logo at right* | | | |
| SD 1330 [S] | Western Suite | 1960 | 30.00 |
| *—Multicolor label, white "fan" logo at right* | | | |

**CAPITOL**

| Number | Title (A Side/B Side) | Yr | NM |
|---|---|---|---|
| H 549 [10] | Jimmy Giuffre | 1954 | 250.00 |
| T 549 [M] | Jimmy Giuffre | 1955 | 120.00 |
| T 634 [M] | Tangents in Jazz | 1955 | 120.00 |

**COLUMBIA**

| Number | Title (A Side/B Side) | Yr | NM |
|---|---|---|---|
| CS 8764 [S] | Free Fall | 1963 | 20.00 |

**VERVE**

| Number | Title (A Side/B Side) | Yr | NM |
|---|---|---|---|
| MGVS-6039 [S] | Seven Pieces | 1960 | 30.00 |
| MGVS-6095 [S] | The Easy Way | 1960 | 30.00 |
| MGVS-6130 [S] | Ad Lib | 1960 | 30.00 |
| MGV-8307 [M] | Seven Pieces | 1959 | 40.00 |
| V-8307 [M] | Seven Pieces | 1961 | 20.00 |
| MGV-8337 [M] | The Easy Way | 1960 | 40.00 |
| V-8337 [M] | The Easy Way | 1961 | 20.00 |
| MGV-8361 [M] | Ad Lib | 1960 | 40.00 |
| V-8361 [M] | Ad Lib | 1961 | 20.00 |
| MGV-8387 [M] | The Jimmy Giuffre Quartet In Person | 1961 | 40.00 |
| V-8387 [M] | The Jimmy Giuffre Quartet In Person | 1961 | 20.00 |
| V6-8387 [S] | The Jimmy Giuffre Quartet In Person | 1961 | 25.00 |
| MGV-8395 [M] | Piece for Clarinet and String Orchestra | 1961 | 40.00 |
| V-8395 [M] | Piece for Clarinet and String Orchestra | 1961 | 20.00 |
| V6-8395 [S] | Piece for Clarinet and String Orchestra | 1961 | 25.00 |
| MGV-8397 [M] | Fusion | 1961 | 40.00 |
| V-8397 [M] | Fusion | 1961 | 20.00 |
| V6-8397 [S] | Fusion | 1961 | 25.00 |
| MGV-8402 [M] | Thesis | 1961 | 40.00 |
| V-8402 [M] | Thesis | 1961 | 20.00 |
| V6-8402 [S] | Thesis | 1961 | 25.00 |

### GLACIERS, THE

**MERCURY**

| Number | Title (A Side/B Side) | Yr | NM |
|---|---|---|---|
| MG-20895 [M] | From Sea to Ski | 1964 | 50.00 |
| SR-60895 [S] | From Sea to Ski | 1964 | 60.00 |

### GLAD, THE

**ABC**

| Number | Title (A Side/B Side) | Yr | NM |
|---|---|---|---|
| S-655 | Feelin' Glad | 1969 | 25.00 |

### GLASEL, JOHN

**ABC-PARAMOUNT**

| Number | Title (A Side/B Side) | Yr | NM |
|---|---|---|---|
| ABC-165 [M] | Jazz Session | 1957 | 50.00 |

**GOLDEN CREST**

| Number | Title (A Side/B Side) | Yr | NM |
|---|---|---|---|
| 1002 [M] | Jazz Unlimited | 1960 | 30.00 |

### GLASER, JIM

**MCA**

| Number | Title (A Side/B Side) | Yr | NM |
|---|---|---|---|
| 5612 | Past the Point of No Return | 1985 | 8.00 |
| 5723 | Everybody Knows I'm Yours | 1986 | 8.00 |

**NOBLE VISION**

| Number | Title (A Side/B Side) | Yr | NM |
|---|---|---|---|
| 2001 | The Man in the Mirror | 1983 | 10.00 |

**STARDAY**

| Number | Title (A Side/B Side) | Yr | NM |
|---|---|---|---|
| SLP-149 [M] | Old Time Christmas Singing | 1960 | 70.00 |
| SLP-158 [M] | Just Looking for a Home | 1961 | 60.00 |

### GLASS HARP

**DECCA**

| Number | Title (A Side/B Side) | Yr | NM |
|---|---|---|---|
| DL 75261 | Glass Harp | 1971 | 25.00 |

| Number | Title (A Side/B Side) | Yr | NM |
|---|---|---|---|
| ❑ DL 75306 | Synergy | 1971 | 25.00 |
| ❑ DL 75358 | It Makes Me Glad | 1972 | 25.00 |

MCA

| Number | Title (A Side/B Side) | Yr | NM |
|---|---|---|---|
| ❑ 293 | Glass Harp | 1974 | 10.00 |

*—Reissue of Decca 75261*

## GLAZER, TOM

UNITED ARTISTS

| Number | Title (A Side/B Side) | Yr | NM |
|---|---|---|---|
| ❑ UAL 3540 [M] | Tom Glazer Sings the Ballad of Namu the Killer Whale and Other Ballads of Adventure | 1966 | 25.00 |
| ❑ UAS 6540 [S] | Tom Glazer Sings the Ballad of Namu the Killer Whale and Other Ballads of Adventure | 1966 | 30.00 |

WASHINGTON

| Number | Title (A Side/B Side) | Yr | NM |
|---|---|---|---|
| ❑ WC-301 [M] | The Tom Glazer Concert For and With Children | 1959 | 25.00 |

## GLEASON, JACKIE

CAPITOL

| Number | Title (A Side/B Side) | Yr | NM |
|---|---|---|---|
| ❑ SW-106 | Irving Berlin's Music | 1968 | 12.00 |
| ❑ SKAO-146 | The Best of Jackie Gleason (Vol. 2) | 1968 | 12.00 |
| ❑ SWBB-256 [(2)] | Close-Up | 1969 | 15.00 |
| *—Reissue of Capitol DW 352 and DW 509 in one package* | | | |
| ❑ STBB-346 [(2)] | All I Want for Christmas | 1969 | 15.00 |
| ❑ H 352 [10] | Music for Lovers Only | 1952 | 30.00 |
| ❑ SM-352 | Music for Lovers Only | 197? | 10.00 |
| *—Reissue* | | | |
| ❑ SW 352 [S] | Music for Lovers Only | 1959 | 15.00 |
| *—Re-recorded version of W 352; black rainbow label, Capitol logo at left* | | | |
| ❑ SW 352 [S] | Music for Lovers Only | 1963 | 10.00 |
| *—Re-recorded version; black rainbow label, Capitol logo at top* | | | |
| ❑ W 352 [M] | Music for Lovers Only | 1953 | 25.00 |
| ❑ H 366 [10] | Lover's Rhapsody | 1953 | 30.00 |
| ❑ ST-398 | Romeo and Juliet | 1970 | 12.00 |
| ❑ DW 455 [R] | Music to Make You Misty | 196? | 10.00 |
| ❑ H 455 [10] | Music to Make You Misty | 1954 | 30.00 |
| ❑ SM-455 | Music to Make You Misty | 197? | 10.00 |
| *—Reissue* | | | |
| ❑ W 455 [M] | Music to Make You Misty | 1954 | 25.00 |
| ❑ L 471 [10] | Tawny | 1954 | 30.00 |
| ❑ W 471 [M] | Tawny | 1954 | 25.00 |
| ❑ WAO 475 [(2)M] | Music for Lovers Only/Music to Make You Misty | 1954 | 40.00 |
| ❑ ST-480 | Come Saturday Morning | 1970 | 12.00 |
| ❑ H1-509 [10] | Music, Martini and Memories Part 1 | 1954 | 30.00 |
| ❑ H2-509 [10] | Music, Martini and Memories Part 2 | 1954 | 30.00 |
| ❑ SM-509 | Music, Martini and Memories | 197? | 10.00 |
| *—Reissue* | | | |
| ❑ SW 509 [S] | Music, Martini and Memories | 196? | 15.00 |
| *—Re-recorded for stereo* | | | |
| ❑ W 509 [M] | Music, Martini and Memories | 1954 | 25.00 |
| ❑ STBB-510 [(2)] | Tenderly/Laura | 1971 | 15.00 |
| ❑ H 511 [10] | And Awaaay We Go! | 1954 | 80.00 |
| ❑ W 511 [M] | And Awaaay We Go! | 1955 | 40.00 |
| ❑ W 568 [M] | Jackie Gleason Plays Romantic Jazz | 1955 | 25.00 |
| ❑ DW 570 [R] | Music to Remember Her | 196? | 10.00 |
| ❑ W 570 [M] | Music to Remember Her | 1955 | 25.00 |
| ❑ DW 627 [R] | Lonesome Echo | 196? | 10.00 |
| ❑ H 627 [10] | Lonesome Echo | 1955 | 30.00 |
| ❑ W 627 [M] | Lonesome Echo | 1955 | 25.00 |
| ❑ DW 632 [R] | Music to Change Her Mind | 196? | 10.00 |
| ❑ W 632 [M] | Music to Change Her Mind | 1956 | 25.00 |
| ❑ ST-693 | Words of Love | 1971 | 12.00 |
| ❑ DW 717 [R] | Night Winds | 196? | 10.00 |
| ❑ W 717 [M] | Night Winds | 1956 | 25.00 |
| ❑ DW 758 [R] | Merry Christmas | 196? | 10.00 |
| ❑ W 758 [M] | Merry Christmas | 1956 | 25.00 |
| ❑ DW 816 [R] | Music for the Love Hours | 196? | 10.00 |
| ❑ W 816 [M] | Music for the Love Hours | 1957 | 25.00 |
| ❑ SM-859 | Velvet Brass | 197? | 10.00 |
| *—Reissue* | | | |
| ❑ SW 859 [S] | Velvet Brass | 1959 | 25.00 |
| *—We haven't confirmed if this is in true stereo or not.* | | | |
| ❑ W 859 [M] | Velvet Brass | 1957 | 25.00 |
| ❑ SW 905 [S] | Jackie Gleason Presents "Oooo!" | 1959 | 25.00 |
| *—We haven't confirmed if this is in true stereo or not.* | | | |
| ❑ W 905 [M] | Jackie Gleason Presents "Oooo!" | 1957 | 25.00 |
| ❑ SW 961 [S] | The Torch with Blue Flame | 1959 | 25.00 |
| ❑ W 961 [M] | The Torch with Blue Flame | 1958 | 20.00 |
| ❑ SW 1020 [S] | Riff Jazz | 1959 | 25.00 |
| ❑ W 1020 [M] | Riff Jazz | 1958 | 20.00 |
| ❑ SW 1075 [S] | Rebound | 1959 | 25.00 |
| ❑ W 1075 [M] | Rebound | 1959 | 20.00 |
| ❑ SW 1147 [S] | That Moment | 1959 | 25.00 |
| ❑ W 1147 [M] | That Moment | 1959 | 20.00 |
| ❑ SW 1250 [S] | Aphrodisia | 1960 | 25.00 |
| ❑ W 1250 [M] | Aphrodisia | 1960 | 20.00 |
| ❑ SW 1315 [S] | Opiate D'Amour | 1960 | 20.00 |
| ❑ W 1315 [M] | Opiate D'Amour | 1960 | 15.00 |
| ❑ SW 1439 [S] | Lazy Lively Love | 1961 | 25.00 |
| ❑ W 1439 [M] | Lazy Lively Love | 1961 | 20.00 |
| ❑ SW 1519 [S] | The Gentle Touch | 1961 | 25.00 |
| ❑ W 1519 [M] | The Gentle Touch | 1961 | 20.00 |
| ❑ SWBO 1619 [(2)S] | A Lover's Portfolio | 1962 | 25.00 |
| ❑ WBO 1619 [(2)M] | A Lover's Portfolio | 1962 | 20.00 |
| ❑ SW 1689 [S] | Love, Embers and Flame | 1962 | 20.00 |
| ❑ W 1689 [M] | Love, Embers and Flame | 1962 | 15.00 |
| ❑ SW 1830 [S] | Champagne, Candlelight & Kisses | 1963 | 15.00 |
| ❑ W 1830 [M] | Champagne, Candlelight & Kisses | 1963 | 12.00 |
| ❑ SW 1877 [S] | Movie Themes — For Lovers Only | 1963 | 15.00 |
| ❑ W 1877 [M] | Movie Themes — For Lovers Only | 1963 | 12.00 |
| ❑ SW 1978 [S] | Today's Romantic Hits/For Lovers Only | 1963 | 15.00 |
| ❑ W 1978 [M] | Today's Romantic Hits/For Lovers Only | 1963 | 12.00 |
| ❑ SW 1979 [S] | A Lover's Portfolio, Vol. 1 (Music for Sippin' and Dancin') | 1963 | 15.00 |
| ❑ W 1979 [M] | A Lover's Portfolio, Vol. 1 (Music for Sippin' and Dancin') | 1963 | 12.00 |
| ❑ SW 1980 [S] | A Lover's Portfolio, Vol. 2 (Music for Listenin' and Lovin') | 1963 | 15.00 |
| ❑ W 1980 [M] | A Lover's Portfolio, Vol. 2 (Music for Listenin' and Lovin') | 1963 | 12.00 |
| ❑ SW 2056 [S] | Today's Romantic Hits/For Lovers Only, Vol. 2 | 1964 | 15.00 |
| ❑ W 2056 [M] | Today's Romantic Hits/For Lovers Only, Vol. 2 | 1964 | 12.00 |
| ❑ SW 2144 [S] | Last Dance For Lovers Only | 1964 | 15.00 |
| ❑ W 2144 [M] | Last Dance For Lovers Only | 1964 | 12.00 |
| ❑ SW 2409 [S] | Silk 'N' Brass | 1966 | 15.00 |
| ❑ W 2409 [M] | Silk 'N' Brass | 1966 | 12.00 |
| ❑ SW 2471 [S] | Music Around the World — For Lovers Only | 1966 | 15.00 |
| ❑ W 2471 [M] | Music Around the World — For Lovers Only | 1966 | 12.00 |
| ❑ SW 2582 [S] | How Sweet It Is For Lovers Only | 1966 | 15.00 |
| ❑ W 2582 [M] | How Sweet It Is For Lovers Only | 1966 | 12.00 |
| ❑ SW 2684 [S] | A Taste of Brass For Lovers Only | 1967 | 15.00 |
| ❑ W 2684 [M] | A Taste of Brass For Lovers Only | 1967 | 12.00 |
| ❑ ST 2791 [S] | 'Tis the Season | 1967 | 15.00 |
| ❑ T 2791 [M] | 'Tis the Season | 1967 | 20.00 |
| ❑ SM-2796 | The Best of Jackie Gleason | 197? | 10.00 |
| *—Reissue* | | | |
| ❑ SW 2796 [S] | The Best of Jackie Gleason | 1967 | 15.00 |
| ❑ W 2796 [M] | The Best of Jackie Gleason | 1967 | 15.00 |
| ❑ STCL 2816 [(3)S] | The Jackie Gleason Deluxe Set | 1968 | 25.00 |
| *—Reissue of three complete LPs (titles unknown)* | | | |
| ❑ TCL 2816 [(3)M] | The Jackie Gleason Deluxe Set | 1968 | 25.00 |
| ❑ SW 2880 | Doublin' in Brass | 1968 | 15.00 |
| ❑ SW 2935 | The Now Sound ... For Today's Lovers | 1968 | 15.00 |
| ❑ SQBO 91546 [(2)] | Velvet & Gold: For Lovers Only | 196? | 20.00 |

*—Capitol Record Club exclusive*

PAIR

| Number | Title (A Side/B Side) | Yr | NM |
|---|---|---|---|
| ❑ PDL2-1069 [(2)] | Lush Moods | 1986 | 12.00 |

PICKWICK

| Number | Title (A Side/B Side) | Yr | NM |
|---|---|---|---|
| ❑ SPC-1008 | White Christmas | 197? | 10.00 |
| *—Abridged version of Capitol ST 2791* | | | |
| ❑ SPC-2004 | Romantic Moods | 197? | 10.00 |
| ❑ SPC-2029 | The More I See You | 197? | 10.00 |
| ❑ SPC-3064 | Plays Pretty for the People | 196? | 10.00 |
| ❑ SPC-3218 | Shangri-La | 197? | 10.00 |

## GLENN, DARRELL

NRC

| Number | Title (A Side/B Side) | Yr | NM |
|---|---|---|---|
| ❑ LPA-5 [M] | Crying in the Chapel | 1959 | 25.00 |
| ❑ SLPA-5 [S] | Crying in the Chapel | 1959 | 30.00 |

## GLENN, LLOYD

ALADDIN

| Number | Title (A Side/B Side) | Yr | NM |
|---|---|---|---|
| ❑ LP-808 [M] | Chica-Boo | 1956 | 1000. |
| *—Black vinyl* | | | |
| ❑ LP-808 [M] | Chica-Boo | 1956 | 2000. |

*—Red vinyl; VG value 1000; VG+ value 1500*

BLACK & BLUE

| Number | Title (A Side/B Side) | Yr | NM |
|---|---|---|---|
| ❑ 33077 | Old Time Shuffle | 1977 | 12.00 |

IMPERIAL

| Number | Title (A Side/B Side) | Yr | NM |
|---|---|---|---|
| ❑ LP-9174 [M] | Chica-Boo | 1962 | 150.00 |
| ❑ LP-9175 [M] | After Hours | 1962 | 150.00 |
| ❑ LP-12174 [S] | Chica-Boo | 1962 | 200.00 |
| ❑ LP-12175 [S] | After Hours | 1962 | 200.00 |

SCORE

| Number | Title (A Side/B Side) | Yr | NM |
|---|---|---|---|
| ❑ SLP-4006 [M] | Lloyd Glenn | 1957 | 1000. |
| ❑ SLP-4020 [M] | After Hours | 1958 | 1000. |

SWING TIME

| Number | Title (A Side/B Side) | Yr | NM |
|---|---|---|---|
| ❑ 1901 [10] | Lloyd Glenn Presents All Time Favorites | 1954 | 3000. |

*—VG value 1500; VG+ value 2250*

## GLENN, TYREE

ROULETTE

| Number | Title (A Side/B Side) | Yr | NM |
|---|---|---|---|
| ❑ R-25009 [M] | Tyree Glenn at the Embers | 1957 | 40.00 |
| ❑ R-25050 [M] | Tyree Glenn at the Roundtable | 1959 | 40.00 |
| ❑ SR-25050 [S] | Tyree Glenn at the Roundtable | 1959 | 30.00 |
| ❑ R-25075 [M] | Try a Little Tenderness | 1959 | 40.00 |
| ❑ SR-25075 [S] | Try a Little Tenderness | 1959 | 30.00 |
| ❑ R-25115 [M] | Let's Have a Ball | 1960 | 25.00 |
| ❑ SR-25115 [S] | Let's Have a Ball | 1960 | 30.00 |
| ❑ R-25138 [M] | Tyree Glenn at London House in Chicago | 1961 | 20.00 |
| ❑ SR-25138 [S] | Tyree Glenn at London House in Chicago | 1961 | 25.00 |
| ❑ R-25184 [M] | The Trombone Artistry of Tyree Glenn | 1962 | 20.00 |
| ❑ SR-25184 [S] | The Trombone Artistry of Tyree Glenn | 1962 | 25.00 |

## GLITTERHOUSE

DYNOVOICE

| Number | Title (A Side/B Side) | Yr | NM |
|---|---|---|---|
| ❑ 31905 | Color Bland | 1968 | 20.00 |

## GLOBETROTTERS, THE

KIRSHNER

| Number | Title (A Side/B Side) | Yr | NM |
|---|---|---|---|
| ❑ KES-108 | The Globetrotters | 1970 | 20.00 |

## GLORY (2)

TEXAS REVOLUTION

| Number | Title (A Side/B Side) | Yr | NM |
|---|---|---|---|
| ❑ CFS-2531 | A Meat Music Sampler | 1969 | 100.00 |

## GO-GO'S, THE

RCA VICTOR

| Number | Title (A Side/B Side) | Yr | NM |
|---|---|---|---|
| ❑ LPM-2930 [M] | Swim with the Go-Go's | 1964 | 25.00 |
| ❑ LSP-2930 [S] | Swim with the Go-Go's | 1964 | 30.00 |

## GODCHAUX, KEITH AND DONNA

See KEITH AND DONNA.

## GODZ, THE

ESP-DISK'

| Number | Title (A Side/B Side) | Yr | NM |
|---|---|---|---|
| ❑ 1037 [M] | Contact High with the Godz | 1967 | 60.00 |
| ❑ S-1037 [S] | Contact High with the Godz | 1967 | 50.00 |
| ❑ 1047 | Godz 2 | 1968 | 50.00 |
| ❑ 1077 | Third Testament | 1969 | 50.00 |
| ❑ 2017 | Godzundheit | 1970 | 50.00 |

## GOLD, SANFORD

PRESTIGE

| Number | Title (A Side/B Side) | Yr | NM |
|---|---|---|---|
| ❑ PRLP-7019 [M] | Piano d'Or | 1956 | 60.00 |

## GOLDBERG, BARRY

ATCO

| Number | Title (A Side/B Side) | Yr | NM |
|---|---|---|---|
| ❑ SD 7040 | Barry Goldberg | 1974 | 12.00 |

BUDDAH

| Number | Title (A Side/B Side) | Yr | NM |
|---|---|---|---|
| ❑ BDM-1012 [M] | The Barry Goldberg Reunion | 1968 | 50.00 |
| *—White-label promo in stereo cover with "mono" sticker* | | | |
| ❑ BDS-5012 [S] | The Barry Goldberg Reunion | 1968 | 25.00 |
| ❑ BDS-5029 | Two Jews Blues | 1969 | 25.00 |
| ❑ BDS-5051 | Street Man | 1970 | 15.00 |
| ❑ BDS-5081 | Blast from My Past | 1974 | 15.00 |

EPIC

| Number | Title (A Side/B Side) | Yr | NM |
|---|---|---|---|
| ❑ LN 24199 [M] | Blowing My Mind | 1966 | 30.00 |
| ❑ BN 26199 [S] | Blowing My Mind | 1966 | 40.00 |

RECORD MAN

| Number | Title (A Side/B Side) | Yr | NM |
|---|---|---|---|
| ❑ CR 5015 | Barry Goldberg and Friends | 1972 | 15.00 |

## GOLDEBRIARS, THE

EPIC

| Number | Title (A Side/B Side) | Yr | NM |
|---|---|---|---|
| ❑ LN 24087 [M] | The Goldebriars | 1964 | 15.00 |
| ❑ LN 24114 [M] | Straight Ahead | 1964 | 15.00 |
| ❑ BN 26087 [S] | The Goldebriars | 1964 | 20.00 |
| ❑ BN 26114 [S] | Straight Ahead | 1964 | 20.00 |

## GOLDEN DAWN

INTERNATIONAL ARTISTS

| Number | Title (A Side/B Side) | Yr | NM |
|---|---|---|---|
| ❑ 4 | Power Plant | 1968 | 100.00 |
| ❑ 4 | Power Plant | 1979 | 15.00 |

*—Reissue with "Masterfonics" in trail-off wax*

## GOLDEN EARRING

ATLANTIC

| Number | Title (A Side/B Side) | Yr | NM |
|---|---|---|---|
| ❑ SD 8244 | Eight Miles High | 1970 | 25.00 |

CAPITOL

| Number | Title (A Side/B Side) | Yr | NM |
|---|---|---|---|
| ❑ ST-164 | Miracle Mirror | 1969 | 40.00 |
| ❑ ST 2823 [S] | Winter Harvest | 1967 | 25.00 |
| ❑ T 2823 [M] | Winter Harvest | 1967 | 50.00 |
| ❑ ST-11315 | The Golden Earring | 1974 | 12.00 |

DWARF

| Number | Title (A Side/B Side) | Yr | NM |
|---|---|---|---|
| ❑ 2000 | Golden Earring | 1971 | 25.00 |

MCA

| Number | Title (A Side/B Side) | Yr | NM |
|---|---|---|---|
| ❑ 703 | Grab It For a Second | 198? | 8.00 |

*—Reissue of 3057*

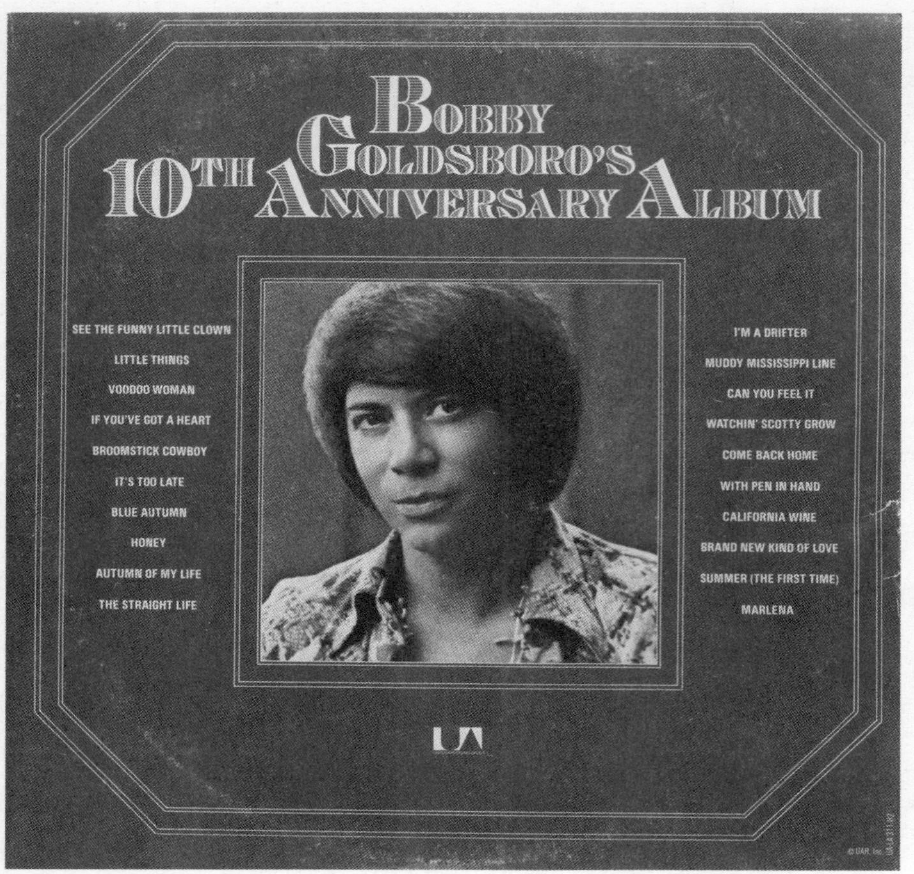


Bobby Goldsboro, *Bobby Goldsboro's 10th Anniversary Album,* United Artists UA-LA311-H2, 1974, 2 records, $20.

| Number | Title (A Side/B Side) | Yr | NM |
|---|---|---|---|
| ❑ 827 | Switch | 198? | 8.00 |
| *—Reissue of 2139* | | | |
| ❑ 2139 | Switch | 197? | 10.00 |
| *—Reissue of Track 2139* | | | |
| ❑ 2183 | To the Hilt | 1976 | 12.00 |
| ❑ 2254 | Mad Love | 1977 | 12.00 |
| ❑ 2352 | Moontan | 1978 | 10.00 |
| *—Reissue of Track 396* | | | |
| ❑ 3057 | Grab It For a Second | 1978 | 12.00 |
| ❑ 6004 [(2)] | Golden Earring Live! | 198? | 10.00 |
| *—Reissue of 8009* | | | |
| ❑ 8009 [(2)] | Golden Earring Live! | 1977 | 15.00 |
| ❑ 37172 | Moontan | 198? | 8.00 |
| *—Reissue of 2352* | | | |

POLYDOR

| Number | Title (A Side/B Side) | Yr | NM |
|---|---|---|---|
| ❑ PD-1-6223 | No Promises...No Debts | 1979 | 12.00 |
| ❑ PD-1-6303 | Long Blond Animal | 1980 | 12.00 |

TRACK

| Number | Title (A Side/B Side) | Yr | NM |
|---|---|---|---|
| ❑ 396 | Moontan | 1974 | 15.00 |
| *—Reissue cover with close-up of earring in ear* | | | |
| ❑ 396 | Moontan | 1974 | 25.00 |
| *—Original cover with nude dancer* | | | |
| ❑ 2139 | Switch | 1975 | 15.00 |

21 RECORDS

| Number | Title (A Side/B Side) | Yr | NM |
|---|---|---|---|
| ❑ T1-1-9004 | Cut | 1982 | 10.00 |
| ❑ T1-1-9008 | N.E.W.S. | 1984 | 10.00 |
| ❑ 90514 | The Hole | 1986 | 10.00 |
| ❑ 817585-1 | Cut | 1985 | 8.00 |
| *—Reissue* | | | |
| ❑ 823717-1 | Something Heavy Going Down —Live from the Twilight Zone | 1984 | 10.00 |

### GOLDEN GATE QUARTET, THE

COLUMBIA

| Number | Title (A Side/B Side) | Yr | NM |
|---|---|---|---|
| ❑ CL 6102 [10] | Golden Gate Spirituals | 1950 | 150.00 |

HARMONY

| Number | Title (A Side/B Side) | Yr | NM |
|---|---|---|---|
| ❑ HL 7018 [M] | The Golden Chariot | 195? | 25.00 |
| *—Second pressing has black labels* | | | |
| ❑ HL 7018 [M] | The Golden Chariot | 1957 | 80.00 |
| *—Original pressing has maroon labels* | | | |

MERCURY

| Number | Title (A Side/B Side) | Yr | NM |
|---|---|---|---|
| ❑ MG-25063 [10] | Spirituals | 1951 | 150.00 |

RCA CAMDEN

| Number | Title (A Side/B Side) | Yr | NM |
|---|---|---|---|
| ❑ CAL-308 [M] | The Golden Gate Quartet | 1956 | 80.00 |

### GOLDEN GATE STRINGS, THE

EPIC

| Number | Title (A Side/B Side) | Yr | NM |
|---|---|---|---|
| ❑ LN 24158 [M] | The Bob Dylan Song Book | 1965 | 12.00 |
| ❑ LN 24160 [M] | A String of Hits | 1965 | 12.00 |
| ❑ LN 24248 [M] | The Monkees Song Book | 1967 | 12.00 |
| ❑ BN 26158 [S] | The Bob Dylan Song Book | 1965 | 15.00 |
| ❑ BN 26160 [S] | A String of Hits | 1965 | 15.00 |
| ❑ BN 26248 [S] | The Monkees Song Book | 1967 | 15.00 |

### GOLDENROD

CHARTMAKER

| Number | Title (A Side/B Side) | Yr | NM |
|---|---|---|---|
| ❑ CSG-1101 | Goldenrod | 1968 | 200.00 |

### GOLDIE, DON

ARGO

| Number | Title (A Side/B Side) | Yr | NM |
|---|---|---|---|
| ❑ LP-708 [M] | Trumpet Caliente | 1963 | 25.00 |
| ❑ LPS-708 [S] | Trumpet Caliente | 1963 | 30.00 |
| ❑ LP-4010 [M] | Brilliant! | 1961 | 25.00 |
| ❑ LPS-4010 [S] | Brilliant! | 1961 | 30.00 |

VERVE

| Number | Title (A Side/B Side) | Yr | NM |
|---|---|---|---|
| ❑ V-8475 [M] | Trumpet Exodus | 1962 | 25.00 |
| ❑ V6-8475 [S] | Trumpet Exodus | 1962 | 30.00 |

### GOLDKETTE, JEAN

"X"

| Number | Title (A Side/B Side) | Yr | NM |
|---|---|---|---|
| ❑ LVA-3017 [10] | Jean Goldkette and His Orchestra Featuring Bix Beiderbecke | 1954 | 60.00 |

### GOLDSBORO, BOBBY

CURB

| Number | Title (A Side/B Side) | Yr | NM |
|---|---|---|---|
| ❑ JZ 36822 | Bobby Goldsboro | 1980 | 12.00 |
| ❑ FZ 37734 | Round-Up Saloon | 1982 | 10.00 |

EPIC

| Number | Title (A Side/B Side) | Yr | NM |
|---|---|---|---|
| ❑ PE 34703 | Goldsboro | 1977 | 12.00 |

LIBERTY

| Number | Title (A Side/B Side) | Yr | NM |
|---|---|---|---|
| ❑ LMAS-5502 | Bobby Goldsboro's Greatest Hits | 1981 | 8.00 |
| *—Reissue of United Artists 5502* | | | |
| ❑ LN-10007 | Bobby Goldsboro's 10th Anniversary Album, Volume 1 | 1981 | 8.00 |
| ❑ LN-10047 | Bobby Goldsboro's 10th Anniversary Album, Volume 2 | 1981 | 8.00 |
| ❑ LN-10114 | The Best of Bobby Goldsboro | 1981 | 8.00 |

SUNSET

| Number | Title (A Side/B Side) | Yr | NM |
|---|---|---|---|
| ❑ SUS-5236 | This Is Bobby Goldsboro | 1969 | 12.00 |
| ❑ SUS-5284 | Pledge of Love | 1970 | 12.00 |
| ❑ SUS-5313 | Autumn of My Life | 1971 | 12.00 |

UNITED ARTISTS

| Number | Title (A Side/B Side) | Yr | NM |
|---|---|---|---|
| ❑ UA-LA019-F | Brand New Kind of Love | 1972 | 15.00 |
| ❑ SP-58 [DJ] | The Bobby Goldsboro Family Album | 1971 | 50.00 |
| *—Promo-only compilation* | | | |
| ❑ UA-LA124-F | Summer (The First Time) | 1973 | 15.00 |
| ❑ UA-LA311-H2 [(2)] | Bobby Goldsboro's 10th Anniversary Album | 1974 | 20.00 |
| ❑ UA-LA424-G | Through the Eyes of a Man | 1975 | 12.00 |
| ❑ UA-LA639-G | Butterfly for Bucky | 1976 | 12.00 |
| ❑ UAL 3358 [M] | The Bobby Goldsbob Album | 1964 | 20.00 |
| ❑ UAL 3381 [M] | I Can't Stop Loving You | 1964 | 20.00 |
| ❑ UAL 3425 [M] | Little Things | 1965 | 20.00 |
| ❑ UAL 3471 [M] | Broomstick Cowboy | 1966 | 20.00 |
| ❑ UAL 3486 [M] | It's Too Late | 1966 | 20.00 |
| ❑ UAL 3552 [M] | Blue Autumn | 1967 | 20.00 |
| ❑ UAL 3561 [M] | Sold Goldsboro/Bobby Goldsboro's Greatest Hits | 1967 | 20.00 |
| ❑ UAL 3599 [M] | Romantic, Soulful, Wacky | 1967 | 20.00 |
| ❑ UAL 3642 [M] | Honey | 1968 | 40.00 |
| *—Some, if not all, copies of this have the title "Pledge of Love" on the label* | | | |
| ❑ UAS 5502 | Bobby Goldsboro's Greatest Hits | 1970 | 20.00 |
| ❑ UAS 5516 | Come Back Home | 1971 | 15.00 |
| ❑ UAS-5578 | California Wine | 1972 | 15.00 |
| ❑ UAS 6358 [S] | I Can't Stop Loving You | 1964 | 25.00 |
| ❑ UAS 6358 [S] | The Bobby Goldsbob Album | 1964 | 25.00 |
| ❑ UAS 6425 [S] | Little Things | 1965 | 25.00 |
| ❑ UAS 6471 [S] | Broomstick Cowboy | 1966 | 25.00 |
| ❑ UAS 6486 [S] | It's Too Late | 1966 | 25.00 |
| ❑ UAS 6552 [S] | Blue Autumn | 1967 | 25.00 |
| ❑ UAS 6561 [S] | Sold Goldsboro/Bobby Goldsboro's Greatest Hits | 1967 | 20.00 |
| ❑ UAS 6599 [S] | Romantic, Soulful, Wacky | 1967 | 20.00 |
| ❑ UAL 6642 [S] | Honey | 1968 | 30.00 |
| *—Early copies of this have the title "Pledge of Love" on the label* | | | |
| ❑ UAS 6642 [S] | Honey | 1968 | 20.00 |
| *—Later copies have the correct title "Honey" on the label* | | | |
| ❑ UAS 6657 | Word Pictures Featuring Autumn of My Life | 1968 | 20.00 |
| ❑ UAS 6704 | Today | 1969 | 20.00 |
| ❑ UAS 6735 | Muddy Mississippi Line | 1969 | 20.00 |
| ❑ UAS 6777 | We Gotta Start Lovin' | 1970 | 20.00 |
| ❑ UAS 6777 | Watching Scotty Grow | 1971 | 15.00 |
| *—Retitled version of above* | | | |
| ❑ ST-91460 | Honey | 1968 | 25.00 |
| *—Capitol Record Club edition* | | | |
| ❑ SKAO-91543 | Word Pictures Featuring Autumn of My Life | 1968 | 25.00 |
| *—Capitol Record Club edition* | | | |

### GOLDTONES, THE

LABREA

| Number | Title (A Side/B Side) | Yr | NM |
|---|---|---|---|
| ❑ L-8011 [M] | The Goldtones | 1961 | 40.00 |
| ❑ LS-8011 [S] | The Goldtones | 1961 | 50.00 |

### GOLIA, VINNY

NINE WINDS

| Number | Title (A Side/B Side) | Yr | NM |
|---|---|---|---|
| ❑ NW 0110 [(3)] | Compositions for Large Ensemble | 1984 | 20.00 |

### GOLLIWOGS, THE Early CREEDENCE CLEARWATER REVIVAL.

FANTASY

| Number | Title (A Side/B Side) | Yr | NM |
|---|---|---|---|
| ❑ F-9474 | Pre-Creedence | 1975 | 30.00 |
| *—Reissue of Fantasy and Scorpio sides* | | | |

### GOLSON, BENNY

ARGO

| Number | Title (A Side/B Side) | Yr | NM |
|---|---|---|---|
| ❑ LP-681 [M] | Take a Number from 1 to 10 | 1961 | 30.00 |
| ❑ LPS-681 [S] | Take a Number from 1 to 10 | 1961 | 40.00 |
| ❑ LP-716 [M] | Free | 1963 | 50.00 |
| ❑ LPS-716 [S] | Free | 1963 | 60.00 |

AUDIO FIDELITY

| Number | Title (A Side/B Side) | Yr | NM |
|---|---|---|---|
| ❑ AFSD-5978 [S] | Pop + Jazz = Swing | 1962 | 40.00 |
| ❑ AFSD-6150 [S] | Just Jazz | 1966 | 40.00 |

CONTEMPORARY

| Number | Title (A Side/B Side) | Yr | NM |
|---|---|---|---|
| ❑ C-3552 [M] | Benny Golson's New York Scene | 1958 | 80.00 |

JAZZLAND

| Number | Title (A Side/B Side) | Yr | NM |
|---|---|---|---|
| ❑ JLP-85 [M] | Reunion | 1962 | 60.00 |
| ❑ JLP-985 [S] | Reunion | 1962 | 50.00 |

MERCURY

| Number | Title (A Side/B Side) | Yr | NM |
|---|---|---|---|
| ❑ SR-60801 [S] | Turning Point | 1963 | 40.00 |

NEW JAZZ

| Number | Title (A Side/B Side) | Yr | NM |
|---|---|---|---|
| ❑ NJLP-8220 [M] | Groovin' with Golson | 1959 | 120.00 |
| *—Purple label* | | | |
| ❑ NJLP-8220 [M] | Groovin' with Golson | 1965 | 40.00 |
| *—Blue label, trident logo at right* | | | |
| ❑ NJLP-8235 [M] | Gone with Golson | 1960 | 120.00 |
| *—Purple label* | | | |



**Except when noted otherwise, VG = 25% of NM, and VG+ = 50% of NM. (Example: VG = $2.00, VG+ = $4.00 and NM = $8.00.)**

❑ NJLP-8235 [M] Gone with Golson 1965 40.00
*—Blue label, trident logo at right*
❑ NJLP-8248 [M] Gettin' With It 1960 120.00
*—Purple label*
❑ NJLP-8248 [M] Gettin' With It 1965 40.00
*—Blue label, trident logo at right*

PRESTIGE
❑ PRLP-7361 [M] Stockholm Sojourn 1965 30.00
❑ PRST-7361 [S] Stockholm Sojourn 1965 40.00

RIVERSIDE
❑ RLP 12-256 [M] The Modern Touch of Benny Golson 1957 100.00
❑ RLP 12-290 [M] The Other Side of Benny Golson 1958 100.00

UNITED ARTISTS
❑ UAL-4020 [M] Benny Golson and the Philadelphians 1959 100.00
❑ UAS-5020 [S] Benny Golson and the Philadelphians 1959 80.00

VERVE
❑ V-8710 [M] Tune In, Turn On 1967 40.00

**GOMEZ, VICENTE**

DECCA
❑ DL 4088 [M] Concerto Flamenco 1960 15.00
❑ DL 4156 [M] Rio Flameneo 1961 15.00
❑ DL 4312 [M] Guitar Extraordinary 1962 15.00
❑ DL 8017 [M] Spanish Guitar Recital 195? 30.00
*—Black label, silver print*
❑ DL 8439 [M] Romantic Guitar 1957 25.00
*—Black label, silver print*
❑ DL 8918 [M] Vicente Gomez 1959 20.00
*—Black label, silver print*
❑ DL 8965 [M] The Artistry of Vicente Gomez 1959 20.00
*—Black label, silver print*
❑ DL 74088 [S] Concerto Flamenco 1960 20.00
❑ DL 74156 [S] Rio Flamenco 1961 20.00
❑ DL 74312 [S] Guitar Extraordinary 1962 20.00
❑ DL 78918 [S] Vicente Gomez 1959 25.00
*—Maroon or black label*
❑ DL 78965 [S] The Artistry of Vicente Gomez 1959 25.00
*—Maroon or black label*

**GONSALVES, PAUL**

ARGO
❑ LP-626 [M] Cookin' 1958 50.00
❑ LPS-626 [S] Cookin' 1959 40.00

IMPULSE!
❑ A-41 [M] Cleopatra Feelin' Jazzy 1963 25.00
❑ AS-41 [S] Cleopatra Feelin' Jazzy 1963 30.00
❑ A-52 [M] Salt and Pepper 1963 25.00
❑ AS-52 [S] Salt and Pepper 1963 30.00
❑ A-55 [M] Tell It the Way It Is 1963 25.00
❑ AS-55 [S] Tell It the Way It Is 1963 30.00

JAZZLAND
❑ JLP-36 [M] Gettin' Together 1961 30.00
❑ JLP-936 [S] Gettin' Together 1961 40.00

**GONSALVES, VIRGIL**

LIBERTY
❑ LJH-6010 [M] Jazz San Francisco Style 1956 50.00

NOCTURNE
❑ NLP-8 [10] Virgil Gonsalves 1954 80.00

OMEGA
❑ OML-1047 [M] Jazz at Monterey 1959 40.00

**GONZALES, BABS**

DAUNTLESS
❑ DM-4311 [M] Sunday Afternoon at Small's Paradise 1963 40.00
❑ DS-6311 [S] Sunday Afternoon at Small's Paradise 1963 50.00

HOPE
❑ 001 [M] Voila! 1958 150.00

JARO
❑ JAM-5000 [M] Cool Philosophy 1959 80.00
❑ JAS-8000 [S] Cool Philosophy 1959 100.00

**GOO GOO DOLLS**

ENIGMA
❑ 7 73406-1 JED 1989 20.00

MERCENARY
❑ MER-2102 Goo Goo Dolls 1987 30.00

**GOOD AND PLENTY**

SENATE
❑ LP-21001 [M] The World of Good and Plenty 1967 30.00
❑ LPS-21001 [S] The World of Good and Plenty 1967 30.00

**GOOD GUYS, THE**

GNP CRESCENDO
❑ GNP-2001 [M] Sidewalk Surfing 1964 30.00
❑ GNPS-2001 [S] Sidewalk Surfing 1964 40.00

UNITED ARTISTS
❑ UAL-3370 [M] The Good Guys Sing 1964 15.00
❑ UAS-6370 [S] The Good Guys Sing 1964 20.00

**GOOD RATS, THE**

KAPP
❑ KS-3580 The Good Rats 1969 40.00

PASSPORT
❑ SP-20 [DJ] Rats the Way You Like It (Live) 1978 60.00
❑ PB-9825 From Rats to Riches 1978 12.00
❑ PB-9830 Birth Comes to Us All 1978 12.00

RAT CITY
❑ 998 [(2)] Live at Last 1979 15.00
❑ RCR-8001 Rat City in Blue 1975 20.00
❑ RCR-8002 Tasty 1978 12.00
❑ RCR-8003 Great American Music 1981 12.00

WARNER BROS.
❑ BS 2813 Tasty 1974 30.00

**GOOD TIMES, THE**

KAMA SUTRA
❑ KLP-8052 [M] The Good Times 1966 15.00
❑ KSLP-8052 [S] The Good Times 1966 20.00

**GOODEES, THE**

HIP
❑ HIS-7002 Candy Coated Goodees 1969 30.00

**GOODMAN, BENNY**

BRUNSWICK
❑ BL 54010 [M] Benny Goodman 1927-34 1954 30.00
❑ BL 58015 [10] Chicago Jazz Classics 1950 50.00

CAPITOL
❑ H 202 [10] Session for Six 1950 50.00
❑ H 295 [10] Easy Does It 1952 50.00
❑ H 343 [10] The Benny Goodman Trio 1952 50.00
❑ T 395 [M] Session for Six 1953 40.00
*—Turquoise label*
❑ T 395 [M] Session for Six 1958 20.00
*—Black label with colorband, Capitol logo on left*
❑ H 409 [10] The Benny Goodman Band 1953 50.00
❑ T 409 [M] The Benny Goodman Band 1953 40.00
*—Turquoise label*
❑ T 409 [M] The Benny Goodman Band 1958 20.00
*—Black label with colorband, Capitol logo on left*
❑ H 441 [10] The Goodman Touch 1953 50.00
❑ T 441 [M] The Goodman Touch 1953 40.00
*—Turquoise label*
❑ T 441 [M] The Goodman Touch 1958 20.00
*—Black label with colorband, Capitol logo on left*
❑ H 479 [10] Small Combo 1947 1954 50.00
❑ H1-565 [10] B.G. in Hi-Fi (Volume 1) 1955 30.00
❑ H2-565 [10] B.G. in Hi-Fi (Volume 2) 1955 30.00
❑ W 565 [M] B.G. in Hi-Fi 1955 40.00
*—Gray label*
❑ W 565 [M] B.G. in Hi-Fi 1958 20.00
*—Black label with colorband, Capitol logo on left*
❑ T 668 [M] Mostly Sextets 1956 30.00
*—Turquoise label*
❑ T 668 [M] Mostly Sextets 1958 20.00
*—Black label with colorband, Capitol logo on left*
❑ T 669 [M] Benny Goodman Combos 1956 30.00
*—Turquoise label*
❑ T 669 [M] Benny Goodman Combos 1958 20.00
*—Black label with colorband, Capitol logo on left*
❑ S 706 [M] Selections Featured in "The Benny Goodman Story" 1956 30.00
*—Turquoise label*
❑ S 706 [M] Selections Featured in "The Benny Goodman Story" 1958 20.00
*—Black label with colorband, Capitol logo on left*
❑ T 1514 [M] The Hits of Benny Goodman 1961 20.00
*—Black label with colorband, Capitol logo on left*

CENTURY
❑ 1150 The King of Swing Direct to Disc 1979 30.00
*—Direct-to-disc audiophile recording*

CHESS
❑ LP-1440 [DJ] Benny Rides Again 1960 100.00
*—Multi-color swirl vinyl*
❑ LP-1440 [M] Benny Rides Again 1960 50.00
❑ LPS-1440 [S] Benny Rides Again 1960 30.00
❑ CH-9161 Benny Rides Again 1984 10.00
*—Reissue*

CLASSICS RECORD LIBRARY
❑ RL-7673 [(3)M] An Album of Swing Classics 1967 50.00
❑ SRL-7673 [(3)S] An Album of Swing Classics 1967 40.00
*—Above two were compiled for Book-of-the-Month Club*

COLUMBIA
❑ C2L 16 [(2)M] Benny in Brussels 195? 40.00
*—Red and black label with six white "eye" logos*
❑ GL 102 [10] Let's Hear the Melody 1950 60.00
❑ CL 500 [M] Combos 1952 40.00
*—Maroon label with gold print*
❑ CL 500 [M] Combos 1955 30.00
*—Red and black label with six "eye" logos*
❑ GL 500 [M] Combos 1951 50.00
*—Black label, silver print*
❑ CL 501 [M] The Golden Era Series Presents Benny Goodman and His Orchestra 1952 40.00
*—Maroon label with gold print*
❑ CL 501 [M] The Golden Era Series Presents Benny Goodman and His Orchestra 1955 30.00
*—Red and black label with six "eye" logos*
❑ GL 501 [M] The Golden Era Series Presents Benny Goodman and His Orchestra 1951 50.00
*—Black label, silver print*
❑ CL 516 [M] The Benny Goodman Trio Plays for the Fletcher Henderson Fund 1953 40.00
*—Maroon label with gold print*
❑ CL 516 [M] The Benny Goodman Trio Plays for the Fletcher Henderson Fund 1955 30.00
*—Red and black label with six "eye" logos*
❑ GL 516 [M] The Benny Goodman Trio Plays for the Fletcher Henderson Fund 1952 50.00
*—Reissue of Martin Block 1000; black label, silver print*
❑ CL 523 [M] Benny Goodman Presents Eddie Sauter Arrangements 1953 40.00
*—Maroon label with gold print*
❑ CL 523 [M] Benny Goodman Presents Eddie Sauter Arrangements 1955 30.00
*—Red and black label with six "eye" logos*
❑ GL 523 [M] Benny Goodman Presents Eddie Sauter Arrangements 1953 50.00
*—Black label, silver print*
❑ CL 524 [M] Benny Goodman Presents Fletcher Henderson Arrangements 1953 30.00
*—Red and black label with six "eye" logos*
❑ CL 524 [M] Benny Goodman Presents Fletcher Henderson Arrangements 1954 40.00
*—Maroon label with gold print*
❑ GL 524 [M] Benny Goodman Presents Fletcher Henderson Arrangements 1953 50.00
*—Black label, silver print*
❑ CL 534 [M] Benny Goodman and His Orchestra 1953 40.00
*—Maroon label with gold print*
❑ CL 534 [M] Benny Goodman and His Orchestra 1955 30.00
*—Red and black label with six "eye" logos*
❑ CL 552 [M] The New Benny Goodman Sextet 1954 40.00
*—Maroon label with gold print*
❑ CL 552 [M] The New Benny Goodman Sextet 1955 30.00
*—Red and black label with six "eye" logos*
❑ CL 652 [M] The Benny Goodman Sextet and Orchestra with Charlie Christian 1955 30.00
*—Red and black label with six "eye" logos*
❑ CL 652 [M] The Benny Goodman Sextet and Orchestra with Charlie Christian 1963 20.00
*—Red label with "Guaranteed High Fidelity" or "Mono" at bottom*
❑ CL 814 [M] Carnegie Hall Jazz Concert, Volume 1 1956 30.00
*—Red and black label with six "eye" logos*
❑ CL 814 [M] Carnegie Hall Jazz Concert, Volume 1 1963 20.00
*—Red label with "Guaranteed High Fidelity" or "Mono" at bottom*
❑ CL 815 [M] Carnegie Hall Jazz Concert, Volume 2 1956 30.00
*—Red and black label with six "eye" logos*
❑ CL 815 [M] Carnegie Hall Jazz Concert, Volume 2 1963 20.00
*—Red label with "Guaranteed High Fidelity" or "Mono" at bottom*
❑ CL 815 [M] Carnegie Hall Jazz Concert, Volume 2 197? 12.00
*—Orange label with "Mono" under "CL 815" at left*
❑ CL 816 [M] Carnegie Hall Jazz Concert, Volume 3 1956 30.00
*—Red and black label with six "eye" logos*
❑ CL 816 [M] Carnegie Hall Jazz Concert, Volume 3 1963 20.00
*—Red label with "Guaranteed High Fidelity" or "Mono" at bottom*
❑ CL 817 [M] The King of Swing, Volume 1 1956 30.00
❑ CL 818 [M] The King of Swing, Volume 2 1956 30.00
❑ CL 819 [M] The King of Swing, Volume 3 1956 30.00
❑ CL 820 [M] The Great Benny Goodman 1956 30.00
*—Red and black label with six "eye" logos*
❑ CL 820 [M] The Great Benny Goodman 1963 20.00
*—Red label with "Guaranteed High Fidelity" or "Mono" at bottom*
❑ CL 821 [M] Vintage Goodman 1956 30.00
❑ CL 1247 [M] Benny in Brussels, Vol. I 1958 30.00
❑ CL 1248 [M] Benny in Brussels, Vol. II 1958 30.00
❑ CL 1324 [M] The Happy Session 1959 30.00
❑ CL 1579 [M] Benny Goodman Swings Again 1960 30.00
❑ CL 2533 [10] Benny at the Ballroom 1955 40.00
*—Retitled reissue of 6100*
❑ CL 2564 [10] The B.G. Six 1955 40.00
*—Retitled reissue of 6052*

| Number | Title (A Side/B Side) | Yr | NM |
|---|---|---|---|
| ❑ CL 6033 [10] | Benny Goodman and Peggy Lee | 1949 | 80.00 |
| ❑ CL 6048 [10] | Dance Parade | 1949 | 50.00 |
| ❑ CL 6052 [10] | Goodman Sextet Session | 1949 | 50.00 |
| ❑ CL 6100 [10] | Dance Parade, Volume 2 | 1950 | 50.00 |
| ❑ CL 6302 [10] | Let's Hear the Melody | 1951 | 50.00 |
| *—Reissue of GL 102* | | | |
| ❑ CS 8075 [S] | Benny in Brussels, Vol. I | 1959 | 40.00 |
| ❑ CS 8076 [S] | Benny in Brussels, Vol. II | 1959 | 40.00 |
| ❑ CS 8129 [S] | The Happy Session | 1959 | 25.00 |
| ❑ CS 8379 [S] | Benny Goodman Swings Again | 1960 | 25.00 |
| ❑ XTV 28995/6 [M] | Swing Into Spring | 1959 | 20.00 |
| *—Special item made for Texaco service stations* | | | |
| **COLUMBIA MASTERWORKS** | | | |
| ❑ OSL 160 [(2)M] | The Famous 1938 Carnegie Hall Jazz Concert | 1956 | 75.00 |
| *—Gray and black labels with six "eye" logos* | | | |
| ❑ OSL 160 [(2)M] | The Famous 1938 Carnegie Hall Jazz Concert | 1963 | 40.00 |
| *—Gray labels with "Columbia" at top* | | | |
| ❑ OSL 160 [(2)M] | The Famous 1938 Carnegie Hall Jazz Concert | 1970 | 20.00 |
| *—Olive labels with "Columbia" circling edge* | | | |
| ❑ SL 160 [(2)M] | The Famous 1938 Carnegie Hall Jazz Concert | 1950 | 100.00 |
| *—Green labels* | | | |
| ❑ SL 176 [(6)M] | King of Swing | 1950 | 150.00 |
| ❑ OSL 180 [(2)M] | The King of Swing | 1956 | 75.00 |
| *—Gray and black labels with six "eye" logos* | | | |
| ❑ OSL 180 [(2)M] | The King of Swing | 1963 | 40.00 |
| *—Gray labels with "Columbia" at top* | | | |
| ❑ SL 180 [(2)M] | 1937-38 Jazz Concert No. 2 | 1950 | 75.00 |
| ❑ ML 4358 [M] | Carnegie Hall Jazz Concert, Volume 1 | 1950 | 40.00 |
| ❑ ML 4359 [M] | Carnegie Hall Jazz Concert, Volume 2 | 1950 | 40.00 |
| ❑ ML 4590 [M] | 1937-38 Jazz Concert No. 2, Volume 1 | 1950 | 40.00 |
| ❑ ML 4591 [M] | 1937-38 Jazz Concert No. 2, Volume 2 | 1950 | 40.00 |
| ❑ ML 4613 [M] | King of Swing, Volume 1 | 1950 | 40.00 |
| ❑ ML 4614 [M] | King of Swing, Volume 2 | 1950 | 40.00 |
| ❑ MS 6805 [S] | Meeting at the Summit | 1961 | 20.00 |
| *—With the Columbia Jazz Combo and the Columbia Orchestra* | | | |
| **COLUMBIA MUSICAL TREASURY** | | | |
| ❑ P4M 5678 [(4)] | The Best of Benny Goodman | 197? | 30.00 |
| *—Issued by Columbia House* | | | |
| **DECCA** | | | |
| ❑ DXB 188 [(2)M] | The Benny Goodman Story | 1956 | 60.00 |
| *—Black label, silver print* | | | |
| ❑ DXB 188 [(2)M] | The Benny Goodman Story | 1961 | 40.00 |
| *—Black label with color bars* | | | |
| ❑ DL 8252 [M] | The Benny Goodman Story, Volume 1 | 1956 | 30.00 |
| *—Black label, silver print* | | | |
| ❑ DL 8252 [M] | The Benny Goodman Story, Volume 1 | 1961 | 20.00 |
| *—Black label with color bars* | | | |
| ❑ DL 8253 [M] | The Benny Goodman Story, Volume 2 | 1956 | 30.00 |
| *—Black label, silver print* | | | |
| ❑ DL 8253 [M] | The Benny Goodman Story, Volume 2 | 1961 | 20.00 |
| *—Black label with color bars* | | | |
| **HARMONY** | | | |
| ❑ HL 7005 [M] | Peggy Lee Sings with Benny Goodman | 1957 | 20.00 |
| **MARTIN BLOCK** | | | |
| ❑ MB-1000 [M] | The Benny Goodman Trio Plays for the Fletcher Henderson Fund | 1951 | 60.00 |
| **MGM** | | | |
| ❑ 3E-9 [(3)M] | The Benny Goodman Treasure Chest | 1959 | 150.00 |
| ❑ E-3788 [M] | Performance Recordings, Volume 1 | 1959 | 25.00 |
| ❑ E-3789 [M] | Performance Recordings, Volume 2 | 1959 | 25.00 |
| ❑ E-3790 [M] | Performance Recordings, Volume 3 | 1959 | 25.00 |
| ❑ E-3810 [M] | The Sound of Music | 1960 | 20.00 |
| ❑ SE-3810 [S] | The Sound of Music | 1960 | 25.00 |
| **MOSAIC** | | | |
| ❑ MQ6-148 [(6)] | The Complete Capitol Small Group Recordings of Benny Goodman 1944-1955 | 199? | 100.00 |
| **RCA VICTOR** | | | |
| ❑ WPT 12 [10] | Benny Goodman | 1951 | 50.00 |
| ❑ LPT-17 [10] | A Treasury of Immortal Performances | 1951 | 50.00 |
| ❑ WPT 26 [10] | Immortal Performances | 1952 | 50.00 |
| ❑ LPT-1005 [M] | Benny Goodman | 1954 | 40.00 |
| ❑ LPM-1099 [M] | The Golden Age of Benny Goodman | 1956 | 40.00 |
| ❑ LPM-1226 [M] | The Benny Goodman Trio/ Quartet/Quintet | 1956 | 40.00 |
| ❑ LPM-1239 [M] | This Is Benny Goodman | 1956 | 40.00 |
| ❑ LPM-2247 [M] | The Kingdom of Swing | 1960 | 20.00 |
| ❑ LSP-2247 [S] | The Kingdom of Swing | 1960 | 25.00 |
| ❑ LSP-2698 [S] | Together Again | 1964 | 20.00 |
| ❑ LPT-3004 [10] | Benny Goodman Quartet | 1952 | 50.00 |
| ❑ LPT-3056 [10] | This Is Benny Goodman and His Orchestra | 1954 | 50.00 |
| ❑ LOC-6008 [(2)M] | Benny Goodman in Moscow | 1962 | 20.00 |
| ❑ LSO-6008 [(2)S] | Benny Goodman in Moscow | 1962 | 25.00 |
| ❑ LPT-6703 [(5)M] | The Golden Age of Swing | 1956 | 600.00 |
| *—Five-record set in white vinyl binder with bound-in booklet* | | | |
| **SUNBEAM** | | | |
| ❑ 116 | At the Madhattan Room Oct. 13, 1937 | 197? | 12.00 |
| ❑ 128/32 [(5)] | From the Congress Hotel, Chicago, 1935-36 | 197? | 25.00 |
| **WESTINGHOUSE** | | | |
| ❑ (no #) [(5)M] | Benny in Brussels | 1958 | 100.00 |
| ❑ XTV 27713/4 [M] | Benny Goodman Plays World Favorites in High Fidelity | 1958 | 30.00 |
| *—No number on cover or label; these numbers come from the trail-off wax* | | | |

## GOODMAN, DICKIE

| Number | Title (A Side/B Side) | Yr | NM |
|---|---|---|---|
| **CASH** | | | |
| ❑ CR 6000 | Mr. Jaws and Other Fables | 1975 | 25.00 |
| **COMET** | | | |
| ❑ 69 | My Son, the Joke | 1963 | 40.00 |
| **IX CHAINS** | | | |
| ❑ NCS 9000 | The Original Flying Saucers | 1973 | 40.00 |
| **RHINO** | | | |
| ❑ RNLP-811 | Dickie Goodman's Greatest Hits | 1983 | 15.00 |
| **RORI** | | | |
| ❑ 3301 | The Many Heads of Dickie Goodman | 1962 | 80.00 |

## GOODMAN, DODY

| Number | Title (A Side/B Side) | Yr | NM |
|---|---|---|---|
| **CORAL** | | | |
| ❑ CRL 57196 [M] | Dody Goodman Sings? | 1958 | 30.00 |

## GOODWIN, RON

| Number | Title (A Side/B Side) | Yr | NM |
|---|---|---|---|
| **CAPITOL** | | | |
| ❑ T 10078 [M] | It Can't Be Wrong | 1957 | 20.00 |
| ❑ T 10177 [M] | Swinging Sweethearts | 1958 | 20.00 |
| ❑ ST 10188 [S] | Music in Orbit | 1958 | 40.00 |
| ❑ T 10188 [M] | Music in Orbit | 1958 | 30.00 |
| ❑ ST 10251 [S] | Music for an Arabian Night | 1959 | 30.00 |
| ❑ T 10251 [M] | Music for an Arabian Night | 1959 | 25.00 |
| ❑ SP-10560 | Jet Flight to Beirut | 196? | 20.00 |
| ❑ ST-11012 | Ron Goodwin Plays Someone Named Burt Bacharach | 1972 | 10.00 |

## GORDIAN KNOT, THE

| Number | Title (A Side/B Side) | Yr | NM |
|---|---|---|---|
| **VERVE** | | | |
| ❑ V-5062 [M] | Tones | 1968 | 30.00 |
| *—White label promo only (no stock copies were issued in mono)* | | | |
| ❑ V6-5062 [S] | Tones | 1968 | 15.00 |

## GORDON, BARRY

| Number | Title (A Side/B Side) | Yr | NM |
|---|---|---|---|
| **UNITED ARTISTS** | | | |
| ❑ UAS 6491 [S] | Yes Sir, That's My Baby | 1966 | 20.00 |

## GORDON, BOB

| Number | Title (A Side/B Side) | Yr | NM |
|---|---|---|---|
| **PACIFIC JAZZ** | | | |
| ❑ PJLP-12 [10] | Meet Mr. Gordon | 1954 | 200.00 |
| **TAMPA** | | | |
| ❑ TP-26 [M] | Jazz Impressions | 1957 | 120.00 |
| *—Red vinyl* | | | |
| ❑ TP-26 [M] | Jazz Impressions | 1958 | 60.00 |
| *—Black vinyl* | | | |

## GORDON, BOB/CLIFFORD BROWN

| Number | Title (A Side/B Side) | Yr | NM |
|---|---|---|---|
| **PACIFIC JAZZ** | | | |
| ❑ PJ-3 [M] | Jazz Immortal | 1960 | 50.00 |
| ❑ PJ-1214 [M] | The Bob Gordon Quintet/The Clifford Brown Ensemble | 1956 | 100.00 |

## GORDON, DEXTER

| Number | Title (A Side/B Side) | Yr | NM |
|---|---|---|---|
| **BETHLEHEM** | | | |
| ❑ BCP-36 [M] | Daddy Plays the Horn | 1956 | 120.00 |
| **BLUE NOTE** | | | |
| ❑ BLP-4077 [M] | Doin' Allright | 1961 | 250.00 |
| *—With W. 63rd St. addresss on label* | | | |
| ❑ BLP-4077 [M] | Doin' Allright | 1963 | 150.00 |
| *—With "New York, USA" address on label* | | | |
| ❑ BLP-4083 [M] | Dexter Calling | 1961 | 200.00 |
| *—With W. 63rd St. address on label* | | | |
| ❑ BLP-4083 [M] | Dexter Calling | 1963 | 150.00 |
| *—With "New York, USA" address on label* | | | |
| ❑ BLP-4112 [M] | Go | 1962 | 150.00 |
| *—With "New York, USA" address on label* | | | |
| ❑ BLP-4133 [M] | A Swingin' Affair | 1963 | 120.00 |
| *—With "New York, USA" address on label* | | | |
| ❑ BLP-4146 [M] | Our Man in Paris | 1963 | 80.00 |
| *—With "New York, USA" address on label* | | | |
| ❑ BLP-4176 [M] | One Flight Up | 1964 | 80.00 |
| *—With "New York, USA" address on label* | | | |
| ❑ BLP-4204 [M] | Gettin' Around | 1965 | 80.00 |
| *—With "New York, USA" address on label* | | | |
| ❑ BST-84077 [S] | Doin' Allright | 1961 | 300.00 |
| *—With W. 63rd St. addresss on label* | | | |
| ❑ BST-84077 [S] | Doin' Allright | 1963 | 200.00 |
| *—With "New York, USA" address on label* | | | |
| ❑ BST-84083 [S] | Dexter Calling | 1961 | 200.00 |
| *—With W. 63rd St. address on label* | | | |
| ❑ BST-84083 [S] | Dexter Calling | 1963 | 150.00 |
| *—With "New York, USA" address on label* | | | |
| ❑ BST-84112 [S] | Go | 1962 | 120.00 |
| *—With "New York, USA" address on label* | | | |
| ❑ BST-84133 | A Swingin' Affair | 199? | 30.00 |
| *—Classic Records 180-gram audiophile reissue* | | | |
| ❑ BST-84133 [S] | A Swingin' Affair | 1963 | 150.00 |
| *—With "New York, USA" address on label* | | | |
| ❑ BST-84146 [S] | Our Man in Paris | 1963 | 100.00 |
| *—With "New York, USA" address on label* | | | |
| ❑ BST-84176 [S] | One Flight Up | 1964 | 80.00 |
| *—With "New York, USA" address on label* | | | |
| ❑ BST-84204 [S] | Gettin' Around | 1965 | 80.00 |
| *—With "New York, USA" address on label* | | | |
| **COLUMBIA** | | | |
| ❑ JC 36853 | Gotham City | 2000 | 12.00 |
| *—180-gram reissue* | | | |
| **DIAL** | | | |
| ❑ LP-204 [10] | Dexter Gordon Quintet | 1950 | 400.00 |
| **DOOTO** | | | |
| ❑ DL-207 [M] | Dexter Blows Hot and Cool | 196? | 400.00 |
| *—Maroon label with "Dooto"* | | | |
| **DOOTONE** | | | |
| ❑ DL-207 [M] | Dexter Blows Hot and Cool | 1956 | 2000. |
| *—Red vinyl* | | | |
| ❑ DL-207 [M] | Dexter Blows Hot and Cool | 1957 | 1200. |
| *—Black vinyl; "Dootone" label with no zip code* | | | |
| ❑ DL-207 [M] | Dexter Blows Hot and Cool | 197? | 100.00 |
| *—Maroon label with zip code* | | | |
| **JAZZLAND** | | | |
| ❑ JLP-29 [M] | The Resurgence of Dexter Gordon | 1960 | 50.00 |
| ❑ JLP-929 [S] | The Resurgence of Dexter Gordon | 1960 | 60.00 |
| **PRESTIGE** | | | |
| ❑ PRST-7623 | The Tower of Power | 1969 | 20.00 |
| ❑ PRST-7680 | More Power | 1969 | 20.00 |
| ❑ PRST-7763 | A Day in Copenhagen | 1970 | 20.00 |
| ❑ PRST-7829 | Panther! | 1971 | 20.00 |
| **SAVOY** | | | |
| ❑ MG-9003 [10] | All Star Series — Dexter Gordon | 1951 | 250.00 |
| ❑ MG-9016 [10] | New Trends in Modern Jazz, Volume 3 | 1952 | 250.00 |
| ❑ MG-12130 [M] | Dexter Rides Again | 1958 | 100.00 |

## GORDON, DEXTER/HOWARD MCGHEE

| Number | Title (A Side/B Side) | Yr | NM |
|---|---|---|---|
| **JAZZTONE** | | | |
| ❑ J-1235 [M] | The Chase | 1956 | 40.00 |

## GORDON, HONI

| Number | Title (A Side/B Side) | Yr | NM |
|---|---|---|---|
| **PRESTIGE** | | | |
| ❑ PRLP-7230 [M] | Honi Gordon Sings | 1962 | 40.00 |
| ❑ PRST-7230 [S] | Honi Gordon Sings | 1962 | 50.00 |

## GORDON, JOE

| Number | Title (A Side/B Side) | Yr | NM |
|---|---|---|---|
| **CONTEMPORARY** | | | |
| ❑ M-3597 [M] | Lookin' Good | 1961 | 30.00 |
| ❑ S-7597 [S] | Lookin' Good | 1961 | 40.00 |
| **EMARCY** | | | |
| ❑ MG-26046 [10] | Introducing Joe Gordon | 1954 | 150.00 |
| ❑ MG-36025 [M] | Introducing Joe Gordon | 1955 | 100.00 |

## GORDON, JOHN

| Number | Title (A Side/B Side) | Yr | NM |
|---|---|---|---|
| **STRATA-EAST** | | | |
| ❑ SES-19760 | Step by Step | 197? | 20.00 |

## GORDON, JUSTIN

| Number | Title (A Side/B Side) | Yr | NM |
|---|---|---|---|
| **DOT** | | | |
| ❑ DLP-3214 [M] | Justin Gordon Swings | 1959 | 40.00 |

## GORDON, KELLY

| Number | Title (A Side/B Side) | Yr | NM |
|---|---|---|---|
| **CAPITOL** | | | |
| ❑ ST-201 | Defunked | 1969 | 20.00 |

## GORDON, ROBERT

| Number | Title (A Side/B Side) | Yr | NM |
|---|---|---|---|
| **PRIVATE STOCK** | | | |
| ❑ PS-2030 | Robert Gordon with Link Wray | 1977 | 16.00 |
| *—Formerly with Tuff Darts* | | | |
| ❑ PS-7008 | Fresh Fish Special | 1978 | 16.00 |
| **RCA VICTOR** | | | |
| ❑ AFL1-3294 | Rock Billy Boogie | 1979 | 12.00 |
| ❑ AFL1-3294 | Rock Billy Boogie | 1979 | 20.00 |
| *—Original pressing on white vinyl* | | | |
| ❑ AFL1-3296 | Robert Gordon with Link Wray | 1979 | 12.00 |
| *—Reissue* | | | |



**Except when noted otherwise, VG = 25% of NM, and VG+ = 50% of NM. (Example: VG = $2.00, VG+ = $4.00 and NM = $8.00.)**

| Number | Title (A Side/B Side) | Yr | NM |
|---|---|---|---|
| ❑ AFL1-3299 | Fresh Fish Special | 1979 | 12.00 |
| *—Reissue* | | | |
| ❑ DJL1-3411 [DJ] | Essential Robert Gordon | 1979 | 30.00 |
| *—Promo-only live album with tracks from Tuff Darts* | | | |
| ❑ AFL1-3523 | Bad Boy | 1980 | 12.00 |
| ❑ AFL1-3773 | Are You Gonna Be the One | 1981 | 12.00 |
| ❑ AFL1-4380 | Too Fast to Live, Too Young to Die | 1982 | 12.00 |

### GORDON 'N ROGERS' INTER-URBAN ELECTRIC A&E PIT CREW & RHYTHM BAND

CAPITOL

| Number | Title (A Side/B Side) | Yr | NM |
|---|---|---|---|
| ❑ STAO-276 | Bug In! | 1969 | 20.00 |

### GORE, CHARLIE

AUDIO LAB

| Number | Title (A Side/B Side) | Yr | NM |
|---|---|---|---|
| ❑ AL-1526 [M] | The Country Gentleman | 1959 | 200.00 |

### GORE, LESLEY

A&M

| Number | Title (A Side/B Side) | Yr | NM |
|---|---|---|---|
| ❑ SP-4564 | Love Me by Name | 1975 | 15.00 |

MERCURY

| Number | Title (A Side/B Side) | Yr | NM |
|---|---|---|---|
| ❑ ML-8016 | I'll Cry If I Want To | 1980 | 10.00 |
| *—Reissue of 60805* | | | |
| ❑ MG 20805 [M] | I'll Cry If I Want To | 1963 | 30.00 |
| *—With no blurb for "It's My Party"* | | | |
| ❑ MG 20805 [M] | I'll Cry If I Want To | 1964 | 20.00 |
| *—With blurb for "It's My Party"* | | | |
| ❑ MG 20849 [M] | Lesley Gore Sings of Mixed-Up Hearts | 1963 | 30.00 |
| ❑ MG 20901 [M] | Boys, Boys, Boys | 1964 | 30.00 |
| ❑ MG 20943 [M] | Girl Talk | 1964 | 30.00 |
| ❑ MG 21024 [M] | The Golden Hits of Lesley Gore | 1965 | 30.00 |
| ❑ MG 21042 [M] | My Town, My Guy & Me | 1965 | 30.00 |
| ❑ MG 21066 [M] | All About Love | 1966 | 30.00 |
| ❑ MG 21120 [M] | California Nights | 1967 | 30.00 |
| ❑ SR 60805 [S] | I'll Cry If I Want To | 1963 | 40.00 |
| *—With no blurb for "It's My Party"* | | | |
| ❑ SR 60805 [S] | I'll Cry If I Want To | 1964 | 30.00 |
| *—With blurb for "It's My Party"* | | | |
| ❑ SR 60849 [S] | Lesley Gore Sings of Mixed-Up Hearts | 1963 | 40.00 |
| ❑ SR 60901 [S] | Boys, Boys, Boys | 1964 | 40.00 |
| ❑ SR 60943 [S] | Girl Talk | 1964 | 40.00 |
| ❑ SR 61024 [S] | The Golden Hits of Lesley Gore | 196? | 15.00 |
| *—Reissues have 10 tracks* | | | |
| ❑ SR 61024 [S] | The Golden Hits of Lesley Gore | 1965 | 40.00 |
| *—Originals have 12 tracks* | | | |
| ❑ SR 61042 [S] | My Town, My Guy & Me | 1965 | 40.00 |
| ❑ SR 61066 [S] | All About Love | 1966 | 40.00 |
| *—Stereo version has a different cover and liner notes than the mono version* | | | |
| ❑ SR 61120 [S] | California Nights | 1967 | 40.00 |
| ❑ SR 61185 | Golden Hits Vol. 2 | 1968 | 40.00 |
| ❑ 810370-1 | The Golden Hits of Lesley Gore | 1983 | 10.00 |
| *—Reissue of 61024* | | | |

MOWEST

| Number | Title (A Side/B Side) | Yr | NM |
|---|---|---|---|
| ❑ MW 117L | Someplace Else Now | 1972 | 15.00 |

RHINO

| Number | Title (A Side/B Side) | Yr | NM |
|---|---|---|---|
| ❑ RNFP-71496 [(2)] | The Lesley Gore Anthology (1963-1968) | 1986 | 15.00 |

WING

| Number | Title (A Side/B Side) | Yr | NM |
|---|---|---|---|
| ❑ PRW-2-119 [(2)] | The Sound of Young Love | 1969 | 20.00 |
| ❑ SRW-16350 | Girl Talk | 1968 | 15.00 |
| ❑ SRW-16382 | Love, Love, Love | 1968 | 15.00 |

### GORME, EYDIE

ABC-PARAMOUNT

| Number | Title (A Side/B Side) | Yr | NM |
|---|---|---|---|
| ❑ 150 [M] | Eydie Gorme | 1957 | 30.00 |
| ❑ 192 [M] | Eydie Swings the Blues | 1957 | 30.00 |
| ❑ 218 [M] | Eydie Gorme Vamps the Roaring 20's | 1958 | 30.00 |
| ❑ S-218 [S] | Eydie Gorme Vamps the Roaring 20's | 196? | 12.00 |
| ❑ 246 [M] | Eydie in Love | 1958 | 30.00 |
| ❑ S-246 [S] | Eydie in Love | 196? | 12.00 |
| ❑ 254 [M] | Show Stoppers | 1959 | 25.00 |
| ❑ S-254 [S] | Show Stoppers | 1959 | 30.00 |
| ❑ 273 [M] | Love Is a Season | 1959 | 25.00 |
| ❑ S-273 [S] | Love Is a Season | 1959 | 30.00 |
| ❑ 307 [M] | On Stage | 1959 | 25.00 |
| ❑ S-307 [S] | On Stage | 1959 | 30.00 |
| ❑ 343 [M] | Eydie in Dixieland | 1960 | 25.00 |
| ❑ S-343 [S] | Eydie in Dixieland | 1960 | 30.00 |
| ❑ 512 [M] | The Best of Romance, Ballads, Blues, Dixieland, Roaring 20's, Showstoppers | 1965 | 15.00 |
| ❑ S-512 [S] | The Best of Romance, Ballads, Blues, Dixieland, Roaring 20's, Showstoppers | 1965 | 20.00 |

COLUMBIA

| Number | Title (A Side/B Side) | Yr | NM |
|---|---|---|---|
| ❑ CL 2012 [M] | Blame It on the Bossa Nova | 1963 | 15.00 |
| ❑ CL 2065 [M] | Let the Good Times Roll | 1963 | 15.00 |
| ❑ CL 2120 [M] | Gorme Country Style | 1964 | 15.00 |
| ❑ CL 2203 [M] | Amor | 1964 | 15.00 |
| ❑ CL 2300 [M] | The Sound of Music (And Other Broadway Hits) | 1965 | 15.00 |

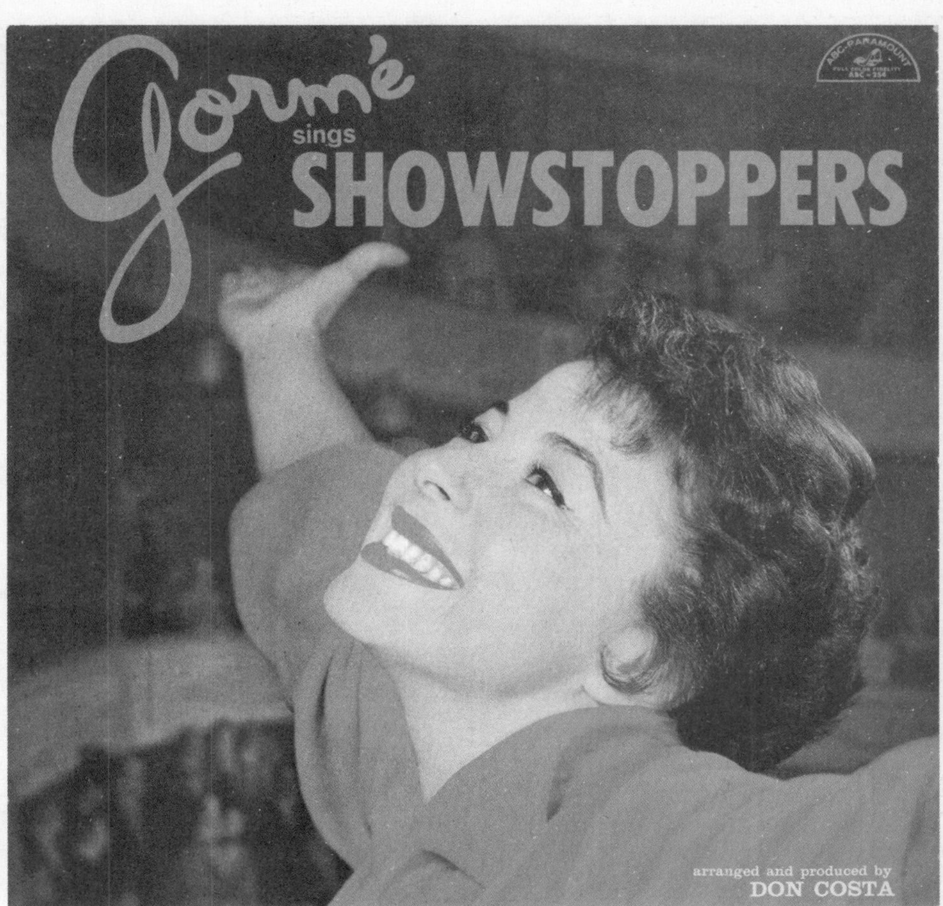


Eydie Gorme, *Showstoppers,* ABC-Paramount ABC-254, 1959, mono, $25.

| Number | Title (A Side/B Side) | Yr | NM |
|---|---|---|---|
| ❑ CL 2376 [M] | More Amor | 1965 | 15.00 |
| ❑ CL 2476 [M] | Don't Go to Strangers | 1966 | 15.00 |
| ❑ CL 2557 [M] | Navidad Means Christmas | 1966 | 15.00 |
| *—With Trio Los Panchos* | | | |
| ❑ CL 2594 [M] | Softly, As I Leave You | 1967 | 15.00 |
| ❑ CL 2764 [M] | Eydie Gorme's Greatest Hits | 1967 | 20.00 |
| ❑ CS 8812 [S] | Blame It on the Bossa Nova | 1963 | 20.00 |
| ❑ CS 8865 [S] | Let the Good Times Roll | 1963 | 20.00 |
| ❑ CS 8920 [S] | Gorme Country Style | 1964 | 20.00 |
| ❑ CS 9003 [S] | Amor | 1964 | 20.00 |
| ❑ PC 9003 | Amor | 198? | 8.00 |
| *—Budget-line reissue* | | | |
| ❑ CS 9100 [S] | The Sound of Music (And Other Broadway Hits) | 1965 | 20.00 |
| ❑ CS 9176 [S] | More Amor | 1965 | 20.00 |
| ❑ CS 9276 [S] | Don't Go to Strangers | 1966 | 20.00 |
| ❑ CS 9357 [S] | Navidad Means Christmas | 1966 | 20.00 |
| *—With Trio Los Panchos* | | | |
| ❑ CS 9394 [S] | Softly, As I Leave You | 1967 | 20.00 |
| ❑ CS 9564 [S] | Eydie Gorme's Greatest Hits | 1967 | 15.00 |
| ❑ PC 9564 | Eydie Gorme's Greatest Hits | 198? | 8.00 |
| *—Budget-line reissue* | | | |
| ❑ CS 9652 [M] | The Look of Love | 1968 | 30.00 |
| *—White label promo; "Special Mono Radio Station Copy" sticker on front of stereo jacket* | | | |
| ❑ CS 9652 [S] | The Look of Love | 1968 | 15.00 |

CORAL

| Number | Title (A Side/B Side) | Yr | NM |
|---|---|---|---|
| ❑ CRL 57109 [M] | Delight | 1957 | 40.00 |

HARMONY

| Number | Title (A Side/B Side) | Yr | NM |
|---|---|---|---|
| ❑ HS 11361 | Yes Indeed! | 1970 | 10.00 |
| ❑ KH 30319 | If He Walked Into My Life | 1971 | 10.00 |

MGM

| Number | Title (A Side/B Side) | Yr | NM |
|---|---|---|---|
| ❑ SE-4780 | It Was a Good Time | 1971 | 12.00 |

RCA VICTOR

| Number | Title (A Side/B Side) | Yr | NM |
|---|---|---|---|
| ❑ LSP-4093 | Eydie | 1968 | 12.00 |
| ❑ LSP-4303 | Tonight I'll Say a Prayer | 1970 | 12.00 |

UNITED ARTISTS

| Number | Title (A Side/B Side) | Yr | NM |
|---|---|---|---|
| ❑ UAL 3143 [M] | Come Sing with Me | 1961 | 20.00 |
| ❑ UAL 3152 [M] | I Feel So Spanish | 1961 | 20.00 |
| ❑ UAL 3189 [M] | The Very Best of Eydie | 1962 | 20.00 |
| ❑ UAS 6143 [S] | Come Sing with Me | 1961 | 25.00 |
| ❑ UAS 6152 [S] | I Feel So Spanish | 1961 | 25.00 |
| ❑ UAS 6189 [S] | The Very Best of Eydie | 1962 | 25.00 |

VOCALION

| Number | Title (A Side/B Side) | Yr | NM |
|---|---|---|---|
| ❑ VL 3708 [M] | Here's Eydie Gorme | 196? | 15.00 |
| ❑ VL 73708 [R] | Here's Eydie Gorme | 196? | 12.00 |

### GOSDIN, VERN

AMI

| Number | Title (A Side/B Side) | Yr | NM |
|---|---|---|---|
| ❑ 1502 | Today My World Slipped Away | 1983 | 12.00 |

COLUMBIA

| Number | Title (A Side/B Side) | Yr | NM |
|---|---|---|---|
| ❑ 1P 8037 | 10 Years of Greatest Hits — Newly Recorded | 1990 | 20.00 |
| *—Columbia House vinyl edition (only U.S. version)* | | | |
| ❑ FC 40982 | Chiseled in Stone | 1988 | 8.00 |
| ❑ FC 45104 | Alone | 1989 | 12.00 |

COMPLEAT

| Number | Title (A Side/B Side) | Yr | NM |
|---|---|---|---|
| ❑ 1004 | If You're Gonna Do Me Wrong (Do It Right) | 1983 | 10.00 |
| ❑ 1008 | There Is a Season | 1984 | 10.00 |
| ❑ 671012 | Time Stood Still | 1984 | 10.00 |
| ❑ 671022 | Greatest Hits | 1986 | 10.00 |

ELEKTRA

| Number | Title (A Side/B Side) | Yr | NM |
|---|---|---|---|
| ❑ 6E-124 | Never My Love | 1978 | 10.00 |
| ❑ 6E-180 | You've Got Somebody | 1979 | 10.00 |
| ❑ 6E-228 | The Best of Vern Gosdin | 1979 | 10.00 |
| ❑ 7E-1112 | Till the End | 1977 | 10.00 |

### GOSDIN BROTHERS, THE Also see GENE CLARK.

CAPITOL

| Number | Title (A Side/B Side) | Yr | NM |
|---|---|---|---|
| ❑ ST 2852 | Sounds of Goodbye | 1968 | 20.00 |

### GOSPEL STARS, THE

TAMLA

| Number | Title (A Side/B Side) | Yr | NM |
|---|---|---|---|
| ❑ TM-222 [M] | The Great Gospel Stars | 1961 | 3000. |
| *—VG value 1000; VG+ value 2000* | | | |

### GOSSETT, LOU

B.T. PUPPY

| Number | Title (A Side/B Side) | Yr | NM |
|---|---|---|---|
| ❑ BTS-1013 | From Me to You | 1970 | 40.00 |

### GOSSEZ, PIERRE

VANGUARD CARDINAL

| Number | Title (A Side/B Side) | Yr | NM |
|---|---|---|---|
| ❑ C-10061 | Bach Takes a Trip | 1969 | 20.00 |

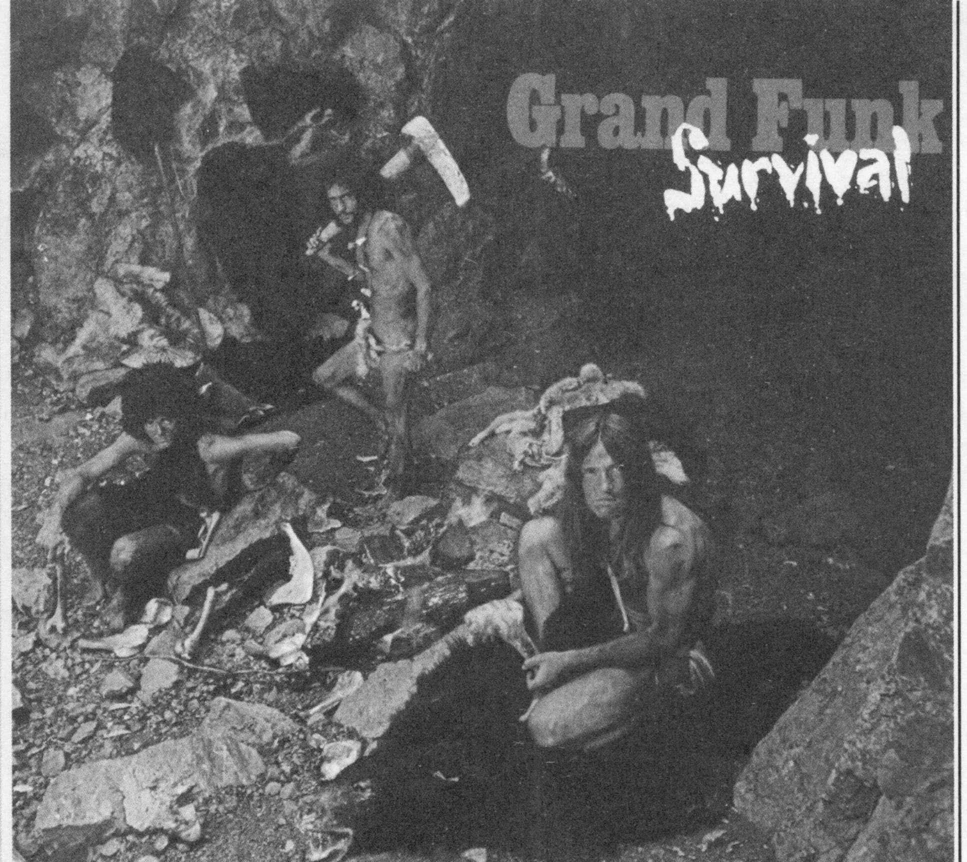


Grand Funk, *Survival,* Capitol SW-764, 1971, green label $15, red label $12, orange label $10.

**Number — Title (A Side/B Side) — Yr — NM**

**GOULD, CHUCK**

VIK
❑ LX-1123 [M] Chuck Gould Plays A La Fletcher Henderson 1957 50.00

**GOULD, MORTON**

COLUMBIA MASTERWORKS
❑ ML 2065 [10] Christmas Music for Orchestra 1949 40.00

RCA VICTOR RED SEAL
❑ LSC-1994 [S] Jungle Drums 1958 30.00
*—Original with "shaded dog" label*
❑ LSC-2080 [S] Brass and Percussion 1958 20.00
*—Original with "shaded dog" label*
❑ LSC-2104 [S] Blues in the Night 1958 30.00
*—Original with "shaded dog" label*
❑ LSC-2195 [S] Copland: Billy the Kid; Rodeo 1959 40.00
*—Original with "shaded dog" label*
❑ LSC-2195 [S] Copland: Billy the Kid; Rodeo 1964 30.00
*—Second edition with "white dog" label*
❑ LSC-2217 [S] Baton and Bows 1959 25.00
*—Original with "shaded dog" label*
❑ LSC-2224 [S] Where's the Melody? 1959 20.00
*—Original with "shaded dog" label*
❑ LSC-2232 [S] Moon, Wind and Stars 1959 20.00
*—Original with "shaded dog" label*
❑ LSC-2308 [S] Doubling in Brass 1959 50.00
*—Original with "shaded dog" label*
❑ LSC-2317 [S] Living Strings 1959 25.00
*—Original with "shaded dog" label*
❑ LSC-2345 [S] Tchaikovsky: 1812 Overture; Ravel: Bolero 1960 20.00
*—Original with "shaded dog" label*
❑ LSC-2437 [S] Bizet: Carmen for Orchestra 1960 40.00
*—Original with "shaded dog" label*
❑ LSC-2532 [S] Fall River Legend 1961 25.00
*—Original with "shaded dog" label*
❑ LSC-2559 [S] Jerome Kern and Cole Porter Favorites 1961 20.00
*—Original with "shaded dog" label*
❑ LSC-2579 [S] Piano Favorites 1962 50.00
*—Original with "shaded dog" label*
❑ LSC-2686 [S] Spirituals for Strings 1962 30.00
*—Original with "shaded dog" label*

**GOULDMAN, GRAHAM**

RCA VICTOR
❑ LPM-3954 [M] The Graham Gouldman Thing 1968 50.00
❑ LSP-3954 [S] The Graham Gouldman Thing 1968 50.00

**GOWANS, BRAD**

RCA VICTOR
❑ LJM-3000 [10] Brad Gowans' New York Nine 1954 50.00

**GOZZO, CONRAD**

RCA VICTOR
❑ LPM-1124 [M] Goz the Great 1955 50.00

**GRAAS, JOHN**

ANDEX
❑ A-3003 [M] Premiere in Jazz 1958 50.00
❑ AS-3003 [S] Premiere in Jazz 1959 40.00

DECCA
❑ DL 8079 [M] Jazz Studio 2 1954 50.00
❑ DL 8104 [M] Jazz Studio 3 1955 50.00
❑ DL 8343 [M] Jazz Lab 1 1956 50.00
❑ DL 8478 [M] Jazz Lab 2 1957 50.00
❑ DL 8677 [M] Jazzmantics 1958 50.00

EMARCY
❑ MG-36117 [M] Coup de Graas 1958 50.00

KAPP
❑ KL-1046 [M] French Horn Jazz 1957 50.00

MERCURY
❑ SR-80020 [S] Coup de Graas 1959 40.00

TREND
❑ TL-1005 [10] French Horn Jazz 1954 120.00

**GRACEN, THELMA**

EMARCY
❑ MG-36096 [M] Thelma Gracen 1956 200.00

WING
❑ MGW-60005 [M]Thelma Gracen 1956 150.00

**GRACIOUS** PAUL DAVIS was in this group.

CAPITOL
❑ ST-602 Gracious 1970 40.00

**GRAFFITI**

ABC
❑ S-663 Graffiti 1968 60.00

**GRAFFMAN, GARY**

RCA VICTOR RED SEAL
❑ LSC-2274 [S] Brahms: Piano Concerto No. 1 1959 25.00
*—With Charles Munch/Boston Symphony Orchestra; original with "shaded dog" label*
❑ LSC-2304 [S] Chopin: Ballades 1959 20.00
*—Original with "shaded dog" label*
❑ LSC-2396 [S] Beethoven: Piano Concerto No. 3 1960 300.00
*—Original with "shaded dog" label*
❑ LSC-2468 [S] Chopin: Concerto No. 1; Mendelssohn: Capriccio Brilliant 1961 100.00
*—Original with "shaded dog" label*

**GRAHAM, ED**

M&K REALTIME
❑ 106 Hot Stix 1980 40.00
*—Direct-to-disc recording; plays at 45 rpm*

**GRAMERCY SIX, THE**

EDISON INTERNATIONAL
❑ P-502 [M] Great Swinging Sounds Vol. 1 1959 30.00

**GRAMMER, BILLY**

DECCA
❑ DL 4212 [M] Gospel Guitar 1962 15.00
❑ DL 4460 [M] Golden Gospel Favorites 1964 12.00
❑ DL 4542 [M] Gotta Travel On 1965 12.00
❑ DL 4642 [M] Country Guitar 1965 12.00
❑ DL 74212 [S] Gospel Guitar 1962 20.00
❑ DL 74460 [S] Golden Gospel Favorites 1964 15.00
❑ DL 74542 [S] Gotta Travel On 1965 15.00
❑ DL 74642 [S] Country Guitar 1965 15.00

EPIC
❑ LN 24233 [M] Sunday Guitar 1967 15.00
❑ BN 26233 [S] Sunday Guitar 1967 15.00

MONUMENT
❑ MLP-4000 [M] Travelin' On 1959 40.00
❑ MLP-8039 [M] Travelin' On 1965 25.00
❑ SLP-18039 [P] Travelin' On 1965 30.00

VOCALION
❑ VL 73826 Favorites 1968 12.00

**GRANATA, ROCCO**

LAURIE
❑ LLP-2003 [M] Marina and Other Italian Favorites 1960 25.00

**GRAND FUNK RAILROAD**

CAPITOL
❑ ST-307 On Time 1969 15.00
❑ SKAO-406 Grand Funk 1970 15.00
❑ SKAO-471 Closer to Home 1970 15.00
❑ SWBB-633 [(2)]Live Album 1970 15.00
*—Includes poster*
❑ SW-764 Survival 1971 12.00
*—Red "target" label; add $5 if individual photos of the band members are included*
❑ SW-764 Survival 1971 15.00
*—Lime-green label; add $5 if individual photos of the band members are included*
❑ SW-764 Survival 1973 10.00
*—Orange label, "Capitol" at bottom*
❑ SW-853 E Pluribus Funk 1971 15.00
*—Round cover designed like a coin*
❑ SABB-11042 [(2)]Mark, Don and Mel 1969-71 1972 15.00
❑ SMAS-11099 Phoenix 1972 12.00
❑ SMAS-11207 We're An American Band 1973 10.00
*—Black vinyl*
❑ SMAS-11207 We're An American Band 1973 20.00
*—Gold vinyl without sheet of four stickers*
❑ SMAS-11207 We're An American Band 1973 30.00
*—Gold vinyl with sheet of four stickers*
❑ SWAE-11278 Shinin' On 1974 8.00
*—With 3-D glasses missing and no poster*
❑ SWAE-11278 Shinin' On 1974 12.00
*—With 3-D glasses attached to cover and with 3-D poster*
❑ SO-11356 All the Girls in the World Beware!!! 1974 15.00
*—With poster (deduct 33% if missing)*
❑ SABB-11445 Caught in the Act 1975 10.00
❑ ST-11482 Born to Die 1976 10.00
❑ ST-11579 Grand Funk Hits 1976 10.00
❑ SN-16138 Grand Funk Hits 1981 8.00
❑ SN-16176 Closer to Home 1981 8.00
❑ SN-16177 Grand Funk 1981 8.00
❑ SN-16178 On Time 1981 8.00
❑ 21692 We're An American Band 1999 25.00
*—Limited-edition reissue on 180-gram gold vinyl with original 1973 packaging*

FULL MOON
❑ HS 3625 Grand Funk Lives 1981 10.00
❑ 23750 What's Funk 1983 10.00

MCA
❑ 2216 Good Singin' Good Playin' 1976 12.00
*—Produced by Frank Zappa*

| Number | Title (A Side/B Side) | Yr | NM |
|---|---|---|---|
| **GRANDMA'S ROCKERS** | | | |
| FREDLO | | | |
| ❑ 6727 | Homemade Apple Pie | 1967 | 1500. |
| *—VG value 500; VG+ value 1000* | | | |
| **GRANDMASTER FLASH** | | | |
| ELEKTRA | | | |
| ❑ 60389 | They Said It Couldn't Be Done | 1985 | 12.00 |
| ❑ 60723 | Ba-Dop-Boom-Bang | 1987 | 10.00 |
| ❑ 60769 | On the Strength | 1988 | 12.00 |
| SUGAR HILL | | | |
| ❑ SH 268 | The Message | 1982 | 20.00 |
| *—Note: This album has been reissued to look like the original* | | | |
| ❑ SH 9121 | Greatest Messages | 1984 | 20.00 |
| **GRANT, AMY** | | | |
| A&M | | | |
| ❑ SP-3900 | The Collection | 1986 | 8.00 |
| *—Issued simultaneously with Myrrh 684306* | | | |
| ❑ SP-5051 | Amy Grant | 1985 | 8.00 |
| *—Reissue of Myrrh 6586 with new cover* | | | |
| ❑ SP-5052 | My Father's Eyes | 1985 | 8.00 |
| *—Reissue of Myrrh 6625* | | | |
| ❑ SP-5053 | Never Alone | 1985 | 8.00 |
| *—Reissue of Myrrh 6645* | | | |
| ❑ SP-5054 | Amy Grant In Concert | 1985 | 8.00 |
| *—Reissue of Myrrh 6668* | | | |
| ❑ SP-5055 | Amy Grant In Concert, Volume Two | 1985 | 8.00 |
| *—Reissue of Myrrh 6677* | | | |
| ❑ SP-5056 | Age to Age | 1985 | 8.00 |
| *—Reissue of Myrrh 6697* | | | |
| ❑ SP-5057 | A Christmas Album | 1985 | 10.00 |
| *—Reissue of Myrrh 6768* | | | |
| ❑ SP-5058 | Straight Ahead | 1985 | 8.00 |
| *—Reissue of Myrrh 675706* | | | |
| ❑ SP-5060 | Unguarded | 1985 | 8.00 |
| *—Issued simultaneously with Myrrh 680606, and with four different covers; "D" on spine* | | | |
| ❑ SP-5060 | Unguarded | 1985 | 8.00 |
| *—Issued simultaneously with Myrrh 680606, and with four different covers; "O" on spine* | | | |
| ❑ SP-5060 | Unguarded | 1985 | 8.00 |
| *—Issued simultaneously with Myrrh 680606, and with four different covers; "R" on spine* | | | |
| ❑ SP-5060 | Unguarded | 1985 | 8.00 |
| *—Issued simultaneously with Myrrh 680606, and with four different covers; "W" on spine* | | | |
| ❑ SP-5199 | Lead Me On | 1988 | 8.00 |
| *—Issued simultaneously with Myrrh 687106* | | | |
| ❑ 75021 5321 1 | Heart in Motion | 1991 | 15.00 |
| MYRRH | | | |
| ❑ MSB-6586 | Amy Grant | 1977 | 20.00 |
| *—With colorized "ugly cover" of Amy's head and shoulders; "Amy Grant" at upper left* | | | |
| ❑ MSB-6586 | Amy Grant | 198? | 10.00 |
| *—With new cover of Amy in natural color; "Amy Grant" at upper right* | | | |
| ❑ MSB-6625 | My Father's Eyes | 1979 | 12.00 |
| ❑ MSB-6645 | Never Alone | 1980 | 12.00 |
| ❑ MSB-6668 | Amy Grant In Concert | 1981 | 12.00 |
| ❑ MSB-6677 | Amy Grant In Concert, Volume Two | 1981 | 12.00 |
| ❑ MSB-6697 | Age to Age | 1982 | 12.00 |
| ❑ MSB-6768 | A Christmas Album | 1983 | 12.00 |
| ❑ 901-611135-2 [DJ] | A Christmas Album | 1983 | 80.00 |
| *—Promo-only picture disc in die-cut sleeve* | | | |
| ❑ 901-622335-5 [DJ] | Straight Ahead | 1984 | 100.00 |
| *—Promo-only music and interview album for Christian radio stations* | | | |
| ❑ 701-675706-4 | Straight Ahead | 1984 | 10.00 |
| ❑ 701-680606-5 | Unguarded | 1985 | 10.00 |
| *—Issued simultaneously with A&M 5060, and with four different covers; "D" on spine* | | | |
| ❑ 701-680606-5 | Unguarded | 1985 | 10.00 |
| *—Issued simultaneously with A&M 5060, and with four different covers; "O" on spine* | | | |
| ❑ 701-680606-5 | Unguarded | 1985 | 10.00 |
| *—Issued simultaneously with A&M 5060, and with four different covers; "R" on spine* | | | |
| ❑ 701-680606-5 | Unguarded | 1985 | 10.00 |
| *—Issued simultaneously with A&M 5060, and with four different covers; "W" on spine* | | | |
| ❑ 701-684306-8 | The Collection | 1986 | 10.00 |
| *—Issued simultaneously with A&M 3900* | | | |
| ❑ 701-687106-1 | Lead Me On | 1988 | 10.00 |
| *—Issued simultaneously with A&M 5199* | | | |
| **GRANT, EARL** | | | |
| DECCA | | | |
| ❑ DL 4044 [M] | The Magic of Earl Grant | 1960 | 12.00 |
| ❑ DL 4165 [M] | Ebb Tide | 1961 | 12.00 |
| ❑ DL 4188 [M] | Earl After Dark | 1961 | 12.00 |
| ❑ DL 4231 [M] | Beyond the Reef | 1962 | 12.00 |
| ❑ DL 4299 [M] | Earl Grant at Basin Street East | 1962 | 12.00 |
| ❑ DL 4338 [M] | Midnight Sun | 1963 | 12.00 |
| ❑ DL 4405 [M] | Yes Sirree | 1963 | 12.00 |
| ❑ DL 4454 [M] | Fly Me to the Moon | 1963 | 12.00 |
| ❑ DL 4506 [M] | Just for a Thrill | 1964 | 12.00 |
| ❑ DL 4576 [M] | Just One More Time | 1964 | 12.00 |
| ❑ DL 4623 [M] | Trade Winds | 1965 | 12.00 |
| ❑ DL 4624 [M] | Spotlight on Earl Grant | 1965 | 12.00 |

DS 50047
Golden Grass, The Grassroots
Their Greatest Hits
STEREO
DUNHILL
Midnight Confessions · Let's Live For Today · Feelings · Bella Linda
Things I Should Have Said · Where Were You When I Needed You


The Grass Roots, *Golden Grass,* ABC-Dunhill DS-50047, 1968, $20.

| Number | Title (A Side/B Side) | Yr | NM |
|---|---|---|---|
| ❑ DL 4677 [M] | Winter Wonderland | 1965 | 12.00 |
| ❑ DL 4729 [M] | Songs Made Famous by Nat Cole | 1966 | 12.00 |
| ❑ DL 4738 [M] | Stand By Me | 1966 | 12.00 |
| ❑ DL 4806 [M] | Bali Ha'I | 1967 | 12.00 |
| ❑ DL 4811 [M] | Just a Closer Walk with Thee | 1967 | 15.00 |
| ❑ DL 4813 [M] | Earl Grant's Greatest Hits | 1967 | 15.00 |
| ❑ DL 4937 [M] | Gently Swingin' | 1968 | 20.00 |
| ❑ DL 4974 [M] | Spanish Eyes | 1968 | 25.00 |
| ❑ DXS 7204 [(2)] | The Best of Earl Grant | 1969 | 20.00 |
| ❑ DL 8672 [M] | The Versatile Earl Grant | 1958 | 20.00 |
| ❑ DL 8830 [M] | The End | 1959 | 15.00 |
| ❑ DL 8905 [M] | Grant Takes Rhythm | 1959 | 15.00 |
| ❑ DL 8916 [M] | Nothing But the Blues | 1960 | 15.00 |
| ❑ DL 8935 [M] | Paris Is My Beat | 1960 | 15.00 |
| ❑ DL 74044 [S] | The Magic of Earl Grant | 1960 | 15.00 |
| ❑ DL 74165 [S] | Ebb Tide | 1961 | 15.00 |
| ❑ DL 74188 [S] | Earl After Dark | 1961 | 15.00 |
| ❑ DL 74231 [S] | Beyond the Reef | 1962 | 15.00 |
| ❑ DL 74299 [S] | Earl Grant at Basin Street East | 1962 | 15.00 |
| ❑ DL 74338 [S] | Midnight Sun | 1963 | 15.00 |
| ❑ DL 74405 [S] | Yes Sirree | 1963 | 15.00 |
| ❑ DL 74454 [S] | Fly Me to the Moon | 1963 | 15.00 |
| ❑ DL 74506 [S] | Just for a Thrill | 1964 | 15.00 |
| ❑ DL 74576 [S] | Just One More Time | 1964 | 15.00 |
| ❑ DL 74623 [S] | Trade Winds | 1965 | 15.00 |
| ❑ DL 74624 [S] | Spotlight on Earl Grant | 1965 | 15.00 |
| ❑ DL 74677 [S] | Winter Wonderland | 1965 | 15.00 |
| ❑ DL 74729 [S] | Songs Made Famous by Nat Cole | 1966 | 15.00 |
| ❑ DL 74738 [S] | Stand By Me | 1966 | 15.00 |
| ❑ DL 74806 [S] | Bali Ha'I | 1967 | 15.00 |
| ❑ DL 74811 [S] | Just a Closer Walk with Thee | 1967 | 15.00 |
| ❑ DL 74813 [S] | Earl Grant's Greatest Hits | 1967 | 15.00 |
| ❑ DL 74937 [S] | Gently Swingin' | 1968 | 15.00 |
| ❑ DL 74974 [S] | Spanish Eyes | 1968 | 15.00 |
| ❑ DL 75052 | In Motion | 1969 | 15.00 |
| ❑ DL 75108 | This Magic Moment | 1970 | 15.00 |
| ❑ DL 75158 | A Time for Us | 1970 | 12.00 |
| ❑ DL 75223 | Earl Grant | 1970 | 12.00 |
| ❑ DL 78830 [S] | The End | 1959 | 20.00 |
| ❑ DL 78905 [S] | Grant Takes Rhythm | 1959 | 20.00 |
| ❑ DL 78916 [S] | Nothing But the Blues | 1960 | 20.00 |
| ❑ DL 78935 [S] | Paris Is My Beat | 1960 | 20.00 |
| VOCALION | | | |
| ❑ VL 3793 [M] | It's So Good | 1967 | 12.00 |
| ❑ VL 73793 [S] | It's So Good | 1967 | 12.00 |

| Number | Title (A Side/B Side) | Yr | NM |
|---|---|---|---|
| ❑ VL 73860 | Send for Me | 1969 | 12.00 |
| ❑ VL 73893 | One for My Baby | 1969 | 12.00 |
| **GRANT, GOGI** | | | |
| ERA | | | |
| ❑ EL-106 [M] | The Wayward Wind | 196? | 25.00 |
| ❑ 20001 [M] | Suddenly There's Gogi Grant | 1956 | 60.00 |
| *—Black vinyl* | | | |
| ❑ 20001 [M] | Suddenly There's Gogi Grant | 1956 | 100.00 |
| *—Red vinyl* | | | |
| LIBERTY | | | |
| ❑ LRP-3144 [M] | If You Want to Get to Heaven, Shout | 1960 | 30.00 |
| ❑ LST-7144 [S] | If You Want to Get to Heaven, Shout | 1960 | 40.00 |
| PETE | | | |
| ❑ S-1101 | Gogi Grant | 1968 | 15.00 |
| ❑ S-1111 | The Way a Woman Feels | 1970 | 15.00 |
| RCA VICTOR | | | |
| ❑ LOC-1030 [M] | The Helen Morgan Story | 1957 | 60.00 |
| ❑ LPM-1717 [M] | Welcome to My Heart | 1958 | 40.00 |
| ❑ LPM-1940 [M] | Torch Time | 1959 | 30.00 |
| ❑ LSP-1940 [S] | Torch Time | 1959 | 40.00 |
| ❑ LPM-2000 [M] | Granted… It's Gogi | 1960 | 30.00 |
| ❑ LSP-2000 [S] | Granted… It's Gogi | 1960 | 40.00 |
| **GRAPEFRUIT** | | | |
| ABC DUNHILL | | | |
| ❑ DS-50050 | Around Grapefruit | 1968 | 40.00 |
| RCA VICTOR | | | |
| ❑ LSP-4215 | Deep Water | 1969 | 30.00 |
| **GRAPPELLI, STEPHANE** | | | |
| ATLANTIC | | | |
| ❑ SD 1391 [S] | Feeling + Finesse = Jazz | 1962 | 20.00 |
| BARCLAY | | | |
| ❑ 820007 | Music to Pass the Time | 196? | 20.00 |
| BLACK LION | | | |
| ❑ 047 [(2)] | I Got Rhythm | 1974 | 20.00 |
| CLASSIC JAZZ | | | |
| ❑ 23 [(2)] | Homage to Django | 197? | 20.00 |
| EMARCY | | | |
| ❑ MG-36120 [M] | Improvisations | 1957 | 60.00 |

Grateful Dead, *American Beauty,* Warner Bros. WS 1893, 1971, green label, $25.

| Number | Title (A Side/B Side) | Yr | NM |
|---|---|---|---|

## GRAPPELLI, STEPHANE, AND BARNEY KESSEL

### MOBILE FIDELITY

❑ 1-111 I Remember Django 1984 50.00
*—Audiophile vinyl*

## GRASS ROOTS, THE

### ABC

❑ AC-30003 The ABC Collection 1976 15.00

### ABC DUNHILL

❑ DS-50027 Feelings 1968 15.00
*—Reissue with ABC logo*
❑ DS-50047 Golden Grass 1968 20.00
❑ DS-50052 Lovin' Things 1969 20.00
❑ DS-50067 Leaving It All Behind 1969 20.00
❑ DS-50087 More Golden Grass 1970 20.00
❑ DSX-50107 Their 16 Greatest Hits 1971 20.00
❑ DSX-50112 Move Along 1972 15.00
❑ DSX-50137 A Lotta Mileage 1973 15.00

### COMMAND

❑ QD-40013 [Q] Their 16 Greatest Hits 1974 30.00

### DUNHILL

❑ D-50011 [M] Where Were You When I Needed You 1966 150.00
❑ DS-50011 [S] Where Were You When I Needed You 1966 100.00
❑ D-50020 [M] Let's Live for Today 1967 25.00
❑ DS-50020 [S] Let's Live for Today 1967 30.00
❑ D-50027 [M] Feelings 1968 30.00
❑ DS-50027 [S] Feelings 1968 20.00

### HAVEN

❑ ST-9204 The Grass Roots 1975 15.00

### MCA

❑ 5331 Powers of the Night 1982 12.00
❑ 37154 Their 16 Greatest Hits 198? 8.00
*—Budget-line reissue of ABC Dunhill 50107*

## GRATEFUL DEAD, THE

Also see JERRY GARCIA; MICKEY HART; KEITH AND DONNA; BOB WEIR.

### ARISTA

❑ SP-35 [DJ] Grateful Dead Sampler 1978 30.00
❑ AB 4198 Shakedown Street 1978 12.00
❑ AL 7001 Terrapin Station 1977 15.00
❑ AL 7001 [DJ] Terrapin Station 1977 50.00
*—Radio station promos are banded for airplay*
❑ AL 8112 [(2)] Dead Set 198? 10.00
*—Budget-line reissue of 8606*
❑ AL 8321 Shakedown Street 198? 8.00
*—Budget-line reissue of 4198*
❑ AL 8329 Terrapin Station 198? 8.00
*—Budget-line reissue of 7001*
❑ AL 8332 Go to Heaven 198? 8.00
*—Budget-line reissue of 9508*
❑ AL 8452 In the Dark 1987 10.00
❑ AL 8575 Built to Last 1989 10.00
❑ A2L 8604 [(2)] Reckoning 1981 15.00
❑ A2L 8606 [(2)] Dead Set 1981 15.00
❑ AL3 8634 [(3)] Without a Net 1990 25.00
❑ AL 9508 Go to Heaven 1980 12.00

### DIRECT DISK

❑ SD-16619 Terrapin Station 1980 100.00
*—Audiophile vinyl*

### GRATEFUL DEAD

❑ GD-01 Wake of the Flood 1973 20.00
*—With no contributing artists on back cover*
❑ GD-01 Wake of the Flood 1975 15.00
*—With contributing artists on back cover and United Artists distribution*
❑ GD-01 [DJ] Wake of the Flood 1973 400.00
*—Green vinyl meant for fan-club members; ironically, most copies were damaged in a flood before distribution*
❑ GD-102 Grateful Dead from the Mars Hotel 1974 20.00
*—Without United Artists distribution*
❑ GD-102 Grateful Dead from the Mars Hotel 1975 15.00
*—With United Artists distribution and "Grateful Dead" label*
❑ GD-LA494-G Blues for Allah 1975 20.00
❑ GD-LA620-J2 [(2)] Steal Your Face 1976 25.00

### MOBILE FIDELITY

❑ 1-014 American Beauty 1980 50.00
*—Audiophile vinyl*
❑ 1-172 Grateful Dead from the Mars Hotel 1984 40.00
*—Audiophile vinyl*

### PAIR

❑ PDL2-1053 [(2)] For the Faithful... 1986 12.00

### RHINO

❑ R1-74395 [(2)] Live/Dead 2003 25.00
*—Reissue on 180-gram vinyl*
❑ R1-74396 Workingman's Dead 2003 15.00
*—Reissue on 180-gram vinyl*
❑ R1-74397 American Beauty 2003 15.00
*—Reissue on 180-gram vinyl*

### SUNFLOWER

❑ SUN-5001 Vintage Dead 1970 40.00
*—Album has been counterfeited, but bogus covers are 1/4" shorter than normal LP cover*
❑ SNF-5004 Historic Dead 1971 40.00

### UNITED ARTISTS

❑ GD-102 Grateful Dead from the Mars Hotel 1978 15.00
*—With United Artists "sunrise" label*

### WARNER BROS.

❑ W 1689 [M] The Grateful Dead 1967 200.00
❑ WS 1689 [S] The Grateful Dead 1967 80.00
*—Gold label*
❑ WS 1689 [S] The Grateful Dead 1968 25.00
*—Green label with "W7" logo*
❑ WS 1689 [S] The Grateful Dead 1970 15.00
*—Green label with "WB" logo*
❑ WS 1689 [S] The Grateful Dead 1973 12.00
*—"Burbank" palm-trees label*
❑ WS 1689 [S] The Grateful Dead 1979 8.00
*—White or tan label*
❑ WS 1749 Anthem of the Sun 1968 30.00
*—Green label with "W7" logo*
❑ WS 1749 Anthem of the Sun 197? 50.00
*—Green label with "WB" logo, white background on cover with radically remixed version of LP*
❑ WS 1749 Anthem of the Sun 1970 15.00
*—Green label with "WB" logo, purple cover*
❑ WS 1749 Anthem of the Sun 1973 12.00
*—"Burbank" palm-trees label*
❑ WS 1749 Anthem of the Sun 1979 8.00
*—White or tan label*
❑ WS 1790 Aoxomoxoa 1969 30.00
*—Green label with "W7" logo*
❑ WS 1790 Aoxomoxoa 1970 15.00
*—Green label with "WB" logo*
❑ WS 1790 Aoxomoxoa 1973 12.00
*—"Burbank" palm-trees label*
❑ WS 1790 Aoxomoxoa 1979 8.00
*—White or tan label*
❑ 2WS 1830 [(2)] Live/Dead 1969 40.00
*—Green labels with "W7" logo*
❑ 2WS 1830 [(2)] Live/Dead 1970 20.00
*—Green labels with "WB" logo*
❑ 2WS 1830 [(2)] Live/Dead 1973 15.00
*—"Burbank" palm-trees labels*
❑ 2WS 1830 [(2)] Live/Dead 1979 10.00
*—White or tan labels*
❑ WS 1869 Workingman's Dead 1970 25.00
*—Green label with "WB" logo; textured cover with back cover slick upside down*
❑ WS 1869 Workingman's Dead 1973 12.00
*—"Burbank" palm-trees label; standard cover with back cover right side up*
❑ WS 1869 Workingman's Dead 1979 8.00
*—White or tan label*
❑ WS 1893 American Beauty 1970 25.00
*—Green label with "WB" logo*
❑ WS 1893 American Beauty 1973 12.00
*—"Burbank" palm-trees label*
❑ WS 1893 American Beauty 1979 8.00
*—White or tan label*
❑ 2WS 1935 [(2)] Grateful Dead 1971 30.00
*—Green labels with "WB" logo*
❑ 2WS 1935 [(2)] Grateful Dead 1973 15.00
*—"Burbank" palm-trees labels*
❑ 2WS 1935 [(2)] Grateful Dead 1979 10.00
*—White or tan labels*
❑ 3WX 2668 [(3)] Europe '72 1972 40.00
*—Green labels with "WB" logo*
❑ 3WX 2668 [(3)] Europe '72 1973 20.00
*—"Burbank" palm-trees labels*
❑ 3WX 2668 [(3)] Europe '72 1979 12.00
*—White or tan labels*
❑ BS 2721 History of the Grateful Dead, Vol. 1 (Bear's Choice) 1973 20.00
*—"Burbank" palm-trees labels*
❑ BS 2721 History of the Grateful Dead, Vol. 1 (Bear's Choice) 1978 8.00
*—White or tan labels*
❑ W 2764 The Best of/Skeletons from the Closet 1974 20.00
*—"Burbank" palm-trees labels*
❑ W 2764 The Best of/Skeletons from the Closet 1979 8.00
*—White or tan labels*
❑ 2WS 3091 [(2)] What a Long Strange Trip It's Been: The Best of the Grateful Dead 1977 20.00
*—"Burbank" palm-trees labels*
❑ 2WS 3091 [(2)] What a Long Strange Trip It's Been: The Best of the Grateful Dead 1979 10.00
*—White or tan labels*
❑ ST-93416 American Beauty 1970 50.00
*—Capitol Record Club edition; green label with "W7" logo*

## GRAVES, CONLEY

### DECCA

❑ DL 8220 [M] Genius at Work 1956 40.00



**Except when noted otherwise, VG = 25% of NM, and VG+ = 50% of NM. (Example: VG = $2.00, VG+ = $4.00 and NM = $8.00.)**

| Number | Title (A Side/B Side) | Yr | NM |
|---|---|---|---|
| ❑ DL 8412 [M] | Piano Dynamics | 1957 | 40.00 |
| ❑ DL 8475 [M] | Rendezvous in Paris | 1957 | 40.00 |
| **LIBERTY** | | | |
| ❑ LRP-3007 [M] | V.I.P. (Very Important Pianist) | 1956 | 40.00 |
| **NOCTURNE** | | | |
| ❑ NLP-4 [10] | Piano Artistry | 1954 | 100.00 |

### GRAVES, JOE

| Number | Title (A Side/B Side) | Yr | NM |
|---|---|---|---|
| **CAPITOL** | | | |
| ❑ ST 1977 [S] | The Great New Swingers | 1963 | 30.00 |
| ❑ T 1977 [M] | The Great New Swingers | 1963 | 25.00 |

### GRAVES, MILFORD

| Number | Title (A Side/B Side) | Yr | NM |
|---|---|---|---|
| **ESP-DISK'** | | | |
| ❑ 1015 [M] | Milford Graves Percussion Ensemble | 1966 | 20.00 |
| ❑ S-1015 [S] | Milford Graves Percussion Ensemble | 1966 | 25.00 |

### GRAVES, TERESA

| Number | Title (A Side/B Side) | Yr | NM |
|---|---|---|---|
| **KIRSHNER** | | | |
| ❑ KOS-104 | Teresa Graves | 1970 | 25.00 |

### GRAVITY ADJUSTERS EXPANSION BAND

| Number | Title (A Side/B Side) | Yr | NM |
|---|---|---|---|
| **NOCTURNE** | | | |
| ❑ NRS-302 | One | 1973 | 300.00 |

### GRAY, BILLY

| Number | Title (A Side/B Side) | Yr | NM |
|---|---|---|---|
| **DECCA** | | | |
| ❑ DL 5567 [10] | Dance-O-Rama | 1956 | 200.00 |

### GRAY, CLAUDE

| Number | Title (A Side/B Side) | Yr | NM |
|---|---|---|---|
| **DECCA** | | | |
| ❑ DL 4882 [M] | Claude Gray Sings | 1967 | 25.00 |
| ❑ DL 74882 [S] | Claude Gray Sings | 1967 | 20.00 |
| ❑ DL 74963 | The Easy Way of Claude Gray | 1968 | 20.00 |
| **HILLTOP** | | | |
| ❑ JM-6051 [M] | Treasure of Love | 1967 | 15.00 |
| ❑ JS-6051 [S] | Treasure of Love | 1967 | 12.00 |
| **MERCURY** | | | |
| ❑ MG-20658 [M] | Songs of Broken Love Affairs | 1962 | 20.00 |
| ❑ MG-20718 [M] | Country Goes to Town | 1962 | 20.00 |
| ❑ SR-60658 [S] | Songs of Broken Love Affairs | 1962 | 25.00 |
| ❑ SR-60718 [S] | Country Goes to Town | 1962 | 25.00 |

### GRAY, DOBIE

| Number | Title (A Side/B Side) | Yr | NM |
|---|---|---|---|
| **CAPITOL** | | | |
| ❑ ST-12489 | From Where I Stand | 1986 | 10.00 |
| **CAPRICORN** | | | |
| ❑ CP 0163 | New Ray of Sunshine | 1976 | 10.00 |
| **CHARGER** | | | |
| ❑ CHR-M-2002 [M] | Dobie Gray Sings for "In" Crowders That Go "Go Go" | 1965 | 40.00 |
| ❑ CHR-S-2002 [S] | Dobie Gray Sings for "In" Crowders That Go "Go Go" | 1965 | 120.00 |
| **DECCA** | | | |
| ❑ DL 75397 | Drift Away | 1973 | 12.00 |
| **INFINITY** | | | |
| ❑ INF-9001 | Midnight Diamond | 1979 | 10.00 |
| **MCA** | | | |
| ❑ 371 | Loving Arms | 1973 | 10.00 |
| ❑ 449 | Hey Dixie | 1974 | 10.00 |
| ❑ 515 | Drift Away | 1974 | 10.00 |
| *—Reissue of Decca 75397* | | | |
| **ROBOX** | | | |
| ❑ RBX 8102 | Welcome Home | 1981 | 10.00 |
| **STRIPE** | | | |
| ❑ LPM 2001 [M] | Look — Dobie Gray | 1963 | 100.00 |

### GRAY, DOLORES

| Number | Title (A Side/B Side) | Yr | NM |
|---|---|---|---|
| **CAPITOL** | | | |
| ❑ T 897 [M] | Warm Brandy | 1957 | 30.00 |

### GRAY, GLEN

| Number | Title (A Side/B Side) | Yr | NM |
|---|---|---|---|
| **CAPITOL** | | | |
| ❑ W 747 [M] | Casa Loma in Hi-Fi! | 1956 | 25.00 |
| **CORAL** | | | |
| ❑ CRL 56006 [10] | Hoagy Carmichael Songs | 1950 | 50.00 |
| ❑ CRL 56009 [10] | Glen Gray Souvenirs | 1950 | 50.00 |
| **DECCA** | | | |
| ❑ DL 5089 [10] | Musical Smoke Rings | 1950 | 50.00 |
| ❑ DL 5397 [10] | No-Name Jive | 1953 | 50.00 |
| ❑ DL 8570 [M] | Smoke Rings | 1957 | 20.00 |
| **HARMONY** | | | |
| ❑ HL 7045 [M] | The Great Recordings of Glen Gray | 1957 | 20.00 |

### GRAY, JERRY

| Number | Title (A Side/B Side) | Yr | NM |
|---|---|---|---|
| **CRAFTSMAN** | | | |
| ❑ 8035 [M] | More Miller Hits | 195? | 20.00 |
| **DECCA** | | | |
| ❑ DL 5266 [10] | Dance to the Music of Gray | 1950 | 50.00 |
| ❑ DL 5312 [10] | In the Mood ... | 1951 | 50.00 |
| ❑ DL 5375 [10] | A Tribute to Glenn Miller | 1951 | 50.00 |
| ❑ DL 5478 [10] | Dance Time | 1952 | 50.00 |
| ❑ DL 8101 [M] | Jerry Gray and His Orchestra | 1955 | 40.00 |
| **LIBERTY** | | | |
| ❑ LRP-3038 [M] | Hi-Fi Shades of Gray | 1956 | 40.00 |
| ❑ LRP-3089 [M] | Jerry Gray at the Hollywood Palladium | 1958 | 40.00 |
| ❑ LST-7002 [S] | Hi-Fi Shades of Gray | 1958 | 40.00 |
| ❑ LST-7013 [S] | Jerry Gray at the Hollywood Palladium | 1958 | 40.00 |
| **TOPS** | | | |
| ❑ L-1627 [M] | A Salute to Glenn Miller | 1958 | 20.00 |
| ❑ L-1640 [M] | Glenn Miller Greats | 1958 | 20.00 |
| **VOCALION** | | | |
| ❑ VL 3602 [M] | A Tribute to Glenn Miller | 196? | 20.00 |
| **WARNER BROS.** | | | |
| ❑ W 1446 [M] | Singin' and Swingin' | 1962 | 20.00 |
| ❑ WS 1446 [S] | Singin' and Swingin' | 1962 | 25.00 |

### GRAY, WARDELL

| Number | Title (A Side/B Side) | Yr | NM |
|---|---|---|---|
| **CROWN** | | | |
| ❑ CST-278 [R] | Way Out Wardell | 1962 | 12.00 |
| ❑ CLP-5004 [M] | Way Out Wardell | 1957 | 40.00 |
| *—Originals have a black label with the word "crown" in small letters at top* | | | |
| ❑ CLP-5278 [M] | Way Out Wardell | 1962 | 20.00 |
| **MODERN** | | | |
| ❑ MLP-1204 [M] | Way Out Wardell | 1956 | 300.00 |
| **PRESTIGE** | | | |
| ❑ PRLP-115 [10] | Wardell Gray Tenor Sax | 1951 | 250.00 |
| ❑ PRLP-128 [10] | Jazz Concert | 1952 | 250.00 |
| ❑ PRLP-147 [10] | Wardell Gray's Los Angeles Stars | 1953 | 250.00 |
| ❑ PRLP-7008 [M] | Wardell Gray Memorial, Volume 1 | 1955 | 100.00 |
| ❑ PRLP-7009 [M] | Wardell Gray Memorial, Volume 2 | 1955 | 100.00 |
| ❑ PRLP-7343 [(2)M] | Wardell Gray Memorial Album | 1964 | 50.00 |
| ❑ PRST-7343 [(2)R] | Wardell Gray Memorial Album | 1964 | 25.00 |

### GRAY, WARDELL, AND DEXTER GORDON

| Number | Title (A Side/B Side) | Yr | NM |
|---|---|---|---|
| **DECCA** | | | |
| ❑ DL 7025 [10] | The Chase and the Steeple Chase | 1952 | 250.00 |
| **JAZZTONE** | | | |
| ❑ J-1235 [M] | The Chase and the Steeple Chase | 1956 | 50.00 |

### GREAT JAZZ TRIO, THE

| Number | Title (A Side/B Side) | Yr | NM |
|---|---|---|---|
| **EAST WIND** | | | |
| ❑ 10005 | Direct from L.A. | 1978 | 25.00 |
| *—Direct-to-disc recording* | | | |

### GREAT SOCIETY, THE

| Number | Title (A Side/B Side) | Yr | NM |
|---|---|---|---|
| **COLUMBIA** | | | |
| ❑ CS 9627 [M] | Conspicuous Only In Its Absence | 1968 | 50.00 |
| *—White label promo only; "Special Mono Radio Station Copy" sticker on front; same number as stereo version* | | | |
| ❑ CS 9627 [S] | Conspicuous Only In Its Absence | 1968 | 25.00 |
| *—Red label, "360 Sound Stereo"* | | | |
| ❑ CS 9702 | How It Was | 1968 | 25.00 |
| *—Red label, "360 Sound Stereo"* | | | |
| ❑ G 30459 [(2)] | The Great Society Collectors Item | 1971 | 15.00 |
| **HARMONY** | | | |
| ❑ KH 30391 | Somebody to Love | 1970 | 12.00 |

### GREAT SPECKLED BIRD

| Number | Title (A Side/B Side) | Yr | NM |
|---|---|---|---|
| **AMPEX** | | | |
| ❑ A-10103 | Great Speckled Bird | 1970 | 20.00 |

### GREAVES, R.B.

| Number | Title (A Side/B Side) | Yr | NM |
|---|---|---|---|
| **ATCO** | | | |
| ❑ SD 33-311 | R.B. Greaves | 1969 | 20.00 |
| **INTERMEDIA** | | | |
| ❑ QS-5032 | Rock and Roll | 198? | 10.00 |

### GRECO, BUDDY

| Number | Title (A Side/B Side) | Yr | NM |
|---|---|---|---|
| **APPLAUSE** | | | |
| ❑ APLP-1004 | Hot Nights | 1982 | 10.00 |
| **BAINBRIDGE** | | | |
| ❑ 8004 [(2)] | Greatest Hits | 198? | 15.00 |
| **CORAL** | | | |
| ❑ CRL 57022 [M] | Buddy Greco at Mister Kelly's | 1956 | 25.00 |
| **EPIC** | | | |
| ❑ BN 557 [S] | My Buddy | 1960 | 15.00 |
| ❑ BN 585 [S] | Songs for Swinging Losers | 1960 | 15.00 |
| ❑ BN 593 [S] | Buddy's Back in Town | 1961 | 15.00 |
| ❑ BN 602 [S] | I Like It Swinging | 1961 | 15.00 |
| ❑ BN 615 [S] | Let's Love | 1961 | 15.00 |
| ❑ LN 3660 [M] | My Buddy | 1960 | 12.00 |
| ❑ LN 3746 [M] | Songs for Swinging Losers | 1960 | 12.00 |
| ❑ LN 3771 [M] | Buddy's Back in Town | 1961 | 12.00 |
| ❑ LN 3793 [M] | I Like It Swinging | 1961 | 12.00 |
| ❑ LN 3820 [M] | Let's Love | 1961 | 12.00 |
| ❑ LN 24010 [M] | Buddy and Soul | 1962 | 12.00 |
| ❑ LN 24032 [M] | Soft and Gentle | 1962 | 12.00 |
| ❑ LN 24043 [M] | Buddy Greco's Greatest Hits | 1963 | 12.00 |
| ❑ LN 24057 [M] | Buddy Greco Sings for Intimate Moments | 1963 | 12.00 |
| ❑ LN 24088 [M] | My Last Night in Rome | 1964 | 12.00 |
| ❑ LN 24116 [M] | On Stage | 1964 | 12.00 |
| ❑ LN 24130 [M] | Modern Sounds of Hank Williams | 1965 | 12.00 |
| ❑ LN 24181 [M] | From the Wrists Down | 1965 | 12.00 |
| ❑ BN 26010 [S] | Buddy and Soul | 1962 | 15.00 |
| ❑ BN 26032 [S] | Soft and Gentle | 1962 | 15.00 |
| ❑ BN 26043 [S] | Buddy Greco's Greatest Hits | 1963 | 15.00 |
| ❑ BN 26057 [S] | Buddy Greco Sings for Intimate Moments | 1963 | 15.00 |
| ❑ BN 26088 [S] | My Last Night in Rome | 1964 | 15.00 |
| ❑ BN 26116 [S] | On Stage | 1964 | 15.00 |
| ❑ BN 26130 [S] | Modern Sounds of Hank Williams | 1965 | 15.00 |
| ❑ BN 26181 [S] | From the Wrists Down | 1965 | 15.00 |
| **HARMONY** | | | |
| ❑ HL 7448 [M] | You're Something Else | 196? | 10.00 |
| ❑ HS 11248 [S] | You're Something Else | 196? | 12.00 |
| **KAPP** | | | |
| ❑ KL-1033 [M] | Broadway Melodies | 1956 | 20.00 |
| ❑ KL-1107 [M] | Buddy | 1958 | 20.00 |
| ❑ KL-1231 [M] | The Best of Buddy Greco | 1961 | 15.00 |
| **PROJECT 3** | | | |
| ❑ PR 5105 | For Once in My Life: In Concert | 1980 | 10.00 |
| **REPRISE** | | | |
| ❑ R-6220 [M] | Big Band and Ballads | 1966 | 12.00 |
| ❑ RS-6220 [S] | Big Band and Ballads | 1966 | 15.00 |
| ❑ R-6230 [M] | Buddy's in a Brand New Bag | 1966 | 12.00 |
| ❑ RS-6230 [S] | Buddy's in a Brand New Bag | 1966 | 15.00 |
| ❑ R-6256 [M] | Away We Go! | 1967 | 15.00 |
| ❑ RS-6256 [S] | Away We Go! | 1967 | 12.00 |
| **SCEPTER** | | | |
| ❑ SPS-579 | Let the Sunshine In | 1969 | 12.00 |
| **SUTTON** | | | |
| ❑ SSU 282 [M] | All Time Favorites Featuring Buddy Greco | 196? | 10.00 |
| **VOCALION** | | | |
| ❑ VL 3706 [M] | Here's Buddy Greco | 1964 | 12.00 |
| ❑ VL 73706 [R] | Here's Buddy Greco | 1964 | 10.00 |

### GRECO, JULIETTE

| Number | Title (A Side/B Side) | Yr | NM |
|---|---|---|---|
| **COLUMBIA** | | | |
| ❑ CL 569 [M] | St. Germain-des-Pres | 1954 | 30.00 |
| *—Maroon label, gold print* | | | |

### GREEK FOUNTAIN RIVER FRONT BAND, THE

| Number | Title (A Side/B Side) | Yr | NM |
|---|---|---|---|
| **MONTEL** | | | |
| ❑ 110 [M] | The Greek Fountain River Band Takes Requests | 1965 | 120.00 |

### GREELEY, GEORGE

| Number | Title (A Side/B Side) | Yr | NM |
|---|---|---|---|
| **CAPITOL** | | | |
| ❑ H 438 [10] | Piano Demitasse | 1954 | 30.00 |
| **REPRISE** | | | |
| ❑ R 6092 [M] | Piano Rhapsodies of Love | 1964 | 10.00 |
| ❑ RS 6092 [S] | Piano Rhapsodies of Love | 1964 | 12.00 |
| **WARNER BROS.** | | | |
| ❑ W 1249 [M] | The World's Greatest Popular Piano Concertos | 1958 | 15.00 |
| ❑ WS 1249 [S] | The World's Greatest Popular Piano Concertos | 1959 | 20.00 |
| ❑ W 1291 [M] | World Renowned Popular Piano Concertos | 1959 | 15.00 |
| ❑ WS 1291 [S] | World Renowned Popular Piano Concertos | 1959 | 20.00 |
| ❑ W 1319 [M] | The Greatest Motion Picture Piano Concertos | 1959 | 15.00 |
| ❑ WS 1319 [S] | The Greatest Motion Picture Piano Concertos | 1959 | 20.00 |
| ❑ WS 1338 [S] | 22 Best Loved Christmas Piano Concertos | 1959 | 20.00 |
| ❑ W 1366 [M] | The Most Beautiful Music of Hawaii | 1960 | 12.00 |
| ❑ WS 1366 [S] | The Most Beautiful Music of Hawaii | 1960 | 15.00 |
| ❑ W 1387 [M] | The World's Greatest Love Themes | 1960 | 12.00 |
| ❑ WS 1387 [S] | The World's Greatest Love Themes | 1960 | 15.00 |
| ❑ W 1402 [M] | Piano Italiano | 1961 | 12.00 |
| ❑ WS 1402 [S] | Piano Italiano | 1961 | 15.00 |
| ❑ W 1410 [M] | The Best of the Popular Piano Concertos | 1961 | 12.00 |
| ❑ WS 1410 [S] | The Best of the Popular Piano Concertos | 1961 | 15.00 |
| ❑ W 1415 [M] | Great Broadway Musicals | 1961 | 12.00 |

| Number | Title (A Side/B Side) | Yr | NM |
|---|---|---|---|
| ❑ WS 1415 [S] | Great Broadway Musicals | 1961 | 15.00 |
| ❑ W 1427 [M] | Famous Film Themes | 1961 | 12.00 |
| ❑ WS 1427 [S] | Famous Film Themes | 1961 | 15.00 |
| ❑ W 1451 [M] | George Greeley Plays George Gershwin | 1962 | 12.00 |
| ❑ WS 1451 [S] | George Greeley Plays George Gershwin | 1962 | 15.00 |
| ❑ W 1476 [M] | Themes from Mutiny on the Bounty and Other Great Films | 1962 | 12.00 |
| ❑ WS 1476 [S] | Themes from Mutiny on the Bounty and Other Great Films | 1962 | 15.00 |
| ❑ W 1503 [M] | A Classic Affair | 1963 | 12.00 |
| ❑ WS 1503 [S] | A Classic Affair | 1963 | 15.00 |
| ❑ W 1560 [M] | Best Loved Christmas Piano Concertos | 1965 | 12.00 |
| ❑ WS 1560 [S] | Best Loved Christmas Piano Concertos | 1965 | 15.00 |

## GREEN, AL

### A&M

| Number | Title (A Side/B Side) | Yr | NM |
|---|---|---|---|
| ❑ SP-5150 | Soul Survivor | 1987 | 10.00 |
| ❑ SP-5228 | I Get Joy | 1989 | 10.00 |

### BELL

| Number | Title (A Side/B Side) | Yr | NM |
|---|---|---|---|
| ❑ 6076 | Al Green | 1972 | 20.00 |
| *—Reissue of Hot Line LP* | | | |

### BLUE NOTE

| Number | Title (A Side/B Side) | Yr | NM |
|---|---|---|---|
| ❑ BTE 74584 | Everything's OK | 2005 | 15.00 |
| ❑ 93556 [(2)] | I Can't Stop | 2003 | 15.00 |

### DCC COMPACT CLASSICS

| Number | Title (A Side/B Side) | Yr | NM |
|---|---|---|---|
| ❑ LPZ-2058 | Greatest Hits | 1998 | 30.00 |
| *—Audiophile vinyl* | | | |

### HI

| Number | Title (A Side/B Side) | Yr | NM |
|---|---|---|---|
| ❑ 6004 | The Belle Album | 1977 | 12.00 |
| ❑ 6009 | Truth 'N' Time | 1978 | 12.00 |
| ❑ 8000 | Tired of Being Alone | 1977 | 12.00 |
| ❑ 8001 | Al Green Gets Next to You | 1977 | 12.00 |
| ❑ 8007 | Let's Stay Together | 1977 | 12.00 |
| ❑ SHL-32055 | Green Is Blues | 1969 | 15.00 |
| ❑ SHL-32062 | Al Green Gets Next to You | 1971 | 15.00 |
| ❑ SHL-32070 | Let's Stay Together | 1972 | 15.00 |
| ❑ SHL-32074 | I'm Still in Love with You | 1972 | 15.00 |
| ❑ SHL-32077 | Call Me | 1973 | 15.00 |
| ❑ SHL-32082 | Livin' for You | 1973 | 15.00 |
| ❑ SHL-32087 | Al Green Explores Your Mind | 1974 | 15.00 |
| ❑ SHL-32089 | Al Green/Greatest Hits | 1975 | 15.00 |
| ❑ SHL-32092 | Al Green Is Love | 1975 | 15.00 |
| ❑ SHL-32097 | Full of Fire | 1976 | 15.00 |
| ❑ SHL-32103 | Have a Good Time | 1976 | 15.00 |
| ❑ SHL-32105 | Al Green's Greatest Hits, Volume II | 1977 | 15.00 |

### HOT LINE

| Number | Title (A Side/B Side) | Yr | NM |
|---|---|---|---|
| ❑ 1500 [M] | Back Up Train | 1967 | 50.00 |
| *—As "Al Greene"* | | | |
| ❑ S-1500 [S] | Back Up Train | 1967 | 80.00 |
| *—As "Al Greene"* | | | |

### KORY

| Number | Title (A Side/B Side) | Yr | NM |
|---|---|---|---|
| ❑ 1005 | Al Green | 1977 | 10.00 |
| *—Reissue of Bell LP* | | | |

### MCA

| Number | Title (A Side/B Side) | Yr | NM |
|---|---|---|---|
| ❑ 42308 | Love Ritual | 1988 | 10.00 |

### MOTOWN

| Number | Title (A Side/B Side) | Yr | NM |
|---|---|---|---|
| ❑ 5283 ML | Al Green/Greatest Hits | 198? | 10.00 |
| *—Reissue of Hi 32089* | | | |
| ❑ 5284 ML | I'm Still in Love with You | 198? | 10.00 |
| *—Reissue of Hi 32074* | | | |
| ❑ 5290 ML | Let's Stay Together | 198? | 10.00 |
| *—Reissue of Hi 32070* | | | |
| ❑ 5291 ML | Al Green's Greatest Hits, Volume II | 198? | 10.00 |
| *—Reissue of Hi 32105* | | | |
| ❑ 5317 ML | Truth N' Time | 198? | 10.00 |

### MYRRH

| Number | Title (A Side/B Side) | Yr | NM |
|---|---|---|---|
| ❑ MSB-6661 | The Lord Will Make a Way | 1980 | 10.00 |
| ❑ MSB-6671 | Higher Plane | 1981 | 10.00 |
| ❑ MSB-6702 | Precious Lord | 1981 | 10.00 |
| ❑ MSB-6747 | I'll Rise Again | 1982 | 10.00 |
| ❑ MSB-6774 | Al Green and the Full Gospel Tabernacle Choir | 1984 | 10.00 |
| ❑ WR-8113 | The Lord Will Make a Way | 1985 | 8.00 |
| *—Reissue with new number and A&M logo* | | | |
| ❑ WR-8114 | Higher Plane | 1985 | 8.00 |
| *—Reissue with new number and A&M logo* | | | |
| ❑ WR-8115 | Precious Lord | 1985 | 8.00 |
| *—Reissue with new number and A&M logo* | | | |
| ❑ WR-8116 | I'll Rise Again | 1985 | 8.00 |
| *—Reissue with new number and A&M logo* | | | |
| ❑ WR-8117 | White Christmas | 1985 | 10.00 |
| *—Reissue with new number and A&M logo* | | | |
| ❑ WR-8118 | Trust in God | 1985 | 8.00 |
| *—Reissue with new number and A&M logo* | | | |
| ❑ WR-8209 | Al Green and the Full Gospel Tabernacle Choir | 1986 | 8.00 |
| *—Reissue with new number and A&M logo* | | | |
| ❑ 7-01-678006-6 | White Christmas | 1984 | 12.00 |
| ❑ 7-01-678306-? | Trust in God | 1984 | 10.00 |

### THE RIGHT STUFF

| Number | Title (A Side/B Side) | Yr | NM |
|---|---|---|---|
| ❑ T1-27121 | Let's Stay Together | 1995 | 15.00 |
| *—Green vinyl reissue* | | | |
| ❑ T1-27627 | I'm Still in Love with You | 1995 | 15.00 |
| *—Green vinyl reissue* | | | |

### WORD

| Number | Title (A Side/B Side) | Yr | NM |
|---|---|---|---|
| ❑ E 77000 | One in a Million | 1991 | 12.00 |

## GREEN, BENNIE

### BARBARY

| Number | Title (A Side/B Side) | Yr | NM |
|---|---|---|---|
| ❑ M 33015 [M] | Play More Than You Can Stand | 196? | 25.00 |

### BETHLEHEM

| Number | Title (A Side/B Side) | Yr | NM |
|---|---|---|---|
| ❑ BCP-4019 [M] | Hornful of Soul | 196? | 20.00 |
| *—Reissue of 6054* | | | |
| ❑ BCP-6054 [M] | Hornful of Soul | 1961 | 30.00 |

### BLUE NOTE

| Number | Title (A Side/B Side) | Yr | NM |
|---|---|---|---|
| ❑ BLP-1587 [M] | Back on the Scene | 1958 | 80.00 |
| *—Regular version with W. 63rd St. addresss on label* | | | |
| ❑ BLP-1587 [M] | Back on the Scene | 1958 | 120.00 |
| *—"Deep groove" version (deep indentation under label on both sides)* | | | |
| ❑ BLP-1587 [M] | Back on the Scene | 1963 | 25.00 |
| *—With "New York, USA" address on label* | | | |
| ❑ BST-1587 [S] | Back on the Scene | 1959 | 60.00 |
| *—Regular version with W. 63rd St. addresss on label* | | | |
| ❑ BST-1587 [S] | Back on the Scene | 1959 | 80.00 |
| *—"Deep groove" version (deep indentation under label on both sides)* | | | |
| ❑ BLP-1599 [M] | Soul Stirrin' | 1958 | 80.00 |
| *—Regular version with W. 63rd St. addresss on label* | | | |
| ❑ BLP-1599 [M] | Soul Stirrin' | 1958 | 120.00 |
| *—"Deep groove" version (deep indentation under label on both sides)* | | | |
| ❑ BLP-1599 [M] | Soul Stirrin' | 1963 | 25.00 |
| *—With "New York, USA" address on label* | | | |
| ❑ BST-1599 [S] | Soul Stirrin' | 1959 | 60.00 |
| *—Regular version with W. 63rd St. addresss on label* | | | |
| ❑ BST-1599 [S] | Soul Stirrin' | 1959 | 80.00 |
| *—"Deep groove" version (deep indentation under label on both sides)* | | | |
| ❑ BLP-4010 [M] | Walkin' and Talkin' | 1959 | 80.00 |
| *—Regular version with W. 63rd St. addresss on label* | | | |
| ❑ BLP-4010 [M] | Walkin' and Talkin' | 1959 | 120.00 |
| *—"Deep groove" version (deep indentation under label on both sides)* | | | |
| ❑ BLP-4010 [M] | Walkin' and Talkin' | 1963 | 25.00 |
| *—With "New York, USA" address on label* | | | |
| ❑ BST-4010 [S] | Walkin' and Talkin' | 1959 | 60.00 |
| *—Regular version with W. 63rd St. addresss on label* | | | |
| ❑ BST-4010 [S] | Walkin' and Talkin' | 1959 | 80.00 |
| *—"Deep groove" version (deep indentation under label on both sides)* | | | |
| ❑ BST-81587 [S] | Back on the Scene | 1963 | 20.00 |
| *—With "New York, USA" address on label* | | | |
| ❑ BST-81599 [S] | Soul Stirrin' | 1963 | 20.00 |
| *—With "New York, USA" address on label* | | | |
| ❑ BST-84010 [S] | Walkin' and Talkin' | 1963 | 20.00 |
| *—With "New York, USA" address on label* | | | |

### ENRICA

| Number | Title (A Side/B Side) | Yr | NM |
|---|---|---|---|
| ❑ 2002 [M] | Bennie Green Swings the Blues | 1960 | 30.00 |
| ❑ S-2002 [S] | Bennie Green Swings the Blues | 1960 | 40.00 |

### JAZZLAND

| Number | Title (A Side/B Side) | Yr | NM |
|---|---|---|---|
| ❑ JLP-43 [M] | Glidin' Along | 1961 | 25.00 |
| ❑ JLP-943 [S] | Glidin' Along | 1961 | 30.00 |

### PRESTIGE

| Number | Title (A Side/B Side) | Yr | NM |
|---|---|---|---|
| ❑ PRLP-210 [10] | Bennie Blows His Horn | 1955 | 150.00 |
| ❑ PRLP-7041 [M] | Bennie Green and Art Farmer | 1956 | 100.00 |
| ❑ PRLP-7049 [M] | Walking Down | 1956 | 100.00 |
| ❑ PRLP-7052 [M] | Bennie Green Blows His Horn | 1956 | 100.00 |
| ❑ PRLP-7160 [M] | Bennie Green Blows His Horn | 1959 | 80.00 |

### RCA VICTOR

| Number | Title (A Side/B Side) | Yr | NM |
|---|---|---|---|
| ❑ LPM-2376 [M] | Futura | 1961 | 25.00 |
| ❑ LSP-2376 [S] | Futura | 1961 | 30.00 |

### TIME

| Number | Title (A Side/B Side) | Yr | NM |
|---|---|---|---|
| ❑ S-2021 [S] | Bennie Green | 1960 | 50.00 |
| ❑ 52021 [M] | Bennie Green | 1960 | 40.00 |

### VEE JAY

| Number | Title (A Side/B Side) | Yr | NM |
|---|---|---|---|
| ❑ LP-1005 [M] | The Swingin'est | 1959 | 50.00 |
| ❑ SR-1005 [S] | The Swingin'est | 1959 | 50.00 |
| *—This LP was reissued as "Juggin' Around" by GENE AMMONS on Vee Jay 3024* | | | |

## GREEN, BENNIE/PAUL QUINICHETTE

### DECCA

| Number | Title (A Side/B Side) | Yr | NM |
|---|---|---|---|
| ❑ DL 8176 [M] | Blow Your Horn | 1955 | 50.00 |

## GREEN, BERNIE

### RCA VICTOR

| Number | Title (A Side/B Side) | Yr | NM |
|---|---|---|---|
| ❑ LPM-1929 [M] | Musically Mad | 1959 | 60.00 |
| ❑ LSP-1929 [S] | Musically Mad | 1959 | 100.00 |
| ❑ LSA-2376 [S] | Futura | 1961 | 50.00 |

### SAN FRANCISCO

| Number | Title (A Side/B Side) | Yr | NM |
|---|---|---|---|
| ❑ M-33015 [M] | Bernie Green Plays More Than You Can Stand in Hi-Fi | 1957 | 50.00 |

## GREEN, BUNKY

### ARGO

| Number | Title (A Side/B Side) | Yr | NM |
|---|---|---|---|
| ❑ LP-753 [M] | Testifyin' Time | 1965 | 25.00 |
| ❑ LPS-753 [S] | Testifyin' Time | 1965 | 30.00 |

### CADET

| Number | Title (A Side/B Side) | Yr | NM |
|---|---|---|---|
| ❑ LPS-753 [S] | Testifyin' Time | 1966 | 20.00 |
| ❑ LP-766 [M] | Playin' for Keeps | 1966 | 25.00 |
| ❑ LPS-766 [S] | Playin' for Keeps | 1966 | 30.00 |
| ❑ LP-780 [M] | The Latinization of Bunky Green | 1967 | 30.00 |
| ❑ LPS-780 [S] | The Latinization of Bunky Green | 1967 | 25.00 |

## GREEN, BYRDIE

### PRESTIGE

| Number | Title (A Side/B Side) | Yr | NM |
|---|---|---|---|
| ❑ PRLP-7503 [M] | The Golden Thrush Speaks | 1967 | 20.00 |
| ❑ PRLP-7509 [M] | I Got It Bad | 1967 | 20.00 |

## GREEN, FREDDIE

### RCA VICTOR

| Number | Title (A Side/B Side) | Yr | NM |
|---|---|---|---|
| ❑ LPM-1210 [M] | Mr. Rhythm | 1956 | 50.00 |

## GREEN, GARLAND

### RCA VICTOR

| Number | Title (A Side/B Side) | Yr | NM |
|---|---|---|---|
| ❑ APL1-2351 | Love Is What We Came Here For | 1977 | 12.00 |

### UNI

| Number | Title (A Side/B Side) | Yr | NM |
|---|---|---|---|
| ❑ 73073 | Jealous Kind of Fellow | 1969 | 20.00 |

## GREEN, GRANT

### BLUE NOTE

| Number | Title (A Side/B Side) | Yr | NM |
|---|---|---|---|
| ❑ BN-LA037-G2 [(2)] | Live at the Lighthouse | 1973 | 50.00 |
| ❑ BLP-4064 [M] | Grant's First Stand | 1961 | 200.00 |
| *—With W. 63rd St. address on label* | | | |
| ❑ BLP-4064 [M] | Grant's First Stand | 1963 | 50.00 |
| *—With New York, USA address on label* | | | |
| ❑ BLP-4071 [M] | Green Street | 1961 | 200.00 |
| *—With W. 63rd St. address on label* | | | |
| ❑ BLP-4071 [M] | Green Street | 1963 | 60.00 |
| *—With New York, USA address on label* | | | |
| ❑ BLP-4086 [M] | Grant Stand | 1962 | 200.00 |
| *—With W. 63rd St. address on label* | | | |
| ❑ BLP-4086 [M] | Grant Stand | 1963 | 100.00 |
| *—With New York, USA address on label* | | | |
| ❑ BLP-4099 [M] | Sunday Mornin' | 1962 | 200.00 |
| *—With W. 63rd St. address on label* | | | |
| ❑ BLP-4099 [M] | Sunday Mornin' | 1963 | 150.00 |
| *—With New York, USA address on label* | | | |
| ❑ BLP-4111 [M] | The Latin Bit | 1962 | 100.00 |
| *—With "New York, USA" on label* | | | |
| ❑ BLP-4132 [M] | Feelin' the Spirit | 1963 | 40.00 |
| ❑ BLP-4139 [M] | Am I Blue | 1963 | 100.00 |
| *—With "New York, USA" on label* | | | |
| ❑ BLP-4154 [M] | Idle Moments | 1964 | 40.00 |
| ❑ BLP-4183 [M] | Talkin' About! | 1964 | 40.00 |
| ❑ BLP-4202 [M] | I Want to Hold Your Hand | 1964 | 40.00 |
| ❑ BLP-4253 [M] | Street of Dreams | 1967 | 100.00 |
| *—"A Division of Liberty Records" on label* | | | |
| ❑ BLP-84064 [S] | Grant's First Stand | 1961 | 150.00 |
| *—With W. 63rd St. address on label* | | | |
| ❑ BLP-84064 [S] | Grant's First Stand | 1963 | 80.00 |
| *—With New York, USA address on label* | | | |
| ❑ BLP-84071 [S] | Green Street | 1961 | 150.00 |
| *—With W. 63rd St. address on label* | | | |
| ❑ BLP-84071 [S] | Green Street | 1963 | 60.00 |
| *—With New York, USA address on label* | | | |
| ❑ BLP-84086 [S] | Grant Stand | 1962 | 150.00 |
| *—With W. 63rd St. address on label* | | | |
| ❑ BLP-84086 [S] | Grant Stand | 1963 | 100.00 |
| *—With New York, USA address on label* | | | |
| ❑ BLP-84099 [S] | Sunday Mornin' | 1962 | 150.00 |
| *—With W. 63rd St. address on label* | | | |
| ❑ BLP-84099 [S] | Sunday Mornin' | 1963 | 120.00 |
| *—With New York, USA address on label* | | | |
| ❑ BLP-84111 [S] | The Latin Bit | 1962 | 100.00 |
| *—With New York, USA address on label; reproductions exist* | | | |
| ❑ BLP-84132 [S] | Feelin' the Spirit | 1963 | 100.00 |
| *—With New York, USA address on label* | | | |
| ❑ BLP-84139 [S] | Am I Blue | 1963 | 100.00 |
| *—With New York, USA address on label* | | | |
| ❑ BLP-84154 [S] | Idle Moments | 1964 | 100.00 |
| *—With New York, USA address on label* | | | |
| ❑ BLP-84183 [S] | Talkin' About! | 1964 | 100.00 |
| *—With New York, USA address on label* | | | |
| ❑ BLP-84202 [S] | I Want to Hold Your Hand | 1964 | 100.00 |
| *—With New York, USA address on label* | | | |
| ❑ BLP-84253 [S] | Street of Dreams | 1967 | 80.00 |
| *—"A Division of Liberty Records" on label* | | | |
| ❑ BLP-84310 | Goin' West | 1969 | 100.00 |
| *—"A Division of Liberty Records" on label* | | | |
| ❑ BLP-84327 | Carryin' On | 1969 | 100.00 |
| *—"A Division of Liberty Records" on label* | | | |
| ❑ BLP-84342 | Green Is Beautiful | 1970 | 60.00 |
| *—"A Division of Liberty Records" on label* | | | |
| ❑ BLP-84360 | Alive! | 1970 | 60.00 |
| *—We're not sure what the original label is; it could be the blue and white label with "A Division of Liberty Records," the mostly black label with "Liberty/UA," or the blue and white label with "A Division of United Artists Records"* | | | |



Except when noted otherwise, VG = 25% of NM, and VG+ = 50% of NM. (Example: VG = $2.00, VG+ = $4.00 and NM = $8.00.)

Number Title (A Side/B Side) Yr NM
Number Title (A Side/B Side) Yr NM

❑ BLP-84360 Alive! 1973 25.00
*—Dark blue label with black stylized "b" at upper right*
❑ BLP-84373 Visions 1971 80.00
❑ BLP-84413 Shades of Green 1972 80.00
*—"A Division of United Artists Records" on blue and white label*
❑ BLP-84415 The Final Comedown 1972 80.00
*—"A Division of United Artists Records" on blue and white label*

DELMARK
❑ DL-404 [M] All the Gin Is Gone 1966 25.00
❑ DS-404 [S] All the Gin Is Gone 1966 25.00
❑ DL-427 [M] Black Forrest 1966 25.00
❑ DS-427 [S] Black Forrest 1966 25.00

MOSAIC
❑ MR5-133 [(5)] The Complete Blue Note Recordings of Grant Green with Sonny Clark 199? 300.00

VERVE
❑ V-8627 [M] His Majesty, King Funk 1965 100.00
❑ V6-8627 [S] His Majesty, King Funk 1965 120.00

**GREEN, LLOYD**

CHART
❑ CHM-1006 [M] Mr. Nashville Sound 1968 50.00
❑ CHS-1006 [S] Mr. Nashville Sound 1968 25.00
❑ CHS-1010 Cool Steel Man 1969 25.00
❑ 1024 Moody River 1970 25.00

GRT
❑ 8018 Feelings 1977 12.00

LITTLE DARLIN'
❑ LD-4002 Day for Decision 196? 25.00
❑ LD 4005 The Hit Sounds of Lloyd Green 196? 25.00

MONUMENT
❑ KZ 32532 Shades of Steel 1973 15.00
❑ KZ 33368 Steel Rides 1975 15.00

TIME
❑ ST-2152 [S] Big Steel Guitar 1964 40.00
❑ T-2152 [M] Big Steel Guitar 1964 30.00

**GREEN, PETER** Also see FLEETWOOD MAC.

REPRISE
❑ RS 6436 The End of the Game 1970 20.00

SAIL
❑ 0110 In the Skies 1979 10.00
❑ 0112 Little Dreamer 1980 10.00

**GREEN, PHIL**

LONDON
❑ LPB-17 [10] Rhythm on Reeds 1950 50.00

**GREEN, URBIE**

ABC-PARAMOUNT
❑ ABC-101 [M] Blues and Other Shades of Green 1955 60.00
❑ ABC-137 [M] All About Urbie Green 1956 50.00

BETHLEHEM
❑ BCP-14 [M] East Coast Jazz, Volume 6 1955 80.00

BLUE NOTE
❑ BLP-5036 [10] Urbie Green Septet 1954 250.00

RCA VICTOR
❑ LPM-1667 [M] Let's Face the Music and Dance 1958 40.00
❑ LSP-1667 [S] Let's Face the Music and Dance 1958 40.00
❑ LPM-1741 [M] Jimmy McHugh in Hi-Fi 1958 50.00
❑ LSP-1741 [S] Jimmy McHugh in Hi-Fi 1958 60.00
❑ LPM-1969 [M] Best of the New Broadway Show Hits 1959 40.00
❑ LSP-1969 [S] Best of the New Broadway Show Hits 1959 40.00

VANGUARD
❑ VRS-8010 [10] Urbie Green and His Band 1954 120.00

"X"
❑ LXA-3026 [10] A Cool Yuletide 1954 120.00

**GREEN, URBIE/VIC DICKENSON**

JAZZTONE
❑ J-1259 [M] Urbie Green Octet/Slidin' Swing 1957 40.00

**GREEN, WILLIAM**

EVEREST
❑ SDBR-1213 [S] Shades of Green 1963 20.00

**GREEN BULLFROG**

DECCA
❑ DL 75269 Green Bullfrog 1971 25.00

**GREEN DAY**

ADELINE
❑ 012-1 Warning: 2000 12.00
❑ AR033-1 [(2)] American Idiot 2006 30.00

LOOKOUT!
❑ 22 39/Smooth 1990 10.00
❑ 46 Kerplunk 1992 10.00

REPRISE
❑ 45529 Dookie 1994 15.00
*—Original stock issue on black vinyl*
❑ 45529 Dookie 1995 10.00
*—Reissue on pink vinyl*
❑ 45529 [DJ] Dookie 1994 30.00
*—Promo version on milky pale-green vinyl*
❑ 45529 [DJ] Dookie 1994 35.00
*—Promo version on clear green vinyl in plain white cover*
❑ 46046 Insomniac 1995 10.00

**GREEN RIVER** Members of this band later joined MOTHER LOVE BONE, MUDHONEY and PEARL JAM.

HOMESTEAD
❑ 031 Come On Down 198? 12.00
*—Originals do not have a UPC code (deduct 25% if UPC is there)*

SUB POP
❑ 11 [EP] Dry as a Bone 1987 35.00
*—Later copies have pink inserts*
❑ 11 [EP] Dry as a Bone 1987 50.00
*—First 2,000 copies have yellow inserts*
❑ 15 [EP] Rehab Doll 1988 25.00
❑ 15 [EP] Rehab Doll 1988 35.00
*—First 1,000 copies on green vinyl*

**GREENBAUM, NORMAN** Also see DR. WEST'S MEDICINE SHOW AND JUG BAND.

REPRISE
❑ MS 2048 Petaluma 1972 15.00
❑ RS 6365 Spirit in the Sky 1969 20.00
❑ RS 6422 Back Home Again 1970 15.00

**GREENBRIAR BOYS, THE**

ELEKTRA
❑ EKL-233 [M] Dian and the Greenbriar Boys 1963 25.00
❑ EKS-7233 [S] Dian and the Greenbriar Boys 1963 30.00

VANGUARD
❑ VRS-9104 [M] The Greenbriar Boys 1962 25.00
❑ VRS-9159 [M] Ragged But Right 1964 20.00
❑ VRS-9233 [M] Better Late Than Never 1966 20.00
❑ VSD-79159 [S] Ragged But Right 1964 25.00
❑ VSD-79233 [S] Better Late Than Never 1966 25.00

**GREENE, BURTON**

ESP-DISK'
❑ 1024 [M] Burton Greene 1966 25.00
❑ S-1024 [S] Burton Greene 1966 20.00
❑ S-1074 Burton Greene Concert Tour 1968 25.00

**GREENE, DODO**

BLUE NOTE
❑ BLP-9001 [M] My Hour of Need 1962 50.00
*—With W. 63rd St. addresss on label*
❑ BLP-9001 [M] My Hour of Need 1963 25.00
*—With "New York, USA" address on label*
❑ BST-89001 [S] My Hour of Need 1967 20.00
*—With "A Division of Liberty Records" on label*

**GREENE, JACK**

DECCA
❑ DL 4845 [M] There Goes My Everything 1967 20.00
❑ DL 4904 [M] All the Time 1967 20.00
❑ DL 4939 [M] What Locks the Door 1968 25.00
❑ DL 4979 [M] You Are My Treasure 1968 30.00
❑ DL 74845 [S] There Goes My Everything 1967 15.00
❑ DL 74904 [S] All the Time 1967 15.00
❑ DL 74939 [S] What Locks the Door 1968 15.00
❑ DL 74979 [S] You Are My Treasure 1968 15.00
❑ DL 75080 I Am Not Alone 1969 15.00
❑ DL 75124 Statue of a Fool 1969 15.00
❑ DL 75156 Back in the Arms of Love 1969 15.00
❑ DL 75188 Lord Is That Me 1970 15.00
❑ DL 75208 Greatest Hits 1970 15.00
❑ DL 75283 There's a Whole Lot About a Woman 1971 15.00
❑ DL 75308 Greene Country 1972 15.00
❑ ST-91433 [S] What Locks the Door 1968 20.00
*—Capitol Record Club edition*
❑ T-91433 [M] What Locks the Door 1968 40.00
*—Capitol Record Club edition*

MCA
❑ 291 Greatest Hits 1973 12.00
*—Reissue of Decca 75208*
❑ 295 Greene Country 1973 12.00
*—Reissue of Decca 75308*

PICKWICK
❑ SPC-6173 I Never Had It So Good 197? 10.00

**GREENE, LORNE**

RCA CAMDEN
❑ CAS-2391 Five Card Stud 1970 25.00

RCA VICTOR
❑ SP-33-327 [DJ] Palaver with The Man 1965 50.00
*—Promo-only interview record with script*
❑ LPM-2661 [M] Young at Heart 1963 25.00
❑ LSP-2661 [S] Young at Heart 1963 30.00
❑ LPM-2843 [M] Welcome to the Ponderosa 1964 25.00
❑ LSP-2843 [S] Welcome to the Ponderosa 1964 30.00
❑ LPM-3302 [M] The Man 1965 25.00
❑ LSP-3302 [S] The Man 1965 30.00
❑ LPM-3409 [M] Lorne Greene's American West 1965 25.00
❑ LSP-3409 [S] Lorne Greene's American West 1965 30.00
❑ LPM-3410 [M] Have a Happy Holiday 1965 25.00
❑ LSP-3410 [S] Have a Happy Holiday 1965 30.00
❑ LPM-3678 [M] Portrait of the West 1966 25.00
❑ LSP-3678 [S] Portrait of the West 1966 30.00

RCA VICTOR RED SEAL
❑ LM-2783 [M] Peter and the Wolf 1964 25.00
❑ LSC-2783 [S] Peter and the Wolf 1964 30.00
*—Above with the London Symphony Orchestra*

**GREENE, LORNE; MICHAEL LANDON; DAN BLOCKER**

RCA VICTOR
❑ LPM-2583 [M] Bonanza — Ponderosa Party Time! 1962 30.00
❑ LSP-2583 [S] Bonanza — Ponderosa Party Time! 1962 40.00
❑ LPM-2757 [M] Christmas on the Ponderosa 1963 25.00
❑ LSP-2757 [S] Christmas on the Ponderosa 1963 30.00

**GREENSLEEVES, EDDIE**

CAMEO
❑ C-1031 [M] Humorous Folk Songs 1963 20.00
❑ SC-1031 [S] Humorous Folk Songs 1963 25.00

**GREENWICH, ELLIE** Also see THE RAINDROPS.

UNITED ARTISTS
❑ UAS-6648 Ellie Greenwich Composes, Produces and Sings 1968 50.00

VERVE
❑ V6-5091 Let It Be Written, Let It Be Sung 1973 25.00

**GREER, PAULA**

WORKSHOP JAZZ
❑ WSJ 203 [M] Introducing Miss Paula Greer 1963 250.00

**GREGG, BOBBY**

EPIC
❑ LN 24051 [M] Let's Stomp and Wild Weekend 1963 30.00
❑ BN 26051 [S] Let's Stomp and Wild Weekend 1963 40.00

**GREGORY, DICK**

COLPIX
❑ CP 417 [M] In Living Black and White 1961 25.00
❑ CP 420 [M] East and West 1961 25.00
❑ CP 480 [M] We All Have Problems 1964 25.00

GATEWAY
❑ GLP 9007 [M] My Brother's Keeper 1963 40.00

POPPY
❑ PP-LA176-G2 [(2)] Caught in the Act 1973 15.00
❑ PYS 40008 Dick Gregory On... 1970 15.00
❑ PYS 40011 Dick Gregory at the Village Gate 1972 15.00
❑ PYS 60001 [(2)] The Light Side: The Dark Side 1969 20.00
❑ PYS 60004 [(2)] Frankenstein 1970 15.00
❑ PYS 60005 [(2)] Dick Gregory at Kent State 1971 15.00

TOMATO
❑ 9001 [(3)] The Best of Dick Gregory 1978 20.00

VEE JAY
❑ LP 1093 [M] Running for President 1964 25.00
❑ LP 4001 [M] Dick Gregory Talks Turkey 1962 25.00
❑ LP 4005 [M] Two Sides of Dick Gregory 1963 25.00

**GRENFELL, JOYCE**

ELEKTRA
❑ EKL-184 [M] Presenting Joyce Grenfell 1960 30.00

**GREY, AL**

ARGO
❑ LP-653 [M] The Last of the Big Plungers 1960 25.00
❑ LPS-653 [S] The Last of the Big Plungers 1960 25.00
❑ LP-677 [M] The Thinking Man's Trombone 1961 20.00
❑ LPS-677 [S] The Thinking Man's Trombone 1961 25.00
❑ LP-689 [M] Al Grey and the Billy Mitchell Sextet 1962 20.00
❑ LPS-689 [S] Al Grey and the Billy Mitchell Sextet 1962 25.00
❑ LP-700 [M] Snap Your Fingers 1962 20.00
❑ LPS-700 [S] Snap Your Fingers 1962 25.00
❑ LP-711 [M] Night Song 1963 20.00
❑ LPS-711 [S] Night Song 1963 25.00
❑ LP-718 [M] Having a Ball 1963 20.00
❑ LPS-718 [S] Having a Ball 1963 25.00
❑ LP-731 [M] Boss Bones 1964 20.00
❑ LPS-731 [S] Boss Bones 1964 25.00

TANGERINE
❑ TRCS-1504 [S] Shades of Grey 1965 20.00

**GRIER, ROOSEVELT**

RIC
❑ M-1008 [M] Soul City 1964 20.00
❑ S-1008 [S] Soul City 1964 25.00

Number | Title (A Side/B Side) | Yr | NM

WORD
❑ WR-8342 Committed 1986 12.00

### GRIFF, RAY
ABC DOT
❑ DOSD-2011 Expressions 1974 12.00
CAPITOL
❑ ST-11486 Ray Griff 1976 10.00
❑ ST-11566 The Last of the Winfield Amateurs 1976 10.00
❑ ST-11718 Raymond's Place 1977 10.00
DOT
❑ DLP-25868 A Ray of Sunshine 1968 20.00
❑ DOS-26013 Songs for Everyone 1973 15.00
ROYAL AMERICAN
❑ RAS 1007 Ray Griff Sings 1972 15.00

### GRIFFIN, DICK
STRATA-EAST
❑ SES-19747 The Eighth Wonder 1975 20.00

### GRIFFIN, JIMMY
POLYDOR
❑ PD 6018 James Griffin and Co. 1973 15.00
REPRISE
❑ R-6091 [M] Summer Holiday 1963 50.00
❑ R9-6091 [S] Summer Holiday 1963 60.00

### GRIFFIN, JOHNNY
ARGO
❑ LP-624 [M] Johnny Griffin Quartet 1958 50.00
BLUE NOTE
❑ BLP-1533 [M] Introducing Johnny Griffin 1956 150.00
*—Regular version, Lexington Ave. address on label*
❑ BLP-1533 [M] Introducing Johnny Griffin 1956 200.00
*—"Deep groove" version (deep indentation under label on both sides)*
❑ BLP-1533 [M] Introducing Johnny Griffin 1957 60.00
*—With "W. 63rd St." address on label*
❑ BLP-1533 [M] Introducing Johnny Griffin 1963 25.00
*—With "New York, USA" address on label*
❑ BLP-1559 [M] A Blowing Session 1957 100.00
*—Regular version, "W. 63rd St." address on label*
❑ BLP-1559 [M] A Blowing Session 1957 150.00
*—"Deep groove" version (deep indentation under label on both sides)*
❑ BLP-1559 [M] A Blowing Session 1963 25.00
*—With "New York, USA" address on label*
❑ BLP-1580 [M] The Congregation 1958 80.00
*—Regular version, "W. 63rd St." address on label*
❑ BLP-1580 [M] The Congregation 1958 120.00
*—"Deep groove" version (deep indentation under label on both sides)*
❑ BLP-1580 [M] The Congregation 1963 25.00
*—With "New York, USA" address on label*
❑ BST-1580 [S] The Congregation 1959 60.00
*—Regular version, "W. 63rd St." address on label*
❑ BST-1580 [S] The Congregation 1959 80.00
*—"Deep groove" version (deep indentation under label on both sides)*
❑ BST-1580 [S] The Congregation 1963 20.00
*—With "New York, USA" address on label*
EMARCY
❑ MG-26001 [M] Night Lady 1967 40.00
❑ SR-66001 [S] Night Lady 1967 25.00
INNER CITY
❑ IC-6042 [(2)] Live Tokyo 197? 20.00
JAZZLAND
❑ JLP-93 [M] The Little Giant 1961 40.00
❑ JLP-993 [S] The Little Giant 1961 30.00
MILESTONE
❑ 47014 [(2)] Big Soul 197? 20.00
RIVERSIDE
❑ RLP 12-264 [M]Johnny Griffin Sextet 1958 50.00
❑ RLP 12-274 [M]Way Out! 1958 50.00
❑ RLP 12-304 [M]The Little Giant 1959 50.00
❑ RLP 12-331 [M]The Big Soul-Band 1960 40.00
❑ RLP-338 [M] Studio Jazz Party 1960 40.00
❑ RLP-368 [M] Change of Pace 1961 30.00
❑ RLP-387 [M] White Gardenia 1961 30.00
❑ RLP-420 [M] The Kerry Dancers 1962 25.00
❑ RLP-437 [M] Grab This! 1962 25.00
❑ RLP-462 [M] Do Nothing 'Til You Hear from Me 1963 25.00
❑ RLP-479 [M] Wade in the Water 1964 20.00
❑ RLP-1149 [S] The Little Giant 1959 40.00
❑ RLP-1171 [S] The Big Soul-Band 1960 30.00
❑ RS-9338 [S] Studio Jazz Party 1960 30.00
❑ RS-9368 [S] Change of Pace 1961 30.00
❑ RS-9387 [S] White Gardenia 1961 30.00
❑ RS-9420 [S] The Kerry Dancers 1962 30.00
❑ RS-9437 [S] Grab This! 1962 30.00
❑ RS-9462 [S] Do Nothing 'Til You Hear from Me 1963 30.00
❑ RS-9479 [S] Wade in the Water 1964 25.00

### GRIFFIN, JOHNNY, AND MATTHEW GEE
ATLANTIC
❑ 1431 [M] Soul Groove 1965 20.00
❑ SD 1431 [S] Soul Groove 1965 25.00

### GRIFFIN, KEN
COLUMBIA
❑ CL 692 [M] The Organ Plays at Christmas 1955 25.00
*—Red and black label with six "eye" logos*
❑ CL 6130 [10] Christmas Carols by Ken Griffin 1950 30.00

### GRIFFIN, MERV
CAMEO
❑ C-1060 [M] My Favorite Songs 1964 20.00
❑ SC-1060 [S] My Favorite Songs 1964 25.00
CARLTON
❑ LP-12-134 [M] Merv Griffin's Dance Party 1961 30.00
❑ STLP-12-134 [S]Merv Griffin's Dance Party 1961 40.00
51 WEST
❑ Q 16281 P.S. I Love You 198? 8.00
GRIFFIN
❑ G3G-1501 As Time Goes By 1973 12.00
METROMEDIA
❑ MD 1023 Appearing Nightly 1969 12.00
MGM
❑ E-4326 [M] A Tinkling Piano in the Next Apartment 1965 12.00
❑ SE-4326 [S] A Tinkling Piano in the Next Apartment 1965 15.00
❑ E-4381 [M] 'Alf and 'Alf: Songs of the British Music Hall 1966 15.00
*—With Arthur Treacher*
❑ SE-4381 [S] 'Alf and 'Alf: Songs of the British Music Hall 1966 20.00
*—With Arthur Treacher*
❑ E-4401 [M] And a Sled .... And a Catcher's Mitt ... And a Puppy ... And a Popgun ... And a Big Christmas Album from Merv Griffin and His TV Family 1966 20.00
❑ SE-4401 [S] And a Sled .... And a Catcher's Mitt ... And a Puppy ... And a Popgun ... And a Big Christmas Album from Merv Griffin and His TV Family 1966 25.00
❑ SE-4562 [S] Irving Berlin Songs 1968 —
*—Canceled*

### GRIFFITH, ANDY
CAPITOL
❑ T 962 [M] Just for Laughs 1958 40.00
❑ ST 1105 [S] Andy Griffith Shouts the Blues and Old Timey Songs 1959 50.00
❑ T 1105 [M] Andy Griffith Shouts the Blues and Old Timey Songs 1959 40.00
❑ ST 1215 [S] This Here Andy Griffith 1959 40.00
❑ T 1215 [M] This Here Andy Griffith 1959 30.00
❑ ST 1611 [S] Songs, Themes and Laughs from The Andy Griffith Show 1961 120.00
❑ T 1611 [M] Songs, Themes and Laughs from The Andy Griffith Show 1961 80.00
❑ ST 2066 [S] Andy and Cleopatra 1964 25.00
❑ T 2066 [M] Andy and Cleopatra 1964 20.00

### GRIFFITH, JOHNNY, TRIO
WORKSHOP JAZZ
❑ WSJ 205 [M] Jazz 1963 200.00

### GRIFFITH, NANCI
B.F. DEAL
❑ BFD 9 There's a Light Beyond These Woods 1978 50.00
ELEKTRA
❑ 62015 Blue Roses from the Moons 1997 12.00
FEATHERBED
❑ FB 902 Poet in My Window 1982 20.00
❑ FB 903 There's a Light Beyond These Woods 1982 20.00
MCA
❑ 5927 Lone Star State of Mind 1987 8.00
❑ 6319 Storms 1989 10.00
❑ 42102 Little Love Affairs 1988 8.00
❑ 42255 One Fair Summer Evening 1988 8.00
PHILO
❑ PH-1096 Once in a Very Blue Moon 1984 12.00
❑ PH-1097 There's a Light Beyond These Woods 1986 12.00
❑ PH-1098 Poet in My Window 1986 12.00
❑ PH-1109 Last of the True Believers 1986 12.00

### GRIFFITH, SHIRLEY
BLUESVILLE
❑ BVLP-1087 [M]The Blues of Shirley Griffith 1964 25.00
*—Blue label, trident logo at right*
❑ BVLP-1087 [M]The Blues of Shirley Griffith 1964 50.00
*—Blue label, silver print*

### GRIMES, GARY
DIRECT DISK
❑ SD-16630 Starhand Visions 198? 30.00
*—Audiophile vinyl*

### GRIMES, HENRY
ESP-DISK'
❑ 1027 [M] Henry Grimes Trio 1966 20.00
❑ S-1027 [S] Henry Grimes Trio 1966 25.00

### GRIMES, TINY
PRESTIGE
❑ PRLP-7138 [M]Blues Grooves 1958 100.00
*—Yellow label*
❑ PRLP-7144 [M]Callin' the Blues 1958 100.00
SWINGVILLE
❑ SVLP-2002 [M]Tiny in Swingville 1960 50.00
*—Purple label*
❑ SVLP-2002 [M]Tiny in Swingville 1965 25.00
*—Blue label, trident logo at right*
❑ SVLP-2004 [M]Callin' the Blues 1960 50.00
*—Purple label*
❑ SVLP-2004 [M]Callin' the Blues 1965 25.00
*—Blue label, trident logo at right*
UNITED ARTISTS
❑ UAL-3232 [M] Big Time Guitar 1962 25.00
❑ UAS-6232 [S] Big Time Guitar 1962 30.00

### GRISMAN, DAVID
KALEIDOSCOPE
❑ 5 David Grisman Quintet 1977 20.00

### GRISSOM, JIMMY
ARGO
❑ LP-729 [M] World of Trouble 1963 25.00
❑ LPS-729 [S] World of Trouble 1963 30.00

### GRODECK WHIPPERJENNY
PEOPLE
❑ 3000 Grodeck Whipperjenny 1969 200.00

### GROOV-U
GATEWAY
❑ GLP-3010 Groov-U On Campus 196? 40.00

### GROOVE COLLECTIVE, THE
REPRISE
❑ 45541 [(2)] The Groove Collective 1994 20.00

### GROOVIE GOOLIES, THE
RCA VICTOR
❑ LSP-4420 The Groovie Goolies 1970 25.00

### GROSZ, MARTY
RIVERSIDE
❑ RLP 12-268 [M]Hurrah for Bix 1958 40.00
❑ RLP-1109 [S] Hurrah for Bix 1959 30.00

### GROUNDHOGS, THE
CLEVE
❑ CH-82871 The Groundhogs with John Lee Hooker and John Mayall 196? 100.00
IMPERIAL
❑ LP-12452 Blues Obituary 1969 40.00
LIBERTY
❑ LST-7644 Thank Christ for the Bomb 1970 30.00
UNITED ARTISTS
❑ UA-LA008-F Hogwash 1973 20.00
❑ UA-LA603-G Crosscut Saw 1976 20.00
❑ UA-LA680-G Black Diamond 1976 20.00
❑ UAS-5513 The Groundhogs Split 1971 20.00
❑ UAS-5570 Who Will Save the World 1972 20.00
WORLD PACIFIC
❑ WPS-21892 Scratching the Surface 1968 40.00

### GROUP, THE
BELL
❑ 6038 The Group 1970 20.00
RCA VICTOR
❑ LPM-2663 [M] The Group 1963 20.00
❑ LSP-2663 [S] The Group 1963 25.00

### GROUP IMAGE, THE
COMMUNITY
❑ A-101 A Mouth in the Clouds 1968 30.00

### GROUP ONE
RCA VICTOR
❑ LPM-3524 [M] Brothers Go to Mothers and Others 1966 15.00
❑ LSP-3524 [S] Brothers Go to Mothers and Others 1966 20.00

### GROUP THERAPY
PHILIPS
❑ PHS 600303 37 Minutes of Group Therapy 1969 15.00
RCA VICTOR
❑ LPM-3976 [M] People Get Ready for Group Therapy 1968 40.00
❑ LSP-3976 [S] People Get Ready for Group Therapy 1968 20.00

| Number | Title (A Side/B Side) | Yr | NM |
|---|---|---|---|
| **GROVE, BOBBY** | | | |
| KING | | | |
| ❑ 831 [M] | It Was for You | 1963 | 40.00 |
| **GROVE, DICK** | | | |
| PACIFIC JAZZ | | | |
| ❑ PJ-74 [M] | Little Bird Suite | 1963 | 20.00 |
| ❑ ST-74 [S] | Little Bird Suite | 1963 | 25.00 |
| **GROWING CONCERN, THE** | | | |
| MAINSTREAM | | | |
| ❑ S-6108 [S] | The Growing Concern | 1968 | 120.00 |
| ❑ 56108 [M] | The Growing Concern | 1968 | 80.00 |
| **GROWL** | | | |
| DISCREET | | | |
| ❑ DS 2209 | Growl | 1974 | 20.00 |
| **GRUNTZ, GEORGE** | | | |
| PHILIPS | | | |
| ❑ PHS 600162 [S] | Bach Humbug | 1964 | 20.00 |
| **GRUSIN, DAVE** | | | |
| COLUMBIA | | | |
| ❑ CL 2344 [M] | Kaleidoscope | 1965 | 20.00 |
| ❑ CS 9144 [S] | Kaleidoscope | 1965 | 25.00 |
| EPIC | | | |
| ❑ BN 622 [S] | Subways Are for Sleeping | 1962 | 50.00 |
| ❑ LN 3829 [M] | Subways Are for Sleeping | 1962 | 40.00 |
| ❑ LN 24023 [M] | Piano Strings and Moonlight | 1962 | 40.00 |
| ❑ BN 26023 [S] | Piano Strings and Moonlight | 1962 | 50.00 |
| SHEFFIELD LABS | | | |
| ❑ SL-5 | Discovered Again! | 1976 | 25.00 |
| *—Direct-to-disc recording* | | | |
| SHEFFIELD TREASURY | | | |
| ❑ ST-500 | Discovered Again! | 198? | 20.00 |
| *—Reissue of Sheffield Labs 5* | | | |
| VERSATILE | | | |
| ❑ NED 1135 | Don't Touch | 1977 | 20.00 |
| **GRYCE, GIGI** | | | |
| BLUE NOTE | | | |
| ❑ BLP-5049 [10] | Gigi Gryce's Jazztime Paris | 1954 | 300.00 |
| ❑ BLP-5050 [10] | Gigi Gryce and His Little Band, Volume 2 | 1954 | 300.00 |
| ❑ BLP-5051 [10] | Gigi Gryce Qunitet/Sextet, Volume 3 | 1954 | 300.00 |
| MERCURY | | | |
| ❑ MG-20628 [M] | Reminiscin' | 1961 | 30.00 |
| ❑ SR-60628 [S] | Reminiscin' | 1961 | 40.00 |
| METROJAZZ | | | |
| ❑ E-1006 [M] | Gigi Gryce | 1958 | 80.00 |
| ❑ SE-1006 [S] | Gigi Gryce | 1959 | 60.00 |
| NEW JAZZ | | | |
| ❑ NJLP-8230 [M] | Sayin' Somethin'! | 1959 | 50.00 |
| *—Purple label* | | | |
| ❑ NJLP-8230 [M] | Sayin' Somethin'! | 1965 | 25.00 |
| *—Blue label, trident logo at right* | | | |
| ❑ NJLP-8246 [M] | The Hap'nin's | 1960 | 50.00 |
| *—Purple label* | | | |
| ❑ NJLP-8246 [M] | The Hap'nin's | 1965 | 25.00 |
| *—Blue label, trident logo at right* | | | |
| ❑ NJLP-8262 [M] | The Rat Race Blues | 1961 | 50.00 |
| *—Purple label* | | | |
| ❑ NJLP-8262 [M] | The Rat Race Blues | 1965 | 25.00 |
| *—Blue label, trident logo at right* | | | |
| SAVOY | | | |
| ❑ MG-12137 [M] | Nica's Tempo | 1958 | 80.00 |
| SIGNAL | | | |
| ❑ S-1201 [M] | Gigi Gryce Quartet | 1955 | 300.00 |
| **GRYCE, GIGI, AND CLIFFORD BROWN** | | | |
| BLUE NOTE | | | |
| ❑ BLP-5048 [10] | Gigi Gryce-Clifford Brown Sextet | 1954 | 400.00 |
| **GRYPHON** | | | |
| (NO LABEL) | | | |
| ❑ 12497 | Gryphon | 197? | 80.00 |
| BELL | | | |
| ❑ 1316 | Red Queen to Gryphon Three | 1974 | 15.00 |
| **GUADALCANAL DIARY** | | | |
| DB | | | |
| ❑ 73 | Walking in the Shadow of the Big Man | 1984 | 15.00 |
| ELEKTRA | | | |
| ❑ 60429 | Walking in the Shadow of the Big Man | 1985 | 10.00 |
| ❑ 60478 | Jamboree | 1986 | 10.00 |
| ❑ 60752 | 2X4 | 1987 | 10.00 |
| ❑ 60848 | Flip-Flop | 1989 | 10.00 |
| ❑ 60848 [DJ] | Flip-Flop | 1989 | 12.00 |
| *—Promo-only white label audiophile vinyl* | | | |
| ENTERTAINMENT ON DISC | | | |
| ❑ EOD 102 [EP] | Watusi Rodeo | 1983 | 25.00 |

The Guess Who, *Road Food,* RCA Victor APL1-0405, 1974, $15.

| Number | Title (A Side/B Side) | Yr | NM |
|---|---|---|---|
| **GUARALDI, VINCE** | | | |
| FANTASY | | | |
| ❑ 3213 [M] | Modern Music from San Francisco | 195? | 25.00 |
| *—Black vinyl, red label, non-flexible vinyl* | | | |
| ❑ 3213 [M] | Modern Music from San Francisco | 1956 | 50.00 |
| *—Red vinyl* | | | |
| ❑ 3225 [M] | Vince Guaraldi Trio | 195? | 25.00 |
| *—Black vinyl, red label, non-flexible vinyl* | | | |
| ❑ 3225 [M] | Vince Guaraldi Trio | 1956 | 50.00 |
| *—Red vinyl* | | | |
| ❑ 3257 [M] | A Flower Is a Lovesome Thing | 195? | 25.00 |
| *—Black vinyl, red label, non-flexible vinyl* | | | |
| ❑ 3257 [M] | A Flower Is a Lovesome Thing | 1958 | 40.00 |
| *—Red vinyl* | | | |
| ❑ 3337 [M] | Jazz Impressions of Black Orpheus (Cast Your Fate to the Wind) | 1962 | 25.00 |
| *—Black vinyl, red label, non-flexible vinyl* | | | |
| ❑ 3337 [M] | Jazz Impressions of Black Orpheus (Cast Your Fate to the Wind) | 1962 | 40.00 |
| *—Red vinyl* | | | |
| ❑ 3352 [M] | Vince Guaraldi in Person | 1963 | 25.00 |
| ❑ 3356 [M] | Vince Guaraldi and Bola Sete and Friends | 1964 | 25.00 |
| ❑ 3358 [M] | Tour de Force | 1964 | 25.00 |
| ❑ 3359 [M] | Jazz Impressions | 1965 | 25.00 |
| ❑ 3360 [M] | The Latin Side of Vince Guaraldi | 1965 | 25.00 |
| ❑ 3362 [M] | From All Sides | 1966 | 20.00 |
| ❑ 3367 [M] | Vince Guaraldi at Grace Cathedral | 1967 | 20.00 |
| ❑ 3371 [M] | Live at the El Matador | 1967 | 20.00 |
| ❑ 5019 [M] | A Charlie Brown Christmas | 1964 | 30.00 |
| ❑ 8089 [S] | Jazz Impressions of Black Orpheus (Cast Your Fate to the Wind) | 1962 | 25.00 |
| *—Black vinyl, blue label, non-flexible vinyl* | | | |
| ❑ 8089 [S] | Jazz Impressions of Black Orpheus (Cast Your Fate to the Wind) | 1962 | 40.00 |
| *—Blue vinyl* | | | |
| ❑ 8356 [S] | Vince Guaraldi and Bola Sete and Friends | 1964 | 25.00 |
| ❑ 8358 [S] | Tour de Force | 1964 | 25.00 |
| ❑ 8359 [S] | Jazz Impressions | 1965 | 25.00 |
| ❑ 8360 [S] | The Latin Side of Vince Guaraldi | 1965 | 25.00 |
| ❑ 8362 [S] | From All Sides | 1966 | 20.00 |
| ❑ 8367 [S] | Vince Guaraldi at Grace Cathedral | 1967 | 20.00 |
| ❑ 8371 [S] | Live at the El Matador | 1967 | 20.00 |
| ❑ 8377 | Live-Live-Live | 1968 | 20.00 |
| ❑ 8430 | A Boy Named Charlie Brown — Jazz Impressions | 1971 | 20.00 |
| *—Reissue of 85017* | | | |
| ❑ 8431 | A Charlie Brown Christmas | 1971 | 25.00 |
| *—Reissue of 85019; dark blue label* | | | |
| ❑ 85017 | A Boy Named Charlie Brown — Jazz Impressions | 196? | 25.00 |
| ❑ 85019 [S] | A Charlie Brown Christmas | 1964 | 40.00 |
| MOBILE FIDELITY | | | |
| ❑ 1-112 | Jazz Impressions of Black Orpheus (Cast Your Fate to the Wind) | 1983 | 50.00 |
| *—Audiophile vinyl* | | | |
| WARNER BROS. | | | |
| ❑ WS 1747 | Oh Good Grief! | 1968 | 20.00 |
| **GUARD, DAVE, AND THE WHISKEYHILL SINGERS** | | | |
| CAPITOL | | | |
| ❑ ST 1728 [S] | Dave Guard and the Whiskeyhill Singers | 1962 | 25.00 |
| ❑ T 1728 [M] | Dave Guard and the Whiskeyhill Singers | 1962 | 20.00 |
| **GUARNIERI, JOHNNY** | | | |
| CORAL | | | |
| ❑ CRL 57085 [M] | Songs of Hudson and DeLange | 1957 | 40.00 |
| ❑ CRL 57086 [M] | The Duke Again | 1957 | 40.00 |
| GOLDEN CREST | | | |
| ❑ GC-3020 [M] | Johnny Guarnieri Plays Johnny Guarnieri | 1958 | 40.00 |
| ROYALE | | | |
| ❑ 1296 [M] | An Hour of Modern Music | 1952 | 40.00 |
| ❑ VLP 6047 [10] | Johnny Guarnieri/Tony Mottola/Bob Haggart/Cozy Cole | 195? | 50.00 |
| SAVOY | | | |
| ❑ MG-15007 [10] | Hot Piano | 1951 | 80.00 |

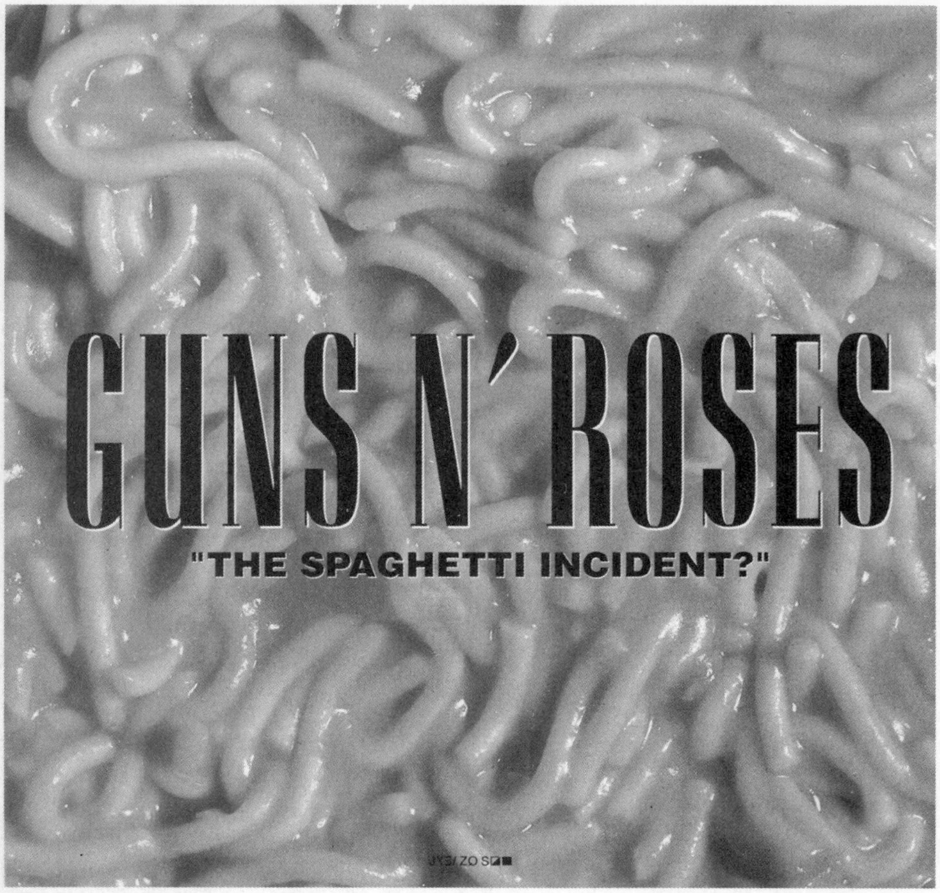

Guns N' Roses, *The Spaghetti Incident?,* Geffen GEF 24617, 1993, orange vinyl, $15.

**GUESS WHO, THE**

| Number | Title (A Side/B Side) | Yr | NM |
|---|---|---|---|
| COMPLEAT | | | |
| ❑ 672012-1 [(2)] | The Best of the Gues Who, Live | 1986 | 20.00 |
| HILLTAK | | | |
| ❑ HT 19227 | All This for a Song | 1979 | 12.00 |
| MGM | | | |
| ❑ SE-4645 | The Guess Who | 1969 | 15.00 |
| *—Compilation of pre-RCA Victor recordings* | | | |
| P.I.P. | | | |
| ❑ 6806 | The Guess Who Play Pure Guess Who | 197? | 12.00 |
| PICKWICK | | | |
| ❑ SPC-3246 | The Guess Who | 1970 | 10.00 |
| PRIDE | | | |
| ❑ PRD 0012 | The History of the Guess Who | 197? | 12.00 |
| RCA | | | |
| ❑ 7622-1-R | The Greatest of the Guess Who | 1987 | 10.00 |
| *—Late reissue* | | | |
| RCA VICTOR | | | |
| ❑ APD1-0130 [Q] | #10 | 1974 | 25.00 |
| ❑ APL1-0130 | #10 | 1973 | 15.00 |
| ❑ AFL1-0269 | The Best of the Guess Who, Volume II | 1977 | 10.00 |
| *—Reissue with new prefix* | | | |
| ❑ APD1-0269 [Q] | The Best of the Guess Who, Volume II | 1974 | 25.00 |
| ❑ APL1-0269 | The Best of the Guess Who, Volume II | 1973 | 15.00 |
| ❑ APD1-0405 [Q] | Road Food | 1974 | 25.00 |
| ❑ APL1-0405 | Road Food | 1974 | 15.00 |
| ❑ CPD1-0636 [Q] | Flavours | 1975 | 25.00 |
| ❑ CPL1-0636 | Flavours | 1975 | 15.00 |
| ❑ ANL1-0983 | Canned Wheat Packed By the Guess Who | 1975 | 10.00 |
| *—Reissue of LSP-4157* | | | |
| ❑ APD1-0995 [Q] | Power in the Music | 1975 | 25.00 |
| ❑ APL1-0995 | Power in the Music | 1975 | 15.00 |
| ❑ LSPX-1004 | The Best of the Guess Who | 1971 | 15.00 |
| ❑ ANL1-1117 | Wheatfield Soul | 1975 | 10.00 |
| *—Reissue of LSP-4141* | | | |
| ❑ APL1-1778 | The Way They Were | 1976 | 15.00 |
| ❑ APL1-2253 | The Greatest of the Guess Who | 1977 | 15.00 |
| ❑ AFL1-2594 | The Best of the Guess Who | 1978 | 10.00 |
| *—Reissue of LSPX-1004* | | | |
| ❑ AYL1-3662 | The Best of the Guess Who | 1979 | 8.00 |
| *—"Best Buy Series" reissue* | | | |
| ❑ AYL1-3673 | American Woman | 1979 | 8.00 |
| *—"Best Buy Series" reissue* | | | |
| ❑ AYL1-3746 | The Greatest of the Guess Who | 1980 | 8.00 |
| *—"Best Buy Series" reissue* | | | |
| ❑ LSP-4141 | Wheatfield Soul | 1969 | 20.00 |
| *—Orange label, non-flexible vinyl* | | | |
| ❑ LSP-4141 | Wheatfield Soul | 1971 | 12.00 |
| *—Orange label, flexible vinyl* | | | |
| ❑ LSP-4157 | Canned Wheat Packed By the Guess Who | 1969 | 20.00 |
| *—Orange label, non-flexible vinyl* | | | |
| ❑ LSP-4157 | Canned Wheat Packed By the Guess Who | 1971 | 12.00 |
| *—Orange label, flexible vinyl* | | | |
| ❑ AFL1-4266 | American Woman | 1977 | 10.00 |
| *—Reissue with new prefix* | | | |
| ❑ LSP-4266 | American Woman | 1970 | 20.00 |
| *—Orange label, non-flexible vinyl* | | | |
| ❑ LSP-4266 | American Woman | 1971 | 12.00 |
| *—Orange label, flexible vinyl* | | | |
| ❑ LSP-4359 | Share the Land | 1970 | 20.00 |
| *—Orange label, non-flexible vinyl* | | | |
| ❑ LSP-4359 | Share the Land | 1971 | 12.00 |
| *—Orange label, flexible vinyl* | | | |
| ❑ LSP-4574 | So Long, Bannatyne | 1971 | 15.00 |
| ❑ LSP-4602 | Rockin' | 1972 | 15.00 |
| ❑ LSP-4779 | Live at the Paramount (Seattle) | 1972 | 25.00 |
| ❑ LSP-4830 | Artificial Paradise | 1973 | 15.00 |
| *—Add 1/3 if paper bag is with package* | | | |
| SCEPTER | | | |
| ❑ SP-533 [M] | Shakin' All Over | 1966 | 40.00 |
| ❑ SPS-533 [P] | Shakin' All Over | 1966 | 25.00 |
| *—The above lists the artist as "The Guess Who's Chad Allan & The Expressions" on the cover* | | | |
| SPRINGBOARD | | | |
| ❑ SPB-4022 | Shakin' All Over | 1972 | 10.00 |
| SUNDAZED | | | |
| ❑ LP 5113 [(2)] | Shakin' All Over | 2001 | 15.00 |
| WAND | | | |
| ❑ WDS-691 [P] | Born in Canada | 1969 | 15.00 |
| *—Reissue of Scepter LP; three tracks are rechanneled* | | | |

**GUIDED BY VOICES**

| Number | Title (A Side/B Side) | Yr | NM |
|---|---|---|---|
| E RECORDS | | | |
| ❑ GBV 0001 | Devil Between My Toes | 1987 | 120.00 |
| HALO | | | |
| ❑ 1 | Sandbox | 1987 | 40.00 |
| ❑ 2 | Self Inflicted Aerial Nostalgia | 1989 | 40.00 |
| I WANNA | | | |
| ❑ (no #) [EP] | Forever Since Breakfast | 1986 | 100.00 |
| MATADOR | | | |
| ❑ OLE-123 | Alien Lanes | 1995 | 10.00 |
| ❑ OLE-161 [(2)] | Under the Bushes, Under the Stars | 1996 | 12.00 |
| *—One side of Record 2 is blank* | | | |
| ❑ OLE-185 [EP] | Sunfish Holy Breakfast | 1996 | 10.00 |
| ❑ OLE-241 | Mag Earwhig! | 1997 | 10.00 |
| ROCKATHON | | | |
| ❑ (no #) | Propeller | 1992 | 50.00 |
| *—Hand-colored cover with nature-book paste-on* | | | |
| ❑ 02 | Tonics & Twisted Chasers | 1997 | 12.00 |
| *—1,000 copies were pressed on various colors of vinyl* | | | |
| ROCKATHON/FADING CAPTAIN SERIES | | | |
| ❑ 7 | Suitcase Abridged: Drinks and Deliveries | 2000 | 12.00 |
| *—500 copies were pressed* | | | |
| ❑ 10 | Daredevil Stamp Collector: Do the Collapse B-Sides | 2001 | 12.00 |
| *—1,000 copies were pressed* | | | |
| ROCKET #9 | | | |
| ❑ (no #) | Same Place the Fly Got Smashed | 1990 | 40.00 |
| SCAT | | | |
| ❑ 31 | Vampire on Titus | 1993 | 15.00 |
| ❑ 35 | Bee Thousand | 1994 | 12.00 |
| ❑ 40 [(6)] | Box | 1994 | 60.00 |
| TVT | | | |
| ❑ 1980 | Do the Collapse | 1999 | 10.00 |
| ❑ 2160 | Isolation Drills | 2001 | 10.00 |

**GUITAR, BONNIE**

| Number | Title (A Side/B Side) | Yr | NM |
|---|---|---|---|
| DOT | | | |
| ❑ DLP-3069 [M] | Moonlight and Shadows | 1957 | 50.00 |
| ❑ DLP-3151 [M] | Whispering Hope | 1958 | 40.00 |
| ❑ DLP-3335 [M] | Dark Moon | 1961 | 25.00 |
| ❑ DLP-3696 [M] | Two Worlds | 1966 | 20.00 |
| ❑ DLP-3737 [M] | Miss Bonnie Guitar | 1966 | 20.00 |
| ❑ DLP-3746 [M] | Merry Christmas from Bonnie Guitar | 1966 | 20.00 |
| ❑ DLP-3793 [M] | Award Winner | 1967 | 20.00 |
| ❑ DLP-25069 [R] | Moonlight and Shadows | 196? | 15.00 |
| ❑ DLP-25151 [S] | Whispering Hope | 1958 | 50.00 |
| ❑ DLP-25335 [R] | Dark Moon | 196? | 15.00 |
| ❑ DLP-25696 [S] | Two Worlds | 1966 | 25.00 |
| ❑ DLP-25737 [S] | Miss Bonnie Guitar | 1966 | 25.00 |
| ❑ DLP-25746 [S] | Merry Christmas from Bonnie Guitar | 1966 | 25.00 |
| ❑ DLP-25793 [S] | Award Winner | 1967 | 20.00 |
| ❑ DLP-25840 | Bonnie Guitar | 1968 | 20.00 |
| ❑ DLP-25892 | Leaves Are the Tears of Autumn | 1968 | 20.00 |
| ❑ DLP-25947 | Affair! | 1969 | 20.00 |
| PARAMOUNT | | | |
| ❑ PAS-5018 | Allegheny | 1970 | 15.00 |
| PICKWICK | | | |
| ❑ SPC-3086 | Favorite Lady of Song | 196? | 12.00 |
| ❑ SPC-3144 | Green, Green Grass of Home | 196? | 12.00 |
| RCA CAMDEN | | | |
| ❑ CAS-2339 | Night Train to Memphis | 1969 | 15.00 |

**GUITAR RAMBLERS, THE**

| Number | Title (A Side/B Side) | Yr | NM |
|---|---|---|---|
| COLUMBIA | | | |
| ❑ CL 2067 [M] | The Happy, Youthful New Sounds of the Guitar Ramblers | 1964 | 25.00 |
| ❑ CS 8867 [S] | The Happy, Youthful New Sounds of the Guitar Ramblers | 1964 | 30.00 |

**GUITAR SLIM**

| Number | Title (A Side/B Side) | Yr | NM |
|---|---|---|---|
| ATLANTIC | | | |
| ❑ 81760 | The Atco Sessions | 1987 | 10.00 |
| SPECIALTY | | | |
| ❑ SP-2130 | Things That I Used to Do | 1969 | 20.00 |

**GULDA, FRIEDRICH**

| Number | Title (A Side/B Side) | Yr | NM |
|---|---|---|---|
| RCA VICTOR | | | |
| ❑ LPM-1355 [M] | Friedrich Gulda at Birdland | 1957 | 50.00 |

**GULLIN, LARS**

| Number | Title (A Side/B Side) | Yr | NM |
|---|---|---|---|
| ATLANTIC | | | |
| ❑ 1246 [M] | Baritone Sax | 1956 | 120.00 |
| *—Black label* | | | |

| Number | Title (A Side/B Side) | Yr | NM |
|---|---|---|---|
| ❑ 1246 [M] | Baritone Sax | 1960 | 50.00 |
| *—Multicolor label, white "fan" logo at right* | | | |
| CONTEMPORARY | | | |
| ❑ C-2505 [10] | Modern Sounds | 1953 | 250.00 |
| EASTWEST | | | |
| ❑ 4003 [M] | Lars Gullin Swings | 196? | 40.00 |
| EMARCY | | | |
| ❑ MG-26041 [10] | Lars Gullin Quartet | 1954 | 200.00 |
| ❑ MG-26044 [10] | Gullin's Garden | 1954 | 200.00 |
| ❑ MG-36012 [M] | Lars Gullin | 1955 | 120.00 |
| ❑ MG-36059 [M] | Lars Gullin with the Moretone Singers | 1955 | 120.00 |
| PRESTIGE | | | |
| ❑ PRLP-144 [10] | New Sounds from Sweden, Volume 5 | 1953 | 200.00 |
| ❑ PRLP-151 [10] | New Sounds from Sweden, Volume 7 | 1953 | 200.00 |

**GULLIVER** With Daryl Hall. John Oates joined later, but is not on these records.

| Number | Title (A Side/B Side) | Yr | NM |
|---|---|---|---|
| ELEKTRA | | | |
| ❑ EKS-74070 | Gulliver | 1970 | 20.00 |

**GUN**

| Number | Title (A Side/B Side) | Yr | NM |
|---|---|---|---|
| EPIC | | | |
| ❑ BN 26468 | Gun | 1969 | 20.00 |
| ❑ BN 26551 | Gunsight | 1970 | 25.00 |

**GUNS & BUTTER**

| Number | Title (A Side/B Side) | Yr | NM |
|---|---|---|---|
| COTILLION | | | |
| ❑ SD 9901 | Guns & Butter | 1972 | 20.00 |

**GUNS N' ROSES** Also see VELVET REVOLVER.

| Number | Title (A Side/B Side) | Yr | NM |
|---|---|---|---|
| GEFFEN | | | |
| ❑ GHS 24148 | Appetite for Destruction | 1987 | 10.00 |
| ❑ XXXG 24148 | Appetite for Destruction | 1987 | 40.00 |
| *—Original "rape cover"; the XXXG prefix is on the cover only; all copies of the record use the GHS prefix* | | | |
| ❑ GHS 24198 | G N' R Lies | 1988 | 12.00 |
| ❑ GEF 24415 [(2)] | Use Your Illusion I | 1991 | 25.00 |
| ❑ GEF 24420 [(2)] | Use Your Illusion II | 1991 | 25.00 |
| ❑ GEF 24617 | The Spaghetti Incident? | 1993 | 15.00 |
| *—Orange vinyl* | | | |
| ❑ R 100805 | G N' R Lies | 1988 | 12.00 |
| *—BMG Direct Marketing edition* | | | |
| ❑ R 170348 | Appetite for Destruction | 1987 | 12.00 |
| *—BMG Direct Marketing edition* | | | |
| ❑ 490514-1 [(4)] | Live Era '87-'93 | 1999 | 120.00 |
| UZI SUICIDE | | | |
| ❑ USR 001 [EP] | Live ?!*@ Like a Suicide | 1986 | 200.00 |

**GUNTER, ARTHUR**

| Number | Title (A Side/B Side) | Yr | NM |
|---|---|---|---|
| EXCELLO | | | |
| ❑ LPS-8017 | Black and Blues | 1971 | 25.00 |

**GURU**

| Number | Title (A Side/B Side) | Yr | NM |
|---|---|---|---|
| CHRYSALIS | | | |
| ❑ F1-21998 | Jazzmatazz Vol. 1 | 1993 | 20.00 |
| ❑ F1-34290 [(2)] | Jazzmatazz Vol. 2: The New Reality | 1995 | 15.00 |
| VIRGIN | | | |
| ❑ 50188 [(2)] | Jazzmatazz Vol. 3: Streetsoul | 2000 | 15.00 |

**GUTHRIE, ARLO**

| Number | Title (A Side/B Side) | Yr | NM |
|---|---|---|---|
| REPRISE | | | |
| ❑ MS 2060 | Hobo's Lullabye | 1972 | 12.00 |
| ❑ MS 2142 | Last of the Brooklyn Cowboys | 1973 | 12.00 |
| ❑ MS4 2142 [Q] | Last of the Brooklyn Cowboys | 1973 | 20.00 |
| ❑ MS 2183 | Arlo Guthrie | 1974 | 12.00 |
| ❑ MS 2239 | Amigo | 1976 | 12.00 |
| ❑ R 6267 [M] | Alice's Restaurant | 1967 | 20.00 |
| ❑ RS 6267 [S] | Alice's Restaurant | 1967 | 15.00 |
| *—Pink, green and gold label* | | | |
| ❑ RS 6267 [S] | Alice's Restaurant | 1968 | 12.00 |
| *—With "W7" and "r:" logos on two-tone orange label* | | | |
| ❑ RS 6267 [S] | Alice's Restaurant | 1970 | 10.00 |
| *—With only "r:" logo on all-orange (tan) label* | | | |
| ❑ RS 6299 | Arlo | 1968 | 15.00 |
| *—With "W7" and "r:" logos on two-tone orange label* | | | |
| ❑ RS 6299 | Arlo | 1970 | 10.00 |
| *—With only "r:" logo on all-orange (tan) label* | | | |
| ❑ RS 6346 | Running Down the Road | 1969 | 15.00 |
| *—With "W7" and "r:" logos on two-tone orange label* | | | |
| ❑ RS 6346 | Running Down the Road | 1970 | 10.00 |
| *—With only "r:" logo on all-orange (tan) label* | | | |
| ❑ RS 6411 | Washington County | 1970 | 12.00 |
| WARNER BROS. | | | |
| ❑ BSK 3117 | The Best of Arlo Guthrie | 1977 | 10.00 |
| *—"Burbank" palm trees label* | | | |
| ❑ BSK 3117 | The Best of Arlo Guthrie | 1979 | 8.00 |
| *—White or tan label* | | | |
| ❑ BSK 3232 | One Night | 1978 | 10.00 |
| ❑ BSK 3336 | Outlasting the Blues | 1979 | 10.00 |
| ❑ BSK 3558 | Power of Love | 1981 | 10.00 |

**GUTHRIE, JACK**

| Number | Title (A Side/B Side) | Yr | NM |
|---|---|---|---|
| CAPITOL | | | |
| ❑ T 2456 [M] | Jack Guthrie's Greatest Songs | 1966 | 25.00 |

Arlo Guthrie, *Amigo,* Reprise MS 2239, 1976, $12.

**GUTHRIE, WOODY**

| Number | Title (A Side/B Side) | Yr | NM |
|---|---|---|---|
| COLLECTABLES | | | |
| ❑ COL-5095 | Golden Classics Vol. 1: Worried Man Blues | 198? | 12.00 |
| ❑ COL-5098 | Golden Classics Vol. 2: Immortal | 198? | 12.00 |
| ELEKTRA | | | |
| ❑ EKL-271/2 [(3)M] | The Library of Congress Recordings | 1964 | 40.00 |
| *—Original pressing has "guitar player" labels* | | | |
| EVEREST ARCHIVE OF FOLK & JAZZ | | | |
| ❑ 204 | Woody Guthrie | 1966 | 12.00 |
| FOLKWAYS | | | |
| ❑ FP-11 [10] | Dust Bowl Ballads | 1950 | 600.00 |
| ❑ FP-715 [10] | Songs to Grow On For Mother and Child | 195? | 600.00 |
| ❑ FA-2011 [10] | Dust Bowl Ballads | 195? | 500.00 |
| *—Reissue of FP-11* | | | |
| ❑ FA-2481 [M] | Bound for Glory: Songs and Stories of Woody Guthrie | 1956 | 150.00 |
| ❑ FA-2483 [M] | Woody Guthrie Sings Folk Songs | 1964 | 50.00 |
| ❑ FA-2484 [M] | Woody Guthrie Sings Folk Songs, Vol. 2 | 1964 | 50.00 |
| ❑ FA-2485 [M] | Struggle | 1964 | 50.00 |
| ❑ FH-5212 [M] | Dust Bowl Ballads | 1964 | 30.00 |
| ❑ FH-5485 [M] | Ballds of Sacco and Vanzetti | 196? | 30.00 |
| ❑ FC-7005 [10] | Songs to Grow On | 1950 | 500.00 |
| ❑ FC-7015 [10] | Songs to Grow On For Mother and Child | 1953 | 500.00 |
| *—Reissue of FP-715* | | | |
| ❑ FC-7027 [10] | Songs to Grow On Vol. 3 | 1951 | 500.00 |
| ❑ 31001 [R] | This Land Is Your Land | 196? | 12.00 |
| RCA VICTOR | | | |
| ❑ LPV-502 [M] | Dust Bowl Ballads | 1964 | 25.00 |
| ROUNDER | | | |
| ❑ 1036 | Columbia River Collection | 1987 | 10.00 |
| ❑ 1040 | Dust Bowl Ballads | 1988 | 10.00 |
| ❑ 1041/2/3 [(3)] | The Library of Congress Recordings | 1988 | 20.00 |
| SMITHSONIAN FOLKWAYS | | | |
| ❑ SF-40007 | Woody Guthrie Sings Folk Songs | 1989 | 12.00 |
| ❑ SF-40025 | Struggle | 1989 | 12.00 |
| VERVE FOLKWAYS | | | |
| ❑ FV-9007 [M] | Bed on the Floor | 1965 | 30.00 |
| ❑ FVS-9007 [R] | Bed on the Floor | 1965 | 20.00 |
| ❑ FV-9036 [M] | Bonneville Dam & Other Columbia River Songs | 1965 | 30.00 |
| ❑ FVS-9036 [R] | Bonneville Dam & Other Columbia River Songs | 1965 | 20.00 |

**GUTHRIE, WOODY, AND CISCO HOUSTON**

| Number | Title (A Side/B Side) | Yr | NM |
|---|---|---|---|
| STINSON | | | |
| ❑ SLP-32 [10] | Cowboy Songs | 195? | 200.00 |
| ❑ SLP-44 [10] | Folk Songs, Vol. 1 | 195? | 200.00 |
| ❑ SLP-53 [10] | More Songs | 195? | 200.00 |

**GUTHRIE, WOODY; SONNY TERRY; ALEX STEWART**

| Number | Title (A Side/B Side) | Yr | NM |
|---|---|---|---|
| STINSON | | | |
| ❑ SLP-7 [10] | Chain Gang, Vol. 1 | 195? | 200.00 |
| ❑ SLP-8 [10] | Chain Gang, Vol. 2 | 195? | 200.00 |

**GUY, BUDDY**

| Number | Title (A Side/B Side) | Yr | NM |
|---|---|---|---|
| BLUE THUMB | | | |
| ❑ BTS 20 | Buddy and the Juniors | 1970 | 25.00 |
| CHESS | | | |
| ❑ LP-409 | I Was Walking Through the Woods | 1970 | 20.00 |
| ❑ LP-1527 [M] | I Left My Blues in San Francisco | 1968 | 30.00 |
| ❑ CH-9115 | Buddy Guy | 1984 | 8.00 |
| MCA | | | |
| ❑ 11165 | I Was Walking Through the Woods | 1995 | 25.00 |
| *—"Heavy Vinyl" audiophile reissue* | | | |
| VANGUARD | | | |
| ❑ VSD-79272 | A Man and the Blues | 1968 | 25.00 |
| ❑ VSD-79290 | This Is Buddy Guy | 1969 | 25.00 |
| ❑ VSD-79323 | Hold That Plane! | 1972 | 20.00 |

**GUY, CHARLES**

| Number | Title (A Side/B Side) | Yr | NM |
|---|---|---|---|
| CAPITOL | | | |
| ❑ ST 1920 [S] | Prisoner's Dream | 1963 | 25.00 |
| ❑ T 1920 [M] | Prisoner's Dream | 1963 | 20.00 |

**GWALTNEY, TOMMY**

| Number | Title (A Side/B Side) | Yr | NM |
|---|---|---|---|
| RIVERSIDE | | | |
| ❑ RLP-353 [M] | Goin' to Kansas City | 1960 | 30.00 |
| ❑ RS-9353 [S] | Goin' to Kansas City | 1960 | 40.00 |

| Number | Title (A Side/B Side) | Yr | NM |
|---|---|---|---|
| **GYPSY** | | | |
| METROMEDIA | | | |
| ❑ MD-1031 [(2)] | Gypsy | 1970 | 20.00 |
| ❑ MD 1044 | In the Garden | 1971 | 15.00 |
| RCA VICTOR | | | |
| ❑ APL1-0093 | Unlock the Gates | 1973 | 15.00 |
| ❑ LSP-4775 | Antithesis | 1972 | 15.00 |

# H

| Number | Title (A Side/B Side) | Yr | NM |
|---|---|---|---|
| **H.P. LOVECRAFT** | | | |
| MERCURY | | | |
| ❑ SRM-1-1041 | We Love You | 1975 | 15.00 |
| PHILIPS | | | |
| ❑ PHM 200252 [M] | H.P. Lovecraft | 1967 | 20.00 |
| ❑ PHS 600252 [S] | H.P. Lovecraft | 1967 | 25.00 |
| ❑ PHS 600279 | Lovecraft II | 1968 | 25.00 |
| REPRISE | | | |
| ❑ RS 6419 | Valley of the Moon | 1970 | 20.00 |
| SUNDAZED | | | |
| ❑ LP-5004 | Live May 11, 1968 | 199? | 10.00 |
| **H.Y. SLEDGE** | | | |
| SSS INTERNATIONAL | | | |
| ❑ 22 | Bootleg Music | 1971 | 20.00 |
| **HA'PENNYS, THE** | | | |
| FERSCH | | | |
| ❑ FL-1110 | Love Is Not the Same | 1968 | 200.00 |
| **HACKETT, BOBBY** | | | |
| BRUNSWICK | | | |
| ❑ BL 56014 [10] | Trumpet Solos | 1950 | 50.00 |
| CAPITOL | | | |
| ❑ H 458 [10] | Soft Lights | 1954 | 50.00 |
| ❑ T 458 [M] | Soft Lights | 1955 | 25.00 |
| *—Black colorband label, logo at left* | | | |
| ❑ T 458 [M] | Soft Lights | 1955 | 40.00 |
| *—Turquoise or gray label* | | | |
| ❑ T 575 [M] | In a Mellow Mood | 1955 | 25.00 |
| *—Black colorband label, logo at left* | | | |
| ❑ T 575 [M] | In a Mellow Mood | 1955 | 40.00 |
| *—Turquoise or gray label* | | | |
| ❑ T 692 [M] | Coast Concert | 1956 | 25.00 |
| *—Black colorband label, logo at left* | | | |
| ❑ T 692 [M] | Coast Concert | 1956 | 40.00 |
| *—Turquoise or gray label* | | | |
| ❑ T 719 [M] | Rendezvous | 1956 | 25.00 |
| *—Black colorband label, logo at left* | | | |
| ❑ T 719 [M] | Rendezvous | 1956 | 40.00 |
| *—Turquoise or gray label* | | | |
| ❑ T 857 [M] | Gotham Jazz Scene | 1957 | 25.00 |
| *—Black colorband label, logo at left* | | | |
| ❑ T 857 [M] | Gotham Jazz Scene | 1957 | 40.00 |
| *—Turquoise or gray label* | | | |
| ❑ ST 933 [S] | Jazz Ultimate | 1959 | 30.00 |
| *—Black colorband label, logo at left* | | | |
| ❑ T 933 [M] | Jazz Ultimate | 1958 | 25.00 |
| *—Black colorband label, logo at left* | | | |
| ❑ T 933 [M] | Jazz Ultimate | 1958 | 40.00 |
| *—Turquoise or gray label* | | | |
| ❑ T 1002 [M] | Don't Take Your Love from Me | 1958 | 25.00 |
| *—Black colorband label, logo at left* | | | |
| ❑ T 1002 [M] | Don't Take Your Love from Me | 1958 | 40.00 |
| *—Turquoise or gray label* | | | |
| ❑ ST 1077 [S] | Bobby Hackett at the Embers | 1958 | 30.00 |
| *—Black colorband label, logo at left* | | | |
| ❑ ST 1077 [S] | Bobby Hackett at the Embers | 1962 | 20.00 |
| *—Black colorband label, logo at top* | | | |
| ❑ T 1077 [M] | Bobby Hackett at the Embers | 1958 | 25.00 |
| *—Black colorband label, logo at left* | | | |
| ❑ T 1077 [M] | Bobby Hackett at the Embers | 1962 | 15.00 |
| *—Black colorband label, logo at top* | | | |
| ❑ ST 1172 [S] | Blues with a Kick | 1959 | 30.00 |
| ❑ T 1172 [M] | Blues with a Kick | 1959 | 25.00 |
| ❑ ST 1235 [S] | Bobby Hackett Quartet | 1959 | 30.00 |
| ❑ T 1235 [M] | Bobby Hackett Quartet | 1959 | 25.00 |
| ❑ ST 1413 [S] | Easy Beat | 1960 | 25.00 |
| ❑ T 1413 [M] | Easy Beat | 1960 | 20.00 |
| COLUMBIA | | | |
| ❑ CL 1602 [M] | Dream Awhile | 1961 | 20.00 |
| ❑ CL 1729 [M] | The Most Beautiful Horn in the World | 1962 | 20.00 |
| ❑ CL 2566 [10] | The Bobby Hackett Horn | 1955 | 50.00 |
| ❑ CL 6156 [10] | Jazz Session | 1951 | 50.00 |
| ❑ CS 8402 [S] | Dream Awhile | 1961 | 25.00 |
| ❑ CS 8529 [S] | The Most Beautiful Horn in the World | 1962 | 25.00 |
| ❑ CS 8695 [S] | Night Love | 1962 | 20.00 |
| COMMODORE | | | |
| ❑ FL-20016 [10] | Horn A Plenty | 1951 | 50.00 |
| EPIC | | | |
| ❑ LN 3106 [M] | The Hackett Horn | 1956 | 40.00 |
| ❑ FLS 15107 [S] | The Swingin'est Gals in Town | 196? | 20.00 |
| SESAC | | | |
| ❑ N-4101 [M] | The Spirit Swings Me | 1960 | 25.00 |
| ❑ SN-4101 [S] | The Spirit Swings Me | 1960 | 30.00 |
| ❑ N-4105 [M] | Candlelight and Romance | 1960 | 25.00 |
| ❑ SN-4105 [S] | Candlelight and Romance | 1960 | 30.00 |
| **HACKETT, BOBBY/MAX KAMINSKY** | | | |
| BRUNSWICK | | | |
| ❑ BL 58043 [10] | Battle of Jazz, Vol. 5 | 1953 | 50.00 |
| **HADEN, CHARLIE** | | | |
| ABC IMPULSE! | | | |
| ❑ AS-9183 | Liberation Music Orchestra | 1973 | 40.00 |
| **HAGAR, ERNIE** | | | |
| SAGE AND SAND | | | |
| ❑ C-42 [M] | Swinging Steel Guitar | 1965 | 30.00 |
| **HAGGARD, MERLE** | | | |
| CAPITOL | | | |
| ❑ SKAO-168 | Pride In What I Am | 1969 | 25.00 |
| ❑ SM-168 | Pride In What I Am | 197? | 10.00 |
| *—Reissue with new prefix* | | | |
| ❑ SWBB-223 [(2)] | Same Train, A Different Time | 1969 | 30.00 |
| ❑ SWBB-259 [(2)] | Close-Up | 1969 | 30.00 |
| *—Reissue in one package of "Strangers" and "Swinging Doors"* | | | |
| ❑ ST-319 | A Portrait of Merle Haggard | 1969 | 20.00 |
| ❑ ST-384 | Okie from Muskogee | 1970 | 20.00 |
| ❑ ST-451 | The Fightin' Side of Me | 1970 | 20.00 |
| ❑ ST-638 | A Tribute to the Best Damn Fiddle Player in the World (Or, My Salute to Bob Wills) | 1970 | 25.00 |
| ❑ STBB-707 [(2)] | Sing a Sad Song/High on a Hilltop | 1971 | 30.00 |
| ❑ ST-735 | Hag | 1971 | 15.00 |
| ❑ SWBO-803 [(2)] | The Land of Many Churches | 1971 | 60.00 |
| ❑ ST-823 | Truly the Best of Merle Haggard | 1971 | 40.00 |
| ❑ ST-835 | Someday We'll Look Back | 1971 | 20.00 |
| ❑ ST-882 | Let Me Tell You About a Song | 1972 | 20.00 |
| ❑ ST 2373 [S] | Strangers | 1965 | 30.00 |
| ❑ T 2373 [M] | Strangers | 1965 | 25.00 |
| ❑ SM-2585 | Swinging Doors | 197? | 10.00 |
| *—Reissue with new prefix* | | | |
| ❑ ST 2585 [S] | Swinging Doors | 1966 | 30.00 |
| ❑ T 2585 [M] | Swinging Doors | 1966 | 25.00 |
| ❑ SM-2702 | I'm a Lonesome Fugitive | 197? | 10.00 |
| *—Reissue with new prefix* | | | |
| ❑ ST 2702 [S] | I'm a Lonesome Fugitive | 1967 | 30.00 |
| ❑ T 2702 [M] | I'm a Lonesome Fugitive | 1967 | 25.00 |
| ❑ ST 2789 [S] | Branded Man | 1967 | 30.00 |
| ❑ T 2789 [M] | Branded Man | 1967 | 25.00 |
| ❑ ST 2848 [S] | Sing Me Back Home | 1968 | 25.00 |
| ❑ T 2848 [M] | Sing Me Back Home | 1968 | 30.00 |
| ❑ ST 2912 | The Legend of Bonnie and Clyde | 1968 | 25.00 |
| ❑ SKAO 2951 | The Best of Merle Haggard | 1968 | 25.00 |
| ❑ ST 2972 | Mama Tried | 1968 | 25.00 |
| ❑ ST-11082 | The Best of the Best of Merle Haggard | 1972 | 15.00 |
| ❑ ST-11127 | It's Not Love | 1972 | 12.00 |
| ❑ ST-11141 | Totally Instrumental with One Exception | 1973 | 15.00 |
| ❑ ST-11200 | I Love Dixie Blues...So I Recorded "Live" in New Orleans | 1973 | 12.00 |
| ❑ ST-11230 | Merle Haggard's Christmas Present (Something Old, Something New) | 1973 | 12.00 |
| ❑ ST-11276 | If We Make It Through December | 1974 | 12.00 |
| ❑ ST-11331 | Merle Haggard Presents His 30th Album | 1974 | 12.00 |
| ❑ ST-11365 | Keep Movin' On | 1975 | 12.00 |
| ❑ ST-11483 | It's All in the Movies | 1975 | 12.00 |
| ❑ SABB-11531 [(2)] | Songs I'll Always Sing | 1976 | 15.00 |
| ❑ ST-11544 | My Love Affair with Trains | 1976 | 12.00 |
| ❑ ST-11586 | The Roots of My Raising | 1976 | 12.00 |
| ❑ ST-11693 | A Working Man Can't Get Nowhere Today | 1977 | 12.00 |
| ❑ ST-11745 | Eleven Winners | 1977 | 12.00 |
| ❑ SM-11823 | My Love Affair with Trains | 1978 | 10.00 |
| *—Reissue* | | | |
| ❑ SW-11839 | The Way It Was | 1978 | 12.00 |
| ❑ SM-12036 | It's All in the Movies | 1979 | 10.00 |
| *—Reissue* | | | |
| ❑ SN-16052 | Sing a Sad Song | 1979 | 8.00 |
| *—Budget-line reissue* | | | |
| ❑ SN-16053 | High on a Hilltop | 1979 | 8.00 |
| *—Budget-line reissue* | | | |
| ❑ SN-16054 | The Best of Merle Haggard | 1979 | 8.00 |
| *—Budget-line reissue* | | | |
| ❑ SN-16277 | Okie from Muskogee | 1982 | 8.00 |
| *—Budget-line reissue* | | | |
| ❑ SN-16278 | The Fightin' Side of Me | 1982 | 8.00 |
| *—Budget-line reissue* | | | |
| ❑ SN-16279 | A Tribute to the Best Damn Fiddle Player in the World (Or, My Salute to Bob Wills) | 1982 | 8.00 |
| *—Budget-line reissue* | | | |
| ❑ SN-16303 | Eleven Winners | 1984 | 8.00 |
| *—Budget-line reissue* | | | |
| CAPITOL SPECIAL MARKETS | | | |
| ❑ SL-8086 [(2)] | Songs I'll Always Sing | 1977 | 20.00 |
| ❑ SLB-8137 [(2)] | Merle Haggard Salutes the Greats | 1980 | 15.00 |
| EPIC | | | |
| ❑ FE 37593 | Big City | 1981 | 10.00 |
| ❑ PE 37593 | Big City | 1985 | 8.00 |
| *—Budget-line reissue* | | | |
| ❑ FE 38092 | Going Where the Lonely Go | 1982 | 10.00 |
| ❑ PE 38092 | Going Where the Lonely Go | 1985 | 8.00 |
| *—Budget-line reissue* | | | |
| ❑ PE 38307 | Goin' Home for Christmas | 1982 | 10.00 |
| ❑ FE 38815 | That's the Way Love Goes | 1983 | 10.00 |
| ❑ FE 39159 | The Epic Collection | 1983 | 10.00 |
| ❑ PE 39159 | The Epic Collection | 1985 | 8.00 |
| *—Budget-line reissue* | | | |
| ❑ FE 39364 | It's All in the Game | 1984 | 10.00 |
| ❑ FE 39545 | His Epic Hits: The First 11 | 1985 | 10.00 |
| ❑ FE 39602 | Kern River | 1985 | 10.00 |
| ❑ FE 40107 | Out Among the Stars | 1986 | 10.00 |
| ❑ PE 40107 | Out Among the Stars | 1986 | 8.00 |
| *—Budget-line reissue* | | | |
| ❑ FE 40224 | Amber Waves of Grain | 1985 | 10.00 |
| ❑ FE 40286 | A Friend in California | 1986 | 10.00 |
| ❑ FE 40986 | Chill Factor | 1988 | 10.00 |
| ❑ FE 44283 | 5:01 Blues | 1989 | 10.00 |
| MCA | | | |
| ❑ 2267 | Ramblin' Fever | 1977 | 12.00 |
| ❑ 2314 | My Farewell to Elvis | 1977 | 15.00 |
| ❑ 2375 | I'm Always on a Mountain | 1978 | 12.00 |
| ❑ 3089 | Serving 190 Proof | 1979 | 12.00 |
| ❑ 3229 | The Way I Am | 1980 | 12.00 |
| ❑ 5139 | Back to the Barrooms | 1980 | 12.00 |
| ❑ 5250 | Songs for the Mamma | 1981 | 12.00 |
| ❑ 5386 | Greatest Hits | 1982 | 12.00 |
| ❑ 5573 | His Best | 1985 | 10.00 |
| ❑ 37138 | Ramblin' Fever | 1980 | 8.00 |
| *—Budget-line reissue* | | | |
| ❑ 37139 | My Farewell to Elvis | 1980 | 8.00 |
| *—Budget-line reissue* | | | |
| ❑ 37140 | I'm Always on a Mountain | 1980 | 8.00 |
| *—Budget-line reissue* | | | |
| ❑ 37141 | Serving 190 Proof | 1980 | 8.00 |
| *—Budget-line reissue* | | | |
| ❑ 37207 | The Way I Am | 1982 | 8.00 |
| *—Budget-line reissue* | | | |
| **HAGGARD, MERLE, AND BONNIE OWENS** | | | |
| CAPITOL | | | |
| ❑ ST 2453 [S] | Just Between the Two of Us | 1966 | 30.00 |
| ❑ T 2453 [M] | Just Between the Two of Us | 1966 | 25.00 |
| **HAHN, JERRY** | | | |
| CHANGES | | | |
| ❑ LP-7001 | Arabein | 1968 | 20.00 |
| **HAIG, AL** | | | |
| COUNTERPOINT | | | |
| ❑ C-551 [M] | Jazz Will o' the Wisp | 1957 | 100.00 |
| ESOTERIC | | | |
| ❑ ESJ-7 [10] | Al Haig Trio | 1954 | 200.00 |
| MINT | | | |
| ❑ AL-711 [M] | Al Haig Today | 1964 | 150.00 |
| PACIFIC JAZZ | | | |
| ❑ PJLP-18 [10] | Al Haig Trio | 1955 | 150.00 |
| PERIOD | | | |
| ❑ SPL-1104 [10] | Al Haig Quartet | 1954 | 150.00 |
| SEECO | | | |
| ❑ SLP-7 [10] | Highlights in Modern Jazz | 195? | 120.00 |
| **HAIG, AL/MARY LOU WILLIAMS** | | | |
| PRESTIGE | | | |
| ❑ PRLP-175 [10] | Piano Moderns | 1953 | 200.00 |
| **HAINES, CONNIE** | | | |
| CORAL | | | |
| ❑ CRL 56055 [10] | Connie Haines Sings | 1955 | 120.00 |
| RCA VICTOR | | | |
| ❑ LPM-2264 [M] | Faith, Hope and Charity | 1961 | 20.00 |
| ❑ LSP-2264 [S] | Faith, Hope and Charity | 1961 | 30.00 |
| TOPS | | | |
| ❑ L-1606 [M] | Connie Haines Sings Helen Morgan | 1959 | 30.00 |
| **HALE, CORKY** | | | |
| GENE NORMAN | | | |
| ❑ GNP-17 [M] | Corky Hale | 1956 | 50.00 |
| **HALEN, CARL** | | | |
| EMPIRICAL | | | |
| ❑ LP-101 [10] | Gin Bottle Seven | 1957 | 50.00 |
| RIVERSIDE | | | |
| ❑ RLP 12-231 [M] | Gin Bottle Jazz | 1958 | 60.00 |
| *—White label, blue print* | | | |



**Except when noted otherwise, VG = 25% of NM, and VG+ = 50% of NM. (Example: VG = $2.00, VG+ = $4.00 and NM = $8.00.)**

| Number | Title (A Side/B Side) | Yr | NM |
|---|---|---|---|
| ❑ RLP 12-231 [M] | Gin Bottle Jazz | 1959 | 30.00 |
| *—Blue label, microphone logo at top* | | | |
| ❑ RLP 12-261 [M] | Whoopee Makers' Jazz | 1958 | 40.00 |
| ❑ RLP-1103 [S] | Whoopee Makers' Jazz | 1958 | 30.00 |
| **HALEY, BILL, AND HIS COMETS** | | | |
| ACCORD | | | |
| ❑ SN-7125 | Rockin' and Rollin' | 1981 | 10.00 |
| DECCA | | | |
| ❑ DL 5560 [10] | Shake, Rattle and Roll | 1955 | 800.00 |
| ❑ DXSE-7211 [(2)] | Bill Haley's Golden Hits | 1972 | 15.00 |
| ❑ DL 8225 [M] | Rock Around the Clock | 1955 | 150.00 |
| *—All-black label with silver print* | | | |
| ❑ DL 8225 [M] | Rock Around the Clock | 1960 | 50.00 |
| *—Black label with colorband, no mention of MCA on label* | | | |
| ❑ DL 8225 [M] | Rock Around the Clock | 1967 | 30.00 |
| *—Black label with colorband, "A Division of MCA" on label* | | | |
| ❑ DL 8315 [M] | Music for the Boyfriend | 1956 | 150.00 |
| ❑ DL 8345 [M] | Rock 'n Roll Stage Show | 1956 | 150.00 |
| ❑ DL 8569 [M] | Rockin' the Oldies | 1957 | 150.00 |
| ❑ DL 8692 [M] | Rockin' Around the World | 1958 | 150.00 |
| ❑ DL 8775 [M] | Rockin' the Joint | 1958 | 150.00 |
| ❑ DL 8821 [M] | Bill Haley's Chicks | 1959 | 100.00 |
| ❑ DL 8964 [M] | Strictly Instrumental | 1960 | 100.00 |
| ❑ DL 75027 | Bill Haley's Greatest Hits | 1968 | 15.00 |
| ❑ DL 78225 [R] | Rock Around the Clock | 1959 | 75.00 |
| *—All-black label with silver print* | | | |
| ❑ DL 78225 [R] | Rock Around the Clock | 1960 | 25.00 |
| *—Black label with colorband, no mention of MCA on label* | | | |
| ❑ DL 78225 [R] | Rock Around the Clock | 1967 | 15.00 |
| *—Black label with colorband, "A Division of MCA" on label* | | | |
| ❑ DL 78821 [S] | Bill Haley's Chicks | 1959 | 150.00 |
| ❑ DL 78964 [S] | Strictly Instrumental | 1960 | 150.00 |
| ESSEX | | | |
| ❑ LP 202 [M] | Rock with Bill Haley and the Comets | 1955 | 500.00 |
| 51 WEST | | | |
| ❑ Q 16120 | Live in New York/Greatest Hits | 1981 | 10.00 |
| *—"All selections under license from Buddah Records"* | | | |
| GNP CRESCENDO | | | |
| ❑ GNPS-2077 | Rock 'N' Roll | 1973 | 12.00 |
| ❑ GNPS-2097 | Rock Around the Country | 1976 | 12.00 |
| GREAT NORTHWEST | | | |
| ❑ GNW 4015 | Interviewed by Red Robinson | 1981 | 12.00 |
| JANUS | | | |
| ❑ 3035 | Travelin' Band | 1972 | 25.00 |
| ❑ 7003 [(2)] | Razzle-Dazzle | 1972 | 15.00 |
| KAMA SUTRA | | | |
| ❑ KLPS-2014 | Scrapbook | 1970 | 30.00 |
| MCA | | | |
| ❑ 161 | Bill Haley's Greatest Hits | 1973 | 10.00 |
| *—Reissue of Decca 75027* | | | |
| ❑ 4010 [(2)] | Bill Haley's Golden Hits | 1973 | 12.00 |
| *—Reissue of Decca 7211* | | | |
| ❑ 5539 [(2)] | From the Original Master Tapes | 1987 | 12.00 |
| PAIR | | | |
| ❑ MSM2-35069 [(2)] | Rock and Roll Giant | 1986 | 12.00 |
| PICCADILLY | | | |
| ❑ PIC-3408 | Greatest Hits | 1980 | 10.00 |
| PICKWICK | | | |
| ❑ PTP-2077 [(2)] | Rock 'N' Roll | 197? | 12.00 |
| ❑ SPC-3256 | Bill Haley and the Comets | 1970 | 10.00 |
| ❑ SPC-3280 | Rock 'N' Roll Revival | 197? | 10.00 |
| ROULETTE | | | |
| ❑ R 25174 [M] | Twistin' Knights at the Roundtable | 1962 | 80.00 |
| ❑ SR 25174 [S] | Twistin' Knights at the Roundtable | 1962 | 100.00 |
| SOMERSET | | | |
| ❑ P-4600 [M] | Rock with Bill Haley and the Comets | 1958 | 150.00 |
| TRANS WORLD | | | |
| ❑ LP 202 [M] | Rock with Bill Haley and the Comets | 1956 | 300.00 |
| VOCALION | | | |
| ❑ VL 3696 [M] | Bill Haley and the Comets | 1963 | 25.00 |
| WARNER BROS. | | | |
| ❑ W 1378 [M] | Bill Haley and His Comets | 1959 | 50.00 |
| ❑ WS 1378 [S] | Bill Haley and His Comets | 1959 | 70.00 |
| ❑ W 1391 [M] | Bill Haley's Jukebox | 1960 | 50.00 |
| ❑ WS 1391 [S] | Bill Haley's Jukebox | 1960 | 70.00 |
| ❑ WS 1831 | Rock 'N' Roll Revival | 1970 | 15.00 |
| ❑ ST-93103 | Rock 'N' Roll Revival | 1970 | 25.00 |
| *—Capitol Record Club edition* | | | |
| **HALFNELSON** See SPARKS. | | | |
| **HALL, ADELAIDE** | | | |
| MONMOUTH-EVERGREEN | | | |
| ❑ 7080 | That Wonderful... | 1970 | 20.00 |

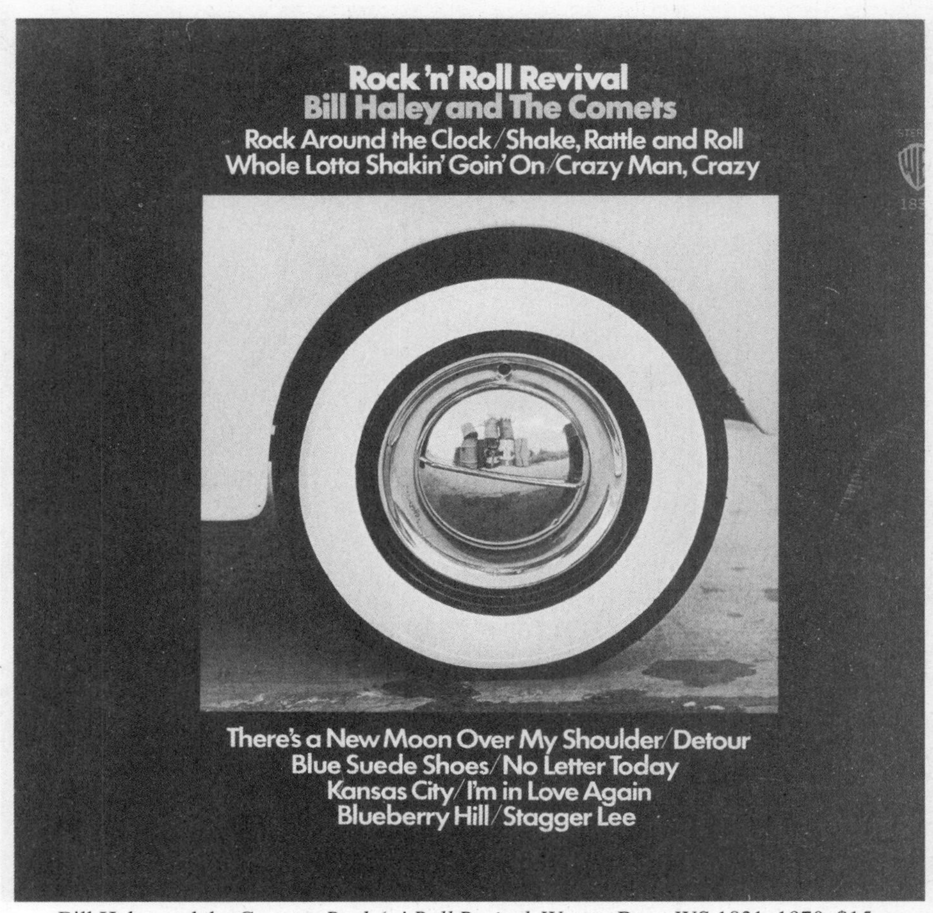


Bill Haley and the Comets, *Rock 'n' Roll Revival,* Warner Bros. WS 1831, 1970, $15.

| Number | Title (A Side/B Side) | Yr | NM |
|---|---|---|---|
| **HALL, BECKY** | | | |
| AAMCO | | | |
| ❑ ALP-324 [M] | A Tribute to Bessie Smith | 1958 | 30.00 |
| **HALL, CONNIE** | | | |
| DECCA | | | |
| ❑ DL 4217 [M] | Connie Hall | 1962 | 25.00 |
| ❑ DL 74217 [S] | Connie Hall | 1962 | 30.00 |
| VOCALION | | | |
| ❑ VL 3752 [M] | Country Songs | 1965 | 20.00 |
| ❑ VL 3801 [M] | Country Style | 1968 | 20.00 |
| ❑ VL 73752 [S] | Country Songs | 1965 | 25.00 |
| ❑ VL 73801 [S] | Country Style | 1968 | 20.00 |
| **HALL, DARYL, AND JOHN OATES** | | | |
| ALLEGIANCE | | | |
| ❑ AV-5014 | Nucleus | 198? | 8.00 |
| ARISTA | | | |
| ❑ AL-8539 | Ooh Yeah! | 1988 | 10.00 |
| ❑ AL-8614 | Change of Season | 1989 | 12.00 |
| ATLANTIC | | | |
| ❑ 7242 [M] | Whole Oats | 1972 | 60.00 |
| *—White label promo only with "d/j copy monaural" sticker on cover* | | | |
| ❑ SD 7242 | Whole Oats | 1972 | 12.00 |
| ❑ SD 7269 | Abandoned Luncheonette | 1973 | 12.00 |
| ❑ SD 18109 | War Babies | 1974 | 12.00 |
| ❑ SD 18213 | No Goodbyes | 1977 | 10.00 |
| ❑ SD 19139 | Abandoned Luncheonette | 1977 | 8.00 |
| CHELSEA | | | |
| ❑ CHL-547 | Past Times Behind | 1976 | 12.00 |
| INTERMEDIA | | | |
| ❑ QS-5040 | The Early Years | 198? | 8.00 |
| JEM | | | |
| ❑ 55002 | Early Years | 198? | 8.00 |
| MOBILE FIDELITY | | | |
| ❑ 1-069 | Abandoned Luncheonette | 1982 | 20.00 |
| *—Audiophile vinyl* | | | |
| RCA VICTOR | | | |
| ❑ APL1-1144 | Daryl Hall & John Oates | 1976 | 10.00 |
| ❑ APL1-1467 | Bigger Than Both of Us | 1976 | 10.00 |
| ❑ AFL1-2300 | Beauty on a Back Street | 1977 | 10.00 |
| ❑ AFL1-2802 | Livetime! | 1978 | 10.00 |

| Number | Title (A Side/B Side) | Yr | NM |
|---|---|---|---|
| ❑ AFL1-2804 | Along the Red Ledge | 1978 | 10.00 |
| ❑ AFL1-2804 | Along the Red Ledge | 1978 | 15.00 |
| *—Red vinyl* | | | |
| ❑ ANL1-3463 | Daryl Hall & John Oates | 1979 | 8.00 |
| ❑ AFL1-3494 | X-Static | 1979 | 10.00 |
| ❑ DJL1-3512 [DJ] | Post Static | 1979 | 20.00 |
| *—Promo-only one-sided 4-song sampler* | | | |
| ❑ AQL1-3646 | Voices | 1980 | 8.00 |
| *—"RE 4" on back cover: Color photo of Hall and Oates on each side* | | | |
| ❑ AQL1-3646 | Voices | 1980 | 10.00 |
| *—"RE 2" on back cover: Cover not embossed; Hall's head 3 inches-plus below "Voices" on front cover* | | | |
| ❑ AQL1-3646 | Voices | 1980 | 12.00 |
| *—No "RE" of any type on back cover: Embossed lettering and sound waves, Hall's head almost touches the word "Voices" on front* | | | |
| ❑ AQL1-3646 | Voices | 1980 | 12.00 |
| *—"RE 3" on back cover: Cover lettering in black* | | | |
| ❑ AQL1-3646 | Voices | 1980 | 12.00 |
| *—"RE" on back cover: Variation unknown* | | | |
| ❑ AQL1-3646 | Voices | 1981 | 8.00 |
| *—"RE 5" on back cover: Variation unknown* | | | |
| ❑ AQL1-3646 | Voices | 1981 | 8.00 |
| *—"RE 6" on back cover: Bar code on upper left back cover* | | | |
| ❑ DJL1-3832 | RCA Radio Special Interview Series | 1980 | 15.00 |
| ❑ AYL1-3836 | Daryl Hall & John Oates | 1980 | 8.00 |
| ❑ AYL1-3866 | Bigger Than Both of Us | 1980 | 8.00 |
| ❑ AFL1-4028 | Private Eyes | 1981 | 10.00 |
| ❑ DJL1-4179 | Special Radio Series | 1981 | 15.00 |
| ❑ AYL1-4230 | Beauty on a Back Street | 1981 | 8.00 |
| ❑ AYL1-4231 | Along the Red Ledge | 1981 | 8.00 |
| ❑ AYL1-4303 | X-Static | 1982 | 8.00 |
| ❑ AFL1-4383 | H2O | 1982 | 10.00 |
| ❑ AYL1-4722 | Livetime! | 1983 | 8.00 |
| ❑ CPL1-4858 | Rock 'n Soul Part 1 | 1983 | 8.00 |
| *—"RE 2" on lower left back: Variation unknown* | | | |
| ❑ CPL1-4858 | Rock 'n Soul Part 1 | 1983 | 10.00 |
| *—"RE" on lower left back: back cover says "Plus Two New Songs (Recorded September 1983)," then mentions "Say It Isn't So" and "Adult Education"* | | | |
| ❑ CPL1-4858 | Rock 'n Soul Part 1 | 1983 | 12.00 |
| *—Original cover: back cover says "Plus Two New Songs (Recorded September 1983)" WITHOUT mentioning what the songs are* | | | |
| ❑ AFL1-5309 | Big Bam Boom | 1984 | 12.00 |
| ❑ AJL1-5336 | Big Bam Boom | 1984 | 10.00 |
| ❑ AFL1-7035 | Live at the Apollo | 1985 | 10.00 |

Daryl Hall and John Oates, *Whole Oats,* Atlantic SD 7242, 1972, stereo, $15.

### HALL, DICKSON

EPIC

| Number | Title (A Side/B Side) | Yr | NM |
|---|---|---|---|
| ❑ LN 3427 [M] | 25 All-Time Country and Western Hits | 1958 | 25.00 |

KAPP

| Number | Title (A Side/B Side) | Yr | NM |
|---|---|---|---|
| ❑ KL-1067 [M] | Fabulous Country Hits Way Out West | 1957 | 30.00 |
| ❑ KL-1464 [M] | 24 Fabulous Country Hits | 1966 | 20.00 |
| ❑ KS-3464 [S] | 24 Fabulous Country Hits | 1966 | 25.00 |

MGM

| Number | Title (A Side/B Side) | Yr | NM |
|---|---|---|---|
| ❑ E-329 [10] | Outlaws of the Old West | 1954 | 60.00 |
| ❑ E-3263 [M] | Outlaws of the Old West | 1956 | 40.00 |

PERFECT

| Number | Title (A Side/B Side) | Yr | NM |
|---|---|---|---|
| ❑ P-14016 [M] | Country & Western Million Sellers | 1960 | 20.00 |
| ❑ PS-14016 [S] | Country & Western Million Sellers | 1960 | 25.00 |

### HALL, EDMOND

BLUE NOTE

| Number | Title (A Side/B Side) | Yr | NM |
|---|---|---|---|
| ❑ B-6505 [M] | Celestial Express | 1969 | 20.00 |

MOSAIC

| Number | Title (A Side/B Side) | Yr | NM |
|---|---|---|---|
| ❑ MR6-109 [(6)] | The Complete Edmond Hall/ James P. Johnson/Sidney De Paris/Vic Dickenson Blue Note Sessions | 199? | 100.00 |

UNITED ARTISTS

| Number | Title (A Side/B Side) | Yr | NM |
|---|---|---|---|
| ❑ UAL-4028 [M] | Petite Fleur | 1959 | 40.00 |
| ❑ UAS-5028 [S] | Petite Fleur | 1959 | 30.00 |

### HALL, EDMOND/SIDNEY DEPARIS

BLUE NOTE

| Number | Title (A Side/B Side) | Yr | NM |
|---|---|---|---|
| ❑ BLP-7007 [10] | Jamming in Jazz Hall | 1951 | 200.00 |

### HALL, EDMOND/ART HODES

BLUE NOTE

| Number | Title (A Side/B Side) | Yr | NM |
|---|---|---|---|
| ❑ B-6504 [M] | Original Blue Note Jazz, Volume 1 | 1969 | 20.00 |

### HALL, JIM

PACIFIC JAZZ

| Number | Title (A Side/B Side) | Yr | NM |
|---|---|---|---|
| ❑ PJ-10 [M] | Good Friday Blues | 1960 | 40.00 |
| ❑ PJ-79 [M] | Jazz Guitar | 1963 | 30.00 |
| ❑ ST-79 [S] | Jazz Guitar | 1963 | 25.00 |
| ❑ PJ-1227 [M] | Jazz Guitar | 1957 | 80.00 |

WORLD PACIFIC

| Number | Title (A Side/B Side) | Yr | NM |
|---|---|---|---|
| ❑ WP-1227 [M] | Jazz Guitar | 1958 | 50.00 |

### HALL, JOANIE

SAGE AND SAND

| Number | Title (A Side/B Side) | Yr | NM |
|---|---|---|---|
| ❑ C-34 [M] | Western Meets Country | 1962 | 25.00 |

### HALL, JUANITA

COUNTERPOINT

| Number | Title (A Side/B Side) | Yr | NM |
|---|---|---|---|
| ❑ 558 [S] | Juanita Hall Sings the Blues | 1959 | 150.00 |

### HALL, LARRY

STRAND

| Number | Title (A Side/B Side) | Yr | NM |
|---|---|---|---|
| ❑ SL-1005 [M] | Sandy | 1960 | 150.00 |
| ❑ SLS-1005 [S] | Sandy | 1960 | 200.00 |

### HALL, TOM T.

MERCURY

| Number | Title (A Side/B Side) | Yr | NM |
|---|---|---|---|
| ❑ SRM-1-500 | Songs of Fox Hollow | 1975 | 12.00 |
| ❑ SRM-1-668 | The Rhymer and Other Five and Dimers | 1973 | 12.00 |
| ❑ SRM-1-687 | For the People in the Last Hard Town | 1974 | 12.00 |
| ❑ SRM-1-1009 | Country Is | 1974 | 12.00 |
| ❑ SRM-1-1033 | I Wrote | 1975 | 12.00 |
| ❑ SRM-1-1044 | Greatest Hits, Volume 2 | 1975 | 12.00 |
| ❑ SRM-1-1076 | Faster Horses | 1976 | 12.00 |
| ❑ SRM-1-1111 | Magnificent Music | 1977 | 12.00 |
| ❑ SRM-1-1139 | About Love | 1977 | 12.00 |
| ❑ SRM-1-5008 | Greatest Hits, Volume 3 | 1978 | 12.00 |
| ❑ SR-61211 | Ballad of Forty Dollars and His Other Great Songs | 1969 | 20.00 |
| ❑ SR-61247 | Homecoming | 1969 | 20.00 |
| ❑ SR-61277 | Witness Life | 1970 | 20.00 |
| ❑ SR-61307 | 100 Children | 1970 | 20.00 |
| ❑ SR-61350 | In Search of a Song | 1971 | 15.00 |
| ❑ SR-61362 | We All Got Together And… | 1972 | 15.00 |
| ❑ SR-61369 | Greatest Hits | 1972 | 15.00 |
| ❑ 814025-1 | Jesus to Jack Daniels | 1983 | 8.00 |
| ❑ 822425-1 | Natural Dreams | 1984 | 8.00 |
| ❑ 822500-1 | In Search of a Song | 1987 | 8.00 |
| ❑ 824143-1 | Greatest Hits | 1985 | 8.00 |
| *—Reissue* | | | |
| ❑ 824144-1 | Greatest Hits, Volume 2 | 1985 | 8.00 |
| *—Reissue* | | | |
| ❑ 824145-1 | Greatest Hits, Volume 3 | 1985 | 8.00 |
| *—Reissue* | | | |
| ❑ 824508-1 | Song in a Seashell | 1985 | 8.00 |
| ❑ 832350-1 | Songs of Fox Hollow | 1987 | 8.00 |
| *—Reissue* | | | |
| ❑ 834779-1 | Country Songs for Children | 1988 | 8.00 |
| *—Reissue* | | | |

PICCADILLY

| Number | Title (A Side/B Side) | Yr | NM |
|---|---|---|---|
| ❑ 3558 | I Like Beer | 198? | 8.00 |

RCA VICTOR

| Number | Title (A Side/B Side) | Yr | NM |
|---|---|---|---|
| ❑ AHL1-2622 | New Train | 1978 | 10.00 |
| ❑ AHL1-3018 | Places I've Been | 1979 | 10.00 |
| ❑ AHL1-3495 | T's in Town | 1979 | 10.00 |
| ❑ AHL1-3685 | Soldier of Fortune | 1980 | 10.00 |
| ❑ AHL1-4749 | In Concert: Recorded Live at the Grand Ole Opry | 1983 | 10.00 |
| ❑ AYL1-5432 | In Concert: Recorded Live at the Grand Ole Opry | 1985 | 8.00 |
| *—"Best Buy Series" reissue* | | | |

### HALLBERG, BENGT

EPIC

| Number | Title (A Side/B Side) | Yr | NM |
|---|---|---|---|
| ❑ LN 3375 [M] | Bengt Hallberg | 1957 | 120.00 |

PRESTIGE

| Number | Title (A Side/B Side) | Yr | NM |
|---|---|---|---|
| ❑ PRLP-176 [10] | Bengt Hallberg's Swedish All-Stars | 1953 | 350.00 |

### HALLBERG, BENGT/ARNE DOMNERUS

PRESTIGE

| Number | Title (A Side/B Side) | Yr | NM |
|---|---|---|---|
| ❑ PRLP-145 [10] | New Sounds from Sweden, Volume 6 | 1953 | 400.00 |

### HALLBERG, BENGT/LARS GULLIN

PRESTIGE

| Number | Title (A Side/B Side) | Yr | NM |
|---|---|---|---|
| ❑ PRLP-121 [10] | New Sounds from Sweden, Volume 2 | 1952 | 400.00 |

### HALLE ORCHESTRA (JOHN BARBIROLLI, CONDUCTOR)

MERCURY LIVING PRESENCE

| Number | Title (A Side/B Side) | Yr | NM |
|---|---|---|---|
| ❑ SR 90115 [S] | Williams, Vaughan: Symphony No. 8; Bax: Garden of Fand; Butterworth: Shropshire Lad | 1960 | 25.00 |
| *—Maroon label, no "Vendor: Mercury Record Corporation"* | | | |
| ❑ SR 90124 [S] | Viennese Night at the Proms | 1960 | 30.00 |
| *—Maroon label, no "Vendor: Mercury Record Corporation"* | | | |
| ❑ SR 90125 [S] | Elgar: Enigma Variations; Purcell: Suite for Strings | 1960 | 20.00 |
| *—Maroon label, no "Vendor: Mercury Record Corporation"* | | | |
| ❑ SR 90160 [S] | Suppe: Overtures | 196? | 50.00 |
| *—Maroon label, no "Vendor: Mercury Record Corporation"* | | | |
| ❑ SR 90161 [S] | Encore Please, Sir John! | 196? | 200.00 |
| *—Maroon label, no "Vendor: Mercury Record Corporation"* | | | |
| ❑ SR 90164 [S] | Grieg: Peer Gynt Suite; Symphonic Dances; Elegiac Melodies | 196? | 80.00 |
| *—Maroon label, no "Vendor: Mercury Record Corporation"* | | | |

### HALLE ORCHESTRA (GEORGE WELDON, CONDUCTOR)

MERCURY LIVING PRESENCE

| Number | Title (A Side/B Side) | Yr | NM |
|---|---|---|---|
| ❑ SR 90137 [S] | Khachaturian: Gayne Ballet Suite; Mussorgsky: Night on Bare Mountain | 196? | 30.00 |
| *—Maroon label, no "Vendor: Mercury Record Corporation"* | | | |

### HALLYDAY, JOHNNY

PHILIPS

| Number | Title (A Side/B Side) | Yr | NM |
|---|---|---|---|
| ❑ PHM 200019 [M] | America's Rockin' Hits | 1962 | 80.00 |
| ❑ PHS 600019 [S] | America's Rockin' Hits | 1962 | 100.00 |

### HALOS, THE

WARWICK

| Number | Title (A Side/B Side) | Yr | NM |
|---|---|---|---|
| ❑ W-2046 [M] | The Halos | 1962 | 400.00 |

### HAMBLEN, STUART

COLUMBIA

| Number | Title (A Side/B Side) | Yr | NM |
|---|---|---|---|
| ❑ CL 1588 [M] | The Spell of the Yukon | 1961 | 20.00 |
| ❑ CL 1769 [M] | Of God I Sing | 1962 | 20.00 |
| ❑ CS 8388 [S] | The Spell of the Yukon | 1961 | 25.00 |
| ❑ CS 8569 [S] | Of God I Sing | 1962 | 25.00 |

CORAL

| Number | Title (A Side/B Side) | Yr | NM |
|---|---|---|---|
| ❑ CRL 57254 [M] | Remember Me | 1960 | 25.00 |

HARMONY

| Number | Title (A Side/B Side) | Yr | NM |
|---|---|---|---|
| ❑ HL 7009 [M] | Hymns | 1957 | 25.00 |

RCA CAMDEN

| Number | Title (A Side/B Side) | Yr | NM |
|---|---|---|---|
| ❑ CAL-537 [M] | Beyond the Sun | 1959 | 25.00 |

RCA VICTOR

| Number | Title (A Side/B Side) | Yr | NM |
|---|---|---|---|
| ❑ LPM-1253 [M] | It Is No Secret | 1956 | 40.00 |
| ❑ LPM-1436 [M] | Grand Old Hymns | 1957 | 40.00 |
| ❑ LPM-3265 [10] | It Is No Secret | 1954 | 60.00 |

### HAMBRO, LENNY

COLUMBIA

| Number | Title (A Side/B Side) | Yr | NM |
|---|---|---|---|
| ❑ CL 757 [M] | Message from Hambro | 1956 | 40.00 |

EPIC

| Number | Title (A Side/B Side) | Yr | NM |
|---|---|---|---|
| ❑ LN 3361 [M] | The Nature of Things | 1956 | 40.00 |

| Number | Title (A Side/B Side) | Yr | NM |
|---|---|---|---|
| **SAVOY** | | | |
| ❑ MG-15031 [10] | Mambo Hambro | 1954 | 50.00 |

## HAMILTON, CHICO

| Number | Title (A Side/B Side) | Yr | NM |
|---|---|---|---|
| **ABC IMPULSE!** | | | |
| ❑ AS-9213 [(2)] | His Great Hits | 1971 | 20.00 |
| **COLUMBIA** | | | |
| ❑ CL 1590 [M] | Selections from "Bye Bye Birdie" | 1961 | 20.00 |
| ❑ CL 1619 [M] | Chico Hamilton Special | 1961 | 20.00 |
| ❑ CL 1807 [M] | Drumfusion | 1962 | 20.00 |
| ❑ CS 8390 [S] | Selections from "Bye Bye Birdie" | 1961 | 25.00 |
| ❑ CS 8419 [S] | Chico Hamilton Special | 1961 | 25.00 |
| ❑ CS 8607 [S] | Drumfusion | 1962 | 25.00 |
| **DECCA** | | | |
| ❑ DL 8614 [M] | Jazz from the Sweet Smell of Success | 1957 | 50.00 |
| **IMPULSE!** | | | |
| ❑ A-29 [M] | Passin' Thru | 1963 | 25.00 |
| ❑ AS-29 [S] | Passin' Thru | 1963 | 30.00 |
| ❑ A-59 [M] | Man from Two Worlds | 1964 | 25.00 |
| ❑ AS-59 [S] | Man from Two Worlds | 1964 | 30.00 |
| ❑ A-82 [M] | Chi Chi Chico | 1965 | 20.00 |
| ❑ AS-82 [S] | Chi Chi Chico | 1965 | 25.00 |
| ❑ A-9102 [M] | El Chico | 1965 | 20.00 |
| ❑ AS-9102 [S] | El Chico | 1965 | 25.00 |
| ❑ A-9114 [M] | The Further Adventures of El Chico | 1966 | 20.00 |
| ❑ AS-9114 [S] | The Further Adventures of El Chico | 1966 | 25.00 |
| ❑ A-9130 [M] | The Dealer | 1966 | 20.00 |
| ❑ AS-9130 [S] | The Dealer | 1966 | 25.00 |
| **JAZZTONE** | | | |
| ❑ J-1264 [M] | Delightfully Modern | 1957 | 40.00 |
| **NAUTILUS** | | | |
| ❑ NR-13 | Reaching for the Top | 1981 | 30.00 |
| *—Audiophile vinyl* | | | |
| **PACIFIC JAZZ** | | | |
| ❑ PJLP-17 [10] | Chico Hamilton Trio | 1955 | 100.00 |
| ❑ PJ-39 [M] | Spectacular | 1962 | 25.00 |
| *—Reissue of 1209* | | | |
| ❑ PJ-1209 [M] | Chico Hamilton Quintet | 1955 | 75.00 |
| ❑ PJ-1216 [M] | Chico Hamilton Quintet In Hi-Fi | 1956 | 75.00 |
| ❑ PJ-1220 [M] | Chico Hamilton Trio | 1956 | 75.00 |
| ❑ PJ-1225 [M] | Chico Hamilton Quintet | 1957 | 75.00 |
| ❑ PJ-1231 [M] | Chico Hamilton Plays the Music of Fred Katz | 1957 | 75.00 |
| **REPRISE** | | | |
| ❑ R-6078 [M] | A Different Journey | 1963 | 30.00 |
| ❑ R9-6078 [S] | A Different Journey | 1963 | 40.00 |
| **WARNER BROS.** | | | |
| ❑ W 1245 [M] | Chico Hamilton Quintet with Strings Attached | 1958 | 50.00 |
| ❑ WS 1245 [S] | Chico Hamilton Quintet with Strings Attached | 1958 | 60.00 |
| ❑ W 1271 [M] | Gongs East | 1958 | 50.00 |
| ❑ WS 1271 [S] | Gongs East | 1958 | 60.00 |
| ❑ W 1344 [M] | The Three Faces of Chico | 1959 | 50.00 |
| ❑ WS 1344 [S] | The Three Faces of Chico | 1959 | 60.00 |
| **WORLD PACIFIC** | | | |
| ❑ ST-1003 [S] | South Pacific in Hi-Fi | 1958 | 40.00 |
| ❑ ST-1005 [S] | Chico Hamilton Quintet | 1958 | 40.00 |
| ❑ ST-1008 [S] | The Chico Hamilton Trio Featuring Freddie Gambrell | 1958 | 40.00 |
| ❑ ST-1016 [S] | Ellington Suite | 1959 | 40.00 |
| ❑ WP-1216 [M] | Chico Hamilton Quintet In Hi-Fi | 1958 | 50.00 |
| ❑ WP-1225 [M] | Chico Hamilton Quintet | 1958 | 50.00 |
| ❑ WP-1231 [M] | Chico Hamilton Plays the Music of Fred Katz | 1958 | 50.00 |
| ❑ PJ-1238 [M] | South Pacific in Hi-Fi | 1957 | 50.00 |
| ❑ WP-1238 [M] | South Pacific in Hi-Fi | 1958 | 40.00 |
| ❑ PJ-1242 [M] | The Chico Hamilton Trio Featuring Freddie Gambrell | 1957 | 50.00 |
| ❑ WP-1242 [M] | The Chico Hamilton Trio Featuring Freddie Gambrell | 1958 | 40.00 |
| ❑ WP-1258 [M] | Ellington Suite | 1959 | 50.00 |
| ❑ WP-1287 [M] | The Original Hamilton Quintet | 1960 | 50.00 |

## HAMILTON, DAVE

| Number | Title (A Side/B Side) | Yr | NM |
|---|---|---|---|
| **WORKSHOP JAZZ** | | | |
| ❑ WSJ-206 [M] | Blue Vibrations | 1963 | 80.00 |

## HAMILTON, GEORGE

| Number | Title (A Side/B Side) | Yr | NM |
|---|---|---|---|
| **ABC-PARAMOUNT** | | | |
| ❑ 535 [M] | By George | 1966 | 20.00 |
| ❑ S-535 [S] | By George | 1966 | 25.00 |

## HAMILTON, GEORGE, IV

| Number | Title (A Side/B Side) | Yr | NM |
|---|---|---|---|
| **ABC** | | | |
| ❑ X-750 | 16 Greatest Hits | 1972 | 10.00 |
| ❑ AC-30032 | The ABC Collection | 1975 | 12.00 |
| **ABC-PARAMOUNT** | | | |
| ❑ 220 [M] | On Campus | 1958 | 40.00 |
| ❑ S-220 [S] | On Campus | 1958 | 50.00 |
| ❑ 251 [M] | Sing Me a Sad Song (A Tribute to Hank Williams) | 1958 | 40.00 |
| ❑ S-251 [S] | Sing Me a Sad Song (A Tribute to Hank Williams) | 1958 | 50.00 |
| ❑ 461 [M] | George Hamilton IV's Big 15 | 1963 | 30.00 |
| ❑ S-461 [P] | George Hamilton IV's Big 15 | 1963 | 40.00 |
| **ABC/DOT** | | | |
| ❑ DO-2081 | Fine Lace | 1977 | 10.00 |
| **DOT** | | | |
| ❑ 39033 | George Hamilton IV | 1985 | 10.00 |
| **HARMONY** | | | |
| ❑ HS 11379 | Your Cheatin' Heart | 1970 | 10.00 |
| **LAMB AND LION** | | | |
| ❑ 1015 | Bluegrass Gospel | 1974 | 12.00 |
| **MCA** | | | |
| ❑ 705 | Forever Young | 198? | 8.00 |
| *—Reissue of 3206* | | | |
| ❑ 3206 | Forever Young | 1980 | 10.00 |
| **RCA CAMDEN** | | | |
| ❑ ACL1-0242 | Singin' on the Mountains | 1973 | 10.00 |
| ❑ CAL-2200 [M] | A Rose and a Baby Ruth | 1967 | 15.00 |
| ❑ CAS-2200 [S] | A Rose and a Baby Ruth | 1967 | 10.00 |
| ❑ CAS-2468 | Early Morning Rain | 1971 | 10.00 |
| **RCA VICTOR** | | | |
| ❑ APL1-0455 | Greatest Hits | 1974 | 12.00 |
| ❑ LPM-2373 [M] | To You and Yours from Me and Mine | 1961 | 25.00 |
| ❑ LSP-2373 [S] | To You and Yours from Me and Mine | 1961 | 30.00 |
| ❑ LPM-2778 [M] | Abilene | 1963 | 25.00 |
| ❑ LSP-2778 [S] | Abilene | 1963 | 30.00 |
| ❑ LPM-2972 [M] | Fort Worth, Dallas or Houston | 1964 | 25.00 |
| ❑ LSP-2972 [S] | Fort Worth, Dallas or Houston | 1964 | 30.00 |
| ❑ LPM-3371 [M] | Mister Sincerity... A Tribute to Ernest Tubb | 1965 | 25.00 |
| ❑ LSP-3371 [S] | Mister Sincerity... A Tribute to Ernest Tubb | 1965 | 30.00 |
| ❑ LPM-3510 [M] | Coast Country | 1966 | 25.00 |
| ❑ LSP-3510 [S] | Coast Country | 1966 | 30.00 |
| ❑ LPM-3601 [M] | Steel Rail Blues | 1966 | 20.00 |
| ❑ LSP-3601 [S] | Steel Rail Blues | 1966 | 20.00 |
| ❑ LPM-3752 [M] | Folk Country Classics | 1967 | 25.00 |
| ❑ LSP-3752 [S] | Folk Country Classics | 1967 | 20.00 |
| ❑ LPM-3854 [M] | Folksy | 1967 | 25.00 |
| ❑ LSP-3854 [S] | Folksy | 1967 | 20.00 |
| ❑ LPM-3962 [M] | The Gentle Country Sound of George Hamilton IV | 1968 | 40.00 |
| ❑ LSP-3962 [S] | The Gentle Country Sound of George Hamilton IV | 1968 | 20.00 |
| ❑ LSP-4066 | In the 4th Dimension | 1968 | 20.00 |
| ❑ LSP-4164 | Canadian Pacific | 1969 | 15.00 |
| ❑ LSP-4265 | The Best of George Hamilton IV | 1970 | 15.00 |
| ❑ LSP-4342 | Back Where It's At | 1970 | 15.00 |
| ❑ LSP-4435 | Down Home in the Country | 1971 | 15.00 |
| ❑ LSP-4517 | North Country | 1971 | 15.00 |
| ❑ LSP-4609 | West Texas Highway | 1971 | 15.00 |
| ❑ LSP-4700 | Country Music in My Soul | 1972 | 12.00 |
| ❑ LSP-4772 | Travelin' Light | 1972 | 12.00 |
| ❑ LSP-4826 | International Ambassador | 1973 | 12.00 |

## HAMILTON, JIMMY

| Number | Title (A Side/B Side) | Yr | NM |
|---|---|---|---|
| **EVEREST** | | | |
| ❑ SDBR-1100 [S] | Swing Low, Sweet Chariot | 1960 | 30.00 |
| ❑ LPBR-5100 [M] | Swing Low, Sweet Chariot | 1960 | 25.00 |
| **SWINGVILLE** | | | |
| ❑ SVLP-2022 [M] | It's About Time | 1961 | 50.00 |
| *—Purple label* | | | |
| ❑ SVLP-2022 [M] | It's About Time | 1965 | 25.00 |
| *—Blue label, trident logo at right* | | | |
| ❑ SVLP-2028 [M] | Can't Help Swingin' | 1961 | 50.00 |
| *—Purple label* | | | |
| ❑ SVLP-2028 [M] | Can't Help Swingin' | 1965 | 25.00 |
| *—Blue label, trident logo at right* | | | |
| **URANIA** | | | |
| ❑ UJLP-1003 [10] | Clarinet in Hi-Fi | 1954 | 120.00 |
| ❑ UJLP-1204 [M] | Accent on Clarinet | 1955 | 50.00 |
| ❑ UJLP-1208 [M] | Clarinet in Hi-Fi | 1955 | 50.00 |

## HAMILTON, ROY

| Number | Title (A Side/B Side) | Yr | NM |
|---|---|---|---|
| **EPIC** | | | |
| ❑ BN 518 [S] | With All My Love | 1958 | 40.00 |
| ❑ BN 525 [S] | Why Fight The Feeling? | 1959 | 30.00 |
| ❑ BN 530 [S] | Come Out Swingin' | 1959 | 30.00 |
| ❑ BN 535 [S] | Have Blues, Must Travel | 1959 | 30.00 |
| ❑ BN 551 [S] | Spirituals | 1960 | 30.00 |
| ❑ BN 578 [S] | Soft 'n Warm | 1960 | 30.00 |
| ❑ BN 595 [S] | You Can Have Her | 1961 | 40.00 |
| ❑ BN 610 [S] | Only You | 1961 | 30.00 |
| ❑ BN 632 [R] | You'll Never Walk Alone | 1962 | 20.00 |
| ❑ LN 1023 [10] | You'll Never Walk Alone | 1954 | 200.00 |
| ❑ LN 1103 [10] | The Voice of Roy Hamilton | 1954 | 200.00 |
| ❑ LN 3176 [M] | Roy Hamilton | 1955 | 60.00 |
| ❑ LN 3294 [M] | You'll Never Walk Alone | 1956 | 70.00 |
| ❑ LN 3364 [M] | Golden Boy | 1957 | 50.00 |
| ❑ LN 3519 [M] | With All My Love | 1958 | 30.00 |
| ❑ LN 3545 [M] | Why Fight The Feeling? | 1959 | 25.00 |
| ❑ LN 3561 [M] | Come Out Swingin' | 1959 | 25.00 |
| ❑ LN 3580 [M] | Have Blues, Must Travel | 1959 | 25.00 |
| ❑ LN 3628 [M] | Roy Hamilton At His Best | 1960 | 40.00 |
| ❑ LN 3654 [M] | Spirituals | 1960 | 25.00 |
| ❑ LN 3717 [M] | Soft 'n Warm | 1960 | 25.00 |
| ❑ LN 3775 [M] | You Can Have Her | 1961 | 30.00 |
| ❑ LN 3807 [M] | Only You | 1961 | 25.00 |
| ❑ LN 24000 [M] | Mr. Rock and Soul | 1962 | 25.00 |
| ❑ LN 24009 [M] | Roy Hamilton's Greatest Hits | 1962 | 20.00 |
| ❑ LN 24316 [M] | Roy Hamilton's Greatest Hits, Vol. 2 | 1967 | 20.00 |
| ❑ BN 26000 [S] | Mr. Rock and Soul | 1962 | 30.00 |
| ❑ BN 26009 [S] | Roy Hamilton's Greatest Hits | 1962 | 25.00 |
| ❑ BN 26316 [S] | Roy Hamilton's Greatest Hits, Vol. 2 | 1967 | 25.00 |
| **MGM** | | | |
| ❑ E-4139 [M] | Warm and Soul | 1963 | 15.00 |
| ❑ SE-4139 [S] | Warm and Soul | 1963 | 20.00 |
| ❑ E-4233 [M] | Sentimental, Lonely & Blue | 1964 | 15.00 |
| ❑ SE-4233 [S] | Sentimental, Lonely & Blue | 1964 | 20.00 |
| **RCA VICTOR** | | | |
| ❑ LPM-3552 [M] | The Impossible Dream | 1966 | 15.00 |
| ❑ LSP-3552 [S] | The Impossible Dream | 1966 | 20.00 |

## HAMILTON, RUSS

| Number | Title (A Side/B Side) | Yr | NM |
|---|---|---|---|
| **KAPP** | | | |
| ❑ KL-1076 [M] | Rainbow | 1957 | 80.00 |

## HAMILTON, SCOTT

| Number | Title (A Side/B Side) | Yr | NM |
|---|---|---|---|
| **FAMOUS DOOR** | | | |
| ❑ 119 | The Swinging Young Scott | 197? | 20.00 |

## HAMILTON STREETCAR

| Number | Title (A Side/B Side) | Yr | NM |
|---|---|---|---|
| **DOT** | | | |
| ❑ DLP-25939 | Hamilton Streetcar | 1969 | 25.00 |

## HAMLIN, JOHNNY

| Number | Title (A Side/B Side) | Yr | NM |
|---|---|---|---|
| **ARGO** | | | |
| ❑ LP-4001 [M] | Johnny Hamiln Quintet | 1961 | 25.00 |
| ❑ LPS-4001 [S] | Johnny Hamiln Quintet | 1961 | 30.00 |

## HAMMACK, BOBBY

| Number | Title (A Side/B Side) | Yr | NM |
|---|---|---|---|
| **LIBERTY** | | | |
| ❑ LRP-3016 [M] | Power House | 1956 | 40.00 |

## HAMMER

| Number | Title (A Side/B Side) | Yr | NM |
|---|---|---|---|
| **SAN FRANCISCO** | | | |
| ❑ SD 203 | Hammer | 1970 | 20.00 |

## HAMMER, BOB

| Number | Title (A Side/B Side) | Yr | NM |
|---|---|---|---|
| **ABC-PARAMOUNT** | | | |
| ❑ ABC-497 [M] | Beatle Jazz | 1964 | 30.00 |
| ❑ ABCS-497 [S] | Beatle Jazz | 1964 | 40.00 |

## HAMMER, JACK

| Number | Title (A Side/B Side) | Yr | NM |
|---|---|---|---|
| **WARWICK** | | | |
| ❑ W-2014 [M] | Rebellion: Jack Hammer Sings and Reads Songs and Poems of the Beat Generation | 1960 | 80.00 |

## HAMMER, MC

| Number | Title (A Side/B Side) | Yr | NM |
|---|---|---|---|
| **BUSTIN'** | | | |
| ❑ BR-LP-001 | Feel My Power | 1987 | 25.00 |
| **CAPITOL** | | | |
| ❑ SPRO-79080 [EP] | A Bit Legit | 1991 | 8.00 |
| *—Promo-only three-track sampler* | | | |
| ❑ C1-90924 | Let's Get It Started | 1988 | 10.00 |
| ❑ C1-92857 | Please Hammer Don't Hurt 'Em | 1990 | 15.00 |
| ❑ C1-98151 [(2)] | Too Legit to Quit | 1991 | 15.00 |
| **GIANT** | | | |
| ❑ PRO-A-6798 [(2)DJ] | The Funky Headhunter | 1994 | 20.00 |
| *—Vinyl version is promo only* | | | |

## HAMMOND, JOHN

| Number | Title (A Side/B Side) | Yr | NM |
|---|---|---|---|
| **ATLANTIC** | | | |
| ❑ 8152 [M] | I Can Tell | 1967 | 30.00 |
| ❑ SD 8152 [S] | I Can Tell | 1967 | 30.00 |
| ❑ SD 8206 | Sooner or Later | 1968 | 15.00 |
| ❑ SD 8251 | Southern Fried | 1969 | 15.00 |
| **CAPRICORN** | | | |
| ❑ CP 0153 | Can't Beat the Kid | 1975 | 12.00 |
| **COLUMBIA** | | | |
| ❑ C 30458 | Source Point | 1971 | 12.00 |
| ❑ KC 31318 | I'm Satisfied | 1972 | 12.00 |
| **FLYING FISH** | | | |
| ❑ FF-502 | Nobody But You | 1988 | 10.00 |
| **ROUNDER** | | | |
| ❑ 3042 | Mileage | 1980 | 10.00 |
| ❑ 3060 | Frogs for Snakes | 1982 | 10.00 |
| ❑ 3074 | John Hammond Live | 1984 | 10.00 |
| **VANGUARD** | | | |
| ❑ VSD 11/12 [(2)] | The Best of John Hammond | 1970 | 15.00 |
| ❑ VSD-2148 [S] | John Hammond | 1964 | 40.00 |

| Number | Title (A Side/B Side) | Yr | NM |
|---|---|---|---|
| ❑ VRS-9132 [M] | John Hammond | 1964 | 30.00 |
| ❑ VRS-9153 [M] | Big City Blues | 1964 | 30.00 |
| ❑ VRS-9178 [M] | So Many Roads | 1965 | 30.00 |
| ❑ VRS-9198 [M] | Country Blues | 1966 | 30.00 |
| ❑ VRS-9245 [M] | Mirrors | 1967 | 30.00 |
| ❑ VSD-79153 [S] | Big City Blues | 1964 | 40.00 |
| ❑ VSD-79178 [S] | So Many Roads | 1965 | 40.00 |
| ❑ VSD-79198 [S] | Country Blues | 1966 | 40.00 |
| ❑ VSD-79245 [S] | Mirrors | 1967 | 30.00 |
| ❑ VSD-79380 | Solo | 1976 | 10.00 |
| ❑ VSD-79400 | Footwork | 1978 | 10.00 |
| ❑ VSD-79424 | Hot Tracks | 1979 | 10.00 |

### HAMMOND, JOHNNY

**NEW JAZZ**

| Number | Title (A Side/B Side) | Yr | NM |
|---|---|---|---|
| ❑ NJLP-8221 [M] | All Soul *—Purple label* | 1959 | 50.00 |
| ❑ NJLP-8221 [M] | All Soul *—Blue label with trident logo* | 1965 | 25.00 |
| ❑ NJLP-8229 [M] | That Good Feelin' *—Purple label* | 1959 | 50.00 |
| ❑ NJLP-8229 [M] | That Good Feelin' *—Blue label with trident logo* | 1965 | 25.00 |
| ❑ NJLP-8241 [M] | Talk That Talk *—Purple label* | 1960 | 50.00 |
| ❑ NJLP-8241 [M] | Talk That Talk *—Blue label with trident logo* | 1965 | 25.00 |
| ❑ NJLP-8288 [M] | Look Out! *—Purple label* | 1962 | 50.00 |
| ❑ NJLP-8288 [M] | Look Out! *—Blue label with trident logo* | 1965 | 25.00 |

**PRESTIGE**

| Number | Title (A Side/B Side) | Yr | NM |
|---|---|---|---|
| ❑ PRLP-7203 [M] | Stimulation *—Yellow label* | 1961 | 40.00 |
| ❑ PRLP-7203 [M] | Stimulation *—Blue label with trident logo* | 1965 | 25.00 |
| ❑ PRLP-7217 [M] | Gettin' the Message *—Yellow label* | 1961 | 40.00 |
| ❑ PRLP-7217 [M] | Gettin' the Message *—Blue label with trident logo* | 1965 | 25.00 |
| ❑ PRLP-7408 [M] | The Stinger | 1965 | 20.00 |
| ❑ PRST-7408 [S] | The Stinger | 1965 | 25.00 |
| ❑ PRLP-7420 [M] | Opus de Funk | 1966 | 20.00 |
| ❑ PRST-7420 [S] | Opus de Funk | 1966 | 25.00 |
| ❑ PRLP-7464 [M] | The Stinger Meets the Golden Thrush | 1966 | 20.00 |
| ❑ PRST-7464 [S] | The Stinger Meets the Golden Thrush | 1966 | 25.00 |
| ❑ PRLP-7482 [M] | Love Potion #9 | 1967 | 25.00 |
| ❑ PRST-7482 [S] | Love Potion #9 | 1967 | 20.00 |
| ❑ PRLP-7494 [M] | Ebb Tide | 1967 | 25.00 |
| ❑ PRST-7494 [S] | Ebb Tide | 1967 | 20.00 |
| ❑ PRST-7549 | Soul Flowers | 1968 | 20.00 |
| ❑ PRST-7564 | Dirty Grape | 1968 | 20.00 |
| ❑ PRST-7588 | Nasty | 1968 | 20.00 |
| ❑ PRST-7681 | Soul Talk | 1969 | 20.00 |

**RIVERSIDE**

| Number | Title (A Side/B Side) | Yr | NM |
|---|---|---|---|
| ❑ RLP-442 [M] | Black Coffee | 1963 | 25.00 |
| ❑ RLP-466 [M] | Mr. Wonderful | 1963 | 25.00 |
| ❑ RLP-482 [M] | Open House! | 1965 | 20.00 |
| ❑ RLP-496 [M] | A Little Taste | 1965 | 20.00 |
| ❑ RS-9442 [S] | Black Coffee | 1963 | 30.00 |
| ❑ RS-9466 [S] | Mr. Wonderful | 1963 | 30.00 |
| ❑ RS-9482 [S] | Open House! | 1965 | 25.00 |
| ❑ RS-9496 [S] | A Little Taste | 1965 | 25.00 |

**SALVATION**

| Number | Title (A Side/B Side) | Yr | NM |
|---|---|---|---|
| ❑ 702 | A Gambler's Life | 1974 | 12.00 |

### HAMPEL, GUNTER

**BIRTH**

| Number | Title (A Side/B Side) | Yr | NM |
|---|---|---|---|
| ❑ 001 | The 8th of July, 1969 | 1969 | 40.00 |
| ❑ 002 | Dances | 1970 | 30.00 |
| ❑ 003 | Symphony No. 5 and 6 | 1970 | 30.00 |
| ❑ 005 | People Symphony | 1970 | 30.00 |
| ❑ 007 | Spirits | 1971 | 20.00 |
| ❑ 008 | Familie | 1972 | 20.00 |
| ❑ 009 | Angel | 1972 | 20.00 |
| ❑ 0010 | Waltz for 3 Universes in a Corridor | 1972 | 20.00 |
| ❑ 0011 | Broadway/Folksong | 1972 | 20.00 |
| ❑ 0012 | I Love Being with You | 1972 | 20.00 |
| ❑ 0013 | Unity Dance | 1973 | 20.00 |
| ❑ 0016 | Out from Under | 1974 | 20.00 |
| ❑ 0017 | Journey to the Song Within | 1974 | 20.00 |
| ❑ 0021/0022 [(2)] | Celebrations | 1974 | 30.00 |
| ❑ 0023 | Ruomi | 1975 | 20.00 |
| ❑ 0024 | Cosmic Dancer | 1975 | 20.00 |
| ❑ 0025 | Enfant Terrible | 1976 | 20.00 |
| ❑ 0026 | Transformation | 1976 | 20.00 |
| ❑ 0027 | That Came Down on Me | 1978 | 20.00 |
| ❑ 0028 | All Is Real | 1978 | 20.00 |
| ❑ 0029 | Vogelfrei | 1978 | 20.00 |
| ❑ 0030 | Freedom of the Universe | 1978 | 20.00 |
| ❑ 0031 | All the Things You Could Be If Charles Mingus Was Your Daddy | 1980 | 20.00 |
| ❑ 0032 | A Place to Be with Us | 1981 | 20.00 |
| ❑ 0033 | Life on This Planet 1981 | 1981 | 20.00 |
| ❑ 0034 | Cavana | 1982 | 20.00 |
| ❑ 0035 | Generator | 1982 | 20.00 |
| ❑ 0036 | Companion | 1983 | 20.00 |
| ❑ 0038 | Jubilation | 1984 | 20.00 |
| ❑ 0039 | Fresh Heat | 1985 | 20.00 |

**ESP-DISK'**

| Number | Title (A Side/B Side) | Yr | NM |
|---|---|---|---|
| ❑ 1042 [M] | Music from Europe | 1967 | 25.00 |
| ❑ S-1042 [S] | Music from Europe | 1967 | 20.00 |

**FLYING DUTCHMAN**

| Number | Title (A Side/B Side) | Yr | NM |
|---|---|---|---|
| ❑ 126 | The 8th of July, 1969 | 1970 | 40.00 |
| ❑ FD-10126 | The 8th of July, 1969 | 1971 | 20.00 |

**HORO**

| Number | Title (A Side/B Side) | Yr | NM |
|---|---|---|---|
| ❑ 33/34 [(2)] | Oasis | 1978 | 30.00 |

### HAMPEL, GUNTER, AND BOULOU FERRE

**BIRTH**

| Number | Title (A Side/B Side) | Yr | NM |
|---|---|---|---|
| ❑ 006 | Espace | 1970 | 25.00 |

### HAMPTON, LIONEL

**AMERICAN RECORDING SOCIETY**

| Number | Title (A Side/B Side) | Yr | NM |
|---|---|---|---|
| ❑ G-403 [M] | The Swinging Jazz of Lionel Hampton | 1956 | 40.00 |

**AUDIO FIDELITY**

| Number | Title (A Side/B Side) | Yr | NM |
|---|---|---|---|
| ❑ AFLP-1849 [M] | Lionel | 1957 | 30.00 |
| ❑ AFLP-1913 [M] | Hamp's Big Band | 1958 | 30.00 |
| ❑ AFSD-5849 [S] | Lionel | 1958 | 40.00 |
| ❑ AFSD-5913 [S] | Hamp's Big Band | 1958 | 40.00 |

**BLUE NOTE**

| Number | Title (A Side/B Side) | Yr | NM |
|---|---|---|---|
| ❑ BLP-5046 [10] | Rockin' and Groovin' | 1954 | 300.00 |

**BLUEBIRD**

| Number | Title (A Side/B Side) | Yr | NM |
|---|---|---|---|
| ❑ AXM6-5536 [(6)] | The Complete Lionel Hampton 1937-1941 | 1976 | 50.00 |

**CLEF**

| Number | Title (A Side/B Side) | Yr | NM |
|---|---|---|---|
| ❑ MGC-142 [10] | The Lionel Hampton Quartet | 1953 | 120.00 |
| ❑ MGC-611 [M] | The Lionel Hampton Quartet | 1954 | 80.00 |
| ❑ MGC-628 [M] | The Lionel Hampton Quintet | 1954 | 80.00 |
| ❑ MGC-642 [M] | The Lionel Hampton Quintet, Volume 2 | 1955 | 100.00 |
| ❑ MGC-667 [M] | The Lionel Hampton Quartet and Quintet | 1955 | 100.00 |
| ❑ MGC-670 [M] | Lionel Hampton Big Band | 1955 | 100.00 |
| ❑ MGC-673 [M] | The Lionel Hampton Quartet | 1955 | 80.00 |
| ❑ MGC-714 [M] | Lionel Hampton Plays Love Songs | 1956 | 70.00 |
| ❑ MGC-726 [M] | King of the Vibes | 1956 | 70.00 |
| ❑ MGC-727 [M] | Air Mail Special | 1956 | 70.00 |
| ❑ MGC-735 [M] | Flying Home | 1956 | 70.00 |
| ❑ MGC-736 [M] | Swingin' with Hamp | 1956 | 70.00 |
| ❑ MGC-738 [M] | Hamp! | 1956 | 70.00 |
| ❑ MGC-744 [M] | Hamp's Big Four | 1956 | 70.00 |

**COLUMBIA**

| Number | Title (A Side/B Side) | Yr | NM |
|---|---|---|---|
| ❑ CL 711 [M] | Wailin' at the Trianon | 1956 | 40.00 |
| ❑ CL 1304 [M] | Golden Vibes | 1959 | 25.00 |
| ❑ CL 1486 [M] | Silver Vibes | 1960 | 25.00 |
| ❑ CL 1661 [M] | Soft Vibes | 1961 | 20.00 |
| ❑ CS 8110 [S] | Golden Vibes | 1959 | 20.00 |
| ❑ CS 8277 [S] | Silver Vibes | 1960 | 20.00 |
| ❑ CS 8461 [S] | Soft Vibes | 1961 | 20.00 |

**CONTEMPORARY**

| Number | Title (A Side/B Side) | Yr | NM |
|---|---|---|---|
| ❑ C-3502 [M] | Hampton in Paris | 1955 | 50.00 |

**CORONET**

| Number | Title (A Side/B Side) | Yr | NM |
|---|---|---|---|
| ❑ CX-159 [M] | Lionel Hampton | 196? | 12.00 |
| ❑ CXS-159 [S] | Lionel Hampton | 196? | 12.00 |

**DECCA**

| Number | Title (A Side/B Side) | Yr | NM |
|---|---|---|---|
| ❑ DL 5230 [10] | Boogie Woogie | 1950 | 80.00 |
| ❑ DL 5297 [10] | Moonglow | 1951 | 80.00 |
| ❑ DL 7013 [10] | Just Jazz | 1962 | 80.00 |
| ❑ DL 8088 [M] | All American Award Concert at Carnegie Hall *—Black label, silver print* | 1955 | 50.00 |
| ❑ DL 8088 [M] | All American Award Concert at Carnegie Hall *—Black label with color bars* | 196? | 20.00 |
| ❑ DL 8230 [M] | Moonglow *—Black label, silver print* | 1956 | 50.00 |
| ❑ DL 8230 [M] | Moonglow *—Black label with color bars* | 196? | 20.00 |
| ❑ DL 9055 [M] | Just Jazz | 1958 | 50.00 |
| ❑ DL 74194 [S] | The Original Star Dust | 1962 | 20.00 |
| ❑ DL 74296 [S] | Hamp's Golden Favorites | 1962 | 20.00 |
| ❑ DL 79244 [R] | Stepping Out Volume 1 1942-1945 | 197? | 12.00 |

**EMARCY**

| Number | Title (A Side/B Side) | Yr | NM |
|---|---|---|---|
| ❑ MG-27537 [10] | Hamp in Paris | 1954 | 100.00 |
| ❑ MG-27538 [10] | Crazy Hamp | 1954 | 100.00 |
| ❑ MG-36032 [M] | Hamp in Paris | 1955 | 50.00 |
| ❑ MG-36034 [M] | Crazy Rhythm | 1955 | 50.00 |
| ❑ MG-36035 [M] | Jam Session in Paris | 1955 | 50.00 |

**EPIC**

| Number | Title (A Side/B Side) | Yr | NM |
|---|---|---|---|
| ❑ LN 3190 [M] | Apollo Hall Concert 1954 | 1955 | 50.00 |
| ❑ LA 16027 [M] | Many Splendored Vibes | 1962 | 20.00 |
| ❑ BA 17027 [S] | Many Splendored Vibes | 1962 | 25.00 |

**GENE NORMAN**

| Number | Title (A Side/B Side) | Yr | NM |
|---|---|---|---|
| ❑ GNP-15 [M] | Lionel Hampton with the Just Jazz All-Stars | 1956 | 50.00 |

**GLAD HAMP**

| Number | Title (A Side/B Side) | Yr | NM |
|---|---|---|---|
| ❑ GH-1001 [M] | The Many Sides of Lionel Hampton | 1961 | 25.00 |
| ❑ GHS-1001 [S] | The Many Sides of Lionel Hampton | 1961 | 30.00 |
| ❑ GH-1003 [M] | The Exciting Hamp in Europe | 1962 | 25.00 |
| ❑ GHS-1003 [S] | The Exciting Hamp in Europe | 1962 | 30.00 |
| ❑ GH-1004 [M] | Bossa Nova Jazz | 1963 | 25.00 |
| ❑ GHS-1004 [S] | Bossa Nova Jazz | 1963 | 30.00 |
| ❑ GH-1005 [M] | Lionel Hampton on Tour | 1963 | 25.00 |
| ❑ GHS-1005 [S] | Lionel Hampton on Tour | 1963 | 30.00 |
| ❑ GH-1006 [M] | Hamp in Japan | 1964 | 25.00 |
| ❑ GHS-1006 [S] | Hamp in Japan | 1964 | 30.00 |
| ❑ GH-1007 [M] | East Meets West | 1965 | 25.00 |
| ❑ GHS-1007 [S] | East Meets West | 1965 | 30.00 |
| ❑ GH-1009 [M] | A Taste of Hamp | 1965 | 25.00 |
| ❑ GHS-1009 [S] | A Taste of Hamp | 1965 | 30.00 |
| ❑ GH-3050 [M] | All That Twistin' Jazz | 1962 | 25.00 |
| ❑ GHS-3050 [S] | All That Twistin' Jazz | 1962 | 30.00 |

**GNP CRESCENDO**

| Number | Title (A Side/B Side) | Yr | NM |
|---|---|---|---|
| ❑ GNP-15 [M] | Lionel Hampton with the Just Jazz All-Stars | 196? | 20.00 |

**HARMONY**

| Number | Title (A Side/B Side) | Yr | NM |
|---|---|---|---|
| ❑ HL 7115 [M] | Hamp in Hi-Fi | 1958 | 20.00 |
| ❑ HL 7281 [M] | The One and Only Lionel Hampton | 1961 | 20.00 |

**IMPULSE!**

| Number | Title (A Side/B Side) | Yr | NM |
|---|---|---|---|
| ❑ A-78 [M] | You Better Know It | 1965 | 25.00 |
| ❑ AS-78 [S] | You Better Know It | 1965 | 30.00 |

**JAZZTONE**

| Number | Title (A Side/B Side) | Yr | NM |
|---|---|---|---|
| ❑ J-1040 [10] | Visit on a Skyscraper | 195? | 50.00 |
| ❑ J-1238 [M] | The Fabulous Lionel Hampton and His All-Stars | 1957 | 40.00 |
| ❑ J-1246 [M] | Lionel Hampton's All Star Groups | 1957 | 40.00 |

**LION**

| Number | Title (A Side/B Side) | Yr | NM |
|---|---|---|---|
| ❑ L-70064 [M] | Lionel Hampton and His Orchestra | 1958 | 20.00 |

**MGM**

| Number | Title (A Side/B Side) | Yr | NM |
|---|---|---|---|
| ❑ E-285 [10] | Oh, Rock | 1954 | 120.00 |
| ❑ E-3386 [M] | Oh, Rock | 1956 | 50.00 |

**NORGRAN**

| Number | Title (A Side/B Side) | Yr | NM |
|---|---|---|---|
| ❑ MGN-1080 [M] | Lionel Hampton and His Giants | 1956 | 100.00 |

**PERFECT**

| Number | Title (A Side/B Side) | Yr | NM |
|---|---|---|---|
| ❑ 12002 [M] | Lionel Hampton Swings | 1959 | 30.00 |
| ❑ 14002 [S] | Lionel Hampton Swings | 1959 | 40.00 |

**RCA CAMDEN**

| Number | Title (A Side/B Side) | Yr | NM |
|---|---|---|---|
| ❑ CAL-317 [M] | Open House | 1957 | 20.00 |
| ❑ CAL-402 [M] | Jivin' the Vibes | 1958 | 20.00 |

**RCA VICTOR**

| Number | Title (A Side/B Side) | Yr | NM |
|---|---|---|---|
| ❑ LPT-18 [10] | A Treasury of Immortal Performances | 1951 | 100.00 |
| ❑ LJM-1000 [M] | Hot Mallets | 1954 | 50.00 |
| ❑ LPM-1422 [M] | Jazz Flamenco | 1957 | 50.00 |
| ❑ LPM-2318 [M] | Swing Classics | 1961 | 25.00 |
| ❑ LPM-3917 [M] | Lionel Hampton Plays Bert Kaempfert | 1968 | 25.00 |

**VERVE**

| Number | Title (A Side/B Side) | Yr | NM |
|---|---|---|---|
| ❑ MGV-2018 [M] | Lionel Hampton Plays Love Songs | 1957 | 50.00 |
| ❑ V-2018 [M] | Lionel Hampton Plays Love Songs | 1961 | 20.00 |
| ❑ MGV-8019 [M] | Travelin' Band | 1957 | 50.00 |
| ❑ V-8019 [M] | Travelin' Band | 1961 | 20.00 |
| ❑ MGV-8105 [M] | King of the Vibes | 1957 | 50.00 |
| ❑ V-8105 [M] | King of the Vibes | 1961 | 20.00 |
| ❑ MGV-8106 [M] | Air Mail Special | 1957 | 50.00 |
| ❑ V-8106 [M] | Air Mail Special | 1961 | 20.00 |
| ❑ MGV-8112 [M] | Flying Home | 1957 | 50.00 |
| ❑ V-8112 [M] | Flying Home | 1961 | 20.00 |
| ❑ MGV-8113 [M] | Swingin' with Hamp | 1957 | 50.00 |
| ❑ V-8113 [M] | Swingin' with Hamp | 1961 | 20.00 |
| ❑ MGV-8114 [M] | Hamp! | 1957 | 50.00 |
| ❑ V-8114 [M] | Hamp! | 1961 | 20.00 |
| ❑ MGV-8117 [M] | Hamp's Big Four | 1957 | 50.00 |
| ❑ V-8117 [M] | Hamp's Big Four | 1961 | 20.00 |
| ❑ MGV-8170 [M] | Lionel Hampton and His Giants | 1957 | 50.00 |
| ❑ V-8170 [M] | Lionel Hampton and His Giants | 1961 | 20.00 |
| ❑ MGV-8215 [M] | The Genius of Lionel Hampton | 1958 | 50.00 |
| ❑ V-8215 [M] | The Genius of Lionel Hampton | 1961 | 20.00 |
| ❑ MGV-8223 [M] | Lionel Hampton '58 | 1958 | 50.00 |
| ❑ V-8223 [M] | Lionel Hampton '58 | 1961 | 20.00 |
| ❑ MGV-8226 [M] | Hallelujah Hamp | 1958 | 50.00 |
| ❑ V-8226 [M] | Hallelujah Hamp | 1961 | 20.00 |
| ❑ MGV-8228 [M] | The High and the Mighty | 1958 | 50.00 |
| ❑ V-8228 [M] | The High and the Mighty | 1961 | 20.00 |

### HAMPTON, LIONEL, AND STAN GETZ

**NORGRAN**

| Number | Title (A Side/B Side) | Yr | NM |
|---|---|---|---|
| ❑ MGN-1037 [M] | Hamp and Getz | 1955 | 100.00 |

**VERVE**

| Number | Title (A Side/B Side) | Yr | NM |
|---|---|---|---|
| ❑ MGV-8128 [M] | Hamp and Getz | 1957 | 50.00 |
| ❑ V-8128 [M] | Hamp and Getz | 1961 | 20.00 |

| Number | Title (A Side/B Side) | Yr | NM |
|---|---|---|---|
| **HAMPTON, LIONEL; ART TATUM; BUDDY RICH** | | | |
| CLEF | | | |
| ❑ MGC-709 [M] | The Hampton-Tatum-Rich Trio | 1956 | 80.00 |
| VERVE | | | |
| ❑ MGV-8093 [M] | The Hampton-Tatum-Rich Trio | 1957 | 50.00 |
| ❑ V-8093 [M] | The Hampton-Tatum-Rich Trio | 1961 | 20.00 |
| **HAMPTON, LIONEL, AND CHARLIE TEAGARDEN** | | | |
| CORAL | | | |
| ❑ CRL 57438 [M] | The Great Hamp and Little T. | 1963 | 20.00 |
| ❑ CRL 757438 [S] | The Great Hamp and Little T. | 1963 | 25.00 |
| **HAMPTON, SLIDE** | | | |
| ATLANTIC | | | |
| ❑ 1339 [M] | Sister Salvation | 1960 | 30.00 |
| *—Multicolor label, white "fan" logo at right* | | | |
| ❑ SD 1339 [S] | Sister Salvation | 1960 | 40.00 |
| *—Multicolor label, white "fan" logo at right* | | | |
| ❑ 1362 [M] | Somethin' Sanctified | 1961 | 30.00 |
| *—Multicolor label, white "fan" logo at right* | | | |
| ❑ SD 1362 [S] | Somethin' Sanctified | 1961 | 40.00 |
| *—Multicolor label, white "fan" logo at right* | | | |
| ❑ 1379 [M] | Jazz with a Twist | 1962 | 25.00 |
| ❑ SD 1379 [S] | Jazz with a Twist | 1962 | 30.00 |
| ❑ 1396 [M] | Explosion! | 1962 | 20.00 |
| ❑ SD 1396 [S] | Explosion! | 1962 | 25.00 |
| CHARLIE PARKER | | | |
| ❑ PLP-803 [M] | Two Sides of Slide | 1962 | 25.00 |
| ❑ PLP-803S [S] | Two Sides of Slide | 1962 | 25.00 |
| EPIC | | | |
| ❑ LA 16030 [M] | Drum Suite | 1963 | 20.00 |
| ❑ BA 17030 [S] | Drum Suite | 1963 | 25.00 |
| STRAND | | | |
| ❑ SL-1006 [M] | Slide Hampton and His Horn of Plenty | 1959 | 40.00 |
| ❑ SLS-1006 [S] | Slide Hampton and His Horn of Plenty | 1959 | 40.00 |
| **HANCOCK, HERBIE** | | | |
| BLUE NOTE | | | |
| ❑ BLP-4109 [M] | Takin' Off | 1962 | 50.00 |
| ❑ BLP-4126 [M] | My Point of View | 1963 | 35.00 |
| ❑ BLP-4147 [M] | Inventions and Dimensions | 1963 | 35.00 |
| ❑ BLP-4175 [M] | Empyrean Isles | 1964 | 35.00 |
| ❑ BLP-4195 [M] | Maiden Voyage | 1965 | 35.00 |
| ❑ B1-46339 | Maiden Voyage | 1997 | 20.00 |
| *—Audiophile reissue* | | | |
| ❑ BST-84109 [S] | Takin' Off | 1962 | 40.00 |
| *—With New York, USA address on label* | | | |
| ❑ BST-84126 [S] | My Point of View | 1963 | 35.00 |
| *—With New York, USA address on label* | | | |
| ❑ BST-84147 [S] | Inventions and Dimensions | 1963 | 35.00 |
| *—With New York, USA address on label* | | | |
| ❑ BST-84175 [S] | Empyrean Isles | 1964 | 35.00 |
| *—With New York, USA address on label* | | | |
| ❑ BST-84195 [S] | Maiden Voyage | 1965 | 35.00 |
| *—With New York, USA address on label* | | | |
| COLUMBIA | | | |
| ❑ CQ 32371 [Q] | Head Hunters | 1973 | 25.00 |
| ❑ PCQ 32965 [Q] | Thrust | 1974 | 25.00 |
| ❑ PCQ 34280 [Q] | Secrets | 1976 | 25.00 |
| MGM | | | |
| ❑ E-4447 [M] | Blow-Up | 1967 | 40.00 |
| ❑ SE-4447 [S] | Blow-Up | 1967 | 50.00 |
| *—Also includes one track by the Yardbirds* | | | |
| **HANDSOME BOY MODELING SCHOOL** | | | |
| ELEKTRA | | | |
| ❑ 62941 [(2)] | White People | 2004 | 15.00 |
| TOMMY BOY | | | |
| ❑ TB 1258 [(2)] | So...How's Your Girl? | 1999 | 25.00 |
| **HANDY, CAP'N JOHN** | | | |
| RCA VICTOR | | | |
| ❑ LPM-3762 [M] | Introducing Cap'n John Handy | 1967 | 25.00 |
| **HANDY, GEORGE** | | | |
| "X" | | | |
| ❑ LXA-1004 [M] | Handyland, U.S.A. | 1954 | 100.00 |
| "X" | | | |
| ❑ LXA-1032 [M] | By George! Handy, Of Course | 1954 | 80.00 |
| **HANDY, JOHN** | | | |
| ROULETTE | | | |
| ❑ RE-132 [(2)] | In the Vernacular | 197? | 20.00 |
| *—Compilation of earlier material* | | | |
| ❑ R 52042 [M] | In the Ver-nac'-u-lar | 1960 | 20.00 |
| ❑ SR 52042 [S] | In the Ver-nac'-u-lar | 1960 | 25.00 |
| ❑ R 52088 [M] | No Coast Jazz | 1962 | 30.00 |
| ❑ SR 52088 [S] | No Coast Jazz | 1962 | 40.00 |
| ❑ SR 52121 [S] | John Handy Jazz | 1964 | 40.00 |
| ❑ SR 52124 [S] | Quote, Unquote | 1964 | 40.00 |
| **HANDY, W.C.** | | | |
| HERITAGE | | | |
| ❑ 0052 [10] | Blues Revisited | 195? | 120.00 |
| **HANGMEN, THE** | | | |
| MONUMENT | | | |
| ❑ MLP-8077 [M] | Bitter Sweet | 1967 | 30.00 |
| ❑ SLP-18077 [S] | Bitter Sweet | 1967 | 40.00 |
| **HANKINS, ESCO** | | | |
| AUDIO LAB | | | |
| ❑ AL-1547 [M] | Country Style | 1961 | 200.00 |
| **HANNA, KEN** | | | |
| CAPITOL | | | |
| ❑ T 6512 [M] | Jazz for Dancers | 1955 | 40.00 |
| **HANNA, ROLAND** | | | |
| ATCO | | | |
| ❑ 33-108 [M] | Destry Rides Again | 1959 | 40.00 |
| ❑ SD 33-108 [S] | Destry Rides Again | 1959 | 40.00 |
| ❑ 33-121 [M] | Easy to Love | 1960 | 30.00 |
| ❑ SD 33-121 [S] | Easy to Love | 1960 | 40.00 |
| BASF | | | |
| ❑ 20875 | Child of Gemini | 1972 | 25.00 |
| **HANRAHAN, KIP** | | | |
| PANGAEA | | | |
| ❑ 42137 | Days & Nights of Blue Luck Inverted | 1988 | 20.00 |
| **HAPPENINGS, THE** | | | |
| B.T. PUPPY | | | |
| ❑ BTP-1001 [M] | The Happenings (Bye-Bye, So Long, Farewell...See You in September) | 1966 | 25.00 |
| ❑ BTS-1001 [S] | The Happenings (Bye-Bye, So Long, Farewell...See You in September) | 1966 | 30.00 |
| ❑ BTP-1003 [M] | Psycle | 1967 | 25.00 |
| ❑ BTPS-1003 [S] | Psycle | 1967 | 30.00 |
| ❑ BTS-1004 | The Happenings Golden Hits! | 1968 | 40.00 |
| JUBILEE | | | |
| ❑ JGS-8028 | Piece of Mind | 1969 | 25.00 |
| ❑ JGS-8030 | The Happenings' Greatest Hits | 1969 | 25.00 |
| **HAPPY CHIPMUNKS, THE** | | | |
| HOLIDAY | | | |
| ❑ HDY-1950 | Merry Christmas from the Happy Chipmunks | 1982 | 25.00 |
| *—Record quickly pulled from market because of unauthorized use of the name "Chipmunks"* | | | |
| **HAPPY DRAGON BAND, THE** | | | |
| FIDDLER'S MUSIC | | | |
| ❑ 1157 | The Happy Dragon Band | 1977 | 80.00 |
| **HAPSHASH AND THE COLOURED COAT** | | | |
| IMPERIAL | | | |
| ❑ LP-9377 [M] | Hapshash and the Coloured Coat | 1968 | 50.00 |
| ❑ LP-12377 [S] | Hapshash and the Coloured Coat | 1968 | 40.00 |
| ❑ LP-12430 | Western Flyer | 1969 | 40.00 |
| **HARD TIMES, THE** | | | |
| WORLD PACIFIC | | | |
| ❑ WP-1867 [M] | Blew Mind | 1968 | 25.00 |
| ❑ WPS-21867 [S] | Blew Mind | 1968 | 30.00 |
| **HARDAWAY, BOB** | | | |
| BETHLEHEM | | | |
| ❑ BCP-1028 [10] | Bob Hardaway | 1955 | 120.00 |
| **HARDEN, ARLENE** | | | |
| COLUMBIA | | | |
| ❑ CL 2833 [M] | Sing Me Back Home | 1967 | 30.00 |
| ❑ CS 9633 [S] | Sing Me Back Home | 1967 | 20.00 |
| ❑ CS 9674 | What Can I Say | 1968 | 20.00 |
| **HARDEN, WILBUR** | | | |
| SAVOY | | | |
| ❑ MG-12127 [M] | Mainstream 1958/The East Coast Jazz Scene Featuring John Coltrane | 1958 | 60.00 |
| ❑ MG-12131 [M] | Jazz Way Out | 1958 | 50.00 |
| ❑ MG-12134 [M] | The King and I | 1958 | 50.00 |
| ❑ MG-12136 [M] | Tanganyika Suite | 1958 | 50.00 |
| ❑ SST-13002 [S] | The King and I | 1959 | 40.00 |
| ❑ SST-13004 [S] | Jazz Way Out | 1959 | 40.00 |
| ❑ SST-13005 [S] | Tanganyika Suite | 1959 | 40.00 |
| **HARDEN TRIO, THE** | | | |
| COLUMBIA | | | |
| ❑ CL 2506 [M] | Tippy Toeing | 1966 | 20.00 |
| ❑ CS 9306 [S] | Tippy Toeing | 1966 | 25.00 |
| **HARDIN, TIM** | | | |
| ANTILLES | | | |
| ❑ 7023 | Nine | 1974 | 15.00 |
| ATCO | | | |
| ❑ 33-210 [M] | This Is Tim Hardin | 1967 | 25.00 |
| ❑ SD 33-210 [R] | This Is Tim Hardin | 1967 | 15.00 |
| COLUMBIA | | | |
| ❑ CS 9787 | Suite for Susan Moore and Damion — We Are — One, One, All in One | 1969 | 25.00 |
| *—"360 Sound" label* | | | |
| ❑ C 30551 | Bird on a Wire | 1971 | 20.00 |
| ❑ KC 31764 | Painted Head | 1972 | 20.00 |
| ❑ PC 37164 | The Shock of Grace | 1981 | 12.00 |
| MGM | | | |
| ❑ GAS-104 | Tim Hardin (Golden Archive Series) | 1970 | 20.00 |
| ❑ M3G-4952 | Archetypes | 1974 | 15.00 |
| POLYDOR | | | |
| ❑ PD-1-6333 | Memorial Album | 1981 | 12.00 |
| VERVE FOLKWAYS | | | |
| ❑ FT-3004 [M] | Tim Hardin/1 | 1966 | 25.00 |
| ❑ FTS-3004 [S] | Tim Hardin/1 | 1966 | 30.00 |
| VERVE FORECAST | | | |
| ❑ FT-3004 [M] | Tim Hardin/1 | 1967 | 15.00 |
| ❑ FTS-3004 [S] | Tim Hardin/1 | 1967 | 20.00 |
| ❑ FTS-3022 | Tim Hardin/2 | 1967 | 25.00 |
| ❑ FTS-3049 | Tim Hardin/3 — Live in Concert | 1968 | 25.00 |
| ❑ FTS-3064 | Tim Hardin/4 | 1969 | 25.00 |
| ❑ FTS-3078 | The Best of Tim Hardin | 1970 | 20.00 |
| **HARDMAN, BILL** | | | |
| SAVOY | | | |
| ❑ MG-12170 [M] | Bill Hardman Quintet | 1961 | 60.00 |
| **HARDWATER** | | | |
| CAPITOL | | | |
| ❑ ST-2954 | Hardwater | 1968 | 40.00 |
| **HARDY, FRANCOISE** | | | |
| 4 CORNERS OF THE WORLD | | | |
| ❑ FCL-4208 [M] | The "Yeh Yeh" Girl from Paris! | 196? | 20.00 |
| ❑ FCS-4208 [S] | The "Yeh Yeh" Girl from Paris! | 196? | 25.00 |
| ❑ FCL-4219 [M] | Maid in Paris | 196? | 20.00 |
| ❑ FCS-4219 [S] | Maid in Paris | 196? | 25.00 |
| ❑ FCL-4231 [M] | Francoise... | 196? | 20.00 |
| ❑ FCS-4231 [S] | Francoise... | 196? | 25.00 |
| ❑ FCL-4238 [M] | Je Vous Aime | 196? | 20.00 |
| ❑ FCS-4238 [S] | Je Vous Aime | 196? | 25.00 |
| ❑ FCS-4255 [S] | The Best of Francoise Hardy | 196? | 20.00 |
| REPRISE | | | |
| ❑ RS 6290 | Francoise Hardy | 1968 | 25.00 |
| ❑ RS 6318 | Loving | 1969 | 20.00 |
| ❑ RS 6345 | Mon Amour, Adieu | 1969 | 20.00 |
| **HARDY BOYS, THE** | | | |
| RCA VICTOR | | | |
| ❑ LSP-4217 | Here Come the Hardy Boys | 1969 | 20.00 |
| ❑ LSP-4315 | Wheels | 1970 | 20.00 |
| **HARIAN, KENT** | | | |
| CARAVAN | | | |
| ❑ LP-15611 [M] | Echoes of Joy | 1956 | 250.00 |
| **HARLEY, RUFUS** | | | |
| ATLANTIC | | | |
| ❑ 3001 [M] | Bagpipe Blues | 1967 | 25.00 |
| **HARMONAIRES MALE QUINTET, THE** | | | |
| VARSITY | | | |
| ❑ 6915 [10] | Spirituals | 195? | 80.00 |
| **HARMONY BLAZERS, THE** | | | |
| HARMONY | | | |
| ❑ HL 7103 [M] | Ten Big Hits | 1959 | 40.00 |
| ❑ HL 7126 [M] | Rock & Roll Vol. II | 1959 | 40.00 |
| ❑ HL 7200 [M] | The Big Ten | 1959 | 40.00 |
| **HARNELL, JOE** | | | |
| CAPITOL | | | |
| ❑ ST-11657 | Harnell | 1977 | 12.00 |
| COLUMBIA | | | |
| ❑ CL 2466 [M] | Golden Piano Hits | 1966 | 12.00 |
| ❑ CL 2699 [M] | Bossa Now | 1967 | 15.00 |
| ❑ CS 9266 [S] | Golden Piano Hits | 1966 | 15.00 |
| ❑ CS 9499 [S] | Bossa Now | 1967 | 12.00 |
| EPIC | | | |
| ❑ LN (# unknown) [M] | I Want to Be Happy | 1960 | 15.00 |
| ❑ BN 573 [S] | I Want to Be Happy | 1960 | 20.00 |
| JUBILEE | | | |
| ❑ JLP-1015 [M] | Piano Inventions of Jo Harnell | 1956 | 50.00 |
| ❑ JGM-5020 [M] | Joe Harnell and His Trio | 1963 | 15.00 |
| *—Reissue of 1015* | | | |

**KAPP**

| Number | Title (A Side/B Side) | Yr | NM |
|---|---|---|---|
| ❑ KL 1318 [M] | Fly Me to the Moon and the Bossa Nova Pops | 1962 | 15.00 |
| ❑ KL 1325 [M] | More Joe Harnell, More Bossa Nova Pops | 1963 | 15.00 |
| ❑ KL 1339 [M] | Joe Harnell | 1963 | 15.00 |
| ❑ KL 1416 [M] | The Rhythm and the Fire | 1965 | 12.00 |
| ❑ KL 1480 [M] | The Best of Joe Harnell | 1966 | 12.00 |
| ❑ KS 3318 [S] | Fly Me to the Moon and the Bossa Nova Pops | 1962 | 20.00 |
| ❑ KS 3325 [S] | More Joe Harnell, More Bossa Nova Pops | 1963 | 20.00 |
| ❑ KS 3339 [S] | Joe Harnell | 1963 | 20.00 |
| ❑ KS 3416 [S] | The Rhythm and the Fire | 1965 | 15.00 |
| ❑ KS 3480 [S] | The Best of Joe Harnell | 1966 | 15.00 |

**MOTOWN**

| Number | Title (A Side/B Side) | Yr | NM |
|---|---|---|---|
| ❑ MS-698 | Moving On!! | 1969 | 40.00 |

### HARPER, BEN

**CARDAS**

| Number | Title (A Side/B Side) | Yr | NM |
|---|---|---|---|
| ❑ CR 5818 | Pleasure and Pain | 1992 | 500.00 |
| *—With Tom Freund* | | | |

**VIRGIN**

| Number | Title (A Side/B Side) | Yr | NM |
|---|---|---|---|
| ❑ 10079 [(4)] | Live from Mars | 2001 | 100.00 |
| *—As "Ben Harper and the Innocent Criminals"* | | | |
| ❑ 48151 [(2)] | Burn to Shine | 1999 | 50.00 |
| *—As "Ben Harper and the Innocent Criminals"* | | | |
| ❑ 71206 | There Will Be a Light | 2005 | 20.00 |
| *—With the Blind Boys of Alabama* | | | |
| ❑ 83003 [(2)] | Diamonds on the Inside | 2003 | 20.00 |

### HARPER, BILLY

**STRATA-EAST**

| Number | Title (A Side/B Side) | Yr | NM |
|---|---|---|---|
| ❑ SES-19739 | Capra Black | 1973 | 40.00 |

### HARPER, HERBIE

**BETHLEHEM**

| Number | Title (A Side/B Side) | Yr | NM |
|---|---|---|---|
| ❑ BCP-1025 [10] | Herbie Harper | 1955 | 120.00 |

**LIBERTY**

| Number | Title (A Side/B Side) | Yr | NM |
|---|---|---|---|
| ❑ LRP-6003 [M] | Herbie Harper | 1956 | 80.00 |

**MODE**

| Number | Title (A Side/B Side) | Yr | NM |
|---|---|---|---|
| ❑ LP-100 [M] | Herbie Harper Sextet | 1957 | 100.00 |

**NOCTURNE**

| Number | Title (A Side/B Side) | Yr | NM |
|---|---|---|---|
| ❑ NLP-1 [10] | Herbie Harper Quintet | 1954 | 150.00 |
| ❑ NLP-7 [10] | Herbie Harper | 1954 | 150.00 |

**TAMPA**

| Number | Title (A Side/B Side) | Yr | NM |
|---|---|---|---|
| ❑ TP-11 [M] | Herbie Harper Quintet | 1957 | 100.00 |
| *—Red vinyl* | | | |
| ❑ TP-11 [M] | Herbie Harper Quintet | 1958 | 50.00 |
| *—Black vinyl* | | | |

### HARPER, JANICE

**CAPITOL**

| Number | Title (A Side/B Side) | Yr | NM |
|---|---|---|---|
| ❑ ST 1337 [S] | Embers of Love | 1960 | 25.00 |
| ❑ T 1337 [M] | Embers of Love | 1960 | 20.00 |

### HARPER, ROY

**CHRYSALIS**

| Number | Title (A Side/B Side) | Yr | NM |
|---|---|---|---|
| ❑ PRO-620 [DJ] | Introduction to Roy Harper | 1976 | 30.00 |
| ❑ CHR 1105 | When An Old Cricketer Leaves the Crease | 1976 | 15.00 |
| ❑ CHR 1139 | One of Those Days in England | 1977 | 15.00 |
| ❑ CHR 1160 | Flat Baroque and Berserk | 1978 | 12.00 |
| *—Reissue of Harvest LP* | | | |
| ❑ CHR 1161 | Stormcock | 1978 | 12.00 |
| *—Released in the UK in 1971* | | | |
| ❑ CHR 1162 | Lifemask | 1978 | 12.00 |
| *—Released in the UK in 1973* | | | |
| ❑ CHR 1163 | Valentine | 1978 | 12.00 |
| *—Released in the UK in 1974* | | | |
| ❑ CH2 1164 [(2)] | Flashes from the Archives of Oblivion | 1978 | 15.00 |
| *—Released in the UK in 1974* | | | |

**HARVEST**

| Number | Title (A Side/B Side) | Yr | NM |
|---|---|---|---|
| ❑ SKAO-418 | Flat Baroque and Berserk | 1970 | 20.00 |

**PVC**

| Number | Title (A Side/B Side) | Yr | NM |
|---|---|---|---|
| ❑ 8937 | Whatever Happened to Jugula | 198? | 12.00 |

**WORLD PACIFIC**

| Number | Title (A Side/B Side) | Yr | NM |
|---|---|---|---|
| ❑ WPS-21888 | Folkjokeopus | 1969 | 25.00 |

### HARPER, TONI

**RCA VICTOR**

| Number | Title (A Side/B Side) | Yr | NM |
|---|---|---|---|
| ❑ LPM-2092 [M] | Lady Lonely | 1960 | 30.00 |
| ❑ LSP-2092 [S] | Lady Lonely | 1960 | 40.00 |
| ❑ LPM-2253 [M] | Night Mood | 1960 | 30.00 |
| ❑ LSP-2253 [S] | Night Mood | 1960 | 40.00 |

**VERVE**

| Number | Title (A Side/B Side) | Yr | NM |
|---|---|---|---|
| ❑ MGV-2001 [M] | Toni Harper Sings | 1956 | 150.00 |
| ❑ V-2001 [M] | Toni Harper Sings | 1961 | 50.00 |

### HARPER, WALT

**GATEWAY**

| Number | Title (A Side/B Side) | Yr | NM |
|---|---|---|---|
| ❑ 7016 [M] | On the Road | 1966 | 20.00 |

### HARPERS BIZARRE

**FOREST BAY**

| Number | Title (A Side/B Side) | Yr | NM |
|---|---|---|---|
| ❑ 7545 | As Time Goes By | 1976 | 15.00 |

**WARNER BROS.**

| Number | Title (A Side/B Side) | Yr | NM |
|---|---|---|---|
| ❑ W 1693 [M] | Feelin' Groovy | 1967 | 25.00 |
| ❑ WS 1693 [S] | Feelin' Groovy | 1967 | 20.00 |
| *—Gold label* | | | |
| ❑ WS 1693 [S] | Feelin' Groovy | 1968 | 15.00 |
| *—Green "W7" label* | | | |
| ❑ WS 1716 | Anything Goes | 1967 | 20.00 |
| ❑ WS 1739 | The Secret Life of Harpers Bizarre | 1968 | 20.00 |
| ❑ WS 1784 | Harpers Bizarre Four | 1969 | 20.00 |
| ❑ ST-91351 | Anything Goes | 1968 | 25.00 |
| *—Capitol Record Club edition* | | | |

### HARPO, SLIM

**EXCELLO**

| Number | Title (A Side/B Side) | Yr | NM |
|---|---|---|---|
| ❑ LP-8003 [M] | Raining in My Heart | 1961 | 250.00 |
| *—Orange and blue label* | | | |
| ❑ LPS-8003 [M] | Raining in My Heart | 196? | 100.00 |
| *—All-blue label* | | | |
| ❑ LP-8005 [M] | Baby Scratch My Back | 1966 | 200.00 |
| *—Orange and blue label* | | | |
| ❑ LPS-8005 [M] | Baby Scratch My Back | 196? | 100.00 |
| *—All-blue label* | | | |
| ❑ LPS-8008 [M] | Tip On In | 1968 | 50.00 |
| ❑ LPS-8010 [M] | The Best of Slim Harpo | 1969 | 50.00 |
| ❑ LPS-8013 [M] | Slim Harpo Knew the Blues | 1970 | 50.00 |

**RHINO**

| Number | Title (A Side/B Side) | Yr | NM |
|---|---|---|---|
| ❑ RNLP-106 | The Best of Slim Harpo | 198? | 15.00 |
| ❑ R1-70169 | Scratch My Back: The Best of Slim Harpo | 1989 | 12.00 |

### HARRIOTT, JOE

**CAPITOL**

| Number | Title (A Side/B Side) | Yr | NM |
|---|---|---|---|
| ❑ T 10351 [M] | Abstract | 1962 | 20.00 |

**JAZZLAND**

| Number | Title (A Side/B Side) | Yr | NM |
|---|---|---|---|
| ❑ JLP-37 [M] | Southern Horizons | 1961 | 25.00 |
| ❑ JLP-49 [M] | Free Form | 1961 | 25.00 |
| ❑ JLP-937 [S] | Southern Horizons | 1961 | 30.00 |
| ❑ JLP-949 [S] | Free Form | 1961 | 30.00 |

### HARRIS, ART

**KAPP**

| Number | Title (A Side/B Side) | Yr | NM |
|---|---|---|---|
| ❑ KL-1015 [M] | Jazz Goes to Post-Graduate School | 1956 | 40.00 |

### HARRIS, ART, AND MITCH LEIGH

**EPIC**

| Number | Title (A Side/B Side) | Yr | NM |
|---|---|---|---|
| ❑ LG 1010 [10] | Modern Woodwind Expressions | 1954 | 50.00 |
| ❑ LN 3200 [M] | New Jazz in Hi-Fi | 1956 | 40.00 |

**KAPP**

| Number | Title (A Side/B Side) | Yr | NM |
|---|---|---|---|
| ❑ KL-1011 [M] | Baroque Band and Brass Choir — Jazz 1775 | 1956 | 40.00 |

### HARRIS, BARRY

**ARGO**

| Number | Title (A Side/B Side) | Yr | NM |
|---|---|---|---|
| ❑ LP-644 [M] | Breakin' It Up | 1959 | 40.00 |
| ❑ LPS-644 [S] | Breakin' It Up | 1959 | 30.00 |

**CADET**

| Number | Title (A Side/B Side) | Yr | NM |
|---|---|---|---|
| ❑ LP-644 [M] | Breakin' It Up | 1966 | 20.00 |

**PRESTIGE**

| Number | Title (A Side/B Side) | Yr | NM |
|---|---|---|---|
| ❑ PRLP-7498 [M] | Luminescence | 1967 | 30.00 |
| ❑ PRST-7498 [S] | Luminescence | 1967 | 20.00 |
| ❑ PRST-7600 | Bull's Eye | 1969 | 20.00 |
| ❑ PRST-7733 | Magnificent! | 1970 | 20.00 |

**RIVERSIDE**

| Number | Title (A Side/B Side) | Yr | NM |
|---|---|---|---|
| ❑ RLP 12-326 [M] | Barry Harris at the Jazz Workshop | 1960 | 30.00 |
| ❑ RLP-354 [M] | Preminado | 1961 | 30.00 |
| ❑ RLP-392 [M] | Listen to Barry Harris | 1961 | 30.00 |
| ❑ RLP-413 [M] | Newer Than New | 1962 | 25.00 |
| ❑ RLP-435 [M] | Chasin' the Bird | 1962 | 25.00 |
| ❑ RLP-1177 [S] | Barry Harris at the Jazz Workshop | 1960 | 40.00 |
| ❑ RS-9354 [S] | Preminado | 1961 | 40.00 |
| ❑ RS-9392 [S] | Listen to Barry Harris | 1961 | 40.00 |
| ❑ RS-9413 [S] | Newer Than New | 1962 | 30.00 |
| ❑ RS-9435 [S] | Chasin' the Bird | 1962 | 30.00 |

### HARRIS, BILL (1)

**CLEF**

| Number | Title (A Side/B Side) | Yr | NM |
|---|---|---|---|
| ❑ MGC-125 [10] | Bill Harris Collates | 1953 | 150.00 |

**FANTASY**

| Number | Title (A Side/B Side) | Yr | NM |
|---|---|---|---|
| ❑ 3263 [M] | Bill Harris and Friends | 1958 | 40.00 |
| *—Red vinyl* | | | |
| ❑ 3263 [M] | Bill Harris and Friends | 1959 | 25.00 |
| *—Black vinyl* | | | |

**NORGRAN**

| Number | Title (A Side/B Side) | Yr | NM |
|---|---|---|---|
| ❑ MGN-1062 [M] | The Bill Harris Herd | 1956 | 120.00 |

### HARRIS, BILL (2)

**EMARCY**

| Number | Title (A Side/B Side) | Yr | NM |
|---|---|---|---|
| ❑ MG-36097 [M] | Bill Harris | 1956 | 40.00 |
| ❑ MG-36113 [M] | The Harris Touch | 1957 | 40.00 |

**MERCURY**

| Number | Title (A Side/B Side) | Yr | NM |
|---|---|---|---|
| ❑ MG-20552 [M] | The Harris Touch | 1960 | 30.00 |
| ❑ SR-60552 [S] | The Harris Touch | 1960 | 25.00 |

**WING**

| Number | Title (A Side/B Side) | Yr | NM |
|---|---|---|---|
| ❑ MGW-12220 [M] | Great Guitar Sounds | 1963 | 20.00 |

### HARRIS, EDDIE

**ATLANTIC**

| Number | Title (A Side/B Side) | Yr | NM |
|---|---|---|---|
| ❑ 1545 [M] | The Best of Eddie Harris | 1970 | 25.00 |
| *—Promo-only white label mono pressing* | | | |

**COLUMBIA**

| Number | Title (A Side/B Side) | Yr | NM |
|---|---|---|---|
| ❑ CS 8968 [S] | Cool Sax, Warm Heart | 1964 | 20.00 |
| ❑ CS 9095 [S] | Cool Sax from Hollywood to Broadway | 1965 | 20.00 |
| ❑ CS 9681 [M] | Here Comes the Judge | 1968 | 25.00 |
| *—Mono copies are promo only* | | | |

**VEE JAY**

| Number | Title (A Side/B Side) | Yr | NM |
|---|---|---|---|
| ❑ VJLPS 1081 [S] | The Theme from Exodus and Other Film Spectaculars | 1964 | 20.00 |
| ❑ LP 3016 [M] | Exodus to Jazz | 1961 | 30.00 |
| ❑ SR 3016 [S] | Exodus to Jazz | 1961 | 40.00 |
| ❑ LP 3025 [M] | Mighty Like a Rose | 1961 | 30.00 |
| ❑ SR 3025 [S] | Mighty Like a Rose | 1961 | 40.00 |
| ❑ LP 3027 [M] | Jazz for "Breakfast at Tiffany's" | 1961 | 30.00 |
| ❑ SR 3027 [S] | Jazz for "Breakfast at Tiffany's" | 1961 | 40.00 |
| ❑ LP 3028 [M] | A Study in Jazz | 1962 | 20.00 |
| ❑ SR 3028 [S] | A Study in Jazz | 1962 | 30.00 |
| ❑ LP 3031 [M] | Eddie Harris Goes to the Movies | 1962 | 20.00 |
| ❑ SR 3031 [S] | Eddie Harris Goes to the Movies | 1962 | 30.00 |
| ❑ LP 3034 [M] | Bossa Nova | 1963 | 20.00 |
| ❑ SR 3034 [S] | Bossa Nova | 1963 | 30.00 |
| ❑ LP 3037 [M] | Half and Half | 1963 | 25.00 |
| ❑ SR 3037 [S] | Half and Half | 1963 | 30.00 |

### HARRIS, EMMYLOU

**JUBILEE**

| Number | Title (A Side/B Side) | Yr | NM |
|---|---|---|---|
| ❑ JGS-8031 | Gliding Bird | 1969 | 120.00 |
| *—Originals have color covers; counterfeit covers are black and white* | | | |

**MOBILE FIDELITY**

| Number | Title (A Side/B Side) | Yr | NM |
|---|---|---|---|
| ❑ 1-015 | Quarter Moon in a Ten Cent Town | 1979 | 40.00 |
| *—Audiophile vinyl* | | | |

**REPRISE**

| Number | Title (A Side/B Side) | Yr | NM |
|---|---|---|---|
| ❑ MS 2213 | Pieces of the Sky | 1975 | 10.00 |
| ❑ MS 2236 | Elite Hotel | 1976 | 10.00 |
| ❑ MSK 2284 | Pieces of the Sky | 1977 | 8.00 |
| *—Reissue of 2213* | | | |
| ❑ MSK 2286 | Elite Hotel | 1977 | 8.00 |
| *—Reissue of 2236* | | | |
| ❑ 25776 | Bluebird | 1989 | 12.00 |

**WARNER BROS.**

| Number | Title (A Side/B Side) | Yr | NM |
|---|---|---|---|
| ❑ BS 2998 | Luxury Liner | 1977 | 12.00 |
| ❑ BSK 3115 | Luxury Liner | 1977 | 10.00 |
| *—Reissue of 2998* | | | |
| ❑ BSK 3141 | Quarter Moon in a Ten Cent Town | 1978 | 10.00 |
| ❑ BSK 3258 | Profile/Best of Emmylou Harris | 1978 | 10.00 |
| ❑ BSK 3318 | Blue Kentucky Girl | 1979 | 10.00 |
| ❑ BSK 3422 | Roses in the Snow | 1980 | 10.00 |
| ❑ BSK 3484 | Light of the Stable: The Christmas Album | 1980 | 10.00 |
| ❑ BSK 3508 | Evangeline | 1981 | 10.00 |
| ❑ BSK 3603 | Cimarron | 1981 | 10.00 |
| ❑ 23740 | Last Date | 1982 | 10.00 |
| ❑ 23961 | White Shoes | 1983 | 10.00 |
| ❑ 25161 | Profile II — The Best of Emmylou Harris | 1984 | 10.00 |
| ❑ 25205 | The Ballad of Sally Rose | 1985 | 10.00 |
| ❑ 25352 | Thirteen | 1986 | 10.00 |
| ❑ 25585 | Angel Band | 1987 | 10.00 |

### HARRIS, GENE

**BLUE NOTE**

| Number | Title (A Side/B Side) | Yr | NM |
|---|---|---|---|
| ❑ BN-LA141-G [(2)] | Yesterday, Today and Tomorrow | 1973 | 25.00 |
| ❑ BN-LA313-G | Astral Signal | 1974 | 20.00 |
| ❑ BST-84378 | The Three Sounds | 1971 | 20.00 |
| ❑ BST-84423 | Gene Harris of the Three Sounds | 1972 | 20.00 |

**JUBILEE**

| Number | Title (A Side/B Side) | Yr | NM |
|---|---|---|---|
| ❑ JLP-1005 [M] | Our Love Is Here to Stay | 1955 | 50.00 |
| ❑ JGM-1115 [M] | Genie in My Soul | 1959 | 40.00 |

### HARRIS, HAROLD

**VEE JAY**

| Number | Title (A Side/B Side) | Yr | NM |
|---|---|---|---|
| ❑ LP-3018 [M] | Here's Harold | 1962 | 25.00 |
| ❑ SR-3018 [S] | Here's Harold | 1962 | 30.00 |
| ❑ LP-3036 [M] | Harold Harris at the Playboy Club | 1963 | 25.00 |
| ❑ SR-3036 [S] | Harold Harris at the Playboy Club | 1963 | 30.00 |

### HARRIS, PEPPERMINT

**TIME**

| Number | Title (A Side/B Side) | Yr | NM |
|---|---|---|---|
| ❑ 5 [M] | Peppermint Harris | 1962 | 200.00 |

### HARRIS, PHIL

**MEGA**

| Number | Title (A Side/B Side) | Yr | NM |
|---|---|---|---|
| ❑ MLPS-608 | Southern Comfort ... The Best of Phil Harris | 1974 | 15.00 |

| Number | Title (A Side/B Side) | Yr | NM |
|---|---|---|---|
| **RCA CAMDEN** | | | |
| ❑ CAL-456 [M] | That's What I Like About the South | 1963 | 15.00 |
| ❑ CAS-456(e) [R] | That's What I Like About the South | 1963 | 10.00 |
| **RCA VICTOR** | | | |
| ❑ LPM-1985 [M] | The South Shall Rise Again | 1959 | 25.00 |
| ❑ LSP-1985 [S] | The South Shall Rise Again | 1959 | 30.00 |
| ❑ LPM-3037 [10] | Phil Harris On the Record | 1952 | 40.00 |
| **SUNBEAM** | | | |
| ❑ HB 302 | Broadcasts from the Cocoanut Grove, L.A., 1932 | 198? | 10.00 |

## HARRIS, RICHARD

| Number | Title (A Side/B Side) | Yr | NM |
|---|---|---|---|
| **ABC DUNHILL** | | | |
| ❑ DS-50032 | A Tramp Shining | 1968 | 15.00 |
| ❑ DS-50042 | The Yard Went On Forever | 1968 | 15.00 |
| ❑ DS-50074 | The Love Album | 1970 | 15.00 |
| ❑ DSX-50116 | My Boy | 1971 | 12.00 |
| ❑ DSX-50133 | Slides | 1972 | 12.00 |
| ❑ DSX-50139 | The Great Performances | 1973 | 12.00 |
| ❑ DSX-50159 | I, In the Membership | 1974 | 12.00 |
| ❑ DSX-50160 | Jonathan Livingston Seagull | 1973 | 12.00 |
| *—Spoken-word recording* | | | |
| **ATLANTIC** | | | |
| ❑ QD 18120 [Q] | The Prophet by Kahlil Gibran | 1974 | 20.00 |
| *—Spoken-word recording* | | | |
| ❑ SD 18120 | The Prophet by Kahlil Gibran | 1974 | 12.00 |
| *—Spoken-word recording* | | | |
| **MCA** | | | |
| ❑ 27016 | A Tramp Shining | 198? | 8.00 |
| *—Budget-line reissue* | | | |
| **PICKWICK** | | | |
| ❑ SPC-3626 | A Tramp Shining | 1978 | 10.00 |

## HARRIS, ROLF

| Number | Title (A Side/B Side) | Yr | NM |
|---|---|---|---|
| **EPIC** | | | |
| ❑ LN 24053 [M] | Tie Me Kangaroo Down, Sport & Sun Arise | 1963 | 20.00 |
| ❑ LN 24110 [M] | Join Rolf Harris Singing The Count of King Caractacus (And Other Fun Songs) | 1964 | 20.00 |
| ❑ BN 26053 [S] | Tie Me Kangaroo Down, Sport & Sun Arise | 1963 | 25.00 |
| ❑ BN 26110 [S] | Join Rolf Harris Singing The Count of King Caractacus (And Other Fun Songs) | 1964 | 25.00 |

## HARRIS, SHAUN

Also see THE WEST COAST POP ART EXPERIMENTAL BAND.

| Number | Title (A Side/B Side) | Yr | NM |
|---|---|---|---|
| **CAPITOL** | | | |
| ❑ ST-11168 | Shaun Harris | 1973 | 30.00 |

## HARRIS, WYNONIE

| Number | Title (A Side/B Side) | Yr | NM |
|---|---|---|---|
| **KING** | | | |
| ❑ KS-1086 | Good Rockin' Blues | 1970 | 25.00 |

## HARRISON, CASS

| Number | Title (A Side/B Side) | Yr | NM |
|---|---|---|---|
| **MGM** | | | |
| ❑ E-3388 [M] | The Duke and I | 1956 | 40.00 |
| ❑ E-3495 [M] | Wrappin' It Up | 1957 | 40.00 |

## HARRISON, GEORGE

Also see THE BEATLES; TRAVELING WILBURYS.

| Number | Title (A Side/B Side) | Yr | NM |
|---|---|---|---|
| **APPLE** | | | |
| ❑ STCH-639 [(3)] | All Things Must Pass | 1970 | 40.00 |
| *—Apple labels on first two records and "Apple Jam" labels on third; includes poster and lyric innersleeves* | | | |
| ❑ ST-3350 | Wonderwall Music Bonus Photo | 1968 | 5.00 |
| ❑ ST-3350 | Wonderwall Music | 1968 | 25.00 |
| *—With "Mfd. by Apple" on label* | | | |
| ❑ ST-3350 | Wonderwall Music | 1968 | 150.00 |
| *—With Capitol logo on Side 2 bottom* | | | |
| ❑ SMAS-3410 | Living in the Material World | 1973 | 15.00 |
| ❑ SMAS-3418 | Dark Horse | 1974 | 15.00 |
| ❑ SW-3420 | Extra Texture (Read All About It) | 1975 | 15.00 |
| **CAPITOL** | | | |
| ❑ STCH-639 [(3)] | All Things Must Pass | 1976 | 30.00 |
| *—Orange labels with poster and lyric innersleeves* | | | |
| ❑ STCH-639 [(3)] | All Things Must Pass | 1978 | 25.00 |
| *—Purple labels with poster and lyric innersleeves* | | | |
| ❑ STCH-639 [(3)] | All Things Must Pass | 1983 | 100.00 |
| *—Black labels, print in colorband, with poster and lyric innersleeves* | | | |
| ❑ ST-11578 | The Best of George Harrison | 1976 | 15.00 |
| *—Custom label, no bar code on back* | | | |
| ❑ ST-11578 | The Best of George Harrison | 1976 | 180.00 |
| *—Orange label* | | | |
| ❑ ST-11578 | The Best of George Harrison | 1978 | 10.00 |
| *—Purple label, large Capitol logo* | | | |
| ❑ ST-11578 | The Best of George Harrison | 1983 | 25.00 |
| *—Black label, print in colorband* | | | |
| ❑ ST-11578 | The Best of George Harrison | 1988 | 25.00 |
| *—Odd reissue with custom label; large stand-alone "S" in trail-off area; bar code on cover* | | | |
| ❑ ST-11578 | The Best of George Harrison | 1989 | 80.00 |
| *—Purple label, small Capitol logo* | | | |

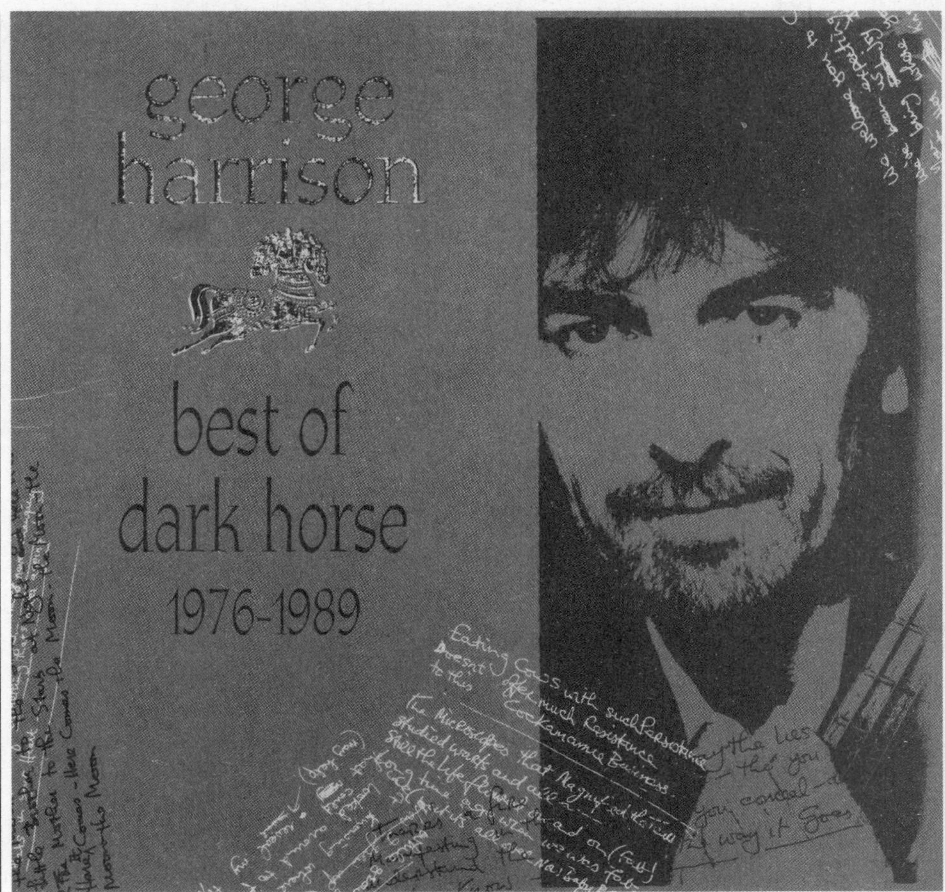


George Harrison, *Best of Dark Horse 1976-1989,* Dark Horse 25726, 1990, $25.

| Number | Title (A Side/B Side) | Yr | NM |
|---|---|---|---|
| ❑ SN-16055 | Dark Horse | 1980 | 15.00 |
| *—Budget-line reissue; reverses front and back covers* | | | |
| ❑ SN-16216 | Living in the Material World | 1980 | 20.00 |
| *—Budget-line reissue* | | | |
| ❑ SN-16217 | Extra Texture (Read All About It) | 1980 | 25.00 |
| *—Budget-line reissue* | | | |
| **CAPITOL/APPLE** | | | |
| ❑ STCH-639 [(3)] | All Things Must Pass | 1988 | 80.00 |
| *—Odd pressing with Apple labels and Capitol cover (look for stand-alone "S" in trail-off wax); with large sticker on back cover* | | | |
| **DARK HORSE** | | | |
| ❑ (no #) [DJ] | Dark Horse Radio Special | 1974 | 400.00 |
| *—Promo-only; George Harrison introduces his new record label and artists* | | | |
| ❑ PRO 649 [DJ] | A Personal Music Dialogue at Thirty Three and 1/3 | 1976 | 50.00 |
| ❑ DH 3005 | Thirty Three and 1/3 | 1976 | 10.00 |
| *—Deduct 30% for cut-outs* | | | |
| ❑ DHK 3255 | George Harrison | 1979 | 10.00 |
| *—Deduct 30% for cut-outs* | | | |
| ❑ DHK 3255 | George Harrison | 1979 | 40.00 |
| *—Columbia House edition (back cover says "Manufactured by Columbia House Under License"* | | | |
| ❑ DHK 3492 | Somewhere in England | 1981 | 10.00 |
| *—Deduct 30% for cut-outs* | | | |
| ❑ 23724 | Gone Troppo | 1982 | 10.00 |
| *—Deduct 30% for cut-outs* | | | |
| ❑ 23724 [DJ] | Gone Troppo | 1982 | 25.00 |
| *—Promo on Quiex II vinyl* | | | |
| ❑ 25643 | Cloud Nine | 1987 | 10.00 |
| ❑ W1-25643 | Cloud Nine | 1987 | 12.00 |
| *—Columbia House edition* | | | |
| ❑ 25726 | Best of Dark Horse 1976-1989 | 1989 | 25.00 |
| ❑ W1-25726 | Best of Dark Horse 1976-1989 | 1989 | 15.00 |
| *—Columbia House edition* | | | |
| ❑ R 174328 | Cloud Nine | 1987 | 15.00 |
| *—BMG Direct Marketing edition* | | | |
| ❑ R 180307 | Best of Dark Horse 1976-1989 | 1989 | 15.00 |
| *—BMG Direct Marketing edition* | | | |
| **ZAPPLE** | | | |
| ❑ ST-3358 | Electronic Sound | 1969 | 40.00 |

## HARRISON, GEORGE, AND FRIENDS

The "Friends" include BADFINGER; ERIC CLAPTON; BOB DYLAN; BILLY PRESTON; LEON RUSSELL; RAVI SHANKAR; RINGO STARR.

| Number | Title (A Side/B Side) | Yr | NM |
|---|---|---|---|
| **APPLE** | | | |
| ❑ STCX-3385 [(3)] | The Concert for Bangla Desh | 1971 | 40.00 |
| *—With 64-page booklet and custom innersleeves* | | | |
| ❑ STCX-3385 [(3)] | The Concert for Bangla Desh | 1975 | 50.00 |
| *—As above, but with "All Rights Reserved" on labels* | | | |
| **CAPITOL** | | | |
| ❑ SABB-12248 [(2)] | The Concert for Bangla Desh | 1982 | 300.00 |
| *—Scheduled reissue that was never officially released, though a few copies got out by mistake* | | | |

## HARRISON, NOEL

| Number | Title (A Side/B Side) | Yr | NM |
|---|---|---|---|
| **LONDON** | | | |
| ❑ PS 459 [S] | Noel Harrison | 1966 | 25.00 |
| ❑ LL 3459 [M] | Noel Harrison | 1966 | 20.00 |
| **REPRISE** | | | |
| ❑ R-6263 [M] | Collage | 1967 | 15.00 |
| ❑ RS-6263 [S] | Collage | 1967 | 20.00 |
| ❑ R-6295 [M] | Santa Monica Pier | 1968 | 40.00 |
| *—White label promo only* | | | |
| ❑ RS-6295 [S] | Santa Monica Pier | 1968 | 15.00 |
| ❑ RS-6321 | The Great Electric Experiment Is Over | 1969 | 15.00 |

## HARRISON, WENDELL

| Number | Title (A Side/B Side) | Yr | NM |
|---|---|---|---|
| **TRIBE** | | | |
| ❑ PRSD-2212 | Evening with the Devil | 197? | 100.00 |
| ❑ PRSD-4002 | Message from the Tribe, Vol. 3 | 197? | 100.00 |
| **WENHA** | | | |
| ❑ 015 | Dreams of a Love Supreme | 198? | 50.00 |
| ❑ 016 | Organic Dream | 198? | 40.00 |
| ❑ 2212 | Evening with the Devil | 198? | 20.00 |
| *—Reissue of Tribe 2212* | | | |
| ❑ 4002 | Message from the Tribe | 198? | 20.00 |
| *—Reissue of Tribe 4002* | | | |

## HARRISON, WES

| Number | Title (A Side/B Side) | Yr | NM |
|---|---|---|---|
| **PHILIPS** | | | |
| ❑ PHM 200103 [M] | You Won't Believe Your Ears | 1963 | 20.00 |
| ❑ PHS 600103 [S] | You Won't Believe Your Ears | 1963 | 25.00 |

## HARRISON, WILBERT

| Number | Title (A Side/B Side) | Yr | NM |
|---|---|---|---|
| **BUDDAH** | | | |
| ❑ BDS-5002 | Wilbert Harrison | 1971 | 30.00 |
| **CHELSEA** | | | |
| ❑ CH 523 | Wilbert Harrison | 1977 | 20.00 |
| **JUGGERNAUT** | | | |
| ❑ ST-8803 | Shoot You Full of Love | 1971 | 50.00 |

| Number | Title (A Side/B Side) | Yr | NM |
|---|---|---|---|
| SAVOY JAZZ | | | |
| SJL-1182 | Listen to My Song | 1987 | 12.00 |
| SPHERE SOUND | | | |
| SSR-7000 [M] | Kansas City | 1965 | 250.00 |
| SSSR-7000 [R] | Kansas City | 1965 | 200.00 |
| SUE | | | |
| SSLP-8801 | Let's Work Together | 1970 | 50.00 |
| WET SOUL | | | |
| 1001 | Anything You Want | 197? | 50.00 |
| **HARROW, NANCY** | | | |
| ATLANTIC | | | |
| 8075 [M] | You Never Know | 1963 | 25.00 |
| SD 8075 [S] | You Never Know | 1963 | 30.00 |
| CANDID | | | |
| CD-8008 [M] | Wild Women Don't Have the Blues | 1962 | 30.00 |
| CD-9008 [S] | Wild Women Don't Have the Blues | 1962 | 40.00 |
| **HART, FREDDIE** | | | |
| CAPITOL | | | |
| ST-469 | New Sounds | 1970 | 12.00 |
| ST-593 | California Grapevine | 1970 | 12.00 |
| ST-838 | Easy Loving | 1971 | 12.00 |
| ST-11014 | My Hang-Up Is You | 1972 | 12.00 |
| ST-11073 | Bless Your Heart | 1972 | 12.00 |
| ST-11107 | Got the All-Overs | 1972 | 12.00 |
| ST-11156 | Super Kind of Woman | 1973 | 12.00 |
| ST-11197 | Trip to Heaven | 1973 | 12.00 |
| ST-11252 | If You Can't Feel It | 1974 | 12.00 |
| ST-11296 | Hang In There Girl | 1974 | 12.00 |
| ST-11353 | Country Heart 'N' Soul | 1975 | 12.00 |
| ST-11374 | Greatest Hits | 1975 | 12.00 |
| ST-11449 | The First Time | 1975 | 10.00 |
| ST-11504 | People Put to Music | 1976 | 10.00 |
| ST-11568 | That Look in Her Eyes | 1976 | 10.00 |
| ST-11626 | The Pleasure's Been All Mine | 1977 | 10.00 |
| ST-11724 | Only You | 1978 | 10.00 |
| COLUMBIA | | | |
| CL 1792 [M] | The Spirited Freddie Hart | 1962 | 40.00 |
| G 31550 [(2)] | The World of Freddie Hart | 1972 | 15.00 |
| HARMONY | | | |
| HL 7412 [M] | The Best of Freddie Hart | 1967 | 12.00 |
| HS 11212 [S] | The Best of Freddie Hart | 1967 | 12.00 |
| KH 31165 | Lonesome Love | 1972 | 10.00 |
| KH 32467 | You Are My World | 1973 | 10.00 |
| HILLTOP | | | |
| 6117 | From Canada to Tennessee | 1972 | 10.00 |
| KAPP | | | |
| KL-1456 [M] | The Hart of Country Music | 1966 | 15.00 |
| KL-1492 [M] | Straight from the Heart | 1966 | 15.00 |
| KL-1513 [M] | Hurtin' Man | 1967 | 20.00 |
| KL-1539 [M] | The Neon and the Rain | 1967 | 20.00 |
| KS-3456 [S] | The Hart of Country Music | 1966 | 20.00 |
| KS-3492 [S] | Straight from the Heart | 1966 | 20.00 |
| KS-3513 [S] | Hurtin' Man | 1967 | 20.00 |
| KS-3539 [S] | The Neon and the Rain | 1967 | 20.00 |
| KS-3546 | Togetherness | 1968 | 20.00 |
| KS-3568 | Born a Fool | 1968 | 20.00 |
| KS-3592 | Greatest Hits | 1969 | 15.00 |
| MCA | | | |
| 4088 [(2)] | The Best of Freddie Hart | 1975 | 15.00 |
| SUNBIRD | | | |
| ST-50100 | Sure Thing | 1980 | 12.00 |
| **HART, MICKEY** Also see THE GRATEFUL DEAD. | | | |
| RELIX | | | |
| 2026 | Rolling Thunder | 1987 | 12.00 |
| WARNER BROS. | | | |
| BS 2635 | Rolling Thunder | 1972 | 30.00 |
| **HARTFORD, JOHN** | | | |
| FLYING FISH | | | |
| FF-020 | Mark Twang | 1976 | 10.00 |
| FF-028 | Nobody Knows What You Do | 1977 | 10.00 |
| FF-044 | All in the Name of Love | 1983 | 10.00 |
| FF-063 | Headin' Down Into the Mystery Below | 1978 | 10.00 |
| FF-095 | Slumberin' on the Cumberland | 1979 | 10.00 |
| *—With Pat Burton and Benny Martin* | | | |
| FF-228 | You and Me at Home | 1980 | 10.00 |
| FF-259 | Catalogue | 1982 | 10.00 |
| FF-289 | Gum Tree Canoe | 1984 | 10.00 |
| FF-440 | Me Oh My, How Time Flies | 1987 | 10.00 |
| MCA | | | |
| 5861 | Annual Waltz | 1987 | 8.00 |
| RCA VICTOR | | | |
| LPM-3687 [M] | John Hartford Looks at Life | 1966 | 20.00 |
| LSP-3687 [S] | John Hartford Looks at Life | 1966 | 15.00 |
| LPM-3796 [M] | Earthwords and Music | 1967 | 25.00 |
| LSP-3796 [S] | Earthwords and Music | 1967 | 15.00 |
| LPM-3884 [M] | The Love Album | 1967 | 25.00 |
| LSP-3884 [S] | The Love Album | 1967 | 15.00 |
| LPM-3998 [M] | Housing Project | 1968 | 50.00 |
| LSP-3998 [S] | Housing Project | 1968 | 15.00 |
| LSP-4068 | Gentle on My Mind and Other Originals | 1968 | 15.00 |
| LSP-4156 | John Hartford | 1969 | 15.00 |
| LSP-4337 | Iron Mountain Depot | 1970 | 15.00 |
| WARNER BROS. | | | |
| WS 1916 | Aereo-Plain | 1971 | 12.00 |
| BS 2651 | Morning Bugle | 1972 | 12.00 |
| **HARTMAN, JOHNNY** | | | |
| ABC-PARAMOUNT | | | |
| ABC-574 [M] | The Unforgettable Johnny Hartman | 1966 | 30.00 |
| ABCS-574 [S] | The Unforgettable Johnny Hartman | 1966 | 40.00 |
| BETHLEHEM | | | |
| BCP-43 [M] | Songs from the Heart | 1956 | 80.00 |
| BCP-6014 [M] | All of Me: The Debonair Mr. Hartman | 1957 | 80.00 |
| IMPULSE! | | | |
| A-57 [M] | I Just Dropped By to Say Hello | 1964 | 30.00 |
| AS-57 [S] | I Just Dropped By to Say Hello | 1964 | 40.00 |
| A-74 [M] | The Voice That Is | 1965 | 30.00 |
| AS-74 [S] | The Voice That Is | 1965 | 40.00 |
| REGENT | | | |
| MG-6014 [M] | Just You, Just Me | 1956 | 80.00 |
| **HARTMAN, LISA** | | | |
| KIRSHNER | | | |
| PZ 34109 | Lisa Hartman | 1976 | 40.00 |
| JZ 35609 | Hold On | 1978 | 20.00 |
| **HARUMI** | | | |
| VERVE FORECAST | | | |
| FTS-3030 | Harumi | 1968 | 25.00 |
| **HARVEY, LAURENCE** | | | |
| ATLANTIC | | | |
| 1367 [M] | This Is My Beloved | 1962 | 40.00 |
| SD 1367 [S] | This Is My Beloved | 1962 | 50.00 |
| **HASKELL, JACK** | | | |
| STRAND | | | |
| SL-1020 [M] | Jack Haskell Swings for Jack Paar | 1961 | 20.00 |
| SLS-1020 [S] | Jack Haskell Swings for Jack Paar | 1961 | 30.00 |
| **HASKELL, JIMMIE** | | | |
| IMPERIAL | | | |
| LP-9068 [M] | Countdown | 1959 | 30.00 |
| LP-12015 [S] | Countdown | 1959 | 50.00 |
| **HASKILL, CLARA** | | | |
| MERCURY LIVING PRESENCE | | | |
| SR 90413 [S] | Mozart: Piano Concertos No. 20 and 23; Rondo in A | 196? | 30.00 |
| *—Maroon label, no "Vendor: Mercury Record Corporation"* | | | |
| SR 90413 [S] | Mozart: Piano Concertos No. 20 and 23; Rondo in A | 196? | 80.00 |
| *—Maroon label, with "Vendor: Mercury Record Corporation" (second edition is more sought after than the first)* | | | |
| **HASSLES, THE** BILLY JOEL was in this group. | | | |
| LIBERTY | | | |
| LN-10138 | The Hassles | 1981 | 12.00 |
| LN-10139 | Hour of the Wolf | 1981 | 12.00 |
| UNITED ARTISTS | | | |
| UAS-6631 | The Hassles | 1968 | 25.00 |
| UAS-6699 | Hour of the Wolf | 1969 | 25.00 |
| **HATZA, GREG** | | | |
| CORAL | | | |
| CRL 757495 [S] | Organized Jazz | 1963 | 20.00 |
| **HAVENS, RICHIE** | | | |
| A&M | | | |
| SP-4598 | The End of the Beginning | 1976 | 10.00 |
| SP-4641 | Mirage | 1977 | 10.00 |
| DOUGLAS | | | |
| D-779 [M] | Richie Havens' Record | 1966 | 15.00 |
| SD-779 [S] | Richie Havens' Record | 1966 | 20.00 |
| D-780 [M] | Electric Havens | 1966 | 25.00 |
| SD-780 [S] | Electric Havens | 1966 | 20.00 |
| ELEKTRA | | | |
| 6E-242 | Connections | 1980 | 10.00 |
| MGM | | | |
| SE-4698 | Mixed Bag | 1970 | 15.00 |
| *—Reissue of Verve Forecast 3006* | | | |
| SE-4699 | Something Else Again | 1970 | 15.00 |
| *—Reissue of Verve Forecast 3034* | | | |
| SE-4700 [(2)] | Richard P. Havens, 1963 | 1970 | 20.00 |
| *—Reissue of Verve Forecast 3047* | | | |
| RBI | | | |
| 400 | Simple Things | 1987 | 10.00 |
| STORMY FOREST | | | |
| SFS-6001 | Stonehenge | 1969 | 15.00 |
| SFS-6005 | Alarm Clock | 1970 | 12.00 |
| SFS-6010 | The Great Blind Degree | 1971 | 12.00 |
| SFS-6012 [(2)] | Richie Havens On Stage | 1972 | 15.00 |
| SFS-6013 | Portfolio | 1973 | 12.00 |
| SFS-6201 | Mixed Bag II | 1974 | 12.00 |
| VERVE FOLKWAYS | | | |
| FT-3006 [M] | Mixed Bag | 1967 | 25.00 |
| FTS-3006 [S] | Mixed Bag | 1967 | 20.00 |
| VERVE FORECAST | | | |
| FTS-3006 | Mixed Bag | 1968 | 15.00 |
| FT-3034 [M] | Something Else Again | 1968 | 40.00 |
| FTS-3034 [S] | Something Else Again | 1968 | 20.00 |
| FTS-3047 [(2)] | Richard P. Havens, 1983 | 1968 | 25.00 |
| FTS-3061 | Richie Havens | 1969 | — |
| *—Canceled* | | | |
| **HAWES, HAMPTON** | | | |
| CONTEMPORARY | | | |
| C-3505 [M] | Hampton Hawes | 1955 | 100.00 |
| C-3515 [M] | This Is Hampton Hawes | 1956 | 100.00 |
| C-3523 [M] | Everybody Likes Hampton Hawes | 1956 | 80.00 |
| C-3545 [M] | All Night Session! Volume 1 | 1958 | 80.00 |
| C-3546 [M] | All Night Session! Volume 2 | 1958 | 80.00 |
| C-3547 [M] | All Night Session! Volume 3 | 1958 | 80.00 |
| C-3553 [M] | Four! Hampton Hawes!!! | 1958 | 80.00 |
| M-3589 [M] | For Real! | 1959 | 60.00 |
| M-3614 [M] | The Green Leaves of Summer | 1964 | 50.00 |
| M-3616 [M] | Here and Now | 1965 | 50.00 |
| M-3621 [M] | The Seance | 1966 | 40.00 |
| M-3631 [M] | I'm All Smiles | 1967 | 60.00 |
| S-7545 [S] | All Night Session! Volume 1 | 1960 | 70.00 |
| S-7546 [S] | All Night Session! Volume 2 | 1960 | 70.00 |
| S-7547 [S] | All Night Session! Volume 3 | 1960 | 70.00 |
| S-7553 [S] | Four! Hampton Hawes!!! | 1960 | 70.00 |
| S-7589 [S] | For Real! | 1959 | 50.00 |
| S-7614 [S] | The Green Leaves of Summer | 1964 | 50.00 |
| S-7616 [S] | Here and Now | 1965 | 40.00 |
| S-7621 [S] | The Seance | 1966 | 40.00 |
| S-7631 [S] | I'm All Smiles | 1967 | 30.00 |
| PRESTIGE | | | |
| PRLP-212 [10] | Hampton Hawes Quartet | 1955 | 200.00 |
| STEREO RECORDS | | | |
| S-7026 [S] | Four! Hampton Hawes!!! | 1959 | 100.00 |
| VANTAGE | | | |
| VLP-1 [10] | Hamp Hawes | 1954 | 300.00 |
| VAULT | | | |
| LPS-9009 | Hampton Hawes Plays Movie Musicals | 1969 | 20.00 |
| LPS-9010 | High in the Sky | 1970 | 25.00 |
| **HAWKINS, COLEMAN** | | | |
| ADVANCE | | | |
| LSP-9 [10] | Coleman Hawkins Favorites | 1951 | 300.00 |
| AMERICAN RECORDING SOCIETY | | | |
| G-316 [M] | Coleman Hawkins and His Orchestra | 1956 | 50.00 |
| APOLLO | | | |
| LAP-101 [10] | Coleman Hawkins All Stars | 1951 | 300.00 |
| BRUNSWICK | | | |
| BL 58030 [10] | Tenor Sax | 1952 | 200.00 |
| CAPITOL | | | |
| H 327 [10] | Classics in Jazz | 1952 | 250.00 |
| T 819 [M] | Gilded Hawk | 1957 | 80.00 |
| COMMODORE | | | |
| FL-20025 [10] | King of the Tenor Sax | 1952 | 300.00 |
| CONCERT HALL JAZZ | | | |
| J-1201 [M] | Improvisations Unlimited | 1955 | 60.00 |
| CONTINENTAL | | | |
| 16006 [M] | On the Bean | 1962 | 25.00 |
| S-16006 [S] | On the Bean | 1962 | 30.00 |
| CROWN | | | |
| CLP-5181 [M] | Coleman Hawkins and His Orchestra | 1960 | 20.00 |
| CLP-5207 [M] | The Hawk Swing | 1961 | 20.00 |
| DECCA | | | |
| DL 4081 [M] | The Hawk Blows at Midnight | 1961 | 30.00 |
| DL 8127 [M] | The Hawk Talks | 1955 | 80.00 |
| DL 74081 [S] | The Hawk Blows at Midnight | 1961 | 40.00 |
| EMARCY | | | |
| MG-26013 [10] | The Bean | 1954 | 200.00 |
| FELSTED | | | |
| SJA-2005 [S] | The High and Mighty Hawk | 1959 | 80.00 |
| FAJ-7005 [M] | The High and Mighty Hawk | 1959 | 60.00 |

| Number | Title (A Side/B Side) | Yr | NM |
|---|---|---|---|
| **IMPULSE!** | | | |
| ❑ A-26 [M] | Duke Ellington Meets Coleman Hawkins | 1962 | 25.00 |
| ❑ AS-26 [S] | Duke Ellington Meets Coleman Hawkins | 1962 | 30.00 |
| ❑ A-28 [M] | Desafinado | 1963 | 25.00 |
| ❑ AS-28 [S] | Desafinado | 1963 | 30.00 |
| ❑ A-34 [M] | Today and Now | 1963 | 25.00 |
| ❑ AS-34 [S] | Today and Now | 1963 | 30.00 |
| ❑ A-87 [M] | Wrapped Tight | 1965 | 25.00 |
| ❑ AS-87 [S] | Wrapped Tight | 1965 | 30.00 |
| **JAZZTONE** | | | |
| ❑ J-1201 [M] | Timeless Jazz | 1955 | 50.00 |
| *—Reissue of Concert Hall Jazz 1201* | | | |
| **MAINSTREAM** | | | |
| ❑ 56037 [M] | Meditations | 1965 | 25.00 |
| **MOODSVILLE** | | | |
| ❑ MVLP-7 [M] | At Ease with Coleman Hawkins | 1960 | 50.00 |
| *—Green label* | | | |
| ❑ MVLP-7 [M] | At Ease with Coleman Hawkins | 1965 | 25.00 |
| *—Blue label, trident logo at right* | | | |
| ❑ MVLP-15 [M] | The Hawk Relaxes | 1961 | 50.00 |
| *—Green label* | | | |
| ❑ MVLP-15 [M] | The Hawk Relaxes | 1965 | 25.00 |
| *—Blue label, trident logo at right* | | | |
| ❑ MVLP-23 [M] | Good Old Broadway | 1962 | 40.00 |
| *—Gren label* | | | |
| ❑ MVLP-23 [M] | Good Old Broadway | 1965 | 20.00 |
| *—Blue label, trident logo at right* | | | |
| ❑ MVST-23 [S] | Good Old Broadway | 1962 | 50.00 |
| *—Green label* | | | |
| ❑ MVST-23 [S] | Good Old Broadway | 1965 | 25.00 |
| *—Blue label, trident logo at right* | | | |
| ❑ MVLP-25 [M] | The Jazz Version of No Strings | 1962 | 40.00 |
| *—Green label* | | | |
| ❑ MVLP-25 [M] | The Jazz Version of No Strings | 1965 | 20.00 |
| *—Blue label, trident logo at right* | | | |
| ❑ MVST-25 [S] | The Jazz Version of No Strings | 1962 | 50.00 |
| *—Green label* | | | |
| ❑ MVST-25 [S] | The Jazz Version of No Strings | 1965 | 25.00 |
| *—Blue label, trident logo at right* | | | |
| ❑ MVLP-31 [M] | Make Someone Happy | 1963 | 40.00 |
| *—Green label* | | | |
| ❑ MVLP-31 [M] | Make Someone Happy | 1965 | 20.00 |
| *—Blue label, trident logo at right* | | | |
| ❑ MVST-31 [S] | Make Someone Happy | 1963 | 50.00 |
| *—Green label* | | | |
| ❑ MVST-31 [S] | Make Someone Happy | 1965 | 25.00 |
| *—Blue label, trident logo at right* | | | |
| **PHILIPS** | | | |
| ❑ PHM 200022 [M] | Jazz at the Metropole | 1962 | 20.00 |
| ❑ PHS 600022 [S] | Jazz at the Metropole | 1962 | 25.00 |
| **PRESTIGE** | | | |
| ❑ PRLP-7149 [M] | Soul | 1958 | 80.00 |
| ❑ PRLP-7156 [M] | Hawk Eyes | 1958 | 80.00 |
| **RCA VICTOR** | | | |
| ❑ LPV-501 [M] | Body and Soul | 1965 | 20.00 |
| ❑ LJM-1017 [M] | Hawk In Flight | 1955 | 80.00 |
| ❑ LPM-1281 [M] | Hawk in Hi-Fi | 1956 | 80.00 |
| **RIVERSIDE** | | | |
| ❑ RLP 12-117/8 [(2)M] | Coleman Hawkins: A Documentary | 1956 | 200.00 |
| ❑ RLP 12-233 [M] | The Hawk Flies High | 1957 | 100.00 |
| *—White label, blue print* | | | |
| ❑ RLP 12-233 [M] | The Hawk Flies High | 1959 | 50.00 |
| *—Blue label, microphone logo at top* | | | |
| **SAVOY** | | | |
| ❑ MG-12013 [M] | The Hawk Returns | 1955 | 120.00 |
| ❑ MG-15039 [10] | The Hawk Talks | 1954 | 200.00 |
| **STINSON** | | | |
| ❑ SLP-22 [10] | Originals with Hawkins | 1950 | 300.00 |
| ❑ SLP-22 [M] | Originals with Hawkins | 195? | 40.00 |
| **SWINGVILLE** | | | |
| ❑ SVLP-2001 [M] | Coleman Hawkins Plus the Red Garland Trio | 1960 | 50.00 |
| *—Purple label* | | | |
| ❑ SVLP-2001 [M] | Coleman Hawkins Plus the Red Garland Trio | 1965 | 25.00 |
| *—Blue label, trident logo at right* | | | |
| ❑ SVLP-2005 [M] | The Coleman Hawkins All Stars | 1960 | 50.00 |
| *—Purple label* | | | |
| ❑ SVLP-2005 [M] | The Coleman Hawkins All Stars | 1965 | 25.00 |
| *—Blue label, trident logo at right* | | | |
| ❑ SVLP-2016 [M] | Night Hawk | 1961 | 50.00 |
| *—Purple label* | | | |
| ❑ SVLP-2016 [M] | Night Hawk | 1965 | 25.00 |
| *—Blue label, trident logo at right* | | | |
| ❑ SVLP-2024 [M] | Things Ain't What They Used to Be | 1961 | 40.00 |
| *—Purple label* | | | |
| ❑ SVLP-2024 [M] | Things Ain't What They Used to Be | 1965 | 20.00 |
| *—Blue label, trident logo at right* | | | |
| ❑ SVST-2024 [S] | Things Ain't What They Used to Be | 1961 | 50.00 |
| *—Red label* | | | |
| ❑ SVST-2024 [S] | Things Ain't What They Used to Be | 1965 | 25.00 |
| *—Blue label, trident logo at right* | | | |
| ❑ SVLP-2025 [M] | Years Ago | 1961 | 40.00 |
| *—Purple label* | | | |
| ❑ SVLP-2025 [M] | Years Ago | 1965 | 20.00 |
| *—Blue label, trident logo at right* | | | |
| ❑ SVST-2025 [S] | Years Ago | 1961 | 50.00 |
| *—Red label* | | | |
| ❑ SVST-2025 [S] | Years Ago | 1965 | 25.00 |
| *—Blue label, trident logo at right* | | | |
| ❑ SVLP-2035 [M] | Blues Groove | 1962 | 50.00 |
| *—Purple label* | | | |
| ❑ SVLP-2035 [M] | Blues Groove | 1965 | 25.00 |
| *—Blue label, trident logo at right* | | | |
| ❑ SVST-2035 [S] | Blues Groove | 1962 | 40.00 |
| *—Red label* | | | |
| ❑ SVST-2035 [S] | Blues Groove | 1965 | 20.00 |
| *—Blue label, trident logo at right* | | | |
| ❑ SVLP-2038 [M] | Soul | 1962 | 50.00 |
| *—Purple label* | | | |
| ❑ SVLP-2038 [M] | Soul | 1965 | 25.00 |
| *—Blue label, trident logo at right* | | | |
| ❑ SVST-2038 [S] | Soul | 1962 | 40.00 |
| *—Red label* | | | |
| ❑ SVST-2038 [S] | Soul | 1965 | 20.00 |
| *—Blue label, trident logo at right* | | | |
| ❑ SVLP-2039 [M] | Hawk Eyes | 1962 | 50.00 |
| *—Purple label* | | | |
| ❑ SVLP-2039 [M] | Hawk Eyes | 1965 | 25.00 |
| *—Blue label, trident logo at right* | | | |
| ❑ SVST-2039 [S] | Hawk Eyes | 1962 | 40.00 |
| *—Red label* | | | |
| ❑ SVST-2039 [S] | Hawk Eyes | 1965 | 20.00 |
| *—Blue label, trident logo at right* | | | |
| **URANIA** | | | |
| ❑ UJLP-1201 [M] | Accent on Tenor Sax | 1955 | 100.00 |
| ❑ UJLP-41201 [R] | Accent on Tenor Sax | 196? | 20.00 |
| **VERVE** | | | |
| ❑ MGVS-6033 [S] | The Genius of Coleman Hawkins | 1960 | 40.00 |
| ❑ MGVS-6066 [S] | Coleman Hawkins Encounters Ben Webster | 1960 | 40.00 |
| ❑ MGVS-6066 [S] | Coleman Hawkins Encounters Ben Webster | 199? | 25.00 |
| *—Classic Records reissue on audiophile vinyl* | | | |
| ❑ MGVS-6110 [S] | Coleman Hawkins and His Confreres with the Oscar Peterson Trio | 1960 | 40.00 |
| ❑ MGV-8261 [M] | The Genius of Coleman Hawkins | 1958 | 50.00 |
| ❑ V-8261 [M] | The Genius of Coleman Hawkins | 1961 | 25.00 |
| ❑ V6-8261 [S] | The Genius of Coleman Hawkins | 1961 | 20.00 |
| ❑ MGV-8327 [M] | Coleman Hawkins Encounters Ben Webster | 1959 | 50.00 |
| ❑ V-8327 [M] | Coleman Hawkins Encounters Ben Webster | 1961 | 25.00 |
| ❑ V6-8327 [S] | Coleman Hawkins Encounters Ben Webster | 1961 | 20.00 |
| ❑ MGV-8346 [M] | Coleman Hawkins and His Confreres with the Oscar Peterson Trio | 1959 | 50.00 |
| ❑ V-8346 [M] | Coleman Hawkins and His Confreres with the Oscar Peterson Trio | 1961 | 25.00 |
| ❑ V6-8346 [S] | Coleman Hawkins and His Confreres with the Oscar Peterson Trio | 1961 | 20.00 |
| ❑ V-8509 [M] | Hawkins! Alive! At the Village Gate | 1963 | 25.00 |
| ❑ V6-8509 [S] | Hawkins! Alive! At the Village Gate | 1963 | 30.00 |
| ❑ V-8568 [M] | The Essential Coleman Hawkins | 1964 | 20.00 |
| ❑ V6-8568 [S] | The Essential Coleman Hawkins | 1964 | 25.00 |
| **VIK** | | | |
| ❑ LX-1059 [M] | The Hawk in Paris | 1957 | 80.00 |
| **WORLD WIDE** | | | |
| ❑ MGS-20001 [S] | Coleman Hawkins with the Basie Saxophone Section | 1958 | 50.00 |

## HAWKINS, COLEMAN/GEORGIE AULD

| Number | Title (A Side/B Side) | Yr | NM |
|---|---|---|---|
| **GRAND AWARD** | | | |
| ❑ GA 33-316 [M] | Jazz Concert | 1955 | 50.00 |
| *—Without wrap-around cover* | | | |
| ❑ GA 33-316 [M] | Jazz Concert | 1955 | 100.00 |
| *—With wrap-around cover intact* | | | |

## HAWKINS, COLEMAN, AND ROY ELDREDGE

| Number | Title (A Side/B Side) | Yr | NM |
|---|---|---|---|
| **VERVE** | | | |
| ❑ MGVS-6028 [S] | At the Opera House | 1960 | 40.00 |
| ❑ MGV-8266 [M] | At the Opera House | 1958 | 50.00 |
| ❑ V-8266 [M] | At the Opera House | 1961 | 25.00 |
| ❑ V6-8266 [S] | At the Opera House | 1961 | 20.00 |

## HAWKINS, COLEMAN; ROY ELDREDGE; PETE BROWN; JO JONES

| Number | Title (A Side/B Side) | Yr | NM |
|---|---|---|---|
| **VERVE** | | | |
| ❑ MGV-8240 [M] | All Stars at Newport | 1958 | 50.00 |
| ❑ V-8240 [M] | All Stars at Newport | 1961 | 20.00 |

## HAWKINS, COLEMAN; ROY ELDREDGE; JOHNNY HODGES

| Number | Title (A Side/B Side) | Yr | NM |
|---|---|---|---|
| **VERVE** | | | |
| ❑ V-8509 [M] | Alive at the Village Gate | 1963 | 20.00 |
| ❑ V6-8509 [S] | Alive at the Village Gate | 1963 | 25.00 |
| ❑ V6-8509 [S] | Alive at the Village Gate | 199? | 25.00 |
| *—Classic Records reissue on audiophile vinyl* | | | |

## HAWKINS, COLEMAN, AND FRANK HUNTER

| Number | Title (A Side/B Side) | Yr | NM |
|---|---|---|---|
| **MIRA** | | | |
| ❑ M-3003 [M] | The Hawk and the Hunter | 1965 | 20.00 |
| ❑ MS-3003 [S] | The Hawk and the Hunter | 1965 | 25.00 |

## HAWKINS, COLEMAN, AND PEE WEE RUSSELL

| Number | Title (A Side/B Side) | Yr | NM |
|---|---|---|---|
| **CANDID** | | | |
| ❑ CD-8020 [M] | Jazz Reunion | 1960 | 40.00 |
| ❑ CS-9020 [S] | Jazz Reunion | 1960 | 40.00 |

## HAWKINS, COLEMAN, AND CLARK TERRY

| Number | Title (A Side/B Side) | Yr | NM |
|---|---|---|---|
| **COLUMBIA** | | | |
| ❑ CS 8791 [S] | Back in Bean's Bag | 1963 | 20.00 |
| ❑ CS 8791 [S] | Back in Bean's Bag | 1999 | 25.00 |
| *—Classic Records reissue on audiophile vinyl* | | | |

## HAWKINS, COLEMAN/BEN WEBSTER

| Number | Title (A Side/B Side) | Yr | NM |
|---|---|---|---|
| **BRUNSWICK** | | | |
| ❑ BL 54016 [M] | The Big Sounds of Coleman Hawkins and Ben Webster | 1956 | 80.00 |

## HAWKINS, DALE

| Number | Title (A Side/B Side) | Yr | NM |
|---|---|---|---|
| **BELL** | | | |
| ❑ 6036 | L.A., Memphis and Tyler, Texas | 1969 | 40.00 |
| **CHESS** | | | |
| ❑ ACRR-706 | Dale Hawkins | 1976 | 15.00 |
| ❑ LP-1429 [M] | Oh! Susie-Q | 1958 | 1500. |
| *—VG value 500; VG+ value 1000* | | | |
| **ROULETTE** | | | |
| ❑ R 25175 [M] | Let's All Twist at the Miami Beach Peppermint Lounge | 1962 | 200.00 |
| ❑ SR 25175 [S] | Let's All Twist at the Miami Beach Peppermint Lounge | 1962 | 300.00 |

## HAWKINS, DOLORES

| Number | Title (A Side/B Side) | Yr | NM |
|---|---|---|---|
| **EPIC** | | | |
| ❑ LN 1119 [M] | Meet Dolores Hawkins | 1955 | 40.00 |
| ❑ LN 3250 [M] | Dolores | 1957 | 40.00 |

## HAWKINS, ERSKINE

| Number | Title (A Side/B Side) | Yr | NM |
|---|---|---|---|
| **CORAL** | | | |
| ❑ CRL 56051 [10] | After Hours | 1954 | 120.00 |
| **DECCA** | | | |
| ❑ DL 4081 [M] | The Hawk Blows at Midnight | 1960 | 30.00 |
| ❑ DL 74081 [S] | The Hawk Blows at Midnight | 1960 | 40.00 |
| **IMPERIAL** | | | |
| ❑ LP-9191 [M] | 25 Golden Years of Jazz, Volume 1 | 1962 | 25.00 |
| ❑ LP-9197 [M] | 25 Golden Years of Jazz, Volume 2 | 1962 | 25.00 |
| ❑ LP-12191 [S] | 25 Golden Years of Jazz, Volume 1 | 1962 | 30.00 |
| ❑ LP-12197 [S] | 25 Golden Years of Jazz, Volume 2 | 1962 | 30.00 |
| **RCA VICTOR** | | | |
| ❑ LPM-2227 [M] | After Hours | 1960 | 40.00 |

## HAWKINS, HAWKSHAW

| Number | Title (A Side/B Side) | Yr | NM |
|---|---|---|---|
| **GLADWYNNE** | | | |
| ❑ G-2006 [M] | Country Western Cavalcade with Hawkshaw Hawkins | 195? | 120.00 |
| **HARMONY** | | | |
| ❑ HL 7301 [M] | The Great Hawkshaw Hawkins | 1963 | 20.00 |
| ❑ HS 11044 [R] | The Great Hawkshaw Hawkins | 1963 | 15.00 |
| **KING** | | | |
| ❑ 587 [M] | Hawkshaw Hawkins | 1958 | 100.00 |
| ❑ 592 [M] | Grand Ole Opry Favorites | 1958 | 100.00 |
| ❑ 599 [M] | Hawkshaw Hawkins | 1959 | 100.00 |
| ❑ 808 [M] | The All New Hawkshaw Hawkins | 1963 | 80.00 |
| ❑ KS-808 [S] | The All New Hawkshaw Hawkins | 1963 | 100.00 |
| ❑ 858 [M] | Taken From Our Vaults, Volume 1 | 1963 | 40.00 |
| ❑ 870 [M] | Taken From Our Vaults, Volume 2 | 1963 | 40.00 |
| ❑ 873 [M] | Taken From Our Vaults, Volume 3 | 1964 | 40.00 |
| **LABREA** | | | |
| ❑ 8020 [M] | Hawkshaw Hawkins | 195? | 100.00 |
| **RCA CAMDEN** | | | |
| ❑ CAL-808 [M] | Hawkshaw Hawkins Sings | 1964 | 20.00 |
| ❑ CAS-808 [R] | Hawkshaw Hawkins Sings | 1964 | 15.00 |
| ❑ CAL-931 [M] | The Country Gentleman | 1966 | 20.00 |
| ❑ CAS-931 [R] | The Country Gentleman | 1966 | 15.00 |

SHAFT-Music from the Soundtrack
Composed and Performed by ISAAC HAYES
MGM's
SHAFT
ENS-2-5002
STEREO
ENTERPRISE


Isaac Hayes, *Shaft,* Enterprise ENS-2-5002, 1971, 2 records, $20.

| Number | Title (A Side/B Side) | Yr | NM |
|---|---|---|---|
| **HAWKINS, JENNELL** | | | |
| AMAZON | | | |
| ❑ 1001 [M] | The Many Moods of Jenny | 1961 | 150.00 |
| ❑ 1002 [M] | Moments to Remember | 1962 | 150.00 |
| **HAWKINS, RONNIE** | | | |
| ACCORD | | | |
| ❑ SN-7213 | Premonition | 1983 | 10.00 |
| COTILLION | | | |
| ❑ SD 9019 | Ronnie Hawkins | 1970 | 15.00 |
| ❑ SD 9039 | The Hawk | 1971 | 15.00 |
| MONUMENT | | | |
| ❑ KZ 31330 | Rock and Roll Resurrection | 1972 | 12.00 |
| ❑ KZ 32940 | The Giant of Rock 'n' Roll | 1974 | 12.00 |
| ❑ ZG 33855 [(2)] | Rock and Roll Resurrection/ The Ghost of Rock and Roll | 1976 | 15.00 |
| ROULETTE | | | |
| ❑ R 25078 [M] | Ronnie Hawkins | 1959 | 150.00 |
| *—White label with spokes* | | | |
| ❑ R 25078 [M] | Ronnie Hawkins | 1964 | 50.00 |
| *—Orange/yellow label* | | | |
| ❑ SR 25078 [S] | Ronnie Hawkins | 1959 | 200.00 |
| *—White label with spokes; black vinyl* | | | |
| ❑ SR 25078 [S] | Ronnie Hawkins | 1959 | 600.00 |
| *—White label with spokes; red vinyl* | | | |
| ❑ SR 25078 [S] | Ronnie Hawkins | 1964 | 60.00 |
| *—Orange/yellow label* | | | |
| ❑ R 25102 [M] | Mr. Dynamo | 1960 | 150.00 |
| ❑ SR 25102 [S] | Mr. Dynamo | 1960 | 200.00 |
| *—Black vinyl* | | | |
| ❑ SR 25102 [S] | Mr. Dynamo | 1960 | 600.00 |
| *—Red vinyl* | | | |
| ❑ R 25120 [M] | The Folk Ballads of Ronnie Hawkins | 1960 | 100.00 |
| ❑ SR 25120 [S] | The Folk Ballads of Ronnie Hawkins | 1960 | 150.00 |
| ❑ R 25137 [M] | Ronnie Hawkins Sings the Songs of Hank Williams | 1960 | 100.00 |
| ❑ SR 25137 [S] | Ronnie Hawkins Sings the Songs of Hank Williams | 1960 | 150.00 |
| ❑ SR 42045 | The Best of Ronnie Hawkins and His Band | 1970 | 25.00 |
| UNITED ARTISTS | | | |
| ❑ UA-LA968-H | The Hawk | 1979 | 10.00 |

| Number | Title (A Side/B Side) | Yr | NM |
|---|---|---|---|
| **HAWKINS, SCREAMIN' JAY** | | | |
| EPIC | | | |
| ❑ LN 3448 [M] | At Home with Screamin' Jay Hawkins | 1958 | 1200. |
| ❑ LN 3457 [M] | I Put a Spell on You | 1958 | 500.00 |
| ❑ BN 26457 [R] | I Put a Spell on You | 1969 | 60.00 |
| PHILIPS | | | |
| ❑ PHS 600319 | What That Is | 1969 | 40.00 |
| ❑ PHS 600336 | Screamin' Jay Hawkins | 1970 | 40.00 |
| SOUNDS OF HAWAII | | | |
| ❑ 5015 | A Night at Forbidden City | 196? | 50.00 |
| **HAWKS, BILLY** | | | |
| PRESTIGE | | | |
| ❑ PRLP-7501 [M] | New Genius of the Blues | 1967 | 25.00 |
| ❑ PRST-7501 [S] | New Genius of the Blues | 1967 | 20.00 |
| ❑ PRST-7556 | More Heavy Soul | 1968 | 20.00 |
| **HAWKWIND** | | | |
| ATCO | | | |
| ❑ SD 36-115 | Warrior on the Edge of Time | 1975 | 15.00 |
| GWR | | | |
| ❑ 1237 [(2)] | Live Chronicles | 1986 | 12.00 |
| LIBERTY | | | |
| ❑ LWB-120 [(2)] | Space Ritual/Alive in Liverpool and London | 1981 | 12.00 |
| *—Reissue of United Artists 120* | | | |
| ❑ LW-5567 | In Search of Space | 1981 | 8.00 |
| *—Reissue of United Artists 5567* | | | |
| SIRE | | | |
| ❑ SRK 6047 | Quark Strangeness and Charm | 1978 | 12.00 |
| UNITED ARTISTS | | | |
| ❑ UA-LA001-F | Doremi Fasol Latido | 1973 | 15.00 |
| ❑ UA-LA120-H [(2)] | Space Ritual/Alive in Liverpool and London | 1973 | 20.00 |
| ❑ UA-LA328-G | Hall of the Mountain Grill | 1974 | 15.00 |
| ❑ UAS-5519 | Hawkwind | 1971 | 15.00 |
| ❑ UAS-5567 | In Search of Space | 1972 | 15.00 |
| **HAWN, GOLDIE** | | | |
| REPRISE | | | |
| ❑ MS 2061 | Goldie | 1972 | 25.00 |

| Number | Title (A Side/B Side) | Yr | NM |
|---|---|---|---|
| **HAYDEN, WILLIE** | | | |
| DOOTO | | | |
| ❑ DTL-293 [M] | Blame It on the Blues | 196? | 200.00 |
| *—Multi-color label* | | | |
| ❑ DTL-293 [M] | Blame It on the Blues | 1960 | 500.00 |
| *—Maroon label* | | | |
| **HAYES, BILL** | | | |
| ABC-PARAMOUNT | | | |
| ❑ 194 [M] | Bill Hayes Sings the Best of Disney | 1957 | 40.00 |
| DAYBREAK | | | |
| ❑ DR-2020 | The Look of Love | 1972 | 25.00 |
| KAPP | | | |
| ❑ KL-1106 [M] | Jimmy Crack Corn | 1958 | 25.00 |
| **HAYES, CLANCY** | | | |
| DELMARK | | | |
| ❑ DS-210 [M] | Oh By Jingo | 1965 | 20.00 |
| ❑ DS-9210 [S] | Oh By Jingo | 1965 | 25.00 |
| DOWN HOME | | | |
| ❑ MGD-3 [M] | Clancy Hayes Sings | 1956 | 60.00 |
| GOOD TIME JAZZ | | | |
| ❑ S-10050 [S] | Swingin' Minstrel | 1963 | 25.00 |
| ❑ L-12050 [M] | Swingin' Minstrel | 1963 | 20.00 |
| VERVE | | | |
| ❑ MGV-1003 [M] | Clancy Hayes Sings | 1957 | 40.00 |
| **HAYES, ISAAC** | | | |
| ABC/HBS | | | |
| ❑ D-874 | Chocolate Chip | 1975 | 15.00 |
| ❑ D-923 | Disco Connection | 1975 | 12.00 |
| ❑ D-925 | Groove-a-Thon | 1976 | 12.00 |
| ❑ D-953 | Juicy Fruit (Disco Freak) | 1976 | 12.00 |
| ATLANTIC | | | |
| ❑ SD 1599 | In the Beginning | 1972 | 15.00 |
| *—Reissue of Enterprise 100* | | | |
| COLUMBIA | | | |
| ❑ FC 40316 | U-Turn | 1986 | 10.00 |
| ❑ FC 40941 | Love Attack | 1988 | 10.00 |
| ENTERPRISE | | | |
| ❑ E-100 [M] | Presenting Isaac Hayes | 1968 | 40.00 |
| ❑ ES-100 [S] | Presenting Isaac Hayes | 1968 | 30.00 |
| ❑ ENS-1001 | Hot Buttered Soul | 1969 | 20.00 |
| ❑ ENS-1010 | The Isaac Hayes Movement | 1970 | 20.00 |
| ❑ ENS-1014 | To Be Continued | 1970 | 20.00 |
| ❑ ENS-5002 [(2)] | Shaft | 1971 | 20.00 |
| ❑ EQS-2-5002 [(2)Q] | Shaft | 1971 | 40.00 |
| ❑ ENS-5003 [(2)] | Black Moses | 1971 | 20.00 |
| ❑ ENS-5005 [(2)] | Live at the Sahara Tahoe | 1973 | 15.00 |
| ❑ XQS-5005 [(2)Q] | Live at the Sahara Tahoe | 1973 | 30.00 |
| ❑ ENS-5007 | Joy | 1973 | 12.00 |
| ❑ EQS-5007 [Q] | Joy | 1973 | 20.00 |
| ❑ ENS-7504 | Tough Guys | 1974 | 12.00 |
| ❑ EQS-7504 [Q] | Tough Guys | 1974 | 20.00 |
| ❑ ENS-7507 [(2)] | Truck Turner | 1974 | 15.00 |
| ❑ ENS-7510 | The Best of Isaac Hayes | 1975 | 12.00 |
| MOBILE FIDELITY | | | |
| ❑ MFSL 1-273 | Hot Buttered Soul | 2003 | 25.00 |
| *—"Original Master Recording" at top of front cover* | | | |
| POINTBLANK | | | |
| ❑ SPRO-12787 [DJ] | Funky Junky | 1995 | 15.00 |
| *—Vinyl is promo only* | | | |
| POLYDOR | | | |
| ❑ PD-1-6120 | New Horizon | 1977 | 10.00 |
| ❑ PD-1-6164 | For the Sake of Love | 1978 | 10.00 |
| ❑ PD-1-6224 | Don't Let Go | 1979 | 10.00 |
| ❑ PD-1-6269 | And Once Again | 1980 | 10.00 |
| STAX | | | |
| ❑ STX-4102 | Hotbed | 197? | 10.00 |
| ❑ STX-4114 | Hot Buttered Soul | 1978 | 10.00 |
| *—Reissue of Enterprise 1001* | | | |
| ❑ STX-4129 | The Isaac Hayes Movement | 197? | 10.00 |
| *—Reissue of Enterprise 1010* | | | |
| ❑ STX-4133 | To Be Continued | 197? | 10.00 |
| *—Reissue of Enterprise 1014* | | | |
| ❑ MPS-8509 | Excerpts from Black Moses | 1981 | 10.00 |
| ❑ MPS-8515 | His Greatest Hit Singles | 1982 | 10.00 |
| ❑ MPS-8530 | Joy | 1984 | 10.00 |
| *—Reissue of Enterprise 5007* | | | |
| ❑ STX-88002 [(2)] | Shaft | 1979 | 12.00 |
| *—Reissue of Enterprise 5002* | | | |
| ❑ STX-88003 [(2)] | Enterprise: His Greatest Hits | 1980 | 12.00 |
| ❑ STX-88004 [(2)] | Live at the Sahara Tahoe | 198? | 12.00 |
| *—Reissue of Enterprise 5005* | | | |
| **HAYES, LOUIS** | | | |
| VEE JAY | | | |
| ❑ LP-3010 [M] | Louis Hayes | 1960 | 80.00 |
| ❑ SR-3010 [S] | Louis Hayes | 1960 | 150.00 |
| **HAYES, MARTHA** | | | |
| JUBILEE | | | |
| ❑ JLP-1023 [M] | A Hayes Named Martha | 1956 | 50.00 |

### HAYES, RICHARD

**ABC-PARAMOUNT**

| Number | Title (A Side/B Side) | Yr | NM |
|---|---|---|---|
| ❑ ABC-131 [M] | Richard Hayes | 1956 | 40.00 |

**MALA**

| Number | Title (A Side/B Side) | Yr | NM |
|---|---|---|---|
| ❑ MLP-25 [M] | Love on the Rocks | 1959 | 30.00 |

### HAYES, ROLAND

**VANGUARD**

| Number | Title (A Side/B Side) | Yr | NM |
|---|---|---|---|
| ❑ VRS-462 [M] | The Life of Christ in Folk Song | 1954 | 30.00 |
| ❑ VRS-494 [M] | My Songs, Aframerican Religious Folk Songs | 1955 | 30.00 |
| ❑ VRS-7016 [10] | Christmas Carols of the Nations | 195? | 50.00 |

### HAYES, TUBBY

**EPIC**

| Number | Title (A Side/B Side) | Yr | NM |
|---|---|---|---|
| ❑ LA 16019 [M] | Introducing Tubby | 1961 | 40.00 |
| ❑ LA 16023 [M] | Tubby the Tenor | 1962 | 40.00 |
| ❑ BA 17019 [S] | Introducing Tubby | 1961 | 50.00 |
| ❑ BA 17023 [S] | Tubby the Tenor | 1962 | 50.00 |
| ❑ BA 17023 [S] | Tubby the Tenor | 199? | 25.00 |

*—Classic Records reissue on audiophile vinyl*

**IMPERIAL**

| Number | Title (A Side/B Side) | Yr | NM |
|---|---|---|---|
| ❑ LP-9046 [M] | Little Giant of Jazz | 1957 | 80.00 |

**SMASH**

| Number | Title (A Side/B Side) | Yr | NM |
|---|---|---|---|
| ❑ MGS-27026 [M] | Tubby's Back in Town | 1963 | 40.00 |
| ❑ SRS-67026 [S] | Tubby's Back in Town | 1963 | 50.00 |

### HAYMARKET SQUARE

**CHAPARRAL**

| Number | Title (A Side/B Side) | Yr | NM |
|---|---|---|---|
| ❑ 201 | Magic Lantern | 1968 | 1500. |

### HAYMES, DICK

**AUDIOPHILE**

| Number | Title (A Side/B Side) | Yr | NM |
|---|---|---|---|
| ❑ AP-79 | Imagination | 1978 | 12.00 |
| ❑ AP-130 | For You, For Me, Forevermore | 197? | 12.00 |
| ❑ AP-200 | Keep It Simple | 198? | 12.00 |

**BALLAD**

| Number | Title (A Side/B Side) | Yr | NM |
|---|---|---|---|
| ❑ DHS-6 | As Time Goes By | 1978 | 15.00 |
| ❑ DHS-7 | Last Goodbye | 1980 | 15.00 |
| ❑ DHS-8 | Rare Dick Haymes | 198? | 15.00 |

**CAPITOL**

| Number | Title (A Side/B Side) | Yr | NM |
|---|---|---|---|
| ❑ T 713 [M] | Rain or Shine | 1956 | 30.00 |
| *—Turquoise label* | | | |
| ❑ T 787 [M] | Moondreams | 1956 | 30.00 |
| *—Turquoise label* | | | |

**DAYBREAK**

| Number | Title (A Side/B Side) | Yr | NM |
|---|---|---|---|
| ❑ DR 2016 | Dick Haymes Comes Home | 1973 | 15.00 |

**DECCA**

| Number | Title (A Side/B Side) | Yr | NM |
|---|---|---|---|
| ❑ DL 5012 [10] | Souvenir Album | 1949 | 50.00 |
| ❑ DL 5022 [10] | Christmas Songs | 1949 | 50.00 |
| ❑ DL 5023 [10] | Dick Haymes Sings Irving Berlin | 1949 | 50.00 |
| ❑ DL 5038 [10] | Little Shamrocks | 1950 | 50.00 |
| ❑ DL 5243 [10] | Dick Haymes Sings with Helen Forrest, Volume 1 | 195? | 50.00 |
| ❑ DL 5291 [10] | Sentimental Songs | 195? | 50.00 |
| ❑ DL 5335 [10] | Sweethearts | 195? | 50.00 |
| ❑ DL 8773 [M] | Little White Lies | 1959 | 40.00 |

**MCA**

| Number | Title (A Side/B Side) | Yr | NM |
|---|---|---|---|
| ❑ 2-4097 [(2)] | The Best of Dick Haymes | 1976 | 15.00 |

*—Black labels with rainbow*

**MCA CORAL**

| Number | Title (A Side/B Side) | Yr | NM |
|---|---|---|---|
| ❑ CB-20016 | Easy | 1973 | 10.00 |

**VOCALION**

| Number | Title (A Side/B Side) | Yr | NM |
|---|---|---|---|
| ❑ VL 3616 [M] | Dick Haymes | 196? | 15.00 |

**WARWICK**

| Number | Title (A Side/B Side) | Yr | NM |
|---|---|---|---|
| ❑ W-2023 [M] | Richard the Lion-Hearted | 1960 | 30.00 |

### HAYNES, ROY

**EMARCY**

| Number | Title (A Side/B Side) | Yr | NM |
|---|---|---|---|
| ❑ MG-26048 [10] | Bushman's Holiday | 1954 | 150.00 |

**IMPULSE!**

| Number | Title (A Side/B Side) | Yr | NM |
|---|---|---|---|
| ❑ A-23 [M] | Out of the Afternoon | 1962 | 60.00 |
| ❑ AS-23 [S] | Out of the Afternoon | 1962 | 80.00 |

**MAINSTREAM**

| Number | Title (A Side/B Side) | Yr | NM |
|---|---|---|---|
| ❑ MRL-313 | Hip Ensemble | 1971 | 20.00 |
| ❑ MRL-351 | Senyah | 1972 | 20.00 |

**NEW JAZZ**

| Number | Title (A Side/B Side) | Yr | NM |
|---|---|---|---|
| ❑ NJLP-8245 [M] | Just Us | 1960 | 80.00 |
| *—Purple label* | | | |
| ❑ NJLP-8245 [M] | Just Us | 1965 | 25.00 |
| *—Blue label, trident logo at right* | | | |
| ❑ NJLP-8286 [M] | Cracklin' | 1962 | 80.00 |
| *—Purple label* | | | |
| ❑ NJLP-8286 [M] | Cracklin' | 1965 | 25.00 |
| *—Blue label, trident logo at right* | | | |
| ❑ NJLP-8287 [M] | Cymbalism | 1962 | 80.00 |
| *—Purple label* | | | |
| ❑ NJLP-8287 [M] | Cymbalism | 1965 | 25.00 |
| *—Blue label, trident logo at right* | | | |

**PACIFIC JAZZ**

| Number | Title (A Side/B Side) | Yr | NM |
|---|---|---|---|
| ❑ PJ-82 [M] | People | 1964 | 30.00 |
| ❑ ST-82 [S] | People | 1964 | 40.00 |

### HAYNES, ROY/QUINCY JONES

**EMARCY**

| Number | Title (A Side/B Side) | Yr | NM |
|---|---|---|---|
| ❑ MG-36083 [M] | Jazz Abroad | 1956 | 100.00 |

### HAYNES, ROY; PHINEAS NEWBORN; PAUL CHAMBERS

**NEW JAZZ**

| Number | Title (A Side/B Side) | Yr | NM |
|---|---|---|---|
| ❑ NJLP-8210 [M] | We Three | 1958 | 100.00 |

### HAYWARD, JUSTIN, AND JOHN LODGE

Also see THE MOODY BLUES.

**THRESHOLD**

| Number | Title (A Side/B Side) | Yr | NM |
|---|---|---|---|
| ❑ THS 14 | Blue Jays | 1975 | 15.00 |
| ❑ THSX 101 [DJ] | Blue Jays | 1975 | 50.00 |

*—Open-end interview with script; used to promote the LP of the same name*

### HAYWOOD, LEON

**COLUMBIA**

| Number | Title (A Side/B Side) | Yr | NM |
|---|---|---|---|
| ❑ PC 34363 | Intimate | 1976 | 10.00 |

**DECCA**

| Number | Title (A Side/B Side) | Yr | NM |
|---|---|---|---|
| ❑ DL 74949 | It's Got to Be Mellow | 1969 | 20.00 |

**FAT FISH**

| Number | Title (A Side/B Side) | Yr | NM |
|---|---|---|---|
| ❑ LP 2525 | Soul Cargo | 1966 | 60.00 |

**GALAXY**

| Number | Title (A Side/B Side) | Yr | NM |
|---|---|---|---|
| ❑ 8206 | Mellow, Mellow | 196? | 20.00 |

**MCA**

| Number | Title (A Side/B Side) | Yr | NM |
|---|---|---|---|
| ❑ 2322 | Double My Pleasure | 1978 | 10.00 |
| ❑ 3090 | Energy | 1979 | 10.00 |

**20TH CENTURY**

| Number | Title (A Side/B Side) | Yr | NM |
|---|---|---|---|
| ❑ T-411 | Back to Stay | 1973 | 12.00 |
| ❑ T-440 | Keep It in the Family | 1974 | 12.00 |
| ❑ T-476 | Come and Get Yourself Some | 1975 | 10.00 |
| ❑ T-613 | Naturally | 1980 | 10.00 |

### HAZEL, EDDIE

Member of PARLIAMENT/FUNKADELIC.

**WARNER BROS.**

| Number | Title (A Side/B Side) | Yr | NM |
|---|---|---|---|
| ❑ BSK 3058 | Games, Dames and Guitar Thangs | 1977 | 40.00 |

### HAZEL, MONK

**SOUTHLAND**

| Number | Title (A Side/B Side) | Yr | NM |
|---|---|---|---|
| ❑ SLP-217 [M] | Monk Hazel | 1956 | 40.00 |

### HAZLEWOOD, LEE

Also see ANN-MARGRET; NANCY SINATRA.

**CAPITOL**

| Number | Title (A Side/B Side) | Yr | NM |
|---|---|---|---|
| ❑ ST-11171 | Poet, Fool or Bum | 1973 | 40.00 |

**HARMONY**

| Number | Title (A Side/B Side) | Yr | NM |
|---|---|---|---|
| ❑ HS 11290 [S] | Houston | 196? | 20.00 |

*—Reissue of Reprise 6163*

**LHI**

| Number | Title (A Side/B Side) | Yr | NM |
|---|---|---|---|
| ❑ S-12006 | Trouble Is a Lonesome Town | 1969 | 20.00 |
| *—Reissue of Mercury 60860* | | | |
| ❑ S-12009 | Forty | 1969 | 40.00 |

**MERCURY**

| Number | Title (A Side/B Side) | Yr | NM |
|---|---|---|---|
| ❑ MG-20860 [M] | Trouble Is a Lonesome Town | 1964 | 25.00 |
| ❑ SR-60860 [S] | Trouble Is a Lonesome Town | 1964 | 30.00 |

**MGM**

| Number | Title (A Side/B Side) | Yr | NM |
|---|---|---|---|
| ❑ E-4362 [M] | The Very Special World of Lee Hazlewood | 1966 | 25.00 |
| ❑ SE-4362 [S] | The Very Special World of Lee Hazlewood | 1966 | 30.00 |
| ❑ E-4403 [M] | Lee Hazlewoodism - Its Cause and Cure | 1966 | 30.00 |
| ❑ SE-4403 [S] | Lee Hazlewoodism - Its Cause and Cure | 1966 | 40.00 |

**REPRISE**

| Number | Title (A Side/B Side) | Yr | NM |
|---|---|---|---|
| ❑ R-6133 [M] | The N.S.V.I.P.'s | 1965 | 30.00 |
| ❑ RS-6133 [S] | The N.S.V.I.P.'s | 1965 | 40.00 |
| ❑ R-6163 [M] | Friday's Child | 1965 | 25.00 |
| ❑ RS-6163 [S] | Friday's Child | 1965 | 30.00 |
| ❑ RS-6297 | Love and Other Crimes | 1968 | 40.00 |

**SMELLS LIKE**

| Number | Title (A Side/B Side) | Yr | NM |
|---|---|---|---|
| ❑ SLR-30 | Cowboy in Sweden | 1999 | 15.00 |
| ❑ SLR-37 | Trouble Is a Lonesome Town | 1999 | 15.00 |
| ❑ SLR-38 | Requiem for an Almost Lady | 1999 | 15.00 |
| ❑ SLR-40 | 13 | 2000 | 15.00 |

### HEE

**BUDDAH**

| Number | Title (A Side/B Side) | Yr | NM |
|---|---|---|---|
| ❑ BDS-5062 | Head | 1970 | 30.00 |

*—With coloring book (deduct 1/3 if missing)*

### HEAD, JIM, AND HIS DEL RAYS

**HP**

| Number | Title (A Side/B Side) | Yr | NM |
|---|---|---|---|
| ❑ 22893 [M] | Jim Head and His Del Rays | 1963 | 300.00 |

### HEAD, ROY

**ABC**

| Number | Title (A Side/B Side) | Yr | NM |
|---|---|---|---|
| ❑ AB-1054 | Tonight's the Night | 1978 | 10.00 |

**ABC DOT**

| Number | Title (A Side/B Side) | Yr | NM |
|---|---|---|---|
| ❑ DO-2051 | Head First | 1976 | 12.00 |
| ❑ DO-2066 | A Head of His Time | 1977 | 12.00 |

**ABC DUNHILL**

| Number | Title (A Side/B Side) | Yr | NM |
|---|---|---|---|
| ❑ DS-50080 | Same People | 1970 | 20.00 |

**ELEKTRA**

| Number | Title (A Side/B Side) | Yr | NM |
|---|---|---|---|
| ❑ 6E-234 | In Our Room | 1979 | 10.00 |
| ❑ 6E-298 | The Many Sides of Roy Head | 1980 | 10.00 |

**MCA**

| Number | Title (A Side/B Side) | Yr | NM |
|---|---|---|---|
| ❑ 796 | Tonight's the Night | 1980 | 8.00 |

*—Reissue of ABC album*

**SCEPTER**

| Number | Title (A Side/B Side) | Yr | NM |
|---|---|---|---|
| ❑ S-532 [M] | Treat Me Right | 1965 | 30.00 |
| ❑ SS-532 [S] | Treat Me Right | 1965 | 40.00 |

**TMI**

| Number | Title (A Side/B Side) | Yr | NM |
|---|---|---|---|
| ❑ 1000 | Dismal Prisoner | 1972 | 15.00 |

**TNT**

| Number | Title (A Side/B Side) | Yr | NM |
|---|---|---|---|
| ❑ 101 [M] | Roy Head and the Traits | 1965 | 150.00 |

*—Counterfeit alert: Authentics do NOT contain the hit "Treat Her Right."*

### HEAD OVER HEELS

**CAPITOL**

| Number | Title (A Side/B Side) | Yr | NM |
|---|---|---|---|
| ❑ ST-797 | Head Over Heels | 1971 | 30.00 |

### HEAD SHOP, THE

**EPIC**

| Number | Title (A Side/B Side) | Yr | NM |
|---|---|---|---|
| ❑ BN 26476 | The Head Shop | 1969 | 60.00 |

### HEADS, THE

**LIBERTY**

| Number | Title (A Side/B Side) | Yr | NM |
|---|---|---|---|
| ❑ LST-7581 | Heads Up | 1968 | 25.00 |

### HEADS, HANDS AND FEET

**ATCO**

| Number | Title (A Side/B Side) | Yr | NM |
|---|---|---|---|
| ❑ SD 7025 | Old Soldiers Never Die | 1973 | 20.00 |

**CAPITOL**

| Number | Title (A Side/B Side) | Yr | NM |
|---|---|---|---|
| ❑ SVBB-680 [(2)] | Heads, Hands and Feet | 1971 | 25.00 |
| ❑ ST-11051 | Tracks | 1972 | 20.00 |

### HEADSTONE

**STARR**

| Number | Title (A Side/B Side) | Yr | NM |
|---|---|---|---|
| ❑ (# unknown) | Still Looking | 1974 | 150.00 |

### HEALY, PAT

**WORLD PACIFIC**

| Number | Title (A Side/B Side) | Yr | NM |
|---|---|---|---|
| ❑ WP-409 [M] | Just Before Dawn | 1958 | 80.00 |

### HEARD, J.C.

**ARGO**

| Number | Title (A Side/B Side) | Yr | NM |
|---|---|---|---|
| ❑ LP-633 [M] | This Is Me, J.C. | 1958 | 40.00 |
| ❑ LPS-633 [S] | This Is Me, J.C. | 1959 | 30.00 |

### HEART

**CAPITOL**

| Number | Title (A Side/B Side) | Yr | NM |
|---|---|---|---|
| ❑ ST-12410 | Heart | 1985 | 10.00 |
| *—With remix of "Never." Side one trail-off wax has an "RE-1"* | | | |
| ❑ ST-12410 | Heart | 1985 | 15.00 |
| *—With original mix of "Never"* | | | |
| ❑ SQ-12500 | Dreamboat Annie | 1986 | 8.00 |
| ❑ SQ-12501 | Magazine | 1986 | 8.00 |
| ❑ PJ-12546 | Bad Animals | 1987 | 8.00 |
| ❑ 72435-21184-1 | Dreamboat Annie | 1999 | 15.00 |
| *—180-gram audiophile reissue* | | | |
| ❑ C1-91820 | Brigade | 1990 | 12.00 |
| ❑ R 153552 | Bad Animals | 1987 | 10.00 |
| *—BMG Direct Marketing edition* | | | |
| ❑ ST-512410 | Heart | 1985 | 15.00 |
| *—Columbia House edition; has original mix of "Never"* | | | |
| ❑ PJ-512546 | Bad Animals | 1987 | 10.00 |
| *—Columbia House edition* | | | |
| ❑ C1-591820 | Brigade | 1990 | 12.00 |
| *—Columbia House edition* | | | |

**EPIC**

| Number | Title (A Side/B Side) | Yr | NM |
|---|---|---|---|
| ❑ AS 884 [DJ] | Heart | 1980 | 20.00 |
| *—Promo-only sampler from "Greatest Hits/Live"* | | | |
| ❑ FE 36371 | Bebe Le Strange | 1980 | 10.00 |
| ❑ KE2 36888 [(2)] | Greatest Hits/Live | 1980 | 12.00 |
| ❑ FE 38049 | Private Audition | 1982 | 10.00 |
| ❑ PE 38049 | Private Audition | 1985 | 8.00 |
| ❑ PE 38800 | Passionworks | 1985 | 8.00 |
| ❑ QE 38800 | Passionworks | 1983 | 10.00 |

**MUSHROOM**

| Number | Title (A Side/B Side) | Yr | NM |
|---|---|---|---|
| ❑ MRS-1-SP [PD] | Magazine | 1978 | 20.00 |
| ❑ MRS-2-SP [PD] | Dreamboat Annie | 1978 | 25.00 |
| ❑ MRS-5005 | Dreamboat Annie | 1976 | 10.00 |
| ❑ MRS-5008 | Magazine | 1977 | 60.00 |
| *—Original issue, quickly recalled; "Magazine" is the last song on side 1; Side 2, Track 3 is "Blues Medley (Mother Earth) (You Shook Me Babe)"; at the bottom of the back cover is "Mushroom Records regrets that a contractual dispute has made it necessary to complete this record without the cooperation or endorsement of the group Heart, who have expressly disclaimed artistic involvement in completing this record."* | | | |
| ❑ MRS-5008 | Magazine | 1978 | 10.00 |
| *—Authorized edition; Side 2, Track 3 is "Mother Earth Blues"* | | | |

Heart, *Magazine,* Mushroom MRS-5008, 1977, with "contractual dispute" disclaimer on back cover, $60.

| Number | Title (A Side/B Side) | Yr | NM |
|---|---|---|---|
| **NAUTILUS** | | | |
| ❑ NR-3 | Dreamboat Annie | 1980 | 40.00 |
| *—Audiophile pressing* | | | |
| **PORTRAIT** | | | |
| ❑ JR 34799 | Little Queen | 1977 | 10.00 |
| ❑ PR 34799 | Little Queen | 1984 | 8.00 |
| ❑ FR 35555 | Dog and Butterfly | 1978 | 10.00 |
| ❑ PR 35555 | Dog and Butterfly | 1981 | 8.00 |
| ❑ HR 44799 | Little Queen | 1981 | 50.00 |
| *—Half-speed mastered edition* | | | |

### HEARTBEATS, THE

| Number | Title (A Side/B Side) | Yr | NM |
|---|---|---|---|
| **EMUS** | | | |
| ❑ ES-12033 | A Thousand Miles Away | 1979 | 25.00 |
| **ROULETTE** | | | |
| ❑ R 25107 [M] | A Thousand Miles Away | 1960 | 400.00 |

### HEARTS, THE

| Number | Title (A Side/B Side) | Yr | NM |
|---|---|---|---|
| **ZELLA** | | | |
| ❑ 337 [M] | I Feel Good | 1963 | 400.00 |

### HEARTS AND FLOWERS

| Number | Title (A Side/B Side) | Yr | NM |
|---|---|---|---|
| **CAPITOL** | | | |
| ❑ ST 2762 [S] | Now Is the Time for Hearts and Flowers | 1967 | 40.00 |
| ❑ T 2762 [M] | Now Is the Time for Hearts and Flowers | 1967 | 40.00 |
| ❑ ST 2868 | Of Horses, Kids and Forgotten Women | 1968 | 50.00 |

### HEARTS OF STONE

| Number | Title (A Side/B Side) | Yr | NM |
|---|---|---|---|
| **V.I.P.** | | | |
| ❑ VIPS-404 | Stop the World... We Wanna Get On | 1970 | 40.00 |

### HEATH, ALBERT

| Number | Title (A Side/B Side) | Yr | NM |
|---|---|---|---|
| **MUSE** | | | |
| ❑ MR-5031 | Kwanza (The First) | 1974 | 20.00 |
| **O'BE** | | | |
| ❑ LP-301 | Kawaida | 1969 | 40.00 |
| **TRIP** | | | |
| ❑ 5032 | Kawaida | 1974 | 25.00 |
| *—As "Kuumba Toudie Heath"* | | | |

### HEATH, JIMMY

| Number | Title (A Side/B Side) | Yr | NM |
|---|---|---|---|
| **RIVERSIDE** | | | |
| ❑ RLP 12-314 [M] | The Thumper | 1960 | 40.00 |
| ❑ RLP 12-333 [M] | Really Big | 1960 | 30.00 |
| ❑ RLP-372 [M] | The Quota | 1961 | 30.00 |
| ❑ RLP-400 [M] | Triple Threat | 1962 | 30.00 |
| ❑ RLP-465 [M] | Swamp Soul | 1963 | 30.00 |
| ❑ RLP-486 [M] | On the Trail | 1965 | 20.00 |
| ❑ RLP-1160 [S] | The Thumper | 1960 | 40.00 |
| ❑ RLP-1188 [S] | Really Big | 1960 | 40.00 |
| ❑ RS-9372 [S] | The Quota | 1961 | 40.00 |
| ❑ RS-9400 [S] | Triple Threat | 1962 | 40.00 |
| ❑ RS-9465 [S] | Swamp Soul | 1963 | 40.00 |
| ❑ RS-9486 [S] | On the Trail | 1965 | 25.00 |

### HEATH, TED

| Number | Title (A Side/B Side) | Yr | NM |
|---|---|---|---|
| **LONDON** | | | |
| ❑ PS 116 [S] | Hits I Missed | 1958 | 25.00 |
| ❑ PS 117 [S] | All Time Top Twelve | 1958 | 25.00 |
| *—Re-recorded version of LL 1716* | | | |
| ❑ PS 138 [S] | Swing Session | 1958 | 25.00 |
| *—New stereo recordings of the same material as appears on LL 802* | | | |
| ❑ PS 140 [S] | Ted Heath Swings in High Stereo | 1958 | 25.00 |
| ❑ PS 148 [S] | Shall We Dance | 1959 | 25.00 |
| ❑ PS 159 [S] | Great Film Hits | 1959 | 25.00 |
| ❑ PS 171 [S] | Pop Hits from the Classics | 1959 | 25.00 |
| ❑ PS 172 [S] | Big Band Blues | 1959 | 25.00 |
| ❑ PS 174 [S] | My Very Good Friends The Bandleaders | 1959 | 25.00 |
| ❑ PS 175 [S] | The Hits of the Twenties | 1960 | 20.00 |
| ❑ PS 184 [S] | The Big Band Dixie Sound | 1960 | 20.00 |
| ❑ PS 187 [S] | Ted Heath in Concert | 1960 | 20.00 |
| ❑ PS 190 [S] | Songs for the Young at Heart | 1960 | 20.00 |
| ❑ PS 216 [S] | The Hits of the Thirties | 1961 | 20.00 |
| ❑ PS 219 [S] | Latin Swingers | 1961 | 20.00 |
| ❑ LPB-340 [10] | Tempo for Dancing | 195? | 40.00 |
| ❑ LPB-374 [10] | Ted Heath and His Orchestra | 195? | 40.00 |
| ❑ LB-511 [10] | Listen to My Music | 195? | 40.00 |
| ❑ LB-732 [10] | Black and White Magic | 195? | 40.00 |
| ❑ LL 750 [M] | Ted Heath Strikes Up the Band | 1953 | 20.00 |
| ❑ LL 802 [M] | Ted Heath at the London Palladium | 1953 | 20.00 |
| ❑ LL 978 [M] | Ted Heath Plays the Music of Fats Waller | 1954 | 20.00 |
| ❑ LL 1000 [M] | The 100th London Palladium Concert | 1955 | 20.00 |
| ❑ LL 1211 [M] | Jazz Concert at the London Palladium, Vol. 3 | 1955 | 20.00 |
| ❑ LL 1217 [M] | Gershwin for Moderns | 1956 | 20.00 |
| ❑ LL 1279 [M] | Kern for Moderns | 1956 | 20.00 |
| ❑ LL 1379 [M] | Jazz Concert at the London Palladium, Vol. 4 | 1956 | 20.00 |
| ❑ LL 1475 [M] | Ted Heath Swings in Hi-Fi | 1956 | 20.00 |
| ❑ LL 1500 [M] | Rodgers for Moderns | 1956 | 20.00 |
| ❑ LL 1564 [M] | Ted Heath's First American Tour | 1956 | 20.00 |
| ❑ LL 1566 [M] | Ted Heath at Carnegie Hall | 1956 | 20.00 |
| ❑ LL 1676 [M] | A Yank in Europe | 1956 | 20.00 |
| ❑ LL 1716 [M] | All Time Top Twelve | 1957 | 20.00 |
| ❑ LL 1721 [M] | Spotlight on Sidemen | 1957 | 20.00 |
| ❑ LL 1737 [M] | Showcase | 1957 | 20.00 |
| ❑ LL 1743 [M] | Tribute to the Fabulous Dorseys | 1957 | 20.00 |
| ❑ LL 1749 [M] | Rhapsody in Blue | 1957 | 20.00 |
| ❑ LL 3047 [M] | Things to Come | 1958 | 20.00 |
| ❑ LL 3057 [M] | Hits I Missed | 1958 | 20.00 |
| ❑ LL 3058 [M] | Old English | 1958 | 20.00 |
| ❑ LL 3062 [M] | Shall We Dance | 1959 | 20.00 |
| ❑ LL 3106 [M] | Great Film Hits | 1959 | 20.00 |
| ❑ LL 3124 [M] | Pop Hits from the Classics | 1959 | 20.00 |
| ❑ LL 3125 [M] | Big Band Blues | 1959 | 20.00 |
| ❑ LL 3127 [M] | My Very Good Friends The Bandleaders | 1959 | 20.00 |

### HEATH BROTHERS, THE

| Number | Title (A Side/B Side) | Yr | NM |
|---|---|---|---|
| **STRATA-EAST** | | | |
| ❑ SES-19766 | Marchin' On | 1975 | 25.00 |

### HEATHER BLACK

| Number | Title (A Side/B Side) | Yr | NM |
|---|---|---|---|
| **AMERICAN PLAYBOY** | | | |
| ❑ 1001 | Heather Black Live | 197? | 60.00 |
| ❑ 1001 [(2)] | Heather Black Live | 197? | 150.00 |
| *—Evidently, some copies of this were 2-record sets* | | | |
| **DOUBLE BAYOU** | | | |
| ❑ 2000 | Heather Black | 197? | 30.00 |

### HEATS, THE

| Number | Title (A Side/B Side) | Yr | NM |
|---|---|---|---|
| **ALBATROSS** | | | |
| ❑ 1001 | The Heats | 1980 | 25.00 |

### HEAVY BALLOON, THE

| Number | Title (A Side/B Side) | Yr | NM |
|---|---|---|---|
| **ELEPHANT** | | | |
| ❑ EVS-104 | 32,000 Lbs. | 1969 | 70.00 |

### HEBB, BOBBY

| Number | Title (A Side/B Side) | Yr | NM |
|---|---|---|---|
| **EPIC** | | | |
| ❑ BN 26523 | Love Games | 1970 | 12.00 |
| **PHILIPS** | | | |
| ❑ PHM 200212 [M] | Sunny | 1966 | 25.00 |
| *—With "200-212" in trail-off; this record is mono* | | | |
| ❑ PHM 200212 [S] | Sunny | 1966 | 25.00 |
| *—With "2/600-212" in trail-off; this record plays stereo, though labeled mono* | | | |
| ❑ PHS 600212 [S] | Sunny | 1966 | 30.00 |

### HECKMAN, DON

| Number | Title (A Side/B Side) | Yr | NM |
|---|---|---|---|
| **ICTUS** | | | |
| ❑ 101 | Summerlin Improvisational Jazz Workshop | 1967 | 60.00 |

### HEFTI, NEAL

| Number | Title (A Side/B Side) | Yr | NM |
|---|---|---|---|
| **COLUMBIA** | | | |
| ❑ CL 1516 [M] | Light and Right | 1960 | 20.00 |
| ❑ CS 8316 [S] | Light and Right | 1960 | 25.00 |
| **CORAL** | | | |
| ❑ 7CX 2 [(2)S] | Hollywood Song Book | 1959 | 60.00 |
| ❑ CX 2 [(2)M] | Hollywood Song Book | 1959 | 40.00 |
| ❑ CRL 56083 [10] | Swingin' on a Coral Reef | 1953 | 50.00 |
| ❑ CRL 57241 [M] | Hollywood Song Book, Volume 1 | 1958 | 20.00 |
| ❑ CRL 57242 [M] | Hollywood Song Book, Volume 2 | 1958 | 20.00 |
| ❑ CRL 57256 [M] | Music U.S.A. | 1959 | 20.00 |
| ❑ CRL 757241 [S] | Hollywood Song Book, Volume 1 | 1959 | 30.00 |
| ❑ CRL 757242 [S] | Hollywood Song Book, Volume 2 | 1959 | 30.00 |
| ❑ CRL 757256 [S] | Music U.S.A. | 1959 | 30.00 |
| **EPIC** | | | |
| ❑ LG 1013 [10] | Singing Instrumentals | 1955 | 60.00 |
| ❑ LN 3113 [M] | Singing Instrumentals | 1956 | 50.00 |
| ❑ LN 3440 [M] | Singing Instrumentals | 1958 | 30.00 |
| ❑ LN 3481 [M] | Pardon My Do-Wah | 1958 | 30.00 |
| **RCA VICTOR** | | | |
| ❑ LPM-3573 [M] | Batman Theme (and 11 Other Bat-Songs) | 1966 | 50.00 |
| ❑ LSP-3573 [S] | Batman Theme (and 11 Other Bat-Songs) | 1966 | 60.00 |
| ❑ LPM-3621 [M] | Hefti in Gotham City | 1966 | 50.00 |
| ❑ LSP-3621 [S] | Hefti in Gotham City | 1966 | 60.00 |

| Number | Title (A Side/B Side) | Yr | NM |
|---|---|---|---|
| **REPRISE** | | | |
| ❑ R-6018 [M] | Themes from TV's Top 12 | 1962 | 25.00 |
| ❑ R9-6018 [S] | Themes from TV's Top 12 | 1962 | 30.00 |
| ❑ R-6039 [M] | Jazz Pops | 1962 | 20.00 |
| ❑ R9-6039 [S] | Jazz Pops | 1962 | 25.00 |
| **VIK** | | | |
| ❑ LX-1092 [M] | Concert Miniatures | 1957 | 60.00 |
| **"X"** | | | |
| ❑ LXA-3021 [10] | Music of Rudolf Frimi | 1954 | 50.00 |

### HEIFETZ, JASCHA

| Number | Title (A Side/B Side) | Yr | NM |
|---|---|---|---|
| **RCA VICTOR RED SEAL** | | | |
| ❑ LSC-1903 [S] | Brahms: Violin Concerto | 1958 | 50.00 |
| *—With Fritz Reiner/Chicago Symphony Orchestra; original with "shaded dog" label* | | | |
| ❑ LSC-1992 [S] | Beethoven: Violin Concerto in D | 1958 | 50.00 |
| *—With Charles Munch/Boston Symphony Orchestra* | | | |
| ❑ LSC-2129 [S] | Tchaikovsky: Violin Concerto | 1958 | 40.00 |
| *—With Fritz Reiner/Chicago Symphony Orchestra; original with "shaded dog" label* | | | |
| ❑ LSC-2129 [S] | Tchaikovsky: Violin Concerto | 1999 | 25.00 |
| *—Classic Records reissue* | | | |
| ❑ LSC-2314 [S] | Mendelssohn: Violin Concerto in E; Prokofiev: Violin Concerton in G | 1959 | 30.00 |
| *—With Charles Munch/Boston Symphony Orchestra* | | | |
| ❑ LSC-2435 [S] | Sibelius: Violin Concerto | 1960 | 40.00 |
| *—Originals with "shaded dog" label* | | | |
| ❑ LSC-2577 [S] | Bach: Concerto for Two Violins; Beethoven: Kreutzer Sonata | 1962 | 70.00 |
| *—Original with "shaded dog" label* | | | |
| ❑ LSC-2603 [S] | Bruch: Scottish Fantasy; Vieuxtemps; Violin Concerto No. 5 | 1962 | 50.00 |
| *—Original with "shaded dog" label* | | | |
| ❑ LSC-2652 [S] | Bruch: Violin Concerto No. 1 in G; Mozart: Violin Concerto No. 4 in D | 1962 | 60.00 |
| *—Original with "shaded dog" label* | | | |
| ❑ LSC-2734 [S] | Glazunov: Violin Concerto; Mozart: Sinfonia Concertante | 1963 | 100.00 |
| *—Original with "shaded dog" label* | | | |

### HEIFETZ, JASCHA, AND GREGOR PIATIGORSKI

| Number | Title (A Side/B Side) | Yr | NM |
|---|---|---|---|
| **RCA VICTOR RED SEAL** | | | |
| ❑ LDS-2513 [S] | Brahms: Double Concerto | 1961 | 40.00 |
| *—Originals with "shaded dog" label* | | | |

### HEIFETZ, JASCHA; WILLIAM PRIMROSE; GREGOR PIATIGORSKI

| Number | Title (A Side/B Side) | Yr | NM |
|---|---|---|---|
| **RCA VICTOR RED SEAL** | | | |
| ❑ LSC-2550 [S] | Beethoven: Serenade, op. 8; Kodaly: Duo | 1961 | 40.00 |
| *—Originals with "shaded dog" label* | | | |
| ❑ LSC-2563 [S] | Beethoven: Trio in D; Bach: Three Sinfonias; Schubert: Trio No. 2 | 1961 | 40.00 |
| *—Original with "shaded dog" label* | | | |

### HEINDORF, RAY

| Number | Title (A Side/B Side) | Yr | NM |
|---|---|---|---|
| **DCC COMPACT CLASSICS** | | | |
| ❑ LPZ-2023 | For Whom the Bell Tolls | 1996 | 25.00 |
| *—Audiophile vinyl* | | | |
| **WARNER BROS.** | | | |
| ❑ B 1201 [M] | For Whom the Bell Tolls | 1958 | 30.00 |
| *—Re-recording of 1943 movie score; the first LP on Warner Bros. Records* | | | |
| ❑ BS 1201 [S] | For Whom the Bell Tolls | 1959 | 40.00 |
| *—Gold label* | | | |
| ❑ W 1213 [M] | Spellbound | 1958 | 30.00 |
| *—Re-recording of 1945 movie score* | | | |
| ❑ WS 1213 [S] | Spellbound | 1959 | 40.00 |
| *—Gold label* | | | |

### HELL, RICHARD, AND THE VOIDOIDS

| Number | Title (A Side/B Side) | Yr | NM |
|---|---|---|---|
| **RED STAR** | | | |
| ❑ RED 801 | Destiny Street | 1982 | 15.00 |
| *—Richard Hell solo* | | | |
| **SIRE** | | | |
| ❑ SRK 6037 | Blank Generation | 1977 | 25.00 |

### HELLBORG, JONAS

| Number | Title (A Side/B Side) | Yr | NM |
|---|---|---|---|
| **DAY EIGHT** | | | |
| ❑ DEM 001 | The Bassic Thing | 1982 | 20.00 |

### HELLERS, THE

| Number | Title (A Side/B Side) | Yr | NM |
|---|---|---|---|
| **COMMAND** | | | |
| ❑ RS 934 SD | Singers, Talkers, Players, Swingers and Doers | 1968 | 40.00 |

### HELLO PEOPLE, THE

| Number | Title (A Side/B Side) | Yr | NM |
|---|---|---|---|
| **ABC** | | | |
| ❑ D-882 | Bricks | 1975 | 10.00 |
| **ABC DUNHILL** | | | |
| ❑ DS-50184 | The Handsome Devils | 1974 | 10.00 |
| **MEDIARTS** | | | |
| ❑ 41-8 | Have You Seen the Light | 1970 | 12.00 |
| **PHILIPS** | | | |
| ❑ PHS 200265 [M] | The Hello People | 1968 | 25.00 |
| *—Possibly white label promo only* | | | |
| ❑ PHS 600265 [S] | The Hello People | 1968 | 15.00 |
| ❑ PHS 600276 | Fusion | 1969 | 15.00 |

### HELM, BOB

| Number | Title (A Side/B Side) | Yr | NM |
|---|---|---|---|
| **RIVERSIDE** | | | |
| ❑ RLP-2510 [10] | Bob Helm | 1954 | 80.00 |

### HELM, BOB/LU WATTERS

| Number | Title (A Side/B Side) | Yr | NM |
|---|---|---|---|
| **RIVERSIDE** | | | |
| ❑ RLP 12-213 [M] | San Francisco Style | 1956 | 60.00 |

### HELMS, BOBBY

| Number | Title (A Side/B Side) | Yr | NM |
|---|---|---|---|
| **COLUMBIA** | | | |
| ❑ CL 2060 [M] | The Best of Bobby Helms | 1963 | 25.00 |
| ❑ CS 8860 [S] | The Best of Bobby Helms | 1963 | 30.00 |
| **DECCA** | | | |
| ❑ DL 8638 [M] | Bobby Helms Sings to My Special Angel | 1957 | 120.00 |
| **HARMONY** | | | |
| ❑ HL 7409 [M] | Fraulein | 1967 | 12.00 |
| ❑ HS 11209 [S] | Fraulein | 1967 | 12.00 |
| **KAPP** | | | |
| ❑ KL 1463 [M] | I'm the Man | 1966 | 15.00 |
| ❑ KL 1505 [M] | Sorry My Name Isn't Fred | 1966 | 15.00 |
| ❑ KS 3463 [S] | I'm the Man | 1966 | 20.00 |
| ❑ KS 3505 [S] | Sorry My Name Isn't Fred | 1966 | 20.00 |
| **LITTLE DARLIN'** | | | |
| ❑ 8088 | All New Just for You | 1968 | 25.00 |
| **MISTLETOE** | | | |
| ❑ MLP-1206 | Jingle Bell Rock | 197? | 12.00 |
| **POWER PAK** | | | |
| ❑ 283 | Greatest Hits | 197? | 10.00 |
| **VOCALION** | | | |
| ❑ VL 3743 [M] | Someone Already There | 1965 | 15.00 |
| ❑ VL 73743 [R] | Someone Already There | 1965 | 12.00 |
| ❑ VL 73874 | My Special Angel | 1969 | 12.00 |

### HELMS, DON

| Number | Title (A Side/B Side) | Yr | NM |
|---|---|---|---|
| **SMASH** | | | |
| ❑ MGS-27001 [M] | The Steel Guitar Sounds of Hank Williams | 1962 | 20.00 |
| ❑ MGS-27019 [M] | Don Helms' Steel Guitar | 1962 | 20.00 |
| ❑ SRS-67001 [S] | The Steel Guitar Sounds of Hank Williams | 1962 | 25.00 |
| ❑ SRS-67019 [S] | Don Helms' Steel Guitar | 1962 | 25.00 |

### HELP

| Number | Title (A Side/B Side) | Yr | NM |
|---|---|---|---|
| **DECCA** | | | |
| ❑ DL 75257 | Help | 1970 | 30.00 |
| ❑ DL 75304 | Second Coming | 1971 | 30.00 |

### HEMPHILL, JULIUS

| Number | Title (A Side/B Side) | Yr | NM |
|---|---|---|---|
| **ARISTA FREEDOM** | | | |
| ❑ AL 1012 | 'Coon Bid'ness | 1975 | 20.00 |
| ❑ AL 1028 | Dogon A.D. | 1976 | 25.00 |
| **MBARI** | | | |
| ❑ (# unknown) | 'Coon Bid'ness | 1974 | 40.00 |
| ❑ (# unknown) [(2)] | Blue Boye | 1977 | 60.00 |
| ❑ 5001 | Dogon A.D. | 1972 | 50.00 |

### HENDERSON, BILL

| Number | Title (A Side/B Side) | Yr | NM |
|---|---|---|---|
| **MGM** | | | |
| ❑ E-4128 [M] | Bill Henderson with the Oscar Peterson Trio | 1963 | 25.00 |
| ❑ SE-4128 [S] | Bill Henderson with the Oscar Peterson Trio | 1963 | 30.00 |
| **VEE JAY** | | | |
| ❑ LP-1015 [M] | Bill Henderson Sings | 1959 | 25.00 |
| ❑ SR-1015 [S] | Bill Henderson Sings | 1959 | 40.00 |
| ❑ LP-1031 [M] | Bill Henderson | 1961 | 25.00 |
| ❑ SR-1031 [S] | Bill Henderson | 1961 | 40.00 |
| **VERVE** | | | |
| ❑ V-8619 [M] | When My Dreamboat Comes Home | 1965 | 20.00 |
| ❑ V6-8619 [S] | When My Dreamboat Comes Home | 1965 | 25.00 |

### HENDERSON, BOBBY

| Number | Title (A Side/B Side) | Yr | NM |
|---|---|---|---|
| **HALCYON** | | | |
| ❑ 102 | Home in the Clouds | 1970 | 20.00 |
| **VANGUARD** | | | |
| ❑ VRS-8511 [M] | Handful of Keys | 1955 | 40.00 |

### HENDERSON, BUGS

| Number | Title (A Side/B Side) | Yr | NM |
|---|---|---|---|
| **ARMADILLO** | | | |
| ❑ LP-78-1 | The Bugs Henderson Group At Last | 1978 | 40.00 |

### HENDERSON, EDDIE

| Number | Title (A Side/B Side) | Yr | NM |
|---|---|---|---|
| **BLUE NOTE** | | | |
| ❑ BN-LA464-G | Sunburst | 1975 | 20.00 |
| ❑ BN-LA636-G | Heritage | 1976 | 20.00 |

### HENDERSON, FLETCHER

| Number | Title (A Side/B Side) | Yr | NM |
|---|---|---|---|
| **COLUMBIA** | | | |
| ❑ C4L 19 [(4)M] | The Fletcher Henderson Story | 1961 | 100.00 |
| *—Box set with booklet; red and black labels with six "eye" logos* | | | |
| ❑ C4L 19 [(4)M] | The Fletcher Henderson Story | 1963 | 50.00 |
| *—Red "Guaranteed High Fidelity" labels* | | | |
| ❑ C4L 19 [(4)M] | The Fletcher Henderson Story | 1966 | 30.00 |
| *—Red "360 Sound Mono" labels* | | | |
| **DECCA** | | | |
| ❑ DL 6025 [10] | Fletcher Henderson Memorial Album | 1952 | 150.00 |
| ❑ DL 9227 [M] | Fletcher Henderson: First Impression (Vol. 1 1924-1931) | 1958 | 50.00 |
| *—Black label, silver print* | | | |
| ❑ DL 9227 [M] | Fletcher Henderson: First Impression (Vol. 1 1924-1931) | 1961 | 30.00 |
| *—Black label with color bars* | | | |
| ❑ DL 9228 [M] | Fletcher Henderson: The Swing's the Thing (Vol. 2 1931-1934) | 1958 | 50.00 |
| *—Black label, silver print* | | | |
| ❑ DL 9228 [M] | Fletcher Henderson: The Swing's the Thing (Vol. 2 1931-1934) | 1961 | 30.00 |
| *—Black label with color bars* | | | |
| **HISTORICAL** | | | |
| ❑ 13 | Fletcher Henderson 1923-24 | 1967 | 20.00 |
| ❑ 18 | Fletcher Henderson Volume 2: 1923-25 | 1967 | 20.00 |
| **JAZZTONE** | | | |
| ❑ J-1285 [M] | The Big Reunion | 1958 | 30.00 |
| **MILESTONE** | | | |
| ❑ M-2005 | The Immortal Fletcher Henderson | 196? | 25.00 |
| **RIVERSIDE** | | | |
| ❑ RLP-1055 [10] | Fletcher Henderson | 1954 | 150.00 |
| **SUTTON** | | | |
| ❑ SSL-286 [M] | Fletcher Henderson with Slam Stewart | 195? | 25.00 |
| **"X"** | | | |
| ❑ LVA-3013 [10] | Fletcher Henderson and His Connie's Inn Orchestra | 1954 | 150.00 |

### HENDERSON, JOE

| Number | Title (A Side/B Side) | Yr | NM |
|---|---|---|---|
| **BLUE NOTE** | | | |
| ❑ BLP-4140 [M] | Page One | 1963 | 25.00 |
| ❑ BLP-4152 [M] | Our Thing | 1963 | 25.00 |
| ❑ BLP-4166 [M] | In 'n Out | 1964 | 25.00 |
| ❑ BLP-4189 [M] | Inner Urge | 1965 | 25.00 |
| ❑ BLP-4227 [M] | Mode for Joe | 1966 | 25.00 |
| ❑ BST-84140 [S] | Page One | 1963 | 30.00 |
| *—"New York, USA" address on label* | | | |
| ❑ BST-84152 [S] | Our Thing | 1963 | 30.00 |
| *—"New York, USA" address on label* | | | |
| ❑ BST-84166 [S] | In 'n Out | 1964 | 30.00 |
| *—"New York, USA" address on label* | | | |
| ❑ BST-84189 [S] | Inner Urge | 1965 | 30.00 |
| *—"New York, USA" address on label* | | | |
| ❑ BST-84227 [S] | Mode for Joe | 1966 | 30.00 |
| *—"New York, USA" address on label* | | | |
| **FONTANA** | | | |
| ❑ SRF-67590 | Hits, Hits, Hits! | 1969 | 30.00 |
| **MILESTONE** | | | |
| ❑ M-9008 | The Kicker | 1968 | 20.00 |
| ❑ M-9017 | Tetragon | 1969 | 20.00 |
| ❑ M-9024 | Power to the People | 1970 | 20.00 |
| ❑ M-9028 | If You're Not Part | 1970 | 20.00 |
| ❑ M-9034 | In Pursuit of Blackness | 1971 | 20.00 |
| ❑ M-9040 | Black Is the Color | 1972 | 20.00 |
| ❑ M-9047 | Joe Henderson In Japan | 1972 | 20.00 |
| **TODD** | | | |
| ❑ MT-2701 [M] | Snap Your Fingers | 1962 | 50.00 |
| ❑ ST-2701 [S] | Snap Your Fingers | 1962 | 70.00 |

### HENDERSON, SKITCH

| Number | Title (A Side/B Side) | Yr | NM |
|---|---|---|---|
| **CAPITOL** | | | |
| ❑ H 110 [10] | Keyboard Sketches | 1950 | 50.00 |

### HENDRICKS, JON

| Number | Title (A Side/B Side) | Yr | NM |
|---|---|---|---|
| **COLUMBIA** | | | |
| ❑ CL 1583 [M] | Evolution of the Blues | 1961 | 30.00 |
| ❑ CL 1805 [M] | Fast Livin' Blues | 1962 | 30.00 |
| ❑ CS 8383 [S] | Evolution of the Blues | 1961 | 40.00 |
| ❑ CS 8605 [S] | Fast Livin' Blues | 1962 | 40.00 |
| **REPRISE** | | | |
| ❑ R-6089 [M] | Salud! | 1964 | 25.00 |
| ❑ R9-6089 [S] | Salud! | 1964 | 30.00 |
| **SMASH** | | | |
| ❑ MGS-27069 [M] | Recorded In Person at the Trident | 1963 | 25.00 |
| ❑ SRS-67069 [S] | Recorded In Person at the Trident | 1963 | 30.00 |

Jimi Hendrix, *Rainbow Bridge,* Reprise MS 2040, 1971, $20.

| Number | Title (A Side/B Side) | Yr | NM |
|---|---|---|---|
| **WORLD PACIFIC** | | | |
| ❑ WP-1283 [M] | A Good Git-Together | 1959 | 80.00 |

**HENDRIX, JIMI**

| Number | Title (A Side/B Side) | Yr | NM |
|---|---|---|---|
| **ACCORD** | | | |
| ❑ SN-7101 | Kaleidoscope | 1981 | 10.00 |
| ❑ SN-7112 | Before London | 1981 | 10.00 |
| ❑ SN-7139 | Cosmic Feeling | 1981 | 10.00 |
| **CAPITOL** | | | |
| ❑ STAO-472 | Band of Gypsys | 1970 | 20.00 |
| ❑ SWBB-659 [(2)] | Get That Feeling/Flashing | 1971 | 25.00 |
| ❑ ST 2856 [S] | Get That Feeling | 1967 | 40.00 |
| ❑ T 2856 [M] | Get That Feeling | 1967 | 80.00 |
| ❑ ST 2894 [S] | Flashing | 1968 | 40.00 |
| ❑ T 2894 [M] | Flashing | 1968 | 100.00 |
| ❑ SJ-12416 | Band of Gypsys 2 | 1986 | 10.00 |
| *—Side 2 lists, and plays, three songs* | | | |
| ❑ SJ-12416 | Band of Gypsys 2 | 1986 | 150.00 |
| *—Side 2 lists three songs, but plays four completely different songs. Four bands are visible on the record.* | | | |
| ❑ MLP-15022 [EP] | Johnny B. Goode | 1986 | 8.00 |
| ❑ SN-16319 | Band of Gypsys | 1985 | 10.00 |
| *—Budget-line reissue* | | | |
| ❑ C1-96414 | Band of Gypsys | 1995 | 15.00 |
| *—Numbered reissue* | | | |
| **EXPERIENCE HENDRIX/CAPITOL** | | | |
| ❑ ST-472 | Band of Gypsys | 1997 | 25.00 |
| *—Limited edition on "heavy vinyl" with booklet; distributed by Classic Records* | | | |
| **EXPERIENCE HENDRIX/CLASSIC** | | | |
| ❑ B0000698-01 [(2)] | Martin Scorsese Presents the Blues: Jimi Hendrix | 2004 | 40.00 |
| *—Regular edition on black vinyl* | | | |
| ❑ B0000698-01 [(2)] | Martin Scorsese Presents the Blues: Jimi Hendrix | 2004 | 50.00 |
| *—Limited edition of 1,000 on blue vinyl* | | | |
| ❑ RTH 2006 [(2)] | Blues | 2002 | 60.00 |
| *—Limited edition on 200-gram blue vinyl* | | | |
| ❑ RTH 2006 [(2)] | Blues | 2003 | 40.00 |
| *—Limited edition on 200-gram black vinyl* | | | |
| ❑ RTH-2016 [(4)] | Voodoo Child: The Jimi Hendrix Collection | 2005 | 40.00 |
| *—Box set; red vinyl* | | | |
| ❑ RTH-2016 [(4)] | Voodoo Child: The Jimi Hendrix Collection | 2005 | 80.00 |
| *—Black 200-gram vinyl* | | | |

| Number | Title (A Side/B Side) | Yr | NM |
|---|---|---|---|
| **EXPERIENCE HENDRIX/MCA** | | | |
| ❑ B0001159-01 [(2)] | Live at Berkeley | 2003 | 25.00 |
| ❑ 11599 [(2)] | First Rays of the New Rising Sun | 1997 | 50.00 |
| *—Limited edition on "heavy vinyl" with booklet* | | | |
| ❑ 11600 [(2)] | Electric Ladyland | 1997 | 40.00 |
| *—Limited edition on "heavy vinyl" with booklet* | | | |
| ❑ 11601 | Axis: Bold As Love | 1997 | 50.00 |
| *—Limited edition on "heavy vinyl" with booklet* | | | |
| ❑ 11602 [(2)] | Are You Experienced? | 1997 | 50.00 |
| *—Limited edition on "heavy vinyl" with booklet* | | | |
| ❑ 11607 | Band of Gypsys | 1997 | 25.00 |
| *—Limited edition on "heavy vinyl" with booklet; pressed in U.S. for export to Europe* | | | |
| ❑ 11608 | Are You Experienced? | 1997 | 40.00 |
| *—Limited edition on "heavy vinyl" with booklet; pressed in U.S. for export to Europe; has different cover than US version* | | | |
| ❑ 11671 [(2)] | Experience Hendrix: The Best of Jimi Hendrix | 1998 | 25.00 |
| *—Despite lower number, was released after South Saturn Delta* | | | |
| ❑ 11684 [(2)] | South Saturn Delta | 1997 | 25.00 |
| *—Numbered, limited edition on "heavy vinyl"* | | | |
| ❑ 11742 [(3)] | BBC Sessions | 1998 | 30.00 |
| ❑ 11931 [(3)] | Live at the Fillmore East | 1999 | 30.00 |
| ❑ 11987 [(3)] | Live at Woodstock | 1999 | 30.00 |
| ❑ 112316 [(8)] | The Jimi Hendrix Experience | 2000 | 70.00 |
| *—Limited edition of 5,000 in purple felt box* | | | |
| ❑ 112984 | Smash Hits | 2002 | 15.00 |
| *—Limited edition on "heavy vinyl"* | | | |
| ❑ 113086-1 [(3)] | Blue Wild Angel: Jimi Hendrix Live at the Isle of Wight | 2002 | 40.00 |
| **NUTMEG** | | | |
| ❑ 1001 | High, Live 'N' Dirty | 1978 | 25.00 |
| *—Black vinyl* | | | |
| ❑ 1001 | High, Live 'N' Dirty | 1978 | 25.00 |
| *—Red vinyl* | | | |
| ❑ 1002 | Cosmic Turnaround | 1981 | 12.00 |
| **PHOENIX 10** | | | |
| ❑ PHX 320 | Rare Hendrix | 1981 | 8.00 |
| ❑ PHX 324 | Roots of Hendrix | 1981 | 8.00 |
| **PICKWICK** | | | |
| ❑ SPC-3528 | Jimi | 197? | 10.00 |
| **REPRISE** | | | |
| ❑ MS 2025 | Smash Hits | 1969 | 40.00 |
| *—With "W7" and "r:" logos on two-tone orange label* | | | |
| ❑ MS 2025 | Smash Hits Bonus Poster | 1969 | 40.00 |

| Number | Title (A Side/B Side) | Yr | NM |
|---|---|---|---|
| ❑ MS 2025 | Smash Hits | 1970 | 12.00 |
| *—With only "r:" logo on all-orange (tan) label* | | | |
| ❑ MS 2025 | Smash Hits | 198? | 8.00 |
| *—Red and black label or gold and light blue label* | | | |
| ❑ MS 2029 | Historic Performances As Recorded at the Monterey International Pop Festival | 1970 | 20.00 |
| *—Side 1: Jimi Hendrix; Side 2: Otis Redding; with only "r:" logo on all-orange (tan) label* | | | |
| ❑ MS 2029 | Historic Performances As Recorded at the Monterey International Pop Festival | 1970 | 200.00 |
| *—Side 1: Jimi Hendrix; Side 2: Otis Redding; with "W7" and "r:" logos on two-tone orange label* | | | |
| ❑ MS 2034 | The Cry of Love | 1971 | 15.00 |
| *—With only "r:" logo on all-orange (tan) label* | | | |
| ❑ MS 2034 | The Cry of Love | 1971 | 500.00 |
| *—With "W7" and "r:" logos on two-tone orange label* | | | |
| ❑ MS 2040 | Rainbow Bridge | 1971 | 20.00 |
| ❑ MS 2049 | Hendrix in the West | 1972 | 20.00 |
| ❑ MS 2103 | War Heroes | 1972 | 20.00 |
| ❑ MS 2204 | Crash Landing | 1975 | 15.00 |
| ❑ MS 2229 | Midnight Lightning | 1975 | 15.00 |
| ❑ 2RS 2245 [(2)] | The Essential Jimi Hendrix | 1978 | 20.00 |
| ❑ MSK 2276 | Smash Hits | 1977 | 10.00 |
| *—Reissue* | | | |
| ❑ HS 2293 | The Essential Jimi Hendrix Volume Two | 1979 | 15.00 |
| *—Add 100% if bonus single of "Gloria" with picture sleeve is enclosed* | | | |
| ❑ HS 2299 | Nine to the Universe | 1980 | 10.00 |
| ❑ R 6261 [M] | Are You Experienced? | 1967 | 200.00 |
| ❑ RS 6261 [S] | Are You Experienced? | 1967 | 50.00 |
| *—Pink, gold and green label* | | | |
| ❑ RS 6261 [S] | Are You Experienced? | 1968 | 25.00 |
| *—With "W7" and "r:" logos on two-tone orange label* | | | |
| ❑ RS 6261 [S] | Are You Experienced? | 1970 | 12.00 |
| *—With only "r:" logo on all-orange (tan) label* | | | |
| ❑ RS 6261 [S] | Are You Experienced? | 198? | 8.00 |
| *—Red and black label or gold and light blue label* | | | |
| ❑ R 6281 [M] | Axis: Bold As Love | 1968 | 2500. |
| ❑ RS 6281 [S] | Axis: Bold As Love | 1968 | 25.00 |
| *—With "W7" and "r:" logos on two-tone orange label* | | | |
| ❑ RS 6281 [S] | Axis: Bold As Love | 1968 | 80.00 |
| *—Pink, gold and green label* | | | |
| ❑ RS 6281 [S] | Axis: Bold As Love | 1970 | 12.00 |
| *—With only "r:" logo on all-orange (tan) label* | | | |
| ❑ RS 6281 [S] | Axis: Bold As Love | 198? | 8.00 |
| *—Red and black label or gold and light blue label* | | | |
| ❑ 2R 6307 [(2)M] | Electric Ladyland | 1968 | 4000. |
| *—Mono is promo only; VG value 2000; VG+ value 3000* | | | |
| ❑ 2RS 6307 [(2)S] | Electric Ladyland | 1968 | 100.00 |
| *—With "W7" and "r:" logos on two-tone orange label* | | | |
| ❑ 2RS 6307 [(2)S] | Electric Ladyland | 1970 | 15.00 |
| *—With only "r:" logo on all-orange (tan) label* | | | |
| ❑ 2RS 6307 [(2)S] | Electric Ladyland | 198? | 12.00 |
| *—Red and black label or gold and light blue label* | | | |
| ❑ 2RS 6481 [(2)] | Soundtrack Recordings from the Film Jimi Hendrix | 1973 | 25.00 |
| ❑ 22306 [(2)] | The Jimi Hendrix Concerts | 1982 | 12.00 |
| ❑ 25119 | Kiss the Sky | 1984 | 10.00 |
| ❑ 25358 | Jimi Plays Monterey | 1986 | 10.00 |
| ❑ SKAO-91441 | Axis: Bold As Love | 1968 | 40.00 |
| *—Capitol Record Club edition; two-tone orange label with "W7" and "r:" at top* | | | |
| ❑ STBO-91568 [(2)] | Electric Ladyland | 1968 | 150.00 |
| *—Capitol Record Club edition* | | | |
| ❑ SMAS-93467 | The Cry of Love | 1971 | 60.00 |
| *—Capitol Record Club edition* | | | |
| ❑ SMAS-93972 | Rainbow Bridge | 1971 | 50.00 |
| *—Capitol Record Club edition* | | | |
| **RHINO** | | | |
| ❑ RNDF-254 [PD] | The Jimi Hendrix Interview | 1982 | 25.00 |
| **RYKO ANALOGUE** | | | |
| ❑ RALP-0038 [(2)] | Live at Winterland | 1988 | 15.00 |
| ❑ RALP-0078 [(2)] | Radio One | 1988 | 15.00 |
| *—Clear vinyl* | | | |
| **SPRINGBOARD** | | | |
| ❑ SPB-4010 | Jimi Hendrix | 197? | 10.00 |
| **TRACK** | | | |
| ❑ 612003 [M] | Axis: Bold As Love | 2000 | 25.00 |
| *—Classic Records issue of the original U.K. mono mix, on a reproduction of the original British label* | | | |
| **TRIP** | | | |
| ❑ 3509 [(2)] | Superpak | 197? | 15.00 |
| ❑ TLP-9500 | Rare Hendrix | 1972 | 15.00 |
| ❑ TLP-9501 | Roots of Hendrix | 1972 | 12.00 |
| ❑ TLP-9512 | Moods | 1973 | 12.00 |
| ❑ TLP-9523 | The Genius of Jimi Hendrix | 1973 | 12.00 |
| **UNITED ARTISTS** | | | |
| ❑ UA-LA505-E | The Very Best of Jimi Hendrix | 1975 | 12.00 |
| **WARNER BROS.** | | | |
| ❑ HS 2299 | Nine to the Universe | 1980 | 12.00 |
| *—Reprise cover, Warner Bros. tan "pinstripe" label; possibly Columbia House edition?* | | | |

**HENDRIX, JIMI, AND LONNIE YOUNGBLOOD**

| Number | Title (A Side/B Side) | Yr | NM |
|---|---|---|---|
| **MAPLE** | | | |
| ❑ 6004 | Two Great Experiences Together | 1971 | 50.00 |

### HENKE, MEL

**CONTEMPORARY**

| Number | Title (A Side/B Side) | Yr | NM |
|---|---|---|---|
| ❑ C-5001 [M] | Dig Mel Henke | 1955 | 50.00 |
| ❑ C-5003 [M] | Now Spin This | 1956 | 50.00 |

**WARNER BROS.**

| Number | Title (A Side/B Side) | Yr | NM |
|---|---|---|---|
| ❑ W 1472 [M] | La Dolce Henke | 1962 | 40.00 |
| ❑ WS 1472 [S] | La Dolce Henke | 1962 | 50.00 |

### HENRIQUE, LUIZ

**FONTANA**

| Number | Title (A Side/B Side) | Yr | NM |
|---|---|---|---|
| ❑ MGF-27553 [M] | Listen to Me | 1966 | 20.00 |
| ❑ SRF-67553 [S] | Listen to Me | 1966 | 25.00 |

**VERVE**

| Number | Title (A Side/B Side) | Yr | NM |
|---|---|---|---|
| ❑ V-8697 [M] | Barra Limpa | 1967 | 30.00 |
| ❑ V6-8697 [S] | Barra Limpa | 1967 | 20.00 |

### HENRY, CLARENCE

**ARGO**

| Number | Title (A Side/B Side) | Yr | NM |
|---|---|---|---|
| ❑ LP-4009 [M] | You Always Hurt the One You Love | 1961 | 250.00 |

**CADET**

| Number | Title (A Side/B Side) | Yr | NM |
|---|---|---|---|
| ❑ LP-4009 [M] | You Always Hurt the One You Love | 1966 | 50.00 |

*—Includes copies of Cadet LP in Argo sleeves*

**ROULETTE**

| Number | Title (A Side/B Side) | Yr | NM |
|---|---|---|---|
| ❑ SR 42039 | Alive and Well and Living in New Orleans | 1969 | 25.00 |

### HENRY, ERNIE

**RIVERSIDE**

| Number | Title (A Side/B Side) | Yr | NM |
|---|---|---|---|
| ❑ RLP 12-222 [M] | Presenting Ernie Henry | 1956 | 180.00 |

### HENRY TREE

**MAINSTREAM**

| Number | Title (A Side/B Side) | Yr | NM |
|---|---|---|---|
| ❑ S-6129 | Electric Holy Man | 1968 | 30.00 |

### HENSKE, JUDY

**ELEKTRA**

| Number | Title (A Side/B Side) | Yr | NM |
|---|---|---|---|
| ❑ EKL-231 [M] | Judy Henske | 1963 | 20.00 |
| ❑ EKL-241 [M] | High Flying Bird | 1964 | 20.00 |
| ❑ EKS-7231 [S] | Judy Henske | 1963 | 25.00 |
| ❑ EKL-7241 [S] | High Flying Bird | 1964 | 25.00 |

**MERCURY**

| Number | Title (A Side/B Side) | Yr | NM |
|---|---|---|---|
| ❑ MG-21010 [M] | Little Bit of Sunshine…Little Bit of Rain | 1965 | 20.00 |
| ❑ SR-61010 [S] | Little Bit of Sunshine…Little Bit of Rain | 1965 | 25.00 |

**REPRISE**

| Number | Title (A Side/B Side) | Yr | NM |
|---|---|---|---|
| ❑ R-6203 [M] | The Death Defying Judy Henske: The First Concert Album | 1966 | 20.00 |
| ❑ RS-6203 [S] | The Death Defying Judy Henske: The First Concert Album | 1966 | 25.00 |

### HENSKE, JUDY, AND JERRY YESTER

**REPRISE**

| Number | Title (A Side/B Side) | Yr | NM |
|---|---|---|---|
| ❑ RS-6388 | Farewell Aldebaran | 1969 | 20.00 |

**STRAIGHT**

| Number | Title (A Side/B Side) | Yr | NM |
|---|---|---|---|
| ❑ STS-1052 | Farewell Aldebaran | 1968 | 30.00 |

### HENSLEY, WALTER

**CAPITOL**

| Number | Title (A Side/B Side) | Yr | NM |
|---|---|---|---|
| ❑ ST 2149 [S] | The Five-String Banjo Today | 1964 | 20.00 |
| ❑ T 2149 [M] | The Five-String Banjo Today | 1964 | 15.00 |

### HERBERT, MORT

**SAVOY**

| Number | Title (A Side/B Side) | Yr | NM |
|---|---|---|---|
| ❑ MG-12073 [M] | Night People | 1956 | 40.00 |

### HERD, THE

**FONTANA**

| Number | Title (A Side/B Side) | Yr | NM |
|---|---|---|---|
| ❑ SRF-67579 | Lookin' Thru You | 1968 | 25.00 |

### HERDSMEN, THE

**FANTASY**

| Number | Title (A Side/B Side) | Yr | NM |
|---|---|---|---|
| ❑ 3201 [M] | The Herdsmen Play Paris | 1955 | 40.00 |

*—Black vinyl*

| Number | Title (A Side/B Side) | Yr | NM |
|---|---|---|---|
| ❑ 3201 [M] | The Herdsmen Play Paris | 1955 | 80.00 |

*—Green vinyl*

### HERMAN, JERRY

**UNITED ARTISTS**

| Number | Title (A Side/B Side) | Yr | NM |
|---|---|---|---|
| ❑ UAL-3432 [M] | Hello, Jerry! | 1965 | 20.00 |
| ❑ UAS-6432 [S] | Hello, Jerry! | 1965 | 25.00 |

### HERMAN, WOODY

**AMERICAN RECORDING SOCIETY**

| Number | Title (A Side/B Side) | Yr | NM |
|---|---|---|---|
| ❑ G-410 [M] | The Progressive Big Band Sound | 1956 | 40.00 |

**ATLANTIC**

| Number | Title (A Side/B Side) | Yr | NM |
|---|---|---|---|
| ❑ 1328 [M] | Woody Herman at the Monterey Jazz Festival | 1960 | 40.00 |
| ❑ SD 1328 [S] | Woody Herman at the Monterey Jazz Festival | 1960 | 30.00 |

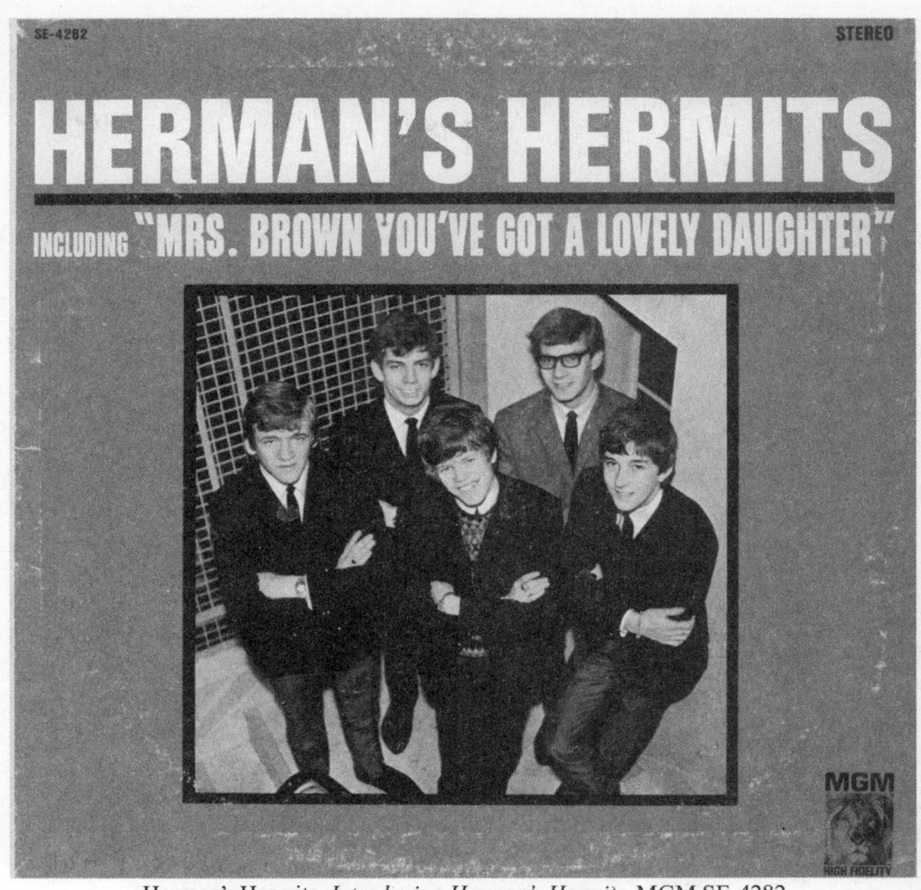


Herman's Hermits, *Introducing Herman's Hermits,* MGM SE-4282, 1965, mono, "Mrs. Brown You've Got a Lovely Daughter" mentioned on front cover, $15.

**BRUNSWICK**

| Number | Title (A Side/B Side) | Yr | NM |
|---|---|---|---|
| ❑ BL 54024 [M] | The Swinging Herman Herd | 1957 | 40.00 |

**CAPITOL**

| Number | Title (A Side/B Side) | Yr | NM |
|---|---|---|---|
| ❑ H 324 [10] | Classics in Jazz | 1952 | 70.00 |
| ❑ T 324 [M] | Classics in Jazz | 1955 | 40.00 |
| ❑ T 560 [M] | The Woody Herman Band | 1955 | 40.00 |
| ❑ T 658 [M] | Road Band | 1955 | 40.00 |
| ❑ T 748 [M] | Jackpot! | 1956 | 40.00 |
| ❑ T 784 [M] | Blues Groove | 1956 | 40.00 |
| ❑ T 1554 [M] | The Hits of Woody Herman | 1961 | 20.00 |

**CENTURY**

| Number | Title (A Side/B Side) | Yr | NM |
|---|---|---|---|
| ❑ CRDD-1080 | Road Father | 1979 | 25.00 |

*—Direct-to-disc recording*

**CLEF**

| Number | Title (A Side/B Side) | Yr | NM |
|---|---|---|---|
| ❑ MGC-745 [M] | Jazz, the Utmost! | 1956 | 80.00 |

**COLUMBIA**

| Number | Title (A Side/B Side) | Yr | NM |
|---|---|---|---|
| ❑ C3L 25 [(3)M] | The Thundering Herds | 1963 | 50.00 |
| ❑ CL 592 [M] | The Three Herds | 1955 | 50.00 |

*—Maroon label with gold print*

| Number | Title (A Side/B Side) | Yr | NM |
|---|---|---|---|
| ❑ CL 592 [M] | The Three Herds | 1956 | 30.00 |

*—Red and black label with six "eye" logos*

| Number | Title (A Side/B Side) | Yr | NM |
|---|---|---|---|
| ❑ CL 651 [M] | Music for Tired Lovers | 1955 | 40.00 |
| ❑ CL 683 [M] | Twelve Shades of Blue | 1956 | 30.00 |
| ❑ CL 2509 [10] | Ridin' Herd | 1955 | 60.00 |
| ❑ CL 2563 [10] | Woody! | 1955 | 60.00 |
| ❑ CL 6026 [10] | Sequence in Jazz | 1949 | 70.00 |
| ❑ CL 6049 [10] | Dance Parade | 1949 | 70.00 |
| ❑ CL 6092 [10] | Woody Herman and His Woodchoppers | 1950 | 70.00 |

**CORAL**

| Number | Title (A Side/B Side) | Yr | NM |
|---|---|---|---|
| ❑ CRL 56005 [10] | Blue Prelude | 1950 | 70.00 |
| ❑ CRL 56010 [10] | Woody Herman Souvenirs | 1950 | 70.00 |
| ❑ CRL 56090 [10] | Woody's Best | 1953 | 70.00 |

**CROWN**

| Number | Title (A Side/B Side) | Yr | NM |
|---|---|---|---|
| ❑ CST 205 [S] | The New Swingin' Herman Herd | 1960 | 20.00 |
| ❑ CLP 5180 [M] | The New Swingin' Herman Band | 1960 | 20.00 |

**DECCA**

| Number | Title (A Side/B Side) | Yr | NM |
|---|---|---|---|
| ❑ DL 8133 [M] | Woodchopper's Ball | 1955 | 40.00 |

**DIAL**

| Number | Title (A Side/B Side) | Yr | NM |
|---|---|---|---|
| ❑ LP-210 [10] | Swinging with the Woodchoppers | 1950 | 150.00 |

**EVEREST**

| Number | Title (A Side/B Side) | Yr | NM |
|---|---|---|---|
| ❑ SDBR-1003 [S] | The Herd Rides Again…In Stereo | 1958 | 40.00 |
| ❑ SDBR-1032 [S] | Moody Woody | 1958 | 40.00 |
| ❑ LPBR-5003 [M] | The Herd Rides Again | 1958 | 30.00 |
| ❑ LPBR-5032 [M] | Moody Woody | 1958 | 30.00 |

**FANTASY**

| Number | Title (A Side/B Side) | Yr | NM |
|---|---|---|---|
| ❑ FPM-4003 [Q] | Children of Lima | 1975 | 20.00 |

**FORUM**

| Number | Title (A Side/B Side) | Yr | NM |
|---|---|---|---|
| ❑ F-9016 [M] | Woody Herman Sextet at the Round Table | 196? | 20.00 |
| ❑ FS-9016 [S] | Woody Herman Sextet at the Round Table | 196? | 25.00 |

**HARMONY**

| Number | Title (A Side/B Side) | Yr | NM |
|---|---|---|---|
| ❑ HL 7013 [M] | Bijou | 1957 | 20.00 |
| ❑ HL 7093 [M] | Summer Sequence | 1957 | 20.00 |

**JAZZLAND**

| Number | Title (A Side/B Side) | Yr | NM |
|---|---|---|---|
| ❑ JLP-17 [M] | The Fourth Herd | 1960 | 25.00 |
| ❑ JLP-917 [S] | The Fourth Herd | 1960 | 25.00 |

**LION**

| Number | Title (A Side/B Side) | Yr | NM |
|---|---|---|---|
| ❑ L-70059 [M] | The Herman Herd at Carnegie Hall | 1958 | 25.00 |

**MARS**

| Number | Title (A Side/B Side) | Yr | NM |
|---|---|---|---|
| ❑ MRX-1 [10] | Dance Date on Mars | 1952 | 250.00 |
| ❑ MRX-2 [10] | Woody Herman Goes Native | 1953 | 250.00 |

**MGM**

| Number | Title (A Side/B Side) | Yr | NM |
|---|---|---|---|
| ❑ E-158 [10] | Woody Herman at Carnegie Hall, 1946, Vol. 1 | 1952 | 70.00 |
| ❑ E-159 [10] | Woody Herman at Carnegie Hall, 1946, Vol. 2 | 1952 | 70.00 |
| ❑ E-192 [10] | The Third Herd | 1953 | 70.00 |
| ❑ E-284 [10] | Blue Flame | 1955 | 70.00 |
| ❑ E-3043 [M] | Carnegie Hall 1946 | 1953 | 50.00 |

*—Compiles 158 and 159 on one 12-inch LP*

| Number | Title (A Side/B Side) | Yr | NM |
|---|---|---|---|
| ❑ E-3385 [M] | Hi-Fi-ing Herd | 1956 | 40.00 |

**MOBILE FIDELITY**

| Number | Title (A Side/B Side) | Yr | NM |
|---|---|---|---|
| ❑ 1-219 | The Fourth Herd | 1994 | 30.00 |

*—Audiophile vinyl*

| Number | Title (A Side/B Side) | Yr | NM |
|---|---|---|---|
| **PHILIPS** | | | |
| ❑ PHS 600065 [S] | Woody Herman 1963 | 1963 | 20.00 |
| ❑ PHS 600092 [S] | Encore: Woody Herman 1963 | 1963 | 20.00 |
| ❑ PHS 600118 [S] | Woody Herman: 1964 | 1964 | 20.00 |
| ❑ PHS 600131 [S] | The Swinging Herman Herd Recorded Live | 1964 | 20.00 |
| ❑ PHS 600171 [S] | Woody's Big Band Goodies | 1965 | 20.00 |
| **ROULETTE** | | | |
| ❑ R 25067 [M] | Woody Herman Sextet at the Round Table | 1959 | 30.00 |
| ❑ SR 25067 [S] | Woody Herman Sextet at the Round Table | 1959 | 40.00 |
| **VERVE** | | | |
| ❑ MGV-2030 [M] | Early Autumn | 1957 | 40.00 |
| ❑ MGV-2069 [M] | Songs for Hip Lovers | 1957 | 40.00 |
| ❑ MGV-2096 [M] | Love Is the Sweetest Thing — Sometimes | 1958 | 40.00 |
| ❑ MGV-8014 [M] | Jazz, the Utmost! | 1957 | 40.00 |
| *—Reissue of Clef LP* | | | |
| ❑ MGV-8216 [M] | Men from Mars | 1958 | 40.00 |
| ❑ MGV-8255 [M] | Woody Herman '58 | 1958 | 40.00 |
| ❑ V-8558 [M] | Hey! Heard the Herd? | 1963 | 20.00 |
| *—Reissue of Verve 8216* | | | |
| ❑ V6-8764 | Concerto for Herd | 1968 | 20.00 |

## HERMAN, WOODY/TITO PUENTE

| Number | Title (A Side/B Side) | Yr | NM |
|---|---|---|---|
| **EVEREST** | | | |
| ❑ SDBR-1010 [S] | Herman's Beat of Puente | 1958 | 40.00 |
| ❑ LPBR-5010 [M] | Herman's Beat of Puente | 1958 | 40.00 |

## HERMAN'S HERMITS

| Number | Title (A Side/B Side) | Yr | NM |
|---|---|---|---|
| **ABKCO** | | | |
| ❑ 4227-1 | Their Greatest Hits | 1988 | 8.00 |
| *—Abridged version of AB 4227* | | | |
| ❑ AB-4227 [(2)] | XX (Greatest Hits) | 1973 | 12.00 |
| **MGM** | | | |
| ❑ E-4282 [M] | Introducing Herman's Hermits | 1965 | 15.00 |
| *—Version 3: With "Including 'Mrs. Brown You've Got a Lovely Daughter' " on front cover* | | | |
| ❑ E-4282 [M] | Introducing Herman's Hermits | 1965 | 20.00 |
| *—Version 2: Same as above, but with a sticker that says "Featuring "Mrs. Brown You Have a Lovely Daughter'."* | | | |
| ❑ E-4282 [M] | Introducing Herman's Hermits | 1965 | 25.00 |
| *—Version 1: With "Including Their Hit Single 'I'm Into Something Good' " on front cover* | | | |
| ❑ SE-4282 [R] | Introducing Herman's Hermits | 1965 | 10.00 |
| *—Version 3: With "Including 'Mrs. Brown You've Got a Lovely Daughter' " on front cover* | | | |
| ❑ SE-4282 [R] | Introducing Herman's Hermits | 1965 | 15.00 |
| *—Version 2: Same as above, but with a sticker that says "Featuring "Mrs. Brown You Have a Lovely Daughter'."* | | | |
| ❑ SE-4282 [R] | Introducing Herman's Hermits | 1965 | 20.00 |
| *—Version 1: With "Including Their Hit Single 'I'm Into Something Good' " on front cover* | | | |
| ❑ E-4295 [M] | Herman's Hermits On Tour | 1965 | 12.00 |
| ❑ SE-4295 [R] | Herman's Hermits On Tour | 1965 | 10.00 |
| ❑ E-4315 [M] | The Best of Herman's Hermits | 1965 | 12.00 |
| ❑ SE-4315 [R] | The Best of Herman's Hermits | 1965 | 10.00 |
| ❑ E-4342 [M] | Hold On! | 1966 | 10.00 |
| ❑ SE-4342 [P] | Hold On! | 1966 | 12.00 |
| ❑ E-4386 [M] | Both Sides of Herman's Hermits | 1966 | 10.00 |
| ❑ SE-4386 [R] | Both Sides of Herman's Hermits | 1966 | 8.00 |
| ❑ E-4416 [M] | The Best of Herman's Hermits, Volume 2 | 1966 | 12.00 |
| *—Add 50% if bonus photo of Herman is included* | | | |
| ❑ SE-4416 [P] | The Best of Herman's Hermits, Volume 2 | 1966 | 10.00 |
| *—Add 50% if bonus photo of Herman is included. "Hold On" and "Leaning on the Lamp Post" are in true stereo.* | | | |
| ❑ E-4438 [M] | There's a Kind of Hush All Over the World | 1967 | 10.00 |
| ❑ SE-4438 [R] | There's a Kind of Hush All Over the World | 1967 | 8.00 |
| ❑ E-4478 [M] | Blaze | 1967 | 10.00 |
| ❑ SE-4478 [S] | Blaze | 1967 | 10.00 |
| ❑ E-4505 [M] | The Best of Herman's Hermits, Volume 3 | 1967 | 10.00 |
| ❑ SE-4505 [P] | The Best of Herman's Hermits, Volume 3 | 1967 | 10.00 |
| *—"Don't Go Out Into the Rain," "Museum," "Last Bus Home" and "Mum and Dad" are in true stereo.* | | | |
| ❑ SE-4548 [P] | Mrs. Brown You've Got a Lovely Daughter | 1968 | 10.00 |
| *—"Mrs. Brown You've Got a Lovely Daughter" and "There's a Kind of Hush" are rechanneled* | | | |
| ❑ ST-90416 [R] | Introducing Herman's Hermits | 1965 | 20.00 |
| *—Capitol Record Club edition* | | | |
| ❑ T-90416 [M] | Introducing Herman's Hermits | 1965 | 25.00 |
| *—Capitol Record Club edition* | | | |
| ❑ ST-90421 [R] | Herman's Hermits On Tour | 1965 | 20.00 |
| *—Capitol Record Club edition* | | | |
| ❑ T-90421 [M] | Herman's Hermits On Tour | 1965 | 25.00 |
| *—Capitol Record Club edition* | | | |
| ❑ KAO-90613 [M] | The Best of Herman's Hermits | 1966 | 15.00 |
| *—Capitol Record Club edition* | | | |
| ❑ ST-90646 [R] | Hold On! | 1966 | 20.00 |
| *—Capitol Record Club edition* | | | |
| ❑ T-90646 [M] | Hold On! | 1966 | 25.00 |
| *—Capitol Record Club edition* | | | |
| ❑ ST-91286 [S] | Blaze | 1967 | 20.00 |
| *—Capitol Record Club edition* | | | |
| ❑ T-91286 [M] | Blaze | 1967 | 30.00 |
| *—Capitol Record Club edition* | | | |

## HERON, MIKE

| Number | Title (A Side/B Side) | Yr | NM |
|---|---|---|---|
| **ELEKTRA** | | | |
| ❑ EKS-74093 | Smiling Men with Bad Reputations | 1971 | 20.00 |

## HERRMANN, BERNARD

| Number | Title (A Side/B Side) | Yr | NM |
|---|---|---|---|
| **MOBILE FIDELITY** | | | |
| ❑ 1-240 | The Fantasy Film World of Bernard Herrmann | 1996 | 20.00 |
| *—Audiophile vinyl* | | | |
| ❑ 1-255 | The Four Faces of Jazz | 1996 | 20.00 |
| *—Audiophile vinyl* | | | |

## HERSCH, FRED

| Number | Title (A Side/B Side) | Yr | NM |
|---|---|---|---|
| **CHESKY** | | | |
| ❑ 90 | Dancing in the Dark | 1993 | 20.00 |

## HESITATIONS, THE

| Number | Title (A Side/B Side) | Yr | NM |
|---|---|---|---|
| **KAPP** | | | |
| ❑ KL-1525 [M] | Soul Superman | 1967 | 30.00 |
| ❑ KS-3525 [S] | Soul Superman | 1967 | 25.00 |
| ❑ KS-3548 | The New Born Free | 1968 | 25.00 |
| ❑ KS-3561 | Where We're At | 1968 | 25.00 |
| ❑ KS-3574 | Solid Gold | 1969 | 25.00 |

## HESS, CHUCK

| Number | Title (A Side/B Side) | Yr | NM |
|---|---|---|---|
| **STRAND** | | | |
| ❑ SL-1084 [M] | Country & Western Favorites | 1960 | 20.00 |
| ❑ SLS-1084 [S] | Country & Western Favorites | 1960 | 25.00 |

## HESTER, CAROLYN

| Number | Title (A Side/B Side) | Yr | NM |
|---|---|---|---|
| **COLUMBIA** | | | |
| ❑ CL 1796 [M] | Carolyn Hester | 1962 | 60.00 |
| *—With Bob Dylan on harmonica on three tracks; black and red label with six "eye" logos* | | | |
| ❑ CL 1796 [M] | Carolyn Hester | 1963 | 20.00 |
| *—Red label with "Guaranteed High Fidelity"* | | | |
| ❑ CL 2032 [M] | This Life I'm Living | 1963 | 20.00 |
| ❑ CS 8596 [S] | Carolyn Hester | 1962 | 80.00 |
| *—With Bob Dylan on harmonica on three tracks; black and red label with six "eye" logos* | | | |
| ❑ CS 8596 [S] | Carolyn Hester | 1963 | 25.00 |
| *—Red label, "360 Sound Stereo" in black* | | | |
| ❑ CS 8832 [S] | This Life I'm Living | 1963 | 25.00 |
| **CORAL** | | | |
| ❑ CRL 57143 [M] | Scarlet Ribbons | 1957 | 50.00 |
| **DOT** | | | |
| ❑ DLP-3604 [M] | That's My Song | 1964 | 15.00 |
| ❑ DLP-3638 [M] | Carolyn Hester at Town Hall One | 1965 | 15.00 |
| ❑ DLP-3649 [M] | Carolyn Hester at Town Hall Two | 1965 | 15.00 |
| ❑ DLP-25604 [S] | That's My Song | 1964 | 20.00 |
| ❑ DLP-25638 [S] | Carolyn Hester at Town Hall One | 1965 | 20.00 |
| ❑ DLP-25649 [S] | Carolyn Hester at Town Hall Two | 1965 | 20.00 |
| **FOLK ODYSSEY** | | | |
| ❑ 32160264 | Simply Carolyn Hester | 196? | 20.00 |
| **METROMEDIA** | | | |
| ❑ MD-1001 | The Carolyn Hester Coalition | 1969 | 20.00 |
| ❑ MD-1022 | Magazine | 1970 | 60.00 |
| **RCA VICTOR** | | | |
| ❑ APD1-0086 [Q] | Carolyn Hester | 1973 | 20.00 |
| *—Only released in quadraphonic* | | | |
| **TRADITION** | | | |
| ❑ TLP-1043 [M] | Carolyn Hester | 1961 | 40.00 |

## HEYWARD, NICK

| Number | Title (A Side/B Side) | Yr | NM |
|---|---|---|---|
| **REPRISE** | | | |
| ❑ PRO-A-3384 [DJ] | Words and Music | 1988 | 20.00 |
| *—Promo-only interview record* | | | |

## HEYWOOD, EDDIE

| Number | Title (A Side/B Side) | Yr | NM |
|---|---|---|---|
| **BRUNSWICK** | | | |
| ❑ BL 58036 [10] | Eddie Heywood '45 | 1953 | 50.00 |
| **COLUMBIA** | | | |
| ❑ CL 6157 [10] | Piano Moods | 1951 | 50.00 |
| **COMMODORE** | | | |
| ❑ FL-20007 [10] | Eight Selections | 1950 | 75.00 |
| **CORAL** | | | |
| ❑ CRL 57095 [M] | Featuring Eddie Heywood | 1957 | 40.00 |
| **DECCA** | | | |
| ❑ DL 8202 [M] | Lightly and Politely | 1956 | 30.00 |
| ❑ DL 8270 [M] | Swing Low Sweet Heywood | 1956 | 30.00 |
| **EMARCY** | | | |
| ❑ MG-36042 [M] | Eddie Heywood | 1955 | 40.00 |
| **EPIC** | | | |
| ❑ LN 3327 [M] | Eddie Heywood at Twilight | 1956 | 30.00 |
| **MERCURY** | | | |
| ❑ MG-20445 [M] | Breezin' Along with the Breeze | 1959 | 20.00 |
| ❑ MG-20590 [M] | Eddie Heywood at the Piano | 1960 | 20.00 |
| ❑ MG-20632 [M] | One for My Baby | 1960 | 20.00 |
| ❑ SR-60115 [S] | Breezin' Along with the Breeze | 1959 | 25.00 |
| ❑ SR-60248 [S] | Eddie Heywood at the Piano | 1960 | 25.00 |
| ❑ SR-60632 [S] | One for My Baby | 1960 | 25.00 |
| **MGM** | | | |
| ❑ E-135 [10] | It's Easy to Remember | 1952 | 50.00 |
| ❑ E-3093 [M] | Pianorama | 1955 | 40.00 |
| ❑ E-3260 [M] | Eddie Heywood | 1956 | 40.00 |
| **RCA VICTOR** | | | |
| ❑ LPM-1466 [M] | The Touch of Eddie Heywood | 1957 | 30.00 |
| ❑ LPM-1529 [M] | Canadian Sunset | 1957 | 30.00 |
| ❑ LSP-1529 [S] | Canadian Sunset | 1958 | 40.00 |
| ❑ LPM-1900 [M] | The Keys and I | 1958 | 30.00 |

## HI-LITES, THE (2)

| Number | Title (A Side/B Side) | Yr | NM |
|---|---|---|---|
| **DANDEE** | | | |
| ❑ DLP-206 [M] | For Your Precious Love | 1961 | 2000. |

## HI-LO'S, THE

| Number | Title (A Side/B Side) | Yr | NM |
|---|---|---|---|
| **COLUMBIA** | | | |
| ❑ CL 952 [M] | Suddenly It's the Hi-Lo's | 1957 | 30.00 |
| ❑ CL 1023 [M] | Now Hear This | 1957 | 30.00 |
| ❑ CL 1259 [M] | The Hi-Lo's and All That Jazz | 1958 | 30.00 |
| ❑ CL 1416 [M] | Broadway Playbill | 1959 | 30.00 |
| ❑ CL 1509 [M] | All Over the Place | 1960 | 25.00 |
| ❑ CL 1723 [M] | This Time It's Love | 1962 | 25.00 |
| ❑ CS 8057 [S] | Love Nest | 1958 | 40.00 |
| ❑ CS 8077 [S] | The Hi-Lo's and All That Jazz | 1958 | 40.00 |
| ❑ CS 8213 [S] | Broadway Playbill | 1959 | 40.00 |
| ❑ CS 8300 [S] | All Over the Place | 1960 | 30.00 |
| ❑ CS 8523 [S] | This Time It's Love | 1962 | 30.00 |
| **KAPP** | | | |
| ❑ KL 1027 [M] | The Hi-Lo's and the Jerry Fielding Band | 1956 | 30.00 |
| ❑ KL 1184 [M] | Under Glass | 1959 | 25.00 |
| *—Reissue of Starlite 7005* | | | |
| ❑ KL 1194 [M] | On Hand | 1960 | 25.00 |
| *—Reissue of Starlite 7008* | | | |
| **OMEGA** | | | |
| ❑ OSL-11 [S] | The Hi-Lo's in Stereo | 195? | 30.00 |
| **REPRISE** | | | |
| ❑ R-6066 [M] | The Hi-Lo's Happen to Bossa Nova | 1963 | 20.00 |
| ❑ R9-6066 [S] | The Hi-Lo's Happen to Bossa Nova | 1963 | 25.00 |
| **STARLITE** | | | |
| ❑ 6004 [10] | Listen! | 1955 | 60.00 |
| ❑ 6005 [10] | The Hi-Lo's, I Presume | 1955 | 60.00 |
| ❑ 7005 [M] | Under Glass | 1956 | 40.00 |
| ❑ 7006 [M] | Listen! | 1956 | 40.00 |
| *—Reissue of 6004* | | | |
| ❑ 7007 [M] | The Hi-Lo's. I Presume | 1956 | 40.00 |
| *—Reissue of 6005* | | | |
| ❑ 7008 [M] | On Hand | 1956 | 40.00 |

## HI-TONES, THE

| Number | Title (A Side/B Side) | Yr | NM |
|---|---|---|---|
| **HI** | | | |
| ❑ HL-31011 [M] | Raunchy Sounds | 1963 | 20.00 |
| ❑ SHL-32011 [S] | Raunchy Sounds | 1963 | 25.00 |
| **L&M** | | | |
| ❑ 223 | I'm So Sorry | 196? | 200.00 |

## HIATT, JOHN

| Number | Title (A Side/B Side) | Yr | NM |
|---|---|---|---|
| **A&M** | | | |
| ❑ SP-5158 | Bring the Family | 1987 | 10.00 |
| ❑ SP-5206 | Slow Turning | 1988 | 10.00 |
| ❑ 75021 5310 1 | Stolen Moments | 1990 | 12.00 |
| **EPIC** | | | |
| ❑ KE 32688 | Hangin' Around the Observatory | 1974 | 15.00 |
| ❑ KE 33190 | Overcoats | 1975 | 15.00 |
| ❑ PE 33190 | Overcoats | 198? | 8.00 |
| *—Budget-line reissue* | | | |
| **GEFFEN** | | | |
| ❑ GHS 2009 | All of a Sudden | 1982 | 12.00 |
| ❑ GHS 4017 | Riding with the King | 1983 | 12.00 |
| ❑ GHS 24055 | Warming Up to the Ice Age | 1984 | 12.00 |
| **MCA** | | | |
| ❑ 741 | Two-Bit Monster | 198? | 8.00 |
| *—Reissue* | | | |
| ❑ 747 | Slug Line | 198? | 8.00 |
| *—Reissue* | | | |
| ❑ 3088 | Slug Line | 1979 | 12.00 |
| ❑ 5123 | Two-Bit Monster | 1980 | 12.00 |
| **MOBILE FIDEILTY** | | | |
| ❑ 1-210 | Bring the Family | 1994 | 50.00 |
| *—Audiophile vinyl* | | | |

## HIBBLER, AL

| Number | Title (A Side/B Side) | Yr | NM |
|---|---|---|---|
| **ARGO** | | | |
| ❑ LP-601 [M] | Melodies by Al Hibbler | 1956 | 40.00 |
| *—Reissue of Marterry LP* | | | |
| **ATLANTIC** | | | |
| ❑ 1251 [M] | After the Lights Go Down Low | 1957 | 50.00 |
| *—Black label* | | | |
| ❑ 1251 [M] | After the Lights Go Down Low | 1961 | 25.00 |
| *—Mostly red label, white fan logo* | | | |
| ❑ 1251 [M] | After the Lights Go Down Low | 1963 | 20.00 |
| *—Mostly red label, black fan logo* | | | |
| **BRUNSWICK** | | | |
| ❑ BL 54036 [M] | Al Hibbler with the Ellingtonians | 1957 | 50.00 |
| **DECCA** | | | |
| ❑ DL 8328 [M] | Starring Al Hibbler | 1956 | 30.00 |
| ❑ DL 8420 [M] | Here's Hibbler | 1957 | 30.00 |
| ❑ DL 8697 [M] | Torchy and Blue | 1958 | 30.00 |
| ❑ DL 8757 [M] | Hits by Hibbler | 1958 | 30.00 |
| ❑ DL 8862 [M] | Al Hibbler Remembers the Big Songs of the Big Bands | 1959 | 30.00 |
| ❑ DL 78862 [S] | Al Hibbler Remembers the Big Songs of the Big Bands | 1959 | 40.00 |
| **DISCOVERY** | | | |
| ❑ 842 | It's Monday Every Day | 198? | 12.00 |
| *—Reissue of Reprise LP* | | | |
| **LMI** | | | |
| ❑ 10001 [M] | Early One Morning | 1964 | 30.00 |
| **MARTERRY** | | | |
| ❑ LP-601 [M] | Melodies by Al Hibbler | 1956 | 80.00 |
| **MCA** | | | |
| ❑ 4098 [(2)] | The Best of Al Hibbler | 197? | 15.00 |
| **NORGRAN** | | | |
| ❑ MGN-4 [10] | Al Hibbler Favorites | 1954 | 150.00 |
| ❑ MGN-15 [10] | Al Hibbler Sings Duke Ellington | 1954 | 150.00 |
| **OPEN SKY** | | | |
| ❑ OSR-3126 | For Sentimental Reasons | 1986 | 12.00 |
| **REPRISE** | | | |
| ❑ R-2005 [M] | It's Monday Every Day | 1961 | 30.00 |
| ❑ R9-2005 [S] | It's Monday Every Day | 1961 | 40.00 |
| **SCORE** | | | |
| ❑ SLP-4013 [M] | I Surrender, Dear | 1957 | 100.00 |
| **VERVE** | | | |
| ❑ MGV-4000 [M] | Al Hibbler Sings Love Songs | 1956 | 60.00 |
| ❑ V-4000 [M] | Al Hibbler Sings Love Songs | 1961 | 20.00 |

## HICKEY, ERSEL

| Number | Title (A Side/B Side) | Yr | NM |
|---|---|---|---|
| **BACK-TRAC** | | | |
| ❑ P 18750 | The Rockin' Bluebird | 1985 | 60.00 |
| *—Allegedly, only 200 copies of this were pressed* | | | |

## HICKMAN, DWAYNE

| Number | Title (A Side/B Side) | Yr | NM |
|---|---|---|---|
| **CAPITOL** | | | |
| ❑ ST 1441 [S] | Dobie! | 1960 | 50.00 |
| ❑ T 1441 [M] | Dobie! | 1960 | 40.00 |

## HIGGINS, CHUCK

| Number | Title (A Side/B Side) | Yr | NM |
|---|---|---|---|
| **COMBO** | | | |
| ❑ LP-300 [M] | Pachuko Hop | 195? | 40.00 |
| *—Chuck Higgins on cover, fully clothed* | | | |
| ❑ LP-300 [M] | Pachuko Hop | 195? | 800.00 |
| *—"Naked woman" cover (well, she's wearing a scarf)* | | | |

## HIGGINS, EDDIE

| Number | Title (A Side/B Side) | Yr | NM |
|---|---|---|---|
| **ATLANTIC** | | | |
| ❑ SD 1446 [S] | Soulero | 1966 | 20.00 |
| **VEE JAY** | | | |
| ❑ LP-3017 [M] | Eddie Higgins | 1961 | 30.00 |
| ❑ SR-3017 [S] | Eddie Higgins | 1961 | 40.00 |

## HIGH TIDE

| Number | Title (A Side/B Side) | Yr | NM |
|---|---|---|---|
| **LIBERTY** | | | |
| ❑ LST-7638 | Sea Shanties | 1969 | 25.00 |

## HIGH TREASON

| Number | Title (A Side/B Side) | Yr | NM |
|---|---|---|---|
| **ABBOTT** | | | |
| ❑ ABS-1209 | High Treason | 1968 | 60.00 |

## HIGHTOWER, DEAN

| Number | Title (A Side/B Side) | Yr | NM |
|---|---|---|---|
| **ABC-PARAMOUNT** | | | |
| ❑ ABC-312 [M] | Twangy Guitar with a Beat | 1959 | 25.00 |
| ❑ ABCS-312 [S] | Twangy Guitar with a Beat | 1959 | 30.00 |

## HIGHTOWER, DONNA

| Number | Title (A Side/B Side) | Yr | NM |
|---|---|---|---|
| **CAPITOL** | | | |
| ❑ ST 1133 [S] | Take One | 1959 | 50.00 |
| ❑ T 1133 [M] | Take One | 1959 | 40.00 |
| ❑ ST 1273 [S] | Gee Baby...Ain't I Good to You | 1959 | 50.00 |
| ❑ T 1273 [M] | Gee Baby...Ain't I Good to You | 1959 | 40.00 |

## HIGHTOWER, WILLIE

| Number | Title (A Side/B Side) | Yr | NM |
|---|---|---|---|
| **CAPITOL** | | | |
| ❑ ST-367 | If I Had a Hammer | 1969 | 100.00 |
| **COLLECTABLES** | | | |
| ❑ COL-5170 | Golden Classics | 198? | 10.00 |

## HIGHWAYMEN, THE

| Number | Title (A Side/B Side) | Yr | NM |
|---|---|---|---|
| **ABC-PARAMOUNT** | | | |
| ❑ 522 [M] | On a New Road | 1965 | 12.00 |
| ❑ S-522 [S] | On a New Road | 1965 | 15.00 |
| **UNITED ARTISTS** | | | |
| ❑ UAL 3125 [M] | The Highwaymen | 1961 | 15.00 |
| ❑ UAL 3168 [M] | Standing Room Only! | 1962 | 15.00 |
| ❑ UAL 3225 [M] | Encore! | 1962 | 15.00 |
| ❑ UAL 3245 [M] | March On, Brothers | 1963 | 15.00 |
| ❑ UAL 3294 [M] | Hootenanny with the Highwaymen | 1963 | 15.00 |
| ❑ UAL 3323 [M] | One More Time | 1964 | 15.00 |
| ❑ UAL 3348 [M] | Homecoming | 1964 | 15.00 |
| ❑ UAS 6125 [S] | The Highwaymen | 1961 | 20.00 |
| ❑ UAS 6168 [S] | Standing Room Only! | 1962 | 20.00 |
| ❑ UAS 6225 [S] | Encore! | 1962 | 20.00 |
| ❑ UAS 6245 [S] | March On, Brothers | 1963 | 20.00 |
| ❑ UAS 6294 [S] | Hootenanny with the Highwaymen | 1963 | 20.00 |
| ❑ UAS 6323 [S] | One More Time | 1964 | 20.00 |
| ❑ UAS 6348 [S] | Homecoming | 1964 | 20.00 |

## HILDEGARDE

| Number | Title (A Side/B Side) | Yr | NM |
|---|---|---|---|
| **DECCA** | | | |
| ❑ DL 8656 [M] | Souvenir Album | 1958 | 30.00 |
| *—Black label, silver print* | | | |

## HILDINGER, DAVE

| Number | Title (A Side/B Side) | Yr | NM |
|---|---|---|---|
| **BATON** | | | |
| ❑ 1204 [M] | The Young Moderns | 1957 | 40.00 |

## HILL, ANDREW

| Number | Title (A Side/B Side) | Yr | NM |
|---|---|---|---|
| **BLUE NOTE** | | | |
| ❑ BN-LA459-H2 [(2)] | One for One | 1975 | 20.00 |
| ❑ BLP-4151 [M] | Black Fire | 1963 | 30.00 |
| ❑ BLP-4159 [M] | Judgment! | 1964 | 30.00 |
| ❑ BLP-4160 [M] | Smoke Stack | 1964 | 30.00 |
| ❑ BLP-4167 [M] | Point of Departure | 1964 | 30.00 |
| ❑ BLP-4217 [M] | Compulsion | 1965 | 25.00 |
| ❑ BST-84151 [S] | Black Fire | 1963 | 40.00 |
| *—With "New York, USA" address on label* | | | |
| ❑ BST-84159 [S] | Judgment! | 1964 | 40.00 |
| *—With "New York, USA" address on label* | | | |
| ❑ BST-84160 [S] | Smoke Stack | 1964 | 40.00 |
| *—With "New York, USA" address on label* | | | |
| ❑ BST-84167 [S] | Point of Departure | 1964 | 40.00 |
| *—With "New York, USA" address on label* | | | |
| ❑ BST-84203 [S] | Andrew!!! — The Music of Andrew Hill | 1967 | 25.00 |
| *—With "A Division of Liberty Records" on label; version with "New York, USA" on label not known to exist* | | | |
| ❑ BST-84217 [S] | Compulsion | 1965 | 30.00 |
| *—With "New York, USA" address on label* | | | |
| ❑ BST-84303 | Grass Roots | 1968 | 20.00 |
| ❑ BST-84330 | Lift Every Voice | 1969 | 20.00 |
| **MOSAIC** | | | |
| ❑ MQ10-161 [(10)] | The Complete Andrew Hill Blue Note Sessions | 199? | 180.00 |
| **WARWICK** | | | |
| ❑ W-2002 [M] | So in Love | 1960 | 60.00 |
| ❑ W-2002ST [S] | So in Love | 1960 | 80.00 |

## HILL, GOLDIE

| Number | Title (A Side/B Side) | Yr | NM |
|---|---|---|---|
| **DECCA** | | | |
| ❑ DL 4034 [M] | Goldie Hill | 1960 | 25.00 |
| ❑ DL 4148 [M] | Lonely Heartaches | 1961 | 20.00 |
| ❑ DL 4219 [M] | According to My Heart | 1962 | 20.00 |
| ❑ DL 4492 [M] | Country Hit Parade | 1964 | 20.00 |
| ❑ DL 74034 [S] | Goldie Hill | 1960 | 30.00 |
| ❑ DL 74148 [S] | Lonely Heartaches | 1961 | 25.00 |
| ❑ DL 74219 [S] | According to My Heart | 1962 | 25.00 |
| ❑ DL 74492 [S] | Country Hit Parade | 1964 | 25.00 |
| **VOCALION** | | | |
| ❑ VL 73800 | Country Songs | 196? | 12.00 |

## HILL, TINY

| Number | Title (A Side/B Side) | Yr | NM |
|---|---|---|---|
| **HINDSIGHT** | | | |
| ❑ HSR-159 | The Uncollected Tiny Hill and His Orchestra, 1944 | 1980 | 10.00 |
| **MERCURY** | | | |
| ❑ MG-20630 [M] | Dancin' and Singin' with Tiny Hill | 195? | 25.00 |
| ❑ MG-20631 [M] | Golden Hits | 195? | 25.00 |
| ❑ MG-25126 [10] | Tiny Hill | 1952 | 50.00 |
| ❑ SR-60631 [R] | Golden Hits | 196? | 15.00 |

## HILL, VINCE

| Number | Title (A Side/B Side) | Yr | NM |
|---|---|---|---|
| **TOWER** | | | |
| ❑ T 5064 [M] | At the Club | 1966 | 25.00 |

## HILL, VINSON

| Number | Title (A Side/B Side) | Yr | NM |
|---|---|---|---|
| **SAVOY** | | | |
| ❑ MG-12187 [M] | The Vinson Hill Trio | 1966 | 30.00 |

## HILLMEN, THE

| Number | Title (A Side/B Side) | Yr | NM |
|---|---|---|---|
| **TOGETHER** | | | |
| ❑ STT-1012 | The Hillmen | 1970 | 80.00 |

## HILLOW HAMMET

| Number | Title (A Side/B Side) | Yr | NM |
|---|---|---|---|
| **HOUSE OF FOX** | | | |
| ❑ 2 | Hammer | 1968 | 150.00 |

## HILLTOPPERS, THE

| Number | Title (A Side/B Side) | Yr | NM |
|---|---|---|---|
| **DOT** | | | |
| ❑ DLP-105 [10] | The Hilltoppers | 1954 | 60.00 |
| ❑ DLP-106 [10] | The Hilltoppers | 1954 | 60.00 |
| ❑ DLP-3003 [M] | The Hilltoppers Present Tops in Pops | 1955 | 50.00 |
| *—Cartoon of female fan on cover* | | | |
| ❑ DLP-3003 [M] | The Hilltoppers Present Tops in Pops | 1956 | 30.00 |
| *—Four caps with "W" on them on cover* | | | |
| ❑ DLP-3029 [M] | The Towering Hilltoppers | 1957 | 30.00 |
| ❑ DLP-3073 [M] | Love in Bloom | 1958 | 30.00 |

## HINES, EARL "FATHA"

| Number | Title (A Side/B Side) | Yr | NM |
|---|---|---|---|
| **ADVANCE** | | | |
| ❑ 4 [10] | Fats Waller Memorial Set | 1951 | 150.00 |
| **ATLANTIC** | | | |
| ❑ ALS-120 [10] | Earl Hines: QRS Solos | 1952 | 200.00 |
| **BRUNSWICK** | | | |
| ❑ BL 58035 [10] | Earl Hines Plays Fats Waller | 1953 | 120.00 |
| **CAPITOL** | | | |
| ❑ ST 1971 [S] | Earl "Fatha" Hines | 1963 | 30.00 |
| ❑ T 1971 [M] | Earl "Fatha" Hines | 1963 | 25.00 |
| **CHIAROSCURO** | | | |
| ❑ 116 [(2)] | An Evening with Hines | 1972 | 20.00 |
| **COLUMBIA** | | | |
| ❑ CL 2320 [M] | The New Earl Hines Trio | 1965 | 20.00 |
| ❑ CL 6171 [10] | Piano Moods | 1951 | 120.00 |
| ❑ CS 9120 [S] | The New Earl Hines Trio | 1965 | 25.00 |
| **CONTACT** | | | |
| ❑ 2 [M] | Spontaneous Explorations | 1964 | 25.00 |
| ❑ S-2 [S] | Spontaneous Explorations | 1964 | 30.00 |
| **CRAFTSMEN** | | | |
| ❑ 8041 [M] | Swingin' and Singin' | 1960 | 25.00 |
| **DECCA** | | | |
| ❑ DL 9221 [M] | Southside Swing (1934-35) | 1967 | 25.00 |
| ❑ DL 9235 [M] | Earl Hines at the Apex Club | 1968 | 25.00 |
| **DIAL** | | | |
| ❑ LP-303 [10] | Earl Hines Trio | 1952 | 250.00 |
| ❑ LP-306 [10] | Earl Hines All Stars | 1953 | 250.00 |
| **ENSIGN** | | | |
| ❑ 22021 | Earl Hines Rhythm | 1969 | 20.00 |
| **EPIC** | | | |
| ❑ LN 3223 [M] | Oh, Fatha! | 1956 | 50.00 |
| ❑ LN 3501 [M] | Earl "Fatha" Hines | 1958 | 50.00 |
| **FANTASY** | | | |
| ❑ 3217 [M] | "Fatha" Plays "Fats" | 195? | 50.00 |
| *—Black vinyl* | | | |
| ❑ 3217 [M] | "Fatha" Plays "Fats" | 1956 | 100.00 |
| *—Red vinyl* | | | |
| ❑ 3238 [M] | Earl "Fatha" Hines Solo | 195? | 50.00 |
| *—Black vinyl* | | | |
| ❑ 3238 [M] | Earl "Fatha" Hines Solo | 1956 | 100.00 |
| *—Red vinyl* | | | |
| **FOCUS** | | | |
| ❑ FM-335 [M] | The Real Earl Hines In Concert | 1965 | 25.00 |
| ❑ FS-335 [S] | The Real Earl Hines In Concert | 1965 | 30.00 |
| **HALCYON** | | | |
| ❑ 101 | The Quintessential Recording Session | 196? | 20.00 |
| **IMPULSE!** | | | |
| ❑ A-9108 [M] | Once Upon a Time | 1966 | 25.00 |
| ❑ AS-9108 [S] | Once Upon a Time | 1966 | 30.00 |
| **JAZZ PANORAMA** | | | |
| ❑ 7 [M] | All Stars | 1961 | 40.00 |
| **M&K** | | | |
| ❑ 105 | "Fatha" | 1979 | 25.00 |
| *—Direct-to-disc recording* | | | |
| **MASTER JAZZ** | | | |
| ❑ 8126 [(2)] | Earl Hines Plays Duke Ellington, Volumes 2 and 3 | 1973 | 20.00 |
| **MERCURY** | | | |
| ❑ MG-25018 [10] | Earl Hines and the All Stars | 1950 | 250.00 |
| **MGM** | | | |
| ❑ E-3832 [M] | Earl's Pearls | 1960 | 25.00 |
| ❑ SE-3832 [S] | Earl's Pearls | 1960 | 30.00 |
| **NOCTURNE** | | | |
| ❑ NLP-5 [10] | Earl "Fatha" Hines | 1954 | 150.00 |
| **RCA VICTOR** | | | |
| ❑ LPT-20 [10] | Earl Hines with Billy Eckstine | 1953 | 120.00 |
| ❑ LPV-512 [M] | The Grand Terrace Band | 1965 | 25.00 |
| ❑ LPM-3380 [M] | Up to Date | 1965 | 20.00 |
| ❑ LSP-3380 [S] | Up to Date | 1965 | 25.00 |

| Number | Title (A Side/B Side) | Yr | NM |
|---|---|---|---|
| **RIVERSIDE** | | | |
| ❑ RLP-398 [M] | A Monday Date | 1961 | 30.00 |
| ❑ RS-9398 [R] | A Monday Date | 196? | 20.00 |
| **ROYALE** | | | |
| ❑ 18166 [10] | Eal "Fatha" Hines — Great Piano Solos | 195? | 120.00 |
| **TIARA** | | | |
| ❑ TMT-7524 [M] | Earl "Fatha" Hines with Buck Clayton | 195? | 20.00 |
| **TOPS** | | | |
| ❑ L-1599 [M] | "Fatha" | 195? | 30.00 |
| **VERVE** | | | |
| ❑ VSP-35 [M] | Life with Fatha | 1966 | 20.00 |
| **"X"** | | | |
| ❑ LVA-3023 [10] | Piano Solos | 1954 | 120.00 |

### HINES, EARL "FATHA," AND ROY ELDRIDGE

| Number | Title (A Side/B Side) | Yr | NM |
|---|---|---|---|
| **LIMELIGHT** | | | |
| ❑ LM-82028 [M] | The Grand Reunion, Volume 2 | 1965 | 20.00 |
| ❑ LS-86028 [S] | The Grand Reunion, Volume 2 | 1965 | 25.00 |

### HINES, EARL "FATHA," AND COLEMAN HAWKINS

| Number | Title (A Side/B Side) | Yr | NM |
|---|---|---|---|
| **LIMELIGHT** | | | |
| ❑ LM-82020 [M] | The Grand Reunion | 1965 | 20.00 |
| ❑ LS-86020 [S] | The Grand Reunion | 1965 | 25.00 |

### HINES, ERNIE

| Number | Title (A Side/B Side) | Yr | NM |
|---|---|---|---|
| **WE PRODUCE** | | | |
| ❑ 1902 | Electrified | 1972 | 50.00 |

### HINES, MIMI

| Number | Title (A Side/B Side) | Yr | NM |
|---|---|---|---|
| **DECCA** | | | |
| ❑ DL 4709 [M] | Mimi Hines Sings | 1966 | 20.00 |
| ❑ DL 4834 [M] | Mimi Hines Is a Happening | 1967 | 25.00 |
| ❑ DL 74709 [S] | Mimi Hines Sings | 1966 | 25.00 |
| ❑ DL 74834 [S] | Mimi Hines Is a Happening | 1967 | 20.00 |

### HINES, HINES & DAD

| Number | Title (A Side/B Side) | Yr | NM |
|---|---|---|---|
| **COLUMBIA** | | | |
| ❑ CS 9679 | Pandemonium | 1968 | 20.00 |

### HINSON, DON, AND THE RIGAMORTICIANS

| Number | Title (A Side/B Side) | Yr | NM |
|---|---|---|---|
| **CAPITOL** | | | |
| ❑ ST 2219 [S] | Monster Dance Party | 1964 | 40.00 |
| ❑ T 2219 [M] | Monster Dance Party | 1964 | 30.00 |

### HINTON, JOE

| Number | Title (A Side/B Side) | Yr | NM |
|---|---|---|---|
| **BACK BEAT** | | | |
| ❑ B-60 [M] | Funny (How Time Slips Away) | 1965 | 50.00 |
| ❑ BS-60 [S] | Funny (How Time Slips Away) | 1965 | 70.00 |
| **DUKE** | | | |
| ❑ DLPS-91 | Duke-Peacock Remembers Joe Hinton | 1969 | 20.00 |

### HINTON, MILT

| Number | Title (A Side/B Side) | Yr | NM |
|---|---|---|---|
| **BETHLEHEM** | | | |
| ❑ BCP-10 [M] | East Coast Jazz Series #5 | 1957 | 50.00 |
| ❑ BCP-1020 [10] | Milt Hinton Quartet | 1955 | 80.00 |
| **EPIC** | | | |
| ❑ LN 3271 [M] | The Rhythm Section | 1956 | 50.00 |

### HINTON, MILT; WENDELL MARSHALL; BULL RUTHER

| Number | Title (A Side/B Side) | Yr | NM |
|---|---|---|---|
| **RCA VICTOR** | | | |
| ❑ LPM-1107 [M] | Basses Loaded! | 1955 | 80.00 |

### HINTON, SAM

| Number | Title (A Side/B Side) | Yr | NM |
|---|---|---|---|
| **DECCA** | | | |
| ❑ DL 8108 [M] | Singing Across the Land | 1955 | 40.00 |
| ❑ DL 8418 [M] | A Family Tree of Folk Songs | 1957 | 30.00 |

### HIPP, JUTTA

| Number | Title (A Side/B Side) | Yr | NM |
|---|---|---|---|
| **BLUE NOTE** | | | |
| ❑ BLP-1515 [M] | Jutta Hipp at the Hickory House, Volume 1 | 1956 | 400.00 |
| *—"Deep groove" version, W. 63rd St. address on label* | | | |
| ❑ BLP-1515 [M] | Jutta Hipp at the Hickory House, Volume 1 | 1956 | 600.00 |
| *—"Deep groove" version, Lexington Ave. address on label* | | | |
| ❑ BLP-1515 [M] | Jutta Hipp at the Hickory House, Volume 1 | 1963 | 50.00 |
| *—With "New York, USA" address on label* | | | |
| ❑ BLP-1516 [M] | Jutta Hipp at the Hickory House, Volume 2 | 1956 | 400.00 |
| *—"Deep groove" version, W. 63rd St. address on label* | | | |
| ❑ BLP-1516 [M] | Jutta Hipp at the Hickory House, Volume 2 | 1956 | 600.00 |
| *—"Deep groove" version, Lexington Ave. address on label* | | | |
| ❑ BLP-1516 [M] | Jutta Hipp at the Hickory House, Volume 2 | 1963 | 50.00 |
| *—With "New York, USA" address on label* | | | |
| ❑ BLP-1530 [M] | Jutta Hipp with Zoot Sims | 1956 | 400.00 |
| *—"Deep groove" version, W. 63sr St. address on label* | | | |
| ❑ BLP-1530 [M] | Jutta Hipp with Zoot Sims | 1956 | 600.00 |
| *—"Deep groove" version; Lexington Ave. address on label* | | | |
| ❑ BLP-1530 [M] | Jutta Hipp with Zoot Sims | 1963 | 40.00 |
| *—With "New York, USA" address on label* | | | |
| ❑ BLP-1530 [M] | Jutta Hipp with Zoot Sims | 1971 | 20.00 |
| *—"A Division of United Artists" on label* | | | |
| ❑ BLP-1530 [M] | Jutta Hipp with Zoot Sims | 2003 | 30.00 |
| *—200-gram reissue; distributed by Classic Records* | | | |
| ❑ BLP-5056 [10] | Jutta — New Faces, New Sounds from Germany | 1955 | 800.00 |
| **MGM** | | | |
| ❑ E-3157 [M] | Cool Europe | 1955 | 150.00 |

### HIRT, AL

| Number | Title (A Side/B Side) | Yr | NM |
|---|---|---|---|
| **AUDIO FIDELITY** | | | |
| ❑ AFSD-5877 [S] | Swingin' Dixie (At Dan's Pier 600 in New Orleans) | 1959 | 20.00 |
| ❑ AFSD-5878 [S] | Swingin' Dixie | 1959 | 20.00 |
| ❑ AFSD-5926 [S] | Swingin' Dixie (Vol. 3) | 1961 | 20.00 |
| ❑ AFSD-5927 [S] | Swingin' Dixie (Vol. 4) | 1961 | 20.00 |
| **RCA VICTOR** | | | |
| ❑ LSC-2729 [S] | "Pops" Goes the Trumpet | 1964 | 20.00 |
| *—With the Boston Pops Orchestra conducted by Arthur Fiedler* | | | |
| ❑ LPM-3917 [M] | Al Hirt Plays Bert Kaempfert | 1968 | 20.00 |
| ❑ LPM-3979 [M] | Unforgettable | 1968 | 25.00 |
| **VERVE** | | | |
| ❑ MGV-1012 [M] | Swinging Dixie from Dan's Pier 600 | 1957 | 50.00 |
| ❑ MGV-1027 [M] | Blockbustin' Dixie! | 195? | 40.00 |
| ❑ V-1027 [M] | Blockbustin' Dixie! | 1961 | 20.00 |

### HIRT, AL, AND ANN-MARGRET

| Number | Title (A Side/B Side) | Yr | NM |
|---|---|---|---|
| **RCA VICTOR** | | | |
| ❑ LPM-2690 [M] | Beauty and the Beard | 1964 | 25.00 |
| ❑ LSP-2690 [S] | Beauty and the Beard | 1964 | 30.00 |

### HITCHCOCK, ROBYN, AND THE EGYPTIANS

| Number | Title (A Side/B Side) | Yr | NM |
|---|---|---|---|
| **A&M** | | | |
| ❑ SP-5182 | Globe of Frogs | 1988 | 12.00 |
| ❑ SP-5241 | Queen Elvis | 1989 | 12.00 |
| ❑ 75021 5368 1 | Perspex Island | 1991 | 20.00 |
| **RELATIVITY** | | | |
| ❑ EMC 8056 | Gotta Let This Hen Out | 1985 | 12.00 |
| ❑ 8074 [EP] | Exploding in Silence | 1986 | 25.00 |
| *—Picture disc* | | | |
| ❑ 88561-8082-1 | I Often Dream of Trains | 1986 | 12.00 |
| *—First U.S. issue of U.K. album* | | | |
| ❑ 88561-8083-1 | Groovy Decoy | 1986 | 12.00 |
| *—First U.S. issue of U.K. album* | | | |
| ❑ 88561-8088-1 | Black Snake Diamond Role | 1986 | 12.00 |
| *—First U.S. issue of U.K. album* | | | |
| ❑ 88561-8089-1 | Invisible Hitchcock | 1986 | 12.00 |
| ❑ 88561-8130-1 | Element of Light | 1987 | 12.00 |
| **SLASH** | | | |
| ❑ 25316 | Fegmania! | 1985 | 12.00 |
| **WARNER BROS.** | | | |
| ❑ 46399 | Mossy Liquor | 1996 | 30.00 |
| *—Collection of demos; released only on vinyl* | | | |
| ❑ 47147 [(2)] | Storefront Hitchcock | 1998 | 20.00 |

### HITCHCOCK, STAN

| Number | Title (A Side/B Side) | Yr | NM |
|---|---|---|---|
| **AUDIOGRAPH** | | | |
| ❑ 6004 | Stan Hitchcock | 1982 | 10.00 |
| **CINNAMON** | | | |
| ❑ CIN 5001 | Stan Hitchcock Country | 1973 | 15.00 |
| **EPIC** | | | |
| ❑ LN 24138 [M] | Just Call Me Lonesome | 1965 | 20.00 |
| ❑ BN 26138 [S] | Just Call Me Lonesome | 1965 | 25.00 |
| ❑ BN 26408 [M] | I'm Easy to Love | 1968 | 40.00 |
| *—White label promo with stereo number; "Epic Mono" sticker on front cover* | | | |
| ❑ BN 26408 [S] | I'm Easy to Love | 1968 | 20.00 |
| ❑ BN 26438 | Softly and Tenderly | 1969 | 20.00 |
| ❑ BN 26530 | Honey, I'm Home | 1969 | 15.00 |
| **GRT** | | | |
| ❑ 20001 | Dixie Belle | 1970 | 15.00 |

### HIVES, THE

| Number | Title (A Side/B Side) | Yr | NM |
|---|---|---|---|
| **GEARHEAD** | | | |
| ❑ RPM 30 | Barely Legal❑ RPM 30Barely Legal | 2000 | 15.00 |
| ❑ RPM 40 | Veni Vidi Vicious | 2001 | 12.00 |
| **INTERSCOPE** | | | |
| ❑ B0002756-01 [(2)] | Tyrannosaurus Hives | 2004 | 20.00 |

### HOBBITS, THE

| Number | Title (A Side/B Side) | Yr | NM |
|---|---|---|---|
| **DECCA** | | | |
| ❑ DL 4920 [M] | Down to Middle-Earth | 1967 | 40.00 |
| ❑ DL 5009 [M] | Men and Doors | 1968 | 80.00 |
| ❑ DL 74920 [S] | Down to Middle-Earth | 1967 | 50.00 |
| ❑ DL 75009 [S] | Men and Doors | 1968 | 30.00 |

### HODEIR, ANDRE

| Number | Title (A Side/B Side) | Yr | NM |
|---|---|---|---|
| **PHILIPS** | | | |
| ❑ PHM 200073 [M] | Jazz Et Al | 1963 | 25.00 |
| ❑ PHS 600073 [S] | Jazz Et Al | 1963 | 30.00 |
| **SAVOY** | | | |
| ❑ MG-12104 [M] | American Jazzmen Play Andre Hodeir | 1957 | 40.00 |
| ❑ MG-12113 [M] | Andre Hodeir Presents the Paris Scene | 1957 | 40.00 |

### HODES, ART

| Number | Title (A Side/B Side) | Yr | NM |
|---|---|---|---|
| **BLUE NOTE** | | | |
| ❑ B-6502 [M] | The Funky Piano of Art Hodes | 1969 | 25.00 |
| *—"A Division of Liberty Records" on label* | | | |
| ❑ B-6508 [M] | Sittin' In | 1969 | 25.00 |
| ❑ BLP-7004 [10] | The Best in Two-Beat | 1950 | 500.00 |
| ❑ BLP-7005 [10] | Art Hodes' Hot Five | 1950 | 500.00 |
| ❑ BLP-7006 [10] | Dixieland Jubilee | 1950 | 500.00 |
| ❑ BLP-7015 [10] | Dixieland Clambake | 1951 | 500.00 |
| ❑ BLP-7021 [10] | Out of the Backroom | 1952 | 500.00 |
| **DOTTED EIGHTH** | | | |
| ❑ 1000 [M] | Art for Art's Sake | 195? | 50.00 |
| **EMARCY** | | | |
| ❑ MG-26104 [10] | Jazz Chicago Style | 1954 | 150.00 |
| ❑ SRE-66005 | Plain Old Blues | 196? | 20.00 |
| **JAZZOLOGY** | | | |
| ❑ J-46 [M] | For Art's Sake | 196? | 20.00 |
| **MERCURY** | | | |
| ❑ MG-20185 [M] | Chicago Style Jazz | 1957 | 60.00 |
| **MOSAIC** | | | |
| ❑ MR5-114 [(5)] | The Complete Art Hodes Blue Note Sessions | 199? | 200.00 |
| *—Limited edition of 7,500* | | | |
| **PARAMOUNT** | | | |
| ❑ LP-113 [M] | The Trios | 1955 | 150.00 |
| **RIVERSIDE** | | | |
| ❑ RLP-1012 [10] | Chicago Rhythm Kings | 1953 | 150.00 |

### HODGES, JOHNNY

| Number | Title (A Side/B Side) | Yr | NM |
|---|---|---|---|
| **AMERICAN RECORDING SOCIETY** | | | |
| ❑ G-421 [M] | Johnny Hodges and the Ellington All-Stars | 195? | 40.00 |
| **CLEF** | | | |
| ❑ MGC-111 [10] | Johnny Hodges Collates | 1953 | 150.00 |
| ❑ MGC-128 [10] | Johnny Hodges Collates #2 | 1953 | 200.00 |
| **EPIC** | | | |
| ❑ LN 3105 [M] | Hodge Podge | 1955 | 60.00 |
| **FLYING DUTCHMAN** | | | |
| ❑ 120 | Three Shades of Blue | 1971 | 20.00 |
| **IMPULSE!** | | | |
| ❑ A-61 [M] | Everybody Knows | 1964 | 25.00 |
| ❑ AS-61 [S] | Everybody Knows | 1964 | 30.00 |
| **JAZZ PANORAMA** | | | |
| ❑ 1806 [10] | Johnny Hodges | 1951 | 150.00 |
| **MERCER** | | | |
| ❑ LP-1000 [10] | Johnny Hodges, Vol. 1 | 1951 | 150.00 |
| ❑ LP-1006 [10] | Johnny Hodges, Vol. 2 | 1951 | 150.00 |
| **MERCURY** | | | |
| ❑ MGC-111 [10] | Johnny Hodges Collates | 1952 | 250.00 |
| **MOSAIC** | | | |
| ❑ MR6-126 [(6)] | The Complete Johnny Hodges Sessions 1951-1955 | 199? | 150.00 |
| **NORGRAN** | | | |
| ❑ MGN-1 [10] | Swing with Johnny Hodges | 1954 | 200.00 |
| ❑ MGN-1004 [M] | Memories of Ellington | 1954 | 150.00 |
| ❑ MGN-1009 [M] | More of Johnny Hodges | 1954 | 150.00 |
| ❑ MGN-1024 [M] | Johnny Hodges Dance Bash | 1955 | 150.00 |
| ❑ MGN-1045 [M] | Creamy | 1955 | 150.00 |
| ❑ MGN-1048 [M] | Castle Rock | 1955 | 120.00 |
| ❑ MGN-1055 [M] | Ellingtonia '56 | 1956 | 100.00 |
| ❑ MGN-1059 [M] | In a Tender Mood | 1956 | 100.00 |
| ❑ MGN-1060 [M] | Used to Be Duke | 1956 | 100.00 |
| ❑ MGN-1061 [M] | The Blues | 1956 | 100.00 |
| ❑ MGN-1091 [M] | Perdido | 1956 | 100.00 |
| ❑ MGN-1092 [M] | In a Mellow Tone | 1956 | 100.00 |
| **RCA VICTOR** | | | |
| ❑ LPV-533 [M] | Things Ain't What They Used to Be | 1966 | 20.00 |
| ❑ LPT-3000 [10] | Alto Sax | 1952 | 150.00 |
| ❑ LPM-3867 [M] | Triple Play | 1967 | 30.00 |
| ❑ LSP-3867 [S] | Triple Play | 1967 | 20.00 |
| **VERVE** | | | |
| ❑ MGVS-6017 [S] | The Big Sound | 1960 | 40.00 |
| ❑ MGVS-6048 [S] | The Prettiest Gershwin | 1960 | 40.00 |
| ❑ MGVS-6055 [S] | Back to Back — Duke Ellington and Johnny Hodges Play the Blues | 1960 | 40.00 |
| ❑ MGVS-6109 [S] | Side by Side | 1960 | 40.00 |
| ❑ MGVS-6109 [S] | Side by Side | 199? | 25.00 |
| *—Classic Records reissue on audiophile vinyl* | | | |
| ❑ MGV-8136 [M] | Creamy | 1957 | 50.00 |
| *—Reissue of Norgran 1045* | | | |
| ❑ V-8136 [M] | Creamy | 1961 | 20.00 |
| ❑ MGV-8139 [M] | Castle Rock | 1957 | 50.00 |
| *—Reissue of Norgran 1048* | | | |

| Number | Title (A Side/B Side) | Yr | NM |
|---|---|---|---|
| ❑ V-8139 [M] | Castle Rock | 1961 | 20.00 |
| ❑ MGV-8145 [M] | Ellingtonia '56 | 1957 | 50.00 |
| *—Reissue of Norgran 1055* | | | |
| ❑ V-8145 [M] | Ellingtonia '56 | 1961 | 20.00 |
| ❑ MGV-8149 [M] | In a Tender Mood | 1957 | 50.00 |
| *—Reissue of Norgran 1059* | | | |
| ❑ V-8149 [M] | In a Tender Mood | 1961 | 20.00 |
| ❑ MGV-8150 [M] | Used to Be Duke | 1957 | 50.00 |
| *—Reissue of Norgran 1060* | | | |
| ❑ V-8150 [M] | Used to Be Duke | 1961 | 20.00 |
| ❑ MGV-8151 [M] | The Blues | 1957 | 50.00 |
| *—Reissue of Norgran 1061* | | | |
| ❑ V-8151 [M] | The Blues | 1961 | 20.00 |
| ❑ MGV-8179 [M] | Perdido | 1957 | 50.00 |
| *—Reissue of Norgran 1091* | | | |
| ❑ V-8179 [M] | Perdido | 1961 | 20.00 |
| ❑ MGV-8180 [M] | In a Mellow Tone | 1957 | 50.00 |
| *—Reissue of Norgran 1092* | | | |
| ❑ V-8180 [M] | In a Mellow Tone | 1961 | 20.00 |
| ❑ MGV-8203 [M] | Duke's in Bed | 1957 | 50.00 |
| ❑ V-8203 [M] | Duke's in Bed | 1961 | 20.00 |
| ❑ MGV-8271 [M] | The Big Sound | 1958 | 50.00 |
| ❑ V-8271 [M] | The Big Sound | 1961 | 20.00 |
| ❑ V6-8271 [S] | The Big Sound | 1961 | 20.00 |
| ❑ MGV-8314 [M] | The Prettiest Gershwin | 1959 | 50.00 |
| ❑ V-8314 [M] | The Prettiest Gershwin | 1961 | 20.00 |
| ❑ V6-8314 [S] | The Prettiest Gershwin | 1961 | 20.00 |
| ❑ MGV-8317 [M] | Back to Back — Duke Ellington and Johnny Hodges Play the Blues | 1959 | 50.00 |
| ❑ V-8317 [M] | Back to Back — Duke Ellington and Johnny Hodges Play the Blues | 1961 | 20.00 |
| ❑ V6-8317 [S] | Back to Back — Duke Ellington and Johnny Hodges Play the Blues | 1961 | 20.00 |
| ❑ MGV-8345 [M] | Side by Side | 1959 | 50.00 |
| ❑ V-8345 [M] | Side by Side | 1961 | 20.00 |
| ❑ V6-8345 [S] | Side by Side | 1961 | 20.00 |
| ❑ MGV-8355 [M] | Not So Dukish | 1960 | 50.00 |
| ❑ V-8355 [M] | Not So Dukish | 1961 | 20.00 |
| ❑ MGV-8358 [M] | Blues-a-Plenty | 1960 | 50.00 |
| ❑ V-8358 [M] | Blues-a-Plenty | 1961 | 20.00 |
| ❑ V6-8358 [S] | Blues-a-Plenty | 1961 | 20.00 |
| ❑ V6-8358 [S] | Blues-a-Plenty | 199? | 25.00 |
| *—Classic Records reissue on audiophile vinyl* | | | |
| ❑ V-8452 [M] | Johnny Hodges with Billy Strayhorn | 1962 | 25.00 |
| ❑ V6-8452 [S] | Johnny Hodges with Billy Strayhorn | 1962 | 30.00 |
| ❑ V-8492 [M] | The Eleventh Hour | 1962 | 25.00 |
| ❑ V6-8492 [S] | The Eleventh Hour | 1962 | 30.00 |
| ❑ V-8561 [M] | Sandy's Gone | 1963 | 25.00 |
| ❑ V6-8561 [S] | Sandy's Gone | 1963 | 30.00 |
| ❑ V6-8680 [S] | Blue Notes | 1966 | 20.00 |
| ❑ V-8726v [M] | Don't Sleep in the Subway | 1967 | 20.00 |

### HODGES, JOHNNY, AND WILD BILL DAVIS

**RCA VICTOR**

| Number | Title (A Side/B Side) | Yr | NM |
|---|---|---|---|
| ❑ LPM-3393 [M] | Con-Soul and Sax | 1965 | 20.00 |
| ❑ LSP-3393 [S] | Con-Soul and Sax | 1965 | 25.00 |
| ❑ LSP-3706 [S] | Eddie Hodges and Wild Bill Davis In Atlantic City | 1966 | 20.00 |

**VERVE**

| Number | Title (A Side/B Side) | Yr | NM |
|---|---|---|---|
| ❑ V-8406 [M] | Blue Hodges | 1961 | 20.00 |
| ❑ V6-8406 [S] | Blue Hodges | 1961 | 25.00 |
| ❑ V-8570 [M] | A Mess of Blues | 1964 | 20.00 |
| ❑ V6-8570 [S] | A Mess of Blues | 1964 | 25.00 |
| ❑ V-8599 [M] | Blue Rabbit | 1964 | 20.00 |
| ❑ V6-8599 [S] | Blue Rabbit | 1964 | 25.00 |
| ❑ V-8617 [M] | Joe's Blues | 1965 | 20.00 |
| ❑ V6-8617 [S] | Joe's Blues | 1965 | 25.00 |
| ❑ V-8630 [M] | Wings and Things | 1965 | 20.00 |
| ❑ V6-8630 [S] | Wings and Things | 1965 | 25.00 |
| ❑ V-8635 [M] | Blue Pyramid | 1965 | 20.00 |
| ❑ V6-8635 [S] | Blue Pyramid | 1965 | 25.00 |

### HODGES, JOHNNY, AND EARL "FATHA" HINES

**VERVE**

| Number | Title (A Side/B Side) | Yr | NM |
|---|---|---|---|
| ❑ V-8647 [M] | Stride Right | 1966 | 20.00 |
| ❑ V6-8647 [S] | Stride Right | 1966 | 25.00 |
| ❑ V-8732 [M] | Swing's Our Thing | 1967 | 25.00 |

### HOFFMAN, ABBIE

**BIG TOE**

| Number | Title (A Side/B Side) | Yr | NM |
|---|---|---|---|
| ❑ 1 | Wake Up, America! | 196? | 30.00 |

### HOFNER, ADOLPH

**COLUMBIA**

| Number | Title (A Side/B Side) | Yr | NM |
|---|---|---|---|
| ❑ CL 9017 [10] | Dude Ranch Dances | 1951 | 200.00 |

**DECCA**

| Number | Title (A Side/B Side) | Yr | NM |
|---|---|---|---|
| ❑ DL 5564 [10] | Dance-O-Rama | 1955 | 400.00 |

### HOG HEAVEN The Shondells after Tommy James went solo.

**ROULETTE**

| Number | Title (A Side/B Side) | Yr | NM |
|---|---|---|---|
| ❑ SR 42057 | Hog Heaven | 1971 | 20.00 |

### HOGAN, CLAIRE

**MGM**

| Number | Title (A Side/B Side) | Yr | NM |
|---|---|---|---|
| ❑ E-4501 [M] | Boozers and Losers | 1967 | 20.00 |
| ❑ SE-4501 [S] | Boozers and Losers | 1967 | 25.00 |

### HOGAN, SILAS

**EXCELLO**

| Number | Title (A Side/B Side) | Yr | NM |
|---|---|---|---|
| ❑ LPS-8019 | Trouble at Home | 1972 | 20.00 |

### HOGG, SMOKEY

**CROWN**

| Number | Title (A Side/B Side) | Yr | NM |
|---|---|---|---|
| ❑ CLP-5226 [M] | Smokey Hogg Sings the Blues | 1962 | 50.00 |

**TIME**

| Number | Title (A Side/B Side) | Yr | NM |
|---|---|---|---|
| ❑ 6 [M] | Smokey Hogg | 1962 | 80.00 |

**UNITED**

| Number | Title (A Side/B Side) | Yr | NM |
|---|---|---|---|
| ❑ US-7745 | Smokey Hogg | 1970 | 12.00 |

### HOLDEN, RANDY

**HOBBIT**

| Number | Title (A Side/B Side) | Yr | NM |
|---|---|---|---|
| ❑ 5002 | Population II | 1968 | 200.00 |

### HOLDEN, RON

**DONNA**

| Number | Title (A Side/B Side) | Yr | NM |
|---|---|---|---|
| ❑ DLP-2111 [M] | I Love You So | 1960 | 250.00 |
| ❑ DLPS-2111 [M] | I Love You So | 1960 | 300.00 |
| *—Stereo records not known to exist; this is for a mono record in a stereo cover* | | | |

### HOLIDAY, BILLIE

**AMERICAN RECORDING SOCIETY**

| Number | Title (A Side/B Side) | Yr | NM |
|---|---|---|---|
| ❑ G-409 [M] | Billie Holiday Sings | 1956 | 60.00 |
| *—Reissue of Clef 713* | | | |
| ❑ G-431 [M] | Lady Sings the Blues | 1957 | 60.00 |
| *—Reissue of Clef 721* | | | |

**CLEF**

| Number | Title (A Side/B Side) | Yr | NM |
|---|---|---|---|
| ❑ MGC-118 [10] | Billie Holiday Sings | 1953 | 180.00 |
| ❑ MGC-144 [10] | An Evening with Billie Holiday | 1954 | 180.00 |
| ❑ MGC-161 [10] | Billie Holiday Favorites | 1954 | 180.00 |
| ❑ MGC-169 [10] | Billie Holiday at Jazz at the Philharmonic | 1955 | 180.00 |
| ❑ MGC-669 [M] | Music for Torching | 1955 | 100.00 |
| ❑ MGC-686 [M] | A Recital by Billie Holiday | 1956 | 120.00 |
| *—Reissue of 144 and 161 as one 12-inch LP* | | | |
| ❑ MGC-690 [M] | Solitude — Songs by Billie Holiday | 1956 | 120.00 |
| *—Reissue of 118* | | | |
| ❑ MGC-713 [M] | Velvet Moods | 1956 | 120.00 |
| ❑ MGC-721 [M] | Lady Sings the Blues | 1956 | 120.00 |

**COLUMBIA**

| Number | Title (A Side/B Side) | Yr | NM |
|---|---|---|---|
| ❑ C3L 21 [(3)M] | The Golden Years | 1962 | 50.00 |
| *—Red and black label with six "eye" logos* | | | |
| ❑ C3L 21 [(3)M] | The Golden Years | 1963 | 25.00 |
| *—Red "Guaranteed High Fidelity" or "360 Sound" label* | | | |
| ❑ C3L 40 [(3)M] | The Golden Years, Volume 2 | 1966 | 30.00 |
| *—Red label, "Mono" at bottom* | | | |
| ❑ C3L 40 [(3)M] | The Golden Years, Volume 2 | 197? | 20.00 |
| *—Orange labels* | | | |
| ❑ CL 637 [M] | Lady Day | 1954 | 70.00 |
| *—Maroon label, gold print* | | | |
| ❑ CL 637 [M] | Lady Day | 1956 | 40.00 |
| *—Red and black label with six "eye" logos* | | | |
| ❑ CL 1157 [M] | Lady in Satin | 1958 | 40.00 |
| *—Red and black label with six "eye" logos* | | | |
| ❑ CL 6129 [10] | Billie Holiday Sings | 1950 | 200.00 |
| ❑ CL 6163 [10] | Billie Holiday Favorites | 1951 | 200.00 |
| ❑ CS 8048 [S] | Lady in Satin | 1958 | 40.00 |
| *—Red and black label with six "eye" logos* | | | |
| ❑ CS 8048 [S] | Lady in Satin | 1999 | 25.00 |
| *—Classic Records reissue on audiophile vinyl* | | | |
| ❑ G 30782 [(2)] | God Bless the Child | 1972 | 20.00 |

**COLUMBIA MUSICAL TREASURY**

| Number | Title (A Side/B Side) | Yr | NM |
|---|---|---|---|
| ❑ P3M 5869 [(3)] | The Golden Years | 197? | 20.00 |

**COMMODORE**

| Number | Title (A Side/B Side) | Yr | NM |
|---|---|---|---|
| ❑ FL-20005 [10] | Billie Holiday, Volume 1 | 1950 | 250.00 |
| ❑ FL-20006 [10] | Billie Holiday, Volume 2 | 1950 | 250.00 |
| ❑ FL-30008 [M] | Billie Holiday | 1959 | 50.00 |
| *—Reissue of 20006* | | | |
| ❑ FL-30011 [M] | Billie Holiday with Eddie Heywood and His Orchestra | 1959 | 50.00 |
| *—Reissue of 20005* | | | |

**CROWN**

| Number | Title (A Side/B Side) | Yr | NM |
|---|---|---|---|
| ❑ CLP-5380 [M] | Billie Holiday & Vivian Fears | 196? | 20.00 |

**DECCA**

| Number | Title (A Side/B Side) | Yr | NM |
|---|---|---|---|
| ❑ DXB-161 [(2)M] | The Billie Holiday Story | 1959 | 20.00 |
| ❑ DL 5345 [10] | Lover Man | 1951 | 200.00 |
| ❑ DL 8215 [M] | The Lady Sings | 1956 | 60.00 |
| ❑ DL 8701 [M] | The Blues Are Brewin' | 1958 | 60.00 |
| ❑ DL 8702 [M] | Lover Man | 1958 | 60.00 |

**JAZZTONE**

| Number | Title (A Side/B Side) | Yr | NM |
|---|---|---|---|
| ❑ J-1209 [M] | Billie Holiday Sings | 1955 | 50.00 |
| *—Reissue of Commodore 20005* | | | |

**JOLLY ROGER**

| Number | Title (A Side/B Side) | Yr | NM |
|---|---|---|---|
| ❑ 5020 [10] | Billie Holiday, Volume 1 | 1954 | 100.00 |
| ❑ 5021 [10] | Billie Holiday, Volume 2 | 1954 | 100.00 |
| ❑ 5022 [10] | Billie Holiday, Volume 3 | 1954 | 100.00 |

**MAINSTREAM**

| Number | Title (A Side/B Side) | Yr | NM |
|---|---|---|---|
| ❑ 56000 [M] | The Commodore Recordings | 1965 | 25.00 |
| ❑ 56022 [M] | Once Upon a Time | 1965 | 25.00 |

**MGM**

| Number | Title (A Side/B Side) | Yr | NM |
|---|---|---|---|
| ❑ E-3764 [M] | Billie Holiday | 1959 | 40.00 |
| ❑ SE-3764 [S] | Billie Holiday | 1959 | 50.00 |

**MOBILE FIDELITY**

| Number | Title (A Side/B Side) | Yr | NM |
|---|---|---|---|
| ❑ 1-247 | Body and Soul | 1996 | 120.00 |
| *—Audiophile vinyl* | | | |

**RIC**

| Number | Title (A Side/B Side) | Yr | NM |
|---|---|---|---|
| ❑ M-2001 [M] | Rare Live Recording | 1964 | 25.00 |

**SCORE**

| Number | Title (A Side/B Side) | Yr | NM |
|---|---|---|---|
| ❑ SLP-4014 [M] | Billie Holiday Sings the Blues | 1957 | 120.00 |

**UNITED ARTISTS**

| Number | Title (A Side/B Side) | Yr | NM |
|---|---|---|---|
| ❑ UAJ-14014 [M] | Lady Love | 1962 | 40.00 |
| ❑ UASJ-15014 [S] | Lady Love | 1962 | 50.00 |

**VERVE**

| Number | Title (A Side/B Side) | Yr | NM |
|---|---|---|---|
| ❑ MGVS-6021 [S] | Songs for Distingue Lovers | 1960 | 60.00 |
| ❑ MGVS-6021 [S] | Songs for Distingue Lovers | 199? | 25.00 |
| *—Classic Records reissue on audiophile vinyl* | | | |
| ❑ MGVS-6021-45 [(2)S] | Songs for Distingue Lovers | 1999 | 20.00 |
| *—Classic Records reissue on two 12-inch 45-rpm records* | | | |
| ❑ MGV-8026 [M] | Music for Torching | 1957 | 40.00 |
| *—Reissue of Clef 669* | | | |
| ❑ V-8026 [M] | Music for Torching | 1961 | 20.00 |
| ❑ MGV-8027 [M] | A Recital by Billie Holiday | 1957 | 40.00 |
| *—Reissue of Clef 686* | | | |
| ❑ V-8027 [M] | A Recital by Billie Holiday | 1961 | 20.00 |
| ❑ MGV-8074 [M] | Solitude — Songs by Billie Holiday | 1957 | 40.00 |
| *—Reissue of Clef 690* | | | |
| ❑ V-8074 [M] | Solitude — Songs by Billie Holiday | 1961 | 20.00 |
| ❑ MGV-8096 [M] | Velvet Moods | 1957 | 40.00 |
| *—Reissue of Clef 713* | | | |
| ❑ V-8096 [M] | Velvet Moods | 1961 | 20.00 |
| ❑ MGV-8099 [M] | Lady Sings the Blues | 1957 | 40.00 |
| *—Reissue of Clef 721* | | | |
| ❑ V-8099 [M] | Lady Sings the Blues | 1957 | 20.00 |
| ❑ MGV-8197 [M] | Body and Soul | 1957 | 60.00 |
| ❑ V-8197 [M] | Body and Soul | 1961 | 20.00 |
| ❑ MGV-8257 [M] | Songs for Distingue Lovers | 1958 | 60.00 |
| ❑ V-8257 [M] | Songs for Distingue Lovers | 1961 | 20.00 |
| ❑ V6-8257 [S] | Songs for Distingue Lovers | 1961 | 25.00 |
| ❑ MGV-8302 [M] | Stay with Me | 1959 | 50.00 |
| ❑ V-8302 [M] | Stay with Me | 1961 | 20.00 |
| ❑ MGV-8329 [M] | All or Nothing at All | 1959 | 50.00 |
| ❑ V-8329 [M] | All or Nothing at All | 1959 | 20.00 |
| ❑ MGV-8338-2 [(2)M] | The Unforgettable Lady Day | 1959 | 80.00 |
| ❑ V-8338-2 [(2)M] | The Unforgettable Lady Day | 1961 | 25.00 |
| ❑ V-8410 [M] | The Essential Billie Holiday | 1961 | 20.00 |
| ❑ V-8505 [M] | The Essential Jazz Vocals | 1963 | 20.00 |

### HOLIDAY, BILLIE, AND STAN GETZ

**DALE**

| Number | Title (A Side/B Side) | Yr | NM |
|---|---|---|---|
| ❑ 25 [10] | Billie and Stan | 1951 | 400.00 |

### HOLIDAY, BILLIE/AL HIBBLER

**IMPERIAL**

| Number | Title (A Side/B Side) | Yr | NM |
|---|---|---|---|
| ❑ LP-9185 [M] | Billie Holiday, Al Hibbler and the Blues | 1962 | 50.00 |
| ❑ LP-12185 [R] | Billie Holiday, Al Hibbler and the Blues | 196? | 30.00 |

### HOLIDAY, JIMMY

**MINIT**

| Number | Title (A Side/B Side) | Yr | NM |
|---|---|---|---|
| ❑ LP-24005 [M] | Turning Point | 1966 | 30.00 |
| ❑ LP-40005 [S] | Turning Point | 1966 | 40.00 |

### HOLIDAY, JOE

**DECCA**

| Number | Title (A Side/B Side) | Yr | NM |
|---|---|---|---|
| ❑ DL 8487 [M] | Holiday for Jazz | 1957 | 60.00 |

**PRESTIGE**

| Number | Title (A Side/B Side) | Yr | NM |
|---|---|---|---|
| ❑ PRLP-131 [10] | Joe Holiday | 1952 | 200.00 |

### HOLIDAY, JOE/BILLY TAYLOR

**PRESTIGE**

| Number | Title (A Side/B Side) | Yr | NM |
|---|---|---|---|
| ❑ PRLP-171 [10] | Mambo Jazz | 1953 | 150.00 |

### HOLLAND, EDDIE

**MOTOWN**

| Number | Title (A Side/B Side) | Yr | NM |
|---|---|---|---|
| ❑ 604 [M] | Eddie Holland | 1963 | 400.00 |

### HOLLIDAY, JUDY

**COLUMBIA**

| Number | Title (A Side/B Side) | Yr | NM |
|---|---|---|---|
| ❑ CL 1153 [M] | Trouble Is a Man | 1958 | 30.00 |
| ❑ CS 8041 [S] | Trouble Is a Man | 1959 | 40.00 |

### HOLLIES, THE

**ATLANTIC**

| Number | Title (A Side/B Side) | Yr | NM |
|---|---|---|---|
| ❑ 80076 | What Goes Around | 1983 | 10.00 |

**CAPITOL**

| Number | Title (A Side/B Side) | Yr | NM |
|---|---|---|---|
| ❑ N-16056 | Hollies' Greatest | 1980 | 8.00 |

**COLUMBIA LIMITED EDITION**

| Number | Title (A Side/B Side) | Yr | NM |
|---|---|---|---|
| ❑ LE 10178 | He Ain't Heavy, He's My Brother | 1976 | 12.00 |

The Buddy Holly Story
CORAL RECORDS
CRL 57279


Buddy Holly, *The Buddy Holly Story,*
Coral CRL 57279, 1959, mono, all-black print on back cover, $150.

| Number | Title (A Side/B Side) | Yr | NM |
|---|---|---|---|
| **EMI AMERICA** | | | |
| ❑ SN-16397 | More Great Hits (1963-1968) | 1986 | 8.00 |
| **EPIC** | | | |
| ❑ AS 138 [DJ] | Everything You Always Wanted to Hear by the Hollies But Were Afraid to Ask For | 1976 | 20.00 |
| *—Promo-only sampler album* | | | |
| ❑ LN 24315 [M] | Evolution | 1967 | 30.00 |
| ❑ LN 24344 [M] | Dear Eloise/King Midas in Reverse | 1967 | 30.00 |
| ❑ BN 26315 [S] | Evolution | 1967 | 25.00 |
| ❑ BN 26344 [S] | Dear Eloise/King Midas in Reverse | 1967 | 25.00 |
| ❑ BN 26447 | Words and Music by Bob Dylan | 1969 | 15.00 |
| *—Yellow label* | | | |
| ❑ BN 26447 | Words and Music by Bob Dylan | 1973 | 10.00 |
| *—Orange label* | | | |
| ❑ BN 26538 | He Ain't Heavy, He's My Brother | 1970 | 20.00 |
| ❑ E 30255 | Moving Finger | 1971 | 20.00 |
| ❑ KE 30958 | Distant Light | 1972 | 15.00 |
| *—Yellow label* | | | |
| ❑ KE 30958 | Distant Light | 1974 | 10.00 |
| *—Orange label* | | | |
| ❑ PE 30958 | Distant Light | 1986 | 8.00 |
| *—Blue label* | | | |
| ❑ KE 31992 | Romany | 1972 | 12.00 |
| *—Yellow label* | | | |
| ❑ KE 31992 | Romany | 1974 | 10.00 |
| *—Orange label* | | | |
| ❑ KE 32061 | The Hollies' Greatest Hits | 1973 | 12.00 |
| *—Yellow label* | | | |
| ❑ KE 32061 | The Hollies' Greatest Hits | 1974 | 10.00 |
| *—Orange label* | | | |
| ❑ PE 32061 | The Hollies' Greatest Hits | 1979 | 8.00 |
| *—Blue label* | | | |
| ❑ KE 32574 | Hollies | 1974 | 10.00 |
| ❑ PE 33387 | Another Night | 1975 | 10.00 |
| ❑ PE 34714 | Clarke, Hicks, Sylvester, Calvert & Elliot | 1977 | 10.00 |
| ❑ JE 35334 | A Crazy Steal | 1978 | 10.00 |
| **IMPERIAL** | | | |
| ❑ LP-9265 [M] | Here I Go Again | 1964 | 50.00 |
| *—Black and pink label* | | | |
| ❑ LP-9265 [M] | Here I Go Again | 1964 | 150.00 |
| *—Black label with stars* | | | |
| ❑ LP-9299 [M] | Hear! Here! | 1965 | 50.00 |
| ❑ LP-9312 [M] | The Hollies — Beat Group | 1966 | 30.00 |
| ❑ LP-9330 [M] | Bus Stop | 1966 | 25.00 |
| *—Black and green label* | | | |
| ❑ LP-9330 [M] | Bus Stop | 1966 | 30.00 |
| *—Black and pink label* | | | |
| ❑ LP-9339 [M] | Stop! Stop! Stop! | 1966 | 25.00 |
| ❑ LP-9350 [M] | The Hollies' Greatest Hits | 1967 | 20.00 |
| ❑ LP-12265 [R] | Here I Go Again | 1964 | 30.00 |
| *—Black and pink label* | | | |
| ❑ LP-12265 [R] | Here I Go Again | 1964 | 100.00 |
| *—Black label with silver print* | | | |
| ❑ LP-12299 [R] | Hear! Here! | 1965 | 30.00 |
| ❑ LP-12312 [S] | The Hollies — Beat Group | 1966 | 40.00 |
| ❑ LP-12330 [R] | Bus Stop | 1966 | 20.00 |
| *—Black and green label* | | | |
| ❑ LP-12330 [R] | Bus Stop | 1966 | 25.00 |
| *—Black and pink label* | | | |
| ❑ LP-12339 [S] | Stop! Stop! Stop! | 1966 | 30.00 |
| ❑ LP-12350 [P] | The Hollies' Greatest Hits | 1967 | 25.00 |
| **LIBERTY** | | | |
| ❑ LN-10216 | Pay You Back with Interest | 1982 | 8.00 |
| **PAIR** | | | |
| ❑ PDL2-1041 [(2)] | Hottest Hits | 1986 | 15.00 |
| **REALM** | | | |
| ❑ 2V-8026 [(2)] | The Hollies, Volume 1 | 1976 | 15.00 |
| *—Two-record TV package* | | | |
| ❑ 1V-8027 | The Hollies, Volume 2 | 1976 | 12.00 |
| *—TV package sold with Realm 8026* | | | |
| **UNITED ARTISTS** | | | |
| ❑ UA-LA329-E | The Very Best of the Hollies | 1975 | 10.00 |

## HOLLOWAY, BRENDA

| Number | Title (A Side/B Side) | Yr | NM |
|---|---|---|---|
| **MOTOWN** | | | |
| ❑ 5242 ML | Every Little Bit Hurts | 1982 | 12.00 |
| **TAMLA** | | | |
| ❑ T 257 [M] | Every Little Bit Hurts | 1964 | 200.00 |
| ❑ TS 257 [R] | Every Little Bit Hurts | 1964 | 150.00 |

## HOLLOWAY, LOLEATTA

| Number | Title (A Side/B Side) | Yr | NM |
|---|---|---|---|
| **GOLD MIND** | | | |
| ❑ 7500 | Loleatta | 1977 | 20.00 |
| ❑ A-9501 | Queen of the Night | 1978 | 20.00 |
| ❑ GA-9506 | Love Sensation | 1979 | 20.00 |

## HOLLOWAY, RED

| Number | Title (A Side/B Side) | Yr | NM |
|---|---|---|---|
| **PRESTIGE** | | | |
| ❑ PRLP-7299 [M] | Burner | 1964 | 50.00 |
| *—Yellow label, Bergenfield, N.J. address* | | | |
| ❑ PRLP-7299 [M] | Burner | 1965 | 25.00 |
| *—Blue label, trident logo at right* | | | |
| ❑ PRST-7299 [S] | Burner | 1964 | 50.00 |
| *—Yellow label, Bergenfield, N.J. address* | | | |
| ❑ PRST-7299 [S] | Burner | 1965 | 25.00 |
| *—Blue label, trident logo at right* | | | |
| ❑ PRLP-7325 [M] | Cookin' Together | 1964 | 30.00 |
| ❑ PRST-7325 [S] | Cookin' Together | 1964 | 40.00 |
| ❑ PRLP-7390 [M] | Sax, Strings and Soul | 1965 | 20.00 |
| ❑ PRST-7390 [S] | Sax, Strings and Soul | 1965 | 25.00 |
| ❑ PRLP-7473 [M] | Red Soul | 1966 | 20.00 |
| ❑ PRST-7473 [S] | Red Soul | 1966 | 25.00 |

## HOLLY, BUDDY

| Number | Title (A Side/B Side) | Yr | NM |
|---|---|---|---|
| **CORAL** | | | |
| ❑ CXB 8 [(2)M] | The Best of Buddy Holly | 1966 | 80.00 |
| ❑ CXSB 8 [(2)R] | The Best of Buddy Holly | 1966 | 50.00 |
| ❑ CRL 57210 [M] | Buddy Holly | 1958 | 400.00 |
| *—Maroon label* | | | |
| ❑ CRL 57210 [M] | Buddy Holly | 1964 | 100.00 |
| *—Black label with color bars* | | | |
| ❑ CRL 57279 [M] | The Buddy Holly Story | 1959 | 150.00 |
| *—Maroon label; back color print in all black* | | | |
| ❑ CRL 57279 [M] | The Buddy Holly Story | 1959 | 300.00 |
| *—Maroon label; back color print in black and red* | | | |
| ❑ CRL 57279 [M] | The Buddy Holly Story | 1963 | 80.00 |
| *—Black label with color bars* | | | |
| ❑ CRL 57326 [M] | The Buddy Holly Story, Vol. 2 | 1959 | 200.00 |
| *—Maroon label* | | | |
| ❑ CRL 57326 [M] | The Buddy Holly Story, Vol. 2 | 1963 | 80.00 |
| *—Black label with color bars* | | | |
| ❑ CRL 57405 [M] | Buddy Holly and the Crickets | 1962 | 150.00 |
| *—Reissue of the Crickets LP on Brunswick 54038* | | | |
| ❑ CRL 57426 [M] | Reminiscing | 1963 | 200.00 |
| *—Maroon label* | | | |
| ❑ CRL 57426 [M] | Reminiscing | 1964 | 80.00 |
| *—Black label with color bars* | | | |
| ❑ CRL 57450 [M] | Buddy Holly Showcase | 1964 | 100.00 |
| ❑ CRL 57463 [M] | Holly in the Hills | 1965 | 120.00 |
| ❑ CRL 57492 [M] | Buddy Holly's Greatest Hits | 1967 | 80.00 |
| ❑ CRL 757279 [R] | The Buddy Holly Story | 1963 | 40.00 |
| ❑ CRL 757326 [R] | The Buddy Holly Story, Vol. 2 | 1963 | 40.00 |
| ❑ CRL 757405 [R] | Buddy Holly and the Crickets | 1963 | 40.00 |
| ❑ CRL 757426 [R] | Reminiscing | 1964 | 40.00 |
| ❑ CRL 757450 [R] | Buddy Holly Showcase | 1964 | 80.00 |
| ❑ CRL 757463 [R] | Holly in the Hills | 1965 | 100.00 |
| ❑ CRL 757492 [P] | Buddy Holly's Greatest Hits | 1967 | 50.00 |
| ❑ CRL 757504 [S] | Giant | 1969 | 50.00 |
| **CRICKET** | | | |
| ❑ C001000 | Buddy Holly Live — Volume 1 | 197? | 20.00 |
| ❑ C001001 | Buddy Holly Live — Volume 1 | 197? | 20.00 |
| **DECCA** | | | |
| ❑ DXSE 7207 [(2)] | A Rock 'n' Roll Collection | 1972 | 40.00 |
| ❑ DL 8707 [M] | That'll Be the Day | 1958 | 1500. |
| *—Black label with silver print* | | | |
| ❑ DL 8707 [M] | That'll Be the Day | 1961 | 300.00 |
| *—Black label with color bars* | | | |
| **GREAT NORTHWEST** | | | |
| ❑ GNW-4014 | Visions of Buddy | 197? | 10.00 |
| *—Interview album* | | | |
| **MCA** | | | |
| ❑ 737 | The Great Buddy Holly | 197? | 10.00 |
| *—Reissue of MCA Coral LP* | | | |
| ❑ 1484 | Buddy Holly/The Crickets 20 Golden Greats | 198? | 8.00 |
| *—Reissue of 3040* | | | |
| ❑ 3040 | Buddy Holly/The Crickets 20 Golden Greats | 1978 | 15.00 |
| ❑ 4009 [(2)] | A Rock 'n' Roll Collection | 1973 | 20.00 |
| *—Black labels with rainbow* | | | |
| ❑ 4009 [(2)] | A Rock 'n' Roll Collection | 1978 | 12.00 |
| *—Later pressings on tan or blue/rainbow labels* | | | |
| ❑ 4184 [(2)] | Legend | 1985 | 20.00 |
| ❑ 5540 [(2)] | From the Original Master Tapes | 1986 | 25.00 |
| ❑ 11161 | Buddy Holly | 1995 | 40.00 |
| *—Audiophile "Heavy Vinyl" reissue with gatefold cover* | | | |
| ❑ 25239 | Buddy Holly | 1989 | 12.00 |
| *—Reissue of Coral 57210* | | | |
| ❑ 27059 | For the First Time Anywhere | 1983 | 10.00 |
| ❑ 80000 [(6)] | The Complete Buddy Holly | 1981 | 80.00 |
| *—Box set with booklet and custom innersleeves* | | | |
| **MCA CORAL** | | | |
| ❑ CD-20101 | The Great Buddy Holly | 1973 | 12.00 |
| **VOCALION** | | | |
| ❑ VL 3811 [M] | The Great Buddy Holly | 1967 | 80.00 |
| ❑ VL 73811 [R] | The Great Buddy Holly | 1967 | 50.00 |
| ❑ VL 73923 | Good Rockin' | 1971 | 120.00 |

## HOLLYRIDGE STRINGS, THE

| Number | Title (A Side/B Side) | Yr | NM |
|---|---|---|---|
| **CAPITOL** | | | |
| ❑ ST-883 | Hits of the 70's | 1971 | 12.00 |
| ❑ SM-2116 | The Beatles Song Book | 197? | 10.00 |
| ❑ ST 2116 [S] | The Beatles Song Book | 1964 | 20.00 |



**Except when noted otherwise, VG = 25% of NM, and VG+ = 50% of NM. (Example: VG = $2.00, VG+ = $4.00 and NM = $8.00.)**

| Number | Title (A Side/B Side) | Yr | NM |
|---|---|---|---|
| ❑ T 2116 [M] | The Beatles Song Book | 1964 | 15.00 |
| ❑ SM-2156 | The Beach Boys Song Book | 197? | 10.00 |
| ❑ ST 2156 [S] | The Beach Boys Song Book | 1964 | 20.00 |
| ❑ T 2156 [M] | The Beach Boys Song Book | 1964 | 15.00 |
| ❑ ST 2199 [S] | Hits Made Famous by the Four Seasons | 1965 | 20.00 |
| ❑ T 2199 [M] | Hits Made Famous by the Four Seasons | 1965 | 15.00 |
| ❑ ST 2202 [S] | The Beatles Song Book, Vol. 2 | 1965 | 20.00 |
| ❑ T 2202 [M] | The Beatles Song Book, Vol. 2 | 1965 | 15.00 |
| ❑ ST 2221 [S] | Hits Made Famous by Elvis Presley | 1965 | 20.00 |
| ❑ T 2221 [M] | Hits Made Famous by Elvis Presley | 1965 | 15.00 |
| ❑ ST 2310 [S] | The Nat King Cole Song Book | 1965 | 20.00 |
| ❑ T 2310 [M] | The Nat King Cole Song Book | 1965 | 15.00 |
| ❑ ST 2404 [S] | Christmas Favorites by the Hollyridge Strings | 1965 | 15.00 |
| ❑ T 2404 [M] | Christmas Favorites by the Hollyridge Strings | 1965 | 12.00 |
| ❑ SM-2429 | The New Beatles Song Book | 197? | 10.00 |
| ❑ ST 2429 [S] | The New Beatles Song Book | 1966 | 20.00 |
| ❑ T 2429 [M] | The New Beatles Song Book | 1966 | 15.00 |
| ❑ ST 2564 [S] | Oldies But Goldies | 1966 | 20.00 |
| ❑ T 2564 [M] | Oldies But Goldies | 1966 | 15.00 |
| ❑ ST 2611 [S] | Skyscraper | 1966 | 20.00 |
| ❑ T 2611 [M] | Skyscraper | 1966 | 15.00 |
| ❑ ST 2656 [S] | The Beatles Song Book, Vol. 4 | 1967 | 15.00 |
| ❑ T 2656 [M] | The Beatles Song Book, Vol. 4 | 1967 | 20.00 |
| ❑ ST 2749 [S] | The Beach Boys Song Book, Vol. 2 | 1967 | 15.00 |
| ❑ T 2749 [M] | The Beach Boys Song Book, Vol. 2 | 1967 | 20.00 |
| ❑ ST 2998 | Hits Made Famous by Simon and Garfunkel | 1968 | 15.00 |
| ❑ SM-11830 | Christmas Favorites by the Hollyridge Strings | 1978 | 10.00 |

*—Abridged reissue of ST 2404*

### HOLLYWOOD ARGYLES, THE

LUTE

| Number | Title (A Side/B Side) | Yr | NM |
|---|---|---|---|
| ❑ L-9001 [M] | The Hollywood Argyles (Alley Oop) | 1960 | 700.00 |

### HOLLYWOOD PERSUADERS, THE

ORIGINAL SOUND

| Number | Title (A Side/B Side) | Yr | NM |
|---|---|---|---|
| ❑ LPM-5013 [M] | Drums a-Go-Go | 1965 | 50.00 |
| ❑ LPS-8874 [S] | Drums a-Go-Go | 1965 | 60.00 |

### HOLLYWOOD SAXOPHONE QUARTET, THE

LIBERTY

| Number | Title (A Side/B Side) | Yr | NM |
|---|---|---|---|
| ❑ LRP-3047 [M] | Gold Rush Suite | 1957 | 40.00 |
| ❑ LRP-3080 [M] | Sax Appeal | 1958 | 30.00 |
| ❑ LRP-6005 [M] | The Hollywood Saxophone Quartet | 1955 | 40.00 |

### HOLMAN, BILL

| Number | Title (A Side/B Side) | Yr | NM |
|---|---|---|---|
| ANDEX | | | |
| ❑ A-3004 [M] | In a Jazz Orbit | 1958 | 40.00 |
| ❑ AS-3004 [S] | In a Jazz Orbit | 1959 | 30.00 |
| ❑ A-3005 [M] | Jive for Five | 1958 | 40.00 |
| ❑ AS-3005 [S] | Jive for Five | 1959 | 30.00 |
| CAPITOL | | | |
| ❑ ST 1464 [S] | Great Big Band | 1960 | 30.00 |
| ❑ T 1464 [M] | Great Big Band | 1960 | 25.00 |
| ❑ H 6500 [10] | The Bill Holman Octet | 1954 | 120.00 |
| CORAL | | | |
| ❑ CRL 57188 [M] | The Fabulous Bill Holman | 1958 | 80.00 |

### HOLMAN, EDDIE

| Number | Title (A Side/B Side) | Yr | NM |
|---|---|---|---|
| ABC | | | |
| ❑ S-701 | I Love You | 1970 | 30.00 |
| SALSOUL | | | |
| ❑ 5511 | A Night to Remember | 1977 | 10.00 |

### HOLMBERG, JIM

ESP-DISK'

| Number | Title (A Side/B Side) | Yr | NM |
|---|---|---|---|
| ❑ 1098 | MIJ | 196? | 20.00 |

### HOLMES, JAKE

| Number | Title (A Side/B Side) | Yr | NM |
|---|---|---|---|
| COLUMBIA | | | |
| ❑ C 30996 | Jake Holmes | 1972 | 12.00 |
| POLYDOR | | | |
| ❑ 24-4007 | Jake Holmes | 1969 | 12.00 |
| ❑ 24-4034 | So Close, So Very Far to Go | 1970 | 12.00 |
| TOWER | | | |
| ❑ DT 5079 [R] | Above Ground | 1967 | 15.00 |
| ❑ T 5079 [M] | Above Ground | 1967 | 20.00 |
| ❑ ST 5127 | Letter to Katherine December | 1968 | 15.00 |

### HOLMES, MARVIN

| Number | Title (A Side/B Side) | Yr | NM |
|---|---|---|---|
| BROWN DOOR | | | |
| ❑ MH-6573 | Summer of '73 | 1973 | 50.00 |
| ❑ MH-6581 | Honor Thy Father | 1975 | 50.00 |
| UNI | | | |
| ❑ 73046 | Ooh, Ooh, The Dragon And Other Monsters | 1969 | 100.00 |

*—Reproductions exist*

### HOLMES, RICHARD "GROOVE"

| Number | Title (A Side/B Side) | Yr | NM |
|---|---|---|---|
| PACIFIC JAZZ | | | |
| ❑ PJ-23 [M] | Richard "Groove" Holmes | 1961 | 25.00 |
| ❑ ST-23 [S] | Richard "Groove" Holmes | 1961 | 30.00 |
| ❑ PJ-32 [M] | Groovin' with Jug | 1961 | 30.00 |
| ❑ ST-32 [S] | Groovin' with Jug | 1961 | 40.00 |
| ❑ PJ-51 [M] | Somethin' Special | 1962 | 20.00 |
| ❑ ST-51 [S] | Somethin' Special | 1962 | 25.00 |
| ❑ PJ-59 [M] | After Hours | 1962 | 20.00 |
| ❑ ST-59 [S] | After Hours | 1962 | 25.00 |
| ❑ ST-20105 [S] | Tell It Like It Tis | 1966 | 20.00 |
| PRESTIGE | | | |
| ❑ PRST-7435 [S] | Soul Message | 1966 | 20.00 |
| ❑ PRST-7468 [S] | Living Soul | 1966 | 20.00 |
| ❑ PRST-7485 [S] | Misty | 1966 | 20.00 |
| ❑ PRLP-7493 [M] | Spicy | 1967 | 20.00 |
| ❑ PRLP-7497 [M] | Super Cool | 1967 | 20.00 |
| ❑ PRLP-7514 [M] | Get Up and Get It | 1967 | 20.00 |
| WARNER BROS. | | | |
| ❑ W 1553 [M] | Book of the Blues | 1964 | 20.00 |
| ❑ WS 1553 [S] | Book of the Blues | 1964 | 25.00 |
| WORLD PACIFIC | | | |
| ❑ ST-20147 | Welcome Home | 1968 | 20.00 |

### HOLT, RED

ARGO

| Number | Title (A Side/B Side) | Yr | NM |
|---|---|---|---|
| ❑ LP-696 [M] | Look Out! Look Out! | 1962 | 20.00 |
| ❑ LPS-696 [S] | Look Out! Look Out! | 1962 | 25.00 |

### HOLY MACKEREL, THE

REPRISE

| Number | Title (A Side/B Side) | Yr | NM |
|---|---|---|---|
| ❑ RS-6311 | The Holy Mackerel | 1968 | 25.00 |

### HOLY MODAL ROUNDERS, THE

| Number | Title (A Side/B Side) | Yr | NM |
|---|---|---|---|
| ADELPHIA | | | |
| ❑ 1030 | Last Round | 198? | 10.00 |
| ELEKTRA | | | |
| ❑ EKS-74026 | The Moray Eels Eat the Holy Modal Rounders | 1968 | 30.00 |
| ESP-DISK' | | | |
| ❑ 1068 [M] | Indian War Whoop | 1967 | 40.00 |
| ❑ 1068-S [S] | Indian War Whoop | 1967 | 40.00 |
| FANTASY | | | |
| ❑ F-24711 | Stampfel and Weber | 1972 | 20.00 |
| FOLKLORE | | | |
| ❑ FRLP-14031 [M] | The Holy Modal Rounders | 1964 | 80.00 |
| METROMEDIA | | | |
| ❑ MD-1039 | Good Taste Is Timeless | 1970 | 30.00 |
| PRESTIGE | | | |
| ❑ PRLP-7410 [M] | The Holy Modal Rounders 2 | 1965 | 40.00 |
| ❑ PRLP-7451 [M] | The Holy Modal Rounders | 1966 | 40.00 |
| *—Reissue of Folklore LP* | | | |
| ❑ PR-7720 | The Holy Modal Rounders | 1969 | 25.00 |
| ROUNDER | | | |
| ❑ 3004 | Alleged in Their Own Time | 198? | 10.00 |
| SUNDAZED | | | |
| ❑ LP 5126 | The Moray Eels Eat the Holy Modal Rounders | 2002 | 12.00 |

*—Reissue on 180-gram vinyl*

### HOMBRES, THE

VERVE FORECAST

| Number | Title (A Side/B Side) | Yr | NM |
|---|---|---|---|
| ❑ FT-3036 [M] | Let It Out (Let It All Hang Out) | 1967 | 30.00 |
| ❑ FTS-3036 [S] | Let It Out (Let It All Hang Out) | 1967 | 25.00 |
| ❑ FTS-3068 | The Hombres | 1968 | — |

*—Canceled*

### HOMER

UNITED

| Number | Title (A Side/B Side) | Yr | NM |
|---|---|---|---|
| ❑ HS-101 | Grown in U.S.A. | 1970 | 250.00 |

### HOMER AND JETHRO

| Number | Title (A Side/B Side) | Yr | NM |
|---|---|---|---|
| AUDIO LAB | | | |
| ❑ AL-1513 [M] | Musical Madness | 1958 | 100.00 |
| KING | | | |
| ❑ 639 [M] | They Sure Are Corny | 1959 | 100.00 |
| ❑ 848 [M] | Cornier Than Corn | 1963 | 70.00 |
| ❑ KS-1005 | 24 Great Songs in the Homer & Jethro Style | 1967 | 20.00 |
| RCA CAMDEN | | | |
| ❑ CAL-707 [M] | Homer and Jethro Strike Back | 1961 | 15.00 |
| RCA VICTOR | | | |
| ❑ LPM-1412 [M] | Barefoot Ballads | 1957 | 50.00 |
| ❑ LPM-1560 [M] | The Worst of Homer & Jethro | 1958 | 50.00 |
| ❑ LPM-1880 [M] | Life Can Be Miserable | 1958 | 30.00 |
| ❑ LSP-1880 [S] | Life Can Be Miserable | 1958 | 50.00 |
| ❑ LPM-2181 [M] | Homer and Jethro at the Country Club | 1960 | 25.00 |
| ❑ LSP-2181 [S] | Homer and Jethro at the Country Club | 1960 | 40.00 |
| ❑ LPM-2286 [M] | Songs My Mother Never Sang | 1961 | 25.00 |
| ❑ LSP-2286 [S] | Songs My Mother Never Sang | 1961 | 30.00 |
| ❑ LPM-2455 [M] | Zany Songs of the '30s | 1962 | 25.00 |
| ❑ LSP-2455 [S] | Zany Songs of the '30s | 1962 | 30.00 |
| ❑ LPM-2459 [M] | Playing It Straight | 1962 | 25.00 |
| ❑ LSP-2459 [S] | Playing It Straight | 1962 | 30.00 |
| ❑ LPM-2492 [M] | Homer and Jethro at the Convention | 1962 | 25.00 |
| ❑ LSP-2492 [S] | Homer and Jethro at the Convention | 1962 | 30.00 |
| ❑ LPM-2674 [M] | Homer and Jethro Go West | 1963 | 25.00 |
| ❑ LSP-2674 [S] | Homer and Jethro Go West | 1963 | 30.00 |
| ❑ LPM-2743 [M] | Ooh, That's Corny | 1963 | 25.00 |
| ❑ LSP-2743 [S] | Ooh, That's Corny | 1963 | 30.00 |
| ❑ LPM-2928 [M] | Cornfucius Say | 1964 | 25.00 |
| ❑ LSP-2928 [S] | Cornfucius Say | 1964 | 30.00 |
| ❑ LPM-2954 [M] | Fractured Folk Songs | 1964 | 25.00 |
| ❑ LSP-2954 [S] | Fractured Folk Songs | 1964 | 30.00 |
| ❑ LPM-3112 [10] | Homer & Jethro Fracture Frank Loesser | 1953 | 150.00 |
| ❑ LPM-3357 [M] | Homer and Jethro Sing Tenderly | 1965 | 25.00 |
| ❑ LSP-3357 [S] | Homer and Jethro Sing Tenderly | 1965 | 30.00 |
| ❑ LPM-3462 [M] | The Old Crusty Minstrels | 1965 | 25.00 |
| ❑ LSP-3462 [S] | The Old Crusty Minstrels | 1965 | 30.00 |
| ❑ LPM-3474 [M] | The Best of Homer and Jethro | 1966 | 25.00 |
| ❑ LSP-3474 [S] | The Best of Homer and Jethro | 1966 | 30.00 |
| ❑ LPM-3538 [M] | Any News from Nashville? | 1966 | 25.00 |
| ❑ LSP-3538 [S] | Any News from Nashville? | 1966 | 30.00 |
| ❑ LPM-3673 [M] | Wanted for Murder | 1966 | 25.00 |
| ❑ LSP-3673 [S] | Wanted for Murder | 1966 | 30.00 |
| ❑ LPM-3701 [M] | It Ain't Necessarily Square | 1967 | 30.00 |
| ❑ LSP-3701 [S] | It Ain't Necessarily Square | 1967 | 25.00 |
| ❑ LPM-3822 [M] | Nashville Cats | 1967 | 40.00 |
| ❑ LSP-3822 [S] | Nashville Cats | 1967 | 25.00 |
| ❑ LPM-3877 [M] | Somethin' Stupid | 1967 | 50.00 |
| ❑ LSP-3877 [S] | Somethin' Stupid | 1967 | 25.00 |
| ❑ LPM-3973 [M] | There's Nothing Like an Old Hippie | 1968 | 100.00 |
| ❑ LSP-3973 [S] | There's Nothing Like an Old Hippie | 1968 | 25.00 |
| ❑ LSP-4001 | Cool, Crazy Christmas | 1968 | 20.00 |
| ❑ LSP-4024 | Homer and Jethro at Vanderbilt U. | 1969 | 20.00 |
| ❑ LSP-4148 | Homer and Jethro's Next Album | 1969 | 20.00 |

### HOMESICK JAMES

PRESTIGE

| Number | Title (A Side/B Side) | Yr | NM |
|---|---|---|---|
| ❑ PRLP-7388 [M] | Homesick James | 1965 | 30.00 |

### HONDELLS, THE

MERCURY

| Number | Title (A Side/B Side) | Yr | NM |
|---|---|---|---|
| ❑ MG-20940 [M] | Go Little Honda | 1964 | 40.00 |
| ❑ MG-20982 [M] | The Hondells | 1965 | 50.00 |
| ❑ SR-60940 [S] | Go Little Honda | 1964 | 60.00 |
| ❑ SR-60982 [S] | The Hondells | 1965 | 80.00 |

### HONEY AND THE BEES

JOSIE

| Number | Title (A Side/B Side) | Yr | NM |
|---|---|---|---|
| ❑ JOS-4013 | Love | 1970 | 20.00 |

### HONEY DREAMERS, THE

FANTASY

| Number | Title (A Side/B Side) | Yr | NM |
|---|---|---|---|
| ❑ 3207 [M] | The Honey Dreamers Sing Gershwin | 195? | 40.00 |
| *—Black vinyl* | | | |
| ❑ 3207 [M] | The Honey Dreamers Sing Gershwin | 1956 | 80.00 |

*—Red vinyl*

### HONEYCOMBS, THE

| Number | Title (A Side/B Side) | Yr | NM |
|---|---|---|---|
| INTERPHON | | | |
| ❑ IN-88001 [M] | Here Are the Honeycombs | 1964 | 40.00 |
| ❑ IN-88001 [R] | Here Are the Honeycombs | 1964 | 30.00 |
| VEE JAY | | | |
| ❑ IN-88001 [M] | Here Are the Honeycombs | 1964 | 50.00 |
| ❑ IN-88001 [R] | Here Are the Honeycombs | 1964 | 40.00 |

### HOODOO RHYTHM DEVILS, THE

CAPITOL

| Number | Title (A Side/B Side) | Yr | NM |
|---|---|---|---|
| ❑ ST-842 | The Hoodoo Rhythm Devils | 1971 | 20.00 |

### HOOK, THE

UNI

| Number | Title (A Side/B Side) | Yr | NM |
|---|---|---|---|
| ❑ 73023 | The Hook Will Grab You | 1968 | 25.00 |
| ❑ 73038 | Hooked | 1969 | 25.00 |

### HOOKER, EARL

| Number | Title (A Side/B Side) | Yr | NM |
|---|---|---|---|
| ARHOOLIE | | | |
| ❑ LP 1044 | 2 Bugs and a Roach | 1968 | 25.00 |
| ❑ LP 1051 | Hooker and Steve | 1969 | 25.00 |
| ❑ LP 1066 | His First and Last Recordings | 1970 | 25.00 |
| BLUE THUMB | | | |
| ❑ BTS 12 | Sweet Black Angel | 1969 | 30.00 |

Hooters,. *Amore,* Antenna HOO 83, 1983, $20.

| Number | Title (A Side/B Side) | Yr | NM |
|---|---|---|---|
| **BLUES ON BLUES** | | | |
| ❑ 10002 | The Last of the Great Earl Hooker | 197? | 20.00 |
| **BLUESWAY** | | | |
| ❑ BLS-6032 | Don't Have to Worry | 1969 | 25.00 |
| ❑ BLS-6038 | If You Miss Him | 1970 | 25.00 |
| ❑ BLS-6072 | Do You Remember the Great Earl Hooker | 1973 | 15.00 |
| **CUCA** | | | |
| ❑ 3400 [M] | The Genius of Earl Hooker | 1965 | 250.00 |

## HOOKER, JOHN LEE

| Number | Title (A Side/B Side) | Yr | NM |
|---|---|---|---|
| **ABC** | | | |
| ❑ S-720 [(2)] | Endless Boogie | 1971 | 20.00 |
| ❑ X-736 | Never Get Out of These Blues Alive | 1972 | 20.00 |
| ❑ XQ-736 [Q] | Never Get Out of These Blues Alive | 1974 | 25.00 |
| ❑ X-761 | Live at Soledad Prison | 1972 | 20.00 |
| ❑ XQ-761 [Q] | Live at Soledad Prison | 1974 | 25.00 |
| ❑ X-768 | Born in Mississippi, Raised Up in Tennessee | 1973 | 20.00 |
| ❑ XQ-768 [Q] | Born in Mississippi, Raised Up in Tennessee | 1974 | 25.00 |
| ❑ X-838 | Free Beer and Chicken | 1974 | 15.00 |
| ❑ XQ-838 [Q] | Free Beer and Chicken | 1974 | 25.00 |
| **ATCO** | | | |
| ❑ 33-151 [M] | Don't Turn Me From Your Door | 1963 | 100.00 |
| ❑ SD 33-151 [R] | Don't Turn Me From Your Door | 1967 | 50.00 |
| **ATLANTIC** | | | |
| ❑ SD 7228 | Detroit Special | 1972 | 20.00 |
| **BATTLE** | | | |
| ❑ BLP-6113 [M] | John Lee Hooker | 196? | 150.00 |
| ❑ BLP-6114 [M] | How Long Blues | 196? | 150.00 |
| **BLUESWAY** | | | |
| ❑ BL-6002 [M] | Live at Café A-Go-Go | 1967 | 25.00 |
| ❑ BLS-6002 [S] | Live at Café A-Go-Go | 1967 | 20.00 |
| ❑ BL-6012 [M] | Urban Blues | 1967 | 25.00 |
| ❑ BLS-6012 [S] | Urban Blues | 1967 | 20.00 |
| ❑ BLS-6023 | Simply the Truth | 1968 | 20.00 |
| ❑ BLS-6038 | If You Miss 'Em | 1969 | 20.00 |
| ❑ BLQ-6052 [Q] | Live at Kabuki-Wuki | 1974 | 25.00 |
| ❑ BLS-6052 | Live at Kabuki-Wuki | 1973 | 15.00 |

| Number | Title (A Side/B Side) | Yr | NM |
|---|---|---|---|
| **BUDDAH** | | | |
| ❑ BDS-4002 | The Very Best of John Lee Hooker | 1970 | 15.00 |
| ❑ BDS-7506 | Big Band Blues | 1970 | 15.00 |
| **CHAMELEON** | | | |
| ❑ D1-74794 | The Hook | 1989 | 10.00 |
| ❑ D1-74808 | The Healer | 1989 | 10.00 |
| **CHESS** | | | |
| ❑ LP-1438 [M] | House of the Blues | 1960 | 300.00 |
| *—Black label* | | | |
| ❑ LP-1438 [M] | House of the Blues | 1966 | 50.00 |
| *—Blue and white label* | | | |
| ❑ LP-1454 [M] | John Lee Hooker Plays and Sings the Blues | 1961 | 300.00 |
| *—Black label* | | | |
| ❑ LP-1454 [M] | John Lee Hooker Plays and Sings the Blues | 1966 | 50.00 |
| *—Blue and white label* | | | |
| ❑ LP-1508 [M] | Real Folk Blues | 1966 | 50.00 |
| ❑ LPS-1508 [R] | Real Folk Blues | 1966 | 30.00 |
| ❑ CH-9199 | John Lee Hooker Plays and Sings the Blues | 1986 | 8.00 |
| *—Reissue* | | | |
| ❑ CH-9258 | House of the Blues | 1987 | 8.00 |
| ❑ CH-9271 | The Real Folk Blues | 1988 | 8.00 |
| ❑ 60011 [(2)] | Mad Man Blues | 1973 | 20.00 |
| ❑ CH2-92507 [(2)] | Mad Man Blues | 198? | 12.00 |
| **COLLECTABLES** | | | |
| ❑ COL-5151 | Golden Classics | 198? | 12.00 |
| **CROWN** | | | |
| ❑ CLP-5157 [M] | The Blues | 196? | 12.00 |
| *—Black label with multi-color "Crown"* | | | |
| ❑ CLP-5157 [M] | The Blues | 1960 | 100.00 |
| *—Black label with silver "Crown"* | | | |
| ❑ CLP-5157 [M] | The Blues | 1962 | 30.00 |
| *—Gray label* | | | |
| ❑ CLP-5232 [M] | John Lee Hooker Sings the Blues | 196? | 12.00 |
| *—Black label with multi-color "Crown"* | | | |
| ❑ CLP-5232 [M] | John Lee Hooker Sings the Blues | 1962 | 30.00 |
| *—Gray label* | | | |
| ❑ CLP-5232 [M] | John Lee Hooker Sings the Blues | 1962 | 100.00 |
| *—Black label with silver "Crown"* | | | |

| Number | Title (A Side/B Side) | Yr | NM |
|---|---|---|---|
| ❑ CLP-5295 [M] | Folk Blues | 1962 | 12.00 |
| *—Black label with multi-color "Crown"* | | | |
| ❑ CLP-5295 [M] | Folk Blues | 1962 | 30.00 |
| *—Gray label* | | | |
| ❑ CLP-5353 [M] | The Great John Lee Hooker | 1963 | 12.00 |
| *—Black label with multi-color "Crown"* | | | |
| ❑ CLP-5353 [M] | The Great John Lee Hooker | 1963 | 30.00 |
| *—Gray label* | | | |
| **EVEREST ARCHIVE OF FOLK & JAZZ** | | | |
| ❑ 222 | John Lee Hooker | 1968 | 12.00 |
| ❑ 347 | Hooked On Blues | 1980 | 12.00 |
| **EXODUS** | | | |
| ❑ 325 [M] | Is He the World's Greatest Blues Singer? | 1966 | 25.00 |
| **FANTASY** | | | |
| ❑ 24706 [(2)] | Boogie Chillun | 1972 | 15.00 |
| ❑ 24722 [(2)] | Black Snake | 197? | 15.00 |
| **GALAXY** | | | |
| ❑ 201 [M] | I'm John Lee Hooker | 1961 | 250.00 |
| ❑ 205 [M] | Live at Sugar Hill | 1962 | 250.00 |
| ❑ 8205 [S] | Live at Sugar Hill | 1962 | 250.00 |
| **GNP CRESCENDO** | | | |
| ❑ GNPS-10007 [(2)] | The Best of John Lee Hooker | 1974 | 15.00 |
| **GREENE BOTTLE** | | | |
| ❑ 3130 [(2)] | Johnny Lee | 1972 | 15.00 |
| **IMPULSE!** | | | |
| ❑ A-9103 [M] | It Serves You Right to Suffer | 1966 | 30.00 |
| ❑ AS-9103 [S] | It Serves You Right to Suffer | 1966 | 40.00 |
| **JEWEL** | | | |
| ❑ 5005 | I Feel Good | 1971 | 15.00 |
| **KING** | | | |
| ❑ 727 [M] | John Lee Hooker Sings the Blues | 1960 | 500.00 |
| ❑ KLP-727 | John Lee Hooker Sings the Blues | 1988 | 8.00 |
| *—Reissue of earlier 727* | | | |
| ❑ KS-1085 | Moanin' and Stompin' Blues | 1970 | 25.00 |
| **LABOR** | | | |
| ❑ 4 | Alone | 1982 | 10.00 |
| **MUSE** | | | |
| ❑ 5205 | Sittin' Here Thinkin' | 1980 | 12.00 |
| **PAUSA** | | | |
| ❑ PR-7197 | Jealous | 1986 | 10.00 |
| **RIVERSIDE** | | | |
| ❑ RLP 12-321 [M] | That's My Story | 1960 | 100.00 |
| ❑ RLP 12-838 [M] | The Country Blues of John Lee Hooker | 1959 | 100.00 |
| **SPECIALTY** | | | |
| ❑ SPS-2125 | Alone | 1970 | 30.00 |
| ❑ SPS-2127 | Going Down Highway 51 | 1970 | 30.00 |
| **STAX** | | | |
| ❑ STS-2013 | That's Where It's At | 1970 | 15.00 |
| ❑ STX-4134 | That's Where It's At | 1979 | 10.00 |
| *—Reissue of 2013* | | | |
| **TOMATO** | | | |
| ❑ 7009 [(2)] | The Cream | 1978 | 15.00 |
| **TRADITION** | | | |
| ❑ 2089 | Real Blues | 1970 | 15.00 |
| **UNITED ARTISTS** | | | |
| ❑ UA-LA127-J [(3)] | John Lee Hooker's Detroit | 1974 | 25.00 |
| ❑ UAS-5512 | Coast to Coast Blues Band | 1971 | 15.00 |
| **VEE JAY** | | | |
| ❑ LP-1007 [M] | I'm John Lee Hooker | 1959 | 300.00 |
| *—Maroon label* | | | |
| ❑ LP-1007 [M] | I'm John Lee Hooker | 1960 | 80.00 |
| *—Black label with colorband* | | | |
| ❑ VJLP-1007 | I'm John Lee Hooker | 1986 | 8.00 |
| *—Reissue of original on flimsier vinyl* | | | |
| ❑ LP-1023 [M] | Travelin' | 1960 | 80.00 |
| ❑ LP-1033 [M] | The Folk Lore of John Lee Hooker | 1961 | 50.00 |
| ❑ SR-1033 [S] | The Folk Lore of John Lee Hooker | 1961 | 80.00 |
| ❑ LP-1043 [M] | Burnin' | 1962 | 50.00 |
| ❑ SR-1043 [S] | Burnin' | 1962 | 150.00 |
| ❑ LP-1049 [M] | The Best of John Lee Hooker | 1962 | 50.00 |
| ❑ SR-1049 [P] | The Best of John Lee Hooker | 1962 | 80.00 |
| ❑ VJLP-1049 | The Best of John Lee Hooker | 1986 | 8.00 |
| *—Reissue of original on flimsier vinyl* | | | |
| ❑ LP-1058 [M] | The Big Soul of John Lee Hooker | 1963 | 50.00 |
| ❑ SR-1058 [S] | The Big Soul of John Lee Hooker | 1963 | 150.00 |
| ❑ VJLP-1058 | The Big Soul of John Lee Hooker | 1986 | 8.00 |
| *—Reissue of original on flimsier vinyl* | | | |
| ❑ LP-1066 [M] | John Lee Hooker On Campus | 1963 | 50.00 |
| ❑ SR-1066 [S] | John Lee Hooker On Campus | 1963 | 150.00 |
| ❑ LP-1078 [M] | John Lee Hooker at Newport | 1964 | 50.00 |
| ❑ SR-1078 [S] | John Lee Hooker at Newport | 1964 | 150.00 |

| Number | Title (A Side/B Side) | Yr | NM |
|---|---|---|---|
| ❑ VJLP-1078 | John Lee Hooker at Newport | 1986 | 8.00 |
| *—Reissue of original on flimsier vinyl* | | | |
| ❑ DY-7301 | John Lee Hooker In Person | 198? | 8.00 |
| ❑ LP-8502 [M] | Is He the World's Greatest Blues Singer? | 1965 | 40.00 |
| *—This is the title on the cover; the label calls it "Is He Really the World's Greatest Blues Singer?"* | | | |
| ❑ VJLP-8502 | Is He the World's Greatest Blues Singer? | 1986 | 8.00 |
| *—Reissue of original on flimsier vinyl; this is the title on the cover; the label calls it "Is He Really the World's Greatest Blues Singer?"* | | | |
| **VERVE FOLKWAYS** | | | |
| ❑ FT-3003 [M] | John Lee Hooker and Seven Nights | 1965 | 25.00 |
| ❑ FTS-3003 [S] | John Lee Hooker and Seven Nights | 1965 | 40.00 |
| **WAND** | | | |
| ❑ WDS-689 | On the Waterfront | 1972 | 15.00 |

## HOOKER, JOHN LEE, AND CANNED HEAT

| Number | Title (A Side/B Side) | Yr | NM |
|---|---|---|---|
| **LIBERTY** | | | |
| ❑ 35002 | Hooker 'n' Heat | 1971 | 20.00 |
| **RHINO** | | | |
| ❑ RNLP-801 | Recorded Live at the Fox Venice Theatre | 1985 | 12.00 |
| ❑ RNDA-71105 | Infinite Boogie | 1987 | 12.00 |

## HOOTCH

| Number | Title (A Side/B Side) | Yr | NM |
|---|---|---|---|
| **PROGRESS** | | | |
| ❑ PRS-4844 | Hootch | 1974 | 600.00 |

## HOOTERS

| Number | Title (A Side/B Side) | Yr | NM |
|---|---|---|---|
| **ANTENNA** | | | |
| ❑ HOO 83 | Amore | 1983 | 20.00 |
| **COLUMBIA** | | | |
| ❑ BFC 39912 | Nervous Night | 1985 | 12.00 |
| ❑ FC 39912 | Nervous Night | 1985 | 10.00 |
| *—Reissue with new prefix* | | | |
| ❑ OC 40659 | One Way Home | 1987 | 10.00 |
| ❑ C 45058 | Zig Zag | 1989 | 10.00 |

## HOOTIE & THE BLOWFISH

| Number | Title (A Side/B Side) | Yr | NM |
|---|---|---|---|
| **ATLANTIC** | | | |
| ❑ 82613 | Cracked Rear View | 1995 | 100.00 |
| *—Red vinyl* | | | |
| ❑ 82886 | Fairweather Johnson | 1996 | 20.00 |
| ❑ 83136 | Musical Chairs | 1998 | 15.00 |

## HOPE, BOB

| Number | Title (A Side/B Side) | Yr | NM |
|---|---|---|---|
| **CADET** | | | |
| ❑ LP-4046 | On the Road to Vietnam | 1965 | 15.00 |
| **CAPITOL** | | | |
| ❑ ST-11538 | America Is 200 Years Old ... And There's Still Hope! | 1976 | 12.00 |
| **DECCA** | | | |
| ❑ DL 4396 [M] | Hope in Russia and One Other Place | 1963 | 20.00 |
| ❑ DL 74396 [S] | Hope in Russia and One Other Place | 1963 | 25.00 |
| **MCA** | | | |
| ❑ 906 | Bob Hope in Hollywood | 1984 | 12.00 |
| **RADIOLA** | | | |
| ❑ MR-1060 | The Bob Hope Radio Show | 197? | 10.00 |
| *—Includes two radio shows: October 23, 1945 and December 18, 1945* | | | |
| **RCA VICTOR** | | | |
| ❑ LOC-1055 [M] | Not So Long Ago: NBC Project Twenty | 1960 | 20.00 |
| ❑ LSO-1055 [S] | Not So Long Ago: NBC Project Twenty | 1960 | 25.00 |
| **SPEAR** | | | |
| ❑ 4700 | Holidays | 1973 | 15.00 |

## HOPE, ELMO

| Number | Title (A Side/B Side) | Yr | NM |
|---|---|---|---|
| **AUDIO FIDELITY** | | | |
| ❑ AFLP-2119 [M] | Sounds from Riker's Island | 1963 | 30.00 |
| ❑ AFSD-6119 [S] | Sounds from Riker's Island | 1963 | 40.00 |
| **BEACON** | | | |
| ❑ B-401 [M] | High Hopes | 1961 | 30.00 |
| ❑ BS-401 [S] | High Hopes | 1961 | 40.00 |
| **BLUE NOTE** | | | |
| ❑ BLP-5029 [10] | Elmo Hope Trio | 1953 | 300.00 |
| ❑ BLP-5044 [10] | Elmo Hope Quintet | 1954 | 300.00 |
| **CELEBRITY** | | | |
| ❑ 209 [M] | Elmo Hope Trio | 1962 | 25.00 |
| ❑ S-209 [S] | Elmo Hope Trio | 1962 | 30.00 |
| **CONTEMPORARY** | | | |
| ❑ M-3620 [M] | The Elmo Hope Trio | 1966 | 25.00 |
| ❑ S-7620 [S] | The Elmo Hope Trio | 1966 | 30.00 |
| **HIFI** | | | |
| ❑ J-616 [M] | Elmo Hope | 1960 | 40.00 |
| ❑ JS-616 [S] | Elmo Hope | 1960 | 50.00 |
| **PRESTIGE** | | | |
| ❑ PRLP-7010 [M] | Meditations | 1956 | 120.00 |
| ❑ PRLP-7021 [M] | Hope Meets Foster | 1956 | 120.00 |
| ❑ PRLP-7021 [M] | Wail, Frank, Wail | 1957 | 80.00 |
| *—Retitled reissue of above album* | | | |
| ❑ PRLP-7043 [M] | Informal Jazz | 1956 | 120.00 |
| **RIVERSIDE** | | | |
| ❑ RLP-381 [M] | Homecoming! | 1961 | 40.00 |
| ❑ RLP-408 [M] | Hope-Full | 1962 | 25.00 |
| ❑ RS-9381 [S] | Homecoming! | 1961 | 50.00 |
| ❑ RS-9408 [S] | Hope-Full | 1962 | 30.00 |

## HOPE, LYNN

| Number | Title (A Side/B Side) | Yr | NM |
|---|---|---|---|
| **ALADDIN** | | | |
| ❑ LP-707 [10] | Lynn Hope and His Tenor Sax | 1953 | 600.00 |
| ❑ LP-805 [M] | Lynn Hope and His Tenor Sax | 1955 | 500.00 |
| **IMPERIAL** | | | |
| ❑ LP-9177-A [M] | Tenderly | 1962 | 40.00 |
| ❑ LP-12177-A [S] | Tenderly | 1962 | 60.00 |
| **KING** | | | |
| ❑ 717 [M] | Maharajah of the Saxophone | 1961 | 120.00 |
| **SCORE** | | | |
| ❑ SLP-4015 [M] | Tenderly | 1957 | 200.00 |

## HOPKIN, MARY

| Number | Title (A Side/B Side) | Yr | NM |
|---|---|---|---|
| **APPLE** | | | |
| ❑ ST-3351 | Post Card | 1969 | 25.00 |
| ❑ ST-5-3351 | Post Card | 1969 | 30.00 |
| *—Capitol Record Club edition* | | | |
| ❑ SMAS-3381 | Earth Song/Ocean Song | 1970 | 25.00 |
| ❑ SW-3395 | Those Were the Days | 1972 | 40.00 |

## HOPKINS, CLAUDE

| Number | Title (A Side/B Side) | Yr | NM |
|---|---|---|---|
| **DESIGN** | | | |
| ❑ DLP-30 [M] | Golden Era of Dixieland Jazz 1887-1937 | 1957 | 25.00 |
| **SWINGVILLE** | | | |
| ❑ SVLP-2009 [M] | Yes Indeed | 1960 | 50.00 |
| *—Purple label* | | | |
| ❑ SVLP-2009 [M] | Yes Indeed | 1965 | 25.00 |
| *—Blue label, trident logo at right* | | | |
| ❑ SVLP-2020 [M] | Let's Jam | 1961 | 50.00 |
| *—Purple label* | | | |
| ❑ SVLP-2020 [M] | Let's Jam | 1965 | 25.00 |
| *—Blue label, trident logo at right* | | | |
| ❑ SVLP-2041 [M] | Swing Time | 1962 | 50.00 |
| *—Purple label* | | | |
| ❑ SVLP-2041 [M] | Swing Time | 1965 | 25.00 |
| *—Blue label, trident logo at right* | | | |

## HOPKINS, KENYON

| Number | Title (A Side/B Side) | Yr | NM |
|---|---|---|---|
| **VERVE** | | | |
| ❑ V-8694 [M] | Dream Songs | 1967 | 20.00 |

## HOPKINS, LIGHTNIN'

| Number | Title (A Side/B Side) | Yr | NM |
|---|---|---|---|
| **ANALOGUE PRODUCTIONS** | | | |
| ❑ AAPB-014 | Goin' Away | 199? | 40.00 |
| *—Audiophile reissue* | | | |
| **ARHOOLIE** | | | |
| ❑ 1011 | Lightnin' Hopkins and His Guitar | 196? | 20.00 |
| ❑ 1022 | Lightnin' Hopkins, His Brother and Barbara Dane | 196? | 20.00 |
| ❑ 1030 | Blues Festival | 196? | 15.00 |
| ❑ 1034 | Texas Blues Man | 1968 | 15.00 |
| ❑ 1063 | Lightnin' Hopkins in Berkeley | 1969 | 15.00 |
| ❑ 1087 | Poor Lightnin' | 1970 | 15.00 |
| ❑ 2007 | Early Recordings | 197? | 15.00 |
| ❑ 2010 | Early Recordings Volume 2 | 197? | 15.00 |
| **BARNABY** | | | |
| ❑ Z 30247 | Lightnin' Hopkins in New York | 1970 | 15.00 |
| **BLUES CLASSICS** | | | |
| ❑ 30 | Historic Recordings 1952-1953 | 1986 | 12.00 |
| **BLUESVILLE** | | | |
| ❑ BVLP-1019 [M] | Lightnin' | 1961 | 100.00 |
| *—Blue label, silver print* | | | |
| ❑ BVLP-1019 [M] | Lightnin' | 1964 | 30.00 |
| *—Blue label, trident logo on right* | | | |
| ❑ BVLP-1029 [M] | Last Night Blues | 1961 | 100.00 |
| *—Blue label, silver print* | | | |
| ❑ BVLP-1045 [M] | Blues in My Bottle | 1962 | 100.00 |
| *—Blue label, silver print* | | | |
| ❑ BVLP-1045 [M] | Blues in My Bottle | 1964 | 30.00 |
| *—Blue label, trident logo on right* | | | |
| ❑ BVLP-1057 [M] | Walkin' This Street | 1962 | 100.00 |
| *—Blue label, silver print* | | | |
| ❑ BVLP-1057 [M] | Walkin' This Street | 1964 | 30.00 |
| *—Blue label, trident logo on right* | | | |
| ❑ BVLP-1061 [M] | Lightnin' & Co. | 1963 | 100.00 |
| *—Blue label, silver print* | | | |
| ❑ BVLP-1061 [M] | Lightnin' & Co. | 1964 | 30.00 |
| *—Blue label, trident logo on right* | | | |
| ❑ BVLP-1070 [M] | Smokes Like Lightnin' | 1963 | 100.00 |
| *—Blue label, silver print* | | | |
| ❑ BVLP-1070 [M] | Smokes Like Lightnin' | 1964 | 30.00 |
| *—Blue label, trident logo on right* | | | |
| ❑ BVLP-1073 [M] | Goin' Away | 1963 | 100.00 |
| *—Blue label, silver print* | | | |
| ❑ BVLP-1073 [M] | Goin' Away | 1964 | 30.00 |
| *—Blue label, trident logo on right* | | | |
| ❑ BVLP-1081 [M] | Gotta Move Your Baby | 1964 | 30.00 |
| *—Blue label, trident logo on right* | | | |
| ❑ BVLP-1084 [M] | Lightnin' Hopkins' Greatest Hits | 1964 | 40.00 |
| ❑ BVLP-1086 [M] | Down Home Blues | 1964 | 25.00 |
| **BLUESWAY** | | | |
| ❑ S-6039 | If You Miss 'Im | 1969 | 20.00 |
| **BULLDOG** | | | |
| ❑ 1010 | The Texas Bluesman | 1965 | 15.00 |
| **CANDID** | | | |
| ❑ CM-8010 [M] | Lightnin' in New York | 1961 | 120.00 |
| ❑ CS-9010 [S] | Lightnin' in New York | 1961 | 150.00 |
| **COLLECTABLES** | | | |
| ❑ COL-5111 | Golden Classics — Mojo Hand | 198? | 10.00 |
| ❑ COL-5121 | The Herald Recordings/1954 | 198? | 10.00 |
| ❑ COL-5143 | Golden Classics, Part 1: Drinkin' the Blues | 198? | 10.00 |
| ❑ COL-5144 | Golden Classics, Part 2: Prison Blues | 198? | 10.00 |
| ❑ COL-5145 | Golden Classics, Part 3: Mama and Papa Hopkins | 198? | 10.00 |
| ❑ COL-5146 | Golden Classics, Part 4: Nothin' But the Blues | 198? | 10.00 |
| ❑ COL-5203 | The Lost Texas Tapes, Vol. 1 | 198? | 10.00 |
| ❑ COL-5204 | The Lost Texas Tapes, Vol. 2 | 198? | 10.00 |
| ❑ COL-5205 | The Lost Texas Tapes, Vol. 3 | 198? | 10.00 |
| ❑ COL-5206 | The Lost Texas Tapes, Vol. 4 | 198? | 10.00 |
| ❑ COL-5207 | The Lost Texas Tapes, Vol. 5 | 198? | 10.00 |
| **CROWN** | | | |
| ❑ CLP-5224 [M] | Lightnin' Hopkins Sings the Blues | 196? | 25.00 |
| *—Black label, multi-color logo* | | | |
| ❑ CLP-5224 [M] | Lightnin' Hopkins Sings the Blues | 1962 | 50.00 |
| *—Gray label* | | | |
| ❑ CLP-5224 [M] | Lightnin' Hopkins Sings the Blues | 1962 | 100.00 |
| *—Black label, silver "Crown"* | | | |
| **DART** | | | |
| ❑ D-8000 [M] | Blues Underground | 196? | 200.00 |
| *—Retitled version of above* | | | |
| ❑ D-8000 [M] | Lightning Strikes Again | 1960 | 400.00 |
| **DCC COMPACT CLASSICS** | | | |
| ❑ LPZ-2007 | Blues Hoot | 1996 | 30.00 |
| *—Audiophile vinyl* | | | |
| **EVEREST ARCHIVE OF FOLK & JAZZ** | | | |
| ❑ 241 | Lightnin' Hopkins | 1969 | 15.00 |
| ❑ 313 | Lightnin' Hopkins, Vol. 2 | 197? | 15.00 |
| ❑ 342 | Autobiography in Blues | 1979 | 12.00 |
| **FANTASY** | | | |
| ❑ OBC-506 | Blues in My Bottle | 198? | 12.00 |
| ❑ OBC-522 | Goin' Away | 1988 | 12.00 |
| ❑ OBC-532 | Lightnin' | 1990 | 12.00 |
| ❑ 24702 [(2)] | Double Blues | 1972 | 20.00 |
| ❑ 24725 [(2)] | How Many More Years | 1981 | 15.00 |
| **FIRE** | | | |
| ❑ FLP 104 [M] | Mojo Hand | 1960 | 1500. |
| **FOLKLORE** | | | |
| ❑ FRLP-14021 [M] | Hootin' the Blues | 1964 | 60.00 |
| ❑ FRST-14021 [S] | Hootin' the Blues | 1964 | 70.00 |
| **FOLKWAYS** | | | |
| ❑ FS-3822 [M] | Lightnin' Hopkins | 1962 | 40.00 |
| ❑ 31011 | Roots | 196? | 15.00 |
| **GNP CRESCENDO** | | | |
| ❑ 10022 | Legacy of the Blues, Volume 12 | 1978 | 12.00 |
| **GUEST STAR** | | | |
| ❑ G-1459 [M] | "Live" at the Bird Lounge, Houston, Texas | 1964 | 30.00 |
| ❑ GS-1459 [R] | "Live" at the Bird Lounge, Houston, Texas | 1964 | 20.00 |
| **HERALD** | | | |
| ❑ LP 1012 [M] | Lightnin' and the Blues | 1959 | 800.00 |
| *—Yellow label* | | | |
| ❑ LP 1012 [M] | Lightnin' and the Blues | 1959 | 1500. |
| *—Black label; VG value 750; VG+ value 1125* | | | |
| ❑ LP 1012 [M] | Lightnin' and the Blues | 196? | 500.00 |
| *—Multi-color label* | | | |
| **IMPERIAL** | | | |
| ❑ LP-9180 [M] | Lightnin' Hopkins On Stage | 1962 | 300.00 |
| ❑ LP-9186 [M] | Lightnin' Hopkins Sings the Blues | 1962 | 300.00 |
| ❑ LP-9211 [M] | Lightnin' Hopkins and the Blues | 1963 | 200.00 |
| ❑ LP-12211 [R] | Lightnin' Hopkins and the Blues | 1963 | 100.00 |
| **INTERNATIONAL ARTISTS** | | | |
| ❑ IA-6 | Free Form Patterns | 1968 | 50.00 |
| *—With psychedelic art on cover* | | | |
| ❑ IA-6 | Free Form Patterns | 1968 | 200.00 |
| *—With photo on cover* | | | |

| Number | Title (A Side/B Side) | Yr | NM |
|---|---|---|---|
| **JAZZ MAN** | | | |
| ❑ BLZ-5502 | Lightnin' in New York | 1982 | 10.00 |
| **JEWEL** | | | |
| ❑ 5000 | Blue Lightnin' | 1967 | 15.00 |
| ❑ 5001 | Talkin' Some Sense | 1968 | 15.00 |
| ❑ 5015 | Great Electric Show and Dance | 1970 | 15.00 |
| **KING** | | | |
| ❑ KS-1085 | Moanin' Blues | 1969 | 15.00 |
| **MAINSTREAM** | | | |
| ❑ 311 | The Blues | 1971 | 15.00 |
| ❑ 326 | Dirty Blues | 197? | 15.00 |
| ❑ 405 | Low Down Dirty Blues | 1974 | 15.00 |
| ❑ S-6040 [S] | Blues | 196? | 30.00 |
| ❑ 56040 [M] | Blues | 196? | 25.00 |
| **MOUNT VERNON** | | | |
| ❑ 104 [M] | Nothin' But the Blues | 196? | 25.00 |
| **OLYMPIC GOLD MEDAL** | | | |
| ❑ 7110 | Blues Giant | 1974 | 12.00 |
| **POPPY** | | | |
| ❑ 60002 [(2)] | Lightnin'! | 1969 | 25.00 |
| **PRESTIGE** | | | |
| ❑ PRLPT-7370 [(2)M] | My Life with the Blues | 1965 | 60.00 |
| ❑ PRST-7370 [(2)S] | My Life with the Blues | 1965 | 70.00 |
| ❑ PRLP-7377 [M] | Soul Blues | 1966 | 50.00 |
| ❑ PRST-7377 [S] | Soul Blues | 1966 | 60.00 |
| ❑ PRST-7592 | Lightnin' Hopkins' Greatest Hits | 1969 | 15.00 |
| ❑ PRST-7714 | The Best of Lightnin' Hopkins & His Texas Blues Band | 1969 | 15.00 |
| ❑ PRST-7806 | Hootin' the Blues | 1969 | 15.00 |
| ❑ PRST-7811 | The Blues of Lightnin' Hopkins | 1969 | 15.00 |
| ❑ PRST-7831 | Gotta Move Your Baby | 1970 | 15.00 |
| **RHINO** | | | |
| ❑ RNLP 103 | Los Angeles Blues | 1982 | 10.00 |
| **SCORE** | | | |
| ❑ SLP-4022 [M] | Lightnin' Hopkins Strums the Blues | 1958 | 1200. |
| **SMITHSONIAN FOLKWAYS** | | | |
| ❑ SF-40019 | Lightnin' Hopkins | 1990 | 12.00 |
| **SPHERE SOUND** | | | |
| ❑ SSR-7001 [M] | Lightnin' Hopkins | 1964 | 400.00 |
| ❑ SSSR-7001 [R] | Lightnin' Hopkins | 1964 | 300.00 |
| **TIME** | | | |
| ❑ 1 [M] | Blues/Folk | 1960 | 120.00 |
| ❑ 2 [M] | Blues/Folk Volume 2 | 1960 | 120.00 |
| ❑ ST-70004 [S] | Last of the Great Blues Singers | 1962 | 120.00 |
| ❑ T-70004 [M] | Last of the Great Blues Singers | 1962 | 120.00 |
| **TOMATO** | | | |
| ❑ 7004 [(2)] | Lightnin'! | 1977 | 15.00 |
| **TRADITION** | | | |
| ❑ TLP-1035 [M] | Country Blues | 1960 | 30.00 |
| ❑ TLP-1040 [M] | Autobiography in Blues | 1961 | 30.00 |
| ❑ TLP-2056 [M] | The Best of Lightnin' Hopkins | 1967 | 20.00 |
| ❑ TLP-2103 [M] | Lightnin' Strikes | 1972 | 15.00 |
| **TRIP** | | | |
| ❑ TLP-8015 | Lightnin' Hopkins | 1971 | 12.00 |
| **UNITED** | | | |
| ❑ US-7713 | Lightnin' Hopkins Sings the Blues | 196? | 15.00 |
| ❑ US-7744 | Original Folk Blues | 196? | 15.00 |
| ❑ US-7785 | A Legend in His Time | 196? | 15.00 |
| **UNITED ARTISTS** | | | |
| ❑ UAS-5512 | Coast to Coast Blues Band | 197? | 15.00 |
| **UP FRONT** | | | |
| ❑ 158 | Lightnin' Blues | 1973 | 12.00 |
| **VAULT** | | | |
| ❑ 129 | California Mudslide | 1969 | 25.00 |
| **VEE JAY** | | | |
| ❑ LP 1044 [M] | Lightnin' Strikes | 1962 | 50.00 |
| **VERVE** | | | |
| ❑ V-8453 [M] | Fast Life Woman | 1962 | 40.00 |
| **VERVE FOLKWAYS** | | | |
| ❑ FV-9000 [M] | The Roots of Lightnin' Hopkins | 1965 | 25.00 |
| ❑ FVS-9000 [S] | The Roots of Lightnin' Hopkins | 1965 | 30.00 |
| ❑ FV-9022 [M] | Lightnin' Strikes | 1965 | 25.00 |
| ❑ FVS-9022 [S] | Lightnin' Strikes | 1965 | 30.00 |
| **VERVE FORECAST** | | | |
| ❑ FT-3013 [M] | Something Blue | 1967 | 20.00 |
| ❑ FTS-3013 [S] | Something Blue | 1967 | 25.00 |
| ❑ FTS-3031 | Lightnin' Strikes | 1968 | 20.00 |
| **WORLD PACIFIC** | | | |
| ❑ ST-1817 [S] | First Meetin' | 1963 | 40.00 |
| *—Black vinyl* | | | |
| ❑ ST-1817 [S] | First Meetin' | 1963 | 80.00 |
| *—Red vinyl* | | | |
| ❑ WP-1817 [M] | First Meetin' | 1963 | 30.00 |

### HOPKINS, NICKY

| Number | Title (A Side/B Side) | Yr | NM |
|---|---|---|---|
| **COLUMBIA** | | | |
| ❑ KC 32074 | The Tin Man Was a Dreamer | 1973 | 20.00 |

### HOPNEY

| Number | Title (A Side/B Side) | Yr | NM |
|---|---|---|---|
| **ILLUSION** | | | |
| ❑ CM-1032 | Ends and Means | 1979 | 250.00 |
| ❑ CM-1033 | Perils of Love | 1978 | 250.00 |
| ❑ CM-1034 | Cosmic Rockout | 1977 | 500.00 |

### HORN, PAUL

| Number | Title (A Side/B Side) | Yr | NM |
|---|---|---|---|
| **COLUMBIA** | | | |
| ❑ CL 1677 [M] | The Sound of Paul Horn | 1961 | 25.00 |
| ❑ CS 8477 [S] | The Sound of Paul Horn | 1961 | 30.00 |
| ❑ CS 8722 [S] | Profile of a Jazz Musician | 1962 | 20.00 |
| ❑ CS 8850 [S] | Impressions of "Cleopatra" | 1963 | 20.00 |
| **DOT** | | | |
| ❑ DLP-3091 [M] | House of Horn | 1957 | 50.00 |
| ❑ DLP-9002 [M] | Plenty of Horn | 1958 | 50.00 |
| ❑ DLP-29002 [S] | Plenty of Horn | 1959 | 40.00 |
| **HIFI** | | | |
| ❑ J-615 [M] | Something Blue | 1960 | 30.00 |
| ❑ JS-615 [S] | Something Blue | 1960 | 40.00 |
| **ISLAND** | | | |
| ❑ ILSD 6 [(2)] | Special Edition | 197? | 20.00 |
| **KUCKUCK** | | | |
| ❑ KU-060/061 [(2)] | Inside the Great Pyramid | 198? | 20.00 |
| **RCA VICTOR** | | | |
| ❑ LSP-3386 [S] | Cycle | 1965 | 20.00 |
| ❑ LSP-3414 [S] | Jazz Suite on the Mass Texts | 1965 | 20.00 |
| ❑ LSP-3519 [S] | Here's That Rainy Day | 1966 | 20.00 |
| ❑ LSP-3613 [S] | Monday, Monday | 1966 | 20.00 |
| **WORLD PACIFIC** | | | |
| ❑ WP-1266 [M] | Impressions | 1959 | 50.00 |

### HORN, SHIRLEY

| Number | Title (A Side/B Side) | Yr | NM |
|---|---|---|---|
| **ABC-PARAMOUNT** | | | |
| ❑ ABC-538 [M] | Travelin' Light | 1965 | 40.00 |
| ❑ ABCS-538 [S] | Travelin' Light | 1965 | 50.00 |
| **MERCURY** | | | |
| ❑ MG-20761 [M] | Loads of Love | 1963 | 50.00 |
| ❑ MG-20835 [M] | Shirley Horn with Horns | 1963 | 50.00 |
| ❑ SR-60761 [S] | Loads of Love | 1963 | 60.00 |
| ❑ SR-60835 [S] | Shirley Horn with Horns | 1963 | 60.00 |
| ❑ SR-60835 [S] | Shirley Horn with Horns | 199? | 25.00 |
| *—Classic Records reissue on audiophile vinyl* | | | |
| **STEREO-CRAFT** | | | |
| ❑ RTN-16 [M] | Embers and Ashes | 1961 | 60.00 |
| ❑ RTS-16 [S] | Embers and Ashes | 1961 | 80.00 |

### HORNE, JIMMY "BO"

| Number | Title (A Side/B Side) | Yr | NM |
|---|---|---|---|
| **SUNSHINE SOUND** | | | |
| ❑ SSE-7801 | Dance Across the Floor | 1978 | 20.00 |
| ❑ SSE-7805 | Goin' Home for Love | 1979 | 15.00 |

### HORNE, LENA

| Number | Title (A Side/B Side) | Yr | NM |
|---|---|---|---|
| **CHARTER** | | | |
| ❑ CLS-101 [S] | Lena Sings Your Requests | 1963 | 20.00 |
| ❑ CLS-106 [S] | Like Latin | 1964 | 20.00 |
| **JAZZTONE** | | | |
| ❑ J-1262 [M] | Lena and Ivie | 1957 | 50.00 |
| **LION** | | | |
| ❑ L-70050 [M] | I Feel So Smoochie | 1959 | 20.00 |
| **MGM** | | | |
| ❑ E-545 [10] | Lena Horne Sings | 1952 | 50.00 |
| **MOBILE FIDELITY** | | | |
| ❑ 2-094 [(2)] | Lena Horne: The Lady and Her Music | 1982 | 40.00 |
| *—Audiophile vinyl* | | | |
| **MOVIETONE** | | | |
| ❑ MTS 72005 [S] | Once in a Lifetime | 196? | 20.00 |
| **RCA VICTOR** | | | |
| ❑ LOC-1028 [M] | Lena Horne at the Waldorf Astoria | 1957 | 30.00 |
| ❑ LSO-1028 [S] | Lena Horne at the Waldorf Astoria | 1957 | 40.00 |
| ❑ LPM-1148 [M] | It's Love | 1955 | 50.00 |
| ❑ LPM-1375 [M] | Stormy Weather | 1956 | 50.00 |
| ❑ LPM-1879 [M] | Give the Lady What She Wants | 1958 | 30.00 |
| ❑ LSP-1879 [S] | Give the Lady What She Wants | 1958 | 40.00 |
| ❑ LPM-1895 [M] | Songs of Burke and Van Heusen | 1959 | 30.00 |
| ❑ LSP-1895 [S] | Songs of Burke and Van Heusen | 1959 | 40.00 |
| ❑ LPM-2364 [M] | Lena Horne at the Sands | 1961 | 25.00 |
| ❑ LSP-2364 [S] | Lena Horne at the Sands | 1961 | 30.00 |
| ❑ LPM-2465 [M] | Lena on the Blue Side | 1962 | 25.00 |
| ❑ LSP-2465 [S] | Lena on the Blue Side | 1962 | 30.00 |
| ❑ LPM-2587 [M] | Lena...Lovely and Alive | 1963 | 25.00 |
| ❑ LSP-2587 [S] | Lena...Lovely and Alive | 1963 | 30.00 |
| ❑ LPT-3061 [10] | This Is Lena Horne | 1952 | 50.00 |
| **TOPS** | | | |
| ❑ L-910 [10] | Moanin' Low | 195? | 40.00 |
| ❑ L-931 [10] | Lena Horne Sings | 195? | 40.00 |
| ❑ L-1502 [M] | Lena Horne | 1958 | 20.00 |
| **20TH CENTURY FOX** | | | |
| ❑ TFS-4115 [S] | Here's Lena Now | 1964 | 20.00 |
| **UNITED ARTISTS** | | | |
| ❑ UAS 6433 [S] | Feelin' Good | 1965 | 20.00 |
| ❑ UAS 6470 [S] | Lena in Hollywood | 1966 | 20.00 |
| ❑ UAS 6496 [S] | Soul | 1966 | 20.00 |

### HORNE, LENA, AND HARRY BELAFONTE

| Number | Title (A Side/B Side) | Yr | NM |
|---|---|---|---|
| **RCA VICTOR** | | | |
| ❑ LOC-1507 [M] | Porgy and Bess | 1959 | 25.00 |
| ❑ LSO-1507 [S] | Porgy and Bess | 1959 | 40.00 |

### HORNETS, THE

| Number | Title (A Side/B Side) | Yr | NM |
|---|---|---|---|
| **LIBERTY** | | | |
| ❑ LRP-3348 [M] | Motorcycles U.S.A. | 1963 | 40.00 |
| ❑ LRP-3364 [M] | Big Drag Boats U.S.A. | 1964 | 50.00 |
| ❑ LST-7348 [S] | Motorcycles U.S.A. | 1963 | 50.00 |
| ❑ LST-7364 [S] | Big Drag Boats U.S.A. | 1964 | 60.00 |

### HOROWITZ, VLADIMIR

| Number | Title (A Side/B Side) | Yr | NM |
|---|---|---|---|
| **RCA VICTOR RED SEAL** | | | |
| ❑ LSC-2366 [S] | Beethoven: Piano Sonata in D "Appassionata" | 1960 | 20.00 |
| *—Originals with "shaded dog" label* | | | |

### HORSES

Don Johnson of "Miami Vice" and "Nash Bridges" fame was supposedly in this band.

| Number | Title (A Side/B Side) | Yr | NM |
|---|---|---|---|
| **WHITE WHALE** | | | |
| ❑ WWS-7121 | Horses | 1970 | 40.00 |

### HORTON, JOHNNY

| Number | Title (A Side/B Side) | Yr | NM |
|---|---|---|---|
| **BRIAR** | | | |
| ❑ 104 [M] | Done Rovin' | 196? | 150.00 |
| **COLUMBIA** | | | |
| ❑ CL 1362 [M] | The Spectacular Johnny Horton | 1959 | 30.00 |
| ❑ CL 1478 [M] | Johnny Horton Makes History | 1960 | 30.00 |
| ❑ 1596/8396 | Johnny Horton's Greatest Hits Bonus Photo | 1961 | 10.00 |
| ❑ CL 1596 [M] | Johnny Horton's Greatest Hits | 1961 | 25.00 |
| ❑ CL 1721 [M] | Honky-Tonk Man | 1962 | 30.00 |
| ❑ CL 2299 [M] | I Can't Forget You | 1965 | 25.00 |
| ❑ CL 2566 [M] | Johnny Horton on Stage at the Louisiana Hayride | 1966 | 20.00 |
| ❑ CS 8167 [S] | The Spectacular Johnny Horton | 1959 | 40.00 |
| ❑ CS 8269 [S] | Johnny Horton Makes History | 1960 | 40.00 |
| ❑ CS 8396 [S] | Johnny Horton's Greatest Hits | 1961 | 30.00 |
| ❑ PC 8396 | Johnny Horton's Greatest Hits | 198? | 8.00 |
| *—Budget-line reissue* | | | |
| ❑ CS 8779 [R] | Honky-Tonk Man | 1962 | 15.00 |
| ❑ CS 9099 [R] | I Can't Forget You | 1965 | 15.00 |
| ❑ CS 9366 [S] | Johnny Horton on Stage at the Louisiana Hayride | 1966 | 25.00 |
| ❑ CS 9940 | Johnny Horton On the Road | 1969 | 15.00 |
| ❑ G 30884 [(2)] | The World of Johnny Horton | 1971 | 15.00 |
| **DOT** | | | |
| ❑ DLP 3221 [M] | Johnny Horton | 1962 | 30.00 |
| ❑ DLP 25221 [R] | Johnny Horton | 1962 | 15.00 |
| **HARMONY** | | | |
| ❑ HS 11291 [R] | The Unforgettable Johnny Horton | 196? | 12.00 |
| ❑ HS 11384 | The Legendary Johnny Horton | 1970 | 12.00 |
| ❑ KH 30394 | The Battle of New Orleans | 1971 | 12.00 |
| **HILLTOP** | | | |
| ❑ 6012 | The Voice of Johnny Horton | 196? | 12.00 |
| ❑ JS-6060 | All for the Love of a Girl | 196? | 12.00 |
| **MERCURY** | | | |
| ❑ MG-20478 [M] | The Fantastic Johnny Horton | 1959 | 50.00 |
| **SESAC** | | | |
| ❑ 1201 [M] | Free and Easy Songs | 1959 | 150.00 |

### HORTON, ROBERT

| Number | Title (A Side/B Side) | Yr | NM |
|---|---|---|---|
| **COLUMBIA** | | | |
| ❑ CL 2202 [M] | The Very Thought of You | 1964 | 25.00 |
| ❑ CL 2408 [M] | A Man Called Shenandoah | 1966 | 25.00 |
| ❑ CS 9002 [S] | The Very Thought of You | 1964 | 30.00 |
| ❑ CS 9208 [S] | A Man Called Shenandoah | 1966 | 30.00 |

### HORTON, WALTER "SHAKEY"

| Number | Title (A Side/B Side) | Yr | NM |
|---|---|---|---|
| **ARGO** | | | |
| ❑ LP-4037 [M] | The Soul of Blues Harmonica | 1964 | 150.00 |
| ❑ LPS-4037 [S] | The Soul of Blues Harmonica | 1964 | 250.00 |

### HOT BUTTER

| Number | Title (A Side/B Side) | Yr | NM |
|---|---|---|---|
| **MUSICOR** | | | |
| ❑ MS-3242 | Popcorn | 1972 | 12.00 |
| *—Regular cover* | | | |
| ❑ MS-3242 | Popcorn | 1972 | 20.00 |
| *—Die-cut cover* | | | |

### HOT DOGGERS, THE

| Number | Title (A Side/B Side) | Yr | NM |
|---|---|---|---|
| **EPIC** | | | |
| ❑ LN 24054 [M] | Surfin' U.S.A. | 1963 | 150.00 |
| ❑ BN 26054 [S] | Surfin' U.S.A. | 1963 | 200.00 |

| Number | Title (A Side/B Side) | Yr | NM |
|---|---|---|---|
| **HOT POOP** | | | |
| HOT POOP | | | |
| ❑ 3072 | Hot Poop Does Their Own Thing | 1971 | 300.00 |
| **HOT RODDERS, THE** | | | |
| CROWN | | | |
| ❑ CST-378 [S] | Big Hot Rod | 1963 | 25.00 |
| ❑ CLP-5378 [M] | Big Hot Rod | 1963 | 20.00 |
| **HOT TUNA** Offshoot of JEFFERSON AIRPLANE. | | | |
| GRUNT | | | |
| ❑ BFL1-0348 | The Phosphorescent Rat | 1974 | 15.00 |
| ❑ BFD1-0820 [Q] | America's Choice | 1975 | 25.00 |
| ❑ BFL1-0820 | America's Choice | 1975 | 15.00 |
| ❑ FTR-1004 | Burgers | 1972 | 15.00 |
| ❑ BFD1-1238 [Q] | Yellow Fever | 1975 | 25.00 |
| ❑ BFL1-1238 | Yellow Fever | 1975 | 15.00 |
| ❑ BFL1-1920 | Hoppkorv | 1976 | 15.00 |
| ❑ CYL2-2545 [(2)] | Double Dose | 1978 | 20.00 |
| ❑ BXL1-2591 | Burgers | 1978 | 12.00 |
| *—Reissue of 1004* | | | |
| ❑ DJL1-2852 [DJ] | The Last Interview? A Live Hot Tuna Radio Classic | 1978 | 30.00 |
| ❑ BXL1-3357 | Final Vinyl | 1979 | 12.00 |
| RCA VICTOR | | | |
| ❑ AYL1-3864 | Hot Tuna | 1981 | 8.00 |
| *—"Best Buy Series" reissue* | | | |
| ❑ AYL1-3865 | First Pull Up Then Pull Down | 1981 | 8.00 |
| *—"Best Buy Series" reissue* | | | |
| ❑ AYL1-3951 | Burgers | 1981 | 8.00 |
| *—"Best Buy Series" reissue* | | | |
| ❑ LSP-4353 | Hot Tuna | 1970 | 15.00 |
| ❑ LSP-4550 | First Pull Up Then Pull Down | 1971 | 15.00 |
| **HOTHOUSE FLOWERS** | | | |
| LONDON | | | |
| ❑ 085 [DJ] | Conversation and Music with Hothouse Flowers | 1988 | 15.00 |
| ❑ PRO 884-1 [DJ] | Live | 1990 | 25.00 |
| *—Six-song promo-only live EP* | | | |
| ❑ 828101-1 | People | 1988 | 12.00 |
| **HOTLEGS** Early incarnation of 10CC. Also see GRAHAM GOULDMAN. | | | |
| CAPITOL | | | |
| ❑ ST-587 | Hotlegs Thinks: School Stinks | 1970 | 25.00 |
| **HOUK, RALPH** | | | |
| CARLTON | | | |
| ❑ HH-16 [M] | Hear How to Play Better Baseball | 1961 | 40.00 |
| **HOUR GLASS, THE** | | | |
| LIBERTY | | | |
| ❑ LRP-3536 [M] | The Hour Glass | 1967 | 25.00 |
| ❑ LST-7536 [S] | The Hour Glass | 1967 | 30.00 |
| ❑ LST-7555 | The Power of Love | 1968 | 30.00 |
| SPRINGBOARD | | | |
| ❑ SPB-4016 | Duane and Gregg Allman with the Hour Glass | 1976 | 10.00 |
| UNITED ARTISTS | | | |
| ❑ UA-LA013-G2 [(2)] | The Hour Glass | 1973 | 15.00 |
| **HOUSE, SON** | | | |
| COLUMBIA | | | |
| ❑ CL 2417 [M] | Father of the Folk Blues | 1965 | 20.00 |
| ❑ CS 9217 [S] | Father of the Folk Blues | 1965 | 25.00 |
| *—Red "360 Sound" label* | | | |
| **HOUSE, SON, AND J.D. SHORT** | | | |
| VERVE FOLKWAYS | | | |
| ❑ FV-9035 [M] | Blues from the Mississippi Delta | 1966 | 40.00 |
| ❑ FVS-9035 [R] | Blues from the Mississippi Delta | 1966 | 20.00 |
| **HOUSE OF PAIN** Also see EVERLAST. | | | |
| TOMMY BOY | | | |
| ❑ TB 1056 | House of Pain (Fine Malt Lyrics) | 1992 | 40.00 |
| ❑ TB 1161 | Truth Crushed to Earth Shall Rise Again | 1996 | 30.00 |
| **HOUSTON, DAVID** | | | |
| EPIC | | | |
| ❑ EGP 502 [(2)] | The World of David Houston | 1970 | 20.00 |
| ❑ LN 24112 [M] | New Voice from Nashville | 1964 | 15.00 |
| ❑ LN 24156 [M] | 12 Great Country Hits | 1965 | 15.00 |
| ❑ LN 24213 [M] | Almost Persuaded | 1966 | 15.00 |
| ❑ LN 24303 [M] | A Loser's Cathedral | 1967 | 20.00 |
| ❑ LN 24320 [M] | Golden Hymns | 1967 | 20.00 |
| ❑ LN 24338 [M] | You Mean the World to Me | 1967 | 20.00 |
| ❑ LN 24342 [M] | David Houston's Greatest Hits | 1968 | 30.00 |
| ❑ BN 26112 [S] | New Voice from Nashville | 1964 | 20.00 |
| ❑ BN 26156 [S] | 12 Great Country Hits | 1965 | 20.00 |
| ❑ BN 26213 [S] | Almost Persuaded | 1966 | 20.00 |

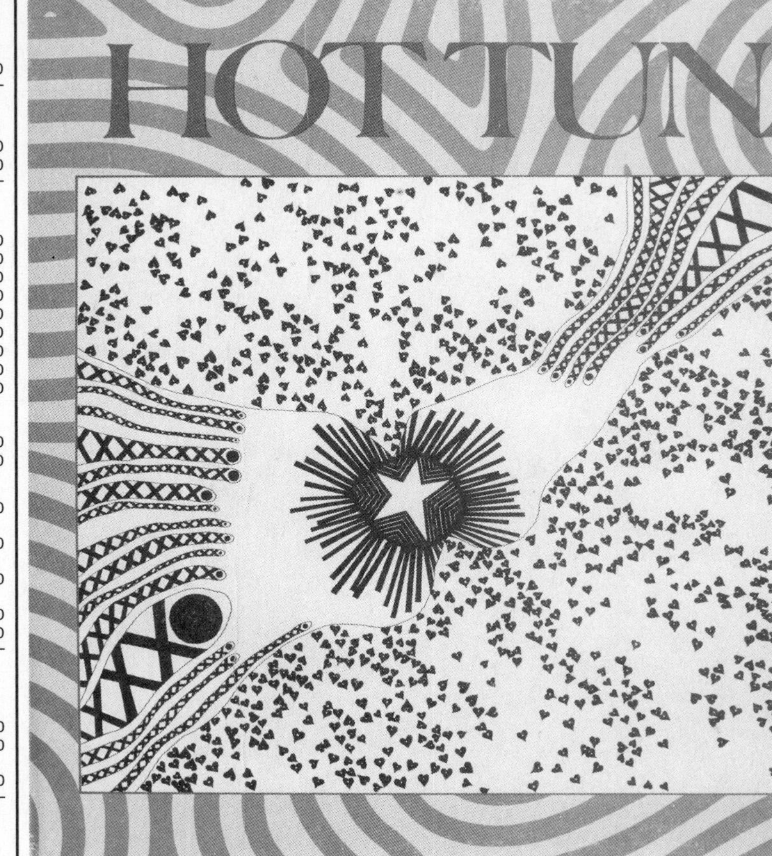


Hot Tuna, *First Pull Up, Then Pull Down,* RCA Victor LSP-4550, 1971, $15.

| Number | Title (A Side/B Side) | Yr | NM |
|---|---|---|---|
| ❑ BN 26303 [S] | A Loser's Cathedral | 1967 | 15.00 |
| ❑ BN 26320 [S] | Golden Hymns | 1967 | 15.00 |
| ❑ BN 26338 [S] | You Mean the World to Me | 1967 | 15.00 |
| ❑ BN 26342 [S] | David Houston's Greatest Hits | 1968 | 15.00 |
| ❑ BN 26391 | Already It's Heaven | 1968 | 15.00 |
| ❑ BN 26432 | Where Love Used to Live | 1969 | 15.00 |
| ❑ BN 26482 | David | 1969 | 15.00 |
| ❑ BN 26539 | Baby, Baby | 1970 | 15.00 |
| ❑ E 30108 | Wonders of the Wine | 1970 | 15.00 |
| ❑ E 30437 | Sweet Lovin' | 1971 | 15.00 |
| ❑ E 30602 | David Houston's Greatest Hits, Volume 2 | 1971 | 15.00 |
| ❑ E 30657 | A Woman Always Knows | 1971 | 15.00 |
| ❑ KE 31385 | The Day Love Walked In | 1972 | 12.00 |
| ❑ KE 32189 | Good Things | 1973 | 12.00 |
| ❑ KE 33350 | A Man Needs Love | 1975 | 12.00 |
| ❑ KE 33948 | What a Night | 1976 | 12.00 |
| GUSTO | | | |
| ❑ 0012 | The Best of David Houston | 1978 | 10.00 |
| HARMONY | | | |
| ❑ HS 11412 | David Houston | 1970 | 10.00 |
| ❑ KH 31778 | The Many Sides of David Houston | 1972 | 10.00 |
| ❑ KH 32287 | Old Time Religion | 1973 | 10.00 |
| RCA CAMDEN | | | |
| ❑ CAL-2126 [M] | David Houston Sings | 1966 | 15.00 |
| ❑ CAS-2126 [R] | David Houston Sings | 1966 | 10.00 |
| STARDAY | | | |
| ❑ 990 | David Houston | 1978 | 10.00 |
| **HOUSTON, DAVID, AND TAMMY WYNETTE** | | | |
| EPIC | | | |
| ❑ LN 24325 [M] | My Elusive Dreams | 1967 | 20.00 |
| ❑ BN 26325 [S] | My Elusive Dreams | 1967 | 15.00 |
| **HOUSTON, JOE** | | | |
| COMBO | | | |
| ❑ LP-100 [M] | Joe Houston | 195? | 400.00 |
| *—Color photo of Joe Houston on cover* | | | |
| ❑ LP-100 [M] | Joe Houston | 195? | 400.00 |
| *—Silver cover with "J" in the shape of a saxophone* | | | |
| ❑ LP-400 [M] | Rockin' at the Drive In | 195? | 200.00 |
| *—Blue ink on front and back covers* | | | |
| ❑ LP-400 [M] | Rockin' at the Drive In | 195? | 300.00 |
| *—Black ink on front and back covers* | | | |

| Number | Title (A Side/B Side) | Yr | NM |
|---|---|---|---|
| CROWN | | | |
| ❑ CST-313 [R] | Surf Rockin' | 1963 | 30.00 |
| ❑ CST-319 [R] | Limbo | 1963 | 30.00 |
| ❑ CLP-5006 [M] | Joe Houston Rock and Rolls All Night Long | 195? | 100.00 |
| *—Black label, gold print* | | | |
| ❑ CLP-5006 [M] | Joe Houston Rock and Rolls All Night Long | 196? | 40.00 |
| *—Gray label, black print* | | | |
| ❑ CLP-5203 [M] | Wild Man of the Tenor Sax | 1962 | 40.00 |
| ❑ CLP-5246 [M] | Doin' the Twist | 1962 | 40.00 |
| ❑ CLP-5313 [M] | Surf Rockin' | 1963 | 40.00 |
| ❑ CLP-5319 [M] | Limbo | 1963 | 40.00 |
| MODERN | | | |
| ❑ LMP-1206 [M] | Joe Houston Blows All Night Long | 1956 | 300.00 |
| TOPS | | | |
| ❑ L-1518 [M] | Rock and Roll | 195? | 80.00 |
| **HOUSTON, THELMA** | | | |
| ABC DUNHILL | | | |
| ❑ DS-50054 | Sun Shower | 1969 | 25.00 |
| MCA | | | |
| ❑ 5395 | Thelma Houston | 1983 | 10.00 |
| ❑ 5527 | Qualifying Heat | 1984 | 10.00 |
| MOTOWN | | | |
| ❑ M5-120V1 | Superstar Series, Vol. 20 | 1981 | 10.00 |
| ❑ M5-127V1 | Sunshower | 1981 | 8.00 |
| ❑ M5-226V1 | Any Way You Like It | 1982 | 10.00 |
| MOWEST | | | |
| ❑ MW-102 | Thelma Houston | 1972 | 20.00 |
| RCA VICTOR | | | |
| ❑ AFL1-3500 | Breakwater Cat | 1980 | 10.00 |
| ❑ AFL1-3842 | Never Gonna Be Another One | 1981 | 10.00 |
| REPRISE | | | |
| ❑ 26234 | Throw You Down | 1990 | 15.00 |
| SHEFFIELD LABS | | | |
| ❑ 2 | I've Got the Music In Me | 1975 | 40.00 |
| SHEFFIELD TREASURY | | | |
| ❑ ST-200 | I've Got the Music In Me | 1983 | 20.00 |
| *—Reissue of Sheffield Labs 2* | | | |

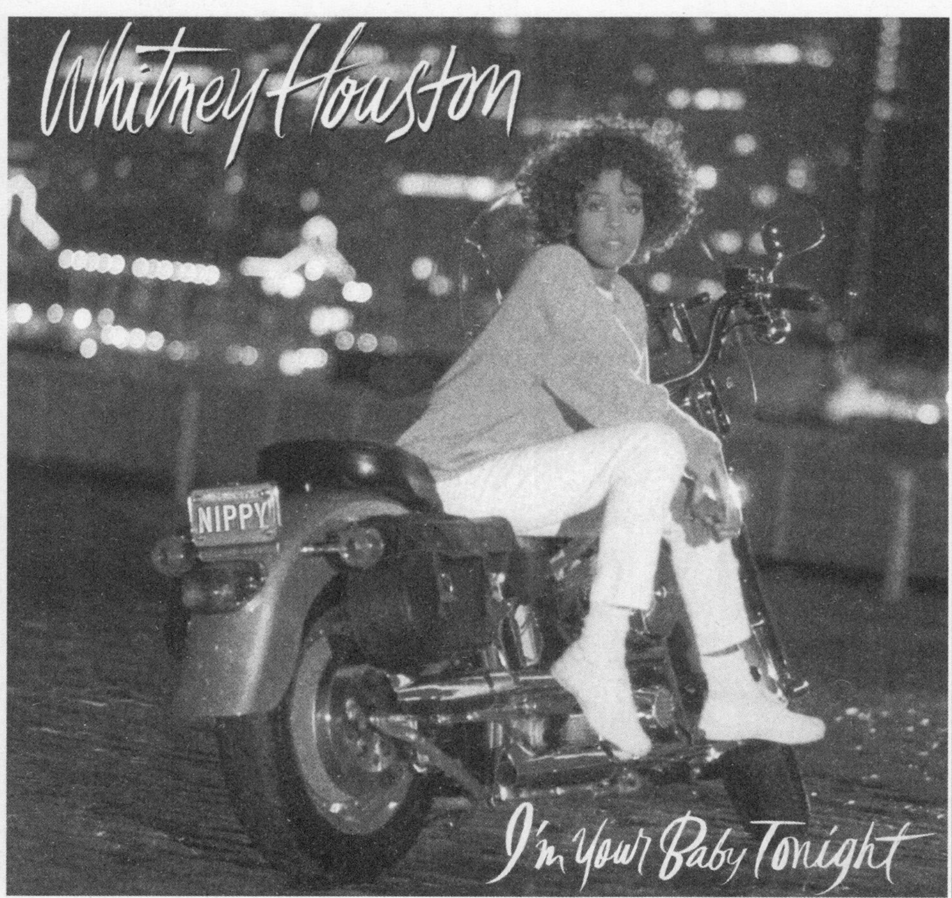


Whitney Houston, *I'm Your Baby Tonight,* Arista AL-8616, 1990, $10.

| Number | Title (A Side/B Side) | Yr | NM |
|---|---|---|---|
| **TAMLA** | | | |
| ❑ T6-345R1 | Any Way You Like It | 1976 | 12.00 |
| ❑ T7-358R1 | The Devil in Me | 1977 | 10.00 |
| ❑ T7-361R1 | Ready to Roll | 1978 | 10.00 |

## HOUSTON, WHITNEY

| Number | Title (A Side/B Side) | Yr | NM |
|---|---|---|---|
| **ARISTA** | | | |
| ❑ AL 8212 | Whitney Houston | 1985 | 8.00 |
| ❑ AL 8405 | Whitney | 1987 | 8.00 |
| ❑ 14652 [(4)] | The Unreleased Mixes | 2000 | 20.00 |
| *—Box set of 12-inch single remixes* | | | |
| ❑ AL 18616 | I'm Your Baby Tonight | 1990 | 10.00 |
| ❑ 19037 [(2)] | My Love Is Your Love | 1998 | 12.00 |

## HOUSTON FEARLESS

| Number | Title (A Side/B Side) | Yr | NM |
|---|---|---|---|
| **IMPERIAL** | | | |
| ❑ LP-12421 | Houston Fearless | 1969 | 20.00 |

## HOWARD, DAVE

| Number | Title (A Side/B Side) | Yr | NM |
|---|---|---|---|
| **CHOREO** | | | |
| ❑ C-5 [M] | I Love Everybody | 1961 | 25.00 |
| ❑ CS-5 [S] | I Love Everybody | 1961 | 30.00 |

## HOWARD, EDDY

| Number | Title (A Side/B Side) | Yr | NM |
|---|---|---|---|
| **CIRCLE** | | | |
| ❑ 29 | Eddy Howard 1949-1952 | 198? | 10.00 |
| ❑ 79 | Eddy Howard 1949-1953 | 1985 | 10.00 |
| **COLUMBIA** | | | |
| ❑ CL 6067 [10] | Eddy Howard | 1949 | 60.00 |
| **HINDSIGHT** | | | |
| ❑ HSR-119 | Eddy Howard 1946-1951 | 198? | 10.00 |
| ❑ HSR-156 | Eddy Howard 1945-1948 | 198? | 10.00 |
| ❑ HSR-405 [(2)] | Eddy Howard and His Orchestra Play 22 Original Big Band Favorites | 198? | 12.00 |
| **INSIGHT** | | | |
| ❑ 205 | Eddy Howard and His Orchestra 1945-1951 | 198? | 10.00 |
| **MERCURY** | | | |
| ❑ MG-20112 [M] | Singing in the Rain | 195? | 25.00 |
| ❑ MG-20312 [M] | Paradise Isle | 195? | 25.00 |
| ❑ MG-20432 [M] | Great for Dancing | 1958 | 20.00 |
| ❑ MG-20562 [M] | Eddy Howard's Golden Hits | 1961 | 15.00 |
| ❑ MG-20593 [M] | More Eddy Howard's Golden Hits | 1962 | 15.00 |
| ❑ MG-20665 [M] | Eddy Howard Sings and Plays the Great Old Waltzes | 1962 | 15.00 |
| ❑ MG-20817 [M] | Eddy Howard Sings and Plays the Great Band Hits | 196? | 15.00 |
| ❑ MG-20910 [M] | Intimately Yours | 1965 | 15.00 |
| ❑ MG-21014 [M] | Softly and Sincerely | 196? | 15.00 |
| ❑ MG-25011 [10] | Selected Song Favorites | 1949 | 50.00 |
| *—Title appears only on label; cover simply states "Eddy Howard and His Orchestra"* | | | |
| ❑ SR-60104 [S] | Great for Dancing | 1959 | 25.00 |
| ❑ SR-60562 [S] | Eddy Howard's Golden Hits | 1961 | 20.00 |
| ❑ SR-60593 [S] | More Eddy Howard's Golden Hits | 1962 | 20.00 |
| ❑ SR-60665 [S] | Eddy Howard Sings and Plays the Great Old Waltzes | 1962 | 20.00 |
| ❑ SR-60817 [S] | Eddy Howard Sings and Plays the Great Band Hits | 196? | 20.00 |
| ❑ SR-60910 [S] | Intimately Yours | 1965 | 20.00 |
| ❑ SR-61014 [S] | Softly and Sincerely | 196? | 20.00 |
| **WING** | | | |
| ❑ MGW-12104 [M] | Saturday Night Dance Date | 196? | 12.00 |
| ❑ MGW-12171 [M] | Eddy Howard Sings Words of Love | 196? | 12.00 |
| ❑ MGW-12171 [M] | Words of Love | 196? | 12.00 |
| ❑ MGW-12194 [M] | Sleepy Serenade | 196? | 12.00 |
| ❑ MGW-12249 [M] | The Velvet Voice | 196? | 12.00 |
| ❑ SRW-16104 [S] | Saturday Night Dance Date | 196? | 12.00 |
| ❑ SRW-16171 [S] | Eddy Howard Sings Words of Love | 196? | 12.00 |
| ❑ SRW-16171 [S] | Words of Love | 196? | 12.00 |
| ❑ SRW-16194 [S] | Sleepy Serenade | 196? | 12.00 |
| ❑ SRW-16249 [S] | The Velvet Voice | 196? | 12.00 |

## HOWARD, HARLAN

| Number | Title (A Side/B Side) | Yr | NM |
|---|---|---|---|
| **CAPITOL** | | | |
| ❑ ST 1631 [S] | Harlan Howard Sings Harlan Howard | 1961 | 40.00 |
| ❑ T 1631 [M] | Harlan Howard Sings Harlan Howard | 1961 | 30.00 |
| **MONUMENT** | | | |
| ❑ MLP-8038 [M] | All-Time Favorite Country Songwriter | 1965 | 25.00 |
| ❑ SLP-18038 [S] | All-Time Favorite Country Songwriter | 1965 | 30.00 |
| **RCA VICTOR** | | | |
| ❑ LPM-3729 [M] | Mr. Songwriter | 1967 | 25.00 |
| ❑ LSP-3729 [S] | Mr. Songwriter | 1967 | 20.00 |
| ❑ LPM-3886 [M] | Down to Earth | 1968 | 50.00 |
| ❑ LSP-3886 [S] | Down to Earth | 1968 | 20.00 |

## HOWARD, JAN

| Number | Title (A Side/B Side) | Yr | NM |
|---|---|---|---|
| **CAPITOL** | | | |
| ❑ ST 1779 [S] | Sweet and Sentimental | 1962 | 25.00 |
| ❑ T 1779 [M] | Sweet and Sentimental | 1962 | 20.00 |
| **DECCA** | | | |
| ❑ DL 4793 [M] | Jan Howard Sings Evil on Your Mind | 1966 | 15.00 |
| ❑ DL 4832 [M] | Bad Seed | 1966 | 15.00 |
| ❑ DL 4931 [M] | This Is Jan Howard Country | 1967 | 25.00 |
| ❑ DL 5012 [M] | Count Your Blessings, Woman | 1968 | 40.00 |
| *—White label promo only* | | | |
| ❑ DL 74793 [S] | Jan Howard Sings Evil on Your Mind | 1966 | 20.00 |
| ❑ DL 74832 [S] | Bad Seed | 1966 | 20.00 |
| ❑ DL 74931 [S] | This Is Jan Howard Country | 1967 | 20.00 |
| ❑ DL 75012 [S] | Count Your Blessings, Woman | 1968 | 20.00 |
| ❑ DL 75130 | Jan Howard | 1969 | 20.00 |
| ❑ DL 75166 | For God and Country | 1969 | 25.00 |
| ❑ DL 75207 | Rock Me Back to Little Rock | 1970 | 20.00 |
| ❑ DL 75293 | Love Is Like a Spinning Wheel | 1972 | 20.00 |
| **PICKWICK** | | | |
| ❑ JS 6174 | Rock Me Back to Little Rock! | 197? | 10.00 |
| **TOWER** | | | |
| ❑ ST 5068 [S] | Lonely Country | 1967 | 20.00 |
| ❑ T 5068 [M] | Lonely Country | 1967 | 20.00 |
| ❑ DT 5119 [R] | The Real Me | 1968 | 15.00 |
| **WRANGLER** | | | |
| ❑ 1005 [M] | Jan Howard | 1962 | 25.00 |
| ❑ S-1005 [S] | Jan Howard | 1962 | 30.00 |

## HOWARD, JOE

| Number | Title (A Side/B Side) | Yr | NM |
|---|---|---|---|
| **KING** | | | |
| ❑ 661 [M] | The Golden Sound | 1959 | 50.00 |
| **SUNSET** | | | |
| ❑ SU-3001 [M] | Patterns for Trombone | 1955 | 40.00 |

## HOWARD, NOAH

| Number | Title (A Side/B Side) | Yr | NM |
|---|---|---|---|
| **ESP-DISK'** | | | |
| ❑ 1031 [M] | Noah Howard Quartet | 1966 | 20.00 |
| ❑ S-1031 [S] | Noah Howard Quartet | 1966 | 25.00 |
| ❑ S-1064 [S] | Live at Judson Hall | 1969 | 20.00 |

## HOWL THE GOOD

| Number | Title (A Side/B Side) | Yr | NM |
|---|---|---|---|
| **RARE EARTH** | | | |
| ❑ RS-537 | Howl the Good | 1972 | 20.00 |

## HOWLIN' WOLF

| Number | Title (A Side/B Side) | Yr | NM |
|---|---|---|---|
| **CADET** | | | |
| ❑ LPS-319 | This Is Howlin' Wolf's New Album | 1969 | 25.00 |
| **CHESS** | | | |
| ❑ 201 [(2)] | Howlin' Wolf | 1976 | 15.00 |
| ❑ LP-1434 [M] | Moanin' in the Moonlight | 1958 | 600.00 |
| ❑ LP-1469 [M] | Howlin' Wolf | 1962 | 600.00 |
| ❑ LP-1502 [M] | The Real Folk Blues | 1966 | 50.00 |
| ❑ LP-1512 [M] | More Real Folk Blues | 1966 | 50.00 |
| ❑ LP-1540 | Evil | 1969 | 25.00 |
| ❑ CH-9107 | His Greatest Sides, Vol. 1 | 1985 | 10.00 |
| ❑ CH-9182 | Chicago — 26 Golden Years | 1985 | 10.00 |
| ❑ CH-9195 | Moanin' in the Moonlight | 1986 | 8.00 |
| *—Reissue of 1434* | | | |
| ❑ CH-9273 | The Real Folk Blues | 1988 | 10.00 |
| *—Reissue of 1502* | | | |
| ❑ CH-9279 | More Real Folk Blues | 1988 | 10.00 |
| *—Reissue of 1512* | | | |
| ❑ CH-9297 | The London Howlin' Wolf Sessions | 1989 | 10.00 |
| *—Reissue of 60008* | | | |
| ❑ CH5-9332 [(5)] | The Chess Box | 1991 | 40.00 |
| ❑ CH-50002 | Message to the Young | 1971 | 20.00 |
| ❑ CH-50015 | Live and Cookin' | 1972 | 20.00 |
| ❑ CH-50045 | Back Door Wolf | 1974 | 20.00 |
| ❑ CH-60008 | The London Howlin' Wolf Sessions | 1971 | 20.00 |
| ❑ CH-60016 [(2)] | Howlin' Wolk, AKA Chester Burnett | 1972 | 25.00 |
| ❑ CH-93001 | Change My Way | 198? | 10.00 |
| **CROWN** | | | |
| ❑ CLP-5240 [M] | Howlin' Wolf Sings the Blues | 1962 | 25.00 |
| **CUSTOM** | | | |
| ❑ CM-2055 [M] | Big City Blues | 196? | 40.00 |
| ❑ CS-2055 [R] | Big City Blues | 196? | 20.00 |
| **KENT** | | | |
| ❑ KLP-526 [M] | Original Folk Blues | 1967 | 15.00 |
| ❑ KST-526 [R] | Original Folk Blues | 1967 | 12.00 |
| ❑ KST-527 | Howlin' Wolf's 20 Greatest R&B Hits | 1968 | 12.00 |
| ❑ KST-535 | Underground Blues | 1968 | 12.00 |



**Except when noted otherwise, VG = 25% of NM, and VG+ = 50% of NM. (Example: VG = $2.00, VG+ = $4.00 and NM = $8.00.)**

| Number | Title (A Side/B Side) | Yr | NM |
|---|---|---|---|
| **ROUNDER** | | | |
| ❑ SS-28 | Cadillac Daddy: Memphis Recordings, 1952 | 1989 | 12.00 |

### HUBBARD, FREDDIE

| Number | Title (A Side/B Side) | Yr | NM |
|---|---|---|---|
| **ATLANTIC** | | | |
| ❑ 1477 [M] | Backlash | 1967 | 25.00 |
| **BLUE NOTE** | | | |
| ❑ BLP-4040 [M] | Open Sesame | 1960 | 80.00 |
| *—Regular version with W. 63rd St. address on label* | | | |
| ❑ BLP-4040 [M] | Open Sesame | 1960 | 120.00 |
| *—"Deep groove" version (deep indentation under label on both sides)* | | | |
| ❑ BLP-4040 [M] | Open Sesame | 1963 | 20.00 |
| *—With New York, USA address on label* | | | |
| ❑ BLP-4056 [M] | Goin' Up | 1960 | 80.00 |
| *—With W. 63rd St. address on label* | | | |
| ❑ BLP-4056 [M] | Goin' Up | 1963 | 20.00 |
| *—With New York, USA address on label* | | | |
| ❑ BLP-4073 [M] | Hub Cap | 1961 | 80.00 |
| *—With W. 63rd St. address on label* | | | |
| ❑ BLP-4073 [M] | Hub Cap | 1963 | 20.00 |
| *—With New York, USA address on label* | | | |
| ❑ BLP-4085 [M] | Ready for Freddie | 1961 | 80.00 |
| *—With 61st St. address on label* | | | |
| ❑ BLP-4085 [M] | Ready for Freddie | 1963 | 20.00 |
| *—With New York, USA address on label* | | | |
| ❑ BLP-4115 [M] | Hub Tones | 1962 | 25.00 |
| ❑ BLP-4172 [M] | Breaking Point | 1964 | 25.00 |
| ❑ BLP-4196 [M] | Blue Spirits | 1965 | 25.00 |
| ❑ BLP-4207 [M] | The Night of the Cookers — Live at Club Le Marchal, Vol. 1 | 1965 | 25.00 |
| ❑ BLP-4208 [M] | The Night of the Cookers — Live at Club Le Marchal, Vol. 2 | 1965 | 25.00 |
| ❑ BST-84040 [S] | Open Sesame | 1960 | 60.00 |
| *—With W. 63rd St. addresss on label* | | | |
| ❑ BST-84040 [S] | Open Sesame | 1963 | 25.00 |
| *—With New York, USA address on label* | | | |
| ❑ BST-84040 [S] | Open Sesame | 199? | 25.00 |
| *—Classic Records reissue on audiophile vinyl* | | | |
| ❑ BST-84056 [S] | Goin' Up | 1960 | 60.00 |
| *—With W. 63rd St. address on label* | | | |
| ❑ BST-84056 [S] | Goin' Up | 1963 | 25.00 |
| *—With New York, USA address on label* | | | |
| ❑ BST-84073 [S] | Hub Cap | 1961 | 60.00 |
| *—With W. 63rd St. address on label* | | | |
| ❑ BST-84073 [S] | Hub Cap | 1963 | 25.00 |
| *—With New York, USA address on label* | | | |
| ❑ BST-84085 [S] | Ready for Freddie | 1961 | 60.00 |
| *—With 61st St. addresss on label* | | | |
| ❑ BST-84085 [S] | Ready for Freddie | 1963 | 25.00 |
| *—With New York, USA address on label* | | | |
| ❑ BST-84115 [S] | Hub-Tones | 1962 | 30.00 |
| *—With New York, USA address on label* | | | |
| ❑ BST-84172 [S] | Breaking Point | 1964 | 30.00 |
| *—With New York, USA address on label* | | | |
| ❑ BST-84196 [S] | Blue Spirits | 1965 | 30.00 |
| *—With New York, USA address on label* | | | |
| ❑ BST-84207 [S] | The Night of the Cookers — Live at Club Le Marchal, Vol. 1 | 1965 | 30.00 |
| *—With New York, USA address on label* | | | |
| ❑ BST-84208 [S] | The Night of the Cookers — Live at Club Le Marchal, Vol. 2 | 1965 | 30.00 |
| *—With New York, USA address on label* | | | |
| **IMPULSE!** | | | |
| ❑ A-27 [M] | The Artistry of Freddie Hubbard | 1962 | 25.00 |
| ❑ AS-27 [S] | The Artistry of Freddie Hubbard | 1962 | 30.00 |
| ❑ A-38 [M] | The Body and Soul of Freddie Hubbard | 1963 | 25.00 |
| ❑ AS-38 [S] | The Body and Soul of Freddie Hubbard | 1963 | 30.00 |

### HUCKO, PEANUTS

| Number | Title (A Side/B Side) | Yr | NM |
|---|---|---|---|
| **GRAND AWARD** | | | |
| ❑ GA 33-331 [M] | Tribute to Benny Goodman | 1956 | 40.00 |
| **WALDORF MUSIC HALL** | | | |
| ❑ MH 33-153 [10] | A Tribute to Benny Goodman | 1956 | 30.00 |

### HUCKO, PEANUTS/RAY MCKINLEY

| Number | Title (A Side/B Side) | Yr | NM |
|---|---|---|---|
| **GRAND AWARD** | | | |
| ❑ GA 33-333 [M] | The Swingin' 30s | 1956 | 40.00 |

### HUDSON, ROCK

| Number | Title (A Side/B Side) | Yr | NM |
|---|---|---|---|
| **STANYAN** | | | |
| ❑ SR-10014 | Rock Gently | 1971 | 25.00 |

### HUDSON AND LANDRY

| Number | Title (A Side/B Side) | Yr | NM |
|---|---|---|---|
| **DORE** | | | |
| ❑ 324 | Hanging In There | 1971 | 20.00 |
| ❑ 326 | Losing Their Heads | 1971 | 20.00 |
| ❑ 329 | Right-Off! | 1972 | 20.00 |
| ❑ 331 | Weird Kingdom | 1973 | 20.00 |
| ❑ 333 | The Best of Hudson and Landry | 1974 | 15.00 |
| ❑ 334 | The Best of Hudson and Landry 2 | 1975 | 15.00 |

### HUG, ARMAND

| Number | Title (A Side/B Side) | Yr | NM |
|---|---|---|---|
| **CIRCLE** | | | |
| ❑ L-411 [10] | New Orleans 88 | 1951 | 60.00 |
| **PARAMOUNT** | | | |
| ❑ LP-114 [10] | Armand Hug Plays Armand Piron | 1954 | 50.00 |

### HUGHES, FREDDIE

| Number | Title (A Side/B Side) | Yr | NM |
|---|---|---|---|
| **WAND** | | | |
| ❑ WDS-664 | Send My Baby Back | 1968 | 25.00 |
| *—The numbering system suggests this would have been issued in 1965, but the singles from this LP were issued in 1968, thus we use the later date.* | | | |

### HUGHES, JIMMY

| Number | Title (A Side/B Side) | Yr | NM |
|---|---|---|---|
| **ATCO** | | | |
| ❑ 33-209 [M] | Why Not Tonight | 1967 | 20.00 |
| ❑ SD 33-209 [S] | Why Not Tonight | 1967 | 20.00 |
| **VEE JAY** | | | |
| ❑ VJ-1102 [M] | Steal Away | 1965 | 25.00 |
| ❑ VJS-1102 [R] | Steal Away | 1965 | 25.00 |
| **VOLT** | | | |
| ❑ VOS-6003 | Something Special | 1969 | 20.00 |

### HUGHES, LANGSTON

| Number | Title (A Side/B Side) | Yr | NM |
|---|---|---|---|
| **FOLKWAYS** | | | |
| ❑ FA-7312 [10] | The Story of Jazz for Children | 1954 | 50.00 |
| *—With booklet* | | | |
| **MGM** | | | |
| ❑ E-3697 [M] | The Weary Blues | 1958 | 50.00 |
| *—Yellow label* | | | |
| **VERVE** | | | |
| ❑ VSP-36 [M] | The Weary Blues | 1966 | 20.00 |
| ❑ VSPS-36 [R] | The Weary Blues | 1966 | 12.00 |

### HUGHES, RHETA

| Number | Title (A Side/B Side) | Yr | NM |
|---|---|---|---|
| **COLUMBIA** | | | |
| ❑ CL 2385 [M] | Introducing An Electrifying New Star | 1965 | 30.00 |
| ❑ CS 9185 [S] | Introducing An Electrifying New Star | 1965 | 40.00 |

### HUGO AND LUIGI

| Number | Title (A Side/B Side) | Yr | NM |
|---|---|---|---|
| **RCA VICTOR** | | | |
| ❑ LPM-2254 [M] | The Sound of Children at Christmas | 1960 | 15.00 |
| ❑ LSP-2254 [S] | The Sound of Children at Christmas | 1960 | 20.00 |
| ❑ LPM-2641 [M] | The Cascading Voices of the Hugo & Luigi Chorus | 1963 | 10.00 |
| ❑ LSP-2641 [S] | The Cascading Voices of the Hugo & Luigi Chorus | 1963 | 12.00 |
| ❑ LPM-2717 [M] | Let's Fall in Love | 1963 | 10.00 |
| ❑ LSP-2717 [S] | Let's Fall in Love | 1963 | 12.00 |
| ❑ LPM-2789 [M] | The Cascading Voices of the Hugo & Luigi Chorus — With Brass | 1964 | 10.00 |
| ❑ LSP-2789 [S] | The Cascading Voices of the Hugo & Luigi Chorus — With Brass | 1964 | 12.00 |
| ❑ LPM-2863 [M] | The Cascading Voices of the Hugo & Luigi Chorus — With Strings | 1964 | 10.00 |
| ❑ LSP-2863 [S] | The Cascading Voices of the Hugo & Luigi Chorus — With Strings | 1964 | 12.00 |
| ❑ LSP-4083 | Maggie Flynn | 1968 | 10.00 |
| **ROULETTE** | | | |
| ❑ R-25044 [M] | When Good Fellows Get Together | 1959 | 20.00 |
| ❑ R-25283 [M] | Cascading Voices | 1965 | 12.00 |
| ❑ SR-25283 [S] | Cascading Voices | 1965 | 15.00 |
| **WING** | | | |
| ❑ MGW 12207 [M] | Sing Along by the Fireside | 195? | 12.00 |

### HULLABALLOOS, THE

| Number | Title (A Side/B Side) | Yr | NM |
|---|---|---|---|
| **ROULETTE** | | | |
| ❑ R-25297 [M] | England's Newest Singing Sensations | 1965 | 50.00 |
| ❑ SR-25297 [P] | England's Newest Singing Sensations | 1965 | 75.00 |
| ❑ R-25310 [M] | The Hullabaloos on Hullabaloo | 1965 | 50.00 |
| ❑ SR-25310 [P] | The Hullabaloos on Hullabaloo | 1965 | 75.00 |

### HULLABALOO SINGERS AND ORCHESTRA, THE

| Number | Title (A Side/B Side) | Yr | NM |
|---|---|---|---|
| **COLUMBIA** | | | |
| ❑ CL 2410 [M] | The Hullabaloo Show | 1965 | 20.00 |
| ❑ CS 9210 [S] | The Hullabaloo Show | 1965 | 25.00 |

### HUMAN BEINZ, THE

| Number | Title (A Side/B Side) | Yr | NM |
|---|---|---|---|
| **CAPITOL** | | | |
| ❑ ST 2906 | Nobody But Me | 1968 | 30.00 |
| ❑ ST 2926 | Evolutions | 1968 | 40.00 |
| **GATEWAY** | | | |
| ❑ GLP-3012 | Nobody But Me | 1968 | 40.00 |
| *—With added tracks by The Mammals* | | | |

### HUMBLE PIE

| Number | Title (A Side/B Side) | Yr | NM |
|---|---|---|---|
| **A&M** | | | |
| ❑ SP-3127 | Humble Pie | 1981 | 8.00 |
| *—Budget-line reissue* | | | |
| ❑ SP-3132 | Smokin' | 1981 | 8.00 |
| *—Budget-line reissue* | | | |
| ❑ SP-3208 | The Best of Humble Pie | 1982 | 10.00 |
| ❑ SP-3506 [(2)] | Performance — Rockin' the Fillmore | 1971 | 15.00 |
| ❑ SP-3513 [(2)] | Lost and Found | 1972 | 15.00 |
| ❑ SP-3611 | Thunderbox | 1974 | 12.00 |
| ❑ SP-3701 [(2)] | Eat It | 1973 | 15.00 |
| ❑ SP-4270 | Humble Pie | 1970 | 12.00 |
| ❑ SP-4301 | Rock On | 1971 | 12.00 |
| ❑ SP-4342 | Smokin' | 1972 | 12.00 |
| ❑ SP-4514 | Street Rats | 1975 | 12.00 |
| ❑ SP-6008 [(2)] | Performance — Rockin' the Fillmore | 1981 | 10.00 |
| *—Budget-line reissue* | | | |
| ❑ SP-6009 [(2)] | Lost and Found | 1981 | 10.00 |
| *—Budget-line reissue* | | | |
| ❑ SP-6503 [(2)] | Eat It | 1981 | 10.00 |
| *—Budget-line reissue* | | | |
| **ACCORD** | | | |
| ❑ SN-7192 | Recaptured | 1981 | 10.00 |
| **ATCO** | | | |
| ❑ SD 38-122 | On to Victory | 1980 | 10.00 |
| ❑ SD 38-131 | Go for the Throat | 1981 | 10.00 |
| **COMPLEAT** | | | |
| ❑ 672009-1 [(2)] | A Slice of Humble Pie | 1985 | 12.00 |
| **IMMEDIATE** | | | |
| ❑ IMOCS-101 | As Safe As Yesterday Is | 1969 | 25.00 |

### HUMBLEBUMS, THE GERRY RAFFERTY was in this group.

| Number | Title (A Side/B Side) | Yr | NM |
|---|---|---|---|
| **LIBERTY** | | | |
| ❑ LST-7636 | The Humblebums | 1969 | 30.00 |
| ❑ LST-7656 | Open Up the Door | 1970 | 30.00 |

### HUMES, ANITA See THE ESSEX.

### HUMES, HELEN

| Number | Title (A Side/B Side) | Yr | NM |
|---|---|---|---|
| **CONTEMPORARY** | | | |
| ❑ M-3571 [M] | 'Tain't Nobody's Biz-Ness If I Do | 1960 | 50.00 |
| ❑ M-3582 [M] | Songs I Like to Sing | 1960 | 50.00 |
| ❑ M-3598 [M] | Swingin' with Humes | 1961 | 40.00 |
| ❑ S-7571 [S] | 'Tain't Nobody's Biz-Ness If I Do | 1960 | 50.00 |
| ❑ S-7582 [S] | Songs I Like to Sing | 1960 | 50.00 |
| ❑ S-7598 [S] | Swingin' with Humes | 1961 | 50.00 |

### HUMPERDINCK, ENGELBERT

| Number | Title (A Side/B Side) | Yr | NM |
|---|---|---|---|
| **EPIC** | | | |
| ❑ (no #) [PD] | Last of the Romantics | 1978 | 25.00 |
| ❑ PE 34381 | After the Lovin' | 1976 | 10.00 |
| *—Orange label* | | | |
| ❑ PE 34381 | After the Lovin' | 1979 | 8.00 |
| *—Dark blue label; back cover does not yet have bar code* | | | |
| ❑ PE 34381 | After the Lovin' | 198? | 6.00 |
| *—Dark blue label; back cover has bar code* | | | |
| ❑ E 34436 | The Ultimate | 1977 | 10.00 |
| *—Orange label* | | | |
| ❑ PE 34436 | The Ultimate | 198? | 8.00 |
| *—Reissue with bar code; dark blue label* | | | |
| ❑ E 34719 | Golden Love Songs | 1977 | 10.00 |
| *—Orange label* | | | |
| ❑ PE 34719 | Golden Love Songs | 198? | 8.00 |
| *—Reissue with bar code; dark blue label* | | | |
| ❑ PE 34730 | Miracles | 1977 | 10.00 |
| *—Orange label* | | | |
| ❑ PE 34730 | Miracles | 198? | 8.00 |
| *—Reissue with bar code; dark blue label* | | | |
| ❑ JE 35020 | Last of the Romantics | 1978 | 10.00 |
| *—Orange label* | | | |
| ❑ PE 35020 | Last of the Romantics | 198? | 8.00 |
| *—Reissue with bar code; dark blue label* | | | |
| ❑ PE 35031 | Christmas Tyme | 1977 | 12.00 |
| ❑ JE 35791 | This Moment in Time | 1979 | 10.00 |
| ❑ PE 35791 | This Moment in Time | 198? | 8.00 |
| *—Budget-line reissue* | | | |
| ❑ JE 36431 | Love's Only Love | 1980 | 10.00 |
| ❑ PE 36765 | A Merry Christmas with Engelbert Humperdinck | 1980 | 10.00 |
| *—Some copies of the record have a "JE" prefix* | | | |
| ❑ E2X 36782 [(2)] | All of Me/Live in Concert | 1980 | 12.00 |
| ❑ FE 37128 | Don't You Love Me Anymore | 1981 | 10.00 |
| ❑ PE 37128 | Don't You Love Me Anymore | 1983 | 8.00 |
| *—Budget-line reissue* | | | |
| ❑ FE 38087 | You and Your Lover | 1983 | 10.00 |
| ❑ PE 39469 | White Christmas | 1984 | 10.00 |
| **LONDON** | | | |
| ❑ BP 688/9 [(2)] | Engelbert Humperdinck Sings for You | 1977 | 15.00 |
| ❑ PS 709 | Love Letters | 1978 | 10.00 |
| **PARROT** | | | |
| ❑ PA 61012 [M] | Release Me | 1967 | 20.00 |

| Number | Title (A Side/B Side) | Yr | NM |
|---|---|---|---|
| ❑ PA 61015 [M] | The Last Waltz | 1967 | 20.00 |
| ❑ PAS 71012 [S] | Release Me | 1967 | 15.00 |
| ❑ PAS 71015 [S] | The Last Waltz | 1967 | 15.00 |
| ❑ PAS 71022 | A Man Without Love | 1968 | 15.00 |
| ❑ PAS 71026 | Engelbert | 1969 | 15.00 |
| ❑ XPAS 71030 | Engelbert Humperdinck | 1969 | 15.00 |
| ❑ XPAS 71038 | We Made It Happen | 1970 | 15.00 |
| ❑ XPAS 71043 | Sweetheart | 1971 | 15.00 |
| ❑ XPAS 71048 | Another Time, Another Place | 1971 | 15.00 |
| ❑ XPAS 71051 | Live at the Riviera, Las Vegas | 1971 | 15.00 |
| ❑ XPAS 71056 | In Time | 1972 | 15.00 |
| ❑ XPAS 71061 | King of Hearts | 1973 | 15.00 |
| ❑ APAS 71065 | My Love | 1974 | 15.00 |
| ❑ PAS 71067 | His Greatest Hits | 1974 | 15.00 |
| ❑ SW-93216 | We Made It Happen | 1970 | 20.00 |
| *—Capitol Record Club edition* | | | |

**SILVER EAGLE**

| Number | Title (A Side/B Side) | Yr | NM |
|---|---|---|---|
| ❑ SE 1034 [(2)] | A Lovely Way to Spend an Evening | 1985 | 15.00 |
| *—Mail-order offer* | | | |

### HUMPHREY, PERCY

**RIVERSIDE**

| Number | Title (A Side/B Side) | Yr | NM |
|---|---|---|---|
| ❑ RLP-378 [M] | Percy Humphrey's Crescent City Joymakers | 1961 | 30.00 |

### HUNGER

**PUBLIC**

| Number | Title (A Side/B Side) | Yr | NM |
|---|---|---|---|
| ❑ 1006 | Strictly from Hunger | 1969 | 600.00 |

### HUNT, PEE WEE

**ALLEGRO**

| Number | Title (A Side/B Side) | Yr | NM |
|---|---|---|---|
| ❑ 1633 [M] | Dixieland | 1956 | 25.00 |

**CAPITOL**

| Number | Title (A Side/B Side) | Yr | NM |
|---|---|---|---|
| ❑ H 203 [10] | Straight from Dixie | 1950 | 40.00 |
| ❑ T 203 [M] | Straight from Dixie | 195? | 30.00 |
| ❑ H 312 [10] | Dixieland Detour | 1952 | 50.00 |
| ❑ H 492 [10] | Swingin' Around | 1954 | 40.00 |
| ❑ T 573 [M] | Dixieland Classics | 1955 | 30.00 |
| ❑ T 783 [M] | Pee Wee and Fingers | 1956 | 30.00 |
| ❑ T 984 [M] | Cole Porter Ala Dixie | 1957 | 30.00 |
| *—Turquoise label* | | | |
| ❑ T 1144 [M] | The Blues A La Dixie | 1958 | 25.00 |
| ❑ ST 1265 [S] | Dixieland Kickoff | 1959 | 30.00 |
| ❑ T 1265 [M] | Dixieland Kickoff | 1959 | 25.00 |
| ❑ T 1362 [M] | Pee Wee Hunt's Dance Party | 1960 | 15.00 |

**ROYALE**

| Number | Title (A Side/B Side) | Yr | NM |
|---|---|---|---|
| ❑ 18153 [10] | Pee Wee Hunt and His Dixieland Band | 195? | 40.00 |

**SOLITAIRE**

| Number | Title (A Side/B Side) | Yr | NM |
|---|---|---|---|
| ❑ 507 [10] | Dixieland Capers | 195? | 30.00 |

### HUNT, PEE WEE/PEE WEE RUSSELL

**RONDO-LETTE**

| Number | Title (A Side/B Side) | Yr | NM |
|---|---|---|---|
| ❑ A 2 [M] | Dixieland: Pee Wee Hunt and Pee Wee Russell | 195? | 25.00 |

### HUNT, TOMMY

**DYNAMO**

| Number | Title (A Side/B Side) | Yr | NM |
|---|---|---|---|
| ❑ D-7001 [M] | Tommy Hunt's Greatest Hits | 1967 | 20.00 |
| ❑ DS-8001 [S] | Tommy Hunt's Greatest Hits | 1967 | 25.00 |

**SCEPTER**

| Number | Title (A Side/B Side) | Yr | NM |
|---|---|---|---|
| ❑ 506 [M] | I Just Don't Know What to Do with Myself | 1962 | 50.00 |
| ❑ SS-506 [S] | I Just Don't Know What to Do with Myself | 1962 | 60.00 |

### HUNTER, ALBERTA

**RIVERSIDE**

| Number | Title (A Side/B Side) | Yr | NM |
|---|---|---|---|
| ❑ RLP-418 [M] | Alberta Hunter with Lovie Austin's Blues Serenaders | 1962 | 30.00 |

### HUNTER, FRANK

**JUBILEE**

| Number | Title (A Side/B Side) | Yr | NM |
|---|---|---|---|
| ❑ JLP-1020 [M] | Sounds of Hunter | 1956 | 50.00 |

### HUNTER, IVORY JOE

**ATLANTIC**

| Number | Title (A Side/B Side) | Yr | NM |
|---|---|---|---|
| ❑ 8008 [M] | Ivory Joe Hunter | 1957 | 200.00 |
| *—Black label* | | | |
| ❑ 8008 [M] | Ivory Joe Hunter | 1960 | 100.00 |
| *—Purple and red label* | | | |
| ❑ 8015 [M] | The Old and the New | 1958 | 200.00 |
| *—Black label* | | | |
| ❑ 8015 [M] | The Old and the New | 1960 | 100.00 |
| *—Purple and red label* | | | |

**DOT**

| Number | Title (A Side/B Side) | Yr | NM |
|---|---|---|---|
| ❑ DLP-3569 [M] | This Is Ivory Joe Hunter | 1964 | 40.00 |
| ❑ DLP-25569 [S] | This Is Ivory Joe Hunter | 1964 | 50.00 |

**EPIC**

| Number | Title (A Side/B Side) | Yr | NM |
|---|---|---|---|
| ❑ E 30348 | The Return of Ivory Joe Hunter | 1971 | 20.00 |

**EVEREST ARCHIVE OF FOLK & JAZZ**

| Number | Title (A Side/B Side) | Yr | NM |
|---|---|---|---|
| ❑ 289 | Ivory Joe Hunter | 1974 | 12.00 |

**GOLDISC**

| Number | Title (A Side/B Side) | Yr | NM |
|---|---|---|---|
| ❑ 403 [M] | The Fabulous Ivory Joe Hunter | 1961 | 60.00 |

**HOME COOKING**

| Number | Title (A Side/B Side) | Yr | NM |
|---|---|---|---|
| ❑ 112 | I'm Coming Down with the Blues | 1989 | 12.00 |

**KING**

| Number | Title (A Side/B Side) | Yr | NM |
|---|---|---|---|
| ❑ 605 [M] | 16 of His Greatest Hits | 1958 | 400.00 |

**LION**

| Number | Title (A Side/B Side) | Yr | NM |
|---|---|---|---|
| ❑ L-70068 [M] | I Need You So | 1959 | 60.00 |

**MGM**

| Number | Title (A Side/B Side) | Yr | NM |
|---|---|---|---|
| ❑ E-3488 [M] | I Get That Lonesome Feeling | 1957 | 300.00 |

**PARAMOUNT**

| Number | Title (A Side/B Side) | Yr | NM |
|---|---|---|---|
| ❑ PAS-6080 | I've Always Been Country | 1974 | 12.00 |

**POLYDOR**

| Number | Title (A Side/B Side) | Yr | NM |
|---|---|---|---|
| ❑ 830897-1 | Since I Met You Baby | 1987 | 12.00 |

**SMASH**

| Number | Title (A Side/B Side) | Yr | NM |
|---|---|---|---|
| ❑ MGS-27037 [M] | Ivory Joe Hunter's Golden Hits | 1963 | 40.00 |
| ❑ SRS-67037 [S] | Ivory Joe Hunter's Golden Hits | 1963 | 50.00 |

**SOUND**

| Number | Title (A Side/B Side) | Yr | NM |
|---|---|---|---|
| ❑ M-603 [M] | Ivory Joe Hunter | 1959 | 150.00 |

**STRAND**

| Number | Title (A Side/B Side) | Yr | NM |
|---|---|---|---|
| ❑ SL-1123 [M] | The Artistry of Ivory Joe Hunter | 196? | 40.00 |
| ❑ SLS-1123 [S] | The Artistry of Ivory Joe Hunter | 196? | 50.00 |

### HUNTER, LURLEAN

**ATLANTIC**

| Number | Title (A Side/B Side) | Yr | NM |
|---|---|---|---|
| ❑ 1344 [M] | Blue and Sentimental | 1960 | 50.00 |
| ❑ SD 1344 [S] | Blue and Sentimental | 1960 | 60.00 |

**RCA VICTOR**

| Number | Title (A Side/B Side) | Yr | NM |
|---|---|---|---|
| ❑ LPM-1151 [M] | Lonesome Gal | 1955 | 100.00 |

**VIK**

| Number | Title (A Side/B Side) | Yr | NM |
|---|---|---|---|
| ❑ LX-1061 [M] | Night Life | 1956 | 80.00 |
| ❑ LX-1116 [M] | Stepping Out | 1957 | 80.00 |

### HUNTER, ROBERT

**RELIX**

| Number | Title (A Side/B Side) | Yr | NM |
|---|---|---|---|
| ❑ 2002 [PD] | Promontory Rider | 1982 | 20.00 |
| *—Limited edition of 1,000 picture discs* | | | |

**ROUND**

| Number | Title (A Side/B Side) | Yr | NM |
|---|---|---|---|
| ❑ RX-101 | Tales of the Great Rum Runners | 1974 | 40.00 |
| ❑ RX-105 | Tiger Rose | 1975 | 40.00 |

### HUNTER, STAN, AND SONNY FORTUNE

**PRESTIGE**

| Number | Title (A Side/B Side) | Yr | NM |
|---|---|---|---|
| ❑ PRLP-7458 [M] | Trip on the Strip | 1967 | 30.00 |
| ❑ PRST-7458 [S] | Trip on the Strip | 1967 | 20.00 |

### HUNTER, TAB

**DOT**

| Number | Title (A Side/B Side) | Yr | NM |
|---|---|---|---|
| ❑ DLP-3370 [M] | Young Love | 1961 | 30.00 |
| ❑ DLP-25370 [S] | Young Love | 1961 | 30.00 |

**WARNER BROS.**

| Number | Title (A Side/B Side) | Yr | NM |
|---|---|---|---|
| ❑ W 1221 [M] | Tab Hunter | 1958 | 30.00 |
| ❑ WS 1221 [S] | Tab Hunter | 1958 | 40.00 |
| ❑ W 1292 [M] | When I Fall in Love | 1959 | 30.00 |
| ❑ WS 1292 [S] | When I Fall in Love | 1959 | 40.00 |
| ❑ W 1367 [M] | R.F.D. Tab Hunter | 1960 | 30.00 |
| ❑ WS 1367 [S] | R.F.D. Tab Hunter | 1960 | 40.00 |

### HUNTER MUSKETT

**BRADLEY**

| Number | Title (A Side/B Side) | Yr | NM |
|---|---|---|---|
| ❑ 1003 | Hunter Muskett | 1973 | 80.00 |

### HURT, MISSISSIPPI JOHN

**BIOGRAPH**

| Number | Title (A Side/B Side) | Yr | NM |
|---|---|---|---|
| ❑ C-4 [M] | 1928: His First Recordings | 1972 | 25.00 |

**PIEDMONT**

| Number | Title (A Side/B Side) | Yr | NM |
|---|---|---|---|
| ❑ PLP-13157 [M] | Folk Songs and Blues | 1963 | 80.00 |
| ❑ PLP-13181 [M] | Worried Blues | 1964 | 80.00 |

**VANGUARD**

| Number | Title (A Side/B Side) | Yr | NM |
|---|---|---|---|
| ❑ VSD-19/20 [(2)] | The Best of Missisippi John Hurt | 197? | 25.00 |
| ❑ VRS-9145 [M] | Blues at Newport | 1965 | 25.00 |
| ❑ VRS-9220 [M] | Mississippi John Hurt/Today | 1966 | 25.00 |
| ❑ VRS-9248 [M] | The Immortal Mississippi John Hurt | 1967 | 25.00 |
| ❑ VSD-79145 [S] | Blues at Newport | 1965 | 30.00 |
| ❑ VSD-79220 [S] | Mississippi John Hurt/Today | 1966 | 30.00 |
| ❑ VSD-79248 [S] | The Immortal Mississippi John Hurt | 1967 | 30.00 |
| ❑ VSD-79327 | The Last Session | 1972 | 20.00 |

### HURVITZ, SANDY

**VERVE**

| Number | Title (A Side/B Side) | Yr | NM |
|---|---|---|---|
| ❑ V6-5064 | Sandy's Album Is Here at Last | 1968 | 30.00 |
| *—Produced by FRANK ZAPPA* | | | |

### HUSKER DU

**NEW ALLIANCE**

| Number | Title (A Side/B Side) | Yr | NM |
|---|---|---|---|
| ❑ 007 | Land Speed Record | 1982 | 12.00 |
| *—Second pressing, "Marketed by SST" on cover* | | | |
| ❑ 007 | Land Speed Record | 1982 | 25.00 |
| *—No reference to SST on cover* | | | |

**REFLEX**

| Number | Title (A Side/B Side) | Yr | NM |
|---|---|---|---|
| ❑ #D | Everything Falls Apart | 1982 | 40.00 |

**SST**

| Number | Title (A Side/B Side) | Yr | NM |
|---|---|---|---|
| ❑ 020 [EP] | Metal Circus | 1983 | 8.00 |
| ❑ 027 [(2)] | Zen Arcade | 1984 | 15.00 |
| ❑ PSST E-27 [DJ] | Eight Miles High/6 from Zen Arcade | 1984 | 30.00 |
| *—Promo sampler, etched design on side 1, sticker cover* | | | |
| ❑ 031 | New Day Rising | 1985 | 10.00 |
| ❑ 055 | Flip Your Wig | 1985 | 10.00 |
| ❑ 195 | Land Speed Record | 198? | 10.00 |
| *—Reissue of New Alliance 007* | | | |
| ❑ 908 [10] | Metal Circus | 199? | 8.00 |
| ❑ 915 [10] | Eight Miles High/Makes No Sense at All | 199? | 8.00 |

**WARNER BROS.**

| Number | Title (A Side/B Side) | Yr | NM |
|---|---|---|---|
| ❑ WBMS-145 [DJ] | The Warehouse Interview | 1987 | 25.00 |
| *—Promo only, part of the Warner Bros. Music Show series* | | | |
| ❑ PRO-A-2719 [DJ] | Warehouse: Songs and Stories | 1987 | 8.00 |
| *—Promo-only four-song sampler* | | | |
| ❑ 25385 | Candy Apple Grey | 1986 | 12.00 |
| ❑ 25544 [(2)] | Warehouse: Songs and Stories | 1987 | 12.00 |

### HUSKY, FERLIN

**ABC**

| Number | Title (A Side/B Side) | Yr | NM |
|---|---|---|---|
| ❑ X-776 | True True Lovin' | 1973 | 12.00 |
| ❑ X-803 | Sweet Honky Tonk | 1974 | 12.00 |
| ❑ X-818 | Freckles and Polliwog Days | 1974 | 12.00 |
| ❑ X-849 | Champagne Ladies and Blue Ribbon Babies | 1974 | 12.00 |
| ❑ X-884 | The Foster-Rice Songbook | 1975 | 12.00 |

**CAPITOL**

| Number | Title (A Side/B Side) | Yr | NM |
|---|---|---|---|
| ❑ ST-115 | White Fences and Evergreen Trees | 1968 | 15.00 |
| ❑ SKAO-143 | The Best of Ferlin Husky | 1969 | 15.00 |
| ❑ SM-143 | The Best of Ferlin Husky | 197? | 10.00 |
| *—Reissue with new prefix* | | | |
| ❑ ST-239 | That's Why I Love You So Much | 1969 | 15.00 |
| ❑ ST-433 | Your Love Is Heavenly Sunshine | 1970 | 15.00 |
| ❑ ST-591 | Your Sweet Love Lifted Me | 1970 | 15.00 |
| ❑ T 718 [M] | Songs of the Home and Heart | 1956 | 60.00 |
| *—Turquoise label* | | | |
| ❑ T 718 [M] | Songs of the Home and Heart | 1959 | 40.00 |
| *—Black colorband label, Capitol logo at left* | | | |
| ❑ T 718 [M] | Songs of the Home and Heart | 1962 | 25.00 |
| *—Black colorband label, Capitol logo at top* | | | |
| ❑ ST-768 | One More Time | 1971 | 15.00 |
| ❑ T 880 [M] | Boulevard of Broken Dreams | 1957 | 60.00 |
| *—Turquoise label* | | | |
| ❑ T 880 [M] | Boulevard of Broken Dreams | 1958 | 40.00 |
| *—Black colorband label, Capitol logo at left* | | | |
| ❑ T 976 [M] | Sittin' On a Rainbow | 1958 | 60.00 |
| *—Turquoise label* | | | |
| ❑ T 1204 [M] | Born to Lose | 1959 | 40.00 |
| *—Black colorband label, Capitol logo at left* | | | |
| ❑ T 1204 [M] | Born to Lose | 1962 | 25.00 |
| *—Black colorband label, Capitol logo at top* | | | |
| ❑ T 1280 [M] | Ferlin's Favorites | 1960 | 40.00 |
| *—Black colorband label, Capitol logo at left* | | | |
| ❑ T 1280 [M] | Ferlin's Favorites | 1962 | 25.00 |
| *—Black colorband label, Capitol logo at top* | | | |
| ❑ DT 1383 [R] | Gone | 196? | 12.00 |
| ❑ T 1383 [M] | Gone | 196? | 20.00 |
| *—Gold "The Star Line" label; "The Star Line" logo on cover* | | | |
| ❑ T 1383 [M] | Gone | 1960 | 40.00 |
| *—Black colorband label, Capitol logo at left* | | | |
| ❑ T 1383 [M] | Gone | 1962 | 25.00 |
| *—Black colorband label, Capitol logo at top* | | | |
| ❑ ST 1546 [S] | Walkin' and Hummin' | 1961 | 30.00 |
| *—Black colorband label, Capitol logo at left* | | | |
| ❑ ST 1546 [S] | Walkin' and Hummin' | 1962 | 20.00 |
| *—Black colorband label, Capitol logo at top* | | | |
| ❑ T 1546 [M] | Walkin' and Hummin' | 1961 | 25.00 |
| *—Black colorband label, Capitol logo at left* | | | |
| ❑ T 1546 [M] | Walkin' and Hummin' | 1962 | 15.00 |
| *—Black colorband label, Capitol logo at top* | | | |
| ❑ ST 1633 [S] | Memories of Home | 1961 | 30.00 |
| *—Black colorband label, Capitol logo at left* | | | |
| ❑ ST 1633 [S] | Memories of Home | 1962 | 20.00 |
| *—Black colorband label, Capitol logo at top* | | | |
| ❑ T 1633 [M] | Memories of Home | 1961 | 25.00 |
| *—Black colorband label, Capitol logo at left* | | | |
| ❑ T 1633 [M] | Memories of Home | 1962 | 15.00 |
| *—Black colorband label, Capitol logo at top* | | | |
| ❑ ST 1720 [S] | Some of My Favorites | 1962 | 20.00 |
| ❑ T 1720 [M] | Some of My Favorites | 1962 | 15.00 |
| ❑ ST 1885 [S] | The Heart and Soul of Ferlin Husky | 1963 | 20.00 |
| ❑ T 1885 [M] | The Heart and Soul of Ferlin Husky | 1963 | 15.00 |
| ❑ DT 1991 [R] | The Hits of Ferlin Husky | 1963 | 12.00 |
| ❑ T 1991 [M] | The Hits of Ferlin Husky | 1963 | 15.00 |
| ❑ ST 2101 [S] | By Request | 1964 | 20.00 |
| ❑ T 2101 [M] | By Request | 1964 | 15.00 |
| ❑ ST 2305 [S] | True, True Lovin' | 1965 | 20.00 |
| ❑ T 2305 [M] | True, True Lovin' | 1965 | 15.00 |
| ❑ ST 2439 [S] | Ferlin Husky Sings the Songs of Music City, U.S.A. | 1966 | 20.00 |

| Number | Title (A Side/B Side) | Yr | NM |
|---|---|---|---|
| ❑ T 2439 [M] | Ferlin Husky Sings the Songs of Music City, U.S.A. | 1966 | 15.00 |
| ❑ ST 2548 [S] | I Could Sing All Night | 1966 | 20.00 |
| ❑ T 2548 [M] | I Could Sing All Night | 1966 | 15.00 |
| ❑ ST 2705 [S] | What Am I Gonna Do Now? | 1967 | 15.00 |
| ❑ T 2705 [M] | What Am I Gonna Do Now? | 1967 | 20.00 |
| ❑ ST 2793 [S] | Christmas All Year Long | 1967 | 15.00 |
| ❑ T 2793 [M] | Christmas All Year Long | 1967 | 15.00 |
| ❑ ST 2870 [S] | Just for You | 1968 | 15.00 |
| ❑ T 2870 [M] | Just for You | 1968 | 30.00 |
| ❑ ST 2913 | Where No One Stands Alone | 1968 | 15.00 |
| ❑ ST-11069 | Just Plain Lonely | 1972 | 15.00 |

**HILLTOP**

| Number | Title (A Side/B Side) | Yr | NM |
|---|---|---|---|
| ❑ 6005 | Ole Opry Favorites | 196? | 12.00 |
| ❑ 6086 | Green, Green Grass of Home | 1970 | 12.00 |
| ❑ 6099 | Wings of a Dove | 197? | 12.00 |

**KING**

| Number | Title (A Side/B Side) | Yr | NM |
|---|---|---|---|
| ❑ 647 [M] | Country Tunes Sung from the Heart | 1959 | 70.00 |
| ❑ 728 [M] | Easy Livin' | 1960 | 70.00 |

**STARDAY**

| Number | Title (A Side/B Side) | Yr | NM |
|---|---|---|---|
| ❑ 3018 | Greatest Hits | 197? | 12.00 |

### HUTCHERSON, BOBBY

**BLUE NOTE**

| Number | Title (A Side/B Side) | Yr | NM |
|---|---|---|---|
| ❑ BLP-4198 [M] | Dialogue | 1965 | 25.00 |
| ❑ BLP-4213 [M] | Components | 1966 | 25.00 |
| ❑ BLP-4231 [M] | Happenings | 1967 | 30.00 |
| ❑ BST-84198 [S] | Dialogue | 1965 | 30.00 |
| *—With "New York, USA" address on label* | | | |
| ❑ BST-84213 [S] | Components | 1966 | 30.00 |
| *—With "New York, USA" address on label* | | | |
| ❑ BST-84231 [S] | Happenings | 1967 | 25.00 |
| *—With "New York, USA" address on label* | | | |
| ❑ BST-84244 [S] | Stick-Up! | 1968 | 20.00 |
| *—With "A Division of Liberty Records" on label* | | | |
| ❑ BST-84291 | Total Eclipse | 1969 | 20.00 |
| *—With "A Division of Liberty Records" on label* | | | |
| ❑ BST-84333 | Bobby Hutcherson Now | 1969 | 20.00 |
| *—With "A Division of Liberty Records" on label* | | | |
| ❑ BST-84362 | San Francisco | 1970 | 20.00 |

### HUTTON, BETTY

**CAPITOL**

| Number | Title (A Side/B Side) | Yr | NM |
|---|---|---|---|
| ❑ H 256 [10] | Square in the Social Circle | 1950 | 60.00 |

**WARNER BROS.**

| Number | Title (A Side/B Side) | Yr | NM |
|---|---|---|---|
| ❑ W 1267 [M] | Betty Hutton at the Saints and Sinners Ball | 1959 | 20.00 |
| ❑ WS 1267 [S] | Betty Hutton at the Saints and Sinners Ball | 1959 | 25.00 |

### HUTTON, DANNY Also see THREE DOG NIGHT.

**MGM**

| Number | Title (A Side/B Side) | Yr | NM |
|---|---|---|---|
| ❑ SE-4664 | Pre-Dog Night | 1970 | 30.00 |

### HYLAND, BRIAN

**ABC-PARAMOUNT**

| Number | Title (A Side/B Side) | Yr | NM |
|---|---|---|---|
| ❑ 400 [M] | Let Me Belong to You | 1961 | 30.00 |
| ❑ S-400 [S] | Let Me Belong to You | 1961 | 40.00 |
| ❑ 431 [M] | Sealed with a Kiss | 1962 | 30.00 |
| ❑ S-431 [S] | Sealed with a Kiss | 1962 | 40.00 |
| ❑ 463 [M] | Country Meets Folk | 1964 | 30.00 |
| ❑ S-463 [S] | Country Meets Folk | 1964 | 40.00 |

**DOT**

| Number | Title (A Side/B Side) | Yr | NM |
|---|---|---|---|
| ❑ DLP 25926 | Tragedy/A Million to One | 1969 | 15.00 |
| ❑ DLP 25954 | Stay and Love Me All Summer | 1969 | 15.00 |

**KAPP**

| Number | Title (A Side/B Side) | Yr | NM |
|---|---|---|---|
| ❑ KL 1202 [M] | The Bashful Blonde | 1960 | 50.00 |
| ❑ KS 3202 [S] | The Bashful Blonde | 1960 | 80.00 |

**PHILIPS**

| Number | Title (A Side/B Side) | Yr | NM |
|---|---|---|---|
| ❑ PHM 200136 [M] | Here's to Our Love | 1964 | 20.00 |
| ❑ PHM 200158 [M] | Rockin' Folk | 1965 | 20.00 |
| ❑ PHM 200217 [M] | Run, Run, Look and See/The Joker Went Wild | 1966 | 20.00 |
| *—With "200-217" in trail-off; this record plays mono* | | | |
| ❑ PHM 200217 [S] | Run, Run, Look and See/The Joker Went Wild | 1966 | 20.00 |
| *—With "2/600-217" in trail-off; this record plays stereo, though labeled mono* | | | |
| ❑ PHS 600136 [S] | Here's to Our Love | 1964 | 25.00 |
| ❑ PHS 600158 [S] | Rockin' Folk | 1965 | 25.00 |
| ❑ PHS 600217 [S] | Run, Run, Look and See/The Joker Went Wild | 1966 | 25.00 |

**PICKWICK**

| Number | Title (A Side/B Side) | Yr | NM |
|---|---|---|---|
| ❑ SPC-3261 | Young Years | 197? | 10.00 |

**PRIVATE STOCK**

| Number | Title (A Side/B Side) | Yr | NM |
|---|---|---|---|
| ❑ PS-7003 | In a State of Bayou | 1977 | 12.00 |

**RHINO**

| Number | Title (A Side/B Side) | Yr | NM |
|---|---|---|---|
| ❑ RNLP-70226 | Greatest Hits | 1987 | 10.00 |

**UNI**

| Number | Title (A Side/B Side) | Yr | NM |
|---|---|---|---|
| ❑ 73097 | Brian Hyland | 1970 | 15.00 |
| *—The album is listed as "stereo," but "Gypsy Woman" is rechanneled* | | | |

**WING**

| Number | Title (A Side/B Side) | Yr | NM |
|---|---|---|---|
| ❑ MGW-12341 [M] | Here's to Our Love | 1967 | 12.00 |
| ❑ SRW-16341 [S] | Here's to Our Love | 1967 | 12.00 |

### HYMAN, DICK

**ATLANTIC**

| Number | Title (A Side/B Side) | Yr | NM |
|---|---|---|---|
| ❑ SD 1671 | Satchmo Remembered | 1975 | 10.00 |

**COMMAND**

| Number | Title (A Side/B Side) | Yr | NM |
|---|---|---|---|
| ❑ RS 811 SD [S] | Provocative Piano | 1960 | 20.00 |
| ❑ RS 824 SD [S] | Provocative Piano Volume 2 | 1961 | 20.00 |
| ❑ RS 832 SD [S] | The Dick Hyman Trio | 1961 | 20.00 |
| ❑ RS 856 SD [S] | Electrodynamics | 1963 | 20.00 |
| ❑ RS 862 SD [S] | Fabulous | 1963 | 20.00 |
| ❑ RS 875 SD [S] | Keyboard Kaleidoscope | 1964 | 20.00 |
| ❑ RS 891 SD [S] | The Man from O.R.G.A.N. | 1965 | 50.00 |
| ❑ RS 33-891 [M] | The Man from O.R.G.A.N. | 1965 | 40.00 |
| ❑ RS 899 SD [S] | Happening! | 1966 | 20.00 |
| ❑ RS 911 SD [S] | Brazilian Impressions | 1966 | 20.00 |
| ❑ RS 924 SD | Mirrors | 1967 | 20.00 |
| ❑ RS 933 SD | Sweet Sweet Soul | 1968 | 25.00 |
| ❑ RS 938 SD | Moog — The Electric Eclectics of Dick Hyman | 1968 | 30.00 |
| ❑ RS 946 SD | The Age of Electronicus | 1969 | 40.00 |
| ❑ RS 951 SD | Concerto Electro | 1970 | 30.00 |
| ❑ RSSD 968/2 [(2)] | The Synthesizer | 1973 | 40.00 |
| *—Reissue of "Electric Eclectics" and "Age of Electronicus"* | | | |
| ❑ RSSD 973/2 [(2)] | The Kaleidoscopic Keyboard | 1974 | 20.00 |
| ❑ RSSD 980/2 [(2)] | Organ Antics | 1974 | 20.00 |

**LION**

| Number | Title (A Side/B Side) | Yr | NM |
|---|---|---|---|
| ❑ L-70067 [M] | Swingin' Double Date | 1958 | 15.00 |

**MGM**

| Number | Title (A Side/B Side) | Yr | NM |
|---|---|---|---|
| ❑ E-289 [10] | The "Unforgettable" Sound of the Dick Hyman Trio | 1955 | 40.00 |
| ❑ E-3280 [M] | The Dick Hyman Trio Swings | 1954 | 25.00 |
| *—Yellow label* | | | |
| ❑ E-3329 [M] | The "Unforgettable" Sound of the Dick Hyman Trio | 1955 | 25.00 |
| *—Yellow label* | | | |
| ❑ E-3379 [M] | Behind a Shady Nook | 1956 | 25.00 |
| *—Yellow label* | | | |
| ❑ E-3483 [M] | Red Sails in the Sunset | 1957 | 25.00 |
| *—Yellow label* | | | |
| ❑ E-3494 [M] | Hi-Fi Suite | 1957 | 25.00 |
| *—Yellow label* | | | |
| ❑ E-3535 [M] | 60 Great All-Time Songs, Vol. 1 | 1957 | 20.00 |
| *—Yellow label* | | | |
| ❑ E-3536 [M] | 60 Great All-Time Songs, Vol. 2 | 1957 | 20.00 |
| *—Yellow label* | | | |
| ❑ E-3537 [M] | 60 Great All-Time Songs, Vol. 3 | 1957 | 20.00 |
| *—Yellow label* | | | |
| ❑ E-3553 [M] | Rockin' Sax and Rollin' Organ | 1958 | 25.00 |
| *—Yellow label* | | | |
| ❑ E-3586 [M] | 60 Great All-Time Songs, Vol. 4 | 1958 | 20.00 |
| *—Yellow label* | | | |
| ❑ E-3587 [M] | 60 Great All-Time Songs, Vol. 5 | 1958 | 20.00 |
| *—Yellow label* | | | |
| ❑ E-3588 [M] | 60 Great All-Time Songs, Vol. 6 | 1958 | 20.00 |
| *—Yellow label* | | | |
| ❑ E-3606 [M] | Dick Hyman and Harpsichord in Hi-Fi | 1958 | 20.00 |
| *—Yellow label* | | | |
| ❑ E-3642 [M] | Gigi | 1958 | 20.00 |
| *—Yellow label* | | | |
| ❑ E-3724 [M] | 60 Great Songs That Say "I Love You" | 1959 | 20.00 |
| *—Yellow label* | | | |
| ❑ E-3725 [M] | 60 Great Songs from Broadway Musicals | 1959 | 20.00 |
| *—Yellow label* | | | |
| ❑ E-3726 [M] | 60 Great Continental and Classical Favorites | 1959 | 20.00 |
| ❑ E-3747 [M] | Whoop-Up! | 1959 | 20.00 |
| *—Yellow label* | | | |
| ❑ SE-3747 [S] | Whoop-Up! | 1959 | 30.00 |
| ❑ E-3808 [M] | Strictly Organic | 1960 | 20.00 |
| ❑ SE-3808 [S] | Strictly Organic | 1960 | 30.00 |
| ❑ E-3821 [M] | After Six | 1960 | 20.00 |
| ❑ SE-3821 [S] | After Six | 1960 | 25.00 |
| ❑ E-4119 [M] | Moon Gas | 1963 | 20.00 |
| ❑ SE-4119 [S] | Moon Gas | 1963 | 30.00 |

**MUSICAL HERITAGE SOCIETY**

| Number | Title (A Side/B Side) | Yr | NM |
|---|---|---|---|
| ❑ MHS 912213K | Face the Music: Irving Berlin | 198? | 10.00 |

**RCA VICTOR GOLD SEAL**

| Number | Title (A Side/B Side) | Yr | NM |
|---|---|---|---|
| ❑ AGL1-3651 | Scott Joplin: 16 Classic Rags | 1980 | 8.00 |
| *—Reissue* | | | |

**RCA VICTOR RED SEAL**

| Number | Title (A Side/B Side) | Yr | NM |
|---|---|---|---|
| ❑ ARL1-1257 | Scott Joplin: 16 Classic Rags | 1976 | 10.00 |
| ❑ XRL1-4746 | Kitten on the Keys: Music of Zez Confrey | 1983 | 10.00 |

**REFERENCE RECORDINGS**

| Number | Title (A Side/B Side) | Yr | NM |
|---|---|---|---|
| ❑ RR-33 | Dick Hyman Plays Fats Waller | 1991 | 25.00 |

## I

### IAN, JANIS

**ANALOGUE PRODUCTIONS**

| Number | Title (A Side/B Side) | Yr | NM |
|---|---|---|---|
| ❑ AAP 027 | Breaking Silence | 1995 | 25.00 |
| *—Audiophile vinyl* | | | |

**CAPITOL**

| Number | Title (A Side/B Side) | Yr | NM |
|---|---|---|---|
| ❑ SKAO-683 | Present Company | 1971 | 15.00 |
| ❑ SN-683 | Present Company | 1975 | 10.00 |

**COLUMBIA**

| Number | Title (A Side/B Side) | Yr | NM |
|---|---|---|---|
| ❑ KC 32857 | Stars | 1974 | 10.00 |
| ❑ PC 32857 | Stars | 197? | 8.00 |
| ❑ PC 33394 | Between the Lines | 1975 | 10.00 |
| *—No bar code on cover* | | | |
| ❑ PC 33394 | Between the Lines | 1979 | 8.00 |
| *—With bar code on cover* | | | |
| ❑ PCQ 33394 [Q] | Between the Lines | 1975 | 15.00 |
| ❑ PC 33919 | Aftertones | 1976 | 10.00 |
| *—No bar code on cover* | | | |
| ❑ PC 33919 | Aftertones | 1979 | 8.00 |
| *—With bar code on cover* | | | |
| ❑ PCQ 33919 [Q] | Aftertones | 1976 | 15.00 |
| ❑ JC 34440 | Miracle Row | 1977 | 10.00 |
| ❑ JC 35325 | Janis Ian | 1978 | 10.00 |
| ❑ JC 36139 | Night Rains | 1979 | 10.00 |
| ❑ PC 36139 | Night Rains | 198? | 8.00 |
| ❑ FC 37360 | Restless Eyes | 1981 | 10.00 |

**MGM**

| Number | Title (A Side/B Side) | Yr | NM |
|---|---|---|---|
| ❑ GAS-121 | Janis Ian (Golden Archive Series) | 1970 | 25.00 |

**POLYDOR**

| Number | Title (A Side/B Side) | Yr | NM |
|---|---|---|---|
| ❑ PD-6058 | Janis Ian | 1976 | 10.00 |

**VERVE**

| Number | Title (A Side/B Side) | Yr | NM |
|---|---|---|---|
| ❑ V/VS-5027 | Janis Ian | 1967 | — |
| *—Scheduled, possibly not released; same LP is Verve Forecast 3017* | | | |

**VERVE FOLKWAYS**

| Number | Title (A Side/B Side) | Yr | NM |
|---|---|---|---|
| ❑ FT-3017 [M] | Janis Ian | 1967 | 30.00 |
| ❑ FTS-3017 [S] | Janis Ian | 1967 | 30.00 |

**VERVE FORECAST**

| Number | Title (A Side/B Side) | Yr | NM |
|---|---|---|---|
| ❑ FT-3017 [M] | Janis Ian | 1967 | 20.00 |
| ❑ FTS-3017 [S] | Janis Ian | 1967 | 15.00 |
| ❑ FT-3024 [M] | For All the Seasons of Your Mind | 1967 | 20.00 |
| ❑ FTS-3024 [S] | For All the Seasons of Your Mind | 1967 | 15.00 |
| ❑ FTS-3048 | The Secret Life of J. Eddy Fink | 1968 | 15.00 |
| ❑ FTS-3063 | Who Really Cares? | 1969 | 15.00 |

### IAN AND SYLVIA

**AMPEX**

| Number | Title (A Side/B Side) | Yr | NM |
|---|---|---|---|
| ❑ A-10103 | Great Speckled Bird | 1970 | 20.00 |

**COLUMBIA**

| Number | Title (A Side/B Side) | Yr | NM |
|---|---|---|---|
| ❑ C 30736 | Ian and Sylvia | 1971 | 12.00 |
| ❑ KC 31337 | You Were On My Mind | 1972 | 12.00 |
| ❑ G 32516 [(2)] | The Best of Ian and Sylvia | 1973 | 15.00 |

**MGM**

| Number | Title (A Side/B Side) | Yr | NM |
|---|---|---|---|
| ❑ GAS-115 | Ian and Sylvia (Golden Archive Series) | 1970 | 15.00 |
| ❑ E-4388 [M] | Lovin' Sound | 1967 | 20.00 |
| ❑ SE-4388 [S] | Lovin' Sound | 1967 | 15.00 |
| ❑ E-4550 [M] | Full Circle | 1968 | 40.00 |
| *—Mono is yellow label promo only; cover has "DJ Monaural" sticker on front* | | | |
| ❑ SE-4550 [S] | Full Circle | 1968 | 20.00 |

**VANGUARD**

| Number | Title (A Side/B Side) | Yr | NM |
|---|---|---|---|
| ❑ VSD-5/6 [(2)] | Ian and Sylvia's Greatest Hits | 1969 | 15.00 |
| ❑ VSD-23/24 [(2)] | Ian and Sylvia's Greatest Hits, Vol. 2 | 1970 | 15.00 |
| ❑ VSD-2113 [S] | Ian and Sylvia | 1963 | 30.00 |
| ❑ VSD-2149 [S] | Four Strong Winds | 1963 | 25.00 |
| ❑ VRS-9109 [M] | Ian and Sylvia | 1963 | 25.00 |
| ❑ VRS-9133 [M] | Four Strong Winds | 1963 | 20.00 |
| ❑ VRS-9154 [M] | Northern Journey | 1964 | 20.00 |
| ❑ VRS-9175 [M] | Early Morning Rain | 1965 | 20.00 |
| ❑ VRS-9215 [M] | Play One More | 1966 | 20.00 |
| ❑ VRS-9241 [M] | So Much for Dreaming | 1967 | 20.00 |
| ❑ VSD-73114 | Greatest Hits | 1985 | 10.00 |
| ❑ VSD-79154 [S] | Northern Journey | 1964 | 25.00 |
| ❑ VSD-79175 [S] | Early Morning Rain | 1965 | 25.00 |
| ❑ VSD-79215 [S] | Play One More | 1966 | 25.00 |
| ❑ VSD-79241 [S] | So Much for Dreaming | 1967 | 25.00 |
| ❑ VSD-79269 | The Best of Ian & Sylvia | 1968 | 15.00 |
| ❑ VSD-79284 | Nashville | 1968 | 15.00 |

### IAN AND THE ZODIACS

**PHILIPS**

| Number | Title (A Side/B Side) | Yr | NM |
|---|---|---|---|
| ❑ PHM 200176 [M] | Ian and the Zodiacs | 1965 | 40.00 |
| ❑ PHS 600176 [S] | Ian and the Zodiacs | 1965 | 50.00 |

### IBRAHIM, ABDULLAH Originally recorded as "Dollar Brand," which is the name on these records.

**REPRISE**

| Number | Title (A Side/B Side) | Yr | NM |
|---|---|---|---|
| ❑ R-6111 [M] | Duke Ellington Presents the Dollar Brand Trio | 1965 | 20.00 |
| ❑ RS-6111 [S] | Duke Ellington Presents the Dollar Brand Trio | 1965 | 25.00 |

### ICE-T

**ATOMIC POP**

| Number | Title (A Side/B Side) | Yr | NM |
|---|---|---|---|
| ❑ AP 0011 [(2)] | Greatest Hits: The Evidence | 2000 | 20.00 |

The Illusion, *Together (As a Way of Life)*, Steed ST 37005, 1969, $15.

| Number | Title (A Side/B Side) | Yr | NM |
|---|---|---|---|
| RHYME SYNDICATE | | | |
| ❑ 53858 | Home Invasion | 1993 | 10.00 |
| SIRE | | | |
| ❑ PRO-A-4959 [(2)DJ] | O.G. Original Gangster | 1991 | 25.00 |
| *—Promo-only radio-ready version of album otherwise unavailable on U.S. vinyl* | | | |
| ❑ 25602 | Rhyme Pays | 1987 | 10.00 |
| ❑ 25765 | Power | 1988 | 12.00 |
| ❑ 26028 | The Iceberg/Freedom of Speech...Just Watch What You Say | 1989 | 12.00 |
| **ID, THE** Two different groups. | | | |
| AURA | | | |
| ❑ 1000 | Where Are We Going? | 1976 | 50.00 |
| RCA VICTOR | | | |
| ❑ LPM-3805 [M] | The Inner Sounds of the Id | 1967 | 40.00 |
| ❑ LSP-3805 [S] | The Inner Sounds of the Id | 1967 | 40.00 |
| **IDES OF MARCH, THE** | | | |
| RCA VICTOR | | | |
| ❑ APL1-0143 | Midnight Oil | 1973 | 15.00 |
| ❑ LSP-4812 | World Woven | 1972 | 15.00 |
| SUNDAZED | | | |
| ❑ LP-5032 | Ideology | 199? | 12.00 |
| WARNER BROS. | | | |
| ❑ WS 1863 | Vehicle | 1970 | 15.00 |
| *—Green "WB" label* | | | |
| ❑ WS 1863 | Vehicle | 1970 | 20.00 |
| *—Green "W7" label* | | | |
| ❑ WS 1896 | Common Bond | 1971 | 15.00 |
| **IDLE RACE, THE** Jeff Lynne, later of THE MOVE and ELECTRIC LIGHT ORCHESTRA, was in this group. | | | |
| LIBERTY | | | |
| ❑ LST-7603 | Birthday Party | 1969 | 50.00 |
| **IF** | | | |
| CAPITOL | | | |
| ❑ ST-539 | If | 1970 | 20.00 |
| ❑ SW-676 | If2 | 1971 | 20.00 |
| ❑ SMAS-820 | If3 | 1971 | 20.00 |
| ❑ ST-11299 | Not Just Another Bunch of Pretty Faces | 1974 | 12.00 |

| Number | Title (A Side/B Side) | Yr | NM |
|---|---|---|---|
| ❑ ST-11344 | Tea Break Over — Back On Your 'Eads! | 1974 | 12.00 |
| METROMEDIA | | | |
| ❑ BML1-0174 | Double Diamond | 1973 | 12.00 |
| ❑ KMD-1057 | Waterfall | 1972 | 12.00 |
| **IFIELD, FRANK** | | | |
| CAPITOL | | | |
| ❑ ST 10356 [S] | I'm Confessin' | 1963 | 25.00 |
| ❑ T 10356 [M] | I'm Confessin' | 1963 | 20.00 |
| HICKORY | | | |
| ❑ LPM-132 [M] | The Best of Frank Ifield | 1966 | 20.00 |
| ❑ LPS-132 [P] | The Best of Frank Ifield | 1966 | 20.00 |
| ❑ LPM-136 [M] | Tale of Two Cities | 1967 | 15.00 |
| ❑ LPS-136 [S] | Tale of Two Cities | 1967 | 20.00 |
| ❑ ST-90753 [S] | The Best of Frank Ifield | 1966 | 25.00 |
| *—Capitol Record Club edition* | | | |
| ❑ T-90753 [M] | The Best of Frank Ifield | 1966 | 25.00 |
| *—Capitol Record Club edition* | | | |
| VEE JAY | | | |
| ❑ LP 1054 [M] | I Remember You | 1962 | 30.00 |
| ❑ SR 1054 [S] | I Remember You | 1962 | 50.00 |
| **IGGY AND THE STOOGES** Includes records as "The Stooges." Also see IGGY POP. | | | |
| BOMP! | | | |
| ❑ 1018 | Kill City | 1978 | 8.00 |
| *—By "Iggy Pop and James Williamson"* | | | |
| COLUMBIA | | | |
| ❑ KC 32111 | Raw Power | 1973 | 50.00 |
| ELEKTRA | | | |
| ❑ EKS 74051 | The Stooges | 1969 | 50.00 |
| *—By "The Stooges"; red label with large stylized "E" (butterfly label, deduct 60%)* | | | |
| ❑ EKS 74101 | Fun House | 1970 | 50.00 |
| *—By "The Stooges"; red label with large stylized "E" (butterfly label, deduct 60%)* | | | |
| IMPORT/BOMP! | | | |
| ❑ 1015 | Metallic K.O. | 1977 | 18.00 |
| ❑ 1018 | Kill City | 1978 | 12.00 |
| *—By "Iggy Pop and James Williamson"; original issue on green vinyl* | | | |
| SUNDAZED | | | |
| ❑ LP 5149 | The Stooges | 2002 | 15.00 |
| *—By "The Stooges"; reissue on 180-gram vinyl* | | | |

| Number | Title (A Side/B Side) | Yr | NM |
|---|---|---|---|
| ❑ LP 5150 | Fun House | 2002 | 15.00 |
| *—By "The Stooges"; reissue on 180-gram vinyl* | | | |
| **IGGY POP** Also see IGGY AND THE STOOGES. | | | |
| A&M | | | |
| ❑ SP-5145 | Blah Blah Blah | 1986 | 10.00 |
| ❑ SP-5198 | Instinct | 1988 | 10.00 |
| ❑ SP-17641 [DJ] | Live at the Channel 7/19/88 | 1988 | 40.00 |
| *—Numbered, rubber-stamped promo-only edition* | | | |
| ❑ R 134099 | Blah Blah Blah | 1986 | 12.00 |
| *—RCA Music Service edition* | | | |
| ANIMAL | | | |
| ❑ 6000 | Zombie Birdhouse | 1982 | 12.00 |
| ❑ FV 41399 | Zombie Birdhouse | 1983 | 8.00 |
| *—Reissue* | | | |
| ARISTA | | | |
| ❑ SP-115 [EP] | Special Rock Club Versions | 1981 | 18.00 |
| *—Promo-only remixes of 4 songs from the "Party" LP* | | | |
| ❑ AL 4237 | New Values | 1979 | 15.00 |
| ❑ AB 4259 | Soldier | 1980 | 12.00 |
| ❑ AL5-8172 | Soldier | 198? | 8.00 |
| *—Reissue* | | | |
| ❑ AL5-8189 | Party | 198? | 8.00 |
| *—Reissue* | | | |
| ❑ AL 9572 | Party | 1981 | 12.00 |
| PAIR | | | |
| ❑ PDL2-1051 [(2)] | Iggy Pop | 1986 | 12.00 |
| *—Compilation of RCA Victor material* | | | |
| RCA VICTOR | | | |
| ❑ APL1-2275 | The Idiot | 1977 | 18.00 |
| ❑ AFL1-2488 | Lust for Life | 1977 | 18.00 |
| ❑ AFL1-2796 | TV Eye — 1977 Live | 1978 | 12.00 |
| ❑ AFL1-4957 | Choice Cuts | 1984 | 15.00 |
| SUNDAZED | | | |
| ❑ LP 5039 | New Values | 200? | 12.00 |
| *—Reissue on 180-gram vinyl* | | | |
| ❑ LP 5041 | Soldier | 200? | 12.00 |
| *—Reissue on 180-gram vinyl* | | | |
| VIRGIN | | | |
| ❑ 91381 | Brick by Brick | 1990 | 10.00 |
| **IKETTES, THE** | | | |
| MODERN | | | |
| ❑ M-102 [M] | Soul Hits | 1965 | 30.00 |
| ❑ MST-102 [S] | Soul Hits | 1965 | 40.00 |
| UNITED ARTISTS | | | |
| ❑ UA-LA190-F | (G)Old and New | 1973 | 12.00 |
| **ILL WIND, THE** | | | |
| ABC | | | |
| ❑ S-641 | Flashes | 1968 | 100.00 |
| **ILLUSION, THE** | | | |
| STEED | | | |
| ❑ ST-37003 | The Illusion | 1969 | 20.00 |
| ❑ ST-37005 | Together (As a Way of Life) | 1969 | 15.00 |
| ❑ ST-37006 | If It's So | 1970 | 15.00 |
| **ILLUSTRATION** | | | |
| JANUS | | | |
| ❑ JLP-3010 | Illustration | 1969 | 25.00 |
| **ILMO SMOKEHOUSE** | | | |
| BEAUTIFUL SOUND | | | |
| ❑ 3002 | Ilmo Smokehouse | 1971 | 40.00 |
| ROULETTE | | | |
| ❑ RS-3002 | Ilmo Smokehouse | 1971 | 20.00 |
| **ILORI, SOLOMON** | | | |
| BLUE NOTE | | | |
| ❑ BLP-4136 [M] | African High Life | 1963 | 60.00 |
| ❑ BST-84136 [S] | African High Life | 1963 | 80.00 |
| *—With "New York, USA" address on label* | | | |
| ❑ BST-84136 [S] | African High Life | 1967 | 25.00 |
| *—With "A Division of Liberty Records" on label* | | | |
| **IMPACS, THE** | | | |
| KING | | | |
| ❑ 886 [M] | Impact! | 1964 | 200.00 |
| ❑ KS-886 [S] | Impact! | 1964 | 300.00 |
| ❑ 916 [M] | A Weekend with the Impacs | 1964 | 200.00 |
| ❑ KS-916 [S] | A Weekend with the Impacs | 1964 | 300.00 |
| **IMPACTS, THE** | | | |
| DEL-FI | | | |
| ❑ DFLP-1234 [M] | Wipe Out | 1963 | 60.00 |
| ❑ DFS-1234 [S] | Wipe Out | 1963 | 80.00 |
| ❑ DLF-1234 | Wipe Out | 199? | 12.00 |
| *—Reissue with bar code* | | | |
| **IMPALA SYNDROME, THE** | | | |
| PARALLAX | | | |
| ❑ 4002 | The Impala Syndrome | 1970 | 100.00 |
| **IMPALAS, THE** | | | |
| CUB | | | |
| ❑ 8003 [M] | Sorry (I Ran All the Way Home) | 1959 | 400.00 |
| ❑ S-8003 [S] | Sorry (I Ran All the Way Home) | 1959 | 600.00 |

**IMPRESSIONS, THE** Also see JERRY BUTLER; CURTIS MAYFIELD.

ABC

| Number | Title (A Side/B Side) | Yr | NM |
|---|---|---|---|
| ❑ 606 [M] | The Fabulous Impressions | 1967 | 25.00 |
| ❑ S-606 [S] | The Fabulous Impressions | 1967 | 20.00 |
| ❑ S-635 | We're a Winner | 1968 | 15.00 |
| ❑ S-654 | The Best of the Impressions | 1968 | 15.00 |
| ❑ S-668 | The Versatile Impressions | 1969 | 15.00 |
| ❑ S-727 | 16 Greatest Hits | 1971 | 12.00 |
| ❑ D-780 [(2)] | Curtis Mayfield/His Early Years with the Impressions | 1973 | 20.00 |
| ❑ ST-91540 | The Best of the Impressions | 1968 | 20.00 |
| *—Capitol Record Club edition* | | | |

ABC-PARAMOUNT

| Number | Title (A Side/B Side) | Yr | NM |
|---|---|---|---|
| ❑ 450 [M] | The Impressions | 1963 | 30.00 |
| ❑ S-450 [S] | The Impressions | 1963 | 40.00 |
| ❑ 468 [M] | The Never Ending Impressions | 1964 | 30.00 |
| ❑ S-468 [S] | The Never Ending Impressions | 1964 | 40.00 |
| ❑ 493 [M] | Keep On Pushing | 1964 | 30.00 |
| ❑ S-493 [S] | Keep On Pushing | 1964 | 40.00 |
| ❑ 505 [M] | People Get Ready | 1965 | 30.00 |
| ❑ S-505 [S] | People Get Ready | 1965 | 40.00 |
| ❑ 515 [M] | The Impressions' Greatest Hits | 1965 | 20.00 |
| ❑ S-515 [S] | The Impressions' Greatest Hits | 1965 | 25.00 |
| ❑ 523 [M] | One By One | 1965 | 20.00 |
| ❑ S-523 [S] | One By One | 1965 | 25.00 |
| ❑ 545 [M] | Ridin' High | 1966 | 20.00 |
| ❑ S-545 [S] | Ridin' High | 1966 | 25.00 |
| ❑ ST-90097 [S] | People Get Ready | 1965 | 50.00 |
| *—Capitol Record Club edition* | | | |
| ❑ ST-90106 [S] | Keep On Pushing | 1965 | 50.00 |
| *—Capitol Record Club edition* | | | |
| ❑ T-90472 [M] | The Impressions | 1965 | 40.00 |
| *—Capitol Record Club edition* | | | |
| ❑ ST-90492 [S] | The Never Ending Impressions | 1965 | 50.00 |
| *—Capitol Record Club edition* | | | |
| ❑ ST-90520 [S] | One By One | 1965 | 30.00 |
| *—Capitol Record Club edition* | | | |
| ❑ T-90520 [M] | One By One | 1965 | 25.00 |
| *—Capitol Record Club edition* | | | |

CHI-SOUND

| Number | Title (A Side/B Side) | Yr | NM |
|---|---|---|---|
| ❑ T-596 | Come to My Party | 1979 | 10.00 |
| ❑ T-624 | Fan the Fire | 1981 | 10.00 |

COTILLION

| Number | Title (A Side/B Side) | Yr | NM |
|---|---|---|---|
| ❑ SD 9912 | It's About Time | 1976 | 12.00 |

CURTOM

| Number | Title (A Side/B Side) | Yr | NM |
|---|---|---|---|
| ❑ CUR-2006 | Lasting Impressions | 198? | 10.00 |
| ❑ CU 5003 | First Impressions | 1975 | 12.00 |
| ❑ CU 5009 | Loving Power | 1976 | 12.00 |
| ❑ CRS-8001 | This Is My Country | 1968 | 15.00 |
| ❑ CRS-8003 | The Young Mods' Forgotten Story | 1969 | 15.00 |
| ❑ CRS-8004 | Best Impressions — Curtis, Sam, Dave | 1969 | 15.00 |
| ❑ CRS-8006 | Check Out Your Mind | 1970 | 15.00 |
| ❑ CRS-8012 | Times Have Changed | 1972 | 15.00 |
| ❑ CRS-8016 | Preacher Man | 1973 | 15.00 |
| ❑ CRS-8019 | Finally Got Myself Together | 1974 | 15.00 |

LOST-NITE

| Number | Title (A Side/B Side) | Yr | NM |
|---|---|---|---|
| ❑ LLP-22 [10] | Jerry Butler and the Impressions | 1981 | 15.00 |
| *—Red vinyl* | | | |

MCA

| Number | Title (A Side/B Side) | Yr | NM |
|---|---|---|---|
| ❑ 1500 | The Impressions Greatest Hits | 1982 | 8.00 |
| ❑ 5373 | In the Heat of the Night | 1982 | 10.00 |

PICKWICK

| Number | Title (A Side/B Side) | Yr | NM |
|---|---|---|---|
| ❑ SPC-3602 | The Impressions | 1978 | 8.00 |

SCEPTER CITATION

| Number | Title (A Side/B Side) | Yr | NM |
|---|---|---|---|
| ❑ CTN-18018 | The Best of Curtis Mayfield and the Impressions | 1972 | 10.00 |

SIRE

| Number | Title (A Side/B Side) | Yr | NM |
|---|---|---|---|
| ❑ SASH-3717 [(2)] | The Vintage Years | 1977 | 15.00 |
| *—Includes solo hits by Jerry Butler and Curtis Mayfield* | | | |

**IMPROVISATION CHAMBER ENSEMBLE**

RCA VICTOR RED SEAL

| Number | Title (A Side/B Side) | Yr | NM |
|---|---|---|---|
| ❑ LSC-2558 [S] | Studies in Improvisation | 1961 | 30.00 |
| *—Original with "shaded dog" label* | | | |

**IMUS, DON**

BANG

| Number | Title (A Side/B Side) | Yr | NM |
|---|---|---|---|
| ❑ 407 | This Honky's Nuts | 1974 | 25.00 |

RCA VICTOR

| Number | Title (A Side/B Side) | Yr | NM |
|---|---|---|---|
| ❑ LSP-4699 | 1200 Hamburgers to Go | 1972 | 25.00 |
| *—As "Imus in the Morning"* | | | |
| ❑ LSP-4819 | One Sacred Chicken to Go | 1973 | 25.00 |

**IN GROUP, THE**

IN

| Number | Title (A Side/B Side) | Yr | NM |
|---|---|---|---|
| ❑ I-1002 [M] | Swinging 12 String | 1964 | 20.00 |
| ❑ IS-1002 [S] | Swinging 12 String | 1964 | 25.00 |

Indigo Girls, *Nomads – Indians – Saints,* Epic E 46820, 1991, $20.

**IN-SECT, THE**

RCA CAMDEN

| Number | Title (A Side/B Side) | Yr | NM |
|---|---|---|---|
| ❑ CAL-909 [M] | Introducing the In-Sect Direct from England | 1964 | 40.00 |
| ❑ CAS-909 [S] | Introducing the In-Sect Direct from England | 1964 | 50.00 |

**INCREDIBLE STRING BAND, THE**

CARTHAGE

| Number | Title (A Side/B Side) | Yr | NM |
|---|---|---|---|
| ❑ CGLP-4421 | The Hangman's Beautiful Daughter | 198? | 12.00 |

ELEKTRA

| Number | Title (A Side/B Side) | Yr | NM |
|---|---|---|---|
| ❑ EKM-322 [M] | The Incredible String Band | 1967 | 30.00 |
| ❑ 7E-2002 [(2)] | 'U' | 1971 | 25.00 |
| *—Butterfly label* | | | |
| ❑ 7E-2004 [(2)] | Relics of the Incredible String Band | 1971 | 20.00 |
| *—Butterfly label* | | | |
| ❑ EKM-4010 [M] | The 5,000 Spirits | 1967 | 30.00 |
| ❑ EKS-7322 | The Incredible String Band | 1969 | 15.00 |
| *—Red label, large stylized "E"* | | | |
| ❑ EKS-7322 | The Incredible String Band | 1971 | 12.00 |
| *—Butterfly label* | | | |
| ❑ EKS-7322 [S] | The Incredible String Band | 1967 | 20.00 |
| *—Brown label* | | | |
| ❑ EKS-74010 | The 5,000 Spirits | 1969 | 15.00 |
| *—Red label, large stylized "E"* | | | |
| ❑ EKS-74010 | The 5,000 Spirits | 1971 | 12.00 |
| *—Butterfly label* | | | |
| ❑ EKS-74010 [S] | The 5,000 Spirits | 1967 | 20.00 |
| *—Brown label* | | | |
| ❑ EKS-74021 | The Hangman's Beautiful Daughter | 1968 | 20.00 |
| *—Brown label* | | | |
| ❑ EKS-74021 | The Hangman's Beautiful Daughter | 1969 | 15.00 |
| *—Red label, large stylized "E"* | | | |
| ❑ EKS-74021 | The Hangman's Beautiful Daughter | 1971 | 12.00 |
| *—Butterfly label* | | | |
| ❑ EKS-74036 | Wee Tam | 1969 | 15.00 |
| *—Red label, large stylized "E"* | | | |
| ❑ EKS-74036 | Wee Tam | 1969 | 20.00 |
| *—Brown label* | | | |
| ❑ EKS-74036 | Wee Tam | 1971 | 12.00 |
| *—Butterfly label* | | | |
| ❑ EKS-74037 | The Big Huge | 1969 | 15.00 |
| *—Red label, large stylized "E"* | | | |
| ❑ EKS-74037 | The Big Huge | 1969 | 20.00 |
| *—Brown label* | | | |
| ❑ EKS-74037 | The Big Huge | 1971 | 12.00 |
| *—Butterfly label* | | | |
| ❑ EKS-74057 | Changing Horses | 1969 | 15.00 |
| *—Red label, large stylized "E"* | | | |
| ❑ EKS-74057 | Changing Horses | 1971 | 12.00 |
| *—Butterfly label* | | | |
| ❑ EKS-74061 | I Looked Up | 1970 | 15.00 |
| *—Red label, large stylized "E"* | | | |
| ❑ EKS-74061 | I Looked Up | 1971 | 12.00 |
| *—Butterfly label* | | | |
| ❑ EKS-74112 | Liquid Acrobat As Regards the Air | 1972 | 15.00 |
| *—Butterfly label* | | | |

REPRISE

| Number | Title (A Side/B Side) | Yr | NM |
|---|---|---|---|
| ❑ MS 2122 | Earthspan | 1973 | 12.00 |
| ❑ MS 2139 | No Ruinous Feud | 1973 | 12.00 |
| ❑ MS 2198 | Hard Rope and Silver Twine | 1974 | 12.00 |

SUNDAZED

| Number | Title (A Side/B Side) | Yr | NM |
|---|---|---|---|
| ❑ LP 5127 [S] | The Incredible String Band | 2003 | 12.00 |
| *—Reissue on 180-gram vinyl* | | | |
| ❑ LP 5128 [S] | The 5,000 Spirits | 2003 | 12.00 |
| *—Reissue on 180-gram vinyl* | | | |
| ❑ LP 5129 [S] | The Hangman's Beautiful Daughter | 2003 | 12.00 |
| *—Reissue on 180-gram vinyl* | | | |

**INCREDIBLES, THE**

AUDIO ARTS

| Number | Title (A Side/B Side) | Yr | NM |
|---|---|---|---|
| ❑ AAS-7000 | Heart and Soul | 1970 | 20.00 |

**IND, PETER**

WAVE

| Number | Title (A Side/B Side) | Yr | NM |
|---|---|---|---|
| ❑ W-1 [M] | Looking Out | 1961 | 25.00 |
| ❑ WS-1 [S] | Looking Out | 1961 | 30.00 |

**INDEPENDENTS, THE**

WAND

| Number | Title (A Side/B Side) | Yr | NM |
|---|---|---|---|
| ❑ WDS-694 | The First Time We Met | 1973 | 25.00 |
| ❑ WDS-696 | The Independents | 1973 | 25.00 |
| ❑ WDS-699 | Discs of Gold | 1974 | 25.00 |

**INDEX**

DC
❑ 71 The Index 1968 3000.
*—Black label; issued with black and white jacket; number is from deal wax; VG value 1500; VG+ value 2250*
❑ 4736 The Index 1968 2000.
*—Red label; issued with generic white jacket, though sometimes found in first LP's jacket; number in dead wax; VG value 1000; VG+ value 1500*

**INDIAN SUMMER**

RCA/NEON
❑ NE-3 Indian Summer 1971 20.00

**INDIGO GIRLS**

DRAGON PATH
❑ LMM-I [EP] Indigo Girls 1986 150.00
*—Black vinyl*
❑ LMM-I [EP] Indigo Girls 1986 200.00
*—Blue or clear vinyl (each of equal value)*

EPIC
❑ EAS 1481 [EP] Indigo Girls Sampler 1989 15.00
*—Promo-only with tour-dates sticker on white cardboard cover; includes Kid Fears/Closer to Fine/Center Stage/Prince of Darkness*
❑ EAS 1861 [EP] Land of Canaan Plus Five Live 1989 30.00
*—Promo-only item with five live tracks on B-side*
❑ EAS 2201 [DJ] Shades of Indigo: An Interview by Shawn Colvin 1990 70.00
❑ EAS 4020 [DJ] Indigo Girls Live 1991 40.00
*—Promo-only version of "Back on the Bus Y'All"*
❑ FE 45044 Indigo Girls 1989 15.00
❑ FE 45427 Strange Fire 1989 15.00
*—Reissue of Indigo release*
❑ E 46820 Nomads*Indians*Saints 1990 20.00
❑ E 57621 Swamp Ophelia 1994 40.00
*—Black vinyl; all copies autographed on the label by the Indigo Girls*
❑ E 57621 Swamp Ophelia 1994 40.00
*—Green vinyl; all copies autographed on the label by the Indigo Girls*

INDIGO
❑ LMM-II Strange Fire 1987 200.00
*—Blue, clear or red vinyl (each of equal value)*
❑ LMM-II Strange Fire 1987 150.00
*—Black vinyl*

**INFLUENCE**

ABC
❑ ABCS-630 Influence 1968 30.00

**INGMANN, JORGEN**

ATCO
❑ 33-130 [M] Apache 1961 40.00
❑ 33-139 [M] The Many Guitars of Jorgen Ingmann 1962 40.00

MERCURY
❑ MG-20200 [M] Swinging Guitar 1956 60.00
❑ MG-20292 [M] Swing Softly 1956 60.00

UNITED ARTISTS
❑ UAS-6785 El Condor Pasa 1970 20.00

**INK SPOTS**

COLORTONE
❑ 4901 [M] The Ink Spots 1958 60.00
❑ 4947 [M] The Ink Spots, Vol. 2 1959 60.00

CROWN
❑ CST-144 [S] The Ink Spots' Greatest Hits 1959 25.00
*—Black vinyl*
❑ CST-144 [S] The Ink Spots' Greatest Hits 1959 50.00
*—Red vinyl*
❑ CST-175 [S] The Ink Spots 1961 25.00
*—Black vinyl*
❑ CST-175 [S] The Ink Spots 1961 50.00
*—Red vinyl*
❑ CST-217 [S] The Sensational Ink Spots 1962 25.00
*—Black vinyl*
❑ CST-217 [S] The Sensational Ink Spots 1962 50.00
*—Red vinyl*
❑ CLP-5112 [M] The Ink Spots' Greatest Hits 1959 20.00
❑ CLP-5142 [M] The Ink Spots 1961 20.00
❑ CLP-5187 [M] The Sensational Ink Spots 1962 20.00
❑ CLP 5221 [M] More Ink Spots 196? 15.00

DECCA
❑ DXB 182 [(2)M] The Best of the Ink Spots 1965 30.00
❑ DL 4297 [M] Our Golden Favorites 1962 25.00
❑ DL 5056 [10] The Ink Spots 1950 50.00
❑ DL 5071 [10] The Ink Spots, Vol. 2 1950 50.00
❑ DL 5333 [10] Precious Memories 1951 50.00
❑ DL 5541 [10] Street of Dreams 1954 50.00
❑ DXSB 7182 [(2)P] The Best of the Ink Spots 1965 20.00
❑ DL 8154 [M] The Best of the Ink Spots 1955 40.00
*—Black label, silver print*
❑ DL 8232 [M] Time Our for Tears 1956 40.00
*—Black label, silver print*
❑ DL 8768 [M] Torch Time 1958 40.00
*—Black label, silver print*
❑ DL 74297 [S] Our Golden Favorites 1962 20.00

EVEREST ARCHIVE OF FOLK & JAZZ
❑ 350 The Ink Spots in London 197? 10.00

GOLDEN TONE
❑ C4024 The Fabulous Ink Spots 195? 12.00
❑ C4037 Ink Spots Vol. II 195? 12.00

GRAND AWARD
❑ GA 232 SD [S] The Ink Spots' Greatest, Volume 3 1959 40.00
❑ GA 33-328 [M] The Ink Spots' Greatest, Volume 1 1958 25.00
❑ GA 33-354 [M] The Ink Spots' Greatest, Volume 2 1958 25.00
❑ GA 33-396 [M] The Ink Spots' Greatest, Volume 3 1959 25.00

KING
❑ 535 [M] Something Old, Something New 1956 400.00
❑ 642 [M] Songs That Will Live Forever 1959 300.00
*—Reissue of 535*
❑ 5001 18 Hits by the Ink Spots 197? 10.00

LONGINES SYMPHONETTE
❑ SYS 5830 10 of the Best Ink Spots Hits 197? 10.00
*—Label calls this "The Best of the Ink Spots"; also on label is "New Premium for Mills Bros. V&R Offer"*

MCA
❑ 4005 [(2)] The Best of the Ink Spots 197? 12.00
❑ MSM2-35253 [(2)] The Beautiful Music Company Presents the Ink Spots 1991 20.00

OPEN SKY
❑ 3125 Just Like Old Times 198? 10.00

PAULA
❑ 2212 The Ink Spots Sing Country 1972 10.00

RONDO
❑ R-2010 [M] The Ink Spots in the Spotlite 1963 12.00
❑ RS-2010 [S] The Ink Spots in the Spotlite 1963 15.00
*—Title on label is "The Ink Spots"*

TOPS
❑ L-1561 [M] The Ink Spots 1957 40.00
❑ L-1668 [M] The Ink Spots, Vol. 2 1959 40.00

VERVE
❑ MGV-2124 [M] The Ink Spots' Favorites 1959 25.00
❑ MGVS-6096 [S] The Ink Spots' Favorites 1959 40.00

VOCALION
❑ VL 3606 [M] Sincerely Yours 196? 12.00
❑ VL 3725 [M] Lost in a Dream 1965 12.00
❑ VL 73606 [R] Sincerely Yours 196? 10.00
❑ VL 73725 [R] Lost in a Dream 1965 10.00

WALDORF MUSIC HALL
❑ MH 33-144 [10] Songs of the South Seas 195? 80.00
❑ MH 33-152 [10] The Ink Spots Quartet 195? 80.00

**INMAN, AUTRY**

EPIC
❑ BN 26428 Ballad of Two Brothers 1968 20.00

JUBILEE
❑ JGM-2055 [M] Riscotheque Saturday Night 1964 20.00
❑ JGS-2055 [S] Riscotheque Saturday Night 1964 25.00
❑ JGM-2056 [M] New Year's Eve with Autry Inman 1964 20.00
❑ JGS-2056 [S] New Year's Eve with Autry Inman 1964 25.00

MOUNTAIN DEW
❑ 7022 [M] Autry Inman 1963 20.00
❑ S-7022 [S] Autry Inman 1963 25.00

SIMS
❑ 107 [M] Autry Inman at the Frontier Club 1964 20.00
❑ S-107 [S] Autry Inman at the Frontier Club 1964 25.00

**INMAN, JERRY**

COLUMBIA
❑ CL 2793 [M] Lennon-McCartney Country Style R.F.D. 1967 30.00
❑ CS 9593 [S] Lennon-McCartney Country Style R.F.D. 1967 20.00

ELEKTRA
❑ 7E-1068 You Betchum! 1976 12.00

**INNOCENCE, THE**

KAMA SUTRA
❑ KLP-8059 [M] The Innocence 1967 20.00
❑ KLPS-8059 [S] The Innocence 1967 30.00

**INNOCENT, THE** With Trent Reznor, pre-NINE INCH NAILS.

RED LABEL
❑ 7300 Livin' in the Street 1985 60.00

**INNOCENTS, THE**

INDIGO
❑ 503 [M] Inocently Yours 1961 80.00
❑ 503 [M] Inocently Yours 1961 500.00
*—Plain white cover; promo only*

**INSECT TRUST, THE**

ATCO
❑ SD 33-313 Hoboken Saturday Night 1970 40.00

CAPITOL
❑ SKAO-109 The Insect Trust 1968 40.00

**INSIDE OUT**

FREDLO
❑ 6834 Bringing It All Back 1968 200.00

**INSTANT COMPOSERS POOL (ICP ORCHESTRA)**

ICP
❑ 020 Tetterettet 1977 25.00
❑ 022 Live Soncino 1980 25.00

**INTERNATIONAL SUBMARINE BAND, THE** With Gram Parsons, later of THE BYRDS and THE FLYING BURRITO BROTHERS.

LHI
❑ 12001 Safe at Home 1968 100.00
*—Counterfeits have white labels, legitimate copies have multi-color labels*

RHINO
❑ RNLP 069 Safe at Home 1985 25.00

SUNDAZED
❑ LP 5112 Safe at Home 2001 12.00
*—Reissue on 180-gram vinyl*

**INTERPRETERS, THE**

CADET
❑ LP-762 [M] The Knack 1966 15.00
❑ LPS-762 [S] The Knack 1966 20.00

**INTRIGUES, THE**

YEW
❑ YS-777 In a Moment 1970 30.00

**INTRUDERS, THE (1)**

GAMBLE
❑ G-5001 [M] The Intruders Are Together 1967 40.00
❑ GS-5001 [S] The Intruders Are Together 1967 50.00
❑ GS-5004 Cowboys to Girls 1968 50.00
❑ GS-5005 The Intruders Greatest Hits 1969 40.00
❑ GS-5008 When We Get Married 1970 50.00
❑ KZ 31991 Save the Children 1973 20.00
❑ KZ 32131 Super Hits 1973 20.00

PHILADELPHIA INT'L.
❑ PZ 32131 Super Hits 198? 8.00
*—Reissue of Gamble 32131*

TSOP
❑ KZ 33149 Energy of Love 1974 15.00

**INVADERS, THE**

JUSTICE
❑ JLP-125 On the Right Track 196? 300.00

**INVICTAS, THE**

INVICTAS
❑ M80P-5816/7 [M] The Invictas 196? 250.00

SAHARA
❑ 101 [M] The Invictas A-Go-Go 1965 120.00

20TH CENTURY FOX
❑ TCF-3152 [M] The Invictas 1964 40.00

**INVISIBLE MAN'S BAND, THE** Successor to THE FIVE STAIRSTEPS.

BOARDWALK
❑ NB1-33238 Really Wanna See Ya 1981 20.00

**INXS**

ATCO
❑ 90072 Shabooh Shoobah 1983 12.00
❑ 90115 [EP] Dekadance 1983 15.00
❑ 90160 The Swing 1984 12.00
❑ 90184 INXS 1984 12.00
*—U.S. issue of 1980 Australian album*
❑ 90185 Underneath the Colours 1984 12.00
*—U.S. issue of 1981 Australian album*

ATLANTIC
❑ 81277 Listen Like Thieves 1985 10.00
❑ 81796 Kick 1987 10.00
❑ 82140 X 1990 10.00
❑ A1-82294 Live Baby Live 1991 25.00
*—Columbia House version (only U.S. vinyl pressing)*
❑ R 114468 Listen Like Thieves 1985 12.00
*—RCA Music Service edition*
❑ R 153606 Kick 1987 12.00
*—BMG Direct Marketing edition*
❑ R 164378 X 1990 12.00
*—BMG Direct Marketing edition*

**IRISH ROVERS, THE**

DECCA
❑ DL 4835 [M] First 1967 20.00




**Except when noted otherwise, VG = 25% of NM, and VG+ = 50% of NM. (Example: VG = $2.00, VG+ = $4.00 and NM = $8.00.)**

| Number | Title (A Side/B Side) | Yr | NM |
|---|---|---|---|
| ❑ DL 4951 [M] | The Unicorn | 1968 | 25.00 |
| ❑ DL 74835 [S] | First | 1967 | 15.00 |
| ❑ DL 74951 [S] | The Unicorn | 1968 | 15.00 |
| ❑ DL 75037 | All Hung Up | 1968 | 15.00 |
| ❑ DL 75081 | Tales to Warm Your Mind | 1969 | 15.00 |
| ❑ DL 75157 | Life of the Rover | 1969 | 15.00 |
| ❑ DL 75302 | On the Shores of Americay | 1971 | 15.00 |

MCA

| Number | Title (A Side/B Side) | Yr | NM |
|---|---|---|---|
| ❑ 15 | The Unicorn | 1973 | 10.00 |
| *—Reissue of Decca 74951* | | | |
| ❑ 175 | On the Shores of Americay | 1973 | 10.00 |
| *—Reissue of Decca 75302* | | | |
| ❑ 249 | First | 1973 | 10.00 |
| *—Reissue of Decca 74835* | | | |
| ❑ 284 | Life of the Rover | 1973 | 10.00 |
| *—Reissue of Decca 75157* | | | |
| ❑ 4066 [(2)] | Greatest Hits | 1976 | 15.00 |

**IRON BUTTERFLY**

ATCO

| Number | Title (A Side/B Side) | Yr | NM |
|---|---|---|---|
| ❑ 33-227 [M] | Heavy | 1967 | 30.00 |
| ❑ SD 33-227 [S] | Heavy | 1967 | 25.00 |
| *—Brown and purple label* | | | |
| ❑ SD 33-227 [S] | Heavy | 1969 | 15.00 |
| *—Yellow label* | | | |
| ❑ 33-250 [M] | In-A-Gadda-Da-Vida | 1968 | 50.00 |
| ❑ SD 33-250 [S] | In-A-Gadda-Da-Vida | 1968 | 25.00 |
| *—Brown and purple label* | | | |
| ❑ SD 33-250 [S] | In-A-Gadda-Da-Vida | 1969 | 15.00 |
| *—Yellow label* | | | |
| ❑ SD 33-250 [S] | In-A-Gadda-Da-Vida | 197? | 10.00 |
| *—Any later Atco label; LP was in print into the late 1980s* | | | |
| ❑ SD 33-280 | Ball | 1969 | 15.00 |
| ❑ SD 33-318 | Iron Butterfly Live | 197? | 10.00 |
| *—Any later Atco label; LP was in print into the late 1980s* | | | |
| ❑ SD 33-318 | Iron Butterfly Live | 1970 | 15.00 |
| *—Yellow label* | | | |
| ❑ SD 33-339 | Metamorphosis | 1970 | 15.00 |
| ❑ SD 33-369 | The Best of Iron Butterfly/ Evolution | 1971 | 15.00 |

MCA

| Number | Title (A Side/B Side) | Yr | NM |
|---|---|---|---|
| ❑ 465 | Scorching Beauty | 1975 | 12.00 |
| ❑ 2164 | Sun and Steel | 1976 | 12.00 |

PAIR

| Number | Title (A Side/B Side) | Yr | NM |
|---|---|---|---|
| ❑ PDL2-1065 [(2)] | Rare Flight | 1986 | 15.00 |

**IRON MAIDEN**

CAPITOL

| Number | Title (A Side/B Side) | Yr | NM |
|---|---|---|---|
| ❑ ST-12094 | Iron Maiden | 198? | 8.00 |
| *—Reissue of Harvest 12094* | | | |
| ❑ ST-12141 | Killers | 198? | 8.00 |
| *—Reissue of Harvest 12141* | | | |
| ❑ ST-12202 | The Number of the Beast | 1982 | 8.00 |
| ❑ SEAX-12219 [PD] | The Number of the Beast | 1982 | 50.00 |
| ❑ ST-12274 | Piece of Mind | 1983 | 8.00 |
| ❑ SEAX-12306 [PD] | Piece of Mind | 1983 | 60.00 |
| ❑ SJ-12321 | Powerslave | 1984 | 8.00 |
| ❑ SABB-12441 [(2)] | Live After Death | 1985 | 10.00 |
| ❑ SJ-12524 | Somewhere in Time | 1986 | 8.00 |
| ❑ SQ-15017 [EP] | Maiden Japan | 198? | 6.00 |
| *—Reissue of Harvest 15000* | | | |
| ❑ 53185 [(4)] | Best of the Beast | 1996 | 80.00 |
| *—Box set with booklet; probably a UK pressing stickered with US bar code* | | | |
| ❑ C1-90258 | Seventh Son of a Seventh Son | 1988 | 10.00 |

EPIC

| Number | Title (A Side/B Side) | Yr | NM |
|---|---|---|---|
| ❑ E 46905 | No Prayer for the Dying | 1990 | 25.00 |
| *—Red vinyl* | | | |

HARVEST

| Number | Title (A Side/B Side) | Yr | NM |
|---|---|---|---|
| ❑ ST-12094 | Iron Maiden | 1980 | 12.00 |
| ❑ ST-12141 | Killers | 1981 | 12.00 |
| ❑ MLP-15000 [EP] | Maiden Japan | 1981 | 8.00 |

**IRVINE, WELDON**

BMG SPECIAL PRODUCTS

| Number | Title (A Side/B Side) | Yr | NM |
|---|---|---|---|
| ❑ DRL1-1794 | Cosmic Vortex | 199? | 15.00 |
| *—Reissue* | | | |
| ❑ DRL1-1795 | Sinbad | 199? | 15.00 |
| *—Reissue* | | | |
| ❑ DRL1-1796 | Spirit Man | 199? | 15.00 |
| *—Reissue* | | | |

NODLEW

| Number | Title (A Side/B Side) | Yr | NM |
|---|---|---|---|
| ❑ 1001 | Liberated Brother | 1972 | 300.00 |
| ❑ 1002 | Time Capsule | 1973 | 300.00 |
| *—Reproductions exist* | | | |

RCA VICTOR

| Number | Title (A Side/B Side) | Yr | NM |
|---|---|---|---|
| ❑ APL1-0703 | Cosmic Vortex | 1974 | 120.00 |
| ❑ APL1-0909 | Spirit Man | 1975 | 120.00 |
| ❑ APL1-1363 | Sinbad | 1976 | 150.00 |

STRATA-EAST

| Number | Title (A Side/B Side) | Yr | NM |
|---|---|---|---|
| ❑ SES-19479 | In Harmony | 1974 | 120.00 |

**ISLEY BROTHERS, THE**

BUDDAH

| Number | Title (A Side/B Side) | Yr | NM |
|---|---|---|---|
| ❑ BDS-5652 [(2)] | The Best of the Isley Brothers | 1976 | 15.00 |

COLLECTABLES

| Number | Title (A Side/B Side) | Yr | NM |
|---|---|---|---|
| ❑ COL-5103 | Shout! | 198? | 10.00 |

DEF SOUL

| Number | Title (A Side/B Side) | Yr | NM |
|---|---|---|---|
| ❑ B0004812-01 [(2)] | Baby Makin' Music | 2006 | 15.00 |

ISLAND

| Number | Title (A Side/B Side) | Yr | NM |
|---|---|---|---|
| ❑ 7243 [(2)DJ] | Mission to Please | 1996 | 20.00 |
| *—Promo-only vinyl in generic cover* | | | |

MOTOWN

| Number | Title (A Side/B Side) | Yr | NM |
|---|---|---|---|
| ❑ M5-106V1 | Motown Superstar Series, Volume 6 | 1981 | 8.00 |
| ❑ M5-128V1 | This Old Heart of Mine | 1981 | 8.00 |
| *—Reissue of Tamla 269* | | | |
| ❑ M5-143V1 | Doin' Their Thing (Best of the Isley Brothers) | 1981 | 8.00 |
| *—Reissue of Tamla 287* | | | |

PICKWICK

| Number | Title (A Side/B Side) | Yr | NM |
|---|---|---|---|
| ❑ SPC-3331 | Soul Shout! | 197? | 10.00 |

RCA CAMDEN

| Number | Title (A Side/B Side) | Yr | NM |
|---|---|---|---|
| ❑ ACL1-0126 | Rock On Brother | 1973 | 12.00 |
| ❑ ACL1-0861 | Rock Around the Clock | 1975 | 12.00 |

RCA VICTOR

| Number | Title (A Side/B Side) | Yr | NM |
|---|---|---|---|
| ❑ LPM-2156 [M] | Shout! | 1959 | 120.00 |
| *—"Long Play" label* | | | |
| ❑ LSP-2156 [S] | Shout! | 1959 | 200.00 |
| *—"Living Stereo" label* | | | |

SCEPTER

| Number | Title (A Side/B Side) | Yr | NM |
|---|---|---|---|
| ❑ SC-552 [M] | Take Some Time Out for the Isley Brothers | 1966 | 30.00 |
| ❑ SCS-552 [S] | Take Some Time Out for the Isley Brothers | 1966 | 40.00 |

SUNSET

| Number | Title (A Side/B Side) | Yr | NM |
|---|---|---|---|
| ❑ SUS-5257 | The Isley Brothers Do Their Thing | 1969 | 15.00 |

T-NECK

| Number | Title (A Side/B Side) | Yr | NM |
|---|---|---|---|
| ❑ ASZ 137 [DJ] | Everything You Always Wanted to Hear by the Isley Brothers But Were Afraid to Ask For | 1976 | 20.00 |
| *—Promo-only compilation* | | | |
| ❑ TNS-3001 | It's Our Thing | 1969 | 20.00 |
| ❑ TNS-3002 | The Brothers: Isley | 1969 | 20.00 |
| ❑ TNS-3006 | Get Into Something | 1970 | 15.00 |
| ❑ TNS-3007 | In the Beginning (With Jimi Hendrix) | 1970 | 20.00 |
| ❑ TNS-3008 | Givin' It Back | 1971 | 15.00 |
| ❑ TNS-3009 | Brother, Brother, Brother | 1972 | 15.00 |
| ❑ TNS-3010 [(2)] | The Isleys Live | 1973 | 20.00 |
| ❑ TNS-3011 | Isleys' Greatest Hits | 1973 | 15.00 |
| ❑ KZ 32453 | 3 + 3 | 1973 | 12.00 |
| ❑ PZ 32453 | 3 + 3 | 197? | 8.00 |
| *—Reissue with new prefix* | | | |
| ❑ ZQ 32453 [Q] | 3 + 3 | 1974 | 20.00 |
| ❑ PZ 33070 | Live It Up | 1974 | 12.00 |
| *—No bar code on cover* | | | |
| ❑ PZQ 33070 [Q] | Live It Up | 1974 | 20.00 |
| ❑ PZ 33536 | The Heat Is On | 1975 | 12.00 |
| *—No bar code on cover* | | | |
| ❑ PZ 33536 | The Heat Is On | 198? | 8.00 |
| *—Budget-line reissue with bar code* | | | |
| ❑ PZ 33809 | Harvest for the World | 1976 | 12.00 |
| *—No bar code on cover* | | | |
| ❑ PZQ 33809 [Q] | Harvest for the World | 1976 | 20.00 |
| ❑ PZ 34432 | Go for Your Guns | 1977 | 12.00 |
| *—No bar code on cover* | | | |
| ❑ PZ 34432 | Go for Your Guns | 198? | 8.00 |
| *—Budget-line reissue with bar code* | | | |
| ❑ PZQ 34432 [Q] | Go for Your Guns | 1977 | 20.00 |
| ❑ PZ 34452 | Forever Gold | 1977 | 10.00 |
| ❑ JZ 34930 | Showdown | 1978 | 10.00 |
| ❑ PZ 34930 | Showdown | 198? | 8.00 |
| *—Budget-line reissue* | | | |
| ❑ KZ2 35650 [(2)] | Timeless | 1978 | 12.00 |
| ❑ PZ2 36077 [(2)] | Winner Takes All | 1979 | 12.00 |
| ❑ FZ 36305 | Go All the Way | 1980 | 10.00 |
| ❑ PZ 36305 | Go All the Way | 198? | 8.00 |
| *—Budget-line reissue* | | | |
| ❑ FZ 37080 | Grand Slam | 1981 | 10.00 |
| ❑ PZ 37080 | Grand Slam | 198? | 8.00 |
| *—Budget-line reissue* | | | |
| ❑ FZ 37533 | Inside You | 1981 | 10.00 |
| ❑ FZ 38047 | The Real Deal | 1982 | 10.00 |
| ❑ FZ 38674 | Between the Sheets | 1983 | 10.00 |
| ❑ PZ 38674 | Between the Sheets | 1985 | 8.00 |
| *—Budget-line reissue* | | | |
| ❑ FZ 39240 | Greatest Hits, Vol. 1 | 1984 | 10.00 |
| ❑ PZ 39240 | Greatest Hits, Vol. 1 | 1985 | 8.00 |
| *—Budget-line reissue* | | | |

TAMLA

| Number | Title (A Side/B Side) | Yr | NM |
|---|---|---|---|
| ❑ T-269 [M] | This Old Heart of Mine | 1966 | 25.00 |
| ❑ TS-269 [S] | This Old Heart of Mine | 1966 | 30.00 |
| ❑ T-275 [M] | Soul on the Rocks | 1967 | 25.00 |
| ❑ TS-275 [S] | Soul on the Rocks | 1967 | 30.00 |
| ❑ TS-287 | Doin' Their Thing (Best of the Isley Brothers) | 1969 | 20.00 |

UNITED ARTISTS

| Number | Title (A Side/B Side) | Yr | NM |
|---|---|---|---|
| ❑ UA-LA500-E | The Very Best of the Isley Brothers | 1975 | 10.00 |
| ❑ UAL-3313 [M] | The Famous Isley Brothers | 1963 | 50.00 |
| ❑ UAS-6313 [S] | The Famous Isley Brothers | 1963 | 60.00 |

WAND

| Number | Title (A Side/B Side) | Yr | NM |
|---|---|---|---|
| ❑ WD-653 [M] | Twist & Shout | 1962 | 80.00 |
| ❑ WDS-653 [S] | Twist & Shout | 1962 | 100.00 |

WARNER BROS.

| Number | Title (A Side/B Side) | Yr | NM |
|---|---|---|---|
| ❑ 25347 | Masterpiece | 1985 | 10.00 |
| ❑ 25586 | Smooth Sailin' | 1987 | 10.00 |
| ❑ 25940 | Spend the Night | 1989 | 10.00 |

**IT'S A BEAUTIFUL DAY**

COLUMBIA

| Number | Title (A Side/B Side) | Yr | NM |
|---|---|---|---|
| ❑ CS 1058 | Marrying Maiden | 1970 | 15.00 |
| *—Orange label* | | | |
| ❑ CS 1058 | Marrying Maiden | 1970 | 30.00 |
| *—Red "360 Sound" label* | | | |
| ❑ CS 9768 | It's A Beautiful Day | 1969 | 30.00 |
| *—Red "360 Sound" label* | | | |
| ❑ CS 9768 | It's A Beautiful Day | 1970 | 20.00 |
| *—Orange label* | | | |
| ❑ C 30734 | Choice Quality Stuff/Anytime | 1971 | 15.00 |
| ❑ KC 31338 | It's a Beautiful Day at Carnegie Hall | 1972 | 15.00 |
| ❑ KC 32181 | It's a Beautiful Day...Today | 1973 | 15.00 |
| ❑ KC 32660 [DJ] | A Thousand and One Nights | 1973 | 50.00 |
| *—Canceled before commercial release?* | | | |

SAN FRANCISCO SOUND

| Number | Title (A Side/B Side) | Yr | NM |
|---|---|---|---|
| ❑ 11790 | It's A Beautiful Day | 1985 | 25.00 |
| *—Limited reissue* | | | |

**IVERS, PETER**

EPIC

| Number | Title (A Side/B Side) | Yr | NM |
|---|---|---|---|
| ❑ BN 26500 | Knight of the Blue Communion | 1970 | 40.00 |

WARNER BROS.

| Number | Title (A Side/B Side) | Yr | NM |
|---|---|---|---|
| ❑ BS 2804 | Terminal Love | 1974 | 12.00 |
| ❑ BS 2930 | Peter Ivers | 1976 | 12.00 |

**IVES, BURL**

BELL

| Number | Title (A Side/B Side) | Yr | NM |
|---|---|---|---|
| ❑ 6055 | Time | 1971 | 10.00 |

COLUMBIA

| Number | Title (A Side/B Side) | Yr | NM |
|---|---|---|---|
| ❑ CL 628 [M] | The Wayfaring Stranger | 1955 | 30.00 |
| ❑ CL 980 [M] | Burl Ives Sings Songs for All Ages | 1956 | 30.00 |
| ❑ CL 1459 [M] | Return of the Wayfaring Stranger | 1960 | 30.00 |
| ❑ CL 2570 [10] | Children's Favorites | 1955 | 40.00 |
| *—"House Party Series" issue* | | | |
| ❑ CL 6058 [10] | The Return of the Wayfaring Stranger | 1949 | 50.00 |
| ❑ CL 6109 [10] | The Wayfaring Stranger | 1950 | 50.00 |
| ❑ CL 6144 [10] | More Folk Songs | 1950 | 50.00 |
| ❑ CS 9041 [R] | The Wayfaring Stranger | 1964 | 12.00 |
| ❑ CS 9675 | The Times They Are a-Changin' | 1969 | 12.00 |
| ❑ CS 9728 | Burl Ives Christmas Album | 1968 | 12.00 |
| ❑ CS 9925 | Softly and Tenderly | 1969 | 12.00 |

DECCA

| Number | Title (A Side/B Side) | Yr | NM |
|---|---|---|---|
| ❑ DXB 167 [(2)M] | The Best of Burl Ives | 1961 | 25.00 |
| ❑ DL 4152 [M] | The Versatile Burl Ives | 1961 | 15.00 |
| ❑ DL 4179 [M] | Songs of the West | 1961 | 15.00 |
| ❑ DL 4279 [M] | It's Just My Funny Way of Laughin' | 1962 | 15.00 |
| ❑ DL 4304 [M] | Sing Out, Sweet Land | 1962 | 15.00 |
| ❑ DL 4320 [M] | Sunshine in My Soul | 1962 | 15.00 |
| ❑ DL 4361 [M] | Burl | 1963 | 15.00 |
| ❑ DL 4390 [M] | The Best of Burl's for Boys and Girls | 1963 | 15.00 |
| ❑ DL 4433 [M] | Singin' Easy | 1964 | 15.00 |
| ❑ DL 4533 [M] | True Love | 1964 | 15.00 |
| ❑ DL 4578 [M] | Pearly Shells | 1964 | 15.00 |
| ❑ DL 4606 [M] | My Gal Sal | 1965 | 12.00 |
| ❑ DL 4668 [M] | On the Beach at Waikiki | 1965 | 12.00 |
| ❑ DL 4689 [M] | Have a Holly Jolly Christmas | 1965 | 12.00 |
| ❑ DL 4734 [M] | Burl's Choice | 1966 | 12.00 |
| ❑ DL 4789 [M] | Something Special | 1966 | 12.00 |
| ❑ DL 4850 [M] | Burl Ives' Greatest Hits | 1967 | 15.00 |
| ❑ DL 4876 [M] | Broadway | 1967 | 15.00 |
| ❑ DL 4972 [M] | Big Country Hits | 1968 | 15.00 |
| ❑ DL 5013 [10] | Ballads and Folk Songs, Volume II | 1949 | 50.00 |
| ❑ DL 5080 [10] | A Collection of Ballads and Folk Songs, Volume One | 1949 | 50.00 |
| ❑ DL 5093 [10] | Ballads, Folk and Country Songs | 1949 | 50.00 |
| ❑ DL 5428 [10] | Christmas Day in the Morning | 1952 | 50.00 |
| ❑ DL 5467 [10] | Folk Songs Dramatic and Dangerous | 1953 | 50.00 |
| ❑ DL 5490 [10] | Women: Folk Songs About the Fair Sex | 1954 | 50.00 |
| ❑ DXSB 7167 [(2)S] | The Best of Burl Ives | 1961 | 30.00 |
| ❑ DL 8080 [M] | Coronation Concert | 1953 | 40.00 |
| ❑ DL 8107 [M] | The Wild Side of Life | 1955 | 25.00 |
| ❑ DL 8125 [M] | Men | 1956 | 25.00 |
| ❑ DL 8245 [M] | Down to the Sea in Ships | 1956 | 25.00 |
| ❑ DL 8246 [M] | Women | 1956 | 25.00 |
| ❑ DL 8247 [M] | In the Quiet of Night | 1956 | 25.00 |
| ❑ DL 8248 [M] | Burl Ives Sings for Fun | 1956 | 25.00 |
| ❑ DL 8391 [M] | Christmas Eve | 1957 | 25.00 |

| Number | Title (A Side/B Side) | Yr | NM |
|---|---|---|---|
| ❑ DL 8444 [M] | Songs of Ireland | 1958 | 25.00 |
| ❑ DL 8587 [M] | Captain Burl Ives' Ark | 1958 | 25.00 |
| ❑ DL 8637 [M] | Old Time Varieties | 1958 | 25.00 |
| ❑ DL 8749 [M] | Australian Folk Songs | 1959 | 25.00 |
| ❑ DL 8886 [M] | Cheers | 1959 | 25.00 |
| ❑ DL 74152 [S] | The Versatile Burl Ives | 1961 | 20.00 |
| ❑ DL 74179 [S] | Songs of the West | 1961 | 20.00 |
| ❑ DL 74279 [S] | It's Just My Funny Way of Laughin' | 1962 | 20.00 |
| ❑ DL 74304 [S] | Sing Out, Sweet Land | 1962 | 20.00 |
| ❑ DL 74320 [S] | Sunshine in My Soul | 1962 | 20.00 |
| ❑ DL 74361 [S] | Burl | 1963 | 20.00 |
| ❑ DL 74390 [S] | The Best of Burl's for Boys and Girls | 1963 | 20.00 |
| ❑ DL 74433 [S] | Singin' Easy | 1964 | 20.00 |
| ❑ DL 74533 [S] | True Love | 1964 | 20.00 |
| ❑ DL 74578 [S] | Pearly Shells | 1964 | 20.00 |
| ❑ DL 74606 [S] | My Gal Sal | 1965 | 15.00 |
| ❑ DL 74668 [S] | On the Beach at Waikiki | 1965 | 15.00 |
| ❑ DL 74689 [S] | Have a Holly Jolly Christmas | 1965 | 15.00 |
| ❑ DL 74734 [S] | Burl's Choice | 1966 | 15.00 |
| ❑ DL 74789 [S] | Something Special | 1966 | 15.00 |
| ❑ DL 74850 [S] | Burl Ives' Greatest Hits | 1967 | 12.00 |
| ❑ DL 74876 [S] | Broadway | 1967 | 12.00 |
| ❑ DL 74972 [S] | Big Country Hits | 1968 | 12.00 |
| ❑ DL 78391 [R] | Christmas Eve | 196? | 10.00 |
| ❑ DL 78886 [S] | Cheers | 1959 | 30.00 |

**DISNEYLAND**

| Number | Title (A Side/B Side) | Yr | NM |
|---|---|---|---|
| ❑ ST-3927 [M] | Chim Chim Chiree and Other Children's Choices | 1964 | 15.00 |
| ❑ STER-3927 [S] | Chim Chim Chiree and Other Children's Choices | 1964 | 20.00 |

**EVEREST ARCHIVE OF FOLK & JAZZ**

| Number | Title (A Side/B Side) | Yr | NM |
|---|---|---|---|
| ❑ 340 | Burl Ives Live | 1978 | 10.00 |

**HARMONY**

| Number | Title (A Side/B Side) | Yr | NM |
|---|---|---|---|
| ❑ HL 9507 [M] | The Little White Duck | 196? | 15.00 |
| ❑ HL 9551 [M] | The Lollipop Tree | 196? | 15.00 |
| ❑ HS 11275 | Got the World by the Tail | 196? | 10.00 |

**MCA**

| Number | Title (A Side/B Side) | Yr | NM |
|---|---|---|---|
| ❑ 114 | Burl Ives' Greatest Hits | 1973 | 10.00 |
| *—Reissue of Decca 74850* | | | |
| ❑ 318 | Paying My Dues Again | 1973 | 10.00 |
| ❑ 4034 [(2)] | The Best of Burl Ives | 197? | 12.00 |
| ❑ 4089 [(2)] | The Best of Burl Ives Volume 2 | 197? | 12.00 |
| ❑ 15002 | Have a Holly Jolly Christmas | 1973 | 12.00 |
| *—Reissue of Decca 74689; black label with rainbow* | | | |
| ❑ 15002 | Have a Holly Jolly Christmas | 1980 | 8.00 |
| *—Blue label with rainbow* | | | |
| ❑ 15030 | Santa Claus Is Coming to Town | 198? | 10.00 |

**NATIONAL GEOGRAPHIC**

| Number | Title (A Side/B Side) | Yr | NM |
|---|---|---|---|
| ❑ 07806 | We Americans | 1978 | 12.00 |

**PICKWICK**

| Number | Title (A Side/B Side) | Yr | NM |
|---|---|---|---|
| ❑ SPC-1018 | Twelve Days of Christmas | 197? | 10.00 |

**STINSON**

| Number | Title (A Side/B Side) | Yr | NM |
|---|---|---|---|
| ❑ SLP-1 [10] | The Wayfaring Stranger | 1949 | 60.00 |

**SUNSET**

| Number | Title (A Side/B Side) | Yr | NM |
|---|---|---|---|
| ❑ SUS-5280 | Favorites | 1970 | 10.00 |

**UNITED ARTISTS**

| Number | Title (A Side/B Side) | Yr | NM |
|---|---|---|---|
| ❑ UAL 3060 [M] | Ballads | 1959 | 15.00 |
| ❑ UAS 6060 [S] | Ballads | 1959 | 20.00 |

**WORD**

| Number | Title (A Side/B Side) | Yr | NM |
|---|---|---|---|
| ❑ 3259 [M] | Faith and Joy | 196? | 15.00 |
| ❑ 3339 [M] | Shall We Gather at the River | 1966 | 12.00 |
| ❑ 3391 [M] | I Do Believe | 1967 | 12.00 |
| ❑ 8140 [S] | Faith and Joy | 196? | 20.00 |
| ❑ 8339 [S] | Shall We Gather at the River | 1966 | 15.00 |
| ❑ 8391 [S] | I Do Believe | 1967 | 15.00 |
| ❑ 8537 | How Great Thou Art | 1971 | 12.00 |

### IVEYS, THE
See BADFINGER.

### IVORY

**PLAYBOY**

| Number | Title (A Side/B Side) | Yr | NM |
|---|---|---|---|
| ❑ 115 | Ivory | 1973 | 12.00 |

**TETRAGRAMMATON**

| Number | Title (A Side/B Side) | Yr | NM |
|---|---|---|---|
| ❑ T-104 | Ivory | 1968 | 20.00 |

### IVORY, JACKIE

**ATCO**

| Number | Title (A Side/B Side) | Yr | NM |
|---|---|---|---|
| ❑ 33-178 [M] | Soul Discovery | 1965 | 20.00 |
| ❑ SD 33-178 [S] | Soul Discovery | 1965 | 25.00 |

### IVY LEAGUE, THE

**CAMEO**

| Number | Title (A Side/B Side) | Yr | NM |
|---|---|---|---|
| ❑ C 2000 [M] | Tossing and Turning | 1965 | 30.00 |
| ❑ CS 2000 [R] | Tossing and Turning | 1965 | 30.00 |

### IVY LEAGUE TRIO, THE

**CORAL**

| Number | Title (A Side/B Side) | Yr | NM |
|---|---|---|---|
| ❑ CRL 57399 [M] | On and Off Campus | 1962 | 15.00 |
| ❑ CRL 57404 [M] | Rare and Well Done | 1962 | 15.00 |
| ❑ CRL 757399 [S] | On and Off Campus | 1962 | 20.00 |
| ❑ CRL 757404 [S] | Rare and Well Done | 1962 | 20.00 |

**REPRISE**

| Number | Title (A Side/B Side) | Yr | NM |
|---|---|---|---|
| ❑ R-6087 [M] | Folk Ballads from the World of Edgar Allan Poe | 1963 | 20.00 |
| ❑ R9-6087 [R] | Folk Ballads from the World of Edgar Allan Poe | 1963 | 30.00 |

# J

### J.B.'S, THE
See FRED WESLEY.

### J.F.K. QUINTET, THE

**RIVERSIDE**

| Number | Title (A Side/B Side) | Yr | NM |
|---|---|---|---|
| ❑ RLP-396 [M] | New Frontiers from Washington | 1961 | 30.00 |
| ❑ RLP-424 [M] | Young Ideas | 1962 | 30.00 |
| ❑ RS-9396 [S] | New Frontiers from Washington | 1961 | 40.00 |
| ❑ RS-9424 [S] | Young Ideas | 1962 | 40.00 |

### J.K. AND COMPANY

**BEAT ROCKET**

| Number | Title (A Side/B Side) | Yr | NM |
|---|---|---|---|
| ❑ BR-126 | Suddenly One Summer | 2000 | 12.00 |
| *—Reissue on 180-gram vinyl* | | | |

**WHITE WHALE**

| Number | Title (A Side/B Side) | Yr | NM |
|---|---|---|---|
| ❑ WWS-7117 | Suddenly One Summer | 1969 | 25.00 |

### J'S WITH JAMIE, THE

**COLUMBIA**

| Number | Title (A Side/B Side) | Yr | NM |
|---|---|---|---|
| ❑ CL 2005 [M] | Hey, Look Us Over! | 1963 | 30.00 |
| ❑ CL 2149 [M] | The Remarkable J's with Jamie | 1964 | 30.00 |
| ❑ CS 8805 [S] | Hey, Look Us Over! | 1963 | 40.00 |
| ❑ CS 8949 [S] | The Remarkable J's with Jamie | 1964 | 40.00 |

### JACINTHA

**GROOVE NOTE**

| Number | Title (A Side/B Side) | Yr | NM |
|---|---|---|---|
| ❑ 2001 | Here's to Ben | 1999 | 25.00 |
| *—Audiophile vinyl* | | | |

### JACKIE AND ROY
See JACKIE CAIN AND ROY KRAL.

### JACKS, THE

**CROWN**

| Number | Title (A Side/B Side) | Yr | NM |
|---|---|---|---|
| ❑ CST-372 [R] | Jumpin' with the Jacks | 1962 | 50.00 |
| ❑ CLP-5021 [M] | Jumpin' with the Jacks | 1960 | 200.00 |
| ❑ CLP-5372 [M] | Jumpin' with the Jacks | 1962 | 100.00 |

**RELIC**

| Number | Title (A Side/B Side) | Yr | NM |
|---|---|---|---|
| ❑ 5023 | The Jacks' Greatest Hits | 198? | 10.00 |

**RPM**

| Number | Title (A Side/B Side) | Yr | NM |
|---|---|---|---|
| ❑ LRP-3006 [M] | Jumpin' with the Jacks | 1956 | 2000. |
| *—VG value 1000; VG+ value 1500* | | | |

**UNITED**

| Number | Title (A Side/B Side) | Yr | NM |
|---|---|---|---|
| ❑ US-7797 | Rock 'n' Roll Hits of the 50's | 197? | 15.00 |

### JACKSON, ALAN

**ARISTA**

| Number | Title (A Side/B Side) | Yr | NM |
|---|---|---|---|
| ❑ AL 8623 | Here in the Real World | 1990 | 20.00 |
| ❑ AL 8681 | Don't Rock the Jukebox | 1991 | 25.00 |
| *—Columbia House vinyl edition* | | | |
| ❑ R 143877 | Don't Rock the Jukebox | 1991 | 25.00 |
| *—BMG Direct Marketing vinyl version* | | | |

### JACKSON, BULL MOOSE

**AUDIO LAB**

| Number | Title (A Side/B Side) | Yr | NM |
|---|---|---|---|
| ❑ AL-1524 [M] | Bull Moose Jackson | 1959 | 600.00 |

**BOGUS**

| Number | Title (A Side/B Side) | Yr | NM |
|---|---|---|---|
| ❑ 6-0214851 | Moosemania! | 1985 | 10.00 |

### JACKSON, CALVIN

**COLUMBIA**

| Number | Title (A Side/B Side) | Yr | NM |
|---|---|---|---|
| ❑ CL 756 [M] | Calvin Jackson and the All Stars Quartet | 1956 | 50.00 |
| ❑ CL 824 [M] | Rave Notice | 1956 | 50.00 |

**LIBERTY**

| Number | Title (A Side/B Side) | Yr | NM |
|---|---|---|---|
| ❑ LRP-3071 [M] | Jazz Variations | 1957 | 40.00 |

**"X"**

| Number | Title (A Side/B Side) | Yr | NM |
|---|---|---|---|
| ❑ LXA-1005 [M] | Calvin Jackson at the Plaza | 1954 | 50.00 |

### JACKSON, CHUBBY

**ARGO**

| Number | Title (A Side/B Side) | Yr | NM |
|---|---|---|---|
| ❑ LP-614 [M] | Chubby's Back | 1957 | 80.00 |
| ❑ LPS-614 [S] | Chubby's Back | 1959 | 70.00 |
| ❑ LP-625 [M] | I'm Entitled to You | 1958 | 80.00 |

**EVEREST**

| Number | Title (A Side/B Side) | Yr | NM |
|---|---|---|---|
| ❑ SDBR-1009 [S] | Chubby Takes Over | 1959 | 40.00 |
| ❑ SDBR-1029 [S] | The Big Three | 1959 | 40.00 |
| ❑ SDBR-1041 [S] | Jazz Then Till Now | 1960 | 40.00 |
| ❑ LPBR-5009 [M] | Chubby Takes Over | 1959 | 30.00 |
| ❑ LPBR-5029 [M] | The Big Three | 1959 | 30.00 |
| ❑ LPBR-5041 [M] | Jazz Then Till Now | 1960 | 30.00 |

**LAURIE**

| Number | Title (A Side/B Side) | Yr | NM |
|---|---|---|---|
| ❑ LLP-2011 [M] | Twist Calling | 1962 | 30.00 |

**NEW JAZZ**

| Number | Title (A Side/B Side) | Yr | NM |
|---|---|---|---|
| ❑ NJLP-105 [10] | Chubby Jackson and His All Star Band | 1950 | 800.00 |
| *—Original; reissued as Prestige 105* | | | |

**PRESTIGE**

| Number | Title (A Side/B Side) | Yr | NM |
|---|---|---|---|
| ❑ PRLP-105 [10] | Chubby Jackson and His All Star Band | 1951 | 600.00 |
| ❑ PRST-7641 | Chubby Jackson Sextet and Big Band | 1969 | 20.00 |

**RAINBOW**

| Number | Title (A Side/B Side) | Yr | NM |
|---|---|---|---|
| ❑ 708 [10] | Chubby Jackson | 1951 | 400.00 |

**STEREO-CRAFT**

| Number | Title (A Side/B Side) | Yr | NM |
|---|---|---|---|
| ❑ RTN-108 [M] | The Big Three | 195? | 50.00 |
| ❑ RTS-108 [S] | The Big Three | 195? | 50.00 |

### JACKSON, CHUBBY, AND BILL HARRIS

**EMARCY**

| Number | Title (A Side/B Side) | Yr | NM |
|---|---|---|---|
| ❑ MG-26003 [10] | The Small Herd | 1954 | 200.00 |
| ❑ MG-26012 [M] | Out of the Herd | 1965 | 20.00 |

**MERCURY**

| Number | Title (A Side/B Side) | Yr | NM |
|---|---|---|---|
| ❑ MG-25076 [10] | Jazz Journey | 1950 | 300.00 |

### JACKSON, CHUCK

**ABC**

| Number | Title (A Side/B Side) | Yr | NM |
|---|---|---|---|
| ❑ X-798 | Through All Times | 1973 | 15.00 |

**ALL PLATINUM**

| Number | Title (A Side/B Side) | Yr | NM |
|---|---|---|---|
| ❑ 3014 | Needing You, Wanting You | 1976 | 15.00 |

**COLLECTABLES**

| Number | Title (A Side/B Side) | Yr | NM |
|---|---|---|---|
| ❑ COL-5115 | Golden Classics | 198? | 10.00 |

**EMI AMERICA**

| Number | Title (A Side/B Side) | Yr | NM |
|---|---|---|---|
| ❑ SW-17031 | I Wanna Give You Some Love | 1980 | 10.00 |

**GUEST STAR**

| Number | Title (A Side/B Side) | Yr | NM |
|---|---|---|---|
| ❑ GS-1912 [M] | Chuck Jackson | 196? | 20.00 |
| ❑ GSS-1912 [R] | Chuck Jackson | 196? | 12.00 |

**MOTOWN**

| Number | Title (A Side/B Side) | Yr | NM |
|---|---|---|---|
| ❑ M-667 [M] | Chuck Jackson Arrives! | 1967 | 40.00 |
| ❑ MS-667 [S] | Chuck Jackson Arrives! | 1967 | 25.00 |
| ❑ MS-687 | Goin' Back to Chuck Jackson | 1969 | 25.00 |

**SCEPTER**

| Number | Title (A Side/B Side) | Yr | NM |
|---|---|---|---|
| ❑ 5100 | A Tribute to Burt Bacharach | 1972 | 15.00 |

**SPIN-O-RAMA**

| Number | Title (A Side/B Side) | Yr | NM |
|---|---|---|---|
| ❑ 123 [M] | Starring Chuck Jackson | 196? | 20.00 |
| ❑ S-123 [R] | Starring Chuck Jackson | 196? | 12.00 |

**STRAND**

| Number | Title (A Side/B Side) | Yr | NM |
|---|---|---|---|
| ❑ SL-1125 [M] | The Great Chuck Jackson | 196? | 25.00 |
| ❑ SLS-1125 [S] | The Great Chuck Jackson | 196? | 30.00 |

**UNITED ARTISTS**

| Number | Title (A Side/B Side) | Yr | NM |
|---|---|---|---|
| ❑ UA-LA499-E | The Very Best of Chuck Jackson | 1974 | 10.00 |

**V.I.P.**

| Number | Title (A Side/B Side) | Yr | NM |
|---|---|---|---|
| ❑ 403 | Teardrops Keep Fallin' on My Heart | 1970 | 40.00 |

**WAND**

| Number | Title (A Side/B Side) | Yr | NM |
|---|---|---|---|
| ❑ LP-650 [M] | I Don't Want to Cry | 1961 | 40.00 |
| ❑ LP-654 [M] | Any Day Now | 1962 | 40.00 |
| ❑ WD-655 [M] | Encore | 1963 | 40.00 |
| ❑ WD-658 [M] | Chuck Jackson On Tour | 1964 | 40.00 |
| ❑ WDM-667 [M] | Mr. Everything | 1965 | 30.00 |
| ❑ WDS-667 [S] | Mr. Everything | 1965 | 40.00 |
| ❑ WD-673 [M] | A Tribute to Rhythm and Blues | 1966 | 30.00 |
| ❑ WDS-673 [S] | A Tribute to Rhythm and Blues | 1966 | 40.00 |
| ❑ WD-676 [M] | A Tribute to Rhythm and Blues, Volume 2 | 1966 | 30.00 |
| ❑ WDS-676 [S] | A Tribute to Rhythm and Blues, Volume 2 | 1966 | 40.00 |
| ❑ WD-680 [M] | Dedicated to the King!! | 1966 | 40.00 |
| ❑ WDS-680 [S] | Dedicated to the King!! | 1966 | 50.00 |
| ❑ WD-683 [M] | Chuck Jackson's Greatest Hits | 1967 | 20.00 |
| ❑ WDS-683 [S] | Chuck Jackson's Greatest Hits | 1967 | 25.00 |

### JACKSON, CHUCK, AND MAXINE BROWN
Also see each artist's individual listings.

**WAND**

| Number | Title (A Side/B Side) | Yr | NM |
|---|---|---|---|
| ❑ WD-669 [M] | Say Something | 1965 | 30.00 |
| ❑ WDS-669 [S] | Say Something | 1965 | 40.00 |
| ❑ WD-678 [M] | Hold On, We're Coming | 1966 | 30.00 |
| ❑ WDS-678 [S] | Hold On, We're Coming | 1966 | 40.00 |

### JACKSON, CHUCK, AND TAMMI TERRELL
Also see each artist's individual listings.

**WAND**

| Number | Title (A Side/B Side) | Yr | NM |
|---|---|---|---|
| ❑ WD-682 [M] | The Early Show | 1967 | 30.00 |
| ❑ WDS-682 [S] | The Early Show | 1967 | 30.00 |

### JACKSON, DEON

**ATCO**

| Number | Title (A Side/B Side) | Yr | NM |
|---|---|---|---|
| ❑ 33-188 [M] | Love Makes the World Go Round | 1966 | 30.00 |
| ❑ SD 33-188 [S] | Love Makes the World Go Round | 1966 | 40.00 |

**COLLECTABLES**

| Number | Title (A Side/B Side) | Yr | NM |
|---|---|---|---|
| ❑ COL-5106 | Golden Classics | 198? | 10.00 |

### JACKSON, FRANZ

**PINNACLE**

| Number | Title (A Side/B Side) | Yr | NM |
|---|---|---|---|
| ❑ 102 [M] | No Saints | 1961 | 20.00 |
| ❑ S-104 [S] | Night at Red Arrow | 196? | 20.00 |
| ❑ 109 [M] | Franz Jackson | 1966 | 20.00 |



Except when noted otherwise, VG = 25% of NM, and VG+ = 50% of NM. (Example: VG = $2.00, VG+ = $4.00 and NM = $8.00.)

| Number | Title (A Side/B Side) | Yr | NM |
|---|---|---|---|
| **RIVERSIDE** | | | |
| ❑ RLP-406 [M] | Franz Jackson and the Original Jass All-Stars | 1962 | 30.00 |

## JACKSON, FRED

| Number | Title (A Side/B Side) | Yr | NM |
|---|---|---|---|
| **BLUE NOTE** | | | |
| ❑ BLP-4094 [M] | Hootin' 'N Tootin' | 1962 | 60.00 |
| *—With 61st St. address on label* | | | |
| ❑ BLP-4094 [M] | Hootin' 'N Tootin' | 1963 | 25.00 |
| *—With "New York, USA" address on label* | | | |
| ❑ BST-84094 [S] | Hootin' 'N Tootin' | 1962 | 80.00 |
| *—With 61st St. address on label* | | | |
| ❑ BST-84094 [S] | Hootin' 'N Tootin' | 1963 | 30.00 |
| *—With "New York, USA" address on label* | | | |
| ❑ BST-84094 [S] | Hootin' 'N Tootin' | 1967 | 20.00 |
| *—With "A Division of Liberty Records" on label* | | | |

## JACKSON, J.J.

| Number | Title (A Side/B Side) | Yr | NM |
|---|---|---|---|
| **CALLA** | | | |
| ❑ C-1101 [M] | But It's Alright/I Dig Girls | 1967 | 20.00 |
| ❑ CS-1101 [S] | But It's Alright/I Dig Girls | 1967 | 25.00 |
| **CONGRESS** | | | |
| ❑ CS-7000 | The Greatest Little Soul Band in the World | 1968 | 25.00 |
| **PERCEPTION** | | | |
| ❑ 3 | J.J. Jackson's Dilemma | 1970 | 15.00 |
| **WARNER BROS.** | | | |
| ❑ WS 1797 | The Great J.J. Jackson | 1969 | 20.00 |

## JACKSON, JOE

| Number | Title (A Side/B Side) | Yr | NM |
|---|---|---|---|
| **A&M** | | | |
| ❑ SP-3187 | Look Sharp! | 198? | 8.00 |
| *—Reissue of SP-4743* | | | |
| ❑ SP-3221 | I'm the Man | 198? | 8.00 |
| *—Reissue of SP-4794* | | | |
| ❑ SP-3241 | Beat Crazy | 198? | 8.00 |
| *—Reissue of SP-4837* | | | |
| ❑ SP-3271 | Joe Jackson's Jumpin' Jive | 198? | 8.00 |
| *—Reissue of SP-4871* | | | |
| ❑ SP-3286 | Body and Soul | 1986 | 8.00 |
| *—Reissue of SP-5000* | | | |
| ❑ SP-3666 [(2)] | Look Sharp! | 1979 | 20.00 |
| *—Two 10-inch records in gatefold sleeve with button* | | | |
| ❑ SP-3908 | Will Power | 1987 | 12.00 |
| ❑ SP-4743 | Look Sharp! | 1979 | 12.00 |
| ❑ SP-4794 | I'm the Man | 1979 | 10.00 |
| ❑ SP-4837 | Beat Crazy | 1980 | 10.00 |
| ❑ SP-4871 | Joe Jackson's Jumpin' Jive | 1981 | 10.00 |
| ❑ SP-4906 | Night and Day | 1982 | 10.00 |
| ❑ SP-4931 | Mike's Murder [Soundtrack] | 1983 | 12.00 |
| ❑ SP-5000 | Body and Soul | 1984 | 10.00 |
| ❑ SP-5249 | Blaze of Glory | 1989 | 10.00 |
| ❑ SP-6021 [(2)] | Big World | 1986 | 15.00 |
| ❑ SP-6706 [(2)] | Live: 1980-1986 | 1988 | 15.00 |
| ❑ R 101141 | Blaze of Glory | 1989 | 12.00 |
| *—BMG Direct Marketing edition* | | | |
| ❑ R 209597 [(2)] | Live 1980-1986 | 1987 | 15.00 |
| *—BMG Direct Marketing edition* | | | |
| ❑ R 244331 [(2)] | Big World | 1986 | 15.00 |
| *—RCA Music Service edition* | | | |
| **MOBILE FIDELITY** | | | |
| ❑ 1-080 | Night and Day | 1982 | 30.00 |
| *—Audiophile vinyl* | | | |

## JACKSON, LIL' SON

| Number | Title (A Side/B Side) | Yr | NM |
|---|---|---|---|
| **ARHOOLIE** | | | |
| ❑ 1004 [M] | Lil' Son Jackson | 1960 | 25.00 |
| **IMPERIAL** | | | |
| ❑ LP-9142 [M] | Rockin' and Rollin' | 1961 | 400.00 |

## JACKSON, MAHALIA

| Number | Title (A Side/B Side) | Yr | NM |
|---|---|---|---|
| **APOLLO** | | | |
| ❑ 201/202 [M] | Spirituals | 1954 | 30.00 |
| ❑ 482 [M] | No Matter How You Pray | 1959 | 25.00 |
| ❑ 499 [M] | Mahalia Jackson | 1962 | 25.00 |
| ❑ 1001/2 [M] | Command Performance | 1961 | 25.00 |
| **COLUMBIA** | | | |
| ❑ CL 644 [M] | Mahalia Jackson | 1955 | 40.00 |
| ❑ CL 702 [M] | Sweet Little Jesus Boy | 1955 | 40.00 |
| ❑ CL 899 [M] | Bless This House | 1956 | 30.00 |
| ❑ CL 1244 [M] | Newport 1958 | 1959 | 20.00 |
| ❑ CL 1343 [M] | That Great Gettin' Up Morning | 1959 | 20.00 |
| ❑ CL 1428 [M] | Come On Children, Let's Sing | 1960 | 20.00 |
| ❑ CL 1473 [M] | The Power and the Glory | 1960 | 20.00 |
| ❑ CL 1549 [M] | I Believe | 1960 | 15.00 |
| ❑ CL 1643 [M] | Every Time I Feel the Spirit | 1961 | 15.00 |
| ❑ CL 1726 [M] | Recorded in Europe During Her Latest Concert Tour | 1962 | 15.00 |
| ❑ CL 1824 [M] | Great Songs of Love and Faith | 1962 | 15.00 |
| ❑ CL 1903 [M] | Silent Night | 1962 | 15.00 |
| ❑ CL 1936 [M] | Make a Joyful Noise Unto the Lord | 1962 | 15.00 |
| ❑ CL 2004 [M] | Mahalia Jackson's Greatest Hits | 1963 | 12.00 |
| ❑ CL 2130 [M] | Let's Pray Together | 1964 | 12.00 |
| ❑ CL 2452 [M] | Mahalia Sings | 1966 | 12.00 |
| ❑ CL 2546 [M] | Garden of Prayer | 1967 | 15.00 |
| ❑ CL 2552 [10] | You'll Never Walk Alone | 1955 | 50.00 |

Michael Jackson, *Dangerous,* Epic E2 45400, 1991, 2 records, $15.

| Number | Title (A Side/B Side) | Yr | NM |
|---|---|---|---|
| ❑ CL 2605 [M] | My Faith | 1967 | 15.00 |
| ❑ CL 2690 [M] | Mahalia Jackson In Concert, Easter Sunday 1967 | 1967 | 15.00 |
| ❑ CS 8071 [S] | Newport 1958 | 1959 | 30.00 |
| ❑ CS 8153 [S] | That Great Gettin' Up Morning | 1959 | 25.00 |
| ❑ CS 8225 [S] | Come On Children, Let's Sing | 1960 | 25.00 |
| ❑ CS 8264 [S] | The Power and the Glory | 1960 | 25.00 |
| ❑ CS 8349 [S] | I Believe | 1960 | 20.00 |
| ❑ CS 8443 [S] | Every Time I Feel the Spirit | 1961 | 20.00 |
| ❑ CS 8526 [S] | Recorded in Europe During Her Latest Concert Tour | 1962 | 20.00 |
| ❑ CS 8624 [S] | Great Songs of Love and Faith | 1962 | 20.00 |
| ❑ CS 8703 [S] | Silent Night | 1962 | 20.00 |
| ❑ CS 8736 [S] | Make a Joyful Noise Unto the Lord | 1962 | 20.00 |
| ❑ CS 8759 [R] | Mahalia Jackson | 1963 | 12.00 |
| ❑ CS 8761 [R] | Bless This House | 1963 | 12.00 |
| ❑ PC 8761 | Bless This House | 198? | 8.00 |
| *—Budget-line reissue* | | | |
| ❑ CS 8804 [S] | Mahalia Jackson's Greatest Hits | 1963 | 15.00 |
| ❑ CS 8930 [S] | Let's Pray Together | 1964 | 15.00 |
| ❑ CS 9252 [S] | Mahalia Sings | 1966 | 15.00 |
| ❑ CS 9346 [S] | Garden of Prayer | 1967 | 12.00 |
| ❑ CS 9405 [S] | My Faith | 1967 | 12.00 |
| ❑ CS 9490 [S] | Mahalia Jackson In Concert, Easter Sunday 1967 | 1967 | 12.00 |
| ❑ CS 9659 | A Mighty Fortress | 1968 | 12.00 |
| ❑ CS 9686 | The Best-Loved Hymns of Dr. Martin Luther King Jr. | 1968 | 15.00 |
| ❑ PC 9686 | The Best-Loved Hymns of Dr. Martin Luther King Jr. | 198? | 8.00 |
| *—Budget-line reissue* | | | |
| ❑ CS 9727 | Christmas with Mahalia | 1968 | 12.00 |
| ❑ CS 9813 | Right Out of the Church | 1969 | 12.00 |
| ❑ CS 9950 | What the World Needs Now | 1970 | 12.00 |
| ❑ CG 30744 [(2)] | America's Favorite Hymns | 1971 | 15.00 |
| ❑ KG 31379 [(2)] | The Great Mahalia Jackson | 1972 | 15.00 |
| ❑ KC 34073 | How I Got Over | 1976 | 10.00 |
| ❑ PC 37710 | Mahalia Jackson's Greatest Hits | 198? | 8.00 |
| ❑ 3C 38304 | Silent Night | 1982 | 8.00 |
| *—Reissue* | | | |
| **COLUMBIA SPECIAL PRODUCTS** | | | |
| ❑ P2 13200 [(2)] | (HRB Music Proudly Presents) The Best of Mahalia Jackson: Hymns, Spirituals & Songs of Inspiration | 1976 | 15.00 |
| **FOLKWAYS** | | | |
| ❑ 31101 | I Sing Because I'm Happy, Volume 1 | 198? | 10.00 |
| ❑ 31102 | I Sing Because I'm Happy, Volume 2 | 198? | 10.00 |
| **GRAND AWARD** | | | |
| ❑ GA 265 SD | I Believe | 1966 | 15.00 |
| *—Reissue of 326* | | | |
| ❑ GA 33-326 [M] | Mahalia Jackson | 1955 | 30.00 |
| ❑ GA 33-390 [M] | Mahalia Jackson | 195? | 30.00 |
| **HARMONY** | | | |
| ❑ HS 11279 | You'll Never Walk Alone | 196? | 10.00 |
| ❑ HS 11372 | Abide with Me | 1970 | 10.00 |
| ❑ H 30019 | Sunrise, Sunset | 1970 | 10.00 |
| ❑ KH 31111 | Lord Don't Let Me Fall | 1972 | 10.00 |
| **KENWOOD** | | | |
| ❑ 474 | In the Upper Room | 196? | 15.00 |
| ❑ 479 | Just As I Am | 196? | 15.00 |
| ❑ 482 | No Matter How You Pray | 196? | 15.00 |
| ❑ 486 | Mahalia | 196? | 15.00 |
| ❑ 489 | Mahalia Jackson With the Greatest Spiritual Singers | 196? | 15.00 |
| ❑ 500 | The Best of Mahalia Jackson | 196? | 15.00 |
| ❑ 501 | I Lift My Voice | 196? | 15.00 |
| ❑ 502 | Sing Out | 196? | 15.00 |
| ❑ 1001/2 [(2)] | Command Performance | 196? | 20.00 |
| **PICKWICK** | | | |
| ❑ SPC-3510 | I Believe | 197? | 10.00 |
| **PRIORITY** | | | |
| ❑ PU 37710 | Mahalia Jackson's Greatest Hits | 1981 | 10.00 |

## JACKSON, MARY ANNE

| Number | Title (A Side/B Side) | Yr | NM |
|---|---|---|---|
| **HANOVER** | | | |
| ❑ HM-8009 [M] | The Wild Piano of Mary Anne Jackson | 1959 | 80.00 |

## JACKSON, MICHAEL Also see THE JACKSONS.

| Number | Title (A Side/B Side) | Yr | NM |
|---|---|---|---|
| **EPIC** | | | |
| ❑ FE 35745 | Off the Wall | 1979 | 8.00 |
| ❑ QE 38112 | Thriller | 1982 | 8.00 |
| ❑ 8E8 38867 [PD] | Thriller | 1983 | 20.00 |
| ❑ OE 40600 | Bad | 1987 | 8.00 |
| ❑ 9E9 44043 [PD] | Bad | 1987 | 12.00 |
| ❑ E2 45400 [(2)] | Dangerous | 1991 | 15.00 |

Wanda Jackson, *Wonderful Wanda,* Capitol T 1776, 1962, mono, $25.

| Number | Title (A Side/B Side) | Yr | NM |
|---|---|---|---|
| ❑ HE 47545 | Off the Wall | 1982 | 40.00 |
| *—Half-speed mastered edition* | | | |
| ❑ HE 48112 | Thriller | 1982 | 40.00 |
| *—Half-speed mastered edition* | | | |
| ❑ E3 59000 [(3)] | HIStory: Past, Present and Future — Book I | 1995 | 20.00 |
| *—Box set with 12x12 booklet* | | | |
| ❑ E2 68000 [(2)] | Blood on the Dance Floor: HIStory in the Mix | 1997 | 15.00 |
| ❑ E2 69400 [(2)] | Invincible | 2001 | 15.00 |
| **MOTOWN** | | | |
| ❑ M5-107V1 | Motown Superstar Series, Vol. 7 | 1981 | 8.00 |
| ❑ M5-130V1 | Got to Be There | 1981 | 10.00 |
| *—Reissue of Motown 747* | | | |
| ❑ M5-153V1 | Ben | 1981 | 10.00 |
| *—Reissue of Motown 755* | | | |
| ❑ M5-194V1 | The Best of Michael Jackson | 1981 | 10.00 |
| *—Reissue of Motown 851* | | | |
| ❑ M 747 | Got to Be There | 1972 | 15.00 |
| ❑ M 755 | Ben | 1972 | 15.00 |
| *—With only Michael Jackson on front cover* | | | |
| ❑ M 755 | Ben | 1972 | 60.00 |
| *—With Michael Jackson on top half of cover, rats on the bottom half* | | | |
| ❑ M 767 | Music and Me | 1973 | 15.00 |
| ❑ M6-825S | Forever, Michael | 1975 | 12.00 |
| ❑ M6-851S | The Best of Michael Jackson | 1975 | 12.00 |
| ❑ M8-956M1 | One Day in Your Life | 1981 | 10.00 |
| ❑ 6099 ML | Michael Jackson and The Jackson 5 — 14 Greatest Hits | 1984 | 10.00 |
| *—Picture disc packaged with one glove* | | | |
| ❑ 6101 ML | Farewell My Summer Love 1984 | 1984 | 10.00 |

## JACKSON, MICHAEL GREGORY

| Number | Title (A Side/B Side) | Yr | NM |
|---|---|---|---|
| **BIJA** | | | |
| ❑ 1000 | Clarity | 1976 | 25.00 |
| **IAI** | | | |
| ❑ 373857 | Karmonic Suite | 1978 | 20.00 |

## JACKSON, MILT

| Number | Title (A Side/B Side) | Yr | NM |
|---|---|---|---|
| **ABC IMPULSE!** | | | |
| ❑ AS-9189 | That's the Way It Is | 1969 | 20.00 |
| ❑ AS-9193 | Memphis Jackson | 1969 | 20.00 |
| **ATLANTIC** | | | |
| ❑ 1242 [M] | Ballads and Blues | 1956 | 40.00 |
| *—Black label* | | | |
| ❑ 1242 [M] | Ballads and Blues | 1961 | 20.00 |
| *—Multicolor label, white "fan" logo at right* | | | |
| ❑ 1269 [M] | Plenty, Plenty Soul | 1957 | 40.00 |
| *—Black label* | | | |
| ❑ 1269 [M] | Plenty, Plenty Soul | 1961 | 20.00 |
| *—Multicolor label, white "fan" logo at right* | | | |
| ❑ SD 1269 [S] | Plenty, Plenty Soul | 1959 | 40.00 |
| *—Green label* | | | |
| ❑ SD 1269 [S] | Plenty, Plenty Soul | 1961 | 20.00 |
| *—Multicolor label, white "fan" logo at right* | | | |
| ❑ 1294 [M] | Bags & Flutes | 1958 | 40.00 |
| *—Black label* | | | |
| ❑ 1294 [M] | Bags & Flutes | 1961 | 20.00 |
| *—Multicolor label, white "fan" logo at right* | | | |
| ❑ SD 1294 [S] | Bags & Flutes | 1959 | 40.00 |
| *—Green label* | | | |
| ❑ SD 1294 [S] | Bags & Flutes | 1961 | 20.00 |
| *—Multicolor label, white "fan" logo at right* | | | |
| ❑ 1316 [M] | Bean Bags | 1959 | 40.00 |
| *—Black label* | | | |
| ❑ 1316 [M] | Bean Bags | 1961 | 20.00 |
| *—Multicolor label, white "fan" logo at right* | | | |
| ❑ SD 1316 [S] | Bean Bags | 1959 | 40.00 |
| *—Green label* | | | |
| ❑ SD 1316 [S] | Bean Bags | 1961 | 20.00 |
| *—Multicolor label, white "fan" logo at right* | | | |
| ❑ 1342 [M] | Ballad Artistry | 1960 | 20.00 |
| *—Multicolor label, white "fan" logo at right* | | | |
| ❑ SD 1342 [S] | Ballad Artistry | 1960 | 25.00 |
| *—Multicolor label, white "fan" logo at right* | | | |
| ❑ SD 1417 [S] | Vibrations | 1964 | 20.00 |
| **BLUE NOTE** | | | |
| ❑ BLP-1509 [M] | Milt Jackson | 1956 | 100.00 |
| *—Regular version with Lexington Ave. address on label* | | | |
| ❑ BLP-1509 [M] | Milt Jackson | 1956 | 150.00 |
| *—"Deep groove" version (deep indentation under label on both sides)* | | | |
| ❑ BLP-1509 [M] | Milt Jackson | 1963 | 25.00 |
| *—With "New York, USA" address on label* | | | |
| ❑ BLP-5011 [10] | Wizard of the Vibes | 1952 | 300.00 |
| **DEE GEE** | | | |
| ❑ 1002 [10] | Milt Jackson | 1952 | 300.00 |
| **IMPULSE!** | | | |
| ❑ A-14 [M] | Statements | 1962 | 25.00 |
| ❑ AS-14 [S] | Statements | 1962 | 30.00 |
| ❑ A-70 [M] | Jazz n' Samba | 1964 | 25.00 |
| ❑ AS-70 [S] | Jazz n' Samba | 1964 | 30.00 |
| **LIMELIGHT** | | | |
| ❑ LM-82006 [M] | In a New Setting | 1964 | 20.00 |
| ❑ LM-82024 [M] | At the Museum of Modern Art | 1965 | 20.00 |
| ❑ LM-82045 [M] | Born Free | 1966 | 20.00 |
| ❑ LS-86006 [S] | In a New Setting | 1964 | 25.00 |
| ❑ LS-86024 [S] | At the Museum of Modern Art | 1965 | 25.00 |
| ❑ LS-86045 [S] | Born Free | 1966 | 25.00 |
| **PRESTIGE** | | | |
| ❑ PRLP-183 [10] | Milt Jackson Quintet | 1954 | 200.00 |
| ❑ PRLP-7003 [M] | Milt Jackson | 1955 | 120.00 |
| ❑ PRLP-7224 [M] | Soul Pioneers | 1962 | 40.00 |
| **RIVERSIDE** | | | |
| ❑ RLP-429 [M] | Big Bags | 1962 | 20.00 |
| ❑ RLP-446 [M] | Invitation | 1963 | 20.00 |
| ❑ RLP-478 [M] | For Someone I Love | 1966 | 20.00 |
| ❑ RLP-495 [M] | "Live" at the Village Gate | 1967 | 25.00 |
| ❑ RS-9429 [S] | Big Bags | 1962 | 25.00 |
| ❑ RS-9446 [S] | Invitation | 1963 | 25.00 |
| ❑ RS-9478 [S] | For Someone I Love | 1966 | 25.00 |
| ❑ RS-9495 [S] | "Live" at the Village Gate | 1967 | 20.00 |
| **SAVOY** | | | |
| ❑ MG-12042 [M] | Roll 'Em Bags | 1955 | 50.00 |
| ❑ MG-12046 [M] | Milt Jackson Quartette | 1955 | 50.00 |
| ❑ MG-12061 [M] | Meet Milt | 1956 | 50.00 |
| ❑ MG-12070 [M] | Jazz Skyline | 1956 | 50.00 |
| ❑ MG-12080 [M] | Jackson's Ville | 1956 | 50.00 |
| ❑ MG-15058 [10] | Milt Jackson | 1954 | 150.00 |
| **UNITED ARTISTS** | | | |
| ❑ UAL-4022 [M] | Bags' Opus | 1959 | 40.00 |
| ❑ UAS-5022 [S] | Bags' Opus | 1959 | 30.00 |

## JACKSON, MILT, AND JOHN COLTRANE
Also see each artist's individual listings.

| Number | Title (A Side/B Side) | Yr | NM |
|---|---|---|---|
| **ATLANTIC** | | | |
| ❑ 1368 [M] | Bags and Trane | 1961 | 30.00 |
| *—Multicolor label, white "fan" logo at right* | | | |
| ❑ 1368 [M] | Bags and Trane | 1963 | 20.00 |
| *—Multicolor label, black "fan" logo at right* | | | |
| ❑ SD 1368 [S] | Bags and Trane | 1961 | 40.00 |
| *—Multicolor label, white "fan" logo at right* | | | |
| ❑ SD 1368 [S] | Bags and Trane | 1963 | 25.00 |
| *—Multicolor label, black "fan" logo at right* | | | |

## JACKSON, MILT, AND WES MONTGOMERY
Also see each artist's individual listings.

| Number | Title (A Side/B Side) | Yr | NM |
|---|---|---|---|
| **RIVERSIDE** | | | |
| ❑ RLP-407 [M] | Bags Meets Wes | 1962 | 20.00 |
| ❑ RS-9407 [S] | Bags Meets Wes | 1962 | 25.00 |

## JACKSON, RONALD SHANNON

| Number | Title (A Side/B Side) | Yr | NM |
|---|---|---|---|
| **ABOUT TIME** | | | |
| ❑ AT-1003 | Eye on You | 1980 | 20.00 |
| **MOERS** | | | |
| ❑ 01081 | Street Priest | 1981 | 20.00 |
| ❑ 01086 | Nasty | 1981 | 20.00 |

## JACKSON, SAMMY

| Number | Title (A Side/B Side) | Yr | NM |
|---|---|---|---|
| **ARVEE** | | | |
| ❑ A-434 [M] | Ladies Man | 1962 | 50.00 |
| ❑ SA-434 [S] | Ladies Man | 1962 | 60.00 |

## JACKSON, SHOT

| Number | Title (A Side/B Side) | Yr | NM |
|---|---|---|---|
| **CUMBERLAND** | | | |
| ❑ MGC-29513 [M] | Bluegrass Dobro | 1965 | 20.00 |
| ❑ SRC-69513 [S] | Bluegrass Dobro | 1965 | 25.00 |
| **STARDAY** | | | |
| ❑ SLP-230 [M] | The Singing Strings of Steel Guitar and Dobro | 1962 | 30.00 |

## JACKSON, STONEWALL

| Number | Title (A Side/B Side) | Yr | NM |
|---|---|---|---|
| **COLUMBIA** | | | |
| ❑ CL 1391 [M] | The Dynamic Stonewall Jackson | 1959 | 25.00 |
| ❑ CL 1770 [M] | Sadness in a Song | 1962 | 20.00 |
| ❑ CL 2059 [M] | I Love a Song | 1963 | 20.00 |
| ❑ CL 2278 [M] | Trouble & Me | 1964 | 15.00 |
| ❑ CL 2377 [M] | Stonewall Jackson's Greatest Hits | 1965 | 15.00 |
| ❑ CL 2509 [M] | All's Fair in Love 'n' War | 1966 | 15.00 |
| ❑ CL 2674 [M] | Help Stamp Out Loneliness | 1967 | 25.00 |
| ❑ CL 2762 [M] | Stonewall Jackson Country | 1967 | 25.00 |
| ❑ CS 8186 [S] | The Dynamic Stonewall Jackson | 1959 | 30.00 |
| ❑ CS 8570 [S] | Sadness in a Song | 1962 | 25.00 |
| ❑ CS 8859 [S] | I Love a Song | 1963 | 25.00 |
| ❑ CS 9078 [S] | Trouble & Me | 1964 | 20.00 |
| ❑ CS 9177 [S] | Stonewall Jackson's Greatest Hits | 1965 | 20.00 |
| ❑ CS 9309 [S] | All's Fair in Love 'n' War | 1966 | 20.00 |
| ❑ CS 9474 [S] | Help Stamp Out Loneliness | 1967 | 20.00 |
| ❑ CS 9562 [S] | Stonewall Jackson Country | 1967 | 20.00 |

| Number | Title (A Side/B Side) | Yr | NM |
|---|---|---|---|
| ❑ CS 9669 | Nothing Takes the Place of Loving You | 1968 | 20.00 |
| ❑ CS 9708 | The Great Old Songs | 1968 | 20.00 |
| ❑ CS 9754 | The Old Country Church | 1969 | 25.00 |
| ❑ CS 9880 | Tribute to Hank Williams | 1969 | 20.00 |
| ❑ C 30254 | The Real Thing | 1971 | 15.00 |

HARMONY

| Number | Title (A Side/B Side) | Yr | NM |
|---|---|---|---|
| ❑ HS 11187 | The Exciting Stonewall Jackson | 196? | 12.00 |

**JACKSON, TOMMY**

DECCA

| Number | Title (A Side/B Side) | Yr | NM |
|---|---|---|---|
| ❑ DL 8950 [M] | Square Dances Without Calls | 1959 | 20.00 |
| ❑ DL 78950 [S] | Square Dances Without Calls | 1959 | 25.00 |

DOT

| Number | Title (A Side/B Side) | Yr | NM |
|---|---|---|---|
| ❑ DLP-3015 [M] | Popular Square Dance Music | 1957 | 30.00 |
| ❑ DLP-3085 [M] | Square Dance Tonight! | 1958 | 25.00 |
| ❑ DLP-3163 [M] | Do-Si-Do | 1959 | 20.00 |
| ❑ DLP-3330 [M] | Square Dance Festival, Vol. 1 | 1960 | 20.00 |
| ❑ DLP-3331 [M] | Square Dance Festival, Vol. 2 | 1960 | 20.00 |
| ❑ DLP-3454 [M] | Swing Your Partner | 1962 | 15.00 |
| ❑ DLP-3471 [M] | Greatest Bluegrass Hits | 1962 | 20.00 |
| ❑ DLP-3532 [M] | Square Dance Festival, Vol. 3 | 1961 | 20.00 |
| ❑ DLP-3580 [M] | Square Dances | 1963 | 15.00 |
| ❑ DLP-25380 [S] | Square Dances | 1963 | 20.00 |
| ❑ DLP-25454 [S] | Swing Your Partner | 1962 | 20.00 |
| ❑ DLP-25471 [S] | Greatest Bluegrass Hits | 1962 | 25.00 |

MERCURY

| Number | Title (A Side/B Side) | Yr | NM |
|---|---|---|---|
| ❑ MG-20346 [M] | Square Dance Fiddle Favorites | 1958 | 25.00 |

**JACKSON, WALTER**

CHI-SOUND

| Number | Title (A Side/B Side) | Yr | NM |
|---|---|---|---|
| ❑ CS-LA656-G | Feeling Good | 1976 | 12.00 |
| ❑ CS-LA733-G | I Want to Come Back As A Song | 1977 | 12.00 |
| ❑ CS-LA844-G | Good to See You | 1978 | 12.00 |

COLUMBIA

| Number | Title (A Side/B Side) | Yr | NM |
|---|---|---|---|
| ❑ FC 37132 | Tell Me Where It Hurts | 1981 | 10.00 |

EPIC

| Number | Title (A Side/B Side) | Yr | NM |
|---|---|---|---|
| ❑ E 34657 | Greatest Hits | 1977 | 10.00 |
| ❑ PE 40434 | Greatest Hits | 1987 | 8.00 |

OKEH

| Number | Title (A Side/B Side) | Yr | NM |
|---|---|---|---|
| ❑ OKM 12107 [M] | It's All Over | 1965 | 25.00 |
| ❑ OKM 12108 [M] | Welcome Home | 1966 | 25.00 |
| ❑ OKM 12120 [M] | Speak Her Name | 1967 | 25.00 |
| ❑ OKS 14107 [S] | It's All Over | 1965 | 30.00 |
| ❑ OKS 14108 [S] | Welcome Home | 1966 | 30.00 |
| ❑ OKS 14120 [S] | Speak Her Name | 1967 | 30.00 |
| ❑ OKS 14128 | Walter Jackson's Greatest Hits | 1969 | 15.00 |

**JACKSON, WANDA**

CAPITOL

| Number | Title (A Side/B Side) | Yr | NM |
|---|---|---|---|
| ❑ ST-129 | The Many Moods of Wanda Jackson | 1969 | 15.00 |
| ❑ ST-238 | The Happy Side of Wanda Jackson | 1969 | 15.00 |
| ❑ ST 8-0345 | Wanda Jackson In Person | 1970 | 20.00 |
| *—Capitol Record Club edition* | | | |
| ❑ ST-345 | Wanda Jackson In Person | 1970 | 15.00 |
| ❑ ST-434 | Wanda Jackson Country! | 1970 | 15.00 |
| ❑ ST-554 | A Woman Lives for Love | 1970 | 15.00 |
| ❑ ST-669 | I've Gotta Sing! | 1971 | 15.00 |
| ❑ T 1041 [M] | Wanda Jackson | 1958 | 300.00 |
| *—Black colorband label, Capitol logo at left* | | | |
| ❑ T 1041 [M] | Wanda Jackson | 1962 | 100.00 |
| *—Black colorband label, Capitol logo at top* | | | |
| ❑ T 1384 [M] | Rockin' with Wanda | 1960 | 400.00 |
| *—Black colorband label, Capitol logo at left* | | | |
| ❑ T 1384 [M] | Rockin' with Wanda | 1962 | 250.00 |
| *—Gold "Star Line" label* | | | |
| ❑ T 1384 [M] | Rockin' with Wanda | 1963 | 150.00 |
| *—Black "Star Line" label* | | | |
| ❑ ST 1511 [S] | There's a Party Goin' On | 1961 | 400.00 |
| *—Black colorband label, Capitol logo at left* | | | |
| ❑ T 1511 [M] | There's a Party Goin' On | 1961 | 250.00 |
| *—Black colorband label, Capitol logo at left* | | | |
| ❑ ST 1596 [S] | Right or Wrong | 1961 | 50.00 |
| *—Black colorband label, Capitol logo at left* | | | |
| ❑ ST 1596 [S] | Right or Wrong | 1962 | 25.00 |
| *—Black colorband label, Capitol logo at top* | | | |
| ❑ T 1596 [M] | Right or Wrong | 1961 | 40.00 |
| *—Black colorband label, Capitol logo at left* | | | |
| ❑ T 1596 [M] | Right or Wrong | 1962 | 20.00 |
| *—Black colorband label, Capitol logo at top* | | | |
| ❑ ST 1776 [S] | Wonderful Wanda | 1962 | 30.00 |
| ❑ T 1776 [M] | Wonderful Wanda | 1962 | 25.00 |
| ❑ ST 1911 [S] | Love Me Forever | 1963 | 30.00 |
| ❑ T 1911 [M] | Love Me Forever | 1963 | 25.00 |
| ❑ ST 2030 [S] | Two Sides of Wanda | 1964 | 30.00 |
| ❑ T 2030 [M] | Two Sides of Wanda | 1964 | 25.00 |
| ❑ ST 2306 [S] | Blues in My Heart | 1965 | 30.00 |
| ❑ T 2306 [M] | Blues in My Heart | 1965 | 25.00 |
| ❑ ST 2438 [S] | Wanda Jackson Sings Country Songs | 1965 | 30.00 |
| ❑ T 2438 [M] | Wanda Jackson Sings Country Songs | 1965 | 25.00 |
| ❑ ST 2606 [S] | Wanda Jackson Salutes the Country Music Hall of Fame | 1966 | 20.00 |

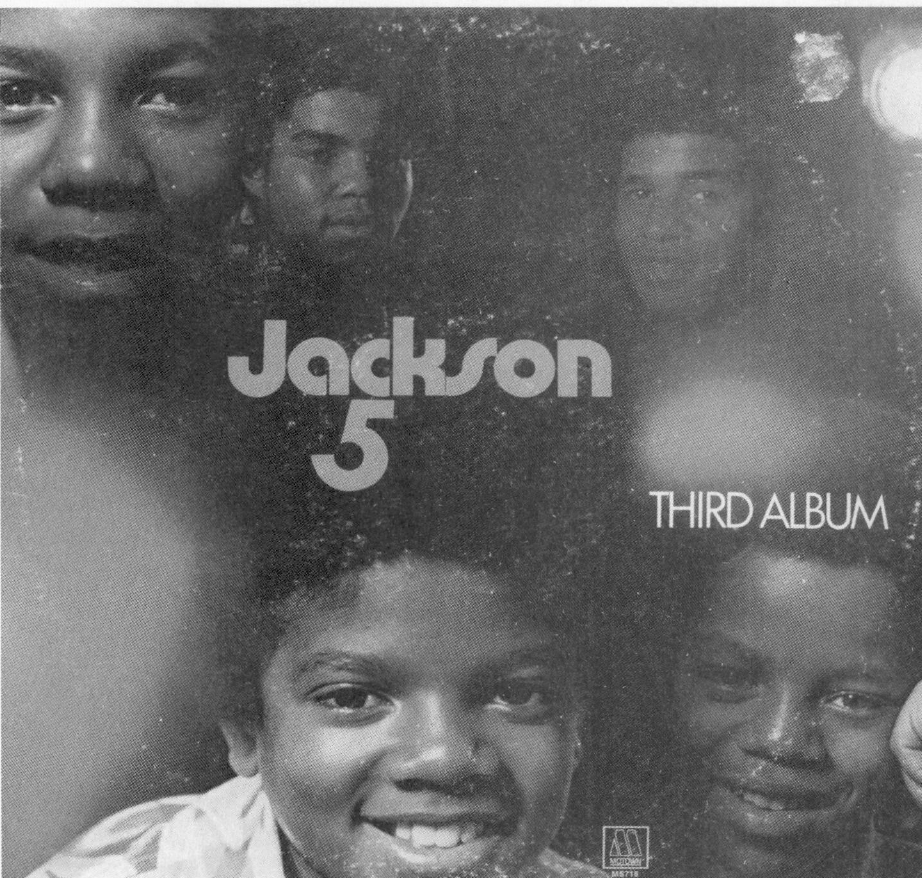


The Jackson Five, *Third Album,* Motown MS 718, 1970, $15.

| Number | Title (A Side/B Side) | Yr | NM |
|---|---|---|---|
| ❑ T 2606 [M] | Wanda Jackson Salutes the Country Music Hall of Fame | 1966 | 15.00 |
| ❑ ST 2704 [S] | Reckless Love Affair | 1967 | 15.00 |
| ❑ T 2704 [M] | Reckless Love Affair | 1967 | 20.00 |
| ❑ ST 2812 [S] | You'll Always Have My Love | 1967 | 15.00 |
| ❑ T 2812 [M] | You'll Always Have My Love | 1967 | 20.00 |
| ❑ ST 2883 [S] | The Best of Wanda Jackson | 1968 | 15.00 |
| ❑ T 2883 [M] | The Best of Wanda Jackson | 1968 | 40.00 |
| *—Red and white "Starline" label* | | | |
| ❑ ST 2976 | Cream of the Crop | 1968 | 15.00 |
| ❑ ST-11023 | Praise the Lord | 1972 | 15.00 |
| ❑ ST-11096 | I Wouldn't Want You Any Other Way | 1972 | 15.00 |
| ❑ ST-11161 | Country Keepsakes | 1973 | 15.00 |

DECCA

| Number | Title (A Side/B Side) | Yr | NM |
|---|---|---|---|
| ❑ DL 4224 [M] | Lovin' Country Style | 1962 | 50.00 |

GUSTO

| Number | Title (A Side/B Side) | Yr | NM |
|---|---|---|---|
| ❑ GT 0057 | Greatest Hits | 1980 | 10.00 |

HILLTOP

| Number | Title (A Side/B Side) | Yr | NM |
|---|---|---|---|
| ❑ 6058 | Please Help Me I'm Falling | 1968 | 10.00 |
| ❑ 6074 | Leave My Baby Alone | 1969 | 12.00 |
| ❑ 6116 | We'll Sing in the Sunshine | 1972 | 12.00 |
| ❑ 6123 | By the Time I Get to Phoenix | 1973 | 10.00 |
| ❑ 6182 | Tears at the Grand Ole Opry | 1974 | 10.00 |

MYRRH

| Number | Title (A Side/B Side) | Yr | NM |
|---|---|---|---|
| ❑ MSB-6513 | When It's Time to Fall in Love Again | 1974 | 12.00 |
| ❑ MSB-6533 | Now I Have Everything | 1975 | 12.00 |
| ❑ MSB-6556 | Make Me Like a Child Again | 1976 | 12.00 |

PICKWICK

| Number | Title (A Side/B Side) | Yr | NM |
|---|---|---|---|
| ❑ PTP-2053 [(2)] | Wanda Jackson | 1974 | 12.00 |

SYMPATHY FOR THE RECORD INDUSTRY

| Number | Title (A Side/B Side) | Yr | NM |
|---|---|---|---|
| ❑ SFTRI-724 | Heart Trouble | 2003 | 12.00 |

VARRICK

| Number | Title (A Side/B Side) | Yr | NM |
|---|---|---|---|
| ❑ VR-025 | Rock 'n' Roll Away Your Blues | 1987 | 12.00 |

VOCALION

| Number | Title (A Side/B Side) | Yr | NM |
|---|---|---|---|
| ❑ VL 73861 [R] | Nobody's Darlin' | 1968 | 12.00 |

WORD

| Number | Title (A Side/B Side) | Yr | NM |
|---|---|---|---|
| ❑ WST-8614 | Country Gospel | 1973 | 12.00 |
| ❑ WST-8781 | Closer to Jesus | 1977 | 12.00 |

**JACKSON, WILLIS**

CADET

| Number | Title (A Side/B Side) | Yr | NM |
|---|---|---|---|
| ❑ LPS-763 [S] | Smoking with Willis | 1966 | 20.00 |

MOODSVILLE

| Number | Title (A Side/B Side) | Yr | NM |
|---|---|---|---|
| ❑ MVLP-17 [M] | In My Solitude | 1961 | 50.00 |
| *—Green label* | | | |
| ❑ MVLP-17 [M] | In My Solitude | 1965 | 25.00 |
| *—Blue label, trident logo at right* | | | |

PRESTIGE

| Number | Title (A Side/B Side) | Yr | NM |
|---|---|---|---|
| ❑ PRLP-7162 [M] | Please, Mr. Jackson | 1959 | 50.00 |
| ❑ PRLP-7172 [M] | Cool Gator | 1959 | 50.00 |
| ❑ PRLP-7183 [M] | Blue Gator | 1960 | 50.00 |
| ❑ PRLP-7196 [M] | Really Groovin' | 1961 | 50.00 |
| ❑ PRLP-7211 [M] | Cookin' Sherry | 1961 | 30.00 |
| ❑ PRST-7211 [S] | Cookin' Sherry | 1961 | 40.00 |
| ❑ PRLP-7232 [M] | Thunderbird | 1962 | 30.00 |
| ❑ PRST-7232 [S] | Thunderbird | 1962 | 40.00 |
| ❑ PRLP-7260 [M] | Bossa Nova Plus | 1962 | 30.00 |
| ❑ PRST-7260 [S] | Bossa Nova Plus | 1962 | 40.00 |
| ❑ PRLP-7264 [M] | Neapolitan Nights | 1963 | 30.00 |
| ❑ PRST-7264 [S] | Neapolitan Nights | 1963 | 40.00 |
| ❑ PRLP-7273 [M] | Loose... | 1963 | 30.00 |
| ❑ PRST-7273 [S] | Loose... | 1963 | 40.00 |
| ❑ PRLP-7285 [M] | Grease 'n' Gravy | 1963 | 30.00 |
| ❑ PRST-7285 [S] | Grease 'n' Gravy | 1963 | 40.00 |
| ❑ PRLP-7296 [M] | The Good Life | 1964 | 30.00 |
| ❑ PRST-7296 [S] | The Good Life | 1964 | 40.00 |
| ❑ PRLP-7317 [M] | More Gravy | 1964 | 30.00 |
| ❑ PRST-7317 [S] | More Gravy | 1964 | 40.00 |
| ❑ PRLP-7329 [M] | Boss Shoutin' | 1964 | 25.00 |
| ❑ PRST-7329 [S] | Boss Shoutin' | 1964 | 30.00 |
| ❑ PRLP-7348 [M] | Live! Jackson's Action | 1965 | 25.00 |
| ❑ PRST-7348 [S] | Live! Jackson's Action | 1965 | 30.00 |
| ❑ PRLP-7364 [M] | Together Again | 1965 | 25.00 |
| ❑ PRST-7364 [S] | Together Again | 1965 | 30.00 |
| ❑ PRLP-7380 [M] | Live! Action | 1965 | 25.00 |
| ❑ PRST-7380 [S] | Live! Action | 1965 | 30.00 |
| ❑ PRLP-7396 [M] | Soul Night — Live! | 1965 | 25.00 |
| ❑ PRST-7396 [S] | Soul Night — Live! | 1965 | 30.00 |
| ❑ PRLP-7412 [M] | Tell It... | 1966 | 20.00 |
| ❑ PRST-7412 [S] | Tell It... | 1966 | 25.00 |
| ❑ PRLP-7428 [M] | Together Again...Again | 1966 | 20.00 |
| ❑ PRST-7428 [S] | Together Again...Again | 1966 | 25.00 |
| ❑ PRST-7551 | Soul Grabber | 1968 | 20.00 |
| ❑ PRST-7571 | Star Bag | 1968 | 20.00 |

| Number | Title (A Side/B Side) | Yr | NM |
|---|---|---|---|
| ❑ PRST-7602 | Swivel Hips | 1969 | 20.00 |
| ❑ PRST-7648 | Gator's Groove | 1969 | 20.00 |
| ❑ PRST-7783 | Please Mr. Jackson | 1970 | 20.00 |
| ❑ PRST-7830 | Keep On a-Blowing | 1971 | 20.00 |
| **VERVE** | | | |
| ❑ V6-8589 [S] | 'Gator Tails | 1964 | 20.00 |

### JACKSON HEIGHTS

| Number | Title (A Side/B Side) | Yr | NM |
|---|---|---|---|
| **MERCURY** | | | |
| ❑ SR-61331 | King Progress | 1970 | 25.00 |
| **VERVE** | | | |
| ❑ V6-5089 | Jackson Heights | 1973 | 20.00 |

### JACKSONS, THE
Includes records as "The Jackson Five." Also see MICHAEL JACKSON.

| Number | Title (A Side/B Side) | Yr | NM |
|---|---|---|---|
| **EPIC** | | | |
| ❑ PE 34229 | The Jacksons | 1976 | 10.00 |
| *—Orange label* | | | |
| ❑ PE 34229 | The Jacksons | 198? | 6.00 |
| *—Budget-line reissue with bar code and dark blue label* | | | |
| ❑ JE 34835 | Goin' Places | 1977 | 10.00 |
| *—Orange label* | | | |
| ❑ PE 34835 | Goin' Places | 198? | 6.00 |
| *—Budget-line reissue* | | | |
| ❑ JE 35552 | Destiny | 1978 | 10.00 |
| *—Orange label* | | | |
| ❑ JE 35552 | Destiny | 1979 | 8.00 |
| *—Dark blue label* | | | |
| ❑ FE 36424 | Triumph | 1980 | 8.00 |
| ❑ KE2 37545 [(2)] | Jacksons Live | 1981 | 12.00 |
| ❑ QE 38946 | Victory | 1984 | 8.00 |
| ❑ 8E8 39576 [PD] | Victory | 1984 | 15.00 |
| ❑ OE 40911 | 2300 Jackson Street | 1989 | 8.00 |
| ❑ HE 46424 | Triumph | 1982 | 60.00 |
| *—Half-speed mastered edition* | | | |
| **MOTOWN** | | | |
| ❑ M5-112V1 | Motown Superstar Series, Vol. 12 | 1981 | 10.00 |
| ❑ M5-129V1 | Diana Ross Presents the Jackson Five | 1981 | 8.00 |
| ❑ M5-152V1 | ABC | 1981 | 8.00 |
| ❑ M5-157V1 | Third Album | 1981 | 8.00 |
| ❑ M5-201V1 | Jackson 5 Greatest Hits | 1981 | 8.00 |
| ❑ MS 700 | Diana Ross Presents the Jackson 5 | 1969 | 25.00 |
| ❑ MS 709 | ABC | 1970 | 25.00 |
| ❑ MS 713 | Christmas Album | 1970 | 25.00 |
| ❑ MS 718 | Third Album | 1970 | 15.00 |
| ❑ M-735 | Maybe Tomorrow | 1971 | 15.00 |
| ❑ M-741 | Jackson 5 Greatest Hits | 1971 | 15.00 |
| ❑ M-742 | Goin' Back to Indiana | 1971 | 15.00 |
| ❑ M-750 | Lookin' Through the Windows | 1972 | 15.00 |
| ❑ M-761 | Skywriter | 1973 | 12.00 |
| ❑ M6-780 | Dancing Machine | 1974 | 12.00 |
| ❑ M6-783 | Get It Together | 1973 | 12.00 |
| ❑ M6-829 | Moving Violation | 1975 | 12.00 |
| ❑ M6-865 | Joyful Jukebox Music | 1976 | 12.00 |
| ❑ M7-868 [(3)] | Anthology | 1976 | 20.00 |
| ❑ 37463 1294-1 [DJ] | Soulsation! | 1995 | 20.00 |
| *—Vinyl is promo only; 4-song sampler from box set* | | | |
| ❑ 5228 ML | Maybe Tomorrow | 1982 | 8.00 |
| ❑ 5250 ML | Christmas Album | 1982 | 8.00 |
| *—Reissue of Motown 713* | | | |

### JACOBI, LOU

| Number | Title (A Side/B Side) | Yr | NM |
|---|---|---|---|
| **CAPITOL** | | | |
| ❑ ST 2596 [S] | Al Tijuana and His Jewish Brass | 1966 | 20.00 |
| ❑ T 2596 [M] | Al Tijuana and His Jewish Brass | 1966 | 15.00 |

### JACOBS, DICK

| Number | Title (A Side/B Side) | Yr | NM |
|---|---|---|---|
| **CORAL** | | | |
| ❑ CRL 57381 [M] | The Electro-Sonic Orchestra Presenting a New Concept in Sound | 1958 | 20.00 |
| ❑ CRL 757381 [S] | The Electro-Sonic Orchestra Presenting a New Concept in Sound | 1958 | 30.00 |

### JACOBS, FREDDIE

| Number | Title (A Side/B Side) | Yr | NM |
|---|---|---|---|
| **WESTMINSTER** | | | |
| ❑ WP-6087 [M] | Swingin' Folk Tunes | 195? | 30.00 |

### JACOBS, HANK

| Number | Title (A Side/B Side) | Yr | NM |
|---|---|---|---|
| **SUE** | | | |
| ❑ LP-1023 [M] | So Far Away | 1964 | 80.00 |

### JACOBY, DON

| Number | Title (A Side/B Side) | Yr | NM |
|---|---|---|---|
| **DECCA** | | | |
| ❑ DL 74241 [S] | The Swinging Big Sound | 1963 | 20.00 |

### JACQUET, ILLINOIS

| Number | Title (A Side/B Side) | Yr | NM |
|---|---|---|---|
| **ALADDIN** | | | |
| ❑ LP-708 [10] | Illinois Jacquet and His Tenor Sax | 1954 | 500.00 |
| ❑ LP-803 [M] | Illinois Jacquet and His Tenor Sax | 1956 | 200.00 |
| **APOLLO** | | | |
| ❑ LP-104 [10] | Illinois Jacquet Jam Session | 1951 | 600.00 |
| **ARGO** | | | |
| ❑ LP-722 [M] | The Message | 1963 | 40.00 |
| ❑ LPS-722 [S] | The Message | 1963 | 50.00 |
| ❑ LP-735 [M] | Desert Winds | 1964 | 40.00 |
| ❑ LPS-735 [S] | Desert Winds | 1964 | 50.00 |
| ❑ LP-746 [M] | Bosses of the Ballad | 1964 | 40.00 |
| ❑ LPS-746 [S] | Illinois Jacquet Plays Cole Porter | 1964 | 50.00 |
| **CADET** | | | |
| ❑ CA-722 [S] | The Message | 197? | 20.00 |
| *—Yellow and red label* | | | |
| ❑ LPS-722 [S] | The Message | 1966 | 30.00 |
| *—Reissue of Argo 722; fading blue label* | | | |
| ❑ LPS-735 [S] | Desert Winds | 1966 | 25.00 |
| *—Reissue of Argo 735; fading blue label* | | | |
| ❑ LPS-746 [S] | Bosses of the Ballad | 1966 | 25.00 |
| *—Reissue of Argo 746; fading blue label* | | | |
| ❑ LP-754 [M] | Spectrum | 1965 | 40.00 |
| ❑ LPS-754 [S] | Spectrum | 1965 | 50.00 |
| ❑ LP-773 [M] | Go Power! | 1966 | 40.00 |
| ❑ LPS-773 [S] | Go Power! | 1966 | 50.00 |
| **CLEF** | | | |
| ❑ MGC-112 [10] | Illinois Jacquet Collates | 1953 | 300.00 |
| ❑ MGC-129 [10] | Illinois Jacquet Collates #2 | 1953 | 300.00 |
| ❑ MGC-167 [10] | Jazz by Jacquet | 1954 | 300.00 |
| ❑ MGC-622 [M] | Jazz Moods | 1955 | 200.00 |
| ❑ MGC-676 [M] | Illinois Jacquet Septet | 1955 | 200.00 |
| ❑ MGC-700 [M] | Jazz Moods by Illinois Jacquet | 1956 | 150.00 |
| ❑ MGC-701 [M] | Port of Rico | 1956 | 150.00 |
| ❑ MGC-702 [M] | Groovin' with Jacquet | 1956 | 200.00 |
| ❑ MGC-750 [M] | Swing's the Thing | 1956 | 150.00 |
| **EPIC** | | | |
| ❑ LA 16033 [M] | Illinois Jacquet | 1963 | 40.00 |
| ❑ BA 17033 [S] | Illinois Jacquet | 1963 | 50.00 |
| ❑ BA 17033 [S] | Illinois Jacquet | 199? | 25.00 |
| *—Classic Records reissue on audiophile vinyl* | | | |
| **GROOVE NOTE** | | | |
| ❑ 2003 [(2)] | Birthday Party | 1999 | 50.00 |
| *—Audiophile vinyl; one record has the entire album, the other has two tracks at 45 rpm* | | | |
| **IMPERIAL** | | | |
| ❑ LP-9184 [M] | Flying Home | 1962 | 30.00 |
| ❑ LP-12184 [S] | Flying Home | 1962 | 40.00 |
| **MERCURY** | | | |
| ❑ MGC-112 [10] | Illinois Jacquet Collates | 1952 | 500.00 |
| **MOSAIC** | | | |
| ❑ MQ6-165 [(6)] | The Complete Illinois Jacquet Sessions 1945-50 | 199? | 100.00 |
| **PRESTIGE** | | | |
| ❑ PRST-7575 | Bottoms Up! | 1968 | 40.00 |
| ❑ PRST-7597 | The King! | 1968 | 40.00 |
| ❑ PRST-7629 | The Soul Explosion | 1969 | 40.00 |
| ❑ PRST-7731 | The Blues — That's Me | 1969 | 40.00 |
| **RCA VICTOR** | | | |
| ❑ LPM-3236 [10] | Black Velvet | 1954 | 500.00 |
| **ROULETTE** | | | |
| ❑ R-52035 [M] | Illinois Jacquet Flies Again | 1959 | 70.00 |
| ❑ SR-52035 [S] | Illinois Jacquet Flies Again | 1959 | 60.00 |
| **SAVOY** | | | |
| ❑ MG-15024 [10] | Tenor Sax | 1953 | 400.00 |
| **VERVE** | | | |
| ❑ MGV-8023 [M] | Swing's the Thing | 1957 | 60.00 |
| *—Reissue of Clef 750* | | | |
| ❑ V-8023 [M] | Swing's the Thing | 1961 | 25.00 |
| ❑ MGV-8061 [M] | Illinois Jacquet and His Orchestra | 1957 | 60.00 |
| *—Reissue of Clef 676* | | | |
| ❑ V-8061 [M] | Illinois Jacquet and His Orchestra | 1961 | 25.00 |
| ❑ MGV-8084 [M] | Jazz Moods by Illinois Jacquet | 1957 | 60.00 |
| *—Reissue of Clef 700* | | | |
| ❑ V-8084 [M] | Jazz Moods by Illinois Jacquet | 1961 | 25.00 |
| ❑ MGV-8085 [M] | Port of Rico | 1957 | 60.00 |
| *—Reissue of Clef 701* | | | |
| ❑ V-8085 [M] | Port of Rico | 1961 | 25.00 |
| ❑ MGV-8086 [M] | Groovin' with Jacquet | 1957 | 60.00 |
| *—Reissue of Clef 702* | | | |
| ❑ V-8086 [M] | Groovin' with Jacquet | 1961 | 25.00 |

### JACQUET, ILLINOIS, AND BEN WEBSTER

| Number | Title (A Side/B Side) | Yr | NM |
|---|---|---|---|
| **CLEF** | | | |
| ❑ MGC-680 [M] | "The Kid" and "The Brute" | 1955 | 200.00 |
| **VERVE** | | | |
| ❑ MGV-8065 [M] | "The Kid" and "The Brute" | 1957 | 60.00 |
| *—Reissue of Clef 680* | | | |
| ❑ V-8065 [M] | "The Kid" and "The Brute" | 1961 | 20.00 |

### JACQUET, ILLINOIS, AND LESTER YOUNG

| Number | Title (A Side/B Side) | Yr | NM |
|---|---|---|---|
| **ALADDIN** | | | |
| ❑ LP-701 [10] | Battle of the Saxes | 1953 | 1200. |

### JACQUET, RUSSELL

| Number | Title (A Side/B Side) | Yr | NM |
|---|---|---|---|
| **KING** | | | |
| ❑ 295-81 [10] | Russell Jacquet and His All Stars | 1954 | 250.00 |

### JADE

| Number | Title (A Side/B Side) | Yr | NM |
|---|---|---|---|
| **GENERAL AMERICAN** | | | |
| ❑ 11311 | The Faces of Jade | 1968 | 80.00 |

### JADE, FAINE

| Number | Title (A Side/B Side) | Yr | NM |
|---|---|---|---|
| **RSVP** | | | |
| ❑ 8002 | Introspection: A Faine Jade Recital | 1968 | 400.00 |

### JADES, THE

| Number | Title (A Side/B Side) | Yr | NM |
|---|---|---|---|
| **JARRETT** | | | |
| ❑ 21517 [M] | Live at the Disco a-Go-Go | 1965 | 120.00 |

### JAG PANZER

| Number | Title (A Side/B Side) | Yr | NM |
|---|---|---|---|
| **AZRA IRON WORKS** | | | |
| ❑ 1001 [PD] | Ample Destruction | 1985 | 25.00 |
| *—Allegedly, 250 were pressed as picture discs* | | | |

### JAGGERZ, THE

| Number | Title (A Side/B Side) | Yr | NM |
|---|---|---|---|
| **GAMBLE** | | | |
| ❑ GS-5006 | Introducing the Jaggerz | 1969 | 20.00 |
| **KAMA SUTRA** | | | |
| ❑ KSBS-2017 | We Went to Different Schools Together | 1970 | 15.00 |
| **WOODEN NICKEL** | | | |
| ❑ BWL1-0772 | Come Again | 1975 | 12.00 |

### JAIM

| Number | Title (A Side/B Side) | Yr | NM |
|---|---|---|---|
| **ETHEREAL** | | | |
| ❑ 1001 | Prophecy Fulfilled | 1970 | 50.00 |

### JALOPY FIVE, THE

| Number | Title (A Side/B Side) | Yr | NM |
|---|---|---|---|
| **MODERN SOUND** | | | |
| ❑ M-561 [M] | I Love That West Coast Sound | 1965 | 50.00 |
| ❑ MS-561 [S] | I Love That West Coast Sound | 1965 | 50.00 |

### JAM, THE

| Number | Title (A Side/B Side) | Yr | NM |
|---|---|---|---|
| **POLYDOR** | | | |
| ❑ PX1-503 [EP] | The Jam | 1982 | 12.00 |
| ❑ PX1-506 [EP] | The Bitterest Pill | 1982 | 12.00 |
| ❑ PD1-6110 | In the City | 1977 | 25.00 |
| ❑ PD1-6129 | This Is the Modern World | 1978 | 20.00 |
| ❑ PD1-6188 | All Mod Cons | 1979 | 15.00 |
| ❑ PD1-6249 | Setting Sons | 1980 | 15.00 |
| ❑ PD1-6315 | Sound Affects | 1981 | 15.00 |
| ❑ PD1-6349 | The Gift | 1982 | 12.00 |
| ❑ PD1-6365 | Dig the New Breed | 1982 | 10.00 |
| ❑ 810751-1 [EP] | Beat Surrender | 1982 | 10.00 |
| ❑ 815537-1 [(2)] | Snap! | 1983 | 15.00 |
| ❑ 817124-1 | In the City | 198? | 10.00 |
| *—Reissue* | | | |
| ❑ 823281-1 | This Is the Modern World | 198? | 10.00 |
| *—Reissue* | | | |

### JAMAL, AHMAD

| Number | Title (A Side/B Side) | Yr | NM |
|---|---|---|---|
| **ARGO** | | | |
| ❑ LP-602 [M] | Chamber Music of the New Jazz | 1956 | 30.00 |
| *—Dark green label, gold or silver print* | | | |
| ❑ LP-602 [M] | Chamber Music of the New Jazz | 1956 | 50.00 |
| *—With "Creative Hi-Fidelity Modern Music" on cover; "ship" label; reissue of Parrot LP* | | | |
| ❑ LP-610 [M] | Count 'Em 88 | 1957 | 30.00 |
| ❑ LP-628 [M] | But Not for Me/Ahmad Jamal at the Pershing | 1958 | 30.00 |
| ❑ LPS-628 [S] | But Not for Me/Ahmad Jamal at the Pershing | 1958 | 40.00 |
| ❑ LP-636 [M] | Ahmad Jamal, Volume IV | 1958 | 30.00 |
| ❑ LPS-636 [S] | Ahmad Jamal, Volume IV | 1958 | 40.00 |
| ❑ LP-646 [M] | Jamal at the Penthouse | 1959 | 30.00 |
| ❑ LPS-646 [S] | Jamal at the Penthouse | 1959 | 40.00 |
| ❑ LP-662 [M] | Happy Moods | 1960 | 20.00 |
| ❑ LPS-662 [S] | Happy Moods | 1960 | 25.00 |
| ❑ LP-667 [M] | Ahmad Jamal at the Pershing Volume 2 | 1961 | 20.00 |
| ❑ LPS-667 [S] | Ahmad Jamal at the Pershing Volume 2 | 1961 | 25.00 |
| ❑ LP-673 [M] | Listen to Ahmad Jamal | 1961 | 20.00 |
| ❑ LPS-673 [S] | Listen to Ahmad Jamal | 1961 | 25.00 |
| ❑ LP-685 [M] | Alhambra | 1961 | 20.00 |
| ❑ LPS-685 [S] | Alhambra | 1961 | 25.00 |
| ❑ LP-691 [M] | All of You | 1962 | 20.00 |
| ❑ LPS-691 [S] | All of You | 1962 | 25.00 |
| ❑ LP-703 [M] | Ahmad Jamal at the Blackhawk | 1962 | 20.00 |
| ❑ LPS-703 [S] | Ahmad Jamal at the Blackhawk | 1962 | 25.00 |
| ❑ LP-712 [M] | Macanudo | 1963 | 20.00 |
| ❑ LPS-712 [S] | Macanudo | 1963 | 25.00 |
| ❑ LP-719 [M] | Poin'-ci-an'a | 1963 | 20.00 |
| ❑ LPS-719 [S] | Poin'-ci-an'a | 1963 | 25.00 |
| ❑ LP-733 [M] | "Naked City" Theme | 1964 | 20.00 |
| ❑ LPS-733 [S] | "Naked City" Theme | 1964 | 25.00 |

| Number | Title (A Side/B Side) | Yr | NM |
|---|---|---|---|
| ❑ LP-751 [M] | The Roar of the Greasepaint | 1965 | 20.00 |
| ❑ LPS-751 [S] | The Roar of the Greasepaint | 1965 | 25.00 |
| ❑ LP-758 [M] | Extensions | 1965 | 20.00 |
| ❑ LPS-758 [S] | Extensions | 1965 | 25.00 |
| ❑ LP-2638 [(2)M] | Portfolio of Ahmad Jamal | 1959 | 40.00 |
| *—Textured cover with raised image of Jamal; limited, numbered edition* | | | |
| ❑ LPS-2638 [(2)S] | Portfolio of Ahmad Jamal | 1959 | 50.00 |
| **CADET** | | | |
| ❑ LPS-764 [S] | Rhapsody | 1966 | 20.00 |
| ❑ LPS-777 [S] | Heat Wave | 1966 | 20.00 |
| *—Original with fading blue label* | | | |
| ❑ LPS-777 [S] | Heat Wave | 1977 | 12.00 |
| *—Reissue, "a division of All Platinum Record Group" on back cover* | | | |
| ❑ LPS-786 [S] | Standard Eyes | 1967 | 20.00 |
| ❑ LP-792 [M] | Cry Young | 1967 | 20.00 |
| ❑ LPS-2638 [(2)S] | Portfolio of Ahmad Jamal | 1966 | 20.00 |
| *—Cadet issues generally did not have embossed covers* | | | |
| **EPIC** | | | |
| ❑ BN 627 [R] | Ahmad Jamal Trio | 196? | 20.00 |
| ❑ BN 634 [S] | The Piano Scene of Ahmad Jamal | 1959 | 20.00 |
| ❑ LN 3212 [M] | Ahmad Jamal Trio | 1956 | 50.00 |
| *—Yellow label with lines around rim* | | | |
| ❑ LN 3212 [M] | Ahmad Jamal Trio | 1963 | 25.00 |
| *—Yellow label, no lines around rim* | | | |
| ❑ LN 3631 [M] | The Piano Scene of Ahmad Jamal | 1959 | 30.00 |
| **PARROT** | | | |
| ❑ 55-245/6 [M] | Ahmad Jamal Plays | 1955 | 1500. |
| *—VG value 500; VG+ value 1000* | | | |

### JAMES, BOB

| Number | Title (A Side/B Side) | Yr | NM |
|---|---|---|---|
| **ESP-DISK'** | | | |
| ❑ 1009 [M] | Explosions | 1965 | 40.00 |
| ❑ S-1009 [S] | Explosions | 1965 | 50.00 |
| **MERCURY** | | | |
| ❑ MG-20768 [M] | Bold Conceptions | 1963 | 40.00 |
| ❑ SR-60768 [S] | Bold Conceptions | 1963 | 50.00 |
| **TAPPAN ZEE** | | | |
| ❑ HC 45594 | Touchdown | 1982 | 30.00 |
| *—Half-speed mastered edition* | | | |
| ❑ HC 47495 | Sign of the Times | 1982 | 30.00 |
| *—Half-speed mastered edition* | | | |

### JAMES, BOB, AND EARL KLUGH

| Number | Title (A Side/B Side) | Yr | NM |
|---|---|---|---|
| **MOBILE FIDELITY** | | | |
| ❑ 1-124 | Two of a Kind | 1984 | 40.00 |
| *—"Original Master Recording" banner across top of front cover* | | | |
| **TAPPAN ZEE** | | | |
| ❑ HC 46241 | One on One | 198? | 30.00 |
| *—Half-speed mastered edition* | | | |

### JAMES, DENNIS

| Number | Title (A Side/B Side) | Yr | NM |
|---|---|---|---|
| **KAPP** | | | |
| ❑ KL-1009 [M] | Let's All Sing a Song for Christmas | 1955 | 30.00 |

### JAMES, ELMORE

| Number | Title (A Side/B Side) | Yr | NM |
|---|---|---|---|
| **BELL** | | | |
| ❑ 6037 | Elmore James | 1969 | 25.00 |
| **CHESS** | | | |
| ❑ LP-1537 | Whose Muddy Shoes | 1969 | 25.00 |
| **COLLECTABLES** | | | |
| ❑ COL-5112 | Golden Classics | 198? | 12.00 |
| ❑ COL-5184 | The Complete Fire and Enjoy Sessions, Part 1 | 198? | 10.00 |
| ❑ COL-5185 | The Complete Fire and Enjoy Sessions, Part 2 | 198? | 10.00 |
| ❑ COL-5186 | The Complete Fire and Enjoy Sessions, Part 3 | 198? | 10.00 |
| ❑ COL-5187 | The Complete Fire and Enjoy Sessions, Part 4 | 198? | 10.00 |
| **CROWN** | | | |
| ❑ CLP-5168 [M] | Blues After Hours | 1961 | 250.00 |
| *—Black label, silver "Crown"* | | | |
| ❑ CLP-5168 [M] | Blues After Hours | 1962 | 50.00 |
| *—Gray label* | | | |
| **INTERMEDIA** | | | |
| ❑ QS-5034 | Red Hot Blues | 198? | 10.00 |
| **KENT** | | | |
| ❑ KST-522 [R] | Original Folk Blues | 1964 | 25.00 |
| ❑ KLP-5022 [M] | Original Folk Blues | 1964 | 40.00 |
| ❑ KLP-9001 | Anthology of the Blues Legend | 196? | 25.00 |
| ❑ KLP-9010 | The Resurrection of Elmore James | 196? | 25.00 |
| **SPHERE SOUND** | | | |
| ❑ SR-7002 [M] | The Sky Is Crying | 1965 | 180.00 |
| ❑ SSR-7002 [R] | The Sky Is Crying | 1965 | 120.00 |
| ❑ SR-7008 [M] | I Need You | 1966 | 150.00 |
| ❑ SSR-7008 [R] | I Need You | 1966 | 120.00 |
| **UP FRONT** | | | |
| ❑ UP-122 | The Great Elmore James | 1970 | 12.00 |

### JAMES, ETTA

| Number | Title (A Side/B Side) | Yr | NM |
|---|---|---|---|
| **ARGO** | | | |
| ❑ LP-4003 [M] | At Last! | 1961 | 40.00 |
| ❑ LPS-4003 [S] | At Last! | 1961 | 60.00 |
| ❑ LP-4011 [M] | The Second Time Around | 1961 | 30.00 |
| ❑ LPS-4011 [S] | The Second Time Around | 1961 | 40.00 |
| ❑ LP-4013 [M] | Etta James | 1962 | 30.00 |
| ❑ LPS-4013 [P] | Etta James | 1962 | 40.00 |
| *—Two duets with Harvey Fuqua are rechanneled* | | | |
| ❑ LP-4018 [M] | Etta James Sings for Lovers | 1962 | 30.00 |
| ❑ LPS-4018 [S] | Etta James Sings for Lovers | 1962 | 40.00 |
| ❑ LP-4025 [M] | Etta James Top Ten | 1963 | 30.00 |
| ❑ LPS-4025 [S] | Etta James Top Ten | 1963 | 40.00 |
| ❑ LP-4032 [M] | Etta James Rocks the House | 1964 | 100.00 |
| ❑ LPS-4032 [S] | Etta James Rocks the House | 1964 | 150.00 |
| ❑ LP-4040 [M] | The Queen of Soul | 1965 | 30.00 |
| ❑ LPS-4040 [S] | The Queen of Soul | 1965 | 40.00 |
| **CADET** | | | |
| ❑ LP-802 [M] | Tell Mama | 1968 | 25.00 |
| ❑ LPS-802 [S] | Tell Mama | 1968 | 20.00 |
| ❑ LPS-832 | Etta James Sings Funk | 1969 | 20.00 |
| ❑ LPS-847 | Losers Weepers | 1970 | 15.00 |
| ❑ LP-4003 [M] | At Last! | 1966 | 12.00 |
| ❑ LPS-4003 [S] | At Last! | 1966 | 15.00 |
| ❑ LP-4011 [M] | The Second Time Around | 1966 | 12.00 |
| ❑ LPS-4011 [S] | The Second Time Around | 1966 | 15.00 |
| ❑ LP-4013 [M] | Etta James | 1966 | 12.00 |
| ❑ LPS-4013 [S] | Etta James | 1966 | 15.00 |
| ❑ LP-4018 [M] | Etta James Sings for Lovers | 1966 | 12.00 |
| ❑ LPS-4018 [S] | Etta James Sings for Lovers | 1966 | 15.00 |
| ❑ LP-4025 [M] | Etta James Top Ten | 1966 | 12.00 |
| ❑ LPS-4025 [S] | Etta James Top Ten | 1966 | 15.00 |
| ❑ LP-4040 [M] | The Queen of Soul | 1966 | 12.00 |
| ❑ LPS-4040 [S] | The Queen of Soul | 1966 | 15.00 |
| ❑ LP-4055 [M] | Call My Name | 1967 | 15.00 |
| ❑ LPS-4055 [S] | Call My Name | 1967 | 20.00 |
| **CHESS** | | | |
| ❑ CH2-6028 [(2)] | The Sweetest Peaches | 1989 | 12.00 |
| ❑ CH-9110 | Her Greatest Sides, Vol. 1 | 1984 | 10.00 |
| ❑ CH-9184 | Etta James Rocks the House | 1986 | 8.00 |
| *—Reissue* | | | |
| ❑ CH-9266 | At Last! | 1987 | 8.00 |
| *—Reissue* | | | |
| ❑ CH-9269 | Tell Mama | 1987 | 8.00 |
| *—Reissue* | | | |
| ❑ CH-9287 | The Second Time Around | 1989 | 8.00 |
| *—Reissue* | | | |
| ❑ ACH-19003 | Etta Is Betta Than Evvah! | 1976 | 15.00 |
| ❑ CH-50042 | Etta James | 1973 | 15.00 |
| ❑ 2CH-60004 [(2)] | Peaches | 1971 | 20.00 |
| ❑ CH-60029 | Come a Little Closer | 1974 | 15.00 |
| ❑ CH-91509 | Come a Little Closer | 198? | 8.00 |
| *—Reissue* | | | |
| **CROWN** | | | |
| ❑ CST-360 [R] | Etta James | 1963 | 20.00 |
| *—With Etta smiling on cover* | | | |
| ❑ CST-360 [R] | Etta James | 1963 | 20.00 |
| *—With Etta somber on cover* | | | |
| ❑ CLP-5209 [M] | Miss Etta James | 1961 | 100.00 |
| *—First edition, with framed picture on cover* | | | |
| ❑ CLP-5209 [M] | Miss Etta James | 1962 | 60.00 |
| *—Second edition, all-white cover with "Miss Etta James"* | | | |
| ❑ CLP-5234 [M] | The Best of Etta James | 1962 | 60.00 |
| *—Black label* | | | |
| ❑ CLP-5234 [M] | The Best of Etta James | 1963 | 30.00 |
| *—Gray label* | | | |
| ❑ CLP-5250 [M] | Twist with Etta James | 1962 | 60.00 |
| *—Black label* | | | |
| ❑ CLP-5250 [M] | Twist with Etta James | 1963 | 30.00 |
| *—Gray label* | | | |
| ❑ CLP-5360 [M] | Etta James | 1963 | 30.00 |
| *—With Etta smiling on cover* | | | |
| ❑ CLP-5360 [M] | Etta James | 1963 | 30.00 |
| *—With Etta somber on cover* | | | |
| **INTERMEDIA** | | | |
| ❑ QS-5014 | Etta, Red Hot 'N' Live! | 198? | 10.00 |
| **ISLAND** | | | |
| ❑ 91018 | Seven Year Itch | 1988 | 10.00 |
| ❑ 842926-1 | Sticking to My Guns | 1990 | 12.00 |
| **KENT** | | | |
| ❑ KST-500 [R] | Miss Etta James | 1964 | 25.00 |
| *—Black vinyl* | | | |
| ❑ KST-500 [R] | Miss Etta James | 1964 | 80.00 |
| *—Red vinyl* | | | |
| ❑ KLP-5000 [M] | Miss Etta James | 1964 | 30.00 |
| **UNITED** | | | |
| ❑ US 7712 | Etta James Sings | 197? | 10.00 |
| **WARNER BROS.** | | | |
| ❑ BSK 3156 | Deep in the Night | 1978 | 12.00 |

### JAMES, HARRY

On items with asterisks (*), at least one track has FRANK SINATRA as lead vocalist.

| Number | Title (A Side/B Side) | Yr | NM |
|---|---|---|---|
| **CAPITOL** | | | |
| ❑ W 654 [M] | Harry James in Hi-Fi | 1955 | 30.00 |
| ❑ W 712 [M] | More Harry James in Hi-Fi | 1956 | 30.00 |
| ❑ T 874 [M] | Wild About Harry | 1957 | 30.00 |
| ❑ T 1037 [M] | The New James | 1958 | 30.00 |
| ❑ T 1093 [M] | Harry's Choice | 1958 | 30.00 |
| ❑ T 1515 [M] | The Hits of Harry James | 1961 | 20.00 |
| *—Black colorband label, logo at left* | | | |
| **COLUMBIA** | | | |
| ❑ CL 522 [M] | One Night Stand | 1953 | 40.00 |
| *—Maroon label, gold print* | | | |
| ❑ GL 522 [M] | One Night Stand | 1953 | 50.00 |
| *—Black label, silver print* | | | |
| ❑ CL 553 [M] | Trumpet After Midnight | 1954 | 40.00 |
| *—Maroon label, gold print* | | | |
| ❑ CL 562 [M] | Dancing in Person with Harry James at the Hollywood Palladium | 1954 | 40.00 |
| *—Maroon label, gold print* | | | |
| ❑ CL 581 [M] | Soft Lights, Sweet Trumpet | 1954 | 40.00 |
| *—Maroon label, gold print* | | | |
| ❑ CL 615 [M] | Juke Box Jamboree | 1955 | 40.00 |
| *—Maroon label, gold print* | | | |
| ❑ CL 655 [M] | *All Time Favorites | 1955 | 40.00 |
| *—Maroon label, gold print* | | | |
| ❑ CL 669 [M] | Jazz Session | 1955 | 40.00 |
| ❑ CL 2527 [10] | The Man with the Horn | 1955 | 50.00 |
| ❑ CL 2630 [M] | *Harry James' Greatest Hits | 1967 | 20.00 |
| ❑ CL 6009 [10] | *All Time Favorites | 1949 | 50.00 |
| ❑ CL 6044 [10] | Trumpet Time | 1950 | 50.00 |
| ❑ CL 6088 [10] | Dance Parade | 1950 | 50.00 |
| ❑ CL 6138 [10] | Your Dance Date | 1951 | 50.00 |
| ❑ CL 6207 [10] | Soft Lights, Sweet Trumpet | 1952 | 50.00 |
| **LONGINES SYMPHONETTE** | | | |
| ❑ LS-217 [(5)] | Harry James Dance Band Spectacular | 196? | 30.00 |
| **MGM** | | | |
| ❑ E-3778 [M] | Harry James and His New Swingin' Band | 1959 | 20.00 |
| ❑ SE-3778 [S] | Harry James and His New Swingin' Band | 1959 | 25.00 |
| ❑ E-3848 [M] | Harry James Today | 1960 | 20.00 |
| ❑ SE-3848 [S] | Harry James Today | 1960 | 25.00 |
| ❑ E-4003 [M] | Requests on the Road | 1961 | 20.00 |
| ❑ SE-4003 [S] | Requests on the Road | 1961 | 25.00 |
| ❑ SE-4058 [S] | The Solid Gold Trumpet | 1962 | 20.00 |
| ❑ SE-4137 [S] | Double Dixie | 1963 | 20.00 |

### JAMES, JIMMY, AND THE VAGABONDS

| Number | Title (A Side/B Side) | Yr | NM |
|---|---|---|---|
| **ATCO** | | | |
| ❑ 33-222 [M] | The New Religion | 1967 | 20.00 |
| ❑ SD 33-222 [S] | The New Religion | 1967 | 20.00 |
| **PYE** | | | |
| ❑ 12111 | You Don't Stand a Chance If You Can't Dance | 1975 | 10.00 |

### JAMES, JONI

| Number | Title (A Side/B Side) | Yr | NM |
|---|---|---|---|
| **MGM** | | | |
| ❑ E-222 [10] | Let There Be Love | 1953 | 200.00 |
| ❑ E-234 [10] | Award Winning Album | 1954 | 200.00 |
| ❑ E-272 [10] | Little Girl Blue | 1955 | 200.00 |
| ❑ E-3240 [M] | When I Fall in Love | 1955 | 80.00 |
| *—Yellow label* | | | |
| ❑ E-3240 [M] | When I Fall in Love | 1960 | 40.00 |
| *—Black label* | | | |
| ❑ E-3328 [M] | In the Still of the Night | 1956 | 80.00 |
| *—Yellow label* | | | |
| ❑ E-3328 [M] | In the Still of the Night | 1960 | 40.00 |
| *—Black label* | | | |
| ❑ E-3346 [M] | Award Winning Album | 1956 | 80.00 |
| *—Yellow label* | | | |
| ❑ E-3346 [M] | Award Winning Album | 1960 | 40.00 |
| *—Black label* | | | |
| ❑ E-3347 [M] | Little Girl Blue | 1956 | 80.00 |
| *—Yellow label* | | | |
| ❑ E-3347 [M] | Little Girl Blue | 1960 | 40.00 |
| *—Black label* | | | |
| ❑ E-3348 [M] | Let There Be Love | 1956 | 80.00 |
| *—Yellow label* | | | |
| ❑ E-3348 [M] | Let There Be Love | 1960 | 40.00 |
| *—Black label* | | | |
| ❑ E-3449 [M] | Songs by Victor Young and Frank Loesser | 1956 | 80.00 |
| *—Yellow label* | | | |
| ❑ E-3449 [M] | Songs by Victor Young and Frank Loesser | 1960 | 40.00 |
| *—Black label* | | | |
| ❑ E-3468 [M] | Merry Christmas from Joni | 1956 | 120.00 |
| *—Yellow label original* | | | |
| ❑ E-3468 [M] | Merry Christmas from Joni | 1960 | 60.00 |
| *—Black label reissue* | | | |
| ❑ E-3528 [M] | Give Us This Day | 1957 | 80.00 |
| *—Yellow label* | | | |
| ❑ E-3528 [M] | Give Us This Day | 1960 | 40.00 |
| *—Black label* | | | |
| ❑ E-3533 [M] | Songs by Jerome Kern and Harry Warren | 1957 | 80.00 |
| *—Yellow label* | | | |
| ❑ E-3533 [M] | Songs by Jerome Kern and Harry Warren | 1960 | 40.00 |
| *—Black label* | | | |
| ❑ E-3602 [M] | Among My Souvenirs | 1958 | 80.00 |
| *—Yellow label* | | | |

Joni James, *Folk Songs by Joni James,* MGM E 3958, 1961, mono, $50.

| Number | Title (A Side/B Side) | Yr | NM |
|---|---|---|---|
| ❑ E-3602 [M] | Among My Souvenirs | 1960 | 40.00 |
| *—Black label* | | | |
| ❑ E-3623 [M] | Ti Voglio Bene | 1958 | 80.00 |
| *—Yellow label* | | | |
| ❑ E-3623 [M] | Ti Voglio Bene | 1960 | 40.00 |
| *—Black label* | | | |
| ❑ E-3706 [M] | Award Winning Album, Volume 2 | 1958 | 80.00 |
| *—Yellow label* | | | |
| ❑ E-3706 [M] | Award Winning Album, Volume 2 | 1960 | 40.00 |
| *—Black label* | | | |
| ❑ E-3718 [M] | Je T'aime (I Love You) | 1958 | 80.00 |
| *—Yellow label* | | | |
| ❑ E-3718 [M] | Je T'aime (I Love You) | 1960 | 40.00 |
| *—Black label* | | | |
| ❑ SE-3718 [S] | Je T'aime (I Love You) | 1958 | 120.00 |
| *—Yellow label* | | | |
| ❑ SE-3718 [S] | Je T'aime (I Love You) | 1960 | 50.00 |
| *—Black label* | | | |
| ❑ E-3739 [M] | Songs of Hank Williams | 1959 | 80.00 |
| *—Yellow label* | | | |
| ❑ E-3739 [M] | Songs of Hank Williams | 1960 | 40.00 |
| *—Black label* | | | |
| ❑ SE-3739 [S] | Songs of Hank Williams | 1959 | 120.00 |
| *—Yellow label* | | | |
| ❑ SE-3739 [S] | Songs of Hank Williams | 1960 | 50.00 |
| *—Black label* | | | |
| ❑ E-3749 [M] | Irish Favorites | 1959 | 80.00 |
| *—Yellow label* | | | |
| ❑ E-3749 [M] | Irish Favorites | 1960 | 40.00 |
| *—Black label* | | | |
| ❑ SE-3749 [S] | Irish Favorites | 1959 | 120.00 |
| *—Yellow label* | | | |
| ❑ SE-3749 [S] | Irish Favorites | 1960 | 50.00 |
| *—Black label* | | | |
| ❑ E-3755 [M] | 100 Strings and Joni | 1959 | 80.00 |
| *—Yellow label* | | | |
| ❑ E-3755 [M] | 100 Strings and Joni | 1960 | 40.00 |
| *—Black label* | | | |
| ❑ SE-3755 [S] | 100 Strings and Joni | 1959 | 120.00 |
| *—Yellow label* | | | |
| ❑ SE-3755 [S] | 100 Strings and Joni | 1960 | 50.00 |
| *—Black label* | | | |
| ❑ E-3772 [M] | Joni James Swings Sweet | 1959 | 60.00 |
| ❑ SE-3772 [S] | Joni James Swings Sweet | 1959 | 80.00 |
| ❑ E-3800 [M] | Joni James at Carnegie Hall | 1959 | 60.00 |
| ❑ SE-3800 [S] | Joni James at Carnegie Hall | 1959 | 80.00 |
| ❑ E-3837 [M] | I'm in the Mood for Love | 1960 | 60.00 |
| ❑ SE-3837 [S] | I'm in the Mood for Love | 1960 | 80.00 |

| Number | Title (A Side/B Side) | Yr | NM |
|---|---|---|---|
| ❑ E-3839 [M] | 100 Strings and Joni On Broadway | 1960 | 60.00 |
| ❑ SE-3839 [S] | 100 Strings and Joni On Broadway | 1960 | 70.00 |
| ❑ E-3840 [M] | 100 Strings and Joni In Hollywood | 1960 | 60.00 |
| ❑ SE-3840 [S] | 100 Strings and Joni In Hollywood | 1960 | 70.00 |
| ❑ E-3885 [M] | More Joni Hits | 1960 | 50.00 |
| ❑ SE-3885 [S] | More Joni Hits | 1960 | 60.00 |
| ❑ E-3892 [M] | 100 Voices, 100 Strings | 1960 | 50.00 |
| ❑ SE-3892 [S] | 100 Voices, 100 Strings | 1960 | 60.00 |
| ❑ E-3958 [M] | Folk Songs by Joni James | 1961 | 50.00 |
| ❑ SE-3958 [S] | Folk Songs by Joni James | 1961 | 60.00 |
| ❑ E-3987 [M] | The Mood Is Swinging | 1961 | 50.00 |
| ❑ SE-3987 [S] | The Mood Is Swinging | 1961 | 60.00 |
| ❑ E-3990 [M] | The Mood Is Romance | 1961 | 50.00 |
| ❑ SE-3990 [S] | The Mood Is Romance | 1961 | 60.00 |
| ❑ E-3991 [M] | The Mood Is Blue | 1961 | 50.00 |
| ❑ SE-3991 [S] | The Mood Is Blue | 1961 | 60.00 |
| ❑ E-4008 [M] | After Hours | 1962 | 50.00 |
| ❑ SE-4008 [S] | After Hours | 1962 | 60.00 |
| ❑ E-4053 [M] | I Feel a Song Comin' On | 1962 | 50.00 |
| ❑ SE-4053 [S] | I Feel a Song Comin' On | 1962 | 60.00 |
| ❑ E-4054 [M] | I'm Your Girl | 1962 | 50.00 |
| ❑ SE-4054 [S] | I'm Your Girl | 1962 | 60.00 |
| ❑ E-4101 [M] | Country Girl Style | 1962 | 50.00 |
| ❑ SE-4101 [S] | Country Girl Style | 1962 | 60.00 |
| ❑ E-4151 [M] | The Very Best of Joni James | 1963 | 40.00 |
| ❑ SE-4151 [S] | The Very Best of Joni James | 1963 | 50.00 |
| ❑ E-4158 [M] | Something for the Boys | 1963 | 40.00 |
| ❑ SE-4158 [S] | Something for the Boys | 1963 | 50.00 |
| ❑ E-4182 [M] | Three O'Clock in the Morning | 1963 | 40.00 |
| ❑ SE-4182 [S] | Three O'Clock in the Morning | 1963 | 50.00 |
| ❑ E-4200 [M] | My Favorite Things | 1963 | 40.00 |
| ❑ SE-4200 [S] | My Favorite Things | 1963 | 50.00 |
| ❑ E-4208 [M] | Italianissime! | 1963 | 40.00 |
| ❑ SE-4208 [S] | Italianissime! | 1963 | 50.00 |
| ❑ E-4248 [M] | Put On a Happy Face | 1964 | 40.00 |
| ❑ SE-4248 [S] | Put On a Happy Face | 1964 | 50.00 |
| ❑ E-4255 [M] | Joni James Sings the Gershwins | 1964 | 40.00 |
| ❑ SE-4255 [S] | Joni James Sings the Gershwins | 1964 | 50.00 |
| ❑ E-4263 [M] | Beyond the Reef | 1964 | 40.00 |
| ❑ SE-4263 [S] | Beyond the Reef | 1964 | 50.00 |
| ❑ E-4286 [M] | Bossa Nova Style | 1965 | 40.00 |
| ❑ SE-4286 [S] | Bossa Nova Style | 1965 | 50.00 |

| Number | Title (A Side/B Side) | Yr | NM |
|---|---|---|---|
| **JAMES, LEONARD** | | | |
| DECCA | | | |
| ❑ DL 8772 [M] | Boppin' and a-Strollin' | 1958 | 50.00 |
| **JAMES, SKIP** | | | |
| VANGUARD | | | |
| ❑ VRS-9219 [M] | Skip James Today! | 1966 | 30.00 |
| ❑ VSD-79219 [S] | Skip James Today! | 1966 | 25.00 |
| ❑ VSD-79273 | Devil Got My Woman | 1968 | 25.00 |
| **JAMES, SONNY** | | | |
| ABC | | | |
| ❑ AC-30027 | The ABC Collection | 1976 | 12.00 |
| CAPITOL | | | |
| ❑ ST-111 | Born to Be with You | 1968 | 15.00 |
| ❑ SKAO-144 | The Best of Sonny James Vol. 2 | 1969 | 15.00 |
| ❑ ST 8-0193 | Only the Lonely | 1969 | 20.00 |
| *—Capitol Record Club edition* | | | |
| ❑ ST-193 | Only the Lonely | 1969 | 15.00 |
| ❑ SWBB-258 [(2)] | Close-Up | 1969 | 20.00 |
| *—Combines ST 2500 and ST 2788 in one package* | | | |
| ❑ ST-320 | The Astrodome Presents In Person Sonny James | 1969 | 15.00 |
| ❑ ST 8-0432 | It's Just a Matter of Time | 1970 | 20.00 |
| *—Capitol Record Club edition* | | | |
| ❑ ST-432 | It's Just a Matter of Time | 1970 | 15.00 |
| ❑ ST-478 | My Love/Don't Keep Me Hangin' On | 1970 | 15.00 |
| ❑ STBB-535 [(2)] | You're the Only World I Know/ I'll Never Find Another You | 1970 | 20.00 |
| *—Combines the two listed albums in one package* | | | |
| ❑ ST-629 | #1 | 1970 | 15.00 |
| ❑ ST-734 | Empty Arms | 1971 | 15.00 |
| ❑ T 779 [M] | The Southern Gentleman | 1957 | 50.00 |
| *—Turquoise label* | | | |
| ❑ T 779 [M] | The Southern Gentleman | 1964 | 20.00 |
| *—Black label with colorband, logo on top* | | | |
| ❑ ST-804 | The Sensational Sonny James | 1971 | 15.00 |
| ❑ ST-849 | Here Comes Honey Again | 1971 | 15.00 |
| ❑ T 867 [M] | Sonny | 1957 | 50.00 |
| *—Turquoise label* | | | |
| ❑ T 867 [M] | Sonny | 1964 | 20.00 |
| *—Black label with colorband, logo on top* | | | |
| ❑ T 988 [M] | Honey | 1958 | 50.00 |
| *—Turquoise label* | | | |
| ❑ T 988 [M] | Honey | 1964 | 20.00 |
| *—Black label with colorband, logo on top* | | | |
| ❑ T 1178 [M] | This Is Sonny James | 1959 | 40.00 |
| *—Black label with colorband, logo at left* | | | |
| ❑ T 1178 [M] | This Is Sonny James | 1964 | 20.00 |
| *—Black label with colorband, logo on top* | | | |
| ❑ ST 2017 [S] | The Minute You're Gone | 1964 | 25.00 |
| ❑ T 2017 [M] | The Minute You're Gone | 1964 | 20.00 |
| ❑ ST 2209 [S] | You're the Only World I Know | 1965 | 25.00 |
| ❑ T 2209 [M] | You're the Only World I Know | 1965 | 20.00 |
| ❑ ST 2317 [S] | I'll Keep Holding On | 1965 | 25.00 |
| ❑ T 2317 [M] | I'll Keep Holding On | 1965 | 20.00 |
| ❑ ST 2415 [S] | Behind the Tear | 1965 | 25.00 |
| ❑ T 2415 [M] | Behind the Tear | 1965 | 20.00 |
| ❑ ST 2500 [S] | True Love's a Blessing | 1966 | 25.00 |
| ❑ T 2500 [M] | True Love's a Blessing | 1966 | 20.00 |
| ❑ ST 2561 [S] | Till the Last Leaf Shall Fall | 1966 | 25.00 |
| ❑ T 2561 [M] | Till the Last Leaf Shall Fall | 1966 | 20.00 |
| ❑ ST 2589 [S] | My Christmas Dream | 1966 | 25.00 |
| ❑ T 2589 [M] | My Christmas Dream | 1966 | 20.00 |
| ❑ SM-2615 | The Best of Sonny James | 197? | 10.00 |
| ❑ ST 2615 [S] | The Best of Sonny James | 1966 | 20.00 |
| *—Black Starline label* | | | |
| ❑ T 2615 [M] | The Best of Sonny James | 1966 | 15.00 |
| ❑ ST 2703 [S] | Need You | 1967 | 15.00 |
| ❑ T 2703 [M] | Need You | 1967 | 20.00 |
| ❑ ST 2788 [S] | I'll Never Find Another You | 1967 | 15.00 |
| ❑ T 2788 [M] | I'll Never Find Another You | 1967 | 20.00 |
| ❑ ST 2884 [S] | A World of Our Own | 1968 | 15.00 |
| ❑ T 2884 [M] | A World of Our Own | 1968 | 25.00 |
| ❑ ST 2937 | Heaven Says Hello | 1968 | 15.00 |
| ❑ SM-11013 | The Biggest Hits of Sonny James | 197? | 10.00 |
| ❑ ST-11013 | The Biggest Hits of Sonny James | 1972 | 15.00 |
| ❑ ST-11067 | That's Why I Love You Like I Do | 1972 | 15.00 |
| ❑ ST-11108 | Traces | 1972 | 12.00 |
| ❑ ST-11144 | The Gentleman from the South | 1973 | 12.00 |
| ❑ ST-11196 | Young Love | 1973 | 12.00 |
| ❑ SQBO-91357 [(2)] | That Special Country Feeling | 196? | 30.00 |
| *—Capitol Record Club exclusive* | | | |
| COLUMBIA | | | |
| ❑ KC 31646 | When the Snow Is On the Roses | 1972 | 12.00 |
| ❑ KC 32028 | Sonny James Sings the Greatest Country Hits of '72 | 1973 | 12.00 |
| ❑ KC 32291 | If She Just Helps Me Get Over You | 1973 | 12.00 |
| ❑ KC 32805 | Is It Wrong | 1974 | 12.00 |
| ❑ KC 33056 | A Mi Esposa Con Amor (To My Wife with Love) | 1974 | 12.00 |
| ❑ KC 33428 | A Little Bit South of Saskatoon/ Little Band of Gold | 1975 | 12.00 |
| ❑ KC 33477 | The Guitars of Sonny James | 1975 | 12.00 |



Except when noted otherwise, VG = 25% of NM, and VG+ = 50% of NM. (Example: VG = $2.00, VG+ = $4.00 and NM = $8.00.)

| Number | Title (A Side/B Side) | Yr | NM |
|---|---|---|---|
| ❑ CG 33627 [(2)] | When the Snow Is On the Roses/If She Just Helps Me Get Over You | 1975 | 15.00 |
| ❑ PC 33846 | Country Male Artist of the Decade | 1975 | 12.00 |
| ❑ PC 34035 | 200 Years of Country Music | 1976 | 12.00 |
| ❑ PC 34309 | When Something Is Wrong with My Baby | 1976 | 12.00 |
| ❑ PC 34472 | You're Free to Go | 1977 | 12.00 |
| ❑ PC 34706 | Sonny James In Prison, In Person | 1977 | 12.00 |
| ❑ KC 35379 | This Is the Love | 1978 | 12.00 |
| ❑ KC 35626 | Sonny James' Greatest Hits | 1978 | 12.00 |
| DOT | | | |
| ❑ DLP 3462 [M] | Young Love | 1962 | 40.00 |
| ❑ DLP 25462 [S] | Young Love | 1962 | 50.00 |
| DOT/MCA | | | |
| ❑ 39087 | Sonny James | 198? | 10.00 |
| HILLTOP | | | |
| ❑ 6067 | Invisible Tears | 1969 | 10.00 |
| ❑ 6079 | Timberline | 1969 | 10.00 |
| PICKWICK | | | |
| ❑ SPC-3594 | Young Love | 1977 | 8.00 |
| RCA CAMDEN | | | |
| ❑ CAL-2140 [M] | Young Love | 1967 | 15.00 |
| ❑ CAS-2140 [S] | Young Love | 1967 | 12.00 |

**JAMES, TOMMY, AND THE SHONDELLS**

| Number | Title (A Side/B Side) | Yr | NM |
|---|---|---|---|
| RHINO | | | |
| ❑ R1-70920 [(2)] | Anthology | 1989 | 15.00 |
| ROULETTE | | | |
| ❑ R 25336 [M] | Hanky Panky | 1966 | 20.00 |
| ❑ SR 25336 [P] | Hanky Panky | 1966 | 25.00 |
| *—"Hanky Panky" is rechanneled* | | | |
| ❑ R 25344 [M] | It's Only Love | 1967 | 30.00 |
| ❑ SR 25344 [S] | It's Only Love | 1967 | 25.00 |
| ❑ R 25353 [M] | I Think We're Alone Now | 1967 | 30.00 |
| ❑ SR 25353 [P] | I Think We're Alone Now | 1967 | 15.00 |
| *—Photo cover* | | | |
| ❑ SR 25353 [P] | I Think We're Alone Now | 1967 | 25.00 |
| *—Footprints cover; "I Think We're Alone Now" is rechanneled* | | | |
| ❑ R 25355 [M] | Something Special! The Best of Tommy James & The Shondells | 1968 | 50.00 |
| ❑ SR 25355 [S] | Something Special! The Best of Tommy James & The Shondells | 1968 | 25.00 |
| ❑ R 25357 [M] | Gettin' Together | 1968 | 40.00 |
| ❑ SR 25357 [S] | Gettin' Together | 1968 | 25.00 |
| ❑ SR 42005 | Something Special! The Best of Tommy James & The Shondells | 1968 | 15.00 |
| ❑ SR 42012 | Mony Mony | 1968 | 20.00 |
| ❑ SR 42023 | Crimson and Clover | 1969 | 20.00 |
| ❑ SR 42030 | Cellophane Symphony | 1969 | 20.00 |
| ❑ SR 42040 | The Best of Tommy James & The Shondells | 1969 | 20.00 |
| *—Original versions are in a Unipak (gatefold must be opened to remove record)* | | | |
| ❑ SR 42040 | The Best of Tommy James & The Shondells | 197? | 15.00 |
| *—Later versions have gatefold covers, but record can be removed without opening it* | | | |
| ❑ SR 42044 | Travelin' | 1970 | 15.00 |
| SCEPTER CITATION | | | |
| ❑ CTN-18025 | The Best of Tommy James and the Shondells | 1973 | 10.00 |

**JAMES GANG, THE (1)**

| Number | Title (A Side/B Side) | Yr | NM |
|---|---|---|---|
| ABC | | | |
| ❑ S-688 | Yer' Album | 1970 | 12.00 |
| ❑ S-711 | James Gang Rides Again | 1970 | 12.00 |
| *—Standard pressing without "Bolero" as part of "The Bomber"; "RE-1" in trail-off wax* | | | |
| ❑ S-711 | James Gang Rides Again | 1970 | 25.00 |
| *—First pressing with a short version of Ravel's "Bolero" as part of the song "The Bomber"; exists on both promos and early stock copies; no "RE-1" in trail-off wax* | | | |
| ❑ X-721 | Thirds | 1971 | 12.00 |
| ❑ X-733 | James Gang Live in Concert | 1971 | 12.00 |
| ❑ X-741 | Straight Shooter | 1972 | 12.00 |
| ❑ X-760 | Passin' Thru | 1972 | 12.00 |
| ❑ ABCX-774 | The Best of the James Gang Featuring Joe Walsh | 1973 | 12.00 |
| *—Most copies of this LP contain the edited version of "The Bomber." The full title of the LP is on the spine, and the record's trail-off wax has the number "ABCX-774-A-RE-1".* | | | |
| ❑ ABCX-774 | The Best of the James Gang Featuring Joe Walsh | 1973 | 20.00 |
| *—A few copies of this LP contain the full version of "The Bomber" with the "Bolero" excerpt. The words "The Best Of" do NOT appear on the spine, and the record's trail-off wax has the number "ABCX-774-A".* | | | |
| ❑ X-801 [(2)] | 16 Greatest Hits | 1973 | 15.00 |
| ATCO | | | |
| ❑ SD 36-102 | Miami | 1974 | 10.00 |
| ❑ SD 36-112 | Newborn | 1975 | 10.00 |

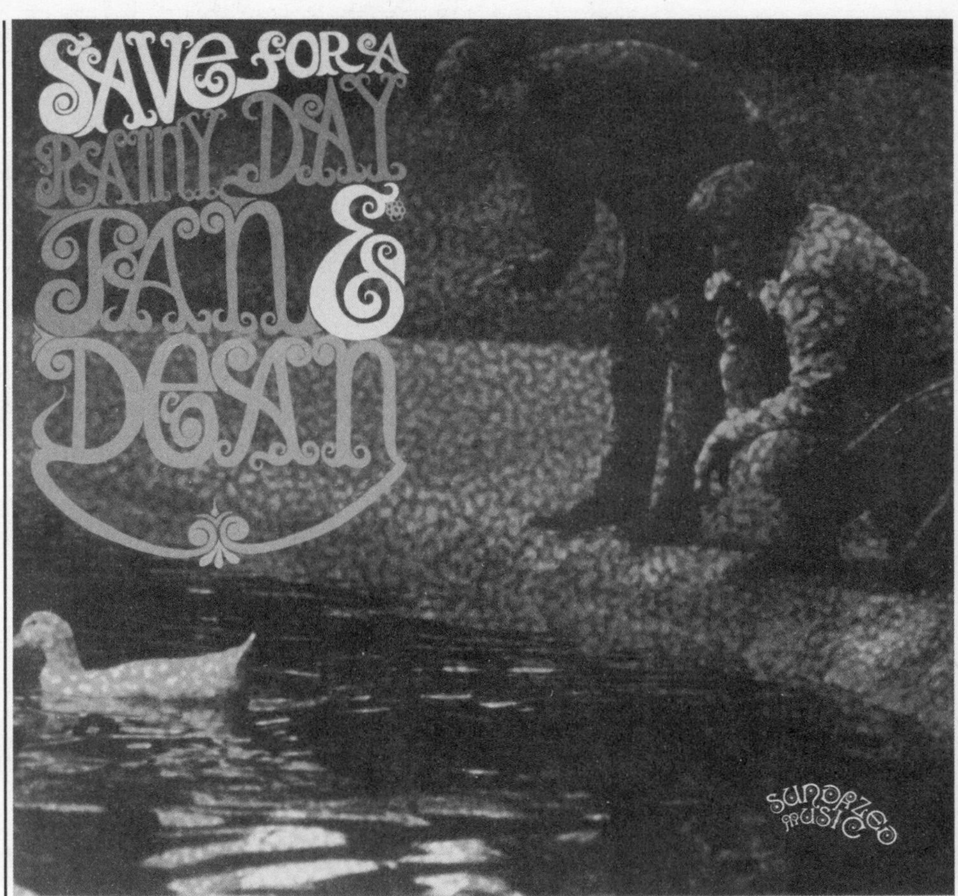


Jan and Dean, *Save for a Rainy Day,* Sundazed LP 5022, 1996, 2 records, $15.

| Number | Title (A Side/B Side) | Yr | NM |
|---|---|---|---|
| ❑ SD 36-141 | Jesse Come Home | 1976 | 10.00 |
| ❑ SD 7037 | Bang | 1973 | 10.00 |
| BLUESWAY | | | |
| ❑ BLS-6034 | Yer' Album | 1969 | 15.00 |
| MCA | | | |
| ❑ 6012 [(2)] | 16 Greatest Hits | 1980 | 10.00 |
| *—Reissue* | | | |
| ❑ 37111 | James Gang Rides Again | 1980 | 8.00 |
| *—Reissue* | | | |
| ❑ 37112 | The Best of the James Gang Featuring Joe Walsh | 1980 | 8.00 |
| *—Reissue* | | | |

**JAMME**

| Number | Title (A Side/B Side) | Yr | NM |
|---|---|---|---|
| ABC DUNHILL | | | |
| ❑ DS-50072 | Jamme | 1970 | 20.00 |

**JAN AND DEAN**

| Number | Title (A Side/B Side) | Yr | NM |
|---|---|---|---|
| COLUMBIA | | | |
| ❑ CL 2661 [M] | Save for a Rainy Day | 1967 | — |
| *—Canceled* | | | |
| ❑ CS 9461 [S] | Save for a Rainy Day | 1967 | 4000. |
| *—LP not known to exist, but an acetate does, and possibly an import on this label and number; VG value 2000; VG+ value 3000* | | | |
| DEADMAN'S CURVE | | | |
| ❑ (no #) | Live at the Keystone Berkeley | 1981 | 25.00 |
| *—With front and back covers pasted on* | | | |
| ❑ (no #) | Live at the Keystone Berkeley | 1981 | 50.00 |
| *—Plain jacket with front and back cover inserts* | | | |
| DORE | | | |
| ❑ LP-101 | Jan and Dean Bonus Photo | 1960 | 120.00 |
| ❑ LP-101 | Jan and Dean | 197? | 15.00 |
| *—Reissue with black label* | | | |
| ❑ LP-101 [M] | Jan and Dean | 1960 | 400.00 |
| *—Original with blue label* | | | |
| J&D | | | |
| ❑ 101 [M] | Save for a Rainy Day | 1967 | 300.00 |
| *—Private pressing by Dean Torrence of unreleased Columbia album* | | | |
| LIBERTY | | | |
| ❑ LRP-3248 [M] | Jan and Dean's Golden Hits | 1962 | 30.00 |
| ❑ LRP-3294 [M] | Jan and Dean Take Linda Surfin' | 1963 | 50.00 |
| ❑ LRP-3314 [M] | Surf City and Other Swingin' Cities | 1963 | 40.00 |
| ❑ LRP-3339 [M] | Drag City | 1963 | 40.00 |
| ❑ LRP-3361 [M] | The New Girl in School/Dead Man's Curve | 1964 | 20.00 |
| *—Reissue with reversed title* | | | |
| ❑ LRP-3361 [M] | Dead Man's Curve/The New Girl in School | 1964 | 30.00 |
| *—Full-color cover* | | | |
| ❑ LRP-3361 [M] | Dead Man's Curve/The New Girl in School | 1964 | 40.00 |
| *—Black and white cover with pink tint* | | | |
| ❑ LRP-3368 [M] | Ride the Wild Surf | 1964 | 30.00 |
| ❑ LRP-3377 [M] | The Little Old Lady from Pasadena | 1964 | 30.00 |
| ❑ LRP-3403 [M] | Command Performance/Live in Person | 1965 | 30.00 |
| ❑ LRP-3417 [M] | Jan and Dean's Golden Hits, Volume 2 | 1965 | 25.00 |
| ❑ LRP-3431 [M] | Folk 'N' Roll | 1965 | 30.00 |
| ❑ LRP-3441 [M] | Filet of Soul | 1966 | 30.00 |
| ❑ LRP-3444 [M] | Jan and Dean Meet Batman | 1966 | 50.00 |
| ❑ LRP-3458 [M] | Popsicle | 1966 | 30.00 |
| ❑ LRP-3460 [M] | Jan and Dean's Golden Hits, Volume 3 | 1966 | 25.00 |
| ❑ LST-7248 [S] | Jan and Dean's Golden Hits | 1962 | 40.00 |
| ❑ LST-7294 [S] | Jan and Dean Take Linda Surfin' | 1963 | 80.00 |
| ❑ LST-7314 [S] | Surf City and Other Swingin' Cities | 1963 | 50.00 |
| ❑ LST-7339 [S] | Drag City | 1963 | 50.00 |
| ❑ LST-7361 [S] | The New Girl in School/Dead Man's Curve | 1964 | 30.00 |
| *—Reissue with reversed title* | | | |
| ❑ LST-7361 [S] | Dead Man's Curve/The New Girl in School | 1964 | 40.00 |
| *—Full-color cover* | | | |
| ❑ LST-7361 [S] | Dead Man's Curve/The New Girl in School | 1964 | 50.00 |
| *—Black and white cover with pink tint* | | | |
| ❑ LST-7368 [S] | Ride the Wild Surf | 1964 | 40.00 |
| ❑ LST-7377 [S] | The Little Old Lady from Pasadena | 1964 | 40.00 |
| ❑ LST-7403 [S] | Command Performance/Live in Person | 1965 | 40.00 |
| ❑ LST-7417 [S] | Jan and Dean's Golden Hits, Volume 2 | 1965 | 30.00 |
| ❑ LST-7431 [S] | Folk 'N' Roll | 1965 | 40.00 |
| ❑ LST-7441 [S] | Filet of Soul | 1966 | 40.00 |
| ❑ LST-7444 [S] | Jan and Dean Meet Batman | 1966 | 70.00 |

❑ LST-7458 [S] Popsicle 1966 40.00
❑ LST-7460 [S] Jan and Dean's Golden Hits, Volume 3 1966 30.00
❑ LN-10011 Dead Man's Curve 1980 8.00
*—Budget-line reissue*
❑ LN-10115 The Best of Jan and Dean 1981 8.00
❑ LN-10151 The Little Old Lady from Pasadena 1982 8.00
*—Budget-line reissue*

PAIR
❑ PDL2-1071 [(2)]California Gold 1986 12.00

RHINO
❑ RNDA 1498 [(2)]One Summer Night — Live 1982 20.00

SUNDAZED
❑ LP 5022 [(2)] Save for a Rainy Day 1996 15.00
*—First release to the general public; colored vinyl*
❑ LP 5040 Jan and Dean (The Dore Album) 1996 10.00
*—Reissue of Dore LP on colored vinyl with extra tracks and poster*

SUNSET
❑ SUM-1156 [M] Jan and Dean 1967 15.00
❑ SUS-5156 [S] Jan and Dean 1967 15.00

UNITED ARTISTS
❑ UA-LA341-H2 [(2)]Gotta Take That One Last Ride 1974 15.00
❑ UA-LA443-E The Very Best of Jan and Dean 1975 10.00
❑ UA-LA515-E The Very Best of Jan and Dean, Volume 2 1975 10.00
❑ UAS-9961 [(2)] Anthology (Legendary Masters Series, Vol. 3) 1971 25.00

**JAN AND KJELD**

KAPP
❑ KL-1190 [M] Banjo Boy 1960 30.00

**JAN AND LORRAINE**

ABC
❑ S-691 Gypsy People 1969 25.00

**JANE'S ADDICTION**

TRIPLE X
❑ 51004 Jane's Addiction 1987 15.00

WARNER BROS.
❑ PRO-A-3369 [DJ]Words and Music 1988 40.00
*—Promo-only interview album*
❑ 25727 Nothing's Shocking 1988 12.00
❑ 25993 Ritual de lo Habitual 1990 12.00
*—First cover, with drawing*
❑ 26223 Ritual de lo Habitual 1990 10.00
*—Second cover, all white with text of First Amendment*

**JANIGRO, ANTONIO**

RCA VICTOR RED SEAL
❑ LSC-2365 [S] Cello Concertos 1960 30.00
*—Original with "shaded dog" label*
❑ LSC-2460 [S] Bach: Suite No. 2 in B; Brandenburg Concerto No. 5 1961 20.00
*—Original with "shaded dog" label*
❑ LSC-2653 [S] Music for Strings 1962 40.00
*—Original with "shaded dog" label*

**JANIS, BYRON**

MERCURY LIVING PRSENSCE
❑ SR 90260 [S] Rachmaninoff: Piano Concerto No. 2; Preludes in C# and E-flat 196? 25.00
*—With Antal Dorati/Minneapolis Symphony Orchestra; maroon label, with "Vendor: Mercury Record Corporation"*
❑ SR 90260 [S] Rachmaninoff: Piano Concerto No. 2; Preludes in C# and E-flat 196? 60.00
*—With Antal Dorati/Minneapolis Symphony Orchestra; maroon label, no "Vendor: Mercury Record Corporation"*
❑ SR 90266 [S] Tchaikovsky: Piano Concerto No. 1 196? 25.00
*—With Herbert Menges/London Symphony Orchestra; maroon label, with "Vendor: Mercury Record Corporation"*
❑ SR 90266 [S] Tchaikovsky: Piano Concerto No. 1 196? 50.00
*—With Herbert Menges/London Symphony Orchestra; maroon label, no "Vendor: Mercury Record Corporation"*
❑ SR 90283 [S] Rachmaninoff: Piano Concerto No. 3 196? 40.00
*—With Antal Dorati/London Symphony Orchestra; maroon label, with "Vendor: Mercury Record Corporation"*
❑ SR 90283 [S] Rachmaninoff: Piano Concerto No. 3 196? 100.00
*—With Antal Dorati/London Symphony Orchestra; maroon label, no "Vendor: Mercury Record Corporation"*
❑ SR 90300 [S] Prokofiev: Piano Concerto No. 2; Rachmaninoff: Piano Concerto No. 1 196? 20.00
*—Third edition: Dark red (not maroon) label*
❑ SR 90300 [S] Prokofiev: Piano Concerto No. 2; Rachmaninoff: Piano Concerto No. 1 196? 25.00
*—Maroon label, with "Vendor: Mercury Record Corporation"*
❑ SR 90300 [S] Prokofiev: Piano Concerto No. 2; Rachmaninoff: Piano Concerto No. 1 196? 40.00
*—Maroon label, no "Vendor: Mercury Record Corporation"*
❑ SR 90305 [S] Encore 196? 150.00
*—Maroon label, no "Vendor: Mercury Record Corporation"*
❑ SR 90329 [S] Liszt: Piano Concertos No. 1 and 2 196? 50.00
*—Maroon label, no "Vendor: Mercury Record Corporation"*
❑ SR 90383 [S] Schumann: Piano Concerto; Arabesque; Wieck Variations 196? 30.00
*—With Stanislaw Skrowaczewski/London Symphony Orchestra; maroon label, no "Vendor: Mercury Record Corporation"*

RCA VICTOR RED SEAL
❑ LSC-2237 [S] Rachmaninoff: Piano Concerto No. 3 1959 200.00
*—With Charles Munch/Boston Symphony Orchestra; original with "shaded dog" label*
❑ LSC-2541 [S] Liszt: Todtentanz; Rachmaninoff: Piano Concerto No. 1 1961 25.00
*—With Fritz Reiner/Chicago Symphony Orch.; Classic Records reissue*
❑ LSC-2541 [S] Liszt: Todtentanz; Rachmaninoff: Piano Concerto No. 1 1961 100.00
*—With Fritz Reiner/Chicago Symphony Orch.; originals with "shaded dog" label*

**JANIS, CONRAD**

CIRCLE
❑ L-404 [10] Conrad Janis' Tailgate Jazz Band 1951 50.00

JUBILEE
❑ JLP-7 [10] Conrad Janis and His Tailgaters 1954 50.00
❑ JLP-1010 [M] Conrad Janis and His Tailgate Five 1955 40.00

RIVERSIDE
❑ RLP 12-215 [M]Dixieland Jam Session 1956 50.00
*—White label, blue print*
❑ RLP 12-215 [M]Dixieland Jam Session 1959 30.00
*—Blue label, microphone label at top*

**JANIS, JOHNNY**

ABC-PARAMOUNT
❑ ABC-140 [M] For the First Time 1956 60.00

COLUMBIA
❑ CL 1674 [M] The Start of Something Big 1961 25.00
❑ CS 8474 [S] The Start of Something Big 1961 30.00

MONUMENT
❑ MLP-8036 [M] Once in a Blue Moon 1965 15.00
❑ SLP-18036 [S] Once in a Blue Moon 1965 20.00

**JANSSEN, DAVID**

EPIC
❑ LN 24150 [M] Hidden Island 1965 20.00
❑ BN 26150 [S] Hidden Island 1965 25.00

**JARMAN, JOSEPH**

DELMARK
❑ DS-410 Song for 1968 20.00
❑ DS-417 As If It Were the Seasons 1969 20.00

**JARMAN, JOSEPH, AND DON MOYE**

INDIA NAVIGATION
❑ IN-1033 [(2)] Egwu-Anwu 1978 20.00

**JARRE, JEAN-MICHEL**

MOBILE FIDELITY
❑ 1-212 Oxygene 1995 20.00
*—Audiophile vinyl*
❑ 1-227 Equinoxe 1995 20.00
*—Audiophile vinyl*

**JARREAU, AL**

MOBILE FIDELITY
❑ 1-019 All Fly Home 1980 20.00
*—Audiophile vinyl*

**JARRETT, KEITH**

ECM
❑ 1035/6/7 ST [(3)]Solo Concerts 1974 25.00
*—Original issue, made in Germany?*
❑ ECM-3-1035 [(3)]Solo Concerts 197? 20.00
*—Distributed by Polydor*
❑ 1100 [(10)] The Sun Bear Concerts 1977 150.00
*—Made in Germany*
❑ ECM3-1227 [(3)]Concerts 1982 20.00
*—Distributed by Warner Bros.; box set*

VORTEX
❑ 2006 Life Between the Exit Signs 1969 40.00
❑ 2008 Restoration Ruin 1969 40.00
❑ 2012 Somewhere Before 1970 40.00

**JARVIS, JOHN**

CRYSTAL CLEAR
❑ 8004 Evolutions 1980 20.00
*—Direct-to-disc recording*

**JASPAR, BOBBY**

EMARCY
❑ MG-36105 [M] Bobby Jaspar and His All Stars 1957 80.00

RIVERSIDE
❑ RLP 12-240 [M]Bobby Jaspar 1957 80.00
*—White label, blue print*
❑ RLP 12-240 [M]Bobby Jaspar 1959 40.00
*—Blue label, microphone label at top*

**JASPER WRATH**

SUNFLOWER
❑ SNF-5003 Jasper Wrath 1971 40.00

**JAUME, ANDRE**

HAT HUT
❑ 1989/90 [(2)] Musique Pour 8: L'oc 1981 20.00

**JAUME, ANDRE, AND JOE MCPHEE**

HAT HUT
❑ 12 [(2)] Tales and Prophecies 1980 20.00

**JAY AND THE AMERICANS**

LIBERTY
❑ LM-1010 Jay and the Americans Greatest Hits 1981 8.00
*—Another reissue*

RHINO
❑ RNLP 70224 All-Time Greatest Hits 1986 12.00

SUNSET
❑ SUS-5252 Jay and the Americans!! 1968 12.00
❑ SUS-5278 Early American Hits 1969 15.00

UNART
❑ M-20018 [M] Jay and the Americans!! 196? 12.00
❑ MS-21018 [S] Jay and the Americans!! 196? 12.00

UNITED ARTISTS
❑ UA-LA357-E The Very Best of Jay and the Americans 1975 12.00
❑ LM-1010 Jay and the Americans Greatest Hits 1980 10.00
*—Reissue*
❑ UAL-3222 [M] She Cried 1962 50.00
❑ UAL-3300 [M] At the Café Wha? 1963 50.00
❑ UAL-3407 [M] Come a Little Bit Closer 1964 25.00
❑ UAL-3417 [M] Blockbusters 1965 25.00
❑ UAL-3453 [M] Jay and the Americans Greatest Hits 1965 20.00
❑ UAL-3474 [M] Sunday and Me 1966 20.00
❑ UAL-3534 [M] Livin' Above Your Head 1966 20.00
❑ UAL-3555 [M] Jay and the Americans Greatest Hits, Volume 2 1966 20.00
❑ UAL-3562 [M] Try Some of This! 1967 20.00
❑ UAS-6222 [S] She Cried 1962 100.00
❑ UAS-6300 [S] At the Café Wha? 1963 100.00
❑ UAS-6407 [S] Come a Little Bit Closer 1964 30.00
❑ UAS-6417 [S] Blockbusters 1965 30.00
❑ UAS-6453 [S] Jay and the Americans Greatest Hits 1965 25.00
❑ UAS-6474 [S] Sunday and Me 1966 25.00
❑ UAS-6534 [S] Livin' Above Your Head 1966 25.00
❑ UAS-6555 [S] Jay and the Americans Greatest Hits, Volume 2 1966 20.00
❑ UAS-6562 [S] Try Some of This! 1967 20.00
❑ UAS-6671 Sands of Time 1969 20.00
❑ UAS-6719 Wax Museum 1970 20.00
❑ UAS-6751 Wax Museum, Volume 2 1970 20.00
❑ UAS-6762 Capture the Moment 1970 20.00
❑ ST-90814 [S] Jay and the Americans Greatest Hits 1966 30.00
*—Capitol Record Club edition*
❑ ST-90815 [S] Jay and the Americans Greatest Hits, Volume 2 1966 30.00
*—Capitol Record Club edition*

**JAY AND THE TECHNIQUES**

SMASH
❑ MGS-27095 [M]Apples, Peaches, Pumpkin Pie 1967 30.00
❑ MGS-27102 [M]Love Lost and Found 1968 60.00
*—Mono may be white-label promo only*
❑ SRS-67095 [S] Apples, Peaches, Pumpkin Pie 1967 30.00
*—First cover with "live" photo of the band*
❑ SRS-67095 [S] Apples, Peaches, Pumpkin Pie 1968 20.00
*—Second cover with "posed" photo of the band*
❑ SRS-67102 [S] Love Lost and Found 1968 30.00

**JAYE, JERRY**

HI
❑ HL-12038 [M] My Girl Josephine 1967 20.00
❑ SHL-32038 [S] My Girl Josephine 1967 20.00
❑ SHL-32102 Honky Tonk Women Love Redneck Men 1976 12.00

**JAYHAWKS, THE** This is the alt-country group, not the 1950s vocal group.

AMERICAN
❑ 43006 Tomorrow the Green Grass 1995 10.00
❑ 43114 Sound of Lies 1997 12.00

| Number | Title (A Side/B Side) | Yr | NM |
|---|---|---|---|
| BUNKHOUSE | | | |
| ❑ 7001 | The Jayhawks | 1986 | 80.00 |
| TWIN/TONE | | | |
| ❑ TTR 89151 | Blue Earth | 1989 | 15.00 |
| **JAYNETTS, THE** | | | |
| TUFF | | | |
| ❑ LP 13 [M] | Sally Go 'Round the Roses | 1963 | 300.00 |
| **JAZZ ARTISTS GUILD, THE** | | | |
| CANDID | | | |
| ❑ CD-8022 [M] | Newport Rebels | 1960 | 40.00 |
| ❑ CS-9022 [S] | Newport Rebels | 1960 | 50.00 |
| **JAZZ BROTHERS, THE** | | | |
| RIVERSIDE | | | |
| ❑ RLP-335 [M] | Jazz Brothers | 1960 | 25.00 |
| ❑ RLP-371 [M] | Hey, Baby! | 1961 | 25.00 |
| ❑ RLP-405 [M] | Spring Fever | 1962 | 25.00 |
| ❑ RS-9335 [S] | Jazz Brothers | 1960 | 30.00 |
| ❑ RS-9371 [S] | Hey, Baby! | 1961 | 30.00 |
| ❑ RS-9405 [S] | Spring Fever | 1962 | 30.00 |
| **JAZZ CITY** | | | |
| RAHMP | | | |
| ❑ 2 | Jazz City | 197? | 20.00 |
| **JAZZ CITY ALL-STARS, THE** | | | |
| BETHLEHEM | | | |
| ❑ BCP-79 [M] | Jazz City Presents the Jazz City All-Stars | 1957 | 50.00 |
| **JAZZ COMPOSERS ORCHESTRA** | | | |
| JCOA | | | |
| ❑ LP-1001/2 [(2)] | Jazz Composers Orchestra | 1968 | 60.00 |
| **JAZZ CORPS, THE** | | | |
| PACIFIC JAZZ | | | |
| ❑ PJ-10116 [M] | The Jazz Corps Under the Direction of Tommy Peltier | 1967 | 25.00 |
| **JAZZ COURIERS, THE** | | | |
| CARLTON | | | |
| ❑ LP 12-116 [M] | The Couriers of Jazz | 1959 | 50.00 |
| ❑ ST 12-116 [S] | The Couriers of Jazz | 1959 | 40.00 |
| JAZZLAND | | | |
| ❑ JLP-34 [M] | Message from Britain | 1961 | 25.00 |
| ❑ JLP-934 [S] | Message from Britain | 1961 | 30.00 |
| WHIPPET | | | |
| ❑ WLP-700 [M] | The Jazz Couriers | 1956 | 120.00 |
| **JAZZ CRUSADERS, THE** See THE CRUSADERS. | | | |
| **JAZZ EXPONENTS, THE** | | | |
| ARGO | | | |
| ❑ LP-622 [M] | The Jazz Exponents | 1958 | 40.00 |
| **JAZZ FIVE, THE** | | | |
| RIVERSIDE | | | |
| ❑ RLP-361 [M] | The Hooter | 1961 | 25.00 |
| ❑ RS-9361 [S] | The Hooter | 1961 | 30.00 |
| **JAZZ INTERACTIONS ORCHESTRA, THE** | | | |
| VERVE | | | |
| ❑ V-8731 [M] | Jazzhattan Suite | 1967 | 20.00 |
| **JAZZ LAB, THE** | | | |
| COLUMBIA | | | |
| ❑ CL 998 [M] | Jazz Lab | 1957 | 150.00 |
| ❑ CL 1058 [M] | Modern Jazz Perspective/Jazz Lab, Volume 2 | 1957 | 150.00 |
| JAZZLAND | | | |
| ❑ JLP-1 [M] | Jazz Lab | 1960 | 50.00 |
| ❑ JLP-901 [S] | Jazz Lab | 1960 | 60.00 |
| JOSIE | | | |
| ❑ JOZ-3500 [M] | Gigi Gryce and Donald Byrd | 1962 | 40.00 |
| *—Reissue of Jubilee album* | | | |
| ❑ JS-3500 [R] | Gigi Gryce and Donald Byrd | 196? | 20.00 |
| JUBILEE | | | |
| ❑ JLP-1059 [M] | Jazz Lab | 1958 | 100.00 |
| RIVERSIDE | | | |
| ❑ RLP 12-229 [M] | Gigi Gryce and the Jazz Lab Quintet | 1957 | 100.00 |
| *—White label, blue print* | | | |
| ❑ RLP 12-229 [M] | Gigi Gryce and the Jazz Lab Quintet | 1959 | 50.00 |
| *—Blue label, microphone logo at top* | | | |
| ❑ RLP-1110 [S] | Gigi Gryce and the Jazz Lab Quintet | 1959 | 50.00 |
| **JAZZ MESSENGERS, THE** See ART BLAKEY. | | | |
| **JAZZ SYMPHONICS** | | | |
| RENFRO | | | |
| ❑ LP-12369 | The Beginning | 1968 | 60.00 |

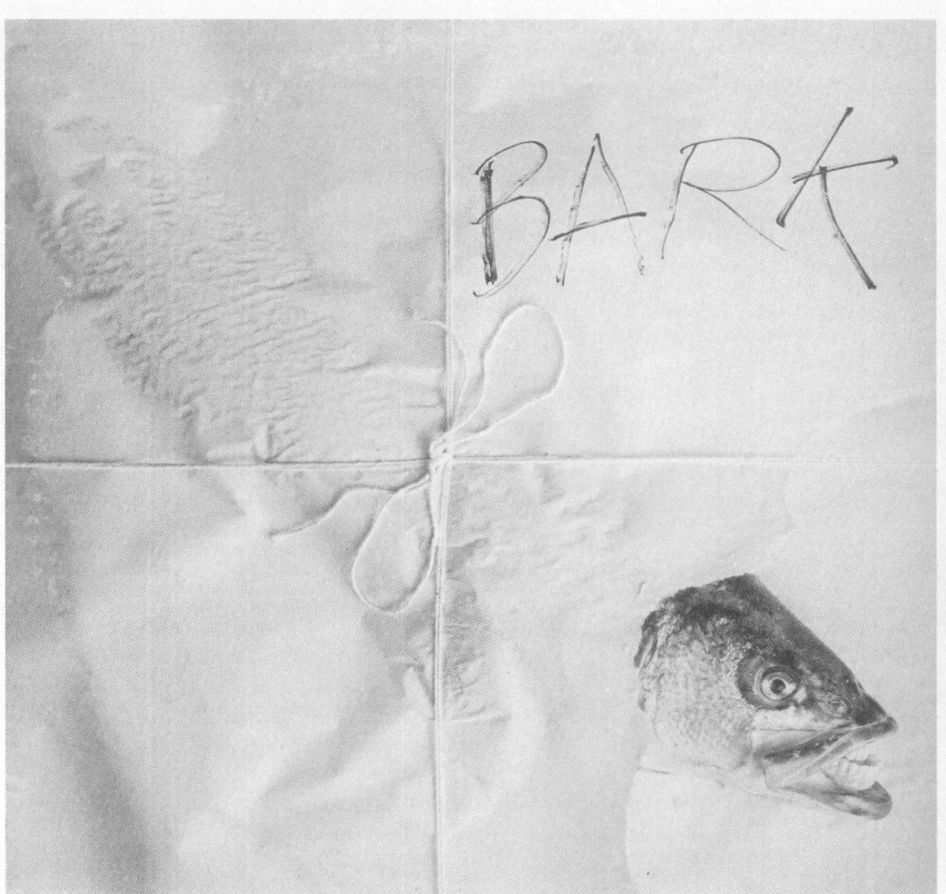


Jefferson Airplane, *Bark*, Grunt FTR-1001, 1971, without brown paper bag, $10.

| Number | Title (A Side/B Side) | Yr | NM |
|---|---|---|---|
| **JAZZPICKERS, THE** | | | |
| EMARCY | | | |
| ❑ MG-36111 [M] | The Jazzpickers | 1957 | 50.00 |
| ❑ MG-36123 [M] | Command Performance | 1958 | 50.00 |
| MERCURY | | | |
| ❑ SR-80013 [S] | For Moderns Only | 1959 | 40.00 |
| **JAZZTET, THE** | | | |
| ARGO | | | |
| ❑ LP-664 [M] | Meet the Jazztet | 1960 | 50.00 |
| ❑ LPS-664 [S] | Meet the Jazztet | 1960 | 60.00 |
| ❑ LP-672 [M] | Big City Sounds | 1961 | 40.00 |
| ❑ LPS-672 [S] | Big City Sounds | 1961 | 50.00 |
| ❑ LP-684 [M] | The Jazztet and John Lewis | 1961 | 40.00 |
| ❑ LPS-684 [S] | The Jazztet and John Lewis | 1961 | 50.00 |
| ❑ LP-688 [M] | The Jazztet at Birdhouse | 1961 | 40.00 |
| ❑ LPS-688 [S] | The Jazztet at Birdhouse | 1961 | 50.00 |
| CADET | | | |
| ❑ CA-664 [S] | Meet the Jazztet | 197? | 20.00 |
| *—Yellow and red label* | | | |
| ❑ LPS-664 [S] | Meet the Jazztet | 1966 | 30.00 |
| *—Fading blue label* | | | |
| CHESS | | | |
| ❑ CH-9159 | Meet the Jazztet | 198? | 12.00 |
| *—Reissue* | | | |
| MERCURY | | | |
| ❑ MG-20698 [M] | Here and Now | 1962 | 40.00 |
| ❑ MG-20737 [M] | Another Git-Together | 1962 | 40.00 |
| ❑ SR-60698 [S] | Here and Now | 1962 | 50.00 |
| ❑ SR-60737 [S] | Another Git-Together | 1962 | 50.00 |
| **JAZZY JEFF AND FRESH PRINCE** | | | |
| JIVE | | | |
| ❑ 1026-1-J | Rock the House | 1986 | 10.00 |
| *—Reissued in 1989 with same catalog number and one new track* | | | |
| ❑ 1091-1-J [(2)] | He's the D.J., I'm the Rapper | 1988 | 12.00 |
| *—Without "Nightmare on My Street" disclaimer on cover* | | | |
| ❑ 1091-1-J RE [(2)] | He's the D.J., I'm the Rapper | 1988 | 16.00 |
| *—With "Nightmare on My Street" disclaimer on cover (much scarcer than original)* | | | |
| ❑ 1188-1-J | And in This Corner... | 1989 | 10.00 |
| ❑ 1392-1-J | Homebase | 1991 | 12.00 |
| ❑ JL6-8399 | On Fire | 1985 | 12.00 |

| Number | Title (A Side/B Side) | Yr | NM |
|---|---|---|---|
| ❑ 41489-1 | Code Red | 1993 | 12.00 |
| *—LP in generic black cover with center hole and sticker* | | | |
| WORD UP | | | |
| ❑ WDLP-0001 | Rock the House | 1985 | 25.00 |
| **JEFFERSON** | | | |
| JANUS | | | |
| ❑ JLS-3006 | Jefferson | 1969 | 25.00 |
| **JEFFERSON, BLIND LEMON** | | | |
| MILESTONE | | | |
| ❑ MLP-2004 [M] | The Immortal Blind Lemon Jefferson | 1968 | 25.00 |
| ❑ MLP-2007 [M] | The Immortal Blind Lemon Jefferson, Vol. 2 | 1969 | 25.00 |
| ❑ MLP-2013 [M] | Black Snake Moan | 1970 | 25.00 |
| RIVERSIDE | | | |
| ❑ RLP 12-125 [M] | Blind Lemon Jefferson — Classic Folk Blues | 1957 | 120.00 |
| ❑ RLP 12-136 [M] | Blind Lemon Jefferson, Volume 2 | 1958 | 120.00 |
| ❑ 1014 [10] | The Folk Blues of Blind Lemon Jefferson | 1953 | 250.00 |
| ❑ 1053 [10] | Penitentiary Blues | 1955 | 250.00 |
| **JEFFERSON, EDDIE** | | | |
| PRESTIGE | | | |
| ❑ PRST-7619 | Body and Soul | 1969 | 20.00 |
| ❑ PRST-7698 | Come Along with Me | 1969 | 20.00 |
| RIVERSIDE | | | |
| ❑ RLP-411 [M] | Letter from Home | 1962 | 30.00 |
| ❑ RS-9411 [S] | Letter from Home | 1962 | 40.00 |
| **JEFFERSON, RON** | | | |
| PACIFIC JAZZ | | | |
| ❑ PJ-36 [M] | Love Lifted Me | 1962 | 30.00 |
| ❑ ST-36 [S] | Love Lifted Me | 1962 | 40.00 |
| **JEFFERSON AIRPLANE** Also see MARTY BALIN; HOT TUNA; JEFFERSON STARSHIP; PAUL KANTNER; GRACE SLICK. | | | |
| DCC COMPACT CLASSICS | | | |
| ❑ LPZ-2033 | Surrealistic Pillow | 1997 | 25.00 |
| *—Audiophile vinyl* | | | |

| Number | Title (A Side/B Side) | Yr | NM |
|---|---|---|---|
| **EPIC** | | | |
| ❑ OE 45271 | Jefferson Airplane | 1989 | 15.00 |
| **GRUNT** | | | |
| ❑ BFL1-0147 | Thirty Seconds Over Winterland | 1973 | 12.00 |
| ❑ APL1-0437 | Early Flight | 1974 | 12.00 |
| ❑ FTR-1001 | Bark | 1971 | 10.00 |
| *—Without brown paper bag* | | | |
| ❑ FTR-1001 | Bark | 1971 | 15.00 |
| *—With brown paper bag* | | | |
| ❑ FTR-1007 | Long John Silver | 1972 | 12.00 |
| ❑ CYL2-1255 [(2)] | Flight Log 1966-1976 | 1977 | 12.00 |
| ❑ AYL1-4386 | Bark | 1981 | 8.00 |
| ❑ AYL1-4391 | Thirty Seconds Over Winterland | 1981 | 8.00 |
| **MOBILE FIDELITY** | | | |
| ❑ 1-148 | Crown of Creation | 1984 | 20.00 |
| *—Audiophile vinyl* | | | |
| **PAIR** | | | |
| ❑ PDL2-1090 [(2)] | Time Machine | 1986 | 12.00 |
| **RCA** | | | |
| ❑ 5724-1-R [(2)] | 2400 Fulton Street: An Anthology | 1987 | 15.00 |
| **RCA VICTOR** | | | |
| ❑ APD1-0320 [Q] | Volunteers | 1973 | 80.00 |
| *—Yellow/orange label* | | | |
| ❑ APD1-0320 [Q] | Volunteers | 1975 | 50.00 |
| *—Tan label* | | | |
| ❑ LOP-1511 [M] | After Bathing at Baxter's | 1967 | 50.00 |
| ❑ LSO-1511 [S] | After Bathing at Baxter's | 1967 | 20.00 |
| *—Black label, dog on top* | | | |
| ❑ LSO-1511 [S] | After Bathing at Baxter's | 1969 | 12.00 |
| *—Orange label* | | | |
| ❑ LSO-1511 [S] | After Bathing at Baxter's | 1975 | 10.00 |
| *—Tan label* | | | |
| ❑ LPM-3584 [M] | Jefferson Airplane Takes Off! | 1966 | 25.00 |
| *—Version 3: No "Runnin' 'Round This World", altered lyrics to "Let Me In" ("Don't tell me it's so funny") and "Run Around ("That sway as you stay here by me"). All later versions confirm to Version 3.* | | | |
| ❑ LPM-3584 [M] | Jefferson Airplane Takes Off! | 1966 | 1000. |
| *—Version 2: No "Runnin' 'Round This World", but "questionable" lyrics remain in "Let Me In" ("Don't tell me you want money") and "Run Around" ("That sway as you lay under me"). Until the exact matrix numbers are known, it must be heard to confirm.* | | | |
| ❑ LPM-3584 [M] | Jefferson Airplane Takes Off! | 1966 | 3000. |
| *—Version 1: With "Runnin' 'Round This World" as last song on side 1. Count the number of bands on Side 1 of the record; don't rely on the cover listing, as some jackets list the title when it's not on the record; VG value 1500; VG+ value 2250* | | | |
| ❑ LSP-3584 [S] | Jefferson Airplane Takes Off! | 1966 | 25.00 |
| *—Version 3: See Version 3 note under mono version* | | | |
| ❑ LSP-3584 [S] | Jefferson Airplane Takes Off! | 1966 | 1800. |
| *—Version 2: See Version 2 note under mono version* | | | |
| ❑ LSP-3584 [S] | Jefferson Airplane Takes Off! | 1966 | 5000. |
| *—Version 1: See Version 1 note under mono version; VG value 2000; VG+ value 3500* | | | |
| ❑ LSP-3584 [S] | Jefferson Airplane Takes Off! | 1969 | 12.00 |
| *—Orange label* | | | |
| ❑ LSP-3584 [S] | Jefferson Airplane Takes Off! | 1975 | 10.00 |
| *—Tan label* | | | |
| ❑ AYL1-3661 | The Worst of Jefferson Airplane | 1980 | 8.00 |
| ❑ AYL1-3738 | Surrealistic Pillow | 1980 | 8.00 |
| ❑ AYL1-3739 | Jefferson Airplane Takes Off! | 1980 | 8.00 |
| ❑ LPM-3766 [M] | Surrealistic Pillow | 1967 | 60.00 |
| ❑ LSP-3766 [S] | Surrealistic Pillow | 1967 | 30.00 |
| *—Black label, dog on top* | | | |
| ❑ LSP-3766 [S] | Surrealistic Pillow | 1969 | 12.00 |
| *—Orange label* | | | |
| ❑ LSP-3766 [S] | Surrealistic Pillow | 1975 | 10.00 |
| *—Tan label* | | | |
| ❑ AYL1-3797 | Crown of Creation | 1980 | 8.00 |
| ❑ AYL1-3798 | Bless Its Pointed Little Head | 1980 | 8.00 |
| ❑ AYL1-3867 | Volunteers | 1980 | 8.00 |
| ❑ LSP-4058 | Crown of Creation | 1968 | 30.00 |
| *—Black label, dog on top* | | | |
| ❑ LSP-4058 | Crown of Creation | 1969 | 12.00 |
| *—Orange label* | | | |
| ❑ LSP-4058 | Crown of Creation | 1975 | 10.00 |
| *—Tan label* | | | |
| ❑ LSP-4133 | Bless Its Pointed Little Head | 1969 | 12.00 |
| *—Orange label* | | | |
| ❑ LSP-4133 | Bless Its Pointed Little Head | 1975 | 10.00 |
| *—Tan label* | | | |
| ❑ LSP-4238 | Volunteers | 1969 | 12.00 |
| *—Orange label* | | | |
| ❑ LSP-4238 | Volunteers | 1975 | 10.00 |
| *—Tan label* | | | |
| ❑ LSP-4459 | The Worst of Jefferson Airplane | 1970 | 12.00 |
| ❑ AFL1-4545 | After Bathing at Baxter's | 1981 | 8.00 |
| ❑ AYL1-4718 | After Bathing at Baxter's | 1983 | 8.00 |
| **SUNDAZED** | | | |
| ❑ LP 5186 [M] | Jefferson Airplane Takes Off | 2005 | 15.00 |
| *—Reissue on 180-gram vinyl* | | | |
| ❑ LP 5187 [M] | After Bathing at Baxter's | 2005 | 15.00 |
| *—Reissue on 180-gram vinyl* | | | |

## JEFFERSON STARSHIP
See cross-references under JEFFERSON AIRPLANE.

| Number | Title (A Side/B Side) | Yr | NM |
|---|---|---|---|
| **DCC COMPACT CLASSICS** | | | |
| ❑ LPZ-2036 | Red Octopus | 1997 | 25.00 |
| *—Audiophile vinyl* | | | |
| **GRUNT** | | | |
| ❑ BFD1-0717 [Q] | Dragon Fly | 1974 | 15.00 |
| ❑ BFL1-0717 | Dragon Fly | 1974 | 10.00 |
| ❑ BFD1-0999 [Q] | Red Octopus | 1975 | 15.00 |
| ❑ BFL1-0999 | Red Octopus | 1975 | 10.00 |
| ❑ BFD1-1557 [Q] | Spitfire | 1976 | 15.00 |
| ❑ BFL1-1557 | Spitfire | 1976 | 10.00 |
| ❑ BXL1-2515 | Earth | 1978 | 10.00 |
| ❑ BZL1-3247 | Gold | 1978 | 10.00 |
| ❑ DJL1-3363 [PD] | Gold | 1978 | 15.00 |
| *—Promo-only picture disc* | | | |
| ❑ BZL1-3452 | Freedom at Point Zero | 1979 | 10.00 |
| ❑ AYL1-3660 | Red Octopus | 1980 | 8.00 |
| ❑ AYL1-3796 | Dragon Fly | 1980 | 8.00 |
| ❑ BZL1-3848 | Modern Times | 1981 | 10.00 |
| ❑ AYL1-3953 | Spitfire | 1981 | 8.00 |
| ❑ AYL1-4172 | Earth | 1981 | 8.00 |
| ❑ BXL1-4372 | Winds of Change | 1982 | 10.00 |
| ❑ BXL1-4921 | Nuclear Furniture | 1984 | 10.00 |
| ❑ AYL1-5161 | Freedom at Point Zero | 1984 | 8.00 |

## JEFFREY, JOE, GROUP

| Number | Title (A Side/B Side) | Yr | NM |
|---|---|---|---|
| **WAND** | | | |
| ❑ WDS-686 | My Pledge of Love | 1969 | 30.00 |

## JEFFREY, PAUL

| Number | Title (A Side/B Side) | Yr | NM |
|---|---|---|---|
| **SAVOY** | | | |
| ❑ MG-12192 [M] | Electrifying Sounds | 1968 | 20.00 |

## JEFFRIES, FRAN

| Number | Title (A Side/B Side) | Yr | NM |
|---|---|---|---|
| **MONUMENT** | | | |
| ❑ MLP-8069 [M] | This Is Fran Jeffries | 1967 | 30.00 |
| ❑ SLP-18069 [S] | This Is Fran Jeffries | 1967 | 25.00 |
| **WARWICK** | | | |
| ❑ W-2020 [M] | Fran Can Really Hang You Up the Most | 1960 | 20.00 |

## JEFFRIES, HERB

| Number | Title (A Side/B Side) | Yr | NM |
|---|---|---|---|
| **BETHLEHEM** | | | |
| ❑ BCP-72 [M] | Say It Isn't So | 1957 | 60.00 |
| **CORAL** | | | |
| ❑ CRL 56044 [10] | Time on My Hands | 1951 | 100.00 |
| ❑ CRL 56066 [10] | Herb Jeffries Sings Flamingo and Other Songs in a Mellow Mood | 1952 | 120.00 |
| **DOBRE** | | | |
| ❑ DR-1047 | I Remember the Bing | 1978 | 15.00 |
| **GOLDEN TONE** | | | |
| ❑ C-4066 [M] | The Devil Is a Woman | 196? | 12.00 |
| ❑ 14066 [S] | The Devil Is a Woman | 196? | 12.00 |
| **HARMONY** | | | |
| ❑ HL 7048 [M] | Herb Jeffries | 195? | 15.00 |
| **MERCURY** | | | |
| ❑ MG-25089 [10] | Magenta Moods | 1950 | 100.00 |
| ❑ MG-25090 [10] | Herb Jeffries Sings | 1950 | 100.00 |
| ❑ MG-25091 [10] | Just Jeffries | 1950 | 100.00 |
| **RCA VICTOR** | | | |
| ❑ LPM-1608 [M] | Senor Flamingo | 1957 | 40.00 |
| **RKO UNIQUE** | | | |
| ❑ ULP-128 [M] | Jamaica | 1956 | 30.00 |

## JELLY BEAN BANDITS, THE

| Number | Title (A Side/B Side) | Yr | NM |
|---|---|---|---|
| **MAINSTREAM** | | | |
| ❑ S-6103 [S] | The Jelly Bean Bandits | 1967 | 150.00 |
| ❑ 56103 [M] | The Jelly Bean Bandits | 1967 | 100.00 |

## JELLYBREAD

| Number | Title (A Side/B Side) | Yr | NM |
|---|---|---|---|
| **BLUE HORIZON** | | | |
| ❑ BH-4801 | First Slice | 1970 | 30.00 |

## JELVING, AKE

| Number | Title (A Side/B Side) | Yr | NM |
|---|---|---|---|
| **CAPITOL** | | | |
| ❑ T 10079 [M] | Christmas in Sweden | 195? | 20.00 |
| *—Black label with colorband, logo on left* | | | |
| ❑ T 10079 [M] | Christmas in Sweden | 1957 | 30.00 |
| *—Turquoise label* | | | |

## JENKINS, FLORENCE FOSTER
One of the worst singers ever to be recorded — and unlike MRS. MILLER, Jenkins sang arias!

| Number | Title (A Side/B Side) | Yr | NM |
|---|---|---|---|
| **RCA VICTOR** | | | |
| ❑ LM-2597 [M] | The Glory (????) of the Human Voice | 1961 | 20.00 |
| ❑ LRT-7001 [10] | A Florence! Foster!! Jenkins!!! Recital!!!! | 195? | 50.00 |

## JENKINS, GORDON

| Number | Title (A Side/B Side) | Yr | NM |
|---|---|---|---|
| **BAINBRIDGE** | | | |
| ❑ BT-1022 [S] | Soul of a People | 1980 | 10.00 |
| **CAPITOL** | | | |
| ❑ DT 766 [R] | The Complete Manhattan Tower | 196? | 12.00 |
| ❑ T 766 [M] | The Complete Manhattan Tower | 1956 | 30.00 |
| *—Turquoise label* | | | |
| ❑ T 781 [M] | Night Dreams | 1956 | 30.00 |
| *—Turquoise label* | | | |
| ❑ ST 884 [S] | Stolen Hours | 1959 | 30.00 |
| ❑ T 884 [M] | Stolen Hours | 1956 | 30.00 |
| *—Turquoise label* | | | |
| ❑ T 1023 [M] | Dream Dust | 1958 | 25.00 |
| ❑ ST 1048 [S] | Tropicana Holiday | 1958 | 30.00 |
| ❑ T 1048 [M] | Tropicana Holiday | 1958 | 25.00 |
| **COLUMBIA** | | | |
| ❑ CL 1764 [M] | Hawaiian Wedding Songs | 1962 | 12.00 |
| ❑ CL 1882 [M] | The Magic World of Gordon Jenkins | 1962 | 12.00 |
| ❑ CL 2009 [M] | In a Tender Mood | 1963 | 12.00 |
| ❑ CS 8564 [S] | Hawaiian Wedding Songs | 1962 | 15.00 |
| ❑ CS 8682 [S] | The Magic World of Gordon Jenkins | 1962 | 15.00 |
| ❑ CS 8809 [S] | In a Tender Mood | 1963 | 15.00 |
| **DECCA** | | | |
| ❑ DL 4714 [M] | My Heart Sings | 1966 | 12.00 |
| ❑ DL 5275 [10] | Playing His Compositions | 195? | 40.00 |
| ❑ DL 5307 [10] | For You | 195? | 40.00 |
| ❑ DL 5469 [10] | Me and Juliet/Can-Can | 1953 | 40.00 |
| ❑ DL 8011 [M] | Manhattan Tower/California (The Golden State) | 1951 | 30.00 |
| *—Black label, gold print* | | | |
| ❑ DL 8077 [M] | In the Still of the Night | 195? | 25.00 |
| ❑ DL 8109 [M] | P.S. I Love You | 195? | 25.00 |
| ❑ DL 8116 [M] | Heartbeats | 195? | 25.00 |
| ❑ DL 8313 [M] | He Likes to Go Dancing: Music for the Boy Friend | 195? | 25.00 |
| ❑ DL 74714 [S] | My Heart Sings | 1966 | 15.00 |
| ❑ DL 78011 [R] | Manhattan Tower/California (The Golden State) | 196? | 12.00 |
| **DOT** | | | |
| ❑ DLP-3752 [M] | Soft Soul | 1966 | 12.00 |
| ❑ DLP-25752 [S] | Soft Soul | 1966 | 15.00 |
| **GWP** | | | |
| ❑ 2035 | Way Back Now | 1971 | 10.00 |
| **KAPP** | | | |
| ❑ KL 1361 [M] | I Live Alone | 196? | 12.00 |
| ❑ KS 3361 [S] | I Live Alone | 196? | 15.00 |
| **MAINSTREAM** | | | |
| ❑ S-6093 [S] | Soul of a People | 196? | 12.00 |
| *—Reissue of Time S-2050* | | | |
| ❑ 56093 [M] | Soul of a People | 196? | 10.00 |
| *—Reissue of Time 52050* | | | |
| **MCA** | | | |
| ❑ 166 | Manhattan Tower/California (The Golden State) | 1973 | 10.00 |
| *—Black label with rainbow* | | | |
| **MCA CORAL** | | | |
| ❑ CB-20030 | Romance | 1973 | 10.00 |
| **PICKWICK** | | | |
| ❑ PC-3005 [M] | Yours — The Magic of Gordon Jenkins | 196? | 12.00 |
| ❑ SPC-3005 [S] | Yours — The Magic of Gordon Jenkins | 196? | 12.00 |
| **SEARS** | | | |
| ❑ SPS-403 [S] | The Romantic Moods of Gordon Jenkins | 196? | 15.00 |
| **SUNSET** | | | |
| ❑ SUM-1149 [M] | Blue Prelude | 196? | 15.00 |
| ❑ SUS-5149 [S] | Blue Prelude | 196? | 12.00 |
| **TIME** | | | |
| ❑ S-2050 [S] | Soul of a People | 196? | 15.00 |
| ❑ S-2061 [S] | France | 196? | 15.00 |
| ❑ S-2130 [S] | Paris, I Wish You Love | 196? | 15.00 |
| ❑ 52050 [M] | Soul of a People | 196? | 12.00 |
| ❑ 52061 [M] | France | 196? | 12.00 |
| ❑ 52130 [M] | Paris, I Wish You Love | 196? | 12.00 |
| **VEE JAY** | | | |
| ❑ VJLP-1089 [M] | The Great Movie Themes of the 30s, 40s and 50s | 1964 | 12.00 |
| ❑ VJLPS-1089 [S] | The Great Movie Themes of the 30s, 40s and 50s | 1964 | 20.00 |
| **VOCALION** | | | |
| ❑ VL 3615 [M] | Dreamer's Holiday | 196? | 15.00 |
| **WARNER BROS.** | | | |
| ❑ W 1464 [M] | Let's Duet | 1963 | 12.00 |
| ❑ WS 1464 [S] | Let's Duet | 1963 | 15.00 |

## JENKINS, JOHN

| Number | Title (A Side/B Side) | Yr | NM |
|---|---|---|---|
| **BLUE NOTE** | | | |
| ❑ BLP-1573 [M] | John Jenkins with Kenny Burrell | 1958 | 200.00 |
| *—Regular version with W. 63rd St., New York address on label* | | | |
| ❑ BLP-1573 [M] | John Jenkins with Kenny Burrell | 1958 | 300.00 |
| *—"Deep groove" version; W. 63rd St. address on label* | | | |
| ❑ BLP-1573 [M] | John Jenkins with Kenny Burrell | 1963 | 40.00 |
| *—With "New York, USA" address on label* | | | |

| Number | Title (A Side/B Side) | Yr | NM |
|---|---|---|---|
| ❑ BST-1573 [S] | John Jenkins with Kenny Burrell | 1959 | 120.00 |

*—Regular version with W. 63rd St., New York address on label*

| Number | Title (A Side/B Side) | Yr | NM |
|---|---|---|---|
| ❑ BST-1573 [S] | John Jenkins with Kenny Burrell | 1959 | 200.00 |

*—"Deep groove" version; W. 63rd St. address on label*

| Number | Title (A Side/B Side) | Yr | NM |
|---|---|---|---|
| ❑ BST-1573 [S] | John Jenkins with Kenny Burrell | 1963 | 40.00 |

*—With "New York, USA" address on label*

REGENT

| Number | Title (A Side/B Side) | Yr | NM |
|---|---|---|---|
| ❑ MG-6056 [M] | Jazz Eyes | 1957 | 150.00 |

SAVOY

| Number | Title (A Side/B Side) | Yr | NM |
|---|---|---|---|
| ❑ MG-12201 [M] | Jazz Eyes | 196? | 40.00 |

### JENKINS, JOHN; CLIFF JORDAN; BOBBY TIMMONS

NEW JAZZ

| Number | Title (A Side/B Side) | Yr | NM |
|---|---|---|---|
| ❑ NJLP-8232 [M] | Jenkins, Jordan and Timmons | 1960 | 150.00 |

*—Purple label*

| Number | Title (A Side/B Side) | Yr | NM |
|---|---|---|---|
| ❑ NJLP-8232 [M] | Jenkins, Jordan and Timmons | 1965 | 50.00 |

*—Blue label with trident logo*

### JENKINS, MARV

OROVOX

| Number | Title (A Side/B Side) | Yr | NM |
|---|---|---|---|
| ❑ 1001 [M] | Marv Jenkins Arrives | 196? | 40.00 |
| ❑ S-1001 [S] | Marv Jenkins Arrives | 196? | 40.00 |

REPRISE

| Number | Title (A Side/B Side) | Yr | NM |
|---|---|---|---|
| ❑ R-6077 [M] | Good Little Man at the Rubaiyat Room | 1963 | 20.00 |
| ❑ R9-6077 [S] | Good Little Man at the Rubaiyat Room | 1963 | 25.00 |

### JENNEY, JACK

COLUMBIA

| Number | Title (A Side/B Side) | Yr | NM |
|---|---|---|---|
| ❑ GL 100 [10] | The Golden Era | 1949 | 50.00 |

COLUMBIA MASTERWORKS

| Number | Title (A Side/B Side) | Yr | NM |
|---|---|---|---|
| ❑ ML 4803 [M] | Jack Jenney | 195? | 80.00 |

**JENNIFER** See JENNIFER WARNES.

### JENNINGS, BILL

AUDIO LAB

| Number | Title (A Side/B Side) | Yr | NM |
|---|---|---|---|
| ❑ AL-1514 [M] | Guitar/Vibes | 1959 | 100.00 |

KING

| Number | Title (A Side/B Side) | Yr | NM |
|---|---|---|---|
| ❑ 295-105 [10] | Jazz Interlude | 195? | 250.00 |
| ❑ 295-106 [10] | The Fabulous Guitar of Bill Jennings | 195? | 250.00 |
| ❑ 398-508 [M] | Mood Indigo | 1955 | 100.00 |
| ❑ 398-527 [M] | Billy in the Lion's Den | 1956 | 100.00 |

PRESTIGE

| Number | Title (A Side/B Side) | Yr | NM |
|---|---|---|---|
| ❑ PRLP-7164 [M] | Enough Said! | 1959 | 50.00 |
| ❑ PRLP-7177 [M] | Glide On | 1960 | 50.00 |

### JENNINGS, WAYLON

A&M

| Number | Title (A Side/B Side) | Yr | NM |
|---|---|---|---|
| ❑ SP-4238 | Don't Think Twice | 1969 | 40.00 |

BAT

| Number | Title (A Side/B Side) | Yr | NM |
|---|---|---|---|
| ❑ 1001 [M] | Waylon Jennings at JD's | 1964 | 700.00 |

*—Approximately 500 copies pressed*

MCA

| Number | Title (A Side/B Side) | Yr | NM |
|---|---|---|---|
| ❑ 731 | Waylon Jennings | 198? | 12.00 |

*—Reissue of Vocalion LP*

| Number | Title (A Side/B Side) | Yr | NM |
|---|---|---|---|
| ❑ 5688 | Will the Wolf Survive | 1986 | 10.00 |
| ❑ 5911 | Hangin' Tough | 1987 | 10.00 |
| ❑ 42038 | A Man Called Hoss | 1987 | 10.00 |
| ❑ 42038 [DJ] | A Man Called Hoss | 1987 | 60.00 |

*—Promo-only edition with letter and 48-page book*

| Number | Title (A Side/B Side) | Yr | NM |
|---|---|---|---|
| ❑ 42222 | Full Circle | 1988 | 10.00 |
| ❑ 42287 | New Classic Waylon | 1989 | 10.00 |

PAIR

| Number | Title (A Side/B Side) | Yr | NM |
|---|---|---|---|
| ❑ PDL1-1005 [(2)] | Waylon! | 1986 | 12.00 |
| ❑ PDL1-1033 [(2)] | A Couple More Years | 1986 | 12.00 |
| ❑ PDL1-1110 [(2)] | Honly Tonk Hero | 1986 | 12.00 |

PICKWICK

| Number | Title (A Side/B Side) | Yr | NM |
|---|---|---|---|
| ❑ ACL-0306 | Only Daddy That'll Walk the Line | 197? | 8.00 |

*—Reissue of RCA Camden LP*

| Number | Title (A Side/B Side) | Yr | NM |
|---|---|---|---|
| ❑ CAS-2556 | Heartaches by the Number | 197? | 8.00 |

*—Reissue of RCA Camden CAS-2556*

| Number | Title (A Side/B Side) | Yr | NM |
|---|---|---|---|
| ❑ ACL-7019 [S] | The Dark Side of Fame | 1976 | 10.00 |

*—Reissue of RCA Camden CAS-2183*

RCA

| Number | Title (A Side/B Side) | Yr | NM |
|---|---|---|---|
| ❑ 5620-1-RB | The Best of Waylon | 1987 | 10.00 |
| ❑ 9561-1-R | The Early Years (1965-1969) | 1989 | 10.00 |

RCA CAMDEN

| Number | Title (A Side/B Side) | Yr | NM |
|---|---|---|---|
| ❑ ACL1-0306 | Only Daddy That'll Walk the Line | 1973 | 10.00 |
| ❑ CAL-2183 [M] | The One and Only Waylon Jennings | 1967 | 15.00 |
| ❑ CAS-2183 [S] | The One and Only Waylon Jennings | 1967 | 12.00 |
| ❑ CAS-2556 | Heartaches by the Number | 1972 | 12.00 |
| ❑ CAS-2608 | Ruby, Don't Take Your Love to Town | 1972 | 12.00 |

Jethro Tull, *Aqualung,* Reprise MS 2035, 1971, $15.

RCA VICTOR

| Number | Title (A Side/B Side) | Yr | NM |
|---|---|---|---|
| ❑ APL1-0240 | Honky Tonk Heroes | 1973 | 15.00 |
| ❑ APL1-0539 | This Time | 1974 | 12.00 |
| ❑ APL1-0734 | The Ramblin' Man | 1974 | 12.00 |
| ❑ APL1-1062 | Dreaming My Dreams | 1975 | 10.00 |
| ❑ APL1-1108 | Waylon Live | 1976 | 10.00 |
| ❑ AFL1-1816 | Are You Ready for the Country | 1977 | 8.00 |

*—Black label, dog near side; new prefix*

| Number | Title (A Side/B Side) | Yr | NM |
|---|---|---|---|
| ❑ APL1-1816 | Are You Ready for the Country | 1976 | 10.00 |
| ❑ AAL1-2317 | Ol' Waylon | 198? | 8.00 |

*—Reissue*

| Number | Title (A Side/B Side) | Yr | NM |
|---|---|---|---|
| ❑ APL1-2317 | Ol' Waylon | 1977 | 10.00 |
| ❑ AFL1-2979 | I've Always Been Crazy | 1978 | 10.00 |
| ❑ AHL1-3378 | Greatest Hits | 1979 | 10.00 |
| ❑ AHL1-3493 | What Goes Around Comes Around | 1979 | 10.00 |
| ❑ LPM-3523 [M] | Folk-Country | 1966 | 30.00 |
| ❑ LSP-3523 [S] | Folk-Country | 1966 | 40.00 |
| ❑ AHL1-3602 | Music Man | 1980 | 10.00 |
| ❑ LPM-3620 [M] | Leavin' Town | 1966 | 30.00 |
| ❑ LSP-3620 [S] | Leavin' Town | 1966 | 40.00 |
| ❑ LPM-3660 [M] | Waylon Sings Ol' Harlan | 1967 | 30.00 |
| ❑ LSP-3660 [S] | Waylon Sings Ol' Harlan | 1967 | 40.00 |
| ❑ AYL1-3663 | Are You Ready for the Country | 1980 | 8.00 |

*—Budget-line reissue*

| Number | Title (A Side/B Side) | Yr | NM |
|---|---|---|---|
| ❑ LPM-3736 [M] | Nashville Rebel | 1967 | 40.00 |
| ❑ LSP-3736 [S] | Nashville Rebel | 1967 | 50.00 |
| ❑ LPM-3825 [M] | Love of the Common People | 1967 | 30.00 |
| ❑ LSP-3825 [S] | Love of the Common People | 1967 | 25.00 |
| ❑ AYL1-3897 | Honky Tonk Heroes | 1980 | 8.00 |

*—Budget-line reissue*

| Number | Title (A Side/B Side) | Yr | NM |
|---|---|---|---|
| ❑ LPM-3918 [M] | Hangin' On | 1968 | 100.00 |
| ❑ LSP-3918 [S] | Hangin' On | 1968 | 25.00 |
| ❑ LPM-4023 [M] | Only the Greatest | 1968 | 150.00 |
| ❑ LSP-4023 [S] | Only the Greatest | 1968 | 25.00 |
| ❑ AYL1-4072 | Dreaming My Dreams | 1981 | 8.00 |

*—Budget-line reissue*

| Number | Title (A Side/B Side) | Yr | NM |
|---|---|---|---|
| ❑ AYL1-4073 | The Ramblin' Man | 1981 | 8.00 |

*—Budget-line reissue*

| Number | Title (A Side/B Side) | Yr | NM |
|---|---|---|---|
| ❑ LSP-4085 | Jewels | 1968 | 25.00 |
| ❑ LSP-4137 | Just to Satisfy You | 1969 | 25.00 |
| ❑ AYL1-4163 | Waylon Live | 1981 | 8.00 |

*—Budget-line reissue*

| Number | Title (A Side/B Side) | Yr | NM |
|---|---|---|---|
| ❑ AYL1-4164 | I've Always Been Crazy | 1981 | 8.00 |

*—Budget-line reissue*

| Number | Title (A Side/B Side) | Yr | NM |
|---|---|---|---|
| ❑ LSP-4180 | Country-Folk | 1969 | 25.00 |
| ❑ AHL1-4247 | Black On Black | 1982 | 10.00 |
| ❑ AYL1-4250 | Music Man | 1982 | 8.00 |

*—Budget-line reissue*

| Number | Title (A Side/B Side) | Yr | NM |
|---|---|---|---|
| ❑ LSP-4260 | Waylon | 1970 | 20.00 |
| ❑ LSP-4341 | The Best of Waylon Jennings | 1970 | 20.00 |
| ❑ LSP-4418 | Singer of Sad Songs | 1970 | 20.00 |
| ❑ LSP-4487 | The Taker/Tulsa | 1971 | 20.00 |
| ❑ LSP-4567 | Cedartown, Georgia | 1971 | 20.00 |
| ❑ LSP-4647 | Good Hearted Woman | 1972 | 20.00 |
| ❑ AHL1-4673 | It's Only Rock & Roll | 1983 | 10.00 |
| ❑ LSP-4751 | Ladies Love Outlaws | 1972 | 20.00 |
| ❑ AHL1-4826 | Waylon and Company | 1983 | 10.00 |
| ❑ AYL1-4828 | The Best of Waylon Jennings | 1983 | 8.00 |

*—Budget-line reissue*

| Number | Title (A Side/B Side) | Yr | NM |
|---|---|---|---|
| ❑ LSP-4854 | Lonesome, On'ry and Mean | 1973 | 15.00 |
| ❑ AHL1-5017 | Never Could Toe the Mark | 1984 | 10.00 |
| ❑ AYL1-5126 | Ol' Waylon | 1984 | 8.00 |

*—Budget-line reissue*

| Number | Title (A Side/B Side) | Yr | NM |
|---|---|---|---|
| ❑ AHL1-5325 | Waylon's Greatest Hits, Vol. 2 | 1984 | 10.00 |
| ❑ AHL1-5428 | Turn the Page | 1985 | 10.00 |
| ❑ AYL1-5433 | Waylon and Company | 1985 | 8.00 |

*—Budget-line reissue*

| Number | Title (A Side/B Side) | Yr | NM |
|---|---|---|---|
| ❑ AHL1-5473 | Collector's Series | 1985 | 10.00 |
| ❑ AYL1-7046 | Never Could Toe the Mark | 1985 | 8.00 |

*—Budget-line reissue*

| Number | Title (A Side/B Side) | Yr | NM |
|---|---|---|---|
| ❑ AHL1-7184 | Sweet Mother Texas | 1986 | 10.00 |

SOUNDS

| Number | Title (A Side/B Side) | Yr | NM |
|---|---|---|---|
| ❑ 1001 [M] | Waylon Jennings at JD's | 1964 | 500.00 |

*—Approximately 500 copies pressed; reissue of Bat 1001*

TIME-LIFE

| Number | Title (A Side/B Side) | Yr | NM |
|---|---|---|---|
| ❑ STW-102 | Country Music | 1981 | 10.00 |

VOCALION

| Number | Title (A Side/B Side) | Yr | NM |
|---|---|---|---|
| ❑ VL 73873 | Waylon Jennings | 1969 | 25.00 |

### JENSEN, KRIS

HICKORY

| Number | Title (A Side/B Side) | Yr | NM |
|---|---|---|---|
| ❑ LP 110 [M] | Torture | 1963 | 80.00 |

### JENSEN, KURT

HOLLYWOOD

| Number | Title (A Side/B Side) | Yr | NM |
|---|---|---|---|
| ❑ LPH-137 [M] | An Evening with Jayne | 195? | 60.00 |

*—Collectible for its "cheesecake" cover of Jayne Mansfield*

### JEREMY AND THE SATYRS

REPRISE

| Number | Title (A Side/B Side) | Yr | NM |
|---|---|---|---|
| ❑ R-6282 [M] | Jeremy and the Satyrs | 1968 | 40.00 |

*—Mono is white label promo only*

| Number | Title (A Side/B Side) | Yr | NM |
|---|---|---|---|
| ❑ RS-6282 [S] | Jeremy and the Satyrs | 1968 | 20.00 |

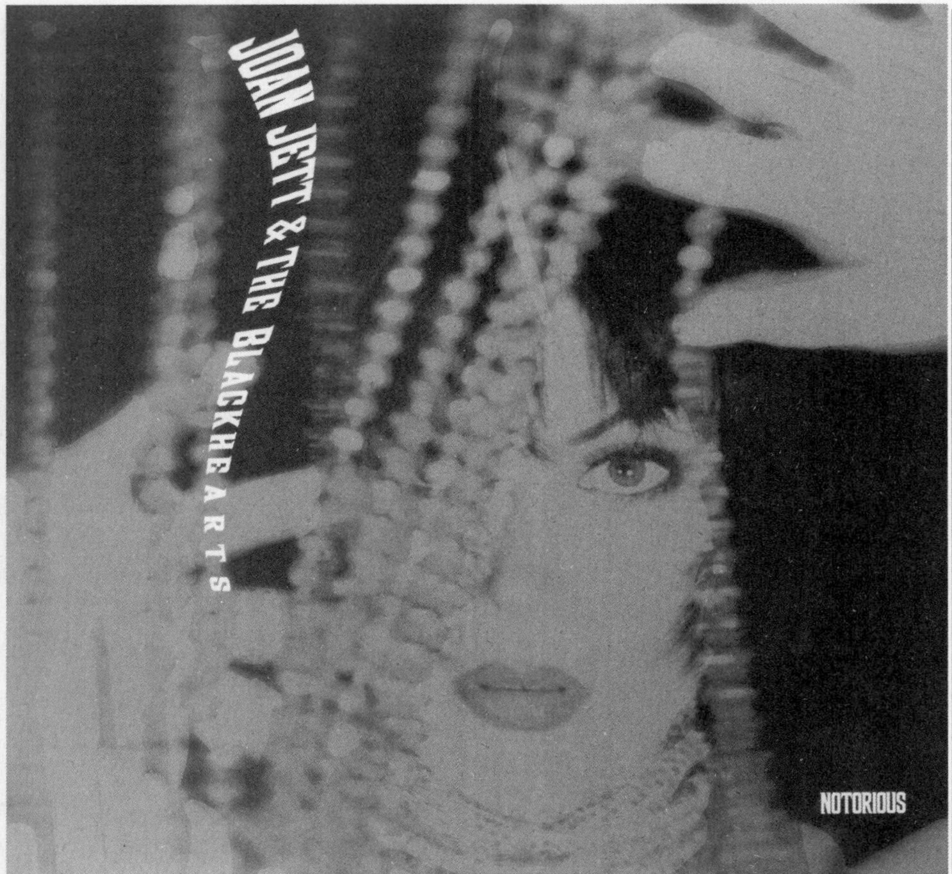


Joan Jett and the Blackhearts, *Notorious,* Blackheart Z 47488, 1991, $30.

## JEREMY'S FRIENDS

### WARWICK

| Number | Title (A Side/B Side) | Yr | NM |
|---|---|---|---|
| ❑ W-2019 [M] | Jeremy's Friends | 1960 | 50.00 |

## JERICHO

### AMPEX

| Number | Title (A Side/B Side) | Yr | NM |
|---|---|---|---|
| ❑ A-10112 | Jericho | 1971 | 25.00 |

## JESSE J. AND THE BANDITS

### RECAR

| Number | Title (A Side/B Side) | Yr | NM |
|---|---|---|---|
| ❑ 2011 [M] | Top Teen Hits | 1965 | 100.00 |

## JESUS JONES

### SBK

| Number | Title (A Side/B Side) | Yr | NM |
|---|---|---|---|
| ❑ SPRO-05348/9 [DJ] | A Conversation with Jesus | 1990 | 20.00 |
| *—Generic cover with sticker* | | | |
| ❑ K1-94480 | Liquidizer | 1989 | 15.00 |

## JETHRO TULL

### CHRYSALIS

| Number | Title (A Side/B Side) | Yr | NM |
|---|---|---|---|
| ❑ PRO 623 [DJ] | The Jethro Tull Radio Show | 1975 | 50.00 |
| ❑ CHR 1003 | Thick as a Brick | 1973 | 12.00 |
| *—Green label, "3300 Warner Blvd." address* | | | |
| ❑ CHR 1003 | Thick as a Brick | 1977 | 10.00 |
| *—Blue label, New York address* | | | |
| ❑ 2CH 1035 [(2)] | Living in the Past | 1972 | 20.00 |
| *—Two-record set with booklet; green labels* | | | |
| ❑ CHR 1035 [(2)] | Living in the Past | 1977 | 15.00 |
| *—Blue label, New York address* | | | |
| ❑ CHR 1040 | A Passion Play | 1973 | 12.00 |
| *—Green label, "3300 Warner Blvd." address* | | | |
| ❑ CHR 1040 | A Passion Play | 1977 | 10.00 |
| *—Blue label, New York address* | | | |
| ❑ CHR 1041 | This Was | 1973 | 12.00 |
| *—Green label, "3300 Warner Blvd." address* | | | |
| ❑ CHR 1041 | This Was | 1977 | 10.00 |
| *—Blue label, New York address* | | | |
| ❑ CHR 1042 | Stand Up | 1973 | 12.00 |
| *—Green label, "3300 Warner Blvd." address* | | | |
| ❑ CHR 1042 | Stand Up | 1977 | 10.00 |
| *—Blue label, New York address* | | | |
| ❑ CHR 1043 | Benefit | 1973 | 12.00 |
| *—Green label, "3300 Warner Blvd." address* | | | |
| ❑ CHR 1043 | Benefit | 1977 | 10.00 |
| *—Blue label, New York address* | | | |
| ❑ CH4 1044 [Q] | Aqualung | 1974 | 40.00 |
| ❑ CHR 1044 | Aqualung | 1973 | 12.00 |
| *—Green label, "3300 Warner Blvd." address* | | | |
| ❑ CHR 1044 | Aqualung | 1977 | 10.00 |
| *—Blue label, New York address* | | | |
| ❑ CH4 1067 [Q] | War Child | 1974 | 40.00 |
| ❑ CHR 1067 | War Child | 1974 | 10.00 |
| *—Blue label, New York address* | | | |
| ❑ CHR 1067 | War Child | 1974 | 12.00 |
| *—Green label, "3300 Warner Blvd." address* | | | |
| ❑ CHR 1078 | M.U. — The Best of Jethro Tull | 1975 | 12.00 |
| *—Green label, "3300 Warner Blvd." address* | | | |
| ❑ CHR 1078 | M.U. — The Best of Jethro Tull | 1977 | 10.00 |
| *—Blue label, New York address* | | | |
| ❑ CHR 1082 | Minstrel in the Gallery | 1975 | 12.00 |
| *—Green label, "3300 Warner Blvd." address* | | | |
| ❑ CHR 1082 | Minstrel in the Gallery | 1977 | 10.00 |
| *—Blue label, New York address* | | | |
| ❑ CHR 1111 | Too Old to Rock 'N' Roll; Too Young to Die! | 1976 | 12.00 |
| *—Green label, "3300 Warner Blvd." address* | | | |
| ❑ CHR 1111 | Too Old to Rock 'N' Roll; Too Young to Die! | 1977 | 10.00 |
| *—Blue label, New York address* | | | |
| ❑ CHR 1132 | Songs from the Wood | 1977 | 10.00 |
| ❑ CHR 1135 | Repeat — The Best of Jethro Tull, Vol. II | 1977 | 10.00 |
| ❑ CHR 1175 | Heavy Horses | 1978 | 10.00 |
| ❑ CHR2 1201 [(2)] | Jethro Tull Live — Bursting Out | 1978 | 12.00 |
| ❑ CHR 1238 | Stormwatch | 1979 | 10.00 |
| ❑ CHR 1301 | "A" | 1980 | 10.00 |
| ❑ CHR 1380 | The Broadsword and the Beast | 1982 | 10.00 |
| ❑ F1-21708 | Rock Island | 1989 | 10.00 |
| ❑ FV 41003 | Thick as a Brick | 1983 | 8.00 |
| ❑ PV 41003 | Thick as a Brick | 1986 | 8.00 |
| ❑ KV2 41035 [(2)] | Living in the Past | 1983 | 12.00 |
| ❑ PV 41040 | A Passion Play | 1983 | 8.00 |
| ❑ PV 41041 | This Was | 1983 | 8.00 |
| ❑ PV 41042 | Stand Up | 1983 | 8.00 |
| ❑ PV 41043 | Benefit | 1983 | 8.00 |
| ❑ FV 41044 | Aqualung | 1983 | 8.00 |
| ❑ PV 41067 | War Child | 1983 | 8.00 |
| ❑ FV 41078 | M.U. — The Best of Jethro Tull | 1983 | 8.00 |
| ❑ PV 41082 | Minstrel in the Gallery | 1983 | 8.00 |
| ❑ PV 41111 | Too Old to Rock 'N' Roll; Too Young to Die! | 1983 | 8.00 |
| ❑ PV 41132 | Songs from the Wood | 1983 | 8.00 |
| ❑ FV 41135 | Repeat — The Best of Jethro Tull, Vol. II | 1983 | 8.00 |
| ❑ PV 41135 | Repeat — The Best of Jethro Tull, Vol. II | 1986 | 8.00 |
| ❑ PV 41175 | Heavy Horses | 1983 | 8.00 |
| ❑ V2X 41201 [(2)] | Jethro Tull Live — Bursting Out | 1983 | 12.00 |
| ❑ PV 41238 | Stormwatch | 1983 | 8.00 |
| ❑ PV 41301 | "A" | 1983 | 8.00 |
| ❑ FV 41380 | The Broadsword and the Beast | 1983 | 8.00 |
| ❑ PV 41380 | The Broadsword and the Beast | 1986 | 8.00 |
| ❑ FV 41461 | Under Wraps | 1984 | 10.00 |
| ❑ PV 41461 | Under Wraps | 1986 | 8.00 |
| ❑ FV 41515 | Original Masters | 1985 | 10.00 |
| ❑ FV 41590 | Crest of a Knave | 1987 | 10.00 |
| ❑ V5X 41653 [(5)] | 20 Years of Jethro Tull | 1988 | 80.00 |
| ❑ VX2 41655 [(2)] | 20 Years of Jethro Tull | 1989 | 25.00 |
| *—Abridged version of Chrysalis 41653* | | | |

### DCC COMPACT CLASSICS

| Number | Title (A Side/B Side) | Yr | NM |
|---|---|---|---|
| ❑ LPZ 2033 | Aqualung | 1997 | 100.00 |
| *—Audiophile vinyl* | | | |
| ❑ LPZ-2059 | Original Masters | 1998 | 40.00 |
| *—Audiophile vinyl* | | | |

### MOBILE FIDELITY

| Number | Title (A Side/B Side) | Yr | NM |
|---|---|---|---|
| ❑ 1-061 | Aqualung | 1980 | 70.00 |
| *—Audiophile vinyl* | | | |
| ❑ 1-092 | The Broadsword and the Beast | 1982 | 40.00 |
| *—Audiophile vinyl* | | | |
| ❑ 1-187 | Thick as a Brick | 1985 | 30.00 |
| *—Audiophile vinyl* | | | |

### REPRISE

| Number | Title (A Side/B Side) | Yr | NM |
|---|---|---|---|
| ❑ MS 2035 | Aqualung | 1971 | 15.00 |
| ❑ MS 2072 | Thick as a Brick | 1972 | 15.00 |
| ❑ 2MS 2106 [(2)] | Living in the Past | 1972 | 25.00 |
| *—Two-record set with booklet; original edition, rather than using cardboard outer sleeve for the records, has record sleeves attached to enclosed booklet, and thus is difficult to find intact* | | | |
| ❑ RS 6336 | This Was | 1969 | 20.00 |
| *—Two-tone orange label with "r:" and "W7" logos on label* | | | |
| ❑ RS 6336 | This Was | 1970 | 15.00 |
| *—All-one-color (orange/brown) label with no "W7" on label* | | | |
| ❑ RS 6360 | Stand Up | 1969 | 20.00 |
| *—Two-tone orange label with "r:" and "W7" logos on label; band "stands up" when gatefold is opened* | | | |
| ❑ RS 6360 | Stand Up | 1970 | 15.00 |
| *—All-one-color (orange/brown) label with no "W7" on label* | | | |
| ❑ RS 6400 | Benefit | 1970 | 15.00 |
| *—All-one-color (orange/brown) label with no "W7" on label* | | | |
| ❑ RS 6400 | Benefit | 1970 | 20.00 |
| *—Two-tone orange label with "r:" and "W7" logos on label* | | | |

## JETT, JOAN, AND THE BLACKHEARTS

### BLACKHEART

| Number | Title (A Side/B Side) | Yr | NM |
|---|---|---|---|
| ❑ JJ 707 | Joan Jett | 1980 | 60.00 |
| ❑ BFZ 40544 | Good Music | 1986 | 12.00 |
| ❑ FZ 44146 | Up Your Alley | 1988 | 10.00 |
| ❑ Z 45473 | The Hit List | 1990 | 15.00 |
| ❑ Z 47488 | Notorious | 1991 | 30.00 |

### BOARDWALK

| Number | Title (A Side/B Side) | Yr | NM |
|---|---|---|---|
| ❑ NB1-33243 | I Love Rock-n-Roll | 1982 | 10.00 |
| *—First pressing contains "Little Drummer Boy," which was replaced on second pressings* | | | |
| ❑ NB1-33243 | I Love Rock-n-Roll | 1982 | 12.00 |
| *—Second pressing, with "Oh Woe Is Me"* | | | |
| ❑ NB1-33251 | Bad Reputation | 1982 | 10.00 |
| *—Reissue of FW 37065* | | | |
| ❑ FW 37065 | Bad Reputation | 1981 | 12.00 |
| *—Essentially a reissue of Blackheart JJ 707* | | | |

### MCA

| Number | Title (A Side/B Side) | Yr | NM |
|---|---|---|---|
| ❑ 5437 | Album | 1983 | 12.00 |
| ❑ 5476 | Glorious Results of a Misspent Youth | 1984 | 12.00 |
| ❑ R 163731 | Glorious Results of a Misspent Youth | 1984 | 16.00 |
| *—RCA Music Service edition* | | | |

### REPRISE

| Number | Title (A Side/B Side) | Yr | NM |
|---|---|---|---|
| ❑ 45567 | Pure and Simple | 1994 | 20.00 |

## JEWEL

### ATLANTIC

| Number | Title (A Side/B Side) | Yr | NM |
|---|---|---|---|
| ❑ 82700 [(2)] | Pieces of You | 1997 | 25.00 |
| *—Contains five songs not on the 1995 CD of the same name* | | | |
| ❑ 82950 [(2)] | Spirit | 1998 | 30.00 |
| ❑ 83519-1 [(2)] | This Way | 2001 | 50.00 |

## JIM & JESSE

### COLUMBIA LIMITED EDITION

| Number | Title (A Side/B Side) | Yr | NM |
|---|---|---|---|
| ❑ LE 10542 | All-Time Great Country Instrumentals | 197? | 10.00 |

### EPIC

| Number | Title (A Side/B Side) | Yr | NM |
|---|---|---|---|
| ❑ LN 24031 [M] | Bluegrass Special | 1963 | 20.00 |
| ❑ LN 24074 [M] | Bluegrass Classics | 1963 | 20.00 |
| ❑ LN 24107 [M] | The Old Country Church | 1964 | 20.00 |
| ❑ LN 24144 [M] | Y'All Come | 1964 | 20.00 |
| ❑ LN 24176 [M] | Berry Pickin' the Country | 1965 | 20.00 |
| ❑ LN 24204 [M] | Sing Unto Him | 1966 | 20.00 |
| ❑ LN 24314 [M] | Diesel on My Tail | 1967 | 20.00 |
| ❑ BN 26031 [S] | Bluegrass Special | 1963 | 25.00 |

| Number | Title (A Side/B Side) | Yr | NM |
|---|---|---|---|
| ❑ BN 26074 [S] | Bluegrass Classics | 1963 | 25.00 |
| ❑ BN 26107 [S] | The Old Country Church | 1964 | 25.00 |
| ❑ BN 26144 [S] | Y'All Come | 1964 | 25.00 |
| ❑ BN 26176 [S] | Berry Pickin' the Country | 1965 | 25.00 |
| ❑ BN 26204 [S] | Sing Unto Him | 1966 | 25.00 |
| ❑ BN 26314 [S] | Diesel on My Tail | 1967 | 25.00 |
| ❑ BN 26394 | All-Time Great Country Instrumentals | 1968 | 20.00 |
| ❑ BN 26465 | Saluting the Louvin Brothers | 1969 | 20.00 |

**JIMENEZ, JOSE**

A&M

| Number | Title (A Side/B Side) | Yr | NM |
|---|---|---|---|
| ❑ SP-4144 | Mashuganishi Yogi | 1968 | 15.00 |

CAPITOL

| Number | Title (A Side/B Side) | Yr | NM |
|---|---|---|---|
| ❑ ST-464 | Hoo Ha! Direct from Noshville | 1970 | 15.00 |

KAPP

| Number | Title (A Side/B Side) | Yr | NM |
|---|---|---|---|
| ❑ KL 1215 [M] | More Jose Jimenez | 1961 | 20.00 |
| ❑ KL 1215 [M] | Jose Jimenez the Submarine Officer | 1961 | 25.00 |
| *—Original title* | | | |
| ❑ KL 1238 [M] | Jose Jimenez at the Hungry I | 196? | 15.00 |
| *—Reissue with new title* | | | |
| ❑ KL 1238 [M] | Jose Jimenez — The Astronaut (The First Man in Space) | 1961 | 20.00 |
| ❑ KL-1257 [M] | Jose Jimenez in Orbit — Bill Dana on Earth | 1961 | 20.00 |
| ❑ KL 1304 [M] | Jose Jimenez Talks to Teenagers of All Ages | 1962 | 20.00 |
| ❑ KL-1320 [M] | Jose Jimenez — Our Secret Weapon | 1963 | 20.00 |
| ❑ KL-1332 [M] | Jose Jimenez in Jollywood | 1963 | 20.00 |
| ❑ KL-1402 [M] | Bill Dana in Las Vegas | 1964 | 20.00 |
| ❑ KS 3238 [S] | Jose Jimenez at the Hungry I | 196? | 15.00 |
| *—Reissue with new title* | | | |
| ❑ KS 3238 [S] | Jose Jimenez — The Astronaut (The First Man in Space) | 1961 | 25.00 |
| ❑ KS-3257 [S] | Jose Jimenez in Orbit — Bill Dana on Earth | 1961 | 25.00 |
| ❑ KS 3304 [S] | Jose Jimenez Talks to Teenagers of All Ages | 1962 | 25.00 |
| ❑ KS-3332 [S] | Jose Jimenez in Jollywood | 1963 | 25.00 |

ROULETTE

| Number | Title (A Side/B Side) | Yr | NM |
|---|---|---|---|
| ❑ R 25161 [M] | My Name...Jose Jimenez | 1961 | 20.00 |
| *—Reissue of Signature LP* | | | |

SIGNATURE

| Number | Title (A Side/B Side) | Yr | NM |
|---|---|---|---|
| ❑ SM 1013 [M] | My Name...Jose Jimenez | 1960 | 25.00 |

**JIVE FIVE, THE**

AMBIENT SOUND

| Number | Title (A Side/B Side) | Yr | NM |
|---|---|---|---|
| ❑ FZ 37717 | Here We Are | 1982 | 15.00 |

AMBIENT SOUND/ROUNDER

| Number | Title (A Side/B Side) | Yr | NM |
|---|---|---|---|
| ❑ ASR-801 | Way Back | 1985 | 12.00 |

COLLECTABLES

| Number | Title (A Side/B Side) | Yr | NM |
|---|---|---|---|
| ❑ COL-5022 | Greatest Hits | 198? | 10.00 |

RELIC

| Number | Title (A Side/B Side) | Yr | NM |
|---|---|---|---|
| ❑ 5020 | The Jive Five's Greatest Hits (1961-1963) | 198? | 10.00 |

UNITED ARTISTS

| Number | Title (A Side/B Side) | Yr | NM |
|---|---|---|---|
| ❑ UAL-3455 [M] | The Jive Five | 1965 | 50.00 |
| ❑ UAS-6455 [S] | The Jive Five | 1965 | 75.00 |

**JOBIM, ANTONIO CARLOS**

WARNER BROS.

| Number | Title (A Side/B Side) | Yr | NM |
|---|---|---|---|
| ❑ WS 1611 [S] | The Wonderful World of Antonio Carlos Jobim | 1966 | 20.00 |
| ❑ WS 1636 [S] | Love, Strings | 1966 | 20.00 |
| *—Gold label* | | | |

**JOE & EDDIE**

GNP CRESCENDO

| Number | Title (A Side/B Side) | Yr | NM |
|---|---|---|---|
| ❑ GNP-75 [M] | Joe & Eddie | 1963 | 20.00 |
| ❑ GNP-86 [M] | There's a Meetin' Here Tonite | 1963 | 20.00 |
| ❑ GNP-96 [M] | Coast to Coast | 1964 | 20.00 |
| ❑ GNPS-96 [S] | Coast to Coast | 1964 | 25.00 |
| ❑ GNP-99 [M] | Joe & Eddie, Volume 4 | 1964 | 20.00 |
| ❑ GNPS-99 [S] | Joe & Eddie, Volume 4 | 1964 | 25.00 |
| ❑ GNP-2005 [M] | Tear Down the Walls | 1965 | 15.00 |
| ❑ GNPS-2005 [S] | Tear Down the Walls | 1965 | 20.00 |
| ❑ GNP-2007 [M] | Joe & Eddie Live in Hollywood | 1965 | 15.00 |
| ❑ GNPS-2007 [S] | Joe & Eddie Live in Hollywood | 1965 | 20.00 |
| ❑ GNP-2014 [M] | Walkin' Down the Line | 1965 | 15.00 |
| ❑ GNPS-2014 [S] | Walkin' Down the Line | 1965 | 20.00 |
| ❑ GNP-2021 [M] | The Magic of Their Singing | 1966 | 15.00 |
| ❑ GNPS-2021 [S] | The Magic of Their Singing | 1966 | 20.00 |
| ❑ GNP-2032 [M] | The Best of Joe & Eddie | 1966 | 15.00 |
| ❑ GNPS-2032 [S] | The Best of Joe & Eddie | 1966 | 20.00 |

**JOEL, BILLY**

COLUMBIA

| Number | Title (A Side/B Side) | Yr | NM |
|---|---|---|---|
| ❑ AS 326 [DJ] | Souvenir | 1976 | 30.00 |
| *—Promo-only LP with one side live, one side a compilation of studio tracks* | | | |
| ❑ AS 402 [DJ] | Inter Chords/Billy Joel Interview | 1977 | 25.00 |
| *—Promo-only interview album* | | | |
| ❑ AS 1343 [DJ] | Billy Joel Interview | 1982 | 25.00 |
| ❑ CQ 32544 [Q] | Piano Man | 1974 | 20.00 |

Elton John, *Empty Sky,* MCA 2130, 1975, black label, $10.

| Number | Title (A Side/B Side) | Yr | NM |
|---|---|---|---|
| ❑ KC 32544 | Piano Man | 1973 | 12.00 |
| *—Some copies have the first song spelled "Travelin' Prayer," others have it "Travellin' Prayer." No difference in value.* | | | |
| ❑ PC 32544 | Piano Man | 1976 | 10.00 |
| *—No bar code on back cover* | | | |
| ❑ PC 32544 | Piano Man | 1979 | 8.00 |
| *—With bar code on back cover* | | | |
| ❑ PC 33146 | Streetlife Serenade | 1975 | 10.00 |
| *—No bar code on back cover* | | | |
| ❑ PC 33146 | Streetlife Serenade | 1979 | 8.00 |
| *—With bar code on back cover* | | | |
| ❑ PCQ 33146 [Q] | Streetlife Serenade | 1975 | 20.00 |
| ❑ PC 33848 | Turnstiles | 1976 | 8.00 |
| *—With bar code on back cover* | | | |
| ❑ PC 33848 | Turnstiles | 1976 | 10.00 |
| *—No bar code on back cover* | | | |
| ❑ PCQ 33848 [Q] | Turnstiles | 1976 | 20.00 |
| ❑ HC 34987 | The Stranger | 1981 | 30.00 |
| *—Original pressing of half-speed mastered edition* | | | |
| ❑ JC 34987 | The Stranger | 1977 | 10.00 |
| ❑ PC 34987 | The Stranger | 1979 | 8.00 |
| ❑ FC 35609 | 52nd Street | 1978 | 10.00 |
| ❑ PC 35609 | 52nd Street | 1985 | 8.00 |
| ❑ FC 36384 | Glass Houses | 1980 | 10.00 |
| ❑ PC 36384 | Glass Houses | 1986 | 8.00 |
| ❑ PC 37461 | Songs in the Attic | 1984 | 8.00 |
| ❑ TC 37461 | Songs in the Attic | 1981 | 10.00 |
| ❑ QC 38200 | The Nylon Curtain | 1982 | 10.00 |
| ❑ QC 38837 | An Innocent Man | 1983 | 10.00 |
| ❑ PC 38984 | Cold Spring Harbor | 1983 | 8.00 |
| *—Remixed, remastered version of Family Productions album* | | | |
| ❑ C2 40121 [(2)] | Greatest Hits, Volumes 1 and 2 | 1985 | 12.00 |
| ❑ OC 40402 | The Bridge | 1986 | 10.00 |
| ❑ C2 40996 [(2)] | KOHUEPT | 1987 | 15.00 |
| ❑ OC 44366 | Storm Front | 1989 | 12.00 |
| ❑ HC 44987 | The Stranger | 1982 | 25.00 |
| *—Half-speed mastered edition (reissue)* | | | |
| ❑ HC 45609 | 52nd Street | 1982 | 25.00 |
| *—Half-speed mastered edition* | | | |
| ❑ HC 47461 | Songs in the Attic | 1982 | 70.00 |
| *—Half-speed mastered edition* | | | |
| ❑ HC 48837 | An Innocent Man | 1983 | 30.00 |
| *—Half-speed mastered edition* | | | |

FAMILY PRODUCTIONS

| Number | Title (A Side/B Side) | Yr | NM |
|---|---|---|---|
| ❑ FPS-2700 | Cold Spring Harbor | 1971 | 40.00 |
| *—Authentic copies have mostly dark blue labels; when reissued on Columbia, the entire LP was remixed and remastered, and "You Can Make Me Free" was shortened by three minutes* | | | |

**JOHANSEN, DAVID** Also see NEW YORK DOLLS.

BLUE SKY

| Number | Title (A Side/B Side) | Yr | NM |
|---|---|---|---|
| ❑ AS 519 [DJ] | The David Johansen Group Live | 1978 | 30.00 |
| ❑ AS 1281 [DJ] | Live and Sampler | 1981 | 12.00 |
| *—Promo-only four-song sampler* | | | |
| ❑ JZ 34926 | David Johansen | 1978 | 10.00 |
| ❑ JZ 36082 | In Style | 1979 | 10.00 |
| ❑ FZ 36589 | Here Comes the Night | 1981 | 10.00 |
| ❑ ARZ 38004 | Live It Up | 1982 | 10.00 |

PASSPORT

| Number | Title (A Side/B Side) | Yr | NM |
|---|---|---|---|
| ❑ PB-6043 | Sweet Revenge | 1984 | 10.00 |

**JOHANSSON, JAN**

DOT

| Number | Title (A Side/B Side) | Yr | NM |
|---|---|---|---|
| ❑ DLP-3416 [M] | Sweden Non-Stop | 1962 | 20.00 |
| ❑ DLP-25416 [S] | Sweden Non-Stop | 1962 | 25.00 |

**JOHN, ELTON**

COLUMBIA SPECIAL PRODUCTS

| Number | Title (A Side/B Side) | Yr | NM |
|---|---|---|---|
| ❑ P 16196 | The Best of Elton John, Volume One | 1981 | 12.00 |
| ❑ P 16197 | The Best of Elton John, Volume Two | 1981 | 12.00 |
| *—Both of the above "Distributed Exclusively by Scott Distributing Corp."* | | | |

DCC COMPACT CLASSICS

| Number | Title (A Side/B Side) | Yr | NM |
|---|---|---|---|
| ❑ LPZ-2004 | Madman Across the Water | 1994 | 120.00 |
| *—Audiophile vinyl* | | | |
| ❑ LPZ-2013 | Elton John's Greatest Hits | 1995 | 100.00 |
| *—Audiophile vinyl* | | | |
| ❑ LPZ-2020 | Elton John's Greatest Hits, Volume 2 | 1996 | — |
| *—Canceled* | | | |

DIRECT DISC

| Number | Title (A Side/B Side) | Yr | NM |
|---|---|---|---|
| ❑ SD-16614 [(2)] | Goodbye Yellow Brick Road | 1980 | 50.00 |
| *—Audiophile vinyl* | | | |

GEFFEN

| Number | Title (A Side/B Side) | Yr | NM |
|---|---|---|---|
| ❑ GHS 2002 | The Fox | 1981 | 10.00 |
| ❑ GHS 2013 | Jump Up! | 1982 | 10.00 |
| ❑ GHS 4006 | Too Low for Zero | 1983 | 10.00 |
| ❑ GHS 24031 | Breaking Hearts | 1984 | 10.00 |
| ❑ GHS 24031 [DJ] | Breaking Hearts | 1984 | 20.00 |
| *—Promo pressing on Quiex II vinyl* | | | |

Elton John, *Greatest Hits Volumes One and Two,* MCA R231711, 1980s, 2 records, RCA Music Service exclusive, $15.

| Number | Title (A Side/B Side) | Yr | NM |
|---|---|---|---|
| ❑ GHS 24077 | Ice on Fire | 1985 | 10.00 |
| ❑ GHS 24114 | Leather Jackets | 1986 | 10.00 |
| ❑ GHS 24153 | Elton John's Greatest Hits, Vol. 3, 1979-1987 | 1987 | 10.00 |

MCA

| Number | Title (A Side/B Side) | Yr | NM |
|---|---|---|---|
| ❑ 619 | 11-17-70 | 1979 | 8.00 |
| ❑ 620 | Empty Sky | 1979 | 8.00 |
| ❑ 621 | Rock of the Westies | 1979 | 8.00 |
| ❑ 622 | Here and There | 1979 | 8.00 |
| ❑ 771 | Victim of Love | 1981 | 8.00 |
| ❑ 772 | 21 at 33 | 1981 | 8.00 |
| ❑ 1689 | Elton John's Greatest Hits | 198? | 8.00 |
| ❑ 4L33-1848 [(4)DJ] | Victim of Love | 1979 | 100.00 |
| *—Promo-only collection of the entire album as four 12-inch singles* | | | |
| ❑ L33-1995 [PD] | A Single Man | 1978 | 40.00 |
| *—Promo picture disc* | | | |
| ❑ 2012 | Elton John | 1973 | 10.00 |
| ❑ 2014 | Tumbleweed Connection | 1973 | 10.00 |
| *—With booklet* | | | |
| ❑ 2015 | 11-17-70 | 1973 | 10.00 |
| ❑ 2016 | Madman Across the Water | 1973 | 10.00 |
| *—With booklet* | | | |
| ❑ 2017 | Honky Chateau | 1973 | 10.00 |
| ❑ 2100 | Don't Shoot Me, I'm Only the Piano Player | 1973 | 10.00 |
| *—With black rainbow label and booklet* | | | |
| ❑ 2100 | Don't Shoot Me, I'm Only the Piano Player | 1973 | 20.00 |
| *—With all-black label (no rainbow) and booklet* | | | |
| ❑ 2116 | Caribou | 1974 | 10.00 |
| ❑ 2128 | Elton John's Greatest Hits | 1974 | 10.00 |
| ❑ 2130 | Empty Sky | 1975 | 10.00 |
| *—First American issue of his 1969 debut* | | | |
| ❑ 2142 | Captain Fantastic and the Brown Dirt Cowboy | 1975 | 12.00 |
| *—With custom label, two booklets and poster* | | | |
| ❑ 2142 [DJ] | Captain Fantastic and the Brown Dirt Cowboy | 1975 | 300.00 |
| *—Brown vinyl promo, autographed by Elton John and Bernie Taupin* | | | |
| ❑ 2163 | Rock of the Westies | 1975 | 10.00 |
| ❑ 2197 | Here and There | 1976 | 10.00 |
| ❑ 3001 | Tumbleweed Connection | 1977 | 8.00 |
| ❑ 3003 | Madman Across the Water | 1977 | 8.00 |
| ❑ 3027 | Elton John's Greatest Hits, Volume 2 | 1977 | 10.00 |
| ❑ 3065 | A Single Man | 1978 | 10.00 |
| ❑ 5104 | Victim of Love | 1979 | 10.00 |
| ❑ 5121 | 21 at 33 | 1980 | 10.00 |
| *—Originals have custom labels* | | | |
| ❑ 5224 | Elton John's Greatest Hits | 1981 | 8.00 |
| ❑ 5225 | Elton John's Greatest Hits, Volume 2 | 1981 | 8.00 |
| ❑ 6011 [(2)] | Blue Moves | 1979 | 10.00 |
| ❑ 6240 | Reg Strikes Back | 1988 | 10.00 |
| ❑ 6321 | Sleeping with the Past | 1989 | 10.00 |
| ❑ 6894 [(2)] | Goodbye Yellow Brick Road | 1980 | 10.00 |
| ❑ 8022 [(2)] | Live in Australia with the Melbourne Symphony Orchestra | 1987 | 15.00 |
| ❑ 2-10003 [(2)] | Goodbye Yellow Brick Road | 1973 | 15.00 |
| ❑ 13921 [EP] | The Thom Bell Sessions | 1979 | 8.00 |
| ❑ 14951 [PD] | A Single Man | 1978 | 20.00 |
| *—Stock picture disc* | | | |
| ❑ 37064 | Honky Chateau | 1979 | 8.00 |
| ❑ 37065 | Caribou | 1979 | 8.00 |
| ❑ 37066 | Captain Fantastic and the Brown Dirt Cowboy | 1979 | 8.00 |
| ❑ 37067 | Elton John | 1979 | 8.00 |
| ❑ 37068 | A Single Man | 1979 | 8.00 |
| ❑ 37113 | Don't Shoot Me, I'm Only the Piano Player | 1979 | 8.00 |
| ❑ 37199 | Tumbleweed Connection | 1982 | 8.00 |
| ❑ 37200 | Madman Across the Water | 1982 | 8.00 |
| ❑ 37215 | Elton John's Greatest Hits | 1983 | 8.00 |
| ❑ 37216 | Elton John's Greatest Hits | 1983 | 8.00 |
| ❑ 37266 | Your Songs | 1986 | 10.00 |
| ❑ 39115 | The Complete Thom Bell Sessions | 1989 | 30.00 |
| ❑ R231711 [(2)] | Greatest Hits Volumes One and Two | 198? | 15.00 |
| *—RCA Music Service exclusive; combines both MCA greatest-hits sets* | | | |

MOBILE FIDELITY

| Number | Title (A Side/B Side) | Yr | NM |
|---|---|---|---|
| ❑ 2-160 [(2)] | Goodbye Yellow Brick Road | 1984 | 40.00 |
| *—Audiophile vinyl* | | | |

NAUTILUS

| Number | Title (A Side/B Side) | Yr | NM |
|---|---|---|---|
| ❑ NR-42 | Elton John's Greatest Hits | 198? | 100.00 |
| *—Audiophile vinyl* | | | |

PARAMOUNT

| Number | Title (A Side/B Side) | Yr | NM |
|---|---|---|---|
| ❑ PAS 6004 | Friends (Soundtrack) | 1971 | 20.00 |
| *—Whitish gray label original* | | | |
| ❑ PAS 6004 | Friends (Soundtrack) | 1975 | 25.00 |
| *—Dark blue label with "Paramount" logo at top and ABC Records reference along edge; much rarer than the original* | | | |

ROCKET

| Number | Title (A Side/B Side) | Yr | NM |
|---|---|---|---|
| ❑ L33-1173/4 [DJ] | Get Up and Dance | 1977 | 100.00 |
| *—Promo-only sampler from "Blue Moves" LP; blue vinyl* | | | |
| ❑ 2-11004 [(2)] | Blue Moves | 1976 | 15.00 |
| *—Originals have light blue labels with a train at the top of the label* | | | |
| ❑ 526915-1 | Made in England | 1995 | 20.00 |
| *—U.S. version is on 180-gram vinyl, distributed by Classic Records* | | | |

UNI

| Number | Title (A Side/B Side) | Yr | NM |
|---|---|---|---|
| ❑ 73090 | Elton John | 1970 | 15.00 |
| ❑ 73096 | Tumbleweed Connection | 1971 | 15.00 |
| *—With booklet* | | | |
| ❑ 93090 | Elton John | 1971 | 12.00 |
| ❑ 93096 | Tumbleweed Connection | 1971 | 12.00 |
| *—With booklet* | | | |
| ❑ 93105 | 11-17-70 | 1971 | 15.00 |
| ❑ 93120 | Madman Across the Water | 1971 | 15.00 |
| *—With booklet* | | | |
| ❑ 93135 | Honky Chateau | 1972 | 15.00 |
| *—With "(P) 1972 This Record Co., Ltd." on label* | | | |
| ❑ 93135 | Honky Chateau | 1972 | 20.00 |
| *—With "(P) 1972 MCA Records, Inc." on label* | | | |

## JOHN, LITTLE WILLIE

BLUESWAY

| Number | Title (A Side/B Side) | Yr | NM |
|---|---|---|---|
| ❑ BLS-6069 | Free at Last | 1973 | 25.00 |

KING

| Number | Title (A Side/B Side) | Yr | NM |
|---|---|---|---|
| ❑ 564 [M] | Fever | 1957 | 600.00 |
| *—White cover with "Fever" in large colorful letters* | | | |
| ❑ 395-564 [M] | Fever | 1956 | 1000. |
| *—"Nurse with thermometer" cover* | | | |
| ❑ 596 [M] | Talk to Me | 1958 | 300.00 |
| ❑ 603 [M] | Mister Little Willie John | 1958 | 250.00 |
| ❑ 691 [M] | Little Willie John In Action | 1960 | 250.00 |
| ❑ 739 [M] | Sure Things | 1961 | 150.00 |
| ❑ 767 [M] | The Sweet, the Hot, the Teenage Beat | 1961 | 150.00 |
| ❑ 802 [M] | Come On and Join Little Willie John | 1962 | 120.00 |
| ❑ 895 [M] | These Are My Favorite Songs | 1964 | 100.00 |
| ❑ 949 [M] | Little Willie Sings All Originals | 1966 | 100.00 |
| ❑ KS-949 [S] | Little Willie Sings All Originals | 1966 | 150.00 |
| ❑ KS-1081 | Free at Last | 1970 | 40.00 |

## JOHN, ROBERT

COLUMBIA

| Number | Title (A Side/B Side) | Yr | NM |
|---|---|---|---|
| ❑ CS 9687 [M] | If You Don't Want My Love | 1968 | 50.00 |
| *—Mono is white label promo only with stereo number; "Special Mono Radio Station Copy" sticker is on front cover* | | | |
| ❑ CS 9687 [S] | If You Don't Want My Love | 1968 | 20.00 |

EMI AMERICA

| Number | Title (A Side/B Side) | Yr | NM |
|---|---|---|---|
| ❑ SW-17007 | Robert John | 1979 | 10.00 |
| ❑ SW-17027 | Back on the Street | 1980 | 10.00 |

HARMONY

| Number | Title (A Side/B Side) | Yr | NM |
|---|---|---|---|
| ❑ KH 31353 | On the Way Up | 1972 | 12.00 |

## JOHN'S CHILDREN

WHITE WHALE

| Number | Title (A Side/B Side) | Yr | NM |
|---|---|---|---|
| ❑ WWS 7128 | Orgasm | 1970 | 200.00 |

## JOHNNIE AND JACK

DECCA

| Number | Title (A Side/B Side) | Yr | NM |
|---|---|---|---|
| ❑ DL 4308 [M] | Smiles and Tears | 1962 | 20.00 |
| ❑ DL 74308 [S] | Smiles and Tears | 1962 | 25.00 |

RCA CAMDEN

| Number | Title (A Side/B Side) | Yr | NM |
|---|---|---|---|
| ❑ CAL-747 [M] | Johnny & Jack Sing "Poison Love" and Other Country Favorites | 1963 | 25.00 |
| ❑ CAS-747 [R] | Johnny & Jack Sing "Poison Love" and Other Country Favorites | 1963 | 12.00 |
| ❑ CAL-822 [M] | Sincerely | 1964 | 25.00 |
| ❑ CAS-822 [R] | Sincerely | 1964 | 12.00 |

RCA VICTOR

| Number | Title (A Side/B Side) | Yr | NM |
|---|---|---|---|
| ❑ LPM-1587 [M] | The Tennessee Mountain Boys | 1957 | 40.00 |
| ❑ LPM-2017 [M] | Hits by Johnnie & Jack | 1959 | 30.00 |
| ❑ LSP-2017 [R] | Hits by Johnnie & Jack | 1959 | 20.00 |
| ❑ VPM-6022 [(2)] | All the Best of Johnnie & Jack | 1970 | 25.00 |

## JOHNNY AND THE BLUE BEATS

WINSOR

| Number | Title (A Side/B Side) | Yr | NM |
|---|---|---|---|
| ❑ 1001 | Smile | 196? | 40.00 |

## JOHNNY AND THE HURRICANES

ATILA

| Number | Title (A Side/B Side) | Yr | NM |
|---|---|---|---|
| ❑ 1030 [M] | Live at the Star-Club | 1964 | 300.00 |

BIG TOP

| Number | Title (A Side/B Side) | Yr | NM |
|---|---|---|---|
| ❑ 12-1302 [M] | The Big Sound of Johnny and the Hurricanes | 1960 | 250.00 |
| ❑ ST 12-1302 [S] | The Big Sound of Johnny and the Hurricanes | 1960 | 300.00 |

WARWICK

| Number | Title (A Side/B Side) | Yr | NM |
|---|---|---|---|
| ❑ W-2007 [M] | Johnny and the Hurricanes | 1959 | 150.00 |
| ❑ W-2007ST [S] | Johnny and the Hurricanes | 1959 | 300.00 |
| ❑ W-2010 [M] | Stormsville | 1960 | 150.00 |
| ❑ W-2010ST [S] | Stormsville | 1960 | 250.00 |

**Number | Title (A Side/B Side) | Yr | NM**

### JOHNSON, BETTY

ATLANTIC
❑ 8017 [M] Betty Johnson 1958 50.00
❑ 8027 [M] The Song You Heard When You Fell in Love 1959 50.00
*—Black label*
❑ 8027 [M] The Song You Heard When You Fell in Love 1960 20.00
*—White "fan" logo on right*
❑ SD 8027 [S] The Song You Heard When You Fell in Love 1959 80.00
*—Green label*
❑ SD 8027 [S] The Song You Heard When You Fell in Love 1960 25.00
*—White "fan" logo on right*

### JOHNSON, BLIND WILLIE

FOLKWAYS
❑ FG-3585 [M] Blind Willie Johnson: His Story 1957 100.00

RBF
❑ 10 [M] Blind Willie Johnson 1927-1930 1965 70.00

### JOHNSON, BOB, AND THE LONESOME TRAVELERS

PARKWAY
❑ P-7017 [M] 12 Shades of Bluegrass 1962 50.00

### JOHNSON, BUBBER

KING
❑ 569 [M] Come Home 1957 200.00
❑ 624 [M] Bubber Johnson Sings Sweet Love Songs 1959 150.00

### JOHNSON, BUDD

ARGO
❑ LP-721 [M] French Cookin' 1963 25.00
❑ LPS-721 [S] French Cookin' 1963 30.00
❑ LP-736 [M] Ya! Ya! 1964 25.00
❑ LPS-736 [S] Ya! Ya! 1964 30.00
❑ LP-748 [M] Off the Wall 1965 25.00
❑ LPS-748 [S] Off the Wall 1965 30.00

FELSTED
❑ SJA-2007 [S] Blues A La Mode 1959 80.00
❑ FAJ-7007 [M] Blues A La Mode 1959 60.00

RIVERSIDE
❑ RLP-343 [M] Budd Johnson and the Four Brass Giants 1960 40.00
❑ RS-9343 [S] Budd Johnson and the Four Brass Giants 1960 50.00

SWINGVILLE
❑ SVLP-2015 [M] Let's Swing 1961 50.00
*—Purple label*
❑ SVLP-2015 [M] Let's Swing 1965 25.00
*—Blue label, trident logo at right*

### JOHNSON, BUDDY

MERCURY
❑ MG-20209 [M] Rock 'N' Roll 195? 80.00
❑ MG-20322 [M] Walkin' 195? 80.00
❑ MG-20330 [M] Buddy Johnson Wails 195? 80.00
❑ MG-20347 [M] Swing Me 195? 80.00
❑ SR-60072 [S] Buddy Johnson Wails 195? 100.00

WING
❑ MGW-12005 [M] Rock 'N' Roll 1956 150.00
❑ MGW-12111 [M] Rock 'n' Roll Stage Show 1963 40.00
❑ MGW-12234 [M] Buddy Johnson Wails 196? 30.00

### JOHNSON, BUDDY & ELLA

MERCURY
❑ MG-20347 [M] Swing Me 195? 80.00

ROULETTE
❑ R 25085 [M] Go Ahead and Rock and Roll 1959 80.00
❑ SR 25085 [S] Go Ahead and Rock and Roll 1959 120.00

### JOHNSON, BUNK

AMERICAN MUSIC
❑ 638 [10] Bunk Plays the Blues — The Spirituals 1951 60.00
❑ 644 [10] Bunk Johnson Talking 1952 60.00

COLUMBIA
❑ CL 520 [M] Bunk Johnson and His Band 1953 50.00
*—Maroon label, gold print*
❑ CL 520 [M] Bunk Johnson and His Band 1955 40.00
*—Red and black label with six "eye" logos*
❑ GL 520 [M] Bunk Johnson and His Band 1952 60.00
*—Black label, silver print*
❑ CL 829 [M] Bunk Johnson 1955 40.00
*—Red and black label with six "eye" logos*

COLUMBIA MASTERWORKS
❑ ML 4802 [M] The Last Testament of a Great New Orleans Jazzman 1950 80.00

COMMODORE
❑ DL-30007 [M] The Bunk Johnson Band 1952 50.00

**Number | Title (A Side/B Side) | Yr | NM**

GOOD TIME JAZZ
❑ L-17 [10] Bunk Johnson and the Yerba Buena Jazz Band 1953 50.00
❑ L-12048 [M] Bunk Johnson and His Superior Jazz Band 1962 30.00

MAINSTREAM
❑ 56039 [M] Bunk Johnson — A Legend 1965 20.00

### JOHNSON, BUNK, AND LU WATTERS

GOOD TIME JAZZ
❑ L-12024 [M] Bunk and Lu 195? 40.00

### JOHNSON, CANDY

CANJO
❑ LP-1001 [M] The Candy Johnson Show 1964 40.00
❑ LP-1002 [M] Bikini Beach 1964 40.00

### JOHNSON, CHARLIE

"X"
❑ LVA-3026 [10] Harlem in the Twenties, Vol. 2 1954 60.00

### JOHNSON, DICK

EMARCY
❑ MG-36081 [M] Music for Swinging Moderns 1956 100.00

RIVERSIDE
❑ RLP 12-253 [M] Most Likely... 1957 80.00

### JOHNSON, J.J.

BLUE NOTE
❑ BLP-1505 [M] The Eminent Jay Jay Johnson, Volume 1 1955 300.00
*—"Deep groove" version; Lexington Ave. address on label*
❑ BLP-1505 [M] The Eminent Jay Jay Johnson, Volume 1 1958 200.00
*—"Deep groove" version, W. 63rd St. address on label*
❑ BLP-1505 [M] The Eminent Jay Jay Johnson, Volume 1 1963 50.00
*—"New York, USA" address on label*
❑ BLP-1506 [M] The Eminent Jay Jay Johnson, Volume 2 1955 300.00
*—"Deep groove" version; Lexington Ave. address on label*
❑ BLP-1506 [M] The Eminent Jay Jay Johnson, Volume 2 1958 200.00
*—"Deep groove" version, W. 63rd St. address on label*
❑ BLP-1506 [M] The Eminent Jay Jay Johnson, Volume 2 1963 50.00
*—"New York, USA" address on label*
❑ BLP-5028 [10] Jay Jay Johnson All Stars 1953 700.00
❑ BLP-5057 [10] Jay Jay Johnson, Volume 2 1955 700.00
❑ BLP-5070 [10] Jay Jay Johnson, Volume 3 1955 700.00

COLUMBIA
❑ CL 935 [M] "J" Is for Jazz 1956 50.00
*—Red and black label with six "eye" logos*
❑ CL 1030 [M] First Place 1957 50.00
*—Red and black label with six "eye" logos*
❑ CL 1084 [M] Dial J.J. 5 1957 50.00
*—Red and black label with six "eye" logos*
❑ CL 1161 [M] J.J. In Person 1958 50.00
*—Red and black label with six "eye" logos*
❑ CL 1303 [M] Blue Trombone 1959 40.00
*—Red and black label with six "eye" logos*
❑ CL 1383 [M] Really Livin' 1959 40.00
*—Red and black label with six "eye" logos*
❑ CL 1547 [M] Trombones and Voices 1960 30.00
*—Red and black label with six "eye" logos*
❑ CL 1606 [M] J.J. Inc 1961 30.00
*—Red and black label with six "eye" logos*
❑ CL 1737 [M] A Touch of Satin 1962 40.00
*—Red and black label with six "eye" logos*
❑ CS 8009 [S] J.J. In Person 1959 40.00
*—Red and black label with six "eye" logos*
❑ CS 8109 [S] Blue Trombone 1959 50.00
*—Red and black label with six "eye" logos*
❑ CS 8178 [S] Really Livin' 1959 50.00
*—Red and black label with six "eye" logos*
❑ CS 8347 [S] Trombones and Voices 1960 40.00
*—Red and black label with six "eye" logos*
❑ CS 8406 [S] J.J. Inc 1961 40.00
*—Red and black label with six "eye" logos*
❑ CS 8537 [S] A Touch of Satin 1962 50.00
*—Red and black label with six "eye" logos*
❑ CS 8537 [S] A Touch of Satin 1963 20.00
*—Red label with "360 Sound Stereo" in black or white at bottom*

IMPULSE!
❑ A-68 [M] Proof Positive 1965 40.00
❑ AS-68 [S] Proof Positive 1965 50.00

MOSAIC
❑ MQ11-169 [(11)] The Complete Columbia J.J. Johnson Small Group Sessions 199? 300.00

RCA VICTOR
❑ LPM-3350 [M] J.J.! 1965 20.00
❑ LSP-3350 [S] J.J.! 1965 25.00
❑ LPM-3458 [M] Goodies 1965 20.00
❑ LSP-3458 [S] Goodies 1965 25.00
❑ LPM-3544 [M] Broadway Express 1966 20.00
❑ LSP-3544 [S] Broadway Express 1966 25.00
❑ LPM-3833 [M] The Total J.J. Johnson 1967 30.00

**Number | Title (A Side/B Side) | Yr | NM**

❑ LSP-3833 [S] The Total J.J. Johnson 1967 20.00

REGENT
❑ MG-6001 [M] Jazz South Pacific 1956 50.00

SAVOY
❑ MG-12205 [M] Jazz South Pacific 196? 20.00
*—Reissue of Regent 6001*

VERVE
❑ V-8530 [M] J.J.'s Broadway 1963 20.00
❑ V6-8530 [S] J.J.'s Broadway 1963 25.00

### JOHNSON, J.J./BENNIE GREEN

PRESTIGE
❑ PRLP-123 [10] Modern Jazz Trombones, Volume 2 1952 200.00

### JOHNSON, J.J., AND KAI WINDING

A&M
❑ SP-3008 Israel 1968 20.00
*—As "K. & J.J."*
❑ SP9-3008 Israel 1983 15.00
*—As "K. & J.J."; "Audio Master Plus" reissue*
❑ SP-3016 Betwixt and Between 1969 20.00
*—As "J & K"*

BETHLEHEM
❑ BCP-13 [M] K + J.J. (East Coast Jazz/7) 1955 100.00
*—With "BCP 13" on the label as well as the cover*
❑ BCP-6001 [M] K + J.J. (East Coast Jazz/7) 1955 50.00
*—With the number "BCP 13" on the upper right corner of the front cover and "BCP 6001" stickers on the back cover and "BCP 6001" on the labels*

COLUMBIA
❑ CL 742 [M] Trombone for Two 1956 50.00
*—Red label with "360 Sound Stereo" in black or white at bottom*
❑ CL 742 [M] Trombone for Two 1963 20.00
*—Red label with "Guaranteed High Fidelity" or "360 Sound Mono" at bottom*
❑ CL 892 [M] J.J. Johnson, Kai Winding + 6 1956 50.00
*—Red and black "6-eye" label*
❑ CL 892 [M] J.J. Johnson, Kai Winding + 6 1963 20.00
*—Red label with "Guaranteed High Fidelity" or "360 Sound Mono" at bottom*
❑ CL 973 [M] Jay and Kai 1957 50.00
*—Red and black label with six "eye" logos*
❑ CL 973 [M] Jay and Kai 1963 20.00
*—Red label with "Guaranteed High Fidelity" or "360 Sound Mono" at bottom*
❑ CL 2573 [10] Kai + J.J. 1955 80.00

IMPULSE!
❑ A-1 [M] The Great Kai & J.J. 1961 40.00
❑ AS-1 [S] The Great Kai & J.J. 1961 50.00

PRESTIGE
❑ PRLP-109 [10] Modern Jazz Trombones 1951 200.00
❑ PRLP-195 [10] Jay and Kai 1954 200.00
❑ PRLP-7253 [M] Looking Back 1963 50.00
❑ PRST-7253 [R] Looking Back 1963 30.00

SAVOY
❑ MG-12010 [M] Jay and Kai 1955 80.00
❑ MG-12106 [M] J.J. Johnson's Jazz Quintets 1957 80.00
❑ MG-15038 [10] Jay and Kai 1954 120.00
❑ MG-15048 [10] Jay and Kai, Volume 2 1955 100.00
❑ MG-15049 [10] Jay and Kai, Volume 3 1955 100.00

"X"
❑ LXA-1040 [M] An Afternoon at Birdland 1956 80.00

### JOHNSON, J.J.; KAI WINDING; BENNIE GREEN

DEBUT
❑ DLP-5 [10] Jazz Workshop, Volume 1 1953 200.00
❑ DLP-14 [10] Jazz Workshop, Volume 2 1955 200.00
❑ DEB-126 [M] Four Trombones 1958 100.00

FANTASY
❑ 6005 [M] Four Trombones 1963 30.00
*—Black vinyl*
❑ 6005 [M] Four Trombones 1963 50.00
*—Red vinyl*
❑ 86005 [R] Four Trombones 1963 20.00
*—Black vinyl*
❑ 86005 [R] Four Trombones 1963 40.00
*—Blue vinyl*

PRESTIGE
❑ 16-4 [M] Trombone by Three 1956 500.00
*—This album plays at 16 2/3 rpm and is marked as such; white label*
❑ PRLP-7023 [M] Trombone by Three 1956 150.00
*—Yellow label with W. 50th St. address*
❑ PRLP-7030 [M] J.J. Johnson, Kai Winding, Bennie Green 1956 150.00
*—Yellow label with W. 50th St. address*

### JOHNSON, JAMES P.

BLUE NOTE
❑ BLP-7011 [10] Stomps, Rags and Blues 1951 300.00
❑ BLP-7012 [10] Jazz Band Ball 1951 300.00

COLUMBIA
❑ CL 1780 [M] Father of the Stride Piano 1961 25.00
*—Red and black label with six "eye" logos*

| Number | Title (A Side/B Side) | Yr | NM |
|---|---|---|---|
| **DECCA** | | | |
| ❑ DL 5190 [10] | The Daddy of the Piano | 1950 | 100.00 |
| ❑ DL 5228 [10] | James P. Johnson Plays Fats Waller Favorites | 1951 | 100.00 |
| **FOLKWAYS** | | | |
| ❑ FJ-2816 | Striding in Dixieland | 196? | 20.00 |
| ❑ FJ-2842 [M] | Yamekraw | 1962 | 20.00 |
| ❑ FJ-2850 | The Original James P. Johnson | 196? | 20.00 |
| **RIVERSIDE** | | | |
| ❑ RLP 12-105 [M] | Rediscovered Early Solos | 1955 | 60.00 |
| *—White label, blue print* | | | |
| ❑ RLP 12-105 [M] | Rediscovered Early Solos | 1959 | 40.00 |
| *—Blue label, microphone logo at top* | | | |
| ❑ RLP 12-151 [M] | Backwater Blues | 1955 | 60.00 |
| *—White label, blue print* | | | |
| ❑ RLP 12-151 [M] | Backwater Blues | 1959 | 40.00 |
| *—Blue label, microphone logo at top* | | | |
| ❑ RLP-1011 [10] | Rent Party | 1953 | 120.00 |
| ❑ RLP-1046 [10] | Early Harlem Piano, Vol. 2 | 1954 | 120.00 |
| ❑ RLP-1056 [10] | Harlem Rent Party | 1955 | 100.00 |
| **STINSON** | | | |
| ❑ SLP-21 [10] | New York Jazz | 1950 | 120.00 |
| ❑ SLP-21 [M] | New York Jazz | 195? | 50.00 |

## JOHNSON, KEITH

| Number | Title (A Side/B Side) | Yr | NM |
|---|---|---|---|
| **REFERENCE RECORDINGS** | | | |
| ❑ RR-7 | Prof. Johnson's Astounding Sound Show | 198? | 20.00 |
| *—Plays at 45 rpm* | | | |

## JOHNSON, LAURIE

| Number | Title (A Side/B Side) | Yr | NM |
|---|---|---|---|
| **COLPIX** | | | |
| ❑ CP 471 [M] | England's New Big Band | 1964 | 20.00 |

## JOHNSON, LONNIE

| Number | Title (A Side/B Side) | Yr | NM |
|---|---|---|---|
| **BLUESVILLE** | | | |
| ❑ BVLP-1007 [M] | Blues by Lonnie | 1960 | 200.00 |
| *—Blue label, silver print* | | | |
| ❑ BVLP-1007 [M] | Blues by Lonnie | 1964 | 60.00 |
| *—Blue label with trident logo at right* | | | |
| ❑ BVLP-1011 [M] | Blues and Ballads | 1960 | 200.00 |
| *—Blue label, silver print* | | | |
| ❑ BVLP-1011 [M] | Blues and Ballads | 1964 | 60.00 |
| *—Blue label with trident logo at right* | | | |
| ❑ BVLP-1024 [M] | Losing Game | 1961 | 200.00 |
| *—Blue label, silver print* | | | |
| ❑ BVLP-1024 [M] | Losing Game | 1964 | 60.00 |
| *—Blue label with trident logo at right* | | | |
| ❑ BVLP-1062 [M] | Another Night to Cry | 1963 | 200.00 |
| *—Blue label, silver print* | | | |
| ❑ BVLP-1062 [M] | Another Night to Cry | 1964 | 60.00 |
| *—Blue label with trident logo at right* | | | |
| **COLUMBIA** | | | |
| ❑ C 46221 | Steppin' On the Blues | 1990 | 20.00 |
| **FANTASY** | | | |
| ❑ OBC-502 | Blues by Lonnie | 198? | 12.00 |
| ❑ OBC-531 | Blues and Ballads | 1990 | 12.00 |
| **KING** | | | |
| ❑ 520 [M] | Lonesome Road | 1958 | 2000. |
| *—VG value 750; VG+ value 1375* | | | |
| ❑ 958 [M] | Lonnie Johnson 24 Twelve-Bar Blues | 1966 | 60.00 |
| ❑ KS-958 [R] | Lonnie Johnson 24 Twelve-Bar Blues | 1966 | 60.00 |
| ❑ KS-1083 | Tomorrow Night | 1970 | 25.00 |
| **PRESTIGE** | | | |
| ❑ PRST-7724 | The Blues of Lonnie Johnson | 1970 | 20.00 |

## JOHNSON, LONNIE, AND VICTORIA SPIVEY

| Number | Title (A Side/B Side) | Yr | NM |
|---|---|---|---|
| **BLUESVILLE** | | | |
| ❑ BVLP-1044 [M] | Idle Hours | 1962 | 150.00 |
| *—Blue label, silver print* | | | |
| ❑ BVLP-1044 [M] | Idle Hours | 1964 | 50.00 |
| *—Blue label with trident logo at right* | | | |
| ❑ BVLP-1054 [M] | Woman Blues | 1962 | 150.00 |
| *—Blue label, silver print* | | | |
| ❑ BVLP-1054 [M] | Woman Blues | 1964 | 50.00 |
| *—Blue label with trident logo at right* | | | |
| **FANTASY** | | | |
| ❑ OBC-518 | Idle Hours | 198? | 12.00 |

## JOHNSON, MARV

| Number | Title (A Side/B Side) | Yr | NM |
|---|---|---|---|
| **UNITED ARTISTS** | | | |
| ❑ UAL 3081 [M] | Marvelous Marv Johnson | 1960 | 150.00 |
| ❑ UAL 3118 [M] | More Marv Johnson | 1961 | 150.00 |
| ❑ UAL 3187 [M] | I Believe | 1962 | 150.00 |
| ❑ UAS 6081 [S] | Marvelous Marv Johnson | 1960 | 200.00 |
| ❑ UAS 6118 [S] | More Marv Johnson | 1961 | 200.00 |
| ❑ UAS 6187 [S] | I Believe | 1962 | 200.00 |

## JOHNSON, OSIE

| Number | Title (A Side/B Side) | Yr | NM |
|---|---|---|---|
| **BETHLEHEM** | | | |
| ❑ BCP-66 [M] | The Happy Jazz of Osie Johnson | 1957 | 50.00 |
| **PERIOD** | | | |
| ❑ SPL-1108 [10] | Osie's Oasis | 1955 | 80.00 |
| ❑ SPL-1112 [10] | Johnson's Whacks | 1955 | 80.00 |
| **RCA VICTOR** | | | |
| ❑ LPM-1369 [M] | A Bit of the Blues | 1957 | 40.00 |

## JOHNSON, PETE

| Number | Title (A Side/B Side) | Yr | NM |
|---|---|---|---|
| **BLUE NOTE** | | | |
| ❑ BLP-7019 [10] | Boogie Woogie Blues and Skiffle | 1952 | 300.00 |
| **BRUNSWICK** | | | |
| ❑ BL 58041 [10] | Boogie Woogie Mood | 1953 | 80.00 |
| **MOSAIC** | | | |
| ❑ MR1-119 | The Pete Johnson/Earl Hines/Teddy Bunn Blue Note Sessions | 199? | 20.00 |
| **RIVERSIDE** | | | |
| ❑ RLP-1056 [10] | Jumpin' with Pete Johnson | 1955 | 80.00 |
| **SAVOY** | | | |
| ❑ MG-14018 [M] | Pete's Blues | 1958 | 120.00 |

## JOHNSON, PETE/HADDA BROOKS

| Number | Title (A Side/B Side) | Yr | NM |
|---|---|---|---|
| **CROWN** | | | |
| ❑ CLP-5058 [M] | Boogie | 195? | 20.00 |

## JOHNSON, PLAS

| Number | Title (A Side/B Side) | Yr | NM |
|---|---|---|---|
| **CAPITOL** | | | |
| ❑ ST 1281 [S] | This Must Be the Plas! | 1960 | 30.00 |
| ❑ T 1281 [M] | This Must Be the Plas! | 1960 | 25.00 |
| ❑ ST 1503 [S] | Mood for the Blues | 1961 | 30.00 |
| ❑ T 1503 [M] | Mood for the Blues | 1961 | 25.00 |
| **TAMPA** | | | |
| ❑ TP-24 [M] | Bop Me, Daddy | 1957 | 100.00 |
| *—Colored vinyl* | | | |
| ❑ TP-24 [M] | Bop Me, Daddy | 1958 | 50.00 |
| *—Black vinyl* | | | |

## JOHNSON, ROBERT

| Number | Title (A Side/B Side) | Yr | NM |
|---|---|---|---|
| **COLUMBIA** | | | |
| ❑ CL 1654 [M] | King of the Delta Blues Singers | 1961 | 500.00 |
| *—Red and black label with six "eye" logos* | | | |
| ❑ CL 1654 [M] | King of the Delta Blues Singers | 1963 | 50.00 |
| *—"Guaranteed High Fidelity" label* | | | |
| ❑ CL 1654 [M] | King of the Delta Blues Singers | 1965 | 25.00 |
| *—"360 Sound Mono" label* | | | |
| ❑ CL 1654 [M] | King of the Delta Blues Singers | 1970 | 12.00 |
| *—Orange label with "Columbia" circling the edge* | | | |
| ❑ CL 1654 [M] | King of the Delta Blues Singers | 1998 | 10.00 |
| *—Red label, "Columbia" in white at top, "Sony Music" under side numbers* | | | |
| ❑ CL 1654 [M] | King of the Delta Blues Singers | 2001 | 15.00 |
| *—Reissue on 180-gram vinyl (sealed copies have a sticker indicating this)* | | | |
| ❑ C 30034 [M] | King of the Delta Blues Singers, Volume 2 | 1970 | 20.00 |
| ❑ PC 30034 [M] | King of the Delta Blues Singers, Volume 2 | 1979 | 10.00 |
| ❑ C3 46222 [(3)] | Robert Johnson — The Complete Recordings | 1990 | 50.00 |

## JOHNSON, RUDOLPH

| Number | Title (A Side/B Side) | Yr | NM |
|---|---|---|---|
| **BLACK JAZZ** | | | |
| ❑ 4 | Spring Rain | 1971 | 25.00 |
| ❑ 11 | Second Coming | 1972 | 25.00 |

## JOHNSON, SYL

| Number | Title (A Side/B Side) | Yr | NM |
|---|---|---|---|
| **TWINIGHT** | | | |
| ❑ LPS-1002 | Is It Because I'm Black? | 1968 | 30.00 |

## JOHNSON AND DRAKE

| Number | Title (A Side/B Side) | Yr | NM |
|---|---|---|---|
| **OVATION** | | | |
| ❑ OVQD-1434 [Q] | Carry It On | 1973 | 20.00 |

## JOHNSON FAMILY SINGERS, THE

| Number | Title (A Side/B Side) | Yr | NM |
|---|---|---|---|
| **RCA VICTOR** | | | |
| ❑ LPM-1128 [M] | Old Time Religion | 1955 | 25.00 |

## JOHNSTON, BRUCE

| Number | Title (A Side/B Side) | Yr | NM |
|---|---|---|---|
| **COLUMBIA** | | | |
| ❑ CL 2057 [M] | Surfin' 'Round the World | 1963 | 150.00 |
| ❑ CS 8857 [S] | Surfin' 'Round the World | 1963 | 300.00 |
| ❑ PC 34459 | Going Public | 1976 | 15.00 |
| **DEL-FI** | | | |
| ❑ DFLP-1228 [M] | Surfers' Pajama Party | 1963 | 100.00 |
| ❑ DFST-1228 [S] | Surfers' Pajama Party | 1963 | 200.00 |

## JOHNSTON, COLONEL JUBILATION B., AND THE MYSTIC KNIGHTS BAND AND STREET SINGERS

| Number | Title (A Side/B Side) | Yr | NM |
|---|---|---|---|
| **COLUMBIA** | | | |
| ❑ CL 2532 [M] | Moldy Goldies | 1966 | 25.00 |
| ❑ CS 9332 [S] | Moldy Goldies | 1966 | 30.00 |

## JOLLY, PETE

| Number | Title (A Side/B Side) | Yr | NM |
|---|---|---|---|
| **AVA** | | | |
| ❑ A-22 [M] | Little Bird | 1963 | 20.00 |
| ❑ AS-22 [S] | Little Bird | 1963 | 25.00 |
| ❑ A-39 [M] | Sweet September | 1963 | 20.00 |
| ❑ AS-39 [S] | Sweet September | 1963 | 25.00 |
| ❑ A-51 [M] | Hello Jolly | 1964 | 20.00 |
| ❑ AS-51 [S] | Hello Jolly | 1964 | 25.00 |
| **CHARLIE PARKER** | | | |
| ❑ PLP-825 [M] | Pete Jolly Gasses Everybody | 1962 | 20.00 |
| ❑ PLP-825S [S] | Pete Jolly Gasses Everybody | 1962 | 25.00 |
| **COLUMBIA** | | | |
| ❑ CL 2397 [M] | Too Much, Baby | 1965 | 20.00 |
| ❑ CS 9197 [S] | Too Much, Baby | 1965 | 25.00 |
| **METROJAZZ** | | | |
| ❑ E-1014 [M] | Impossible | 1958 | 35.00 |
| ❑ SE-1014 [S] | Impossible | 1958 | 35.00 |
| **MGM** | | | |
| ❑ E-4127 [M] | 5 O'Clock Shadows | 1963 | 20.00 |
| ❑ SE-4127 [S] | 5 O'Clock Shadows | 1963 | 25.00 |
| **RCA VICTOR** | | | |
| ❑ LPM-1105 [M] | Jolly Jumps In | 1955 | 50.00 |
| ❑ LPM-1125 [M] | Duo, Trio, Quartet | 1955 | 50.00 |
| ❑ LPM-1367 [M] | When Lights Are Low | 1957 | 50.00 |
| **STEREO FIDELITY** | | | |
| ❑ SFS-11000 [S] | Continental Jazz | 1960 | 25.00 |

## JOLSON, AL

| Number | Title (A Side/B Side) | Yr | NM |
|---|---|---|---|
| **DECCA** | | | |
| ❑ DXA 169 [(2)M] | The Best of Jolson | 196? | 25.00 |
| ❑ DLP 5006 [10] | Jolson Sings Again | 1949 | 30.00 |
| ❑ DLP 5026 [10] | Al Jolson In Songs He Made Famous | 1949 | 30.00 |
| ❑ DLP 5029 [10] | Souvenir Album, Vol. II | 1949 | 30.00 |
| ❑ DLP 5030 [10] | Al Jolson, Vol. III | 1949 | 30.00 |
| ❑ DLP 5031 [10] | Souvenir Album, Vol. IV | 1949 | 30.00 |
| ❑ DL 5308 [10] | Stephen Foster Songs | 1950 | 100.00 |
| ❑ DL 5314 [10] | Souvenir Album, Vol. V | 1951 | 30.00 |
| ❑ DL 5315 [10] | Souvenir Album, Vol. VI | 1951 | 30.00 |
| ❑ DXSA 7169 [(2)R] | The Best of Jolson | 196? | 15.00 |
| ❑ DL 9034 [M] | You Made Me Love You | 1957 | 25.00 |
| *—Black label, silver print* | | | |
| ❑ DL 9034 [M] | You Made Me Love You | 196? | 15.00 |
| *—Black label with color bars* | | | |
| ❑ DL 9035 [M] | Rock-a-Bye Your Baby | 1957 | 25.00 |
| *—Black label, silver print* | | | |
| ❑ DL 9035 [M] | Rock-a-Bye Your Baby | 196? | 15.00 |
| *—Black label with color bars* | | | |
| ❑ DL 9036 [M] | Rainbow 'Round My Shoulder | 1957 | 25.00 |
| *—Black label, silver print* | | | |
| ❑ DL 9036 [M] | Rainbow 'Round My Shoulder | 196? | 15.00 |
| *—Black label with color bars* | | | |
| ❑ DL 9037 [M] | You Ain't Heard Nothin' Yet! | 1957 | 15.00 |
| *—Black label with color bars* | | | |
| ❑ DL 9037 [M] | You Ain't Heard Nothin' Yet! | 1957 | 25.00 |
| *—Black label, silver print* | | | |
| ❑ DL 9038 [M] | Memories | 1957 | 15.00 |
| *—Black label with color bars* | | | |
| ❑ DL 9038 [M] | Memories | 1957 | 25.00 |
| *—Black label, silver print* | | | |
| ❑ DL 9050 [M] | Among My Souvenirs | 1957 | 25.00 |
| *—Black label, silver print* | | | |
| ❑ DL 9050 [M] | Among My Souvenirs | 196? | 15.00 |
| *—Black label with color bars* | | | |
| ❑ DL 9063 [M] | The Immortal Al Jolson | 1958 | 25.00 |
| *—Maroon label, silver print* | | | |
| ❑ DL 9063 [M] | The Immortal Al Jolson | 196? | 15.00 |
| *—Black label with color bars* | | | |
| ❑ DL 9070 [M] | Overseas | 1959 | 30.00 |
| *—Black label, silver print* | | | |
| ❑ DL 9070 [M] | Overseas | 196? | 15.00 |
| *—Black label with color bars* | | | |
| ❑ DL 9074 [M] | The World's Greatest Entertainer | 1959 | 25.00 |
| *—Black label, silver print* | | | |
| ❑ DL 9074 [M] | The World's Greatest Entertainer | 196? | 15.00 |
| *—Black label with color bars* | | | |
| ❑ DL 9095 [M] | Al Jolson with Oscar Levant at the Piano | 1961 | 30.00 |
| ❑ DL 9099 [M] | Jolie | 196? | 25.00 |
| *—Black label, silver print* | | | |
| ❑ DL 79034 [R] | You Made Me Love You | 196? | 12.00 |
| ❑ DL 79035 [R] | Rock-a-Bye Your Baby | 196? | 12.00 |
| ❑ DL 79036 [R] | Rainbow 'Round My Shoulder | 196? | 12.00 |
| ❑ DL 79037 [R] | You Ain't Heard Nothin' Yet! | 196? | 12.00 |
| ❑ DL 79038 [R] | Memories | 196? | 12.00 |
| ❑ DL 79050 [R] | Among My Souvenirs | 196? | 12.00 |
| ❑ DL 79070 [R] | Overseas | 196? | 12.00 |
| ❑ DL 79074 [R] | The World's Greatest Entertainer | 196? | 12.00 |
| ❑ DL 79095 [R] | Al Jolson with Oscar Levant at the Piano | 196? | 12.00 |
| **MCA** | | | |
| ❑ 2057 | You Made Me Love You | 197? | 10.00 |
| ❑ 2058 | Rock-a-Bye Your Baby | 197? | 10.00 |
| ❑ 2059 | Rainbow 'Round My Shoulder | 197? | 10.00 |
| ❑ 2060 | You Ain't Heard Nothin' Yet! | 197? | 10.00 |
| ❑ 2061 | Memories | 197? | 10.00 |
| ❑ 2064 | Among My Souvenirs | 197? | 10.00 |
| ❑ 2066 | The Immortal Al Jolson | 197? | 10.00 |
| ❑ 2067 | The World's Greatest Entertainer | 197? | 10.00 |
| ❑ 10002 [(2)] | The Best of Jolson | 1973 | 12.00 |
| ❑ 27051 | You Made Me Love You | 198? | 8.00 |

| Number | Title (A Side/B Side) | Yr | NM |
|---|---|---|---|
| ❑ 27052 | Rock-a-Bye Your Baby | 198? | 8.00 |
| ❑ 27053 | Rainbow 'Round My Shoulder | 198? | 8.00 |
| ❑ 27054 | You Ain't Heard Nothin' Yet! | 198? | 8.00 |
| ❑ 27055 | Memories | 198? | 8.00 |
| ❑ 27057 | The Immortal Al Jolson | 198? | 8.00 |
| ❑ 27058 | The World's Greatest Entertainer | 198? | 8.00 |
| SUNBEAM | | | |
| ❑ 503 | Steppin' Out | 197? | 10.00 |
| ❑ 505 | California, Here I Come | 197? | 10.00 |
| TOTEM | | | |
| ❑ 1006 | Al Jolson On the Air, Volume 1 | 197? | 10.00 |
| ❑ 1012 | Al Jolson On the Air, Volume 2 | 197? | 10.00 |
| ❑ 1019 | Al Jolson On the Air, Volume 3 | 197? | 10.00 |
| ❑ 1030 | Al Jolson On the Air, Volume 4 | 197? | 10.00 |
| ❑ 1040 | Al Jolson On the Air, Volume 5 | 197? | 10.00 |
| **JON AND ROBIN AND THE IN CROWD** | | | |
| ABNAK | | | |
| ❑ ABM-2068 [M] | Soul of a Boy and Girl | 1967 | 20.00 |
| ❑ ABST-2068 [S] | Soul of a Boy and Girl | 1967 | 20.00 |
| ❑ ABST-2070 | Elastic Event | 1968 | 20.00 |
| **JONES, ANN, AND HER AMERICAN SWEETHEARTS** | | | |
| AUDIO LAB | | | |
| ❑ AL-1521 [M] | Ann Jones and Her American Sweethearts | 1959 | 150.00 |
| ❑ AL-1556 [M] | Hit and Run | 1960 | 150.00 |
| **JONES, BOOGALOO JOE** | | | |
| PRESTIGE | | | |
| ❑ PRST-7557 | Mind Bender | 1968 | 20.00 |
| ❑ PRST-7617 | My Fire! More of the Psychedelic Soul Jazz Guitar of Joe Jones | 1968 | 20.00 |
| *—As "Joe Jones"* | | | |
| ❑ PRST-7697 | Boogaloo Joe | 1969 | 20.00 |
| ❑ PRST-7766 | Right On Brother! | 1970 | 20.00 |
| ❑ 10004 | No Way! | 1971 | 25.00 |
| ❑ 10035 | What It Is | 1971 | 30.00 |
| ❑ 10056 | Snake Rhythm Rock | 1972 | 30.00 |
| ❑ 10072 | Black Whip | 1973 | 30.00 |
| **JONES, BRIAN** | | | |
| ROLLING STONES | | | |
| ❑ COC 49100 | Brian Jones Presents the Pipes of Pan at Joujouka | 1971 | 60.00 |
| **JONES, CARMELL** | | | |
| PACIFIC JAZZ | | | |
| ❑ PJ-29 [M] | The Remarkable Carmell Jones | 1961 | 40.00 |
| ❑ ST-29 [S] | The Remarkable Carmell Jones | 1961 | 50.00 |
| ❑ PJ-53 [M] | Business Meetin' | 1962 | 40.00 |
| ❑ ST-53 [S] | Business Meetin' | 1962 | 50.00 |
| *—Black vinyl* | | | |
| ❑ ST-53 [S] | Business Meetin' | 1962 | 80.00 |
| *—Yellow vinyl* | | | |
| PRESTIGE | | | |
| ❑ PRLP-7401 [M] | Jay Hawk Talk | 1965 | 30.00 |
| ❑ PRST-7401 [S] | Jay Hawk Talk | 1965 | 40.00 |
| ❑ PRST-7669 | Carmell Jones in Europe | 1969 | 20.00 |
| **JONES, CURTIS** | | | |
| BLUESVILLE | | | |
| ❑ BVLP-1022 [M] | Trouble Blues | 1961 | 80.00 |
| *—Blue label, silver print* | | | |
| ❑ BVLP-1022 [M] | Trouble Blues | 1964 | 25.00 |
| *—Blue label, trident logo at right* | | | |
| DELMARK | | | |
| ❑ DL-605 [M] | Lonesome Bedroom Blues | 1963 | 40.00 |
| **JONES, DAVY** Also see THE MONKEES. | | | |
| BELL | | | |
| ❑ 6067 | Davy Jones | 1971 | 20.00 |
| COLPIX | | | |
| ❑ CP 493 [M] | David Jones | 1965 | 25.00 |
| ❑ CPS 493 [S] | David Jones | 1965 | 40.00 |
| *—This album charted in 1967 thanks to the singer's membership in The Monkees* | | | |
| **JONES, DEAN** | | | |
| VALIANT | | | |
| ❑ VLM-407 [M] | Introducing Dean Jones | 196? | 20.00 |
| ❑ VLS-407 [S] | Introducing Dean Jones | 196? | 20.00 |
| **JONES, ELVIN** | | | |
| ABC IMPULSE! | | | |
| ❑ AS-9160 | Heavy Sounds | 1968 | 20.00 |
| ATLANTIC | | | |
| ❑ 1443 [M] | And Then Again | 1965 | 20.00 |
| ❑ SD 1443 [S] | And Then Again | 1965 | 25.00 |
| ❑ 1485 [M] | Midnight Walk | 1967 | 20.00 |
| ❑ SD 1485 [S] | Midnight Walk | 1967 | 25.00 |

| Number | Title (A Side/B Side) | Yr | NM |
|---|---|---|---|
| BLUE NOTE | | | |
| ❑ BN-LA015-G [(2)] | Live at the Lighthouse | 1973 | 20.00 |
| ❑ BN-LA506-H2 [(2)] | Prime Element | 1976 | 20.00 |
| ❑ BST-84282 | Puttin' It Together | 1968 | 25.00 |
| ❑ BST-84305 | The Ultimate Elvin Jones | 1969 | 25.00 |
| ❑ BST-84331 | Poly-Currents | 1969 | 25.00 |
| ❑ BST-84361 | Coalition | 1970 | 25.00 |
| ❑ BST-84369 | Genesis | 1971 | 20.00 |
| ❑ BST-84414 | Elvin Jones | 1972 | 20.00 |
| IMPULSE! | | | |
| ❑ A-88 [M] | Dear John C. | 1965 | 25.00 |
| ❑ AS-88 [S] | Dear John C. | 1965 | 30.00 |
| RIVERSIDE | | | |
| ❑ RLP-409 [M] | Elvin! | 1962 | 25.00 |
| ❑ RS-9409 [S] | Elvin! | 1962 | 30.00 |
| **JONES, ELVIN, AND THE JIMMY GARRISON SEXTETTE** | | | |
| IMPULSE! | | | |
| ❑ A-49 [M] | Illumination | 1963 | 25.00 |
| ❑ AS-49 [S] | Illumination | 1963 | 30.00 |
| **JONES, ETTA** | | | |
| KING | | | |
| ❑ 544 [M] | The Jones Girl...Etta | 1956 | 150.00 |
| ❑ 707 [M] | Etta Jones Sings | 1960 | 80.00 |
| PRESTIGE | | | |
| ❑ PRLP-7186 [M] | Don't Go to Strangers | 1960 | 40.00 |
| *—Yellow label* | | | |
| ❑ PRLP-7186 [M] | Don't Go to Strangers | 1964 | 20.00 |
| *—Blue label, trident logo at right* | | | |
| ❑ PRST-7186 [S] | Don't Go to Strangers | 1960 | 50.00 |
| *—Silver label* | | | |
| ❑ PRST-7186 [S] | Don't Go to Strangers | 1964 | 25.00 |
| *—Blue label, trident logo at right* | | | |
| ❑ PRLP-7194 [M] | Something Nice | 1961 | 50.00 |
| *—Yellow label* | | | |
| ❑ PRLP-7194 [M] | Something Nice | 1964 | 25.00 |
| *—Blue label, trident logo at right* | | | |
| ❑ PRLP-7204 [M] | So Warm — Etta Jones and Strings | 1961 | 40.00 |
| *—Yellow label* | | | |
| ❑ PRLP-7204 [M] | So Warm — Etta Jones and Strings | 1964 | 20.00 |
| *—Blue label, trident logo at right* | | | |
| ❑ PRST-7204 [S] | So Warm — Etta Jones and Strings | 1961 | 50.00 |
| *—Silver label* | | | |
| ❑ PRST-7204 [S] | So Warm — Etta Jones and Strings | 1964 | 25.00 |
| *—Blue label, trident logo at right* | | | |
| ❑ PRLP-7214 [M] | From the Heart | 1961 | 40.00 |
| *—Yellow label* | | | |
| ❑ PRLP-7214 [M] | From the Heart | 1964 | 20.00 |
| *—Blue label, trident logo at right* | | | |
| ❑ PRST-7214 [S] | From the Heart | 1961 | 50.00 |
| *—Silver label* | | | |
| ❑ PRST-7214 [S] | From the Heart | 1964 | 25.00 |
| *—Blue label, trident logo at right* | | | |
| ❑ PRLP-7241 [M] | Lonely and Blue | 1962 | 40.00 |
| *—Yellow label* | | | |
| ❑ PRLP-7241 [M] | Lonely and Blue | 1964 | 20.00 |
| *—Blue label, trident logo at right* | | | |
| ❑ PRST-7241 [S] | Lonely and Blue | 1962 | 50.00 |
| *—Silver label* | | | |
| ❑ PRST-7241 [S] | Lonely and Blue | 1964 | 25.00 |
| *—Blue label, trident logo at right* | | | |
| ❑ PRLP-7272 [M] | Love Shout | 1963 | 40.00 |
| *—Yellow label* | | | |
| ❑ PRLP-7272 [M] | Love Shout | 1964 | 20.00 |
| *—Blue label, trident logo at right* | | | |
| ❑ PRST-7272 [S] | Love Shout | 1963 | 50.00 |
| *—Silver label* | | | |
| ❑ PRST-7272 [S] | Love Shout | 1964 | 25.00 |
| *—Blue label, trident logo at right* | | | |
| ❑ PRLP-7284 [M] | Holler! | 1963 | 40.00 |
| *—Yellow label* | | | |
| ❑ PRLP-7284 [M] | Holler! | 1964 | 20.00 |
| *—Blue label, trident logo at right* | | | |
| ❑ PRST-7284 [S] | Holler! | 1963 | 50.00 |
| *—Silver label* | | | |
| ❑ PRST-7284 [S] | Holler! | 1964 | 25.00 |
| *—Blue label, trident logo at right* | | | |
| ❑ PRLP-7443 [M] | Etta Jones' Greatest Hits | 1967 | 25.00 |
| ❑ PRST-7443 [S] | Etta Jones' Greatest Hits | 1967 | 20.00 |
| ROULETTE | | | |
| ❑ R-25329 [M] | Etta Jones Sings | 1965 | 20.00 |
| ❑ SR-25329 [S] | Etta Jones Sings | 1965 | 25.00 |
| WESTBOUND | | | |
| ❑ 203 | Etta Jones '75 | 1975 | 20.00 |
| **JONES, GEORGE** | | | |
| ACCORD | | | |
| ❑ SN-7201 | Tender Years | 1982 | 10.00 |
| ALLEGIANCE | | | |
| ❑ AV-5015 | Cold Cold Heart | 198? | 10.00 |
| BULLDOG | | | |
| ❑ BDL-2009 | 20 Golden Pieces of George Jones | 198? | 10.00 |

| Number | Title (A Side/B Side) | Yr | NM |
|---|---|---|---|
| EPIC | | | |
| ❑ KE 31321 | George Jones | 1972 | 15.00 |
| *—Yellow label* | | | |
| ❑ KE 31321 | George Jones | 1973 | 12.00 |
| *—Orange label* | | | |
| ❑ KE 31718 | A Picture of Me (Without You) | 1972 | 15.00 |
| *—Yellow label* | | | |
| ❑ KE 31718 | A Picture of Me (Without You) | 1973 | 12.00 |
| *—Orange label* | | | |
| ❑ KE 32412 | Nothing Ever Hurt Me (Half As Bad As Losing You) | 1973 | 15.00 |
| ❑ KE 32563 | In a Gospel Way | 1974 | 15.00 |
| ❑ KE 33083 | The Grand Tour | 1974 | 15.00 |
| ❑ KE 33352 | The Best of George Jones | 1975 | 15.00 |
| ❑ PE 33352 | The Best of George Jones | 1981 | 8.00 |
| *—Budget-line reissue* | | | |
| ❑ KE 33547 | Memories of Us | 1975 | 15.00 |
| ❑ BG 33749 [(2)] | George Jones/A Picture of Me (Without You) | 1976 | 15.00 |
| ❑ KE 34034 | The Battle | 1976 | 12.00 |
| ❑ KE 34290 | Alone Again | 1976 | 12.00 |
| ❑ PE 34692 | All-Time Greatest Hits Volume 1 | 1977 | 12.00 |
| *—Orange label* | | | |
| ❑ PE 34692 | All-Time Greatest Hits Volume 1 | 198? | 8.00 |
| *—Dark blue label* | | | |
| ❑ PE 34717 | I Wanta Sing | 1977 | 12.00 |
| *—Orange label* | | | |
| ❑ PE 34717 | I Wanta Sing | 198? | 8.00 |
| *—Dark blue label* | | | |
| ❑ KE 35414 | Bartender's Blues | 1978 | 12.00 |
| ❑ PE 35414 | Bartender's Blues | 198? | 8.00 |
| *—Budget-line reissue* | | | |
| ❑ JE 35544 | My Very Special Guests | 1979 | 12.00 |
| ❑ PE 35544 | My Very Special Guests | 198? | 8.00 |
| *—Budget-line reissue* | | | |
| ❑ JE 36586 | I Am What I Am | 1980 | 12.00 |
| ❑ FE 37106 | Still the Same Old Me | 1981 | 10.00 |
| ❑ PE 37106 | Still the Same Ole Me | 198? | 8.00 |
| *—Budget-line reissue* | | | |
| ❑ FE 37346 | Encore | 1981 | 10.00 |
| ❑ KE2 38323 [(2)] | Anniversary — 10 Years of Hits | 1982 | 12.00 |
| ❑ FE 38406 | Shine On | 1983 | 10.00 |
| ❑ PE 38406 | Shine On | 198? | 8.00 |
| *—Budget-line reissue* | | | |
| ❑ FE 38978 | Jones Country | 1983 | 10.00 |
| ❑ PE 38978 | Jones Country | 1985 | 8.00 |
| *—Budget-line reissue* | | | |
| ❑ FE 39002 | You've Still Got a Place in My Heart | 1984 | 10.00 |
| ❑ FE 39272 | Ladies' Choice | 1984 | 10.00 |
| ❑ FE 39546 | By Request | 1984 | 10.00 |
| ❑ FE 39598 | Who's Gonna Fill Their Shoes | 1985 | 10.00 |
| ❑ FE 39899 | First Time Live! | 1985 | 10.00 |
| ❑ FE 40413 | Wine Colored Roses | 1986 | 10.00 |
| ❑ FE 40776 | Super Hits | 1987 | 10.00 |
| ❑ FE 40781 | Too Wild Too Long | 1988 | 10.00 |
| ❑ FE 44078 | One Woman Man | 1989 | 10.00 |
| EVEREST ARCHIVE OF FOLK & JAZZ | | | |
| ❑ 353 | George Jones Sings Country Hits | 198? | 10.00 |
| HILLTOP | | | |
| ❑ 6048 | You're In My Heart | 1968 | 15.00 |
| ❑ 6092 | Heartaches by the Number | 1969 | 15.00 |
| ❑ 6133 | Oh Lonesome Me | 1970 | 15.00 |
| INTERMEDIA | | | |
| ❑ QS-5044 | I Can't Change Overnight | 198? | 10.00 |
| ❑ QS-5061 | How I Love These Old Songs | 198? | 10.00 |
| LIBERTY | | | |
| ❑ LN-10167 | Trouble in Mind | 1981 | 8.00 |
| ❑ LN-10168 | I Get Lonely in a Hurry | 1981 | 8.00 |
| MCA | | | |
| ❑ 10398 | And Along Came Jones | 1991 | 20.00 |
| *—Vinyl issued only through Columbia House* | | | |
| MERCURY | | | |
| ❑ ML-8014 | Greatest Hits | 1980 | 12.00 |
| ❑ MG-20282 [M] | Hillbilly Hit Parade, Volume 1 | 1957 | 150.00 |
| *—Five tracks by George Jones, one by George Jones with Benny Barnes, and four by other artists* | | | |
| ❑ MG-20306 [M] | 14 Country Favorites | 1957 | 150.00 |
| ❑ MG-20462 [M] | Country Church Time | 1959 | 200.00 |
| ❑ MG-20477 [M] | George Jones Sings White Lightning and Other Favorites | 1959 | 150.00 |
| ❑ MG-20596 [M] | George Jones Salutes Hank Williams | 1960 | 80.00 |
| ❑ MG-20621 [M] | George Jones' Greatest Hits | 1961 | 40.00 |
| ❑ MG-20624 [M] | Country and Western Hits | 1961 | 40.00 |
| ❑ MG-20694 [M] | George Jones Sings From the Heart | 1962 | 40.00 |
| ❑ MG-20793 [M] | The Novelty Side of George Jones | 1963 | 80.00 |
| ❑ MG-20836 [M] | The Ballad Side of George Jones | 1963 | 40.00 |
| ❑ MG-20906 [M] | Blue and Lonesome | 1964 | 25.00 |
| ❑ MG-20937 [M] | Country and Western No. 1 Male Singer | 1964 | 25.00 |
| ❑ MG-20990 [M] | Heartaches and Tears | 1965 | 25.00 |
| ❑ MG-21029 [M] | Singing the Blues | 1965 | 25.00 |

| Number | Title (A Side/B Side) | Yr | NM |
|---|---|---|---|
| ❑ MG-21048 [M] | George Jones' Greatest Hits Volume 2 | 1965 | 25.00 |
| ❑ SR-60257 [S] | George Jones Salutes Hank Williams | 1960 | 100.00 |
| ❑ SR-60621 [P] | George Jones' Greatest Hits | 1961 | 50.00 |
| ❑ SR-60624 [P] | Country and Western Hits | 1961 | 50.00 |
| ❑ SR-60694 [S] | George Jones Sings From the Heart | 1962 | 50.00 |
| ❑ SR-60793 [S] | The Novelty Side of George Jones | 1963 | 100.00 |
| ❑ SR-60836 [S] | The Ballad Side of George Jones | 1963 | 50.00 |
| ❑ SR-60906 [S] | Blue and Lonesome | 1964 | 30.00 |
| ❑ SR-60937 [S] | Country and Western No. 1 Male Singer | 1964 | 30.00 |
| ❑ SR-60990 [S] | Heartaches and Tears | 1965 | 30.00 |
| ❑ SR-61029 [S] | Singing the Blues | 1965 | 30.00 |
| ❑ SR-61048 [S] | George Jones' Greatest Hits Volume 2 | 1965 | 30.00 |
| ❑ 822646-1 | George Jones Salutes Hank Williams | 1985 | 10.00 |
| ❑ 826095-1 | Rockin' the Country | 1985 | 10.00 |
| ❑ 826248-1 | Greatest Hits | 1986 | 10.00 |
| **MUSICOR** | | | |
| ❑ MM-2046 [M] | Mr. Country and Western Music | 1965 | 30.00 |
| ❑ MM-2060 [M] | New Country Hits | 1965 | 30.00 |
| ❑ MM-2061 [M] | Old Brush Arbors | 1966 | 30.00 |
| ❑ MM-2088 [M] | Love Bug | 1966 | 30.00 |
| ❑ MM-2099 [M] | I'm a People | 1966 | 25.00 |
| ❑ MM-2106 [M] | We Found Heaven Right Here on Earth | 1966 | 25.00 |
| ❑ MM-2116 [M] | George Jones' Greatest Hits | 1967 | 25.00 |
| ❑ MM-2119 [M] | Walk Through This World with Me | 1967 | 30.00 |
| ❑ MM-2124 [M] | Cup of Loneliness | 1967 | 30.00 |
| ❑ MM-2128 [M] | Hits by George | 1967 | 30.00 |
| ❑ MS-3046 [S] | Mr. Country and Western Music | 1965 | 40.00 |
| ❑ MS-3060 [S] | New Country Hits | 1965 | 40.00 |
| ❑ MS-3061 [S] | Old Brush Arbors | 1966 | 40.00 |
| ❑ MS-3088 [S] | Love Bug | 1966 | 40.00 |
| ❑ MS-3099 [S] | I'm a People | 1966 | 30.00 |
| ❑ MS-3106 [S] | We Found Heaven Right Here on Earth | 1966 | 30.00 |
| ❑ MS-3116 [S] | George Jones' Greatest Hits | 1967 | 25.00 |
| ❑ MS-3119 [S] | Walk Through This World with Me | 1967 | 20.00 |
| ❑ MS-3124 [S] | Cup of Loneliness | 1967 | 20.00 |
| ❑ MS-3128 [S] | Hits by George | 1967 | 20.00 |
| ❑ MS-3149 | The Songs of Dallas Frazier | 1968 | 20.00 |
| ❑ MS-3158 | If My Heart Had Windows | 1968 | 20.00 |
| ❑ M2S-3159 [(2)] | The George Jones Story: The Musical Loves, Life and Sorrows of America's Great Country Star | 1968 | 30.00 |
| ❑ M2S-3169 [(2)] | My Country | 1969 | 30.00 |
| ❑ MS-3177 | I'll Share My World with You | 1969 | 20.00 |
| ❑ MS-3181 | Where Grass Won't Grow | 1969 | 20.00 |
| ❑ MS-3188 | Will You Visit Me on Sunday? | 1970 | 20.00 |
| ❑ MS-3191 | The Best of George Jones | 1970 | 20.00 |
| ❑ MS-3194 | George Jones With Love | 1971 | 20.00 |
| ❑ MS-3203 | The Best of Sacred Music | 1971 | 20.00 |
| ❑ MS-3204 | The Great Songs of Leon Payne | 1971 | 20.00 |
| **NASHVILLE** | | | |
| ❑ 2076 | Seasons of My Heart | 1970 | 15.00 |
| **PAIR** | | | |
| ❑ PDL2-1074 [(2)] | The Best of George Jones | 1986 | 12.00 |
| ❑ PDL2-1080 [(2)] | Country, By George! | 1986 | 12.00 |
| **POWER PAK** | | | |
| ❑ 271 | The Crown Prince of Country Music | 197? | 10.00 |
| **QUICKSILVER** | | | |
| ❑ QS-1011 | Frozen in Time | 198? | 10.00 |
| ❑ QS-1012 | If My Heart Had Windows | 198? | 10.00 |
| **RCA CAMDEN** | | | |
| ❑ ACL1-0377 | The Race Is On | 1973 | 12.00 |
| ❑ CAS-2591 | Flowers for Mama | 1973 | 12.00 |
| **RCA VICTOR** | | | |
| ❑ APL1-0316 | Best of George Jones Vol. II | 1973 | 15.00 |
| ❑ APL1-0486 | You Gotta Be My Baby | 1974 | 15.00 |
| ❑ APL1-0612 | His Songs | 1974 | 15.00 |
| ❑ APL1-0815 | I Can Love You Enough | 1974 | 15.00 |
| ❑ APL1-1113 | The Best of the Best | 1975 | 15.00 |
| ❑ LSP-4672 | First in the Hearts of Country Music Lovers | 1972 | 15.00 |
| ❑ LSP-4716 | Best of George Jones Vol. I | 1972 | 15.00 |
| ❑ LSP-4725 | Poor Man's Riches | 1972 | 15.00 |
| ❑ LSP-4726 | I Made Leaving (Easy for You) | 1972 | 15.00 |
| ❑ LSP-4727 | Country Singer | 1972 | 15.00 |
| ❑ LSP-4733 | George Jones And Friends | 1972 | 15.00 |
| ❑ LSP-4785 | Four-O Thirty-Three | 1972 | 15.00 |
| ❑ LSP-4786 | Tender Years | 1972 | 15.00 |
| ❑ LSP-4787 | Take Me | 1972 | 15.00 |
| ❑ LSP-4801 | Wrapped Around Her Finger | 1973 | 15.00 |
| ❑ LSP-4847 | I Can Still See Him | 1973 | 15.00 |
| **ROUNDER** | | | |
| ❑ SS-15 | Burn the Honky Tonk Down | 198? | 10.00 |
| ❑ SS-17 | Heartaches & Hangovers | 198? | 10.00 |
| **SEARS** | | | |
| ❑ SPS-125 | Maybe, Little Baby | 196? | 20.00 |
| **STARDAY** | | | |
| ❑ SLP 101 [M] | The Grand Ole Opry's New Star | 1958 | 1200. |
| ❑ SLP 125 [M] | The Crown Prince of Country Music | 1960 | 160.00 |
| ❑ SLP 150 [M] | George Jones Sings His Greatest Hits | 1962 | 50.00 |
| ❑ SLP 151 [M] | The Fabulous Country Music Sound of George Jones | 1962 | 50.00 |
| ❑ SLP 335 [M] | George Jones | 1965 | 40.00 |
| ❑ SLP 344 [M] | Long Live King George | 1965 | 40.00 |
| ❑ SLP 366 | The George Jones Story Bonus Photo | 1966 | 20.00 |
| ❑ SLP 366 [(2)M] | The George Jones Story | 1966 | 30.00 |
| ❑ SLP 401 | The George Jones Song Book & Picture Album | 1967 | 50.00 |
| *—With book* | | | |
| ❑ SLP 401 [M] | The George Jones Song Book & Picture Album | 1967 | 30.00 |
| *—Without book* | | | |
| ❑ SLP 440 [M] | The Golden Country Hits of George Jones | 1969 | 30.00 |
| ❑ 3021 | 16 Greatest Hits | 197? | 10.00 |
| ❑ DT-90080 [R] | George Jones Sings His Greatest Hits | 1964 | 80.00 |
| *—Capitol Record Club edition* | | | |
| ❑ DT-90611 [R] | The Crown Prince of Country Music | 196? | 40.00 |
| *—Capitol Record Club edition* | | | |
| **TIME-LIFE** | | | |
| ❑ STW-103 | Country Music | 1981 | 10.00 |
| **UNITED ARTISTS** | | | |
| ❑ UXS-85 [(2)] | George Jones Superpak | 1972 | 20.00 |
| ❑ UAL-3193 [M] | The New Favorites of George Jones | 1962 | 30.00 |
| ❑ UAL-3218 [M] | George Jones Sings the Hits of His Country Cousins | 1962 | 30.00 |
| ❑ UAL-3219 [M] | Homecoming in Heaven | 1962 | 30.00 |
| ❑ UAL-3220 [M] | My Favorites of Hank Williams | 1962 | 30.00 |
| ❑ UAL-3221 [M] | George Jones Sings Bob Wills | 1962 | 40.00 |
| ❑ UAL-3270 [M] | I Wish the Night Would Never End | 1963 | 25.00 |
| ❑ UAL-3291 [M] | The Best of George Jones | 1963 | 25.00 |
| ❑ UAL-3338 [M] | More New Favorites | 1964 | 25.00 |
| ❑ UAL-3364 [M] | George Jones Sings Like the Dickens | 1964 | 40.00 |
| ❑ UAL-3388 [M] | I Get Lonely in a Hurry | 1964 | 30.00 |
| ❑ UAL-3408 [M] | Trouble in Mind | 1965 | 30.00 |
| ❑ UAL-3422 [M] | The Race Is On | 1965 | 20.00 |
| *—With cartoon on front* | | | |
| ❑ UAL-3422 [M] | The Race Is On | 1965 | 30.00 |
| *—With photo of George Jones on front* | | | |
| ❑ UAL-3442 [M] | King of Broken Hearts | 1965 | 30.00 |
| ❑ UAL-3457 [M] | The Great George Jones | 1966 | 30.00 |
| ❑ UAL-3532 [M] | George Jones' Golden Hits, Volume 1 | 1966 | 20.00 |
| ❑ UAL-3558 [M] | The Young George Jones | 1967 | 30.00 |
| ❑ UAL-3566 [M] | George Jones' Golden Hits, Volume 2 | 1967 | 30.00 |
| ❑ UAS-6193 [S] | The New Favorites of George Jones | 1962 | 40.00 |
| ❑ UAS-6218 [S] | George Jones Sings the Hits of His Country Cousins | 1962 | 40.00 |
| ❑ UAS-6219 [S] | Homecoming in Heaven | 1962 | 40.00 |
| ❑ UAS-6220 [S] | My Favorites of Hank Williams | 1962 | 40.00 |
| ❑ UAS-6221 [S] | George Jones Sings Bob Wills | 1962 | 50.00 |
| ❑ UAS-6270 [S] | I Wish the Night Would Never End | 1963 | 30.00 |
| ❑ UAS-6291 [S] | The Best of George Jones | 1963 | 30.00 |
| ❑ UAS-6328 [S] | More New Favorites | 1964 | 30.00 |
| ❑ UAS-6364 [S] | George Jones Sings Like the Dickens | 1964 | 50.00 |
| ❑ UAS-6388 [S] | I Get Lonely in a Hurry | 1964 | 40.00 |
| ❑ UAS-6408 [S] | Trouble in Mind | 1965 | 40.00 |
| ❑ UAS-6422 [S] | The Race Is On | 1965 | 25.00 |
| *—With cartoon on front* | | | |
| ❑ UAS-6422 [S] | The Race Is On | 1965 | 40.00 |
| *—With photo of George Jones on front* | | | |
| ❑ UAS-6442 [S] | King of Broken Hearts | 1965 | 40.00 |
| ❑ UAS-6457 [S] | The Great George Jones | 1966 | 40.00 |
| ❑ UAS-6532 [S] | George Jones' Golden Hits, Volume 1 | 1966 | 25.00 |
| ❑ UAS-6558 [S] | The Young George Jones | 1967 | 20.00 |
| ❑ UAS-6566 [S] | George Jones' Golden Hits, Volume 2 | 1967 | 20.00 |
| ❑ UAS-6696 | George Jones' Golden Hits, Volume 3 | 1968 | 20.00 |
| ❑ ST-90829 [S] | The Race Is On | 1965 | 40.00 |
| *—Capitol Record Club edition; photo on front* | | | |
| ❑ T-90829 [M] | The Race Is On | 1965 | 30.00 |
| *—Capitol Record Club edition; photo on front* | | | |
| **WING** | | | |
| ❑ MGW-12266 [M] | The Great George Jones | 196? | 15.00 |
| ❑ SRW-16266 [S] | The Great George Jones | 196? | 15.00 |

### JONES, GEORGE, AND MELBA MONTGOMERY

| Number | Title (A Side/B Side) | Yr | NM |
|---|---|---|---|
| **GUEST STAR** | | | |
| ❑ GS 1465 [M] | George Jones and Melba Montgomery | 196? | 12.00 |
| *—Contains two solo records by each artist (no duets!) and assorted stuff by others* | | | |
| **LIBERTY** | | | |
| ❑ LN-10169 | Singing What's In Our Hearts | 1981 | 8.00 |
| **MUSICOR** | | | |
| ❑ MM-2109 [M] | Close Together (As You and Me) | 1966 | 20.00 |
| ❑ MM-2127 [M] | Let's Get Together/Boy Meets Girl | 1967 | 30.00 |
| ❑ MM-2127 [M] | Party Pickin' | 1967 | 30.00 |
| *—Alternate title* | | | |
| ❑ MS-3109 [S] | Close Together (As You and Me) | 1966 | 25.00 |
| ❑ MS-3127 [S] | Let's Get Together/Boy Meets Girl | 1967 | 20.00 |
| ❑ MS-3127 [S] | Party Pickin' | 1967 | 20.00 |
| *—Alternate title* | | | |
| **UNITED ARTISTS** | | | |
| ❑ UAL-3301 [M] | Singing What's In Our Hearts | 1963 | 25.00 |
| ❑ UAL-3352 [M] | Bluegrass Hootenanny | 1964 | 25.00 |
| ❑ UAL-3472 [M] | Blue Moon of Kentucky | 1966 | 20.00 |
| ❑ UAS-6301 [S] | Singing What's In Our Hearts | 1963 | 30.00 |
| ❑ UAS-6352 [S] | Bluegrass Hootenanny | 1964 | 30.00 |
| ❑ UAS-6472 [S] | Blue Moon of Kentucky | 1966 | 25.00 |
| ❑ T-90832 [M] | Blue Moon of Kentucky | 1966 | 25.00 |
| *—Capitol Record Club edition* | | | |

### JONES, GEORGE; MELBA MONTGOMERY; JUDY LYNN

| Number | Title (A Side/B Side) | Yr | NM |
|---|---|---|---|
| **UNITED ARTISTS** | | | |
| ❑ UAL-3367 [M] | A King and Two Queens | 1964 | 20.00 |
| ❑ UAS-6367 [S] | A King and Two Queens | 1964 | 25.00 |

### JONES, GEORGE; MELBA MONTGOMERY; GENE PITNEY

| Number | Title (A Side/B Side) | Yr | NM |
|---|---|---|---|
| **MUSICOR** | | | |
| ❑ MM-2079 [M] | Famous Country Duets | 1965 | 20.00 |
| ❑ MS-3079 [S] | Famous Country Duets | 1965 | 25.00 |

### JONES, GEORGE, AND MARGIE SINGLETON

| Number | Title (A Side/B Side) | Yr | NM |
|---|---|---|---|
| **MERCURY** | | | |
| ❑ MG-20747 [M] | Duets Country Style | 1962 | 30.00 |
| ❑ SR-60747 [S] | Duets Country Style | 1962 | 40.00 |

### JONES, GRANDPA

| Number | Title (A Side/B Side) | Yr | NM |
|---|---|---|---|
| **DECCA** | | | |
| ❑ DL 4364 [M] | An Evening with Grandpa Jones | 1963 | 25.00 |
| ❑ DL 74364 [S] | An Evening with Grandpa Jones | 1963 | 30.00 |
| **KING** | | | |
| ❑ 554 [M] | Grandpa Jones Sings His Biggest Hits | 1958 | 100.00 |
| ❑ 625 [M] | Strictly Country Tunes | 1959 | 100.00 |
| ❑ 809 [M] | Rollin' Along with Grandpa Jones | 1963 | 60.00 |
| ❑ 822 [M] | 16 Sacred Gospel Songs | 1963 | 60.00 |
| ❑ 845 [M] | Do You Remember? | 1963 | 60.00 |
| ❑ 888 [M] | The Other Side of Grandpa Jones | 1964 | 60.00 |
| ❑ KS-1042 | The Living Legend of Country Music | 1969 | 20.00 |
| **MONUMENT** | | | |
| ❑ MLP-4006 [M] | Grandpa Jones Makes the Rafters Ring | 1962 | 25.00 |
| ❑ MLP-8001 [M] | Yodeling Hits | 1963 | 20.00 |
| ❑ MLP-8021 [M] | Real Folk Songs | 1964 | 20.00 |
| ❑ MLP-8041 [M] | Grandpa Jones Remembers the Brown's Ferry Four | 1966 | 25.00 |
| ❑ SLP-14006 [S] | Grandpa Jones Makes the Rafters Ring | 1962 | 30.00 |
| ❑ SLP-18001 [S] | Yodeling Hits | 1963 | 25.00 |
| ❑ SLP-18021 [S] | Real Folk Songs | 1964 | 25.00 |
| ❑ SLP-18041 [S] | Grandpa Jones Remembers the Brown's Ferry Four | 1966 | 30.00 |
| ❑ SLP-18083 | Everybody's Grandpa | 1968 | 20.00 |
| ❑ SLP-18131 | Grandpa Jones Sings Hits from Hee Haw | 1969 | 20.00 |

### JONES, HANK

| Number | Title (A Side/B Side) | Yr | NM |
|---|---|---|---|
| **ABC-PARAMOUNT** | | | |
| ❑ ABC-496 [M] | This Is Ragtime Now | 1964 | 20.00 |
| ❑ ABCS-496 [S] | This Is Ragtime Now | 1964 | 25.00 |
| **ARGO** | | | |
| ❑ LP-728 [M] | Here's Love | 1963 | 20.00 |
| ❑ LPS-728 [S] | Here's Love | 1963 | 25.00 |
| **CAPITOL** | | | |
| ❑ ST 1044 [S] | The Talented Touch of Hank Jones | 1958 | 30.00 |
| ❑ T 1044 [M] | The Talented Touch of Hank Jones | 1958 | 40.00 |



**Except when noted otherwise, VG = 25% of NM, and VG+ = 50% of NM. (Example: VG = $2.00, VG+ = $4.00 and NM = $8.00.)**

| Number | Title (A Side/B Side) | Yr | NM |
|---|---|---|---|
| ❑ ST 1175 [S] | Porgy and Bess | 1959 | 30.00 |
| ❑ T 1175 [M] | Porgy and Bess | 1959 | 40.00 |
| **CLEF** | | | |
| ❑ MGC-100 [10] | Hank Jones Piano | 1953 | 120.00 |
| ❑ MGC-707 [M] | Urbanity — Piano Solos by Hank Jones | 1956 | 100.00 |
| **GOLDEN CREST** | | | |
| ❑ GC-3042 [M] | Hank Jones Swings "Gigi" | 1958 | 50.00 |
| ❑ GCS-3042 [S] | Hank Jones Swings "Gigi" | 196? | 20.00 |
| ❑ GC-5002 [S] | Hank Jones Swings "Gigi" | 1959 | 40.00 |
| **MERCURY** | | | |
| ❑ MGC-100 [10] | Hank Jones Piano | 195? | 150.00 |
| ❑ MG-25022 [10] | Hank Jones Piano | 1950 | 200.00 |
| ❑ MG-35014 [10] | Hank Jones Piano | 1950 | 200.00 |
| **RCA VICTOR** | | | |
| ❑ LPM-2570 [M] | Arrival Time | 1962 | 25.00 |
| ❑ LSP-2570 [S] | Arrival Time | 1962 | 30.00 |
| **SAVOY** | | | |
| ❑ MG-12037 [M] | Hank Jones Quartet-Quintet | 1955 | 80.00 |
| ❑ MG-12053 [M] | The Trio | 1956 | 80.00 |
| ❑ MG-12084 [M] | Have You Met Hank Jones | 1956 | 80.00 |
| ❑ MG-12087 [M] | Hank Jones Trio | 1956 | 80.00 |
| **VERVE** | | | |
| ❑ MGV-8091 [M] | Urbanity — Piano Solos by Hank Jones | 1957 | 80.00 |
| ❑ V-8091 [M] | Urbanity — Piano Solos by Hank Jones | 1961 | 25.00 |

### JONES, ISHAM

| Number | Title (A Side/B Side) | Yr | NM |
|---|---|---|---|
| **RCA VICTOR** | | | |
| ❑ LPV-504 [M] | The Great Isham Jones and His Orchestra | 1966 | 20.00 |

### JONES, JACK

| Number | Title (A Side/B Side) | Yr | NM |
|---|---|---|---|
| **CAPITOL** | | | |
| ❑ ST 1274 [S] | This Love of Mine | 1959 | 30.00 |
| ❑ T 1274 [M] | This Love of Mine | 1959 | 25.00 |
| ❑ ST 2100 [S] | In Love | 1964 | 20.00 |
| *—Reissue of 1274* | | | |
| ❑ T 2100 [M] | In Love | 1964 | 15.00 |
| **KAPP** | | | |
| ❑ KL-1228 [M] | Shall We Dance | 1961 | 12.00 |
| ❑ KL-1259 [M] | Lollipops and Roses | 196? | 12.00 |
| *—Revised title* | | | |
| ❑ KL-1259 [M] | This Was My Love | 1962 | 20.00 |
| *—Original title* | | | |
| ❑ KL-1265 [M] | I've Got a Lot of Livin' to Do | 1962 | 12.00 |
| ❑ KL-1328 [M] | Call Me Irresponsible | 1963 | 12.00 |
| ❑ KL-1337 [M] | She Loves Me | 1963 | 12.00 |
| ❑ KL-1352 [M] | Wives and Lovers | 1963 | 12.00 |
| ❑ KL-1365 [M] | Bewitched | 1964 | 12.00 |
| ❑ KL-1396 [M] | Where Love Has Gone | 1964 | 12.00 |
| ❑ KL 1399 [M] | The Jack Jones Christmas Album | 1964 | 12.00 |
| ❑ KL-1415 [M] | Dear Heart | 1964 | 12.00 |
| ❑ KL-1433 [M] | My Kind of Town | 1965 | 12.00 |
| ❑ KL-1435 [M] | There's Love & There's Love & There's Love | 1965 | 12.00 |
| ❑ KL-1465 [M] | For the "In" Crowd | 1966 | 12.00 |
| ❑ KL-1486 [M] | The Impossible Dream | 1966 | 12.00 |
| ❑ KL-1500 [M] | Jack Jones Sings | 1966 | 12.00 |
| ❑ KL-1511 [M] | Lady | 1967 | 15.00 |
| ❑ KL-1531 [M] | Our Song | 1967 | 15.00 |
| ❑ KL-1551 [M] | What the World Needs Now Is Love! | 1968 | 20.00 |
| *—May only exist as a white label promo; covers are stereo with "Mono" sticker* | | | |
| ❑ KL-1559 [M] | Greatest Hits | 1968 | 20.00 |
| *—May exist only as a white label promo; covers are stereo with a "Mono" sticker* | | | |
| ❑ KS-3228 [S] | Shall We Dance | 1961 | 15.00 |
| ❑ KS-3259 [S] | Lollipops and Roses | 196? | 15.00 |
| *—Revised title* | | | |
| ❑ KS-3259 [S] | This Was My Love | 1962 | 25.00 |
| *—Original title* | | | |
| ❑ KS-3265 [S] | I've Got a Lot of Livin' to Do | 1962 | 15.00 |
| ❑ KS-3328 [S] | Call Me Irresponsible | 1963 | 15.00 |
| ❑ KS-3337 [S] | She Loves Me | 1963 | 15.00 |
| ❑ KS-3352 [S] | Wives and Lovers | 1963 | 15.00 |
| ❑ KS-3365 [S] | Bewitched | 1964 | 15.00 |
| ❑ KS-3396 [S] | Where Love Has Gone | 1964 | 15.00 |
| ❑ KS 3399 [S] | The Jack Jones Christmas Album | 1964 | 15.00 |
| ❑ KS-3415 [S] | Dear Heart | 1964 | 15.00 |
| ❑ KS-3433 [S] | My Kind of Town | 1965 | 15.00 |
| ❑ KS-3435 [S] | There's Love & There's Love & There's Love | 1965 | 15.00 |
| ❑ KS-3465 [S] | For the "In" Crowd | 1966 | 15.00 |
| ❑ KS-3486 [S] | The Impossible Dream | 1966 | 15.00 |
| ❑ KS-3500 [S] | Jack Jones Sings | 1966 | 15.00 |
| ❑ KS-3511 [S] | Lady | 1967 | 12.00 |
| ❑ KS-3531 [S] | Our Song | 1967 | 12.00 |
| ❑ KS-3551 [S] | What the World Needs Now Is Love! | 1968 | 12.00 |
| ❑ KS-3559 | Greatest Hits | 1968 | 12.00 |
| ❑ KS-3566 | Curtain Time | 1968 | 12.00 |
| ❑ KS-3590 | Jack Jones in Hollywood | 1969 | 12.00 |
| ❑ KS-3602 | Greatest Hits Vol. 2 | 1970 | 12.00 |
| ❑ KXS-5009 [(2)] | The Best of Jack Jones | 196? | 15.00 |
| **MCA** | | | |
| ❑ 4115 [(2)] | The Best of Jack Jones | 197? | 12.00 |
| *—Reissue of Kapp KXS-5009* | | | |
| ❑ 15014 | The Jack Jones Christmas Album | 197? | 10.00 |
| *—Reissue* | | | |
| ❑ 15036 | White Christmas | 198? | 8.00 |
| **MGM** | | | |
| ❑ MG-1-5023 | Nobody Does It Better | 1979 | 10.00 |
| ❑ MG-1-5024 | Don't Stop Now | 1980 | 10.00 |
| **PICKWICK** | | | |
| ❑ PC-3001 [M] | This Love of Mine | 196? | 12.00 |
| ❑ SPC-3001 [S] | This Love of Mine | 196? | 12.00 |
| ❑ SPC-3041 | A Very Precious Love | 196? | 10.00 |
| **RCA CAMDEN** | | | |
| ❑ ACL1-0255 | Christmas with Jack Jones | 1973 | 12.00 |
| *—Reissue of RCA Victor LSP-4234* | | | |
| **RCA VICTOR** | | | |
| ❑ APL1-0139 | Together | 1973 | 10.00 |
| ❑ APL1-0408 | Harbour | 1974 | 10.00 |
| ❑ APL1-0773 | Write Me a Love Song, Charlie | 1975 | 10.00 |
| ❑ ANL1-1081 | Jack Jones Sings Michel Legrand | 1975 | 8.00 |
| *—Reissue* | | | |
| ❑ APL1-1111 | What I Did for Love | 1975 | 10.00 |
| ❑ APL1-2067 | The Full Life | 1976 | 10.00 |
| ❑ APL1-2361 | With One More Look at You | 1977 | 10.00 |
| ❑ LPM-3911 [M] | Without Her | 1967 | 20.00 |
| ❑ LSP-3911 [S] | Without Her | 1967 | 12.00 |
| ❑ LPM-3969 [M] | If You Ever Leave Me | 1968 | 20.00 |
| ❑ LSP-3969 [S] | If You Ever Leave Me | 1968 | 12.00 |
| ❑ LSP-4048 | Where Is Love | 1968 | 12.00 |
| ❑ LSP-4108 | L.A. Break Down | 1969 | 12.00 |
| ❑ LSP-4209 | A Time for Us | 1969 | 12.00 |
| ❑ LSP-4234 | A Jack Jones Christmas | 1969 | 15.00 |
| ❑ LSP-4413 | In Person at the Sands, Las Vegas | 1970 | 12.00 |
| ❑ LSP-4480 | Jack Jones Sings Michel Legrand | 1970 | 12.00 |
| ❑ LSP-4613 | A Song for You | 1971 | 12.00 |
| ❑ LSP-4692 | Bread Winners | 1972 | 10.00 |
| **VOCALION** | | | |
| ❑ VL 73913 | Jack Jones Showcase | 1970 | 10.00 |

### JONES, JIMMY

| Number | Title (A Side/B Side) | Yr | NM |
|---|---|---|---|
| **JEN JILLUS** | | | |
| ❑ 1001 | The Handy Man's Back in Town | 1977 | 12.00 |
| **MGM** | | | |
| ❑ E-3847 [M] | Good Timin' | 1960 | 120.00 |
| ❑ SE-3847 [S] | Good Timin' | 1960 | 160.00 |

### JONES, JO

| Number | Title (A Side/B Side) | Yr | NM |
|---|---|---|---|
| **EVEREST** | | | |
| ❑ SDBR-1023 [S] | Jo Jones Trio | 1959 | 30.00 |
| ❑ SDBR-1099 [S] | Vamp Till Ready | 1960 | 30.00 |
| ❑ SDBR-1110 [S] | Percussion and Bass | 1960 | 30.00 |
| ❑ LPBR-5023 [M] | Jo Jones Trio | 1959 | 25.00 |
| ❑ LPBR-5099 [M] | Vamp Till Ready | 1960 | 25.00 |
| ❑ LPBR-5110 [M] | Percussion and Bass | 1960 | 25.00 |
| **JAZZTONE** | | | |
| ❑ J-1242 [M] | Jo Jones Special | 1956 | 50.00 |
| **VANGUARD** | | | |
| ❑ VSD-2031 [S] | Jo Jones Plus Two | 1959 | 30.00 |
| ❑ VRS-8503 [M] | Jo Jones Special | 1955 | 60.00 |
| ❑ VRS-8525 [M] | Jo Jones Plus Two | 1959 | 40.00 |

### JONES, JOE

| Number | Title (A Side/B Side) | Yr | NM |
|---|---|---|---|
| **ROULETTE** | | | |
| ❑ R 25143 [M] | You Talk Too Much | 1961 | 150.00 |
| ❑ SR 25143 [R] | You Talk Too Much | 1961 | 100.00 |

### JONES, JOHN PAUL

Also see LED ZEPPELIN.

| Number | Title (A Side/B Side) | Yr | NM |
|---|---|---|---|
| **COLUMBIA** | | | |
| ❑ KC 32047 | John Paul Jones | 1973 | 20.00 |

### JONES, JONAH

| Number | Title (A Side/B Side) | Yr | NM |
|---|---|---|---|
| **ANGEL** | | | |
| ❑ ANG.60005 [10] | Jonah Wails — 1st Blast | 1954 | 75.00 |
| ❑ ANG.60006 [10] | Jonah Wails — 2nd Blast | 1954 | 75.00 |
| **BETHLEHEM** | | | |
| ❑ BCP-1014 [10] | Jonah Jones Sextet | 1954 | 80.00 |
| **CAPITOL** | | | |
| ❑ T 839 [M] | Muted Jazz | 1957 | 40.00 |
| ❑ T 963 [M] | Swingin' On Broadway | 1958 | 40.00 |
| ❑ ST 1039 [S] | Jumpin' with Jonah | 1958 | 30.00 |
| ❑ T 1039 [M] | Jumpin' with Jonah | 1958 | 25.00 |
| ❑ ST 1083 [S] | Swingin' at the Cinema | 1958 | 30.00 |
| ❑ T 1083 [M] | Swingin' at the Cinema | 1958 | 25.00 |
| ❑ ST 1115 [S] | Jonah Jumps Again | 1959 | 30.00 |
| ❑ T 1115 [M] | Jonah Jumps Again | 1959 | 25.00 |
| ❑ ST 1193 [S] | I Dig Chicks | 1959 | 25.00 |
| ❑ T 1193 [M] | I Dig Chicks | 1959 | 20.00 |
| ❑ ST 1237 [S] | Swingin' 'Round the World | 1959 | 25.00 |
| ❑ T 1237 [M] | Swingin' 'Round the World | 1959 | 20.00 |
| ❑ ST 1375 [S] | Hit Me Again! | 1960 | 25.00 |
| ❑ T 1375 [M] | Hit Me Again! | 1960 | 20.00 |
| ❑ ST 1404 [S] | Jumpin' with a Shuffle | 1960 | 25.00 |
| ❑ T 1404 [M] | Jumpin' with a Shuffle | 1960 | 20.00 |
| ❑ ST 1405 [S] | A Touch of Blue | 1960 | 25.00 |
| ❑ T 1405 [M] | A Touch of Blue | 1960 | 20.00 |
| ❑ ST 1532 [S] | The Unsinkable Molly Brown | 1961 | 25.00 |
| ❑ T 1532 [M] | The Unsinkable Molly Brown | 1961 | 20.00 |
| ❑ ST 1557 [S] | Great Instrumental Hits Styled by Jonah Jones | 1961 | 25.00 |
| ❑ T 1557 [M] | Great Instrumental Hits Styled by Jonah Jones | 1961 | 20.00 |
| ❑ ST 1641 [S] | Broadway Swings Again | 1961 | 25.00 |
| ❑ T 1641 [M] | Broadway Swings Again | 1961 | 20.00 |
| ❑ ST 1660 [S] | Jonah Jones/Glenn Gray | 1961 | 25.00 |
| ❑ T 1660 [M] | Jonah Jones/Glenn Gray | 1961 | 20.00 |
| ❑ ST 1773 [S] | Jazz Bonus | 1962 | 20.00 |
| ❑ ST 1948 [S] | And Now, In Person — Jonah Jones | 1963 | 20.00 |
| ❑ ST 2087 [S] | Blowin' Up a Storm | 1964 | 20.00 |
| **GROOVE** | | | |
| ❑ LG-1001 [M] | Jonah Jones at the Embers | 1956 | 50.00 |
| **MOTOWN** | | | |
| ❑ M-683 | Along Came Jonah | 1969 | 40.00 |
| ❑ M-690 | Little Dis, Little Dat | 1970 | 40.00 |
| **RCA VICTOR** | | | |
| ❑ LPM-2004 [M] | Jonah Jones at the Embers | 1959 | 40.00 |
| *—Reissue of Groove and Vik LP* | | | |
| **VIK** | | | |
| ❑ LXA-1135 [M] | Jonah Jones at the Embers | 1958 | 40.00 |
| *—Reissue of Groove LP* | | | |

### JONES, JONAH/CHARLIE SHAVERS

| Number | Title (A Side/B Side) | Yr | NM |
|---|---|---|---|
| **BETHLEHEM** | | | |
| ❑ BCP-6034 [M] | Sounds of the Trumpets | 1959 | 40.00 |

### JONES, LINDA

| Number | Title (A Side/B Side) | Yr | NM |
|---|---|---|---|
| **LOMA** | | | |
| ❑ 5907 | Hypnotized | 1967 | 30.00 |
| **TURBO** | | | |
| ❑ 7007 | Your Precious Love | 1972 | 20.00 |

### JONES, NORAH

| Number | Title (A Side/B Side) | Yr | NM |
|---|---|---|---|
| **BLUE NOTE** | | | |
| ❑ BTE 32088 | Come Away with Me | 2004 | 15.00 |
| *—Standard-weight issue with lyrics on back cover; "Manufactured by Caroline Distribution" on back* | | | |
| ❑ BTE 84800 | Feels Like Home | 2004 | 15.00 |
| *—Standard-weight edition; "Manufactured by Caroline Distribution" on back cover* | | | |
| **CLASSICRECORDS.COM** | | | |
| ❑ JP-5004 | Come Away with Me | 2002 | 25.00 |
| *—Audiophile pressing; heavyweight vinyl with gatefold cover* | | | |

### JONES, PAUL

Original lead singer for MANFRED MANN.

| Number | Title (A Side/B Side) | Yr | NM |
|---|---|---|---|
| **CAPITOL** | | | |
| ❑ ST 2795 [S] | Paul Jones Sings Songs from the Film "Privilege" and Others | 1967 | 30.00 |
| ❑ T 2795 [M] | Paul Jones Sings Songs from the Film "Privilege" and Others | 1967 | 30.00 |
| **LONDON** | | | |
| ❑ XPS 605 | Crucifix in a Horseshoe | 1971 | 12.00 |

### JONES, PHILLY JOE

| Number | Title (A Side/B Side) | Yr | NM |
|---|---|---|---|
| **ATLANTIC** | | | |
| ❑ 1340 [M] | Philly Joe's Beat | 1960 | 25.00 |
| *—Multicolor label, white "fan" logo on right* | | | |
| ❑ SD 1340 [S] | Philly Joe's Beat | 1960 | 30.00 |
| *—Multicolor label, white "fan" logo on right* | | | |
| **RIVERSIDE** | | | |
| ❑ RLP 12-282 [M] | Blues for Dracula | 1958 | 50.00 |
| ❑ RLP 12-302 [M] | Drums Around the World | 1959 | 50.00 |
| ❑ RLP 12-313 [M] | Showcase | 1959 | 50.00 |
| ❑ RLP-1147 [S] | Drums Around the World | 1959 | 40.00 |
| ❑ RLP-1159 [S] | Showcase | 1959 | 40.00 |

### JONES, PHILLY JOE, AND ELVIN JONES

| Number | Title (A Side/B Side) | Yr | NM |
|---|---|---|---|
| **ATLANTIC** | | | |
| ❑ 1428 [M] | Together | 1964 | 25.00 |
| ❑ SD 1428 [S] | Together | 1964 | 30.00 |

### JONES, QUINCY

| Number | Title (A Side/B Side) | Yr | NM |
|---|---|---|---|
| **A&M** | | | |
| ❑ QU-53041 [Q] | You've Got It Bad Girl | 1974 | 20.00 |
| ❑ QU-53617 [Q] | Body Heat | 1974 | 20.00 |
| ❑ QU-54526 [Q] | Mellow Madness | 1975 | 20.00 |
| **ABC-PARAMOUNT** | | | |
| ❑ 149 [M] | This Is How I Feel About Jazz | 1956 | 100.00 |
| ❑ 186 [M] | Go West, Man! | 1957 | 100.00 |

Rickie Lee Jones, *Flying Cowboys,* Geffen GHS 24246, 1989, $10.

| Number | Title (A Side/B Side) | Yr | NM |
|---|---|---|---|
| **COLGEMS** | | | |
| ❑ COM-107 [M] | In Cold Blood | 1967 | 20.00 |
| ❑ COS-107 [S] | In Cold Blood | 1967 | 25.00 |
| **EMARCY** | | | |
| ❑ MG-36083 [M] | Jazz Abroad | 1956 | 100.00 |
| **IMPULSE!** | | | |
| ❑ A-11 [M] | The Quintessence | 1962 | 30.00 |
| ❑ AS-11 [S] | The Quintessence | 1962 | 40.00 |
| **LIBERTY** | | | |
| ❑ LOM-16004 [M] | Enter Laughing | 1967 | 25.00 |
| ❑ LOS-17004 [S] | Enter Laughing | 1967 | 30.00 |
| **MERCURY** | | | |
| ❑ PPS-2014 [M] | Around the World | 1961 | 30.00 |
| ❑ PPS-6014 [S] | Around the World | 1961 | 40.00 |
| ❑ MG-20444 [M] | Birth of a Band | 1959 | 50.00 |
| ❑ MG-20561 [M] | The Great, Wide World of Quincy Jones | 1960 | 50.00 |
| ❑ MG-20612 [M] | I Dig Dancers | 1960 | 40.00 |
| ❑ MG-20653 [M] | Quincy Jones at Newport '61 | 1961 | 30.00 |
| ❑ MG-20751 [M] | Big Band Bossa Nova | 1962 | 30.00 |
| ❑ MG-20799 [M] | Quincy Jones Plays Hip Hits | 1963 | 30.00 |
| ❑ MG-20863 [M] | Quincy Jones Explores the Music of Henry Mancini | 1964 | 20.00 |
| ❑ MG-20938 [M] | Golden Boy | 1964 | 20.00 |
| ❑ MG-21011 [M] | The Pawnbroker | 1964 | 20.00 |
| ❑ MG-21025 [M] | Mirage | 1965 | 20.00 |
| ❑ MG-21050 [M] | Quincy Jones Plays for Pussycats | 1965 | 20.00 |
| ❑ MG-21063 [M] | Quincy's Got a Brand New Bag | 1965 | 20.00 |
| ❑ MG-21070 [M] | Slender Thread | 1966 | 20.00 |
| ❑ SR-60129 [S] | Birth of a Band | 1959 | 60.00 |
| ❑ SR-60221 [S] | The Great, Wide World of Quincy Jones | 1960 | 60.00 |
| ❑ SR-60612 [S] | I Dig Dancers | 1960 | 50.00 |
| ❑ SR-60653 [S] | Quincy Jones at Newport '61 | 1961 | 40.00 |
| ❑ SR-60751 [S] | Big Band Bossa Nova | 1962 | 40.00 |
| ❑ SR-60799 [S] | Quincy Jones Plays Hip Hits | 1963 | 40.00 |
| ❑ SR-60863 [S] | Quincy Jones Explores the Music of Henry Mancini | 1964 | 25.00 |
| ❑ SR-60938 [S] | Golden Boy | 1964 | 25.00 |
| ❑ SR-61011 [S] | The Pawnbroker | 1964 | 25.00 |
| ❑ SR-61025 [S] | Mirage | 1965 | 25.00 |
| ❑ SR-61050 [S] | Quincy Jones Plays for Pussycats | 1965 | 25.00 |
| ❑ SR-61063 [S] | Quincy's Got a Brand New Bag | 1965 | 25.00 |
| ❑ SR-61070 [S] | Slender Thread | 1966 | 25.00 |
| **MOBILE FIDELITY** | | | |
| ❑ 1-078 | You've Got It Bad Girl | 1981 | 25.00 |
| *—Audiophile vinyl* | | | |
| **NAUTILUS** | | | |
| ❑ NR-52 | The Dude | 198? | 40.00 |
| *—Audiophile vinyl* | | | |
| **PRESTIGE** | | | |
| ❑ PRLP-172 [10] | Quincy Jones with the Swedish-American All Stars | 1953 | 200.00 |
| **QWEST** | | | |
| ❑ 25356 [(2)] | The Color Purple | 1985 | 20.00 |
| *—Boxed set on purple vinyl* | | | |
| **UNITED ARTISTS** | | | |
| ❑ UAS-5214 | They Call Me Mister Tibbs | 1970 | 25.00 |

**JONES, RICHARD**

| Number | Title (A Side/B Side) | Yr | NM |
|---|---|---|---|
| **PAX** | | | |
| ❑ 6010 [10] | New Orleans Style | 1954 | 80.00 |
| **RIVERSIDE** | | | |
| ❑ RLP-1017 [10] | Richard P. Jones and Clarence Williams | 1953 | 80.00 |

**JONES, RICKIE LEE**

| Number | Title (A Side/B Side) | Yr | NM |
|---|---|---|---|
| **GEFFEN** | | | |
| ❑ GHS 24246 | Flying Cowboys | 1989 | 10.00 |
| **MOBILE FIDELITY** | | | |
| ❑ 1-089 | Rickie Lee Jones | 1982 | 200.00 |
| *—Audiophile vinyl* | | | |
| **WARNER BROS.** | | | |
| ❑ BSK 3296 | Rickie Lee Jones | 1979 | 8.00 |
| ❑ BSK 3432 | Pirates | 1981 | 8.00 |
| ❑ 23805 [10] | Girl at Her Volcano | 1983 | 8.00 |
| ❑ 23805 [10] | Girl at Her Volcano | 1983 | 15.00 |
| *—Promo-only version on Quiex II vinyl* | | | |
| ❑ 25117 | The Magazine | 1984 | 8.00 |

**JONES, RUFUS**

| Number | Title (A Side/B Side) | Yr | NM |
|---|---|---|---|
| **CAMEO** | | | |
| ❑ C-1076 [M] | Five on Eight | 1964 | 25.00 |
| ❑ SC-1076 [S] | Five on Eight | 1964 | 30.00 |

**JONES, SAM**

| Number | Title (A Side/B Side) | Yr | NM |
|---|---|---|---|
| **RIVERSIDE** | | | |
| ❑ RLP 12-324 [M] | The Soul Society | 1960 | 40.00 |
| ❑ RLP-358 [M] | The Chant! | 1961 | 30.00 |
| ❑ RLP-432 [M] | Down Home | 1962 | 30.00 |
| ❑ RLP-1172 [S] | The Soul Society | 1960 | 40.00 |
| ❑ RS-9358 [S] | The Chant! | 1961 | 40.00 |
| ❑ RS-9432 [S] | Down Home | 1962 | 40.00 |

**JONES, SPIKE, AND THE CITY SLICKERS**

| Number | Title (A Side/B Side) | Yr | NM |
|---|---|---|---|
| **CORNOGRAPHIC** | | | |
| ❑ 1001 | King of Corn | 197? | 10.00 |
| **GOLDBERG & O'REILY** | | | |
| ❑ MF 205/4 [(3)] | The Craziest Show on Earth | 1977 | 20.00 |
| *—Collection of radio show performances* | | | |
| **HINDSIGHT** | | | |
| ❑ HSR-185 | The Uncollected Spike Jones 1946 | 198? | 10.00 |
| **LIBERTY** | | | |
| ❑ LRP-3140 [M] | Omnibust | 1959 | 50.00 |
| ❑ LRP-3154 [M] | 60 Years of Music America Hates Best | 1960 | 50.00 |
| ❑ LRP-3338 [M] | Washington Square | 1963 | 20.00 |
| ❑ LRP-3349 [M] | Spike Jones' New Band | 1964 | 30.00 |
| ❑ LRP-3370 [M] | My Man | 1964 | 20.00 |
| ❑ LRP-3401 [M] | Spike Jones Plays Hank Williams Hits | 1965 | 20.00 |
| ❑ LST-7140 [S] | Omnibust | 1959 | 75.00 |
| *—Black vinyl* | | | |
| ❑ LST-7140 [S] | Omnibust | 1959 | 150.00 |
| *—Red vinyl* | | | |
| ❑ LST-7154 [S] | 60 Years of Music America Hates Best | 1960 | 75.00 |
| ❑ LST-7338 [S] | Washington Square | 1963 | 25.00 |
| ❑ LST-7349 [S] | Spike Jones' New Band | 1964 | 40.00 |
| ❑ LST-7370 [S] | My Man | 1964 | 25.00 |
| ❑ LST-7401 [S] | Spike Jones Plays Hank Williams Hits | 1965 | 25.00 |
| **RCA GOLD SEAL** | | | |
| ❑ AGL1-4142 | Spike Jones Is Murdering the Classics! | 1982 | 8.00 |
| *—Reissue* | | | |
| **RCA RED SEAL** | | | |
| ❑ LSC-3235 [R] | Spike Jones Is Murdering the Classics! | 1971 | 20.00 |
| **RCA VICTOR** | | | |
| ❑ LPT-18 [10] | Spike Jones Plays the Charleston | 1952 | 200.00 |
| ❑ ANL1-1035 | The Best of Spike Jones | 1975 | 10.00 |
| *—Reissue* | | | |
| ❑ LPM-2224 [M] | Thank You Music Lovers | 1960 | 50.00 |
| *—"RCA Victor" in silver above dog, "Long 33 1/3 Play" at bottom of label* | | | |
| ❑ LPM-2224 [M] | Thank You Music Lovers | 1965 | 25.00 |
| *—"RCA Victor" in white above dog, "Monaural" at bottom of label* | | | |
| ❑ ANL1-2312 | The Best of Spike Jones, Volume 2 | 1977 | 10.00 |
| *—Reissue* | | | |
| ❑ LPM-3054 [10] | Bottoms Up | 1952 | 200.00 |
| ❑ LPM-3128 [10] | Spike Jones Murders Carmen and Kids the Classics | 1953 | 200.00 |
| ❑ AYL1-3748 | The Best of Spike Jones, Volume 1 | 1980 | 8.00 |
| *—"Best Buy Series" reissue* | | | |
| ❑ LPM-3849 [M] | The Best of Spike Jones | 1967 | 25.00 |
| ❑ LSP-3849 [R] | The Best of Spike Jones | 1967 | 20.00 |
| ❑ AYL1-3870 | The Best of Spike Jones, Volume 2 | 1981 | 8.00 |
| *—"Best Buy Series" reissue* | | | |
| **RHINO** | | | |
| ❑ R1 70196 | It's a Spike Jones Christmas | 1988 | 12.00 |
| ❑ R1 70261 | Dinner Music...For People Who Aren't Very Hungry | 1988 | 12.00 |
| **UNITED ARTISTS** | | | |
| ❑ UA-LA439-E | The Very Best of Spike Jones | 1975 | 12.00 |
| **VERVE** | | | |
| ❑ MGV-2021 [M] | Let's Sing a Song for Christmas | 1956 | 50.00 |
| ❑ V-2021 [M] | Let's Sing a Song for Christmas | 1961 | 30.00 |
| ❑ MGV-4005 [M] | Dinner Music...For People Who Aren't Very Hungry | 1957 | 50.00 |
| ❑ V-4005 [M] | Dinner Music...For People Who Aren't Very Hungry | 1961 | 25.00 |
| **WARNER BROS.** | | | |
| ❑ W 1332 [M] | Spike Jones in Hi-Fi | 1959 | 40.00 |
| ❑ WS 1332 [S] | Spike Jones in Hi-Fi | 1959 | 50.00 |
| *—This is the title on the front of the LP cover, but the spine says "Spike Jones in Stereo"* | | | |

**JONES, STAN**

| Number | Title (A Side/B Side) | Yr | NM |
|---|---|---|---|
| **BUENA VISTA** | | | |
| ❑ BV-3306 [M] | Ghost Riders in the Sky | 1961 | 25.00 |
| *—Reissue of Disneyland WDL-3015* | | | |
| **DISNEYLAND** | | | |
| ❑ WDL-1005 [M] | Songs of the National Parks | 1958 | 40.00 |
| *—Sold only at national parks* | | | |
| ❑ WDL-3015 [M] | Creakin' Leather | 1958 | 40.00 |
| ❑ WDL-3033 [M] | This Was the West — The Story and the Songs | 1958 | 40.00 |



**Except when noted otherwise, VG = 25% of NM, and VG+ = 50% of NM. (Example: VG = $2.00, VG+ = $4.00 and NM = $8.00.)**

## JONES, TAMIKO

| Number | Title (A Side/B Side) | Yr | NM |
|---|---|---|---|
| **A&M** | | | |
| ❑ SP-3011 | I'll Be Anything for You | 1969 | 25.00 |
| **ARISTA** | | | |
| ❑ AL-4040 | Love Trip | 1975 | 25.00 |
| **DECEMBER** | | | |
| ❑ DR-8500 | Tamiko | 1968 | 30.00 |
| **METROMEDIA** | | | |
| ❑ MD 1030 | Tamiko Jones in Muscle Shoals | 1970 | 25.00 |

## JONES, THAD

| Number | Title (A Side/B Side) | Yr | NM |
|---|---|---|---|
| **BLUE NOTE** | | | |
| ❑ BLP-1513 [M] | Detroit-New York Junction | 1956 | 500.00 |
| *—"Deep groove" version; Lexington Ave. address on label* | | | |
| ❑ BLP-1513 [M] | Detroit-New York Junction | 1958 | 300.00 |
| *—"Deep groove" version, W. 63rd St. address on label* | | | |
| ❑ BLP-1513 [M] | Detroit-New York Junction | 1963 | 50.00 |
| *—With "New York, USA" address on label* | | | |
| ❑ BLP-1527 [M] | The Magnificent Thad Jones | 1956 | 150.00 |
| *—"Deep groove" version, W. 63rd St. address on label* | | | |
| ❑ BLP-1527 [M] | The Magnificent Thad Jones | 1956 | 500.00 |
| *—"Deep groove" version; Lexington Ave. address on label* | | | |
| ❑ BLP-1527 [M] | The Magnificent Thad Jones | 1963 | 50.00 |
| *—With "New York, USA" address on label* | | | |
| ❑ BLP-1546 [M] | The Magnificent Thad Jones, Volume 3 | 1957 | 200.00 |
| *—Regular version, W. 63rd St., NY address on label* | | | |
| ❑ BLP-1546 [M] | The Magnificent Thad Jones, Volume 3 | 1957 | 400.00 |
| *—"Deep groove" version; W. 63rd St. address on label* | | | |
| ❑ BLP-1546 [M] | The Magnificent Thad Jones, Volume 3 | 1963 | 50.00 |
| *—With "New York, USA" address on label* | | | |
| **DEBUT** | | | |
| ❑ DLP-12 [10] | The Fabulous Thad Jones | 1954 | 600.00 |
| ❑ DLP-17 [10] | Jazz Collaborations | 1954 | 600.00 |
| ❑ DEB-127 [M] | Thad Jones | 1958 | 300.00 |
| **FANTASY** | | | |
| ❑ 6004 [M] | The Fabulous Thad Jones | 1962 | 25.00 |
| *—Black vinyl* | | | |
| ❑ 6004 [M] | The Fabulous Thad Jones | 1962 | 50.00 |
| *—Red vinyl* | | | |
| ❑ 86004 [R] | The Fabulous Thad Jones | 1962 | 30.00 |
| *—Blue vinyl* | | | |
| **MOSAIC** | | | |
| ❑ MQ5-172 [(5)] | The Complete Blue Note/UA/ Roulette Recordings of Thad Jones | 199? | 100.00 |
| **PERIOD** | | | |
| ❑ SPL-1208 [M] | Mad Thad | 1956 | 250.00 |
| **PRESTIGE** | | | |
| ❑ PRLP-7118 [M] | After Hours | 1957 | 200.00 |
| *—Yellow label with W. 50th St. address* | | | |
| **UNITED ARTISTS** | | | |
| ❑ UAL-4025 [M] | Motor City Scene | 1959 | 80.00 |
| ❑ UAS-5025 [S] | Motor City Scene | 1959 | 60.00 |

## JONES, THAD, AND PEPPER ADAMS

| Number | Title (A Side/B Side) | Yr | NM |
|---|---|---|---|
| **MILESTONE** | | | |
| ❑ MLP-1001 [M] | Mean What You Say | 1966 | 20.00 |
| ❑ MSP-9001 [S] | Mean What You Say | 1966 | 25.00 |

## JONES, THAD, AND MEL LEWIS

| Number | Title (A Side/B Side) | Yr | NM |
|---|---|---|---|
| **BLUE NOTE** | | | |
| ❑ BST-84346 | Consummation | 1970 | 30.00 |
| ❑ BST-89905 [(2)] | The Jazz Wave Ltd. On Tour (Volume 1) | 1970 | 25.00 |
| **MOSAIC** | | | |
| ❑ MQ7-151 [(7)] | The Complete Solid State Recordings of the Thad Jones-Mel Lewis Orchestra | 199? | 150.00 |
| **SOLID STATE** | | | |
| ❑ SM-17003 [M] | Presenting Thad Jones, Mel Lewis and the Jazz Orchestra | 1966 | 20.00 |
| ❑ SM-17016 [M] | Live at the Village Vanguard | 1967 | 30.00 |
| ❑ SS-18003 [S] | Presenting Thad Jones, Mel Lewis and the Jazz Orchestra | 1966 | 20.00 |

## JONES, TOM

| Number | Title (A Side/B Side) | Yr | NM |
|---|---|---|---|
| **EPIC** | | | |
| ❑ PE 34383 | Classic Tom Jones | 1976 | 12.00 |
| ❑ PE 34468 | Say You'll Stay Until Tomorrow | 1977 | 12.00 |
| ❑ PE 34720 | Tom Is Love | 1977 | 10.00 |
| ❑ JE 35023 | What a Night | 1978 | 10.00 |
| **JIVE** | | | |
| ❑ 1214-1-J | Move Closer | 1989 | 12.00 |
| **LONDON** | | | |
| ❑ PS 717 | The Country Side of Tom Jones | 1978 | 10.00 |
| ❑ LC-50002 | Tom Jones' Greatest Hits | 1977 | 12.00 |
| ❑ 820234-1 | This Is Tom Jones | 1985 | 8.00 |
| ❑ 820319-1 | Tom Jones' Greatest Hits | 1985 | 10.00 |
| **MCA** | | | |
| ❑ 3182 | Tom Jones | 1979 | 10.00 |
| ❑ 37114 | Rescue Me | 1980 | 8.00 |
| **MERCURY** | | | |
| ❑ SRM-1-4010 | Darlin' | 1981 | 10.00 |
| ❑ SRM-1-4062 | Tom Jones Country | 1982 | 10.00 |
| ❑ 814448-1 | Don't Let Our Dreams Die Young | 1983 | 10.00 |
| ❑ 822701-1 | Love Is on the Radio | 1984 | 10.00 |
| ❑ 826140-1 | Tender Loving Care | 1985 | 10.00 |
| ❑ 830409-1 | Things That Matter Most to Me | 1987 | 10.00 |
| **PARROT** | | | |
| ❑ XPAS-1 [DJ] | Special Tom Jones Interview | 1970 | 100.00 |
| *—Promo-only open-end interview with gatefold cover and script* | | | |
| ❑ PA 61004 [M] | It's Not Unusual | 1965 | 15.00 |
| ❑ PA 61006 [M] | What's New Pussycat? | 1965 | 15.00 |
| ❑ PA 61007 [M] | A-Tom-Ic Jones | 1966 | 15.00 |
| ❑ PA 61009 [M] | Green, Green Grass of Home | 1967 | 15.00 |
| ❑ PA 61011 [M] | Funny Familiar Forgotten Feelings | 1967 | 15.00 |
| ❑ PA 61014 [M] | Tom Jones Live | 1967 | 15.00 |
| ❑ PAS 71004 [S] | It's Not Unusual | 1965 | 15.00 |
| ❑ PAS 71006 [S] | What's New Pussycat? | 1965 | 15.00 |
| ❑ PAS 71007 [S] | A-Tom-Ic Jones | 1966 | 15.00 |
| ❑ PAS 71009 [S] | Green, Green Grass of Home | 1967 | 15.00 |
| ❑ PAS 71011 [S] | Funny Familiar Forgotten Feelings | 1967 | 15.00 |
| ❑ PAS 71014 [S] | Tom Jones Live | 1967 | 15.00 |
| ❑ PAS 71019 | The Tom Jones Fever Zone | 1968 | 12.00 |
| ❑ PAS 71025 | Help Yourself | 1969 | 12.00 |
| ❑ PAS 71028 | This Is Tom Jones | 1969 | 12.00 |
| ❑ PAS 71031 | Live in Las Vegas | 1969 | 12.00 |
| ❑ PAS 71037 | Tom | 1970 | 12.00 |
| ❑ PAS 71039 | I (Who Have Nothing) | 1970 | 12.00 |
| ❑ PAS 71046 | She's a Lady | 1971 | 12.00 |
| ❑ 2XPAS 71049/50 [(2)] | Live at Caesar's Palace | 1971 | 12.00 |
| ❑ XPAS 71055 | Close Up | 1972 | 12.00 |
| ❑ XPAS 71060 | The Body and Soul of Tom Jones | 197? | 12.00 |
| ❑ XPAS 71062 | Tom Jones' Greatest Hits | 1973 | 12.00 |
| ❑ PAS 71066 | Somethin' 'Bout You Baby I Like | 1974 | 12.00 |
| ❑ PAS 71068 | Memories Don't Leave Like People Do | 197? | 12.00 |
| ❑ ST-92025 | This Is Tom Jones | 1969 | 15.00 |
| *—Capitol Record Club edition* | | | |
| ❑ SW-93186 | Tom | 197? | 15.00 |
| *—Capitol Record Club edition* | | | |

## JONES BOYS, THE

| Number | Title (A Side/B Side) | Yr | NM |
|---|---|---|---|
| **MUSICOR** | | | |
| ❑ MM-2017 [M] | Country and Western Songbook | 1964 | 25.00 |
| ❑ MS-3017 [S] | Country and Western Songbook | 1964 | 30.00 |
| ❑ MS-3182 | My Boys, the Jones Boys | 1970 | 20.00 |

## JONES BOYS, THE (2)

All-star jazz group of musicians with the last name of Jones, none of whom were related.

| Number | Title (A Side/B Side) | Yr | NM |
|---|---|---|---|
| **PERIOD** | | | |
| ❑ SPL-1210 [M] | The Jones Bash | 1954 | 80.00 |

## JONES BROTHERS, THE

| Number | Title (A Side/B Side) | Yr | NM |
|---|---|---|---|
| **METROJAZZ** | | | |
| ❑ E-1003 [M] | Keepin' Up with the Joneses | 1958 | 80.00 |
| ❑ SE-1003 [S] | Keepin' Up with the Joneses | 1958 | 60.00 |

## JOPLIN, JANIS

Also see BIG BROTHER AND THE HOLDING COMPANY.

| Number | Title (A Side/B Side) | Yr | NM |
|---|---|---|---|
| **COLUMBIA** | | | |
| ❑ AS 1377 [DJ] | A Collection | 1982 | 20.00 |
| ❑ KCS 9913 | I Got Dem Ol' Kozmik Blues Again Mama! | 1969 | 20.00 |
| *—"360 Sound Stereo" on label* | | | |
| ❑ KCS 9913 | I Got Dem Ol' Kozmik Blues Again Mama! | 1970 | 12.00 |
| *—Orange label* | | | |
| ❑ PC 9913 | I Got Dem Ol' Kozmik Blues Again Mama! | 198? | 8.00 |
| *—Budget-line reissue* | | | |
| ❑ CQ 30322 [Q] | Pearl | 1974 | 20.00 |
| ❑ KC 30322 | Pearl | 1971 | 15.00 |
| ❑ PC 30322 | Pearl | 1975 | 12.00 |
| *—Reissue without bar code* | | | |
| ❑ PC 30322 | Pearl | 198? | 8.00 |
| *—Reissue with bar code* | | | |
| ❑ C2X 31160 [(2)] | Joplin in Concert | 1972 | 20.00 |
| ❑ CG 31160 | Joplin in Concert | 198? | 12.00 |
| ❑ KC 32168 | Janis Joplin's Greatest Hits | 1973 | 15.00 |
| ❑ PC 32168 | Janis Joplin's Greatest Hits | 197? | 8.00 |
| ❑ CG 33345 [(2)] | Janis | 198? | 12.00 |
| ❑ PG 33345 [(2)] | Janis | 1975 | 15.00 |
| ❑ PC 37569 | Farewell Song | 1982 | 10.00 |
| **COLUMBIA SPECIAL PRODUCTS** | | | |
| ❑ 2P 13792 [(2)] | The Greatest Hits of Janis Joplin | 1977 | 20.00 |

## JORDAN, CLIFFORD

| Number | Title (A Side/B Side) | Yr | NM |
|---|---|---|---|
| **ATLANTIC** | | | |
| ❑ 1444 [M] | These Are My Roots | 1965 | 25.00 |
| ❑ SD 1444 [S] | These Are My Roots | 1965 | 30.00 |
| **BLUE NOTE** | | | |
| ❑ BLP-1549 [M] | Blowing In from Chicago | 1957 | 80.00 |
| *—Regular version, W. 63rd St., NY address on label* | | | |
| ❑ BLP-1549 [M] | Blowing In from Chicago | 1957 | 120.00 |
| *—"Deep groove" version (deep indentation under label on both sides)* | | | |
| ❑ BLP-1549 [M] | Blowing In from Chicago | 1963 | 25.00 |
| *—With "New York, USA" address on label* | | | |
| ❑ BLP-1565 [M] | Clifford Jordan | 1957 | 80.00 |
| *—Regular version, W. 63rd St., NY address on label* | | | |
| ❑ BLP-1565 [M] | Clifford Jordan | 1957 | 120.00 |
| *—"Deep groove" version (deep indentation under label on both sides)* | | | |
| ❑ BLP-1565 [M] | Clifford Jordan | 1963 | 25.00 |
| *—With "New York, USA" address on label* | | | |
| ❑ BST-1565 [S] | Clifford Jordan | 1959 | 60.00 |
| *—Regular version, W. 63rd St., NY address on label* | | | |
| ❑ BST-1565 [S] | Clifford Jordan | 1959 | 80.00 |
| *—"Deep groove" version (deep indentation under label on both sides)* | | | |
| ❑ BST-1565 [S] | Clifford Jordan | 1963 | 20.00 |
| *—With "New York, USA" address on label* | | | |
| ❑ BLP-1582 [M] | Cliff Craft | 1958 | 80.00 |
| *—Regular version, W. 63rd St., NY address on label* | | | |
| ❑ BLP-1582 [M] | Cliff Craft | 1958 | 120.00 |
| *—"Deep groove" version (deep indentation under label on both sides)* | | | |
| ❑ BLP-1582 [M] | Cliff Craft | 1963 | 25.00 |
| *—With "New York, USA" address on label* | | | |
| ❑ BST-1582 [S] | Cliff Craft | 1959 | 60.00 |
| *—Regular version, W. 63rd St., NY address on label* | | | |
| ❑ BST-1582 [S] | Cliff Craft | 1959 | 80.00 |
| *—"Deep groove" version (deep indentation under label on both sides)* | | | |
| ❑ BST-1582 [S] | Cliff Craft | 1963 | 20.00 |
| *—With "New York, USA" address on label* | | | |
| ❑ BST-81582 [S] | Cliff Craft | 199? | 25.00 |
| *—Classic Records reissue on audiophile vinyl* | | | |
| **JAZZLAND** | | | |
| ❑ JLP-40 [M] | A Story Tale | 1961 | 30.00 |
| ❑ JLP-52 [M] | Starting Time | 1961 | 30.00 |
| ❑ JLP-69 [M] | Bearcat | 1962 | 30.00 |
| ❑ JLP-940 [S] | A Story Tale | 1961 | 40.00 |
| ❑ JLP-952 [S] | Starting Time | 1961 | 40.00 |
| ❑ JLP-969 [S] | Bearcat | 1962 | 40.00 |
| **RIVERSIDE** | | | |
| ❑ RLP-340 [M] | Spellbound | 1960 | 40.00 |
| ❑ RS-9340 [S] | Spellbound | 1960 | 30.00 |
| **STRATA-EAST** | | | |
| ❑ SES 1972-1 | In the World | 1972 | 20.00 |
| ❑ SES 19737/8 [(2)] | Glass Bead Games | 1974 | 25.00 |
| **VORTEX** | | | |
| ❑ 2010 | Soul Fountain | 1970 | 20.00 |

## JORDAN, DUKE

| Number | Title (A Side/B Side) | Yr | NM |
|---|---|---|---|
| **BLUE NOTE** | | | |
| ❑ BLP-4046 [M] | Flight to Jordan | 1960 | 80.00 |
| *—With W. 63rd St., NY address on label* | | | |
| ❑ BLP-4046 [M] | Flight to Jordan | 1963 | 25.00 |
| *—With "New York, USA" address on label* | | | |
| ❑ BST-84046 [S] | Flight to Jordan | 1960 | 60.00 |
| *—With W. 63rd St., NY address on label* | | | |
| ❑ BST-84046 [S] | Flight to Jordan | 1963 | 20.00 |
| *—With "New York, USA" address on label* | | | |
| **CHARLIE PARKER** | | | |
| ❑ PLP-805 [M] | East and West of Jazz | 1962 | 25.00 |
| ❑ PLP-805S [S] | East and West of Jazz | 1962 | 30.00 |
| **NEW JAZZ** | | | |
| ❑ NJ-810 [10] | Jordu | 195? | 200.00 |
| **SAVOY** | | | |
| ❑ MG-12149 [M] | Duke Jordan | 1959 | 80.00 |
| **SIGNAL** | | | |
| ❑ S-1202 [M] | Duke Jordan | 1955 | 250.00 |

## JORDAN, DUKE/HALL OVERTON

| Number | Title (A Side/B Side) | Yr | NM |
|---|---|---|---|
| **SAVOY** | | | |
| ❑ MG-12145 [M] | Do It Yourself Jazz | 1959 | 100.00 |
| ❑ MG-12146 [M] | Jazz Laboratory Series | 1959 | 100.00 |
| **SIGNAL** | | | |
| ❑ S-101/2 [M] | Jazz Laboratory Series | 1955 | 250.00 |
| *—Deduct 20 percent if book is missing* | | | |

## JORDAN, KING

| Number | Title (A Side/B Side) | Yr | NM |
|---|---|---|---|
| **CORAL** | | | |
| ❑ CRL 57372 [M] | Phantom Guitar | 1962 | 20.00 |
| ❑ CRL 757372 [S] | Phantom Guitar | 1962 | 25.00 |

## JORDAN, LOUIS

| Number | Title (A Side/B Side) | Yr | NM |
|---|---|---|---|
| **DECCA** | | | |
| ❑ DL 5035 [M] | Greatest Hits | 1968 | 30.00 |
| ❑ DL 8551 [M] | Let the Good Times Roll | 1958 | 100.00 |
| *—Black label, silver print* | | | |
| **MERCURY** | | | |
| ❑ MG-20242 [M] | Somebody Up There Digs Me | 1957 | 120.00 |
| ❑ MG-20331 [M] | Man, We're Wailin' | 1958 | 120.00 |

Journey, *Next,* Columbia PC 34311, 1977, no bar code, $10.

**SCORE**

| Number | Title (A Side/B Side) | Yr | NM |
|---|---|---|---|
| ❑ SLP-4007 [M] | Go Blow Your Horn | 1957 | 200.00 |

**TANGERINE**

| Number | Title (A Side/B Side) | Yr | NM |
|---|---|---|---|
| ❑ 1503 [M] | Hallelujah | 1964 | 20.00 |
| ❑ S-1503 [S] | Hallelujah | 1964 | 25.00 |

**WING**

| Number | Title (A Side/B Side) | Yr | NM |
|---|---|---|---|
| ❑ MGW-12126 [M] | Somebody Up There Digs Me | 1962 | 25.00 |

### JORDAN, SHEILA

**BLUE NOTE**

| Number | Title (A Side/B Side) | Yr | NM |
|---|---|---|---|
| ❑ BLP-9002 [M] | Portrait of Sheila Jordan | 1962 | 150.00 |
| *—With W. 63rd St., NY address on label* | | | |
| ❑ BLP-9002 [M] | Portrait of Sheila Jordan | 1963 | 25.00 |
| *—With "New York, USA" address on label* | | | |

**WAVE**

| Number | Title (A Side/B Side) | Yr | NM |
|---|---|---|---|
| ❑ W-1 [M] | Looking Out | 1961 | 60.00 |
| ❑ WS-1 [S] | Looking Out | 1961 | 80.00 |

### JORDAN, TAFT

**MERCURY**

| Number | Title (A Side/B Side) | Yr | NM |
|---|---|---|---|
| ❑ MG-20429 [M] | The Moods of Taft Jordan | 1959 | 40.00 |
| ❑ SR-60101 [S] | The Moods of Taft Jordan | 1959 | 40.00 |

**MOODSVILLE**

| Number | Title (A Side/B Side) | Yr | NM |
|---|---|---|---|
| ❑ MVLP-21 [M] | Mood Indigo — Taft Jordan Plays Duke Ellington | 1961 | 50.00 |
| *—Green label* | | | |
| ❑ MVLP-21 [M] | Mood Indigo — Taft Jordan Plays Duke Ellington | 1965 | 25.00 |
| *—Blue label, trident logo at right* | | | |

**STATUS**

| Number | Title (A Side/B Side) | Yr | NM |
|---|---|---|---|
| ❑ 21 [M] | Mood Indigo — Taft Jordan Plays Duke Ellington | 196? | 25.00 |
| *—Reissue of Moodsville 21* | | | |

### JORDAN BROTHERS, THE

**JBP**

| Number | Title (A Side/B Side) | Yr | NM |
|---|---|---|---|
| ❑ ASM-416 | Today's Yesterdays Volume 1 | 1980 | 30.00 |

### JORDANAIRES, THE

**CAPITOL**

| Number | Title (A Side/B Side) | Yr | NM |
|---|---|---|---|
| ❑ T 1011 [M] | Heavenly Spirit | 1958 | 40.00 |
| ❑ T 1167 [M] | Gloryland | 1959 | 40.00 |
| ❑ ST 1311 [S] | Land of Jordan | 1960 | 40.00 |
| ❑ T 1311 [M] | Land of Jordan | 1960 | 30.00 |
| ❑ ST 1559 [S] | To God Be the Glory | 1961 | 25.00 |
| ❑ T 1559 [M] | To God Be the Glory | 1961 | 20.00 |
| ❑ ST 1742 [S] | Spotlight on the Jordanaires | 1962 | 30.00 |
| ❑ T 1742 [M] | Spotlight on the Jordanaires | 1962 | 25.00 |

**CLASSIC**

| Number | Title (A Side/B Side) | Yr | NM |
|---|---|---|---|
| ❑ CCR 1935 | Christmas to Elvis from the Jordanaires | 1978 | 12.00 |

**COLUMBIA**

| Number | Title (A Side/B Side) | Yr | NM |
|---|---|---|---|
| ❑ CL 2214 [M] | This Land | 1964 | 20.00 |
| ❑ CL 2458 [M] | The Big Country Hits | 1966 | 20.00 |
| ❑ CS 9014 [S] | This Land | 1964 | 25.00 |
| ❑ CS 9258 [S] | The Big Country Hits | 1966 | 25.00 |

**DECCA**

| Number | Title (A Side/B Side) | Yr | NM |
|---|---|---|---|
| ❑ DL 8681 [M] | Peace in the Valley | 1957 | 50.00 |

**RCA VICTOR**

| Number | Title (A Side/B Side) | Yr | NM |
|---|---|---|---|
| ❑ LPM-3081 [10] | Beautiful City | 1953 | 100.00 |

**SESAC**

| Number | Title (A Side/B Side) | Yr | NM |
|---|---|---|---|
| ❑ 1401/2 [M] | Of Rivers and Plains | 195? | 80.00 |

### JORGENSON, CHRISTINE

**J RECORDS**

| Number | Title (A Side/B Side) | Yr | NM |
|---|---|---|---|
| ❑ J-1 [M] | Christine Jorgenson Reveals | 1958 | 50.00 |

### JOSEFUS

**HOOKAH**

| Number | Title (A Side/B Side) | Yr | NM |
|---|---|---|---|
| ❑ 330 | Dead Man | 1969 | 300.00 |

**MAINSTREAM**

| Number | Title (A Side/B Side) | Yr | NM |
|---|---|---|---|
| ❑ S-6127 | Josefus | 1970 | 100.00 |

### JOSEPH

**SCEPTER**

| Number | Title (A Side/B Side) | Yr | NM |
|---|---|---|---|
| ❑ SRS-674 | Stoned Age Man | 1970 | 80.00 |

### JOSEPH, MARGIE

**ATLANTIC**

| Number | Title (A Side/B Side) | Yr | NM |
|---|---|---|---|
| ❑ SD 7248 | Margie Joseph | 1973 | 50.00 |
| ❑ SD 7277 | Sweet Surrender | 1974 | 25.00 |
| ❑ SD 18126 | Margie | 1975 | 25.00 |
| ❑ SD 19182 | Feeling My Way | 1978 | 30.00 |

**COTILLION**

| Number | Title (A Side/B Side) | Yr | NM |
|---|---|---|---|
| ❑ SD 9906 | Hear the Words, Feel the Feeling | 1976 | 25.00 |
| ❑ 90158 | Ready for the Night | 1984 | 15.00 |

**H.C.R.C.**

| Number | Title (A Side/B Side) | Yr | NM |
|---|---|---|---|
| ❑ HLP-20009 | Knockout | 1983 | 12.00 |

**ICHIBAN**

| Number | Title (A Side/B Side) | Yr | NM |
|---|---|---|---|
| ❑ 1027 | Stay | 1988 | 15.00 |

**VOLT**

| Number | Title (A Side/B Side) | Yr | NM |
|---|---|---|---|
| ❑ VOS-6012 | Margie Joseph Makes a New Impression | 1971 | 25.00 |
| ❑ VOS-6016 | Phase II | 1971 | 30.00 |

### JOSHUA FOX

**TETRAGRAMMATON**

| Number | Title (A Side/B Side) | Yr | NM |
|---|---|---|---|
| ❑ T-125 | Joshua Fox | 1969 | 30.00 |

### JOSIE AND THE PUSSYCATS

**CAPITOL**

| Number | Title (A Side/B Side) | Yr | NM |
|---|---|---|---|
| ❑ ST-665 | Josie and the Pussycats | 1970 | 200.00 |

### JOURNEY

**COLUMBIA**

| Number | Title (A Side/B Side) | Yr | NM |
|---|---|---|---|
| ❑ AS 914 [DJ] | Journey | 1981 | 15.00 |
| *—Promo-only four-song sampler* | | | |
| ❑ AS 1606 [DJ] | A Candid Conversation with Journey | 1983 | 20.00 |
| *—Promo-only interview and songs LP* | | | |
| ❑ PC 33388 | Journey | 1975 | 10.00 |
| *—No bar code on cover* | | | |
| ❑ PC 33388 | Journey | 198? | 6.00 |
| *—With bar code on cover* | | | |
| ❑ PC 33904 | Look Into the Future | 1976 | 10.00 |
| *—No bar code on cover* | | | |
| ❑ PC 33904 | Look Into the Future | 198? | 6.00 |
| *—With bar code on cover* | | | |
| ❑ PCQ 33904 [Q] | Look Into the Future | 1976 | — |
| *—Not released* | | | |
| ❑ PC 34311 | Next | 1977 | 10.00 |
| *—No bar code on cover* | | | |
| ❑ PC 34311 | Next | 198? | 6.00 |
| *—With bar code on cover* | | | |
| ❑ JC 34912 | Infinity | 1978 | 10.00 |
| *—No bar code on cover* | | | |
| ❑ JC 34912 | Infinity | 1979 | 6.00 |
| *—With bar code on cover* | | | |
| ❑ FC 35797 | Evolution | 1979 | 8.00 |
| ❑ PC 35797 | Evolution | 1985 | 6.00 |
| *—Budget-line reissue* | | | |
| ❑ C2 36324 [(2)] | In the Beginning | 1979 | 10.00 |
| ❑ FC 36339 | Departure | 1980 | 8.00 |
| ❑ KC2 37016 [(2)] | Captured | 1981 | 10.00 |
| ❑ TC 37408 | Escape | 1981 | 8.00 |
| ❑ FC 37998 | Dream After Dream | 1982 | 12.00 |
| ❑ PC 37998 | Dream After Dream | 1986 | 8.00 |
| *—Budget-line reissue* | | | |
| ❑ QC 38504 | Frontiers | 1983 | 8.00 |
| ❑ OC 39936 | Raised on Radio | 1986 | 8.00 |
| ❑ OC 44493 | Greatest Hits | 1988 | 10.00 |
| ❑ HC 44912 | Infinity | 1982 | 30.00 |
| *—Half-speed mastered edition* | | | |
| ❑ HC 46339 | Departure | 1980 | 20.00 |
| *—Half-speed mastered edition* | | | |
| ❑ HC 47408 | Escape | 1982 | 20.00 |
| *—Half-speed mastered edition* | | | |
| ❑ HC 47998 | Dream After Dream | 1982 | 30.00 |
| *—Half-speed mastered edition* | | | |
| ❑ HC 48504 | Frontiers | 1983 | 30.00 |
| *—Half-speed mastered edition* | | | |

**MOBILE FIDELITY**

| Number | Title (A Side/B Side) | Yr | NM |
|---|---|---|---|
| ❑ 1-144 | Escape | 1984 | 200.00 |
| *—Audiophile vinyl* | | | |

### JOURNEYMEN, THE (1)

**CAPITOL**

| Number | Title (A Side/B Side) | Yr | NM |
|---|---|---|---|
| ❑ ST 1629 [S] | The Journeymen | 1961 | 30.00 |
| ❑ T 1629 [M] | The Journeymen | 1961 | 25.00 |
| ❑ ST 1770 [S] | Coming Attraction — Live! | 1962 | 30.00 |
| ❑ T 1770 [M] | Coming Attraction — Live! | 1962 | 25.00 |
| ❑ ST 1951 [S] | New Directions in Folk Music | 1963 | 30.00 |
| ❑ T 1951 [M] | New Directions in Folk Music | 1963 | 25.00 |

### JOY DIVISION

**FACTORY**

| Number | Title (A Side/B Side) | Yr | NM |
|---|---|---|---|
| ❑ FACT US 1 | Unknown Pleasures | 1979 | 20.00 |
| ❑ FACT US 6 | Closer | 1980 | 25.00 |
| *—Red tint vinyl* | | | |
| ❑ FACT US 6 | Closer | 1980 | 50.00 |
| *—Purple tint vinyl* | | | |

**QWEST**

| Number | Title (A Side/B Side) | Yr | NM |
|---|---|---|---|
| ❑ 25747 | Substance | 1988 | 30.00 |
| ❑ 25840 | Unknown Pleasures | 1989 | 15.00 |
| *—Reissue of FACT US 1* | | | |
| ❑ 25841 | Closer | 1989 | 15.00 |
| *—Reissue of FACT US 6* | | | |

### JOY STRINGS, THE

**EPIC**

| Number | Title (A Side/B Side) | Yr | NM |
|---|---|---|---|
| ❑ LN 24321 [M] | Well Seasoned | 1967 | 20.00 |
| ❑ BN 26321 [S] | Well Seasoned | 1967 | 20.00 |

| Number | Title (A Side/B Side) | Yr | NM |
|---|---|---|---|

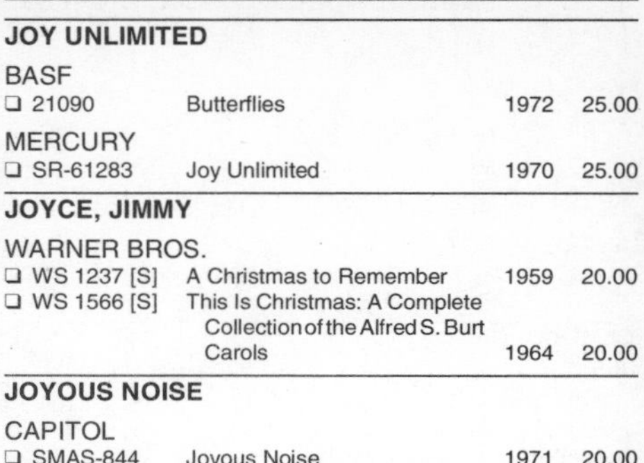

**JOY UNLIMITED**

BASF

| ❑ 21090 | Butterflies | 1972 | 25.00 |
|---|---|---|---|

MERCURY

| ❑ SR-61283 | Joy Unlimited | 1970 | 25.00 |
|---|---|---|---|

**JOYCE, JIMMY**

WARNER BROS.

| ❑ WS 1237 [S] | A Christmas to Remember | 1959 | 20.00 |
|---|---|---|---|
| ❑ WS 1566 [S] | This Is Christmas: A Complete Collection of the Alfred S. Burt Carols | 1964 | 20.00 |

**JOYOUS NOISE**

CAPITOL

| ❑ SMAS-844 | Joyous Noise | 1971 | 20.00 |
|---|---|---|---|

**JUDAS PRIEST**

COLUMBIA

| ❑ AS99 1543 [DJ] | Screaming for Vengeance | 1982 | 20.00 |
|---|---|---|---|

*—Promo-only "world tour" picture disc; plays the correct LP*

| ❑ AS99 1543 [DJ] | Screaming for Vengeance | 1982 | 30.00 |
|---|---|---|---|

*—Promo-only "world tour" picture disc; plays Neil Diamond's "Heartlight" LP in error*

| ❑ PC 34787 | Sin After Sin | 1977 | 12.00 |
|---|---|---|---|

*—Originals have no bar code on back cover*

| ❑ PC 34787 | Sin After Sin | 198? | 6.00 |
|---|---|---|---|

*—Reissue; bar code on back cover*

| ❑ JC 35296 | Stained Class | 1978 | 8.00 |
|---|---|---|---|
| ❑ PC 35296 | Stained Class | 198? | 6.00 |

*—Budget-line reissue*

| ❑ JC 35706 | Hell Bent for Leather | 1979 | 8.00 |
|---|---|---|---|
| ❑ JC 36179 | Unleashed in the East (Live in Japan) | 1979 | 8.00 |
| ❑ PC 36179 | Unleashed in the East (Live in Japan) | 1985 | 6.00 |

*—Budget-line reissue with new prefix*

| ❑ JC 36443 | British Steel | 1980 | 8.00 |
|---|---|---|---|
| ❑ FC 37052 | Point of Entry | 1981 | 8.00 |
| ❑ FC 38160 | Screaming for Vengeance | 1982 | 8.00 |
| ❑ FC 38219 | Defenders of the Faith | 1984 | 8.00 |
| ❑ 9C9 39926 [PD] | Great Vinyl and Concert Hits | 1984 | 60.00 |
| ❑ OC 40158 | Turbo | 1986 | 8.00 |
| ❑ C2 40794 [(2)] | Priest ... Live! | 1987 | 10.00 |
| ❑ FC 44244 | Ram It Down | 1988 | 8.00 |

GULL

| ❑ GU6-403S1 | Rocka-Rolla | 1975 | — |
|---|---|---|---|

*—Canceled*

JANUS

| ❑ JXS-7019 | Sad Wings of Destiny | 1976 | 25.00 |
|---|---|---|---|
| ❑ JXS-7019 [DJ] | Sad Wings of Destiny | 1976 | 30.00 |

*—Promo version, with "Specially faded for easier programming" sticker on cover*

OVATION

| ❑ OV-1751 | Sad Wings of Destiny | 1980 | 15.00 |
|---|---|---|---|

RCA VICTOR

| ❑ AYL1-4747 | Sad Wings of Destiny | 1983 | 10.00 |
|---|---|---|---|

*—Reissue of Ovation LP*

| ❑ AYL1-4933 | The Best of Judas Priest | 1984 | 8.00 |
|---|---|---|---|
| ❑ AYL1-5041 | Rocka-Rolla | 1984 | 10.00 |

*—Reissue of Visa 7001 with new cover*

| ❑ CYL1-5399 [(2)] | Hero, Hero | 1985 | 12.00 |
|---|---|---|---|

VISA

| ❑ IMP-7001 | Rocka Rolla | 1979 | 15.00 |
|---|---|---|---|

*—First U.S. issue of unreleased Gull LP; front cover has a bottle-cap motif*

**JUDD, WYNONNA**

MCA

| ❑ 1P-8201 | Wynonna | 1992 | 25.00 |
|---|---|---|---|

*—Only released on vinyl through Columbia House; label misspells her name as "Wyonna"!*

**JUDDS, THE**

HEARTLAND

| ❑ HL-2041 [(2)] | Classic Gold | 1992 | 20.00 |
|---|---|---|---|

RCA

| ❑ 5916-1-R | Heartland | 1987 | 10.00 |
|---|---|---|---|
| ❑ 6422-1-R | Christmas Time with the Judds | 1987 | 10.00 |
| ❑ 8318-1-R | Greatest Hits | 1988 | 10.00 |
| ❑ 9595-1-R | River of Time | 1989 | 12.00 |

RCA VICTOR

| ❑ AHL1-5319 | Why Not Me | 1984 | 10.00 |
|---|---|---|---|
| ❑ AHL1-7042 | Rockin' with the Rhythm | 1985 | 10.00 |
| ❑ MHL1-8515 [EP] | The Judds | 1984 | 8.00 |

**JULIAN'S TREATMENT**

DECCA

| ❑ DL 75224 | A Time Before This | 1970 | 20.00 |
|---|---|---|---|

**JULLIARD STRING QUARTET**

RCA VICTOR RED SEAL

| ❑ LSC-2378 [S] | Schubert: String Quartet No. 14 "Death and the Maiden" | 1960 | 80.00 |
|---|---|---|---|

*—Original with "shaded dog" label*

Joy Division, *Substance,* Qwest 25747, 1988, $30.

| Number | Title (A Side/B Side) | Yr | NM |
|---|---|---|---|
| ❑ LSC-2413 [S] | Debussy: String Quartet in G; Ravel: String Quartet in F | 1960 | 150.00 |

*—Original with "shaded dog" label*

| ❑ LSC-2481 [S] | Carter: String Quartet No. 2; Schuman: String Quartet No. 3 | 1961 | 40.00 |
|---|---|---|---|

*—Original with "shaded dog" label*

| ❑ LSC-2524 [S] | Dvorak: String Quartet in C; Wolf: Italian Serenade | 1961 | 25.00 |
|---|---|---|---|

*—Originals with "shaded dog" label*

| ❑ LSC-2531 [S] | Berg: Lyric Suite; Webern: 5 Pieces; Six Bagatelles | 1961 | 50.00 |
|---|---|---|---|

*—Originals with "shaded dog" label*

| ❑ LSC-2626 [S] | Beethoven: String Quartet in C# Minor | 1962 | 30.00 |
|---|---|---|---|

*—Original with "shaded dog" label*

| ❑ LSC-2626 [S] | Beethoven: String Quartet in C# Minor | 1964 | 50.00 |
|---|---|---|---|

*—Second edition with "white dog" label; a rare instance where the later pressing is more sought after than the original*

| ❑ LSC-2632 [S] | Beethoven: String Quartet in F, Op. 95; String Quartet in F, Op. 135 | 1962 | 60.00 |
|---|---|---|---|

*—Original with "shaded dog" label*

**JULY**

EPIC

| ❑ BN 26416 | July | 1969 | 200.00 |
|---|---|---|---|

**JUNIOR'S EYES**

A&M

| ❑ SP-4189 | Junior's Eyes | 1970 | 20.00 |
|---|---|---|---|

**JUST IV**

LIBERTY

| ❑ LRP-3340 [M] | First Twelve Sides | 1964 | 20.00 |
|---|---|---|---|
| ❑ LST-7340 [S] | First Twelve Sides | 1964 | 25.00 |

**JUST US**

KAPP

| ❑ KL-1502 [M] | I Can't Grow Peaches on a Cherry Tree | 1966 | 20.00 |
|---|---|---|---|
| ❑ KS-3502 [S] | I Can't Grow Peaches on a Cherry Tree | 1966 | 25.00 |

**JUSTICE, JIMMY**

KAPP

| ❑ KL-1308 [M] | Justice for All | 1963 | 25.00 |
|---|---|---|---|

| Number | Title (A Side/B Side) | Yr | NM |
|---|---|---|---|
| ❑ KS-3308 [S] | Justice for All | 1963 | 40.00 |

**JUSTIS, BILL**

HARMONY

| ❑ KH 31189 | Enchanted Sea | 1972 | 12.00 |
|---|---|---|---|

MONUMENT

| ❑ MLP 8078 [M] | The Eternal Sea | 1967 | 15.00 |
|---|---|---|---|
| ❑ SLP 18078 [S] | The Eternal Sea | 1967 | 15.00 |

PHILLIPS INTERNATIONAL

| ❑ PLP-1950 [M] | Cloud Nine | 1959 | 400.00 |
|---|---|---|---|

SMASH

| ❑ MGS-27021 [M] | Bill Justis Plays 12 Big Instrumental Hits (Alley Cat/ Green Onions) | 1962 | 15.00 |
|---|---|---|---|
| ❑ MGS-27030 [M] | Bill Justis Plays 12 More Big Instrumental Hits (Telstar/ The Lonely Bull) | 1963 | 15.00 |
| ❑ MGS-27031 [M] | Bill Justis Plays 12 Smash Instrumental Hits | 1963 | 15.00 |
| ❑ MGS-27036 [M] | Bill Justis Plays 12 Top Tunes | 1963 | 15.00 |
| ❑ MGS-27043 [M] | Bill Justis Plays 12 Other Instrumental Hits | 1964 | 15.00 |
| ❑ MGS-27047 [M] | Dixieland Folk Style | 1964 | 15.00 |
| ❑ MGS-27065 [M] | More Instrumental Hits | 1965 | 15.00 |
| ❑ MGS-27077 [M] | Taste of Honey/The "In" Crowd | 1966 | 15.00 |
| ❑ SRS-67021 [S] | Bill Justis Plays 12 Big Instrumental Hits (Alley Cat/ Green Onions) | 1962 | 20.00 |
| ❑ SRS-67030 [S] | Bill Justis Plays 12 More Big Instrumental Hits (Telstar/ The Lonely Bull) | 1963 | 20.00 |
| ❑ SRS-67031 [S] | Bill Justis Plays 12 Smash Instrumental Hits | 1963 | 20.00 |
| ❑ SRS-67036 [S] | Bill Justis Plays 12 Top Tunes | 1963 | 20.00 |
| ❑ SRS-67043 [S] | Bill Justis Plays 12 Other Instrumental Hits | 1964 | 20.00 |
| ❑ SRS-67047 [S] | Dixieland Folk Style | 1964 | 20.00 |
| ❑ SRS-67065 [S] | More Instrumental Hits | 1965 | 20.00 |
| ❑ SRS-67077 [S] | Taste of Honey/The "In" Crowd | 1966 | 20.00 |
| ❑ 830898-1 | Raunchy | 1987 | 10.00 |

SUN

| ❑ LP-109 | Raunchy | 1969 | 12.00 |
|---|---|---|---|

Number | Title (A Side/B Side) | Yr | NM

# K

## K-DOE, ERNIE

### JANUS
❑ JLS-3030 Ernie K-Doe 1971 25.00

### MINIT
❑ LP-0002 [M] Mother-in-Law 1961 200.00
*—Orange label*
❑ LP-24002 [R] Mother-in-Law 196? 150.00
*—Black label, not issued until after Imperial bought Minit*

## KAEMPFERT, BERT

### DECCA
❑ DL 4101 [M] Wonderland by Night 1960 15.00
❑ DL 4117 [M] The Wonderland of Bert Kaempfert 1961 15.00
❑ DL 4161 [M] Dancing in Wonderland 1961 15.00
❑ DL 4228 [M] With a "Sound" in My Heart 1962 12.00
❑ DL 4265 [M] Lights Out, Sweet Dreams 1963 12.00
❑ DL 4273 [M] Afrikaan Beat and Other Favorites 1962 12.00
❑ DL 4305 [M] That Happy Feeling 1962 12.00
❑ DL 4374 [M] Living It Up! 1963 12.00
❑ DL 4441 [M] Christmas Wonderland 1963 15.00
❑ DL 4490 [M] That Latin Feeling 1964 12.00
❑ DL 4569 [M] Blue Midnight 1965 12.00
❑ DL 4616 [M] The Magic Music of Far Away Places 1965 12.00
❑ DL 4670 [M] Three O'Clock in the Morning 1965 12.00
❑ DL 4693 [M] Bye Bye Blues 1966 12.00
❑ DL 4795 [M] Strangers in the Night 1966 12.00
❑ DL 4810 [M] Bert Kaempfert's Greatest Hits 1966 12.00
❑ DL 4860 [M] Hold Me 1967 12.00
❑ DL 4925 [M] The World We Knew 1967 20.00
❑ DL 4986 [M] Love That 1968 20.00
❑ DXS 7200 [(2)] The Best of Bert Kaempfert 197? 20.00
❑ DL 8881 [M] April in Portugal 1959 15.00
❑ DL 34485 [M] Bert Kaempfert's Best 1966 15.00
*—Special Decca Custom Division edition*
❑ DL 74101 [S] Wonderland by Night 1960 20.00
❑ DL 74117 [S] The Wonderland of Bert Kaempfert 1961 20.00
❑ DL 74161 [S] Dancing in Wonderland 1961 20.00
❑ DL 74228 [S] With a "Sound" in My Heart 1962 15.00
❑ DL 74265 [S] Lights Out, Sweet Dreams 1963 15.00
❑ DL 74273 [S] Afrikaan Beat and Other Favorites 1962 15.00
❑ DL 74305 [S] That Happy Feeling 1962 15.00
❑ DL 74374 [S] Living It Up! 1963 15.00
❑ DL 74441 [S] Christmas Wonderland 1963 16.00
*—Same as above, but in stereo*
❑ DL 74490 [S] That Latin Feeling 1964 15.00
❑ DL 74569 [S] Blue Midnight 1965 15.00
❑ DL 74616 [S] The Magic Music of Far Away Places 1965 15.00
❑ DL 74670 [S] Three O'Clock in the Morning 1965 15.00
❑ DL 74693 [S] Bye Bye Blues 1966 15.00
❑ DL 74795 [S] Strangers in the Night 1966 15.00
❑ DL 74810 [S] Bert Kaempfert's Greatest Hits 1966 15.00
❑ DL 74860 [S] Hold Me 1967 15.00
❑ DL 74925 [S] The World We Knew 1967 15.00
❑ DL 74986 [S] Love That 1968 15.00
❑ DL 75059 My Way of Life 1968 15.00
❑ DL 75089 Warm and Wonderful 1969 15.00
❑ DL 75140 Traces of Love 1969 15.00
❑ DL 75175 The Kaempfert Touch 1970 15.00
❑ DL 75234 Free and Easy 1970 15.00
❑ DL 75256 Orange Colored Sky 1971 15.00
❑ DL 75305 Bert Kaempfert Now! 1971 15.00
❑ DL 75322 Six Plus Six 1972 15.00
❑ DL 75367 Bert Kaempfert's Greatest Hits, Volume 2 1972 15.00
❑ DL 78881 [S] April in Portugal 1959 20.00
❑ T-90995 [M] Strangers in the Night 1966 15.00
*—Capitol Record Club edition*
❑ ST-91165 Blue Midnight 196? 18.00
*—Capitol Record Club edition*
❑ ST-91502 Love That 1968 18.00
*—Capitol Record Club edition*
❑ ST-93495 Orange Colored Sky 1971 18.00
*—Capitol Record Club edition*
❑ DL 734485 [S] Bert Kaempfert's Best 1966 20.00
*—Special Decca Custom Division edition*

### LONGINES SYMPHONETTE
❑ LWS 299/300/1/2/3 [(5)] Strangers in the Night 196? 30.00
❑ LWS 304 Sweet and Gentle 196? 10.00

### MCA
❑ 11 Bert Kaempfert's Greatest Hits 1973 10.00
*—Reissue of Decca 74810*
❑ 214 Christmas Wonderland 1973 12.00
*—First MCA reissue of Decca 74441*
❑ 314 The Fabulous Fifties 1973 12.00
❑ 368 To the Good Life 1973 12.00
❑ 402 The Most Beautiful Girl 1974 12.00
❑ 447 Gallery 1974 12.00
❑ 466 Golden Memories 1974 12.00
❑ 489 Moon Over Miami 1975 12.00
❑ 4043 [(2)] The Best of Bert Kaempfert 197? 15.00
*—Reissue of Decca 7200; black label with rainbow*
❑ 4100 [(2)] The Best of Bert Kaempfert, Volume 2 197? 15.00
*—Black label with rainbow*
❑ 15020 Christmas Wonderland 197? 10.00
*—Reissue; black label with rainbow*
❑ 15020 Christmas Wonderland 198? 8.00
*—Reissue; blue label with rainbow*

### POLYDOR
❑ K2M 5051 [(2)M] The Happy Wonderland of Bert Kaempfert 1966 15.00
*—Columbia Record Club exclusive*
❑ K2S 5052 [(2)S] The Happy Wonderland of Bert Kaempfert 1966 15.00
*—Columbia Record Club exclusive*
❑ SPH 37553 Wonderland by Night 1967 12.00
*—Columbia Record Club edition*
❑ SPH 37556 Afrikaan Beat and Other Favorites 1967 12.00
*—Columbia Record Club edition*
❑ SPH 37580 With a "Sound" in My Heart 1967 12.00
*—Columbia Record Club edition*
❑ SPH 37598 Lights Out, Sweet Dreams 1967 12.00
*—Columbia Record Club edition*
❑ SPH 37599 Living It Up! 1967 12.00
*—Columbia Record Club exclusive*

## KAK

### EPIC
❑ BN 26429 Kak 1969 250.00
*—Beware -- a reissue that looks almost identical to the original and sells for around $12 appeared in stores in 2000-2001*

## KALABASH CORP., THE

### UNCLE BILL
❑ KB-3114 The Kalabash Corp. 1970 80.00

## KALEIDOSCOPE, THE

### EPIC
❑ LN 24304 [M] Side Trips 1967 30.00
❑ LN 24333 [M] Beacon from Mars 1967 60.00
❑ BN 26304 [S] Side Trips 1967 40.00
❑ BN 26333 [S] Beacon from Mars 1967 100.00
❑ BN 26467 Incredible Kaleidoscope 1969 30.00
❑ BN 26508 Bernice 1970 30.00

### PACIFIC ARTS
❑ 102 When Scopes Collide 1978 12.00

## KALIN TWINS, THE

### DECCA
❑ DL 8812 [M] The Kalin Twins 1959 100.00

### VOCALION
❑ VL 3771 [M] When 1966 15.00
❑ VL 73771 [R] When 1966 12.00

## KALLAO, ALEX

### BATON
❑ BL-1205 [M] Alex Kallao in Concert, University of Ottawa 1957 60.00

### RCA VICTOR
❑ LJM-1011 [M] Evening at the Embers 1954 50.00

## KALLEN, KITTY

### COLUMBIA
❑ CL 1404 [M] If I Give My Heart to You 1960 20.00
❑ CL 1662 [M] Honky Tonk Angel 1961 20.00
❑ CS 8204 [S] If I Give My Heart to You 1960 25.00
❑ CS 8462 [S] Honky Tonk Angel 1961 25.00

### DECCA
❑ DL 8397 [M] It's a Lonesome Old Town 1958 40.00

### MERCURY
❑ MG 25206 [10] Pretty Kitty Kallen Sings 1955 50.00

### MOVIETONE
❑ 71026 [M] Delightfully 1967 15.00
❑ S-72026 [S] Delightfully 1967 15.00

### RCA VICTOR
❑ LPM-2640 [M] My Coloring Book 1963 20.00
❑ LSP-2640 [S] My Coloring Book 1963 25.00

### VOCALION
❑ VL 3679 [M] Little Things Mean a Lot 1959 25.00

### WING
❑ MGW-12241 [M] Kitty Kallen Sings 196? 15.00
❑ SRW-16241 [R] Kitty Kallen Sings 196? 12.00

## KALLMAN, DICK

### RCA VICTOR
❑ LPM-3485 [M] Dick Kallman Drops In as Hank 1966 20.00
❑ LSP-3485 [S] Dick Kallman Drops In as Hank 1966 25.00

## KAMINSKY, MAX

### COMMODORE
❑ FL-20019 [10] Max Kaminsky 1952 50.00

### CONCERT HALL JAZZ
❑ 1009 [10] Windy City Jazz 1955 50.00

### JAZZTONE
❑ J-1208 [M] Chicago Style 1955 40.00

### MGM
❑ E-261 [10] When the Saints Go Marching In 1954 50.00

### RCA VICTOR
❑ LJM-3003 [10] Jazz on the Campus, Ltd. 1954 50.00

### UNITED ARTISTS
❑ UAL-3174 [M] Max Goes East 1961 20.00
❑ UAS-6174 [S] Max Goes East 1961 25.00

## KAMUCA, RICHIE

### HIFI
❑ R-604 [M] Jazz Erotica 1957 200.00
❑ J-609 [M] West Coast Jazz in Hi-Fi 1959 60.00
❑ JS-609 [S] West Coast Jazz in Hi-Fi 1959 50.00

### MODE
❑ LP-102 [M] Richie Kamuka Quartet 1957 200.00

## KANE, BIG DADDY

### COLD CHILLIN'
❑ PRO-A-5205 [(2)DJ] Prince of Darkness 1991 30.00
*—Vinyl is promo only*
❑ 25731 Long Live the Kane 1988 40.00
❑ 25941 It's a Big Daddy Thing 1989 30.00
❑ 26303 Taste of Chocolate 1990 20.00

## KANE'S COUSINS

### SHOVE LOVE
❑ 9827 Undergum Bubbleground 1969 40.00

## KANGAROO

### MGM
❑ SE-4586 Kangaroo 1968 25.00

## KANNIBAL KOMIX

### COLOSSUS
❑ 1004 Kannibal Komix 1970 20.00

## KANSAS

### CBS ASSOCIATED
❑ QZ 38733 Drastic Measures 1983 8.00
❑ QZ 39283 The Best of Kansas 1984 8.00

### KIRSHNER
❑ AS 555 [DJ] Two for the Show (Sampler) 1978 20.00
*—Promo-only single disc of selections from 35660*
❑ KZ 32817 Kansas 1974 12.00
❑ PZ 32817 Kansas 197? 8.00
*—Reissue*
❑ PZ 33385 Song for America 1975 12.00
*—Without bar code on cover*
❑ PZ 33385 Song for America 198? 8.00
*—With bar code on cover*
❑ PZ 33806 Masque 1975 12.00
*—Without bar code on cover*
❑ PZ 33806 Masque 198? 8.00
*—With bar code on cover*
❑ JZ 34224 Leftoverture 1976 10.00
❑ PZ 34224 Leftoverture 198? 8.00
*—Budget-line reissue*
❑ JZ 34929 Point of Know Return 1977 10.00
❑ PZ2 35660 [(2)] Two for the Show 1978 15.00
❑ FZ 36008 Monolith 1979 10.00
❑ PZ 36008 Monolith 198? 8.00
*—Budget-line reissue*
❑ FZ 36588 Audio-Visions 1980 10.00
❑ PZ 36588 Audio-Visions 198? 8.00
*—Budget-line reissue*
❑ FZ 38002 Vinyl Confessions 1982 10.00
❑ PZ 38002 Vinyl Confessions 198? 8.00
*—Budget-line reissue*
❑ HZ 44224 Leftoverture 1982 40.00
*—Half-speed mastered edition*
❑ HZ 44929 Point of Know Return 1982 40.00
*—Half-speed mastered edition*
❑ HZ 46008 Monolith 1982 50.00
*—Half-speed mastered edition*
❑ HZ 48002 Vinyl Confessions 1982 100.00
*—Half-speed mastered edition*

### MCA
❑ 5838 Power 1986 8.00
❑ 6254 In the Spirit of Things 1988 8.00

## KANTNER, PAUL/JEFFERSON STARSHIP

### RCA VICTOR
❑ AYL1-3868 Blows Against the Empire 1981 8.00
*—Budget-line reissue*
❑ AFL1-4448 Blows Against the Empire 1977 10.00
*—Reissue of LSP-4448*
❑ LSP-4448 Blows Against the Empire 1970 15.00
❑ LSP-4448 [DJ] Blows Against the Empire 1970 150.00
*—Clear vinyl promo*

## KAPLAN, ARTIE

### HOPI
❑ VHS 901 Confessions of a Male Chauvinist Pig 1971 25.00



Except when noted otherwise, VG = 25% of NM, and VG+ = 50% of NM. (Example: VG = $2.00, VG+ = $4.00 and NM = $8.00.)

| Number | Title (A Side/B Side) | Yr | NM |
|---|---|---|---|
| **KARAS, ANTON** | | | |
| COLUMBIA | | | |
| ❑ CL 2576 [M] | Rendezvous in Vienna | 1967 | 12.00 |
| ❑ CS 9376 [S] | Rendezvous in Vienna | 1967 | 15.00 |
| DESIGN | | | |
| ❑ DLP-120 [M] | The Viennese Strings of Anton Karas | 1959 | 15.00 |
| LONDON | | | |
| ❑ PS 319 [S] | Vienna, City of Dreams | 1963 | 15.00 |
| ❑ LL 1560 [M] | "The Third Man" Theme | 1959 | 25.00 |
| ❑ LL 3319 [M] | Vienna, City of Dreams | 1963 | 12.00 |
| PERIOD | | | |
| ❑ SPL-1917 | Viennese Bonbons | 196? | 10.00 |
| ❑ SPL-1918 | Viennese Bonbons Volume II | 196? | 10.00 |
| SURREY | | | |
| ❑ S-1001 [M] | Zither Magic | 196? | 12.00 |
| ❑ SS-1001 [S] | Zither Magic | 196? | 12.00 |
| VOX | | | |
| ❑ VX-25180 [10] | Movie Cocktails | 1954 | 30.00 |
| **KARLOFF, BORIS** | | | |
| CAEDMON | | | |
| ❑ TC-1038 [M] | Just So Stories and Other Tales | 195? | 25.00 |
| ❑ TC-1074 [M] | The Reluctant Dragon | 196? | 25.00 |
| ❑ TC-1075 [M] | The Pied Piper; The Hunting of the Snarks | 196? | 25.00 |
| ❑ TC-1088 [M] | More of Kipling's Just So Stories | 196? | 25.00 |
| ❑ TC-1100 [M] | Kipling's Jungle Books: How Fear Came | 196? | 25.00 |
| ❑ TC-1109 [M] | The Ugly Duckling and Other Tales | 196? | 25.00 |
| ❑ TC-1117 [M] | The Little Match Girl and Other Tales | 196? | 25.00 |
| ❑ TC-1129 [M] | The Three Bears, Henny Penny and Other Fairy Tales | 1962 | 25.00 |
| ❑ TC-1139 [M] | The Cat That Walked By Herself | 196? | 25.00 |
| ❑ TC-1176 [M] | Kipling's Jungle Books: Toomai of the Elephants | 196? | 25.00 |
| ❑ TC-1221 [M] | Aesop's Fables | 1967 | 20.00 |
| DECCA | | | |
| ❑ DL 4833 [M] | An Evening with Boris Karloff and His Friends | 1967 | 20.00 |
| ❑ DL 74833 [S] | An Evening with Boris Karloff and His Friends | 1967 | 25.00 |
| MERCURY | | | |
| ❑ MG-20815 [M] | Tales of the Frightened, Volume 1 | 1963 | 40.00 |
| ❑ MG-20816 [M] | Tales of the Frightened, Volume 2 | 1963 | 40.00 |
| ❑ SR-60815 [S] | Tales of the Frightened, Volume 1 | 1963 | 50.00 |
| ❑ SR-60816 [S] | Tales of the Frightened, Volume 2 | 1963 | 50.00 |
| **KARMEN, STEVE** | | | |
| JUBILEE | | | |
| ❑ JGM-2048 [M] | This Is a City? | 1963 | 20.00 |
| STRUTTIN' | | | |
| ❑ STR-104 | Reconnecting | 1977 | 12.00 |
| **KASSEL, ART** | | | |
| KAPP | | | |
| ❑ KL-1248 [M] | Dance to the Music of Art Kassel | 1962 | 20.00 |
| ❑ KS-3248 [S] | Dance to the Music of Art Kassel | 1962 | 25.00 |
| **KAT MANDU** | | | |
| MARLIN | | | |
| ❑ 2233 | Kat Mandu | 1979 | 20.00 |
| **KATMANDU** | | | |
| MAINSTREAM | | | |
| ❑ S-6131 | Katmandu | 1971 | 40.00 |
| **KATZ, DICK** | | | |
| ATLANTIC | | | |
| ❑ 1314 [M] | Piano and Pin | 1959 | 40.00 |
| *—Black label* | | | |
| ❑ 1314 [M] | Piano and Pin | 1961 | 25.00 |
| *—Multicolor label, white "fan" logo at right* | | | |
| ❑ SD 1314 [S] | Piano and Pin | 1959 | 40.00 |
| *—Green label* | | | |
| ❑ SD 1314 [S] | Piano and Pin | 1961 | 20.00 |
| *—Multicolor label, white "fan" logo at right* | | | |
| **KATZ, DICK; DEREK SMITH; RENE URTREGER** | | | |
| ATLANTIC | | | |
| ❑ 1287 [M] | John Lewis Presents Jazz Piano International | 1958 | 40.00 |
| *—Black label* | | | |
| ❑ 1287 [M] | John Lewis Presents Jazz Piano International | 1961 | 25.00 |
| *—Multicolor label, white "fan" logo at right* | | | |

| Number | Title (A Side/B Side) | Yr | NM |
|---|---|---|---|
| **KATZ, FRED** | | | |
| DECCA | | | |
| ❑ DL 9202 [M] | Soulo Cello | 1958 | 40.00 |
| ❑ DL 9213 [M] | 4-5-6 Trio | 1958 | 40.00 |
| ❑ DL 9217 [M] | Fred Katz and Jammers | 1958 | 40.00 |
| ❑ DL 79202 [S] | Soulo Cello | 1958 | 30.00 |
| ❑ DL 79213 [S] | 4-5-6 Trio | 1958 | 30.00 |
| ❑ DL 79217 [S] | Fred Katz and Jammers | 1958 | 30.00 |
| WARNER BROS. | | | |
| ❑ W 1277 [M] | Folk Songs for Far Out Folks | 1959 | 25.00 |
| ❑ WS 1277 [S] | Folk Songs for Far Out Folks | 1959 | 30.00 |
| **KATZ, MICKEY** | | | |
| CAPITOL | | | |
| ❑ H 298 [10] | Mickey Katz: The Star of Broadway's Borschtcapades | 195? | 40.00 |
| ❑ T 298 [M] | The Very Best of Mickey Katz | 195? | 30.00 |
| *—Turquoise or gray label* | | | |
| ❑ H 457 [10] | The Family Danced | 195? | 40.00 |
| ❑ T 799 [M] | Mish Mosh | 1957 | 30.00 |
| *—Turquoise or gray label* | | | |
| ❑ T 934 [M] | Katz Puts On the Dog | 1958 | 30.00 |
| *—Turquoise or gray label* | | | |
| ❑ T 1021 [M] | Katz Plays Music for Weddings, Bar Mitzvahs and Brisses | 1958 | 30.00 |
| *—Turquoise or gray label* | | | |
| ❑ T 1102 [M] | The Most Mishige | 1959 | 25.00 |
| *—Black colorband label, logo at left* | | | |
| ❑ W 1257 [M] | Katz Pajamas | 1959 | 25.00 |
| *—Black colorband label, logo at left* | | | |
| ❑ W 1307 [M] | Comin' Round the Katzkills | 1959 | 25.00 |
| *—Black colorband label, logo at left* | | | |
| ❑ ST 1445 [S] | The Borscht Jester | 1960 | 25.00 |
| *—Black colorband label, logo at left* | | | |
| ❑ T 1445 [M] | The Borscht Jester | 1960 | 20.00 |
| *—Black colorband label, logo at left* | | | |
| ❑ ST 1603 [S] | At the U.N. | 1961 | 25.00 |
| *—Black colorband label, logo at left* | | | |
| ❑ T 1603 [M] | At the U.N. | 1961 | 20.00 |
| *—Black colorband label, logo at left* | | | |
| ❑ ST 1744 [S] | Sing Along with Mickele | 1962 | 25.00 |
| ❑ T 1744 [M] | Sing Along with Mickele | 1962 | 20.00 |
| RCA VICTOR | | | |
| ❑ LPM-3193 [10] | Borscht | 1954 | 40.00 |
| **KAUFMANN, BOB** | | | |
| LHI | | | |
| ❑ 12002 | Trip Through a Blown Mind | 1967 | 60.00 |
| **KAY, JOHN, AND SPARROW** See SPARROW. | | | |
| **KAY, JOHN, AND STEPPENWOLF** See STEPPENWOLF. | | | |
| **KAYAK** | | | |
| HARVEST | | | |
| ❑ ST-11305 | See See the Sun | 1973 | 15.00 |
| JANUS | | | |
| ❑ (no #) [PD] | Phantom of the Night | 1979 | 25.00 |
| *—Numbered limited edition of 3,000* | | | |
| ❑ NXS-7023 | Royal Bed Bouncer | 1975 | 10.00 |
| ❑ NXS-7034 | Starlight Dancer | 1978 | 10.00 |
| ❑ NXS-7039 | Phantom of the Night | 1979 | 10.00 |
| MERCURY | | | |
| ❑ SRM-1-3824 | Periscope Life | 1980 | 10.00 |
| **KAYE, DANNY** | | | |
| CAPITOL | | | |
| ❑ T 937 [M] | Mommy Gimme a Drinka Water | 1958 | 40.00 |
| COLUMBIA | | | |
| ❑ CL 6023 [10] | Danny Kaye | 1949 | 50.00 |
| ❑ CL 6249 [10] | Danny Kaye Entertains | 195? | 50.00 |
| DECCA | | | |
| ❑ DSXB 175 [(2)R] | The Best of Danny Kaye | 1965 | 15.00 |
| ❑ DXB 175 [(2)M] | The Best of Danny Kaye | 1965 | 25.00 |
| ❑ DLP 5033 [10] | Danny Kaye | 1950 | 50.00 |
| ❑ DL 5094 [10] | Gilbert and Sullivan and Danny Kaye | 1950 | 50.00 |
| ❑ DL 8212 [M] | The Court Jester | 1955 | 50.00 |
| *—Black label, silver print* | | | |
| ❑ DL 8461 [M] | Danny at the Palace | 1957 | 50.00 |
| *—Black label, silver print* | | | |
| ❑ DL 8461 [M] | Danny at the Palace | 1960 | 25.00 |
| *—Black label with color bars* | | | |
| ❑ DL 8726 [M] | Danny Kaye for Children | 1959 | 30.00 |
| *—Black label, silver print* | | | |
| ❑ DL 8726 [M] | Danny Kaye for Children | 1960 | 25.00 |
| *—Black label with color bars* | | | |
| **KAYE, MARY, TRIO** | | | |
| COLUMBIA | | | |
| ❑ CL 1910 [M] | Our Hawaii | 1962 | 15.00 |
| ❑ CS 8710 [S] | Our Hawaii | 1962 | 20.00 |
| DECCA | | | |
| ❑ DL 8238 [M] | The Mary Kaye Trio | 1956 | 30.00 |
| ❑ DL 8434 [M] | Music on a Silver Platter | 1957 | 30.00 |
| ❑ DL 8650 [M] | You Don't Know What Love Is | 1958 | 30.00 |

| Number | Title (A Side/B Side) | Yr | NM |
|---|---|---|---|
| MOVIETONE | | | |
| ❑ 71027 [M] | Just Us | 1967 | 12.00 |
| ❑ S 72027 [S] | Just Us | 1967 | 12.00 |
| 20TH CENTURY FOX | | | |
| ❑ TFM-3117 [M] | Night Life | 1964 | 12.00 |
| ❑ TFS-4117 [S] | Night Life | 1964 | 15.00 |
| VERVE | | | |
| ❑ MGV-2142 [M] | Up Front! | 1960 | 40.00 |
| ❑ V-8446 [M] | For the Record | 1962 | 20.00 |
| ❑ V6-8446 [S] | For the Record | 1962 | 25.00 |
| WARNER BROS. | | | |
| ❑ B 1222 [M] | Too Much! | 1958 | 20.00 |
| ❑ W 1263 [M] | Jackpot | 1959 | 20.00 |
| ❑ WS 1263 [S] | Jackpot | 1959 | 25.00 |
| ❑ W 1342 [M] | The Mary Kaye Trio on the Sunset Strip | 1959 | 20.00 |
| ❑ WS 1342 [S] | The Mary Kaye Trio on the Sunset Strip | 1959 | 25.00 |
| **KAYE, SAMMY** | | | |
| COLUMBIA | | | |
| ❑ CL 561 [M] | Swing and Sway with Sammy Kaye | 195? | 30.00 |
| ❑ CL 668 [M] | Music, Maestro, Please! | 195? | 30.00 |
| ❑ CL 885 [M] | My Fair Lady (For Dancing) | 1956 | 20.00 |
| ❑ CL 891 [M] | What Makes Sammy Swing and Sway | 1956 | 20.00 |
| ❑ CL 964 [M] | Sunday Serenade | 1957 | 20.00 |
| ❑ CL 1018 [M] | Popular American Waltzes | 1957 | 20.00 |
| ❑ CL 1571 [M] | Dancing on a Silken Cloud | 1960 | 15.00 |
| ❑ CL 2541 [10] | Christmas Serenade | 1955 | 40.00 |
| *—"House Party Series" issue* | | | |
| ❑ CL 6155 [10] | Sunday Serenade | 1953 | 40.00 |
| ❑ CS 8371 [S] | Dancing on a Silken Cloud | 1960 | 20.00 |
| RCA CAMDEN | | | |
| ❑ CAL-355 [M] | Swing and Sway with Sammy Kaye | 1957 | 20.00 |
| RCA VICTOR | | | |
| ❑ LPM 15 [10] | Sammy Kaye Plays Irving Berlin for Dancing | 1950 | 50.00 |
| ❑ LPM-3966 [M] | The Best of Sammy Kaye | 1967 | 20.00 |
| **KAZ, FRED** | | | |
| ATLANTIC | | | |
| ❑ 1335 [M] | Eastern Exposure | 1960 | 25.00 |
| *—Multicolor label, white "fan" logo at right* | | | |
| ❑ SD 1335 [S] | Eastern Exposure | 1960 | 30.00 |
| *—Multicolor label, white "fan" logo at right* | | | |
| **KAZAN, LAINIE** | | | |
| MGM | | | |
| ❑ E-4340 [M] | Right Now | 1966 | 20.00 |
| ❑ SE-4340 [S] | Right Now | 1966 | 25.00 |
| ❑ E-4385 [M] | Lainie Kazan | 1966 | 20.00 |
| ❑ SE-4385 [S] | Lainie Kazan | 1966 | 25.00 |
| ❑ E-4451 [M] | The Love Album | 1967 | 25.00 |
| ❑ SE-4451 [S] | The Love Album | 1967 | 20.00 |
| ❑ SE-4496 | Love Is | 1968 | 20.00 |
| ❑ SE-4631 | The Best of Lainie Kazan | 1969 | 20.00 |
| **KEATING, JOHNNY** | | | |
| BALLY | | | |
| ❑ BAL-12001 [M] | English Jazz | 1956 | 50.00 |
| DOT | | | |
| ❑ DLP-3066 [M] | Swinging Scots | 1957 | 40.00 |
| **KEENE, BOB** | | | |
| ANDEX | | | |
| ❑ S-4001 [M] | Solo for 7 | 1958 | 50.00 |
| DEL-FI | | | |
| ❑ DFLP-1202 [M] | Unforgettable Love Songs of the 50's | 1959 | 40.00 |
| ❑ DFLP-1222 [M] | Twist to Radio KRLA | 1962 | 30.00 |
| GENE NORMAN | | | |
| ❑ GNP-149 [10] | Bob Keene | 1954 | 50.00 |
| **KEITH** | | | |
| MERCURY | | | |
| ❑ MG-21102 [M] | 98.6/Ain't Gonna Lie | 1967 | 15.00 |
| ❑ MG-21129 [M] | Out of Crank | 1967 | 15.00 |
| ❑ SR-61102 [S] | 98.6/Ain't Gonna Lie | 1967 | 20.00 |
| ❑ SR-61129 [S] | Out of Crank | 1967 | 20.00 |
| RCA VICTOR | | | |
| ❑ LSP-4143 | The Adventures of Keith | 1969 | 20.00 |
| **KEITH AND DONNA** Also see THE GRATEFUL DEAD. | | | |
| ROUND | | | |
| ❑ RX-104 | Keith and Donna | 1975 | 30.00 |
| **KELLAWAY, ROGER** | | | |
| DISCWASHER | | | |
| ❑ 003 | Nostalgia Suite | 1979 | 20.00 |
| PACIFIC JAZZ | | | |
| ❑ PJ-10122 [M] | Spirit Feel | 196? | 20.00 |

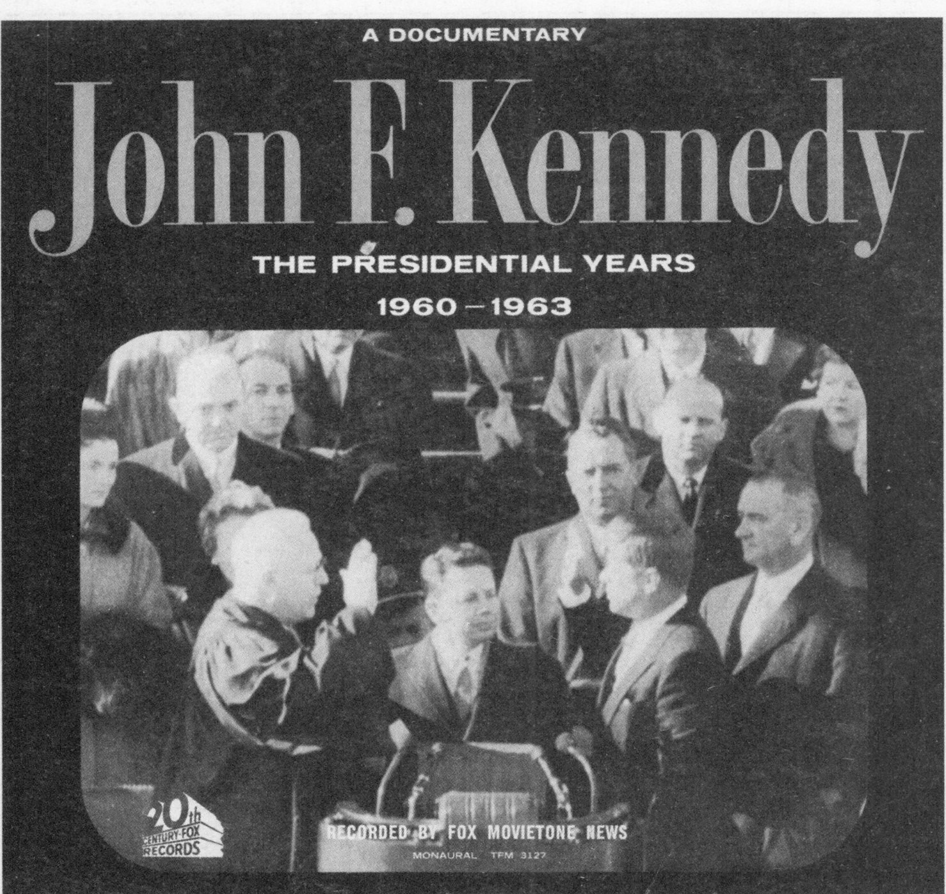

A DOCUMENTARY
John F. Kennedy
THE PRESIDENTIAL YEARS
1960 – 1963
20th Century-Fox Records
RECORDED BY FOX MOVIETONE NEWS
MONAURAL TFM 3127


John F. Kennedy, *The Presidential Years 1960-1963,* 20th Century Fox TFM 3127, 1963, mono, $20.

| Number | Title (A Side/B Side) | Yr | NM |
|---|---|---|---|
| PRESTIGE | | | |
| ❑ PRLP-7399 [M] | The Roger Kellaway Trio | 1965 | 25.00 |
| ❑ PRST-7399 [S] | The Roger Kellaway Trio | 1965 | 30.00 |
| REGINA | | | |
| ❑ R-298 [M] | Portraits | 1964 | 20.00 |
| ❑ RS-298 [S] | Portraits | 1964 | 25.00 |
| WORLD PACIFIC | | | |
| ❑ WP-21861 [M] | Stride | 1967 | 20.00 |

**KELLER, ALLEN**

| Number | Title (A Side/B Side) | Yr | NM |
|---|---|---|---|
| CHARLIE PARKER | | | |
| ❑ PLP-817 [M] | A New Look at the World | 1962 | 25.00 |
| ❑ PLP-817S [S] | A New Look at the World | 1962 | 30.00 |

**KELLER, HAL**

| Number | Title (A Side/B Side) | Yr | NM |
|---|---|---|---|
| SAND | | | |
| ❑ 7 [M] | Hal Keller Debut | 1957 | 50.00 |
| SOUND | | | |
| ❑ 602 [M] | Hal Keller Debut | 1959 | 40.00 |

**KELLER, JERRY**

| Number | Title (A Side/B Side) | Yr | NM |
|---|---|---|---|
| KAPP | | | |
| ❑ KL-1178 [M] | Here Comes Jerry Keller | 1959 | 40.00 |
| ❑ KS-3178 [S] | Here Comes Jerry Keller | 1959 | 50.00 |

**KELLERMAN, SALLY**

| Number | Title (A Side/B Side) | Yr | NM |
|---|---|---|---|
| DECCA | | | |
| ❑ DL 75359 | Roll with the Feelin' | 1972 | 20.00 |

**KELLIN, MIKE**

| Number | Title (A Side/B Side) | Yr | NM |
|---|---|---|---|
| VERVE FORECAST | | | |
| ❑ FT-3028 [M] | Mike Kellin | 1967 | 25.00 |
| ❑ FTS-3028 [S] | Mike Kellin | 1967 | 25.00 |

**KELLY, BEVERLY**

| Number | Title (A Side/B Side) | Yr | NM |
|---|---|---|---|
| AUDIO FIDELITY | | | |
| ❑ AFLP-1874 [M] | Beverly Kelly Sings | 1958 | 30.00 |
| ❑ AFSD-5874 [S] | Beverly Kelly Sings | 1958 | 40.00 |
| RIVERSIDE | | | |
| ❑ RLP-328 [M] | Love Locked Out | 1960 | 25.00 |
| ❑ RLP-345 [M] | Bev Kelly In Person | 1960 | 25.00 |
| ❑ RS-9328 [S] | Love Locked Out | 1960 | 30.00 |
| ❑ RS-9345 [S] | Bev Kelly In Person | 1960 | 30.00 |

**KELLY, EMMETT**

| Number | Title (A Side/B Side) | Yr | NM |
|---|---|---|---|
| ROULETTE | | | |
| ❑ R-25130 [M] | Sing Along with Emmett Kelly | 1962 | 25.00 |
| ❑ SR-25130 [S] | Sing Along with Emmett Kelly | 1962 | 30.00 |

**KELLY, JACK**

| Number | Title (A Side/B Side) | Yr | NM |
|---|---|---|---|
| JUBILEE | | | |
| ❑ JLP-21 [10] | Jack Kelly's Badinage | 1955 | 50.00 |

**KELLY, MONTY**

| Number | Title (A Side/B Side) | Yr | NM |
|---|---|---|---|
| ALSHIRE | | | |
| ❑ SAS 610 | Passport to Romance | 196? | 10.00 |
| CARLTON | | | |
| ❑ LP 12-111 [M] | Porgy and Bess | 1959 | 20.00 |
| ❑ STLP 12-111 [S] | Porgy and Bess | 1959 | 25.00 |
| ❑ LP 12-123 [M] | Summer Set | 1960 | 20.00 |
| ❑ STLP 12-123 [S] | Summer Set | 1960 | 25.00 |
| ESSEX | | | |
| ❑ ESLP-106 [10] | I Love | 1954 | 30.00 |
| ❑ ESLP-108 [10] | Monty Kelly Takes Me to Far Away Places | 1954 | 30.00 |
| ❑ ESLP-203 [M] | Tropicana | 1955 | 25.00 |
| SOMERSET | | | |
| ❑ P 7300 [M] | Tropicana | 196? | 10.00 |
| *—Reissue of Trans World 203* | | | |
| TRANS WORLD | | | |
| ❑ TWLP-203 [M] | Tropicana | 1956 | 20.00 |
| *—Reissue of Essex 203* | | | |

**KELLY, WYNTON**

| Number | Title (A Side/B Side) | Yr | NM |
|---|---|---|---|
| BLUE NOTE | | | |
| ❑ BLP-5025 [10] | Piano Interpretations by Wynton Kelly | 1953 | 400.00 |
| JAZZLAND | | | |
| ❑ JLP-83 [M] | Whisper Not | 1962 | 40.00 |
| ❑ JLP-983 [S] | Whisper Not | 1962 | 50.00 |
| RIVERSIDE | | | |
| ❑ RLP 12-254 [M] | Wynton Kelly Piano | 1957 | 70.00 |
| ❑ RLP 12-298 [M] | Kelly Blue | 1959 | 60.00 |
| ❑ RLP-1142 [S] | Kelly Blue | 1959 | 50.00 |
| VEE JAY | | | |
| ❑ LP-1016 [M] | Kelly Great | 1960 | 80.00 |
| ❑ SR-1016 [S] | Kelly Great | 1960 | 100.00 |
| ❑ VJ-1086 [M] | Best of Wynton Kelly | 1964 | 40.00 |
| ❑ VJS-1086 [S] | Best of Wynton Kelly | 1964 | 50.00 |
| ❑ LP-3004 [M] | Kelly Great | 1960 | 60.00 |
| *—Reissue of LP-1016* | | | |
| ❑ SR-3004 [S] | Kelly Great | 1960 | 80.00 |
| *—Reissue of SR-1016* | | | |
| ❑ LP-3011 [M] | Kelly at Midnite | 1960 | 80.00 |
| ❑ SR-3011 [S] | Kelly at Midnite | 1960 | 100.00 |
| ❑ LP-3022 [M] | Wynton Kelly | 1961 | 50.00 |
| ❑ SR-3022 [S] | Wynton Kelly | 1961 | 60.00 |
| ❑ VJS-3072-2 [(2)] | Final Notes | 1977 | 25.00 |
| VERVE | | | |
| ❑ V6-8576 [S] | Comin' In the Back Door | 1964 | 40.00 |
| ❑ V6-8588 [S] | It's All Right | 1964 | 30.00 |
| ❑ V6-8622 [S] | Undiluted | 1965 | 50.00 |
| ❑ V6-8633 [S] | Smokin' at the Half Note | 1965 | 25.00 |

**KELLY BROTHERS, THE**

| Number | Title (A Side/B Side) | Yr | NM |
|---|---|---|---|
| EXCELLO | | | |
| ❑ LPS-8007 | Sweet Soul | 1968 | 50.00 |
| KING | | | |
| ❑ 810 [M] | The Kelly Brothers Sing a Page of Songs from the Good Book | 1962 | 100.00 |

**KENDALLS, THE**

| Number | Title (A Side/B Side) | Yr | NM |
|---|---|---|---|
| DOT | | | |
| ❑ DLP-26001 | Two Divided by Love | 1972 | 15.00 |
| EPIC | | | |
| ❑ E2 45249 [(2)] | 20 Favorites | 1989 | 15.00 |
| GUSTO | | | |
| ❑ GT 0001 | 1978 Grammy Award Winners — Best Country Duo | 1978 | 10.00 |
| MCA | | | |
| ❑ 27021 | Never Ending Song of Love | 198? | 10.00 |
| MCA CURB | | | |
| ❑ 5724 | Fire at First Sight | 1986 | 8.00 |
| MERCURY | | | |
| ❑ SRM-1-4046 | Stickin' Together | 1982 | 10.00 |
| ❑ SRM-1-6005 | Lettin' You In on a Feelin' | 1981 | 10.00 |
| ❑ 812779-1 | Movin' Train | 1983 | 8.00 |
| ❑ 824250-1 | Two Heart Harmony | 1985 | 8.00 |
| ❑ 826307-1 | Thank God for the Radio... And All the Hits | 1986 | 8.00 |
| OVATION | | | |
| ❑ 1719 | Heaven's Just a Sin Away | 1977 | 12.00 |
| ❑ 1733 | Old Fashioned Love | 1978 | 12.00 |
| ❑ 1739 | Just Like Real People | 1979 | 12.00 |
| ❑ 1746 | Heart of the Matter | 1979 | 12.00 |
| ❑ 1756 | The Best of the Kendalls | 1980 | 12.00 |
| POWER PAK | | | |
| ❑ PO-216 | Leavin' on a Jet Plane | 197? | 10.00 |
| STEP ONE | | | |
| ❑ 0023 | Break the Routine | 1987 | 10.00 |
| STOP | | | |
| ❑ 1020 | Meet the Kendalls | 1970 | 20.00 |

**KENNEDY, DAVE**

| Number | Title (A Side/B Side) | Yr | NM |
|---|---|---|---|
| COULEE | | | |
| ❑ 1001 [M] | Breaking Up Is Hard to Do | 1964 | 50.00 |

**KENNEDY, JERRY** Also see TOM AND JERRY (2).

| Number | Title (A Side/B Side) | Yr | NM |
|---|---|---|---|
| SMASH | | | |
| ❑ MGS-27004 [M] | Dancing Guitars Rock Elvis' Hits | 1962 | 30.00 |
| ❑ MGS-27024 [M] | Jerry Kennedy's Guitars and Strings Play the Golden Standards | 1963 | 20.00 |
| ❑ MGS-27066 [M] | From Nashville to Soulville | 1965 | 20.00 |
| ❑ SRS-67004 [S] | Dancing Guitars Rock Elvis' Hits | 1962 | 40.00 |
| ❑ SRS-67024 [S] | Jerry Kennedy's Guitars and Strings Play the Golden Standards | 1963 | 25.00 |
| ❑ SRS-67066 [S] | From Nashville to Soulville | 1965 | 25.00 |

**KENNEDY, JOHN FITZGERALD** Various tribute records, most of which were released in the immediate aftermath of his assassination in 1963.

| Number | Title (A Side/B Side) | Yr | NM |
|---|---|---|---|
| CAEDMON | | | |
| ❑ TC-2021 [(2)] | Self-Portrait | 196? | 20.00 |
| CAPITOL | | | |
| ❑ ST 2486 [S] | Years of Lightning, Day of Drums | 1966 | 30.00 |
| ❑ T 2486 [M] | Years of Lightning, Day of Drums | 1966 | 20.00 |
| *—Narrated by Gregory Peck; U.S. Information Agency movie soundtrack* | | | |
| COLPIX | | | |
| ❑ CP 2500 [M] | Four Days That Shocked the World | 1964 | 50.00 |
| *—Narrated by Reid Collins; covers Nov. 22-25, 1963* | | | |

Number | Title (A Side/B Side) | Yr | NM

DECCA
❑ DL 9116 [M] That Was The Week That Was 1963 20.00
*—BBC show's tribute to JFK, broadcast Nov. 23, 1963*
DIPLOMAT
❑ 10000 [M] John F. Kennedy — A Memorial Album 1963 15.00
DOCUMENTARIES UNLIMITED
❑ (no #) [M] JFK The Man, The President 1963 20.00
*—Narrated by Barry Gray*
HARMONICA
❑ HLP-3005 [M] Kennedy Speaks 1963 20.00
LEGACY
❑ L2L 1017 [(2)M]John Fitzgerald Kennedy...As We Remember Him 1965 25.00
*—Narrated by Charles Kuralt; with 240-page book*
PICKWICK
❑ 169 [M] The Presidential Years (1960-1963) 1963 15.00
PREMIER
❑ 2099 [M] A Memorial Album 1963 20.00
*—From WMCA Radio, New York, Nov. 22, 1963*
RCA VICTOR
❑ VDM-101 [M] The Kennedy Wit 1964 15.00
*—Narrated by David Brinkley with introduction by Adlai E. Stevenson*
SOMERSET
❑ 16100 [M] Actual Speeches of Franklin D. Roosevelt and John F. Kennedy 1963 15.00
*—One side has FDR speeches, the other, JFK speeches*
20TH CENTURY
❑ TCF 3127 [M] The Presidential Years 1960-1963 1963 20.00
*—Narrated by David Teig*

**KENNEDY, MIKE** Also see LOS BRAVOS.
ABC
❑ ABCX-754 Louisianna 1972 20.00

**KENNEDY, ROBERT FRANCIS** Tribute album released shortly after his death.
COLUMBIA
❑ C2S 792 [(2)] A Memorial 1968 20.00

**KENNER, CHRIS**
ATLANTIC
❑ 8117 [M] Land of 1,000 Dances 1965 80.00
COLLECTABLES
❑ COL-5116 Golden Classics: I Like It Like That 198? 12.00

**KENNEY, BEVERLY**
DECCA
❑ DL 8743 [M] Beverly Kenney Sings for Playboys 1958 400.00
❑ DL 8850 [M] Born to Be Blue 1959 250.00
❑ DL 8948 [M] Like Yesterday 1960 200.00
❑ DL 78948 [S] Like Yesterday 1960 300.00
ROOST
❑ RST-2206 [M] Beverly Kenney Sings for Johnny Smith 1956 300.00
❑ RST-2212 [M] Come Swing with Me 1956 300.00
❑ RST-2218 [M] Beverly Kenney with Jimmy Jones and the Basie-ites 1957 300.00

**KENNY, BILL**
WARWICK
❑ W-2021 [M] Mr. Ink Spot 1960 25.00

**KENNY AND THE KASUALS**
MARK
❑ 5000 [M] The Impact Sound of Kenny and the Kasuals Live at the Studio Club 1966 1000.
❑ 5000 [M] The Impact Sound of Kenny and the Kasuals Live at the Studio Club 1977 25.00
*—"Reissue, 1977" appears on cover*
❑ 6000 [M] Teen Dreams 1978 250.00
*—Red vinyl; numbered, signed limited edition*
❑ 7000 [S] Garage Kings 1979 25.00

**KENSINGTON MARKET**
WARNER BROS.
❑ WS 1754 Avenue Road 1968 20.00
❑ WS 1780 Aardvark 1969 20.00

**KENT, GEORGE**
SHANNON
❑ 1003 George Kent 1974 20.00

**KENTON, STAN**
CAPITOL
❑ H 155 [10] Encores 1950 60.00

Number | Title (A Side/B Side) | Yr | NM

❑ T 155 [M] Encores 195? 40.00
*—Turquoise label*
❑ H 167 [10] Artistry in Rhythm 1950 60.00
❑ T 167 [M] Artistry in Rhythm 195? 40.00
*—Turquoise label*
❑ H 172 [10] A Presentation of Progressive Jazz 1950 60.00
❑ T 172 [M] A Presentation of Progressive Jazz 195? 40.00
❑ P 189 [10] Innovations in Modern Music 1950 60.00
❑ H 190 [10] Milestones 1950 60.00
❑ T 190 [M] Milestones 195? 40.00
*—Turquoise label*
❑ T 190 [M] Milestones 196? 25.00
*—Black colorband label, logo at left*
❑ PRO-206/7 [DJ]The Kenton Era (Excerpts) 1955 40.00
❑ L 248 [10] Stan Kenton Presents 1951 60.00
❑ T 248 [M] Stan Kenton Presents 195? 40.00
*—Turquoise label*
❑ T 248 [M] Stan Kenton Presents 196? 15.00
*—Black colorband label, logo at top*
❑ T 248 [M] Stan Kenton Presents 196? 25.00
*—Black colorband label, logo at left*
❑ H 353 [10] City of Glass 1952 60.00
❑ H 358 [10] Classics 1952 60.00
❑ T 358 [M] Classics 195? 40.00
*—Turquoise label*
❑ H 383 [10] New Concepts of Artistry in Rhythm 1953 60.00
❑ T 383 [M] New Concepts of Artistry in Rhythm 195? 40.00
*—Turquoise label*
❑ H 386 [10] Prologue: This Is an Orchestra 1953 60.00
❑ H 421 [10] Popular Favorites 1953 60.00
❑ T 421 [M] Popular Favorites 195? 40.00
*—Turquoise label*
❑ H 426 [10] Sketches on Standards 1953 60.00
❑ T 426 [M] Sketches on Standards 195? 40.00
*—Turquoise label*
❑ H 460 [10] This Modern World 1953 60.00
❑ H 462 [10] Portraits on Standards 1953 60.00
❑ T 462 [M] Portraits on Standards 195? 40.00
*—Turquoise label*
❑ T 462 [M] Portraits on Standards 196? 25.00
*—Black colorband label, logo at left*
❑ W 524 [M] Kenton Showcase 1954 40.00
❑ H 525 [10] Kenton Showcase — The Music of Bill Russo 1954 60.00
❑ H 526 [10] Kenton Showcase — The Music of Bill Holman 1954 60.00
❑ TDB 569 [(4)M]The Kenton Era 1955 100.00
*—Box set with 44-page book*
❑ WDX 569 [(4)M]The Kenton Era 196? 70.00
*—Box set with 44-page book; limited edition reissue with black label, Capitol logo at left*
❑ STCL-575 [(3)] Stan Kenton 1970 20.00
❑ T 656 [M] Duet 1955 40.00
*—With June Christy; turquoise label*
❑ T 666 [M] Contemporary Concepts 1955 40.00
*—Turquoise label*
❑ SW 724 [S] Kenton in Hi-Fi 1959 50.00
*—Black label with colorband, logo at left; one fewer track than mono version*
❑ SW 724 [S] Kenton in Hi-Fi 1962 30.00
*—Black label with colorband, logo at top; one fewer track than mono version*
❑ W 724 [M] Kenton in Hi-Fi 1956 40.00
*—Gray label*
❑ W 724 [M] Kenton in Hi-Fi 1959 20.00
*—Black label with colorband, logo at left*
❑ T 731 [M] Cuban Fire! 1956 40.00
*—Turquoise label*
❑ T 731 [M] Cuban Fire! 1959 20.00
*—Black label with colorband, Capitol logo at left*
❑ T 736 [M] City of Glass/This Modern World 1956 40.00
*—Combination of 353 and 460 onto one 12-inch LP, turquoise label*
❑ T 810 [M] Kenton with Voices 1957 40.00
*—Turquoise label*
❑ T 932 [M] Rendezvous with Kenton 1957 40.00
*—Turquoise label*
❑ T 995 [M] Back to Balboa 1958 40.00
*—Turquoise label*
❑ ST 1068 [S] The Ballad Style of Stan Kenton 1959 20.00
*—Black label with colorband, Capitol logo at left*
❑ T 1068 [M] The Ballad Style of Stan Kenton 1959 25.00
*—Black label with colorband, Capitol logo at left*
❑ ST 1130 [S] Lush Interlude 1959 20.00
*—Black label with colorband, Capitol logo at left*
❑ T 1130 [M] Lush Interlude 1959 25.00
*—Black label with colorband, Capitol logo at left*
❑ ST 1166 [S] The Stage Door Swings 1959 20.00
*—Black label with colorband, Capitol logo at left*
❑ T 1166 [M] The Stage Door Swings 1959 25.00
*—Black label with colorband, Capitol logo at left*
❑ ST 1276 [S] The Kenton Touch 1960 20.00
*—Black label with colorband, Capitol logo at left*
❑ T 1276 [M] The Kenton Touch 1960 25.00
*—Black label with colorband, Capitol logo at left*
❑ SW 1305 [S] Viva Kenton! 1960 20.00
*—Black label with colorband, Capitol logo at left*
❑ W 1305 [M] Viva Kenton! 1960 25.00
*—Black label with colorband, Capitol logo at left*

Number | Title (A Side/B Side) | Yr | NM

❑ STBO 1327 [(2)S]Road Show 1960 30.00
*—Black label with colorband, Capitol logo at left*
❑ TBO 1327 [(2)M]Road Show 1960 40.00
*—Black label with colorband, Capitol logo at left*
❑ TBO 1327 [(2)M]Road Show 1962 20.00
*—Black label with colorband, Capitol logo at top*
❑ ST 1394 [S] Standards in Silhouette 1960 20.00
*—Black label with colorband, Capitol logo at left*
❑ T 1394 [M] Standards in Silhouette 1960 25.00
*—Black label with colorband, Capitol logo at left*
❑ ST 1460 [S] Kenton at the Las Vegas Tropicana 1961 20.00
*—Black label with colorband, Capitol logo at left*
❑ T 1460 [M] Kenton at the Las Vegas Tropicana 1961 25.00
*—Black label with colorband, Capitol logo at left*
❑ ST 1533 [S] The Romantic Approach 1961 20.00
*—Black label with colorband, Capitol logo at left*
❑ T 1533 [M] The Romantic Approach 1961 25.00
*—Black label with colorband, Capitol logo at left*
❑ ST 1609 [S] Kenton's West Side Story 1961 12.00
*—Black label with colorband, Capitol logo at top*
❑ ST 1609 [S] Kenton's West Side Story 1961 20.00
*—Black label with colorband, Capitol logo at left*
❑ T 1609 [M] Kenton's West Side Story 1961 25.00
*—Black label with colorband, Capitol logo at left*
❑ STCL 2989 [(3)]The Stan Kenton Deluxe Set 1968 20.00
CREATIVE WORLD
❑ ST 1030 [(4)R] The Kenton Era 197? 20.00
*—Reissue of Capitol TDB 569*
❑ ST 1058 [(2)Q] Live at Butler University 1972 20.00
❑ ST 1059 [(2)Q] Stan Kenton with the Four Freshmen at Butler University 1972 20.00
❑ ST 1060 [(2)Q] National Anthems of the World 1972 20.00
DECCA
❑ DL 8259 [M] Stan Kenton — Formative Years 195? 25.00
*—All-black label with silver print*
LONDON PHASE 4
❑ BP 44179/80 [(2)]Stan Kenton Today 1972 40.00
MOBILE FIDELITY
❑ 1-091 Kenton Plays Wagner 1982 25.00
*—Audiophile vinyl*
MOSAIC
❑ MR6-136 [(6)] The Complete Capitol Recordings of the Holmanand Russo Charts 199? 120.00
❑ MQ10-163 [(10)]The Complete Capitol Studio Recordings of Stan Kenton 1943-47 199? 200.00

**KENTON, STAN, AND TEX RITTER** Also see each artist's individual listings.
CAPITOL
❑ ST 1757 [S] Stan Kenton/Tex Ritter 1962 80.00
❑ T 1757 [M] Stan Kenton/Tex Ritter 1962 60.00

**KENTUCKY COLONELS, THE**
BRIAR
❑ 109 The New Sounds of Bluegrass America 1976 40.00
❑ BT-7202 Livin' in the Past 1975 30.00
WORLD PACIFIC
❑ ST 1821 [S] Appalachian Swing 1964 60.00
❑ T 1821 [M] Appalachian Swing 1964 50.00

**KENYATTA, ROBIN**
ATLANTIC
❑ SD 1633 Gypsy Man 1972 20.00
ECM
❑ 1008 The Girl from Martinique 197? 20.00
VORTEX
❑ 2005 Until 1969 20.00

**KEROUAC, JACK**
DOT
❑ DLP-3154 [M] Poetry for the Beat Generation 1959 10000.
*—Acknowledged to be extremely rare; approximately 130 copies were distributed and only a small handful are known to exist today; the same performance is on Hanover 5000; VG value 5000; VG+ value 7500*
HANOVER
❑ HML-5000 [M] Poetry for the Beat Generation 1959 400.00
*—Reissue of Dot LP with new cover; STEVE ALLEN plays piano on this record*
❑ HML-5006 [M] Blues and Haikus 1959 250.00
*—AL COHN and ZOOT SIMS play saxophones behind Kerouac on this album*
RHINO
❑ R1-70939 [(4)] The Jack Kerouac Collection 1990 60.00
*—Box set compiling the Hanover and Verve LPs plus an LP of unreleased material*
VERVE
❑ MGV-15005 [M]Readings on the Beat Generation 1960 250.00

## KERR, ANITA, SINGERS

| Number | Title (A Side/B Side) | Yr | NM |
|---|---|---|---|
| **AMPEX** | | | |
| ❑ A-10136 | Grow to Know Me | 1971 | 10.00 |
| ❑ A-10142 | A Christmas Story | 1971 | 12.00 |
| *—With the Royal Philharmonic Orchestra* | | | |
| **BAINBRIDGE** | | | |
| ❑ 6224 | Slightly Baroque | 1981 | 10.00 |
| ❑ 6226 | I Sang with Jim Reeves | 1981 | 10.00 |
| ❑ 6227 | The Simon and Garfunkel Songbook | 1981 | 10.00 |
| ❑ 6228 | 'Round Midnight | 1981 | 10.00 |
| **CENTURY** | | | |
| ❑ 1160 | Anita Kerr Performs Wonder's | 1979 | 10.00 |
| **DECCA** | | | |
| ❑ DL 4061 [M] | For You, For Me, Forevermore | 1960 | 15.00 |
| ❑ DL 8647 [M] | Quartet Voices in Hi-Fi | 1958 | 15.00 |
| ❑ DL 74061 [S] | For You, For Me, Forevermore | 1960 | 20.00 |
| ❑ DL 75159 | Till the End of Time | 1970 | 10.00 |
| **DOT** | | | |
| ❑ DLP 25906 | The Anita Kerr Singers Reflect on the Hits of Burt Bacharach & Hal David | 1969 | 10.00 |
| ❑ DLP 25944 | Precious Teresa | 1969 | 10.00 |
| ❑ DLP 25961 | Velvet Voices and Bold Brass | 1969 | 10.00 |
| ❑ DLP 25970 | Touchlove | 1970 | 10.00 |
| **RCA CAMDEN** | | | |
| ❑ CAS-2209 | Georgia on My Mind | 1968 | 10.00 |
| **RCA VICTOR** | | | |
| ❑ APL1-1166 | The Anita Kerr Singers | 1975 | 10.00 |
| ❑ APL1-2298 | Anite Kerr and the French Connection | 1977 | 10.00 |
| ❑ LPM-2480 [M] | From Nashville…The Hit Sound | 1962 | 12.00 |
| ❑ LSP-2480 [S] | From Nashville…The Hit Sound | 1962 | 15.00 |
| ❑ LPM-2581 [M] | "The Genius" In Harmony | 1962 | 12.00 |
| ❑ LSP-2581 [S] | "The Genius" In Harmony | 1962 | 15.00 |
| ❑ LPM-2679 [M] | Tender Words | 1963 | 12.00 |
| ❑ LSP-2679 [S] | Tender Words | 1963 | 15.00 |
| ❑ LPM-3322 [M] | Mellow Moods of Love | 1965 | 12.00 |
| ❑ LSP-3322 [S] | Mellow Moods of Love | 1965 | 15.00 |
| ❑ LPM-3428 [M] | We Dig Mancini | 1965 | 12.00 |
| ❑ LSP-3428 [S] | We Dig Mancini | 1965 | 15.00 |
| ❑ LPM-3485 [M] | Sunday Serenade | 1966 | 12.00 |
| ❑ LSP-3485 [S] | Sunday Serenade | 1966 | 15.00 |
| **VOCALION** | | | |
| ❑ VL 73899 | For You | 1969 | 10.00 |
| **WARNER BROS.** | | | |
| ❑ W 1665 [M] | Slightly Baroque | 1966 | 12.00 |
| ❑ WS 1665 [S] | Slightly Baroque | 1966 | 15.00 |
| ❑ W 1707 [M] | Bert Kaempfert Turns Us On! | 1967 | 15.00 |
| ❑ WS 1707 [S] | Bert Kaempfert Turns Us On! | 1967 | 12.00 |
| ❑ W 1724 [M] | All You Need Is Love | 1967 | 15.00 |
| ❑ WS 1724 [S] | All You Need Is Love | 1967 | 12.00 |
| **WORD** | | | |
| ❑ 8647 | Hallelujah Brass | 197? | 10.00 |
| ❑ 8692 | Hymns | 197? | 10.00 |
| *—With Kurt Kaiser* | | | |
| ❑ 8696 | Walk a Little Slower | 197? | 10.00 |
| ❑ 8706 | Precious Memories | 1977 | 10.00 |
| ❑ 8707 | Hallelujah Guitars | 197? | 10.00 |
| ❑ 8741 | Hallelujah Woodwinds | 197? | 10.00 |
| ❑ 8808 | Hallelujah Voices | 197? | 10.00 |

## KERSHAW, DOUG

| Number | Title (A Side/B Side) | Yr | NM |
|---|---|---|---|
| **SCOTTI BROTHERS** | | | |
| ❑ SB 7115 | Instant Hero | 1981 | 12.00 |
| ❑ FZ 37428 | Instant Hero | 1981 | 10.00 |
| **WARNER BROS.** | | | |
| ❑ WS 1820 | Cajun Way | 1969 | 20.00 |
| *—Green label, "W7" box logo at top* | | | |
| ❑ WS 1820 | Cajun Way | 1970 | 15.00 |
| *—Green label, "WB" shield logo at top* | | | |
| ❑ WS 1861 | Spanish Moss | 1970 | 15.00 |
| *—Green label* | | | |
| ❑ WS 1906 | Doug Kershaw | 1971 | 15.00 |
| *—Green label* | | | |
| ❑ BS 2581 | Swamp Grass | 1972 | 15.00 |
| *—Green label* | | | |
| ❑ BS 2649 | Devil's Elbow | 1973 | 15.00 |
| ❑ BS 2725 | Douglas James Kershaw | 1973 | 15.00 |
| ❑ BS 2793 | Mama Kershaw's Boy | 1974 | 15.00 |
| ❑ BS 2851 | Alive & Pickin' | 1975 | 12.00 |
| ❑ BS 2910 | Ragin' Cajun | 1976 | 12.00 |
| ❑ BS 3025 | Flip, Flop & Fly | 1977 | 12.00 |
| ❑ BSK 3166 | Louisiana Man | 1978 | 12.00 |

## KERSHAW, RUSTY AND DOUG

| Number | Title (A Side/B Side) | Yr | NM |
|---|---|---|---|
| **HICKORY** | | | |
| ❑ LPM-103 [M] | Rusty and Doug Sing Louisiana Man | 1960 | 120.00 |
| **HICKORY/MGM** | | | |
| ❑ H3G-4506 | Louisiana Man | 1974 | 20.00 |

## KESEY, KEN

| Number | Title (A Side/B Side) | Yr | NM |
|---|---|---|---|
| **SOUND CITY** | | | |
| ❑ 27690 [M] | The Acid Test | 1967 | 300.00 |
| *—THE GRATEFUL DEAD appear on this LP* | | | |

## KESNER, DICK

| Number | Title (A Side/B Side) | Yr | NM |
|---|---|---|---|
| **BRUNSWICK** | | | |
| ❑ BL 54044 [M] | Lawrence Welk Presents Dick Kesner | 1958 | 20.00 |
| ❑ BL 54051 [M] | Dick Kesner and His Magic Stradivarius | 1959 | 15.00 |
| ❑ BL 54054 [M] | Intermezzo | 1960 | 15.00 |
| ❑ BL 754044 [S] | Lawrence Welk Presents Dick Kesner | 1959 | 25.00 |
| ❑ BL 754051 [S] | Dick Kesner and His Magic Stradivarius | 1959 | 20.00 |
| ❑ BL 754054 [S] | Intermezzo | 1960 | 20.00 |
| **CORAL** | | | |
| ❑ CRL 57352 [M] | Music of Hawaii | 1960 | 12.00 |
| ❑ CRL 57360 [M] | A "New" Old Refrain | 1961 | 12.00 |
| ❑ CRL 57376 [M] | The Sound of Gypsy Music | 1961 | 12.00 |
| ❑ CRL 57393 [M] | Amor Latino | 1962 | 12.00 |
| ❑ CRL 57435 [M] | Golden Favorites | 1964 | 12.00 |
| ❑ CRL 757352 [S] | Music of Hawaii | 1960 | 15.00 |
| ❑ CRL 757360 [S] | A "New" Old Refrain | 1961 | 15.00 |
| ❑ CRL 757376 [S] | The Sound of Gypsy Music | 1961 | 15.00 |
| ❑ CRL 757393 [S] | Amor Latino | 1962 | 15.00 |
| ❑ CRL 757435 [S] | Golden Favorites | 1964 | 15.00 |
| **VOCALION** | | | |
| ❑ VL 3777 [M] | Latin Favorites | 196? | 12.00 |
| ❑ VL 73777 [S] | Latin Favorites | 196? | 15.00 |

## KESSEL, BARNEY

| Number | Title (A Side/B Side) | Yr | NM |
|---|---|---|---|
| **CONTEMPORARY** | | | |
| ❑ C-2508 [10] | Barney Kessel, Volume 1 | 1953 | 120.00 |
| ❑ C-2514 [10] | Barney Kessel, Volume 2 | 1954 | 120.00 |
| ❑ C-3511 [M] | Easy Like | 1956 | 80.00 |
| ❑ C-3512 [M] | Kessel Plays Standards | 1956 | 80.00 |
| ❑ C-3513 [M] | To Swing or Not to Swing | 1956 | 80.00 |
| ❑ C-3521 [M] | Music to Listen to Barney Kessel By | 1956 | 60.00 |
| ❑ M-3563 [M] | Barney Kessel Plays "Carmen" | 1959 | 40.00 |
| ❑ M-3565 [M] | Some Like It Hot | 1959 | 40.00 |
| ❑ M-3585 [M] | Workin' Out! | 1960 | 40.00 |
| ❑ M-3603 [M] | Let's Cook! | 1962 | 25.00 |
| ❑ M-3613 [M] | Swingin' Party | 1963 | 20.00 |
| ❑ M-3618 [M] | Feeling Free | 1965 | 20.00 |
| ❑ S-7521 [S] | Music to Listen to Barney Kessel By | 1959 | 40.00 |
| ❑ S-7563 [S] | Barney Kessel Plays "Carmen" | 1959 | 30.00 |
| ❑ S-7565 [S] | Some Like It Hot | 1959 | 30.00 |
| ❑ S-7585 [S] | Workin' Out! | 1960 | 30.00 |
| ❑ S-7603 [S] | Let's Cook! | 1962 | 25.00 |
| ❑ S-7613 [S] | Swingin' Party | 1963 | 25.00 |
| ❑ S-7618 [S] | Feeling Free | 1965 | 25.00 |
| **EMERALD** | | | |
| ❑ 2401 [S] | On Fire | 1965 | 20.00 |
| **REPRISE** | | | |
| ❑ R9-6019 [S] | Breakfast at Tiffany's | 1961 | 20.00 |
| ❑ R9-6049 [S] | Bossa Nova | 1962 | 20.00 |
| ❑ R9-6073 [S] | Kessel/Jazz | 1963 | 20.00 |
| **STEREO RECORDS** | | | |
| ❑ S-7001 [S] | Music to Listen to Barney Kessel By | 1958 | 50.00 |

## KEYMEN, THE

| Number | Title (A Side/B Side) | Yr | NM |
|---|---|---|---|
| **ABC-PARAMOUNT** | | | |
| ❑ 258 [M] | Dance with Dick Clark | 1958 | 30.00 |
| ❑ S-258 [S] | Dance with Dick Clark | 1958 | 50.00 |
| ❑ 288 [M] | Dance with Dick Clark, Volume 2 | 1959 | 30.00 |
| ❑ S-288 [S] | Dance with Dick Clark, Volume 2 | 1959 | 50.00 |
| **CORAL** | | | |
| ❑ CRL 57112 [M] | Vocal Sounds of the Keymen | 1957 | 30.00 |
| **GOLDUST** | | | |
| ❑ LPS-153 [M] | The Keymen Live | 196? | 50.00 |

## KEYS, CALVIN

| Number | Title (A Side/B Side) | Yr | NM |
|---|---|---|---|
| **BLACK JAZZ** | | | |
| ❑ 5 | Shawn-neeq | 1972 | 20.00 |

## KHAZAD DOOM

| Number | Title (A Side/B Side) | Yr | NM |
|---|---|---|---|
| **LPL** | | | |
| ❑ 892 | Level 6 1/2 | 1970 | 1000. |

## KICKSTANDS, THE

| Number | Title (A Side/B Side) | Yr | NM |
|---|---|---|---|
| **CAPITOL** | | | |
| ❑ ST 2078 [S] | Black Boots and Bikes | 1964 | 150.00 |
| ❑ T 2078 [M] | Black Boots and Bikes | 1964 | 120.00 |
| ❑ T/ST 2078 | Black Boots and Bikes Bonus Fold-Out | 1964 | 50.00 |

## KID ROCK

| Number | Title (A Side/B Side) | Yr | NM |
|---|---|---|---|
| **ATLANTIC** | | | |
| ❑ 83119 [(2)] | Devil Without a Cause | 1999 | 20.00 |
| ❑ 83314 [(2)] | The History of Rock | 2000 | 20.00 |
| ❑ 83482 [(2)] | Cocky | 2001 | 20.00 |
| ❑ 83685 [(2)] | Kid Rock | 2003 | 15.00 |
| **JIVE** | | | |
| ❑ 1409-1 | Grits Sandwiches for Breakfast | 1990 | 20.00 |

## KID THOMAS

| Number | Title (A Side/B Side) | Yr | NM |
|---|---|---|---|
| **AMERICAN MUSIC** | | | |
| ❑ 642 [10] | Kid Thomas | 1952 | 50.00 |
| **GHB** | | | |
| ❑ GHB-24 [M] | Kid Thomas + The Hall Brothers Jazz Band | 196? | 20.00 |
| **RIVERSIDE** | | | |
| ❑ RLP-365 [M] | Kid Thomas and His Algiers Stompers | 1961 | 30.00 |
| ❑ RLP-386 [M] | Kid Thomas and His Algiers Stompers | 1961 | 30.00 |
| ❑ RS-9365 [R] | Kid Thomas and His Algiers Stompers | 1961 | 20.00 |
| ❑ RS-9386 [R] | Kid Thomas and His Algiers Stompers | 1961 | 20.00 |

## KILGORE, MERLE

| Number | Title (A Side/B Side) | Yr | NM |
|---|---|---|---|
| **STARDAY** | | | |
| ❑ SLP-251 [M] | There's Gold in Them Thar Hills | 1963 | 30.00 |
| **WING** | | | |
| ❑ MGW-12316 [M] | Tall Texan | 196? | 15.00 |
| ❑ SRW-16316 [S] | Tall Texan | 196? | 12.00 |

## KILLING FLOOR

| Number | Title (A Side/B Side) | Yr | NM |
|---|---|---|---|
| **SIRE** | | | |
| ❑ SES-97019 | Killing Floor | 1970 | 50.00 |

## KINCAID, BRADLEY

| Number | Title (A Side/B Side) | Yr | NM |
|---|---|---|---|
| **VARSITY** | | | |
| ❑ 34 [M] | Bradley Kincaid Sings American Ballads and Folk Songs | 1957 | 40.00 |
| ❑ 6988 [10] | American Ballads | 1955 | 60.00 |

## KINCAIDE, DEAN

| Number | Title (A Side/B Side) | Yr | NM |
|---|---|---|---|
| **WEATHERS** | | | |
| ❑ 5610 [M] | Arranged for You | 1954 | 50.00 |

## KINES, TOM

| Number | Title (A Side/B Side) | Yr | NM |
|---|---|---|---|
| **ELEKTRA** | | | |
| ❑ EKL-137 [M] | Of Maids and Mistresses | 1958 | 30.00 |

## KING, ALBERT

| Number | Title (A Side/B Side) | Yr | NM |
|---|---|---|---|
| **ATLANTIC** | | | |
| ❑ SD 8213 | King of the Blues Guitar | 1969 | 25.00 |
| **FANTASY** | | | |
| ❑ 9627 | San Francisco '83 | 1983 | 10.00 |
| ❑ 9633 | I'm in a Phone Booth, Baby | 1984 | 10.00 |
| **KING** | | | |
| ❑ 852 [M] | Big Blues | 1963 | 500.00 |
| ❑ KS-1060 | Travelin' to California | 1969 | 25.00 |
| **MODERN BLUES** | | | |
| ❑ MBLP-723 | Let's Have a Natural Ball | 198? | 10.00 |
| **STAX** | | | |
| ❑ ST-723 [M] | Born Under a Bad Sign | 1967 | 80.00 |
| ❑ STS-723 [S] | Born Under a Bad Sign | 1967 | 120.00 |
| ❑ STS-2003 | Live Wire/Blues Power | 1968 | 50.00 |
| ❑ STS-2010 | Years Gone By | 1969 | 25.00 |
| ❑ STS-2015 | King Does the King's Thing | 1969 | 25.00 |
| ❑ STS-2040 | Lovejoy | 1971 | 20.00 |
| ❑ STS-3009 | I'll Play the Blues for You | 1972 | 20.00 |
| ❑ STX-4101 | The Pinch | 1977 | 12.00 |
| ❑ STX-4128 | Live Wire/Blues Power | 1979 | 10.00 |
| *—Reissue of 2003* | | | |
| ❑ STX-4132 | Montreux Festival | 1980 | 10.00 |
| *—Retitled reissue of 5520* | | | |
| ❑ STS-5505 | I Wanna Get Funky | 1974 | 15.00 |
| ❑ STS-5520 | Montreux Festival | 1975 | 15.00 |
| ❑ MPS-8504 | Blues for Elvis | 1981 | 10.00 |
| *—Retitled reissue of 2015* | | | |
| ❑ MPS-8513 | I'll Play the Blues for You | 1981 | 10.00 |
| *—Reissue of 3309* | | | |
| ❑ MPS-8517 | Lovejoy | 1981 | 10.00 |
| *—Reissue of 2040* | | | |
| ❑ MPS-8522 | Years Gone By | 1982 | 10.00 |
| *—Reissue of 2010* | | | |
| ❑ MPS-8534 | The Lost Session | 1986 | 10.00 |
| ❑ MPS-8536 | I Wanna Get Funky | 1987 | 10.00 |
| *—Reissue of 5505* | | | |
| ❑ MPS-8546 | Blues at Sunrise | 1988 | 10.00 |
| ❑ MPS-8556 | Wednesday Night in San Francisco | 1990 | 10.00 |
| ❑ MPS-8557 | Tuesday Night in San Francisco | 1990 | 10.00 |
| **SUNDAZED** | | | |
| ❑ LP 5031 | Born Under a Bad Sign | 1999 | 15.00 |
| *—Reissue on 180-gram vinyl* | | | |



**Except when noted otherwise, VG = 25% of NM, and VG+ = 50% of NM. (Example: VG = $2.00, VG+ = $4.00 and NM = $8.00.)**

| Number | Title (A Side/B Side) | Yr | NM |
|---|---|---|---|
| TOMATO | | | |
| ❑ TOM-6002 | King Albert | 1978 | 12.00 |
| ❑ TOM-7022 | New Orleans Heat | 1979 | 12.00 |
| UTOPIA | | | |
| ❑ BUL1-1387 | Truckload of Lovin' | 1976 | 12.00 |
| ❑ BUL1-1731 | Albert | 1976 | 12.00 |
| ❑ CUL2-2205 [(2)] | Albert Live | 1977 | 15.00 |
| **KING, ALBERT/STEVE CROPPER/POP STAPLES** | | | |
| STAX | | | |
| ❑ STS-2020 | Jammed Together | 1969 | 25.00 |
| ❑ MPS-8544 | Jammed Together | 1988 | 10.00 |
| *—Reissue* | | | |
| **KING, ALBERT/OTIS RUSH** | | | |
| CHESS | | | |
| ❑ LPS 1538 | Door to Door | 1969 | 25.00 |
| ❑ CH-9322 | Door to Door | 1990 | 10.00 |
| *—Reissue* | | | |
| **KING, ANNA** | | | |
| SMASH | | | |
| ❑ MGS-27059 [M] | Back to Soul | 1964 | 100.00 |
| ❑ SRS-67059 [S] | Back to Soul | 1964 | 120.00 |
| **KING, B.B.** | | | |
| ABC | | | |
| ❑ D-704 | Blues Is King | 1970 | 12.00 |
| *—Reissue of BluesWay 6001* | | | |
| ❑ D-709 | Blues on Top of Blues | 1970 | 12.00 |
| *—Reissue of BluesWay 6011* | | | |
| ❑ D-712 | Lucille | 1970 | 12.00 |
| *—Reissue of BluesWay 6016* | | | |
| ❑ D-713 | Indianola Mississippi Seeds | 1970 | 12.00 |
| ❑ D-723 | Live in Cook County Jail | 1971 | 12.00 |
| ❑ D-724 | Live at the Regal | 1971 | 12.00 |
| *—Reissue of ABC-Paramount 509* | | | |
| ❑ D-730 | B.B. King in London | 1971 | 12.00 |
| ❑ D-743 | L.A. Midnight | 1972 | 12.00 |
| ❑ X-759 | Guess Who | 1972 | 12.00 |
| ❑ X-767 | The Best of B.B. King | 1973 | 12.00 |
| ❑ X-794 | To Know You Is to Love You | 1973 | 12.00 |
| ❑ D-813 | His Best/The Electric B.B. King | 1974 | 12.00 |
| *—Reissue of BluesWay 6022* | | | |
| ❑ D-819 | Live and Well | 1974 | 12.00 |
| *—Reissue of BluesWay 6031* | | | |
| ❑ D-825 | Friends | 1974 | 12.00 |
| ❑ D-868 | Completely Well | 1975 | 12.00 |
| *—Reissue of BluesWay 6037* | | | |
| ❑ D-878 | Back in the Alley | 1975 | 12.00 |
| *—Reissue of BluesWay 6050* | | | |
| ❑ D-898 | Lucille Talks Back | 1975 | 12.00 |
| ❑ AB-977 | King Size | 1977 | 12.00 |
| ❑ AA-1061 | Midnight Believer | 1978 | 12.00 |
| ABC-PARAMOUNT | | | |
| ❑ 456 [M] | Mr. Blues | 1963 | 30.00 |
| ❑ S-456 [S] | Mr. Blues | 1963 | 40.00 |
| ❑ 509 [M] | Live at the Regal | 1965 | 40.00 |
| ❑ S-509 [S] | Live at the Regal | 1965 | 50.00 |
| ❑ 528 [M] | Confessin' the Blues | 1965 | 30.00 |
| ❑ S-528 [S] | Confessin' the Blues | 1965 | 40.00 |
| BLUESWAY | | | |
| ❑ BL-6001 [M] | Blues Is King | 1967 | 40.00 |
| ❑ BLS-6001 [S] | Blues Is King | 1967 | 25.00 |
| ❑ BL-6011 [M] | Blues on Top of Blues | 1968 | 50.00 |
| *—Mono is white label promo only* | | | |
| ❑ BLS-6011 [S] | Blues on Top of Blues | 1968 | 25.00 |
| ❑ BLS-6016 | Lucille | 1968 | 25.00 |
| ❑ BLS-6022 | His Best/The Electric B.B. King | 1969 | 20.00 |
| ❑ BLS-6031 | Live and Well | 1969 | 20.00 |
| ❑ BLS-6037 | Completely Well | 1969 | 20.00 |
| ❑ BLS-6050 | Back in the Alley | 1970 | 20.00 |
| COMMAND | | | |
| ❑ CQD-40022 [Q] | Friends | 1974 | 20.00 |
| CROWN | | | |
| ❑ CST-147 [R] | B.B. King Wails | 1960 | 12.00 |
| *—Black vinyl* | | | |
| ❑ CST-147 [R] | B.B. King Wails | 1960 | 100.00 |
| *—Red vinyl* | | | |
| ❑ CST-152 [R] | B.B. King Sings Spirituals | 1960 | 12.00 |
| *—Black vinyl* | | | |
| ❑ CST-152 [R] | B.B. King Sings Spirituals | 1960 | 100.00 |
| *—Red vinyl* | | | |
| ❑ CST-195 [S] | King of the Blues | 1961 | 20.00 |
| *—Black vinyl; this album is in true stereo, contrary to prior reports* | | | |
| ❑ CST-195 [S] | King of the Blues | 1961 | 120.00 |
| *—Red vinyl; this album is in true stereo, contrary to prior reports* | | | |
| ❑ CST-309 [R] | Blues in My Heart | 1963 | 12.00 |
| ❑ CST-359 [P] | B.B. King | 1963 | 12.00 |
| *—Half of the album is in stereo, half is rechanneled* | | | |
| ❑ CLP-5020 [M] | Singin' the Blues | 1957 | 100.00 |
| *—Black label, silver "Crown"* | | | |
| ❑ CLP-5020 [M] | Singin' the Blues | 196? | 12.00 |
| *—Black label, multi-color "Crown"* | | | |
| ❑ CLP-5020 [M] | Singin' the Blues | 1963 | 20.00 |
| *—Gray label, black "Crown"* | | | |
| ❑ CLP-5063 [M] | The Blues | 1958 | 80.00 |
| *—Black label, silver "Crown"* | | | |
| ❑ CLP-5063 [M] | The Blues | 196? | 12.00 |
| *—Black label, multi-color "Crown"* | | | |
| ❑ CLP-5063 [M] | The Blues | 1963 | 20.00 |
| *—Gray label, black "Crown"* | | | |
| ❑ CLP-5115 [M] | B.B. King Wails | 1959 | 80.00 |
| *—Black label, silver "Crown"* | | | |
| ❑ CLP-5115 [M] | B.B. King Wails | 196? | 12.00 |
| *—Black label, multi-color "Crown"* | | | |
| ❑ CLP-5115 [M] | B.B. King Wails | 1963 | 20.00 |
| *—Gray label, black "Crown"* | | | |
| ❑ CLP-5119 [M] | B.B. King Sings Spirituals | 196? | 12.00 |
| *—Black label, multi-color "Crown"* | | | |
| ❑ CLP-5119 [M] | B.B. King Sings Spirituals | 1960 | 60.00 |
| *—Gray label, black "Crown"* | | | |
| ❑ CLP-5143 [M] | The Great B.B. King | 196? | 12.00 |
| *—Black label, multi-color "Crown"* | | | |
| ❑ CLP-5143 [M] | The Great B.B. King | 1961 | 60.00 |
| *—Gray label, black "Crown"* | | | |
| ❑ CLP-5167 [M] | King of the Blues | 196? | 12.00 |
| *—Black label, multi-color "Crown"* | | | |
| ❑ CLP-5167 [M] | King of the Blues | 1961 | 60.00 |
| *—Gray label, black "Crown"* | | | |
| ❑ CLP-5188 [M] | My Kind of Blues | 196? | 12.00 |
| *—Black label, multi-color "Crown"* | | | |
| ❑ CLP-5188 [M] | My Kind of Blues | 1961 | 60.00 |
| *—Gray label, black "Crown"* | | | |
| ❑ CLP-5230 [M] | More B.B. King | 196? | 12.00 |
| *—Black label, multi-color "Crown"* | | | |
| ❑ CLP-5230 [M] | More B.B. King | 1962 | 60.00 |
| *—Gray label, black "Crown"* | | | |
| ❑ CLP-5248 [M] | Twist with B.B. King | 196? | 12.00 |
| *—Black label, multi-color "Crown"* | | | |
| ❑ CLP-5248 [M] | Twist with B.B. King | 1962 | 60.00 |
| *—Gray label, black "Crown"* | | | |
| ❑ CLP-5286 [M] | Easy Listening Blues | 196? | 12.00 |
| *—Black label, multi-color "Crown"* | | | |
| ❑ CLP-5286 [M] | Easy Listening Blues | 1962 | 60.00 |
| *—Gray label, black "Crown"* | | | |
| ❑ CLP-5309 [M] | Blues in My Heart | 196? | 12.00 |
| *—Black label, multi-color "Crown"* | | | |
| ❑ CLP-5309 [M] | Blues in My Heart | 1963 | 40.00 |
| *—Gray label, black "Crown"* | | | |
| ❑ CLP-5359 [M] | B.B. King | 196? | 12.00 |
| *—Black label, multi-color "Crown"* | | | |
| ❑ CLP-5359 [M] | B.B. King | 1963 | 40.00 |
| *—Gray label, black "Crown"* | | | |
| CRUSADERS | | | |
| ❑ 16013 | Live in London | 1982 | 25.00 |
| *—Part of MCA's "Audiophile Series"* | | | |
| CUSTOM | | | |
| ❑ CM-2046 [M] | Blues for Me | 196? | 12.00 |
| ❑ CM-2049 [M] | I Love You So | 196? | 12.00 |
| ❑ CM-2052 [M] | The Soul of B.B. King | 196? | 12.00 |
| DIRECT DISK | | | |
| ❑ SD-16616 | Midnight Believer | 1980 | 50.00 |
| *—Audiophile vinyl* | | | |
| GALAXY | | | |
| ❑ 202 [M] | 16 Greatest Hits | 1963 | 60.00 |
| ❑ 8202 [S] | 16 Greatest Hits | 1963 | 80.00 |
| GRP | | | |
| ❑ GR-9637 | Live at the Apollo | 1991 | 15.00 |
| KENT | | | |
| ❑ KST-512 [R] | Rock Me Baby | 1964 | 15.00 |
| ❑ KST-513 [R] | Let Me Love You | 1965 | 15.00 |
| ❑ KST-515 [R] | B.B. King Live on Stage | 1965 | 15.00 |
| ❑ KST-516 [R] | The Soul of B.B. King | 1966 | 15.00 |
| ❑ KST-517 [R] | Pure Soul | 1966 | 15.00 |
| ❑ KST-521 [R] | The Jungle | 1967 | 15.00 |
| ❑ KST-529 [R] | Boss of the Blues | 1968 | 15.00 |
| ❑ KST-533 [(2)] | From the Beginning | 1969 | 20.00 |
| ❑ KST-535 | Underground Blues | 1969 | 15.00 |
| ❑ KST-539 | The Incredible Soul of B.B. King | 1970 | 15.00 |
| ❑ KST-548 | Turn On to B.B. King | 1970 | 15.00 |
| ❑ KST-552 | Greatest Hits, Volume 1 | 1971 | 15.00 |
| ❑ KST-561 | Better Than Ever | 1971 | 15.00 |
| ❑ KST-563 | Doing My Thing, Lord | 1971 | 15.00 |
| ❑ KST-565 | B.B. King Live | 1972 | 15.00 |
| ❑ KST-568 | The Original Sweet Sixteen | 1972 | 15.00 |
| ❑ KLP-2008 | Incredible Soul of B.B. King | 1987 | 12.00 |
| ❑ KLP-5012 [M] | Rock Me Baby | 1964 | 20.00 |
| ❑ KLP-5013 [M] | Let Me Love You | 1965 | 20.00 |
| ❑ KLP-5015 [M] | B.B. King Live on Stage | 1965 | 20.00 |
| ❑ KLP-5016 [M] | The Soul of B.B. King | 1966 | 20.00 |
| ❑ KLP-5017 [M] | Pure Soul | 1966 | 20.00 |
| ❑ KLP-5021 [M] | The Jungle | 1967 | 20.00 |
| ❑ KLP-5029 [M] | Boss of the Blues | 1968 | 20.00 |
| MCA | | | |
| ❑ 3151 | Take It Home | 1979 | 10.00 |
| ❑ 5162 | There Must Be a Better World Somewhere | 1981 | 10.00 |
| ❑ 5307 | Love Me Tender | 1982 | 10.00 |
| ❑ 5413 | Blues 'N' Jazz | 1983 | 10.00 |
| ❑ 5616 | Six Silver Strings | 1985 | 10.00 |
| ❑ 6455 | Live at San Quentin | 1990 | 12.00 |
| ❑ 2-8016 [(2)] | "Now Appearing" at Ole Miss | 1980 | 12.00 |
| ❑ 27005 | Live in Cook County Jail | 1980 | 8.00 |
| *—Reissue of ABC 723* | | | |
| ❑ 27006 | Live at the Regal | 1980 | 8.00 |
| *—Reissue of ABC 724* | | | |
| ❑ 27007 | His Best/The Electric B.B. King | 1980 | 8.00 |
| *—Reissue of ABC 813* | | | |
| ❑ 27008 | Live and Well | 1980 | 8.00 |
| *—Reissue of ABC 819* | | | |
| ❑ 27009 | Completely Well | 1980 | 8.00 |
| *—Reissue of ABC 868* | | | |
| ❑ 27010 | Back in the Alley | 1980 | 8.00 |
| *—Reissue of ABC 878* | | | |
| ❑ 27011 | Midnight Believer | 1980 | 8.00 |
| *—Reissue of ABC 1061* | | | |
| ❑ 27028 | Take It Home | 1981 | 8.00 |
| *—Reissue of MCA 3151* | | | |
| ❑ 27034 | There Must Be a Better World Somewhere | 1983 | 8.00 |
| *—Reissue of MCA 5162* | | | |
| ❑ 27074 | The Best of B.B. King | 1984 | 8.00 |
| *—Reissue of ABC 767* | | | |
| ❑ 42183 | The King of the Blues: 1989 | 1989 | 10.00 |
| MCA IMPULSE! | | | |
| ❑ MCA2-4124 [(2)] | Great Moments with B.B. King | 1981 | 12.00 |
| MOBILE FIDELITY | | | |
| ❑ 1-235 | Lucille | 1995 | 25.00 |
| *—Audiophile vinyl* | | | |
| PICKWICK | | | |
| ❑ SPC-3593 | Live at the Regal | 197? | 8.00 |
| ❑ SPC-3654 | Live in Cook County Jail | 197? | 8.00 |
| STAX | | | |
| ❑ ORS-4508 | 16 Original Big Hits | 198? | 8.00 |
| UNITED | | | |
| ❑ US-7703 | Heart Full of Blues | 197? | 8.00 |
| ❑ US-7705 | Easy Listening Blues | 197? | 8.00 |
| *—Reissue of Crown 5286* | | | |
| ❑ US-7708 | Blues for Me | 197? | 8.00 |
| *—Reissue of Custom 2046* | | | |
| ❑ US-7711 | I Love You So | 197? | 8.00 |
| *—Reissue of Custom 2049* | | | |
| ❑ US-7714 | The Soul of B.B. King | 197? | 8.00 |
| *—Reissue of Custom 2052* | | | |
| ❑ US-7721 | Swing Low | 197? | 8.00 |
| ❑ US-7724 | My Kind of Blues | 197? | 8.00 |
| *—Reissue of Crown 5188* | | | |
| ❑ US-7726 | Singin' the Blues | 197? | 8.00 |
| *—Reissue of Crown 5020* | | | |
| ❑ US-7728 | The Great B.B. King | 197? | 8.00 |
| *—Reissue of Crown 5143* | | | |
| ❑ US-7732 | The Blues | 197? | 8.00 |
| *—Reissue of Crown 5063* | | | |
| ❑ US-7733 | Rock Me, Baby | 197? | 8.00 |
| *—Reissue of Kent 5012* | | | |
| ❑ US-7734 | Let Me Love You | 197? | 8.00 |
| *—Reissue of Kent 513* | | | |
| ❑ US-7736 | B.B. King Live on Stage | 197? | 8.00 |
| *—Reissue of Kent 515* | | | |
| ❑ US-7742 | The Jungle | 197? | 8.00 |
| *—Reissue of Kent 521* | | | |
| ❑ US-7750 | Boss of the Blues | 197? | 8.00 |
| *—Reissue of Kent 529* | | | |
| ❑ US-7756 | The Incredible Soul of B.B. King | 197? | 8.00 |
| *—Reissue of Kent 539* | | | |
| ❑ US-7763 | Turn On with B.B. King | 197? | 8.00 |
| *—Reissue of Kent 548* | | | |
| ❑ US-7766 | Greatest Hits, Volume 1 | 197? | 8.00 |
| *—Reissue of Kent 552* | | | |
| ❑ US-7773 | The Original Sweet Sixteen | 197? | 8.00 |
| *—Reissue of Kent 568* | | | |
| ❑ US-7788 | 9 x 9 | 197? | 8.00 |
| **KING, BEN E.** Also see AVERAGE WHITE BAND; THE DRIFTERS. | | | |
| ATCO | | | |
| ❑ 33-133 [M] | Spanish Harlem | 1961 | 100.00 |
| *—Yellow label with harp* | | | |
| ❑ 33-133 [M] | Spanish Harlem | 1962 | 40.00 |
| *—Gold and gray label* | | | |
| ❑ SD 33-133 [S] | Spanish Harlem | 1961 | 150.00 |
| *—Yellow label with harp* | | | |
| ❑ SD 33-133 [S] | Spanish Harlem | 1962 | 50.00 |
| *—Purple and brown label* | | | |
| ❑ 33-137 [M] | Ben E. King Sings for Soulful Lovers | 1962 | 40.00 |
| ❑ SD 33-137 [S] | Ben E. King Sings for Soulful Lovers | 1962 | 60.00 |
| ❑ 33-142 [M] | Don't Play That Song | 1962 | 40.00 |
| ❑ SD 33-142 [S] | Don't Play That Song | 1962 | 60.00 |
| ❑ 33-165 [M] | Ben E. King's Greatest Hits | 1964 | 30.00 |
| ❑ SD 33-165 [S] | Ben E. King's Greatest Hits | 1964 | 40.00 |
| *—Purple and brown label* | | | |
| ❑ SD 33-165 [S] | Ben E. King's Greatest Hits | 1969 | 12.00 |
| *—Yellow label* | | | |
| ❑ SD 33-165 [S] | Ben E. King's Greatest Hits | 197? | 8.00 |
| *—Any other color label* | | | |
| ❑ 33-174 [M] | Seven Letters | 1965 | 40.00 |
| ❑ SD 33-174 [S] | Seven Letters | 1965 | 50.00 |
| ATLANTIC | | | |
| ❑ SD 18132 | Supernatural | 1975 | 12.00 |
| ❑ SD 18169 | I Have a Love | 1976 | 12.00 |
| ❑ SD 18191 | Rhapsody | 1976 | 12.00 |
| ❑ SD 19200 | Let Me Live in Your Life | 1978 | 12.00 |
| ❑ SD 19269 | Music Trance | 1980 | 10.00 |

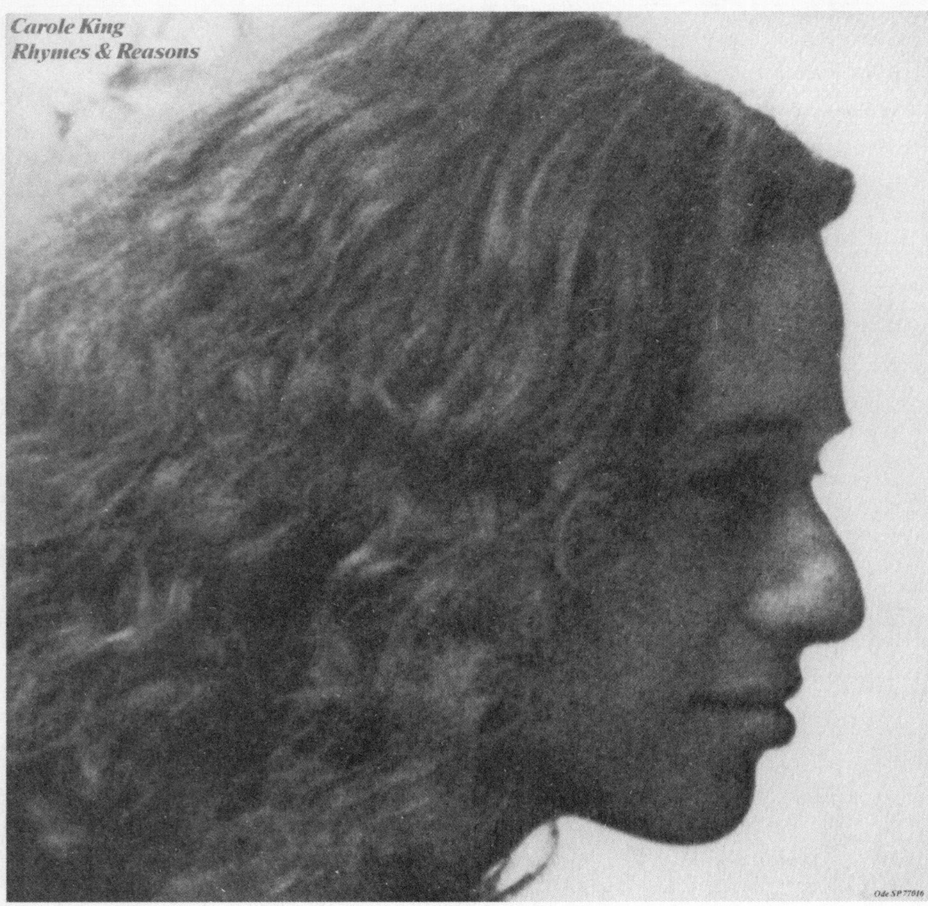


Carole King, *Rhymes & Reasons,* Ode SP-77016, 1972, $12.

| Number | Title (A Side/B Side) | Yr | NM |
|---|---|---|---|
| ❑ SD 19300 | Street Tough | 1981 | 10.00 |
| ❑ 81716 | Stand By Me: The Best of Ben E. King | 1987 | 8.00 |
| *—Includes seven Ben E. King tracks and three by the Drifters* | | | |
| **CLARION** | | | |
| ❑ 606 [M] | Young Boy Blues | 1966 | 25.00 |
| ❑ SD 606 [S] | Young Boy Blues | 1966 | 30.00 |
| **MANDALA** | | | |
| ❑ MLP 3007 | The Beginning of It All for Ben E. King | 1972 | 20.00 |
| ❑ MLP-3008 [DJ] | Audio Biography | 1972 | 30.00 |
| *—Promo-only interview by Richard Robinson* | | | |
| **MAXWELL** | | | |
| ❑ ML-88001 | Rough Edges | 1969 | 20.00 |

### KING, CAROLE

| Number | Title (A Side/B Side) | Yr | NM |
|---|---|---|---|
| **ATLANTIC** | | | |
| ❑ SD 19344 | One to One | 1982 | 10.00 |
| ❑ 80118 | Speeding Time | 1983 | 10.00 |
| **CAPITOL** | | | |
| ❑ SPRO-9103/4 [EP] | Touch the Sky Sampler | 1979 | 15.00 |
| *—Promo-only four-song excerpt from "Touch the Sky"* | | | |
| ❑ SMAS-11667 | Simple Things | 1977 | 10.00 |
| ❑ SW-11785 | Welcome Home | 1978 | 10.00 |
| ❑ SW-11785 | Welcome Home | 1978 | 10.00 |
| ❑ ST-11953 | Touch the Sky | 1979 | 10.00 |
| ❑ SWAK-11963 | Touch the Sky | 1979 | 10.00 |
| ❑ SOO-12073 | Pearls — Songs of Goffin and King | 1980 | 10.00 |
| ❑ SN-16057 | Simple Things | 1980 | 8.00 |
| *—Budget-line reissue* | | | |
| ❑ SN-16058 | Welcome Home | 1980 | 8.00 |
| *—Budget-line reissue* | | | |
| ❑ SN-16059 | Touch the Sky | 1980 | 8.00 |
| *—Budget-line reissue* | | | |
| ❑ C1-90885 | City Streets | 1989 | 12.00 |
| **ODE** | | | |
| ❑ PE 34944 | Carole King: Writer | 1977 | 10.00 |
| *—Reissue of 77006* | | | |
| ❑ FE 34946 | Tapestry | 1979 | 10.00 |
| *—Reissue with new prefix* | | | |
| ❑ PE 34946 | Tapestry | 1977 | 10.00 |
| *—Reissue of 77009* | | | |
| ❑ PE 34949 | Music | 1977 | 10.00 |
| *—Reissue of 77013* | | | |
| ❑ PE 34950 | Rhymes and Reasons | 1977 | 10.00 |
| *—Reissue of 77016* | | | |
| ❑ PE 34953 | Wrap Around Joy | 1977 | 10.00 |
| *—Reissue of 77024* | | | |
| ❑ PE 34955 | Really Rosie | 1977 | 10.00 |
| *—Reissue of 77027* | | | |
| ❑ PE 34962 | Fantasy | 1977 | 10.00 |
| *—Reissue of 77018* | | | |
| ❑ PE 34963 | Thoroughbred | 1977 | 10.00 |
| *—Reissue of 77034* | | | |
| ❑ JE 34967 | Her Greatest Hits | 1978 | 10.00 |
| ❑ HE 44946 | Tapestry | 1980 | 50.00 |
| *—Half-speed mastered edition* | | | |
| ❑ SP-77006 | Writer: Carole King | 1970 | 12.00 |
| ❑ SP-77009 | Tapestry | 1971 | 12.00 |
| ❑ SP-77013 | Music | 1971 | 12.00 |
| ❑ SP-77016 | Rhymes and Reasons | 1972 | 12.00 |
| ❑ SP-77018 | Fantasy | 1973 | 12.00 |
| ❑ SP-77024 | Wrap Around Joy | 1974 | 12.00 |
| ❑ SP-77027 | Really Rosie | 1975 | 12.00 |
| ❑ SP-77034 | Thoroughbred | 1976 | 12.00 |
| ❑ QU-88013 [Q] | Music | 1974 | 20.00 |

### KING, CLAUDE

| Number | Title (A Side/B Side) | Yr | NM |
|---|---|---|---|
| **COLUMBIA** | | | |
| ❑ CS 1024 | Friend, Lover, Woman, Wife | 1970 | 15.00 |
| ❑ CL 1810 [M] | Meet Claude King | 1962 | 25.00 |
| *—Six "eye" logos on label* | | | |
| ❑ CL 1810 [M] | Meet Claude King | 1963 | 15.00 |
| *—"Guaranteed High Fidelity" or "Mono" on red label* | | | |
| ❑ CL 2415 [M] | Tiger Woman | 1965 | 20.00 |
| ❑ CS 8610 [S] | Meet Claude King | 1962 | 40.00 |
| *—Six "eye" logos on label* | | | |
| ❑ CS 8610 [S] | Meet Claude King | 1963 | 20.00 |
| *—"360 Sound Stereo" on red label* | | | |
| ❑ CS 9215 [S] | Tiger Woman | 1965 | 25.00 |
| *—"360 Sound Stereo" on red label* | | | |
| ❑ CS 9789 | I Remember Johnny Horton | 1968 | 15.00 |
| *—"360 Sound Stereo" on red label* | | | |
| ❑ C 30804 | Chip 'n' Dale's Place | 1971 | 15.00 |
| **HARMONY** | | | |
| ❑ HS 11300 | The Best of Claude King | 1969 | 12.00 |

### KING, FREDDIE

| Number | Title (A Side/B Side) | Yr | NM |
|---|---|---|---|
| **COTILLION** | | | |
| ❑ SD 9004 | Freddie King Is a Blues Master | 1969 | 25.00 |
| ❑ SD 9016 | My Feeling for the Blues | 1970 | 25.00 |
| **KING** | | | |
| ❑ 762 [M] | Freddie King Sings the Blues | 1961 | 250.00 |
| ❑ 773 [M] | Let's Hide Away and Dance Away | 1961 | 250.00 |
| ❑ 821 [M] | Bossa Nova and Blues | 1962 | 150.00 |
| ❑ 856 [M] | Freddie King Goes Surfin' | 1963 | 80.00 |
| ❑ KS-856 [S] | Freddie King Goes Surfin' | 1963 | 120.00 |
| ❑ 928 [M] | A Bonanza of Instrumentals | 1965 | 50.00 |
| ❑ KS-928 [S] | A Bonanza of Instrumentals | 1965 | 60.00 |
| ❑ 964 [M] | 24 Vocals and Instrumentals | 1966 | 25.00 |
| ❑ KS-1059 | Hide Away | 1969 | 15.00 |
| **MCA** | | | |
| ❑ 690 | The Best of Freddie King | 1979 | 8.00 |
| *—Reissue of Shelter 52021* | | | |
| **MODERN BLUES** | | | |
| ❑ MB2LP-721 [(2)] | Just Pickin' | 198? | 15.00 |
| ❑ MBLP-722 | Freddie King Sings | 198? | 10.00 |
| **RSO** | | | |
| ❑ RS-1-3025 | Freddie King 1934-1976 | 1977 | 12.00 |
| ❑ SD 4803 | Burglar | 1974 | 12.00 |
| ❑ SD 4811 | Larger Than Life | 1975 | 12.00 |
| **SHELTER** | | | |
| ❑ 2140 | The Best of Freddie King | 1975 | 15.00 |
| *—Original with MCA distribution* | | | |
| ❑ SW-8905 | Getting Ready | 1971 | 15.00 |
| ❑ SW-8913 | Texas Cannonball | 1972 | 15.00 |
| ❑ SW-8919 | Woman Across the River | 1973 | 15.00 |
| ❑ SRL 52021 | The Best of Freddie King | 1977 | 12.00 |
| *—Second edition with ABC distribution* | | | |
| **STARDAY/GUSTO** | | | |
| ❑ 5012 | 17 Original Hits | 1977 | 10.00 |
| ❑ 5033 | Hide Away | 1978 | 10.00 |

### KING, FREDDIE/LULA REED/BOBBY THOMPSON

| Number | Title (A Side/B Side) | Yr | NM |
|---|---|---|---|
| **KING** | | | |
| ❑ 777 [M] | Boy-Girl-Boy | 1962 | 250.00 |

### KING, JEAN

| Number | Title (A Side/B Side) | Yr | NM |
|---|---|---|---|
| **HANNA-BARBERA** | | | |
| ❑ HLP-8505 [M] | Jean King Sings for the In Crowd | 1966 | 20.00 |

### KING, JONATHAN

| Number | Title (A Side/B Side) | Yr | NM |
|---|---|---|---|
| **PARROT** | | | |
| ❑ PA 61013 [M] | Jonathan King Or Then Again.... | 1967 | 40.00 |
| ❑ PAS 71013 [P] | Jonathan King Or Then Again.... | 1967 | 50.00 |
| *—Only "Where the Sun Has Never Shown" is rechanneled.* | | | |
| **U.K.** | | | |
| ❑ 53101 | Bubble Rock Is Here to Stay | 1972 | 25.00 |
| ❑ 53104 | Pandora's Box | 1973 | 25.00 |

### KING, MORGANA

| Number | Title (A Side/B Side) | Yr | NM |
|---|---|---|---|
| **ASCOT** | | | |
| ❑ AM 13014 [M] | The Winter of My Discontent | 1964 | 25.00 |
| ❑ AM 13019 [M] | The End of a Love Affair | 1965 | 25.00 |
| *—Reissue of United Artists 30020* | | | |
| ❑ AM 13020 [M] | Everybody Loves Saturday Night | 1965 | 25.00 |
| ❑ AM 13025 [M] | More Morgana | 1965 | 25.00 |
| ❑ AS 16014 [S] | The Winter of My Discontent | 1964 | 30.00 |
| ❑ AS 16019 [S] | The End of a Love Affair | 1965 | 30.00 |
| *—Reissue of United Artists 40020* | | | |
| ❑ AS 16020 [S] | Everybody Loves Saturday Night | 1965 | 30.00 |
| ❑ AS 16025 [S] | More Morgana | 1965 | 30.00 |
| **EMARCY** | | | |
| ❑ MG-36079 [M] | For You, For Me, For Evermore | 1956 | 120.00 |
| **MAINSTREAM** | | | |
| ❑ S-6015 [S] | With a Taste of Honey | 1964 | 25.00 |
| ❑ S-6052 [S] | Miss Morgana King | 1965 | 25.00 |
| ❑ 56015 [M] | With a Taste of Honey | 1964 | 20.00 |
| ❑ 56052 [M] | Miss Morgana King | 1965 | 20.00 |
| **MERCURY** | | | |
| ❑ MG-20231 [M] | Morgana King Sings the Blues | 1958 | 80.00 |
| **RCA CAMDEN** | | | |
| ❑ CAL-543 [M] | The Greatest Songs Ever Swung | 1959 | 20.00 |
| ❑ CAS-543 [S] | The Greatest Songs Ever Swung | 1959 | 30.00 |
| **REPRISE** | | | |
| ❑ R 6192 [M] | It's a Quiet Thing | 1966 | 20.00 |
| ❑ RS 6192 [S] | It's a Quiet Thing | 1966 | 25.00 |
| ❑ R 6205 [M] | Wild Is Love | 1966 | 20.00 |
| ❑ RS 6205 [S] | Wild Is Love | 1966 | 25.00 |
| ❑ R 6257 [M] | Gemini Changes | 1967 | 20.00 |
| ❑ RS 6257 [S] | Gemini Changes | 1967 | 25.00 |
| **UNITED ARTISTS** | | | |
| ❑ UAL 3028 [M] | Folk Songs A La King | 1960 | 80.00 |
| ❑ UAS 6028 [S] | Folk Songs A La King | 1960 | 100.00 |
| ❑ UAL 30020 [M] | Let Me Love You | 1960 | 100.00 |
| ❑ UAS 30020-S [S] | Let Me Love You | 1960 | 120.00 |



**Except when noted otherwise, VG = 25% of NM, and VG+ = 50% of NM. (Example: VG = $2.00, VG+ = $4.00 and NM = $8.00.)**

| Number | Title (A Side/B Side) | Yr | NM |
|---|---|---|---|
| **VERVE** | | | |
| ❑ V-5061 [M] | I Know How It Feels | 1968 | 25.00 |
| ❑ V6-5061 [S] | I Know How It Feels | 1968 | 25.00 |
| **WING** | | | |
| ❑ SRW-16307 [S] | More Morgana King | 1965 | 20.00 |

**KING, PEE WEE**

| Number | Title (A Side/B Side) | Yr | NM |
|---|---|---|---|
| **BRIAR** | | | |
| ❑ 102 | Golden Olde Tyme Dances | 1975 | 60.00 |
| **LONGHORN** | | | |
| ❑ 1236 [M] | The Legendary Pee Wee King | 1967 | 25.00 |
| **RCA CAMDEN** | | | |
| ❑ CAL-876 [M] | Country Barn Dance | 1965 | 20.00 |
| ❑ CAS-876 [R] | Country Barn Dance | 1965 | 12.00 |
| **RCA VICTOR** | | | |
| ❑ LPM-1237 [M] | Swing West | 1956 | 40.00 |
| ❑ LPM-3028 [10] | Pee Wee King | 195? | 80.00 |
| ❑ LPM-3071 [10] | Western Hits | 195? | 80.00 |
| ❑ LPM-3109 [10] | Waltzes | 195? | 80.00 |
| ❑ LPM-3280 [10] | Swing West | 195? | 80.00 |
| **STARDAY** | | | |
| ❑ SLP-284 [M] | Back Again with the Songs That Made Them Famous | 1964 | 30.00 |

**KING, PEGGY**

| Number | Title (A Side/B Side) | Yr | NM |
|---|---|---|---|
| **COLUMBIA** | | | |
| ❑ CL 2549 [10] | Wish Upon a Star | 1955 | 50.00 |
| **IMPERIAL** | | | |
| ❑ LP-9078 [M] | Lazy Afternoon | 1959 | 20.00 |
| ❑ LP-12026 [S] | Lazy Afternoon | 1959 | 30.00 |
| **STASH** | | | |
| ❑ 246 | Peggy King Sings Jerome Kern: Till the Clouds Roll By | 198? | 8.00 |

**KING, REV. MARTIN LUTHER** The 1968 releases are posthumous tributes.

| Number | Title (A Side/B Side) | Yr | NM |
|---|---|---|---|
| **BUDDAH** | | | |
| ❑ BDS-2002 | Man of Love | 1968 | 20.00 |
| **CREED** | | | |
| ❑ 3201 [M] | I Have a Dream | 1968 | 20.00 |
| **DOOTO** | | | |
| ❑ DTL-831 [M] | Martin Luther King at Zion Hill | 1962 | 30.00 |
| ❑ DTL-841 | The American Dream | 1968 | 20.00 |
| **GORDY** | | | |
| ❑ G-906 [M] | The Great March to Freedom | 1963 | 40.00 |
| *—"Gordy" in script at top of label* | | | |
| ❑ G-906 [M] | The Great March to Freedom | 1968 | 15.00 |
| *—Later pressings* | | | |
| ❑ G-908 [M] | The Great March on Washington | 1963 | 40.00 |
| *—"Gordy" in script at top of label* | | | |
| ❑ G-908 [M] | The Great March on Washington | 1968 | 15.00 |
| *—Later pressings* | | | |
| ❑ G-929 | ...Free at Last | 1968 | 30.00 |
| *—Original with gatefold cover* | | | |
| **MERCURY** | | | |
| ❑ SR-61170 | In Search of Freedom | 1968 | 20.00 |
| **MR. MAESTRO** | | | |
| ❑ 1000 [M] | The March on Washington | 1963 | 30.00 |
| **SUNSET** | | | |
| ❑ 21033 | The Struggle for Freedom | 1968 | 15.00 |
| **20TH CENTURY** | | | |
| ❑ TCF-3110 [M] | Freedom March on Washington | 1963 | 30.00 |
| ❑ S-3201 | The Rev. Dr. Martin Luther King, Jr. | 1968 | 20.00 |
| **UNART** | | | |
| ❑ S 21033 | In the Struggle for Freedom and Human Dignity | 1968 | 20.00 |

**KING, TEDDI**

| Number | Title (A Side/B Side) | Yr | NM |
|---|---|---|---|
| **CORAL** | | | |
| ❑ CRL 57278 [M] | All the King's Songs | 1959 | 60.00 |
| ❑ CRL 757278 [S] | All the King's Songs | 1959 | 80.00 |
| **RCA VICTOR** | | | |
| ❑ LPM-1147 [M] | Bidin' My Time | 1956 | 80.00 |
| ❑ LPM-1313 [M] | To You from Teddi King | 1957 | 100.00 |
| ❑ LPM-1454 [M] | A Girl and Her Songs | 1957 | 80.00 |
| **STORYVILLE** | | | |
| ❑ STLP-302 [10] | 'Round Midnight | 1954 | 250.00 |
| ❑ STLP-314 [10] | Storyville Presents Teddi King | 1954 | 200.00 |
| ❑ STLP-903 [M] | Now In Vogue | 1956 | 150.00 |

**KING CRIMSON**

| Number | Title (A Side/B Side) | Yr | NM |
|---|---|---|---|
| **ATLANTIC** | | | |
| ❑ SD 7212 | Islands | 1972 | 20.00 |
| ❑ SD 7263 | Larks' Tongues in Aspic | 1973 | 20.00 |
| ❑ SD 7298 | Starless and Bible Black | 1974 | 20.00 |

King Curtis, *Arthur Murray's Music for Dancing: The Twist*, RCA Victor LSP-2494, 1962, stereo, $30.

| Number | Title (A Side/B Side) | Yr | NM |
|---|---|---|---|
| ❑ 8245 [M] | In the Court of the Crimson King — An Observation by King Crimson | 1969 | 50.00 |
| *—Mono is white label promo only; comes in stereo cover with "DJ Copy Monaural" sticker on front* | | | |
| ❑ SD 8245 | In the Court of the Crimson King — An Observation by King Crimson | 1969 | 20.00 |
| ❑ SD 8266 | In the Wake of Poseidon | 1970 | 20.00 |
| ❑ SD 8278 | Lizard | 1971 | 20.00 |
| ❑ SD 18110 | Red | 1974 | 15.00 |
| ❑ SD 18136 | USA | 1975 | 15.00 |
| ❑ SD 19155 | In the Court of the Crimson King — An Observation by King Crimson | 1978 | 12.00 |
| *—Reissue of Atlantic 8245* | | | |
| **EDITIONS EG** | | | |
| ❑ EGKC-1 | In the Court of the Crimson King — An Observation by King Crimson | 1985 | 10.00 |
| *—Reissue of Atlantic 19155* | | | |
| ❑ EGKC-2 | In the Wake of Poseidon | 1985 | 10.00 |
| *—Reissue of Atlantic 8266* | | | |
| ❑ EGKC-3 | Lizard | 1985 | 10.00 |
| *—Reissue of Atlantic 8278* | | | |
| ❑ EGKC-4 | Islands | 1985 | 10.00 |
| *—Reissue of Atlantic 7212* | | | |
| ❑ EGKC-6 | Lark's Tongue in Aspic | 1985 | 10.00 |
| *—Reissue of Atlantic 7263* | | | |
| ❑ EGKC-7 | Starless and Bible Black | 1985 | 10.00 |
| *—Reissue of Atlantic 7298* | | | |
| ❑ EGKC-8 | Red | 1985 | 10.00 |
| *—Reissue of Atlantic 18110* | | | |
| ❑ EGKC-9 | USA | 1985 | 10.00 |
| *—Reissue of Atlantic 18135* | | | |
| ❑ EGKC-10 [(2)] | The Young Person's Guide to King Crimson | 1985 | 15.00 |
| **MOBILE FIDELITY** | | | |
| ❑ 1-075 | In the Court of the Crimson King — An Observation by King Crimson | 1981 | 80.00 |
| *—Audiophile vinyl* | | | |
| **WARNER BROS.** | | | |
| ❑ WBMS-119 [DJ] | The Return of King Crimson | 1981 | 60.00 |
| *—Promo-only interview and music show* | | | |
| ❑ BSK 3629 | Discipline | 1981 | 10.00 |
| ❑ 23692 | Beat | 1982 | 10.00 |
| ❑ 25071 | Three of a Perfect Pair | 1984 | 10.00 |

**KING CURTIS**

| Number | Title (A Side/B Side) | Yr | NM |
|---|---|---|---|
| **ATCO** | | | |
| ❑ 33-113 [M] | Have Tenor Sax, Will Blow | 1959 | 40.00 |
| ❑ SD 33-113 [S] | Have Tenor Sax, Will Blow | 1959 | 60.00 |
| ❑ 33-189 [M] | That Lovin' Feeling | 1966 | 20.00 |
| ❑ SD 33-189 [S] | That Lovin' Feeling | 1966 | 25.00 |
| ❑ 33-198 [M] | Live at Small's Paradise | 1966 | 20.00 |
| ❑ SD 33-198 [S] | Live at Small's Paradise | 1966 | 25.00 |
| ❑ 33-211 [M] | The Great Memphis Hits | 1967 | 20.00 |
| ❑ SD 33-211 [S] | The Great Memphis Hits | 1967 | 25.00 |
| ❑ 33-231 [M] | King Size Soul | 1967 | 25.00 |
| ❑ SD 33-231 [S] | King Size Soul | 1967 | 20.00 |
| ❑ 33-247 [M] | Sweet Soul | 1968 | 30.00 |
| ❑ SD 33-247 [S] | Sweet Soul | 1968 | 20.00 |
| ❑ SD 33-266 | The Best of King Curtis | 1968 | 20.00 |
| ❑ SD 33-293 | Instant Groove | 1969 | 20.00 |
| ❑ SD 33-338 | Get Ready | 1970 | 20.00 |
| ❑ SD 33-359 | Live at Fillmore West | 1971 | 20.00 |
| ❑ SD 33-385 | Everybody's Talkin' | 1972 | 20.00 |
| **ATLANTIC** | | | |
| ❑ SD 1637 | Blues Montreux | 1973 | 12.00 |
| **CAPITOL** | | | |
| ❑ ST 1756 [S] | Country Soul | 1963 | 40.00 |
| ❑ T 1756 [M] | Country Soul | 1963 | 30.00 |
| ❑ ST 2095 [S] | Soul Serenade | 1964 | 30.00 |
| ❑ T 2095 [M] | Soul Serenade | 1964 | 25.00 |
| ❑ ST 2341 [S] | King Curtis Plays the Hits Made Famous by Sam Cooke | 1965 | 30.00 |
| ❑ T 2341 [M] | King Curtis Plays the Hits Made Famous by Sam Cooke | 1965 | 25.00 |
| ❑ ST 2858 [S] | The Best of King Curtis | 1968 | 25.00 |
| ❑ T 2858 [M] | The Best of King Curtis | 1968 | 50.00 |
| *—Red and white "Starline" label; may be promo only* | | | |
| ❑ SM-11798 | Soul Serenade | 1978 | 10.00 |
| *—Reissue* | | | |
| ❑ SM-11963 | The Best of King Curtis | 1979 | 10.00 |
| *—Reissue* | | | |
| **CLARION** | | | |
| ❑ 615 [M] | The Great "K" Curtis | 1966 | 20.00 |
| ❑ SD 615 [S] | The Great "K" Curtis | 1966 | 25.00 |
| **COLLECTABLES** | | | |
| ❑ COL-5119 | Soul Twist | 198? | 10.00 |
| ❑ COL-5156 | Golden Classics: Enjoy…The Best of King Curtis | 198? | 10.00 |

ENJOY

| Number | Title (A Side/B Side) | Yr | NM |
|---|---|---|---|
| ENLP-2001 [M] | Soul Twist | 1962 | 50.00 |

EVEREST

| Number | Title (A Side/B Side) | Yr | NM |
|---|---|---|---|
| SDBR-1121 [S] | Azure | 1961 | 75.00 |
| LPBR-5121 [M] | Azure | 1961 | 50.00 |

FANTASY

| Number | Title (A Side/B Side) | Yr | NM |
|---|---|---|---|
| OJC-198 | The New Scene of King Curtis | 1985 | 10.00 |
| *—Reissue of New Jazz 8237* | | | |
| OBC-512 | Trouble in Mind | 1988 | 10.00 |
| *—Reissue of Tru-Sound 15001* | | | |

NEW JAZZ

| Number | Title (A Side/B Side) | Yr | NM |
|---|---|---|---|
| NJLP-8237 [M] | The New Scene of King Curtis | 1960 | 60.00 |
| *—Purple label* | | | |
| NJLP-8237 [M] | The New Scene of King Curtis | 1965 | 30.00 |
| *—Blue label with trident logo on right* | | | |

PRESTIGE

| Number | Title (A Side/B Side) | Yr | NM |
|---|---|---|---|
| PRLP-7222 [M] | Soul Meeting | 1962 | 50.00 |
| PRST-7222 [S] | Soul Meeting | 1962 | 75.00 |
| PRST-7709 | The Best of King Curtis | 1969 | 15.00 |
| PRST-7775 | The Best of King Curtis — One More Time | 1970 | 15.00 |
| PRST-7789 | King Soul | 1970 | 15.00 |
| PRST-7833 | Soul Meeting | 1971 | 15.00 |
| *—Reissue of 7222* | | | |
| 24033 [(2)] | Jazz Groove | 198? | 15.00 |

RCA CAMDEN

| Number | Title (A Side/B Side) | Yr | NM |
|---|---|---|---|
| CAS-2242 | Sax in Motion | 1968 | 15.00 |

RCA VICTOR

| Number | Title (A Side/B Side) | Yr | NM |
|---|---|---|---|
| LPM-2494 [M] | Arthur Murray's Music for Dancing: The Twist! | 1962 | 25.00 |
| LSP-2494 [S] | Arthur Murray's Music for Dancing: The Twist! | 1962 | 30.00 |

TRU-SOUND

| Number | Title (A Side/B Side) | Yr | NM |
|---|---|---|---|
| TS-15001 [M] | Trouble in Mind | 1961 | 50.00 |
| TS-15008 [M] | It's Party Time | 1962 | 50.00 |
| TS-15009 [M] | Doin' the Dixie Twist | 1962 | 50.00 |

### KING PINS, THE (1)

KING

| Number | Title (A Side/B Side) | Yr | NM |
|---|---|---|---|
| 865 [M] | It Won't Be This Way Always | 1963 | 300.00 |

### KING PLEASURE

EVEREST ARCHIVE OF FOLK AND JAZZ

| Number | Title (A Side/B Side) | Yr | NM |
|---|---|---|---|
| FS-262 [M] | King Pleasure | 197? | 12.00 |

FANTASY

| Number | Title (A Side/B Side) | Yr | NM |
|---|---|---|---|
| OJC-1771 [S] | Golden Days | 1991 | 15.00 |

HIFI

| Number | Title (A Side/B Side) | Yr | NM |
|---|---|---|---|
| J-425 [M] | Golden Days | 1960 | 40.00 |
| JS-425 [S] | Golden Days | 1960 | 50.00 |

PRESTIGE

| Number | Title (A Side/B Side) | Yr | NM |
|---|---|---|---|
| PRLP-208 [10] | King Pleasure Sings | 1955 | 500.00 |
| PRLP-7586 | Original Moody's Mood | 1968 | 30.00 |
| PR-24017 [(2)] | The Source | 1972 | 25.00 |

SOLID STATE

| Number | Title (A Side/B Side) | Yr | NM |
|---|---|---|---|
| SS-18021 [S] | Mr. Jazz | 1968 | 25.00 |
| *—Reissue of United Artists 15031* | | | |

UNITED ARTISTS

| Number | Title (A Side/B Side) | Yr | NM |
|---|---|---|---|
| UAS-5634 [S] | Moody's Mood for Love | 1972 | 20.00 |
| UAJ-14031 [M] | Mr. Jazz | 1962 | 40.00 |
| UAJS-15031 [S] | Mr. Jazz | 1962 | 50.00 |

### KING PLEASURE/ANNIE ROSS

FANTASY

| Number | Title (A Side/B Side) | Yr | NM |
|---|---|---|---|
| OJC-217 [M] | King Pleasure Sings/Annie Ross Sings | 198? | 12.00 |

PRESTIGE

| Number | Title (A Side/B Side) | Yr | NM |
|---|---|---|---|
| PRLP-7128 [M] | King Pleasure Sings/Annie Ross Sings | 1957 | 150.00 |
| *—Yellow label, W. 50th Street address on label* | | | |
| PRLP-7128 [M] | King Pleasure Sings/Annie Ross Sings | 1958 | 80.00 |
| *—Yellow label, Bergenfield, N.J. address on label* | | | |
| PRLP-7128 [M] | King Pleasure Sings/Annie Ross Sings | 1965 | 40.00 |
| *—Blue label, trident logo at right* | | | |

### KING SISTERS, THE

CAPITOL

| Number | Title (A Side/B Side) | Yr | NM |
|---|---|---|---|
| T 808 [M] | Aloha | 1957 | 25.00 |
| *—Turquoise or gray label* | | | |
| T 919 [M] | Imagination | 1958 | 25.00 |
| *—Turquoise or gray label* | | | |
| ST 1205 [S] | Warm and Wonderful | 1959 | 30.00 |
| *—Black colorband label, logo at left* | | | |
| T 1205 [M] | Warm and Wonderful | 1959 | 20.00 |
| *—Black colorband label, logo at left* | | | |

### KING'S MEN FIVE, THE

CUCA

| Number | Title (A Side/B Side) | Yr | NM |
|---|---|---|---|
| 1130 [M] | The King's Men Five | 1965 | 20.00 |

### KINGDOM

SPECIALTY

| Number | Title (A Side/B Side) | Yr | NM |
|---|---|---|---|
| SPS-2135 | Kingdom | 1970 | 60.00 |

### KINGFISH With Bob Weir of THE GRATEFUL DEAD.

ROUND

| Number | Title (A Side/B Side) | Yr | NM |
|---|---|---|---|
| RX-108 | Kingfish | 1976 | 25.00 |

### KINGS, THE

ELEKTRA

| Number | Title (A Side/B Side) | Yr | NM |
|---|---|---|---|
| 6E-277 | The Kings Are Here | 1980 | 30.00 |
| 5E-543 | Amazon Beach | 1981 | 12.00 |

### KINGSLEY, GERSHON Also see PERREY-KINGSLEY.

AUDIO FIDELITY

| Number | Title (A Side/B Side) | Yr | NM |
|---|---|---|---|
| AFSD-6222 | Music to Moog By | 1969 | 40.00 |

### KINGSMEN, THE (1)

RHINO

| Number | Title (A Side/B Side) | Yr | NM |
|---|---|---|---|
| RNLP-126 | The Best of the Kingsmen | 1985 | 10.00 |

SCEPTER

| Number | Title (A Side/B Side) | Yr | NM |
|---|---|---|---|
| CTN-18002 | The Best of the Kingsmen | 1972 | 10.00 |

WAND

| Number | Title (A Side/B Side) | Yr | NM |
|---|---|---|---|
| WDM-657 [M] | The Kingsmen In Person | 1964 | 30.00 |
| WDS-657 [P] | The Kingsmen In Person | 1964 | 40.00 |
| WDM-659 [M] | The Kingsmen, Volume II | 1964 | 30.00 |
| *—With "Death of an Angel"* | | | |
| WDM-659 [M] | The Kingsmen, Volume II | 1964 | 40.00 |
| *—Without "Death of an Angel" (replaced by untitled instrumental)* | | | |
| WDS-659 [S] | The Kingsmen, Volume II | 1964 | 40.00 |
| *—With "Death of an Angel"* | | | |
| WDS-659 [S] | The Kingsmen, Volume II | 1964 | 50.00 |
| *—Without "Death of an Angel" (replaced by untitled instrumental)* | | | |
| WDM-662 [M] | The Kingsmen, Volume 3 | 1965 | 25.00 |
| WDS-662 [S] | The Kingsmen, Volume 3 | 1965 | 30.00 |
| WDM-670 [M] | The Kingsmen On Campus | 1965 | 25.00 |
| WDS-670 [S] | The Kingsmen On Campus | 1965 | 30.00 |
| WDM-674 [M] | 15 Great Hits | 1966 | 20.00 |
| WDS-674 [P] | 15 Great Hits | 1966 | 25.00 |
| WDM-675 [M] | Up and Away | 1966 | 20.00 |
| WDS-675 [S] | Up and Away | 1966 | 25.00 |
| WDM-681 [M] | The Kingsmen's Greatest Hits | 1967 | 15.00 |
| WDS-681 [S] | The Kingsmen's Greatest Hits | 1967 | 20.00 |
| ST-91011 [S] | Up and Away | 1966 | 30.00 |
| *—Capitol Record Club edition* | | | |

### KINGSTON TRIO, THE Also see DAVE GUARD AND THE WHISKEYHILL SINGERS; JOHN STEWART.

CAPITOL

| Number | Title (A Side/B Side) | Yr | NM |
|---|---|---|---|
| STBB-513 [(2)] | Tom Dooley/Scarlet Ribbons | 1970 | 20.00 |
| DT 996 [R] | The Kingston Trio | 196? | 12.00 |
| T 996 [M] | The Kingston Trio | 1958 | 40.00 |
| *—Black label with colorband, Capitol logo at left* | | | |
| T 996 [M] | The Kingston Trio | 1958 | 50.00 |
| *—Turquoise label* | | | |
| T 996 [M] | The Kingston Trio | 1962 | 20.00 |
| *—Black label with colorband, Capitol logo at top* | | | |
| T 1107 [M] | From the Hungry I | 1959 | 40.00 |
| *—Black label with colorband, Capitol logo at left* | | | |
| T 1107 [M] | From the Hungry I | 1962 | 20.00 |
| *—Black label with colorband, Capitol logo at top* | | | |
| ST 1183 [S] | Stereo Concert | 1959 | 50.00 |
| *—Black label with colorband, Capitol logo at left* | | | |
| ST 1183 [S] | Stereo Concert | 1962 | 25.00 |
| *—Black label with colorband, Capitol logo at top* | | | |
| ST 1199 [S] | The Kingston Trio at Large | 1959 | 40.00 |
| *—Black label with colorband, Capitol logo at left* | | | |
| ST 1199 [S] | The Kingston Trio at Large | 1962 | 20.00 |
| *—Black label with colorband, Capitol logo at top* | | | |
| T 1199 [M] | The Kingston Trio at Large | 1959 | 30.00 |
| *—Black label with colorband, Capitol logo at left, "Long Playing High-Fidelity"* | | | |
| T 1199 [M] | The Kingston Trio at Large | 1960 | 25.00 |
| *—Black label with colorband, Capitol logo at left, white line replaces "Long Playing High-Fidelity"* | | | |
| T 1199 [M] | The Kingston Trio at Large | 1962 | 15.00 |
| *—Black label with colorband, Capitol logo at top* | | | |
| ST 1258 [S] | Here We Go Again! | 1959 | 40.00 |
| *—Black label with colorband, Capitol logo at left* | | | |
| ST 1258 [S] | Here We Go Again! | 1962 | 20.00 |
| *—Black label with colorband, Capitol logo at top* | | | |
| T 1258 [M] | Here We Go Again! | 1959 | 30.00 |
| *—Black label with colorband, Capitol logo at left* | | | |
| T 1258 [M] | Here We Go Again! | 1962 | 15.00 |
| *—Black label with colorband, Capitol logo at top* | | | |
| ST 1352 [S] | Sold Out | 1960 | 40.00 |
| *—Black label with colorband, Capitol logo at left* | | | |
| ST 1352 [S] | Sold Out | 1962 | 20.00 |
| *—Black label with colorband, Capitol logo at top* | | | |
| T 1352 [M] | Sold Out | 1960 | 30.00 |
| *—Black label with colorband, Capitol logo at left* | | | |
| T 1352 [M] | Sold Out | 1962 | 15.00 |
| *—Black label with colorband, Capitol logo at top* | | | |
| ST 1407 [S] | String Along | 1960 | 40.00 |
| *—Black label with colorband, Capitol logo at left* | | | |
| ST 1407 [S] | String Along | 1962 | 20.00 |
| *—Black label with colorband, Capitol logo at top* | | | |
| T 1407 [M] | String Along | 1960 | 30.00 |
| *—Black label with colorband, Capitol logo at left* | | | |
| T 1407 [M] | String Along | 1962 | 15.00 |
| *—Black label with colorband, Capitol logo at top* | | | |
| ST 1446 [S] | The Last Month of the Year | 1960 | 40.00 |
| *—Same as above, but in stereo* | | | |
| T 1446 [M] | The Last Month of the Year | 1960 | 30.00 |
| ST 1474 [S] | Make Way! | 1961 | 40.00 |
| *—Black label with colorband, Capitol logo at left* | | | |
| ST 1474 [S] | Make Way! | 1962 | 20.00 |
| *—Black label with colorband, Capitol logo at top* | | | |
| T 1474 [M] | Make Way! | 1961 | 30.00 |
| *—Black label with colorband, Capitol logo at left* | | | |
| T 1474 [M] | Make Way! | 1962 | 15.00 |
| *—Black label with colorband, Capitol logo at top* | | | |
| ST 1564 [S] | Goin' Places | 1961 | 40.00 |
| *—Black label with colorband, Capitol logo at left* | | | |
| ST 1564 [S] | Goin' Places | 1962 | 20.00 |
| *—Black label with colorband, Capitol logo at top* | | | |
| T 1564 [M] | Goin' Places | 1961 | 30.00 |
| *—Black label with colorband, Capitol logo at left* | | | |
| T 1564 [M] | Goin' Places | 1962 | 15.00 |
| *—Black label with colorband, Capitol logo at top* | | | |
| DT 1612 [R] | Encores | 1961 | 20.00 |
| *—Black label with colorband, Capitol logo at left* | | | |
| DT 1612 [R] | Encores | 1962 | 10.00 |
| *—Black label with colorband, Capitol logo at top* | | | |
| T 1612 [M] | Encores | 1961 | 30.00 |
| *—Black label with colorband, Capitol logo at left* | | | |
| T 1612 [M] | Encores | 1962 | 15.00 |
| *—Black label with colorband, Capitol logo at top* | | | |
| ST 1642 [S] | Close-Up | 1961 | 40.00 |
| *—Black label with colorband, Capitol logo at left* | | | |
| ST 1642 [S] | Close-Up | 1962 | 20.00 |
| *—Black label with colorband, Capitol logo at top* | | | |
| T 1642 [M] | Close-Up | 1961 | 30.00 |
| *—Black label with colorband, Capitol logo at left* | | | |
| T 1642 [M] | Close-Up | 1962 | 15.00 |
| *—Black label with colorband, Capitol logo at top* | | | |
| ST 1658 [S] | College Concert | 1962 | 25.00 |
| T 1658 [M] | College Concert | 1962 | 20.00 |
| SM-1705 | The Best of the Kingston Trio | 197? | 10.00 |
| ST 1705 [P] | The Best of the Kingston Trio | 1962 | 20.00 |
| T 1705 [M] | The Best of the Kingston Trio | 1962 | 20.00 |
| ST 1747 [S] | Something Special | 1962 | 25.00 |
| T 1747 [M] | Something Special | 1962 | 20.00 |
| ST 1809 [S] | New Frontier | 1962 | 25.00 |
| T 1809 [M] | New Frontier | 1962 | 20.00 |
| ST 1871 [S] | The Kingston Trio #16 | 1963 | 25.00 |
| T 1871 [M] | The Kingston Trio #16 | 1963 | 20.00 |
| ST 1935 [S] | Sunny Side! | 1963 | 25.00 |
| T 1935 [M] | Sunny Side! | 1963 | 20.00 |
| KAO 2005 [M] | Sing a Song with the Kingston Trio | 1963 | 25.00 |
| SKAO 2005 [S] | Sing a Song with the Kingston Trio | 1963 | 30.00 |
| ST 2011 [S] | Time to Think | 1964 | 20.00 |
| T 2011 [M] | Time to Think | 1964 | 15.00 |
| ST 2081 [S] | Back in Town | 1964 | 20.00 |
| T 2081 [M] | Back in Town | 1964 | 15.00 |
| STCL 2180 [(3)S] | The Folk Era | 1964 | 50.00 |
| *—Box set with booklet* | | | |
| TCL 2180 [(3)M] | The Folk Era | 1964 | 40.00 |
| *—Box set with booklet* | | | |
| SM-2280 | The Best of the Kingston Trio, Volume 2 | 197? | 10.00 |
| ST 2280 [S] | The Best of the Kingston Trio, Volume 2 | 1965 | 20.00 |
| T 2280 [M] | The Best of the Kingston Trio, Volume 2 | 1965 | 15.00 |
| SM-2614 | The Best of the Kingston Trio, Volume 3 | 197? | 10.00 |
| ST 2614 [S] | The Best of the Kingston Trio, Volume 3 | 1966 | 20.00 |
| T 2614 [M] | The Best of the Kingston Trio, Volume 3 | 1966 | 15.00 |
| M-11577 | The Kingston Trio | 1976 | 10.00 |
| M-11968 | From the Hungry I | 1979 | 10.00 |
| SN-16183 | The Best of the Kingston Trio | 1981 | 8.00 |
| *—Budget-line reissue* | | | |
| SN-16184 | The Best of the Kingston Trio, Volume 2 | 1981 | 8.00 |
| *—Budget-line reissue* | | | |
| N-16185 | Tom Dooley | 1981 | 8.00 |
| SN-16186 | Scarlet Ribbons | 1981 | 8.00 |

DECCA

| Number | Title (A Side/B Side) | Yr | NM |
|---|---|---|---|
| DL 4613 [M] | The Kingston Trio (Nick-Bob-John) | 1965 | 25.00 |
| DL 4656 [M] | Stay Awhile | 1965 | 25.00 |
| DL 4694 [M] | Somethin' Else | 1965 | 25.00 |
| DL 4758 [M] | Children of the Morning | 1966 | 25.00 |
| DL 74613 [S] | The Kingston Trio (Nick-Bob-John) | 1965 | 30.00 |
| DL 74656 [S] | Stay Awhile | 1965 | 30.00 |
| DL 74694 [S] | Somethin' Else | 1965 | 30.00 |
| DL 74758 [S] | Children of the Morning | 1966 | 30.00 |

FOLK ERA

| Number | Title (A Side/B Side) | Yr | NM |
|---|---|---|---|
| FE-2001 | Rediscover the Kingston Trio | 198? | 10.00 |
| FE-2036 | Hidden Treasures | 198? | 10.00 |

NAUTILUS

| Number | Title (A Side/B Side) | Yr | NM |
|---|---|---|---|
| NR-2 | Aspen Gold | 1979 | 40.00 |
| *—Audiophile vinyl* | | | |

PAIR

| Number | Title (A Side/B Side) | Yr | NM |
|---|---|---|---|
| PDL2-1067 [(2)] | Early American Heroes | 1986 | 12.00 |

PICKWICK

| Number | Title (A Side/B Side) | Yr | NM |
|---|---|---|---|
| SPC-3260 | Tom Dooley | 196? | 12.00 |



**Except when noted otherwise, VG = 25% of NM, and VG+ = 50% of NM. (Example: VG = $2.00, VG+ = $4.00 and NM = $8.00.)**

| Number | Title (A Side/B Side) | Yr | NM |
|---|---|---|---|
| TETRAGRAMMATON | | | |
| ❑ T-5101 [(2)] | Once Upon a Time | 1969 | 25.00 |
| XERES | | | |
| ❑ 1-10001 | 25 Years Non-Stop | 1982 | 12.00 |
| **KINKS, THE** | | | |
| ARISTA | | | |
| ❑ SP-69 [DJ] | Low Budget Radio Interview | 1979 | 40.00 |
| *—Promo-only radio show featuring Ray Davies* | | | |
| ❑ SP-85 [EP] | A Fistful of Kinks | 1980 | 25.00 |
| *—Promo-only four-song sampler from "One for the Road"* | | | |
| ❑ AL 4106 | Sleepwalker | 1977 | 10.00 |
| ❑ AL 4106 [DJ] | Sleepwalker | 1977 | 30.00 |
| *—White label promo* | | | |
| ❑ AL 4167 | Misfits | 1978 | 10.00 |
| ❑ AL 4167 [DJ] | Misfits | 1978 | 30.00 |
| *—White label promo* | | | |
| ❑ AB 4240 | Low Budget | 1979 | 10.00 |
| ❑ AL 8-8018 | State of Confusion | 1983 | 10.00 |
| ❑ AL13 8041 [(2)] | One for the Road | 1983 | 10.00 |
| *—Reissue of 8609* | | | |
| ❑ AL 8264 | Word of Mouth | 1984 | 10.00 |
| ❑ ALB6 8300 | Low Budget | 1985 | 8.00 |
| *—Budget-line reissue* | | | |
| ❑ ALB6 8328 | Give the People What They Want | 1985 | 8.00 |
| *—Budget-line reissue* | | | |
| ❑ ALB6 8375 | Sleepwalker | 1985 | 8.00 |
| *—Budget-line reissue* | | | |
| ❑ ALB6 8377 | Misfits | 1985 | 8.00 |
| *—Budget-line reissue* | | | |
| ❑ A2L 8401 [(2)] | One for the Road | 1980 | 15.00 |
| *—Original edition has this number* | | | |
| ❑ AL11 8428 [(2)] | Come Dancing with the Kinks | 1986 | 12.00 |
| ❑ A2L 8609 [(2)] | One for the Road | 198? | 12.00 |
| *—Second edition of 8401* | | | |
| ❑ AL 9567 | Give the People What They Want | 1981 | 10.00 |
| COMPLEAT | | | |
| ❑ CPL2-2001 [(2)] | A Compleat Collection | 1984 | 12.00 |
| ❑ CPL2-2003 [(2)] | 20th Anniversary Edition | 1984 | 12.00 |
| MCA | | | |
| ❑ 5822 | Think Visual | 1987 | 10.00 |
| ❑ 6337 | UK Jive | 1989 | 12.00 |
| ❑ L33-17281 [DJ] | A Look at "Think Visual" | 1987 | 50.00 |
| *—Promo only in white jacket* | | | |
| ❑ 42107 | Live: The Road | 1988 | 10.00 |
| MOBILE FIDELITY | | | |
| ❑ 1-070 | Misfits | 1981 | 20.00 |
| *—Audiophile vinyl* | | | |
| PICKWICK | | | |
| ❑ ACL-7072 | Preservation Act 1 | 197? | 12.00 |
| *—Reissue of RCA Victor LPL1-5002* | | | |
| PYE | | | |
| ❑ 505 | The Kinks | 1975 | 12.00 |
| ❑ 509 | The Kinks, Vol. 2 | 1976 | 12.00 |
| RCA VICTOR | | | |
| ❑ APL1-1743 | Celluloid Heroes (The Kinks' Greatest) | 1976 | 10.00 |
| ❑ APL1-3520 | Second Time Around | 1980 | 10.00 |
| ❑ AYL1-3749 | Schoolboys in Disgrace | 1980 | 8.00 |
| *—Budget-line reissue* | | | |
| ❑ AYL1-3750 | Soap Opera | 1980 | 8.00 |
| *—Budget-line reissue* | | | |
| ❑ AYL1-3869 | Celluloid Heroes (The Kinks' Greatest) | 1981 | 8.00 |
| *—Budget-line reissue* | | | |
| ❑ AYL1-4558 | Muswell Hillbillies | 1982 | 8.00 |
| *—Budget-line reissue* | | | |
| ❑ LSP-4644 | Muswell Hillbillies | 1971 | 30.00 |
| ❑ AYL1-4719 | Second Time Around | 1983 | 8.00 |
| *—Budget-line reissue* | | | |
| ❑ LPL1-5002 | Preservation Act 1 | 1973 | 15.00 |
| ❑ CPL2-5040 [(2)] | Preservation Act 2 | 1974 | 20.00 |
| ❑ LPL1-5081 | Soap Opera | 1975 | 10.00 |
| *—Brown label* | | | |
| ❑ LPL1-5081 | Soap Opera | 1975 | 15.00 |
| *—Orange label* | | | |
| ❑ LPL1-5102 | Schoolboys in Disgrace | 1975 | 10.00 |
| ❑ VPS-6065 [(2)] | Everybody's in Showbiz | 1972 | 20.00 |
| *—Orange label* | | | |
| ❑ VPS-6065 [(2)] | Everybody's in Showbiz | 1975 | 12.00 |
| *—Brown label* | | | |
| REPRISE | | | |
| ❑ PRO 328 [P] | Then Now and In Between | 1969 | 50.00 |
| *—Album that came with above box is sometimes found by itself without all the other goodies.* | | | |
| ❑ PRO 328 [P] | God Save the Kinks | 1969 | 500.00 |
| *—Mail-order box with decal, postcard, bag of grass, two pins, letter, Kinks consumer guide and "Then Now and In Between" LP. Price is for complete package.* | | | |
| ❑ MS-2127 | The Great Lost Kinks Album | 1973 | 50.00 |
| ❑ R-6143 [M] | You Really Got Me | 1965 | 60.00 |
| ❑ R-6143 [M] | You Really Got Me | 1965 | 400.00 |
| *—White label promo* | | | |
| ❑ RS-6143 [P] | You Really Got Me | 1965 | 80.00 |
| *—Pink, gold and green label* | | | |
| ❑ RS-6143 [P] | You Really Got Me | 1971 | 10.00 |
| *—Orange label with "r:" and steamboat at top* | | | |

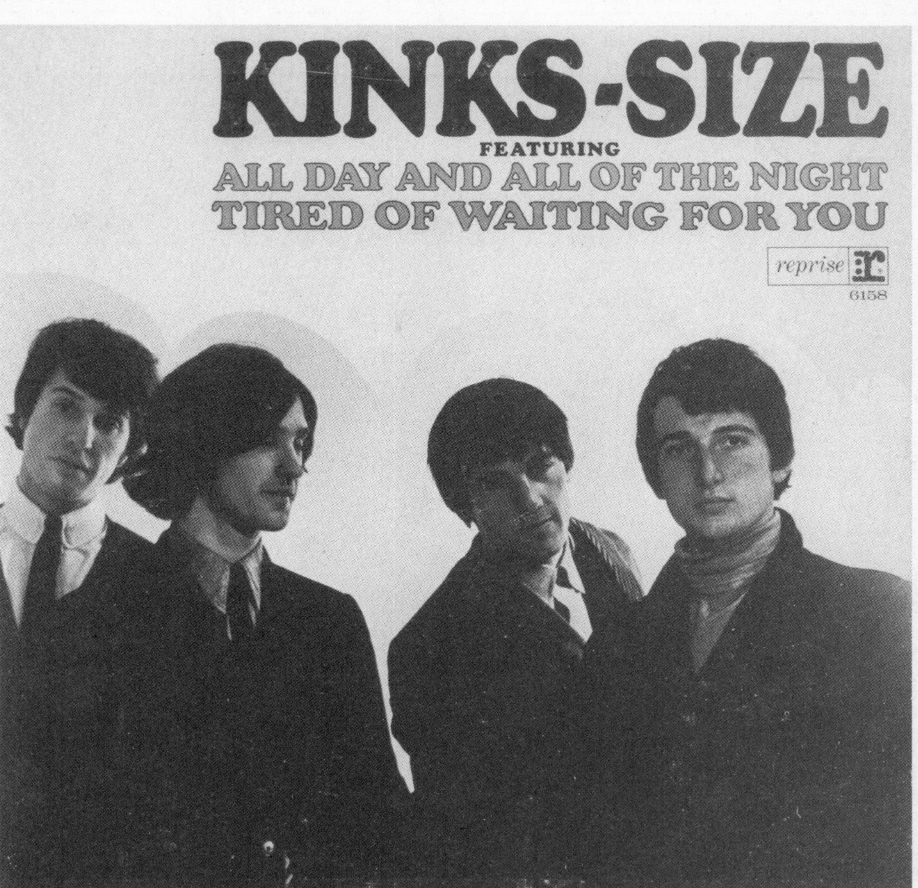


The Kinks, *Kinks-Size,* Reprise R 6158, 1965, mono, $50.

| Number | Title (A Side/B Side) | Yr | NM |
|---|---|---|---|
| ❑ R-6158 [M] | Kinks-Size | 1965 | 50.00 |
| ❑ R-6158 [M] | Kinks-Size | 1965 | 200.00 |
| *—White label promo* | | | |
| ❑ RS-6158 [R] | Kinks-Size | 1965 | 30.00 |
| ❑ R-6173 [M] | Kinda Kinks | 1965 | 50.00 |
| ❑ R-6173 [M] | Kinda Kinks | 1965 | 200.00 |
| *—White label promo* | | | |
| ❑ RS-6173 [R] | Kinda Kinks | 1965 | 30.00 |
| ❑ R-6184 [M] | Kinks Kinkdom | 1965 | 50.00 |
| ❑ R-6184 [M] | Kinks Kinkdom | 1965 | 200.00 |
| *—White label promo* | | | |
| ❑ RS-6184 [R] | Kinks Kinkdom | 1965 | 30.00 |
| ❑ R-6197 [M] | The Kink Kontroversy | 1966 | 50.00 |
| ❑ R-6197 [M] | The Kink Kontroversy | 1966 | 200.00 |
| *—White label promo* | | | |
| ❑ RS-6197 [R] | The Kink Kontroversy | 1966 | 30.00 |
| ❑ R-6217 [M] | The Kinks Greatest Hits! | 1966 | 40.00 |
| ❑ RS-6217 [R] | The Kinks Greatest Hits! | 1966 | 25.00 |
| *—Pink, gold and green label* | | | |
| ❑ RS-6217 [R] | The Kinks Greatest Hits! | 1971 | 10.00 |
| *—Orange label with "r:" and steamboat at top* | | | |
| ❑ R-6228 [M] | Face to Face | 1967 | 40.00 |
| ❑ RS-6228 [P] | Face to Face | 1967 | 30.00 |
| *—Pink, gold and green label* | | | |
| ❑ RS-6228 [P] | Face to Face | 1971 | 10.00 |
| *—Orange label with "r:" and steamboat at top* | | | |
| ❑ R-6260 [M] | The Live Kinks | 1967 | 35.00 |
| ❑ RS-6260 [S] | The Live Kinks | 1967 | 25.00 |
| *—Pink, gold and green label* | | | |
| ❑ RS-6260 [S] | The Live Kinks | 1971 | 10.00 |
| *—Orange label with "r:" and steamboat at top* | | | |
| ❑ R-6279 [M] | Something Else by the Kinks | 1968 | 300.00 |
| *—White label promo; no stock copies were issued in mono* | | | |
| ❑ RS-6279 [S] | Something Else by the Kinks | 1968 | 20.00 |
| *—Two-tone orange label with "r: and "W7" logos with steamboat* | | | |
| ❑ RS-6279 [S] | Something Else by the Kinks | 1968 | 30.00 |
| *—Pink, gold and green label* | | | |
| ❑ RS-6279 [S] | Something Else by the Kinks | 1971 | 10.00 |
| *—Orange label with "r:" and steamboat at top* | | | |
| ❑ RS-6327 | The Kinks Are the Village Green Preservation Society | 1969 | 30.00 |
| *—Two-tone orange label with "r: and "W7" logos with steamboat* | | | |
| ❑ RS-6327 | The Kinks Are the Village Green Preservation Society | 1971 | 10.00 |
| *—Orange label with "r:" and steamboat at top* | | | |
| ❑ RS-6366 | Arthur (Or The Decline and Fall of the British Empire) | 1969 | 25.00 |
| *—Two-tone orange label with "r: and "W7" logos with steamboat* | | | |

| Number | Title (A Side/B Side) | Yr | NM |
|---|---|---|---|
| ❑ RS-6366 | Arthur (Or The Decline and Fall of the British Empire) | 1971 | 10.00 |
| *—Orange label with "r:" and steamboat at top* | | | |
| ❑ RS-6423 | Lola Versus Powerman and the Moneygoround, Part One | 1970 | 15.00 |
| *—Original pressings have blue printing on a white cover* | | | |
| ❑ RS-6423 | Lola Versus Powerman and the Moneygoround, Part One | 1971 | 10.00 |
| *—Later pressings have black printing on a white cover* | | | |
| ❑ 2XS-6454 [(2)] | The Kink Kronicles | 1972 | 15.00 |
| ❑ SMAS-93034 | Arthur (Or The Decline and Fall of the British Empire) | 1970 | 40.00 |
| *—Capitol Record Club edition* | | | |
| RHINO | | | |
| ❑ R1 70086 | The Kinks Greatest Hits! Vol. 1 | 1989 | 12.00 |
| ❑ R1 70315 | You Really Got Me | 1988 | 12.00 |
| ❑ R1 70316 | Kinda Kinks | 1988 | 12.00 |
| ❑ R1 70317 | Kinks-Size | 1988 | 12.00 |
| ❑ R1 70318 | Kinks Kinkdom | 1988 | 12.00 |
| **KINSEY, TONY** | | | |
| LONDON | | | |
| ❑ LL 1672 [M] | Kinsey Come On | 1957 | 50.00 |
| **KIRBY, GEORGE** | | | |
| ARGO | | | |
| ❑ LP-4045 [M] | The Real George Kirby | 1965 | 30.00 |
| ❑ LPS-4045 [S] | The Real George Kirby | 1965 | 40.00 |
| DOOTO | | | |
| ❑ DTL-250 [M] | A Night in Hollywood | 196? | 20.00 |
| **KIRBY, JOHN** | | | |
| COLUMBIA | | | |
| ❑ CL 502 [M] | John Kirby and His Orchestra | 1953 | 40.00 |
| *—Maroon label, gold print* | | | |
| ❑ GL 502 [M] | John Kirby and His Orchestra | 1951 | 50.00 |
| *—Black label, silver print* | | | |
| COLUMBIA MASTERWORKS | | | |
| ❑ ML 4801 [10] | John Kirby and His Orchestra | 195? | 60.00 |
| HARMONY | | | |
| ❑ HL 7124 [M] | Intimate Swing | 1958 | 20.00 |
| **KIRK, ANDY** | | | |
| CORAL | | | |
| ❑ CRL 56019 [10] | Andy Kirk Souvenir Album — Vol. 1 | 1951 | 100.00 |

Kiss, *Hotter Than Hell,* Casablanca NBLP 7006, 1974, blue label, $30.

| Number | Title (A Side/B Side) | Yr | NM |
|---|---|---|---|
| RCA VICTOR | | | |
| ❑ LPM-1302 [M] | A Mellow Bit of Rhythm | 1956 | 40.00 |
| **KIRK, RAHSAAN ROLAND** | | | |
| ARGO | | | |
| ❑ LP-669 [M] | Introducing Roland Kirk | 1960 | 60.00 |
| ❑ LPS-669 [S] | Introducing Roland Kirk | 1960 | 80.00 |
| ATLANTIC | | | |
| ❑ SD 2-303 [(2)] | The Art of Rahsaan Roland Kirk | 1973 | 20.00 |
| ❑ SD 2-907 [(2)] | Bright Moments | 1974 | 20.00 |
| ❑ 1502 [M] | The Inflated Tear | 1968 | 25.00 |
| ❑ 3007 [M] | Here Comes the Whistle Man | 1967 | 25.00 |
| BETHLEHEM | | | |
| ❑ BCP-6064 [M] | Third Dimension | 1962 | 250.00 |
| KING | | | |
| ❑ 539 [M] | Triple Threat | 1956 | 400.00 |
| PRESTIGE | | | |
| ❑ PRLP-7210 [M] | Kirk's Work | 1961 | 100.00 |
| ❑ PRLP-7450 [M] | Funk Underneath | 1967 | 50.00 |
| VERVE | | | |
| ❑ V-8709 [M] | Now Please Don't You Cry, Beautiful Edith | 1967 | 100.00 |
| ❑ V6-8709 [S] | Now Please Don't You Cry, Beautiful Edith | 1967 | 80.00 |
| **KIRKLAND, LEROY** | | | |
| IMPERIAL | | | |
| ❑ LP-12198 [S] | Twistin', Mashin' and All That Jazz | 1962 | 20.00 |
| **KISS** Also see PETER CRISS; ACE FREHLEY; GENE SIMMONS; PAUL STANLEY. | | | |
| CASABLANCA | | | |
| ❑ Kiss '76 [DJ] | Special Kiss Tour Album | 1976 | 80.00 |
| *—Special four-track sampler* | | | |
| ❑ NBLP 737 [DJ] | Rock and Roll Over Special Edition | 1977 | 120.00 |
| *—Five-track sampler from the LP* | | | |
| ❑ NBLP 7001 | Kiss | 1974 | 30.00 |
| *—All renumbered versions have "Kissin' Time"; dark blue label* | | | |
| ❑ NBLP 7001 | Kiss | 1976 | 15.00 |
| *—Tan label with desert scene, "Casablanca" label* | | | |
| ❑ NBLP 7001 | Kiss | 1977 | 12.00 |
| *—Tan label with desert scene, "Casablanca Record and FilmWorks" label* | | | |

| Number | Title (A Side/B Side) | Yr | NM |
|---|---|---|---|
| ❑ NBLP 7006 | Hotter Than Hell | 1974 | 30.00 |
| *—Dark blue label* | | | |
| ❑ NBLP 7006 | Hotter Than Hell | 1976 | 15.00 |
| *—Tan label with desert scene, "Casablanca" label* | | | |
| ❑ NBLP 7006 | Hotter Than Hell | 1977 | 12.00 |
| *—Tan label with desert scene, "Casablanca Record and FilmWorks" label* | | | |
| ❑ NBLP 7016 | Dressed to Kill | 1975 | 30.00 |
| *—Dark blue label* | | | |
| ❑ NBLP 7016 | Dressed to Kill | 1976 | 15.00 |
| *—Tan label with desert scene, "Casablanca" label* | | | |
| ❑ NBLP 7016 | Dressed to Kill | 1977 | 12.00 |
| *—Tan label with desert scene, "Casablanca Record and FilmWorks" label* | | | |
| ❑ NBLP 7020 [(2)] | Alive! | 1975 | 40.00 |
| *—Dark blue labels; with booklet* | | | |
| ❑ NBLP 7020 [(2)] | Alive! | 1976 | 20.00 |
| *—Tan labels with desert scene, "Casablanca" label* | | | |
| ❑ NBLP 7020 [(2)] | Alive! | 1977 | 15.00 |
| *—Tan labels with desert scene, "Casablanca Record and FilmWorks" label* | | | |
| ❑ NBLP 7025 | Destroyer | 1976 | 15.00 |
| *—Tan label with desert scene, "Casablanca" label* | | | |
| ❑ NBLP 7025 | Destroyer | 1976 | 30.00 |
| *—Dark blue label* | | | |
| ❑ NBLP 7025 | Destroyer | 1977 | 12.00 |
| *—Tan label with desert scene, "Casablanca Record and FilmWorks" label* | | | |
| ❑ NBLP 7032 [(3)] | The Originals | 1976 | 100.00 |
| *—Tan label with desert scene, "Casablanca" label; without extras* | | | |
| ❑ NBLP 7032 [(3)] | The Originals | 1976 | 150.00 |
| *—Tan label with desert scene, "Casablanca" label; with booklet, six Kiss cards, a Kiss Army sticker* | | | |
| ❑ NBLP 7032 [(3)] | The Originals | 1977 | 50.00 |
| *—Tan label with desert scene, "Casablanca Record and FilmWorks" label; "Second Printing" on cover; without extras* | | | |
| ❑ NBLP 7032 [(3)] | The Originals | 1977 | 100.00 |
| *—Tan label with desert scene, "Casablanca Record and FilmWorks" label; "Second Printing" on cover; with extras listed above* | | | |
| ❑ NBLP 7037 | Rock and Roll Over | 1976 | 20.00 |
| *—Tan label with desert scene, "Casablanca" label; comes with sticker and Kiss Army paraphenalia order form* | | | |
| ❑ NBLP 7037 | Rock and Roll Over | 1977 | 12.00 |
| *—Tan label with desert scene, "Casablanca Record and FilmWorks" label, with inserts* | | | |
| ❑ NBLP 7057 | Love Gun | 1977 | 12.00 |
| *—Without inserts* | | | |

| Number | Title (A Side/B Side) | Yr | NM |
|---|---|---|---|
| ❑ NBLP 7057 | Love Gun | 1977 | 40.00 |
| *—with "Hot Goods from the Supply Depot" order form, unpunched-out cardboard gun and "Bang!" sticker. All items must be intact to get top dollar for this.* | | | |
| ❑ NBLP 7076 [(2)] | Alive II | 1977 | 15.00 |
| *—Without inserts* | | | |
| ❑ NBLP 7076 [(2)] | Alive II | 1977 | 40.00 |
| *—With 8-page booklet, tattoo insert and "Combat Gear" order form; back cover contents are correct* | | | |
| ❑ NBLP 7076 [(2)] | Alive II | 1977 | 400.00 |
| *—With 8-page booklet, tattoo insert and "Combat Gear" order form; back cover lists three tracks -- "Take Me," "Hooligan" and "Do You Love Me" -- that were not included on the record; no records with these tracks were made; perhaps as few as 50 copies of this cover were made* | | | |
| ❑ NBLP 7100 [(2)] | Double Platinum | 1978 | 15.00 |
| *—Without inserts* | | | |
| ❑ NBLP 7100 [(2)] | Double Platinum | 1978 | 40.00 |
| *—With "platinum award" cardboard insert and "Double Platinum Kiss Gear" order form* | | | |
| ❑ NBLP 7152 | Dynasty | 1979 | 10.00 |
| *—With neither poster nor order form* | | | |
| ❑ NBLP 7152 | Dynasty | 1979 | 15.00 |
| *—With poster and merchandise order form* | | | |
| ❑ NBLP 7225 | Kiss Unmasked | 1980 | 10.00 |
| *—With neither poster nor order form* | | | |
| ❑ NBLP 7225 | Kiss Unmasked | 1980 | 15.00 |
| *—With poster and "Kiss Essential Gear" order form* | | | |
| ❑ NBLP 7261 | Music from The Elder | 1981 | 30.00 |
| *—Various editions have paper or plastic innersleeves, lyric sheets, even incorrect track listings on the back cover; no difference in value is noted between variations* | | | |
| ❑ NBLP 7270 | Creatures of the Night | 1982 | 40.00 |
| *—Original version has band with makeup* | | | |
| ❑ NB 9001 | Kiss | 1974 | 50.00 |
| *—Second Warner Bros.-distributed version DOES have "Kissin' Time" on Side 2 (RE-1 on label)* | | | |
| ❑ NB 9001 | Kiss | 1974 | 80.00 |
| *—First Warner Bros.-distributed version does NOT have "Kissin' Time"* | | | |
| ❑ NB 20128 [DJ] | A Taste of Platinum | 1978 | 50.00 |
| *—Promo-only sampler from Double Platinum* | | | |
| ❑ NB 20137 [DJ] | Peter Criss, Ace Frehley, Gene Simmons, Paul Stanley | 1978 | 40.00 |
| *—Promo-only sampler from the band's solo albums* | | | |
| ❑ 812770-1 | Dynasty | 1983 | 8.00 |
| *—Reissue* | | | |
| ❑ 822780-1 [(2)] | Alive! | 1984 | 10.00 |
| *—Reissue* | | | |
| ❑ 822781-1 [(2)] | Alive II | 1984 | 10.00 |
| *—Reissue* | | | |
| ❑ 824146-1 | Kiss | 1984 | 8.00 |
| *—Reissue* | | | |
| ❑ 824147-1 | Hotter Than Hell | 1984 | 8.00 |
| *—Reissue* | | | |
| ❑ 824148-1 | Dressed to Kill | 1984 | 8.00 |
| *—Reissue* | | | |
| ❑ 824149-1 | Destroyer | 1984 | 8.00 |
| *—Reissue* | | | |
| ❑ 824150-1 | Rock and Roll Over | 1984 | 8.00 |
| *—Reissue* | | | |
| ❑ 824151-1 | Love Gun | 1984 | 8.00 |
| *—Reissue* | | | |
| ❑ 824153-1 | Music from The Elder | 1984 | 8.00 |
| *—Reissue* | | | |
| ❑ 824154-1 | Creatures of the Night | 1984 | 8.00 |
| *—Reissue; features band without its makeup on cover* | | | |
| ❑ 824154-1 | Creatures of the Night | 1994 | 25.00 |
| *—Reissue; glow-in-the-dark vinyl; gatefold edition; makeup cover restored* | | | |
| ❑ 824155-1 [(2)] | Double Platinum | 1984 | 10.00 |
| *—Reissue* | | | |
| ❑ 826242-1 | Unmasked | 1985 | 8.00 |
| *—Reissue* | | | |
| MERCURY | | | |
| ❑ 792-1 [DJ] | First Kiss, Last Licks | 1990 | 100.00 |
| *—Promo-only sampler* | | | |
| ❑ 522647-1 [(2)] | Alive III | 1994 | 25.00 |
| *—Limited edition black vinyl* | | | |
| ❑ 522647-1 [(2)] | Alive III | 1994 | 25.00 |
| *—Limited edition blue vinyl* | | | |
| ❑ 522647-1 [(2)] | Alive III | 1994 | 25.00 |
| *—Limited edition red vinyl* | | | |
| ❑ 522647-1 [(2)] | Alive III | 1994 | 25.00 |
| *—Limited edition white vinyl* | | | |
| ❑ 528674-1 [PD] | Creatures of the Night | 1995 | 25.00 |
| *—Reissue; picture disc of makeup cover* | | | |
| ❑ 528950-1 [(2)] | MTV Unplugged | 1996 | 20.00 |
| *—First editions are on black vinyl* | | | |
| ❑ 528950-1 [(2)] | MTV Unplugged | 1996 | 20.00 |
| *—Second editions are on yellow marbled vinyl* | | | |
| ❑ 532741-1 [(2)] | You Wanted the Best, You Got the Best!! | 1996 | 20.00 |
| ❑ 814297-1 | Lick It Up | 1983 | 12.00 |
| ❑ 822495-1 | Animalize | 1984 | 12.00 |
| ❑ 826099-1 | Asylum | 1985 | 10.00 |
| ❑ 832632-1 | Crazy Nights | 1987 | 10.00 |
| ❑ 832903-1 [PD] | Crazy Nights | 1987 | 25.00 |
| ❑ 836427-1 | Smashes, Thrashes and Hits | 1988 | 10.00 |
| ❑ 836887-1 [PD] | Smashes, Thrashes and Hits | 1988 | 25.00 |
| ❑ 838913-1 | Hot in the Shade | 1989 | 10.00 |

## ORIGINAL CAST ALBUMS

**The first full-length original Broadway cast album was made in 1943, during the 78 rpm era. For the next quarter century, these albums remained a staple. Some of these are below.**

*Carousel,* Decca DL 8003, 1949, original issue, $40.

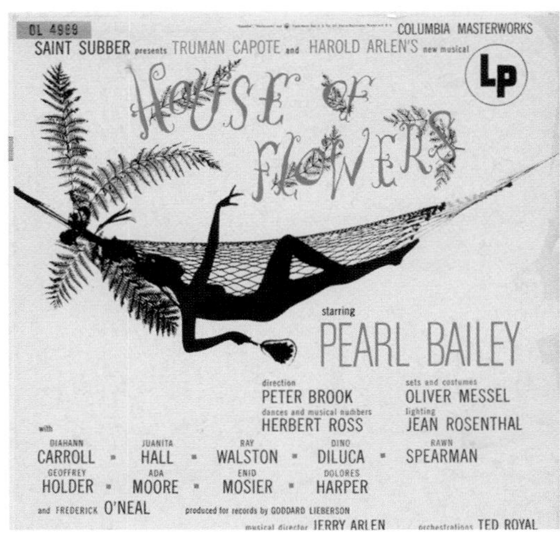


*House of Flowers,*
Columbia Masterworks OL 4969, 1954, $40.

*Me and Juliet,* RCA Victor LOC-1012, 1953, $70.

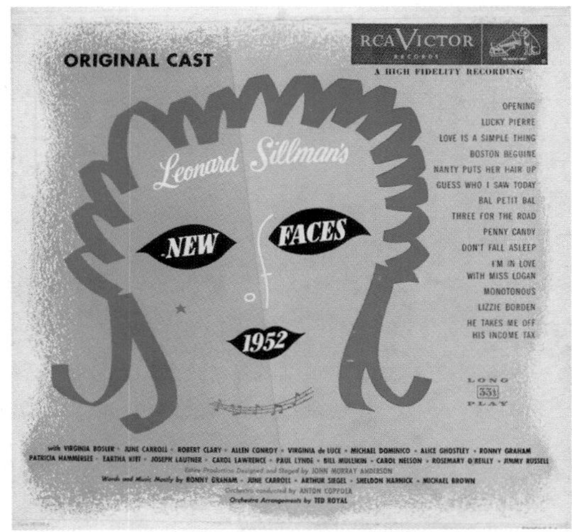


*New Faces of 1952,* RCA Victor LOC-1008, 1952, $25.

*Peter Pan,* RCA Victor LOC-1019, 1954, $40.

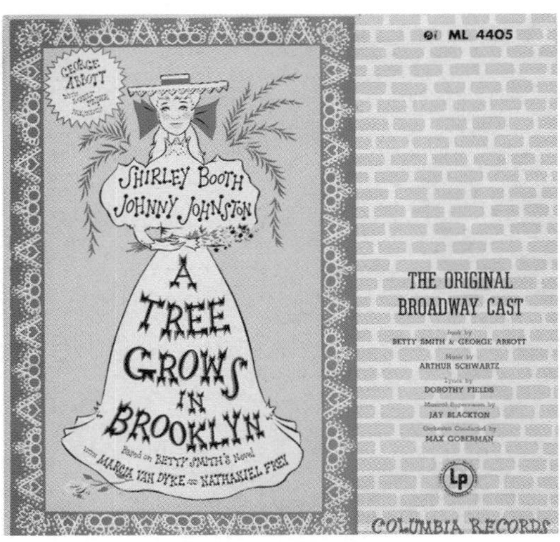


*A Tree Grows in Brooklyn,*
Columbia Masterworks ML 4405, 1951, $30.

## SOUNDS OF THE 1950s

**Most of the biggest albums of the 1950s were by pop vocalists, but they were far from the only albums to be issued. Here's a cross-section of pop and other types of LPs.**

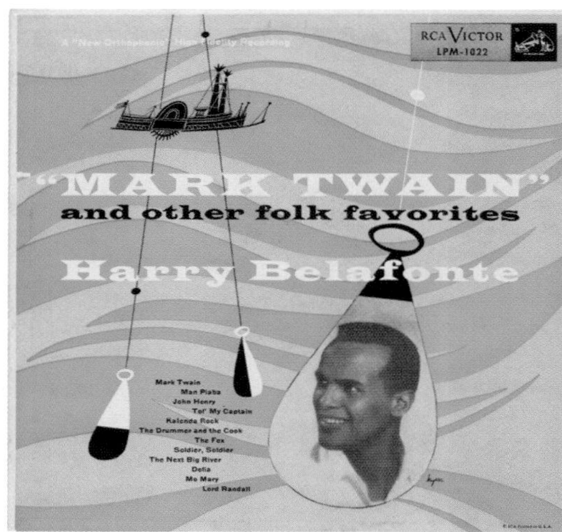


Harry Belafonte, *"Mark Twain" and Other Folk Favorites,* RCA Victor LPM-1022, 1954, mono, $50.

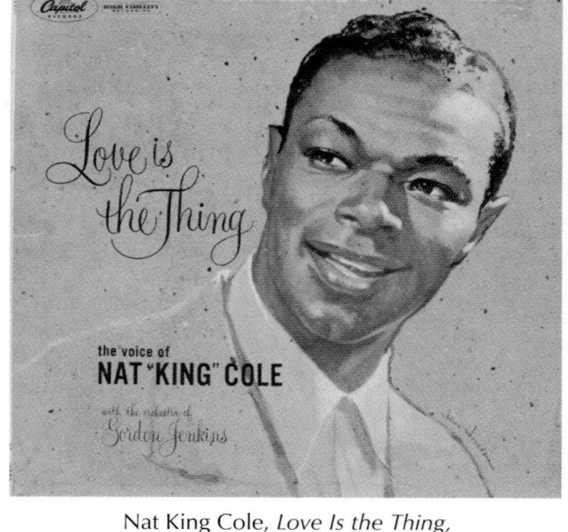


Nat King Cole, *Love Is the Thing,* Capitol W 824, 1957, mono, gray label, $40.

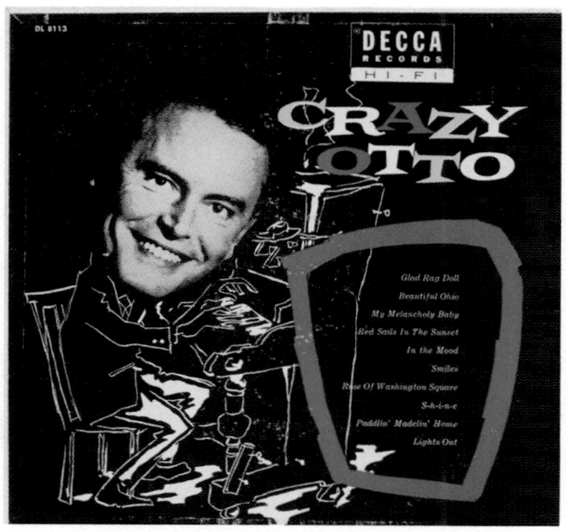


Crazy Otto, *Crazy Otto,* Decca DL 8113, 1955, mono, black label $20, black label with color bars $12.

Bill Doggett, *Everybody Dance the Honky Tonk,* King 395-531, 1958, mono, $50.

Eddie Fisher, *I Love You,* RCA Victor LPM-1097, 1955, $30.

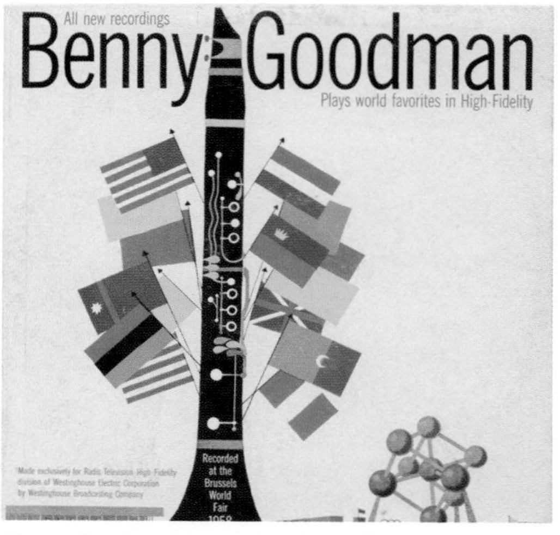


Benny Goodman, *Benny Goodman Plays World Favorites in Hi-Fi,* Westinghouse XTV 27713/4, 1958, mono, $30.

Burl Ives, *The Wayfaring Stranger,*
Columbia CL 628, mono, maroon label, gold print, $30.

Joni James, *Joni James,* MGM E-3346,
mono, yellow label, 1956, $80.

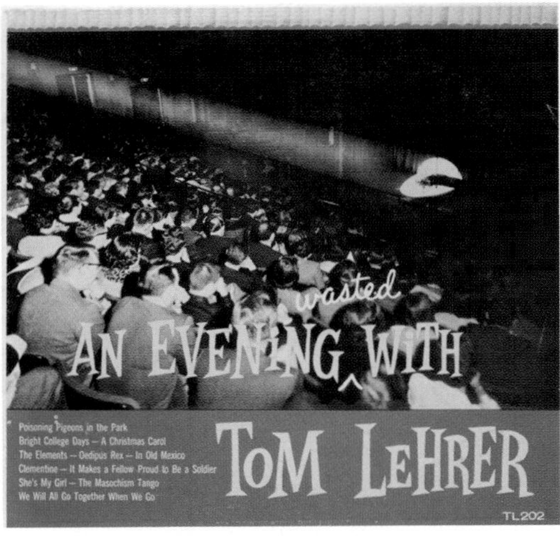


Tom Lehrer, *An Evening Wasted with Tom Lehrer,*
Lehrer TL 202, 1959, mono, $25.

Liberace, *South Pacific,* Columbia
CL 1118, 1957, mono, $30.

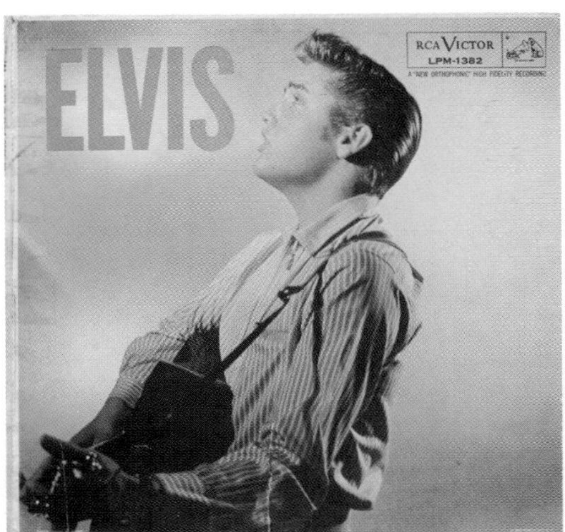


Elvis Presley, *Elvis,* RCA Victor LPM-1382, 1956, mono, $300-$800
depending on certain characteristics; see listings for more details.

Frank Sinatra, *Swing Easy/Songs for Young Lovers,*
Capitol W 587, 1955, mono, gray label, $40.

## SOUNDS OF THE 1960s

**Almost literally, there was something for everyone in the music of the 1960s. Some of the many examples are on the next two pages.**

Big Brother and the Holding Company, *Cheap Thrills,* Columbia KCS 9700, 1968, stereo, red "360 Sound" label, $25.

Glen Campbell, *A New Place in the Sun,* Capitol ST 2907, 1968, stereo, $15.

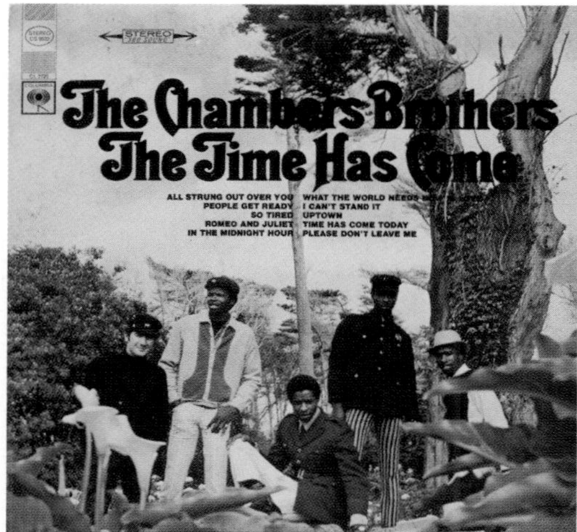


The Chambers Brothers, *The Time Has Come,* Columbia CS 9522, 1967, stereo, red "360 Sound" label, $20.

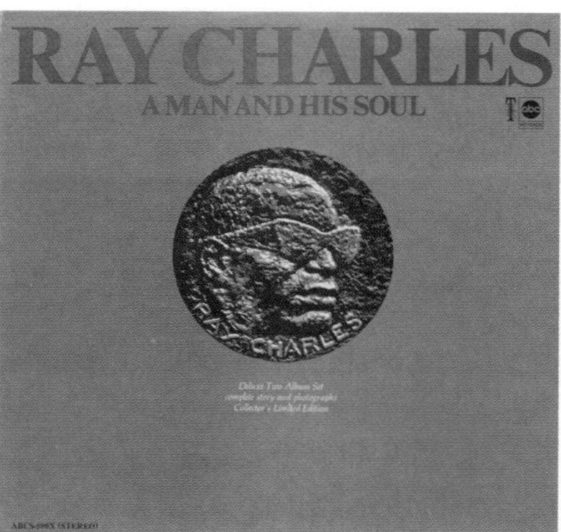


Ray Charles, *A Man and His Soul,* ABC ABCS-590X, 2 records, 1967, stereo, $20.

Four Tops, *Reach Out,* Motown MS 660, 1967, stereo, $25.

Jefferson Airplane, *Surrealistic Pillow,* RCA Victor LPM-3766, 1967, mono, $60.

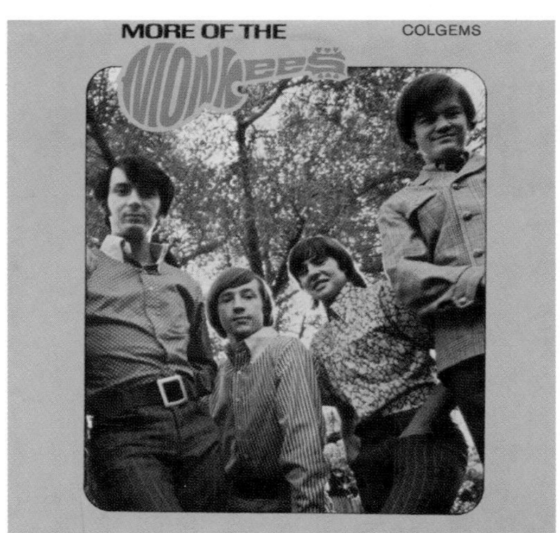


The Monkees, *More of the Monkees,* Colgems COM-102, 1966, mono, $20.

The Rolling Stones, *Through the Past, Darkly,* London NPS-3, 1969, hexagonal cover, $10.

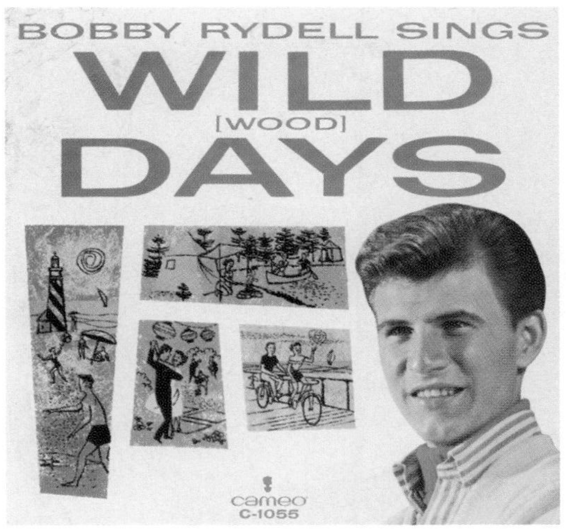


Bobby Rydell, *Wild (Wood) Days,* Cameo C-1055, 1963, mono, $20.

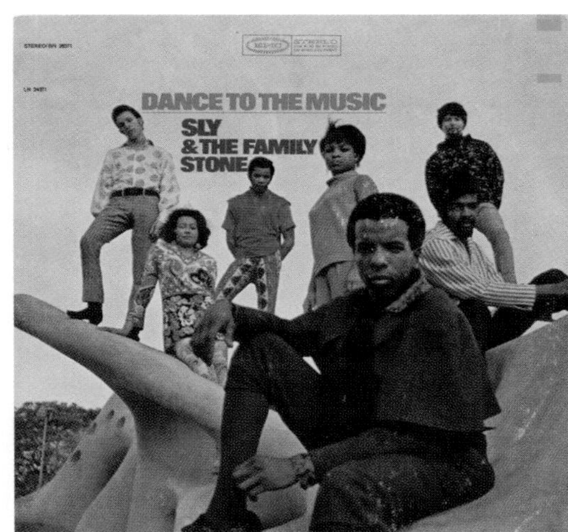


Sly and the Family Stone, *Dance to the Music,* Epic BN 26371, 1968, stereo, yellow label, $15.

Joanie Sommers, *Johnny Get Angry,* Warner Bros. W 1470, 1962, mono, $40.

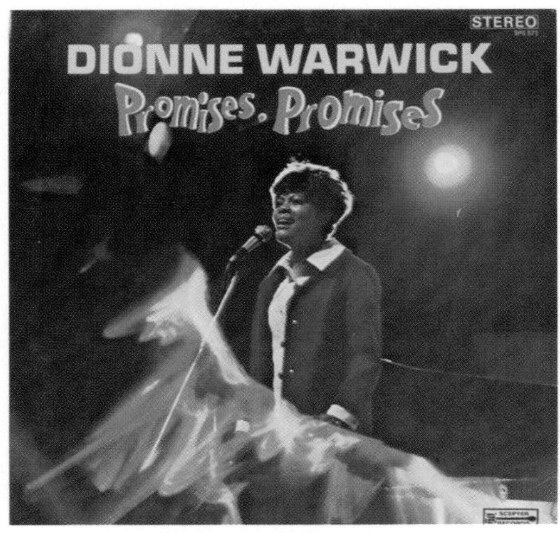


Dionne Warwick, *Promises, Promises,* Scepter SPS 571, 1968, stereo, $15.

## SOUNDS OF THE 1970s

**Here is a sampling of both common and collectible albums from a diverse musical decade.**

The Average White Band,
*Show Your Hand,* MCA 345, 1973, $25.

Brownsville Station, *Brownsville Station,*
Palladium P-1004, 1970, $30.

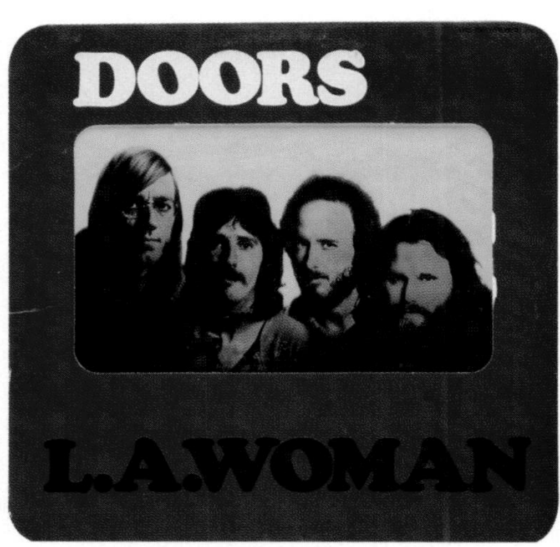


The Doors, *L.A. Woman,* Elektra EKS-75011, 1971, butterfly label, cover has rounded corners, cellophane window and original yellow inner sleeve, $50.

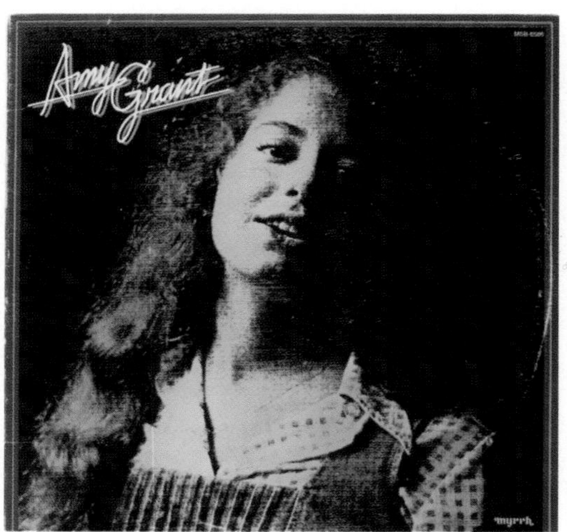


Amy Grant, *Amy Grant,* Myrrh MSB-6586,
1977, original "ugly cover," $25.

The Jackson Five, *ABC,* Motown MS 709, 1970, $25.

Elton John, *Goodbye Yellow Brick Road,*
MCA 2-10003, 1973, 2-record set, $15.

Led Zeppelin, *Houses of the Holy,* Atlantic SD 7255, 1973, $15.

John Lennon, *Walls and Bridges,* Apple SW-3416, 1973, with segmented front cover, $20.

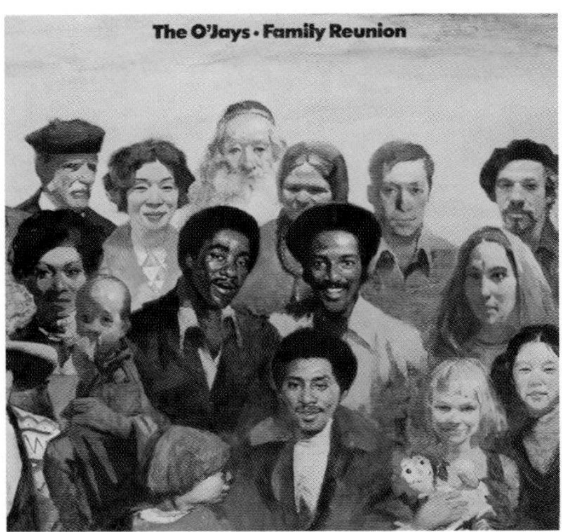


The O'Jays, *Family Reunion,* Philadelphia International PZ 33807, 1975, no bar code on cover, $10.

Queen, *Queen,* Elektra EKS-75064, 1973, butterfly label, "Queen" embossed in gold on cover, $30.

Diana Ross, *Touch Me in the Morning,* Motown M772L, 1973, $15.

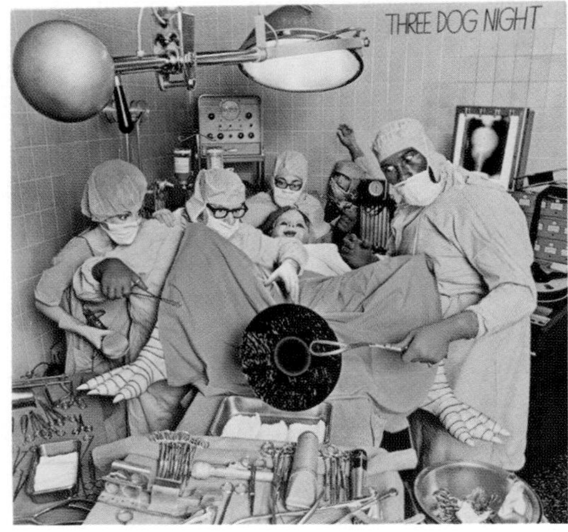


Three Dog Night, *Hard Labor,* ABC-Dunhill DSD 50168, 1974, with uncensored "childbirth" cover, $30.

## BEACH BOYS ALBUMS

**The Beach Boys are one of the most collectible groups in the world. Here is a cross-section of some of their LP covers.**

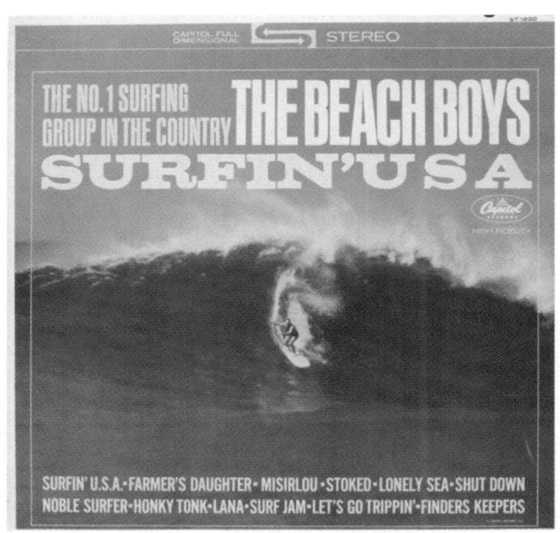


*Surfin' U.S.A.,* Capitol ST 1890, 1963, stereo, $50.

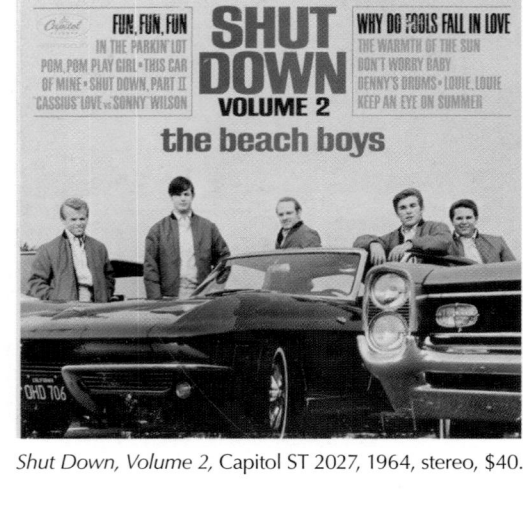

*Shut Down, Volume 2,* Capitol ST 2027, 1964, stereo, $40.

*Beach Boys Concert,* Capitol TAO 2198, 1964, mono, with bound-in booklet, $30.

*Smiley Smile,* Brother ST 9001, 1967, stereo, no mention of Barry Turnbull on back cover, $20.

*Friends,* Capitol ST 2895, 1968, stereo, $20.

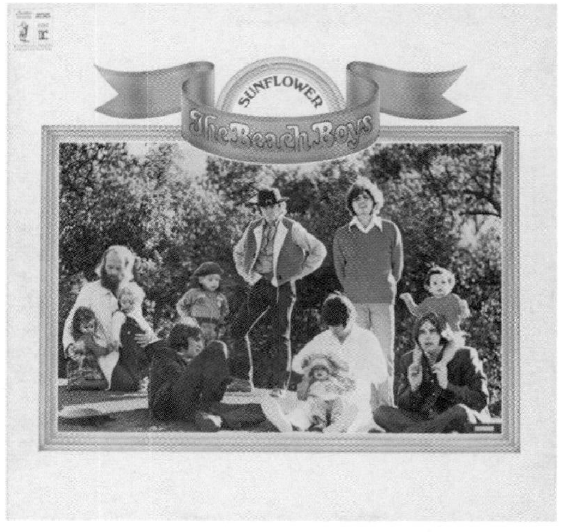


*Sunflower,* Brother/Reprise RS 6382, 1970, $25.

*Good Vibrations – Best of the Beach Boys,*
Brother/Reprise MS 2223, 1975, $12.

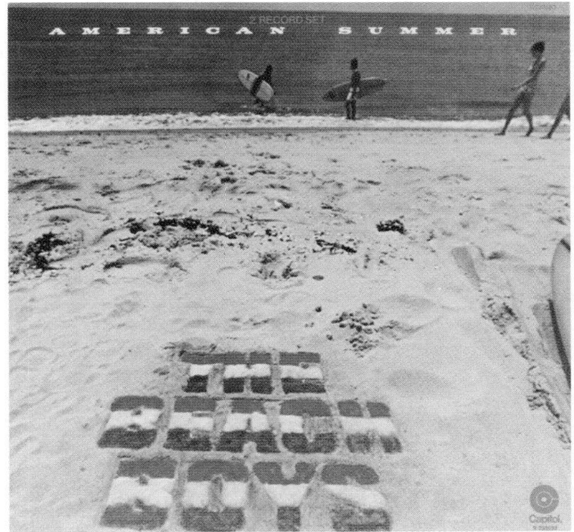


*American Summer,* Capitol R233593, 1975,
2-record set, RCA Music Service exclusive, $25.

*The Beach Boys Love You,*
Brother/Reprise MSK 2258, 1977, $12.

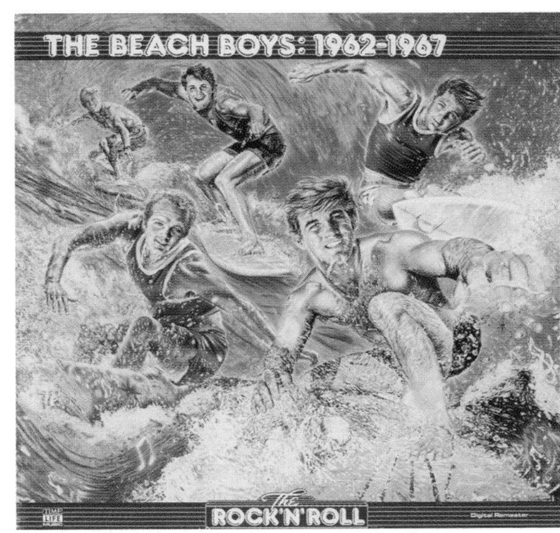


*The Beach Boys: 1962-1967,* Time-Life SRNR 03, 1986, boxed
2-record set, original cover with the group on surfboards, $25.

*Still Cruisin',* Capitol C1-92639, 1989, $12.

*Lost & Found!,* Sundazed LP 5005, 1991, gold vinyl, $12.

## SOUNDS OF THE 1980s

**The 1980s were the last decade when vinyl was commonly available at average retail stores, and the prices of most of the LPs of the period reflect that.**

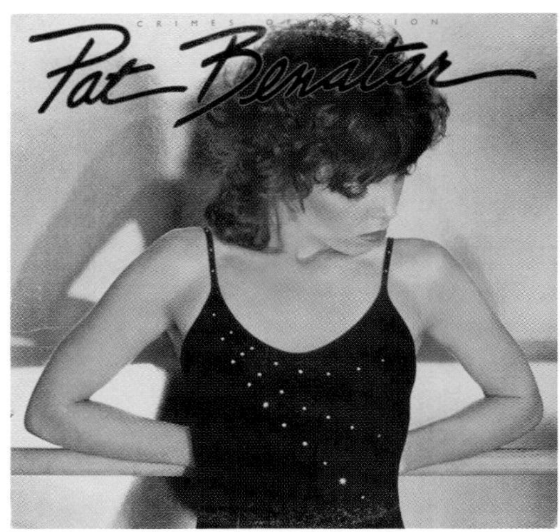


Pat Benatar, *Crimes of Passion,* Chrysalis CHE 1275, 1980, with blue label, $8; with white label, $30.

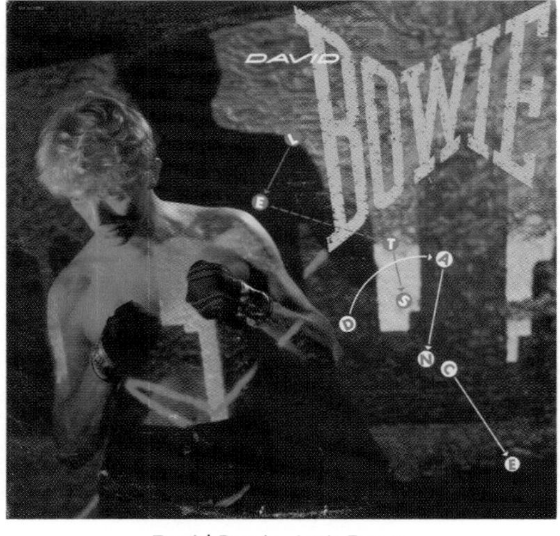


David Bowie, *Let's Dance,* EMI America SO-17093, 1983, $10.

Jimmy Buffett, *Last Mango in Paris,* MCA 5600, 1985, $10.

George Harrison, *Gone Troppo,* Dark Horse 23734, 1982, "Quiex II" promo version, $25.

Husker Du, *Candy Apple Grey,* Warner Bros. 25385, 1986, $12.

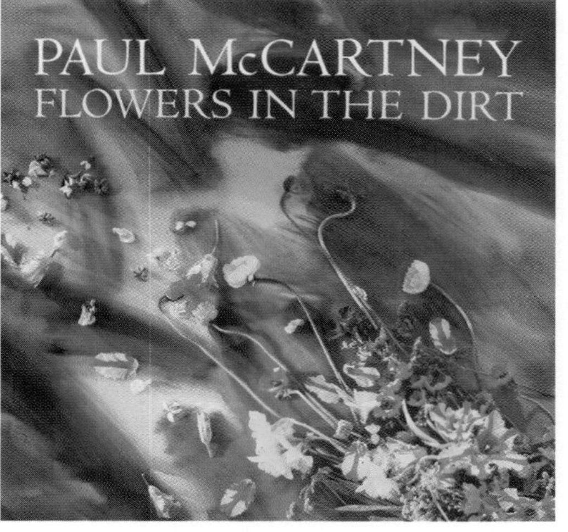


Paul McCartney, *Flowers in the Dirt,* Capitol C1-91653, 1989, $20.

Motley Crue, *Theatre of Pain,* Elektra 60418, 1985, $8.

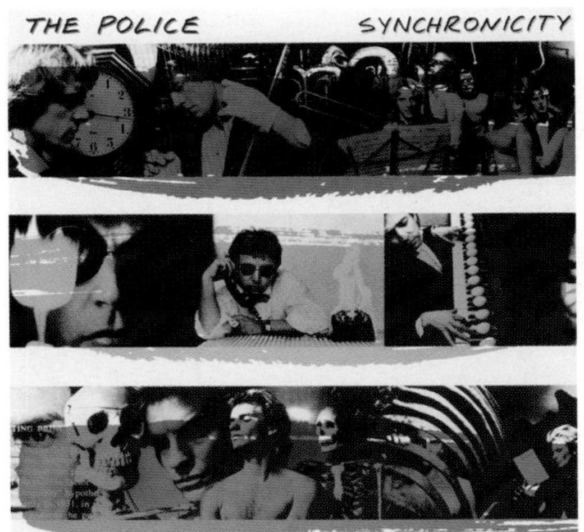

The Police, *Synchronicity,* A&M SP-3735, 1983, with gold, silver and bronze stripes on cover, $40.

R.E.M., *Green,* Warner Bros. 25795, 1989, $12.

Scorpions, *Love at First Sting,*
Mercury 814 981-1, 1984, first cover, $10.

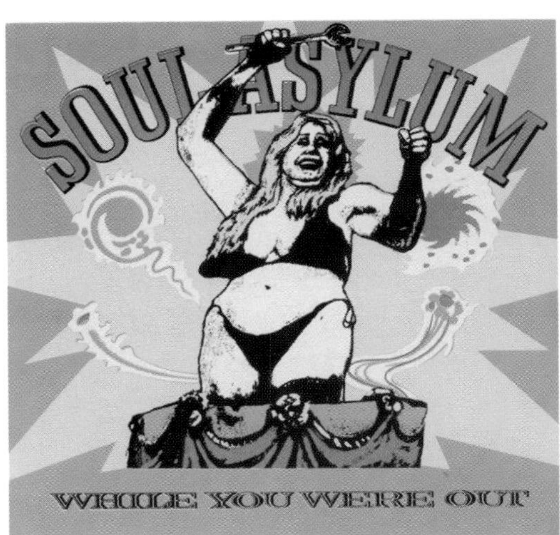

Soul Asylum, *While You Were Out,*
Twin/Tone TTR 8691, 1986, $15.

XTC, *Oranges and Lemons,*
Geffen GHS 24218, 1989, 2-record set, $15.

## SOUNDS OF THE 1990s

**Vinyl albums all but disappeared from regular retail stores in the 1990s as U.S. record labels stopped making them routinely. As a result, many LPs from the decade are hard to find.**

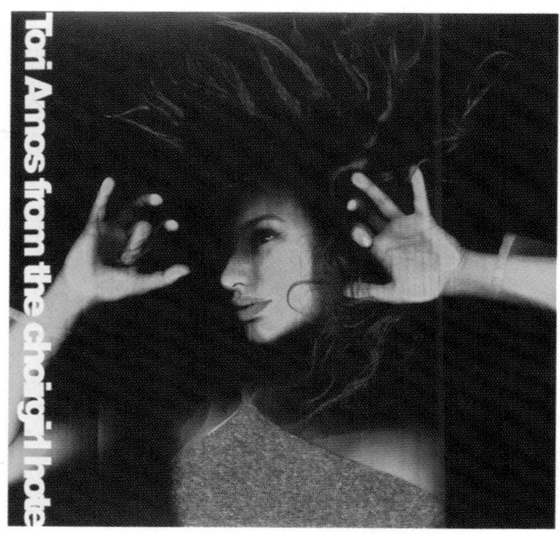


Tori Amos, *From the Choirgirl Hotel,* Atlantic 83095, 1998, 2 records, $25.

Tony Bennett,. *Bennett Sings Ellington Hot & Cool,* Columbia C 63668, 1999, $12.

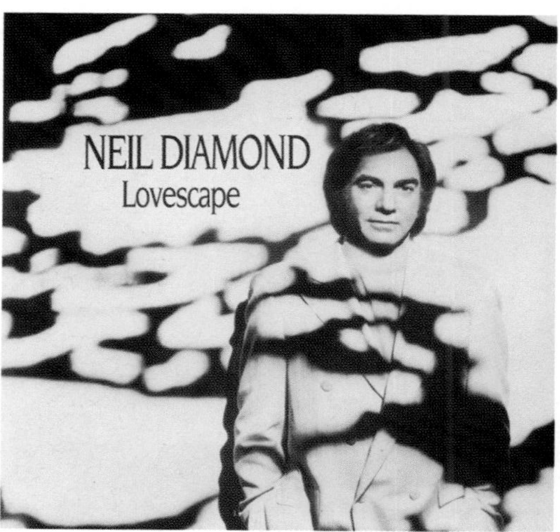


Neil Diamond, *Lovescape,* Columbia C 48610, 1991, $25.

Hammer, *The Funky Headhunter,* Giant PRO-A-6798, 1994, 2 records, promo only, $20.

Jewel, *Pieces of You,* Atlantic 82700, 1996, 2 records, $25.

John Mellencamp, *John Mellencamp,* Columbia C 69602, 1998, $15.

Dolly Parton, *Eagle When She Flies,* Columbia C 46682, 1991, Columbia House exclusive, $20.

The Simpsons, *The Simpsons Sing the Blues,* Geffen GHS 24308, 1990, $25.

Bruce Springsteen, *18 Tracks,* Columbia C2 69476, 1999, 2 records, $15.

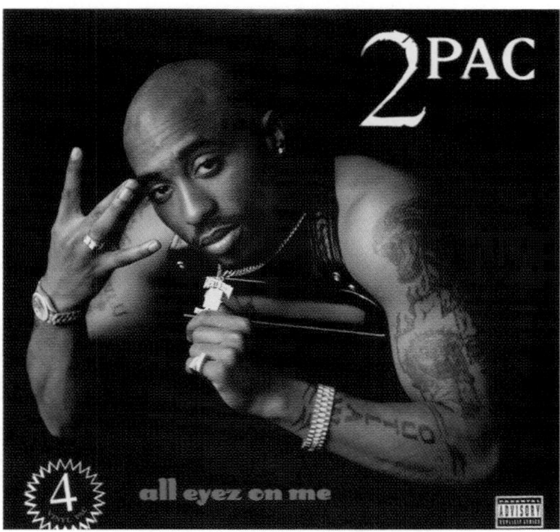


2Pac, *All Eyez on Me,* Death Row/Interscope 314-524 204-1, 1996, 4 records, original edition, $30.

Wilco, *A.M.,* Sire 45857, 1995, red vinyl, $80.

Neil Young and Crazy Horse, *Sleeps with Angels,* Reprise 45749, 1994, 2 records, $25.

## SOUNDS OF THE 2000s

**On the next two pages is a mere sampling of the new American vinyl releases from years starting with the number "2." Many of these are from 2006 and 2007.**

Big Star, *In Space,* DBK Works DBK-115, 2005, $15.

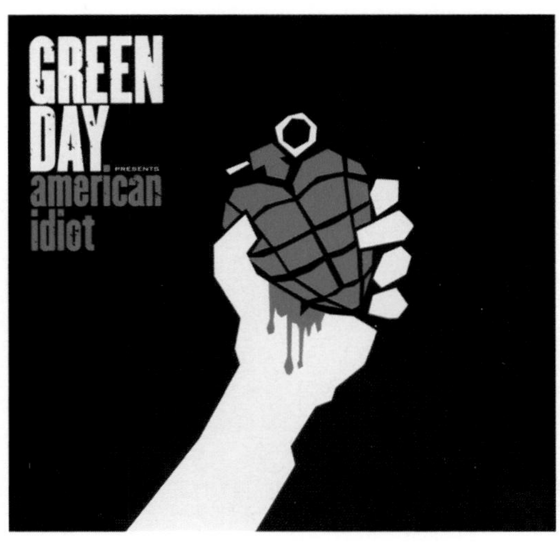


Green Day, *American Idiot,* Adeline AR 033, 2006, 2 records, $30.

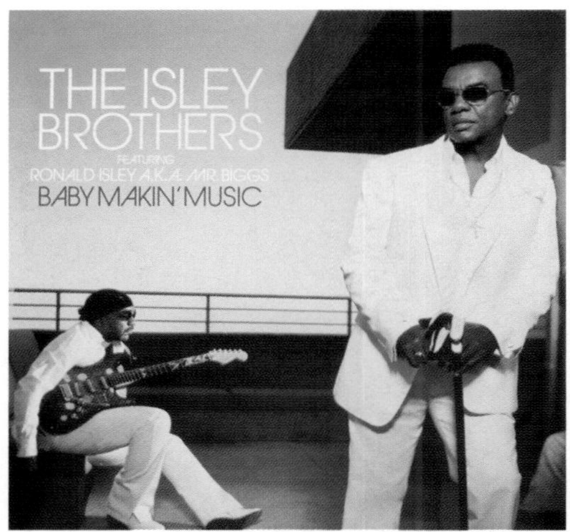


The Isley Brothers, *Baby Makin' Music,* Def Soul B0004812-01, 2006, 2 records, $15.

Meat Loaf, *Bat Out of Hell III: The Monster Is Loose,* Virgin 0946 3 63147 1 6, 2006, 2 records, $20.

Pearl Jam, *Pearl Jam,* J 82876-71467-1, 2006, 2 records, with book, numbers nowhere on sleeve or records except in the trail-off wax, $20.

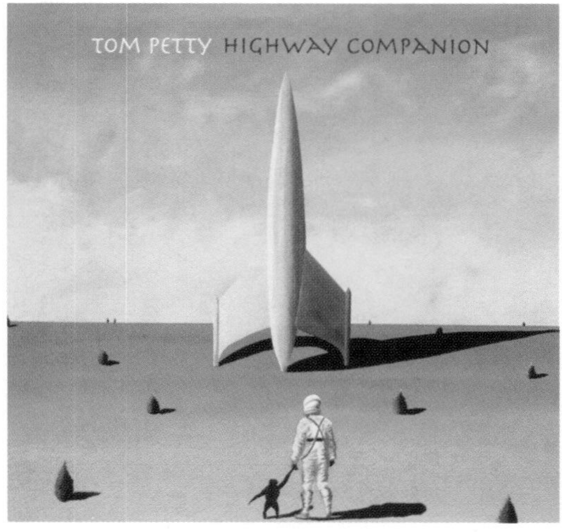


Tom Petty, *Highway Companion,* American 44285, 2007, 2 records, $25.

Red Hot Chili Peppers, *Stadium Arcadium,* Warner Bros. 49996, 2006, 4 records, 180-gram boxed set, $80.

Paul Simon, *Surprise,* Warner Bros. 49982, 2006, $15.

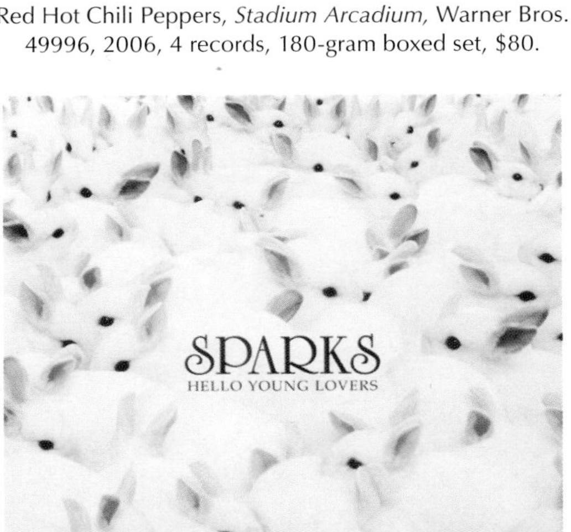


Sparks, Hello *Young Lovers,*
In the Red ITR 131, 2006, $12.

Tool, *Lateralus,* Volcano
31160-1, 2006, 2 records, $40.

Brian Wilson, *Gettin' In Over My Head,*
Rhino R1-76471, 2004, $20.

Soundtrack, *Masked and Anonymous,*
Columbia CSK 90618-1, 2006, $30.

## BEE GEES ALBUMS

**Here is a selection of the Bee Gees' American vinyl albums, which came out from 1967 through 1989.**

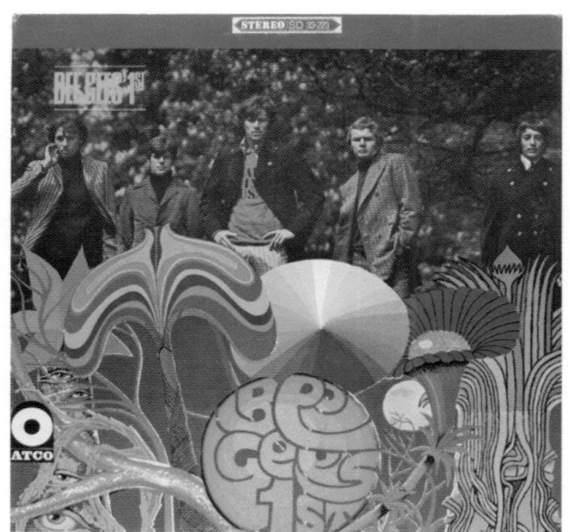


*Bee Gees' 1st,* Atco SD 33-223, 1967, stereo, brown and purple label, $20.

*Horizontal,* Atco 33-233, 1967, mono, $30.

*Cucumber Castle,* Atco SD 33-327, 1970, $12.

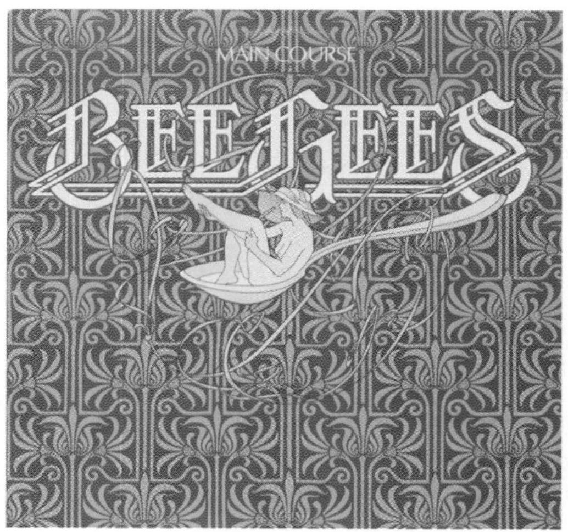


*Main Course,* RSO SO 4807, 1975, $10.

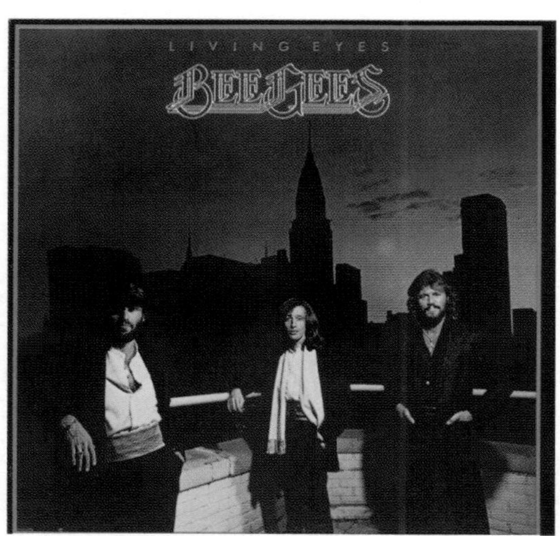


*Living Eyes,* RSO RX-1-3098, 1981, $10.

*One,* Warner Bros. 25887, 1989, $12.

**KIT KATS, THE**

JAMIE
❑ LPM-3029 [M] It's Just a Matter of Time 1966 25.00
❑ LPS-3029 [S] It's Just a Matter of Time 1966 30.00
❑ LPM-3032 [M] The Kit Kats Do Their Thing — Live! 1967 30.00
❑ LPS-3032 [S] The Kit Kats Do Their Thing — Live! 1967 40.00
❑ JLPS-3034 To Understand Is to Love 1970 30.00
*—As "New Hope"*

**KITAEV, ANDREI, AND BILL DOUGLASS**

REFERENCE RECORDINGS
❑ RR-6 First Takes 198? 20.00

**KITCHEN CINQ, THE**

LHI
❑ E-12000 [M] Everything But the Kitchen Cinq 1967 30.00
❑ E7-12000 [S] Everything But the Kitchen Cinq 1967 40.00

**KITT, EARTHA**

CAEDMON
❑ TC-1267 Folk Tales of the Tribes of Africa 1969 20.00

DECCA
❑ DL 4635 [M] Eartha Kitt Sings in Spanish 1965 30.00
❑ DL 74635 [S] Eartha Kitt Sings in Spanish 1965 40.00

GNP CRESCENDO
❑ GNP-2008 [M] At the Plaza 1965 15.00
❑ GNPS-2008 [S] At the Plaza 1965 20.00

KAPP
❑ KL-1162 [M] The Fabulous Eartha Kitt 1959 25.00
❑ KL-1192 [M] Eartha Kitt Revisited 1960 25.00
❑ KS-3046 [S] The Fabulous Eartha Kitt 1959 30.00
❑ KS-3192 [S] Eartha Kitt Revisited 1960 30.00

MGM
❑ E-4009 [M] Bad But Beautiful 1962 25.00
❑ SE-4009 [S] Bad But Beautiful 1962 30.00

RCA VICTOR
❑ LPM-1109 [M] Down to Eartha 1955 50.00
❑ LPM-1153 [M] That Bad Eartha 1955 50.00
❑ LPM-1300 [M] Thursday's Child 1956 50.00
❑ LPM-1661 [M] St. Louis Blues 1958 40.00
❑ LSP-1661 [S] St. Louis Blues 1958 50.00
❑ LPM-3062 [10] RCA Victor Presents Eartha Kitt 1953 80.00
❑ LPM-3187 [10] That Bad Eartha 1953 80.00

STANYAN
❑ SR-10037 Best of All Possible Worlds 1972 15.00
❑ SR-10040 For Always 1975 15.00

SUNNYVIEW
❑ SUN-4902 I Love Men 1984 10.00

**KLARK KENT** Stewart Copeland of THE POLICE in disguise.

KRYPTONE/I.R.S.
❑ SP 70600 [EP] Music Madness from the Kinetic Kid 1980 20.00
*—Green vinyl 10" in die-cut 12" sleeve*

**KLEMMER, JOHN**

CADET
❑ CA-797 [S] Involvement 197? 15.00
*—Pink and yellow label reissue*
❑ LP 797 [M] Involvement 1967 40.00
❑ LPS 797 [S] Involvement 1967 20.00
*—Fading blue label*
❑ LPS 808 And We Were Lovers 1968 20.00

CADET CONCEPT
❑ LPS 321 Blowin' Gold 1969 30.00
❑ LPS 326 All the Children Cried 1970 20.00
❑ LPS 330 Eruptions 1971 20.00

MCA
❑ 1654 Touch 198? 8.00
*—Reissue of MCA 37152*

MOBILE FIDELITY
❑ 1-006 Touch 1979 30.00
*—"Original Master Recording" at top of front cover; audiophile vinyl*

NAUTILUS
❑ NR-4 Straight from the Heart 1980 80.00
*—"Super Disc" audiophile vinyl*
❑ NR-22 Finesse 1981 80.00
*—"SuperDisc" audiophile vinyl*

**KLEMMER, JOHN, AND EDDIE HARRIS**

CRUSADERS
❑ 16015 Two Tone 1982 30.00
*—Part of MCA's "Audiophile Series"*

**KLINK, AL/BOB ALEXANDER**

GRAND AWARD
❑ GA 33-525 [M] Progressive Jazz 1956 30.00
*—Without removable outer cover*
❑ GA 33-525 [M] Progressive Jazz 1956 80.00
*—With removable outer cover*

Number | Title (A Side/B Side) | Yr | NM

**KLOSS, ERIC**

COBBLESTONE
❑ 9006 Doors 1972 20.00

PRESTIGE
❑ PRLP-7442 [M] Introducing Eric Kloss 1966 20.00
❑ PRST-7442 [S] Introducing Eric Kloss 1966 25.00
❑ PRLP-7469 [M] Love and All That Jazz 1966 20.00
❑ PRST-7469 [S] Love and All That Jazz 1966 25.00
❑ PRLP-7486 [M] Grits & Gravy 1967 25.00
❑ PRST-7486 [S] Grits & Gravy 1967 20.00
❑ PRLP-7520 [M] First Class Kloss 1967 30.00
❑ PRST-7520 [S] First Class Kloss 1967 20.00
❑ PRST-7535 Life Force 1968 20.00

**KLUGH, EARL**

MOBILE FIDELITY
❑ 1-025 Finger Paintings 1979 30.00
*—Audiophile vinyl*
❑ UHQR 1-025 Finger Paintings 1982 120.00
*—"Ultra High Quality" audiophile vinyl in box*
❑ 1-076 Late Night Guitar 1981 50.00
*—Audiophile vinyl*

NAUTILUS
❑ NR-46 Crazy for You 198? 40.00
*—Audiophile vinyl*

**KNEPPER, JIMMY**

BETHLEHEM
❑ BCP-77 [M] A Swinging Introduction to Jimmy Knepper 1957 60.00

**KNICKERBOCKERS, THE**

CHALLENGE
❑ CH-621 [M] Jerk and Twine Time 1965 400.00
❑ CH-622 [M] Lies 1966 100.00
❑ CHS-622 [S] Lies 1966 200.00
❑ LP-12664 [M] Llyod Thaxton Presents the Knickerbockers 1965 200.00

SUNDAZED
❑ LP-5000 The Great Lost Knickerbockers Album 1990 12.00
*—Blue vinyl*
❑ LP-5154 Rockin' with the Knickerbockers 2003 12.00

**KNIGHT, CHRIS, AND MAUREEN MCCORMICK** Also see THE BRADY BUNCH.

PARAMOUNT
❑ PAS-6062 Chris Knight and Maureen McCormick 1973 120.00

**KNIGHT, FREDERICK**

STAX
❑ STS-3011 I've Been Lonely So Long 1973 20.00

**KNIGHT, GLADYS, AND THE PIPS**

ACCORD
❑ SN-7103 Every Beat of My Heart 1981 10.00
❑ SN-7105 Letter Full of Tears 1981 10.00
❑ SN-7131 I Feel a Song 1981 10.00
❑ SN-7188 It's Showtime 1982 10.00

ALLEGIANCE
❑ AV-5002 Glad to Be... 198? 10.00

BELL
❑ 1323 In the Beginning 1975 12.00
❑ 6013 Tastiest Hits 1968 20.00

BUDDAH
❑ BDS-5141 Imagination 1973 12.00
❑ BDS-5602 Claudine 1974 30.00
❑ BDS-5612 I Feel a Song 1974 12.00
❑ BDS-5639 2nd Anniversary 1975 12.00
❑ BDS-5653 The Best of Gladys Knight & The Pips 1976 12.00
❑ BDS-5676 Pipe Dreams 1976 12.00
❑ BDS-5689 Still Together 1977 12.00
❑ BDS-5701 The One and Only 1978 12.00
❑ BDS-5714 Miss Gladys Knight 1978 12.00

CASABLANCA
❑ NBLP 7081 At Last...The Pips 1977 10.00
*—As "The Pips"*
❑ NBLP 7113 Callin' 1978 10.00
*—As "The Pips"*

COLLECTABLES
❑ COL-5154 Golden Classics: Letter Full of Tears 198? 10.00

COLUMBIA
❑ JC 35704 Gladys Knight 1979 10.00
❑ PC 35704 Gladys Knight 198? 8.00
*—Budget-line reissue*
❑ JC 36387 About Love 1980 10.00
❑ PC 36387 About Love 198? 8.00
*—Budget-line reissue*
❑ FC 37086 Touch 1981 10.00

Number | Title (A Side/B Side) | Yr | NM

❑ PC 37086 Touch 198? 8.00
*—Budget-line reissue*
❑ FC 38114 That Special Time of Year 1982 10.00
❑ PC 38114 That Special Time of Year 1983 8.00
*—Same as above with new prefix*
❑ FC 38205 Visions 1983 10.00
❑ PC 38205 Visions 198? 8.00
*—Budget-line reissue*
❑ FC 39423 Life 1985 10.00
❑ PC 39423 Life 198? 8.00
*—Budget-line reissue*
❑ FC 40376 Greatest Hits 1986 10.00
❑ FC 40878 The Best of Gladys Knight and the Pips/The Columbia Years 1988 10.00

FURY
❑ 1003 [M] Letter Full of Tears 1962 500.00

LOST-NITE
❑ LLP-17 [10] The Best of Gladys Knight and the Pips 1981 12.00
*—Red vinyl*

MAXX
❑ 3000 [M] Gladys Knight and the Pips 1964 150.00

MCA
❑ 10329 Good Woman 1991 15.00
❑ 42004 All Our Love 1987 10.00

MOTOWN
❑ M5-113V Motown Superstar Series, Vol. 13 1981 10.00
❑ M5-126V1 Everybody Needs Love 1981 12.00
*—Reissue of Soul 706*
❑ M5-148V1 Nitty Gritty 1981 12.00
*—Reissue of Soul 713*
❑ M5-193V1 Neither One of Us 1981 12.00
*—Reissue of Soul 737*
❑ M 792S2 [(2)] Anthology 1974 15.00
❑ MOT 5303 All the Great Hits of Gladys Knight and the Pips 198? 8.00

NATURAL RESOURCES
❑ NR 4004T1 Silk N' Soul 1978 10.00
*—Reissue of Soul 711*

PAIR
❑ PDL2-1198 The Best of Gladys Knight and the Pips 1987 12.00

PICKWICK
❑ SPC-3349 Every Beat of My Heart 197? 10.00

SOUL
❑ S 706 [M] Everybody Needs Love 1967 20.00
❑ SS 706 [S] Everybody Needs Love 1967 25.00
❑ S 707 [M] Feelin' Bluesy 1968 40.00
*—Mono copies are white label promo only; cover has "Monaural Record DJ Copy" sticker*
❑ SS 707 [S] Feelin' Bluesy 1968 25.00
❑ SS 711 Silk N' Soul 1968 25.00
❑ SS 713 Nitty Gritty 1969 25.00
❑ SS 723 Gladys Knight and the Pips Greatest Hits 1970 15.00
❑ SS 730 All in a Knight's Work 1970 15.00
❑ SS 731 If I Were Your Woman 1971 15.00
❑ S 736L Standing Ovation 1971 15.00
❑ S 737L Neither One of Us 1973 15.00
❑ S 739L All I Need Is Time 1973 15.00
❑ S 741 Knight Time 1974 12.00
❑ S 744 A Little Knight Music 1975 12.00

SPHERE SOUND
❑ SR-7006 [M] Gladys Knight and the Pips 196? 200.00
❑ SSR-7006 [R] Gladys Knight and the Pips 196? 120.00

SPRINGBOARD
❑ SPB-4035 Early Hits 1972 10.00
❑ SPB-4050 How Do You Say Goodbye 1973 10.00

TRIP
❑ TLP-9509 It Hurt Me So Bad 1973 10.00

UNITED ARTISTS
❑ UA-LA503-E The Very Best of Gladys Knight and the Pips 1975 12.00

UPFRONT
❑ UPF 130 Gladys Knight and the Pips 197? 10.00
❑ UPF 185 Gladys Knight and the Pips 197? 10.00

VEE JAY
❑ D1-74796 Every Beat of My Heart: The Greatest Hits of the Early Years 1989 15.00

**KNIGHT, JEAN**

COTILLION
❑ SD 5230 Jean Knight and Premium 1981 15.00

MIRAGE
❑ 90282 My Toot Toot 1985 10.00

STAX
❑ STS-2045 Mr. Big Stuff 1971 40.00
❑ MPS-8554 Mr. Big Stuff 198? 10.00

Number | Title (A Side/B Side) | Yr | NM

**KNIGHT, ROBERT**

RISING SONS
❑ RSM-7000 [M] Everlasting Love 1967 30.00
❑ RSS-17000 [S] Everlasting Love 1967 40.00

**KNIGHT, SONNY**

AURA
❑ AR-3001 [M] If You Want This Love 1964 25.00
❑ AS-3001 [S] If You Want This Love 1964 30.00

**KNIGHT, TED**

RANWOOD
❑ R-8149 Hi Guys! 1976 20.00

**KNIGHT, TERRY, AND THE PACK**

ABKCO
❑ AB-4217 [(2)] Mark, Don and Terry 1966-67 1972 20.00

CAMEO
❑ C 2007 [M] Reflections 1967 20.00
*—Reissue of Lucky Eleven LE-8001*
❑ CS 2007 [S] Reflections 1967 25.00
*—Reissue of Lucky Eleven LES-8001*

LUCKY ELEVEN
❑ LE-8000 [M] Terry Knight and the Pack 1966 40.00
❑ LES-8000 [R] Terry Knight and the Pack 1966 25.00
❑ LE-8001 [M] Reflections 1967 25.00
❑ LES-8001 [S] Reflections 1967 40.00

**KNIGHTS, THE** At least two, and possibly three, different groups.

ACE
❑ 4763 Cold Days, Hot Knights 196? 400.00
❑ 200854 Across the Board 1966 400.00
❑ 201302 The Knights 1967 1967 400.00

CAPITOL
❑ DT 2189 [R] Hot Rod High 1964 400.00
❑ T 2189 [M] Hot Rod High 1964 400.00

JUSTICE
❑ JLP-156 On the Move 196? 300.00

**KNOCKOUTS, THE (1)**

TRIBUTE
❑ 1202 [M] Go Ape with the Knockouts 1964 200.00

**KNOPF, PAUL**

PLAYBACK
❑ PLP-500 [M] The Outcat 1959 40.00
❑ PLP-500ST [S] The Outcat 1959 50.00
❑ PLP-501 [M] Enigma of a Day 1959 40.00
❑ PLP-501ST [S] Enigma of a Day 1959 50.00
❑ PLP-502 [M] And the Walls Came Tumbling Down 1960 40.00
❑ PLP-502ST [S] And the Walls Came Tumbling Down 1960 50.00
❑ PLP-503 [M] Paul Knoft Trio 1960 40.00
❑ PLP-503ST [S] Paul Knoft Trio 1960 50.00
❑ PLP-600 [M] Music from the Morgue 1961 40.00
❑ PLP-600ST [S] Music from the Morgue 1961 50.00

**KNOWBODY ELSE** Members were later in BLACK OAK ARKANSAS.

HIP
❑ HIS-7003 Knowbody Else 1969 40.00

**KNOX, BUDDY**

ACCORD
❑ SN-7218 Party Doll and Other Hits 1981 10.00

LIBERTY
❑ LRP-3251 [M] Buddy Knox's Golden Hits 1962 30.00
❑ LST-7251 [S] Buddy Knox's Golden Hits 1962 40.00

ROULETTE
❑ R 25003 [M] Buddy Knox 1957 150.00
*—Black label, red and silver print*
❑ R 25003 [M] Buddy Knox 1957 200.00
*—Black label, all silver print (original)*
❑ R 25003 [M] Buddy Knox 1959 100.00
*—White label with colored spokes*
❑ R 25048 [M] Buddy Knox and Jimmy Bowen 1959 100.00
*—White label with colored spokes*
❑ R 25048 [M] Buddy Knox and Jimmy Bowen 1959 200.00
*—Black label, red and silver print*

UNITED ARTISTS
❑ UAS 6689 Gypsy Man 1969 25.00

**KOALA, THE**

CAPITOL
❑ SKAO-176 The Koala 1969 60.00

**KODAKS, THE / THE STARLITES**

SPHERE SOUND
❑ SSR-7005 [M] The Kodaks Vs. the Starlites 1965 200.00

**KOERNER, SPIDER JOHN**

ELEKTRA
❑ EKL-290 [M] Spider Blues 1965 20.00
❑ EKS-7290 [S] Spider Blues 1965 25.00

SWEET JANE
❑ SJL-1074 Some American Folksongs Like They Used To 1974 30.00
❑ SJL-5872 Music Is Just a Bunch of Notes 1972 100.00
*—With Willie and the Bumblebees and BONNIE RAITT*

**KOERNER, SPIDER JOHN, AND WILLIE MURPHY**

ELEKTRA
❑ EKS-74041 Running, Jumping, Standing Still 1969 20.00

**KOERNER, RAY AND GLOVER**

AUDIOPHILE
❑ AP-78 [M] Blues, Rags and Hollers 1963 50.00
*—Includes four songs not on the Elektra reissue*

ELEKTRA
❑ EKL-240 [M] Blues, Rags and Hollers 1963 25.00
*—Not issued in stereo on Elektra*
❑ EKL-267 [M] Lots More Blues, Rags and Hollers 1964 20.00
❑ EKL-305 [M] The Return of Koerner, Ray and Glover 1965 20.00
❑ EKS-7267 [S] Lots More Blues, Rags and Hollers 1964 25.00
❑ EKS-7305 [S] The Return of Koerner, Ray and Glover 1965 25.00

**KOFFMAN, MOE**

ASCOT
❑ AM 13001 [M] Moe Koffman Plays for the Teens 1962 20.00
❑ AS 16001 [S] Moe Koffman Plays for the Teens 1962 25.00

JANUS
❑ 7037 Museum Pieces 1978 15.00

JUBILEE
❑ JLP-1037 [M] Cool and Hot Sax 1957 40.00
❑ JLP-1074 [M] The Shepherd Swings Again 1958 40.00
❑ JGS-8009 Moe Koffman Goes Electric 1968 30.00
❑ JGS-8016 Turned On 1968 25.00

KAMA SUTRA
❑ KSBS-2018 Moe's Curried Soul 1970 20.00

UNITED ARTISTS
❑ UAJ-14029 [M] Tales of Koffman 1963 25.00
❑ UAJS-15029 [S] Tales of Koffman 1963 30.00

**KOHLMAN, FREDDIE**

MGM
❑ E-297 [10] New Orleans Now — New Orleans Then 1955 80.00

**KOKI, SAM, AND THE PARADISE ISLANDERS**

KAPP
❑ KL-1321 [M] Surfin' at Waikiki 1963 15.00
❑ KS-3321 [S] Surfin' at Waikiki 1963 20.00

**KOKOMO (1)**

FELSTED
❑ FL 7513 [M] Asia Minor 1961 40.00
❑ FS 17513 [S] Asia Minor 1961 50.00

**KOLE, JERRY, AND THE STRINGERS**

CROWN
❑ CST-385 [S] Hot Rod Alley 1963 40.00
❑ CLP-5385 [M] Hot Rod Alley 1963 30.00

**KOLLER, HANS**

DISCOVERY
❑ DL-2005 [10] Hans Koller 1954 80.00

VANGUARD
❑ VRS-8509 [M] Hans Across the Sea 1956 50.00

**KOLOC, BONNIE**

OVATION
❑ OVQD 14-21 [Q] After All This Time 1971 25.00
❑ OVQD 14-26 [Q] Hold On to Me 1972 25.00
❑ OVQD 14-29 [Q] Bonnie Koloc 1973 25.00
❑ OVQD 14-38 [Q] You're Gonna Love Yourself in the Morning 1974 25.00

**KOMACK, JAMES**

RCA VICTOR
❑ LPM-1501 [M] Inside Me 1957 30.00

**KONITZ, LEE**

ATLANTIC
❑ 1217 [M] Lee Konitz with Warne Marsh 1955 80.00
*—Black label*
❑ 1217 [M] Lee Konitz with Warne Marsh 1961 25.00
*—Multicolor label, white "fan" logo at right*
❑ 1258 [M] Inside Hi-Fi 1957 60.00
*—Black label*
❑ 1258 [M] Inside Hi-Fi 1961 25.00
*—Multicolor label, white "fan" logo at right*
❑ SD 1258 [S] Inside Hi-Fi 1958 60.00
*—Green label*
❑ SD 1258 [S] Inside Hi-Fi 1961 20.00
*—Multicolor label, white "fan" logo at right*
❑ 1273 [M] The Real Lee Konitz 1958 50.00
*—Black label*
❑ 1273 [M] The Real Lee Konitz 1961 25.00
*—Multicolor label, white "fan" logo at right*

GROOVE MERCHANT
❑ GM-3306 Chicago 'n All That Jazz! 1975 20.00

JAZZTONE
❑ J-1275 [M] Jazz at Storyville❑ Jazz at Storyville 1957 40.00

MILESTONE
❑ MSP-9013 The Lee Konitz Duets 1968 20.00
❑ MSP-9025 Peacemeal 1968 20.00
❑ MSP-9038 Spirits 1969 20.00
❑ MSP-9060 Satori 1975 20.00

PRESTIGE
❑ PRLP-116 [10] Lee Konitz — The New Sounds 1951 400.00
❑ PRLP-7004 [M] Lee Konitz Groups 1955 150.00
❑ PRLP-7250 [M] Subconscious-Lee 1962 50.00

ROOST
❑ LP-416 [10] Originalee 1953 200.00

STORYVILLE
❑ STLP-304 [10] Lee Konitz at Storyville 1954 250.00
❑ STLP-313 [10] Konitz 1954 250.00
❑ STLP-323 [10] Lee Konitz in Harvard Square 1955 200.00
❑ STLP-901 [M] Lee Konitz at Storyville 1956 120.00

VERVE
❑ MGVS-6035 [S] An Image — Lee Konitz with Strings 1959 30.00
❑ MGVS-6073 [S] Lee Konitz Meets Jimmy Giuffre 1959 30.00
❑ MGVS-6131 [S] You and Lee 1960 30.00
❑ MGV-8209 [M] Very Cool 1958 50.00
❑ V-8209 [M] Very Cool 1961 25.00
❑ MGV-8281 [M] Tranquility 1958 50.00
❑ V-8281 [M] Tranquility 1961 25.00
❑ MGV-8286 [M] An Image — Lee Konitz with Strings 1958 40.00
❑ V-8286 [M] An Image — Lee Konitz with Strings 1961 25.00
❑ V6-8286 [S] An Image — Lee Konitz with Strings 1961 20.00
❑ MGV-8335 [M] Lee Konitz Meets Jimmy Giuffre 1959 40.00
❑ V-8335 [M] Lee Konitz Meets Jimmy Giuffre 1961 20.00
❑ MGV-8362 [M] You and Lee 1960 40.00
❑ V-8362 [M] You and Lee 1961 20.00
❑ V-8399 [M] Motion 1961 20.00
❑ V6-8399 [S] Motion 1961 25.00

**KONITZ, LEE/MILES DAVIS/TEDDY CHARLES**

NEW JAZZ
❑ NJLP-8295 [M] Ezz-Thetic 1962 50.00
*—Purple label*
❑ NJLP-8295 [M] Ezz-Thetic 1965 25.00
*—Blue label, trident logo at right*

**KOOL AND THE GANG**

DE-LITE
❑ MK-48 [DJ] History of Kool and the Gang 1979 15.00
❑ 2003 Kool and the Gang 1969 25.00
❑ 2008 Live at the Sex Machine 1971 12.00
❑ 2009 The Best of Kool and the Gang 1971 12.00
❑ 2010 Live at PJ's 1971 12.00
❑ 2011 Music Is the Message 1972 12.00
❑ 2012 Good Times 1973 12.00
❑ 2013 Wild and Peaceful 1973 10.00
❑ 2014 Light of Worlds 1974 10.00
❑ 2015 Kool & The Gang Greatest Hits! 1975 10.00
❑ 2016 Spirit of the Boogie 1975 10.00
❑ 2018 Love and Understanding 1976 10.00
❑ 2023 Open Sesame 1976 10.00
❑ 4001 Kool Jazz 1973 10.00
❑ 8502 Something Special 1981 10.00
❑ 8505 As One 1982 10.00
❑ 8508 In the Heart 1983 10.00
❑ 9501 The Force 1978 10.00
❑ 9507 Kool & The Gang Spin Their Top Ten Hits 1978 10.00
❑ 9509 Everybody's Dancin' 1979 10.00
❑ 9513 Ladies Night 1979 10.00
❑ 9518 Celebrate! 1980 10.00
❑ 814351-1 In the Heart 1984 8.00
*—Reissue*
❑ 822534-1 Something Special 1984 8.00
*—Reissue*
❑ 822535-1 As One 1984 8.00
*—Reissue*
❑ 822536-1 Kool & The Gang Spin Their Top Ten Hits 1984 8.00
*—Reissue*
❑ 822537-1 Ladies Night 1984 8.00
*—Reissue*

| Number | Title (A Side/B Side) | Yr | NM |
|---|---|---|---|
| ❑ 822538-1 | Celebrate! | 1984 | 8.00 |
| —Reissue | | | |
| ❑ 822943-1 | Emergency | 1984 | 8.00 |

MERCURY

| Number | Title (A Side/B Side) | Yr | NM |
|---|---|---|---|
| ❑ 830398-1 | Forever | 1986 | 8.00 |
| ❑ 834780-1 | Everything's Kool & the Gang: Greatest Hits & More | 1988 | 8.00 |
| ❑ 838233-1 | Sweat | 1989 | 8.00 |

**KOOPER, AL** Also see BLOOD, SWEAT AND TEARS; MIKE BLOOMFIELD; THE BLUES PROJECT.

COLUMBIA

| Number | Title (A Side/B Side) | Yr | NM |
|---|---|---|---|
| ❑ CS 9718 | I Stand Alone | 1969 | 15.00 |
| —"360 Sound" label | | | |
| ❑ CS 9718 | I Stand Alone | 1970 | 10.00 |
| —Orange label | | | |
| ❑ CS 9855 | You Never Know Who Your Friends Are | 1969 | 15.00 |
| —"360 Sound" label | | | |
| ❑ CS 9855 | You Never Know Who Your Friends Are | 1970 | 10.00 |
| —Orange label | | | |
| ❑ CS 9951 | Kooper Session | 1970 | 10.00 |
| —With Shuggie Otis; orange label | | | |
| ❑ CS 9951 | Kooper Session | 1970 | 15.00 |
| —With Shuggie Otis; "360 Sound" label | | | |
| ❑ G 30031 [(2)] | Easy Does It | 1970 | 20.00 |
| ❑ KC 30506 | New York City (You're a Woman) | 1971 | 15.00 |
| ❑ KC 31159 | A Possible Projection of the Future/Childhood's End | 1972 | 15.00 |
| ❑ KC 31723 | Naked Songs | 1973 | 15.00 |
| ❑ PG 33169 [(2)] | Unclaimed Freight (Al's Big Deal) | 1975 | 15.00 |
| ❑ FC 38137 | Championship Wrestling | 1982 | 10.00 |

UNITED ARTISTS

| Number | Title (A Side/B Side) | Yr | NM |
|---|---|---|---|
| ❑ UA-LA702-G | Act Like Nothing's Wrong | 1976 | 12.00 |

**KORNER, ALEXIS**

COLUMBIA

| Number | Title (A Side/B Side) | Yr | NM |
|---|---|---|---|
| ❑ PC 33427 | Get Off of My Cloud | 1975 | 15.00 |

JUST SUNSHINE

| Number | Title (A Side/B Side) | Yr | NM |
|---|---|---|---|
| ❑ 13 | All Star Blues Incorporated | 1974 | 12.00 |

MOBILE FIDELITY

| Number | Title (A Side/B Side) | Yr | NM |
|---|---|---|---|
| ❑ 1-265 | Blues at the Marquee | 1996 | 20.00 |
| —Audiophile vinyl | | | |

WARNER BROS.

| Number | Title (A Side/B Side) | Yr | NM |
|---|---|---|---|
| ❑ 2XS 1966 [(2)] | Bootleg Him | 1972 | 25.00 |
| ❑ BS 2647 | Accidentally Borne in New Orleans | 1972 | 15.00 |

**KOSTELANETZ, ANDRE**

COLUMBIA

| Number | Title (A Side/B Side) | Yr | NM |
|---|---|---|---|
| ❑ AK 1 [M] | Musical Tour of the World | 195? | 20.00 |
| ❑ KZ 1 [M] | Meet Andre Kostelanetz | 1955 | 20.00 |
| —Red and black label with six "eye" logos | | | |
| ❑ GP 10 [(2)] | Sounds of Love | 1969 | 12.00 |
| ❑ C2L 11 [M] | The Romantic Music of Tchaikovsky | 195? | 25.00 |
| —Red and black label with six "eye" logos | | | |
| ❑ CL 704 [M] | Mood for Love | 1956 | 20.00 |
| —Red and black label with six "eye" logos | | | |
| ❑ CL 720 [M] | Peter and the Wolf; Carnival of the Animals | 1956 | 20.00 |
| —Red and black label with six "eye" logos | | | |
| ❑ CL 734 [M] | The Music of Victor Youmans | 1956 | 20.00 |
| —Red and black label with six "eye" logos | | | |
| ❑ CL 758 [M] | Bravo! | 1956 | 20.00 |
| —Red and black label with six "eye" logos | | | |
| ❑ CL 765 [M] | The Music of Victor Herbert | 1956 | 20.00 |
| —Red and black label with six "eye" logos | | | |
| ❑ CL 768 [M] | Music of Irving Berlin | 1956 | 20.00 |
| —Red and black label with six "eye" logos | | | |
| ❑ CL 780 [M] | Lure of the Tropics | 1956 | 20.00 |
| —Red and black label with six "eye" logos | | | |
| ❑ CL 781 [M] | Stardust | 1956 | 20.00 |
| —Red and black label with six "eye" logos | | | |
| ❑ CL 797 [M] | La Boheme for Orchestra | 1956 | 20.00 |
| —Red and black label with six "eye" logos | | | |
| ❑ CL 806 [M] | Show Boat/South Pacific/Slaughter on 10th Avenue | 1956 | 20.00 |
| —Red and black label with six "eye" logos | | | |
| ❑ CL 811 [M] | Calendar Girl | 1956 | 20.00 |
| —Red and black label with six "eye" logos | | | |
| ❑ CL 843 [M] | The Very Thought of You | 1956 | 20.00 |
| —Red and black label with six "eye" logos | | | |
| ❑ CL 863 [M] | Café Continental | 1956 | 20.00 |
| —Red and black label with six "eye" logos | | | |
| ❑ CL 864 [M] | Beautiful Dreamer | 1956 | 20.00 |
| —Red and black label with six "eye" logos | | | |
| ❑ CL 1199 [M] | Theatre Party | 1958 | 15.00 |
| ❑ CL 1220 [M] | Romantic Music of... | 1958 | 15.00 |
| ❑ CL 1335 [M] | The Lure of Paradise | 1959 | 12.00 |
| ❑ CL 1354 [M] | Strauss Waltzes | 1959 | 12.00 |
| ❑ CL 1431 [M] | Gypsy Passion | 1960 | 12.00 |
| ❑ CL 1495 [M] | Gershwin: Rhapsody in Blue; Previn: Concerto in F | 1960 | 12.00 |
| ❑ CL 1528 [M] | Joy to the World: Music for Christmas | 1959 | 15.00 |
| ❑ CL 1657 [M] | Wonderland of Sound | 1961 | 12.00 |
| ❑ CL 1718 [M] | Star-Spangled Marches | 1962 | 12.00 |
| ❑ CL 1827 [M] | Wonderland of Sound (Broadway's Greatest Hits) | 1962 | 12.00 |
| ❑ CL 1898 [M] | Wonderland of Sound (Fire and Jealousy) | 1962 | 12.00 |
| ❑ CL 1938 [M] | Wonderland of Sound (The World's Greatest Waltzes) | 1963 | 10.00 |
| ❑ CL 1995 [M] | Wonderland of Opera | 1963 | 10.00 |
| ❑ CL 2039 [M] | Wonderland of Golden Hits | 1963 | 10.00 |
| ❑ CL 2068 [M] | Wonderland of Christmas | 1963 | 12.00 |
| ❑ CL 2078 [M] | Kostelanetz in Wonderland | 1964 | 10.00 |
| ❑ CL 2133 [M] | Gershwin Wonderland | 1964 | 10.00 |
| ❑ CL 2138 [M] | New York Wonderland | 1964 | 10.00 |
| ❑ CL 2185 [M] | I Wish You Love | 1964 | 10.00 |
| ❑ CL 2250 [M] | New Orleans Wonderland | 1965 | 10.00 |
| ❑ CL 2359 [M] | Thunder (The Spectacular Sound of John Philip Sousa) | 1965 | 10.00 |
| ❑ CL 2467 [M] | The Shadow of Your Smile and Other Great Movie Themes | 1966 | 10.00 |
| ❑ CL 2534 [M] | Today's Golden Hits | 1966 | 10.00 |
| ❑ CL 2581 [M] | Exotic Nights | 1966 | 10.00 |
| ❑ CL 2609 [M] | The Kostelanetz Sound of Today | 1967 | 10.00 |
| ❑ CL 2688 [M] | Concert in the Park | 1967 | 10.00 |
| ❑ CL 2756 [M] | Today's Greatest Movie Hits | 1967 | 12.00 |
| ❑ CL 2823 [M] | Scarborough Fair | 1968 | 15.00 |
| ❑ CL 2891 [M] | For the Young at Heart | 1968 | 15.00 |
| ❑ CS 8144 [S] | The Lure of Paradise | 1959 | 15.00 |
| ❑ CS 8162 [S] | Strauss Waltzes | 1959 | 15.00 |
| ❑ CS 8228 [S] | Gypsy Passion | 1960 | 15.00 |
| ❑ CS 8286 [S] | Gershwin: Rhapsody in Blue; Previn: Concerto in F | 1960 | 15.00 |
| ❑ CS 8328 [S] | Joy to the World: Music for Christmas | 1959 | 20.00 |
| —Red and black label with six "eye" logos | | | |
| ❑ CS 8457 [S] | Wonderland of Sound | 1961 | 15.00 |
| ❑ CS 8518 [S] | Star-Spangled Marches | 1962 | 15.00 |
| ❑ CS 8627 [S] | Wonderland of Sound (Broadway's Greatest Hits) | 1962 | 15.00 |
| ❑ CS 8698 [S] | Wonderland of Sound (Fire and Jealousy) | 1962 | 15.00 |
| ❑ CS 8738 [S] | Wonderland of Sound (The World's Greatest Waltzes) | 1963 | 12.00 |
| ❑ CS 8795 [S] | Wonderland of Opera | 1963 | 12.00 |
| ❑ CS 8839 [S] | Wonderland of Golden Hits | 1963 | 12.00 |
| ❑ CS 8868 [S] | Wonderland of Christmas | 1963 | 15.00 |
| ❑ CS 8878 [S] | Kostelanetz in Wonderland | 1964 | 12.00 |
| ❑ CS 8933 [S] | Gershwin Wonderland | 1964 | 12.00 |
| ❑ CS 8938 [S] | New York Wonderland | 1964 | 12.00 |
| ❑ CS 8985 [S] | I Wish You Love | 1964 | 12.00 |
| ❑ CS 9050 [S] | New Orleans Wonderland | 1965 | 12.00 |
| ❑ CS 9159 [S] | Thunder (The Spectacular Sound of John Philip Sousa) | 1965 | 12.00 |
| ❑ CS 9267 [S] | The Shadow of Your Smile and Other Great Movie Themes | 1966 | 10.00 |
| ❑ CS 9334 [S] | Today's Golden Hits | 1966 | 12.00 |
| ❑ CS 9381 [S] | Exotic Nights | 1966 | 10.00 |
| ❑ CS 9409 [S] | The Kostelanetz Sound of Today | 1967 | 10.00 |
| ❑ CS 9488 [S] | Concert in the Park | 1967 | 10.00 |
| ❑ CS 9556 [S] | Today's Greatest Movie Hits | 1967 | 10.00 |
| ❑ CS 9623 [S] | Scarborough Fair | 1968 | 10.00 |
| ❑ CS 9691 [S] | For the Young at Heart | 1968 | 10.00 |
| ❑ CS 9724 | Hits from Funny Girl, Finian's Rainbow, and Star! | 1968 | 10.00 |
| ❑ CS 9740 | Andre Kostelanetz' Greatest Hits | 1969 | 10.00 |
| ❑ CS 9823 | Traces | 1969 | 10.00 |
| ❑ CS 9973 | Greatest Hits of the 60's | 1970 | 10.00 |
| ❑ CS 9998 | I'll Never Fall in Love Again | 1970 | 10.00 |
| ❑ C 30037 | Everything Is Beautiful | 1970 | 10.00 |
| ❑ C 30501 | Love Story | 1971 | 10.00 |
| ❑ C 30672 | For All We Know | 1971 | 10.00 |
| ❑ C 31002 | Kostelanetz Plays Chicago | 1971 | 10.00 |
| ❑ KG 31491 [(2)] | Andre Kostelanetz Plays Cole Porter | 1972 | 15.00 |
| ❑ KG 32002 [(2)] | The World's Greatest Love Songs | 1973 | 12.00 |
| ❑ CQ 32147 [Q] | A Quadraphonic Concert | 1972 | 15.00 |
| ❑ KC 32187 | Last Tango in Paris | 1973 | 10.00 |
| ❑ KC 32451 | Kostelanetz Plays Great Hits of Today | 1973 | 10.00 |
| ❑ KC 32580 | Andre Kostelanetz Plays Legrand's Greatest Hits | 1974 | 10.00 |
| ❑ KG 32825 [(2)] | Andre Kostelanetz Plays Gershwin | 1974 | 12.00 |
| ❑ CQ 32856 [Q] | Quadraphonic Pop Concert | 1973 | 15.00 |
| ❑ KC 33061 | Musical Reflections of Broadway and Hollywood | 1974 | 10.00 |
| ❑ KG 33065 [(2)] | Strike Up the Band | 1974 | 12.00 |
| ❑ KC 33437 | Orient Express | 1975 | 10.00 |
| ❑ C 33550 | Never Can Say Goodbye | 1975 | 8.00 |
| ❑ KC 33550 | Never Can Say Goodbye | 1975 | 10.00 |
| ❑ KC 33954 | Music from A Chorus Line and Treemonisha | 1975 | 10.00 |
| ❑ KC 34157 | I'm Easy and Other Themes | 1976 | 10.00 |
| ❑ PC 34352 | Dance with Me | 1977 | 10.00 |
| ❑ PC 34660 | Music of Charlie Chaplin and Duke Ellington | 1977 | 10.00 |
| ❑ JC 35328 | You Light Up My Life | 1978 | 10.00 |
| ❑ JC 35788 | Superman | 1979 | 8.00 |
| ❑ JC 36382 | Various Themes | 1980 | 8.00 |

COLUMBIA LIMITED EDITION

| Number | Title (A Side/B Side) | Yr | NM |
|---|---|---|---|
| ❑ LE 10083 | Joy to the World: Music for Christmas | 197? | 10.00 |
| —Reissue of CS 8328 | | | |
| ❑ LE 10086 | Wonderland of Christmas | 197? | 10.00 |
| —Reissue of CS 8868 | | | |

COLUMBIA MASTERWORKS

| Number | Title (A Side/B Side) | Yr | NM |
|---|---|---|---|
| ❑ ML 2007 [10] | Music of Stephen Foster | 195? | 25.00 |
| ❑ ML 2011 [10] | Waltzes of Johann Strauss | 195? | 25.00 |
| ❑ ML 2014 [10] | Songs of Cole Porter | 195? | 30.00 |
| ❑ ML 2022 [10] | Motion Picture Favorites | 195? | 25.00 |
| ❑ ML 2056 [10] | Chopin-Kostelanetz | 195? | 25.00 |
| ❑ ML 4065 [M] | Favorites | 195? | 20.00 |
| ❑ ML 4066 [M] | Clair de Lune | 195? | 20.00 |
| ❑ ML 4082 [M] | Carnival Tropicana | 195? | 20.00 |
| ❑ ML 4253 [M] | Music of Fritz Kreisler and Sigmund Romberg | 195? | 20.00 |
| ❑ ML 4308 [M] | Swan Lake (Highlights) | 195? | 20.00 |
| ❑ ML 4409 [M] | Bizet: L'arlesienne Suites 1 & 2 | 195? | 20.00 |
| ❑ ML 4455 [M] | An American in Paris | 195? | 20.00 |
| ❑ ML 4822 [M] | Lure of the Tropics | 1956 | 20.00 |
| ❑ MS 6106 [S] | Offenbach: Gaite Parisienne; Bizet: Carmen (Highlights) | 195? | 20.00 |
| ❑ ML 6111 [M] | Romantic Strings | 1960 | 12.00 |
| ❑ ML 6129 [M] | Showstoppers | 1960 | 12.00 |
| ❑ ML 6179 [M] | Wishing You a Merry Christmas | 1960 | 12.00 |
| ❑ ML 6206 [M] | Promenade Favorites | 1966 | 12.00 |
| ❑ ML 6224 [M] | Romantic Waltzes of Tchaikovsky | 1961 | 12.00 |
| ❑ ML 6226 [M] | Favorite Romantic Concertos | 1961 | 12.00 |
| ❑ MS 6711 [S] | Romantic Strings | 1960 | 15.00 |
| ❑ MS 6729 [S] | Showstoppers | 1960 | 15.00 |
| ❑ MS 6779 [S] | Wishing You a Merry Christmas | 1960 | 15.00 |
| ❑ MS 6806 [S] | Promenade Favorites | 1966 | 15.00 |
| ❑ MS 6824 [S] | Romantic Waltzes of Tchaikovsky | 1961 | 15.00 |
| ❑ MS 6826 [S] | Favorite Romantic Concertos | 1961 | 15.00 |
| ❑ MS 7087 | Vienna, City of Dreams | 1968 | 12.00 |
| ❑ MS 7108 [S] | Andre Kostelanetz Conducts Great Romantic Ballads | 196? | 10.00 |
| ❑ MS 7319 | Musical Evenings | 1969 | 10.00 |
| ❑ MS 7427 | Extravaganza | 1970 | 10.00 |
| ❑ M 30075 | Music for Strings | 1970 | 10.00 |
| ❑ M 35114 | Festive Overtures | 1978 | 8.00 |

COLUMBIA SPECIAL PRODUCTS

| Number | Title (A Side/B Side) | Yr | NM |
|---|---|---|---|
| ❑ C 10975 | Wishing You a Merry Christmas | 1972 | 10.00 |
| —Reissue of Columbia Masterworks MS 6779 | | | |
| ❑ P 13286 | Scarborough Fair | 197? | 8.00 |

HARMONY

| Number | Title (A Side/B Side) | Yr | NM |
|---|---|---|---|
| ❑ HL 7368 [M] | You and the Night and the Music | 196? | 10.00 |
| ❑ HL 7371 [M] | Broadway Theatre Party | 196? | 10.00 |
| ❑ HL 7395 [M] | Grand Canyon Suite | 196? | 10.00 |
| ❑ HL 7432 [M] | Joy to the World: Music for Christmas | 1967 | 12.00 |
| —Reissue of Columbia 1528 | | | |
| ❑ HS 11168 [S] | You and the Night and the Music | 196? | 10.00 |
| ❑ HS 11171 [S] | Broadway Theatre Party | 196? | 10.00 |
| ❑ HS 11195 [S] | Grand Canyon Suite | 196? | 10.00 |
| ❑ HS 11232 [S] | Joy to the World: Music for Christmas | 1967 | 12.00 |
| —Reissue of Columbia 8328 | | | |
| ❑ HS 11281 | The Magic of Music | 1968 | 10.00 |
| ❑ H 30014 | Be My Love | 1970 | 10.00 |
| ❑ KH 31414 | Greatest Hits of Broadway and Hollywood | 1972 | 10.00 |
| ❑ KH 31500 | Love Theme from "The Godfather" | 1972 | 10.00 |
| ❑ KH 31571 | Andre Kostelanetz Plays Richard Rogers | 1973 | 10.00 |
| ❑ KH 32170 | Strike Up the Band | 1973 | 10.00 |

READER'S DIGEST

| Number | Title (A Side/B Side) | Yr | NM |
|---|---|---|---|
| ❑ RD-120-A [(8)] | The Best of Andre Kostelanetz | 197? | 30.00 |

**KOTTKE, LEO**

CAPITOL

| Number | Title (A Side/B Side) | Yr | NM |
|---|---|---|---|
| ❑ ST-682 | Mudlark | 1971 | 12.00 |
| ❑ ST-11000 | Greenhouse | 1972 | 10.00 |
| ❑ ST-11164 | My Feet Are Smiling | 1973 | 10.00 |
| ❑ ST-11262 | Ice Water | 1974 | 10.00 |
| ❑ ST-11335 | Dreams and All That Stuff | 1974 | 10.00 |
| ❑ ST-11446 | Chewing Pine | 1975 | 10.00 |
| ❑ ST-11576 | Leo Kottke 1971-1976 — Did You Hear Me? | 1976 | 10.00 |
| ❑ SWBC-11867 [(2)] | The Best of Leo Kottke | 1979 | 12.00 |
| ❑ SN-16063 | Mudlark | 1979 | 8.00 |
| —Budget-line reissue | | | |
| ❑ SN-16064 | Ice Water | 1979 | 8.00 |
| —Budget-line reissue | | | |
| ❑ SN-16065 | Greenhouse | 1979 | 8.00 |
| —Budget-line reissue | | | |
| ❑ SN-16187 | Dreams and All That Stuff | 1980 | 8.00 |
| —Budget-line reissue | | | |

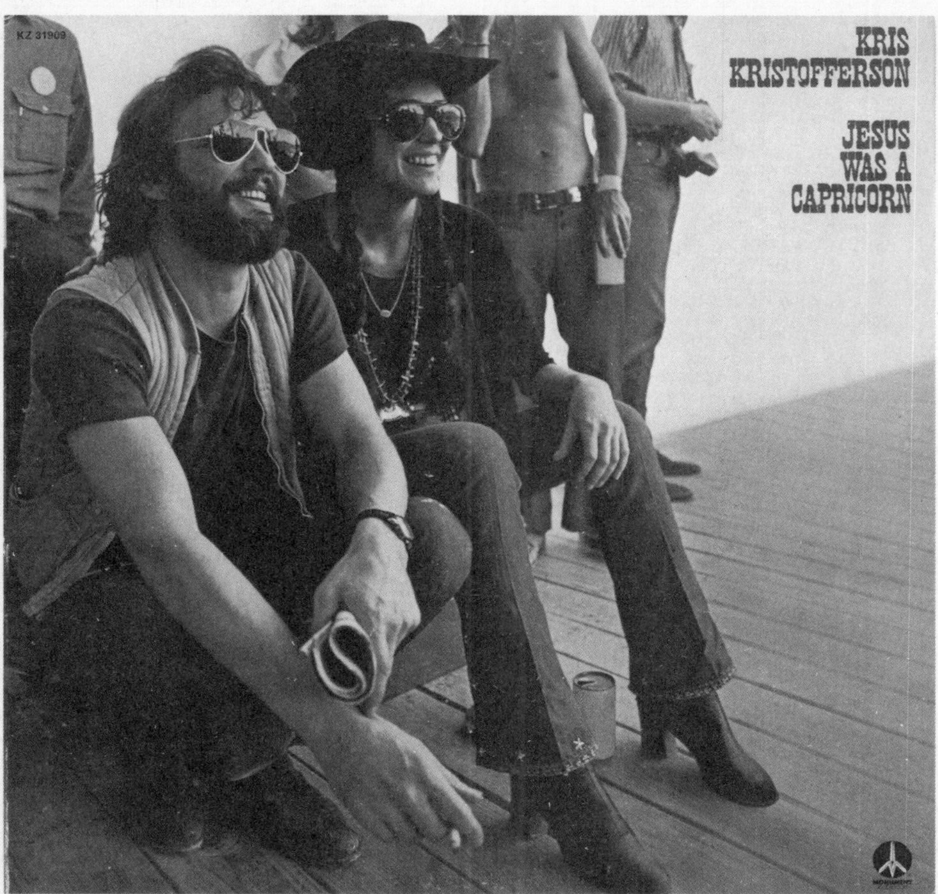


Kris Kristofferson, *Jesus Was a Capricorn,* Monument KZ 31909, 1972, $12.

| Number | Title (A Side/B Side) | Yr | NM |
|---|---|---|---|
| ❑ SN-16188 | Chewing Pine | 1980 | 8.00 |
| *—Budget-line reissue* | | | |
| ❑ SN-16189 | Leo Kottke 1971-1976 — Did You Hear Me? | 1980 | 8.00 |
| *—Budget-line reissue* | | | |

CHRYSALIS

| Number | Title (A Side/B Side) | Yr | NM |
|---|---|---|---|
| ❑ CHR 1106 | Leo Kottke | 1977 | 10.00 |
| ❑ CHR 1191 | Burnt Lips | 1978 | 10.00 |
| ❑ CHR 1234 | Balance | 1979 | 10.00 |
| ❑ CHR 1328 | Guitar Music | 1981 | 10.00 |
| ❑ PV 41106 | Leo Kottke | 1985 | 8.00 |
| *—Budget-line reissue* | | | |
| ❑ PV 41191 | Burnt Lips | 1985 | 8.00 |
| *—Budget-line reissue* | | | |
| ❑ PV 41234 | Balance | 1985 | 8.00 |
| *—Budget-line reissue* | | | |
| ❑ PV 41328 | Guitar Music | 1983 | 8.00 |
| *—Budget-line reissue* | | | |
| ❑ FV 41411 | Time Step | 1983 | 10.00 |
| ❑ PV 41411 | Time Step | 1986 | 8.00 |
| *—Budget-line reissue* | | | |

OBLIVION

| Number | Title (A Side/B Side) | Yr | NM |
|---|---|---|---|
| ❑ S-1 | 12-String Blues/Live at the Scholar Coffee House | 1969 | 25.00 |

PRIVATE MUSIC

| Number | Title (A Side/B Side) | Yr | NM |
|---|---|---|---|
| ❑ 2007-1-P | A Shout Toward Noon | 1986 | 10.00 |
| ❑ 2025-1-P | Regards from Chuck Pink | 1988 | 10.00 |
| ❑ 2050-1-P | My Father's Face | 1989 | 10.00 |

SYMPOSIUM

| Number | Title (A Side/B Side) | Yr | NM |
|---|---|---|---|
| ❑ 2001 | Circle Round the Sun | 1970 | 12.00 |

TAKOMA

| Number | Title (A Side/B Side) | Yr | NM |
|---|---|---|---|
| ❑ 1024 | 6 and 12 String Guitar | 1969 | 12.00 |

**KRAFTWERK**

ASTRALWERKS

| Number | Title (A Side/B Side) | Yr | NM |
|---|---|---|---|
| ❑ ASW 60611 [(4)] | Minimum-Maximum | 2005 | 50.00 |
| *—Box set; each LP is in a cardboard inner sleeve and paper sleeve* | | | |

CAPITOL

| Number | Title (A Side/B Side) | Yr | NM |
|---|---|---|---|
| ❑ ST-11457 | Radio-Activity | 1975 | 16.00 |
| ❑ SW 11603 | Trans-Europe Express | 1977 | 16.00 |
| ❑ SW-11728 | The Man-Machine | 1978 | 16.00 |
| ❑ SN-16301 | Trans-Europe Express | 198? | 10.00 |
| *—Reissue* | | | |
| ❑ SN-16302 | The Man-Machine | 198? | 10.00 |
| *—Reissue* | | | |
| ❑ SN-16380 | Radio-Activity | 1986 | 10.00 |
| *—Reissue* | | | |

ELEKTRA

| Number | Title (A Side/B Side) | Yr | NM |
|---|---|---|---|
| ❑ 60789 | Computer World | 1988 | 8.00 |
| *—Reissue* | | | |
| ❑ 60797 | Autobahn | 1988 | 8.00 |
| *—Still another reissue of this album* | | | |
| ❑ 60798 | Electric Cafe | 1988 | 8.00 |
| *—Reissue* | | | |
| ❑ 60869 [(2)] | The Mix | 1991 | 12.00 |

MERCURY

| Number | Title (A Side/B Side) | Yr | NM |
|---|---|---|---|
| ❑ SRM-1-3704 | Autobahn | 1977 | 15.00 |
| *—Reissue of Vertigo VEL-2003* | | | |

VERTIGO

| Number | Title (A Side/B Side) | Yr | NM |
|---|---|---|---|
| ❑ VEL-2003 | Autobahn | 1974 | 20.00 |
| ❑ VEL-2006 | Ralf & Florian | 1976 | 16.00 |
| *—Recorded in 1973* | | | |

WARNER BROS.

| Number | Title (A Side/B Side) | Yr | NM |
|---|---|---|---|
| ❑ HS 3549 | Computer World | 1981 | 10.00 |
| ❑ 25326 | Autobahn | 1985 | 12.00 |
| *—Another reissue of Vertigo VEL-2003* | | | |
| ❑ 25525 | Electric Cafe | 1986 | 12.00 |

**KRAINIA CONSORT**

MERCURY LIVING PRESENCE

| Number | Title (A Side/B Side) | Yr | NM |
|---|---|---|---|
| ❑ SR 90397 [S] | Music in Shakespeare's England | 196? | 20.00 |
| *—Maroon label, with "Vendor: Mercury Record Corporation"* | | | |
| ❑ SR 90397 [S] | Music in Shakespeare's England | 196? | 60.00 |
| *—Maroon label, no "Vendor: Mercury Record Corporation"* | | | |

**KRAINIS, BERNARD**

MERCURY LIVING PRESENCE

| Number | Title (A Side/B Side) | Yr | NM |
|---|---|---|---|
| ❑ SR 90443 [S] | Concertos for Recorder and Strings | 1965 | 25.00 |
| *—Maroon label, with "Vendor: Mercury Record Corporation"* | | | |

**KRAL, IRENE**

AVA

| Number | Title (A Side/B Side) | Yr | NM |
|---|---|---|---|
| ❑ A-33 [M] | Better Than Anything | 1963 | 40.00 |
| ❑ AS-33 [S] | Better Than Anything | 1963 | 50.00 |

MAINSTREAM

| Number | Title (A Side/B Side) | Yr | NM |
|---|---|---|---|
| ❑ S-6058 [S] | Wonderful Life | 1965 | 40.00 |
| ❑ 56058 [M] | Wonderful Life | 1965 | 30.00 |

UNITED ARTISTS

| Number | Title (A Side/B Side) | Yr | NM |
|---|---|---|---|
| ❑ UAL-3052 [M] | Steve Irene O! | 1959 | 120.00 |
| ❑ UAL-4016 [M] | The Band and I | 1959 | 120.00 |
| ❑ UAS-5016 [S] | The Band and I | 1959 | 150.00 |
| ❑ UAS-6052 [S] | Steve Irene O! | 1959 | 150.00 |

**KRAMER, BILLY J., AND THE DAKOTAS**

CAPITOL

| Number | Title (A Side/B Side) | Yr | NM |
|---|---|---|---|
| ❑ SM-11897 [P] | The Best of Billy J. Kramer and the Dakotas | 1979 | 10.00 |

IMPERIAL

| Number | Title (A Side/B Side) | Yr | NM |
|---|---|---|---|
| ❑ LP 9267 [M] | Little Children | 1964 | 30.00 |
| *—Black and pink label* | | | |
| ❑ LP 9267 [M] | Little Children | 1964 | 50.00 |
| *—Black label with stars* | | | |
| ❑ LP 9273 [M] | I'll Keep You Satisfied/From a Window | 1964 | 30.00 |
| ❑ LP 9291 [M] | Trains and Boats and Planes | 1965 | 30.00 |
| ❑ LP 12267 [P] | Little Children | 1964 | 40.00 |
| *—Black and pink label* | | | |
| ❑ LP 12267 [P] | Little Children | 1964 | 80.00 |
| *—Black label with silver print* | | | |
| ❑ LP 12273 [P] | I'll Keep You Satisfied/From a Window | 1964 | 40.00 |
| ❑ LP 12921 [R] | Trains and Boats and Planes | 1965 | 25.00 |

**KRAUSS, ALISON, AND UNION STATION**

MOBILE FIDELITY

| Number | Title (A Side/B Side) | Yr | NM |
|---|---|---|---|
| ❑ MFSL 2-276 [(2)] | So Long, So Wrong | 2004 | 40.00 |
| *—"Original Master Recording" at top of cover* | | | |

ROUNDER

| Number | Title (A Side/B Side) | Yr | NM |
|---|---|---|---|
| ❑ 0235 | Too Late to Cry | 1987 | 12.00 |
| ❑ 0265 | Two Highways | 1989 | 12.00 |
| ❑ 0275 | I've Got That Old Feeling | 1990 | 12.00 |
| ❑ 0325 | Now That I've Found You: A Collection | 1995 | 12.00 |

**KRAVITZ, LENNY**

VIRGIN

| Number | Title (A Side/B Side) | Yr | NM |
|---|---|---|---|
| ❑ 39169 | Are You Gonna Go My Way | 1993 | 25.00 |
| *—Clear-vinyl LP plus bonus CD with 8 unreleased tracks* | | | |
| ❑ 91290 | Let Love Rule | 1989 | 12.00 |

**KRAZY KATS, THE**

DAMON

| Number | Title (A Side/B Side) | Yr | NM |
|---|---|---|---|
| ❑ 12478 [M] | Movin' Out!! With the Krazy Kats | 1964 | 120.00 |

**KREED**

VISION OF SOUND

| Number | Title (A Side/B Side) | Yr | NM |
|---|---|---|---|
| ❑ 71-56 | Kreed | 1971 | 1200. |

**KRESS, CARL**

CAPITOL

| Number | Title (A Side/B Side) | Yr | NM |
|---|---|---|---|
| ❑ H 368 [10] | Classics in Jazz | 1953 | 50.00 |

**KRISTOFFERSON, KRIS**

COLUMBIA

| Number | Title (A Side/B Side) | Yr | NM |
|---|---|---|---|
| ❑ PZ 30679 | The Silver Tongued Devil and I | 1976 | 8.00 |
| *—Reissue* | | | |
| ❑ PZ 30817 | Me and Bobby McGee | 1976 | 8.00 |
| *—Reissue* | | | |
| ❑ PZ 31302 | Border Lord | 1976 | 8.00 |
| *—Reissue* | | | |
| ❑ PZ 31909 | Jesus Was a Capricorn | 1976 | 8.00 |
| *—Reissue* | | | |
| ❑ PZ 32914 | Spooky Lady's Sideshow | 1976 | 8.00 |
| *—Reissue* | | | |
| ❑ PZ 33379 | Who's to Bless…And Who's to Blame | 1976 | 8.00 |
| *—Reissue* | | | |
| ❑ PZ 34687 | Songs of Kristofferson | 1977 | 12.00 |
| ❑ JZ 35310 | Easter Island | 1978 | 12.00 |
| ❑ JZ 36135 | Shake Hands with the Devil | 1979 | 12.00 |
| ❑ JZ 36885 | To the Bone | 1980 | 12.00 |

MERCURY

| Number | Title (A Side/B Side) | Yr | NM |
|---|---|---|---|
| ❑ 830406-1 | Repossessed | 1987 | 10.00 |

MONUMENT

| Number | Title (A Side/B Side) | Yr | NM |
|---|---|---|---|
| ❑ SLP-18139 | Kristofferson | 1970 | 25.00 |
| *—Original label is light green with a yellow ring* | | | |
| ❑ Z 30679 | The Silver Tongued Devil and I | 1971 | 12.00 |
| ❑ ZQ 30679 [Q] | The Silver Tongued Devil and I | 1972 | 20.00 |
| ❑ Z 30817 | Me and Bobby McGee | 1971 | 12.00 |
| *—Reissue of 18139 with new title* | | | |
| ❑ KZ 31302 | Border Lord | 1972 | 12.00 |
| ❑ ZQ 31302 [Q] | Border Lord | 1972 | 20.00 |
| ❑ KZ 31909 | Jesus Was a Capricorn | 1972 | 12.00 |
| ❑ ZQ 31909 [Q] | Jesus Was a Capricorn | 1973 | 20.00 |
| ❑ PZ 32914 | Spooky Lady's Sideshow | 1974 | 12.00 |
| ❑ PZQ 32914 [Q] | Spooky Lady's Sideshow | 1974 | 20.00 |
| ❑ PZ 33379 | Who's to Bless…And Who's to Blame | 1975 | 12.00 |
| ❑ PZ 34254 | Surreal Thing | 1976 | 12.00 |
| ❑ PW 38392 | Songs of Kristofferson | 1982 | 8.00 |
| *—Reissue of 34687* | | | |

PAIR

| Number | Title (A Side/B Side) | Yr | NM |
|---|---|---|---|
| ❑ PDL2-1078 [(2)] | My Songs | 1986 | 12.00 |

| Number | Title (A Side/B Side) | Yr | NM |
|---|---|---|---|
| **KRISTYL** | | | |
| (NO LABEL) | | | |
| ❑ (no #) | Kristyl | 1975 | 200.00 |
| **KRONOS QUARTET** | | | |
| REFERENCE RECORDINGS | | | |
| ❑ RR-9 | In Formation | 198? | 25.00 |
| *—Audiophile vinyl* | | | |
| **KRUPA, GENE** | | | |
| AMERICAN RECORDING SOCIETY | | | |
| ❑ L-411 [M] | Gene Krupa Quartet | 1956 | 40.00 |
| ❑ L-427 [M] | Drummer Man | 1957 | 40.00 |
| CLEF | | | |
| ❑ MGC-121 [10] | The Gene Krupa Trio Collates | 1953 | 80.00 |
| *—With either Clef or Mercury cover* | | | |
| ❑ MGC-147 [10] | The Gene Krupa Sextet #1 | 1954 | 80.00 |
| ❑ MGC-152 [10] | The Gene Krupa Sextet #2 | 1954 | 80.00 |
| ❑ MGC-500 [M] | The Gene Krupa Trio at Jazz at the Philharmonic | 1953 | 60.00 |
| ❑ MGC-514 [10] | Gene Krupa Trio | 1953 | 80.00 |
| ❑ MGC-627 [M] | Sing, Sing, Sing — The Rocking Mr. Krupa and His Orchestra | 1954 | 60.00 |
| ❑ MGC-631 [M] | The Gene Krupa Sextet #3 | 1954 | 60.00 |
| ❑ MGC-668 [M] | The Gene Krupa Quartet | 1955 | 60.00 |
| ❑ MGC-684 [M] | Krupa and Rich | 1955 | 60.00 |
| ❑ MGC-687 [M] | The Exciting Gene Krupa and His Quartet | 1956 | 60.00 |
| ❑ MGC-703 [M] | Drum Boogie | 1956 | 60.00 |
| ❑ MGC-728 [M] | The Driving Gene Krupa Plays with His Sextet | 1956 | 60.00 |
| COLUMBIA | | | |
| ❑ C2L 29 [(2)M] | Drummin' Man | 1962 | 50.00 |
| *—Red and black labels with six "eye" logos; box set with booklet; deduct 20 percent if book is missing* | | | |
| ❑ C2L 29 [(2)M] | Drummin' Man | 1963 | 20.00 |
| *—Red labels, "Guaranteed High Fidelity" or "360 Sound Mono" on label* | | | |
| ❑ CL 641 [M] | Gene Krupa's Sidekicks | 1955 | 30.00 |
| *—Red and black label with six "eye" logos* | | | |
| ❑ CL 641 [M] | Gene Krupa's Sidekicks | 1955 | 40.00 |
| *—Maroon label, gold print* | | | |
| ❑ CL 735 [M] | Gene Krupa | 1956 | 30.00 |
| *—Red and black label with six "eye" logos* | | | |
| ❑ CL 2515 [10] | Drummin' Man | 1955 | 50.00 |
| ❑ CL 6017 [10] | Gene Krupa | 1949 | 100.00 |
| ❑ CL 6066 [10] | Dance Parade | 1949 | 100.00 |
| MERCURY | | | |
| ❑ MGC-500 [M] | The Gene Krupa Trio at Jazz at the Philharmonic | 1953 | 80.00 |
| ❑ MGC-514 [10] | Gene Krupa Trio | 1953 | 120.00 |
| RCA CAMDEN | | | |
| ❑ CAL-340 [M] | Mutiny in the Parlor | 1958 | 20.00 |
| VERVE | | | |
| ❑ MGV-2008 [M] | Drummer Man — Gene Krupa in Highest-Fi | 1956 | 60.00 |
| *—Orange label* | | | |
| ❑ MGV-2008 [M] | Drummer Man — Gene Krupa in Highest-Fi | 1957 | 50.00 |
| *—Black label* | | | |
| ❑ V-2008 [M] | Drummer Man — Gene Krupa in Highest-Fi | 1961 | 25.00 |
| ❑ MGVS-6008 [S] | Gene Krupa Plays Gerry Mulligan Arrangements | 1959 | 40.00 |
| ❑ MGVS-6042 [S] | Big Noise from Winnetka — Gene Krupa at the London House | 1960 | 40.00 |
| ❑ MGV-8031 [M] | The Gene Krupa Trio | 1957 | 50.00 |
| ❑ V-8031 [M] | The Gene Krupa Trio | 1961 | 25.00 |
| ❑ MGV-8069 [M] | Krupa and Rich | 1957 | 50.00 |
| ❑ V-8069 [M] | Krupa and Rich | 1961 | 25.00 |
| ❑ MGV-8071 [M] | The Exciting Gene Krupa and His Quartet | 1957 | 50.00 |
| ❑ V-8071 [M] | The Exciting Gene Krupa and His Quartet | 1961 | 25.00 |
| ❑ MGV-8087 [M] | Drum Boogie | 1957 | 50.00 |
| ❑ V-8087 [M] | Drum Boogie | 1961 | 25.00 |
| ❑ MGV-8107 [M] | The Driving Gene Krupa | 1957 | 50.00 |
| ❑ V-8107 [M] | The Driving Gene Krupa | 1961 | 25.00 |
| ❑ MGV-8190 [M] | Sing, Sing, Sing | 1957 | 50.00 |
| ❑ V-8190 [M] | Sing, Sing, Sing | 1961 | 25.00 |
| ❑ MGV-8204 [M] | The Jazz Rhythms of Gene Krupa | 1957 | 50.00 |
| ❑ V-8204 [M] | The Jazz Rhythms of Gene Krupa | 1961 | 25.00 |
| ❑ MGV-8276 [M] | Krupa Rocks | 1958 | 50.00 |
| ❑ V-8276 [M] | Krupa Rocks | 1961 | 25.00 |
| ❑ MGV-8292 [M] | Gene Krupa Plays Gerry Mulligan Arrangements | 1958 | 50.00 |
| ❑ V-8292 [M] | Gene Krupa Plays Gerry Mulligan Arrangements | 1961 | 25.00 |
| ❑ V6-8292 [S] | Gene Krupa Plays Gerry Mulligan Arrangements | 1961 | 20.00 |
| ❑ MGV-8300 [M] | Hey! Here's Gene Krupa | 1959 | 50.00 |
| ❑ V-8300 [M] | Hey! Here's Gene Krupa | 1961 | 25.00 |
| ❑ MGV-8310 [M] | Big Noise from Winnetka — Gene Krupa at the London House | 1959 | 50.00 |
| ❑ V-8310 [M] | Big Noise from Winnetka — Gene Krupa at the London House | 1961 | 25.00 |
| ❑ V6-8310 [S] | Big Noise from Winnetka — Gene Krupa at the London House | 1961 | 20.00 |
| ❑ MGV-8369 [M] | The Drum Battle | 1960 | 50.00 |
| ❑ V-8400 [M] | Krupa and Rich | 1961 | 25.00 |
| ❑ V6-8400 [S] | Krupa and Rich | 1961 | 20.00 |
| ❑ V6-8414 [S] | Percussion King | 1961 | 20.00 |
| ❑ V6-8450 [S] | Classics in Percussion | 1962 | 20.00 |
| ❑ V6-8571 [S] | Let Me Off Uptown — The Essential Gene Krupa | 1964 | 20.00 |
| ❑ V6-8584 [S] | The Great New Gene Krupa Quartet Featuring Charlie Ventura | 1964 | 20.00 |
| **KRUPA, GENE; LIONEL HAMPTON; TEDDY WILSON** | | | |
| CLEF | | | |
| ❑ MGC-681 [M] | Selections from "The Benny Goodman Story" | 1956 | 80.00 |
| VERVE | | | |
| ❑ MGV-8066 [M] | Gene Krupa-Lionel Hampton-Teddy Wilson with Red Callender | 1957 | 50.00 |
| *—Reissue of Clef 681 with new title* | | | |
| ❑ V-8066 [M] | Gene Krupa-Lionel Hampton-Teddy Wilson with Red Callender | 1961 | 25.00 |
| **KRUPA, GENE, AND CHARLIE VENTURA** | | | |
| COMMODORE | | | |
| ❑ FL-20028 [10] | The Krupa-Ventura Trio | 1950 | 100.00 |
| **KUBAN, BOB, AND THE IN-MEN** | | | |
| MUSICLAND U.S.A. | | | |
| ❑ LP-3500 [M] | Look Out for the Cheater | 1966 | 30.00 |
| ❑ SLP-3500 [S] | Look Out for the Cheater | 1966 | 40.00 |
| **KUHN, ROLF** | | | |
| URANIA | | | |
| ❑ US-1220 [M] | Sound of Jazz | 1962 | 25.00 |
| ❑ US-41220 [S] | Sound of Jazz | 1962 | 30.00 |
| VANGUARD | | | |
| ❑ VRS-8510 [M] | Streamline | 1955 | 40.00 |
| **KUHN, ROLF AND JOACHIM** | | | |
| ABC IMPULSE! | | | |
| ❑ AS-9150 | Impressions of New York | 1968 | 20.00 |
| **KUHN, STEVE** | | | |
| CONTACT | | | |
| ❑ CM-5 [M] | Steve Kuhn Trio Featuring Steve Swallow and Pete LaRoca | 1965 | 20.00 |
| ❑ CS-5 [S] | Steve Kuhn Trio Featuring Steve Swallow and Pete LaRoca | 1965 | 25.00 |
| IMPULSE! | | | |
| ❑ A-9136 [M] | The October Suite | 1967 | 40.00 |
| ❑ AS-9136 [S] | The October Suite | 1967 | 25.00 |
| **KUHN, STEVE, AND TOSHIKO AKIYOSHI** | | | |
| DAUNTLESS | | | |
| ❑ DM-4308 [M] | The Country & Western Sound for Jazz Pianos | 1963 | 20.00 |
| ❑ DS-6308 [S] | The Country & Western Sound for Jazz Pianos | 1963 | 25.00 |
| **KUSTOM KINGS, THE** | | | |
| SMASH | | | |
| ❑ MGS-27051 [M] | Kustom City, U.S.A. | 1964 | 120.00 |
| ❑ SRS-67051 [S] | Kustom City, U.S.A. | 1964 | 200.00 |
| **KWESKIN, JIM** | | | |
| MOUNTAIN RAILROAD | | | |
| ❑ MR-52672 | Jug Band Blues | 198? | 10.00 |
| ❑ MR-52782 | Jim Kweskin Lives Again | 198? | 10.00 |
| ❑ MR-52790 | Side by Side | 198? | 10.00 |
| ❑ MR-52793 | Swing on a Star | 198? | 10.00 |
| REPRISE | | | |
| ❑ R 6266 [M] | Garden of Joy | 1967 | 20.00 |
| ❑ RS 6266 [S] | Garden of Joy | 1967 | 15.00 |
| ❑ RS 6464 | America | 1971 | 15.00 |
| VANGUARD | | | |
| ❑ VSD 13/14 [(2)] | Greatest Hits | 1970 | 15.00 |
| ❑ VSD-2158 [S] | Jim Kweskin and the Jug Band | 1963 | 25.00 |
| ❑ VRS-9139 [M] | Jim Kweskin and the Jug Band | 1963 | 20.00 |
| ❑ VRS-9163 [M] | Jug Band Music | 1965 | 20.00 |
| ❑ VRS-9188 [M] | Relax Your Mind | 1966 | 20.00 |
| ❑ VRS-9234 [M] | See Reverse Side for Title | 1967 | 20.00 |
| ❑ VRS-9243 [M] | Jump for Joy | 1967 | 20.00 |
| ❑ VRS-9270 [M] | The Best of Jim Kweskin and the Jug Band | 1968 | 40.00 |
| ❑ VSD-79163 [S] | Jug Band Music | 1965 | 25.00 |
| ❑ VSD-79188 [S] | Relax Your Mind | 1966 | 25.00 |
| ❑ VSD-79234 [S] | See Reverse Side for Title | 1967 | 25.00 |
| ❑ VSD-79243 [S] | Jump for Joy | 1967 | 20.00 |
| ❑ VSD-79270 [S] | The Best of Jim Kweskin and the Jug Band | 1968 | 15.00 |
| **KYNARD, CHARLES** | | | |
| MAINSTREAM | | | |
| ❑ MRL-331 | Charles Kynard | 1972 | 20.00 |
| ❑ MRL-366 | Woga | 1973 | 20.00 |
| ❑ MRL-389 | Your Mama Don't Dance | 1973 | 20.00 |
| PACIFIC JAZZ | | | |
| ❑ PJ-72 [M] | Where It's At! | 1963 | 30.00 |
| ❑ ST-72 [S] | Where It's At! | 1963 | 40.00 |
| PRESTIGE | | | |
| ❑ PRST-7599 | Professor Soul | 1968 | 20.00 |
| ❑ PRST-7630 | The Soul Brotherhood | 1969 | 20.00 |
| ❑ PRST-7688 | Reelin' with the Feelin' | 1969 | 20.00 |
| ❑ PRST-7796 | Afro-disiac | 1970 | 20.00 |
| ❑ 10008 | Wa-tu-wa-zui | 1971 | 20.00 |
| WORLD PACIFIC | | | |
| ❑ ST-1823 [S] | Warm Winds | 1964 | 30.00 |
| ❑ WP-1823 [M] | Warm Winds | 1964 | 25.00 |
| **KYSER, KAY** | | | |
| CAPITOL | | | |
| ❑ ST 1692 [S] | Kay Kyser's Greatest Hits | 196? | 15.00 |
| ❑ T 1692 [M] | Kay Kyser's Greatest Hits | 196? | 12.00 |
| COLUMBIA | | | |
| ❑ CL 6012 [10] | Campus Favorites | 1948 | 80.00 |
| ❑ CG 33572 [(2)] | The World of Kay Kyser | 1976 | 15.00 |
| HARMONY | | | |
| ❑ HL 7041 [M] | Kay Kyser | 196? | 15.00 |
| ❑ HL 7136 [M] | Campus Rally | 196? | 15.00 |
| SUNBEAM | | | |
| ❑ SB-218 [M] | Kay Kyser and His Orchestra 1935-39 | 198? | 12.00 |

# L

| Number | Title (A Side/B Side) | Yr | NM |
|---|---|---|---|
| **L.A. 4** | | | |
| CONCORD JAZZ | | | |
| ❑ CJ-1001 | Just Friends | 1980 | 20.00 |
| *—Direct-to-disc recording* | | | |
| EAST WIND | | | |
| ❑ 10003 | Pavanne Pour Une Infante Defunte | 197? | 30.00 |
| *—Audiophile issue* | | | |
| ❑ 10004 | Going Home | 197? | 30.00 |
| *—Audiophile issue* | | | |
| **L.A. JAZZ CHOIR, THE** | | | |
| MOBILE FIDELITY | | | |
| ❑ 1-096 | Listen | 1982 | 80.00 |
| *—Audiophile vinyl* | | | |
| **L7** | | | |
| EPITAPH | | | |
| ❑ 86401 | L7 | 1988 | 50.00 |
| *—Original press with Donita Sparks' head cut off* | | | |
| SLASH | | | |
| ❑ 45624 | Hungry for Stink | 1994 | 12.00 |
| SUB POP | | | |
| ❑ 79 [EP] | Smell the Magic | 1990 | 12.00 |
| ❑ 79 [EP] | Smell the Magic | 1990 | 40.00 |
| *—First 1,000 on purple vinyl* | | | |
| **LA LUPE** | | | |
| ROULETTE | | | |
| ❑ SR-42024 | The Queen Does Her Thing | 1969 | 30.00 |
| **LABEEF, SLEEPY** | | | |
| ROUNDER | | | |
| ❑ 3052 | It Ain't What You Eat... | 198? | 10.00 |
| ❑ 3070 | Electricity | 198? | 10.00 |
| ❑ 3072 | Nothin' But the Truth | 198? | 10.00 |
| SUN | | | |
| ❑ 130 | Bull's Night Out | 1974 | 12.00 |
| ❑ 138 | Western Gold | 197? | 12.00 |
| ❑ 1004 | Rockabilly 1977 | 1977 | 12.00 |
| ❑ 1018 | Downtown Rockabilly | 1978 | 12.00 |
| **LABELLE, PATTI, AND THE BLUE BELLES** | | | |
| ATLANTIC | | | |
| ❑ 8119 [M] | Over the Rainbow | 1966 | 30.00 |
| ❑ SD 8119 [S] | Over the Rainbow | 1966 | 40.00 |
| ❑ 8147 [M] | Dreamer | 1967 | 30.00 |
| ❑ SD 8147 [S] | Dreamer | 1967 | 40.00 |

| Number | Title (A Side/B Side) | Yr | NM |
|---|---|---|---|
| **MISTLETOE** | | | |
| ❑ MLP-1204 | Merry Christmas from LaBelle | 1976 | 20.00 |
| **NEWTOWN** | | | |
| ❑ 631 [M] | Sweethearts of the Apollo | 1963 | 400.00 |
| ❑ 632 [M] | Sleigh Bells, Jingle Bells and Blue Bells | 1963 | 300.00 |
| **PARKWAY** | | | |
| ❑ P-7043 [M] | The Bluebelles On Stage | 1965 | 120.00 |
| *—Without bonus single* | | | |
| ❑ P-7043 [M] | The Bluebelles On Stage | 1965 | 150.00 |
| *—With bonus single* | | | |
| **TRIP** | | | |
| ❑ 3508 | Patti LaBelle and the Bluebelles | 197? | 10.00 |
| ❑ 8000 | Patti LaBelle and the Bluebelles' Greatest Hits | 1971 | 10.00 |
| ❑ 9525 | Early Hits | 197? | 10.00 |
| **UNITED ARTISTS** | | | |
| ❑ UA-LA504-E | The Very Best of Patti LaBelle and the Bluebelles | 1975 | 10.00 |

### LACEWING

| Number | Title (A Side/B Side) | Yr | NM |
|---|---|---|---|
| **MAINSTREAM** | | | |
| ❑ S-6132 | Lacewing | 1971 | 50.00 |

### LACY, STEVE

| Number | Title (A Side/B Side) | Yr | NM |
|---|---|---|---|
| **CANDID** | | | |
| ❑ CD-8007 [M] | The Straight Horn of Steve Lacy | 1960 | 40.00 |
| ❑ CS-9007 [S] | The Straight Horn of Steve Lacy | 1960 | 50.00 |
| **ESP-DISK'** | | | |
| ❑ 1060 [M] | The Forest and the Zoo | 1967 | 60.00 |
| ❑ S-1060 [S] | The Forest and the Zoo | 1967 | 50.00 |
| **HAT HUT** | | | |
| ❑ K/L [(2)] | Stamps | 1978 | 20.00 |
| ❑ 03 [(2)] | The Way | 1979 | 20.00 |
| **NEW JAZZ** | | | |
| ❑ NJLP-8206 [M] | Reflections: Steve Lacy Plays Thelonious Monk | 1958 | 200.00 |
| *—Purple label* | | | |
| ❑ NJLP-8206 [M] | Reflections: Steve Lacy Plays Thelonious Monk | 1965 | 50.00 |
| *—Blue label, trident logo at right* | | | |
| ❑ NJLP-8271 [M] | Evidence | 1962 | 150.00 |
| *—Purple label* | | | |
| ❑ NJLP-8271 [M] | Evidence | 1965 | 50.00 |
| *—Blue label, trident logo at right* | | | |
| **PRESTIGE** | | | |
| ❑ PRLP-7125 [M] | Steve Lacy Soprano Sax | 1956 | 200.00 |
| **STATUS** | | | |
| ❑ ST-8308 [M] | Wynton Kelly with Steve Lacy | 1965 | 60.00 |

### LADNIER, TOMMY

| Number | Title (A Side/B Side) | Yr | NM |
|---|---|---|---|
| **RIVERSIDE** | | | |
| ❑ RLP-1019 [10] | Ida Cox with Tommy Ladnier | 1953 | 100.00 |
| ❑ RLP-1026 [10] | Early Ladnier | 1954 | 100.00 |
| ❑ RLP-1044 [10] | Tommy Ladnier Plays the Blues | 1954 | 100.00 |
| **"X"** | | | |
| ❑ LVA-3027 [M] | Tommy Ladnier | 1954 | 60.00 |

### LAFARGE, PETER

| Number | Title (A Side/B Side) | Yr | NM |
|---|---|---|---|
| **COLUMBIA** | | | |
| ❑ CL 1795 [M] | Ira Hayes and Other Ballads | 1962 | 20.00 |
| ❑ CS 8595 [S] | Ira Hayes and Other Ballads | 1962 | 25.00 |
| **VERVE FOLKWAYS** | | | |
| ❑ FV-9004 [M] | Peter LaFarge Sings Women Blues | 1965 | 20.00 |
| ❑ FVS-9004 [S] | Peter LaFarge Sings Women Blues | 1965 | 25.00 |

### LAFORGE, JACK

| Number | Title (A Side/B Side) | Yr | NM |
|---|---|---|---|
| **AUDIO FIDELITY** | | | |
| ❑ AFSD-6161 [S] | Hit the Road Jack | 196? | 20.00 |
| **REGINA** | | | |
| ❑ R-282 [M] | I Remember You | 196? | 20.00 |
| ❑ RS-282 [S] | I Remember You | 196? | 25.00 |
| ❑ R-288 [M] | Unchain My Heart | 196? | 20.00 |
| ❑ RS-288 [S] | Unchain My Heart | 196? | 25.00 |
| ❑ R-301 [M] | You Fascinate Me So | 196? | 20.00 |
| ❑ RS-301 [S] | You Fascinate Me So | 196? | 25.00 |
| ❑ R-309 [M] | Comin' Home Baby | 196? | 20.00 |
| ❑ RS-309 [S] | Comin' Home Baby | 196? | 25.00 |
| ❑ R-313 [M] | Promise Her Anything | 196? | 20.00 |
| ❑ RS-313 [S] | Promise Her Anything | 196? | 25.00 |
| ❑ R-314 [M] | Jazz Portrait of Jack LaForge | 196? | 20.00 |
| ❑ RS-314 [S] | Jazz Portrait of Jack LaForge | 196? | 25.00 |
| ❑ R-319 [M] | Goldfinger | 1965 | 20.00 |
| ❑ RS-319 [S] | Goldfinger | 1965 | 25.00 |
| ❑ R-327 [M] | Our Crazy Affair | 196? | 20.00 |
| ❑ RS-327 [S] | Our Crazy Affair | 196? | 25.00 |
| ❑ R-716 [M] | Hawaii and I | 196? | 20.00 |
| ❑ RS-716 [S] | Hawaii and I | 196? | 25.00 |

### LAINE, CLEO

| Number | Title (A Side/B Side) | Yr | NM |
|---|---|---|---|
| **FONTANA** | | | |
| ❑ MGF-27552 [M] | Woman to Woman | 1967 | 20.00 |
| ❑ SRF-67531 [S] | Shakespeare and All That Jazz | 1966 | 20.00 |

### LAINE, FRANKIE

| Number | Title (A Side/B Side) | Yr | NM |
|---|---|---|---|
| **ABC** | | | |
| ❑ 604 [M] | I'll Take Care of Your Cares | 1967 | 12.00 |
| ❑ S-604 [S] | I'll Take Care of Your Cares | 1967 | 15.00 |
| ❑ 608 [M] | I Wanted Someone to Love | 1967 | 12.00 |
| ❑ S-608 [S] | I Wanted Someone to Love | 1967 | 15.00 |
| ❑ 628 [M] | To Each His Own | 1968 | 20.00 |
| ❑ S-628 [S] | To Each His Own | 1968 | 15.00 |
| ❑ S-657 | Take Me Back to Laine Country | 1968 | 15.00 |
| ❑ S-682 | You Gave Me a Mountain | 1969 | 15.00 |
| **AMOS** | | | |
| ❑ 7009 | Frankie Laine's Greatest Hits | 1970 | 12.00 |
| ❑ 7013 | Brand New Day | 1971 | 12.00 |
| **BULLDOG** | | | |
| ❑ BDL-1035 | All of Me | 198? | 10.00 |
| **CAPITOL** | | | |
| ❑ ST 2277 [S] | I Believe | 1965 | 15.00 |
| ❑ T 2277 [M] | I Believe | 1965 | 12.00 |
| **COLUMBIA** | | | |
| ❑ CL 625 [M] | Command Performance | 1954 | 40.00 |
| ❑ CL 808 [M] | Jazz Spectacular | 1956 | 30.00 |
| ❑ CL 975 [M] | Rockin' | 1957 | 30.00 |
| ❑ CL 1116 [M] | Foreign Affair | 1958 | 30.00 |
| ❑ CL 1176 [M] | Torchin' | 1959 | 20.00 |
| ❑ CL 1231 [M] | Frankie Laine's Greatest Hits | 1958 | 25.00 |
| *—Red and black label with six "eye" logos* | | | |
| ❑ CL 1231 [M] | Frankie Laine's Greatest Hits | 1962 | 15.00 |
| *—"Guaranteed High Fidelity" or "360 Sound Mono" label* | | | |
| ❑ CL 1277 [M] | Reunion in Rhythm | 1959 | 20.00 |
| ❑ CL 1317 [M] | You Are My Love | 1960 | 20.00 |
| ❑ CL 1393 [M] | Frankie Laine, Balladeer | 1960 | 20.00 |
| ❑ CL 1615 [M] | Hell Bent for Leather! | 1961 | 20.00 |
| *—Red and black label with six "eye" logos* | | | |
| ❑ CL 1615 [M] | Hell Bent for Leather! | 1962 | 15.00 |
| *—"Guaranteed High Fidelity" or "360 Sound Mono" label* | | | |
| ❑ CL 1696 [M] | Deuces Wild | 1962 | 15.00 |
| *—"Guaranteed High Fidelity" or "360 Sound Mono" label* | | | |
| ❑ CL 1696 [M] | Deuces Wild | 1962 | 20.00 |
| *—Red and black label with six "eye" logos* | | | |
| ❑ CL 1829 [M] | Call of the Wild | 1962 | 15.00 |
| ❑ CL 1962 [M] | Wanderlust | 1963 | 15.00 |
| ❑ CL 2504 [10] | Lover's Laine | 1955 | 40.00 |
| ❑ CL 2548 [10] | One for My Baby | 1955 | 40.00 |
| ❑ CL 6200 [10] | One for My Baby | 1952 | 50.00 |
| ❑ CL 6278 [10] | Mr. Rhythm | 1954 | 50.00 |
| ❑ CS 8024 [S] | Torchin' | 1959 | 30.00 |
| ❑ CS 8087 [S] | Reunion in Rhythm | 1959 | 30.00 |
| ❑ CS 8119 [S] | You Are My Love | 1960 | 25.00 |
| ❑ CS 8188 [S] | Frankie Laine, Balladeer | 1960 | 25.00 |
| ❑ CS 8415 [S] | Hell Bent for Leather! | 1961 | 30.00 |
| *—Red and black label with six "eye" logos* | | | |
| ❑ CS 8415 [S] | Hell Bent for Leather! | 1962 | 20.00 |
| *—"360 Sound Stereo" label* | | | |
| ❑ CS 8496 [S] | Deuces Wild | 1962 | 20.00 |
| *—"360 Sound Stereo" label* | | | |
| ❑ CS 8496 [S] | Deuces Wild | 1962 | 25.00 |
| *—Red and black label with six "eye" logos* | | | |
| ❑ CS 8629 [S] | Call of the Wild | 1962 | 20.00 |
| ❑ CS 8636 [R] | Frankie Laine's Greatest Hits | 1963 | 12.00 |
| ❑ PC 8636 | Frankie Laine's Greatest Hits | 198? | 8.00 |
| *—Reissue with new prefix* | | | |
| ❑ CS 8762 [S] | Wanderlust | 1963 | 20.00 |
| **GALAXY SERIES** | | | |
| ❑ 4821 [M] | Frankie Laine Sings | 195? | 12.00 |
| **HARMONY** | | | |
| ❑ HL 7329 [M] | Roving Gambler | 196? | 12.00 |
| ❑ HL 7382 [M] | That's My Desire | 196? | 12.00 |
| ❑ HL 7425 [M] | Memories | 196? | 12.00 |
| ❑ HS 11129 [S] | Roving Gambler | 196? | 12.00 |
| ❑ HS 11182 [S] | That's My Desire | 196? | 12.00 |
| ❑ HS 11225 [S] | Memories | 196? | 12.00 |
| ❑ HS 11345 | I'm Gonna Live 'Til I Die | 1969 | 12.00 |
| ❑ H 30406 | High Noon | 1971 | 12.00 |
| **HINDSIGHT** | | | |
| ❑ HSR-216 | Frankie Laine with Carl Fischer and His Orchestra, 1947 | 1985 | 10.00 |
| **MERCURY** | | | |
| ❑ PKW-2-111 [(2)] | The Great Years | 1969 | 15.00 |
| ❑ MG-20069 [M] | Songs by Frankie Laine | 1956 | 40.00 |
| ❑ MG-20080 [M] | That's My Desire | 1957 | 40.00 |
| ❑ MG-20083 [M] | Frankie Laine Sings For Us | 1957 | 40.00 |
| ❑ MG-20085 [M] | Concert Date | 1957 | 40.00 |
| ❑ MG-20105 [M] | With All My Heart | 1957 | 40.00 |
| ❑ MG-20587 [M] | Frankie Laine's Golden Hits | 1960 | 25.00 |
| ❑ MG-25007 [10] | Favorites | 1949 | 50.00 |
| ❑ MG-25024 [10] | Songs from the Heart | 1950 | 50.00 |
| ❑ MG-25025 [10] | Frankie Laine | 1950 | 50.00 |
| ❑ MG-25026 [10] | Frankie Laine | 1950 | 50.00 |
| ❑ MG-25027 [10] | Frankie Laine | 1950 | 50.00 |
| ❑ MG-25082 [10] | Christmas Favorites | 1951 | 50.00 |
| ❑ MG-25097 [10] | Mr. Rhythm Sings | 1951 | 50.00 |
| ❑ MG-25124 [10] | Listen to Laine | 1952 | 50.00 |
| ❑ SR-60587 [R] | Frankie Laine's Golden Hits | 196? | 12.00 |
| **PICKWICK** | | | |
| ❑ SPC-3526 | That Lucky Old Sun | 197? | 10.00 |
| ❑ SPC-3601 | You Gave Me a Mountain | 197? | 10.00 |
| **TOWER** | | | |
| ❑ ST 5092 [S] | Memory Laine | 1967 | 15.00 |
| ❑ T 5092 [M] | Memory Laine | 1967 | 12.00 |
| **WING** | | | |
| ❑ MGW 12110 [M] | All-Time Favorites | 196? | 15.00 |
| ❑ MGW 12158 [M] | Singing the Blues | 196? | 15.00 |
| ❑ MGW 12202 [M] | That's My Desire | 196? | 15.00 |
| ❑ SRW 16110 [R] | All-Time Favorites | 196? | 12.00 |
| ❑ SRW 16158 [R] | Singing the Blues | 196? | 12.00 |
| ❑ SRW 16202 [R] | That's My Desire | 196? | 12.00 |

### LAMARE, NAPPY, AND KID ORY

| Number | Title (A Side/B Side) | Yr | NM |
|---|---|---|---|
| **MODERN** | | | |
| ❑ 2010 [10] | Modern Records Volume 10 | 195? | 60.00 |
| *—No printing on back cover* | | | |

### LAMAS, FERNANDO

| Number | Title (A Side/B Side) | Yr | NM |
|---|---|---|---|
| **ROULETTE** | | | |
| ❑ R-25041 [M] | With Love, Fernando Lamas | 1958 | 40.00 |

### LAMB

| Number | Title (A Side/B Side) | Yr | NM |
|---|---|---|---|
| **FILLMORE** | | | |
| ❑ F 30003 | Sign of Change | 1970 | 20.00 |
| **WARNER BROS.** | | | |
| ❑ WS 1920 | Cross Between | 1971 | 20.00 |
| ❑ WS 1952 | Bring Out the Sun | 1972 | 20.00 |

### LAMB, JOSEPH

| Number | Title (A Side/B Side) | Yr | NM |
|---|---|---|---|
| **FOLKWAYS** | | | |
| ❑ FJ-3562 [M] | Classic Ragtime | 1960 | 20.00 |

### LAMBERT, DAVE

| Number | Title (A Side/B Side) | Yr | NM |
|---|---|---|---|
| **UNITED ARTISTS** | | | |
| ❑ UAL-3084 [M] | Dave Lambert Sings and Swings Alone | 1959 | 40.00 |
| ❑ UAS-6084 [S] | Dave Lambert Sings and Swings Alone | 1959 | 50.00 |

### LAMBERT, HENDRICKS AND BAVAN

| Number | Title (A Side/B Side) | Yr | NM |
|---|---|---|---|
| **RCA VICTOR** | | | |
| ❑ LPM-2635 [M] | Live at Basin Street East | 1963 | 30.00 |
| ❑ LSP-2635 [S] | Live at Basin Street East | 1963 | 40.00 |
| ❑ LPM-2747 [M] | Lambert, Hendricks and Bavan at Newport | 1963 | 30.00 |
| ❑ LSP-2747 [S] | Lambert, Hendricks and Bavan at Newport | 1963 | 40.00 |
| ❑ LPM-2861 [M] | Lambert, Hendricks and Bavan at the Village Gate | 1964 | 30.00 |
| ❑ LSP-2861 [S] | Lambert, Hendricks and Bavan at the Village Gate | 1964 | 40.00 |

### LAMBERT, HENDRICKS AND ROSS

| Number | Title (A Side/B Side) | Yr | NM |
|---|---|---|---|
| **ABC-PARAMOUNT** | | | |
| ❑ ABC-223 [M] | Sing a Song of Basie | 1958 | 50.00 |
| ❑ ABCS-223 [S] | Sing a Song of Basie | 1958 | 50.00 |
| **COLUMBIA** | | | |
| ❑ CL 1403 [M] | The Hottest New Group in Jazz | 1959 | 30.00 |
| *—Black and red label with six "eye" logos* | | | |
| ❑ CL 1510 [M] | Lambert, Hendricks and Ross Sing Ellington | 1960 | 30.00 |
| *—Black and red label with six "eye" logos* | | | |
| ❑ CL 1675 [M] | High Flying | 1961 | 30.00 |
| *—Black and red label with six "eye" logos* | | | |
| ❑ CS 8198 [S] | The Hottest New Group in Jazz | 1959 | 40.00 |
| *—Black and red label with six "eye" logos* | | | |
| ❑ CS 8198 [S] | The Hottest New Group in Jazz | 1963 | 20.00 |
| *—Red label with "360 Sound Stereo" at bottom* | | | |
| ❑ CS 8310 [S] | Lambert, Hendricks and Ross Sing Ellington | 1960 | 40.00 |
| *—Black and red label with six "eye" logos* | | | |
| ❑ CS 8310 [S] | Lambert, Hendricks and Ross Sing Ellington | 1963 | 20.00 |
| *—Red label with "360 Sound Stereo" at bottom* | | | |
| ❑ CS 8475 [S] | High Flying | 1961 | 40.00 |
| *—Black and red label with six "eye" logos* | | | |
| ❑ CS 8475 [S] | High Flying | 1963 | 20.00 |
| *—Red label with "360 Sound Stereo" at bottom* | | | |
| **IMPULSE!** | | | |
| ❑ A-83 [M] | Sing a Song of Basie | 1965 | 25.00 |
| *—Reissue of ABC-Paramount ABC-223* | | | |
| ❑ AS-83 [S] | Sing a Song of Basie | 1965 | 30.00 |
| *—Reissue of ABC-Paramount ABCS-223* | | | |
| **ROULETTE** | | | |
| ❑ R-52018 [M] | Sing Along with Basie | 1959 | 40.00 |
| ❑ SR-52018 [S] | Sing Along with Basie | 1959 | 50.00 |
| **WORLD PACIFIC** | | | |
| ❑ ST-1025 [S] | The Swingers! | 1959 | 50.00 |
| ❑ WP-1264 [M] | The Swingers! | 1959 | 40.00 |

### LAMEGO, DANNY, AND HIS JUMPIN' JACKS

| Number | Title (A Side/B Side) | Yr | NM |
|---|---|---|---|
| **FORGET-ME-NOT** | | | |
| ❑ 105 [M] | The Big Weekend | 1964 | 100.00 |

### LAMOND, DON

| Number | Title (A Side/B Side) | Yr | NM |
|---|---|---|---|
| **COMMAND** | | | |
| ❑ RS 832 SD [S] | Off Beat Percussion | 1962 | 20.00 |

### LAMONT, CHARLES

| Number | Title (A Side/B Side) | Yr | NM |
|---|---|---|---|
| **UNI** | | | |
| 73076 | A Legend in His Own Mind | 1970 | 25.00 |
| *—As "Lamont"* | | | |

### LAMOUR, DOROTHY

| Number | Title (A Side/B Side) | Yr | NM |
|---|---|---|---|
| **DECCA** | | | |
| DL 5115 [10] | Favorite Hawaiian Songs | 1950 | 80.00 |

### LANCASTER, BYARD

| Number | Title (A Side/B Side) | Yr | NM |
|---|---|---|---|
| **VORTEX** | | | |
| 2003 | It's Not Up to Us | 1968 | 30.00 |

### LANCE, HERB

| Number | Title (A Side/B Side) | Yr | NM |
|---|---|---|---|
| **CHESS** | | | |
| LP-1506 [M] | The Comeback | 1966 | 25.00 |
| LPS-1506 [S] | The Comeback | 1966 | 30.00 |

### LANCE, MAJOR

| Number | Title (A Side/B Side) | Yr | NM |
|---|---|---|---|
| **KAT FAMILY** | | | |
| FZ 38898 | The Major's Back | 1983 | 12.00 |
| **OKEH** | | | |
| OKM-12105 [M] | The Monkey Time | 1963 | 40.00 |
| OKM-12106 [M] | Um, Um, Um, Um, Um, Um | 1964 | 40.00 |
| OKM-12110 [M] | Major's Greatest Hits | 1965 | 30.00 |
| OKS-14105 [S] | The Monkey Time | 1963 | 50.00 |
| OKS-14106 [S] | Um, Um, Um, Um, Um, Um | 1964 | 50.00 |
| OKS-14110 [S] | Major's Greatest Hits | 1965 | 40.00 |
| **SOUL** | | | |
| S7-751 | Now Arriving | 1978 | 12.00 |

### LANCELOT LINK AND THE EVOLUTION REVOLUTION

| Number | Title (A Side/B Side) | Yr | NM |
|---|---|---|---|
| **ABC** | | | |
| S-715 | Lancelot Link and the Evolution Revolution | 1970 | 40.00 |

### LANCERS, THE

| Number | Title (A Side/B Side) | Yr | NM |
|---|---|---|---|
| **CORAL** | | | |
| CRL 57100 [M] | Dixieland Ball | 1957 | 25.00 |
| **IMPERIAL** | | | |
| LP-9075 [M] | Concert in Contrasts | 1959 | 30.00 |
| LP-12023 [S] | Concert in Contrasts | 1959 | 40.00 |
| **TREND** | | | |
| TL-1009 [10] | The Lancers | 1954 | 40.00 |

### LANCHESTER, ELSA

| Number | Title (A Side/B Side) | Yr | NM |
|---|---|---|---|
| **HIFI** | | | |
| 405 [M] | Songs for a Smoke-Filled Room | 1957 | 20.00 |
| 406 [M] | Songs for a Shuttered Parlor | 1958 | 20.00 |
| **VERVE** | | | |
| MGV-15015 [M] | Cockney London | 1960 | 30.00 |
| MGV-15024 [M] | Herself | 1962 | 30.00 |

### LAND, HAROLD

| Number | Title (A Side/B Side) | Yr | NM |
|---|---|---|---|
| **CONTEMPORARY** | | | |
| C-3550 [M] | Harold in the Land of Hi-Fi | 1958 | 80.00 |
| M-3550 [M] | Grooveyard | 1959 | 60.00 |
| *—Reissue with new title* | | | |
| M-3619 [M] | The Fox | 1965 | 20.00 |
| S-7550 [S] | Grooveyard | 1959 | 50.00 |
| S-7619 [S] | The Fox | 1965 | 25.00 |
| **HIFI** | | | |
| J-612 [M] | The Fox | 1960 | 60.00 |
| SJ-612 [S] | The Fox | 1960 | 80.00 |
| **IMPERIAL** | | | |
| LP-9247 [M] | Jazz Impressions of Folk Music | 1963 | 25.00 |
| LP-12247 [S] | Jazz Impressions of Folk Music | 1963 | 30.00 |
| **JAZZLAND** | | | |
| JLP-20 [M] | West Coast Blues! | 1960 | 40.00 |
| JLP-33 [M] | Eastward Ho! Harold Land in New York | 1961 | 40.00 |
| JLP-920 [S] | West Coast Blues! | 1960 | 50.00 |
| JLP-933 [S] | Eastward Ho! Harold Land in New York | 1961 | 50.00 |

### LANDSLIDE

| Number | Title (A Side/B Side) | Yr | NM |
|---|---|---|---|
| **CAPITOL** | | | |
| ST-11006 | Two-Sided Fantasy | 1972 | 40.00 |

### LANE, ABBE

| Number | Title (A Side/B Side) | Yr | NM |
|---|---|---|---|
| **MERCURY** | | | |
| MG-20643 [M] | Abbe Lane with Xavier Cugat and His Orchestra | 1961 | 25.00 |
| MG-20930 [M] | The Many Sides of Abbe Lane | 1964 | 20.00 |
| SR-60643 [S] | Abbe Lane with Xavier Cugat and His Orchestra | 1961 | 30.00 |
| SR-60930 [S] | The Many Sides of Abbe Lane | 1964 | 25.00 |
| **RCA VICTOR** | | | |
| LPM-1554 [M] | Be Mine Tonight | 1957 | 30.00 |
| LSP-1554 [S] | Be Mine Tonight | 1958 | 40.00 |
| LPM-1688 [M] | The Lady in Red | 1958 | 30.00 |
| LSP-1688 [S] | The Lady in Red | 1958 | 40.00 |

### LANE, CRISTY

| Number | Title (A Side/B Side) | Yr | NM |
|---|---|---|---|
| **ARRIVAL** | | | |
| NU 9640 | One Day at a Time: 14 Songs of Inspiration and Harmony | 1983 | 10.00 |
| **LANE** | | | |
| LPS-101 | Cristy Lane Salutes the G.I.'s of Vietnam | 197? | 25.00 |
| **LIBERTY** | | | |
| LT-978 | Simple Little Words | 1981 | 8.00 |
| *—Reissue of United Artists 978* | | | |
| LT-1023 | Ask Me to Dance | 1981 | 8.00 |
| *—Reissue of United Artists 1023* | | | |
| LT-1083 | I Have a Dream | 1981 | 8.00 |
| LN-10226 | Christmas with Cristy | 198? | 10.00 |
| LN-10239 | Amazing Grace | 198? | 6.00 |
| *—Budget-line reissue* | | | |
| LN-10306 | Footprints in the Sand | 1986 | 6.00 |
| *—Budget-line reissue* | | | |
| LN-10309 | Cristy Lane At Her Best | 1986 | 6.00 |
| *—Budget-line reissue* | | | |
| LT-51112 | Fragile — Handle with Care | 1981 | 8.00 |
| LT-51117 | Amazing Grace | 1982 | 8.00 |
| LT-51137 | Here's to Us | 1982 | 8.00 |
| LT-51148 | Footprints in the Sand | 1983 | 8.00 |
| LT-51153 | Cristy Lane At Her Best | 1984 | 8.00 |
| **LS** | | | |
| 1001 | Easy to Love | 198? | 10.00 |
| 1987 | Christmas Gold | 1987 | 10.00 |
| 2002 | Country Classics Vol. 2 | 198? | 10.00 |
| 2003 | Country Classics Vol. 3 | 198? | 10.00 |
| 8027 | Cristy Lane Is the Name | 1978 | 12.00 |
| 8028 | Love Lies | 1979 | 12.00 |
| SLL-8334 | The Sweetest Voice This Side of Heaven | 198? | 10.00 |
| SLL-8358 | Christmas Is the Man from Galilee | 1983 | 10.00 |
| SLL-8385 | Greatest Hits | 198? | 10.00 |
| SLL-8386 | One Day at a Time | 198? | 10.00 |
| 9227 | Cristy Lane Salutes the G.I.'s of Vietnam | 198? | 10.00 |
| **RIVERSONG** | | | |
| 2413 | 14 Golden Hymns | 198? | 10.00 |
| **SUFFOLK MARKETING** | | | |
| SLL-8289 | One Day at a Time | 198? | 10.00 |
| **UNITED ARTISTS** | | | |
| UA-LA978-H | Simple Little Words | 1979 | 10.00 |
| LT-1023 | Ask Me to Dance | 1980 | 10.00 |

### LANEGAN, MARK Also see SCREAMING TREES.

| Number | Title (A Side/B Side) | Yr | NM |
|---|---|---|---|
| **SUB POP** | | | |
| SP 61 | The Winding Sheet | 1990 | 10.00 |
| *—Black vinyl. Among the backing musicians are Kurt Cobain and Krist Novoselic of NIRVANA.* | | | |
| SP 61 | The Winding Sheet | 1990 | 25.00 |
| *—First 1,000 on red vinyl* | | | |
| SP 132 | Whisky for the Holy Ghost | 1994 | 12.00 |
| SP 419 | Scraps at Midnight | 1998 | 12.00 |

### LANG, K.D.

| Number | Title (A Side/B Side) | Yr | NM |
|---|---|---|---|
| **BUMSTEAD** | | | |
| BUM-86 | A Truly Western Experience | 1984 | 25.00 |
| *—Canadian import; reissue of Bumstead 842* | | | |
| BUM-842 | A Truly Western Experience | 1984 | 60.00 |
| *—Canadian import; first issue* | | | |
| **SIRE** | | | |
| PRO-A-3120 [DJ] | The Making of Shadowland | 1988 | 30.00 |
| *—Interview album* | | | |
| 25441 | Angel with a Lariat | 1987 | 10.00 |
| 25724 | Shadowland | 1988 | 10.00 |
| 25877 | Absolute Torch and Twang | 1989 | 12.00 |
| R 134567 | Shadowland | 1988 | 12.00 |
| *—BMG Direct Marketing edition* | | | |
| R 160100 | Angel with a Lariat | 1987 | 12.00 |
| *—BMG Direct Marketing edition* | | | |
| **WARNER BROS.** | | | |
| 46034 | All You Can Eat | 1995 | 20.00 |

### LANG, RONNIE

| Number | Title (A Side/B Side) | Yr | NM |
|---|---|---|---|
| **TOPS** | | | |
| L-1521 [M] | Modern Jazz | 1958 | 25.00 |

### LANGDON, DORY

| Number | Title (A Side/B Side) | Yr | NM |
|---|---|---|---|
| **VERVE** | | | |
| MGV-2101 [M] | Leprechauns Are Upon Me | 1957 | 40.00 |

### LANGDON, JIM

| Number | Title (A Side/B Side) | Yr | NM |
|---|---|---|---|
| **CUCA** | | | |
| 1100 [M] | Jim Langdon Trio | 1965 | 20.00 |

### LANGNER SISTERS, THE

| Number | Title (A Side/B Side) | Yr | NM |
|---|---|---|---|
| **STUDIO CITY** | | | |
| 9011 | The Langner Sisters | 1966 | 30.00 |
| 9012 | It's the Country Life for Me | 1967 | 30.00 |

### LANIN, LESTER

| Number | Title (A Side/B Side) | Yr | NM |
|---|---|---|---|
| **AUDIO FIDELITY** | | | |
| AFLP-2180 [M] | Thoroughly Modern | 1968 | 15.00 |
| AFSD-6180 [S] | Thoroughly Modern | 1968 | 12.00 |
| **EPIC** | | | |
| BSN 146 [(2)S] | The Dance Album | 1964 | 20.00 |
| BN 501 [S] | Lester Lanin Goes to College | 1959 | 20.00 |
| BN 505 [S] | Lester Lanin at the Tiffany Ball | 1959 | 20.00 |
| BN 516 [S] | Cocktail Dancing | 1959 | 20.00 |
| BN 517 [S] | Have Band, Will Travel | 1959 | 20.00 |
| BN 547 [S] | Christmas Dance Party (Volume 9) | 1959 | 20.00 |
| BN 556 [S] | Dance to the Lester Lanin Beat | 1960 | 20.00 |
| BN 570 [S] | High Society | 1961 | 15.00 |
| BN 620 [S] | Twistin' in High Society! | 1961 | 15.00 |
| BN 628 [R] | Lester Lanin and His Orchestra | 1962 | 12.00 |
| BN 633 [R] | Dance to the Music of Lester Lanin | 1962 | 12.00 |
| LN 3242 [M] | Lester Lanin and His Orchestra | 1956 | 15.00 |
| LN 3340 [M] | Dance to the Music of Lester Lanin | 1957 | 15.00 |
| LN 3410 [M] | Lester Lanin at the Tiffany Ball | 1957 | 15.00 |
| LN 3474 [M] | Lester Lanin Goes to College | 1958 | 15.00 |
| LN 3525 [M] | Have Band, Will Travel | 1958 | 15.00 |
| LN 3531 [M] | Cocktail Dancing | 1959 | 15.00 |
| LN 3617 [M] | Christmas Dance Party (Volume 9) | 1959 | 15.00 |
| LN 3656 [M] | Dance to the Lester Lanin Beat | 1960 | 15.00 |
| LN 3699 [M] | High Society | 1961 | 12.00 |
| LN 3825 [M] | Twistin' in High Society! | 1961 | 12.00 |
| SN 6046 [(2)M] | The Dance Album | 1964 | 15.00 |
| LN 24016 [M] | Dancing Theatre Party | 1962 | 12.00 |
| LN 24105 [M] | Richard Rogers Hits | 1964 | 12.00 |
| LN 24317 [M] | Cole Porter's Greatest Hits | 1967 | 12.00 |
| BN 26016 [S] | Dancing Theatre Party | 1962 | 15.00 |
| BN 26105 [S] | Richard Rogers Hits | 1964 | 15.00 |
| BN 26317 [S] | Cole Porter's Greatest Hits | 1967 | 12.00 |
| **HARMONY** | | | |
| HS 11262 | Everybody Dance | 1968 | 10.00 |
| **HINDSIGHT** | | | |
| HSR-210 | Dance Instrumentals: 1960-1962 | 198? | 8.00 |
| **METROMEDIA** | | | |
| MD-1006 | Narrowing the Generation Gap | 1969 | 12.00 |
| **PHILIPS** | | | |
| PHM 200132 [M] | Lester Lanin Plays for Dancing | 1964 | 10.00 |
| PHM 200145 [M] | Dancing at the Discotheque | 1964 | 10.00 |
| PHM 200165 [M] | I Had a Ball | 1965 | 10.00 |
| PHM 200181 [M] | Hits for Dancing | 1965 | 10.00 |
| PHM 200192 [M] | Lester Lanin at the Country Club | 1966 | 10.00 |
| PHM 200211 [M] | Forty Beatles Hits | 1966 | 12.00 |
| PHS 600132 [S] | Lester Lanin Plays for Dancing | 1964 | 12.00 |
| PHS 600145 [S] | Dancing at the Discotheque | 1964 | 12.00 |
| PHS 600165 [S] | I Had a Ball | 1965 | 12.00 |
| PHS 600181 [S] | Hits for Dancing | 1965 | 12.00 |
| PHS 600192 [S] | Lester Lanin at the Country Club | 1966 | 12.00 |
| PHS 600211 [S] | Forty Beatles Hits | 1966 | 15.00 |

### LANZA, MARIO

| Number | Title (A Side/B Side) | Yr | NM |
|---|---|---|---|
| **PAIR** | | | |
| PDL2-1059 [(2)] | The Voice of the Century | 1986 | 12.00 |
| **PICKWICK** | | | |
| CAS-777(e) [R] | Christmas Hymns and Carols | 1977 | 8.00 |
| *—Same contents as RCA Camden CAS-777(e)* | | | |
| **RCA CAMDEN** | | | |
| CAL-450 [M] | You Do Something to Me | 195? | 15.00 |
| CAS-450(e) [R] | You Do Something to Me | 195? | 12.00 |
| CAL-777 [M] | Christmas Hymns and Carols | 196? | 15.00 |
| CAS-777(e) [R] | Christmas Hymns and Carols | 196? | 12.00 |
| **RCA RED SEAL** | | | |
| ARL1-0134 | Lanza Sings Caruso | 1973 | 10.00 |
| CRL1-1750 | A Legendary Performer | 1976 | 10.00 |
| ANL1-2874 | Pure Gold | 1978 | 10.00 |
| CRM5-4158 [(5)] | The Mario Lanza Collection | 1981 | 60.00 |
| ARL1-4405 | The Great Caruso | 198? | 8.00 |
| VCS-6192 [(3)] | Mario Lanza's Greatest Hits | 1970 | 25.00 |
| VCS-7073 [(2)] | Opera's Greatest Hits | 1971 | 18.00 |
| **RCA VICTOR RED SEAL** | | | |
| LM-155 [10] | Mario Lanza Sings Christmas Songs | 1951 | 50.00 |
| LM-1127 [M] | The Great Caruso | 195? | 40.00 |
| LSC-1127(e) [R] | The Great Caruso | 196? | 12.00 |
| LM-1188 [M] | Love Songs and a Neapolitan Serenade | 195? | 40.00 |
| LSC-1188(e) [R] | Love Songs and a Neapolitan Serenade | 196? | 12.00 |
| LM 1837 [M] | Mario Lanza Sings the Hit Songs from "The Student Prince" and Other Great Musical Comedies | 1955 | 40.00 |

The Great Caruso Lanza
RCA Victor
LM-1127
RED SEAL


Mario Lanza, *The Great Caruso,* RCA Victor Red Seal LM-1127, 1950s, $40.

| Number | Title (A Side/B Side) | Yr | NM |
|---|---|---|---|
| LSC 1837(e) [R] | Mario Lanza Sings the Hit Songs from "The Student Prince" and Other Great Musical Comedies | 196? | 12.00 |
| LM-1860 [M] | "A Kiss" and Other Love Songs | 1955 | 40.00 |
| LSC-1860(e) [R] | "A Kiss" and Other Love Songs | 196? | 12.00 |
| LM-1927 [M] | The Touch of Your Hand | 1955 | 40.00 |
| LSC-1927(e) [R] | The Touch of Your Hand | 196? | 12.00 |
| LM-1943 [M] | Magic Mario | 1955 | 40.00 |
| LM-1996 [M] | Serenade | 1956 | 40.00 |
| LM-2070 [M] | Lanza on Broadway | 1956 | 30.00 |
| LSC-2070(e) [R] | Lanza on Broadway | 196? | 12.00 |
| LM-2090 [M] | Cavalcade of Show Tunes | 1957 | 30.00 |
| LSC-2090(e) [R] | Cavalcade of Show Tunes | 196? | 12.00 |
| LM-2211 [M] | Seven Hills of Rome | 1958 | 30.00 |
| LM-2331 [M] | Mario | 1959 | 20.00 |
| LSC-2331 [S] | Mario! | 1959 | 30.00 |
| LM-2333 [M] | Lanza Sings Christmas Carols | 1959 | 15.00 |
| LSC-2333 [S] | Lanza Sings Christmas Carols | 1959 | 20.00 |
| *—Original copies have "shaded dog" on labels* | | | |
| LM-2338 [M] | For the First Time | 1959 | 15.00 |
| LSC-2338 [S] | For the First Time | 1959 | 20.00 |
| LM-2339 [M] | The Student Prince | 1959 | 15.00 |
| LSC-2339 [S] | The Student Prince | 1959 | 20.00 |
| LM-2393 [M] | Mario Lanza Sings Caruso Favorites | 1960 | 15.00 |
| LSC-2393 [S] | Mario Lanza Sings Caruso Favorites | 1960 | 20.00 |
| LM-2422 [M] | Double Feature — Mario Lanza | 1960 | 20.00 |
| LM-2440 [M] | The Desert Song | 1960 | 15.00 |
| LSC-2440 [S] | The Desert Song | 1960 | 20.00 |
| LM-2454 [M] | A Mario Lanza Program | 1960 | 15.00 |
| LSC-2454 [S] | A Mario Lanza Program | 1960 | 20.00 |
| LM-2509 [M] | The Vagabond King | 1961 | 15.00 |
| LSC-2509 [S] | The Vagabond King | 1961 | 20.00 |
| LM-2607 [M] | I'll Walk with God | 1962 | 20.00 |
| LSC-2607(e) [R] | I'll Walk with God | 1962 | 12.00 |
| LM-2720 [M] | I'll See You in My Dreams | 1964 | 12.00 |
| LSC-2720 [S] | I'll See You in My Dreams | 1964 | 15.00 |
| LM-2748 [M] | The Best of Mario Lanza | 1964 | 12.00 |
| LSC-2748 [S] | The Best of Mario Lanza | 1964 | 15.00 |
| LM-2790 [M] | If You Are But a Dream | 196? | 12.00 |
| LSC-2790 [S] | If You Are But a Dream | 196? | 15.00 |
| LM-2932 [M] | His Favorite Arias | 196? | 12.00 |
| LSC-2932 [S] | His Favorite Arias | 196? | 15.00 |
| LM-2998 [M] | The Best of Mario Lanza, Volume 2 | 1968 | 20.00 |
| LSC-2998 [S] | The Best of Mario Lanza, Volume 2 | 1968 | 15.00 |
| LSC-3049 | Younger Than Springtime | 1968 | 12.00 |
| LSC-3101 | Mario Lanza in Opera | 1969 | 15.00 |
| LSC-3102 | Mario Lanza Memories | 1969 | 15.00 |
| LSC-3103 | Mario Lanza...Speak to Me of Love | 1969 | 15.00 |
| LSC-3216 | The Student Prince | 1971 | 12.00 |
| LSC-3289 | Be My Love | 1972 | 12.00 |

**LAPORTA, JOHN**

| Number | Title (A Side/B Side) | Yr | NM |
|---|---|---|---|
| **DEBUT** | | | |
| DLP-10 [10] | The John LaPorta Quintet | 1954 | 400.00 |
| DEB-122 [M] | Three Moods | 1955 | 300.00 |
| **EVEREST** | | | |
| SDBR-1037 [S] | The Most Minor | 1959 | 60.00 |
| LPBR-5037 [M] | The Most Minor | 1959 | 50.00 |
| **FANTASY** | | | |
| 3228 [M] | Conceptions | 1956 | 40.00 |
| *—Black vinyl* | | | |
| 3228 [M] | Conceptions | 1956 | 80.00 |
| *—Red vinyl* | | | |
| 3237 [M] | South American Brothers | 1956 | 40.00 |
| *—Black vinyl* | | | |
| 3237 [M] | South American Brothers | 1956 | 80.00 |
| *—Red vinyl* | | | |
| 3248 [M] | The Clarinet Artistry of John LaPorta | 1957 | 40.00 |
| *—Black vinyl* | | | |
| 3248 [M] | The Clarinet Artistry of John LaPorta | 1957 | 80.00 |
| *—Red vinyl* | | | |
| **MUSIC MINUS ONE** | | | |
| 4003 [M] | Eight Men In Search of a Drummer | 1961 | 25.00 |

**LAREDO, JAIME**

| Number | Title (A Side/B Side) | Yr | NM |
|---|---|---|---|
| **RCA VICTOR RED SEAL** | | | |
| LSC-2373 [S] | Presenting Jaime Laredo | 1960 | 40.00 |
| *—Original with "shaded dog" label* | | | |
| LSC-2414 [S] | Brahms: Violin Sonata No. 3; Bach: Partita No. 3 | 1960 | 80.00 |
| *—Original with "shaded dog" label* | | | |
| LSC-2472 [S] | Bruch: Violin Concerto No. 1; Mozart: Violin Concerto No. 3 | 1961 | 40.00 |
| *—Original with "shaded dog" label* | | | |

**LARKIN, BILLY**

| Number | Title (A Side/B Side) | Yr | NM |
|---|---|---|---|
| **AURA** | | | |
| 23002 [S] | Pigmy | 1964 | 25.00 |
| *—As "The Delegates"* | | | |
| 83002 [M] | Pigmy | 1964 | 20.00 |
| *—As "The Delegates"* | | | |
| **WORLD PACIFIC** | | | |
| WP-1837 [M] | Hole in the Wall | 1966 | 20.00 |
| WP-1843 [M] | Ain't That a Groove | 1966 | 20.00 |
| WP-1850 [M] | Hold On | 1967 | 20.00 |
| WPS-21837 [S] | Hole in the Wall | 1966 | 25.00 |
| WPS-21843 [S] | Ain't That a Groove | 1966 | 25.00 |
| WPS-21850 [S] | Hold On | 1967 | 25.00 |

**LARKINS, ELLIS**

| Number | Title (A Side/B Side) | Yr | NM |
|---|---|---|---|
| **DECCA** | | | |
| DL 5391 [10] | Blues in the Night | 1952 | 50.00 |
| DL 8303 [M] | Manhattan at Midnight | 1956 | 40.00 |
| DL 9205 [M] | The Soft Touch | 1958 | 30.00 |
| DL 9211 [M] | Blue and Sentimental | 1958 | 30.00 |
| DL 79205 [S] | The Soft Touch | 1958 | 25.00 |
| DL 79211 [S] | Blue and Sentimental | 1958 | 25.00 |
| **STORYVILLE** | | | |
| STLP-316 [10] | Perfume and Rain | 1955 | 80.00 |
| STLP-913 [M] | Do Nothin' Till You Hear from Me | 1956 | 50.00 |

**LARKINS, ELLIS/LEE WILEY**

| Number | Title (A Side/B Side) | Yr | NM |
|---|---|---|---|
| **STORYVILLE** | | | |
| STLP-911 [M] | Duologue | 1956 | 60.00 |

**LARKS, THE (1)**

| Number | Title (A Side/B Side) | Yr | NM |
|---|---|---|---|
| **COLLECTABLES** | | | |
| COL-5176 | Golden Classics: The Jerk | 198? | 10.00 |
| **MONEY** | | | |
| LP-1102 [M] | The Jerk | 1965 | 40.00 |
| ST-1102 [S] | The Jerk | 1965 | 50.00 |
| LP-1107 [M] | Soul Kaleidoscope | 1966 | 40.00 |
| ST-1107 [S] | Soul Kaleidoscope | 1966 | 50.00 |
| LP-1110 [M] | Superslick | 1967 | 40.00 |
| ST-1110 [S] | Superslick | 1967 | 50.00 |

**LAROCA, PETE**

| Number | Title (A Side/B Side) | Yr | NM |
|---|---|---|---|
| **BLUE NOTE** | | | |
| BLP-4205 [M] | Basra | 1965 | 30.00 |
| BST-84205 [S] | Basra | 1965 | 40.00 |
| *—With "New York, USA" address on label* | | | |

**LAROCCA, NICK**

| Number | Title (A Side/B Side) | Yr | NM |
|---|---|---|---|
| **SOUTHLAND** | | | |
| 230 [M] | Nick LaRocca and His Dixieland Band | 196? | 20.00 |

**LAROSA, JULIUS**

| Number | Title (A Side/B Side) | Yr | NM |
|---|---|---|---|
| **AUDIOPHILE** | | | |
| AP-190 | It's a Wrap! | 1985 | 12.00 |
| **CADENCE** | | | |
| CLP 1007 [M] | Julius LaRosa (Julie's Best) | 1955 | 40.00 |
| **FORUM** | | | |
| F-16012 [M] | Just Say I Love Her | 1960 | 15.00 |
| FS-16012 [S] | Just Say I Love Her | 1960 | 20.00 |
| **KAPP** | | | |
| KL-1245 [M] | The New Julie LaRosa | 1961 | 15.00 |
| KS-3245 [S] | The New Julie LaRosa | 1961 | 20.00 |
| **METROMEDIA** | | | |
| MD-1036 | Words | 1971 | 12.00 |
| **MGM** | | | |
| E-4398 [M] | You're Gonna Hear From Me | 1966 | 12.00 |
| SE-4398 [S] | You're Gonna Hear From Me | 1966 | 15.00 |
| E-4437 [M] | Hey Look Me Over | 1967 | 12.00 |
| SE-4437 [S] | Hey Look Me Over | 1967 | 15.00 |
| **RCA VICTOR** | | | |
| LPM-1299 [M] | Julius LaRosa | 1956 | 40.00 |
| **ROULETTE** | | | |
| R 25054 [M] | Love Songs A LaRosa | 1959 | 20.00 |
| SR 25054 [S] | Love Songs A LaRosa | 1959 | 25.00 |
| R 25083 [M] | On the Sunny Side | 1960 | 20.00 |
| SR 25083 [S] | On the Sunny Side | 1960 | 25.00 |

**LARRY AND HANK**

| Number | Title (A Side/B Side) | Yr | NM |
|---|---|---|---|
| **PRESTIGE** | | | |
| PRLP-7472 [M] | The Blues/A New Generation | 1965 | 20.00 |
| PRST-7472 [S] | The Blues/A New Generation | 1965 | 25.00 |

**LARRY AND LENORE**

| Number | Title (A Side/B Side) | Yr | NM |
|---|---|---|---|
| **REQUEST** | | | |
| 10037 [M] | Traveling Guitars | 1959 | 100.00 |

**LASHA, PRINCE**

| Number | Title (A Side/B Side) | Yr | NM |
|---|---|---|---|
| **CONTEMPORARY** | | | |
| M-3610 [M] | The Cry | 1963 | 25.00 |
| S-7610 [S] | The Cry | 1963 | 30.00 |
| S-7617 | Firebirds | 1968 | 25.00 |



Except when noted otherwise, VG = 25% of NM, and VG+ = 50% of NM. (Example: VG = $2.00, VG+ = $4.00 and NM = $8.00.)

**LAST CALL OF SHILOH, THE**

LAST CALL
❑ 5136 The Last Call 196? 200.00

**LAST EXIT**

ENEMY
❑ 88561-8176-1 Last Exit 1986 20.00

**LAST POETS, THE**

BLUE THUMB
❑ BT-39 Chastisement 1972 30.00
❑ BT-52 At Last 1973 30.00

CASABLANCA
❑ NBLP 7051 Delights of the Garden 1977 25.00

CELLULOID
❑ 6101 The Last Poets 198? 10.00
❑ 6105 This Is Madness 198? 10.00
❑ 6108 Oh My People 198? 10.00
❑ 6136 Delights of the Garden 198? 10.00

COLLECTABLES
❑ COL-6500 Right On! 198? 10.00

DOUGLAS
❑ 3 The Last Poets 1970 50.00
❑ Z 30583 This Is Madness 1971 50.00
❑ Z 30811 The Last Poets 1971 40.00

JUGGERNAUT
❑ 8802 Right On! 1971 50.00
*—As "The Original Last Poets"*

**LATEEF, YUSEF**

ARGO
❑ LP-634 [M] Live at Cranbrook 1959 80.00

CHARLIE PARKER
❑ PLP-814 [M] Lost in Sound 1962 50.00
❑ PLP-814S [S] Lost in Sound 1962 60.00

DELMARK
❑ DL-407 [M] Yusef! 1965 40.00
❑ DS-407 [S] Yusef! 1965 50.00

IMPULSE!
❑ A-56 [M] Jazz Around the World 1963 40.00
❑ AS-56 [S] Jazz Around the World 1963 50.00
❑ A-69 [M] Live at Pep's 1964 50.00
❑ AS-69 [S] Live at Pep's 1964 60.00
❑ A-84 [M] 1984 1965 30.00
❑ AS-84 [S] 1984 1965 40.00
❑ A-92 [M] Psychicemotus 1966 50.00
❑ AS-92 [S] Psychicemotus 1966 60.00
❑ A-9117 [M] A Flat, G Flat and C 1966 50.00
❑ AS-9117 [S] A Flat, G Flat and C 1966 60.00
❑ A-9125 [M] The Golden Flute 1966 50.00
❑ AS-9125 [S] The Golden Flute 1966 60.00
❑ MAS-90216 [M] Live at Pep's 1964 60.00
*—Capitol Record Club edition*

MOODSVILLE
❑ MVLP-22 [M] Eastern Sounds 1961 100.00
*—Green label, silver print*
❑ MVST-22 [S] Eastern Sounds 1961 120.00
*—Green label, silver print*

NEW JAZZ
❑ NJLP-8218 [M] Other Sounds 1959 200.00
*—Purple label*
❑ NJLP-8218 [M] Other Sounds 1965 80.00
*—Blue label, trident logo at right*
❑ NJLP-8234 [M] Cry! Tender 1960 200.00
*—Purple label*
❑ NJLP-8234 [M] Cry! Tender 1965 80.00
*—Blue label, trident logo at right*
❑ NJLP-8261 [M] The Sounds of Yusef 1961 100.00
*—Reissue of Prestige 7122; purple label*
❑ NJLP-8261 [M] The Sounds of Yusef 1965 50.00
*—Blue label, trident logo at right*
❑ NJLP-8272 [M] Into Something 1962 200.00
*—Purple label*
❑ NJLP-8272 [M] Into Something 1965 80.00
*—Blue label, trident logo at right*

PRESTIGE
❑ PRLP-7122 [M] The Sounds of Yusef 1957 200.00
*—Yellow label*
❑ PRLP-7319 [M] Eastern Sounds 1964 60.00
❑ PRST-7319 [S] Eastern Sounds 1964 70.00
*—Reissue of Moodsville 22*
❑ PRLP-7398 [M] The Sounds of Yusef 1966 30.00
❑ PRST-7398 [S] The Sounds of Yusef Lateef 1966 40.00
❑ PRLP-7447 [M] Yusef Lateef Plays for Lovers 1967 30.00
❑ PRST-7447 [S] Yusef Lateef Plays for Lovers 1967 30.00

RIVERSIDE
❑ RLP 12-325 [M] Three Faces of Yusef Lateef 1960 200.00
❑ RLP-337 [M] The Centaur and the Phoenix 1960 80.00
❑ RLP-1176 [S] Three Faces of Yusef Lateef 1960 150.00
❑ RLP-9337 [S] The Centaur and the Phoenix 1960 60.00

SAVOY
❑ MG-12103 [M] Jazz Mood 1957 100.00
❑ MG-12109 [M] Jazz for the Thinker 1957 100.00
❑ MG-12117 [M] Prayer to the East 1957 100.00
❑ MG-12120 [M] Jazz and the Sounds of Nature 1958 100.00
❑ MG-12139 [M] The Dreamer 1958 100.00
❑ MG-12140 [M] The Fabric of Jazz 1958 100.00
❑ SR-13007 [S] The Dreamer 1959 100.00
❑ SR-13008 [S] The Fabric of Jazz 1959 100.00

VERVE
❑ MGV-8217 [M] Before Dawn 1958 200.00
❑ V-8217 [M] Before Dawn 1961 40.00

VJ INTERNATIONAL
❑ VJS-3052 [M] Contemplation 1974 50.00
*—Reissue of Vee-Jay 3010, which was originally credited to LOUIS HAYES.*

**LATIN ALL-STARS, THE**

CROWN
❑ CLP 5159 [M] Jazz Heat-Bongo Beat 1959 25.00

**LATIN JAZZ QUINTET, THE**

NEW JAZZ
❑ NJLP-8251 [M] Caribe 1960 50.00
*—Purple label*
❑ NJLP-8251 [M] Caribe 1965 25.00
*—Blue label, trident logo at right*

STATUS
❑ ST-8321 [M] Latin Soul 1965 40.00

TRU-SOUND
❑ TRU-15003 [M] Hot Sauce 1962 40.00
❑ TRU-15012 [M] The Latin Jazz Quintet 1962 40.00

UNITED ARTISTS
❑ UAL-4071 [M] The Latin Jazz Quintet 1960 30.00
❑ UAS-5071 [S] The Latin Jazz Quintet 1960 40.00

**LATIN SOULS, THE**

KAPP
❑ KL-1524 [M] Boo-Ga-Loo and Shing-a-Ling 1967 25.00
❑ KS-3524 [S] Boo-Ga-Loo and Shing-a-Ling 1967 20.00
❑ KS-3553 Tigar Boo-Ga-Loo 1968 20.00

**LAUGHTON, CHARLES**

CAPITOL
❑ STBO 1650 [(2)S] The Story Teller 1962 30.00
❑ TBO 1650 [(2)M] The Story Teller 1962 25.00

DECCA
❑ DLP 8010 [M] A Christmas Carol/Mr. Pickwick's Christmas 1955 20.00
*—A-side read by Ronald Colman*
❑ DL 8031 [M] Readings from the Bible 195? 30.00

MCA
❑ 15010 A Christmas Carol/Mr. Pickwick's Christmas 1955 20.00
*—A-side read by Ronald Colman; reissue of Decca LP*

**LAUPER, CYNDI** Also see BLUE ANGEL.

EPIC
❑ OE 44318 A Night to Remember 1989 10.00

PORTRAIT
❑ BFR 38930 She's So Unusual 1983 12.00
❑ FR 38930 She's So Unusual 1984 8.00
*—Reissue with new prefix*
❑ 9R9 39610 She's So Unusual 1984 30.00
*—Picture disc in plastic sleeve with sticker*
❑ OR 40313 True Colors 1986 10.00

**LAUREN, ROD**

RCA VICTOR
❑ LPM-2176 [M] I'm Rod Lauren 1961 40.00
❑ LSP-2176 [S] I'm Rod Lauren 1961 50.00

**LAURIE, ANNIE**

AUDIO LAB
❑ AL-1510 [M] It Hurts to Be in Love 1959 300.00

**LAURIE SISTERS, THE**

RCA CAMDEN
❑ CAL-545 [M] Hits of the Great Girl Groups 1960 25.00
❑ CAS-545 [S] Hits of the Great Girl Groups 1960 30.00

**LAWRENCE, ARNIE**

EMBRYO
❑ SD 525 Inside an Hour Glass 1970 20.00

PROJECT 3
❑ PR-5011 You're Gonna Hear From Me 1967 20.00
❑ PR-5028 Look Toward a Dream 1968 20.00

**LAWRENCE, BILL**

TOPS
❑ L-1576 [M] Bill Lawrence Sings I'm in the Mood for Love 1957 20.00

**LAWRENCE, CAROL**

CAMEO
❑ C-1077 [M] An Evening with Carol Lawrence 1964 20.00
❑ SC-1077 [S] An Evening with Carol Lawrence 1964 25.00

CHANCELLOR
❑ CHL-5015 [M] Tonight at 8:30 1960 20.00
❑ CHLS-5015 [S] Tonight at 8:30 1960 30.00

**LAWRENCE, EDDIE**

CORAL
❑ CRL 57103 [M] The Old Philosopher 1956 30.00
❑ CRL 57155 [M] Eddie "The Old Philosopher" Lawrence 1957 30.00
❑ CRL 57203 [M] The Kingdom of Eddie Lawrence 1958 30.00
❑ CRL 57371 [M] The Side Splitting Personality of Eddie Lawrence 1961 30.00
❑ CRL 57411 [M] Seven Characters In Search of Eddie Lawrence 1962 30.00
❑ CRL 757411 [S] Seven Characters In Search of Eddie Lawrence 1962 40.00

EPIC
❑ LN 24149 [M] Is That What's Bothering You Bunkie? 1965 30.00
❑ BN 26149 [S] Is That What's Bothering You Bunkie? 1965 40.00

SIGNATURE
❑ SM-1003 [M] The Garden of Eddie Lawrence 1960 40.00

**LAWRENCE, ELLIOT**

DECCA
❑ DL 5274 [10] College Prom 1950 50.00
❑ DL 5353 [10] Moonlight on the Campus 1951 50.00

FANTASY
❑ 3206 [M] Elliot Lawrence Plays Gerry Mulligan Arrangements 1956 30.00
*—Black vinyl, red label, non-flexible vinyl*
❑ 3206 [M] Elliot Lawrence Plays Gerry Mulligan Arrangements 196? 20.00
*—Black vinyl, red label, flexible vinyl*
❑ 3206 [M] Elliot Lawrence Plays Gerry Mulligan Arrangements 1956 50.00
*—Red vinyl*
❑ 3219 [M] Elliot Lawrence Plays Tiny Kahn and Johnny Mandel Arrangements 1956 30.00
*—Black vinyl, red label, non-flexible vinyl*
❑ 3219 [M] Elliot Lawrence Plays Tiny Kahn and Johnny Mandel Arrangements 1956 50.00
*—Red vinyl*
❑ 3219 [M] Elliot Lawrence Plays Tiny Kahn and Johnny Mandel Arrangements 196? 20.00
*—Black vinyl, red label, flexible vinyl*
❑ 3226 [M] Dream 1956 30.00
*—Black vinyl, red label, non-flexible vinyl*
❑ 3226 [M] Dream 1956 50.00
*—Red vinyl*
❑ 3226 [M] Dream 196? 20.00
*—Black vinyl, red label, flexible vinyl*
❑ 3236 [M] Swinging at the Steel Pier 1956 30.00
*—Black vinyl, red label, non-flexible vinyl*
❑ 3236 [M] Swinging at the Steel Pier 1956 50.00
*—Red vinyl*
❑ 3236 [M] Swinging at the Steel Pier 196? 20.00
*—Black vinyl, red label, flexible vinyl*
❑ 3246 [M] Elliot Lawrence Plays for Swinging Dancers 1957 25.00
*—Black vinyl, red label, non-flexible vinyl*
❑ 3246 [M] Elliot Lawrence Plays for Swinging Dancers 1957 40.00
*—Red vinyl*
❑ 3261 [M] Dream On — Dance On 1958 25.00
*—Black vinyl, red label, non-flexible vinyl*
❑ 3261 [M] Dream On — Dance On 1958 40.00
*—Red vinyl*
❑ 3290 [M] Big Band Sound 1959 25.00
*—Black vinyl, red label, non-flexible vinyl*
❑ 3290 [M] Big Band Sound 1959 40.00
*—Red vinyl*
❑ 8002 [S] Dream On — Dance On 196? 20.00
*—Black vinyl, blue label, non-flexible vinyl*
❑ 8002 [S] Dream On — Dance On 196? 30.00
*—Blue vinyl*
❑ 8021 [S] Elliot Lawrence Plays for Swinging Dancers 196? 20.00
*—Black vinyl, blue label, non-flexible vinyl*
❑ 8021 [S] Elliot Lawrence Plays for Swinging Dancers 196? 30.00
*—Blue vinyl*
❑ 8031 [S] Big Band Sound 196? 20.00
*—Black vinyl, blue label, non-flexible vinyl*
❑ 8031 [S] Big Band Sound 196? 30.00
*—Blue vinyl*

JAZZTONE
❑ J-1279 [M] Big Band Modern 1958 60.00

MOBILE FIDELITY
❑ 2-229 [(2)] The Music of Elliot Lawrence 1995 40.00
*—"Original Master Recording" at top of cover*

SESAC
❑ N-1153 [M] Jump Steady 1960 30.00
❑ SN-1153 [S] Jump Steady 1960 40.00

| Number | Title (A Side/B Side) | Yr | NM |
|---|---|---|---|
| **SURREY** | | | |
| ❑ S-1019 [M] | Winds on Velvet | 196? | 12.00 |
| ❑ SS-1019 [S] | Winds on Velvet | 196? | 15.00 |
| **TOP RANK** | | | |
| ❑ RM-304 [M] | Music for Trapping (Tender, That Is) | 1959 | 60.00 |
| **VIK** | | | |
| ❑ LX-1113 [M] | Jazz Goes Broadway | 1958 | 60.00 |
| ❑ LX-1124 [M] | Hi-Fi-ing Winds | 1958 | 40.00 |
| **LAWRENCE, GERTRUDE** | | | |
| **DECCA** | | | |
| ❑ DL 5418 [10] | Souvenir Album | 1952 | 50.00 |
| ❑ DL 8673 [M] | A Remembrance | 1958 | 30.00 |
| *—Black label, silver print* | | | |
| **LAWRENCE, STEVE** | | | |
| **ABC-PARAMOUNT** | | | |
| ❑ 290 [M] | Swing Softly with Me | 1959 | 25.00 |
| ❑ S-290 [S] | Swing Softly with Me | 1959 | 30.00 |
| ❑ 392 [M] | The Best of Steve Lawrence | 1960 | 20.00 |
| ❑ S-392 [S] | The Best of Steve Lawrence | 1960 | 25.00 |
| **APPLAUSE** | | | |
| ❑ 1001 | Take It On Home | 1981 | 10.00 |
| **COLUMBIA** | | | |
| ❑ CL 1953 [M] | Winners! | 1963 | 12.00 |
| ❑ CL 2121 [M] | Academy Award Losers | 1964 | 12.00 |
| ❑ CL 2227 [M] | Everybody Knows | 1964 | 12.00 |
| ❑ CL 2419 [M] | The Steve Lawrence Show | 1965 | 12.00 |
| ❑ CL 2540 [M] | Of Love and... Sad Young Men | 1966 | 12.00 |
| ❑ CS 8753 [S] | Winners! | 1963 | 15.00 |
| ❑ CS 8921 [S] | Academy Award Losers | 1964 | 15.00 |
| ❑ CS 9027 [S] | Everybody Knows | 1964 | 15.00 |
| ❑ CS 9219 [S] | The Steve Lawrence Show | 1965 | 15.00 |
| ❑ CS 9340 [S] | Of Love and... Sad Young Men | 1966 | 15.00 |
| ❑ CS 9565 | Greatest Hits | 1968 | 12.00 |
| ❑ PC 9565 | Greatest Hits | 198? | 8.00 |
| *—Reissue with new prefix* | | | |
| **CORAL** | | | |
| ❑ CRL 57050 [M] | About That Girl | 1956 | 40.00 |
| ❑ CRL 57182 [M] | Songs by Steve Lawrence | 1957 | 40.00 |
| ❑ CRL 57204 [M] | Here's Steve Lawrence | 1958 | 40.00 |
| ❑ CRL 57268 [M] | All About Love | 1959 | 30.00 |
| ❑ CRL 57434 [M] | Songs Everybody Knows | 1963 | 25.00 |
| ❑ CRL 757268 [S] | All About Love | 1959 | 40.00 |
| ❑ CRL 757434 [S] | Songs Everybody Knows | 1963 | 30.00 |
| **HARMONY** | | | |
| ❑ HS 11257 | Moon River | 196? | 10.00 |
| ❑ HS 11327 | Ramblin' Rose | 1969 | 10.00 |
| ❑ HS 11397 | Love Me | 1970 | 10.00 |
| **KING** | | | |
| ❑ 593 [M] | Steve Lawrence | 1959 | 80.00 |
| **MGM** | | | |
| ❑ SE-4824 | Portrait | 1973 | 10.00 |
| **RCA VICTOR** | | | |
| ❑ LSP-4167 | I've Gotta Be Me | 1969 | 12.00 |
| ❑ LSP-4347 | On a Clear Day | 1970 | 12.00 |
| **UNITED ARTISTS** | | | |
| ❑ UAL-3098 [M] | The Steve Lawrence Sound | 1960 | 20.00 |
| ❑ UAL-3114 [M] | Steve Lawrence Goes Latin | 1960 | 20.00 |
| ❑ UAL-3150 [M] | Portrait of My Love | 1961 | 20.00 |
| ❑ UAL-3190 [M] | The Very Best of Steve Lawrence | 1962 | 20.00 |
| ❑ UAL-3265 [M] | People Will Say We're in Love | 1963 | 20.00 |
| ❑ UAL-3368 [M] | Steve Lawrence Conquers Broadway | 1964 | 15.00 |
| ❑ UAS-6098 [S] | The Steve Lawrence Sound | 1960 | 25.00 |
| ❑ UAS-6114 [S] | Steve Lawrence Goes Latin | 1960 | 25.00 |
| ❑ UAS-6150 [S] | Portrait of My Love | 1961 | 25.00 |
| ❑ UAS-6190 [S] | The Very Best of Steve Lawrence | 1962 | 25.00 |
| ❑ UAS-6265 [S] | People Will Say We're in Love | 1963 | 25.00 |
| ❑ UAS-6368 [S] | Steve Lawrence Conquers Broadway | 1964 | 20.00 |
| **VOCALION** | | | |
| ❑ VL 3775 [M] | Here's Steve Lawrence | 196? | 12.00 |
| ❑ VL 73775 [R] | Here's Steve Lawrence | 196? | 10.00 |
| ❑ VL 73886 | The More I See You | 1970 | 10.00 |
| **LAWRENCE, STEVE, AND EYDIE GORME** Also see each artist's individual listings. | | | |
| **ABC** | | | |
| ❑ X-764 [(2)] | 20 Golden Performances | 1974 | 12.00 |
| **ABC-PARAMOUNT** | | | |
| ❑ 300 [M] | We Got Us | 1960 | 20.00 |
| ❑ S-300 [S] | We Got Us | 1960 | 25.00 |
| ❑ 311 [M] | Steve and Eydie Sing the Golden Hits | 1960 | 20.00 |
| ❑ S-311 [S] | Steve and Eydie Sing the Golden Hits | 1960 | 25.00 |
| ❑ 469 [M] | Our Best to You | 1964 | 15.00 |
| ❑ S-469 [S] | Our Best to You | 1964 | 20.00 |
| **CALENDAR** | | | |
| ❑ KOM-1001 [M] | Golden Rainbow | 1968 | 30.00 |
| ❑ KOS-1001 [S] | Golden Rainbow | 1968 | 40.00 |
| **COLUMBIA** | | | |
| ❑ CL 2021 [M] | Steve and Eydie at the Movies | 1964 | 12.00 |
| ❑ CL 2262 [M] | That Holiday Feeling | 1964 | 12.00 |
| ❑ CL 2636 [M] | Steve and Eydie Together On Broadway | 1967 | 12.00 |
| ❑ CL 2730 [M] | Bonfa and Brazil | 1968 | 15.00 |
| ❑ CS 8821 [S] | Steve and Eydie at the Movies | 1964 | 15.00 |
| ❑ CS 9062 [S] | That Holiday Feeling | 1964 | 15.00 |
| ❑ CS 9436 [S] | Steve and Eydie Together On Broadway | 1967 | 15.00 |
| ❑ CS 9530 [S] | Bonfa and Brazil | 1968 | 12.00 |
| **CORAL** | | | |
| ❑ CRL 57336 [M] | Steve and Eydie | 1962 | 20.00 |
| **HARMONY** | | | |
| ❑ H 30292 | Something's Gotta Give | 1971 | 10.00 |
| **MATI-MOR** | | | |
| ❑ 8003 | It's Us Again | 196? | 20.00 |
| *—Promotional item for Silvirkin shampoo* | | | |
| **MGM** | | | |
| ❑ SE-4803 | The World of Steve Lawrence and Eydie Gorme | 1972 | 10.00 |
| ❑ SE-4881 | Feelin' | 1973 | 10.00 |
| **RCA VICTOR** | | | |
| ❑ LSP-4107 | Real True Lovin' | 1969 | 12.00 |
| ❑ LSP-4115 | What It Was, Was Love | 1969 | 12.00 |
| ❑ LSP-4393 | A Man and a Woman | 1971 | 12.00 |
| ❑ VPS-6035 [(2)] | This Is Steve Lawrence and Eydie Gorme | 1971 | 15.00 |
| ❑ VPS-6050 [(2)] | This Is Steve Lawrence and Eydie Gorme, Vol. 2 | 1972 | 15.00 |
| **STAGE 2** | | | |
| ❑ 712 | Hallelujah | 198? | 10.00 |
| **UNITED ARTISTS** | | | |
| ❑ UAL-3191 [M] | The Very Best of Eydie and Steve | 1962 | 20.00 |
| ❑ UAL-3268 [M] | Two on the Aisle | 1963 | 20.00 |
| ❑ WWL-4509 [M] | Cozy | 1961 | 20.00 |
| ❑ UAS-6191 [S] | The Very Best of Eydie and Steve | 1962 | 25.00 |
| ❑ UAS-6268 [S] | Two on the Aisle | 1963 | 25.00 |
| ❑ WWS-8509 [S] | Cozy | 1961 | 25.00 |
| **VOCALION** | | | |
| ❑ VL 3825 [M] | Presenting Steve and Eydie | 1968 | 12.00 |
| ❑ VL 73825 [R] | Presenting Steve and Eydie | 1968 | 10.00 |
| **LAWS, HUBERT** | | | |
| **CTI** | | | |
| ❑ 1002 | Crying Song | 1970 | 30.00 |
| *—Original issue* | | | |
| **LAWSON, DEE** | | | |
| **ROULETTE** | | | |
| ❑ R-52017 [M] | 'Round Midnight | 1958 | 30.00 |
| ❑ SR-52017 [S] | 'Round Midnight | 1958 | 40.00 |
| **LAWSON, YANK** | | | |
| **ABC-PARAMOUNT** | | | |
| ❑ ABCS-518 [S] | Big Yank Is Here | 1965 | 20.00 |
| ❑ ABCS-567 [S] | Ole Dixie | 1965 | 20.00 |
| **BRUNSWICK** | | | |
| ❑ BL 58035 [10] | Yank Lawson | 1953 | 60.00 |
| **RIVERSIDE** | | | |
| ❑ RLP-2509 [10] | Yank Lawson's Dixieland Jazz | 1954 | 80.00 |
| **LAWSON, YANK, AND BOB HAGGART** | | | |
| **DECCA** | | | |
| ❑ DL 5368 [10] | Lawson-Haggart Band Play Jelly Roll's Jazz | 1952 | 60.00 |
| ❑ DL 5427 [10] | College Fight Songs | 1952 | 60.00 |
| ❑ DL 5437 [10] | Lawson-Haggart Band Play King Oliver's Jazz | 1952 | 60.00 |
| ❑ DL 5439 [10] | Lawson-Haggart Band | 1952 | 60.00 |
| ❑ DL 5456 [10] | Blues on the River | 1952 | 60.00 |
| ❑ DL 5502 [10] | Windy City Jazz | 1953 | 60.00 |
| ❑ DL 5529 [10] | South of the Mason-Dixon Line | 1954 | 60.00 |
| ❑ DL 5533 [10] | Louis' Hot Fives and Sevens | 1954 | 60.00 |
| ❑ DL 8182 [M] | Lawson-Haggart Band Play Jelly Roll's Jazz | 1955 | 40.00 |
| ❑ DL 8195 [M] | Lawson-Haggart Band Play King Oliver's Jazz | 1955 | 40.00 |
| ❑ DL 8196 [M] | Blues on the River | 1955 | 40.00 |
| ❑ DL 8197 [M] | South of the Mason-Dixon Line | 1955 | 40.00 |
| ❑ DL 8198 [M] | Windy City Jazz | 1955 | 40.00 |
| ❑ DL 8200 [M] | Louis' Hot Fives and Sevens | 1955 | 40.00 |
| ❑ DL 8453 [M] | Hold That Tiger | 1956 | 30.00 |
| ❑ DL 8801 [M] | Boppin' at the Hop | 1959 | 30.00 |
| ❑ DL 78801 [S] | Boppin' at the Hop | 1959 | 40.00 |
| **EVEREST** | | | |
| ❑ SDBR-1040 [S] | Junior Prom | 1959 | 20.00 |
| ❑ SDBR-1084 [S] | Dixieland Goes West | 1960 | 25.00 |
| ❑ LPBR-5040 [M] | Junior Prom | 1959 | 25.00 |
| ❑ LPBR-5084 [M] | Dixieland Goes West | 1960 | 20.00 |
| **PROJECT 3** | | | |
| ❑ PR-5033 | The World's Greatest Jazz Band | 1968 | 20.00 |
| ❑ PR-5039 | Extra | 1969 | 20.00 |
| **STINSON** | | | |
| ❑ SLP-59 [10] | Lawson-Haggart with Jerry Jerome and His Orchestra | 1957 | 25.00 |
| **LAZAR, SAM** | | | |
| **ARGO** | | | |
| ❑ LP-714 [M] | Soul Merchant | 1963 | 25.00 |
| ❑ LPS-714 [S] | Soul Merchant | 1963 | 30.00 |
| ❑ LP-4002 [M] | Space Flight | 1961 | 30.00 |
| ❑ LPS-4002 [S] | Space Flight | 1961 | 40.00 |
| ❑ LP-4015 [M] | Playback | 1962 | 30.00 |
| ❑ LPS-4015 [S] | Playback | 1962 | 40.00 |
| **LAZARUS** | | | |
| **AMAZON** | | | |
| ❑ 1001 | Lazarus | 1970 | 20.00 |
| **LAZY LESTER** | | | |
| **EXCELLO** | | | |
| ❑ LP-8006 [M] | True Blues | 1967 | 400.00 |
| ❑ LPS-8006 [M] | True Blues | 196? | 60.00 |
| *—Says "Stereo" but plays mono* | | | |
| **LAZY SMOKE** | | | |
| **ONYX** | | | |
| ❑ 6003 | Corridor of Faces | 1967 | 1200. |
| **LEA, BARBARA** | | | |
| **PRESTIGE** | | | |
| ❑ PRLP-7065 [M] | Barbara Lea | 1956 | 150.00 |
| ❑ PRLP-7100 [M] | Lea in Love | 1957 | 150.00 |
| **RIVERSIDE** | | | |
| ❑ RLP-2518 [10] | A Woman in Love | 1955 | 200.00 |
| **LEA, TERREA** | | | |
| **ABC-PARAMOUNT** | | | |
| ❑ ABC-141 [M] | Terrea Lea and Her Singing Guitar | 1956 | 30.00 |
| **HIFI** | | | |
| ❑ R-404 [M] | Folk Songs and Ballads | 1957 | 30.00 |
| **LEACH, CURTIS** | | | |
| **LONGHORN** | | | |
| ❑ 003 | Indescribable | 1965 | 50.00 |
| **LEADBELLY** | | | |
| **ALLEGRO** | | | |
| ❑ L-4027 [10] | Sinful Songs | 195? | 250.00 |
| **CAPITOL** | | | |
| ❑ H 369 [10] | Classics in Jazz | 1953 | 250.00 |
| ❑ T 1821 [M] | Leadbelly: Huddie Ledbetter's Best | 1962 | 40.00 |
| **ELEKTRA** | | | |
| ❑ EKL-301/2 [(2)] | The Library of Congress Recordings | 1966 | 25.00 |
| **FOLKWAYS** | | | |
| ❑ FP-4 [10] | Lead Belly's Legacy, Vol. 1: Take This Hammer | 1950 | 120.00 |
| ❑ FP-14 [10] | Lead Belly's Legacy, Vol. 2: Rock Island Line | 1951 | 120.00 |
| ❑ FP-24 [10] | Lead Belly's Legacy, Vol. 3: Early Recordings | 1951 | 120.00 |
| ❑ FP-34 [10] | Lead Belly's Legacy, Vol. 4: Easy Rider | 1951 | 120.00 |
| ❑ FP-241 [(2)M] | Leadbelly's Last Sessions, Vol. 1 | 196? | 40.00 |
| ❑ FP-242 [(2)M] | Leadbelly's Last Sessions, Vol. 2 | 196? | 40.00 |
| ❑ FA-2004 [10] | Lead Belly's Legacy, Vol. 1: Take This Hammer | 195? | 50.00 |
| *—Reissue of FP-4* | | | |
| ❑ FA-2014 [10] | Lead Belly's Legacy, Vol. 2: Rock Island Line | 195? | 50.00 |
| *—Reissue of FP-14* | | | |
| ❑ FA-2024 [10] | Lead Belly's Legacy, Vol. 3: Early Recordings | 195? | 50.00 |
| *—Reissue of FP-24* | | | |
| ❑ FA-2034 [10] | Lead Belly's Legacy, Vol. 4: Easy Rider | 195? | 50.00 |
| *—Reissue of FP-34* | | | |
| ❑ FA-2941 [M] | Leadbelly's Last Sessions, Vol. 3 | 196? | 25.00 |
| ❑ FA-2942 [M] | Leadbelly's Last Sessions, Vol. 4 | 196? | 25.00 |
| ❑ FA-3106 [M] | Leadbelly Sings Folk Songs | 196? | 25.00 |
| **RCA VICTOR** | | | |
| ❑ LPV-505 [M] | Midnight Special | 1964 | 40.00 |
| **ROYALE** | | | |
| ❑ 18131 [10] | Blues Songs | 1954 | 120.00 |
| *—As "The Lonesome Blues Singer"* | | | |
| **VERVE FOLKWAYS** | | | |
| ❑ FT-3019 [M] | From the Last Sessions | 1967 | 25.00 |

| Number | Title (A Side/B Side) | Yr | NM |
|---|---|---|---|
| ❑ FTS-3019 [R] | From the Last Sessions | 1967 | 15.00 |
| ❑ FV-9001 [M] | Take This Hammer | 1965 | 25.00 |
| ❑ FVS-9001 [R] | Take This Hammer | 1965 | 15.00 |
| ❑ FV-9021 [M] | Keep Your Hands Off Her | 1965 | 25.00 |
| ❑ FVS-9021 [R] | Keep Your Hands Off Her | 1965 | 15.00 |

**LEAHY, JOE**

TOWER
❑ ST 5014 [S] Tabasco and Trumpets 1966 25.00
❑ T 5014 [M] Tabasco and Trumpets 1966 20.00
❑ ST 5057 [S] A Taste of Trumpets, A Touch of Voices 1967 25.00
❑ T 5057 [M] A Taste of Trumpets, A Touch of Voices 1967 20.00

**LEAPER, BOB**

LONDON
❑ LL 3391 [M] Big Band Beatle Songs 1964 30.00
❑ SP 44056 [S] Big Band Beatle Songs 1964 40.00

**LEAPY LEE**

DECCA
❑ DL 75076 Little Arrows 1968 20.00
❑ DL 75237 Leapy Lee 1970 15.00

**LEARY, DR. TIMOTHY**

DOUGLAS
❑ 1 You Can Be Anyone This Time Around 1969 100.00

ESP-DISK'
❑ 1027 [M] Turn On, Tune In, Drop Out 1966 150.00

MERCURY
❑ MG-21131 [M] Turn On, Tune In, Drop Out 1967 40.00
❑ SR-61131 [S] Turn On, Tune In, Drop Out 1967 50.00

PIXIE
❑ CA-1069 [M] L.S.D. 1966 80.00

**LEATHERCOATED MINDS, THE**

VIVA
❑ V-6003 [M] Trip Down Sunset Strip 1967 60.00
❑ V-36003 [S] Trip Down Sunset Strip 1967 80.00

**LEAVES, THE**

CAPITOL
❑ ST 2638 [S] All the Good That's Happening 1967 30.00
❑ T 2638 [M] All the Good That's Happening 1967 25.00

MIRA
❑ LP-3005 [M] Hey Joe 1966 40.00
❑ LPS-3005 [S] Hey Joe 1966 50.00

SURREY
❑ LPS-3005 Hey Joe 196? 150.00
*—Issued in Mira jackets*

**LED ZEPPELIN** Also see JOHN PAUL JONES; JIMMY PAGE; ROBERT PLANT.

ATLANTIC
❑ 7201 [M] Led Zeppelin III 1970 200.00
*—White label promo only*
❑ SD 7201 [DJ] Led Zeppelin III 1970 200.00
*—Stereo white label promo*
❑ SD 7201 [S] Led Zeppelin III 1970 15.00
*—Die-cut cover with movable wheel; "1841 Broadway" address on label*
❑ SD 7201 [S] Led Zeppelin III 1974 10.00
*—"75 Rockefeller Plaza" address on label*
❑ SD 7201 [S] Led Zeppelin III 2001 25.00
*—Classic Records reissue on audiophile vinyl*
❑ 7208 [M] Led Zeppelin (IV) (Runes) 1971 300.00
*—White label promo only*
❑ SD 7208 [DJ] Led Zeppelin (IV) (Runes) 1971 150.00
*—Stereo white label promo*
❑ SD 7208 [S] Led Zeppelin (IV) (Runes) 1971 12.00
*—"1841 Broadway" address on label*
❑ SD 7208 [S] Led Zeppelin (IV) (Runes) 1974 10.00
*—"75 Rockefeller Plaza" address on label*
❑ SD 7208 [S] Led Zeppelin (IV) (Runes) 2001 25.00
*—Classic Records reissue on audiophile vinyl*
❑ 7255 [M] Houses of the Holy 1973 1000.
*—White label promo only*
❑ SD 7255 [S] Houses of the Holy 1973 12.00
*—"1841 Broadway" address on label*
❑ SD 7255 [S] Houses of the Holy 1974 10.00
*—"75 Rockefeller Plaza" address on label*
❑ SD 7255 [S] Houses of the Holy 2001 25.00
*—Classic Records reissue on audiophile vinyl*
❑ 8216 [M] Led Zeppelin 1969 400.00
*—White label promo only*
❑ SD 8216 [DJ] Led Zeppelin 1969 200.00
*—Stereo white label promo*
❑ SD 8216 [S] Led Zeppelin 1969 20.00
*—"1841 Broadway" address on label*
❑ SD 8216 [S] Led Zeppelin 1969 250.00
*—Possible mispress with purple and brown labels*
❑ SD 8216 [S] Led Zeppelin 1974 10.00
*—"75 Rockefeller Plaza" address on label*
❑ SD 8216 [S] Led Zeppelin 2000 25.00
*—Classic Records reissue on audiophile vinyl*
❑ 8236 [M] Led Zeppelin II 1969 200.00
*—White label promo only*

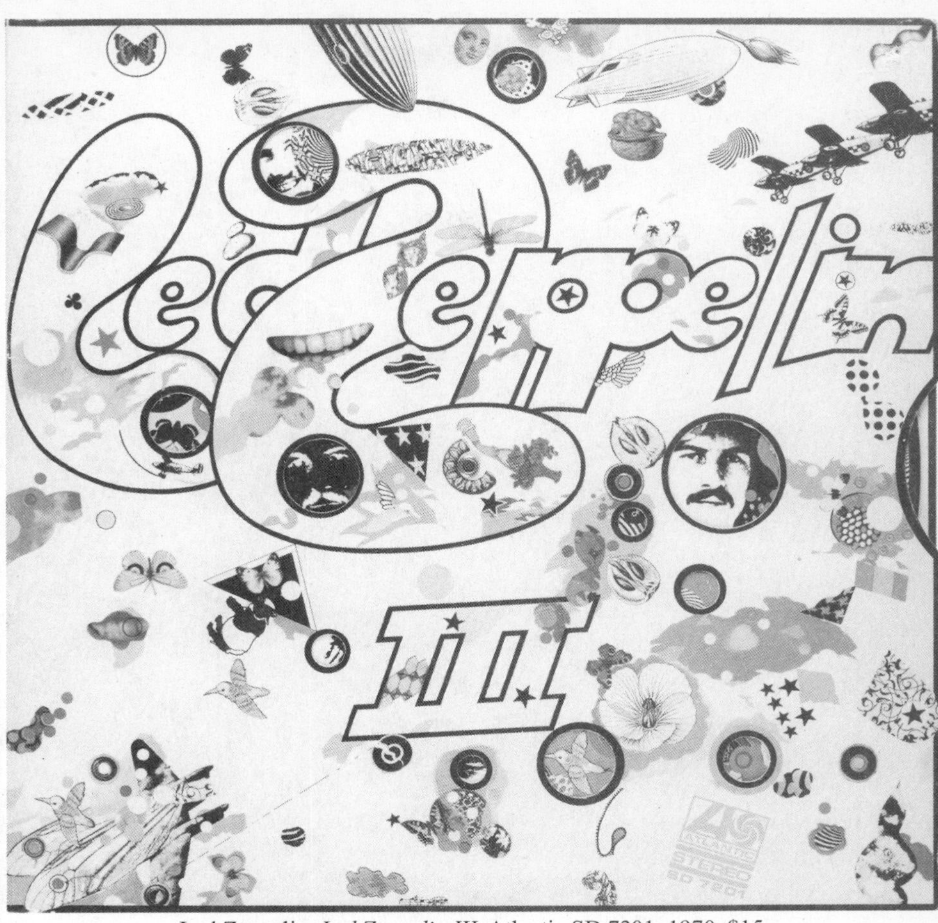


Led Zeppelin, *Led Zeppelin III,* Atlantic SD 7201, 1970, $15.

| Number | Title (A Side/B Side) | Yr | NM |
|---|---|---|---|

❑ SD 8236 [DJ] Led Zeppelin II 1969 300.00
*—Stereo white label promo*
❑ SD 8236 [S] Led Zeppelin II 1969 20.00
*—"1841 Broadway" address on label*
❑ SD 8236 [S] Led Zeppelin II 1974 10.00
*—"75 Rockefeller Plaza" address on label*
❑ SD 8236 [S] Led Zeppelin II 2000 25.00
*—Classic Records reissue on audiophile vinyl*
❑ SD 19126 Led Zeppelin 1977 8.00
❑ SD 19127 Led Zeppelin II 1977 8.00
❑ SD 19128 Led Zeppelin III 1977 8.00
❑ SD 19129 Led Zeppelin (IV) (Runes) 1977 8.00
❑ SD 19130 Houses of the Holy 1977 8.00
❑ 82144 [(6)] Led Zeppelin (Box Set) 1990 100.00
❑ 83061 [(4)] BBC Sessions 2000 60.00
*—Classic Records limited edition; each LP is in its own cardboard sleeve inside a box with a sheet of liner notes*
❑ 83268 [(2)] Early Days: The Best of Led Zeppelin Vol. 1 1999 15.00
❑ 83278 [(2)] Latter Days: The Best of Led Zeppelin Vol. 2 2000 15.00
❑ SMAS-94019 Led Zeppelin (IV) (Runes) 1972 40.00
*—Capitol Record Club edition*

MOBILE FIDELITY
❑ 1-065 Led Zeppelin II 1981 80.00
*—Audiophile vinyl*

SWAN SONG
❑ SS 2-200 [(2)] Physical Graffiti 1975 15.00
❑ SS 2-200 [(2)] Physical Graffiti 2002 40.00
*—Classic Records reissue on audiophile vinyl*
❑ SS 2-201 [(2)] The Song Remains the Same 1976 15.00
❑ SS 2-201 [(2)] The Song Remains the Same 2003 40.00
*—Classic Records edition on 200-gram vinyl*
❑ SS 8416 Presence 1976 10.00
❑ SS 8416 Presence 2002 25.00
*—Classic Records reissue on audiophile vinyl*
❑ SS 16002 In Through the Out Door 1979 10.00
*—Letter "B" on spine; add 50% if brown paper bag is still with jacket*
❑ SS 16002 In Through the Out Door 1979 10.00
*—Letter "C" on spine; add 50% if brown paper bag is still with jacket*
❑ SS 16002 In Through the Out Door 1979 10.00
*—Letter "D" on spine; add 50% if brown paper bag is still with jacket*
❑ SS 16002 In Through the Out Door 1979 10.00
*—Letter "E" on spine; add 50% if brown paper bag is still with jacket*
❑ SS 16002 In Through the Out Door 1979 10.00
*—Letter "F" on spine; add 50% if brown paper bag is still with jacket*
❑ SS 16002 In Through the Out Door 1979 10.00
*—Letter "A" on spine; add 50% if brown paper bag is still with jacket*
❑ SS 16002 In Through the Out Door 2003 30.00
*—Classic Records reissue on 200-gram vinyl; contains a 12-page insert with all six covers; we don't know if the label actually pressed these with six different covers*
❑ 90051 Coda 1982 10.00

**LEDOUX, CHRIS**

AMERICAN COWBOY SONGS
❑ ACS 17001 Thirty Dollar Cowboy 1983 25.00
❑ ACS 20001 Melodies and Memories 1984 30.00
❑ ACS 23001 Chris LeDoux and the Saddle Boogie Band 198? 20.00

LUCKY MAN
❑ NR 4249 Rodeo Songs Old and New 1973 30.00
❑ ACS 5524 Sing Me a Song, Mr. Rodeo Man 197? 30.00
❑ NR 7648 Songs of the American West 1976 30.00
❑ NR 9175 Chris LeDoux Sings Western Country 1978 30.00
❑ LM 10193 Paint Me Back Home in Wyoming 1978 30.00
❑ LM 10194 Western Tunesmith 1980 30.00

**LEE, ARTHUR** Also see LOVE.

A&M
❑ SP-4356 Vindicator 1972 30.00

RHINO
❑ RNLP 020 Arthur Lee 1981 10.00

**LEE, BRENDA**

DECCA
❑ DL 4039 [M] Brenda Lee 1960 25.00
❑ DL 4082 [M] This Is...Brenda 1960 25.00
❑ DL 4104 [M] Emotions 1961 25.00
❑ DL 4176 [M] All the Way 1961 25.00
❑ DL 4216 [M] Sincerely 1962 25.00
❑ DL 4326 [M] Brenda, That's All 1962 25.00
❑ DL 4370 [M] All Alone Am I 1963 25.00
❑ DL 4439 [M] Let Me Sing 1963 25.00
❑ DL 4509 [M] By Request 1964 20.00

Peggy Lee, *Is That All There Is?,* Capitol ST-386, 1969, $12.

| Number | Title (A Side/B Side) | Yr | NM |
|---|---|---|---|
| ❑ DL 4583 [M] | Merry Christmas from Brenda Lee | 1964 | 20.00 |
| ❑ DL 4626 [M] | Top Teen Hits | 1965 | 20.00 |
| ❑ DL 4661 [M] | The Versatile Brenda Lee | 1965 | 20.00 |
| ❑ DL 4684 [M] | Too Many Rivers | 1965 | 20.00 |
| ❑ DL 4755 [M] | Bye Bye Blues | 1966 | 20.00 |
| ❑ DL 4757 [M] | 10 Golden Years | 196? | 15.00 |
| *—With regular cover* | | | |
| ❑ DL 4757 [M] | 10 Golden Years | 1966 | 25.00 |
| *—With gatefold cover* | | | |
| ❑ DL 4825 [M] | Coming On Strong | 1966 | 15.00 |
| ❑ DL 4941 [M] | Reflections in Blue | 1967 | 20.00 |
| ❑ DL 8873 [M] | Grandma, What Great Songs You Sang | 1960 | 40.00 |
| ❑ DL 74039 [S] | Brenda Lee | 1960 | 30.00 |
| ❑ DL 74082 [S] | This Is…Brenda | 1960 | 30.00 |
| ❑ DL 74104 [S] | Emotions | 1961 | 30.00 |
| ❑ DL 74176 [S] | All the Way | 1961 | 30.00 |
| ❑ DL 74216 [S] | Sincerely | 1962 | 30.00 |
| ❑ DL 74326 [S] | Brenda, That's All | 1962 | 30.00 |
| ❑ DL 74370 [S] | All Alone Am I | 1963 | 30.00 |
| ❑ DL 74439 [S] | Let Me Sing | 1963 | 30.00 |
| ❑ DL 74509 [S] | By Request | 1964 | 25.00 |
| ❑ DL 74583 [S] | Merry Christmas from Brenda Lee | 1964 | 25.00 |
| ❑ DL 74626 [S] | Top Teen Hits | 1965 | 25.00 |
| ❑ DL 74661 [S] | The Versatile Brenda Lee | 1965 | 25.00 |
| ❑ DL 74684 [S] | Too Many Rivers | 1965 | 25.00 |
| ❑ DL 74755 [S] | Bye Bye Blues | 1966 | 25.00 |
| ❑ DL 74757 [S] | 10 Golden Years | 196? | 20.00 |
| *—With regular cover* | | | |
| ❑ DL 74757 [S] | 10 Golden Years | 1966 | 30.00 |
| *—With gatefold cover* | | | |
| ❑ DL 74825 [S] | Coming On Strong | 1966 | 20.00 |
| ❑ DL 74941 [S] | Reflections in Blue | 1967 | 15.00 |
| ❑ DL 74955 | For the First Time | 1968 | 15.00 |
| *—With Pete Fountain* | | | |
| ❑ DL 75111 | Johnny One Time | 1969 | 15.00 |
| ❑ DL 75232 | Memphis Portrait | 1970 | 15.00 |
| ❑ DL 78873 [S] | Grandma, What Great Songs You Sang | 1960 | 50.00 |
| ❑ ST-90997 [S] | 10 Golden Years | 1966 | 25.00 |
| *—Capitol Record Club edition* | | | |
| ❑ ST-92062 | Johnny One Time | 1969 | 20.00 |
| *—Capitol Record Club edition* | | | |
| ❑ R 103619 [S] | Merry Christmas from Brenda Lee | 1971 | 20.00 |
| *—RCA Music Service edition* | | | |

| Number | Title (A Side/B Side) | Yr | NM |
|---|---|---|---|
| **MCA** | | | |
| ❑ 232 [S] | Merry Christmas from Brenda Lee | 1973 | 12.00 |
| ❑ 305 | Brenda | 1973 | 15.00 |
| ❑ 373 | New Sunrise | 1973 | 12.00 |
| ❑ 433 | Brenda Lee Now | 1974 | 12.00 |
| ❑ 477 | Sincerely, Brenda Lee | 1975 | 10.00 |
| ❑ 758 | Even Better | 198? | 8.00 |
| *—Reissue of 3211* | | | |
| ❑ 824 | Only When I Laugh | 1982 | 8.00 |
| *—Reissue of 5278* | | | |
| ❑ 2233 | L.A. Sessions | 1976 | 10.00 |
| ❑ 3211 | Even Better | 1979 | 10.00 |
| ❑ 2-4012 [(2)] | The Brenda Lee Story — Her Greatest Hits | 1973 | 20.00 |
| ❑ 5143 | Take Me Back | 1980 | 10.00 |
| ❑ 5278 | Only When I Laugh | 1981 | 10.00 |
| ❑ 5342 | Greatest Country Hits | 1982 | 10.00 |
| ❑ 5626 | Feels So Right | 1985 | 10.00 |
| ❑ 15021 [S] | Merry Christmas from Brenda Lee | 197? | 10.00 |
| ❑ 15038 | Rockin' Around the Christmas Tree | 198? | 10.00 |
| **MCA CORAL** | | | |
| ❑ CB-20044 | Let It Be Me | 197? | 10.00 |
| **VOCALION** | | | |
| ❑ VL 3795 [M] | Here's Brenda Lee | 1967 | 12.00 |
| ❑ VL 73795 [S] | Here's Brenda Lee | 1967 | 12.00 |
| ❑ VL 73890 | Let It Be Me | 1970 | 12.00 |

**LEE, BYRON, AND THE DRAGONAIRES**

| Number | Title (A Side/B Side) | Yr | NM |
|---|---|---|---|
| **ATCO** | | | |
| ❑ 33-182 [M] | Jump Up | 1966 | 20.00 |
| ❑ SD 33-182 [S] | Jump Up | 1966 | 25.00 |
| **BMN** | | | |
| ❑ 004 | Dance the Ska | 196? | 20.00 |
| **JAD** | | | |
| ❑ JS-1004 | Byron Lee and the Dragonaires | 1968 | 20.00 |
| **TOWERS HALL** | | | |
| ❑ 006 | The Sounds of Jamaica | 196? | 20.00 |

**LEE, DICKEY**

| Number | Title (A Side/B Side) | Yr | NM |
|---|---|---|---|
| **MERCURY** | | | |
| ❑ SRM-1-5020 | Dickey Lee | 1979 | 10.00 |
| ❑ SRM-1-5026 | Dickey Lee Again | 1980 | 10.00 |
| **RCA VICTOR** | | | |
| ❑ APL1-0311 | Sparklin' Brown Eyes | 1974 | 12.00 |
| ❑ APL1-1243 | Rocky | 1975 | 12.00 |
| ❑ APL1-1725 | Angels, Roses and Rain | 1976 | 12.00 |
| ❑ LSP-4637 | Never Ending Song of Love | 1971 | 12.00 |
| ❑ LSP-4715 | Ashes of Love | 1972 | 12.00 |
| ❑ LSP-4791 | Baby, Bye Bye | 1972 | 12.00 |
| ❑ LSP-4857 | Crying Over You | 1973 | 12.00 |
| **SMASH** | | | |
| ❑ MGS-27020 [M] | The Tale of Patches | 1962 | 30.00 |
| ❑ SRS-67020 [S] | The Tale of Patches | 1962 | 40.00 |
| **TCF HALL** | | | |
| ❑ TCF-8001 [M] | Dickey Lee Sings "Laurie" and "The Girl from Peyton Place" | 1965 | 20.00 |
| ❑ TCF-9001 [S] | Dickey Lee Sings "Laurie" and "The Girl from Peyton Place" | 1965 | 25.00 |

**LEE, EDDIE**

| Number | Title (A Side/B Side) | Yr | NM |
|---|---|---|---|
| **GEORGIAN** | | | |
| ❑ GR 2001 [M] | Windy City Profile | 1958 | 40.00 |

**LEE, JACKIE (1)**

| Number | Title (A Side/B Side) | Yr | NM |
|---|---|---|---|
| **MIRWOOD** | | | |
| ❑ MW-7000 [M] | The Duck | 1966 | 20.00 |
| ❑ SW-7000 [S] | The Duck | 1966 | 25.00 |

**LEE, JEANNE, AND RAN BLAKE**

| Number | Title (A Side/B Side) | Yr | NM |
|---|---|---|---|
| **RCA VICTOR** | | | |
| ❑ LPM-2500 [M] | The Newest Sound Around | 1962 | 30.00 |
| ❑ LSP-2500 [S] | The Newest Sound Around | 1962 | 40.00 |

**LEE, JULIA**

| Number | Title (A Side/B Side) | Yr | NM |
|---|---|---|---|
| **CAPITOL** | | | |
| ❑ H 228 [10] | Party Time | 1950 | 120.00 |
| ❑ T 228 [M] | Party Time | 195? | 80.00 |

**LEE, KATIE**

| Number | Title (A Side/B Side) | Yr | NM |
|---|---|---|---|
| **HORIZON** | | | |
| ❑ WP-1604 [M] | The Best of Katie Lee | 1962 | 20.00 |
| ❑ WP-1604 Stereo [S] | The Best of Katie Lee | 1962 | 25.00 |
| **REPRISE** | | | |
| ❑ R-6025 [M] | Songs of Coach and Consultation | 1961 | 25.00 |
| **SPECIALTY** | | | |
| ❑ SP-5000 [M] | Spicy Songs for Cool Knights | 1959 | 30.00 |

**LEE, LAURA**

| Number | Title (A Side/B Side) | Yr | NM |
|---|---|---|---|
| **CHESS** | | | |
| ❑ CH-50031 | Love More Than Pride | 1972 | 20.00 |
| **HOT WAX** | | | |
| ❑ HA-708 | Women's Love Rights | 1971 | 15.00 |
| ❑ HA-714 | Laura Lee | 1972 | 15.00 |
| ❑ HA-715 | The Best of Laura Lee | 1973 | 15.00 |
| **INVICTUS** | | | |
| ❑ KZ 33133 | Laura Lee | 1974 | 10.00 |

**LEE, PEGGY**

| Number | Title (A Side/B Side) | Yr | NM |
|---|---|---|---|
| **A&M** | | | |
| ❑ SP-4547 | Mirrors | 1975 | 12.00 |
| **ATLANTIC** | | | |
| ❑ SD 18108 | Let's Love | 1974 | 12.00 |
| **CAPITOL** | | | |
| ❑ ST-105 | Two Shows Nightly | 1969 | 500.00 |
| *—Withdrawn immediately after release; most of the known copies have the word "FREE" stamped diagonally in the upper right corner of the cover* | | | |
| ❑ H 151 [10] | Rendezvous with Peggy Lee | 1952 | 100.00 |
| ❑ T 151 [M] | Rendezvous with Peggy Lee | 1954 | 50.00 |
| *—Turquoise or gray label* | | | |
| ❑ T 151 [M] | Rendezvous with Peggy Lee | 1959 | 25.00 |
| *—Black label with colorband, Capitol logo at left* | | | |
| ❑ ST-183 | A Natural Woman | 1969 | 15.00 |
| ❑ H 204 [10] | My Best to You | 1952 | 100.00 |
| ❑ T 204 [M] | My Best to You | 1954 | 50.00 |
| *—Turquoise or gray label* | | | |
| ❑ T 204 [M] | My Best to You | 1959 | 25.00 |
| *—Black label with colorband, Capitol logo at left* | | | |
| ❑ DKAO-377 | Peggy Lee's Greatest | 1969 | 12.00 |
| ❑ SM-386 | Is That All There Is? | 197? | 10.00 |
| *—Reissue with new prefix* | | | |
| ❑ ST-386 | Is That All There Is? | 1969 | 12.00 |
| ❑ ST-463 | Bridge Over Troubled Water | 1970 | 12.00 |
| ❑ STBB-517 [(2)] | Folks Who Live on the Hill/ Broadway Ala Lee | 1970 | 15.00 |
| ❑ STCL-576 [(3)] | Peggy Lee | 1970 | 25.00 |
| ❑ ST-622 | Make It with You | 1970 | 12.00 |
| ❑ ST-810 | Where Did They Go | 1971 | 12.00 |
| ❑ ST 864 [S] | The Man I Love | 1959 | 30.00 |
| ❑ T 864 [M] | The Man I Love | 1957 | 50.00 |
| *—Turquoise label* | | | |
| ❑ T 864 [M] | The Man I Love | 1959 | 25.00 |
| *—Black label with colorband, Capitol logo at left* | | | |
| ❑ ST 979 [S] | Jump for Joy | 1959 | 30.00 |
| ❑ T 979 [M] | Jump for Joy | 1958 | 40.00 |
| *—Turquoise or gray label* | | | |
| ❑ T 979 [M] | Jump for Joy | 1959 | 25.00 |
| *—Black label with colorband, Capitol logo at left* | | | |
| ❑ ST 1049 [S] | Things Are Swingin' | 1959 | 30.00 |



Except when noted otherwise, VG = 25% of NM, and VG+ = 50% of NM. (Example: VG = $2.00, VG+ = $4.00 and NM = $8.00.)

| Number | Title (A Side/B Side) | Yr | NM |
|---|---|---|---|
| ❑ T 1049 [M] | Things Are Swingin' | 1958 | 25.00 |
| ❑ ST 1131 [S] | I Like Men | 1959 | 30.00 |
| ❑ T 1131 [M] | I Like Men | 1959 | 25.00 |
| ❑ ST 1213 [S] | Alright, Okay, You Win | 1959 | 30.00 |
| ❑ T 1213 [M] | Alright, Okay, You Win | 1959 | 25.00 |
| ❑ ST 1219 [S] | Beauty and the Beat | 1959 | 30.00 |
| *—With George Shearing; black label with colorband, Capitol logo at left* | | | |
| ❑ ST 1219 [S] | Beauty and the Beat | 1962 | 20.00 |
| *—With George Shearing; black label with colorband, Capitol logo at top* | | | |
| ❑ T 1219 [M] | Beauty and the Beat | 1959 | 25.00 |
| *—With George Shearing; black label with colorband, Capitol logo at left* | | | |
| ❑ T 1219 [M] | Beauty and the Beat | 1962 | 15.00 |
| *—With George Shearing; black label with colorband, Capitol logo at top* | | | |
| ❑ SM-1290 | Latin Ala Lee! | 1977 | 10.00 |
| *—Reissue with new prefix* | | | |
| ❑ ST 1290 [S] | Latin Ala Lee! | 1960 | 25.00 |
| *—Black label with colorband, Capitol logo at left* | | | |
| ❑ ST 1290 [S] | Latin Ala Lee! | 1962 | 15.00 |
| *—Black label with colorband, Capitol logo at top* | | | |
| ❑ T 1290 [M] | Latin Ala Lee! | 1960 | 20.00 |
| *—Black label with colorband, Capitol logo at left* | | | |
| ❑ T 1290 [M] | Latin Ala Lee! | 1962 | 12.00 |
| *—Black label with colorband, Capitol logo at top* | | | |
| ❑ ST 1366 [S] | All Aglow Again | 1960 | 25.00 |
| *—Black label with colorband, Capitol logo at left* | | | |
| ❑ ST 1366 [S] | All Aglow Again | 1962 | 15.00 |
| *—Black label with colorband, Capitol logo at top* | | | |
| ❑ T 1366 [M] | All Aglow Again | 1960 | 20.00 |
| *—Black label with colorband, Capitol logo at left* | | | |
| ❑ T 1366 [M] | All Aglow Again | 1962 | 12.00 |
| *—Black label with colorband, Capitol logo at top* | | | |
| ❑ ST 1401 [S] | Pretty Eyes | 1960 | 25.00 |
| *—Black label with colorband, Capitol logo at left* | | | |
| ❑ ST 1401 [S] | Pretty Eyes | 1962 | 15.00 |
| *—Black label with colorband, Capitol logo at top* | | | |
| ❑ T 1401 [M] | Pretty Eyes | 1960 | 20.00 |
| *—Black label with colorband, Capitol logo at left* | | | |
| ❑ T 1401 [M] | Pretty Eyes | 1962 | 12.00 |
| *—Black label with colorband, Capitol logo at top* | | | |
| ❑ ST 1423 [S] | Christmas Carousel | 1960 | 25.00 |
| ❑ T 1423 [M] | Christmas Carousel | 1960 | 20.00 |
| ❑ ST 1475 [S] | Ole Ala Lee! | 1961 | 25.00 |
| ❑ T 1475 [M] | Ole Ala Lee! | 1961 | 20.00 |
| ❑ SM-1520 | Basin Street East | 1977 | 10.00 |
| *—Reissue with new prefix* | | | |
| ❑ ST 1520 [S] | Basin Street East | 1961 | 25.00 |
| *—Black label with colorband, Capitol logo at left* | | | |
| ❑ ST 1520 [S] | Basin Street East | 1962 | 15.00 |
| *—Black label with colorband, Capitol logo at top* | | | |
| ❑ T 1520 [M] | Basin Street East | 1961 | 20.00 |
| *—Black label with colorband, Capitol logo at left* | | | |
| ❑ T 1520 [M] | Basin Street East | 1962 | 12.00 |
| *—Black label with colorband, Capitol logo at top* | | | |
| ❑ ST 1630 [S] | If You Go | 1962 | 25.00 |
| ❑ T 1630 [M] | If You Go | 1962 | 20.00 |
| ❑ ST 1671 [S] | Blue Cross Country | 1962 | 25.00 |
| ❑ T 1671 [M] | Blue Cross Country | 1962 | 20.00 |
| ❑ DT 1743 [R] | Bewitching-Lee! | 1962 | 15.00 |
| ❑ T 1743 [M] | Bewitching-Lee! | 1962 | 25.00 |
| *—Black "The Star Line" label* | | | |
| ❑ ST 1772 [S] | Sugar 'n' Spice | 1962 | 25.00 |
| ❑ T 1772 [M] | Sugar 'n' Spice | 1962 | 20.00 |
| ❑ ST 1850 [S] | Mink Jazz | 1963 | 25.00 |
| ❑ T 1850 [M] | Mink Jazz | 1963 | 20.00 |
| ❑ SM-1857 | I'm a Woman | 1977 | 10.00 |
| *—Reissue with new prefix* | | | |
| ❑ ST 1857 [S] | I'm a Woman | 1963 | 25.00 |
| ❑ T 1857 [M] | I'm a Woman | 1963 | 20.00 |
| ❑ ST 1969 [S] | In Love Again | 1963 | 25.00 |
| ❑ T 1969 [M] | In Love Again | 1963 | 20.00 |
| ❑ ST 2096 [S] | In the Name of Love | 1964 | 20.00 |
| ❑ T 2096 [M] | In the Name of Love | 1964 | 15.00 |
| ❑ ST 2320 [S] | Pass Me By | 1965 | 20.00 |
| ❑ T 2320 [M] | Pass Me By | 1965 | 15.00 |
| ❑ ST 2388 [S] | That Was Then, Now Is Now | 1965 | 20.00 |
| ❑ T 2388 [M] | That Was Then, Now Is Now | 1965 | 15.00 |
| ❑ ST 2390 [S] | Happy Holiday | 1965 | 15.00 |
| ❑ T 2390 [M] | Happy Holiday | 1965 | 12.00 |
| ❑ ST 2469 [S] | Guitars Ala Lee | 1966 | 20.00 |
| ❑ T 2469 [M] | Guitars Ala Lee | 1966 | 15.00 |
| ❑ ST 2475 [S] | Big $pender | 1966 | 20.00 |
| ❑ T 2475 [M] | Big $pender | 1966 | 15.00 |
| ❑ ST 2732 [S] | Extra Special | 1967 | 15.00 |
| ❑ T 2732 [M] | Extra Special | 1967 | 20.00 |
| ❑ ST 2781 | Somethin' Groovy | 1968 | 15.00 |
| ❑ ST 2887 | The Hits of Peggy Lee | 1968 | 15.00 |
| ❑ ST-11077 | Norma Deloris Egstrom from Jamestown, North Dakota | 1972 | 12.00 |
| ❑ SN-16140 | Peggy Lee Sings Songs of Cy Coleman | 198? | 8.00 |
| **COLUMBIA** | | | |
| ❑ CL 6033 [10] | Benny Goodman and Peggy Lee | 1949 | 60.00 |
| **DECCA** | | | |
| ❑ DXB 164 [(2)M] | The Best of Peggy Lee | 1964 | 30.00 |
| ❑ DL 4458 [M] | Lover | 1964 | 25.00 |
| ❑ DL 4461 [M] | The Fabulous Peggy Lee | 1964 | 25.00 |

| Number | Title (A Side/B Side) | Yr | NM |
|---|---|---|---|
| ❑ DL 5482 [10] | Black Coffee | 1953 | 100.00 |
| ❑ DL 5539 [10] | Songs in an Intimate Style | 1953 | 80.00 |
| ❑ DXSB 7164 [(2)R] | The Best of Peggy Lee | 1964 | 20.00 |
| ❑ DL 8358 [M] | Black Coffee | 1956 | 60.00 |
| ❑ DL 8411 [M] | Dream Street | 1957 | 60.00 |
| ❑ DL 8591 [M] | Sea Shells | 1958 | 60.00 |
| ❑ DL 8816 [M] | Miss Wonderful | 1959 | 60.00 |
| ❑ DL 74458 [R] | Lover | 1964 | 15.00 |
| ❑ DL 74461 [R] | The Fabulous Peggy Lee | 1964 | 15.00 |
| **DRG** | | | |
| ❑ SL-5190 | Close Enough for Love | 1979 | 12.00 |
| **EVEREST ARCHIVE OF FOLK & JAZZ** | | | |
| ❑ 294 | Peggy Lee | 197? | 10.00 |
| **GLENDALE** | | | |
| ❑ 6023 | You Can Depend on Me | 1982 | 10.00 |
| **HARMONY** | | | |
| ❑ HL 7005 [M] | Peggy Lee Sings with Benny Goodman | 195? | 25.00 |
| ❑ H 30024 | Miss Peggy Lee | 1970 | 10.00 |
| **HINDSIGHT** | | | |
| ❑ HSR-220 | Peggy Lee with the David Barbour and Billy May Bands, 1948 | 1985 | 10.00 |
| **MCA** | | | |
| ❑ 4049 [(2)] | The Best of Peggy Lee | 197? | 12.00 |
| **MERCURY** | | | |
| ❑ SRM-1-1172 | Live in London | 1977 | 12.00 |
| **MUSICMASTERS** | | | |
| ❑ 5005 | Peggy Sings the Blues | 1988 | 12.00 |
| **PAUSA** | | | |
| ❑ PR-9043 | Sugar 'n' Spice | 1985 | 10.00 |
| **PICKWICK** | | | |
| ❑ SPC-3090 | Once More with Feeling | 196? | 10.00 |
| ❑ SPC-3192 | I've Got the World | 1971 | 10.00 |
| **S&P** | | | |
| ❑ 502 | Bewitching-Lee! | 2003 | 25.00 |
| *—Reissue on 180-gram vinyl* | | | |
| ❑ 504 | Latin Ala Lee! | 2004 | 25.00 |
| *—Reissue on 180-gram vinyl* | | | |
| **TIME-LIFE** | | | |
| ❑ SLGD-07 [(2)] | Legendary Singers: Peggy Lee | 1985 | 15.00 |
| **VOCALION** | | | |
| ❑ VL 3776 [M] | So Blue | 1966 | 15.00 |
| ❑ VL 73776 [R] | So Blue | 1966 | 10.00 |
| ❑ VL 73903 | Crazy in the Heart | 1969 | 10.00 |
| **LEE, PERRY** | | | |
| **ROULETTE** | | | |
| ❑ R-52080 [M] | A Night at Count Basie's | 1962 | 15.00 |
| ❑ SR-52080 [S] | A Night at Count Basie's | 1962 | 20.00 |
| **LEE, PINKY** | | | |
| **DECCA** | | | |
| ❑ DL 8421 [M] | The Surprise Party | 1957 | 40.00 |
| **LEE, ROBIN** | | | |
| **DOT** | | | |
| ❑ DLP-3661 [M] | Robin Lee | 1965 | 25.00 |
| **LEFEVERE, KAMIEL** | | | |
| **MERCURY LIVING PRESENCE** | | | |
| ❑ SR 90189 [S] | The Magic of the Bells | 196? | 50.00 |
| *—Maroon label, no "Vendor: Mercury Record Corporation"* | | | |
| **LEFEVRE, RAYMOND** | | | |
| **ATLANTIC** | | | |
| ❑ 8044 [M] | Romantica | 1961 | 20.00 |
| ❑ SD 8044 [S] | Romantica | 1961 | 25.00 |
| **BUDDAH** | | | |
| ❑ BDS-5095 | Raymond Lefevre | 1971 | 10.00 |
| ❑ BDS-5109 | Oh Happy Day | 1972 | 10.00 |
| **4 CORNERS OF THE WORLD** | | | |
| ❑ FCL-4239 [M] | Love Me, Please Love Me | 1967 | 12.00 |
| ❑ FCS-4239 [S] | Love Me, Please Love Me | 1967 | 12.00 |
| ❑ FCS-4244 | Soal Coaxing (Ame Caline) | 1968 | 12.00 |
| ❑ FCS-4250 | La La La (He Gives Me Love) | 1968 | 12.00 |
| ❑ FCS-4257 | Merry Christmas | 1968 | 12.00 |
| **KAPP** | | | |
| ❑ KL-1510 [M] | You Don't Have to Stay | 1967 | 15.00 |
| ❑ KS-3510 [S] | You Don't Have to Stay | 1967 | 12.00 |
| **MONUMENT** | | | |
| ❑ MLP-8067 [M] | Paris Cancan | 1967 | 15.00 |
| ❑ SLP-18067 [S] | Paris Cancan | 1967 | 12.00 |
| **LEFT BANKE, THE** | | | |
| **RHINO** | | | |
| ❑ RNLP-123 | History of the Left Banke | 1985 | 10.00 |
| **SMASH** | | | |
| ❑ MGS-27088 [M] | Walk Away Renee/Pretty Ballerina | 1967 | 40.00 |

| Number | Title (A Side/B Side) | Yr | NM |
|---|---|---|---|
| ❑ SRS-67088 | Walk Away Renee/Pretty Ballerina | 198? | 10.00 |
| *—Reissue with thinner vinyl* | | | |
| ❑ SRS-67088 [S] | Walk Away Renee/Pretty Ballerina | 1967 | 40.00 |
| ❑ SRS-67113 | The Left Banke, Too | 1968 | 50.00 |
| **LEGEND** Probably two different groups. | | | |
| **BELL** | | | |
| ❑ 6027 | Legend | 1969 | 40.00 |
| **MEGAPHONE** | | | |
| ❑ 101 | Legend | 1970 | 80.00 |
| **LEGENDS, THE** | | | |
| **CAPITOL** | | | |
| ❑ ST 1925 [S] | The Legends Let Loose | 1963 | 80.00 |
| ❑ T 1925 [M] | The Legends Let Loose | 1963 | 60.00 |
| **COLUMBIA** | | | |
| ❑ CL 1707 [M] | Hit Sounds of Today's Smash Hit Combos | 1961 | 30.00 |
| ❑ CS 8507 [S] | Hit Sounds of Today's Smash Hit Combos | 1961 | 40.00 |
| **ERMINE** | | | |
| ❑ LP-101 [M] | The Legends Let Loose | 1963 | 200.00 |
| **LEGGE, WADE** | | | |
| **BLUE NOTE** | | | |
| ❑ BLP-5031 [10] | New Faces New Sounds | 1953 | 600.00 |
| **LEGGIO, CARMEN** | | | |
| **GOLDEN CREST** | | | |
| ❑ GCS-1000 | Jazz | 196? | 20.00 |
| **LEGRAND, MICHEL** | | | |
| **COLUMBIA** | | | |
| ❑ CL 555 [M] | I Love Paris | 1954 | 40.00 |
| ❑ CL 647 [M] | Holiday in Rome | 1955 | 25.00 |
| ❑ CL 706 [M] | Vienna Holiday | 1955 | 25.00 |
| ❑ CL 888 [M] | Castles in Spain | 1956 | 25.00 |
| ❑ CL 1115 [M] | Michel Legrand Plays Cole Porter | 1957 | 25.00 |
| ❑ CL 1139 [M] | Legrand in Rio | 1957 | 25.00 |
| ❑ CL 1250 [M] | Legrand Jazz | 1958 | 40.00 |
| *—Miles Davis appears on this record* | | | |
| ❑ CL 1437 [M] | I Love Paris | 1960 | 25.00 |
| ❑ CS 8079 [S] | Legrand Jazz | 1959 | 40.00 |
| *—Miles Davis appears on this record* | | | |
| ❑ CS 8237 [S] | I Love Paris | 1960 | 20.00 |
| **MERCURY** | | | |
| ❑ MG 20342 [M] | C'est Magnifique | 1958 | 20.00 |
| **MOBILE FIDELITY** | | | |
| ❑ 1-504 | Jazz Grand | 198? | 50.00 |
| *—Audiophile vinyl* | | | |
| **PHILIPS** | | | |
| ❑ PHM 200074 [M] | The Michel Legrand Big Band Plays Richard Rogers | 1963 | 20.00 |
| ❑ PHM 200143 [M] | Michel Legrand Sings | 1964 | 25.00 |
| ❑ PHS 600074 [S] | The Michel Legrand Big Band Plays Richard Rogers | 1963 | 25.00 |
| ❑ PHS 600143 [S] | Michel Legrand Sings | 1964 | 30.00 |
| **LEGS DIAMOND** | | | |
| **CREAM** | | | |
| ❑ CR 1010 | Firepower | 1979 | 25.00 |
| **MERCURY** | | | |
| ❑ SRM-1-1136 | Legs Diamond | 1977 | 30.00 |
| ❑ SRM-1-1191 | A Diamond Is a Hard Rock | 1977 | 30.00 |
| **LEHRER, TOM** | | | |
| **LEHRER** | | | |
| ❑ TLP-1 [10] | Songs by Tom Lehrer | 1953 | 100.00 |
| ❑ TL-101 [M] | Songs by Tom Lehrer | 1959 | 40.00 |
| ❑ TL-102 [M] | More of Tom Lehrer | 1958 | 40.00 |
| ❑ TL-102S [S] | More of Tom Lehrer | 1959 | 40.00 |
| ❑ TL-201 [M] | Tom Lehrer Revisited | 1959 | 25.00 |
| ❑ TL-202 [M] | An Evening Wasted with Tom Lehrer | 1959 | 25.00 |
| ❑ TL-202S [S] | An Evening Wasted with Tom Lehrer | 1959 | 40.00 |
| **REPRISE** | | | |
| ❑ R-6179 [M] | That Was the Year That Was | 1965 | 20.00 |
| ❑ RS-6179 [S] | That Was the Year That Was | 1965 | 25.00 |
| *—Pink, yellow and green label* | | | |
| ❑ RS-6179 [S] | That Was the Year That Was | 1968 | 15.00 |
| *—Two-tone orange label with "W7" and "r:" logos* | | | |
| ❑ RS-6179 [S] | That Was the Year That Was | 1970 | 10.00 |
| *—Orange/tan label with "r:" logo* | | | |
| ❑ R 6199 [M] | An Evening Wasted with Tom Lehrer | 1966 | 20.00 |
| *—Reissue of Lehrer 202* | | | |
| ❑ RS 6199 [S] | An Evening Wasted with Tom Lehrer | 1966 | 25.00 |
| *—Reissue of Lehrer 202* | | | |
| ❑ R-6216 [M] | Songs by Tom Lehrer | 1966 | 20.00 |
| ❑ RS-6216 [S] | Songs by Tom Lehrer | 1966 | 25.00 |

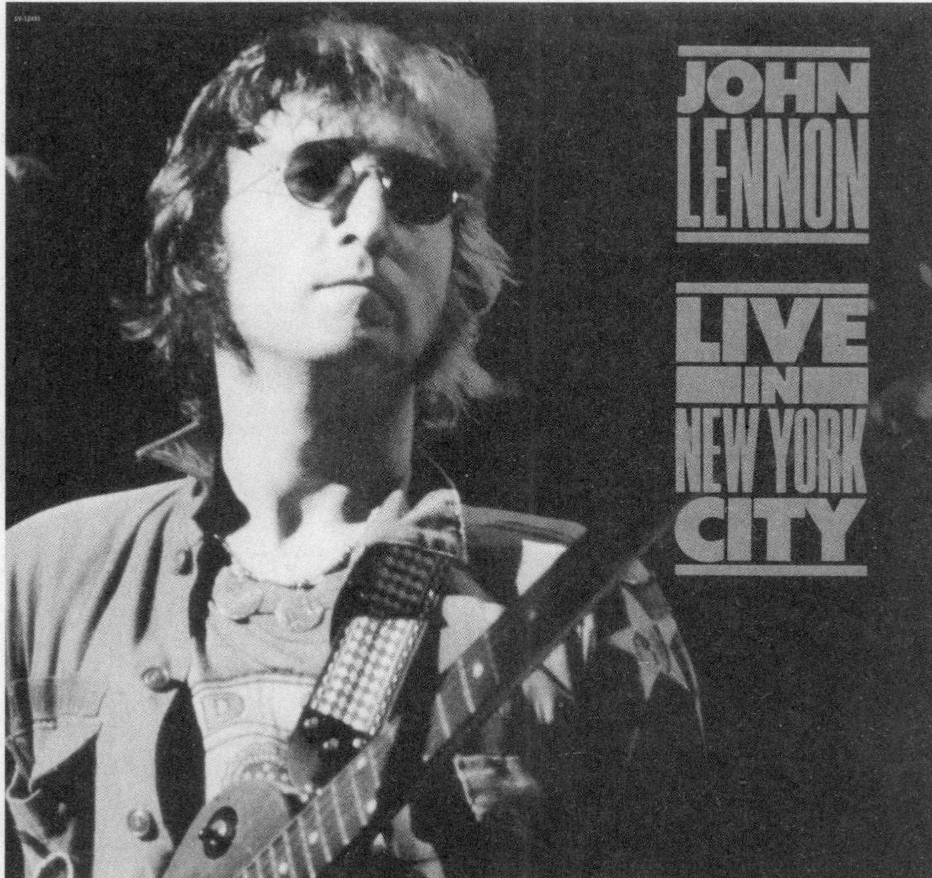


John Lennon, *Live in New York City,* Capitol SV-12451, 1986, $12.

**Number — Title (A Side/B Side) — Yr — NM**

**LEIBER, JERRY**

KAPP
❑ KL-1127 [M] Scooby-Doo 1959 50.00

**LEIBER AND STOLLER BIG BAND, THE**

ATLANTIC
❑ 8047 [M] Yakety Yak 1960 40.00
*—White "fan" logo on right side of label*
❑ 8047 [M] Yakety Yak 1962 20.00
*—Black "fan" logo on right side of label*
❑ SD 8047 [S] Yakety Yak 1960 50.00
*—White "fan" logo on right side of label*
❑ SD 8047 [S] Yakety Yak 1962 25.00
*—Black "fan" logo on right side of label*

**LEIBERT, DICK**

WESTMINSTER
❑ WST 15006 [S] Leibert Takes Broadway 195? 20.00
❑ WST 15009 [S] Leibert Takes Richmond 195? 20.00
❑ WST 15020 [S] A Merry Wurlitzer Christmas 195? 20.00
❑ WST 15034 [S] Leibert Takes a Holiday 195? 20.00
❑ WST 15043 [S] Leibert Takes You Dancing 195? 20.00
❑ WST 15050 [S] Sing a Song with Leibert 195? 20.00

**LEIGHTON, BERNIE**

COLUMBIA
❑ CL 6112 [10] East Side Rendezvous 1950 80.00

**LEIGHTON, BERNIE/JOHNNY GUARNIERI**

EMARCY
❑ MG-26018 [10] Piano Stylings 1954 80.00

**LEMER, PETER**

ESP-DISK'
❑ 1057 Local Colour 1968 25.00

**LEMMON, JACK**

CAPITOL
❑ ST 1943 [S] Jack Lemmon Plays Piano Selections from Irma La Douce 1963 60.00
❑ T 1943 [M] Jack Lemmon Plays Piano Selections from Irma La Douce 1963 50.00

EPIC
❑ BN 523 [S] A Twist of Lemmon 1959 50.00

**Number — Title (A Side/B Side) — Yr — NM**

❑ BN 528 [S] Jack Lemmon Sings and Plays Music from Some Like It Hot 1959 50.00
❑ LN 3491 [M] A Twist of Lemmon 1959 40.00
❑ LN 3559 [M] Jack Lemmon Sings and Plays Music from Some Like It Hot 1959 40.00

**LEMON PIPERS, THE**

BUDDAH
❑ BDM-1009 [M] Green Tambourine 1968 25.00
❑ BDM-1016 [M] Jungle Marmalade 1968 40.00
*—Mono is promo only; in stereo cover with "Mono" sticker*
❑ BDS-5009 [S] Green Tambourine 1968 25.00
❑ BDS-5016 [S] Jungle Marmalade 1968 25.00

**LEMONGELLO, PETER**

RAPP
❑ LR 8899 Love '76 1976 30.00

**LEMONHEADS, THE**

ATLANTIC
❑ 82137 Lovey 1990 20.00
*—U.S. edition; imports with a similar number go for less*
❑ 82537 Come On Feel the Lemonheads 1993 25.00
*—5,000 copies pressed, all on green vinyl; imports sell for less*

TAANG!
❑ 15 Hate Your Friends 1987 12.00
*—Any edition not listed among the first five pressings above*
❑ 15 Hate Your Friends 1987 20.00
*—Fifth pressing: Yellow vinyl, yellow lettering on sleeve, yellow label*
❑ 15 Hate Your Friends 1987 25.00
*—Fourth pressing: Black vinyl, red lettering on sleeve, blue and green label*
❑ 15 Hate Your Friends 1987 25.00
*—Third pressing: Black vinyl, red lettering on sleeve, red label*
❑ 15 Hate Your Friends 1987 30.00
*—The second 2,000 are on black vinyl, red lettering on sleeve, yellow label*
❑ 15 Hate Your Friends 1987 40.00
*—The first 3,000 were on black vinyl, yellow lettering on sleeve, yellow label*
❑ 23 Creator 1988 15.00
❑ 32 Lick 1989 15.00

**Number — Title (A Side/B Side) — Yr — NM**

**LENNON, JOHN** Includes records as "Plastic Ono Band," "John Ono Lennon," "John Lennon/Plastic Ono Band" and other records he made with Yoko Ono. Also see THE BEATLES.

ADAM VIII
❑ A-8018 John Lennon Sings the Great Rock & Roll Hits (Roots) 1975 1000.
*—Counterfeits abound. On authentic copies, cover is posterboard (not slicks); labels are normal size (not overly large); printing on cover is sharp, not blurry; the word "Greatest" does NOT appear on the spine. Authentic copies usually have ad sleeve also.*

APPLE
❑ SMAX-3361 Wedding Album 1969 150.00
*—With photo strip, postcard, poster of wedding photos, poster of lithographs, "Bagism" bag, booklet, photo of slice of wedding cake. Missing inserts reduce the value.*
❑ SW-3362 Live Peace in Toronto 1969 1970 15.00
*—By "The Plastic Ono Band" -- without calendar*
❑ SW-3362 Live Peace in Toronto 1969 1970 20.00
*—By "The Plastic Ono Band"; with calendar*
❑ SW-3372 John Lennon Plastic Ono Band 1970 20.00
❑ SW-3379 Imagine 1971 20.00
*—With either of two postcard inserts, lyric sleeve, poster*
❑ SW-3379 Imagine 1975 20.00
*—"All Rights Reserved" label*
❑ SVBB-3392 [(2)] Some Time in New York City 1972 30.00
*—By John and Yoko; with photo card and petition*
❑ SVBB-3392 [(2)DJ] Some Time in New York City 1972 1000.
*—White label promo*
❑ SW-3414 Mind Games 1973 20.00
❑ SW-3416 Walls and Bridges 1974 20.00
*—With fold-open segmented front cover*
❑ SK-3419 Rock 'N' Roll 1975 20.00
❑ SW-3421 Shaved Fish 1975 20.00
❑ T-5001 Two Virgins — Unfinished Music No. 1 1968 50.00
*—With Yoko Ono; without brown bag*
❑ T-5001 Two Virgins — Unfinished Music No. 1 1968 150.00
*—With Yoko Ono; with die-cut bag*
❑ T-5001 Two Virgins — Unfinished Music No. 1 1968 150.00
*—With Yoko Ono; price with brown bag*
❑ T-5001 Two Virgins — Unfinished Music No. 1 1985 15.00
*—With Yoko Ono; reissue, flat label*

CAPITOL
❑ SW-3372 John Lennon Plastic Ono Band 1978 12.00
*—Purple label, large Capitol logo*
❑ SW-3372 John Lennon Plastic Ono Band 1982 20.00
*—Black label, print in colorband*
❑ SW-3372 John Lennon Plastic Ono Band 1988 30.00
*—Purple label, small Capitol logo*
❑ SW-3379 Imagine 1978 10.00
*—Purple label, large Capitol logo*
❑ SW-3379 Imagine 1986 30.00
*—Black label, print in colorband*
❑ SW-3379 Imagine 1987 25.00
*—Black label, print in colorband; "Digitally Re-Mastered" at top of front cover*
❑ SW-3379 Imagine 1988 30.00
*—Purple label, small Capitol logo*
❑ SVBB-3392 [(2)] Some Time in New York City 197? 25.00
*—By John and Yoko; purple label, large Capitol logo*
❑ SVBB-3392 [(2)] Some Time in New York City 197? 100.00
*—Both discs in single-pocket gatefold (the other pocket is glued shut)*
❑ SW-3414 Mind Games 1978 40.00
*—Purple label, large Capitol logo*
❑ SW-3416 Walls and Bridges 1978 15.00
*—Purple label, large Capitol logo; standard front cover*
❑ SW-3416 Walls and Bridges 1982 30.00
*—Black label, print in colorband*
❑ SW-3416 Walls and Bridges 1989 30.00
*—Purple label, small Capitol logo*
❑ SK-3419 Rock 'N' Roll 1978 40.00
*—Purple label, large Capitol logo*
❑ SW-3421 Shaved Fish 1978 12.00
*—Purple Capitol label with Apple logo on cover*
❑ SW-3421 Shaved Fish 1978 40.00
*—Purple Capitol label with Capitol logo on cover*
❑ SW-3421 Shaved Fish 1983 20.00
*—Black Capitol label with Apple logo on cover*
❑ SW-3421 Shaved Fish 1983 40.00
*—Black Capitol label with Capitol logo on cover*
❑ SW-3421 Shaved Fish 1989 40.00
*—Purple Capitol label (small logo) with Capitol logo on cover*
❑ ST-12239 Live Peace in Toronto 1969 1982 10.00
*—By "The Plastic Ono Band"; reissue, purple Capitol label*
❑ ST-12239 Live Peace in Toronto 1969 1983 50.00
*—By "The Plastic Ono Band"; reissue, black Capitol label*
❑ SV-12451 Live in New York City 1986 12.00
❑ SJ-12533 Menlove Ave. 1986 15.00
❑ SN-16068 Mind Games 1980 12.00
*—Budget-line reissue*
❑ SN-16069 Rock 'N' Roll 1980 12.00
*—Budget-line reissue*
❑ C1-90803 [(2)] Imagine: Music from the Motion Picture 1988 20.00
❑ C1-91425 Double Fantasy 1989 20.00
*—Very briefly available reissue*

| Number | Title (A Side/B Side) | Yr | NM |
|---|---|---|---|
| R 144136 | Menlove Ave. | 198? | 50.00 |
| *—BMG Direct Marketing edition* | | | |
| R 144136 | Menlove Ave. | 1986 | 50.00 |
| *—RCA Music Service edition* | | | |
| R 144497 | Live in New York City | 1986 | 15.00 |
| *—RCA Music Service edition* | | | |
| SV-512451 | Live in New York City | 1986 | 15.00 |
| *—Columbia House edition* | | | |
| C1-591425 | Double Fantasy | 1989 | 60.00 |
| *—Columbia House edition of reissue* | | | |
| **GEFFEN** | | | |
| GHS 2001 | Double Fantasy | 1980 | 10.00 |
| *—Seven tracks by John, seven by Yoko; off-white label; titles on back cover out of order* | | | |
| GHS 2001 | Double Fantasy | 1981 | 12.00 |
| *—Columbia House edition (all have corrected back cover) without "CH" on label* | | | |
| GHS 2001 | Double Fantasy | 1981 | 12.00 |
| *—Off-white label, titles in order on the back cover* | | | |
| GHS 2001 | Double Fantasy | 1981 | 75.00 |
| *—Columbia House edition (all have corrected back cover) with "CH" on label* | | | |
| GHS 2001 | Double Fantasy | 1986 | 50.00 |
| *—Same as above, but with black Geffen label* | | | |
| GHSP 2023 | The John Lennon Collection | 1982 | 20.00 |
| GHSP 2023 [DJ] | The John Lennon Collection | 1982 | 50.00 |
| *—Promo only on Quiex II audiophile vinyl* | | | |
| R 104689 | Double Fantasy | 1981 | 40.00 |
| *—RCA Music Service edition* | | | |
| **MOBILE FIDELITY** | | | |
| 1-153 | Imagine | 1984 | 50.00 |
| *—Audiophile vinyl* | | | |
| MFSL 1-277 | Imagine | 2004 | 25.00 |
| *—"Original Master Recording" at top of front cover* | | | |
| MFSL 1-280 | John Lennon Plastic Ono Band | 2004 | 25.00 |
| *—"Original Master Recording" at top of front cover* | | | |
| **NAUTILUS** | | | |
| NR-47 | Double Fantasy | 1982 | 80.00 |
| *—Half-speed master* | | | |
| NR-47 | Double Fantasy | 1982 | 2000. |
| *—Half-speed master; alternate experimental cover with yellow and red added to black and white front* | | | |
| **PARLOPHONE** | | | |
| 21954 [(2)] | Lennon Legend | 1998 | 20.00 |
| *—"Made in U.S.A." on back cover* | | | |
| **POLYDOR** | | | |
| 817160-1 | Milk and Honey | 1983 | 10.00 |
| *—Six tracks by John, six by Yoko* | | | |
| 817160-1 | Milk and Honey | 1984 | 150.00 |
| *—Yellow or green vinyl; unauthorized "inside jobs"* | | | |
| 817238-1 | Heart Play (Unfinished Dialogue) | 1983 | 12.00 |
| *—Interviews with John Lennon and Yoko Ono* | | | |
| **SILHOUETTE** | | | |
| SM-10012 [(2)] | Reflections and Poetry | 1984 | 25.00 |
| **ZAPPLE** | | | |
| ST-3357 | Life with the Lions — Unfinished Music No. 2 | 1969 | 20.00 |
| *—With Yoko Ono* | | | |

### LENNON, JULIAN

| Number | Title (A Side/B Side) | Yr | NM |
|---|---|---|---|
| **ATLANTIC** | | | |
| PR 2693 [DJ] | Mr. Jordan According to Mr. Lennon | 1989 | 20.00 |
| *—Promo-only interview album* | | | |
| 81084 | Valotte | 1984 | 10.00 |
| 81640 | The Secret Value of Daydreaming | 1986 | 10.00 |
| 81928 | Mr. Jordan | 1989 | 10.00 |

### LENNON SISTERS, THE

| Number | Title (A Side/B Side) | Yr | NM |
|---|---|---|---|
| **BRUNSWICK** | | | |
| BL 54031 [M] | Let's Get Acquainted | 1957 | 25.00 |
| BL 54039 [M] | Lawrence Welk Presents the Lennon Sisters | 1958 | 25.00 |
| **DOT** | | | |
| DLP-3250 [M] | Best-Loved Catholic Hymns | 1959 | 15.00 |
| DLP-3292 [M] | The Lennon Sisters Sing 12 Great Hits | 1960 | 15.00 |
| DLP 3343 [M] | Christmas with the Lennon Sisters | 1961 | 15.00 |
| DLP-3398 [M] | Sad Movies (Make Me Cry) | 1961 | 15.00 |
| DLP-3417 [M] | Can't Help Falling in Love | 1962 | 12.00 |
| DLP-3481 [M] | The Lennon Sisters' Favorites | 1963 | 12.00 |
| DLP-3557 [M] | Dominique and Other Great Folk Songs | 1964 | 12.00 |
| DLP-3589 [M] | No. 1 Hits of the 1960s | 1964 | 12.00 |
| DLP-3622 [M] | Twelve Great Hits, Volume 2 | 1965 | 12.00 |
| DLP-3659 [M] | Solos | 1965 | 12.00 |
| DLP-3797 [M] | Somethin' Stupid | 1967 | 15.00 |
| DLP-25250 [S] | Best-Loved Catholic Hymns | 1959 | 20.00 |
| DLP-25292 [S] | The Lennon Sisters Sing 12 Great Hits | 1960 | 20.00 |
| DLP 25343 [S] | Christmas with the Lennon Sisters | 1961 | 20.00 |
| DLP-25398 [S] | Sad Movies (Make Me Cry) | 1961 | 20.00 |
| DLP-25417 [S] | Can't Help Falling in Love | 1962 | 15.00 |

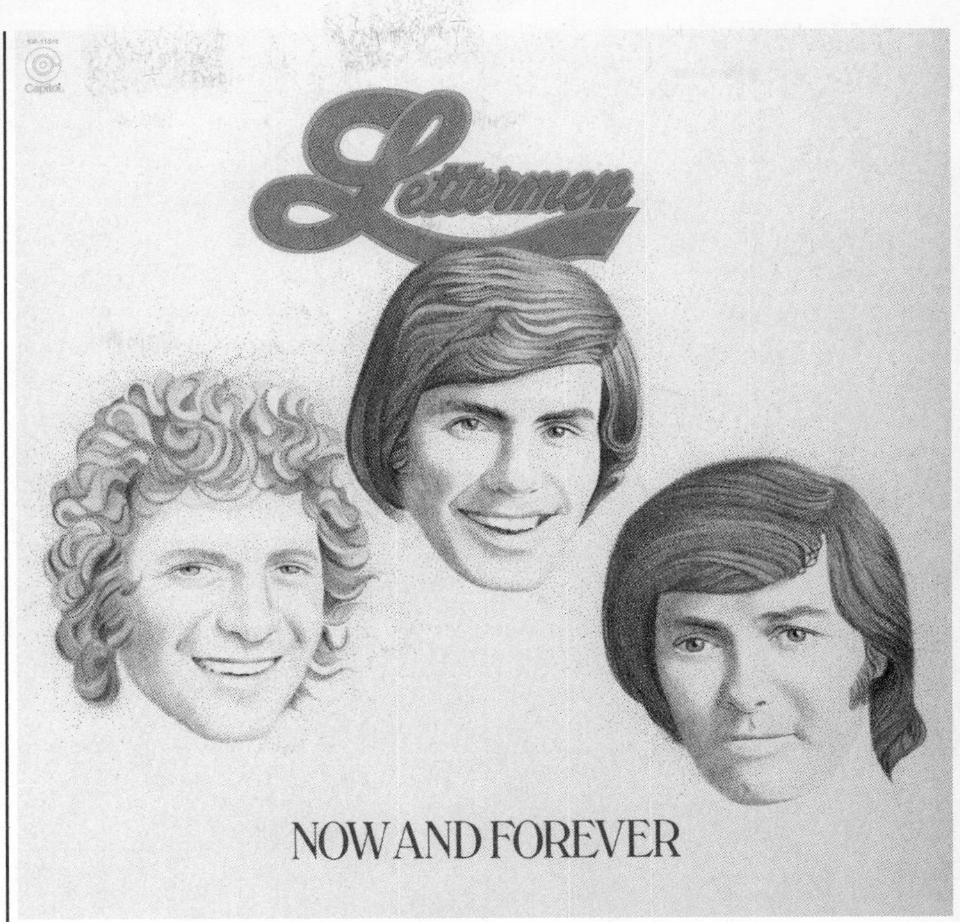

The Lettermen, *Now and Forever,* Capitol SW-11319, 1974, $10.

| Number | Title (A Side/B Side) | Yr | NM |
|---|---|---|---|
| DLP-25481 [S] | The Lennon Sisters' Favorites | 1963 | 15.00 |
| DLP-25557 [S] | Dominique and Other Great Folk Songs | 1964 | 15.00 |
| DLP-25589 [S] | No. 1 Hits of the 1960s | 1964 | 15.00 |
| DLP-25622 [S] | Twelve Great Hits, Volume 2 | 1965 | 15.00 |
| DLP-25659 [S] | Solos | 1965 | 15.00 |
| DLP-25797 [S] | Somethin' Stupid | 1967 | 12.00 |
| **HAMILTON** | | | |
| HLP-119 [M] | Melody of Love | 196? | 12.00 |
| HLP-12119 [S] | Melody of Love | 196? | 12.00 |
| **MERCURY** | | | |
| SR-61164 | The Lennon Sisters Today!! | 1968 | 12.00 |
| SR-61201 | Pop Country | 1969 | 12.00 |
| **PICKWICK** | | | |
| PTP-2014 [(2)] | America's Sweethearts | 1973 | 12.00 |
| SPC-3084 | Our Favorite Songs | 196? | 10.00 |
| SPC-3110 | Goodnight Sweetheart | 197? | 10.00 |
| **RANWOOD** | | | |
| 7027 [(2)] | 22 Songs of Faith and Inspiration | 198? | 10.00 |
| 8205 | Best of the Lennon Sisters | 198? | 8.00 |
| 8212 | How Great Thou Art | 198? | 8.00 |
| **VOCALION** | | | |
| VL 73864 | Too Marvelous for Words | 1969 | 10.00 |
| VL 73887 | The Lennon Sisters with Lawrence Welk | 1970 | 10.00 |

### LENOIR, J.B.

| Number | Title (A Side/B Side) | Yr | NM |
|---|---|---|---|
| **CHESS** | | | |
| LP-410 | Natural Man | 1970 | 40.00 |
| CH-9323 | Natural Man | 1990 | 12.00 |
| **POLYDOR** | | | |
| 24-4011 | J.B. Lenoir | 1970 | 15.00 |

### LENYA, LOTTE

| Number | Title (A Side/B Side) | Yr | NM |
|---|---|---|---|
| **COLUMBIA MASTERWORKS** | | | |
| ML 5056 [M] | Berlin Theater Songs by Kurt Weill | 1957 | 30.00 |
| KL 5229 [M] | September Song | 1958 | 30.00 |

### LEONARD, HARLAN

| Number | Title (A Side/B Side) | Yr | NM |
|---|---|---|---|
| **RCA VICTOR** | | | |
| LPV-531 [M] | Harlan Leonard and His Rockets | 1965 | 25.00 |

### LEONARD, HARVEY

| Number | Title (A Side/B Side) | Yr | NM |
|---|---|---|---|
| **KEYNOTE** | | | |
| 1102 [M] | Jazz Ecstasy | 1955 | 50.00 |

### LEONARD, JACK E.

| Number | Title (A Side/B Side) | Yr | NM |
|---|---|---|---|
| **VIK** | | | |
| LX-1080 [M] | Rock 'n Roll for People Over Sixteen | 1957 | 40.00 |

### LEOPARDS, THE

| Number | Title (A Side/B Side) | Yr | NM |
|---|---|---|---|
| **MOON** | | | |
| (# unknown) | Kansas City Slickers | 1977 | 25.00 |

### LES JAZZ MODES

| Number | Title (A Side/B Side) | Yr | NM |
|---|---|---|---|
| **ATLANTIC** | | | |
| 1280 [M] | The Most Happy Fella | 1958 | 80.00 |
| *—Black label* | | | |
| 1280 [M] | The Most Happy Fella | 1961 | 30.00 |
| *—Multicolor label, white "fan" logo at right* | | | |
| 1306 [M] | Les Jazz Modes | 1959 | 60.00 |
| *—Black label* | | | |
| 1306 [M] | Les Jazz Modes | 1961 | 30.00 |
| *—Multicolor label, white "fan" logo at right* | | | |
| SD-1306 [S] | Les Jazz Modes | 1959 | 60.00 |
| *—Green label* | | | |
| SD-1306 [S] | Les Jazz Modes | 1961 | 30.00 |
| *—Multicolor label, white "fan" logo at right* | | | |
| **DAWN** | | | |
| DLP-1101 [M] | Jazzville | 1956 | 100.00 |
| DLP-1108 [M] | Les Jazz Modes | 1956 | 100.00 |
| DLP-1117 [M] | Mood in Scarlet | 1957 | 100.00 |
| **SEECO** | | | |
| CELP-466 [M] | Smart Jazz for the Smart Set | 1960 | 30.00 |

### LESLIE, BILL

| Number | Title (A Side/B Side) | Yr | NM |
|---|---|---|---|
| **ARGO** | | | |
| LP-710 [M] | Diggin' the Chicks | 1962 | 25.00 |
| LPS-710 [S] | Diggin' the Chicks | 1962 | 30.00 |

| Number | Title (A Side/B Side) | Yr | NM |
|---|---|---|---|
| **LESTER, KETTY** | | | |
| AVI | | | |
| ❑ 6116 | A Collection of Her Best | 1982 | 15.00 |
| ERA | | | |
| ❑ EL-108 [M] | Love Letters | 1962 | 40.00 |
| ❑ ES-108 [S] | Love Letters | 1962 | 60.00 |
| PETE | | | |
| ❑ 1109 | Ketty Lester | 1969 | 15.00 |
| RCA VICTOR | | | |
| ❑ LPM-2945 [M] | The Soul of Me | 1964 | 25.00 |
| ❑ LSP-2945 [S] | The Soul of Me | 1964 | 30.00 |
| ❑ LPM-3326 [M] | Where Is Love | 1965 | 25.00 |
| ❑ LSP-3326 [S] | Where Is Love | 1965 | 30.00 |
| SHEFFIELD | | | |
| ❑ 15 | Ketty Lester In Concert | 1977 | 15.00 |
| TOWER | | | |
| ❑ ST 5029 [S] | When a Woman Loves a Man | 1966 | 25.00 |
| ❑ T 5029 [M] | When a Woman Loves a Man | 1966 | 25.00 |
| **LETMAN, JOHN** | | | |
| BETHLEHEM | | | |
| ❑ BCP-6053 [M] | The Many Angles of John Letman | 1961 | 30.00 |
| ❑ SBCP-6053 [S] | The Many Angles of John Letman | 1961 | 40.00 |
| **LETTERMEN, THE** | | | |
| APPLAUSE | | | |
| ❑ 1006 | Love Is... | 198? | 10.00 |
| CAPITOL | | | |
| ❑ SKAO-138 | The Best of the Lettermen, Vol. 2 | 1969 | 12.00 |
| ❑ SM-147 | Put Your Head on My Shoulder | 1977 | 8.00 |
| *—Reissue with new prefix* | | | |
| ❑ ST-147 | Put Your Head on My Shoulder | 1968 | 15.00 |
| ❑ ST-202 | I Have Dreamed | 1969 | 12.00 |
| ❑ SWBB-251 [(2)] | Close-Up | 1969 | 15.00 |
| *—Reissue of ST 2013 and ST 2083 in one package* | | | |
| ❑ ST 8-0269 | Hurt So Bad | 1969 | 15.00 |
| *—Capitol Record Club edition* | | | |
| ❑ ST-269 | Hurt So Bad | 1969 | 12.00 |
| ❑ ST-390 | Traces/Memories | 1970 | 12.00 |
| ❑ ST 8-0496 | Reflections | 1970 | 15.00 |
| *—Capitol Record Club edition* | | | |
| ❑ ST-496 | Reflections | 1970 | 12.00 |
| ❑ STCL-577 [(3)] | The Lettermen | 1970 | 25.00 |
| ❑ ST-634 | Everything's Good About You | 1971 | 12.00 |
| ❑ STBB-710 [(2)] | Let It Be Me/And I Love Her | 1971 | 15.00 |
| ❑ SW-781 | Feelings | 1971 | 12.00 |
| ❑ ST-836 | Love Book | 1971 | 12.00 |
| ❑ ST 1669 [S] | A Song for Young Love | 1962 | 20.00 |
| ❑ T 1669 [M] | A Song for Young Love | 1962 | 15.00 |
| ❑ ST 1711 [S] | Once Upon a Time | 1962 | 20.00 |
| ❑ T 1711 [M] | Once Upon a Time | 1962 | 15.00 |
| ❑ ST 1761 [S] | Jim, Tony and Bob | 1962 | 20.00 |
| ❑ T 1761 [M] | Jim, Tony and Bob | 1962 | 15.00 |
| ❑ ST 1829 [S] | College Standards | 1963 | 20.00 |
| ❑ T 1829 [M] | College Standards | 1963 | 15.00 |
| ❑ ST 1936 [S] | The Lettermen In Concert | 1963 | 20.00 |
| ❑ T 1936 [M] | The Lettermen In Concert | 1963 | 15.00 |
| ❑ ST 2013 [S] | A Lettermen Kind of Love | 1964 | 15.00 |
| ❑ T 2013 [M] | A Lettermen Kind of Love | 1964 | 12.00 |
| ❑ ST 2083 [S] | The Lettermen Look at Love | 1964 | 15.00 |
| ❑ T 2083 [M] | The Lettermen Look at Love | 1964 | 12.00 |
| ❑ ST 2142 [S] | She Cried | 1964 | 15.00 |
| ❑ T 2142 [M] | She Cried | 1964 | 12.00 |
| ❑ ST 2213 [S] | You'll Never Walk Alone | 1965 | 15.00 |
| ❑ T 2213 [M] | You'll Never Walk Alone | 1965 | 12.00 |
| ❑ ST 2270 [S] | Portrait of My Love | 1965 | 15.00 |
| ❑ T 2270 [M] | Portrait of My Love | 1965 | 12.00 |
| ❑ ST 2359 [S] | The Hit Sounds of the Lettermen | 1965 | 15.00 |
| ❑ T 2359 [M] | The Hit Sounds of the Lettermen | 1965 | 12.00 |
| ❑ ST 2428 [S] | More Hit Sounds of the Lettermen! | 1966 | 15.00 |
| ❑ T 2428 [M] | More Hit Sounds of the Lettermen! | 1966 | 12.00 |
| ❑ ST 2496 [S] | A New Song for Young Love | 1966 | 15.00 |
| ❑ T 2496 [M] | A New Song for Young Love | 1966 | 12.00 |
| ❑ ST 2554 [S] | The Best of the Lettermen | 1966 | 15.00 |
| ❑ T 2554 [M] | The Best of the Lettermen | 1966 | 12.00 |
| ❑ ST 2587 [S] | For Christmas This Year | 1966 | 15.00 |
| ❑ ST-8-2587 [S] | For Christmas This Year | 1966 | 20.00 |
| *—Capitol Record Club edition* | | | |
| ❑ T 2587 [M] | For Christmas This Year | 1966 | 12.00 |
| ❑ ST 2633 [S] | Warm | 1967 | 15.00 |
| ❑ T 2633 [M] | Warm | 1967 | 15.00 |
| ❑ SM-2711 | Spring! | 1977 | 8.00 |
| *—Reissue with new prefix* | | | |
| ❑ ST 2711 [S] | Spring! | 1967 | 15.00 |
| ❑ T 2711 [M] | Spring! | 1967 | 15.00 |
| ❑ ST 2758 [S] | The Lettermen!!!... And "Live!" | 1967 | 15.00 |
| ❑ T 2758 [M] | The Lettermen!!!... And "Live!" | 1967 | 20.00 |
| ❑ ST 2865 | Goin' Out of My Head | 1968 | 15.00 |

| Number | Title (A Side/B Side) | Yr | NM |
|---|---|---|---|
| ❑ ST 2934 | Special Request | 1968 | 15.00 |
| ❑ SPRO-4798/9 [DJ] | A Collection of Their Finest Songs | 1969 | 25.00 |
| *—Promo-only collection of excerpts of 20 songs* | | | |
| ❑ SW-11010 | Lettermen 1 | 1972 | 10.00 |
| ❑ SW-11124 | Spin Away | 1972 | 10.00 |
| ❑ SW-11183 | "Alive" Again ... Naturally | 1973 | 10.00 |
| ❑ SW-11249 | All-Time Greatest Hits | 1973 | 10.00 |
| ❑ SW-11319 | Now and Forever | 1974 | 10.00 |
| ❑ SW-11364 | There Is No Greater Love | 1974 | 10.00 |
| ❑ SW-11424 | Make Time | 1975 | 10.00 |
| ❑ SW-11470 | The Time Is Right | 1975 | 10.00 |
| ❑ SW-11508 | Kind of Country | 1976 | 10.00 |
| ❑ SM-11678 | Hurt So Bad | 1977 | 8.00 |
| *—Reissue of 269* | | | |
| ❑ SM-11814 | The Lettermen!!! ... And "Live!" | 1978 | 8.00 |
| *—Reissue of 2758* | | | |
| ❑ SM-11970 | Goin' Out of My Head | 1979 | 8.00 |
| *—Reissue of 2865* | | | |
| ❑ SN-16071 | The Best of the Lettermen | 1980 | 8.00 |
| *—Budget-line reissue* | | | |
| ❑ SN-16190 | Let It Be Me | 1981 | 8.00 |
| *—Budget-line reissue* | | | |
| ❑ SN-16191 | And I Love Her | 1981 | 8.00 |
| *—Budget-line reissue* | | | |
| ❑ SN-16222 | The Best of the Lettermen, Vol. 2 | 198? | 8.00 |
| *—Budget-line reissue* | | | |
| ❑ SN-16312 | All-Time Greatest Hits | 198? | 8.00 |
| *—Budget-line reissue* | | | |
| LONGINES SYMPHONETTE | | | |
| ❑ 220 [(5)] | A Time for Us | 1972 | 30.00 |
| PICKWICK | | | |
| ❑ SPC-3294 | Soft Hits | 1972 | 10.00 |
| ❑ SPC-3565 | With Love | 1978 | 8.00 |
| **LEVEY, STAN** | | | |
| BETHLEHEM | | | |
| ❑ BCP-37 [M] | This Time the Dream's On Me | 1956 | 50.00 |
| ❑ BCP-71 [M] | Grand Stan | 1957 | 50.00 |
| ❑ BCP-1017 [10] | Stan Levey Plays | 1954 | 120.00 |
| MODE | | | |
| ❑ LP-101 [M] | Stan Levey Quartet | 1957 | 80.00 |
| **LEVIATHAN** | | | |
| MACH | | | |
| ❑ XMA-12501 | Leviathan | 1974 | 40.00 |
| **LEVIN, MARC** | | | |
| SAVOY | | | |
| ❑ MG-12190 [M] | The Dragon Suite | 1967 | 25.00 |
| SWEET DRAGON | | | |
| ❑ 1 | Songs, Dances and Prayers | 197? | 20.00 |
| **LEVINE, HENRY** | | | |
| RCA CAMDEN | | | |
| ❑ CAL-321 [M] | Lower Basin Street | 1958 | 25.00 |
| RCA VICTOR | | | |
| ❑ LPM-1283 [M] | Dixieland Jazz Band | 1956 | 50.00 |
| **LEVINSON, MARK** | | | |
| MARK LEVINSON | | | |
| ❑ 7 | Jazz at Long Wharf | 1979 | 30.00 |
| *—Audiophile edition pressed at 45 rpm* | | | |
| **LEVISTER, ALONZO** | | | |
| DEBUT | | | |
| ❑ DEB-125 [M] | Manhattan Moondrama | 1956 | 150.00 |
| **LEVITT, ROD** | | | |
| RCA VICTOR | | | |
| ❑ LSP-3372 [S] | Insight | 1965 | 20.00 |
| ❑ LSP-3448 [S] | Solid Ground | 1965 | 20.00 |
| ❑ LSP-3615 [S] | 42nd Street | 1966 | 20.00 |
| RIVERSIDE | | | |
| ❑ RS-9471 [S] | The Dynamic Sound Patterns of the Rod Levitt Orchestra | 1964 | 20.00 |
| **LEVITTS, THE** | | | |
| ESP-DISK' | | | |
| ❑ S-1095 | We Are the Levitts | 1970 | 25.00 |
| **LEVY, LOU** | | | |
| JUBILEE | | | |
| ❑ JLP-1101 [M] | Lou Levy Plays Baby Grand Jazz | 1959 | 40.00 |
| ❑ SDJLP-1101 [S] | Lou Levy Plays Baby Grand Jazz | 1959 | 40.00 |
| NOCTURNE | | | |
| ❑ NLP-10 [10] | Lou Levy Trio | 1954 | 100.00 |
| PHILIPS | | | |
| ❑ PHS 600056 [S] | The Hymn | 1962 | 20.00 |
| RCA VICTOR | | | |
| ❑ LPM-1267 [M] | Solo Scene | 1956 | 50.00 |

| Number | Title (A Side/B Side) | Yr | NM |
|---|---|---|---|
| ❑ LPM-1319 [M] | Jazz in Four Colors | 1956 | 50.00 |
| ❑ LPM-1491 [M] | A Most Musical Fella | 1957 | 50.00 |
| **LEVY, LOU/CONTE CANDOLI** | | | |
| ATLANTIC | | | |
| ❑ 1268 [M] | West Coast Wailers | 1957 | 50.00 |
| *—Black label* | | | |
| ❑ 1268 [M] | West Coast Wailers | 1961 | 25.00 |
| *—Multicolor label, white "fan" logo at right* | | | |
| **LEVY, O'DONEL** | | | |
| GROOVE MERCHANT | | | |
| ❑ 501 | Black Velvet | 1971 | 25.00 |
| ❑ 507 | Breeding of Mind | 1972 | 25.00 |
| ❑ 518 | Dawn of a New Day | 1973 | 25.00 |
| ❑ 526 | Simba | 1974 | 30.00 |
| ❑ 535 | Everything I Do Gonna Be Funky | 1975 | 30.00 |
| ❑ 3313 | Windows | 197? | 20.00 |
| ❑ 4408 [(2)] | Hands of Fire | 197? | 25.00 |
| **LEWD** | | | |
| ICI | | | |
| ❑ CF 200 | American Wino | 1982 | 40.00 |
| **LEWIS, BARBARA** | | | |
| ATLANTIC | | | |
| ❑ 8086 [M] | Hello Stranger | 1963 | 40.00 |
| ❑ SD 8086 [S] | Hello Stranger | 1963 | 50.00 |
| ❑ 8090 [M] | Snap Your Fingers | 1964 | 40.00 |
| ❑ SD 8090 [S] | Snap Your Fingers | 1964 | 50.00 |
| ❑ 8110 [M] | Baby, I'm Yours | 1965 | 40.00 |
| ❑ SD 8110 [S] | Baby, I'm Yours | 1965 | 50.00 |
| ❑ 8118 [M] | It's Magic | 1966 | 30.00 |
| ❑ SD 8118 [S] | It's Magic | 1966 | 40.00 |
| ❑ SD 8173 | Workin' on a Groovy Thing | 1968 | 25.00 |
| ❑ 8286 [M] | The Best of Barbara Lewis | 1971 | 40.00 |
| *—Mono is white label promo only; front cover has "d/j copy monaural" sticker* | | | |
| ❑ SD 8286 [S] | The Best of Barbara Lewis | 1971 | 20.00 |
| COLLECTABLES | | | |
| ❑ COL-5104 | Golden Classics | 198? | 10.00 |
| ENTERPRISE | | | |
| ❑ ENS-1006 | The Many Grooves of Barbara Lewis | 1970 | 25.00 |
| **LEWIS, BOBBY (1)** R&B singer. | | | |
| BELTONE | | | |
| ❑ 4000 [M] | Tossin' and Turnin' | 1961 | 200.00 |
| **LEWIS, BOBBY (2)** Country singer. | | | |
| ACE OF HEARTS | | | |
| ❑ 1002 | Too Many Memories | 1974 | 15.00 |
| RPA | | | |
| ❑ 1002 | Portrait in Love | 1976 | 10.00 |
| ❑ 1013 | Soul Full of Music | 1977 | 10.00 |
| UNITED ARTISTS | | | |
| ❑ UAL-3582 [M] | How Long Has It Been | 1967 | 25.00 |
| ❑ UAS-6582 [S] | How Long Has It Been | 1967 | 25.00 |
| ❑ UAS-6616 | A World of Love from Bobby Lewis | 1967 | 20.00 |
| ❑ UAS-6629 | An Ordinary Miracle | 1968 | 20.00 |
| ❑ UAS-6673 | From Heaven to Heartache | 1968 | 20.00 |
| ❑ UAS-6717 | Thanks for You and I | 1969 | 20.00 |
| ❑ UAS-6760 | The Best of Bobby Lewis, Vol. 1 | 1970 | 15.00 |
| **LEWIS, DAVE** | | | |
| A&M | | | |
| ❑ LP-105 [M] | Little Green Thing | 1964 | 20.00 |
| ❑ SP-4105 [S] | Little Green Thing | 1964 | 25.00 |
| JERDEN | | | |
| ❑ JRL-7006 [M] | Dave Lewis Plays Herb Alpert and the Tijuana Brass | 1966 | 20.00 |
| ❑ JRLS-7006 [S] | Dave Lewis Plays Herb Alpert and the Tijuana Brass | 1966 | 25.00 |
| **LEWIS, FURRY** | | | |
| AMPEX | | | |
| ❑ A-10140 | Live at the Gaslight | 1971 | 25.00 |
| BLUESVILLE | | | |
| ❑ BVLP-1036 [M] | Back on My Feet Again | 1961 | 100.00 |
| *—Blue label, silver print* | | | |
| ❑ BVLP-1036 [M] | Back on My Feet Again | 1964 | 30.00 |
| *—Blue label, trident logo at right* | | | |
| ❑ BVLP-1037 [M] | Done Changed My Mind | 1961 | 100.00 |
| *—Blue label, silver print* | | | |
| ❑ BVLP-1037 [M] | Done Changed My Mind | 1964 | 30.00 |
| *—Blue label, trident logo at right* | | | |
| **LEWIS, GARY, AND THE PLAYBOYS** | | | |
| LIBERTY | | | |
| ❑ LM-1003 | This Diamond Ring | 1981 | 8.00 |
| *—Reissue of United Artists 1008* | | | |
| ❑ LRP-3408 [M] | This Diamond Ring | 1965 | 20.00 |
| ❑ LRP-3419 [M] | A Session with Gary Lewis and the Playboys | 1965 | 20.00 |



**Except when noted otherwise, VG = 25% of NM, and VG+ = 50% of NM. (Example: VG = $2.00, VG+ = $4.00 and NM = $8.00.)**

| Number | Title (A Side/B Side) | Yr | NM |
|---|---|---|---|
| ❑ LRP-3428 [M] | Everybody Loves a Clown | 1965 | 20.00 |
| ❑ LRP-3435 [M] | She's Just My Style | 1966 | 15.00 |
| ❑ LRP-3452 [M] | Hits Again! | 1966 | 15.00 |
| ❑ LRP-3468 [M] | Golden Greats | 1966 | 15.00 |
| ❑ LRP-3487 [M] | (You Don't Have to) Paint Me a Picture | 1967 | 15.00 |
| *—Side 1 plays as listed* | | | |
| ❑ LRP-3487 [M] | (You Don't Have to) Paint Me a Picture | 1967 | 20.00 |
| *—Side 1, Song 4 claims to be "Tina" but plays "Ice Melts in the Sun"* | | | |
| ❑ LRP-3519 [M] | New Directions | 1967 | 15.00 |
| ❑ LRP-3524 [M] | Listen | 1967 | 15.00 |
| ❑ LST-7408 [S] | This Diamond Ring | 1965 | 25.00 |
| ❑ LST-7419 [S] | A Session with Gary Lewis and the Playboys | 1965 | 25.00 |
| ❑ LST-7428 [S] | Everybody Loves a Clown | 1965 | 25.00 |
| ❑ LST-7435 [S] | She's Just My Style | 1966 | 20.00 |
| ❑ LST-7452 [S] | Hits Again! | 1966 | 20.00 |
| ❑ LST-7468 [S] | Golden Greats | 1966 | 20.00 |
| *—Side 2 plays as listed* | | | |
| ❑ LST-7468 [S] | Golden Greats | 1966 | 30.00 |
| *—Side 2, Song 2 claims to be "I Won't Make That Mistake Again" but it plays "You've Got to Hide Your Love Away"* | | | |
| ❑ LST-7487 [S] | (You Don't Have to) Paint Me a Picture | 1967 | 20.00 |
| *—Side 1 plays as listed* | | | |
| ❑ LST-7487 [S] | (You Don't Have to) Paint Me a Picture | 1967 | 25.00 |
| *—Side 1, Song 4 claims to be "Tina" but plays "Ice Melts in the Sun"* | | | |
| ❑ LST-7519 [S] | New Directions | 1967 | 15.00 |
| ❑ LST-7524 [S] | Listen | 1967 | 15.00 |
| ❑ LST-7568 | Gary Lewis Now! | 1968 | 15.00 |
| ❑ LST-7589 | More Golden Greats | 1968 | 15.00 |
| ❑ LST-7606 | Close Cover Before Playing | 1969 | 15.00 |
| ❑ LST-7623 | Rhythm of the Rain | 1969 | 15.00 |
| ❑ LST-7633 | I'm On the Right Road Now | 1970 | 15.00 |
| ❑ LN-10241 | Golden Greats | 198? | 8.00 |
| *—Budget-line reissue* | | | |
| RHINO | | | |
| ❑ RNLP-163 | Greatest Hits (1965-1968) | 1985 | 10.00 |
| SUNSET | | | |
| ❑ SUM-1168 [M] | Gary Lewis and the Playboys | 1967 | 12.00 |
| ❑ SUS-5168 [S] | Gary Lewis and the Playboys | 1967 | 12.00 |
| ❑ SUS-5262 | Rhythm! | 1969 | 12.00 |
| UNITED ARTISTS | | | |
| ❑ UA-LA430-E | The Very Best of Gary Lewis and the Playboys | 1975 | 10.00 |
| ❑ LM-1003 | This Diamond Ring | 1980 | 10.00 |
| *—Edited reissue of Liberty 7408* | | | |

## LEWIS, GEORGE (1)

| Number | Title (A Side/B Side) | Yr | NM |
|---|---|---|---|
| AMERICAN MUSIC | | | |
| ❑ 639 [10] | The George Lewis Band in the French Quarter | 1951 | 80.00 |
| ❑ 645 [10] | George Lewis with Kid Shots Madison | 1952 | 80.00 |
| ATLANTIC | | | |
| ❑ SD 1411 [S] | The George Lewis Band | 1963 | 20.00 |
| BLUE NOTE | | | |
| ❑ BLP-1205 [M] | George Lewis and His New Orleans Stompers, Volume 1 | 1955 | 100.00 |
| *—Regular version, Lexington Ave. address on label* | | | |
| ❑ BLP-1205 [M] | George Lewis and His New Orleans Stompers, Volume 1 | 1955 | 150.00 |
| *—"Deep groove" version (deep indentation under label on both sides)* | | | |
| ❑ BLP-1205 [M] | George Lewis and His New Orleans Stompers, Volume 1 | 1963 | 25.00 |
| *—With "New York, USA" address on label* | | | |
| ❑ BLP-1206 [M] | George Lewis and His New Orleans Stompers, Volume 2 | 1955 | 100.00 |
| *—Regular version, Lexington Ave. address on label* | | | |
| ❑ BLP-1206 [M] | George Lewis and His New Orleans Stompers, Volume 2 | 1955 | 150.00 |
| *—"Deep groove" version (deep indentation under label on both sides)* | | | |
| ❑ BLP-1206 [M] | George Lewis and His New Orleans Stompers, Volume 2 | 1963 | 25.00 |
| *—With "New York, USA" address on label* | | | |
| ❑ BLP-1208 [M] | George Lewis Concert! | 1955 | 100.00 |
| *—Regular version, Lexington Ave. address on label* | | | |
| ❑ BLP-1208 [M] | George Lewis Concert! | 1955 | 150.00 |
| *—"Deep groove" version (deep indentation under label on both sides)* | | | |
| ❑ BLP-1208 [M] | George Lewis Concert! | 1963 | 25.00 |
| *—With "New York, USA" address on label* | | | |
| ❑ BLP-7010 [10] | George Lewis' New Orleans Stompers, Volume 1 | 1951 | 250.00 |
| ❑ BLP-7013 [10] | George Lewis' New Orleans Stompers, Volume 2 | 1951 | 250.00 |
| ❑ BLP-7027 [10] | George Lewis' New Orleans Stompers, Volume 3 | 1954 | 250.00 |
| ❑ BLP-7028 [10] | George Lewis' New Orleans Stompers, Volume 4 | 1954 | 250.00 |
| CAVALIER | | | |
| ❑ CVLP-6004 [M] | George Lewis in Hi-Fi | 1956 | 60.00 |
| CIRCLE | | | |
| ❑ L-421 [10] | George Lewis and His New Orleans All-Stars | 1951 | 80.00 |
| DELMAR | | | |
| ❑ DL-201 [M] | Doctor Jazz | 195? | 50.00 |
| ❑ DL-202 [M] | On Parade | 195? | 50.00 |
| DELMARK | | | |
| ❑ DL-202 | George Lewis' New Orleans Stompers | 196? | 25.00 |
| ❑ DL-203 | George Lewis Memorial Album | 196? | 20.00 |
| DISC JOCKEY | | | |
| ❑ DDL-100 [(2)M] | Jazz at Ohio Union | 195? | 1200. |
| *—Box set with booklet* | | | |
| EMPIRICAL | | | |
| ❑ EM-107 [10] | Spirituals in Ragtime | 1956 | 80.00 |
| JAZZ MAN | | | |
| ❑ LP-1 [10] | George Lewis' Ragtime Band | 1953 | 80.00 |
| *—"Limited First Pressing Dec. 25, 1953" on label at left* | | | |
| ❑ LJ-331 [10] | New Orleans Music | 1954 | 80.00 |
| MOSAIC | | | |
| ❑ MR5-132 [(5)] | The Complete Blue Note Recordings of George Lewis | 199? | 100.00 |
| PARADOX | | | |
| ❑ LP-6001 [10] | George Lewis | 1951 | 80.00 |
| RIVERSIDE | | | |
| ❑ RLP 12-207 [M] | Jazz in the Classic New Orleans Tradition | 1956 | 50.00 |
| *—White label, blue print* | | | |
| ❑ RLP 12-207 [M] | Jazz in the Classic New Orleans Tradition | 1959 | 30.00 |
| *—Blue label, microphone logo at top* | | | |
| ❑ RLP 12-230 [M] | Jazz at Vespers | 1957 | 50.00 |
| *—White label, blue print* | | | |
| ❑ RLP 12-230 [M] | Jazz at Vespers | 1959 | 30.00 |
| *—Blue label, microphone logo at top* | | | |
| ❑ RLP 12-283 [M] | George Lewis of New Orleans | 1958 | 40.00 |
| ❑ RLP-2507 [10] | George Lewis | 1954 | 100.00 |
| ❑ RLP-2512 [10] | George Lewis with Guest Artist Red Allen | 1955 | 100.00 |
| SOUTHLAND | | | |
| ❑ SLP-208 [10] | George Lewis | 1955 | 80.00 |
| VERVE | | | |
| ❑ MGV-1019 [M] | Blues from the Bayou | 1957 | 50.00 |
| ❑ V-1019 [M] | Blues from the Bayou | 1961 | 20.00 |
| ❑ MGV-1021 [M] | Doctor Jazz | 1957 | 50.00 |
| ❑ V-1021 [M] | Doctor Jazz | 1961 | 20.00 |
| ❑ MGV-1024 [M] | Hot Time in the Old Town Tonight | 1957 | 50.00 |
| ❑ V-1024 [M] | Hot Time in the Old Town Tonight | 1961 | 20.00 |
| ❑ V6-1024 [S] | Hot Time in the Old Town Tonight | 1961 | 20.00 |
| ❑ MGV-1027 [M] | George Lewis' Dixieland Band | 1957 | 50.00 |
| ❑ V-1027 [M] | George Lewis' Dixieland Band | 1961 | 20.00 |
| ❑ MGVS-6064 [S] | Oh, Didn't He Ramble | 1960 | 40.00 |
| ❑ MGVS-6113 [S] | Blues from the Bayou | 1960 | 40.00 |
| ❑ MGVS-6122 [S] | Doctor Jazz | 1960 | 40.00 |
| ❑ MGV-8232 [M] | George Lewis and Turk Murphy at Newport | 1958 | 50.00 |
| ❑ V-8232 [M] | George Lewis and Turk Murphy at Newport | 1961 | 20.00 |
| ❑ MGV-8277 [M] | The Perennial George Lewis | 1958 | 50.00 |
| ❑ V-8277 [M] | The Perennial George Lewis | 1961 | 20.00 |
| ❑ MGV-8303 [M] | On Stage: George Lewis Concert, Volume 1 | 1959 | 50.00 |
| ❑ V-8303 [M] | On Stage: George Lewis Concert, Volume 1 | 1961 | 20.00 |
| ❑ MGV-8304 [M] | On Stage: George Lewis Concert, Volume 2 | 1959 | 50.00 |
| ❑ V-8304 [M] | On Stage: George Lewis Concert, Volume 2 | 1961 | 20.00 |
| ❑ MGV-8325 [M] | Oh, Didn't He Ramble | 1959 | 50.00 |
| ❑ V-8325 [M] | Oh, Didn't He Ramble | 1961 | 20.00 |

## LEWIS, HUEY, AND THE NEWS

| Number | Title (A Side/B Side) | Yr | NM |
|---|---|---|---|
| CHRYSALIS | | | |
| ❑ CHR 1292 | Huey Lewis and the News | 1980 | 12.00 |
| ❑ CHR 1340 | Picture This | 1982 | 10.00 |
| ❑ FV 41292 | Huey Lewis and the News | 1983 | 8.00 |
| *—Reissue of 1292* | | | |
| ❑ PV 41292 | Huey Lewis and the News | 198? | 6.00 |
| *—Reissue with new prefix* | | | |
| ❑ FV 41340 | Picture This | 1983 | 8.00 |
| *—Reissue of 1340* | | | |
| ❑ FV 41412 | Sports | 1983 | 8.00 |
| ❑ OV 41412 | Sports | 198? | 6.00 |
| *—Reissue with new prefix* | | | |
| ❑ OV 41534 | Fore! | 1986 | 8.00 |
| ❑ OV 41622 | Small World | 1988 | 8.00 |
| ❑ 8V8 42795 [EP] | 84 Sports Tour | 1984 | 15.00 |
| *—Three-song picture disc numbered as if it were a single* | | | |
| MOBILE FIDELITY | | | |
| ❑ 1-181 | Sports | 1985 | 30.00 |
| *—"Original Master Recording" on front cover* | | | |

## LEWIS, HUGH X.

| Number | Title (A Side/B Side) | Yr | NM |
|---|---|---|---|
| KAPP | | | |
| ❑ KL-1462 [M] | The Hugh X. Lewis Album | 1966 | 20.00 |
| ❑ KL-1494 [M] | Just Before Dawn | 1966 | 20.00 |
| ❑ KL-1522 [M] | My Kind of Country | 1967 | 30.00 |
| ❑ KS-3462 [S] | The Hugh X. Lewis Album | 1966 | 25.00 |
| ❑ KS-3494 [S] | Just Before Dawn | 1966 | 25.00 |
| ❑ KS-3522 [S] | My Kind of Country | 1967 | 25.00 |
| ❑ KS-3545 | Just a Prayer Away | 1968 | 25.00 |
| ❑ KS-3563 | Country Fever | 1968 | 25.00 |

## LEWIS, JERRY

| Number | Title (A Side/B Side) | Yr | NM |
|---|---|---|---|
| DECCA | | | |
| ❑ DL 8410 [M] | Jerry Lewis Just Sings | 1956 | 60.00 |
| ❑ DL 8595 [M] | More Jerry Lewis | 1957 | 60.00 |
| ❑ DL 8936 [M] | Big Songs for Little People | 1959 | 50.00 |
| ❑ DL 78936 [S] | Big Songs for Little People | 1959 | 60.00 |
| DOT | | | |
| ❑ DLP 3664 [M] | The Jerry Lewis Singers | 1964 | 15.00 |
| ❑ DLP 25664 [S] | The Jerry Lewis Singers | 1964 | 20.00 |

## LEWIS, JERRY LEE

| Number | Title (A Side/B Side) | Yr | NM |
|---|---|---|---|
| ACCORD | | | |
| ❑ SN-7133 | I Walk the Line | 1981 | 10.00 |
| DESIGN | | | |
| ❑ DLP-165 [M] | Rockin' with Jerry Lee Lewis | 1963 | 25.00 |
| ❑ DST-165 [R] | Rockin' with Jerry Lee Lewis | 1963 | 20.00 |
| ELEKTRA | | | |
| ❑ 6E-184 | Jerry Lee Lewis | 1979 | 12.00 |
| ❑ 6E-254 | When Two Worlds Collide | 1980 | 12.00 |
| ❑ 6E-291 | Killer Country | 1980 | 12.00 |
| ❑ 60191 | The Best of Jerry Lee Lewis Featuring 39 and Holding | 1982 | 10.00 |
| HILLTOP | | | |
| ❑ 6102 | Sunday After Church | 1971 | 10.00 |
| ❑ 6110 | Roll Over Beethoven | 1972 | 10.00 |
| ❑ 6120 | Rural Route #1 | 1972 | 10.00 |
| MCA | | | |
| ❑ 5387 | My Fingers Do the Talkin' | 1983 | 10.00 |
| ❑ 5478 | I Am What I Am | 1984 | 10.00 |
| MERCURY | | | |
| ❑ SRM-1-637 | The "Killer" Rocks On | 1972 | 15.00 |
| ❑ SRM-1-677 | Sometimes a Memory Ain't Enough | 1973 | 15.00 |
| ❑ 690 [DJ] | A Jerry Lee Lewis Radio Special | 1973 | 50.00 |
| ❑ SRM-1-690 | Southern Roots — Back Home to Memphis | 1973 | 15.00 |
| ❑ SRM-1-710 | I-40 Country | 1974 | 15.00 |
| ❑ SRM-2-803 [(2)] | The Session | 1973 | 20.00 |
| ❑ SRM-1-1030 | Boogie Woogie Country Man | 1975 | 15.00 |
| ❑ SRM-1-1064 | Odd Man In | 1975 | 15.00 |
| ❑ SRM-1-1109 | Country Class | 1976 | 15.00 |
| ❑ SRM-1-5004 | Country Memories | 1977 | 15.00 |
| ❑ SRM-1-5006 | The Best of Jerry Lee Lewis Volume II | 1978 | 15.00 |
| ❑ SRM-1-5010 | Jerry Lee Lewis Keeps Rockin' | 1978 | 15.00 |
| ❑ SR-61278 | Live at the International, Las Vegas | 1970 | 15.00 |
| ❑ SR-61318 | In Loving Memories | 1970 | 30.00 |
| ❑ SR-61323 | There Must Be More to Love Than This | 1971 | 15.00 |
| ❑ SR-61343 | Touching Home | 1971 | 15.00 |
| *—With photo of Jerry Lee in front of a brick wall* | | | |
| ❑ SR-61343 | Touching Home | 1971 | 20.00 |
| *—With drawing on cover and small photo of Jerry Lee* | | | |
| ❑ SR-61346 | Would You Take Another Chance on Me? | 1971 | 15.00 |
| ❑ SR-61366 | Who's Gonna Play This Old Piano... (Think About It Darlin') | 1972 | 15.00 |
| ❑ 822789-1 | The Best of Jerry Lee Lewis Volume II | 198? | 10.00 |
| ❑ 826251-1 | Greatest Hits | 198? | 10.00 |
| ❑ 830399-1 | Would You Take Another Chance on Me | 1987 | 10.00 |
| *—Reissue of 61346* | | | |
| ❑ 836935-1 | Killer: The Mercury Years Volume One, 1963-1968 | 1989 | 12.00 |
| ❑ 836938-1 | Killer: The Mercury Years Volume Two, 1969-1972 | 1989 | 12.00 |
| ❑ 836941-1 | Killer: The Mercury Years Volume Three, 1973-1977 | 1989 | 12.00 |
| PAIR | | | |
| ❑ PDL2-1132 [(2)] | Solid Gold | 1986 | 12.00 |
| PICKWICK | | | |
| ❑ PTP-2055 [(2)] | Jerry Lee Lewis | 1973 | 12.00 |
| ❑ SPC-3224 | High Heel Sneakers | 1970 | 10.00 |
| ❑ SPC-3344 | Drinking Wine Spo-Dee-O-Dee | 1973 | 10.00 |
| POLYDOR | | | |
| ❑ 826139-1 | I'm on Fire | 1985 | 10.00 |
| ❑ 839516-1 | Great Balls of Fire! | 1989 | 12.00 |
| POWER PAK | | | |
| ❑ 247 | From the Vaults of Sun | 1974 | 10.00 |

RHINO

| Number | Title (A Side/B Side) | Yr | NM |
|---|---|---|---|
| ❑ RNDF-255 [PD] | Original Sun Greatest Hits | 1983 | 15.00 |
| ❑ RNDA-1499 [(2)] | Milestones | 1985 | 15.00 |
| ❑ R1-70255 | Original Sun Greatest Hits | 1989 | 10.00 |

*—Reissue of 255 on black vinyl*

| Number | Title (A Side/B Side) | Yr | NM |
|---|---|---|---|
| ❑ R1-70656 | Jerry Lee Lewis | 1989 | 12.00 |

*—Reissue of Sun 1230*

| Number | Title (A Side/B Side) | Yr | NM |
|---|---|---|---|
| ❑ R1-70657 | Jerry Lee's Greatest | 1989 | 12.00 |

*—Reissue of Sun 1265*

| Number | Title (A Side/B Side) | Yr | NM |
|---|---|---|---|
| ❑ R1-70899 | Wild One: Rare Tracks from Jerry Lee Lewis | 1989 | 12.00 |
| ❑ R1-71499 [(2)] | Milestones | 1989 | 12.00 |

*—Reissue of 1499*

SEARS

| Number | Title (A Side/B Side) | Yr | NM |
|---|---|---|---|
| ❑ SPS-610 | Hound Dog | 1970 | 25.00 |

SMASH

| Number | Title (A Side/B Side) | Yr | NM |
|---|---|---|---|
| ❑ SL-7001 | Golden Hits | 1980 | 12.00 |
| ❑ MGS-27040 [M] | The Golden Hits of Jerry Lee Lewis | 1964 | 25.00 |
| ❑ MGS-27056 [M] | The Greatest Live Show on Earth | 1964 | 100.00 |
| ❑ MGS-27063 [M] | The Return of Rock | 1965 | 30.00 |
| ❑ MGS-27071 [M] | Country Songs for City Folks | 1965 | 25.00 |
| ❑ MGS-27079 [M] | Memphis Beat | 1966 | 25.00 |
| ❑ MGS-27086 [M] | By Request — More of the Greatest Live Show on Earth | 1966 | 30.00 |
| ❑ MGS-27097 [M] | Soul My Way | 1967 | 30.00 |
| ❑ SRS-67040 [S] | The Golden Hits of Jerry Lee Lewis | 1964 | 30.00 |
| ❑ SRS-67040 [S] | The Golden Rock Hits of Jerry Lee Lewis | 1969 | 15.00 |

*—Retitled reissue*

| Number | Title (A Side/B Side) | Yr | NM |
|---|---|---|---|
| ❑ SRS-67056 [S] | The Greatest Live Show on Earth | 1964 | 150.00 |
| ❑ SRS-67063 [S] | The Return of Rock | 1965 | 40.00 |
| ❑ SRS-67071 | All Country | 1969 | 15.00 |

*—Retitled reissue*

| Number | Title (A Side/B Side) | Yr | NM |
|---|---|---|---|
| ❑ SRS-67071 [S] | Country Songs for City Folks | 1965 | 30.00 |
| ❑ SRS-67079 [S] | Memphis Beat | 1966 | 30.00 |
| ❑ SRS-67086 [S] | By Request — More of the Greatest Live Show on Earth | 1966 | 40.00 |
| ❑ SRS-67097 [S] | Soul My Way | 1967 | 40.00 |
| ❑ SRS-67104 | Another Place Another Time | 1968 | 20.00 |
| ❑ SRS-67112 | She Still Comes Around (To Love What's Left of Me) | 1969 | 20.00 |
| ❑ SRS-67117 | Jerry Lee Lewis Sings the Country Music Hall of Fame Hits, Vol. 1 | 1969 | 20.00 |
| ❑ SRS-67118 | Jerry Lee Lewis Sings the Country Music Hall of Fame Hits, Vol. 2 | 1969 | 20.00 |
| ❑ SRS-67128 | She Even Woke Me Up to Say Goodbye | 1970 | 20.00 |
| ❑ SRS-67131 | The Best of Jerry Lee Lewis | 1970 | 20.00 |

SUN

| Number | Title (A Side/B Side) | Yr | NM |
|---|---|---|---|
| ❑ LP-102 | Original Golden Hits — Volume 1 | 1969 | 15.00 |
| ❑ LP-103 | Original Golden Hits — Volume 2 | 1969 | 15.00 |
| ❑ LP-107 | Rockin' Rhythm and Blues | 1969 | 15.00 |
| ❑ SUN-108 | The Golden Cream of the Country | 1969 | 15.00 |
| ❑ SUN-108 [M] | The Golden Cream of the Country | 1969 | 40.00 |

*—Mono version is white label promo only; the word "MONO" appears at 9 o'clock on the label*

| Number | Title (A Side/B Side) | Yr | NM |
|---|---|---|---|
| ❑ LP-114 | A Taste of Country | 1970 | 15.00 |
| ❑ LP-121 | Ole Tyme Country Music | 1971 | 15.00 |
| ❑ LP-124 | Monsters | 1971 | 15.00 |
| ❑ LP-128 | Original Golden Hits — Volume 3 | 1972 | 15.00 |
| ❑ SUN-145 | Roots | 1982 | 12.00 |
| ❑ 1005 | The Original | 1978 | 12.00 |
| ❑ SUN-1011 | Duets | 1978 | 15.00 |

*—As "Jerry Lee Lewis and Friends"; gold vinyl*

| Number | Title (A Side/B Side) | Yr | NM |
|---|---|---|---|
| ❑ 1018 | Trio + | 1979 | 12.00 |

*—With Carl Perkins, Charlie Rich and (uncredited) Orion*

| Number | Title (A Side/B Side) | Yr | NM |
|---|---|---|---|
| ❑ SLP-1230 [M] | Jerry Lee Lewis | 1958 | 200.00 |
| ❑ SLP-1265 [M] | Jerry Lee's Greatest | 1961 | 250.00 |
| ❑ SLP-1265 [M] | Jerry Lee's Greatest | 1961 | 800.00 |

*—White label promo*

SUNNYVALE

| Number | Title (A Side/B Side) | Yr | NM |
|---|---|---|---|
| ❑ 905 | The Sun Story, Vol. 5 | 1977 | 10.00 |

WING

| Number | Title (A Side/B Side) | Yr | NM |
|---|---|---|---|
| ❑ PKW2-125 [(2)] | The Legend of Jerry Lee Lewis | 1969 | 25.00 |
| ❑ MGW-12340 [M] | The Return of Rock | 1967 | 12.00 |
| ❑ SRW-16340 | In Demand | 1968 | 10.00 |
| ❑ SRW-16340 [S] | The Return of Rock | 1967 | 12.00 |
| ❑ SRW-16406 | Unlimited | 1968 | 12.00 |

## LEWIS, JERRY LEE, AND LINDA GAIL LEWIS

SMASH

| Number | Title (A Side/B Side) | Yr | NM |
|---|---|---|---|
| ❑ SRS-67126 | Together | 1969 | 20.00 |

## LEWIS, JOHN

ATLANTIC

| Number | Title (A Side/B Side) | Yr | NM |
|---|---|---|---|
| ❑ 1272 [M] | The John Lewis Piano | 1958 | 40.00 |

*—Black label*

| Number | Title (A Side/B Side) | Yr | NM |
|---|---|---|---|
| ❑ 1272 [M] | The John Lewis Piano | 1961 | 20.00 |

*—Multicolor label, white "fan" logo at right*

| Number | Title (A Side/B Side) | Yr | NM |
|---|---|---|---|
| ❑ 1313 [M] | Improvised Meditations and Excursions | 1959 | 40.00 |

*—Black label*

| Number | Title (A Side/B Side) | Yr | NM |
|---|---|---|---|
| ❑ 1313 [M] | Improvised Meditations and Excursions | 1961 | 20.00 |

*—Multicolor label, white "fan" logo at right*

| Number | Title (A Side/B Side) | Yr | NM |
|---|---|---|---|
| ❑ SD 1313 [S] | Improvised Meditations and Excursions | 1959 | 50.00 |

*—Green label*

| Number | Title (A Side/B Side) | Yr | NM |
|---|---|---|---|
| ❑ SD 1313 [S] | Improvised Meditations and Excursions | 1961 | 20.00 |

*—Multicolor label, white "fan" logo at right*

| Number | Title (A Side/B Side) | Yr | NM |
|---|---|---|---|
| ❑ 1334 [M] | The Golden Striker | 1960 | 25.00 |

*—Multicolor label, white "fan" logo at right*

| Number | Title (A Side/B Side) | Yr | NM |
|---|---|---|---|
| ❑ SD 1334 [S] | The Golden Striker | 1960 | 30.00 |

*—Multicolor label, white "fan" logo at right*

| Number | Title (A Side/B Side) | Yr | NM |
|---|---|---|---|
| ❑ 1365 [M] | John Lewis Presents Jazz Abstractions | 1961 | 25.00 |

*—Multicolor label, white "fan" logo at right*

| Number | Title (A Side/B Side) | Yr | NM |
|---|---|---|---|
| ❑ SD 1365 [S] | John Lewis Presents Jazz Abstractions | 1961 | 30.00 |

*—Multicolor label, white "fan" logo at right*

| Number | Title (A Side/B Side) | Yr | NM |
|---|---|---|---|
| ❑ SD 1365 [S] | John Lewis Presents Jazz Abstractions | 1964 | 20.00 |

*—Multicolor label, black "fan" logo at right*

| Number | Title (A Side/B Side) | Yr | NM |
|---|---|---|---|
| ❑ 1370 [M] | Original Sin | 1961 | 25.00 |

*—Multicolor label, white "fan" logo at right*

| Number | Title (A Side/B Side) | Yr | NM |
|---|---|---|---|
| ❑ SD 1370 [S] | Original Sin | 1961 | 30.00 |

*—Multicolor label, white "fan" logo at right*

| Number | Title (A Side/B Side) | Yr | NM |
|---|---|---|---|
| ❑ SD 1370 [S] | Original Sin | 1964 | 20.00 |

*—Multicolor label, black "fan" logo at right*

| Number | Title (A Side/B Side) | Yr | NM |
|---|---|---|---|
| ❑ 1375 [M] | The Wonderful World of Jazz | 1961 | 25.00 |

*—Multicolor label, white "fan" logo at right*

| Number | Title (A Side/B Side) | Yr | NM |
|---|---|---|---|
| ❑ SD 1375 [S] | The Wonderful World of Jazz | 1961 | 30.00 |

*—Multicolor label, white "fan" logo at right*

| Number | Title (A Side/B Side) | Yr | NM |
|---|---|---|---|
| ❑ SD 1375 [S] | The Wonderful World of Jazz | 1964 | 20.00 |

*—Multicolor label, black "fan" logo at right*

| Number | Title (A Side/B Side) | Yr | NM |
|---|---|---|---|
| ❑ SD 1392 [S] | European Encounter | 1963 | 20.00 |
| ❑ SD 1402 [S] | Animal Dance | 1963 | 20.00 |
| ❑ SD 1425 [S] | Essence | 1964 | 20.00 |

RCA VICTOR

| Number | Title (A Side/B Side) | Yr | NM |
|---|---|---|---|
| ❑ LPM-1742 [M] | European Windows | 1958 | 50.00 |

## LEWIS, JOHN, AND SACHA DISTEL

ATLANTIC

| Number | Title (A Side/B Side) | Yr | NM |
|---|---|---|---|
| ❑ 1267 [M] | Afternoon in Paris | 1957 | 40.00 |

*—Black label*

| Number | Title (A Side/B Side) | Yr | NM |
|---|---|---|---|
| ❑ 1267 [M] | Afternoon in Paris | 1964 | 15.00 |

*—Multicolor label, black "fan" logo at right*

## LEWIS, JOHN, AND BILL PERKINS

PACIFIC JAZZ

| Number | Title (A Side/B Side) | Yr | NM |
|---|---|---|---|
| ❑ PJ-44 [M] | Grand Encounter: 2' East, 3' West | 1962 | 60.00 |

*—Reissue with new number*

| Number | Title (A Side/B Side) | Yr | NM |
|---|---|---|---|
| ❑ PJ-1217 [M] | Grand Encounter: 2' East, 3' West | 1956 | 200.00 |

WORLD PACIFIC

| Number | Title (A Side/B Side) | Yr | NM |
|---|---|---|---|
| ❑ WP-1217 [M] | Grand Encounter: 2' East, 3' West | 1959 | 120.00 |

## LEWIS, KATHARINE HANDY

FOLKWAYS

| Number | Title (A Side/B Side) | Yr | NM |
|---|---|---|---|
| ❑ FJ-3540 [M] | W.C. Handy Blues | 1958 | 30.00 |

## LEWIS, LINDA GAIL

SMASH

| Number | Title (A Side/B Side) | Yr | NM |
|---|---|---|---|
| ❑ SRS-67119 | Two Sides of Linda Gail Lewis | 1969 | 25.00 |

## LEWIS, MEADE LUX

ABC-PARAMOUNT

| Number | Title (A Side/B Side) | Yr | NM |
|---|---|---|---|
| ❑ ABC-164 [M] | Out of the Roaring 20's | 1956 | 50.00 |

ATLANTIC

| Number | Title (A Side/B Side) | Yr | NM |
|---|---|---|---|
| ❑ ALS-133 [10] | Boogie-Woogie Interpretations | 1952 | 250.00 |

BLUE NOTE

| Number | Title (A Side/B Side) | Yr | NM |
|---|---|---|---|
| ❑ BLP-7018 [10] | Boogie-Woogie Classics | 1952 | 600.00 |

DISC

| Number | Title (A Side/B Side) | Yr | NM |
|---|---|---|---|
| ❑ DLP-352 [10] | Meade Lux Lewis at the Philharmonic | 195? | 400.00 |

DOWN HOME

| Number | Title (A Side/B Side) | Yr | NM |
|---|---|---|---|
| ❑ MGD-7 [M] | Yancey's Last Ride | 1956 | 60.00 |

MERCURY

| Number | Title (A Side/B Side) | Yr | NM |
|---|---|---|---|
| ❑ MG-25158 [10] | Meade Lux Lewis | 1951 | 250.00 |

PHILIPS

| Number | Title (A Side/B Side) | Yr | NM |
|---|---|---|---|
| ❑ PHM 200044 [M] | Boogie Woogie House Party | 196? | 20.00 |
| ❑ PHS 600044 [S] | Boogie Woogie House Party | 196? | 25.00 |

RIVERSIDE

| Number | Title (A Side/B Side) | Yr | NM |
|---|---|---|---|
| ❑ RLP-402 [M] | The Blues Piano Artistry of Meade Lux Lewis | 1962 | 40.00 |
| ❑ RS-9402 [S] | The Blues Piano Artistry of Meade Lux Lewis | 1962 | 40.00 |

STINSON

| Number | Title (A Side/B Side) | Yr | NM |
|---|---|---|---|
| ❑ 25 [M] | Meade Lux Lewis | 196? | 30.00 |

TOPS

| Number | Title (A Side/B Side) | Yr | NM |
|---|---|---|---|
| ❑ L-1533 [M] | Barrelhouse Piano | 195? | 40.00 |

VERVE

| Number | Title (A Side/B Side) | Yr | NM |
|---|---|---|---|
| ❑ MGV-1006 [M] | Cat House Piano | 1957 | 80.00 |
| ❑ V-1006 [M] | Cat House Piano | 1961 | 40.00 |
| ❑ MGV-1007 [M] | Meade Lux Lewis | 1957 | 70.00 |
| ❑ V-1007 [M] | Meade Lux Lewis | 1961 | 30.00 |

## LEWIS, MEADE LUX, AND LOUIS BELLSON

CLEF

| Number | Title (A Side/B Side) | Yr | NM |
|---|---|---|---|
| ❑ MGC-632 [M] | Boogie Woogie Piano and Drums | 1954 | 80.00 |

## LEWIS, MEL

MODE

| Number | Title (A Side/B Side) | Yr | NM |
|---|---|---|---|
| ❑ LP-103 [M] | Mel Lewis Sextet | 1957 | 120.00 |

SAN FRANCISCO

| Number | Title (A Side/B Side) | Yr | NM |
|---|---|---|---|
| ❑ 2 [M] | Got 'Cha | 1957 | 150.00 |

VEE JAY

| Number | Title (A Side/B Side) | Yr | NM |
|---|---|---|---|
| ❑ VJS-3062 | Gettin' Together | 1974 | 20.00 |

## LEWIS, RAMSEY

Includes releases by "Ramsey Lewis Trio."

ARGO

| Number | Title (A Side/B Side) | Yr | NM |
|---|---|---|---|
| ❑ LP-611 [M] | Gentleman of Swing | 1958 | 50.00 |
| ❑ LPS-611 [S] | Gentleman of Swing | 1959 | 60.00 |
| ❑ LP-627 [M] | Gentleman of Jazz | 1958 | 50.00 |
| ❑ LPS-627 [S] | Gentleman of Jazz | 1959 | 60.00 |
| ❑ LP-642 [M] | The Ramsey Lewis Trio with Lee Winchester | 1959 | 40.00 |
| ❑ LPS-642 [S] | The Ramsey Lewis Trio with Lee Winchester | 1959 | 50.00 |
| ❑ LP-645 [M] | An Hour with the Ramsey Lewis Trio | 1959 | 40.00 |
| ❑ LPS-645 [S] | An Hour with the Ramsey Lewis Trio | 1959 | 50.00 |
| ❑ LP-665 [M] | Stretching Out | 1960 | 40.00 |
| ❑ LPS-665 [S] | Stretching Out | 1960 | 50.00 |
| ❑ LP-671 [M] | The Ramsey Lewis Trio in Chicago | 1961 | 40.00 |
| ❑ LPS-671 [S] | The Ramsey Lewis Trio in Chicago | 1961 | 50.00 |
| ❑ LP-680 [M] | More Music from the Soil | 1961 | 40.00 |
| ❑ LPS-680 [S] | More Music from the Soil | 1961 | 50.00 |
| ❑ LP-687 [M] | Sound of Christmas | 1961 | 40.00 |
| ❑ LPS-687 [S] | Sound of Christmas | 1961 | 50.00 |
| ❑ LP-693 [M] | The Sound of Spring | 1962 | 25.00 |
| ❑ LPS-693 [S] | The Sound of Spring | 1962 | 30.00 |
| ❑ LP-701 [M] | Country Meets the Blues | 1962 | 25.00 |
| ❑ LPS-701 [S] | Country Meets the Blues | 1962 | 30.00 |
| ❑ LP-705 [M] | Bossa Nova | 1962 | 25.00 |
| ❑ LPS-705 [S] | Bossa Nova | 1962 | 30.00 |
| ❑ LP-715 [M] | Pot Luck | 1963 | 25.00 |
| ❑ LPS-715 [S] | Pot Luck | 1963 | 30.00 |
| ❑ LP-723 [M] | Barefoot Sunday Blues | 1963 | 25.00 |
| ❑ LPS-723 [S] | Barefoot Sunday Blues | 1963 | 30.00 |
| ❑ LP-732 [M] | Bach to the Blues | 1964 | 25.00 |
| ❑ LPS-732 [S] | Bach to the Blues | 1964 | 30.00 |
| ❑ LP-741 [M] | The Ramsey Lewis Trio at the Bohemian Caverns | 1964 | 25.00 |
| ❑ LPS-741 [S] | The Ramsey Lewis Trio at the Bohemian Caverns | 1964 | 30.00 |
| ❑ LP-745 [M] | More Sounds of Christmas | 1964 | 25.00 |
| ❑ LPS-745 [S] | More Sounds of Christmas | 1964 | 30.00 |
| ❑ LP-755 [M] | Choice! The Best of the Ramsey Lewis Trio | 1965 | 30.00 |
| ❑ LPS-755 [S] | Choice! The Best of the Ramsey Lewis Trio | 1965 | 40.00 |
| ❑ LP-757 [M] | The In Crowd | 1965 | 25.00 |
| ❑ LPS-757 [S] | The In Crowd | 1965 | 30.00 |

CADET

| Number | Title (A Side/B Side) | Yr | NM |
|---|---|---|---|
| ❑ LP-687X [M] | Sound of Christmas | 1966 | 20.00 |

*—Reissue of Argo 687*

| Number | Title (A Side/B Side) | Yr | NM |
|---|---|---|---|
| ❑ LPS-687X [S] | Sound of Christmas | 1966 | 20.00 |

*—Reissue of Argo 687-S*

| Number | Title (A Side/B Side) | Yr | NM |
|---|---|---|---|
| ❑ LPS-745 [S] | More Sounds of Christmas | 1966 | 20.00 |
| ❑ LPS-755 [S] | Choice! The Best of the Ramsey Lewis Trio | 1965 | 20.00 |
| ❑ LPS-761 [S] | Hang On Ramsey! | 1966 | 20.00 |
| ❑ LPS-771 [S] | Swingin' | 1966 | 20.00 |
| ❑ LPS-774 [S] | Wade in the Water | 1966 | 20.00 |
| ❑ LP-782 [M] | The Movie Album | 1967 | 20.00 |
| ❑ LP-790 [M] | Goin' Latin | 1967 | 20.00 |
| ❑ LP-794 [M] | Dancing in the Street | 1967 | 20.00 |

COLUMBIA

| Number | Title (A Side/B Side) | Yr | NM |
|---|---|---|---|
| ❑ HC 47687 | Live at the Savoy | 1982 | 80.00 |

*—Half-speed mastered edition*

EMARCY

| Number | Title (A Side/B Side) | Yr | NM |
|---|---|---|---|
| ❑ MG-36150 [M] | Down to Earth | 1958 | 40.00 |
| ❑ SR-80029 [S] | Down to Earth | 1958 | 50.00 |

MERCURY

| Number | Title (A Side/B Side) | Yr | NM |
|---|---|---|---|
| ❑ MG-20536 [M] | Down to Earth | 1965 | 20.00 |
| ❑ SR-60536 [S] | Down to Earth | 1965 | 25.00 |

## LEWIS, RAMSEY, AND JEAN DUSHON

ARGO

| Number | Title (A Side/B Side) | Yr | NM |
|---|---|---|---|
| ❑ 750 [M] | You Better Believe Me | 1965 | 25.00 |
| ❑ 750S [S] | You Better Believe Me | 1965 | 30.00 |



**Except when noted otherwise, VG = 25% of NM, and VG+ = 50% of NM. (Example: VG = $2.00, VG+ = $4.00 and NM = $8.00.)**

| Number | Title (A Side/B Side) | Yr | NM |
|---|---|---|---|

**LEWIS, ROBERT Q.**

ATCO

| Number | Title (A Side/B Side) | Yr | NM |
|---|---|---|---|
| ❑ 33-212 [M] | I'm Just Wild About Vaudeville | 1963 | 25.00 |
| ❑ SD 33-212 [S] | I'm Just Wild About Vaudeville | 1963 | 30.00 |

"X"

| Number | Title (A Side/B Side) | Yr | NM |
|---|---|---|---|
| ❑ LXA-1033 [M] | Robert Q. Lewis and His Gang | 1956 | 50.00 |

**LEWIS, SHARI**

RCA CAMDEN

| Number | Title (A Side/B Side) | Yr | NM |
|---|---|---|---|
| ❑ CAL-1052 [M] | Jack and the Beanstalk and Other Stories | 1964 | 30.00 |
| ❑ CAS-1052 [S] | Jack and the Beanstalk and Other Stories | 1964 | 30.00 |

RCA VICTOR

| Number | Title (A Side/B Side) | Yr | NM |
|---|---|---|---|
| ❑ LBY-1006 [M] | Fun in Shariland | 1954 | 80.00 |

**LEWIS, SMILEY**

IMPERIAL

| Number | Title (A Side/B Side) | Yr | NM |
|---|---|---|---|
| ❑ LP-9141 [M] | I Hear You Knocking | 1961 | 600.00 |
| *—Black vinyl* | | | |
| ❑ LP-9141 [M] | I Hear You Knocking | 1961 | 6000. |
| *—Green vinyl (one copy known)* | | | |

**LEWIS, TED**

COLUMBIA

| Number | Title (A Side/B Side) | Yr | NM |
|---|---|---|---|
| ❑ CL 6127 [10] | Classic Jazz | 1950 | 50.00 |

DECCA

| Number | Title (A Side/B Side) | Yr | NM |
|---|---|---|---|
| ❑ DL 4905 [M] | Ted Lewis' Greatest Hits | 1967 | 25.00 |
| ❑ DL 5114 [10] | Ted Lewis and His Orchestra | 195? | 50.00 |
| ❑ DL 8321 [M] | Is Everybody Happy? | 1956 | 40.00 |
| ❑ DL 8322 [M] | The Medicine Man for the Blues | 1956 | 40.00 |

EPIC

| Number | Title (A Side/B Side) | Yr | NM |
|---|---|---|---|
| ❑ LN 3170 [M] | Everybody's Happy! | 1955 | 40.00 |

**LEWIS AND CLARKE EXPEDITION, THE**

COLGEMS

| Number | Title (A Side/B Side) | Yr | NM |
|---|---|---|---|
| ❑ COM-105 [M] | The Lewis and Clarke Expedition | 1967 | 25.00 |
| ❑ COS-105 [S] | The Lewis and Clarke Expedition | 1967 | 30.00 |

**LEWIS CONNECTION, THE** Minneapolis group; PRINCE is featured on one track.

(NO LABEL)

| Number | Title (A Side/B Side) | Yr | NM |
|---|---|---|---|
| ❑ (no #) | The Lewis Connection | 1979 | 400.00 |

**LEWIS FAMILY, THE**

STARDAY

| Number | Title (A Side/B Side) | Yr | NM |
|---|---|---|---|
| ❑ SLP-121 [M] | Singin' Time Down South | 1960 | 30.00 |
| ❑ SLP-161 [M] | Anniversary Celebration | 1962 | 30.00 |
| ❑ SLP-193 [M] | Gospel Special | 1962 | 30.00 |
| ❑ SLP-238 [M] | Sing Me a Gospel Song | 1962 | 30.00 |
| ❑ SLP-252 [M] | All Night Singing Convention | 1963 | 30.00 |
| ❑ SLP-289 [M] | Singin' in My Soul | 1964 | 30.00 |
| ❑ SLP-331 [M] | The First Family of Gospel Music | 1965 | 30.00 |
| ❑ SLP-364 [M] | The Lewis Family Sings the Gospel with Carl Story | 1965 | 30.00 |
| ❑ SLP-381 [M] | The Lewis Family Album | 1965 | 30.00 |
| ❑ SLP-395 [M] | Shall We Gather at the River | 1966 | 25.00 |
| ❑ SLP-408 [M] | Time Is Moving On | 1966 | 25.00 |
| ❑ SLP-422 | Golden Gospel Banjo | 1968 | 20.00 |
| ❑ SLP-433 | Did You Ever Go Sailing | 1969 | 20.00 |
| ❑ SLP-450 | Golden Gospel of the Lewis Family | 1970 | 20.00 |

**LIBBY, JERRY**

SABRINA

| Number | Title (A Side/B Side) | Yr | NM |
|---|---|---|---|
| ❑ SA-100 [M] | Live? At Wilkins | 1964 | 20.00 |

**LIBERACE**

ABC

| Number | Title (A Side/B Side) | Yr | NM |
|---|---|---|---|
| ❑ 4002 | 16 Great Performances | 1974 | 12.00 |

AVI

| Number | Title (A Side/B Side) | Yr | NM |
|---|---|---|---|
| ❑ 1023 | Candlelight Classics | 1973 | 12.00 |
| ❑ 1029 | The World of Liberace | 1974 | 12.00 |

CBS

| Number | Title (A Side/B Side) | Yr | NM |
|---|---|---|---|
| ❑ FM 42244 | Concert Favorites | 1986 | 10.00 |

COLUMBIA

| Number | Title (A Side/B Side) | Yr | NM |
|---|---|---|---|
| ❑ CL 575 [M] | Liberace at the Piano | 1954 | 40.00 |
| *—Maroon label, gold print* | | | |
| ❑ CL 589 [M] | Christmas at Liberace's | 1954 | 50.00 |
| *—Maroon label, gold print* | | | |
| ❑ CL 600 [M] | Liberace at the Hollywood Bowl | 1955 | 40.00 |
| ❑ CL 645 [M] | Hollywood Bowl Encore | 1955 | 40.00 |
| ❑ CL 661 [M] | Liberace by Candlelight | 1955 | 40.00 |
| ❑ CL 800 [M] | Sincerely Yours | 1956 | 50.00 |
| ❑ CL 896 [M] | Liberace at Home | 1956 | 50.00 |
| ❑ CL 1118 [M] | South Pacific | 1957 | 30.00 |
| ❑ CL 2516 [10] | Piano Reverie | 1955 | 60.00 |
| ❑ CL 2592 [10] | Kiddin' on the Keys | 1955 | 60.00 |
| ❑ CL 6217 [10] | Liberace at the Piano | 1952 | 80.00 |
| ❑ CL 6239 [10] | An Evening with Liberace | 1953 | 80.00 |
| ❑ CL 6251 [10] | Liberace by Candlelight | 1953 | 80.00 |

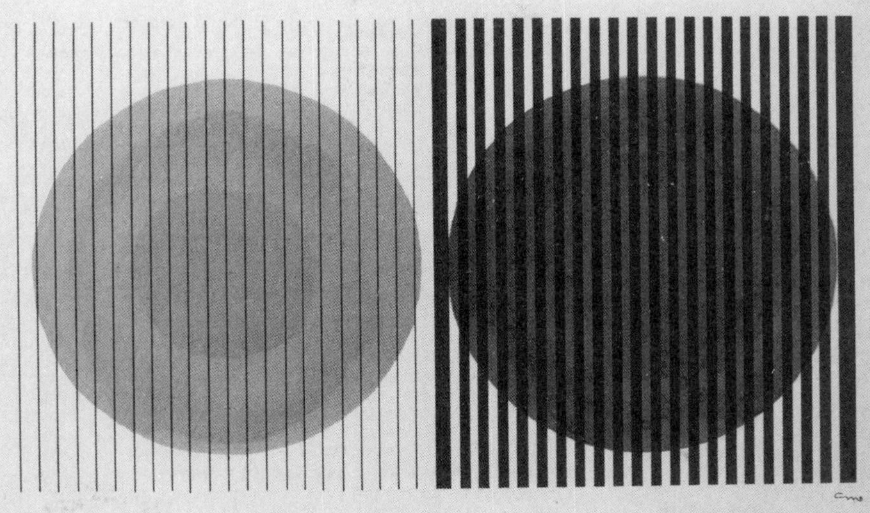

STEREO
RS 868SD
Command records
ENOCH LIGHT
COMMAND PERFORMANCES
Personally selected by Enoch Light and especially arranged for dynamic stereo performances.


Enoch Light, *Command Performances,* Command RS 868SD, 1964, $15.

| Number | Title (A Side/B Side) | Yr | NM |
|---|---|---|---|
| ❑ CL 6269 [10] | Concertos for You | 1953 | 80.00 |
| ❑ CL 6283 [10] | Concertos for You, Volume 2 | 1953 | 80.00 |
| ❑ CL 6327 [10] | Liberace Plays Chopin | 1954 | 80.00 |
| ❑ CL 6328 [10] | Liberace Plays Chopin, Volume 2 | 1954 | 80.00 |
| ❑ CS 9845 | Liberace's Greatest Hits | 1969 | 12.00 |
| *—Red "360 Sound" label* | | | |
| ❑ CS 9845 | Liberace's Greatest Hits | 1970 | 10.00 |
| *—Orange label* | | | |

CORAL

| Number | Title (A Side/B Side) | Yr | NM |
|---|---|---|---|
| ❑ 7CXB 9 [(2)S] | The Best of Liberace | 1965 | 20.00 |
| ❑ CXB 9 [(2)M] | The Best of Liberace | 1965 | 15.00 |
| ❑ CRL 57292 [M] | Piano Song Book — Movie Themes | 1959 | 15.00 |
| ❑ CRL 57305 [M] | The Magic Pianos of Liberace | 1960 | 12.00 |
| ❑ CRL 57305 [M] | The Magic Pianos of Liberace | 1960 | 15.00 |
| ❑ CRL 57344 [M] | My Inspiration | 1961 | 12.00 |
| ❑ CRL 57346 [M] | Liberace at the Palladium | 1961 | 12.00 |
| ❑ CRL 57377 [M] | My Parade of Golden Favorites | 1961 | 12.00 |
| ❑ CRL 57392 [M] | As Time Goes By | 1962 | 12.00 |
| ❑ CRL 57395 [M] | Rhapsody by Candlelight | 1962 | 12.00 |
| ❑ CRL 57452 [M] | Golden Themes from Hollywood | 1964 | 12.00 |
| ❑ CRL 757292 [S] | Piano Song Book — Movie Themes | 1959 | 20.00 |
| ❑ CRL 757305 [S] | The Magic Pianos of Liberace | 1960 | 15.00 |
| ❑ CRL 757305 [S] | The Magic Pianos of Liberace | 1960 | 20.00 |
| ❑ CRL 757344 [S] | My Inspiration | 1961 | 15.00 |
| ❑ CRL 757346 [S] | Liberace at the Palladium | 1961 | 15.00 |
| ❑ CRL 757377 [S] | My Parade of Golden Favorites | 1961 | 15.00 |
| ❑ CRL 757392 [S] | As Time Goes By | 1962 | 15.00 |
| ❑ CRL 757395 [S] | Rhapsody by Candlelight | 1962 | 15.00 |
| ❑ CRL 757452 [S] | Golden Themes from Hollywood | 1964 | 15.00 |

DOT

| Number | Title (A Side/B Side) | Yr | NM |
|---|---|---|---|
| ❑ DLP-3547 [M] | Mr. Showmanship | 1964 | 12.00 |
| ❑ DLP-3550 [M] | A Liberace Christmas | 1964 | 12.00 |
| ❑ DLP-3563 [M] | My Most Requested | 1965 | 12.00 |
| ❑ DLP-3595 [M] | Liberace at the Americana, Volume 1 | 1965 | 12.00 |
| ❑ DLP-3596 [M] | Liberace at the Americana, Volume 2 | 1965 | 12.00 |
| ❑ DLP-3755 [M] | New Sounds | 1966 | 12.00 |
| ❑ DLP-3816 [M] | Liberace Now! | 1967 | 15.00 |
| ❑ DLP-9502 [M] | Silver Anniversary | 1965 | 12.00 |
| ❑ DLP-25547 [S] | Mr. Showmanship | 1964 | 15.00 |
| ❑ DLP-25550 [S] | A Liberace Christmas | 1964 | 15.00 |
| ❑ DLP-25563 [S] | My Most Requested | 1965 | 15.00 |
| ❑ DLP-25595 [S] | Liberace at the Americana, Volume 1 | 1965 | 15.00 |
| ❑ DLP-25596 [S] | Liberace at the Americana, Volume 2 | 1965 | 15.00 |
| ❑ DLP-25755 [S] | New Sounds | 1966 | 15.00 |
| ❑ DLP-25816 [S] | Liberace Now! | 1967 | 15.00 |
| ❑ DLP-25858 | The Love Album | 1968 | 12.00 |
| ❑ DLP-25901 | Sound of Love | 1969 | 12.00 |
| ❑ DLP-29502 [S] | Silver Anniversary | 1965 | 15.00 |

HARMONY

| Number | Title (A Side/B Side) | Yr | NM |
|---|---|---|---|
| ❑ HL 7154 [M] | The Liberace Show | 1959 | 15.00 |
| ❑ HL 7237 [M] | Rhapsody in Blue | 196? | 12.00 |
| ❑ HL 7361 [M] | Concerto by Candlelight | 196? | 12.00 |
| ❑ HS 11054 [R] | The Liberace Show | 196? | 10.00 |
| ❑ HS 11161 [R] | Concerto by Candlelight | 196? | 12.00 |
| ❑ HL 11175 [R] | Rhapsody in Blue | 196? | 10.00 |
| ❑ HS 11325 | Tenderly | 1969 | 10.00 |
| ❑ HS 11391 | The Very Thought of You | 1970 | 10.00 |

MCA

| Number | Title (A Side/B Side) | Yr | NM |
|---|---|---|---|
| ❑ 740 | Here's Liberace | 198? | 8.00 |
| *—Reissue of Vocalion 73821* | | | |
| ❑ 4060 [(2)] | The Best of Liberace | 197? | 12.00 |
| ❑ 4167 [(2)] | The Artistry of Liberace | 198? | 12.00 |

MISTLETOE

| Number | Title (A Side/B Side) | Yr | NM |
|---|---|---|---|
| ❑ MLP-1208 | Twas the Night Before Christmas | 1974 | 10.00 |

PARAMOUNT

| Number | Title (A Side/B Side) | Yr | NM |
|---|---|---|---|
| ❑ PAS-1009 | The Best of Liberace | 1973 | 12.00 |
| ❑ PAS-1032 [(2)] | Liberace In Concert | 1974 | 15.00 |

PICKWICK

| Number | Title (A Side/B Side) | Yr | NM |
|---|---|---|---|
| ❑ SPC-3085 | You Made Me Love You | 196? | 10.00 |
| ❑ SPC-3124 | Strangers in the Night | 196? | 10.00 |
| ❑ SPC-3159 | What Now My Love | 1969 | 10.00 |
| ❑ SPC-3208 | By the Time I Get to Phoenix | 197? | 10.00 |

VOCALION

| Number | Title (A Side/B Side) | Yr | NM |
|---|---|---|---|
| ❑ VL 3821 [M] | Here's Liberace | 196? | 12.00 |
| ❑ VL 73821 [R] | Here's Liberace | 196? | 12.00 |

WARNER BROS.

| Number | Title (A Side/B Side) | Yr | NM |
|---|---|---|---|
| ❑ WS 1847 | A Brand New Me | 1969 | 12.00 |
| ❑ WS 1889 | Love and Music Festival "Live" | 1970 | 12.00 |

| Number | Title (A Side/B Side) | Yr | NM |
|---|---|---|---|

## LIBERACE, GEORGE

### COLUMBIA

| Number | Title (A Side/B Side) | Yr | NM |
|---|---|---|---|
| ❑ CL 587 [M] | A Musical Journey with George Liberace | 1954 | 40.00 |
| *—Maroon label, gold print* | | | |

### CROWN

| Number | Title (A Side/B Side) | Yr | NM |
|---|---|---|---|
| ❑ CST-218 [S] | Hawaiian Paradise | 196? | 25.00 |
| *—Black label; red vinyl* | | | |

### IMPERIAL

| Number | Title (A Side/B Side) | Yr | NM |
|---|---|---|---|
| ❑ LP-9039 [M] | George Liberace Goes Teenage | 1957 | 50.00 |

## LIBERMAN, JEFFERY

### LIBRAH

| Number | Title (A Side/B Side) | Yr | NM |
|---|---|---|---|
| ❑ 1545 | Jeffery Liberman | 1975 | 80.00 |
| ❑ 6969 | Solitude Within | 1975 | 120.00 |
| ❑ 12157 | Synergy | 1976 | 120.00 |

## LIDSTROM, JACK

### WORLD PACIFIC

| Number | Title (A Side/B Side) | Yr | NM |
|---|---|---|---|
| ❑ PJ-1235 [M] | Look, Dad! They're Comin' Down the Street in Hi-Fi | 1957 | 40.00 |

## LIGGINS, JOE

### MERCURY

| Number | Title (A Side/B Side) | Yr | NM |
|---|---|---|---|
| ❑ MG-20731 [M] | Honeydripper | 1962 | 80.00 |
| ❑ SR-60731 [S] | Honeydripper | 1962 | 100.00 |

## LIGHT, ENOCH

### ABC WESTMINSTER/GRAND AWARD

| Number | Title (A Side/B Side) | Yr | NM |
|---|---|---|---|
| ❑ 68008 | Sing Along with the Original Roaring 20's | 1974 | 10.00 |
| ❑ 68009 | The Flirty 30's | 1974 | 10.00 |
| ❑ 68012 | The Torchy Thirties | 1974 | 10.00 |

### COMMAND

| Number | Title (A Side/B Side) | Yr | NM |
|---|---|---|---|
| ❑ 800 SD [S] | Persuasive Percussion | 1960 | 15.00 |
| *—By "Terry Snyder and the All-Stars"* | | | |
| ❑ 33-800 [M] | Persuasive Percussion | 1960 | 12.00 |
| *—By "Terry Snyder and the All-Stars"* | | | |
| ❑ 804 SD [S] | The Sound of Strings | 1960 | 15.00 |
| ❑ 33-804 [M] | The Sound of Strings | 1960 | 12.00 |
| ❑ 805 SD [S] | Paperback Ballet | 1960 | 15.00 |
| ❑ 33-805 [M] | Paperback Ballet | 1960 | 12.00 |
| ❑ 806 SD [S] | Provocative Percussion | 1960 | 15.00 |
| *—By "The Command All-Stars"* | | | |
| ❑ 33-806 [M] | Provocative Percussion | 1960 | 12.00 |
| *—By "The Command All-Stars"* | | | |
| ❑ 808 SD [S] | Persuasive Percussion, Volume 2 | 1960 | 15.00 |
| *—By "Terry Snyder and the All-Stars"* | | | |
| ❑ 33-808 [M] | Persuasive Percussion, Volume 2 | 1960 | 12.00 |
| *—By "Terry Snyder and the All-Stars"* | | | |
| ❑ 810 SD [S] | Provocative Percussion, Volume 2 | 1960 | 15.00 |
| ❑ 33-810 [M] | Provocative Percussion, Volume 2 | 1960 | 12.00 |
| ❑ 814 SD [S] | Pertinent Percussion Cha-Cha's | 1960 | 15.00 |
| ❑ 33-814 [M] | Pertinent Percussion Cha-Cha's | 1960 | 12.00 |
| ❑ 817 SD [S] | Persuasive Percussion, Volume 3 | 1961 | 15.00 |
| *—By "The Command All-Stars"* | | | |
| ❑ 33-817 [M] | Persuasive Percussion, Volume 3 | 1961 | 12.00 |
| *—By "The Command All-Stars"* | | | |
| ❑ 818 SD [S] | Big Bold and Brassy | 1961 | 15.00 |
| ❑ 33-818 [M] | Big Bold and Brassy | 1961 | 12.00 |
| ❑ 821 SD [S] | Provocative Percussion, Volume 3 | 1961 | 15.00 |
| ❑ 33-821 [M] | Provocative Percussion, Volume 3 | 1961 | 12.00 |
| ❑ 822 SD [S] | Far Away Places | 1961 | 15.00 |
| ❑ 33-822 [M] | Far Away Places | 1961 | 12.00 |
| ❑ 826 SD [S] | Stereo 35/MM | 1961 | 15.00 |
| ❑ 830 SD [S] | Persuasive Percussion, Volume 4 | 1962 | 15.00 |
| ❑ 33-830 [M] | Persuasive Percussion, Volume 4 | 1962 | 12.00 |
| ❑ 831 SD [S] | Stereo 35/MM, Volume Two | 1962 | 15.00 |
| ❑ 833 SD [S] | Vibrations | 1962 | 15.00 |
| ❑ 33-833 [M] | Vibrations | 1962 | 12.00 |
| ❑ 834 SD [S] | Provocative Percussion, Volume 4 | 1962 | 15.00 |
| ❑ 33-834 [M] | Provocative Percussion, Volume 4 | 1962 | 12.00 |
| ❑ 835 SD [S] | Great Themes from Hit Films | 1962 | 15.00 |
| ❑ 33-835 [M] | Great Themes from Hit Films | 1962 | 12.00 |
| ❑ 840 SD [S] | Enoch Light and His Orchestra At Carnegie Hall Play Irving Berlin | 1962 | 15.00 |
| ❑ 33-840 [M] | Enoch Light and His Orchestra At Carnegie Hall Play Irving Berlin | 1962 | 12.00 |
| ❑ 844 SD [S] | Big Band Bossa Nova | 1962 | 15.00 |
| ❑ 33-844 [M] | Big Band Bossa Nova | 1962 | 12.00 |
| ❑ 850 SD [S] | Far Away Places, Volume 2 | 1963 | 15.00 |
| ❑ 33-850 [M] | Far Away Places, Volume 2 | 1963 | 12.00 |
| ❑ 851 SD [S] | Let's Dance the Bossa Nova | 1963 | 15.00 |
| ❑ 33-851 [M] | Let's Dance the Bossa Nova | 1963 | 12.00 |
| ❑ 854 SD [S] | 1963 — The Year's Most Popular Themes | 1963 | 15.00 |
| ❑ 33-854 [M] | 1963 — The Year's Most Popular Themes | 1963 | 12.00 |
| ❑ 863 SD [S] | Rome 35/MM | 1964 | 15.00 |
| ❑ 33-863 [M] | Rome 35/MM | 1964 | 12.00 |
| ❑ 867 SD [S] | Dimension "3" | 1964 | 15.00 |
| ❑ 33-867 [M] | Dimension "3" | 1964 | 12.00 |
| ❑ 868 SD [S] | Command Performances | 1964 | 15.00 |
| ❑ 33-868 [M] | Command Performances | 1964 | 12.00 |
| ❑ 871 SD [S] | Great Themes from Hit Films | 1964 | 15.00 |
| ❑ 33-871 [M] | Great Themes from Hit Films | 1964 | 12.00 |
| ❑ 873 SD [S] | Discotheque Dance...Dance...Dance | 1964 | 15.00 |
| ❑ 33-873 [M] | Discotheque Dance...Dance...Dance | 1964 | 12.00 |
| ❑ 879 SD [S] | Great Cole Porter Songs | 1965 | 15.00 |
| ❑ 33-879 [M] | Great Cole Porter Songs | 1965 | 12.00 |
| ❑ 882 SD [S] | Discotheque Dance...Dance...Dance, Volume 2 | 1965 | 15.00 |
| ❑ 33-882 [M] | Discotheque Dance...Dance...Dance, Volume 2 | 1965 | 12.00 |
| ❑ 887 SD [S] | Magnificent Movie Themes | 1965 | 15.00 |
| ❑ 33-887 [M] | Magnificent Movie Themes | 1965 | 12.00 |
| ❑ 895 SD [S] | Persuasive Percussion 1966 | 1966 | 15.00 |
| ❑ 33-895 [M] | Persuasive Percussion 1966 | 1966 | 12.00 |
| ❑ 915 SD | Command Performances, Volume 2 | 1969 | 15.00 |
| ❑ QD-40002 [Q] | A New Concept | 1972 | 15.00 |

### GRAND AWARD

| Number | Title (A Side/B Side) | Yr | NM |
|---|---|---|---|
| ❑ GA-201 SD [S] | The Roaring Twenties | 1958 | 25.00 |
| ❑ GA-202 SD [S] | The Flirty Thirties | 1958 | 25.00 |
| ❑ GA-203 SD [S] | Waltzes for Dancing | 1958 | 25.00 |
| ❑ GA-206 SD [S] | Tommy Dorsey's Song Hits | 1958 | 25.00 |
| ❑ GA-207 SD [S] | Glenn Miller's Song Hits | 1958 | 25.00 |
| ❑ GA-211 SD [S] | The Roaring Twenties, Volume 2 | 1958 | 25.00 |
| ❑ GA-214 SD [S] | Around the World in 80 Days | 1958 | 25.00 |
| ❑ GA-215 SD [S] | Gigi | 1958 | 25.00 |
| ❑ GA-216 SD [S] | My Fair Lady | 1958 | 25.00 |
| ❑ GA-217 SD [S] | Oklahoma/South Pacific | 1958 | 25.00 |
| ❑ GA-220 SD [S] | The Torchy Thirties | 1958 | 25.00 |
| ❑ GA-222 SD [S] | I Want to Be Happy Cha Cha's | 1959 | 25.00 |
| ❑ GA-224 SD [S] | New World Symphony | 1958 | 25.00 |
| ❑ GA-225 SD [S] | The Great Themes of America's Great Bands | 1958 | 25.00 |
| ❑ GA-227 SD [S] | Happy Cha Cha's, Vol. 2 | 1959 | 25.00 |
| ❑ GA-228 SD [S] | Show Spectacular | 1959 | 25.00 |
| ❑ GA-229 SD [S] | The Roaring Twenties, Volume 3 | 1959 | 25.00 |
| ❑ GA-236 SD [S] | All the Things You Are | 1959 | 25.00 |
| ❑ GA-237 SD [S] | Come to Hawaii | 1959 | 25.00 |
| ❑ GA-238 SD [S] | With My Eyes Wide Open I'm Dreaming | 1959 | 25.00 |
| ❑ GA-242 SD [S] | Something to Remember You By | 1959 | 25.00 |
| ❑ GA-246 SD [S] | Just for Kicks | 1959 | 25.00 |
| ❑ GA-251 SD [S] | Sing Along with the Original Roaring 20's | 1959 | 25.00 |
| ❑ GA 33-327 [M] | The Roaring Twenties | 1958 | 20.00 |
| ❑ GA 33-353 [M] | The Roaring Twenties, Volume 3 | 1959 | 20.00 |
| ❑ GA 33-371 [M] | The Flirty Thirties | 1958 | 20.00 |
| ❑ GA 33-372 [M] | Waltzes for Dancing | 1958 | 20.00 |
| ❑ GA 33-380 [M] | Paris Spectacular | 1958 | 20.00 |
| ❑ GA 33-381 [M] | Glenn Miller's Song Hits | 1958 | 20.00 |
| ❑ GA 33-382 [M] | Tommy Dorsey's Song Hits | 1958 | 20.00 |
| ❑ GA 33-388 [M] | I Want to Be Happy Cha Cha's | 1959 | 20.00 |
| ❑ GA 33-391 [M] | Happy Cha Cha's, Vol. 2 | 1959 | 20.00 |
| ❑ GA 33-392 [M] | The Great Themes of America's Great Bands | 1958 | 20.00 |
| ❑ GA 33-399 [M] | All the Things You Are | 1959 | 20.00 |
| ❑ GA 33-405 [M] | Come to Hawaii | 1959 | 20.00 |
| ❑ GA 33-406 [M] | With My Eyes Wide Open I'm Dreaming | 1959 | 20.00 |
| ❑ GA 33-410 [M] | Something to Remember You By | 1959 | 20.00 |
| ❑ GA 33-419 [M] | Sing Along with the Original Roaring 20's | 1959 | 20.00 |

### PROJECT 3

| Number | Title (A Side/B Side) | Yr | NM |
|---|---|---|---|
| ❑ PR-5000 SD | Spanish Strings | 1967 | 12.00 |
| ❑ PR4C-5000 [Q] | Spanish Strings | 1973 | 15.00 |
| ❑ PR-5004 SD | It's Happening | 1967 | 12.00 |
| ❑ PR-5005 SD | Film on Film — Great Movie Themes | 1967 | 12.00 |
| ❑ PR-5013 SD | Film Fame | 1968 | 12.00 |
| ❑ PR-5021 SD | Twelve Smash Hits | 1968 | 12.00 |
| ❑ PR-5027 SD | The Best of Hollywood '68-'69 | 1968 | 12.00 |
| ❑ PR-5030 SD | Whoever You Are, I Love You | 1968 | 12.00 |
| ❑ PR-5036 SD | Enoch Light and the Brass Menagerie | 1969 | 12.00 |
| ❑ PR4C-5036 [Q] | Enoch Light and the Brass Menagerie | 1973 | 15.00 |
| ❑ PR-5038 SD | Glittering Guitars | 1969 | 12.00 |
| ❑ PR-5042 SD | Enoch Light and the Brass Menagerie, Volume 2 | 1969 | 12.00 |
| ❑ PR4C-5042 [Q] | Enoch Light and the Brass Menagerie, Volume 2 | 1973 | 15.00 |
| ❑ PR-5043 SD | Spaced Out | 1970 | 12.00 |
| ❑ PR4C-5043 [Q] | Spaced Out | 1973 | 15.00 |
| ❑ PR-5046 SD | Best of the Movie Themes 1970 | 1970 | 12.00 |
| ❑ PR4C-5046 [Q] | Best of the Movie Themes 1970 | 1973 | 15.00 |
| ❑ PR-5048 SD | Permissive Polyphonics | 1970 | 12.00 |
| ❑ PR4C-5048 [Q] | Permissive Polyphonics | 1973 | 15.00 |
| ❑ PR-5049 SD | Big Band Hits of the 30's | 1971 | 12.00 |
| ❑ PR4C-5049 [Q] | Big Band Hits of the 30's | 1973 | 15.00 |
| ❑ PR-5051 SD | Hit Movie Themes | 1971 | 12.00 |
| ❑ PR4C-5051 [Q] | Hit Movie Themes | 1973 | 15.00 |
| ❑ PR-5056 SD | Big Band Hits of the 30's & 40's! | 1971 | 12.00 |
| ❑ PR4C-5056 [Q] | Big Band Hits of the 30's & 40's! | 1973 | 15.00 |
| ❑ PR-5059 SD | Big Hits of the 20's | 1971 | 12.00 |
| ❑ PR4C-5059 [Q] | Big Hits of the 20's | 1973 | 15.00 |
| ❑ PR-5060 SD | Enoch Light and the Brass Menagerie 1973 | 1972 | 12.00 |
| ❑ PR4C-5060 [Q] | Enoch Light and the Brass Menagerie 1973 | 1973 | 15.00 |
| ❑ PR-5063 SD | Movie Hits! | 1972 | 12.00 |
| ❑ PR4C-5063 [Q] | Movie Hits! | 1973 | 15.00 |
| ❑ PR4C-5068 [Q] | 4 Channel Dynamite! | 1973 | 15.00 |
| ❑ PR4C-5073 [Q] | Charge! | 1973 | 15.00 |
| ❑ PR4C-5076 [Q] | Big Band Hits of the 40's & 50's | 1973 | 15.00 |
| ❑ PR4C-5077 [Q] | Future Sound Shock | 1973 | 15.00 |
| ❑ PR-5084 SD | Beatles Classics | 1974 | 12.00 |
| ❑ PR4C-5084 [Q] | Beatles Classics | 1974 | 15.00 |
| ❑ PR-5086 SD | Great Hits from the Gatsby Era | 1974 | 12.00 |
| ❑ PR4C-5086 [Q] | Great Hits from the Gatsby Era | 1974 | 15.00 |
| ❑ PR-5089 SD | Big Band Hits of the 30's, Volume 2 | 1975 | 12.00 |
| ❑ PR4C-5089 [Q] | Big Band Hits of the 30's, Volume 2 | 1975 | 15.00 |
| ❑ PR-5092 SD | Disco Disque | 197? | 12.00 |
| ❑ PR4C-5092 [Q] | Disco Disque | 197? | 15.00 |
| ❑ PR-5100 | Let It Be | 197? | 12.00 |
| ❑ PR-5109 | The Most Beautiful Music in the World | 1981 | 12.00 |
| ❑ PR-6003/4 [(2)] | Big Hits of the Seventies | 1974 | 15.00 |
| ❑ PR4C-6003/4 [(2)Q] | Big Hits of the Seventies | 1974 | 20.00 |
| ❑ PR-6005/6 [(2)] | Big Band Hits of the 30's, 40's & 50's | 1974 | 15.00 |
| ❑ PR4C-6005/6 [(2)Q] | Big Band Hits of the 30's, 40's & 50's | 1974 | 20.00 |
| ❑ PR-6011/12 [(2)] | Music Maestro, Please | 197? | 15.00 |
| ❑ PR-6013/14 [(2)] | Big Band Hits of the 30's and 40's | 197? | 15.00 |
| ❑ PR4C-6013/14 [(2)Q] | Big Band Hits of the 30's and 40's | 197? | 20.00 |
| ❑ PR-6034 [(2)] | 20 Great Movie Themes | 1980 | 15.00 |

### SEAGULL

| Number | Title (A Side/B Side) | Yr | NM |
|---|---|---|---|
| ❑ LG-8204 | Blowin' in the Wind | 198? | 10.00 |
| ❑ LG-8207 | Music from the Movies | 198? | 10.00 |

## LIGHT CRUST DOUGHBOYS, THE

### AUDIO LAB

| Number | Title (A Side/B Side) | Yr | NM |
|---|---|---|---|
| ❑ AL-1525 [M] | The Light Crust Doughboys | 1959 | 150.00 |

## LIGHTFOOT, GORDON

### LIBERTY

| Number | Title (A Side/B Side) | Yr | NM |
|---|---|---|---|
| ❑ LN-10038 | The Best of Lightfoot | 198? | 8.00 |
| *—Budget-line reissue* | | | |
| ❑ LN-10039 | Sunday Concert | 198? | 8.00 |
| *—Budget-line reissue* | | | |
| ❑ LN-10040 | Back Here on Earth | 198? | 8.00 |
| *—Budget-line reissue* | | | |
| ❑ LN-10041 | Did She Mention My Name | 198? | 8.00 |
| *—Budget-line reissue* | | | |
| ❑ LN-10043 | The Way I Feel | 198? | 8.00 |
| *—Budget-line reissue* | | | |
| ❑ LN-10044 | Lightfoot | 198? | 8.00 |
| *—Budget-line reissue* | | | |

### MOBILE FIDELITY

| Number | Title (A Side/B Side) | Yr | NM |
|---|---|---|---|
| ❑ 1-018 | Sundown | 1979 | 40.00 |
| *—Audiophile vinyl* | | | |

### PAIR

| Number | Title (A Side/B Side) | Yr | NM |
|---|---|---|---|
| ❑ PDL2-1081 [(2)] | Songbook | 1986 | 12.00 |

### REPRISE

| Number | Title (A Side/B Side) | Yr | NM |
|---|---|---|---|
| ❑ MS 2037 | Summer Side of Life | 1971 | 12.00 |
| ❑ MS 2056 | Don Quixote | 1972 | 12.00 |
| ❑ MS 2116 | Old Dan's Records | 1972 | 12.00 |
| ❑ MS 2177 | Sundown | 1974 | 12.00 |
| ❑ MS4-2177 [Q] | Sundown | 1974 | 20.00 |
| ❑ MS 2206 | Cold on the Shoulder | 1975 | 12.00 |
| ❑ MS4-2206 [Q] | Cold on the Shoulder | 1975 | 20.00 |
| ❑ 2RS 2237 [(2)] | Gord's Gold | 1975 | 15.00 |
| ❑ MS 2246 | Summertime Dream | 1976 | 12.00 |
| ❑ RS 6392 | Sit Down Young Stranger | 1970 | 15.00 |
| ❑ RS 6392 | If You Could Read My Mind | 1971 | 10.00 |
| *—Retitled version* | | | |
| ❑ ST-93228 | Sit Down Young Stranger | 1970 | 20.00 |
| *—Capitol Record Club edition* | | | |

### UNITED ARTISTS

| Number | Title (A Side/B Side) | Yr | NM |
|---|---|---|---|
| ❑ UA-LA243-G | The Very Best of Gordon Lightfoot | 1974 | 12.00 |
| ❑ UAL-3487 [M] | Lightfoot | 1966 | 20.00 |
| ❑ UAL-3587 [M] | The Way I Feel | 1967 | 20.00 |

| Number | Title (A Side/B Side) | Yr | NM |
|---|---|---|---|
| ❑ UAS-5510 | Classic Lightfoot (The Best of Lightfoot/Volume 2) | 1971 | 15.00 |
| ❑ UAS-6487 [S] | Lightfoot | 1966 | 25.00 |
| ❑ UAS-6587 [S] | The Way I Feel | 1967 | 25.00 |
| ❑ UAS-6649 | Did She Mention My Name | 1968 | 20.00 |
| ❑ UAS-6672 | Back Here on Earth | 1969 | 20.00 |
| ❑ UAS-6714 | Sunday Concert | 1969 | 15.00 |
| ❑ UAS-6754 | The Best of Gordon Lightfoot | 1970 | 15.00 |

WARNER BROS.

| Number | Title (A Side/B Side) | Yr | NM |
|---|---|---|---|
| ❑ BSK 3149 | Endless Wire | 1978 | 10.00 |
| ❑ HS 3426 | Dream Street Rose | 1980 | 10.00 |
| ❑ BSK 3633 | Shadows | 1982 | 10.00 |
| ❑ 23901 | Salute | 1983 | 10.00 |
| ❑ 25482 | East of Midnight | 1986 | 10.00 |
| ❑ 25784 | Gord's Gold, Volume II | 1989 | 12.00 |

### LIGHTHOUSE

EVOLUTION

| Number | Title (A Side/B Side) | Yr | NM |
|---|---|---|---|
| ❑ 3007 | One Fine Morning | 1971 | 15.00 |
| ❑ 3010 | Thoughts of Movin' On | 1972 | 15.00 |
| ❑ 3014 [(2)] | Lighthouse Live! | 1972 | 20.00 |
| ❑ 3016 | Sunny Days | 1973 | 15.00 |

JANUS

| Number | Title (A Side/B Side) | Yr | NM |
|---|---|---|---|
| ❑ JSX-7025 | The Best of Lighthouse | 1976 | 12.00 |

POLYDOR

| Number | Title (A Side/B Side) | Yr | NM |
|---|---|---|---|
| ❑ PD-5056 | Can You Feel It | 1973 | 12.00 |
| ❑ PD-1-6028 | Good Day | 1974 | 12.00 |

RCA VICTOR

| Number | Title (A Side/B Side) | Yr | NM |
|---|---|---|---|
| ❑ LSP-4173 | Lighthouse | 1969 | 15.00 |
| ❑ LSP-4241 | Suite Feeling | 1969 | 15.00 |
| ❑ LSP-4325 | Peacing It All Together | 1970 | 15.00 |

### LIGHTNIN' SLIM

EXCELLO

| Number | Title (A Side/B Side) | Yr | NM |
|---|---|---|---|
| ❑ LP 8000 [M] | Rooster Blues | 1960 | 800.00 |
| ❑ LPS 8000 [M] | Rooster Blues | 196? | 50.00 |
| *—Thogh labeled "Electronic Stereo," this record is mono* | | | |
| ❑ LP 8004 [M] | Lightnin' Slim's Bell Ringer | 1965 | 300.00 |
| ❑ LPS 8004 [M] | Lightnin' Slim's Bell Ringer | 196? | 50.00 |
| *—Thogh labeled "Electronic Stereo," this record is mono* | | | |
| ❑ LPS 8018 | High and Low Down | 1971 | 15.00 |
| ❑ LPS 8023 | London Gumbo | 1972 | 15.00 |

INTERMEDIA

| Number | Title (A Side/B Side) | Yr | NM |
|---|---|---|---|
| ❑ QS-5062 | That's All Right | 198? | 10.00 |

### LIGHTNING

P.I.P.

| Number | Title (A Side/B Side) | Yr | NM |
|---|---|---|---|
| ❑ 6807 | Lightning | 1971 | 30.00 |

### LIL' KIM

UNDEAS

| Number | Title (A Side/B Side) | Yr | NM |
|---|---|---|---|
| ❑ 92733 [(2)] | Hard Core | 1996 | 20.00 |
| ❑ 92840 [(2)] | The Notorious K.I.M. | 2000 | 15.00 |

### LILLIE, BEATRICE

DECCA

| Number | Title (A Side/B Side) | Yr | NM |
|---|---|---|---|
| ❑ DL 5453 [10] | Souvenir Album | 1954 | 50.00 |

LIBERTY MUSIC SHOP

| Number | Title (A Side/B Side) | Yr | NM |
|---|---|---|---|
| ❑ 1002 [10] | Thirty Minutes with Bea Lillie | 1954 | 50.00 |

LONDON

| Number | Title (A Side/B Side) | Yr | NM |
|---|---|---|---|
| ❑ LL 1373 [M] | An Evening with Bea Little | 1956 | 30.00 |
| ❑ 5471 [M] | Auntie Bea | 1959 | 30.00 |

### LILLY BROTHERS, THE

FOLKLORE

| Number | Title (A Side/B Side) | Yr | NM |
|---|---|---|---|
| ❑ FL-14010 [M] | Bluegrass Breakdown | 1963 | 20.00 |
| ❑ FLS-14010 [S] | Bluegrass Breakdown | 1963 | 25.00 |
| ❑ FL-14035 [M] | Country Songs | 1964 | 20.00 |
| ❑ FLS-14035 [S] | Country Songs | 1964 | 25.00 |

FOLKWAYS

| Number | Title (A Side/B Side) | Yr | NM |
|---|---|---|---|
| ❑ FA-2433 [M] | Folk Songs from the Southern Mountains | 196? | 20.00 |

### LIMELITERS, THE Also see GLENN YARBROUGH.

ELEKTRA

| Number | Title (A Side/B Side) | Yr | NM |
|---|---|---|---|
| ❑ EKM-180 [M] | The Limeliters | 1960 | 20.00 |
| ❑ EKS-7180 [S] | The Limeliters | 1960 | 25.00 |

GNP CRESCENDO

| Number | Title (A Side/B Side) | Yr | NM |
|---|---|---|---|
| ❑ GNPS-2188 | Alive! In Concert, Vol. 1 | 1986 | 10.00 |
| ❑ GNPS-2190 | Alive! In Concert, Vol. 2 | 1987 | 10.00 |

LEGACY

| Number | Title (A Side/B Side) | Yr | NM |
|---|---|---|---|
| ❑ 113 | Their First Historic Album | 1970 | 12.00 |

RCA CAMDEN

| Number | Title (A Side/B Side) | Yr | NM |
|---|---|---|---|
| ❑ ACL1-0602 | This Train | 1974 | 10.00 |

RCA VICTOR

| Number | Title (A Side/B Side) | Yr | NM |
|---|---|---|---|
| ❑ LPM-2272 [M] | Tonight: In Person | 1961 | 20.00 |
| ❑ LSP-2272 [S] | Tonight: In Person | 1961 | 25.00 |
| ❑ ANL1-2336 | Pure Gold | 1977 | 8.00 |
| ❑ LPM-2393 [M] | The Slightly Fabulous Limeliters | 1961 | 20.00 |
| ❑ LSP-2393 [S] | The Slightly Fabulous Limeliters | 1961 | 25.00 |
| ❑ LPM-2445 [M] | Sing Out! | 1962 | 20.00 |
| ❑ LSP-2445 [S] | Sing Out! | 1962 | 25.00 |
| ❑ LPM-2512 [M] | Through Children's Eyes | 1962 | 20.00 |
| ❑ LSP-2512 [S] | Through Children's Eyes | 1962 | 25.00 |
| ❑ LPM-2547 [M] | Folk Matinee | 1962 | 20.00 |
| ❑ LSP-2547 [S] | Folk Matinee | 1962 | 25.00 |
| ❑ LPM-2588 [M] | Makin' a Joyful Noise | 1963 | 20.00 |
| ❑ LSP-2588 [S] | Makin' a Joyful Noise | 1963 | 25.00 |
| ❑ LPM-2609 [M] | Our Men in San Francisco | 1963 | 20.00 |
| ❑ LSP-2609 [S] | Our Men in San Francisco | 1963 | 25.00 |
| ❑ LPM-2671 [M] | Fourteen 14K Folk Songs | 1963 | 20.00 |
| ❑ LSP-2671 [S] | Fourteen 14K Folk Songs | 1963 | 25.00 |
| ❑ LPM-2844 [M] | More of Everything! | 1964 | 15.00 |
| ❑ LSP-2844 [S] | More of Everything! | 1964 | 20.00 |
| ❑ LPM-2889 [M] | The Best of the Limeliters | 1964 | 15.00 |
| ❑ LSP-2889 [S] | The Best of the Limeliters | 1964 | 20.00 |
| ❑ LPM-2906 [M] | Leave It to the Limeliters | 1964 | 15.00 |
| ❑ LSP-2906 [S] | Leave It to the Limeliters | 1964 | 20.00 |
| ❑ LPM-2907 [M] | London Concert | 1964 | 15.00 |
| ❑ LSP-2907 [S] | London Concert | 1964 | 20.00 |
| ❑ LPM-3385 [M] | The Limeliters Look at Love... In Depth | 1965 | 15.00 |
| ❑ LSP-3385 [S] | The Limeliters Look at Love... In Depth | 1965 | 20.00 |
| ❑ LSP-4100 | The Original "Those Were the Days" | 1969 | 15.00 |

WEST KNOLL

| Number | Title (A Side/B Side) | Yr | NM |
|---|---|---|---|
| ❑ WK-1001 | Alive! In Concert, Vol. 1 | 198? | 10.00 |
| ❑ WK-1002 | Alive! In Concert, Vol. 2 | 198? | 10.00 |

### LIMOUSINE

GSF

| Number | Title (A Side/B Side) | Yr | NM |
|---|---|---|---|
| ❑ 1002 | Limousine | 1972 | 20.00 |

### LINCOLN, ABBEY

CANDID

| Number | Title (A Side/B Side) | Yr | NM |
|---|---|---|---|
| ❑ CD-8015 [M] | Straight Ahead | 1960 | 80.00 |
| ❑ CS-9015 [S] | Straight Ahead | 1960 | 100.00 |

LIBERTY

| Number | Title (A Side/B Side) | Yr | NM |
|---|---|---|---|
| ❑ LRP-3025 [M] | Abbey Lincoln's Affair | 1957 | 70.00 |

RIVERSIDE

| Number | Title (A Side/B Side) | Yr | NM |
|---|---|---|---|
| ❑ RLP 12-251 [M] | That's Him! | 1957 | 50.00 |
| ❑ RLP 12-277 [M] | It's Magic | 1958 | 50.00 |
| ❑ RLP 12-308 [M] | Abbey Is Blue | 1959 | 60.00 |
| ❑ RLP-1107 [S] | That's Him! | 1958 | 40.00 |
| ❑ RLP-1153 [S] | Abbey Is Blue | 1959 | 80.00 |

### LINCOLN, PHILAMORE

EPIC

| Number | Title (A Side/B Side) | Yr | NM |
|---|---|---|---|
| ❑ BN 26497 | North Wind Blew South | 1970 | 25.00 |

### LINCOLN STREET EXIT

MAINSTREAM

| Number | Title (A Side/B Side) | Yr | NM |
|---|---|---|---|
| ❑ S-6126 | Drive It | 1970 | 100.00 |

### LIND, BOB

CAPITOL

| Number | Title (A Side/B Side) | Yr | NM |
|---|---|---|---|
| ❑ ST-780 | Since There Were Circles | 1971 | 15.00 |

VERVE FOLKWAYS

| Number | Title (A Side/B Side) | Yr | NM |
|---|---|---|---|
| ❑ FT-3005 [M] | The Elusive Bob Lind | 1966 | 25.00 |
| ❑ FTS-3005 [S] | The Elusive Bob Lind | 1966 | 30.00 |

WORLD PACIFIC

| Number | Title (A Side/B Side) | Yr | NM |
|---|---|---|---|
| ❑ WP-1841 [M] | Don't Be Concerned | 1966 | 20.00 |
| ❑ WP-1851 [M] | Photographs of Feeling | 1966 | 20.00 |
| ❑ ST-21841 [S] | Don't Be Concerned | 1966 | 25.00 |
| ❑ ST-21851 [S] | Photographs of Feeling | 1966 | 25.00 |

### LINDBERG, NILS

CAPITOL

| Number | Title (A Side/B Side) | Yr | NM |
|---|---|---|---|
| ❑ ST 10363 [S] | Trisection | 196? | 25.00 |
| ❑ T 10363 [M] | Trisection | 196? | 20.00 |

### LINDE, DENNIS

INTREPID

| Number | Title (A Side/B Side) | Yr | NM |
|---|---|---|---|
| ❑ 4004 [M] | Linde Manor | 1966 | 20.00 |
| ❑ 74004 [S] | Linde Manor | 1966 | 25.00 |

### LINDEN, KATHY

FELSTED

| Number | Title (A Side/B Side) | Yr | NM |
|---|---|---|---|
| ❑ 7501 [M] | That Certain Boy | 1959 | 60.00 |

### LINDH, JAYSON

JAS

| Number | Title (A Side/B Side) | Yr | NM |
|---|---|---|---|
| ❑ JAS-4000 | Second Carneval | 1975 | 20.00 |

METRONOME

| Number | Title (A Side/B Side) | Yr | NM |
|---|---|---|---|
| ❑ DIX-3000 | Ramadan | 1972 | 25.00 |
| ❑ DIX-3001 | Cous-Cous | 1973 | 25.00 |
| ❑ DIX-3002 | Sissel | 1974 | 25.00 |

### LINDSEY, GEORGE

CAPITOL

| Number | Title (A Side/B Side) | Yr | NM |
|---|---|---|---|
| ❑ ST-230 | 96 Miles to Bakersfield | 1969 | 25.00 |
| ❑ ST 2965 | Goober Sings! | 1968 | 25.00 |

### LINKLETTER, ART

COLUMBIA

| Number | Title (A Side/B Side) | Yr | NM |
|---|---|---|---|
| ❑ CL 703 [M] | Howlers, Boners and Shockers | 1956 | 40.00 |

### LINN, RAY

TREND

| Number | Title (A Side/B Side) | Yr | NM |
|---|---|---|---|
| ❑ 515 | Chicago Jazz | 1980 | 20.00 |
| *—Direct-to-disc recording* | | | |

### LINN COUNTY

MERCURY

| Number | Title (A Side/B Side) | Yr | NM |
|---|---|---|---|
| ❑ SR-61181 | Proud Flesh Soothseer | 1968 | 20.00 |
| ❑ SR-61218 | Fever Shot | 1969 | 20.00 |

PHILIPS

| Number | Title (A Side/B Side) | Yr | NM |
|---|---|---|---|
| ❑ PHS 600326 | Till the Break of Dawn | 1970 | 15.00 |

### LINTON, SHERWIN

BLACK GOLD

| Number | Title (A Side/B Side) | Yr | NM |
|---|---|---|---|
| ❑ 7116 | I'm Not Johnny Cash | 1972 | 25.00 |

BREAKER

| Number | Title (A Side/B Side) | Yr | NM |
|---|---|---|---|
| ❑ BR-4001 | Christmas Memories | 1987 | 12.00 |

RE-CAR

| Number | Title (A Side/B Side) | Yr | NM |
|---|---|---|---|
| ❑ 2108 | Sherwin Linton and the Cotton Kings | 1968 | 60.00 |

### LIPSCOMB, MANCE

ARHOOLIE

| Number | Title (A Side/B Side) | Yr | NM |
|---|---|---|---|
| ❑ 1001 [M] | Texas Sharecropper and Songster | 1960 | 50.00 |
| ❑ 1023 [M] | Texas Songster, Vol. 2 | 1963 | 40.00 |
| ❑ 1026 [M] | Texas Songster, Vol. 3 | 1965 | 40.00 |
| ❑ 1033 [M] | Mance Lipscomb, Vol. 4 | 1966 | 40.00 |
| ❑ 1049 | Mance Lipscomb, Vol. 5 | 1970 | 25.00 |
| ❑ 1069 | Mance Lipscomb, Vol. 6 | 1975 | 25.00 |

REPRISE

| Number | Title (A Side/B Side) | Yr | NM |
|---|---|---|---|
| ❑ R-2012 [M] | Trouble in Mind | 1961 | 100.00 |
| ❑ R9-2012 [S] | Trouble in Mind | 1961 | 150.00 |
| ❑ RS-6404 | Trouble in Mind | 1969 | 30.00 |

### LIPSTIQUE

TOM N JERRY

| Number | Title (A Side/B Side) | Yr | NM |
|---|---|---|---|
| ❑ TJ-4701 | At the Discotheque | 1978 | 20.00 |

### LIPTON, PEGGY

ODE

| Number | Title (A Side/B Side) | Yr | NM |
|---|---|---|---|
| ❑ Z12 44006 | Peggy Lipton | 1968 | 25.00 |

### LIQUID SMOKE

AVCO EMBASSY

| Number | Title (A Side/B Side) | Yr | NM |
|---|---|---|---|
| ❑ AVE-33005 | Liquid Smoke | 1970 | 25.00 |

### LIST, EUGENE

MERCURY LIVING PRESENCE

| Number | Title (A Side/B Side) | Yr | NM |
|---|---|---|---|
| ❑ SR 90290 [S] | Gershwin Favorites | 196? | 20.00 |
| *—Maroon label, no "Vendor: Mercury Record Corporation"* | | | |

### LISTENING

VANGUARD

| Number | Title (A Side/B Side) | Yr | NM |
|---|---|---|---|
| ❑ VSD-6504 | Listening | 1968 | 60.00 |

### LISTON, MELBA

METROJAZZ

| Number | Title (A Side/B Side) | Yr | NM |
|---|---|---|---|
| ❑ E-1013 [M] | Melba Liston and Her Bones | 1958 | 80.00 |
| ❑ SE-1013 [S] | Melba Liston and Her Bones | 1958 | 60.00 |

### LITE STORM, THE

BEVERLY HILLS

| Number | Title (A Side/B Side) | Yr | NM |
|---|---|---|---|
| ❑ 1135 | Lite Storm Warning | 1973 | 60.00 |

### LITTER

EVA

| Number | Title (A Side/B Side) | Yr | NM |
|---|---|---|---|
| ❑ 12013 | Rare Tracks | 1983 | 15.00 |

HEXAGON

| Number | Title (A Side/B Side) | Yr | NM |
|---|---|---|---|
| ❑ 681 | $100 Fine | 1968 | 400.00 |

PROBE

| Number | Title (A Side/B Side) | Yr | NM |
|---|---|---|---|
| ❑ 4504 | Emerge | 1969 | 50.00 |

WARICK

| Number | Title (A Side/B Side) | Yr | NM |
|---|---|---|---|
| ❑ 671 | Distortions | 1967 | 500.00 |

### LITTLE, BOOKER

BETHLEHEM

| Number | Title (A Side/B Side) | Yr | NM |
|---|---|---|---|
| ❑ BCP-6061 [M] | Booker Little and Friends | 1962 | 80.00 |

CANDID

| Number | Title (A Side/B Side) | Yr | NM |
|---|---|---|---|
| ❑ CD-8027 [M] | Out Front | 1961 | 60.00 |
| ❑ CS-9027 [S] | Out Front | 1961 | 80.00 |

TIME

| Number | Title (A Side/B Side) | Yr | NM |
|---|---|---|---|
| ❑ S-2011 [S] | Booker Little | 1960 | 80.00 |
| ❑ 52011 [M] | Booker Little | 1960 | 60.00 |

UNITED ARTISTS

| Number | Title (A Side/B Side) | Yr | NM |
|---|---|---|---|
| ❑ UAL-4034 [M] | The Booker Little Four | 1959 | 120.00 |
| ❑ UAS-5034 [S] | The Booker Little Four | 1959 | 100.00 |

### LITTLE, BOOKER, AND BOOKER ERVIN

TCB

| Number | Title (A Side/B Side) | Yr | NM |
|---|---|---|---|
| ❑ 1003 | Sounds of Inner City | 197? | 40.00 |

## LITTLE ANTHONY AND THE IMPERIALS

### ACCORD

| Number | Title (A Side/B Side) | Yr | NM |
|---|---|---|---|
| ❑ SN-7216 | Tears on My Pillow | 1983 | 10.00 |

### AVCO

| Number | Title (A Side/B Side) | Yr | NM |
|---|---|---|---|
| ❑ AV-11012 | On a New Street | 1973 | 20.00 |

### DCP

| Number | Title (A Side/B Side) | Yr | NM |
|---|---|---|---|
| ❑ DCL-3801 [M] | I'm On the Outside Looking In | 1964 | 25.00 |
| ❑ DCL-3808 [M] | Goin' Out of My Head | 1965 | 25.00 |
| ❑ DCL-3809 [M] | The Best of Little Anthony and the Imperials | 1965 | 20.00 |
| ❑ DCS-6801 [S] | I'm On the Outside Looking In | 1964 | 30.00 |
| ❑ DCS-6808 [S] | Goin' Out of My Head | 1965 | 30.00 |
| ❑ DCS-6809 [S] | The Best of Little Anthony and the Imperials | 1965 | 25.00 |

### END

| Number | Title (A Side/B Side) | Yr | NM |
|---|---|---|---|
| ❑ LP 303 [M] | We Are The Imperials Featuring Little Anthony | 1959 | 250.00 |
| ❑ LP 311 [M] | Shades of the 40's | 1960 | 200.00 |

### FORUM

| Number | Title (A Side/B Side) | Yr | NM |
|---|---|---|---|
| ❑ F-9107 [M] | Little Anthony and the 'Imperials' Greatest Hits | 196? | 15.00 |
| ❑ FS-9107 [R] | Little Anthony and the Imperials' Greatest Hits | 196? | 12.00 |

### LIBERTY

| Number | Title (A Side/B Side) | Yr | NM |
|---|---|---|---|
| ❑ LM-1017 | Out of Sight, Out of Mind | 1981 | 8.00 |
| *—Reissue of United Artists 1017* | | | |
| ❑ LN-10133 | The Best of Little Anthony and the Imperials | 1981 | 8.00 |
| *—Budget-line reissue* | | | |

### PICKWICK

| Number | Title (A Side/B Side) | Yr | NM |
|---|---|---|---|
| ❑ SPC-3029 | The Hits of Little Anthony and the Imperials | 196? | 12.00 |

### RHINO

| Number | Title (A Side/B Side) | Yr | NM |
|---|---|---|---|
| ❑ R1-70919 | The Best of Little Anthony and the Imperials | 1989 | 12.00 |

### ROULETTE

| Number | Title (A Side/B Side) | Yr | NM |
|---|---|---|---|
| ❑ R-25294 [M] | Little Anthony and the Imperials' Greatest Hits | 1965 | 25.00 |
| ❑ SR-25294 [R] | Little Anthony and the Imperials' Greatest Hits | 1965 | 20.00 |
| ❑ SR-42007 | Forever Yours | 1968 | 15.00 |

### SONGBIRD

| Number | Title (A Side/B Side) | Yr | NM |
|---|---|---|---|
| ❑ 3245 | Daylight | 1980 | 10.00 |

### SUNSET

| Number | Title (A Side/B Side) | Yr | NM |
|---|---|---|---|
| ❑ SUS-5287 | Little Anthony and the Imperials | 1970 | 15.00 |

### UNITED ARTISTS

| Number | Title (A Side/B Side) | Yr | NM |
|---|---|---|---|
| ❑ UA-LA026-G [(2)] | Legendary Masters Series | 1972 | 25.00 |
| ❑ UA-LA255-G | The Very Best of Little Anthony and the Imperials | 1974 | 10.00 |
| ❑ LM-1017 | Out of Sight, Out of Mind | 1980 | 10.00 |
| *—Reissue of United Artists 6720* | | | |
| ❑ UAS 6720 | Out of Sight, Out of Mind | 1969 | 20.00 |

### VEEP

| Number | Title (A Side/B Side) | Yr | NM |
|---|---|---|---|
| ❑ VP 13510 [M] | I'm On the Outside Looking In | 1966 | 15.00 |
| ❑ VP 13511 [M] | Goin' Out of My Head | 1966 | 15.00 |
| ❑ VP 13512 [M] | The Best of Little Anthony and the Imperials | 1966 | 15.00 |
| ❑ VP 13513 [M] | Payin' Our Dues | 1966 | 15.00 |
| ❑ VP 13514 [M] | Reflections | 1967 | 15.00 |
| ❑ VP 13516 [M] | Movie Grabbers | 1967 | 15.00 |
| ❑ VPS 16510 [S] | I'm On the Outside Looking In | 1966 | 20.00 |
| ❑ VPS 16511 [S] | Goin' Out of My Head | 1966 | 20.00 |
| ❑ VPS 16512 [S] | The Best of Little Anthony and the Imperials | 1966 | 20.00 |
| ❑ VPS 16513 [S] | Payin' Our Dues | 1966 | 20.00 |
| ❑ VPS 16514 [S] | Reflections | 1967 | 20.00 |
| ❑ VPS 16516 [S] | Movie Grabbers | 1967 | 20.00 |
| ❑ VPS 16519 | The Best of Little Anthony, Volume 2 | 1968 | 15.00 |
| ❑ ST-90840 [S] | The Best of Little Anthony and the Imperials | 1966 | 25.00 |
| *—Capitol Record Club edition* | | | |

## LITTLE BILL AND THE BLUENOTES

### CAMELOT

| Number | Title (A Side/B Side) | Yr | NM |
|---|---|---|---|
| ❑ 102 [M] | The Fiesta Club Presents Little Bill and the Bluenotes | 1960 | 400.00 |

## LITTLE BOY BLUES

### FONTANA

| Number | Title (A Side/B Side) | Yr | NM |
|---|---|---|---|
| ❑ SRF-67578 | In the Woodland of Weir | 1968 | 30.00 |

## LITTLE CAESAR AND THE ROMANS

### DEL-FI

| Number | Title (A Side/B Side) | Yr | NM |
|---|---|---|---|
| ❑ DFLP-1218 [M] | Memories of Those Oldies But Goodies | 1961 | 300.00 |

## LITTLE ESTHER

See LITTLE ESTHER PHILLIPS.

## LITTLE EVA

### DIMENSION

| Number | Title (A Side/B Side) | Yr | NM |
|---|---|---|---|
| ❑ DLP-6000 [M] | LLLLLoco-Motion | 1962 | 150.00 |
| *—Without "Keep Your Hands Off My Baby"* | | | |
| ❑ DLP-6000 [M] | LLLLLoco-Motion | 1962 | 200.00 |
| *—With "Keep Your Hands Off My Baby"* | | | |
| ❑ DLPS-6000 [R] | LLLLLoco-Motion | 1962 | 150.00 |
| *—Without "Keep Your Hands Off My Baby"* | | | |
| ❑ DLPS-6000 [R] | LLLLLoco-Motion | 1962 | 200.00 |
| *—With "Keep Your Hands Off My Baby"* | | | |

## LITTLE FEAT

### MOBILE FIDELITY

| Number | Title (A Side/B Side) | Yr | NM |
|---|---|---|---|
| ❑ 1-013 [(2)] | Waiting for Columbus | 1979 | 80.00 |
| *—Audiophile vinyl* | | | |

### NAUTILUS

| Number | Title (A Side/B Side) | Yr | NM |
|---|---|---|---|
| ❑ NR-24 | Time Loves a Hero | 198? | 50.00 |
| *—Audiophile vinyl* | | | |

### WARNER BROS.

| Number | Title (A Side/B Side) | Yr | NM |
|---|---|---|---|
| ❑ PRO-A-984 [DJ] | Hoy-Hoy! | 1981 | 20.00 |
| *—Single-album sampler of 2-LP set* | | | |
| ❑ WS 1890 | Little Feat | 1971 | 15.00 |
| *—Green "WB" label; without photo on back cover* | | | |
| ❑ WS 1890 | Little Feat | 1971 | 20.00 |
| *—Green "WB" label; with photo on back cover* | | | |
| ❑ WS 1890 | Little Feat | 1973 | 10.00 |
| *—"Burbank" palm trees label* | | | |
| ❑ WS 1890 | Little Feat | 1979 | 8.00 |
| *—Tan or white label* | | | |
| ❑ BS 2600 | Sailin' Shoes | 1972 | 15.00 |
| *—Green "WB" label* | | | |
| ❑ BS 2600 | Sailin' Shoes | 1973 | 10.00 |
| *—"Burbank" palm trees label* | | | |
| ❑ BS 2600 | Sailin' Shoes | 1979 | 8.00 |
| *—Tan or white label* | | | |
| ❑ BS 2686 | Dixie Chicken | 1973 | 15.00 |
| *—"Burbank" palm trees label* | | | |
| ❑ BS 2686 | Dixie Chicken | 1979 | 8.00 |
| *—Tan or white label* | | | |
| ❑ BS 2748 | Feats Don't Fail Me Now | 1974 | 15.00 |
| *—"Burbank" palm trees label* | | | |
| ❑ BS 2748 | Feats Don't Fail Me Now | 1979 | 8.00 |
| *—Tan or white label* | | | |
| ❑ BS 2884 | The Last Record Album | 1975 | 15.00 |
| *—"Burbank" palm trees label* | | | |
| ❑ BS 2884 | The Last Record Album | 1979 | 8.00 |
| *—Tan or white label* | | | |
| ❑ BS 3015 | Time Loves a Hero | 1977 | 12.00 |
| *—"Burbank" palm trees label* | | | |
| ❑ BS 3015 | Time Loves a Hero | 1979 | 8.00 |
| *—Tan or white label* | | | |
| ❑ 2WS 3140 [(2)] | Waiting for Columbus | 1978 | 15.00 |
| *—"Burbank" palm trees label* | | | |
| ❑ 2WS 3140 [(2)] | Waiting for Columbus | 1979 | 10.00 |
| *—Tan or white label* | | | |
| ❑ HS 3345 | Down on the Farm | 1979 | 10.00 |
| ❑ 2BSK 3538 [(2)] | Hoy-Hoy! | 1981 | 12.00 |
| ❑ 25750 | Let It Roll | 1988 | 10.00 |
| ❑ 26263 | Representing the Mambo | 1990 | 15.00 |

### ZOO/CLASSIC

| Number | Title (A Side/B Side) | Yr | NM |
|---|---|---|---|
| ❑ 11097 [(2)] | Ain't Had Enough Fun | 1995 | 18.00 |
| *—150-gram vinyl* | | | |
| ❑ 11097 [(2)] | Ain't Had Enough Fun | 1995 | 20.00 |
| *—180-gram vinyl* | | | |

## LITTLE GIRLS

### FTM ENTERPRISES

| Number | Title (A Side/B Side) | Yr | NM |
|---|---|---|---|
| ❑ (no #) [EP] | Little Girls 1985 | 1985 | 100.00 |
| *—Promo-only three-song EP, with all songs on same side, on clear vinyl in clear plastic sleeve; also contains two black & white photos of the group and three pages of biographical notes and reviews; 100 pressed* | | | |

### PVC

| Number | Title (A Side/B Side) | Yr | NM |
|---|---|---|---|
| ❑ 5904 [EP] | Thank Heaven! | 1983 | 20.00 |

## LITTLE JOE

### BRUNSWICK

| Number | Title (A Side/B Side) | Yr | NM |
|---|---|---|---|
| ❑ BL 754135 | Little Joe (Sure Can Sing) | 1968 | 20.00 |

## LITTLE MILTON

### CHECKER

| Number | Title (A Side/B Side) | Yr | NM |
|---|---|---|---|
| ❑ LP-2995 [M] | We're Gonna Make It | 196? | 25.00 |
| *—Blue, fading to white, label* | | | |
| ❑ LP-2995 [M] | We're Gonna Make It | 1965 | 100.00 |
| *—Black label* | | | |
| ❑ LP-2995 [M] | We're Gonna Make It | 1966 | 70.00 |
| *—Blue label with red and black checkers* | | | |
| ❑ LP-3002 [M] | Little Milton Sings Big Blues | 1966 | 50.00 |
| ❑ LP-3011 | Grits Ain't Groceries | 1969 | 25.00 |
| ❑ LP-3012 | If Walls Could Talk | 1970 | 25.00 |

### CHESS

| Number | Title (A Side/B Side) | Yr | NM |
|---|---|---|---|
| ❑ 204 [(2)] | Little Milton | 1976 | 15.00 |
| ❑ CH-9252 | We're Gonna Make It | 1986 | 10.00 |
| *—Reissue of Checker 2995* | | | |
| ❑ CH-9265 | Little Milton Sings Big Blues | 1987 | 10.00 |
| *—Reissue of Checker 3002* | | | |
| ❑ CH-9289 | If Walls Could Talk | 1989 | 10.00 |
| *—Reissue of Checker 3012* | | | |
| ❑ CH-50013 | Little Milton's Greatest Hits | 1972 | 15.00 |

### GLADES

| Number | Title (A Side/B Side) | Yr | NM |
|---|---|---|---|
| ❑ 7508 | Friend of Mine | 1976 | 12.00 |
| ❑ 7511 | Me for You, You for Me | 1977 | 12.00 |

### MALACO

| Number | Title (A Side/B Side) | Yr | NM |
|---|---|---|---|
| ❑ 7419 | Playin' for Keeps | 198? | 12.00 |
| ❑ 7427 | I Will Survive | 198? | 12.00 |
| ❑ 7435 | Annie Mae's Café | 198? | 12.00 |
| ❑ 7445 | Movin' to the Country | 198? | 12.00 |
| ❑ 7448 | Back to Back | 198? | 12.00 |
| ❑ 7453 | Too Much Pain | 198? | 12.00 |

### MCA

| Number | Title (A Side/B Side) | Yr | NM |
|---|---|---|---|
| ❑ 5414 | Age Ain't Nothin' But a Number | 1983 | 10.00 |

### ROUNDER

| Number | Title (A Side/B Side) | Yr | NM |
|---|---|---|---|
| ❑ SS-35 | The Sun Masters | 198? | 12.00 |

### STAX

| Number | Title (A Side/B Side) | Yr | NM |
|---|---|---|---|
| ❑ STS-3012 | Waiting for Little Milton | 1973 | 20.00 |
| ❑ 4117 | Waiting for Little Milton | 1978 | 12.00 |
| *—Reissue of 3012* | | | |
| ❑ 5514 | Blues 'n' Soul | 1974 | 20.00 |
| ❑ MPS-8514 | Walking the Back Streets | 1981 | 10.00 |
| ❑ MPS-8518 | Blues 'n' Soul | 1981 | 10.00 |
| *—Reissue of 5514* | | | |
| ❑ MPS-8529 | Grits Ain't Groceries | 198? | 10.00 |
| *—Despite the title, this is NOT a reissue of Checker 3011, but a later live recording* | | | |
| ❑ MPS-8550 | What It Is | 198? | 10.00 |

## LITTLE MISS CORNSHUCKS

### CHESS

| Number | Title (A Side/B Side) | Yr | NM |
|---|---|---|---|
| ❑ LP-1453 [M] | The Loneliest Gal in Town | 1961 | 200.00 |

## LITTLE RICHARD

### ACCORD

| Number | Title (A Side/B Side) | Yr | NM |
|---|---|---|---|
| ❑ SN-7123 | Tutti Frutti | 1981 | 10.00 |

### AUDIO ENCORES

| Number | Title (A Side/B Side) | Yr | NM |
|---|---|---|---|
| ❑ 1002 | Little Richard | 1980 | 25.00 |

### BUDDAH

| Number | Title (A Side/B Side) | Yr | NM |
|---|---|---|---|
| ❑ BDS-7501 | Little Richard | 1969 | 30.00 |

### CORAL

| Number | Title (A Side/B Side) | Yr | NM |
|---|---|---|---|
| ❑ CRL 57446 [M] | Coming Home | 1963 | 40.00 |
| ❑ CRL 757446 [S] | Coming Home | 1963 | 50.00 |

### CROWN

| Number | Title (A Side/B Side) | Yr | NM |
|---|---|---|---|
| ❑ CLP-5362 [M] | Little Richard Sings Freedom Songs | 1963 | 20.00 |

### CUSTOM

| Number | Title (A Side/B Side) | Yr | NM |
|---|---|---|---|
| ❑ 2061 [M] | Little Richard Sings Spirituals | 196? | 12.00 |

### EPIC

| Number | Title (A Side/B Side) | Yr | NM |
|---|---|---|---|
| ❑ EG 30428 [(2)] | Cast a Long Shadow | 1971 | 20.00 |
| ❑ PE 40389 | Little Richard's Greatest Hits | 1986 | 10.00 |
| ❑ PE 40390 | The Explosive Little Richard | 1986 | 10.00 |

### EXACT

| Number | Title (A Side/B Side) | Yr | NM |
|---|---|---|---|
| ❑ 206 | The Best of Little Richard | 1980 | 10.00 |

### GNP CRESCENDO

| Number | Title (A Side/B Side) | Yr | NM |
|---|---|---|---|
| ❑ GNP-9033 | The Big Hits | 1974 | 12.00 |

### GRT

| Number | Title (A Side/B Side) | Yr | NM |
|---|---|---|---|
| ❑ 2103 | The Original Little Richard | 1977 | 10.00 |

### GUEST STAR

| Number | Title (A Side/B Side) | Yr | NM |
|---|---|---|---|
| ❑ GS-1429 [M] | Little Richard with Sister Rosetta Tharpe | 196? | 12.00 |
| ❑ GSS-1429 [R] | Little Richard with Sister Rosetta Tharpe | 196? | 12.00 |

### KAMA SUTRA

| Number | Title (A Side/B Side) | Yr | NM |
|---|---|---|---|
| ❑ KSBS-2023 | Little Richard | 1970 | 25.00 |

### MERCURY

| Number | Title (A Side/B Side) | Yr | NM |
|---|---|---|---|
| ❑ MG-20656 [M] | It's Real | 1961 | 50.00 |
| ❑ SR-60656 [S] | It's Real | 1961 | 60.00 |

### MODERN

| Number | Title (A Side/B Side) | Yr | NM |
|---|---|---|---|
| ❑ 100 [M] | His Greatest Hits/Recorded Live | 1966 | 20.00 |
| ❑ 103 [M] | The Explosive Little Richard | 1966 | 20.00 |
| ❑ 1000 [S] | His Greatest Hits/Recorded Live | 1966 | 25.00 |
| ❑ 1003 [S] | The Explosive Little Richard | 1966 | 25.00 |

### OKEH

| Number | Title (A Side/B Side) | Yr | NM |
|---|---|---|---|
| ❑ OKM 12117 [M] | The Explosive Little Richard | 1967 | 25.00 |
| ❑ OKM 12121 [M] | Little Richard's Greatest Hits | 1967 | 25.00 |
| ❑ OKS 14117 [S] | The Explosive Little Richard | 1967 | 20.00 |
| ❑ OKS 14121 [S] | Little Richard's Greatest Hits | 1967 | 20.00 |

### PICKWICK

| Number | Title (A Side/B Side) | Yr | NM |
|---|---|---|---|
| ❑ SPC-3258 | King of the Gospel Singers | 197? | 10.00 |

### RCA CAMDEN

| Number | Title (A Side/B Side) | Yr | NM |
|---|---|---|---|
| ❑ CAL-420 [M] | Little Richard | 1956 | 200.00 |
| ❑ CAS-2430(e) | Every Hour with Little Richard | 1970 | 12.00 |

### REPRISE

| Number | Title (A Side/B Side) | Yr | NM |
|---|---|---|---|
| ❑ MS 2107 | The Second Coming | 1973 | 20.00 |
| ❑ RS 6406 | The Rill Thing | 1971 | 20.00 |
| ❑ RS 6462 | King of Rock and Roll | 1972 | 20.00 |

### RHINO

| Number | Title (A Side/B Side) | Yr | NM |
|---|---|---|---|
| ❑ R1-70236 | Shut Up! A Collection of Rare Tracks, 1951-1964 | 1988 | 12.00 |

### SCEPTER CITATION

| Number | Title (A Side/B Side) | Yr | NM |
|---|---|---|---|
| ❑ CTN-18020 | The Best of Little Richard | 1972 | 12.00 |

### SPECIALTY

| Number | Title (A Side/B Side) | Yr | NM |
|---|---|---|---|
| ❑ 100 [M] | Here's Little Richard | 1957 | 700.00 |



**Except when noted otherwise, VG = 25% of NM, and VG+ = 50% of NM. (Example: VG = $2.00, VG+ = $4.00 and NM = $8.00.)**

| Number | Title (A Side/B Side) | Yr | NM |
|---|---|---|---|
| ❑ SP-2100 [M] | Here's Little Richard | 1957 | 200.00 |
| *—Thick vinyl* | | | |
| ❑ SP-2103 [M] | Little Richard | 1958 | 150.00 |
| *—Front cover photo occupies the entire cover* | | | |
| ❑ SP-2103 [M] | Little Richard | 196? | 100.00 |
| *—Front cover photo partially obscured by a black triangle at uper right; thick vinyl* | | | |
| ❑ SP-2103 [M] | Little Richard | 197? | 20.00 |
| *—Reissue with thinner vinyl* | | | |
| ❑ SP-2104 [M] | The Fabulous Little Richard | 1958 | 150.00 |
| *—Thick vinyl* | | | |
| ❑ SP-2104 [M] | The Fabulous Little Richard | 197? | 20.00 |
| *—Reissue with thinner vinyl* | | | |
| ❑ SP-2111 | Little Richard — His Biggest Hits | 1963 | 50.00 |
| *—Thick vinyl* | | | |
| ❑ SP-2111 [M] | Little Richard — His Biggest Hits | 197? | 20.00 |
| *—Reissue with thinner vinyl* | | | |
| ❑ SP-2113 | Little Richard's Grooviest 17 Original Hits | 1968 | 25.00 |
| *—Thick vinyl* | | | |
| ❑ SP-2136 | Well Alright! | 1970 | 20.00 |
| ❑ SP-8508 [(5)] | The Specialty Sessions | 1989 | 40.00 |
| **SPIN-O-RAMA** | | | |
| ❑ 119 [M] | Clap Your Hands | 196? | 12.00 |
| **TRIP** | | | |
| ❑ 8013 [(2)] | Greatest Hits | 1972 | 12.00 |
| **20TH FOX** | | | |
| ❑ FXG-5010 [M] | Little Richard Sings Gospel | 1959 | 100.00 |
| ❑ SGM-5010 [S] | Little Richard Sings Gospel | 1959 | 150.00 |
| **UNITED** | | | |
| ❑ US-7775 | His Greatest Hits/Recorded Live | 197? | 10.00 |
| ❑ US-7777 | The Wild and Frantic Little Richard | 197? | 10.00 |
| **UNITED ARTISTS** | | | |
| ❑ UA-LA497-E | The Very Best of Little Richard | 1975 | 10.00 |
| **UPFRONT** | | | |
| ❑ UPF-123 | The Best of Little Richard | 197? | 10.00 |
| ❑ UPF-197 | Little Richard Sings Gospel | 197? | 10.00 |
| **VEE JAY** | | | |
| ❑ LP-1107 [M] | Little Richard Is Back! | 1964 | 50.00 |
| ❑ LPS-1107 [S] | Little Richard Is Back! | 1964 | 70.00 |
| ❑ VJLP-1107 | Little Richard's Back | 198? | 10.00 |
| *—Reissue with thin vinyl* | | | |
| ❑ LP-1124 [M] | Little Richard's Greatest Hits | 1965 | 25.00 |
| ❑ LPS-1124 [S] | Little Richard's Greatest Hits | 1965 | 40.00 |
| ❑ VJLP-1124 | Little Richard's Greatest Hits | 198? | 10.00 |
| *—Reissue with thin vinyl* | | | |
| ❑ DY-7304 | Talkin' 'Bout Soul | 198? | 12.00 |
| **VEE JAY/CHAMELEON** | | | |
| ❑ D1-74797 | Rip It Up | 1989 | 12.00 |
| **WARNER BROS.** | | | |
| ❑ 25529 | Lifetime Friend | 1986 | 12.00 |
| **WING** | | | |
| ❑ MGW-12288 [M] | King of the Gospel Singers | 1964 | 15.00 |
| ❑ SRW-16288 [S] | King of the Gospel Singers | 1964 | 20.00 |

### LITTLE RIVER BAND

| Number | Title (A Side/B Side) | Yr | NM |
|---|---|---|---|
| **CAPITOL** | | | |
| ❑ SOO-11954 | First Under the Wire | 1979 | 8.00 |
| ❑ SWBK-12061 [(2)] | Backstage Pass | 1980 | 10.00 |
| ❑ ST-12163 | Time Exposure | 1981 | 8.00 |
| ❑ ST-12247 | Greatest Hits | 1982 | 8.00 |
| ❑ ST-12273 | The Net | 1983 | 8.00 |
| ❑ SJ-12365 | Playing to Win | 1985 | 8.00 |
| *—As "LRB"* | | | |
| ❑ ST-12480 | No Reins | 1986 | 8.00 |
| ❑ SN-16072 | After Hours | 1979 | 10.00 |
| *—First U.S. issue of their second Australian LP* | | | |
| ❑ SN-16141 | Beginnings | 1980 | 10.00 |
| ❑ SN-16142 | Beginnings, Vol. 2 | 1980 | 10.00 |
| ❑ SN-16345 | First Under the Wire | 198? | 6.00 |
| *—Budget-line reissue* | | | |
| ❑ SN-16346 | Time Exposure | 198? | 6.00 |
| *—Budget-line reissue* | | | |
| ❑ SN-16454 | Little River Band | 1987 | 6.00 |
| *—Budget-line reissue* | | | |
| ❑ SN-16455 | Diamantina Cocktail | 1987 | 6.00 |
| *—Budget-line reissue* | | | |
| ❑ SN-16456 | Sleeper Catcher | 1987 | 6.00 |
| *—Budget-line reissue* | | | |
| ❑ SN-16457 | Greatest Hits | 1987 | 6.00 |
| *—Budget-line reissue* | | | |
| **HARVEST** | | | |
| ❑ ST-11512 | Little River Band | 1976 | 10.00 |
| ❑ SW-11645 | Diamantina Cocktail | 1977 | 10.00 |
| ❑ SW-11783 | Sleeper Catcher | 1978 | 10.00 |
| **MCA** | | | |
| ❑ 6269 | Get Lucky | 1990 | 12.00 |
| ❑ 42193 | Monsoon | 1989 | 10.00 |

Live, *Throwing Copper,* Radioactive RAR-10997, 1994, clear vinyl, $60.

| Number | Title (A Side/B Side) | Yr | NM |
|---|---|---|---|
| **MOBILE FIDELITY** | | | |
| ❑ 1-036 | First Under the Wire | 1980 | 25.00 |
| *—Audiophile vinyl* | | | |

### LITTLE SISTERS, THE

| Number | Title (A Side/B Side) | Yr | NM |
|---|---|---|---|
| **MGM** | | | |
| ❑ E-4116 [M] | The Joys of Love | 1963 | 25.00 |
| ❑ SE-4116 [S] | The Joys of Love | 1963 | 30.00 |

### LITTLE SONNY

| Number | Title (A Side/B Side) | Yr | NM |
|---|---|---|---|
| **ENTERPRISE** | | | |
| ❑ ENS-1005 | New King of the Blues Harmonica | 1970 | 40.00 |
| ❑ ENS-1018 | Black and Blue | 1971 | 40.00 |
| ❑ ENS-1036 | Hard Goin' Up | 1973 | 40.00 |

### LITTLE WALTER

| Number | Title (A Side/B Side) | Yr | NM |
|---|---|---|---|
| **CHECKER** | | | |
| ❑ LP-1428 [M] | The Best of Little Walter | 1957 | 500.00 |
| *—Black or maroon label* | | | |
| ❑ LP-3004 [M] | The Best of Little Walter | 1967 | 50.00 |
| *—Reissue of 1428* | | | |
| **CHESS** | | | |
| ❑ 2ACMB-202 [(2)] | Little Walter | 1976 | 20.00 |
| *—Reissue of 60014* | | | |
| ❑ CHV-416 [M] | Confessin' the Blues | 1974 | 12.00 |
| ❑ LP-1535 [M] | Hate to See You Go | 1969 | 25.00 |
| ❑ 2CH-60014 [(2)] | Boss Blues Harmonica | 1972 | 20.00 |

### LIVE

| Number | Title (A Side/B Side) | Yr | NM |
|---|---|---|---|
| **RADIOACTIVE** | | | |
| ❑ RAR-10997 | Throwing Copper | 1994 | 20.00 |
| *—Black vinyl* | | | |
| ❑ RAR-10997 | Throwing Copper | 1994 | 60.00 |
| *—Clear vinyl* | | | |
| ❑ RAR2-11590 [(2)] | Secret Samadhi | 1997 | 15.00 |
| *—White vinyl; includes poster* | | | |
| ❑ RAR2-11590 [(2)] | Secret Samadhi | 1997 | 15.00 |
| *—Clear vinyl; includes poster* | | | |

### LIVELY ONES, THE

| Number | Title (A Side/B Side) | Yr | NM |
|---|---|---|---|
| **DEL-FI** | | | |
| ❑ DFLP-1226 [M] | Surf Rider | 1963 | 100.00 |
| ❑ DFST-1226 [S] | Surf Rider | 1963 | 150.00 |
| ❑ DFLP-1231 [M] | Surf Drums | 1963 | 50.00 |
| ❑ DFST-1231 [S] | Surf Drums | 1963 | 70.00 |
| ❑ DLF 1231 | Surf Drums | 1997 | 12.00 |
| ❑ DFLP-1237 [M] | Surf City | 1963 | 40.00 |
| ❑ DFST-1237 [S] | Surf City | 1963 | 50.00 |
| ❑ DLF 1237 | Surf City | 1997 | 12.00 |
| ❑ DFLP-1240 [M] | Surfin' South of the Border | 1964 | 40.00 |
| ❑ DFST-1240 [S] | Surfin' South of the Border | 1964 | 50.00 |
| **MGM** | | | |
| ❑ E-4449 [M] | Bugalu Party | 1967 | 20.00 |
| ❑ SE-4449 [S] | Bugalu Party | 1967 | 25.00 |

### LIVERPOOL BEATS, THE

| Number | Title (A Side/B Side) | Yr | NM |
|---|---|---|---|
| **RONDO** | | | |
| ❑ 2026 [M] | The New Merseyside Sound | 1964 | 30.00 |

### LIVERPOOL FIVE, THE

| Number | Title (A Side/B Side) | Yr | NM |
|---|---|---|---|
| **RCA VICTOR** | | | |
| ❑ LPM-3583 [M] | The Liverpool Five Arrive | 1966 | 25.00 |
| ❑ LSP-3583 [S] | The Liverpool Five Arrive | 1966 | 30.00 |
| ❑ LPM-3682 [M] | Out of Sight | 1967 | 25.00 |
| ❑ LSP-3682 [S] | Out of Sight | 1967 | 30.00 |

### LIVERPOOL SCENE, THE

| Number | Title (A Side/B Side) | Yr | NM |
|---|---|---|---|
| **EPIC** | | | |
| ❑ LN 24336 [M] | The Incredible New Liverpool Scene | 1967 | 25.00 |
| ❑ BN 26336 [S] | The Incredible New Liverpool Scene | 1967 | 30.00 |

### LIVERPOOLS, THE

| Number | Title (A Side/B Side) | Yr | NM |
|---|---|---|---|
| **WYNCOTE** | | | |
| ❑ SW-9001 [S] | Beatle Mania! In the U.S.A. | 1964 | 25.00 |
| ❑ W-9001 [M] | Beatle Mania! In the U.S.A. | 1964 | 20.00 |
| ❑ SW-9061 [S] | The Hit Sounds from England | 1964 | 20.00 |
| ❑ W-9061 [M] | The Hit Sounds from England | 1964 | 15.00 |

### LIVIN' BLUES

| Number | Title (A Side/B Side) | Yr | NM |
|---|---|---|---|
| **DWARF** | | | |
| ❑ 2003 | Dutch Treat | 1971 | 30.00 |

### LIVING COLOUR

| Number | Title (A Side/B Side) | Yr | NM |
|---|---|---|---|
| **EPIC** | | | |
| ❑ FE 44099 | Vivid | 1988 | 12.00 |
| ❑ E 46202 | Time's Up | 1990 | 20.00 |
| *—Yellow vinyl* | | | |

## LLOYD, CHARLES

**ATLANTIC**

| Number | Title (A Side/B Side) | Yr | NM |
|---|---|---|---|
| ❑ SD 1459 [S] | Dream Weaver | 1966 | 20.00 |
| *—Blue and green label* | | | |
| ❑ SD 1459 [S] | Dream Weaver | 1969 | 12.00 |
| *—Red and green label, white stripe through center hole* | | | |
| ❑ SD 1473 [S] | Forest Flower | 1967 | 25.00 |
| ❑ 1481 [M] | Love-In | 1967 | 40.00 |

**COLUMBIA**

| Number | Title (A Side/B Side) | Yr | NM |
|---|---|---|---|
| ❑ CL 2267 [M] | Discovery! | 1965 | 25.00 |
| ❑ CL 2412 [M] | Of Course, Of Course | 1966 | 25.00 |
| ❑ CS 9067 [S] | Discovery! | 1965 | 30.00 |
| ❑ CS 9212 [S] | Of Course, Of Course | 1966 | 30.00 |
| ❑ CS 9609 [M] | Nirvana | 1968 | 50.00 |
| *—White label promo; "Special Mono Radio Station Copy" sticker on stereo cover* | | | |
| ❑ CS 9609 [S] | Nirvana | 1968 | 25.00 |

## LLOYD, DAVID

**EPIC**

| Number | Title (A Side/B Side) | Yr | NM |
|---|---|---|---|
| ❑ LN 24151 [M] | Confidential (Sounds for a Secret Agent) | 1965 | 20.00 |
| ❑ BN 26151 [S] | Confidential (Sounds for a Secret Agent) | 1965 | 25.00 |

## LLOYD, HAROLD, JR.

**CORAL**

| Number | Title (A Side/B Side) | Yr | NM |
|---|---|---|---|
| ❑ CRL 57471 [M] | The Intimate Style of Harold Lloyd, Jr. | 1963 | 15.00 |
| ❑ CRL 757471 [S] | The Intimate Style of Harold Lloyd, Jr. | 1963 | 20.00 |

## LOADING ZONE, THE

**RCA VICTOR**

| Number | Title (A Side/B Side) | Yr | NM |
|---|---|---|---|
| ❑ LSP-3959 | The Loading Zone | 1968 | 25.00 |

**UMBRELLA**

| Number | Title (A Side/B Side) | Yr | NM |
|---|---|---|---|
| ❑ US-101 | One for All | 1967 | 80.00 |

## LOBO (2)

Jazz guitarist and singer named Edu Lobo. No relation to the 1970s pop singer, whose real name is Kent Lavoie.

**A&M**

| Number | Title (A Side/B Side) | Yr | NM |
|---|---|---|---|
| ❑ SP-3035 | Sergio Mendes Presents Lobo | 1970 | 25.00 |

## LOCKLIN, HANK

**DESIGN**

| Number | Title (A Side/B Side) | Yr | NM |
|---|---|---|---|
| ❑ DLP-603 [M] | Hank Locklin | 196? | 15.00 |

**HILLTOP**

| Number | Title (A Side/B Side) | Yr | NM |
|---|---|---|---|
| ❑ JM-6003 | Born to Ramble | 196? | 15.00 |
| ❑ JM-6041 [M] | Hank Locklin Sings Hank Locklin | 196? | 15.00 |
| ❑ JS-6041 [R] | Hank Locklin Sings Hank Locklin | 196? | 12.00 |
| ❑ JM-6083 | Queen of Hearts | 196? | 15.00 |

**KING**

| Number | Title (A Side/B Side) | Yr | NM |
|---|---|---|---|
| ❑ 672 [M] | The Best of Hank Locklin | 1961 | 60.00 |
| ❑ 738 [M] | Encores | 1961 | 60.00 |

**METRO**

| Number | Title (A Side/B Side) | Yr | NM |
|---|---|---|---|
| ❑ M 541 [M] | Down Texas Way | 196? | 15.00 |
| ❑ MS 541 [R] | Down Texas Way | 196? | 12.00 |

**RCA CAMDEN**

| Number | Title (A Side/B Side) | Yr | NM |
|---|---|---|---|
| ❑ CAL-705 [M] | Hank Locklin | 1962 | 15.00 |
| ❑ CAL-912 [M] | My Kind of Country Music | 196? | 15.00 |
| ❑ CAS-912 [R] | My Kind of Country Music | 196? | 12.00 |

**RCA VICTOR**

| Number | Title (A Side/B Side) | Yr | NM |
|---|---|---|---|
| ❑ LPM-1673 [M] | Foreign Love | 1958 | 60.00 |
| ❑ LPM-2291 [M] | Please Help Me, I'm Falling | 1960 | 30.00 |
| ❑ LSP-2291 [S] | Please Help Me, I'm Falling | 1960 | 40.00 |
| ❑ LPM-2464 [M] | Happy Journey | 1962 | 25.00 |
| ❑ LSP-2464 [S] | Happy Journey | 1962 | 30.00 |
| ❑ LPM-2597 [M] | A Tribute to Roy Acuff, the King of Country Music | 1962 | 25.00 |
| ❑ LSP-2597 [S] | A Tribute to Roy Acuff, the King of Country Music | 1962 | 30.00 |
| ❑ LPM-2680 [M] | The Ways of Life | 1963 | 25.00 |
| ❑ LSP-2680 [S] | The Ways of Life | 1963 | 30.00 |
| ❑ LPM-2801 [M] | Irish Songs, Country Style | 1964 | 20.00 |
| ❑ LSP-2801 [S] | Irish Songs, Country Style | 1964 | 25.00 |
| ❑ LPM-2997 [M] | Hank Locklin Sings Hank Williams | 1964 | 20.00 |
| ❑ LSP-2997 [S] | Hank Locklin Sings Hank Williams | 1964 | 25.00 |
| ❑ LPM-3391 [M] | Hank Locklin Sings Eddy Arnold | 1965 | 20.00 |
| ❑ LSP-3391 [S] | Hank Locklin Sings Eddy Arnold | 1965 | 25.00 |
| ❑ LPM-3465 [M] | Once Over Lightly | 1965 | 20.00 |
| ❑ LSP-3465 [S] | Once Over Lightly | 1965 | 25.00 |
| ❑ LPM-3559 [M] | The Best of Hank Locklin | 1966 | 20.00 |
| ❑ LSP-3559 [S] | The Best of Hank Locklin | 1966 | 25.00 |
| ❑ LPM-3588 [M] | The Girls Get Prettier | 1966 | 20.00 |
| ❑ LSP-3588 [S] | The Girls Get Prettier | 1966 | 25.00 |
| ❑ LPM-3656 [M] | The Gloryland Way | 1966 | 20.00 |
| ❑ LSP-3656 [S] | The Gloryland Way | 1966 | 25.00 |
| ❑ LPM-3770 [M] | Send Me the Pillow You Dream On | 1967 | 25.00 |
| ❑ LSP-3770 [S] | Send Me the Pillow You Dream On | 1967 | 20.00 |
| ❑ LPM-3841 [M] | Nashville Women | 1967 | 25.00 |
| ❑ LSP-3841 [S] | Nashville Women | 1967 | 20.00 |
| ❑ LPM-3946 [M] | Country Hall of Fame | 1968 | 100.00 |
| ❑ LSP-3946 [S] | Country Hall of Fame | 1968 | 20.00 |
| ❑ LSP-4030 | My Love Song for You | 1968 | 20.00 |
| ❑ LSP-4113 | Softly | 1969 | 20.00 |
| ❑ LSP-4191 | Lookin' Back | 1969 | 15.00 |

**SEARS**

| Number | Title (A Side/B Side) | Yr | NM |
|---|---|---|---|
| ❑ SPS-104 | Send Me the Pillow You Dream On | 196? | 25.00 |

**STEREO-SPECTRUM**

| Number | Title (A Side/B Side) | Yr | NM |
|---|---|---|---|
| ❑ SDLP-603 [R] | Hank Locklin | 196? | 12.00 |
| *—"Stereo" version of Design DLP-603* | | | |

**WRANGLER**

| Number | Title (A Side/B Side) | Yr | NM |
|---|---|---|---|
| ❑ 1004 [M] | Hank Locklin | 1962 | 25.00 |

## LOCKWOOD, ROBERT, JR.

**TRIX**

| Number | Title (A Side/B Side) | Yr | NM |
|---|---|---|---|
| ❑ 3307 | Contrasts | 197? | 20.00 |

## LOCO, JOE

**FANTASY**

| Number | Title (A Side/B Side) | Yr | NM |
|---|---|---|---|
| ❑ 3215 [M] | Invitation to the Mambo | 1956 | 20.00 |
| *—Black vinyl, red label, non-flexible vinyl* | | | |
| ❑ 3215 [M] | Invitation to the Mambo | 1956 | 30.00 |
| *—Red vinyl* | | | |
| ❑ 3215 [M] | Invitation to the Mambo | 196? | 15.00 |
| *—Black vinyl, red label, flexible vinyl* | | | |
| ❑ 3277 [M] | Cha-Cha-Cha | 1958 | 20.00 |
| *—Black vinyl, red label, non-flexible vinyl* | | | |
| ❑ 3277 [M] | Cha-Cha-Cha | 1958 | 30.00 |
| *—Red vinyl* | | | |
| ❑ 3277 [M] | Cha-Cha-Cha | 196? | 15.00 |
| *—Black vinyl, red label, flexible vinyl* | | | |
| ❑ 3280 [M] | Going Loco | 1958 | 20.00 |
| *—Black vinyl, red label, non-flexible vinyl* | | | |
| ❑ 3280 [M] | Going Loco | 1958 | 30.00 |
| *—Red vinyl* | | | |
| ❑ 3280 [M] | Going Loco | 196? | 15.00 |
| *—Black vinyl, red label, flexible vinyl* | | | |
| ❑ 3285 [M] | Ole, Ole, Ole | 1959 | 20.00 |
| *—Black vinyl, red label, non-flexible vinyl* | | | |
| ❑ 3285 [M] | Ole, Ole, Ole | 1959 | 30.00 |
| *—Red vinyl* | | | |
| ❑ 3285 [M] | Ole, Ole, Ole | 196? | 15.00 |
| *—Black vinyl, red label, flexible vinyl* | | | |
| ❑ 3294 [M] | Latin Jewels | 1959 | 20.00 |
| *—Black vinyl, red label, non-flexible vinyl* | | | |
| ❑ 3294 [M] | Latin Jewels | 1959 | 30.00 |
| *—Red vinyl* | | | |
| ❑ 3294 [M] | Latin Jewels | 196? | 15.00 |
| *—Black vinyl, red label, flexible vinyl* | | | |
| ❑ 3303 [M] | The Best of Joe Loco | 196? | 15.00 |
| *—Black vinyl, red label, flexible vinyl* | | | |
| ❑ 3303 [M] | The Best of Joe Loco | 1960 | 20.00 |
| *—Black vinyl, red label, non-flexible vinyl* | | | |
| ❑ 3303 [M] | The Best of Joe Loco | 1960 | 30.00 |
| *—Red vinyl* | | | |
| ❑ 3321 [M] | Pachanga with Joe Loco | 196? | 15.00 |
| *—Black vinyl, red label, flexible vinyl* | | | |
| ❑ 3321 [M] | Pachanga with Joe Loco | 1961 | 20.00 |
| *—Black vinyl, red label, non-flexible vinyl* | | | |
| ❑ 3321 [M] | Pachanga with Joe Loco | 1961 | 30.00 |
| *—Red vinyl* | | | |
| ❑ 8022 [S] | Cha-Cha-Cha | 196? | 15.00 |
| *—Black vinyl, blue label, flexible vinyl* | | | |
| ❑ 8022 [S] | Cha-Cha-Cha | 1962 | 20.00 |
| *—Black vinyl, blue label, non-flexible vinyl* | | | |
| ❑ 8022 [S] | Cha-Cha-Cha | 1962 | 30.00 |
| *—Blue vinyl* | | | |
| ❑ 8028 [S] | Ole, Ole, Ole | 196? | 15.00 |
| *—Black vinyl, blue label, flexible vinyl* | | | |
| ❑ 8028 [S] | Ole, Ole, Ole | 1962 | 20.00 |
| *—Black vinyl, blue label, non-flexible vinyl* | | | |
| ❑ 8028 [S] | Ole, Ole, Ole | 1962 | 30.00 |
| *—Blue vinyl* | | | |
| ❑ 8041 [S] | Latin Jewels | 196? | 15.00 |
| *—Black vinyl, blue label, flexible vinyl* | | | |
| ❑ 8041 [S] | Latin Jewels | 1962 | 20.00 |
| *—Black vinyl, blue label, non-flexible vinyl* | | | |
| ❑ 8041 [S] | Latin Jewels | 1962 | 30.00 |
| *—Blue vinyl* | | | |
| ❑ 8042 [S] | Going Loco | 196? | 15.00 |
| *—Black vinyl, blue label, flexible vinyl* | | | |
| ❑ 8042 [S] | Going Loco | 1962 | 20.00 |
| *—Black vinyl, blue label, non-flexible vinyl* | | | |
| ❑ 8042 [S] | Going Loco | 1962 | 30.00 |
| *—Blue vinyl* | | | |
| ❑ 8048 [S] | The Best of Joe Loco | 196? | 15.00 |
| *—Black vinyl, blue label, flexible vinyl* | | | |
| ❑ 8048 [S] | The Best of Joe Loco | 1962 | 20.00 |
| *—Black vinyl, blue label, non-flexible vinyl* | | | |
| ❑ 8048 [S] | The Best of Joe Loco | 1962 | 30.00 |
| *—Blue vinyl* | | | |
| ❑ 8064 [S] | Pachanga with Joe Loco | 196? | 15.00 |
| *—Black vinyl, blue label, flexible vinyl* | | | |
| ❑ 8064 [S] | Pachanga with Joe Loco | 1962 | 20.00 |
| *—Black vinyl, blue label, non-flexible vinyl* | | | |
| ❑ 8064 [S] | Pachanga with Joe Loco | 1962 | 30.00 |
| *—Blue vinyl* | | | |

**IMPERIAL**

| Number | Title (A Side/B Side) | Yr | NM |
|---|---|---|---|
| ❑ LP-9070 [M] | Let's Go Loco | 1959 | 20.00 |
| ❑ LP-9073 [M] | Happy Go Loco | 1959 | 20.00 |
| ❑ LP-9166 [M] | Pachanga Twist | 1962 | 20.00 |
| ❑ LP-12014 [S] | Let's Go Loco | 1959 | 25.00 |
| ❑ LP-12019 [S] | Happy Go Loco | 1959 | 25.00 |
| ❑ LP-12079 [S] | Pachanga Twist | 1962 | 25.00 |

**TICO**

| Number | Title (A Side/B Side) | Yr | NM |
|---|---|---|---|
| ❑ LP-109 [10] | Mambos, Vol. 1 | 195? | 40.00 |
| ❑ LP-111 [10] | Mambos, Vol. 2 | 195? | 40.00 |
| ❑ LP-121 [10] | Mambos, Vol. 3 | 195? | 40.00 |
| ❑ LP-122 [10] | Mambos, Vol. 4 | 195? | 40.00 |
| ❑ LP-123 [10] | Mambo Dance Favorites, Vol. 5 | 195? | 40.00 |
| ❑ LP-129 [10] | Mambo U.S.A. | 1954 | 40.00 |
| ❑ LP-132 [10] | Instrumental Mambos (Vol. 7) | 1955 | 40.00 |
| ❑ LP-1006 [M] | Mambo Moods | 1955 | 30.00 |
| ❑ LP-1008 [M] | Make Mine Mambo | 1955 | 30.00 |
| ❑ LP-1012 [M] | Mambo Fantasy | 1956 | 30.00 |
| ❑ LP-1013 [M] | Viva Mambo! | 1956 | 30.00 |

## LODI

**MOWEST**

| Number | Title (A Side/B Side) | Yr | NM |
|---|---|---|---|
| ❑ MW 101L | Happiness | 1972 | 25.00 |

## LOFGREN, NILS

**A&M**

| Number | Title (A Side/B Side) | Yr | NM |
|---|---|---|---|
| ❑ SP-3145 | Cry Tough | 198? | 8.00 |
| *—Reissue of 4573* | | | |
| ❑ SP-3201 | The Best | 1982 | 10.00 |
| ❑ SP-3707 [(2)] | Night After Night | 1977 | 12.00 |
| ❑ SP-4509 | Nils Lofgren | 1975 | 10.00 |
| ❑ SP-4573 | Cry Tough | 1976 | 10.00 |
| ❑ SP-4628 | I Came to Dance | 1977 | 10.00 |
| ❑ SP-4756 | Nils | 1979 | 10.00 |
| ❑ SP-6509 [(2)] | Night After Night | 198? | 10.00 |
| *—Reissue of 3707* | | | |
| ❑ SP-8362 [DJ] | Authorized Bootleg | 1976 | 25.00 |

**BACKSTREET**

| Number | Title (A Side/B Side) | Yr | NM |
|---|---|---|---|
| ❑ 5251 | Night Fades Away | 1981 | 10.00 |
| ❑ 5421 | Wonderland | 1983 | 10.00 |

**COLUMBIA**

| Number | Title (A Side/B Side) | Yr | NM |
|---|---|---|---|
| ❑ BFC 39982 | Flip | 1985 | 10.00 |

## LOFTON, CLARENCE

**RIVERSIDE**

| Number | Title (A Side/B Side) | Yr | NM |
|---|---|---|---|
| ❑ RLP-1037 [10] | Honky-Tonk and Boogie-Woogie Piano | 1954 | 80.00 |

## LOFTON, TRICKY, AND CARMELL JONES

**PACIFIC JAZZ**

| Number | Title (A Side/B Side) | Yr | NM |
|---|---|---|---|
| ❑ PJ-49 [M] | Brass Bag | 1962 | 40.00 |
| ❑ ST-49 [S] | Brass Bag | 1962 | 50.00 |

## LOGAN, GIUSEPPI

**ESP-DISK'**

| Number | Title (A Side/B Side) | Yr | NM |
|---|---|---|---|
| ❑ S-1007 [S] | Giuseppi Logan Quartet | 1965 | 20.00 |
| ❑ S-1013 [S] | More Giuseppi Logan | 1965 | 20.00 |

## LOGGINS, KENNY

**COLUMBIA**

| Number | Title (A Side/B Side) | Yr | NM |
|---|---|---|---|
| ❑ AS 569 [DJ] | Kenny Loggins Live | 1979 | 15.00 |
| *—One-sided promo with three otherwise unavailable live recordings* | | | |
| ❑ AS 946 [DJ] | For Radio Only | 1980 | 15.00 |
| *—Promo-only four-song sampler from "Kenny Loggins Alive"* | | | |
| ❑ PC 34655 | Celebrate Me Home | 1977 | 10.00 |
| *—Originals have no bar code* | | | |
| ❑ PC 34655 | Celebrate Me Home | 1979 | 8.00 |
| *—Reissues have bar code* | | | |
| ❑ JC 35387 | Nightwatch | 1978 | 10.00 |
| *—Originals have no bar code* | | | |
| ❑ PC 35387 | Nightwatch | 198? | 8.00 |
| *—Reissue with new prefix* | | | |
| ❑ JC 36172 | Keep the Fire | 1979 | 10.00 |
| ❑ PC 36172 | Keep the Fire | 198? | 8.00 |
| *—Budget-line reissue* | | | |
| ❑ C2X 36738 [(2)] | Kenny Loggins Alive | 1980 | 12.00 |
| ❑ TC 38127 | High Adventure | 1982 | 10.00 |
| ❑ FC 39174 | Vox Humana | 1985 | 8.00 |
| ❑ OC 40535 | Back to Avalon | 1988 | 10.00 |
| ❑ HC 45387 | Nightwatch | 198? | 70.00 |
| *—Half-speed mastered edition* | | | |

## LOGGINS AND MESSINA

Also see KENNY LOGGINS; JIM MESSINA.

**COLUMBIA**

| Number | Title (A Side/B Side) | Yr | NM |
|---|---|---|---|
| ❑ C 31044 | Kenny Loggins with Jim Messina Sittin' In | 1972 | 10.00 |
| ❑ PC 31044 | Kenny Loggins with Jim Messina Sittin' In | 197? | 8.00 |
| *—Reissue with new prefix* | | | |
| ❑ CQ 31748 [Q] | Loggins and Messina | 1973 | 15.00 |
| ❑ KC 31748 | Loggins and Messina | 1972 | 10.00 |
| ❑ PC 31748 | Loggins and Messina | 197? | 8.00 |
| *—Reissue with new prefix* | | | |
| ❑ CQ 32540 [Q] | Full Sail | 1973 | 15.00 |
| ❑ KC 32540 | Full Sail | 1973 | 10.00 |
| ❑ PC 32540 | Full Sail | 197? | 8.00 |
| *—Reissue with new prefix* | | | |

| Number | Title (A Side/B Side) | Yr | NM |
|---|---|---|---|
| ❑ PG 32848 [(2)] | On Stage | 1974 | 12.00 |
| —Original with no bar code | | | |
| ❑ PG 32848 [(2)] | On Stage | 198? | 10.00 |
| —With bar code | | | |
| ❑ PC 33175 | Mother Lode | 1974 | 10.00 |
| —Original with no bar code | | | |
| ❑ PC 33175 | Mother Lode | 198? | 8.00 |
| —With bar code | | | |
| ❑ PC 33578 | Native Sons | 1976 | 10.00 |
| —Original with no bar code | | | |
| ❑ PC 33578 | Native Sons | 198? | 8.00 |
| —With bar code | | | |
| ❑ PCQ 33578 [Q] | Native Sons | 1976 | 15.00 |
| ❑ PC 33810 | So Fine | 1975 | 10.00 |
| —Original with no bar code | | | |
| ❑ PC 33810 | So Fine | 198? | 8.00 |
| —With bar code | | | |
| ❑ JG 34167 [(2)] | Finale | 1977 | 12.00 |
| ❑ PC 34388 | The Best of Friends | 1976 | 10.00 |
| —Original with no bar code | | | |
| ❑ PC 34388 | The Best of Friends | 198? | 8.00 |
| —With bar code | | | |
| ❑ HC 44388 | The Best of Friends | 1982 | 50.00 |
| —Half-speed mastered edition | | | |

DIRECT DISC

| Number | Title (A Side/B Side) | Yr | NM |
|---|---|---|---|
| ❑ SD 16606 | Full Sail | 198? | 30.00 |
| —Audiophile vinyl | | | |

EPIC

| Number | Title (A Side/B Side) | Yr | NM |
|---|---|---|---|
| ❑ PC 34388 | The Best of Friends | 1976 | 20.00 |
| —Mispressing with wrong label | | | |

### LOGSDON, JIMMIE

KING

| Number | Title (A Side/B Side) | Yr | NM |
|---|---|---|---|
| ❑ 843 [M] | Howdy Neighbors | 1963 | 60.00 |

### LOLITA

KAPP

| Number | Title (A Side/B Side) | Yr | NM |
|---|---|---|---|
| ❑ KL-1219 [M] | Sailor | 1961 | 25.00 |
| ❑ KL-1229 [M] | Songs You Will Never Forget | 1961 | 25.00 |
| ❑ KS-3219 [S] | Sailor | 1961 | 30.00 |
| ❑ KS-3229 [S] | Songs You Will Never Forget | 1961 | 30.00 |

### LOLLIPOP SHOPPE, THE

UNI

| Number | Title (A Side/B Side) | Yr | NM |
|---|---|---|---|
| ❑ 73019 | The Lollipop Shoppe | 1968 | 80.00 |

### LOMAX, JACKIE

APPLE

| Number | Title (A Side/B Side) | Yr | NM |
|---|---|---|---|
| ❑ ST-3354 | Is This What You Want? | 1969 | 25.00 |

CAPITOL

| Number | Title (A Side/B Side) | Yr | NM |
|---|---|---|---|
| ❑ ST-11558 | Livin' for Lovin' | 1976 | 10.00 |
| ❑ ST-11668 | Did You Ever | 1977 | 10.00 |

WARNER BROS.

| Number | Title (A Side/B Side) | Yr | NM |
|---|---|---|---|
| ❑ PRO 520 [DJ] | An Interview with Jackie Lomax | 1972 | 40.00 |
| ❑ WS 1914 | Home Is In My Head | 1971 | 12.00 |
| ❑ BS 2591 | Three | 1972 | 12.00 |

### LOMBARDO, GUY

CAPITOL

| Number | Title (A Side/B Side) | Yr | NM |
|---|---|---|---|
| ❑ STCL-578 [(3)] | Guy Lombardo | 1970 | 25.00 |
| ❑ W 738 [M] | Lombardo in Hi-Fi | 1956 | 20.00 |
| —Gray label | | | |
| ❑ T 739 [M] | Your Guy Lombardo Medley | 1956 | 20.00 |
| —Turquoise label | | | |
| ❑ T 788 [M] | A Decade on Broadway 1946-56 | 1956 | 20.00 |
| —Turquoise label | | | |
| ❑ T 892 [M] | Lively Guy | 1957 | 20.00 |
| —Turquoise label | | | |
| ❑ T 916 [M] | A Decade on Broadway 1935-45 | 1958 | 20.00 |
| —Turquoise label | | | |
| ❑ ST 1019 [S] | Berlin by Lombardo | 1959 | 25.00 |
| —Black colorband label, logo at left | | | |
| ❑ T 1019 [M] | Berlin by Lombardo | 1958 | 20.00 |
| —Turquoise or gray label | | | |
| ❑ ST 1121 [S] | Dancing Room Only | 1959 | 20.00 |
| —Black colorband label, logo at left | | | |
| ❑ ST 1244 [S] | Your Guy Lombardo Medley, Vol. 2 | 1960 | 20.00 |
| —Black colorband label, logo at left | | | |
| ❑ ST 1306 [S] | The Sweetest Waltzes This Side of Heaven | 1960 | 20.00 |
| —Black colorband label, logo at left | | | |
| ❑ ST 1393 [S] | Guy Lombardo at Harrah's Club | 1960 | 20.00 |
| ❑ T 1393 [M] | Guy Lombardo at Harrah's Club | 1960 | 15.00 |
| ❑ SKAO 1443 [S] | Sing the Songs of Christmas | 1960 | 20.00 |
| —Black colorband label, logo at left | | | |
| ❑ T 1461 [M] | The Best of Guy Lombardo | 1961 | 20.00 |
| —Black colorband label, logo at left | | | |
| ❑ ST 1593 [S] | Drifting and Dreaming | 1961 | 20.00 |
| —Black colorband label, logo at left | | | |
| ❑ ST 1598 [S] | Your Guy Lombardo Medley, Vol. 3 | 1961 | 20.00 |
| —Black colorband label, logo at left | | | |
| ❑ STDL 2181 [(4)S] | The Lombardo Years | 1964 | 30.00 |
| ❑ TDL 2181 [(4)M] | The Lombardo Years | 1964 | 25.00 |

DECCA

| Number | Title (A Side/B Side) | Yr | NM |
|---|---|---|---|
| ❑ DXB 185 [(2)M] | The Best of Guy Lombardo | 1964 | 20.00 |
| ❑ DL 5002 [10] | The Twin Pianos — Vol. 1 | 195? | 30.00 |
| —Record has "DL" prefix; sleeve may or may not have "DL" | | | |
| ❑ DLP 5002 [10] | The Twin Pianos — Vol. 1 | 1949 | 40.00 |
| —Both record and sleeve have "DLP" prefix | | | |
| ❑ DL 5003 [10] | The Twin Pianos — Vol. 2 | 195? | 30.00 |
| —Record has "DL" prefix; sleeve may or may not have "DL" | | | |
| ❑ DLP 5003 [10] | The Twin Pianos — Vol. 2 | 1949 | 40.00 |
| —Both record and sleeve have "DLP" prefix | | | |
| ❑ DL 5024 [10] | Sidewalks of New York | 1949 | 40.00 |
| ❑ DL 5041 [10] | Lombardoland | 1949 | 40.00 |
| ❑ DL 5097 [10] | Song Hits from Broadway Shows | 1949 | 40.00 |
| ❑ DL 5127 [10] | Latin Rhythms | 195? | 30.00 |
| ❑ DL 5156 [10] | Hawaiian Songs | 1950 | 30.00 |
| ❑ DL 5193 [10] | Waltzes | 195? | 30.00 |
| ❑ DL 5235 [10] | Silver Jubilee — 1925-1950 | 1950 | 30.00 |
| ❑ DL 5277 [10] | Square Dances (Without Calls) | 195? | 30.00 |
| ❑ DL 5322 [10] | Souvenirs | 195? | 30.00 |
| ❑ DL 5325 [10] | Waltzland | 195? | 30.00 |
| ❑ DL 5328 [10] | Lombardoland, Vol. 2 | 195? | 30.00 |
| ❑ DL 5329 [10] | Enjoy Yourself | 195? | 30.00 |
| ❑ DL 5330 [10] | The Sweetest Music This Side of Heaven | 195? | 30.00 |
| ❑ DL 5430 [10] | Jingle Bells | 1952 | 30.00 |
| ❑ DL 5434 [10] | Everybody Dance to the Music of Guy Lombardo | 1952 | 30.00 |
| ❑ DL 5447 [10] | Twin Piano Magic | 195? | 30.00 |
| ❑ DL 8070 [M] | A Night at the Roosevelt | 195? | 20.00 |
| —Black label, silver print | | | |
| ❑ DL 8097 [M] | Lombardoland, U.S.A. | 195? | 20.00 |
| —Black label, silver print | | | |
| ❑ DL 8119 [M] | Twin Pianos | 195? | 20.00 |
| —Black label, silver print | | | |
| ❑ DL 8135 [M] | Soft and Sweet | 1955 | 20.00 |
| —Black label, silver print | | | |
| ❑ DL 8136 [M] | Enjoy Yourself | 1955 | 20.00 |
| —Black label, silver print | | | |
| ❑ DL 8205 [M] | Waltz Time | 1955 | 20.00 |
| —Black label, silver print | | | |
| ❑ DL 8208 [M] | The Band Played On | 1955 | 20.00 |
| —Black label, silver print | | | |
| ❑ DL 8249 [M] | Lombardoland | 1956 | 20.00 |
| —Black label, silver print | | | |
| ❑ DL 8251 [M] | Twin Piano Magic | 1956 | 20.00 |
| —Black label, silver print | | | |
| ❑ DL 8254 [M] | Everybody Dance | 1956 | 20.00 |
| —Black label, silver print | | | |
| ❑ DL 8255 [M] | Oh! How We Danced | 1956 | 20.00 |
| —Black label, silver print | | | |
| ❑ DL 8256 [M] | Waltzland | 1956 | 20.00 |
| —Black label, silver print | | | |
| ❑ DL 8333 [M] | Silver Jubilee | 1956 | 20.00 |
| —Black label, silver print | | | |
| ❑ DL 8354 [M] | Jingle Bells | 1956 | 20.00 |
| —Black label, silver print | | | |
| ❑ DL 8843 [M] | Instrumentally Yours | 1959 | 20.00 |
| —Black label, silver print | | | |
| ❑ DL 8894 [M] | The Sidewalks of New York | 1959 | 20.00 |
| —Black label, silver print | | | |
| ❑ DL 78962 [S] | The Sweetest Music This Side of Heaven (A Musical Biography 1926-1932) | 1960 | 20.00 |
| —Black label, silver print | | | |

### LONDON, JULIE

LIBERTY

| Number | Title (A Side/B Side) | Yr | NM |
|---|---|---|---|
| ❑ MCR-1 [M] | By Myself | 196? | 25.00 |
| —Columbia Record Club exclusive | | | |
| ❑ SCR-1 [S] | By Myself | 196? | 30.00 |
| —Columbia Record Club exclusive | | | |
| ❑ LRP-3006 [M] | Julie Is Her Name | 1956 | 50.00 |
| —Green label | | | |
| ❑ LRP-3006 [M] | Julie Is Her Name | 1960 | 20.00 |
| —Black label, colorband and logo at left | | | |
| ❑ LRP-3012 [M] | Lonely Girl | 1956 | 50.00 |
| —Green label | | | |
| ❑ LRP-3012 [M] | Lonely Girl | 1960 | 20.00 |
| —Black label, colorband and logo at left | | | |
| ❑ LRP-3043 [M] | About the Blues | 1957 | 40.00 |
| —Green label | | | |
| ❑ LRP-3043 [M] | About the Blues | 1960 | 20.00 |
| —Black label, colorband and logo at left | | | |
| ❑ LRP-3060 [M] | Make Love to Me | 1957 | 40.00 |
| —Green label | | | |
| ❑ LRP-3060 [M] | Make Love to Me | 1960 | 20.00 |
| —Black label, colorband and logo at left | | | |
| ❑ LRP-3096 [M] | Julie | 1957 | 40.00 |
| —Green label | | | |
| ❑ LRP-3100 [M] | Julie Is Her Name, Volume 2 | 1958 | 40.00 |
| —Green label | | | |
| ❑ LRP-3100 [M] | Julie Is Her Name, Volume 2 | 1960 | 20.00 |
| —Black label, colorband and logo at left | | | |
| ❑ LRP-3105 [M] | London By Night | 1958 | 30.00 |
| —Green label | | | |
| ❑ LRP-3119 [M] | Swing Me an Old Song | 1959 | 30.00 |
| —Green label | | | |
| ❑ LRP-3130 [M] | Your Number Please | 1959 | 30.00 |
| —Green label | | | |
| ❑ LRP-3130 [M] | Your Number Please | 1960 | 20.00 |
| —Black label, colorband and logo at left | | | |
| ❑ LRP-3152 [M] | Julie…At Home | 1960 | 30.00 |
| ❑ LRP-3164 [M] | Around Midnight | 1960 | 30.00 |
| ❑ LRP-3171 [M] | Send for Me | 1961 | 30.00 |
| ❑ LRP-3192 [M] | Whatever Julie Wants | 1961 | 30.00 |
| ❑ LRP-3203 [M] | Sophisticated Lady | 1962 | 25.00 |
| ❑ LRP-3231 [M] | Love Letters | 1962 | 25.00 |
| ❑ LRP-3249 [M] | Love on the Rocks | 1963 | 25.00 |
| ❑ LRP-3278 [M] | Latin in a Satin Mood | 1963 | 25.00 |
| ❑ LRP-3291 [M] | Julie's Golden Greats | 1963 | 25.00 |
| —Black cover | | | |
| ❑ LRP-3291 [M] | Julie's Golden Greats | 1963 | 25.00 |
| —White cover | | | |
| ❑ LRP-3300 [M] | The End of the World | 1963 | 25.00 |
| ❑ LRP-3324 [M] | The Wonderful World of Julie London | 1963 | 25.00 |
| ❑ LRP-3342 [M] | Julie London | 1964 | 25.00 |
| ❑ LRP-3375 [M] | Julie London In Person at the Americana | 1964 | 25.00 |
| ❑ LRP-3392 [M] | Our Fair Lady | 1965 | 25.00 |
| ❑ LRP-3416 [M] | Feeling Good | 1965 | 25.00 |
| ❑ LRP-3434 [M] | All Through the Night | 1965 | 25.00 |
| ❑ LRP-3478 [M] | For the Night People | 1966 | 25.00 |
| ❑ LRP-3493 [M] | Nice Girls Don't Stay for Breakfast | 1967 | 25.00 |
| ❑ LRP-3514 [M] | With Body and Soul | 1967 | 30.00 |
| ❑ L-5501 [M] | The Best of Julie London | 1962 | 30.00 |
| ❑ S-6601 [S] | The Best of Julie London | 1962 | 40.00 |
| ❑ LST-7004 [S] | Julie | 1958 | 70.00 |
| —Black label, silver print | | | |
| ❑ LST-7012 [S] | About the Blues | 1958 | 70.00 |
| —Black label, silver print | | | |
| ❑ LST-7012 [S] | About the Blues | 1960 | 25.00 |
| —Black label, colorband and logo at left | | | |
| ❑ LST-7027 [S] | Julie Is Her Name | 1958 | 40.00 |
| —Black label, silver print | | | |
| ❑ LST-7027 [S] | Julie Is Her Name | 1958 | 100.00 |
| —Blue vinyl | | | |
| ❑ LST-7027 [S] | Julie Is Her Name | 1958 | 100.00 |
| —Red vinyl | | | |
| ❑ LST-7027 [S] | Julie Is Her Name | 1960 | 25.00 |
| —Black label, colorband and logo at left | | | |
| ❑ LST-7029 [S] | Lonely Girl | 1958 | 40.00 |
| —Black label, silver print | | | |
| ❑ LST-7029 [S] | Lonely Girl | 1960 | 25.00 |
| —Black label, colorband and logo at left | | | |
| ❑ LST-7060 [S] | Make Love to Me | 1958 | 40.00 |
| —Black label, silver print | | | |
| ❑ LST-7060 [S] | Make Love to Me | 1960 | 25.00 |
| —Black label, colorband and logo at left | | | |
| ❑ LST-7100 [S] | Julie Is Her Name, Volume 2 | 1958 | 40.00 |
| —Black label, silver print | | | |
| ❑ LST-7100 [S] | Julie Is Her Name, Volume 2 | 1960 | 25.00 |
| —Black label, colorband and logo at left | | | |
| ❑ LST-7105 [S] | London By Night | 1958 | 40.00 |
| —Black label, silver print | | | |
| ❑ LST-7119 [S] | Swing Me an Old Song | 1959 | 40.00 |
| —Black label, silver print | | | |
| ❑ LST-7130 [S] | Your Number Please | 1959 | 40.00 |
| —Black label, silver print | | | |
| ❑ LST-7130 [S] | Your Number Please | 1960 | 25.00 |
| —Black label, colorband and logo at left | | | |
| ❑ LST-7152 [S] | Julie…At Home | 1960 | 40.00 |
| —Black vinyl | | | |
| ❑ LST-7152 [S] | Julie…At Home | 1960 | 100.00 |
| —Blue vinyl | | | |
| ❑ LST-7164 [S] | Around Midnight | 1960 | 40.00 |
| ❑ LST-7171 [S] | Send for Me | 1961 | 40.00 |
| ❑ LST-7192 [S] | Whatever Julie Wants | 1961 | 40.00 |
| ❑ LST-7203 [S] | Sophisticated Lady | 1962 | 30.00 |
| ❑ LST-7231 [S] | Love Letters | 1962 | 30.00 |
| ❑ LST-7249 [S] | Love on the Rocks | 1963 | 30.00 |
| ❑ LST-7278 [S] | Latin in a Satin Mood | 1963 | 30.00 |
| ❑ LST-7291 [S] | Julie's Golden Greats | 1963 | 30.00 |
| —Black cover | | | |
| ❑ LST-7291 [S] | Julie's Golden Greats | 1963 | 30.00 |
| —White cover | | | |
| ❑ LST-7300 [S] | The End of the World | 1963 | 30.00 |
| ❑ LST-7324 [S] | The Wonderful World of Julie London | 1963 | 30.00 |
| ❑ LST-7342 [S] | Julie London | 1964 | 30.00 |
| ❑ LST-7375 [S] | Julie London In Person at the Americana | 1964 | 30.00 |
| ❑ LST-7392 [S] | Our Fair Lady | 1965 | 30.00 |
| ❑ LST-7416 [S] | Feeling Good | 1965 | 30.00 |
| ❑ LST-7434 [S] | All Through the Night | 1965 | 30.00 |
| ❑ LST-7478 [S] | For the Night People | 1966 | 30.00 |
| ❑ LST-7493 [S] | Nice Girls Don't Stay for Breakfast | 1967 | 25.00 |
| ❑ LST-7514 [S] | With Body and Soul | 1967 | 25.00 |
| ❑ LST-7546 | Easy Does It | 1968 | 20.00 |
| ❑ LST-7609 | Yummy, Yummy, Yummy | 1969 | 20.00 |
| ❑ SL-9002 [M] | Calendar Girl | 1956 | 100.00 |

SUNSET

| Number | Title (A Side/B Side) | Yr | NM |
|---|---|---|---|
| ❑ SUM-1104 [M] | Julie London | 196? | 12.00 |
| ❑ SUM-1161 [M] | Soft and Sweet | 196? | 12.00 |
| ❑ SUS-5104 [S] | Julie London | 196? | 15.00 |
| ❑ SUS-5161 [S] | Soft and Sweet | 196? | 15.00 |
| ❑ SUS-5207 | Gone with the Wind | 196? | 12.00 |

UNITED ARTISTS

| Number | Title (A Side/B Side) | Yr | NM |
|---|---|---|---|
| ❑ UA-LA437-E | The Very Best of Julie London | 1975 | 12.00 |

### LONDON, LAURIE

CAPITOL

| Number | Title (A Side/B Side) | Yr | NM |
|---|---|---|---|
| ❑ T 10169 [M] | England's 14 Year Old Singing Sensation — Laurie London | 1958 | 50.00 |

**LONDON POPS ORCHESTRA (FREDERICK FENNELL, CONDUCTOR)**

MERCURY LIVING PRESENCE

❑ SR 90439 [S] Coates: Three Elizabeths; London Suite; Four Ways Suite 1965 20.00
*—Maroon label, with "Vendor: Mercury Record Corporation"*

**LONDON PROMS SYMPHONY ORCHESTRA (RAYMOND AGOULT, CONDUCTOR)**

RCA VICTOR RED SEAL

❑ LSC-2326 [S] Clair de Lune 1960 220.00
*—Original with "shaded dog" label*
❑ LSC-2326 [S] Clair de Lune 199? 25.00
*—Classic Records reissue*

**LONDON PROMS SYMPHONY ORCHESTRA (CHARLES MACKERRAS, CONDUCTOR)**

RCA VICTOR RED SEAL

❑ LSC-2336 [S] Sibelius: Finlandia 1960 40.00
*—Original with "shaded dog" label*
❑ LSC-2336 [S] Sibelius: Finlandia 199? 25.00
*—Classic Records reissue*

**LONDON PROMS SYMPHONY ORCHESTRA (ROBERT SHARPLES, CONDUCTOR)**

RCA VICTOR RED SEAL

❑ LSC-2299 [S] Lehar: Waltzes 1959 25.00
*—Original with "shaded dog" label*

**LONDON SOUND 70 ORCHESTRA AND CHORUS**

DECCA

❑ DEB 7-7 [(3)] The Sounds of Christmas 1970 25.00

**LONDON SYMPHONY ORCHESTRA (ARTHUR BLISS, CONDUCTOR)**

RCA VICTOR RED SEAL

❑ LSC-2257 [S] Elgar: Pomp and Circumstance Marches 1-5 1959 100.00
*—Original with "shaded dog" label*

**LONDON SYMPHONY ORCHESTRA (ANTAL DORATI, CONDUCTOR)**

MERCURY LIVING PRESENCE

❑ SR 90006 [S] Prokofiev: Love for Three Oranges Suite; Scythian Suite 195? 300.00
❑ SR 90006 [S] Prokofiev: Love for Three Oranges Suite; Scythian Suite 199? 25.00
*—Classic Records reissue*
❑ SR 90122 [S] Borodin: Polovetsian Dances; Rimsky-Korsakov: Coq d-Or 1960 25.00
*—Maroon label, no "Vendor: Mercury Record Corporation"*
❑ SR 90123 [S] Mendelssohn: Symphony No. 3; Fingel's Cave Overture 1960 40.00
*—Maroon label, no "Vendor: Mercury Record Corporation"*
❑ SR 90153 [S] Respighi: The Birds; Brazilian Impressions 196? 50.00
*—Maroon label, with "Vendor: Mercury Record Corporation"*
❑ SR 90153 [S] Respighi: The Birds; Brazilian Impressions 196? 200.00
*—Maroon label, no "Vendor: Mercury Record Corporation"*
❑ SR 90154 [S] Brahms: Haydn Variations; Hungarian Dances 196? 30.00
*—Maroon label, no "Vendor: Mercury Record Corporation"*
❑ SR 90155 [S] Haydn: Symphonies 100 and 101 196? 100.00
*—Maroon label, no "Vendor: Mercury Record Corporation"*
❑ SR 90156 [S] Verdi: Overtures 196? 20.00
*—Maroon label, no "Vendor: Mercury Record Corporation"*
❑ SR 90158 [S] Handel-Harty: Water Music Suite; Royal Fireworks Music 196? 50.00
*—Maroon label, no "Vendor: Mercury Record Corporation"*
❑ SR 90209 [S] Khachaturian: Gayne Ballet Suite; Tchaikovsky: Romeo and Juliet 196? 30.00
*—Maroon label, no "Vendor: Mercury Record Corporation"*
❑ SR 90209 [S] Khachaturian: Gayne Ballet Suite; Tchaikovsky: Romeo and Juliet 196? 30.00
*—Maroon label, with "Vendor: Mercury Record Corporation"*
❑ SR 90214 [S] Lizst: Les Preludes; Smetana: The Moldau; Mussorgsky: Night on Bald Mountain; Sibelius: Valse Triste 196? 40.00
*—Maroon label, no "Vendor: Mercury Record Corporation"*
❑ SR 90226 [S] Stravinsky: The Firebird 196? 25.00
*—Third edition: Dark red (not maroon) label*
❑ SR 90226 [S] Stravinsky: The Firebird 196? 30.00
*—Maroon label, with "Vendor: Mercury Record Corporation"*
❑ SR 90226 [S] Stravinsky: The Firebird 196? 250.00
*—Maroon label, no "Vendor: Mercury Record Corporation"*
❑ SR 90226 [S] Stravinsky: The Firebird 199? 25.00
*—Classic Records reissue*
❑ SR 90234 [S] Wagner: Tristan und Isolde Prelude and Liebestod; Tannhauser Overture; Lohengrin Prelude 196? 25.00
*—Maroon label, no "Vendor: Mercury Record Corporation"*
❑ SR 90235 [S] Liszt: Hungarian Rhapsodies No. 2 and 3; Enescu: Rumanian Rhapsodies No. 1 and 2 196? 20.00
*—Third edition: Dark red (not maroon) label*
❑ SR 90235 [S] Liszt: Hungarian Rhapsodies No. 2 and 3; Enescu: Rumanian Rhapsodies No. 1 and 2 196? 60.00
*—Maroon label, no "Vendor: Mercury Record Corporation"*
❑ SR 90235 [S] Liszt: Hungarian Rhapsodies No. 2 and 3; Enescu: Rumanian Rhapsodies No. 1 and 2 196? 60.00
*—Maroon label, with "Vendor: Mercury Record Corporation"*
❑ SR 90236 [S] Dvorak: Symphony No. 4 (8) in G; Carnaval Overture 196? 120.00
*—Maroon label, no "Vendor: Mercury Record Corporation"*
❑ SR 90246 [S] Copland: Appalachian Spring; Billy the Kid 196? 20.00
*—Third edition: Dark red (not maroon) label*
❑ SR 90246 [S] Copland: Appalachian Spring; Billy the Kid 196? 80.00
*—Maroon label, no "Vendor: Mercury Record Corporation"*
❑ SR 90246 [S] Copland: Appalachian Spring; Billy the Kid 196? 80.00
*—Maroon label, with "Vendor: Mercury Record Corporation"*
❑ SR 90255 [S] Tchaikovsky: Symphony No. 5 196? 150.00
*—Maroon label, no "Vendor: Mercury Record Corporation"*
❑ SR 90265 [S] Rimsky-Korsakov: Capriccio Espagnol; Russian Easter Overture; Borodin: Prince Igor Overture 196? 50.00
*—Maroon label, no "Vendor: Mercury Record Corporation"*
❑ SR 90268 [S] Brahms: Symphony No. 1 196? 50.00
*—Maroon label, no "Vendor: Mercury Record Corporation"*
❑ SR 90278 [S] Berg: Suites from Lulu and Wozzeck 196? 25.00
*—Maroon label, with "Vendor: Mercury Record Corporation"*
❑ SR 90278 [S] Berg: Suites from Lulu and Wozzeck 196? 60.00
*—Maroon label, no "Vendor: Mercury Record Corporation"*
❑ SR 90279 [S] Tchakiovsky: Symphony No. 4 in F 196? 300.00
*—Maroon label, no "Vendor: Mercury Record Corporation"*
❑ SR 90280 [S] Mozart: Symphony No. 40; Haydn: Symphony No. 45 196? 20.00
*—Maroon label, no "Vendor: Mercury Record Corporation"*
❑ SR 90287 [S] Wagner: Mesitersinger Prelude; Tannhauser Overture; Parsifal; Lohengrin Selections 196? 30.00
*—Maroon label, with "Vendor: Mercury Record Corporation"*
❑ SR 90287 [S] Wagner: Mesitersinger Prelude; Tannhauser Overture; Parsifal; Lohengrin Selections 196? 40.00
*—Maroon label, no "Vendor: Mercury Record Corporation"*
❑ SR 90311 [S] Bartok: Bluebeard's Castle 196? 20.00
*—Maroon label, no "Vendor: Mercury Record Corporation"*
❑ SR 90312 [S] Tchakovsky: Symphony No. 6 196? 50.00
*—Maroon label, no "Vendor: Mercury Record Corporation"*
❑ SR 90312 [S] Tchakovsky: Symphony No. 6 196? 50.00
*—Maroon label, with "Vendor: Mercury Record Corporation"*
❑ SR 90316 [S] Vienna 1908-1914 196? 120.00
*—Maroon label, with "Vendor: Mercury Record Corporation"*
❑ SR 90316 [S] Vienna 1908-1914 196? 200.00
*—Maroon label, no "Vendor: Mercury Record Corporation"*
❑ SR 90317 [S] Beethoven: Symphony No. 5; Egmont Overture; Consecration of the House Overture 196? 25.00
*—Maroon label, with "Vendor: Mercury Record Corporation"*
❑ SR 90317 [S] Beethoven: Symphony No. 5; Egmont Overture; Consecration of the House Overture 196? 80.00
*—Maroon label, no "Vendor: Mercury Record Corporation"*
❑ SR 90371 [S] Liszt: Hungarian Rhapsodies Nos. 1, 4, 5 and 6 196? 30.00
*—Third edition: Dark red (not maroon) label*
❑ SR 90371 [S] Liszt: Hungarian Rhapsodies Nos. 1, 4, 5 and 6 196? 60.00
*—Maroon label, with "Vendor: Mercury Record Corporation"*
❑ SR 90371 [S] Liszt: Hungarian Rhapsodies Nos. 1, 4, 5 and 6 196? 400.00
*—Maroon label, no "Vendor: Mercury Record Corporation"*
❑ SR 90378 [S] Bartok: Concerto for Orchestra 196? 400.00
*—Maroon label, no "Vendor: Mercury Record Corporation"*
❑ SR 90387 [S] Stravnisky: Song of the Nightingale; Fireworks; Scherzo; Four Etudes 196? 40.00
*—Maroon label, with "Vendor: Mercury Record Corporation"*
❑ SR 90387 [S] Stravnisky: Song of the Nightingale; Fireworks; Scherzo; Four Etudes 196? 100.00
*—Maroon label, no "Vendor: Mercury Record Corporation"*
❑ SR 90409 [S] Tchaikovsky: Rococo Variations; Saint-Saens: Cello Concerto No. 1 196? 40.00
*—Maroon label, with "Vendor: Mercury Record Corporation"*
❑ SR 90409 [S] Tchaikovsky: Rococo Variations; Saint-Saens: Cello Concerto No. 1 196? 100.00
*—Maroon label, no "Vendor: Mercury Record Corporation"*
❑ SR 90415 [S] Haydn: Symphony No. 100 in G; Beethoven: Symphony No. 6 in F 196? 20.00
*—Maroon label, no "Vendor: Mercury Record Corporation"*
❑ SR 90426 [S] Bartok: The Wooden Prince 196? 20.00
*—Maroon label, with "Vendor: Mercury Record Corporation"*
❑ SR 90426 [S] Bartok: The Wooden Prince 196? 40.00
*—Maroon label, no "Vendor: Mercury Record Corporation"*
❑ SR 90435 [S] Paris 1917-1938 196? 20.00
*—Maroon label, oval "Mercury" logo*
❑ SR 90435 [S] Paris 1917-1938 1965 100.00
*—Maroon label, with "Vendor: Mercury Record Corporation"*
❑ SR 90437 [S] Brahms: 16 Hungarian Dances 1965 20.00
*—Maroon label, with "Vendor: Mercury Record Corporation"*

**LONDON SYMPHONY ORCHESTRA (ALEXANDER GIBSON, CONDUCTOR)**

RCA VICTOR RED SEAL

❑ LSC-2405 [S] Sibelius: Symphony No. 5 1960 220.00
*—Original with "shaded dog" label*
❑ LSC-2405 [S] Sibelius: Symphony No. 5 199? 25.00
*—Classic Records reissue*

**LONDON SYMPHONY ORCHESTRA (JEAN MARTINON, CONDUCTOR)**

RCA VICTOR RED SEAL

❑ LSC-2298 [S] Borodin: Symphony No. 2; Rimsky-Korsakov: Capriccio Espagnole 1960 70.00
*—Original with "shaded dog" label*
❑ LSC-2298 [S] Borodin: Symphony No. 2; Rimsky-Korsakov: Capriccio Espagnole 199? 25.00
*—Classic Records reissue*
❑ LSC-2322 [S] Shostakovich: Symphony No. 1 1960 100.00
*—Original with "shaded dog" label*
❑ LSC-2322 [S] Shostakovich: Symphony No. 1 199? 25.00
*—Classic Records reissue*
❑ LSC-2419 [S] Dvorak: Slavonic Dances 1960 180.00
*—Original with "shaded dog" label*
❑ LSC-2419 [S] Dvorak: Slavonic Dances 199? 25.00
*—Classic Records reissue*

**LONDON SYMPHONY ORCHESTRA (PIERRE MONTEUX, CONDUCTOR)**

RCA VICTOR RED SEAL

❑ LSC-2177 [S] Tchaikovsky: Sleeping Beauty (Excerpts) 1959 25.00
*—Original with "shaded dog" label*
❑ LSC-2208 [S] Rimsky-Korsakov: Scheherazade 1959 30.00
*—Original with "shaded dog" label*
❑ LSC-2342 [S] Sibelius: Symphony No. 2 1960 20.00
*—Original with "shaded dog" label*
❑ LSC-2342 [S] Sibelius: Symphony No. 2 199? 25.00
*—Classic Records reissue*
❑ LSC-2418 [S] Elgar: Enigma Variations 1960 80.00
*—Original with "shaded dog" label*
❑ LSC-2418 [S] Elgar: Enigma Variations 199? 25.00
*—Classic Records reissue*
❑ LSC-2489 [S] Dvorak: Symphony No. 2 196? 25.00
*—Original with "shaded dog" label*
❑ LSC-2489 [S] Dvorak: Symphony No. 2 199? 25.00
*—Classic Records reissue*

**LONDON SYMPHONY ORCHESTRA (HANS SCHMIDT-ISSERSTEDT, CONDUCTOR)**

MERCURY LIVING PRESENCE

❑ SR 90184 [S] Mozart: Symphonies No. 39 and 41 196? 30.00
*—Maroon label, with "Vendor: Mercury Record Corporation"*
❑ SR 90184 [S] Mozart: Symphonies No. 39 and 41 196? 120.00
*—Maroon label, no "Vendor: Mercury Record Corporation"*

**LONDON SYMPHONY ORCHESTRA (WALTER SUSSKIND, HANS SCHMIDT-ISSERSTEDT, CONDUCTORS)**

MERCURY LIVING PRESENCE

❑ SR 90196 [S] Schubert: Symphonies No. 4 and 6 196? 20.00
*—Maroon label, no "Vendor: Mercury Record Corporation"*

**LONE STAR RAMBLERS, THE**

LONGHORN

❑ LP-600 [M] Texas Square Dancing with Red at the 60 Club 196? 25.00

**LONESOME BLUES SINGER, THE** See LEADBELLY.

**LONESOME PINE FIDDLERS, THE**

STARDAY

❑ SLP-155 [M] 14 Mountain Songs Featuring 5-String Banjo 1961 40.00
❑ SLP-194 [M] Bluegrass 1962 40.00
❑ SLP-222 [M] More Bluegrass 1963 40.00

## LONESOME RHODES

**RCA VICTOR**

| Number | Title (A Side/B Side) | Yr | NM |
|---|---|---|---|
| ❑ LPM-3759 [M] | Lonesome Rhodes | 1967 | 30.00 |
| ❑ LSP-3759 [S] | Lonesome Rhodes | 1967 | 20.00 |

## LONESOME SUNDOWN

**EXCELLO**

| Number | Title (A Side/B Side) | Yr | NM |
|---|---|---|---|
| ❑ LPS-8012 | Lonesome Lonely Blues | 1970 | 25.00 |

## LONG, BARBARA

**SAVOY**

| Number | Title (A Side/B Side) | Yr | NM |
|---|---|---|---|
| ❑ MG-12161 [M] | Soul | 1961 | 30.00 |

## LONG, DANNY

**CAPITOL**

| Number | Title (A Side/B Side) | Yr | NM |
|---|---|---|---|
| ❑ ST 1988 [S] | Jazz Furlough | 1963 | 20.00 |

## LONG, SHORTY (1) R&B singer.

**SOUL**

| Number | Title (A Side/B Side) | Yr | NM |
|---|---|---|---|
| ❑ SM-709 [M] | Here Comes the Judge | 1968 | 50.00 |
| *—Mono is white label promo only; mono sticker on stereo cover* | | | |
| ❑ SS-709 [S] | Here Comes the Judge | 1968 | 20.00 |
| ❑ SS-719 | The Prime of Shorty Long | 1969 | 15.00 |

## LONG, SHORTY (2) C&W singer.

**FORD**

| Number | Title (A Side/B Side) | Yr | NM |
|---|---|---|---|
| ❑ FXM-712 [M] | Country Jamboree | 1963 | 20.00 |

## LONGBRANCH PENNYWHISTLE

**AMOS**

| Number | Title (A Side/B Side) | Yr | NM |
|---|---|---|---|
| ❑ AAS-7007 | Longbranch Pennywhistle | 1969 | 50.00 |

## LONGMIRE, WILBERT

**PACIFIC JAZZ**

| Number | Title (A Side/B Side) | Yr | NM |
|---|---|---|---|
| ❑ ST-20161 | Revolution | 1969 | 20.00 |

## LONGO, MIKE

**GROOVE MERCHANT**

| Number | Title (A Side/B Side) | Yr | NM |
|---|---|---|---|
| ❑ 525 | Funkia | 1974 | 20.00 |

## LONZO AND OSCAR

**COLUMBIA**

| Number | Title (A Side/B Side) | Yr | NM |
|---|---|---|---|
| ❑ CS 9587 | Mountain Dew | 1968 | 20.00 |

**DECCA**

| Number | Title (A Side/B Side) | Yr | NM |
|---|---|---|---|
| ❑ DL 4363 [M] | Country Comedy Time | 1963 | 20.00 |

**STARDAY**

| Number | Title (A Side/B Side) | Yr | NM |
|---|---|---|---|
| ❑ SLP-119 [M] | America's Greatest Country Comedians | 1960 | 40.00 |
| ❑ SLP-244 [M] | Country Music Time | 1963 | 40.00 |

## LOOKOFSKY, HARRY

**ATLANTIC**

| Number | Title (A Side/B Side) | Yr | NM |
|---|---|---|---|
| ❑ 1319 [M] | Stringville | 1959 | 40.00 |
| *—Black label* | | | |
| ❑ 1319 [M] | Stringville | 1961 | 20.00 |
| *—Multicolor label, white "fan" logo at right* | | | |
| ❑ SD 1319 [S] | Stringville | 1959 | 40.00 |
| *—Green label* | | | |

## LOOSE

**NOCTURNE**

| Number | Title (A Side/B Side) | Yr | NM |
|---|---|---|---|
| ❑ 906 | Freaky Billie, The Wheelie King | 1970 | 30.00 |

## LOOSE FUR

**DRAG CITY**

| Number | Title (A Side/B Side) | Yr | NM |
|---|---|---|---|
| ❑ DC 203 | Loose Fur | 2003 | 25.00 |

## LOPEZ, TRINI

**CAPITOL**

| Number | Title (A Side/B Side) | Yr | NM |
|---|---|---|---|
| ❑ SK 11009 | Viva | 1972 | 10.00 |

**GUEST STAR**

| Number | Title (A Side/B Side) | Yr | NM |
|---|---|---|---|
| ❑ GS-1499 [M] | Trini Lopez and Scott Gregory | 1964 | 50.00 |
| *—"Scott Gregory" is said to be a pseudonym for BILL HALEY.* | | | |

**HARMONY**

| Number | Title (A Side/B Side) | Yr | NM |
|---|---|---|---|
| ❑ H 30012 | Bye Bye Love | 1970 | 10.00 |

**KING**

| Number | Title (A Side/B Side) | Yr | NM |
|---|---|---|---|
| ❑ 863 [M] | Teenage Love Songs | 1963 | 60.00 |
| ❑ 877 [M] | More of Trini Lopez | 1964 | 60.00 |
| ❑ 962 [M] | 24 Songs by the Great Trini Lopez | 1966 | 30.00 |

**REPRISE**

| Number | Title (A Side/B Side) | Yr | NM |
|---|---|---|---|
| ❑ R-6093 [M] | Trini Lopez at PJ's | 1963 | 12.00 |
| ❑ R9-6093 [S] | Trini Lopez at PJ's | 1963 | 15.00 |
| ❑ R-6103 [M] | More Trini Lopez at PJ's | 1963 | 12.00 |
| ❑ RS-6103 [S] | More Trini Lopez at PJ's | 1963 | 15.00 |
| ❑ R-6112 [M] | On the Move | 1964 | 12.00 |
| ❑ RS-6112 [S] | On the Move | 1964 | 15.00 |
| ❑ R-6125 [M] | The Latin Album | 1964 | 12.00 |
| ❑ RS-6125 [S] | The Latin Album | 1964 | 15.00 |
| ❑ R-6134 [M] | Live at Basin St. East | 1964 | 12.00 |
| ❑ RS-6134 [S] | Live at Basin St. East | 1964 | 15.00 |
| ❑ R-6147 [M] | The Folk Album | 1965 | 12.00 |
| ❑ RS-6147 [S] | The Folk Album | 1965 | 15.00 |
| ❑ R-6165 [M] | The Love Album | 1965 | 12.00 |
| ❑ RS-6165 [S] | The Love Album | 1965 | 15.00 |
| ❑ R-6171 [M] | The Rhythm & Blues Album | 1965 | 12.00 |
| ❑ RS-6171 [S] | The Rhythm & Blues Album | 1965 | 15.00 |
| ❑ R-6183 [M] | The Sing-Along World of Trini Lopez | 1965 | 12.00 |
| ❑ RS-6183 [S] | The Sing-Along World of Trini Lopez | 1965 | 15.00 |
| ❑ R-6196 [M] | Trini | 1966 | 12.00 |
| ❑ RS-6196 [S] | Trini | 1966 | 15.00 |
| ❑ R-6215 [M] | The Second Latin Album | 1966 | 12.00 |
| ❑ RS-6215 [S] | The Second Latin Album | 1966 | 15.00 |
| ❑ R-6226 [M] | Greatest Hits! | 1966 | 12.00 |
| ❑ RS-6226 [S] | Greatest Hits! | 1966 | 15.00 |
| ❑ R-6238 [M] | Trini Lopez in London | 1967 | 15.00 |
| ❑ RS-6238 [S] | Trini Lopez in London | 1967 | 12.00 |
| ❑ R-6255 [M] | Trini Lopez — Now! | 1967 | 15.00 |
| ❑ RS-6255 [S] | Trini Lopez — Now! | 1967 | 12.00 |
| ❑ R-6285 [M] | It's a Great Life | 1968 | 25.00 |
| *—Mono is white label promo only* | | | |
| ❑ RS-6285 [S] | It's a Great Life | 1968 | 12.00 |
| ❑ RS-6300 | Welcome to Trini Country | 1968 | 12.00 |
| ❑ RS-6337 | The Whole Enchilada | 1969 | 12.00 |
| ❑ RS-6361 | The Trini Lopez Show | 1970 | 15.00 |

**ROULETTE**

| Number | Title (A Side/B Side) | Yr | NM |
|---|---|---|---|
| ❑ 3020 | Transformed by Time | 1978 | 10.00 |

## LORD, BOBBY

**DECCA**

| Number | Title (A Side/B Side) | Yr | NM |
|---|---|---|---|
| ❑ DL 75246 | Bobby Lord | 1970 | 12.00 |

**HARMONY**

| Number | Title (A Side/B Side) | Yr | NM |
|---|---|---|---|
| ❑ HL 7322 [M] | Bobby Lord's Best | 1964 | 25.00 |

**HICKORY**

| Number | Title (A Side/B Side) | Yr | NM |
|---|---|---|---|
| ❑ LP-126 [M] | The Bobby Lord Show | 1965 | 20.00 |

## LORD SITAR

**CAPITOL**

| Number | Title (A Side/B Side) | Yr | NM |
|---|---|---|---|
| ❑ ST 2916 | Lord Sitar | 1968 | 30.00 |

## LOREN, DONNA

**CAPITOL**

| Number | Title (A Side/B Side) | Yr | NM |
|---|---|---|---|
| ❑ ST 2323 [S] | Beach Blanket Bingo | 1965 | 50.00 |
| ❑ T 2323 [M] | Beach Blanket Bingo | 1965 | 40.00 |

## LORING, GLORIA

**ATLANTIC**

| Number | Title (A Side/B Side) | Yr | NM |
|---|---|---|---|
| ❑ 81679 | Gloria Loring | 1986 | 8.00 |
| ❑ 81852 | Full Moon, No Hesitation | 1988 | 8.00 |

**MGM**

| Number | Title (A Side/B Side) | Yr | NM |
|---|---|---|---|
| ❑ SE-4499 | Today | 1968 | 20.00 |

## LOS ANGELES PHILHARMONIC (ZUBIN MEHTA, CONDUCTOR)

**MOBILE FIDELITY**

| Number | Title (A Side/B Side) | Yr | NM |
|---|---|---|---|
| ❑ 1-008 | Suites from "Star Wars" and "Close Encounters of the Third Kind" | 1979 | 50.00 |
| *—Audiophile vinyl* | | | |

## LOS BRAVOS Also see MIKE KENNEDY.

**PARROT**

| Number | Title (A Side/B Side) | Yr | NM |
|---|---|---|---|
| ❑ PAS 71021 | Bring a Little Lovin' | 1968 | 80.00 |
| *—Among the other tracks, "Black Is Black" in in true stereo.* | | | |

**PRESS**

| Number | Title (A Side/B Side) | Yr | NM |
|---|---|---|---|
| ❑ PR 73003 [M] | Black Is Black | 1966 | 50.00 |
| ❑ PRS 83003 [R] | Black Is Black | 1966 | 30.00 |

## LOS INDIOS TABAJARAS

**RCA CAMDEN**

| Number | Title (A Side/B Side) | Yr | NM |
|---|---|---|---|
| ❑ CXS-9031 [(2)] | Los Indios Tabajaras | 1973 | 15.00 |

**RCA INTERNATIONAL**

| Number | Title (A Side/B Side) | Yr | NM |
|---|---|---|---|
| ❑ IL5-7367 | Los Grandes Exitos | 198? | 12.00 |

**RCA VICTOR**

| Number | Title (A Side/B Side) | Yr | NM |
|---|---|---|---|
| ❑ AFL1-0210 | Favorite Movie Themes | 1977 | 10.00 |
| *—Reissue with new prefix* | | | |
| ❑ APL1-0210 | Favorite Movie Themes | 1973 | 12.00 |
| ❑ FSP-296 | Maria Elena | 1971 | 12.00 |
| ❑ FSP-300 | Siempre En Mi Corazon | 1972 | 12.00 |
| ❑ FSP-310 | Softly | 1972 | 12.00 |
| ❑ AFL1-0668 | Classical Guitars | 1977 | 10.00 |
| *—Reissue with new prefix* | | | |
| ❑ CPL1-0668 | Classical Guitars | 1974 | 12.00 |
| ❑ AFL1-1033 | Secret Love | 1977 | 10.00 |
| *—Reissue with new prefix* | | | |
| ❑ APL1-1033 | Secret Love | 1975 | 12.00 |
| ❑ ANL1-1179 | Maria Elena | 1976 | 10.00 |
| *—Reissue* | | | |
| ❑ LPM-1788 [M] | Sweet and Savage | 1958 | 40.00 |
| ❑ LSP-1788 [S] | Sweet and Savage | 1958 | 50.00 |
| ❑ APL1-2082 | Mellow Nostalgia | 1977 | 12.00 |
| ❑ ANL1-2321 | In a Sentimental Mood | 1977 | 10.00 |
| ❑ AFL1-2526 | Masterpieces | 1978 | 12.00 |
| ❑ LPM-2822 [M] | Maria Elena | 1963 | 20.00 |
| *—Reissue of LPM-1788* | | | |
| ❑ LSP-2822 [S] | Maria Elena | 1963 | 25.00 |
| *—Reissue of LSP-1788* | | | |
| ❑ AFL1-2912 | Always in My Heart | 1977 | 10.00 |
| *—Reissue with new prefix* | | | |
| ❑ LPM-2912 [M] | Always in My Heart | 1964 | 15.00 |
| ❑ LSP-2912 [S] | Always in My Heart | 1964 | 20.00 |
| ❑ LPM-2959 [M] | Twin Guitar Moods | 1964 | 15.00 |
| ❑ LSP-2959 [S] | Twin Guitar Moods | 1964 | 20.00 |
| ❑ AFL1-3241 | Two Guitars | 1979 | 10.00 |
| ❑ LPM-3413 [M] | Many-Splendored Guitars | 1965 | 15.00 |
| ❑ LSP-3413 [S] | Many-Splendored Guitars | 1965 | 20.00 |
| ❑ AFL1-3505 | Casually Classical | 1977 | 10.00 |
| *—Reissue with new prefix* | | | |
| ❑ LPM-3505 [M] | Casually Classical | 1966 | 15.00 |
| ❑ LSP-3505 [S] | Casually Classical | 1966 | 20.00 |
| ❑ AFL1-3535 | Rainbows | 1980 | 10.00 |
| ❑ LPM-3611 [M] | Twin Guitars — In a Mood for Lovers | 1966 | 15.00 |
| ❑ LSP-3611 [S] | Twin Guitars — In a Mood for Lovers | 1966 | 20.00 |
| ❑ LPM-3723 [M] | Their Very Special Touch | 1967 | 15.00 |
| ❑ LSP-3723 [S] | Their Very Special Touch | 1967 | 20.00 |
| ❑ LPM-3909 [M] | Fascinating Rhythms of Their Brazil | 1968 | 20.00 |
| ❑ LSP-3909 [S] | Fascinating Rhythms of Their Brazil | 1968 | 15.00 |
| ❑ AFL1-3990 | Beautiful Sounds | 1981 | 10.00 |
| ❑ AFL1-4007 | The Best of Los Indios Tabajaras | 1977 | 10.00 |
| *—Reissue with new prefix* | | | |
| ❑ LSP-4007 | The Best of Los Indios Tabajaras | 1968 | 15.00 |
| ❑ LSP-4013 | In a Sentimental Mood | 1968 | 15.00 |
| ❑ LSP-4129 | Song of the Islands | 1969 | 15.00 |
| ❑ AFL1-4273 | Music for Romance | 1982 | 10.00 |
| ❑ LSP-4365 | Dreams of Love | 1970 | 15.00 |
| ❑ LSP-4496 | The Very Thought of You | 1971 | 15.00 |
| ❑ LSP-4615 | What the World Needs Now | 1971 | 12.00 |
| ❑ AFL1-4649 | Guitars on the Go | 1983 | 10.00 |

## LOS LOBOS

**NEW VISTAS**

| Number | Title (A Side/B Side) | Yr | NM |
|---|---|---|---|
| ❑ 1001 | Just Another Band from East L.A. | 1978 | 250.00 |

**SLASH**

| Number | Title (A Side/B Side) | Yr | NM |
|---|---|---|---|
| ❑ 23963 [EP] | And a Time to Dance | 1983 | 12.00 |
| ❑ 25177 | How Will the Wolf Survive? | 1984 | 10.00 |
| ❑ 25523 | By the Light of the Moon | 1987 | 10.00 |
| ❑ 25790 | La Pistola y El Corazon | 1988 | 15.00 |
| ❑ 26131 | The Neighborhood | 1990 | 20.00 |
| ❑ R 144507 | By the Light of the Moon | 1987 | 12.00 |
| *—RCA Music Service edition* | | | |

## LOS LOCOS DEL RITMO

**DIMSA**

| Number | Title (A Side/B Side) | Yr | NM |
|---|---|---|---|
| ❑ 8178 | Rock! | 196? | 100.00 |

## LOS SEVEN DAYS

**ECO**

| Number | Title (A Side/B Side) | Yr | NM |
|---|---|---|---|
| ❑ 314 | Sha-La-La | 196? | 50.00 |

## LOST & FOUND

**INTERNATIONAL ARTISTS**

| Number | Title (A Side/B Side) | Yr | NM |
|---|---|---|---|
| ❑ IA-3 | Everybody's Here | 1968 | 100.00 |
| *—Original pressing, no "Masterfonics" in dead wax* | | | |
| ❑ IA-3 | Everybody's Here | 1979 | 15.00 |
| *—Reissue with "Masterfonics" in trail-off wax* | | | |

## LOST NATION, THE

**RARE EARTH**

| Number | Title (A Side/B Side) | Yr | NM |
|---|---|---|---|
| ❑ RS-518 | Paradise Lost | 1970 | 20.00 |

## LOTHAR AND THE HAND PEOPLE

**CAPITOL**

| Number | Title (A Side/B Side) | Yr | NM |
|---|---|---|---|
| ❑ ST-247 | Space Hymn | 1969 | 40.00 |
| ❑ SM-2997 | Presenting Lothar and the Hand People | 1977 | 8.00 |
| *—Reissue with new prefix* | | | |
| ❑ ST 2997 | Presenting Lothar and the Hand People | 1968 | 40.00 |

## LOUDERMILK, JOHN D.

**RCA VICTOR**

| Number | Title (A Side/B Side) | Yr | NM |
|---|---|---|---|
| ❑ LPM-2434 [M] | Language of Love | 1961 | 25.00 |
| ❑ LSP-2434 [S] | Language of Love | 1961 | 30.00 |
| ❑ LPM-2539 [M] | Twelve Sides of Loudermilk | 1962 | 20.00 |
| ❑ LSP-2539 [S] | Twelve Sides of Loudermilk | 1962 | 25.00 |
| ❑ LPM-3497 [M] | A Bizarre Collection of the Most Unusual Songs | 1965 | 20.00 |
| ❑ LSP-3497 [S] | A Bizarre Collection of the Most Unusual Songs | 1965 | 25.00 |
| ❑ LPM-3807 [M] | Suburban Attitudes in Country Music | 1967 | 25.00 |
| ❑ LSP-3807 [S] | Suburban Attitudes in Country Music | 1967 | 20.00 |
| ❑ LSP-4040 | Country Love Songs | 1968 | 20.00 |
| ❑ LSP-4097 | The Open Mind of John D. Loudermilk | 1968 | 20.00 |

**WARNER BROS.**

| Number | Title (A Side/B Side) | Yr | NM |
|---|---|---|---|
| ❑ WS 1922 | Volume 1, Elloree | 1971 | 15.00 |

| Number | Title (A Side/B Side) | Yr | NM |
|---|---|---|---|

### LOUDON, DOROTHY

CORAL

| Number | Title | Yr | NM |
|---|---|---|---|
| ❑ CRL 57265 [M] | At the Blue Angel | 1959 | 20.00 |
| ❑ CRL 757265 [S] | At the Blue Angel | 1959 | 25.00 |

### LOUIE AND THE LOVERS

EPIC

| Number | Title | Yr | NM |
|---|---|---|---|
| ❑ E 30026 | Rise | 1970 | 20.00 |

### LOUISE, TINA

CONCERT HALL

| Number | Title | Yr | NM |
|---|---|---|---|
| ❑ H-1503 [M] | Her Portrait in Hi-Fi | 1958 | 50.00 |
| ❑ H-1521 [M] | It's Time for Tina | 1958 | 200.00 |

URANIA

| Number | Title | Yr | NM |
|---|---|---|---|
| ❑ ULM-2005 [M] | It's Time for Tina | 1959 | 200.00 |
| ❑ USD-2005 [S] | It's Time for Tina | 1959 | 300.00 |

### LOUISIANA HONEY DRIPPERS, THE

PRESTIGE

| Number | Title | Yr | NM |
|---|---|---|---|
| ❑ PR-13035 [M] | Bluegrass | 1961 | 25.00 |

### LOUISIANA RED

ROULETTE

| Number | Title | Yr | NM |
|---|---|---|---|
| ❑ R-25200 [M] | The Lowdown Back Porch Blues | 1963 | 40.00 |

### LOUSSIER, JACQUES

LONDON

| Number | Title | Yr | NM |
|---|---|---|---|
| ❑ PS 454/5 [(2)S] | Bach Jazz | 1965 | 20.00 |

### LOUVIN, CHARLIE

Also see JIM AND JESSE; THE LOUVIN BROTHERS.

CAPITOL

| Number | Title | Yr | NM |
|---|---|---|---|
| ❑ ST-142 | Hey Daddy | 1969 | 20.00 |
| ❑ ST-8-0142 | Hey Daddy | 1969 | 25.00 |
| *—Capitol Record Club edition* | | | |
| ❑ ST-248 | The Kind of Man I Am | 1969 | 20.00 |
| ❑ ST-416 | Here's a Toast to Mama | 1970 | 20.00 |
| ❑ ST-555 | Ten Times Charlie | 1970 | 20.00 |
| ❑ ST 2208 [S] | Less and Less and I Don't Love You Anymore | 1965 | 25.00 |
| ❑ T 2208 [M] | Less and Less and I Don't Love You Anymore | 1965 | 20.00 |
| ❑ ST 2437 [S] | The Many Moods of Charlie Louvin | 1966 | 25.00 |
| ❑ T 2437 [M] | The Many Moods of Charlie Louvin | 1966 | 20.00 |
| ❑ ST 2482 [S] | Lonesome Is Me | 1966 | 25.00 |
| ❑ T 2482 [M] | Lonesome Is Me | 1966 | 20.00 |
| ❑ ST 2689 [S] | I'll Remember Always | 1967 | 20.00 |
| ❑ T 2689 [M] | I'll Remember Always | 1967 | 25.00 |
| ❑ ST 2787 [S] | I Forgot to Cry | 1967 | 20.00 |
| ❑ T 2787 [M] | I Forgot to Cry | 1967 | 25.00 |
| ❑ ST 2958 | Will You Visit Me on Sundays | 1968 | 20.00 |

UNITED ARTISTS

| Number | Title | Yr | NM |
|---|---|---|---|
| ❑ UA-LA248-G | It Almost Felt Like Love | 1974 | 15.00 |

### LOUVIN, CHARLIE, AND MELBA MONTGOMERY

CAPITOL

| Number | Title | Yr | NM |
|---|---|---|---|
| ❑ ST-686 | Somethin' to Brag About | 1971 | 20.00 |
| ❑ ST-808 | Baby, You've Got What It Takes | 1971 | 20.00 |

### LOUVIN, IRA

Also see THE LOUVIN BROTHERS.

CAPITOL

| Number | Title | Yr | NM |
|---|---|---|---|
| ❑ ST 2413 [S] | The Unforgettable Ira Louvin | 1965 | 30.00 |
| ❑ T 2413 [M] | The Unforgettable Ira Louvin | 1965 | 25.00 |

### LOUVIN BROTHERS, THE

Also see CHARLIE LOUVIN; IRA LOUVIN.

CAPITOL

| Number | Title | Yr | NM |
|---|---|---|---|
| ❑ DT 769 [R] | Tragic Songs of Life | 196? | 20.00 |
| ❑ T 769 [M] | Tragic Songs of Life | 1956 | 100.00 |
| *—Turquoise label* | | | |
| ❑ T 769 [M] | Tragic Songs of Life | 1959 | 40.00 |
| *—Black colorband label, logo at left* | | | |
| ❑ T 769 [M] | Tragic Songs of Life | 1962 | 25.00 |
| *—Black colorband label, logo at top* | | | |
| ❑ T 825 [M] | Nearer My God to Thee | 1957 | 100.00 |
| *—Turquoise label* | | | |
| ❑ T 825 [M] | Nearer My God to Thee | 1959 | 40.00 |
| *—Black colorband label, logo at left* | | | |
| ❑ T 825 [M] | Nearer My God to Thee | 1962 | 25.00 |
| *—Black colorband label, logo at top* | | | |
| ❑ T 910 [M] | Ira and Charlie | 1958 | 100.00 |
| *—Turquoise label* | | | |
| ❑ T 910 [M] | Ira and Charlie | 1959 | 40.00 |
| *—Black colorband label, logo at left* | | | |
| ❑ T 910 [M] | Ira and Charlie | 1962 | 25.00 |
| *—Black colorband label, logo at top* | | | |
| ❑ DT 1061 [R] | The Family Who Prays | 196? | 20.00 |
| ❑ T 1061 [M] | The Family Who Prays | 1958 | 80.00 |
| *—Black colorband label, logo at left* | | | |
| ❑ T 1061 [M] | The Family Who Prays | 1962 | 25.00 |
| *—Black colorband label, logo at top* | | | |
| ❑ T 1106 [M] | Country Love Ballads | 1959 | 80.00 |
| *—Black colorband label, logo at left* | | | |
| ❑ T 1106 [M] | Country Love Ballads | 1962 | 25.00 |
| *—Black colorband label, logo at top* | | | |
| ❑ T 1277 [M] | Satan Is Real | 1960 | 80.00 |
| *—Black colorband label, logo at left* | | | |
| ❑ T 1277 [M] | Satan Is Real | 1962 | 25.00 |
| *—Black colorband label, logo at top* | | | |
| ❑ T 1385 [M] | My Baby's Gone | 1960 | 80.00 |
| *—Black colorband label, logo at left* | | | |
| ❑ T 1385 [M] | My Baby's Gone | 1962 | 25.00 |
| *—Black colorband label, logo at top* | | | |
| ❑ T 1449 [M] | A Tribute to the Delmore Brothers | 1960 | 80.00 |
| *—Black colorband label, logo at left* | | | |
| ❑ T 1449 [M] | A Tribute to the Delmore Brothers | 1962 | 25.00 |
| *—Black colorband label, logo at top* | | | |
| ❑ T 1547 [M] | Encore | 1961 | 80.00 |
| *—Black colorband label, logo at left* | | | |
| ❑ T 1547 [M] | Encore | 1962 | 25.00 |
| *—Black colorband label, logo at top* | | | |
| ❑ ST 1616 [S] | Country Christmas | 1961 | 80.00 |
| *—Black rainbow label with "Capitol" at left* | | | |
| ❑ ST 1616 [S] | Country Christmas | 1962 | 25.00 |
| *—Black rainbow label with "Capitol" at top* | | | |
| ❑ T 1616 [M] | Country Christmas | 1961 | 50.00 |
| *—Black rainbow label with "Capitol" at left* | | | |
| ❑ T 1616 [M] | Country Christmas | 1962 | 20.00 |
| *—Black rainbow label with "Capitol" at top* | | | |
| ❑ ST 1721 [S] | Weapon of Prayer | 1962 | 50.00 |
| ❑ T 1721 [M] | Weapon of Prayer | 1962 | 40.00 |
| ❑ ST 1834 [S] | Keep Your Eyes on Jesus | 1963 | 50.00 |
| ❑ T 1834 [M] | Keep Your Eyes on Jesus | 1963 | 40.00 |
| ❑ ST 2091 [S] | The Louvin Brothers Sing and Play Their Current Hits | 1964 | 30.00 |
| ❑ T 2091 [M] | The Louvin Brothers Sing and Play Their Current Hits | 1964 | 25.00 |
| ❑ ST 2331 [S] | Thank God for My Christian Home | 1965 | 30.00 |
| ❑ T 2331 [M] | Thank God for My Christian Home | 1965 | 25.00 |
| ❑ ST 2827 [S] | The Great Roy Acuff Songs | 1967 | 30.00 |
| ❑ T 2827 [M] | The Great Roy Acuff Songs | 1967 | 40.00 |

METRO

| Number | Title | Yr | NM |
|---|---|---|---|
| ❑ M-598 [M] | The Louvin Brothers | 1966 | 25.00 |
| ❑ MS-598 [R] | The Louvin Brothers | 1966 | 20.00 |

MGM

| Number | Title | Yr | NM |
|---|---|---|---|
| ❑ E-3426 [M] | The Louvin Brothers | 1957 | 200.00 |

SEARS

| Number | Title | Yr | NM |
|---|---|---|---|
| ❑ SP-119 [M] | Ira & Charles Louvin | 196? | 20.00 |
| ❑ SPS-119 [R] | Ira & Charles Louvin | 196? | 15.00 |

TOWER

| Number | Title | Yr | NM |
|---|---|---|---|
| ❑ DT 5038 [R] | Two Different Worlds | 1966 | 20.00 |
| ❑ T 5038 [M] | Two Different Worlds | 1966 | 30.00 |
| ❑ DT 5122 | Country Heart and Soul | 1968 | 20.00 |

### LOVE

Also see ARTHUR LEE.

BLUE THUMB

| Number | Title | Yr | NM |
|---|---|---|---|
| ❑ BTS-8822 | False Start | 1970 | 20.00 |
| ❑ BTS-9000 [(2)] | Out Here | 1969 | 25.00 |

ELEKTRA

| Number | Title | Yr | NM |
|---|---|---|---|
| ❑ EKL-4001 [M] | Love | 1966 | 100.00 |
| ❑ EKL-4001 [M] | Love | 1966 | 300.00 |
| *—White label promo* | | | |
| ❑ EKL-4005 [M] | Da Capo | 1967 | 100.00 |
| ❑ EKL-4013 [M] | Forever Changes | 1967 | 50.00 |
| ❑ EKL-4013 [M] | Forever Changes | 1967 | 150.00 |
| *—White label promo* | | | |
| ❑ EKS-74001 [S] | Love | 1966 | 50.00 |
| *—Brown label* | | | |
| ❑ EKS-74001 [S] | Love | 1969 | 15.00 |
| *—Red label with large stylized "E"* | | | |
| ❑ EKS-74001 [S] | Love | 1971 | 12.00 |
| *—Butterfly label* | | | |
| ❑ EKS-74005 [S] | Da Capo | 1967 | 40.00 |
| *—Brown label* | | | |
| ❑ EKS-74005 [S] | Da Capo | 1969 | 15.00 |
| *—Red label with large stylized "E"* | | | |
| ❑ EKS-74005 [S] | Da Capo | 1971 | 12.00 |
| *—Butterfly label* | | | |
| ❑ EKS-74013 [S] | Forever Changes | 1967 | 30.00 |
| *—Brown label* | | | |
| ❑ EKS-74013 [S] | Forever Changes | 1969 | 15.00 |
| *—Red label with large stylized "E"* | | | |
| ❑ EKS-74013 [S] | Forever Changes | 1971 | 12.00 |
| *—Butterfly label* | | | |
| ❑ EKS-74013 [S] | Forever Changes | 1980 | 10.00 |
| *—Red label, small "E," Warner Communications logo on label* | | | |
| ❑ EKS-74013 [S] | Forever Changes | 1984 | 8.00 |
| *—Red and black label* | | | |
| ❑ EKS-74049 | Four Sail | 1969 | 25.00 |
| *—Red label with large stylized "E"* | | | |
| ❑ EKS-74049 | Four Sail | 1971 | 12.00 |
| *—Butterfly label* | | | |
| ❑ EKS-74049 [DJ] | Four Sail | 1969 | 80.00 |
| *—White label promo* | | | |
| ❑ EKS-74058 | Revisited | 1970 | 25.00 |
| *—Red label with large stylized "E"* | | | |
| ❑ EKS-74058 | Revisited | 1971 | 12.00 |
| *—Butterfly label* | | | |
| ❑ EKS-74058 | Revisited | 198? | 10.00 |
| *—Red label, small "E," Warner Communications logo on label* | | | |
| ❑ EKS-74058 | Revisited | 1984 | 8.00 |
| *—Red and black label* | | | |

MCA

| Number | Title | Yr | NM |
|---|---|---|---|
| ❑ 27025 | Studio/Live | 1982 | 10.00 |

RHINO

| Number | Title | Yr | NM |
|---|---|---|---|
| ❑ RNDF-251 [PD] | Love Live | 1981 | 15.00 |
| ❑ RNLP-800 | Best of Love | 1980 | 10.00 |
| ❑ RNLP-70175 | The Best of Love (1966-1969) (Golden Archive Series) | 1987 | 10.00 |

RSO

| Number | Title | Yr | NM |
|---|---|---|---|
| ❑ SO 4804 | Reel to Real | 1974 | 15.00 |

SUNDAZED

| Number | Title | Yr | NM |
|---|---|---|---|
| ❑ LP 5100 | Love | 2001 | 12.00 |
| *—Reissue on 180-gram vinyl* | | | |
| ❑ LP 5101 | Da Capo | 2001 | 12.00 |
| *—Reissue on 180-gram vinyl* | | | |
| ❑ LP 5102 | Forever Changes | 2001 | 12.00 |
| *—Reissue on 180-gram vinyl* | | | |
| ❑ LP 5103 | Four Sail | 2004 | 12.00 |
| ❑ LP 5104 | Revisited | 2001 | 12.00 |
| *—Reissue on 180-gram vinyl* | | | |

### LOVE, HOLLY

ACE

| Number | Title | Yr | NM |
|---|---|---|---|
| ❑ LP-1022 [M] | My Love Confessions | 1962 | 30.00 |

### LOVE, PRESTON

KENT

| Number | Title | Yr | NM |
|---|---|---|---|
| ❑ KST-540 | Omaha Bar-B-Q | 1968 | 20.00 |

### LOVE EXCHANGE, THE

TOWER

| Number | Title | Yr | NM |
|---|---|---|---|
| ❑ ST 5115 [S] | The Love Exchange | 1968 | 25.00 |
| ❑ T 5115 [M] | The Love Exchange | 1968 | 60.00 |

### LOVE GENERATION, THE

IMPERIAL

| Number | Title | Yr | NM |
|---|---|---|---|
| ❑ LP-9351 [M] | The Love Generation | 1967 | 20.00 |
| ❑ LP-12351 [S] | The Love Generation | 1967 | 20.00 |
| ❑ LP-12364 | A Generation of Love | 1968 | 20.00 |
| ❑ LP-12408 | Montage | 1968 | 20.00 |

### LOVE SCULPTURE

EMI AMERICA

| Number | Title | Yr | NM |
|---|---|---|---|
| ❑ SQ-17208 | Blues Helping | 1986 | 12.00 |
| *—Reissue of Rare Earth LP* | | | |

PARROT

| Number | Title | Yr | NM |
|---|---|---|---|
| ❑ PAS 71035 | Forms and Feelings | 1970 | 25.00 |

RARE EARTH

| Number | Title | Yr | NM |
|---|---|---|---|
| ❑ RS-505 | Blues Helping | 1969 | 40.00 |

### LOVECRAFT

See H.P. LOVECRAFT.

### LOVELITES, THE

UNI

| Number | Title | Yr | NM |
|---|---|---|---|
| ❑ 73081 | The Lovelites | 1970 | 25.00 |

### LOVETT, LEE

STRAND

| Number | Title | Yr | NM |
|---|---|---|---|
| ❑ SL-1055 [M] | Jazz Dance Party | 1962 | 20.00 |
| ❑ SLS-1055 [S] | Jazz Dance Party | 1962 | 25.00 |
| ❑ SL-1059 [M] | Misty | 1962 | 20.00 |
| ❑ SLS-1059 [S] | Misty | 1962 | 25.00 |

WYNNE

| Number | Title | Yr | NM |
|---|---|---|---|
| ❑ WLP-108 [M] | Jazz Dance Party | 195? | 30.00 |

### LOVICH, LENE

STIFF/EPIC

| Number | Title | Yr | NM |
|---|---|---|---|
| ❑ JE 36102 | Stateless | 1979 | 12.00 |
| ❑ JE 36102 | Stateless | 1979 | 20.00 |
| *—Red vinyl* | | | |
| ❑ JE 36308 | Flex | 1980 | 12.00 |
| ❑ 5E 37452 [EP] | New Toy | 1981 | 15.00 |
| ❑ ARE 38399 | No Man's Land | 1983 | 10.00 |

### LOVIN' SPOONFUL, THE

Also see JOHN SEBASTIAN; ZALMAN YANOVSKY.

ACCORD

| Number | Title | Yr | NM |
|---|---|---|---|
| ❑ SN-7196 | Distant Echoes | 1981 | 10.00 |

BUDDAH

| Number | Title | Yr | NM |
|---|---|---|---|
| ❑ BDM-5706 | The Best of the Lovin' Spoonful | 197? | 12.00 |
| ❑ BLB6-8339 | The Best of the Lovin' Spoonful | 198? | 10.00 |
| *—Reissue of 5706* | | | |

51 WEST

| Number | Title | Yr | NM |
|---|---|---|---|
| ❑ Q 16023 | ... So Nice | 1979 | 10.00 |

KAMA SUTRA

| Number | Title | Yr | NM |
|---|---|---|---|
| ❑ KLPS-750-2 [(2)] | 24 Karat Hits | 1968 | 20.00 |
| ❑ KSBS-2011 | The John Sebastian Song Book | 1970 | 15.00 |
| ❑ KSBS-2013 | The Very Best of the Lovin' Spoonful | 1970 | 15.00 |
| ❑ KSBS-2029 | Once Upon a Time | 1971 | 15.00 |
| ❑ KSBS-2608 [(2)] | The Best...Lovin' Spoonful | 1976 | 20.00 |
| ❑ KLP-8050 [M] | Do You Believe in Magic | 1965 | 20.00 |
| ❑ KLPS-8050 [S] | Do You Believe in Magic | 1965 | 30.00 |
| ❑ KLP-8051 [M] | Daydream | 1966 | 20.00 |
| ❑ KLPS-8051 [S] | Daydream | 1966 | 30.00 |
| ❑ KLP-8053 [M] | What's Up, Tiger Lily? | 1966 | 20.00 |

| Number | Title (A Side/B Side) | Yr | NM |
|---|---|---|---|
| ❑ KLPS-8053 [S] | What's Up, Tiger Lily? | 1966 | 30.00 |
| ❑ KLP-8054 [M] | Hums of the Lovin' Spoonful | 1966 | 20.00 |
| ❑ KLPS-8054 [S] | Hums of the Lovin' Spoonful | 1966 | 30.00 |
| ❑ KLP-8056 [M] | The Best of the Lovin' Spoonful | 1967 | 15.00 |
| *—Came with four bonus photos of the band, which are priced separately* | | | |
| ❑ KLP/S-8056 | The Best of the Lovin' Spoonful Bonus Photos (4) | 1967 | 10.00 |
| ❑ KLPS-8056 [S] | The Best of the Lovin' Spoonful | 1967 | 15.00 |
| *—Came with four bonus photos of the band, which are priced separately* | | | |
| ❑ KLP-8058 [M] | You're a Big Boy Now | 1967 | 20.00 |
| ❑ KLPS-8058 [S] | You're a Big Boy Now | 1967 | 20.00 |
| ❑ KLP-8061 [M] | Everything Playing | 1968 | 30.00 |
| ❑ KLPS-8061 [S] | Everything Playing | 1968 | 20.00 |
| ❑ KLP-8064 [M] | The Best of the Lovin' Spoonful, Volume 2 | 1968 | 50.00 |
| ❑ KLPS-8064 [S] | The Best of the Lovin' Spoonful, Volume 2 | 1968 | 20.00 |
| ❑ KLPS-8073 | Revelation: Revolution '69 | 1969 | 25.00 |
| ❑ ST-90597 [S] | Do You Believe in Magic | 1965 | 40.00 |
| *—Capitol Record Club edition* | | | |
| ❑ T-90597 [M] | Do You Believe in Magic | 1965 | 30.00 |
| *—Capitol Record Club edition* | | | |
| ❑ ST-90675 [S] | Daydream | 1966 | 40.00 |
| *—Capitol Record Club edition* | | | |
| ❑ T-90675 [M] | Daydream | 1966 | 25.00 |
| *—Capitol Record Club edition* | | | |
| ❑ ST-90988 [S] | Hums of the Lovin' Spoonful | 1966 | 40.00 |
| *—Capitol Record Club edition* | | | |
| ❑ KAO-91102 [M] | The Best of the Lovin' Spoonful | 1967 | 25.00 |
| *—Capitol Record Club edition* | | | |
| ❑ SKAO-91102 [S] | The Best of the Lovin' Spoonful | 1967 | 20.00 |
| *—Capitol Record Club edition* | | | |
| ❑ ST-91198 [S] | You're a Big Boy Now | 1967 | 25.00 |
| *—Capitol Record Club edition* | | | |
| KOALA | | | |
| ❑ KO 14221 | Day Dream | 1979 | 10.00 |
| PAIR | | | |
| ❑ PDL2-1200 [(2)] | The Best of the Lovin' Spoonful | 1986 | 12.00 |
| RHINO | | | |
| ❑ RNLP-114 | The Best of the Lovin' Spoonful, Vol. 2 | 1985 | 10.00 |
| SUNDAZED | | | |
| ❑ LP 5159 | Do You Believe in Magic | 2002 | 15.00 |
| *—Reissue on 180-gram vinyl* | | | |
| ❑ LP 5160 | Daydream | 2002 | 15.00 |
| *—Reissue on 180-gram vinyl* | | | |
| ❑ LP 5166 | Hums of the Lovin' Spoonful | 2003 | 15.00 |
| *—Reissue on 180-gram vinyl* | | | |
| **LOWE, BERNIE, ORCHESTRA** | | | |
| CAMEO | | | |
| ❑ C-1057 [M] | Encore | 1963 | 20.00 |
| ❑ C-4005 [M] | If the Big Bands Were Here Today | 1962 | 20.00 |
| ❑ SC-4005 [S] | If the Big Bands Were Here Today | 1962 | 25.00 |
| ❑ C-4007 [M] | If the Big Bands Were Here Today, Vol. 2 | 1962 | 20.00 |
| ❑ SC-4007 [S] | If the Big Bands Were Here Today, Vol. 2 | 1962 | 25.00 |
| **LOWE, FRANK** | | | |
| ESP-DISK' | | | |
| ❑ 3013 | Black Beings | 197? | 25.00 |
| **LOWE, JIM** | | | |
| DOT | | | |
| ❑ DLP-3051 [M] | The Green Door | 1956 | 150.00 |
| ❑ DLP-3114 [M] | Wicked Women | 1958 | 100.00 |
| ❑ DLP-3681 [M] | Songs They Sing Behind the Green Door | 1965 | 25.00 |
| ❑ DLP-25881 [S] | Songs They Sing Behind the Green Door | 1965 | 30.00 |
| MERCURY | | | |
| ❑ MG-20246 [M] | The Door of Fame | 1957 | 150.00 |
| **LOWE, MUNDELL** | | | |
| CHARLIE PARKER | | | |
| ❑ PLP-822 [M] | Blues for a Stripper | 1962 | 40.00 |
| ❑ PLP-822S [S] | Blues for a Stripper | 1962 | 50.00 |
| FAMOUS DOOR | | | |
| ❑ HL-102 | California Guitar | 1974 | 25.00 |
| JAZZLAND | | | |
| ❑ JLP-8 [M] | Low-Down Guitar | 1960 | 60.00 |
| OFFBEAT | | | |
| ❑ OLP-3010 [M] | Tacet for Neurotics | 1960 | 80.00 |
| ❑ OS-93010 [S] | Tacet for Neurotics | 1960 | 100.00 |
| RCA CAMDEN | | | |
| ❑ CAL-490 [M] | Porgy and Bess | 1959 | 15.00 |
| ❑ CAS-490 [S] | Porgy and Bess | 1959 | 20.00 |
| ❑ CAL-522 [M] | TV Action Jazz! | 1959 | 15.00 |
| ❑ CAS-522 [S] | TV Action Jazz! | 1959 | 20.00 |
| ❑ CAL-627 [M] | TV Action Jazz! — Volume 2 | 1960 | 25.00 |

The Lovin' Spoonful, *The Best of the Lovin' Spoonful,* Kama Sutra KLP-8056, 1967, $15.

| Number | Title (A Side/B Side) | Yr | NM |
|---|---|---|---|
| ❑ CAS-627 [S] | TV Action Jazz! — Volume 2 | 1960 | 30.00 |
| RCA VICTOR | | | |
| ❑ LJM-3002 [10] | The Mundell Lowe Quintet | 1954 | 120.00 |
| RIVERSIDE | | | |
| ❑ RLP 12-204 [M] | The Mundell Lowe Quartet | 1956 | 80.00 |
| *—White label, blue print* | | | |
| ❑ RLP 12-204 [M] | The Mundell Lowe Quartet | 1959 | 50.00 |
| *—Blue label, microphone logo at top* | | | |
| ❑ RLP 12-208 [M] | Guitar Moods | 1956 | 60.00 |
| *—White label, blue print* | | | |
| ❑ RLP 12-208 [M] | Guitar Moods | 1959 | 50.00 |
| *—Blue label, microphone logo at top* | | | |
| ❑ RLP 12-219 [M] | New Music of Alec Wilder | 1956 | 80.00 |
| *—White label, blue print* | | | |
| ❑ RLP 12-219 [M] | New Music of Alec Wilder | 1959 | 50.00 |
| *—Blue label, microphone logo at top* | | | |
| ❑ RLP 12-238 [M] | A Grand Night for Swinging | 1957 | 80.00 |
| *—White label, blue print* | | | |
| ❑ RLP 12-238 [M] | A Grand Night for Swinging | 1959 | 50.00 |
| *—Blue label, microphone logo at top* | | | |
| **LOWE, NICK** | | | |
| COLUMBIA | | | |
| ❑ AS 1400 [DJ] | An Interrogation of Nick Lowe | 1990 | 25.00 |
| *—Promo-only interview album* | | | |
| ❑ JC 35529 | Pure Pop for Now People | 1978 | 20.00 |
| ❑ PC 35529 | Pure Pop for Now People | 198? | 8.00 |
| *—Budget-line reissue* | | | |
| ❑ JC 36087 | Labour of Lust | 1979 | 10.00 |
| ❑ PC 36087 | Labour of Lust | 198? | 8.00 |
| *—Budget-line reissue* | | | |
| ❑ FC 37932 | Nick the Knife | 1982 | 12.00 |
| ❑ PC 37932 | Nick the Knife | 198? | 8.00 |
| *—Budget-line reissue* | | | |
| ❑ FC 38589 | The Abominable Showman | 1983 | 12.00 |
| ❑ PC 38589 | The Abominable Showman | 1986 | 8.00 |
| *—Budget-line reissue* | | | |
| ❑ FC 39371 | Nick Lowe and His Cowboy Outfit | 1984 | 12.00 |
| ❑ PC 39371 | Nick Lowe and His Cowboy Outfit | 1986 | 8.00 |
| *—Budget-line reissue* | | | |
| ❑ FC 39958 | The Rose of England | 1985 | 12.00 |
| ❑ FC 40381 | Pinker and Prouder Than Previous | 1988 | 14.00 |
| REPRISE | | | |
| ❑ 26132 | Party of One | 1990 | 12.00 |

| Number | Title (A Side/B Side) | Yr | NM |
|---|---|---|---|
| **LOWE, SAMMY** | | | |
| RCA VICTOR | | | |
| ❑ LPM-2770 [M] | Hitsville U.S.A. | 1963 | 20.00 |
| ❑ LSP-2770 [S] | Hitsville U.S.A. | 1963 | 25.00 |
| **LRY** | | | |
| CONGRESS OF THE CROW | | | |
| ❑ 8031002 | The LRY Record | 1968 | 200.00 |
| **LUBOFF, NORMAN, CHOIR** | | | |
| COLUMBIA | | | |
| ❑ CL 545 [M] | Easy to Remember | 1954 | 20.00 |
| *—Maroon label, gold print* | | | |
| ❑ CL 2545 [10] | Carols for Christmas | 1955 | 30.00 |
| *—"House Party Series"* | | | |
| ❑ CL 6272 [10] | Christmas Carols | 1953 | 40.00 |
| **LUCAS, BUDDY** | | | |
| UNITED ARTISTS | | | |
| ❑ UAL-3482 [M] | Fifty Fabulous Harmonica Favorites | 1966 | 20.00 |
| ❑ UAS-6482 [S] | Fifty Fabulous Harmonica Favorites | 1966 | 25.00 |
| **LUCAS, NICK** | | | |
| CAVALIER | | | |
| ❑ CAV-5003 [10] | Tip-Toe Thru the Tulips | 195? | 80.00 |
| *—Green vinyl* | | | |
| DECCA | | | |
| ❑ DL 8653 [M] | Painting the Clouds with Sunshine | 1957 | 40.00 |
| **LUCEY, CHRIS** | | | |
| SURREY | | | |
| ❑ SS-1027 [M] | Songs of Protest and Anti-Protest | 197? | 40.00 |
| **LUCRAFT, HOWARD** | | | |
| DECCA | | | |
| ❑ DL 8679 [M] | Showcase for Modern Jazz | 1958 | 30.00 |
| **LUDDEN, ALLEN** | | | |
| RCA VICTOR | | | |
| ❑ LPM-2934 [M] | Allen Ludden Sings His Favorite Songs | 1964 | 20.00 |
| ❑ LSP-2934 [S] | Allen Ludden Sings His Favorite Songs | 1964 | 25.00 |

Lulu, *Melody Fair,* Atco 33-330, 1970, special mono promo copy, $30.

## LULU

| Number | Title (A Side/B Side) | Yr | NM |
|---|---|---|---|
| **ALFA** | | | |
| ❑ 10006 | Lulu | 1981 | 12.00 |
| **ATCO** | | | |
| ❑ 33-310 [M] | New Routes | 1970 | 30.00 |
| *—White label promo; no stock copies were issued in mono* | | | |
| ❑ SD 33-310 [S] | New Routes | 1970 | 12.00 |
| ❑ 33-330 [M] | Melody Fair | 1970 | 30.00 |
| *—White label promo, "DJ Copy Monaural" on cover; no stock copies were issued in mono* | | | |
| ❑ SD 33-330 [S] | Melody Fair | 1970 | 12.00 |
| **CHELSEA** | | | |
| ❑ BCL1-0144 | Lulu | 1973 | 12.00 |
| ❑ CHL-518 | Heaven and Earth and the Stars | 1976 | 20.00 |
| **EPIC** | | | |
| ❑ LN 24339 [M] | To Sir with Love | 1967 | 25.00 |
| ❑ BN 26339 [P] | To Sir with Love | 1967 | 30.00 |
| ❑ BN 26536 | It's Lulu | 1970 | 12.00 |
| **HARMONY** | | | |
| ❑ H 30249 | To Love Somebody | 1970 | 20.00 |
| **PARROT** | | | |
| ❑ PA 61016 [M] | From Lulu with Love | 1967 | 60.00 |
| ❑ PAS 71016 [S] | From Lulu with Love | 1967 | 80.00 |
| **PICKWICK** | | | |
| ❑ SPC-3237 | Lulu | 1973 | 8.00 |
| **ROCKET** | | | |
| ❑ BXL1-3073 | Don't Take Love for Granted | 1978 | 12.00 |

## LULU BELLE AND SCOTTY

| Number | Title (A Side/B Side) | Yr | NM |
|---|---|---|---|
| **STARDAY** | | | |
| ❑ SLP-206 [M] | The Sweethearts of Country Music | 1963 | 40.00 |
| ❑ SLP-285 [M] | Down Memory Lane | 1964 | 40.00 |
| ❑ SLP-351 [M] | Lulu Belle & Scotty | 1965 | 40.00 |
| **SUPER** | | | |
| ❑ 6201 [M] | Lule Belle & Scotty | 1963 | 50.00 |

## LUMAN, BOB

| Number | Title (A Side/B Side) | Yr | NM |
|---|---|---|---|
| **EPIC** | | | |
| ❑ BN 26393 | Ain't Got Time to Be Unhappy | 1968 | 20.00 |
| ❑ BN 26463 | Come On Home and Sing the Blues | 1969 | 20.00 |
| ❑ BN 26541 | Gettin' Back | 1970 | 20.00 |
| ❑ E 30617 | Is It Any Wonder | 1971 | 20.00 |
| ❑ E 30923 | Chain Don't Take to Me | 1972 | 20.00 |
| ❑ KE 31375 | When You Say Love | 1972 | 20.00 |
| ❑ KE 31746 | Lonely Women Make Good Lovers | 1972 | 20.00 |
| ❑ KE 32192 | Neither One of Us | 1973 | 15.00 |
| ❑ KE 32759 | Bob Luman's Greatest Hits | 1974 | 15.00 |
| ❑ KE 33942 | Satisfied Mind | 1975 | 12.00 |
| ❑ KE 34445 | Alive and Well! | 1976 | 12.00 |
| **HARMONY** | | | |
| ❑ KH 32006 | Bob Luman | 1973 | 12.00 |
| **HICKORY** | | | |
| ❑ LPM-124 [M] | Livin' Lovin' Sounds | 1965 | 25.00 |
| ❑ LPS-124 [S] | Livin' Lovin' Sounds | 1965 | 30.00 |
| **HICKORY/MGM** | | | |
| ❑ H3G-4508 | Still Loving You | 1974 | 15.00 |
| **POLYDOR** | | | |
| ❑ PD-1-6135 | Bob Luman | 1978 | 12.00 |
| **WARNER BROS.** | | | |
| ❑ W 1396 [M] | Let's Think About Livin' | 1960 | 50.00 |
| ❑ WS 1396 [S] | Let's Think About Livin' | 1960 | 70.00 |

## LUMLEY, RUFUS

| Number | Title (A Side/B Side) | Yr | NM |
|---|---|---|---|
| **RCA VICTOR** | | | |
| ❑ LPM-3898 [M] | Rufus Lumley | 1967 | 50.00 |
| ❑ LSP-3898 [S] | Rufus Lumley | 1967 | 40.00 |

## LUNA

| Number | Title (A Side/B Side) | Yr | NM |
|---|---|---|---|
| **ARHOOLIE** | | | |
| ❑ ST-8001 | Space Swell | 1968 | 20.00 |

## LUNCEFORD, JIMMIE

| Number | Title (A Side/B Side) | Yr | NM |
|---|---|---|---|
| **ALLEGRO ELITE** | | | |
| ❑ (# unknown) [10] | Jimmie Lunceford Plays | 195? | 40.00 |
| **COLUMBIA** | | | |
| ❑ GL 104 [10] | Lunceford Special | 1950 | 80.00 |
| ❑ CL 634 [M] | Lunceford Special | 1955 | 50.00 |
| *—Maroon label, gold print* | | | |
| ❑ CL 634 [M] | Lunceford Special | 1956 | 40.00 |
| *—Red and black label with six "eye" logos* | | | |
| ❑ CL 2715 [M] | Lunceford Special | 1967 | 30.00 |
| **COLUMBIA MASTERWORKS** | | | |
| ❑ ML 4804 [M] | Lunceford Special | 195? | 60.00 |
| **DECCA** | | | |
| ❑ DL 5393 [10] | For Dancers Only | 1952 | 60.00 |
| ❑ DL 8050 [M] | Jimmie Lunceford and His Orchestra | 1954 | 40.00 |
| ❑ DL 9237 [M] | Rhythm Is Our Business | 1968 | 40.00 |
| ❑ DL 9238 [M] | Harlem Shout | 1968 | 40.00 |
| ❑ DL 79237 [R] | Rhythm Is Our Business | 1968 | 20.00 |
| ❑ DL 79238 [R] | Harlem Shout | 1968 | 20.00 |
| **"X"** | | | |
| ❑ LX-3002 [M] | Jimmie Lunceford and His Chickasaw Syncopators | 1954 | 60.00 |

## LUNCH, LYDIA

| Number | Title (A Side/B Side) | Yr | NM |
|---|---|---|---|
| **RUBY** | | | |
| ❑ JRR 806 | 13.13 | 1982 | 30.00 |
| **ZE/BUDDAH** | | | |
| ❑ 33006 | Queen of Siam | 1980 | 30.00 |

## LUND, GARRETT

| Number | Title (A Side/B Side) | Yr | NM |
|---|---|---|---|
| **(NO LABEL)** | | | |
| ❑ (no #) | Almost Grown | 1975 | 300.00 |

## LUNDY, PAT

| Number | Title (A Side/B Side) | Yr | NM |
|---|---|---|---|
| **COLUMBIA** | | | |
| ❑ CS 9588 | Soul Ain't Nothin' But the Blues | 1968 | 20.00 |

## LUNN, ROBERT

| Number | Title (A Side/B Side) | Yr | NM |
|---|---|---|---|
| **STARDAY** | | | |
| ❑ SLP-228 [M] | The Original Talking Blues Man | 1962 | 30.00 |

## LUTCHER, NELLIE

| Number | Title (A Side/B Side) | Yr | NM |
|---|---|---|---|
| **CAPITOL** | | | |
| ❑ H 232 [10] | Real Gone | 1950 | 60.00 |
| ❑ T 232 [M] | Real Gone | 1955 | 40.00 |
| **EPIC** | | | |
| ❑ LN 1108 [10] | Whee! Nellie | 1955 | 50.00 |
| **LIBERTY** | | | |
| ❑ LRP-3014 [M] | Our New Nellie | 1956 | 40.00 |

## LYMAN, ARTHUR

| Number | Title (A Side/B Side) | Yr | NM |
|---|---|---|---|
| **GNP CRESCENDO** | | | |
| ❑ GNP-605 [M] | Exotic Sounds | 1963 | 15.00 |
| ❑ GNPS-605 [S] | Exotic Sounds | 1963 | 20.00 |
| ❑ GNP-606 [M] | Paradise | 1964 | 15.00 |
| ❑ GNPS-606 [S] | Paradise | 1964 | 20.00 |
| ❑ GNP-607 [M] | Cast Your Fate to the Wind | 1965 | 15.00 |
| ❑ GNPS-607 [S] | Cast Your Fate to the Wind | 1965 | 20.00 |
| ❑ GNPS-2091 | Puka Shells | 1975 | 10.00 |
| **HIFI** | | | |
| ❑ R-607 [M] | Leis of Jazz | 1958 | 20.00 |
| ❑ SR-607 [S] | Leis of Jazz | 1958 | 30.00 |
| ❑ R-806 [M] | Taboo | 1958 | 20.00 |
| ❑ SR-806 [S] | Taboo | 1958 | 30.00 |
| ❑ R-807 [M] | Hawaiian Sunset | 1959 | 20.00 |
| ❑ SR-807 [S] | Hawaiian Sunset | 1959 | 30.00 |
| ❑ R-808 [M] | Bwan-A | 1959 | 20.00 |
| ❑ SR-808 [S] | Bwan-A | 1959 | 30.00 |
| ❑ R-813 [M] | The Legend of Pele | 1959 | 20.00 |
| ❑ SR-813 [S] | The Legend of Pele | 1959 | 30.00 |
| ❑ R-815 [M] | Bahia | 1959 | 20.00 |
| ❑ SR-815 [S] | Bahia | 1959 | 30.00 |
| ❑ R-818 [M] | Arthur Lyman On Broadway | 1960 | 20.00 |
| ❑ SR-818 [S] | Arthur Lyman On Broadway | 1960 | 30.00 |
| ❑ R-822 [M] | Taboo (Volume 2) | 1960 | 20.00 |
| ❑ SR-822 [S] | Taboo (Volume 2) | 1960 | 30.00 |
| **LIFE** | | | |
| ❑ L 1004 [M] | Yellow Bird | 1961 | 20.00 |
| *—Reissue with new title reflecting the hit single* | | | |
| ❑ L 1004 [M] | Percussion Spectacular | 1961 | 30.00 |
| ❑ SL 1004 [S] | Yellow Bird | 1961 | 25.00 |
| *—Reissue with new title reflecting the hit single* | | | |
| ❑ SL 1004 [S] | Percussion Spectacular | 1961 | 40.00 |
| ❑ L 1005 [M] | The Colorful Percussions of Arthur Lyman | 1962 | 20.00 |
| ❑ SL 1005 [S] | The Colorful Percussions of Arthur Lyman | 1962 | 25.00 |
| ❑ L 1007 [M] | The Many Moods of Arthur Lyman | 1962 | 20.00 |
| ❑ SL 1007 [S] | The Many Moods of Arthur Lyman | 1962 | 25.00 |
| ❑ L 1009 [M] | I Wish You Love | 1963 | 20.00 |
| ❑ L 1009 [M] | Love for Sale! | 1963 | 25.00 |
| *—Alternate title* | | | |
| ❑ SL 1009 [S] | I Wish You Love | 1963 | 25.00 |
| ❑ SL 1009 [S] | Love for Sale! | 1963 | 30.00 |
| *—Alternate title* | | | |
| ❑ L 1010 [M] | Cotton Fields | 1963 | 20.00 |
| ❑ SL 1010 [S] | Cotton Fields | 1963 | 25.00 |
| ❑ L 1014 [M] | Blowin' in the Wind | 1963 | 20.00 |
| ❑ SL 1014 [S] | Blowin' in the Wind | 1963 | 25.00 |
| ❑ L 1018 [M] | Mele Kalikimaka (Merry Christmas) | 1963 | 20.00 |

| Number | Title (A Side/B Side) | Yr | NM |
|---|---|---|---|
| ❑ SL 1018 [S] | Mele Kalikimaka (Merry Christmas) | 1963 | 25.00 |
| ❑ L 1023 [M] | Isle of Enchantment | 1964 | 20.00 |
| ❑ SL 1023 [S] | Isle of Enchantment | 1964 | 25.00 |
| ❑ L 1024 [M] | Call of the Midnight Sun | 1964 | 20.00 |
| ❑ SL 1024 [S] | Call of the Midnight Sun | 1964 | 25.00 |
| ❑ L 1025 [M] | Hawaiian Sunset, Volume 2 | 1965 | 15.00 |
| ❑ SL 1025 [S] | Hawaiian Sunset, Volume 2 | 1965 | 20.00 |
| ❑ L 1027 [M] | Polynesia | 1965 | 15.00 |
| ❑ SL 1027 [S] | Polynesia | 1965 | 20.00 |
| ❑ L 1030 [M] | Greatest Hits | 1965 | 12.00 |
| ❑ SL 1030 [S] | Greatest Hits | 1965 | 15.00 |
| ❑ L 1031 [M] | Lyman '66 | 1965 | 15.00 |
| ❑ SL 1031 [S] | Lyman '66 | 1965 | 20.00 |
| ❑ L 1033 [M] | The Shadow of Your Smile | 1966 | 15.00 |
| ❑ SL 1033 [S] | The Shadow of Your Smile | 1966 | 20.00 |
| ❑ L 1034 [M] | Aloha, Amigo | 1966 | 15.00 |
| ❑ SL 1034 [S] | Aloha, Amigo | 1966 | 20.00 |
| ❑ L 1035 [M] | Ilikai | 1967 | 15.00 |
| ❑ SL 1035 [S] | Ilikai | 1967 | 20.00 |
| ❑ L 1036 [M] | Arthur Lyman at the Port of L.A. | 1967 | 15.00 |
| ❑ SL 1036 [S] | Arthur Lyman at the Port of L.A. | 1967 | 20.00 |
| ❑ SL 1037 | Latitude 20 | 1968 | 15.00 |
| ❑ SL 1038 | Aphrodisia | 1968 | 15.00 |
| ❑ SL 1039 | Winner's Circle | 1969 | 15.00 |
| ❑ SL 1040 | Today's Greatest Hits | 1970 | 15.00 |

**LYMON, FRANKIE**

GUEST STAR

❑ GS-1406 [M] Teen Time Tunes Starring Frankie Lymon 1959 40.00
*—Various-artists compilation; color cover*
❑ GS-1406 [M] Rock & Roll Party Starring Frankie Lymon 196? 25.00
*—Various-artists compilation; retitled, black and white cover*

ROULETTE

❑ R-25013 [M] Frankie Lymon at the London Palladium 1958 300.00
❑ R-25036 [M] Rock 'N' Roll 1958 300.00
❑ R-25250 [M] Frankie Lymon's Greatest 1964 30.00
❑ SR-25250 [R] Frankie Lymon's Greatest 1964 25.00

**LYMON, FRANKIE, AND THE TEENAGERS**

ACCORD

❑ SN-7203 Why Do Fools Fall in Love 1982 10.00

GEE

❑ GLP-701 [M] The Teenagers Featuring Frankie Lymon 1956 500.00
*—Red label*
❑ GLP-701 [M] The Teenagers Featuring Frankie Lymon 1961 150.00
*—Gray label*
❑ GLP-701 [M] The Teenagers Featuring Frankie Lymon 197? 12.00
*—White label on thinner vinyl*

MURRAY HILL

❑ 148 [(5)] Frankie Lymon and the Teenagers 198? 70.00

RHINO

❑ R1-70918 The Best of Frankie Lymon and the Teenagers 1989 12.00

**LYNN, BARBARA**

ATLANTIC

❑ 8171 [M] Here Is Barbara Lynn 1968 50.00
❑ SD 8171 [S] Here Is Barbara Lynn 1968 40.00

JAMIE

❑ JLP-3023 [M] You'll Lose a Good Thing 1962 50.00
❑ JLPS-3023 [R] You'll Lose a Good Thing 1962 50.00
❑ JLP-3026 [M] Sister of Soul 1964 —
*—Canceled*
❑ JLPS-3026 [S] Sister of Soul 1964 —
*—Canceled*

**LYNN, DIANA**

CAPITOL

❑ H 180 [10] Piano Moods 1950 60.00

**LYNN, DONNA**

CAPITOL

❑ ST 2085 [S] Java Jones/My Boyfriend Got a Beatle Haircut 1964 30.00
❑ T 2085 [M] Java Jones/My Boyfriend Got a Beatle Haircut 1964 20.00

**LYNN, JUDY**

AMARET

❑ ST-5011 Parts of Love 1971 15.00
❑ AST-5014 Naturally 197? 15.00

COLUMBIA

❑ CS 9879 Judy Lynn Sings at Caesar's Palace 1968 15.00

MUSICOR

❑ MM-2096 [M] The Judy Lynn Show Plays Again 1966 15.00
❑ MM-2112 [M] Honey Stuff 1966 15.00
❑ MM-2126 [M] Golden Nuggets 1967 15.00
❑ MS-3096 [S] The Judy Lynn Show Plays Again 1966 20.00
❑ MS-3112 [S] Honey Stuff 1966 20.00
❑ MS-3126 [S] Golden Nuggets 1967 15.00

UNART

❑ 20009 [M] Judy Lynn in Las Vegas 1967 15.00
❑ 21009 [S] Judy Lynn in Las Vegas 1967 12.00

UNITED ARTISTS

❑ UAL-3226 [M] Judy Lynn Sings at the Golden Nugget 1962 20.00
❑ UAL-3288 [M] Here Is Our Gal, Judy Lynn 1963 15.00
❑ UAL-3342 [M] America's Number One Most Promising Country and Western Girl Singer 1964 15.00
❑ UAL-3390 [M] The Judy Lynn Show 1964 15.00
❑ UAL-3443 [M] The Judy Lynn Show Act 2 1965 15.00
❑ UAL-3461 [M] The Best of Judy Lynn 1966 15.00
❑ UAS-6226 [S] Judy Lynn Sings at the Golden Nugget 1962 25.00
❑ UAS-6288 [S] Here Is Our Gal, Judy Lynn 1963 20.00
❑ UAS-6342 [S] America's Number One Most Promising Country and Western Girl Singer 1964 20.00
❑ UAS-6390 [S] The Judy Lynn Show 1964 20.00
❑ UAS-6443 [S] The Judy Lynn Show Act 2 1965 20.00
❑ UAS-6461 [S] The Best of Judy Lynn 1966 20.00

**LYNN, LORETTA**

DECCA

❑ DL 4457 [M] Loretta Lynn Sings 1963 60.00
❑ DL 4541 [M] Before I'm Over You 1964 30.00
❑ DL 4620 [M] Songs from My Heart 1965 30.00
❑ DL 4665 [M] Blue Kentucky Girl 1965 30.00
❑ DL 4695 [M] Hymns 1965 30.00
❑ DL 4744 [M] I Like 'Em Country 1966 25.00
❑ DL 4783 [M] You Ain't Woman Enough 1966 25.00
❑ DL 4817 [M] Country Christmas 1966 25.00
❑ DL 4842 [M] Don't Come Home a-Drinkin' (With Lovin' on Your Mind) 1967 30.00
❑ DL 4928 [M] Who Says God Is Dead! 1967 40.00
❑ DL 4930 [M] Singin' with Feelin' 1967 30.00
❑ DL 4997 [M] Fist City 1968 50.00
*—Mono version appears to exist only as a white label promo*
❑ DL 74457 [S] Loretta Lynn Sings 1963 80.00
❑ DL 74541 [S] Before I'm Over You 1964 40.00
❑ DL 74620 [S] Songs from My Heart 1965 40.00
❑ DL 74665 [S] Blue Kentucky Girl 1965 40.00
❑ DL 74695 [S] Hymns 1965 40.00
❑ DL 74744 [S] I Like 'Em Country 1966 30.00
❑ DL 74783 [S] You Ain't Woman Enough 1966 30.00
❑ DL 74817 [S] Country Christmas 1966 30.00
❑ DL 74842 [S] Don't Come Home a-Drinkin' (With Lovin' on Your Mind) 1967 25.00
❑ DL 74928 [S] Who Says God Is Dead! 1967 25.00
❑ DL 74930 [S] Singin' with Feelin' 1967 25.00
❑ DL 74997 [S] Fist City 1968 25.00
❑ DL 75000 Loretta Lynn's Greatest Hits 1968 25.00
❑ DL 75084 Your Squaw Is On the Warpath 1969 25.00
*—Later editions delete the track "Barney"*
❑ DL 75084 Your Squaw Is On the Warpath 1969 40.00
*—First editions had a track called "Barney"*
❑ DL 75113 Woman of the World/To Make a Man 1969 25.00
❑ DL 75163 Wings Upon Your Horns 1970 25.00
❑ DL 75198 Loretta Lynn Writes 'Em and Sings 'Em 1970 25.00
❑ DL 75253 Coal Miner's Daughter 1971 20.00
❑ DL 75282 I Wanna Be Free 1971 20.00
❑ DL 75310 You're Lookin' at Country 1971 20.00
❑ DL 75334 One's On the Way 1972 20.00
❑ DL 75351 God Bless America Again 1972 20.00
❑ DL 75381 Here I Am Again 1972 20.00
❑ ST-91604 Loretta Lynn's Greatest Hits 1968 30.00
*—Capitol Record Club edition*

MCA

❑ 1 Loretta Lynn's Greatest Hits 1973 15.00
*—Reissue of Decca 75000*
❑ 5 Hymns 1973 15.00
*—Reissue of Decca 74695*
❑ 6 You Ain't Woman Enough 1973 15.00
*—Reissue of Decca 74783*
❑ 7 Who Says God Is Dead! 1973 15.00
*—Reissue of Decca 74928*
❑ 58 Here I Am Again 1973 15.00
*—Reissue of Decca 75381*
❑ 113 Don't Come Home a-Drinkin' (With Lovin' on Your Mind) 1973 15.00
*—Reissue of Decca 74842*
❑ 248 Country Christmas 1973 15.00
*—First reissue of Decca LP*
❑ 300 Entertainer of the Year — Loretta 1973 15.00
❑ 355 Love Is the Foundation 1973 15.00
❑ 420 Loretta Lynn's Greatest Hits Vol. II 1974 15.00
❑ 444 They Don't Make 'Em Like My Daddy 1974 15.00
❑ 471 Back to the Country 1975 12.00
❑ 628 When the Tingle Becomes a Chill 198? 8.00
*—Budget-line reissue*
❑ 630 Somebody Somewhere 198? 8.00
*—Budget-line reissue*
❑ 721 We've Come a Long Way, Baby 198? 8.00
*—Budget-line reissue*
❑ 735 Alone with You 198? 10.00
❑ L33-1934 [DJ] Loretta Lynn 1974 40.00
*—Promo-only compilation*
❑ 2146 Home 1975 12.00
❑ 2179 When the Tingle Becomes a Chill 1976 12.00
❑ 2228 Somebody Somewhere 1976 12.00
❑ 2265 I Remember Patsy 1977 12.00
❑ 2330 Out of My Head and Back in My Bed 1978 12.00
❑ 2341 Loretta Lynn's Greatest Hits 1978 12.00
*—Reissue of MCA 1*
❑ 2342 Coal Miner's Daughter 1978 12.00
*—Reissue*
❑ 2353 Loretta Lynn's Greatest Hits Vol. II 1978 12.00
*—Reissue of MCA 420*
❑ 3073 We've Come a Long Way, Baby 1979 12.00
❑ 3217 Loretta 1980 10.00
❑ 5148 Lookin' Good 1980 10.00
❑ 5293 I Lie 1982 10.00
❑ 5426 Lyin', Cheatin', Woman Chasin', Honky Tonkin', Whiskey Drinkin' You 1983 10.00
❑ 5613 Just a Woman 1985 10.00
❑ 15022 Country Christmas 1974 12.00
*—Second reissue of Decca LP; black rainbow label*
❑ 15022 Country Christmas 1980 10.00
*—Blue rainbow label*
❑ 15032 Christmas Without Daddy 198? 12.00
❑ 35013 Allis-Chalmers Presents Loretta Lynn 1978 40.00
*—Special products compilation*
❑ 35018 Crisco Presents Loretta Lynn's Country Classics 1979 40.00
*—Special products compilation*
❑ 37080 I Remember Patsy Cline 198? 8.00
*—Budget-line reissue*
❑ 37165 Loretta 198? 8.00
*—Budget-line reissue*
❑ 37205 Loretta Lynn's Greatest Hits Vol. II 198? 8.00
*—Budget-line reissue*
❑ 37235 Loretta Lynn's Greatest Hits 198? 8.00
*—Budget-line reissue*
❑ 37236 Coal Miner's Daughter 198? 8.00
*—Budget-line reissue*
❑ 42174 Who Was That Stranger 1988 10.00

VOCALION

❑ VL 73853 Here's Loretta Lynn 1968 15.00

**LYNN, LORETTA, AND ERNEST TUBB** See ERNEST TUBB AND LORETTA LYNN.

**LYNN, LORETTA, AND CONWAY TWITTY** See CONWAY TWITTY AND LORETTA LYNN.

**LYNN, VERA**

LONDON

❑ LPB-58 [10] Sincerely Yours 195? 60.00
❑ PS 156 [S] Vera Lynn Sings Songs of the Twenties 196? 30.00
❑ PS 359 [S] Wonderful Vera 1964 20.00
❑ LB-690 [10] Sincerely Yours Vol. 2 195? 60.00
❑ LL 1306 [M] Vera Lynn Concert 195? 20.00
❑ LL 1510 [M] If I Am Dreaming 195? 20.00
❑ LL 3142 [M] Vera Lynn Sings Songs of the Twenties 196? 20.00
❑ LL 3294 [M] Golden Hits 196? 20.00
❑ LL 3359 [M] Wonderful Vera 1964 20.00

MGM

❑ E-3887 [M] Yours 1961 20.00
❑ SE-3887 [S] Yours 1961 25.00
❑ E-3889 [M] As Time Goes By 1961 20.00
❑ SE-3889 [S] As Time Goes By 1961 25.00

STANYAN

❑ 10032 When the Lights Go On Again 197? 15.00
❑ 10080 Vera Lynn Remembers the World at War 197? 15.00
❑ 10123 Among My Souvenirs 197? 15.00

SUFFOLK MARKETING

❑ SMI-1-28 All My Best (Her World Famous Recordings) 198? 10.00

UNITED ARTISTS

❑ UAL-3591 [M] It Hurts to Say Goodbye 1967 25.00
❑ UAS-6591 [S] It Hurts to Say Goodbye 1967 15.00

**LYNNE, GLORIA**

ABC IMPULSE!

❑ ASD-9311 I Don't Know How to Love Him 1976 12.00

CANYON

❑ 7709 Happy and In Love 1970 15.00

Lynyrd Skynyrd, *Lynyrd Skynyrd 1991,* Atlantic A1-82258, 1991, $20.

| Number | Title (A Side/B Side) | Yr | NM |
|---|---|---|---|
| **COLLECTABLES** | | | |
| COL-5138 | Golden Classics | 198? | 10.00 |
| **DESIGN** | | | |
| D-177 [M] | My Funny Valentine | 196? | 10.00 |
| DS-177 [S] | My Funny Valentine | 196? | 12.00 |
| **EVEREST** | | | |
| ES-1001 [S] | Gloria Lynne Live! Take 1 | 1959 | 40.00 |
| SDBR-1022 [S] | Miss Gloria Lynne | 1959 | 30.00 |
| SDBR-1063 [S] | Lonely and Sentimental | 1960 | 30.00 |
| SDBR-1090 [S] | Try a Little Tenderness | 1960 | 30.00 |
| SDBR-1101 [S] | Day In, Day Out | 1961 | 30.00 |
| SDBR-1126 [S] | I'm Glad There Is You | 1961 | 30.00 |
| SDBR-1128 [S] | He Needs Me | 1961 | 30.00 |
| SDBR-1131 [S] | This Little Boy of Mine | 1961 | 30.00 |
| SDBR-1132 [S] | Gloria Lynne at Basin Street East | 1962 | 30.00 |
| SDBR-1203 [S] | Gloria Blue | 1962 | 30.00 |
| SDBR-1208 [S] | Gloria Lynne at the Las Vegas Thunderbird | 1963 | 30.00 |
| EV-1220 [S] | Gloria, Marty & Strings | 1963 | 30.00 |
| EV-1226 [S] | I Wish You Love | 1964 | 25.00 |
| EV-1228 [S] | Glorious Gloria Lynne | 1964 | 25.00 |
| EV-1230 [S] | After Hours | 1965 | 25.00 |
| EV-1231 [S] | The Best of Gloria Lynne | 1965 | 20.00 |
| EV-1237 [S] | Go! Go! Go! | 1965 | 20.00 |
| EV-1238 [S] | Gloria Lynne '66 | 1966 | 20.00 |
| E-5001 [M] | Gloria Lynne Live! Take 1 | 1959 | 30.00 |
| LPBR-5022 [M] | Miss Gloria Lynne | 1959 | 20.00 |
| LPBR-5063 [M] | Lonely and Sentimental | 1960 | 20.00 |
| LPBR-5090 [M] | Try a Little Tenderness | 1960 | 20.00 |
| LPBR-5101 [M] | Day In, Day Out | 1961 | 20.00 |
| LPBR-5126 [M] | I'm Glad There Is You | 1961 | 20.00 |
| LPBR-5128 [M] | He Needs Me | 1961 | 20.00 |
| LPBR-5131 [M] | This Little Boy of Mine | 1961 | 20.00 |
| LPBR-5132 [M] | Gloria Lynne at Basin Street East | 1962 | 20.00 |
| LPBR-5203 [M] | Gloria Blue | 1962 | 20.00 |
| LPBR-5208 [M] | Gloria Lynne at the Las Vegas Thunderbird | 1963 | 20.00 |
| EV-5220 [M] | Gloria, Marty & Strings | 1963 | 20.00 |
| EV-5226 [M] | I Wish You Love | 1964 | 20.00 |
| EV-5228 [M] | Glorious Gloria Lynne | 1964 | 20.00 |
| EV-5230 [M] | After Hours | 1965 | 20.00 |
| EV-5231 [M] | The Best of Gloria Lynne | 1965 | 15.00 |
| EV-5237 [M] | Go! Go! Go! | 1965 | 15.00 |
| EV-5238 [M] | Gloria Lynne '66 | 1966 | 15.00 |
| ST-90057 [M] | I Wish You Love | 196? | 25.00 |
| *—Capitol Record Club edition* | | | |
| **FONTANA** | | | |
| MGF-27528 [M] | Intimate Moments | 1964 | 15.00 |
| MGF-27541 [M] | Soul Serenade | 1965 | 15.00 |
| MGF-27546 [M] | Love and a Woman | 1965 | 15.00 |
| MGF-27555 [M] | Where It's At | 1966 | 15.00 |
| MGF-27561 [M] | Gloria | 1966 | 15.00 |
| MGF-27571 [M] | The Other Side of Gloria Lynne | 1967 | 20.00 |
| SRF-67528 [S] | Intimate Moments | 1964 | 20.00 |
| SRF-67541 [S] | Soul Serenade | 1965 | 20.00 |
| SRF-67546 [S] | Love and a Woman | 1965 | 20.00 |
| SRF-67555 [S] | Where It's At | 1966 | 20.00 |
| SRF-67561 [S] | Gloria | 1966 | 20.00 |
| SRF-67571 [S] | The Other Side of Gloria Lynne | 1967 | 15.00 |
| SRF-67577 | Here, There and Everywhere | 1968 | 15.00 |
| **HIFI** | | | |
| L-440 [M] | The Gloria Lynne Calendar | 1966 | 15.00 |
| SL-440 [S] | The Gloria Lynne Calendar | 1966 | 20.00 |
| SR-441 | Greatest Hits | 1969 | 15.00 |
| **INTERMEDIA** | | | |
| QS-5069 | Classics | 198? | 10.00 |
| **MERCURY** | | | |
| SRM-1-633 | A Very Gentle Sound | 1972 | 15.00 |
| **MUSE** | | | |
| MR-5381 | A Time for Love | 198? | 10.00 |
| **SUNSET** | | | |
| SUM-1145 [M] | Gloria Lynne | 1966 | 12.00 |
| SUM-1171 [M] | I Wish You Love | 1967 | 12.00 |
| SUS-5145 [S] | Gloria Lynne | 1966 | 12.00 |
| SUS-5171 [S] | I Wish You Love | 1967 | 12.00 |
| SUS-5221 | Golden Greats | 1968 | 12.00 |
| **UPFRONT** | | | |
| 146 | Gloria Lynne | 197? | 12.00 |

**LYNYRD SKYNYRD**

| Number | Title (A Side/B Side) | Yr | NM |
|---|---|---|---|
| **ATLANTIC** | | | |
| A1-82258 | Lynyrd Skynyrd 1991 | 1991 | 20.00 |
| *—The only U.S. vinyl version was released through Columbia House* | | | |
| **MCA** | | | |
| 363 | (pronounced leh-nerd skin-nerd) | 1975 | 12.00 |
| *—Reissue on black rainbow label* | | | |
| 413 | Second Helping | 1975 | 12.00 |
| *—Reissue on black rainbow label* | | | |
| 1448 | Best of the Rest | 1985 | 8.00 |
| L33-1946 [(2)DJ] | One More From the Road | 1976 | 25.00 |
| *—Promo only on black vinyl* | | | |
| L33-1946 [(2)DJ] | One More From the Road | 1976 | 50.00 |
| *—Promo on blue, gold, purple or red vinyl (each has the same value)* | | | |
| L33-1988 [DJ] | Skynyrd's First and…Last | 1978 | 25.00 |
| *—Promo sampler* | | | |
| 2137 | Nuthin' Fancy | 1975 | 12.00 |
| 2170 | Gimme Back My Bullets | 1976 | 12.00 |
| 3019 | (pronounced leh-nerd skin-nerd) | 1976 | 10.00 |
| *—Second reissue with new number on black rainbow label* | | | |
| 3020 | Second Helping | 1976 | 10.00 |
| *—Second reissue with new number on black rainbow label* | | | |
| 3021 | Nuthin' Fancy | 1976 | 10.00 |
| *—Reissue with new number on black rainbow label* | | | |
| 3022 | Gimme Back My Bullets | 1977 | 10.00 |
| *—Reissue with new number on black rainbow label* | | | |
| 3029 | Street Survivors | 1977 | 10.00 |
| *—After the band's plane crash, the "flames" photo was replaced with the back cover photo; the back cover is black with only the song titles* | | | |
| 3029 | Street Survivors | 1977 | 25.00 |
| *—Originals with the band in flames on the front cover and a smaller band photo on the back cover* | | | |
| 3047 | Skynyrd's First and…Last | 1978 | 12.00 |
| *—Originals with tan labels and gatefold cover* | | | |
| 5221 | (pronounced leh-nerd skin-nerd) | 1980 | 8.00 |
| 5222 | Second Helping | 1980 | 8.00 |
| 5223 | Street Survivors | 1980 | 8.00 |
| 5370 | Best of the Rest | 1982 | 10.00 |
| *—Original version* | | | |
| 6001 [(2)] | One More From the Road | 1976 | 15.00 |
| *—Originals with black rainbow label and gatefold cover* | | | |
| 6897 [(2)] | One More From the Road | 1985 | 10.00 |
| *—Most, if not all, of these pressings have no gatefold* | | | |
| 6898 [(2)] | Gold & Platinum | 1985 | 10.00 |
| *—Most, if not all, of these pressings have no gatefold* | | | |
| 8011 [(2)] | One More From the Road | 1977 | 12.00 |
| *—First reissue with new number* | | | |
| 8027 [(2)] | Southern by the Grace of God | 1988 | 12.00 |
| 10014 [(2)] | One More From the Road | 1980 | 10.00 |
| *—Second reissue* | | | |
| 11008 [(2)] | Gold & Platinum | 1979 | 12.00 |
| *—Originals with embossed gatefold cover* | | | |
| 37069 | Gimme Back My Bullets | 1980 | 8.00 |
| 37070 | Nuthin' Fancy | 1980 | 8.00 |
| 37071 | Skynyrd's First and…Last | 1980 | 8.00 |
| 37211 | (pronounced leh-nerd skin-nerd) | 1985 | 8.00 |
| 37212 | Second Helping | 1985 | 8.00 |
| 37213 | Street Survivors | 1985 | 8.00 |
| 42084 | Legend | 1987 | 10.00 |
| 42293 | Skynyrd's Innyrds | 1989 | 12.00 |
| **SOUNDS OF THE SOUTH** | | | |
| 363 | (pronounced leh-nerd skin-nerd) | 1973 | 20.00 |
| 413 | Second Helping | 1974 | 20.00 |
| *—Both of the above are original pressings with yellow labels* | | | |

**LYONS, JIMMY**

| Number | Title (A Side/B Side) | Yr | NM |
|---|---|---|---|
| **HAT HUT** | | | |
| Y/Z/Z [(3)] | Push | 1979 | 25.00 |
| 21 [(2)] | Jump Up/What to Do About | 198? | 20.00 |

**LYTLE, JOHNNY**

| Number | Title (A Side/B Side) | Yr | NM |
|---|---|---|---|
| **JAZZLAND** | | | |
| JLP-22 [M] | Blue Vibes | 1960 | 25.00 |
| JLP-44 [M] | Happy Ground | 1961 | 25.00 |
| JLP-67 [M] | Nice and Easy | 1962 | 25.00 |
| JLP-81 [M] | Moon Child | 1962 | 25.00 |
| JLP-922 [S] | Blue Vibes | 1960 | 30.00 |
| JLP-944 [S] | Happy Ground | 1961 | 30.00 |
| JLP-967 [S] | Nice and Easy | 1962 | 30.00 |
| JLP-981 [S] | Moon Child | 1962 | 30.00 |
| **RIVERSIDE** | | | |
| RLP-456 [M] | Got That Feeling | 1963 | 20.00 |
| RLP-470 [M] | Happy Ground | 1964 | 20.00 |
| RLP-480 [M] | The Village Caller | 1965 | 20.00 |
| RM-3003 [M] | A Groove | 1967 | 30.00 |
| RS-3003 [S] | A Groove | 1967 | 20.00 |
| RS-9456 [S] | Got That Feeling | 1963 | 25.00 |
| RS-9470 [S] | Happy Ground | 1964 | 25.00 |
| RS-9480 [S] | The Village Caller | 1965 | 25.00 |
| **SOLID STATE** | | | |
| SS-18014 | A Man and a Woman | 1967 | 20.00 |
| SS-18044 | Be Proud | 1969 | 20.00 |
| SS-18056 | Close Enough | 1969 | 20.00 |

**LYTTELTON, HUMPHREY**

| Number | Title (A Side/B Side) | Yr | NM |
|---|---|---|---|
| **ANGEL** | | | |
| ANG.60008 [10] | Some Like It Hot | 1955 | 60.00 |
| **BETHLEHEM** | | | |
| BCP-6063 [M] | Humph Plays Standards | 1961 | 30.00 |
| **LONDON** | | | |
| PS 178 [S] | Humph Dedicates | 1959 | 25.00 |
| LL 3101 [M] | I Play As I Please | 195? | 30.00 |
| LL 3132 [M] | Humph Dedicates | 195? | 30.00 |



**Except when noted otherwise, VG = 25% of NM, and VG+ = 50% of NM. (Example: VG = $2.00, VG+ = $4.00 and NM = $8.00.)**

# M

## MABERN, HAROLD

PRESTIGE

| Number | Title (A Side/B Side) | Yr | NM |
|---|---|---|---|
| ❑ PRST-7568 | A Few Miles from Memphis | 1968 | 20.00 |
| ❑ PRST-7624 | Rakin' and Scrapin' | 1969 | 20.00 |
| ❑ PRST-7687 | Workin' and Wailin' | 1969 | 20.00 |
| ❑ PRST-7764 | Greasy Kid Stuff | 1970 | 20.00 |

## MABLEY, MOMS

CHESS

| Number | Title (A Side/B Side) | Yr | NM |
|---|---|---|---|
| ❑ LP-1447 [M] | Moms Mabley, Funniest Woman in the World, Onstage | 1961 | 25.00 |
| ❑ LP-1452 [M] | Moms Mabley at the "UN" | 1961 | 25.00 |
| ❑ LP-1460 [M] | Moms Mabley at the Playboy Club | 1961 | 25.00 |
| ❑ LP-1463 [M] | Moms Mabley at Geneva Conference | 1962 | 25.00 |
| ❑ LP-1472 [M] | Moms Mabley Breaks It Up | 1962 | 25.00 |
| ❑ LP-1477 [M] | Young Men, Si — Old Men, No | 1962 | 25.00 |
| ❑ LP-1479 [M] | I Got Somethin' to Tell You! | 1963 | 25.00 |
| ❑ LP-1482 [M] | The Funny Sides of Moms Mabley | 1963 | 25.00 |
| ❑ LP-1486 [M] | Moms Wows | 1964 | 25.00 |
| ❑ LP-1487 [M] | The Best of Moms | 1964 | 25.00 |
| ❑ LP-1497 [M] | The Man in My Life | 1965 | 20.00 |
| ❑ LPS-1525 | Moms Mabley Breaks Up the Network | 1968 | 20.00 |
| ❑ LPS-1530 | Moms Mabley Sings | 1969 | 20.00 |

MERCURY

| Number | Title (A Side/B Side) | Yr | NM |
|---|---|---|---|
| ❑ MG-20889 [M] | Out on a Limb | 1964 | 15.00 |
| ❑ MG-20907 [M] | Moms the Word | 1964 | 15.00 |
| ❑ MG-21012 [M] | Now Hear This | 1965 | 15.00 |
| ❑ MG-21090 [M] | Moms Mabley at the White House | 1966 | 15.00 |
| ❑ MG-21139 [M] | The Best of Moms Mabley | 1967 | 25.00 |
| ❑ SR-60889 [S] | Out on a Limb | 1964 | 20.00 |
| ❑ SR-60907 [S] | Moms the Word | 1964 | 20.00 |
| ❑ SR-61012 [S] | Now Hear This | 1965 | 20.00 |
| ❑ SR-61090 [S] | Moms Mabley at the White House | 1966 | 20.00 |
| ❑ SR-61139 [S] | The Best of Moms Mabley | 1967 | 15.00 |
| ❑ SR-61205 | Her Young Thing | 1969 | 15.00 |
| ❑ SR-61229 | The Youngest Teenager | 1969 | 15.00 |
| ❑ SR-61235 | Abraham, Martin and John | 1969 | 15.00 |
| ❑ SR-61263 | Live at Sing Sing | 1970 | 15.00 |

## MABON, WILLIE

CHESS

| Number | Title (A Side/B Side) | Yr | NM |
|---|---|---|---|
| ❑ LP-1439 [M] | Willie Mabon | 1958 | 400.00 |

*—Black label*

## MACARTHUR, DOUGLAS

ATCO

| Number | Title (A Side/B Side) | Yr | NM |
|---|---|---|---|
| ❑ 8095 [M] | The Life of General MacArthur | 1964 | 40.00 |

## MACDONALD, JEANETTE, AND NELSON EDDY

RCA VICTOR

| Number | Title (A Side/B Side) | Yr | NM |
|---|---|---|---|
| ❑ LPT-16 [10] | Rose Marie | 1952 | 60.00 |
| ❑ LPV-526 [M] | Rose Marie | 1965 | 25.00 |
| ❑ LPM-1738 [M] | Favorites in Hi-Fi | 1958 | 40.00 |

## MACEO AND ALL THE KING'S MEN

EXCELLO

| Number | Title (A Side/B Side) | Yr | NM |
|---|---|---|---|
| ❑ LPS-8022 | Funky Music Machine | 1972 | 30.00 |

HOUSE OF FOX

| Number | Title (A Side/B Side) | Yr | NM |
|---|---|---|---|
| ❑ LP-1 | Doing Their Own Thing | 1971 | 30.00 |

## MACEO AND THE MACKS

PEOPLE

| Number | Title (A Side/B Side) | Yr | NM |
|---|---|---|---|
| ❑ PE-6601 | Us | 1973 | 30.00 |

## MACERO, TEO

COLUMBIA

| Number | Title (A Side/B Side) | Yr | NM |
|---|---|---|---|
| ❑ CL 842 [M] | What's New? | 1956 | 80.00 |

*—Red and black label with six "eye" logos*

DEBUT

| Number | Title (A Side/B Side) | Yr | NM |
|---|---|---|---|
| ❑ DLP-6 [10] | Explorations by Teo Macero | 1954 | 500.00 |

PRESTIGE

| Number | Title (A Side/B Side) | Yr | NM |
|---|---|---|---|
| ❑ PRLP-7104 [M] | Teo — Teo Macero with the Prestige Jazz Quartet | 1957 | 150.00 |

## MACHITO

CLEF

| Number | Title (A Side/B Side) | Yr | NM |
|---|---|---|---|
| ❑ MGC-505 [10] | Afro-Cuban Jazz | 1953 | 150.00 |
| ❑ MGC-511 [10] | Machito Jazz with Flip and Bird | 1953 | 150.00 |
| ❑ MGC-689 [M] | Afro-Cuban Jazz | 1956 | 100.00 |

CORAL

| Number | Title (A Side/B Side) | Yr | NM |
|---|---|---|---|
| ❑ CRL 57258 [M] | Vacation at the Concord | 1959 | 40.00 |
| ❑ CRL 757258 [S] | Vacation at the Concord | 1959 | 30.00 |

DECCA

| Number | Title (A Side/B Side) | Yr | NM |
|---|---|---|---|
| ❑ DL 5157 [10] | Machito's Afro-Cuban | 1950 | 200.00 |

MERCURY

| Number | Title (A Side/B Side) | Yr | NM |
|---|---|---|---|
| ❑ MGC-505 [10] | Afro-Cuban Jazz | 1951 | 200.00 |
| ❑ MGC-511 [10] | Machito Jazz with Flip and Bird | 1952 | 200.00 |
| ❑ MG-25009 [10] | Jungle Drums | 1950 | 200.00 |
| ❑ MG-25020 [10] | Rhumbas | 1950 | 200.00 |

RCA VICTOR

| Number | Title (A Side/B Side) | Yr | NM |
|---|---|---|---|
| ❑ LPM-3944 [M] | Machito Goes Memphis | 1968 | 40.00 |
| ❑ LSP-3944 [S] | Machito Goes Memphis | 1968 | 20.00 |

ROULETTE

| Number | Title (A Side/B Side) | Yr | NM |
|---|---|---|---|
| ❑ R-52006 [M] | Kenya | 1958 | 40.00 |
| ❑ SR-52006 [S] | Kenya | 1958 | 30.00 |
| ❑ R-52026 [M] | With Flute to Boot | 1959 | 40.00 |
| ❑ SR-52026 [S] | With Flute to Boot | 1959 | 30.00 |

TICO

| Number | Title (A Side/B Side) | Yr | NM |
|---|---|---|---|
| ❑ LP-138 [10] | El Niche | 1956 | 150.00 |
| ❑ LP-1002 [M] | Cha Cha Cha at the Palladium | 1955 | 80.00 |
| ❑ LP-1029 [M] | Asia Minor Cha Cha Cha | 1956 | 80.00 |
| ❑ LP-1033 [M] | Si Si, No No | 1957 | 80.00 |
| ❑ LP-1045 [M] | Inspired by "The Sun Also Rises" | 1957 | 80.00 |
| ❑ LP-1053 [M] | Mi Amigo, Machito | 1959 | 60.00 |
| ❑ LP-1062 [M] | Irving Berlin in Latin America | 1959 | 60.00 |
| ❑ LP-1074 [M] | A Night with Machito | 1960 | 50.00 |
| ❑ LPS-1074 [S] | A Night with Machito | 1960 | 60.00 |
| ❑ LP-1084 [M] | The New Sound of Machito (El Sonido Nuevo de Machito) | 1962 | 40.00 |
| ❑ LPS-1084 [S] | The New Sound of Machito (El Sonido Nuevo de Machito) | 1962 | 50.00 |
| ❑ LP-1090 [M] | Variedades | 1963 | 40.00 |
| ❑ LPS-1090 [S] | Variedades | 1963 | 50.00 |
| ❑ LP-1094 [M] | Tremendo Cumban! | 1963 | 40.00 |
| ❑ LPS-1094 [S] | Tremendo Cumban! | 1963 | 50.00 |
| ❑ CLP-1314 | Latin Soul Plus Jazz | 1973 | 20.00 |
| ❑ CLP-1328 | Lo Mejor De Machito Y Sus AfroCubans Con Graciela | 1974 | 20.00 |

VERVE

| Number | Title (A Side/B Side) | Yr | NM |
|---|---|---|---|
| ❑ VSP-19 [M] | Soul Source | 1966 | 20.00 |
| ❑ MGV-8073 [M] | Afro-Cuban Jazz | 1957 | 50.00 |
| ❑ V-8073 [M] | Afro-Cuban Jazz | 1961 | 20.00 |

## MACK, DAVID

SEREMUS

| Number | Title (A Side/B Side) | Yr | NM |
|---|---|---|---|
| ❑ SRE-1009 [M] | New Directions | 1965 | 20.00 |
| ❑ SRS-12009 [S] | New Directions | 1965 | 25.00 |

## MACK, LONNIE

ALLIGATOR

| Number | Title (A Side/B Side) | Yr | NM |
|---|---|---|---|
| ❑ AL-3903 | The Wham of That Memphis Man | 1987 | 10.00 |

*—Reissue of Fraternity LP*

| Number | Title (A Side/B Side) | Yr | NM |
|---|---|---|---|
| ❑ AL-4739 | Strike Like Lightning | 1985 | 10.00 |
| ❑ AL-4750 | Second Sight | 1987 | 10.00 |
| ❑ AL-4786 | Live!: Attack of the Killer V | 1990 | 12.00 |

CAPITOL

| Number | Title (A Side/B Side) | Yr | NM |
|---|---|---|---|
| ❑ ST-11619 | Home at Last | 1976 | 12.00 |
| ❑ ST-11703 | Lonnie Mack and Pismo | 1977 | 12.00 |

ELEKTRA

| Number | Title (A Side/B Side) | Yr | NM |
|---|---|---|---|
| ❑ EKS-74040 | Glad I'm In the Band | 1969 | 25.00 |
| ❑ EKS-74050 | Whatever's Right | 1969 | 25.00 |
| ❑ EKS-74077 | For Collectors Only | 1970 | 25.00 |
| ❑ EKS-74102 | The Hills of Indiana | 1971 | 25.00 |

EPIC

| Number | Title (A Side/B Side) | Yr | NM |
|---|---|---|---|
| ❑ FE 44075 | Roadhouses and Dance Halls | 1989 | 12.00 |

FRATERNITY

| Number | Title (A Side/B Side) | Yr | NM |
|---|---|---|---|
| ❑ SF-1014 [M] | The Wham of That Memphis Man | 1963 | 120.00 |
| ❑ SSF-1014 [S] | The Wham of That Memphis Man | 1963 | 300.00 |

TRIP

| Number | Title (A Side/B Side) | Yr | NM |
|---|---|---|---|
| ❑ TLX-9522 [(2)] | The Memphis Sounds of Lonnie Mack | 1975 | 12.00 |

## MACK, WARNER

DECCA

| Number | Title (A Side/B Side) | Yr | NM |
|---|---|---|---|
| ❑ DL 4692 [M] | The Bridge Washed Out | 1965 | 20.00 |
| ❑ DL 4766 [M] | The Country Touch | 1966 | 20.00 |
| ❑ DL 4883 [M] | Drifting Apart | 1967 | 25.00 |
| ❑ DL 4912 [M] | Songs We Sand in Church and Home | 1967 | 25.00 |
| ❑ DL 74692 [S] | The Bridge Washed Out | 1965 | 25.00 |
| ❑ DL 74766 [S] | The Country Touch | 1966 | 25.00 |
| ❑ DL 74883 [S] | Drifting Apart | 1967 | 20.00 |
| ❑ DL 74912 [S] | Songs We Sand in Church and Home | 1967 | 20.00 |
| ❑ DL 74995 | The Many Country Moods of Warner Mack | 1968 | 20.00 |
| ❑ DL 75092 | The Country Beat of Warner Mack | 1969 | 20.00 |
| ❑ DL 75165 | I'll Still Be Missing You | 1969 | 20.00 |

KAPP

| Number | Title (A Side/B Side) | Yr | NM |
|---|---|---|---|
| ❑ KL-1255 [M] | Golden Country Hits | 1961 | 20.00 |
| ❑ KL-1279 [M] | Golden Country Hits, Vol. 2 | 1962 | 20.00 |
| ❑ KL-1461 [M] | Everybody's Country Favorites | 196? | 15.00 |
| ❑ KS-3255 [S] | Golden Country Hits | 1961 | 25.00 |
| ❑ KS-3279 [S] | Golden Country Hits, Vol. 2 | 1962 | 25.00 |
| ❑ KS-3461 [S] | Everybody's Country Favorites | 196? | 20.00 |

## MACKAY, BRUCE

ORO

| Number | Title (A Side/B Side) | Yr | NM |
|---|---|---|---|
| ❑ 1 | Bruce Mackay | 196? | 20.00 |

## MACKAY, DAVID, AND VICKI HAMILTON

ABC IMPULSE!

| Number | Title (A Side/B Side) | Yr | NM |
|---|---|---|---|
| ❑ AS-9184 | David MacKay and Vicki Hamilton | 1969 | 20.00 |

## MACKENZIE, GISELE

EVEREST

| Number | Title (A Side/B Side) | Yr | NM |
|---|---|---|---|
| ❑ SDBR-1069 [S] | In Person at the Empire Room | 1959 | 30.00 |
| ❑ LPBR-5069 [M] | In Person at the Empire Room | 1959 | 25.00 |

GLENDALE

| Number | Title (A Side/B Side) | Yr | NM |
|---|---|---|---|
| ❑ GL-6017 | Gisele MacKenzie Sings | 1978 | 12.00 |

RCA VICTOR

| Number | Title (A Side/B Side) | Yr | NM |
|---|---|---|---|
| ❑ LPM-1790 [M] | Gisele | 1958 | 30.00 |
| ❑ LSP-1790 [S] | Gisele | 1958 | 40.00 |
| ❑ LPM-2006 [M] | Christmas with Gisele | 1959 | 30.00 |
| ❑ LSP-2006 [S] | Christmas with Gisele | 1959 | 40.00 |

SUNSET

| Number | Title (A Side/B Side) | Yr | NM |
|---|---|---|---|
| ❑ SUM-1155 [M] | In Person at the Empire Room | 196? | 12.00 |
| ❑ SUS-5155 [S] | In Person at the Empire Room | 196? | 15.00 |

VIK

| Number | Title (A Side/B Side) | Yr | NM |
|---|---|---|---|
| ❑ LX-1055 [M] | Gisele MacKenzie | 1956 | 40.00 |
| ❑ LX-1075 [M] | Mam'selle MacKenzie | 1956 | 40.00 |
| ❑ LX-1099 [M] | Christmas with Gisele | 1957 | 40.00 |

## MACON, UNCLE DAVE

DECCA

| Number | Title (A Side/B Side) | Yr | NM |
|---|---|---|---|
| ❑ DL 4760 [M] | Uncle Dave Macon | 1966 | 30.00 |

## MACRAE, GORDON

ALLEGRO ROYALE

| Number | Title (A Side/B Side) | Yr | NM |
|---|---|---|---|
| ❑ 1606 [M] | Gordon MacRae | 1952 | 20.00 |

ANGEL

| Number | Title (A Side/B Side) | Yr | NM |
|---|---|---|---|
| ❑ S 37318 | The Student Prince | 1973 | 10.00 |

*—Operetta with Dorothy Kirsten; reissue of Capitol SW 1841*

| Number | Title (A Side/B Side) | Yr | NM |
|---|---|---|---|
| ❑ S 37319 | The Desert Song | 1973 | 10.00 |

*—Operetta with Dorothy Kirsten; reissue of Capitol SW 1842*

| Number | Title (A Side/B Side) | Yr | NM |
|---|---|---|---|
| ❑ S 37320 | The New Moon | 1973 | 10.00 |

*—Operetta with Dorothy Kirsten; reissue of Capitol SW 1966*

CAPITOL

| Number | Title (A Side/B Side) | Yr | NM |
|---|---|---|---|
| ❑ ST-125 | Only Love | 1969 | 12.00 |
| ❑ H 218 [10] | The Vagabond King | 1951 | 50.00 |

*—Operetta with Lucille Norman*

| Number | Title (A Side/B Side) | Yr | NM |
|---|---|---|---|
| ❑ P 219 [M] | New Moon and The Vagabond King | 1951 | 30.00 |

*—Operettas with Lucille Norman; original*

| Number | Title (A Side/B Side) | Yr | NM |
|---|---|---|---|
| ❑ T 219 [M] | New Moon and The Vagabond King | 195? | 30.00 |

*—Operettas with Lucille Norman; turquoise label*

| Number | Title (A Side/B Side) | Yr | NM |
|---|---|---|---|
| ❑ H 231 [10] | Gordon MacRae Sings | 1951 | 40.00 |
| ❑ L 334 [10] | Roberta | 1952 | 40.00 |

*—Operetta with Lucille Norman and Anne Triola*

| Number | Title (A Side/B Side) | Yr | NM |
|---|---|---|---|
| ❑ L 335 [10] | The Merry Widow | 1952 | 40.00 |

*—With Lucille Norman*

| Number | Title (A Side/B Side) | Yr | NM |
|---|---|---|---|
| ❑ L 351 [10] | The Desert Song | 1953 | 40.00 |

*—Operetta with Lucille Norman and Bob Sands*

| Number | Title (A Side/B Side) | Yr | NM |
|---|---|---|---|
| ❑ T 394 [M] | The Desert Song and Roberta | 195? | 30.00 |

*—Turquoise label original*

| Number | Title (A Side/B Side) | Yr | NM |
|---|---|---|---|
| ❑ L 407 [10] | The Student Prince | 1953 | 40.00 |

*—Operetta with Dorothy Warenskjold and Harry Stanton*

| Number | Title (A Side/B Side) | Yr | NM |
|---|---|---|---|
| ❑ H 422 [10] | By the Light of the Silvery Moon | 1953 | 40.00 |

*—With June Hutton; not the soundtrack from the movie because MacRae and movie co-star Doris Day were on different labels*

| Number | Title (A Side/B Side) | Yr | NM |
|---|---|---|---|
| ❑ P 437 [M] | The Student Prince and The Merry Widow | 1953 | 40.00 |

*—Original*

| Number | Title (A Side/B Side) | Yr | NM |
|---|---|---|---|
| ❑ T 437 [M] | The Student Prince and The Merry Widow | 195? | 30.00 |

*—Turqiouse label original*

| Number | Title (A Side/B Side) | Yr | NM |
|---|---|---|---|
| ❑ L 468 [10] | Naughty Marietta | 1954 | 40.00 |

*—Operetta with Marguerite Piazza*

| Number | Title (A Side/B Side) | Yr | NM |
|---|---|---|---|
| ❑ L 485 [10] | 3 Sailors and a Girl | 1953 | 60.00 |

*—With Jane Powell and Gene Nelson*

| Number | Title (A Side/B Side) | Yr | NM |
|---|---|---|---|
| ❑ L 530 [10] | The Red Mill | 1954 | 40.00 |

*—Operetta with Lucille Norman*

| Number | Title (A Side/B Side) | Yr | NM |
|---|---|---|---|
| ❑ T 537 [M] | Romantic Ballads | 1955 | 30.00 |

*—Turquoise or gray label*

| Number | Title (A Side/B Side) | Yr | NM |
|---|---|---|---|
| ❑ T 551 [M] | Naughty Marietta and The Red Mill | 1955 | 30.00 |

*—Turquoise label original*

| Number | Title (A Side/B Side) | Yr | NM |
|---|---|---|---|
| ❑ T 681 [M] | Operetta Favorites | 1956 | 30.00 |

*—Turquoise or gray label*

| Number | Title (A Side/B Side) | Yr | NM |
|---|---|---|---|
| ❑ T 765 [M] | The Best Things in Life Are Free | 1956 | 30.00 |

*—Turquoise or gray label*

| Number | Title (A Side/B Side) | Yr | NM |
|---|---|---|---|
| ❑ T 834 [M] | Cowboy's Lament | 1957 | 30.00 |

*—Turquoise or gray label*

| Number | Title (A Side/B Side) | Yr | NM |
|---|---|---|---|
| ❑ T 875 [M] | Motion Picture Soundstage | 1957 | 30.00 |

*—Turquoise or gray label*

| Number | Title (A Side/B Side) | Yr | NM |
|---|---|---|---|
| ❑ ST 980 [S] | Gordon MacRae in Concert | 1959 | 40.00 |

*—Black colorband label, logo at left*

| Number | Title (A Side/B Side) | Yr | NM |
|---|---|---|---|
| ❑ T 980 [M] | Gordon MacRae in Concert | 1957 | 30.00 |

*—Turquoise or gray label*

Number | Title (A Side/B Side) | Yr | NM

❑ T 1050 [M] This Is Gordon MacRae 1958 30.00
*—Turquoise label*
❑ ST 1146 [S] The Seasons of Love 1959 20.00
*—Black colorband label, Capitol logo at left*
❑ T 1146 [M] The Seasons of Love 1959 15.00
*—Black colorband label, Capitol logo at left*
❑ ST 1251 [S] Songs for an Evening at Home 1959 20.00
*—Black colorband label, Capitol logo at left*
❑ T 1251 [M] Songs for an Evening at Home 1959 15.00
*—Black colorband label, Capitol logo at left*
❑ ST 1353 [S] Our Love Story 1960 20.00
*—With Sheila MacRae; black colorband label, Capitol logo at left*
❑ T 1353 [M] Our Love Story 1960 15.00
*—With Sheila MacRae; black colorband label, Capitol logo at left*
❑ ST 1466 [S] Hallowed Be Thy Name 1960 20.00
*—Black colorband label, Capitol logo at left*
❑ T 1466 [M] Hallowed Be Thy Name 1960 15.00
*—Black colorband label, Capitol logo at left*
❑ SW 1841 [S] The Student Prince 1963 15.00
*—Operetta with Dorothy Kirsten*
❑ W 1841 [M] The Student Prince 1963 12.00
*—Opertta with Dorothy Kirsten*
❑ SW 1842 [S] The Desert Song 1963 15.00
*—Operetta with Dorothy Kirsten*
❑ W 1842 [M] The Desert Song 1963 12.00
*—Operetta with Dorothy Kirsten*
❑ SW 1966 [S] The New Moon 1963 15.00
*—Operetta with Dorothy Kirsten*
❑ W 1966 [M] The New Moon 1963 12.00
*—Operetta with Dorothy Kirsten*
❑ SW 2022 [S] Kismet 1964 15.00
*—Operetta with Dorothy Kirsten*
❑ W 2022 [M] Kismet 1964 12.00
*—Operetta with Dorothy Kirsten*
❑ ST 2578 [S] If She Walked Into My Life 1966 15.00
❑ T 2578 [M] If She Walked Into My Life 1966 12.00

COLORTONE
❑ 4939 [M] Gordon MacRae Sings 1958 15.00

EVON
❑ 320 [M] Gordon MacRae Sings 1958 15.00
*—Reissue of Allegro Royale LP*

GALAXY
❑ 4805 [M] Gordon MacRae 1958 15.00
*—Reissue of Allegro Royale LP*

RONDO-LETTE
❑ A5 [M] Gordon MacRae 1958 15.00
*—Reissue of Allegro Royale LP*

ROYALE
❑ 18106 [10] Gordon MacRae and Walter Gross Orchestra 195? 30.00
❑ 18155 [10] Gordon MacRae and Orchestra 195? 30.00

SUTTON
❑ SSU 292 [R] Gordon MacRae Sings Broadway's Best! 196? 10.00
❑ SU 292 [M] Gordon MacRae Sings Broadway's Best! 196? 10.00

**MACRAE, GORDON, AND JO STAFFORD** See JO STAFFORD AND GORDON MacRAE.

**MACRAE, SHEILA**

ABC
❑ ABCS-611 How Sweet She Is 1968 25.00

**MAD LADS, THE**

STAX
❑ MPS-8525 The Best of the Mad Lads 198? 10.00

VOLT
❑ 414 [M] The Mad Lads In Action 1966 30.00
❑ S-414 [S] The Mad Lads In Action 1966 40.00
❑ VOS-6005 The Mad, Mad, Mad, Mad, Mad Lads 1969 30.00
❑ VOS-6020 A New Beginning 1973 20.00

**MAD RIVER**

CAPITOL
❑ ST-185 Paradise Bar and Grill 1969 40.00
❑ ST 2985 Mad River 1968 50.00

**MADDOX, JOHNNY**

DOT
❑ DLP-102 [10] Authentic Ragtime 1952 40.00
❑ DLP-3000 [M] Ragtime Melodies 1955 25.00
❑ DLP-3005 [M] Johnny Maddox Plays 1956 25.00
❑ DLP-3008 [M] Tap Dance Rhythms 1956 25.00
❑ DLP-3044 [M] King of Ragtime 1957 20.00
❑ DLP-3063 [M] The Thirties in Ragtime 1957 20.00
❑ DLP-3067 [M] My Old Flames 1957 20.00
❑ DLP-3108 [M] Ragtime Piano 1917-18 1958 15.00
❑ DLP-3122 [M] Johnny Maddox Plays the Million Sellers 1958 15.00
❑ DLP-3131 [M] Dieieland Blues 1959 15.00
❑ DLP-3198 [M] Old Fashioned Love 1959 15.00
❑ DLP-3289 [M] Crazy Otto Piano 1960 12.00
❑ DLP-3314 [M] Johnny Maddox Plays More Million Sellers 1960 12.00
❑ DLP-3321 [M] The World's Greatest Piano Rolls 1960 12.00
❑ DLP-3334 [M] Near You 1960 12.00
❑ DLP-3378 [M] Sabre Dance 1961 12.00
❑ DLP-3476 [M] World's Greatest Piano Rolls, Volume 2 1962 12.00
❑ DLP-3477 [M] World's Greatest Piano Rolls, Volume 3 1962 12.00
❑ DLP-3478 [M] World's Greatest Piano Rolls, Volume 4 1962 12.00
❑ DLP-3493 [M] Ragtime Twenties 1963 12.00
❑ DLP-3521 [M] Ragtime Duets 1963 12.00
*—With Glenn Rowell*
❑ DLP-3539 [M] Memphis 1963 12.00
❑ DLP-3549 [M] Johnny Maddox Plays the Million Sellers, Volume 3 1963 12.00
❑ DLP-3621 [M] Raggin' the Hits 1965 12.00
❑ DLP-3633 [M] Ragtime by Request 1965 12.00
❑ DLP-3645 [M] More Ragtime Twenties 1965 12.00
❑ DLP-3720 [M] World's Greatest Piano Rolls, Volume 5 1966 12.00
❑ DLP-3721 [M] World's Greatest Piano Rolls, Volume 6 1966 12.00
❑ DLP-3722 [M] World's Greatest Piano Rolls, Volume 7 1966 12.00
❑ DLP-3724 [M] Ragtime Memories 1966 12.00
❑ DLP-3739 [M] Ragtime Piano Man 1966 12.00
❑ DLP-3817 [M] Second Hand Rose 1967 15.00
❑ DLP-25122 [S] Johnny Maddox Plays the Million Sellers 1959 20.00
❑ DLP-25131 [S] Dieieland Blues 1959 20.00
❑ DLP-25198 [S] Old Fashioned Love 1959 20.00
❑ DLP-25289 [S] Crazy Otto Piano 1960 15.00
❑ DLP-25314 [S] Johnny Maddox Plays More Million Sellers 1960 15.00
❑ DLP-25321 [S] The World's Greatest Piano Rolls 1960 15.00
❑ DLP-25378 [S] Sabre Dance 1961 15.00
❑ DLP-25476 [S] World's Greatest Piano Rolls, Volume 2 1962 15.00
❑ DLP-25477 [S] World's Greatest Piano Rolls, Volume 3 1962 12.00
❑ DLP-25478 [S] World's Greatest Piano Rolls, Volume 4 1962 15.00
❑ DLP-25493 [S] Ragtime Twenties 1963 15.00
❑ DLP-25521 [S] Ragtime Duets 1963 15.00
*—With Glenn Rowell*
❑ DLP-25539 [S] Memphis 1963 15.00
❑ DLP-25549 [S] Johnny Maddox Plays the Million Sellers, Volume 3 1963 15.00
❑ DLP-25621 [M] Raggin' the Hits 1965 15.00
❑ DLP-25633 [S] Ragtime by Request 1965 15.00
❑ DLP-25645 [S] More Ragtime Twenties 1965 15.00
❑ DLP-25720 [S] World's Greatest Piano Rolls, Volume 5 1966 15.00
❑ DLP-25721 [S] World's Greatest Piano Rolls, Volume 6 1966 15.00
❑ DLP-25722 [S] World's Greatest Piano Rolls, Volume 7 1966 15.00
❑ DLP-25724 [S] Ragtime Memories 1966 15.00
❑ DLP-25739 [S] Ragtime Piano Man 1966 15.00
❑ DLP-25817 [S] Second Hand Rose 1967 15.00

HAMILTON
❑ HLP-115 [M] 12 Ragtime Greats 1964 10.00
❑ HLP-150 [M] Great Marches and Waltzes 1964 10.00
❑ HLP-12115 [S] 12 Ragtime Greats 1964 12.00
❑ HLP-12150 [S] Great Marches and Waltzes 1964 12.00

PARAMOUNT
❑ PAS-2-1029 [(2)]Piano Roll Greats 1974 12.00

PICKWICK
❑ PC-3097 [M] Alley Cat and Other Piano Roll Favorites 196? 12.00
❑ SPC-3097 [S] Alley Cat and Other Piano Roll Favorites 196? 10.00

**MADDOX, LESTER**

LEFEVRE
❑ MLSP-3485 God, Family and Country 197? 40.00

**MADDOX, ROSE** Also see THE MADDOX BROTHERS AND ROSE.

CAPITOL
❑ ST 1312 [S] The One Rose 1960 40.00
❑ T 1312 [M] The One Rose 1960 30.00
❑ ST 1437 [S] Glorybound Train 1960 40.00
❑ T 1437 [M] Glorybound Train 1960 30.00
❑ ST 1548 [S] A Big Bouquet of Roses 1961 40.00
❑ T 1548 [M] A Big Bouquet of Roses 1961 30.00
❑ ST 1799 [S] Rose Maddox Sings Bluegrass 1962 50.00
❑ T 1799 [M] Rose Maddox Sings Bluegrass 1962 40.00
❑ ST 1993 [S] Alone with You 1963 40.00
❑ T 1993 [M] Alone with You 1963 30.00

COLUMBIA
❑ CL 1159 [M] Precious Memories 1958 40.00

**MADDOX BROTHERS AND ROSE** Also see ROSE MADDOX.

KING
❑ 669 [M] A Collection of Standard Sacred Songs 1959 150.00
❑ 677 [M] The Maddox Brothers and Rose 1960 120.00
❑ 752 [M] I'll Write Your Name in the Sand 1961 120.00

WRANGLER
❑ W-1003 [M] The Maddox Brothers and Rose 1962 30.00
❑ WS-1003 [S] The Maddox Brothers and Rose 1962 40.00

**MADIGAN, BETTY**

MGM
❑ E-3448 [M] Am I Blue? 1956 40.00

**MADISON, AL**

GOLDEN CREST
❑ GC-3048 [M] Meet Al Madison 196? 25.00

**MADONNA**

MAVERICK
❑ PRO-A-5904 [(2)DJ]Erotica 1992 60.00
*—Vinyl is promo only*
❑ PRO-A-7311 [(2)DJ]Bedtime Stories 1994 80.00
*—Promo only on pink vinyl*
❑ PRO-A-9378 [(2)DJ]Ray of Light 1998 60.00
*—Vinyl is promo only; generic cover with sticker*
❑ PRO-A-100500-A [(2)DJ]Music 2000 50.00
*—Vinyl is promo only; generic white die-cut sleeve*
❑ PRO-A-100871 [(3)DJ]GHV2 Remixed — The Best of 1991-2001 2001 40.00
*—Promo-only remixes of 12 songs from the "GHV2" CD; comes in generic black jacket with hole in center*

SIRE
❑ PRO-A-2892 You Can Dance 1987 30.00
*—Promo-only; contains single edits of the seven songs on the stock editions*
❑ 23867 Madonna 1983 10.00
*—Second pressing with 3:49 version of "Burning Up"*
❑ 23867 Madonna 1983 20.00
*—First pressing with 4:48 version of "Burning Up"; this version has only been found on copies with a gold promo stamp on the cover*
❑ W1-23867 Madonna 1984 15.00
*—Columbia House edition*
❑ 25157 Like a Virgin 1984 50.00
*—White vinyl with cream colored spine*
❑ 25157 Like a Virgin 1984 60.00
*—White vinyl with silver colored spine*
❑ 25157 Like a Virgin 1984 10.00
❑ W1-25157 Like a Virgin 1985 15.00
*—Columbia House edition*
❑ 25442 True Blue 1986 8.00
*—Without poster*
❑ 25442 True Blue 1986 12.00
*—With poster*
❑ W1-25442 True Blue 1986 15.00
*—Columbia House edition; issued with poster*
❑ 25535 You Can Dance 1987 8.00
*—Without gold obi*
❑ 25535 You Can Dance 1987 12.00
*—With gold obi "Madonna and Dancing"*
❑ W1-25535 You Can Dance 1987 15.00
*—Columbia House edition; not issued with obi*
❑ 25844 Like a Prayer 1989 10.00
❑ W1-25844 Like a Prayer 1989 15.00
*—Columbia House edition*
❑ 26209 I'm Breathless 1990 10.00
❑ W1-26209 I'm Breathless 1990 15.00
*—Columbia House edition*
❑ 26440 [(2)] The Immaculate Collection 1990 15.00
❑ W1-26440 [(2)] The Immaculate Collection 1990 20.00
*—Columbia House edition*
❑ R 100572 I'm Breathless 1990 15.00
*—BMG Direct Marketing edition*
❑ R 101029 Like a Prayer 1989 15.00
*—BMG Direct Marketing edition*
❑ R 134536 You Can Dance 1987 15.00
*—RCA Music Service edition; not issued with obi*
❑ R 143811 True Blue 1986 15.00
*—RCA Music Service edition; issued with poster*
❑ R 161153 Like a Virgin 1985 15.00
*—RCA Music Service edition*
❑ R 164288 Madonna 1984 15.00
*—RCA Music Service edition*
❑ R 254164 [(2)] The Immaculate Collection 1990 20.00
*—BMG Direct Marketing edition*

WARNER BROS.
❑ 42916-0 [(3)] Confessions Remixed 2005 40.00
*—Six remixes of five different songs from "Confessions on a Dance Floor"*
❑ 49460-1 [(2)] Confessions on a Dance Floor 2005 40.00
*—All copies on pink vinyl*

**MADRIGAL**

SSS INTERNATIONAL
❑ 18 Madrigal 1971 30.00

**MADURA**

COLUMBIA
❑ G 30794 [(2)] Madura 1971 20.00
❑ KC 32545 Madura II 1973 15.00

| Number | Title (A Side/B Side) | Yr | NM |
|---|---|---|---|
| **MAESTRO, JOHNNY** Also see THE CRESTS. | | | |
| BUDDAH | | | |
| ❑ BDS-5091 | The Johnny Maestro Story | 1971 | 40.00 |
| *—With inserts; deduct 40% if missing* | | | |
| **MAGI, THE** | | | |
| UNCLE DIRTY | | | |
| ❑ 6102-N13 | Win or Lose | 1975 | 300.00 |
| **MAGIC** May be two different groups. | | | |
| ARMADILLO | | | |
| ❑ 8031 | Enclosed | 1970 | 400.00 |
| RARE EARTH | | | |
| ❑ RS-527 | Magic | 1971 | 25.00 |
| **MAGIC FERN, THE** | | | |
| PANORAMA | | | |
| ❑ 108 | The Magic Fern | 1980 | 150.00 |
| **MAGIC LANTERNS** | | | |
| ATLANTIC | | | |
| ❑ SD 8217 | Shame, Shame | 1969 | 20.00 |
| **MAGIC SAM** | | | |
| DELMARK | | | |
| ❑ DL-615 | West Side Soul | 1968 | 50.00 |
| ❑ DL-620 | Black Magic | 1969 | 50.00 |
| **MAGIC SAND** | | | |
| UNI | | | |
| ❑ 73094 | Magic Sand | 1971 | 25.00 |
| **MAGNIFICENT MEN, THE** | | | |
| CAPITOL | | | |
| ❑ ST 2678 [S] | The Magnificent Men | 1967 | 15.00 |
| ❑ T 2678 [M] | The Magnificent Men | 1967 | 20.00 |
| ❑ ST 2775 [S] | The Magnificent Men "Live!" | 1967 | 15.00 |
| ❑ T 2775 [M] | The Magnificent Men "Live!" | 1967 | 20.00 |
| ❑ ST 2846 [S] | World of Soul | 1968 | 15.00 |
| ❑ T 2846 [M] | World of Soul | 1968 | 20.00 |
| MERCURY | | | |
| ❑ SR-61252 | Better Than a Ten Cent Movie | 1970 | 15.00 |
| **MAHAL, TAJ** | | | |
| COLUMBIA | | | |
| ❑ CG 18 [(2)] | Giant Step/De Ole Folks at Home | 198? | 10.00 |
| *—Reissue with new prefix* | | | |
| ❑ GP 18 [(2)] | Giant Step/De Ole Folks at Home | 1969 | 20.00 |
| *—Red "360 Sound" label* | | | |
| ❑ GP 18 [(2)] | Giant Step/De Ole Folks at Home | 1971 | 15.00 |
| *—Orange label* | | | |
| ❑ CL 2779 [M] | Taj Mahal | 1967 | 30.00 |
| ❑ CS 9579 [S] | Taj Mahal | 1967 | 15.00 |
| *—Red "360 Sound" label* | | | |
| ❑ CS 9579 [S] | Taj Mahal | 1971 | 12.00 |
| *—Orange label* | | | |
| ❑ PC 9579 [S] | Taj Mahal | 198? | 8.00 |
| *—Reissue with new prefix* | | | |
| ❑ CS 9698 | The Natch'l Blues | 1968 | 15.00 |
| *—Red "360 Sound" label* | | | |
| ❑ CS 9698 | The Natch'l Blues | 1971 | 12.00 |
| *—Orange label* | | | |
| ❑ PC 9698 | The Natch'l Blues | 198? | 8.00 |
| *—Reissue with new prefix* | | | |
| ❑ CG 30619 [(2)] | The Real Thing | 198? | 10.00 |
| *—Reissue with new prefix* | | | |
| ❑ G 30619 [(2)] | The Real Thing | 1971 | 20.00 |
| ❑ C 30767 | Happy to Be Like I Am | 1971 | 12.00 |
| ❑ PC 30767 | Happy to Be Like I Am | 198? | 8.00 |
| *—Budget-line reissue* | | | |
| ❑ KC 31605 | Recycling the Blues & Other Related Stuff | 1972 | 12.00 |
| ❑ PC 31605 | Recycling the Blues & Other Related Stuff | 198? | 8.00 |
| *—Budget-line reissue* | | | |
| ❑ KC 32600 | Oooh So Good 'N Blues | 1973 | 12.00 |
| ❑ PC 32600 | Oooh So Good 'N Blues | 198? | 8.00 |
| *—Budget-line reissue* | | | |
| ❑ KC 33051 | Mo' Roots | 1974 | 12.00 |
| ❑ PC 33051 | Mo' Roots | 198? | 8.00 |
| *—Budget-line reissue* | | | |
| ❑ PC 33801 | Music Keeps Me Together | 1975 | 12.00 |
| ❑ PC 34103 | Satisfied & Tickled Too | 1976 | 12.00 |
| ❑ PC 34466 | Anthology Volume 1 | 1977 | 12.00 |
| ❑ FC 36528 | The Best of Taj Mahal | 1981 | 10.00 |
| ❑ PC 36528 | The Best of Taj Mahal | 198? | 8.00 |
| *—Budget-line reissue* | | | |
| CRYSTAL CLEAR | | | |
| ❑ 5011 | Live and Direct | 1980 | 25.00 |
| *—Direct-to-disc recording* | | | |
| WARNER BROS. | | | |
| ❑ BS 2994 | Music Fuh Ya' (Musica Para Tu) | 1977 | 10.00 |
| ❑ BS 3024 | Brothers | 1977 | 10.00 |
| ❑ BS 3094 | Evolution (Recent) | 1978 | 10.00 |
| **MAHAN, LARRY** | | | |
| WARNER BROS. | | | |
| ❑ BS 2959 | King of the Rodeo | 1976 | 20.00 |
| **MAHAVISHNU ORCHESTRA** | | | |
| COLUMBIA | | | |
| ❑ CQ 31996 [Q] | Birds of Fire | 1973 | 20.00 |
| ❑ CQ 32766 [Q] | Between Nothingness and Eternity | 1973 | 25.00 |
| **MAHOGANY RUSH** | | | |
| COLUMBIA | | | |
| ❑ PC 34190 | Mahogany Rush IV | 1976 | 15.00 |
| *—Original with no bar code* | | | |
| ❑ PC 34190 | Mahogany Rush IV | 198? | 8.00 |
| *—Reissue with bar code* | | | |
| ❑ PC 34677 | World Anthem | 1977 | 15.00 |
| *—Original with no bar code* | | | |
| ❑ PC 34677 | World Anthem | 198? | 8.00 |
| *—Reissue with bar code* | | | |
| ❑ JC 35257 | Frank Marino & Mahogany Rush Live | 1978 | 15.00 |
| ❑ PC 35257 | Frank Marino & Mahogany Rush Live | 198? | 8.00 |
| *—Budget-line reissue* | | | |
| ❑ JC 35753 | Tales of the Unexpected | 1979 | 15.00 |
| ❑ PC 35753 | Tales of the Unexpected | 198? | 8.00 |
| *—Budget-line reissue* | | | |
| ❑ JC 36204 | What's Next | 1980 | 15.00 |
| ❑ PC 36204 | What's Next | 198? | 8.00 |
| *—Budget-line reissue* | | | |
| NINE | | | |
| ❑ 936 | Maxoom | 1973 | 50.00 |
| 20TH CENTURY | | | |
| ❑ T-451 | Child of the Novelty | 1974 | 25.00 |
| ❑ T-463 | Maxoom | 1975 | 25.00 |
| *—Reissue of Nine 936* | | | |
| ❑ T-482 | Strange Universe | 1975 | 20.00 |
| **MAHONES, GILDO** | | | |
| PRESTIGE | | | |
| ❑ PRLP-7339 [(2)M] | The Soulful Piano of Gildo Mahones | 1964 | 30.00 |
| ❑ PRST-7339 [(2)S] | The Soulful Piano of Gildo Mahones | 1964 | 40.00 |
| ❑ PRLP-16004 [M] | Shooting High | 1964 | 40.00 |
| **MAIDEN, SIDNEY** | | | |
| BLUESVILLE | | | |
| ❑ BVLP-1035 [M] | Trouble An' Blues | 1961 | 80.00 |
| *—Blue label, silver print* | | | |
| ❑ BVLP-1035 [M] | Trouble An' Blues | 1964 | 20.00 |
| *—Blue label, trident logo at right* | | | |
| **MAIN ATTRACTION, THE** | | | |
| TOWER | | | |
| ❑ ST-5117 [S] | And Now...The Main Attraction | 1968 | 25.00 |
| ❑ T-5117 [M] | And Now...The Main Attraction | 1968 | 50.00 |
| **MAINER, J.E.** | | | |
| ARHOOLIE | | | |
| ❑ F 5002 | J.E. Mainer's Mountaineers | 197? | 12.00 |
| BLUE JAY | | | |
| ❑ 101 | 70th Happy Birthday | 1968 | 20.00 |
| ❑ 102 | Precious Memories | 1968 | 20.00 |
| KING | | | |
| ❑ 666 | Good Ole Mountain Music | 197? | 12.00 |
| *—Gusto reissue* | | | |
| ❑ 666 [M] | Good Ole Mountain Music | 1960 | 100.00 |
| ❑ 765 [M] | Variety Album | 1961 | 100.00 |
| OLD HOMESTEAD | | | |
| ❑ 146 | J.E. Mainer at Home with Family and Friends, Vol. 1 | 197? | 15.00 |
| OLD TIMEY | | | |
| ❑ 107 | J.E. Mainer's Mountaineers, Vol. 2 | 197? | 12.00 |
| RURAL RHYTHM | | | |
| ❑ RRJE-185 | The Legendary J.E. Mainer and His Mountaineers | 198? | 12.00 |
| ❑ RRJE-191 | More Old Time Mountain Music | 198? | 12.00 |
| ❑ RRJE-198 | The Legendary J.E. Mainer, Vol. 3 | 198? | 12.00 |
| ❑ RRJE-225 | The Legendary J.E. Mainer, Vol. 7 | 198? | 12.00 |
| ❑ RRJE-246 | The Legendary J.E. Mainer, Vol. 16 | 198? | 12.00 |
| ❑ RRJE-250 | The Legendary J.E. Mainer, Vol. 20 | 198? | 12.00 |
| **MAINER, WADE** | | | |
| KING | | | |
| ❑ 769 [M] | Soulful Sacred Songs | 1961 | 100.00 |
| OLD HOMESTEAD | | | |
| ❑ 4000 [(2)] | From the Maple to the Hill | 1976 | 20.00 |
| ❑ 90001 | Sacred Songs of Mother and Home | 1971 | 15.00 |
| ❑ 90016 | Sacred Songs Mountain Style | 197? | 15.00 |
| ❑ 90123 | Old Time Songs | 1980 | 15.00 |
| **MAINIERI, MIKE** | | | |
| ARGO | | | |
| ❑ LP-706 [M] | Blues on the Other Side | 1963 | 25.00 |
| ❑ LPS-706 [S] | Blues on the Other Side | 1963 | 30.00 |
| SOLID STATE | | | |
| ❑ SS-18029 | Insight | 1968 | 20.00 |
| ❑ SS-18049 | Journey Thru an Electric Tube | 1969 | 20.00 |
| **MAIZE, JOE** | | | |
| DECCA | | | |
| ❑ DL 4555 [M] | Isle of Dreams | 1965 | 20.00 |
| ❑ DL 8590 [M] | Presenting Joe Maize and His Cordsmen | 1958 | 30.00 |
| ❑ DL 8817 [M] | Hawaiian Dreams | 1959 | 20.00 |
| ❑ DL 74555 [S] | Isle of Dreams | 1965 | 25.00 |
| ❑ DL 78817 [S] | Hawaiian Dreams | 1959 | 25.00 |
| **MAJIC SHIP, THE** | | | |
| BEL AMI | | | |
| ❑ BA-711 | The Majic Ship | 1968 | 500.00 |
| **MAJORS, THE (1)** | | | |
| IMPERIAL | | | |
| ❑ LP-9222 [M] | Meet the Majors | 1963 | 150.00 |
| ❑ LP-12222 [S] | Meet the Majors | 1963 | 300.00 |
| **MAKEBA, MIRIAM** | | | |
| KAPP | | | |
| ❑ KL-1274 [M] | The Many Voices of Miriam Makeba | 1962 | 20.00 |
| ❑ KS-3274 [S] | The Many Voices of Miriam Makeba | 1962 | 25.00 |
| MERCURY | | | |
| ❑ MG-21082 [M] | The Magnificent Miriam Makeba | 1966 | 12.00 |
| ❑ MG-21095 [M] | All About Miriam | 1967 | 12.00 |
| ❑ SR-61082 [S] | The Magnificent Miriam Makeba | 1966 | 15.00 |
| ❑ SR-61095 [S] | All About Miriam | 1967 | 15.00 |
| MERCURY/URBAN AFRICA | | | |
| ❑ 838208-1 | Welela | 1989 | 12.00 |
| PETERS INT'L. | | | |
| ❑ PLD 2082 | Miriam Makeba in Concert | 1977 | 12.00 |
| RCA VICTOR | | | |
| ❑ LPM-2267 [M] | Miriam Makeba | 1960 | 20.00 |
| ❑ LSP-2267 [S] | Miriam Makeba | 1960 | 25.00 |
| ❑ LPM-2750 [M] | The World of Miriam Makeba | 1963 | 15.00 |
| ❑ LSP-2750 [S] | The World of Miriam Makeba | 1963 | 20.00 |
| ❑ LPM-2845 [M] | The Voice of Africa | 1964 | 15.00 |
| ❑ LSP-2845 [S] | The Voice of Africa | 1964 | 20.00 |
| ❑ LPM-3321 [M] | Makeba Sings | 1965 | 15.00 |
| ❑ LSP-3321 [S] | Makeba Sings | 1965 | 20.00 |
| ❑ LPM-3512 [M] | The Magic of Makeba | 1966 | 15.00 |
| ❑ LSP-3512 [S] | The Magic of Makeba | 1966 | 20.00 |
| ❑ LPM-3982 [M] | The Best of Miriam Makeba | 1968 | 25.00 |
| ❑ LSP-3982 [S] | The Best of Miriam Makeba | 1968 | 12.00 |
| REPRISE | | | |
| ❑ R-6253 [M] | Miriam Makeba In Concert! | 1967 | 15.00 |
| ❑ RS-6253 [S] | Miriam Makeba In Concert! | 1967 | 12.00 |
| ❑ R-6274 [M] | Pata Pata | 1967 | 15.00 |
| ❑ RS-6274 [S] | Pata Pata | 1967 | 12.00 |
| ❑ RS-6310 | Makeba! | 1968 | 12.00 |
| ❑ RS-6381 | Keep Me in Mind | 1970 | 12.00 |
| WARNER BROS. | | | |
| ❑ 25673 | Sangoma | 1988 | 10.00 |
| **MAKEM, TOMMY** | | | |
| TRADITION | | | |
| ❑ TLP-1044 [M] | Songs of Tommy Makem | 1961 | 30.00 |
| ❑ TLPS-1044 [S] | Songs of Tommy Makem | 1961 | 40.00 |
| **MAKOWICZ, ADAM** | | | |
| SHEFFIELD LABS | | | |
| ❑ 21 | The Name Is Makowicz (ma-ko-vitch) | 1984 | 20.00 |
| *—Audiophile vinyl* | | | |
| **MALACHI** | | | |
| VERVE | | | |
| ❑ V-5024 [M] | Holy Music | 1967 | 30.00 |
| ❑ V6-5024 [S] | Holy Music | 1967 | 40.00 |
| **MALCOLM X** | | | |
| DOUGLAS | | | |
| ❑ SD 795 [M] | Malcolm X Talks to Young People | 1968 | 30.00 |
| ❑ SD 797 | His Wit and Wisdom | 196? | 30.00 |
| ❑ Z 30743 [M] | By Any Means Necessary | 1971 | 30.00 |
| PAUL WINLEY | | | |
| ❑ 135 | The Ballot or the Bullet | 197? | 20.00 |

The Mamas and the Papas, *The Mamas and the Papas Deliver,* Dunhill DS-50014, 1967, stereo, $25.

| Number | Title (A Side/B Side) | Yr | NM |
|---|---|---|---|
| **RCA** | | | |
| ❑ 66132 | Words from the Frontlines: Excerpts from the Great Speeches of Malcolm X | 1992 | 20.00 |
| **UPFRONT** | | | |
| ❑ UPF-152 | Malcolm X Speaks to the People in Harlem | 197? | 15.00 |
| **WARNER BROS.** | | | |
| ❑ BS 2619 | Malcolm X | 1972 | 25.00 |
| ❑ PRO-A-5943 [DJ] | Malcolm X Speaks | 1992 | 20.00 |
| ❑ PRO-A-5957 [DJ] | Music and Dialog from the Historic 1992 Documentary Film Malcolm X | 1992 | 20.00 |

## MALTBY, RICHARD

| Number | Title (A Side/B Side) | Yr | NM |
|---|---|---|---|
| **COLUMBIA** | | | |
| ❑ CL 1271 [M] | Swingin' Down the Lane | 1959 | 20.00 |
| ❑ CL 1341 [M] | Hello Young Lovers | 1959 | 20.00 |
| ❑ CS 8083 [S] | Swingin' Down the Lane | 1959 | 25.00 |
| ❑ CS 8151 [S] | Hello Young Lovers | 1959 | 25.00 |
| **RCA CAMDEN** | | | |
| ❑ CAL-526 [M] | A Bow to the Big Name Bands | 1959 | 20.00 |
| ❑ CAL-600 [M] | Music from Mr. Lucky | 1960 | 20.00 |
| ❑ CAL-711 [M] | Most Requested | 1961 | 20.00 |
| **ROULETTE** | | | |
| ❑ R-25129 [M] | Richard Maltby Swings for Dancers | 1960 | 20.00 |
| ❑ R-25148 [M] | Swing Folksongs | 1961 | 20.00 |
| ❑ SR-25148 [S] | Swing Folksongs | 1961 | 25.00 |
| ❑ R-25178 [M] | Brilliant Big Band Ballads and Blues | 1962 | 20.00 |
| ❑ SR-25178 [S] | Brilliant Big Band Ballads and Blues | 1962 | 25.00 |
| **VIK** | | | |
| ❑ LX-1051 [M] | Hue-Fi Moods by Maltby | 1957 | 30.00 |
| ❑ LX-1068 [M] | Manhattan Bandstand | 1957 | 30.00 |
| ❑ LX-1071 [M] | Maltby with Strings Attached | 1958 | 30.00 |
| **"X"** | | | |
| ❑ LX-1038 [M] | Make Mine Maltby | 1956 | 30.00 |

## MALVIN, ARTIE

| Number | Title (A Side/B Side) | Yr | NM |
|---|---|---|---|
| **WALDORF MUSIC HALL** | | | |
| ❑ 33-149 [10] | Rock and Roll | 1955 | 120.00 |

## MAMA CASS See CASS ELLIOT.

## MAMA LION

| Number | Title (A Side/B Side) | Yr | NM |
|---|---|---|---|
| **FAMILY PRODUCTIONS** | | | |
| ❑ FPS-2702 | Mama Lion | 1972 | 20.00 |
| ❑ FPS-2713 | Give It Everything I've Got | 1973 | 20.00 |

## MAMAS AND THE PAPAS, THE

| Number | Title (A Side/B Side) | Yr | NM |
|---|---|---|---|
| **ABC** | | | |
| ❑ AC-30005 | The ABC Collection | 1976 | 15.00 |
| **ABC DUNHILL** | | | |
| ❑ DS-50006 | If You Can Believe Your Eyes and Ears | 1968 | 12.00 |
| ❑ DS-50010 | The Mamas and the Papas | 1968 | 12.00 |
| ❑ DS-50014 | The Mamas and the Papas Deliver | 1968 | 12.00 |
| ❑ DS-50025 | Farewell to the First Golden Era | 1968 | 12.00 |
| ❑ DS-50031 | The Papas and the Mamas | 1968 | 15.00 |
| *—The five LPs above are reissues of records originally without the ABC logo* | | | |
| ❑ DS-50038 | Golden Era, Volume 2 | 1968 | 20.00 |
| ❑ DS-50064 | 16 of Their Greatest Hits | 1969 | 15.00 |
| ❑ DS-50073 [(2)] | A Gathering of Flowers | 1970 | 25.00 |
| ❑ DSX-50100 | Monterey International Pop Festival | 1970 | 15.00 |
| ❑ DSX-50106 | People Like Us | 1971 | 12.00 |
| ❑ DSX-50145 [(2)] | 20 Golden Hits | 1973 | 20.00 |
| ❑ SMAS-93470 | Monterey International Pop Festival | 1970 | 25.00 |
| *—Capitol Record Club edition; label has the old-style "Dunhill" logo without the "ABC" as part of it* | | | |
| **DUNHILL** | | | |
| ❑ D-50006 [M] | If You Can Believe Your Eyes and Ears | 1966 | 20.00 |
| *—With scroll over toilet* | | | |
| ❑ D-50006 [M] | If You Can Believe Your Eyes and Ears | 1966 | 40.00 |
| *—Black cover with photo cropped to render toilet invisible* | | | |
| ❑ D-50006 [M] | If You Can Believe Your Eyes and Ears | 1966 | 80.00 |
| *—With toilet completely visible in lower right* | | | |
| ❑ DS-50006 [S] | If You Can Believe Your Eyes and Ears | 1966 | 25.00 |
| *—With scroll over toilet proclaiming "Includes California Dreamin' "* | | | |
| ❑ DS-50006 [S] | If You Can Believe Your Eyes and Ears | 1966 | 25.00 |
| *—With scroll over toilet proclaiming "Includes California Dreamin'... Monday Monday... I Call Your Name"* | | | |
| ❑ DS-50006 [S] | If You Can Believe Your Eyes and Ears | 1966 | 50.00 |
| *—Black cover with photo cropped to render toilet invisible* | | | |
| ❑ DS-50006 [S] | If You Can Believe Your Eyes and Ears | 1966 | 100.00 |
| *—With toilet completely visible in lower right* | | | |
| ❑ D-50010 [M] | The Mamas and the Papas | 1966 | 20.00 |
| ❑ DS-50010 [S] | The Mamas and the Papas | 1966 | 25.00 |
| ❑ D-50014 [M] | The Mamas and the Papas Deliver | 1967 | 20.00 |
| ❑ DS-50014 [S] | The Mamas and the Papas Deliver | 1967 | 25.00 |
| ❑ D-50025 [M] | Farewell to the First Golden Era | 1967 | 20.00 |
| ❑ DS-50025 [S] | Farewell to the First Golden Era | 1967 | 20.00 |
| ❑ DS-50031 | The Papas and the Mamas | 1968 | 25.00 |
| ❑ ST-90797 [S] | If You Can Believe Your Eyes and Ears | 1966 | 50.00 |
| *—Capitol Record Club edition; known copies have scroll proclaiming "Includes California Dreamin'."* | | | |
| ❑ T-90797 [M] | If You Can Believe Your Eyes and Ears | 1966 | 50.00 |
| *—Capitol Record Club edition; known copies have scroll proclaiming "Includes California Dreamin'."* | | | |
| ❑ ST-90924 [S] | The Mamas and the Papas | 1966 | 40.00 |
| *—Capitol Record Club edition* | | | |
| ❑ T-90924 [M] | The Mamas and the Papas | 1966 | 30.00 |
| *—Capitol Record Club edition* | | | |
| **MCA** | | | |
| ❑ 709 | Farewell to the First Golden Era | 1980 | 8.00 |
| ❑ 710 | The Papas and the Mamas | 1980 | 8.00 |
| ❑ 6019 [(2)] | The Best of the Mamas and the Papas | 1986 | 12.00 |
| ❑ 37145 | 16 of Their Greatest Hits | 1980 | 8.00 |
| **PICKWICK** | | | |
| ❑ SPC-3352 | California Dreaming | 1972 | 12.00 |

## MAN

| Number | Title (A Side/B Side) | Yr | NM |
|---|---|---|---|
| **PHILIPS** | | | |
| ❑ PHS 600313 | Revelation | 1969 | 20.00 |
| *—As "Manpower"* | | | |

## MANCE, JUNIOR

| Number | Title (A Side/B Side) | Yr | NM |
|---|---|---|---|
| **ATLANTIC** | | | |
| ❑ 1479 [M] | Harlem Lullaby | 1967 | 20.00 |
| ❑ 1496 [M] | I Believe to My Soul | 1968 | 25.00 |
| **CAPITOL** | | | |
| ❑ ST 2092 [S] | Get Ready, Set, Jump! | 1964 | 25.00 |
| ❑ T 2092 [M] | Get Ready, Set, Jump! | 1964 | 20.00 |
| ❑ ST 2218 [S] | Straight Ahead | 1965 | 20.00 |
| ❑ ST 2393 [S] | That's Where It Is | 1965 | 20.00 |
| **JAZZLAND** | | | |
| ❑ JLP-30 [M] | The Soulful Piano of Junior Mance | 1960 | 25.00 |
| ❑ JLP-41 [M] | Junior Mance Trio at the Village Vanguard | 1961 | 25.00 |
| ❑ JLP-53 [M] | Big Chief! | 1961 | 25.00 |
| ❑ JLP-63 [M] | The Jazz Soul of Hollywood | 1961 | 25.00 |
| ❑ JLP-77 [M] | Happy Time | 1962 | 25.00 |
| ❑ JLP-930 [S] | The Soulful Piano of Junior Mance | 1960 | 30.00 |
| ❑ JLP-941 [S] | Junior Mance Trio at the Village Vanguard | 1961 | 30.00 |
| ❑ JLP-953 [S] | Big Chief! | 1961 | 30.00 |
| ❑ JLP-963 [S] | The Jazz Soul of Hollywood | 1961 | 30.00 |
| ❑ JLP-977 [S] | Happy Time | 1962 | 30.00 |
| **RIVERSIDE** | | | |
| ❑ RLP-447 [M] | Junior's Blues | 1963 | 25.00 |
| ❑ RS-9447 [S] | Junior's Blues | 1963 | 30.00 |
| **VERVE** | | | |
| ❑ MGVS-6057 [S] | Junior | 1960 | 30.00 |
| ❑ MGV-8319 [M] | Junior | 1959 | 40.00 |
| ❑ V-8319 [M] | Junior | 1961 | 20.00 |

## MANCHESTER, MELISSA

| Number | Title (A Side/B Side) | Yr | NM |
|---|---|---|---|
| **ARISTA** | | | |
| ❑ AL 4006 | Home to Myself | 1975 | 10.00 |
| *—Reissue of Bell 1123* | | | |
| ❑ AL 4011 | Bright Eyes | 1975 | 10.00 |
| *—Reissue of Bell 1303* | | | |
| ❑ AL 4031 | Melissa | 1975 | 10.00 |
| ❑ AQ 4031 [Q] | Melissa | 1975 | 15.00 |
| ❑ AL 4067 | Better Days & Happy Endings | 1976 | 10.00 |
| ❑ AQ 4067 [Q] | Better Days & Happy Endings | 1976 | 15.00 |
| ❑ AL 4095 | Help Is On the Way | 1976 | 10.00 |
| ❑ AL 4136 | Singin' | 1977 | 10.00 |
| ❑ AB 4186 | Don't Cry Out Loud | 1978 | 10.00 |
| ❑ AL 8055 | Melissa | 1983 | 8.00 |
| *—Budget-line reissue of 4031* | | | |
| ❑ AL 8094 | Emergency | 1983 | 10.00 |
| ❑ AL 8293 | Greatest Hits | 198? | 8.00 |
| *—Budget-line reissue of 9611* | | | |
| ❑ AL 8350 | Hey Ricky | 198? | 8.00 |
| *—Budget-line reissue of 9574* | | | |

| Number | Title (A Side/B Side) | Yr | NM |
|---|---|---|---|
| ❑ AL 8373 | Don't Cry Out Loud | 198? | 8.00 |
| *—Budget-line reissue of 4186* | | | |
| ❑ AL 9506 | Melissa Manchester | 1979 | 10.00 |
| ❑ AL 9533 | For the Working Girl | 1980 | 10.00 |
| ❑ AL 9574 | Hey Ricky | 1982 | 10.00 |
| ❑ AL 9611 | Greatest Hits | 1983 | 10.00 |
| **BELL** | | | |
| ❑ 1123 | Home to Myself | 1973 | 12.00 |
| ❑ 1303 | Bright Eyes | 1974 | 12.00 |
| **MCA** | | | |
| ❑ 5587 | Mathematics | 1985 | 10.00 |
| **MIKA** | | | |
| ❑ 841273-1 | Tribute | 1989 | 12.00 |
| **MOBILE FIDELITY** | | | |
| ❑ 1-028 | Melissa | 1980 | 20.00 |
| *—Audiophile vinyl* | | | |
| **NAUTILUS** | | | |
| ❑ NR-33 | Don't Cry Out Loud | 198? | 40.00 |
| *--Audiophile vinyl* | | | |
| **PAIR** | | | |
| ❑ PDL2-1086 [(2)] | The Many Moods of Melissa Manchester | 1986 | 12.00 |

## MANCHESTERS, THE (1)

| Number | Title (A Side/B Side) | Yr | NM |
|---|---|---|---|
| **DIPLOMAT** | | | |
| ❑ D-2307 [M] | Beatlerama | 1964 | 15.00 |
| *—No artist credited on label or cover* | | | |
| ❑ D-2307 [M] | Beatlerama | 1964 | 15.00 |
| *—With artist credited* | | | |
| ❑ DS-2307 [S] | Beatlerama | 1964 | 20.00 |
| *—No artist credited on label or cover* | | | |
| ❑ DS-2307 [S] | Beatlerama | 1964 | 20.00 |
| *—With artist credited* | | | |
| **GUEST STAR** | | | |
| ❑ G-2307 [M] | Beatlerama | 1964 | 15.00 |
| ❑ GS-2307 [S] | Beatlerama | 1964 | 20.00 |

## MANCINI, HENRY

| Number | Title (A Side/B Side) | Yr | NM |
|---|---|---|---|
| **AVCO EMBASSY** | | | |
| ❑ AVE 0110 | Sunflower | 1970 | 15.00 |
| **DECCA** | | | |
| ❑ DL 79185 | Sometimes a Great Notion | 1971 | 15.00 |
| **LIBERTY** | | | |
| ❑ LRP-3121 [M] | The Versatile Henry Mancini | 1959 | 20.00 |
| ❑ LST-7121 [S] | The Versatile Henry Mancini | 1959 | 30.00 |
| ❑ LT-51135 | Trail of the Pink Panther | 1982 | 10.00 |
| **MCA** | | | |
| ❑ 2085 | The Great Waldo Pepper | 1975 | 12.00 |
| ❑ 6222 | The Glass Menagerie | 1987 | 10.00 |
| **PAIR** | | | |
| ❑ PDL2-1092 [(2)] | The Mancini Collection (Film Music) | 1986 | 12.00 |
| **PARAMOUNT** | | | |
| ❑ PAS-6000 | The Molly Maguires | 1970 | 20.00 |
| **RCA CAMDEN** | | | |
| ❑ ACL2-0293 [(2)] | Film Music | 1973 | 12.00 |
| ❑ CAL-928 [M] | The Second Time Around and Others | 1966 | 12.00 |
| ❑ CAS-928 [S] | The Second Time Around and Others | 1966 | 12.00 |
| ❑ CAL-2158 [M] | Mancini Plays Mancini and Other Composers | 1968 | 12.00 |
| ❑ CAS-2158 [S] | Mancini Plays Mancini and Other Composers | 1968 | 10.00 |
| ❑ CAS-2510 | Dream of You | 1971 | 10.00 |
| ❑ CXS-9005 [(2)] | Mancini Magic | 1971 | 12.00 |
| ❑ CXS-9034 | Everybody's Favorite | 1972 | 10.00 |
| **RCA SPECIAL PRODUCTS** | | | |
| ❑ DPL1-0678 | Taking It Easy | 1984 | 15.00 |
| *—Manufactured for Abbott Laboratories* | | | |
| **RCA VICTOR** | | | |
| ❑ APD1-0013 [Q] | Mancini Salutes Sousa | 1973 | 18.00 |
| ❑ APL1-0013 | Mancini Salutes Sousa | 1972 | 12.00 |
| ❑ APD1-0098 [Q] | Brass, Ivory and Strings | 1973 | 18.00 |
| ❑ APL1-0098 | Brass, Ivory and Strings | 1973 | 12.00 |
| ❑ PRM-175 [M] | Academy Award Songs, Volume Two | 1965 | 15.00 |
| *—Made for the B.F. Goodrich tire company* | | | |
| ❑ PRS-175 [S] | Academy Award Songs, Volume Two | 1965 | 20.00 |
| *—Made for the B.F. Goodrich tire company* | | | |
| ❑ ABL1-0231 | Visions of Eight | 1973 | 12.00 |
| ❑ AFL1-0270 | Country Gentlemen | 1977 | 10.00 |
| *—Reissue with new prefix* | | | |
| ❑ APD1-0270 [Q] | Country Gentlemen | 1973 | 18.00 |
| ❑ APL1-0270 | Country Gentlemen | 1973 | 12.00 |
| ❑ APL1-0271 | Oklahoma Crude | 1973 | 12.00 |
| ❑ AFL1-0672 | Hangin' Out | 1977 | 10.00 |
| *—Reissue with new prefix* | | | |
| ❑ APD1-0672 [Q] | Hangin' Out | 1974 | 18.00 |
| ❑ CPL1-0672 | Hangin' Out | 1974 | 12.00 |
| ❑ ABD1-0968 [Q] | Return of the Pink Panther | 1975 | 18.00 |

Henry Mancini, *Encore! More of the Concert Sound of Henry Mancini,* RCA Victor LSP-3887, 1967, stereo, $15.

| Number | Title (A Side/B Side) | Yr | NM |
|---|---|---|---|
| ❑ ABL1-0968 | Return of the Pink Panther | 1975 | 12.00 |
| ❑ ANL1-0980 | Pure Gold | 1975 | 10.00 |
| ❑ AFL1-1025 | Symphonic Soul | 1977 | 8.00 |
| *—Reissue with new prefix* | | | |
| ❑ APD1-1025 [Q] | Symphonic Soul | 1975 | 18.00 |
| ❑ APL1-1025 | Symphonic Soul | 1975 | 10.00 |
| ❑ APL1-1379 | Concert of Film Music | 1975 | 10.00 |
| ❑ CPL1-1843 | A Legendary Performer | 1976 | 10.00 |
| ❑ APL1-1896 | Cop Show Themes | 1976 | 10.00 |
| ❑ ANL1-1928 [S] | A Merry Mancini Christmas | 1976 | 8.00 |
| *—Reissue with new number and new front cover* | | | |
| ❑ LPM-1956 [M] | The Music from Peter Gunn | 1959 | 12.00 |
| *—Second reissue cover is green/blue on front with huge "Peter Gunn" in center; back cover has a figure with a gun and a large photo of Henry Mancini at the upper left; catalog number on back is followed by "RE 2"* | | | |
| ❑ LPM-1956 [M] | The Music from Peter Gunn | 1959 | 20.00 |
| *—First reissue cover is green/blue on front with huge "Peter Gunn" in center; back cover has a figure with a gun and a small photo of Henry Mancini at the lower left positioned so that it appears the gun is aimed at his head; catalog number on back cover is followed by "RE"* | | | |
| ❑ LPM-1956 [M] | The Music from Peter Gunn | 1959 | 40.00 |
| *—Original cover is a "block" design with "Peter Gunn" at top* | | | |
| ❑ LSP-1956 [S] | The Music from Peter Gunn | 1959 | 15.00 |
| *—Second reissue cover is green/blue on front with huge "Peter Gunn" in center; back cover has a figure with a gun and a large photo of Henry Mancini at the upper left; catalog number on back is followed by "RE 2"* | | | |
| ❑ LSP-1956 [S] | The Music from Peter Gunn | 1959 | 25.00 |
| *—First reissue cover is green/blue on front with huge "Peter Gunn" in center; back cover has a figure with a gun and a small photo of Henry Mancini at the lower left positioned so that it appears the gun is aimed at his head; catalog number on back cover is followed by "RE"* | | | |
| ❑ LSP-1956 [S] | The Music from Peter Gunn | 1959 | 50.00 |
| *—Original cover is a "block" design with "Peter Gunn" at top* | | | |
| ❑ LPM-2040 [M] | More Music from Peter Gunn | 1959 | 20.00 |
| ❑ LSP-2040 [S] | More Music from Peter Gunn | 1959 | 25.00 |
| ❑ LPM-2101 [M] | The Mancini Touch | 1959 | 20.00 |
| ❑ LSP-2101 [S] | The Mancini Touch | 1959 | 25.00 |
| ❑ LPM-2147 [M] | The Blues and the Beat | 1960 | 25.00 |
| ❑ LSP-2147 [S] | The Blues and the Beat | 1960 | 30.00 |
| ❑ LPM-2198 [M] | Music from Mr. Lucky | 1960 | 20.00 |
| ❑ LSP-2198 [S] | Music from Mr. Lucky | 1960 | 25.00 |
| ❑ LPM-2258 [M] | Combo! | 1960 | 20.00 |
| ❑ LSP-2258 [S] | Combo! | 1960 | 25.00 |
| ❑ APL1-2290 | Mancini's Angels | 1977 | 10.00 |
| ❑ LPM-2360 [M] | Mr. Lucky Goes Latin | 1961 | 20.00 |

| Number | Title (A Side/B Side) | Yr | NM |
|---|---|---|---|
| ❑ LSP-2360 [S] | Mr. Lucky Goes Latin | 1961 | 25.00 |
| ❑ LPM-2362 [M] | Breakfast at Tiffany's | 1961 | 20.00 |
| ❑ LSP-2362 [S] | Breakfast at Tiffany's | 1961 | 25.00 |
| ❑ LPM-2442 [M] | Experiment in Terror | 1962 | 20.00 |
| *—Reissue cover has two mannequins* | | | |
| ❑ LPM-2442 [M] | Experiment in Terror | 1962 | 25.00 |
| *—Original cover has Lee Remick under attack* | | | |
| ❑ LSP-2442 [S] | Experiment in Terror | 1962 | 25.00 |
| *—Reissue cover has two mannequins* | | | |
| ❑ LSP-2442 [S] | Experiment in Terror | 1962 | 40.00 |
| *—Original cover has Lee Remick under attack* | | | |
| ❑ ANL1-2484 | Mancini Plays the Theme from Love Story | 1977 | 10.00 |
| *—Reissue of LSP-4466* | | | |
| ❑ LPM-2559 [M] | Hatari! | 1962 | 20.00 |
| ❑ LSP-2559 [S] | Hatari! | 1962 | 25.00 |
| ❑ LPM-2604 [M] | Our Man in Hollywood | 1963 | 15.00 |
| ❑ LSP-2604 [S] | Our Man in Hollywood | 1963 | 20.00 |
| ❑ LPM-2692 [M] | Uniquely Mancini | 1963 | 15.00 |
| ❑ LSP-2692 [S] | Uniquely Mancini | 1963 | 20.00 |
| ❑ AFL1-2693 | The Best of Mancini | 1977 | 10.00 |
| *—Reissue with new prefix* | | | |
| ❑ LPM-2693 [M] | The Best of Mancini | 1964 | 12.00 |
| ❑ LSP-2693 [S] | The Best of Mancini | 1964 | 15.00 |
| ❑ LPM-2755 [M] | Charade | 1963 | 15.00 |
| ❑ LSP-2755 [S] | Charade | 1963 | 20.00 |
| ❑ LPM-2795 [M] | The Pink Panther | 1964 | 15.00 |
| ❑ LSP-2795 [S] | The Pink Panther | 1964 | 20.00 |
| ❑ LPM-2897 [M] | The Concert Sound of Henry Mancini | 1964 | 12.00 |
| ❑ LSP-2897 [S] | The Concert Sound of Henry Mancini | 1964 | 15.00 |
| ❑ LPM-2990 [M] | Dear Heart and Other Songs About Love | 1965 | 12.00 |
| ❑ LSP-2990 [S] | Dear Heart and Other Songs About Love | 1965 | 15.00 |
| ❑ AQL1-3052 | The Theme Scene | 1978 | 10.00 |
| ❑ AQL1-3347 | The Best of Mancini, Volume 3 | 1979 | 10.00 |
| ❑ LPM-3356 [M] | The Latin Sound of Henry Mancini | 1965 | 12.00 |
| ❑ LSP-3356 [S] | The Latin Sound of Henry Mancini | 1965 | 15.00 |
| ❑ LPM-3402 [M] | The Great Race | 1965 | 12.00 |
| ❑ LSP-3402 [S] | The Great Race | 1965 | 15.00 |
| ❑ AFL1-3557 | The Best of Mancini, Volume 2 | 1977 | 10.00 |
| *—Reissue with new prefix* | | | |
| ❑ LPM-3557 [M] | The Best of Mancini, Volume 2 | 1966 | 12.00 |
| ❑ LSP-3557 [S] | The Best of Mancini, Volume 2 | 1966 | 15.00 |

| Number | Title (A Side/B Side) | Yr | NM |
|---|---|---|---|
| ❑ LPM-3612 [M] | A Merry Mancini Christmas | 1966 | 10.00 |
| *—Original front cover has a photo of Henry Mancini and family* | | | |
| ❑ LSP-3612 [S] | A Merry Mancini Christmas | 1966 | 12.00 |
| *—Same as above, but in stereo* | | | |
| ❑ LPM-3623 [M] | Arabesque | 1966 | 12.00 |
| ❑ LSP-3623 [S] | Arabesque | 1966 | 15.00 |
| ❑ LPM-3648 [M] | What Did You Do in the War, Daddy? | 1966 | 12.00 |
| ❑ LSP-3648 [S] | What Did You Do in the War, Daddy? | 1966 | 15.00 |
| ❑ AYL1-3667 | Pure Gold | 1980 | 8.00 |
| *—"Best Buy Series" reissue* | | | |
| ❑ AYL1-3668 | Mancini Country | 1980 | 8.00 |
| *—"Best Buy Series" reissue* | | | |
| ❑ LPM-3694 [M] | Mancini '67 | 1967 | 15.00 |
| ❑ LSP-3694 [S] | Mancini '67 | 1967 | 15.00 |
| ❑ AFL1-3713 | Music of Hawaii | 1977 | 10.00 |
| *—Reissue with new prefix* | | | |
| ❑ LPM-3713 [M] | Music of Hawaii | 1966 | 12.00 |
| ❑ LSP-3713 [S] | Music of Hawaii | 1966 | 15.00 |
| ❑ AYL1-3756 | Brass on Ivory | 1980 | 8.00 |
| *—"Best Buy Series" reissue* | | | |
| ❑ AYL1-3757 | A Warm Shade of Ivory | 1980 | 8.00 |
| *—"Best Buy Series" reissue* | | | |
| ❑ LPM-3802 [M] | Two for the Road | 1967 | 20.00 |
| ❑ LSP-3802 [S] | Two for the Road | 1967 | 15.00 |
| ❑ AYL1-3822 | The Best of Mancini | 1981 | 8.00 |
| *—"Best Buy Series" reissue* | | | |
| ❑ LPM-3840 [M] | Gunn | 1967 | 20.00 |
| ❑ LSP-3840 [S] | Gunn | 1967 | 30.00 |
| ❑ AYL1-3877 | Music of Hawaii | 1981 | 8.00 |
| *—"Best Buy Series" reissue* | | | |
| ❑ LPM-3887 [M] | Encore! More of the Concert Sound of Henry Mancini | 1967 | 20.00 |
| ❑ LSP-3887 [S] | Encore! More of the Concert Sound of Henry Mancini | 1967 | 15.00 |
| ❑ LPM-3943 [M] | The Mancini Sound | 1968 | 20.00 |
| ❑ LSP-3943 [S] | The Mancini Sound | 1968 | 15.00 |
| ❑ AYL1-3954 | Country Gentlemen | 1981 | 8.00 |
| *—"Best Buy Series" reissue* | | | |
| ❑ LPM-3997 [M] | Party | 1968 | 25.00 |
| ❑ LSP-3997 [S] | Party | 1968 | 15.00 |
| ❑ LSP-4049 | The Big Latin Band of Henry Mancini | 1968 | 15.00 |
| ❑ AFL1-4140 | A Warm Shade of Ivory | 1977 | 8.00 |
| *—Reissue with new prefix* | | | |
| ❑ LSP-4140 | A Warm Shade of Ivory | 1969 | 15.00 |
| ❑ LSP-4239 | Six Hours Past Sunset | 1969 | 15.00 |
| ❑ AFL1-4307 | Mancini Country | 1977 | 10.00 |
| *—Reissue with new prefix* | | | |
| ❑ LSP-4307 | Mancini Country | 1970 | 15.00 |
| ❑ LSP-4350 | Theme from "Z" and Other Film Music | 1970 | 15.00 |
| ❑ LSP-4466 | Mancini Plays the Theme from Love Story | 1971 | 15.00 |
| ❑ AFL1-4542 | Mancini Concert | 1977 | 10.00 |
| *—Reissue with new prefix* | | | |
| ❑ LSP-4542 | Mancini Concert | 1971 | 15.00 |
| ❑ AFL1-4629 | Brass on Ivory | 1977 | 8.00 |
| *—Reissue with new prefix* | | | |
| ❑ LSP-4629 | Brass on Ivory | 1972 | 12.00 |
| ❑ LSP-4630 | Big Screen — Little Screen | 1972 | 15.00 |
| ❑ LSP-4689 | The Mancini Generation | 1972 | 12.00 |
| ❑ LPM-6013 [(2)M] | The Academy Award Songs | 1966 | 15.00 |
| ❑ LSP-6013 [(2)S] | The Academy Award Songs | 1966 | 20.00 |
| ❑ VPS-6029 [(2)] | This Is Henry Mancini | 1970 | 20.00 |
| ❑ VPS-6053 [(2)] | This Is Henry Mancini, Volume 2 | 1972 | 20.00 |

### SUNSET

| Number | Title (A Side/B Side) | Yr | NM |
|---|---|---|---|
| ❑ SUM-1105 [M] | Sounds and Voices | 1966 | 12.00 |
| ❑ SUS-5105 [S] | Sounds and Voices | 1966 | 12.00 |

### UNITED ARTISTS

| Number | Title (A Side/B Side) | Yr | NM |
|---|---|---|---|
| ❑ UA-LA694-G | The Pink Panther Strikes Again | 1976 | 15.00 |
| ❑ UAS-5210 | The Hawaiians | 1970 | 12.00 |
| ❑ SW-93297 | The Hawaiians | 1970 | 20.00 |
| *—Capitol Record Club edition* | | | |

### WARNER BROS.

| Number | Title (A Side/B Side) | Yr | NM |
|---|---|---|---|
| ❑ W 1312 [M] | March Step in Hi-Fi | 1959 | 20.00 |
| ❑ WS 1312 [S] | March Step in Stereo | 1959 | 30.00 |
| ❑ W 1465 [M] | Sousa's Greatest Marches | 1962 | 15.00 |
| ❑ WS 1465 [S] | Sousa's Greatest Marches | 1962 | 20.00 |
| ❑ W 1491 [M] | Marches | 1963 | 15.00 |
| ❑ WS 1491 [S] | Marches | 1963 | 20.00 |
| ❑ BS 2700 | The Thief Who Came to Dinner | 1973 | 15.00 |
| ❑ BSK 3399 | 10 | 1979 | 15.00 |

## MANCUSO, GUS

### FANTASY

| Number | Title (A Side/B Side) | Yr | NM |
|---|---|---|---|
| ❑ 3223 [M] | Introducing Gus Mancuso | 1956 | 40.00 |
| *—Black vinyl* | | | |
| ❑ 3223 [M] | Introducing Gus Mancuso | 1956 | 60.00 |
| *—Red vinyl* | | | |
| ❑ 3282 [M] | Music from New Faces | 1958 | 20.00 |
| *—Black vinyl* | | | |
| ❑ 3282 [M] | Music from New Faces | 1958 | 40.00 |
| *—Red vinyl* | | | |
| ❑ 8025 [S] | Music from New Faces | 1960 | 30.00 |
| *—Blue vinyl* | | | |

## MANDEL, HARVEY

### EDITIONS EG

| Number | Title (A Side/B Side) | Yr | NM |
|---|---|---|---|
| ❑ CAROL-1535-1 | Cristo Redentor | 198? | 10.00 |
| *—Reissue of Philips 600-281* | | | |

### JANUS

| Number | Title (A Side/B Side) | Yr | NM |
|---|---|---|---|
| ❑ JLS-3017 | Baby Batter | 1970 | 12.00 |
| ❑ JLS-3037 | The Snake | 1972 | 12.00 |
| ❑ JLS-3047 | Shangrenade | 1973 | 12.00 |
| ❑ JSX-3067 | Feel the Sound of Harvey Mandel | 1974 | 12.00 |
| ❑ JXS-7014 | The Best of Harvey Mandel | 1975 | 12.00 |

### OVATION

| Number | Title (A Side/B Side) | Yr | NM |
|---|---|---|---|
| ❑ OV-1415 | Get Off in Chicago | 1971 | 15.00 |

### PHILIPS

| Number | Title (A Side/B Side) | Yr | NM |
|---|---|---|---|
| ❑ PHS 600281 | Cristo Redentor | 1969 | 25.00 |
| ❑ PHS 600306 | Righteous | 1969 | 25.00 |
| ❑ PHS 600325 | Games Guitars Play | 1970 | 25.00 |

## MANDO AND THE CHILI PEPPERS

### GOLDEN CREST

| Number | Title (A Side/B Side) | Yr | NM |
|---|---|---|---|
| ❑ CR-3023 [M] | On the Road with Rock and Roll | 1957 | 500.00 |

## MANDRAKE MEMORIAL

### POPPY

| Number | Title (A Side/B Side) | Yr | NM |
|---|---|---|---|
| ❑ PYS 40002 | Mandrake Memorial | 1968 | 40.00 |
| ❑ PYS 40003 | Medium | 1969 | 40.00 |
| ❑ PYS 40006 | Puzzle | 1970 | 40.00 |

## MANDRELL, BARBARA

### ABC

| Number | Title (A Side/B Side) | Yr | NM |
|---|---|---|---|
| ❑ AB-1088 | Moods | 1978 | 12.00 |
| ❑ AB-1119 | The Best of Barbara Mandrell | 1979 | 12.00 |

### ABC DOT

| Number | Title (A Side/B Side) | Yr | NM |
|---|---|---|---|
| ❑ DOSD-2045 | This Is Barbara Mandrell | 1976 | 12.00 |
| ❑ DOSD-2067 | Midnight Angel | 1976 | 12.00 |
| ❑ DO-2076 | Lovers, Friends and Strangers | 1977 | 12.00 |
| ❑ DO-2098 | Love's Ups and Downs | 1977 | 12.00 |

### CAPITOL

| Number | Title (A Side/B Side) | Yr | NM |
|---|---|---|---|
| ❑ C1-90416 | I'll Be Your Jukebox Tonight | 1988 | 10.00 |
| ❑ C1-91977 | Morning Sun | 1990 | 12.00 |

### COLUMBIA

| Number | Title (A Side/B Side) | Yr | NM |
|---|---|---|---|
| ❑ C 30967 | Treat Him Right | 1971 | 20.00 |
| ❑ KC 32743 | The Midnight Oil | 1973 | 15.00 |
| ❑ PC 32743 | The Midnight Oil | 198? | 8.00 |
| *—Budget-line reissue* | | | |
| ❑ KC 32959 | This Time I Almost Made It | 1974 | 15.00 |
| ❑ PC 34876 | The Best of Barbara Mandrell | 1977 | 12.00 |
| *—No bar code on cover* | | | |
| ❑ PC 34876 | The Best of Barbara Mandrell | 198? | 8.00 |
| *—Reissue with bar code on cover* | | | |
| ❑ FC 37437 | Looking Back | 1982 | 10.00 |
| ❑ PC 37437 | Looking Back | 198? | 8.00 |
| *—Budget-line reissue* | | | |

### COLUMBIA LIMITED EDITION

| Number | Title (A Side/B Side) | Yr | NM |
|---|---|---|---|
| ❑ LE 10550 | Treat Him Right | 197? | 10.00 |

### EMI AMERICA

| Number | Title (A Side/B Side) | Yr | NM |
|---|---|---|---|
| ❑ ET-46956 | Sure Feels Good | 1987 | 10.00 |

### MCA

| Number | Title (A Side/B Side) | Yr | NM |
|---|---|---|---|
| ❑ 641 | Midnight Angel | 198? | 8.00 |
| *—Reissue of ABC Dot 2067* | | | |
| ❑ 672 | This Is Barbara Mandrell | 198? | 8.00 |
| *—Reissue of ABC Dot 2045* | | | |
| ❑ 673 | Lovers, Friends and Strangers | 198? | 8.00 |
| *—Reissue of ABC Dot 2076* | | | |
| ❑ 674 | Love's Ups and Downs | 198? | 8.00 |
| *—Reissue of ABC Dot 2098* | | | |
| ❑ 3165 | Just for the Record | 1979 | 10.00 |
| ❑ 3280 | Moods | 1980 | 8.00 |
| *—Reissue of ABC 1088* | | | |
| ❑ 5136 | Love Is Fair | 1980 | 10.00 |
| ❑ 5243 | Barbara Mandrell Live | 1981 | 10.00 |
| ❑ 5295 | ...In Black and White | 1982 | 10.00 |
| ❑ 5330 | He Set My Life to Music | 1982 | 10.00 |
| ❑ 5377 | Spun Gold | 1983 | 10.00 |
| ❑ 5474 | Clean Cut | 1984 | 10.00 |
| ❑ 5519 | Christmas at Our House | 1984 | 12.00 |
| ❑ 5566 | Greatest Hits | 1985 | 10.00 |
| ❑ 5619 | Get to the Heart | 1985 | 10.00 |
| ❑ 37173 | Just for the Record | 198? | 8.00 |
| *—Budget-line reissue* | | | |
| ❑ 37202 | Moods | 198? | 6.00 |
| *—Budget-line reissue* | | | |
| ❑ 37224 | Barbara Mandrell Live | 198? | 8.00 |
| *—Budget-line reissue* | | | |

### PAIR

| Number | Title (A Side/B Side) | Yr | NM |
|---|---|---|---|
| ❑ PDL1-1079 [(2)] | The Best of Barbara Mandrell | 1986 | 12.00 |

### TIME-LIFE

| Number | Title (A Side/B Side) | Yr | NM |
|---|---|---|---|
| ❑ STW-104 | Country Music | 1981 | 10.00 |

## MANGIONE, CHUCK

### JAZZLAND

| Number | Title (A Side/B Side) | Yr | NM |
|---|---|---|---|
| ❑ JLP-84 [M] | Recuerdo | 1962 | 40.00 |
| ❑ JLP-984 [S] | Recuerdo | 1962 | 50.00 |

### MOBILE FIDELITY

| Number | Title (A Side/B Side) | Yr | NM |
|---|---|---|---|
| ❑ 1-068 | Feels So Good | 1981 | 25.00 |
| *—Audiophile vinyl* | | | |

## MANGIONE, GAP

### GRC

| Number | Title (A Side/B Side) | Yr | NM |
|---|---|---|---|
| ❑ 9001 | Diana in the Autumn Wind | 1968 | 25.00 |

## MANHATTAN JAZZ ALL-STARS, THE

### COLUMBIA

| Number | Title (A Side/B Side) | Yr | NM |
|---|---|---|---|
| ❑ CL 1426 [M] | Swinging Guys and Dolls | 1960 | 25.00 |
| ❑ CS 8223 [S] | Swinging Guys and Dolls | 1960 | 30.00 |

## MANHATTAN JAZZ SEPTETTE, THE

### CORAL

| Number | Title (A Side/B Side) | Yr | NM |
|---|---|---|---|
| ❑ CRL 57090 [M] | The Manhattan Jazz Septette | 1956 | 80.00 |

## MANHATTAN TRANSFER

### ATLANTIC

| Number | Title (A Side/B Side) | Yr | NM |
|---|---|---|---|
| ❑ SD 16036 | Mecca for Moderns | 1981 | 10.00 |
| ❑ SD 18133 | The Manhattan Transfer | 1975 | 10.00 |
| ❑ SD 18183 | Coming Out | 1976 | 10.00 |
| ❑ SD 19163 | Pastiche | 1978 | 10.00 |
| ❑ SD 19258 | Extensions | 1979 | 10.00 |
| ❑ SD 19319 | The Best of the Manhattan Transfer | 1981 | 10.00 |
| ❑ 80104 | Bodies and Souls | 1983 | 10.00 |
| ❑ 81233 | Bop Doo-Wopp | 1984 | 12.00 |
| ❑ 81266 | Vocalese | 1985 | 10.00 |
| ❑ 81723 | Live | 1987 | 10.00 |
| ❑ 81803 | Brasil | 1987 | 10.00 |

### CAPITOL

| Number | Title (A Side/B Side) | Yr | NM |
|---|---|---|---|
| ❑ ST-778 | Jukin' | 1971 | 15.00 |
| *—With Gene Pistilli* | | | |
| ❑ ST-11405 | Jukin' | 1975 | 10.00 |
| *—With Gene Pistilli; reissue of 778* | | | |
| ❑ SN-16223 | Jukin' | 198? | 8.00 |
| *—With Gene Pistilli; budget-line reissue* | | | |

### COLUMBIA

| Number | Title (A Side/B Side) | Yr | NM |
|---|---|---|---|
| ❑ C 47079 | The Offbeat of Avenues | 1991 | 15.00 |

### MOBILE FIDELITY

| Number | Title (A Side/B Side) | Yr | NM |
|---|---|---|---|
| ❑ 1-022 | Manhattan Transfer Live | 1979 | 20.00 |
| *—Audiophile vinyl* | | | |
| ❑ 1-199 | Extensions | 1994 | 25.00 |
| *—Audiophile vinyl* | | | |

## MANHATTANS, THE (1)

### CARNIVAL

| Number | Title (A Side/B Side) | Yr | NM |
|---|---|---|---|
| ❑ CMLP-201 [M] | Dedicated to You | 1966 | 250.00 |
| ❑ CSLP-201 [S] | Dedicated to You | 1966 | 500.00 |
| ❑ CMLP-202 [M] | For You and Yours | 1967 | 150.00 |
| ❑ CSLP-202 [S] | For You and Yours | 1967 | 300.00 |

### COLLECTABLES

| Number | Title (A Side/B Side) | Yr | NM |
|---|---|---|---|
| ❑ COL-5135 | Dedicated to You: Golden Carnival Classics, Part One | 198? | 10.00 |
| ❑ COL-5136 | For You and Yours: Golden Carnival Classics, Part Two | 198? | 10.00 |

### COLUMBIA

| Number | Title (A Side/B Side) | Yr | NM |
|---|---|---|---|
| ❑ KC 32444 | There's No Me Without You | 1973 | 15.00 |
| ❑ PC 32444 | There's No Me Without You | 198? | 8.00 |
| *—Budget-line reissue* | | | |
| ❑ KC 33064 | That's How Much I Love You | 1975 | 15.00 |
| ❑ PC 33820 | The Manhattans | 1976 | 12.00 |
| *—No bar code on back cover* | | | |
| ❑ PC 33820 | The Manhattans | 198? | 8.00 |
| *—With bar code on back cover* | | | |
| ❑ PC 34450 | It Feels So Good | 1977 | 12.00 |
| *—No bar code on back cover* | | | |
| ❑ PC 34450 | It Feels So Good | 198? | 8.00 |
| *—With bar code on back cover* | | | |
| ❑ PCQ 34450 [Q] | It Feels So Good | 1977 | 20.00 |
| ❑ JC 35252 | There's No Good in Goodbye | 1978 | 12.00 |
| ❑ JC 35693 | Love Talk | 1979 | 12.00 |
| ❑ PC 35693 | After Midnight | 198? | 8.00 |
| *—Budget-line reissue* | | | |
| ❑ JC 36411 | After Midnight | 1980 | 12.00 |
| ❑ JC 36861 | Manhattans Greatest Hits | 1980 | 12.00 |
| ❑ FC 37156 | Black Tie | 1981 | 10.00 |
| ❑ PC 37156 | Black Tie | 198? | 8.00 |
| *—Budget-line reissue* | | | |
| ❑ FC 38600 | Forever By Your Side | 1983 | 10.00 |
| ❑ FC 39277 | Too Hot to Stop It | 1985 | 10.00 |

### DELUXE

| Number | Title (A Side/B Side) | Yr | NM |
|---|---|---|---|
| ❑ 12000 | With These Hands | 1971 | 25.00 |
| ❑ 12004 | A Million to One | 1972 | 25.00 |

### SOLID SMOKE

| Number | Title (A Side/B Side) | Yr | NM |
|---|---|---|---|
| ❑ 8007 | Follow Your Heart | 1981 | 10.00 |

### VALLEY VUE

| Number | Title (A Side/B Side) | Yr | NM |
|---|---|---|---|
| ❑ D1-72946 | Sweet Talk | 1989 | 12.00 |

## MANILLA ROAD

### ROADSTER

| Number | Title (A Side/B Side) | Yr | NM |
|---|---|---|---|
| ❑ MR 1001 | Invasion | 1980 | 100.00 |
| ❑ MR 1002 | Metal | 1982 | 100.00 |
| ❑ MR 1003 | Crystal Logic | 1983 | 50.00 |

## MANILOW, BARRY

### ARISTA

| Number | Title (A Side/B Side) | Yr | NM |
|---|---|---|---|
| ❑ AB 2500 [EP] | Oh, Julie! | 1982 | 20.00 |
| ❑ AB 4007 | Barry Manilow I | 1977 | 8.00 |
| *—Reissue of AL 4007 with new prefix* | | | |
| ❑ AL 4007 | Barry Manilow I | 1975 | 10.00 |
| *—Revised version of Bell 1129 with new cover; "Could It Be Magic" especially is noticeably different between the Bell and Arista versions* | | | |



Except when noted otherwise, VG = 25% of NM, and VG+ = 50% of NM. (Example: VG = $2.00, VG+ = $4.00 and NM = $8.00.)

| Number | Title (A Side/B Side) | Yr | NM |
|---|---|---|---|
| ❑ AB 4016 | Barry Manilow II | 1977 | 8.00 |
| *—Reissue of AL 4016 with new prefix* | | | |
| ❑ AL 4016 | Barry Manilow II | 1975 | 10.00 |
| *—Reissue of Bell 1314* | | | |
| ❑ AQ 4016 [Q] | Barry Manilow II | 1975 | 15.00 |
| ❑ AB 4060 | Tryin' to Get the Feeling | 1977 | 8.00 |
| *—Reissue of AL 4060 with new prefix* | | | |
| ❑ AL 4060 | Tryin' to Get the Feeling | 1975 | 10.00 |
| ❑ AQ 4060 [Q] | Tryin' to Get the Feeling | 1975 | 15.00 |
| ❑ AB 4090 | This One's for You | 1977 | 8.00 |
| *—Reissue of AL 4090 with new prefix* | | | |
| ❑ AL 4090 | This One's for You | 1976 | 10.00 |
| ❑ AQ 4090 [Q] | This One's for You | 1976 | 20.00 |
| ❑ AB 4164 | Even Now | 1978 | 8.00 |
| ❑ AL8-8003 | Here Comes the Night | 198? | 6.00 |
| *—Reissue of 9610* | | | |
| ❑ AL13-8039 [(2)] | Greatest Hits | 1983 | 10.00 |
| ❑ AL5-8046 | One Voice | 198? | 6.00 |
| *—Reissue of 9505* | | | |
| ❑ AL13-8049 [(2)] | Barry Manilow/Live | 1983 | 10.00 |
| ❑ AL5-8052 | Even Now | 198? | 6.00 |
| *—Reissue of 8322* | | | |
| ❑ AL5-8070 | Tryin' to Get the Feeling | 198? | 6.00 |
| *—Reissue of 8336* | | | |
| ❑ AL5-8085 | Barry Manilow II | 198? | 6.00 |
| *—Reissue of 8370* | | | |
| ❑ AL8-8102 | Barry Manilow/Greatest Hits, Vol. II | 1983 | 8.00 |
| ❑ AL8-8117 | Barry | 198? | 6.00 |
| *—Reissue of 9537* | | | |
| ❑ AL8-8123 | If I Should Love Again | 198? | 6.00 |
| *—Reissue of 9573* | | | |
| ❑ AL5-8153 | Barry Manilow I | 198? | 6.00 |
| *—Reissue of 8372* | | | |
| ❑ AL5-8160 | This One's for You | 198? | 6.00 |
| *—Reissue of 8331* | | | |
| ❑ AL8-8254 | 2:00 A.M. Paradise Café | 1984 | 8.00 |
| ❑ AL9-8274 | The Manilow Collection — 20 Classic Hits | 1985 | 8.00 |
| ❑ AL8-8291 | Barry Manilow/Greatest Hits, Vol. II | 1985 | 6.00 |
| ❑ AL8-8322 | Even Now | 1985 | 6.00 |
| ❑ AL8-8331 | This One's for You | 1985 | 6.00 |
| ❑ AL8-8336 | Tryin' to Get the Feeling | 1985 | 6.00 |
| ❑ AL8-8370 | Barry Manilow II | 1985 | 6.00 |
| ❑ AL8-8372 | Barry Manilow I | 1985 | 6.00 |
| ❑ AL 8500 [(2)] | Barry Manilow/Live | 1977 | 12.00 |
| ❑ AL-8527 | Swing Street | 1987 | 8.00 |
| ❑ AL-8570 | Barry Manilow | 1989 | 8.00 |
| ❑ AL-8598 | Greatest Hits, Vol. 1 | 1989 | 10.00 |
| ❑ AL-8599 | Greatest Hits, Vol. 2 | 1989 | 10.00 |
| ❑ AL-8600 | Greatest Hits, Vol. 3 | 1989 | 10.00 |
| ❑ A2L 8601 [(2)] | Greatest Hits | 1978 | 12.00 |
| ❑ A2L 8601 [(2)PD] | Greatest Hits | 1979 | 40.00 |
| *—Entire contents on two picture discs (yes, it has the same number as the regular issue)* | | | |
| ❑ AL-8638 [(2)] | Live on Broadway | 1990 | 20.00 |
| ❑ AL-8644 | Because It's Christmas | 1990 | 15.00 |
| ❑ AL 9505 | One Voice | 1979 | 8.00 |
| ❑ AL 9537 | Barry | 1980 | 8.00 |
| ❑ AL 9573 | If I Should Love Again | 1981 | 8.00 |
| ❑ AL-9610 | Here Comes the Night | 1982 | 8.00 |
| ❑ NU 9740 | Manilow Magic | 1982 | 12.00 |
| *—Manufactured by K-Tel* | | | |

BELL

| Number | Title (A Side/B Side) | Yr | NM |
|---|---|---|---|
| ❑ 1129 | Barry Manilow | 1973 | 25.00 |
| ❑ 1314 | Barry Manilow II | 1974 | 15.00 |

MOBILE FIDELITY

| Number | Title (A Side/B Side) | Yr | NM |
|---|---|---|---|
| ❑ 1-097 | Barry Manilow I | 1981 | 20.00 |
| *—Audiophile vinyl* | | | |

RCA VICTOR

| Number | Title (A Side/B Side) | Yr | NM |
|---|---|---|---|
| ❑ AFL1-7044 | Manilow | 1985 | 8.00 |

## MANN, AIMEE

MOBILE FIDELITY

| Number | Title (A Side/B Side) | Yr | NM |
|---|---|---|---|
| ❑ MFSL 1-278 | Lost in Space | 2003 | 25.00 |
| *—"Original Master Recording" at top of front cover* | | | |

## MANN, BARRY

ABC-PARAMOUNT

| Number | Title (A Side/B Side) | Yr | NM |
|---|---|---|---|
| ❑ 399 [M] | Who Put the Bomp | 1963 | 120.00 |
| ❑ S-399 [S] | Who Put the Bomp | 1963 | 300.00 |

CASABLANCA

| Number | Title (A Side/B Side) | Yr | NM |
|---|---|---|---|
| ❑ NBLP 7226 | Barry Mann | 1980 | 10.00 |

NEW DESIGN

| Number | Title (A Side/B Side) | Yr | NM |
|---|---|---|---|
| ❑ Z 30876 | Lay It All Out | 1971 | 12.00 |

RCA VICTOR

| Number | Title (A Side/B Side) | Yr | NM |
|---|---|---|---|
| ❑ APL1-0860 | Survivor | 1975 | 12.00 |
| ❑ DJL1-1162 [DJ] | Flo and Eddie Interview Barry Mann | 1975 | 50.00 |

## MANN, CARL

PHILLIPS INT'L.

| Number | Title (A Side/B Side) | Yr | NM |
|---|---|---|---|
| ❑ PLP-1960 [M] | Like Mann | 1960 | 600.00 |

## MANN, HERBIE

ATLANTIC

| Number | Title (A Side/B Side) | Yr | NM |
|---|---|---|---|
| ❑ SD 1343 [S] | The Common Ground | 1960 | 20.00 |
| ❑ SD 1371 [S] | The Family of Mann | 1961 | 20.00 |
| ❑ SD 1380 [S] | Herbie Mann at the Village Gate | 1962 | 20.00 |
| ❑ SD 1384 [S] | Right Now | 1962 | 20.00 |
| ❑ SD 1397 [S] | Do the Bossa Nova with Herbie Mann | 1962 | 20.00 |
| ❑ SD 1407 [S] | Herbie Mann Returns to the Village Gate | 1963 | 20.00 |
| ❑ SD 1413 [S] | Herbie Mann Live at Newport | 1963 | 20.00 |
| ❑ SD 1422 [S] | Latin Fever | 1964 | 20.00 |
| ❑ SD 1426 [S] | Nirvana | 1964 | 20.00 |
| ❑ SD 1433 [S] | My Kinda Groove | 1965 | 20.00 |
| ❑ SD 1437 [S] | The Roar of the Greasepaint, The Smell of the Crowd | 1965 | 20.00 |
| ❑ SD 1445 [S] | Standing Ovation at Newport | 1965 | 20.00 |
| ❑ SD 1454 [S] | Herbie Mann Today | 1966 | 20.00 |
| ❑ SD 1462 [S] | Monday Night at the Village Gate | 1966 | 20.00 |
| ❑ SD 1464 [S] | Our Mann Flute | 1966 | 20.00 |
| ❑ 1471 [M] | New Mann at Newport | 1967 | 20.00 |
| ❑ 1475 [M] | Impressions of the Middle East | 1967 | 20.00 |
| ❑ 1483 [M] | The Beat Goes On | 1967 | 20.00 |
| ❑ 1490 [M] | The Herbie Mann String Album | 1968 | 25.00 |
| ❑ QD 1632 [Q] | Hold On, I'm Comin' | 1973 | 20.00 |
| ❑ 8141 [M] | Mann and a Woman | 1967 | 20.00 |

BETHLEHEM

| Number | Title (A Side/B Side) | Yr | NM |
|---|---|---|---|
| ❑ BCP-24 [M] | Flamingo, My Goodness — Four Flutes, Vol. 2 | 1955 | 50.00 |
| ❑ BCP-40 [M] | The Herbie Mann-Sam Most Quintet | 1956 | 50.00 |
| ❑ BCP-58 [M] | Herbie Mann Plays | 1956 | 50.00 |
| ❑ BCP-63 [M] | Love and the Weather | 1956 | 50.00 |
| ❑ BCP-1018 [10] | East Coast Jazz 4 | 1954 | 120.00 |
| ❑ BCP-6011 | Early Mann | 1976 | 10.00 |
| *—Reissue of older material; distributed by Caytronics* | | | |
| ❑ BCP-6020 [M] | The Mann with the Most | 1960 | 40.00 |
| ❑ BCP-6067 [M] | The Epitome of Jazz | 1963 | 30.00 |

COLUMBIA

| Number | Title (A Side/B Side) | Yr | NM |
|---|---|---|---|
| ❑ CS 9188 [S] | Latin Mann | 1965 | 20.00 |

EPIC

| Number | Title (A Side/B Side) | Yr | NM |
|---|---|---|---|
| ❑ LN 3395 [M] | Salute to the Flute | 1957 | 60.00 |
| ❑ LN 3499 [M] | Herbie Mann with the Ilcken Trio | 1958 | 60.00 |

JAZZLAND

| Number | Title (A Side/B Side) | Yr | NM |
|---|---|---|---|
| ❑ JLP-5 [M] | Herbie Mann Quintet | 1960 | 30.00 |
| *—Reissue of Riverside 245* | | | |

NEW JAZZ

| Number | Title (A Side/B Side) | Yr | NM |
|---|---|---|---|
| ❑ NJLP-8211 [M] | Just Walkin' | 1958 | 50.00 |
| *—Purple label* | | | |
| ❑ NJLP-8211 [M] | Just Walkin' | 1964 | 25.00 |
| *—Blue label with trident logo* | | | |

PRESTIGE

| Number | Title (A Side/B Side) | Yr | NM |
|---|---|---|---|
| ❑ PRLP-7101 [M] | Flute Souffle | 1957 | 80.00 |
| ❑ PRLP-7124 [M] | Flute Flight | 1957 | 80.00 |
| ❑ PRLP-7136 [M] | Mann in the Morning | 1958 | 80.00 |

RIVERSIDE

| Number | Title (A Side/B Side) | Yr | NM |
|---|---|---|---|
| ❑ RLP 12-234 [M] | Sultry Serenade | 1957 | 60.00 |
| *—Blue on white label* | | | |
| ❑ RLP 12-234 [M] | Sultry Serenade | 1958 | 40.00 |
| *—Blue label with reel and microphone logo* | | | |
| ❑ RLP 12-245 [M] | Great Ideas of Western Mann | 1957 | 40.00 |

SAVOY

| Number | Title (A Side/B Side) | Yr | NM |
|---|---|---|---|
| ❑ MG-12102 [M] | Flute Suite | 1957 | 50.00 |
| ❑ MG-12107 [M] | Mann Alone | 1957 | 50.00 |
| ❑ MG-12108 [M] | Yardbird Suite | 1957 | 50.00 |

SURREY

| Number | Title (A Side/B Side) | Yr | NM |
|---|---|---|---|
| ❑ SS-1015 [S] | Big Band | 1965 | 20.00 |

UNITED ARTISTS

| Number | Title (A Side/B Side) | Yr | NM |
|---|---|---|---|
| ❑ UAL-4042 [M] | African Suite | 1959 | 30.00 |
| ❑ UAS-5042 [S] | African Suite | 1959 | 40.00 |
| ❑ UAJ-14009 [M] | Brasil, Bossa Nova and Blue | 1962 | 30.00 |
| ❑ UAJ-14022 [M] | St. Thomas | 1962 | 30.00 |
| ❑ UAJS-15009 [S] | Brasil, Bossa Nova and Blue | 1962 | 40.00 |
| ❑ UAJS-15022 [S] | St. Thomas | 1962 | 40.00 |

VERVE

| Number | Title (A Side/B Side) | Yr | NM |
|---|---|---|---|
| ❑ MGVS-6074 [S] | Flautista! — Herbie Mann Plays Afro-Cuban Jazz | 1960 | 30.00 |
| ❑ MGV-8247 [M] | The Magic Flute of Herbie Mann | 1958 | 40.00 |
| ❑ V-8247 [M] | The Magic Flute of Herbie Mann | 1961 | 20.00 |
| ❑ MGV-8336 [M] | Flautista! — Herbie Mann Plays Afro-Cuban Jazz | 1959 | 40.00 |
| ❑ V-8336 [M] | Flautista! — Herbie Mann Plays Afro-Cuban Jazz | 1961 | 20.00 |
| ❑ MGV-8392 [M] | Flute, Brass, Vibes and Percussion | 1960 | 30.00 |
| ❑ V-8392 [M] | Flute, Brass, Vibes and Percussion | 1961 | 20.00 |
| ❑ V-8527 [M] | The Sound of Mann | 1963 | 20.00 |

## MANN, HERBIE, AND BUDDY COLLETTE

INTERLUDE

| Number | Title (A Side/B Side) | Yr | NM |
|---|---|---|---|
| ❑ MO-503 [M] | Flute Fraternity | 1959 | 40.00 |
| *—Reissue of Mode 114* | | | |
| ❑ ST-1103 [S] | Flute Fraternity | 1959 | 30.00 |

MODE

| Number | Title (A Side/B Side) | Yr | NM |
|---|---|---|---|
| ❑ LP-114 [M] | Flute Fraternity | 1957 | 70.00 |

## MANN, HERBIE, AND JOAO GILBERTO

ATLANTIC

| Number | Title (A Side/B Side) | Yr | NM |
|---|---|---|---|
| ❑ SD 8105 [S] | Herbie Mann and Joao Gilberto with Antonio Carlos Jobim | 1965 | 20.00 |

## MANN, HERBIE, AND MACHITO

ROULETTE

| Number | Title (A Side/B Side) | Yr | NM |
|---|---|---|---|
| ❑ SR-52122 [S] | Afro-Jazziac | 1963 | 20.00 |

## MANN, JOHNNY, SINGERS

EPIC

| Number | Title (A Side/B Side) | Yr | NM |
|---|---|---|---|
| ❑ KE 31954 | Stand Up and Cheer! | 1973 | 12.00 |

LIBERTY

| Number | Title (A Side/B Side) | Yr | NM |
|---|---|---|---|
| ❑ LRP-3134 [M] | Alma Mater | 1959 | 15.00 |
| ❑ LRP-3149 [M] | Roar Along with the Singing Twenties | 1960 | 15.00 |
| ❑ LRP-3156 [M] | Swing Along with the Singing Thirties | 1960 | 15.00 |
| ❑ LRP-3198 [M] | Ballads of the King | 1961 | 15.00 |
| ❑ LRP-3217 [M] | Ballads of the King, Volume 2 | 1961 | 15.00 |
| ❑ LRP-3253 [M] | Golden Folk Song Hits | 1963 | 12.00 |
| ❑ LRP-3296 [M] | Golden Folk Song Hits, Volume 2 | 1963 | 12.00 |
| ❑ LRP-3355 [M] | Golden Folk Song Hits, Volume 3 | 1964 | 12.00 |
| ❑ LRP-3387 [M] | Invisible Tears | 1964 | 12.00 |
| ❑ LRP-3391 [M] | The Ballad Sound (Beatle Songs) | 1964 | 15.00 |
| ❑ LRP-3411 [M] | If I Loved You | 1965 | 12.00 |
| ❑ LRP-3436 [M] | I'll Remember You | 1965 | 12.00 |
| ❑ LRP-3447 [M] | Daydream | 1966 | 12.00 |
| ❑ LRP-3522 [M] | We Wish You a Merry Christmas | 1967 | 15.00 |
| ❑ LRP-3523 [M] | We Can Fly! Up-Up and Away | 1967 | 12.00 |
| ❑ LST-7134 [S] | Alma Mater | 1959 | 20.00 |
| ❑ LST-7149 [S] | Roar Along with the Singing Twenties | 1960 | 20.00 |
| ❑ LST-7156 [S] | Swing Along with the Singing Thirties | 1960 | 20.00 |
| ❑ LST-7198 [S] | Ballads of the King | 1961 | 20.00 |
| ❑ LST-7217 [S] | Ballads of the King, Volume 2 | 1961 | 20.00 |
| ❑ LST-7253 [S] | Golden Folk Song Hits | 1963 | 15.00 |
| ❑ LST-7296 [S] | Golden Folk Song Hits, Volume 2 | 1963 | 15.00 |
| ❑ LST-7355 [S] | Golden Folk Song Hits, Volume 3 | 1964 | 15.00 |
| ❑ LST-7387 [S] | Invisible Tears | 1964 | 15.00 |
| ❑ LST-7391 [S] | The Ballad Sound (Beatle Songs) | 1964 | 20.00 |
| ❑ LST-7411 [S] | If I Loved You | 1965 | 15.00 |
| ❑ LST-7426 [S] | I'll Remember You | 1965 | 15.00 |
| ❑ LST-7447 [S] | Daydream | 1966 | 15.00 |
| ❑ LST-7522 [S] | We Wish You a Merry Christmas | 1967 | 15.00 |
| ❑ LST-7523 [S] | We Can Fly! Up-Up and Away | 1967 | 15.00 |
| ❑ LST-7629 | Golden | 1969 | 12.00 |
| ❑ LMM-13017 [M] | The Great Bands with Great Voices Swing the Great Voices of the Great Bands | 1962 | 15.00 |
| ❑ LSS-14017 [S] | The Great Bands with Great Voices Swing the Great Voices of the Great Bands | 1962 | 20.00 |

SUNSET

| Number | Title (A Side/B Side) | Yr | NM |
|---|---|---|---|
| ❑ SUM-1115 [M] | The Flowing Voices of the Johnny Mann Singers | 196? | 10.00 |
| ❑ SUS-5115 [S] | The Flowing Voices of the Johnny Mann Singers | 196? | 12.00 |
| ❑ SUS-5196 | Heart Full of Song | 1968 | 12.00 |
| ❑ SUS-5231 | Country Style | 1969 | 12.00 |
| ❑ SUS-5288 | At Our Best | 1970 | 12.00 |

UNITED ARTISTS

| Number | Title (A Side/B Side) | Yr | NM |
|---|---|---|---|
| ❑ UXS-87 [(2)] | The Johnny Mann Singers Superpak | 1972 | 15.00 |

## MANN, MANFRED

ASCOT

| Number | Title (A Side/B Side) | Yr | NM |
|---|---|---|---|
| ❑ AM-13015 [M] | The Manfred Mann Album | 1964 | 40.00 |
| ❑ AM-13018 [M] | The Five Faces of Manfred Mann | 1965 | 40.00 |
| ❑ AM-13021 [M] | My Little Red Book of Winners | 1965 | 40.00 |
| ❑ AM-13024 [M] | Mann Made | 1966 | 40.00 |
| ❑ AS-16015 [P] | The Manfred Mann Album | 1964 | 50.00 |
| ❑ AS-16018 [P] | The Five Faces of Manfred Mann | 1965 | 50.00 |
| ❑ AS-16021 [S] | My Little Red Book of Winners | 1965 | 50.00 |
| ❑ AS-16024 [S] | Mann Made | 1966 | 50.00 |

CAPITOL

| Number | Title (A Side/B Side) | Yr | NM |
|---|---|---|---|
| ❑ SM-11688 | The Best of Manfred Mann | 1977 | 10.00 |
| ❑ SN-16073 | The Best of Manfred Mann | 1980 | 8.00 |

JANUS

| Number | Title (A Side/B Side) | Yr | NM |
|---|---|---|---|
| ❑ JXS-3064 | The Best of Manfred Mann | 1974 | 12.00 |

the MANFRED MANN album
featuring DO WAH DIDDY DIDDY
DON'T ASK ME WHAT I SAY • IT'S GONNA WORK OUT FINE • BRING IT TO JEROME
DOWN THE ROAD APIECE • SACK O' WOE • WHAT YOU GONNA DO?
UNTIE ME • SMOKESTACK LIGHTNING • GOT MY MOJO WORKING
WITHOUT YOU • I'M YOUR HOOCHIE COOCHE MAN
ASCOT
HIGH FIDELITY THE MANFRED MANN ALBUM • ASCOT • AM 13015


Manfred Mann, *The Manfred Mann Album,* Ascot AM 13015, 1964, mono, $40.

| Number | Title (A Side/B Side) | Yr | NM |
|---|---|---|---|
| **MERCURY** | | | |
| ❑ SR-61168 | The Mighty Quinn | 1968 | 25.00 |
| **POLYDOR** | | | |
| ❑ 24-4013 | Chapter Three | 1970 | 15.00 |
| **UNITED ARTISTS** | | | |
| ❑ 94 [DJ] | Manfred Mann Interview | 1966 | 200.00 |
| *—Promotional album in plain white jacket* | | | |
| ❑ UAL 3549 [M] | Pretty Flamingo | 1966 | 30.00 |
| ❑ UAL 3551 [M] | Manfred Mann's Greatest Hits | 1966 | 30.00 |
| ❑ UAS 6549 [S] | Pretty Flamingo | 1966 | 40.00 |
| ❑ UAS 6551 [P] | Manfred Mann's Greatest Hits | 1966 | 40.00 |
| *—"Do Wah Diddy Diddy," "Sha La La," "I Got You Babe" and "Satisfaction" are rechanneled.* | | | |

### MANN, REV. COLUMBUS

| Number | Title (A Side/B Side) | Yr | NM |
|---|---|---|---|
| **TAMLA** | | | |
| ❑ T-227 [M] | They Shall Be Mine | 1962 | 4000. |
| *—VG value 2000; VG+ value 3000* | | | |
| **WINGATE** | | | |
| ❑ 701 [M] | He Satisfies Me | 196? | 900.00 |

### MANN, SHADOW

| Number | Title (A Side/B Side) | Yr | NM |
|---|---|---|---|
| **TOMORROW** | | | |
| ❑ TPS-69001 | Come Live with Me | 1974 | 60.00 |

### MANNA, CHARLIE

| Number | Title (A Side/B Side) | Yr | NM |
|---|---|---|---|
| **DECCA** | | | |
| ❑ DL 4159 [M] | Manna Overboard!! | 1961 | 25.00 |
| ❑ DL 4213 [M] | Manna Live!! | 1962 | 25.00 |
| ❑ DL 74159 [R] | Manna Overboard!! | 1961 | 15.00 |
| ❑ DL 74213 [R] | Manna Live!! | 1962 | 15.00 |
| **VERVE** | | | |
| ❑ V-15051 [M] | The Rise and Fall of the Great Society | 1966 | 12.00 |
| ❑ V6-15051 [S] | The Rise and Fall of the Great Society | 1966 | 15.00 |

### MANNE, SHELLY

| Number | Title (A Side/B Side) | Yr | NM |
|---|---|---|---|
| **ATLANTIC** | | | |
| ❑ 1487 [M] | Jazz Gunn | 1967 | 20.00 |
| ❑ 8157 [M] | Daktari | 1968 | 25.00 |
| **CAPITOL** | | | |
| ❑ ST 2173 [S] | "My Fair Lady" with Un-Original Cast | 1964 | 20.00 |
| ❑ ST 2313 [S] | Manne, That's Gershwin | 1965 | 20.00 |
| **CONTEMPORARY** | | | |
| ❑ C-2503 [10] | Shelly Manne and His Men | 1953 | 150.00 |
| ❑ C-2511 [10] | Shelly Manne and His Men, Volume 2 | 1954 | 150.00 |
| ❑ C-2516 [10] | The Three | 1954 | 150.00 |
| ❑ C-2518 [10] | The Two | 1954 | 150.00 |
| ❑ C-3507 [M] | The West Coast Sound | 1955 | 60.00 |
| ❑ C-3516 [M] | Swinging Sounds, Vol. 4 | 1956 | 70.00 |
| ❑ C-3519 [M] | More Swinging Sounds, Vol. 5 | 1957 | 70.00 |
| ❑ C-3525 [M] | Shelly Manne and His Friends | 1957 | 50.00 |
| ❑ C-3527 [M] | Modern Jazz Performance of Songs from "My Fair Lady" | 1957 | 50.00 |
| ❑ C-3533 [M] | Li'l Abner | 1957 | 50.00 |
| ❑ C-3536 [M] | Concerto for Clarinet and Combo | 1957 | 50.00 |
| ❑ C-3557 [M] | The Gambit | 1958 | 50.00 |
| ❑ C-3559 [M] | Bells Are Ringing | 1958 | 40.00 |
| ❑ C-3560 [M] | Shelly Manne Plays "Peter Gunn" | 1958 | 50.00 |
| ❑ M-3566 [M] | Son of Gunn | 1959 | 40.00 |
| ❑ M-3577 [M] | Shelly Manne and His Men at the Black Hawk, Vol. 1 | 1960 | 40.00 |
| ❑ M-3578 [M] | Shelly Manne and His Men at the Black Hawk, Vol. 2 | 1960 | 40.00 |
| ❑ M-3579 [M] | Shelly Manne and His Men at the Black Hawk, Vol. 3 | 1960 | 40.00 |
| ❑ M-3580 [M] | Shelly Manne and His Men at the Black Hawk, Vol. 4 | 1960 | 40.00 |
| ❑ M-3584 [M] | The Three and The Two | 1960 | 30.00 |
| ❑ M-3593/4 [(2)M] | Live! Shelly Manne and His Men at the Manne-Hole | 1961 | 40.00 |
| ❑ M-3599 [M] | Checkmate | 1961 | 25.00 |
| ❑ M-3609 [M] | My Son, the Jazz Drummer! | 1962 | 25.00 |
| ❑ M-3624 [M] | Outside | 1966 | 25.00 |
| ❑ M-5006 [M] | Sounds Unheard Of | 1962 | 30.00 |
| ❑ S-7025 [S] | Shelly Manne Plays "Peter Gunn" | 1959 | 40.00 |
| ❑ S-7519 [S] | Swinging Sounds in Stereo | 1959 | 50.00 |
| ❑ S-7527 [S] | Modern Jazz Performance of Songs from "My Fair Lady" | 1959 | 40.00 |
| ❑ S-7533 [S] | Li'l Abner | 1959 | 40.00 |
| ❑ S-7557 [S] | The Gambit | 1959 | 40.00 |
| ❑ S-7559 [S] | Bells Are Ringing | 1959 | 30.00 |
| ❑ S-7566 [S] | Son of Gunn | 1959 | 30.00 |
| ❑ S-7577 [S] | Shelly Manne and His Men at the Black Hawk, Vol. 1 | 1960 | 30.00 |
| ❑ S-7578 [S] | Shelly Manne and His Men at the Black Hawk, Vol. 2 | 1960 | 30.00 |
| ❑ S-7579 [S] | Shelly Manne and His Men at the Black Hawk, Vol. 3 | 1960 | 30.00 |
| ❑ S-7580 [S] | Shelly Manne and His Men at the Black Hawk, Vol. 4 | 1960 | 30.00 |
| ❑ S-7593/4 [(2)S] | Live! Shelly Manne and His Men at the Manne-Hole | 1961 | 50.00 |
| ❑ S-7599 [S] | Checkmate | 1961 | 30.00 |
| ❑ S-7609 [S] | My Son, the Jazz Drummer! | 1962 | 30.00 |
| ❑ S-7624 [S] | Outside | 1966 | 30.00 |
| ❑ S-9006 [S] | Sounds Unheard Of | 1962 | 40.00 |
| **DEE GEE** | | | |
| ❑ 1003 [10] | Here's That Manne | 1952 | 300.00 |
| **IMPULSE!** | | | |
| ❑ A-20 [M] | 2 3 4 | 1962 | 40.00 |
| ❑ AS-20 [S] | 2 3 4 | 1962 | 60.00 |
| **STEREO RECORDS** | | | |
| ❑ S-7002 [S] | Modern Jazz Performance of Songs from "My Fair Lady" | 1958 | 50.00 |
| ❑ S-7007 [S] | Swinging Sounds in Stereo | 1958 | 80.00 |
| ❑ S-7019 [S] | Li'l Abner | 1958 | 50.00 |
| ❑ S-7025 [S] | Shelly Manne Plays "Peter Gunn" | 1958 | 50.00 |
| ❑ S-7030 [S] | The Gambit | 1958 | 50.00 |

### MANNE, SHELLY/BILL RUSSO

| Number | Title (A Side/B Side) | Yr | NM |
|---|---|---|---|
| **SAVOY** | | | |
| ❑ MG-12045 [M] | Deep Purple | 1955 | 50.00 |

### MANNING, TERRY

| Number | Title (A Side/B Side) | Yr | NM |
|---|---|---|---|
| **ENTERPRISE** | | | |
| ❑ ENS-1008 | Home Sweet Home | 1969 | 40.00 |

### MANONE, WINGY

| Number | Title (A Side/B Side) | Yr | NM |
|---|---|---|---|
| **DECCA** | | | |
| ❑ DL 8473 [M] | Trumpet on the Wing | 1957 | 40.00 |
| **IMPERIAL** | | | |
| ❑ LP-12190 [S] | Wingy Manone on the Jazzband Bus | 1962 | 40.00 |
| **MCA** | | | |
| ❑ 1364 | Jam and Jive | 1983 | 12.00 |
| **RCA VICTOR** | | | |
| ❑ LPV-563 [M] | Wingy Manone, Volume 1 | 1969 | 20.00 |
| **"X"** | | | |
| ❑ LVA-3014 [10] | Wingy Manone, Vol. 1 | 1954 | 50.00 |

**MANPOWER** See MAN.

### MANSFIELD, JAYNE

| Number | Title (A Side/B Side) | Yr | NM |
|---|---|---|---|
| **MGM** | | | |
| ❑ E-4202 [M] | Shakespeare, Tchaikovsky and Me | 1964 | 40.00 |
| ❑ SE-4202 [S] | Shakespeare, Tchaikovsky and Me | 1964 | 60.00 |
| **20TH CENTURY** | | | |
| ❑ FOX-3049 [M] | Jayne Mansfield Busts Up Las Vegas | 1961 | 200.00 |

### MANSON, CHARLES

| Number | Title (A Side/B Side) | Yr | NM |
|---|---|---|---|
| **AWARENESS** | | | |
| ❑ 08903-1056 | Lie: The Love and Terror Cult | 1987 | 20.00 |
| ❑ LP-2144 | Lie: The Love and Terror Cult | 197? | 40.00 |
| **ESP-DISK'** | | | |
| ❑ 2003 | Lie: The Love and Terror Cult | 1970 | 200.00 |

### MANSON, MARILYN

| Number | Title (A Side/B Side) | Yr | NM |
|---|---|---|---|
| **NOTHING** | | | |
| ❑ 90273 [(2)] | Mechanical Animals | 1998 | 25.00 |
| *—One record on blue vinyl, the other on red; packaged in two separate cardboard covers in the same shrink wrap* | | | |
| ❑ 069 490790-1 [(2)] | Holywood | 2000 | 25.00 |

### MANTLE, MICKEY

| Number | Title (A Side/B Side) | Yr | NM |
|---|---|---|---|
| **RCA VICTOR** | | | |
| ❑ LPM-1704 [M] | My Favorite Hits | 1958 | 400.00 |

### MANTLER, MICHAEL

| Number | Title (A Side/B Side) | Yr | NM |
|---|---|---|---|
| **WATT** | | | |
| ❑ 2 | No Answer | 197? | 20.00 |
| ❑ 3 | 13 & 3/4 | 197? | 20.00 |
| ❑ 4 | Hapless Child | 197? | 20.00 |
| ❑ 5 | Silence | 197? | 20.00 |

### MANTOVANI

| Number | Title (A Side/B Side) | Yr | NM |
|---|---|---|---|
| **BAINBRIDGE** | | | |
| ❑ BT-6277 | Mantovani's Italia | 1988 | 8.00 |
| ❑ 8001 [(2)] | The Magic of Mantovani: Live at the Royal Festival Hall | 1982 | 12.00 |
| **FLEETWOOD** | | | |
| ❑ FMS 1019 | 90 Minutes with Mantovani | 1978 | 12.00 |
| *—Side 1: Great Songs of Christmas (reissue of London recordings); Side 2: Great Songs for All Seasons* | | | |
| **HOLIDAY** | | | |
| ❑ HDY 1928 | Holy Night | 1981 | 10.00 |

| Number | Title (A Side/B Side) | Yr | NM |
|---|---|---|---|
| LONDON | | | |
| ❑ SS 1 [S] | Mantovani Stereo Showcase | 1959 | 20.00 |
| ❑ PS 106 [S] | Gems Forever | 1959 | 20.00 |
| ❑ PS 112 [S] | Music from the Films | 1959 | 15.00 |
| ❑ PS 118 [S] | Strauss Waltzes | 1959 | 20.00 |
| ❑ PS 119 [S] | Waltz Encores | 1959 | 20.00 |
| ❑ PS 124 [S] | Film Encores | 1959 | 15.00 |
| ❑ PS 125 [S] | Song Hits from Theatreland | 1959 | 15.00 |
| ❑ PS 133 [S] | Concert Encores | 1959 | 20.00 |
| ❑ PS 142 [S] | Christmas Carols | 1959 | 20.00 |
| *—Originals have blue back cover, "Stereophonic" on upper left front cover and dark blue "FFSS" labels* | | | |
| ❑ PS 142 [S] | Christmas Carols | 196? | 15.00 |
| *—Reissue with white back cover* | | | |
| ❑ PS 147 [S] | Continental Encores | 1959 | 20.00 |
| ❑ PS 164 [S] | Film Encores, Vol. 2 | 1959 | 20.00 |
| ❑ PS 165 [S] | The Music of Victor Herbert and Sigmund Romberg | 1959 | 20.00 |
| ❑ PS 165/6 [(2)S] | All-American Showcase | 1959 | 25.00 |
| ❑ PS 166 [S] | The Music of Irving Berlin and Rudolf Friml | 1959 | 20.00 |
| ❑ PS 182 [S] | The American Scene | 1960 | 15.00 |
| ❑ PS 193 [S] | Songs to Remember | 1960 | 15.00 |
| ❑ PS 202 [S] | Operetta Memories | 1960 | 15.00 |
| ❑ PS 224 [S] | Mantovani Plays Music from Exodus and Other Great Themes | 1960 | 15.00 |
| ❑ PS 232 [S] | Italia Mia | 1961 | 15.00 |
| ❑ PS 242 [S] | Themes from Broadway (Carnival) | 1961 | 15.00 |
| ❑ PS 245 [S] | Songs of Praise | 1961 | 12.00 |
| ❑ PS 248 [S] | American Waltzes | 1962 | 12.00 |
| ❑ PS 249 [S] | Moon River and Other Great Film Themes | 1962 | 12.00 |
| ❑ PS 269 [S] | Classical Encores | 1963 | 12.00 |
| ❑ PS 270 [S] | Stop the World—I Want to Get Off/Oliver | 1962 | 12.00 |
| ❑ PS 280 [S] | The World's Great Love Songs | 1963 | 12.00 |
| ❑ PS 295 [S] | Latin Rendezvous | 1963 | 12.00 |
| ❑ PS 328 [S] | Mantovani/Manhattan | 1963 | 12.00 |
| ❑ PS 338 [S] | Christmas Greetings from Mantovani | 1963 | 15.00 |
| ❑ PS 360 [S] | Folk Songs Around the World | 1964 | 12.00 |
| ❑ PS 392 [S] | The Incomparable Mantovani | 1964 | 12.00 |
| ❑ PS 419 [S] | The Mantovani Sound — Big Hits from Broadway and Hollywood | 1965 | 12.00 |
| ❑ PS 422 [S] | Mantovani Ole | 1965 | 12.00 |
| ❑ PS 448 [S] | Mantovani Magic | 1966 | 12.00 |
| ❑ PS 474 [S] | Mr. Music...Mantovani | 1966 | 12.00 |
| ❑ PS 483 [S] | Mantovani's Golden Hits | 1967 | 12.00 |
| ❑ PS 516 [S] | Mantovani/Hollywood | 1967 | 12.00 |
| ❑ PS 526 [S] | The Mantovani Touch | 1968 | 12.00 |
| ❑ PS 532 [S] | Mantovani/Tango | 1968 | 12.00 |
| ❑ PS 542 [S] | Mantovani...Memories | 1968 | 12.00 |
| ❑ PS 548 [S] | The Mantovani Scene | 1969 | 12.00 |
| ❑ PS 565 [S] | The World of Mantovani | 1969 | 12.00 |
| ❑ LL 570 [M] | Greensleeves (A Selection of Favorite Waltzes) | 1952 | 20.00 |
| ❑ PS 570 | Greensleeves | 1970 | 12.00 |
| ❑ PS 572 [S] | Mantovani Today | 1970 | 12.00 |
| ❑ PS 578 [S] | Mantovani In Concert | 1970 | 12.00 |
| ❑ XPS 585/6 [(2)S] | From Monty with Love | 1971 | 15.00 |
| ❑ XPS 598 [S] | To Lovers Everywhere U.S.A. | 1971 | 12.00 |
| ❑ XPS 610 [S] | Annunzio Paolo Mantovani (25th Anniversary) | 1972 | 12.00 |
| ❑ LL 685 [M] | Strauss Waltzes | 1953 | 20.00 |
| ❑ BP 720/1 [(2)] | Christmas Favorites | 19?? | 15.00 |
| ❑ LL 766 [M] | An Enchanted Evening with Mantovani | 1953 | 20.00 |
| ❑ LL 768 [M] | Mantovani Plays Tangos | 1953 | 20.00 |
| ❑ XPS 900 | Gypsy Soul | 1972 | 10.00 |
| ❑ XPS 902 | An Evening with Mantovani | 1973 | 10.00 |
| ❑ XPS 906 | All-Time Greatest Hits, Volume 1 | 1973 | 10.00 |
| ❑ APS 907 | Musical Moments | 1974 | 10.00 |
| ❑ BP 910/1 [(2)] | Romantic Hits | 197? | 12.00 |
| ❑ LL 913 [M] | Christmas Carols | 1953 | 15.00 |
| *—Original recordings in mono* | | | |
| ❑ LL 913 [M] | Christmas Carols | 1959 | 12.00 |
| *—Mono versions of stereo re-recordings* | | | |
| ❑ XPS 913 | The Greatest Gift Is Love | 197? | 10.00 |
| ❑ XPS 914 | More Golden Hits | 197? | 10.00 |
| ❑ XPS 915 | American Encores | 1976 | 10.00 |
| ❑ XPS 917 | Strictly Mantovani | 1977 | 10.00 |
| ❑ PS 921 | Favorite Melodies from Opera | 1978 | 10.00 |
| ❑ LL 979 [M] | Romantic Melodies | 1954 | 20.00 |
| ❑ LL 1094 [M] | Waltz Time | 1954 | 20.00 |
| ❑ LL 1150 [M] | The Music of Rudolf Friml | 1955 | 20.00 |
| ❑ LL 1219 [M] | Song Hits from Theatreland | 1955 | 20.00 |
| ❑ LL 1259 [M] | Lonely Ballerina (Musical Modes) | 1956 | 20.00 |
| ❑ LL 1262 [M] | Gershwin: Concerto | 1955 | 20.00 |
| ❑ LL 1262 [M] | Gershwin: Rhapsody in Blue | 1955 | 20.00 |
| ❑ LL 1331 [M] | Operatic Arias | 1955 | 20.00 |
| ❑ LL 1452 [M] | Waltzes of Irving Berlin | 1956 | 20.00 |
| ❑ LL 1502 [M] | Candlelight | 195? | 15.00 |
| ❑ LL 1513 [M] | Music from the Films | 1956 | 20.00 |
| ❑ LL 1525 [M] | Music from the Ballet | 1956 | 20.00 |
| ❑ LL 1700 [M] | Film Encores | 1957 | 20.00 |
| ❑ LL 1748 [M] | The World's Favorite Love Songs | 1957 | 20.00 |
| ❑ LL 3004 [M] | Concert Encores | 1958 | 15.00 |
| ❑ LL 3032 [M] | Gems Forever | 1958 | 15.00 |
| ❑ LL 3095 [M] | Continental Encores | 1959 | 15.00 |
| ❑ LL 3117 [M] | Film Encores, Vol. 2 | 1959 | 15.00 |
| ❑ LL 3122 [M] | The Music of Victor Herbert and Sigmund Romberg | 1959 | 15.00 |
| ❑ LL 3122/3 [(2)M] | All-American Showcase | 1959 | 20.00 |
| ❑ LL 3123 [M] | The Music of Irving Berlin and Rudolf Friml | 1959 | 15.00 |
| ❑ LL 3136 [M] | The American Scene | 1960 | 12.00 |
| ❑ LL 3149 [M] | Songs to Remember | 1960 | 12.00 |
| ❑ LL 3181 [M] | Operetta Memories | 1960 | 12.00 |
| ❑ LL 3231 [M] | Mantovani Plays Music from Exodus and Other Great Themes | 1960 | 12.00 |
| ❑ LL 3239 [M] | Italia Mia | 1961 | 12.00 |
| ❑ LL 3250 [M] | Themes from Broadway (Carnival) | 1961 | 12.00 |
| ❑ LL 3251 [M] | Songs of Praise | 1961 | 10.00 |
| ❑ LL 3260 [M] | American Waltzes | 1962 | 10.00 |
| ❑ LL 3261 [M] | Moon River and Other Great Film Themes | 1962 | 10.00 |
| ❑ LL 3269 [M] | Classical Encores | 1963 | 10.00 |
| ❑ LL 3270 [M] | Stop the World—I Want to Get Off/Oliver | 1962 | 10.00 |
| ❑ LL 3280 [M] | The World's Great Love Songs | 1963 | 10.00 |
| ❑ LL 3295 [M] | Latin Rendezvous | 1963 | 10.00 |
| ❑ LL 3328 [M] | Mantovani/Manhattan | 1963 | 10.00 |
| ❑ LL 3338 [M] | Christmas Greetings from Mantovani | 1963 | 12.00 |
| ❑ LL 3360 [M] | Folk Songs Around the World | 1964 | 10.00 |
| ❑ LL 3392 [M] | The Incomparable Mantovani | 1964 | 10.00 |
| ❑ LL 3419 [M] | The Mantovani Sound — Big Hits from Broadway and Hollywood | 1965 | 10.00 |
| ❑ LL 3422 [M] | Mantovani Ole | 1965 | 10.00 |
| ❑ LL 3448 [M] | Mantovani Magic | 1966 | 10.00 |
| ❑ LL 3474 [M] | Mr. Music...Mantovani | 1966 | 10.00 |
| ❑ LL 3483 [M] | Mantovani's Golden Hits | 1967 | 12.00 |
| ❑ LL 3516 [M] | Mantovani/Hollywood | 1967 | 12.00 |
| ❑ LL 3526 [M] | The Mantovani Touch | 1968 | 15.00 |
| ❑ PM 55001 [M] | Kismet | 1964 | 12.00 |
| ❑ 820085-1 | Mantovani's Golden Hits | 198? | 8.00 |
| *—Reissue of 483* | | | |
| ❑ 820333-1 | Mantovani/Tango | 198? | 8.00 |
| *—Reissue of 532* | | | |
| ❑ 820334-1 | The Incomparable Mantovani | 198? | 8.00 |
| *—Reissue of 392* | | | |
| LONDON PHASE 4 | | | |
| ❑ SP-44043 [S] | Kismet | 1964 | 15.00 |
| ❑ BP 44302/3 [(2)] | Million Sellers | 1978 | 12.00 |

**MAPHIS, JOE**

| Number | Title (A Side/B Side) | Yr | NM |
|---|---|---|---|
| COLUMBIA | | | |
| ❑ CL 1005 [M] | Fire on the Strings | 1957 | 100.00 |
| HARMONY | | | |
| ❑ HL 7180 [M] | Hi-Fi Holiday for Banjo | 1959 | 25.00 |
| ❑ HS 11032 [S] | Hi-Fi Holiday for Banjo | 1959 | 30.00 |
| KAPP | | | |
| ❑ KL-1347 [M] | Hootenanny Star | 1964 | 20.00 |
| ❑ KS-3347 [S] | Hootenanny Star | 1964 | 25.00 |
| MACGREGOR | | | |
| ❑ MGR-1205 [M] | King of the Strings | 196? | 80.00 |
| MOSRITE | | | |
| ❑ MA-400 [M] | The New Sound of Joe Maphis | 1967 | 30.00 |
| ❑ MS-400 [S] | The New Sound of Joe Maphis | 1967 | 30.00 |
| STARDAY | | | |
| ❑ SLP-316 [M] | King of the Strings | 1966 | 50.00 |
| ❑ SLP-373 [M] | Country Guitar Goes to the Jimmy Dean Show | 1966 | 60.00 |
| *—Deduct 1/3 if instruction book is missing* | | | |

**MAPHIS, JOE AND ROSE LEE**

| Number | Title (A Side/B Side) | Yr | NM |
|---|---|---|---|
| CAPITOL | | | |
| ❑ ST 1778 [S] | Rose Lee and Joe Maphis | 1962 | 40.00 |
| ❑ T 1778 [M] | Rose Lee and Joe Maphis | 1962 | 30.00 |
| STARDAY | | | |
| ❑ SLP-286 [M] | Mr. and Mrs. Country Music | 1964 | 30.00 |
| ❑ SLP-322 [M] | Golden Gospel | 1966 | 30.00 |

**MAPHIS, ROSE LEE**

| Number | Title (A Side/B Side) | Yr | NM |
|---|---|---|---|
| COLUMBIA | | | |
| ❑ CL 1598 [M] | Rose Lee Maphis | 1961 | 30.00 |
| ❑ CS 8398 [S] | Rose Lee Maphis | 1961 | 40.00 |

**MAR-KEYS**

| Number | Title (A Side/B Side) | Yr | NM |
|---|---|---|---|
| ATLANTIC | | | |
| ❑ 8055 [M] | Last Night | 1961 | 100.00 |
| *—White "fan" logo on right* | | | |
| ❑ 8055 [M] | Last Night | 1962 | 50.00 |
| *—Black "fan" logo on right* | | | |
| ❑ SD 8055 [R] | Last Night | 1966 | 40.00 |
| ❑ 8062 [M] | Do the Pop-Eye with the Mar-Keys | 1962 | 50.00 |
| ❑ SD 8062 [R] | Do the Pop-Eye with the Mar-Keys | 1966 | 40.00 |
| STAX | | | |
| ❑ ST-707 [M] | The Great Memphis Sound | 1966 | 50.00 |
| ❑ STS-707 [R] | The Great Memphis Sound | 1966 | 40.00 |
| ❑ STS-2025 | Damifiknew | 1969 | 20.00 |
| ❑ STS-2036 | Memphis Experience | 1971 | 20.00 |

**MAR-KEYS/BOOKER T. AND THE MG'S** Also see each artist's individual listings.

| Number | Title (A Side/B Side) | Yr | NM |
|---|---|---|---|
| STAX | | | |
| ❑ ST-720 [M] | Back to Back | 1967 | 20.00 |
| ❑ STS-720 [S] | Back to Back | 1967 | 25.00 |

**MARABLE, LAWRENCE**

| Number | Title (A Side/B Side) | Yr | NM |
|---|---|---|---|
| JAZZ WEST | | | |
| ❑ LP-8 [M] | Tenor Man | 1956 | 300.00 |

**MARAIS, JOSEPH**

| Number | Title (A Side/B Side) | Yr | NM |
|---|---|---|---|
| DECCA | | | |
| ❑ DL 5014 [10] | South African Veld | 1949 | 50.00 |
| ❑ DL 5083 [10] | Songs from the Veld, Vol. 2 | 1950 | 50.00 |
| ❑ DL 5106 [10] | Songs of Many Lands | 1950 | 50.00 |

**MARAIS, JOSEPH, AND MIRANDA**

| Number | Title (A Side/B Side) | Yr | NM |
|---|---|---|---|
| DECCA | | | |
| ❑ DL 5268 [10] | Ballads of Many Lands | 1950 | 50.00 |
| ❑ DL 8711 [M] | Sundown Songs | 1957 | 25.00 |
| ❑ DL 9026 [M] | Marais and Miranda In Person, Vol. 1 | 1955 | 30.00 |
| ❑ DL 9027 [M] | Marais and Miranda In Person, Vol. 2 | 1955 | 30.00 |
| ❑ DL 9030 [M] | Christmas with Joseph and Miranda | 1955 | 30.00 |
| ❑ DL 9047 [M] | Africana Suite and Songs of Spirit and Humor | 1956 | 30.00 |

**MARATHONS, THE (1)**

| Number | Title (A Side/B Side) | Yr | NM |
|---|---|---|---|
| ARVEE | | | |
| ❑ A-428 [M] | Peanut Butter | 1961 | 180.00 |

**MARBLE PHROGG, THE**

| Number | Title (A Side/B Side) | Yr | NM |
|---|---|---|---|
| DERRICK | | | |
| ❑ 8868 | The Marble Phrogg | 1968 | 1000. |

**MARCEAU, MARCEL**

| Number | Title (A Side/B Side) | Yr | NM |
|---|---|---|---|
| GONE | | | |
| ❑ LP 1F | The Best of Marcel Marceau | 196? | 50.00 |
| MGM | | | |
| ❑ SE-4 | The Best of Marcel Marceau | 196? | 40.00 |
| *—The above records are identical: 38 minutes of silence and 2 minutes of applause!* | | | |

**MARCELS, THE**

| Number | Title (A Side/B Side) | Yr | NM |
|---|---|---|---|
| COLPIX | | | |
| ❑ CP-416 [M] | Blue Moon | 1961 | 350.00 |
| *—Gold label* | | | |
| ❑ CP-416 [M] | Blue Moon | 1963 | 120.00 |
| *—Blue label* | | | |

**MARCH, HAL**

| Number | Title (A Side/B Side) | Yr | NM |
|---|---|---|---|
| DOT | | | |
| ❑ DLP-3092 [M] | The Moods of March | 1958 | 30.00 |
| ❑ DLP-25092 [S] | The Moods of March | 1958 | 40.00 |
| HAMILTON | | | |
| ❑ HLP-101 [M] | Hal March Conducts | 1960 | 15.00 |
| ❑ HLP-12101 [S] | Hal March Conducts | 1960 | 20.00 |
| *—Reissue of Dot LP* | | | |

**MARCH, LITTLE PEGGY**

| Number | Title (A Side/B Side) | Yr | NM |
|---|---|---|---|
| RCA VICTOR | | | |
| ❑ LPM-2732 [M] | I Will Follow Him | 1963 | 60.00 |
| ❑ LSP-2732 [S] | I Will Follow Him | 1963 | 80.00 |
| ❑ LPM-3883 [M] | No Foolin' | 1968 | 40.00 |
| ❑ LSP-3883 [S] | No Foolin' | 1968 | 25.00 |

**MARCH, LITTLE PEGGY/BENNIE THOMAS**

| Number | Title (A Side/B Side) | Yr | NM |
|---|---|---|---|
| RCA VICTOR | | | |
| ❑ LPM-3408 [M] | In Our Fashion | 1965 | 40.00 |
| ❑ LSP-3408 [S] | In Our Fashion | 1965 | 50.00 |

**MARCHAN, BOBBY**

| Number | Title (A Side/B Side) | Yr | NM |
|---|---|---|---|
| COLLECTABLES | | | |
| ❑ COL-5113 | Golden Classics | 198? | 10.00 |
| SPHERE SOUND | | | |
| ❑ SSR-7004 [M] | There's Something on Your Mind | 1964 | 300.00 |

**MARCUS, LEW**

| Number | Title (A Side/B Side) | Yr | NM |
|---|---|---|---|
| SAVOY | | | |
| ❑ MG-15006 [10] | Back Room Piano | 1951 | 50.00 |

**MARCUS, STEVE**

| Number | Title (A Side/B Side) | Yr | NM |
|---|---|---|---|
| VORTEX | | | |
| ❑ 2001 | Tomorrow Never Knows | 1968 | 25.00 |
| ❑ 2009 | The Count's Rock Band | 1969 | 25.00 |
| ❑ 2013 | The Lord's Prayer | 1969 | 25.00 |

**MARESCA, ERNIE**

SEVILLE

| Number | Title (A Side/B Side) | Yr | NM |
|---|---|---|---|
| ❑ SV 77001 [M] | Shout! Shout! Knock Yourself Out | 1962 | 120.00 |
| ❑ SV 87001 [S] | Shout! Shout! Knock Yourself Out | 1962 | 200.00 |

**MARGOLIN, STUART**

WARNER BROS.

| Number | Title (A Side/B Side) | Yr | NM |
|---|---|---|---|
| ❑ BSK 3439 | And the Angel Sings | 1980 | 20.00 |

**MARGULIS, CHARLIE**

CARLTON

| Number | Title (A Side/B Side) | Yr | NM |
|---|---|---|---|
| ❑ LP 12-103 [M] | Marvelous Margulis | 1958 | 25.00 |
| ❑ STLP 12-103 [S] | Marvelous Margulis | 1959 | 30.00 |

**MARIANI**

SONOBEAT

| Number | Title (A Side/B Side) | Yr | NM |
|---|---|---|---|
| ❑ HEC 411/2 | Perpetuum Mobile | 197? | 2500. |
| *—Issued in generic white cover; the band and label names are stamped on the jacket, and each of the 50 copies is numbered and autographed by the members of the band; VG value 1000; VG+ value 1750* | | | |

**MARIANO, CHARLIE**

BETHLEHEM

| Number | Title (A Side/B Side) | Yr | NM |
|---|---|---|---|
| ❑ BCP-25 [M] | Alto Sax for Young Moderns | 1956 | 100.00 |
| ❑ BCP-49 [M] | Charlie Mariano Plays Chloe | 1957 | 100.00 |
| ❑ BCP-1022 [10] | Charlie Mariano Sextet | 1955 | 150.00 |

FANTASY

| Number | Title (A Side/B Side) | Yr | NM |
|---|---|---|---|
| ❑ 3-10 [10] | Charlie Mariano Sextet | 1953 | 180.00 |

IMPERIAL

| Number | Title (A Side/B Side) | Yr | NM |
|---|---|---|---|
| ❑ IMP-3006 [10] | Charlie Mariano Quintet Volume 1 | 1955 | 150.00 |
| ❑ IMP-3007 [10] | Charlie Mariano Quintet Volume 2 | 1955 | 150.00 |

PRESTIGE

| Number | Title (A Side/B Side) | Yr | NM |
|---|---|---|---|
| ❑ PRLP-130 [10] | Charlie Mariano | 1952 | 200.00 |
| ❑ PRLP-153 [10] | Charlie Mariano Boston All Stars | 1953 | 200.00 |

REGINA

| Number | Title (A Side/B Side) | Yr | NM |
|---|---|---|---|
| ❑ R-286 [M] | A Jazz Portrait of Charlie Mariano | 1963 | 25.00 |
| ❑ RS-286 [S] | A Jazz Portrait of Charlie Mariano | 1963 | 30.00 |

**MARIANO, CHARLIE, AND JERRY DODGION**

WORLD PACIFIC

| Number | Title (A Side/B Side) | Yr | NM |
|---|---|---|---|
| ❑ WP-1245 [M] | Beauties of 1918 | 1958 | 50.00 |

**MARIANO, TOSHIKO** See TOSHIKO AKIYOSHI.

**MARINERS, THE**

CADENCE

| Number | Title (A Side/B Side) | Yr | NM |
|---|---|---|---|
| ❑ CLP-1008 [M] | The Mariners Sing Spirituals | 1956 | 40.00 |

COLUMBIA

| Number | Title (A Side/B Side) | Yr | NM |
|---|---|---|---|
| ❑ CL 609 [M] | Hymns | 1955 | 40.00 |

**MARINO, FRANK, AND MAHOGANY RUSH** See MAHOGANY RUSH.

**MARKETTS, THE**

LIBERTY

| Number | Title (A Side/B Side) | Yr | NM |
|---|---|---|---|
| ❑ LRP-3226 [M] | The Surfing Scene | 196? | 30.00 |
| *—Retitled version of above* | | | |
| ❑ LRP-3226 [M] | Surfer's Stomp | 1962 | 40.00 |
| *—Add 20% if "Surfer's Stomp" instruction sheet is enclosed* | | | |
| ❑ LST-7226 [S] | The Surfing Scene | 196? | 40.00 |
| *—Retitled version of above* | | | |
| ❑ LST-7226 [S] | Surfer's Stomp | 1962 | 50.00 |
| *—Add 20% if "Surfer's Stomp" instruction sheet is enclosed* | | | |

MERCURY

| Number | Title (A Side/B Side) | Yr | NM |
|---|---|---|---|
| ❑ SRM-1-679 | AM, FM, Etc. | 1973 | 15.00 |

WARNER BROS.

| Number | Title (A Side/B Side) | Yr | NM |
|---|---|---|---|
| ❑ W 1509 [M] | The Marketts Take to Wheels | 1963 | 40.00 |
| ❑ WS 1509 [S] | The Marketts Take to Wheels | 1963 | 50.00 |
| ❑ W 1537 [M] | Out of Limits! | 1964 | 30.00 |
| ❑ WS 1537 [S] | Out of Limits! | 1964 | 40.00 |
| ❑ W 1642 [M] | The Batman Theme | 1966 | 40.00 |
| ❑ WS 1642 [S] | The Batman Theme | 1966 | 50.00 |

WORLD PACIFIC

| Number | Title (A Side/B Side) | Yr | NM |
|---|---|---|---|
| ❑ WP-1870 [M] | Sun Power | 1967 | 25.00 |
| ❑ WPS-21870 [S] | Sun Power | 1967 | 20.00 |

**MARKEWICH, REESE**

MODERN AGE

| Number | Title (A Side/B Side) | Yr | NM |
|---|---|---|---|
| ❑ MA-134 [M] | New Designs in Jazz | 1958 | 50.00 |

**MARKHAM, PIGMEAT**

CHESS

| Number | Title (A Side/B Side) | Yr | NM |
|---|---|---|---|
| ❑ LP-1451 [M] | The Trial | 1961 | 25.00 |
| ❑ LP-1462 [M] | Pigmeat Markham At the Party | 1962 | 25.00 |
| ❑ LP-1467 [M] | Anything Goes | 1962 | 25.00 |
| ❑ LP-1475 [M] | The World's Greatest Clown | 1963 | 25.00 |
| ❑ LP-1484 [M] | Open the Door, Richard | 1964 | 25.00 |
| ❑ LP-1493 [M] | Mr. Funny Man | 1965 | 25.00 |
| ❑ LP-1500 [M] | This'll Kill Ya | 1965 | 25.00 |
| ❑ LP-1505 [M] | If You Can't Be Good, Be Careful | 1966 | 15.00 |
| ❑ LPS-1505 [S] | If You Can't Be Good, Be Careful | 1966 | 20.00 |
| ❑ LP-1515 [M] | Mr. Vaudeville | 1967 | 15.00 |
| ❑ LPS-1515 [S] | Mr. Vaudeville | 1967 | 20.00 |
| ❑ LP-1517 [M] | Save Your Soul, Baby | 1967 | 20.00 |
| ❑ LPS-1517 [S] | Save Your Soul, Baby | 1967 | 20.00 |
| ❑ LP-1521 [M] | Backstage | 1968 | 20.00 |
| ❑ LPS-1521 [S] | Backstage | 1968 | 20.00 |
| ❑ LPS-1525 | Here Comes the Judge | 1968 | 20.00 |
| ❑ LPS-1526 | Tune Me In | 1968 | 15.00 |
| ❑ LPS-1529 | Hustlers | 1969 | 15.00 |
| ❑ LPS-1534 | Bag | 1970 | 15.00 |
| ❑ CH-9166 | Here Comes the Judge | 1985 | 10.00 |
| *—Reissue of 1525* | | | |

JEWEL

| Number | Title (A Side/B Side) | Yr | NM |
|---|---|---|---|
| ❑ 5007 | Crap-Shootin' Rev | 1972 | 12.00 |
| ❑ 5012 | Will the Real Pigmeat Markham Please Sit Down | 1973 | 12.00 |

**MARKLEY**

FORWARD

| Number | Title (A Side/B Side) | Yr | NM |
|---|---|---|---|
| ❑ 1007 | A Group | 1969 | 30.00 |

**MARKS, GUY**

ABC

| Number | Title (A Side/B Side) | Yr | NM |
|---|---|---|---|
| ❑ 549 [M] | Hollywood Sings | 1966 | 15.00 |
| ❑ S-549 [S] | Hollywood Sings | 1966 | 15.00 |
| ❑ S-648 | Loving You Has Made Me Bananas | 1968 | 20.00 |

**MARKS, J., AND SHIPEN LEBZELTER**

COLUMBIA MASTERWORKS

| Number | Title (A Side/B Side) | Yr | NM |
|---|---|---|---|
| ❑ MS 7193 | Rock and Other Four-Letter Words | 1969 | 30.00 |
| ❑ M 30006 | First National Nothing | 1970 | 20.00 |

**MARLEY, BOB, AND THE WAILERS**

ACCORD

| Number | Title (A Side/B Side) | Yr | NM |
|---|---|---|---|
| ❑ SN-7211 | Jamaican Storm | 1982 | 10.00 |

CALLA

| Number | Title (A Side/B Side) | Yr | NM |
|---|---|---|---|
| ❑ CAS-1240 [(2)] | The Birth of a Legend | 1976 | 15.00 |
| ❑ ZX 34759 | The Birth of a Legend | 1977 | 10.00 |
| *—Reissue of Record 1 of Calla 1240* | | | |
| ❑ ZX 34760 | Early Music | 1977 | 10.00 |
| *—Reissue of Record 2 of Calla 1240* | | | |

COLUMBIA

| Number | Title (A Side/B Side) | Yr | NM |
|---|---|---|---|
| ❑ PZ 34759 | The Birth of a Legend | 198? | 8.00 |
| *—Budget-line reissue of Calla 34759* | | | |
| ❑ PZ 34760 | Early Music | 198? | 8.00 |
| *—Budget-line reissue of Calla 34760* | | | |

COTILLION

| Number | Title (A Side/B Side) | Yr | NM |
|---|---|---|---|
| ❑ SD 5228 | Chances Are | 1981 | 10.00 |

ISLAND

| Number | Title (A Side/B Side) | Yr | NM |
|---|---|---|---|
| ❑ ISLD 11 [(2)] | Babylon by Bus | 1978 | 15.00 |
| *—Island distribution* | | | |
| ❑ ISLD 11 [(2)] | Babylon by Bus | 1979 | 12.00 |
| *—Warner Bros. distribution* | | | |
| ❑ ILPS 9241 | Catch a Fire | 1975 | 15.00 |
| *—Reissue with standard cover; Island distribution* | | | |
| ❑ ILPS 9241 | Catch a Fire | 1978 | 12.00 |
| *—Reissue; Warner Bros. distribution* | | | |
| ❑ ILPS 9256 | Burnin' | 1974 | 15.00 |
| *—Island distribution* | | | |
| ❑ ILPS 9256 | Burnin' | 1978 | 12.00 |
| *—Warner Bros. distribution* | | | |
| ❑ ILPS 9281 | Natty Dread | 1974 | 15.00 |
| *—Island distribution* | | | |
| ❑ ILPS 9281 | Natty Dread | 1978 | 12.00 |
| *—Warner Bros. distribution* | | | |
| ❑ SW-9329 | Catch a Fire | 1973 | 50.00 |
| *—"Cigarette lighter" cover with flip-open top; Capitol distribution* | | | |
| ❑ SMAS-9338 | Burnin' | 1973 | 20.00 |
| *—Capitol distribution* | | | |
| ❑ ILPS 9376 | Live! | 1975 | 12.00 |
| *—Island distribution* | | | |
| ❑ ILPS 9376 | Live! | 1978 | 10.00 |
| *—Warner Bros. distribution* | | | |
| ❑ ILPS 9383 | Rastaman Vibration | 1976 | 12.00 |
| *—Island distribution* | | | |
| ❑ ILPS 9383 | Rastaman Vibration | 1978 | 10.00 |
| *—Warner Bros. distribution* | | | |
| ❑ ILPS 9383 [DJ] | Rastaman Vibration | 1976 | 100.00 |
| *—Promotional package with burlap box and press kit* | | | |
| ❑ ILPS 9498 | Exodus | 1977 | 12.00 |
| *—Island distribution (all have multicolor labels)* | | | |
| ❑ ILPS 9498 | Exodus | 1978 | 10.00 |
| *—Warner Bros. distribution* | | | |
| ❑ ILPS 9517 | Kaya | 1978 | 12.00 |
| *—Island distribution* | | | |
| ❑ ILPS 9517 | Kaya | 1979 | 10.00 |
| *—Warner Bros. distribution* | | | |
| ❑ ILPS 9542 | Survival | 1979 | 12.00 |
| ❑ ILPS 9596 | Uprising | 1980 | 12.00 |
| ❑ 90029 [(2)] | Babylon by Bus | 1983 | 12.00 |
| ❑ 90030 | Catch a Fire | 1983 | 8.00 |
| ❑ 90031 | Burnin' | 1983 | 8.00 |
| ❑ 90032 | Live! | 1983 | 8.00 |
| ❑ 90033 | Rastaman Vibration | 1983 | 8.00 |
| ❑ 90034 | Exodus | 1983 | 8.00 |
| ❑ 90035 | Kaya | 1983 | 8.00 |
| ❑ 90036 | Uprising | 1983 | 8.00 |
| ❑ 90037 | Natty Dread | 1983 | 8.00 |
| *—90029-90037 are reissues with Atco distribution* | | | |
| ❑ 90085 | Confrontation | 1983 | 10.00 |
| ❑ 90169 | Legend | 1984 | 10.00 |
| ❑ 90520 | Rebel Music | 1986 | 10.00 |
| ❑ 524419-1 | Dreams of Freedom | 1997 | 12.00 |
| ❑ 546404-1 | Chant Down Babylon | 1999 | 12.00 |

MOBILE FIDELITY

| Number | Title (A Side/B Side) | Yr | NM |
|---|---|---|---|
| ❑ 1-221 | Exodus | 1995 | 25.00 |
| *—Audiophile vinyl* | | | |
| ❑ 1-236 | Catch a Fire | 1995 | 25.00 |
| *—Audiophile vinyl* | | | |

TUFF GONG

| Number | Title (A Side/B Side) | Yr | NM |
|---|---|---|---|
| ❑ 524103-1 | Natural Mystic | 1995 | 15.00 |
| ❑ 846197-1 [(2)] | Babylon by Bus | 1990 | 15.00 |
| ❑ 846200-1 | Burnin' | 1990 | 12.00 |
| ❑ 846201-1 | Catch a Fire | 1990 | 12.00 |
| ❑ 846202-1 | Survival | 1990 | 12.00 |
| ❑ 846203-1 | Live! | 1990 | 12.00 |
| ❑ 846204-1 | Natty Dread | 1990 | 12.00 |
| ❑ 846205-1 | Rastaman Vibration | 1990 | 12.00 |
| ❑ 846206-1 | Rebel Music | 1990 | 12.00 |
| ❑ 846207-1 | Confrontation | 1990 | 12.00 |
| ❑ 846208-1 | Exodus | 1990 | 12.00 |
| ❑ 846209-1 | Kaya | 1990 | 12.00 |
| ❑ 846210-1 | Legend | 1990 | 12.00 |
| ❑ 846211-1 | Uprising | 1990 | 12.00 |
| ❑ 848243-1 | Talkin' Blues | 1991 | 12.00 |

**MARLO, MICKI**

ABC-PARAMOUNT

| Number | Title (A Side/B Side) | Yr | NM |
|---|---|---|---|
| ❑ 295 [M] | Married I Can Always Get | 1959 | 20.00 |
| ❑ S-295 [S] | Married I Can Always Get | 1959 | 25.00 |

**MARLOWE, MARION, AND FRANK PARKER**

COLUMBIA

| Number | Title (A Side/B Side) | Yr | NM |
|---|---|---|---|
| ❑ CL 576 [M] | Arthur Godfrey's TV Sweethearts | 1954 | 30.00 |
| *—Maroon label, gold print* | | | |

**MARLOWE, MEXIE**

KING

| Number | Title (A Side/B Side) | Yr | NM |
|---|---|---|---|
| ❑ 799 [M] | Meet Mexie Marlowe | 1962 | 100.00 |

**MARMALADE, THE**

EPIC

| Number | Title (A Side/B Side) | Yr | NM |
|---|---|---|---|
| ❑ BN 26553 | The Best of the Marmalade | 1970 | 20.00 |

LONDON

| Number | Title (A Side/B Side) | Yr | NM |
|---|---|---|---|
| ❑ PS 575 | Reflections of My Life | 1970 | 20.00 |

**MARMAROSA, DODO**

ARGO

| Number | Title (A Side/B Side) | Yr | NM |
|---|---|---|---|
| ❑ LP-4012 [M] | Dodo's Back | 1961 | 25.00 |
| ❑ LPS-4012 [S] | Dodo's Back | 1961 | 30.00 |

**MARMAROSA, DODO/ERROLL GARNER**

CONCERT HALL JAZZ

| Number | Title (A Side/B Side) | Yr | NM |
|---|---|---|---|
| ❑ 1001 [10] | Piano Contrasts | 1955 | 50.00 |

DIAL

| Number | Title (A Side/B Side) | Yr | NM |
|---|---|---|---|
| ❑ LP-208 [10] | Piano Contrasts | 1950 | 250.00 |

**MARR, HANK**

KING

| Number | Title (A Side/B Side) | Yr | NM |
|---|---|---|---|
| ❑ 829 [M] | Teentime Dance Steps | 1963 | 30.00 |
| ❑ 899 [M] | Live at Club 502 | 1964 | 40.00 |
| ❑ 933 [M] | On and Off Stage | 1965 | 30.00 |
| ❑ 1011 [M] | Hank Marr Plays 24 Originals | 1966 | 20.00 |
| ❑ 1025 [M] | Sounds from the Marr-Ket Place | 1968 | 20.00 |
| ❑ KSD-1061 | Greasy Spoon | 1969 | 20.00 |

**MARS, CHRIS** Also see THE REPLACEMENTS.

SMASH

| Number | Title (A Side/B Side) | Yr | NM |
|---|---|---|---|
| ❑ 513198-1 [DJ] | Horseshoes and Hand Grenades | 1992 | 20.00 |
| *—Vinyl is promo only* | | | |

**MARS, SYLVIA**

LYRIC

| Number | Title (A Side/B Side) | Yr | NM |
|---|---|---|---|
| ❑ 124 | Blues Walk Right In | 196? | 60.00 |

**MARSALA, JOE/BUD FREEMAN**

BRUNSWICK

| Number | Title (A Side/B Side) | Yr | NM |
|---|---|---|---|
| ❑ BL 58037 [10] | Battle of Jazz, Vol. 1 | 1953 | 50.00 |

**MARSALIS, BRANFORD**

JAZZ PLANET

| Number | Title (A Side/B Side) | Yr | NM |
|---|---|---|---|
| ❑ JP-5004 [(2)] | The Dark Keys | 1996 | 30.00 |

**MARSALIS, WYNTON**

COLUMBIA

| Number | Title (A Side/B Side) | Yr | NM |
|---|---|---|---|
| ❑ HC 47574 | Wynton Marsalis | 198? | 30.00 |
| *—Half-speed mastered edition* | | | |

## MARSH, MILTON

### STRATA-EAST

| Number | Title (A Side/B Side) | Yr | NM |
|---|---|---|---|
| ❑ SES-19758 | Monism | 1975 | 20.00 |

## MARSH, WARNE

### ATLANTIC

| Number | Title (A Side/B Side) | Yr | NM |
|---|---|---|---|
| ❑ 1291 [M] | Warne Marsh | 1958 | 50.00 |
| *—Black label* | | | |
| ❑ 1291 [M] | Warne Marsh | 1961 | 25.00 |
| *—Multicolor label, white "fan" logo at right* | | | |
| ❑ SD 1291 [S] | Warne Marsh | 1958 | 50.00 |
| *—Green label* | | | |
| ❑ SD 1291 [S] | Warne Marsh | 1961 | 20.00 |
| *—Multicolor label, white "fan" logo at right* | | | |

### IMPERIAL

| Number | Title (A Side/B Side) | Yr | NM |
|---|---|---|---|
| ❑ LP-9027 [M] | Jazz of Two Cities | 1957 | 80.00 |
| ❑ LP-12013 [S] | The Winds of Warne Marsh | 1959 | 60.00 |
| *—Retitled version in stereo?* | | | |

### MODE

| Number | Title (A Side/B Side) | Yr | NM |
|---|---|---|---|
| ❑ LP-125 [M] | Music for Prancing | 1957 | 80.00 |

### REVELATION

| Number | Title (A Side/B Side) | Yr | NM |
|---|---|---|---|
| ❑ R-12 | Ne Plus Ultra | 1970 | 20.00 |

## MARSHALL, CHUCK

### DECCA

| Number | Title (A Side/B Side) | Yr | NM |
|---|---|---|---|
| ❑ DL 4267 [M] | Twist to Songs Everybody Knows | 1962 | 15.00 |
| ❑ DL 74267 [S] | Twist to Songs Everybody Knows | 1962 | 20.00 |

## MARSHALL, JACK

### CAPITOL

| Number | Title (A Side/B Side) | Yr | NM |
|---|---|---|---|
| ❑ ST 1108 [S] | 18th Century Jazz | 1959 | 25.00 |
| ❑ T 1108 [M] | 18th Century Jazz | 1959 | 20.00 |
| ❑ ST 1194 [S] | Soundsville! | 1959 | 25.00 |
| ❑ T 1194 [M] | Soundsville! | 1959 | 20.00 |
| ❑ ST 1351 [S] | The Marshall Swings | 1960 | 25.00 |
| ❑ T 1351 [M] | The Marshall Swings | 1960 | 20.00 |
| ❑ ST 1601 [S] | Songs Without Words | 1961 | 25.00 |
| ❑ T 1601 [M] | Songs Without Words | 1961 | 20.00 |
| ❑ ST 1727 [S] | The Twangy, Shoutin', Fantastic Big-Band Sounds of Tuff Jack | 1962 | 40.00 |
| ❑ T 1727 [M] | The Twangy, Shoutin', Fantastic Big-Band Sounds of Tuff Jack | 1962 | 30.00 |
| ❑ ST 1939 [S] | My Son the Surf Nut | 1963 | 40.00 |
| ❑ T 1939 [M] | My Son the Surf Nut | 1963 | 30.00 |

## MARSHALL, PENNY, AND CINDY WILLIAMS

### ATLANTIC

| Number | Title (A Side/B Side) | Yr | NM |
|---|---|---|---|
| ❑ SD 18203 | Laverne and Shirley Sing | 1979 | 25.00 |

## MARSHALL, PETER

### DOT

| Number | Title (A Side/B Side) | Yr | NM |
|---|---|---|---|
| ❑ DLP-25930 | For the Love of Pete | 1969 | 25.00 |

## MARSHMALLOW WAY

### UNITED ARTISTS

| Number | Title (A Side/B Side) | Yr | NM |
|---|---|---|---|
| ❑ UAS-6708 | Marshmallow Way | 1969 | 20.00 |

## MARTERIE, RALPH

### AMBASSADOR

| Number | Title (A Side/B Side) | Yr | NM |
|---|---|---|---|
| ❑ S-98058 | Big Band Man/On the Sunny Side of the Street | 196? | 10.00 |

### MERCURY

| Number | Title (A Side/B Side) | Yr | NM |
|---|---|---|---|
| ❑ SRW-16238 [S] | Music for a Private Eye | 196? | 15.00 |
| ❑ MG-20010 [M] | Sweet and Lovely | 195? | 20.00 |
| ❑ MG-20054 [M] | Alone Together | 195? | 20.00 |
| ❑ MG-20066 [M] | Dance Band in Town | 195? | 20.00 |
| ❑ MG-20124 [M] | Swing Baby | 195? | 20.00 |
| ❑ MG-20125 [M] | On Bandstand No. 1 | 195? | 20.00 |
| ❑ MG-20128 [M] | Salute to the Aragon Ballroom | 195? | 20.00 |
| ❑ MG-20174 [M] | Love Themes from the Classics | 195? | 20.00 |
| ❑ MG-20198 [M] | Young America Dances | 195? | 20.00 |
| ❑ MG-20253 [M] | Dance Date | 195? | 20.00 |
| ❑ MG-20294 [M] | College Dance Favorites | 1959 | 20.00 |
| *—Revised title* | | | |
| ❑ MG-20336 [M] | Hits That Made Ralph Marterie and His Orchestra Famous | 195? | 20.00 |
| ❑ MG-20395 [M] | Dance Party | 195? | 15.00 |
| ❑ MG-20397 [M] | Hi-Fidelity Concert | 195? | 15.00 |
| ❑ MG-20437 [M] | Music for a Private Eye | 1960 | 20.00 |
| ❑ MG-20506 [M] | Big Band Man | 1960 | 15.00 |
| ❑ MG-25085 [10] | Ralph Marterie and His Orchestra | 195? | 40.00 |
| ❑ MG-25102 [10] | Moods for Dancing | 195? | 50.00 |
| ❑ MG-25121 [10] | Junior Prom | 195? | 50.00 |
| ❑ MG-25171 [10] | Dancing on the Down Beat | 195? | 50.00 |
| ❑ SR-60034 [S] | Dance Party | 1959 | 25.00 |
| ❑ SR-60035 [S] | College Dance Favorites | 1959 | 25.00 |
| ❑ SR-60036 [S] | Hi-Fidelity Concert | 1959 | 20.00 |
| ❑ SR-60109 [S] | Music for a Private Eye | 1960 | 25.00 |
| ❑ SR-60183 [S] | Big Band Man | 1960 | 20.00 |

### MUSICOR

| Number | Title (A Side/B Side) | Yr | NM |
|---|---|---|---|
| ❑ MS-3011 | 51 Discotheque Dance Favorites | 196? | 10.00 |
| ❑ MS-3049 | Motion Picture Hits | 196? | 12.00 |

### UNITED ARTISTS

| Number | Title (A Side/B Side) | Yr | NM |
|---|---|---|---|
| ❑ UAL-3223 [M] | Ralph Marterie Plays Again | 196? | 12.00 |
| ❑ UAL-3235 [M] | Dance to the Music Man | 1962 | 12.00 |
| ❑ UAL-3285 [M] | Dancers Choice | 196? | 12.00 |
| ❑ UAL-3349 [M] | 50 Fabulous Dance Favorites | 196? | 12.00 |
| ❑ WWR 3506 [M] | 88 Strings | 196? | 12.00 |
| ❑ UAS-6223 [S] | Ralph Marterie Plays Again | 196? | 15.00 |
| ❑ UAS-6285 [S] | Dancers Choice | 196? | 15.00 |
| ❑ UAS-6325 [S] | Dance to the Music Man | 1962 | 15.00 |
| ❑ UAS-6349 [S] | 50 Fabulous Dance Favorites | 196? | 15.00 |
| ❑ WWS 8506 [S] | 88 Strings | 196? | 15.00 |

### WING

| Number | Title (A Side/B Side) | Yr | NM |
|---|---|---|---|
| ❑ MGW-12117 [M] | Dance Date | 195? | 12.00 |
| ❑ MGW-12154 [M] | Marvelous Marterie | 195? | 12.00 |
| ❑ MGW-12155 [M] | Trumpeters Lullaby | 195? | 12.00 |
| ❑ MGW-12160 [M] | Love Themes from the Classics | 195? | 12.00 |
| ❑ MGW-12179 [M] | Dance Album | 195? | 12.00 |
| ❑ MGW-12185 [M] | Soft Tender Trumpet | 195? | 12.00 |
| ❑ MGW-12238 [M] | Music for a Private Eye | 196? | 12.00 |
| ❑ MGW-12259 [M] | Dance Party | 196? | 12.00 |
| ❑ SRW-12511 [S] | Marvelous Marterie | 1959 | 15.00 |
| ❑ SRW-16269 [S] | Dance Party | 196? | 12.00 |

## MARTHA AND THE VANDELLAS

### GORDY

| Number | Title (A Side/B Side) | Yr | NM |
|---|---|---|---|
| ❑ G-902 [M] | Come and Get These Memories | 1963 | 400.00 |
| ❑ GS-902 [S] | Come and Get These Memories | 1963 | 800.00 |
| ❑ G-907 [M] | Heat Wave | 1963 | 150.00 |
| ❑ GS-907 [R] | Heat Wave | 1963 | 150.00 |
| *—"Stereo" banner pre-printed on cover* | | | |
| ❑ GS-907 [S] | Heat Wave | 1963 | 400.00 |
| *—Mono cover with "Stereo" sticker* | | | |
| ❑ G-915 [M] | Dance Party | 1965 | 40.00 |
| ❑ GS-915 [S] | Dance Party | 1965 | 60.00 |
| ❑ G-917 [M] | Greatest Hits | 1966 | 25.00 |
| ❑ GS-917 [S] | Greatest Hits | 1966 | 30.00 |
| ❑ G-920 [M] | Watchout! | 1966 | 25.00 |
| ❑ GS-920 [S] | Watchout! | 1966 | 30.00 |
| ❑ G-925 [M] | Martha and the Vandellas Live! | 1967 | 30.00 |
| ❑ GS-925 [S] | Martha and the Vandellas Live! | 1967 | 25.00 |
| ❑ G-926 [M] | Ridin' High | 1968 | 40.00 |
| *—Mono is promo only* | | | |
| ❑ GS-926 [S] | Ridin' High | 1968 | 20.00 |
| ❑ GS-944 | Sugar 'N Spice | 1969 | 20.00 |
| ❑ GS-952 | Natural Resources | 1970 | 20.00 |
| ❑ GS-958 | Black Magic | 1972 | 20.00 |

### MOTOWN

| Number | Title (A Side/B Side) | Yr | NM |
|---|---|---|---|
| ❑ M5-111V1 | Motown Superstar Series, Vol. 11 | 1981 | 10.00 |
| ❑ M5-145V1 | Heat Wave | 1981 | 10.00 |
| *—Reissue of Gordy 907* | | | |
| ❑ M5-204V1 | Greatest Hits | 1981 | 10.00 |
| *—Reissue of Gordy 917* | | | |
| ❑ M7-778 [(2)] | Anthology | 1974 | 15.00 |

## MARTIN, ARCH

### ZEPHYR

| Number | Title (A Side/B Side) | Yr | NM |
|---|---|---|---|
| ❑ 12009 [M] | Arch Martin Quintet | 1959 | 30.00 |

## MARTIN, BENNY

### STARDAY

| Number | Title (A Side/B Side) | Yr | NM |
|---|---|---|---|
| ❑ SLP-131 [M] | Country Music's Sensational Entertainer | 1961 | 50.00 |

## MARTIN, BOBBI

### BUDDAH

| Number | Title (A Side/B Side) | Yr | NM |
|---|---|---|---|
| ❑ BDS-5090 | Tomorrow | 1971 | 12.00 |

### CORAL

| Number | Title (A Side/B Side) | Yr | NM |
|---|---|---|---|
| ❑ CRL 57472 [M] | Don't Forget I Still Love You | 1965 | 15.00 |
| ❑ CRL 57478 [M] | I Love You So | 1965 | 15.00 |
| ❑ CRL 757472 [S] | Don't Forget I Still Love You | 1965 | 20.00 |
| ❑ CRL 757478 [S] | I Love You So | 1965 | 20.00 |

### SUNSET

| Number | Title (A Side/B Side) | Yr | NM |
|---|---|---|---|
| ❑ SUS-5319 | Thinking of You | 197? | 10.00 |

### UNITED ARTISTS

| Number | Title (A Side/B Side) | Yr | NM |
|---|---|---|---|
| ❑ UAS-6668 | Harper Valley P.T.A. | 1968 | 12.00 |
| ❑ UAS-6700 | For the Love of Him | 1969 | 12.00 |
| ❑ UAS-6755 | With Love | 1970 | 12.00 |

### VOCALION

| Number | Title (A Side/B Side) | Yr | NM |
|---|---|---|---|
| ❑ VL 73906 | Have You Ever Been Lonely | 196? | 10.00 |

## MARTIN, DEAN

### CAPITOL

| Number | Title (A Side/B Side) | Yr | NM |
|---|---|---|---|
| ❑ SKAO-140 | The Best of Dean Martin, Vol. 2 | 1968 | 15.00 |
| ❑ H 401 [10] | Dean Martin Sings | 1953 | 100.00 |
| ❑ T 401 [M] | Dean Martin Sings | 1953 | 50.00 |
| ❑ STBB-523 [(2)] | You're Nobody 'Til Somebody Loves You/Return to Me | 1970 | 20.00 |
| ❑ T 576 [M] | Swingin' Down Yonder | 1955 | 30.00 |
| ❑ T 849 [M] | Pretty Baby | 1957 | 30.00 |
| ❑ DT 1047 [R] | This Is Dean Martin | 196? | 12.00 |
| ❑ T 1047 [M] | This Is Dean Martin | 1958 | 30.00 |
| ❑ ST 1150 [S] | Sleep Warm | 1959 | 30.00 |
| ❑ T 1150 [M] | Sleep Warm | 1959 | 25.00 |
| ❑ ST 1285 [S] | A Winter Romance | 1959 | 30.00 |
| ❑ T 1285 [M] | A Winter Romance | 1959 | 20.00 |
| ❑ ST 1442 [S] | This Time I'm Swingin' | 1961 | 30.00 |
| ❑ T 1442 [M] | This Time I'm Swingin' | 1961 | 20.00 |
| ❑ SW 1580 [S] | Dean Martin | 1961 | 30.00 |
| ❑ W 1580 [M] | Dean Martin | 1961 | 20.00 |
| ❑ SM-1659 | Dino — Italian Love Songs | 197? | 10.00 |
| *—Reissue with new prefix* | | | |
| ❑ ST 1659 [S] | Dino — Italian Love Songs | 1962 | 30.00 |
| ❑ T 1659 [M] | Dino — Italian Love Songs | 1962 | 20.00 |
| ❑ ST 1702 [S] | Cha Cha De Amor | 1962 | 30.00 |
| ❑ T 1702 [M] | Cha Cha De Amor | 1962 | 20.00 |
| ❑ DT 2212 [R] | Hey Brother Pour the Wine | 1964 | 12.00 |
| ❑ T 2212 [M] | Hey Brother Pour the Wine | 1964 | 20.00 |
| ❑ ST 2297 [S] | Dean Martin Sings — Sinatra Conducts | 1965 | 20.00 |
| ❑ T 2297 [M] | Dean Martin Sings — Sinatra Conducts | 1965 | 15.00 |
| ❑ DT 2333 [R] | Dean Martin — Southern Style | 1965 | 12.00 |
| ❑ T 2333 [M] | Dean Martin — Southern Style | 1965 | 15.00 |
| ❑ STT 2343 [S] | Holiday Cheer | 1965 | 20.00 |
| *—Some copies of this LP have labels that state the title as "Baby, It's Cold Outside."* | | | |
| ❑ TT 2343 [M] | Holiday Cheer | 1965 | 15.00 |
| *—Reissue of 1285 with one fewer track* | | | |
| ❑ DT 2601 [R] | The Best of Dean Martin | 1966 | 12.00 |
| ❑ SM-2601 | The Best of Dean Martin | 197? | 10.00 |
| *—Reissue with new prefix* | | | |
| ❑ T 2601 [M] | The Best of Dean Martin | 1966 | 15.00 |
| ❑ DTCL 2815 [(3)R] | The Dean Martin Deluxe Set | 1967 | 20.00 |
| ❑ TCL 2815 [(3)M] | The Dean Martin Deluxe Set | 1967 | 30.00 |

### LONGINES SYMPHONETTE

| Number | Title (A Side/B Side) | Yr | NM |
|---|---|---|---|
| ❑ LS-124A [(5)] | Memories Are Made of This | 197? | 25.00 |
| *—Records are indiividually numbered SYS 5230, 5231, 5232, 5233 and 5234* | | | |

### PAIR

| Number | Title (A Side/B Side) | Yr | NM |
|---|---|---|---|
| ❑ PDL2-1029 [(2)] | Dreams and Memories | 1986 | 12.00 |

### PICKWICK

| Number | Title (A Side/B Side) | Yr | NM |
|---|---|---|---|
| ❑ PTP-2051 [(2)] | Dean Martin | 197? | 12.00 |
| ❑ SPC-3057 | You Can't Love 'Em All | 196? | 10.00 |
| ❑ SPC-3089 | I Can't Give You Anything But Love | 196? | 10.00 |
| ❑ SPC-3136 | Young and Foolish | 196? | 10.00 |
| ❑ SPC-3175 | You Were Made for Love | 197? | 10.00 |
| ❑ SPC-3283 | Deluxe | 197? | 10.00 |

### REPRISE

| Number | Title (A Side/B Side) | Yr | NM |
|---|---|---|---|
| ❑ MS 2053 | Dino | 1972 | 15.00 |
| ❑ MS 2113 | Sittin' on Top of the World | 1973 | 15.00 |
| ❑ MS 2174 | You're the Best Thing That Ever Happened to Me | 1973 | 15.00 |
| ❑ MS 2267 | Once in a Lifetime | 1978 | 12.00 |
| ❑ R-6021 [M] | French Style | 1962 | 15.00 |
| ❑ R9-6021 [S] | French Style | 1962 | 20.00 |
| ❑ R-6054 [M] | Dino Latino | 1962 | 15.00 |
| ❑ R9-6054 [S] | Dino Latino | 1962 | 20.00 |
| ❑ R-6061 [M] | Country Style | 1963 | 15.00 |
| ❑ R9-6061 [S] | Country Style | 1963 | 20.00 |
| ❑ R-6085 [M] | Dean "Tex" Martin Rides Again | 1963 | 15.00 |
| ❑ R9-6085 [S] | Dean "Tex" Martin Rides Again | 1963 | 20.00 |
| ❑ R-6123 [M] | Dream with Dean | 1964 | 12.00 |
| ❑ RS-6123 [S] | Dream with Dean | 1964 | 15.00 |
| ❑ R-6130 [M] | Everybody Loves Somebody | 1964 | 12.00 |
| ❑ RS-6130 [S] | Everybody Loves Somebody | 1964 | 15.00 |
| ❑ R-6140 [M] | The Door Is Still Open to My Heart | 1964 | 12.00 |
| ❑ RS-6140 [S] | The Door Is Still Open to My Heart | 1964 | 15.00 |
| ❑ R-6146 [M] | Dean Martin Hits Again | 1965 | 12.00 |
| ❑ RS-6146 [S] | Dean Martin Hits Again | 1965 | 15.00 |
| ❑ R-6170 [M] | (Remember Me) I'm the One Who Loves You | 1965 | 12.00 |
| ❑ RS-6170 [S] | (Remember Me) I'm the One Who Loves You | 1965 | 15.00 |
| ❑ R-6181 [M] | Houston | 1965 | 12.00 |
| ❑ RS-6181 [S] | Houston | 1965 | 15.00 |
| ❑ R-6201 [M] | Somewhere There's a Someone | 1966 | 12.00 |
| ❑ RS-6201 [S] | Somewhere There's a Someone | 1966 | 15.00 |
| ❑ R-6211 [M] | The Silencers | 1966 | 20.00 |
| ❑ RS-6211 [S] | The Silencers | 1966 | 25.00 |
| ❑ R-6213 [M] | The Hit Sound of Dean Martin | 1966 | 12.00 |
| ❑ RS-6213 [S] | The Hit Sound of Dean Martin | 1966 | 15.00 |
| ❑ R 6222 [M] | The Dean Martin Christmas Album | 1966 | 15.00 |
| ❑ RS 6222 [S] | The Dean Martin Christmas Album | 1966 | 20.00 |
| ❑ R-6233 [M] | The Dean Martin TV Show | 1966 | 12.00 |
| ❑ RS-6233 [S] | The Dean Martin TV Show | 1966 | 15.00 |
| ❑ R-6242 [M] | Happiness Is Dean Martin | 1967 | 15.00 |
| ❑ RS-6242 [S] | Happiness Is Dean Martin | 1967 | 15.00 |
| ❑ R-6250 [M] | Welcome to My World | 1967 | 15.00 |
| ❑ RS-6250 [S] | Welcome to My World | 1967 | 15.00 |
| ❑ RS-6301 | Dean Martin's Greatest Hits! Vol. 1 | 1968 | 15.00 |
| ❑ RS-6320 | Dean Martin's Greatest Hits! Vol. 2 | 1968 | 15.00 |

| Number | Title (A Side/B Side) | Yr | NM |
|---|---|---|---|
| ❑ R-6330 [M] | Gentle on My Mind | 1968 | 30.00 |
| ❑ RS-6330 [S] | Gentle on My Mind | 1968 | 15.00 |
| ❑ RS-6338 | I Take a Lot of Pride in What I Am | 1969 | 15.00 |
| ❑ RS-6403 | My Woman, My Woman, My Wife | 1970 | 15.00 |
| ❑ RS-6428 | For the Good Times | 1971 | 15.00 |
| ❑ SW-94345 | Dino | 1972 | 20.00 |

*—Capitol Record Club edition*

TOWER

| Number | Title (A Side/B Side) | Yr | NM |
|---|---|---|---|
| ❑ DT 5006 [R] | The Lush Years | 1965 | 15.00 |
| ❑ T 5006 [M] | The Lush Years | 1965 | 20.00 |
| ❑ DT 5018 [R] | Relaxin' | 1966 | 15.00 |
| ❑ T 5018 [M] | Relaxin' | 1966 | 20.00 |
| ❑ ST 5036 [S] | Happy in Love | 1966 | 20.00 |
| ❑ T 5036 [M] | Happy in Love | 1966 | 15.00 |

WARNER BROS.

| Number | Title (A Side/B Side) | Yr | NM |
|---|---|---|---|
| ❑ 23870 | The Nashville Sessions | 1983 | 12.00 |

## MARTIN, DEWEY, AND MEDICINE BALL

Dewey is a former member of BUFFALO SPRINGFIELD.

UNI

| Number | Title (A Side/B Side) | Yr | NM |
|---|---|---|---|
| ❑ 73088 | Dewey Martin and Medicine Ball | 1970 | 25.00 |

## MARTIN, FREDDY

RCA VICTOR

| Number | Title (A Side/B Side) | Yr | NM |
|---|---|---|---|
| ❑ LPM-1414 [M] | Freddy Martin at the Cocoanut Grove | 1957 | 20.00 |

## MARTIN, GEORGE

UNITED ARTISTS

| Number | Title (A Side/B Side) | Yr | NM |
|---|---|---|---|
| ❑ UAL 3377 [M] | Off the Beatle Track | 1964 | 80.00 |
| ❑ UAL 3383 [M] | A Hard Day's Night | 1964 | 40.00 |
| ❑ UAL 3420 [M] | George Martin | 1965 | 40.00 |
| ❑ UAL 3448 [M] | George Martin Plays "Help" | 1965 | 50.00 |
| ❑ UAL 3539 [M] | George Martin Salutes the Beatle Girls | 1966 | 50.00 |
| ❑ UAL 3647 [M] | London by George | 1967 | 30.00 |
| ❑ UAS 6377 [S] | Off the Beatle Track | 1964 | 100.00 |
| ❑ UAS 6383 [S] | A Hard Day's Night | 1964 | 50.00 |
| ❑ UAS 6420 [S] | George Martin | 1965 | 50.00 |
| ❑ UAS 6448 [S] | George Martin Plays "Help" | 1965 | 80.00 |
| ❑ UAS 6539 [S] | George Martin Salutes the Beatle Girls | 1966 | 80.00 |
| ❑ UAS 6647 [S] | London by George | 1967 | 40.00 |

## MARTIN, GRADY

DECCA

| Number | Title (A Side/B Side) | Yr | NM |
|---|---|---|---|
| ❑ DL 4072 [M] | Big City Lights | 1960 | 20.00 |
| ❑ DL 4286 [M] | Swingin' Down the River | 1962 | 15.00 |
| ❑ DL 4476 [M] | Songs Everybody Knows | 1963 | 15.00 |
| ❑ DL 5566 [10] | Dance-O-Rama | 1955 | 200.00 |
| ❑ DL 8181 [M] | Powerhouse Dance Party | 1955 | 30.00 |
| ❑ DL 8292 [M] | Juke Box Jamboree | 1956 | 30.00 |
| ❑ DL 8648 [M] | The Roaring Twenties | 1957 | 30.00 |
| ❑ DL 8883 [M] | Hot Time Tonight | 1959 | 20.00 |
| ❑ DL 74072 [S] | Big City Lights | 1960 | 25.00 |
| ❑ DL 74286 [S] | Swingin' Down the River | 1962 | 20.00 |
| ❑ DL 74476 [S] | Songs Everybody Knows | 1963 | 20.00 |
| ❑ DL 78883 [S] | Hot Time Tonight | 1959 | 25.00 |

## MARTIN, JIMMY

DECCA

| Number | Title (A Side/B Side) | Yr | NM |
|---|---|---|---|
| ❑ DL 4016 [M] | Good 'n Country | 1960 | 25.00 |
| ❑ DL 4285 [M] | Country Music Time | 1962 | 25.00 |
| ❑ DL 4360 [M] | This World Is Not My Home | 1963 | 25.00 |
| ❑ DL 4536 [M] | Widow Maker | 1964 | 20.00 |
| ❑ DL 4643 [M] | Sunny Side of the Mountain | 1965 | 20.00 |
| ❑ DL 4769 [M] | Mr. Good 'n Country Music | 1966 | 20.00 |
| ❑ DL 4891 [M] | Big and Country Instrumentals | 1967 | 20.00 |
| ❑ DL 4996 [M] | Tennessee | 1968 | 60.00 |

*—Mono is white label promo only*

| Number | Title (A Side/B Side) | Yr | NM |
|---|---|---|---|
| ❑ DL 74016 [S] | Good 'n Country | 1960 | 30.00 |
| ❑ DL 74285 [S] | Country Music Time | 1962 | 30.00 |
| ❑ DL 74360 [S] | This World Is Not My Home | 1963 | 30.00 |
| ❑ DL 74536 [S] | Widow Maker | 1964 | 25.00 |
| ❑ DL 74643 [S] | Sunny Side of the Mountain | 1965 | 25.00 |
| ❑ DL 74769 [S] | Mr. Good 'n Country Music | 1966 | 25.00 |
| ❑ DL 74891 [S] | Big and Country Instrumentals | 1967 | 20.00 |
| ❑ DL 74996 [S] | Tennessee | 1968 | 20.00 |

## MARTIN, MARTY

See BOXCAR WILLIE.

## MARTIN, MARY

COLUMBIA MASTERWORKS

| Number | Title (A Side/B Side) | Yr | NM |
|---|---|---|---|
| ❑ ML 2061 [10] | Mary Martin Sings for You | 1949 | 50.00 |

DISNEYLAND

| Number | Title (A Side/B Side) | Yr | NM |
|---|---|---|---|
| ❑ WDL-1038 [M] | Hi-Ho—Mary Martin Sings and Swings Walt Disney Favorites | 1958 | 20.00 |
| ❑ DQ-1296 [M] | Mary Martin Songs from Rodgers and Hammerstein's The Sound of Music | 1966 | 15.00 |
| ❑ STER-1296 [S] | Mary Martin Songs from Rodgers and Hammerstein's The Sound of Music | 1966 | 20.00 |
| ❑ ST-2002 [M] | The Little Lame Lamb | 1958 | 50.00 |
| ❑ STER-3031 [S] | Mary Martin Sings a Musical Love Story | 1959 | 25.00 |
| ❑ WD-3031 [M] | Mary Martin Sings a Musical Love Story | 1958 | 20.00 |
| ❑ STER-3038 [S] | Hi-Ho! | 1959 | 25.00 |
| ❑ WD-3038 [M] | Hi-Ho! | 1958 | 20.00 |
| ❑ ST-3911 [M] | The Story of Sleeping Beauty | 1958 | 30.00 |

*—Back cover art features Sleeping Beauty and prince*

| Number | Title (A Side/B Side) | Yr | NM |
|---|---|---|---|
| ❑ ST-3911 [M] | The Story of Sleeping Beauty | 1969 | 20.00 |

*—Back cover art features pictures from the booklet*

| Number | Title (A Side/B Side) | Yr | NM |
|---|---|---|---|
| ❑ ST-3936 [M] | Mary Martin Songs from Rodgers and Hammerstein's The Sound of Music | 1966 | 15.00 |
| ❑ STER-3936 [S] | Mary Martin Songs from Rodgers and Hammerstein's The Sound of Music | 1966 | 20.00 |
| ❑ STER-4016 [S] | Hi-Ho! | 1959 | 30.00 |
| ❑ WDL-4016 [M] | Hi-Ho! | 1958 | 20.00 |

## MARTIN, TONY

APPLAUSE

| Number | Title (A Side/B Side) | Yr | NM |
|---|---|---|---|
| ❑ APLP-1003 | I'll See You in My Dreams | 1982 | 10.00 |
| ❑ R 134276 | I'll See You in My Dreams | 1982 | 12.00 |

*—RCA Music Service edition*

AUDIO FIDELITY

| Number | Title (A Side/B Side) | Yr | NM |
|---|---|---|---|
| ❑ AFSD-6200 | Tony Martin | 1968 | 15.00 |

CHART

| Number | Title (A Side/B Side) | Yr | NM |
|---|---|---|---|
| ❑ CHS-1029 | Tony Martin in Nashville | 1970 | 20.00 |

DECCA

| Number | Title (A Side/B Side) | Yr | NM |
|---|---|---|---|
| ❑ DL 5189 [10] | Tony Martin Sings, Vol. 1 | 1950 | 40.00 |
| ❑ DL 8286 [M] | Melody Lane | 195? | 25.00 |

*—Black label, silver print*

| Number | Title (A Side/B Side) | Yr | NM |
|---|---|---|---|
| ❑ DL 8287 [M] | Our Love Affair | 195? | 25.00 |

*—Black label, silver print*

| Number | Title (A Side/B Side) | Yr | NM |
|---|---|---|---|
| ❑ DL 8366 [M] | In the Spotlight | 195? | 25.00 |

*—Black label, silver print*

DOT

| Number | Title (A Side/B Side) | Yr | NM |
|---|---|---|---|
| ❑ DLP-3360 [M] | His Greatest Hits | 1961 | 15.00 |
| ❑ DLP-25360 [S] | His Greatest Hits | 1961 | 20.00 |

KOALA

| Number | Title (A Side/B Side) | Yr | NM |
|---|---|---|---|
| ❑ KO 14140 | I'm Always Chasing Rainbows | 198? | 12.00 |

MCA

| Number | Title (A Side/B Side) | Yr | NM |
|---|---|---|---|
| ❑ 1515 [M] | Tony Martin Collectibles | 198? | 12.00 |

MCA CORAL

| Number | Title (A Side/B Side) | Yr | NM |
|---|---|---|---|
| ❑ CB-20019 | Melody | 1973 | 12.00 |

MERCURY

| Number | Title (A Side/B Side) | Yr | NM |
|---|---|---|---|
| ❑ MG-20075 [M] | Mr. Song Man | 195? | 25.00 |
| ❑ MG-20079 [M] | Dream Music | 195? | 25.00 |
| ❑ MG-20644 [M] | Golden Hits by Tony Martin | 1961 | 15.00 |
| ❑ MG-25004 [10] | Tony Martin | 1950 | 40.00 |
| ❑ MG-60644 [S] | Golden Hits by Tony Martin | 1961 | 15.00 |

MOTOWN

| Number | Title (A Side/B Side) | Yr | NM |
|---|---|---|---|
| ❑ MS-645 [S] | Live! At the Americana | 1966 | — |

*—Canceled*

| Number | Title (A Side/B Side) | Yr | NM |
|---|---|---|---|
| ❑ MT-645 [M] | Live! At the Americana | 1966 | — |

*—Canceled*

MOVIETONE

| Number | Title (A Side/B Side) | Yr | NM |
|---|---|---|---|
| ❑ MTM-1007 [M] | Live at Carnegie Hall | 196? | 10.00 |

*—Reissue of 20th Century Fox 3138*

| Number | Title (A Side/B Side) | Yr | NM |
|---|---|---|---|
| ❑ MTS-2007 [S] | Live at Carnegie Hall | 196? | 12.00 |

*—Reissue of 20th Century Fox 4138*

RCA CAMDEN

| Number | Title (A Side/B Side) | Yr | NM |
|---|---|---|---|
| ❑ CAL-412 [M] | I Get Ideas | 195? | 15.00 |
| ❑ CAL-484 [M] | Tony Martin Sings of Love | 195? | 15.00 |
| ❑ CAL-576 [M] | Tonight | 195? | 15.00 |

RCA SPECIAL PRODUCTS

| Number | Title (A Side/B Side) | Yr | NM |
|---|---|---|---|
| ❑ DML2-0999 [(2)] | The Greatest Singer of Them All! | 1991 | 15.00 |

RCA VICTOR

| Number | Title (A Side/B Side) | Yr | NM |
|---|---|---|---|
| ❑ LPM-1218 [M] | The Night Was Made for Love | 1956 | 25.00 |
| ❑ LPM-1263 [M] | Speak to Me of Love | 1956 | 25.00 |
| ❑ LPM-1357 [M] | A Night at the Copacabana with Tony Martin | 1956 | 25.00 |
| ❑ LPM-2107 [M] | Dream a Little Dream | 1960 | 20.00 |
| ❑ LSP-2107 [S] | Dream a Little Dream | 1960 | 30.00 |
| ❑ LPM-2146 [M] | Tony Martin at the Desert Inn | 1960 | 20.00 |
| ❑ LSP-2146 [S] | Tony Martin at the Desert Inn | 1960 | 25.00 |
| ❑ LPM-3126 [10] | World-Wide Favorites | 195? | 40.00 |
| ❑ LPM-3136 [10] | One for My Baby | 195? | 40.00 |

20TH CENTURY FOX

| Number | Title (A Side/B Side) | Yr | NM |
|---|---|---|---|
| ❑ TFM-3138 [M] | Live at Carnegie Hall | 1964 | 12.00 |
| ❑ TFS-4138 [S] | Live at Carnegie Hall | 1964 | 15.00 |

VOCALION

| Number | Title (A Side/B Side) | Yr | NM |
|---|---|---|---|
| ❑ VL 3610 [M] | Tony Martin | 196? | 15.00 |

WING

| Number | Title (A Side/B Side) | Yr | NM |
|---|---|---|---|
| ❑ MGW-12203 [M] | Mr. Song Man | 196? | 12.00 |

## MARTIN, VINCE, AND FRED NEIL

ELEKTRA

| Number | Title (A Side/B Side) | Yr | NM |
|---|---|---|---|
| ❑ EKL-248 [M] | Tear Down the Walls | 1964 | 50.00 |
| ❑ EKS-7248 [S] | Tear Down the Walls | 1964 | 60.00 |

## MARTINDALE, WINK

DOT

| Number | Title (A Side/B Side) | Yr | NM |
|---|---|---|---|
| ❑ DLP-3245 [M] | Deck of Cards | 1960 | 20.00 |
| ❑ DLP-3293 [M] | The Bible Story | 1960 | 15.00 |
| ❑ DLP-3403 [M] | Big Bad John | 1962 | 15.00 |
| ❑ DLP-3571 [M] | My True Love | 1964 | 15.00 |
| ❑ DLP-3692 [M] | Giddyup Go | 1966 | 15.00 |
| ❑ DLP-25245 [S] | Deck of Cards | 1960 | 25.00 |
| ❑ DLP-25293 [S] | The Bible Story | 1960 | 20.00 |
| ❑ DLP-25403 [S] | Big Bad John | 1962 | 20.00 |
| ❑ DLP-25571 [S] | My True Love | 1964 | 20.00 |
| ❑ DLP-25692 [S] | Giddyup Go | 1966 | 20.00 |

## MARTINEZ, TONY

DEL-FI

| Number | Title (A Side/B Side) | Yr | NM |
|---|---|---|---|
| ❑ DFLP-1205 [M] | The Many Sides of Pepino | 1959 | 30.00 |
| ❑ DFLP-1205S [S] | The Many Sides of Pepino | 1959 | 40.00 |

## MARTINO, AL

CAPITOL

| Number | Title (A Side/B Side) | Yr | NM |
|---|---|---|---|
| ❑ ST-180 | Sausalito | 1969 | 12.00 |
| ❑ ST-379 | Jean | 1969 | 12.00 |
| ❑ ST-405 | Can't Help Falling in Love | 1970 | 12.00 |
| ❑ ST-497 | My Heart Sings | 1970 | 12.00 |
| ❑ STBB-526 [(2)] | Here in My Heart/Yesterday | 1970 | 15.00 |
| ❑ STCL-572 [(3)] | Al Martino | 1971 | 25.00 |
| ❑ STBB-713 [(2)] | I Wish You Love/Losing You | 1971 | 15.00 |
| ❑ ST-793 | Summer of '42 | 1971 | 12.00 |
| ❑ ST 1774 [S] | The Exciting Voice of Al Martino | 1962 | 20.00 |
| ❑ T 1774 [M] | The Exciting Voice of Al Martino | 1962 | 15.00 |
| ❑ ST 1907 [S] | The Italian Voice of Al Martino | 1963 | 20.00 |
| ❑ T 1907 [M] | The Italian Voice of Al Martino | 1963 | 15.00 |
| ❑ ST 1914 [S] | I Love You Because | 1963 | 15.00 |
| ❑ T 1914 [M] | I Love You Because | 1963 | 12.00 |
| ❑ ST 1975 [S] | Painted, Tainted Rose | 1963 | 15.00 |
| ❑ T 1975 [M] | Painted, Tainted Rose | 1963 | 12.00 |
| ❑ ST 2040 [S] | Living a Lie | 1964 | 15.00 |
| ❑ T 2040 [M] | Living a Lie | 1964 | 12.00 |
| ❑ ST 2107 [S] | I Love You More and More Every Day/Tears and Roses | 1964 | 15.00 |
| ❑ T 2107 [M] | I Love You More and More Every Day/Tears and Roses | 1964 | 12.00 |
| ❑ ST 2165 [S] | A Merry Christmas from Al Martino | 1964 | 15.00 |
| ❑ T 2165 [M] | A Merry Christmas from Al Martino | 1964 | 12.00 |
| ❑ ST 2200 [S] | We Could | 1964 | 15.00 |
| ❑ T 2200 [M] | We Could | 1964 | 12.00 |
| ❑ ST 2312 [S] | Somebody Else Is Taking My Place | 1965 | 15.00 |
| ❑ T 2312 [M] | Somebody Else Is Taking My Place | 1965 | 12.00 |
| ❑ ST 2362 [S] | My Cherie | 1965 | 15.00 |
| ❑ T 2362 [M] | My Cherie | 1965 | 12.00 |
| ❑ ST 2435 [S] | Spanish Eyes | 1966 | 15.00 |
| ❑ T 2435 [M] | Spanish Eyes | 1966 | 12.00 |
| ❑ ST 2528 [S] | Think I'll Go Somewhere and Cry Myself to Sleep | 1966 | 15.00 |
| ❑ T 2528 [M] | Think I'll Go Somewhere and Cry Myself to Sleep | 1966 | 12.00 |
| ❑ ST 2592 [S] | This Is Love | 1966 | 15.00 |
| ❑ T 2592 [M] | This Is Love | 1966 | 12.00 |
| ❑ ST 2654 [S] | This Love for You | 1967 | 15.00 |
| ❑ T 2654 [M] | This Love for You | 1967 | 15.00 |
| ❑ ST 2733 [S] | Daddy's Little Girl | 1967 | 15.00 |
| ❑ T 2733 [M] | Daddy's Little Girl | 1967 | 15.00 |
| ❑ ST 2780 [S] | Mary in the Morning | 1967 | 15.00 |
| ❑ T 2780 [M] | Mary in the Morning | 1967 | 15.00 |
| ❑ ST 2843 | This Is Al Martino | 1968 | 15.00 |
| ❑ ST 2908 | Love Is Blue | 1968 | 15.00 |
| ❑ SKAO 2946 | The Best of Al Martino | 1968 | 15.00 |
| ❑ SM-2946 | The Best of Al Martino | 197? | 10.00 |

*—Reissue with new prefix*

| Number | Title (A Side/B Side) | Yr | NM |
|---|---|---|---|
| ❑ ST 2983 | Wake Up to Me Gentle | 1968 | 15.00 |
| ❑ SM-11071 | Love Theme from "The Godfather" | 1977 | 8.00 |

*—Reissue with new prefix*

| Number | Title (A Side/B Side) | Yr | NM |
|---|---|---|---|
| ❑ ST-11071 | Love Theme from "The Godfather" | 1972 | 10.00 |
| ❑ ST-11302 | I Won't Last a Day Without You | 1974 | 10.00 |
| ❑ ST-11366 | To the Door of the Sun | 1975 | 10.00 |
| ❑ ST-11572 | Sing My Love Songs | 1976 | 10.00 |
| ❑ SM-11679 | To the Door of the Sun | 1977 | 8.00 |

*—Reissue of 11366*

| Number | Title (A Side/B Side) | Yr | NM |
|---|---|---|---|
| ❑ ST-11741 | The Next Hundred Years | 1978 | 10.00 |
| ❑ SN-16074 | The Best of Al Martino | 1981 | 8.00 |

*—Budget-line reissue*

| Number | Title (A Side/B Side) | Yr | NM |
|---|---|---|---|
| ❑ SQBO-91280 [(2)] | The Romantic World of Al Martino | 196? | 20.00 |

*—Capitol Record Club exclusive*

MOVIETONE

| Number | Title (A Side/B Side) | Yr | NM |
|---|---|---|---|
| ❑ MTM 2002 [M] | That Old Feeling | 196? | 15.00 |
| ❑ MTM 2015 [M] | All of Me | 1967 | 20.00 |
| ❑ MTS 72002 [S] | That Old Feeling | 196? | 20.00 |
| ❑ MTS 72015 [S] | All of Me | 1967 | 15.00 |

PICKWICK

| Number | Title (A Side/B Side) | Yr | NM |
|---|---|---|---|
| ❑ SPC-3049 | Don't Go to Strangers | 196? | 12.00 |
| ❑ SPC-3276 | Mary in the Morning | 197? | 10.00 |

| Number | Title (A Side/B Side) | Yr | NM |
|---|---|---|---|
| SPRINGBOARD | | | |
| ❑ 4074 | Time After Time | 1978 | 8.00 |
| 20TH CENTURY FOX | | | |
| ❑ SF-3025 [M] | Al Martino | 1959 | 25.00 |
| ❑ SFX-3025 [S] | Al Martino | 1959 | 30.00 |
| ❑ SF-3032 [M] | Sing Along with Al Martino | 1959 | 25.00 |
| ❑ SFX-3032 [S] | Sing Along with Al Martino | 1959 | 30.00 |
| ❑ TF-4168 [M] | Al Martino Sings | 196? | 20.00 |
| ❑ TFS-4168 [S] | Al Martino Sings | 196? | 25.00 |
| ❑ SXG-5009 [S] | When Your Lover Has Gone | 1963 | 25.00 |
| ❑ XG-5009 [M] | When Your Lover Has Gone | 1963 | 20.00 |
| **MARTINO, PAT** | | | |
| COBBLESTONE | | | |
| ❑ 9015 | The Visit | 1972 | 20.00 |
| PRESTIGE | | | |
| ❑ PRLP-7513 [M] | El Hombre | 1967 | 25.00 |
| ❑ PRLP-7547 [M] | Strings! | 1967 | 25.00 |
| **MARVELETTES, THE** | | | |
| MOTOWN | | | |
| ❑ M5-180V1 | Greatest Hits | 1981 | 10.00 |
| *—Reissue of Tamla 253* | | | |
| ❑ M7-827 [(2)] | Anthology | 1975 | 15.00 |
| ❑ 5266 ML | Please Mr. Postman | 1982 | 10.00 |
| *—Reissue of Tamla 228* | | | |
| TAMLA | | | |
| ❑ T-228 [M] | Please Mr. Postman | 1961 | 600.00 |
| *—White label* | | | |
| ❑ T-228 [M] | Please Mr. Postman | 1963 | 300.00 |
| *—Yellow label with globes logo* | | | |
| ❑ T-229 [M] | The Marveletts Sing | 1962 | 500.00 |
| *—Title as listed on front cover (misspelled); all-black cover with white circles* | | | |
| ❑ T-229 [M] | Smash Hits of 62' | 1962 | 1200. |
| *—Title as listed on front cover; large black "M" with song titles in circles; VG value 600; VG+ value 900* | | | |
| ❑ T-229 [M] | The Marveletts Sing | 1963 | 250.00 |
| *—Yellow label with side-by-side globes logo* | | | |
| ❑ T-231 [M] | Playboy | 1962 | 500.00 |
| *—Yellow label with overlapping record and globe logo* | | | |
| ❑ T-231 [M] | Playboy | 1962 | 600.00 |
| *—White label* | | | |
| ❑ T-231 [M] | Playboy | 1963 | 250.00 |
| *—Yellow label with side-by-side globes logo* | | | |
| ❑ T-237 [M] | The Marvelous Marvelettes | 1963 | 150.00 |
| ❑ T-243 [M] | Recorded Live on Stage | 1963 | 80.00 |
| ❑ T-253 [M] | Greatest Hits | 1966 | 30.00 |
| *—Yellow cover* | | | |
| ❑ T-253 [M] | Greatest Hits | 1967 | 25.00 |
| *—Green cover* | | | |
| ❑ TS-253 [S] | Greatest Hits | 1966 | 40.00 |
| *—Yellow cover* | | | |
| ❑ TS-253 [S] | Greatest Hits | 1967 | 20.00 |
| *—Green cover* | | | |
| ❑ T-274 [M] | The Marvelettes | 1967 | 30.00 |
| ❑ TS-274 [S] | The Marvelettes | 1967 | 20.00 |
| ❑ T-286 [M] | Sophisticated Soul | 1968 | 40.00 |
| ❑ TS-286 [S] | Sophisticated Soul | 1968 | 20.00 |
| ❑ TS-288 | In Full Bloom | 1969 | 15.00 |
| ❑ TS-305 | Return of the Marvelettes | 1970 | 15.00 |
| **MARVELOWS, THE** | | | |
| ABC | | | |
| ❑ S-643 | The Mighty Marvelows | 1968 | 30.00 |
| **MARVIN AND JOHNNY** | | | |
| CROWN | | | |
| ❑ CST-381 [R] | Marvin and Johnny | 1963 | 12.00 |
| ❑ CLP-5381 [M] | Marvin and Johnny | 1963 | 50.00 |
| **MARX, BILL** | | | |
| VEE JAY | | | |
| ❑ LP-3032 [M] | Jazz Kaleidoscope | 1962 | 20.00 |
| ❑ SR-3032 [S] | Jazz Kaleidoscope | 1962 | 25.00 |
| ❑ LP-3035 [M] | My Son, the Folk Swinger | 1963 | 20.00 |
| ❑ SR-3035 [S] | My Son, the Folk Swinger | 1963 | 25.00 |
| **MARX, DICK** | | | |
| OMEGA | | | |
| ❑ OSL-2 [S] | Marx Makes Broadway | 1959 | 30.00 |
| *—The front cover of the above LP spells his last name "Marks," though it is spelled correctly on the label and back cover* | | | |
| ❑ OML-1002 [M] | Marx Makes Broadway | 1958 | 40.00 |
| **MARX, DICK, AND JOHN FRIGO** | | | |
| BRUNSWICK | | | |
| ❑ BL 54006 [M] | Two Much Piano | 1955 | 40.00 |
| **MARX, GROUCHO** | | | |
| DECCA | | | |
| ❑ DL 5405 [10] | Hooray for Captain Spaulding | 1954 | 250.00 |
| **MARX, HARPO** | | | |
| MERCURY | | | |
| ❑ MG-20232 [M] | Harpo in Hi-Fi | 1957 | 100.00 |
| ❑ MG-20363 [M] | Harpo at Work! | 1959 | 80.00 |
| ❑ SR-60016 [S] | Harpo at Work! | 1959 | 100.00 |
| RCA VICTOR | | | |
| ❑ LPM-27 [10] | Harp by Harpo | 1952 | 250.00 |
| WING | | | |
| ❑ MGW-12164 [M] | Harpo | 1960 | 40.00 |
| **MARY BUTTERWORTH** | | | |
| CUSTOM FIDELITY | | | |
| ❑ 2092 | Mary Butterworth | 1969 | 300.00 |
| **MASEKELA, HUGH** | | | |
| MERCURY | | | |
| ❑ SR-60797 [S] | The Trumpet of Hugh Masekela | 1963 | 20.00 |
| UNI | | | |
| ❑ 3015 [M] | Hugh Masekela Is Alive and Well at the Whisky | 1967 | 20.00 |
| **MASKED MARAUDERS, THE** Fictional supergroup from a Rolling Stone magazine album review, which noted the presence of Bob Dylan, Mick Jagger, John Lennon and Paul McCartney. The below, recorded using the bogus review as a guide, was actually THE CLEANLINESS AND GODLINESS SKIFFLE BAND. | | | |
| DEITY | | | |
| ❑ RS 6378 | The Masked Marauders | 1969 | 20.00 |
| **MASON, BARBARA** | | | |
| ARCTIC | | | |
| ❑ ALP-1000 [M] | Yes, I'm Ready | 1965 | 80.00 |
| ❑ ALPS-1000 [P] | Yes, I'm Ready | 1965 | 120.00 |
| ❑ ALPS-1004 | Oh, How It Hurts | 1968 | 80.00 |
| BUDDAH | | | |
| ❑ BDS-5117 | Give Me Your Love | 1972 | 15.00 |
| ❑ BDS-5140 | Lady Love | 1973 | 20.00 |
| ❑ BDS-5610 | Transition | 1974 | 20.00 |
| ❑ BDS-5628 | Love's the Thing | 1975 | 20.00 |
| NATIONAL GENERAL | | | |
| ❑ 2001 | If You Knew Him Like I Do | 1970 | 60.00 |
| PRELUDE | | | |
| ❑ 12159 | I Am Your Woman, She Is Your Wife | 1978 | 20.00 |
| **MASON, BARBARA, AND BUNNY SIGLER** | | | |
| CURTOM | | | |
| ❑ CU 5014 | Locked in This Position | 1977 | 15.00 |
| **MASON, DAVE** | | | |
| BLUE THUMB | | | |
| ❑ BTS-19 | Alone Together | 1970 | 20.00 |
| *—Originals on multicolored vinyl* | | | |
| ❑ BTS-19 | All Together | 1970 | 200.00 |
| *—Erroneous pressing of "Alone Together"* | | | |
| ❑ BTS-19 | Alone Together | 1975 | 12.00 |
| *—Multicolor label with "ABC" logo* | | | |
| ❑ BTS-34 | Headkeeper | 1972 | 15.00 |
| ❑ BTS-54 | Dave Mason Is Alive! | 1973 | 15.00 |
| ❑ ABCD-880 | Dave Mason At His Best | 1975 | 10.00 |
| ❑ BT-6013 | The Best of Dave Mason | 1974 | 10.00 |
| ❑ BT-6032 | Very Best of Dave Mason | 1978 | 10.00 |
| ❑ BTS-8819 | Alone Together | 1971 | 50.00 |
| *—Capitol-distributed black vinyl reissue* | | | |
| CHUMLEY | | | |
| ❑ 00101 | Some Assembly Required | 1987 | 10.00 |
| COLUMBIA | | | |
| ❑ CQ 31721 [Q] | It's Like You Never Left | 1973 | 18.00 |
| ❑ KC 31721 | It's Like You Never Left | 1973 | 10.00 |
| ❑ PC 31721 | It's Like You Never Left | 197? | 8.00 |
| *—Reissue with new prefix* | | | |
| ❑ PC 33096 | Dave Mason | 1974 | 10.00 |
| *—No bar code on cover* | | | |
| ❑ PC 33096 | Dave Mason | 198? | 8.00 |
| *—Budget-line reissue with bar code* | | | |
| ❑ PCQ 33096 [Q] | Dave Mason | 1974 | 18.00 |
| ❑ PC 33698 | Split Coconut | 1975 | 10.00 |
| ❑ PCQ 33698 [Q] | Split Coconut | 1975 | 18.00 |
| ❑ PG 34174 [(2)] | Certified Live | 1976 | 12.00 |
| ❑ PC 34680 | Let It Flow | 1977 | 10.00 |
| *—No bar code on cover* | | | |
| ❑ PC 34680 | Let It Flow | 198? | 8.00 |
| *—Budget-line reissue with bar code* | | | |
| ❑ JC 35285 | Mariposa de Oro | 1978 | 10.00 |
| ❑ JC 36144 | Old Crest on a New Wave | 1980 | 10.00 |
| ❑ FC 37089 | The Best of Dave Mason | 1981 | 10.00 |
| ❑ PC 37089 | The Best of Dave Mason | 1983 | 8.00 |
| *—Budget-line reissue* | | | |
| MCA | | | |
| ❑ 712 | Headkeeper | 198? | 8.00 |
| *—Reissue of Blue Thumb 34* | | | |
| ❑ 713 | Dave Mason Is Alive | 198? | 8.00 |
| *—Reissue of Blue Thumb 54* | | | |
| ❑ 714 | Dave Mason At His Best | 198? | 8.00 |
| *—Reissue of Blue Thumb 880* | | | |
| ❑ 715 | Very Best of Dave Mason | 198? | 8.00 |
| *—Reissue of Blue Thumb 6032* | | | |
| ❑ 800 | The Best of Dave Mason | 1981 | 8.00 |
| *—Reissue of Blue Thumb 6013* | | | |
| ❑ 11319 | Alone Together | 1995 | 20.00 |
| *—"Heavy Vinyl" gatefold reissue* | | | |
| ❑ 27035 | Alone Together | 198? | 8.00 |
| *—Reissue of Blue Thumb 19* | | | |
| ❑ 42086 | Two Hearts | 1988 | 10.00 |
| S&P | | | |
| ❑ 503 | It's Like You Never Left | 2003 | 20.00 |
| *—Reissue on 180-gram vinyl* | | | |
| **MASON, DAVE, AND CASS ELLIOT** Also see each artist's individual listings. | | | |
| BLUE THUMB | | | |
| ❑ BTS-8825 | Dave Mason and Cass Elliot | 1971 | 20.00 |
| **MASON, JACKIE** | | | |
| VERVE | | | |
| ❑ V-15033 [M] | I'm the Greatest Comedian in the World Only Nobody Knows It Yet | 1962 | 20.00 |
| ❑ V-15034 [M] | I Want to Leave You with the Words of a Great Comedian | 1963 | 20.00 |
| ❑ V-15045 [M] | Great Moments in Comedy | 1964 | 20.00 |
| WARNER BROS. | | | |
| ❑ 25603 | The World According to Me! | 1987 | 10.00 |
| **MASON PROFFIT** | | | |
| AMPEX | | | |
| ❑ A-10138 | Last Night I Had the Strangest Dream | 1971 | 30.00 |
| HAPPY TIGER | | | |
| ❑ HT-1009 | Wanted! Mason Proffit | 1970 | 25.00 |
| ❑ HT-1019 | Movin' Toward Happiness | 1971 | 20.00 |
| WARNER BROS. | | | |
| ❑ BS 2657 | Rockfish Crossing | 1972 | 15.00 |
| ❑ BS 2704 | Bareback Rider | 1973 | 15.00 |
| ❑ 2WS 2746 [(2)] | Come and Gone | 1974 | 20.00 |
| **MASTER CYLINDER** | | | |
| INNER CITY | | | |
| ❑ IC-1112 | Elsewhere | 198? | 30.00 |
| **MASTER FLEET** | | | |
| SUSSEX | | | |
| ❑ SRA-8028 | High on the Sea | 1974 | 40.00 |
| **MASTERS, JOE** | | | |
| COLUMBIA | | | |
| ❑ CL 2598 [M] | The Jazz Mass | 1967 | 25.00 |
| ❑ CS 9398 [S] | The Jazz Mass | 1967 | 20.00 |
| **MASTERSOUNDS, THE** | | | |
| FANTASY | | | |
| ❑ 3305 [M] | Swingin' with the Mastersounds | 1960 | 40.00 |
| *—Red vinyl* | | | |
| ❑ 3305 [M] | Swingin' with the Mastersounds | 1962 | 25.00 |
| *—Black vinyl* | | | |
| ❑ 3316 [M] | A Date with the Mastersounds | 1961 | 40.00 |
| *—Red vinyl* | | | |
| ❑ 3316 [M] | A Date with the Mastersounds | 1962 | 25.00 |
| *—Black vinyl* | | | |
| ❑ 3327 [M] | The Mastersounds on Tour | 1961 | 40.00 |
| *—Red vinyl* | | | |
| ❑ 3327 [M] | The Mastersounds on Tour | 1962 | 25.00 |
| *—Black vinyl* | | | |
| ❑ 8050 [S] | Swingin' with the Mastersounds | 1961 | 30.00 |
| *—Blue vinyl* | | | |
| ❑ 8050 [S] | Swingin' with the Mastersounds | 1962 | 20.00 |
| *—Black vinyl* | | | |
| ❑ 8062 [S] | A Date with the Mastersounds | 1961 | 30.00 |
| *—Blue vinyl* | | | |
| ❑ 8062 [S] | A Date with the Mastersounds | 1962 | 20.00 |
| *—Black vinyl* | | | |
| ❑ 8066 [S] | The Mastersounds on Tour | 1961 | 30.00 |
| *—Blue vinyl* | | | |
| ❑ 8066 [S] | The Mastersounds on Tour | 1962 | 20.00 |
| *—Black vinyl* | | | |
| PACIFIC JAZZ | | | |
| ❑ PJM-403 [M] | Introducing the Mastersounds | 1957 | 50.00 |
| ❑ PJM-405 [M] | The King and I | 1958 | 50.00 |
| WORLD PACIFIC | | | |
| ❑ ST-1010 [S] | Kismet | 1958 | 30.00 |
| ❑ ST-1012 [S] | Flower Drum Song | 1958 | 30.00 |
| ❑ ST-1017 [S] | The King and I | 1959 | 30.00 |
| ❑ ST-1019 [S] | Ballads and Blues | 1959 | 30.00 |
| ❑ ST-1026 [S] | The Mastersounds in Concert | 1959 | 30.00 |
| ❑ ST-1030 [S] | Happy Holidays from Many Lands | 1959 | 30.00 |
| ❑ WP-1243 [M] | Kismet | 1958 | 40.00 |
| ❑ WP-1252 [M] | Flower Drum Song | 1958 | 40.00 |
| ❑ WP-1260 [M] | Ballads and Blues | 1959 | 40.00 |
| ❑ WP-1269 [M] | The Mastersounds in Concert | 1959 | 40.00 |
| ❑ WP-1271 [M] | Jazz Showcase | 1959 | 30.00 |
| *—Reissue of Pacific Jazz 403* | | | |
| ❑ WP-1272 [M] | The King and I | 1959 | 30.00 |
| *—Reissue of Pacific Jazz 405* | | | |
| ❑ WP-1280 [M] | Happy Holidays from Many Lands | 1959 | 40.00 |
| ❑ ST-1284 [S] | The Mastersounds Play Horace Silver | 1960 | 30.00 |
| ❑ WP-1284 [M] | The Mastersounds Play Horace Silver | 1960 | 40.00 |

CL 1133
JOHNNY'S
GREATEST HITS
JOHNNY MATHIS
COLUMBIA Lp
GUARANTEED HIGH FIDELITY
Chances Are · All the Time · The Twelfth of Never
When Sunny Gets Blue · When I Am with You
Wonderful! Wonderful! · It's Not for Me to Say
Come to Me · Wild Is the Wind
Warm and Tender · No Love · I Look at You


Johnny Mathis, *Johnny's Greatest Hits,*
Columbia CL 1133, 1958, mono, red and black "6 eye" label, $30.

| Number | Title (A Side/B Side) | Yr | NM |
|---|---|---|---|
| **MATHEWS, MAT** | | | |
| BRUNSWICK | | | |
| ❑ BL 54013 [M] | Bag's Groove | 1956 | 80.00 |
| DAWN | | | |
| ❑ DLP-1104 [M] | The Modern Art of Jazz | 1956 | 100.00 |
| **MATHEWS, RONNIE** | | | |
| PRESTIGE | | | |
| ❑ PRLP-7303 [M] | Doin' the Thang | 1964 | 30.00 |
| ❑ PRST-7303 [S] | Doin' the Thang | 1964 | 40.00 |
| **MATHIS, COUNTRY JOHNNY** The "original" Johnny Mathis, the "Country" prefix was added to his name after the "other" Johnny Mathis became far more popular. | | | |
| HILLTOP GOSPEL | | | |
| ❑ GS-7004 | Country Johnny Mathis | 1965 | 25.00 |
| LITTLE DARLIN' | | | |
| ❑ 8007 | He Keeps Me Singin' | 1967 | 20.00 |
| **MATHIS, JOHNNY** | | | |
| COLUMBIA | | | |
| ❑ GP 2 [(2)] | Warm/Open Fire, Two Guitars | 1969 | 15.00 |
| ❑ C2L 17 [(2)M] | The Rhythms and Ballads of Broadway | 1960 | 25.00 |
| *—Red and black label with six "eye" logos* | | | |
| ❑ C2L 17 [(2)M] | The Rhythms and Ballads of Broadway | 1962 | 20.00 |
| *—Red label with either "Guaranteed High Fidelity" or "360 Sound Mono"* | | | |
| ❑ C2L 34 [(2)M] | The Great Years | 1964 | 15.00 |
| ❑ C2S 803 [(2)S] | The Rhythms and Ballads of Broadway | 1960 | 30.00 |
| *—Red and black label with six "eye" logos* | | | |
| ❑ C2S 803 [(2)S] | The Rhythms and Ballads of Broadway | 1962 | 25.00 |
| *—Red "360 Sound" label* | | | |
| ❑ C2S 834 [(2)S] | The Great Years | 1964 | 20.00 |
| *—Red "360 Sound" label* | | | |
| ❑ CL 887 [M] | Johnny Mathis | 1957 | 50.00 |
| ❑ CS 1005 | Raindrops Keep Fallin' on My Head | 1970 | 12.00 |
| ❑ CL 1028 [M] | Wonderful Wonderful | 1957 | 30.00 |
| *—Red and black label with six "eye" logos* | | | |
| ❑ CL 1028 [M] | Wonderful Wonderful | 1962 | 15.00 |
| *—Red label with either "Guaranteed High Fidelity" or "360 Sound Mono"* | | | |

| Number | Title (A Side/B Side) | Yr | NM |
|---|---|---|---|
| ❑ CL 1078 [M] | Warm | 1957 | 30.00 |
| *—Red and black label with six "eye" logos* | | | |
| ❑ CL 1078 [M] | Warm | 1962 | 15.00 |
| *—Red label with either "Guaranteed High Fidelity" or "360 Sound Mono"* | | | |
| ❑ CL 1119 [M] | Good Night, Dear Lord | 1958 | 30.00 |
| *—Red and black label with six "eye" logos* | | | |
| ❑ CL 1119 [M] | Good Night, Dear Lord | 1962 | 15.00 |
| *—Red label with either "Guaranteed High Fidelity" or "360 Sound Mono"* | | | |
| ❑ CL 1133 [M] | Johnny's Greatest Hits | 1958 | 30.00 |
| *—Red and black label with six "eye" logos* | | | |
| ❑ CL 1133 [M] | Johnny's Greatest Hits | 1962 | 15.00 |
| *—Red label with either "Guaranteed High Fidelity" or "360 Sound Mono"* | | | |
| ❑ CL 1165 [M] | Swing Softly | 1958 | 30.00 |
| *—Red and black label with six "eye" logos* | | | |
| ❑ CL 1165 [M] | Swing Softly | 1962 | 15.00 |
| *—Red label with either "Guaranteed High Fidelity" or "360 Sound Mono"* | | | |
| ❑ CL 1195 [M] | Merry Christmas | 1958 | 40.00 |
| *—Original cover has Johnny standing, holding skis and poles* | | | |
| ❑ CL 1195 [M] | Merry Christmas | 196? | 30.00 |
| *—Second cover has Johnny sitting, with skis and poles in snow* | | | |
| ❑ CL 1270 [M] | Open Fire, Two Guitars | 1959 | 30.00 |
| *—Red and black label with six "eye" logos* | | | |
| ❑ CL 1270 [M] | Open Fire, Two Guitars | 1962 | 15.00 |
| *—Red label with either "Guaranteed High Fidelity" or "360 Sound Mono"* | | | |
| ❑ CL 1344 [M] | More Johnny's Greatest Hits | 1959 | 25.00 |
| *—Red and black label with six "eye" logos* | | | |
| ❑ CL 1344 [M] | More Johnny's Greatest Hits | 1962 | 15.00 |
| *—Red label with either "Guaranteed High Fidelity" or "360 Sound Mono"* | | | |
| ❑ CL 1351 [M] | Heavenly | 1959 | 20.00 |
| *—Red and black label with six "eye" logos* | | | |
| ❑ CL 1351 [M] | Heavenly | 1962 | 15.00 |
| *—Red label with either "Guaranteed High Fidelity" or "360 Sound Mono"* | | | |
| ❑ CL 1422 [M] | Faithfully | 1959 | 20.00 |
| *—Red and black label with six "eye" logos* | | | |
| ❑ CL 1422 [M] | Faithfully | 1962 | 15.00 |
| *—Red label with either "Guaranteed High Fidelity" or "360 Sound Mono"* | | | |
| ❑ CL 1526 [M] | Johnny's Mood | 1960 | 20.00 |
| *—Red and black label with six "eye" logos* | | | |
| ❑ CL 1526 [M] | Johnny's Mood | 1962 | 15.00 |
| *—Red label with either "Guaranteed High Fidelity" or "360 Sound Mono"* | | | |

| Number | Title (A Side/B Side) | Yr | NM |
|---|---|---|---|
| ❑ CL 1623 [M] | I'll Buy You a Star | 1961 | 15.00 |
| *—Red and black label with six "eye" logos* | | | |
| ❑ CL 1623 [M] | I'll Buy You a Star | 1962 | 12.00 |
| *—Red label with either "Guaranteed High Fidelity" or "360 Sound Mono"* | | | |
| ❑ CL 1644 [M] | Portrait of Johnny | 1961 | 15.00 |
| *—Red and black label with six "eye" logos; add 1/3 if portrait is there* | | | |
| ❑ CL 1644 [M] | Portrait of Johnny | 1962 | 12.00 |
| *—Red label with either "Guaranteed High Fidelity" or "360 Sound Mono"* | | | |
| ❑ CL 1711 [M] | Live It Up! | 1962 | 12.00 |
| *—Red label with either "Guaranteed High Fidelity" or "360 Sound Mono"* | | | |
| ❑ CL 1711 [M] | Live It Up! | 1962 | 15.00 |
| *—Red and black label with six "eye" logos* | | | |
| ❑ CL 1915 [M] | Rapture | 1962 | 12.00 |
| ❑ CL 2016 [M] | Johnny's Newest Hits | 1963 | 12.00 |
| ❑ CL 2044 [M] | Johnny | 1963 | 12.00 |
| ❑ CL 2098 [M] | Romantically | 1963 | 12.00 |
| ❑ CL 2143 [M] | I'll Search My Heart and Other Great Hits | 1964 | 12.00 |
| ❑ CL 2223 [M] | The Ballads of Broadway | 1964 | 12.00 |
| ❑ CL 2224 [M] | The Rhythms of Broadway | 1964 | 12.00 |
| ❑ CL 2726 [M] | Up, Up and Away | 1967 | 15.00 |
| ❑ CL 2837 [M] | Love Is Blue | 1968 | 25.00 |
| ❑ CL 2905 [M] | Those Were the Days | 1968 | 40.00 |
| ❑ CS 8012 [S] | Good Night, Dear Lord | 1958 | 40.00 |
| *—Red and black label with six "eye" logos* | | | |
| ❑ CS 8012 [S] | Good Night, Dear Lord | 1962 | 20.00 |
| *—Red "360 Sound" label* | | | |
| ❑ CS 8021 [S] | Merry Christmas | 1959 | 25.00 |
| *—Original cover has Johnny standing, holding skis and poles; red and black label with six "eye" logos* | | | |
| ❑ CS 8021 [S] | Merry Christmas | 196? | 20.00 |
| *—Second cover has Johnny sitting, with skis and poles in snow* | | | |
| ❑ PC 8021 [S] | Merry Christmas | 198? | 6.00 |
| *—New prefix; original "standing" cover; bar code on back cover with "02" suffix* | | | |
| ❑ CS 8023 [S] | Swing Softly | 1958 | 40.00 |
| *—Red and black label with six "eye" logos* | | | |
| ❑ CS 8039 [S] | Warm | 1958 | 40.00 |
| *—Red and black label with six "eye" logos* | | | |
| ❑ CS 8039 [S] | Warm | 1962 | 20.00 |
| *—Red "360 Sound" label* | | | |
| ❑ CS 8056 [S] | Open Fire, Two Guitars | 1959 | 40.00 |
| *—Red and black label with six "eye" logos* | | | |
| ❑ CS 8056 [S] | Open Fire, Two Guitars | 1962 | 20.00 |
| *—Red "360 Sound" label* | | | |
| ❑ CS 8150 [S] | More Johnny's Greatest Hits | 1959 | 30.00 |
| *—Red and black label with six "eye" logos* | | | |
| ❑ CS 8150 [S] | More Johnny's Greatest Hits | 1962 | 20.00 |
| *—Red "360 Sound" label* | | | |
| ❑ CS 8150 [S] | More Johnny's Greatest Hits | 1971 | 10.00 |
| *—Orange label* | | | |
| ❑ PC 8150 [S] | More Johnny's Greatest Hits | 198? | 6.00 |
| *—Reissue with new prefix* | | | |
| ❑ CS 8152 [S] | Heavenly | 1959 | 30.00 |
| *—Red and black label with six "eye" logos* | | | |
| ❑ CS 8152 [S] | Heavenly | 1962 | 20.00 |
| *—Red "360 Sound" label* | | | |
| ❑ CS 8152 [S] | Heavenly | 1971 | 10.00 |
| *—Orange label* | | | |
| ❑ PC 8152 [S] | Heavenly | 198? | 6.00 |
| *—Reissue with new prefix* | | | |
| ❑ CS 8219 [S] | Faithfully | 1959 | 25.00 |
| *—Red and black label with six "eye" logos* | | | |
| ❑ CS 8219 [S] | Faithfully | 1962 | 20.00 |
| *—Red "360 Sound" label* | | | |
| ❑ CS 8326 [S] | Johnny's Mood | 1960 | 25.00 |
| *—Red and black label with six "eye" logos* | | | |
| ❑ CS 8326 [S] | Johnny's Mood | 1962 | 20.00 |
| *—Red "360 Sound" label* | | | |
| ❑ CS 8423 [S] | I'll Buy You a Star | 1961 | 20.00 |
| *—Red and black label with six "eye" logos* | | | |
| ❑ CS 8423 [S] | I'll Buy You a Star | 1962 | 15.00 |
| *—Red "360 Sound" label* | | | |
| ❑ CS 8444 [S] | Portrait of Johnny | 1961 | 20.00 |
| *—Red and black label with six "eye" logos; add 1/3 if portrait is there* | | | |
| ❑ CS 8444 [S] | Portrait of Johnny | 1962 | 15.00 |
| *—Red "360 Sound" label* | | | |
| ❑ CS 8511 [S] | Live It Up! | 1962 | 15.00 |
| *—Red "360 Sound" label* | | | |
| ❑ CS 8511 [S] | Live It Up! | 1962 | 20.00 |
| *—Red and black label with six "eye" logos; add 1/3 if portrait is there* | | | |
| ❑ CS 8634 [R] | Johnny's Greatest Hits | 1963 | 12.00 |
| ❑ CS 8715 [S] | Rapture | 1962 | 15.00 |
| *—Red "360 Sound" label* | | | |
| ❑ CS 8816 [S] | Johnny's Newest Hits | 1963 | 15.00 |
| *—Red "360 Sound" label* | | | |
| ❑ CS 8844 [S] | Johnny | 1963 | 15.00 |
| *—Red "360 Sound" label* | | | |
| ❑ CS 8898 [S] | Romantically | 1963 | 15.00 |
| *—Red "360 Sound" label* | | | |
| ❑ CS 8943 [S] | I'll Search My Heart and Other Great Hits | 1964 | 15.00 |
| *—Red "360 Sound" label* | | | |
| ❑ CS 9023 [S] | The Ballads of Broadway | 1964 | 15.00 |
| *—Red "360 Sound" label* | | | |
| ❑ CS 9024 [S] | The Ballads of Broadway | 1964 | 15.00 |
| *—Red "360 Sound" label* | | | |
| ❑ CS 9046 [R] | Wonderful Wonderful | 1964 | 12.00 |



**Except when noted otherwise, VG = 25% of NM, and VG+ = 50% of NM. (Example: VG = $2.00, VG+ = $4.00 and NM = $8.00.)**

| Number | Title (A Side/B Side) | Yr | NM |
|---|---|---|---|
| ❑ CS 9526 [S] | Up, Up and Away | 1967 | 15.00 |
| ❑ CS 9637 [S] | Love Is Blue | 1968 | 15.00 |
| ❑ CS 9705 [S] | Those Were the Days | 1968 | 15.00 |
| ❑ CS 9871 | People | 1969 | 15.00 |
| ❑ CS 9872 | The Impossible Dream | 1969 | 15.00 |
| *—Red "360 Sound" label* | | | |
| ❑ CS 9872 | The Impossible Dream | 1971 | 10.00 |
| *—Orange label* | | | |
| ❑ PC 9872 | The Impossible Dream | 198? | 6.00 |
| *—Reissue with new prefix* | | | |
| ❑ CS 9909 | Love Theme from "Romeo and Juliet" | 1969 | 15.00 |
| *—Red "360 Sound" label* | | | |
| ❑ CS 9909 | Love Theme from "Romeo and Juliet" | 1971 | 10.00 |
| *—Orange label* | | | |
| ❑ PC 9909 | Love Theme from "Romeo and Juliet" | 198? | 6.00 |
| *—Reissue with new prefix* | | | |
| ❑ CS 9923 | Give Me Your Love for Christmas | 1969 | 12.00 |
| ❑ C 30210 | Close to You | 1970 | 12.00 |
| ❑ G 30350 [(2)] | Johnny Mathis Sings the Music of Bacharach & Kaempfert | 1970 | 15.00 |
| ❑ C 30499 | Love Story | 1971 | 12.00 |
| ❑ PC 30499 | Love Story | 198? | 8.00 |
| *—Budget-line reissue* | | | |
| ❑ C 30740 | You've Got a Friend | 1971 | 12.00 |
| ❑ CQ 30740 [Q] | You've Got a Friend | 1972 | 20.00 |
| ❑ PC 30740 | You've Got a Friend | 198? | 8.00 |
| *—Budget-line reissue* | | | |
| ❑ 2CQ 30979 [(2)Q] | Johnny Mathis In Person | 1972 | 25.00 |
| ❑ KG 30979 [(2)] | Johnny Mathis In Person | 1972 | 15.00 |
| ❑ CQ 31342 [Q] | The First Time Ever (I Saw Your Face) | 1972 | 20.00 |
| ❑ KC 31342 | The First Time Ever (I Saw Your Face) | 1972 | 12.00 |
| ❑ PC 31342 | The First Time Ever (I Saw Your Face) | 198? | 8.00 |
| *—Budget-line reissue* | | | |
| ❑ KG 31345 [(2)] | Johnny Mathis' All-Time Greatest Hits | 1972 | 15.00 |
| ❑ CQ 31626 [Q] | Song Sung Blue | 1972 | 20.00 |
| ❑ KC 31626 | Song Sung Blue | 1972 | 12.00 |
| ❑ CQ 32114 [Q] | Me and Mrs. Jones | 1973 | 18.00 |
| ❑ KC 32114 | Me and Mrs. Jones | 1973 | 10.00 |
| ❑ KC 32258 | Killing Me Softly with Her Song | 1973 | 10.00 |
| ❑ CQ 32435 [Q] | I'm Coming Home | 1973 | 18.00 |
| ❑ KC 32435 | I'm Coming Home | 1973 | 10.00 |
| ❑ PC 32435 | I'm Coming Home | 198? | 8.00 |
| *—Budget-line reissue* | | | |
| ❑ C 32963 | What'll I Do | 1974 | 10.00 |
| ❑ KC 33251 | The Heart of a Woman | 1974 | 10.00 |
| ❑ PC 33420 | When Will I See You Again | 1975 | 10.00 |
| ❑ CG 33621 [(2)] | Heavenly/Faithfully | 1975 | 12.00 |
| ❑ PC 33887 | Feelings | 1975 | 10.00 |
| ❑ PC 34117 | I Only Have Eyes for You | 1976 | 10.00 |
| ❑ PC 34441 | Mathis Is… | 1977 | 10.00 |
| ❑ PC 34667 | Johnny Mathis' Greatest Hits | 1977 | 10.00 |
| ❑ PC 34872 | Hold Me, Thrill Me, Kiss Me | 1977 | 10.00 |
| ❑ PC 35259 | You Light Up My Life | 1986 | 8.00 |
| *—Budget-line reissue* | | | |
| ❑ JC 35359 | You Light Up My Life | 1978 | 10.00 |
| ❑ C 35578 | Romantically | 1978 | 8.00 |
| ❑ JC 35649 | The Best Days of My Life | 1979 | 10.00 |
| ❑ PC 35649 | The Best Days of My Life | 1985 | 8.00 |
| *—Budget-line reissue* | | | |
| ❑ JC 36216 | Mathis Magic | 1979 | 10.00 |
| ❑ JC 36505 | Different Kinda Different | 1980 | 10.00 |
| ❑ JC 36871 | The Best of Johnny Mathis 1975-1980 | 1980 | 10.00 |
| ❑ C2X 37440 [(2)] | The First 25 Years — The Silver Anniversary Album | 1981 | 12.00 |
| ❑ FC 37748 | Friends in Love | 1982 | 10.00 |
| ❑ 3C 38306 | Christmas with Johnny Mathis | 1982 | 8.00 |
| *—Reissue of Columbia LE 10196 with same contents* | | | |
| ❑ FC 38699 | Johnny Mathis Live | 1983 | 10.00 |
| ❑ FC 38718 | A Special Part of Me | 1984 | 10.00 |
| ❑ PC 39468 | For Christmas | 1984 | 8.00 |
| ❑ FC 39601 | Right from the Heart | 1985 | 10.00 |
| ❑ FC 40372 | The Hollywood Musicals | 1986 | 10.00 |
| *—With Henry Mancini* | | | |
| ❑ FC 40447 | Christmas Eve with Johnny Mathis | 1986 | 10.00 |
| ❑ OC 44156 | Once in a While | 1988 | 10.00 |
| ❑ OC 44336 | In the Still of the Night | 1989 | 12.00 |

COLUMBIA LIMITED EDITION

| Number | Title (A Side/B Side) | Yr | NM |
|---|---|---|---|
| ❑ LE 10003 | Portrait of Johnny | 197? | 10.00 |
| ❑ LE 10196 | Christmas with Johnny Mathis | 1976 | 10.00 |
| *—Reissue of Harmony KH 30684 with same contents* | | | |

COLUMBIA MUSICAL TREASURY

| Number | Title (A Side/B Side) | Yr | NM |
|---|---|---|---|
| ❑ 6P 6030 [(6)] | The Johnny Mathis Treasury | 197? | 30.00 |

COLUMBIA SPECIAL PRODUCTS

| Number | Title (A Side/B Side) | Yr | NM |
|---|---|---|---|
| ❑ C 10896 | Merry Christmas | 1972 | 12.00 |
| *—Reissue* | | | |
| ❑ P 11477 | Romantically, Johnny Mathis | 197? | 12.00 |
| ❑ P3 11837 [(3)] | Romantically, Johnny Mathis | 197? | 25.00 |
| ❑ P6 14628 [(6)] | Misty Memories: The Complete Johnny Mathis Treasury | 197? | 30.00 |
| *—Maunfactured for Candelite Music* | | | |
| ❑ P 14658 | Holidays at the Fireside | 197? | 20.00 |
| *—Bonus album with box set 14628* | | | |
| ❑ P 14908 | The Heart of Johnny Mathis | 197? | 15.00 |
| *—Bonus album with box set 14628* | | | |
| ❑ P4 14971 [(4)] | Johnny | 197? | 25.00 |

HARMONY

| Number | Title (A Side/B Side) | Yr | NM |
|---|---|---|---|
| ❑ KH 30017 | Johnny Mathis | 1970 | 10.00 |
| ❑ KH 30684 | Christmas with Johnny Mathis | 1971 | 12.00 |
| *—Reissue of Mercury SR 60837 with two fewer tracks* | | | |
| ❑ KH 31935 | Something for Everyone | 1973 | 10.00 |

MERCURY

| Number | Title (A Side/B Side) | Yr | NM |
|---|---|---|---|
| ❑ MG 20837 [M] | Sounds of Christmas | 1963 | 12.00 |
| ❑ MG-20890 [M] | Tender Is the Night | 1964 | 12.00 |
| ❑ MG-20913 [M] | The Wonderful World of Make Believe | 1964 | 12.00 |
| ❑ MG-20942 [M] | This Is Love | 1964 | 12.00 |
| ❑ MG-20988 [M] | Johnny Mathis Ole | 1965 | 12.00 |
| ❑ MG-20991 [M] | Love Is Everything | 1965 | 12.00 |
| ❑ MG-21041 [M] | The Sweetheart Tree | 1965 | 12.00 |
| ❑ MG-21073 [M] | The Shadow of Your Smile | 1966 | 12.00 |
| ❑ MG-21093 [M] | So Nice | 1966 | 12.00 |
| ❑ MG-21107 [M] | Johnny Mathis Sings | 1967 | 15.00 |
| ❑ SR 60837 [S] | Sounds of Christmas | 1963 | 15.00 |
| ❑ SR-60890 [S] | Tender Is the Night | 1964 | 15.00 |
| ❑ SR-60913 [S] | The Wonderful World of Make Believe | 1964 | 15.00 |
| ❑ SR-60942 [S] | This Is Love | 1964 | 15.00 |
| ❑ SR-60988 [S] | Johnny Mathis Ole | 1965 | 15.00 |
| ❑ SR-60991 [S] | Love Is Everything | 1965 | 15.00 |
| ❑ SR-61041 [S] | The Sweetheart Tree | 1965 | 15.00 |
| ❑ SR-61073 [S] | The Shadow of Your Smile | 1966 | 15.00 |
| ❑ SR-61093 [S] | So Nice | 1966 | 15.00 |
| ❑ SR-61107 [S] | Johnny Mathis Sings | 1967 | 15.00 |

MOBILE FIDELITY

| Number | Title (A Side/B Side) | Yr | NM |
|---|---|---|---|
| ❑ 1-171 | Heavenly | 1985 | 25.00 |
| *—Audiophile vinyl* | | | |

READER'S DIGEST

| Number | Title (A Side/B Side) | Yr | NM |
|---|---|---|---|
| ❑ RB4-097 [(6)] | His Greatest Hits and Finest Performances | 198? | 25.00 |

TIME-LIFE

| Number | Title (A Side/B Side) | Yr | NM |
|---|---|---|---|
| ❑ SLGD-08 [(2)] | Legendary Singers: Johnny Mathis | 1985 | 15.00 |

## MATLOCK, MATTY

RCA VICTOR

| Number | Title (A Side/B Side) | Yr | NM |
|---|---|---|---|
| ❑ LPM-1413 [M] | Pete Kelly at Home | 1957 | 40.00 |

WARNER BROS.

| Number | Title (A Side/B Side) | Yr | NM |
|---|---|---|---|
| ❑ W 1280 [M] | Four Button Dixie | 1958 | 30.00 |
| ❑ WS 1280 [S] | Four Button Dixie | 1958 | 40.00 |

"X"

| Number | Title (A Side/B Side) | Yr | NM |
|---|---|---|---|
| ❑ LXA-3035 [10] | Sports Parade | 1955 | 50.00 |

## MATTEA, KATHY

MERCURY

| Number | Title (A Side/B Side) | Yr | NM |
|---|---|---|---|
| ❑ R 110791 | A Collection of Hits | 1990 | 20.00 |
| *—Only released on vinyl by BMG Direct Marketing* | | | |
| ❑ 818560-1 | Kathy Mattea | 1984 | 10.00 |
| ❑ 824308-1 | From My Heart | 1985 | 10.00 |
| ❑ 830405-1 | Walk the Way the Wind Blows | 1986 | 10.00 |
| ❑ 832793-1 | Untasted Honey | 1987 | 10.00 |
| ❑ 836950-1 | Willow in the Wind | 1989 | 12.00 |

## MATTHEWS, DAVE, BAND

RCA

| Number | Title (A Side/B Side) | Yr | NM |
|---|---|---|---|
| ❑ 67660 | Before These Crowded Streets | 1998 | 200.00 |

## MATTHEWS, ONZY

CAPITOL

| Number | Title (A Side/B Side) | Yr | NM |
|---|---|---|---|
| ❑ ST 2099 [S] | Blues with a Touch of Elegance | 1964 | 20.00 |

## MAUDS, THE

MERCURY

| Number | Title (A Side/B Side) | Yr | NM |
|---|---|---|---|
| ❑ MG-21135 [M] | The Mauds Hold On | 1967 | 20.00 |
| ❑ SR-61135 [S] | The Mauds Hold On | 1967 | 25.00 |

## MAULAWI

STRATA-EAST

| Number | Title (A Side/B Side) | Yr | NM |
|---|---|---|---|
| ❑ SES 104-74 | Maulawi | 1974 | 20.00 |

## MAURIAT, PAUL

FANTASY

| Number | Title (A Side/B Side) | Yr | NM |
|---|---|---|---|
| ❑ 8380 | Paris by Night | 1968 | 12.00 |
| ❑ 8389 | Joyeux Noel | 1968 | 12.00 |
| ❑ 8394 | Latin Style | 1969 | 12.00 |

MERCURY

| Number | Title (A Side/B Side) | Yr | NM |
|---|---|---|---|
| ❑ SRM-1-3746 | Overseas | 1978 | 10.00 |

MGM

| Number | Title (A Side/B Side) | Yr | NM |
|---|---|---|---|
| ❑ SE-4838 | Love Theme from "The Godfather" | 1972 | 10.00 |
| ❑ M3G-4999 | Have You Never Been Mellow | 1975 | 10.00 |

PHILIPS

| Number | Title (A Side/B Side) | Yr | NM |
|---|---|---|---|
| ❑ PHM 200197 [M] | Listen Too | 1965 | 12.00 |
| ❑ PHM 200215 [M] | Of Vodka and Caviar | 1966 | 12.00 |
| ❑ PHM 200226 [M] | More Mauriat | 1967 | 15.00 |
| ❑ PHM 200248 [M] | Blooming Hits | 1967 | 20.00 |
| ❑ PHM 200255 [M] | The Christmas Album | 1967 | 20.00 |
| ❑ PHS 600197 [S] | Listen Too | 1965 | 15.00 |
| ❑ PHS 600215 [S] | Of Vodka and Caviar | 1966 | 15.00 |
| ❑ PHS 600226 [S] | More Mauriat | 1967 | 15.00 |
| ❑ PHS 600248 [S] | Blooming Hits | 1967 | 15.00 |
| *—Original copies have no "blurb" for "Love Is Blue" on front cover* | | | |
| ❑ PHS 600248 [S] | Blooming Hits | 1968 | 12.00 |
| *—With blurb for "Love Is Blue" on front cover* | | | |
| ❑ PHS 600255 [S] | The Christmas Album | 1967 | 15.00 |
| ❑ PHS 600270 | Mauriat Magic | 1968 | 15.00 |
| ❑ PHS 600280 | Prevailing Airs | 1968 | 15.00 |
| ❑ PHS 600292 | Doing My Thing | 1969 | 15.00 |
| ❑ PHS 600299 | The Soul of Paul Mauriat | 1969 | 15.00 |
| ❑ PHS 600320 | L-O-V-E | 1969 | 15.00 |
| ❑ PHS 600337 | Midnight Cowboy/Let the Sunshine In | 1970 | 12.00 |
| ❑ PHS 600345 | Gone Is Love | 1970 | 12.00 |
| ❑ PHS 600352 | El Condor Pasa | 1970 | 12.00 |

VERVE

| Number | Title (A Side/B Side) | Yr | NM |
|---|---|---|---|
| ❑ V6-5087 | Theme from "A Summer Place" | 1973 | 10.00 |

## MAXIMILLIAN

ABC

| Number | Title (A Side/B Side) | Yr | NM |
|---|---|---|---|
| ❑ S-696 | Maximillian | 1969 | 40.00 |

## MAXTED, BILLY

BRUNSWICK

| Number | Title (A Side/B Side) | Yr | NM |
|---|---|---|---|
| ❑ BL 58052 [10] | Honky Tonk Piano | 1953 | 60.00 |

CADENCE

| Number | Title (A Side/B Side) | Yr | NM |
|---|---|---|---|
| ❑ CLP-1005 [M] | Billy Maxted Plays Hi-Fi Keyboard | 1955 | 40.00 |
| ❑ CLP-1012 [M] | Jazz at Nick's | 1955 | 40.00 |
| ❑ CLP-1013 [M] | Dixieland Manhattan Style | 1955 | 40.00 |
| ❑ CLP-3013 [M] | Dixieland Manhattan Style | 1958 | 30.00 |

SEECO

| Number | Title (A Side/B Side) | Yr | NM |
|---|---|---|---|
| ❑ CELP-438 [M] | Bourbon St. Billy and the Blues | 1960 | 20.00 |
| ❑ CELP-458 [M] | Art of Jazz | 1960 | 20.00 |
| ❑ CELP-4380 [S] | Bourbon St. Billy and the Blues | 1960 | 25.00 |
| ❑ CELP-4580 [S] | Art of Jazz | 1960 | 25.00 |

## MAXWELL, DIANE

CHALLENGE

| Number | Title (A Side/B Side) | Yr | NM |
|---|---|---|---|
| ❑ CHL-607 [M] | Almost Seventeen | 1959 | 40.00 |
| ❑ CHS-2501 [S] | Almost Seventeen | 1959 | 50.00 |

## MAY, BILLY

BAINBRIDGE

| Number | Title (A Side/B Side) | Yr | NM |
|---|---|---|---|
| ❑ ST 1001 | I Believe in You | 197? | 12.00 |

CAPITOL

| Number | Title (A Side/B Side) | Yr | NM |
|---|---|---|---|
| ❑ H 237 [10] | Join the Band | 1951 | 40.00 |
| ❑ L 329 [10] | Big Band Bash | 1952 | 40.00 |
| ❑ T 329 [M] | Big Band Bash | 195? | 25.00 |
| *—Turquoise label original* | | | |
| ❑ H 349 [10] | A Band Is Born! | 1952 | 40.00 |
| ❑ T 349 [M] | A Band Is Born! | 195? | 25.00 |
| *—Turquoise label original* | | | |
| ❑ H 374 [10] | Bacchanalia! | 1953 | 40.00 |
| ❑ T 374 [M] | Bacchanalia! | 195? | 30.00 |
| *—Turquoise label original* | | | |
| ❑ H 487 [10] | Billy May's Naughty Operetta! | 1953 | 40.00 |
| ❑ T 487 [M] | Billy May's Naughty Operetta! | 195? | 25.00 |
| *—Turquoise label original* | | | |
| ❑ M 562 [M] | Sorta-May | 197? | 10.00 |
| *—Reissue with new prefix* | | | |
| ❑ T 562 [M] | Sorta-May | 195? | 25.00 |
| *—Turqouise label original* | | | |
| ❑ T 677 [M] | Sorta-Dixie! | 195? | 25.00 |
| *—Turquoise label original* | | | |
| ❑ T 771 [M] | Billy May Plays for Fancy Dancin' | 1956 | 25.00 |
| *—Turquoise label original* | | | |
| ❑ STAO 924 [S] | Jimmie Lunceford in Hi-Fi: Authentic Re-Creations of the Lunceford Style | 1958 | 40.00 |
| *—Black colorband label, Capitol logo at left* | | | |
| ❑ TAO 924 [M] | Jimmie Lunceford in Hi-Fi: Authentic Re-Creations of the Lunceford Style | 1958 | 30.00 |
| *—Turquoise label original* | | | |
| ❑ ST 1043 [S] | Big Fat Brass | 1958 | 30.00 |
| *—Black colorband label, Capitol logo at left* | | | |
| ❑ T 1043 [M] | Big Fat Brass | 1958 | 20.00 |
| *—Black colorband label, Capitol logo at left* | | | |
| ❑ ST 1329 [S] | Cha Cha! | 1959 | 25.00 |
| *—Black colorband label, Capitol logo at left* | | | |
| ❑ T 1329 [M] | Cha Cha! | 1959 | 20.00 |
| *—Black colorband label, Capitol logo at left* | | | |
| ❑ T 1367 [M] | Cha Cha Mambos | 1959 | 20.00 |
| *—Black colorband label, logo at left* | | | |
| ❑ T 1377 [M] | Pow! | 1959 | 20.00 |
| *—Gold "The Star Line" label* | | | |
| ❑ ST 1417 [S] | The Girls and Boys on Broadway | 1960 | 20.00 |
| *—Black colorband label, Capitol logo at left* | | | |
| ❑ T 1417 [M] | The Girls and Boys on Broadway | 1960 | 15.00 |
| *—Black colorband label, Capitol logo at left* | | | |

John Mayall, *Thru the Years,* London 2PS 600/1, 1971, 2 records, $12.

| Number | Title (A Side/B Side) | Yr | NM |
|---|---|---|---|
| ❑ ST 1581 [S] | The Great Jimmie Lunceford: Authentic Re-Creations of the Lunceford Style by Billy May | 1961 | 20.00 |
| *—Gold "The Star Line" label* | | | |
| ❑ T 1581 [M] | The Great Jimmie Lunceford: Authentic Re-Creations of the Lunceford Style by Billy May | 1961 | 15.00 |
| *—Gold "The Star Line" label* | | | |
| ❑ ST 1709 [S] | The Sweetest Swingin' Sounds of No Strings | 196? | 20.00 |
| ❑ T 1709 [M] | The Sweetest Swingin' Sounds of No Strings | 196? | 15.00 |
| ❑ ST 1888 [S] | Bill's Bag | 1963 | 20.00 |
| ❑ T 1888 [M] | Bill's Bag | 1963 | 15.00 |
| ❑ ST 2560 [S] | Billy May Today | 1965 | 15.00 |
| ❑ T 2560 [M] | Billy May Today | 1965 | 12.00 |
| ❑ M 11885 [M] | Sorta-Dixie! | 197? | 10.00 |
| *—Reissue of Capitol 677* | | | |
| **CREATIVE WORLD** | | | |
| ❑ ST-1051 [M] | Sorta-May | 197? | 12.00 |
| ❑ ST-1054 | Sorta-Dixie! | 197? | 12.00 |
| **IMPERIAL** | | | |
| ❑ LP-9042 [M] | Fuzzy Pink Nightgown | 1957 | 50.00 |
| *—Movie soundtrack* | | | |
| **PAUSA** | | | |
| ❑ PR 9035 | A Band Is Born! | 198? | 10.00 |
| *—Reissue of Capitol T 349* | | | |
| **PICKWICK** | | | |
| ❑ PC- 3010 [M] | Hey It's May | 196? | 15.00 |
| ❑ SPC- 3010 [R] | Hey It's May | 196? | 8.00 |
| **STEREO SOUNDS** | | | |
| ❑ SA-12 | Music for Uptight Guys | 196? | 15.00 |
| **TIME** | | | |
| ❑ S-2064 [S] | Billy May and His Orchestra | 1962 | 20.00 |
| ❑ 52064 [M] | Billy May and His Orchestra | 1962 | 15.00 |
| **TIME-LIFE** | | | |
| ❑ STL-340 [(3)] | The Swing Era: 1930-1936 | 197? | 20.00 |
| *—Box set with hardcover book; re-creations of original big-band charts, with some contributions by the Glenn Gray Orchestra* | | | |
| ❑ STL-341 [(3)] | The Swing Era: 1936-1937 | 197? | 20.00 |
| *—Box set with hardcover book; re-creations of original big-band charts, with some contributions by the Glenn Gray Orchestra* | | | |
| ❑ STL-342 [(3)] | The Swing Era: 1937-1938 | 197? | 20.00 |
| *—Box set with hardcover book; re-creations of original big-band charts, with some contributions by the Glenn Gray Orchestra* | | | |
| ❑ STL-343 [(3)] | The Swing Era: 1938-1939 | 197? | 20.00 |
| *—Box set with hardcover book; re-creations of original big-band charts, with some contributions by the Glenn Gray Orchestra* | | | |
| ❑ STL-344 [(3)] | The Swing Era: 1939-1940 | 197? | 20.00 |
| *—Box set with hardcover book; re-creations of original big-band charts, with some contributions by the Glenn Gray Orchestra* | | | |
| ❑ STL-345 [(3)] | The Swing Era: 1940-1941 | 197? | 20.00 |
| *—Box set with hardcover book; re-creations of original big-band charts, with some contributions by the Glenn Gray Orchestra* | | | |
| ❑ STL-346 [(3)] | The Swing Era: 1941-1942 | 197? | 20.00 |
| *—Box set with hardcover book; re-creations of original big-band charts, with some contributions by the Glenn Gray Orchestra* | | | |
| ❑ STL-347 [(3)] | The Swing Era: 1942-1944 | 197? | 20.00 |
| *—Box set with hardcover book; re-creations of original big-band charts, with some contributions by the Glenn Gray Orchestra* | | | |
| ❑ STL-348 [(3)] | The Swing Era: 1944-1945 | 197? | 20.00 |
| *—Box set with hardcover book; re-creations of original big-band charts, with some contributions by the Glenn Gray Orchestra* | | | |
| ❑ STL-349 [(3)] | The Swing Era: The Postwar Years | 197? | 20.00 |
| *—Box set with hardcover book; re-creations of original big-band charts, with some contributions by the Glenn Gray Orchestra* | | | |
| ❑ STL-350 [(3)] | The Swing Era: Into the '50s | 197? | 20.00 |
| *—Box set with hardcover book; re-creations of original big-band charts, with some contributions by the Glenn Gray Orchestra* | | | |
| ❑ STL-351 [(3)] | The Swing Era: Encore! | 197? | 20.00 |
| *—Box set with hardcover book; re-creations of original big-band charts, with some contributions by the Glenn Gray Orchestra* | | | |
| ❑ STL-352 [(3)] | The Swing Era: Curtain Call | 197? | 20.00 |
| *—Box set with hardcover book; re-creations of original big-band charts, with some contributions by the Glenn Gray Orchestra* | | | |
| ❑ STL-353 [(3)] | The Swing Era: One More Time | 197? | 20.00 |
| *—Box set with hardcover book; re-creations of original big-band charts, with some contributions by the Glenn Gray Orchestra* | | | |

## MAY BLITZ

| Number | Title (A Side/B Side) | Yr | NM |
|---|---|---|---|
| **PARAMOUNT** | | | |
| ❑ PAS-5020 | May Blitz | 1970 | 20.00 |

## MAYALL, JOHN

| Number | Title (A Side/B Side) | Yr | NM |
|---|---|---|---|
| **ABC** | | | |
| ❑ ABCD-926 | Notice to Appear | 1976 | 10.00 |
| ❑ D-958 | A Banquet in Blues | 1976 | 10.00 |
| ❑ D-992 | Lots of People | 1977 | 10.00 |
| ❑ D-1039 | A Hard Core Package | 1977 | 10.00 |
| ❑ D-1086 | Last of the British Blues | 1978 | 10.00 |
| **ACCORD** | | | |
| ❑ SN-7209 | Roadshow Blues Band | 1982 | 10.00 |
| **BLUE THUMB** | | | |
| ❑ BTS-6019 | New Year, New Band, New Company | 1975 | 10.00 |
| **DECAL** | | | |
| ❑ LIK-1 | Some of My Best Friends Are Blues | 1986 | 10.00 |
| **DJM** | | | |
| ❑ 23 | The Bottom Line | 1979 | 10.00 |
| ❑ 29 | No More Interviews | 1979 | 10.00 |
| **GNP CRESCENDO** | | | |
| ❑ 2184 | Behind the Iron Curtain | 1986 | 10.00 |
| **ISLAND** | | | |
| ❑ 91005 | Chicago Line | 1988 | 10.00 |
| ❑ 842795-1 | A Sense of Place | 1990 | 12.00 |
| **LONDON** | | | |
| ❑ PS 492 [S] | Blues Breakers with Eric Clapton | 1966 | 40.00 |
| ❑ PS 502 [S] | A Hard Road | 1967 | 20.00 |
| ❑ PS 529 [S] | Crusade | 1967 | 20.00 |
| ❑ PS 534 | The Blues Alone | 1968 | 15.00 |
| ❑ PS 537 | Bare Wires | 1968 | 15.00 |
| ❑ PS 543 | Raw Blues | 1968 | 15.00 |
| ❑ PS 545 | Blues from Laurel Canyon | 1969 | 15.00 |
| ❑ PS 562 | Looking Back | 1969 | 15.00 |
| ❑ PS 570 | The Diary of a Band | 1970 | 12.00 |
| ❑ PS 589 | Live in Europe | 1971 | 12.00 |
| ❑ 2PS 600 [(2)] | Through the Years | 1971 | 12.00 |
| ❑ 2PS 618 [(2)] | Down the Line | 1973 | 10.00 |
| ❑ LL 3492 [M] | Blues Breakers with Eric Clapton | 1966 | 30.00 |
| ❑ LL 3502 [M] | A Hard Road | 1967 | 20.00 |
| ❑ LL 3529 [M] | Crusade | 1967 | 20.00 |
| ❑ LC-50009 | Blues Breakers with Eric Clapton | 1977 | 10.00 |
| *—Reissue of London PS 492* | | | |
| ❑ 800086-1 | Blues Breakers with Eric Clapton | 1983 | 8.00 |
| *—Reissue of London 50009* | | | |
| ❑ 820320-1 | Primal Solos | 1985 | 8.00 |
| ❑ 820331-1 | Looking Back | 1985 | 8.00 |
| *—Reissue of London PS 562* | | | |
| ❑ 820342-1 | Raw Blues | 1985 | 8.00 |
| *—Reissue of London PS 543* | | | |
| **MCA** | | | |
| ❑ 716 | Last of the British Blues | 1980 | 8.00 |
| *—Reissue of ABC 1086* | | | |
| ❑ 795 | Hard Core | 1980 | 8.00 |
| *—Reissue of ABC 1039* | | | |
| **MOBILE FIDELITY** | | | |
| ❑ 1-183 | Blues Breakers Featuring Eric Clapton | 1985 | 40.00 |
| *—Audiophile vinyl* | | | |
| ❑ 1-246 | The Blues Alone | 1996 | 30.00 |
| *—Audiophile vinyl* | | | |
| **POLYDOR** | | | |
| ❑ 25-3002 [(2)] | Back to the Roots | 1971 | 12.00 |
| ❑ PD2-3005 [(2)] | Ten Years Are Gone | 1973 | 12.00 |
| ❑ PD2-3006 [(2)] | The Best of John Mayall | 1973 | 12.00 |
| ❑ 24-4004 | The Turning Point | 1970 | 10.00 |
| ❑ 24-4010 | Empty Rooms | 1970 | 10.00 |
| ❑ 24-4022 | U.S.A. Union | 1970 | 10.00 |
| ❑ PD-5012 | Memories | 1971 | 10.00 |
| ❑ PD-5027 | Jazz-Blues Fusion | 1972 | 10.00 |
| ❑ PD-5036 | Moving On | 1972 | 10.00 |
| ❑ PD-6030 | The Latest Edition | 1974 | 12.00 |
| ❑ SKAO-93398 | U.S.A. Union | 1970 | 15.00 |
| *—Capitol Record Club edition* | | | |
| ❑ 823305-1 | The Turning Point | 1985 | 8.00 |
| *—Reissue of Polydor 24-4004* | | | |
| ❑ 837127-1 | Archive to the Eighties | 1988 | 8.00 |

## MAYER, NATHANIEL

| Number | Title (A Side/B Side) | Yr | NM |
|---|---|---|---|
| **FORTUNE** | | | |
| ❑ 8014 [M] | Goin' Back to the Village of Love | 196? | 60.00 |
| *—Yellow label* | | | |
| ❑ 8014 [M] | Goin' Back to the Village of Love | 196? | 150.00 |
| *—Purple label* | | | |
| ❑ 8014 [M] | Goin' Back to the Village of Love | 1964 | 300.00 |
| *—Light blue label* | | | |
| ❑ 8014 [M] | Goin' Back to the Village of Love | 197? | 15.00 |
| *—Bluish purple label, with much more flexible vinyl than earlier pressings* | | | |

## MAYFIELD, CURTIS Also see THE IMPRESSIONS.

| Number | Title (A Side/B Side) | Yr | NM |
|---|---|---|---|
| **BOARDWALK** | | | |
| ❑ NB1-33239 | Love Is the Place | 1981 | 10.00 |
| ❑ NB1-33256 | Honesty | 1982 | 10.00 |
| **CRC** | | | |
| ❑ 2001 | We Come in Peace with a Message of Love | 1985 | 12.00 |
| **CURTOM** | | | |
| ❑ CUR-2003 | There's No Place Like America Today | 198? | 8.00 |
| *—Reissue of 5001* | | | |
| ❑ CUR-2005 | Something to Believe In | 198? | 8.00 |
| *—Reissue of RSO 3077* | | | |
| ❑ CUR-2008 | Take It to the Street | 198? | 10.00 |

| Number | Title (A Side/B Side) | Yr | NM |
|---|---|---|---|
| ❑ CUR-2901 [(2)] | Live in Europe | 198? | 12.00 |
| ❑ CUR-2902 [(2)] | Greatest Hits of All Time (Classic Collection) | 198? | 12.00 |
| ❑ CU 5001 | There's No Place Like America Today | 1975 | 12.00 |
| ❑ CU 5007 | Give, Get, Take and Have | 1976 | 12.00 |
| ❑ CU 5013 | Never Say You Can't Survive | 1977 | 12.00 |
| ❑ CUK 5022 | Do It All Night | 1978 | 12.00 |
| ❑ CRS-8005 | Curtis | 1970 | 15.00 |
| ❑ CRS-8008 [(2)] | Curtis/Live! | 1971 | 20.00 |
| ❑ CRS-8009 | Roots | 1971 | 15.00 |
| ❑ CRS-8014 | Superfly | 1972 | 20.00 |
| ❑ CRS-8015 | Back to the World | 1973 | 15.00 |
| ❑ CRS-8018 | Curtis in Chicago | 1973 | 15.00 |
| ❑ CRS-8601 | Sweet Exorcist | 1974 | 12.00 |
| ❑ CRS-8604 | Got to Find a Way | 1974 | 12.00 |
| RSO | | | |
| ❑ RS-1-3053 | Heartbeat | 1979 | 10.00 |
| ❑ RS-1-3077 | Something to Believe In | 1980 | 10.00 |
| **MAYFIELD, PERCY** | | | |
| BRUNSWICK | | | |
| ❑ BL 754145 | Walking on a Tightrope | 1968 | 20.00 |
| INTERMEDIA | | | |
| ❑ QS-5010 | Please Send Me Someone to Love | 198? | 10.00 |
| RCA VICTOR | | | |
| ❑ LSP-4269 | Percy Mayfield Sings Percy Mayfield | 1970 | 15.00 |
| ❑ LSP-4444 | Weakness Is a Thing Called Man | 1970 | 15.00 |
| ❑ LSP-4558 | Blues And Then Some | 1971 | 15.00 |
| SPECIALTY | | | |
| ❑ SPS-2126 | The Best of Percy Mayfield | 1970 | 20.00 |
| ❑ SP-7001 | Poet of the Blues | 1990 | 15.00 |
| TANGERINE | | | |
| ❑ TRC-1505 [M] | My Jug and I | 1966 | 20.00 |
| ❑ TRCS-1505 [S] | My Jug and I | 1966 | 25.00 |
| ❑ TRC-1510 [M] | Bought Blues | 1967 | 20.00 |
| ❑ TRCS-1510 [S] | Bought Blues | 1967 | 25.00 |
| **MAYPOLE** | | | |
| COLOSSUS | | | |
| ❑ CS-1007 | Maypole | 1971 | 60.00 |
| **MAZE** | | | |
| MTA | | | |
| ❑ 5012 | Armageddon | 1969 | 100.00 |
| **MAZZY STAR** | | | |
| CAPITOL | | | |
| ❑ C1-27224 | Among My Swan | 1996 | 80.00 |
| ROUGH TRADE | | | |
| ❑ RUS 771 | She Hangs Brightly | 1990 | 100.00 |
| **MC5** | | | |
| ALIVE | | | |
| ❑ 0005 [10] | Power Trip | 1994 | 6.00 |
| ❑ 0008 [10] | Ice Pick Slim/Mad Like Eldridge Cleaver | 1994 | 6.00 |
| ATLANTIC | | | |
| ❑ SD 8247 | Back in the USA | 1970 | 50.00 |
| ❑ SD 8285 | High Time | 1971 | 50.00 |
| ELEKTRA | | | |
| ❑ EKS-74042 | Kick Out the Jams | 1969 | 20.00 |
| *—All other editions* | | | |
| ❑ EKS-74042 | Kick Out the Jams | 1969 | 50.00 |
| *—Gatefold cover with John Sinclair liner notes in center spread; brownish label* | | | |
| SUNDAZED | | | |
| ❑ LP 5092 | Kick Out the Jams | 2001 | 15.00 |
| *—Reissue of original Elektra album, complete with uncensored liner notes* | | | |
| ❑ LP 5093 | Back in the USA | 2002 | 12.00 |
| *—Reissue on 180-gram vinyl* | | | |
| ❑ LP 5094 | High Time | 2002 | 12.00 |
| *—Reissue on 180-gram vinyl* | | | |
| TOTAL ENERGY | | | |
| ❑ 2001 [10] | The American Ruse | 1994 | 6.00 |
| **MCAULIFFE, LEON** | | | |
| ABC-PARAMOUNT | | | |
| ❑ ABC-394 [M] | Cozy Inn | 1961 | 40.00 |
| ❑ ABCS-394 [S] | Cozy Inn | 1961 | 60.00 |
| CAPITOL | | | |
| ❑ ST 2016 [S] | The Dancin'est Band Around | 1964 | 40.00 |
| ❑ T 2016 [M] | The Dancin'est Band Around | 1964 | 30.00 |
| ❑ ST 2148 [S] | Everybody Dance! Everybody Swing! | 1964 | 40.00 |
| ❑ T 2148 [M] | Everybody Dance! Everybody Swing! | 1964 | 30.00 |

MC5, *Kick Out the Jams,* Elektra EKS-74042, 1969, gatefold cover with John Sinclair liner notes, $50.

| Number | Title (A Side/B Side) | Yr | NM |
|---|---|---|---|
| CIMARRON | | | |
| ❑ CLP-2002 [M] | The Swingin' Western Strings of Leon McAuliff | 1960 | 50.00 |
| DOT | | | |
| ❑ DLP-3139 [M] | Take Off | 1958 | 60.00 |
| ❑ DLP-3689 [M] | Golden Country Hits | 1966 | 40.00 |
| ❑ DLP-25689 [R] | Golden Country Hits | 1966 | 25.00 |
| SESAC | | | |
| ❑ (# unknown) [M] | Just a Minute | 1957 | 100.00 |
| ❑ 1601 [M] | Points West | 1957 | 100.00 |
| STARDAY | | | |
| ❑ SLP-171 [M] | Mr. Western Swing | 1962 | 50.00 |
| ❑ SLP-280 [M] | The Swingin' West with Leon McAuliff | 1964 | 40.00 |
| ❑ SLP-309 [M] | The Swingin' Western Strings of Leon McAuliff | 1964 | 40.00 |
| **MCBEE, CECIL** | | | |
| STRATA-EAST | | | |
| ❑ SES-7417 | Mutima | 1975 | 25.00 |
| **MCBROWNE, LENNY** | | | |
| PACIFIC JAZZ | | | |
| ❑ PJ-1 [M] | The Four Souls | 1960 | 30.00 |
| ❑ ST-1 [S] | The Four Souls | 1960 | 40.00 |
| RIVERSIDE | | | |
| ❑ RLP-346 [M] | Eastern Lights | 1960 | 30.00 |
| ❑ RS-9346 [S] | Eastern Lights | 1960 | 40.00 |
| **MCCALL, DARRELL** | | | |
| COLUMBIA | | | |
| ❑ KC 34718 | Lily Dale | 1977 | 12.00 |
| WAYSIDE | | | |
| ❑ 1030 | Meet Darrell McCall | 1969 | 20.00 |
| **MCCALL, MARY ANN** | | | |
| CORAL | | | |
| ❑ CRL 57276 [M] | Melancholy Baby | 1959 | 60.00 |
| ❑ CRL 757276 [S] | Melancholy Baby | 1959 | 80.00 |
| DISCOVERY | | | |
| ❑ 3011 [10] | Mary Ann McCall Sings | 1950 | 300.00 |
| JUBILEE | | | |
| ❑ JLP-1078 [M] | Detour to the Moon | 1958 | 60.00 |

| Number | Title (A Side/B Side) | Yr | NM |
|---|---|---|---|
| REGENT | | | |
| ❑ MG-6040 [M] | Easy Living | 1957 | 80.00 |
| **MCCALL, TOUSSAINT** | | | |
| RONN | | | |
| ❑ 7527 [M] | Nothing Can Take the Place of You | 1967 | 30.00 |
| ❑ 7527S [S] | Nothing Can Take the Place of You | 1967 | 40.00 |
| **MCCANN, LES** | | | |
| LIMELIGHT | | | |
| ❑ LM-82043 [M] | Bucket O' Grease | 1967 | 20.00 |
| ❑ LM-82046 [M] | Live at the Bohemian Caverns, Washington, D.C. | 1967 | 20.00 |
| ❑ LS-86016 [S] | But Not Really | 1965 | 20.00 |
| ❑ LS-86025 [S] | Poo Boo | 1965 | 20.00 |
| ❑ LS-86031 [S] | Beaux J. Pooboo | 1966 | 20.00 |
| ❑ LS-86036 [S] | Live at Shelly's Manne-Hole | 1966 | 20.00 |
| ❑ LS-86041 [S] | Les McCann Plays the Hits | 1966 | 20.00 |
| PACIFIC JAZZ | | | |
| ❑ PJ-2 [M] | The Truth | 1960 | 25.00 |
| ❑ ST-2 [S] | The Truth | 1960 | 30.00 |
| ❑ PJ-7 [M] | The Shout | 1960 | 25.00 |
| ❑ ST-7 [S] | The Shout | 1960 | 30.00 |
| ❑ PJ-16 [M] | Les McCann in San Francisco | 1961 | 25.00 |
| ❑ ST-16 [S] | Les McCann in San Francisco | 1961 | 30.00 |
| ❑ PJ-25 [M] | Pretty Lady | 1961 | 20.00 |
| ❑ ST-25 [S] | Pretty Lady | 1961 | 25.00 |
| ❑ PJ-31 [M] | Les McCann Sings | 1961 | 20.00 |
| ❑ ST-31 [S] | Les McCann Sings | 1961 | 25.00 |
| ❑ PJ-45 [M] | Les McCann in New York | 1962 | 20.00 |
| ❑ ST-45 [S] | Les McCann in New York | 1962 | 25.00 |
| ❑ PJ-56 [M] | On Time | 1962 | 20.00 |
| *—Black vinyl* | | | |
| ❑ PJ-56 [M] | On Time | 1962 | 40.00 |
| *—Yellow vinyl* | | | |
| ❑ ST-56 [S] | On Time | 1962 | 25.00 |
| *—Black vinyl* | | | |
| ❑ ST-56 [S] | On Time | 1962 | 50.00 |
| *—Yellow vinyl* | | | |
| ❑ ST-63 [S] | Shampoo | 1962 | 20.00 |
| ❑ ST-69 [S] | The Gospel Truth | 1963 | 20.00 |
| ❑ ST-78 [S] | Soul Hits | 1963 | 20.00 |
| ❑ ST-81 [S] | Jazz Waltz | 1964 | 20.00 |
| ❑ ST-84 [S] | McCanna | 1964 | 20.00 |

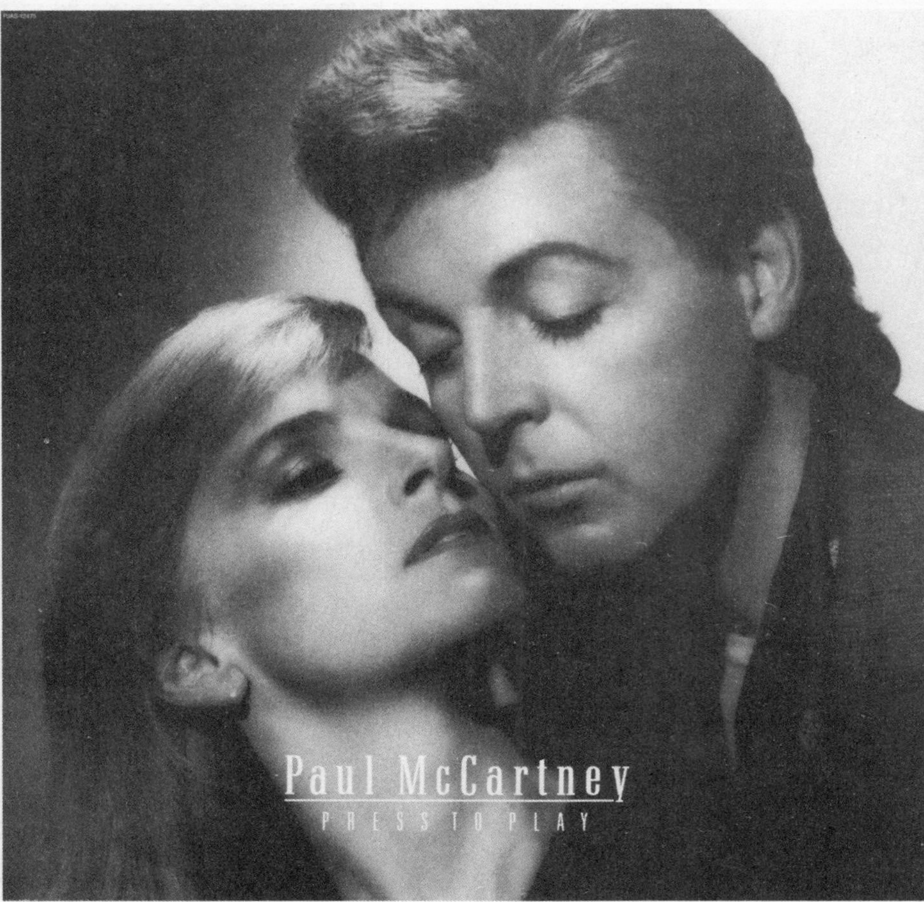


Paul McCartney, *Press to Play,* Capitol PJAS-12475, 1986, $12.

| Number | Title (A Side/B Side) | Yr | NM |
|---|---|---|---|
| ❑ ST-91 [S] | McCann/Wilson | 1965 | 20.00 |
| *—With Gerald Wilson* | | | |
| ❑ ST-20097 [S] | Spanish Onions | 1966 | 20.00 |
| ❑ ST-20107 [S] | A Bag of Gold | 1966 | 20.00 |

**MCCARTNEY, PAUL** Includes Thrillington and Wings. Also see THE BEATLES.

APPLE

| Number | Title (A Side/B Side) | Yr | NM |
|---|---|---|---|
| ❑ SMAS-3363 | McCartney | 197? | 20.00 |
| *—New prefix on label* | | | |
| ❑ SMAS-3363 | McCartney | 1975 | 100.00 |
| *—With "All Rights Reserved" on label* | | | |
| ❑ STAO-3363 | McCartney | 1970 | 20.00 |
| *—Only "McCartney" on label; back cover does NOT say "An Abkco managed company"* | | | |
| ❑ STAO-3363 | McCartney | 1970 | 25.00 |
| *—"McCartney" and "Paul McCartney" on separate lines on label; New York address on back cover* | | | |
| ❑ STAO-3363 | McCartney | 1970 | 25.00 |
| *—Only "McCartney" on label; back cover says "An Abkco managed company"* | | | |
| ❑ STAO-3363 | McCartney | 1970 | 30.00 |
| *—"McCartney" and "Paul McCartney" on separate lines on label; California addess on back cover* | | | |
| ❑ STAO-3363 | McCartney | 1970 | 80.00 |
| *—Apple label with small Capitol logo on B-side* | | | |
| ❑ MAS-3375 [M] | Ram | 1971 | 4000. |
| *—Credited to "Paul and Linda McCartney"; mono record in stereo cover for radio station use only* | | | |
| ❑ SMAS-3375 | Ram | 1971 | 15.00 |
| *—Credited to "Paul and Linda McCartney"; unsliced apple on one label, sliced apple on other* | | | |
| ❑ SMAS-3375 | Ram | 1971 | 30.00 |
| *—Credited to "Paul and Linda McCartney"; unsliced apple on both labels* | | | |
| ❑ SMAS-3375 | Ram | 1971 | 50.00 |
| *—Credited to "Paul and Linda McCartney"; Apple label with small Capitol logo on B-side* | | | |
| ❑ SMAS-3375 | Ram | 1975 | 100.00 |
| *—Credited to "Paul and Linda McCartney"; with "All Rights Reserved" on label* | | | |
| ❑ SW-3386 | Wild Life | 1971 | 15.00 |
| *—Credited to "Wings"* | | | |
| ❑ SMAL-3409 | Red Rose Speedway | 1973 | 20.00 |
| *—Credited to "Paul McCartney and Wings"; with bound-in booklet* | | | |
| ❑ SO-3415 | Band on the Run | 1973 | 20.00 |
| *—Credited to "Paul McCartney and Wings"; with photo innersleeve and poster* | | | |
| ❑ SPRO-6210 [DJ] | Brung to Ewe By | 1971 | 400.00 |
| *—Promo-only radio spots for "Ram"; counterfeits have uneven spacing between tracks* | | | |

CAPITOL

| Number | Title (A Side/B Side) | Yr | NM |
|---|---|---|---|
| ❑ SMAS-3363 | McCartney | 1976 | 20.00 |
| *—Black label, "Manufactured by MPL Communications Inc" at top* | | | |
| ❑ SMAS-3363 | McCartney | 1976 | 25.00 |
| *—Black label, "Manufactured by McCartney Music Inc" at top* | | | |
| ❑ SMAS-3375 | Ram | 197? | 20.00 |
| *—Credited to "Paul and Linda McCartney"; black label, "Manufactured by MPL Communications Inc" at top* | | | |
| ❑ SMAS-3375 | Ram | 197? | 40.00 |
| *—Credited to "Paul and Linda McCartney"; black label, "Manufactured by Capitol RecordsÔ" on label* | | | |
| ❑ SMAS-3375 | Ram | 1976 | 30.00 |
| *—Credited to "Paul and Linda McCartney"; black label, "Manufactured by McCartney Music Inc" at top* | | | |
| ❑ SW-3386 | Wild Life | 197? | 20.00 |
| *—Credited to "Wings"; black label, "Manufactured by MPL Communications Inc" at top* | | | |
| ❑ SW-3386 | Wild Life | 1976 | 30.00 |
| *—Credited to "Wings"; black label, "Manufactured by McCartney Music Inc" at top* | | | |
| ❑ SMAL-3409 | Red Rose Speedway | 197? | 25.00 |
| *—Credited to "Paul McCartney and Wings"; black label, "Manufactured by MPL Communications Inc" at top* | | | |
| ❑ SMAL-3409 | Red Rose Speedway | 1976 | 30.00 |
| *—Credited to "Paul McCartney and Wings"; black label, "Manufactured by McCartney Music Inc" at top* | | | |
| ❑ SO-3415 | Band on the Run | 197? | 20.00 |
| *—Credited to "Paul McCartney and Wings"; black label, "Maunfactured by MPL Communications Inc." at top* | | | |
| ❑ SO-3415 | Band on the Run | 197? | 50.00 |
| *—Credited to "Paul McCartney and Wings"; black label, "Manufactured by Capitol Records..."* | | | |
| ❑ SO-3415 | Band on the Run | 1975 | 20.00 |
| *—Credited to "Paul McCartney and Wings"; custom label with MPL logo* | | | |
| ❑ SMAS-11419 | Venus and Mars | 1975 | 15.00 |
| *—Credited to "Wings"; with two posters and two stickers* | | | |
| ❑ SW-11525 | Wings at the Speed of Sound | 1976 | 10.00 |
| *—Credited to "Wings"; custom label* | | | |
| ❑ SW-11525 [DJ] | Wings at the Speed of Sound | 1976 | 300.00 |
| *—Credited to "Wings"; white label advance promo* | | | |
| ❑ SWCO-11593 [(3)] | Wings Over America | 1976 | 25.00 |
| *—Credited to "Wings"; custom labels with poster* | | | |
| ❑ ST-11642 | Thrillington | 1977 | 100.00 |
| *—Credited to "Percy 'Thrills' Thrillington"; instrumental versions of songs from Ram LP* | | | |
| ❑ SW-11777 | London Town | 1978 | 15.00 |
| *—Credited to "Wings"; custom label with poster* | | | |
| ❑ SEAX-11901 [PD] | Band on the Run | 1978 | 40.00 |
| *—Credited to "Paul McCartney and Wings"; picture disc* | | | |
| ❑ SOO-11905 | Wings Greatest | 1978 | 15.00 |
| *—Credited to "Wings"; custom label with poster* | | | |
| ❑ SOO-11905 [DJ] | Wings Greatest | 1978 | 400.00 |
| *—Credited to "Wings"; white label advance promo/test pressing* | | | |
| ❑ PJAS-12475 | Press to Play | 1986 | 12.00 |
| ❑ CLW-48287 [(2)] | All the Best! | 1987 | 20.00 |
| ❑ C1-56500 | Flaming Pie | 1997 | 30.00 |
| ❑ C1-91653 | Flowers in the Dirt | 1989 | 20.00 |
| ❑ C1-94778 [(3)] | Tripping the Live Fantastic | 1990 | 60.00 |
| ❑ 99176 [(2)] | Band on the Run | 1999 | 40.00 |
| *—Limited-edition 180-gram reissue with original LP on one record and interviews and "The Making of.." on the second* | | | |
| ❑ C1-595379 | Tripping the Live Fantastic — Highlights! | 1990 | 25.00 |
| *—Released on vinyl only through Columbia House; with Canada address on back cover, this was sold in the U.S. by Columbia House* | | | |
| ❑ C1-595379 | Tripping the Live Fantastic — Highlights! | 1990 | 25.00 |
| *—Released on vinyl only through Columbia House; with U.S. address on back cover* | | | |

COLUMBIA

| Number | Title (A Side/B Side) | Yr | NM |
|---|---|---|---|
| ❑ A2S 821 [(2)DJ] | The McCartney Interview | 1980 | 40.00 |
| *—Promo-only set; one LP is the entire interview, the other is banded for airplay; white labels with black print; counterfeits have blank white labels* | | | |
| ❑ FC 36057 | Back to the Egg | 1979 | 10.00 |
| *—Credited to "Wings"; custom label* | | | |
| ❑ FC 36057 [DJ] | Back to the Egg | 1979 | 40.00 |
| *—Credited to "Wings"; "Demonstration -- Not for Sale" on custom label* | | | |
| ❑ PC 36057 | Back to the Egg | 1984 | 30.00 |
| *—Credited to "Wings"; "PC" cover with "FC" label* | | | |
| ❑ PC 36057 | Back to the Egg | 1984 | 40.00 |
| *—Credited to "Wings"; "PC" cover with "PC" label* | | | |
| ❑ JC 36478 | McCartney | 1979 | 15.00 |
| ❑ PC 36478 | McCartney | 1984 | 15.00 |
| *—Budget-line reissue* | | | |
| ❑ JC 36479 | Ram | 1980 | 15.00 |
| *—Credited to "Paul and Linda McCartney"* | | | |
| ❑ PC 36479 | Ram | 1984 | 15.00 |
| *—Credited to "Paul and Linda McCartney"; budget-line reissue* | | | |
| ❑ JC 36480 | Wild Life | 1980 | 15.00 |
| *—Credited to "Wings"* | | | |
| ❑ PC 36480 | Wild Life | 1982 | 15.00 |
| *—Credited to "Wings"; budget-line reissue* | | | |
| ❑ JC 36481 | Red Rose Speedway | 1980 | 15.00 |
| *—Credited to "Paul McCartney and Wings"; flat or glossy cover* | | | |
| ❑ PC 36481 | Red Rose Speedway | 198? | 15.00 |
| *—Credited to "Paul McCartney and Wings"; not issued with booklet* | | | |
| ❑ JC 36482 | Band on the Run | 198? | 100.00 |
| *—Credited to "Paul McCartney and Wings"; white "MPL" logo on lower left front cover* | | | |
| ❑ JC 36482 | Band on the Run | 1980 | 15.00 |
| *—Credited to "Paul McCartney and Wings"; custom label* | | | |
| ❑ PC 36482 | Band on the Run | 198? | 20.00 |
| *—Credited to "Paul McCartney and Wings"; "PC" cover with "JC" label* | | | |
| ❑ PC 36482 | Band on the Run | 198? | 30.00 |
| *—Credited to "Paul McCartney and Wings"; "PC" cover with "PC" label* | | | |
| ❑ FC 36511 | McCartney II | 1980 | 10.00 |
| *—Add 80% if bonus single of "Coming Up (Live at Glasgow)" (AE7 1204) is with package* | | | |
| ❑ FC 36511 [DJ] | McCartney II | 1980 | 30.00 |
| *—White label promo* | | | |
| ❑ PC 36511 | McCartney II | 1984 | 25.00 |
| *—"PC" cover with "FC" label* | | | |
| ❑ PC 36511 | McCartney II | 1984 | 100.00 |
| *—"PC" cover with "PC" label* | | | |
| ❑ JC 36801 | Venus and Mars | 1980 | 15.00 |
| *—Credited to "Wings"; with one poster and two stickers* | | | |
| ❑ PC 36801 | Venus and Mars | 1982 | 15.00 |
| *—Credited to "Wings"; budget-line reissue, not issued with inserts* | | | |
| ❑ PC 36987 | The McCartney Interview | 1980 | 12.00 |
| *—Stock release of interview originally intended for promotional use only* | | | |
| ❑ FC 37409 | Wings at the Speed of Sound | 1981 | 15.00 |
| *—Credited to "Wings"; custom label* | | | |
| ❑ PC 37409 | Wings at the Speed of Sound | 1982 | 15.00 |
| *—Credited to "Wings"; regular Columbia label, budget-line reissue* | | | |
| ❑ PC 37462 | Tug of War | 1984 | 30.00 |
| *—Custom label; "PC" cover with "TC" label* | | | |
| ❑ PC 37462 | Tug of War | 1984 | 100.00 |
| *—Regular Columbia label; "PC" cover with "PC" label* | | | |
| ❑ TC 37462 | Tug of War | 1982 | 10.00 |
| ❑ C3X 37990 [(3)] | Wings Over America | 1982 | 50.00 |
| *—Credited to "Wings"; custom labels, no poster* | | | |
| ❑ QC 39149 | Pipes of Peace | 1983 | 12.00 |
| ❑ SC 39613 | Give My Regards to Broad Street | 1984 | 15.00 |
| ❑ HC 46382 | Band on the Run | 1981 | 50.00 |
| *—Credited to "Paul McCartney and Wings"; half-speed mastered edition* | | | |

| Number | Title (A Side/B Side) | Yr | NM |
|---|---|---|---|
| **MPL/PARLOPHONE** | | | |
| ❑ 96413 | Unplugged (The Official Bootleg) | 1991 | 75.00 |
| *—No U.S. pressings; "American" copies were U.K. imports with liner notes in Spanish!* | | | |
| **NATIONAL FEATURES CORP.** | | | |
| ❑ 2955/6 | Band on the Run Radio Interview Special | 1973 | 1500. |
| *—Promo-only interview disc* | | | |

### MCCLINTON, DELBERT

| Number | Title (A Side/B Side) | Yr | NM |
|---|---|---|---|
| **ABC** | | | |
| ❑ ABCD-907 | Victim of Life's Circumstances | 1975 | 20.00 |
| ❑ ABCD-959 | Genuine Cowhide | 1976 | 20.00 |
| ❑ AB-991 | Love Rustler | 1977 | 20.00 |
| **ACCORD** | | | |
| ❑ SN-7145 | Wake Up Baby | 198? | 10.00 |
| **ALLIGATOR** | | | |
| ❑ AL-3902 | Honky Tonkin' (I Done Me Some) | 1986 | 10.00 |
| ❑ AL-4773 | Live from Austin | 1989 | 12.00 |
| **CAPITOL/MSS** | | | |
| ❑ ST-12115 | The Jealous Kind | 1980 | 12.00 |
| ❑ ST-12188 | Playin' from the Heart | 1981 | 12.00 |
| **CAPRICORN** | | | |
| ❑ CPN-0201 | Second Wind | 1978 | 20.00 |
| ❑ CPN-0223 | Keeper of the Flame | 1979 | 15.00 |
| **INTERMEDIA** | | | |
| ❑ QS-5029 | Feelin' Alright! | 198? | 10.00 |
| **MCA** | | | |
| ❑ 5197 | The Best of Delbert McClinton | 1981 | 10.00 |

### MCCLINTON, O.B.

| Number | Title (A Side/B Side) | Yr | NM |
|---|---|---|---|
| **ENTERPRISE** | | | |
| ❑ ENS-1023 | Country | 1972 | 30.00 |
| ❑ ENS-1029 | Obie from Senatobie | 1973 | 30.00 |
| ❑ ENS-1037 | Live at Randy's Rodeo | 1973 | 30.00 |
| ❑ ENS-7506 | If You Loved Her That Way | 1974 | 25.00 |
| **EPIC** | | | |
| ❑ FE 40674 | The Only One | 1987 | 10.00 |
| **HOMETOWN** | | | |
| ❑ 104 | Album No. 1 | 198? | 12.00 |

### MCCORMICK BROTHERS, THE

| Number | Title (A Side/B Side) | Yr | NM |
|---|---|---|---|
| **HICKORY** | | | |
| ❑ LP-102 [M] | Songs for Home Folks | 1961 | 80.00 |
| ❑ LP-108 [M] | Authentic Bluegrass Hits | 1962 | 60.00 |
| **METROMEDIA** | | | |
| ❑ MM-1019 | Grass Meets Brass | 1969 | 20.00 |

### MCCOY, CLYDE

| Number | Title (A Side/B Side) | Yr | NM |
|---|---|---|---|
| **CAPITOL** | | | |
| ❑ H 311 [10] | Sugar Blues | 195? | 100.00 |
| ❑ T 311 [M] | Sugar Blues | 1955 | 50.00 |
| *—Turquoise or gray label* | | | |
| ❑ T 311 [M] | Sugar Blues | 1959 | 40.00 |
| *—Black colorband label, logo at left* | | | |
| ❑ T 311 [M] | Sugar Blues | 1963 | 25.00 |
| *—Black colorband label, logo at top* | | | |
| **MERCURY** | | | |
| ❑ MG-20110 [M] | The Blues | 195? | 40.00 |
| ❑ SR-60677 [S] | Really McCoy | 1961 | 20.00 |
| ❑ SR-60730 [S] | Blue Prelude | 1962 | 20.00 |
| **TOP RANK** | | | |
| ❑ RM-350 [M] | Dixieland's Best Friend | 1961 | 30.00 |
| ❑ RS-650 [S] | Dixieland's Best Friend | 1961 | 40.00 |

### MCCOY, FREDDIE

| Number | Title (A Side/B Side) | Yr | NM |
|---|---|---|---|
| **COBBLESTONE** | | | |
| ❑ 9004 | Gimme Some | 1972 | 20.00 |
| **PRESTIGE** | | | |
| ❑ PRLP-7395 [M] | Lonely Avenue | 1965 | 20.00 |
| ❑ PRST-7395 [S] | Lonely Avenue | 1965 | 25.00 |
| ❑ PRLP-7444 [M] | Spider Man | 1966 | 20.00 |
| ❑ PRST-7444 [S] | Spider Man | 1966 | 25.00 |
| ❑ PRLP-7470 [M] | Funk Drops | 1967 | 25.00 |
| ❑ PRST-7470 [S] | Funk Drops | 1967 | 25.00 |
| ❑ PRLP-7487 [M] | Peas 'N' Rice | 1967 | 30.00 |
| ❑ PRST-7487 [S] | Peas 'N' Rice | 1967 | 25.00 |
| ❑ PRST-7542 | Beans and Greens | 1968 | 25.00 |
| ❑ PRST-7561 | Soul Yogi | 1968 | 25.00 |
| ❑ PRST-7582 | Listen Here | 1968 | 25.00 |
| ❑ PRST-7706 | The Best of Freddie McCoy | 1969 | 20.00 |

### MCCOY, VAN

| Number | Title (A Side/B Side) | Yr | NM |
|---|---|---|---|
| **AVCO** | | | |
| ❑ AV-69002 | Love Is the Answer | 1974 | 10.00 |
| ❑ AV-69006 | Disco Baby | 1975 | 10.00 |
| ❑ AV-69009 | The Disco Kid | 1975 | 10.00 |
| **BUDDAH** | | | |
| ❑ BDS-5103 | Soul Improvisations | 1971 | 15.00 |
| ❑ BDS-5648 | From Disco to Love | 1975 | 10.00 |
| *—Retitled reissue of 5103* | | | |
| **COLUMBIA** | | | |
| ❑ CL 2497 [M] | Night Time Is the Lonely Time | 1966 | 20.00 |
| ❑ CS 9297 [S] | Night Time Is the Lonely Time | 1966 | 25.00 |
| **H&L** | | | |
| ❑ HL-69002 | Love Is the Answer | 1976 | 8.00 |
| *—Reissue of Avco 69002* | | | |
| ❑ HL-69006 | Disco Baby | 1976 | 8.00 |
| *—Reissue of Avco 69006* | | | |
| ❑ HL-69009 | The Disco Kid | 1976 | 8.00 |
| *—Reissue of Avco 69009* | | | |
| ❑ HL-69012 | The Real McCoy | 1976 | 10.00 |
| ❑ HL-69014 | Rhythms of the World | 1976 | 10.00 |
| ❑ HL-69016 | The Hustle and Best of Van McCoy | 1976 | 10.00 |
| ❑ HL-69022 | Van McCoy and His Magnificent Movie Machine | 1977 | 10.00 |
| **MCA** | | | |
| ❑ 3036 | My Favorite Fantasy | 1978 | 10.00 |
| ❑ 3054 | A Woman Called Moses | 1978 | 10.00 |
| ❑ 3071 | Lovely Dancer | 1979 | 10.00 |

### MCCOYS, THE

| Number | Title (A Side/B Side) | Yr | NM |
|---|---|---|---|
| **BANG** | | | |
| ❑ BLP-212 [M] | Hang On Sloopy | 1965 | 30.00 |
| ❑ BLPS-212 [S] | Hang On Sloopy | 1965 | 40.00 |
| ❑ BLP-213 [M] | You Make Me Feel So Good | 1966 | 30.00 |
| ❑ BLPS-213 [S] | You Make Me Feel So Good | 1966 | 40.00 |
| **MERCURY** | | | |
| ❑ SR-61163 | Infinite McCoys | 1968 | 25.00 |
| ❑ SR-61207 | Human Ball | 1969 | 25.00 |

### MCCRACKLIN, JIMMY

| Number | Title (A Side/B Side) | Yr | NM |
|---|---|---|---|
| **CHESS** | | | |
| ❑ LP-1464 [M] | Jimmy McCracklin Sings | 1961 | 120.00 |
| **CROWN** | | | |
| ❑ CLP-5244 [M] | Twist with Jimmy McCracklin | 196? | 15.00 |
| *—Black label, multi-color "Crown"* | | | |
| ❑ CLP-5244 [M] | Twist with Jimmy McCracklin | 1962 | 25.00 |
| *—Gray label* | | | |
| ❑ CLP-5244 [M] | Twist with Jimmy McCracklin | 1962 | 50.00 |
| *—Black label, silver "Crown"* | | | |
| **EVEJIM** | | | |
| ❑ EJR-4013 | Same Lovin' | 198? | 12.00 |
| **IMPERIAL** | | | |
| ❑ LP-9219 [M] | I Just Gotta Know | 1964 | 25.00 |
| ❑ LP-9285 [M] | Every Night, Every Day | 1965 | 25.00 |
| ❑ LP-9297 [M] | Think | 1965 | 25.00 |
| ❑ LP-9306 [M] | My Answer | 1966 | 25.00 |
| ❑ LP-9316 [M] | The New Soul of Jimmy McCracklin | 1966 | 25.00 |
| ❑ LP-12219 [S] | I Just Gotta Know | 1964 | 30.00 |
| ❑ LP-12285 [S] | Every Night, Every Day | 1965 | 30.00 |
| ❑ LP-12297 [S] | Think | 1965 | 30.00 |
| ❑ LP-12306 [S] | My Answer | 1966 | 30.00 |
| ❑ LP-12316 [S] | The New Soul of Jimmy McCracklin | 1966 | 30.00 |
| **MINIT** | | | |
| ❑ LP-4009 [M] | The Best of Jimmy McCracklin | 1967 | 30.00 |
| ❑ LP-24009 [S] | The Best of Jimmy McCracklin | 1967 | 25.00 |
| ❑ LP-24011 | Let's Get Together | 1968 | 25.00 |
| ❑ LP-24017 | Stinger Man | 1969 | 25.00 |
| **STAX** | | | |
| ❑ STS-2047 | Yesterday Is Gone | 1972 | 20.00 |
| ❑ MPS-8506 | High on the Blues | 1980 | 10.00 |

### MCCULLOCH, DANNY

| Number | Title (A Side/B Side) | Yr | NM |
|---|---|---|---|
| **CAPITOL** | | | |
| ❑ ST-174 | Wings of a Man | 1969 | 20.00 |

### MCCURDY, ED

| Number | Title (A Side/B Side) | Yr | NM |
|---|---|---|---|
| **DAWN** | | | |
| ❑ DLP-1127 [M] | The Folk Singer | 195? | 30.00 |
| **ELEKTRA** | | | |
| ❑ EKL-24 [10] | Sin Songs — Pro and Con | 1955 | 40.00 |
| ❑ EKL-108 [M] | Blood Booze 'n' Bones | 1956 | 30.00 |
| ❑ EKL-110 [M] | When Dalliance Was In Flower 1 | 1956 | 30.00 |
| ❑ EKL-112 [M] | Songs of the Old West | 1956 | 30.00 |
| ❑ EKL-124 [M] | Sin Songs — Pro and Con | 1957 | 30.00 |
| *—Reissue of EKL-24 with extra tracks* | | | |
| ❑ EKL-140 [M] | When Dalliance Was In Flower 2 | 1958 | 30.00 |
| ❑ EKL-160 [M] | When Dalliance Was In Flower 3 | 1959 | 30.00 |
| ❑ EKL-170 [M] | Son of Dalliance | 1959 | 30.00 |
| ❑ EKL-205 [M] | A Treasure Chest of American Folk Song | 1961 | 25.00 |
| ❑ EKL-213 [(2)M] | The Best of Dalliance | 1961 | 30.00 |
| ❑ EKS-7160 [S] | When Dalliance Was In Flower 3 | 1959 | 40.00 |
| **RIVERSIDE** | | | |
| ❑ RLP 12-601 [M] | The Ballad Record | 195? | 30.00 |
| **TRADITION** | | | |
| ❑ TLP-1003 [M] | A Ballad Singer's Choice | 195? | 30.00 |
| ❑ TLP-1027 [M] | Children's Songs | 195? | 30.00 |
| ❑ TLP-2061 [M] | Songs of the West | 196? | 20.00 |

### MCCURDY, ED; JACK ELLIOTT; OSCAR BRAND

| Number | Title (A Side/B Side) | Yr | NM |
|---|---|---|---|
| **ELEKTRA** | | | |
| ❑ EKL-14 [10] | Badmen and Heroes | 1955 | 50.00 |

### MCCURDY, ED; JACK ELLIOTT; OSCAR BRAND; DICK WILDER

| Number | Title (A Side/B Side) | Yr | NM |
|---|---|---|---|
| **ELEKTRA** | | | |
| ❑ EKL-129 [M] | Badmen, Heroes and Pirate Songs | 1957 | 30.00 |

### MCCURN, GEORGE

| Number | Title (A Side/B Side) | Yr | NM |
|---|---|---|---|
| **A&M** | | | |
| ❑ LP-102 [M] | Country Boy Goes to Town!!!!! | 1963 | 25.00 |

### MCDANIEL, WILLARD

| Number | Title (A Side/B Side) | Yr | NM |
|---|---|---|---|
| **CROWN** | | | |
| ❑ CLP-5024 [M] | 88 A La Carte | 1958 | 100.00 |

### MCDANIELS, GENE

| Number | Title (A Side/B Side) | Yr | NM |
|---|---|---|---|
| **ATLANTIC** | | | |
| ❑ SD 8259 | Outlaw | 1970 | 15.00 |
| ❑ SD 8281 | Headless Heroes | 1971 | 15.00 |
| **LIBERTY** | | | |
| ❑ LRP-3146 [M] | In Times Like These | 1960 | 30.00 |
| ❑ LRP-3175 [M] | Sometimes I'm Happy, Sometimes I'm Blue | 1960 | 30.00 |
| ❑ LRP-3191 [M] | 100 Lbs. of Clay! | 1961 | 30.00 |
| ❑ LRP-3204 [M] | Gene McDaniels Sings Movie Memories | 1962 | 30.00 |
| ❑ LRP-3215 [M] | Tower of Strength | 1962 | 30.00 |
| ❑ LRP-3258 [M] | Hit After Hit | 1962 | 30.00 |
| ❑ LRP-3275 [M] | Spanish Lace | 1963 | 25.00 |
| ❑ LRP-3311 [M] | The Wonderful World of Gene McDaniels | 1963 | 25.00 |
| ❑ LST-7146 [S] | In Times Like These | 1960 | 40.00 |
| *—Black vinyl* | | | |
| ❑ LST-7146 [S] | In Times Like These | 1960 | 200.00 |
| *—Blue vinyl* | | | |
| ❑ LST-7175 [S] | Sometimes I'm Happy, Sometimes I'm Blue | 1960 | 40.00 |
| ❑ LST-7191 [S] | 100 Lbs. of Clay! | 1961 | 40.00 |
| ❑ LST-7204 [S] | Gene McDaniels Sings Movie Memories | 1962 | 40.00 |
| ❑ LST-7215 [S] | Tower of Strength | 1962 | 40.00 |
| ❑ LST-7258 [S] | Hit After Hit | 1962 | 40.00 |
| ❑ LST-7275 [S] | Spanish Lace | 1963 | 30.00 |
| ❑ LST-7311 [S] | The Wonderful World of Gene McDaniels | 1963 | 30.00 |
| **ODE** | | | |
| ❑ SP-77028 | Natural Juices | 1975 | 12.00 |
| **SUNSET** | | | |
| ❑ SUM-1122 [M] | Facts of Life | 1967 | 12.00 |
| ❑ SUS-5122 [S] | Facts of Life | 1967 | 15.00 |
| **UNITED ARTISTS** | | | |
| ❑ UA-LA447-E | The Very Best of Gene McDaniels | 1975 | 10.00 |

### MCDONALD, COUNTRY JOE See COUNTRY JOE AND THE FISH.

### MCDONALD, KATHI

| Number | Title (A Side/B Side) | Yr | NM |
|---|---|---|---|
| **CAPITOL** | | | |
| ❑ ST-11224 | Insane Asylum | 1974 | 30.00 |

### MCDONALD, MARIE

| Number | Title (A Side/B Side) | Yr | NM |
|---|---|---|---|
| **RCA VICTOR** | | | |
| ❑ LPM-1585 [M] | The Body Sings!, The | 1957 | 50.00 |

### MCDONALD, MICHAEL Also see THE DOOBIE BROTHERS.

| Number | Title (A Side/B Side) | Yr | NM |
|---|---|---|---|
| **ARISTA** | | | |
| ❑ ABM-2006 | That Was Then — The Early Recordings of Michael McDonald | 1982 | 50.00 |
| **MOBILE FIDELITY** | | | |
| ❑ 1-149 | If That's What It Takes | 1985 | 40.00 |
| *—Audiophile vinyl* | | | |
| **REPRISE** | | | |
| ❑ 25979 | Take It to Heart | 1990 | 15.00 |
| **WARNER BROS.** | | | |
| ❑ 23703 | If That's What It Takes | 1982 | 10.00 |
| ❑ 25291 | No Lookin' Back | 1985 | 10.00 |

### MCDONALD, SKEETS

| Number | Title (A Side/B Side) | Yr | NM |
|---|---|---|---|
| **CAPITOL** | | | |
| ❑ T 1040 [M] | Goin' Steady with the Blues | 1958 | 80.00 |
| **COLUMBIA** | | | |
| ❑ CL 2170 [M] | Call Me Skeets | 1964 | 25.00 |
| ❑ CS 8970 [S] | Call Me Skeets | 1964 | 30.00 |

**FORTUNE**

| Number | Title (A Side/B Side) | Yr | NM |
|---|---|---|---|
| ❑ 3001 | The Tattooed Lady and Other Songs | 1969 | 50.00 |

**SEARS**

| Number | Title (A Side/B Side) | Yr | NM |
|---|---|---|---|
| ❑ SPS-116 [R] | Skeets | 196? | 25.00 |

## MCDOWELL, MISSISSIPPI FRED

**ARHOOLIE**

| Number | Title (A Side/B Side) | Yr | NM |
|---|---|---|---|
| ❑ F-1021 [M] | Delta Blues | 1964 | 50.00 |
| ❑ F-1027 [M] | Delta Blues, Volume 2 | 1966 | 50.00 |
| ❑ F-1046 | Mississippi Fred McDowell and His Blues Boys | 1970 | 30.00 |
| ❑ F-1068 | Keep Your Lamp Trimmed and Burning | 1973 | 20.00 |

**CAPITOL**

| Number | Title (A Side/B Side) | Yr | NM |
|---|---|---|---|
| ❑ ST-403 | I Do Not Play No Rock and Roll | 1970 | 25.00 |

**JUST SUNSHINE**

| Number | Title (A Side/B Side) | Yr | NM |
|---|---|---|---|
| ❑ JSS-4 | Mississippi Fred McDowell 1904-1972 | 1973 | 15.00 |

**MILESTONE**

| Number | Title (A Side/B Side) | Yr | NM |
|---|---|---|---|
| ❑ MLP-3003 [M] | Long Way from Home | 1966 | 30.00 |
| ❑ MLS-93003 [S] | Long Way from Home | 1966 | 40.00 |

**SIRE**

| Number | Title (A Side/B Side) | Yr | NM |
|---|---|---|---|
| ❑ SES-97018 | Mississippi Fred McDowell in London | 1970 | 30.00 |

## MCDOWELL, RONNIE

**CURB**

| Number | Title (A Side/B Side) | Yr | NM |
|---|---|---|---|
| ❑ 10602 | I'm Still Missing You | 1988 | 8.00 |

**EPIC**

| Number | Title (A Side/B Side) | Yr | NM |
|---|---|---|---|
| ❑ JE 36142 | Rockin' You Easy, Lovin' You Slow | 1979 | 10.00 |
| ❑ PE 36142 | Rockin' You Easy, Lovin' You Slow | 198? | 8.00 |
| *—Budget-line reissue with new prefix* | | | |
| ❑ JE 36336 | Love So Many Ways | 1980 | 10.00 |
| ❑ JE 36821 | Going, Going ... Gone | 1980 | 10.00 |
| ❑ PE 36821 | Going, Going ... Gone | 198? | 8.00 |
| *—Budget-line reissue with new prefix* | | | |
| ❑ FE 37399 | Good Time Lovin' Man | 1981 | 10.00 |
| ❑ PE 37399 | Good Time Lovin' Man | 198? | 8.00 |
| *—Budget-line reissue with new prefix* | | | |
| ❑ FE 38017 | Love to Burn | 1982 | 10.00 |
| ❑ PE 38017 | Love to Burn | 198? | 8.00 |
| *—Budget-line reissue with new prefix* | | | |
| ❑ FE 38314 | Greatest Hits | 1983 | 10.00 |
| ❑ FE 38514 | Personally | 1983 | 10.00 |
| ❑ PE 38514 | Personally | 1985 | 8.00 |
| *—Budget-line reissue with new prefix* | | | |
| ❑ FE 38981 | Country Boy's Heart | 1983 | 10.00 |
| ❑ PE 38981 | Country Boy's Heart | 1985 | 8.00 |
| *—Budget-line reissue with new prefix* | | | |
| ❑ FE 39329 | Willing | 1984 | 10.00 |
| ❑ FE 39954 | In a New York Minute | 1985 | 10.00 |
| ❑ PE 40643 | Older Women and Other Greatest Hits | 1987 | 10.00 |

**MCA CURB**

| Number | Title (A Side/B Side) | Yr | NM |
|---|---|---|---|
| ❑ 5725 | All Tied Up in Love | 1986 | 8.00 |

**SCORPION**

| Number | Title (A Side/B Side) | Yr | NM |
|---|---|---|---|
| ❑ 0010 | Live at the Fox | 1978 | 15.00 |
| ❑ 8021 | The King Is Gone | 1977 | 20.00 |
| ❑ 8028 | I Love You, I Love You, I Love You | 1978 | 15.00 |

## MCDUFF, JACK

**ATLANTIC**

| Number | Title (A Side/B Side) | Yr | NM |
|---|---|---|---|
| ❑ SD 1463 [S] | A Change Is Gonna Come | 1966 | 20.00 |
| ❑ 1472 [M] | Tobacco Road | 1967 | 20.00 |

**PRESTIGE**

| Number | Title (A Side/B Side) | Yr | NM |
|---|---|---|---|
| ❑ PRLP-7174 [M] | Brother Jack | 1960 | 50.00 |
| ❑ PRLP-7185 [M] | Tough 'Duff | 1960 | 50.00 |
| ❑ PRLP-7199 [M] | The Honeydripper | 1961 | 50.00 |
| ❑ PRLP-7220 [M] | Goodnight, It's Time to Go | 1961 | 40.00 |
| ❑ PRST-7220 [S] | Goodnight, It's Time to Go | 1961 | 40.00 |
| ❑ PRLP-7228 [M] | Mellow Gravy — Brother Jack Meets the Boss | 1962 | 40.00 |
| ❑ PRST-7228 [S] | Mellow Gravy — Brother Jack Meets the Boss | 1962 | 40.00 |
| ❑ PRLP-7259 [M] | Screamin' | 1963 | 40.00 |
| ❑ PRST-7259 [S] | Screamin' | 1963 | 40.00 |
| ❑ PRLP-7265 [M] | Somethin' Slick! | 1963 | 40.00 |
| ❑ PRST-7265 [S] | Somethin' Slick! | 1963 | 40.00 |
| ❑ PRLP-7274 [M] | Live! | 1963 | 40.00 |
| ❑ PRST-7274 [S] | Live! | 1963 | 40.00 |
| ❑ PRLP-7286 [M] | Live! At the Jazz Workshop | 1964 | 40.00 |
| ❑ PRST-7286 [S] | Live! At the Jazz Workshop | 1964 | 40.00 |
| ❑ PRLP-7323 [M] | The Dynamic Jack McDuff | 1964 | 40.00 |
| ❑ PRST-7323 [S] | The Dynamic Jack McDuff | 1964 | 40.00 |
| ❑ PRLP-7333 [M] | Prelude | 1964 | 25.00 |
| ❑ PRST-7333 [S] | Prelude | 1964 | 30.00 |
| ❑ PRLP-7362 [M] | The Concert McDuff Recorded Live! | 1965 | 25.00 |
| ❑ PRST-7362 [S] | The Concert McDuff Recorded Live! | 1965 | 30.00 |
| ❑ PRLP-7404 [M] | Silk and Soul | 1965 | 25.00 |
| ❑ PRST-7404 [S] | Silk and Soul | 1965 | 30.00 |
| ❑ PRLP-7422 [M] | Hot Barbeque | 1966 | 20.00 |
| ❑ PRST-7422 [S] | Hot Barbeque | 1966 | 25.00 |
| ❑ PRLP-7476 [M] | Walk On By | 1967 | 25.00 |
| ❑ PRST-7476 [S] | Walk On By | 1967 | 20.00 |
| ❑ PRLP-7481 [M] | Brother Jack McDuff's Greatest Hits | 1967 | 25.00 |
| ❑ PRST-7481 [S] | Brother Jack McDuff's Greatest Hits | 1967 | 20.00 |
| ❑ PRLP-7492 [M] | Hallelujah Time! | 1967 | 25.00 |
| ❑ PRST-7492 [S] | Hallelujah Time! | 1967 | 20.00 |
| ❑ PRST-7529 | The Midnight Sun | 1968 | 20.00 |
| ❑ PRST-7567 | Soul Circle | 1968 | 20.00 |
| ❑ PRST-7596 | Jack McDuff Plays for Beautiful People | 1969 | 20.00 |
| ❑ PRST-7642 | I Got a Woman | 1969 | 20.00 |
| ❑ PRST-7666 | Steppin' Out | 1969 | 20.00 |
| ❑ PRST-7703 | Live! The Best of Brother Jack McDuff | 1969 | 20.00 |

## MCENTIRE, REBA

**MCA**

| Number | Title (A Side/B Side) | Yr | NM |
|---|---|---|---|
| ❑ 5475 | Just a Little Love | 1984 | 8.00 |
| ❑ 5516 | My Kind of Country | 1984 | 8.00 |
| ❑ 5585 | Have I Got a Deal for You | 1985 | 8.00 |
| ❑ 5691 | Whoever's in New England | 1986 | 8.00 |
| ❑ 5807 | What Am I Gonna Do About You | 1986 | 8.00 |
| ❑ 5979 | Reba McEntire's Greatest Hits | 1987 | 8.00 |
| ❑ 6294 | Sweet Sixteen | 1989 | 10.00 |
| ❑ 2P-7933 [(2)] | Reba Live | 1989 | 25.00 |
| *—Columbia House edition; no regular retail version* | | | |
| ❑ 1P-8162 | For My Broken Heart | 1991 | 25.00 |
| *—Only released on vinyl through Columbia House* | | | |
| ❑ 10016 | Rumor Has It | 1990 | 20.00 |
| ❑ 42030 | The Last One to Know | 1987 | 8.00 |
| ❑ 42031 | Merry Christmas to You | 1987 | 10.00 |
| ❑ 42134 | Reba | 1988 | 8.00 |
| ❑ R 164184 | Merry Christmas to You | 1987 | 12.00 |
| *—BMG Direct Marketing edition* | | | |
| ❑ R 244602 [(2)] | Reba Live | 1989 | 25.00 |
| *—BMG Direct Marketing version; no regular retail version* | | | |

**MERCURY**

| Number | Title (A Side/B Side) | Yr | NM |
|---|---|---|---|
| ❑ SRM-1-1177 | Reba McEntire | 1977 | 100.00 |
| ❑ SRM-1-4047 | Unlimited | 1982 | 25.00 |
| ❑ SRM-1-5002 | Reba McEntire | 1977 | 40.00 |
| *—Reissue of 1177* | | | |
| ❑ SRM-1-5017 | Out of a Dream | 1979 | 40.00 |
| ❑ SRM-1-5029 | Feel the Fire | 1980 | 30.00 |
| ❑ SRM-1-6003 | Heart to Heart | 1981 | 30.00 |
| ❑ 812781-1 | Behind the Scene | 1983 | 20.00 |
| ❑ 822455-1 | Reba Nell McEntire | 1986 | 10.00 |
| ❑ 822882-1 | Unlimited | 1986 | 10.00 |
| *—Reissue* | | | |
| ❑ 822887-1 | Feel the Fire | 1986 | 10.00 |
| *—Reissue* | | | |
| ❑ 824342-1 | The Best of Reba McEntire | 1985 | 10.00 |

## MCFADDEN, BOB

**BRUNSWICK**

| Number | Title (A Side/B Side) | Yr | NM |
|---|---|---|---|
| ❑ BL 54056 [M] | Songs Our Mummy Taught Us | 1959 | 200.00 |
| ❑ BL 754056 [S] | Songs Our Mummy Taught Us | 1959 | 300.00 |

## MCFARLAND, GARY

**IMPULSE!**

| Number | Title (A Side/B Side) | Yr | NM |
|---|---|---|---|
| ❑ A-46 [M] | Point of Departure | 1963 | 30.00 |
| ❑ AS-46 [S] | Points of Departure | 1963 | 40.00 |
| ❑ A-9104 [M] | Tijuana Jazz | 1966 | 20.00 |
| ❑ AS-9104 [S] | Tijuana Jazz | 1966 | 25.00 |
| ❑ A-9112 [M] | Profiles | 1966 | 30.00 |
| ❑ AS-9112 [S] | Profiles | 1966 | 40.00 |
| ❑ A-9122 [M] | Simpatico | 1966 | 30.00 |
| ❑ AS-9122 [S] | Simpatico | 1966 | 40.00 |

**VERVE**

| Number | Title (A Side/B Side) | Yr | NM |
|---|---|---|---|
| ❑ V6-8443 [S] | How to Succeed in Business Without Really Trying | 1962 | 25.00 |
| ❑ V6-8518 [S] | The Gary McFarland Orchestra with Special Guest Soloist Bill Evans | 1963 | 30.00 |
| ❑ V6-8603 [S] | Soft Samba | 1964 | 30.00 |
| ❑ V6-8632 [S] | The "In" Sound | 1965 | 50.00 |
| ❑ V6-8682 [S] | Soft Samba Strings | 1966 | 30.00 |
| ❑ V-8738 [M] | Scorpio and Other Signs | 1967 | 50.00 |

## MCGARITY, LOU

**ARGO**

| Number | Title (A Side/B Side) | Yr | NM |
|---|---|---|---|
| ❑ LP-654 [M] | Blue Lou | 1960 | 30.00 |
| ❑ LPS-654 [S] | Blue Lou | 1960 | 40.00 |

**JUBILEE**

| Number | Title (A Side/B Side) | Yr | NM |
|---|---|---|---|
| ❑ JGM-1108 [M] | Some Like It Hot | 1959 | 50.00 |

## MCGEE, SAM AND KIRK, AND THE CROOK BROTHERS

**STARDAY**

| Number | Title (A Side/B Side) | Yr | NM |
|---|---|---|---|
| ❑ SLP-182 [M] | Opry Old Timers | 1962 | 40.00 |

## MCGHEE, BROWNIE

**BLUESVILLE**

| Number | Title (A Side/B Side) | Yr | NM |
|---|---|---|---|
| ❑ BVLP-1042 [M] | Brownie's Blues | 1962 | 80.00 |
| *—Blue label, silver print* | | | |
| ❑ BVLP-1042 [M] | Brownie's Blues | 1964 | 25.00 |
| *—Blue label, trident logo at right* | | | |

**FANTASY**

| Number | Title (A Side/B Side) | Yr | NM |
|---|---|---|---|
| ❑ OBC-505 | Brownie's Blues | 198? | 12.00 |

**FOLKWAYS**

| Number | Title (A Side/B Side) | Yr | NM |
|---|---|---|---|
| ❑ FP-30 [10] | Brownie McGhee Blues | 1951 | 120.00 |
| ❑ FA-2030 [10] | Brownie McGhee Blues | 1951 | 100.00 |
| ❑ 2421/2 [(2)] | Traditional Blues Vol. 1 and 2 | 197? | 15.00 |
| ❑ 3557 | Brownie McGhee Sings the Blues | 197? | 12.00 |

**SAVOY JAZZ**

| Number | Title (A Side/B Side) | Yr | NM |
|---|---|---|---|
| ❑ SJL-1204 | Jumpin' the Blues | 1989 | 12.00 |

## MCGHEE, BROWNIE, AND SONNY TERRY

See SONNY TERRY AND BROWNIE McGHEE.

## MCGHEE, HOWARD

**ARGO**

| Number | Title (A Side/B Side) | Yr | NM |
|---|---|---|---|
| ❑ LP-4020 [M] | House Warmin' | 1963 | 25.00 |
| ❑ LPS-4020 [S] | House Warmin' | 1963 | 30.00 |

**BETHLEHEM**

| Number | Title (A Side/B Side) | Yr | NM |
|---|---|---|---|
| ❑ BCP-42 [M] | The Return of Howard McGhee | 1956 | 80.00 |
| ❑ BCP-61 [M] | Life Is Just a Bowl of Cherries | 1957 | 80.00 |
| ❑ BCP-6055 [M] | Dusty Blue | 1961 | 50.00 |
| ❑ BCPS-6055 [S] | Dusty Blue | 1961 | 60.00 |

**BLUE NOTE**

| Number | Title (A Side/B Side) | Yr | NM |
|---|---|---|---|
| ❑ BLP-5012 [10] | Howard McGhee's All Stars/ Howard McGhee-Fats Navarro Sextet | 1952 | 300.00 |
| ❑ BLP-5024 [10] | Howard McGhee, Volume 2 | 1953 | 300.00 |

**CONTEMPORARY**

| Number | Title (A Side/B Side) | Yr | NM |
|---|---|---|---|
| ❑ M-3596 [M] | Maggie's Back in Town | 1961 | 40.00 |
| ❑ S-7596 [S] | Maggie's Back in Town | 1961 | 50.00 |

**DIAL**

| Number | Title (A Side/B Side) | Yr | NM |
|---|---|---|---|
| ❑ LP-217 [10] | Night Music | 1951 | 300.00 |

**HI-LO**

| Number | Title (A Side/B Side) | Yr | NM |
|---|---|---|---|
| ❑ HL-6001 [10] | Jazz Goes to the Battlefront, Vol. 1 | 1952 | 250.00 |
| ❑ HL-6002 [10] | Jazz Goes to the Battlefront, Vol. 2 | 1952 | 250.00 |

**SAVOY**

| Number | Title (A Side/B Side) | Yr | NM |
|---|---|---|---|
| ❑ MG-12026 [M] | Howard McGhee and Milt Jackson | 1955 | 80.00 |

**UNITED ARTISTS**

| Number | Title (A Side/B Side) | Yr | NM |
|---|---|---|---|
| ❑ UAJ-14028 [M] | Nobody Knows You When You're Down and Out | 1963 | 30.00 |
| ❑ UAJS-15028 [S] | Nobody Knows You When You're Down and Out | 1963 | 40.00 |

## MCGHEE, STICK, AND JOHN LEE HOOKER

**AUDIO LAB**

| Number | Title (A Side/B Side) | Yr | NM |
|---|---|---|---|
| ❑ AL-1520 [M] | Highway of Blues | 1959 | 350.00 |

## MCGOVERN, PATTY, AND THOMAS TALBERT

**ATLANTIC**

| Number | Title (A Side/B Side) | Yr | NM |
|---|---|---|---|
| ❑ 1245 [M] | Wednesday's Child | 1956 | 50.00 |
| *—Black label* | | | |
| ❑ 1245 [M] | Wednesday's Child | 1961 | 25.00 |
| *—Multicolor label, white "fan" logo at right* | | | |

## MCGRAW, TIM

**CURB**

| Number | Title (A Side/B Side) | Yr | NM |
|---|---|---|---|
| ❑ 77886-2P [DJ] | Everywhere | 1997 | 25.00 |
| *—Promo-only picture disc* | | | |

## MCGRIFF, JIMMY

**SOLID STATE**

| Number | Title (A Side/B Side) | Yr | NM |
|---|---|---|---|
| ❑ SM-17006 [M] | Cherry | 1967 | 20.00 |
| ❑ SS-18001 [S] | The Big Band of Jimmy McGriff | 1966 | 20.00 |
| ❑ SS-18002 [S] | A Bag Full of Soul | 1966 | 20.00 |
| ❑ SS-18006 [S] | Cherry | 1967 | 20.00 |
| ❑ SS-18017 | A Bag Full of Blues | 1968 | 20.00 |
| ❑ SS-18030 | I've Got a New Woman | 1968 | 20.00 |
| ❑ SS-18036 | Honey | 1968 | 20.00 |
| ❑ SS-18045 | The Worm | 1968 | 20.00 |
| ❑ SS-18053 | Step I | 1969 | 20.00 |
| ❑ SS-18060 | A Thing to Come By | 1969 | 20.00 |
| ❑ SS-18063 | The Way You Look Tonight | 1970 | 20.00 |

**SUE**

| Number | Title (A Side/B Side) | Yr | NM |
|---|---|---|---|
| ❑ LP-1012 [M] | I've Got a Woman | 1962 | 30.00 |
| ❑ STLP-1012 [S] | I've Got a Woman | 1962 | 40.00 |
| ❑ LP-1013 [M] | One of Mine | 1963 | 30.00 |
| ❑ STLP-1013 [S] | One of Mine | 1963 | 40.00 |
| ❑ LP-1017 [M] | Jimmy McGriff at the Apollo | 1963 | 30.00 |
| ❑ STLP-1017 [S] | Jimmy McGriff at the Apollo | 1963 | 40.00 |
| ❑ LP-1018 [M] | Christmas with McGriff | 1963 | 30.00 |
| ❑ STLP-1018 [S] | Christmas with McGriff | 1963 | 40.00 |
| ❑ LP-1020 [M] | Jimmy McGriff at the Organ | 1963 | 30.00 |
| ❑ STLP-1020 [S] | Jimmy McGriff at the Organ | 1963 | 40.00 |
| ❑ LP-1033 [M] | Topkapi | 1964 | 30.00 |
| ❑ STLP-1033 [S] | Topkapi | 1964 | 40.00 |
| ❑ LP-1039 [M] | Blues for Mister Jimmy | 1965 | 30.00 |
| ❑ STLP-1039 [S] | Blues for Mister Jimmy | 1965 | 40.00 |
| ❑ LP-1043 [M] | Toast to Greatest Hits | 1966 | 20.00 |

| Number | Title (A Side/B Side) | Yr | NM |
|---|---|---|---|
| ❑ STLP-1043 [S] | Toast to Greatest Hits | 1966 | 25.00 |
| **VEEP** | | | |
| ❑ VP-13515 [M] | Live Where the Action Is | 1966 | 20.00 |
| ❑ VP-13522 [M] | Greatest Organ Hits | 1967 | 25.00 |
| ❑ VPS-16515 [S] | Live Where the Action Is | 1966 | 25.00 |
| ❑ VPS-16522 [S] | Greatest Organ Hits | 1967 | 20.00 |
| **MCGUINN, ROGER** Also see THE BYRDS. | | | |
| **ARISTA** | | | |
| ❑ AL 8648 | Back from Rio | 1991 | 15.00 |
| **COLUMBIA** | | | |
| ❑ AS 353 [DJ] | The Roger McGuinn Airplay Anthology | 1977 | 30.00 |
| *—Promo only; also includes Byrds tracks* | | | |
| ❑ KC 31946 | Roger McGuinn | 1973 | 12.00 |
| ❑ KC 32956 | Peace On You | 1974 | 12.00 |
| ❑ PC 33541 | Roger McGuinn & Band | 1975 | 12.00 |
| ❑ PC 34154 | Cardiff Rose | 1976 | 12.00 |
| ❑ PC 34656 | Thunderbyrd | 1977 | 12.00 |
| **MCGUIRE, BARRY** Also see THE NEW CHRISTY MINSTRELS. | | | |
| **ABC DUNHILL** | | | |
| ❑ DS-50033 | The World's Last Private Citizen | 1968 | 25.00 |
| **DUNHILL** | | | |
| ❑ D-50003 [M] | Eve of Destruction | 1965 | 30.00 |
| ❑ DS-50003 [S] | Eve of Destruction | 1965 | 40.00 |
| ❑ D-50005 [M] | This Precious Time | 1966 | 25.00 |
| ❑ DS-50005 [S] | This Precious Time | 1966 | 30.00 |
| **HORIZON** | | | |
| ❑ ST-1636 [S] | The Barry McGuire Album | 1963 | 40.00 |
| ❑ WP-1636 [M] | The Barry McGuire Album | 1963 | 30.00 |
| **MIRA** | | | |
| ❑ LP-3000 [M] | The Barry McGuire Album | 1965 | 20.00 |
| *—Reissue of Horizon LP* | | | |
| ❑ LPS-3000 [S] | The Barry McGuire Album | 1965 | 25.00 |
| *—Reissue of Horizon LP* | | | |
| **MYRRH** | | | |
| ❑ MSA-6519 | Seeds | 1974 | 12.00 |
| ❑ MSA-6531 | Lighten Up | 1975 | 12.00 |
| **ODE** | | | |
| ❑ SP-77004 | Barry McGuire with the Doctor | 1970 | 15.00 |
| **MCGUIRE, BARRY, AND BARRY KANE** | | | |
| **HORIZON** | | | |
| ❑ SWP-1608 [S] | Barry and Barry: Here and Now! | 1962 | 30.00 |
| ❑ WP-1608 [M] | Barry and Barry: Here and Now! | 1962 | 25.00 |
| **MCGUIRE, PHYLLIS** Also see THE McGUIRE SISTERS. | | | |
| **ABC-PARAMOUNT** | | | |
| ❑ 552 [M] | Phyllis McGuire Sings | 1966 | 15.00 |
| ❑ S-552 [S] | Phyllis McGuire Sings | 1966 | 20.00 |
| **MCGUIRE SISTERS, THE** Also see PHYLLIS McGUIRE. | | | |
| **ABC-PARAMOUNT** | | | |
| ❑ 530 [M] | The McGuire Sisters Today | 1966 | 15.00 |
| ❑ S-530 [S] | The McGuire Sisters Today | 1966 | 20.00 |
| **CORAL** | | | |
| ❑ 7CXB 6 [(2)P] | The Best of the McGuire Sisters | 1965 | 25.00 |
| ❑ CXB 6 [(2)M] | The Best of the McGuire Sisters | 1965 | 25.00 |
| ❑ CRL 56123 [10] | By Request | 1955 | 50.00 |
| ❑ CRL 57026 [M] | Do You Remember When | 1956 | 40.00 |
| ❑ CRL 57028 [M] | 'S Wonderful | 1956 | 40.00 |
| ❑ CRL 57033 [M] | He | 1956 | 40.00 |
| ❑ CRL 57052 [M] | Sincerely | 1956 | 40.00 |
| ❑ CRL 57097 [M] | Children's Holiday | 1956 | 40.00 |
| ❑ CRL 57134 [M] | Teenage Party | 1957 | 30.00 |
| ❑ CRL 57145 [M] | While the Lights Are Low | 1957 | 30.00 |
| ❑ CRL 57180 [M] | Musical Magic | 1957 | 30.00 |
| ❑ CRL 57217 [M] | Sugartime | 1958 | 30.00 |
| ❑ CRL 57225 [M] | Greetings from the McGuire Sisters | 1958 | 30.00 |
| ❑ CRL 57296 [M] | May You Always | 1959 | 20.00 |
| ❑ CRL 57303 [M] | In Harmony with Him | 1959 | 25.00 |
| ❑ CRL 57337 [M] | His and Hers | 1960 | 20.00 |
| ❑ CRL 57349 [M] | Our Golden Favorites | 1961 | 20.00 |
| ❑ CRL 57385 [M] | Just for Old Times' Sake | 1961 | 20.00 |
| ❑ CRL 57398 [M] | Subways Are for Sleeping | 1961 | 15.00 |
| ❑ CRL 57415 [M] | Songs Everybody Knows | 1962 | 15.00 |
| ❑ CRL 57443 [M] | Showcase | 196? | 20.00 |
| ❑ CRL 757296 [S] | May You Always | 1959 | 30.00 |
| ❑ CRL 757303 [S] | In Harmony with Him | 1959 | 40.00 |
| ❑ CRL 757337 [S] | His and Hers | 1960 | 30.00 |
| ❑ CRL 757349 [R] | Our Golden Favorites | 196? | 12.00 |
| ❑ CRL 757385 [S] | Just for Old Times' Sake | 1961 | 30.00 |
| ❑ CRL 757398 [S] | Subways Are for Sleeping | 1961 | 20.00 |
| ❑ CRL 757415 [S] | Songs Everybody Knows | 1962 | 20.00 |
| ❑ CRL 757443 [R] | Showcase | 196? | 12.00 |
| **MCA** | | | |
| ❑ 4119 [(2)] | The Best of the McGuire Sisters | 1978 | 12.00 |
| *—Reissue of Coral 6* | | | |
| **VOCALION** | | | |
| ❑ VL 3685 [M] | Children's Holiday | 1960 | 20.00 |

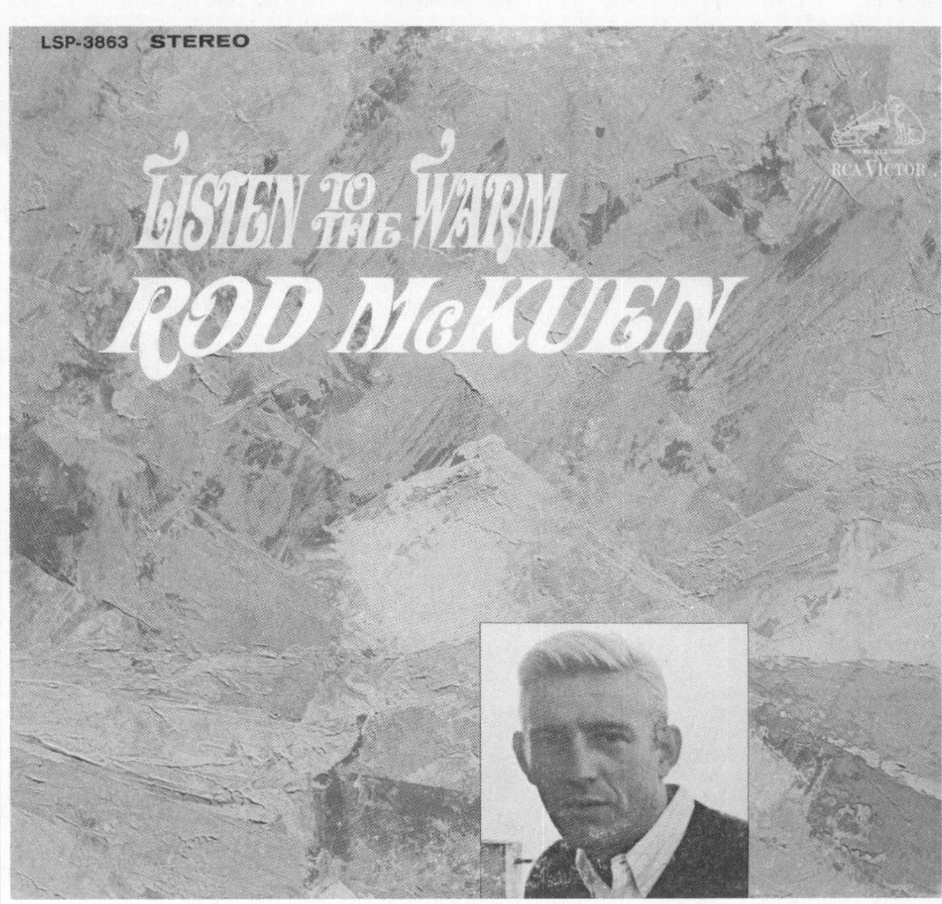


Rod McKuen, *Listen to the Warm,* RCA Victor LSP-3863, 1967, stereo, $15.

| Number | Title (A Side/B Side) | Yr | NM |
|---|---|---|---|
| ❑ VL 3798 [M] | The McGuire Sisters | 1967 | 15.00 |
| ❑ VL 73798 [R] | The McGuire Sisters | 1967 | 12.00 |
| **MCHARGUE, ROSY** | | | |
| **JUMP** | | | |
| ❑ JL-8 [10] | Dixie Combo | 1955 | 50.00 |
| **MCINTYRE, HAL** | | | |
| **COLUMBIA** | | | |
| ❑ CL 6124 [10] | Dance Date | 1950 | 50.00 |
| **ROULETTE** | | | |
| ❑ R-25079 [M] | It Seems Like Only Yesterday | 1959 | 20.00 |
| ❑ SR-25079 [S] | It Seems Like Only Yesterday | 1959 | 25.00 |
| **MCINTYRE, KALAPARUSHA MAURICE** | | | |
| **DELMARK** | | | |
| ❑ DS-419 | Humility | 1969 | 20.00 |
| ❑ DS-425 | Forces and Feelings | 197? | 20.00 |
| **MCINTYRE, KEN** | | | |
| **NEW JAZZ** | | | |
| ❑ NJLP-8247 [M] | Looking Ahead | 1960 | 80.00 |
| *—Purple label* | | | |
| ❑ NJLP-8247 [M] | Looking Ahead | 1965 | 30.00 |
| *—Blue label, trident logo at right* | | | |
| ❑ NJLP-8259 [M] | Stone Blues | 1961 | 80.00 |
| *—Purple label* | | | |
| ❑ NJLP-8259 [M] | Stone Blues | 1965 | 30.00 |
| *—Blue label, trident logo at right* | | | |
| **UNITED ARTISTS** | | | |
| ❑ UAL-3336 [M] | Way Way Out | 1964 | 40.00 |
| ❑ UAS-6336 [S] | Way Way Out | 1964 | 50.00 |
| ❑ UAJ-14015 [M] | Year of the Iron Sheep | 1962 | 50.00 |
| ❑ UAJS-15015 [S] | Year of the Iron Sheep | 1962 | 60.00 |
| **MCKAY, SCOTTY** | | | |
| **ACE** | | | |
| ❑ LP-1017 [M] | Tonight In Person | 1961 | 80.00 |
| **MCKAY, STUART** | | | |
| **RCA VICTOR** | | | |
| ❑ LJM-1021 [M] | Stuart McKay and His Woods | 1955 | 40.00 |
| **MCKENNA, DAVE** | | | |
| **ABC-PARAMOUNT** | | | |
| ❑ ABC-104 [M] | Solo Piano | 1956 | 40.00 |

| Number | Title (A Side/B Side) | Yr | NM |
|---|---|---|---|
| **EPIC** | | | |
| ❑ BN 527 [S] | Dave McKenna | 1959 | 25.00 |
| ❑ LN 3558 [M] | Dave McKenna | 1959 | 30.00 |
| **MCKENNA, DAVE, AND HALL OVERTON** | | | |
| **BETHLEHEM** | | | |
| ❑ BCP-6049 [M] | Dual Piano Jazz | 1960 | 30.00 |
| ❑ BCPS-6049 [S] | Dual Piano Jazz | 1960 | 30.00 |
| **MCKENZIE, SCOTT** | | | |
| **ODE** | | | |
| ❑ Z12 44001 [M] | The Voice of Scott McKenzie | 1967 | 40.00 |
| ❑ Z12 44002 [S] | The Voice of Scott McKenzie | 1967 | 25.00 |
| ❑ SP-77007 | Stained Glass Morning | 1970 | 15.00 |
| **MCKINLEY, RAY** Also see GLENN MILLER ORCHESTRA. | | | |
| **ALLEGRO ELITE** | | | |
| ❑ 4015 [10] | Ray McKinley Plays Sauter and Others | 195? | 50.00 |
| ❑ 4129 [10] | Ray McKinley and His Famous Orchestra | 195? | 100.00 |
| **MCKINLEY, RAY/JOE MARSALA** | | | |
| **DECCA** | | | |
| ❑ DL 5262 [10] | Dixieland Jazz Battle, Vol. 2 | 1950 | 50.00 |
| **MCKINLEY, RAY, AND EDDIE SAUTER** | | | |
| **SAVOY** | | | |
| ❑ MG-12024 [M] | Borderline | 1955 | 50.00 |
| **MCKINNEY, HAROLD** | | | |
| **TRIBE** | | | |
| ❑ 2233 | Voices and Rhythms | 197? | 40.00 |
| **MCKINNEY'S COTTON PICKERS** | | | |
| **RCA VICTOR** | | | |
| ❑ LPT-24 [10] | McKinney's Cotton Pickers | 1952 | 60.00 |
| **"X"** | | | |
| ❑ LVA-3031 [10] | McKinney's Cotton Pickers | 1954 | 50.00 |
| **MCKUEN, ROD** | | | |
| **BUDDAH** | | | |
| ❑ BDS-5138 | Cycles | 197? | 12.00 |
| **CAPITOL** | | | |
| ❑ ST 2079 [S] | Rod McKuen Sings Rod McKuen | 1964 | 20.00 |

| Number | Title (A Side/B Side) | Yr | NM |
|---|---|---|---|
| ❑ T 2079 [M] | Rod McKuen Sings Rod McKuen | 1964 | 15.00 |
| ❑ ST 2838 [S] | Love Movement | 1968 | 15.00 |
| ❑ T 2838 [M] | Love Movement | 1968 | 25.00 |
| **DECCA** | | | |
| ❑ DL 4969 [M] | Very Warm | 1968 | 20.00 |
| ❑ DL 8882 [M] | Anywhere I Wander | 1958 | 20.00 |
| ❑ DL 8946 [M] | Alone After Dark | 1959 | 20.00 |
| ❑ DL 74969 [S] | Very Warm | 1968 | 15.00 |
| ❑ DL 78882 [S] | Anywhere I Wander | 1958 | 30.00 |
| ❑ DL 78946 [S] | Alone After Dark | 1959 | 30.00 |
| **EPIC** | | | |
| ❑ BN 26370 [M] | In Search of Eros | 1968 | 30.00 |
| *—White label promo only; in stereo cover with "Epic Mono" sticker* | | | |
| ❑ BN 26370 [S] | In Search of Eros | 1968 | 15.00 |
| **EVEREST** | | | |
| ❑ 3208 | Desire Has No Special Time | 1968 | 15.00 |
| ❑ 3267 | Life Is | 197? | 15.00 |
| **HIFI** | | | |
| ❑ R 407 [M] | Time of Desire | 1958 | 20.00 |
| ❑ SR 407 [S] | Time of Desire | 1958 | 25.00 |
| ❑ R 419 [M] | Beatsville | 1960 | 20.00 |
| ❑ SR 419 [S] | Beatsville | 1960 | 25.00 |
| **HORIZON** | | | |
| ❑ ST-1612 [S] | New Sounds in Folk Music | 1963 | 25.00 |
| ❑ WP-1612 [M] | New Sounds in Folk Music | 1963 | 20.00 |
| ❑ WPLP-1632 [M] | There's a Hoot Tonight | 1963 | 20.00 |
| ❑ WPLP-1632 [S] | There's a Hoot Tonight | 1963 | 25.00 |
| **IN** | | | |
| ❑ 1003 [M] | Seasons in the Sun | 1964 | 20.00 |
| ❑ S-1003 [S] | Seasons in the Sun | 1964 | 25.00 |
| **JUBILEE** | | | |
| ❑ J-5013 [M] | Mr. Oliver Twist | 1962 | 20.00 |
| ❑ SJ-5013 [S] | Mr. Oliver Twist | 1962 | 25.00 |
| **KAPP** | | | |
| ❑ KL-1538 [M] | In a Lonely Place | 1967 | 20.00 |
| ❑ KS-3538 [S] | In a Lonely Place | 1967 | 15.00 |
| **LIBERTY** | | | |
| ❑ LRP-3011 [M] | Lazy Afternoon | 1956 | 40.00 |
| **RCA VICTOR** | | | |
| ❑ LPM-3424 [M] | Rod McKuen Sings His Own | 1965 | 15.00 |
| ❑ LSP-3424 [S] | Rod McKuen Sings His Own | 1965 | 20.00 |
| ❑ LPM-3508 [M] | The Loner | 1966 | 15.00 |
| ❑ LSP-3508 [S] | The Loner | 1966 | 20.00 |
| ❑ LPM-3635 [M] | Other Kinds of Songs | 1966 | 15.00 |
| ❑ LSP-3635 [S] | Other Kinds of Songs | 1966 | 20.00 |
| ❑ LPM-3786 [M] | Through European Windows | 1967 | 20.00 |
| ❑ LSP-3786 [S] | Through European Windows | 1967 | 15.00 |
| ❑ LPM-3863 [M] | Listen to the Warm | 1967 | 20.00 |
| ❑ LSP-3863 [S] | Listen to the Warm | 1967 | 15.00 |
| ❑ LSP-4010 | A Single Man | 1968 | 15.00 |
| ❑ LSP-4127 | The Best of Rod McKuen | 1969 | 15.00 |
| **STANYAN** | | | |
| ❑ STS-001 | In Concert | 197? | 15.00 |
| *—Originals are numbered, limited editions* | | | |
| ❑ STS-003 | Seasons in the Sun | 197? | 15.00 |
| ❑ 1894 [(2)] | Pastorale | 197? | 12.00 |
| ❑ 2560 | Rod McKuen's Greatest Hits 2 | 197? | 10.00 |
| ❑ 2688 | Rod McKuen's Greatest Hits, Vol. 4 | 197? | 10.00 |
| ❑ 4010 | A Single Man | 197? | 10.00 |
| ❑ 5004 | Seasons in the Sun Vol. 2 | 197? | 12.00 |
| ❑ 5005 | Blessings in Shades of Green | 1970 | 12.00 |
| ❑ 5006 | Folk Album | 1970 | 12.00 |
| ❑ 5009 | Love's Been Good to Me | 1970 | 12.00 |
| ❑ 5010 | A Boy Named Charlie Brown | 1970 | 15.00 |
| ❑ 5016 [(2)] | Live in London! | 1971 | 15.00 |
| ❑ 5020 | Try Rod McKuen in Your Own Home | 197? | 12.00 |
| ❑ 5022 | Rod McKuen Sings Jacques Brel | 197? | 12.00 |
| ❑ 5025 | Rod | 197? | 12.00 |
| ❑ 5031 | Rod McKuen's Greatest Hits, Vol. 3 | 197? | 12.00 |
| ❑ 5032 | Have a Nice Day | 1973 | 12.00 |
| ❑ 5040 | Evening in Vienna | 1972 | 12.00 |
| ❑ 5042 | Rod McKuen Grand Tour, Vol. 3 | 1972 | 12.00 |
| ❑ 5046 [(2)] | Seasons in the Sun Vols. 1 and 2 | 197? | 15.00 |
| ❑ 5047 | Pastures Green | 197? | 12.00 |
| ❑ 5048 [(2)] | Listen to the Warm | 197? | 15.00 |
| ❑ 5051 [(2)] | Amsterdam Concert | 1972 | 15.00 |
| ❑ 5072 | A Portrait of Rod McKuen | 1972 | 12.00 |
| ❑ 5075 | Live at the Sydney Opera House | 197? | 12.00 |
| ❑ 9001 | Concerto No. 1 for Four Harpsichords and Orchestra | 197? | 12.00 |
| ❑ 9005 | Symphony No. 1: "All Men Love Something" | 197? | 12.00 |
| ❑ 9006 | Concerto No. 2 for Guitar and Orchestra; Five Pieces | 197? | 12.00 |
| ❑ 9008 | Piano Variations | 197? | 12.00 |
| ❑ 9010 | McKuen Conducts McKuen | 1972 | 12.00 |
| ❑ 9012 | Concerto No. 3 for Piano and Orchestra | 1972 | 12.00 |
| ❑ 9015 | Seascapes; Plains of My Country | 197? | 12.00 |
| ❑ 10009 | Concerto No. 1; Four Statements | 197? | 12.00 |
| **SUNSET** | | | |
| ❑ SUS-5273 | In the Beginning | 1970 | 10.00 |
| **TRADITION** | | | |
| ❑ 2063 [M] | A San Francisco Hippie Trip | 1967 | 25.00 |
| **WARNER BROS.** | | | |
| ❑ WS 1722 | Beautiful Strangers | 1968 | 15.00 |
| ❑ WS 1758 | Lonesome Cities | 1968 | 15.00 |
| ❑ WS 1772 | Greatest Hits of Rod McKuen | 1969 | 15.00 |
| ❑ 2WS 1794 [(2)] | Rod McKuen at Carnegie Hall | 1969 | 20.00 |
| ❑ WS 1837 | New Ballads | 1970 | 12.00 |
| ❑ 2WS 1894 [(2)] | Pastorale | 1971 | 15.00 |
| ❑ 2WS 1947 [(2)] | Rod McKuen Grand Tour | 1971 | 15.00 |
| ❑ BS 2560 | Rod McKuen's Greatest Hits 2 | 1970 | 12.00 |
| ❑ BS 2638 | Odyssey | 1973 | 12.00 |
| ❑ BS 2688 | Rod McKuen's Greatest Hits, Vol. 4 | 1973 | 12.00 |
| ❑ 2WS 2731 [(2)] | Back to Carnegie Hall | 1973 | 15.00 |
| ❑ BS 2785 | Seasons in the Sun | 1974 | 12.00 |
| ❑ BS 2817 | Alone | 1974 | 12.00 |
| ❑ BS 2931 | McKuen Country | 1976 | 10.00 |
| ❑ ST-92042 | Greatest Hits of Rod McKuen | 1969 | 20.00 |
| *—Capitol Record Club edition* | | | |

## MCKUEN, ROD; TAK SHINDO; JULIE MEREDITH

| Number | Title (A Side/B Side) | Yr | NM |
|---|---|---|---|
| **IMPERIAL** | | | |
| ❑ LP-9092 [M] | The Yellow Unicorn | 1960 | 40.00 |
| ❑ LP-12036 [S] | The Yellow Unicorn | 1960 | 50.00 |

## MCKUSICK, HAL

| Number | Title (A Side/B Side) | Yr | NM |
|---|---|---|---|
| **BETHLEHEM** | | | |
| ❑ BCP-16 [M] | East Coast Jazz/8 | 1955 | 200.00 |
| **CORAL** | | | |
| ❑ CRL 57116 [M] | Jazz at the Academy | 1957 | 80.00 |
| ❑ CRL 57131 [M] | Hal McKusick Quintet | 1957 | 80.00 |
| **DECCA** | | | |
| ❑ DL 9209 [M] | Cross Section — Saxes | 1958 | 50.00 |
| ❑ DL 79209 [S] | Cross Section — Saxes | 1958 | 40.00 |
| **MCA** | | | |
| ❑ 1379 | Hal McKusick Quintet Featuring Art Farmer 1957 | 198? | 12.00 |
| **PRESTIGE** | | | |
| ❑ PRLP-7135 [M] | Triple Exposure | 1957 | 80.00 |
| **RCA VICTOR** | | | |
| ❑ LPM-1164 [M] | Hal McKusick in the 20th Century Drawing Room | 1956 | 80.00 |
| ❑ LPM-1366 [M] | The Jazz Workshop | 1957 | 120.00 |

## MCLACHLAN, SARAH

| Number | Title (A Side/B Side) | Yr | NM |
|---|---|---|---|
| **ARISTA** | | | |
| ❑ RTH-2000 [(2)] | Fumbling Toward Ecstasy and The Freedom Sessions | 1997 | 40.00 |
| *—Audiophile vinyl issue of both CDs on 2-LP set by Classic Records, with one bonus track* | | | |
| ❑ RTH-2004 | Touch | 2002 | 25.00 |
| *—Audiophile vinyl reissue by Classic Records* | | | |
| ❑ RTH-2005 | Solace | 2002 | 25.00 |
| *—Audiophile vinyl reissue by Classic Records* | | | |
| ❑ AL 8594 | Touch | 1989 | 20.00 |
| ❑ RTH-18970 | Surfacing | 1999 | 25.00 |
| *—Audiophile vinyl issue by Classic Records* | | | |

## MCLAIN, DENNY

| Number | Title (A Side/B Side) | Yr | NM |
|---|---|---|---|
| **CAPITOL** | | | |
| ❑ ST-204 | Denny McLain In Las Vegas | 1969 | 25.00 |
| ❑ ST 2881 | Denny McLain at the Organ | 1968 | 25.00 |

## MCLAUGHLIN, JOHN

| Number | Title (A Side/B Side) | Yr | NM |
|---|---|---|---|
| **RYKO ANALOGUE** | | | |
| ❑ RALP-0051 | My Goals Beyond | 1987 | 20.00 |
| *—Clear vinyl; fourth issue of this album* | | | |

## MCLAWLER, SARAH

| Number | Title (A Side/B Side) | Yr | NM |
|---|---|---|---|
| **VEE JAY** | | | |
| ❑ LP-1030 [M] | At the Break of Day | 1961 | 40.00 |
| *—With Richard Otto* | | | |

## MCLEAN, DON

| Number | Title (A Side/B Side) | Yr | NM |
|---|---|---|---|
| **ARISTA** | | | |
| ❑ AL 4149 | Prime Time | 1978 | 10.00 |
| **CAPITOL** | | | |
| ❑ C1-48080 | Love Tracks | 1988 | 10.00 |
| **CASABLANCA** | | | |
| ❑ NBLP 7173 | Chain Lightning | 1979 | — |
| *—Canceled* | | | |
| **EMI AMERICA** | | | |
| ❑ ST-17255 | Don McLean's Greatest Hits, Then and Now | 1987 | 10.00 |
| **LIBERTY** | | | |
| ❑ LN-10037 | American Pie | 1980 | 8.00 |
| *—Reissue of United Artists 5535* | | | |
| ❑ LN-10157 | Tapestry | 1982 | 8.00 |
| *—Reissue of United Artists 5522* | | | |
| ❑ LN-10211 | Homeless Brother | 198? | 8.00 |
| *—Reissue of United Artists 315* | | | |
| **MEDIARTS** | | | |
| ❑ 41-4 | Tapestry | 1970 | 20.00 |
| **MILLENNIUM** | | | |
| ❑ BXL1-7756 | Chain Lightning | 1981 | 10.00 |
| ❑ BXL1-7762 | Believers | 1981 | 10.00 |
| **UNITED ARTISTS** | | | |
| ❑ UA-LA161-F | Playin' Favorites | 1973 | 12.00 |
| ❑ UA-LA315-G | Homeless Brother | 1974 | 12.00 |
| ❑ UA-LA652-H2 [(2)] | Solo | 1976 | 15.00 |
| ❑ UAS-5522 | Tapestry | 1971 | 12.00 |
| *—Reissue of Mediarts LP* | | | |
| ❑ UAS-5535 | American Pie | 1971 | 12.00 |
| ❑ UAS-5651 | Don McLean | 1972 | 12.00 |

## MCLEAN, JACKIE

| Number | Title (A Side/B Side) | Yr | NM |
|---|---|---|---|
| **ADLIB** | | | |
| ❑ ADL-6601 [M] | The Jackie McLean Quintet | 1955 | 2000. |
| **BLUE NOTE** | | | |
| ❑ BLP-4013 [M] | New Soil | 1959 | 300.00 |
| *—Regular version, W. 63rd St. address on label* | | | |
| ❑ BLP-4013 [M] | New Soil | 1959 | 500.00 |
| *—"Deep groove" version; W. 63rd St. address on label* | | | |
| ❑ BLP-4013 [M] | New Soil | 1963 | 50.00 |
| *—With "New York, USA" address on label* | | | |
| ❑ BST-4013 [S] | New Soil | 1959 | 200.00 |
| *—Regular version, W. 63rd St. address on label* | | | |
| ❑ BST-4013 [S] | New Soil | 1959 | 300.00 |
| *—"Deep groove" version; W. 63rd St. address on label* | | | |
| ❑ BST-4013 [S] | New Soil | 1963 | 40.00 |
| *—With "New York, USA" address on label* | | | |
| ❑ BLP-4024 [M] | Swing, Swang, Swingin' | 1959 | 500.00 |
| *—Regular version, W. 63rd St. address on label* | | | |
| ❑ BLP-4024 [M] | Swing, Swang, Swingin' | 1959 | 800.00 |
| *—"Deep groove" version; W. 63rd St. address on label* | | | |
| ❑ BLP-4024 [M] | Swing, Swang, Swingin' | 1963 | 50.00 |
| *—With "New York, USA" address on label* | | | |
| ❑ BLP-4038 [M] | Capuchin Swing | 1960 | 150.00 |
| *—W. 63rd St. address on label, either with no "deep groove" or with the groove on only one side* | | | |
| ❑ BLP-4038 [M] | Capuchin Swing | 1960 | 400.00 |
| *—Deep groove; with "W. 63rd St." address on label* | | | |
| ❑ BLP-4038 [M] | Capuchin Swing | 1963 | 40.00 |
| *—With "New York, USA" address on label* | | | |
| ❑ BLP-4051 [M] | Jackie's Bag | 1960 | 500.00 |
| *—Deep groove; with W. 63rd St. address on label* | | | |
| ❑ BLP-4051 [M] | Jackie's Bag | 1963 | 50.00 |
| *—With "New York, USA" address on label* | | | |
| ❑ BLP-4067 [M] | Bluesnik | 1961 | 400.00 |
| *—With W. 63rd St. address on label* | | | |
| ❑ BLP-4067 [M] | Bluesnik | 1963 | 40.00 |
| *—With "New York, USA" address on label* | | | |
| ❑ BLP-4089 [M] | A Fickle Sonance | 1961 | 400.00 |
| *—With W. 63rd St. address on label* | | | |
| ❑ BLP-4089 [M] | A Fickle Sonance | 1963 | 150.00 |
| *—With "New York, USA" address on label* | | | |
| ❑ BLP-4106 [M] | Let Freedom Ring | 1962 | 300.00 |
| *—With "New York, USA" address on label* | | | |
| ❑ BLP-4137 [M] | One Step Beyond | 1963 | 120.00 |
| *—With "New York, USA" address on label* | | | |
| ❑ BLP-4165 [M] | Destination... Out! | 1964 | 120.00 |
| *—With "New York, USA" address on label* | | | |
| ❑ BLP-4179 [M] | It's Time! | 1964 | 60.00 |
| *—With "New York, USA" address on label* | | | |
| ❑ BLP-4215 [M] | Right Now! | 1965 | 80.00 |
| *—With "New York, USA" address on label* | | | |
| ❑ BLP-4218 [M] | Action Action Action | 1965 | 120.00 |
| *—With "New York, USA" address on label* | | | |
| ❑ BLP-4262 [M] | New and Old Gospel | 1967 | 250.00 |
| *—With "A Division of Liberty Records" on label* | | | |
| ❑ BST-84024 [S] | Swing, Swang, Swingin' | 1959 | 400.00 |
| *—With W. 63rd St. address on label* | | | |
| ❑ BST-84024 [S] | Swing, Swang, Swingin' | 1963 | 80.00 |
| *—With "New York, USA" address on label* | | | |
| ❑ BST-84038 [S] | Capuchin Swing | 1960 | 250.00 |
| *—With W. 63rd St. address on label* | | | |
| ❑ BST-84038 [S] | Capuchin Swing | 1963 | 60.00 |
| *—With "New York, USA" address on label* | | | |
| ❑ BST-84051 [S] | Jackie's Bag | 1960 | 250.00 |
| *—With W. 63rd St. address on label* | | | |
| ❑ BST-84051 [S] | Jackie's Bag | 1963 | 60.00 |
| *—With "New York, USA" address on label* | | | |
| ❑ BST-84067 [S] | Bluesnik | 1961 | 200.00 |
| *—With W. 63rd St. address on label* | | | |
| ❑ BST-84067 [S] | Bluesnik | 1963 | 60.00 |
| *—With "New York, USA" address on label* | | | |
| ❑ BST-84089 [S] | A Fickle Sonance | 1961 | 250.00 |
| *—With W. 63rd St. address on label* | | | |
| ❑ BST-84089 [S] | A Fickle Sonance | 1963 | 100.00 |
| *—With "New York, USA" address on label* | | | |
| ❑ BST-84106 [S] | Let Freedom Ring | 1962 | 200.00 |
| *—With "New York, USA" address on label* | | | |
| ❑ BST-84106 [S] | Let Freedom Ring | 1967 | 40.00 |
| *—With "A Division of Liberty Records" on label* | | | |
| ❑ BST-84137 [S] | One Step Beyond | 1963 | 100.00 |
| *—With "New York, USA" address on label* | | | |

| Number | Title (A Side/B Side) | Yr | NM |
|---|---|---|---|
| ❑ BST-84137 [S] | One Step Beyond | 1967 | 40.00 |
| *—With "A Division of Liberty Records" on label* | | | |
| ❑ BST-84137 [S] | One Step Beyond | 197? | 15.00 |
| *—Dark blue label with black stylized "B"* | | | |
| ❑ BST-84165 [S] | Destination... Out! | 1964 | 100.00 |
| *—With "New York, USA" address on label* | | | |
| ❑ BST-84165 [S] | Destination... Out! | 1967 | 40.00 |
| *—With "A Division of Liberty Records" on label* | | | |
| ❑ BST-84165 [S] | Destination... Out! | 197? | 15.00 |
| *—Dark blue label with white stylized "B"* | | | |
| ❑ BST-84179 [S] | It's Time! | 1964 | 100.00 |
| *—With "New York, USA" address on label* | | | |
| ❑ BST-84179 [S] | It's Time! | 1967 | 25.00 |
| *—With "A Division of Liberty Records" on label* | | | |
| ❑ BST-84215 [S] | Right Now! | 1965 | 100.00 |
| *—With "New York, USA" address on label* | | | |
| ❑ BST-84215 [S] | Right Now! | 1967 | 30.00 |
| *—With "A Division of Liberty Records" on label* | | | |
| ❑ BST-84218 [S] | Action Action Action | 1965 | 100.00 |
| *—With "New York, USA" address on label* | | | |
| ❑ BST-84218 [S] | Action Action Action | 1967 | 30.00 |
| *—With "A Division of Liberty Records" on label* | | | |
| ❑ BST-84262 [S] | New and Old Gospel | 1967 | 120.00 |
| *—With "A Division of Liberty Records" on label* | | | |
| ❑ BST-84284 | 'Bout Soul | 1968 | 80.00 |
| *—With "A Division of Liberty Records" on label* | | | |
| ❑ BST-84345 | Demon's Dance | 1969 | 80.00 |
| *—With "A Division of Liberty Records" on label* | | | |
| **JOSIE** | | | |
| ❑ JJM-3503 [M] | Jackie McLean Sextet | 1963 | 60.00 |
| ❑ JLPS-3503 [S] | Jackie McLean Sextet | 1963 | 40.00 |
| ❑ JJM-3507 [M] | Jackie McLean Sextet | 1963 | 60.00 |
| ❑ JLPS-3507 [S] | Jackie McLean Sextet | 1963 | 40.00 |
| **JUBILEE** | | | |
| ❑ JLP-1064 [M] | The Jackie McLean Quintet | 1958 | 150.00 |
| ❑ JLP-1093 [M] | Jackie McLean Plays Fat Jazz | 1959 | 200.00 |
| **MOSAIC** | | | |
| ❑ MQ6-150 [(6)] | The Complete Blue Note 1964-66 Jackie McLean Sessions | 1993 | 200.00 |
| *—Limited edition of 5,000* | | | |
| **NEW JAZZ** | | | |
| ❑ NJLP-8212 [M] | McLean's Scene | 1958 | 150.00 |
| *—Purple label* | | | |
| ❑ NJLP-8212 [M] | McLean's Scene | 1965 | 40.00 |
| *—Blue label, trident logo at right* | | | |
| ❑ NJLP-8231 [M] | Makin' the Changes | 1960 | 150.00 |
| *—Purple label* | | | |
| ❑ NJLP-8231 [M] | Makin' the Changes | 1965 | 40.00 |
| *—Blue label, trident logo at right* | | | |
| ❑ NJLP-8253 [M] | A Long Drink of the Blues | 1961 | 150.00 |
| *—Purple label* | | | |
| ❑ NJLP-8253 [M] | A Long Drink of the Blues | 1965 | 40.00 |
| *—Blue label, trident logo at right* | | | |
| ❑ NJLP-8263 [M] | Lights Out! | 1961 | 100.00 |
| *—Purple label* | | | |
| ❑ NJLP-8263 [M] | Lights Out! | 1965 | 40.00 |
| *—Blue label, trident logo at right* | | | |
| ❑ NJLP-8279 [M] | 4, 5 and 6 | 1962 | 100.00 |
| *—Purple label* | | | |
| ❑ NJLP-8279 [M] | 4, 5 and 6 | 1965 | 40.00 |
| *—Blue label, trident logo at right* | | | |
| ❑ NJLP-8290 [M] | Steeplechase | 1962 | 100.00 |
| *—Purple label* | | | |
| ❑ NJLP-8290 [M] | Steeplechase | 1965 | 40.00 |
| *—Blue label, trident logo at right* | | | |
| **PRESTIGE** | | | |
| ❑ PRLP-7035 [M] | Lights Out! | 1956 | 300.00 |
| *—"446 W. 50th St., N.Y.C." address on yellow label* | | | |
| ❑ PRLP-7048 [M] | 4, 5 and 6 | 1956 | 300.00 |
| *—"446 W. 50th St., N.Y.C." address on yellow label* | | | |
| ❑ PRLP-7068 [M] | Jackie's Pal — Introducing Bill Hardman | 1956 | 300.00 |
| *—"446 W. 50th St., N.Y.C." address on yellow label* | | | |
| ❑ PRLP-7087 [M] | Jackie McLean & Co. | 1957 | 400.00 |
| *—"446 W. 50th St., N.Y.C." address on label* | | | |
| ❑ PRLP-7114 [M] | Alto Madness | 1957 | 250.00 |
| *—Yellow label* | | | |
| ❑ PRLP-7500 [M] | Strange Blues | 1967 | 40.00 |
| **RCA VICTOR** | | | |
| ❑ AFL1-3230 [S] | Monuments | 1979 | 25.00 |
| **STATUS** | | | |
| ❑ ST-8312 [M] | Alto Madness | 1965 | 60.00 |
| ❑ ST-8323 [M] | Jackie McLean & Co. | 1965 | 60.00 |

### MCLOLLIE, OSCAR

| Number | Title (A Side/B Side) | Yr | NM |
|---|---|---|---|
| **CROWN** | | | |
| ❑ CLP-5016 [M] | Oscar McLollie and His Honey Jumpers | 1956 | 400.00 |
| *—Opinions differ as to whether this LP actually exists. Value is probably conservative.* | | | |

### MCLUHAN

| Number | Title (A Side/B Side) | Yr | NM |
|---|---|---|---|
| **BRUNSWICK** | | | |
| ❑ BL 754177 | Anomaly | 1972 | 20.00 |

### MCLUHAN, MARSHALL

| Number | Title (A Side/B Side) | Yr | NM |
|---|---|---|---|
| **COLUMBIA** | | | |
| ❑ CL 2701 [M] | The Medium Is the Message | 1967 | 25.00 |
| ❑ CS 9501 [S] | The Medium Is the Message | 1967 | 25.00 |

### MCMAHON, ED

| Number | Title (A Side/B Side) | Yr | NM |
|---|---|---|---|
| **CAMEO** | | | |
| ❑ C-2009 [M] | And Me...I'm Ed McMahon | 1967 | 25.00 |
| ❑ SC-2009 [S] | And Me...I'm Ed McMahon | 1967 | 30.00 |
| **RCA CAMDEN** | | | |
| ❑ CAL-1083 [M] | What Do You Want to Be When You Grow Up? | 1965 | 20.00 |
| ❑ CAS-1083 [S] | What Do You Want to Be When You Grow Up? | 1965 | 25.00 |

### MCNABB, TED

| Number | Title (A Side/B Side) | Yr | NM |
|---|---|---|---|
| **EPIC** | | | |
| ❑ BN 558 [S] | Ted McNabb and Company | 1959 | 40.00 |
| ❑ LN 3663 [M] | Ted McNabb and Company | 1959 | 50.00 |

### MCNAIR, BARBARA

| Number | Title (A Side/B Side) | Yr | NM |
|---|---|---|---|
| **AUDIO FIDELITY** | | | |
| ❑ AFSD-6222 | More Today Than Yesterday | 1969 | 20.00 |
| ❑ ST-92074 | More Today Than Yesterday | 1969 | 25.00 |
| *—Capitol Record Club edition* | | | |
| **MOTOWN** | | | |
| ❑ 644 [M] | Here I Am | 1966 | 50.00 |
| ❑ S-644 [S] | Here I Am | 1966 | 60.00 |
| ❑ S-680 | The Real Barbara McNair | 1969 | 30.00 |
| **SIGNATURE** | | | |
| ❑ SM 1042 [M] | Love Talk | 1960 | 40.00 |
| ❑ SS 1042 [S] | Love Talk | 1960 | 50.00 |
| **WARNER BROS.** | | | |
| ❑ W 1541 [M] | I Enjoy Being a Girl | 1964 | 25.00 |
| ❑ WS 1541 [S] | I Enjoy Being a Girl | 1964 | 30.00 |
| ❑ W 1570 [M] | The Livin' End | 1964 | 25.00 |
| ❑ WS 1570 [S] | The Livin' End | 1964 | 30.00 |

### MCNEELY, BIG JAY

| Number | Title (A Side/B Side) | Yr | NM |
|---|---|---|---|
| **COLLECTABLES** | | | |
| ❑ COL-5133 | Golden Classics | 198? | 10.00 |
| **FEDERAL** | | | |
| ❑ 295-96 [10] | Big Jay McNeely | 1955 | 3000. |
| ❑ 395-530 [M] | Big Jay McNeely in 3-D | 1956 | 800.00 |
| **KING** | | | |
| ❑ 650 [M] | Big "J" in 3-D | 1959 | 500.00 |
| **SAVOY** | | | |
| ❑ MG-15045 [10] | A Rhythm and Blues Concert | 1955 | 2000. |
| *—VG value 1000; VG+ value 1500* | | | |
| **WARNER BROS.** | | | |
| ❑ W 1533 [M] | Big Jay McNeely | 1963 | 80.00 |
| ❑ WS 1533 [S] | Big Jay McNeely | 1963 | 100.00 |

### MCNEILL, DON

| Number | Title (A Side/B Side) | Yr | NM |
|---|---|---|---|
| **CORAL** | | | |
| ❑ CRL 57288 [M] | Book, Candle, Prayer | 1958 | 30.00 |
| ❑ CRL 57291 [M] | March Around the Breakfast Table | 1958 | 30.00 |

### MCNICHOL, KRISTY AND JIMMY

| Number | Title (A Side/B Side) | Yr | NM |
|---|---|---|---|
| **RCA VICTOR** | | | |
| ❑ AFL1-2875 | Kristy and Jimmy McNichol | 1978 | 20.00 |

### MCPARTLAND, JIMMY

| Number | Title (A Side/B Side) | Yr | NM |
|---|---|---|---|
| **BRUNSWICK** | | | |
| ❑ BL 54018 [M] | Dixieland Band | 1955 | 50.00 |
| ❑ BL 58049 [10] | Shades of Bix | 1953 | 80.00 |
| **EPIC** | | | |
| ❑ BN 506 [S] | "The Music Man" Goes Dixieland, The | 1958 | 30.00 |
| ❑ LN 3371 [M] | Jimmy McPartland's Dixieland | 1956 | 40.00 |
| ❑ LN 3463 [M] | "The Music Man" Goes Dixieland, The | 1958 | 40.00 |
| **JAZZTONE** | | | |
| ❑ J-1227 [M] | The Middle Road | 1956 | 40.00 |
| **MERCURY** | | | |
| ❑ MG-20460 [M] | Meet Me in Chicago | 1959 | 25.00 |
| ❑ SR-60143 [S] | Meet Me in Chicago | 1959 | 30.00 |
| **RCA CAMDEN** | | | |
| ❑ CAL-549 [M] | That Happy Dixieland Jazz | 1960 | 25.00 |
| **RCA VICTOR** | | | |
| ❑ LPV-549 [M] | That Happy Dixieland Jazz | 1966 | 20.00 |

### MCPARTLAND, JIMMY/PAUL BARBARIN

| Number | Title (A Side/B Side) | Yr | NM |
|---|---|---|---|
| **JAZZTONE** | | | |
| ❑ J-1241 [M] | Dixieland Now and Then | 195? | 30.00 |

### MCPARTLAND, MARIAN

| Number | Title (A Side/B Side) | Yr | NM |
|---|---|---|---|
| **ARGO** | | | |
| ❑ LP-640 [M] | Marion McPartland at the London House | 1959 | 40.00 |
| ❑ LPS-640 [S] | Marion McPartland at the London House | 1959 | 30.00 |
| **CAPITOL** | | | |
| ❑ T 574 [M] | Marion McPartland at the Hickory House | 1955 | 40.00 |
| ❑ T 699 [M] | After Dark | 1956 | 40.00 |
| ❑ T 785 [M] | Marion McPartland Trio | 1957 | 40.00 |
| **SAVOY** | | | |
| ❑ MG-12004 [M] | Marion McPartland in Concert | 1955 | 50.00 |
| ❑ MG-12005 [M] | Lullaby of Birdland | 1955 | 50.00 |
| ❑ MG-15019 [10] | Jazz at Storyville, Volume 3 | 1952 | 80.00 |
| ❑ MG-15021 [10] | Piano Moods | 1952 | 80.00 |
| ❑ MG-15027 [10] | Marion McPartland | 1953 | 80.00 |
| ❑ MG-15032 [10] | Jazz at the Hickory House | 1953 | 80.00 |
| **TIME** | | | |
| ❑ S-2073 [S] | Bossa Nova Plus Soul | 1963 | 30.00 |
| ❑ S-2189 [S] | West Side Story | 196? | 30.00 |
| ❑ 52073 [M] | Bossa Nova Plus Soul | 1963 | 25.00 |
| ❑ 52189 [M] | West Side Story | 196? | 25.00 |

### MCPARTLAND, MARIAN, AND GEORGE SHEARING

| Number | Title (A Side/B Side) | Yr | NM |
|---|---|---|---|
| **SAVOY** | | | |
| ❑ MG-12016 [M] | Great Britain's Marion McPartland and George Shearing | 1955 | 40.00 |

### MCPEAK, CURTIS

| Number | Title (A Side/B Side) | Yr | NM |
|---|---|---|---|
| **ABC-PARAMOUNT** | | | |
| ❑ ABC-446 [M] | Bluegrass Hillbillies | 1963 | 20.00 |
| ❑ ABCS-446 [S] | Bluegrass Hillbillies | 1963 | 25.00 |

### MCPHATTER, CLYDE Also see THE DRIFTERS.

| Number | Title (A Side/B Side) | Yr | NM |
|---|---|---|---|
| **ALLEGIANCE** | | | |
| ❑ AV-5029 | The Pretty One | 198? | 10.00 |
| **ATLANTIC** | | | |
| ❑ 8024 [M] | Love Ballads | 1958 | 500.00 |
| *—Black label* | | | |
| ❑ 8024 [M] | Love Ballads | 1960 | 200.00 |
| *—Brown and purple label* | | | |
| ❑ 8024 [M] | Love Ballads | 1960 | 400.00 |
| *—White "bullseye" label* | | | |
| ❑ 8031 [M] | Clyde | 1959 | 500.00 |
| *—Black label* | | | |
| ❑ 8031 [M] | Clyde | 1960 | 200.00 |
| *—Brown and purple label* | | | |
| ❑ 8031 [M] | Clyde | 1960 | 400.00 |
| *—White "bullseye" label* | | | |
| ❑ 8077 [M] | The Best of Clyde McPhatter | 1963 | 200.00 |
| **DECCA** | | | |
| ❑ DL 75231 | Welcome Home | 1970 | 25.00 |
| **MERCURY** | | | |
| ❑ MG-20597 [M] | Ta Ta | 1960 | 50.00 |
| ❑ MG-20655 [M] | Golden Blues Hits | 1961 | 50.00 |
| ❑ MG-20711 [M] | Lover Please | 1962 | 50.00 |
| ❑ MG-20750 [M] | Rhythm and Soul | 1962 | 50.00 |
| ❑ MG-20783 [M] | Clyde McPhatter's Greatest Hits | 1963 | 30.00 |
| ❑ MG-20902 [M] | Songs of the Big City | 1964 | 30.00 |
| ❑ MG-20915 [M] | Live at the Apollo | 1964 | 30.00 |
| ❑ SR-60262 [S] | Ta Ta | 1960 | 70.00 |
| ❑ SR-60655 [S] | Golden Blues Hits | 1961 | 70.00 |
| ❑ SR-60711 [S] | Lover Please | 1962 | 70.00 |
| ❑ SR-60750 [S] | Rhythm and Soul | 1962 | 70.00 |
| ❑ SR-60783 [S] | Clyde McPhatter's Greatest Hits | 1963 | 40.00 |
| ❑ SR-60902 [S] | Songs of the Big City | 1964 | 40.00 |
| ❑ SR-60915 [S] | Live at the Apollo | 1964 | 40.00 |
| **MGM** | | | |
| ❑ E-3775 [M] | Let's Start Over Again | 1959 | 150.00 |
| ❑ SE-3775 [S] | Let's Start Over Again | 1959 | 200.00 |
| ❑ E-3866 [M] | Clyde McPhatter's Greatest Hits | 1960 | 70.00 |
| ❑ SE-3866 [S] | Clyde McPhatter's Greatest Hits | 1960 | 80.00 |
| **WING** | | | |
| ❑ MGW-12224 [M] | May I Sing for You? | 1962 | 25.00 |
| ❑ SRW-16224 [S] | May I Sing for You? | 1962 | 30.00 |

### MCPHEE, JOE

| Number | Title (A Side/B Side) | Yr | NM |
|---|---|---|---|
| **CJR** | | | |
| ❑ 2 | Nation Time | 197? | 25.00 |
| ❑ 3 | Trinity | 197? | 25.00 |
| ❑ 4 | Pieces of Light | 197? | 25.00 |
| **HAT HUT** | | | |
| ❑ A | Black Magic Man | 1974 | 25.00 |
| ❑ C | Tenor | 1976 | 20.00 |
| ❑ D | Rotation | 1977 | 20.00 |
| ❑ I/J [(2)] | Graphics | 1977 | 30.00 |
| ❑ O | Variations on a Blue Line/'Round Midnight | 1978 | 20.00 |
| ❑ P | Glasses | 1978 | 20.00 |
| ❑ 01 | Old Eyes | 1979 | 20.00 |
| ❑ 1987/8 [(2)] | Topology | 1981 | 25.00 |

### MCPHERSON, CHARLES

| Number | Title (A Side/B Side) | Yr | NM |
|---|---|---|---|
| **PRESTIGE** | | | |
| ❑ PRLP-7359 [M] | Bebop Revisited | 1965 | 30.00 |
| ❑ PRST-7359 [S] | Bebop Revisited | 1965 | 40.00 |
| ❑ PRLP-7427 [M] | Con Alma! | 1966 | 30.00 |
| ❑ PRST-7427 [S] | Con Alma! | 1966 | 40.00 |

❑ PRLP-7480 [M] The Charles McPherson Quintet Live! 1967 40.00
❑ PRST-7480 [S] The Charles McPherson Quintet Live! 1967 30.00
❑ PRST-7559 From This Moment On 1968 30.00
❑ PRST-7603 Horizons 1969 30.00
❑ PRST-7743 McPherson's Mood 1970 20.00

### MCRAE, CARMEN

ATLANTIC
❑ SD 2-904 [(2)] The Great American Songbook 1971 20.00
❑ 8143 [M] For Once in My Life 1967 20.00

BETHLEHEM
❑ BCP-1023 [10] Carmen McRae 1955 100.00

COLUMBIA
❑ CL 1730 [M] Lover Man 1962 20.00
❑ CL 1943 [M] Something Wonderful 1962 20.00
❑ CS 8530 [S] Lover Man 1962 25.00
❑ CS 8743 [S] Something Wonderful 1962 25.00

DECCA
❑ DL 8173 [M] By Special Request 1955 50.00
*—Black label, silver print*
❑ DL 8173 [M] By Special Request 1960 20.00
*—Black label with color bars*
❑ DL 8267 [M] Torchy! 1956 50.00
*—Black label, silver print*
❑ DL 8267 [M] Torchy! 1960 20.00
*—Black label with color bars*
❑ DL 8347 [M] Blue Moon 1957 50.00
*—Black label, silver print*
❑ DL 8347 [M] Blue Moon 1960 20.00
*—Black label with color bars*
❑ DL 8583 [M] After Glow 1957 50.00
*—Black label, silver print*
❑ DL 8583 [M] After Glow 1960 20.00
*—Black label with color bars*
❑ DL 8662 [M] Mad About the Man 1958 50.00
*—Black label, silver print*
❑ DL 8662 [M] Mad About the Man 1960 20.00
*—Black label with color bars*
❑ DL 8738 [M] Carmen for Cool Ones 1958 50.00
*—Black label, silver print*
❑ DL 8738 [M] Carmen for Cool Ones 1960 20.00
*—Black label with color bars*
❑ DL 8815 [M] Birds of a Feather 1959 50.00
*—Black label, silver print*
❑ DL 8815 [M] Birds of a Feather 1960 20.00
*—Black label with color bars*

FOCUS
❑ FS-334 [S] Bittersweet 1964 20.00

HARMONY
❑ HL 7452 [M] Yesterdays 1968 20.00

KAPP
❑ KL-1117 [M] Book of Ballads 1958 25.00
❑ KL-1135 [M] When You're Away 1959 25.00
❑ KL-1169 [M] Something to Swing About 1960 25.00
❑ KL-1541 [M] This Is Carmen McRae 1967 20.00
❑ KS-3000 [S] Book of Ballads 1958 30.00
❑ KS-3018 [S] When You're Away 1959 30.00
❑ KS-3053 [S] Something to Swing About 1960 30.00

MAINSTREAM
❑ S-6028 [S] Second to None 1965 20.00
❑ S-6044 [S] Haven't We Met? 1965 20.00
❑ S-6065 [S] Woman Talk 1966 20.00
❑ S-6084 [S] Alfie 1966 20.00
❑ 56091 [M] In Person/San Francisco 1967 20.00

TIME
❑ S-2104 [S] Live at Sugar Hill 1960 25.00
❑ 52104 [M] Live at Sugar Hill 1960 20.00

### MCRITCHIE, GREG

CADET
❑ LP-4058 [M] Fighting Back 1967 25.00

ZEPHYR
❑ 12005 [M] Easy Jazz on a Fish Beat Bass 1959 250.00

### MCSHANN, JAY

CAPITOL
❑ ST 2645 [S] McShann's Piano 1967 20.00
❑ T 2645 [M] McShann's Piano 1967 20.00

DECCA
❑ DL 5503 [10] Kansas City Memories 1954 500.00
*—CHARLIE PARKER appears on this LP*
❑ DL 9236 [M] Kansas City Memories 1958 200.00

### MCTELL, BLIND WILLIE

BLUESVILLE
❑ BVLP-1040 [M] Last Session 1962 120.00
*—Blue label, silver print*
❑ BVLP-1040 [M] Last Session 1964 30.00
*—Blue label, trident logo at right*

MELODEON
❑ 7323 [M] 1940 1956 150.00

### MCTELL, RALPH

CAPITOL
❑ ST-240 Eight Frames a Second 1969 20.00

REPRISE
❑ MS 2121 Not Till Tomorrow 1973 15.00

### MCWILLIAMS, DAVID

KAPP
❑ KS-3547 Days of Pearly Spencer 1968 25.00

### MEADER, VAUGHN

CADENCE
❑ CLP 3060 [M] The First Family 1962 10.00
❑ CLP 3065 [M] The First Family, Volume Two 1963 20.00
❑ CLP 25065 [S] The First Family, Volume Two 1963 30.00

KAMA SUTRA
❑ KSBS-2038 The Second Coming 1971 15.00

LAURIE
❑ LLP-2035 [M] Take That! 1966 15.00

VERVE
❑ V-15042 [M] Have Some Nuts 1964 15.00
❑ V6-15042 [S] Have Some Nuts 1964 20.00
❑ V-15050 [M] If the Shoe Fits 1965 15.00

### MEADOW Supposedly, Laura Branigan was in this group.

PARAMOUNT
❑ PAS-6066 The Friend Ship 1973 20.00

### MEAT LOAF Also see STONEY AND MEATLOAF.

ATLANTIC
❑ 81698 Blind Before I Stop 1986 8.00

CLEVELAND INT'L.
❑ FE 36007 Dead Ringer 1981 8.00
❑ PE 36007 Dead Ringer 198? 6.00
*—Budget-line reissue*

EPIC
❑ E99 34974 [PD] Bat Out of Hell 1978 20.00
❑ JE 34974 Bat Out of Hell 1979 8.00
*—Dark blue label*
❑ PE 34974 Bat Out of Hell 1977 10.00
*—Orange label; originals do not have bar code on back cover*
❑ PE 34974 Bat Out of Hell 1985 6.00
*—Dark blue label; bar code on cover*
❑ FE 38444 Midnight at the Lost and Found 1983 8.00
❑ HE 44974 Bat Out of Hell 1981 40.00
*—Half-speed mastered edition*

RCA VICTOR
❑ AFL1-5451 Bad Attitude 1985 8.00

VIRGIN
❑ 09463-63147-1 [(2)] Bat Out of Hell III: The Monster Is Loose 2006 20.00

### MEAT PUPPETS

LONDON
❑ 1109 [10] Raw Meat 199? 20.00
*—Promo-only five-song 10-inch EP*
❑ 828484-1 Too High to Die 1994 12.00
*—Includes bonus 10-inch EP (double value for DJ stamp on cover)*

MERCURY
❑ 828665-1 No Joke! 1995 10.00

SST
❑ 009 Meat Puppets 1982 15.00
❑ 019 Meat Puppets II 1984 12.00
❑ 039 Up on the Sun 1985 12.00
❑ 049 [10] Out My Way 1986 8.00
*—10-inch EP*
❑ 100 Mirage 1986 12.00
❑ 150 Huevos 1987 10.00
❑ 253 Monsters 1989 10.00
❑ 265 [(2)] No Strings Attached 1990 16.00

### MECCA, LOU

BLUE NOTE
❑ BLP-5067 [10] Lou Mecca Quartet 1955 300.00

### MECKI MARK MEN, THE

LIMELIGHT
❑ LS-86054 The Mecki Mark Men 1968 25.00
❑ LS-86068 Running in the Summer Night 1969 25.00

### MEDIUM

GAMMA
❑ GS-503 Medium 196? 100.00

### MEDLEY, BILL

A&M
❑ SP-3505 A Song for You 1971 12.00
❑ SP-3517 Smile 1972 12.00

LIBERTY
❑ LT-1097 Sweet Thunder 1981 8.00
*—Reissue of United Artists 1097*

MGM
❑ E-4583 [M] Bill Medley 100% 1968 50.00
*—Mono is yellow label promo only*
❑ SE-4583 [S] Bill Medley 100% 1968 20.00
❑ SE-4603 Soft and Soulful 1969 20.00
❑ SE-4640 Someone Is Standing Outside 1969 20.00
❑ SE-4702 Nobody Knows 1970 15.00
❑ SE-4741 Gone 1970 15.00

RCA VICTOR
❑ BXL1-4434 Right Here and Now 1982 10.00
❑ CPL1-5352 Still Hung Up on You 1984 10.00
❑ MHL1-8519 [EP] I Still Do 1985 8.00

UNITED ARTISTS
❑ UA-LA929-H Lay a Little Lovin' on Me 1978 10.00
❑ LT-1097 Sweet Thunder 1980 10.00

### MEEUWSEN, TERRY ANN

SANDY
❑ SRS-9003 Meet Terry 1976 30.00

### MEHEGAN, JOHN

EPIC
❑ LA 16007 [M] Act of Jazz 1960 20.00
❑ BA 17007 [S] Act of Jazz 1960 25.00

PERSPECTIVE
❑ PR-1 [M] From Barrelhouse to Bop 195? 50.00

SAVOY
❑ MG-12028 [M] Reflections 1956 40.00
❑ MG-15054 [10] The Last Mehegan 1955 60.00

TJ
❑ LP-1 [M] Casual Affair 1959 40.00

### MEHEGAN, JOHN, AND EDDIE COSTA

SAVOY
❑ MG-12049 [M] A Pair of Pianos 1956 40.00

### MEL AND TIM

BAMBOO
❑ BMS-8001 Good Guys Only Win in the Movies 1970 25.00

STAX
❑ STS-3007 Starting All Over Again 1972 20.00
❑ STS-5501 Mel and Tim 1974 20.00

### MELACHRINO, GEORGE

RCA VICTOR
❑ LPM-1000 [M] Music for Dining 195? 25.00
❑ LPM-1001 [M] Music for Relaxation 195? 25.00
❑ LPM-1002 [M] Music for Reading 195? 25.00
❑ LPM-1005 [M] Music for Courage and Confidence 195? 25.00
❑ LPM-1006 [M] Music to Help You Sleep 195? 25.00
❑ LPM-1008 [M] Show Tunes 195? 25.00
❑ LPM-1027 [M] Music for Two People Alone 195? 25.00
❑ LPM-1028 [M] Music for Daydreaming 195? 25.00
❑ LPM-1029 [M] Music to Work or Study By 195? 25.00
❑ LPM-1045 [M] Christmas in High Fidelity 1954 25.00
❑ LPM-1110 [M] Immortal Ladies 1955 20.00
❑ LPM-1184 [M] Masquerade 1955 20.00
❑ LPM-1261 [M] Sounds of Paris 1956 20.00
❑ LPM-1307 [M] Melachrino on Broadway 1956 20.00
❑ LPM-1329 [M] I'll Walk Beside You 1956 20.00
❑ LPM-1330 [M] Those Beautiful Strings 1956 20.00
❑ LPM-1757 [M] Strauss Waltzes 1958 15.00
❑ LSP-1757 [S] Strauss Waltzes 1958 20.00
❑ LPM-1762 [M] Lisbon at Twilight 1958 15.00
❑ LSP-1762 [S] Lisbon at Twilight 1958 20.00

### MELIS, JOSE

DIPLOMAT
❑ D-2260 [M] Jose Melis and the Metropolitan Strings 196? 10.00
❑ DS-2260 [S] Jose Melis and the Metropolitan Strings 196? 10.00

HARMONY
❑ HL 7150 [M] Exciting TV Star Jose Melis 195? 12.00

MERCURY
❑ MG 20008 [M] Classics the South American Way 195? 15.00
❑ MG 20127 [M] Latin American Stylings 195? 15.00
❑ MG 20275 [M] Tonight It's Music 195? 15.00
❑ MG 20610 [M] Jose Melis on Broadway 1961 12.00
❑ MG 20648 [M] Jose Melis in Movieland 1961 12.00
❑ MG 20684 [M] Jose Melis at the Pops Concert 1962 12.00
❑ MG 20709 [M] Jose Melis at the Opera 1962 12.00
❑ MG 20738 [M] Everybody's Favorites 1962 12.00
❑ MG 25035 [10] Jose Melis 195? 30.00
❑ MG 25119 [10] Latin-American Piano 195? 30.00
❑ SR 60610 [S] Jose Melis on Broadway 1961 15.00
❑ SR 60648 [S] Jose Melis in Movieland 1961 15.00
❑ SR 60684 [S] Jose Melis at the Pops Concert 1962 15.00
❑ SR 60709 [S] Jose Melis at the Opera 1962 15.00
❑ SR 60738 [S] Everybody's Favorites 1962 15.00

Number | Title (A Side/B Side) | Yr | NM

MGM
❑ E-262 [10] The Jose Melis Trio 1955 30.00
❑ E-3527 [M] Jose Melis of the Jack Paar Show 1957 15.00

MUSICOR
❑ MM-2071 [M] Piano Classics the South American Way 1967 12.00
❑ MS-3071 [S] Piano Classics the South American Way 1967 12.00

PALACE
❑ P-84 [M] Dance Party with Jose Melis 195? 12.00

SEECO
❑ CELP-411 [M] Tonight with Jose Melis 1958 15.00
❑ CELP-414 [M] Jose Melis at Midnight 1959 15.00
❑ CELP 423 [M] Christmas with Melis 1959 15.00
❑ CELP-436 [M] The Many Moods of Jose Melis 1960 12.00
❑ CELP-445 [M] Jose Melis Plays the Latin Way 1960 12.00
❑ CELP-462 [M] Jose Melis Plays Jack Paar's Favorites 1960 12.00
❑ CELP-471 [M] Our Love 1961 12.00
❑ CELP-4140 [S] Jose Melis at Midnight 1959 20.00
❑ CELP-4360 [S] The Many Moods of Jose Melis 1960 15.00
❑ CELP-4450 [S] Jose Melis Plays the Latin Way 1960 15.00
❑ CELP-4620 [S] Jose Melis Plays Jack Paar's Favorites 1960 15.00
❑ CELP-4710 [S] Our Love 1961 15.00

## MELLE, GIL

BLUE NOTE
❑ BLP-1517 [M] Patterns in Jazz 1956 400.00
*—Regular version, Lexington Ave. address on label*
❑ BLP-1517 [M] Patterns in Jazz 1956 600.00
*—"Deep groove" version; Lexington Ave. address on label*
❑ BLP-5020 [10] Gil Melle Quintet/Sextet 1953 800.00
❑ BLP-5033 [10] Gil Melle Quintet, Volume 2 1953 800.00
❑ BLP-5054 [10] Gil Melle Quintet, Volume 3 1954 800.00
❑ BLP-5063 [10] Gil Melle Quintet, Volume 4 — Five Impressions of Color 1954 800.00

PRESTIGE
❑ PRLP-7040 [M] Melle Plays Primitive Modern 1956 200.00
*—Yellow label with W. 50th St. address*
❑ PRLP-7063 [M] Gil's Guests 1956 150.00
*—Yellow label with W. 50th St. address*
❑ PRLP-7097 [M] Quadrama 1957 150.00
*—Yellow label*

VERVE
❑ V6-8744 Tome VI 1968 40.00

## MELLENCAMP, JOHN

COLUMBIA
❑ C 69602 John Mellencamp 1998 15.00

MCA
❑ 2225 Chestnut Street Incident 1977 25.00
*—As "Johnny Cougar"*

MERCURY
❑ 832465-1 The Lonesome Jubilee 1987 8.00
❑ 838220-1 Big Daddy 1989 10.00

MOBILE FIDELITY
❑ 1-222 The Lonesome Jubilee 1995 20.00
*—Audiophile vinyl*

RIVA
❑ RVL 7401 John Cougar 1979 10.00
*—As "John Cougar"*
❑ RVL 7403 Nothin' Matters and What If It Did 1980 10.00
*—As "John Cougar"*
❑ RVL 7501 American Fool 1982 8.00
*—As "John Cougar"*
❑ RVL 7504 Uh-Huh 1983 8.00
*—As "John Cougar Mellencamp"*
❑ 824865-1 Scarecrow 1985 8.00
*—As "John Cougar Mellencamp"*

## MELLO-KINGS, THE

COLLECTABLES
❑ COL-5020 Greatest Hits 198? 10.00

HERALD
❑ H-1013 [M] Tonight-Tonight 196? 250.00
*—Multi-color label*
❑ H-1013 [M] Tonight-Tonight 1960 500.00
*—Yellow label*

RELIC
❑ LP-5035 Greatest Hits 198? 12.00

## MELLO-LARKS, THE

RCA CAMDEN
❑ CAL-530 [M] Just for a Lark 1959 40.00

## MELROSE, FRANK

ABC-PARAMOUNT
❑ (# unknown) [M] Kansas City Frank Melrose 1956 50.00

## MELTON, LEVY, AND THE DEY BROTHERS

COLUMBIA
❑ KC 31279 Levy Melton and the Dey Brothers 1972 20.00

Harold Melvin and the Blue Notes, *Wake Up Everybody,* Philadelphia International PZ 33808, 1975, $12.

Number | Title (A Side/B Side) | Yr | NM

## MELTZER, DAVID AND TINA

VANGUARD
❑ VSD-6619 Poet Song 1969 25.00

## MELVIN, HAROLD, AND THE BLUE NOTES

ABC
❑ AB-969 Reaching for the World 1977 10.00
❑ AB-1041 Now Is the Time 1978 10.00

MCA
❑ 5261 All Things Happen in Time 1981 10.00

PHILADELPHIA INT'L.
❑ KZ 31648 Harold Melvin and the Blue Notes 1972 12.00
❑ KZ 32407 Black & Blue 1973 12.00
❑ ZQ 32407 [Q] Black & Blue 1973 20.00
❑ PZ 33148 To Be True 1975 12.00
❑ PZ 33808 Wake Up Everybody 1975 12.00
❑ PZQ 33808 [Q] Wake Up Everybody 1975 20.00
❑ PZ 34232 Collector's Item — All Their Greatest Hits! 1976 12.00

PHILLY WORLD
❑ 90187 Talk It Up (Tell Everybody) 1985 10.00

SOURCE
❑ 3197 The Blue Album 1980 10.00

## MEMPHIS SLIM

BATTLE
❑ BM-6118 [M] Alone with My Friends 1963 50.00
❑ BM-6122 [M] Baby Please Come Home 1963 50.00

BLUESVILLE
❑ BVLP-1018 [M] Just Blues 1961 120.00
*—Blue label, silver print*
❑ BVLP-1018 [M] Just Blues 1964 30.00
*—Blue label, trident logo at right*
❑ BVLP-1031 [M] No Strain 1961 120.00
*—Blue label, silver print*
❑ BVLP-1031 [M] No Strain 1964 30.00
*—Blue label, trident logo at right*
❑ BVLP-1053 [M] All Kinds of Blues 1962 100.00
*—Blue label, silver print*
❑ BVLP-1053 [M] All Kinds of Blues 1964 30.00
*—Blue label, trident logo at right*
❑ BVLP-1075 [M] Steady Rollin' Blues 1963 100.00
*—Blue label, silver print*

Number | Title (A Side/B Side) | Yr | NM

❑ BVLP-1075 [M] Steady Rollin' Blues 1964 30.00
*—Blue label, trident logo at right*

BUDDAH
❑ BDS-7505 Mother Earth 1969 20.00

CANDID
❑ CM-8023 [M] Slim's Tribute to Big Bill Broonzy 1961 60.00
❑ CM-8024 [M] Memphis Slim U.S.A. 1962 60.00
❑ CS-9023 [S] Slim's Tribute to Big Bill Broonzy 1961 80.00
❑ CS-9024 [S] Memphis Slim U.S.A. 1962 80.00

CHESS
❑ LP-1455 [M] Memphis Slim 1961 150.00
*—Black label*
❑ LP-1510 [M] The Real Folk Blues 1966 80.00

DISC
❑ D-105 [M] If the Rabbit Had a Gun 1964 40.00

FOLKWAYS
❑ FG-3524 [M] The Real Boogie Woogie 1959 100.00
❑ FG-3535 [M] Memphis Slim...And the Real Honky Tonk 1960 100.00
❑ FG-3536 [M] Chicago Blues 1961 100.00

JUBILEE
❑ JGM-8003 [M] Legend of the Blues 1967 25.00
❑ JGS-8003 [S] Legend of the Blues 1967 25.00

KING
❑ 885 [M] Memphis Slim Sings Folk Blues 1964 50.00

SCEPTER
❑ SM-535 [M] Self Portrait 1966 20.00
❑ SMS-535 [S] Self Portrait 1966 25.00

SPIN-O-RAMA
❑ 149 [M] Lonesome Blues 196? 20.00

STRAND
❑ SL-1046 [M] The World's Foremost Blues Singer 1962 40.00
❑ SLS-1046 [S] The World's Foremost Blues Singer 1962 50.00

UNITED ARTISTS
❑ UAL-3137 [M] Broken Soul Blues 1961 60.00
❑ UAS-6137 [S] Broken Soul Blues 1961 80.00

| Number | Title (A Side/B Side) | Yr | NM |
|---|---|---|---|

VEE JAY

❑ LP-1012 [M] Memphis Slim at the Gate of the Horn 1959 200.00
*—Maroon label*

❑ LP-1012 [M] Memphis Slim at the Gate of the Horn 1961 120.00
*—Black rainbow label, oval logo*

**MEMPHIS WILLIE B**

BLUESVILLE

❑ BVLP-1034 [M] Introducing Memphis Willie B 1961 100.00
*—Blue label, silver print*

❑ BVLP-1034 [M] Introducing Memphis Willie B 1964 30.00
*—Blue label, trident logo at right*

❑ BVLP-1048 [M] Hard Working Man Blues 1962 100.00
*—Blue label, silver print*

❑ BVLP-1048 [M] Hard Working Man Blues 1964 30.00
*—Blue label, trident logo at right*

**MEN, THE**

SNAT-5

❑ 2001 Hermeneutics 1981 25.00

**MEN AT WORK**

COLUMBIA

❑ A2S 1650 [(2)DJ] Cargo (World Premiere Weekend) 1983 20.00
*—Promo-only two-record package of interviews and music*

❑ ARC 37978 Business as Usual 1982 10.00

❑ FC 37978 Business as Usual 1982 8.00
*—New prefix to reflect list-price increase*

❑ PC 38660 Cargo 198? 8.00
*—Reissue with new prefix*

❑ QC 38660 Cargo 1983 10.00

❑ FC 40078 Two Hearts 1985 8.00

❑ HC 47978 Business as Usual 1983 25.00
*—Half-speed mastered edition*

❑ HC 48660 Cargo 1983 25.00
*—Half-speed mastered edition*

**MEN WITHOUT HATS**

BACKSTREET

❑ 5436 Rhythm of Youth 1983 10.00
*—Reissue*

❑ 39002 Rhythm of Youth 1983 12.00

MCA

❑ 5487 Folk of the 80's, Part 3 1984 10.00

MERCURY

❑ 842000-1 In the 21st Century 1989 10.00

STIFF

❑ TEES-12-01 [EP] Folk of the 80's 1981 30.00
*—Reissue of Trend 10-inch EP*

TREND

❑ HATS-001 [10] Folk of the 80's 1981 40.00
*—10-inch four-song EP; possibly released only in Canada*

**MENDES, SERGIO**

ATLANTIC

❑ SD 1466 [S] Great Arrival 1966 20.00

❑ 1480 [M] The Beat of Brazil 1967 20.00

CAPITOL

❑ ST 2294 [S] In a Brazilan Bag 1965 60.00

❑ T 2294 [M] In a Brazilan Bag 1965 50.00

MOBILE FIDELITY

❑ 1-118 Sergio Mendes and Brasil '66 1984 50.00
*—Audiophile vinyl*

PHILIPS

❑ PHM 200263 [M] Quiet Nights 1968 20.00

TOWER

❑ ST 5052 [S] In a Brazilan Bag 1966 50.00
*—Reissue of Capitol 2294*

❑ T 5052 [M] In a Brazilan Bag 1966 40.00
*—Reissue of Capitol 2294*

**MENUHIN, YEHUDI**

MERCURY LIVING PRESENCE

❑ SR 90003 [S] Bartok: Violin Concerto No. 2 1959 70.00
*—With Antal Dorati/Minneapolis Symphony Orch.; maroon label, no "Vendor: Mercury Record Corporation"*

❑ SR 90003 [S] Bartok: Violin Concerto No. 2 196? 30.00
*—With Antal Dorati/Minneapolis Symphony Orch.; maroon label, with "Vendor: Mercury Record Corporation"*

**MEPHISTOPHELES**

REPRISE

❑ RS 6355 In Frustration I Hear Singing 1969 40.00

**MERCER, JOHNNY**

CAPITOL

❑ H 210 [10] Music of Jerome Kern 1950 80.00

❑ H 214 [10] Johnny Mercer Sings 1950 80.00

❑ T 907 [M] Ac-Cent-Tchu-Ate the Positive 1957 50.00

JUPITER

❑ JLP-1001 [M] Johnny Mercer Sings Just for Fun 1956 50.00

PAUSA

❑ PR 9062 Jonny Mercer Sings Jonny Mercer 1986 10.00
*—Name is indeed misspelled on the label as "Jonny"*

**MERCER, MABEL**

ATLANTIC

❑ ALS-402 [10] Songs by Mabel Mercer, Volume 1 1954 80.00

❑ ALS-403 [10] Songs by Mabel Mercer, Volume 2 1954 80.00

❑ 2-602 [(2)M] The Art of Mabel Mercer 1959 60.00
*—Black labels*

❑ 2-602 [(2)M] The Art of Mabel Mercer 1961 30.00
*—Multicolor labels, white "fan" logo at right*

❑ 2-602 [(2)M] The Art of Mabel Mercer 1963 20.00
*—Multicolor labels, black "fan" logo at right*

❑ SD 2-605 [(2)] The Second Town Hall Concert 1969 20.00
*—Red and green label with "1841 Broadway" address*

❑ SD 2-605 [(2)] The Second Town Hall Concert 1975 12.00
*—Red and green label with "75 Rockefeller Plaza" address*

❑ 1213 [M] Mabel Mercer Sings Cole Porter 1955 40.00
*—Black label*

❑ 1213 [M] Mabel Mercer Sings Cole Porter 1961 20.00
*—Multicolor label, white "fan" logo at right*

❑ 1244 [M] Midnight at Mabel Mercer's 1956 40.00
*—Black label*

❑ 1244 [M] Midnight at Mabel Mercer's 1961 20.00
*—Multicolor label, white "fan" logo at right*

❑ 1301 [M] Once in a Blue Moon 1959 40.00
*—Black label*

❑ 1301 [M] Once in a Blue Moon 1961 20.00
*—Multicolor label, white "fan" logo at right*

❑ SD 1301 [S] Once in a Blue Moon 1959 50.00
*—Green label*

❑ SD 1301 [S] Once in a Blue Moon 1961 25.00
*—Multicolor labels, white "fan" logo at right*

❑ SD 1301 [S] Once in a Blue Moon 1963 20.00
*—Multicolor labels, black "fan" logo at right*

❑ 1322 [M] Merely Marvelous Mabel Mercer 1960 40.00
*—Black label*

❑ 1322 [M] Merely Marvelous Mabel Mercer 1961 20.00
*—Multicolor label, white "fan" logo at right*

❑ SD 1322 [S] Merely Marvelous Mabel Mercer 1960 50.00
*—Green label*

❑ SD 1322 [S] Merely Marvelous Mabel Mercer 1961 25.00
*—Multicolor labels, white "fan" logo at right*

❑ SD 1322 [S] Merely Marvelous Mabel Mercer 1963 20.00
*—Multicolor labels, black "fan" logo at right*

DECCA

❑ DL 74472 [S] Mabel Mercer Sings 1964 20.00

**MERCER, MABEL, AND BOBBY SHORT**

ATLANTIC

❑ SD 2-604 [(2)] Mabel Mercer and Bobby Short at Town Hall 1968 20.00

**MERCHANTS OF DREAM, THE**

A&M

❑ SP-4149 Strange Night Voyage 1969 25.00

**MERCY**

SUNDI

❑ SRLP-803 The Mercy & Love (Can Make You Happy) 1969 20.00
*—Has the original version of the title song plus filler instrumentals*

WARNER BROS.

❑ WS 1799 Love (Can Make You Happy) 1969 15.00
*—"Love (Can Make You Happy)" was re-recorded for this LP*

**MERCY DEE**

ARHOOLIE

❑ F-1007 [M] Mercy Dee 1961 60.00

BLUESVILLE

❑ BVLP-1039 [M] A Pity and a Shame 1962 80.00
*—Blue label, silver print*

❑ BVLP-1039 [M] A Pity and a Shame 1964 25.00
*—Blue label, trident logo at right*

**MEREDITH, BUDDY**

STARDAY

❑ SLP-225 [M] Sing Me a Heart Song 1963 30.00

**MEREDITH, BURGESS**

COLPIX

❑ CP-452 [M] Burgess Meredith Sings Songs from "How the West Was Won" 1964 20.00

❑ SCP-452 [S] Burgess Meredith Sings Songs from "How the West Was Won" 1964 25.00

EPIC

❑ BN 590 [S] Songs and Stories of the Gold Rush 1961 30.00

❑ LN 3656 [M] Songs and Stories of the Gold Rush 1961 25.00

**MERIAN, LEON**

SEECO

❑ CELP-4470 [S] This Time the Swing's On Me 1960 20.00

❑ CELP-4590 [S] Fiorello! 1960 20.00

**MERIWETHER, ROY**

CAPITOL

❑ ST-102 Soul Knight 1969 30.00

COLUMBIA

❑ CL 2584 [M] Stone Truth 1967 20.00

❑ CL 2744 [M] Soul Invader 1968 30.00

❑ CS 9233 [S] Soup and Onions (Soul Cookin') 1966 20.00

❑ CS 9298 [S] Popcorn and Soul Groovin' at the Movies 1966 20.00

**MERKIN**

WINDI

❑ 1004/5 Music from Merkin 1972 400.00

**MERMAIDS, THE** See THE MURMAIDS.

**MERMAN, ETHEL**

DECCA

❑ DXA 153 [(2)M] A Musical Autobiography 195? 40.00
*—Black label, silver print*

❑ DL 5053 [10] Songs She Made Famous 1950 60.00

❑ DL 8178 [M] A Musical Autobiography, Volume 1 195? 25.00
*—Black label, silver print*

❑ DL 8179 [M] A Musical Autobiography, Volume 2 195? 25.00
*—Black label, silver print*

❑ DL 9028 [M] Memories 1955 40.00

**MERRILL, HELEN**

ATCO

❑ 33-112 [M] American Country Songs 1959 50.00

EMARCY

❑ MG-36006 [M] Helen Merrill 1955 80.00
*—Blue label with drummer logo*

❑ MG-36057 [M] Helen Merrill with Strings 1955 80.00
*—Blue label with drummer logo*

❑ MG-36078 [M] Dream of You 1956 80.00
*—Blue label with drummer logo*

❑ MG-36078 [M] Dream of You 1958 30.00
*—Blue label, double oval at top, "Emarcy Jazz" between the two ovals under "Mercury"*

❑ MG-36107 [M] Merrill at Midnight 1957 80.00
*—Blue label with drummer logo*

❑ MG-36107 [M] Merrill at Midnight 1958 30.00
*—Blue label, double oval at top, "Emarcy Jazz" between the two ovals under "Mercury"*

❑ MG-36134 [M] The Nearness of You 1958 50.00

MAINSTREAM

❑ S-6014 [S] The Artistry of Helen Merrill 1965 30.00

❑ 56014 [M] The Artistry of Helen Merrill 1965 30.00

MERCURY

❑ 826340-1 [(4)] The Complete Helen Merrill on Mercury 1985 80.00

METROJAZZ

❑ E-1010 [M] You've Got a Date with the Blues 1958 40.00

❑ SE-1010 [S] You've Got a Date with the Blues 1958 50.00

MILESTONE

❑ MLP-1003 [M] The Feeling Is Mutual 1967 40.00

❑ MLS-9003 [S] The Feeling Is Mutual 1967 25.00

❑ M-9019 Shade of Difference 1969 20.00

**MERRILL, TONI**

RAMA

❑ RLP-5004 [M] Songs from the Heart 1957 80.00

**MERRY-GO-ROUND, THE**

A&M

❑ LP-132 [M] The Merry-Go-Round 1967 40.00

❑ SP-4132 [S] The Merry-Go-Round 1967 30.00

RHINO

❑ RNLP 126 The Best of the Merry-Go-Round 1985 10.00

**MERRYWEATHER, NEIL**

CAPITOL

❑ SKAO-220 Merryweather 1969 15.00

❑ STBB-278 [(2)] Word of Mouth 1969 20.00

KENT

❑ KST-546 Neil Merryweather and the Boers 197? 15.00

| Number | Title (A Side/B Side) | Yr | NM |
|---|---|---|---|
| **MERCURY** | | | |
| ❑ SRM-1-1007 | Space Rangers | 1974 | 12.00 |
| ❑ SRM-1-1024 | Kryptonite | 1975 | 12.00 |
| **MERSEYBEATS, THE** | | | |
| ARC INTERNATIONAL | | | |
| ❑ 834 [M] | England's Best Sellers | 1964 | 40.00 |
| **MERSEYBOYS, THE** | | | |
| VEE JAY | | | |
| ❑ VJ-1101 [DJ] | The 15 Greatest Songs of the Beatles | 1964 | 150.00 |
| *—White label, all-blue print; without typographical error on label: "Saluting Their Return To America"* | | | |
| ❑ VJ-1101 [DJ] | The 15 Greatest Songs of the Beatles | 1964 | 150.00 |
| *—White label, blue and black print; with typographical error on label: "Saluting Their Return to Amercia"* | | | |
| ❑ VJ-1101 [M] | The 15 Greatest Songs of the Beatles | 1964 | 100.00 |
| *—With typographical error on label "Saluting Their Return to Amercia"; this album is not known to exist in stereo* | | | |
| ❑ VJ-1101 [M] | The 15 Greatest Songs of the Beatles | 1964 | 100.00 |
| *—Without typographical error on label "Saluting Their Return To America"; this album is not known to exist in stereo* | | | |
| **MESHEL, BILLY** | | | |
| PROBE | | | |
| ❑ CPLP-4502 | The Love Songs of A. Wilbur Meshel | 1969 | 20.00 |
| **MESMERIZING EYE, THE** | | | |
| SMASH | | | |
| ❑ MGS-27090 [M] | Psychedelia — A Musical Light Show | 1967 | 50.00 |
| ❑ SRS-67090 [S] | Psychedelia — A Musical Light Show | 1967 | 60.00 |
| **MESSENGERS, THE (1)** | | | |
| RARE EARTH | | | |
| ❑ RS-509 | The Messengers | 1969 | 20.00 |
| **MESSINA, JIM** Also see BUFFALO SPRINGFIELD; LOGGINS AND MESSINA; POCO. | | | |
| AUDIO FIDELITY | | | |
| ❑ DFM-3037 [M] | The Dragsters | 1964 | 80.00 |
| ❑ DFS-7037 [S] | The Dragsters | 1964 | 100.00 |
| COLUMBIA | | | |
| ❑ JC 36141 | Oasis | 1979 | 10.00 |
| THIMBLE | | | |
| ❑ TLP-3 | Jim Messina | 197? | 15.00 |
| WARNER BROS. | | | |
| ❑ BSK 3559 | Messina | 1981 | 10.00 |
| ❑ BSK 3559 [DJ] | Messina | 1981 | 20.00 |
| *—Promo-only version on Quiex II vinyl* | | | |
| ❑ 23825 | One More Mile | 1983 | 10.00 |
| **METALLICA** | | | |
| ELEKTRA | | | |
| ❑ 60396 | Ride the Lightning | 1984 | 20.00 |
| ❑ 60439 | Master of Puppets | 1986 | 20.00 |
| ❑ 60757 [EP] | Garage Days Re-Revisited | 1987 | 50.00 |
| ❑ 60766 | Kill 'Em All | 1987 | 15.00 |
| *—Reissue of Megaforce 069 with two extra tracks* | | | |
| ❑ 60812 [(2)] | ...And Justice for All | 1988 | 40.00 |
| ❑ 61113 [(2)] | Metallica | 1991 | 60.00 |
| ❑ 61923 [(2)] | Load | 1996 | 20.00 |
| ❑ 62126 [(2)] | Re-Load | 1997 | 30.00 |
| ❑ 62299 [(3)] | Garage Inc. | 1998 | 25.00 |
| ❑ 62504 [(3)] | S&M | 1999 | 20.00 |
| ❑ 62853 [(2)] | St. Anger | 2003 | 30.00 |
| MEGAFORCE | | | |
| ❑ MRI 069 | Kill 'Em All | 1983 | 40.00 |
| ❑ MRI 069 [PD] | Kill 'Em All | 1983 | 50.00 |
| *—Un-numbered version* | | | |
| ❑ MRI 069 [PD] | Kill 'Em All | 1983 | 100.00 |
| *—Numbered limited edition version* | | | |
| ❑ MRI 769 | Ride the Lightning | 1984 | 40.00 |
| RHINO | | | |
| ❑ R1-76156 [(10)] | Vinyl Box Set | 2004 | 200.00 |
| *—Limited edition of 5,000 numbered copies; includes their first four albums pressed on two records each, the "Garage Days Re-Revisited" EP and the picture disc "Creeping Death"* | | | |
| **METERS, THE** | | | |
| JOSIE | | | |
| ❑ JOS-4010 | The Meters | 1969 | 70.00 |
| ❑ JOS-4011 | Look-Ka Py Py | 1970 | 70.00 |
| ❑ JOS-4012 | Struttin' | 1970 | 70.00 |
| REPRISE | | | |
| ❑ MS 2076 | Cabbage Alley | 1972 | 70.00 |
| ❑ MS 2200 | Rejuvenation | 1974 | 50.00 |
| ❑ MS 2228 | Fire on the Bayou | 1975 | 50.00 |
| ❑ MS 2252 | Trick Bag | 1976 | 50.00 |

Metallica, *...And Justice for All*, Elektra 60812, 1988, 2 records, $40.

| Number | Title (A Side/B Side) | Yr | NM |
|---|---|---|---|
| ROUNDER | | | |
| ❑ 2103 | Look-Ka Py Py | 1990 | 20.00 |
| *—Reissue of Josie 4011* | | | |
| ❑ 2104 | Good Old Funky Music | 1990 | 20.00 |
| SUNDAZED | | | |
| ❑ LP 5081 | Kickback | 2001 | 12.00 |
| VIRGO | | | |
| ❑ 12002 | The Best of the Meters | 1972 | 50.00 |
| WARNER BROS. | | | |
| ❑ BS 3042 | New Directions | 1977 | 50.00 |
| **METHENY, MIKE** | | | |
| HEADFIRST | | | |
| ❑ 9712 | Blue Jay Sessions | 198? | 20.00 |
| **METHOD ACTOR** The lead singer was Washington, D.C. cult favorite Eva Cassidy. | | | |
| (LABEL UNKNOWN) | | | |
| ❑ (# unknown) | Method Actor | 1988 | 500.00 |
| **METRONOMES, THE (U)** | | | |
| STRAND | | | |
| ❑ SL-1057 [M] | The Fabulous Metronomes Sing the Standard Hits | 1962 | 30.00 |
| ❑ SLS-1057 [S] | The Fabulous Metronomes Sing the Standard Hits | 1962 | 40.00 |
| WYNNE | | | |
| ❑ 106 [M] | And Now... The Metronomes | 1960 | 120.00 |
| **METROPOLITAN JAZZ OCTET** | | | |
| ARGO | | | |
| ❑ LP-659 [M] | The Legend of Bix | 1960 | 30.00 |
| **METROS, THE (1)** | | | |
| RCA VICTOR | | | |
| ❑ LPM-3776 [M] | Sweetest One | 1967 | 80.00 |
| ❑ LSP-3776 [S] | Sweetest One | 1967 | 100.00 |
| **METROTONES, THE** | | | |
| COLUMBIA | | | |
| ❑ CL 6341 [10] | Tops in Rock and Roll | 1955 | 250.00 |
| **MEYERS, AUGIE** | | | |
| ATLANTIC AMERICA | | | |
| ❑ 90856 | My Main Squeeze | 1988 | 10.00 |

| Number | Title (A Side/B Side) | Yr | NM |
|---|---|---|---|
| PARAMOUNT | | | |
| ❑ PAS-6065 | You Ain't Rollin' Your Roll Rite | 1973 | 20.00 |
| POLYDOR | | | |
| ❑ 24-4069 | Western Head Music Co. | 1971 | 20.00 |
| TEXAS RE-CORD | | | |
| ❑ 1002 | Live at the Longneck | 197? | 30.00 |
| **MEZZROW, MEZZ** | | | |
| BLUE NOTE | | | |
| ❑ BLP-7023 [10] | Mezz Mezzrow and His Band | 1952 | 300.00 |
| LONDON | | | |
| ❑ TKL-93092 [10] | A La Schola Cantorum | 195? | 60.00 |
| RCA VICTOR | | | |
| ❑ LJM-1006 [M] | Mezzin' Around | 1954 | 50.00 |
| "X" | | | |
| ❑ LVA-3015 [10] | Mezz Mezzrow's Swing Session | 1954 | 100.00 |
| "X" | | | |
| ❑ LVA-3027 [10] | Mezz Mezzrow | 1954 | 100.00 |
| **MFG** | | | |
| HAT HUT | | | |
| ❑ S/T [(2)] | MFG in Minnesota | 1978 | 30.00 |
| **MIAMI SOUND MACHINE** | | | |
| AUDIOFON | | | |
| ❑ AUS 5426 | Live Again — Renacer | 1977 | 200.00 |
| *—The rest have a cover with a blue and yellow "tropical" background* | | | |
| ❑ AUS 5426 | Live Again — Renacer | 1977 | 300.00 |
| *—First 600 have a cover where the backdrop is clearly visible* | | | |
| ❑ AUS 5427 | Miami Sound Machine | 1978 | 200.00 |
| *—Spanish-language version* | | | |
| CBS INTERNATIONAL | | | |
| ❑ DML 10306 | Imported | 1980 | 50.00 |
| *—Reissue of 10455* | | | |
| ❑ DHL 10311 | Miami Sound Machine | 1980 | 100.00 |
| *—Different album than Electric Cat 226 and its later issues* | | | |
| ❑ DIL 10320 | Otra Vez | 1981 | 50.00 |
| ❑ DIL 10330 | Rio | 1982 | 50.00 |
| ❑ DSL 10335 | 7Up Presenta Los Hits de Miami Sound Machine | 1983 | 150.00 |
| *—Only available in the Miami area from 7Up dealers* | | | |

❑ DIL 10349 A Toda Maquina 1984 40.00
*—Spanish-language version of "Eyes of Innocence," their first all-English LP*
❑ DIL 10375 Primitive Love 1985 30.00
*—Edition mostly distributed in Puerto Rico, with three Spanish-language tracks replacing three English tracks*
❑ DKL 10455 Imported 1979 100.00
*—Reissue of MSM album*

ELECTRIC CAT
❑ ECS 226 Miami Sound Machine 1978 200.00
*—Mostly English-language version*

EPIC
❑ BFE 39622 Eyes of Innocence 1984 15.00
*—Original issue*
❑ PE 39622 Eyes of Innocence 1986 8.00
*—Reissue with new prefix*
❑ BFE 40131 Primitive Love 1985 12.00
*—The band's breakthrough LP to non-Hispanic audiences, and the last one not to have Gloria Estefan prominently credited; original issue*
❑ FE 40131 Primitive Love 1986 8.00
*—Reissue with new prefix*

MSM
❑ ERK 0714 Imported 1979 200.00

TOP HITS
❑ TH-AM 2185 Live Again — Renacer 1982 80.00
*—Reissue of Audiofon LP of the same name*
❑ TH-AM 2187 Miami Sound Machine 1982 100.00
*—Reissue of Electric Cat LP of the same name*
❑ TH-AM 2228 Lo Mejor De Miami Sound Machine — A Portrait of the Originals 1983 50.00
*—Compilation from first two Spanish-language LPs*

## MICHAELS, LEE

A&M
❑ SP-3158 Lee Michaels 198? 8.00
*—Budget-line reissue*
❑ SP-3518 Live 1973 15.00
❑ SP-4140 Carnival of Life 1968 40.00
❑ SP-4152 Recital 1968 20.00
❑ SP-4199 Lee Michaels 1969 15.00
❑ SP-4249 Barrel 1970 15.00
❑ SP-4302 5th 1971 15.00
❑ SP-4336 Space and First Takes 1972 15.00

COLUMBIA
❑ CQ 32275 [Q] Nice Day for Something 1973 20.00
❑ KC 32275 Nice Day for Something 1973 12.00
❑ KC 32846 Tailface 1974 12.00

## MICKELSON, PAUL

RCA VICTOR
❑ LPM-1115 [M] Christmas Bells 1955 20.00
❑ LPM-1517 [M] The Best of Christmas 1957 20.00

## MICKEY AND SYLVIA Also see MICKEY BAKER; SYLVIA (1).

RCA CAMDEN
❑ CAL-863 [M] Love Is Strange 1965 50.00
❑ CAS-863(e) [R] Love Is Strange 1965 30.00

RCA VICTOR
❑ APM1-0327 Do It Again 1973 12.00

VIK
❑ LX-1102 [M] New Sounds 1957 400.00

## MIDLER, BETTE

ATLANTIC
❑ PR 275 [DJ] Live! At Last Specially Edited for Air Play 1977 15.00
*—Promo-only 14-track sampler*
❑ 7238 [M] The Divine Miss M 1972 30.00
*—Mono is promo only; white label, "dj copy monaural" sticker on stereo cover*
❑ QD 7238 [Q] The Divine Miss M 1973 20.00
❑ SD 7238 [S] The Divine Miss M 1972 10.00
*—"1841 Broadway" address on label*
❑ SD 7270 Bette Midler 1973 12.00
*—"1841 Broadway" address on label; with poster*
❑ SD 2-9000 [(2)] Live! At Last 1977 12.00
❑ SD 16004 Thighs and Whispers 1979 10.00
❑ SD 16010 The Rose 1979 10.00
❑ SD 16022 Divine Madness 1980 10.00
❑ SD 18155 Songs for the New Depression 1976 10.00
❑ SD 19151 Broken Blossom 1977 10.00
❑ 80070 No Frills 1983 10.00
❑ 81291 Mud Will Be Flung Tonight! 1985 10.00
❑ 81933 Beaches 1988 10.00
❑ 82129 Some People's Lives 1990 12.00
❑ SW-95507 Bette Midler 1973 20.00
*—Longines Record Club edition*
❑ R 163898 Mud Will Be Flung Tonight! 1985 12.00
*—RCA Music Service edition*

## MIDNIGHTERS, THE

FEDERAL
❑ 295-90 [10] Their Greatest Hits 1954 8000.
*—VG value 4000; VG+ value 6000*
❑ 541 [M] Their Greatest Hits 1955 1000.
*—Yellow cover*
❑ 541 [M] Their Greatest Hits 1955 1500.
*—Red cover*
❑ 581 [M] The Midnighters, Volume 2 1955 1200.

KING
❑ 541 [M] Their Greatest Jukebox Hits 1958 400.00
*—Crownless black label, "King" is two inches wide on label*
❑ 541 [M] Their Greatest Jukebox Hits 196? 200.00
*—Reissue with Hank Ballard on cover*
❑ 541 [M] Their Greatest Jukebox Hits 196? 300.00
*—Crownless black label, "King" is three inches wide on label. Above two have a girl on the cover.*
❑ 581 [M] The Midnighters, Volume 2 1958 300.00
*—Crownless black label, "King" is two inches wide on label*
❑ 581 [M] The Midnighters, Volume 2 196? 200.00
*—Crownless black label, "King" is three inches wide on label*

## MIGHTY BABY

HEAD
❑ LPS-025 Mighty Baby 1969 60.00

## MIGHTY CLOUDS OF JOY

ABC
❑ D-899 Kickin' 1975 10.00
❑ D-986 The Truth Is the Power 1976 10.00
❑ D-1038 Live and Direct 1977 10.00

ABC DUNHILL
❑ DSX-50177 It's Time 1974 10.00

HOB
❑ 288 "Live" Zion Songs 196? 15.00

KING
❑ SG3-1107 Out Talking to Yourself 1970 15.00

MCA
❑ 1091 [(2)] The Very Best of Mighty Clouds of Joy 198? 10.00
❑ 28008 Family Circle 198? 8.00
*—Reissue of Peacock 114*
❑ 28012 The Bright Side 198? 8.00
*—Reissue of Peacock 121*
❑ 28017 Mighty Clouds of Joy At the Music Hall 198? 8.00
*—Reissue of Peacock 134*
❑ 28019 The Best of Mighty Clouds of Joy 198? 8.00
*—Reissue of Peacock 136*
❑ 28025 The Untouchables 198? 8.00
*—Reissue of Peacock 151*
❑ 28028 Songs of Rev. Julius Cheeks and the Nightingales 198? 8.00
*—Reissue of Peacock 163*
❑ 28030 God Bless America 198? 8.00
*—Reissue of Peacock 170*
❑ 28032 Live at the Apollo 198? 8.00
*—Reissue of Peacock 173*
❑ 28040 The Best of Mighty Clouds of Joy — Volume 2 198? 8.00

MYRRH
❑ MSB-6663 Cloudburst 1980 10.00
❑ MSB-6681 The Truth Is the Power 1981 10.00
❑ MSB-6694 Miracle Man 1982 10.00
❑ MSB-6712 Request Line 1983 10.00
❑ WR-8121 Mighty Clouds Alive 1984 10.00
❑ WR-8122 Sing and Shout 1984 10.00

PEACOCK
❑ 114 Family Circle 196? 20.00
❑ 121 The Bright Side 196? 20.00
❑ 134 Mighty Clouds of Joy At the Music Hall 196? 20.00
❑ 136 The Best of Mighty Clouds of Joy 196? 20.00
❑ 151 The Untouchables 196? 20.00
❑ 161 Out Talking to Yourself 196? 20.00
❑ 163 Songs of Rev. Julius Cheeks and the Nightingales 196? 20.00
❑ 170 God Bless America 1971 15.00
❑ 173 Live at the Apollo 1972 15.00

PRIORITY
❑ RV 37707 Changing Times 1982 10.00

## MIGHTY FAITH INCREASERS, THE

KING
❑ 806 [M] The Mighty Faith Increasers with Willa Dorsey 1962 150.00
❑ 814 [M] A Festival of Spiritual Songs 1962 150.00

## MIGHTY MIGHTY BOSSTONES

BIG RIG
❑ BR 101 [(2)] Don't Know How to Party 1993 50.00
*—Includes one 12-inch plaid picture disc and a 10-inch record called "Skacore"*
❑ BR 102 [(2)10] Question the Answers 1994 50.00
*—Two 10-inch records; includes one song not on the CD version*

BIG RIG/ISLAND
❑ 314 542451-1 [(2)] Pay Attention 2000 30.00

SIDE ONE DUMMY
❑ SDLP- 1234 A Jackknife to a Swan 2002 25.00

TAANG!
❑ 44 Devils Night Out 1991 30.00
❑ 49 More Noise & Other Disturbances 1991 25.00

## MIKE + THE MECHANICS

ATLANTIC
❑ PR 820 [DJ] Mike on Mike 1985 20.00
*—Promo-only music and interviews*
❑ PR 2543 [DJ] Mike on Mike II 1989 15.00
*—Promo-only music and interviews*
❑ 81287 Mike + The Mechanics 1985 10.00
❑ 81923 Living Years 1989 10.00

## MIL-COMBO, THE

CAPITOL
❑ T 579 [M] The Mil-Combo 1955 50.00

## MILANOV, ZINKA

RCA VICTOR RED SEAL
❑ LSC-2303 [S] Operatic Arias by Puccini 1959 40.00
*—Originals on "shaded dog" label*

## MILBURN, AMOS

ALADDIN
❑ LP-704 [10] Rockin' the Boogie 1952 4000.
*—Black vinyl*
❑ LP-704 [10] Rockin' the Boogie 1952 8000.
*—Red vinyl, blue cover*
❑ LP-810 [M] Rockin' the Boogie 1957 —
*—Canceled*

IMPERIAL
❑ LP-9176 [M] Million Sellers 1962 500.00

MOSAIC
❑ MQ10-155 [(10)] The Complete Aladdin Recordings of Amos Milburn 199? 180.00
*—Limited editon of 3,500*

MOTOWN
❑ 608 [M] The Return of Amos Milburn, "The" Blues Boss 1963 900.00

SCORE
❑ LP-4012 [M] Let's Have a Party 1957 800.00
❑ LP-4035 [M] Amos Milburn Sings the Blues 1958 —
*—Canceled*

## MILBURN, AMOS/WYNONIE HARRIS/ETC.

ALADDIN
❑ LP-703 [10] Party After Hours 1952 4000.
*—Black vinyl*
❑ LP-703 [10] Party After Hours 1952 8000.
*—Red vinyl, blue cover*

## MILES, BARRY

CENTURY
❑ 1070 Fusion Is… 1979 20.00
*—Audiophile edition*

CHARLIE PARKER
❑ PLP-804 [M] Miles of Genius 1962 25.00
❑ PLP-804S [S] Miles of Genius 1962 30.00

POPPY
❑ PY-40009 Barry Miles 1970 20.00

## MILES, BUDDY

ATLANTIC
❑ SD 2-4000 [(2)] Sneak Attack 1982 12.00

CASABLANCA
❑ NBLP 7019 More Miles Per Gallon 1975 10.00
❑ NBLP 7024 Bicentennial Gathering of the Tribes 1976 10.00

COLUMBIA
❑ CQ 32048 [Q] Chapter VII 1973 20.00
❑ KC 32048 Chapter VII 1973 12.00
❑ CQ 32694 [Q] Booger Bear 1973 20.00
❑ KC 32694 Booger Bear 1973 12.00
❑ KC 33089 All the Faces 1974 12.00

MERCURY
❑ SRM-1-608 A Message to the People 1971 15.00
❑ SRM-2-7500 [(2)] Buddy Miles Live 1971 15.00
❑ SR-61196 Expressway to Your Skull 1968 20.00
❑ SR-61222 Electric Church 1969 20.00
❑ SR-61280 Them Changes 1970 15.00
❑ SR-61313 We Got to Live Together 1970 15.00

## MILES, LIZZIE

COOK
❑ 1181 [10] Queen Mother of the Rue Royale 1955 80.00
❑ 1182 [M] Moans and Blues 195? 60.00
❑ 1183 [M] Hot Songs My Mother Taught Me 195? 60.00
❑ 1184 [M] Torchy Lullabies My Mother Taught Me 195? 60.00
*—Black vinyl*

| Number | Title (A Side/B Side) | Yr | NM |
|---|---|---|---|
| ❑ 1184 [M] | Torchy Lullabies My Mother Taught Me | 195? | 200.00 |

*—Rose-colored vinyl*

**MILES, LUKE "LONG GONE"**

WORLD PACIFIC

| Number | Title (A Side/B Side) | Yr | NM |
|---|---|---|---|
| ❑ ST-1820 [S] | Country Born | 1964 | 30.00 |
| ❑ WP-1820 [M] | Country Born | 1964 | 25.00 |

**MILKWOOD (1)**

A&M

| Number | Title (A Side/B Side) | Yr | NM |
|---|---|---|---|
| ❑ SP-4226 | Under Milkwood | 1969 | 300.00 |

**MILKWOOD (2)**

PARAMOUNT

| Number | Title (A Side/B Side) | Yr | NM |
|---|---|---|---|
| ❑ PAS-6046 | How's the Weather? | 1973 | 40.00 |

**MILKWOOD TAPESTRY**

METROMEDIA

| Number | Title (A Side/B Side) | Yr | NM |
|---|---|---|---|
| ❑ MD-1007 | Milkwood Tapestry | 1969 | 50.00 |

**MILLARD & DYCE**

KAYMAR

| Number | Title (A Side/B Side) | Yr | NM |
|---|---|---|---|
| ❑ KS-7-265 | Open | 1973 | 60.00 |

**MILLENNIUM**

COLUMBIA

| Number | Title (A Side/B Side) | Yr | NM |
|---|---|---|---|
| ❑ CS 9663 | Begin | 1968 | 30.00 |

**MILLER, CHUCK**

MERCURY

| Number | Title (A Side/B Side) | Yr | NM |
|---|---|---|---|
| ❑ MG-20195 [M] | After Hours | 1956 | 80.00 |

**MILLER, CLARENCE "BIG"**

COLUMBIA

| Number | Title (A Side/B Side) | Yr | NM |
|---|---|---|---|
| ❑ CL 1611 [M] | Revelation and the Blues | 1961 | 25.00 |
| ❑ CL 1808 [M] | Big Miller Sings, Twists, Shouts and Preaches | 1962 | 25.00 |
| ❑ CS 8411 [S] | Revelation and the Blues | 1961 | 30.00 |
| ❑ CS 8608 [S] | Big Miller Sings, Twists, Shouts and Preaches | 1962 | 30.00 |

UNITED ARTISTS

| Number | Title (A Side/B Side) | Yr | NM |
|---|---|---|---|
| ❑ UAL-3047 [M] | Did You Ever Hear the Blues? | 1959 | 40.00 |
| ❑ UAS-6047 [S] | Did You Ever Hear the Blues? | 1959 | 60.00 |

**MILLER, DON**

KING

| Number | Title (A Side/B Side) | Yr | NM |
|---|---|---|---|
| ❑ 712 [M] | The Don Miller Quartet | 1960 | 60.00 |

**MILLER, EDDIE**

CAPITOL

| Number | Title (A Side/B Side) | Yr | NM |
|---|---|---|---|
| ❑ T 614 [M] | Classics in Jazz | 1955 | 50.00 |

**MILLER, EDDIE/GEORGE VAN EPS**

JUMP

| Number | Title (A Side/B Side) | Yr | NM |
|---|---|---|---|
| ❑ JL-5 [10] | Eddie Miller/George Van Eps | 1953 | 50.00 |

**MILLER, FRANKIE**

AUDIO LAB

| Number | Title (A Side/B Side) | Yr | NM |
|---|---|---|---|
| ❑ AL-1562 [M] | The Fine Country Singing of Frankie Miller | 1963 | 150.00 |

STARDAY

| Number | Title (A Side/B Side) | Yr | NM |
|---|---|---|---|
| ❑ SLP-134 [M] | Country Music's Great New Star | 1961 | 100.00 |
| ❑ SLP-199 [M] | The True Country Style of Frankie Miller | 1962 | 100.00 |
| ❑ SLP-339 [M] | Blackland Farmer | 1965 | 60.00 |

**MILLER, GLENN**

BLUEBIRD

| Number | Title (A Side/B Side) | Yr | NM |
|---|---|---|---|
| ❑ 9785-1-RB [(4)] | The Popular Recordings 1938-1942 | 1989 | 25.00 |

EPIC

| Number | Title (A Side/B Side) | Yr | NM |
|---|---|---|---|
| ❑ LA 16002 [M] | Glenn Miller | 1960 | 20.00 |

EVEREST

| Number | Title (A Side/B Side) | Yr | NM |
|---|---|---|---|
| ❑ 4005/5 [(5)] | His Complete Recordings on Columbia (1928-1938) As Player and Conductor | 1982 | 25.00 |

*—Box set with 8-page booklet*

RCA VICTOR

| Number | Title (A Side/B Side) | Yr | NM |
|---|---|---|---|
| ❑ LPT-16 [10] | Glenn Miller Concert — Volume 1 | 1951 | 60.00 |
| ❑ LPT-30 [10] | Glenn Miller Concert — Volume 2 | 1951 | 60.00 |
| ❑ LPT-31 [10] | Glenn Miller | 1951 | 60.00 |
| ❑ PR-114 [M] | Glenn Miller Originals | 1962 | 20.00 |

*—Promotional item for Salada Foods Inc.*

| Number | Title (A Side/B Side) | Yr | NM |
|---|---|---|---|
| ❑ LOP-1005 [M] | The Marvelous Miller Medleys | 1958 | 40.00 |
| ❑ LPT-1016 [M] | Juke Box Saturday Night | 1955 | 40.00 |
| ❑ LPT-1031 [M] | The Nearness of You | 1955 | 40.00 |
| ❑ LPM-1189 [M] | The Sound of Glenn Miller | 1956 | 40.00 |
| ❑ LPM-1190 [M] | This Is Glenn Miller | 1956 | 40.00 |
| ❑ LPM-1192 [M] | Selections from "The Glenn Miller Story" and Other Hits | 1956 | 40.00 |
| ❑ LPM-1193 [M] | Glenn Miller Concert | 1956 | 40.00 |

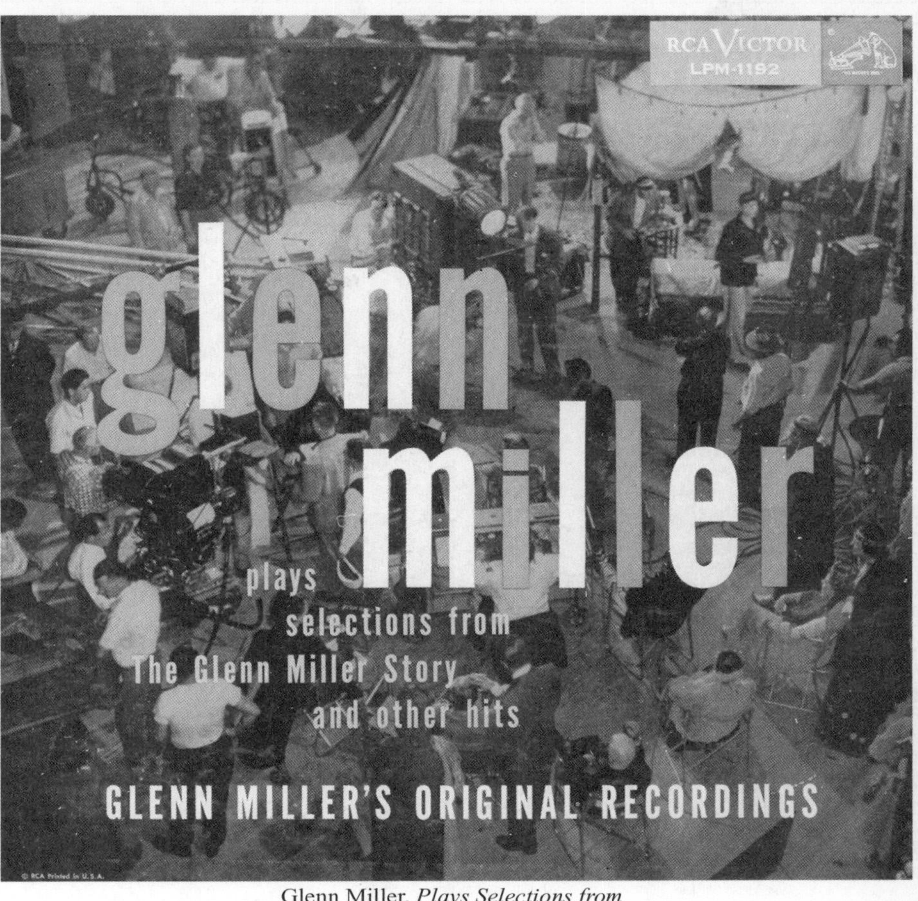


Glenn Miller, *Plays Selections from The Glenn Miller Story and Other Hits*, RCA Victor LPM-1192, 1956, mono, $40.

| Number | Title (A Side/B Side) | Yr | NM |
|---|---|---|---|
| ❑ LPM-1494 [M] | Marvelous Miller Moods | 1957 | 40.00 |
| ❑ LPM-1506 [M] | The Glenn Miller Carnegie Hall Concert | 1957 | 40.00 |
| ❑ LPM-1973 [M] | The Marvelous Miller Medleys | 1959 | 30.00 |
| ❑ LPT-3001 [10] | Glenn Miller Concert — Volume 3 | 195? | 60.00 |
| ❑ LPT-3002 [10] | This Is Glenn Miller | 195? | 60.00 |
| ❑ LPT-3036 [10] | This Is Glenn Miller — Volume 2 | 195? | 60.00 |
| ❑ LPT-3057 [10] | Selections from the Film "The Glenn Miller Story" | 1954 | 60.00 |
| ❑ LPT-3067 [10] | Sunrise Serenade | 1954 | 60.00 |
| ❑ LPM-6100 [(3)M] | For the Very First Time... | 195? | 50.00 |

*—Black "Long Play" labels in leatherette spiral-bound binder*

| Number | Title (A Side/B Side) | Yr | NM |
|---|---|---|---|
| ❑ LPM-6101 [(3)M] | Glenn Miller On the Air | 1963 | 40.00 |
| ❑ LSP-6101 [(3)R] | Glenn Miller On the Air | 1963 | 25.00 |
| ❑ LPT-6700 [(5)M] | Glenn Miller and His Orchestra Limited Edition — Second Pressing | 195? | 60.00 |

*—Black "Long Play" labels in leatherette spiral-bound binder*

| Number | Title (A Side/B Side) | Yr | NM |
|---|---|---|---|
| ❑ LPT-6700 [(5)M] | Glenn Miller and His Orchestra Limited Edition | 1953 | 150.00 |

*—Silver labels with red print in leatherette spiral-bound binder*

| Number | Title (A Side/B Side) | Yr | NM |
|---|---|---|---|
| ❑ LPT-6701 [(5)M] | Glenn Miller and His Orchestra Limited Edition Volume Two — Second Pressing | 195? | 60.00 |

*—Black "Long Play" labels in leatherette spiral-bound binder; identified as "Second Pressing" throughout*

| Number | Title (A Side/B Side) | Yr | NM |
|---|---|---|---|
| ❑ LPT-6701 [(5)M] | Glenn Miller and His Orchestra Limited Edition Volume Two | 1954 | 120.00 |

*—Black "Long Play" labels in leatherette spiral-bound binder*

| Number | Title (A Side/B Side) | Yr | NM |
|---|---|---|---|
| ❑ LPT-6702 [(4)M] | Glenn Miller Army Air Force Band | 195? | 60.00 |

*—Same as above, but in box rather than in binder*

| Number | Title (A Side/B Side) | Yr | NM |
|---|---|---|---|
| ❑ LPT-6702 [(4)M] | Glenn Miller Army Air Force Band | 1955 | 120.00 |

*—Black "Long Play" labels in leatherette spiral-bound binder*

READER'S DIGEST

| Number | Title (A Side/B Side) | Yr | NM |
|---|---|---|---|
| ❑ RD4-64 [(6)R] | The Unforgettable Glenn Miller | 1968 | 20.00 |

20TH FOX

| Number | Title (A Side/B Side) | Yr | NM |
|---|---|---|---|
| ❑ TCF-100-2 [(2)M] | Glenn Miller and His Orchestra Original Film Sound Tracks | 1958 | 30.00 |
| ❑ TCF-100-2S [(2)R] | Glenn Miller and His Orchestra Original Film Sound Tracks | 1961 | 20.00 |

**MILLER, GLENN, ORCHESTRA (BUDDY DEFRANCO, DIRECTOR)**

RCA VICTOR

| Number | Title (A Side/B Side) | Yr | NM |
|---|---|---|---|
| ❑ LPM-3880 [M] | The Glenn Miller Orchestra Returns to the Glen Island Casino | 1968 | 20.00 |
| ❑ LPM-3971 [M] | The Glenn Miller Orchestra Makes the Goin' Great | 1968 | 40.00 |

**MILLER, GLENN, ORCHESTRA (RAY MCKINLEY, DIRECTOR)**

EPIC

| Number | Title (A Side/B Side) | Yr | NM |
|---|---|---|---|
| ❑ BN 26133 [S] | Glenn Miller Time — 1965 | 1965 | 20.00 |
| ❑ BN 26157 [S] | Great Songs of the 60's | 1965 | 20.00 |

RCA VICTOR

| Number | Title (A Side/B Side) | Yr | NM |
|---|---|---|---|
| ❑ LPM-1522 [M] | The New Glenn Miller Orchestra in Hi-Fi | 1957 | 30.00 |
| ❑ LSP-1522 [S] | The New Glenn Miller Orchestra in Hi-Fi | 1958 | 40.00 |
| ❑ LPM-1678 [M] | Something Old, New, Borrowed and Blue | 1958 | 30.00 |
| ❑ LSP-1678 [S] | Something Old, New, Borrowed and Blue | 1958 | 40.00 |
| ❑ LPM-1852 [M] | The Miller Sound | 1959 | 30.00 |
| ❑ LSP-1852 [S] | The Miller Sound | 1959 | 40.00 |
| ❑ LPM-1948 [M] | On Tour with the New Glenn Miller Orchestra | 1959 | 30.00 |
| ❑ LSP-1948 [S] | On Tour with the New Glenn Miller Orchestra | 1959 | 40.00 |
| ❑ LPM-2080 [M] | The Great Dance Bands of the 30's and 40's | 1960 | 25.00 |
| ❑ LSP-2080 [S] | The Great Dance Bands of the 30's and 40's | 1960 | 30.00 |
| ❑ LPM-2193 [M] | Dance, Anyone? | 1960 | 25.00 |
| ❑ LSP-2193 [S] | Dance, Anyone? | 1960 | 30.00 |
| ❑ LPM-2270 [M] | The Authentic Sound of the New Glenn Miller Orchestra — Today | 1961 | 25.00 |
| ❑ LSP-2270 [S] | The Authentic Sound of the New Glenn Miller Orchestra — Today | 1961 | 30.00 |
| ❑ LPM-2436 [M] | Glenn Miller Time | 1961 | 25.00 |
| ❑ LSP-2436 [S] | Glenn Miller Time | 1961 | 30.00 |
| ❑ LPM-2519 [M] | Echoes of Glenn Miller | 1962 | 25.00 |
| ❑ LSP-2519 [S] | Echoes of Glenn Miller | 1962 | 30.00 |

| Number | Title (A Side/B Side) | Yr | NM |
|---|---|---|---|
| ❑ ANL1-2975(e) [S] | The Great Dance Bands of the 30's and 40's | 1978 | 8.00 |
| *—Reissue of LSP-2080* | | | |

## MILLER, JODY

### CAPITOL

| Number | Title (A Side/B Side) | Yr | NM |
|---|---|---|---|
| ❑ ST 1913 [S] | Wednesday's Child Is Full of Woe | 1963 | 40.00 |
| ❑ T 1913 [M] | Wednesday's Child Is Full of Woe | 1963 | 30.00 |
| ❑ ST 2349 [S] | Queen of the House | 1965 | 20.00 |
| ❑ T 2349 [M] | Queen of the House | 1965 | 15.00 |
| ❑ ST 2412 [S] | Home of the Brave | 1965 | 20.00 |
| ❑ T 2412 [M] | Home of the Brave | 1965 | 15.00 |
| ❑ ST 2446 [S] | Jody Miller Sings the Great Hits of Buck Owens | 1966 | 20.00 |
| ❑ T 2446 [M] | Jody Miller Sings the Great Hits of Buck Owens | 1966 | 15.00 |
| ❑ ST 2996 | The Nashville Sound of Jody Miller | 1968 | 15.00 |
| ❑ ST-11169 | The Best of Jody Miller | 1973 | 12.00 |

### EPIC

| Number | Title (A Side/B Side) | Yr | NM |
|---|---|---|---|
| ❑ E 30282 | Look at Mine | 1971 | 12.00 |
| ❑ E 30659 | He's So Fine | 1971 | 12.00 |
| ❑ KE 31706 | There's a Party Goin' On | 1972 | 12.00 |
| ❑ KE 32386 | Good News! | 1973 | 12.00 |
| ❑ KE 32569 | House of the Rising Sun | 1974 | 12.00 |
| ❑ KE 33349 | Country Girl | 1975 | 12.00 |
| ❑ KE 33934 | Will You Love Me Tomorrow? | 1976 | 12.00 |
| ❑ PE 34446 | Here's Jody | 1977 | 12.00 |

## MILLER, MICKEY

### FOLKWAYS

| Number | Title (A Side/B Side) | Yr | NM |
|---|---|---|---|
| ❑ FA-2393 [M] | American Folk Songs | 1959 | 30.00 |

## MILLER, MITCH

### ATLANTIC

| Number | Title (A Side/B Side) | Yr | NM |
|---|---|---|---|
| ❑ SD 8277 | Peace Sing Along with Mitch | 1970 | 12.00 |

### COLUMBIA

| Number | Title (A Side/B Side) | Yr | NM |
|---|---|---|---|
| ❑ CL 601 [M] | Mmmmitch! | 1954 | 20.00 |
| *—Maroon label, gold print* | | | |
| ❑ CL 779 [M] | It's So Peaceful in the Country | 1956 | 20.00 |
| *—Red and black label with 6 "eye" logos* | | | |
| ❑ CL 1102 [M] | Mitch's Marches | 1957 | 15.00 |
| ❑ CL 1160 [M] | Sing Along with Mitch | 1958 | 15.00 |
| ❑ CL 1205 [M] | Christmas Sing Along with Mitch | 1958 | 15.00 |
| *—Originals have gatefold cover with eight detachable lyric sheets inside* | | | |
| ❑ CL 1243 [M] | More Sing Along with Mitch | 1958 | 15.00 |
| ❑ CL 1283 [M] | Still More! Sing Along with Mitch | 1959 | 15.00 |
| ❑ CL 1316 [M] | Folk Songs Sing Along with Mitch | 1959 | 15.00 |
| ❑ CL 1331 [M] | Party Sing Along with Mitch | 1959 | 15.00 |
| ❑ CL 1389 [M] | Fireside Sing Along with Mitch | 1959 | 15.00 |
| ❑ CL 1414 [M] | Saturday Night Sing Along with Mitch | 1960 | 12.00 |
| ❑ CL 1457 [M] | Sentimental Sing Along with Mitch | 1960 | 12.00 |
| ❑ CL 1475 [M] | March Along with Mitch | 1960 | 12.00 |
| ❑ CL 1542 [M] | Memories Sing Along with Mitch | 1960 | 12.00 |
| ❑ CL 1544 [M] | Mitch's Greatest Hits | 1961 | 12.00 |
| ❑ CL 1568 [M] | Happy Times! Sing Along with Mitch | 1961 | 12.00 |
| ❑ CL 1628 [M] | TV Sing Along with Mitch | 1961 | 12.00 |
| ❑ CL 1671 [M] | Your Request Sing Along with Mitch | 1961 | 12.00 |
| ❑ CL 1701 [M] | Holiday Sing Along with Mitch | 1961 | 12.00 |
| ❑ CL 1727 [M] | Rhythm Sing Along with Mitch | 1962 | 12.00 |
| ❑ CL 1773 [M] | Family Sing Along with Mitch | 1962 | 12.00 |
| ❑ CL 1864 [M] | Night Time Sing Along with Mitch | 1963 | 12.00 |
| ❑ CL 2063 [M] | Hymn Sing Along with Mitch | 1963 | 12.00 |
| ❑ CL 6222 [10] | Mitch Miller with Horns and Chorus | 195? | 30.00 |
| ❑ CS 8004 | Sing Along with Mitch | 1963 | 12.00 |
| *—Red label* | | | |
| ❑ CS 8004 | Sing Along with Mitch | 1970 | 8.00 |
| *—Orange label* | | | |
| ❑ CS 8004 [S] | Sing Along with Mitch | 1959 | 20.00 |
| *—Red and black label with 6 "eye" logos* | | | |
| ❑ PC 8004 | Sing Along with Mitch | 198? | 6.00 |
| *—Reissue with new prefix* | | | |
| ❑ CS 8027 [S] | Christmas Sing Along with Mitch | 1959 | 20.00 |
| *—Originals have gatefold cover with eight detachable lyric sheets inside* | | | |
| ❑ CS 8043 [S] | More Sing Along with Mitch | 1959 | 20.00 |
| ❑ CS 8099 [S] | Still More! Sing Along with Mitch | 1959 | 20.00 |
| ❑ CS 8118 [S] | Folk Songs Sing Along with Mitch | 1959 | 20.00 |
| ❑ CS 8138 [S] | Party Sing Along with Mitch | 1959 | 20.00 |
| ❑ CS 8184 [S] | Fireside Sing Along with Mitch | 1959 | 20.00 |
| ❑ CS 8211 [S] | Saturday Night Sing Along with Mitch | 1960 | 15.00 |
| ❑ CS 8251 [S] | Sentimental Sing Along with Mitch | 1960 | 15.00 |
| ❑ CS 8342 [S] | Memories Sing Along with Mitch | 1960 | 15.00 |
| ❑ CS 8368 [S] | Happy Times! Sing Along with Mitch | 1961 | 15.00 |
| ❑ CS 8428 [S] | TV Sing Along with Mitch | 1961 | 15.00 |
| ❑ CS 8471 [S] | Your Request Sing Along with Mitch | 1961 | 15.00 |
| ❑ CS 8501 [S] | Holiday Sing Along with Mitch | 1961 | 15.00 |
| ❑ CS 8527 [S] | Rhythm Sing Along with Mitch | 1962 | 15.00 |
| ❑ CS 8573 [S] | Family Sing Along with Mitch | 1962 | 15.00 |
| ❑ CS 8638 [R] | Mitch's Greatest Hits | 1963 | 10.00 |
| ❑ CS 8664 [S] | Night Time Sing Along with Mitch | 1963 | 15.00 |
| ❑ CS 8863 [S] | Hymn Sing Along with Mitch | 1963 | 15.00 |
| ❑ G 30250 [(2)] | 34 All Time Great Sing Along Selections | 1970 | 12.00 |
| ❑ 3C 39297 | Holiday Sing Along with Mitch | 1984 | 8.00 |
| ❑ PC 39298 | Christmas Sing Along with Mitch | 1984 | 8.00 |

### DECCA

| Number | Title (A Side/B Side) | Yr | NM |
|---|---|---|---|
| ❑ DL 4777 [M] | Dance and Sing Along with Mitch | 1966 | 10.00 |
| ❑ DL 74777 [S] | Dance and Sing Along with Mitch | 1966 | 12.00 |

### HARMONY

| Number | Title (A Side/B Side) | Yr | NM |
|---|---|---|---|
| ❑ HL 7404 [M] | March Along with Mitch | 1967 | 10.00 |
| ❑ HS 11204 [S] | March Along with Mitch | 1967 | 12.00 |
| ❑ HS 11241 | Fireside Sing Along with Mitch | 1968 | 10.00 |
| ❑ HS 11242 | Memories Sing Along with Mitch | 1968 | 10.00 |
| ❑ HS 11273 | Everybody Sing Along with Mitch | 1968 | 10.00 |
| ❑ HS 11354 | Night Time Sing Along with Mitch | 1970 | 10.00 |

## MILLER, MRS.

### AMARET

| Number | Title (A Side/B Side) | Yr | NM |
|---|---|---|---|
| ❑ 5000 | Mrs. Miller Does Her Thing | 1969 | 20.00 |

### CAPITOL

| Number | Title (A Side/B Side) | Yr | NM |
|---|---|---|---|
| ❑ ST 2494 [S] | Mrs. Miller's Greatest Hits | 1966 | 30.00 |
| ❑ T 2494 [M] | Mrs. Miller's Greatest Hits | 1966 | 25.00 |
| ❑ ST 2579 [S] | Will Success Spoil Mrs. Miller? | 1966 | 30.00 |
| ❑ T 2579 [M] | Will Success Spoil Mrs. Miller? | 1966 | 25.00 |
| ❑ ST 2734 [S] | The Country Soul of Mrs. Miller | 1967 | 25.00 |
| ❑ T 2734 [M] | The Country Soul of Mrs. Miller | 1967 | 25.00 |

## MILLER, NED

### CAPITOL

| Number | Title (A Side/B Side) | Yr | NM |
|---|---|---|---|
| ❑ ST 2330 [S] | Ned Miller Sings the Songs of Ned Miller | 1965 | 25.00 |
| ❑ T 2330 [M] | Ned Miller Sings the Songs of Ned Miller | 1965 | 20.00 |
| ❑ ST 2414 [S] | The Best of Ned Miller | 1966 | 20.00 |
| ❑ T 2414 [M] | The Best of Ned Miller | 1966 | 15.00 |
| ❑ ST 2586 [S] | Teardrop Lane | 1967 | 20.00 |
| ❑ T 2586 [M] | Teardrop Lane | 1967 | 20.00 |
| ❑ ST 2914 | In the Name of Love | 1968 | 15.00 |

### FABOR

| Number | Title (A Side/B Side) | Yr | NM |
|---|---|---|---|
| ❑ FLP-1001 [M] | From a Jack to a King | 1963 | 40.00 |
| *—Black vinyl* | | | |
| ❑ FLP-1001 [M] | From a Jack to a King | 1963 | 100.00 |
| *—Colored vinyl* | | | |

## MILLER, PUNCH

### IMPERIAL

| Number | Title (A Side/B Side) | Yr | NM |
|---|---|---|---|
| ❑ LP-9160 [M] | Hongo Fongo | 1962 | 25.00 |

## MILLER, ROGER

### COLUMBIA

| Number | Title (A Side/B Side) | Yr | NM |
|---|---|---|---|
| ❑ KC 32449 | Dear Folks Sorry I Haven't Written Lately | 1973 | 15.00 |
| ❑ KC 33472 | Supersongs | 1975 | 15.00 |

### HILLTOP

| Number | Title (A Side/B Side) | Yr | NM |
|---|---|---|---|
| ❑ 6109 | King of the Road | 197? | 10.00 |
| ❑ 6131 | Little Green Apples | 197? | 10.00 |

### MCA

| Number | Title (A Side/B Side) | Yr | NM |
|---|---|---|---|
| ❑ 5722 | Roger Miller | 1986 | 10.00 |

### MERCURY

| Number | Title (A Side/B Side) | Yr | NM |
|---|---|---|---|
| ❑ SR-61297 | A Trip in the Country | 1970 | 15.00 |
| ❑ SR-61361 | The Best of Roger Miller | 1971 | 15.00 |
| ❑ 826261-1 | Golden Hits | 198? | 8.00 |
| *—Reissue of Smash 67073* | | | |

### NASHVILLE

| Number | Title (A Side/B Side) | Yr | NM |
|---|---|---|---|
| ❑ 2046 | The Amazing Roger Miller | 196? | 12.00 |

### PICKWICK

| Number | Title (A Side/B Side) | Yr | NM |
|---|---|---|---|
| ❑ PTP-2057 [(2)] | King High | 1973 | 12.00 |
| ❑ SPC-3226 | Engine #9 | 197? | 10.00 |

### RCA CAMDEN

| Number | Title (A Side/B Side) | Yr | NM |
|---|---|---|---|
| ❑ CAL-851 [M] | Roger Miller | 1964 | 12.00 |
| ❑ CAS-851 [S] | Roger Miller | 1964 | 15.00 |
| ❑ CAL-903 [M] | The One and Only Roger Miller | 1965 | 12.00 |
| ❑ CAS-903 [S] | The One and Only Roger Miller | 1965 | 15.00 |

### SMASH

| Number | Title (A Side/B Side) | Yr | NM |
|---|---|---|---|
| ❑ MGS-27049 [M] | Dang Me | 196? | 12.00 |
| *—Yet another retitled version of "Roger and Out"* | | | |
| ❑ MGS-27049 [M] | Dang Me/Chug-a-Lug | 196? | 12.00 |
| *—Retitled version of "Roger and Out"* | | | |
| ❑ MGS-27049 [M] | Roger and Out | 1964 | 15.00 |
| ❑ MGS-27061 [M] | The Return of Roger Miller | 1965 | 15.00 |
| ❑ MGS-27068 [M] | The 3rd Time Around | 1965 | 15.00 |
| ❑ MGS-27073 [M] | Golden Hits | 1965 | 15.00 |
| ❑ MGS-27075 [M] | Words and Music | 1966 | 15.00 |
| ❑ MGS-27092 [M] | Walkin' in the Sunshine | 1967 | 20.00 |
| ❑ MGS-27096 [M] | Waterhole #3 | 1967 | 25.00 |
| ❑ SRS-67049 [S] | Dang Me | 196? | 15.00 |
| *—Yet another retitled version of "Roger and Out"* | | | |
| ❑ SRS-67049 [S] | Dang Me/Chug-a-Lug | 196? | 15.00 |
| *—Retitled version of "Roger and Out"* | | | |
| ❑ SRS-67049 [S] | Roger and Out | 1964 | 20.00 |
| ❑ SRS-67061 [S] | The Return of Roger Miller | 1965 | 20.00 |
| ❑ SRS-67068 [S] | The 3rd Time Around | 1965 | 20.00 |
| ❑ SRS-67073 [S] | Golden Hits | 1965 | 20.00 |
| ❑ SRS-67075 [S] | Words and Music | 1966 | 20.00 |
| ❑ SRS-67092 [S] | Walkin' in the Sunshine | 1967 | 20.00 |
| ❑ SRS-67096 [S] | Waterhole #3 | 1967 | 20.00 |
| ❑ SRS-67103 | A Tender Look at Love | 1968 | 20.00 |
| ❑ SRS-67123 | Roger Miller | 1969 | 20.00 |
| ❑ SRS-67129 | Roger Miller 1970 | 1970 | 20.00 |

### STARDAY

| Number | Title (A Side/B Side) | Yr | NM |
|---|---|---|---|
| ❑ SLP-318 [M] | The Country Side of Roger Miller | 196? | 25.00 |
| *—Retitled version of "Wild Child"* | | | |
| ❑ SLP-318 [M] | Wild Child Roger Miller | 1965 | 30.00 |
| ❑ 3011 | Painted Poetry | 1978 | 10.00 |
| ❑ DT-90241 [R] | Wild Child Roger Miller | 1965 | 40.00 |
| *—Capitol Record Club edition* | | | |
| ❑ T-90241 [M] | Wild Child Roger Miller | 1965 | 40.00 |
| *—Capitol Record Club edition* | | | |

### 20TH CENTURY

| Number | Title (A Side/B Side) | Yr | NM |
|---|---|---|---|
| ❑ T-592 | Making a Name for Myself | 1979 | 12.00 |

### WINDSONG

| Number | Title (A Side/B Side) | Yr | NM |
|---|---|---|---|
| ❑ BHL1-2337 | Off the Wall | 1977 | 12.00 |

## MILLER, STEVE, BAND

### CAPITOL

| Number | Title (A Side/B Side) | Yr | NM |
|---|---|---|---|
| ❑ SKAO-184 | Brave New World | 1969 | 20.00 |
| *—Black label with colorband* | | | |
| ❑ SKAO-184 | Brave New World | 1970 | 15.00 |
| *—Green label* | | | |
| ❑ SKAO-8-0184 | Brave New World | 1969 | 25.00 |
| *—Capitol Record Club edition; black label with colorband* | | | |
| ❑ ST-331 | Your Saving Grace | 1969 | 15.00 |
| ❑ SKAO-436 | Number 5 | 1970 | 15.00 |
| ❑ STBB-717 [(2)] | Children of the Future/Living in the U.S.A. | 1971 | 15.00 |
| *—Repackage of 2920 and 2984 (with new title for the latter)* | | | |
| ❑ SW-748 | Rock Love | 1971 | 15.00 |
| ❑ SKAO 2920 | Children of the Future | 1968 | 25.00 |
| *—Black label with colorband* | | | |
| ❑ SKAO 2920 | Children of the Future | 1970 | 15.00 |
| *—Green label* | | | |
| ❑ ST 2984 | Sailor | 1968 | 25.00 |
| *—Black label with colorband* | | | |
| ❑ ST 2984 | Sailor | 1970 | 15.00 |
| *—Green label* | | | |
| ❑ SMAS-11022 | Recall the Beginning...A Journey from Eden | 1972 | 15.00 |
| ❑ SVBB-11114 [(2)] | Anthology | 1972 | 15.00 |
| ❑ SMAS-11235 | The Joker | 1973 | 10.00 |
| ❑ ST-11497 | Fly Like an Eagle | 1976 | 10.00 |
| ❑ SO-11630 | Book of Dreams | 1977 | 10.00 |
| ❑ SOO-11872 | Greatest Hits 1974-1978 | 1978 | 10.00 |
| ❑ SOO-11872 [DJ] | Greatest Hits 1974-1978 | 1978 | 30.00 |
| *—Promo only on blue vinyl* | | | |
| ❑ SEAX-11903 [PD] | Book of Dreams | 1978 | 15.00 |
| ❑ ST-12121 | Circle of Love | 1981 | 10.00 |
| ❑ ST-12216 | Abracadabra | 1982 | 10.00 |
| ❑ ST-12263 | Steve Miller Live | 1983 | 10.00 |
| ❑ SJ-12339 | Italian X-Rays | 1985 | 10.00 |
| ❑ PJ-12445 | Living in the 20th Century | 1987 | 10.00 |
| ❑ SN-16078 | Brave New World | 1980 | 8.00 |
| ❑ SN-16079 | Your Saving Grace | 1980 | 8.00 |
| ❑ SN-16262 | Children of the Future | 1982 | 8.00 |
| ❑ SN-16263 | Sailor | 1982 | 8.00 |
| ❑ SN-16321 | Greatest Hits 1974-1978 | 1984 | 8.00 |
| ❑ SN-16323 | Book of Dreams | 1984 | 8.00 |
| ❑ SN-16339 | Fly Like an Eagle | 1984 | 8.00 |
| ❑ SN-16357 | Circle of Love | 1985 | 8.00 |
| ❑ 21185 | Fly Like an Eagle | 1999 | 20.00 |
| *—Limited-edition reissue on 180-gram vinyl* | | | |
| ❑ C1-48303 | Born 2 B Blue | 1988 | 10.00 |
| ❑ SKAO-80436 | Number 5 | 1970 | 20.00 |
| *—Capitol Record Club edition* | | | |
| ❑ R 223186 [(2)] | Anthology | 197? | 15.00 |
| *—RCA Music Service edition* | | | |

### DCC COMPACT CLASSICS

| Number | Title (A Side/B Side) | Yr | NM |
|---|---|---|---|
| ❑ LPZ-2028 | Greatest Hits 1974-1978 | 1996 | 40.00 |
| *—Audiophile vinyl* | | | |

### MOBILE FIDELITY

| Number | Title (A Side/B Side) | Yr | NM |
|---|---|---|---|
| ❑ 1-021 | Fly Like an Eagle | 1979 | 40.00 |
| *—Audiophile vinyl* | | | |

| Number | Title (A Side/B Side) | Yr | NM |
|---|---|---|---|

### MILLER, STEVE, BAND/QUICKSILVER MESSENGER SERVICE/THE BAND

Also see each artist's individual listings.

**CAPITOL**

| Number | Title (A Side/B Side) | Yr | NM |
|---|---|---|---|
| ❑ STCR-288 [(3)] | Sailor/Quicksilver Messenger Service/Music from Big Pink | 1969 | 40.00 |

*—Special 3-LP box set combining these three LPs, also listed separately in each group's listing, in one package*

### MILLMAN, JACK

**DECCA**

| Number | Title (A Side/B Side) | Yr | NM |
|---|---|---|---|
| ❑ DL 8156 [M] | Jazz Studio 4 | 1955 | 50.00 |

**ERA**

| Number | Title (A Side/B Side) | Yr | NM |
|---|---|---|---|
| ❑ EL-20005 [M] | Blowing Up a Storm *—Black vinyl* | 1956 | 40.00 |
| ❑ EL-20005 [M] | Blowing Up a Storm *—Red vinyl* | 1956 | 60.00 |

**LIBERTY**

| Number | Title (A Side/B Side) | Yr | NM |
|---|---|---|---|
| ❑ LJH-6007 [M] | Shades of Things to Come | 1956 | 50.00 |

### MILLS, ALAN

**FOLKWAYS**

| Number | Title (A Side/B Side) | Yr | NM |
|---|---|---|---|
| ❑ FP-29 [10] | Folk Songs of French Canada | 1952 | 50.00 |
| ❑ FP-831 [10] | Folk Songs of Newfoundland | 1953 | 50.00 |
| ❑ FA-2313 [M] | Songs of the Sea | 1957 | 30.00 |
| ❑ FW-3000 [(2)M] | Canada's Story in Song | 1960 | 40.00 |
| ❑ FW-3001 [M] | O Canada: A History in Song | 1956 | 30.00 |
| ❑ FW-6831 [M] | Folk Songs of Newfoundland | 195? | 30.00 |
| ❑ FW-6929 [M] | Folk Songs of French Canada | 195? | 30.00 |
| ❑ FC-7018 [M] | French Folk Songs for Children in English | 1957 | 30.00 |
| ❑ FC-7208 [M] | French Folk Songs for Children | 1957 | 30.00 |
| ❑ FC-7642 [M] | More Animals, Vol. 2 | 1956 | 30.00 |
| ❑ FC-7677 [M] | Animals, Vol. 1 | 1956 | 30.00 |
| ❑ FC-7750 [M] | Christmas Songs from Many Lands | 1956 | 30.00 |
| ❑ FW-8771 [M] | We'll Rant and We'll Roar: Songs of Newfoundland | 1958 | 30.00 |

**SCHOLASTIC**

| Number | Title (A Side/B Side) | Yr | NM |
|---|---|---|---|
| ❑ FC-7750 [M] | Christmas Songs from Many Lands | 196? | 15.00 |

*—Reissue of Folkways album with same contents*

### MILLS, HAYLEY

**BUENA VISTA**

| Number | Title (A Side/B Side) | Yr | NM |
|---|---|---|---|
| ❑ BV-3311 [M] | Let's Get Together | 1962 | 25.00 |
| ❑ STER-3311 [S] | Let's Get Together | 1962 | 40.00 |

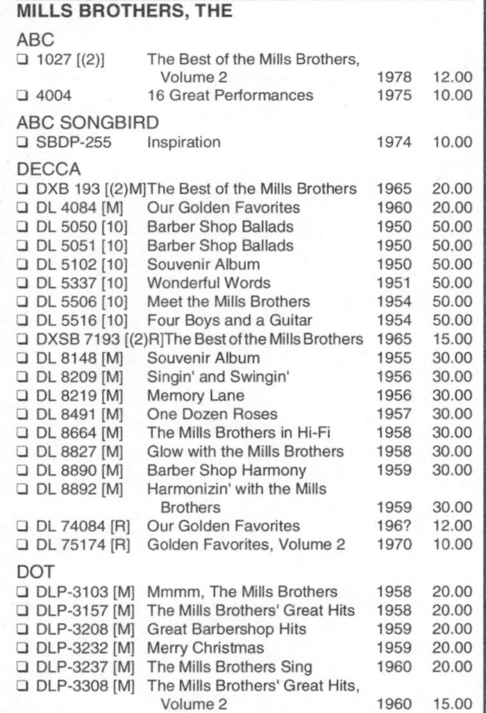

### MILLS BROTHERS, THE

**ABC**

| Number | Title (A Side/B Side) | Yr | NM |
|---|---|---|---|
| ❑ 1027 [(2)] | The Best of the Mills Brothers, Volume 2 | 1978 | 12.00 |
| ❑ 4004 | 16 Great Performances | 1975 | 10.00 |

**ABC SONGBIRD**

| Number | Title (A Side/B Side) | Yr | NM |
|---|---|---|---|
| ❑ SBDP-255 | Inspiration | 1974 | 10.00 |

**DECCA**

| Number | Title (A Side/B Side) | Yr | NM |
|---|---|---|---|
| ❑ DXB 193 [(2)M] | The Best of the Mills Brothers | 1965 | 20.00 |
| ❑ DL 4084 [M] | Our Golden Favorites | 1960 | 20.00 |
| ❑ DL 5050 [10] | Barber Shop Ballads | 1950 | 50.00 |
| ❑ DL 5051 [10] | Barber Shop Ballads | 1950 | 50.00 |
| ❑ DL 5102 [10] | Souvenir Album | 1950 | 50.00 |
| ❑ DL 5337 [10] | Wonderful Words | 1951 | 50.00 |
| ❑ DL 5506 [10] | Meet the Mills Brothers | 1954 | 50.00 |
| ❑ DL 5516 [10] | Four Boys and a Guitar | 1954 | 50.00 |
| ❑ DXSB 7193 [(2)R] | The Best of the Mills Brothers | 1965 | 15.00 |
| ❑ DL 8148 [M] | Souvenir Album | 1955 | 30.00 |
| ❑ DL 8209 [M] | Singin' and Swingin' | 1956 | 30.00 |
| ❑ DL 8219 [M] | Memory Lane | 1956 | 30.00 |
| ❑ DL 8491 [M] | One Dozen Roses | 1957 | 30.00 |
| ❑ DL 8664 [M] | The Mills Brothers in Hi-Fi | 1958 | 30.00 |
| ❑ DL 8827 [M] | Glow with the Mills Brothers | 1958 | 30.00 |
| ❑ DL 8890 [M] | Barber Shop Harmony | 1959 | 30.00 |
| ❑ DL 8892 [M] | Harmonizin' with the Mills Brothers | 1959 | 30.00 |
| ❑ DL 74084 [R] | Our Golden Favorites | 196? | 12.00 |
| ❑ DL 75174 [R] | Golden Favorites, Volume 2 | 1970 | 10.00 |

**DOT**

| Number | Title (A Side/B Side) | Yr | NM |
|---|---|---|---|
| ❑ DLP-3103 [M] | Mmmm, The Mills Brothers | 1958 | 20.00 |
| ❑ DLP-3157 [M] | The Mills Brothers' Great Hits | 1958 | 20.00 |
| ❑ DLP-3208 [M] | Great Barbershop Hits | 1959 | 20.00 |
| ❑ DLP-3232 [M] | Merry Christmas | 1959 | 20.00 |
| ❑ DLP-3237 [M] | The Mills Brothers Sing | 1960 | 20.00 |
| ❑ DLP-3308 [M] | The Mills Brothers' Great Hits, Volume 2 | 1960 | 15.00 |
| ❑ DLP-3338 [M] | Yellow Bird | 1960 | 15.00 |
| ❑ DLP-3363 [M] | San Antonio Rose | 1961 | 15.00 |
| ❑ DLP-3368 [M] | Great Hawaiian Hits | 1961 | 15.00 |
| ❑ DLP-3465 [M] | Beer Barrel Polka and Other Hits | 1962 | 12.00 |
| ❑ DLP-3508 [M] | The End of the World | 1963 | 12.00 |
| ❑ DLP-3565 [M] | Gems by the Mills Brothers | 1964 | 12.00 |
| ❑ DLP-3568 [M] | Hymns We Love | 1964 | 12.00 |
| ❑ DLP-3592 [M] | Say Si Si and Other Great Latin Hits | 1964 | 12.00 |
| ❑ DLP-3652 [M] | Ten Years of Hits 1954-1964 | 1965 | 12.00 |
| ❑ DLP-3699 [M] | These Are the Mills Brothers | 1966 | 12.00 |
| ❑ DLP-3744 [M] | That Country Feeling | 1966 | 12.00 |
| ❑ DL-3766 [M] | The Mills Brothers Today | 1966 | 12.00 |
| ❑ DLP-3783 [M] | The Mills Brothers Live | 1967 | 15.00 |
| ❑ DLP-25103 [S] | Mmmm, The Mills Brothers | 1958 | 30.00 |
| ❑ DLP-25157 [S] | The Mills Brothers' Great Hits *—Blue vinyl* | 195? | 60.00 |
| ❑ DLP-25157 [S] | The Mills Brothers' Great Hits *—Black vinyl* | 1958 | 30.00 |
| ❑ DLP-25208 [S] | Great Barbershop Hits | 1959 | 30.00 |
| ❑ DLP-25232 [S] | Merry Christmas *—Same as above, but in stereo; with cursive "Dot" logo* | 1959 | 30.00 |
| ❑ DLP-25232 [S] | Merry Christmas *—With "Dot"/"Paramount" logo* | 1968 | 12.00 |
| ❑ DLP-25237 [S] | The Mills Brothers Sing | 1960 | 30.00 |
| ❑ DLP-25308 [S] | The Mills Brothers' Great Hits, Volume 2 | 1960 | 20.00 |
| ❑ DLP-25338 [S] | Yellow Bird | 1960 | 20.00 |
| ❑ DLP-25363 [S] | San Antonio Rose | 1961 | 20.00 |
| ❑ DLP-25368 [S] | Great Hawaiian Hits | 1961 | 20.00 |
| ❑ DLP-25465 [S] | Beer Barrel Polka and Other Hits | 1962 | 15.00 |
| ❑ DLP-25508 [S] | The End of the World | 1963 | 15.00 |
| ❑ DLP-25565 [S] | Gems by the Mills Brothers | 1964 | 15.00 |
| ❑ DLP-25568 [S] | Hymns We Love | 1964 | 15.00 |
| ❑ DLP-25592 [S] | Say Si Si and Other Great Latin Hits | 1964 | 15.00 |
| ❑ DLP-25652 [S] | Ten Years of Hits 1954-1964 | 1965 | 15.00 |
| ❑ DLP-25699 [S] | These Are the Mills Brothers | 1966 | 15.00 |
| ❑ DLP-25744 [S] | That Country Feeling | 1966 | 15.00 |
| ❑ DLP-25766 [S] | The Mills Brothers Today | 1966 | 15.00 |
| ❑ DLP-25783 [S] | The Mills Brothers Live | 1967 | 15.00 |
| ❑ DLP-25809 | Fortuosity | 1968 | 15.00 |
| ❑ DLP-25872 | My Shy Violet | 1968 | 15.00 |
| ❑ DLP-25927 | Dream | 1969 | 15.00 |
| ❑ DLP-25960 | The Mills Brothers In Motion | 1970 | 15.00 |

**EVEREST ARCHIVE OF FOLK & JAZZ**

| Number | Title (A Side/B Side) | Yr | NM |
|---|---|---|---|
| ❑ 300 | The Mills Brothers | 197? | 10.00 |
| ❑ 328 | The Mills Brothers, Volume 2 | 197? | 10.00 |

**GNP CRESCENDO**

| Number | Title (A Side/B Side) | Yr | NM |
|---|---|---|---|
| ❑ GNP-9106 | Four Boys and a Guitar | 197? | 10.00 |

**HAMILTON**

| Number | Title (A Side/B Side) | Yr | NM |
|---|---|---|---|
| ❑ HL-116 [M] | The Mills Brothers Sing for You | 1964 | 12.00 |
| ❑ HS-12116 [S] | The Mills Brothers Sing for You | 1964 | 12.00 |

**MARK 56**

| Number | Title (A Side/B Side) | Yr | NM |
|---|---|---|---|
| ❑ 709 | Original Radio Broadcasts | 197? | 10.00 |

**MCA**

| Number | Title (A Side/B Side) | Yr | NM |
|---|---|---|---|
| ❑ 132 | Golden Favorites, Volume 2 | 1973 | 10.00 |
| ❑ 188 | Old Golden Favorites | 1973 | 10.00 |
| ❑ 717 | 16 Great Performances | 1980 | 8.00 |
| ❑ 1556 | The Mills Brothers | 198? | 10.00 |
| ❑ 4039 [(2)] | The Best of the Mills Brothers | 197? | 12.00 |
| ❑ 15029 | Merry Christmas | 198? | 10.00 |
| ❑ 27083 | The Mills Brothers Great Hits | 1980 | 8.00 |
| ❑ 28116 | Were You There | 198? | 8.00 |

**MCA SPECIAL MARKETS**

| Number | Title (A Side/B Side) | Yr | NM |
|---|---|---|---|
| ❑ MSM2-35067 [(2)] | Classic Mills Brothers | 198? | 10.00 |

**PARAMOUNT**

| Number | Title (A Side/B Side) | Yr | NM |
|---|---|---|---|
| ❑ PAS-1010 | The Best of the Mills Brothers | 1973 | 12.00 |
| ❑ PAS-1027 [(2)] | The Best of the Mills Brothers, Volume 2 | 1974 | 15.00 |
| ❑ PAS-5025 | No Turnin' Back | 1971 | 12.00 |
| ❑ PAS-6024 | What a Wonderful World | 1972 | 12.00 |
| ❑ PAS-6038 | A Donut and a Dream | 1973 | 12.00 |

**PICKWICK**

| Number | Title (A Side/B Side) | Yr | NM |
|---|---|---|---|
| ❑ SPC-1025 | Merry Christmas *—Reissue of Dot album with one fewer track* | 1979 | 10.00 |
| ❑ 2008 | Songs You Remember | 197? | 10.00 |
| ❑ 2030 | The Mills Brothers | 1973 | 10.00 |
| ❑ SPC-3076 | 14 Karat Gold | 196? | 10.00 |
| ❑ SPC-3107 | Anytime | 197? | 10.00 |
| ❑ SPC-3137 | Dream a Little Dream | 197? | 10.00 |
| ❑ SPC-3158 | Till We Meet Again | 197? | 10.00 |
| ❑ SPC-3220 | Cab Driver | 197? | 10.00 |
| ❑ SPC-3556 | The Mills Brothers | 1976 | 8.00 |

**RANWOOD**

| Number | Title (A Side/B Side) | Yr | NM |
|---|---|---|---|
| ❑ 7035 [(2)] | 22 Great Hits | 1985 | 10.00 |
| ❑ 8123 | Cab Driver | 197? | 10.00 |
| ❑ 8133 | The Mills Brothers Story | 197? | 10.00 |
| ❑ 8139 | Country's Greatest Hits | 197? | 10.00 |
| ❑ 8152 | 50th Anniversary | 197? | 10.00 |
| ❑ 8198 | Command Performance | 198? | 8.00 |

**SUNNYVALE**

| Number | Title (A Side/B Side) | Yr | NM |
|---|---|---|---|
| ❑ 1023 | Timeless | 1978 | 10.00 |

**VOCALION**

| Number | Title (A Side/B Side) | Yr | NM |
|---|---|---|---|
| ❑ VL 3607 [M] | In a Mellow Tone | 196? | 12.00 |
| ❑ VL 73607 [R] | In a Mellow Tone | 196? | 10.00 |
| ❑ VL 73859 [R] | Such Sweet Singing | 1969 | 10.00 |

The Steve Miller Band, *Children of the Future,* Capitol SKAO-2920, 1968, black label with colorband, $25.

DOT
STEREO
DLP 25927
DREAM
THE MILLS BROTHERS
FEATURING THE JIMTOWN ROAD
THE JIMTOWN ROAD ◦ DREAM ◦ THE STRAIGHT LIFE ◦ BABY DREAM YOUR DREAM (from the Broadway Show "Sweet Charity")
WHEN,WHEN,WHEN ◦ FLIT AROUND ◦ WHAT HAVE I DONE FOR HER LATELY ◦ HAPPY GO LUCKY ME ◦ DIDN'T WE ◦ GUY ON THE GO


The Mills Brothers, *Dream,* Dot DLP-25927, 1969, $15.

## MILSAP, RONNIE

**PAIR**

| Number | Title (A Side/B Side) | Yr | NM |
|---|---|---|---|
| ❑ PDL2-1031 [(2)] | Believe It! | 1986 | 12.00 |
| ❑ PDL2-1105 [(2)] | Back on My Mind Again | 1986 | 12.00 |

**PICKWICK**

| Number | Title (A Side/B Side) | Yr | NM |
|---|---|---|---|
| ❑ JS-6179 | Plain and Simple | 197? | 10.00 |

**RCA**

| Number | Title (A Side/B Side) | Yr | NM |
|---|---|---|---|
| ❑ 9588-1-R | Stranger Things Have Happened | 1989 | 10.00 |
| ❑ R 183710 | Back to the Grindstone | 1991 | 20.00 |
| *—Only released on vinyl through BMG Direct Marketing* | | | |

**RCA VICTOR**

| Number | Title (A Side/B Side) | Yr | NM |
|---|---|---|---|
| ❑ APL1-0338 | Where My Heart Is | 1973 | 20.00 |
| ❑ APD1-0500 [Q] | Pure Love | 1974 | 20.00 |
| ❑ APL1-0500 | Pure Love | 1974 | 15.00 |
| ❑ APD1-0846 [Q] | A Legend in My Time | 1975 | 20.00 |
| ❑ APL1-0846 | A Legend in My Time | 1975 | 15.00 |
| ❑ APL1-1223 | Night Things | 1975 | 15.00 |
| ❑ APL1-1666 | 20-20 Vision | 1976 | 12.00 |
| ❑ APL1-2043 | Ronnie Milsap Live | 1976 | 12.00 |
| ❑ AFL1-2439 | It Was Almost Like a Song | 1977 | 12.00 |
| ❑ AFL1-2780 | Only One Love in My Life | 1978 | 12.00 |
| ❑ AHL1-3346 | Images | 1979 | 12.00 |
| ❑ AHL1-3563 | Milsap Magic | 1980 | 10.00 |
| ❑ AYL1-3760 | Where My Heart Is | 1980 | 8.00 |
| *—"Best Buy Series" reissue* | | | |
| ❑ AHL1-3772 | Greatest Hits | 1980 | 10.00 |
| ❑ AYL1-3899 | Pure Love | 1981 | 8.00 |
| *—"Best Buy Series" reissue* | | | |
| ❑ AAL1-3932 | Out Where the Bright Lights Are Glowing | 1981 | 10.00 |
| ❑ AHL1-4060 | There's No Gettin' Over Me | 1981 | 10.00 |
| ❑ AYL1-4171 | Images | 1981 | 8.00 |
| *—"Best Buy Series" reissue* | | | |
| ❑ AYL1-4255 | Ronnie Milsap Live | 1982 | 8.00 |
| *—"Best Buy Series" reissue* | | | |
| ❑ AHL1-4311 | Inside Ronnie Milsap | 1982 | 10.00 |
| ❑ AHL1-4670 | Keyed Up | 1983 | 10.00 |
| ❑ AHL1-5016 | One More Try for Love | 1984 | 10.00 |
| ❑ AYL1-5139 | It Was Almost Like a Song | 1984 | 8.00 |
| *—"Best Buy Series" reissue* | | | |
| ❑ AYL1-5140 | There's No Gettin' Over Me | 1984 | 8.00 |
| *—"Best Buy Series" reissue* | | | |
| ❑ AYL1-5142 | Inside Ronnie Milsap | 1984 | 8.00 |
| *—"Best Buy Series" reissue* | | | |
| ❑ AHL1-5425 | Greatest Hits, Vol. 2 | 1985 | 10.00 |
| ❑ AYL1-5435 | Keyed Up | 1985 | 8.00 |
| *—"Best Buy Series" reissue* | | | |
| ❑ 5624-1-R | Christmas with Ronnie Milsap | 1986 | 10.00 |
| ❑ 6425-1-R | Heart and Soul | 1987 | 10.00 |
| ❑ CPL1-7166 | Collector's Series | 1986 | 8.00 |
| ❑ AHL1-7194 | Lost in the Fifties Tonight | 1986 | 10.00 |
| ❑ 7618-1-R | Heart and Soul | 1988 | 8.00 |
| *—Reissue of 6245* | | | |

**TIME-LIFE**

| Number | Title (A Side/B Side) | Yr | NM |
|---|---|---|---|
| ❑ STW-110 | Country Music | 1981 | 10.00 |

**WARNER BROS.**

| Number | Title (A Side/B Side) | Yr | NM |
|---|---|---|---|
| ❑ WS 1934 | Ronnie Milsap | 1971 | 20.00 |
| ❑ BS 2870 | A Rose By Any Other Name | 1975 | 15.00 |

## MILTON, ROY

**KENT**

| Number | Title (A Side/B Side) | Yr | NM |
|---|---|---|---|
| ❑ KST-554 [R] | The Great Roy Milton | 196? | 30.00 |
| ❑ KLP-5054 [M] | The Great Roy Milton | 1963 | 50.00 |

## MIMMS, GARNET, AND THE ENCHANTERS

**ARISTA**

| Number | Title (A Side/B Side) | Yr | NM |
|---|---|---|---|
| ❑ AL 4153 | Garnet Mimms Has It All | 1978 | 12.00 |

**UNITED ARTISTS**

| Number | Title (A Side/B Side) | Yr | NM |
|---|---|---|---|
| ❑ UAL 3305 [M] | Cry Baby and 11 Other Hits | 1963 | 80.00 |
| ❑ UAL 3396 [M] | As Long As I Have You | 1964 | 50.00 |
| ❑ UAL 3498 [M] | I'll Take Good Care of You | 1966 | 50.00 |
| ❑ UAS 6305 [S] | Cry Baby and 11 Other Hits | 1963 | 100.00 |
| ❑ UAS 6396 [S] | As Long As I Have You | 1964 | 70.00 |
| ❑ UAS 6498 [S] | I'll Take Good Care of You | 1966 | 70.00 |

## MIND EXPANDERS, THE

**DOT**

| Number | Title (A Side/B Side) | Yr | NM |
|---|---|---|---|
| ❑ DLP-3773 [M] | What's Happening | 1967 | 100.00 |
| ❑ DLP-25773 [S] | What's Happening | 1967 | 80.00 |

## MIND GARAGE, THE

**RCA VICTOR**

| Number | Title (A Side/B Side) | Yr | NM |
|---|---|---|---|
| ❑ LSP-4218 | The Mind Garage | 1969 | 20.00 |
| ❑ LSP-4319 | The Mind Garage Again! | 1970 | 20.00 |

## MINDBENDERS, THE

**FONTANA**

| Number | Title (A Side/B Side) | Yr | NM |
|---|---|---|---|
| ❑ MGF-27554 [M] | A Groovy Kind of Love | 1966 | 25.00 |
| *—With "Ashes to Ashes"* | | | |
| ❑ MGF-27554 [M] | A Groovy Kind of Love | 1966 | 30.00 |
| *—With "Don't Cry No More"* | | | |
| ❑ SRF-67554 [R] | A Groovy Kind of Love | 1966 | 20.00 |
| *—With "Ashes to Ashes"* | | | |
| ❑ SRF-67554 [R] | A Groovy Kind of Love | 1966 | 25.00 |
| *—With "Don't Cry No More"* | | | |

## MINEO, SAL

**EPIC**

| Number | Title (A Side/B Side) | Yr | NM |
|---|---|---|---|
| ❑ LN 3405 [M] | Sal | 1958 | 150.00 |

## MINGUS, CHARLES

**ABC IMPULSE!**

| Number | Title (A Side/B Side) | Yr | NM |
|---|---|---|---|
| ❑ AS-35 [S] | Black Saint and Sinner Lady | 1968 | 20.00 |
| *—Black label with red ring* | | | |
| ❑ AS-54 [S] | Mingus, Mingus, Mingus, Mingus, Mingus | 1968 | 20.00 |
| *—Black label with red ring* | | | |
| ❑ AS-60 [S] | Charlie Mingus Plays Piano | 1968 | 20.00 |
| *—Black label with red ring* | | | |

**ATLANTIC**

| Number | Title (A Side/B Side) | Yr | NM |
|---|---|---|---|
| ❑ SD 3-600 [(3)] | Passions of a Man: The Charles Mingus Anthology | 1980 | 20.00 |
| ❑ 1237 [M] | Pithecanthropus Erectus | 1956 | 80.00 |
| *—Black label* | | | |
| ❑ 1237 [M] | Pithecanthropus Erectus | 1961 | 25.00 |
| *—Multicolor label, white "fan" logo at right* | | | |
| ❑ 1237 [M] | Pithecanthropus Erectus | 1964 | 20.00 |
| *—Multicolor label, black "fan" logo at right* | | | |
| ❑ 1260 [M] | The Clown | 1957 | 80.00 |
| *—Black label* | | | |
| ❑ 1260 [M] | The Clown | 1961 | 25.00 |
| *—Multicolor label, white "fan" logo at right* | | | |
| ❑ 1260 [M] | The Clown | 1964 | 20.00 |
| *—Multicolor label, black "fan" logo at right* | | | |
| ❑ 1305 [M] | Blues & Roots | 1959 | 80.00 |
| *—White "bullseye" label* | | | |
| ❑ 1305 [M] | Blues & Roots | 1961 | 30.00 |
| *—Multicolor label, white "fan" logo at right* | | | |
| ❑ 1305 [M] | Blues & Roots | 1964 | 25.00 |
| *—Multicolor label, black "fan" logo at right* | | | |
| ❑ SD 1305 [S] | Blues & Roots | 1959 | 80.00 |
| *—White "bullseye" label* | | | |
| ❑ SD 1305 [S] | Blues & Roots | 1961 | 30.00 |
| *—Multicolor label, white "fan" logo at right* | | | |
| ❑ 1377 [M] | Oh, Yeah | 1961 | 30.00 |
| *—Multicolor label, white "fan" logo at right* | | | |
| ❑ SD 1377 [S] | Oh, Yeah | 1961 | 40.00 |
| *—Multicolor label, white "fan" logo at right* | | | |
| ❑ SD 1377 [S] | Oh, Yeah | 1964 | 25.00 |
| *—Multicolor label, black "fan" logo at right* | | | |
| ❑ 1417 [M] | Tonight at Noon | 1964 | 25.00 |
| ❑ SD 1417 [S] | Tonight at Noon | 1964 | 30.00 |

**BETHLEHEM**

| Number | Title (A Side/B Side) | Yr | NM |
|---|---|---|---|
| ❑ BCP-65 [M] | The Jazz Experiment of Charlie Mingus | 1956 | 100.00 |
| ❑ BCP-6019 [M] | East Coasting | 1957 | 100.00 |
| ❑ BCP-6026 [M] | A Modern Jazz Symposium of Jazz and Poetry | 1958 | 100.00 |

**CANDID**

| Number | Title (A Side/B Side) | Yr | NM |
|---|---|---|---|
| ❑ CD-8005 [M] | Charles Mingus Presents Charles Mingus | 1960 | 40.00 |
| ❑ CD-8021 [M] | Mingus | 1960 | 40.00 |
| ❑ CS-9005 [S] | Charles Mingus Presents Charles Mingus | 1960 | 50.00 |
| ❑ CS-9021 [S] | Mingus | 1960 | 50.00 |

**CHARLES MINGUS**

| Number | Title (A Side/B Side) | Yr | NM |
|---|---|---|---|
| ❑ JWS-001/2 [(2)] | Mingus at Monterey | 1966 | 300.00 |
| *—Gatefold jacket with color photo on front; "This album can be purchased only by mail" on back cover* | | | |
| ❑ JWS-001/2 [(2)] | Mingus at Monterey | 1966 | 700.00 |
| *—Single-pocket jacket with sepia-tone photo on front* | | | |
| ❑ JWS-001/2 [(2)] | Mingus at Monterey | 1968 | 60.00 |
| *—Gatefold jacket with color photo on front; distributed by Fantasy* | | | |
| ❑ JWS-005 | My Favorite Quintet | 1966 | 300.00 |
| *—"This album can be purchased only by mail" on back cover* | | | |
| ❑ JWS-009 | Town Hall Concert 1964, Vol. 1 | 1966 | 300.00 |
| *—"This album can be purchased only by mail" on back cover* | | | |
| ❑ JWS-013/14 [(2)] | Special Music Written For (But Not Heard At) Monterey | 1966 | 1000. |
| *—Single-pocket jacket; "This album can be purchased only by mail" on back cover* | | | |

**COLUMBIA**

| Number | Title (A Side/B Side) | Yr | NM |
|---|---|---|---|
| ❑ CL 1370 [M] | Mingus Ah Um | 1959 | 80.00 |
| *—Red and black label with six "eye" logos* | | | |
| ❑ CL 1370 [M] | Mingus Ah Um | 1963 | 40.00 |
| *—Red label with "Guaranteed High Fidelity" at bottom* | | | |
| ❑ CL 1370 [M] | Mingus Ah Um | 1966 | 30.00 |
| *—Red label with "360 Sound Mono" at bottom* | | | |
| ❑ CL 1440 [M] | Mingus Dynasty | 1960 | 30.00 |
| *—Red and black label with six "eye" logos* | | | |
| ❑ CL 1440 [M] | Mingus Dynasty | 1963 | 20.00 |
| *—Red label with "Guaranteed High Fidelity" at bottom* | | | |
| ❑ CS 8171 [S] | Mingus Ah Um | 1959 | 120.00 |
| *—Red and black label with six "eye" logos* | | | |
| ❑ CS 8171 [S] | Mingus Ah Um | 1963 | 50.00 |
| *—Red label with "360 Sound Stereo" in black at bottom* | | | |
| ❑ CS 8171 [S] | Mingus Ah Um | 1966 | 40.00 |
| *—Red label with "360 Sound Stereo" in white at bottom* | | | |
| ❑ CS 8171 [S] | Mingus Ah Um | 199? | 25.00 |
| *—Classic Records reissue on audiophile vinyl* | | | |



Except when noted otherwise, VG = 25% of NM, and VG+ = 50% of NM. (Example: VG = $2.00, VG+ = $4.00 and NM = $8.00.)

| Number | Title (A Side/B Side) | Yr | NM |
|---|---|---|---|
| ❑ CS 8236 [S] | Mingus Dynasty | 1960 | 40.00 |
| *—Red and black label with six "eye" logos* | | | |
| ❑ CS 8236 [S] | Mingus Dynasty | 1963 | 25.00 |
| *—Red label with "360 Sound Stereo" in black at bottom* | | | |
| ❑ CS 8236 [S] | Mingus Dynasty | 1966 | 20.00 |
| *—Red label with "360 Sound Stereo" in white at bottom* | | | |
| ❑ G 30628 [(2)] | Better Git It in Your Soul | 1971 | 20.00 |
| ❑ KG 31814 [(2)] | Charles Mingus and Friends | 1973 | 20.00 |

DEBUT

| Number | Title (A Side/B Side) | Yr | NM |
|---|---|---|---|
| ❑ DLP-1 [10] | Strings and Keys | 1953 | 500.00 |
| ❑ DEB-123 [M] | Mingus at the Bohemia | 1956 | 200.00 |

FANTASY

| Number | Title (A Side/B Side) | Yr | NM |
|---|---|---|---|
| ❑ JWS-001/2 [(2)] | Mingus at Monterey | 1969 | 20.00 |
| *—Reissue of Charles Mingus 001/2* | | | |
| ❑ 6002 [M] | Chazz! | 1962 | 30.00 |
| *—Black vinyl* | | | |
| ❑ 6002 [M] | Chazz! | 1962 | 50.00 |
| *—Red vinyl* | | | |
| ❑ 6009 [M] | The Charlie Mingus Quartet + Max Roach | 1963 | 30.00 |
| ❑ 6017 [M] | Right Now — Live at the Jazz Workshop | 1966 | 25.00 |
| ❑ 86002 [R] | Chazz! | 196? | 25.00 |
| *—Blue vinyl* | | | |
| ❑ 86017 [S] | Right Now — Live at the Jazz Workshop | 1966 | 30.00 |

GRP/IMPULSE!

| Number | Title (A Side/B Side) | Yr | NM |
|---|---|---|---|
| ❑ 217 | Charlie Mingus Plays Piano | 1997 | 20.00 |
| *—Reissue on audioiphile vinyl* | | | |

IMPULSE!

| Number | Title (A Side/B Side) | Yr | NM |
|---|---|---|---|
| ❑ A-35 [M] | Black Saint and Sinner Lady | 1963 | 30.00 |
| ❑ AS-35 [S] | Black Saint and Sinner Lady | 1963 | 40.00 |
| ❑ A-54 [M] | Mingus, Mingus, Mingus, Mingus, Mingus | 1963 | 30.00 |
| ❑ AS-54 [S] | Mingus, Mingus, Mingus, Mingus, Mingus | 1963 | 40.00 |
| ❑ A-60 [M] | Charlie Mingus Plays Piano | 1964 | 30.00 |
| ❑ AS-60 [S] | Charlie Mingus Plays Piano | 1964 | 40.00 |

JAZZTONE

| Number | Title (A Side/B Side) | Yr | NM |
|---|---|---|---|
| ❑ J-1226 [M] | Jazz Experiment | 1956 | 60.00 |
| ❑ J-1271 [M] | The Jazz Experiments of Charlie Mingus | 1957 | 50.00 |

JOSIE

| Number | Title (A Side/B Side) | Yr | NM |
|---|---|---|---|
| ❑ JLPS-3508 [R] | Mingus Three | 1963 | 20.00 |
| ❑ JOZ-3508 [M] | Mingus Three | 1963 | 30.00 |

JUBILEE

| Number | Title (A Side/B Side) | Yr | NM |
|---|---|---|---|
| ❑ JLP-1054 [M] | Mingus Trio | 1958 | 80.00 |

LIMELIGHT

| Number | Title (A Side/B Side) | Yr | NM |
|---|---|---|---|
| ❑ LM-82015 [M] | Mingus Revisited | 1965 | 25.00 |
| ❑ LS-86105 [S] | Mingus Revisited | 1965 | 30.00 |

MERCURY

| Number | Title (A Side/B Side) | Yr | NM |
|---|---|---|---|
| ❑ MG-20627 [M] | Pre-Bird | 1961 | 30.00 |
| ❑ SR-60627 [S] | Pre-Bird | 1961 | 40.00 |

MOSAIC

| Number | Title (A Side/B Side) | Yr | NM |
|---|---|---|---|
| ❑ MR4-111 [(4)] | The Complete Candid Recordings of Charles Mingus | 199? | 200.00 |
| *—Limited editon of 7,500* | | | |
| ❑ MQ4-143 [(4)] | The Complete 1959 CBS Charles Mingus Sessions | 199? | 150.00 |

PERIOD

| Number | Title (A Side/B Side) | Yr | NM |
|---|---|---|---|
| ❑ SPL-1107 [10] | Jazzical Moods, Volume 1 | 1955 | 200.00 |
| ❑ SLP-1111 [10] | Jazzical Moods, Volume 2 | 1955 | 200.00 |

PRESTIGE

| Number | Title (A Side/B Side) | Yr | NM |
|---|---|---|---|
| ❑ 34001 [(3)] | The Great Concert | 197? | 20.00 |

RCA VICTOR

| Number | Title (A Side/B Side) | Yr | NM |
|---|---|---|---|
| ❑ LPM-2533 [M] | Tijuana Moods | 1962 | 40.00 |
| ❑ LSP-2533 [S] | Tijuana Moods | 1962 | 50.00 |
| ❑ LSP-2533 [S] | Tijuana Moods | 199? | 25.00 |
| *—Classic Records reissue on audiophile vinyl* | | | |

SAVOY

| Number | Title (A Side/B Side) | Yr | NM |
|---|---|---|---|
| ❑ MG-12059 [M] | Jazz Composers Workshop | 1956 | 100.00 |
| ❑ MG-15050 [10] | Charlie Mingus | 1955 | 200.00 |

SOLID STATE

| Number | Title (A Side/B Side) | Yr | NM |
|---|---|---|---|
| ❑ SS-18019 | Wonderland | 1968 | 20.00 |
| ❑ SS-18024 | Town Hall Concert | 1968 | 20.00 |

UNITED ARTISTS

| Number | Title (A Side/B Side) | Yr | NM |
|---|---|---|---|
| ❑ UAL-4036 [M] | Jazz Portraits | 1959 | 40.00 |
| ❑ UAS-5036 [S] | Jazz Portraits | 1959 | 50.00 |
| ❑ UAJ-14005 [M] | Wonderland | 1962 | 40.00 |
| ❑ UAJ-14024 [M] | Town Hall Concert | 1963 | 40.00 |
| ❑ UAJS-15005 [S] | Wonderland | 1962 | 50.00 |
| ❑ UAJS-15024 [S] | Town Hall Concert | 1963 | 50.00 |

## MINION, FRANK

BETHLEHEM

| Number | Title (A Side/B Side) | Yr | NM |
|---|---|---|---|
| ❑ BCP-6033 [M] | Forward Sound | 1959 | 40.00 |
| ❑ BCP-6052 [M] | The Soft Land of Make Believe | 1961 | 40.00 |
| ❑ BCPS-6052 [S] | The Soft Land of Make Believe | 1961 | 50.00 |

## MINNEAPOLIS SYMPHONY ORCHESTRA (ANTAL DORATI, CONDUCTOR)

MERCURY LIVING PRESENCE

| Number | Title (A Side/B Side) | Yr | NM |
|---|---|---|---|
| ❑ SR 90007 [S] | Albeniz-Artos: Iberia; Falla: Interlude and Dance | 1959 | 70.00 |
| *—Maroon label, no "Vendor: Mercury Record Corporation"* | | | |
| ❑ SR 90011 [S] | Beethoven: Symphony No. 3 | 1959 | 40.00 |
| *—Maroon label, no "Vendor: Mercury Record Corporation"* | | | |
| ❑ SR 90016 [S] | Offenbach: Gaite Parisienne; Strauss, Johann: Graduation Ball | 1959 | 20.00 |
| *—Maroon label, no "Vendor: Mercury Record Corporation"* | | | |
| ❑ SR 90098 [S] | Bartok: Suite No. 2 | 1959 | 40.00 |
| *—Maroon label, no "Vendor: Mercury Record Corporation"* | | | |
| ❑ SR 90132 [S] | Kodaly: Hary Janos Suite; Bartok: Hungarian Sketches; Rumanian Dances | 196? | 30.00 |
| *—Maroon label, with "Vendor: Mercury Record Corporation"* | | | |
| ❑ SR 90132 [S] | Kodaly: Hary Janos Suite; Bartok: Hungarian Sketches; Rumanian Dances | 1960 | 120.00 |
| *—Maroon label, no "Vendor: Mercury Record Corporation"* | | | |
| ❑ SR 90139 [S] | Rossini: Overtures | 196? | 25.00 |
| *—Maroon label, no "Vendor: Mercury Record Corporation"* | | | |
| ❑ SR 90139 [S] | Rossini: Overtures | 196? | 40.00 |
| *—Maroon label, with "Vendor: Mercury Record Corporation" (a rare case where the second edition is more sought after than the first)* | | | |
| ❑ SR 90171 [S] | Brahms: Symphony No. 2 | 196? | 25.00 |
| *—Maroon label, no "Vendor: Mercury Record Corporation"* | | | |
| ❑ SR 90172 [S] | Copland: Rodeo; El Salon Mexico; Danzon Cubano | 196? | 50.00 |
| *—Maroon label, with "Vendor: Mercury Record Corporation"* | | | |
| ❑ SR 90172 [S] | Copland: Rodeo; El Salon Mexico; Danzon Cubano | 196? | 100.00 |
| *—Maroon label, no "Vendor: Mercury Record Corporation"* | | | |
| ❑ SR 90178 [S] | The Strauss Family Album | 196? | 20.00 |
| *—Maroon label, no "Vendor: Mercury Record Corporation"* | | | |
| ❑ SR 90195 [S] | Rimsky-Korsakov: Scheherazade | 196? | 40.00 |
| *—Maroon label, no "Vendor: Mercury Record Corporation"* | | | |
| ❑ SR 90201 [S] | Tchaikovsky: March Slave; Polonaise and Waltz; Francesca da Rimini | 196? | 30.00 |
| *—Maroon label, with "Vendor: Mercury Record Corporation"* | | | |
| ❑ SR 90201 [S] | Tchaikovsky: March Slave; Polonaise and Waltz; Francesca da Rimini | 196? | 40.00 |
| *—Maroon label, no "Vendor: Mercury Record Corporation"* | | | |
| ❑ SR 90202 [S] | Strauss, Richard: Don Juan; Death and Transfiguration | 196? | 80.00 |
| *—Maroon label, no "Vendor: Mercury Record Corporation"* | | | |
| ❑ SR 90216 [S] | Stravinsky: Petrouchka | 196? | 30.00 |
| *—Maroon label, with "Vendor: Mercury Record Corporation"* | | | |
| ❑ SR 90216 [S] | Stravinsky: Petrouchka | 196? | 80.00 |
| *—Maroon label, no "Vendor: Mercury Record Corporation"* | | | |
| ❑ SR 90217 [S] | Mussorgsky: Pictures at an Exhibition | 196? | 40.00 |
| *—Maroon label, with "Vendor: Mercury Record Corporation"* | | | |
| ❑ SR 90217 [S] | Mussorgsky: Pictures at an Exhibition | 196? | 220.00 |
| *—Maroon label, no "Vendor: Mercury Record Corporation"* | | | |
| ❑ SR 90248 [S] | Dorati: Symphony; Nocturne; Capriccio | 196? | 160.00 |
| *—Maroon label, no "Vendor: Mercury Record Corporation"* | | | |
| ❑ SR 90253 [S] | Stravinsky: Le Sacre du Printemps (The Rite of Spring) | 196? | 20.00 |
| *—Maroon label, with "Vendor: Mercury Record Corporation"* | | | |
| ❑ SR 90253 [S] | Stravinsky: Le Sacre du Printemps (The Rite of Spring) | 196? | 60.00 |
| *—Maroon label, no "Vendor: Mercury Record Corporation"* | | | |
| ❑ SR 90282 [S] | Schuller: Seven Studies on Themes of Paul Klee; Fetler: Contrasts for Orchestra | 196? | 50.00 |
| *—Maroon label, with "Vendor: Mercury Record Corporation"* | | | |
| ❑ SR 90282 [S] | Schuller: Seven Studies on Themes of Paul Klee; Fetler: Contrasts for Orchestra | 196? | 100.00 |
| *—Maroon label, no "Vendor: Mercury Record Corporation"* | | | |
| ❑ SR 90288 [S] | Bloch: Sinfonia Brave; Peterson, Wayne: Free Variations for Orchestra | 196? | 80.00 |
| *—Maroon label, no "Vendor: Mercury Record Corporation"* | | | |
| ❑ SR 90298 [S] | Respighi: Pines and Fountains of Rome | 196? | 30.00 |
| *—Maroon label, with "Vendor: Mercury Record Corporation"* | | | |
| ❑ SR 90298 [S] | Respighi: Pines and Fountains of Rome | 196? | 50.00 |
| *—Maroon label, no "Vendor: Mercury Record Corporation"* | | | |
| ❑ SR 90431 [S] | Offenbach: Gaite Parisienne; Gershwin: An American in Paris | 1965 | 20.00 |
| *—Maroon label, with "Vendor: Mercury Record Corporation"* | | | |
| ❑ SR 90499 [S] | Dorati: Symphony; Nocturne and Capriccio | 196? | 20.00 |
| *—Maroon label, with "Vendor: Mercury Record Corporation"* | | | |

## MINNEAPOLIS SYMPHONY ORCHESTRA (STANISLAW SKROWACZEWSKI, CONDUCTOR)

MERCURY LIVING PRESENCE

| Number | Title (A Side/B Side) | Yr | NM |
|---|---|---|---|
| ❑ SR 90060 [S] | Khachatourian: Gayne Ballet; Shostakovich: Symphony No. 5 | 1960 | 250.00 |
| *—Maroon label, no "Vendor: Mercury Record Corporation"* | | | |
| ❑ SR 90218 [S] | Schubert: Symphony in B "Unfinished" | 196? | 20.00 |
| *—Maroon label, with "Vendor: Mercury Record Corporation"* | | | |
| ❑ SR 90218 [S] | Schubert: Symphony in B "Unfinished" | 196? | 60.00 |
| *—Maroon label, no "Vendor: Mercury Record Corporation"* | | | |
| ❑ SR 90272 [S] | Schubert: Symphony No. 7 (9) in C | 196? | 50.00 |
| *—Maroon label, no "Vendor: Mercury Record Corporation"* | | | |
| ❑ SR 90315 [S] | Prokofiev: Romeo and Juliet Ballet Suites 1 and 2 | 196? | 20.00 |
| *—Maroon label, with "Vendor: Mercury Record Corporation"* | | | |
| ❑ SR 90315 [S] | Prokofiev: Romeo and Juliet Ballet Suites 1 and 2 | 196? | 50.00 |
| *—Maroon label, no "Vendor: Mercury Record Corporation"* | | | |
| ❑ SR 90356 [S] | Mendelssohn: Symphony No. 4; Schubert: Symphony No. 5 | 196? | 25.00 |
| *—Maroon label, no "Vendor: Mercury Record Corporation"* | | | |

## MINNELLI, LIZA

A&M

| Number | Title (A Side/B Side) | Yr | NM |
|---|---|---|---|
| ❑ SP-3524 [(2)] | Liza Minnelli Foursider | 1973 | 15.00 |
| ❑ SP-4141 [M] | Liza Minnelli | 1968 | 25.00 |
| *—Mono copies have stereo numbers, but the labels are mono white label promos* | | | |
| ❑ SP-4141 [S] | Liza Minnelli | 1968 | 15.00 |
| ❑ SP-4164 | Come Saturday Morning | 1969 | 15.00 |
| ❑ SP-4272 | New Feelin' | 1970 | 15.00 |
| ❑ SP-4345 | Live at the Olympia | 1971 | 15.00 |
| ❑ SP-6013 [(2)] | Liza Minnelli Foursider | 198? | 10.00 |
| *—Reissue of 3524* | | | |

CAPITOL

| Number | Title (A Side/B Side) | Yr | NM |
|---|---|---|---|
| ❑ ST 2174 [S] | Liza! Liza! | 1964 | 25.00 |
| ❑ T 2174 [M] | Liza! Liza! | 1964 | 20.00 |
| ❑ SM-2271 | It Amazes Me | 1976 | 10.00 |
| *—Reissue with new prefix* | | | |
| ❑ ST 2271 [S] | It Amazes Me | 1965 | 25.00 |
| ❑ T 2271 [M] | It Amazes Me | 1965 | 20.00 |
| ❑ ST 2448 [S] | There Is a Time | 1966 | 25.00 |
| ❑ T 2448 [M] | There Is a Time | 1966 | 20.00 |
| ❑ SM-11080 | Maybe This Time | 197? | 10.00 |
| *—Reissue with new prefix* | | | |
| ❑ ST-11080 | Maybe This Time | 1972 | 12.00 |
| ❑ SM-11803 | There Is a Time | 1978 | 10.00 |
| *—Reissue of ST 2448* | | | |

COLUMBIA

| Number | Title (A Side/B Side) | Yr | NM |
|---|---|---|---|
| ❑ KC 31762 | Liza with a "Z" | 1972 | 15.00 |
| ❑ PC 31762 | Liza with a "Z" | 198? | 8.00 |
| *—Budget-line reissue* | | | |
| ❑ CQ 32149 [Q] | Liza Minnelli The Singer | 1973 | 20.00 |
| ❑ KC 32149 | Liza Minnelli The Singer | 1973 | 15.00 |
| ❑ PC 32149 | Liza Minnelli The Singer | 198? | 8.00 |
| *—Budget-line reissue* | | | |
| ❑ PC 32854 | Live at the Winter Garden | 1974 | 15.00 |
| ❑ PC 34887 | Tropical Nights | 1977 | 12.00 |

EPIC

| Number | Title (A Side/B Side) | Yr | NM |
|---|---|---|---|
| ❑ OE 45098 | Results | 1989 | 15.00 |

TELARC

| Number | Title (A Side/B Side) | Yr | NM |
|---|---|---|---|
| ❑ 15502 [(2)] | Liza Minnelli at Carnegie Hall | 1987 | 15.00 |

## MINNIE PEARL

STARDAY

| Number | Title (A Side/B Side) | Yr | NM |
|---|---|---|---|
| ❑ SLP-224 [M] | Howdee! | 1963 | 40.00 |
| ❑ SLP-380 [M] | America's Beloved Minnie Pearl | 1965 | 40.00 |
| ❑ SLP-397 [M] | The Country Music Story | 1966 | 30.00 |

## MINOR THREAT

DISCHORD

| Number | Title (A Side/B Side) | Yr | NM |
|---|---|---|---|
| ❑ 10 | Out of Step | 1983 | 20.00 |
| *—Second stock pressing, gray back cover with photos* | | | |
| ❑ 10 | Out of Step | 1983 | 50.00 |
| *—First stock pressing, black back cover with lyrics* | | | |
| ❑ 10 [DJ] | Out of Step | 1983 | 500.00 |
| *—Test pressing of 50; black silkscreen cover with sheep logo; paste-on back cover; blank labels; plain innersleeve with rubber stamp* | | | |
| ❑ 12 [EP] | The First Two 7" On a 12" | 1984 | 15.00 |

## MINT TATTOO

DOT

| Number | Title (A Side/B Side) | Yr | NM |
|---|---|---|---|
| ❑ DLP-25918 | Mint Tattoo | 1969 | 30.00 |

## MINUTEMEN

NEW ALLIANCE

| Number | Title (A Side/B Side) | Yr | NM |
|---|---|---|---|
| ❑ 017 | The Politics of Time | 1984 | 12.00 |

SST

| Number | Title (A Side/B Side) | Yr | NM |
|---|---|---|---|
| ❑ 004 | The Punch Line | 1981 | 12.00 |
| ❑ 004 | The Punch Line | 1981 | 20.00 |
| *—Original copies have white labels* | | | |
| ❑ 014 | What Makes a Man Start Fires? | 1983 | 10.00 |
| ❑ 014 | What Makes a Man Start Fires? | 1983 | 15.00 |
| *—Original version has yellow labels and no UPC code* | | | |
| ❑ 016 [EP] | Buzz or Howl Under the Influence of Heat | 1983 | 10.00 |
| ❑ 028 [(2)] | Double Nickels on the Dime | 1984 | 12.00 |
| ❑ PSST E-28 [DJ] | Excerpts from Double Nickels on the Dime | 1984 | 25.00 |
| *—One-sided promo LP with etched B-side and sticker on blank cover* | | | |
| ❑ 034 [EP] | Project Mersh | 1985 | 10.00 |

The Chad Mitchell Trio, *Reflecting,* Mercury MG-20891, 1964, mono, $15.

| Number | Title (A Side/B Side) | Yr | NM |
|---|---|---|---|
| ❑ 058 | 3-Way Tie (For Last) | 1985 | 12.00 |
| ❑ 068 [(2)] | Ballot Result | 1987 | 12.00 |
| ❑ 277 | The Politics of Time | 198? | 10.00 |
| *—Reissue of New Alliance 017* | | | |

**MIRACLES, THE**

COLUMBIA

| Number | Title (A Side/B Side) | Yr | NM |
|---|---|---|---|
| ❑ PC 34460 | Love Crazy | 1977 | 12.00 |
| ❑ PCQ 34460 [Q] | Love Crazy | 1977 | 20.00 |
| ❑ JC 34910 | The Miracles | 1978 | 12.00 |

MOTOWN

| Number | Title (A Side/B Side) | Yr | NM |
|---|---|---|---|
| ❑ M5-133V1 | Do It Baby | 1981 | 8.00 |
| *—Reissue of Tamla 334* | | | |
| ❑ M5-136V1 | Away We a Go-Go | 1981 | 8.00 |
| *—Reissue of Tamla 271* | | | |
| ❑ M5-156V1 | The Tears of a Clown | 1981 | 8.00 |
| *—Reissue of Tamla 276* | | | |
| ❑ M5-160V1 | Hi, We're the Miracles | 1981 | 8.00 |
| *—Reissue of Tamla 220* | | | |
| ❑ M5-210V1 | Greatest Hits, Vol. 2 | 1981 | 8.00 |
| *—Reissue of Tamla 280* | | | |
| ❑ M5-217V1 | Doin' Mickey's Monkey | 1981 | 8.00 |
| *—Reissue of Tamla 245* | | | |
| ❑ M5-220V1 | Recorded Live on Stage | 1981 | 8.00 |
| *—Reissue of Tamla 241* | | | |
| ❑ M8-238M2 [(2)] | Greatest Hits from the Beginning | 1982 | 12.00 |
| *—Reissue of Tamla 254* | | | |
| ❑ M 793R3 [(3)] | Smokey Robinson and the Miracles Anthology | 1974 | 20.00 |
| ❑ 5253 ML | The Season for Miracles | 1982 | 8.00 |
| *—Reissue of Tamla 307* | | | |
| ❑ 5254 ML | Christmas with the Miracles | 1982 | 8.00 |
| *—Reissue of Tamla 236* | | | |

TAMLA

| Number | Title (A Side/B Side) | Yr | NM |
|---|---|---|---|
| ❑ T 220 [M] | Hi We're the Miracles | 1961 | 600.00 |
| *—White label* | | | |
| ❑ T 223 [M] | Cookin' with the Miracles | 1962 | 800.00 |
| *—White label* | | | |
| ❑ T 230 [M] | I'll Try Something New | 1962 | 600.00 |
| *- -White label* | | | |
| ❑ T 236 [M] | Christmas with the Miracles | 1963 | 300.00 |
| *—Originals have two globes on the top of the label* | | | |
| ❑ T 238 [M] | You've Really Got a Hold on Me | 1963 | 200.00 |
| *—Retitled version of "The Fabulous Miracles"* | | | |
| ❑ T 238 [M] | The Fabulous Miracles | 1963 | 300.00 |
| ❑ T 241 [M] | The Miracles On Stage | 1963 | 200.00 |
| ❑ T 245 [M] | Doin' Mickey's Monkey | 1963 | 200.00 |
| ❑ TS 245 [S] | Doin' Mickey's Monkey | 1963 | 300.00 |
| ❑ T 254 [(2)M] | Greatest Hits from the Beginning | 1965 | 50.00 |
| ❑ TS 254 [(2)P] | Greatest Hits from the Beginning | 1965 | 40.00 |
| ❑ T 267 [M] | Going to a Go-Go | 1966 | 30.00 |
| ❑ TS 267 [S] | Going to a Go-Go | 1966 | 40.00 |
| ❑ T 271 [M] | Away We a Go-Go | 1966 | 25.00 |
| ❑ TS 271 [S] | Away We a Go-Go | 1966 | 30.00 |
| ❑ T 276 [M] | Make It Happen | 1967 | 25.00 |
| ❑ TS 276 [S] | Make It Happen | 1967 | 30.00 |
| ❑ TS 276 [S] | The Tears of a Clown | 1970 | 15.00 |
| *—Retitled version of "Make It Happen"* | | | |
| ❑ TS 280 | Greatest Hits, Vol. 2 | 1968 | 25.00 |
| ❑ TS 289 | Live! | 1969 | 20.00 |
| ❑ T 290 [M] | Special Occasion | 1968 | 50.00 |
| ❑ TS 290 [S] | Special Occasion | 1968 | 20.00 |
| ❑ TS 295 | Time Out for Smokey Robinson & the Miracles | 1969 | 20.00 |
| ❑ TS 297 | Four in Blue | 1969 | 20.00 |
| ❑ TS 301 | What Love Has...Joined Together | 1970 | 15.00 |
| ❑ TS 306 | A Pocket Full of Miracles | 1970 | 15.00 |
| ❑ TS 307 | The Season for Miracles | 1970 | 15.00 |
| ❑ TS 312 | One Dozen Roses | 1971 | 15.00 |
| ❑ TS 318 | Flying High Together | 1972 | 15.00 |
| ❑ TS 320 [(2)] | 1957-1972 | 1972 | 20.00 |
| ❑ T 325F | Renaissance | 1973 | 12.00 |
| ❑ T6-334 | Do It Baby | 1974 | 12.00 |
| ❑ T6-336 | Don't Cha Love It | 1975 | 12.00 |
| ❑ T6-339 | City of Angels | 1975 | 12.00 |
| ❑ T6-344 | The Power of Music | 1976 | 12.00 |
| ❑ T7-357 | Greatest Hits | 1977 | 12.00 |

**MISFITS, THE**

CAROLINE

| Number | Title (A Side/B Side) | Yr | NM |
|---|---|---|---|
| ❑ 7511 | Static Age | 1995 | — |
| *—Canceled; finally released on 7520* | | | |
| ❑ 7515 | Collection II | 1995 | 30.00 |
| *—Green vinyl (3,500 made); sealed copies have bar code roughly 1/4 to 1/2 inch from bottom of back cover* | | | |
| ❑ 7515 | Collection II | 1995 | 40.00 |
| *—Red vinyl (6,000 made); sealed copies have bar code roughly 1 inch from the bottom of back cover* | | | |
| ❑ 7515 | Collection II | 1995 | 100.00 |
| *—Clear vinyl (500 made); sealed copies have bar code at upper right or not at all* | | | |
| ❑ 7520 | Static Age | 1997 | 30.00 |
| *—Yellow vinyl (1,000 made)* | | | |
| ❑ 7520 | Static Age | 1997 | 40.00 |
| *—Red vinyl (2,000 made)* | | | |
| ❑ 7520 | Static Age | 1997 | 100.00 |
| *—Purple vinyl (500 made)* | | | |

GEFFEN

| Number | Title (A Side/B Side) | Yr | NM |
|---|---|---|---|
| ❑ GEF 25126 | American Psycho | 1997 | 20.00 |

PLAN 9

| Number | Title (A Side/B Side) | Yr | NM |
|---|---|---|---|
| ❑ PL9-02 | Earth A.D. | 1983 | 12.00 |
| *—At least 10,000 on black vinyl (distributed by Caroline)* | | | |
| ❑ PL9-02 | Earth A.D. | 1983 | 500.00 |
| *—500 on yellow vinyl* | | | |
| ❑ PL9-02 | Earth A.D. | 1983 | 600.00 |
| *—200 on clear vinyl with red and blue swirls* | | | |
| ❑ PL9-02 | Earth A.D. | 1983 | 800.00 |
| *—200 on dark purple vinyl* | | | |
| ❑ PL9-02 | Earth A.D. | 1983 | 1500. |
| *—100 on green vinyl* | | | |
| ❑ PL9-03 [EP] | Die, Die My Darling | 1984 | 12.00 |
| *—Common issue on black vinyl (distribuled by Caroline)* | | | |
| ❑ PL9-03 [EP] | Die, Die My Darling | 1984 | 250.00 |
| *—500 on purple vinyl* | | | |
| ❑ PL9-03 [EP] | Die, Die My Darling | 1984 | 250.00 |
| *—500 on white vinyl (distributed by Caroline)* | | | |
| ❑ PL9-06 | Legacy of Brutality | 1986 | 20.00 |
| *—Black vinyl (distributed by Caroline)* | | | |
| ❑ PL9-06 | Legacy of Brutality | 1986 | 300.00 |
| *—500 on white vinyl* | | | |
| ❑ PL9-06 | Legacy of Brutality | 1986 | 500.00 |
| *—500 on red vinyl* | | | |
| ❑ PL9-06 | Legacy of Brutality | 1986 | 5000. |
| *—16 (!!) on pink vinyl; VG value 2000; VG+ value 3500* | | | |
| ❑ PL9-08 [EP] | Evilive | 1987 | 20.00 |
| *—Black vinyl (distributed by Caroline)* | | | |
| ❑ PL9-08 [EP] | Evilive | 1987 | 100.00 |
| *—2,000 on green vinyl (distributed by Caroline)* | | | |
| ❑ PL9-09 | Misfits | 1988 | 12.00 |

ROADRUNNER

| Number | Title (A Side/B Side) | Yr | NM |
|---|---|---|---|
| ❑ RR 8658-1 | Famous Monsters | 1999 | 20.00 |
| *—Picture disc* | | | |

RUBY/SLASH

| Number | Title (A Side/B Side) | Yr | NM |
|---|---|---|---|
| ❑ JRR 804 | Walk Among Us | 1982 | 50.00 |
| *—Purple cover with innersleeve and insert* | | | |
| ❑ JRR 804 | Walk Among Us | 1982 | 100.00 |
| *—Original red cover; has custom innersleeve and insert* | | | |

SLASH

| Number | Title (A Side/B Side) | Yr | NM |
|---|---|---|---|
| ❑ 25756 | Walk Among Us | 1988 | 20.00 |
| *—Reissue of JRR 804; some copies came with a Halloween bag, which can double or even triple the value!* | | | |

**MISSOURI**

PANAMA

| Number | Title (A Side/B Side) | Yr | NM |
|---|---|---|---|
| ❑ 1022 | Missouri | 1977 | 30.00 |

**MISSOURIANS, THE**

"X"

| Number | Title (A Side/B Side) | Yr | NM |
|---|---|---|---|
| ❑ LVA-3020 [10] | Harlem in the Twenties, Volume 1 | 1954 | 50.00 |

**MR. GASSER AND THE WEIRDOS**

CAPITOL

| Number | Title (A Side/B Side) | Yr | NM |
|---|---|---|---|
| ❑ ST 2010 [S] | Hot Rod Hootenanny | 1963 | 120.00 |
| ❑ T 2010 [M] | Hot Rod Hootenanny | 1963 | 100.00 |
| ❑ ST 2057 [S] | Rods n' Ratfinks | 1963 | 120.00 |
| *—Add 25% if ratfink decal is enclosed* | | | |
| ❑ T 2057 [M] | Rods n' Ratfinks | 1963 | 100.00 |
| *—Add 25% if ratfink decal is enclosed* | | | |
| ❑ ST 2114 [S] | Surfink! | 1964 | 150.00 |
| *—Without bonus single* | | | |
| ❑ ST 2114 [S] | Surfink! | 1964 | 200.00 |
| *—With bonus single in pocket on cover: "Santa Barbara"/"Midnight Run" by the Super Stocks* | | | |
| ❑ T 2114 [M] | Surfink! | 1964 | 100.00 |
| *—Without bonus single* | | | |
| ❑ T 2114 [M] | Surfink! | 1964 | 150.00 |
| *—With bonus single in pocket on cover: "Santa Barbara"/"Midnight Run" by the Super Stocks* | | | |

**MR. SHORT STUFF**

SPIVEY

| Number | Title (A Side/B Side) | Yr | NM |
|---|---|---|---|
| ❑ 1005 | Mr. Short Stuff | 196? | 20.00 |

**MITCHELL, BILLY**

SMASH

| Number | Title (A Side/B Side) | Yr | NM |
|---|---|---|---|
| ❑ MGS-27027 [M] | This Is Billy Mitchell | 1962 | 25.00 |
| ❑ MGS-27042 [M] | A Little Juicy | 1962 | 25.00 |
| ❑ SRS-67027 [S] | This Is Billy Mitchell | 1962 | 30.00 |
| ❑ SRS-67042 [S] | A Little Juicy | 1962 | 30.00 |

**MITCHELL, BLUE**

BLUE NOTE

| Number | Title (A Side/B Side) | Yr | NM |
|---|---|---|---|
| ❑ BLP-4178 [M] | The Thing to Do | 1964 | 150.00 |
| *—"New York, USA" on label* | | | |
| ❑ BLP-4214 [M] | Down With It | 1965 | 60.00 |
| *—"New York, USA" on label* | | | |

| Number | Title (A Side/B Side) | Yr | NM |
|---|---|---|---|
| ❑ BLP-4228 [M] | Bring It Home to Me | 1966 | 50.00 |
| *—"New York, USA" on label* | | | |
| ❑ BLP-4257 [M] | Boss Horn | 1967 | 50.00 |
| *—With "A Division of Liberty Records" on label* | | | |
| ❑ BST-84178 [S] | The Thing to Do | 1964 | 80.00 |
| *—With "New York, USA" address on label* | | | |
| ❑ BST-84214 [S] | Down With It | 1965 | 50.00 |
| *—With "New York, USA" address on label* | | | |
| ❑ BST-84228 [S] | Bring It Home to Me | 1966 | 50.00 |
| *—With "New York, USA" address on label* | | | |
| ❑ BST-84257 [S] | Boss Horn | 1967 | 30.00 |
| *—With "A Division of Liberty Records" on label* | | | |
| ❑ BST-84272 | Heads Up! | 1968 | 30.00 |
| *—With "A Division of Liberty Records" on label* | | | |
| ❑ BST-84300 | Collision in Black | 1968 | 30.00 |
| *—With "A Division of Liberty Records" on label* | | | |
| ❑ BST-84324 | Bantu Village | 1969 | 40.00 |
| *—With "A Division of Liberty Records" on label* | | | |
| **MOSAIC** | | | |
| ❑ MQ6-178 [(6)] | The Complete Blue Note Sessions | 199? | 100.00 |
| **RIVERSIDE** | | | |
| ❑ RLP 12-273 [M] | The Big Six | 1958 | 100.00 |
| ❑ RLP 12-293 [M] | Out of the Blue | 1958 | 100.00 |
| ❑ RLP 12-309 [M] | Blue Soul | 1959 | 100.00 |
| ❑ RLP-336 [M] | Blue's Moods | 1960 | 80.00 |
| ❑ RLP-367 [M] | Smooth as the Wind | 1961 | 60.00 |
| ❑ RLP-414 [M] | A Sure Thing | 1962 | 60.00 |
| ❑ RLP-439 [M] | The Cup Bearers | 1963 | 60.00 |
| ❑ RLP-1131 [S] | Out of the Blue | 1959 | 80.00 |
| ❑ RLP-1155 [S] | Blue Soul | 1959 | 80.00 |
| ❑ RS-9336 [S] | Blue's Moods | 1960 | 80.00 |
| ❑ RS-9367 [S] | Smooth as the Wind | 1961 | 80.00 |
| ❑ RS-9414 [S] | A Sure Thing | 1962 | 80.00 |
| ❑ RS-9439 [S] | The Cup Bearers | 1963 | 80.00 |

## MITCHELL, CHAD

| Number | Title (A Side/B Side) | Yr | NM |
|---|---|---|---|
| **BELL** | | | |
| ❑ 6028 | Chad | 1969 | 15.00 |
| **WARNER BROS.** | | | |
| ❑ W 1667 [M] | Chad Mitchell Himself | 1966 | 15.00 |
| ❑ WS 1667 [S] | Chad Mitchell Himself | 1966 | 20.00 |
| ❑ W 1706 [M] | A Feeling of Love | 1967 | 20.00 |
| ❑ WS 1706 [S] | A Feeling of Love | 1967 | 15.00 |

## MITCHELL, CHAD, TRIO

| Number | Title (A Side/B Side) | Yr | NM |
|---|---|---|---|
| **COLPIX** | | | |
| ❑ CP-411 [M] | The Chad Mitchell Trio | 1961 | 20.00 |
| ❑ SCP-411 [S] | The Chad Mitchell Trio | 1961 | 30.00 |
| ❑ CP-463 [M] | Everybody's Listening | 1964 | 20.00 |
| ❑ SCP-463 [S] | Everybody's Listening | 1964 | 30.00 |
| **KAPP** | | | |
| ❑ KGP-102 BI [(3)M] | My Gift to You | 196? | 50.00 |
| *—Three-record boxed set containing KL-1262, KL-1281 and KL-1313 on mid-1960s reissue labels (black with white circle and "Kapp" vertical logo at top)* | | | |
| ❑ KL-1262 [M] | Mighty Day on Campus | 1962 | 20.00 |
| ❑ KL-1281 [M] | The Chad Mitchell Trio at the Bitter End | 1962 | 20.00 |
| ❑ KL-1313 [M] | Chad Mitchell Trio In Action | 1963 | 20.00 |
| ❑ KL-1334 [M] | The Best of Chad Mitchell Trio | 1963 | 20.00 |
| ❑ KS-3262 [S] | Mighty Day on Campus | 1962 | 25.00 |
| ❑ KS-3281 [S] | The Chad Mitchell Trio at the Bitter End | 1962 | 25.00 |
| ❑ KS-3313 [S] | Chad Mitchell Trio In Action | 1963 | 25.00 |
| ❑ KS-3334 [S] | The Best of Chad Mitchell Trio | 1963 | 25.00 |
| **MERCURY** | | | |
| ❑ MG-20838 [M] | Singin' Our Mind | 1963 | 15.00 |
| ❑ MG-20891 [M] | Reflecting | 1964 | 15.00 |
| ❑ SR-60838 [S] | Singin' Our Mind | 1963 | 20.00 |
| ❑ SR-60891 [S] | Reflecting | 1964 | 20.00 |

## MITCHELL, FREDDIE

| Number | Title (A Side/B Side) | Yr | NM |
|---|---|---|---|
| **ALLEGRO ROYALE** | | | |
| ❑ 1600 [M] | That Boogie Beat | 195? | 60.00 |

## MITCHELL, GUY

| Number | Title (A Side/B Side) | Yr | NM |
|---|---|---|---|
| **COLUMBIA** | | | |
| ❑ CL 1211 [M] | Guy in Love | 1958 | 40.00 |
| ❑ CL 1226 [M] | Guy's Greatest Hits | 1959 | 50.00 |
| *—Red and black label with six "eye" logos* | | | |
| ❑ CL 1226 [M] | Guy's Greatest Hits | 1962 | 30.00 |
| *—"Guaranteed High Fidelity" on red label* | | | |
| ❑ CL 1226 [M] | Guy's Greatest Hits | 1965 | 20.00 |
| *—"360 Sound Mono" on red label* | | | |
| ❑ CL 1552 [M] | Sunshine Guitar | 1960 | 30.00 |
| ❑ CL 6231 [10] | Open Spaces | 1953 | 70.00 |
| ❑ CS 8011 [S] | Guy in Love | 1959 | 50.00 |
| ❑ CS 8352 [S] | Sunshine Guitar | 1960 | 40.00 |
| **KING** | | | |
| ❑ 644 [M] | Sincerely Yours | 1959 | 300.00 |
| **NASHVILLE** | | | |
| ❑ 2074 | Heartaches | 1970 | 12.00 |
| **STARDAY** | | | |
| ❑ 412 | Traveling Shoes | 1968 | 20.00 |
| ❑ 432 | Singin' Up a Storm | 1969 | 20.00 |

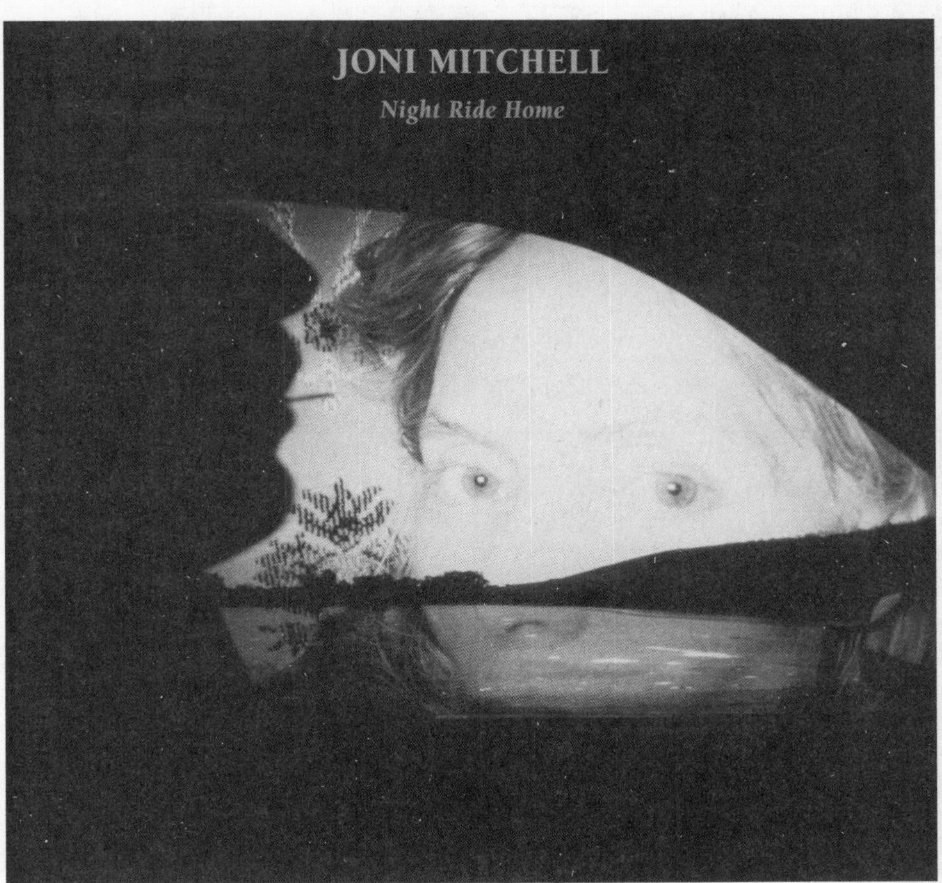


Joni Mitchell, *Night Ride Home,* Geffen GEF-24302, 1991, $15.

## MITCHELL, JONI

| Number | Title (A Side/B Side) | Yr | NM |
|---|---|---|---|
| **ASYLUM** | | | |
| ❑ AB-202 | Miles of Aisles | 1974 | 10.00 |
| ❑ 5E-505 | Mingus | 1979 | 10.00 |
| ❑ BB-701 [(2)] | Don Juan's Reckless Daughter | 1977 | 12.00 |
| ❑ BB-704 [(2)] | Shadows and Light | 1980 | 12.00 |
| ❑ 7E-1001 | Court and Spark | 1974 | 10.00 |
| ❑ EQ-1001 [Q] | Court and Spark | 1974 | 20.00 |
| ❑ 7E-1051 | The Hissing of Summer Lawns | 1975 | 10.00 |
| ❑ EQ-1051 [Q] | The Hissing of Summer Lawns | 1975 | 20.00 |
| ❑ 7E-1087 | Hejira | 1976 | 10.00 |
| ❑ SD 5057 | For the Roses | 1972 | 10.00 |
| **DCC COMPACT CLASSICS** | | | |
| ❑ LPZ-2044 | Court and Spark | 1997 | 120.00 |
| *—Audiophile vinyl* | | | |
| ❑ LPZ-2069 | Blue | 2000 | — |
| *—Audiophile vinyl; canceled* | | | |
| **GEFFEN** | | | |
| ❑ PRO-A-1081 [DJ] | Wild Things Run Fast Sampler | 1982 | 12.00 |
| *—Promo-only 4-song EP* | | | |
| ❑ GHS 2019 | Wild Things Run Fast | 1982 | 8.00 |
| ❑ GHS 24074 | Dog Eat Dog | 1985 | 8.00 |
| ❑ GHS 24172 | Chalk Mark in a Rain Storm | 1988 | 8.00 |
| ❑ GEF 24302 | Night Ride Home | 1991 | 15.00 |
| **NAUTILUS** | | | |
| ❑ NR-11 | Court and Spark | 1980 | 50.00 |
| *—Audiophile vinyl* | | | |
| **REPRISE** | | | |
| ❑ MS 2038 | Blue | 1970 | 15.00 |
| ❑ R 6293 [M] | Joni Mitchell | 1968 | 40.00 |
| *—White label promo; evidently, no stock copies were issued in mono* | | | |
| ❑ RS 6293 [S] | Joni Mitchell | 1968 | 20.00 |
| *—With "W7" and "r:" logos on two-tone orange label* | | | |
| ❑ RS 6293 [S] | Joni Mitchell | 1970 | 12.00 |
| *—With only "r:" logo on all-orange (tan) label* | | | |
| ❑ RS 6341 | Clouds | 1969 | 20.00 |
| *—With "W7" and "r:" logos on two-tone orange label* | | | |
| ❑ RS 6341 | Clouds | 1970 | 12.00 |
| *—With only "r:" logo on all-orange (tan) label* | | | |
| ❑ RS 6376 | Ladies of the Canyon | 1970 | 12.00 |
| *—With only "r:" logo on all-orange (tan) label* | | | |
| ❑ RS 6376 | Ladies of the Canyon | 1970 | 20.00 |
| *—With "W7" and "r:" logos on two-tone orange label* | | | |
| **RHINO VINYL** | | | |
| ❑ 74842 | Blue | 2007 | 25.00 |
| *—Reissue on 180-gram vinyl; has replica Reprise label* | | | |

## MITCHELL, PAUL

| Number | Title (A Side/B Side) | Yr | NM |
|---|---|---|---|
| **VERVE** | | | |
| ❑ V-8713 [M] | Live at the Atlanta Playboy Club | 1967 | 20.00 |

## MITCHELL, RED

| Number | Title (A Side/B Side) | Yr | NM |
|---|---|---|---|
| **BETHLEHEM** | | | |
| ❑ BCP-38 [M] | Jam for Your Bread | 1956 | 100.00 |
| ❑ BCP-1033 [10] | Happy Minors | 1955 | 400.00 |
| **CONTEMPORARY** | | | |
| ❑ C-3538 [M] | Presenting Red Mitchell | 1957 | 120.00 |
| **PACIFIC JAZZ** | | | |
| ❑ PJ-22 [M] | Rejoice | 1961 | 30.00 |
| ❑ ST-22 [S] | Rejoice | 1961 | 40.00 |

## MITCHELL, RED, AND HAROLD LAND

| Number | Title (A Side/B Side) | Yr | NM |
|---|---|---|---|
| **ATLANTIC** | | | |
| ❑ 1376 [M] | Hear Ye! | 1961 | 30.00 |
| *—Multicolor label, white "fan" logo at right* | | | |
| ❑ 1376 [M] | Hear Ye! | 1964 | 20.00 |
| *—Multicolor label, black "fan" logo at right* | | | |
| ❑ SD 1376 [S] | Hear Ye! | 1961 | 40.00 |
| *—Multicolor label, white "fan" logo at right* | | | |
| ❑ SD 1376 [S] | Hear Ye! | 1964 | 25.00 |
| *—Multicolor label, black "fan" logo at right* | | | |

## MITCHELL, ROSCOE

Also see ART ENSEMBLE OF CHICAGO.

| Number | Title (A Side/B Side) | Yr | NM |
|---|---|---|---|
| **DELMARK** | | | |
| ❑ D-408 [M] | Roscoe Mitchell Sextet | 1966 | 25.00 |
| ❑ DS-408 [S] | Roscoe Mitchell Sextet | 1966 | 20.00 |
| **NESSA** | | | |
| ❑ N-2 | Congliptious | 1968 | 25.00 |
| ❑ N-9/10 [(2)] | Nonaah | 1977 | 25.00 |
| ❑ N-14/15 [(2)] | L-R-G/The Maze/S II Examples | 1980 | 20.00 |

## MITCHELL, WHITEY

| Number | Title (A Side/B Side) | Yr | NM |
|---|---|---|---|
| **ABC-PARAMOUNT** | | | |
| ❑ ABC-126 [M] | Whitey Mitchell Sextette | 1956 | 50.00 |

## MITCHELL, WILLIE

| Number | Title (A Side/B Side) | Yr | NM |
|---|---|---|---|
| **BEARSVILLE** | | | |
| ❑ BRK 3520 | ... Listen ... Dance | 1980 | 10.00 |

| Number | Title (A Side/B Side) | Yr | NM |
|---|---|---|---|
| **HI** | | | |
| ❑ 8002 | Willie Mitchell Live | 1977 | 10.00 |
| ❑ HL-32010 [M] | Sunrise Serenade | 1963 | 40.00 |
| ❑ SHL-32010 [S] | Sunrise Serenade | 1963 | 25.00 |
| ❑ HL-32021 [M] | Hold It | 1964 | 25.00 |
| ❑ SHL-32021 [S] | Hold It | 1964 | 30.00 |
| ❑ HL-32026 [M] | It's Dance Time | 1965 | 25.00 |
| ❑ HL-32029 [M] | Driving Beat | 1966 | 25.00 |
| ❑ SHL-32029 [S] | Driving Beat | 1966 | 30.00 |
| ❑ HL-32034 [M] | The Hit Sound of Willie Mitchell | 1967 | 30.00 |
| ❑ SHL-32034 [S] | The Hit Sound of Willie Mitchell | 1967 | 25.00 |
| ❑ SHL-32036 [S] | It's Dance Time | 1965 | 30.00 |
| ❑ HL-32039 [M] | Ooh Baby, You Turn Me On | 1967 | 30.00 |
| ❑ SHL-32039 [S] | Ooh Baby, You Turn Me On | 1967 | 25.00 |
| ❑ SHL-32042 | Willie Mitchell Live | 1968 | 25.00 |
| ❑ SHL-32045 | Solid Soul | 1968 | 25.00 |
| ❑ SHL-32048 | On Top | 1969 | 25.00 |
| ❑ SHL-32050 | Soul Bag | 1969 | 25.00 |
| ❑ SHL-32056 | The Many Moods of Willie Mitchell | 1970 | 25.00 |
| ❑ SHL-32058 | Robin's Nest | 1970 | 25.00 |
| ❑ SHL-32068/9 [(2)] | The Best of Willie Mitchell | 1971 | 30.00 |

**MITCHELL TRIO, THE**

| Number | Title (A Side/B Side) | Yr | NM |
|---|---|---|---|
| **MERCURY** | | | |
| ❑ MG-20944 [M] | The Slightly Irreverent Mitchell Trio | 1964 | 15.00 |
| ❑ MG-20992 [M] | Typical American Boys | 1965 | 15.00 |
| ❑ MG-21049 [M] | That's the Way It's Gonna Be | 1965 | 15.00 |
| ❑ MG-21067 [M] | Violets of Dawn | 1966 | 15.00 |
| ❑ SR-60944 [S] | The Slightly Irreverent Mitchell Trio | 1964 | 20.00 |
| ❑ SR-60992 [S] | Typical American Boys | 1965 | 20.00 |
| ❑ SR-61049 [S] | That's the Way It's Gonna Be | 1965 | 20.00 |
| ❑ SR-61067 [S] | Violets of Dawn | 1966 | 20.00 |
| **REPRISE** | | | |
| ❑ R-6258 [M] | Alive | 1967 | 20.00 |
| ❑ RS-6258 [S] | Alive | 1967 | 15.00 |

**MITCHELL-RUFF DUO, THE**

| Number | Title (A Side/B Side) | Yr | NM |
|---|---|---|---|
| **ATLANTIC** | | | |
| ❑ 1374 [M] | The Catbird Seat | 1961 | 20.00 |
| *—Multicolor label, white "fan" logo at right* | | | |
| ❑ SD 1374 [S] | The Catbird Seat | 1961 | 25.00 |
| *—Multicolor label, white "fan" logo at right* | | | |
| ❑ 1458 [M] | After This Message | 1966 | 20.00 |
| ❑ SD 1458 [S] | After This Message | 1966 | 25.00 |
| **EPIC** | | | |
| ❑ LN 3221 [M] | The Mitchell-Ruff Duo | 1956 | 40.00 |
| ❑ LN 3318 [M] | Campus Concert | 1956 | 40.00 |
| **ROULETTE** | | | |
| ❑ R-52002 [M] | Appearing Nightly | 1958 | 40.00 |
| ❑ SR-52002 [S] | Appearing Nightly | 1959 | 30.00 |
| ❑ R-52013 [M] | The Mitchell-Ruff Duo Plus Strings and Brass | 1958 | 40.00 |
| ❑ SR-52013 [S] | The Mitchell-Ruff Duo Plus Strings and Brass | 1959 | 30.00 |
| ❑ R-52025 [M] | Jazz for Juniors | 1959 | 30.00 |
| ❑ SR-52025 [S] | Jazz for Juniors | 1959 | 25.00 |
| ❑ R-52034 [M] | Jazz Mission to Moscow | 1959 | 30.00 |
| ❑ SR-52034 [S] | Jazz Mission to Moscow | 1959 | 25.00 |
| ❑ R-52037 [M] | The Sound of Music | 1960 | 25.00 |
| ❑ SR-52037 [S] | The Sound of Music | 1960 | 30.00 |

**MITCHELLS, THE**

| Number | Title (A Side/B Side) | Yr | NM |
|---|---|---|---|
| **METROJAZZ** | | | |
| ❑ E-1012 [M] | Get Those Elephants Out'a Here | 1958 | 120.00 |
| ❑ SE-1012 [S] | Get Those Elephants Out'a Here | 1958 | 100.00 |

**MITCHUM, ROBERT**

| Number | Title (A Side/B Side) | Yr | NM |
|---|---|---|---|
| **CAPITOL** | | | |
| ❑ T 853 [M] | Calypso — Is Like So... | 1957 | 100.00 |
| **MONUMENT** | | | |
| ❑ MLP-8066 [M] | That Man, Robert Mitchum, Sings | 1967 | 25.00 |
| ❑ SLP-18066 [S] | That Man, Robert Mitchum, Sings | 1967 | 25.00 |

**MIXTURES, THE (1)**

| Number | Title (A Side/B Side) | Yr | NM |
|---|---|---|---|
| **LINDA** | | | |
| ❑ 3301 [M] | Stompin' at the Rainbow | 1962 | 100.00 |

**MIZE, BILLY**

| Number | Title (A Side/B Side) | Yr | NM |
|---|---|---|---|
| **IMPERIAL** | | | |
| ❑ LP-12441 | This Time and Place | 1969 | 20.00 |
| **UNITED ARTISTS** | | | |
| ❑ UAS-6781 | You're Alright with Me | 1971 | 15.00 |
| **ZODIAC** | | | |
| ❑ 5007 | Love 'n' Stuff | 1976 | 12.00 |

**MJT + 3**

| Number | Title (A Side/B Side) | Yr | NM |
|---|---|---|---|
| **ARGO** | | | |
| ❑ LP-621 [M] | Daddy-O Presents MJT + 3 | 1957 | 40.00 |
| **VEE JAY** | | | |
| ❑ LP-1013 [M] | Walter Perkins' MJT + 3 | 1959 | 30.00 |
| ❑ SR-1013 [S] | Walter Perkins' MJT + 3 | 1959 | 40.00 |
| ❑ LP-3008 [M] | Make Everybody Happy | 1960 | 25.00 |
| ❑ SR-3008 [S] | Make Everybody Happy | 1960 | 30.00 |
| ❑ LP-3014 [M] | MJT + 3 | 1961 | 25.00 |
| ❑ SR-3014 [S] | MJT + 3 | 1961 | 30.00 |

**MOB, THE**

| Number | Title (A Side/B Side) | Yr | NM |
|---|---|---|---|
| **COLOSSUS** | | | |
| ❑ CS-1006 | The Mob | 1971 | 20.00 |
| **MGM** | | | |
| ❑ SE-4839 | The Mob | 1972 | 15.00 |

**MOBLEY, HANK**

| Number | Title (A Side/B Side) | Yr | NM |
|---|---|---|---|
| **BLUE NOTE** | | | |
| ❑ BLP-1540 [M] | Hank Mobley with Donald Byrd and Lee Morgan | 1957 | 500.00 |
| *—"Deep groove" version; W. 63rd St. address on label* | | | |
| ❑ BLP-1540 [M] | Hank Mobley with Donald Byrd and Lee Morgan | 1957 | 1000. |
| *—"Deep groove" version, Lexington Ave. address on label* | | | |
| ❑ BLP-1540 [M] | Hank Mobley with Donald Byrd and Lee Morgan | 1963 | 50.00 |
| *—With "New York, USA" address on label* | | | |
| ❑ BLP-1544 [M] | Hank Mobley and His All Stars | 1957 | 300.00 |
| *—Regular version, W. 63rd St. address on label* | | | |
| ❑ BLP-1544 [M] | Hank Mobley and His All Stars | 1957 | 800.00 |
| *—"Deep groove" version; W. 63rd St. address on label* | | | |
| ❑ BLP-1544 [M] | Hank Mobley and His All Stars | 1963 | 40.00 |
| *—With "New York, USA" address on label* | | | |
| ❑ BLP-1550 [M] | Hank Mobley | 1957 | 300.00 |
| *—Regular version, W. 63rd St. address on label* | | | |
| ❑ BLP-1550 [M] | Hank Mobley | 1957 | 800.00 |
| *—"Deep groove" version; W. 63rd St. address on label* | | | |
| ❑ BLP-1550 [M] | Hank Mobley | 1963 | 40.00 |
| *—With "New York, USA" address on label* | | | |
| ❑ BLP-1560 [M] | Hank | 1957 | 300.00 |
| *—Regular version, W. 63rd St. address on label* | | | |
| ❑ BLP-1560 [M] | Hank | 1957 | 800.00 |
| *—"Deep groove" version (deep indentation under label on both sides)* | | | |
| ❑ BLP-1560 [M] | Hank | 1963 | 40.00 |
| *—With "New York, USA" address on label* | | | |
| ❑ BLP-1568 [M] | Hank Mobley | 1957 | 300.00 |
| *—Regular version, W. 63rd St. address on label* | | | |
| ❑ BLP-1568 [M] | Hank Mobley | 1957 | 1000. |
| *—"Deep groove" version; W. 63rd St. address on label* | | | |
| ❑ BLP-1568 [M] | Hank Mobley | 1963 | 40.00 |
| *—With "New York, USA" address on label* | | | |
| ❑ BLP-1568 [M] | Hank Mobley | 200? | 30.00 |
| *—200-gram reissue, distributed by Classic Records* | | | |
| ❑ BST-1568 [S] | Hank Mobley | 1959 | 200.00 |
| *—Regular version, W. 63rd St. address on label* | | | |
| ❑ BST-1568 [S] | Hank Mobley | 1959 | 400.00 |
| *—"Deep groove" version; W. 63rd St. address on label* | | | |
| ❑ BST-1568 [S] | Hank Mobley | 1963 | 40.00 |
| *—With "New York, USA" address on label* | | | |
| ❑ BLP-1574 [M] | Peckin' Time | 1958 | 300.00 |
| *—Regular version, W. 63rd St. address on label* | | | |
| ❑ BLP-1574 [M] | Peckin' Time | 1958 | 1200. |
| *—"Deep groove" version; W. 63rd St. address on label* | | | |
| ❑ BLP-1574 [M] | Peckin' Time | 1963 | 40.00 |
| *—With "New York, USA" address on label* | | | |
| ❑ BLP-4031 [M] | Soul Station | 1960 | 200.00 |
| *—Regular version, W. 63rd St. address on label* | | | |
| ❑ BLP-4031 [M] | Soul Station | 1960 | 600.00 |
| *—"Deep groove" version; W. 63rd St. address on label* | | | |
| ❑ BLP-4031 [M] | Soul Station | 1963 | 40.00 |
| *—With "New York, USA" address on label* | | | |
| ❑ BLP-4058 [M] | Roll Call | 1961 | 400.00 |
| *—With W. 63rd St. address on label* | | | |
| ❑ BLP-4058 [M] | Roll Call | 1963 | 60.00 |
| *—With "New York, USA" address on label* | | | |
| ❑ BLP-4080 [M] | Workout | 1961 | 400.00 |
| *—With W. 63rd St. address on label* | | | |
| ❑ BLP-4080 [M] | Workout | 1963 | 200.00 |
| *—With "New York, USA" address on label* | | | |
| ❑ BLP-4149 [M] | No Room for Squares | 1963 | 200.00 |
| *—With "New York, USA" address on label* | | | |
| ❑ BLP-4186 [M] | The Turnaround! | 1964 | 200.00 |
| *—With "New York, USA" address on label* | | | |
| ❑ BLP-4209 [M] | Dippin' | 1965 | 150.00 |
| *—With "New York, USA" address on label* | | | |
| ❑ BLP-4230 [M] | A Caddy for Daddy | 1966 | 150.00 |
| *—With "New York, USA" address on label* | | | |
| ❑ BLP-4273 [M] | Hi Voltage | 1968 | 500.00 |
| *—With "A Division of Liberty Records" address on label* | | | |
| ❑ BLP-5066 [10] | Hank Mobley Quartet | 1955 | 1500. |
| ❑ BST-84031 [S] | Soul Station | 1960 | 200.00 |
| *—With W. 63rd St. address on label* | | | |
| ❑ BST-84031 [S] | Soul Station | 1963 | 40.00 |
| *—With "New York, USA" address on label* | | | |
| ❑ BST-84058 | Roll Call | 199? | 25.00 |
| *—180-gram reissue; distributed by Classic Records* | | | |
| ❑ BST-84058 [S] | Roll Call | 1961 | 200.00 |
| *—With W. 63rd St. address on label* | | | |
| ❑ BST-84058 [S] | Roll Call | 1963 | 40.00 |
| *—With "New York, USA" address on label* | | | |
| ❑ BST-84080 [S] | Workout | 1961 | 200.00 |
| *—With W. 63rd St. address on label* | | | |
| ❑ BST-84080 [S] | Workout | 1963 | 150.00 |
| *—With "New York, USA" address on label* | | | |
| ❑ BST-84149 [S] | No Room for Squares | 1963 | 100.00 |
| *—With "New York, USA" address on label* | | | |
| ❑ BST-84149 [S] | No Room for Squares | 1967 | 40.00 |
| *—With "A Division of Liberty Records" on label* | | | |
| ❑ BST-84186 [S] | The Turnaround! | 1964 | 100.00 |
| *—With "New York, USA" address on label* | | | |
| ❑ BST-84186 [S] | The Turnaround! | 1967 | 40.00 |
| *—With "A Division of Liberty Records" on label* | | | |
| ❑ BST-84209 [S] | Dippin' | 1965 | 100.00 |
| *—With "New York, USA" address on label* | | | |
| ❑ BST-84209 [S] | Dippin' | 1967 | 40.00 |
| *—With "A Division of Liberty Records" on label* | | | |
| ❑ BST-84230 [S] | A Caddy for Daddy | 1966 | 100.00 |
| *—With "New York, USA" address on label* | | | |
| ❑ BST-84230 [S] | A Caddy for Daddy | 1967 | 40.00 |
| *—With "A Division of Liberty Records" on label* | | | |
| ❑ BST-84273 [S] | Hi Voltage | 1968 | 100.00 |
| *—With "A Division of Liberty Records" on label* | | | |
| ❑ BST-84288 | Reach Out! | 1968 | 80.00 |
| *—With "A Division of Liberty Records" on label* | | | |
| ❑ BST-84329 | The Flip | 1969 | 80.00 |
| *—With "A Division of Liberty Records" on label* | | | |
| **PRESTIGE** | | | |
| ❑ PRLP-7061 [M] | Mobley's Message | 1956 | 500.00 |
| *—Yellow label with W. 50th St. address* | | | |
| ❑ PRLP-7082 [M] | Mobley's Second Message | 1957 | 500.00 |
| *—Yellow label with W. 50th St. address* | | | |
| **SAVOY** | | | |
| ❑ MG-12092 [M] | Jazz Message #2 | 1956 | 400.00 |
| **STATUS** | | | |
| ❑ ST-8311 [M] | 52nd Street Theme | 1965 | 80.00 |

**MOBY GRAPE** Also see ALEXANDER "SKIP" SPENCE.

| Number | Title (A Side/B Side) | Yr | NM |
|---|---|---|---|
| **COLUMBIA** | | | |
| ❑ MGS 1 | Grape Jam | 1968 | 20.00 |
| ❑ CXS 3 [(2)] | Wow/Grape Jam | 1968 | 30.00 |
| *—Joint release of the two albums under one cover* | | | |
| ❑ CXS 3 [(2)] | Wow/Grape Jam | 1971 | 15.00 |
| *—Orange labels* | | | |
| ❑ 2698/9498 | Moby Grape Poster | 1967 | 8.00 |
| *—Poster has offending finger airbrushed out* | | | |
| ❑ 2698/9498 | Moby Grape Poster | 1967 | 15.00 |
| *—Poster has Don Stephenson "giving the finger" on his washboard* | | | |
| ❑ CL 2698 [M] | Moby Grape | 1967 | 20.00 |
| *—Cover has offending finger airbrushed out* | | | |
| ❑ CL 2698 [M] | Moby Grape | 1967 | 40.00 |
| *—Cover has Don Stephenson "giving the finger" on his washboard* | | | |
| ❑ CS 9498 | Moby Grape | 1971 | 12.00 |
| *—Orange label; with poster* | | | |
| ❑ CS 9498 [S] | Moby Grape | 1967 | 20.00 |
| *—Cover has offending finger airbrushed out* | | | |
| ❑ CS 9498 [S] | Moby Grape | 1967 | 40.00 |
| *—Cover has Don Stephenson "giving the finger" on his washboard* | | | |
| ❑ CS 9613 | Wow | 1968 | 20.00 |
| ❑ CS 9613 [M] | Wow | 1968 | 40.00 |
| *—"Special Mono Radio Station Copy" with white label* | | | |
| ❑ CS 9696 | Moby Grape '69 | 1969 | 20.00 |
| ❑ CS 9912 | Truly Fine Citizen | 1969 | 20.00 |
| ❑ C 31098 | Great Grape | 1972 | 15.00 |
| **ESCAPE** | | | |
| ❑ ESA 1 | Live Grape | 1978 | 15.00 |
| **HARMONY** | | | |
| ❑ KH 30392 | Omaha | 1971 | 15.00 |
| **REPRISE** | | | |
| ❑ RS 6460 | 20 Granite Creek | 1971 | 20.00 |

**MOD AND THE ROCKERS**

| Number | Title (A Side/B Side) | Yr | NM |
|---|---|---|---|
| **JUSTICE** | | | |
| ❑ JLP-153 | Mod and the Rockers Now! | 1967 | 400.00 |

**MODERN FOLK QUARTET, THE**

| Number | Title (A Side/B Side) | Yr | NM |
|---|---|---|---|
| **WARNER BROS.** | | | |
| ❑ W 1511 [M] | The Modern Folk Quartet | 1963 | 25.00 |
| ❑ WS 1511 [S] | The Modern Folk Quartet | 1963 | 30.00 |
| ❑ W 1546 [M] | Changes | 1964 | 25.00 |
| ❑ WS 1546 [S] | Changes | 1964 | 30.00 |

**MODERN JAZZ DISCIPLES, THE**

| Number | Title (A Side/B Side) | Yr | NM |
|---|---|---|---|
| **NEW JAZZ** | | | |
| ❑ NJLP-8222 [M] | Modern Jazz Disciples | 1959 | 50.00 |
| *—Purple label* | | | |
| ❑ NJLP-8222 [M] | Modern Jazz Disciples | 1965 | 25.00 |
| *—Blue label, trident logo at right* | | | |
| ❑ NJLP-8240 [M] | Right Down Front | 1960 | 50.00 |
| *—Purple label* | | | |
| ❑ NJLP-8240 [M] | Right Down Front | 1965 | 25.00 |
| *—Blue label, trident logo at right* | | | |

**MODERN JAZZ QUARTET, THE**

| Number | Title (A Side/B Side) | Yr | NM |
|---|---|---|---|
| **APPLE** | | | |
| ❑ ST-3353 | Under the Jasmine Tree | 1969 | 30.00 |
| ❑ ST-5-3353 | Under the Jasmine Tree | 1969 | 50.00 |
| *—Capitol Record Club edition* | | | |
| ❑ STAO-3360 | Space | 1970 | 30.00 |

**Number — Title (A Side/B Side) — Yr — NM**

❑ STAO-5-3360 Space 1970 50.00
*—Capitol Record Club edition*

ATLANTIC
❑ 2-603 [(2)M] The European Concert 1961 30.00
*—Multicolor labels, white "fan" logo at right*
❑ 2-603 [(2)M] The European Concert 1963 20.00
*—Multicolor labels, black "fan" logo at right*
❑ SD 2-603 [(2)S]The European Concert 1961 40.00
*—Multicolor labels, white "fan" logo at right*
❑ SD 2-603 [(2)S]The European Concert 1963 25.00
*—Multicolor labels, black "fan" logo at right*
❑ SQ 2-909 [(2)Q]The Last Concert 1975 25.00
❑ 1231 [M] Fontessa 1956 40.00
*—Black label*
❑ 1231 [M] Fontessa 1960 20.00
*—Multicolor label, white "fan" logo at right*
❑ SD 1231 [S] Fontessa 1958 30.00
*—Green label*
❑ 1247 [M] The Modern Jazz Quartet at the Music Inn 1956 40.00
*—Black label*
❑ 1247 [M] The Modern Jazz Quartet at the Music Inn 1960 20.00
*—Multicolor label, white "fan" logo at right*
❑ 1265 [M] The Modern Jazz Quartet 1957 40.00
*—Black label*
❑ 1265 [M] The Modern Jazz Quartet 1960 20.00
*—Multicolor label, white "fan" logo at right*
❑ 1284 [M] No Sun in Venice 1958 40.00
*—Black label*
❑ 1284 [M] No Sun in Venice 1960 20.00
*—Multicolor label, white "fan" logo at right*
❑ SD 1284 [S] No Sun in Venice 1958 30.00
*—Green label*
❑ 1299 [M] The Modern Jazz Quartet at the Music Inn, Volume 2 1958 40.00
*—Black label*
❑ 1299 [M] The Modern Jazz Quartet at the Music Inn, Volume 2 1960 20.00
*—Multicolor label, white "fan" logo at right*
❑ SD 1299 [S] The Modern Jazz Quartet at the Music Inn, Volume 2 1958 30.00
*—Green label*
❑ 1325 [M] Pyramid 1960 40.00
*—Black label*
❑ 1325 [M] Pyramid 1961 20.00
*—Multicolor label, white "fan" logo at right*
❑ SD 1325 [S] Pyramid 1960 30.00
*—Green label*
❑ 1345 [M] Third Stream Music 1960 20.00
*—Multicolor label, white "fan" logo at right*
❑ SD 1345 [S] Third Stream Music 1960 25.00
*—Multicolor label, white "fan" logo at right*
❑ 1359 [M] The Modern Jazz Quartet and Orchestra 1961 20.00
*—Multicolor label, white "fan" logo at right*
❑ SD 1359 [S] The Modern Jazz Quartet and Orchestra 1961 25.00
*—Multicolor label, white "fan" logo at right*
❑ SD 1381 [S] Lonely Woman 1962 20.00
*—Multicolor label, black "fan" logo at right*
❑ SD 1385 [S] The European Concert, Volume 1 1962 20.00
*—Multicolor label, black "fan" logo at right*
❑ SD 1386 [S] The European Concert, Volume 2 1962 20.00
*—Multicolor label, black "fan" logo at right*
❑ SD 1390 [S] The Comedy 1963 20.00
*—Multicolor label, black "fan" logo at right*
❑ SD 1414 [S] The Sheriff 1964 20.00
*—Multicolor label, black "fan" logo at right*
❑ SD 1420 [S] A Quartet Is a Quartet Is a Quartet 1964 20.00
*—Multicolor label, black "fan" logo at right*
❑ 1486 [M] Live at the Lighthouse 1967 20.00
❑ SQ 1652 [Q] Blues on Bach 1974 20.00

MOBILE FIDELITY
❑ 1-090 Live at the Lighthouse 1982 50.00
*—Audiophile vinyl*
❑ 1-205 The Modern Jazz Quartet 1994 30.00
*—Audiophile vinyl*
❑ 1-206 Blues at Carnegie Hall 1994 30.00
*—Audiophile vinyl*
❑ 1-228 The Modern Jazz Quartet at the Music Inn, Volume 2 1995 60.00
*—Audiophile vinyl*

PRESTIGE
❑ 16-1 [M] Concorde 1955 500.00
*—This album plays at 16 2/3 rpm and is marked as such; white label; one side has the Modern Jazz Quartet, the other side has Milt Jackson*
❑ PRLP-160 [10] The Modern Jazz Quartet with Milt Jackson 1953 120.00
❑ PRLP-170 [10] The Modern Jazz Quartet, Volume 2 1953 120.00
❑ PRLP-7005 [M]Concorde 1955 70.00
*—Yellow label originals*
❑ PRLP-7057 [M]Django 1956 70.00
*—Yellow label originals*
❑ PRLP-7059 [M]Modern Jazz Quartet/Milt Jackson Quintet 1956 70.00
*—Yellow label originals*
❑ PRLP-7421 [M]The Modern Jazz Quartet Play for Lovers 1966 20.00
❑ PRLP-7425 [M]The Modern Jazz Quartet Plays Jazz Classics 1966 20.00

SAVOY
❑ MG-12046 [M] Modern Jazz Quartet 1955 50.00

UNITED ARTISTS
❑ UAL-4072 [M] Patterns 1960 25.00
❑ UAS-5072 [S] Patterns 1960 30.00

**MODERN JAZZ QUINTET, THE**

SURREY
❑ S-1030 [M] Q.T. Hush 1966 25.00
❑ SS-1030 [S] Q.T. Hush 1966 30.00

**MODERN JAZZ SEXTET, THE**

AMERICAN RECORDING SOCIETY
❑ G-429 [M] The Modern Jazz Sextet 1957 40.00

NORGRAN
❑ MGN-1076 [M] The Modern Jazz Sextet 1956 100.00

VERVE
❑ MGV-8166 [M] The Modern Jazz Sextet 1957 60.00
❑ V-8166 [M] The Modern Jazz Sextet 1961 25.00

**MODERN JAZZ SOCIETY, THE**

AMERICAN RECORDING SOCIETY
❑ G-432 [M] A Concert of Contemporary Music 1957 40.00

NORGRAN
❑ MGN-1040 [M] A Concert of Contemporary Music 1955 100.00

VERVE
❑ VSP-18 [M] Little David's Fugue 1966 20.00
*—As "The Modern Jazz Ensemble"*
❑ MGV-8131 [M] A Concert of Contemporary Music 1957 60.00
❑ V-8131 [M] A Concert of Contemporary Music 1961 25.00

**MODERN JAZZ STARS, THE**

CROWN
❑ CLP-5008 [M] Jazz Surprise 1957 20.00
❑ CLP-5009 [M] Jazz Masquerade 1957 20.00
*—Original edition has black label with silver print*

**MODERN JAZZ TRIO** See MJT + 3.

**MODERN LOVERS, THE** See JONATHAN RICHMAN AND THE MODERN LOVERS.

**MODUGNO, DOMENICO**

DECCA
❑ DL 4133 [M] Viva Italia 1961 30.00
❑ DL 8808 [M] Nel Blu Dipinto Di Blu (Volare) and Other Italian Favorites 1958 50.00
❑ DL 8853 [M] Encore 1959 40.00

**MODULATIONS, THE**

BUDDAH
❑ BDS-5638 It's Rough Out Here 1975 80.00
*—Reproductions exist*

**MOER, PAUL**

DEL-FI
❑ DFLP-1212 [M]Contemporary Jazz Classics 1961 20.00
❑ DFST-1212 [S] Contemporary Jazz Classics 1961 25.00

**MOFFETT, CHARLES**

SAVOY
❑ MG-12194 The Gift 1969 20.00

**MOJO MEN, THE**

GRT
❑ 10003 Mojo Magic 1969 25.00

**MOLE, MIFF/EDMUND HALL**

BRUNSWICK
❑ BL 58042 [10] Battle of Jazz, Volume 4 1953 60.00

**MOLLY HATCHET**

CAPITOL
❑ C1-92114 Lightning Strikes Twice 1989 12.00

EPIC
❑ AS99 694 [DJ] Flirtin' with Disaster 1979 40.00
*—Promo-only picture disc*
❑ AS99 844 [DJ] Beatin' the Odds 1980 40.00
*—Promo-only picture disc*
❑ AS99 1320 [DJ]Take No Prisoners 1981 25.00
*—Promo-only picture disc*
❑ JE 35347 Molly Hatchet 1978 12.00
*—Orange label*
❑ JE 35347 Molly Hatchet 1979 10.00
*—Dark blue label*
❑ PE 35347 Molly Hatchet 198? 8.00
*—Budget-line reissue with new prefix*
❑ JE 36110 Flirtin' with Disaster 1979 10.00
❑ FE 36572 Beatin' the Odds 1980 10.00
❑ FE 37480 Take No Prisoners 1981 10.00
❑ PE 37480 Take No Prisoners 198? 8.00
*—Budget-line reissue with new prefix*
❑ FE 38429 No Guts... No Glory 1983 10.00
❑ PE 38429 No Guts... No Glory 198? 8.00
*—Budget-line reissue with new prefix*
❑ FE 39621 The Deed Is Done 1984 10.00
❑ E2 40137 [(2)] Double Trouble Live 1985 15.00

**MOLOCH**

ENTERPRISE
❑ ENS-1002 Moloch 1969 20.00

**MOM'S APPLE PIE**

BROWN BAG
❑ BB-LA073-F Mom's Apple Pie #2 1973 15.00
❑ 14200 Mom's Apple Pie 1972 20.00
*—With barbed wire wall covering the former opening. This is much rarer than the first version, though less sought-after*
❑ 14200 Mom's Apple Pie 1972 20.00
*—With vulva showing in the apple pie*

**MOMENTS, THE** R&B trio. For legal reasons, their albums on Polydor were issued under the name "Ray, Goodman and Brown."

CHESS
❑ CH2-92517 [(2)]Greatest Hits 198? 12.00

POLYDOR
❑ PD-1-6240 Ray, Goodman & Brown 1979 10.00
❑ PD-1-6299 Ray, Goodman & Brown II 1980 10.00
❑ PD-1-6341 Stay 1981 10.00

STANG
❑ ST-1000 Not On the Outside, But On the Inside Strong 1969 30.00
❑ ST-1002 The Moments On Top 1970 30.00
❑ ST-1003 A Moment with the Moments 1970 30.00
❑ ST-1004 Moments Greatest Hits 1971 20.00
❑ ST-1006 The Moments Live at the New York State Womans Prison 1971 25.00
❑ ST-1009 The Other Side of the Moments 1972 25.00
❑ ST-1015 Live at the Miss Black America Pageant 1972 20.00
❑ ST-1019 The Best of the Moments 1975 15.00
❑ ST-1022 My Thing 1973 15.00
❑ ST-1023 The Sexy Moments 1974 15.00
❑ ST-1026 Look at Me 1975 15.00
❑ ST-1030 Moments With You 1976 15.00
❑ 2ST-1033 [(2)] Greatest Hits 1977 20.00
❑ ST-1034 Sharp 1978 15.00

**MONCUR, GRACHAN, III**

BLUE NOTE
❑ BLP-4153 [M] Evolution 1963 25.00
❑ BLP-4177 [M] Some Other Stuff 1964 25.00
❑ BST-84153 [S] Evolution 1963 30.00
*—With "New York, USA" address on label*
❑ BST-84177 [S] Some Other Stuff 1964 30.00
*—With "New York, USA" address on label*

**MONDAY BLUES**

VAULT
❑ 133 The Phil Spector Song Book 1970 20.00

**MONEY, ZOOT**

EPIC
❑ LN 24241 [M] All Happening Zoot Money's Big Roll Band at Klooks Kleek 1966 20.00

**MONICA, CORBETT**

DOT
❑ DLP-3303 [M] For Laughs1 1960 30.00

**MONITORS, THE (1)**

SOUL
❑ SS-714 Greetings, We're the Monitors 1969 60.00

**MONK, THELONIOUS**

ANALOGUE PRODUCTIONS
❑ AP-37 [(7)] The Riverside Tenor Sessions 1999 250.00

BLUE NOTE
❑ BLP-1510 [M] Genius of Modern Music, Vol. 1 1956 400.00
*—"Deep groove" version; Lexington Ave. address on label*
❑ BLP-1510 [M] Genius of Modern Music, Vol. 1 1958 200.00
*—"Deep groove" edition, W. 63rd St. address on label*
❑ BLP-1510 [M] Genius of Modern Music, Vol. 1 1963 40.00
*—"New York, USA" address on label*
❑ BLP-1511 [M] Genius of Modern Music, Vol. 2 1956 400.00
*—"Deep groove" version; Lexington Ave. address on label*
❑ BLP-1511 [M] Genius of Modern Music, Vol. 2 1958 200.00
*—"Deep groove" edition, W. 63rd St. address on label*
❑ BLP-1511 [M] Genius of Modern Music, Vol. 2 1963 40.00
*—"New York, USA" address on label*
❑ BLP-5002 [10] Genius of Modern Music, Vol. 1 1952 800.00
❑ BLP-5009 [10] Genius of Modern Music, Vol. 2 1952 800.00

COLUMBIA
❑ CL 1965 [M] Monk's Dream 1963 30.00
*—"Guaranteed High Fideilty" on label*

| Number | Title (A Side/B Side) | Yr | NM |
|---|---|---|---|
| ❑ CL 1965 [M] | Monk's Dream | 1966 | 20.00 |
| *—"360 Sound Mono" on label* | | | |
| ❑ CL 2038 [M] | Criss-Cross | 1963 | 30.00 |
| *—"Guaranteed High Fidelity" on label* | | | |
| ❑ CL 2038 [M] | Criss-Cross | 1966 | 20.00 |
| *—"360 Sound Mono" on label* | | | |
| ❑ CL 2164 [M] | Monk Big Band and Quartet In Concert | 1964 | 30.00 |
| *—"Guaranteed High Fidelity" on label* | | | |
| ❑ CL 2164 [M] | Monk Big Band and Quartet In Concert | 1966 | 20.00 |
| *—"360 Sound Mono" on label* | | | |
| ❑ CL 2184 [M] | It's Monk's Time | 1964 | 30.00 |
| *—"Guaranteed High Fidelity" on label* | | | |
| ❑ CL 2184 [M] | It's Monk's Time | 1966 | 20.00 |
| *—"360 Sound Mono" on label* | | | |
| ❑ CL 2291 [M] | Monk | 1965 | 30.00 |
| *—"Guaranteed High Fideilty" on label* | | | |
| ❑ CL 2291 [M] | Monk | 1966 | 20.00 |
| *—"360 Sound Mono" on label* | | | |
| ❑ CL 2349 [M] | Solo Monk | 1965 | 30.00 |
| *—"360 Sound Mono" on label* | | | |
| ❑ CL 2416 [M] | Misterioso | 1966 | 25.00 |
| *—"360 Sound Mono" on label* | | | |
| ❑ CL 2651 [M] | Straight No Chaser | 1967 | 50.00 |
| *—Red label with "Mono"* | | | |
| ❑ CS 8765 [S] | Monk's Dream | 1963 | 70.00 |
| *—"360 Sound Stereo" in black on label* | | | |
| ❑ CS 8765 [S] | Monk's Dream | 1966 | 25.00 |
| *—"360 Sound Stereo" in white on label* | | | |
| ❑ CS 8838 [S] | Criss-Cross | 1963 | 60.00 |
| *—"360 Sound Stereo" in black on label* | | | |
| ❑ CS 8838 [S] | Criss-Cross | 1966 | 25.00 |
| *—"360 Sound Stereo" in white on label* | | | |
| ❑ CS 8964 [S] | Monk Big Band and Quartet In Concert | 1964 | 80.00 |
| *—"360 Sound Stereo" in black on label* | | | |
| ❑ CS 8964 [S] | Monk Big Band and Quartet In Concert | 1966 | 25.00 |
| *—"360 Sound Stereo" in white on label* | | | |
| ❑ CS 8984 [S] | It's Monk's Time | 1964 | 70.00 |
| *—"360 Sound Stereo" in black on label* | | | |
| ❑ CS 8984 [S] | It's Monk's Time | 1966 | 30.00 |
| *—"360 Sound Stereo" in white on label* | | | |
| ❑ CS 9091 [S] | Monk | 1965 | 50.00 |
| *—"360 Sound Stereo" in black on label* | | | |
| ❑ CS 9091 [S] | Monk | 1966 | 25.00 |
| *—"360 Sound Stereo" in white on label* | | | |
| ❑ CS 9149 [S] | Solo Monk | 1965 | 40.00 |
| *—Red "360 Sound" label* | | | |
| ❑ CS 9216 [S] | Misterioso | 1966 | 30.00 |
| *—"360 Sound Stereo" on red label* | | | |
| ❑ CS 9451 [S] | Straight No Chaser | 1967 | 40.00 |
| *—Red "360 Sound" label* | | | |
| ❑ CS 9632 [M] | Underground | 1968 | 50.00 |
| *—White label promo only with stereo number; "Special Mono Radio Station Copy" sticker on stereo cover* | | | |
| ❑ CS 9632 [S] | Underground | 1968 | 30.00 |
| *—Red "360 Sound" label* | | | |
| ❑ CS 9806 | Monk's Blues | 1969 | 80.00 |
| *—Red "360 Sound" label* | | | |

### COLUMBIA MUSICAL TREASURY

| Number | Title (A Side/B Side) | Yr | NM |
|---|---|---|---|
| ❑ DS 338 | Monk's Miracles | 1967 | 30.00 |
| *—Columbia Record Club exclusive* | | | |

### MOSAIC

| Number | Title (A Side/B Side) | Yr | NM |
|---|---|---|---|
| ❑ MR4-101 [(4)] | The Complete Blue Note Recordings of Thelonious Monk | 198? | 200.00 |
| *—Limited edition of 7,500* | | | |
| ❑ MR4-112 [(4)] | The Complete Black Lion and Vogue Recordings | 199? | 250.00 |
| *—Limited edition of 7,500* | | | |

### PRESTIGE

| Number | Title (A Side/B Side) | Yr | NM |
|---|---|---|---|
| ❑ PRLP-142 [10] | Thelonious Monk Trio | 1953 | 800.00 |
| ❑ PRLP-166 [10] | Thelonious Monk Quintet with Sonny Rollins and Julius Watkins | 1953 | 800.00 |
| ❑ PRLP-180 [10] | Thelonious Monk Quintet | 1954 | 800.00 |
| ❑ PRLP-189 [10] | Thelonious Monk Trio | 1954 | 800.00 |
| ❑ PRLP-7027 [M] | Thelonious Monk | 1956 | 300.00 |
| *—Reissue of 142 and 189 on one 12-inch record; yellow label with W. 50th St. address; label calls this "Thelonious Monk Trio"* | | | |
| ❑ PRLP-7053 [M] | Monk | 1956 | 200.00 |
| *—Reissue of 150; yellow label with W. 50th St. address* | | | |
| ❑ PRLP-7075 [M] | Thelonious Monk/Sonny Rollins | 1957 | 200.00 |
| *—Reissue of 166; yellow label with W. 50th St. address* | | | |
| ❑ PRLP-7159 [M] | Monk's Moods | 1959 | 80.00 |
| *—Reissue of 7027; yellow label with Bergenfield, N.J. address* | | | |
| ❑ PRLP-7169 [M] | Work | 1959 | 80.00 |
| *—Reissue of 7075* | | | |
| ❑ PRLP-7245 [M] | We See | 1962 | 80.00 |
| *—Reissue of 7053* | | | |
| ❑ PRLP-7363 [M] | The Golden Monk | 1965 | 30.00 |
| *—Reissue of 7245* | | | |
| ❑ PRLP-7508 [M] | The High Priest | 1967 | 50.00 |
| *—Reissue of 7159* | | | |

### RIVERSIDE

| Number | Title (A Side/B Side) | Yr | NM |
|---|---|---|---|
| ❑ R-022 [(22)] | The Complete Riverside Recordings | 1987 | 500.00 |
| ❑ RLP 12-201 [M] | Thelonious Monk Plays Duke Ellington | 1955 | 600.00 |
| *—White label with blue print* | | | |
| ❑ RLP 12-201 [M] | Thelonious Monk Plays Duke Ellington | 1958 | 100.00 |
| *—Blue label with reel and microphone logo* | | | |
| ❑ RLP 12-209 [M] | The Unique Thelonious Monk | 1956 | 500.00 |
| *—White label with blue print* | | | |
| ❑ RLP 12-209 [M] | The Unique Thelonious Monk | 1958 | 100.00 |
| *—Blue label with reel and microphone logo* | | | |
| ❑ RLP 12-226 [M] | Brilliant Corners | 1957 | 400.00 |
| *—White label with blue print* | | | |
| ❑ RLP 12-226 [M] | Brilliant Corners | 1958 | 100.00 |
| *—Blue label with reel and microphone logo* | | | |
| ❑ RLP 12-235 [M] | Thelonious Himself | 1957 | 400.00 |
| *—White label with blue print* | | | |
| ❑ RLP 12-235 [M] | Thelonious Himself | 1958 | 100.00 |
| *—Blue label with reel and microphone logo* | | | |
| ❑ RLP 12-242 [M] | Monk's Music | 1957 | 400.00 |
| *—White label with blue print* | | | |
| ❑ RLP 12-242 [M] | Monk's Music | 1958 | 100.00 |
| *—Blue label with reel and microphone logo* | | | |
| ❑ RLP 12-247 [M] | Mulligan Meets Monk | 1957 | 400.00 |
| *—White label with blue print* | | | |
| ❑ RLP 12-247 [M] | Mulligan Meets Monk | 1958 | 100.00 |
| *—Blue label with reel and microphone logo* | | | |
| ❑ RLP 12-262 [M] | Thelonious in Action Recorded at the Five Spot Café, New York, With Johnny Griffn | 1958 | 80.00 |
| *—Blue label with reel and microphone logo* | | | |
| ❑ RLP 12-279 [M] | Misterioso | 1958 | 100.00 |
| *—Blue label with reel-and-microphone logo* | | | |
| ❑ RLP 12-300 [M] | The Thelonious Monk Orchestra at Town Hall | 1959 | 60.00 |
| *—Blue label with reel and microphone logo* | | | |
| ❑ RLP 12-305 [M] | 5 By Monk By 5 | 1959 | 60.00 |
| *—Blue label with reel and microphone logo* | | | |
| ❑ RLP 12-312 [M] | Thelonious Alone in San Francisco | 1959 | 60.00 |
| *—Blue label with reel and microphone logo* | | | |
| ❑ RLP 12-323 [M] | Thelonious Monk Quartet Plus Two at the Blackhawk | 1960 | 60.00 |
| *—Blue label with reel and microphone logo* | | | |
| ❑ RLP-421 [M] | Thelonious Monk's Greatest Hits | 1962 | 25.00 |
| ❑ RLP-443 [M] | Thelonious Monk in Italy | 1963 | 30.00 |
| ❑ RLP-460/1 [(2)M] | Two Hours with Thelonious Monk | 1963 | 60.00 |
| ❑ RLP-483 [M] | The Thelonious Monk Story, Volume 1 | 1965 | 30.00 |
| ❑ RLP-483/4 [(2)M] | The Thelonious Monk Story | 1965 | 70.00 |
| ❑ RLP-484 [M] | The Thelonious Monk Story, Volume 2 | 1965 | 30.00 |
| ❑ RLP-491 [M] | Monk in France | 1965 | 30.00 |
| ❑ RLP 1101 [S] | Monk's Music | 1959 | 60.00 |
| *—Black label with reel and microphone logo* | | | |
| ❑ RLP 1106 [S] | Mulligan Meets Monk | 1959 | 60.00 |
| *—Black label with reel and microphone logo* | | | |
| ❑ RLP 1133 [S] | Misterioso | 1958 | 70.00 |
| *—Black label with reel and microphone logo* | | | |
| ❑ RLP 1138 [S] | The Thelonious Monk Orchestra at Town Hall | 1959 | 70.00 |
| *—Black label with reel and microphone logo* | | | |
| ❑ RLP 1150 [S] | 5 By Monk By 5 | 1959 | 80.00 |
| *—Black label with reel and microphone logo* | | | |
| ❑ RLP 1158 [S] | Thelonious Alone in San Francisco | 1959 | 70.00 |
| *—Black label with reel and microphone logo* | | | |
| ❑ RLP 1171 [S] | Thelonious Monk Quartet Plus Two at the Blackhawk | 1960 | 70.00 |
| *—Black label with reel and microphone logo* | | | |
| ❑ RLP 1190 [S] | Thelonious in Action Recorded at the Five Spot Café, New York, With Johnny Griffn | 1960 | 70.00 |
| *—Black label with reel and microphone logo* | | | |
| ❑ RM-3000 [M] | Mighty Monk | 1967 | 40.00 |
| ❑ RM-3004 [M] | Monk's Music | 1967 | 30.00 |
| ❑ RS-9421 [S] | Thelonious Monk's Greatest Hits | 1962 | 30.00 |
| ❑ RS-9443 [S] | Thelonious Monk in Italy | 1963 | 40.00 |
| ❑ RS-9460/1 [(2)S] | Two Hours with Thelonious Monk | 1963 | 80.00 |
| ❑ RS-9483 [S] | The Thelonious Monk Story, Volume 1 | 1965 | 25.00 |
| ❑ RS-9483/4 [(2)S] | The Thelonious Monk Story | 1965 | 60.00 |
| ❑ RS-9484 [S] | The Thelonious Monk Story, Volume 2 | 1965 | 25.00 |
| ❑ RS-9491 [S] | Monk in France | 1965 | 25.00 |

## MONK, THELONIOUS, AND JOHN COLTRANE

### JAZZLAND

| Number | Title (A Side/B Side) | Yr | NM |
|---|---|---|---|
| ❑ JLP-46 [M] | Thelonious Monk with John Coltrane | 1961 | 100.00 |
| ❑ JLP-946 [S] | Thelonious Monk with John Coltrane | 1961 | 80.00 |

### RIVERSIDE

| Number | Title (A Side/B Side) | Yr | NM |
|---|---|---|---|
| ❑ RLP-490 [M] | Thelonious Monk with John Coltrane | 1965 | 50.00 |
| *—Reissue of Jazzland 46* | | | |
| ❑ RS-9490 [S] | Thelonious Monk with John Coltrane | 1965 | 40.00 |
| *—Reissue of Jazzland 946* | | | |

## MONKEES, THE Also see DAVY JONES; MIKE NESMITH.

### ARISTA

| Number | Title (A Side/B Side) | Yr | NM |
|---|---|---|---|
| ❑ AL 4089 | The Monkees' Greatest Hits | 1976 | 12.00 |
| *—Reissue of Bell LP* | | | |
| ❑ AL8-8313 | The Monkees' Greatest Hits | 198? | 8.00 |
| *—Reissue of Arista 4089* | | | |
| ❑ AL9-8432 | Then & Now...The Best of the Monkees | 1986 | 12.00 |
| ❑ AL-8524 | The Monkees | 1988 | 12.00 |
| ❑ AL-8525 | More of the Monkees | 1988 | 12.00 |

### BELL

| Number | Title (A Side/B Side) | Yr | NM |
|---|---|---|---|
| ❑ 6081 | Re-Focus | 1972 | 30.00 |

### COLGEMS

| Number | Title (A Side/B Side) | Yr | NM |
|---|---|---|---|
| ❑ COM-101 [M] | The Monkees | 1966 | 20.00 |
| *—Second pressing: Side 1, Song 5 listed as "Papa Gene's Blues" (RE after number on upper right back cover)* | | | |
| ❑ COM-101 [M] | The Monkees | 1966 | 25.00 |
| *—First pressing: Side 1, Song 5 listed as "Papa Jean's Blues"* | | | |
| ❑ COS-101 [S] | The Monkees | 1966 | 20.00 |
| *—Second pressing: Side 1, Song 5 listed as "Papa Gene's Blues" (RE after number on upper right back cover)* | | | |
| ❑ COS-101 [S] | The Monkees | 1966 | 25.00 |
| *—First pressing: Side 1, Song 5 listed as "Papa Jean's Blues"* | | | |
| ❑ COM-102 [M] | More of the Monkees | 1966 | 20.00 |
| ❑ COS-102 [S] | More of the Monkees | 1966 | 20.00 |
| ❑ COM-103 [M] | The Monkees' Headquarters | 1967 | 20.00 |
| *—First pressing: Back cover, center bottom photo is of two of the LP's producers* | | | |
| ❑ COM-103 [M] | The Monkees' Headquarters | 1967 | 30.00 |
| *—Second pressing: Back cover, center bottom photo is of producers plus the Monkees with beards; "RE" on upper right back cover* | | | |
| ❑ COS-103 [S] | The Monkees' Headquarters | 1967 | 20.00 |
| *—First pressing: Back cover, center bottom photo is of two of the LP's producers* | | | |
| ❑ COS-103 [S] | The Monkees' Headquarters | 1967 | 30.00 |
| *—Second pressing: Back cover, center bottom photo is of producers plus the Monkees with beards; "RE" on upper right back cover* | | | |
| ❑ COM-104 [M] | Pisces, Aquarius, Capricorn & Jones Ltd. | 1967 | 40.00 |
| ❑ COS-104 [S] | Pisces, Aquarius, Capricorn & Jones Ltd. | 1967 | 20.00 |
| ❑ COM-109 [M] | The Birds, the Bees & the Monkees | 1968 | 100.00 |
| ❑ COS-109 [S] | The Birds, the Bees & the Monkees | 1968 | 20.00 |
| ❑ COS-113 | Instant Replay | 1969 | 40.00 |
| ❑ COS-115 | The Monkees Greatest Hits | 1969 | 40.00 |
| ❑ COS-117 | The Monkees Present | 1969 | 50.00 |
| ❑ COS-119 | Changes | 1970 | 80.00 |
| ❑ PRS-329 | The Monkees' Golden Hits | 1971 | 100.00 |
| *—RCA Special Products edition* | | | |
| ❑ SCOS-1001 [(2)] | A Barrel Full of Monkees | 1971 | 75.00 |
| ❑ COSO-5008 | Head | 1968 | 50.00 |

### FSH

| Number | Title (A Side/B Side) | Yr | NM |
|---|---|---|---|
| ❑ 71110 | Live, 20th Anniversary Tour | 1987 | 20.00 |
| *—Live album sold at tour stops* | | | |

### LAURIE HOUSE

| Number | Title (A Side/B Side) | Yr | NM |
|---|---|---|---|
| ❑ LH-8009 | The Monkees | 1974 | 20.00 |
| *—TV mail-order offer* | | | |

### PAIR

| Number | Title (A Side/B Side) | Yr | NM |
|---|---|---|---|
| ❑ ARPDL2-1109 [(2)] | Hit Factory | 1986 | 20.00 |

### RCA SPECIAL PRODUCTS

| Number | Title (A Side/B Side) | Yr | NM |
|---|---|---|---|
| ❑ DPL2-0188 [(2)] | The Monkees | 1976 | 25.00 |
| *—TV mail-order offer* | | | |

### RHINO

| Number | Title (A Side/B Side) | Yr | NM |
|---|---|---|---|
| ❑ RNLP-113 | Monkee Flips | 1984 | 12.00 |
| ❑ RNLP-144 | The Birds, the Bees and the Monkees | 1985 | 12.00 |
| ❑ RNLP-145 | Head | 1985 | 12.00 |
| ❑ RNLP-146 | Instant Replay | 1985 | 12.00 |
| ❑ RNLP-147 | The Monkees Present | 1985 | 12.00 |
| ❑ RNLP-701 [PD] | Monkee Business | 1982 | 15.00 |
| ❑ RNLP-70139 | Live 1967 | 1987 | 12.00 |
| ❑ RNLP-70140 | The Monkees | 1986 | 12.00 |
| ❑ RNLP-70141 | Pisces, Aquarius, Capricorn & Jones Ltd. | 1986 | 12.00 |
| ❑ RNLP-70142 | More of the Monkees | 1986 | 12.00 |
| ❑ RNLP-70143 | The Monkees' Headquarters | 1986 | 12.00 |
| ❑ RNLP-70148 | Changes | 1986 | 12.00 |
| ❑ RNLP-70150 | Missing Links | 1987 | 12.00 |
| ❑ RNIN-70706 | Pool It! | 1987 | 10.00 |

### SILHOUETTE

| Number | Title (A Side/B Side) | Yr | NM |
|---|---|---|---|
| ❑ SM-10012 [PD] | Tails of the Monkees | 1983 | 15.00 |

### SILVER EAGLE

| Number | Title (A Side/B Side) | Yr | NM |
|---|---|---|---|
| ❑ SE-1048 [(2)] | The Best of the Monkees | 1986 | 15.00 |
| *—TV mail-order offer* | | | |

### SUNDAZED

| Number | Title (A Side/B Side) | Yr | NM |
|---|---|---|---|
| ❑ LP 5045 | The Monkees | 1996 | 10.00 |
| ❑ LP 5046 | More of the Monkees | 1996 | 10.00 |
| ❑ LP 5047 | The Monkees Headquarters | 1996 | 10.00 |

| Number | Title (A Side/B Side) | Yr | NM |
|---|---|---|---|
| ❑ LP 5048 | Pisces, Aquarius, Capricorn & Jones Ltd. | 1996 | 10.00 |
| ❑ LP 5049 | The Birds, the Bees, and the Monkees | 1996 | 10.00 |

*—All of the above are on colored vinyl with bonus tracks and posters*

**MONRO, MATT**

CAPITOL

| Number | Title (A Side/B Side) | Yr | NM |
|---|---|---|---|
| ❑ SKAO-152 | Best of Matt Monro | 1969 | 10.00 |
| ❑ ST 2540 [S] | This Is the Life | 1966 | 15.00 |
| ❑ T 2540 [M] | This Is the Life | 1966 | 12.00 |
| ❑ ST 2608 [S] | Here's to My Lady | 1966 | 15.00 |
| ❑ T 2608 [M] | Here's to My Lady | 1966 | 12.00 |
| ❑ ST 2683 [S] | Invitation to Broadway | 1967 | 15.00 |
| ❑ T 2683 [M] | Invitation to Broadway | 1967 | 12.00 |
| ❑ ST 2730 [S] | Invitation to the Movies/Born Free | 1967 | 12.00 |
| ❑ T 2730 [M] | Invitation to the Movies/Born Free | 1967 | 15.00 |
| ❑ ST 2801 [S] | These Years | 1968 | 12.00 |
| ❑ T 2801 [M] | These Years | 1968 | 15.00 |

LIBERTY

| Number | Title (A Side/B Side) | Yr | NM |
|---|---|---|---|
| ❑ LRP-3240 [M] | Matt Monro | 1962 | 15.00 |
| ❑ LRP-3256 [M] | From Hollywood With Love | 1962 | 15.00 |
| ❑ LRP-3402 [M] | Walk Away | 1965 | 12.00 |
| ❑ LRP-3423 [M] | All My Loving | 1965 | 12.00 |
| ❑ LRP-3437 [M] | Yesterday | 1966 | 12.00 |
| ❑ LRP-3459 [M] | Matt Monro's Best | 1966 | 12.00 |
| ❑ LST-7240 [S] | Matt Monro | 1962 | 20.00 |
| ❑ LST-7256 [S] | From Hollywood With Love | 1962 | 20.00 |
| ❑ LST-7402 [S] | Walk Away | 1965 | 15.00 |
| ❑ LST-7423 [S] | All My Loving | 1965 | 15.00 |
| ❑ LST-7437 [S] | Yesterday | 1966 | 15.00 |
| ❑ LST-7459 [S] | Matt Monro's Best | 1966 | 15.00 |

LONDON

| Number | Title (A Side/B Side) | Yr | NM |
|---|---|---|---|
| ❑ LL 1611 [M] | Blue and Sentimental | 1957 | 30.00 |

PICKWICK

| Number | Title (A Side/B Side) | Yr | NM |
|---|---|---|---|
| ❑ SPC-3147 | This Is All I Ask | 197? | 10.00 |

WARWICK

| Number | Title (A Side/B Side) | Yr | NM |
|---|---|---|---|
| ❑ W 2045 [M] | My Kind of Girl | 1961 | 30.00 |
| ❑ WST 2045 [S] | My Kind of Girl | 1961 | 50.00 |

**MONROE, BILL**

COLUMBIA

| Number | Title (A Side/B Side) | Yr | NM |
|---|---|---|---|
| ❑ FC 38904 | Columbia Historic Editions | 1983 | 12.00 |

DECCA

| Number | Title (A Side/B Side) | Yr | NM |
|---|---|---|---|
| ❑ DL 4080 [M] | Mr. Bluegrass | 1960 | 30.00 |
| ❑ DL 4266 [M] | Bluegrass Ramble | 1962 | 30.00 |
| ❑ DL 4327 [M] | My All Time Country Favorites | 1962 | 25.00 |
| ❑ DL 4382 [M] | Bluegrass Special | 1963 | 25.00 |
| ❑ DL 4537 [M] | I'll Meet You in Chuch Sunday Morning | 1964 | 25.00 |
| ❑ DL 4601 [M] | Bluegrass Instrumentals | 1965 | 20.00 |
| ❑ DL 4780 [M] | The High Lonesome Sound of Bill Monroe | 1966 | 20.00 |
| ❑ DL 4896 [M] | Bluegrass Time | 1967 | 30.00 |
| ❑ DL 8731 [M] | Knee Deep in Bluegrass | 1958 | 50.00 |
| ❑ DL 8769 [M] | I Saw the Light | 1959 | 50.00 |
| ❑ DL 74080 [S] | Mr. Bluegrass | 1960 | 40.00 |
| ❑ DL 74266 [S] | Bluegrass Ramble | 1962 | 40.00 |
| ❑ DL 74327 [S] | My All Time Country Favorites | 1962 | 30.00 |
| ❑ DL 74382 [S] | Bluegrass Special | 1963 | 30.00 |
| ❑ DL 74537 [S] | I'll Meet You in Church Sunday Morning | 1964 | 30.00 |
| ❑ DL 74601 [S] | Bluegrass Instrumentals | 1965 | 25.00 |
| ❑ DL 74780 [S] | The High Lonesome Sound of Bill Monroe | 1966 | 25.00 |
| ❑ DL 74896 [S] | Bluegrass Time | 1967 | 20.00 |
| ❑ DL 75010 | Bill Monroe's Greatest Hits | 1968 | 20.00 |
| ❑ DL 75135 | A Voice from On High | 1969 | 20.00 |
| ❑ DL 75213 | Kentucky Bluegrass | 1970 | 20.00 |
| ❑ DL 75281 | Country Music Hall of Fame | 1972 | 20.00 |
| ❑ DL 78731 [S] | Knee Deep in Bluegrass | 1958 | 70.00 |
| ❑ DL 78769 [S] | I Saw the Light | 1959 | 70.00 |

HARMONY

| Number | Title (A Side/B Side) | Yr | NM |
|---|---|---|---|
| ❑ HL 7290 [M] | The Great Bill Monroe and His Bluegrass Boys | 1961 | 25.00 |
| ❑ HL 7315 [M] | Bill Monroe's Best | 1964 | 20.00 |
| ❑ HL 7338 [M] | The Original Bluegrass Sound | 1965 | 20.00 |
| ❑ HS 11335 [R] | The Great Bill Monroe and His Bluegrass Boys | 1969 | 15.00 |

MCA

| Number | Title (A Side/B Side) | Yr | NM |
|---|---|---|---|
| ❑ 17 | Bill Monroe's Greatest Hits | 1973 | 12.00 |
| *—Reissue of Decca 75010* | | | |
| ❑ 82 | Mr. Bluegrass | 1973 | 12.00 |
| *—Reissue of Decca 74080* | | | |
| ❑ 88 | Bluegrass Ramble | 1973 | 12.00 |
| *—Reissue of Decca 74266* | | | |
| ❑ 97 | Bluegrass Special | 1973 | 12.00 |
| *—Reissue of Decca 74382* | | | |
| ❑ 104 | Bluegrass Instrumentals | 1973 | 12.00 |
| *—Reissue of Decca 74601* | | | |
| ❑ 110 | The High Lonesome Sound of Bill Monroe | 1973 | 12.00 |
| *—Reissue of Decca 74780* | | | |

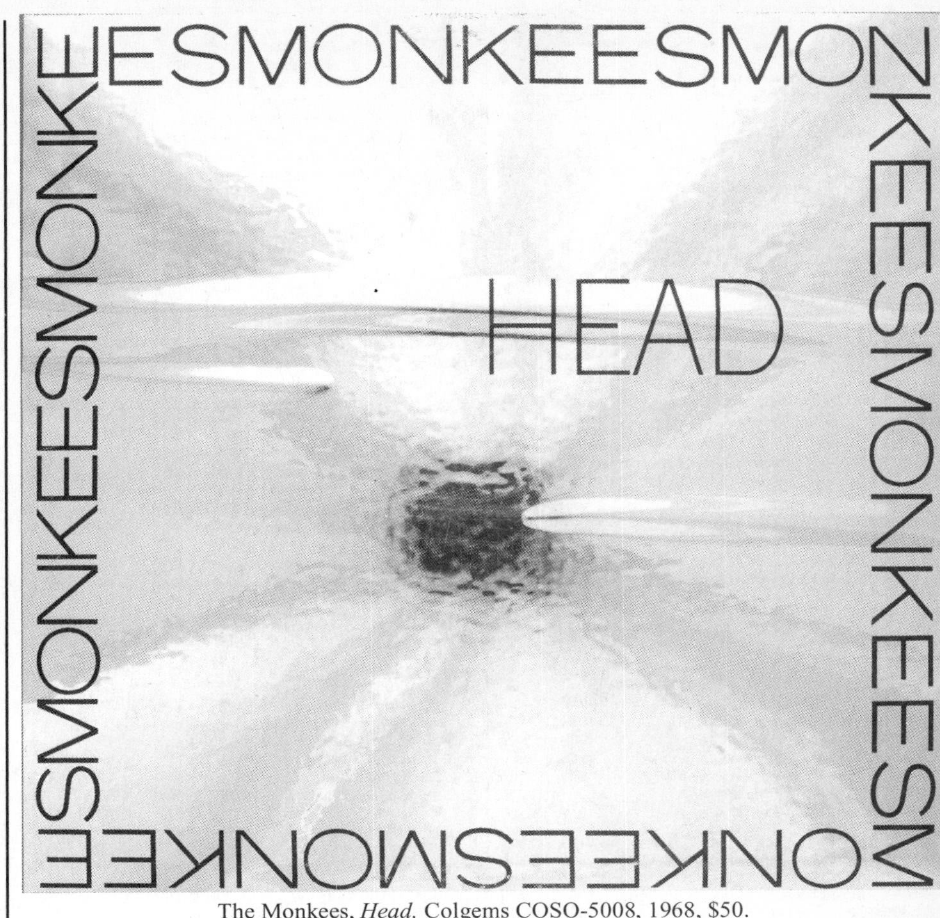


The Monkees, *Head,* Colgems COSO-5008, 1968, $50.

| Number | Title (A Side/B Side) | Yr | NM |
|---|---|---|---|
| ❑ 116 | Bluegrass Time | 1973 | 12.00 |
| *—Reissue of Decca 74896* | | | |
| ❑ 131 | A Voice from On High | 1973 | 12.00 |
| *—Reissue of Decca 75135* | | | |
| ❑ 136 | Kentucky Bluegrass | 1973 | 12.00 |
| *—Reissue of Decca 75213* | | | |
| ❑ 140 | Country Music Hall of Fame | 1973 | 12.00 |
| *—Reissue of Decca 75281* | | | |
| ❑ 226 | I'll Meet You in Church Sunday Morning | 1973 | 12.00 |
| *—Reissue of Decca 74537* | | | |
| ❑ 426 | Road of Life | 1974 | 15.00 |
| ❑ 500 | Uncle Pen | 197? | 12.00 |
| ❑ 527 | I Saw the Light | 197? | 12.00 |
| *—Reissue of Decca 78769* | | | |
| ❑ 707 | Weary Traveler | 198? | 10.00 |
| *—Reissue of 2173* | | | |
| ❑ 708 | Bill Monroe Sings Bluegrass, Body and Soul | 198? | 10.00 |
| *—Reissue of 2251* | | | |
| ❑ 765 | Bean Blossom '79 | 198? | 10.00 |
| *—Reissue of 3209* | | | |
| ❑ 2173 | Weary Traveler | 1976 | 15.00 |
| ❑ 2251 | Bill Monroe Sings Bluegrass, Body and Soul | 1977 | 15.00 |
| ❑ 2315 | Bluegrass Memories | 1978 | 15.00 |
| ❑ 3209 | Bean Blossom '79 | 1979 | 15.00 |
| ❑ 4090 [(2)] | The Best of Bill Monroe | 197? | 15.00 |
| ❑ 5435 | Bill Monroe and Friends | 1984 | 12.00 |
| ❑ 5625 | Bill Monroe and the Stars of the Bluegrass Hall of Fame | 1985 | 12.00 |
| ❑ 8002 [(2)] | Bean Blossom | 1973 | 20.00 |

RCA CAMDEN

| Number | Title (A Side/B Side) | Yr | NM |
|---|---|---|---|
| ❑ CAL-719 [M] | Father of Bluegrass Music | 1962 | 25.00 |

**MONROE, CHARLIE**

STARDAY

| Number | Title (A Side/B Side) | Yr | NM |
|---|---|---|---|
| ❑ SLP-361 [M] | Lord, Build Me a Cabin | 1965 | 25.00 |
| ❑ SLP-372 [M] | Charlie Monroe Sings Again | 1966 | 25.00 |

**MONROE, MARILYN**

ASCOT

| Number | Title (A Side/B Side) | Yr | NM |
|---|---|---|---|
| ❑ AM-13008 [M] | Marilyn Monroe | 1963 | 40.00 |
| ❑ AS-16008 [S] | Marilyn Monroe | 1963 | 50.00 |

MOVIETONE

| Number | Title (A Side/B Side) | Yr | NM |
|---|---|---|---|
| ❑ 1016 [M] | The Unforgettable Marilyn Monroe | 1967 | 25.00 |
| ❑ 72016 [R] | The Unforgettable Marilyn Monroe | 1967 | 20.00 |

SANDY HOOK

| Number | Title (A Side/B Side) | Yr | NM |
|---|---|---|---|
| ❑ SH-2013 [PD] | Rare Recordings 1948-1962 | 1980 | 25.00 |

STET

| Number | Title (A Side/B Side) | Yr | NM |
|---|---|---|---|
| ❑ DS-15005 | Never Before and Never Again | 1980 | 15.00 |

20TH CENTURY

| Number | Title (A Side/B Side) | Yr | NM |
|---|---|---|---|
| ❑ T-901 | Remember Marilyn | 1973 | 25.00 |

20TH FOX

| Number | Title (A Side/B Side) | Yr | NM |
|---|---|---|---|
| ❑ F/SXG-5000 | Marilyn Bonus Photo | 1962 | 50.00 |
| ❑ FXG-5000 [M] | Marilyn | 1962 | 150.00 |
| ❑ SXG-5000 [R] | Marilyn | 1962 | 100.00 |

**MONROE, VAUGHN**

DOT

| Number | Title (A Side/B Side) | Yr | NM |
|---|---|---|---|
| ❑ DLP-3419 [M] | Surfer's Stomp | 1962 | 30.00 |
| ❑ DLP-3431 [M] | His Greatest Hits | 1962 | 12.00 |
| ❑ DLP-3470 [M] | Great Themes of Famous Bands and Famous Singers | 1962 | 12.00 |
| ❑ DLP-3548 [M] | Great Gospels — Great Hymns | 1963 | 12.00 |
| ❑ DLP-3584 [M] | His Greatest Hits, Volume 2 | 1964 | 12.00 |
| ❑ DLP-25419 [S] | Surfer's Stomp | 1962 | 40.00 |
| ❑ DLP-25431 [S] | His Greatest Hits | 1962 | 15.00 |
| ❑ DLP-25470 [S] | Great Themes of Famous Bands and Famous Singers | 1962 | 15.00 |
| ❑ DLP-25548 [S] | Great Gospels — Great Hymns | 1963 | 15.00 |
| ❑ DLP-25584 [S] | His Greatest Hits, Volume 2 | 1964 | 15.00 |

HAMILTON

| Number | Title (A Side/B Side) | Yr | NM |
|---|---|---|---|
| ❑ HLP-137 [M] | Racing with the Moon | 1965 | 10.00 |
| ❑ HLP-12137 [S] | Racing with the Moon | 1965 | 12.00 |

RCA CAMDEN

| Number | Title (A Side/B Side) | Yr | NM |
|---|---|---|---|
| ❑ CAL-329 [M] | Dance with Me | 1956 | 20.00 |
| ❑ CAL-354 [M] | Dreamland Special | 1956 | 20.00 |

RCA VICTOR

| Number | Title (A Side/B Side) | Yr | NM |
|---|---|---|---|
| ❑ LPM-13 [10] | Vaughn Monroe Plays Victor Herbert for Dancing | 1952 | 40.00 |
| ❑ ANL1-1140 | The Best of Vaughn Monroe | 1976 | 8.00 |
| ❑ LPM-1493 [M] | House Party | 1957 | 30.00 |
| ❑ LPM-1799 [M] | There I Sing, Swing It Again | 1958 | 20.00 |
| ❑ LSP-1799 [S] | There I Sing, Swing It Again | 1958 | 30.00 |
| ❑ LPM-3048 [10] | Vaughn Monroe Caravan | 1952 | 40.00 |
| ❑ LPM-3817 [M] | The Best of Vaughn Monroe | 1967 | 20.00 |
| ❑ LSP-3817 [R] | The Best of Vaughn Monroe | 1967 | 12.00 |
| ❑ VPM-6073 [(2)] | This Is Vaughn Monroe | 1972 | 15.00 |

| Number | Title (A Side/B Side) | Yr | NM |
|---|---|---|---|

**MONROES, THE**

ALFA

| | | | |
|---|---|---|---|
| ❑ AAE-15015 [EP] | The Monroes | 1982 | 20.00 |

**MONTAGE**

LAURIE

| | | | |
|---|---|---|---|
| ❑ SLP-2049 | Montage | 1969 | 20.00 |

**MONTANA, PATSY**

SIMS

| | | | |
|---|---|---|---|
| ❑ 122 [M] | The New Sound of Patsy Montana | 1964 | 50.00 |

STARDAY

| | | | |
|---|---|---|---|
| ❑ SLP-376 [M] | Cowboy's Sweetheart | 1966 | 30.00 |

**MONTANA SLIM**

DECCA

| | | | |
|---|---|---|---|
| ❑ DL 4092 [M] | The Dynamite Trail | 1960 | 50.00 |
| ❑ DL 8917 [M] | I'm Ragged But I'm Right | 1959 | 60.00 |
| ❑ DL 74092 [S] | The Dynamite Trail | 1960 | 60.00 |

RCA CAMDEN

| | | | |
|---|---|---|---|
| ❑ CAL-527 [M] | Wilf Carter/Montana Slim | 1958 | 40.00 |
| ❑ CAL-668 [M] | Reminiscin' with Montana Slim | 1962 | 25.00 |
| ❑ CAL-846 [M] | 32 Wonderful Years | 1965 | 20.00 |
| ❑ CAS-846 [R] | 32 Wonderful Years | 1965 | 12.00 |

STARDAY

| | | | |
|---|---|---|---|
| ❑ SLP-300 [M] | Wilf Carter As Montana Slim | 1964 | 30.00 |
| ❑ SLP-389 [M] | Wilf Carter | 1966 | 30.00 |

**MONTE, LOU**

RCA CAMDEN

| | | | |
|---|---|---|---|
| ❑ CAL-455 [M] | Here's Lou Monte | 195? | 12.00 |

RCA VICTOR

| | | | |
|---|---|---|---|
| ❑ LPM-1651 [M] | Lou Monte Sings for You | 1957 | 25.00 |
| ❑ LPM-1877 [M] | Songs for Pizza Lovers | 1958 | 25.00 |
| ❑ LPM-1976 [M] | Italian House Party | 1959 | 20.00 |
| ❑ LSP-1976 [S] | Italian House Party | 1959 | 25.00 |
| ❑ LPM-3672 [M] | The Best of Lou Monte | 1966 | 15.00 |
| ❑ LSP-3672 [S] | The Best of Lou Monte | 1966 | 12.00 |
| ❑ LPM-3705 [M] | Good Time Songs | 1967 | 15.00 |
| ❑ LSP-3705 [S] | Good Time Songs | 1967 | 12.00 |

REPRISE

| | | | |
|---|---|---|---|
| ❑ R-6005 [M] | Great Italian-American Hits | 1961 | 20.00 |
| ❑ R9-6005 [S] | Great Italian-American Hits | 1961 | 25.00 |
| ❑ R-6014 [M] | Live in Person | 1961 | 20.00 |
| ❑ R9-6014 [S] | Live in Person | 1961 | 25.00 |
| ❑ R-6058 [M] | Pepino The Italian Mouse & Other Italian Fun Songs | 1962 | 20.00 |
| ❑ R9-6058 [S] | Pepino The Italian Mouse & Other Italian Fun Songs | 1962 | 25.00 |
| ❑ R-6099 [M] | More Italian Fun Songs | 1963 | 20.00 |
| ❑ R9-6099 [S] | More Italian Fun Songs | 1963 | 25.00 |
| ❑ R-6118 [M] | The Golden Hits of Lou Monte | 1964 | 15.00 |
| ❑ RS-6118 [S] | The Golden Hits of Lou Monte | 1964 | 20.00 |

ROULETTE

| | | | |
|---|---|---|---|
| ❑ R-25126 [M] | Italiano U.S.A. | 1960 | 20.00 |
| ❑ SR-25126 [S] | Italiano U.S.A. | 1960 | 25.00 |
| ❑ R-25257 [M] | The Magic World of Italy | 1963 | 15.00 |
| ❑ SR-25257 [S] | The Magic World of Italy | 1963 | 20.00 |

**MONTEGO JOE**

ESP-DISK'

| | | | |
|---|---|---|---|
| ❑ S-1067 | Montego Joe's HARYOU Percussion Ensemble | 1968 | 25.00 |

PRESTIGE

| | | | |
|---|---|---|---|
| ❑ PRLP-7336 [M] | Arriba Con Montego Joe | 1964 | 25.00 |
| ❑ PRST-7336 [S] | Arriba Con Montego Joe | 1964 | 30.00 |
| ❑ PRLP-7413 [M] | Wild and Warm | 1966 | 25.00 |
| ❑ PRST-7413 [S] | Wild and Warm | 1966 | 30.00 |

**MONTENEGRO, HUGO** Includes some of his soundtracks; others are in the "Soundtracks" and "Television Albums" sections.

BAINBRIDGE

| | | | |
|---|---|---|---|
| ❑ 1002 | American Musical Theatre, Volume 1 (1924-1935) | 198? | 8.00 |
| ❑ 1003 | American Musical Theatre, Volume 2 (1935-1945) | 198? | 8.00 |
| ❑ 1004 | American Musical Theatre, Volume 3 (1946-1952) | 198? | 8.00 |
| ❑ 1005 | American Musical Theatre, Volume 4 (1953-1960) | 198? | 8.00 |
| ❑ 1009 | Big Band Boogie | 198? | 8.00 |
| ❑ 1021 | Camelot | 198? | 8.00 |
| ❑ 1028 | Hugo Montenegro Plays the Movies | 198? | 8.00 |

GWP

| | | | |
|---|---|---|---|
| ❑ 2003 | The Dawn of Dylan | 1971 | 15.00 |

MAINSTREAM

| | | | |
|---|---|---|---|
| ❑ S-6101 [S] | Camelot | 1967 | 12.00 |
| ❑ 56101 [M] | Camelot | 1967 | 15.00 |

RCA CAMDEN

| | | | |
|---|---|---|---|
| ❑ CAL-729 [M] | In a Sentimental Mood | 196? | 12.00 |
| ❑ CAS-729 [S] | In a Sentimental Mood | 196? | 12.00 |
| ❑ CAS-2309 | Hawaiian Wedding Song | 1969 | 10.00 |

RCA VICTOR

| | | | |
|---|---|---|---|
| ❑ ARD1-0001 [Q] | Love Theme from "The Godfather" | 1972 | 12.00 |
| ❑ APD1-0025 [Q] | Scenes and Themes | 1973 | 20.00 |
| ❑ ARD1-0132 [Q] | Neil's Diamonds | 1973 | 15.00 |
| ❑ APL1-0413 | Hugo in Wonderland | 1974 | 12.00 |
| ❑ ARD1-0413 [Q] | Hugo in Wonderland | 1974 | 15.00 |
| ❑ ARD1-0784 [Q] | Others by Brothers | 1974 | 15.00 |
| ❑ APD1-1024 [Q] | Rocket Man | 1975 | 20.00 |
| ❑ APL1-1024 | Rocket Man | 1975 | 12.00 |
| ❑ ANL1-1094 | Music from A Fistful of Dollars & For a Few Dollars More & The Good, The Bad and The Ugly | 1975 | 10.00 |
| ❑ ANL1-2348 | The Neil Diamond Songbook | 1977 | 10.00 |
| ❑ LPM-2958 [M] | The Young Beat of Rome | 1964 | 12.00 |
| ❑ LSP-2958 [S] | The Young Beat of Rome | 1964 | 15.00 |
| ❑ LPM-3540 [M] | Come Spy with Me | 1966 | 12.00 |
| ❑ LSP-3540 [S] | Come Spy with Me | 1966 | 15.00 |
| ❑ LPM-3927 [M] | Music from A Fistful of Dollars & For a Few Dollars More & The Good, The Bad and The Ugly | 1968 | 20.00 |
| ❑ LSP-3927 [S] | Music from A Fistful of Dollars & For a Few Dollars More & The Good, The Bad and The Ugly | 1968 | 15.00 |
| ❑ LPM-4022 [M] | Hang 'Em High | 1968 | 40.00 |
| ❑ LSP-4022 [S] | Hang 'Em High | 1968 | 15.00 |
| ❑ LSP-4104 | Good Vibrations | 1969 | 15.00 |
| ❑ LSP-4170 | Moog Power | 1969 | 20.00 |
| ❑ LSP-4273 | Colours of Love | 1970 | 12.00 |
| ❑ AFL1-4361 | The Best of Hugo Montenegro | 1977 | 10.00 |
| ❑ LSP-4361 | The Best of Hugo Montenegro | 1970 | 12.00 |
| ❑ LSP-4537 | People…One to One | 1971 | 12.00 |
| ❑ LSP-4631 | Mammy Blue | 1971 | 12.00 |
| ❑ VPS-6036 [(2)] | This Is Hugo Montenegro | 1971 | 15.00 |

TIME

| | | | |
|---|---|---|---|
| ❑ S-2018 [S] | Cha Chas for Dancing | 196? | 20.00 |
| ❑ S-2020 [S] | Boogie Woogie and Bongos | 196? | 20.00 |
| ❑ S-2030 [S] | Arriba | 196? | 20.00 |
| ❑ S-2035 [S] | American Musical Theatre, Volume 1 (1924-1935) | 196? | 15.00 |
| ❑ S-2036 [S] | American Musical Theatre, Volume 2 (1935-1945) | 196? | 15.00 |
| ❑ S-2037 [S] | American Musical Theatre, Volume 3 (1946-1952) | 1961 | 15.00 |
| ❑ S-2038 [S] | American Musical Theatre, Volume 4 (1953-1960) | 1961 | 15.00 |
| ❑ S-2044 [S] | Great Songs from Motion Pictures Vol. 1 (1927-1937) | 1961 | 15.00 |
| ❑ S-2045 [S] | Great Songs from Motion Pictures Vol. 2 (1938-1944) | 1961 | 15.00 |
| ❑ S-2046 [S] | Great Songs from Motion Pictures Vol. 3 (1945-1960) | 1961 | 15.00 |
| ❑ S-2051 [S] | Montenegro in Italy | 196? | 15.00 |
| ❑ TDM 3003 [(2)M] | Italy - Ciao | 196? | 15.00 |
| ❑ TDS 3003 [(2)S] | Italy - Ciao | 196? | 20.00 |
| ❑ 52018 [M] | Cha Chas for Dancing | 196? | 15.00 |
| ❑ 52020 [M] | Boogie Woogie and Bongos | 196? | 15.00 |
| ❑ 52030 [M] | Arriba | 196? | 15.00 |
| ❑ 52035 [M] | American Musical Theatre, Volume 1 (1924-1935) | 196? | 12.00 |
| ❑ 52036 [M] | American Musical Theatre, Volume 2 (1935-1945) | 196? | 12.00 |
| ❑ 52037 [M] | American Musical Theatre, Volume 3 (1946-1952) | 1961 | 12.00 |
| ❑ 52038 [M] | American Musical Theatre, Volume 4 (1953-1960) | 1961 | 12.00 |
| ❑ 52044 [M] | Great Songs from Motion Pictures Vol. 1 (1927-1937) | 1961 | 12.00 |
| ❑ 52045 [M] | Great Songs from Motion Pictures Vol. 2 (1938-1944) | 1961 | 12.00 |
| ❑ 52046 [M] | Great Songs from Motion Pictures Vol. 3 (1945-1960) | 1961 | 12.00 |
| ❑ 52051 [M] | Montenegro in Italy | 196? | 12.00 |

20TH CENTURY FOX

| | | | |
|---|---|---|---|
| ❑ S-4204 | Lady in Cement | 1968 | 20.00 |

20TH FOX

| | | | |
|---|---|---|---|
| ❑ 3018 [M] | The 20th Century Strings, Volume 1 | 1959 | 20.00 |

VIK

| | | | |
|---|---|---|---|
| ❑ LX-1089 [M] | Loves of My Life | 1957 | 25.00 |
| ❑ LX-1106 [M] | Ellington Fantasy | 1957 | 25.00 |

**MONTEROSE, J.R.**

BLUE NOTE

| | | | |
|---|---|---|---|
| ❑ BLP-1536 [M] | J.R. Monterose | 1956 | 400.00 |

*—"Deep groove" version, W. 63rd St. address on label*

| | | | |
|---|---|---|---|
| ❑ BLP-1536 [M] | J.R. Monterose | 1956 | 600.00 |

*—"Deep groove" version; Lexington Ave. address on label*

| | | | |
|---|---|---|---|
| ❑ BLP-1536 [M] | J.R. Monterose | 1963 | 50.00 |

*—With "New York, USA" address on label*

| | | | |
|---|---|---|---|
| ❑ BLP-1536 [M] | J.R. Monterose | 2003 | 30.00 |

*—200-gram reissue; distributed by Classic Records*

JARO

| | | | |
|---|---|---|---|
| ❑ JAM-5004 [M] | The Message | 1959 | 800.00 |
| ❑ JAS-8004 [S] | The Message | 1959 | 1000. |

STUDIO 4

| | | | |
|---|---|---|---|
| ❑ 100 [M] | J.R. Monterose in Action | 195? | 1500. |

**MONTEZ, CHRIS**

A&M

| | | | |
|---|---|---|---|
| ❑ LP-115 [M] | The More I See You/Call Me | 1966 | 20.00 |
| ❑ LP-120 [M] | Time After Time | 1966 | 15.00 |
| ❑ LP-128 [M] | Foolin' Around | 1967 | 15.00 |
| ❑ LP-157 [M] | Watch What Happens | 1967 | 15.00 |
| ❑ ST-4115 [S] | The More I See You/Call Me | 1966 | 25.00 |
| ❑ SP-4120 [S] | Time After Time | 1966 | 20.00 |
| ❑ SP-4128 [S] | Foolin' Around | 1967 | 20.00 |
| ❑ SP-4157 [S] | Watch What Happens | 1967 | 20.00 |

MONOGRAM

| | | | |
|---|---|---|---|
| ❑ M-100 [M] | Let's Dance and Have Some Kinda' Fun!!! | 1963 | 400.00 |

**MONTGOMERY, BUDDY**

ABC IMPULSE!

| | | | |
|---|---|---|---|
| ❑ AS-9192 | This Rather Than That | 1970 | 20.00 |

MILESTONE

| | | | |
|---|---|---|---|
| ❑ M-9015 | Two-Sided Album | 1969 | 20.00 |

**MONTGOMERY, DAVID, AND CECIL LYTLE**

SONIC ARTS

| | | | |
|---|---|---|---|
| ❑ 6 | Ragtime Piano for Four Hands | 197? | 20.00 |

*—Direct-to-disc recording*

**MONTGOMERY, LITTLE BROTHER**

BLUESVILLE

| | | | |
|---|---|---|---|
| ❑ BVLP-1012 [M] | Tasty Blues | 1961 | 80.00 |

*—Blue label, silver print*

| | | | |
|---|---|---|---|
| ❑ BVLP-1012 [M] | Tasty Blues | 1964 | 30.00 |

*—Blue label with trident logo at right*

RIVERSIDE

| | | | |
|---|---|---|---|
| ❑ RLP-410 [M] | Little Brother Montgomery, Chicago Living Legend | 1962 | 30.00 |
| ❑ RS-9410 [S] | Little Brother Montgomery, Chicago Living Legend | 1962 | 40.00 |

**MONTGOMERY, MARIAN**

CAPITOL

| | | | |
|---|---|---|---|
| ❑ ST 1884 [S] | Marian Montgomery Swings for Winners and Losers | 1963 | 30.00 |
| ❑ T 1884 [M] | Marian Montgomery Swings for Winners and Losers | 1963 | 25.00 |
| ❑ ST 1962 [S] | Let There Be Love, Let There Be Swing, Let There Be Marian Montgomery | 1963 | 30.00 |
| ❑ T 1962 [M] | Let There Be Love, Let There Be Swing, Let There Be Marian Montgomery | 1963 | 25.00 |
| ❑ ST 2185 [S] | Lovin' Is Livin' | 1964 | 30.00 |
| ❑ T 2185 [M] | Lovin' Is Livin' | 1964 | 25.00 |

DECCA

| | | | |
|---|---|---|---|
| ❑ DL 4773 [M] | What's New? | 1965 | 20.00 |
| ❑ DL 74773 [S] | What's New? | 1965 | 25.00 |

**MONTGOMERY, MELBA** Also see GEORGE JONES AND MELBA MONTGOMERY.

CAPITOL

| | | | |
|---|---|---|---|
| ❑ ST-328 | The Big, Wonderful Country World of Melba Montgomery | 1969 | 15.00 |

*—This is the title on the cover; the label calls this "The Big, Beautiful Country World of Melba Montgomery"*

| | | | |
|---|---|---|---|
| ❑ ST-468 | Don't Keep Me Lonely Too Long | 1970 | 15.00 |

ELEKTRA

| | | | |
|---|---|---|---|
| ❑ CM-2 | Don't Let the Good Times Fool You | 1975 | 10.00 |
| ❑ CM-6 | The Greatest Gift of All | 1975 | 10.00 |
| ❑ EKS-75069 | Melba Montgomery | 1973 | 12.00 |
| ❑ EKS-75079 | No Charge | 1974 | 10.00 |

HILLTOP

| | | | |
|---|---|---|---|
| ❑ JS-6031 | Miss Country Music | 196? | 12.00 |

MUSICOR

| | | | |
|---|---|---|---|
| ❑ MM-2074 [M] | Country Girl | 1966 | 15.00 |
| ❑ MM-2097 [M] | The Hallelujah Road | 1966 | 15.00 |
| ❑ MM-2113 [M] | Melba Toast | 1967 | 20.00 |
| ❑ MM-2114 [M] | Don't Keep Me Lonely Too Long | 1967 | 20.00 |
| ❑ MS-3074 [S] | Country Girl | 1966 | 20.00 |
| ❑ MS-3097 [S] | The Hallelujah Road | 1966 | 20.00 |
| ❑ MS-3113 [S] | Melba Toast | 1967 | 20.00 |
| ❑ MS-3114 [S] | Don't Keep Me Lonely Too Long | 1967 | 20.00 |

STARDAY

| | | | |
|---|---|---|---|
| ❑ SLP-352 [M] | Queen of Country Music | 1965 | 25.00 |

UNITED ARTISTS

| | | | |
|---|---|---|---|
| ❑ UAL-3341 [M] | America's Number One Country and Western Girl Singer | 1964 | 20.00 |
| ❑ UAL-3369 [M] | Down Home | 1964 | 20.00 |
| ❑ UAL-3391 [M] | I Can't Get Used to Being Lonely | 1965 | 20.00 |

Number | Title (A Side/B Side) | Yr | NM

❑ UAS-6341 [S] America's Number One Country and Western Girl Singer 1964 25.00
❑ UAS-6369 [S] Down Home 1964 25.00
❑ UAS-6391 [S] I Can't Get Used to Being Lonely 1965 25.00

**MONTGOMERY, MONK**

CHISA
❑ CS-801 It's Never Too Late 1970 20.00
❑ CS-806 Bass Odyssey 1971 20.00

**MONTGOMERY, WES**

A&M
❑ LP-2001 [M] A Day in the Life 1967 20.00

DCC COMPACT CLASSICS
❑ LPZ-2014 Goin' Out of My Head 1996 40.00
*—Audiophile vinyl*

MOBILE FIDELITY
❑ MFSL-508 Bumpin' 198? 40.00
*—"Original Master Recording" at top of cover*

PACIFIC JAZZ
❑ PJ-5 [M] Montgomeryland 1960 30.00
❑ ST-5 [S] Montgomeryland 1960 40.00
❑ PJ-10130 [M] Kismet 1967 20.00
❑ ST-20104 [S] Easy Groove 1966 20.00

RIVERSIDE
❑ RLP 12-310 [M] A Dynamic New Sound 1959 80.00
❑ RLP 12-320 [M] The Incredible Jazz Guitar of Wes Montgomery 1960 60.00
❑ RLP-342 [M] Movin' Along 1960 25.00
❑ RLP-382 [M] So Much Guitar! 1961 25.00
❑ RLP-434 [M] Full House 1962 30.00
❑ RLP-459 [M] Boss Guitar 1963 80.00
❑ RLP-472 [M] Fusion! Wes Montgomery with Strings 1964 20.00
❑ RLP 1156 [S] New Concepts in Jazz Guitar 1959 30.00
❑ RLP 1169 [S] The Incredible Jazz Guitar of Wes Montgomery 1960 30.00
❑ RS-9342 [S] Movin' Along 1960 25.00
❑ RS-9382 [S] So Much Guitar! 1961 25.00
❑ RS-9434 [S] Full House 1962 30.00
❑ RS-9459 [S] Boss Guitar 1963 25.00
❑ RS-9472 [S] Fusion! Wes Montgomery with Strings 1964 25.00
❑ RS-9492 [S] Portrait of Wes 1965 20.00
❑ RS-9494 [S] Guitar on the Go 1965 20.00

VERVE
❑ V6-8610 [S] Movin' Wes 1965 20.00
❑ V6-8625 [S] Bumpin' 1965 20.00
❑ V6-8642 [S] Goin' Out of My Head 1966 20.00
❑ V6-8653 [S] Tequila 1966 20.00
❑ V-8672 [M] California Dreaming 1967 20.00
❑ V-8714 [M] The Best of Wes Montgomery 1967 20.00

**MONTGOMERY BROTHERS, THE**

FANTASY
❑ 3308 [M] The Montgomery Brothers 1960 30.00
*—Black vinyl*
❑ 3308 [M] The Montgomery Brothers 1960 50.00
*—Red vinyl*
❑ 3323 [M] The Montgomery Brothers in Canada 1961 30.00
*—Black vinyl*
❑ 3323 [M] The Montgomery Brothers in Canada 1961 50.00
*—Red vinyl*
❑ 3376 [M] Wes' Best 1967 20.00
❑ 8052 [S] The Montgomery Brothers 1960 25.00
*—Black vinyl*
❑ 8052 [S] The Montgomery Brothers 1960 40.00
*—Blue vinyl*
❑ 8066 [S] The Montgomery Brothers in Canada 1961 25.00
*—Black vinyl*
❑ 8066 [S] The Montgomery Brothers in Canada 1961 40.00
*—Blue vinyl*

PACIFIC JAZZ
❑ PJ-17 [M] Wes, Buddy and Monk Montgomery 1961 30.00

RIVERSIDE
❑ RLP-362 [M] Groove Yard 1961 25.00
❑ RS-9362 [S] Groove Yard 1961 30.00

WORLD PACIFIC
❑ PJ-1240 [M] The Montgomery Brothers and Five Others 1957 80.00
❑ WP-1240 [M] The Montgomery Brothers and Five Others 1958 60.00
*—Reissue with new prefix*

**MONTROSE, JACK**

ATLANTIC
❑ 1223 [M] Arranged, Played, Composed by Jack Montrose with Bob Gordon 1956 80.00
*—Black label*

Number | Title (A Side/B Side) | Yr | NM

❑ 1223 [M] Arranged, Played, Composed by Jack Montrose with Bob Gordon 1961 25.00
*—Multicolor label, white "fan" logo at right*

PACIFIC JAZZ
❑ PJ-1208 [M] Jack Montrose Sextet 1955 80.00
*—Black vinyl*
❑ PJ-1208 [M] Jack Montrose Sextet 1955 150.00
*—Red vinyl*

RCA VICTOR
❑ LPM-1451 [M] Blues and Vanilla 1957 50.00
❑ LPM-1572 [M] The Horns Full 1957 50.00

WORLD PACIFIC
❑ WP-1208 [M] Jack Montrose Sextet 1958 50.00

**MONTY PYTHON**

ARISTA
❑ SP-101 [DJ] Monty Python's Contractural Obligation Sampler 1980 30.00
*—One side is censored, the other is uncensored*
❑ AL 4039 Matching Tie & Handkerchief 1975 20.00
*—Side 2 is "trick tracked," with two different routines depending on where you place the needle at the start*
❑ AL 4050 The Album of the Soundtrack of the Trailer of the Film of "Monty Python and the Holy Grail" 1975 20.00
❑ AL 4073 Monty Python Live! At City Center 1976 20.00
❑ AL 8296 The Monty Python Instant Record Collection 198? 8.00
*—Reissue*
❑ AL 8343 Monty Python's Contractual Obligation Album 198? 8.00
*—Reissue*
❑ AL 8353 Monty Python Live! At City Center 198? 8.00
*—Reissue*
❑ AL 8355 The Album of the Soundtrack of the Trailer of the Film of "Monty Python and the Holy Grail" 198? 8.00
*—Reissue*
❑ AL 8357 Matching Tie and Handkerchief 198? 8.00
*—Reissue; we don't know whether Side 2 maintains the trick groove on this issue*
❑ AB 9536 Monty Python's Contractual Obligation Album 1980 20.00
❑ AB 9580 The Monty Python Instant Record Collection 1981 15.00

BBC
❑ 22073 Monty Python's Flying Circus 1980 20.00
*—Excerpts from TV shows; pressed by Columbia, possibly for exclusive use by the record club*

BUDDAH
❑ BDS 5656 [(2)] The Worst of Monty Python 1976 20.00
*—Repackage of the two Charisma LPs*

CHARISMA
❑ CAS 1049 Another Monty Python Record 1972 25.00
❑ CAS 1063 Monty Python's Previous Record 1972 25.00

MCA
❑ 6121 Monty Python and the Meaning of Life 1983 12.00

PYE
❑ 12116 Monty Python's Flying Circus 1975 20.00

VIRGIN
❑ 90865 [(2)] The Final Rip Off 1988 20.00

WARNER BROS.
❑ BSK 3396 Life of Brian 1979 15.00

**MOODY, CLYDE**

KING
❑ 891 [M] The Best of Clyde Moody 1964 80.00

OLD HOMESTEAD
❑ 90013 Moody's Blues — Bluesy Bluegrass 197? 15.00

**MOODY, JAMES**

ARGO
❑ LP-603 [M] Flute 'n the Blues 1956 40.00
*—Reissue of Creative 603*
❑ LP-613 [M] Moody's Mood for Love 1957 40.00
❑ LP-637 [M] Last Train from Overbrook 1959 40.00
❑ LPS-637 [S] Last Train from Overbrook 1959 30.00
❑ LP-648 [M] James Moody 1959 40.00
❑ LPS-648 [S] James Moody 1959 30.00
❑ LP-666 [M] Hey! It's James Moody 1960 30.00
❑ LPS-666 [S] Hey! It's James Moody 1960 40.00
❑ LP-679 [M] Moody with Strings 1961 30.00
❑ LPS-679 [S] Moody with Strings 1961 40.00
❑ LP-695 [M] Another Bag 1962 30.00
❑ LPS-695 [S] Another Bag 1962 40.00
❑ LP-725 [M] Great Day 1963 25.00
❑ LPS-725 [S] Great Day 1963 30.00

Number | Title (A Side/B Side) | Yr | NM

❑ LP-740 [M] Comin' On Strong 1964 25.00
❑ LPS-740 [S] Comin' On Strong 1964 30.00

BLUE NOTE
❑ BLP-5005 [10] James Moody with Strings 1952 300.00
❑ BLP-5006 [10] James Moody and His Modernists 1952 300.00

CADET
❑ LP-756 [M] Cookin' the Blues 1965 20.00
❑ LPS-756 [S] Cookin' the Blues 1965 25.00
❑ 2CA-60010 [(2)] Everything About Sax and Flute 1972 20.00

CREATIVE
❑ LP-603 [M] Flute 'n Blues 1956 150.00

DIAL
❑ LP-209 [10] James Moody, His Saxophone and His Band 1950 400.00

EMARCY
❑ MG-26004 [10] The Moody Story 1954 150.00
❑ MG-26040 [10] Moodsville 1954 150.00
❑ MG-36031 [M] The Moody Story 1955 100.00

MILESTONE
❑ M-9005 Brass Figures 1968 20.00
❑ M-9023 Blues and Other Colors 1970 20.00

PRESTIGE
❑ PRLP-110 [10] James Moody Favorites, No. 1 1951 200.00
❑ PRLP-125 [10] James Moody Favorites, No. 2 1952 200.00
❑ PRLP-146 [10] James Moody Favorites, No. 3 1953 200.00
❑ PRLP-157 [10] Moody in France 1953 150.00
❑ PRLP-192 [10] Moody's Mood 1954 150.00
❑ PRLP-198 [10] James Moody and His Band 1954 150.00
❑ PRLP-7011 [M] Hi-Fi Party 1955 100.00
❑ PRLP-7036 [M] Wail, Moody, Wail 1956 100.00
❑ PRLP-7056 [M] James Moody's Moods 1956 100.00
❑ PRLP-7072 [M] Moody 1956 100.00
❑ PRLP-7179 [M] Moody's Workshop 1960 50.00
❑ PRLP-7431 [M] James Moody's Greatest Hits 1967 25.00
❑ PRLP-7441 [M] James Moody's Greatest Hits, Volume 2 1967 25.00

ROOST
❑ RST-405 [10] James Moody in France 1951 250.00

SCEPTER
❑ SPS-525 [S] Running the Gamut 1965 25.00
❑ SRM-525 [M] Running the Gamut 1965 20.00

**MOODY, JAMES/GEORGE WALLINGTON**

BLUE NOTE
❑ B-6503 [M] The Beginning and End of Bop 1969 30.00

**MOODY, PHIL**

SOMERSET
❑ P-10400 [M] Intimate Jazz 1959 30.00

**MOODY BLUES, THE** Also see JUSTIN HAYWARD AND JOHN LODGE; RAY THOMAS.

COMPLEAT
❑ 672008 [(2)] Early Blues 1985 15.00
*—Reissue of London 1964-66 material*

DERAM
❑ DE 16012 [M] Days of Future Passed 1968 250.00
❑ DES 18012 [S] Days of Future Passed 1968 20.00
*—With large "DERAM" on top half of label*
❑ DES 18012 [S] Days of Future Passed 1968 30.00
*—With "LONDON" under "DERAM" on top half of label*
❑ DES 18017 In Search of the Lost Chord 1968 20.00
*—Originals have gatefold covers*
❑ DES 18025 On the Threshold of a Dream 1969 20.00
*—Originals have gatefold covers and lyric booklet*
❑ DES 18051 [R] In the Beginning 1971 20.00
❑ 820006-1 [S] Days of Future Passed 1985 8.00
❑ 820168-1 In Search of the Lost Chord 1985 8.00
❑ 820170-1 On the Threshold of a Dream 1985 8.00

LONDON
❑ PS 428 [R] Go Now — The Moody Blues #1 1965 40.00
❑ PS 690/1 [(2)] Caught Live + 5 1977 12.00
❑ PS 708 Octave 1978 10.00
❑ PS 708 [DJ] Octave 1978 30.00
*—Promo only on blue vinyl*
❑ LL 3428 [M] Go Now — The Moody Blues #1 1965 50.00
❑ 820161-1 [(2)] Caught Live + 5 1985 8.00
❑ 820329-1 Octave 1986 8.00

MOBILE FIDELITY
❑ 1-042 Days of Future Passed 1980 60.00
*—Audiophile vinyl*
❑ 1-151 Seventh Sojourn 1984 70.00
*—Audiophile vinyl*
❑ 1-215 On the Threshold of a Dream 1994 25.00
*—Audiophile vinyl*
❑ 1-232 Every Good Boy Deserves Favour 1995 25.00
*—Audiophile vinyl*
❑ 1-253 To Our Children's Children's Children 1996 60.00
*—Audiophile vinyl*

STEREO DES 18012
DAYS OF FUTURE PASSED
THE MOODY BLUES
WITH
THE LONDON FESTIVAL ORCHESTRA
conducted by PETER KNIGHT

INCLUDING
NIGHTS IN
WHITE SATIN

DERAM
LONDON

THE DAY BEGINS • DAWN: Dawn is a feeling • THE MORNING: Another morning • LUNCH BREAK: Peak hour
THE AFTERNOON: Forever afternoon (Tuesday?) • EVENING: The sun set: Twilight time • THE NIGHT: Nights in white satin

The Moody Blues, *Days of Future Passed,* Deram DES 18012, 1968, stereo, $20.

| Number | Title (A Side/B Side) | Yr | NM |
|---|---|---|---|
| **NAUTILUS** | | | |
| ❑ NR-21 | On the Threshold of a Dream | 1981 | 50.00 |
| *—Audiophile vinyl; DBX-encoded version* | | | |
| ❑ NR-21 | On the Threshold of a Dream | 1981 | 60.00 |
| *—Audiophile vinyl* | | | |
| **POLYDOR** | | | |
| ❑ 829 179-1 | The Other Side of Life | 1986 | 10.00 |
| ❑ 835 756-1 | Sur La Mer | 1988 | 12.00 |
| ❑ 840 659-1 | Greatest Hits (1967-1988) | 1989 | 15.00 |
| **THRESHOLD** | | | |
| ❑ THS 1 | To Our Children's Children's Children | 1969 | 15.00 |
| *—White label with purple logo; gatefold cover* | | | |
| ❑ THS 1 | To Our Children's Children's Children | 197? | 10.00 |
| *—Blue label; no gatefold* | | | |
| ❑ THS 3 | A Question of Balance | 197? | 10.00 |
| *—Blue label; no gatefold* | | | |
| ❑ THS 3 | A Question of Balance | 1970 | 15.00 |
| *—White label with purple logo; gatefold cover* | | | |
| ❑ THS 5 | Every Good Boy Deserves Favour | 197? | 10.00 |
| *—Blue label; no gatefold* | | | |
| ❑ THS 5 | Every Good Boy Deserves Favour | 197? | 12.00 |
| *—Blue label; gatefold cover* | | | |
| ❑ THS 5 | Every Good Boy Deserves Favour | 1971 | 15.00 |
| *—White label with purple logo; gatefold cover* | | | |
| ❑ THS 7 | Seventh Sojourn | 197? | 10.00 |
| *—Blue label; no gatefold* | | | |
| ❑ THS 7 | Seventh Sojourn | 197? | 12.00 |
| *—Blue label; gatefold cover* | | | |
| ❑ THS 7 | Seventh Sojourn | 1972 | 15.00 |
| *—White label with purple logo; gatefold cover* | | | |
| ❑ THS 12/13 [(2)] | This Is the Moody Blues | 1974 | 15.00 |
| ❑ THX-100 [DJ] | Special Interview Kit | 1971 | 150.00 |
| *—Includes script* | | | |
| ❑ TR-1-2901 | Long Distance Voyager | 1981 | 10.00 |
| ❑ TR-1-2902 | The Present | 1982 | 10.00 |
| ❑ SMAS-93329 | A Question of Balance | 1971 | 20.00 |
| *—Capitol Record Club edition* | | | |
| ❑ 810119-1 | The Present | 1983 | 8.00 |
| ❑ 820007-1 [(2)] | This Is the Moody Blues | 1985 | 8.00 |
| ❑ 820105-1 | Long Distance Voyager | 1985 | 8.00 |
| ❑ 820155-1 | Voices in the Sky/The Best of the Moody Blues | 1985 | 10.00 |
| ❑ 820159-1 | Seventh Sojourn | 1985 | 8.00 |
| ❑ 820160-1 | Every Good Boy Deserves Favour | 1985 | 8.00 |
| ❑ 820211-1 | A Question of Balance | 1985 | 8.00 |

## MOOG MACHINE, THE

| Number | Title (A Side/B Side) | Yr | NM |
|---|---|---|---|
| **COLUMBIA** | | | |
| ❑ CS 9921 | Switched-On Rock | 1969 | 20.00 |
| ❑ CS 9959 | Christmas Becomes Electric | 1969 | 20.00 |

## MOON, KEITH

Also see THE WHO.

| Number | Title (A Side/B Side) | Yr | NM |
|---|---|---|---|
| **TRACK/MCA** | | | |
| ❑ 2136 | Two Sides of the Moon | 1975 | 40.00 |

## MOON, THE

| Number | Title (A Side/B Side) | Yr | NM |
|---|---|---|---|
| **IMPERIAL** | | | |
| ❑ LP-12381 | Without Earth | 1968 | 40.00 |
| ❑ LP-12444 | The Moon | 1969 | 40.00 |

## MOONDOG

| Number | Title (A Side/B Side) | Yr | NM |
|---|---|---|---|
| **COLUMBIA** | | | |
| ❑ KC 30897 | Moondog 2 | 1971 | 50.00 |
| *—With booklet (deduct 20 percent if missing)* | | | |
| **COLUMBIA MASTERWORKS** | | | |
| ❑ MS 7335 | Moondog | 1969 | 30.00 |
| *—Gray label with "360 Sound Stereo" at bottom* | | | |
| ❑ MS 7335 | Moondog | 2001 | 12.00 |
| *—180-gram reissue* | | | |
| **EPIC** | | | |
| ❑ LG 1002 [10] | Moondog and His Friends | 1954 | 300.00 |
| **FANTASY** | | | |
| ❑ OJC-1741 | Moondog | 1990 | 15.00 |
| **MOONDOG** | | | |
| ❑ 1 | Snaketime Series by Moondog | 195? | 800.00 |
| *—With paper insert; deduct 25 percent if it is missing* | | | |
| **MUSICAL HERITAGE SOCIETY** | | | |
| ❑ MHS 3803 | Moondog | 1978 | 40.00 |
| **PRESTIGE** | | | |
| ❑ PRLP-7042 [M] | Moondog | 1956 | 200.00 |
| *—Yellow label with W. 50th St. address* | | | |
| ❑ PRLP-7069 [M] | More Moondog | 1957 | 200.00 |
| *—Yellow label with W. 50th St. address* | | | |
| ❑ PRLP-7099 [M] | The Story of Moondog | 1957 | 200.00 |
| *—Yellow label with W. 50th St. address* | | | |

## MOONEY, ART

| Number | Title (A Side/B Side) | Yr | NM |
|---|---|---|---|
| **CORONET** | | | |
| ❑ CX-138 [M] | Cha Cha Cha with Art Mooney | 196? | 10.00 |
| ❑ CXS-138 [S] | Cha Cha Cha with Art Mooney | 196? | 12.00 |
| ❑ CX-220 [M] | Dance and Dream | 196? | 12.00 |
| ❑ CXS-220 [S] | Dance and Dream | 196? | 12.00 |
| **DECCA** | | | |
| ❑ DL 4207 [M] | Songs Everybody Knows | 1962 | 12.00 |
| ❑ DL 74207 [S] | Songs Everybody Knows | 1962 | 15.00 |
| **DIPLOMAT** | | | |
| ❑ DS-2218 [S] | Cha Cha Cha with Art Mooney | 196? | 12.00 |
| ❑ DS-2246 [S] | Sing Along | 196? | 12.00 |
| **HURRAH** | | | |
| ❑ H-1002 [M] | Big Band Dance Time | 1962 | 10.00 |
| ❑ HS-1002 [S] | Big Band Dance Time | 1962 | 12.00 |
| **KAPP** | | | |
| ❑ KL-1405 [M] | Jump for Joy! | 1964 | 12.00 |
| ❑ KL-1421 [M] | Sentimental Love Songs of World War II | 1965 | 12.00 |
| ❑ KS-3405 [S] | Jump for Joy! | 1964 | 15.00 |
| ❑ KS-3421 [S] | Sentimental Love Songs of World War II | 1965 | 15.00 |
| **LION** | | | |
| ❑ L-70062 [M] | Those Happy Banjos | 1958 | 15.00 |
| **MGM** | | | |
| ❑ E-121 [10] | Sunset to Sunrise | 1952 | 30.00 |
| ❑ E-206 [10] | Banjo Bonanza | 1953 | 30.00 |
| ❑ E-3431 [M] | Art Mooney Presents the Happy Minstrels | 1956 | 25.00 |
| ❑ E-3616 [M] | Art Mooney in Hi-Fi Dixieland | 1957 | 20.00 |
| ❑ E-3628 [M] | Sunrise to Sunrise | 1958 | 40.00 |
| *—Quickly deleted and reissued as 3649 with a new title* | | | |
| ❑ E-3649 [M] | Art Mooney and His Orchestra in Hi-Fi Play for Dancing | 1958 | 20.00 |
| *—Reissue of 3628 with new cover and title* | | | |
| ❑ E-3899 [M] | Spectacular Voices with Banjos | 1961 | 12.00 |
| ❑ SE-3899 [S] | Spectacular Voices with Banjos | 1961 | 15.00 |
| **PIROUETTE** | | | |
| ❑ FM-45 [M] | Cha Cha Cha with Art Mooney | 196? | 10.00 |
| **PROMENADE** | | | |
| ❑ 2218 [M] | Cha Cha Cha with Art Mooney | 196? | 10.00 |
| ❑ 2246 [M] | Sing Along | 196? | 10.00 |
| **RCA VICTOR** | | | |
| ❑ LPM-3739 [M] | The Best of Art Mooney | 1967 | 20.00 |
| ❑ LSP-3739 [S] | The Best of Art Mooney | 1967 | 12.00 |
| **SPIN-O-RAMA** | | | |
| ❑ S-45 [S] | Cha Cha Cha with Art Mooney | 196? | 12.00 |
| ❑ M-93 [M] | Dancetime | 196? | 10.00 |
| ❑ MK-3079 [M] | Cha Cha Cha with Art Mooney | 196? | 10.00 |
| **TIARA** | | | |
| ❑ TM-7545 [M] | Cha Cha Cha with Art Mooney | 196? | 10.00 |

## MOONEY, JOE

| Number | Title (A Side/B Side) | Yr | NM |
|---|---|---|---|
| **ATLANTIC** | | | |
| ❑ 1255 [M] | Lush Life | 1958 | 40.00 |
| *—Black label* | | | |
| ❑ 1255 [M] | Lush Life | 1961 | 20.00 |
| *—Multicolor label, white "fan" logo at right* | | | |
| **COLUMBIA** | | | |
| ❑ CS 8986 [S] | The Greatness of Joe Mooney | 1964 | 20.00 |
| **DECCA** | | | |
| ❑ DL 5555 [10] | You Go to My Head | 1955 | 50.00 |
| ❑ DL 8468 [M] | On the Rocks | 1957 | 40.00 |

## MOONGLOWS, THE

| Number | Title (A Side/B Side) | Yr | NM |
|---|---|---|---|
| **CHESS** | | | |
| ❑ LP 1430 [M] | Look! It's the Moonglows | 1959 | 500.00 |
| ❑ LP 1471 [M] | The Best of Bobby Lester & the Moonglows | 1962 | 300.00 |
| *—Black label* | | | |
| ❑ LP 1471 [M] | The Best of Bobby Lester & the Moonglows | 1966 | 50.00 |
| *—Blue, fading to white label* | | | |
| ❑ CH-9111 | Their Greatest Sides | 1986 | 12.00 |
| ❑ CH-9193 | Look! It's the Moonglows | 1987 | 12.00 |
| *—Reissue of 1430* | | | |
| **CONSTELLATION** | | | |
| ❑ C-2 [M] | Collectors Showcase — The Moonglows | 1964 | 50.00 |
| *—Dark blue lettering* | | | |
| ❑ C-2 [M] | Collectors Showcase — The Moonglows | 1964 | 100.00 |
| *—Light blue lettering* | | | |
| **LOST-NITE** | | | |
| ❑ LP-23 [10] | The Moonglows | 1981 | 12.00 |
| **RCA VICTOR** | | | |
| ❑ LSP-4722 | The Return of the Moonglows | 1972 | 15.00 |

## MOONLIGHTERS, THE

| Number | Title (A Side/B Side) | Yr | NM |
|---|---|---|---|
| **CENTURY** | | | |
| ❑ 29132 | An Evening with the Moonlighters | 197? | 20.00 |

| Number | Title (A Side/B Side) | Yr | NM |
|---|---|---|---|
| **MOONRAKERS, THE** | | | |
| SHAMLEY | | | |
| ❑ 704 | Together | 1968 | 40.00 |
| **MOONSHINERS, THE** | | | |
| VILLAGE GATE | | | |
| ❑ 2002 [M] | Breakout! | 1964 | 20.00 |
| **MOOR, DET** Actually producer and composer Robert Mersey. | | | |
| GALLANT | | | |
| ❑ GT 4001 [M] | Great Jazz from Great TV | 1962 | 40.00 |
| **MOORE, ADA** | | | |
| DEBUT | | | |
| ❑ DLP-15 [10] | Jazz Workshop | 1955 | 200.00 |
| **MOORE, BOB** | | | |
| HICKORY | | | |
| ❑ LP-131 [M] | Viva Bob Moore | 1965 | 15.00 |
| ❑ LPS-131 [S] | Viva Bob Moore | 1965 | 20.00 |
| MONUMENT | | | |
| ❑ MLP-4005 [M] | Mexico and Other Great Hits! | 1961 | 20.00 |
| ❑ SLP-4005 [S] | Mexico and Other Great Hits! | 1961 | 25.00 |
| ❑ MLP-8008 [M] | Mexico | 1967 | 12.00 |
| ❑ SLP-18008 [S] | Mexico | 1967 | 15.00 |
| **MOORE, BOBBY, AND THE RHYTHM ACES** | | | |
| CHECKER | | | |
| ❑ LP-3000 [M] | Searching for My Love | 1966 | 30.00 |
| ❑ LPS-3000 [R] | Searching for My Love | 1966 | 20.00 |
| **MOORE, BREW** | | | |
| FANTASY | | | |
| ❑ 3222 [M] *—Black vinyl* | The Brew Moore Quintet | 1956 | 40.00 |
| ❑ 3222 [M] *—Red vinyl* | The Brew Moore Quintet | 1956 | 80.00 |
| ❑ 3264 [M] *—Black vinyl* | Brew Moore | 1958 | 30.00 |
| ❑ 3264 [M] *—Red vinyl* | Brew Moore | 1958 | 50.00 |
| ❑ 6013 [M] *—Black vinyl* | Brew Moore in Europe | 1962 | 25.00 |
| ❑ 6013 [M] *—Red vinyl* | Brew Moore in Europe | 1962 | 40.00 |
| ❑ 86013 [S] *—Black vinyl* | Brew Moore in Europe | 1962 | 20.00 |
| ❑ 86013 [S] *—Blue vinyl* | Brew Moore in Europe | 1962 | 30.00 |
| SAVOY | | | |
| ❑ MG-9028 [10] | Tenor Sax | 1953 | 150.00 |
| **MOORE, CHARLIE, AND BILL NAPIER** | | | |
| KING | | | |
| ❑ 828 [M] | Folk 'n' Hill | 1963 | 50.00 |
| ❑ 880 [M] | The Best of Charlie Moore and Bill Napier | 1964 | 50.00 |
| ❑ 917 [M] | Country Hymnal | 1964 | 40.00 |
| ❑ 936 [M] | Songs of the Lonesome Truck Drivers | 1965 | 30.00 |
| ❑ KS-936 [S] | Songs of the Lonesome Truck Drivers | 1965 | 40.00 |
| ❑ 982 [M] | Country Music Goes to Viet Nam | 1966 | 30.00 |
| ❑ KS-982 [S] | Country Music Goes to Viet Nam | 1966 | 40.00 |
| ❑ 992 [M] | City Folks Back on the Farm | 1966 | 30.00 |
| ❑ KS-992 [S] | City Folks Back on the Farm | 1966 | 40.00 |
| ❑ 1014 [M] | Spectacular Instrumentals | 1967 | 25.00 |
| ❑ KS-1014 [S] | Spectacular Instrumentals | 1967 | 20.00 |
| ❑ 1017 [M] | Gospel and Sacred Songs | 1967 | 25.00 |
| ❑ KS-1017 [S] | Gospel and Sacred Songs | 1967 | 20.00 |
| ❑ 1021 [M] | Brand New Country & Western Songs | 1967 | 25.00 |
| ❑ KS-1021 [S] | Brand New Country & Western Songs | 1967 | 20.00 |
| **MOORE, DANNY** | | | |
| EVEREST | | | |
| ❑ SDBR-1211 [S] | Folk Songs from Here and There | 1963 | 25.00 |
| ❑ LPBR-5211 [M] | Folk Songs from Here and There | 1963 | 20.00 |
| **MOORE, DEBBY** | | | |
| TOP RANK | | | |
| ❑ RM-12-301 [M] | My Kind of Blues | 1959 | 40.00 |
| **MOORE, DUDLEY** | | | |
| ATLANTIC | | | |
| ❑ 1403 [M] | Beyond the Fringe and All That Jazz | 1963 | 25.00 |
| ❑ SD 1403 [S] | Beyond the Fringe and All That Jazz | 1963 | 30.00 |
| LONDON | | | |
| ❑ PS 558 | Dudley Moore Trio | 1969 | 25.00 |

| Number | Title (A Side/B Side) | Yr | NM |
|---|---|---|---|
| **MOORE, GATEMOUTH** | | | |
| AUDIO FIDELITY | | | |
| ❑ AFLP-1921 [M] | Revival! | 196? | 60.00 |
| ❑ AFSD-5921 [S] | Revival! | 196? | 80.00 |
| BLUESWAY | | | |
| ❑ BLS 6074 | After 21 Years | 1973 | 20.00 |
| KING | | | |
| ❑ 684 [M] | Gatemouth Moore Sings Blues | 1960 | 5000. |
| **MOORE, JERRY** | | | |
| ESP-DISK' | | | |
| ❑ 1061 | Life Is a Constant Journey Home | 1968 | 20.00 |
| **MOORE, LATTIE** | | | |
| AUDIO LAB | | | |
| ❑ AL-1555 [M] | The Best of Lattie Moore | 1960 | 200.00 |
| ❑ AL-1573 [M] | Country Side | 1962 | 150.00 |
| DERBYTOWN | | | |
| ❑ 102 [M] | Lattie Moore | 196? | 40.00 |
| **MOORE, MARILYN** | | | |
| BETHLEHEM | | | |
| ❑ BCP-73 [M] | Moody | 1957 | 80.00 |
| **MOORE, OSCAR** | | | |
| CHARLIE PARKER | | | |
| ❑ PLP-830 [M] | The Fabulous Oscar Moore Guitar | 1962 | 25.00 |
| ❑ PLP-830S [S] | The Fabulous Oscar Moore Guitar | 1962 | 30.00 |
| SKYLARK | | | |
| ❑ SKLP-19 [M] | Oscar Moore Trio | 1954 | 100.00 |
| TAMPA | | | |
| ❑ TP-16 [M] *—Colored vinyl* | Oscar Moore Trio | 1957 | 80.00 |
| ❑ TP-16 [M] *—Black vinyl* | Oscar Moore Trio | 1958 | 50.00 |
| ❑ TP-22 [M] *—Colored vinyl* | Galivantin' Guitar | 1957 | 80.00 |
| ❑ TP-22 [M] *—Black vinyl* | Galivantin' Guitar | 1958 | 50.00 |
| **MOORE, PHIL** | | | |
| CLEF | | | |
| ❑ MGC-635 [M] | Music for Moderns | 1954 | 100.00 |
| STRAND | | | |
| ❑ SL-1004 [M] | Polynesian Paradise | 1959 | 40.00 |
| ❑ SLS-1004 [S] | Polynesian Paradise | 1959 | 50.00 |
| **MOORE, REGGIE** | | | |
| MAINSTREAM | | | |
| ❑ MRL-341 | Wishbone | 1971 | 20.00 |
| ❑ MRL-380 | Furioso | 1972 | 20.00 |
| **MOORE, SCOTTY** | | | |
| EPIC | | | |
| ❑ LN 24103 [M] | The Guitar That Changed the World | 1964 | 80.00 |
| ❑ BN 26103 [S] | The Guitar That Changed the World | 1964 | 100.00 |
| GUINNESS | | | |
| ❑ GNS-36038 | What's Left | 1977 | 15.00 |
| **MOORE, SHELLEY** | | | |
| ARGO | | | |
| ❑ LP-4016 [M] | For the First Time | 1962 | 30.00 |
| ❑ LPS-4016 [S] | For the First Time | 1962 | 40.00 |
| **MOORE, TIM** | | | |
| A SMALL RECORD COMPANY | | | |
| ❑ SRS-10001 | Tim Moore | 1974 | 30.00 |
| ABC DUNHILL | | | |
| ❑ DSX-50132 | Of Woodstock and Other Places | 1973 | 12.00 |
| ASYLUM | | | |
| ❑ 6E-179 | High Contrast | 1979 | 10.00 |
| ❑ 7E-1019 | Tim Moore | 1974 | 10.00 |
| ❑ 7E-1042 | Behind the Eyes | 1975 | 10.00 |
| ❑ 7E-1088 | White Shadows | 1977 | 10.00 |
| ELEKTRA | | | |
| ❑ 60463 | Flash Forward | 1985 | 10.00 |
| **MOORE, WILD BILL** | | | |
| JAZZLAND | | | |
| ❑ JLP-38 [M] | Wild Bill's Beat | 1961 | 30.00 |
| ❑ JLP-54 [M] | Bottom Groove | 1961 | 30.00 |
| ❑ JLP-938 [S] | Wild Bill's Beat | 1961 | 40.00 |
| ❑ JLP-954 [S] | Bottom Groove | 1961 | 40.00 |
| **MORAN, PAT** | | | |
| AUDIO FIDELITY | | | |
| ❑ AFLP-1875 [M] | This Is Pat Moran | 1958 | 40.00 |
| ❑ AFSD-5875 [S] | This Is Pat Moran | 1958 | 50.00 |

| Number | Title (A Side/B Side) | Yr | NM |
|---|---|---|---|
| BETHLEHEM | | | |
| ❑ BCP-6007 [M] | Pat Moran Quartet | 1956 | 50.00 |
| ❑ BCP-6018 [M] | While at Birdland | 1957 | 50.00 |
| **MORATH, MAX** | | | |
| EPIC | | | |
| ❑ BN 26066 [S] | Celebrated Maestro | 1963 | 20.00 |
| RCA VICTOR | | | |
| ❑ LSO-1159 | Max Morath at the Turn of the Century | 1969 | 25.00 |
| SAVOY | | | |
| ❑ MG-12091 [M] | Introducing Max Morath | 196? | 20.00 |
| **MOREL, TERRY** | | | |
| BETHLEHEM | | | |
| ❑ BCP-47 [M] | Songs of a Woman in Love | 1956 | 150.00 |
| **MORELLO, JOE** | | | |
| INTRO | | | |
| ❑ 608 [M] | Joe Morello Sextet | 1957 | 150.00 |
| RCA VICTOR | | | |
| ❑ LPM-2486 [M] | It's About Time | 1961 | 25.00 |
| ❑ LSP-2486 [S] | It's About Time | 1961 | 30.00 |
| **MORENO, RITA** | | | |
| STRAND | | | |
| ❑ L-1039 [M] | Rita Moreno Sings | 1962 | 30.00 |
| ❑ SL-1039 [S] | Rita Moreno Sings | 1962 | 40.00 |
| WYNNE | | | |
| ❑ WLP-103 [M] | Warm, Wild, Wonderful | 1964 | 20.00 |
| ❑ WLP-703 [S] | Warm, Wild, Wonderful | 1964 | 25.00 |
| **MOREY STORE BAND, THE** | | | |
| SOUND MACHINE | | | |
| ❑ 49007 | Cry for the Dreamer | 197? | 100.00 |
| **MORGAN, DICK** | | | |
| RIVERSIDE | | | |
| ❑ RLP 12-329 [M] | Dick Morgan at the Showboat | 1960 | 40.00 |
| ❑ RLP-347 [M] | See What I Mean? | 1960 | 30.00 |
| ❑ RLP-383 [M] | Settin' In | 1961 | 30.00 |
| ❑ RLP-1183 [S] | Dick Morgan at the Showboat | 1960 | 40.00 |
| ❑ RS-9347 [S] | See What I Mean? | 1960 | 40.00 |
| ❑ RS-9383 [S] | Settin' In | 1961 | 40.00 |
| **MORGAN, FRANK** | | | |
| GENE NORMAN | | | |
| ❑ GNP-12 [M] *—Red vinyl* | Frank Morgan | 1955 | 120.00 |
| WHIPPET | | | |
| ❑ WLP-704 [M] | Frank Morgan | 1956 | 100.00 |
| **MORGAN, GEORGE** | | | |
| COLUMBIA | | | |
| ❑ CL 1044 [M] | Morgan, By George | 1957 | 50.00 |
| ❑ CL 1631 [M] | Golden Memories | 1961 | 25.00 |
| ❑ CL 2111 [M] | Tender Lovin' Care | 1964 | 20.00 |
| ❑ CL 2333 [M] | Red Roses for a Blue Lady | 1965 | 20.00 |
| ❑ CS 8431 [S] | Golden Memories | 1961 | 30.00 |
| ❑ CS 8911 [S] | Tender Lovin' Care | 1964 | 25.00 |
| ❑ CS 9133 [S] | Red Roses for a Blue Lady | 1965 | 25.00 |
| ❑ PC 33894 | Remembering George Morgan | 1975 | 12.00 |
| 4 STAR | | | |
| ❑ 002 | From This Moment On | 1975 | 12.00 |
| MCA | | | |
| ❑ 422 | Red Rose from the Blue Side of Town/Somewhere Around Midnight | 1974 | 12.00 |
| ❑ 461 | Candy Mountain Melody | 1974 | 12.00 |
| STARDAY | | | |
| ❑ SLP-400 | Candy Kisses | 1967 | 25.00 |
| ❑ SLP-410 | Country Hits by Candlelight | 1967 | 25.00 |
| ❑ SLP-413 | Steal Away | 1968 | 20.00 |
| ❑ SLP-417 | Barbara | 1969 | 20.00 |
| STOP | | | |
| ❑ 10009 | George Morgan Sings Like a Bird | 1969 | 15.00 |
| **MORGAN, JANE** | | | |
| ABC | | | |
| ❑ S-638 | A Jane Morgan Happening | 1968 | 12.00 |
| COLPIX | | | |
| ❑ CP 469 [M] | The Last Time I Saw Paris | 1964 | 20.00 |
| ❑ SCP 469 [S] | The Last Time I Saw Paris | 1964 | 25.00 |
| ❑ CP 497 [M] | The Jane Morgan Album | 1966 | 15.00 |
| ❑ SCP 497 [S] | The Jane Morgan Album | 1966 | 20.00 |
| EPIC | | | |
| ❑ LN 24166 [M] | In My Style | 1965 | 12.00 |
| ❑ LN 24190 [M] | Today's Hits...Tomorrow's Golden Favorites | 1966 | 12.00 |
| ❑ LN 24211 [M] | Fresh Flavor | 1966 | 12.00 |
| ❑ LN 24247 [M] | Kiss Tomorrow Goodbye | 1967 | 15.00 |
| ❑ BN 26166 [S] | In My Style | 1965 | 15.00 |

| Number | Title (A Side/B Side) | Yr | NM |
|---|---|---|---|
| ❑ BN 26190 [S] | Today's Hits...Tomorrow's Golden Favorites | 1966 | 15.00 |
| ❑ BN 26211 [S] | Fresh Flavor | 1966 | 15.00 |
| ❑ BN 26247 [S] | Kiss Tomorrow Goodbye | 1967 | 12.00 |

**HARMONY**

| Number | Title (A Side/B Side) | Yr | NM |
|---|---|---|---|
| ❑ HS 11398 | Sounds of Silence | 1970 | 10.00 |

**KAPP**

| Number | Title (A Side/B Side) | Yr | NM |
|---|---|---|---|
| ❑ KJM-1 [DJ] | Radio Station Sampler | 196? | 25.00 |
| *—Promo only, gatefold cover* | | | |
| ❑ KL-1023 [M] | Jane Morgan | 1956 | 30.00 |
| ❑ KL-1066 [M] | Fascination | 1957 | 30.00 |
| ❑ KL-1080 [M] | All the Way | 1958 | 30.00 |
| ❑ KL-1089 [M] | Something Old, New, Borrowed, Blue | 1958 | 30.00 |
| ❑ KL-1089S [S] | Something Old, New, Borrowed, Blue | 1958 | 40.00 |
| ❑ KL-1093 [M] | Jane Morgan | 1958 | 30.00 |
| ❑ KL-1105 [M] | The Day the Rains Came | 1958 | 30.00 |
| ❑ KL-1105S [S] | The Day the Rains Came | 1958 | 40.00 |
| ❑ KL-1129 [M] | Jane in Spain | 1959 | 25.00 |
| ❑ KL-1170 [M] | Jane Morgan Time | 1959 | 20.00 |
| ❑ KL-1191 [M] | Ballads of Lady Jane | 1960 | 15.00 |
| ❑ KL-1239 [M] | Second Time Around | 1961 | 15.00 |
| ❑ KL-1246 [M] | The Great Golden Hits | 1961 | 15.00 |
| ❑ KL-1247 [M] | Big Hits from Broadway | 1961 | 15.00 |
| ❑ KL-1250 [M] | Love Makes the World Go 'Round | 1961 | 15.00 |
| ❑ KL-1268 [M] | Jane Morgan at the Cocoanut Grove | 1962 | 15.00 |
| ❑ KL-1275 [M] | More Golden Hits | 1962 | 15.00 |
| ❑ KL-1296 [M] | What Now My Love | 1962 | 15.00 |
| ❑ KL-1329 [M] | Jane Morgan's Greatest Hits | 1963 | 12.00 |
| ❑ KS-3001 [S] | Broadway in Stereo | 1959 | 30.00 |
| ❑ KS-3014 [S] | Jane in Spain | 1959 | 30.00 |
| ❑ KS-3017 [S] | Fascination | 1959 | 30.00 |
| ❑ KS-3054 [S] | Jane Morgan Time | 1959 | 25.00 |
| ❑ KS-3066 [S] | Fascination | 1962 | 20.00 |
| ❑ KS-3191 [S] | Ballads of Lady Jane | 1960 | 20.00 |
| ❑ KS-3239 [S] | Second Time Around | 1961 | 20.00 |
| ❑ KS-3246 [S] | The Great Golden Hits | 1961 | 20.00 |
| ❑ KS-3247 [S] | Big Hits from Broadway | 1961 | 20.00 |
| ❑ KS-3250 [S] | Love Makes the World Go 'Round | 1961 | 20.00 |
| ❑ KS-3268 [S] | Jane Morgan at the Cocoanut Grove | 1962 | 20.00 |
| ❑ KS-3275 [S] | More Golden Hits | 1962 | 20.00 |
| ❑ KS-3296 [S] | What Now My Love | 1962 | 20.00 |
| ❑ KS-3329 [S] | Jane Morgan's Greatest Hits | 1963 | 15.00 |
| ❑ UXL-5006 [(2)M] | Great Songs from the Great Shows of the Century | 195? | 40.00 |

**MCA**

| Number | Title (A Side/B Side) | Yr | NM |
|---|---|---|---|
| ❑ 537 | Jane Morgan's Greatest Hits | 197? | 10.00 |

**RCA VICTOR**

| Number | Title (A Side/B Side) | Yr | NM |
|---|---|---|---|
| ❑ LSP-4171 | Traces of Love | 1969 | 12.00 |
| ❑ LSP-4322 | Jane Morgan in Nashville | 1970 | 12.00 |

### MORGAN, JAYE P.

**ALLEGRO ELITE**

| Number | Title (A Side/B Side) | Yr | NM |
|---|---|---|---|
| ❑ 4111 [M] | Jaye P. Morgan Sings | 195? | 12.00 |

**BEVERLY HILLS**

| Number | Title (A Side/B Side) | Yr | NM |
|---|---|---|---|
| ❑ 24 | What Are You Doing the Rest of Your Life | 1970 | 30.00 |

**MAYFAIR**

| Number | Title (A Side/B Side) | Yr | NM |
|---|---|---|---|
| ❑ 9739 [M] | Life Is Just a Bowl of Cherries | 195? | 15.00 |

**MGM**

| Number | Title (A Side/B Side) | Yr | NM |
|---|---|---|---|
| ❑ E-3774 [M] | Slow and Easy | 1959 | 25.00 |
| ❑ SE-3774 [S] | Slow and Easy | 1959 | 30.00 |
| ❑ E-3830 [M] | Up North | 1960 | 25.00 |
| ❑ SE-3830 [S] | Up North | 1960 | 30.00 |
| ❑ E-3867 [M] | Down South | 1960 | 25.00 |
| ❑ SE-3867 [S] | Down South | 1960 | 30.00 |
| ❑ E-3940 [M] | That Country Sound | 1961 | 25.00 |
| ❑ SE-3940 [S] | That Country Sound | 1961 | 30.00 |

**RCA VICTOR**

| Number | Title (A Side/B Side) | Yr | NM |
|---|---|---|---|
| ❑ LPM-1155 [M] | Jaye P. Morgan | 1955 | 50.00 |
| ❑ LPM-1682 [M] | Just You, Just Me | 1958 | 40.00 |

**RONDO-LETTE**

| Number | Title (A Side/B Side) | Yr | NM |
|---|---|---|---|
| ❑ A-13 [M] | Jaye P. Morgan Sings | 1958 | 25.00 |

**ROYALE**

| Number | Title (A Side/B Side) | Yr | NM |
|---|---|---|---|
| ❑ 18147 [10] | Jaye P. Morgan and Orchestra | 195? | 20.00 |

**TOPS**

| Number | Title (A Side/B Side) | Yr | NM |
|---|---|---|---|
| ❑ L-1739 [M] | Life Is Just a Bowl of Cherries | 195? | 15.00 |

### MORGAN, LEE

**BLUE NOTE**

| Number | Title (A Side/B Side) | Yr | NM |
|---|---|---|---|
| ❑ BLP-1538 [M] | Lee Morgan Indeed! | 1957 | 500.00 |
| *—"Deep groove" edition, W. 63rd St. address on label* | | | |
| ❑ BLP-1538 [M] | Lee Morgan Indeed! | 1957 | 1500. |
| *—"Deep groove" version; Lexington Ave. address on label* | | | |
| ❑ BLP-1538 [M] | Lee Morgan Indeed! | 1963 | 50.00 |
| *—"New York, USA" address on label* | | | |
| ❑ BLP-1538 [M] | Lee Morgan Indeed! | 200? | 30.00 |
| *—200-gram edition; distributed by Classic Records* | | | |
| ❑ BLP-1541 [M] | Lee Morgan, Volume 2 | 1957 | 400.00 |
| *—"Deep groove" edition, W. 63rd St. address on label* | | | |
| ❑ BLP-1541 [M] | Lee Morgan, Volume 2 | 1957 | 1000. |
| *—"Deep groove" version; Lexington Ave. address on label* | | | |
| ❑ BLP-1541 [M] | Lee Morgan, Volume 2 | 1963 | 50.00 |
| *—"New York, USA" address on label* | | | |
| ❑ BLP-1557 [M] | Lee Morgan, Volume 3 | 1957 | 300.00 |
| *—Regular edition, W. 63rd St. address on label* | | | |
| ❑ BLP-1557 [M] | Lee Morgan, Volume 3 | 1957 | 900.00 |
| *—"Deep groove" version; W. 63rd St. address on label* | | | |
| ❑ BLP-1557 [M] | Lee Morgan, Volume 3 | 1963 | 50.00 |
| *—"New York, USA" address on label* | | | |
| ❑ BLP-1575 [M] | City Lights | 1958 | 200.00 |
| *—Regular edition, W. 63rd St. address on label* | | | |
| ❑ BLP-1575 [M] | City Lights | 1958 | 600.00 |
| *—"Deep groove" version; W. 63rd St. address on label* | | | |
| ❑ BLP-1575 [M] | City Lights | 1963 | 50.00 |
| *—"New York, USA" address on label* | | | |
| ❑ BST-1575 [S] | City Lights | 1959 | 150.00 |
| *—Regular edition, W. 63rd St. address on label* | | | |
| ❑ BST-1575 [S] | City Lights | 1959 | 300.00 |
| *—"Deep groove" version; W. 63rd St. address on label* | | | |
| ❑ BST-1575 [S] | City Lights | 1963 | 25.00 |
| *—"New York, USA" address on label* | | | |
| ❑ BLP-1578 [M] | The Cooker | 1958 | 200.00 |
| *—Regular edition, W. 63rd St. address on label* | | | |
| ❑ BLP-1578 [M] | The Cooker | 1958 | 400.00 |
| *—"Deep groove" version; W. 63rd St. address on label* | | | |
| ❑ BLP-1578 [M] | The Cooker | 1963 | 50.00 |
| *—"New York, USA" address on label* | | | |
| ❑ BST-1578 [S] | The Cooker | 1959 | 200.00 |
| *—Regular edition, W. 63rd St. address on label* | | | |
| ❑ BST-1578 [S] | The Cooker | 1959 | 300.00 |
| *—"Deep groove" version; W. 63rd St. address on label* | | | |
| ❑ BST-1578 [S] | The Cooker | 1963 | 40.00 |
| *—"New York, USA" address on label* | | | |
| ❑ BLP-1590 [M] | Candy | 1958 | 250.00 |
| *—Regular edition, W. 63rd St. address on label* | | | |
| ❑ BLP-1590 [M] | Candy | 1958 | 500.00 |
| *—"Deep groove" version; W. 63rd St. address on label* | | | |
| ❑ BLP-1590 [M] | Candy | 1963 | 50.00 |
| *—"New York, USA" address on label* | | | |
| ❑ BST-1590 [S] | Candy | 1959 | 200.00 |
| *—Regular edition, W. 63rd St. address on label* | | | |
| ❑ BST-1590 [S] | Candy | 1959 | 300.00 |
| *—"Deep groove" version; W. 63rd St. address on label* | | | |
| ❑ BST-1590 [S] | Candy | 1963 | 40.00 |
| *—"New York, USA" address on label* | | | |
| ❑ BLP-4034 [M] | Lee-Way | 1960 | 300.00 |
| *—Regular edition, W. 63rd St. address on label* | | | |
| ❑ BLP-4034 [M] | Lee-Way | 1960 | 500.00 |
| *—"Deep groove" version; W. 63rd St. address on label* | | | |
| ❑ BLP-4034 [M] | Lee-Way | 1963 | 50.00 |
| *—"New York, USA" address on label* | | | |
| ❑ BLP-4157 [M] | The Sidewinder | 1964 | 100.00 |
| *—"New York, USA" on label* | | | |
| ❑ BLP-4169 [M] | Search for the New Land | 1965 | 120.00 |
| *—"New York, USA" on label* | | | |
| ❑ BLP-4199 [M] | The Rumproller | 1966 | 100.00 |
| *—"New York, USA" on label* | | | |
| ❑ BLP-4212 [M] | The Gigolo | 1966 | 100.00 |
| *—"New York, USA" on label* | | | |
| ❑ BLP-4222 [M] | Cornbread | 1967 | 80.00 |
| *—"New York, USA" on label* | | | |
| ❑ BLP-4243 [M] | Delightfulee Morgan | 1967 | 120.00 |
| ❑ BST-84034 [S] | Lee-Way | 1960 | 150.00 |
| *—Regular edition, W. 63rd St. address on label* | | | |
| ❑ BST-84034 [S] | Lee-Way | 1963 | 40.00 |
| *—"New York, USA" address on label* | | | |
| ❑ BST-84157 [S] | The Sidewinder | 1964 | 80.00 |
| *—"New York, USA" address on label* | | | |
| ❑ BST-84169 [S] | Search for the New Land | 1965 | 80.00 |
| *—"New York, USA" address on label* | | | |
| ❑ BST-84199 [S] | The Rumproller | 1966 | 80.00 |
| *—"New York, USA" address on label* | | | |
| ❑ BST-84212 [S] | The Gigolo | 1966 | 80.00 |
| *—"New York, USA" address on label* | | | |
| ❑ BST-84222 [S] | Cornbread | 1967 | 80.00 |
| *—"New York, USA" address on label* | | | |
| ❑ BST-84243 [S] | Delightfulee Morgan | 1967 | 60.00 |
| *—"New York, USA" address on label* | | | |
| ❑ BST-84289 | Caramba! | 1969 | 80.00 |
| *—"A Division of Liberty Records" on label* | | | |
| ❑ BST-84312 | Charisma | 1969 | 50.00 |
| *—"A Division of Liberty Records" on label* | | | |
| ❑ BST-84335 | The Sixth Sense | 1969 | 60.00 |
| *—"A Division of Liberty Records" on label* | | | |
| ❑ BST-84901 [(2)] | Lee Morgan | 1972 | 30.00 |
| *—"A Division of Unted Artists" on blue and white labels* | | | |
| ❑ BST-89906 [(2)] | Lee Morgan at the Lighthouse | 1970 | 50.00 |

**GNP CRESCENDO**

| Number | Title (A Side/B Side) | Yr | NM |
|---|---|---|---|
| ❑ GNP-2079 [(2)] | Lee Morgan | 1973 | 20.00 |

**JAZZLAND**

| Number | Title (A Side/B Side) | Yr | NM |
|---|---|---|---|
| ❑ JLP-80 [M] | Take Twelve | 1962 | 50.00 |
| ❑ JLP-980 [S] | Take Twelve | 1962 | 60.00 |

**MOSAIC**

| Number | Title (A Side/B Side) | Yr | NM |
|---|---|---|---|
| ❑ MQ6-162 [(6)] | The Complete Blue Note Lee Morgan Fifties Sessions | 1995 | 300.00 |

**SAVOY**

| Number | Title (A Side/B Side) | Yr | NM |
|---|---|---|---|
| ❑ MG-12091 [M] | Introducing Lee Morgan | 1956 | 400.00 |

**VEE JAY**

| Number | Title (A Side/B Side) | Yr | NM |
|---|---|---|---|
| ❑ VJ-2508 [M] | Lee Morgan Quintet | 1965 | 60.00 |
| ❑ VJS-2508 [S] | Lee Morgan Quintet | 1965 | 80.00 |
| ❑ LP-3007 [M] | Here's Lee Morgan | 1960 | 60.00 |
| ❑ SR-3007 [S] | Here's Lee Morgan | 1960 | 80.00 |
| ❑ LP-3015 [M] | Expoobident | 1960 | 80.00 |
| ❑ SR-3015 [S] | Expoobident | 1960 | 120.00 |

### MORGAN, LORRIE

**RCA**

| Number | Title (A Side/B Side) | Yr | NM |
|---|---|---|---|
| ❑ 9594-1-R | Leave the Light On | 1989 | 12.00 |
| ❑ R 183848 | Something in Red | 1991 | 20.00 |
| *—Only available on vinyl through BMG Direct Marketing* | | | |

### MORGAN, RUSS

**DECCA**

| Number | Title (A Side/B Side) | Yr | NM |
|---|---|---|---|
| ❑ DXB 196 [(2)M] | The Best of Russ Morgan | 1965 | 20.00 |
| ❑ DL 5098 [10] | Music in the Morgan Manner | 1950 | 30.00 |
| ❑ DL 5278 [10] | College Marching Songs | 195? | 30.00 |
| ❑ DL 5324 [10] | Morgan-Airs | 1951 | 30.00 |
| ❑ DL 5406 [10] | Everybody Dance to the Music of Russ Morgan | 195? | 30.00 |
| ❑ DL 8332 [M] | Does Your Heart Beat for Me | 1956 | 20.00 |
| *—Black label, silver print* | | | |
| ❑ DL 8336 [M] | Tap Dancing for Pleasure | 1956 | 20.00 |
| *—Black label, silver print* | | | |
| ❑ DL 8337 [M] | Everybody Dance | 1956 | 20.00 |
| *—Black label, silver print* | | | |
| ❑ DL 8423 [M] | A Lovely Way to Spend an Evening (Songs of Jimmy McHugh) | 1957 | 20.00 |
| *—Black label, silver print* | | | |
| ❑ DL 8581 [M] | Cheerful Little Earful (Songs of Harry Warren) | 195? | 20.00 |
| *—Black label, silver print* | | | |
| ❑ DL 8642 [M] | Velvet Violins | 1957 | 20.00 |
| *—Black label, silver print* | | | |
| ❑ DL 8746 [M] | Kitten on the Keys | 195? | 20.00 |
| *—Black label, silver print* | | | |
| ❑ DL 8828 [M] | Songs Everybody Knows | 1958 | 20.00 |
| *—Black label, silver print* | | | |
| ❑ DL 78828 [S] | Songs Everybody Knows | 1958 | 25.00 |
| *—Black label, silver print* | | | |

**VEE JAY**

| Number | Title (A Side/B Side) | Yr | NM |
|---|---|---|---|
| ❑ VJS-1125 [S] | His Greatest Hits | 1964 | 20.00 |
| ❑ VJS-1139 [S] | Red Roses for a Blue Lady | 1965 | 20.00 |

### MORGEN

**PROBE**

| Number | Title (A Side/B Side) | Yr | NM |
|---|---|---|---|
| ❑ CPLP-4507 | Morgen | 1969 | 150.00 |

### MORLY GREY

**STARSHINE**

| Number | Title (A Side/B Side) | Yr | NM |
|---|---|---|---|
| ❑ 69000 | The Only Truth | 1969 | 200.00 |

### MORMON TABERNACLE CHOIR

**BOOK-OF-THE-MONTH**

| Number | Title (A Side/B Side) | Yr | NM |
|---|---|---|---|
| ❑ 71-6406 [(3)] | Christmas Celebration | 1980 | 25.00 |
| *—Contains 20-page lyric booklet* | | | |

**CBS MASTERWORKS**

| Number | Title (A Side/B Side) | Yr | NM |
|---|---|---|---|
| ❑ IM 36661 | The Power and the Glory | 1981 | 10.00 |
| ❑ FM 37200 | When You Wish Upon a Star | 1981 | 10.00 |
| ❑ IM 37206 | Silent Night — The Greatest Hits of Christmas | 1981 | 12.00 |
| ❑ FM 37286 | The Twenties | 1982 | 10.00 |
| ❑ FM 37297 | Gloria! | 1982 | 10.00 |
| ❑ M 37828 | Serenade | 1985 | 10.00 |
| ❑ MG 37853 [(2)] | The Greatest Hits of Christmas | 1982 | 15.00 |
| ❑ XM 38299 | Christmas Carols Around the World | 1982 | 8.00 |
| ❑ IM 39034 | Faith of Our Fathers | 1984 | 10.00 |
| ❑ M2X 39102 [(2)] | The Great Choruses of Bach and Handel | 1984 | 12.00 |

**COLUMBIA HOUSE**

| Number | Title (A Side/B Side) | Yr | NM |
|---|---|---|---|
| ❑ 6P 6007 [(6)] | The Mormon Tabernacle Choir | 1973 | 30.00 |
| ❑ 1P 6008 | What Child Is This | 1973 | 12.00 |
| ❑ 1P 6075 | Christmas with the Mormon Tabernacle Choir | 1973 | 10.00 |
| ❑ 3P 6240 [(3)] | The Mormon Tabernacle Choir's Greatest Hits (Includes Christmas with the Mormon Tabernacle Choir) | 1974 | 18.00 |
| ❑ 2P 7437 [(2)] | The Mormon Tabernacle Choir Christmas Treasury | 1982 | 15.00 |

**COLUMBIA LIMITED EDITION**

| Number | Title (A Side/B Side) | Yr | NM |
|---|---|---|---|
| ❑ LE 10091 | Christmas Carols Around the World | 1976 | 10.00 |
| ❑ LE 10461 | Hymns and Songs of Brotherhood | 197? | 8.00 |

**COLUMBIA MASTERWORKS**

| Number | Title (A Side/B Side) | Yr | NM |
|---|---|---|---|
| ❑ M2L 263 [(2)M] | Handel: Messiah | 1959 | 20.00 |
| *—Gray and black labels with six "eye" logos* | | | |
| ❑ M2L 286 [(2)M] | Brahms: A German Requiem Sung in English | 1963 | 15.00 |
| ❑ M2L 303 [(2)M] | This Is My Country | 1963 | 15.00 |
| ❑ M2S 607 [(2)S] | Handel: Messiah | 1959 | 25.00 |
| *—Gray and black labels with six "eye" logos* | | | |
| ❑ M2S 686 [(2)S] | Brahms: A German Requiem Sung in English | 1963 | 20.00 |
| *—Gray label, "360 Sound Stereo" in black* | | | |
| ❑ M2S 703 [(2)S] | This Is My Country | 1963 | 20.00 |
| *—Gray label, "360 Sound Stereo" in black; not to be confused with the single-record LP of the same name* | | | |

| Number | Title (A Side/B Side) | Yr | NM |
|---|---|---|---|
| ❑ ML 2077 [10] | The Mormon Tabernacle Choir of Salt Lake City | 1949 | 40.00 |
| *—Their first album* | | | |
| ❑ ML 2098 [10] | The Mormon Tabernacle Choir of Salt Lake City Volume II | 1950 | 30.00 |
| ❑ ML 4789 [M] | The Mormon Tabernacle Choir of Salt Lake City | 195? | 25.00 |
| *—Reissue of two 10-inch LPs onto one 12-inch LP* | | | |
| ❑ ML 5048 [M] | Concert of Sacred Music | 1955 | 20.00 |
| ❑ ML 5203 [M] | Songs of Faith and Devotion | 1957 | 20.00 |
| ❑ ML 5222 [M] | The Mormon Tabernacle Choir Sings Christmas Carols | 1957 | 20.00 |
| ❑ ML 5302 [M] | The Lord Is My Shepherd | 1958 | 15.00 |
| *—Gray and black label with six "eye" logos* | | | |
| ❑ ML 5364 [M] | The Beloved Choruses | 1958 | 15.00 |
| *—Gray and black label with six "eye" logos* | | | |
| ❑ ML 5386 [M] | The Lord's Prayer | 1959 | 15.00 |
| *—Gray and black label with six "eye" logos* | | | |
| ❑ ML 5423 [M] | The Spirit of Christmas | 1959 | 12.00 |
| ❑ ML 5497 [M] | A Mighty Fortress | 1960 | 12.00 |
| *—Gray and black label with six "eye" logos* | | | |
| ❑ ML 5592 [M] | The Holly and the Ivy | 1960 | 12.00 |
| ❑ ML 5659 [M] | Songs of the North & South 1861-1865 | 1961 | 12.00 |
| *—Gray and black label with six "eye" logos* | | | |
| ❑ ML 5684 [M] | Christmas Carols Around the World | 1961 | 12.00 |
| ❑ ML 5714 [M] | Hymns and Songs of Brotherhood | 1962 | 12.00 |
| ❑ ML 5767 [M] | The Lord's Prayer Volume II | 1962 | 12.00 |
| ❑ ML 5819 [M] | This Is My Country | 1962 | 12.00 |
| ❑ ML 5899 [M] | The Joy of Christmas | 1963 | 12.00 |
| *—With the New York Philharmonic conducted by Leonard Bernstein* | | | |
| ❑ ML 6019 [M] | The Mormon Tabernacle Choir at the World's Fair | 1964 | 20.00 |
| ❑ MS 6019 [S] | The Lord Is My Shepherd | 1958 | 20.00 |
| *—Gray and black label with six "eye" logos* | | | |
| ❑ MS 6058 [S] | The Beloved Choruses | 1958 | 20.00 |
| *—Gray and black label with six "eye" logos* | | | |
| ❑ MS 6068 [S] | The Lord's Prayer | 1959 | 20.00 |
| *—Gray and black label with six "eye" logos* | | | |
| ❑ ML 6079 [M] | Beloved Choruses Volume Two | 1964 | 12.00 |
| ❑ MS 6100 [S] | The Spirit of Christmas | 1959 | 15.00 |
| *—Same as ML 5500, but in stereo* | | | |
| ❑ ML 6121 [M] | God Bless America | 1965 | 12.00 |
| ❑ ML 6147 [M] | This Land Is Your Land | 1965 | 12.00 |
| ❑ MS 6162 [S] | A Mighty Fortress | 1960 | 15.00 |
| *—Gray and black label with six "eye" logos* | | | |
| ❑ ML 6177 [M] | The Mormon Tabernacle Choir Sings Christmas Carols | 1965 | 12.00 |
| *—A new recording of ML 5222* | | | |
| ❑ MS 6192 [S] | The Holly and the Ivy | 1960 | 15.00 |
| *—Same as ML 5592, but in stereo* | | | |
| ❑ ML 6235 [M] | Bless This House | 1966 | 10.00 |
| ❑ MS 6259 [S] | Songs of the North & South 1861-1865 | 1961 | 15.00 |
| *—Gray and black label with six "eye" logos* | | | |
| ❑ MS 6284 [S] | Christmas Carols Around the World | 1961 | 15.00 |
| *—Same as ML 5684, but in stereo* | | | |
| ❑ ML 6308 [M] | Sing Unto God | 1966 | 10.00 |
| ❑ MS 6314 [S] | Hymns and Songs of Brotherhood | 1962 | 15.00 |
| ❑ ML 6351 [M] | The Mormon Tabernacle Choir's Greatest Hits | 1966 | 10.00 |
| ❑ MS 6367 [S] | The Lord's Prayer Volume II | 1962 | 15.00 |
| ❑ ML 6412 [M] | The Old Beloved Songs | 1967 | 12.00 |
| ❑ MS 6419 [S] | This Is My Country | 1962 | 15.00 |
| ❑ ML 6461 [M] | Anvil Chorus: Favorite Opera Choruses | 1967 | 12.00 |
| ❑ ML 6486 [M] | The Mormon Tabernacle Choir's Greatest Hits, Volume 2 | 1967 | 12.00 |
| ❑ MS 6499 [S] | The Joy of Christmas | 1963 | 15.00 |
| *—Same as ML 5899, but in stereo* | | | |
| ❑ MS 6619 [S] | The Mormon Tabernacle Choir at the World's Fair | 1964 | 25.00 |
| ❑ MS 6679 [S] | Beloved Choruses Volume Two | 1964 | 15.00 |
| ❑ MS 6721 [S] | God Bless America | 1965 | 15.00 |
| ❑ MS 6747 [S] | This Land Is Your Land | 1965 | 15.00 |
| ❑ MS 6777 [S] | The Mormon Tabernacle Choir Sings Christmas Carols | 1965 | 15.00 |
| *—Same as ML 6177, but in stereo* | | | |
| ❑ MS 6835 [S] | Bless This House | 1966 | 12.00 |
| ❑ MS 6908 [S] | Sing Unto God | 1966 | 12.00 |
| ❑ MS 6951 [S] | The Mormon Tabernacle Choir's Greatest Hits | 1966 | 12.00 |
| *—Same as ML 6351, but in stereo* | | | |
| ❑ MS 7012 [S] | The Old Beloved Songs | 1967 | 12.00 |
| ❑ MS 7061 [S] | Anvil Chorus: Favorite Opera Choruses | 1967 | 12.00 |
| ❑ MS 7086 [S] | The Mormon Tabernacle Choir's Greatest Hits, Volume 2 | 1967 | 12.00 |
| ❑ MS 7149 | Beautiful Dreamer | 1968 | 12.00 |
| *—Gray "360 Sound" label* | | | |
| ❑ MS 7292 | Hallelujah Chorus: The Great Handel Choruses | 1969 | 12.00 |
| *—Gray "360 Sound" label* | | | |
| ❑ MS 7399 | The Mormon Tabernacle Choir's Greatest Hits, Volume 3 | 1970 | 12.00 |
| ❑ MS 7405 | Jesu, Joy of Man's Desiring: The Great Bach Choruses | 1970 | 12.00 |
| *—Gray "360 Sound" label* | | | |
| ❑ M 30054 | God of Our Fathers | 1970 | 12.00 |
| ❑ M 30077 | Joy to the World | 1970 | 12.00 |
| ❑ XM 30077 | Joy to the World | 197? | 10.00 |
| *—Reissue of M 30077* | | | |
| ❑ M 30647 | Climb Every Mountain | 1971 | 10.00 |
| ❑ MG 31081 [(2)] | The Mormon Tabernacle Choir Album | 1972 | 15.00 |
| ❑ M 32227 | Cielito Lindo — The Mormon Tabernacle Choir En Espanol | 1973 | 12.00 |
| ❑ M 32298 | Stars & Stripes Forever | 1973 | 10.00 |
| ❑ M 32935 | The Great "Messiah" Choruses | 1974 | 10.00 |
| ❑ M 33440 | Music and the Spoken Word | 1975 | 10.00 |
| ❑ MG 33710 [(2)] | Rock of Ages | 1975 | 12.00 |
| ❑ M 34134 | A Jubilant Song | 1976 | 10.00 |
| ❑ M 34538 | Songs of Thanks | 1977 | 10.00 |
| ❑ M 34546 | White Christmas | 1977 | 12.00 |
| *—In box with insert of Christmas recipes* | | | |
| ❑ M 35120 | Hail to the Victors! | 1978 | 10.00 |
| ❑ M 35148 | Robertson: Oratorio from the Book of Mormon | 1978 | 10.00 |
| ❑ M 35825 | Memories: Songs America Loves Best | 1980 | 10.00 |
| ❑ M 35868 | Beyond the Blue Horizon | 1980 | 10.00 |

COLUMBIA SPECIAL PRODUCTS

| Number | Title (A Side/B Side) | Yr | NM |
|---|---|---|---|
| ❑ CSS 1667 | The Mormon Tabernacle Choir in South Carolina — Tricentennial Concert | 1970 | 20.00 |
| ❑ P 14243 | Nearer My God to Thee | 1977 | 12.00 |
| *—"Mfg by CBS for Covenant Recordings"* | | | |
| ❑ P 14244 | Lift Thine Eyes | 1977 | 12.00 |
| *—"Mfg by CBS for Covenant Recordings"* | | | |
| ❑ P 14245 | For All the Saints | 1977 | 12.00 |
| *—"Mfg by CBS for Covenant Recordings"* | | | |
| ❑ P 14246 | Now the Day Is Over | 1977 | 12.00 |
| *—"Mfg by CBS for Covenant Recordings"* | | | |
| ❑ P 14247 | I Know That My Redeemer Lives | 1977 | 12.00 |
| *—"Mfg by CBS for Covenant Recordings"* | | | |
| ❑ P 14303 | It's Christmas! | 1977 | 12.00 |
| *—"Mfg by CBS for Covenant Recordings"* | | | |
| ❑ P 15935 | Songs of Faith | 1983 | 10.00 |

FRANKLIN MINT

| Number | Title (A Side/B Side) | Yr | NM |
|---|---|---|---|
| ❑ (no #) [(2)] | The Greatest Songs of Christmas | 1980 | 25.00 |
| *—Maroon vinyl; the choir's first digital recording* | | | |

HARMONY

| Number | Title (A Side/B Side) | Yr | NM |
|---|---|---|---|
| ❑ HS 11272 | Onward Christian Soldiers | 1968 | 10.00 |
| ❑ HS 11370 | Faith of Our Fathers | 1970 | 12.00 |
| ❑ KH 30673 | The Mormon Tabernacle Choir Sings Songs of Christmas | 1971 | 10.00 |

READER'S DIGEST

| Number | Title (A Side/B Side) | Yr | NM |
|---|---|---|---|
| ❑ RD4-093 [(5)] | The Mormon Tabernacle Choir Sings | 1973 | 25.00 |
| ❑ RBA-128/A [(4)] | Climb Ev'ry Mountain: The Mormon Tabernacle Choir Sings Great Songs of Inspiration | 1988 | 25.00 |
| ❑ RD4A-221-1 | Merry Christmas from the Mormon Tabernacle Choir | 1981 | 10.00 |
| ❑ P2 15176/7 [(2)] | 50th Anniversary Album | 1980 | 20.00 |

REALM

| Number | Title (A Side/B Side) | Yr | NM |
|---|---|---|---|
| ❑ 3V 8039 [(3)] | The Mormon Tabernacle Choir's Greatest Hits (Includes Christmas with the Mormon Tabernacle Choir) | 197? | 15.00 |
| *—Reissue of Columbia House 6240* | | | |

TIME-LIFE

| Number | Title (A Side/B Side) | Yr | NM |
|---|---|---|---|
| ❑ SMT 104 [(3)] | Christmas Celebration | 1987 | 20.00 |
| *—Same contents as Book-of-the-Month LP. Side 1, 2 and 6 are identical; Side 3 is BOTM's Side 5, Side 4 is BOTM's Side 3, and Side 5 is BOTM's Side 4.* | | | |

## MORMON TABERNACLE ORGAN AND CHIMES

COLUMBIA MASTERWORKS

| Number | Title (A Side/B Side) | Yr | NM |
|---|---|---|---|
| ❑ ML 6037 [M] | Christmas with the Mormon Tabernacle Organ and Chimes | 1964 | 12.00 |
| ❑ MS 6637 [S] | Christmas with the Mormon Tabernacle Organ and Chimes | 1964 | 15.00 |

## MORNING DEW, THE

ROULETTE

| Number | Title (A Side/B Side) | Yr | NM |
|---|---|---|---|
| ❑ SR-42049 | The Morning Dew | 1970 | 300.00 |

## MORNING GLORY

FONTANA

| Number | Title (A Side/B Side) | Yr | NM |
|---|---|---|---|
| ❑ SRF-67573 | Two Suns Worth | 1968 | 25.00 |

## MORNINGLORY

TOYA

| Number | Title (A Side/B Side) | Yr | NM |
|---|---|---|---|
| ❑ STLP-003 | Growing | 1972 | 40.00 |

## MORRIS, AUDREY

BETHLEHEM

| Number | Title (A Side/B Side) | Yr | NM |
|---|---|---|---|
| ❑ BCP-6010 [M] | The Voice of Audrey Morris | 1956 | 120.00 |

## MORRIS, GREG

DOT

| Number | Title (A Side/B Side) | Yr | NM |
|---|---|---|---|
| ❑ DLP-25881 | For You | 1968 | 20.00 |

## MORRIS, MARLOWE

COLUMBIA

| Number | Title (A Side/B Side) | Yr | NM |
|---|---|---|---|
| ❑ CL 1819 [M] | Play the Thing | 1962 | 20.00 |
| ❑ CS 8619 [S] | Play the Thing | 1962 | 25.00 |

## MORRISON, HAROLD

DECCA

| Number | Title (A Side/B Side) | Yr | NM |
|---|---|---|---|
| ❑ DL 4680 [M] | Hoss, He's the Boss | 1965 | 15.00 |
| ❑ DL 74680 [S] | Hoss, He's the Boss | 1965 | 20.00 |

## MORRISON, VAN

BANG

| Number | Title (A Side/B Side) | Yr | NM |
|---|---|---|---|
| ❑ BLB-218 [M] | Blowin' Your Mind | 1968 | 50.00 |
| *—With the censored "Brown Eyed Girl" lyric, "Laughin' and a-runnin', hey hey, behind the stadium with you," part of which was spliced in from another part of the song. This has been confirmed to exist in mono.* | | | |
| ❑ BLBS-218 [S] | Blowin' Your Mind | 1968 | 20.00 |
| *—With the censored "Brown Eyed Girl" lyric, "Laughin' and a-runnin', hey hey, behind the stadium with you," part of which was spliced in from another part of the song!* | | | |
| ❑ BLP-218 [M] | Blowin' Your Mind | 1967 | 30.00 |
| *—With the true "Brown Eyed Girl" lyric, "Makin' love in the green grass behind the stadium with you."* | | | |
| ❑ BLPS-218 [S] | Blowin' Your Mind | 1967 | 40.00 |
| *—With the true "Brown Eyed Girl" lyric, "Makin' love in the green grass behind the stadium with you."* | | | |
| ❑ BLPS-222 | The Best of Van Morrison | 1970 | 15.00 |
| ❑ BLPS-400 | T.B. Sheets | 1973 | 20.00 |

DIRECT DISK

| Number | Title (A Side/B Side) | Yr | NM |
|---|---|---|---|
| ❑ SD-16604 | Moondance | 1981 | 100.00 |
| *—Audiophile vinyl* | | | |

LOST HIGHWAY

| Number | Title (A Side/B Side) | Yr | NM |
|---|---|---|---|
| ❑ B0005968-01 | Pay the Devil | 2006 | 12.00 |

MERCURY

| Number | Title (A Side/B Side) | Yr | NM |
|---|---|---|---|
| ❑ 818336-1 | Live at the Grand Opera House, Belfast | 1985 | 10.00 |
| ❑ 822895-1 | A Sense of Wonder | 1985 | 8.00 |
| ❑ 830077-1 | No Guru, No Method, No Teacher | 1986 | 8.00 |
| ❑ 832585-1 | Poetic Champions Compose | 1987 | 8.00 |
| ❑ 834496-1 | Irish Heartbeat | 1988 | 8.00 |
| *—With the Chieftains* | | | |
| ❑ 839262-1 | Avalon Sunset | 1989 | 10.00 |
| ❑ 841970-1 | The Best of Van Morrison | 1990 | 15.00 |
| ❑ 847100-1 | Enlightenment | 1990 | 15.00 |

WARNER BROS.

| Number | Title (A Side/B Side) | Yr | NM |
|---|---|---|---|
| ❑ WBMS-102 [DJ] | Live at the Roxy | 1978 | 50.00 |
| ❑ WS 1768 | Astral Weeks | 1968 | 25.00 |
| *—With "W7" logo on green label* | | | |
| ❑ WS 1768 | Astral Weeks | 1970 | 12.00 |
| *—With "WB" logo on green label* | | | |
| ❑ WS 1768 | Astral Weeks | 1973 | 10.00 |
| *—"Burbank" palm-tree label* | | | |
| ❑ WS 1768 | Astral Weeks | 1979 | 8.00 |
| *—Later white or tan label* | | | |
| ❑ WS 1835 | Moondance | 1969 | 20.00 |
| *—With "W7" logo on green label* | | | |
| ❑ WS 1835 | Moondance | 1970 | 12.00 |
| *—With "WB" logo on green label* | | | |
| ❑ WS 1835 | Moondance | 1973 | 10.00 |
| *—"Burbank" palm-tree label* | | | |
| ❑ WS 1884 | His Band and the Street Choir | 1970 | 15.00 |
| *—With "WB" logo on green label* | | | |
| ❑ WS 1884 | His Band and the Street Choir | 1973 | 10.00 |
| *—"Burbank" palm-tree label* | | | |
| ❑ WS 1884 | His Band and the Street Choir | 1979 | 8.00 |
| *—Later white or tan label* | | | |
| ❑ WS 1950 | Tupelo Honey | 1971 | 15.00 |
| *—With "WB" logo on green label, plus poster* | | | |
| ❑ WS 1950 | Tupelo Honey | 1973 | 10.00 |
| *—"Burbank" palm-tree label* | | | |
| ❑ WS 1950 | Tupelo Honey | 1979 | 8.00 |
| *—Later white or tan label* | | | |
| ❑ WS 2633 | Saint Dominic's Preview | 1972 | 15.00 |
| *—With "WB" logo on green label* | | | |
| ❑ WS 2633 | Saint Dominic's Preview | 1973 | 10.00 |
| *—"Burbank" palm-tree label* | | | |
| ❑ WS 2633 | Saint Dominic's Preview | 1979 | 8.00 |
| *—Later white or tan label* | | | |
| ❑ BS 2712 | Hard Nose the Highway | 1973 | 12.00 |
| *—"Burbank" palm-tree label* | | | |
| ❑ BS 2712 | Hard Nose the Highway | 1979 | 8.00 |
| *—Later white or tan label* | | | |
| ❑ 2BS 2760 [(2)] | It's Too Late to Stop Now | 1974 | 15.00 |
| *—"Burbank" palm-tree labels* | | | |

Van Morrison, *Tupelo Honey,* Warner Bros. WS 1950, 1971, green label, $15.

| Number | Title (A Side/B Side) | Yr | NM |
|---|---|---|---|
| ❑ 2BS 2760 [(2)] | It's Too Late to Stop Now | 1979 | 8.00 |
| *—Later white or tan label* | | | |
| ❑ BS 2805 | Veedon Fleece | 1974 | 12.00 |
| *—"Burbank" palm-tree labels* | | | |
| ❑ BS 2805 | Veedon Fleece | 1979 | 8.00 |
| *—Later white or tan label* | | | |
| ❑ BS 2987 | A Period of Transition | 1977 | 12.00 |
| *—"Burbank" palm-tree labels* | | | |
| ❑ BS 2987 | A Period of Transition | 1979 | 8.00 |
| *—Later white or tan label* | | | |
| ❑ BSK 3103 | Moondance | 1977 | 10.00 |
| *—Reissue with new number; "Burbank" palm-tree label* | | | |
| ❑ BSK 3103 | Moondance | 1979 | 8.00 |
| *—Later white or tan label* | | | |
| ❑ BSK 3212 | Wavelength | 1978 | 12.00 |
| ❑ HS 3390 | Into the Music | 1979 | 12.00 |
| ❑ BSK 3462 | Common One | 1980 | 12.00 |
| ❑ BSK 3652 | Beautiful Vision | 1981 | 12.00 |
| ❑ 23802 | Inarticulate Speech of the Heart | 1983 | 12.00 |

## MORRISSEY, PAT

MERCURY

| Number | Title (A Side/B Side) | Yr | NM |
|---|---|---|---|
| ❑ MG-20197 [M] | I'm Pat Morrissey, I Sing | 1957 | 100.00 |

## MORROW, BUDDY

EPIC

| Number | Title (A Side/B Side) | Yr | NM |
|---|---|---|---|
| ❑ LN 24095 [M] | Big Band Beatlemania | 1964 | 25.00 |
| ❑ BN 26095 [S] | Big Band Beatlemania | 1964 | 30.00 |

MERCURY

| Number | Title (A Side/B Side) | Yr | NM |
|---|---|---|---|
| ❑ MG-20062 [M] | Shall We Dance? | 195? | 30.00 |
| ❑ MG-20204 [M] | A Salute to the Fabulous Dorseys | 1957 | 30.00 |
| ❑ MG-20221 [M] | Golden Trombone | 1956 | 30.00 |
| ❑ MG-20290 [M] | Tribute to Tommy Dorsey | 1957 | 30.00 |
| ❑ MG-20372 [M] | Just We Two | 195? | 30.00 |
| ❑ MG-20396 [M] | Night Train | 195? | 30.00 |
| ❑ MG-20702 [M] | Night Train Goes to Hollywood | 1962 | 25.00 |
| ❑ SR-60009 [S] | Night Train | 1958 | 40.00 |
| ❑ SR-60018 [S] | Just We Two | 1958 | 40.00 |
| ❑ SR-60702 [S] | Night Train Goes to Hollywood | 1962 | 30.00 |
| ❑ SR-60764 [S] | A Collection of 33 All-Time Dance Favorites | 1963 | 20.00 |

RCA VICTOR

| Number | Title (A Side/B Side) | Yr | NM |
|---|---|---|---|
| ❑ LPM-1427 [M] | Night Train | 1956 | 40.00 |
| ❑ LPM-1925 [M] | Dancing Tonight To Morrow | 1958 | 30.00 |
| ❑ LSP-1925 [S] | Dancing Tonight To Morrow | 1958 | 40.00 |
| ❑ LPM-2018 [M] | Big Band Guitar | 1959 | 30.00 |
| ❑ LSP-2018 [S] | Big Band Guitar | 1959 | 40.00 |
| ❑ LPM-2042 [M] | Impact | 1959 | 30.00 |
| ❑ LSP-2042 [S] | Impact | 1959 | 40.00 |
| ❑ LPM-2180 [M] | Double Impact | 1960 | 30.00 |
| ❑ LSP-2180 [S] | Double Impact | 1960 | 40.00 |
| ❑ LPM-2208 [M] | Poe for Moderns | 1960 | 30.00 |
| ❑ LSP-2208 [S] | Poe for Moderns | 1960 | 40.00 |

## MORSE, ELLA MAE

CAPITOL

| Number | Title (A Side/B Side) | Yr | NM |
|---|---|---|---|
| ❑ H 513 [10] | Barrelhouse Boogie and the Blues | 1954 | 400.00 |
| ❑ T 513 [M] | Barrelhouse Boogie and the Blues | 1955 | 250.00 |
| ❑ T 898 [M] | Morse Code | 1957 | 150.00 |
| *—Turquoise label* | | | |
| ❑ ST 1802 [S] | Hits of Ella Mae Morse and Freddie Slack | 1962 | 120.00 |
| ❑ T 1802 [M] | Hits of Ella Mae Morse and Freddie Slack | 1962 | 100.00 |
| ❑ M-11971 [M] | Hits of Ella Mae Morse and Freddie Slack | 197? | 15.00 |
| *—Reissue* | | | |

## MORSE, ROBERT, AND CHARLES NELSON REILLY

CAPITOL

| Number | Title (A Side/B Side) | Yr | NM |
|---|---|---|---|
| ❑ ST 1862 [S] | A Jolly Theatrical Christmas | 1963 | 25.00 |
| ❑ T 1862 [M] | A Jolly Theatrical Christmas | 1963 | 20.00 |

## MORTIMER

PHILIPS

| Number | Title (A Side/B Side) | Yr | NM |
|---|---|---|---|
| ❑ PHS 600267 | Mortimer | 1969 | 25.00 |

## MORTON, JELLY ROLL

CIRCLE

| Number | Title (A Side/B Side) | Yr | NM |
|---|---|---|---|
| ❑ L-14001 [M] | The Saga of Mr. Jelly Lord Volume 1: Jazz Started in New Orelans | 1951 | 120.00 |
| ❑ L-14002 [M] | The Saga of Mr. Jelly Lord Volume 2: Way Down Yonder | 1951 | 120.00 |
| ❑ L-14003 [M] | The Saga of Mr. Jelly Lord Volume 3: Jazz Is Strictly Music | 1951 | 120.00 |
| ❑ L-14004 [M] | The Saga of Mr. Jelly Lord Volume 4: The Spanish Tinge | 1951 | 120.00 |
| ❑ L-14005 [M] | The Saga of Mr. Jelly Lord Volume 5: Bad Man Ballads | 1951 | 120.00 |
| ❑ L-14006 [M] | The Saga of Mr. Jelly Lord Volume 6: Jazz Piano Soloist #1 | 1951 | 120.00 |
| ❑ L-14007 [M] | The Saga of Mr. Jelly Lord Volume 7: Everyone Had His Style | 1951 | 120.00 |
| ❑ L-14008 [M] | The Saga of Mr. Jelly Lord Volume 8: Jelly and the Blues | 1951 | 120.00 |
| ❑ L-14009 [M] | The Saga of Mr. Jelly Lord Volume 9: Alabama Bound | 1951 | 120.00 |
| ❑ L-14010 [M] | The Saga of Mr. Jelly Lord Volume 10: Jazz Piano Soloist #2 | 1951 | 120.00 |
| ❑ L-14011 [M] | The Saga of Mr. Jelly Lord Volume 11: In New Orleans | 1951 | 120.00 |
| ❑ L-14012 [M] | The Saga of Mr. Jelly Lord Volume 12: I'm the Winin' Boy | 1951 | 120.00 |

COMMODORE

| Number | Title (A Side/B Side) | Yr | NM |
|---|---|---|---|
| ❑ DL-30000 [M] | New Orleans Memories | 1950 | 100.00 |

JAZZ PANORAMA

| Number | Title (A Side/B Side) | Yr | NM |
|---|---|---|---|
| ❑ 1804 [10] | Peppers | 1951 | 100.00 |
| ❑ 1810 [10] | Peppers | 1951 | 100.00 |

MAINSTREAM

| Number | Title (A Side/B Side) | Yr | NM |
|---|---|---|---|
| ❑ 56020 [M] | Jelly Roll Morton | 1965 | 25.00 |

RCA VICTOR

| Number | Title (A Side/B Side) | Yr | NM |
|---|---|---|---|
| ❑ LPT-32 [10] | A Treasury of Immortal Performances | 1952 | 100.00 |
| ❑ LPV-508 [M] | Stomps and Joys | 1965 | 20.00 |
| ❑ LPV-524 [M] | Hot Jazz, Pop Jazz, Hokum and Hilarity | 1965 | 20.00 |
| ❑ LPV-546 [M] | Mr. Jelly Lord | 1966 | 20.00 |
| ❑ LPV-559 [M] | I Thought I Heard Buddy Bolden Say | 1966 | 20.00 |
| ❑ LPM-1649 [M] | The King of New Orleans Jazz | 1957 | 50.00 |

RIVERSIDE

| Number | Title (A Side/B Side) | Yr | NM |
|---|---|---|---|
| ❑ RLP 12-102 [M] | The New Orleans Rhythm Kings with Jelly Roll Morton | 1955 | 50.00 |
| ❑ RLP 12-111 [M] | Classic Piano Solos | 1955 | 50.00 |
| ❑ RLP 12-128 [M] | The Incomparable Jelly Roll Morton | 1956 | 50.00 |
| ❑ RLP 12-132 [M] | Mr. Jelly Lord | 1956 | 50.00 |
| ❑ RLP 12-133 [M] | Jelly Roll Morton Plays and Sings | 1956 | 50.00 |
| ❑ RLP 12-140 [M] | Rags and Blues | 1956 | 50.00 |
| ❑ RLP-1018 [10] | Rediscovered Solos | 1953 | 100.00 |
| ❑ RLP-1027 [10] | Jelly Roll Morton's Kings of Jazz: His Rarest Recordings | 1954 | 100.00 |
| ❑ RLP-1038 [10] | Classic Jazz Piano, Volume 1 | 1954 | 100.00 |
| ❑ RLP-1041 [10] | Classic Jazz Piano, Volume 2 | 1954 | 100.00 |
| ❑ RLP-9001 [M] | Library of Congress Recordings Volume 1 | 1955 | 50.00 |
| ❑ RLP-9002 [M] | Library of Congress Recordings Volume 2 | 1955 | 50.00 |
| ❑ RLP-9003 [M] | Library of Congress Recordings Volume 3 | 1955 | 50.00 |
| ❑ RLP-9004 [M] | Library of Congress Recordings Volume 4 | 1955 | 50.00 |
| ❑ RLP-9005 [M] | Library of Congress Recordings Volume 5 | 1955 | 50.00 |
| ❑ RLP-9006 [M] | Library of Congress Recordings Volume 6 | 1955 | 50.00 |
| ❑ RLP-9007 [M] | Library of Congress Recordings Volume 7 | 1955 | 50.00 |
| ❑ RLP-9008 [M] | Library of Congress Recordings Volume 8 | 1955 | 50.00 |
| ❑ RLP-9009 [M] | Library of Congress Recordings Volume 9 | 1955 | 50.00 |
| ❑ RLP-9010 [M] | Library of Congress Recordings Volume 10 | 1955 | 50.00 |
| ❑ RLP-9011 [M] | Library of Congress Recordings Volume 11 | 1955 | 50.00 |
| ❑ RLP-9012 [M] | Library of Congress Recordings Volume 12 | 1955 | 50.00 |

"X"

| Number | Title (A Side/B Side) | Yr | NM |
|---|---|---|---|
| ❑ LX-3008 [10] | Red Hot Peppers, Volume 1 | 1954 | 100.00 |

"X"

| Number | Title (A Side/B Side) | Yr | NM |
|---|---|---|---|
| ❑ LVA-3028 [10] | Red Hot Peppers, Volume 2 | 1954 | 100.00 |

## MOSBY, JOHNNY AND JONIE

CAPITOL

| Number | Title (A Side/B Side) | Yr | NM |
|---|---|---|---|
| ❑ ST-170 | Just Hold My Hand | 1969 | 15.00 |
| ❑ ST-286 | Hold Me | 1969 | 15.00 |
| ❑ ST-414 | I'll Never Be Free | 1970 | 15.00 |
| ❑ ST-556 | My Happiness | 1970 | 15.00 |
| ❑ ST-737 | Oh, Love of Mine | 1971 | 15.00 |
| ❑ ST 2903 | Make a Left and Then a Right | 1968 | 15.00 |

COLUMBIA

| Number | Title (A Side/B Side) | Yr | NM |
|---|---|---|---|
| ❑ CL 2297 [M] | Mr. & Mrs. Country Music | 1965 | 15.00 |
| ❑ CS 9097 [S] | Mr. & Mrs. Country Music | 1965 | 20.00 |

HARMONY

| Number | Title (A Side/B Side) | Yr | NM |
|---|---|---|---|
| ❑ HS 11389 | Mr. & Mrs. Country Music | 1970 | 10.00 |

STARDAY

| Number | Title (A Side/B Side) | Yr | NM |
|---|---|---|---|
| ❑ SLP-328 [M] | The New Sweethearts of Country Music | 1965 | 30.00 |

### MOSLEY, BOB

| Number | Title (A Side/B Side) | Yr | NM |
|---|---|---|---|
| **REPRISE** | | | |
| ❑ MS 2068 | Bob Mosley | 1972 | 20.00 |

### MOSS, GENE

| Number | Title (A Side/B Side) | Yr | NM |
|---|---|---|---|
| **RCA VICTOR** | | | |
| ❑ LPM-2977 [M] | Dracula's Greatest Hits | 1964 | 30.00 |
| ❑ LSP-2977 [S] | Dracula's Greatest Hits | 1964 | 40.00 |

### MOSSE, SANDY

| Number | Title (A Side/B Side) | Yr | NM |
|---|---|---|---|
| **ARGO** | | | |
| ❑ LP-609 [M] | Chicago Scene | 1957 | 40.00 |
| ❑ LP-639 [M] | Relaxin' with Sandy Mosse | 1959 | 30.00 |
| ❑ LPS-639 [S] | Relaxin' with Sandy Mosse | 1959 | 40.00 |

### MOST, ABE

| Number | Title (A Side/B Side) | Yr | NM |
|---|---|---|---|
| **LIBERTY** | | | |
| ❑ LJH-6004 [M] | Mister Clarinet | 1955 | 50.00 |

### MOST, SAM

| Number | Title (A Side/B Side) | Yr | NM |
|---|---|---|---|
| **BETHLEHEM** | | | |
| ❑ BCP-18 [M] | I'm Nuts About the Most: East Coast Jazz, Volume 7 | 1955 | 50.00 |
| ❑ BCP-75 [M] | Sam Most Plays Bird, Bud, Monk and Miles | 1957 | 50.00 |
| ❑ BCP-78 [M] | The Amazing Sam Most with Strings | 1958 | 50.00 |
| ❑ BCP-6008 [M] | Musically Yours | 1956 | 50.00 |
| **DEBUT** | | | |
| ❑ DLP-11 [10] | Sam Most Sextet | 1954 | 300.00 |
| **VANGUARD** | | | |
| ❑ VRS-8014 [10] | Sam Most Sextet | 1954 | 80.00 |
| **XANADU** | | | |
| ❑ X-3001 | Flute Talk | 1980 | 25.00 |
| *—Audiophile edition* | | | |

### MOTELS, THE Also see MARTHA DAVIS.

| Number | Title (A Side/B Side) | Yr | NM |
|---|---|---|---|
| **CAPITOL** | | | |
| ❑ ST-11996 | The Motels | 1979 | 10.00 |
| ❑ ST-12070 | Careful | 1980 | 10.00 |
| ❑ ST-12177 | All Four One | 1982 | 10.00 |
| ❑ ST-12177 [DJ] | All Four One | 1982 | 20.00 |
| *—Promo-only high-grade vinyl pressing (different front cover)* | | | |
| ❑ ST-12288 | Little Robbers | 1983 | 10.00 |
| ❑ SJ-12378 | Shock | 1985 | 10.00 |
| ❑ SN-16343 | The Motels | 1985 | 8.00 |
| *—Budget-line reissue* | | | |
| ❑ SN-16347 | Careful | 1985 | 8.00 |
| *—Budget-line reissue* | | | |
| ❑ SN-16355 | Little Robbers | 1985 | 8.00 |
| *—Budget-line reissue* | | | |
| ❑ SN-16420 | All Four One | 198? | 8.00 |
| *—Budget-line reissue* | | | |

### MOTEN, BENNIE

| Number | Title (A Side/B Side) | Yr | NM |
|---|---|---|---|
| **HISTORICAL** | | | |
| ❑ 9 | Bennie Moten's Kansas City Orchestra | 1966 | 20.00 |
| **RCA VICTOR** | | | |
| ❑ LPV-514 [M] | Bennie Moten's Great Band of 1930-32 | 1965 | 20.00 |
| **"X"** | | | |
| ❑ LX-3004 [10] | Kansas City Jazz, Volume 1 | 1954 | 60.00 |
| **"X"** | | | |
| ❑ LVA-3025 [10] | Kansas City Jazz, Volume 2 | 1954 | 60.00 |
| **"X"** | | | |
| ❑ LVA-3038 [10] | Kansas City Jazz, Volume 3 | 1954 | 60.00 |

### MOTHER EARTH

| Number | Title (A Side/B Side) | Yr | NM |
|---|---|---|---|
| **MERCURY** | | | |
| ❑ SR-61194 | Living with the Animals | 1968 | 25.00 |
| ❑ SR-61226 | Make a Joyful Noise | 1969 | 20.00 |
| ❑ SR-61230 | Tracy Nelson Country | 1969 | 20.00 |
| ❑ SR-61270 | Satisfied | 1970 | 20.00 |
| **REPRISE** | | | |
| ❑ MS 2054 | Tracy Nelson/Mother Earth | 1972 | 15.00 |
| ❑ RS 6431 | Bring Me Home | 1971 | 15.00 |

### MOTHER LOVE BONE

| Number | Title (A Side/B Side) | Yr | NM |
|---|---|---|---|
| **POLYDOR** | | | |
| ❑ 843191-1 | Apple | 1990 | 50.00 |
| **STARDOG** | | | |
| ❑ 839011-1 [EP] | Shine | 1989 | 50.00 |
| *—Four songs on side one, the same four songs on side two* | | | |

### MOTHERS OF INVENTION, THE See FRANK ZAPPA.

### MOTIONS, THE (3)

| Number | Title (A Side/B Side) | Yr | NM |
|---|---|---|---|
| **PHILIPS** | | | |
| ❑ PHS 600317 | Electric Baby | 1969 | 20.00 |

Mott the Hoople, *Mott,* Columbia KC 32425, 1973, $15.

### MOTLEY CRUE

| Number | Title (A Side/B Side) | Yr | NM |
|---|---|---|---|
| **ELEKTRA** | | | |
| ❑ 60174 | Too Fast for Love | 1982 | 10.00 |
| *—Reissue of Leathur LP with slight revisions* | | | |
| ❑ 60289 | Shout at the Devil | 1982 | 8.00 |
| ❑ 60395 [EP] | Helter Skelter | 1984 | 40.00 |
| *—Picture disc with four songs; includes poster and insert (deduct 50 percent if missing)* | | | |
| ❑ 60418 | Theatre of Pain | 1985 | 8.00 |
| ❑ 60725 | Girls, Girls, Girls | 1987 | 8.00 |
| ❑ 60829 | Dr. Feelgood | 1989 | 12.00 |
| **LEATHUR** | | | |
| ❑ LR-1281 | Too Fast for Love | 1981 | 150.00 |
| *—Second pressing with red lettering on cover. Both Leathur pressings contain "Stick to Your Guns," which was not on the Elektra reissue* | | | |
| ❑ LR-1281 | Too Fast for Love | 1981 | 300.00 |
| *—First pressing with white lettering on cover* | | | |
| **MOTLEY/HIP-O SELECT** | | | |
| ❑ B0004791-01 | Too Fast for Love | 2005 | 20.00 |
| *—Reissue of Leathur LP with bonus 7-inch single, Stick to Your Guns/Toast of the Town* | | | |

### MOTORHEAD

| Number | Title (A Side/B Side) | Yr | NM |
|---|---|---|---|
| **EMI AMERICA** | | | |
| ❑ LN-10340 | On Parole | 1986 | 10.00 |
| *—First U.S. issue of early U.K. LP* | | | |
| **ENIGMA** | | | |
| ❑ D1-73536 | The Birthday Party | 1990 | 12.00 |
| ❑ D1-75405 | No Sleep at All | 1988 | 8.00 |
| **ISLAND** | | | |
| ❑ 90233 [(2)] | No Remorse | 1984 | 12.00 |
| *—Regular cover* | | | |
| ❑ 90236 [(2)] | No Remorse | 1984 | 30.00 |
| *—Leather cover* | | | |
| **MERCURY** | | | |
| ❑ SRM-1-4011 | Ace of Spades | 1980 | 10.00 |
| ❑ SRM-1-4023 | No Sleep 'Til Hammersmith | 1981 | 10.00 |
| ❑ SRM-1-4042 | Iron Fist | 1982 | 10.00 |
| ❑ 811365-1 | Another Perfect Day | 1983 | 8.00 |
| **PROFILE** | | | |
| ❑ PAL-1223 | Orgasmatron | 1986 | 8.00 |
| ❑ PAL-1240 | Rock 'N' Roll | 1987 | 8.00 |
| ❑ PRO-3241 | Overkill | 1986 | 8.00 |
| *—First U.S. issue of early U.K. LP* | | | |
| ❑ PRO-3242 | Bomber | 1986 | 8.00 |
| *—First U.S. issue of early U.K. LP* | | | |
| ❑ PRO-3243 | Ace of Spades | 1986 | 8.00 |
| *—Reissue of Mercury 4011* | | | |
| ❑ PRO-3244 | No Sleep 'Til Hammersmith | 1986 | 8.00 |
| *—Reissue of Mercury 4023* | | | |
| **WTG** | | | |
| ❑ N 46858 | 1916 | 1991 | 12.00 |

### MOTT THE HOOPLE

| Number | Title (A Side/B Side) | Yr | NM |
|---|---|---|---|
| **ATLANTIC** | | | |
| ❑ SD 7297 | Rock and Roll Queen | 1974 | 20.00 |
| ❑ SD 8258 | Mott the Hoople | 1970 | 20.00 |
| *—With "1841 Broadway" address and no mention of Warner Communications on label* | | | |
| ❑ SD 8258 | Mott the Hoople | 198? | 8.00 |
| *—With Warner Communications "W" logo on label* | | | |
| ❑ SD 8272 | Mad Shadows | 1970 | 20.00 |
| ❑ SD 8284 | Wildlife | 1971 | 20.00 |
| ❑ SD 8304 | Brain Capers | 1972 | 20.00 |
| **COLUMBIA** | | | |
| ❑ KC 31750 | All the Young Dudes | 1972 | 15.00 |
| ❑ PC 31750 | All the Young Dudes | 198? | 8.00 |
| *—Budget-line reissue* | | | |
| ❑ KC 32425 | Mott | 1973 | 15.00 |
| ❑ PC 32425 | Mott | 198? | 8.00 |
| *—Budget-line reissue* | | | |
| ❑ PC 32871 | The Hoople | 1974 | 15.00 |
| ❑ PCQ 32871 [Q] | The Hoople | 1974 | 25.00 |
| ❑ PC 33282 | Mott the Hoople Live | 1974 | 15.00 |
| *—No bar code on cover* | | | |
| ❑ PC 33282 | Mott the Hoople Live | 198? | 8.00 |
| *—Reissue with bar code on cover* | | | |
| ❑ PC 33705 | Drive On | 1975 | 15.00 |
| ❑ PC 34236 | Shouting and Pointing | 1976 | 15.00 |
| ❑ PC 34368 | Mott the Hoople's Greatest Hits | 1976 | 12.00 |
| *—No bar code on cover* | | | |
| ❑ PC 34368 | Mott the Hoople's Greatest Hits | 198? | 8.00 |
| *—Reissue with bar code on cover* | | | |

### MOTTOLA, TONY

| Number | Title (A Side/B Side) | Yr | NM |
|---|---|---|---|
| **ABC** | | | |
| ❑ S-738 | 16 Great Performances | 1972 | 10.00 |
| ❑ X-770 | Mister Guitar | 1973 | 10.00 |

| Number | Title (A Side/B Side) | Yr | NM |
|---|---|---|---|
| **COMMAND** | | | |
| ❑ 33-807 [M] | Mr. Big | 1961 | 12.00 |
| ❑ SD 807 [S] | Mr. Big | 1961 | 15.00 |
| ❑ 33-816 [M] | Roman Guitar | 1962 | 12.00 |
| ❑ SD 816 [S] | Roman Guitar | 1962 | 15.00 |
| ❑ 33-823 [M] | Country and Western Folk Songs | 1962 | 12.00 |
| ❑ SD 823 [S] | Country and Western Folk Songs | 1962 | 15.00 |
| ❑ 33-828 [M] | String Band Strum-Along | 1962 | 12.00 |
| ❑ SD 828 [S] | String Band Strum-Along | 1962 | 15.00 |
| ❑ 33-836 [M] | Roman Guitar, Volume Two | 1962 | 12.00 |
| ❑ SD 836 [S] | Roman Guitar, Volume Two | 1962 | 15.00 |
| ❑ 33-841 [M] | Spanish Guitar | 1963 | 12.00 |
| ❑ SD 841 [S] | Spanish Guitar | 1963 | 15.00 |
| ❑ 33-847 [M] | Romantic Guitar | 1963 | 12.00 |
| ❑ SD 847 [S] | Romantic Guitar | 1963 | 15.00 |
| ❑ 33-864 [M] | Sentimental Guitar | 1964 | 12.00 |
| ❑ SD 864 [S] | Sentimental Guitar | 1964 | 15.00 |
| ❑ 33-877 [M] | Guitar — Paris | 1964 | 12.00 |
| ❑ SD 877 [S] | Guitar — Paris | 1964 | 15.00 |
| ❑ 33-885 [M] | Command Performance | 1965 | 12.00 |
| ❑ SD 885 [S] | Command Performance | 1965 | 15.00 |
| ❑ 33-889 [M] | Love Songs — Mexico/S.A. | 1965 | 12.00 |
| ❑ SD 889 [S] | Love Songs — Mexico/S.A. | 1965 | 15.00 |
| ❑ 33-900 [M] | Amor — Mexico/S.A. | 1966 | 12.00 |
| ❑ SD 900 [S] | Amor — Mexico/S.A. | 1966 | 15.00 |
| ❑ 33-908 [M] | Guitar — U.S.A. | 1967 | 15.00 |
| ❑ SD 908 [S] | Guitar — U.S.A. | 1967 | 12.00 |
| ❑ QD-40001 [Q] | Guitar — Paris | 1972 | 20.00 |
| **PICKWICK** | | | |
| ❑ SPC-3610 | Spanish Guitar | 1978 | 8.00 |
| **PROJECT 3** | | | |
| ❑ PR-5003 | Heart and Soul | 1967 | 12.00 |
| ❑ PR-5010 | A Latin Love-In | 1967 | 12.00 |
| ❑ PR4C-5010 [Q] | A Latin Love-In | 1973 | 18.00 |
| ❑ PR-5020 | Lush, Latin & Lovely | 1968 | 12.00 |
| ❑ PR4C-5020 [Q] | Lush, Latin & Lovely | 1973 | 18.00 |
| ❑ PR-5025 | Warm, Wild & Wonderful | 1968 | 12.00 |
| ❑ PR4C-5025 [Q] | Warm, Wild & Wonderful | 1973 | 18.00 |
| ❑ PR-5032 | Roma Oggi/Rome Today | 1969 | 12.00 |
| ❑ PR4C-5032 [Q] | Roma Oggi/Rome Today | 1973 | 18.00 |
| ❑ PR-5035 | Tony Mottola Joins the Guitar Underground | 1969 | 12.00 |
| ❑ PR-5041 | The Tony Touch | 1970 | 12.00 |
| ❑ PR4C-5041 [Q] | The Tony Touch | 1973 | 18.00 |
| ❑ PR-5044 | Tony Mottola's Guitar Factory | 1970 | 12.00 |
| ❑ PR-5050 | Close to You | 1971 | 12.00 |
| ❑ PR-5058 | Warm Feelings | 1971 | 12.00 |
| ❑ PR-5062 | Superstar Guitar | 1972 | 12.00 |
| ❑ PR4C-5062 [Q] | Superstar Guitar | 1973 | 15.00 |
| ❑ PR-5069 | Tony and Strings | 1973 | 12.00 |
| ❑ PR4C-5069 [Q] | Tony and Strings | 1973 | 18.00 |
| ❑ PR-5074 | Two Guitars | 1974 | 10.00 |
| ❑ PR4C-5078 [Q] | Tony Mottola with the Quad Guitars | 1974 | 15.00 |
| ❑ PR-5082 | Tony Mottola with the Brass Menagerie | 1974 | 12.00 |
| ❑ PR-5094 | I Only Have Eyes for You | 197? | 10.00 |
| ❑ PR-5101 | Goin' Out of My Head | 197? | 10.00 |
| ❑ PR-6007/8 [(2)] | Favorite Things: The Best of Tony Mottola | 1975 | 15.00 |
| ❑ PR-6025/6 [(2)] | Feelings | 198? | 12.00 |
| ❑ PR-6031/2 [(2)] | The Best of Tony Mottola | 198? | 12.00 |

### MOULE, KEN

| Number | Title (A Side/B Side) | Yr | NM |
|---|---|---|---|
| **LONDON** | | | |
| ❑ LL 1673 [M] | Ken Moule Arranges for... | 1957 | 50.00 |
| *—Label calls this "Cool Moule"* | | | |

### MOUNT ALVERNIA SEMINARY CHOIR

| Number | Title (A Side/B Side) | Yr | NM |
|---|---|---|---|
| **ABC-PARAMOUNT** | | | |
| ❑ 211 [M] | Christmas in a Monastery: The Sons of St. Francis Sing | 1957 | 20.00 |

### MOUNT RUSHMORE

| Number | Title (A Side/B Side) | Yr | NM |
|---|---|---|---|
| **DOT** | | | |
| ❑ DLP-25898 | High on Mount Rushmore | 1968 | 20.00 |
| ❑ DLP-25934 | Mount Rushmore '69 | 1969 | 20.00 |

### MOUNTAIN

| Number | Title (A Side/B Side) | Yr | NM |
|---|---|---|---|
| **COLUMBIA** | | | |
| ❑ CQ 32079 [Q] | The Best of Mountain | 1973 | 20.00 |
| ❑ KC 32079 | The Best of Mountain | 1973 | 12.00 |
| ❑ PC 32079 | The Best of Mountain | 198? | 8.00 |
| *—Budget-line reissue* | | | |
| ❑ CG 32818 [(2)] | Twin Peaks | 1974 | 15.00 |
| ❑ PG 32818 [(2)] | Twin Peaks | 198? | 10.00 |
| *—Budget-line reissue* | | | |
| ❑ CQ 33008 [Q] | Avalanche | 1974 | 20.00 |
| ❑ KC 33008 | Avalanche | 1974 | 12.00 |
| ❑ PC 33008 | Avalanche | 197? | 8.00 |
| *—Budget-line reissue* | | | |
| **SCOTTI BROTHERS** | | | |
| ❑ FZ 40006 | Go for Your Life | 1985 | 10.00 |
| **WINDFALL** | | | |
| ❑ 4501 | Mountain Climbing! | 1970 | 15.00 |
| ❑ 5500 | Nantucket Sleighride | 1971 | 15.00 |
| *—Deduct 20% if inserts are missing* | | | |
| ❑ 5501 | Flowers of Evil | 1971 | 15.00 |
| ❑ 5502 | Mountain Live (The Road Goes Ever On) | 1972 | 15.00 |

### MOUNTAIN BUS

| Number | Title (A Side/B Side) | Yr | NM |
|---|---|---|---|
| **GOOD** | | | |
| ❑ 101 | Sundance | 1971 | 150.00 |

### MOUNTAIN RAMBLERS, THE

| Number | Title (A Side/B Side) | Yr | NM |
|---|---|---|---|
| **ATLANTIC** | | | |
| ❑ 1347 [M] | Blue Ridge Mountain Music | 1962 | 25.00 |
| ❑ SD 1347 [S] | Blue Ridge Mountain Music | 1962 | 30.00 |

### MOUZON, ALPHONSE

| Number | Title (A Side/B Side) | Yr | NM |
|---|---|---|---|
| **BLUE NOTE** | | | |
| ❑ BN-LA222-G | Funky Snakefoot | 1974 | 20.00 |

### MOVE, THE

| Number | Title (A Side/B Side) | Yr | NM |
|---|---|---|---|
| **A&M** | | | |
| ❑ SP-3181 | Shazam | 1982 | 10.00 |
| *—Budget-line reissue of 4259* | | | |
| ❑ SP-3625 [(2)] | The Best of the Move | 1974 | 15.00 |
| ❑ SP-4259 | Shazam | 1969 | 30.00 |
| **CAPITOL** | | | |
| ❑ ST-658 | Looking On | 1971 | 20.00 |
| ❑ ST-811 | Message from the Country | 1971 | 20.00 |
| **UNITED ARTISTS** | | | |
| ❑ UAS-5666 | Split Ends | 1972 | 15.00 |

### MOVING SIDEWALKS, THE

| Number | Title (A Side/B Side) | Yr | NM |
|---|---|---|---|
| **TANTARA** | | | |
| ❑ 6919 | Flash | 1968 | 300.00 |

### MOZIAN, ROGER KING

| Number | Title (A Side/B Side) | Yr | NM |
|---|---|---|---|
| **CLEF** | | | |
| ❑ MGC-166 [10] | The Colorful Music of Roger King Mozian | 1954 | 100.00 |

### MTUME UMOJA ENSEMBLE

| Number | Title (A Side/B Side) | Yr | NM |
|---|---|---|---|
| **STRATA-EAST** | | | |
| ❑ SES-1972-4 [(2)] | Alkebu-Lan, Land of the Blacks | 1972 | 50.00 |

### MU

| Number | Title (A Side/B Side) | Yr | NM |
|---|---|---|---|
| **CAS** | | | |
| ❑ 300 | Mu | 1971 | 300.00 |

### MUDHONEY

| Number | Title (A Side/B Side) | Yr | NM |
|---|---|---|---|
| **REPRISE** | | | |
| ❑ 45840 | My Brother the Cow | 1994 | 15.00 |
| **SUB POP** | | | |
| ❑ 21 [EP] | Superfuzz Bigmuff | 1988 | 20.00 |
| *—Without poster* | | | |
| ❑ 21 [EP] | Superfuzz Bigmuff | 1988 | 30.00 |
| *—With poster* | | | |
| ❑ 44 | Mudhoney | 1989 | 20.00 |
| *—Without gatefold and poster* | | | |
| ❑ 44 | Mudhoney | 1989 | 30.00 |
| *—First 3,000 have gatefold sleeve and poster* | | | |
| ❑ 105 | Every Good Boy Deserves Fudge | 1991 | 10.00 |
| ❑ 105 PD [PD] | Every Good Boy Deserves Fudge | 1991 | 30.00 |
| *—Picture disc -- limited edition of 2,500* | | | |
| ❑ SP 500 [(3)] | March to Fuzz | 2000 | 25.00 |
| ❑ SP-555 | Since We've Become Translucent | 2002 | 15.00 |
| **SUPER ELECTRO** | | | |
| ❑ SE 10 | Tomorrow Hit Today | 1998 | 12.00 |

### MUGWUMPS, THE

| Number | Title (A Side/B Side) | Yr | NM |
|---|---|---|---|
| **WARNER BROS.** | | | |
| ❑ W 1697 [M] | The Mugwumps | 1967 | 25.00 |
| ❑ WS 1697 [S] | The Mugwumps | 1967 | 30.00 |

### MUHAMMAD, IDRIS

| Number | Title (A Side/B Side) | Yr | NM |
|---|---|---|---|
| **KUDU** | | | |
| ❑ 17 | Power of Soul | 1974 | 25.00 |
| ❑ 27 | House of the Rising Sun | 1976 | 25.00 |
| ❑ 34 | Turn This Mutha Out | 1977 | 20.00 |
| ❑ 38 | Boogie to the Top | 1978 | 20.00 |
| **PRESTIGE** | | | |
| ❑ 10005 | Black Rhythm Revolution | 1971 | 40.00 |
| ❑ 10036 | Peace and Rhythm | 1971 | 30.00 |

### MULCAY, JIMMY AND MILDRED

| Number | Title (A Side/B Side) | Yr | NM |
|---|---|---|---|
| **JUBILEE** | | | |
| ❑ JGM-5017 [M] | Magic Millions | 1962 | 30.00 |

### MULDAUR, GEOFF

| Number | Title (A Side/B Side) | Yr | NM |
|---|---|---|---|
| **FOLKLORE** | | | |
| ❑ FRLP-14004 [M] | Sleepy Man Blues | 1964 | 30.00 |
| ❑ FRST-14004 [S] | Sleepy Man Blues | 1964 | 40.00 |
| **PRESTIGE** | | | |
| ❑ PRST-7727 | Sleepy Man Blues | 1969 | 20.00 |
| *—Reissue of Folklore LP* | | | |

### MULLER, WERNER

| Number | Title (A Side/B Side) | Yr | NM |
|---|---|---|---|
| **DECCA** | | | |
| ❑ DL 8388 [M] | O, Tannenbaum (Christmas on the Rhine) | 1956 | 20.00 |
| *—Black label, silver print* | | | |

### MULLICAN, MOON

| Number | Title (A Side/B Side) | Yr | NM |
|---|---|---|---|
| **AUDIO LAB** | | | |
| ❑ AL-1568 [M] | Instrumentals | 1962 | 150.00 |
| **CORAL** | | | |
| ❑ CRL 57235 [M] | Moon Over Mullican | 1958 | 500.00 |
| **HILLTOP** | | | |
| ❑ JS-6033 | Good Times Gonna Roll Again | 1966 | 25.00 |
| **KAPP** | | | |
| ❑ KS-3600 | Showcase | 1968 | 30.00 |
| **KING** | | | |
| ❑ 555 [M] | Moon Mullican Sings His All-Time Greatest Hits | 1958 | 200.00 |
| ❑ 628 [M] | Moon Mullican Plays and Sings 16 of His Favorite Tunes | 1959 | 150.00 |
| ❑ 681 [M] | The Many Moods of Moon Mullican | 1960 | 150.00 |
| ❑ 937 [M] | Moon Mullican Sings 24 of His Favorite Tunes | 1965 | 50.00 |
| **NASHVILLE** | | | |
| ❑ 2080 | I'll Sail My Ship Alone | 1970 | 20.00 |
| **SPAR** | | | |
| ❑ SP-3005 [M] | Mister Honky Tonk Man | 1965 | 100.00 |
| **STARDAY** | | | |
| ❑ SLP-135 [M] | Playin' and Singin' | 1963 | 100.00 |
| ❑ SLP-267 [M] | Mister Piano Man | 1964 | 50.00 |
| ❑ SLP-398 [M] | The Unforgettable Moon Mullican | 1967 | 40.00 |
| **STERLING** | | | |
| ❑ ST-601 [M] | I'll Sail My Ship Alone | 1958 | 200.00 |

### MULLIGAN, GERRY

| Number | Title (A Side/B Side) | Yr | NM |
|---|---|---|---|
| **CAPITOL** | | | |
| ❑ H 439 [10] | Gerry Mulligan and His Ten-Tette | 1953 | 250.00 |
| **COLUMBIA** | | | |
| ❑ CL 1307 [M] | What Is There to Say? | 1959 | 40.00 |
| *—Red and black label with six "eye" logos* | | | |
| ❑ CL 1932 [M] | Jeru | 1963 | 30.00 |
| *—Red label, "Guaranteed High Fidelity" at bottom* | | | |
| ❑ CL 1932 [M] | Jeru | 1965 | 12.00 |
| *—Red label, "360 Sound Mono" at bottom* | | | |
| ❑ CS 8116 [S] | What Is There to Say? | 1959 | 40.00 |
| *—Red and black label with six "eye" logos* | | | |
| ❑ CS 8732 [S] | Jeru | 1963 | 30.00 |
| *—Red label, "360 Sound Stereo" in black at bottom* | | | |
| **EMARCY** | | | |
| ❑ MG-36056 [M] | Presenting the Gerry Mulligan Sextet | 1955 | 150.00 |
| ❑ MG-36101 [M] | Mainstream of Jazz | 1956 | 150.00 |
| **FANTASY** | | | |
| ❑ 3-6 [10] | Gerry Mulligan Quartet | 1953 | 150.00 |
| *—Black vinyl* | | | |
| ❑ 3-6 [10] | Gerry Mulligan Quartet | 1953 | 200.00 |
| *—Green vinyl* | | | |
| ❑ 3-6 [10] | Gerry Mulligan Quartet | 1953 | 200.00 |
| *—Red vinyl* | | | |
| **GENE NORMAN** | | | |
| ❑ GNP-3 [10] | Gerry Mulligan Quartet | 1952 | 250.00 |
| **LIMELIGHT** | | | |
| ❑ LM-82004 [M] | Butterfly with Hiccups | 1964 | 25.00 |
| ❑ LM-82021 [M] | If You Can't Beat 'Em, Join 'Em | 1965 | 25.00 |
| ❑ LM-82030 [M] | Feelin' Good | 1965 | 25.00 |
| ❑ LM-82040 [M] | Something Borrowed, Something Blue | 1966 | 20.00 |
| ❑ LS-86004 [S] | Butterfly with Hiccups | 1964 | 30.00 |
| ❑ LS-86021 [S] | If You Can't Beat 'Em, Join 'Em | 1965 | 30.00 |
| ❑ LS-86030 [S] | Feelin' Good | 1965 | 30.00 |
| ❑ LS-86040 [S] | Something Borrowed, Something Blue | 1966 | 25.00 |
| **MERCURY** | | | |
| ❑ MG-20453 [M] | A Profile of Gerry Mulligan | 1959 | 60.00 |
| **MOBILE FIDELITY** | | | |
| ❑ 1-179 | At the Village Vanguard | 1985 | 40.00 |
| *—Audiophile vinyl* | | | |
| ❑ 1-234 | Gerry Mulligan Meets Ben Webster | 1995 | 40.00 |
| *—Audiophile vinyl* | | | |
| ❑ 1-241 | Blues in Time | 1996 | 30.00 |
| *—Audiophile vinyl* | | | |



**Except when noted otherwise, VG = 25% of NM, and VG+ = 50% of NM. (Example: VG = $2.00, VG+ = $4.00 and NM = $8.00.)**

| Number | Title (A Side/B Side) | Yr | NM |
|---|---|---|---|
| **MOSAIC** | | | |
| MR5-102 [(5)] | The Complete Pacific Jazz and Capitol Recordings of the Original Gerry Mulligan Quartet and Tentette | 198? | 100.00 |
| **PACIFIC JAZZ** | | | |
| PJLP-1 [10] | Gerry Mulligan Quartet | 1953 | 300.00 |
| PJLP-2 [10] | Lee Konitz Plays with the Gerry Mulligan Quartet | 1953 | 300.00 |
| PJLP-5 [10] | Gerry Mulligan Quartet | 1953 | 300.00 |
| PJ-8 [M] | The Genius of Gerry Mulligan | 1960 | 40.00 |
| PJLP-10 [10] | Lee Konitz and the Gerry Mulligan Quartet | 1954 | 250.00 |
| PJ-38 [M] | Konitz Meets Mulligan | 1962 | 30.00 |
| PJ-47 [M] | Reunion with Chet Baker | 1962 | 30.00 |
| ST-47 [S] | Reunion with Chet Baker | 1962 | 30.00 |
| PJ-50 [M] | California Concerts | 1962 | 30.00 |
| PJ-75 [M] | Timeless | 1963 | 30.00 |
| PJM-406 [M] | Lee Konitz with the Gerry Mulligan Quartet | 1956 | 150.00 |
| PJ-1201 [M] | Gerry Mulligan Sextet | 1955 | 150.00 |
| PJ-1207 [M] | The Original Mulligan Quartet | 1955 | 150.00 |
| PJ-1210 [M] | Paris Concert | 1956 | 150.00 |
| PJ-1228 [M] | Gerry Mulligan at Storyville | 1957 | 150.00 |
| PJ-10102 [M] | Paris Concert | 1966 | 20.00 |
| ST-20102 [S] | Paris Concert | 1966 | 20.00 |
| T 90061 [M] | Reunion with Chet Baker | 196? | 30.00 |
| *—Capitol Record Club edition* | | | |
| **PHILIPS** | | | |
| PHM 200077 [M] | Spring Is Sprung | 1963 | 20.00 |
| PHM 200108 [M] | Night Lights | 1963 | 20.00 |
| PHS 600077 [S] | Spring Is Sprung | 1963 | 25.00 |
| PHS 600108 [S] | Night Lights | 1963 | 25.00 |
| **PRESTIGE** | | | |
| PRLP-120 [10] | Gerry Mulligan Blows | 1952 | 300.00 |
| PRLP-141 [10] | Mulligan Too Blows | 1953 | 300.00 |
| PRLP-7006 [M] | Mulligan Plays Mulligan | 1956 | 100.00 |
| *—Yellow label* | | | |
| PRLP-7251 [M] | Historically Speaking | 1963 | 40.00 |
| *—Yellow label* | | | |
| **UNITED ARTISTS** | | | |
| UAL-4085 [M] | Nightwatch | 1960 | 40.00 |
| UAS-5085 [S] | Nightwatch | 1960 | 50.00 |
| **VERVE** | | | |
| MGVS-6003 [S] | Getz Meets Mulligan in Hi-Fi | 1960 | 40.00 |
| MGVS-6104 [S] | Gerry Mulligan Meets Ben Webster | 1960 | 40.00 |
| MGV-8246 [M] | The Gerry Mulligan-Paul Desmond Quartet | 1958 | 50.00 |
| V-8246 [M] | The Gerry Mulligan-Paul Desmond Quartet | 1961 | 20.00 |
| MGV-8249 [M] | Getz Meets Mulligan in Hi-Fi | 1958 | 40.00 |
| V-8249 [M] | Getz Meets Mulligan in Hi-Fi | 1961 | 20.00 |
| V6-8249 [S] | Getz Meets Mulligan in Hi-Fi | 1961 | 25.00 |
| MGV-8343 [M] | Gerry Mulligan Meets Ben Webster | 1959 | 40.00 |
| V-8343 [M] | Gerry Mulligan Meets Ben Webster | 1961 | 20.00 |
| MGV-8367 [M] | Gerry Mulligan Meets Johnny Hodges | 1960 | 40.00 |
| V-8367 [M] | Gerry Mulligan Meets Johnny Hodges | 1961 | 20.00 |
| V6-8367 [S] | Gerry Mulligan Meets Johnny Hodges | 1961 | 25.00 |
| MGV-8388 [M] | Gerry Mulligan and the Concert Jazz Band | 1960 | 40.00 |
| V-8388 [M] | Gerry Mulligan and the Concert Jazz Band | 1961 | 20.00 |
| V6-8388 [S] | Gerry Mulligan and the Concert Jazz Band | 1961 | 25.00 |
| MGV-8396 [M] | Gerry Mulligan and the Concert Jazz Band at the Village Vanguard | 1960 | 40.00 |
| V-8396 [M] | Gerry Mulligan and the Concert Jazz Band at the Village Vanguard | 1961 | 20.00 |
| V6-8396 [S] | Gerry Mulligan and the Concert Jazz Band at the Village Vanguard | 1961 | 25.00 |
| V-8415 [M] | Gerry Mulligan and the Concert Jazz Band Presents a Concert in Jazz | 1961 | 25.00 |
| V6-8415 [S] | Gerry Mulligan and the Concert Jazz Band Presents a Concert in Jazz | 1961 | 30.00 |
| V-8438 [M] | The Gerry Mulligan Concert Jazz Band On Tour with Guest Soloist Zoot Sims | 1962 | 25.00 |
| V6-8438 [S] | The Gerry Mulligan Concert Jazz Band On Tour with Guest Soloist Zoot Sims | 1962 | 30.00 |
| V-8466 [M] | The Gerry Mulligan Quartet | 1962 | 25.00 |
| V6-8466 [S] | The Gerry Mulligan Quartet | 1962 | 30.00 |
| V-8478 [M] | Blues in Time | 1962 | 20.00 |
| V6-8478 [S] | Blues in Time | 1962 | 25.00 |
| V-8515 [M] | Gerry Mulligan '63 — The Concert Jazz Band | 1963 | 20.00 |

| Number | Title (A Side/B Side) | Yr | NM |
|---|---|---|---|
| V6-8515 [S] | Gerry Mulligan '63 — The Concert Jazz Band | 1963 | 25.00 |
| V6-8534 [S] | Gerry Mulligan Meets Ben Webster | 1963 | 20.00 |
| V6-8535 [S] | Gerry Mulligan Meets Stan Getz | 1963 | 20.00 |
| V6-8536 [S] | Gerry Mulligan Meets Johnny Hodges | 1963 | 20.00 |
| **WORLD PACIFIC** | | | |
| PJM-406 [M] | Lee Konitz with the Gerry Mulligan Quartet | 1958 | 80.00 |
| ST-1001 [S] | The Gerry Mulligan Songbook, Volume 1 | 1958 | 100.00 |
| ST-1006 [S] | Gerry Mulligan at Storyville | 1958 | 100.00 |
| ST-1007 [S] | Reunion with Chet Baker | 1958 | 80.00 |
| WP-1201 [M] | California Concerts | 1958 | 80.00 |
| WP-1207 [M] | The Original Mulligan Quartet | 1958 | 80.00 |
| WP-1210 [M] | Paris Concert | 1958 | 80.00 |
| WP-1228 [M] | Gerry Mulligan at Storyville | 1958 | 80.00 |
| PJ-1237 [M] | The Gerry Mulligan Songbook, Volume 1 | 1957 | 120.00 |
| WP-1237 [M] | The Gerry Mulligan Songbook, Volume 1 | 1958 | 80.00 |
| PJ-1241 [M] | Reunion with Chet Baker | 1957 | 120.00 |
| WP-1241 [M] | Reunion with Chet Baker | 1958 | 80.00 |
| WP-1273 [M] | Lee Konitz Plays with the Gerry Mulligan Quartet | 1959 | 80.00 |
| *—Reissue of 406* | | | |
| **MULLIGAN, GERRY, AND CHET BAKER** | | | |
| **JAZZTONE** | | | |
| J-1253 [M] | Mulligan and Baker! | 1957 | 40.00 |
| **MULLIGAN, GERRY/BUDDY DEFRANCO** | | | |
| **GENE NORMAN** | | | |
| GNP-26 [M] | The Gerry Mulligan Quartet with Chet Baker/Buddy DeFranco Quartet | 1957 | 80.00 |
| *—Combined reissue of two 10-inch LPs* | | | |
| GNP-56 [M] | The Gerry Mulligan Quartet with Chet Baker/Buddy DeFranco Quartet | 196? | 40.00 |
| *—Reissue of 26* | | | |
| **MULLIGAN, GERRY/PAUL DESMOND** | | | |
| **FANTASY** | | | |
| 3220 [M] | Gerry Mulligan Quartet/Paul Desmond Quintet | 1956 | 40.00 |
| *—Black vinyl* | | | |
| 3220 [M] | Gerry Mulligan Quartet/Paul Desmond Quintet | 1956 | 80.00 |
| *—Red vinyl; combined reissue of two 10-inch LPs* | | | |
| **MULLIGAN, GERRY, AND SHORTY ROGERS** | | | |
| **CAPITOL** | | | |
| T 691 [M] | Modern Sounds | 1956 | 80.00 |
| T 2025 [M] | Modern Sounds | 1963 | 20.00 |
| **MULLIGAN, GERRY/KAI WINDING/RED RODNEY** | | | |
| **STATUS** | | | |
| ST-8306 [M] | Broadway | 1965 | 40.00 |
| **MULTIPLICATION ROCK (SOUNDTRACK)** | | | |
| **CAPITOL** | | | |
| SJA-11174 | Multiplication Rock | 1973 | 40.00 |
| **MUMY, BILL** | | | |
| **BB** | | | |
| 103 | Bill Mumy | 1980 | 25.00 |
| **MUNSTERS, THE** | | | |
| **DECCA** | | | |
| DL 4588 [M] | The Munsters | 1964 | 100.00 |
| DL 74588 [S] | The Munsters | 1964 | 150.00 |
| **MURE, BILLY** | | | |
| **EVEREST** | | | |
| SDBR-1067 [S] | A String of Trumpets | 1960 | 30.00 |
| SDBR-1072 [S] | Songs of Hank Williams | 1960 | 30.00 |
| SDBR-1120 [S] | Strictly Cha-Cha-Cha | 1961 | 30.00 |
| LPBR-5067 [M] | A String of Trumpets | 1960 | 20.00 |
| LPBR-5072 [M] | Songs of Hank Williams | 1960 | 20.00 |
| LPBR-5120 [M] | Strictly Cha-Cha-Cha | 1961 | 20.00 |
| **KAPP** | | | |
| KL-1253 [M] | Tough Strings | 1961 | 20.00 |
| KS-3253 [S] | Tough Strings | 1961 | 30.00 |
| **MGM** | | | |
| E-3780 [M] | Supersonic Guitars | 1959 | 30.00 |
| SE-3780 [S] | Supersonic Guitars | 1959 | 50.00 |
| E-3807 [M] | Supersonic Guitars, Vol. 2 | 1959 | 30.00 |
| SE-3807 [S] | Supersonic Guitars, Vol. 2 | 1959 | 50.00 |
| E-4131 [M] | Teen Bossa Nova | 1963 | 20.00 |
| SE-4131 [S] | Teen Bossa Nova | 1963 | 30.00 |
| E-4189 [M] | Maria Elena and Other Great Songs | 1964 | 20.00 |
| SE-4189 [S] | Maria Elena and Other Great Songs | 1964 | 30.00 |

| Number | Title (A Side/B Side) | Yr | NM |
|---|---|---|---|
| E-4406 [M] | Happy Guitars | 1966 | 20.00 |
| SE-4406 [S] | Happy Guitars | 1966 | 25.00 |
| **PREMIER** | | | |
| PM-9014 [M] | Blue Hawaii | 196? | 10.00 |
| *—Side 1 by Billy Mure; Side 2 by Harry Kaapuni and His Royal Hawaiians* | | | |
| **RCA VICTOR** | | | |
| LPM-1536 [M] | Supersonic Guitars in Hi-Fi | 1957 | 40.00 |
| LPM-1694 [M] | Fireworks | 1958 | 30.00 |
| LSP-1694 [S] | Fireworks | 1958 | 40.00 |
| LPM-1869 [M] | Supersonic in Flight | 1959 | 30.00 |
| LSP-1869 [S] | Supersonic in Flight | 1959 | 50.00 |
| **SPIN-O-RAMA** | | | |
| S 147 [M] | Blue Hawaii | 196? | 10.00 |
| *—Side 1 by Billy Mure; Side 2 by Harry Kaapuni and His Royal Hawaiians* | | | |
| S 157 [M] | Hawaiian Moods | 196? | 10.00 |
| *—One side by Billy Mure; one side by Luke Leilani* | | | |
| **STRAND** | | | |
| SL-1010 [M] | Hawaiian Percussion | 1961 | 25.00 |
| SLS-1010 [S] | Hawaiian Percussion | 1961 | 40.00 |
| SL-1021 [M] | 'Round the World in Percussion | 1961 | 25.00 |
| SLS-1021 [S] | 'Round the World in Percussion | 1961 | 40.00 |
| SL-1070 [M] | Pink Hawaii | 1962 | 20.00 |
| SLS-1070 [S] | Pink Hawaii | 1962 | 30.00 |
| **SUNSET** | | | |
| SUS-5173 | Songs of Hank Williams | 196? | 12.00 |
| *—Reissue of Everest SDBR-1072 with fewer tracks* | | | |
| **UNITED ARTISTS** | | | |
| UAL-3031 [M] | Bandstand Record Hop | 1959 | 40.00 |
| UAS-6031 [S] | Bandstand Record Hop | 1959 | 60.00 |
| **MURMAIDS, THE** | | | |
| **CHATTAHOOCHEE** | | | |
| CHLP-628 [M] | The Mermaids Resurface! | 1981 | 30.00 |
| **MURPHY, EDDIE** | | | |
| **COLUMBIA** | | | |
| AS99 1763 [DJ] | Comedian | 1983 | 20.00 |
| *—Promo-only picture disc* | | | |
| FC 39005 | Comedian | 1983 | 10.00 |
| 9C9 39151 | Comedian | 1983 | 15.00 |
| *—Stock version of picture disc* | | | |
| FC 39952 | How Could It Be | 1985 | 10.00 |
| OC 40970 | So Happy | 1989 | 12.00 |
| **THE ENTERTAINMENT COMPANY** | | | |
| AS 1607 [EP] | Special Censored Versions | 1982 | 12.00 |
| *—Promo-only collection of "safe for airplay" routines from FC 38180* | | | |
| FC 38180 | Eddie Murphy | 1982 | 10.00 |
| **MURPHY, ELLIOTT** | | | |
| **POLYDOR** | | | |
| PD-5061 | Aquashow | 1973 | 20.00 |
| *—First edition with "Like a Great Gatsby" listed as a song title* | | | |
| **RCA VICTOR** | | | |
| APL1-0916 | Lost Generation | 1975 | 20.00 |
| *—Orange or tan labels* | | | |
| APL1-1318 | Night Lights | 1976 | 20.00 |
| *—Orange or tan labels* | | | |
| **MURPHY, LYLE** | | | |
| **GENE NORMAN** | | | |
| GNP-9 [10] | Four Saxophones in Twelve Tones | 1954 | 120.00 |
| GNP-33 [M] | New Orbits in Sound | 1957 | 50.00 |
| GNP-152 [M] | Four Saxophones in Twelve Tones | 195? | 50.00 |
| **MURPHY, MARK** | | | |
| **CAPITOL** | | | |
| ST 1177 [S] | This Could Be the Start of Something | 1959 | 30.00 |
| T 1177 [M] | This Could Be the Start of Something | 1959 | 25.00 |
| ST 1299 [S] | Hip Parade | 1960 | 30.00 |
| T 1299 [M] | Hip Parade | 1960 | 25.00 |
| ST 1458 [S] | Playing the Field | 1960 | 30.00 |
| T 1458 [M] | Playing the Field | 1960 | 25.00 |
| **DECCA** | | | |
| DL 8390 [M] | Meet Mark Murphy | 1957 | 50.00 |
| DL 8632 [M] | Let Yourself Go | 1958 | 40.00 |
| **FONTANA** | | | |
| MGF-27537 [M] | A Swingin' Singin' Affair | 1965 | 20.00 |
| SRF-67537 [S] | A Swingin' Singin' Affair | 1965 | 25.00 |
| **RIVERSIDE** | | | |
| RLP-395 [M] | Rah | 1961 | 25.00 |
| RLP-441 [M] | That's How I Love the Blues! | 1962 | 25.00 |
| RS-9395 [S] | Rah | 1961 | 30.00 |
| RS-9441 [S] | That's How I Love the Blues! | 1962 | 30.00 |
| **MURPHY, ROSE** | | | |
| **ROYALE** | | | |
| 1835 [10] | Rose Murphy and Quartette | 195? | 80.00 |

| Number | Title (A Side/B Side) | Yr | NM |
|---|---|---|---|
| ❑ VLP-6079 [10] | Chi-Chi Girl | 195? | 80.00 |

UNITED ARTISTS

| Number | Title (A Side/B Side) | Yr | NM |
|---|---|---|---|
| ❑ UAJ-14025 [M] | Jazz, Joy and Happiness | 1962 | 50.00 |
| ❑ UAJS-15025 [S] | Jazz, Joy and Happiness | 1962 | 60.00 |

VERVE

| Number | Title (A Side/B Side) | Yr | NM |
|---|---|---|---|
| ❑ MGV-2070 [M] | Not Cha-Cha But Chi-Chi | 1957 | 50.00 |
| ❑ V-2070 [M] | Not Cha-Cha But Chi-Chi | 1961 | 25.00 |

**MURPHY, TURK**

COLUMBIA

| Number | Title (A Side/B Side) | Yr | NM |
|---|---|---|---|
| ❑ CL 546 [M] | When the Saints Go Marching In | 1953 | 40.00 |
| *—Maroon label, gold print* | | | |
| ❑ CL 546 [M] | When the Saints Go Marching In | 1955 | 30.00 |
| *—Red and black label with six "eye" logos* | | | |
| ❑ CL 559 [M] | The Music of Jelly Roll Morton | 1954 | 40.00 |
| *—Maroon label, gold print* | | | |
| ❑ CL 559 [M] | The Music of Jelly Roll Morton | 1955 | 30.00 |
| *—Red and black label with six "eye" logos* | | | |
| ❑ CL 595 [M] | Barrelhouse Jazz | 1954 | 40.00 |
| *—Maroon label, gold print* | | | |
| ❑ CL 595 [M] | Barrelhouse Jazz | 1955 | 30.00 |
| *—Red and black label with six "eye" logos* | | | |
| ❑ CL 650 [M] | Dancing Jazz | 1955 | 30.00 |
| *—Red and black label with six "eye" logos* | | | |
| ❑ CL 650 [M] | Dancing Jazz | 1955 | 40.00 |
| *—Maroon label, gold print* | | | |
| ❑ CL 6257 [10] | Barrelhouse Jazz | 1953 | 50.00 |

GOOD TIME JAZZ

| Number | Title (A Side/B Side) | Yr | NM |
|---|---|---|---|
| ❑ L-7 [10] | Turk Murphy with Claire Austin | 1952 | 50.00 |
| ❑ L-12026 [M] | San Francisco Jazz, Volume 1 | 1955 | 40.00 |
| ❑ L-12027 [M] | San Francisco Jazz, Volume 2 | 1955 | 40.00 |

RCA VICTOR

| Number | Title (A Side/B Side) | Yr | NM |
|---|---|---|---|
| ❑ LPM-2501 [M] | Let the Good Times Roll | 1962 | 20.00 |
| ❑ LSP-2501 [S] | Let the Good Times Roll | 1962 | 25.00 |

ROULETTE

| Number | Title (A Side/B Side) | Yr | NM |
|---|---|---|---|
| ❑ R-25076 [M] | Turk Murphy and His Jazz Band at the Roundtable | 1959 | 20.00 |
| ❑ SR-25076 [S] | Turk Murphy and His Jazz Band at the Roundtable | 1959 | 25.00 |
| ❑ R-25088 [M] | Music for Wise Guys | 1960 | 20.00 |
| ❑ SR-25088 [S] | Music for Wise Guys | 1960 | 25.00 |

VERVE

| Number | Title (A Side/B Side) | Yr | NM |
|---|---|---|---|
| ❑ MGV-1013 [M] | Music for Losers | 1957 | 40.00 |
| ❑ V-1013 [M] | Music for Losers | 1961 | 20.00 |
| ❑ MGV-1015 [M] | Turk Murphy on Easy Street | 1957 | 40.00 |
| ❑ V-1015 [M] | Turk Murphy on Easy Street | 1961 | 20.00 |

**MURRAY, ANNE**

CAPITOL

| Number | Title (A Side/B Side) | Yr | NM |
|---|---|---|---|
| ❑ ST-579 | Snowbird | 1970 | 12.00 |
| ❑ ST-667 | Anne Murray | 1971 | 12.00 |
| ❑ ST-821 | Talk It Over in the Morning | 1971 | 12.00 |
| ❑ ST-11024 | Annie | 1972 | 10.00 |
| ❑ ST-11172 | Danny's Song | 1973 | 10.00 |
| ❑ ST-11266 | Love Song | 1974 | 10.00 |
| ❑ ST-11324 | Country | 1974 | 10.00 |
| ❑ ST-11354 | Highly Prized Possession | 1974 | 10.00 |
| ❑ ST-11433 | Together | 1975 | 10.00 |
| ❑ ST-11559 | Keeping in Touch | 1976 | 10.00 |
| ❑ ST-11743 | Let's Keep It That Way | 1978 | 10.00 |
| ❑ SW-11849 | New Kind of Feeling | 1979 | 10.00 |
| ❑ SOO-12012 | I'll Always Love You | 1979 | 10.00 |
| ❑ ST-12039 | A Country Collection | 1980 | 10.00 |
| ❑ SOO-12064 | Somebody's Waiting | 1980 | 10.00 |
| ❑ SOO-12110 | Anne Murray's Greatest Hits | 1980 | 10.00 |
| ❑ SOO-12144 | Where Do You Go When You Dream | 1981 | 10.00 |
| ❑ ST-12225 | The Hottest Night of the Year | 1982 | 10.00 |
| ❑ ST-12301 | A Little Good News | 1983 | 10.00 |
| ❑ SJ-12363 | Heart Over Mind | 1984 | 10.00 |
| ❑ SJ-12466 | Something to Talk About | 1986 | 10.00 |
| ❑ PJ-12562 | Harmony | 1987 | 10.00 |
| ❑ SN-16080 | Talk It Over in the Morning | 1980 | 8.00 |
| *—Budget-line reissue* | | | |
| ❑ SN-16081 | Highly Prized Possession | 1980 | 8.00 |
| *—Budget-line reissue* | | | |
| ❑ SN-16082 | Keeping in Touch | 1980 | 8.00 |
| *—Budget-line reissue* | | | |
| ❑ SN-16211 | Danny's Song | 1981 | 8.00 |
| *—Budget-line reissue* | | | |
| ❑ SN-16212 | Love Song | 1981 | 8.00 |
| *—Budget-line reissue* | | | |
| ❑ SN-16213 | Country | 1981 | 8.00 |
| *—Budget-line reissue* | | | |
| ❑ SN-16232 | Christmas Wishes | 1981 | 10.00 |
| *—Original issue was on the budget-line series* | | | |
| ❑ SN-16233 | There's a Hippo in My Tub | 1981 | 10.00 |
| *—Original issue was on the budget-line series* | | | |
| ❑ SN-16282 | Together | 1982 | 8.00 |
| *—Budget-line reissue* | | | |
| ❑ SN-16283 | New Kind of Feeling | 1982 | 8.00 |
| *—Budget-line reissue* | | | |
| ❑ SN-16338 | A Country Collection | 198? | 8.00 |
| *—Budget-line reissue* | | | |
| ❑ SN-16341 | Let's Keep It That Way | 198? | 8.00 |
| *—Budget-line reissue* | | | |

| Number | Title (A Side/B Side) | Yr | NM |
|---|---|---|---|
| ❑ C1-48764 | As I Am | 1988 | 10.00 |
| ❑ C1-90886 | Christmas | 1987 | 8.00 |
| ❑ C1-92072 | Greatest Hits Volume II | 1989 | 12.00 |

CAPITOL NASHVILLE

| Number | Title (A Side/B Side) | Yr | NM |
|---|---|---|---|
| ❑ R 173232 | You Will | 1990 | 20.00 |
| *—Only released on vinyl through BMG Direct Marketing* | | | |

PICKWICK

| Number | Title (A Side/B Side) | Yr | NM |
|---|---|---|---|
| ❑ SPC-3350 | What About Me | 197? | 8.00 |

**MURRAY, DAVID**

HAT HUT

| Number | Title (A Side/B Side) | Yr | NM |
|---|---|---|---|
| ❑ U/V [(2)] | The Third Family | 1979 | 20.00 |

**MURRAY, SUNNY**

ESP-DISK'

| Number | Title (A Side/B Side) | Yr | NM |
|---|---|---|---|
| ❑ 1032 [M] | Sunny Murray | 1966 | 20.00 |
| ❑ S-1032 [S] | Sunny Murray | 1966 | 25.00 |

JIHAD

| Number | Title (A Side/B Side) | Yr | NM |
|---|---|---|---|
| ❑ 663 [M] | Sunny's Time Now | 1967 | 200.00 |

**MURRAY THE "K"** See VARIOUS ARTISTS COLLECTIONS.

**MUSCLE SHOALS HORNS, THE**

BANG

| Number | Title (A Side/B Side) | Yr | NM |
|---|---|---|---|
| ❑ BLP-403 | Born to Get Down | 1975 | 20.00 |

**MUSIC ASYLUM, THE**

UNITED ARTISTS

| Number | Title (A Side/B Side) | Yr | NM |
|---|---|---|---|
| ❑ UAS-6778 | Commit Thyself | 1970 | 20.00 |

**MUSIC COMPANY, THE**

CRESTVIEW

| Number | Title (A Side/B Side) | Yr | NM |
|---|---|---|---|
| ❑ CRS-3057 | Hard and Heavy | 196? | 25.00 |

MIRWOOD

| Number | Title (A Side/B Side) | Yr | NM |
|---|---|---|---|
| ❑ M-7002 [M] | Rubber Soul Jazz | 1966 | 20.00 |
| ❑ MS-7002 [S] | Rubber Soul Jazz | 1966 | 25.00 |

**MUSIC EMPORIUM, THE**

SENTINEL

| Number | Title (A Side/B Side) | Yr | NM |
|---|---|---|---|
| ❑ 69001 | The Music Emporium | 1969 | 2000. |

SUNDAZED

| Number | Title (A Side/B Side) | Yr | NM |
|---|---|---|---|
| ❑ LP 5078 | The Music Emporium | 2001 | 15.00 |
| *—First legitimate reissue of the original* | | | |

**MUSIC EXPLOSION, THE**

LAURIE

| Number | Title (A Side/B Side) | Yr | NM |
|---|---|---|---|
| ❑ LLP-2040 [M] | Little Bit O'Soul | 1967 | 20.00 |
| ❑ SLLP-2040 [S] | Little Bit O'Soul | 1967 | 25.00 |

**MUSIC MACHINE, THE**

ORIGINAL SOUND

| Number | Title (A Side/B Side) | Yr | NM |
|---|---|---|---|
| ❑ 5015 [M] | (Turn On) The Music Machine | 1966 | 40.00 |
| ❑ 8875 [S] | (Turn On) The Music Machine | 1966 | 50.00 |

SUNDAZED

| Number | Title (A Side/B Side) | Yr | NM |
|---|---|---|---|
| ❑ LP 5038 | Ignition | 2000 | 12.00 |

WARNER BROS.

| Number | Title (A Side/B Side) | Yr | NM |
|---|---|---|---|
| ❑ W 1732 [M] | Bonniwell's Music Machine | 1967 | 25.00 |
| ❑ WS 1732 [S] | Bonniwell's Music Machine | 1967 | 40.00 |

**MUSSELWHITE, CHARLIE**

VANGUARD

| Number | Title (A Side/B Side) | Yr | NM |
|---|---|---|---|
| ❑ VSD-6258 | Tennessee Woman | 1969 | 20.00 |
| ❑ VRS-9232 [M] | Stand Back! Here Comes Charlie Musselwhite's South Side Band | 1966 | 20.00 |
| ❑ VSD-79232 [S] | Stand Back! Here Comes Charlie Musselwhite's South Side Band | 1966 | 25.00 |
| ❑ VSD-79287 | Charlie Musselwhite | 1968 | 20.00 |

**MUSSO, VIDO**

CROWN

| Number | Title (A Side/B Side) | Yr | NM |
|---|---|---|---|
| ❑ CLP-5007 [M] | The Swingin'st | 1957 | 50.00 |
| *—Reissue of Modern LP* | | | |
| ❑ CLP-5029 [M] | Teenage Dance Party | 1957 | 50.00 |

MODERN

| Number | Title (A Side/B Side) | Yr | NM |
|---|---|---|---|
| ❑ MLP-1207 [M] | The Swingin'st | 1956 | 100.00 |

**MUSSULLI, BOOTS**

CAPITOL

| Number | Title (A Side/B Side) | Yr | NM |
|---|---|---|---|
| ❑ H 6506 [10] | Boots Mussulli | 1955 | 120.00 |
| ❑ T 6506 [M] | Boots Mussulli | 1955 | 50.00 |

**MUSTANGS, THE**

PROVIDENCE

| Number | Title (A Side/B Side) | Yr | NM |
|---|---|---|---|
| ❑ PLP-001 [M] | Dartell Stomp | 1964 | 50.00 |

**MUTZIE**

SUSSEX

| Number | Title (A Side/B Side) | Yr | NM |
|---|---|---|---|
| ❑ SUX-7001 | Light of Your Shadow | 1970 | 25.00 |

**MY BLOODY VALENTINE**

CREATION/RELATIVITY

| Number | Title (A Side/B Side) | Yr | NM |
|---|---|---|---|
| ❑ 1006 | Isn't Anything | 1989 | 20.00 |

**MYERS, DAVE**

CAROLE

| Number | Title (A Side/B Side) | Yr | NM |
|---|---|---|---|
| ❑ 8002 [M] | Greatest Racing Themes | 1967 | 50.00 |

DEL-FI

| Number | Title (A Side/B Side) | Yr | NM |
|---|---|---|---|
| ❑ DFLP-1239 [M] | Hangin' Twenty | 1963 | 80.00 |
| ❑ DFST-1239 [S] | Hangin' Twenty | 1963 | 180.00 |
| ❑ DLF-1239 | Hangin' Twenty | 1998 | 12.00 |

**MYERSON, BESS**

MGM

| Number | Title (A Side/B Side) | Yr | NM |
|---|---|---|---|
| ❑ E-3785 [M] | Fashions in Music | 1959 | 30.00 |
| ❑ SE-3785 [S] | Fashions in Music | 1959 | 40.00 |

**MYRICK, BERL**

STRATA-EAST

| Number | Title (A Side/B Side) | Yr | NM |
|---|---|---|---|
| ❑ SES-102-74 | Live 'n Well | 1974 | 30.00 |

**MYRICK, GARY, AND THE FIGURES**

EPIC

| Number | Title (A Side/B Side) | Yr | NM |
|---|---|---|---|
| ❑ AS 912 [DJ] | Talks in Stereo | 1981 | 40.00 |
| *—Side one has studio tracks, side two has live versions of songs on side one* | | | |
| ❑ AS 1389 [DJ] | Live Sampler | 1982 | 16.00 |
| *—Four live tracks, including one unreleased song* | | | |
| ❑ JE 36524 | Gary Myrick and the Figures | 1981 | 10.00 |
| *—Reissue with amended prefix* | | | |
| ❑ NJE 36524 | Gary Myrick and the Figures | 1980 | 12.00 |
| ❑ ARE 37429 | Living in a Movie | 1981 | 10.00 |
| ❑ B5E 38637 [EP] | Language | 1983 | 10.00 |

GEFFEN

| Number | Title (A Side/B Side) | Yr | NM |
|---|---|---|---|
| ❑ GHS 24076 | Stand for Love | 1985 | 10.00 |

**MYSTERIOUS FLYING ORCHESTRA, THE**

RCA VICTOR

| Number | Title (A Side/B Side) | Yr | NM |
|---|---|---|---|
| ❑ APL1-2137 | The Mysterious Flying Orchestra | 1977 | 20.00 |

**MYSTIC ASTROLOGICAL CRYSTAL BAND, THE**

CAROLE

| Number | Title (A Side/B Side) | Yr | NM |
|---|---|---|---|
| ❑ 8001 [M] | Mystic Astrological Crystal Band | 1967 | 25.00 |
| ❑ S-8001 [S] | Mystic Astrological Crystal Band | 1967 | 30.00 |
| ❑ S-8003 | Clip Out, Put On Book | 1968 | 30.00 |

**MYSTIC MOODS ORCHESTRA, THE**

BAINBRIDGE

| Number | Title (A Side/B Side) | Yr | NM |
|---|---|---|---|
| ❑ 6201 | More Than Music | 1982 | 6.00 |
| ❑ 6202 | Moods for a Stormy Night | 1982 | 6.00 |
| *—Reissue of Sound Bird 7504* | | | |
| ❑ 6203 | Mexico! | 1982 | 6.00 |
| ❑ 6204 | Nightide | 1982 | 6.00 |
| *—Reissue of Sound Bird 7502* | | | |
| ❑ 6205 | One Stormy Night | 1982 | 6.00 |
| *—Reissue of Sound Bird 7501* | | | |
| ❑ 6206 | Emotions | 1982 | 6.00 |
| *—Reissue of Sound Bird 7505* | | | |
| ❑ 6207 | Love Token | 1982 | 6.00 |
| ❑ 6208 | Stormy Weekend | 1982 | 6.00 |
| *—Reissue of Sound Bird 7506* | | | |
| ❑ 6209 | Highway One | 1982 | 6.00 |
| ❑ 6210 | English Muffins | 1982 | 6.00 |
| ❑ 6211 | Country Lovin' Folk | 1982 | 6.00 |
| *—Reissue of Sound Bird 8512* | | | |
| ❑ 6212 | Extensions | 1982 | 6.00 |
| ❑ 6215 | Erogenous | 1982 | 6.00 |
| *—Reissue of Sound Bird 7509* | | | |
| ❑ 6216 | Another Stormy Night | 1983 | 8.00 |
| ❑ 6219 | Summer Moods | 1985 | 8.00 |

MOBILE FIDELITY

| Number | Title (A Side/B Side) | Yr | NM |
|---|---|---|---|
| ❑ 1-001 | Emotions | 1979 | 25.00 |
| *—Audiophile vinyl* | | | |
| ❑ 1-002 | Cosmic Forces | 1979 | 25.00 |
| *—Audiophile vinyl* | | | |
| ❑ 1-003 | Stormy Weekend | 1979 | 25.00 |
| *—Audiophile vinyl* | | | |

PHILIPS

| Number | Title (A Side/B Side) | Yr | NM |
|---|---|---|---|
| ❑ PHM 200205 [M] | One Stormy Night | 1966 | 12.00 |
| ❑ PHM 200213 [M] | Nightide | 1966 | 12.00 |
| ❑ PHM 200231 [M] | More Than Music | 1967 | 15.00 |
| ❑ PHM 200250 [M] | Mexican Trip | 1967 | 15.00 |
| ❑ PHM 200260 [M] | The Mystic Moods of Love | 1968 | 15.00 |
| ❑ PHS 600205 [S] | One Stormy Night | 1966 | 15.00 |
| ❑ PHS 600213 [S] | Nightide | 1966 | 15.00 |
| ❑ PHS 600231 [S] | More Than Music | 1967 | 12.00 |
| ❑ PHS 600250 [S] | Mexican Trip | 1967 | 12.00 |
| ❑ PHS 600260 [S] | The Mystic Moods of Love | 1968 | 12.00 |
| ❑ PHS 600277 | Emotions | 1968 | 12.00 |
| ❑ PHS 600301 | Extensions | 1969 | 12.00 |
| ❑ PHS 600321 | Love Token | 1969 | 12.00 |
| ❑ PHS 600342 | Stormy Weekend | 1970 | 12.00 |
| ❑ PHS 600349 | English Muffins | 1970 | 12.00 |
| ❑ PHS 600351 | Country Lovin' Folk | 1971 | 12.00 |

SOUND BIRD

| Number | Title (A Side/B Side) | Yr | NM |
|---|---|---|---|
| ❑ 7501 | One Stormy Night | 1975 | 8.00 |
| *—Reissue of Warner Bros. 2594* | | | |



**Except when noted otherwise, VG = 25% of NM, and VG+ = 50% of NM. (Example: VG = $2.00, VG+ = $4.00 and NM = $8.00.)**

| Number | Title (A Side/B Side) | Yr | NM |
|---|---|---|---|
| ❑ 7502 | Nightide | 1975 | 8.00 |
| *—Reissue of Warner Bros. 2593* | | | |
| ❑ 7503 | Man and… | 1975 | 8.00 |
| ❑ 7504 | Moods for a Stormy Night | 1975 | 8.00 |
| ❑ 7505 | Emotions | 1975 | 8.00 |
| ❑ 7506 | Stormy Weekend | 1975 | 8.00 |
| *—Reissue of Warner Bros. 2596* | | | |
| ❑ 7507 | Touch | 1975 | 8.00 |
| ❑ SQ 7507 [Q] | Touch | 1975 | 12.00 |
| ❑ 7508 | Love the One You're With | 1975 | 8.00 |
| *—Reissue of Warner Bros. 2577* | | | |
| ❑ SQ 7508 [Q] | Love the One You're With | 1975 | 12.00 |
| *—Reissue of Warner Bros. BS4 2577* | | | |
| ❑ 7509 | Erogenous | 1975 | 8.00 |
| *—Reissue of Warner Bros. 2786* | | | |
| ❑ SQ 7509 [Q] | Erogenous | 1975 | 12.00 |
| *—Reissue of Warner Bros. BS4 2786* | | | |
| ❑ 7510 | Being with You | 1976 | 10.00 |
| ❑ SQ 7510 [Q] | Being with You | 1976 | 16.00 |
| ❑ 8503 | Misty | 1978 | 8.00 |
| ❑ 8505 | Midnight | 1978 | 8.00 |
| ❑ 8508 | Alone Together | 1978 | 8.00 |
| ❑ 8510 | Being with You | 1978 | 8.00 |
| *—Reissue of Sound Bird 7510* | | | |
| ❑ 8511 | Cosmic Forces | 1978 | 8.00 |
| ❑ 8512 | Country Lovin' Folk | 1978 | 8.00 |
| ❑ 8514 | Simple | 1978 | 8.00 |

#### WARNER BROS.

| Number | Title (A Side/B Side) | Yr | NM |
|---|---|---|---|
| ❑ BS 2577 | Love the One You're With | 1972 | 12.00 |
| ❑ BS4 2577 [Q] | Love the One You're With | 1974 | 16.00 |
| ❑ BS 2593 | Nightide | 1972 | 10.00 |
| *—Reissue of Philips 600-213* | | | |
| ❑ BS 2594 | One Stormy Night | 1972 | 10.00 |
| *—Reissue of Philips 600-205* | | | |
| ❑ BS 2595 | Love Token | 1972 | 10.00 |
| *—Reissue of Philips 600-321* | | | |
| ❑ BS 2596 | Stormy Weekend | 1972 | 10.00 |
| *—Reissue of Philips 600-342* | | | |
| ❑ BS 2597 | Emotions | 1972 | 10.00 |
| *—Reissue of Philips 600-277* | | | |
| ❑ BS 2598 | The Mystic Moods of Love | 1972 | 10.00 |
| *—Reissue of Philips 600-260* | | | |
| ❑ BS 2648 | Highway One | 1973 | 12.00 |
| ❑ BS4 2648 [Q] | Highway One | 1974 | 16.00 |
| ❑ BS 2690 | Awakening | 1973 | 12.00 |
| ❑ BS4 2690 [Q] | Awakening | 1974 | 16.00 |
| ❑ BS 2745 | Clear Light | 1974 | 12.00 |
| ❑ BS4 2745 [Q] | Clear Light | 1974 | 16.00 |
| ❑ BS 2786 | Erogenous | 1974 | 10.00 |
| ❑ BS4 2786 [Q] | Erogenous | 1974 | 16.00 |

### MYSTIC NUMBER NATIONAL BANK, THE

#### PROBE

| Number | Title (A Side/B Side) | Yr | NM |
|---|---|---|---|
| ❑ CPLP-4501 | The Mystic Number National Bank | 1969 | 20.00 |

### MYSTIC SIVA

#### VO

| Number | Title (A Side/B Side) | Yr | NM |
|---|---|---|---|
| ❑ 19713 | Mystic Siva | 1971 | 1000. |

# N

### N.E.R.D.

#### VIRGIN

| Number | Title (A Side/B Side) | Yr | NM |
|---|---|---|---|
| ❑ 12622 [(2)] | In Search of… | 2002 | 25.00 |
| ❑ 91457 [(2)] | Fly or Die | 2004 | 15.00 |

### N.W.A.

#### PRIORITY

| Number | Title (A Side/B Side) | Yr | NM |
|---|---|---|---|
| ❑ SPRO 30080 [DJ] | Greatest Hits/In-Store Play | 1996 | 20.00 |
| *—Promo-only "clean" versions for retailer use* | | | |

#### RUTHLESS

| Number | Title (A Side/B Side) | Yr | NM |
|---|---|---|---|
| ❑ MRC 1057 | N.W.A. and the Posse | 1987 | 25.00 |
| ❑ 7224 [EP] | 100 Miles and Runnin' | 1990 | 15.00 |
| ❑ 50561 [(2)] | Greatest Hits | 1996 | 15.00 |
| ❑ 57102 | Straight Outta Compton | 1989 | 20.00 |
| ❑ 57119 | N.W.A. and the Posse | 1990 | 15.00 |
| *—Reissue of MRC 1057* | | | |
| ❑ 57126 | Efil4zaggin (Niggaz4life) | 1991 | 20.00 |

### NABORS, JIM

#### CAPITOL SPECIAL MARKETS

| Number | Title (A Side/B Side) | Yr | NM |
|---|---|---|---|
| ❑ SL-8136 | 20 All-Time Favorites | 1977 | 10.00 |

#### COLUMBIA

| Number | Title (A Side/B Side) | Yr | NM |
|---|---|---|---|
| ❑ CS 1020 | The Jim Nabors Hour | 1970 | 12.00 |
| ❑ CL 2368 [M] | Shazam! (Gomer Pyle, U.S.M.C.) | 1965 | 20.00 |
| ❑ CL 2558 [M] | Jim Nabors Sings Love Me with All Your Heart | 1966 | 12.00 |
| ❑ CL 2665 [M] | Jim Nabors By Request | 1967 | 12.00 |
| ❑ CL 2703 [M] | The Things I Love | 1967 | 12.00 |
| ❑ CL 2731 [M] | Jim Nabors' Christmas Album | 1967 | 12.00 |
| ❑ CS 9168 [S] | Shazam! (Gomer Pyle, U.S.M.C.) | 1965 | 25.00 |
| ❑ CS 9358 [S] | Jim Nabors Sings Love Me with All Your Heart | 1966 | 15.00 |
| ❑ CS 9465 [S] | Jim Nabors By Request | 1967 | 15.00 |
| ❑ CS 9503 [S] | The Things I Love | 1967 | 15.00 |
| ❑ CS 9531 | Jim Nabors' Christmas Album | 1970 | 10.00 |
| *—Later editions with orange label* | | | |
| ❑ CS 9531 [S] | Jim Nabors' Christmas Album | 1967 | 12.00 |
| *—Originals with "360 Sound" label* | | | |
| ❑ CS 9620 | Kiss Me Goodbye | 1968 | 12.00 |
| ❑ CS 9716 | The Lord's Prayer and Other Sacred Songs | 1968 | 12.00 |
| ❑ PC 9716 | The Lord's Prayer | 1979 | 8.00 |
| *—Budget-line reissue* | | | |
| ❑ CS 9817 | Galveston | 1969 | 12.00 |
| ❑ C 30129 | Everything Is Beautiful | 1970 | 12.00 |
| ❑ C 30449 | For the Good Times/The Jim Nabors Hour | 1971 | 12.00 |
| ❑ 3C 30671 | How Great Thou Art | 198? | 8.00 |
| *—Budget-line reissue* | | | |
| ❑ C 30671 | How Great Thou Art | 1971 | 12.00 |
| ❑ C 30810 | Help Me Make It Through the Night | 1971 | 12.00 |
| ❑ CQ 30810 [Q] | Help Me Make It Through the Night | 1971 | 20.00 |
| ❑ KC 31336 | The Way of Love | 1972 | 12.00 |
| ❑ KG 31591 [(2)] | Great Love Songs | 1972 | 15.00 |
| ❑ PG 31591 [(2)] | Great Love Songs | 198? | 10.00 |
| *—Budget-line reissue* | | | |
| ❑ C 31630 | Merry Christmas | 1972 | 10.00 |
| ❑ KG 31973 [(2)] | The World of Jim Nabors | 1972 | 15.00 |
| ❑ PG 31973 [(2)] | The World of Jim Nabors | 1979 | 10.00 |
| *—Budget-line reissue* | | | |
| ❑ KC 32377 | The Twelfth of Never | 1972 | 12.00 |
| ❑ KC 32909 | Peace in the Valley | 1973 | 12.00 |
| ❑ PC 32909 | Peace in the Valley | 1979 | 8.00 |
| *—Budget-line reissue* | | | |
| ❑ KC 32950 | It's My Life | 1973 | 12.00 |
| ❑ KC 33401 | A Very Special Love Song | 1974 | 12.00 |
| ❑ PC 33401 | A Very Special Love Song | 1979 | 8.00 |
| *—Budget-line reissue* | | | |
| ❑ CG 33618 [(2)] | The Lord's Prayer/How Great Thou Art | 1975 | 15.00 |

#### COLUMBIA SPECIAL PRODUCTS

| Number | Title (A Side/B Side) | Yr | NM |
|---|---|---|---|
| ❑ P 13507 | Somewhere My Love | 1977 | 10.00 |

#### HARMONY

| Number | Title (A Side/B Side) | Yr | NM |
|---|---|---|---|
| ❑ KH 30398 | More | 1971 | 10.00 |

#### PAIR

| Number | Title (A Side/B Side) | Yr | NM |
|---|---|---|---|
| ❑ PDL2-1077 [(2)] | The Very Special Warmth of Jim Nabors | 1986 | 12.00 |
| ❑ PDL2-1097 [(2)] | On the Country Side | 1986 | 12.00 |

#### RANWOOD

| Number | Title (A Side/B Side) | Yr | NM |
|---|---|---|---|
| ❑ R-7017 [(2)] | 22 Great Hymn and Country Favorites | 1984 | 12.00 |
| ❑ R-8157 | Old Time Religion | 1976 | 10.00 |
| ❑ R-8164 | Town & Country | 1976 | 10.00 |
| ❑ R-8176 | Sincerely | 1977 | 10.00 |
| ❑ R-8178 | I See God | 1977 | 10.00 |

#### REALM

| Number | Title (A Side/B Side) | Yr | NM |
|---|---|---|---|
| ❑ 1V-8170 | Christmas with Jim Nabors | 1982 | 8.00 |

### NAGLE, RON

#### WARNER BROS.

| Number | Title (A Side/B Side) | Yr | NM |
|---|---|---|---|
| ❑ WS 1902 | Bad Rice | 1970 | 20.00 |

### NAKED RAYGUN

#### CAROLINE

| Number | Title (A Side/B Side) | Yr | NM |
|---|---|---|---|
| ❑ 1348 | Jettison | 1988 | 20.00 |
| ❑ 1371 | Understand? | 1989 | 20.00 |
| ❑ 1642 | Raygun...Naked Raygun | 1990 | 20.00 |

#### HAUNTED TOWN

| Number | Title (A Side/B Side) | Yr | NM |
|---|---|---|---|
| ❑ HTR 11 | Free Shit | 2001 | 10.00 |

#### HOMESTEAD

| Number | Title (A Side/B Side) | Yr | NM |
|---|---|---|---|
| ❑ HMS 008 | Throb Throb | 1984 | 20.00 |
| *—Second edition has lyric innersleeve* | | | |
| ❑ HMS 008 | Throb Throb | 1984 | 30.00 |
| *—First edition has lyric sheet* | | | |
| ❑ HMS 045 | All Rise | 1985 | 30.00 |

#### RUTHLESS

| Number | Title (A Side/B Side) | Yr | NM |
|---|---|---|---|
| ❑ 03 [EP] | Basement Screams | 1983 | 80.00 |

### NANCE, RAY

#### SOLID STATE

| Number | Title (A Side/B Side) | Yr | NM |
|---|---|---|---|
| ❑ SS-18062 | Body and Soul | 1969 | 20.00 |

### NANTON, MORRIS

#### PRESTIGE

| Number | Title (A Side/B Side) | Yr | NM |
|---|---|---|---|
| ❑ PRLP-7345 [M] | Preface | 1964 | 20.00 |
| ❑ PRST-7345 [S] | Preface | 1964 | 25.00 |
| ❑ PRLP-7409 [M] | Something We've Got | 1965 | 20.00 |
| ❑ PRST-7409 [S] | Something We've Got | 1965 | 25.00 |
| ❑ PRLP-7467 [M] | Soul Fingers | 1966 | 20.00 |
| ❑ PRST-7467 [S] | Soul Fingers | 1966 | 25.00 |

#### WARNER BROS.

| Number | Title (A Side/B Side) | Yr | NM |
|---|---|---|---|
| ❑ W-1256 [M] | Flower Drum Song | 1958 | 25.00 |
| ❑ WS-1256 [S] | Flower Drum Song | 1958 | 30.00 |
| ❑ W-1279 [M] | The Original Jazz Performance of "Roberta" | 1959 | 25.00 |
| ❑ WS-1279 [S] | The Original Jazz Performance of "Roberta" | 1959 | 30.00 |

### NAPOLEON, PHIL

#### CAPITOL

| Number | Title (A Side/B Side) | Yr | NM |
|---|---|---|---|
| ❑ ST 1344 [S] | Phil Napoleon and the Memphis Five | 1960 | 20.00 |
| ❑ T 1344 [M] | Phil Napoleon and the Memphis Five | 1960 | 25.00 |
| ❑ ST 1428 [S] | In the Land of Dixie | 1961 | 25.00 |
| ❑ T 1428 [M] | In the Land of Dixie | 1961 | 20.00 |
| ❑ ST 1535 [S] | Tenderloin Dixieland | 1961 | 25.00 |
| ❑ T 1535 [M] | Tenderloin Dixieland | 1961 | 20.00 |

#### COLUMBIA

| Number | Title (A Side/B Side) | Yr | NM |
|---|---|---|---|
| ❑ CL 2505 [10] | Two-Beat | 1955 | 80.00 |

#### EMARCY

| Number | Title (A Side/B Side) | Yr | NM |
|---|---|---|---|
| ❑ MG-26008 [10] | Dixieland Classics Vol. 1 | 1954 | 100.00 |
| ❑ MG-26009 [10] | Dixieland Classics Vol. 2 | 1954 | 100.00 |
| ❑ MG-36033 [M] | Dixieland Classics Vol. 1 | 1955 | 80.00 |

#### JOLLY ROGER

| Number | Title (A Side/B Side) | Yr | NM |
|---|---|---|---|
| ❑ 5006 [10] | Dixieland By Phil Napoleon | 1954 | 50.00 |

#### MERCURY

| Number | Title (A Side/B Side) | Yr | NM |
|---|---|---|---|
| ❑ MG-25078 [10] | Dixieland Classics Vol. 1 | 1953 | 100.00 |
| ❑ MG-25079 [10] | Dixieland Classics Vol. 2 | 1953 | 100.00 |

### NAPOLEON XIV

#### RHINO

| Number | Title (A Side/B Side) | Yr | NM |
|---|---|---|---|
| ❑ RNLP 816 | They're Coming to Take Me Away, Ha-Haaa! | 1985 | 12.00 |

#### WARNER BROS.

| Number | Title (A Side/B Side) | Yr | NM |
|---|---|---|---|
| ❑ W 1661 [M] | They're Coming to Take Me Away, Ha-Haaa! | 1966 | 60.00 |
| ❑ WS 1661 [S] | They're Coming to Take Me Away, Ha-Haaa! | 1966 | 100.00 |

### NARZ, JACK

#### DOT

| Number | Title (A Side/B Side) | Yr | NM |
|---|---|---|---|
| ❑ DLP-3244 [M] | Sing the Folk Hits with Jack Narz | 1960 | 25.00 |
| ❑ DLP-25244 [S] | Sing the Folk Hits with Jack Narz | 1960 | 30.00 |

### NAS

#### COLUMBIA

| Number | Title (A Side/B Side) | Yr | NM |
|---|---|---|---|
| ❑ C2S 41881 [(2)DJ] | I Am | 1999 | 20.00 |
| *—Promo-only version in generic black sleeve* | | | |
| ❑ C 57694 | Illmatic | 1994 | 30.00 |
| ❑ C2 63930 [(2)] | Nastradamus | 1999 | 15.00 |
| ❑ C 67015 | It Was Written | 1996 | 12.00 |
| ❑ C2 68773 [(2)] | I Am | 1999 | 15.00 |
| ❑ C2 85275 [(2)] | The Lost Tapes | 2002 | 15.00 |
| ❑ C2 85736 [(2)] | Stillmatic | 2001 | 15.00 |
| ❑ C2 86930 [(2)] | God's Son | 2002 | 15.00 |
| ❑ C4 92065 [(4)] | Street's Disciple | 2004 | 25.00 |
| ❑ C2 92072 [(2)] | Illmatic | 2004 | 15.00 |
| *—10th anniversary reissue with bonus material* | | | |

### NASCIMENTO, MILTON

#### A&M

| Number | Title (A Side/B Side) | Yr | NM |
|---|---|---|---|
| ❑ LP-(# unknown) [M] | Milton Nascimento | 1967 | 30.00 |
| ❑ SP-(# unknown) [S] | Milton Nascimento | 1967 | 20.00 |
| ❑ SP-3019 | Courage | 1969 | 20.00 |

### NASH, JOHNNY

#### ABC-PARAMOUNT

| Number | Title (A Side/B Side) | Yr | NM |
|---|---|---|---|
| ❑ 244 [M] | Johnny Nash | 1958 | 30.00 |
| ❑ S-244 [S] | Johnny Nash | 1959 | 40.00 |
| ❑ 276 [M] | Quiet Hour | 1959 | 30.00 |
| ❑ S-276 [S] | Quiet Hour | 1959 | 40.00 |
| ❑ 299 [M] | I Got Rhythm | 1959 | 30.00 |
| ❑ S-299 [S] | I Got Rhythm | 1959 | 40.00 |
| ❑ 344 [M] | Let's Get Lost | 1960 | 30.00 |
| ❑ S-344 [S] | Let's Get Lost | 1960 | 40.00 |
| ❑ 383 [M] | Studio Time | 1961 | 30.00 |
| ❑ S-383 [S] | Studio Time | 1961 | 40.00 |

#### ARGO

| Number | Title (A Side/B Side) | Yr | NM |
|---|---|---|---|
| ❑ LP-4038 [M] | Composer's Choice | 1964 | 20.00 |
| ❑ LPS-4038 [S] | Composer's Choice | 1964 | 25.00 |

#### EPIC

| Number | Title (A Side/B Side) | Yr | NM |
|---|---|---|---|
| ❑ KE 31607 | I Can See Clearly Now | 1972 | 15.00 |
| *—Yellow label* | | | |
| ❑ KE 31607 | I Can See Clearly Now | 1973 | 12.00 |
| *—Orange label* | | | |
| ❑ KE 32158 | My Merry-Go-Round | 1973 | 15.00 |
| ❑ PE 32828 | Celebrate Life | 1974 | 15.00 |

#### JAD

| Number | Title (A Side/B Side) | Yr | NM |
|---|---|---|---|
| ❑ JS-1001 | Prince of Peace | 1969 | 25.00 |
| ❑ JS-1006 | Folk Soul | 1970 | 25.00 |
| ❑ JS-1207 | Hold Me Tight | 1968 | 30.00 |

### NASH, TED

#### COLUMBIA

| Number | Title (A Side/B Side) | Yr | NM |
|---|---|---|---|
| ❑ CL 989 [M] | Star Eyes | 1957 | 40.00 |

#### STARLITE

| Number | Title (A Side/B Side) | Yr | NM |
|---|---|---|---|
| ❑ LP-6001 [10] | Ted Nash | 1954 | 50.00 |

| Number | Title (A Side/B Side) | Yr | NM |
|---|---|---|---|

### NASH, TED & DICK
**LIBERTY**
❑ LJH-6011 [M] The Brothers Nash 1956 50.00

### NASHVILLE ALL STARS, THE
**RCA VICTOR**
❑ LPM-2302 [M] After the Riot at Newport 1960 40.00
❑ LSP-2302 [S] After the Riot at Newport 1960 50.00
**RCA VICTOR RECORD CLUB**
❑ CPM-0114 [M] All-Time Country and Western Hits 1966 12.00
❑ CSP-0114 [S] All-Time Country and Western Hits 1966 15.00
❑ CPM-0126 [M] That Happy Nashville Sound 1967 15.00
❑ CSP-0126 [S] That Happy Nashville Sound 1967 12.00

### NASHVILLE GUITARS, THE
**MONUMENT**
❑ MLP-8058 [M] The Nashville Guitars 1966 15.00
❑ SLP-18058 [S] The Nashville Guitars 1966 20.00
❑ MLP-18093 The Nashville Guitars at Home 1968 15.00

### NASHVILLE PUSSY
**AMPHETAMINE REPTILE**
❑ AMREP-69 Let Them Eat Pussy 1999 40.00
**RESERVATION**
❑ REZP-1 [PD] Say Something Nasty 2003 15.00
*—Picture disc; 1,000 pressed*
**TVT**
❑ 3340-1 High as Hell 2000 25.00

### NASHVILLE TEENS, THE
**LONDON**
❑ PS 407 [R] Tobacco Road 1964 80.00
❑ LL 3407 [M] Tobacco Road 1964 100.00

### NASTOS, NICK
**STRAND**
❑ SL-1097 [M] Guitars on Fire 1962 20.00
❑ SLS-1097 [S] Guitars on Fire 1962 25.00

### NATIONAL GALLERY, THE
**PHILIPS**
❑ PHS 600266 The National Gallery (Performing Musical Interpretations of the Paintings of Paul Klee) 1968 30.00

### NATIONAL JAZZ ENSEMBLE
**CHIAROSCURO**
❑ 151 [(2)] National Jazz Ensemble, Volume 2 197? 20.00

### NATIONAL LAMPOON
**BANANA**
❑ BTS 38 Radio Dinner 1972 15.00
❑ BTS 6006 Lemmings 1973 15.00
❑ BTS 6008 Missing White House Tapes 1974 15.00
**EPIC**
❑ PE 33410 Gold Turkey 1974 12.00
*—Orange label*
❑ PE 33410 Gold Turkey 1979 8.00
*—Dark blue label*
❑ PE 33956 Goodbye Pop 1975 12.00
*—Orange label*
❑ PE 33956 Goodbye Pop 1979 8.00
*—Dark blue label*
**LABEL 21**
❑ IMP-2001 That's Not Funny, That's Sick! 1978 10.00
❑ PIC-2001 [PD] That's Not Funny, That's Sick! 1978 20.00
❑ IMP-2002 The White Album 1979 10.00
**MCA**
❑ 27023 Lemmings 198? 8.00
❑ 27024 Radio Dinner 198? 8.00
**PASSPORT**
❑ PB 6018 Sex, Drugs, Rock and Roll and the End of the World 1982 10.00
**VISA**
❑ 2001 That's Not Funny, That's Sick! 198? 8.00
❑ 2002 The White Album 198? 8.00
❑ 7008 Greatest Hits of the National Lampoon 1978 12.00

### NATIONAL SYMPHONY ORCHESTRA (HOWARD MITCHELL, CONDUCTOR)
**RCA VICTOR RED SEAL**
❑ LSC-2261 [S] Shostakovich: Symphony No. 5 1959 50.00
*—Original with "shaded dog" label*

### NATURAL FOUR, THE
**CURTOM**
❑ CU 5004 Heaven Right Here on Earth 1975 20.00
❑ CRT-8600 The Natural Four 1974 20.00

### NAVARRO, FATS
**BLUE NOTE**
❑ BLP-1531 [M] The Fabulous Fats Navarro, Vol. 1 1956 200.00
*—"Deep groove" version, W. 63rd St. address on label*
❑ BLP-1531 [M] The Fabulous Fats Navarro, Vol. 1 1956 500.00
*—"Deep groove" version; Lexington Ave. address on label*
❑ BLP-1531 [M] The Fabulous Fats Navarro, Vol. 1 1963 40.00
*—With "New York, USA" address on label*
❑ BLP-1532 [M] The Fabulous Fats Navarro, Vol. 2 1956 200.00
*—"Deep groove" version, W. 63rd St. address on label*
❑ BLP-1532 [M] The Fabulous Fats Navarro, Vol. 2 1956 500.00
*—"Deep groove" version; Lexington Ave. address on label*
❑ BLP-1532 [M] The Fabulous Fats Navarro, Vol. 2 1963 40.00
*—With "New York, USA" address on label*
❑ BLP-5004 [10] Fats Navarro Memorial Album 1952 1000.
**RIVERSIDE**
❑ RS-3019 Good Bait 1968 20.00
**SAVOY**
❑ MG-9005 [10] New Sounds in Modern Music 1952 400.00
❑ MG-9019 [10] New Trends Of Jazz 1952 400.00
❑ MG-12011 [M] Fats Navarro Memorial 1955 150.00
❑ MG-12133 [M] Nostalgia 1958 100.00

### NAVARRO, FATS/KAI WINDING/BREW MOORE
**SAVOY**
❑ MG-12119 [M] In the Beginning...Bebop 1957 60.00

### NAVARRO, TOMMY, AND THE SUNDIALERS
**URANIA**
❑ UR-900 [M] Twist Around the Town 1961 100.00
❑ US-5900 [S] Twist Around the Town 1961 150.00

### NAZARETH
**A&M**
❑ SP-3109 Close Enough for Rock 'N' Roll 1981 8.00
*—Budget-line reissue*
❑ SP-3168 Exercises 1982 8.00
*—Reissue of Warner Bros. 2639*
❑ SP-3169 Nazareth 1982 8.00
*—Reissue of Warner Bros. 2615*
❑ SP-3225 Hair of the Dog 1984 8.00
*—Budget-line reissue*
❑ SP-3226 Hot Tracks 1984 8.00
*—Budget-line reissue*
❑ SP-3609 Loud 'N' Proud 1974 10.00
❑ SP-3641 Rampant 1974 10.00
❑ SP-4396 Razamanaz 1973 15.00
*—First edition with brown label*
❑ SP-4396 Razamanaz 1974 10.00
❑ SP-4511 Hair of the Dog 1975 10.00
❑ SP-4562 Close Enough for Rock 'N' Roll 1976 10.00
❑ SP-4610 Play 'N' the Game 1976 10.00
❑ SP-4643 Hot Tracks 1977 10.00
❑ SP-4666 Expect No Mercy 1977 10.00
❑ SP-4741 No Mean City 1979 10.00
❑ SP-4799 Malice in Wonderland 1980 10.00
❑ SP-4844 The Fool Circle 1981 10.00
❑ SP-4901 2XS 1982 10.00
❑ SP-6703 [(2)] 'Snaz 1981 12.00
**MCA**
❑ 5458 Sound Elixir 1983 10.00
**WARNER BROS.**
❑ BS 2615 Nazareth 1972 20.00
❑ BS 2639 Exercises 1972 20.00

### NAZZ (1) Also see TODD RUNDGREN.
**RHINO**
❑ RNLP 109 Nazz 1984 10.00
❑ RNLP 110 Nazz Nazz 1984 10.00
❑ RNLP 111 Nazz III 1984 10.00
❑ RNLP 116 The Best of Nazz 1984 10.00
❑ R1 70116 The Best of Nazz 1987 8.00
**SGC**
❑ SD 5001 Nazz 1968 40.00
❑ 5002 [M] Nazz Nazz 1969 80.00
*—Promo-only mono pressing on red vinyl*
❑ SD 5002 [S] Nazz Nazz 1969 40.00
*—Red vinyl*
❑ SD 5002 [S] Nazz Nazz 1969 80.00
*—Black vinyl*
❑ SD 5004 Nazz III 1970 40.00

### NBC SYMPHONY ORCHESTRA (LEOPOLD STOKOWSKI, COND.)
**RCA VICTOR RED SEAL**
❑ LSC-2555 [S] The Sound of Stokowski and Wagner 1961 60.00
*—Originals with "shaded dog" label*
❑ LSC-2555 [S] The Sound of Stokowski and Wagner 1964 25.00
*—Second editions with "white dog" label*

### NDEGEOCELLO, ME'SHELL
**MAVERICK**
❑ PRO-A-6622 [(2)DJ]Plantation Lullabies 1993 20.00
*—Promo-only U.S. vinyl release*

### NECROS
**RESTLESS**
❑ 72203 Tangled Up 1986 12.00
**TOUCH & GO**
❑ 2 Conquest for Death 1983 70.00

### NEELY, JIMMY
**TRU-SOUND**
❑ TRU-15002 [M]Misirlou 1962 40.00

### NEFF, HILDEGARDE
**LONDON**
❑ PS 596 From Here On It Gets Rough 1971 20.00

### NEGATIVLAND
**SEELAND**
❑ 001 Negativland 1981 15.00
*—Every copy has a different cover*
❑ 002 Points 1982 12.00
*—Black vinyl*
❑ 002 Points 1982 15.00
*—Blue vinyl*
❑ 003 A Big 10-8 Place 1985 12.00
**SST**
❑ 133 Escape from Noise 1987 18.00
*—With booklet*
❑ 252 Helter Stupid 1989 12.00
❑ 272 [EP] U2 1990 100.00
*—Withdrawn thanks to pressure from the record company of U2 (the band)*
❑ 292 [EP] Guns 1992 8.00

### NEIGHB'RHOOD CHILDREN
**ACTA**
❑ 8005 [M] The Neighb'rhood Children 1968 80.00
❑ 38005 [S] The Neighb'rhood Children 1968 100.00
**SUNDAZED**
❑ LP 5023 [(2)] Long Years in Space 199? 15.00

### NEIL, FRED
**CAPITOL**
❑ ST-294 Everybody's Talkin' 1969 25.00
❑ ST 2665 [S] Fred Neil 1966 40.00
*—With color photo on back*
❑ ST 2665 [S] Fred Neil 1967 30.00
*—With black & white photo on back*
❑ T 2665 [M] Fred Neil 1966 30.00
❑ ST 2862 [S] Fred Neil Sessions 1968 30.00
❑ T 2862 [M] Fred Neil Sessions 1968 40.00
**ELEKTRA**
❑ EKL-293 [M] Bleecker and MacDougal 1965 30.00
❑ EKS-7293 [S] Bleecker and MacDougal 1965 40.00
❑ EKS-74073 Little Bit of Rain 1970 20.00
*—Reissue of 7293*
**SUNDAZED**
❑ LP 5107 Bleecker and MacDougal 2002 12.00

### NELSON, OLIVER
**ABC IMPULSE!**
❑ AS-9168 [S] Soulful Brass 1968 30.00
*—Black label with red ring*
**ARGO**
❑ LP-737 [M] Fantabulous 1964 50.00
❑ LPS-737 [S] Fantabulous 1964 50.00
**FLYING DUTCHMAN**
❑ FD-116 Black, Brown and Beautiful 1970 60.00
**GRP IMPULSE!**
❑ IMP-212 More Blues and the Abstract Truth 1997 20.00
*—Reissue on audiophile vinyl*
**IMPULSE!**
❑ A-5 [M] The Blues and the Abstract Truth 196? 40.00
*—Later cover has Oliver Nelson clearly indicated as leader and features a photo of him at the right*
❑ A-5 [M] The Blues and the Abstract Truth 1961 100.00
*—Original cover has an abstract painting and lists Bill Evans' name first*
❑ AS-5 [S] The Blues and the Abstract Truth 196? 50.00
*—Later cover has Oliver Nelson clearly indicated as leader and features a photo of him at the right*
❑ AS-5 [S] The Blues and the Abstract Truth 1961 120.00
*—Original cover has an abstract painting and lists Bill Evans' name first*
❑ A-75 [M] More Blues and the Abstract Truth 1964 40.00

| Number | Title (A Side/B Side) | Yr | NM |
|---|---|---|---|
| ❑ AS-75 [S] | More Blues and the Abstract Truth | 1964 | 50.00 |
| ❑ A-9113 [M] | Michelle | 1966 | 30.00 |
| ❑ AS-9113 [S] | Michelle | 1966 | 40.00 |
| ❑ A-9129 [M] | Sound Pieces | 1966 | 40.00 |
| ❑ AS-9129 [S] | Sound Pieces | 1966 | 40.00 |
| ❑ A-9132 [M] | Happenings | 1967 | 40.00 |
| *—With Hank Jones* | | | |
| ❑ AS-9132 [S] | Happenings | 1967 | 30.00 |
| *—With Hank Jones* | | | |
| ❑ A-9144 [M] | The Kennedy Dream | 1967 | 40.00 |
| ❑ AS-9144 [S] | The Kennedy Dream | 1967 | 30.00 |
| ❑ A-9147 [M] | The Spirit of '67 | 1967 | 50.00 |
| *—With Pee Wee Russell* | | | |
| ❑ AS-9147 [S] | The Spirit of '67 | 1967 | 30.00 |
| *—With Pee Wee Russell* | | | |
| ❑ A-9153 [M] | Live From Los Angeles | 1967 | 80.00 |
| ❑ AS-9153 [S] | Live From Los Angeles | 1967 | 30.00 |
| **MOODSVILLE** | | | |
| ❑ MVLP-13 [M] | Nocturne | 1960 | 100.00 |
| *—Green label* | | | |
| ❑ MVLP-13 [M] | Nocturne | 1965 | 50.00 |
| *—Blue label, trident logo at right* | | | |
| **NEW JAZZ** | | | |
| ❑ NJLP-8224 [M] | Meet Oliver Nelson | 1959 | 120.00 |
| *—Purple label* | | | |
| ❑ NJLP-8224 [M] | Meet Oliver Nelson | 1965 | 50.00 |
| *—Blue label, trident logo at right* | | | |
| ❑ NJLP-8233 [M] | Takin' Care of Business | 1960 | 120.00 |
| *—Purple label* | | | |
| ❑ NJLP-8233 [M] | Takin' Care of Business | 1965 | 50.00 |
| *—Blue label, trident logo at right* | | | |
| ❑ NJLP-8243 [M] | Screamin' the Blues | 1960 | 120.00 |
| *—Purple label* | | | |
| ❑ NJLP-8243 [M] | Screamin' the Blues | 1965 | 50.00 |
| *—Blue label, trident logo at right* | | | |
| ❑ NJLP-8255 [M] | Straight Ahead | 1961 | 120.00 |
| *—Purple label* | | | |
| ❑ NJLP-8255 [M] | Straight Ahead | 1965 | 50.00 |
| *—Blue label, trident logo at right* | | | |
| **PRESTIGE** | | | |
| ❑ PRLP-7225 [M] | Afro/American Sketches | 1962 | 50.00 |
| ❑ PRST-7225 [S] | Afro/American Sketches | 1962 | 60.00 |
| ❑ PRLP-7236 [M] | Main Stem | 1962 | 60.00 |
| ❑ PRST-7236 [S] | Main Stem | 1962 | 80.00 |
| **STATUS** | | | |
| ❑ ST-8324 [M] | Screamin' the Blues | 1965 | 50.00 |
| **UNITED ARTISTS** | | | |
| ❑ UAJ-14019 [M] | Impressions of Phaedra | 1962 | 50.00 |
| ❑ UAJS-15019 [S] | Impressions of Phaedra | 1962 | 80.00 |
| **VERVE** | | | |
| ❑ V-8508 [M] | Full Nelson | 1963 | 40.00 |
| ❑ V6-8508 [S] | Full Nelson | 1963 | 50.00 |
| ❑ V6-8743 [S] | Leonard Feather Presents the Sound of Feeling and the Sound of Oliver Nelson | 1968 | 100.00 |

## NELSON, OLIVER; KING CURTIS; JIMMY FORREST

| Number | Title (A Side/B Side) | Yr | NM |
|---|---|---|---|
| **PRESTIGE** | | | |
| ❑ PRLP-7223 [M] | Soul Battle | 1962 | 60.00 |
| *—Yellow label* | | | |
| ❑ PRST-7223 [S] | Soul Battle | 1962 | 70.00 |

## NELSON, RICKY

| Number | Title (A Side/B Side) | Yr | NM |
|---|---|---|---|
| **CAPITOL** | | | |
| ❑ SOO-12109 | Playing to Win | 1981 | 10.00 |
| **DECCA** | | | |
| ❑ DL 4419 [M] | For Your Sweet Love | 1963 | 30.00 |
| ❑ DL 4479 [M] | Rick Nelson Sings "For You" | 1963 | 30.00 |
| ❑ DL 4559 [M] | The Very Thought of You | 1964 | 30.00 |
| ❑ DL 4608 [M] | Spotlight on Rick | 1964 | 30.00 |
| ❑ DL 4660 [M] | Best Always | 1965 | 30.00 |
| ❑ DL 4678 [M] | Love and Kisses | 1965 | 30.00 |
| ❑ DL 4779 [M] | Bright Lights and Country Music | 1966 | 25.00 |
| ❑ DL 4827 [M] | Country Fever | 1967 | 25.00 |
| ❑ DL 4944 [M] | Another Side of Rick | 1967 | 25.00 |
| ❑ DL 5014 [M] | Perspective | 1968 | 50.00 |
| *—Mono copies are promo only* | | | |
| ❑ DL 74419 [S] | For Your Sweet Love | 1963 | 40.00 |
| ❑ DL 74479 [S] | Rick Nelson Sings "For You" | 1963 | 40.00 |
| ❑ DL 74559 [S] | The Very Thought of You | 1964 | 40.00 |
| ❑ DL 74608 [S] | Spotlight on Rick | 1964 | 40.00 |
| ❑ DL 74660 [S] | Best Always | 1965 | 40.00 |
| ❑ DL 74678 [S] | Love and Kisses | 1965 | 40.00 |
| ❑ DL 74779 [S] | Bright Lights and Country Music | 1966 | 30.00 |
| ❑ DL 74827 [S] | Country Fever | 1967 | 30.00 |
| ❑ DL 74944 [S] | Another Side of Rick | 1967 | 30.00 |
| ❑ DL 75014 [S] | Perspective | 1968 | 30.00 |
| ❑ DL 75162 | Rick Nelson In Concert | 1970 | 25.00 |
| ❑ DL 75236 | Rick Sings Nelson | 1970 | 25.00 |
| *—Deduct 20 percent if poster is missing* | | | |
| ❑ DL 75297 | Rudy the Fifth | 1971 | 25.00 |
| ❑ DL 75391 | Garden Party | 1972 | 25.00 |
| **EMI AMERICA** | | | |
| ❑ SQ-17192 | The Very Best of Rick Nelson | 1986 | 10.00 |
| *—Reissue of United Artists UA-LA330* | | | |
| **EPIC** | | | |
| ❑ JE 34420 | Intakes | 1977 | 12.00 |
| ❑ FE 40388 | The Memphis Sessions | 1986 | 10.00 |
| **EPIC/NU-DISK** | | | |
| ❑ 3E 36868 [10] | Four You | 1981 | 12.00 |
| **IMPERIAL** | | | |
| ❑ LP 9048 [M] | Ricky | 1957 | 100.00 |
| *—Black label with stars* | | | |
| ❑ LP 9048 [M] | Ricky | 1964 | 25.00 |
| *—Black label with pink and white at left* | | | |
| ❑ LP 9048 [M] | Ricky | 1966 | 20.00 |
| *—Black label with green and white at left* | | | |
| ❑ LP 9050 [M] | Ricky Nelson | 1958 | 100.00 |
| *—Black label with stars* | | | |
| ❑ LP 9050 [M] | Ricky Nelson | 1964 | 25.00 |
| *—Black label with pink and white at left* | | | |
| ❑ LP 9050 [M] | Ricky Nelson | 1966 | 20.00 |
| *—Black label with green and white at left* | | | |
| ❑ LP 9061 [M] | Ricky Sings Again | 1959 | 100.00 |
| *—Black label with stars* | | | |
| ❑ LP 9061 [M] | Ricky Sings Again | 1964 | 25.00 |
| *—Black label with pink and white at left* | | | |
| ❑ LP 9061 [M] | Ricky Sings Again | 1966 | 20.00 |
| *—Black label with green and white at left* | | | |
| ❑ LP 9082 [M] | Songs by Ricky | 1959 | 75.00 |
| *—Black label with stars* | | | |
| ❑ LP 9082 [M] | Songs by Ricky | 1964 | 25.00 |
| *—Black label with pink and white at left* | | | |
| ❑ LP 9082 [M] | Songs by Ricky | 1966 | 20.00 |
| *—Black label with green and white at left* | | | |
| ❑ LP 9122 [M] | More Songs by Ricky | 1960 | 75.00 |
| *—Black label with stars* | | | |
| ❑ LP 9122 [M] | More Songs by Ricky | 1964 | 25.00 |
| *—Black label with pink and white at left* | | | |
| ❑ LP 9122 [M] | More Songs by Ricky | 1966 | 20.00 |
| *—Black label with green and white at left* | | | |
| ❑ LP 9152 [M] | Rick Is 21 | 1961 | 40.00 |
| *—Black label with stars* | | | |
| ❑ LP 9152 [M] | Rick Is 21 | 1964 | 25.00 |
| *—Black label with pink and white at left* | | | |
| ❑ LP 9152 [M] | Rick Is 21 | 1966 | 20.00 |
| *—Black label with green and white at left* | | | |
| ❑ LP 9167 [M] | Album Seven by Rick | 1962 | 40.00 |
| *—Black label with stars* | | | |
| ❑ LP 9167 [M] | Album Seven by Rick | 1964 | 25.00 |
| *—Black label with pink and white at left* | | | |
| ❑ LP 9167 [M] | Album Seven by Rick | 1966 | 20.00 |
| *—Black label with green and white at left* | | | |
| ❑ LP 9218 [M] | Best Sellers by Rick Nelson | 1963 | 40.00 |
| *—Black label with stars* | | | |
| ❑ LP 9218 [M] | Best Sellers by Rick Nelson | 1964 | 25.00 |
| *—Black label with pink and white at left* | | | |
| ❑ LP 9218 [M] | Best Sellers by Rick Nelson | 1966 | 20.00 |
| *—Black label with green and white at left* | | | |
| ❑ LP 9223 [M] | It's Up to You | 1963 | 40.00 |
| *—Black label with stars* | | | |
| ❑ LP 9223 [M] | It's Up to You | 1964 | 25.00 |
| *—Black label with pink and white at left* | | | |
| ❑ LP 9223 [M] | It's Up to You | 1966 | 20.00 |
| *—Black label with green and white at left* | | | |
| ❑ LP 9232 [M] | Million Sellers | 1963 | 40.00 |
| *—Black label with stars* | | | |
| ❑ LP 9232 [M] | Million Sellers | 1964 | 25.00 |
| *—Black label with pink and white at left* | | | |
| ❑ LP 9232 [M] | Million Sellers | 1966 | 20.00 |
| *—Black label with green and white at left* | | | |
| ❑ LP 9244 [M] | A Long Vacation | 1963 | 40.00 |
| *—Black label with stars* | | | |
| ❑ LP 9244 [M] | A Long Vacation | 1964 | 25.00 |
| *—Black label with pink and white at left* | | | |
| ❑ LP 9244 [M] | A Long Vacation | 1966 | 20.00 |
| *—Black label with green and white at left* | | | |
| ❑ LP 9251 [M] | Rick Nelson Sings for You | 1964 | 25.00 |
| *—Black label with pink and white at left* | | | |
| ❑ LP 9251 [M] | Rick Nelson Sings for You | 1964 | 40.00 |
| *—Black label with stars* | | | |
| ❑ LP 9251 [M] | Rick Nelson Sings for You | 1966 | 20.00 |
| *—Black label with green and white at left* | | | |
| ❑ LP 12030 [S] | Songs by Ricky | 1959 | 200.00 |
| *—Black label with silver print* | | | |
| ❑ LP 12030 [S] | Songs by Ricky | 1964 | 40.00 |
| *—Black label with pink and white at left* | | | |
| ❑ LP 12030 [S] | Songs by Ricky | 1966 | 25.00 |
| *—Black label with green and white at left* | | | |
| ❑ LP 12059 [DJ] | More Songs by Ricky | 1960 | 1000. |
| *—Promo copy on blue vinyl. Add 20 percent for enclosed poster.* | | | |
| ❑ LP 12059 [S] | More Songs by Ricky | 1960 | 100.00 |
| *—Black label with silver print* | | | |
| ❑ LP 12059 [S] | More Songs by Ricky | 1964 | 40.00 |
| *—Black label with pink and white at left* | | | |
| ❑ LP 12059 [S] | More Songs by Ricky | 1966 | 25.00 |
| *—Black label with green and white at left* | | | |
| ❑ LP 12071 [S] | Rick Is 21 | 1961 | 100.00 |
| *—Black label with silver print* | | | |
| ❑ LP 12071 [S] | Rick Is 21 | 1964 | 40.00 |
| *—Black label with pink and white at left* | | | |
| ❑ LP 12071 [S] | Rick Is 21 | 1966 | 25.00 |
| *—Black label with green and white at left* | | | |
| ❑ LP 12082 [S] | Album Seven by Rick | 1962 | 100.00 |
| *—Black label with silver print* | | | |
| ❑ LP 12082 [S] | Album Seven by Rick | 1964 | 40.00 |
| *—Black label with pink and white at left* | | | |
| ❑ LP 12082 [S] | Album Seven by Rick | 1966 | 25.00 |
| *—Black label with green and white at left* | | | |
| ❑ LP 12090 [S] | Ricky Sings Again | 1962 | 150.00 |
| *—Black label with silver print* | | | |
| ❑ LP 12090 [S] | Ricky Sings Again | 1964 | 40.00 |
| *—Black label with pink and white at left* | | | |
| ❑ LP 12090 [S] | Ricky Sings Again | 1966 | 25.00 |
| *—Black label with green and white at left* | | | |
| ❑ LP 12218 [R] | Best Sellers | 1964 | 20.00 |
| *—Black label with pink and white at left* | | | |
| ❑ LP 12218 [R] | Best Sellers | 1966 | 15.00 |
| *—Black label with green and white at left* | | | |
| ❑ LP 12232 [R] | Million Sellers | 1964 | 20.00 |
| *—Black label with pink and white at left* | | | |
| ❑ LP 12232 [R] | Million Sellers | 1966 | 15.00 |
| *—Black label with green and white at left* | | | |
| ❑ LP 12244 [R] | A Long Vacation | 1964 | 20.00 |
| *—Black label with pink and white at left* | | | |
| ❑ LP 12244 [R] | A Long Vacation | 1966 | 15.00 |
| *—Black label with green and white at left* | | | |
| ❑ LP 12251 [R] | Rick Nelson Sings for You | 1964 | 20.00 |
| *—Black label with pink and white at left* | | | |
| ❑ LP 12251 [R] | Rick Nelson Sings for You | 1964 | 25.00 |
| *—Black label with silver print* | | | |
| ❑ LP 12251 [R] | Rick Nelson Sings for You | 1966 | 15.00 |
| *—Black label with green and white at left* | | | |
| ❑ LP 12392 [R] | Ricky | 1968 | 15.00 |
| *—Rechanneled reissue of 9048* | | | |
| ❑ LP 12393 [R] | Ricky Nelson | 1968 | 15.00 |
| *—Rechanneled reissue of 9050* | | | |
| **LIBERTY** | | | |
| ❑ LM-1004 | Ricky | 1981 | 8.00 |
| *—Reissue of United Artists 1004* | | | |
| ❑ LXB-9960 [(2)] | Legendary Masters | 198? | 12.00 |
| *—Reissue of United Artists 9960* | | | |
| ❑ LN-10134 | Ricky Sings Again | 1982 | 10.00 |
| *—Reissue of Imperial 12090* | | | |
| ❑ LN-10205 | Souvenirs | 1983 | 8.00 |
| ❑ LN-10253 | Teen Age Idol | 1984 | 8.00 |
| ❑ LN-10304 | I Need You | 1986 | 8.00 |
| *—Reissue of Sunset 5205* | | | |
| ❑ LN-10305 | Ricky Nelson | 1986 | 8.00 |
| *—Another reissue* | | | |
| ❑ LM-51004 | Ricky | 1983 | 8.00 |
| *—Reissue of Liberty 1004* | | | |
| **MCA** | | | |
| ❑ 3 | Rick Nelson In Concert | 1973 | 12.00 |
| *—Reissue of Decca 75162* | | | |
| ❑ 20 | Rick Sings Nelson | 1973 | 12.00 |
| *—Reissue of Decca 75236* | | | |
| ❑ 37 | Rudy the Fifth | 1973 | 12.00 |
| *—Reissue of Decca 75297* | | | |
| ❑ 62 | Garden Party | 1973 | 12.00 |
| *—Reissue of Decca 75391* | | | |
| ❑ 383 | Windfall | 1974 | 15.00 |
| ❑ 1517 | The Decca Years | 1982 | 8.00 |
| ❑ 2-4004 [(2)] | Rick Nelson Country | 1973 | 15.00 |
| ❑ 6163 | All My Best | 1986 | 10.00 |
| ❑ 25983 | Rick Nelson In Concert The Troubadour, 1969 | 1987 | 10.00 |
| *—Reissue of MCA 3 with revised title* | | | |
| **RHINO** | | | |
| ❑ RNLP 215 | Greatest Hits | 1985 | 12.00 |
| ❑ RNDF 259 [PD] | Greatest Hits | 1985 | 15.00 |
| ❑ R1-70215 | Greatest Hits | 1987 | 10.00 |
| ❑ R1-71114 | Live 1983-1985 | 1989 | 12.00 |
| **SUNSET** | | | |
| ❑ SUM-1118 [M] | Ricky Nelson | 1966 | 15.00 |
| ❑ SUS-5118 [P] | Ricky Nelson | 1966 | 20.00 |
| ❑ SUS-5205 | I Need You | 1968 | 15.00 |
| **TIME-LIFE** | | | |
| ❑ SRNR 31 [(2)] | Rick Nelson: 1957-1972 | 1989 | 15.00 |
| **UNITED ARTISTS** | | | |
| ❑ UA-LA330-E | The Very Best of Rick Nelson | 1974 | 12.00 |
| ❑ LM-1004 | Ricky | 1980 | 10.00 |
| *—Reissue of Imperial 9048* | | | |
| ❑ UAS-9960 [(2)] | Legendary Masters | 1971 | 25.00 |
| **VERVE** | | | |
| ❑ V 2083 [M] | Teen Time | 1957 | 500.00 |
| *—Has three Ricky Nelson songs plus tracks by four others; usually treated as Rick's LP because of his prominence on the cover* | | | |

## NELSON, SANDY

| Number | Title (A Side/B Side) | Yr | NM |
|---|---|---|---|
| **IMPERIAL** | | | |
| ❑ LP 9105 [M] | Sandy Nelson Plays Teen Beat | 1960 | 30.00 |
| ❑ LP 9136 [M] | He's a Drummer Boy | 1961 | 30.00 |
| ❑ LP 9159 [M] | Let There Be Drums | 1962 | 30.00 |
| ❑ LP 9168 [M] | Drums Are My Beat! | 1962 | 20.00 |
| *—Black label with stars* | | | |
| ❑ LP 9168 [M] | Drums Are My Beat! | 1964 | 15.00 |
| *—Pink, white and black label* | | | |
| ❑ LP 9189 [M] | Drummin' Up a Storm | 1962 | 20.00 |
| ❑ LP 9202 [M] | Golden Hits | 1962 | 20.00 |
| ❑ LP 9203 [M] | Country Style | 1962 | 20.00 |
| ❑ LP 9203 [M] | On the Wild Side | 1966 | 15.00 |
| *—Same LP as above, but new title on cover* | | | |
| ❑ LP 9204 [M] | Compelling Percussion | 1962 | 20.00 |
| ❑ LP 9215 [M] | Teenage House Party | 1963 | 20.00 |

| Number | Title (A Side/B Side) | Yr | NM |
|---|---|---|---|
| ❑ LP 9224 [M] | The Best of the Beats | 1963 | 15.00 |
| ❑ LP 9237 [M] | Beat That Drum | 1963 | 15.00 |
| ❑ LP 9249 [M] | Sandy Nelson Plays | 1963 | 15.00 |
| ❑ LP 9258 [M] | Be True to Your School | 1964 | 15.00 |
| ❑ LP 9272 [M] | Live! In Las Vegas | 1964 | 20.00 |
| ❑ LP 9278 [M] | Teen Beat '65 | 1965 | 15.00 |
| ❑ LP 9283 [M] | Drum Discotheque | 1965 | 15.00 |
| ❑ LP 9287 [M] | Drums A Go-Go | 1965 | 15.00 |
| ❑ LP 9298 [M] | Boss Beat | 1965 | 15.00 |
| ❑ LP 9305 [M] | "In" Beat | 1966 | 15.00 |
| ❑ LP 9314 [M] | Super Drums | 1966 | 15.00 |
| ❑ LP 9329 [M] | Beat That #!!@* Drum | 1966 | 12.00 |
| ❑ LP 9340 [M] | Cheetah Beat | 1967 | 12.00 |
| ❑ LP 9345 [M] | The Beat Goes On | 1967 | 12.00 |
| ❑ LP 9362 [M] | Soul Drums | 1967 | 15.00 |
| ❑ LP 12044 [S] | Sandy Nelson Plays Teen Beat | 1960 | 40.00 |
| ❑ LP 12080 [R] | Let There Be Drums | 1962 | 25.00 |
| ❑ LP 12083 [S] | Drums Are My Beat! | 1962 | 25.00 |
| ❑ LP 12089 [R] | He's a Drummer Boy | 1962 | 25.00 |
| ❑ LP 12189 [S] | Drummin' Up a Storm | 1962 | 25.00 |
| ❑ LP 12202 [P] | Golden Hits | 1962 | 25.00 |
| ❑ LP 12203 [S] | Country Style | 1962 | 25.00 |
| ❑ LP 12203 [S] | On the Wild Side | 1966 | 20.00 |
| *—Same LP as above, but new title on cover* | | | |
| ❑ LP 12204 [S] | Compelling Percussion | 1962 | 25.00 |
| ❑ LP 12215 [S] | Teenage House Party | 1963 | 25.00 |
| ❑ LP 12224 [S] | The Best of the Beats | 1963 | 20.00 |
| ❑ LP 12237 [S] | Beat That Drum | 1963 | 20.00 |
| ❑ LP 12249 [S] | Sandy Nelson Plays | 1963 | 20.00 |
| ❑ LP 12258 [S] | Be True to Your School | 1964 | 20.00 |
| ❑ LP 12272 [R] | Live! In Las Vegas | 1964 | 15.00 |
| ❑ LP 12278 [S] | Teen Beat '65 | 1965 | 20.00 |
| ❑ LP 12283 [S] | Drum Discotheque | 1965 | 20.00 |
| ❑ LP 12287 [S] | Drums A Go-Go | 1965 | 20.00 |
| ❑ LP 12298 [S] | Boss Beat | 1965 | 20.00 |
| ❑ LP 12305 [S] | "In" Beat | 1966 | 20.00 |
| ❑ LP 12314 [S] | Super Drums | 1966 | 20.00 |
| ❑ LP 12329 [S] | Beat That #!!@* Drum | 1966 | 15.00 |
| ❑ LP 12340 [S] | Cheetah Beat | 1967 | 15.00 |
| ❑ LP 12345 [S] | The Beat Goes On | 1967 | 15.00 |
| ❑ LP 12362 [S] | Soul Drums | 1967 | 12.00 |
| ❑ LP 12367 | Boogaloo Beat | 1968 | 12.00 |
| ❑ LP 12400 | Rock and Roll Revival | 1968 | 12.00 |
| ❑ LP 12424 | Rebirth of the Beat | 1969 | 12.00 |
| ❑ LP 12439 | Manhattan Spiritual | 1969 | 12.00 |
| ❑ LP 12451 | Groovy | 1970 | 12.00 |

LIBERTY

| Number | Title (A Side/B Side) | Yr | NM |
|---|---|---|---|
| ❑ LN-10172 | The Very Best of Sandy Nelson | 1982 | 8.00 |
| ❑ LN-10209 | Collectors' Gems, Vol. 2 | 1983 | 8.00 |

PICKWICK

| Number | Title (A Side/B Side) | Yr | NM |
|---|---|---|---|
| ❑ SPC-3605 | And Then There Were Drums | 1978 | 10.00 |

SUNSET

| Number | Title (A Side/B Side) | Yr | NM |
|---|---|---|---|
| ❑ SUM-1114 [M] | Walking Beat | 1966 | 10.00 |
| ❑ SUM-1166 [M] | Teen Drums | 1967 | 10.00 |
| ❑ SUS-5114 [S] | Walking Beat | 1966 | 12.00 |
| ❑ SUS-5166 [S] | Teen Drums | 1967 | 12.00 |
| ❑ SUS-5224 | And There Were Drums (Drums and More Drums) | 1968 | 10.00 |
| ❑ SUS-5261 | Heavy Drums | 1969 | 10.00 |
| ❑ SUS-5291 | Sandy Nelson Plays Fats Domino Hits | 1970 | 10.00 |

UNITED ARTISTS

| Number | Title (A Side/B Side) | Yr | NM |
|---|---|---|---|
| ❑ UA-LA440-E | The Very Best of Sandy Nelson | 1975 | 12.00 |

## NELSON, TRACY

ADELPHI

| Number | Title (A Side/B Side) | Yr | NM |
|---|---|---|---|
| ❑ 4119 | Doin' It My Way | 1981 | 10.00 |

ATLANTIC

| Number | Title (A Side/B Side) | Yr | NM |
|---|---|---|---|
| ❑ SD 7310 | Tracy Nelson | 1974 | 12.00 |

COLUMBIA

| Number | Title (A Side/B Side) | Yr | NM |
|---|---|---|---|
| ❑ KC 31759 | Poor Man's Paradise | 1973 | 12.00 |

FLYING FISH

| Number | Title (A Side/B Side) | Yr | NM |
|---|---|---|---|
| ❑ FF-052 | Homemade Songs | 1978 | 10.00 |
| ❑ FF-209 | Come See About Me | 1980 | 10.00 |

MCA

| Number | Title (A Side/B Side) | Yr | NM |
|---|---|---|---|
| ❑ 494 | Sweet Soul Music | 1975 | 12.00 |
| ❑ 2203 | Time Is On My Side | 1976 | 12.00 |

PRESTIGE

| Number | Title (A Side/B Side) | Yr | NM |
|---|---|---|---|
| ❑ PRLP 7393 [M] | Deep Are the Roots | 1965 | 25.00 |
| ❑ PRST 7393 [S] | Deep Are the Roots | 1965 | 30.00 |
| ❑ PRST 7726 | Deep Are the Roots | 1969 | 15.00 |

## NELSON, WILLIE

ALLEGIANCE

| Number | Title (A Side/B Side) | Yr | NM |
|---|---|---|---|
| ❑ AV-5005 | Willie or Won't He | 1983 | 10.00 |
| ❑ AV-5010 | Wild & Willie | 1983 | 10.00 |

ATLANTIC

| Number | Title (A Side/B Side) | Yr | NM |
|---|---|---|---|
| ❑ SD 7262 | Shotgun Willie | 1973 | 20.00 |
| ❑ SD 7291 | Phases and Stages | 1974 | 20.00 |

COLUMBIA

| Number | Title (A Side/B Side) | Yr | NM |
|---|---|---|---|
| ❑ KC 33482 | Red Headed Stranger | 1975 | 15.00 |
| *—No bar code on back cover* | | | |
| ❑ PC 33482 | Red Headed Stranger | 1979 | 8.00 |
| *—With bar code on back cover; budget-line reissue* | | | |
| ❑ PC 34092 | The Sound in Your Mind | 1976 | 12.00 |
| *—No bar code on back cover* | | | |
| ❑ PC 34092 | The Sound in Your Mind | 1979 | 8.00 |
| *—With bar code on back cover; budget-line reissue* | | | |
| ❑ KC 34112 | The Troublemaker | 1976 | 12.00 |
| *—No bar code on back cover* | | | |
| ❑ PC 34112 | The Troublemaker | 1979 | 8.00 |
| *—With bar code on back cover; budget-line reissue* | | | |
| ❑ JC 34695 | To Lefty From Willie | 1977 | 12.00 |
| ❑ PC 34695 | To Lefty From Willie | 1979 | 8.00 |
| *—Budget-line reissue* | | | |
| ❑ JC 35305 | Stardust | 1978 | 10.00 |
| ❑ JC 35305 | Stardust | 2000 | 25.00 |
| *—Classic Records reissue on audiophile vinyl* | | | |
| ❑ KC2 35642 [(2)] | Willie and Family Live | 1978 | 15.00 |
| ❑ JC 36188 | Willie Nelson Sings Kristofferson | 1979 | 10.00 |
| ❑ PC 36188 | Willie Nelson Sings Kristofferson | 1980 | 8.00 |
| *—Budget-line reissue* | | | |
| ❑ JC 36189 | Pretty Paper | 1979 | 10.00 |
| ❑ JS 36327 | The Electric Horseman | 1979 | 10.00 |
| *—Side 2 by Dave Grusin* | | | |
| ❑ S2 36752 [(2)] | Honeysuckle Rose | 1980 | 12.00 |
| *—Over half of the LP is by Willie* | | | |
| ❑ FC 36883 | Somewhere Over the Rainbow | 1981 | 10.00 |
| ❑ KC2 37542 [(2)] | Willie Nelson's Greatest Hits (& Some That Will Be) | 1981 | 12.00 |
| ❑ FC 37951 | Always on My Mind | 1982 | 10.00 |
| ❑ PC 37951 | Always on My Mind | 1984 | 8.00 |
| *—Budget-line reissue* | | | |
| ❑ PC 38248 | Tougher Than Leather | 1984 | 8.00 |
| *—Budget-line reissue* | | | |
| ❑ QC 38248 | Tougher Than Leather | 1983 | 10.00 |
| ❑ CX 38250 [(10)] | Willie Nelson | 1983 | 120.00 |
| ❑ FC 39110 | Without a Song | 1983 | 10.00 |
| ❑ PC 39110 | Without a Song | 1984 | 8.00 |
| *—Budget-line reissue* | | | |
| ❑ FC 39145 | City of New Orleans | 1984 | 10.00 |
| ❑ PC 39145 | City of New Orleans | 1985 | 8.00 |
| *—Budget-line reissue* | | | |
| ❑ FC 39363 | Angel Eyes | 1984 | 10.00 |
| ❑ PC 39363 | Angel Eyes | 1985 | 8.00 |
| *—Budget-line reissue* | | | |
| ❑ FC 39894 | Partners | 1986 | 10.00 |
| ❑ PC 39894 | Partners | 1987 | 8.00 |
| *—Budget-line reissue* | | | |
| ❑ 9C9 39943 [PD] | Always on My Mind | 1985 | 20.00 |
| ❑ FC 39990 | Half Nelson | 1985 | 10.00 |
| *—Duets with 10 different artists* | | | |
| ❑ PC 39990 | Half Nelson | 1986 | 8.00 |
| *—Budget-line reissue* | | | |
| ❑ FC 40008 | Me and Paul | 1985 | 10.00 |
| ❑ PC 40008 | Me and Paul | 1986 | 8.00 |
| *—Budget-line reissue* | | | |
| ❑ FC 40327 | The Promiseland | 1986 | 10.00 |
| ❑ FC 40487 | Island in the Sea | 1987 | 10.00 |
| ❑ HC 43482 | Red Headed Stranger | 1982 | 40.00 |
| *—Half-speed mastered edition* | | | |
| ❑ FC 44431 | What a Wonderful World | 1988 | 10.00 |
| ❑ FC 45046 | A Horse Called Music | 1989 | 10.00 |
| ❑ HC 45305 | Stardust | 1981 | 70.00 |
| *—Half-speed mastered edition* | | | |
| ❑ HC 47951 | Always on My Mind | 1982 | 50.00 |
| *—Half-speed mastered edition* | | | |
| ❑ HC 48248 | Tougher Than Leather | 1983 | 50.00 |
| *—Half-speed mastered edition* | | | |

DELTA

| Number | Title (A Side/B Side) | Yr | NM |
|---|---|---|---|
| ❑ DLP-1157 | Diamonds in the Rough | 1982 | 10.00 |

HEARTLAND

| Number | Title (A Side/B Side) | Yr | NM |
|---|---|---|---|
| ❑ HL 1038/9 [(2)] | The Best of Willie Nelson | 1987 | 15.00 |

LIBERTY

| Number | Title (A Side/B Side) | Yr | NM |
|---|---|---|---|
| ❑ LRP-3239 [M] | ...And Then I Wrote | 1962 | 40.00 |
| ❑ LRP-3308 [M] | Here's Willie Nelson | 1963 | 40.00 |
| ❑ LST-7239 [S] | ...And Then I Wrote | 1962 | 50.00 |
| ❑ LST-7308 [S] | Here's Willie Nelson | 1963 | 50.00 |
| ❑ LN-10013 | Country Willie | 1980 | 8.00 |
| *—Budget-line reissue* | | | |
| ❑ LN-10118 | The Best of Willie Nelson | 1982 | 8.00 |
| *—Budget-line reissue* | | | |

LOST HIGHWAY

| Number | Title (A Side/B Side) | Yr | NM |
|---|---|---|---|
| ❑ B0004706-01 | Countryman | 2005 | 12.00 |
| ❑ B0006079-01 | You Don't Know Me: The Songs of Cindy Walker | 2006 | 12.00 |
| ❑ B0006939-01 | Songbird | 2006 | 15.00 |

PAIR

| Number | Title (A Side/B Side) | Yr | NM |
|---|---|---|---|
| ❑ PDL2-1007 [(2)] | Country Winners | 1986 | 12.00 |
| ❑ PDL2-1032 [(2)] | Once More with Feeling | 1986 | 12.00 |
| ❑ PDL2-1114 [(2)] | Good Hearted Woman | 1986 | 12.00 |

PICKWICK

| Number | Title (A Side/B Side) | Yr | NM |
|---|---|---|---|
| ❑ ACL1-0326 | Country Winners | 1976 | 8.00 |
| ❑ ACL1-0705 | Spotlight on Willie Nelson | 1976 | 8.00 |
| ❑ SPC-3584 | Hello Walls | 1978 | 10.00 |
| ❑ ACL1-7018 | Columbus Stockade Blues | 1976 | 8.00 |

PLANTATION

| Number | Title (A Side/B Side) | Yr | NM |
|---|---|---|---|
| ❑ PLP-24 | The Longhorn Jamboree Presents: Willie Nelson & His Friends | 1976 | 10.00 |
| *—Also includes tracks by David Allan Coe, Jerry Lee Lewis and Carl Perkins* | | | |

RCA CAMDEN

| Number | Title (A Side/B Side) | Yr | NM |
|---|---|---|---|
| ❑ ACL1-0326 | Country Winners | 1973 | 12.00 |
| ❑ ACL1-0705 | Spotlight on Willie Nelson | 1974 | 12.00 |
| ❑ CAS-2444 | Columbus Stockade Blues | 1970 | 15.00 |
| ❑ ACL1-7018 | Columbus Stockade Blues | 1975 | 10.00 |

RCA VICTOR

| Number | Title (A Side/B Side) | Yr | NM |
|---|---|---|---|
| ❑ ANL1-1102 | Yesterday's Wine | 1975 | 10.00 |
| ❑ APL1-1234 | What Can You Do to Me Now | 1975 | 12.00 |
| ❑ APL1-1487 | Willie Nelson Live | 1976 | 12.00 |
| ❑ APL1-2210 | Before His Time | 1977 | 10.00 |
| ❑ AHL1-3243 | Sweet Memories | 1979 | 10.00 |
| ❑ LPM-3418 [M] | Country Willie — His Own Songs | 1965 | 20.00 |
| ❑ LSP-3418 [S] | Country Willie — His Own Songs | 1965 | 25.00 |
| ❑ LPM-3528 [M] | Country Favorites, Willie Nelson Style | 1966 | 20.00 |
| ❑ LSP-3528 [S] | Country Favorites, Willie Nelson Style | 1966 | 25.00 |
| ❑ AHL1-3549 | Danny Davis & Willie Nelson with the Nashville Brass | 1980 | 10.00 |
| ❑ LPM-3659 [M] | Country Music Concert | 1966 | 20.00 |
| ❑ LSP-3659 [S] | Country Music Concert | 1966 | 25.00 |
| ❑ AYL1-3671 | Before His Time | 1980 | 8.00 |
| *—"Best Buy Series" reissue* | | | |
| ❑ LPM-3748 [M] | Make Way for Willie Nelson | 1967 | 20.00 |
| ❑ LSP-3748 [S] | Make Way for Willie Nelson | 1967 | 25.00 |
| ❑ AYL1-3800 | Yesterday's Wine | 1980 | 8.00 |
| *—"Best Buy Series" reissue* | | | |
| ❑ LPM-3858 [M] | The Party's Over and Other Great Willie Nelson Songs | 1967 | 25.00 |
| ❑ LSP-3858 [S] | The Party's Over and Other Great Willie Nelson Songs | 1967 | 20.00 |
| ❑ LPM-3937 [M] | Texas in My Soul | 1968 | 100.00 |
| ❑ LSP-3937 [S] | Texas in My Soul | 1968 | 20.00 |
| ❑ AYL1-3958 | What Can You Do to Me Now | 1981 | 8.00 |
| *—"Best Buy Series" reissue* | | | |
| ❑ AHL1-4045 | The Minstrel Man | 1981 | 10.00 |
| ❑ LSP-4057 | Good Times | 1968 | 20.00 |
| ❑ LSP-4111 | My Own Peculiar Way | 1969 | 20.00 |
| ❑ AYL1-4165 | Willie Nelson Live | 1981 | 8.00 |
| *—"Best Buy Series" reissue* | | | |
| ❑ LSP-4294 | Both Sides Now | 1970 | 20.00 |
| ❑ AYL1-4300 | Sweet Memories | 1982 | 8.00 |
| *—"Best Buy Series" reissue* | | | |
| ❑ LSP-4404 | Laying My Burdens Down | 1970 | 20.00 |
| ❑ AHL1-4420 | The Best of Willie Nelson | 1982 | 10.00 |
| ❑ LSP-4489 | Willie Nelson & Family | 1971 | 20.00 |
| ❑ LSP-4568 | Yesterday's Wine | 1971 | 20.00 |
| ❑ LSP-4653 | The Picture | 1972 | 20.00 |
| ❑ LSP-4760 | The Willie Way | 1972 | 20.00 |
| ❑ AHL1-4819 | My Own Way | 1983 | 10.00 |
| ❑ AYL1-5143 | The Best of Willie Nelson | 1984 | 8.00 |
| *—"Best Buy Series" reissue* | | | |
| ❑ CPL1-5174 | Don't You Ever Get Tired of Hurting Me | 1984 | 10.00 |
| ❑ AYL1-5438 | My Own Way | 1985 | 8.00 |
| *—"Best Buy Series" reissue* | | | |
| ❑ AHL1-5470 | Collector's Series | 1985 | 10.00 |
| ❑ CPL1-7158 | Willie | 1986 | 10.00 |

SONGBIRD

| Number | Title (A Side/B Side) | Yr | NM |
|---|---|---|---|
| ❑ 3258 | Family Bible | 1980 | 10.00 |

SUNSET

| Number | Title (A Side/B Side) | Yr | NM |
|---|---|---|---|
| ❑ SUM-1138 [M] | Hello Walls | 1966 | 15.00 |
| ❑ SUS-5138 [S] | Hello Walls | 1966 | 20.00 |

TAKOMA

| Number | Title (A Side/B Side) | Yr | NM |
|---|---|---|---|
| ❑ TAK-7104 | The Legend Begins | 1983 | 10.00 |

TIME-LIFE

| Number | Title (A Side/B Side) | Yr | NM |
|---|---|---|---|
| ❑ P 16946 [(3)] | Country and Western Classics | 1983 | 20.00 |

UNITED ARTISTS

| Number | Title (A Side/B Side) | Yr | NM |
|---|---|---|---|
| ❑ UA-LA086-E | The Best of Willie Nelson | 1973 | 15.00 |
| *—Reissue of Liberty tracks* | | | |
| ❑ UA-LA410-G | Country Willie | 1975 | 15.00 |
| ❑ UA-LA574-H2 [(2)] | Texas Country | 1975 | 18.00 |
| ❑ UA-LA930-G | There'll Be No Teardrops Tonight | 1978 | 15.00 |

## NEON PHILHARMONIC, THE

Also see TUPPER SAUSSY.

WARNER BROS.

| Number | Title (A Side/B Side) | Yr | NM |
|---|---|---|---|
| ❑ WS 1769 | The Moth Confesses | 1968 | 25.00 |
| ❑ WS 1804 | The Neon Philharmonic | 1969 | 15.00 |

## NEP-TUNES, THE

FAMILY

| Number | Title (A Side/B Side) | Yr | NM |
|---|---|---|---|
| ❑ FLP-152 [M] | Surfer's Holiday | 1963 | 200.00 |
| ❑ SFLP-152 [S] | Surfer's Holiday | 1963 | 300.00 |

## NERO, PAUL

SUNSET

| Number | Title (A Side/B Side) | Yr | NM |
|---|---|---|---|
| ❑ LP-303 [M] | Play the Music of Paul Nero and His Hi-Fiddles | 1956 | 60.00 |

## NERO, PETER

ARISTA

| Number | Title (A Side/B Side) | Yr | NM |
|---|---|---|---|
| ❑ AL 4034 | Disco, Dance and Love Themes | 1976 | 10.00 |

BAINBRIDGE

| Number | Title (A Side/B Side) | Yr | NM |
|---|---|---|---|
| ❑ BT-6268 | The Sounds of Love | 1987 | 10.00 |

COLUMBIA

| Number | Title (A Side/B Side) | Yr | NM |
|---|---|---|---|
| ❑ CS 1009 | I'll Never Fall in Love Again | 1970 | 10.00 |
| ❑ CS 9800 | I've Gotta Be Me | 1969 | 12.00 |
| ❑ C 30586 | Love Story | 1971 | 10.00 |
| ❑ CQ 31105 [Q] | Summer of '42 | 1971 | 15.00 |
| ❑ KC 31105 | Summer of '42 | 1971 | 10.00 |
| ❑ KC 31335 | The First Time Ever (I Saw Your Face) | 1972 | 10.00 |
| ❑ C2 31982 [(2)] | The World of Peter Nero | 1972 | 12.00 |
| ❑ KC 32689 | Say, Has Anybody Seen My Sweet Gypsy Rose | 1973 | 10.00 |
| ❑ PC 33136 | Greatest Hits | 1974 | 10.00 |

CONCORD JAZZ

| Number | Title (A Side/B Side) | Yr | NM |
|---|---|---|---|
| ❑ CJ-48 | Now | 1978 | 10.00 |

CRYSTAL CLEAR

| Number | Title (A Side/B Side) | Yr | NM |
|---|---|---|---|
| ❑ 6001 | The Wiz | 198? | 20.00 |

*—Direct-to-disc recording*

MODE

| Number | Title (A Side/B Side) | Yr | NM |
|---|---|---|---|
| ❑ LP-117 [M] | Bernie Nerow Trio | 1957 | 120.00 |

*—As "Bernie Nerow"*

PREMIER

| Number | Title (A Side/B Side) | Yr | NM |
|---|---|---|---|
| ❑ PM-2011 [M] | Just for You | 1963 | 20.00 |
| ❑ PS-2011 [R] | Just for You | 1963 | 12.00 |

RCA CAMDEN

| Number | Title (A Side/B Side) | Yr | NM |
|---|---|---|---|
| ❑ CAL-2139 [M] | Peter Nero Plays Born Free and Others | 1967 | 15.00 |
| ❑ CAS-2139 [S] | Peter Nero Plays Born Free and Others | 1967 | 12.00 |
| ❑ CAL-2228 [M] | If Ever I Would Leave You | 1968 | 15.00 |
| ❑ CAS-2228 [S] | If Ever I Would Leave You | 1968 | 12.00 |

RCA VICTOR

| Number | Title (A Side/B Side) | Yr | NM |
|---|---|---|---|
| ❑ PRM-241 [M] | Tender Is the Night | 1967 | 15.00 |
| ❑ PRS-241 [S] | Tender Is the Night | 1967 | 20.00 |
| *—Special-products release* | | | |
| ❑ ADL1-0284 [(2)] | Music Festival of Hits | 1973 | 12.00 |
| ❑ LPM-2334 [M] | Piano Forte | 1961 | 15.00 |
| ❑ LSP-2334 [S] | Piano Forte | 1961 | 20.00 |
| ❑ LPM-2383 [M] | New Piano in Town | 1961 | 15.00 |
| ❑ LSP-2383 [S] | New Piano in Town | 1961 | 20.00 |
| ❑ LPM-2484 [M] | Young and Warm and Wonderful | 1962 | 15.00 |
| ❑ LSP-2484 [S] | Young and Warm and Wonderful | 1962 | 20.00 |
| ❑ LPM-2536 [M] | For the Nero-Minded | 1962 | 15.00 |
| ❑ LSP-2536 [S] | For the Nero-Minded | 1962 | 20.00 |
| ❑ LPM-2618 [M] | The Colorful Peter Nero | 1963 | 15.00 |
| ❑ LSP-2618 [S] | The Colorful Peter Nero | 1963 | 20.00 |
| ❑ LPM-2638 [M] | Hail the Conquering Nero | 1963 | 15.00 |
| ❑ LSP-2638 [S] | Hail the Conquering Nero | 1963 | 20.00 |
| ❑ LPM-2710 [M] | Peter Nero in Person | 1963 | 15.00 |
| ❑ LSP-2710 [S] | Peter Nero in Person | 1963 | 20.00 |
| ❑ LPM-2827 [M] | Sunday in New York | 1964 | 15.00 |
| ❑ LSP-2827 [S] | Sunday in New York | 1964 | 20.00 |
| ❑ LPM-2853 [M] | Reflections | 1964 | 15.00 |
| ❑ LSP-2853 [S] | Reflections | 1964 | 20.00 |
| ❑ LPM-2935 [M] | Songs You Won't Forget | 1964 | 15.00 |
| ❑ LSP-2935 [S] | Songs You Won't Forget | 1964 | 20.00 |
| ❑ LPM-2978 [M] | The Best of Peter Nero | 1965 | 15.00 |
| ❑ LSP-2978 [S] | The Best of Peter Nero | 1965 | 20.00 |
| ❑ LPM-3313 [M] | Career Girls | 1965 | 15.00 |
| ❑ LSP-3313 [S] | Career Girls | 1965 | 20.00 |
| ❑ LPM-3496 [M] | The Screen Scene | 1966 | 12.00 |
| ❑ LSP-3496 [S] | The Screen Scene | 1966 | 15.00 |
| ❑ LPM-3550 [M] | Peter Nero — Up Close | 1966 | 12.00 |
| ❑ LSP-3550 [S] | Peter Nero — Up Close | 1966 | 15.00 |
| ❑ LPM-3610 [M] | Peter Nero On Tour | 1966 | 12.00 |
| ❑ LSP-3610 [S] | Peter Nero On Tour | 1966 | 15.00 |
| ❑ LPM-3720 [M] | Plays a Salute to Herb Alpert and the Tijuana Brass | 1967 | 15.00 |
| ❑ LSP-3720 [S] | Plays a Salute to Herb Alpert and the Tijuana Brass | 1967 | 12.00 |
| ❑ LPM-3814 [M] | Xochimilico | 1967 | 15.00 |
| ❑ LSP-3814 [S] | Xochimilico | 1967 | 12.00 |
| ❑ LPM-3871 [M] | Nero-ing In on the Hits | 1968 | 15.00 |
| ❑ LSP-3871 [S] | Nero-ing In on the Hits | 1968 | 12.00 |
| ❑ LPM-3936 [M] | Peter Nero Plays Love Is Blue and Ten Other Great Songs | 1968 | 15.00 |
| ❑ LSP-3936 [S] | Peter Nero Plays Love Is Blue and Ten Other Great Songs | 1968 | 12.00 |
| ❑ LSP-4072 | Impressions (Great Songs of Burt Bacharach and Hal David) | 1968 | 12.00 |
| ❑ LSP-4205 | Love Trip | 1969 | 12.00 |

**NEROW, BERNIE** See PETER NERO.

**NESBITT, JIM**

CHART

| Number | Title (A Side/B Side) | Yr | NM |
|---|---|---|---|
| ❑ CHM-1005 [M] | Truck Drivin' Cat with Nine Wives | 1968 | 30.00 |
| ❑ CHS-1005 [S] | Truck Drivin' Cat with Nine Wives | 1968 | 20.00 |
| ❑ CHS-1031 | Runnin' Bare | 1970 | 20.00 |

The New Colony Six, *Revelations,* Mercury SR-61165, 1968, $30.

**NESMITH, MICHAEL** Also see THE MONKEES.

PACIFIC ARTS

| Number | Title (A Side/B Side) | Yr | NM |
|---|---|---|---|
| ❑ (no #) [DJ] | The Michael Nesmith Radio Special | 1979 | 40.00 |
| ❑ 11-101A | The Prison | 197? | 50.00 |
| *—Boxed set with booklet* | | | |
| ❑ 7-101 | The Prison | 197? | 20.00 |
| *—Standard cover* | | | |
| ❑ 7-106 | Compilation | 1976 | 20.00 |
| ❑ 7-107 | From a Radio Engine to the Photon Wing | 1977 | 12.00 |
| ❑ 7-116 | And the Hits Just Keep On Comin' | 1978 | 15.00 |
| *—Reissue of RCA 4695* | | | |
| ❑ 7-117 | Pretty Much Your Standard Ranch Stash | 1978 | 15.00 |
| *—Reissue of RCA APL1-0164* | | | |
| ❑ 7-118 | Live at the Palais | 1978 | 15.00 |
| ❑ 7-130 | Infinite Rider on the Big Dogma | 1979 | 15.00 |
| ❑ ILPA-9486 | From a Radio Engine to the Photon Wing | 1977 | 15.00 |
| *—Original issue* | | | |

RCA VICTOR

| Number | Title (A Side/B Side) | Yr | NM |
|---|---|---|---|
| ❑ APL1-0164 | Pretty Much Your Standard Ranch Stash | 1973 | 25.00 |
| ❑ LSP-4371 | Magnetic South | 1970 | 30.00 |
| ❑ LSP-4415 | Loose Salute | 1970 | 30.00 |
| ❑ LSP-4497 | Nevada Fighter | 1971 | 25.00 |
| ❑ LSP-4563 | Tantamount to Treason | 1971 | 25.00 |
| ❑ LSP-4695 | And the Hits Just Keep On Comin' | 1972 | 25.00 |

RHINO

| Number | Title (A Side/B Side) | Yr | NM |
|---|---|---|---|
| ❑ R1-70168 | The Newer Stuff | 1989 | 12.00 |

**NESTICO, SAMMY**

MARK

| Number | Title (A Side/B Side) | Yr | NM |
|---|---|---|---|
| ❑ 32244 | Swingaphonic | 1969 | 20.00 |

**NETHERWORLD**

R.E.M.

| Number | Title (A Side/B Side) | Yr | NM |
|---|---|---|---|
| ❑ 4441 | Netherworld | 196? | 60.00 |

**NEVILLE, AARON**

MINIT

| Number | Title (A Side/B Side) | Yr | NM |
|---|---|---|---|
| ❑ LP 24007 [R] | Like It 'Tis | 1967 | 30.00 |
| ❑ LP 40007 [M] | Like It 'Tis | 1967 | 40.00 |

PAR-LO

| Number | Title (A Side/B Side) | Yr | NM |
|---|---|---|---|
| ❑ 1 [M] | Tell It Like It Is | 1967 | 80.00 |
| ❑ 1 [S] | Tell It Like It Is | 1967 | 200.00 |

**NEVILLE BROTHERS, THE** Also see AARON NEVILLE.

CAPITOL

| Number | Title (A Side/B Side) | Yr | NM |
|---|---|---|---|
| ❑ ST-11865 | The Neville Brothers | 1978 | 30.00 |

**NEW APOCALYPSE, THE**

M.T.A.

| Number | Title (A Side/B Side) | Yr | NM |
|---|---|---|---|
| ❑ S-5017 | Stainless Soul | 1970 | 20.00 |

**NEW BIRTH, THE**

ARIOLA AMERICA

| Number | Title (A Side/B Side) | Yr | NM |
|---|---|---|---|
| ❑ SW-50062 | Platinum City | 1979 | 10.00 |

BUDDAH

| Number | Title (A Side/B Side) | Yr | NM |
|---|---|---|---|
| ❑ BDS-5636 | Blind Baby | 1975 | 10.00 |

COLLECTABLES

| Number | Title (A Side/B Side) | Yr | NM |
|---|---|---|---|
| ❑ COL-5100 | Golden Classics | 1988 | 10.00 |

RCA VICTOR

| Number | Title (A Side/B Side) | Yr | NM |
|---|---|---|---|
| ❑ APD1-0285 [Q] | It's Been a Long Time | 1974 | 20.00 |
| ❑ APL1-0285 | It's Been a Long Time | 1974 | 10.00 |
| ❑ APL1-0494 | Comin' From All Ends | 1974 | 10.00 |
| ❑ APL1-1021 | The Best of the New Birth | 1975 | 10.00 |
| ❑ ANL1-2145 | Birth Day | 1977 | 10.00 |
| *—Reissue of 4797* | | | |
| ❑ AFL1-4411 | I'm Back | 1982 | 10.00 |
| ❑ LSP-4450 | The New Birth | 1970 | 15.00 |
| ❑ LSP-4526 | Ain't No Big Thing, But It's Growing | 1971 | 15.00 |
| ❑ LSP-4697 | Coming Together | 1972 | 15.00 |
| ❑ LSP-4797 | Birth Day | 1973 | 12.00 |

WARNER BROS.

| Number | Title (A Side/B Side) | Yr | NM |
|---|---|---|---|
| ❑ BS 2953 | Love Potion | 1976 | 10.00 |
| ❑ BSK 3071 | Behold the Mighty Army | 1977 | 10.00 |

**NEW BLACK EAGLE JAZZ BAND**

DIRTY SHAME

| Number | Title (A Side/B Side) | Yr | NM |
|---|---|---|---|
| ❑ 2002 | On the River | 197? | 20.00 |

**NEW CHRISTY MINSTRELS, THE** At one time or another, KIM CARNES, Gene Clark of THE BYRDS, BARRY McGUIRE, KENNY ROGERS and RANDY SPARKS were members, as were most of the original FIRST EDITION.

COLUMBIA

| Number | Title (A Side/B Side) | Yr | NM |
|---|---|---|---|
| ❑ CL 1872 [M] | The New Christy Minstrels | 1962 | 20.00 |

| Number | Title (A Side/B Side) | Yr | NM |
|---|---|---|---|
| ❑ CL 1941 [M] | The New Christy Minstrels In Person | 1963 | 20.00 |
| ❑ CL 2017 [M] | Tall Tales! Legends & Nonsense | 1963 | 20.00 |
| ❑ CL 2055 [M] | Ramblin' Feturing Green, Green | 1963 | 20.00 |
| ❑ CL 2096 [M] | Merry Christmas | 1963 | 20.00 |
| ❑ CL 2159 [M] | Today | 1964 | 20.00 |
| ❑ CL 2187 [M] | Land of Giants | 1964 | 20.00 |
| ❑ CL 2280 [M] | The Quiet Sides of the New Christy Minstrels | 1965 | 20.00 |
| ❑ CL 2303 [M] | Cowboys and Indians | 1965 | 20.00 |
| ❑ CL 2369 [M] | Chim Chim Cher-ee | 1965 | 20.00 |
| ❑ CL 2384 [M] | The Wandering Minstrels | 1965 | 20.00 |
| ❑ CL 2479 [M] | Greatest Hits | 1966 | 20.00 |
| ❑ CL 2531 [M] | In Italy…In Italian | 1966 | 20.00 |
| ❑ CL 2542 [M] | New Kick | 1967 | 20.00 |
| ❑ CL 2556 [M] | Christmas with the Christies | 1966 | 20.00 |
| ❑ CS 8672 [S] | The New Christy Minstrels | 1962 | 25.00 |
| ❑ CS 8741 [S] | The New Christy Minstrels In Person | 1963 | 25.00 |
| ❑ CS 8817 [S] | Tall Tales! Legends & Nonsense | 1963 | 25.00 |
| ❑ CS 8855 [S] | Ramblin' Feturing Green, Green | 1963 | 25.00 |
| ❑ CS 8896 [S] | Merry Christmas | 1963 | 25.00 |
| ❑ CS 8959 [S] | Today | 1964 | 25.00 |
| ❑ CS 8987 [S] | Land of Giants | 1964 | 25.00 |
| ❑ CS 9080 [S] | The Quiet Sides of the New Christy Minstrels | 1965 | 25.00 |
| ❑ CS 9103 [S] | Cowboys and Indians | 1965 | 25.00 |
| ❑ CS 9169 [S] | Chim Chim Cher-ee | 1965 | 25.00 |
| ❑ CS 9184 [S] | The Wandering Minstrels | 1965 | 25.00 |
| ❑ CS 9279 [S] | Greatest Hits | 1966 | 25.00 |
| ❑ CS 9331 [S] | In Italy...In Italian | 1966 | 25.00 |
| ❑ CS 9342 [S] | New Kick | 1967 | 25.00 |
| ❑ CS 9356 [S] | Christmas with the Christies | 1966 | 25.00 |
| ❑ CS 9616 [M] | On Tour Through Motortown | 1968 | 50.00 |

*—White label promo only; "Special Mono Radio Station Copy" sticker on front*

| Number | Title (A Side/B Side) | Yr | NM |
|---|---|---|---|
| ❑ CS 9616 [S] | On Tour Through Motortown | 1968 | 20.00 |
| ❑ CS 9709 | Chitty Chitty Bang Bang | 1969 | 20.00 |

GREGAR

| Number | Title (A Side/B Side) | Yr | NM |
|---|---|---|---|
| ❑ 102 | You Need Someone to Love | 1970 | 15.00 |

### NEW COLONY SIX, THE

MERCURY

| Number | Title (A Side/B Side) | Yr | NM |
|---|---|---|---|
| ❑ SR-61165 | Revelations | 1968 | 30.00 |
| ❑ SR-61228 | Attacking a Straw Man | 1969 | 30.00 |

SENTAR

| Number | Title (A Side/B Side) | Yr | NM |
|---|---|---|---|
| ❑ LP-101 [M] | Breakthrough | 1966 | 500.00 |
| ❑ SST-3001 [S] | Colonization | 1967 | 60.00 |
| ❑ ST-3001 [M] | Colonization | 1967 | 50.00 |

SUNDAZED

| Number | Title (A Side/B Side) | Yr | NM |
|---|---|---|---|
| ❑ LP 5007 | At the River's Edge | 1995 | 10.00 |

### NEW DAWN, THE

HOOT

| Number | Title (A Side/B Side) | Yr | NM |
|---|---|---|---|
| ❑ GR 704569 | There's a New Dawn | 1970 | 1000. |

### NEW DIMENSIONS, THE

SUNDAZED

| Number | Title (A Side/B Side) | Yr | NM |
|---|---|---|---|
| ❑ LP-5025 | The Best of the New Dimensions | 199? | 10.00 |

SUTTON

| Number | Title (A Side/B Side) | Yr | NM |
|---|---|---|---|
| ❑ SSU-331 [S] | Deuces and Eights | 1963 | 100.00 |
| ❑ SU-331 [M] | Deuces and Eights | 1963 | 80.00 |
| ❑ SSU-332 [S] | Surf 'N' Bongos | 1963 | 50.00 |
| ❑ SU-332 [M] | Surf 'N' Bongos | 1963 | 40.00 |
| ❑ SSU-336 [S] | Soul Surf | 1964 | 50.00 |
| ❑ SU-336 [M] | Soul Surf | 1964 | 40.00 |

**NEW GLENN MILLER ORCHESTRA** See GLENN MILLER ORCHESTRA (in the M's).

### NEW LEGION ROCK SPECTACULAR, THE

SPECTACULAR

| Number | Title (A Side/B Side) | Yr | NM |
|---|---|---|---|
| ❑ 7777 | Wild Ones! | 1975 | 60.00 |

### NEW MIX, THE

UNITED ARTISTS

| Number | Title (A Side/B Side) | Yr | NM |
|---|---|---|---|
| ❑ UAS-6678 | The New Mix | 1968 | 20.00 |

### NEW ORDER

FACTORY

| Number | Title (A Side/B Side) | Yr | NM |
|---|---|---|---|
| ❑ FACTUS 8 [EP] | 1981-1982 | 1983 | 20.00 |
| ❑ FACTUS 12 | Power, Corruption and Lies | 1983 | 20.00 |
| ❑ FACTUS 50 | Movement | 198? | 12.00 |

*—With bar code on cover*

| Number | Title (A Side/B Side) | Yr | NM |
|---|---|---|---|
| ❑ FACTUS 50 | Movement | 1981 | 20.00 |

*—Originals have no bar code*

| Number | Title (A Side/B Side) | Yr | NM |
|---|---|---|---|
| ❑ FACTUS 50 | Movement | 1981 | 50.00 |

*—Purple vinyl (looks more black, but will appear purple when held to a light)*

QWEST

| Number | Title (A Side/B Side) | Yr | NM |
|---|---|---|---|
| ❑ PRO-A-5970 [DJ] | In Order | 1993 | 40.00 |

*—Promo only six-song, 44-minute compilation; orange vinyl*

| Number | Title (A Side/B Side) | Yr | NM |
|---|---|---|---|
| ❑ 25289 | Low Life | 1985 | 10.00 |
| ❑ 25308 | Power, Corruption and Lies | 1985 | 10.00 |

*—Reissue of Factory FACTUS 12*

| Number | Title (A Side/B Side) | Yr | NM |
|---|---|---|---|
| ❑ 25511 | Brotherhood | 1986 | 10.00 |
| ❑ 25621 [(2)] | Substance | 1987 | 15.00 |
| ❑ 25845 | Technique | 1989 | 12.00 |
| ❑ R 100938 | Technique | 1989 | 12.00 |

*—BMG Direct Marketing edition*

### NEW ORLEANS RHYTHM KINGS

BRUNSWICK

| Number | Title (A Side/B Side) | Yr | NM |
|---|---|---|---|
| ❑ BL 58011 [10] | Dixieland Jazz | 1950 | 120.00 |

### NEW ORLEANS SHUFFLERS, THE

KINGSWAY

| Number | Title (A Side/B Side) | Yr | NM |
|---|---|---|---|
| ❑ KL-700 [M] | The New Orleans Shufflers | 1955 | 40.00 |

### NEW RENAISSANCE SOCIETY, THE

HANNA-BARBERA

| Number | Title (A Side/B Side) | Yr | NM |
|---|---|---|---|
| ❑ HLP-9504 [M] | Baroque n' Stones | 1966 | 20.00 |
| ❑ HST-9504 [S] | Baroque n' Stones | 1966 | 25.00 |

### NEW RIDERS OF THE PURPLE SAGE

A&M

| Number | Title (A Side/B Side) | Yr | NM |
|---|---|---|---|
| ❑ SP-4818 | Feelin' All Right | 1981 | 10.00 |

COLUMBIA

| Number | Title (A Side/B Side) | Yr | NM |
|---|---|---|---|
| ❑ KC 30888 | New Riders of the Purple Sage | 1971 | 15.00 |
| ❑ PC 30888 | New Riders of the Purple Sage | 1979 | 8.00 |

*—Budget-line reissue*

| Number | Title (A Side/B Side) | Yr | NM |
|---|---|---|---|
| ❑ KC 31284 | Powerglide | 1972 | 15.00 |
| ❑ PC 31284 | Powerglide | 1979 | 8.00 |

*—Budget-line reissue*

| Number | Title (A Side/B Side) | Yr | NM |
|---|---|---|---|
| ❑ KC 31930 | Gypsy Cowboy | 1972 | 15.00 |
| ❑ PC 31930 | Gypsy Cowboy | 1979 | 8.00 |

*—Budget-line reissue*

| Number | Title (A Side/B Side) | Yr | NM |
|---|---|---|---|
| ❑ CQ 32450 [Q] | The Adventures of Panama Red | 1974 | 20.00 |
| ❑ KC 32450 | The Adventures of Panama Red | 1973 | 15.00 |
| ❑ PC 32450 | The Adventures of Panama Red | 1979 | 8.00 |

*—Budget-line reissue*

| Number | Title (A Side/B Side) | Yr | NM |
|---|---|---|---|
| ❑ PC 32870 | Home, Home on the Road | 1974 | 15.00 |

*—Originals have no bar code*

| Number | Title (A Side/B Side) | Yr | NM |
|---|---|---|---|
| ❑ PC 33145 | Brujo | 1974 | 15.00 |

*—Originals have no bar code*

| Number | Title (A Side/B Side) | Yr | NM |
|---|---|---|---|
| ❑ PC 33688 | Oh, What a Mighty Time | 1975 | 15.00 |

*—Originals have no bar code*

| Number | Title (A Side/B Side) | Yr | NM |
|---|---|---|---|
| ❑ PC 34367 | The Best of New Riders of the Purple Sage | 1976 | 12.00 |

*—Originals have no bar code*

| Number | Title (A Side/B Side) | Yr | NM |
|---|---|---|---|
| ❑ PC 34367 | The Best of New Riders of the Purple Sage | 1979 | 8.00 |

*—Budget-line reissue with bar code*

MCA

| Number | Title (A Side/B Side) | Yr | NM |
|---|---|---|---|
| ❑ 632 | Marin County Line | 1980 | 8.00 |

*—Reissue of 2307*

| Number | Title (A Side/B Side) | Yr | NM |
|---|---|---|---|
| ❑ 2196 | New Riders | 1976 | 12.00 |
| ❑ 2248 | Who Are These Guys | 1977 | 12.00 |
| ❑ 2307 | Marin County Line | 1977 | 12.00 |

RELIX

| Number | Title (A Side/B Side) | Yr | NM |
|---|---|---|---|
| ❑ RRLP-2024 | Before Time Began | 1986 | 8.00 |
| ❑ RRLP-2025 | Vintage NRPS | 1987 | 8.00 |

### NEW SEEKERS, THE

ELEKTRA

| Number | Title (A Side/B Side) | Yr | NM |
|---|---|---|---|
| ❑ EQ-5051 [Q] | The Best of the New Seekers | 1973 | 20.00 |
| ❑ EKS-74088 | Beautiful People | 1971 | 12.00 |
| ❑ EKS-74108 | New Colours | 1971 | 12.00 |
| ❑ EKS-74115 | We'd Like to Teach the World to Sing | 1971 | 12.00 |
| ❑ EKS-75034 | Circles | 1972 | 12.00 |
| ❑ EKS-75051 | The Best of the New Seekers | 1973 | 12.00 |

MGM VERVE

| Number | Title (A Side/B Side) | Yr | NM |
|---|---|---|---|
| ❑ V 5090 | Come Softly to Me | 1972 | 10.00 |
| ❑ V 5095 | The History of the New Seekers | 1973 | 10.00 |
| ❑ V 5098 | Pinball Wizards | 1973 | 10.00 |

### NEW SOCIETY, THE

RCA VICTOR

| Number | Title (A Side/B Side) | Yr | NM |
|---|---|---|---|
| ❑ LPM-3676 [M] | The Barock Sound of the New Society | 1966 | 25.00 |
| ❑ LSP-3676 [S] | The Barock Sound of the New Society | 1966 | 30.00 |

### NEW STRANGERS, THE

FOLKLORE

| Number | Title (A Side/B Side) | Yr | NM |
|---|---|---|---|
| ❑ FRLP-14027 [M] | Meet the New Strangers | 1964 | 20.00 |
| ❑ FRST-14027 [S] | Meet the New Strangers | 1964 | 25.00 |

### NEW SYMPHONY ORCHESTRA OF LONDON (RAYMOND AGOULT, CONDUCTOR)

RCA VICTOR RED SEAL

| Number | Title (A Side/B Side) | Yr | NM |
|---|---|---|---|
| ❑ LSC-2134 [S] | Overture! Overture! | 1959 | 50.00 |

*—Original with "shaded dog" label; issued with two different covers*

| Number | Title (A Side/B Side) | Yr | NM |
|---|---|---|---|
| ❑ LSC-2134 [S] | Overture! Overture! | 199? | 25.00 |

*—Classic Records reissue*

### NEW SYMPHONY ORCHESTRA OF LONDON (RONALD BINGE, CONDUCTOR)

RCA VICTOR RED SEAL

| Number | Title (A Side/B Side) | Yr | NM |
|---|---|---|---|
| ❑ LSC-2399 [S] | Mendelssohniana | 1960 | 300.00 |

*—Originals with "shaded dog" label*

### NEW SYMPHONY ORCHESTRA OF LONDON (ALEXANDER GIBSON, CONDUCTOR)

RCA VICTOR RED SEAL

| Number | Title (A Side/B Side) | Yr | NM |
|---|---|---|---|
| ❑ LSC-2225 [S] | Witches' Brew | 1959 | 400.00 |

*—Original with "shaded dog" label*

| Number | Title (A Side/B Side) | Yr | NM |
|---|---|---|---|
| ❑ LSC-2225 [S] | Witches' Brew | 199? | 25.00 |

*—Classic Records reissue*

### NEW TWEEDY BROTHERS, THE

RIDON

| Number | Title (A Side/B Side) | Yr | NM |
|---|---|---|---|
| ❑ 234 | The New Tweedy Brothers | 1968 | 400.00 |

*—With plain white cover*

| Number | Title (A Side/B Side) | Yr | NM |
|---|---|---|---|
| ❑ 234 | The New Tweedy Brothers | 1968 | 2000. |

*—With oversized hexagonal cover designed to look like a sugar cube*

### NEW WAVE, THE

CANTERBURY

| Number | Title (A Side/B Side) | Yr | NM |
|---|---|---|---|
| ❑ CLPS-1501 | The New Wave | 1967 | 25.00 |

### NEW YORK ART QUARTET, THE

ESP-DISK'

| Number | Title (A Side/B Side) | Yr | NM |
|---|---|---|---|
| ❑ 1004 [M] | The New York Art Quartet | 1965 | 20.00 |
| ❑ S-1004 [S] | The New York Art Quartet | 1965 | 25.00 |

### NEW YORK DOLLS

MERCURY

| Number | Title (A Side/B Side) | Yr | NM |
|---|---|---|---|
| ❑ SRM-1-675 | New York Dolls | 1973 | 40.00 |
| ❑ SRM-1-1001 | In Too Much Too Soon | 1974 | 40.00 |
| ❑ 826094-1 | Night of the Living Dolls | 1985 | 12.00 |

### NEW YORK JAZZ QUARTET, THE (1)

CORAL

| Number | Title (A Side/B Side) | Yr | NM |
|---|---|---|---|
| ❑ CRL 57136 [M] | Music For Suburban Living | 1958 | 200.00 |
| ❑ CRL 757136 [S] | Music For Suburban Living | 1958 | 150.00 |

ELEKTRA

| Number | Title (A Side/B Side) | Yr | NM |
|---|---|---|---|
| ❑ EKL-115 [M] | The New York Jazz Quartet | 1957 | 50.00 |
| ❑ EKL-118 [M] | Gone Native | 1957 | 50.00 |

SAVOY

| Number | Title (A Side/B Side) | Yr | NM |
|---|---|---|---|
| ❑ MG-12172 [M] | Adam's Theme | 1960 | 30.00 |
| ❑ MG-12175 [M] | Gone Native | 1961 | 30.00 |

### NEW YORK JAZZ SEXTET, THE

SCEPTER

| Number | Title (A Side/B Side) | Yr | NM |
|---|---|---|---|
| ❑ S-526 [M] | New York Jazz Sextet | 1964 | 20.00 |
| ❑ SS-526 [S] | New York Jazz Sextet | 1964 | 25.00 |

### NEW YORK ORIGINATORS, THE

PARAMOUNT

| Number | Title (A Side/B Side) | Yr | NM |
|---|---|---|---|
| ❑ RS-201 [10] | The New York Style | 1952 | 60.00 |

### NEW YORK PHILHARMONIC ORCHESTRA (BRUNO WALTER, CONDUCTOR)

COLUMBIA MASTERWORKS

| Number | Title (A Side/B Side) | Yr | NM |
|---|---|---|---|
| ❑ ML 4001 [M] | Mendelssohn: Violin Concerto | 1948 | 40.00 |

*—Violinist: Nathan Milstein; the very first modern microgroove LP!*

| Number | Title (A Side/B Side) | Yr | NM |
|---|---|---|---|
| ❑ ML 4001 [M] | Mendelssohn: Violin Concerto | 1999 | 25.00 |

*—Violinist: Nathan Milstein; Classic Records commemorative reissue*

### NEW YORK PRO MUSICA ANTIQUA

COUNTERPOINT/ESOTERIC

| Number | Title (A Side/B Side) | Yr | NM |
|---|---|---|---|
| ❑ CPT 521 [M] | English Medieval Christmas Carols | 196? | 20.00 |

### NEW YORK SAXOPHONE QUARTET, THE

MARK

| Number | Title (A Side/B Side) | Yr | NM |
|---|---|---|---|
| ❑ 32322 | The New York Saxophone Quartet | 1969 | 20.00 |

20TH CENTURY FOX

| Number | Title (A Side/B Side) | Yr | NM |
|---|---|---|---|
| ❑ TFM-3150 [M] | The New York Saxophone Quartet | 1964 | 20.00 |
| ❑ TFS-3150 [S] | The New York Saxophone Quartet | 1964 | 25.00 |

### NEWBEATS, THE

HICKORY

| Number | Title (A Side/B Side) | Yr | NM |
|---|---|---|---|
| ❑ LPM 120 [M] | Bread and Butter | 1964 | 50.00 |
| ❑ LPS 120 [S] | Bread and Butter | 1964 | 150.00 |
| ❑ LPM 122 [M] | Big Beat Sounds by the Newbeats | 1965 | 50.00 |
| ❑ LPS 122 [S] | Big Beat Sounds by the Newbeats | 1965 | 100.00 |
| ❑ LPM 128 [M] | Run Baby Run | 1965 | 50.00 |
| ❑ LPS 128 [S] | Run Baby Run | 1965 | 100.00 |
| ❑ DT 90701 [R] | Bread and Butter | 1965 | 150.00 |

*—Capitol Record Club edition*

| Number | Title (A Side/B Side) | Yr | NM |
|---|---|---|---|
| ❑ ST 90701 [S] | Bread and Butter | 1965 | 200.00 |

*—Capitol Record Club edition*



Except when noted otherwise, VG = 25% of NM, and VG+ = 50% of NM. (Example: VG = $2.00, VG+ = $4.00 and NM = $8.00.)

| Number | Title (A Side/B Side) | Yr | NM |
|---|---|---|---|
| ❑ T 90701 [M] | Bread and Butter | 1965 | 150.00 |
| *—Capitol Record Club edition* | | | |
| **NEWBORN, PHINEAS** | | | |
| ATLANTIC | | | |
| ❑ 1235 [M] | Here Is Phineas | 1956 | 50.00 |
| *—Black label* | | | |
| ❑ 1235 [M] | Here Is Phineas | 1961 | 20.00 |
| *—Multicolor label, white "fan" logo at right* | | | |
| ❑ SD 1235 [S] | Here Is Phineas | 1958 | 50.00 |
| *—Green label* | | | |
| CONTEMPORARY | | | |
| ❑ M-3600 [M] | The World of Piano! | 1961 | 20.00 |
| ❑ M-3611 [M] | Great Jazz Piano | 1962 | 20.00 |
| ❑ M-3615 [M] | The Newborn Touch | 1964 | 20.00 |
| ❑ S-7600 [S] | The World of Piano! | 1961 | 25.00 |
| ❑ S-7611 [S] | Great Jazz Piano | 1962 | 25.00 |
| ❑ S-7615 [S] | The Newborn Touch | 1964 | 25.00 |
| ❑ S-7622 [S] | Please Send Me Someone to Love | 1969 | 20.00 |
| ❑ C-7648 | Back Home | 198? | 12.00 |
| RCA VICTOR | | | |
| ❑ LPM-1421 [M] | Phineas' Rainbow | 1957 | 50.00 |
| ❑ LPM-1474 [M] | While the Lady Sleeps | 1957 | 50.00 |
| ❑ LPM-1589 [M] | Phineas Newborn Plays Jamaica | 1957 | 50.00 |
| ❑ LPM-1873 [M] | Fabulous Phineas | 1958 | 50.00 |
| ❑ LSP-1873 [S] | Fabulous Phineas | 1958 | 40.00 |
| ROULETTE | | | |
| ❑ R-52031 [M] | Piano Portraits | 1959 | 25.00 |
| ❑ SR-52031 [S] | Piano Portraits | 1959 | 30.00 |
| ❑ R-52043 [M] | I Love a Piano | 1960 | 25.00 |
| ❑ SR-52043 [S] | I Love a Piano | 1960 | 30.00 |
| **NEWBURY, MICKEY** | | | |
| ABC HICKORY | | | |
| ❑ HA-44002 | Rusty Tracks | 1977 | 10.00 |
| ❑ HA-44011 | Eye on the Sparrow | 1978 | 10.00 |
| ❑ HB-44017 | The Sailor | 1979 | 10.00 |
| ELEKTRA | | | |
| ❑ EK-PROMO 20 [DJ] | Recorded Live at Montezuma Hall, San Diego State University, March 6, 1973 | 1973 | 40.00 |
| ❑ 7E-1007 | I Came to Hear the Music | 1974 | 10.00 |
| ❑ 7E-1030 | Lovers | 1975 | 10.00 |
| ❑ EQ-4107 [Q] | 'Frisco Mabel Joy | 1974 | 20.00 |
| ❑ EKS-74107 | 'Frisco Mabel Joy | 1971 | 10.00 |
| ❑ EKS-75055 | Heaven Help the Child | 1973 | 10.00 |
| MCA | | | |
| ❑ 802 | Rusty Tracks | 198? | 8.00 |
| *—Reissue* | | | |
| ❑ 803 | Eye on the Sparrow | 198? | 8.00 |
| *—Reissue* | | | |
| ❑ 804 | The Sailor | 198? | 8.00 |
| *—Reissue* | | | |
| ❑ 945 | Sweet Memories | 1985 | 10.00 |
| MERCURY | | | |
| ❑ SR 61236 | Looks Like Rain | 1969 | 15.00 |
| RCA VICTOR | | | |
| ❑ LSP-4043 | Harlequin Melodies | 1968 | 15.00 |
| **NEWHART, BOB** | | | |
| HARMONY | | | |
| ❑ HS 11344 | The Very Funny Bob Newhart | 196? | 12.00 |
| MURRAY HILL | | | |
| ❑ OP 2529 [(2)] | The Best of the Button-Down Mind | 197? | 20.00 |
| WARNER BROS. | | | |
| ❑ W 1379 [M] | The Button-Down Mind of Bob Newhart | 1960 | 30.00 |
| ❑ WS 1379 [S] | The Button-Down Mind of Bob Newhart | 1960 | 25.00 |
| ❑ W 1393 [M] | The Button-Down Mind Strikes Back! | 1960 | 30.00 |
| ❑ WS 1393 [S] | The Button-Down Mind Strikes Back! | 1960 | 25.00 |
| ❑ 2N 1399 [(2)M] | The Bob Newhart Deluxe Edition | 1961 | 50.00 |
| ❑ 2NS 1399 [(2)S] | The Bob Newhart Deluxe Edition | 1961 | 40.00 |
| ❑ W 1417 [M] | Behind the Button-Down Mind of Bob Newhart | 1961 | 25.00 |
| ❑ WS 1417 [S] | Behind the Button-Down Mind of Bob Newhart | 1961 | 20.00 |
| ❑ W 1467 [M] | The Button-Down Mind on TV | 1962 | 25.00 |
| ❑ WS 1467 [S] | The Button-Down Mind on TV | 1962 | 20.00 |
| ❑ W 1517 [M] | Bob Newhart Faces Bob Newhart (Faces Bob Newhart) | 1964 | 25.00 |
| ❑ W 1588 [M] | The Windmills Are Weakening | 1965 | 30.00 |
| ❑ W 1672 [M] | The Best of Bob Newhart | 1966 | 30.00 |
| ❑ WS 1672 [S] | The Best of Bob Newhart | 1966 | 25.00 |
| *—Gold label* | | | |
| ❑ WS 1672 [S] | The Best of Bob Newhart | 1968 | 20.00 |
| *—Green "W7" label* | | | |
| ❑ WS 1672 [S] | The Best of Bob Newhart | 1970 | 15.00 |
| *—Green "WB" label* | | | |
| ❑ WS 1672 [S] | The Best of Bob Newhart | 1973 | 12.00 |
| *—"Burbank" palm-trees label* | | | |
| ❑ WS 1672 [S] | The Best of Bob Newhart | 1979 | 8.00 |
| *—White or tan label* | | | |
| ❑ W 1717 [M] | This Is It | 1967 | 30.00 |
| **NEWLEY, ANTHONY** | | | |
| LONDON | | | |
| ❑ PS 244 [S] | Tony | 1962 | 25.00 |
| ❑ PS 461 [S] | Genius | 1966 | 15.00 |
| ❑ LL 3156 [M] | Love Is a Now and Then Thing | 1960 | 20.00 |
| ❑ LL 3252 [M] | Tony | 1962 | 15.00 |
| ❑ LL 3262 [M] | This Is Tony Newley | 1962 | 15.00 |
| ❑ LL 3461 [M] | Genius | 1966 | 12.00 |
| RCA VICTOR | | | |
| ❑ LPM-2925 [M] | In My Solitude | 1964 | 15.00 |
| ❑ LSP-2925 [S] | In My Solitude | 1964 | 20.00 |
| ❑ LPM-3347 [M] | Who Can I Turn To | 1965 | 12.00 |
| ❑ LSP-3347 [S] | Who Can I Turn To | 1965 | 15.00 |
| ❑ LPM-3614 [M] | Newly Recorded | 1966 | 12.00 |
| ❑ LSP-3614 [S] | Newly Recorded | 1966 | 15.00 |
| ❑ LPM-3839 [M] | Doctor Dolittle | 1967 | 12.00 |
| ❑ LSP-3839 [S] | Doctor Dolittle | 1967 | 15.00 |
| ❑ LSP-4163 | The Best of Anthony Newley | 1969 | 12.00 |
| **NEWMAN, BOB** | | | |
| AUDIO LAB | | | |
| ❑ AL-1536 [M] | The Kentucky Colonel | 1959 | 200.00 |
| **NEWMAN, DAVID "FATHEAD"** | | | |
| ATLANTIC | | | |
| ❑ 1304 [M] | Ray Charles Presents David "Fathead" Newman | 1959 | 40.00 |
| *—Black label* | | | |
| ❑ SD 1304 [S] | Ray Charles Presents David "Fathead" Newman | 1959 | 50.00 |
| *—Green label* | | | |
| ❑ SD 1304 [S] | Ray Charles Presents David "Fathead" Newman | 1961 | 20.00 |
| *—Multicolor label with white "fan" logo* | | | |
| ❑ 1366 [M] | Straight Ahead | 1961 | 30.00 |
| *—Multicolor label with white "fan" logo* | | | |
| ❑ SD 1366 [S] | Straight Ahead | 1961 | 40.00 |
| *—Multicolor label with white "fan" logo* | | | |
| ❑ 1399 [M] | Fathead Comes On | 1962 | 30.00 |
| ❑ SD 1399 [S] | Fathead Comes On | 1962 | 40.00 |
| ❑ SD 1489 | House of David | 1968 | 20.00 |
| ❑ SD 1505 | Bigger and Better | 1968 | 20.00 |
| COTILLION | | | |
| ❑ SD 18002 | Captain Buckles | 1970 | 20.00 |
| **NEWMAN, JIMMY** | | | |
| DECCA | | | |
| ❑ DL 4221 [M] | Jimmy Newman | 1962 | 25.00 |
| ❑ DL 4398 [M] | Folk Songs of the Bayou Country | 1963 | 40.00 |
| ❑ DL 4748 [M] | Artificial Rose | 1966 | 20.00 |
| ❑ DL 4781 [M] | Jimmy Newman Sings Country Songs | 1966 | 20.00 |
| ❑ DL 4885 [M] | The World of Country Music | 1967 | 25.00 |
| ❑ DL 4960 [M] | The Jimmy Newman Way | 1967 | 25.00 |
| ❑ DL 74221 [S] | Jimmy Newman | 1962 | 30.00 |
| ❑ DL 74398 [S] | Folk Songs of the Bayou Country | 1963 | 50.00 |
| ❑ DL 74748 [S] | Artificial Rose | 1966 | 25.00 |
| ❑ DL 74781 [S] | Jimmy Newman Sings Country Songs | 1966 | 25.00 |
| ❑ DL 74885 [S] | The World of Country Music | 1967 | 20.00 |
| ❑ DL 74960 [S] | The Jimmy Newman Way | 1967 | 20.00 |
| ❑ DL 75065 | Born to Love You | 1968 | 20.00 |
| DOT | | | |
| ❑ DLP-3690 [M] | A Fallen Star | 1965 | 30.00 |
| ❑ DLP-3736 [M] | Country Crossroads | 1966 | 30.00 |
| ❑ DLP-25736 [R] | Country Crossroads | 1966 | 20.00 |
| MGM | | | |
| ❑ E-3777 [M] | This Is Jimmy Newman | 1959 | 25.00 |
| ❑ SE-3777 [S] | This Is Jimmy Newman | 1959 | 30.00 |
| ❑ E-4045 [M] | Songs by Jimmy Newman | 1962 | 25.00 |
| ❑ SE-4045 [S] | Songs by Jimmy Newman | 1962 | 30.00 |
| **NEWMAN, JOE** | | | |
| AMERICAN RECORDING SOCIETY | | | |
| ❑ G-447 [M] | Basically Swing | 1958 | 40.00 |
| ❑ G-451 [M] | New Sounds In Swing | 1958 | 40.00 |
| CORAL | | | |
| ❑ CRL 57121 [M] | The Happy Cats | 1957 | 50.00 |
| ❑ CRL 57208 [M] | Soft Swingin' Jazz | 1958 | 50.00 |
| JAZZTONE | | | |
| ❑ J-1217 [M] | New Sounds In Swing | 1956 | 40.00 |
| ❑ J-1220 [M] | The Count's Men | 1956 | 40.00 |
| ❑ J-1265 [M] | Swing Lightly | 1957 | 40.00 |
| MERCURY | | | |
| ❑ MG-20696 [M] | Joe Newman At Count Basie's | 1962 | 25.00 |
| ❑ SR-60696 [S] | Joe Newman At Count Basie's | 1962 | 30.00 |
| RAMA | | | |
| ❑ LP-1003 [M] | Locking Horns | 1957 | 120.00 |
| RCA VICTOR | | | |
| ❑ LPM-1118 [M] | All I Want To Do Is Swing | 1955 | 100.00 |
| ❑ LPM-1198 [M] | I'm Still Swinging | 1956 | 100.00 |
| ❑ LPM-1324 [M] | Salute To Satch | 1956 | 80.00 |
| ROULETTE | | | |
| ❑ R-52009 [M] | Locking Horns | 1958 | 40.00 |
| ❑ SR-52009 [S] | Locking Horns | 1958 | 30.00 |
| ❑ R-52014 [M] | Joe Newman With Woodwinds | 1958 | 40.00 |
| ❑ SR-52014 [S] | Joe Newman With Woodwinds | 1958 | 30.00 |
| STORYVILLE | | | |
| ❑ STLP-318 [10] | Joe Newman and the Boys In the Band | 1955 | 150.00 |
| ❑ STLP-905 [M] | I Feel Like a Newman | 1956 | 100.00 |
| SWINGVILLE | | | |
| ❑ SVLP-2011 [M] | Jive At Five | 1961 | 50.00 |
| *—Purple label* | | | |
| ❑ SVLP-2011 [M] | Jive At Five | 1965 | 25.00 |
| *—Blue label, trident logo at right* | | | |
| ❑ SVLP-2019 [M] | Good 'N Groovy | 1961 | 50.00 |
| *—Purple label* | | | |
| ❑ SVLP-2019 [M] | Good 'N Groovy | 1965 | 25.00 |
| *—Blue label, trident logo at right* | | | |
| ❑ SVLP-2027 [M] | Joe's Hap'nin's | 1961 | 60.00 |
| *—Purple label* | | | |
| ❑ SVLP-2027 [M] | Joe's Hap'nin's | 1965 | 30.00 |
| *—Blue label, trident logo at right* | | | |
| ❑ SVST-2027 [S] | Joe's Hap'nin's | 1961 | 60.00 |
| *—Red label* | | | |
| ❑ SVST-2027 [S] | Joe's Hap'nin's | 1965 | 30.00 |
| *—Blue label, trident logo at right* | | | |
| TRIP | | | |
| ❑ 5548 | Live at Basie's | 197? | 10.00 |
| VANGUARD | | | |
| ❑ VRS-8007 [10] | Joe Newman and His Band | 1954 | 200.00 |
| VIK | | | |
| ❑ LX-1060 [M] | The Midgets | 1957 | 80.00 |
| WORLD PACIFIC | | | |
| ❑ ST-1288 [S] | Countin' | 1960 | 40.00 |
| ❑ WP-1288 [M] | Countin' | 1960 | 40.00 |
| **NEWMAN, PHYLLIS** | | | |
| SIRE | | | |
| ❑ SES-97002 | Those Were the Days | 1969 | 20.00 |
| **NEWMAN, RANDY** | | | |
| REPRISE | | | |
| ❑ MS 2064 | Sail Away | 1972 | 10.00 |
| *—With song titles listed on back* | | | |
| ❑ MS 2064 | Sail Away | 1972 | 15.00 |
| *—With no song titles listed on back* | | | |
| ❑ MS 2193 | Good Old Boys | 1974 | 10.00 |
| ❑ MS4 2193 [Q] | Good Old Boys | 1974 | 15.00 |
| ❑ RS 6286 | Randy Newman | 1968 | 15.00 |
| *—Cover with close-up of Randy's face; "W7" and "r:" logos on two-tone orange label* | | | |
| ❑ RS 6286 | Randy Newman | 1968 | 20.00 |
| *—Cover with Randy standing in the clouds* | | | |
| ❑ RS 6286 | Randy Newman | 1970 | 12.00 |
| *—With only "r:" logo on all-orange (tan) label* | | | |
| ❑ RS 6373 | 12 Songs | 1970 | 10.00 |
| *—With only "r:" logo on all-orange (tan) label* | | | |
| ❑ RS 6373 | 12 Songs | 1970 | 15.00 |
| *—With "W7" and "r:" logos on two-tone orange label* | | | |
| ❑ RS 6459 | Randy Newman/Live | 1971 | 10.00 |
| ❑ 25773 | Land of Dreams | 1988 | 10.00 |
| WARNER BROS. | | | |
| ❑ BSK 3079 | Little Criminals | 1977 | 10.00 |
| ❑ HS 3346 | Born Again | 1979 | 10.00 |
| ❑ 23755 | Trouble in Paradise | 1983 | 10.00 |
| **NEWTON, JUICE** | | | |
| CAPITOL | | | |
| ❑ ST-11682 | Come to Me | 1977 | 15.00 |
| ❑ ST-11811 | Well-Kept Secret | 1978 | 15.00 |
| ❑ ST-12000 | Take Heart | 1980 | 15.00 |
| ❑ ST-12136 | Juice | 1981 | 10.00 |
| ❑ ST-12210 | Quiet Lies | 1982 | 10.00 |
| ❑ ST-12294 | Dirty Looks | 1983 | 10.00 |
| ❑ SJ-12353 | Greatest Hits | 1984 | 10.00 |
| ❑ SN-16242 | Come to Me | 1982 | 8.00 |
| *—Budget-line reissue* | | | |
| ❑ SN-16243 | Well-Kept Secret | 1982 | 8.00 |
| *—Budget-line reissue* | | | |
| ❑ SN-16244 | Take Heart | 1982 | 8.00 |
| *—Budget-line reissue* | | | |
| ❑ SN-16313 | Juice | 1984 | 8.00 |
| *—Budget-line reissue* | | | |
| ❑ SN-16314 | Quiet Lies | 1984 | 8.00 |
| *—Budget-line reissue* | | | |
| ❑ SN-16356 | Dirty Looks | 1985 | 8.00 |
| *—Budget-line reissue* | | | |
| ❑ SN-16471 | Greatest Hits | 1987 | 8.00 |
| *—Budget-line reissue* | | | |

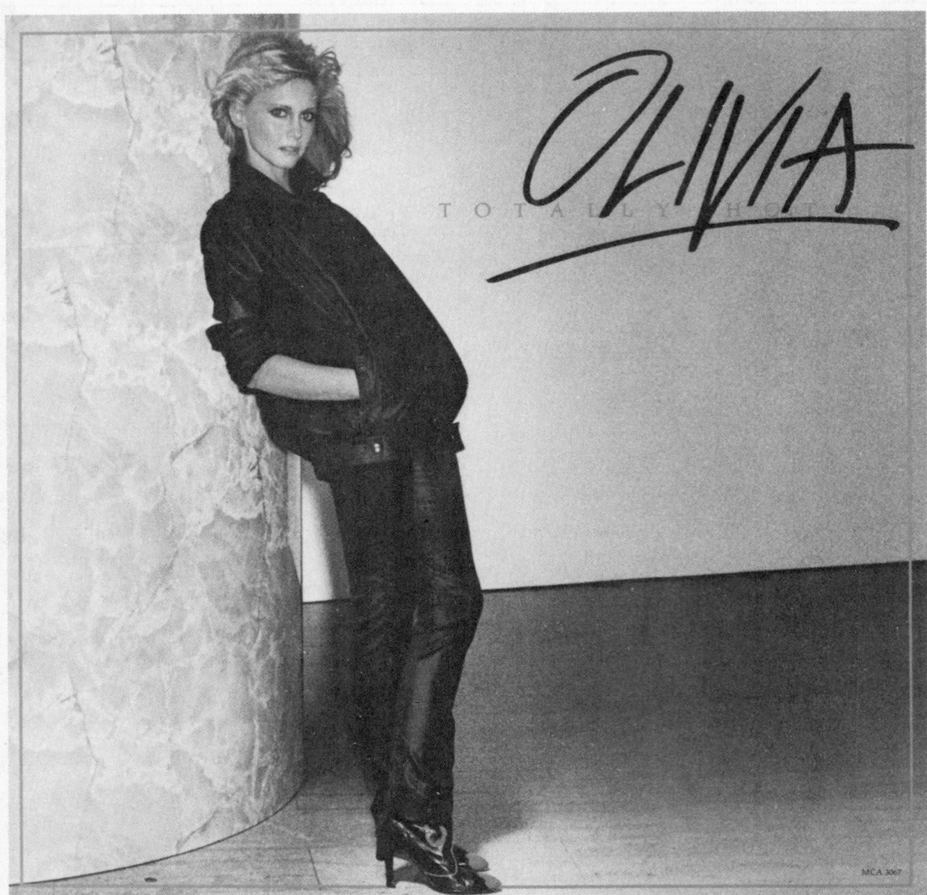


Olivia Newton-John, *Totally Hot,* MCA 3067, 1978, $10.

| Number | Title (A Side/B Side) | Yr | NM |
|---|---|---|---|
| **RCA** | | | |
| ❑ 5646-1-R | Old Flame | 1986 | 10.00 |
| *—Reissue of 5493 with slightly different lineup* | | | |
| ❑ 6371-1-R | Emotion | 1987 | 10.00 |
| ❑ 8376-1-R | Ain't Gonna Cry | 1989 | 10.00 |
| **RCA VICTOR** | | | |
| ❑ APL1-1004 | Juice Newton and Silver Spur | 1975 | 20.00 |
| ❑ APL1-1722 | After Dust Settled | 1977 | 15.00 |
| ❑ AYL1-4037 | Juice Newton and Silver Spur | 1982 | 8.00 |
| *—"Best Buy Series" reissue* | | | |
| ❑ AYL1-4038 | After Dust Settled | 1982 | 8.00 |
| *—"Best Buy Series" reissue* | | | |
| ❑ AFL1-4995 | Can't Wait All Night | 1984 | 10.00 |
| ❑ AFL1-5493 | Old Flame | 1985 | 12.00 |
| **NEWTON, WAYNE** | | | |
| **ARIES II** | | | |
| ❑ WY 201 | Wayne Newton Christmas | 1979 | 10.00 |
| **CAPITOL** | | | |
| ❑ SKAO-137 | The Best of Wayne Newton, Volume 2 | 1968 | 15.00 |
| ❑ STBB-487 [(2)] | Merry Christmas to You | 1970 | 15.00 |
| ❑ ST-617 | How I Got This Way | 1971 | 15.00 |
| ❑ ST 1973 [S] | Danke Schoen | 1963 | 20.00 |
| ❑ T 1973 [M] | Danke Schoen | 1963 | 15.00 |
| ❑ ST 2029 [S] | Wayne Newton In Person | 1964 | 20.00 |
| ❑ T 2029 [M] | Wayne Newton In Person | 1964 | 15.00 |
| ❑ ST 2130 [S] | Wayne Newton Sings Hit Songs | 1964 | 20.00 |
| ❑ T 2130 [M] | Wayne Newton Sings Hit Songs | 1964 | 15.00 |
| ❑ SM-2335 | Red Roses for a Blue Lady | 197? | 10.00 |
| *—Reissue* | | | |
| ❑ ST 2335 [S] | Red Roses for a Blue Lady | 1965 | 20.00 |
| ❑ T 2335 [M] | Red Roses for a Blue Lady | 1965 | 15.00 |
| ❑ ST 2389 [S] | Summer Wind | 1965 | 20.00 |
| ❑ T 2389 [M] | Summer Wind | 1965 | 15.00 |
| ❑ ST 2445 [S] | Wayne Newton — Now! | 1966 | 20.00 |
| ❑ T 2445 [M] | Wayne Newton — Now! | 1966 | 15.00 |
| ❑ SM-2563 | The Old Rugged Cross | 197? | 10.00 |
| *—Reissue* | | | |
| ❑ ST 2563 [S] | The Old Rugged Cross | 1966 | 20.00 |
| ❑ T 2563 [M] | The Old Rugged Cross | 1966 | 15.00 |
| ❑ ST 2588 [S] | Songs for a Merry Christmas | 1966 | 15.00 |
| ❑ T 2588 [M] | Songs for a Merry Christmas | 1966 | 12.00 |
| ❑ ST 2635 [S] | It's Only the Good Times | 1967 | 20.00 |

| Number | Title (A Side/B Side) | Yr | NM |
|---|---|---|---|
| ❑ T 2635 [M] | It's Only the Good Times | 1967 | 15.00 |
| ❑ ST 2714 [S] | Song of the Year...Wayne Newton Style | 1967 | 15.00 |
| ❑ T 2714 [M] | Song of the Year...Wayne Newton Style | 1967 | 20.00 |
| ❑ ST 2797 [S] | The Best of Wayne Newton | 1967 | 15.00 |
| ❑ T 2797 [M] | The Best of Wayne Newton | 1967 | 20.00 |
| ❑ ST 2832 [S] | God Is Alive | 1968 | 15.00 |
| ❑ T 2832 [M] | God Is Alive | 1968 | 20.00 |
| ❑ ST 2847 [S] | Wayne Newton — The Greatest | 1968 | 15.00 |
| ❑ T 2847 [M] | Wayne Newton — The Greatest | 1968 | 20.00 |
| ❑ SM-11972 | Danke Schoen | 1979 | 10.00 |
| *—Reissue* | | | |
| ❑ SN-16083 | The Best of Wayne Newton | 1980 | 8.00 |
| *—Budget-line reissue* | | | |
| **CAPITOL PICKWICK SERIES** | | | |
| ❑ PC-3455 [M] | Somewhere My Love | 196? | 10.00 |
| ❑ SPC-3455 [S] | Somewhere My Love | 196? | 10.00 |
| ❑ PC-3459 [M] | Everybody Loves Somebody | 196? | 10.00 |
| ❑ SPC-3459 [S] | Everybody Loves Somebody | 196? | 10.00 |
| ❑ PC-3461 [M] | Michelle | 196? | 10.00 |
| ❑ SPC-3461 [S] | Michelle | 196? | 10.00 |
| ❑ PC-3464 [M] | Wow! Wayne Newton Live | 196? | 10.00 |
| ❑ SPC-3464 [S] | Wow! Wayne Newton Live | 196? | 10.00 |
| **CHELSEA** | | | |
| ❑ BCL1-0367 | Pour Me a Little More Wine | 1973 | 12.00 |
| ❑ CHL-504 | The Best of Wayne Newton Live | 1974 | 10.00 |
| ❑ CHL-507 | Midnight Idol | 1975 | 10.00 |
| ❑ CHL-512 | Tomorrow | 1976 | 10.00 |
| ❑ CHL-513 | Daddy Don't You Walk So Fast | 1976 | 10.00 |
| *—Reissue of 1001* | | | |
| ❑ CHE 1001 | Daddy Don't You Walk So Fast | 1972 | 12.00 |
| ❑ CHE 1003 | Can't You Hear the Song? | 1972 | 12.00 |
| ❑ CHE 1006 | While We're Still Young | 1973 | 12.00 |
| **CURB** | | | |
| ❑ 10607 | Coming Home | 1989 | 12.00 |
| **MGM** | | | |
| ❑ E-4523 [M] | Walking on New Grass | 1968 | 20.00 |
| ❑ SE-4523 [S] | Walking on New Grass | 1968 | 12.00 |
| ❑ E-4549 [M] | One More Time | 1968 | 20.00 |
| ❑ SE-4549 [S] | One More Time | 1968 | 12.00 |
| ❑ SE-4593 | Christmas Isn't Christmas Without You | 1968 | 12.00 |

| Number | Title (A Side/B Side) | Yr | NM |
|---|---|---|---|
| ❑ SE-4594 | Dreams of the Everyday Housewife/Town and Country | 1969 | 12.00 |
| **20TH CENTURY** | | | |
| ❑ T-576 | Change of Heart | 1979 | 10.00 |
| **WORD** | | | |
| ❑ WST-8586 | Only Believe | 1972 | 12.00 |
| **NEWTON-JOHN, OLIVIA** | | | |
| **GEFFEN** | | | |
| ❑ GHS 24257 | Warm and Tender | 1989 | 12.00 |
| **MCA** | | | |
| ❑ 389 | Let Me Be There | 1973 | 15.00 |
| ❑ 411 | If You Love Me Let Me Know | 1974 | 10.00 |
| *—With corrected song title: "I Honestly Love You"* | | | |
| ❑ 411 | If You Love Me Let Me Know | 1974 | 15.00 |
| *—Originals have incorrect song title: "I Love You, I Honestly Love You"* | | | |
| ❑ 2133 | Have You Never Been Mellow | 1975 | 10.00 |
| ❑ 2148 | Clearly Love | 1975 | 10.00 |
| ❑ 2186 | Come On Over | 1976 | 10.00 |
| ❑ 2223 | Don't Stop Believin' | 1976 | 10.00 |
| ❑ 2280 | Making a Good Thing Better | 1977 | 10.00 |
| ❑ 3012 | Let Me Be There | 1977 | 8.00 |
| *—Reissue* | | | |
| ❑ 3013 | If You Love Me Let Me Know | 1977 | 8.00 |
| *—Reissue* | | | |
| ❑ 3014 | Have You Never Been Mellow | 1977 | 8.00 |
| *—Reissue* | | | |
| ❑ 3015 | Clearly Love | 1977 | 8.00 |
| *—Reissue* | | | |
| ❑ 3016 | Come On Over | 1977 | 8.00 |
| *—Reissue* | | | |
| ❑ 3017 | Don't Stop Believin' | 1977 | 8.00 |
| *—Reissue* | | | |
| ❑ 3018 | Making a Good Thing Better | 1977 | 8.00 |
| *—Reissue* | | | |
| ❑ 3028 | Olivia Newton-John's Greatest Hits | 1977 | 10.00 |
| ❑ 3067 | Totally Hot | 1978 | 10.00 |
| ❑ 5229 | Physical | 1981 | 8.00 |
| ❑ 5347 | Olivia's Greatest Hits, Vol. 2 | 1982 | 8.00 |
| ❑ 6151 | Soul Kiss | 1985 | 8.00 |
| ❑ 6245 | The Rumour | 1988 | 8.00 |
| ❑ 16011 | Physical | 1982 | 25.00 |
| *—Audiophile edition* | | | |
| ❑ 37061 | Clearly Love | 1980 | 8.00 |
| *—Reissue* | | | |
| ❑ 37062 | Come On Over | 1980 | 8.00 |
| *—Reissue* | | | |
| ❑ 37063 | Don't Stop Believin' | 1980 | 8.00 |
| *—Reissue* | | | |
| ❑ 37123 | Totally Hot | 1981 | 8.00 |
| *—Reissue* | | | |
| **MOBILE FIDELITY** | | | |
| ❑ 1-040 | Totally Hot | 1980 | 20.00 |
| *—Audiophile vinyl* | | | |
| **UNI** | | | |
| ❑ 73117 | If Not for You | 1971 | 80.00 |
| **NEXT MORNING, THE** | | | |
| **CALLA** | | | |
| ❑ SC-2002 | The Next Morning | 1972 | 100.00 |
| **NICE, THE** | | | |
| **COLUMBIA SPECIAL PRODUCTS** | | | |
| ❑ P 11633 | Thoughts of Emerlist Davjack | 1973 | 12.00 |
| ❑ P 11634 | Ars Longa Vita Brevis | 1973 | 12.00 |
| ❑ P 11635 | The Nice | 1973 | 12.00 |
| **IMMEDIATE** | | | |
| ❑ Z12 52004 | Thoughts of Emerlist Davjack | 1968 | 20.00 |
| ❑ Z12-52020 | Ars Longa Vita Brevis | 1969 | 20.00 |
| ❑ Z12-52022 | The Nice | 1969 | 15.00 |
| **MERCURY** | | | |
| ❑ SRM-2-6500 [(2)] | Keith Emerson with The Nice | 1972 | 15.00 |
| ❑ SR 61295 | Five Bridges | 1970 | 12.00 |
| ❑ SR 61324 | Elegy | 1971 | 12.00 |
| **SIRE** | | | |
| ❑ SASH-3710 [(2)] | The Vintage Years | 1975 | 15.00 |
| **NICHOLAS, ALBERT** | | | |
| **DELMARK** | | | |
| ❑ DS-209 | Albert Nicholas with Art Hodes' All-Star Stompers | 1964 | 20.00 |
| **NICHOLAS, ALBERT/SIDNEY BECHET** | | | |
| **RIVERSIDE** | | | |
| ❑ RLP-12-216 [M] | Creole Reeds | 1956 | 80.00 |
| *—White label, blue print* | | | |
| ❑ RLP-12-216 [M] | Creole Reeds | 1959 | 40.00 |
| *—Blue label, microphone logo at top* | | | |
| **NICHOLAS, JOSEPH "WOODEN JOE"** | | | |
| **AMERICA MUSIC** | | | |
| ❑ 640 [10] | A Nite at Artesian Hall With Wooden Joe | 1951 | 60.00 |

## NICHOLAS BROTHERS, THE

### MERCURY

| Number | Title (A Side/B Side) | Yr | NM |
|---|---|---|---|
| ❑ MG-20355 [M] | We Do Sing, Too | 1958 | 30.00 |

## NICHOLS, HERBIE

### BETHLEHEM

| Number | Title (A Side/B Side) | Yr | NM |
|---|---|---|---|
| ❑ BCP-81 [M] | Love Gloom Cash and Love | 1957 | 250.00 |

### BLUE NOTE

| Number | Title (A Side/B Side) | Yr | NM |
|---|---|---|---|
| ❑ BLP-1519 [M] | Herbie Nichols Trio | 1956 | 250.00 |
| *—"Deep groove" edition, W. 63rd St. address on label* | | | |
| ❑ BLP-1519 [M] | Herbie Nichols Trio | 1956 | 400.00 |
| *—"Deep groove" version, Lexington Ave. address on label* | | | |
| ❑ BLP-1519 [M] | Herbie Nichols Trio | 1963 | 60.00 |
| *—With "New York, USA" address on label* | | | |
| ❑ BLP-1519 [M] | Herbie Nichols Trio | 1971 | 40.00 |
| *—"A Division of United Artists" on label* | | | |
| ❑ BLP-5068 [10] | The Prophetic Herbie Nichols, Volume 1 | 1955 | 1200. |
| ❑ BLP-5069 [10] | The Prophetic Herbie Nichols, Volume 2 | 1955 | 1200. |

## NICHOLS, MIKE, AND ELAINE MAY

### MERCURY

| Number | Title (A Side/B Side) | Yr | NM |
|---|---|---|---|
| ❑ SRM-2-628 [(2)] | Retrospect | 1972 | 20.00 |
| ❑ OCM 2200 [M] | An Evening with Mike Nichols and Elaine May | 1961 | 30.00 |
| ❑ OCS 6200 [S] | An Evening with Mike Nichols and Elaine May | 1961 | 40.00 |
| ❑ MG 20376 [M] | Improvisations to Music | 1959 | 30.00 |
| ❑ MG 20680 [M] | Nichols and May Examine Doctors | 1962 | 25.00 |
| ❑ MG 20997 [M] | The Best of Nichols and May | 1965 | 20.00 |
| ❑ SR 60040 [S] | Improvisations to Music | 1959 | 40.00 |
| ❑ SR 60680 [S] | Nichols and May Examine Doctors | 1962 | 30.00 |
| ❑ SR 60997 [S] | The Best of Nichols and May | 1965 | 25.00 |

## NICHOLS, NICHELLE

### EPIC

| Number | Title (A Side/B Side) | Yr | NM |
|---|---|---|---|
| ❑ LN 24351 [M] | Down to Earth | 1968 | 80.00 |
| *—White label promo only; in stereo cover with "Mono" sticker* | | | |
| ❑ BN 26351 [S] | Down to Earth | 1968 | 40.00 |

## NICHOLS, RED, AND THE FIVE PENNIES

### AUDIOPHILE

| Number | Title (A Side/B Side) | Yr | NM |
|---|---|---|---|
| ❑ AP-1 [M] | Red Nichols and Band | 195? | 50.00 |
| ❑ AP-7 [M] | Syncopated Chamber Music, Volume 1 | 195? | 50.00 |
| ❑ AP-8 [M] | Syncopated Chamber Music, Volume 2 | 195? | 50.00 |

### BRUNSWICK

| Number | Title (A Side/B Side) | Yr | NM |
|---|---|---|---|
| ❑ BL 54008 [M] | For Collectors Only | 1954 | 50.00 |
| ❑ BL 54047 [M] | The Red Nichols Story | 1959 | 50.00 |
| ❑ BL 58008 [10] | Classics, Volume 1 | 1950 | 80.00 |
| ❑ BL 58009 [10] | Classics, Volume 2 | 1950 | 80.00 |
| ❑ BL 58027 [10] | Volume 3 | 1951 | 80.00 |

### CAPITOL

| Number | Title (A Side/B Side) | Yr | NM |
|---|---|---|---|
| ❑ H 215 [10] | Jazz Time | 1950 | 80.00 |
| ❑ T 775 [M] | Hot Pennies | 1956 | 50.00 |
| ❑ ST 1051 [S] | Parade of the Pennies | 1958 | 30.00 |
| ❑ T 1051 [M] | Parade of the Pennies | 1958 | 20.00 |
| ❑ ST 1297 [S] | Dixieland Dinner Dance | 1960 | 20.00 |
| ❑ ST 1803 [S] | The All-Time Hits of Red Nichols | 1962 | 20.00 |
| ❑ ST 2065 [S] | Blues and Old-Time Rags | 1963 | 20.00 |

### CONCERT DISC

| Number | Title (A Side/B Side) | Yr | NM |
|---|---|---|---|
| ❑ CS-53 | Red Nichols and His Five Pennies | 1961 | 15.00 |

### MOBILE FIDELITY

| Number | Title (A Side/B Side) | Yr | NM |
|---|---|---|---|
| ❑ 1-093 | Red Nichols and the Five Pennies at Marineland | 1982 | 20.00 |
| *—Audiophile vinyl* | | | |

### NAJO

| Number | Title (A Side/B Side) | Yr | NM |
|---|---|---|---|
| ❑ LPS-001 | Nat Nichols Trio | 1967 | 25.00 |
| ❑ LPS-002 | Spring Play | 1967 | 25.00 |

## NICKEL BAG, THE

### KAMA SUTRA

| Number | Title (A Side/B Side) | Yr | NM |
|---|---|---|---|
| ❑ KLP-8066 [M] | Doing Their Love Thing | 1968 | 60.00 |
| *—Both stock and promo copies exist* | | | |
| ❑ KLPS-8066 [S] | Doing Their Love Thing | 1968 | 25.00 |

## NICKS, STEVIE

### ATLANTIC

| Number | Title (A Side/B Side) | Yr | NM |
|---|---|---|---|
| ❑ 1P-8160 | TimeSpace — The Best of Stevie Nicks | 1991 | 20.00 |
| *—Columbia House edition; only US vinyl version* | | | |

### MOBILE FIDELITY

| Number | Title (A Side/B Side) | Yr | NM |
|---|---|---|---|
| ❑ 1-121 | Bella Donna | 1984 | 50.00 |
| *—Audiophile vinyl* | | | |

### MODERN

| Number | Title (A Side/B Side) | Yr | NM |
|---|---|---|---|
| ❑ MR 38-139 | Bella Donna | 1981 | 10.00 |
| ❑ PR-2881 [DJ] | Reflections from the Other Side of the Mirror | 1989 | 40.00 |
| *—Promo-only interview album with script* | | | |
| ❑ 90084 | The Wild Heart | 1983 | 10.00 |
| ❑ 90479 | Rock a Little | 1985 | 10.00 |
| ❑ 91245 | The Other Side of the Mirror | 1989 | 10.00 |

## NICO

### ELEKTRA

| Number | Title (A Side/B Side) | Yr | NM |
|---|---|---|---|
| ❑ EKS-74029 | The Marble Index | 1968 | 25.00 |

### ISLAND

| Number | Title (A Side/B Side) | Yr | NM |
|---|---|---|---|
| ❑ ILPS-9311 | The End | 1975 | 15.00 |

### PVC

| Number | Title (A Side/B Side) | Yr | NM |
|---|---|---|---|
| ❑ 8938 | Camera Obscura | 198? | 12.00 |

### REPRISE

| Number | Title (A Side/B Side) | Yr | NM |
|---|---|---|---|
| ❑ RS 6424 | Desert Shore | 1970 | 20.00 |

### VERVE

| Number | Title (A Side/B Side) | Yr | NM |
|---|---|---|---|
| ❑ V-5032 [M] | Chelsea Girl | 1967 | 30.00 |
| ❑ V6-5032 [S] | Chelsea Girl | 1967 | 40.00 |

## NIEHAUS, LENNIE

### CONTEMPORARY

| Number | Title (A Side/B Side) | Yr | NM |
|---|---|---|---|
| ❑ C-2513 [10] | Lennie Niehaus, Vol. 1: The Quintet | 1954 | 250.00 |
| ❑ C-2517 [10] | Lennie Niehaus, Vol. 2: The Octet | 1954 | 250.00 |
| ❑ C-3503 [M] | Lennie Niehaus, Vol. 3: The Octet No. 2 | 1955 | 150.00 |
| ❑ C-3510 [M] | Lennie Niehaus, Vol. 4: The Quintets & Strings | 1956 | 120.00 |
| ❑ C-3518 [M] | The Lennie Niehaus Quintet | 1956 | 120.00 |
| ❑ C-3524 [M] | Lennie Niehaus, Vol. 5: The Sextet | 1956 | 100.00 |
| ❑ C-3540 [M] | Zounds! Lennie Niehaus, Vol. 2: The Octet | 1957 | 100.00 |

### EMARCY

| Number | Title (A Side/B Side) | Yr | NM |
|---|---|---|---|
| ❑ MG-36118 [M] | I Swing for You | 1957 | 100.00 |

### MERCURY

| Number | Title (A Side/B Side) | Yr | NM |
|---|---|---|---|
| ❑ MG-20555 [M] | I Swing for You | 1960 | 60.00 |
| ❑ SR-60123 [S] | I Swing for You | 1960 | 50.00 |

## NIELSEN, GERTRUDE

### DECCA

| Number | Title (A Side/B Side) | Yr | NM |
|---|---|---|---|
| ❑ DL 5138 [10] | Gertrude Nielsen | 1951 | 50.00 |

## NIEWOOD, GERRY

### A&M

| Number | Title (A Side/B Side) | Yr | NM |
|---|---|---|---|
| ❑ SP-3409 | Slow, Hot Wind | 1977 | 10.00 |

### HORIZON

| Number | Title (A Side/B Side) | Yr | NM |
|---|---|---|---|
| ❑ SP-719 | Gerry Niewood and Timepiece | 1976 | 12.00 |

## NIGHT OWLS, THE

### VALMOR

| Number | Title (A Side/B Side) | Yr | NM |
|---|---|---|---|
| ❑ 79 [M] | Twisting the Oldies | 1962 | 100.00 |

## NIGHT SHADOWS, THE

### HOTTRAX

| Number | Title (A Side/B Side) | Yr | NM |
|---|---|---|---|
| ❑ 1414 | The Square Root of Two | 1979 | 50.00 |
| *—Reissue of Spectrum LP* | | | |
| ❑ 1430 | Live at the Spot | 1981 | 25.00 |
| ❑ 1450 | Invasion of the Acid Eaters | 1982 | 25.00 |

### SPECTRUM

| Number | Title (A Side/B Side) | Yr | NM |
|---|---|---|---|
| ❑ 2001 | The Square Root of Two | 1968 | 1000. |
| *—With neither bonus 45 nor psychedelic poster* | | | |
| ❑ 2001 | The Square Root of Two | 1968 | 1100. |
| *—With bonus 45, but no poster* | | | |
| ❑ 2001 | The Square Root of Two | 1968 | 1200. |
| *—With poster, but no 45* | | | |
| ❑ 2001 | The Square Root of Two | 1968 | 1500. |
| *—With both 45 and poster* | | | |

## NIGHTCAPS, THE

### VANDAN

| Number | Title (A Side/B Side) | Yr | NM |
|---|---|---|---|
| ❑ VRLP-8124 | Wine, Wine, Wine | 196? | 150.00 |

## NIGHTCRAWLERS, THE

### KAPP

| Number | Title (A Side/B Side) | Yr | NM |
|---|---|---|---|
| ❑ KL-1520 [M] | The Little Black Egg | 1967 | 60.00 |
| ❑ KS-3520 [S] | The Little Black Egg | 1967 | 40.00 |

## NIGHTHAWKS, THE

### ALADDIN

| Number | Title (A Side/B Side) | Yr | NM |
|---|---|---|---|
| ❑ LP-101 | Rock and Roll | 197? | 200.00 |

## NILES, JOHN JACOB

### BOONE-TOLLIVER

| Number | Title (A Side/B Side) | Yr | NM |
|---|---|---|---|
| ❑ BTR-22 [10] | American Folk Songs to Dulcimer Accompaniment | 195? | 50.00 |
| ❑ BTR-23 [10] | Ballads | 195? | 50.00 |

### RCA CAMDEN

| Number | Title (A Side/B Side) | Yr | NM |
|---|---|---|---|
| ❑ CAL-219 [M] | American Folk and Gambling Songs | 195? | 25.00 |
| ❑ CAL-245 [M] | American Folk Songs | 195? | 25.00 |
| ❑ CAL-330 [M] | 50th Anniversary Album | 195? | 25.00 |

### TRADITION

| Number | Title (A Side/B Side) | Yr | NM |
|---|---|---|---|
| ❑ TLP-1023 [M] | I Wonder As I Wander | 1957 | 30.00 |
| ❑ TLP-1036 [M] | An Evening with John Jacob Niles | 195? | 30.00 |

## NILSSON

### MUSICOR

| Number | Title (A Side/B Side) | Yr | NM |
|---|---|---|---|
| ❑ MUS-2505 [S] | Early Tymes | 1977 | 15.00 |

### PICKWICK

| Number | Title (A Side/B Side) | Yr | NM |
|---|---|---|---|
| ❑ SPC-3321 | Rock 'N' Roll | 1977 | 10.00 |

### RAPPLE

| Number | Title (A Side/B Side) | Yr | NM |
|---|---|---|---|
| ❑ ABL1-0220 | Son of Dracula | 1974 | 12.00 |

### RCA VICTOR

| Number | Title (A Side/B Side) | Yr | NM |
|---|---|---|---|
| ❑ (no #) [M] | The True One | 1967 | 200.00 |
| *—Boxed set with mono copy of RCA Victor 3874, two photos, button, poster, sticker, bios* | | | |
| ❑ APL1-0097 | A Little Touch of Schmilsson in the Night | 1973 | 12.00 |
| ❑ APL1-0203 | Nilsson Sings Newman | 1974 | 10.00 |
| *—Reissue of LSP-4289* | | | |
| ❑ APD1-0319 [Q] | Nilsson Schmilsson | 1974 | 20.00 |
| ❑ SPS-33-567 [DJ] | Scatalogue | 197? | 100.00 |
| ❑ APD1-0570 [Q] | Pussy Cats | 1974 | 30.00 |
| ❑ CPL1-0570 | Pussy Cats | 1974 | 20.00 |
| ❑ APD1-0817 [Q] | Duit On Mon Dei | 1975 | 20.00 |
| ❑ APL1-0817 | Duit On Mon Dei | 1975 | 12.00 |
| ❑ LSPX-1003 | The Point! | 1971 | 12.00 |
| ❑ APD1-1031 [Q] | Sandman | 1976 | 20.00 |
| ❑ APL1-1031 | Sandman | 1976 | 12.00 |
| ❑ APL1-1119 | That's the Way It Is | 1976 | 12.00 |
| ❑ AFL1-2276 | Knnillssonn | 1977 | 12.00 |
| ❑ AFL1-2798 | Greatest Hits | 1978 | 12.00 |
| ❑ ANL1-3464 | Nilsson Schmilsson | 1979 | 8.00 |
| ❑ AYL1-3761 | A Little Touch of Schmilsson in the Night | 1980 | 8.00 |
| *—"Best Buy Series" reissue* | | | |
| ❑ AYL1-3811 | The Point! | 1980 | 8.00 |
| *—"Best Buy Series" reissue* | | | |
| ❑ AYL1-3812 | Son of Schmilsson | 1980 | 8.00 |
| *—"Best Buy Series" reissue* | | | |
| ❑ LPM-3874 [M] | Pandemonium Shadow Show | 1967 | 40.00 |
| ❑ LSP-3874 [S] | Pandemonium Shadow Show | 1967 | 20.00 |
| *—"Stereo" on black label* | | | |
| ❑ LSP-3874 [S] | Pandemonium Shadow Show | 1969 | 15.00 |
| *—Orange label* | | | |
| ❑ LPM-3956 [M] | Aerial Ballet | 1968 | 50.00 |
| ❑ LSP-3956 [S] | Aerial Ballet | 1968 | 20.00 |
| *—"Stereo" on black label* | | | |
| ❑ LSP-3956 [S] | Aerial Ballet | 1969 | 15.00 |
| *—Orange label, non-flexible vinyl* | | | |
| ❑ LSP-4197 | Harry | 1969 | 15.00 |
| *—Orange label, non-flexible vinyl* | | | |
| ❑ LSP-4289 | Nilsson Sings Newman | 1970 | 12.00 |
| *—Orange label, non-flexible vinyl* | | | |
| ❑ LSP-4417 | The Point! | 1971 | 10.00 |
| *—Reissue of LSPX-1003* | | | |
| ❑ LSP-4515 | Nilsson Schmilsson | 1971 | 12.00 |
| ❑ LSP-4543 | Aerial Pandemonium Ballet | 1971 | 12.00 |
| *—Collection of tracks from 3874 and 3956, remixed with, in some cases, new vocals* | | | |
| ❑ LSP-4717 | Son of Schmilsson | 1972 | 12.00 |
| *—With custom black "Victor" label* | | | |

### TOWER

| Number | Title (A Side/B Side) | Yr | NM |
|---|---|---|---|
| ❑ ST 5095 [S] | Spotlight on Nilsson | 1967 | 20.00 |
| ❑ T 5095 [M] | Spotlight on Nilsson | 1967 | 20.00 |
| ❑ DT 5165 [R] | Spotlight on Nilsson | 1969 | 15.00 |

## NIMMONS, PHIL

### VERVE

| Number | Title (A Side/B Side) | Yr | NM |
|---|---|---|---|
| ❑ MGV-8025 [M] | The Canadian Scene Via Phil Nimmons | 1957 | 25.00 |
| ❑ V-8025 [M] | The Canadian Scene Via Phil Nimmons | 1961 | 20.00 |
| ❑ MGV-8376 [M] | Nimmons 'n' Nine | 1960 | 25.00 |
| ❑ V-8376 [M] | Nimmons 'n' Nine | 1961 | 20.00 |

## NIMOY, LEONARD

### CAEDMON

| Number | Title (A Side/B Side) | Yr | NM |
|---|---|---|---|
| ❑ TC-1466 | The Martian Chronicles | 1976 | 30.00 |
| ❑ TC-1479 | The Illustrated Man | 1976 | 30.00 |
| ❑ TC-1520 | War of the Worlds | 1977 | 30.00 |
| ❑ TC-1526 | Green Hills of Earth | 1977 | 30.00 |

### DOT

| Number | Title (A Side/B Side) | Yr | NM |
|---|---|---|---|
| ❑ DLP 3794 [M] | Mr. Spock's Music from Outer Space | 1967 | 50.00 |
| ❑ DLP 3835 [M] | Two Sides of Leonard Nimoy | 1968 | 50.00 |
| ❑ DLP 3883 [M] | The Way I Feel | 1968 | 80.00 |
| *—Stereo cover with "Monaural" sticker; label is black stock copy* | | | |
| ❑ DLP 25794 [S] | Mr. Spock's Music from Outer Space | 1967 | 80.00 |
| ❑ DLP 25835 [S] | Two Sides of Leonard Nimoy | 1968 | 80.00 |
| ❑ DLP 25883 [S] | The Way I Feel | 1968 | 60.00 |
| ❑ DLP 25910 | The Touch of Leonard Nimoy | 1969 | 60.00 |
| ❑ DLP 25966 | The New World of Leonard Nimoy | 1969 | 60.00 |

### JRT

| Number | Title (A Side/B Side) | Yr | NM |
|---|---|---|---|
| ❑ (# unknown) | The Mysterious Golem | 1982 | 40.00 |

### PARAMOUNT

| Number | Title (A Side/B Side) | Yr | NM |
|---|---|---|---|
| ❑ PAS-1030 [(2)] | Outer Space/Inner Mind | 1970 | 50.00 |

Nirvana, *MTV Unplugged in New York,* DGC 24727, 1994, $20.

**Number | Title (A Side/B Side) | Yr | NM**

PICKWICK
❑ SPC-3199 Space Odyssey 197? 50.00

SEARS
❑ SPS-491 Leonard Nimoy 196? 80.00

**NINE INCH NAILS**

NOTHING/INTERSCOPE
❑ B0004553-01 [(2)]With Teeth 2005 15.00
❑ 490473 [(3)] The Fragile 1999 100.00
*—Also called "Halo Fourteen"*
❑ 490744 [(2)] Things Falling Apart 2000 15.00
*—Also called "Halo Sixteen"*

NOTHING/TVT
❑ 2610 Pretty Hate Machine 1990 10.00
*—Also called "Halo Two"*

NOTHING/TVT/INTERSCOPE
❑ PR 5509 [(2)DJ]The Downward Spiral 1994 50.00
*—Also called "Halo Eight"; vinyl is promo only*

RYKODISC
❑ RLP 10386-1 Pretty Hate Machine 2006 20.00
*—Reissue of TVT album of the same title*

**1910 FRUITGUM COMPANY**

BUDDAH
❑ BDM-5010 [M] Simon Says 1968 50.00
*—Appears to be promo only; "Mono" sticker on stereo cover*
❑ BDS-5010 [S] Simon Says 1968 25.00
❑ BDS-5022 1,2,3 Red Light 1968 25.00
❑ BDS-5027 Goody, Goody Gumdrops 1969 25.00
❑ BDS-5036 Indian Giver 1969 25.00
❑ BDS-5043 Hard Ride 1969 25.00
❑ BDS-5057 Juiciest Fruitgum 1970 25.00

**NINETEENTH WHOLE, THE**

EASTBOUND
❑ EB-9003 Smilin' 1970 200.00

**94 EAST** Early recordings by PRINCE.

HOT PINK
❑ HLP 3223 Minneapolis Genius — 94 East 1977 40.00
*—Deduct 25% for cut-outs*

**NIRVANA** The 1990s grunge group.

DGC
❑ 24425 Nevermind 1991 30.00
*—All copies on black vinyl*

**Number | Title (A Side/B Side) | Yr | NM**

❑ 24504 Incesticide 1992 30.00
*—All copies on blue swirl vinyl*
❑ 24607 In Utero 1993 30.00
*—All copies on clear vinyl*
❑ 24727 MTV Unplugged in New York 1994 20.00
*—Black vinyl, issued simultaneously with white vinyl version; color of vinyl cannot be determined without opening the shrink wrap*
❑ 24727 MTV Unplugged in New York 1994 20.00
*—White vinyl version*
❑ 25105 [(2)] From the Muddy Banks of the Wishkah 1996 15.00

MOBILE FIDELITY
❑ 1-258 Nevermind 1996 200.00
*—Audiophile vinyl*

SUB POP
❑ SP 34 Bleach 1989 20.00
*—Red vinyl*
❑ SP 34 Bleach 1989 60.00
*—Pink vinyl*
❑ SP 34 Bleach 1989 60.00
*—Purple vinyl*
❑ SP 34 Bleach 1989 150.00
*—Red and white swirl vinyl*
❑ SP 34 Bleach 1989 200.00
*—First 1,000 were pressed on white vinyl*
❑ SP 34 Bleach 1989 200.00
*—Second 1,000 were pressed on black vinyl and include a poster*
❑ 70034 Bleach 2000 12.00
*—Reissue*

**NIRVANA (1)** The 1960s psychedelic group.

BELL
❑ 6015 The Story of Simon Simopath 1968 25.00
❑ 6024 All of Us 1969 25.00

**NIRVANA (2)**

METROMEDIA
❑ MD-1018 Nirvana 1970 25.00

**NISTICO, SAL**

JAZZLAND
❑ JLP-66 [M] Heavyweights 1962 30.00
❑ JLP-966 [S] Heavyweights 1962 40.00

RIVERSIDE
❑ RLP-457 [M] Comin' On Up 1963 30.00
❑ RS-9457 [S] Comin' On Up 1963 40.00

**Number | Title (A Side/B Side) | Yr | NM**

**NITTY GRITTY DIRT BAND**

LIBERTY
❑ LWB-184 [(2)] Stars and Stripes Forever 1981 10.00
❑ LKCL-670 [(3)] Dirt, Silver and Gold 1981 12.00
❑ LO-974 An American Dream 1981 8.00
❑ LT-1042 Make a Little Magic 1981 8.00
❑ LRP-3501 [M] The Nitty Gritty Dirt Band 1967 25.00
❑ LRP-3516 [M] Ricochet 1967 25.00
❑ LMAS-5553 All the Good Times 1981 8.00
❑ LST-7501 [S] The Nitty Gritty Dirt Band 1967 30.00
❑ LST-7516 [S] Ricochet 1967 30.00
❑ LST-7540 Rare Junk 1968 25.00
❑ LST-7611 Alive 1969 25.00
❑ LST-7642 Uncle Charlie and His Dog Teddy 1970 25.00
*—Standard issue of LP*
❑ LST-7642 [DJ] Uncle Charlie and His Dog Teddy 1970 120.00
*—Leatherette promo pack with LP, two other discs, photos, booklet*
❑ LTAO-7642 Uncle Charlie and His Dog Teddy 1981 8.00
❑ LT-51146 Let's Go 1982 10.00
❑ LWCL-51158 [(3)]Will the Circle Be Unbroken 1986 15.00

MCA
❑ 6407 The Rest of the Dream 1990 12.00

UNITED ARTISTS
❑ UA-LA184-J2 [(2)]Stars and Stripes Forever 1974 15.00
❑ UA-LA469-G Dream 1975 12.00
❑ UA-LA670-L3 [(3)]Dirt, Silver and Gold 1976 20.00
❑ UA-LA830-H The Chicken Chronicles 1978 10.00
❑ UA-LA854-H The Dirt Band 1978 10.00
❑ UA-LA974-H An American Dream 1979 10.00
❑ LT-1042 Make a Little Magic 1980 10.00
❑ LW-1106 Jealousy 1981 10.00
❑ UAS-5553 All the Good Times 1972 15.00
❑ UAS-9801 [(3)] Will the Circle Be Unbroken 1972 30.00

UNIVERSAL
❑ UVL2-12500 [(2)]Will the Circle Be Unbroken, Volume Two 1989 20.00

WARNER BROS.
❑ 25113 Plain Dirt Fashion 1984 8.00
❑ 25304 Partners, Brothers and Friends 1985 8.00
❑ 25382 Twenty Years of Dirt: The Best of the Nitty Gritty Dirt Band 1986 8.00
❑ 25573 Hold On 1987 8.00
❑ 25722 Workin' Band 1988 8.00
❑ 25830 More Great Dirt: The Best of the Nitty Gritty Dirt Band, Vol. 2 1989 10.00

**NITZSCHE, JACK**

REPRISE
❑ MS 2092 St. Giles Cripplegate 1972 20.00
❑ R 6101 [M] The Lonely Surfer 1963 100.00
❑ R9-6101 [S] The Lonely Surfer 1963 200.00
*—Pink, gold and green label*
❑ RS 6101 [S] The Lonely Surfer 197? 20.00
*—With only "r:" logo on all-orange (tan) label*
❑ R 6115 [M] Dance to the Hits of the Beatles 1964 50.00
❑ RS 6115 [S] Dance to the Hits of the Beatles 1964 60.00
❑ R 6200 [M] Chopin '66 1966 25.00
❑ RS 6200 [S] Chopin '66 1966 30.00

**NKRUMAH, KWAME**

COLUMBIA
❑ CS 9863 Ninth Son 1969 25.00

**NO DOUBT**

TRAUMA/INTERSCOPE
❑ 92580-1 Tragic Kingdom 1995 100.00
❑ 069-490441-1 [(2)]Return of Saturn 2000 15.00
❑ 069-493195-1 [(2)]Rock Steady 2001 40.00

**NOACK, EDDIE**

WIDE WORLD
❑ 2001 Remembering Jimmie Rodgers 1970 25.00

**NOBLE, NICK**

COLUMBIA
❑ CS 9810 I'm Gonna Make You Love Me 1969 15.00

LIBERTY
❑ LRP-3302 [M] Relax 1963 20.00
❑ LST-7302 [M] Relax 1963 25.00

MERCURY
❑ MG-20182 [M] You Don't Know What Love Is 1956 25.00

WING
❑ MGW-12184 [M]Music for Lovers 196? 15.00

**NOBLES, CLIFF**

MOON SHOT
❑ 601 Pony the Horse 1969 40.00

PHIL-L.A. OF SOUL
❑ 4001 The Horse 1968 60.00

### NOGUEZ, JACKY

| Number | Title (A Side/B Side) | Yr | NM |
|---|---|---|---|
| **JAMIE** | | | |
| ❑ JLP-3007 [M] | Chow Chow Bambina | 1959 | 20.00 |
| ❑ JLPS-3007 [S] | Chow Chow Bambina | 1959 | 30.00 |
| ❑ JLP-3012 [M] | Jacky Noguez | 1960 | 20.00 |
| ❑ JLPS-3012 [S] | Jacky Noguez | 1960 | 30.00 |
| ❑ JLP-3013 [M] | Dance Along with Jacky Noguez | 1960 | 20.00 |
| ❑ JLPS-3013 [S] | Dance Along with Jacky Noguez | 1960 | 30.00 |

### NOLAND, TERRY

| Number | Title (A Side/B Side) | Yr | NM |
|---|---|---|---|
| **BRUNSWICK** | | | |
| ❑ BL 54041 [M] | Terry Noland | 1958 | 600.00 |
| *—Buddy Holly plays guitar* | | | |

### NOONE, JIMMIE

| Number | Title (A Side/B Side) | Yr | NM |
|---|---|---|---|
| **BRUNSWICK** | | | |
| ❑ BL 58006 [10] | The Apex Club Orchestra | 1950 | 50.00 |

### NORDINE, KEN

| Number | Title (A Side/B Side) | Yr | NM |
|---|---|---|---|
| **BLUE THUMB** | | | |
| ❑ BTS-33 [(2)] | How Are Things in Your Town? | 1971 | 60.00 |
| ❑ BTS-35 [(2)] | Ken Nordine | 1972 | 50.00 |
| **DECCA** | | | |
| ❑ DL 8550 [M] | Concert in the Sky | 1957 | 60.00 |
| **DOT** | | | |
| ❑ DLP-3075 [M] | Word Jazz | 1958 | 100.00 |
| ❑ DLP-3096 [M] | Son of Word Jazz | 1958 | 100.00 |
| ❑ DLP-3115 [M] | Love Words | 1958 | 100.00 |
| ❑ DLP-3142 [M] | My Baby | 1959 | 50.00 |
| ❑ DLP-3196 [M] | Next! | 1959 | 50.00 |
| ❑ DLP-3301 [M] | Word Jazz, Vol. 2 | 1960 | 60.00 |
| ❑ DLP-25075 [S] | Word Jazz | 1959 | 120.00 |
| ❑ DLP-25096 [S] | Son of Word Jazz | 1959 | 120.00 |
| ❑ DLP-25115 [S] | Love Words | 1959 | 120.00 |
| ❑ DLP-25142 [S] | My Baby | 1959 | 80.00 |
| ❑ DLP-25196 [S] | Next! | 1959 | 80.00 |
| ❑ DLP-25301 [S] | Word Jazz, Vol. 2 | 1960 | 100.00 |
| ❑ DLP-25880 | The Best of Word Jazz | 1968 | 40.00 |
| **FM** | | | |
| ❑ 304 [M] | Passion In the Desert | 1963 | 30.00 |
| ❑ S-304 [S] | Passion In the Desert | 1963 | 40.00 |
| **HAMILTON** | | | |
| ❑ HL-102 [M] | The Voice of Love | 1964 | 30.00 |
| ❑ HL-12102 [S] | The Voice of Love | 1964 | 40.00 |
| **PHILIPS** | | | |
| ❑ PHM 200224 [M] | Colors | 1966 | 80.00 |
| ❑ PHM 200258 [M] | Ken Nordine Does Robert Shure's "Twink" | 1967 | 30.00 |
| ❑ PHS 600224 [S] | Colors | 1966 | 100.00 |
| ❑ PHS 600258 [S] | Ken Nordine Does Robert Shure's "Twink" | 1967 | 40.00 |
| **SNAIL** | | | |
| ❑ SR-1001 | Stare with Your Ears | 1979 | 25.00 |
| ❑ SR-1003 | Grandson of Word Jazz | 1987 | 25.00 |
| **VERSION** | | | |
| ❑ VLP 101 [10] | Passion In the Desert | 1957 | 200.00 |

### NORMA JEAN

| Number | Title (A Side/B Side) | Yr | NM |
|---|---|---|---|
| **HARMONY** | | | |
| ❑ HL 7363 [M] | Country's Favorite | 1966 | 20.00 |
| ❑ HS 11163 [R] | Country's Favorite | 1966 | 15.00 |
| **RCA CAMDEN** | | | |
| ❑ CAL-2218 [M] | Heaven Help the Working Girl | 1968 | 40.00 |
| ❑ CAS-2218 [S] | Heaven Help the Working Girl | 1968 | 15.00 |
| ❑ CAS-2511 | It Wasn't God Who Made Honky Tonk Angels | 1972 | 15.00 |
| **RCA VICTOR** | | | |
| ❑ APL1-0170 | The Only Way to Hold Your Man | 1973 | 15.00 |
| ❑ LPM-2961 [M] | Let's Go All the Way | 1964 | 25.00 |
| ❑ LSP-2961 [S] | Let's Go All the Way | 1964 | 30.00 |
| ❑ LPM-3449 [M] | Pretty Miss Norma Jean | 1965 | 25.00 |
| ❑ LSP-3449 [S] | Pretty Miss Norma Jean | 1965 | 30.00 |
| ❑ LPM-3541 [M] | Please Don't Hurt Me | 1966 | 25.00 |
| ❑ LSP-3541 [S] | Please Don't Hurt Me | 1966 | 30.00 |
| ❑ LPM-3664 [M] | Norma Jean Sings a Tribute to Kitty Wells | 1966 | 25.00 |
| ❑ LSP-3664 [S] | Norma Jean Sings a Tribute to Kitty Wells | 1966 | 30.00 |
| ❑ LPM-3700 [M] | Norma Jean Sings Porter Wagoner | 1967 | 30.00 |
| ❑ LSP-3700 [S] | Norma Jean Sings Porter Wagoner | 1967 | 25.00 |
| ❑ LPM-3836 [M] | Jackson Ain't a Very Big Town | 1967 | 30.00 |
| ❑ LSP-3836 [S] | Jackson Ain't a Very Big Town | 1967 | 25.00 |
| ❑ LPM-3910 [M] | Heaven's Just a Prayer Away | 1967 | 50.00 |
| ❑ LSP-3910 [S] | Heaven's Just a Prayer Away | 1967 | 25.00 |
| ❑ LSP-3977 | Body and Mind | 1968 | 25.00 |
| ❑ LSP-4060 | Love's a Woman's Job | 1968 | 25.00 |
| ❑ LSP-4146 | Country Giants | 1969 | 25.00 |
| ❑ LSP-4227 | The Best of Norma Jean | 1969 | 25.00 |
| ❑ LSP-4341 | Another Man Loved Me Last Night | 1970 | 20.00 |
| ❑ LSP-4446 | It's Time for Norma Jean | 1970 | 25.00 |
| ❑ LSP-4510 | Norma Jean | 1971 | 20.00 |
| ❑ LSP-4587 | Norma Jean Sings | 1971 | 20.00 |
| ❑ LSP-4691 | Thank You for Loving Me | 1972 | 20.00 |
| ❑ LSP-4745 | I Guess That Comes From Being Poor | 1972 | 20.00 |

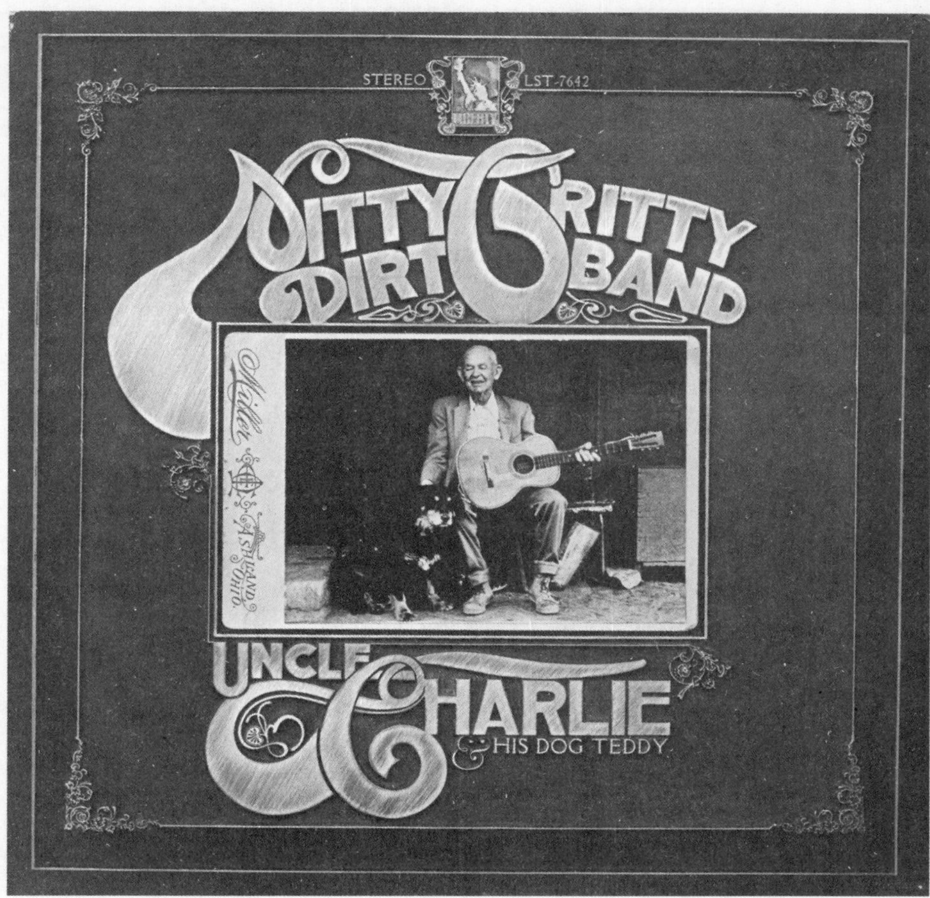


Nitty Gritty Dirt Band, *Uncle Charlie and His Dog Teddy,* Liberty LST-7642, 1970, $25.

### NORMAN, GENE, GROUP

| Number | Title (A Side/B Side) | Yr | NM |
|---|---|---|---|
| **GNP CRESCENDO** | | | |
| ❑ GNP-2015 [M] | Dylan Jazz | 1965 | 20.00 |
| ❑ GNPS-2015 [S] | Dylan Jazz | 1965 | 25.00 |

### NORMAN, LARRY

| Number | Title (A Side/B Side) | Yr | NM |
|---|---|---|---|
| **AB** | | | |
| ❑ 777 | Streams of White Light Into Darkened Corners | 1977 | 25.00 |
| **CAPITOL** | | | |
| ❑ ST-446 | Upon This Rock | 1970 | 30.00 |
| **IMPACT** | | | |
| ❑ 3121 | Upon This Rock | 197? | 20.00 |
| **MGM** | | | |
| ❑ SE-4942 | So Long Ago the Garden | 1974 | 40.00 |
| **ONE WAY** | | | |
| ❑ 900 | Bootleg | 1972 | 30.00 |
| *—Regular cover* | | | |
| ❑ 4847 | Bootleg | 1972 | 40.00 |
| *—Gatefold cover* | | | |
| ❑ 7397 | Street Level | 1971 | 30.00 |
| **PHYDEAUX** | | | |
| ❑ ARF-777-6 | Almost So Long Ago the Garden | 1984 | 12.00 |
| ❑ BONE-777-6 | Almost So Long Ago the Garden | 1981 | 15.00 |
| **SOLID ROCK** | | | |
| ❑ 2001 | In Another Land | 1976 | 15.00 |
| ❑ 2007 | Something New Under the Son | 1981 | 15.00 |
| **STREET LEVEL** | | | |
| ❑ ROCK-888-5 | Only Visiting This Planet | 1978 | 12.00 |
| *—Regular cover* | | | |
| ❑ ROCK-888-5 | Only Visiting This Planet | 1978 | 15.00 |
| *—Gatefold cover* | | | |
| **VERVE** | | | |
| ❑ V6-5092 | Only Visiting This Planet | 1973 | 30.00 |
| *—Tri-fold cover* | | | |
| ❑ V6-5092 | Only Visiting This Planet | 1973 | 40.00 |
| *—Gatefold cover* | | | |

### NORTH, FREDDIE

| Number | Title (A Side/B Side) | Yr | NM |
|---|---|---|---|
| **MANKIND** | | | |
| ❑ 205 | Cuss the Wind | 1973 | 40.00 |

### NORTH, JAY

| Number | Title (A Side/B Side) | Yr | NM |
|---|---|---|---|
| **KEM** | | | |
| ❑ 27 | Look Who's Singing! | 1960 | 100.00 |

### NORTHCOTT, TOM

| Number | Title (A Side/B Side) | Yr | NM |
|---|---|---|---|
| **UNI** | | | |
| ❑ 73108 | Upside Downside | 1971 | 20.00 |

### NORTHERN FRONT

| Number | Title (A Side/B Side) | Yr | NM |
|---|---|---|---|
| **KADER** | | | |
| ❑ (# unknown) | Furniture Store | 1975 | 100.00 |

### NORVO, RED

| Number | Title (A Side/B Side) | Yr | NM |
|---|---|---|---|
| **ALLEGRO** | | | |
| ❑ 1739 [M] | Red Norvo Jazz Trio | 195? | 40.00 |
| **CAPITOL** | | | |
| ❑ T 616 [M] | Classics in Jazz | 1955 | 80.00 |
| **CHARLIE PARKER** | | | |
| ❑ PLP-833 [M] | Pretty Is the Only Way To Fly | 1962 | 25.00 |
| ❑ PLP-833S [S] | Pretty Is the Only Way To Fly | 1962 | 25.00 |
| **COMMODORE** | | | |
| ❑ FL-20023 [10] | Town Hall Concert, Volume 1 | 1952 | 150.00 |
| ❑ FL-20027 [10] | Town Hall Concert, Volume 2 | 1952 | 150.00 |
| **CONTEMPORARY** | | | |
| ❑ C-3534 [M] | Music To Listen To Red Norvo By | 1957 | 50.00 |
| ❑ S-7009 [S] | Music To Listen To Red Norvo By | 1959 | 40.00 |
| **CONTINENTAL** | | | |
| ❑ CS-16005 [S] | Mainstream Jazz | 1962 | 20.00 |
| **DECCA** | | | |
| ❑ DL 5501 [10] | Dancing on the Ceiling | 1953 | 120.00 |

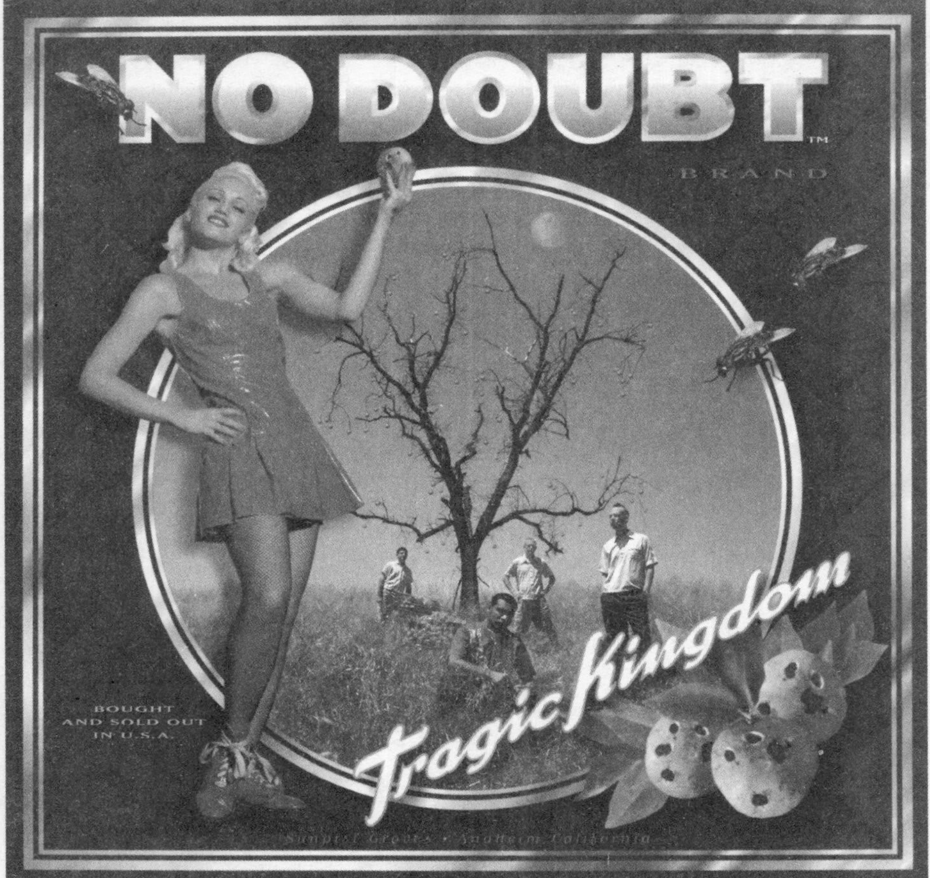


No Doubt, *Tragic Kingdom,* Trauma/Interscope 92580, 1996, $100.

| Number | Title (A Side/B Side) | Yr | NM |
|---|---|---|---|
| DIAL | | | |
| ❑ LP-903 [M] | Fabulous Jazz Session | 1951 | 600.00 |
| DISCOVERY | | | |
| ❑ DL-3012 [10] | Red Norvo Trio | 1950 | 150.00 |
| ❑ DL-3018 [10] | Red Norvo Trio | 1952 | 150.00 |
| ❑ DL-4005 [M] | Red Norvo Trio, Volume 1 | 1951 | 120.00 |
| DOT | | | |
| ❑ DLP-3126 [M] | Windjammer City Style | 1958 | 30.00 |
| ❑ DLP-25126 [S] | Windjammer City Style | 1958 | 40.00 |
| EMARCY | | | |
| ❑ MG-26002 [10] | Improvisation | 1954 | 150.00 |
| EPIC | | | |
| ❑ LN 3128 [M] | Red Norvo and His All Stars | 1955 | 50.00 |
| FANTASY | | | |
| ❑ 3-12 [10] | Red Norvo Trio | 1953 | 100.00 |
| *—Black vinyl* | | | |
| ❑ 3-12 [10] | Red Norvo Trio | 1953 | 150.00 |
| *—Colored vinyl* | | | |
| ❑ 3-19 [M] | Red Norvo Trio | 195? | 40.00 |
| *—Black vinyl* | | | |
| ❑ 3-19 [M] | Red Norvo Trio | 1955 | 80.00 |
| *—Red vinyl* | | | |
| ❑ 3218 [M] | Red Norvo With Strings | 195? | 40.00 |
| *—Black vinyl* | | | |
| ❑ 3244 [M] | The Red Norvo Trios | 195? | 40.00 |
| *—Black vinyl* | | | |
| ❑ 3244 [M] | The Red Norvo Trios | 1957 | 80.00 |
| *—Red vinyl* | | | |
| LIBERTY | | | |
| ❑ LRP-3035 [M] | Ad Lib | 1957 | 40.00 |
| ❑ LJH-6012 [M] | Vibe-rations In Hi-Fi | 1956 | 50.00 |
| RAVE | | | |
| ❑ 101 [M] | Red Norvo Quintet | 1956 | 80.00 |
| RCA VICTOR | | | |
| ❑ LPM-1420 [M] | Hi Five | 1957 | 40.00 |
| ❑ LPM-1449 [M] | Some of My Favorites | 1957 | 40.00 |
| ❑ LSP-1711 [S] | Red Norvo In Stereo | 1958 | 50.00 |
| ❑ LPM-1729 [M] | Red Plays the Blues | 1958 | 40.00 |
| ❑ LSP-1729 [S] | Red Plays the Blues | 1958 | 50.00 |
| REFERENCE RECORDINGS | | | |
| ❑ RR-8 | The Forward Look | 1983 | 20.00 |
| ❑ RR-8-UHGR | The Forward Look | 1983 | 40.00 |
| RONDO-LETTE | | | |
| ❑ A-28 [M] | Red Norvo Trio | 1958 | 25.00 |
| SAVOY | | | |
| ❑ MG-12088 [M] | Move! | 1956 | 80.00 |
| ❑ MG-12093 [M] | Midnight On Cloud 69 | 1956 | 80.00 |
| STEREO RECORDS | | | |
| ❑ S-7009 [S] | Music To Listen To Red Norvo By | 1958 | 50.00 |
| TAMPA | | | |
| ❑ TP-35 [M] | Norvo Naturally | 1957 | 100.00 |
| *—Colored vinyl* | | | |
| ❑ TP-35 [M] | Norvo Naturally | 1958 | 50.00 |
| *—Black vinyl* | | | |
| "X" | | | |
| ❑ LXA-3034 [M] | Red's Blue Room | 1955 | 150.00 |

**NORVO, RED/GEORGIE AULD**

| Number | Title (A Side/B Side) | Yr | NM |
|---|---|---|---|
| GOLDEN ERA | | | |
| ❑ 15016 [M] | The Great Dance Bands, Vol. 2 | 195? | 40.00 |

**NORVO, RED/CAL TJADER**

| Number | Title (A Side/B Side) | Yr | NM |
|---|---|---|---|
| JAZZTONE | | | |
| ❑ J-1277 [M] | Delightfully Light | 195? | 40.00 |

**NORWOOD, DOROTHY**

| Number | Title (A Side/B Side) | Yr | NM |
|---|---|---|---|
| SAVOY | | | |
| ❑ SL-7042 [(2)] | The Mountain Climbers | 1979 | 20.00 |
| ❑ MG 14083 [M] | Johnny and Jesus | 196? | 25.00 |
| ❑ MG 14093 [M] | The Old Lady's House | 196? | 25.00 |
| ❑ MG 14107 [M] | The Bell Didn't Toll | 196? | 25.00 |
| ❑ MG 14127 [M] | He Will Never Let Go My Hand | 196? | 25.00 |
| ❑ MG 14140 [M] | Denied Mother | 196? | 25.00 |
| ❑ MG 14157 [M] | Soldier from Vietnam | 196? | 25.00 |
| ❑ MG 14169 [M] | The Dorothy Norwood Singers | 196? | 25.00 |
| ❑ MG 14175 [M] | The Singing Slave | 196? | 25.00 |
| ❑ MG 14190 [M] | Bereaved Child | 196? | 25.00 |
| ❑ MG 14212 | The Stories Behind the Songs | 196? | 25.00 |
| ❑ MG 14217 | Just in Time | 196? | 25.00 |
| ❑ MG 14244 | Brother Came Too Late | 196? | 25.00 |
| ❑ MG 14259 | Jesus Picked Up the Pieces | 196? | 25.00 |
| ❑ MG 14266 | Despondent Wife | 196? | 25.00 |
| ❑ MG 14282 | Three Little Pigs | 197? | 25.00 |
| *—With Lois Snead* | | | |
| ❑ MG 14295 | Just the Two of Us | 1972 | 25.00 |
| *—With Lois Snead* | | | |
| ❑ MG 14309 | Come By Here | 1973 | 25.00 |

**NOSY PARKER**

| Number | Title (A Side/B Side) | Yr | NM |
|---|---|---|---|
| (NO LABEL) | | | |
| ❑ (no #) | Nosy Parker | 1975 | 250.00 |

**NOTES FROM THE UNDERGROUND**

| Number | Title (A Side/B Side) | Yr | NM |
|---|---|---|---|
| VANGUARD | | | |
| ❑ VSD-6502 | Notes from the Underground | 1970 | 80.00 |

**NOTHING, CHARLIE**

| Number | Title (A Side/B Side) | Yr | NM |
|---|---|---|---|
| TAKOMA | | | |
| ❑ C-1015 | The Psychedelic Saxophone of Charlie Nothing | 1967 | 50.00 |

**NOVA LOCAL, THE**

| Number | Title (A Side/B Side) | Yr | NM |
|---|---|---|---|
| DECCA | | | |
| ❑ DL 74977 | Nova 1 | 1968 | 70.00 |

**NOVAC, JERRY**

| Number | Title (A Side/B Side) | Yr | NM |
|---|---|---|---|
| EMBRYO | | | |
| ❑ 527 | The 5th Word | 1970 | 25.00 |

**NOVELLS, THE**

| Number | Title (A Side/B Side) | Yr | NM |
|---|---|---|---|
| MOTHER'S | | | |
| ❑ MLPS-73 | A Happening | 1968 | 50.00 |

**NOW CREATIVE ARTS JAZZ ENSEMBLE, THE**

| Number | Title (A Side/B Side) | Yr | NM |
|---|---|---|---|
| ARHOOLIE | | | |
| ❑ 8002 | Now | 1969 | 20.00 |

**NOZERO, LARRY**

| Number | Title (A Side/B Side) | Yr | NM |
|---|---|---|---|
| STRATA | | | |
| ❑ 109-75 | Time | 1975 | 20.00 |

**NRBQ**

| Number | Title (A Side/B Side) | Yr | NM |
|---|---|---|---|
| ANNUIT COEPTIS | | | |
| ❑ 1001/2 [(2)] | Scraps/Workshop | 1976 | 20.00 |
| *—Reissue of Kama Sutra LPs* | | | |
| BEARSVILLE | | | |
| ❑ 23817 | Grooves in Orbit | 1983 | 10.00 |
| COLUMBIA | | | |
| ❑ CS 9858 | NRBQ | 1969 | 25.00 |
| *—"360 Sound Stereo" label* | | | |
| ❑ CS 9858 | NRBQ | 1970 | 12.00 |
| *—Orange label* | | | |
| ❑ PC 9858 | NRBQ | 198? | 8.00 |
| *—Budget-line reissue* | | | |
| KAMA SUTRA | | | |
| ❑ KSBS-2045 | Scraps | 1972 | 30.00 |
| ❑ KSBS-2065 | Workshop | 1973 | 40.00 |
| MERCURY | | | |
| ❑ SRM-1-3712 | NRBQ at Yankee Stadium | 1978 | 15.00 |
| ❑ 824462-1 | NRBQ at Yankee Stadlum | 1984 | 10.00 |
| *—Reissue* | | | |
| RED ROOSTER | | | |
| ❑ 101 | All Hopped Up | 1977 | 15.00 |
| ROUNDER | | | |
| ❑ EP-2501 [EP] | Christmas Wish | 1985 | 12.00 |
| ❑ 3029 | All Hopped Up | 1979 | 12.00 |
| ❑ 3030 | Kick Me Hard | 1979 | 12.00 |
| ❑ 3048 | Tiddlywinks | 1980 | 12.00 |
| ❑ 3055 | Scraps | 1982 | 10.00 |
| ❑ 3066 | Tapdancin' Bats | 1983 | 10.00 |
| ❑ 3090 | RC Cola & a Moon Pie | 1987 | 10.00 |
| ❑ 3098 | Lou and the Q | 1986 | 10.00 |
| *—With pro wrestler Captain Lou Albano* | | | |
| ❑ 3108 | God Bless Us All | 1988 | 10.00 |
| ❑ 3109 | Live! Diggin' Uncle Q | 1988 | 10.00 |
| SUNDAZED | | | |
| ❑ LP-5162 | Atsa My Band | 2003 | 15.00 |
| VIRGIN | | | |
| ❑ 91291 | Wild Weekend | 1989 | 10.00 |

**NUBIN, KATI BELL**

| Number | Title (A Side/B Side) | Yr | NM |
|---|---|---|---|
| VERVE | | | |
| ❑ MGV-3004 [M] | Soul, Soul Searchin' | 1960 | 80.00 |
| ❑ V-3004 [M] | Soul, Soul Searchin' | 1961 | 40.00 |
| ❑ V6-3004 [S] | Soul, Soul Searchin' | 1961 | 50.00 |

**NUCLEUS**

| Number | Title (A Side/B Side) | Yr | NM |
|---|---|---|---|
| MAINSTREAM | | | |
| ❑ S-6120 | Nucleus | 1969 | 50.00 |

**NUDIE**

| Number | Title (A Side/B Side) | Yr | NM |
|---|---|---|---|
| NUDIE | | | |
| ❑ 3203 | Nudie and His Mandolin | 196? | 40.00 |

**NUGENT, TED** Also see THE AMBOY DUKES.

| Number | Title (A Side/B Side) | Yr | NM |
|---|---|---|---|
| ATLANTIC | | | |
| ❑ SD 19365 | Nugent | 1982 | 10.00 |
| ❑ 80125 | Penetrator | 1984 | 10.00 |
| ❑ 81632 | Little Miss Dangerous | 1986 | 10.00 |
| ❑ 81812 | If You Can't Lick 'Em...Lick 'Em | 1988 | 10.00 |



**Except when noted otherwise, VG = 25% of NM, and VG+ = 50% of NM. (Example: VG = $2.00, VG+ = $4.00 and NM = $8.00.)**

| Number | Title (A Side/B Side) | Yr | NM |
|---|---|---|---|
| EPIC | | | |
| ❑ AS99-607 [PD] | State of Shock | 1979 | 40.00 |
| *—Promo-only picture disc* | | | |
| ❑ PE 33692 | Ted Nugent | 1975 | 12.00 |
| *—Orange label* | | | |
| ❑ PE 33692 | Ted Nugent | 1979 | 8.00 |
| *—Reissue with dark blue label and bar code* | | | |
| ❑ PE 34121 | Free-for-All | 1976 | 12.00 |
| *—Orange label* | | | |
| ❑ PE 34121 | Free-for-All | 1979 | 8.00 |
| *—Reissue with dark blue label and bar code* | | | |
| ❑ PEQ 34121 [Q] | Free-for-All | 1976 | 20.00 |
| ❑ JE 34700 | Cat Scratch Fever | 1977 | 12.00 |
| *—Orange label* | | | |
| ❑ PE 34700 | Cat Scratch Fever | 198? | 8.00 |
| *—Reissue with dark blue label and bar code* | | | |
| ❑ KE2 35069 [(2)] | Double Live Gonzo! | 1978 | 15.00 |
| *—Orange labels* | | | |
| ❑ FE 35551 | Weekend Warriors | 1978 | 12.00 |
| *—Orange label* | | | |
| ❑ PE 35551 | Weekend Warriors | 198? | 8.00 |
| *—Reissue with dark blue label and bar code* | | | |
| ❑ FE 36000 | State of Shock | 1979 | 10.00 |
| ❑ PE 36000 | State of Shock | 198? | 8.00 |
| *—Budget-line reissue* | | | |
| ❑ FE 36404 | Scream Dream | 1980 | 10.00 |
| ❑ FE 37084 | Intensities in 10 Cities | 1981 | 10.00 |
| ❑ PE 37084 | Intensities in 10 Cities | 198? | 8.00 |
| *—Budget-line reissue* | | | |
| ❑ FE 37667 | Great Gonzos! The Best of Ted Nugent | 1981 | 10.00 |
| ❑ PE 37667 | Great Gonzos! The Best of Ted Nugent | 198? | 8.00 |
| *—Budget-line reissue* | | | |
| **NUTTY SQUIRRELS, THE** | | | |
| COLUMBIA | | | |
| ❑ CL 1589 [M] | Bird Watching | 1961 | 30.00 |
| ❑ CS 8389 [S] | Bird Watching | 1961 | 40.00 |
| HANOVER | | | |
| ❑ HML-8014 [M] | The Nutty Squirrels | 1960 | 50.00 |
| MGM | | | |
| ❑ E-4272 [M] | A Hard Day's Night | 1964 | 25.00 |
| ❑ SE-4272 [S] | A Hard Day's Night | 1964 | 30.00 |
| **NYE, LOUIS** | | | |
| RIVERSIDE | | | |
| ❑ RLP-842 [M] | Heigh-Ho, Madison Avenue | 1960 | 25.00 |
| **NYRO, LAURA** | | | |
| COLUMBIA | | | |
| ❑ CL 2826 [M] | Eli and the Thirteenth Confession | 1968 | 40.00 |
| ❑ CS 9626 | Eli and the Thirteenth Confession | 1970 | 10.00 |
| *—Orange label* | | | |
| ❑ CS 9626 [S] | Eli and the Thirteenth Confession | 1968 | 15.00 |
| *—"360 Sound Stereo" label* | | | |
| ❑ PC 9626 | Eli and the Thirteenth Confession | 198? | 8.00 |
| *—Budget-line reissue* | | | |
| ❑ CS 9737 | New York Tendaberry | 1969 | 15.00 |
| *—"360 Sound Stereo" label* | | | |
| ❑ CS 9737 | New York Tendaberry | 1970 | 10.00 |
| *—Orange label* | | | |
| ❑ PC 9737 | New York Tendaberry | 198? | 8.00 |
| *—Budget-line reissue* | | | |
| ❑ KC 30259 | Christmas and the Beads of Sweat | 1970 | 10.00 |
| *—Orange label* | | | |
| ❑ KC 30259 | Christmas and the Beads of Sweat | 1970 | 15.00 |
| *—"360 Sound Stereo" label* | | | |
| ❑ PC 30259 | Christmas and the Beads of Sweat | 198? | 8.00 |
| *—Budget-line reissue* | | | |
| ❑ KC 30987 | Gonna Take a Miracle | 1971 | 15.00 |
| ❑ PC 30987 | Gonna Take a Miracle | 197? | 8.00 |
| *—Budget-line reissue* | | | |
| ❑ KC 31410 | The First Songs | 1973 | 15.00 |
| *—Reissue of Verve Forecast 3020* | | | |
| ❑ PC 31410 | The First Songs | 197? | 8.00 |
| *—Budget-line reissue* | | | |
| ❑ PC 33912 | Smile | 1976 | 12.00 |
| *—No bar code on cover* | | | |
| ❑ PC2 34331 [(2)DJ] | Season of Lights…Laura Nyro in Concert | 1977 | 50.00 |
| *—Promo only in plain cardboard jacket; this LP was edited to one LP for release* | | | |
| ❑ JC 34786 | Season of Lights…Laura Nyro in Concert | 1977 | 12.00 |
| *—Edited version of above* | | | |
| ❑ JC 35449 | Nested | 1978 | 12.00 |
| ❑ PC 35449 | Nested | 198? | 8.00 |
| *—Budget-line reissue* | | | |
| ❑ FC 39215 | Mother's Spiritual | 1984 | 10.00 |
| VERVE FOLKWAYS | | | |
| ❑ FT-3020 [M] | Laura Nyro — More Than a New Discovery | 1967 | 30.00 |

Laura Nyro, *Christmas and the Beads of Sweat,* Columbia KC 30259, 1970, $10.

| Number | Title (A Side/B Side) | Yr | NM |
|---|---|---|---|
| ❑ FTS-3020 [S] | Laura Nyro — More Than a New Discovery | 1967 | 30.00 |
| VERVE FORECAST | | | |
| ❑ FTS-3020 [S] | Laura Nyro — More Than a New Discovery | 1967 | 20.00 |
| ❑ FTS-3029 | Laura Nyro | 1968 | — |
| *—Canceled* | | | |
| ❑ ST 93036 | Laura Nyro — More Than a New Discovery | 1968 | 25.00 |
| *—Capitol Record Club edition* | | | |

# O

| Number | Title (A Side/B Side) | Yr | NM |
|---|---|---|---|
| **O'BRIAN, HUGH** | | | |
| ABC-PARAMOUNT | | | |
| ❑ ABC-203 [M] | TV's Wyatt Earp Sings | 1957 | 60.00 |
| **O'BRYANT, JOAN** | | | |
| FOLKWAYS | | | |
| ❑ FA-2134 [M] | Folksongs and Ballads of Kansas | 1957 | 30.00 |
| ❑ FA-2338 [M] | American Ballads and Folksongs | 1958 | 30.00 |
| **O'CONNELL, HELEN** | | | |
| MARK 56 | | | |
| ❑ 711 | Christmas with Helen O'Connell | 19?? | 12.00 |
| VIK | | | |
| ❑ LX-1093 [M] | Green Eyes | 1957 | 40.00 |
| **O'CONNOR, CARROLL** | | | |
| A&M | | | |
| ❑ SP-4340 | Remembering You | 1972 | 25.00 |
| AUDIO FIDELITY | | | |
| ❑ AFSD-6727 | Carroll O'Connor Sings for Old P.F.A.R.T.S. | 1976 | 25.00 |
| **O'DAY, ANITA** | | | |
| ADVANCE | | | |
| ❑ LSP-8 [10] | Anita O'Day Specials | 1951 | 250.00 |
| AMERICAN RECORDING SOCIETY | | | |
| ❑ G-426 [M] | For Oscar | 1957 | 40.00 |
| BASF | | | |
| ❑ MB 20750 | Recorded Live at the Berlin Jazz Festival | 1973 | 20.00 |
| CLEF | | | |
| ❑ MGC-130 [10] | Anita O'Day Collates | 1953 | 150.00 |
| CORAL | | | |
| ❑ CRL-56073 [10] | Singin' and Swingin' | 1953 | 150.00 |
| NORGRAN | | | |
| ❑ MGN-30 [10] | Songs By Anita O'Day | 1954 | 150.00 |
| ❑ MGN-1049 [M] | Anita O'Day | 1955 | 120.00 |
| ❑ MGN-1057 [M] | An Evening With Anita O'Day | 1956 | 100.00 |
| VERVE | | | |
| ❑ MGV-2000 [M] | Anita | 1956 | 80.00 |
| ❑ V-2000 [M] | Anita | 1961 | 20.00 |
| ❑ MGV-2043 [M] | Pick Yourself Up With Anita O'Day | 1957 | 80.00 |
| ❑ V-2043 [M] | Pick Yourself Up With Anita O'Day | 1961 | 20.00 |
| ❑ MGV-2049 [M] | The Lady Is a Tramp | 1957 | 60.00 |
| ❑ V-2049 [M] | The Lady Is a Tramp | 1961 | 20.00 |
| ❑ MGV-2050 [M] | An Evening With Anita O'Day | 1957 | 60.00 |
| ❑ V-2050 [M] | An Evening With Anita O'Day | 1961 | 20.00 |
| ❑ MGV-2113 [M] | Anita O'Day At Mr. Kelly's | 1958 | 50.00 |
| ❑ V-2113 [M] | Anita O'Day At Mr. Kelly's | 1961 | 20.00 |
| ❑ V6-2113 [S] | Anita O'Day At Mr. Kelly's | 1961 | 25.00 |
| ❑ MGV-2118 [M] | Anita O'Day Swings Cole Porter | 1959 | 50.00 |
| ❑ V-2118 [M] | Anita O'Day Swings Cole Porter | 1961 | 20.00 |
| ❑ V6-2118 [S] | Anita O'Day Swings Cole Porter | 1961 | 25.00 |
| ❑ MGV-2141 [M] | Anita O'Day and Billy May Swing Rodgers and Hart | 1960 | 60.00 |
| ❑ V-2141 [M] | Anita O'Day and Billy May Swing Rodgers and Hart | 1961 | 20.00 |
| ❑ V6-2141 [S] | Anita O'Day and Billy May Swing Rodgers and Hart | 1961 | 25.00 |
| ❑ MGV-2145 [M] | Waiter, Make Mine Blues | 1960 | 60.00 |
| ❑ V-2145 [M] | Waiter, Make Mine Blues | 1961 | 20.00 |
| ❑ V6-2145 [S] | Waiter, Make Mine Blues | 1961 | 25.00 |
| ❑ MGV-2157 [M] | Trav'lin' Light | 1960 | 50.00 |
| ❑ V-2157 [M] | Trav'lin' Light | 1961 | 20.00 |
| ❑ V6-2157 [S] | Trav'lin' Light | 1961 | 25.00 |
| ❑ MGVS-6002 [S] | Anita O'Day Sings the Winners | 1960 | 60.00 |
| ❑ MGVS-6043 [S] | Anita O'Day At Mr. Kelly's | 1960 | 60.00 |

| Number | Title (A Side/B Side) | Yr | NM |
|---|---|---|---|
| ❑ MGVS-6046 [S] | Cool Heat — Anita O'Day Sings Jimmy Giuffre Arrangements | 1960 | 60.00 |
| ❑ MGVS-6059 [S] | Anita O'Day Swings Cole Porter | 1960 | 60.00 |
| ❑ MGV-8259 [M] | Anita Sings the Most | 1958 | 50.00 |
| ❑ V-8259 [M] | Anita Sings the Most | 1961 | 20.00 |
| ❑ MGV-8283 [M] | Anita O'Day Sings the Winners | 1958 | 50.00 |
| ❑ V-8283 [M] | Anita O'Day Sings the Winners | 1961 | 20.00 |
| ❑ V6-8283 [S] | Anita O'Day Sings the Winners | 1961 | 25.00 |
| ❑ MGV-8312 [M] | Cool Heat — Anita O'Day Sings Jimmy Giuffre Arrangements | 1959 | 50.00 |
| ❑ V-8312 [M] | Cool Heat — Anita O'Day Sings Jimmy Giuffre Arrangements | 1961 | 20.00 |
| ❑ V6-8312 [S] | Cool Heat — Anita O'Day Sings Jimmy Giuffre Arrangements | 1961 | 25.00 |
| ❑ V-8442 [M] | All the Sad Young Men | 1962 | 30.00 |
| ❑ V6-8442 [S] | All the Sad Young Men | 1962 | 40.00 |
| ❑ V-8472 [M] | Time For Two | 1962 | 30.00 |
| ❑ V6-8472 [S] | Time For Two | 1962 | 40.00 |
| ❑ V-8483 [M] | This Is Anita | 1962 | 30.00 |
| ❑ V-8485 [M] | Anita O'Day Sings the Winners | 1962 | 20.00 |
| ❑ V6-8485 [S] | Anita O'Day Sings the Winners | 1962 | 25.00 |
| ❑ V-8514 [M] | Anita O'Day and the Three Sounds | 1963 | 25.00 |
| ❑ V6-8514 [S] | Anita O'Day and the Three Sounds | 1963 | 30.00 |
| ❑ V-8572 [M] | Incomparable! Anita O'Day | 1964 | 25.00 |
| ❑ V6-8572 [S] | Incomparable! Anita O'Day | 1964 | 30.00 |

### O'DAY, MOLLY

| Number | Title (A Side/B Side) | Yr | NM |
|---|---|---|---|
| **AUDIO LAB** | | | |
| ❑ AL-1544 [M] | Music for the Country Folks | 1960 | 30.00 |
| **HARMONY** | | | |
| ❑ HL 7299 [M] | The Unforgettable Molly O'Day | 1963 | 20.00 |
| **STARDAY** | | | |
| ❑ SLP-367 | The Living Legend of Country Music | 1966 | 25.00 |

### O'DELL, DOYE

| Number | Title (A Side/B Side) | Yr | NM |
|---|---|---|---|
| **ERA** | | | |
| ❑ EL-20004 [M] | Doye | 1956 | 30.00 |
| *—Black vinyl* | | | |
| ❑ EL-20004 [M] | Doye | 1956 | 50.00 |
| *—Red vinyl* | | | |
| **SAGE** | | | |
| ❑ C-36 [M] | Crossroads | 195? | 30.00 |

### O'DELL, KENNY

| Number | Title (A Side/B Side) | Yr | NM |
|---|---|---|---|
| **CAPRICORN** | | | |
| ❑ CP 0140 | Kenny O'Dell | 1974 | 12.00 |
| ❑ CPN 0211 | Let's Shake Hands and Come Out Lovin' | 1978 | 12.00 |
| **VEGAS** | | | |
| ❑ 401 | Beautiful People | 1968 | 25.00 |

### O'FARRILL, CHICO

| Number | Title (A Side/B Side) | Yr | NM |
|---|---|---|---|
| **CLEF** | | | |
| ❑ MGC-131 [10] | Afro-Cuban | 1953 | 200.00 |
| ❑ MGC-132 [10] | Chico O'Farrill Jazz | 1953 | 200.00 |
| ❑ MGC-699 [M] | Chico O'Farrill Jazz | 1956 | 80.00 |
| **IMPULSE!** | | | |
| ❑ A-9135 [M] | Nine Flags | 1967 | 25.00 |
| ❑ AS-9135 [S] | Nine Flags | 1967 | 20.00 |
| **NORGRAN** | | | |
| ❑ MGN-9 [10] | The Second Afro-Cuban Jazz Suite | 1954 | 150.00 |
| ❑ MGN-27 [10] | Mambo Dance Sessions | 1954 | 80.00 |
| ❑ MGN-28 [10] | Latino Dance Sessions | 1954 | 80.00 |
| ❑ MGN-31 [10] | Chico O'Farrill | 1954 | 80.00 |
| **VERVE** | | | |
| ❑ MGV-2003 [M] | Mambo/Latino Dances | 1956 | 50.00 |
| ❑ V-2003 [M] | Mambo/Latino Dances | 1961 | 25.00 |
| ❑ MGV-2024 [M] | Music From South America | 1956 | 50.00 |
| ❑ V-2024 [M] | Music From South America | 1961 | 25.00 |
| ❑ MGV-8083 [M] | Jazz North of the Border and South of the Border | 1957 | 50.00 |
| ❑ V-8083 [M] | Jazz North of the Border and South of the Border | 1961 | 25.00 |

### O'GWYNN, JAMES

| Number | Title (A Side/B Side) | Yr | NM |
|---|---|---|---|
| **MERCURY** | | | |
| ❑ MG-20727 [M] | The Best of James O'Gwynn | 1962 | 30.00 |
| ❑ SR-60727 [S] | The Best of James O'Gwynn | 1962 | 40.00 |
| **PLANTATION** | | | |
| ❑ 21 | Greatest Hits | 197? | 12.00 |
| **WING** | | | |
| ❑ MGW-12290 [M] | Heartaches and Memories | 1964 | 20.00 |
| ❑ SRW-16290 [S] | Heartaches and Memories | 1964 | 25.00 |

### O'HARA, MAUREEN

| Number | Title (A Side/B Side) | Yr | NM |
|---|---|---|---|
| **COLUMBIA** | | | |
| ❑ CL 1750 [M] | Maureen O'Hara Sings Her Favorite Irish Songs | 1962 | 40.00 |
| ❑ CS 8550 [S] | Maureen O'Hara Sings Her Favorite Irish Songs | 1962 | 50.00 |

| Number | Title (A Side/B Side) | Yr | NM |
|---|---|---|---|
| **RCA VICTOR** | | | |
| ❑ LPM-1953 [M] | Love Letters | 1959 | 50.00 |
| ❑ LSP-1953 [S] | Love Letters | 1959 | 60.00 |

### O'JAYS, THE

| Number | Title (A Side/B Side) | Yr | NM |
|---|---|---|---|
| **BELL** | | | |
| ❑ 6014 | Back on Top | 1968 | 20.00 |
| ❑ 6082 | The O'Jays | 1973 | 12.00 |
| **EMI** | | | |
| ❑ E1-90921 | Serious | 1989 | 10.00 |
| ❑ E1-93390 | Emotionally Yours | 1991 | 15.00 |
| ❑ E1-96420 | Home for Christmas | 1991 | 15.00 |
| **IMPERIAL** | | | |
| ❑ LP 9290 [M] | Comin' Through | 1965 | 40.00 |
| ❑ LP 12290 [S] | Comin' Through | 1965 | 50.00 |
| **KORY** | | | |
| ❑ 1006 | The O'Jays | 1977 | 10.00 |
| **LIBERTY** | | | |
| ❑ LN-10119 | Greatest Hits | 1980 | 8.00 |
| *—Budget-line reissue of Imperial material* | | | |
| **MINIT** | | | |
| ❑ LP-24008 [S] | Soul Sounds | 1967 | 50.00 |
| ❑ LP-40008 [M] | Soul Sounds | 1967 | 40.00 |
| **NEPTUNE** | | | |
| ❑ 202 | The O'Jays in Philadelphia | 1969 | 30.00 |
| **PHILADELPHIA INT'L.** | | | |
| ❑ ASZ 140 [DJ] | Everything You Always Wanted to Hear by the O'Jays But Were Afraid to Ask For | 1975 | 15.00 |
| ❑ KZ 31712 | Back Stabbers | 1972 | 12.00 |
| ❑ KZ 32120 | The O'Jays in Philadelphia | 1973 | 12.00 |
| *—Reissue of Neptune LP* | | | |
| ❑ KZ 32408 | Ship Ahoy | 1973 | 10.00 |
| ❑ PZ 32408 | Ship Ahoy | 198? | 8.00 |
| *—Budget-line reissue* | | | |
| ❑ PZQ 32408 [Q] | Ship Ahoy | 1974 | 15.00 |
| ❑ KZ 32953 | The O'Jays Live in London | 1974 | 10.00 |
| ❑ PZQ 32953 [Q] | The O'Jays Live in London | 1974 | 15.00 |
| ❑ PZ 33150 | Survival | 1975 | 10.00 |
| ❑ PZ 33807 | Family Reunion | 1975 | 10.00 |
| *—No bar code on back cover* | | | |
| ❑ PZ 33807 | Family Reunion | 198? | 8.00 |
| *—Budget-line reissue with bar code* | | | |
| ❑ PZQ 33807 [Q] | Family Reunion | 1975 | 15.00 |
| ❑ PZ 34245 | Message in the Music | 1976 | 10.00 |
| ❑ PZ 34684 | Travelin' at the Speed of Thought | 1977 | 10.00 |
| ❑ PZG 35024 [(2)] | The O'Jays: Collector's Items | 1978 | 12.00 |
| ❑ Z2 35024 [(2)] | The O'Jays: Collector's Items | 198? | 10.00 |
| *—Reissue* | | | |
| ❑ JZ 35355 | So Full of Love | 1978 | 10.00 |
| ❑ PZ 35355 | So Full of Love | 198? | 8.00 |
| *—Budget-line reissue* | | | |
| ❑ FZ 36027 | Identify Yourself | 1979 | 10.00 |
| ❑ FZ 37999 | My Favorite Person | 1982 | 10.00 |
| ❑ FZ 38518 | When Will I See You Again | 1983 | 10.00 |
| ❑ PZ 38518 | When Will I See You Again | 1985 | 8.00 |
| *—Budget-line reissue* | | | |
| ❑ FZ 39251 | Greatest Hits | 1984 | 10.00 |
| ❑ 53015 | Love Fever | 1985 | 10.00 |
| ❑ 53036 | Let Me Touch You | 1987 | 10.00 |
| **SUNSET** | | | |
| ❑ SUS-5222 | Full of Soul | 1968 | 15.00 |
| *—Reissue of Imperial LP* | | | |
| **TSOP** | | | |
| ❑ FZ 36416 | The Year 2000 | 1980 | 10.00 |
| **UNITED ARTISTS** | | | |
| ❑ UAS-5655 | The O'Jays Greatest Hits | 1972 | 12.00 |
| **VOLCANO** | | | |
| ❑ 31149 | Love You to Tears | 1997 | 15.00 |

### O'KAYSIONS, THE

| Number | Title (A Side/B Side) | Yr | NM |
|---|---|---|---|
| **ABC** | | | |
| ❑ S-664 | Girl Watcher | 1968 | 40.00 |

### O'KEEFE, DANNY

| Number | Title (A Side/B Side) | Yr | NM |
|---|---|---|---|
| **ATLANTIC** | | | |
| ❑ SD 7264 | Breezy Stories | 1973 | 12.00 |
| ❑ SD 18125 | So Long, Harry Truman | 1975 | 12.00 |
| **COTILLION** | | | |
| ❑ SD 9036 | Danny O'Keefe | 1971 | 15.00 |
| **FIRST AMERICAN** | | | |
| ❑ 7700 | The Seattle Tapes | 1977 | 12.00 |
| ❑ 7721 | The Seattle Tapes, Volume 2 | 1979 | 12.00 |
| **PANORAMA** | | | |
| ❑ 105 | Introducing Danny O'Keefe | 1966 | 40.00 |
| **SIGNPOST** | | | |
| ❑ SD 8404 | O'Keefe | 1972 | 12.00 |
| **WARNER BROS.** | | | |
| ❑ PRO 760 [DJ] | The O'Keefe File | 1977 | 15.00 |
| ❑ BS 3050 | American Roulette | 1977 | 10.00 |
| ❑ BSK 3314 | Global Blues | 1978 | 10.00 |

### O'SHEA, MILO

| Number | Title (A Side/B Side) | Yr | NM |
|---|---|---|---|
| **COLUMBIA** | | | |
| ❑ CS 9647 | An Evening in Dublin | 1969 | 20.00 |

### OAK RIDGE BOYS, THE

| Number | Title (A Side/B Side) | Yr | NM |
|---|---|---|---|
| **ABC** | | | |
| ❑ AA-1065 | Room Service | 1978 | 10.00 |
| ❑ AA-1135 | Have Arrived | 1979 | 12.00 |
| **ABC/DOT** | | | |
| ❑ DA-2093 | Y'all Come Back Saloon | 1977 | 10.00 |
| **ACCORD** | | | |
| ❑ SN-7138 | Spiritual Jubilee | 198? | 10.00 |
| ❑ SN-7159 | Spiritual Jubilee — Volume 2 | 198? | 10.00 |
| ❑ SN-7199 | Spiritual Jubilee — Volume 3 | 198? | 10.00 |
| **CADENCE** | | | |
| ❑ CLP-3019 [M] | The Oak Ridge Quartet | 1958 | 60.00 |
| **CANAAN** | | | |
| ❑ 9625 | Together | 1966 | 20.00 |
| *—With the Harvesters* | | | |
| **COLUMBIA** | | | |
| ❑ KC 32742 | The Oak Ridge Boys | 1974 | 12.00 |
| ❑ PC 32742 | The Oak Ridge Boys | 197? | 8.00 |
| *—Reissue* | | | |
| ❑ KC 33057 | Sky High | 1975 | 12.00 |
| ❑ PC 33057 | Sky High | 197? | 8.00 |
| *—Reissue* | | | |
| ❑ KC 33935 | Old Fashioned, Down Home, Hand Clappin', Foot Stompin', Southern Style, Gospel Quartet Music | 1976 | 12.00 |
| ❑ PC 35202 | The Best of the Oak Ridge Boys | 1978 | 10.00 |
| ❑ PC 37711 | Old Fashoned Gospel Quartet Music | 1984 | 8.00 |
| ❑ FC 37737 | All Our Favorite Songs | 1981 | 10.00 |
| ❑ PC 38467 | Smoky Mountain Gospel | 1984 | 8.00 |
| **HEARTWARMING** | | | |
| ❑ HWS 3036 | Thanks | 1971 | 15.00 |
| ❑ HWS 3091 | International | 1971 | 15.00 |
| ❑ HWS 3159 | The Light | 1972 | 15.00 |
| **INTERMEDIA** | | | |
| ❑ QS-5012 | Glory Train | 198? | 10.00 |
| **LIBERTY** | | | |
| ❑ LN-10046 | The Oak Ridge Boys at Their Best | 1981 | 8.00 |
| **MCA** | | | |
| ❑ AA-1135 | Have Arrived | 1979 | 10.00 |
| ❑ L33-2-1276 [(2)DJ] | "Step On Out" World Premiere | 1985 | 25.00 |
| *—Promo-only interview and music LP with no script or cover* | | | |
| ❑ 1446 | Deliver | 1985 | 8.00 |
| *—Budget-line reissue* | | | |
| ❑ 1447 | American Made | 1985 | 8.00 |
| *—Budget-line reissue* | | | |
| ❑ 3220 | Together | 1980 | 10.00 |
| ❑ 5150 | Greatest Hits | 1980 | 10.00 |
| ❑ 5209 | Fancy Free | 1981 | 10.00 |
| ❑ 5294 | Bobbie Sue | 1982 | 10.00 |
| ❑ 5365 | Christmas | 1982 | 10.00 |
| ❑ 5390 | American Made | 1983 | 10.00 |
| ❑ 5455 | Deliver | 1983 | 10.00 |
| ❑ 5496 | Greatest Hits 2 | 1984 | 10.00 |
| ❑ 5555 | Step On Out | 1985 | 10.00 |
| ❑ 5714 | Seasons | 1986 | 10.00 |
| ❑ 5799 | Christmas Again | 1986 | 10.00 |
| ❑ 5945 | Where the Fast Lane Ends | 1987 | 10.00 |
| ❑ 37153 | Room Service | 198? | 8.00 |
| *—Budget-line reissue* | | | |
| ❑ 37221 | Have Arrived | 1984 | 8.00 |
| *—Budget-line reissue* | | | |
| ❑ 37222 | Y'all Come Back Saloon | 1984 | 8.00 |
| *—Budget-line reissue* | | | |
| ❑ 37223 | Together | 1984 | 8.00 |
| *—Budget-line reissue* | | | |
| ❑ 42036 | Heartbeat | 1987 | 10.00 |
| ❑ 42205 | Monongahela | 1988 | 10.00 |
| ❑ 42311 | American Dreams | 1989 | 10.00 |
| **NASHVILLE** | | | |
| ❑ 2086 | Higher Power | 1970 | 15.00 |
| **POWER PAK** | | | |
| ❑ 716 | The Oak Ridge Boys | 197? | 10.00 |
| **PRIORITY** | | | |
| ❑ PU 37711 | Old Fashoned Gospel Quartet Music | 1981 | 10.00 |
| ❑ PU 38467 | Smoky Mountain Gospel | 1983 | 10.00 |
| **RCA** | | | |
| ❑ R 164223 | Unstoppable | 1991 | 15.00 |
| *—Only released on vinyl through BMG Direct Marketing* | | | |
| **SKYLITE** | | | |
| ❑ RLP-6020 [M] | The Oak Ridge Boys Sing for You | 1964 | 20.00 |
| ❑ SRLP-6020 [S] | The Oak Ridge Boys Sing for You | 1964 | 25.00 |

Number | Title (A Side/B Side) | Yr | NM

❑ RLP-6030 [M] I Wouldn't Take Nothing for My Journey Now 1965 20.00
❑ SRLP-6030 [S] I Wouldn't Take Nothing for My Journey Now 1965 25.00
❑ RLP-6040 [M] The Solid Gospel Sound of the Oak Ridge Boys 1966 20.00
❑ SRLP-6040 [S] The Solid Gospel Sound of the Oak Ridge Boys 1966 25.00
❑ RLP-6045 [M] River of Love 1967 20.00
❑ SRLP-6045 [S] River of Love 1967 25.00

### STARDAY
❑ SLP-356 [M] The Sensational Oak Ridge Boys 1965 25.00

### UNITED ARTISTS
❑ UAL 3554 [M] The Oak Ridge Boys at Their Best 1966 20.00
❑ UAS 6554 [S] The Oak Ridge Boys at Their Best 1966 25.00
❑ LN-10046 The Oak Ridge Boys at Their Best 1979 10.00

### WARNER BROS.
❑ W 1497 [M] With Sounds of Nashville 1963 20.00
❑ WS 1497 [S] With Sounds of Nashville 1963 25.00
❑ W 1521 [M] Folk-Minded Spirituals for Spiritual-Minded Folks 1963 20.00
❑ WS 1521 [S] Folk-Minded Spirituals for Spiritual-Minded Folks 1963 25.00

## OASIS

### EPIC
❑ E 94493 Don't Believe the Truth 2005 20.00

### HELTER SKELTER
❑ 88697-00754-1 [(3)]Stop the Clocks 2006 50.00
*—Pressed in Europe but imported by Sony BMG for U.S. distribution*

## OBERNKIRCHEN CHILDREN'S CHOIR

### ANGEL
❑ ANG.65021 [M]Christmas Songs 1955 20.00

## OBOLER, ARCH

### CAPITOL
❑ ST 1763 [S] Drop Dead! An Exercise in Horror 1962 30.00
❑ T 1763 [M] Drop Dead! An Exercise in Horror 1962 25.00

## OCHS, PHIL

### A&M
❑ LP-133 [M] Pleasures of the Harbor 1967 25.00
❑ SP-3125 Phil Ochs Greatest Hits 198? 8.00
*—Budget-line reissue*
❑ SP-4133 [S] Pleasures of the Harbor 1967 20.00
❑ SP-4148 [S] Tape from California 1968 20.00
❑ SP-4181 Rehearsals for Retirement 1969 20.00
❑ SP-4253 Phil Ochs Greatest Hits 1970 20.00
❑ SP-4599 [(2)] Chords of Fame 1974 25.00
*—Original edition*
❑ SP-6511 [(2)] Chords of Fame 1976 15.00
*—Reissue of 4599*

### CARTHAGE
❑ CGLP-4422 I Ain't Marching Anymore 198? 10.00
❑ CGLP-4427 All the News That's Fit to Sing 198? 10.00

### ELEKTRA
❑ EKL-269 [M] All the News That's Fit to Sing 1964 30.00
*—Gold label with "guitar player" logo*
❑ EKL-269 [M] All the News That's Fit to Sing 1966 20.00
*—Gold label with stylized "E" logo*
❑ EKL-287 [M] I Ain't Marching Anymore 1965 30.00
*—Gold label with "guitar player" logo*
❑ EKL-287 [M] I Ain't Marching Anymore 1966 20.00
*—Gold label with stylized "E" logo*
❑ EKL-310 [M] Phil Ochs in Concert 1966 20.00
❑ EKS-7269 [S] All the News That's Fit to Sing 1964 40.00
*—Gold label with "guitar player" logo*
❑ EKS-7269 [S] All the News That's Fit to Sing 1966 25.00
*—Gold label with stylized "E" logo*
❑ EKS-7287 [S] I Ain't Marching Anymore 1965 40.00
*—Gold label with "guitar player" logo*
❑ EKS-7287 [S] I Ain't Marching Anymore 1966 25.00
*—Gold label with stylized "E" logo*
❑ EKS-7287 [S] I Ain't Marching Anymore 1975 12.00
*—Butterfly label with small Warner Communications logo*
❑ EKS-7310 [S] Phil Ochs in Concert 1966 25.00

### FOLKWAYS
❑ FB-5320 Phil Ochs Sings Songs for Broadside (#10) 1976 12.00
❑ FB-5321 Phil Ochs Interviews 197? 12.00
❑ FD-5362 Broadside Tapes 1 (#14) 1979 12.00

### PICKWICK
❑ SPC-3707 Rehearsals for Retirement 197? 10.00

### RHINO
❑ RNLP-70080 A Toast to Those Who Are Gone 1986 10.00

Number | Title (A Side/B Side) | Yr | NM

### SMITHSONIAN/FOLKWAYS
❑ SF-40008 Broadside Tapes 1 (#14) 1989 12.00

## OCTOBER COUNTRY

### EPIC
❑ BN 26381 October Country 1968 20.00

## ODA

### LOUD
❑ A 0011 Oda 1973 200.00

## ODETTA

### ALCAZAR
❑ ALC-104 Christmas Spirituals 198? 10.00

### EVEREST ARCHIVE OF FOLK & JAZZ
❑ 273 Odetta 1973 12.00

### FANTASY
❑ 3-15 [10] Odetta and Larry 1955 50.00
❑ OBC-509 Odetta and the Blues 198? 10.00
*—Reissue of Riverside LP*
❑ F-3252 [M] Odetta and Larry 1957 50.00
*—Dark red vinyl*
❑ F-3252 [M] Odetta and Larry 1958 30.00
❑ F-8345 Odetta and Larry 1963 12.00
*—Reissue of 3252*

### RCA VICTOR
❑ LPM-2573 [M] Sometimes I Feel Like Crying 1962 20.00
❑ LSP-2573 [S] Sometimes I Feel Like Crying 1962 25.00
❑ LPM-2643 [M] Odetta Sings Folk Songs 1963 20.00
❑ LSP-2643 [S] Odetta Sings Folk Songs 1963 25.00
❑ LPM-2792 [M] It's a Mighty World 1964 15.00
❑ LSP-2792 [S] It's a Mighty World 1964 20.00
❑ LPM-2923 [M] Odetta Sings of Many Things 1964 15.00
❑ LSP-2923 [S] Odetta Sings of Many Things 1964 20.00
❑ LPM-3324 [M] Odetta Sings Dylan 1965 15.00
❑ LSP-3324 [S] Odetta Sings Dylan 1965 20.00
❑ LPM-3457 [M] Odetta in Japan 1965 15.00
❑ LSP-3457 [S] Odetta in Japan 1965 20.00

### RIVERSIDE
❑ RLP-417 [M] Odetta and the Blues 1962 25.00
❑ RS-9417 [S] Odetta and the Blues 1962 30.00

### ROSE QUARTZ
❑ RQ-101 Movin' It On 1987 10.00

### TRADITION
❑ TRP-1010 [M] Odetta Sings Ballads and Blues 1957 30.00
❑ TRP-1025 [M] Odetta at the Gate of Horn 1958 30.00
❑ TRP-1052 [M] The Best of Odetta 1967 20.00
❑ TRS-2052 [R] The Best of Odetta 1967 15.00

### VANGUARD
❑ VSD-43/44 [(2)]Essential Odetta 1973 15.00
❑ VSD-2046 [S] My Eyes Have Seen 1960 25.00
❑ VSD-2057 [S] Ballads for Americans 1960 25.00
❑ VSD-2072 [S] Odetta at Carnegie Hall 1961 25.00
❑ VSD-2079 [S] Christmas Spirituals 1961 25.00
❑ VSD-2109 [S] Odetta at Town Hall 1962 25.00
❑ VSD-2153 [S] One Grain of Sand 1963 25.00
❑ VRS-3003 [M] Odetta at Carnegie Hall 1967 15.00
❑ VRS-9059 [M] My Eyes Have Seen 1960 20.00
❑ VRS-9066 [M] Ballads for Americans 1960 20.00
❑ VRS-9076 [M] Odetta at Carnegie Hall 1961 20.00
❑ VRS-9079 [M] Christmas Spirituals 1961 20.00
❑ VRS-9103 [M] Odetta at Town Hall 1962 20.00
❑ VRS-9137 [M] One Grain of Sand 1963 20.00
❑ VSD-73003 [S] Odetta at Carnegie Hall 1967 20.00

## OFF BROADWAY USA

### ATLANTIC
❑ SD 19263 On 1980 20.00
❑ SD 19287 Quick Turns 1981 15.00

## OFFSPRING, THE

### COLUMBIA
❑ C 61419 Conspiracy of One 2000 12.00
❑ C 67810 Ixnay on the Hombre 1997 12.00
❑ C 69661 Americana 1998 12.00
❑ C 89026 Splinter 2003 12.00

### EPITAPH
❑ 86424 Ignition 1992 10.00
❑ 86432 Smash 1994 10.00

### NEMESIS
❑ 6 The Offspring 1989 100.00
*—Original issue, 5,000 copies pressed*

### NITRO
❑ 86460 The Offspring 1995 10.00
*—Reissue of Nemesis LP*

## OGERMAN, CLAUS

### RCA VICTOR
❑ LPM-3366 [M] Soul Searchin' 1965 20.00
❑ LSP-3366 [S] Soul Searchin' 1965 25.00
❑ LPM-3455 [M] Watusi Trumpets 1965 20.00
❑ LSP-3455 [S] Watusi Trumpets 1965 25.00
❑ LPM-3640 [M] Saxes Mexicano 1966 20.00
❑ LSP-3640 [S] Saxes Mexicano 1966 25.00

Number | Title (A Side/B Side) | Yr | NM

### UNITED ARTISTS
❑ UAL-3206 [M] Sing Along in German 1962 20.00
❑ UAS-6206 [S] Sing Along in German 1962 25.00

## OHIO EXPRESS, THE

### BUDDAH
❑ BDM 1018 [M] The Ohio Express 1968 40.00
*—Stereo cover with "mono" sticker attached; white label promo*
❑ BDS 5018 [S] The Ohio Express 1968 20.00
❑ BDS 5026 Chewy, Chewy 1969 20.00
❑ BDS 5037 Mercy 1969 20.00
❑ BDS 5058 The Very Best of the Ohio Express 1970 20.00

### CAMEO
❑ C 20000 [M] Beg, Borrow and Steal 1967 30.00
❑ CS 20000 [S] Beg, Borrow and Steal 1967 40.00

## OHIO PLAYERS, THE

### ACCORD
❑ SN-7102 Young and Ready 1981 8.00

### ARISTA
❑ AB 4226 Everybody Up 1979 8.00

### BOARDWALK
❑ FW 37090 Tenderness 1981 8.00

### CAPITOL
❑ ST-192 Observations in Time 1969 50.00
❑ ST-11291 The Ohio Players 1974 12.00
*—Reissue of 192*

### MERCURY
❑ SRM-1-705 Skin Tight 1974 10.00
*—Chicago skyline label*
❑ SRM-1-705 Skin Tight 1974 12.00
*—Red label*
❑ SRM-1-1013 Fire 1974 10.00
❑ SRM-1-1038 Honey 1975 10.00
❑ SRM-1-1088 Contradiction 1976 10.00
❑ SRM-1-1122 Ohio Players Gold 1976 10.00
❑ SRM-1-3701 Angel 1977 10.00
❑ SRM-1-3707 Mr. Mean 1977 10.00
❑ SRM-1-3730 Jass-Ay-Lay-Dee 1978 10.00
❑ 824461-1 Ohio Players Gold 198? 8.00
*—Reissue of 1122*

### TRACK
❑ TRK 58810 Back 1988 10.00

### TRIP
❑ 8029 First Impression 1972 12.00

### UNITED ARTISTS
❑ UA-LA502-E The Very Best of The Ohio Players 1975 12.00

### WESTBOUND
❑ 211 Rattlesnake 1975 12.00
❑ 219 Pain 1976 12.00
*—Reissue of 2015*
❑ 220 Pleasure 1976 12.00
*—Reissue of 2017*
❑ 222 Ecstasy 1976 12.00
*—Reissue of 2021*
❑ 304 The Best of the Early Years 1977 15.00
❑ 1003 Climax 1974 15.00
❑ 1005 Ohio Players Greatest Hits 1975 15.00
❑ 2015 Pain 1972 20.00
❑ 2017 Pleasure 1973 20.00
❑ 2021 Ecstasy 1973 20.00

## OINGO BOINGO

### A&M
❑ SP-3250 Only a Lad 1984 8.00
*—Reissue of 4863*
❑ SP-3251 Nothing to Fear 1984 8.00
*—Reissue of 4930*
❑ SP-3252 Good for Your Soul 1984 8.00
*—Reissue of 4959*
❑ SP-4863 Only a Lad 1981 10.00
❑ SP-4903 Nothing to Fear 1982 10.00
❑ SP-4959 Good for Your Soul 1983 10.00
❑ SP-5217 Skeletons in the Closet 1988 10.00

### I.R.S.
❑ SP-70400 Oingo Boingo 1980 12.00
*—Limited edition 12" version*
❑ SP-70400 [10] Oingo Boingo 1980 12.00
*—Four-song 10-inch EP*

### MCA
❑ 5665 Dead Man's Party 1985 10.00
❑ 5811 BOI-NGO 1987 10.00
❑ 6365 Dark at the End of the Tunnel 1990 10.00
❑ 8030 [(2)] Boingo Alive 1988 12.00
❑ L33-18137 [DJ]Dark at the End of the Tunnel 1990 40.00
*—Promo-only picture disc*

## OLA AND THE JANGLERS

### GNP CRESCENDO
❑ GNPS-2050 Let's Dance/What a Way to Die 1969 20.00

## OLAY, RUTH

### ABC
❑ ABC-573 [M] Soul In the Night 1966 20.00
❑ ABCS-573 [S] Soul In the Night 1966 25.00

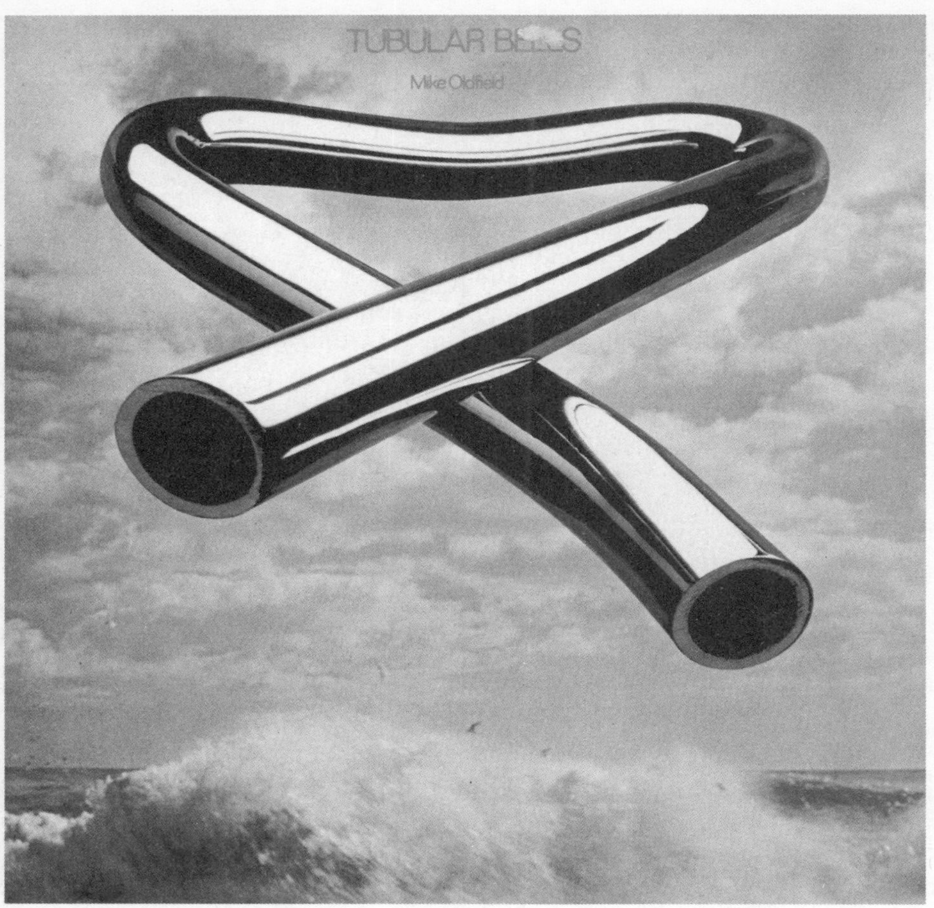


Mike Oldfield, *Tubular Bells,* Virgin VR 13-105, 1973, $15.

| Number | Title (A Side/B Side) | Yr | NM |
|---|---|---|---|
| EMARCY | | | |
| ❑ MG-36125 [M] | Olay! The New Sound Of Ruth Olay | 1958 | 50.00 |
| EVEREST | | | |
| ❑ SDBR-1218 [S] | Olay! OK | 1963 | 30.00 |
| ❑ LPBR-5218 [M] | Olay! OK | 1963 | 25.00 |
| MERCURY | | | |
| ❑ MG-20390 [M] | Easy Living | 1959 | 40.00 |
| ❑ SR-60069 [S] | Easy Living | 1959 | 50.00 |
| UNITED ARTISTS | | | |
| ❑ UAL-3115 [M] | Ruth Olay In Person | 1960 | 30.00 |
| ❑ UAS-4115 [S] | Ruth Olay In Person | 1960 | 40.00 |

**OLD & IN THE WAY**

| Number | Title (A Side/B Side) | Yr | NM |
|---|---|---|---|
| ROUND | | | |
| ❑ RX-103 | Old & In the Way | 1975 | 25.00 |
| SUGAR HILL | | | |
| ❑ SH-3746 | Old & In the Way | 1987 | 10.00 |
| *—Reissue of Round LP* | | | |

**OLDFIELD, MIKE**

| Number | Title (A Side/B Side) | Yr | NM |
|---|---|---|---|
| VIRGIN | | | |
| ❑ QD 13-105 [Q] | Tubular Bells | 1974 | 25.00 |
| ❑ VR 13-105 | Tubular Bells | 1973 | 15.00 |
| *—First stereo issue of this album* | | | |
| ❑ VR 13-109 | Hergest Ridge | 1974 | 12.00 |
| *—First issue of this album* | | | |
| ❑ VR 13-109 [DJ] | Hergest Ridge | 1974 | 20.00 |
| *—Promo only; banded for airplay* | | | |
| ❑ VR 13-115 | The Orchestral Tubular Bells | 1975 | 12.00 |
| ❑ VR 13135 | Tubular Bells | 1979 | 10.00 |
| *—Third stereo issue of this album* | | | |
| ❑ VR 13143 [(2)] | Airborn | 1980 | 15.00 |
| *—U.S.-only compilation, which may make it much more valuable overseas* | | | |
| ❑ PZ 33913 | Ommadawn | 1975 | 12.00 |
| *—Original U.S. issue of this album* | | | |
| ❑ PZ 33913 [DJ] | Ommadawn | 1975 | 20.00 |
| *—Promo only; banded for airplay* | | | |
| ❑ PZQ 33913 [Q] | Ommadawn | 1975 | 20.00 |
| ❑ PZ 34116 | Tubular Bells | 1976 | 12.00 |
| *—Second stereo issue of this album (note the "PZ" prefix)* | | | |
| ❑ 90589 | Tubular Bells | 1987 | 8.00 |
| *—Fifth stereo issue of this album* | | | |
| ❑ 90590 | Hergest Ridge | 1987 | 8.00 |
| *—Reissue of Virgin International 2013* | | | |
| ❑ 90591 | The Killing Fields | 1987 | 10.00 |
| ❑ 90645 | Islands | 1988 | 10.00 |
| ❑ 90894 | The Orchestral Tubular Bells | 1989 | 10.00 |
| *—Reissue of 13-115* | | | |
| ❑ 91270 | Earth Moving | 1990 | 12.00 |
| VIRGIN INTERNATIONAL | | | |
| ❑ VI-2013 | Hergest Ridge | 1979 | 10.00 |
| *—Reissue of 13-109; not to be confused with UK pressings that have only a "V" prefix* | | | |
| ❑ VI-2043 | Ommadawn | 1979 | 10.00 |
| *—Reissue of 33913; not to be confused with UK pressings that have only a "V" prefix* | | | |
| VIRGIN/EPIC | | | |
| ❑ PE 34116 | Tubular Bells | 1982 | 8.00 |
| *—Fourth stereo issue of this album (note the "PE" prefix)* | | | |
| ❑ FE 37358 | QE2 | 1981 | 10.00 |
| ❑ ARE 37983 | Five Miles Out | 1982 | 10.00 |
| ❑ HE 44116 | Tubular Bells | 1982 | 30.00 |
| *—Half-speed mastered edition* | | | |

**OLDHAM, ANDREW**

| Number | Title (A Side/B Side) | Yr | NM |
|---|---|---|---|
| LONDON | | | |
| ❑ PS 457 [S] | The Rolling Stones Songbook | 1965 | 150.00 |
| ❑ LL 3457 [M] | The Rolling Stones Songbook | 1965 | 100.00 |
| PARROT | | | |
| ❑ PA 61003 [M] | East Meets West | 1965 | 80.00 |
| ❑ PAS 71003 [S] | East Meets West | 1965 | 100.00 |

**OLENN, JOHNNY**

| Number | Title (A Side/B Side) | Yr | NM |
|---|---|---|---|
| LIBERTY | | | |
| ❑ LRP-3029 [M] | Just Rollin' with Johnny Olenn | 1956 | 300.00 |

**OLIPHANT, GRASELLA**

| Number | Title (A Side/B Side) | Yr | NM |
|---|---|---|---|
| ATLANTIC | | | |
| ❑ SD-1438 [S] | The Grass Roots | 1965 | 20.00 |

**OLIVA, TONY**

| Number | Title (A Side/B Side) | Yr | NM |
|---|---|---|---|
| KUBANY | | | |
| ❑ SD-600 | My Favorite Music | 1966 | 30.00 |

**OLIVER, JIMMY**

| Number | Title (A Side/B Side) | Yr | NM |
|---|---|---|---|
| SUE | | | |
| ❑ LP-1041 [M] | Hits A-Go-Go | 1966 | 20.00 |
| ❑ STLP-1041 [S] | Hits A-Go-Go | 1966 | 25.00 |

**OLIVER, KING**

| Number | Title (A Side/B Side) | Yr | NM |
|---|---|---|---|
| BRUNSWICK | | | |
| ❑ BL 58020 [10] | King Oliver | 1950 | 120.00 |
| EPIC | | | |
| ❑ LN 3208 [M] | King Oliver Featuring Louis Armstrong | 1956 | 50.00 |
| ❑ LA 16003 [M] | King Oliver and His Orchestra | 1960 | 30.00 |
| ❑ BA 17003 [R] | King Oliver and His Orchestra | 1960 | 20.00 |
| LONDON | | | |
| ❑ AL 3510 [10] | King Oliver Plays the Blues | 195? | 80.00 |
| RCA VICTOR | | | |
| ❑ LPV-529 [M] | King Oliver In New York | 1965 | 25.00 |
| RIVERSIDE | | | |
| ❑ RLP-1007 [10] | King Oliver Plays the Blues | 1953 | 80.00 |
| "X" | | | |
| ❑ LVA-3018 [10] | King Oliver's Uptown Jazz | 1954 | 100.00 |

**OLIVER, SY**

| Number | Title (A Side/B Side) | Yr | NM |
|---|---|---|---|
| MOBILE FIDELITY | | | |
| ❑ 1-242 [(2)] | Oliver's Twist/Easy Walkin' | 1996 | 30.00 |
| *—Audiophile vinyl* | | | |

**OLIVER AND THE TWISTERS**

| Number | Title (A Side/B Side) | Yr | NM |
|---|---|---|---|
| COLPIX | | | |
| ❑ CP-423 [M] | Look Who's Twistin' Everybody | 1961 | 40.00 |

**OLLIE AND THE NIGHTINGALES**

| Number | Title (A Side/B Side) | Yr | NM |
|---|---|---|---|
| STAX | | | |
| ❑ STS-2021 | Ollie and the Nightingales | 1969 | 50.00 |

**OLSEN, DOROTHY**

| Number | Title (A Side/B Side) | Yr | NM |
|---|---|---|---|
| RCA VICTOR | | | |
| ❑ LPM-1606 [M] | I Know Where I'm Going | 1957 | 30.00 |

**OLSEN, GEORGE**

| Number | Title (A Side/B Side) | Yr | NM |
|---|---|---|---|
| RCA VICTOR | | | |
| ❑ LPV-549 [M] | George Olsen and His Music | 1968 | 20.00 |

**OLSHER, LESLEY**

| Number | Title (A Side/B Side) | Yr | NM |
|---|---|---|---|
| VITAL | | | |
| ❑ VTL-011 | Lesley | 1993 | 20.00 |

**OLSSON, NIGEL**

| Number | Title (A Side/B Side) | Yr | NM |
|---|---|---|---|
| BANG | | | |
| ❑ JZ 35792 | Nigel | 1979 | 10.00 |
| ❑ JZ 36491 | Changing Tides | 1980 | 10.00 |
| ROCKET | | | |
| ❑ L33-1962 [DJ] | Drummers Can Sing Too! | 1975 | 20.00 |
| *—Promo-only interview album* | | | |
| ❑ PIG-2158 | Nigel Olsson | 1975 | 12.00 |
| UNI | | | |
| ❑ 73113 | Nigel Olsson's Drum Orchestra | 1971 | 15.00 |

**OLYMPICS, THE**

| Number | Title (A Side/B Side) | Yr | NM |
|---|---|---|---|
| ARVEE | | | |
| ❑ A-423 [M] | Doin' the Hully Gully | 1960 | 160.00 |
| ❑ A-424 [M] | Dance by the Light of the Moon | 1961 | 120.00 |
| ❑ A-429 [M] | Party Time | 1961 | 120.00 |
| EVEREST | | | |
| ❑ 4109 | The Olympics | 1981 | 10.00 |
| MIRWOOD | | | |
| ❑ MS-7003 [S] | Something Old, Something New | 1966 | 50.00 |
| ❑ MW-7003 [M] | Something Old, Something New | 1966 | 40.00 |
| POST | | | |
| ❑ 8000 | The Olympics Sing | 196? | 25.00 |
| RHINO | | | |
| ❑ RNDF-207 | The Official Record Album of the Olympics | 1983 | 12.00 |
| TRI-DISC | | | |
| ❑ 1001 [M] | Do the Bounce | 1963 | 80.00 |

**OMNIBUS**

| Number | Title (A Side/B Side) | Yr | NM |
|---|---|---|---|
| UNITED ARTISTS | | | |
| ❑ UAS-6743 | Omnibus | 1970 | 40.00 |

**ONE**

| Number | Title (A Side/B Side) | Yr | NM |
|---|---|---|---|
| VILLAGE | | | |
| ❑ (# unknown) | Creation Earth | 1977 | 50.00 |
| *—Includes posters* | | | |

**ONENESS OF JUJU**

| Number | Title (A Side/B Side) | Yr | NM |
|---|---|---|---|
| BLACK FIRE | | | |
| ❑ (# unknown) | African Rhythms | 1975 | 60.00 |
| ❑ (# unknown) | Space Jungle Luv | 1976 | 60.00 |
| STRATA-EAST | | | |
| ❑ SES-7420 | Chapter 2: Nia | 1974 | 100.00 |
| *—As "Juju"* | | | |
| ❑ SES-19735 | A Message from Mozambique | 1973 | 100.00 |
| *—As "Juju"* | | | |



**Except when noted otherwise, VG = 25% of NM, and VG+ = 50% of NM. (Example: VG = $2.00, VG+ = $4.00 and NM = $8.00.)**

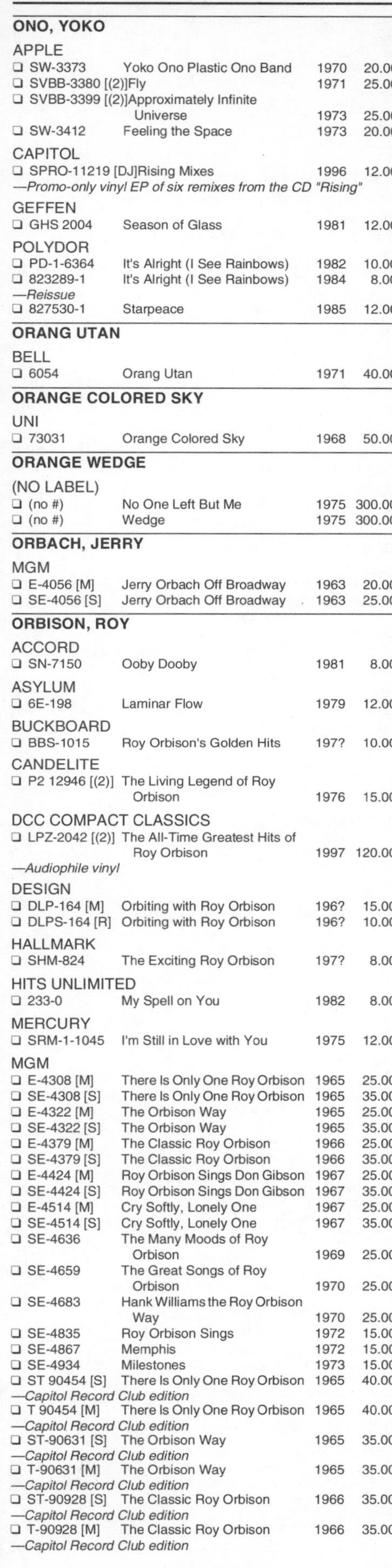

| Number | Title (A Side/B Side) | Yr | NM |
|---|---|---|---|
| **ONO, YOKO** | | | |
| APPLE | | | |
| ❑ SW-3373 | Yoko Ono Plastic Ono Band | 1970 | 20.00 |
| ❑ SVBB-3380 [(2)] | Fly | 1971 | 25.00 |
| ❑ SVBB-3399 [(2)] | Approximately Infinite Universe | 1973 | 25.00 |
| ❑ SW-3412 | Feeling the Space | 1973 | 20.00 |
| CAPITOL | | | |
| ❑ SPRO-11219 [DJ] | Rising Mixes | 1996 | 12.00 |
| *—Promo-only vinyl EP of six remixes from the CD "Rising"* | | | |
| GEFFEN | | | |
| ❑ GHS 2004 | Season of Glass | 1981 | 12.00 |
| POLYDOR | | | |
| ❑ PD-1-6364 | It's Alright (I See Rainbows) | 1982 | 10.00 |
| ❑ 823289-1 | It's Alright (I See Rainbows) | 1984 | 8.00 |
| *—Reissue* | | | |
| ❑ 827530-1 | Starpeace | 1985 | 12.00 |
| **ORANG UTAN** | | | |
| BELL | | | |
| ❑ 6054 | Orang Utan | 1971 | 40.00 |
| **ORANGE COLORED SKY** | | | |
| UNI | | | |
| ❑ 73031 | Orange Colored Sky | 1968 | 50.00 |
| **ORANGE WEDGE** | | | |
| (NO LABEL) | | | |
| ❑ (no #) | No One Left But Me | 1975 | 300.00 |
| ❑ (no #) | Wedge | 1975 | 300.00 |
| **ORBACH, JERRY** | | | |
| MGM | | | |
| ❑ E-4056 [M] | Jerry Orbach Off Broadway | 1963 | 20.00 |
| ❑ SE-4056 [S] | Jerry Orbach Off Broadway | 1963 | 25.00 |
| **ORBISON, ROY** | | | |
| ACCORD | | | |
| ❑ SN-7150 | Ooby Dooby | 1981 | 8.00 |
| ASYLUM | | | |
| ❑ 6E-198 | Laminar Flow | 1979 | 12.00 |
| BUCKBOARD | | | |
| ❑ BBS-1015 | Roy Orbison's Golden Hits | 197? | 10.00 |
| CANDELITE | | | |
| ❑ P2 12946 [(2)] | The Living Legend of Roy Orbison | 1976 | 15.00 |
| DCC COMPACT CLASSICS | | | |
| ❑ LPZ-2042 [(2)] | The All-Time Greatest Hits of Roy Orbison | 1997 | 120.00 |
| *—Audiophile vinyl* | | | |
| DESIGN | | | |
| ❑ DLP-164 [M] | Orbiting with Roy Orbison | 196? | 15.00 |
| ❑ DLPS-164 [R] | Orbiting with Roy Orbison | 196? | 10.00 |
| HALLMARK | | | |
| ❑ SHM-824 | The Exciting Roy Orbison | 197? | 8.00 |
| HITS UNLIMITED | | | |
| ❑ 233-0 | My Spell on You | 1982 | 8.00 |
| MERCURY | | | |
| ❑ SRM-1-1045 | I'm Still in Love with You | 1975 | 12.00 |
| MGM | | | |
| ❑ E-4308 [M] | There Is Only One Roy Orbison | 1965 | 25.00 |
| ❑ SE-4308 [S] | There Is Only One Roy Orbison | 1965 | 35.00 |
| ❑ E-4322 [M] | The Orbison Way | 1965 | 25.00 |
| ❑ SE-4322 [S] | The Orbison Way | 1965 | 35.00 |
| ❑ E-4379 [M] | The Classic Roy Orbison | 1966 | 25.00 |
| ❑ SE-4379 [S] | The Classic Roy Orbison | 1966 | 35.00 |
| ❑ E-4424 [M] | Roy Orbison Sings Don Gibson | 1967 | 25.00 |
| ❑ SE-4424 [S] | Roy Orbison Sings Don Gibson | 1967 | 35.00 |
| ❑ E-4514 [M] | Cry Softly, Lonely One | 1967 | 25.00 |
| ❑ SE-4514 [S] | Cry Softly, Lonely One | 1967 | 35.00 |
| ❑ SE-4636 | The Many Moods of Roy Orbison | 1969 | 25.00 |
| ❑ SE-4659 | The Great Songs of Roy Orbison | 1970 | 25.00 |
| ❑ SE-4683 | Hank Williams the Roy Orbison Way | 1970 | 25.00 |
| ❑ SE-4835 | Roy Orbison Sings | 1972 | 15.00 |
| ❑ SE-4867 | Memphis | 1972 | 15.00 |
| ❑ SE-4934 | Milestones | 1973 | 15.00 |
| ❑ ST 90454 [S] | There Is Only One Roy Orbison | 1965 | 40.00 |
| *—Capitol Record Club edition* | | | |
| ❑ T 90454 [M] | There Is Only One Roy Orbison | 1965 | 40.00 |
| *—Capitol Record Club edition* | | | |
| ❑ ST-90631 [S] | The Orbison Way | 1965 | 35.00 |
| *—Capitol Record Club edition* | | | |
| ❑ T-90631 [M] | The Orbison Way | 1965 | 35.00 |
| *—Capitol Record Club edition* | | | |
| ❑ ST-90928 [S] | The Classic Roy Orbison | 1966 | 35.00 |
| *—Capitol Record Club edition* | | | |
| ❑ T-90928 [M] | The Classic Roy Orbison | 1966 | 35.00 |
| *—Capitol Record Club edition* | | | |

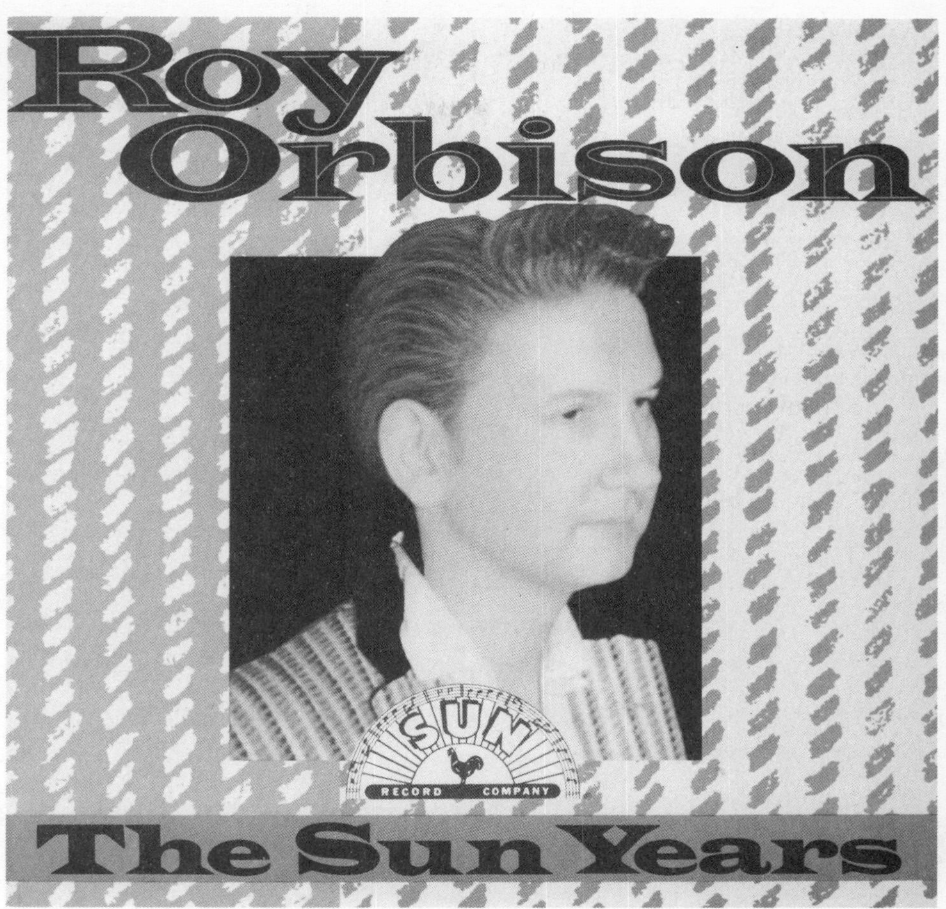


Roy Orbison, *The Sun Years,* Rhino R130965, 1989, BMG Direct Marketing issue, $15.

| Number | Title (A Side/B Side) | Yr | NM |
|---|---|---|---|
| ❑ ST-91173 [S] | Roy Orbison Sings Don Gibson | 1967 | 35.00 |
| *—Capitol Record Club edition* | | | |
| ❑ T-91173 [M] | Roy Orbison Sings Don Gibson | 1967 | 35.00 |
| *—Capitol Record Club edition* | | | |
| MONUMENT | | | |
| ❑ M-4002 [M] | Lonely and Blue | 1961 | 150.00 |
| ❑ M-4007 [M] | Crying | 1962 | 120.00 |
| ❑ M-4009 [M] | Roy Orbison's Greatest Hits | 1962 | 50.00 |
| ❑ MC-6619 | Roy Orbison's Greatest Hits | 1977 | 12.00 |
| ❑ MC-6620 | In Dreams | 1977 | 12.00 |
| ❑ MC-6621 | More of Roy Orbison's Greatest Hits | 1977 | 12.00 |
| ❑ MC-6622 | The Very Best of Roy Orbison | 1977 | 12.00 |
| ❑ MG-7600 | Regeneration | 1976 | 15.00 |
| ❑ MLP-8000 [M] | Roy Orbison's Greatest Hits | 1963 | 30.00 |
| ❑ MLP-8003 [M] | In Dreams | 1963 | 50.00 |
| *—White and rainbow label* | | | |
| ❑ MLP-8003 [M] | In Dreams | 1964 | 30.00 |
| *—Green and gold label* | | | |
| ❑ MLP-8023 [M] | Early Orbison | 1964 | 30.00 |
| ❑ MLP-8024 [M] | More of Roy Orbison's Greatest Hits | 1964 | 30.00 |
| ❑ MLP-8035 [M] | Orbisongs | 1965 | 25.00 |
| ❑ MLP-8045 [M] | The Very Best of Roy Orbison | 1966 | 25.00 |
| ❑ MP-8600 [(2)] | The All-Time Greatest Hits of Roy Orbison | 1977 | 16.00 |
| ❑ SM-14002 [S] | Lonely and Blue | 1961 | 600.00 |
| ❑ SM-14007 [S] | Crying | 1962 | 600.00 |
| ❑ SM-14009 [S] | Roy Orbison's Greatest Hits | 1962 | 80.00 |
| ❑ SLP-18000 [S] | Roy Orbison's Greatest Hits | 1963 | 40.00 |
| ❑ SLP-18003 [S] | In Dreams | 1963 | 100.00 |
| *—White and rainbow label* | | | |
| ❑ SLP-18003 [S] | In Dreams | 1964 | 50.00 |
| *—Green and gold label* | | | |
| ❑ SLP-18023 [S] | Early Orbison | 1964 | 50.00 |
| ❑ SLP-18024 [S] | More of Roy Orbison's Greatest Hits | 1964 | 40.00 |
| ❑ SLP-18035 [S] | Orbisongs | 1965 | 35.00 |
| ❑ SLP-18045 [P] | The Very Best of Roy Orbison | 1966 | 35.00 |
| *—"It's Over" is rechanneled* | | | |
| ❑ KZG 31484 [(2)] | The All-Time Greatest Hits of Roy Orbison | 1972 | 25.00 |
| ❑ KWG 38384 [(2)] | The All-Time Greatest Hits of Roy Orbison | 1982 | 10.00 |
| RHINO | | | |
| ❑ R1 70711 | The Classic Roy Orbison | 1989 | 12.00 |
| ❑ R1 70916 | The Sun Years | 1989 | 15.00 |

| Number | Title (A Side/B Side) | Yr | NM |
|---|---|---|---|
| ❑ R1 71493 [(2)] | For the Lonely: A Roy Orbison Anthology | 1988 | 12.00 |
| S&P | | | |
| ❑ 507 [(2)] | The All-Time Greatest Hits of Roy Orbison | 2004 | 40.00 |
| *—Reissue on 180-gram vinyl* | | | |
| SUN | | | |
| ❑ 113 | The Original Sound | 1969 | 12.00 |
| ❑ LP-1260 [M] | Roy Orbison at the Rock House | 1961 | 600.00 |
| TIME-LIFE | | | |
| ❑ SRNR 34 [(2)] | Roy Orbison 1960-1965 | 1990 | 20.00 |
| *—Box set in "The Rock 'n' Roll Era" series* | | | |
| TRIP | | | |
| ❑ TLX-8505 | The Best of Roy Orbison | 197? | 8.00 |
| VIRGIN | | | |
| ❑ 90604 [(2)] | In Dreams: The Greatest Hits | 1987 | 12.00 |
| *—Re-recordings of his original hits* | | | |
| ❑ 91058 | Mystery Girl | 1989 | 10.00 |
| ❑ 91295 | A Black and White Night | 1990 | 15.00 |
| **ORCHESTRA U.S.A.** | | | |
| COLPIX | | | |
| ❑ CP-448 [M] | Orchestra U.S.A. Debut | 1964 | 40.00 |
| ❑ SCP-448 [S] | Orchestra U.S.A. Debut | 1964 | 50.00 |
| COLUMBIA | | | |
| ❑ CL 2247 [M] | Jazz Journey | 1963 | 25.00 |
| ❑ CS 9047 [S] | Jazz Journey | 1963 | 30.00 |
| RCA VICTOR | | | |
| ❑ LPM-3498 [M] | The Sextet Of Orchestra U.S.A. | 1965 | 20.00 |
| ❑ LSP-3498 [S] | The Sextet Of Orchestra U.S.A. | 1965 | 25.00 |
| **ORCHIDS, THE (U)** | | | |
| ROULETTE | | | |
| ❑ R-25169 [M] | Twistin' at the Roundtable | 1962 | 20.00 |
| ❑ SR-25169 [S] | Twistin' at the Roundtable | 1962 | 25.00 |
| **OREGON** | | | |
| MOBILE FIDELITY | | | |
| ❑ 1-514 | Distant Hills | 198? | 70.00 |
| *—Audiophile vinyl* | | | |
| VANGUARD | | | |
| ❑ VSQ-40031 [Q] | Distant Hills | 1974 | 25.00 |

Number | Title (A Side/B Side) | Yr | NM

**ORGAN GRINDERS, THE**

MERCURY
❑ SR-61282 Out of the Egg 1970 30.00

**ORIENT EXPRESS, THE**

MAINSTREAN
❑ S-6117 The Orient Express 1969 80.00

**ORIGINAL DIXIELAND JAZZ BAND, THE**

RCA VICTOR
❑ LPV-547 [M] The Original Dixieland Jazz Band 1968 20.00

"X"
❑ LX-3007 [M] The Original Dixieland Jazz Band 1954 50.00

**ORIGINAL LAST POETS, THE** See THE LAST POETS.

**ORIGINAL SURFARIS, THE** See THE SURFARIS (2).

**ORIGINAL TWISTERS, THE**

WING
❑ MGW-12217 [M]Come On and Twist 1962 20.00
❑ SRW-16217 [S]Come On and Twist 1962 25.00

**ORIGINAL WASHBOARD BAND, THE**

RCA VICTOR
❑ LPM-1958 [M] Scrubbin' and Pickin' 1959 20.00
❑ LSP-1958 [S] Scrubbin' and Pickin' 1959 25.00

**ORIGINALS, THE (1)**

FANTASY
❑ F-9546 Another Time, Another Place 1978 10.00
❑ F-9577 Come Away with Me 1979 10.00

MOTOWN
❑ M5-110V Motown Superstar Series, Vol. 10 1982 10.00
❑ M7-826 California Sunset 1975 15.00

PHASE II
❑ JW 37075 Yesterday and Today 1981 12.00

SOUL
❑ SS-716 Baby I'm for Real 1969 40.00
❑ SS-724 Portrait of the Originals 1970 25.00
❑ SS-729 Naturally Together 1971 25.00
❑ SS-734 Definitions 1971 20.00
❑ SS-740 The Game Called... 1973 15.00
❑ SS-743 California Sunset 1974 —
*—Unreleased*
❑ S7-746 Communique 1976 15.00
❑ S7-749 Down to Love Town 1977 15.00

**ORIOLES, THE**

BIG A
❑ LP-2001 The Orioles' Greatest All-Time Hits 1969 30.00

CHARLIE PARKER
❑ PLP-816 [M] Modern Sounds of the Orioles 1962 80.00
❑ PLP-816S [S] Modern Sounds of the Orioles 1962 100.00

COLLECTABLES
❑ COL-5014 Sonny Til and the Orioles' Greatest Hits 198? 12.00

MURRAY HILL
❑ M 61234 [(5)] For Collectors Only 1983 40.00

**ORION**

SUN
❑ 1012 Orion Reborn 1978 10.00
*—Blue cover*
❑ 1012 Orion Reborn 1978 30.00
*—White cover, also known as the "coffin cover"*
❑ 1017 Sunrise 1979 10.00
❑ 1019 Orion Country 1980 10.00
❑ 1021 Rockabilly 1981 10.00
❑ 1025 Glory 1982 10.00
❑ 1028 Fresh 1983 10.00

**ORION, P.J., AND THE MAGNATES**

MAGNATE
❑ 122459 P.J. Orion and the Magnates 196? 150.00

**ORION THE HUNTER** With Barry Goudreau, formerly of BOSTON.

PORTRAIT
❑ BFR 39239 Orion the Hunter 1984 20.00

**ORLANDO, TONY**

CASABLANCA
❑ NBLP 7153 I Got Rhythm 1979 10.00
❑ NBLP 7209 Living for the Music 1980 10.00

EPIC
❑ BN 611 [S] Bless You and 11 Other Great Hits 1961 40.00
❑ LN 3808 [M] Bless You and 11 Other Great Hits 1961 30.00

❑ BG 33785 [(2)] Before Dawn 1975 15.00

**ORLONS, THE**

CAMEO
❑ C 1020 [M] The Wah-Watusi 1962 60.00
❑ C 1033 [M] All the Hits by the Orlons 1962 60.00
❑ C 1041 [M] South Street 1963 60.00
❑ C 1054 [M] Not Me 1963 50.00
❑ C 1061 [M] The Orlons' Biggest Hits 1964 50.00
❑ C 1073 [M] Down Memory Lane with the Orlons 1964 50.00

**ORLONS, THE / THE DOVELLS** Also see each artist's individual listings.

CAMEO
❑ C 1067 [M] Golden Hits of the Orlons and the Dovells 1964 50.00

**ORPHAN EGG**

CAROLE
❑ CARS-8004 Orphan Egg 1968 40.00

**ORPHANN**

O.M.I.
❑ 70021 Up for Adoption 1977 100.00

**ORPHEUS**

MGM
❑ E-4524 [M] Orpheus 1968 25.00
❑ SE-4524 [S] Orpheus 1968 20.00
❑ E-4569 [M] Ascending 1968 40.00
*—Known copies are yellow label promos with "DJ Monaural" sticker on stereo cover*
❑ SE-4569 [S] Ascending 1968 20.00
❑ SE-4599 Joyful 1969 20.00

**ORTEGA, ANTHONY**

BETHLEHEM
❑ BCP-79 [M] Jazz For Young Moderns 1957 50.00

HERALD
❑ HLP-0101 [M] A Man and His Horn 1956 60.00

REVELATION
❑ REV-3 [S] New Dance 1968 20.00
❑ REV-M3 [M] New Dance 1968 40.00

VANTAGE
❑ VLP-2 [10] Anthony Ortega 1954 120.00

**ORTEGA, FRANKIE**

IMPERIAL
❑ LP-9025 [M] Piano Stylings 1956 25.00
❑ LP-12011 [S] Piano Stylings 1959 20.00

JUBILEE
❑ JLP-1051 [M] Twinkling Pinkies 1958 25.00
❑ JLP-1080 [M] Swingin' Abroad 1958 20.00
❑ SDJLP-1080 [S]Swingin' Abroad 1958 25.00
❑ JGS-1106 [S] 77 Sunset Strip 1959 40.00
❑ JLP-1106 [M] 77 Sunset Strip 1959 25.00
❑ JGM-1112 [M] Frankie Ortega at the Embers 1960 20.00
❑ JGS-1112 [S] Frankie Ortega at the Embers 1960 25.00

**ORTEGA/DOMANICO/WEST/GOODWIN**

REVELATION
❑ REV-7 [S] Permutations 1969 25.00

**ORY, KID**

COLUMBIA
❑ CL 835 [M] Kid Ory 1955 50.00
❑ CL 6145 [10] Kid Ory & His Creole Dixieland Band 1950 100.00

GOOD TIME JAZZ
❑ L-21 [10] Kid Ory's Creole Jazz Band, 1953 1954 50.00
❑ S-10041/2 [(2)S]Kid Ory's Favorites! 1961 60.00
❑ L-12004 [M] Kid Ory's Creole Jazz Band, 1954 1954 40.00
❑ L-12008 [M] Kid Ory's Creole Jazz Band, 1955 1955 40.00
❑ L-12016 [M] Kid Ory's Creole Jazz Band, 1956 1955 40.00
❑ L-12022 [M] Kid Ory's Creole Jazz Band, 1944-45 1955 40.00
❑ L-12041/2 [(2)M]Kid Ory's Favorites! 1961 50.00
❑ M-12045 [M] This Kid's the Greatest! 1962 30.00

VERVE
❑ MGV-1014 [M] Song of the Wanderer 1957 50.00
❑ V-1014 [M] Song of the Wanderer 1961 20.00
❑ MGV-1016 [M] The Kid From New Orleans 1957 50.00
❑ V-1016 [M] The Kid From New Orleans 1961 20.00
❑ MGV-1017 [M] Kid Ory Plays W.C. Handy 1957 50.00
❑ V-1017 [M] Kid Ory Plays W.C. Handy 1961 20.00
❑ MGV-1022 [M] Dance with Kid Ory or Just Listen 1957 50.00
❑ V-1022 [M] Dance with Kid Ory or Just Listen 1961 20.00
❑ MGV-1023 [M] The Original Jazz 1957 50.00
❑ V-1023 [M] The Original Jazz 1961 20.00
❑ MGV-1026 [M] Dixieland Marching Songs 1957 50.00
❑ V-1026 [M] Dixieland Marching Songs 1961 20.00
❑ MGVS-6011 [S]Song of the Wanderer 1960 40.00
❑ MGVS-6061 [S]Kid Ory Plays W.C. Handy 1960 40.00
❑ MGVS-6125 [S]Dance with Kid Ory or Just Listen 1960 40.00
❑ MGV-8254 [M] Kid Ory In Europe 1958 50.00
❑ V-8254 [M] Kid Ory In Europe 1961 20.00
❑ V-8456 [M] Storyville Nights 1962 25.00
❑ V6-8456 [S] Storyville Nights 1962 20.00

**ORY, KID/JOHNNY WITTWER**

JAZZ MAN
❑ LP-2 [10] Kid Ory's Creole Band/Johnny Wittwer Trio 1954 50.00

**OSBORNE, JIMMIE**

AUDIO LAB
❑ AL-1527 [M] Singing Songs He Wrote 1959 100.00

KING
❑ 730 [M] The Legendary Jimmy Osborne 1961 50.00
❑ 782 [M] Golden Harvest 1963 50.00
❑ 892 [M] The Very Best of Jimmie Osborne 1964 40.00
❑ 941 [M] Jimmie Osborne's Golden Harvest 1965 40.00

**OSBORNE, MARY**

WARWICK
❑ W-2004 [M] A Girl and Her Guitar 1960 100.00
❑ W-2004ST [S] A Girl and Her Guitar 1960 120.00

**OSBORNE BROTHERS, THE**

CMH
❑ 4501 Greatest Bluegrass Hits, Vol. 1 198? 12.00
❑ 6206 #1 197? 12.00
❑ 6231 Bluegrass Concerto 197? 12.00
❑ 6244 Kentucky Calling Me 1980 12.00
❑ 6256 Bobby and His Mandolin 1981 12.00
❑ 9008 [(2)] From Rocky Top to Muddy Bottom 1977 15.00
❑ 9011 [(2)] Bluegrass Collection 1978 15.00
❑ 9016 [(2)] The Essential Bluegrass Album 1979 15.00
*—With MacWiseman*

DECCA
❑ DL 4602 [M] Voices in the Bluegrass 1965 15.00
❑ DL 4767 [M] Up This Hill and Down 1966 15.00
❑ DL 4903 [M] Modern Sounds of Bluegrass Music 1967 15.00
❑ DL 4993 [M] Yesterday, Today and The Osborne Brothers 1968 25.00
❑ DL 74602 [S] Voices in the Bluegrass 1965 20.00
❑ DL 74767 [S] Up This Hill and Down 1966 20.00
❑ DL 74903 [S] Modern Sounds of Bluegrass Music 1967 20.00
❑ DL 74993 [S] Yesterday, Today and The Osborne Brothers 1968 20.00
❑ DL 75079 Favorite Hymns by the Osborne Brothers 1969 20.00
❑ DL 75128 Up to Date and Down to Earth 1969 20.00
❑ DL 75204 Ru-Beeeee 1970 20.00
❑ DL 75271 The Osborne Brothers 1971 15.00
❑ DL 75321 Country Roads 1971 15.00
❑ DL 75356 Bobby & Sonny 1972 15.00

MCA
❑ 105 Voices in the Bluegrass 1973 12.00
*—Reissue of Decca 74602*
❑ 119 Yesterday, Today and The Osborne Brothers 1973 12.00
*—Reissue of Decca 74993*
❑ 125 Favorite Hymns by the Osborne Brothers 1973 12.00
*—Reissue of Decca 75079*
❑ 135 Ru-Beeeee 1973 12.00
*—Reissue of Decca 75204*
❑ 4086 [(2)] The Best of the Osborne Brothers 1974 15.00

MGM
❑ GAS 140 The Osborne Brothers (Golden Archives Series) 1970 20.00
❑ E-3734 [M] Country Pickin' and Hillside Singin' 1959 50.00
❑ E-4018 [M] Bluegrass Music 1962 25.00
❑ SE-4018 [S] Bluegrass Music 1962 30.00
❑ E-4090 [M] Bluegrass Instrumentals 1962 25.00
❑ SE-4090 [S] Bluegrass Instrumentals 1962 30.00
❑ E-4149 [M] Cuttin' Grass 1963 25.00
❑ SE-4149 [S] Cuttin' Grass 1963 30.00

RCA VICTOR
❑ AHL1-4324 Bluegrass Spectacular 1982 10.00
❑ AYL1-5436 Bluegrass Spectacular 1985 8.00
*—"Best Buy Series" reissue*

ROUNDER
❑ SS-03 The Osborne Brothers with Red Allen 1981 12.00
❑ SS-04 The Osborne Brothers 198? 12.00

| Number | Title (A Side/B Side) | Yr | NM |
|---|---|---|---|

SUGAR HILL

| | | | |
|---|---|---|---|
| ❑ SH-3740 | Some Things I Want to Sing About | 1984 | 10.00 |
| ❑ SH-3754 | Once More, Vol. 1 | 1986 | 10.00 |
| ❑ SH-3758 | Once More, Vol. 2 | 1987 | 10.00 |
| ❑ SH-3764 | Singing, Shouting Praises | 1988 | 10.00 |

**OSBOURNE, OZZY**

CBS ASSOCIATED

| | | | |
|---|---|---|---|
| ❑ AS 1828 [DJ] | Interview with Ozzy | 1984 | 30.00 |
| ❑ FZ 38987 | Bark at the Moon | 1983 | 10.00 |
| ❑ PZ 38987 | Bark at the Moon | 1985 | 8.00 |

*—Budget-line reissue with new prefix*

| | | | |
|---|---|---|---|
| ❑ FZ 40026 | The Ultimate Sin | 1986 | 10.00 |
| ❑ 9Z9 40543 [EP] | The Ultimate Live Ozzy | 1986 | 40.00 |

*—Picture disc with live material*

| | | | |
|---|---|---|---|
| ❑ ZX2 40714 | Ozzy Osbourne/Randy Rhoads Tribute | 1987 | 12.00 |
| ❑ FZ 44245 | No Rest for the Wicked | 1988 | 10.00 |
| ❑ Z 46795 | No More Tears | 1991 | 20.00 |

JET

| | | | |
|---|---|---|---|
| ❑ AS99 1372 [PD] | Diary of a Madman | 1981 | 40.00 |

*—Promo-only picture disc*

| | | | |
|---|---|---|---|
| ❑ JZ 36812 | Blizzard of Ozz | 1981 | 10.00 |
| ❑ FZ 37492 | Diary of a Madman | 1981 | 10.00 |
| ❑ 8Z8 37640 [EP] | Mr. Crowley | 1982 | 30.00 |

*—Three-song picture disc with live material*

| | | | |
|---|---|---|---|
| ❑ ZX2 38350 [(2)] | Speak of the Devil | 1982 | 15.00 |

**OSIBISA**

ANTILLES

| | | | |
|---|---|---|---|
| ❑ 7051 | Welcome Home | 1978 | 10.00 |
| ❑ 7058 | Ojah Awake | 1978 | 10.00 |

BUDDAH

| | | | |
|---|---|---|---|
| ❑ BDS-5136 | Super Fly T.N.T. | 1973 | 30.00 |

DECCA

| | | | |
|---|---|---|---|
| ❑ DL 75285 | Osibisa | 1971 | 15.00 |
| ❑ DL 75327 | Woyaya | 1972 | 15.00 |
| ❑ DL 75368 | Heads | 1972 | 15.00 |

ISLAND

| | | | |
|---|---|---|---|
| ❑ ILPS 9355 | Welcome Home | 1976 | 10.00 |
| ❑ ILPS 9411 | Ojah Awake | 1977 | 10.00 |

MCA

| | | | |
|---|---|---|---|
| ❑ 32 | Osibisa | 1973 | 10.00 |

*—Reissue of Decca 75285*

| | | | |
|---|---|---|---|
| ❑ 43 | Woyaya | 1973 | 10.00 |

*—Reissue of Decca 75327*

WARNER BROS.

| | | | |
|---|---|---|---|
| ❑ BS 2732 | Happy Children | 1973 | 10.00 |
| ❑ BS 2802 | Osibirock | 1974 | 10.00 |

**OSIPOV STATE RUSSIAN FOLK ORCHESTRA (VITALY GNUTOV, CONDUCTOR)**

MERCURY LIVING PRESENCE

| | | | |
|---|---|---|---|
| ❑ SR 90310 [S] | Balalaika Favorites | 196? | 30.00 |

*—Third edition: Dark red (not maroon) label*

| | | | |
|---|---|---|---|
| ❑ SR 90310 [S] | Balalaika Favorites | 196? | 50.00 |

*—Maroon label, with "Vendor: Mercury Record Corporation"*

| | | | |
|---|---|---|---|
| ❑ SR 90310 [S] | Balalaika Favorites | 196? | 80.00 |

*—Maroon label, no "Vendor: Mercury Record Corporation"*

| | | | |
|---|---|---|---|
| ❑ SR 90310 [S] | Balalaika Favorites | 1998 | 25.00 |

*—Classic Records reissue*

**OSMONDS, THE** Includes records as "The Osmond Brothers."

ELEKTRA

| | | | |
|---|---|---|---|
| ❑ 60180 | The Osmond Brothers | 1982 | 10.00 |

MERCURY

| | | | |
|---|---|---|---|
| ❑ SRM-1-3766 | Steppin' Out | 1979 | 10.00 |

METRO

| | | | |
|---|---|---|---|
| ❑ M 543 [M] | We Sing You a Merry Christmas | 1965 | 15.00 |

*—Reissue of 4187 with one track missing and remaining contents rearranged*

| | | | |
|---|---|---|---|
| ❑ MS 543 [S] | We Sing You a Merry Christmas | 1965 | 20.00 |

MGM

| | | | |
|---|---|---|---|
| ❑ PM-7 [M] | The Travels of Jaimie McPheeters | 1963 | 50.00 |

*—Side 1: Dialogue from TV show; Side 2: Osmond Brothers tracks. AC Spark Plugs promo.*

| | | | |
|---|---|---|---|
| ❑ PM-9 [M] | We Sing You a Merry Christmas | 1963 | 40.00 |

*—Special-products issue for AC Spark Plug dealers*

| | | | |
|---|---|---|---|
| ❑ E-4146 [M] | Songs We Sang on the Andy Williams Show | 1963 | 25.00 |
| ❑ SE-4146 [S] | Songs We Sang on the Andy Williams Show | 1963 | 30.00 |

*—As "The Osmond Brothers"*

| | | | |
|---|---|---|---|
| ❑ E-4187 [M] | We Sing You a Merry Christmas | 1963 | 25.00 |

*—As "The Osmond Brothers"*

| | | | |
|---|---|---|---|
| ❑ SE-4187 [S] | We Sing You a Merry Christmas | 1963 | 30.00 |
| ❑ E-4235 [M] | The Osmond Brothers Sing the All-Time Hymn Favorites | 1964 | 20.00 |

Ozzy Osbourne, *Blizzard of Ozz,* Jet JZ 36812, 1981, $10.

| Number | Title (A Side/B Side) | Yr | NM |
|---|---|---|---|
| ❑ SE-4235 [S] | The Osmond Brothers Sing the All-Time Hymn Favorites | 1964 | 25.00 |
| ❑ E-4291 [M] | The New Sound of the Osmond Brothers | 1965 | 20.00 |
| ❑ SE-4291 [S] | The New Sound of the Osmond Brothers | 1965 | 25.00 |
| ❑ SE-4724 | Osmonds | 1971 | 12.00 |
| ❑ SE-4770 | Homemade | 1971 | 30.00 |

*—With tear-off poster intact; deduct 60 percent if poster is not attached*

| | | | |
|---|---|---|---|
| ❑ SE-4796 | Phase-III | 1972 | 12.00 |
| ❑ SE-4826 [(2)] | The Osmonds "Live" | 1972 | 15.00 |
| ❑ SE-4851 | Crazy Horses | 1972 | 12.00 |
| ❑ SE-4902 | The Plan | 1973 | 10.00 |
| ❑ M3G-4939 | Love Me for a Reason | 1974 | 10.00 |
| ❑ M3G-4993 | The Proud One | 1975 | 10.00 |
| ❑ MG-2-5012 [(2)] | Around the World — Live in Concert | 1975 | 12.00 |
| ❑ ST 90403 [S] | The New Sound of the Osmond Brothers | 1965 | 40.00 |

*—Capitol Record Club edition*

| | | | |
|---|---|---|---|
| ❑ T 90403 [M] | The New Sound of the Osmond Brothers | 1965 | 40.00 |

*—Capitol Record Club edition*

POLYDOR

| | | | |
|---|---|---|---|
| ❑ PD-1-6077 | Brainstorm | 1976 | 10.00 |
| ❑ PD-2-8001 [(2)] | The Osmond Christmas Album | 1976 | 15.00 |

*—Includes group, solo and duet recordings*

| | | | |
|---|---|---|---|
| ❑ PD-2-9005 | The Osmonds Greatest Hits | 1977 | 12.00 |

WARNER BROS.

| | | | |
|---|---|---|---|
| ❑ 25070 | One Way Rider | 1984 | 8.00 |

**OSTERWALD, HAZY**

BALLY

| | | | |
|---|---|---|---|
| ❑ BAL-12004 [M] | Swiss Jazz | 1956 | 40.00 |

**OSWALD, LEE HARVEY** The below are documentary records, all based on the same radio interview.

EYEWITNESS

| | | | |
|---|---|---|---|
| ❑ 1002 | Lee Harvey Oswald Speaks | 1967 | 80.00 |

INCA

| | | | |
|---|---|---|---|
| ❑ 1001 | Oswald: Self Portrait in Red | 1965 | 100.00 |

KEY

| | | | |
|---|---|---|---|
| ❑ 880 | The President's Assassin Speaks | 1964 | 100.00 |

| Number | Title (A Side/B Side) | Yr | NM |
|---|---|---|---|

**OTHER HALF, THE (1)**

ACTA

| | | | |
|---|---|---|---|
| ❑ 38004 | The Other Half | 1968 | 100.00 |

**OTHER HALF, THE (2)**

7/2

| | | | |
|---|---|---|---|
| ❑ (no #) | The Other Half | 1966 | 1500. |

*—Album has been counterfeited, but those records are translucent when held to a light, originals are not*

**OTIS, JOHNNY**

ALLIGATOR

| | | | |
|---|---|---|---|
| ❑ AL-4726 | The New Johnny Otis Show | 1982 | 10.00 |

CAPITOL

| | | | |
|---|---|---|---|
| ❑ T 940 [M] | The Johnny Otis Show | 1958 | 250.00 |
| ❑ C1-92858 [(2)] | The Capitol Years | 1989 | 15.00 |

DIG

| | | | |
|---|---|---|---|
| ❑ 104 [M] | Rock and Roll Hit Parade, Volume 1 | 1957 | 900.00 |

*—Gold cover with thick cardboard and thick vinyl records. Counterfeits have noticeably thinner vinyl.*

| | | | |
|---|---|---|---|
| ❑ 104 [M] | Rock and Roll Hit Parade, Volume 1 | 1958 | 600.00 |

*—Yellow cover with thick cardboard and thick vinyl records. Counterfeits have noticeably thinner vinyl.*

EPIC

| | | | |
|---|---|---|---|
| ❑ BN 26524 | Cuttin' Up | 1970 | 25.00 |
| ❑ EG 30473 [(2)] | The Johnny Otis Show Live at Monterey | 1971 | 30.00 |

KENT

| | | | |
|---|---|---|---|
| ❑ KST-534 | Cold Shot | 1968 | 25.00 |

SAVOY

| | | | |
|---|---|---|---|
| ❑ SJL-2230 [(2)] | The Original Johnny Otis Show | 1978 | 15.00 |
| ❑ SJL-2252 [(2)] | The Original Johnny Otis Show, Vol. 2 | 1980 | 15.00 |

**OTIS AND CARLA** Also see OTIS REDDING; CARLA THOMAS.

STAX

| | | | |
|---|---|---|---|
| ❑ ST-716 [M] | King and Queen | 1967 | 35.00 |
| ❑ STS-716 [S] | King and Queen | 1967 | 50.00 |

SUNDAZED

| | | | |
|---|---|---|---|
| ❑ LP 5069 [S] | King and Queen | 2001 | 12.00 |

*—Reissue on 180-gram vinyl*

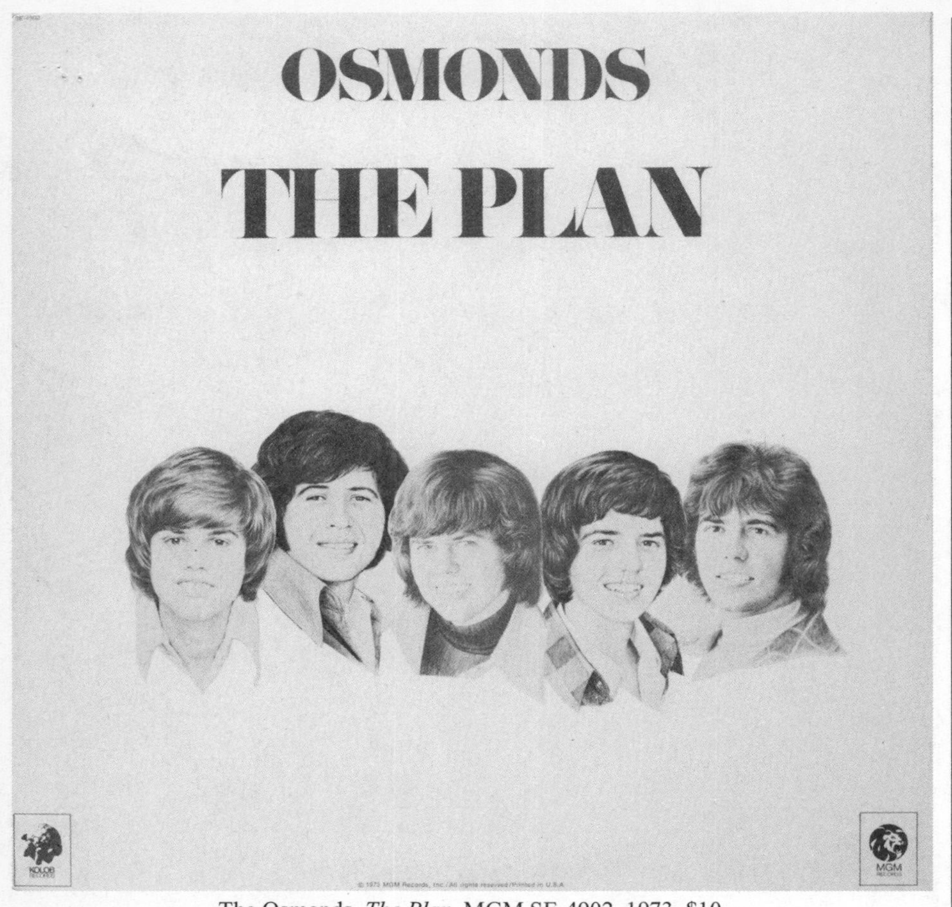


The Osmonds, *The Plan,* MGM SE-4902, 1973, $10.

### OUSLEY, HAROLD

BETHLEHEM

| Number | Title (A Side/B Side) | Yr | NM |
|---|---|---|---|
| ❑ BCP-6059 [M] | Tenor Sax | 1961 | 30.00 |
| ❑ SBCP-6059 [S] | Tenor Sax | 1961 | 40.00 |

COBBLESTONE

| Number | Title (A Side/B Side) | Yr | NM |
|---|---|---|---|
| ❑ 9017 | The Kid! | 1971 | 25.00 |

### OUTLAW BLUES BAND, THE

BLUESWAY

| Number | Title (A Side/B Side) | Yr | NM |
|---|---|---|---|
| ❑ BLS-6020 | Breakin' In | 1969 | 25.00 |
| ❑ BLS-6021 | The Outlaw Blues Band | 1968 | 25.00 |

### OUTLAWS

ARISTA

| Number | Title (A Side/B Side) | Yr | NM |
|---|---|---|---|
| ❑ SP-132 [EP] | Radio Remixes | 1982 | 12.00 |
| *—Promo-only four-song sampler* | | | |
| ❑ AL 4042 | Outlaws | 1975 | 10.00 |
| ❑ AL 4070 | Lady in Waiting | 1976 | 10.00 |
| ❑ AQ 4070 [Q] | Lady in Waiting | 1976 | 15.00 |
| ❑ AL 4135 | Hurry Sundown | 1977 | 10.00 |
| ❑ AB 4205 | Playin' to Win | 1978 | 10.00 |
| ❑ A2L 8114 [(2)] | Bring It Back Alive | 198? | 10.00 |
| *—Second reissue* | | | |
| ❑ A2L 8300 [(2)] | Bring It Back Alive | 1978 | 12.00 |
| ❑ AL 8301 | Outlaws | 198? | 8.00 |
| *—Reissue* | | | |
| ❑ AL 8319 | Greatest Hits of the Outlaws/ High Tides Forever | 198? | 8.00 |
| *—Reissue* | | | |
| ❑ AL 8369 | Hurry Sundown | 198? | 8.00 |
| *—Reissue* | | | |
| ❑ A2L 8608 [(2)] | Bring It Back Alive | 198? | 10.00 |
| *—Reissue* | | | |
| ❑ AL 9507 | In the Eye of the Storm | 1979 | 10.00 |
| ❑ AL 9542 | Ghost Riders | 1980 | 10.00 |
| ❑ AL 9584 | Los Hombres Malo | 1982 | 10.00 |
| ❑ AL 9614 | Greatest Hits of the Outlaws/ High Tides Forever | 1982 | 10.00 |

DIRECT DISC

| Number | Title (A Side/B Side) | Yr | NM |
|---|---|---|---|
| ❑ SD 16617 | Outlaws | 198? | 50.00 |
| *—Audiophile vinyl* | | | |

PAIR

| Number | Title (A Side/B Side) | Yr | NM |
|---|---|---|---|
| ❑ PDL2-1050 [(2)] | The Outlaws | 1986 | 12.00 |

PASHA

| Number | Title (A Side/B Side) | Yr | NM |
|---|---|---|---|
| ❑ BFZ 40512 | Soldiers of Fortune | 1986 | 8.00 |

### OUTSIDERS, THE

CAPITOL

| Number | Title (A Side/B Side) | Yr | NM |
|---|---|---|---|
| ❑ ST 2501 [S] | Time Won't Let Me | 1966 | 30.00 |
| ❑ T 2501 [M] | Time Won't Let Me | 1966 | 25.00 |
| ❑ ST 2558 [S] | The Outsiders Album #2 | 1966 | 30.00 |
| ❑ T 2568 [M] | The Outsiders Album #2 | 1966 | 25.00 |
| ❑ ST 2636 [S] | In | 1967 | 25.00 |
| ❑ T 2636 [M] | In | 1967 | 30.00 |
| ❑ ST 2745 [S] | Happening "Live!" | 1967 | 25.00 |
| ❑ T 2745 [M] | Happening "Live!" | 1967 | 30.00 |

RHINO

| Number | Title (A Side/B Side) | Yr | NM |
|---|---|---|---|
| ❑ RNLP-70132 | The Best of the Outsiders (1965-1968) | 1986 | 10.00 |

### OVATIONS, THE (1)

MGM

| Number | Title (A Side/B Side) | Yr | NM |
|---|---|---|---|
| ❑ SE-4945 | Having a Party | 1973 | 15.00 |

SOUNDS OF MEMPHIS

| Number | Title (A Side/B Side) | Yr | NM |
|---|---|---|---|
| ❑ 7001 | Hooked on a Feeling | 1972 | 20.00 |

### OVERSTREET, TOMMY

ABC

| Number | Title (A Side/B Side) | Yr | NM |
|---|---|---|---|
| ❑ AB-1066 | Better Me | 1978 | 12.00 |

ABC DOT

| Number | Title (A Side/B Side) | Yr | NM |
|---|---|---|---|
| ❑ DOSD-2016 | I'm a Believer | 1975 | 15.00 |
| ❑ DOSD-2027 | Greatest Hits Vol. One | 1975 | 15.00 |
| ❑ DOSD-2038 | The Tommy Overstreet Show Live from the Silver Slipper | 1975 | 15.00 |
| ❑ DOSD-2056 | Turn On to Tommy Overstreet | 1976 | 15.00 |
| ❑ DO-2071 | Vintage '77 | 1977 | 12.00 |
| ❑ DO-2086 | Hangin' 'Round | 1977 | 12.00 |

DOT

| Number | Title (A Side/B Side) | Yr | NM |
|---|---|---|---|
| ❑ DLP-25992 | Gwen (Congratulations) | 1971 | 20.00 |
| ❑ DLP-25994 | This Is Tommy Overstreet | 1972 | 20.00 |
| ❑ DLP-26003 | Heaven Is My Woman's Love | 1972 | 20.00 |
| ❑ DOS-26010 | My Friends Call Me T.O. | 1973 | 20.00 |
| ❑ DOS-26021 | Woman, Your Name Is My Song | 1974 | 20.00 |

ELEKTRA

| Number | Title (A Side/B Side) | Yr | NM |
|---|---|---|---|
| ❑ 6E-178 | I'll Never Let You Down | 1979 | 10.00 |
| ❑ 6E-226 | The Real Tommy Overstreet | 1979 | 10.00 |
| ❑ 6E-292 | The Best of Tommy Overstreet | 1980 | 10.00 |

MCA

| Number | Title (A Side/B Side) | Yr | NM |
|---|---|---|---|
| ❑ 645 | Vintage '77 | 198? | 8.00 |
| *—Reissue* | | | |
| ❑ 646 | Hangin' 'Round | 198? | 8.00 |
| *—Reissue* | | | |
| ❑ 797 | Better Me | 198? | 8.00 |
| *—Reissue* | | | |

### OWEN, JIM

EPIC

| Number | Title (A Side/B Side) | Yr | NM |
|---|---|---|---|
| ❑ PEG 34852 [(2)] | A Song for Us All: A Salute to Hank Williams | 1977 | 20.00 |

### OWEN, REG

DECCA

| Number | Title (A Side/B Side) | Yr | NM |
|---|---|---|---|
| ❑ DL 8859 [M] | Under Paris Skies | 1959 | 20.00 |
| ❑ DL 78859 [S] | Under Paris Skies | 1959 | 25.00 |

PALETTE

| Number | Title (A Side/B Side) | Yr | NM |
|---|---|---|---|
| ❑ 1001 [M] | Manhattan Spiritual | 1959 | 30.00 |
| ❑ S-1001 [S] | Manhattan Spiritual | 1959 | 40.00 |
| ❑ PZ-1004 [M] | Get Happy | 1960 | 20.00 |
| ❑ PZ-1018 [M] | Fiorello! | 1960 | 20.00 |
| ❑ SPZ-31004 [S] | Get Happy | 1960 | 25.00 |
| ❑ SPZ-31018 [S] | Fiorello! | 1960 | 25.00 |

RCA VICTOR

| Number | Title (A Side/B Side) | Yr | NM |
|---|---|---|---|
| ❑ LPM-1542 [M] | The Best of Irving Berlin | 1957 | 25.00 |
| ❑ LPM-1580 [M] | Dreaming | 1958 | 25.00 |
| ❑ LPM-1582 [M] | Coffee Break | 1958 | 20.00 |
| ❑ LSP-1582 [S] | Coffee Break | 1958 | 25.00 |
| ❑ LPM-1597 [M] | Holiday Abroad in Dublin | 1958 | 20.00 |
| ❑ LSP-1597 [S] | Holiday Abroad in Dublin | 1958 | 25.00 |
| ❑ LPM-1599 [M] | Holiday Abroad in London | 1958 | 20.00 |
| ❑ LSP-1599 [S] | Holiday Abroad in London | 1958 | 25.00 |
| ❑ LPM-1675 [M] | The British Isles | 1958 | 20.00 |
| ❑ LSP-1675 [S] | The British Isles | 1958 | 25.00 |
| ❑ LPM-1906 [M] | I'll Sing You 1,000 Love Songs | 1959 | 20.00 |
| ❑ LSP-1906 [S] | I'll Sing You 1,000 Love Songs | 1959 | 25.00 |
| ❑ LPM-1907 [M] | Deep in a Dream | 1959 | 25.00 |
| ❑ LPM-1908 [M] | Girls Were Made to Take Care of Boys | 1959 | 20.00 |
| ❑ LSP-1908 [S] | Girls Were Made to Take Care of Boys | 1959 | 25.00 |
| ❑ LPM-1914 [M] | Cuddle Up a Little Closer | 1959 | 20.00 |
| ❑ LSP-1914 [S] | Cuddle Up a Little Closer | 1959 | 25.00 |
| ❑ LPM-1915 [M] | You Don't Know Paree | 1959 | 25.00 |

### OWEN-B

MUS-I-COL

| Number | Title (A Side/B Side) | Yr | NM |
|---|---|---|---|
| ❑ 101209 | Owen-B | 1970 | 60.00 |

### OWENS, BONNIE

CAPITOL

| Number | Title (A Side/B Side) | Yr | NM |
|---|---|---|---|
| ❑ ST-195 | Lead Me On | 1969 | 25.00 |
| ❑ ST-341 | Hi-Fi to Cry By | 1969 | 25.00 |
| ❑ ST-557 | Mother's Favorite Hymns | 1970 | 25.00 |
| ❑ ST 2403 [S] | Don't Take Advantage of Me | 1965 | 25.00 |
| ❑ T 2403 [M] | Don't Take Advantage of Me | 1965 | 20.00 |
| ❑ ST 2600 [S] | All of Me Belongs to You | 1967 | 25.00 |
| ❑ T 2600 [M] | All of Me Belongs to You | 1967 | 25.00 |
| ❑ ST 2861 | Somewhere Between | 1968 | 25.00 |

### OWENS, BUCK

CAPITOL

| Number | Title (A Side/B Side) | Yr | NM |
|---|---|---|---|
| ❑ ST-131 | I've Got You on My Mind Again | 1969 | 20.00 |
| ❑ SKAO-145 | The Best of Buck Owens, Volume 3 | 1969 | 20.00 |
| ❑ ST-194 | Anywhere U.S.A. | 1969 | 20.00 |
| ❑ ST-212 | Tall Dark Stranger | 1969 | 20.00 |
| ❑ ST 8-0232 | Buck Owens in London | 1969 | 25.00 |
| *—Capitol Record Club edition* | | | |
| ❑ ST-232 | Buck Owens in London | 1969 | 20.00 |
| ❑ SWBB-257 [(2)] | Close-Up | 1969 | 20.00 |
| *—Reissue of "Together Again" and "No One But You"* | | | |
| ❑ ST-439 | Your Mother's Prayer | 1970 | 20.00 |
| ❑ ST-476 | The Kansas City Song | 1970 | 20.00 |
| ❑ STBB-486 [(2)] | A Merry "Hee Haw" Christmas | 1970 | 25.00 |
| ❑ STCL-574 [(3)] | Buck Owens | 1970 | 40.00 |
| ❑ ST-628 | I Wouldn't Live in New York City | 1970 | 20.00 |
| ❑ ST-685 | Bridge Over Troubled Water | 1971 | 15.00 |
| ❑ ST-830 | The Best of Buck Owens, Vol. 4 | 1971 | 15.00 |
| ❑ ST 1482 [S] | Buck Owens Sings Harlan Howard | 1961 | 50.00 |
| ❑ T 1482 [M] | Buck Owens Sings Harlan Howard | 1961 | 40.00 |
| ❑ DT 1489 [R] | Under Your Spell Again | 1968 | 25.00 |
| *—"Duophonic" reissue of mono original with new title* | | | |
| ❑ T 1489 [M] | Buck Owens | 1961 | 40.00 |
| *—Black colorband label, Capitol logo at left* | | | |
| ❑ T 1489 [M] | Buck Owens | 1962 | 30.00 |
| *—Black colorband label, Capitol logo at top* | | | |
| ❑ ST 1777 [S] | You're for Me | 1962 | 50.00 |
| ❑ T 1777 [M] | You're for Me | 1962 | 40.00 |
| ❑ ST 1879 [S] | On the Bandstand | 1963 | 50.00 |
| ❑ T 1879 [M] | On the Bandstand | 1963 | 40.00 |
| ❑ ST 1989 [S] | Buck Owens Sings Tommy Collins | 1963 | 50.00 |



**Except when noted otherwise, VG = 25% of NM, and VG+ = 50% of NM. (Example: VG = $2.00, VG+ = $4.00 and NM = $8.00.)**

| Number | Title (A Side/B Side) | Yr | NM |
|---|---|---|---|
| ❑ T 1989 [M] | Buck Owens Sings Tommy Collins | 1963 | 40.00 |
| ❑ ST 2105 [S] | The Best of Buck Owens | 1964 | 30.00 |
| ❑ T 2105 [M] | The Best of Buck Owens | 1964 | 25.00 |
| ❑ ST 2135 [S] | Together Again/My Heart Skips a Beat | 1964 | 30.00 |
| ❑ T 2135 [M] | Together Again/My Heart Skips a Beat | 1964 | 25.00 |
| ❑ ST 2186 [S] | I Don't Care | 1964 | 30.00 |
| ❑ T 2186 [M] | I Don't Care | 1964 | 25.00 |
| ❑ ST 2283 [S] | I've Got a Tiger by the Tail | 1965 | 30.00 |
| ❑ T 2283 [M] | I've Got a Tiger by the Tail | 1965 | 25.00 |
| ❑ ST 2353 [S] | Before You Go/No One But You | 1965 | 30.00 |
| ❑ T 2353 [M] | Before You Go/No One But You | 1965 | 25.00 |
| ❑ ST 2367 [S] | The Instrumental Hits of Buck Owens & the Buckaroos | 1965 | 30.00 |
| ❑ T 2367 [M] | The Instrumental Hits of Buck Owens & the Buckaroos | 1965 | 25.00 |
| ❑ ST 2396 [S] | Christmas with Buck Owens and His Buckaroos | 1965 | 30.00 |
| ❑ T 2396 [M] | Christmas with Buck Owens and His Buckaroos | 1965 | 20.00 |
| ❑ ST 2443 [S] | Roll Out the Red Carpet for Buck Owens & The Buckaroos | 1966 | 25.00 |
| ❑ T 2443 [M] | Roll Out the Red Carpet for Buck Owens & The Buckaroos | 1966 | 20.00 |
| ❑ ST 2497 [S] | Dust on Mother's Bible | 1966 | 25.00 |
| ❑ T 2497 [M] | Dust on Mother's Bible | 1966 | 20.00 |
| ❑ ST 2556 [S] | Carnegie Hall Concert | 1966 | 25.00 |
| ❑ T 2556 [M] | Carnegie Hall Concert | 1966 | 20.00 |
| ❑ ST 2650 [S] | Open Up Your Heart | 1967 | 25.00 |
| ❑ T 2650 [M] | Open Up Your Heart | 1967 | 20.00 |
| ❑ ST 2715 [S] | Buck Owens and His Buckaroos in Japan | 1967 | 25.00 |
| ❑ T 2715 [M] | Buck Owens and His Buckaroos in Japan | 1967 | 20.00 |
| ❑ ST 2760 [S] | Your Tender Loving Care | 1967 | 25.00 |
| ❑ T 2760 [M] | Your Tender Loving Care | 1967 | 25.00 |
| ❑ ST 2841 [S] | It Takes People Like You to Make People Like Me | 1968 | 25.00 |
| ❑ T 2841 [M] | It Takes People Like You to Make People Like Me | 1968 | 40.00 |
| ❑ ST 2897 | The Best of Buck Owens, Vol. 2 | 1968 | 25.00 |
| ❑ ST 2902 | A Night on the Town | 1968 | 25.00 |
| ❑ ST 2962 | Sweet Rosie Jones | 1968 | 25.00 |
| ❑ ST 2977 | Christmas Shopping | 1968 | 25.00 |
| ❑ SPRO 2980/1 [DJ] | Minute Masters | 1966 | 50.00 |
| *—Promo-only excerpts of 24 songs* | | | |
| ❑ ST 2994 | Buck Owens, The Guitar Player | 1968 | 25.00 |
| ❑ ST-11105 | Live at the White House | 1972 | 15.00 |
| ❑ ST-11136 | In the Palm of Your Hand | 1973 | 15.00 |
| ❑ SMAS-11180 | Ain't It Amazing, Gracie | 1973 | 15.00 |
| ❑ ST-11222 | Arms Full of Empty | 1972 | 15.00 |
| ❑ ST-11273 | The Best of Buck Owens Volume 5 | 1973 | 15.00 |
| ❑ ST-11332 | Monster's Holiday | 1974 | 15.00 |
| ❑ ST-11390 | Weekend Daddy | 1974 | 15.00 |
| ❑ ST-11471 | The Best of Buck Owens, Volume 6 | 1976 | 15.00 |
| ❑ C1-91132 | Hot Dog! | 1988 | 12.00 |
| ❑ C1-92893 | Act Naturally | 1989 | 15.00 |

COUNTRY MUSIC FOUNDATION

| Number | Title (A Side/B Side) | Yr | NM |
|---|---|---|---|
| ❑ CMF-012 | Live at Carnegie Hall | 198? | 12.00 |

LABREA

| Number | Title (A Side/B Side) | Yr | NM |
|---|---|---|---|
| ❑ 1017 [M] | Buck Owens | 1961 | 100.00 |
| ❑ 8017 [S] | Buck Owens | 1961 | 150.00 |

STARDAY

| Number | Title (A Side/B Side) | Yr | NM |
|---|---|---|---|
| ❑ SLP-172 | The Fabulous Country Music Sound of Buck Owens | 1962 | 50.00 |
| ❑ SLP-324 | Coutnry Hit Maker #1 | 1964 | 25.00 |

TIME-LIFE

| Number | Title (A Side/B Side) | Yr | NM |
|---|---|---|---|
| ❑ STW-114 | Country Music | 1981 | 10.00 |

WARNER BROS.

| Number | Title (A Side/B Side) | Yr | NM |
|---|---|---|---|
| ❑ BS 2952 | Buck 'Em | 1976 | 12.00 |
| ❑ BS 3087 | Our Old Mansion | 1977 | 12.00 |

**OWENS, BUCK, AND SUSAN RAYE**

CAPITOL

| Number | Title (A Side/B Side) | Yr | NM |
|---|---|---|---|
| ❑ ST-448 | We're Gonna Get Together | 1970 | 20.00 |
| ❑ ST-558 | Great White Horse | 1970 | 15.00 |
| ❑ ST-837 | Merry Christmas from Buck Owens and Susan Raye | 1971 | 15.00 |
| ❑ ST-11084 | The Best of Buck Owens and Susan Raye | 1972 | 15.00 |
| ❑ ST-11204 | The Good Old Days (Are Here Again) | 1973 | 15.00 |

**OWENS, CHARLES**

VAULT

| Number | Title (A Side/B Side) | Yr | NM |
|---|---|---|---|
| ❑ LP-(# unknown) | I Stand Alone | 196? | 50.00 |

**OWENS, JIMMY**

ATLANTIC

| Number | Title (A Side/B Side) | Yr | NM |
|---|---|---|---|
| ❑ SD 1491 | Jimmy Owens-Kenny Barron Quintet | 1968 | 20.00 |
| *—Multicolor label, black "fan" logo at right* | | | |

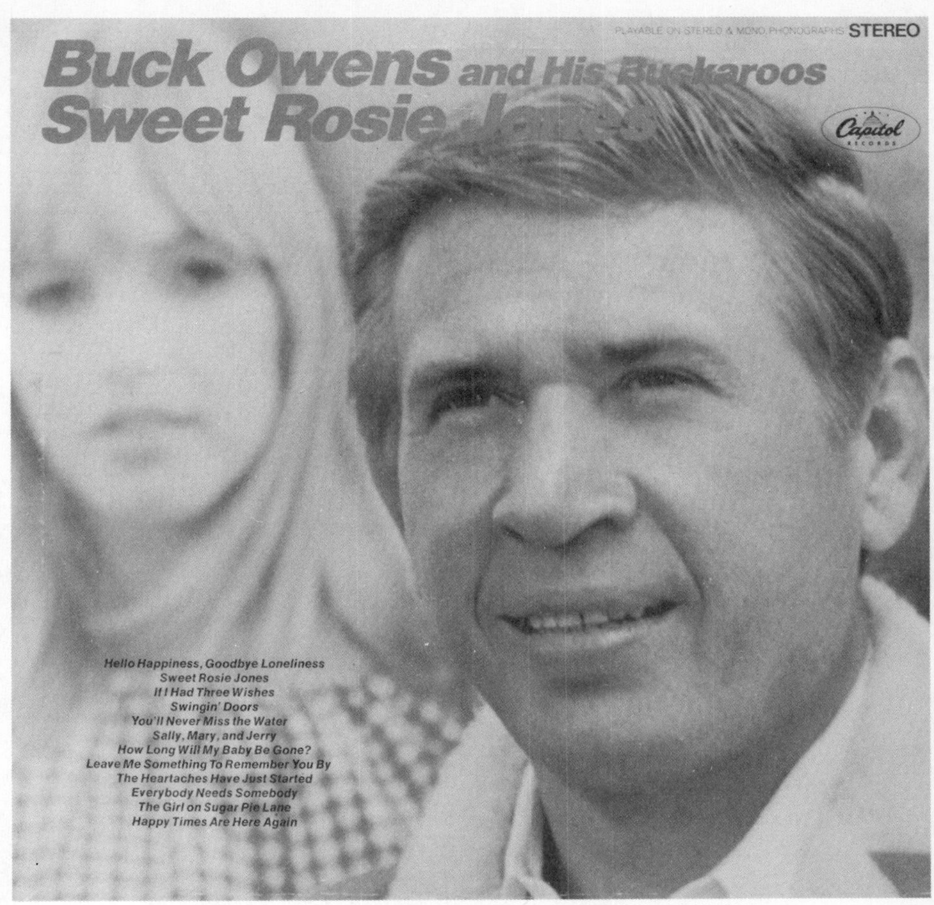


Buck Owens, *Sweet Rosie Jones,* Capitol ST-2962, 1968, $25.

**OXFORD, VERNON**

RCA VICTOR

| Number | Title (A Side/B Side) | Yr | NM |
|---|---|---|---|
| ❑ LPM-3704 [M] | Woman, Let Me Sing You a Song | 1967 | 40.00 |
| ❑ LSP-3704 [S] | Woman, Let Me Sing You a Song | 1967 | 30.00 |

ROUNDER

| Number | Title (A Side/B Side) | Yr | NM |
|---|---|---|---|
| ❑ 0091 | If I Had My Wife to Love Over | 198? | 15.00 |
| ❑ 0123 | His and Hers | 198? | 15.00 |
| ❑ 0156 | Keepin' It Country | 1982 | 15.00 |

**OZ KNOZZ**

OZONE

| Number | Title (A Side/B Side) | Yr | NM |
|---|---|---|---|
| ❑ O2-1000 | Ruff Mix | 1975 | 500.00 |

**OZONE, MAKOTO**

COLUMBIA

| Number | Title (A Side/B Side) | Yr | NM |
|---|---|---|---|
| ❑ FC 40676 | Now You Know | 1987 | 10.00 |

# P

**P.H. PHACTOR**

PICCADILLY

| Number | Title (A Side/B Side) | Yr | NM |
|---|---|---|---|
| ❑ PIC-3343 | Merryjuana | 1980 | 100.00 |
| *—Cover spells the group's name "Factor" but the label has it "Phactor"* | | | |

**P.M. DAWN**

GEE STREET

| Number | Title (A Side/B Side) | Yr | NM |
|---|---|---|---|
| ❑ PRLP-6768-1 [(2)DJ] | The Bliss Album...? | 1993 | 20.00 |
| *—Promo-only vinyl edition* | | | |
| ❑ 524147-1 [(2)] | Jesus Wept | 1995 | 20.00 |

**PABLO CRUISE**

A&M

| Number | Title (A Side/B Side) | Yr | NM |
|---|---|---|---|
| ❑ SP-3111 | Pablo Cruise | 198? | 8.00 |
| *—Budget-line reissue of 4528* | | | |
| ❑ SP-3198 | Worlds Away | 198? | 8.00 |
| *—Budget-line reissue of 4697* | | | |
| ❑ SP-3236 | A Place in the Sun | 198? | 8.00 |
| *—Budget-line reissue of 4625* | | | |
| ❑ SP-3712 | Part of the Game | 1979 | 10.00 |
| ❑ SP-3726 | Reflector | 1981 | 10.00 |
| ❑ SP-4528 | Pablo Cruise | 1975 | 10.00 |
| ❑ SP-4575 | Lifeline | 1976 | 10.00 |
| ❑ SP-4625 | A Place in the Sun | 1977 | 10.00 |
| ❑ SP-4697 | Worlds Away | 1978 | 10.00 |
| ❑ SP-4909 | Out of Our Hands | 1983 | 10.00 |

MOBILE FIDELITY

| Number | Title (A Side/B Side) | Yr | NM |
|---|---|---|---|
| ❑ 1-029 | A Place in the Sun | 1979 | 20.00 |
| *—Audiophile vinyl* | | | |

NAUTILUS

| Number | Title (A Side/B Side) | Yr | NM |
|---|---|---|---|
| ❑ NR-6 | Lifeline | 1980 | 20.00 |
| *—Audiophile vinyl* | | | |
| ❑ NR-28 | Worlds Away | 1981 | 20.00 |
| *—Audiophile vinyl* | | | |

**PACE, JOHNNY**

RIVERSIDE

| Number | Title (A Side/B Side) | Yr | NM |
|---|---|---|---|
| ❑ RLP 12-292 [M] | Chet Baker Introduces Johnny Pace | 1958 | 50.00 |
| ❑ RLP-1130 [S] | Chet Baker Introduces Johnny Pace | 1959 | 50.00 |

**PACERS, THE**

RAZORBACK

| Number | Title (A Side/B Side) | Yr | NM |
|---|---|---|---|
| ❑ 121 [M] | You Asked For It | 1965 | 100.00 |

**PACHECO, MIKE**

INTERLUDE

| Number | Title (A Side/B Side) | Yr | NM |
|---|---|---|---|
| ❑ MO-513 [M] | Hot Skins | 1959 | 40.00 |
| ❑ ST-1013 [S] | Hot Skins | 1959 | 30.00 |

TAMPA

| Number | Title (A Side/B Side) | Yr | NM |
|---|---|---|---|
| ❑ TP-10 [M] | Bongo Skins | 1957 | 100.00 |
| *—Colored vinyl* | | | |
| ❑ TP-10 [M] | Bongo Skins | 1958 | 50.00 |
| *—Black vinyl* | | | |
| ❑ TP-21 [M] | Bongo Session | 1957 | 100.00 |
| *—Colored vinyl* | | | |
| ❑ TP-21 [M] | Bongo Session | 1958 | 50.00 |
| *—Black vinyl* | | | |
| ❑ TP-30 [M] | Bongo Date | 1957 | 100.00 |
| *—Colored vinyl* | | | |
| ❑ TP-30 [M] | Bongo Date | 1958 | 50.00 |
| *—Black vinyl* | | | |

**PACIFIC DRIFT**

DERAM

| Number | Title (A Side/B Side) | Yr | NM |
|---|---|---|---|
| ❑ DES 18040 | Feelin' Free | 1970 | 20.00 |

Pacific Gas & Electric, *Are You Ready,* Columbia CS 1017, 1970, "360 Sound" label, $15.

| Number | Title (A Side/B Side) | Yr | NM |
|---|---|---|---|
| **PACIFIC GAS & ELECTRIC** | | | |
| ABC DUNHILL | | | |
| ❑ DSX-50157 | Pacific Gas and Electric Starring Charlie Allen | 1974 | 12.00 |
| BRIGHT ORANGE | | | |
| ❑ 701 | Get It On | 1968 | 40.00 |
| COLUMBIA | | | |
| ❑ CS 1017 | Are You Ready | 1970 | 12.00 |
| *—Orange label* | | | |
| ❑ CS 1017 | Are You Ready | 1970 | 15.00 |
| *—"360 Sound" label* | | | |
| ❑ CS 9900 | Pacific Gas and Electric | 1969 | 15.00 |
| *—"360 Sound" label* | | | |
| ❑ CS 9900 | Pacific Gas and Electric | 1970 | 12.00 |
| *—Orange label* | | | |
| ❑ C 30362 | PG&E | 1971 | 12.00 |
| ❑ C 32019 | The Best of Pacific Gas & Electric | 1972 | 12.00 |
| POWER | | | |
| ❑ 701 | Get It On | 1969 | 25.00 |
| **PACIFIC OCEAN** | | | |
| V.M.C. | | | |
| ❑ 135 | Pacific Ocean | 1969 | 20.00 |
| **PACK, MARSHALL** | | | |
| STARDAY | | | |
| ❑ SLP-120 [M] | Marshall Pack | 1960 | 40.00 |
| **PACKERS, THE** | | | |
| PURE SOUL MUSIC | | | |
| ❑ 1001 [S] | Hole in the Wall | 1966 | 20.00 |
| **PAGE, HOT LIPS** | | | |
| CONTINENTAL | | | |
| ❑ 16007 [M] | Hot and Cozy | 1962 | 30.00 |
| **PAGE, JIMMY** Also see LED ZEPPELIN; THE YARDBIRDS. | | | |
| GEFFEN | | | |
| ❑ GHS 24188 | Outrider | 1988 | 8.00 |
| SPRINGBOARD | | | |
| ❑ SPB-4038 | Special Early Works | 1972 | 25.00 |

| Number | Title (A Side/B Side) | Yr | NM |
|---|---|---|---|
| **PAGE, PATTI** | | | |
| ACCORD | | | |
| ❑ SN-7206 | Special Thoughts | 1982 | 10.00 |
| COLUMBIA | | | |
| ❑ CL 2049 [M] | Say Wonderful Things | 1963 | 15.00 |
| ❑ CL 2132 [M] | Love After Midnight | 1964 | 15.00 |
| ❑ CL 2353 [M] | Hush, Hush, Sweet Charlotte | 1965 | 15.00 |
| ❑ CL 2414 [M] | Christmas with Patti Page | 1965 | 12.00 |
| ❑ CL 2505 [M] | America's Favorite Hymns | 1966 | 12.00 |
| ❑ CL 2526 [M] | Patti Page's Greatest Hits | 1966 | 12.00 |
| ❑ CL 2761 [M] | Today My Way | 1967 | 20.00 |
| ❑ CS 8849 [S] | Say Wonderful Things | 1963 | 20.00 |
| ❑ CS 8932 [S] | Love After Midnight | 1964 | 20.00 |
| ❑ CS 9153 [S] | Hush, Hush, Sweet Charlotte | 1965 | 20.00 |
| ❑ CS 9214 [S] | Christmas with Patti Page | 1965 | 15.00 |
| ❑ CS 9305 [S] | America's Favorite Hymns | 1966 | 15.00 |
| ❑ CS 9326 | Patti Page's Greatest Hits | 1970 | 10.00 |
| *—Orange label* | | | |
| ❑ CS 9326 [S] | Patti Page's Greatest Hits | 1966 | 15.00 |
| *—"360 Sound" label* | | | |
| ❑ PC 9326 | Patti Page's Greatest Hits | 198? | 8.00 |
| *—Budget-line reissue* | | | |
| ❑ CS 9561 [S] | Today My Way | 1967 | 15.00 |
| ❑ CS 9666 | Gentle on My Mind | 1968 | 15.00 |
| ❑ CS 9999 | Honey Come Back | 1970 | 12.00 |
| EMARCY | | | |
| ❑ MG-36074 [M] | In the Land of Hi-Fi | 1956 | 50.00 |
| ❑ MG-36116 [M] | The East Side | 1957 | 50.00 |
| ❑ MG-36136 [M] | The West Side | 1957 | 50.00 |
| ❑ SR-80000 [S] | In the Land of Hi-Fi | 1959 | 50.00 |
| HARMONY | | | |
| ❑ HS 11381 | Stand By Your Man | 1970 | 10.00 |
| ❑ KH 30407 | Green, Green Grass of Home | 1971 | 10.00 |
| MERCURY | | | |
| ❑ PKW-118 [(2)] | The Most | 1969 | 15.00 |
| ❑ MG-20076 [M] | Romance on the Range | 1955 | 30.00 |
| ❑ MG 20093 [M] | Christmas with Patti Page | 1956 | 30.00 |
| ❑ MG-20095 [M] | Page I | 1955 | 30.00 |
| ❑ MG-20096 [M] | Page II | 1955 | 30.00 |
| ❑ MG-20097 [M] | Page III | 1955 | 30.00 |
| ❑ MG-20098 [M] | You Go to My Head | 1955 | 30.00 |
| ❑ MG-20099 [M] | Music for Two in Love | 1955 | 30.00 |
| ❑ MG-20100 [M] | The Voice of Patti Page | 1955 | 30.00 |
| ❑ MG-20101 [M] | Page IV | 1955 | 30.00 |

| Number | Title (A Side/B Side) | Yr | NM |
|---|---|---|---|
| ❑ MG-20102 [M] | This Is My Song | 1955 | 30.00 |
| ❑ MG-20226 [M] | Manhattan Tower | 1956 | 30.00 |
| ❑ MG-20318 [M] | The Waltz Queen | 1957 | 40.00 |
| *—With one image of Patti Page on cover; "Custom High Fidelity" and Mercury logo at upper right of front cover* | | | |
| ❑ MG-20318 [M] | The Waltz Queen | 1959 | 30.00 |
| *—With two images of Patti Page on cover; Mercury logo at upper left of front cover, "High Custom Fidelity" in white strip along bottom front cover* | | | |
| ❑ MG-20387 [M] | Let's Get Away from It All | 1957 | 30.00 |
| ❑ MG-20388 [M] | I've Heard That Song Before | 1957 | 30.00 |
| ❑ MG-20398 [M] | Patti Page On Camera | 1958 | 30.00 |
| ❑ MG-20405 [M] | Indiscretion | 1959 | 30.00 |
| ❑ MG-20406 [M] | I'll Remember April | 1959 | 30.00 |
| ❑ MG-20417 [M] | Three Little Words | 1960 | 30.00 |
| ❑ MG-20495 [M] | Patti Page's Golden Hits | 1960 | 30.00 |
| ❑ MG-20573 [M] | Just a Closer Walk with Thee | 1960 | 30.00 |
| ❑ MG-20599 [M] | Patti Page Sings and Stars In "Elmer Gantry" | 1960 | 25.00 |
| ❑ MG-20615 [M] | Country & Western Golden Hits | 1961 | 20.00 |
| ❑ MG-20689 [M] | Go On Home | 1962 | 20.00 |
| ❑ MG-20712 [M] | Golden Hits of the Boys | 1962 | 20.00 |
| ❑ MG-20758 [M] | Patti Page On Stage | 1963 | 20.00 |
| ❑ MG-20794 [M] | Patti Page's Golden Hits, Volume 2 | 1963 | 20.00 |
| ❑ MG-20819 [M] | The Singing Rage | 1963 | 20.00 |
| ❑ MG-20909 [M] | Blue Dream Street | 1964 | 20.00 |
| ❑ MG-20952 [M] | The Nearness of You | 1965 | 15.00 |
| ❑ MG-25059 [10] | Songs | 1950 | 40.00 |
| ❑ MG-25101 [10] | Folksong Favorites | 1951 | 40.00 |
| ❑ MG-25109 [10] | Christmas | 1951 | 40.00 |
| ❑ MG-25154 [10] | Tennessee Waltz | 1952 | 40.00 |
| ❑ MG-25185 [10] | Patti Sings for Romance | 1954 | 40.00 |
| ❑ MG-25187 [10] | Song Souvenirs | 1954 | 40.00 |
| ❑ MG-25196 [10] | Just Patti | 1954 | 40.00 |
| ❑ MG-25197 [10] | Patti's Songs | 1954 | 40.00 |
| ❑ MG-25209 [10] | And I Thought About You | 1954 | 40.00 |
| ❑ MG-25210 [10] | So Many Memories | 1954 | 40.00 |
| ❑ SR-60010 [S] | Let's Get Away from It All | 1959 | 40.00 |
| ❑ SR-60011 [S] | I've Heard That Song Before | 1959 | 40.00 |
| ❑ SR-60025 [S] | Patti Page On Camera | 1959 | 40.00 |
| ❑ SR-60037 [S] | Three Little Words | 1960 | 40.00 |
| ❑ SR-60049 [S] | The Waltz Queen | 1959 | 40.00 |
| ❑ SR-60059 [S] | Indiscretion | 1959 | 40.00 |
| ❑ SR-60081 [S] | I'll Remember April | 1959 | 40.00 |
| ❑ SR-60113 [S] | The West Side | 1959 | 50.00 |
| ❑ SR-60114 [S] | The East Side | 1959 | 50.00 |
| ❑ SR-60233 [S] | Just a Closer Walk with Thee | 1960 | 40.00 |
| ❑ SR-60260 [S] | Patti Page Sings and Stars In "Elmer Gantry" | 1960 | 30.00 |
| ❑ SR-60495 [S] | Patti Page's Golden Hits | 196? | 25.00 |
| ❑ SR-60615 [S] | Country & Western Golden Hits | 1961 | 25.00 |
| ❑ SR-60689 [S] | Go On Home | 1962 | 25.00 |
| ❑ SR-60712 [S] | Golden Hits of the Boys | 1962 | 25.00 |
| ❑ SR-60758 [S] | Patti Page On Stage | 1963 | 25.00 |
| ❑ SR-60794 [S] | Patti Page's Golden Hits, Volume 2 | 1963 | 25.00 |
| ❑ SR-60819 [S] | The Singing Rage | 1963 | 25.00 |
| ❑ SR-60909 [S] | Blue Dream Street | 1964 | 25.00 |
| ❑ SR-60952 [S] | The Nearness of You | 1965 | 20.00 |
| ❑ SR-61344 | I'd Rather Be Sorry | 1971 | 12.00 |
| ❑ 822740-1 | Christmas with Patti Page | 1987 | 10.00 |
| *—Reissue* | | | |
| PLANTATION | | | |
| ❑ 548 | Aces | 1981 | 10.00 |
| WING | | | |
| ❑ MGW 12121 [M] | The Waltz Queen | 196? | 12.00 |
| ❑ MGW 12174 [M] | Christmas with Patti Page | 196? | 20.00 |
| *—Same contents and order as Mercury 20093* | | | |
| ❑ MGW 12250 [M] | Let's Get Away from It All | 196? | 12.00 |
| ❑ SRW 16121 [S] | The Waltz Queen | 196? | 15.00 |
| ❑ SRW 16250 [S] | Let's Get Away from It All | 196? | 15.00 |
| **PAICH, MARTY** | | | |
| BETHLEHEM | | | |
| ❑ BCP-44 [M] | Jazz City Workshop | 1956 | 80.00 |
| CADENCE | | | |
| ❑ CLP-3010 [M] | Marty Paich Big Band | 1958 | 50.00 |
| GENE NORMAN | | | |
| ❑ GNP-10 [10] | Marty Paich Octet | 1955 | 120.00 |
| *—Red vinyl* | | | |
| ❑ GNP-21 [M] | Marty Paich Octet | 1956 | 80.00 |
| INTERLUDE | | | |
| ❑ MO-509 [M] | Revel Without a Pause | 1959 | 30.00 |
| ❑ MO-514 [M] | Like Wow — Jazz 1960 | 1960 | 30.00 |
| ❑ ST-1009 [S] | Revel Without a Pause | 1959 | 25.00 |
| ❑ ST-1014 [S] | Like Wow — Jazz 1960 | 1960 | 25.00 |
| MODE | | | |
| ❑ LP-105 [M] | Marty Paich Trio | 1957 | 80.00 |
| ❑ LP-110 [M] | Jazz Band Ball | 1957 | 80.00 |
| RCA VICTOR | | | |
| ❑ LPM-2164 [M] | Piano Quartet | 1960 | 20.00 |
| ❑ LSP-2164 [S] | Piano Quartet | 1960 | 25.00 |
| ❑ LPM-2259 [M] | Piano Quartet | 1960 | 20.00 |
| ❑ LSP-2259 [S] | Piano Quartet | 1960 | 25.00 |

| Number | Title (A Side/B Side) | Yr | NM |
|---|---|---|---|
| **TAMPA** | | | |
| ❑ TP-23 [M] | Hot Piano | 1957 | 150.00 |
| *—Probably the original title* | | | |
| ❑ TP-23 [M] | Jazz for Relaxation | 1957 | 200.00 |
| *—Colored vinyl* | | | |
| ❑ TP-23 [M] | Jazz for Relaxation | 1958 | 100.00 |
| *—Black vinyl* | | | |
| ❑ TP-28 [M] | Marty Paich Quintet Featuring Art Pepper | 1957 | 800.00 |
| *—Red vinyl* | | | |
| ❑ TP-28 [M] | Marty Paich Quintet Featuring Art Pepper | 1958 | 400.00 |
| *—Black vinyl* | | | |
| **WARNER BROS.** | | | |
| ❑ W 1296 [M] | The Broadway Bit | 1959 | 200.00 |
| ❑ WS 1296 [S] | The Broadway Bit | 1959 | 150.00 |
| ❑ W 1349 [M] | I Get A Boot Out of You | 1959 | 150.00 |
| ❑ WS 1349 [S] | I Get A Boot Out of You | 1959 | 180.00 |

**PAIGE, JANIS**

| Number | Title (A Side/B Side) | Yr | NM |
|---|---|---|---|
| **BALLY** | | | |
| ❑ BAL-12008 [M] | Let's Fall in Love | 1957 | 40.00 |

**PAIR, THE**

| Number | Title (A Side/B Side) | Yr | NM |
|---|---|---|---|
| **LIBERTY** | | | |
| ❑ LRP-3410 [M] | The Pair Live! At the Ice House | 1965 | 20.00 |
| ❑ LRP-3440 [M] | The Pair Extraordinaire | 1966 | 15.00 |
| ❑ LRP-3461 [M] | "In"-Citement | 1966 | 15.00 |
| ❑ LRP-3504 [M] | It's a Wonderful World | 1967 | 15.00 |
| ❑ LST-7410 [S] | The Pair Live! At the Ice House | 1965 | 25.00 |
| ❑ LST-7440 [S] | The Pair Extraordinaire | 1966 | 20.00 |
| ❑ LST-7461 [S] | "In"-Citement | 1966 | 20.00 |
| ❑ LST-7504 [S] | It's a Wonderful World | 1967 | 20.00 |

**PAISLEYS, THE**

| Number | Title (A Side/B Side) | Yr | NM |
|---|---|---|---|
| **AUDIO CITY** | | | |
| ❑ 70 | Cosmic Mind at Play | 1970 | 200.00 |

**PALANCE, JACK**

| Number | Title (A Side/B Side) | Yr | NM |
|---|---|---|---|
| **WARNER BROS.** | | | |
| ❑ WS 1865 | Palance | 1970 | 30.00 |

**PALEY, TOM**

| Number | Title (A Side/B Side) | Yr | NM |
|---|---|---|---|
| **ELEKTRA** | | | |
| ❑ EKL-12 [M] | Folk Songs from the Southern Appalachians | 195? | 40.00 |

**PALMER, BRUCE**

| Number | Title (A Side/B Side) | Yr | NM |
|---|---|---|---|
| **VERVE FORECAST** | | | |
| ❑ FTS-3086 | The Cycle Is Complete | 1970 | 20.00 |

**PALMER, EARL**

| Number | Title (A Side/B Side) | Yr | NM |
|---|---|---|---|
| **LIBERTY** | | | |
| ❑ LRP-3201 [M] | Drumsville | 1961 | 30.00 |
| ❑ LRP-3227 [M] | Percolator Twist | 1962 | 30.00 |
| ❑ LST-7201 [S] | Drumsville | 1961 | 40.00 |
| ❑ LST-7227 [S] | Percolator Twist | 1962 | 40.00 |

**PALMER, ROBERT**

| Number | Title (A Side/B Side) | Yr | NM |
|---|---|---|---|
| **EMI MANHATTAN** | | | |
| ❑ E1-48057 | Heavy Nova | 1988 | 10.00 |
| **ISLAND** | | | |
| ❑ PRO-819 [DJ] | Secrets | 1979 | 30.00 |
| *—Promo-only picture disc* | | | |
| ❑ ILPS 9294 | Sneakin' Sally Through the Alley | 1975 | 12.00 |
| ❑ ILPS 9372 | Pressure Drop | 1976 | 12.00 |
| ❑ ILPS 9420 | Some People Can Do What They Like | 1977 | 12.00 |
| ❑ ILPS 9476 | Double Fun | 1978 | 12.00 |
| *—Original copies of the above four albums were NOT distributed by Warner Bros.* | | | |
| ❑ ILPS 9544 | Secrets | 1979 | 10.00 |
| ❑ ILPS 9595 | Clues | 1980 | 10.00 |
| ❑ ILPS 9665 | Maybe It's Live | 1982 | 10.00 |
| ❑ 90065 | Pride | 1983 | 10.00 |
| ❑ 90086 | Sneakin' Sally Through the Alley | 1984 | 8.00 |
| ❑ 90087 | Pressure Drop | 1984 | 8.00 |
| ❑ 90089 | Secrets | 1984 | 8.00 |
| ❑ 90471 | Riptide | 1985 | 10.00 |
| ❑ 90493 | Clues | 1986 | 8.00 |
| ❑ 90494 | Double Fun | 1986 | 8.00 |
| ❑ 91318 | Addictions Volume I | 1989 | 12.00 |
| *—Original pressing available only for a short time* | | | |
| ❑ 842301-1 | Addictions Volume I | 1990 | 10.00 |
| **WARNER BROS.** | | | |
| ❑ WBMS-111 [DJ] | Live in Boston | 1979 | 30.00 |
| *—Part of "The Warner Bros. Music Show"* | | | |

**PALMER, ROY**

| Number | Title (A Side/B Side) | Yr | NM |
|---|---|---|---|
| **RIVERSIDE** | | | |
| ❑ RLP-1020 [10] | Roy Palmer's State Street Ramblers | 1953 | 80.00 |

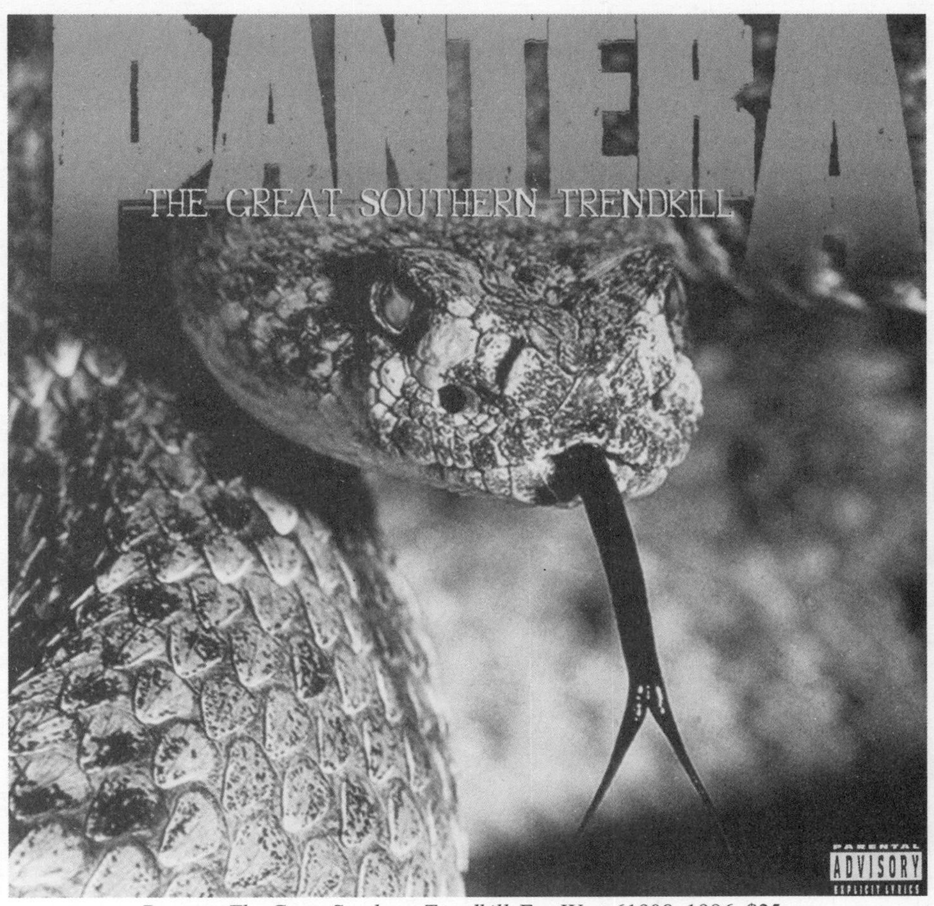


Pantera, *The Great Southern Trendkill,* EastWest 61908, 1996, $25.

**PANDIT, KORLA**

| Number | Title (A Side/B Side) | Yr | NM |
|---|---|---|---|
| **FANTASY** | | | |
| ❑ 3272 [M] | Music of the Exotic East | 1958 | 25.00 |
| *—Black vinyl* | | | |
| ❑ 3272 [M] | Music of the Exotic East | 1958 | 40.00 |
| *—Red vinyl* | | | |
| ❑ 3284 [M] | Latin Holiday | 1959 | 25.00 |
| *—Black vinyl* | | | |
| ❑ 3284 [M] | Latin Holiday | 1959 | 40.00 |
| *—Red vinyl* | | | |
| ❑ 3286 [M] | Korla Pandit at the Pipe Organ | 1959 | 25.00 |
| *—Black vinyl* | | | |
| ❑ 3286 [M] | Korla Pandit at the Pipe Organ | 1959 | 40.00 |
| *—Red vinyl* | | | |
| ❑ 3288 [M] | Tropical Magic | 1959 | 25.00 |
| *—Black vinyl* | | | |
| ❑ 3288 [M] | Tropical Magic | 1959 | 40.00 |
| *—Red vinyl* | | | |
| ❑ 3293 [M] | Speak to Me of Love | 1959 | 25.00 |
| *—Black vinyl* | | | |
| ❑ 3293 [M] | Speak to Me of Love | 1959 | 40.00 |
| *—Red vinyl* | | | |
| ❑ 3304 [M] | Korla Pandit in Concert | 1960 | 25.00 |
| *—Black vinyl* | | | |
| ❑ 3304 [M] | Korla Pandit in Concert | 1960 | 40.00 |
| *—Red vinyl* | | | |
| ❑ 3320 [M] | Music of Mystery and Romance | 1961 | 25.00 |
| *—Black vinyl* | | | |
| ❑ 3320 [M] | Music of Mystery and Romance | 1961 | 40.00 |
| *—Red vinyl* | | | |
| ❑ 3327 [M] | Love Letters | 1961 | 25.00 |
| *—Black vinyl* | | | |
| ❑ 3327 [M] | Love Letters | 1961 | 40.00 |
| *—Red vinyl* | | | |
| ❑ 3329 [M] | Hypnotique | 1961 | 25.00 |
| *—Black vinyl* | | | |
| ❑ 3329 [M] | Hypnotique | 1961 | 40.00 |
| *—Red vinyl* | | | |
| ❑ 3334 [M] | Music of Hollywood | 1962 | 25.00 |
| *—Black vinyl* | | | |
| ❑ 3334 [M] | Music of Hollywood | 1962 | 40.00 |
| *—Red vinyl* | | | |
| ❑ 3342 [M] | Music for Meditation | 1962 | 25.00 |
| *—Black vinyl* | | | |
| ❑ 3342 [M] | Music for Meditation | 1962 | 40.00 |
| *—Red vinyl* | | | |
| ❑ 3347 [M] | Korla Pandit in Paris | 1962 | 25.00 |
| ❑ 3350 [M] | Christmas with Korla Pandit | 1962 | 25.00 |
| *—Black vinyl* | | | |
| ❑ 3350 [M] | Christmas with Korla Pandit | 1962 | 40.00 |
| *—Red vinyl* | | | |
| ❑ 8013 [S] | Music of the Exotic East | 1960 | 30.00 |
| *—Black vinyl* | | | |
| ❑ 8013 [S] | Music of the Exotic East | 1960 | 50.00 |
| *—Blue vinyl* | | | |
| ❑ 8018 [S] | Korla Pandit at the Pipe Organ | 1960 | 30.00 |
| *—Black vinyl* | | | |
| ❑ 8018 [S] | Korla Pandit at the Pipe Organ | 1960 | 50.00 |
| *—Blue vinyl* | | | |
| ❑ 8027 [S] | Latin Holiday | 1960 | 30.00 |
| *—Black vinyl* | | | |
| ❑ 8027 [S] | Latin Holiday | 1960 | 50.00 |
| *—Blue vinyl* | | | |
| ❑ 8034 [S] | Tropical Magic | 1960 | 30.00 |
| *—Black vinyl* | | | |
| ❑ 8034 [S] | Tropical Magic | 1960 | 50.00 |
| *—Blue vinyl* | | | |
| ❑ 8039 [S] | Speak to Me of Love | 1960 | 30.00 |
| *—Black vinyl* | | | |
| ❑ 8039 [S] | Speak to Me of Love | 1960 | 50.00 |
| *—Blue vinyl* | | | |
| ❑ 8049 [S] | Korla Pandit in Concert | 1960 | 30.00 |
| *—Black vinyl* | | | |
| ❑ 8049 [S] | Korla Pandit in Concert | 1960 | 50.00 |
| *—Blue vinyl* | | | |
| ❑ 8061 [S] | Music of Mystery and Romance | 1961 | 30.00 |
| *—Black vinyl* | | | |
| ❑ 8061 [S] | Music of Mystery and Romance | 1961 | 50.00 |
| *—Blue vinyl* | | | |
| ❑ 8070 [S] | Love Letters | 1961 | 30.00 |
| *—Black vinyl* | | | |
| ❑ 8070 [S] | Love Letters | 1961 | 50.00 |
| *—Blue vinyl* | | | |
| ❑ 8075 [S] | Hypnotique | 1961 | 30.00 |
| *—Black vinyl* | | | |
| ❑ 8075 [S] | Hypnotique | 1961 | 50.00 |
| *—Blue vinyl* | | | |
| ❑ 8086 [S] | Music of Hollywood | 1962 | 30.00 |
| *—Black vinyl* | | | |
| ❑ 8086 [S] | Music of Hollywood | 1962 | 50.00 |
| *—Blue vinyl* | | | |
| ❑ 8342 [S] | Music for Meditation | 1962 | 30.00 |
| *—Black vinyl* | | | |
| ❑ 8342 [S] | Music for Meditation | 1962 | 50.00 |
| *—Blue vinyl* | | | |
| ❑ 8347 [S] | Korla Pandit in Paris | 1962 | 30.00 |

| Number | Title (A Side/B Side) | Yr | NM |
|---|---|---|---|
| ❑ 8350 [S] | Christmas with Korla Pandit | 1962 | 30.00 |
| *—Black vinyl* | | | |
| ❑ 8350 [S] | Christmas with Korla Pandit | 1962 | 50.00 |
| *—Blue vinyl* | | | |
| NATIONAL CUSTOM | | | |
| ❑ NCR 12-574 | Fantastique! | 196? | 30.00 |
| SYMPATHY FOR THE RECORD INDUSTRY | | | |
| ❑ SFTRI 387 | Exotica 2000 | 1996 | 12.00 |
| VITA | | | |
| ❑ VLP-14 [10] | Rememb'ring with Korla Pandit | 195? | 80.00 |

**PANICS, THE**

| Number | Title (A Side/B Side) | Yr | NM |
|---|---|---|---|
| CHANCELLOR | | | |
| ❑ CHL-5026 [M] | Panicsville | 1962 | 30.00 |
| ❑ CHLS-5026 [S] | Panicsville | 1962 | 40.00 |
| PHILIPS | | | |
| ❑ PHM 200159 [M] | Discotheque Dance Party | 1964 | 15.00 |
| ❑ PHS 600159 [S] | Discotheque Dance Party | 1964 | 20.00 |

**PANTERA**

| Number | Title (A Side/B Side) | Yr | NM |
|---|---|---|---|
| EASTWEST | | | |
| ❑ 61908 | The Great Southern Trendkill | 1996 | 25.00 |
| ❑ 62068 [(2)] | Official Live: 101 Proof | 1997 | 100.00 |
| ❑ 92302 | Far Beyond Driven | 1994 | 200.00 |
| ELEKTRA | | | |
| ❑ 62451 | Reinventing the Steel | 2000 | 15.00 |
| METAL MAGIC | | | |
| ❑ MMR 1283 | Metal Magic | 1983 | 150.00 |
| ❑ MMR 1984 | Projects in the Jungle | 1984 | 100.00 |
| ❑ MMR 1985 | I Am the Night | 1985 | 80.00 |
| ❑ MMR 1988 | Power Metal | 1988 | 120.00 |

**PAPER GARDEN, THE**

| Number | Title (A Side/B Side) | Yr | NM |
|---|---|---|---|
| MUSICOR | | | |
| ❑ MS-(# unknown) | The Paper Garden | 1968 | 40.00 |

**PARAGONS, THE & THE HARPTONES**

| Number | Title (A Side/B Side) | Yr | NM |
|---|---|---|---|
| MUSICTONE | | | |
| ❑ M-8001 [M] | The Paragons vs. the Harptones | 1964 | 40.00 |

**PARAGONS, THE & THE JESTERS**

| Number | Title (A Side/B Side) | Yr | NM |
|---|---|---|---|
| JOSIE | | | |
| ❑ 4008 [M] | The Paragons Meet the Jesters | 1962 | 200.00 |
| JUBILEE | | | |
| ❑ JLP-1098 [M] | The Paragons Meet the Jesters | 1959 | 300.00 |
| *—Blue label, black vinyl* | | | |
| ❑ JLP-1098 [M] | The Paragons Meet the Jesters | 1959 | 1500. |
| *—Multi-color splash vinyl; VG value 750; VG+ value 1125* | | | |
| ❑ JLP-1098 [M] | The Paragons Meet the Jesters | 196? | 60.00 |
| *—Black label with multi-color logo* | | | |
| ❑ JLP-1098 [M] | The Paragons Meet the Jesters | 196? | 150.00 |
| *—Flat black label* | | | |
| WINLEY | | | |
| ❑ LP-6003 [M] | War! The Jesters vs. the Paragons | 195? | 500.00 |

**PARENTI, TONY**

| Number | Title (A Side/B Side) | Yr | NM |
|---|---|---|---|
| JAZZOLOGY | | | |
| ❑ JCE-1 [10] | Tony Parenti and His New Orleanians | 1962 | 20.00 |
| RIVERSIDE | | | |
| ❑ RLP 12-205 [M] | Ragtime | 195? | 30.00 |
| *—Blue label, microphone logo at top* | | | |
| ❑ RLP 12-205 [M] | Ragtime | 1956 | 60.00 |
| *—White label, blue print* | | | |

**PARENTI, TONY/THE DIXIELAND RHYTHM KINGS**

| Number | Title (A Side/B Side) | Yr | NM |
|---|---|---|---|
| JAZZTONE | | | |
| ❑ J-1273 [M] | Two Beat Bash | 195? | 40.00 |

**PARHAM, TINY**

| Number | Title (A Side/B Side) | Yr | NM |
|---|---|---|---|
| "X" | | | |
| ❑ LVA-3039 [10] | Tiny Parham's South Side Jazz | 1955 | 60.00 |

**PARIS, BOBBY**

| Number | Title (A Side/B Side) | Yr | NM |
|---|---|---|---|
| TETRAGRAMMATON | | | |
| ❑ T-105 [S] | Let Me Show You the Way | 1968 | 40.00 |
| ❑ M-2105 [M] | Let Me Show You the Way | 1968 | 100.00 |

**PARIS, FREDDIE**

| Number | Title (A Side/B Side) | Yr | NM |
|---|---|---|---|
| RCA VICTOR | | | |
| ❑ LSP-4064 | Lovin' Mood | 1968 | 20.00 |

**PARIS, JACKIE**

| Number | Title (A Side/B Side) | Yr | NM |
|---|---|---|---|
| ABC IMPULSE! | | | |
| ❑ AS-17 [S] | The Song Is Paris | 1968 | 20.00 |
| BRUNSWICK | | | |
| ❑ BL-54019 [M] | Skylark | 1957 | 100.00 |
| CORAL | | | |
| ❑ CRL-56118 [10] | That Paris Mood | 195? | 80.00 |
| EASTWEST | | | |
| ❑ 4002 [M] | The Jackie Paris Sound | 1958 | 80.00 |
| EMARCY | | | |
| ❑ MG-36095 [M] | Songs by Jackie Paris | 1956 | 100.00 |
| IMPULSE! | | | |
| ❑ A-17 [M] | The Song Is Paris | 1962 | 30.00 |
| ❑ AS-17 [S] | The Song Is Paris | 1962 | 40.00 |
| TIME | | | |
| ❑ ST-70009 [S] | Jackie Paris Sings the Lyrics of Ira Gershwin | 1959 | 50.00 |
| ❑ T-70009 [M] | Jackie Paris Sings the Lyrics of Ira Gershwin | 1959 | 40.00 |
| WING | | | |
| ❑ MGW-60004 [M] | Songs by Jackie Paris | 1956 | 80.00 |

**PARIS, PRISCILLA** Also see THE PARIS SISTERS.

| Number | Title (A Side/B Side) | Yr | NM |
|---|---|---|---|
| HAPPY TIGER | | | |
| ❑ HT-1002 | Priscilla Loves Billy | 1968 | 40.00 |
| YORK | | | |
| ❑ 4005 [M] | Priscilla Sings Herself | 1967 | 30.00 |
| ❑ 4005-S [S] | Priscilla Sings Herself | 1967 | 40.00 |

**PARIS CONSERVATOIRE ORCHESTRE (ANATOLE FISTOULARI, CONDUCTOR)**

| Number | Title (A Side/B Side) | Yr | NM |
|---|---|---|---|
| RCA VICTOR RED SEAL | | | |
| ❑ LSC-2400 [S] | Ballet Music from the Opera | 1960 | 400.00 |
| *—Original with "shaded dog" label* | | | |
| ❑ LSC-2400 [S] | Ballet Music from the Opera | 199? | 25.00 |
| *—Classic Records reissue* | | | |

**PARIS CONSERVATOIRE ORCHESTRE (JEAN MARTINON, CONDUCTOR)**

| Number | Title (A Side/B Side) | Yr | NM |
|---|---|---|---|
| RCA VICTOR RED SEAL | | | |
| ❑ LSC-2272 [S] | Prokofiev: Symphony No. 5 | 1959 | 80.00 |
| *—Original with "shaded dog" label* | | | |
| ❑ LSC-2288 [S] | Prokofiev: Symphony No. 7 | 1959 | 80.00 |
| *—Original with "shaded dog" label* | | | |
| ❑ LSC-2288 [S] | Prokofiev: Symphony No. 7 | 199? | 25.00 |
| *—Classic Records reissue* | | | |

**PARIS CONSERVATOIRE ORCHESTRE (PIERRE MONTEUX, CONDUCTOR)**

| Number | Title (A Side/B Side) | Yr | NM |
|---|---|---|---|
| RCA VICTOR RED SEAL | | | |
| ❑ LSC-2085 [S] | Stravinsky: The Rite of Spring | 1958 | 50.00 |
| *—Original with "shaded dog" label* | | | |
| ❑ LSC-2085 [S] | Stravinsky: The Rite of Spring | 1964 | 40.00 |
| *—Second issue with "white dog" label* | | | |

**PARIS CONSERVATOIRE ORCHESTRE (JEAN-PAUL MOREL, CONDUCTOR)**

| Number | Title (A Side/B Side) | Yr | NM |
|---|---|---|---|
| RCA VICTOR RED SEAL | | | |
| ❑ LSC-6094 [(2)S] | Albaniz: Iberia; Ravel: Rapsodie Espagnole | 196? | 400.00 |
| *—Original with "shaded dog" label* | | | |

**PARIS CONSERVATOIRE ORCHESTRE (HUGH RIGNOLD, CONDUCTOR)**

| Number | Title (A Side/B Side) | Yr | NM |
|---|---|---|---|
| RCA VICTOR RED SEAL | | | |
| ❑ LSC-2485 [S] | Delibes: Sylvia and Coppelia Ballet Suites | 1961 | 80.00 |
| *—Original with "shaded dog" label* | | | |

**PARIS CONSERVATOIRE ORCHESTRE (ALBERT WOLFF, CONDUCTOR)**

| Number | Title (A Side/B Side) | Yr | NM |
|---|---|---|---|
| RCA VICTOR RED SEAL | | | |
| ❑ LSC-2301 [S] | Adam: Giselle | 1959 | 50.00 |
| *—Original with "shaded dog" label* | | | |

**PARIS PILOT**

| Number | Title (A Side/B Side) | Yr | NM |
|---|---|---|---|
| HIP | | | |
| ❑ 7004 | Paris Pilot | 1970 | 25.00 |

**PARIS SISTERS, THE** Also see PRISCILLA PARIS.

| Number | Title (A Side/B Side) | Yr | NM |
|---|---|---|---|
| REPRISE | | | |
| ❑ R-6259 [M] | Everything Under the Sun | 1967 | 40.00 |
| ❑ RS-6359 [S] | Everything Under the Sun | 1967 | 60.00 |
| SIDEWALK | | | |
| ❑ DT 5906 [R] | Golden Hits of the Paris Sisters | 1967 | 30.00 |
| ❑ T 5906 [M] | Golden Hits of the Paris Sisters | 1967 | 50.00 |
| UNIFILMS | | | |
| ❑ 505 [M] | The Paris Sisters Sing Songs from Glass House | 1966 | 40.00 |
| ❑ S-505 [S] | The Paris Sisters Sing Songs from Glass House | 1966 | 50.00 |

**PARISH HALL**

| Number | Title (A Side/B Side) | Yr | NM |
|---|---|---|---|
| FANTASY | | | |
| ❑ 8398 | Parish Hall | 1969 | 20.00 |

**PARKER, BILLIE JEAN**

| Number | Title (A Side/B Side) | Yr | NM |
|---|---|---|---|
| RCA VICTOR | | | |
| ❑ LPM-3967 [M] | The Truth About Bonnie and Clyde | 1968 | 40.00 |
| ❑ LSP-3967 [S] | The Truth About Bonnie and Clyde | 1968 | 15.00 |

**PARKER, BILLY (2)**

| Number | Title (A Side/B Side) | Yr | NM |
|---|---|---|---|
| STRATA-EAST | | | |
| ❑ SES-19754 | Freedom of Speech | 1975 | 25.00 |

**PARKER, CHARLIE**

| Number | Title (A Side/B Side) | Yr | NM |
|---|---|---|---|
| AMERICAN RECORDING SOCIETY | | | |
| ❑ G-441 [M] | Now's the Time | 1957 | 50.00 |
| BARONET | | | |
| ❑ B-105 [M] | A Handful of Modern Jazz | 1962 | 20.00 |
| ❑ B-107 [M] | The Early Bird | 1962 | 20.00 |
| BIRDLAND | | | |
| ❑ 425 [10] | A Night at Carnegie Hall | 1956 | 300.00 |
| BLUE RIBBON | | | |
| ❑ 8011 [M] | The Early Bird | 1962 | 20.00 |
| CHARLIE PARKER | | | |
| ❑ PLP-401 [M] | Bird Is Free | 1961 | 40.00 |
| ❑ PLP-404 [M] | The Happy Bird | 1961 | 40.00 |
| ❑ PLP-406 [M] | Charlie Parker | 1961 | 40.00 |
| ❑ PLP-407 [M] | Bird Symbols | 1961 | 40.00 |
| ❑ PLP-408 [M] | Once There Was Bird | 1961 | 40.00 |
| ❑ CP-2-502 [(2)M] | Live at Rockland Palace, September 26, 1952 | 1961 | 50.00 |
| ❑ CP-513 [M] | Charlie Parker Plus Strings | 196? | 40.00 |
| ❑ PLP-701 [(3)] | Historical Masterpieces | 196? | 60.00 |
| CLEF | | | |
| ❑ MGC-157 [10] | Charlie Parker | 1954 | 400.00 |
| ❑ MGC-501 [10] | Charlie Parker with Strings | 1954 | 400.00 |
| *—Reissue of Mercury 501* | | | |
| ❑ MGC-509 [10] | Charlie Parker with Strings, No. 2 | 1954 | 400.00 |
| *—Reissue of Mercury 509* | | | |
| ❑ MGC-512 [10] | Bird and Diz | 1954 | 400.00 |
| *—Reissue of Mercury 512* | | | |
| ❑ MGC-513 [10] | South of the Border | 1954 | 400.00 |
| *—Reissue of Mercury 513* | | | |
| ❑ MGC-609 [M] | Charlie Parker Big Band | 1954 | 400.00 |
| ❑ MGC-646 [M] | The Magnificent Charlie Parker | 1955 | 400.00 |
| ❑ MGC-675 [M] | Charlie Parker with Strings | 1955 | 400.00 |
| ❑ MGC-725 [M] | Night and Day | 1956 | 120.00 |
| CONCERT HALL JAZZ | | | |
| ❑ 1004 [10] | The Fabulous Bird | 1955 | 60.00 |
| ❑ 1017 [10] | The Art of Charlie Parker, Vol. 2 | 1955 | 60.00 |
| CONTINENTAL | | | |
| ❑ 16004 [M] | Bird Lives | 1962 | 40.00 |
| DEBUT | | | |
| ❑ DEB-611 [M] | Bird on 52nd Street | 196? | 50.00 |
| DIAL | | | |
| ❑ LP-201 [10] | Charlie Parker Quintet | 1949 | 800.00 |
| ❑ LP-202 [10] | Charlie Parker Quintet | 1949 | 800.00 |
| ❑ LP-203 [10] | Charlie Parker | 1949 | 800.00 |
| ❑ LP-207 [10] | Charlie Parker Sextet | 1949 | 800.00 |
| ❑ LP-901 [M] | The Bird Blows the Blues | 1949 | 4000. |
| *—Limited edition of 300 copies on opaque red vinyl; designed as a mail-order offer; issued with a generic gray cover; also has a pale yellow Dial label similiar to the label's 78 rpm design* | | | |
| ❑ LP-901 [M] | The Bird Blows the Blues | 1950 | 600.00 |
| *—Commercial version of mail-order album* | | | |
| ❑ LP-904 [M] | Alternate Masters | 1951 | 600.00 |
| ❑ LP-905 [M] | Alternate Masters | 1951 | 600.00 |
| ESP-DISK' | | | |
| ❑ ESP-BIRD-2 | Broadcast Performances 1948-1949, Vol. 2 | 1973 | 20.00 |
| FANTASY | | | |
| ❑ 6011 [M] | Bird on 52nd St. | 1964 | 30.00 |
| ❑ 6012 [M] | Bird at St. Nick's | 1964 | 30.00 |
| JAZZ WORKSHOP | | | |
| ❑ JWS-500 [M] | Bird at St. Nick's | 1958 | 120.00 |
| ❑ JWS-501 [M] | Bird on 52nd Street | 1958 | 120.00 |
| JAZZTONE | | | |
| ❑ J-(# unk) [M] | The Art of Charlie Parker, Vol. 2 | 1955 | 50.00 |
| ❑ J-1204 [M] | Giants of Modern Jazz | 1955 | 50.00 |
| ❑ J-1214 [M] | The Fabulous Bird | 1955 | 50.00 |
| ❑ J-1240 [M] | The Saxes of Stan Getz and Charlie Parker | 1957 | 50.00 |
| LES JAZZ COOL | | | |
| ❑ 101 [M] | Les Jazz Cool, Volume 1 | 1960 | 50.00 |
| ❑ 102 [M] | Les Jazz Cool, Volume 2 | 1960 | 50.00 |
| ❑ 103 [M] | Les Jazz Cool, Volume 3 | 1960 | 50.00 |
| MERCURY | | | |
| ❑ MGC-101 [10] | Charlie Parker with Strings | 1950 | 500.00 |
| *—Reissue of 35010* | | | |
| ❑ MGC-109 [10] | Charlie Parker with Strings, Volume 2 | 1950 | 500.00 |
| ❑ MGC-501 [10] | Charlie Parker with Strings | 1951 | 500.00 |
| *—Reissue of 101 with new number* | | | |
| ❑ MGC-509 [10] | Charlie Parker with Strings, Volume 2 | 1952 | 500.00 |
| *—Reissue of 109 with new number* | | | |
| ❑ MGC-512 [10] | Bird and Diz | 1952 | 500.00 |
| ❑ MGC-513 [10] | South of the Border | 1952 | 500.00 |
| ❑ MG-35010 [10] | Charlie Parker with Strings | 1950 | 600.00 |

| Number | Title (A Side/B Side) | Yr | NM |
|---|---|---|---|
| **MOSAIC** | | | |
| ❑ MR10-129 [(10)] | The Complete Dean Benedetti Recordings of Charlie Parker | 199? | 100.00 |
| **ROOST** | | | |
| ❑ LP-2210 [M] | All Star Sextet | 1958 | 120.00 |
| ❑ LP-2257 [M] | The World of Charlie Parker | 1963 | 40.00 |
| **SAVOY** | | | |
| ❑ MG-9000 [10] | Charlie Parker | 1950 | 500.00 |
| ❑ MG-9001 [10] | Charlie Parker, Volume 2 | 1951 | 500.00 |
| ❑ MG-9010 [10] | Charlie Parker, Volume 3 | 1952 | 500.00 |
| ❑ MG-9011 [10] | Charlie Parker, Volume 4 | 1952 | 500.00 |
| ❑ MG-12000 [M] | Charlie Parker Memorial | 1955 | 100.00 |
| ❑ MG-12001 [M] | The Immortal Charlie Parker | 1955 | 100.00 |
| ❑ MG-12009 [M] | Charlie Parker Memorial, Volume 2 | 1955 | 100.00 |
| ❑ MG-12014 [M] | The Genius of Charlie Parker | 1955 | 100.00 |
| ❑ MG-12079 [M] | The Charlie Parker Story | 1956 | 100.00 |
| ❑ MG-12138 [M] | Bird's Night — The Music of Charlie Parker | 1958 | 50.00 |
| ❑ MG-12152 [M] | An Evening at Home with the Bird | 196? | 40.00 |
| ❑ MG-12179 [M] | The "Bird" Returns | 196? | 30.00 |
| ❑ MG-12186 [M] | Newly Discovered Sides by the Immortal Charlie Parker | 1966 | 30.00 |
| **SAVOY JAZZ** | | | |
| ❑ SJL-5500 [(5)] | The Complete Savoy Studio Sessions | 197? | 30.00 |
| **VERVE** | | | |
| ❑ VSP-23 [M] | Bird Wings | 1966 | 20.00 |
| ❑ MGV-8000 [M] | The Charlie Parker Story, Volume 1 | 1957 | 80.00 |
| ❑ V-8000 [M] | The Charlie Parker Story, Volume 1 | 1961 | 25.00 |
| ❑ MGV-8001 [M] | The Charlie Parker Story, Volume 2 | 1957 | 80.00 |
| ❑ V-8001 [M] | The Charlie Parker Story, Volume 2 | 1961 | 25.00 |
| ❑ MGV-8002 [M] | The Charlie Parker Story, Volume 3 | 1957 | 80.00 |
| ❑ V-8002 [M] | The Charlie Parker Story, Volume 3 | 1961 | 25.00 |
| ❑ MGV-8003 [M] | Night and Day (The Genius of Charlie Parker #1) | 1957 | 80.00 |
| ❑ V-8003 [M] | Night and Day (The Genius of Charlie Parker #1) | 1961 | 25.00 |
| ❑ MGV-8004 [M] | April in Paris (The Genius of Charlie Parker #2) | 1957 | 80.00 |
| ❑ V-8004 [M] | April in Paris (The Genius of Charlie Parker #2) | 1961 | 25.00 |
| ❑ MGV-8005 [M] | Now's the Time (The Genius of Charlie Parker #3) | 1957 | 80.00 |
| ❑ V-8005 [M] | Now's the Time (The Genius of Charlie Parker #3) | 1961 | 25.00 |
| ❑ MGV-8006 [M] | Bird and Diz (The Genius of Charlie Parker #4) | 1957 | 80.00 |
| ❑ V-8006 [M] | Bird and Diz (The Genius of Charlie Parker #4) | 1961 | 25.00 |
| ❑ MGV-8007 [M] | Charlie Parker Plays Cole Porter (The Genius of Charlie Parker #5) | 1957 | 80.00 |
| ❑ V-8007 [M] | Charlie Parker Plays Cole Porter (The Genius of Charlie Parker #5) | 1961 | 25.00 |
| ❑ MGV-8008 [M] | Fiesta (The Genius of Charlie Parker #6) | 1957 | 80.00 |
| ❑ V-8008 [M] | Fiesta (The Genius of Charlie Parker #6) | 1961 | 25.00 |
| ❑ MGV-8009 [M] | Jazz Perennial (The Genius of Charlie Parker #7) | 1957 | 80.00 |
| ❑ V-8009 [M] | Jazz Perennial (The Genius of Charlie Parker #7) | 1961 | 25.00 |
| ❑ MGV-8010 [M] | Swedish Schnapps (The Genius of Charlie Parker #8) | 1957 | 80.00 |
| ❑ V-8010 [M] | Swedish Schnapps (The Genius of Charlie Parker #8) | 1961 | 25.00 |
| ❑ MGV-8100-3 [(3)M] | The Charlie Parker Story | 1957 | 150.00 |
| *—Combines 8000, 8001 and 8002 in a box set* | | | |
| ❑ V-8100-3 [(3)M] | The Charlie Parker Story | 1961 | 60.00 |
| *—Combines 8000, 8001 and 8002 in a box set* | | | |
| ❑ V-8409 [M] | The Essential Charlie Parker | 1961 | 25.00 |
| **VOGUE** | | | |
| ❑ LAE-12002 [M] | Memorial Album | 1955 | 150.00 |
| **WARNER BROS.** | | | |
| ❑ 6BS 3159 [(6)] | The Complete Dial Recordings | 1977 | 80.00 |
| *—Limited edition of 4,000 box sets* | | | |
| ❑ 2WB 3198 [(2)] | The Very Best of Bird | 1977 | 20.00 |

### PARKER, CHARLIE; DIZZY GILLESPIE; RED NORVO

| Number | Title (A Side/B Side) | Yr | NM |
|---|---|---|---|
| **DIAL** | | | |
| ❑ LP-903 [M] | Fabulous Jam Session | 1951 | 600.00 |

### PARKER, CHARLIE/DIZZY GILLESPIE/BUD POWELL/MAX ROACH

| Number | Title (A Side/B Side) | Yr | NM |
|---|---|---|---|
| **SAVOY** | | | |
| ❑ MG-9034 [10] | Bird, Diz, Bud, Max | 1953 | 600.00 |

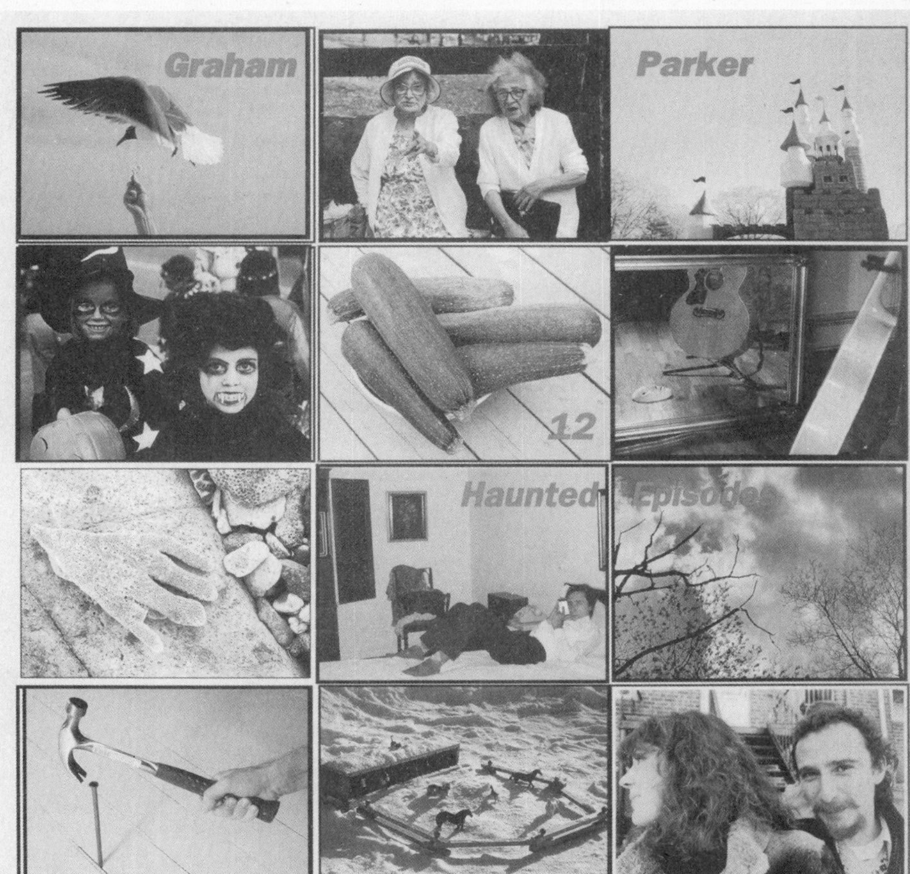


Graham Parker, *12 Haunted Episodes,* Rock the House RTH-2817-1, 1995, $15.

### PARKER, FESS

| Number | Title (A Side/B Side) | Yr | NM |
|---|---|---|---|
| **COLUMBIA** | | | |
| ❑ CL 666 [M] | Walt Disney's Davy Crockett, King of the Wild Frontier | 1955 | 100.00 |
| **DISNEYLAND** | | | |
| ❑ WDL-1007 [M] | Yarns and Songs of the West | 1959 | 30.00 |
| *—Reissue of 3006* | | | |
| ❑ DQ-1269 [M] | Pecos Bill and Other Stories in Song | 1965 | 30.00 |
| ❑ DQ-1315 [M] | Three Adventures of Davy Crockett | 1968 | 25.00 |
| *—Another reissue, this time of 1926* | | | |
| ❑ DQ-1336 | Cowboy and Indian Songs | 1969 | 30.00 |
| ❑ ST-1926 [M] | Three Adventures of Davy Crockett | 1963 | 30.00 |
| *—Reissue of 3602* | | | |
| ❑ WDL-3006 [M] | Yarns and Songs | 1957 | 40.00 |
| ❑ WDL-3041 [M] | Westward Ho the Wagons | 1959 | 30.00 |
| *—Reissue of 4008* | | | |
| ❑ WDA-3602 [M] | Three Adventures of Davy Crockett | 1958 | 50.00 |
| *—Reissue of Columbia 666* | | | |
| ❑ WDL-4006 [M] | Westward Ho the Wagons | 1956 | 80.00 |
| **RCA VICTOR** | | | |
| ❑ LPM-2973 [M] | Fess Parker Sings About Daniel Boone, Davy Crockett and Abe Lincoln | 1964 | 25.00 |
| ❑ LSP-2973 [S] | Fess Parker Sings About Daniel Boone, Davy Crockett and Abe Lincoln | 1964 | 30.00 |

### PARKER, GRAHAM

| Number | Title (A Side/B Side) | Yr | NM |
|---|---|---|---|
| **ARISTA** | | | |
| ❑ SP-63 [DJ] | Live Sparks | 1979 | 30.00 |
| ❑ AL 4223 | Squeezing Out Sparks | 1979 | 12.00 |
| ❑ AL8-8023 | The Real Macaw | 1983 | 10.00 |
| ❑ AL6-8352 | The Real Macaw | 1985 | 8.00 |
| *—Budget-line reissue* | | | |
| ❑ AL6-8356 | The Up Escalator | 1985 | 8.00 |
| *—Budget-line reissue* | | | |
| ❑ AL6-8363 | Squeezing Out Sparks | 1985 | 8.00 |
| *—Budget-line reissue* | | | |
| ❑ AL6-8374 | Another Grey Area | 1985 | 8.00 |
| *—Budget-line reissue* | | | |
| ❑ AL6-8391 | Look Back in Anger | 1985 | 10.00 |
| ❑ AL 9517 | The Up Escalator | 1980 | 10.00 |
| ❑ AL 9589 | Another Grey Area | 1982 | 10.00 |
| **ELEKTRA** | | | |
| ❑ 60388 | Steady Nerves | 1985 | 10.00 |
| **MERCURY** | | | |
| ❑ SRM-2-100 [(2)] | The Parkerilla | 1978 | 18.00 |
| *—Originals have gatefold sleeves* | | | |
| ❑ SRM-1-1095 | Howlin' Wind | 1976 | 15.00 |
| ❑ SRM-1-1117 | Heat Treatment | 1976 | 15.00 |
| ❑ SRM-1-3706 | Stick to Me | 1977 | 15.00 |
| ❑ 824808-1 | Stick to Me | 1985 | 12.00 |
| *—Reissue with new number* | | | |
| ❑ 826097-1 | Pourin' It All Out: The Mercury Years | 1985 | 12.00 |
| **RCA** | | | |
| ❑ 8316-1-R | The Mona Lisa's Sister | 1988 | 10.00 |
| ❑ 9876-1-R | Human Soul | 1989 | 10.00 |
| **ROCK THE HOUSE** | | | |
| ❑ RTH-2817-1 | 12 Haunted Episodes | 1995 | 15.00 |

### PARKER, JACY

| Number | Title (A Side/B Side) | Yr | NM |
|---|---|---|---|
| **VERVE** | | | |
| ❑ V-8424 [M] | Spotlight On Jacy Parker | 1962 | 40.00 |
| ❑ V6-8424 [S] | Spotlight On Jacy Parker | 1962 | 50.00 |

### PARKER, JUNIOR

| Number | Title (A Side/B Side) | Yr | NM |
|---|---|---|---|
| **ABC** | | | |
| ❑ AC-30010 | The ABC Collection | 1976 | 15.00 |
| **ABC DUKE** | | | |
| ❑ DLP-76 | Driving Wheel | 1974 | 15.00 |
| ❑ DLP-83 | The Best of Junior Parker | 1974 | 15.00 |
| **BLUE ROCK** | | | |
| ❑ SRB-64004 | Honey-Drippin' Blues | 1969 | 15.00 |
| **BLUESWAY** | | | |
| ❑ BLS-6066 | Sometime Tomorrow | 1973 | 15.00 |
| **CAPITOL** | | | |
| ❑ ST-564 | Outside Man | 1970 | 15.00 |
| **DUKE** | | | |
| ❑ DLP-76 [M] | Driving Wheel | 196? | 100.00 |
| *—With Wagon Wheel on front cover* | | | |
| ❑ DLP-76 [M] | Driving Wheel | 1962 | 150.00 |
| *—With Cadillac on front cover* | | | |
| ❑ DLP-83 [M] | The Best of Junior Parker | 1967 | 50.00 |

Number | Title (A Side/B Side) | Yr | NM

❑ DLPS-83 [P] The Best of Junior Parker 1967 40.00

GROOVE MERCHANT
❑ 513 Love Ain't Nothin' 1974 15.00

MCA
❑ 27046 The Best of Junior Parker 1980 10.00

MERCURY
❑ MG-21101 [M] Like It Is 1967 30.00
❑ SR-61101 [S] Like It Is 1967 25.00

MINIT
❑ 24024 Blues Man 1969 25.00

UNITED ARTISTS
❑ UAS-6823 I Tell Stories Sad and True 1971 15.00

### PARKER, JUNIOR, AND BOBBY BLAND

ABC DUKE
❑ DLP-72 Blues Consolidated 1974 15.00

DUKE
❑ DLP-72 [M] Blues Consolidated 1961 150.00

### PARKER, KNOCKY

AUDIOPHILE
❑ AP-28 [M] Boogie Woogie Maxine 1956 40.00
❑ AP-102/5 [(4)] The Complete Piano Works of Jelly Roll Morton 196? 50.00
*—In box with booklet; it's unknown whether the volumes also were issued individually*

PROGRESSIVE
❑ PLP-1 [10] New Orleans Stomps 1954 50.00

### PARKER, LEO

BLUE NOTE
❑ BLP-4087 [M] Let Me Tell You 'Bout It 1961 60.00
*—With 61st St. address on label*
❑ BLP-4087 [M] Let Me Tell You 'Bout It 1963 20.00
*—With "New York, USA" address on label*
❑ BST-84087 [S] Let Me Tell You 'Bout It 1961 80.00
*—With 61st St. address on label*
❑ BST-84087 [S] Let Me Tell You 'Bout It 1963 25.00
*—With "New York, USA" address on label*

SAVOY
❑ MG-9009 [10] Leo Parker 1952 250.00
❑ MG-9018 [10] New Trends in Modern Music 1952 250.00

### PARKER, MAYNARD

PRESTIGE
❑ 10054 Midnight Rider 1973 20.00

### PARKER, ROBERT

NOLA
❑ LP-1001 [M] Barefootin' 1966 30.00

### PARKER FAMILY, THE

AUDIO LAB
❑ AL-1548 [M] Songs for Salvation 196? 150.00
❑ AL-1574 [M] Songs for Salvation, Vol. 2 196? 150.00

KING
❑ 932 [M] Just a Real Nice Family 1965 40.00

### PARKINS, LEROY

BETHLEHEM
❑ BCP-6047 [M] LeRoy Parkins and His Yazoo River Band 1960 30.00
❑ SBCP-6047 [S] LeRoy Parkins and His Yazoo River Band 1960 40.00

### PARKS, ANDY

CAPITOL
❑ ST 2799 [S] Sex, School...And Like Other Pressures 1967 20.00
❑ T 2799 [M] Sex, School...And Like Other Pressures 1967 20.00

### PARKS, VAN DYKE

SUNDAZED
❑ LP- 5140 Song Cycle 2002 15.00
*—Reissue on 180-gram vinyl*
❑ LP-5141 Discover America 2002 15.00
*—Reissue on 180-gram vinyl*

WARNER BROS.
❑ WS 1727 Song Cycle 1968 15.00
*—Green label with "W7" box logo*
❑ WS 1727 Song Cycle 1968 25.00
*—Gold label*
❑ WS 1727 Song Cycle 1970 12.00
*—Green label with "WB" shield logo*
❑ BS 2589 Discover America 1972 12.00
❑ BS 2878 Clang of the Yankee Reaper 1975 12.00
❑ 23829 Jump! 1984 12.00
❑ 25968 Tokyo Rose 1989 12.00

### PARLAN, HORACE

BLUE NOTE
❑ BLP-4028 [M] Movin' and Groovin' 1960 80.00
*—Regular version, W. 63rd St. address on label*
❑ BLP-4028 [M] Movin' and Groovin' 1960 100.00
*—"Deep groove" version (deep indentation under label on both sides)*
❑ BLP-4028 [M] Movin' and Groovin' 1963 20.00
*—With "New York, USA" address on label*
❑ BLP-4037 [M] Us Three 1960 80.00
*—Regular version, W. 63rd St. address on label*
❑ BLP-4037 [M] Us Three 1960 100.00
*—"Deep groove" version (deep indentation under label on both sides)*
❑ BLP-4037 [M] Us Three 1963 20.00
*—With "New York, USA" address on label*
❑ BLP-4043 [M] Speakin' My Piece 1960 80.00
*—Regular version, W. 63rd St. address on label*
❑ BLP-4043 [M] Speakin' My Piece 1960 100.00
*—"Deep groove" version (deep indentation under label on both sides)*
❑ BLP-4043 [M] Speakin' My Piece 1963 20.00
*—With "New York, USA" address on label*
❑ BLP-4062 [M] Headin' South 1961 60.00
*—With W. 63rd St. address on label*
❑ BLP-4062 [M] Headin' South 1963 20.00
*—With "New York, USA" address on label*
❑ BLP-4074 [M] On the Spur of the Moment 1961 60.00
*—With 61st St. address on label*
❑ BLP-4074 [M] On the Spur of the Moment 1961 150.00
*—With W. 63rd St. address on label*
❑ BLP-4074 [M] On the Spur of the Moment 1963 20.00
*—With "New York, USA" address on label*
❑ BST-4074 On the Spur of the Moment 199? 25.00
*—Classic Records reissue on audiophile vinyl*
❑ BLP-4082 [M] Up and Down 1961 60.00
*—With 61st St. address on label*
❑ BLP-4082 [M] Up and Down 1963 20.00
*—With "New York, USA" address on label*
❑ BST-84028 [S] Movin' and Groovin' 1960 80.00
*—With W. 63rd St. address on label*
❑ BST-84028 [S] Movin' and Groovin' 1963 25.00
*—With "New York, USA" address on label*
❑ BST-84037 [S] Us Three 1960 80.00
*—With W. 63rd St. address on label*
❑ BST-84037 [S] Us Three 1963 25.00
*—With "New York, USA" address on label*
❑ BST-84043 [S] Speakin' My Piece 1960 80.00
*—With W. 63rd St. address on label*
❑ BST-84043 [S] Speakin' My Piece 1963 25.00
*—With "New York, USA" address on label*
❑ BST-84062 [S] Headin' South 1961 70.00
*—With W. 63rd St. address on label*
❑ BST-84062 [S] Headin' South 1963 25.00
*—With "New York, USA" address on label*
❑ BST-84074 [S] On the Spur of the Moment 1961 70.00
*—With 61st St. address on label*
❑ BST-84074 [S] On the Spur of the Moment 1961 200.00
*—With W. 63rd St. address on label*
❑ BST-84074 [S] On the Spur of the Moment 1963 25.00
*—With "New York, USA" address on label*
❑ BST-84082 [S] Up and Down 1961 70.00
*—With 61st St. address on label*
❑ BST-84082 [S] Up and Down 1963 25.00
*—With "New York, USA" address on label*

MOSAIC
❑ MQ8-197 [(8)] The Complete Horace Parlan Blue Note Sessions 2000 150.00

### PARLET

CASABLANCA
❑ NBLP 7094 Pleasure Principle 1978 20.00
❑ NBLP 7146 Invasion of the Booty Snatchers 1979 20.00

### PARLIAMENT Also see FUNKADELIC.

CASABLANCA
❑ NBLP 7002 Up for the Down Stroke 1974 40.00
❑ NBLP 7014 Chocolate City 1975 40.00
❑ NBLP 7022 Mothership Connection 1976 30.00
❑ NBLP 7034 The Clones of Dr. Funkenstein 1976 30.00
❑ NBLP 7053 [(2)] Parliament Live/P. Funk Earth Tour 1977 40.00
❑ NBLP 7084 Funkentelechy vs. the Placebo Syndrome 1977 30.00
❑ NBLP 7125 Motor-Booty Affair 1978 30.00
❑ NBPIX 7125 [PD] Motor-Booty Affair 1978 40.00
❑ NBLP 7195 Gloryhallastoopid (Or Pin the Tale on the Funky) 1979 30.00
❑ NBLP 7249 Trombipulation 1980 30.00
❑ NBLP 9003 Up for the Down Stroke 1974 50.00
*—Original pressing, distributed by Warner Bros.*
❑ 822637-1 Greatest Hits 1984 15.00
❑ 824501-1 Funkentelechy vs. the Placebo Syndrome 1985 15.00
❑ 824502-1 Mothership Connection 1985 15.00

INVICTUS
❑ ST-7302 Osmium 1970 100.00

### PARSONS, ALAN, PROJECT

ARISTA
❑ SP-68 [(6)DJ] Audio Guide to the Alan Parsons Project 1979 50.00
*—Contains first four APP LPs plus a two-record set of other Parsons work*
❑ SP-140 [(8)DJ] Complete Audio Guide to the Alan Parsons Project 1982 80.00
*—Contains first six APP LPs plus a two-record set of other Parsons work*
❑ AB 4180 Pyramid 1978 10.00
❑ AL 7002 I Robot 1977 10.00
❑ AL 8040 I Robot 1983 8.00
*—Reissue*
❑ AL 8193 The Best of the Alan Parsons Project 1983 8.00
❑ AL 8204 Ammonia Avenue 1984 10.00
❑ AL 8263 Vulture Culture 1985 8.00
❑ ALPD 8263 [DJ] Vulture Culture 1985 25.00
*—Promo-only picture disc*
❑ AL 8289 Ammonia Avenue 1985 8.00
*—Reissue*
❑ AL 8290 Eye in the Sky 1985 8.00
*—Reissue*
❑ AL 8315 The Turn of a Friendly Card 1985 8.00
*—Reissue*
❑ AL 8318 Eve 1985 8.00
*—Reissue*
❑ AL 8320 Pyramid 1985 8.00
*—Reissue*
❑ AL 8384 Stereotomy 1986 8.00
*—With regular LP jacket*
❑ AL 8384 Stereotomy 1986 15.00
*—First editions came in an oversize vinyl jacket*
❑ AL 8448 Gaudi 1987 8.00
❑ AL 8486 The Best of the Alan Parsons Project, Vol. 2 1987 8.00
❑ AL 8487 The Instrumental Works of the Alan Parsons Project 1988 10.00
❑ AB 9504 Eve 1979 10.00
❑ AL 9518 The Turn of a Friendly Card 1980 10.00
❑ AL 9599 Eye in the Sky 1982 10.00

CASABLANCA
❑ 822784-1 Tales of Mystery and Imagination - Edgar Allan Poe 1984 10.00
*—Reissue of 20th Century LP*

MOBILE FIDELITY
❑ 1-084 I Robot 1982 40.00
*—Audiophile vinyl*
❑ MFQR 1-084 I Robot 1982 80.00
*—Audiophile vinyl; Ultra High Quality pressing in box*
❑ 1-204 Tales of Mystery and Imagination - Edgar Allan Poe 1994 20.00
*—Audiophile vinyl*

20TH CENTURY
❑ T-508 Tales of Mystery and Imagination - Edgar Allan Poe 1976 15.00

### PARTON, DOLLY

COLUMBIA
❑ FC 40968 Rainbow 1987 10.00
❑ FC 44384 White Limozeen 1989 12.00
❑ C 46882 Eagle When She Flies 1991 20.00
*—Available on vinyl only through Columbia House*

MONUMENT
❑ 7623 In the Beginning 197? 12.00
❑ MLP-8085 [M] Hello, I'm Dolly 1967 30.00
❑ SLP-18085 [S] Hello, I'm Dolly 1967 40.00
❑ SLP-18136 As Long As I Love 1970 20.00
❑ KZG 31913 [(2)] The World of Dolly 1972 20.00
❑ KZG 33876 [(2)] Hello, I'm Dolly 1975 20.00

PAIR
❑ PDL2-1009 [(2)] Just the Way I Am 1986 12.00
❑ PDL2-1116 [(2)] Portrait 1986 12.00

RCA
❑ 5706-1-R The Best of Dolly Parton, Vol. 3 1987 10.00
❑ 6497-1-R The Best There Is 1987 10.00

RCA CAMDEN
❑ ACL1-0307 Mine 1973 10.00
❑ CAS-2583 Just the Way I Am 1972 10.00

RCA VICTOR
❑ APL1-0033 My Tennessee Mountain Home 1973 12.00
❑ APD1-0286 [Q] Bubbling Over 1974 20.00
❑ APL1-0286 Bubbling Over 1973 12.00
❑ APL1-0473 Jolene 1974 12.00
❑ APL1-0712 Love Is Like a Butterfly 1974 12.00
❑ APL1-0950 The Bargain Store 1975 12.00
❑ APL1-1117 The Best of Dolly Parton 1975 12.00
❑ APL1-1221 Dolly 1975 12.00
❑ APL1-1665 All I Can Do 1976 12.00
❑ APL1-2188 New Harvest...First Gathering 1977 12.00
❑ DJL1-2314 [DJ] Personal Music Dialogue with Dolly Parton 1976 25.00
❑ AFL1-2544 Here You Come Again 1977 12.00
❑ AFL1-2797 Heartbreaker 1978 12.00
❑ AHL1-3361 Great Balls of Fire 1979 12.00
❑ AHL1-3546 Dolly Dolly Dolly 1980 12.00
❑ AYL1-3665 Heartbreaker 1980 8.00
*—"Best Buy Series" reissue*

| Number | Title (A Side/B Side) | Yr | NM |
|---|---|---|---|
| ❑ AYL1-3764 | My Tennessee Mountain Home | 1980 | 8.00 |
| *—"Best Buy Series" reissue* | | | |
| ❑ AHL1-3852 | 9 to 5 and Odd Jobs | 1980 | 12.00 |
| ❑ AYL1-3898 | Jolene | 1981 | 8.00 |
| *—"Best Buy Series" reissue* | | | |
| ❑ LPM-3949 [M] | Just Because I'm a Woman | 1968 | 100.00 |
| ❑ LSP-3949 [S] | Just Because I'm a Woman | 1968 | 20.00 |
| *—Orange label* | | | |
| ❑ LSP-3949 [S] | Just Because I'm a Woman | 1968 | 30.00 |
| *—"Stereo" on black label* | | | |
| ❑ AYL1-3980 | New Harvest | 1981 | 8.00 |
| *—"Best Buy Series" reissue* | | | |
| ❑ LSP-4099 | In the Good Old Days | 1969 | 20.00 |
| ❑ LSP-4188 | My Blue Ridge Mountain Boy | 1969 | 20.00 |
| ❑ LSP-4288 | The Fairest of Them All | 1970 | 20.00 |
| ❑ AHL1-4289 | Heartbreak Express | 1982 | 12.00 |
| ❑ LSP-4387 | A Real Live Dolly | 1970 | 25.00 |
| *—Four songs feature Porter Wagoner* | | | |
| ❑ LSP-4398 | Golden Streets of Glory | 1971 | 20.00 |
| ❑ AHL1-4422 | Greatest Hits | 1982 | 12.00 |
| ❑ LSP-4449 | The Best of Dolly Parton | 1970 | 20.00 |
| ❑ LSP-4507 | Joshua | 1971 | 20.00 |
| ❑ LSP-4603 | Coat of Many Colors | 1971 | 20.00 |
| ❑ LSP-4686 | Touch Your Woman | 1972 | 20.00 |
| ❑ AHL1-4691 | Burlap & Satin | 1983 | 10.00 |
| ❑ LSP-4752 | My Favorite Song Writer: Porter Wagoner | 1972 | 20.00 |
| ❑ LSP-4762 | Dolly Parton Sings | 1972 | 15.00 |
| ❑ AYL1-4829 | Here You Come Again | 1984 | 8.00 |
| *—"Best Buy Series" reissue* | | | |
| ❑ AYL1-4830 | 9 to 5 and Odd Jobs | 1984 | 8.00 |
| *—"Best Buy Series" reissue* | | | |
| ❑ AHL1-4940 | The Great Pretender | 1984 | 10.00 |
| ❑ AYL1-5146 | The Best of Dolly Parton | 1984 | 8.00 |
| *—"Best Buy Series" reissue* | | | |
| ❑ AHL1-5414 | Real Love | 1985 | 10.00 |
| ❑ AYL1-5437 | Burlap & Satin | 1985 | 8.00 |
| *—"Best Buy Series" reissue* | | | |
| ❑ AHL1-5471 | Collector's Series | 1985 | 10.00 |
| ❑ AHL1-9508 | Think About Love | 1986 | 10.00 |

TIME-LIFE

| Number | Title (A Side/B Side) | Yr | NM |
|---|---|---|---|
| ❑ STW-107 | Country Music | 1981 | 10.00 |

**PARTON, DOLLY/GEORGE JONES**

STARDAY

| Number | Title (A Side/B Side) | Yr | NM |
|---|---|---|---|
| ❑ LP 429 [P] | Dolly Parton and George Jones | 1968 | 40.00 |

*—One side of Dolly in stereo, one side of "Possum" in rechanneled stereo*

**PARTON, DOLLY/FAYE TUCKER**

SOMERSET

| Number | Title (A Side/B Side) | Yr | NM |
|---|---|---|---|
| ❑ S-9700 [M] | Hits Made Famous by Country Queens | 1963 | 25.00 |
| ❑ SF-19700 [S] | Hits Made Famous by Country Queens | 1963 | 30.00 |
| *—Dolly Parton sings songs made famous by Kitty Wells* | | | |
| ❑ SF-29400 | Dolly Parton Sings Country Oldies | 1968 | 15.00 |

TIME

| Number | Title (A Side/B Side) | Yr | NM |
|---|---|---|---|
| ❑ 2108 | Country & Western Soul | 1963 | 40.00 |

**PARTON, STELLA**

ELEKTRA

| Number | Title (A Side/B Side) | Yr | NM |
|---|---|---|---|
| ❑ 6E-126 | Stella Parton | 1978 | 12.00 |
| ❑ 6E-191 | Love Ya | 1979 | 12.00 |
| ❑ 6E-229 | The Best of Stella Parton | 1979 | 12.00 |
| ❑ 7E-1111 | Country Sweet | 1977 | 12.00 |

SOUL, COUNTRY & BLUES

| Number | Title (A Side/B Side) | Yr | NM |
|---|---|---|---|
| ❑ 6006 | I Want to Hold You in My Dreams Tonight | 1975 | 20.00 |

TOWN HOUSE

| Number | Title (A Side/B Side) | Yr | NM |
|---|---|---|---|
| ❑ ST-7005 | So Far So Good | 1982 | 12.00 |

**PARTRIDGE FAMILY, THE**

BELL

| Number | Title (A Side/B Side) | Yr | NM |
|---|---|---|---|
| ❑ 1107 | The Partridge Family At Home with Their Greatest Hits | 1972 | 20.00 |
| ❑ 1111 | The Partridge Family Notebook | 1972 | 25.00 |
| ❑ 1122 | Crossword Puzzle | 1973 | 30.00 |
| ❑ 1137 | Bulletin Board | 1973 | 50.00 |
| ❑ 1319 [(2)] | The World of the Partridge Family | 1974 | 40.00 |
| ❑ 6050 | The Partridge Family Album Bonus Photo | 1970 | 10.00 |
| ❑ 6050 | The Partridge Family Album | 1970 | 20.00 |
| ❑ 6059 | Up to Date Book Cover | 1971 | 10.00 |
| ❑ 6059 | Up to Date | 1971 | 20.00 |
| ❑ 6064 | The Partridge Family Sound Magazine | 1971 | 20.00 |
| ❑ 6066 | A Partridge Family Christmas Card | 1971 | 15.00 |
| *—Without Christmas card* | | | |
| ❑ 6066 | A Partridge Family Christmas Card | 1971 | 25.00 |
| *—With attached Christmas card* | | | |
| ❑ 6066 | A Partridge Family Christmas Card | 1971 | 40.00 |
| *—With Christmas card printed on the cover (later pressing)* | | | |

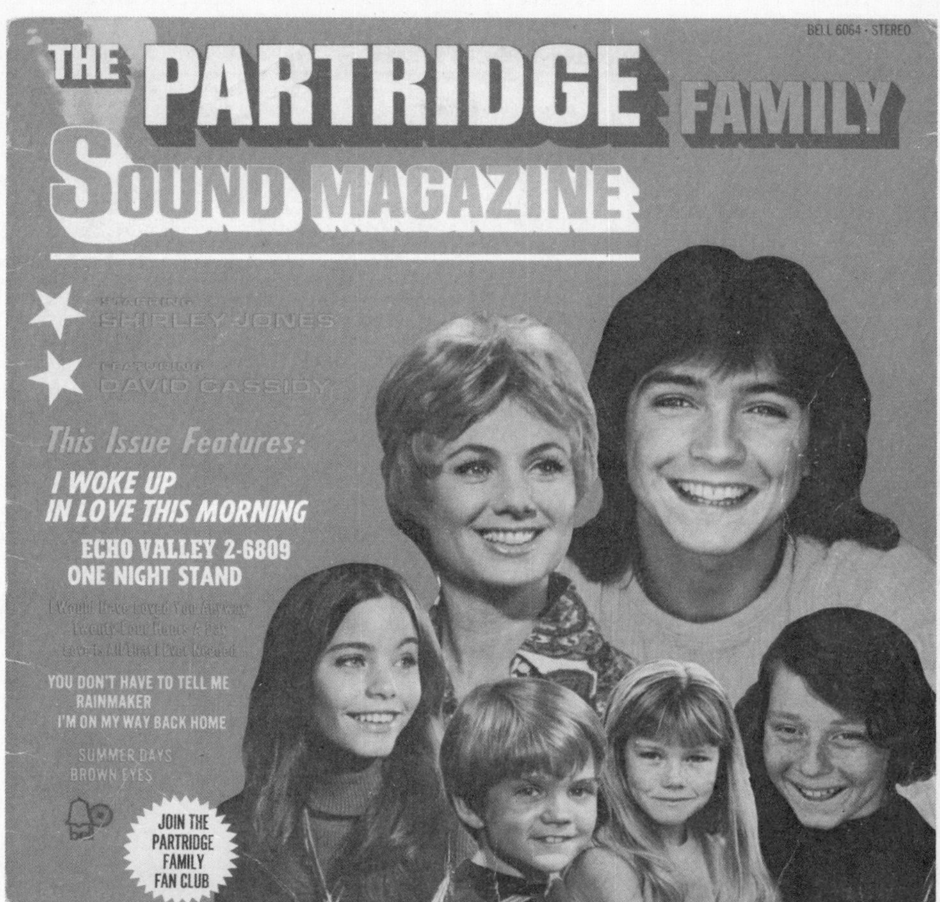


The Partridge Family, *The Partridge Family Sound Magazine,* Bell 6064, 1971, $20.

| Number | Title (A Side/B Side) | Yr | NM |
|---|---|---|---|
| ❑ 6072 | The Partridge Family Shopping Bag Bonus Shopping Bag | 1972 | 10.00 |
| ❑ 6072 | The Partridge Family Shopping Bag | 1972 | 20.00 |

LAURIE HOUSE

| Number | Title (A Side/B Side) | Yr | NM |
|---|---|---|---|
| ❑ H-8014 [(2)] | The Partridge Family | 197? | 50.00 |

**PASS, JOE**

PACIFIC JAZZ

| Number | Title (A Side/B Side) | Yr | NM |
|---|---|---|---|
| ❑ PJ-73 [M] | Catch Me! | 1963 | 25.00 |
| ❑ ST-73 [S] | Catch Me! | 1963 | 30.00 |
| ❑ PJ-85 [M] | For Django | 1964 | 25.00 |
| ❑ ST-85 [S] | For Django | 1964 | 30.00 |

WORLD PACIFIC

| Number | Title (A Side/B Side) | Yr | NM |
|---|---|---|---|
| ❑ WP-1854 [M] | The Stones Jazz | 1967 | 20.00 |
| ❑ WP-1865 [M] | Simplicity | 1967 | 20.00 |
| ❑ ST-21844 [S] | A Sign of the Times | 1966 | 20.00 |
| ❑ ST-21854 [S] | The Stones Jazz | 1967 | 20.00 |

**PASS, JOE, AND ARNOLD ROSS**

PACIFIC JAZZ

| Number | Title (A Side/B Side) | Yr | NM |
|---|---|---|---|
| ❑ PJ-48 [M] | Sounds of Synanon | 1962 | 25.00 |
| ❑ ST-48 [S] | Sounds of Synanon | 1962 | 30.00 |

**PASTEL SIX, THE**

ZEN

| Number | Title (A Side/B Side) | Yr | NM |
|---|---|---|---|
| ❑ 1001 [M] | The Cinnamon Cinder | 1963 | 100.00 |

**PASTOR, TONY**

EVEREST

| Number | Title (A Side/B Side) | Yr | NM |
|---|---|---|---|
| ❑ SDBR-1031 [S] | P.S. — Plays and Sings Shaw | 1959 | 20.00 |

**PASTORIUS, JACO**

IAI

| Number | Title (A Side/B Side) | Yr | NM |
|---|---|---|---|
| ❑ 373846 | Jaco | 1975 | 20.00 |

**PATCHEN, KENNETH, WITH THE CHAMBER JAZZ SEXTET**

CADENCE

| Number | Title (A Side/B Side) | Yr | NM |
|---|---|---|---|
| ❑ CLP-3004 [M] | Kenneth Patchen Reads His Poetry | 1957 | 300.00 |

**PATE, JOHNNY**

GIG

| Number | Title (A Side/B Side) | Yr | NM |
|---|---|---|---|
| ❑ GLP-100 [M] | Subtle Sounds | 1956 | 100.00 |

KING

| Number | Title (A Side/B Side) | Yr | NM |
|---|---|---|---|
| ❑ 561 [M] | Jazz Goes Ivy League | 1958 | 80.00 |
| ❑ 584 [M] | Swingin' Flute | 1958 | 80.00 |
| ❑ 611 [M] | A Date with Johnny Pate | 1959 | 80.00 |

STEPHENY

| Number | Title (A Side/B Side) | Yr | NM |
|---|---|---|---|
| ❑ 4002 [M] | Johnny Pate at the Blue Note | 1957 | 100.00 |

TALISMAN

| Number | Title (A Side/B Side) | Yr | NM |
|---|---|---|---|
| ❑ TLP-1 [10] | Johnny Pate Trio | 1956 | 120.00 |

**PATRON SAINTS, THE**

(NO LABEL)

| Number | Title (A Side/B Side) | Yr | NM |
|---|---|---|---|
| ❑ JT-1001 | Fohhob Bohob | 1969 | 3000. |

*—100 copies were pressed; VG value 1000; VG+ value 2000*

PATRON SAINT

| Number | Title (A Side/B Side) | Yr | NM |
|---|---|---|---|
| ❑ JT-1001 | Fohhob Bohob | 1997 | 25.00 |

*—Authorized reissue with bonus 7-inch single; numbered edition of 500*

**PATTERSON, DON**

CADET

| Number | Title (A Side/B Side) | Yr | NM |
|---|---|---|---|
| ❑ LP-787 [M] | Goin' Down Home | 1967 | 30.00 |
| ❑ LPS-787 [S] | Goin' Down Home | 1967 | 20.00 |

PRESTIGE

| Number | Title (A Side/B Side) | Yr | NM |
|---|---|---|---|
| ❑ PRLP-7331 [M] | The Exiting New Organ of Don Patterson | 1964 | 25.00 |
| ❑ PRST-7331 [S] | The Exciting New Organ of Don Patterson | 1964 | 30.00 |
| ❑ PRLP-7349 [M] | Hip Cake Walk | 1965 | 25.00 |
| ❑ PRST-7349 [S] | Hip Cake Walk | 1965 | 30.00 |
| ❑ PRLP-7381 [M] | Patterson's People | 1965 | 25.00 |
| ❑ PRST-7381 [S] | Patterson's People | 1965 | 30.00 |
| ❑ PRLP-7415 [M] | Holiday Soul | 1966 | 25.00 |
| ❑ PRST-7415 [S] | Holiday Soul | 1965 | 30.00 |
| ❑ PRLP-7430 [M] | Satisfaction | 1966 | 25.00 |
| ❑ PRST-7430 [S] | Satisfaction | 1966 | 30.00 |
| ❑ PRLP-7466 [M] | The Boss Men | 1967 | 30.00 |
| ❑ PRST-7466 [S] | The Boss Men | 1967 | 25.00 |
| ❑ PRLP-7484 [M] | Soul Happening! | 1967 | 25.00 |
| ❑ PRST-7484 [S] | Soul Happening! | 1967 | 20.00 |
| ❑ PRLP-7510 [M] | Mellow Soul | 1967 | 25.00 |
| ❑ PRST-7510 [S] | Mellow Soul | 1967 | 20.00 |
| ❑ PRLP-7533 [M] | Four Dimensions | 1967 | 25.00 |
| ❑ PRST-7533 [S] | Four Dimensions | 1967 | 20.00 |
| ❑ PRST-7563 | Boppin' and Burnin' | 1968 | 20.00 |
| ❑ PRST-7577 | Opus De Don | 1968 | 20.00 |

| Number | Title (A Side/B Side) | Yr | NM |
|---|---|---|---|
| ❑ PRST-7613 | Funk You | 1969 | 20.00 |
| ❑ PRST-7640 | Oh, Happy Days! | 1969 | 20.00 |
| **PATTERSON, KELLEE** | | | |
| BLACK JAZZ | | | |
| ❑ QD-12 | Maiden Voyage | 1974 | 20.00 |
| **PATTERSON SINGERS, THE** | | | |
| ATCO | | | |
| ❑ SD 33-380 | The Patterson Singers | 1972 | 20.00 |
| KING | | | |
| ❑ 763 [M] | Gospel Songs by the Patterson Singers | 1962 | 50.00 |
| ❑ KS-1129 | Jesus Knows | 1971 | 20.00 |
| MINIT | | | |
| ❑ LP-40021 | The Soul of Gospel | 1969 | 20.00 |
| VEE JAY | | | |
| ❑ LP-5017 [M] | My Prayer | 1962 | 25.00 |
| ❑ LP-5032 [M] | The Lord's Prayer | 1963 | 25.00 |
| ❑ LP-5046 [M] | Songs of Faith | 1963 | 20.00 |
| ❑ SR-5046 [S] | Songs of Faith | 1963 | 30.00 |
| ❑ LP-5060 [M] | The Soul of the Patterson Singers | 1964 | 20.00 |
| **PATTO** | | | |
| ISLAND | | | |
| ❑ SW-9322 | Roll 'Em, Smoke 'Em, Put Another Line Out | 1972 | 30.00 |
| VERTIGO | | | |
| ❑ VEL-1001 | Patto | 1971 | 15.00 |
| ❑ VEL-1008 | Hold Your Fire | 1972 | 15.00 |
| **PATTON, "BIG" JOHN** | | | |
| BLUE NOTE | | | |
| ❑ BLP-4130 [M] | Along Came John | 1963 | 30.00 |
| ❑ BLP-4174 [M] | The Way I Feel | 1964 | 25.00 |
| ❑ BLP-4192 [M] | Oh Baby! | 1964 | 25.00 |
| ❑ BLP-4229 [M] | Got a Good Thing Goin' | 1966 | 25.00 |
| ❑ BLP-4239 [M] | Let 'Em Roll | 1966 | 25.00 |
| ❑ BST-84130 [S] | Along Came John | 1963 | 40.00 |
| *—With "New York, USA" address on label* | | | |
| ❑ BST-84174 [S] | The Way I Feel | 1964 | 30.00 |
| *—With "New York, USA" address on label* | | | |
| ❑ BST-84192 [S] | Oh Baby! | 1964 | 30.00 |
| *—With "New York, USA" address on label* | | | |
| ❑ BST-84229 [S] | Got a Good Thing Goin' | 1966 | 30.00 |
| *—With "New York, USA" address on label* | | | |
| ❑ BST-84239 [S] | Let 'Em Roll | 1966 | 30.00 |
| *—With "New York, USA" address on label* | | | |
| ❑ BST-84281 [S] | That Certain Feeling | 1968 | 25.00 |
| *—With "A Division of Liberty Records" on label* | | | |
| ❑ BST-84306 [S] | Understanding | 1969 | 25.00 |
| *—With "A Division of Liberty Records" on label* | | | |
| ❑ BST-84340 [S] | Accent on the Blues | 1970 | 25.00 |
| *—With "A Division of Liberty Records" on label* | | | |
| **PATTON, CHARLEY** | | | |
| ORIGIN JAZZ LIBRARY | | | |
| ❑ OJL-1 [M] | The Immortal Charley Patton No. 1 | 1962 | 25.00 |
| ❑ OJL-7 [M] | The Immortal Charley Patton No. 2 | 1962 | 25.00 |
| YAZOO | | | |
| ❑ 2001 [(2)] | King of the Delta Blues | 197? | 30.00 |
| ❑ 2010 [(2)] | Founder of the Delta Blues | 197? | 30.00 |
| **PATTON, JIMMY** | | | |
| MOON | | | |
| ❑ 101 [M] | Make Room for the Blues | 1966 | 40.00 |
| SIMS | | | |
| ❑ 127 [M] | Blue Darlin' | 1965 | 40.00 |
| SOURDOUGH | | | |
| ❑ 127 [M] | Blue Darlin' | 1965 | 50.00 |
| STEREOPHONIC | | | |
| ❑ LP-1002 [S] | Take 30 Minutes with Jimmy Patton | 196? | 120.00 |
| **PAUL, BILLY** | | | |
| GAMBLE | | | |
| ❑ SG-5002 | Feeling Good at the Cadillac Club | 1968 | 30.00 |
| ICHIBAN | | | |
| ❑ ICH-1025 | Wide Open | 198? | 10.00 |
| NEPTUNE | | | |
| ❑ 201 | Ebony Woman | 1970 | 20.00 |
| PHILADELPHIA INT'L. | | | |
| ❑ Z 30580 | Going East | 1971 | 12.00 |
| ❑ KZ 31793 | 360 Degrees of Billy Paul | 1972 | 12.00 |
| ❑ ZQ 31793 [Q] | 360 Degrees of Billy Paul | 1972 | 20.00 |
| ❑ KZ 32118 | Ebony Woman | 1973 | 12.00 |
| *—Reissue of Neptune LP* | | | |
| ❑ KZ 32119 | Feeling Good at the Cadillac Club | 1973 | 12.00 |
| *—Reissue of Gamble LP* | | | |
| ❑ KZ 32409 | War of the Gods | 1973 | 10.00 |
| ❑ ZQ 32409 [Q] | War of the Gods | 1973 | 20.00 |
| ❑ KZ 32952 | Live in Europe | 1974 | 10.00 |
| ❑ ZQ 32952 [Q] | Live in Europe | 1974 | 20.00 |
| ❑ PZ 33157 | Got My Head On Straight | 1975 | 10.00 |
| ❑ PZ 33843 | When Love Is New | 1975 | 10.00 |
| ❑ PZ 34389 | Let 'Em In | 1976 | 10.00 |
| ❑ PZ 34923 | Only the Strong Survive | 1977 | 10.00 |
| ❑ JZ 35756 | First Class | 1979 | 10.00 |
| ❑ Z2 36314 [(2)] | The Best of Billy Paul | 1980 | 15.00 |
| TOTAL EXPERIENCE | | | |
| ❑ TEL8-5711 | Lately | 1985 | 10.00 |
| **PAUL, LES** | | | |
| CAPITOL | | | |
| ❑ N-16286 | Early Les Paul | 1982 | 8.00 |
| DECCA | | | |
| ❑ DL-5018 [10] | Hawaiian Paradise | 1949 | 100.00 |
| ❑ DL-5376 [10] | Galloping Guitars | 1952 | 100.00 |
| ❑ DL 8589 [M] | More of Les | 1957 | 40.00 |
| GLENDALE | | | |
| ❑ 6014 | The Les Paul Trio | 198? | 10.00 |
| LONDON | | | |
| ❑ 50016 | Multi-Trackin' | 1979 | 12.00 |
| LONDON PHASE 4 | | | |
| ❑ SP-44101 | Les Paul Now! | 1968 | 15.00 |
| VOCALION | | | |
| ❑ VL 3849 [M] | The Guitar Artistry of Les Paul | 196? | 12.00 |
| ❑ VL 73849 [R] | The Guitar Artistry of Les Paul | 196? | 10.00 |
| **PAUL, LES, AND MARY FORD** Also see MARY FORD. | | | |
| CAPITOL | | | |
| ❑ H 226 [10] | The New Sound, Volume 1 | 1950 | 80.00 |
| ❑ T 226 [M] | The New Sound, Volume 1 | 1955 | 50.00 |
| ❑ H 286 [10] | The New Sound, Volume 2 | 1951 | 80.00 |
| ❑ SM-286 | The New Sound, Volume 2 | 197? | 10.00 |
| ❑ T 286 [M] | The New Sound, Volume 2 | 1955 | 50.00 |
| ❑ H 356 [10] | Bye Bye Blues | 1952 | 80.00 |
| ❑ T 356 [M] | Bye Bye Blues | 1955 | 50.00 |
| ❑ H 416 [10] | The Hit Makers | 1953 | 80.00 |
| ❑ T 416 [M] | The Hit Makers | 1955 | 50.00 |
| ❑ H 577 [10] | Les and Mary | 1955 | 80.00 |
| ❑ W 577 [M] | Les and Mary | 1955 | 50.00 |
| ❑ T 802 [M] | Time to Dream | 1956 | 50.00 |
| ❑ DT 1476 [R] | The Hits of Les and Mary | 1960 | 20.00 |
| ❑ T 1476 [M] | The Hits of Les and Mary | 1960 | 25.00 |
| ❑ SM-11308 | The World Is Still Waiting for the Sunrise | 197? | 10.00 |
| *—Reissue with new prefix* | | | |
| ❑ ST-11308 | The World Is Still Waiting for the Sunrise | 1974 | 12.00 |
| CAPITOL SPECIAL MARKETS | | | |
| ❑ SLCR-8130 [(3)] | The All-Time Greatest Hits of Les Paul and Mary Ford | 1980 | 20.00 |
| *—Produced for Murray Hill Records (979462)* | | | |
| COLUMBIA | | | |
| ❑ CL 1276 [M] | Lovers' Luau | 1959 | 20.00 |
| ❑ CL 1688 [M] | Warm and Wonderful | 1962 | 20.00 |
| ❑ CL 1821 [M] | Bouquet of Roses | 1962 | 20.00 |
| ❑ CL 1928 [M] | Swingin' South | 1963 | 15.00 |
| ❑ CS 8086 [S] | Lovers' Luau | 1959 | 30.00 |
| ❑ CS 8488 [S] | Warm and Wonderful | 1962 | 25.00 |
| ❑ CS 8621 [S] | Bouquet of Roses | 1962 | 25.00 |
| ❑ CS 8728 [S] | Swingin' South | 1963 | 20.00 |
| HARMONY | | | |
| ❑ HL 7333 [M] | The Fabulous Les Paul and Mary Ford | 1965 | 12.00 |
| ❑ HS 11133 [S] | The Fabulous Les Paul and Mary Ford | 1965 | 12.00 |
| PICKWICK | | | |
| ❑ SPC-3122 | Brazil | 197? | 10.00 |
| **PAUL AND PAULA** | | | |
| PHILIPS | | | |
| ❑ PHM 200078 [M] | Paul and Paula Sing for Young Lovers | 1963 | 30.00 |
| ❑ PHM 200089 [M] | We Go Together | 1963 | 30.00 |
| ❑ PHM 200101 [M] | Holiday for Teens | 1963 | 30.00 |
| ❑ PHS 600078 [S] | Paul and Paula Sing for Young Lovers | 1963 | 40.00 |
| ❑ PHS 600089 [S] | We Go Together | 1963 | 40.00 |
| ❑ PHS 600101 [S] | Holiday for Teens | 1963 | 40.00 |
| **PAULSON, PAT** | | | |
| RUBICON/MERCURY | | | |
| ❑ SR 61179 | Pat Paulson for President | 1968 | 20.00 |
| ❑ SR 61251 | Live at the Ice House | 1970 | 15.00 |
| **PAUPERS, THE** | | | |
| VERVE FORECAST | | | |
| ❑ FT-3026 [M] | Magic People | 1967 | 20.00 |
| ❑ FTS-3026 [S] | Magic People | 1967 | 20.00 |
| ❑ FTS-3051 | Ellis Island | 1968 | 15.00 |
| **PAVLOV'S DOG** | | | |
| ABC | | | |
| ❑ D-866 | Pampered Menial | 1975 | 25.00 |
| COLUMBIA | | | |
| ❑ PC 33552 | Pampered Menial | 1976 | 12.00 |
| *—Reissue of ABC album* | | | |
| ❑ PC 33964 | At the Sound of the Bell | 1976 | 12.00 |
| **PAVONE, RITA** | | | |
| RCA VICTOR | | | |
| ❑ LPM-2900 [M] | Rita Pavone | 1964 | 15.00 |
| ❑ LSP-2900 [S] | Rita Pavone | 1964 | 20.00 |
| ❑ LPM-2996 [M] | Small Wonder | 1965 | 15.00 |
| ❑ LSP-2996 [S] | Small Wonder | 1965 | 20.00 |
| **PAXTON, TOM** | | | |
| ELEKTRA | | | |
| ❑ EKL-277 [M] | Ramblin' Boy | 1964 | 20.00 |
| ❑ EKL-298 [M] | Ain't That News | 1965 | 20.00 |
| ❑ EKL-317 [M] | Outward Bound | 1966 | 20.00 |
| ❑ 7E-2003 [(2)] | The Compleat Tom Paxton | 1971 | 20.00 |
| ❑ EKS-7277 [S] | Ramblin' Boy | 1964 | 25.00 |
| ❑ EKS-7298 [S] | Ain't That News | 1965 | 25.00 |
| ❑ EKS-7317 [S] | Outward Bound | 1966 | 25.00 |
| ❑ EKS-74019 | Morning Again | 1968 | 20.00 |
| ❑ EKS-74043 | The Things I Notice Now | 1969 | 15.00 |
| ❑ EKS-74066 | Tom Paxton 6 | 1970 | 15.00 |
| FLYING FISH | | | |
| ❑ FF-280 | Even a Gray Day | 1983 | 10.00 |
| ❑ FF-356 | One Million Lawyers...And Other Disasters | 1986 | 10.00 |
| ❑ FF-408 | The Marvellous Toy and Other Gallimaufry | 1987 | 10.00 |
| ❑ FF-414 | And Loving You | 1987 | 10.00 |
| ❑ FF-486 | Politics | 199? | 12.00 |
| ❑ FF-519 | The Very Best of Tom Paxton | 199? | 12.00 |
| GASLIGHT | | | |
| ❑ GV-116 [M] | I'm the Man Who Built the Bridges | 1962 | 80.00 |
| HOGEYE | | | |
| ❑ 004 | Bulletin...We Interrupt This Record | 198? | 10.00 |
| MOUNTAIN RAILROAD | | | |
| ❑ 52792 | Up and Up | 1980 | 12.00 |
| ❑ 52796 | The Paxton Report | 198? | 12.00 |
| PRIVATE STOCK | | | |
| ❑ PS-2002 | Something in My Life | 1975 | 12.00 |
| REPRISE | | | |
| ❑ MS 2096 | Peace Will Come | 1972 | 15.00 |
| ❑ MS 2144 | New Songs for Old Friends | 1973 | 15.00 |
| ❑ RS 6443 | How Come the Sun | 1971 | 15.00 |
| VANGUARD | | | |
| ❑ VSD-79395 | New Songs from the Briarpatch | 1977 | 12.00 |
| ❑ VSD-79411 | Heroes | 1978 | 12.00 |
| **PAYCHECK, JOHNNY** | | | |
| ACCORD | | | |
| ❑ SN-7173 | Extra Special | 1981 | 10.00 |
| ALLEGIANCE | | | |
| ❑ AV-435 | I Don't Need to Know That Right Now | 198? | 8.00 |
| CERTRON | | | |
| ❑ 7002 | Johnny Paycheck Again | 1970 | 15.00 |
| EPIC | | | |
| ❑ E 31141 | She's All I Got | 1971 | 12.00 |
| ❑ KE 31449 | Someone to Give My Love To | 1972 | 12.00 |
| ❑ KE 31702 | Somebody Loves Me | 1972 | 12.00 |
| ❑ KE 32387 | Something About You I Love | 1973 | 12.00 |
| ❑ KE 32570 | Song and Dance Man | 1973 | 12.00 |
| ❑ KE 33091 | Greatest Hits | 1974 | 10.00 |
| ❑ PE 33091 | Greatest Hits | 198? | 8.00 |
| *—Budget-line reissue* | | | |
| ❑ KE 33354 | Loving You Beats All I've Ever Seen | 1975 | 10.00 |
| ❑ KE 33943 | 11 Months and 29 Days | 1975 | 10.00 |
| ❑ PE 34693 | Slide Off of Your Satin Sheets | 1976 | 10.00 |
| ❑ KE 35045 | Take This Job and Shove It | 1977 | 10.00 |
| ❑ PE 35045 | Take This Job and Shove It | 198? | 8.00 |
| *—Budget-line reissue* | | | |
| ❑ KE 35444 | Armed and Crazy | 1978 | 10.00 |
| ❑ KE 35623 | Greatest Hits, Volume 2 | 1978 | 10.00 |
| ❑ PE 35623 | Greatest Hits, Volume 2 | 198? | 8.00 |
| *—Budget-line reissue* | | | |
| ❑ JE 36200 | Everybody's Got a Family — Meet Mine | 1979 | 10.00 |
| ❑ JE 36496 | New York Town | 1980 | 10.00 |
| ❑ FE 36761 | Mr. Hag Told My Story | 1981 | 10.00 |
| ❑ PE 36761 | Mr. Hag Told My Story | 1981 | 8.00 |
| *—Budget-line reissue* | | | |
| ❑ FE 37345 | Encore | 1981 | 10.00 |
| ❑ PE 37345 | Encore | 198? | 8.00 |
| *—Budget-line reissue* | | | |
| ❑ FE 37933 | Lovers and Losers | 1982 | 10.00 |
| ❑ FE 38322 | Johnny Paycheck's Biggest Hits | 1983 | 10.00 |
| ❑ PE 39943 | John Austin Paycheck | 1984 | 8.00 |
| INTERMEDIA | | | |
| ❑ QS-5018 | Back On the Job | 198? | 8.00 |



Except when noted otherwise, VG = 25% of NM, and VG+ = 50% of NM. (Example: VG = $2.00, VG+ = $4.00 and NM = $8.00.)

Number | Title (A Side/B Side) | Yr | NM

LITTLE DARLIN'
❑ LD-4001 [M] Johnny Paycheck at Carnegie Hall 1966 20.00
❑ LD-4003 [M] The Lovin' Machine 1966 20.00
❑ LD-4004 [M] Gospeltime in My Fashion 1967 20.00
❑ LD-4006 [M] Johnny Paycheck Sings Jukebox Charlie 1967 25.00
❑ SLD-8001 [S] Johnny Paycheck at Carnegie Hall 1966 25.00
❑ SLD-8003 [S] The Lovin' Machine 1966 25.00
❑ SLD-8004 [S] Gospeltime in My Fashion 1967 25.00
❑ SLD-8006 [S] Johnny Paycheck Sings Jukebox Charlie 1967 25.00
❑ SLD-8010 Country Soul 1968 25.00
❑ SLD-8012 Johnny Paycheck's Greatest Hits 1968 25.00
❑ SLD-8023 Wherever You Are 1969 25.00

MERCURY
❑ 830404-1 Modern Times 1987 10.00

POWER PAK
❑ PO-284 Johnny Paycheck At His Best 197? 8.00

**PAYNE, BENNIE**

KAPP
❑ KL-1004 [M] Bennie Payne Plays and Sings 1955 80.00

**PAYNE, CECIL**

CHARLIE PARKER
❑ PLP-506 [M] Shaw Nuff 1962 25.00
❑ PLP-506S [S] Shaw Nuff 1962 30.00
❑ PLP-801 [M] Cecil Payne Performing Charlie Parker's Music 1962 40.00
❑ PLP-801S [S] Cecil Payne Performing Charlie Parker's Music 1962 50.00

SAVOY
❑ MG-12147 [M] Patterns of Jazz 1959 80.00

SIGNAL
❑ S-1203 [M] Cecil Payne Quintet and Quartet 1955 200.00

STRATA-EAST
❑ SES-19734 The Zodiac 1973 25.00

**PAYNE, DENNIS, AND THE RENEGADES**

RED MAN
❑ 1492 We're Indian 1969 150.00

**PAYNE, FREDA**

ABC
❑ D-901 Out of Payne Comes Love 1976 12.00

ABC DUNHILL
❑ DSX-50176 Payne and Pleasure 1974 15.00

ABC IMPULSE!
❑ AS-53 [S] After the Lights Go Down Low...And Much More 1968 15.00

CAPITOL
❑ ST-11700 Stares and Whispers 1977 12.00
❑ ST-11864 Supernatural 1978 12.00
❑ ST-12003 Hot 1979 12.00

IMPULSE!
❑ A-53 [M] After the Lights Go Down Low...And Much More 1964 30.00
❑ AS-53 [S] After the Lights Go Down Low...And Much More 1964 40.00

INVICTUS
❑ ST-7301 Band of Gold 1970 15.00
❑ SMAS-7307 Contact 1971 15.00
❑ ST-9804 The Best of Freda Payne 1972 15.00
❑ Z 32493 Reaching Out 1973 15.00

MGM
❑ GAS-128 Freda Payne (Golden Archive Series) 1970 15.00
❑ E-4370 [M] How Do You Say I Don't Love You Anymore 1966 20.00
❑ SE-4370 [S] How Do You Say I Don't Love You Anymore 1966 25.00

**PAYNE, JIMMY**

EPIC
❑ BN 26372 Woman, Woman! What Does It Take? 1968 20.00

**PAYNE, LEON**

STARDAY
❑ SLP-231 [M] Leon Payne: A Living Legend of Country Music 1963 80.00
❑ SLP-236 [M] Americana 1963 50.00

**PEACE, JOE**

RITE
❑ 29917 Finding Peace 1972 200.00

**PEACHES AND HERB**

COLUMBIA
❑ FC 38746 Remember 1983 10.00

Number | Title (A Side/B Side) | Yr | NM

DATE
❑ TEM 3004 [M] Let's Fall in Love 1967 20.00
❑ TEM 3005 [M] For Your Love 1967 25.00
❑ TEM 3007 [M] Golden Duets 1968 30.00
❑ TES 4004 [S] Let's Fall in Love 1967 25.00
❑ TES 4005 [S] For Your Love 1967 20.00
❑ TES 4007 [S] Golden Duets 1968 20.00
❑ TES 4012 Peaches and Herb's Greatest Hits 1968 20.00

EPIC
❑ E 36089 Love Is Strange 1979 10.00
*—Reissue of Date material*
❑ JE 36099 Peaches and Herb's Greatest Hits 1979 10.00
*—Reissue of Date 4012*

MCA
❑ 2261 Peaches and Herb 1977 12.00

POLYDOR
❑ PD-1-6172 2 Hot! 1978 10.00
❑ PD-1-6239 Twice the Fire 1979 10.00
❑ PD-1-6298 Worth the Wait 1980 10.00
❑ PD-1-6332 Sayin' Something! 1981 10.00

**PEANUT BUTTER CONSPIRACY, THE**

CHALLENGE
❑ 2000 For Children of All Ages 1969 30.00

COLUMBIA
❑ CL 2654 [M] The Peanut Butter Conspiracy Is Spreading 1967 30.00
❑ CL 2790 [M] The Great Conspiracy 1968 40.00
❑ CS 9454 [S] The Peanut Butter Conspiracy Is Spreading 1967 30.00
❑ CS 9590 [S] The Great Conspiracy 1968 30.00

**PEARL JAM**

EPIC
❑ E 53136 Vs. 1993 10.00
❑ E2 63365 [(2)] Binaural 2000 12.00
❑ E 66900 Vitalogy 1994 10.00
❑ E 67500 No Code 1996 15.00
*—Includes one of four sets of six 12x12 trading cards*
❑ E 68164 Yield 1998 12.00
❑ E2 69752 [(2)] Live on Two Legs 1998 15.00
❑ E3 85738 [(3)] Lost Dogs 2004 25.00
*—CD version was issued in 2003*
❑ E2 86825 [(2)] Riot Act 2002 12.00
❑ E4 93535 [(4)] Rearviewmirror: Greatest Hits 2004 40.00

EPIC ASSOCIATED
❑ Z 47857 Ten 1991 10.00
*—Album not released on U.S. vinyl until 1994*

J
❑ 82876-71467-1 [(2)]Pearl Jam 2006 20.00
*—With 36-page lyric booklet; number is nowhere on the packaging or labels, but is only in the trail-off wax of the records*

**PEARLS BEFORE SWINE**

ADELPHI
❑ 4111 [(2)] The Best of Pearls Before Swine 198? 15.00

ESP-DISK
❑ 1054 One Nation Under Ground Bonus Poster 1967 25.00
❑ 1054 [M] One Nation Under Ground 1967 50.00
❑ 1054 [S] One Nation Under Ground 1967 50.00
*—Black and white cover*
❑ 1054 [S] One Nation Under Ground 1967 50.00
*—Sepia-tone cover with no border*
❑ 1054 [S] One Nation Under Ground 1967 50.00
*—Sepia-tone cover with white border*
❑ 1054 [S] One Nation Under Ground 1968 30.00
*—Full-color cover*
❑ 1075 Balaklava 1968 40.00

REPRISE
❑ RS 6364 These Things Too 1969 30.00
❑ RS 6405 The Use of Ashes 1970 30.00
❑ RS 6442 City of Gold 1971 40.00
❑ RS 6467 Beautiful Lies You Could Live In 1971 40.00

**PEARSON, ALBIE**

VIBRANT
❑ 1501 Albie Pearson 1973 25.00

**PEARSON, DUKE**

BLUE NOTE
❑ BLP-4022 [M] Profile — Duke Pearson 1959 80.00
*—Regular version with W. 63rd St. address on label*
❑ BLP-4022 [M] Profile — Duke Pearson 1959 120.00
*—"Deep groove" version (deep indentation under label on both sides)*
❑ BLP-4022 [M] Profile — Duke Pearson 1963 25.00
*—With New York, USA address on label*
❑ BLP-4035 [M] Tender Feelin's 1960 80.00
*—Regular version with W. 63rd St. address on label*
❑ BLP-4035 [M] Tender Feelin's 1960 120.00
*—"Deep groove" version (deep indentation under label on both sides)*

Number | Title (A Side/B Side) | Yr | NM

❑ BLP-4035 [M] Tender Feelin's 1963 25.00
*—With New York, USA address on label*
❑ BLP-4191 [M] Wahoo! 1965 30.00
❑ BLP-4252 [M] Sweet Honey Bee 1966 30.00
❑ BST-84022 [S] Profile — Duke Pearson 1959 60.00
*—With W. 63rd St. address on label*
❑ BST-84022 [S] Profile — Duke Pearson 1963 20.00
*—With New York, USA address on label*
❑ BST-84035 [S] Tender Feelin's 1960 60.00
*—With W. 63rd St. address on label*
❑ BST-84035 [S] Tender Feelin's 1963 20.00
*—With New York, USA address on label*
❑ BST-84191 [S] Wahoo! 1965 30.00
*—With New York, USA address on label*
❑ BST-84252 [S] Sweet Honey Bee 1966 30.00
*—With New York, USA address on label*
❑ BST-84267 The Right Touch 1968 25.00
❑ BST-84276 Introducing Duke Pearson's Big Band 1968 25.00
❑ BST-84293 The Phantom 1969 25.00
❑ BST-84308 Now Hear This 1969 25.00
❑ BST-84323 Merry Ole Soul 1970 20.00
❑ BST-84344 How Insensitive 1970 20.00

JAZZTIME
❑ 33-02 [M] Hush! 1962 40.00

**PEBBLES AND BAMM BAMM**

HANNA-BARBERA
❑ HLP-2033 [M] Pebbles and Bamm-Bamm Sing Songs of Christmas 1965 120.00
❑ HLP-2040 [M] On the Good Ship Lollipop 1966 100.00

**PECORA, SANTO**

CLEF
❑ MGC-123 [10] Santo Pecora Collates 1953 100.00
*—With either Mercury or Clef cover; all labels are Clef*

SOUTHLAND
❑ SLP-213 [M] Santo Pecora 1955 50.00

VIK
❑ XLA-1081 [M] Dixieland Mardi Gras 1957 50.00

**PEDICIN, MIKE**

APOLLO
❑ LP-484 [M] Musical Medicine 1957 150.00

**PEEBLES, ANN**

HI
❑ HLP-6002 If This Is Heaven 1977 12.00
❑ HLP-6007 The Handwriting Is On the Wall 1978 12.00
❑ HLP-8005 Part Time Love 197? 12.00
*—Reissue of 32059*
❑ HLP-8009 Straight from the Heart 197? 12.00
*—Reissue of 32065*
❑ SHL-32059 Part Time Love 1971 20.00
❑ SHL-32065 Straight from the Heart 1972 20.00
❑ XSHL-32079 I Can't Stand the Rain 1974 20.00
❑ SHL-32091 Tellin' It 1975 20.00

**PEEL, DAVID**

APPLE
❑ SW-3391 The Pope Smokes Dope 1972 75.00

ELEKTRA
❑ EKS-74032 Have a Marijuana 1968 40.00
❑ EKS-74069 The American Revolution 1970 30.00

**PEELS, THE**

KARATE
❑ 5402 [M] Juanita Banana 1966 80.00

**PEGGY SUE**

DECCA
❑ DL 75153 Dynamite! 1969 25.00
❑ DL 75215 All American Husband 1970 25.00

**PEGGY SUE AND SONNY WRIGHT (2)**

COUNTRY INT'L.
❑ 732 One Side of Peggy Sue and Sonny Wright 198? 20.00

**PEIFFER, BERNARD**

DECCA
❑ DL 8626 [M] The Astounding Bernard Peiffer 1958 50.00
❑ DL 9203 [M] Piano Ala Mood 1958 50.00
❑ DL 9218 [M] The Pied Peiffer of the Piano 1959 50.00
❑ DL 79203 [S] Piano Ala Mood 1958 40.00
❑ DL 79218 [S] The Pied Peiffer of the Piano 1959 40.00

EMARCY
❑ MG-26036 [10] Le Most 1954 80.00
❑ MG-36080 [M] Bernie's Tunes 1956 50.00

LAURIE
❑ LLP-1006 [M] Modern Jazz for People Who Like Original Music 1960 25.00
❑ SLP-1006 [S] Modern Jazz for People Who Like Original Music 1960 30.00
❑ LLP-1008 [M] Cole Porter's "Can Can" 1960 25.00
❑ SLP-1008 [S] Cole Porter's "Can Can" 1960 30.00

NORGRAN
❑ MGN-11 [10] Bernard Peiffer Et Son Trio 1954 80.00

## PELL, DAVE

### ATLANTIC
❑ 1216 [M] Jazz and Romantic Places 1955 100.00
*—Black label*
❑ 1216 [M] Jazz and Romantic Places 1961 30.00
*—Multicolor label, white "fan" logo at right*
❑ 1249 [M] Love Story 1956 80.00
*—Black label*
❑ 1249 [M] Love Story 1961 30.00
*—Multicolor label, white "fan" logo at right*

### CAPITOL
❑ T 925 [M] I Had the Craziest Dream 1958 30.00
*—Turquoise label*
❑ ST 1309 [S] The Big Small Bands 1960 25.00
❑ T 1309 [M] The Big Small Bands 1960 20.00
❑ ST 1512 [S] Old South Wails 1961 25.00
❑ T 1512 [M] Old South Wails 1961 20.00
❑ ST 1687 [S] I Remember John Kirby 1962 25.00
❑ T 1687 [M] I Remember John Kirby 1962 20.00

### CORAL
❑ CRL 57248 [M] Swingin' School Songs 1958 30.00
❑ CRL 757248 [S] Swingin' School Songs 1958 25.00

### KAPP
❑ KL-1025 [M] Dave Pell Plays Rodgers and Hart 1956 30.00
❑ KL-1034 [M] Dave Pell Plays Burke and Van Heusen 1956 40.00
❑ KL-1036 [M] Dave Pell Plays Irving Berlin 1957 40.00

### LIBERTY
❑ LST-7298 [S] Today;s Hits in Jazz 1961 20.00
❑ LST-7321 [S] Jazz Voices in Video 1963 20.00

### PRI
❑ 3002 [M] Dave Pell Plays Harry James' Big Band Sounds 196? 20.00
❑ 3003 [M] Dave Pell Plays Artie Shaw's Big Band Sounds 196? 20.00
❑ 3004 [M] Dave Pell Plays Benny Goodman's Big Band Sounds 196? 20.00
❑ 3005 [M] Dave Pell Plays Lawrence Welk's Big Band Sounds 196? 20.00
❑ 3006 [M] Dave Pell Plays Perez Prado's Big Band Sounds 196? 20.00
❑ 3007 [M] Dave Pell Plays Duke Ellington's Big Band Sounds 196? 20.00
❑ 3009 [M] Dave Pell Plays Mantovani's Big Band Sounds 196? 20.00
❑ 3010 [M] Dave Pell Plays the Dorsey Brothers' Big Band Sounds 196? 20.00
❑ 3011 [M] Dave Pell Plays the Big Band Sounds 196? 20.00

### RCA VICTOR
❑ LPM-1320 [M] Jazz Goes Dancing 1956 50.00
❑ LPM-1394 [M] Swingin' in the Ol' Corral 1957 50.00
❑ LPM-1524 [M] Pell of a Time 1957 50.00
❑ LPM-1662 [M] Campus Hop 1957 50.00

### TREND
❑ TL-1003 [10] Dave Pell Plays Irving Berlin 1953 120.00
❑ TL-1501 [M] Dave Pell Plays Rodgers and Hart 1954 100.00

## PENAZZI, ANDRE

### DAUNTLESS
❑ 7020 [S] Organ Jazz Samba Percussion 1963 20.00

## PENDERGRASS, TEDDY
Also see HAROLD MELVIN AND THE BLUE NOTES.

### ASYLUM
❑ 60317 Love Language 1984 8.00
❑ 60447 Workin' It Back 1985 8.00

### ELEKTRA
❑ 60775 Joy 1988 8.00

### PHILADELPHIA INT'L.
❑ PZ 34390 Teddy Pendergrass 1977 10.00
*—No bar code on back cover*
❑ PZ 34390 Teddy Pendergrass 198? 8.00
*—With bar code on back cover*
❑ PZ 35095 Life Is a Song Worth Singing 1978 10.00
*—No bar code on back cover*
❑ PZ 35095 Life Is a Song Worth Singing 198? 8.00
*—With bar code on back cover*
❑ FZ 36003 Teddy 1979 10.00
❑ PZ 36003 Teddy 198? 8.00
*—Budget-line reissue with new prefix*
❑ KZ2 36294 [(2)] Teddy Live! Coast to Coast 1979 12.00
❑ FZ 36745 TP 1980 10.00
❑ PZ 36745 TP 198? 8.00
*—Budget-line reissue with new prefix*
❑ FZ 37491 It's Time for Love 1981 10.00
❑ PZ 37491 It's Time for Love 198? 8.00
*—Budget-line reissue with new prefix*
❑ FZ 38118 This One's for You 1982 10.00
❑ PZ 38118 This One's for You 198? 8.00
*—Budget-line reissue with new prefix*
❑ FZ 38646 Heaven Only Knows 1983 10.00
❑ PZ 38646 Heaven Only Knows 1985 8.00
*—Budget-line reissue with new prefix*
❑ FZ 39252 Greatest Hits 1984 10.00
❑ HZ 47491 It's Time for Love 198? 40.00
*—Half-speed mastered edition*

## PENGUINS, THE

### COLLECTABLES
❑ COL-5045 Golden Classics 198? 10.00

### DOOTO
❑ DTL-204 [M] The Best Vocal Groups...Rhythm and Blues 1959 200.00
*—Reissue of Dootone 204; blue and yellow label*
❑ DTL-204 [M] The Best Vocal Groups...Rhythm and Blues 196? 100.00
*—Black label with gold/orange/blue ring. This is NOT a counterfeit.*
❑ DTL-242 [M] The Cool, Cool Penguins 1959 700.00
*—Blue and yellow label*
❑ DTL-242 [M] The Cool, Cool Penguins 1959 700.00
*—Red and yellow label*
❑ DTL-242 [M] The Cool, Cool Penguins 196? 200.00
*—Black label with gold/orange/blue ring. This is NOT a counterfeit.*

### DOOTONE
❑ DTL-204 [M] The Best Vocal Groups...Rhythm and Blues 195? 500.00
*—As above; glossy maroon label*
❑ DTL-204 [M] The Best Vocal Groups...Rhythm and Blues 1957 1500.
*—Also includes tracks by the Medallions, Don Julian and the Meadowlarks, and the Dootones. Flat maroon label.*

## PENNY, HANK

### AUDIO LAB
❑ AL-1508 [M] Hank Penny Sings 1959 200.00

## PENNY AND JEAN

### RCA VICTOR
❑ LPM-2244 [M] Two for the Road 1961 20.00
❑ LSP-2244 [S] Two for the Road 1961 25.00

## PENTAGON

### EAST WIND
❑ 10002 Pentagon 1979 20.00

## PENTANGLE, THE

### GREEN LINNET
❑ SIF-3048 So Early in the Spring 1990 12.00

### REPRISE
❑ MS 2100 Solomon's Seal 1972 15.00
❑ RS 6315 The Pentangle 1968 20.00
*—With "W7" and "r:" logos on two-tone orange label*
❑ RS 6315 The Pentangle 1970 15.00
*—With only "r:" logo on all-orange (tan) label*
❑ 2RS 6334 [(2)] Sweet Child 1969 25.00
*—With "W7" and "r:" logos on two-tone orange label*
❑ 2RS 6334 [(2)] Sweet Child 1970 18.00
*—With only "r:" logo on all-orange (tan) label*
❑ RS 6372 Basket of Light 1969 20.00
*—With "W7" and "r:" logos on two-tone orange label*
❑ RS 6372 Basket of Light 1970 15.00
*—With only "r:" logo on all-orange (tan) label*
❑ RS 6430 Cruel Sister 1971 15.00
❑ RS 6463 Reflection 1971 15.00

### SHANACHIE
❑ 79066 A Maid That's Deep in Love 198? 10.00

### VARRICK
❑ VR-017 Open the Door 1985 10.00
❑ VR-026 In the Round 1986 10.00

## PEOPLE

### CAPITOL
❑ ST-151 Both Sides of People 1969 40.00
❑ ST 2924 I Love You 1968 40.00

### PARAMOUNT
❑ PAS-5013 There Are People 1970 20.00

## PEPPER, ART

### ANALOGUE PRODUCTIONS
❑ AP 010 Art Pepper Meets the Rhythm Section 199? 25.00
*—Reissue on audiophile vinyl*
❑ AP 012 Smack Up! 199? 25.00
*—Reissue on audiophile vinyl*
❑ AP 017 Art Pepper + Eleven: Modern Jazz Classics 199? 25.00
*—Reissue on audiophile vinyl*

### CONTEMPORARY
❑ C-3532 [M] Art Pepper Meets the Rhythm Section 1957 100.00
❑ M-3568 [M] Art Pepper + Eleven: Modern Jazz Classics 1959 100.00
❑ M-3573 [M] Gettin' Together! 1960 60.00
❑ M-3602 [M] Smack Up! 1961 60.00
❑ M-3607 [M] Intensity 1963 30.00
❑ S-7532 [S] Art Pepper Meets the Rhythm Section 1959 50.00
❑ S-7568 [S] Art Pepper + Eleven: Modern Jazz Classics 1959 80.00
❑ S-7573 [S] Gettin' Together! 1960 70.00
❑ S-7602 [S] Smack Up! 1961 80.00
❑ S-7607 [S] Intensity 1963 40.00
❑ S-7630 The Way It Was! 1972 30.00
*—Originals have orange labels*

### DISCOVERY
❑ 3019 [10] Art Pepper Quartet 1952 600.00
❑ 3023 [10] Art Pepper Quintet 1954 600.00

### FANTASY
❑ OJC-695 Friday Night at the Village Vanguard 199? 12.00

### INTERLUDE
❑ MO-512 [M] Art Pepper Quartet 1959 50.00
❑ ST-1012 [S] Art Pepper Quartet 1959 40.00

### INTRO
❑ 606 [M] Modern Art 1957 2500.

### JAZZ WEST
❑ JLP-10 [M] The Return of Art Pepper 1956 600.00

### MOSAIC
❑ MR3-105 [(3)] The Complete Pacific Jazz Small Group Recordings of Art Pepper 198? 80.00

### PACIFIC JAZZ
❑ PJ-60 [M] The Artistry of Pepper 1962 40.00

### SAVOY
❑ MG-12089 [M] Surf Ride 1956 100.00

### SCORE
❑ SLP-4030 [M] Modern Art 1958 100.00
❑ SLP-4031 [M] The Art Pepper-Red Norvo Sextet 1958 100.00
❑ SLP-4032 [M] The Return of Art Pepper 1958 100.00

### STEREO RECORDS
❑ S-7018 [S] Art Pepper Meets the Rhythm Section 1958 80.00

### TAMPA
❑ TP-20 [M] Art Pepper Quartet 1957 500.00
*—Red vinyl*
❑ TP-20 [M] Art Pepper Quartet 1958 250.00
*—Black vinyl*
❑ TS-1001 [S] Art Pepper Quartet 1959 1000.

## PEPPER, ART/SHELLY MANNE

### CHARLIE PARKER
❑ PLP-836 [M] Pepper/Manne 1963 25.00
❑ PLP-836S [S] Pepper/Manne 1963 30.00

## PEPPER, ART/SONNY REDD

### REGENT
❑ MG-6069 [M] Two Altos 1959 50.00

### SAVOY
❑ MG-12215 [M] Art Pepper-Sonny Redd 1969 20.00

## PEPPER, JIM

### EMBRYO
❑ SD-731 [(2)] Pepper's Powwow 196? 40.00

## PEPPERMINT, DANNY

### CARLTON
❑ LP-20001 [M] Twist with Danny Peppermint 1962 40.00
❑ STLP-20001 [S] Twist with Danny Peppermint 1962 50.00

## PEPPERMINT RAINBOW, THE

### DECCA
❑ DL 75129 Will You Be Staying After Sunday 1969 20.00

## PEPPERMINT TROLLEY COMPANY, THE

### ACTA
❑ A-8007 [M] The Peppermint Trolley Company 1968 50.00
*—In stereo cover with "Monaural" sticker*
❑ A-38007 [S] The Peppermint Trolley Company 1968 25.00

## PERE UBU

### BLANK
❑ 001 The Modern Dance 1978 40.00

### CHRYSALIS
❑ CHR 1207 Dub Housing 1979 25.00

### ENIGMA
❑ D1-73343 The Tenement Years 1988 12.00

### FONTANA
❑ 838237-1 Cloudland 1989 12.00

### ROUGH TRADE
❑ ROUGH US 4 The Art of Walking 1980 20.00
*—Revised version: Vocal added on "Arabia"; "Miles" is shortened*

| Number | Title (A Side/B Side) | Yr | NM |
|---|---|---|---|
| ❑ ROUGH US 4 | The Art of Walking | 1980 | 40.00 |
| *—First 1,800 were incorrectly mastered* | | | |
| ❑ ROUGH US 7 | The Modern Dance | 1981 | 20.00 |
| *—Reissue of Blank 001* | | | |
| ❑ ROUGH US 10 | 390 Degrees of Simulated Stereo | 1981 | 20.00 |
| ❑ ROUGH US 21 | The Song of the Bailing Man | 1982 | 20.00 |

### PERHACS, LINDA

| Number | Title (A Side/B Side) | Yr | NM |
|---|---|---|---|
| **KAPP** | | | |
| ❑ KS-3636 | Parallelograms | 1970 | 200.00 |

### PERKINS, BILL

| Number | Title (A Side/B Side) | Yr | NM |
|---|---|---|---|
| **LIBERTY** | | | |
| ❑ LRP-3293 [M] | Bossa Nova with Strings Attached | 1963 | 40.00 |
| ❑ LST-7293 [S] | Bossa Nova with Strings Attached | 1963 | 50.00 |
| **PACIFIC JAZZ** | | | |
| ❑ PJ-1221 [M] | The Bill Perkins Octet On Stage | 1956 | 120.00 |
| **RIVERSIDE** | | | |
| ❑ RS-3052 | Quietly There | 1969 | 25.00 |
| **WORLD PACIFIC** | | | |
| ❑ WP-1221 [M] | The Bill Perkins Octet On Stage | 1958 | 80.00 |

### PERKINS, BILL, AND RICHIE KAMUCA

| Number | Title (A Side/B Side) | Yr | NM |
|---|---|---|---|
| **LIBERTY** | | | |
| ❑ LRP-3051 [M] | Tenors Head On | 1957 | 80.00 |

### PERKINS, BILL; ART PEPPER; RICHIE KAMUCA

| Number | Title (A Side/B Side) | Yr | NM |
|---|---|---|---|
| **PACIFIC JAZZ** | | | |
| ❑ PJM-401 [M] | Just Friends | 1956 | 200.00 |
| **WORLD PACIFIC** | | | |
| ❑ PJM-401 [M] | Just Friends | 1958 | 120.00 |

### PERKINS, CARL

| Number | Title (A Side/B Side) | Yr | NM |
|---|---|---|---|
| **ACCORD** | | | |
| ❑ SN-7169 | Presenting Carl Perkins | 1982 | 10.00 |
| **ALBUM GLOBE** | | | |
| ❑ 8118 | Country Soul | 1980 | 10.00 |
| ❑ 9037 | Goin' Back to Memphis | 1980 | 10.00 |
| **ALLEGIANCE** | | | |
| ❑ AV-5001 | The Heart and Soul of Carl Perkins | 198? | 10.00 |
| **BULLDOG** | | | |
| ❑ BDL-2034 | Twenty Golden Pieces | 198? | 10.00 |
| **COLUMBIA** | | | |
| ❑ CL 1234 [DJ] | Whole Lotta Shakin' | 1958 | 800.00 |
| *—White label promo* | | | |
| ❑ CL 1234 [M] | Whole Lotta Shakin' | 1958 | 400.00 |
| ❑ CS 9833 | Carl Perkins' Greatest Hits | 1969 | 25.00 |
| *—Red "360 Sound Stereo" label* | | | |
| ❑ CS 9931 | Carl Perkins On Top | 1969 | 25.00 |
| *—Red "360 Sound Stereo" label* | | | |
| ❑ CS 9981 | Boppin' the Blues | 1970 | 12.00 |
| *—Orange label* | | | |
| ❑ CS 9981 | Boppin' the Blues | 1970 | 25.00 |
| *—Red "360 Sound Stereo" label* | | | |
| ❑ PC 9981 | Boppin' the Blues | 198? | 8.00 |
| *—Budget-line reissue* | | | |
| ❑ FC 37961 | The Survivors | 1982 | 10.00 |
| *—With Johnny Cash and Jerry Lee Lewis* | | | |
| ❑ PC 37961 | The Survivors | 198? | 8.00 |
| *—Budget-line reissue* | | | |
| **COLUMBIA LIMITED EDITION** | | | |
| ❑ LE 10117 | Carl Perkins' Greatest Hits | 1974 | 12.00 |
| *—"Limited Edition" brown label* | | | |
| **DESIGN** | | | |
| ❑ DLP-611 [M] | Tennessee | 1963 | 30.00 |
| ❑ SDLP-611 [R] | Tennessee | 1963 | 20.00 |
| **DOLLIE** | | | |
| ❑ 4001 | Country Boy's Dream | 1967 | 30.00 |
| ❑ ST-91428 | Country Boy's Dream | 1967 | 40.00 |
| *—Capitol Record Club edition* | | | |
| **HARMONY** | | | |
| ❑ HS 11385 | Carl Perkins | 1970 | 15.00 |
| ❑ KH 31179 | Brown Eyed Handsome Man | 1971 | 12.00 |
| ❑ KH 31792 | Greatest Hits | 1972 | 12.00 |
| **HILLTOP** | | | |
| ❑ 6103 | Matchbox | 197? | 12.00 |
| **JET** | | | |
| ❑ JT-LA856-H | Ol' Blue Suede's Back | 1978 | 15.00 |
| ❑ JZ 35604 | Ol' Blue Suede's Back | 1978 | 10.00 |
| **KOALA** | | | |
| ❑ AW 14164 | Country Soul | 198? | 10.00 |
| **MCA DOT** | | | |
| ❑ 39035 | Carl Perkins | 1985 | 10.00 |
| **MERCURY** | | | |
| ❑ SRM-1-691 | My Kind of Country | 1973 | 12.00 |
| **RHINO** | | | |
| ❑ RNLP-70221 | Original Sun Greatest Hits (1955-1957) | 1986 | 12.00 |

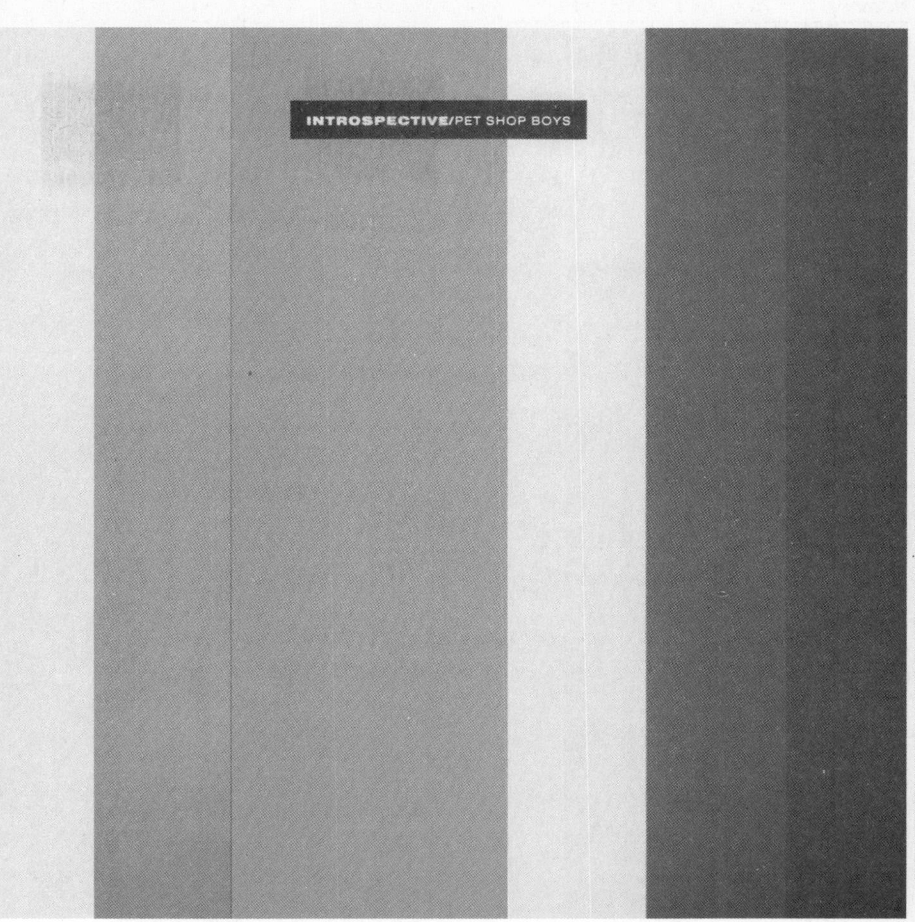


Pet Shop Boys, *Introspective,* EMI Manhattan E1-90868, 1988, $10.

| Number | Title (A Side/B Side) | Yr | NM |
|---|---|---|---|
| **ROUNDER** | | | |
| ❑ SS-27 | Honky Tonk Gal: Rare and Unissued Sun Masters | 1989 | 12.00 |
| **SMASH** | | | |
| ❑ 830002-1 | Class of '55 | 1986 | 12.00 |
| *—With Jerry Lee Lewis, Roy Orbison and Johnny Cash* | | | |
| **SUEDE** | | | |
| ❑ 002 | Live at Austin City Limits | 1981 | 10.00 |
| **SUN** | | | |
| ❑ LP-111 | Original Golden Hits | 1969 | 12.00 |
| ❑ LP-112 | Blue Suede Shoes | 1969 | 12.00 |
| ❑ SLP-1225 [M] | The Dance Album of Carl Perkins | 1957 | 1200. |
| ❑ SLP-1225 [M] | Teen Beat — The Best of Carl Perkins | 1961 | 500.00 |
| *—Reissue with new title* | | | |
| **SUNNYVALE** | | | |
| ❑ 9330803 | The Sun Story, Vol. 3 | 1977 | 12.00 |
| **TRIP** | | | |
| ❑ TLP-8503 [(2)] | The Best of Carl Perkins | 1974 | 12.00 |
| **UNIVERSAL** | | | |
| ❑ UVL-76001 | Born to Rock | 1989 | 15.00 |

### PERKINS, CARL (2) Jazz pianist.

| Number | Title (A Side/B Side) | Yr | NM |
|---|---|---|---|
| **DOOTONE** | | | |
| ❑ DL-211 [M] | Introducing Carl Perkins | 1956 | 120.00 |
| *—Black vinyl* | | | |
| ❑ DL-211 [M] | Introducing Carl Perkins | 1956 | 200.00 |
| *—Red vinyl* | | | |

### PERREY, JEAN-JACQUES

| Number | Title (A Side/B Side) | Yr | NM |
|---|---|---|---|
| **PICKWICK** | | | |
| ❑ PC-3160 [M] | The Happy Moog | 196? | 20.00 |
| ❑ SPC-3160 [S] | The Happy Moog | 196? | 25.00 |
| *—Silver label* | | | |
| **VANGUARD** | | | |
| ❑ VSD-6549 | Moog Indigo | 1969 | 40.00 |
| ❑ VSD-79286 | The Amazing New Electronic Pop Sound of Jean-Jackques Perrey | 1968 | 40.00 |

### PERREY-KINGSLEY

| Number | Title (A Side/B Side) | Yr | NM |
|---|---|---|---|
| **VANGUARD** | | | |
| ❑ VSD-71/72 [(2)] | The Essential Perrey & Kingsley | 197? | 30.00 |
| ❑ VSD-6525 | Kaleidoscopic Vibrations | 1969 | 30.00 |
| ❑ VRS-9222 [M] | The In Sound from Way Out! | 1966 | 30.00 |
| ❑ VSD-79222 [S] | The In Sound from Way Out! | 1966 | 40.00 |

### PERRINE, PEP

| Number | Title (A Side/B Side) | Yr | NM |
|---|---|---|---|
| **HIDEOUT** | | | |
| ❑ 1003 [M] | Pep Perrine Live and In Person | 196? | 120.00 |

### PERSIP, CHARLIE

| Number | Title (A Side/B Side) | Yr | NM |
|---|---|---|---|
| **BETHLEHEM** | | | |
| ❑ BCP-6046 [M] | Charlie Persip and the Jazz Statesmen | 1960 | 40.00 |
| ❑ SBCP-6046 [S] | Charlie Persip and the Jazz Statesmen | 1960 | 40.00 |

### PERSON, HOUSTON

| Number | Title (A Side/B Side) | Yr | NM |
|---|---|---|---|
| **PRESTIGE** | | | |
| ❑ PRLP-7491 [M] | Underground Soul | 1967 | 30.00 |
| ❑ PRST-7491 [S] | Underground Soul | 1967 | 20.00 |
| ❑ PRST-7517 | Chocomotive | 1968 | 20.00 |
| ❑ PRST-7548 | Trust in Me | 1968 | 20.00 |
| ❑ PRST-7566 | Blue Odyssey | 1968 | 20.00 |
| ❑ PRST-7621 | Soul Dance! | 1969 | 20.00 |
| ❑ PRST-7678 | Goodness! | 1969 | 20.00 |
| ❑ PRST-7767 | The Truth! | 1970 | 20.00 |
| ❑ 10003 | Person to Person | 1971 | 25.00 |
| ❑ 10017 | Houston Express | 1971 | 20.00 |
| ❑ 10044 | Broken Windows, Empty Hallways | 1972 | 20.00 |
| ❑ 10055 | Sweet Buns and Barbeque | 1973 | 20.00 |
| **20TH CENTURY** | | | |
| ❑ W-205 | Houston Person | 196? | 25.00 |

### PERSSON, AAKE

| Number | Title (A Side/B Side) | Yr | NM |
|---|---|---|---|
| **EMARCY** | | | |
| ❑ MG-26039 [10] | Swedish Modern | 1954 | 200.00 |

### PERSSON, AAKE/ARNE DOMNERUS

| Number | Title (A Side/B Side) | Yr | NM |
|---|---|---|---|
| **PRESTIGE** | | | |
| ❑ PRLP-173 [10] | Aake Persson Swedish All Stars | 1953 | 250.00 |

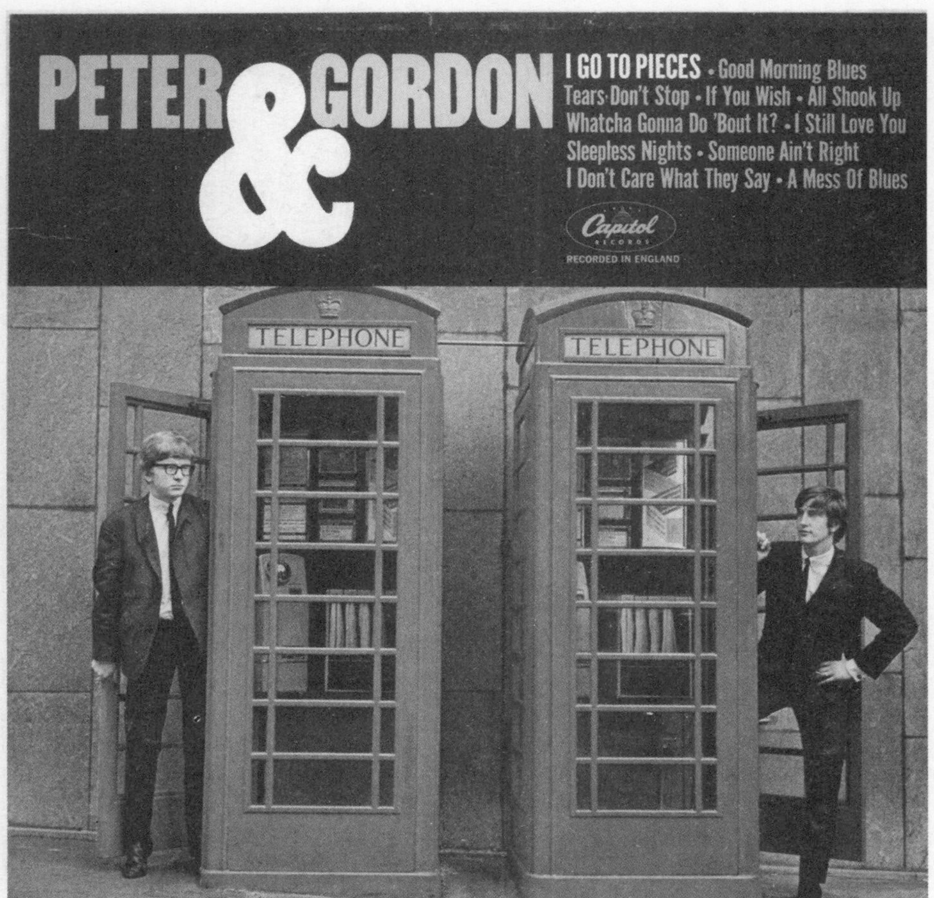


Peter and Gordon, *I Go to Pieces,* Capitol T 2324, 1965, mono, $20.

| Number | Title (A Side/B Side) | Yr | NM |
|---|---|---|---|
| **PERSUADERS, THE** Soul group. | | | |
| ATCO | | | |
| ❑ SD 7021 | The Persuaders | 1973 | 20.00 |
| ❑ SD 7046 | Best Thing That Ever Happened to Me | 1974 | 20.00 |
| CALLA | | | |
| ❑ PZ 34802 | It's All About Love | 1977 | 15.00 |
| COLLECTABLES | | | |
| ❑ COL-5139 | Thin Line Between Love and Hate (Golden Classics) | 198? | 10.00 |
| WIN OR LOSE | | | |
| ❑ SD 33-387 | Thin Line Between Love and Hate | 1972 | 25.00 |
| **PERSUADERS, THE (2)** Surf group. | | | |
| SATURN | | | |
| ❑ SAT-5000 [M] | Surfer's Nightmare | 1963 | 300.00 |
| ❑ SATS-5000 [S] | Surfer's Nightmare | 1963 | 400.00 |
| **PERSUASIONS, THE** | | | |
| A&M | | | |
| ❑ SP-3635 | More Than Before | 1974 | 12.00 |
| ❑ SP-3656 | I Just Want to Sing with My Friends | 1974 | 12.00 |
| CAPITOL | | | |
| ❑ SM-791 | We Came to Play | 197? | 10.00 |
| *—Reissue with new prefix* | | | |
| ❑ ST-791 | We Came to Play | 1971 | 25.00 |
| ❑ ST-872 | Street Corner Symphony | 1972 | 25.00 |
| ❑ ST-11101 | Spread the Word | 1972 | 25.00 |
| CATAMOUNT | | | |
| ❑ 905 | Stardust | 197? | 40.00 |
| ELEKTRA | | | |
| ❑ 7E-1099 | Chirpin' | 1977 | 12.00 |
| FLYING FISH | | | |
| ❑ FF-093 | Comin' At Ya | 1979 | 12.00 |
| MCA | | | |
| ❑ 326 | We Still Ain't Got No Band | 1973 | 15.00 |
| REPRISE | | | |
| ❑ RS 6394 | Acapella | 1970 | 30.00 |

| Number | Title (A Side/B Side) | Yr | NM |
|---|---|---|---|
| ROUNDER | | | |
| ❑ 3053 | Good News | 1981 | 10.00 |
| ❑ 3083 | No Frills | 1984 | 10.00 |
| **PET SHOP BOYS** | | | |
| EMI | | | |
| ❑ E1-28105 | Disco 2 | 1994 | 12.00 |
| ❑ E1-34023 [(3)] | Alternative | 1995 | 60.00 |
| *—Box set pressed in UK for import into the US (regular UK pressings have gatefold sleeves)* | | | |
| EMI AMERICA | | | |
| ❑ PW-17193 | Please | 1986 | 10.00 |
| ❑ SQ-17246 | Disco | 1986 | 10.00 |
| ❑ R 164390 | Please | 1986 | 12.00 |
| *—BMG Direct Marketing edition* | | | |
| EMI MANHATTAN | | | |
| ❑ ELJ-46972 | Actually | 1987 | 10.00 |
| ❑ E1-90263 [(2)] | Actually | 1988 | 20.00 |
| *—Limited set with bonus 12" record of "Always on My Mind" (SPRO-04055/6) included* | | | |
| ❑ E1-90868 | Introspective | 1988 | 10.00 |
| ❑ E1-90868 [(3)DJ] | Special Limited Edition Club Mixes | 1988 | 100.00 |
| *—Promo-only set of three 12-inch singles of remixes, which can also be found separately (SPRO-04231/2; SPRO-04233/41; SPRO-04242/3); this is for the complete package with outer sticker* | | | |
| ❑ R 100681 | Introspective | 1988 | 12.00 |
| *—BMG Direct Marketing edition* | | | |
| ❑ R 153678 | Actually | 1987 | 12.00 |
| *—BMG Direct Marketing edition* | | | |
| **PETER AND GORDON** | | | |
| CAPITOL | | | |
| ❑ ST 2115 [S] | A World Without Love | 1964 | 25.00 |
| ❑ T 2115 [M] | A World Without Love | 1964 | 20.00 |
| ❑ ST 2220 [S] | I Don't Want to See You Again | 1964 | 25.00 |
| ❑ T 2220 [M] | I Don't Want to See You Again | 1964 | 20.00 |
| ❑ ST 2324 [S] | I Go to Pieces | 1965 | 25.00 |
| ❑ T 2324 [M] | I Go to Pieces | 1965 | 20.00 |
| ❑ ST 2368 [S] | True Love Ways | 1965 | 25.00 |
| ❑ T 2368 [M] | True Love Ways | 1965 | 20.00 |
| ❑ ST 2430 [S] | Peter and Gordon Sing the Hits of Nashville | 1966 | 25.00 |
| ❑ T 2430 [M] | Peter and Gordon Sing the Hits of Nashville | 1966 | 20.00 |

| Number | Title (A Side/B Side) | Yr | NM |
|---|---|---|---|
| ❑ ST 2477 [P] | Woman | 1966 | 25.00 |
| *—"Woman" is rechanneled* | | | |
| ❑ T 2477 [M] | Woman | 1966 | 20.00 |
| ❑ ST 2549 [P] | The Best of Peter and Gordon | 1966 | 18.00 |
| *—Black label with colorband; "Woman" is rechanneled* | | | |
| ❑ ST 2549 [P] | The Best of Peter and Gordon | 1967 | 15.00 |
| *—"Starline" label* | | | |
| ❑ T 2549 [M] | The Best of Peter and Gordon | 1966 | 15.00 |
| *—Black label with colorband* | | | |
| ❑ T 2549 [M] | The Best of Peter and Gordon | 1967 | 12.00 |
| *—"Starline" label* | | | |
| ❑ ST 2664 [S] | Lady Godiva | 1967 | 20.00 |
| ❑ T 2664 [M] | Lady Godiva | 1967 | 15.00 |
| ❑ ST 2729 [S] | Knight in Rusty Armour | 1967 | 20.00 |
| ❑ T 2729 [M] | Knight in Rusty Armour | 1967 | 15.00 |
| ❑ ST 2747 [S] | In London for Tea | 1967 | 20.00 |
| ❑ T 2747 [M] | In London for Tea | 1967 | 15.00 |
| ❑ ST 2882 [S] | Hot, Cold and Custard | 1968 | 25.00 |
| ❑ SN-16084 [S] | The Best of Peter and Gordon | 1979 | 8.00 |
| **PETER, PAUL AND MARY** | | | |
| GOLD CASTLE | | | |
| ❑ D1-71301 | No Easy Walk to Freedom | 1988 | 10.00 |
| *—Reissue of 171001* | | | |
| ❑ D1-71316 | A Holiday Celebration | 1988 | 10.00 |
| ❑ R 164086 | A Holiday Celebration | 1988 | 12.00 |
| *—Same as above, except BMG Direct Marketing edition* | | | |
| ❑ 171001 | No Easy Walk to Freedom | 1987 | 12.00 |
| PETER, PAUL AND MARY | | | |
| ❑ 830331 | Such Is Love | 1983 | 20.00 |
| WARNER BROS. | | | |
| ❑ W 1449 [M] | Peter, Paul and Mary | 1962 | 20.00 |
| ❑ WS 1449 [S] | Peter, Paul and Mary | 1962 | 25.00 |
| *—Gold label* | | | |
| ❑ WS 1449 [S] | Peter, Paul and Mary | 1968 | 12.00 |
| *—Green "W7" label* | | | |
| ❑ WS 1449 [S] | Peter, Paul and Mary | 1970 | 10.00 |
| *—Any later Warner Bros. label (green "WB", palm trees, white label)* | | | |
| ❑ W 1473 [M] | (Moving) | 1963 | 20.00 |
| ❑ WS 1473 [S] | (Moving) | 1963 | 25.00 |
| *—Gold label* | | | |
| ❑ WS 1473 [S] | (Moving) | 1968 | 10.00 |
| *—Any later Warner Bros. label (green "W7", green "WB", palm trees, white label)* | | | |
| ❑ W 1507 [M] | In the Wind | 1963 | 20.00 |
| ❑ WS 1507 [S] | In the Wind | 1963 | 25.00 |
| *—Gold label* | | | |
| ❑ WS 1507 [S] | In the Wind | 1968 | 10.00 |
| *—Any later Warner Bros. label* | | | |
| ❑ 2W 1555 [(2)M] | Peter, Paul and Mary In Concert | 1964 | 25.00 |
| ❑ 2WS 1555 [(2)S] | Peter, Paul and Mary In Concert | 1964 | 30.00 |
| *—Gold labels* | | | |
| ❑ 2WS 1555 [(2)S] | Peter, Paul and Mary In Concert | 1968 | 12.00 |
| *—Any later Warner Bros. label* | | | |
| ❑ W 1589 [M] | A Song Will Rise | 1965 | 20.00 |
| ❑ WS 1589 [S] | A Song Will Rise | 1965 | 25.00 |
| *—Gold label* | | | |
| ❑ WS 1589 [S] | A Song Will Rise | 1968 | 10.00 |
| *—Any later Warner Bros. label* | | | |
| ❑ W 1615 [M] | See What Tomorrow Brings | 1965 | 20.00 |
| ❑ WS 1615 [S] | See What Tomorrow Brings | 1965 | 25.00 |
| *—Gold label* | | | |
| ❑ WS 1615 [S] | See What Tomorrow Brings | 1968 | 10.00 |
| *—Any later Warner Bros. label* | | | |
| ❑ W 1648 [M] | Peter, Paul and Mary Album | 1966 | 20.00 |
| ❑ WS 1648 [S] | Peter, Paul and Mary Album | 1966 | 25.00 |
| *—Gold label* | | | |
| ❑ WS 1648 [S] | Peter, Paul and Mary Album | 1968 | 10.00 |
| *—Any later Warner Bros. label* | | | |
| ❑ W 1700 [M] | Album 1700 | 1967 | 25.00 |
| ❑ WS 1700 [S] | Album 1700 | 1967 | 25.00 |
| *—Gold label* | | | |
| ❑ WS 1700 [S] | Album 1700 | 1968 | 12.00 |
| *—Green "W7" label* | | | |
| ❑ WS 1700 [S] | Album 1700 | 1970 | 10.00 |
| *—Any later Warner Bros. label* | | | |
| ❑ WS 1751 | Late Again | 1968 | 15.00 |
| *—Green "W7" label* | | | |
| ❑ WS 1751 | Late Again | 1970 | 10.00 |
| *—Any later Warner Bros. label* | | | |
| ❑ WS 1785 | Peter, Paul and Mommy | 1969 | 15.00 |
| *—Green "W7" label* | | | |
| ❑ WS 1785 | Peter, Paul and Mommy | 1970 | 10.00 |
| *—Any later Warner Bros. label* | | | |
| ❑ BS 2552 | (Ten) Years Together — The Best of Peter, Paul and Mary | 1970 | 15.00 |
| *—Green "WB" label* | | | |
| ❑ BS 2552 | (Ten) Years Together — The Best of Peter, Paul and Mary | 1973 | 12.00 |
| *—"Burbank" palm-trees label* | | | |
| ❑ BSK 3105 | (Ten) Years Together — The Best of Peter, Paul and Mary | 1977 | 10.00 |
| *—"Burbank" palm-trees label* | | | |
| ❑ BSK 3105 | (Ten) Years Together — The Best of Peter, Paul and Mary | 1979 | 8.00 |
| *—White or tan label* | | | |
| ❑ BSK 3231 | Reunion | 1978 | 10.00 |



**Except when noted otherwise, VG = 25% of NM, and VG+ = 50% of NM. (Example: VG = $2.00, VG+ = $4.00 and NM = $8.00.)**

| Number | Title (A Side/B Side) | Yr | NM |
|---|---|---|---|

## PETERS, BROCK

### UNITED ARTISTS

| Number | Title (A Side/B Side) | Yr | NM |
|---|---|---|---|
| ❑ UAL-3041 [M] | Sing'a Man | 1960 | 30.00 |
| ❑ UAL-3062 [M] | Brock Peters at the Village Gate | 1961 | 25.00 |
| ❑ UAL-3127 [M] | Brock Peters | 1963 | 20.00 |
| ❑ UAS-6041 [S] | Sing'a Man | 1960 | 40.00 |
| ❑ UAS-6062 [S] | Brock Peters at the Village Gate | 1961 | 30.00 |
| ❑ UAS-6127 [S] | Brock Peters | 1963 | 25.00 |

## PETERS, RAY

### JCW

| Number | Title (A Side/B Side) | Yr | NM |
|---|---|---|---|
| ❑ 1333 | From the Heart | 1968 | 25.00 |

## PETERS, ROBERTA

### RCA VICTOR RED SEAL

| Number | Title (A Side/B Side) | Yr | NM |
|---|---|---|---|
| ❑ LSC-2379 [S] | Roberta Peters in Recital | 1960 | 20.00 |
| *—Original with "shaded dog" label* | | | |

## PETERSEN, PAUL

### COLPIX

| Number | Title (A Side/B Side) | Yr | NM |
|---|---|---|---|
| ❑ CP-429 [M] | Lollipops and Roses | 1962 | 50.00 |
| ❑ SCP-429 [S] | Lollipops and Roses | 1962 | 60.00 |
| ❑ CP-442 [M] | My Dad | 1963 | 50.00 |
| ❑ SCP-442 [S] | My Dad | 1963 | 60.00 |

## PETERSON, OSCAR

### AMERICAN RECORDING SOCIETY

| Number | Title (A Side/B Side) | Yr | NM |
|---|---|---|---|
| ❑ G-415 [M] | An Oscar for Peterson | 1957 | 40.00 |
| ❑ G-438 [M] | Oscar Peterson Trio at Newport | 1957 | 40.00 |

### CLEF

| Number | Title (A Side/B Side) | Yr | NM |
|---|---|---|---|
| ❑ MGC-106 [10] | Oscar Peterson Piano Solos | 1951 | 100.00 |
| *—Reissue of Mercury 25024* | | | |
| ❑ MGC-107 [10] | Oscar Peterson at Carnegie Hall | 1951 | 100.00 |
| ❑ MGC-110 [10] | Oscar Peterson Collates | 1952 | 100.00 |
| ❑ MGC-116 [10] | The Oscar Peterson Quartet | 1952 | 100.00 |
| ❑ MGC-119 [10] | Oscar Peterson Plays Pretty | 1952 | 100.00 |
| ❑ MGC-127 [10] | Oscar Peterson Collates No. 2 | 1953 | 80.00 |
| ❑ MGC-145 [10] | Oscar Peterson Sings | 1954 | 80.00 |
| ❑ MGC-155 [10] | Oscar Peterson Plays Pretty No. 2 | 1954 | 80.00 |
| ❑ MGC-168 [10] | The Oscar Peterson Quartet No. 2 | 1954 | 80.00 |
| ❑ MGC-603 [M] | Oscar Peterson Plays Cole Porter | 1953 | 60.00 |
| ❑ MGC-604 [M] | Oscar Peterson Plays Irving Berlin | 1953 | 60.00 |
| ❑ MGC-605 [M] | Oscar Peterson Plays George Gershwin | 1953 | 60.00 |
| ❑ MGC-606 [M] | Oscar Peterson Plays Duke Ellington | 1953 | 60.00 |
| ❑ MGC-623 [M] | Oscar Peterson Plays Jerome Kern | 1954 | 50.00 |
| ❑ MGC-624 [M] | Oscar Peterson Plays Richard Rodgers | 1954 | 50.00 |
| ❑ MGC-625 [M] | Oscar Peterson Plays Vincent Youmans | 1954 | 50.00 |
| ❑ MGC-648 [M] | Oscar Peterson Plays Harry Warren | 1955 | 50.00 |
| ❑ MGC-649 [M] | Oscar Peterson Plays Harold Arlen | 1955 | 50.00 |
| ❑ MGC-650 [M] | Oscar Peterson Plays Jimmy McHugh | 1955 | 50.00 |
| ❑ MGC-688 [M] | The Oscar Peterson Quartet | 1956 | 50.00 |
| *—Reissue of 116* | | | |
| ❑ MGC-694 [M] | Recital by Oscar Peterson | 1956 | 50.00 |
| ❑ MGC-695 [M] | Nostalgic Memories by Oscar Peterson | 1956 | 50.00 |
| ❑ MGC-696 [M] | Tenderly — Music by Oscar Peterson | 1956 | 50.00 |
| ❑ MGC-697 [M] | Keyboard Music by Oscar Peterson | 1956 | 50.00 |
| ❑ MGC-698 [M] | An Evening with the Oscar Peterson Duo/Quartet | 1956 | 50.00 |
| ❑ MGC-708 [M] | Oscar Peterson Plays Count Basie | 1956 | 50.00 |

### DCC COMPACT CLASSICS

| Number | Title (A Side/B Side) | Yr | NM |
|---|---|---|---|
| ❑ LPZ-2021 | West Side Story | 1996 | 100.00 |
| *—Audiophile vinyl* | | | |

### LIMELIGHT

| Number | Title (A Side/B Side) | Yr | NM |
|---|---|---|---|
| ❑ LM-82044 [M] | Soul Espanol | 1967 | 20.00 |
| ❑ LS-86010 [S] | Canadiana Suite | 1965 | 20.00 |
| ❑ LS-86023 [S] | Eloquence | 1965 | 20.00 |
| ❑ LS-86029 [S] | With Respect to Nat | 1966 | 20.00 |

### MERCURY

| Number | Title (A Side/B Side) | Yr | NM |
|---|---|---|---|
| ❑ MGC-106 [10] | Oscar Peterson Piano Solos | 1951 | 120.00 |
| ❑ MGC-107 [10] | Oscar Peterson at Carnegie Hall | 1951 | 120.00 |
| ❑ MGC-110 [10] | Oscar Peterson Collates | 1952 | 120.00 |
| ❑ MGC-116 [10] | The Oscar Peterson Quartet | 1952 | 120.00 |
| ❑ MGC-119 [10] | Oscar Peterson Plays Pretty | 1952 | 120.00 |
| ❑ MGC-603 [M] | Oscar Peterson Plays Cole Porter | 1953 | 100.00 |
| ❑ MGC-604 [M] | Oscar Peterson Plays Irving Berlin | 1953 | 100.00 |

Peter, Paul and Mary, *See What Tomorrow Brings,* Warner Bros. WS 1615, 1965, stereo, gold label, $25.

| Number | Title (A Side/B Side) | Yr | NM |
|---|---|---|---|
| ❑ MGC-605 [M] | Oscar Peterson Plays George Gershwin | 1953 | 100.00 |
| ❑ MGC-606 [M] | Oscar Peterson Plays Duke Ellington | 1953 | 100.00 |
| ❑ MG-20975 [M] | Oscar Peterson Trio + One | 1964 | 25.00 |
| ❑ MG-25024 [10] | Oscar Peterson Piano Solos | 1950 | 150.00 |
| ❑ SR-60975 [S] | Oscar Peterson Trio + One | 1964 | 30.00 |

### MOBILE FIDELITY

| Number | Title (A Side/B Side) | Yr | NM |
|---|---|---|---|
| ❑ 1-243 | Very Tall | 1995 | 20.00 |
| *—Audiophile vinyl* | | | |

### RCA VICTOR

| Number | Title (A Side/B Side) | Yr | NM |
|---|---|---|---|
| ❑ LPT-3006 [10] | This Is Oscar Peterson | 1952 | 120.00 |

### VERVE

| Number | Title (A Side/B Side) | Yr | NM |
|---|---|---|---|
| ❑ MGV-2002 [M] | In a Romantic Mood — Oscar Peterson with Strings | 1956 | 40.00 |
| ❑ V-2002 [M] | In a Romantic Mood — Oscar Peterson with Strings | 1961 | 20.00 |
| ❑ MGV-2004 [M] | Pastel Moods by Oscar Peterson | 1956 | 40.00 |
| ❑ V-2004 [M] | Pastel Moods by Oscar Peterson | 1961 | 20.00 |
| ❑ MGV-2012 [M] | Romance — The Vocal Styling of Oscar Peterson | 1956 | 40.00 |
| *—Reissue of Clef 145* | | | |
| ❑ V-2012 [M] | Romance — The Vocal Styling of Oscar Peterson | 1961 | 20.00 |
| ❑ MGV-2044 [M] | Recital by Oscar Peterson | 1957 | 40.00 |
| *—Reissue of Clef 694* | | | |
| ❑ V-2044 [M] | Recital by Oscar Peterson | 1961 | 20.00 |
| ❑ MGV-2045 [M] | Nostalgic Memories by Oscar Peterson | 1957 | 40.00 |
| *—Reissue of Clef 695* | | | |
| ❑ V-2045 [M] | Nostalgic Memories by Oscar Peterson | 1961 | 20.00 |
| ❑ MGV-2046 [M] | Tenderly — Music by Oscar Peterson | 1957 | 40.00 |
| *—Reissue of Clef 696* | | | |
| ❑ V-2046 [M] | Tenderly — Music by Oscar Peterson | 1961 | 20.00 |
| ❑ MGV-2047 [M] | Keyboard Music by Oscar Peterson | 1957 | 40.00 |
| *—Reissue of Clef 697* | | | |
| ❑ V-2047 [M] | Keyboard Music by Oscar Peterson | 1961 | 20.00 |
| ❑ MGV-2048 [M] | An Evening with Oscar Peterson | 1957 | 40.00 |
| *—Reissue of Clef 698* | | | |
| ❑ V-2048 [M] | An Evening with Oscar Peterson | 1961 | 20.00 |
| ❑ MGV-2052 [M] | Oscar Peterson Plays the Cole Porter Songbook | 1957 | 40.00 |
| *—Reissue of Clef 603* | | | |
| ❑ V-2052 [M] | Oscar Peterson Plays the Cole Porter Songbook | 1961 | 20.00 |
| ❑ MGV-2053 [M] | Oscar Peterson Plays the Irving Berlin Songbook | 1957 | 40.00 |
| *—Reissue of Clef 604* | | | |
| ❑ V-2053 [M] | Oscar Peterson Plays the Irving Berlin Songbook | 1961 | 20.00 |
| ❑ MGV-2054 [M] | Oscar Peterson Plays the George Gershwin Songbook | 1957 | 40.00 |
| *—Reissue of Clef 605* | | | |
| ❑ V-2054 [M] | Oscar Peterson Plays the George Gershwin Songbook | 1961 | 20.00 |
| ❑ MGV-2055 [M] | Oscar Peterson Plays the Duke Ellington Songbook | 1957 | 40.00 |
| *—Reissue of Clef 606* | | | |
| ❑ V-2055 [M] | Oscar Peterson Plays the Duke Ellington Songbook | 1961 | 20.00 |
| ❑ MGV-2056 [M] | Oscar Peterson Plays the Jerome Kern Songbook | 1957 | 40.00 |
| *—Reissue of Clef 623* | | | |
| ❑ V-2056 [M] | Oscar Peterson Plays the Jerome Kern Songbook | 1961 | 20.00 |
| ❑ MGV-2057 [M] | Oscar Peterson Plays the Richard Rodgers Songbook | 1957 | 40.00 |
| *—Reissue of Clef 624* | | | |
| ❑ V-2057 [M] | Oscar Peterson Plays the Richard Rodgers Songbook | 1961 | 20.00 |
| ❑ MGV-2059 [M] | Oscar Peterson Plays the Harry Warren Songbook | 1957 | 40.00 |
| *—Reissue of Clef 648* | | | |
| ❑ V-2059 [M] | Oscar Peterson Plays the Harry Warren Songbook | 1961 | 20.00 |
| ❑ MGV-2060 [M] | Oscar Peterson Plays the Harold Arlen Songbook | 1957 | 40.00 |
| *—Reissue of Clef 649* | | | |
| ❑ V-2060 [M] | Oscar Peterson Plays the Harold Arlen Songbook | 1961 | 20.00 |
| ❑ MGV-2061 [M] | Oscar Peterson Plays the Jimmy McHugh Songbook | 1957 | 40.00 |
| *—Reissue of Clef 650* | | | |
| ❑ V-2061 [M] | Oscar Peterson Plays the Jimmy McHugh Songbook | 1961 | 20.00 |
| ❑ MGV-2079 [M] | Soft Sands | 1957 | 40.00 |

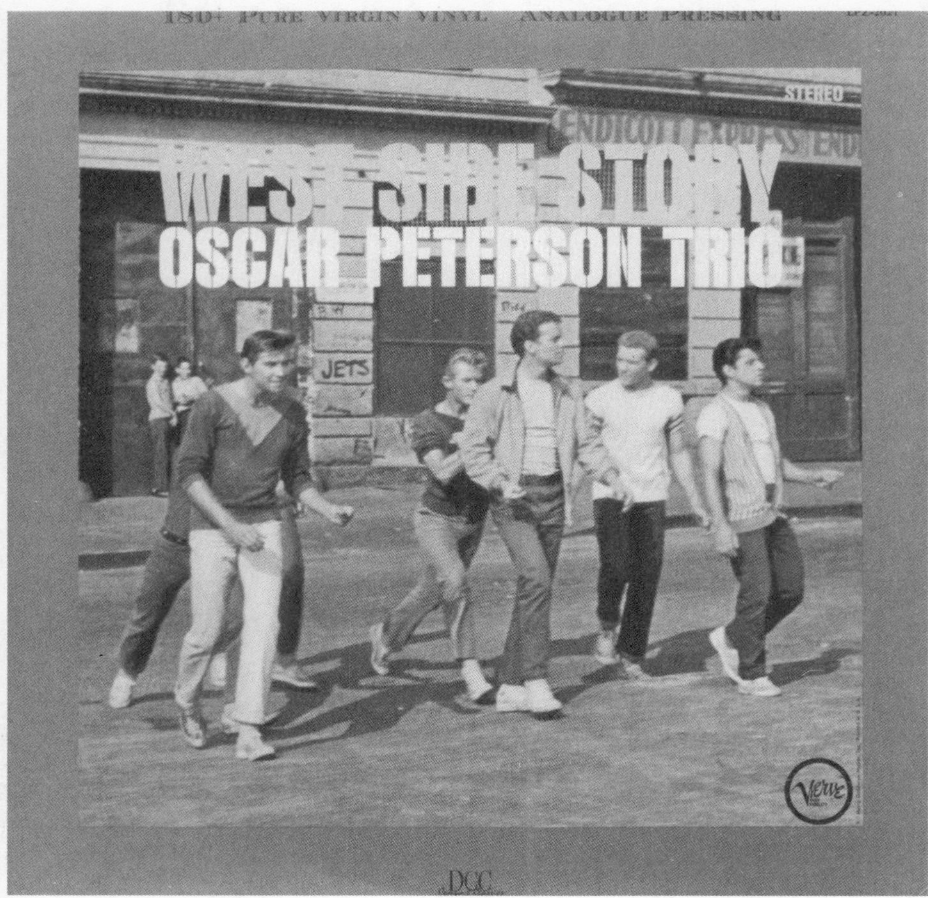


Oscar Peterson, *West Side Story,* DCC Compact Classics LPZ-2021, 1996, $100.

| Number | Title (A Side/B Side) | Yr | NM |
|---|---|---|---|
| ❑ V-2079 [M] | Soft Sands | 1961 | 20.00 |
| ❑ MGV-2119 [M] | Oscar Peterson Plays "My Fair Lady" | 1958 | 40.00 |
| ❑ V-2119 [M] | Oscar Peterson Plays "My Fair Lady" | 1961 | 20.00 |
| ❑ BOMC 70-5601 [S] | Night Train | 197? | 25.00 |
| *—Book-of-the-Month Club edition* | | | |
| ❑ 30-5606 [M] | The Oscar Peterson Quartet #1 | 197? | 12.00 |
| *—Book-of-the-Month Club edition* | | | |
| ❑ MGVS-6060 [S] | Oscar Peterson Plays "My Fair Lady" | 1960 | 30.00 |
| ❑ MGVS-6069 [S] | The Oscar Peterson Trio with the Modern Jazz Quartet at the Opera House | 1960 | 30.00 |
| ❑ MGVS-6071 [S] | Songs for a Swingin' Affair — A Jazz Portrait of Sinatra | 1960 | 40.00 |
| ❑ MGVS-6083 [S] | Oscar Peterson Plays the Cole Porter Songbook | 1960 | 30.00 |
| ❑ MGVS-6084 [S] | Oscar Peterson Plays the Irving Berlin Songbook | 1960 | 30.00 |
| ❑ MGVS-6085 [S] | Oscar Peterson Plays the George Gershwin Songbook | 1960 | 30.00 |
| ❑ MGVS-6086 [S] | Oscar Peterson Plays the Duke Ellington Songbook | 1960 | 30.00 |
| ❑ MGVS-6087 [S] | Oscar Peterson Plays the Jerome Kern Songbook | 1960 | 30.00 |
| ❑ MGVS-6088 [S] | Oscar Peterson Plays the Richard Rodgers Songbook | 1960 | 30.00 |
| ❑ MGVS-6090 [S] | Oscar Peterson Plays the Harry Warren Songbook | 1960 | 30.00 |
| ❑ MGVS-6091 [S] | Oscar Peterson Plays the Harold Arlen Songbook | 1960 | 30.00 |
| ❑ MGVS-6092 [S] | Oscar Peterson Plays the Jimmy McHugh Songbook | 1960 | 30.00 |
| ❑ MGVS-6119 [S] | Swinging Brass with the Oscar Peterson Trio | 1960 | 30.00 |
| ❑ MGV-8024 [M] | The Oscar Peterson Trio at the Stratford Shakespearean Festival | 1957 | 40.00 |
| ❑ V-8024 [M] | The Oscar Peterson Trio at the Stratford Shakespearean Festival | 1961 | 20.00 |
| ❑ MGV-8072 [M] | The Oscar Peterson Quartet No. 1 | 1957 | 40.00 |
| ❑ V-8072 [M] | The Oscar Peterson Quartet No. 1 | 1961 | 20.00 |

| Number | Title (A Side/B Side) | Yr | NM |
|---|---|---|---|
| ❑ MGV-8092 [M] | Oscar Peterson Plays Count Basie | 1957 | 40.00 |
| *—Reissue of Clef 708* | | | |
| ❑ V-8092 [M] | Oscar Peterson Plays Count Basie | 1961 | 20.00 |
| ❑ MGV-8239 [M] | The Oscar Peterson Trio with Sonny Stitt, Roy Eldredge and Jo Jones at Newport | 1958 | 40.00 |
| ❑ V-8239 [M] | The Oscar Peterson Trio with Sonny Stitt, Roy Eldredge and Jo Jones at Newport | 1961 | 20.00 |
| ❑ MGV-8268 [M] | The Oscar Peterson Trio at the Concertgebouw | 1958 | 40.00 |
| ❑ V-8268 [M] | The Oscar Peterson Trio at the Concertgebouw | 1961 | 20.00 |
| ❑ MGV-8269 [M] | The Oscar Peterson Trio with the Modern Jazz Quartet at the Opera House | 1958 | 40.00 |
| ❑ V-8269 [M] | The Oscar Peterson Trio with the Modern Jazz Quartet at the Opera House | 1961 | 20.00 |
| ❑ MGV-8287 [M] | A Night on the Town | 1958 | 40.00 |
| ❑ V-8287 [M] | A Night on the Town | 1961 | 20.00 |
| ❑ MGV-8334 [M] | Songs for a Swingin' Affair — A Jazz Portrait of Sinatra | 1959 | 50.00 |
| ❑ V-8334 [M] | Songs for a Swingin' Affair — A Jazz Portrait of Sinatra | 1961 | 20.00 |
| ❑ MGV-8340 [M] | Porgy and Bess | 1959 | 40.00 |
| ❑ V-8340 [M] | Porgy and Bess | 1961 | 20.00 |
| ❑ MGV-8351 [M] | The Jazz Soul of Oscar Peterson | 1959 | 40.00 |
| ❑ V-8351 [M] | The Jazz Soul of Oscar Peterson | 1961 | 20.00 |
| ❑ MGV-8364 [M] | Swinging Brass with the Oscar Peterson Trio | 1959 | 40.00 |
| ❑ V-8364 [M] | Swinging Brass with the Oscar Peterson Trio | 1961 | 20.00 |
| ❑ MGV-8366 [M] | The Music from "Fiorello!" | 1960 | 40.00 |
| ❑ V-8366 [M] | The Music from "Fiorello!" | 1961 | 20.00 |
| ❑ MGV-8368 [M] | The Oscar Peterson Trio at J.A.T.P. | 1960 | 40.00 |
| ❑ V-8368 [M] | The Oscar Peterson Trio at J.A.T.P. | 1961 | 20.00 |
| ❑ V-8420 [M] | The Trio — Live from Chicago | 1961 | 25.00 |
| ❑ V6-8420 [S] | The Trio — Live from Chicago | 1961 | 30.00 |
| ❑ V-8429 [M] | Very Tall | 1962 | 25.00 |
| ❑ V6-8429 [S] | Very Tall | 1962 | 30.00 |

| Number | Title (A Side/B Side) | Yr | NM |
|---|---|---|---|
| ❑ V-8454 [M] | West Side Story | 1962 | 25.00 |
| ❑ V6-8454 [S] | West Side Story | 1962 | 30.00 |
| ❑ V-8476 [M] | Bursting Out with the All Star Big Band! | 1962 | 25.00 |
| ❑ V6-8476 [S] | Bursting Out with the All Star Big Band! | 1962 | 30.00 |
| ❑ V-8480 [M] | The Sound of the Trio | 1962 | 25.00 |
| ❑ V6-8480 [S] | The Sound of the Trio | 1962 | 30.00 |
| ❑ V-8482 [M] | The Modern Jazz Quartet and the Oscar Petereson Trio at the Opera House | 1962 | 20.00 |
| *—Reissue of 8269* | | | |
| ❑ V6-8482 [S] | The Modern Jazz Quartet and the Oscar Petereson Trio at the Opera House | 1962 | 20.00 |
| *—Reissue of 8269* | | | |
| ❑ V-8516 [M] | Affinity | 1963 | 25.00 |
| ❑ V6-8516 [S] | Affinity | 1963 | 30.00 |
| ❑ V-8538 [M] | Night Train | 1963 | 25.00 |
| ❑ V6-8538 [S] | Night Train | 1963 | 30.00 |
| ❑ V-8562 [M] | The Oscar Peterson Trio with Nelson Riddle | 1963 | 25.00 |
| ❑ V6-8562 [S] | The Oscar Peterson Trio with Nelson Riddle | 1963 | 30.00 |
| ❑ V6-8581 [S] | Oscar Peterson Plays "My Fair Lady" | 1964 | 20.00 |
| ❑ V6-8591 [S] | The Oscar Peterson Trio Plays | 1964 | 20.00 |
| ❑ V6-8606 [S] | We Get Requests | 1965 | 20.00 |
| ❑ V6-8660 [S] | Put On a Happy Face | 1966 | 20.00 |
| ❑ V6-8681 [S] | Something Warm | 1966 | 20.00 |
| ❑ V-8740 [M] | Night Train, Volume 2 | 1967 | 20.00 |

## PETERSON, OSCAR/GERRY MULLIGAN

### VERVE

| Number | Title (A Side/B Side) | Yr | NM |
|---|---|---|---|
| ❑ V-8559 [M] | The Oscar Peterson Trio and the Gerry Mulligan Four at Newport | 1963 | 25.00 |
| ❑ V6-8559 [S] | The Oscar Peterson Trio and the Gerry Mulligan Four at Newport | 1963 | 30.00 |

## PETERSON, RAY

### DECCA

| Number | Title (A Side/B Side) | Yr | NM |
|---|---|---|---|
| ❑ DL 75307 | Ray Peterson Country | 1971 | 20.00 |

### MGM

| Number | Title (A Side/B Side) | Yr | NM |
|---|---|---|---|
| ❑ E-4250 [M] | The Very Best of Ray Peterson | 1964 | 25.00 |
| ❑ SE-4250 [S] | The Very Best of Ray Peterson | 1964 | 30.00 |
| ❑ E-4277 [M] | The Other Side of Ray Peterson | 1965 | 25.00 |
| ❑ SE-4277 [S] | The Other Side of Ray Peterson | 1965 | 30.00 |

### RCA CAMDEN

| Number | Title (A Side/B Side) | Yr | NM |
|---|---|---|---|
| ❑ CAL-2119 [M] | Goodnight My Love | 1966 | 12.00 |
| ❑ CAS-2119 [S] | Goodnight My Love | 1966 | 12.00 |

### RCA VICTOR

| Number | Title (A Side/B Side) | Yr | NM |
|---|---|---|---|
| ❑ LPM-2297 [M] | Tell Laura I Love Her | 1960 | 100.00 |
| ❑ LSP-2297 [S] | Tell Laura I Love Her | 1960 | 150.00 |

### UNI

| Number | Title (A Side/B Side) | Yr | NM |
|---|---|---|---|
| ❑ 73078 | Missing You/Featuring His Greatest Hits! | 1969 | 20.00 |

## PETERSTEIN, SHORTY

### WORLD PACIFIC

| Number | Title (A Side/B Side) | Yr | NM |
|---|---|---|---|
| ❑ WP-1274 [M] | The Wide Weird World of Shorty Petterstein | 1959 | 40.00 |

## PETTIFORD, OSCAR

### ABC-PARAMOUNT

| Number | Title (A Side/B Side) | Yr | NM |
|---|---|---|---|
| ❑ ABC-135 [M] | Oscar Pettiford Orchestra in Hi-Fi | 1956 | 100.00 |
| ❑ ABC-227 [M] | O.P.'s Jazz Men: Oscar Pettiford Orchestra in Hi-Fi, Vol. 2 | 1958 | 120.00 |
| ❑ ABCS-227 [S] | O.P.'s Jazz Men: Oscar Pettiford Orchestra in Hi-Fi, Vol. 2 | 1958 | 100.00 |

### BETHLEHEM

| Number | Title (A Side/B Side) | Yr | NM |
|---|---|---|---|
| ❑ BCP-33 [M] | Oscar Pettiford Sextet | 1955 | 150.00 |
| ❑ BCP-1003 [10] | Oscar Pettiford | 1954 | 250.00 |
| ❑ BCP-1019 [10] | Basically Duke | 1955 | 250.00 |

### DEBUT

| Number | Title (A Side/B Side) | Yr | NM |
|---|---|---|---|
| ❑ DLP-8 [10] | Oscar Pettiford Sextet | 1954 | 500.00 |

### FANTASY

| Number | Title (A Side/B Side) | Yr | NM |
|---|---|---|---|
| ❑ 6010 [M] | My Little Cello | 1964 | 40.00 |
| ❑ 6015 [M] | The Essen Jazz Festival | 1964 | 40.00 |

### JAZZLAND

| Number | Title (A Side/B Side) | Yr | NM |
|---|---|---|---|
| ❑ JLP-64 [M] | Last Recordings by the Late, Great Bassist | 1962 | 60.00 |
| ❑ JLP-964 [R] | Last Recordings by the Late, Great Bassist | 1962 | 40.00 |

## PETTIFORD, OSCAR/VINNIE BURKE

### BETHLEHEM

| Number | Title (A Side/B Side) | Yr | NM |
|---|---|---|---|
| ❑ BCP-6 [M] | Bass by Pettiford/Burke | 1957 | 200.00 |

## PETTIFORD, OSCAR/RED MITCHELL

### BETHLEHEM

| Number | Title (A Side/B Side) | Yr | NM |
|---|---|---|---|
| ❑ BCP-2 [M] | Jazz Mainstream | 1957 | 200.00 |

| Number | Title (A Side/B Side) | Yr | NM |
|---|---|---|---|

### PETTY, NORMAN, TRIO

**COLUMBIA**

| Number | Title (A Side/B Side) | Yr | NM |
|---|---|---|---|
| ❑ CL 1092 [M] | Moondreams | 1958 | 150.00 |

**TOP RANK**

| Number | Title (A Side/B Side) | Yr | NM |
|---|---|---|---|
| ❑ R-639 [M] | Petty for Your Thoughts | 1960 | 30.00 |
| ❑ RS-639 [S] | Petty for Your Thoughts | 1960 | 40.00 |

**VIK**

| Number | Title (A Side/B Side) | Yr | NM |
|---|---|---|---|
| ❑ LX-1073 [M] | Corsage | 1957 | 70.00 |

### PETTY, TOM, AND THE HEARTBREAKERS

**AMERICAN**

| Number | Title (A Side/B Side) | Yr | NM |
|---|---|---|---|
| ❑ 44285-1 [(2)] | Highway Companion | 2007 | 25.00 |
| *—180-gram issue; CD released in 2006* | | | |

**BACKSTREET**

| Number | Title (A Side/B Side) | Yr | NM |
|---|---|---|---|
| ❑ BSR-5105 | Damn the Torpedoes | 1979 | 10.00 |
| ❑ BSR-5160 | Hard Promises | 1981 | 10.00 |
| ❑ BSR-5360 | Long After Dark | 1982 | 10.00 |

**MCA**

| Number | Title (A Side/B Side) | Yr | NM |
|---|---|---|---|
| ❑ 1486 | Damn the Torpedoes | 1987 | 8.00 |
| ❑ 5486 | Southern Accents | 1985 | 10.00 |
| ❑ 5836 | Let Me Up (I've Had Enough) | 1987 | 10.00 |
| ❑ 6253 | Full Moon Fever | 1989 | 10.00 |
| ❑ 2-8021 [(2)] | Pack Up the Plantation — Live! | 1985 | 12.00 |
| ❑ 10317 | Into the Great Wide Open | 1991 | 20.00 |
| ❑ 37116 | You're Gonna Get It! | 1982 | 8.00 |
| ❑ 37143 | Tom Petty and the Heartbreakers | 1982 | 8.00 |
| ❑ 37239 | Hard Promises | 1984 | 8.00 |

**SHELTER**

| Number | Title (A Side/B Side) | Yr | NM |
|---|---|---|---|
| ❑ TP-12677 [DJ] | Official Live 'Leg | 1977 | 40.00 |
| *—Promo-only live album with letter to radio (has been counterfeited)* | | | |
| ❑ SRL-52006 | Tom Petty and the Heartbreakers | 1976 | 15.00 |
| *—Original copies were distributed by ABC* | | | |
| ❑ SRL-52006 | Tom Petty and the Heartbreakers | 1979 | 12.00 |
| *—Later copies were distributed by MCA* | | | |
| ❑ DA-52029 | You're Gonna Get It! | 1978 | 15.00 |
| *—Original copies were distributed by ABC* | | | |
| ❑ DA-52029 | You're Gonna Get It! | 1979 | 12.00 |
| *—Later copies were distributed by MCA* | | | |
| ❑ DA-52029 [DJ] | You're Gonna Get It! | 1978 | 25.00 |
| *—Promo only on red vinyl* | | | |

**WARNER BROS.**

| Number | Title (A Side/B Side) | Yr | NM |
|---|---|---|---|
| ❑ 45759 [(2)] | Wildflowers | 1994 | 20.00 |
| ❑ 46285 | Songs and Music from the Motion Picture "She's the One" | 1996 | 10.00 |
| ❑ 47294 [(2)] | Echo | 1999 | 20.00 |
| ❑ 47955 | The Last DJ | 2002 | 20.00 |

### PHAFNER

**DRAGON**

| Number | Title (A Side/B Side) | Yr | NM |
|---|---|---|---|
| ❑ LP-101 | Overdrive | 1971 | 3000. |
| *—VG value 1000; VG+ value 2000* | | | |

### PHANTOM, THE (2)

**CAPITOL**

| Number | Title (A Side/B Side) | Yr | NM |
|---|---|---|---|
| ❑ ST-11313 | The Phantom's Divine Comedy, Part One | 1974 | 60.00 |

### PHILADELPHIA EXPERIMENT, THE

**ATLANTIC**

| Number | Title (A Side/B Side) | Yr | NM |
|---|---|---|---|
| ❑ 93042 [(2)] | The Philadelphia Experiment | 2001 | 15.00 |

### PHILARMONICS, THE

**CAPRICORN**

| Number | Title (A Side/B Side) | Yr | NM |
|---|---|---|---|
| ❑ CPN 0179 | The Masters in Philadelphia | 1977 | 25.00 |

### PHILBIN, REGIS

**MERCURY**

| Number | Title (A Side/B Side) | Yr | NM |
|---|---|---|---|
| ❑ SR-61169 | It's Time for Regis! | 1968 | 25.00 |

### PHILHARMONIA HUNGARICA (ANTAL DORATI, CONDUCTOR)

**MERCURY LIVING PRESENCE**

| Number | Title (A Side/B Side) | Yr | NM |
|---|---|---|---|
| ❑ SR 90179 [S] | Kodaly: Dances of Galanta; Marosszek Dancves; Bartok-Weiner: Two Romanian Dances | 196? | 40.00 |
| *—Maroon label, no "Vendor: Mercury Record Corporation"* | | | |
| ❑ SR 90183 [S] | Bartok: Dance Suite; Deux Portraits; Mikrokosmos | 196? | 120.00 |
| *—Maroon label, no "Vendor: Mercury Record Corporation"* | | | |
| ❑ SR 90190 [S] | Wienerwalzer Paprika | 196? | 20.00 |
| *—Maroon label, no "Vendor: Mercury Record Corporation"* | | | |
| ❑ SR 90199 [S] | Respighi: Ancient Airs and Dances, Suites 1-3 | 196? | 20.00 |
| *—Third edition: Dark red (not maroon) label* | | | |
| ❑ SR 90199 [S] | Respighi: Ancient Airs and Dances, Suites 1-3 | 196? | 40.00 |
| *—Maroon label, with "Vendor: Mercury Record Corporation"* | | | |
| ❑ SR 90199 [S] | Respighi: Ancient Airs and Dances, Suites 1-3 | 196? | 60.00 |
| *—Maroon label, no "Vendor: Mercury Record Corporation"* | | | |

Tom Petty and the Heartbreakers, *She's the One,* Warner Bros. 46285, 1996, $10.

| Number | Title (A Side/B Side) | Yr | NM |
|---|---|---|---|
| ❑ SR 90200 [S] | Tchaikovsky: Serenade in C; Arensky: Tchaikovsky Variations | 196? | 80.00 |
| *—Maroon label, no "Vendor: Mercury Record Corporation"* | | | |
| ❑ SR 90208 [S] | Haydn: Symphonies 94 and 103 | 196? | 40.00 |
| *—Maroon label, no "Vendor: Mercury Record Corporation"* | | | |

### PHILLIPS, BILL

**DECCA**

| Number | Title (A Side/B Side) | Yr | NM |
|---|---|---|---|
| ❑ DL 4792 [M] | Put It Off Until Tomorrow | 1966 | 30.00 |
| ❑ DL 4897 [M] | Bill Phillips' Style | 1967 | 30.00 |
| ❑ DL 74792 [S] | Put It Off Until Tomorrow | 1966 | 40.00 |
| ❑ DL 74897 [S] | Bill Phillips' Style | 1967 | 25.00 |
| ❑ DL 75022 | Country Action | 1968 | 20.00 |
| ❑ DL 75182 | Little Boy Sad | 1970 | 20.00 |

**HARMONY**

| Number | Title (A Side/B Side) | Yr | NM |
|---|---|---|---|
| ❑ HL 7309 [M] | Bill Phillips' Best | 1964 | 20.00 |

### PHILLIPS, ESTHER

**ATLANTIC**

| Number | Title (A Side/B Side) | Yr | NM |
|---|---|---|---|
| ❑ SD 1565 | Burnin' | 1970 | 25.00 |
| ❑ SD 1680 | Confessin' the Blues | 1975 | 15.00 |
| ❑ 8102 [M] | And I Love Him | 1965 | 50.00 |
| *—Cover has a pink Cupid on it* | | | |
| ❑ 8102 [M] | And I Love Him | 1966 | 30.00 |
| *—Cover has a black photo on it* | | | |
| ❑ SD 8102 [S] | And I Love Him | 1965 | 80.00 |
| *—Cover has a pink Cupid on it* | | | |
| ❑ SD 8102 [S] | And I Love Him | 1966 | 40.00 |
| *—Cover has a black photo on it* | | | |
| ❑ 8122 [M] | Esther | 1966 | 30.00 |
| ❑ SD 8122 [S] | Esther | 1966 | 40.00 |
| ❑ 8130 [M] | The Country Side of Esther Phillips | 1966 | 30.00 |
| *—Reissue of Lenox 227* | | | |
| ❑ SD 8130 [S] | The Country Side of Esther Phillips | 1966 | 40.00 |
| *—Reissue of Lenox S-227* | | | |
| ❑ 90670 | Confessin' the Blues | 1987 | 10.00 |
| *—Reissue of 1680* | | | |

**CBS ASSOCIATED**

| Number | Title (A Side/B Side) | Yr | NM |
|---|---|---|---|
| ❑ PZ 40710 | What a Diff'rence a Day Makes | 1987 | 8.00 |
| *—Reissue of Kudu 23* | | | |
| ❑ PZ 40935 | From a Whisper to a Scream | 1988 | 8.00 |
| *—Reissue of Kudu 05* | | | |

**KING**

| Number | Title (A Side/B Side) | Yr | NM |
|---|---|---|---|
| ❑ 622 [M] | Memory Lane | 1959 | [illegible]000. |

**KUDU**

| Number | Title (A Side/B Side) | Yr | NM |
|---|---|---|---|
| ❑ 05 | From a Whisper to a Scream | 1972 | 12.00 |
| ❑ 09 | Alone Again, Naturally | 1972 | 12.00 |
| ❑ 14 | Black-Eyed Blues | 1973 | 12.00 |
| ❑ 18 | Performance | 1974 | 12.00 |
| ❑ 23 | What a Diff'rence a Day Makes | 1975 | 12.00 |
| ❑ 28 | For All We Know | 1976 | 12.00 |
| ❑ 31 | Capricorn Princess | 1976 | 12.00 |

**LENOX**

| Number | Title (A Side/B Side) | Yr | NM |
|---|---|---|---|
| ❑ 227 [M] | Release Me | 1962 | 100.00 |
| ❑ S-227 [S] | Release Me | 1962 | 200.00 |

**MERCURY**

| Number | Title (A Side/B Side) | Yr | NM |
|---|---|---|---|
| ❑ SRM-1-1187 | You've Come a Long Way, Baby | 1977 | 10.00 |
| ❑ SRM-1-3733 | All About Esther Phillips | 1978 | 10.00 |
| ❑ SRM-1-3769 | Here's Esther — Are You Ready? | 1979 | 10.00 |
| ❑ SRM-1-4005 | A Good Black Is Hard to Crack | 1981 | 10.00 |

**MUSE**

| Number | Title (A Side/B Side) | Yr | NM |
|---|---|---|---|
| ❑ MR-5302 | A Way to Say Goodbye | 1986 | 12.00 |

**SAVOY JAZZ**

| Number | Title (A Side/B Side) | Yr | NM |
|---|---|---|---|
| ❑ SJL-2258 | The Complete Savoy Recordings | 1984 | 10.00 |

### PHILLIPS, FLIP

**BRUNSWICK**

| Number | Title (A Side/B Side) | Yr | NM |
|---|---|---|---|
| ❑ BL 58032 [10] | Tenor Sax Stylings | 1953 | 150.00 |

**CLEF**

| Number | Title (A Side/B Side) | Yr | NM |
|---|---|---|---|
| ❑ MGC-105 [10] | Flip Phillips | 1953 | 200.00 |
| ❑ MGC-109 [10] | Flip Phillips Collates | 1953 | 200.00 |
| ❑ MGC-133 [10] | Flip Phillips Collates No. 2 | 1953 | 250.00 |
| ❑ MGC-158 [10] | Jumping Moods with Flip Phillips | 1954 | 200.00 |
| ❑ MGC-634 [M] | The Flip Phillips-Buddy Rich Trio | 1954 | 120.00 |
| ❑ MGC-637 [M] | The Flip Phillips Quintet | 1954 | 120.00 |
| ❑ MGC-691 [M] | Flip Wails | 1956 | 150.00 |
| ❑ MGC-692 [M] | Swinging with Flip Phillips and His Orchestra | 1956 | 120.00 |
| ❑ MGC-693 [M] | Flip | 1956 | 120.00 |
| ❑ MGC-740 [M] | Rock with Flip | 1956 | 150.00 |

**MERCURY**

| Number | Title (A Side/B Side) | Yr | NM |
|---|---|---|---|
| ❑ MGC-105 [10] | Flip Phillips | 1951 | 250.00 |
| ❑ MGC-109 [10] | Flip Phillips Collates | 1952 | 200.00 |
| ❑ MG-25023 [10] | Flip Phillips Quartet | 1950 | 300.00 |

| Number | Title (A Side/B Side) | Yr | NM |
|---|---|---|---|
| **SUE** | | | |
| ❑ LP-1035 [M] | Flip Phillips Revisited | 1965 | 30.00 |
| ❑ STLP-1035 [S] | Flip Phillips Revisited | 1965 | 40.00 |
| **VERVE** | | | |
| ❑ MGV-8075 [M] | Flip Wails | 1957 | 80.00 |
| ❑ V-8075 [M] | Flip Wails | 1961 | 25.00 |
| ❑ MGV-8076 [M] | Swingin' with Flip | 1957 | 80.00 |
| ❑ V-8076 [M] | Swingin' with Flip | 1961 | 25.00 |
| ❑ MGV-8077 [M] | Flip | 1957 | 80.00 |
| ❑ V-8077 [M] | Flip | 1961 | 25.00 |
| ❑ MGV-8116 [M] | Rock with Flip | 1957 | 80.00 |
| ❑ V-8116 [M] | Rock with Flip | 1961 | 25.00 |

### PHILLIPS, GENE

| Number | Title (A Side/B Side) | Yr | NM |
|---|---|---|---|
| **CROWN** | | | |
| ❑ CLP-5375 [M] | Gene Phillips and the Rockers | 1963 | 30.00 |

### PHILLIPS, SONNY

| Number | Title (A Side/B Side) | Yr | NM |
|---|---|---|---|
| **PRESTIGE** | | | |
| ❑ PRST-7737 | Sure 'Nuff | 1970 | 20.00 |
| ❑ PRST-7799 | Black Magic | 1970 | 20.00 |
| ❑ 10007 | Black On Black | 1971 | 20.00 |

### PHILLIPS, STU

| Number | Title (A Side/B Side) | Yr | NM |
|---|---|---|---|
| **CAPITOL** | | | |
| ❑ ST 2356 [S] | Feels Like Lovin' | 1965 | 30.00 |
| ❑ T 2356 [M] | Feels Like Lovin' | 1965 | 25.00 |
| **RCA VICTOR** | | | |
| ❑ LPM-3619 [M] | Singin' Stu Phillips | 1966 | 20.00 |
| ❑ LSP-3619 [S] | Singin' Stu Phillips | 1966 | 25.00 |
| ❑ LPM-3717 [M] | Grassroots Country | 1967 | 30.00 |
| ❑ LSP-3717 [S] | Grassroots Country | 1967 | 25.00 |
| ❑ LPM-4012 [M] | Our Last Rendezvous | 1968 | 50.00 |
| ❑ LSP-4012 [S] | Our Last Rendezvous | 1968 | 25.00 |

### PHILLIPS, WARREN, AND THE ROCKETS

| Number | Title (A Side/B Side) | Yr | NM |
|---|---|---|---|
| **PARROT** | | | |
| ❑ PAS 71044 | Rocked Out | 1970 | 30.00 |

### PHILLIPS, WOOLF

| Number | Title (A Side/B Side) | Yr | NM |
|---|---|---|---|
| **CORAL** | | | |
| ❑ CRL 56036 [10] | Woolf Phillips Plays Duke Ellington Songs | 1951 | 50.00 |

### PHILOSOPHERS, THE

| Number | Title (A Side/B Side) | Yr | NM |
|---|---|---|---|
| **PHILO** | | | |
| ❑ 1001 | After Sundown | 1969 | 150.00 |

### PHIPPS FAMILY, THE

| Number | Title (A Side/B Side) | Yr | NM |
|---|---|---|---|
| **STARDAY** | | | |
| ❑ SLP-139 [M] | The Phipps Family Sings the Most Requested Sacred Songs of the Carter Family | 1961 | 40.00 |
| ❑ SLP-195 [M] | Old Time Pickin' and Singin' | 1962 | 30.00 |
| ❑ SLP-248 [M] | Echoes of the Carter Family | 1963 | 30.00 |

### PHLUPH

| Number | Title (A Side/B Side) | Yr | NM |
|---|---|---|---|
| **VERVE** | | | |
| ❑ V6-5054 | Phluph | 1968 | 30.00 |

### PIAF, EDITH

| Number | Title (A Side/B Side) | Yr | NM |
|---|---|---|---|
| **CAPITOL** | | | |
| ❑ DTCL 2953 [(3)] | The Edith Piaf Deluxe Set | 1968 | 30.00 |
| ❑ T 10210 [M] | Piaf | 1959 | 25.00 |
| ❑ ST 10283 [S] | Piaf of Paris | 1961 | 20.00 |
| ❑ T 10283 [M] | Piaf of Paris | 1961 | 15.00 |
| ❑ ST 10295 [S] | Potpourri Par Piaf | 1962 | 20.00 |
| ❑ T 10295 [M] | Potpourri Par Piaf | 1962 | 15.00 |
| ❑ ST 10348 [S] | Piaf and Sarapo at the Bobido | 1963 | 20.00 |
| ❑ T 10348 [M] | Piaf and Sarapo at the Bobido | 1963 | 15.00 |
| ❑ ST 10368 [S] | Piaf at the Olympia | 1964 | 20.00 |
| ❑ T 10368 [M] | Piaf at the Olympia | 1964 | 15.00 |
| **COLUMBIA** | | | |
| ❑ CL 898 [M] | La Vie En Rose | 1956 | 40.00 |
| ❑ CL 6223 [10] | Encore Parisiennes | 1952 | 50.00 |
| **DECCA** | | | |
| ❑ DL 6004 [10] | Chansons de Cafes du Paris | 1951 | 60.00 |
| **PHILIPS** | | | |
| ❑ PCC 208 [M] | Adieu, Edith Piaf, Little Sparrow | 1964 | 20.00 |
| **POLYDOR VOX** | | | |
| ❑ PL 3050 [10] | Edith Piaf Sings | 195? | 80.00 |

### PIANO CHOIR, THE

| Number | Title (A Side/B Side) | Yr | NM |
|---|---|---|---|
| **STRATA-EAST** | | | |
| ❑ SES-19730 [(2)] | Handscapes | 1973 | 25.00 |
| ❑ SES-19750 | Handscapes 2 | 1975 | 20.00 |

### PIANO RED

| Number | Title (A Side/B Side) | Yr | NM |
|---|---|---|---|
| **ARHOOLIE** | | | |
| ❑ 1064 | William Perryman (Alone with Piano) | 197? | 12.00 |
| **EUPHONIC** | | | |
| ❑ 1212 | Percussive Piano | 198? | 10.00 |
| **GROOVE** | | | |
| ❑ LG-1001 [M] | Jump Man, Jump | 1956 | — |
| *—The existence of this LP has not been confirmed* | | | |
| ❑ LG-1002 [M] | Piano Red in Concert | 1956 | 600.00 |
| **KING** | | | |
| ❑ KS-1117 | Happiness Is Piano Red | 1970 | 20.00 |
| **RCA CAMDEN** | | | |
| ❑ ACL1-0547 | Rockin' with Red | 1974 | 12.00 |
| **SOUTHLAND** | | | |
| ❑ 8 | Willie Perryman-Piano Red-Dr. Feelgood | 1983 | 15.00 |

### PIATIGORSKI, GREGOR

| Number | Title (A Side/B Side) | Yr | NM |
|---|---|---|---|
| **RCA VICTOR RED SEAL** | | | |
| ❑ LSC-2490 [S] | Dvorak: Cello Concerto | 1961 | 40.00 |
| *—With Charles Munch/Boston Symphony Orch.; original with "shaded dog" label* | | | |
| ❑ LSC-2490 [S] | Dvorak: Cello Concerto | 199? | 25.00 |
| *—With Charles Munch/Boston Symphony Orch.; Classic Records reissue* | | | |

### PICHON, WALTER "FATS"

| Number | Title (A Side/B Side) | Yr | NM |
|---|---|---|---|
| **DECCA** | | | |
| ❑ DL 8390 [M] | Appearing Nightly | 1956 | 40.00 |

### PICKETT, BOBBY "BORIS"

| Number | Title (A Side/B Side) | Yr | NM |
|---|---|---|---|
| **GARPAX** | | | |
| ❑ GPX 57001 [M] | The Original Monster Mash | 1962 | 150.00 |
| ❑ SGP 67001 [S] | The Original Monster Mash | 1962 | 250.00 |
| **PARROT** | | | |
| ❑ XPAS 71063 [R] | The Original Monster Mash | 1973 | 25.00 |
| *—Reissue of Garpax LP with four tracks deleted and one added* | | | |

### PICKETT, WILSON

| Number | Title (A Side/B Side) | Yr | NM |
|---|---|---|---|
| **ATLANTIC** | | | |
| ❑ SD 2-501 [(2)] | Wilson Pickett's Greatest Hits | 1973 | 20.00 |
| ❑ 8114 [M] | In the Midnight Hour | 1965 | 40.00 |
| ❑ SD 8114 [R] | In the Midnight Hour | 1965 | 30.00 |
| ❑ 8129 [M] | The Exciting Wilson Pickett | 1966 | 40.00 |
| ❑ SD 8129 [R] | The Exciting Wilson Pickett | 1966 | 30.00 |
| ❑ 8136 [M] | The Wicked Pickett | 1967 | 40.00 |
| ❑ SD 8136 [R] | The Wicked Pickett | 1967 | 30.00 |
| ❑ 8145 [M] | The Sound of Wilson Pickett | 1967 | 40.00 |
| ❑ SD 8145 [P] | The Sound of Wilson Pickett | 1967 | 40.00 |
| ❑ 8151 [M] | The Best of Wilson Pickett | 1967 | 40.00 |
| ❑ SD 8151 [R] | The Best of Wilson Pickett | 1967 | 20.00 |
| ❑ SD 8175 | I'm in Love | 1968 | 25.00 |
| ❑ SD 8183 | The Midnight Mover | 1968 | 25.00 |
| ❑ SD 8215 | Hey Jude | 1969 | 20.00 |
| ❑ SD 8250 | Right On | 1970 | 20.00 |
| ❑ SD 8270 | Wilson Pickett in Philadelphia | 1970 | 20.00 |
| ❑ 8290 [M] | The Best of Wilson Pickett, Vol. II | 1971 | 25.00 |
| *—Mono copies are promo only* | | | |
| ❑ SD 8290 [S] | The Best of Wilson Pickett, Vol. II | 1971 | 15.00 |
| ❑ SD 8300 | Don't Knock My Love | 1971 | 15.00 |
| ❑ 81283 | The Best of Wilson Pickett | 1985 | 10.00 |
| **BIG TREE** | | | |
| ❑ SD 76011 | Funky Situation | 1978 | 12.00 |
| **DOUBLE-L** | | | |
| ❑ DL-2300 [M] | It's Too Late | 1963 | 50.00 |
| ❑ SDL-8300 [S] | It's Too Late | 1963 | 70.00 |
| **EMI AMERICA** | | | |
| ❑ SW-17019 | I Want You | 1979 | 12.00 |
| ❑ SW-17043 | Right Track | 1981 | 12.00 |
| **MOTOWN** | | | |
| ❑ 6244 ML | American Soul Man | 1987 | 10.00 |
| **RCA VICTOR** | | | |
| ❑ APL1-0312 | Miz Lena's Boy | 1973 | 15.00 |
| ❑ APL1-0495 | Pickett in the Pocket | 1974 | 15.00 |
| ❑ APL1-0856 | Join Me and Let's Be Free | 1975 | 15.00 |
| ❑ ANL1-2149 | Join Me and Let's Be Free | 1977 | 10.00 |
| *—Reissue* | | | |
| ❑ LSP-4858 | Mr. Magic Man | 1973 | 15.00 |
| **TRIP** | | | |
| ❑ 8010 | Wickedness | 1972 | 10.00 |
| **UPFRONT** | | | |
| ❑ UPF-127 [S] | It's Too Late | 197? | 10.00 |
| **WAND** | | | |
| ❑ WD-672 [M] | Great Wilson Pickett Hits | 1966 | 30.00 |
| ❑ WDS-672 [R] | Great Wilson Pickett Hits | 1966 | 20.00 |
| **WICKED** | | | |
| ❑ 9001 | Chocolate Mountain | 1976 | 25.00 |

### PIERCE, BILLIE AND DEDE

| Number | Title (A Side/B Side) | Yr | NM |
|---|---|---|---|
| **RIVERSIDE** | | | |
| ❑ RLP-370 [M] | Blues in the Classic Tradition | 1961 | 30.00 |
| ❑ RLP-394 [M] | Blues and Tonks From the Delta | 1961 | 30.00 |

### PIERCE, NAT

| Number | Title (A Side/B Side) | Yr | NM |
|---|---|---|---|
| **CORAL** | | | |
| ❑ CRL 57091 [M] | Kansas City Memories | 1957 | 50.00 |
| ❑ CRL 57128 [M] | Chamber Music for Moderns | 1957 | 40.00 |
| **FANTASY** | | | |
| ❑ 3-14 [10] | Nat Pierce and the Herdsmen Featuring Dick Collins | 1954 | 80.00 |
| *—Blue vinyl* | | | |
| ❑ 3-14 [10] | Nat Pierce and the Herdsmen Featuring Dick Collins | 1954 | 80.00 |
| *—Red vinyl* | | | |
| **KEYNOTE** | | | |
| ❑ LP-1101 [M] | Nat Pierce Octet and Tentette | 1955 | 80.00 |
| **RCA VICTOR** | | | |
| ❑ LPM-2543 [M] | Big Band at the Savoy Ballroom | 1962 | 25.00 |
| ❑ LSP-2543 [S] | Big Band at the Savoy Ballroom | 1962 | 30.00 |
| **VANGUARD** | | | |
| ❑ VRS-8017 [10] | Nat Pierce Bandstand | 1955 | 80.00 |

### PIERCE, NAT; DICK COLLINS; CHARLIE MARIANO

| Number | Title (A Side/B Side) | Yr | NM |
|---|---|---|---|
| **FANTASY** | | | |
| ❑ 3224 [M] | Nat Pierce-Dick Collins Nonet/ Charlie Mariano Sextet | 195? | 60.00 |
| *—Black vinyl* | | | |
| ❑ 3224 [M] | Nat Pierce-Dick Collins Nonet/ Charlie Mariano Sextet | 1956 | 120.00 |
| *—Red vinyl* | | | |

### PIERCE, NAT; MILT HINTON; BARRY GALBRAITH; OSIE JOHNSON

| Number | Title (A Side/B Side) | Yr | NM |
|---|---|---|---|
| **MUSIC MINUS ONE** | | | |
| ❑ Vol. 1 [M] | Nat Pierce and Milt Hinton and Barry Galbraith and Osie Johnson | 1956 | 30.00 |
| *—With sheet music attached* | | | |

### PIERCE, WEBB

| Number | Title (A Side/B Side) | Yr | NM |
|---|---|---|---|
| **DECCA** | | | |
| ❑ DXB 181 [(2)M] | The Webb Pierce Story | 1964 | 30.00 |
| *—Deduct 25% if booklet is missing* | | | |
| ❑ DL 4015 [M] | Webb with a Beat | 1960 | 30.00 |
| ❑ DL 4079 [M] | Walking the Streets | 1960 | 30.00 |
| ❑ DL 4110 [M] | Golden Favorites | 1961 | 30.00 |
| ❑ DL 4144 [M] | Fallen Angel | 1961 | 30.00 |
| ❑ DL 4218 [M] | Hideaway Heart | 1962 | 30.00 |
| ❑ DL 4294 [M] | Cross Country | 1962 | 30.00 |
| ❑ DL 4358 [M] | I've Got a New Heartache | 1963 | 25.00 |
| ❑ DL 4384 [M] | Bow Thy Head | 1963 | 25.00 |
| ❑ DL 4486 [M] | Sands of Gold | 1964 | 25.00 |
| ❑ DL 4604 [M] | Memory #1 | 1965 | 25.00 |
| ❑ DL 4659 [M] | Country Music Time | 1965 | 25.00 |
| ❑ DL 4739 [M] | Sweet Memories | 1966 | 25.00 |
| ❑ DL 4782 [M] | Webb's Choice | 1966 | 25.00 |
| ❑ DL 4844 [M] | Where'd Ya Stay Last Night | 1967 | 30.00 |
| ❑ DL 4964 [M] | Fool, Fool, Fool | 1968 | 50.00 |
| ❑ DL 5536 [10] | That Wondering Boy | 1954 | 120.00 |
| ❑ DXSB 7181 [(2)S] | The Webb Pierce Story | 1964 | 40.00 |
| *—Deduct 25% if booklet is missing* | | | |
| ❑ DL 8129 [M] | Webb Pierce | 1955 | 60.00 |
| *—Black label, silver print* | | | |
| ❑ DL 8129 [M] | Webb Pierce | 196? | 30.00 |
| *—Black label with color bar* | | | |
| ❑ DL 8295 [M] | That Wondering Boy | 1956 | 60.00 |
| *—Black label, silver print* | | | |
| ❑ DL 8295 [M] | That Wondering Boy | 196? | 30.00 |
| *—Black label with color bar* | | | |
| ❑ DL 8728 [M] | Just Imagination | 1957 | 50.00 |
| *—Black label, silver print* | | | |
| ❑ DL 8728 [M] | Just Imagination | 196? | 30.00 |
| *—Black label with color bar* | | | |
| ❑ DL 8889 [M] | Bound for the Kingdom | 1959 | 40.00 |
| *—Black label, silver print* | | | |
| ❑ DL 8889 [M] | Bound for the Kingdom | 196? | 25.00 |
| *—Black label with color bar* | | | |
| ❑ DL 8899 [M] | Webb! | 1959 | 40.00 |
| *—Black label, silver print* | | | |
| ❑ DL 8899 [M] | Webb! | 196? | 25.00 |
| *—Black label with color bar* | | | |
| ❑ DL 74015 [S] | Webb with a Beat | 1960 | 40.00 |
| ❑ DL 74079 [S] | Walking the Streets | 1960 | 40.00 |
| ❑ DL 74110 [S] | Golden Favorites | 1961 | 40.00 |
| ❑ DL 74144 [S] | Fallen Angel | 1961 | 40.00 |
| ❑ DL 74218 [S] | Hideaway Heart | 1962 | 40.00 |
| ❑ DL 74294 [S] | Cross Country | 1962 | 40.00 |
| ❑ DL 74358 [S] | I've Got a New Heartache | 1963 | 30.00 |
| ❑ DL 74384 [S] | Bow Thy Head | 1963 | 30.00 |
| ❑ DL 74486 [S] | Sands of Gold | 1964 | 30.00 |
| ❑ DL 74604 [S] | Memory #1 | 1965 | 30.00 |
| ❑ DL 74659 [S] | Country Music Time | 1965 | 30.00 |
| ❑ DL 74739 [S] | Sweet Memories | 1966 | 30.00 |
| ❑ DL 74782 [S] | Webb's Choice | 1966 | 30.00 |
| ❑ DL 74844 [S] | Where'd Ya Stay Last Night | 1967 | 25.00 |
| ❑ DL 74964 [S] | Fool, Fool, Fool | 1968 | 25.00 |
| ❑ DL 74999 | Webb Pierce's Greatest Hits | 1968 | 25.00 |
| ❑ DL 75071 | Saturday Night | 1969 | 25.00 |
| ❑ DL 75132 | Webb Pierce Sings This Thing | 1969 | 25.00 |
| ❑ DL 75168 | Love Ain't Never Gonna Be No Better | 1970 | 25.00 |
| ❑ DL 75210 | Merry-Go-Round World | 1970 | 20.00 |
| ❑ DL 75280 | The Webb Pierce Road Show | 1971 | 20.00 |
| ❑ DL 75393 | I'm Gonna Be a Swinger | 1972 | 20.00 |
| ❑ DL 78889 [S] | Bound for the Kingdom | 1959 | 50.00 |
| *—Black label, silver print* | | | |

| Number | Title (A Side/B Side) | Yr | NM |
|---|---|---|---|
| ❑ DL 78889 [S] | Bound for the Kingdom | 196? | 30.00 |
| *—Black label with color bar* | | | |
| ❑ DL 78899 [M] | Webb! | 196? | 30.00 |
| *—Black label with color bar* | | | |
| ❑ DL 78899 [S] | Webb! | 1959 | 50.00 |
| *—Black label, silver print* | | | |
| KING | | | |
| ❑ 648 [M] | The One and Only Webb Pierce | 1959 | 70.00 |
| MCA | | | |
| ❑ 130 | Greatest Hits | 1973 | 12.00 |
| ❑ 513 | I'm Gonna Be a Swinger | 197? | 12.00 |
| *—Reissue of Decca 75393* | | | |
| ❑ 4087 [(2)] | The Best of Webb Pierce | 1974 | 15.00 |
| VOCALION | | | |
| ❑ VL 73830 | Country Songs | 1968 | 12.00 |
| ❑ VL 73911 | Country Favorites | 1970 | 15.00 |
| **PIERCE, WEBB; MARVIN RAINWATER; STUART HAMBLEN** | | | |
| AUDIO LAB | | | |
| ❑ AL-1563 [M] | Sing for You | 1960 | 200.00 |
| **PIKE, DAVE** | | | |
| ATLANTIC | | | |
| ❑ SD 1457 [S] | Jazz for the Jet Set | 1966 | 20.00 |
| BASF | | | |
| ❑ 25112 [(2)] | Riff for Rent | 1973 | 20.00 |
| DECCA | | | |
| ❑ DL 74568 [S] | Manhattan Latin | 1965 | 20.00 |
| EPIC | | | |
| ❑ LA-16025 [M] | Pike's Peak | 1962 | 30.00 |
| ❑ BA-17025 [S] | Pike's Peak | 1962 | 25.00 |
| MOODSVILLE | | | |
| ❑ MVLP-36 [M] | Dave Pike Plays the Jazz Version of "Oliver" | 1963 | 50.00 |
| *—Green label* | | | |
| ❑ MVLP-36 [M] | Dave Pike Plays the Jazz Version of "Oliver" | 1965 | 25.00 |
| *—Blue label, trident logo at right* | | | |
| NEW JAZZ | | | |
| ❑ NJLP-8281 [M] | Bossa Nova Carnival | 1962 | 50.00 |
| *—Purple label* | | | |
| ❑ NJLP-8281 [M] | Bossa Nova Carnival | 1965 | 25.00 |
| *—Blue label, trident logo at right* | | | |
| ❑ NJLP-8284 [M] | Limbo Carnival | 1962 | 50.00 |
| *—Purple label* | | | |
| ❑ NJLP-8284 [M] | Limbo Carnival | 1965 | 25.00 |
| *—Blue label, trident logo at right* | | | |
| RIVERSIDE | | | |
| ❑ RLP-360 [M] | It's Time for David Pike | 1961 | 25.00 |
| ❑ RS-9360 [S] | It's Time for David Pike | 1961 | 30.00 |
| VORTEX | | | |
| ❑ 2007 | The Doors of Perception | 1970 | 20.00 |
| **PIKE, PETE** | | | |
| AUDIO LAB | | | |
| ❑ AL-1559 [M] | Pete Pike | 1960 | 100.00 |
| **PILHOFER, HERB** | | | |
| ARGO | | | |
| ❑ LP-657 [M] | Jazz | 1960 | 25.00 |
| ❑ LPS-657 [S] | Jazz | 1960 | 30.00 |
| ZEPHYR | | | |
| ❑ ZP-12103-G [M] | Dick and Don Maw Present the Herb Pilhofer Octet — Jazz from the North Coast, Volume 2 | 1959 | 60.00 |
| **PILLOW, RAY** | | | |
| ABC | | | |
| ❑ ABCS-665 | Ray Pillow Sings | 1968 | 15.00 |
| ABC DOT | | | |
| ❑ DOSD-2013 | Countryfied | 1975 | 12.00 |
| CAPITOL | | | |
| ❑ ST 2417 [S] | Presenting Ray Pillow | 1965 | 20.00 |
| ❑ T 2417 [M] | Presenting Ray Pillow | 1965 | 15.00 |
| ❑ ST 2738 [S] | Even When It's Bad, It's Good! | 1967 | 15.00 |
| ❑ T 2738 [M] | Even When It's Bad, It's Good! | 1967 | 20.00 |
| HILLTOP | | | |
| ❑ JS-6164 | Wonderful Day | 197? | 12.00 |
| MEGA | | | |
| ❑ 1017 | Slippin' Around with Ray Pillow | 1972 | 15.00 |
| PLANTATION | | | |
| ❑ PLP-6 | People Music | 1970 | 15.00 |
| **PILOT (2)** | | | |
| RCA VICTOR | | | |
| ❑ LSP-4730 | Pilot | 1972 | 12.00 |
| ❑ LSP-4825 | Point of View | 1973 | 20.00 |
| **PINE, COURTNEY** | | | |
| ANTILLES | | | |
| ❑ 510769-1 | Closer to Home | 1992 | 20.00 |

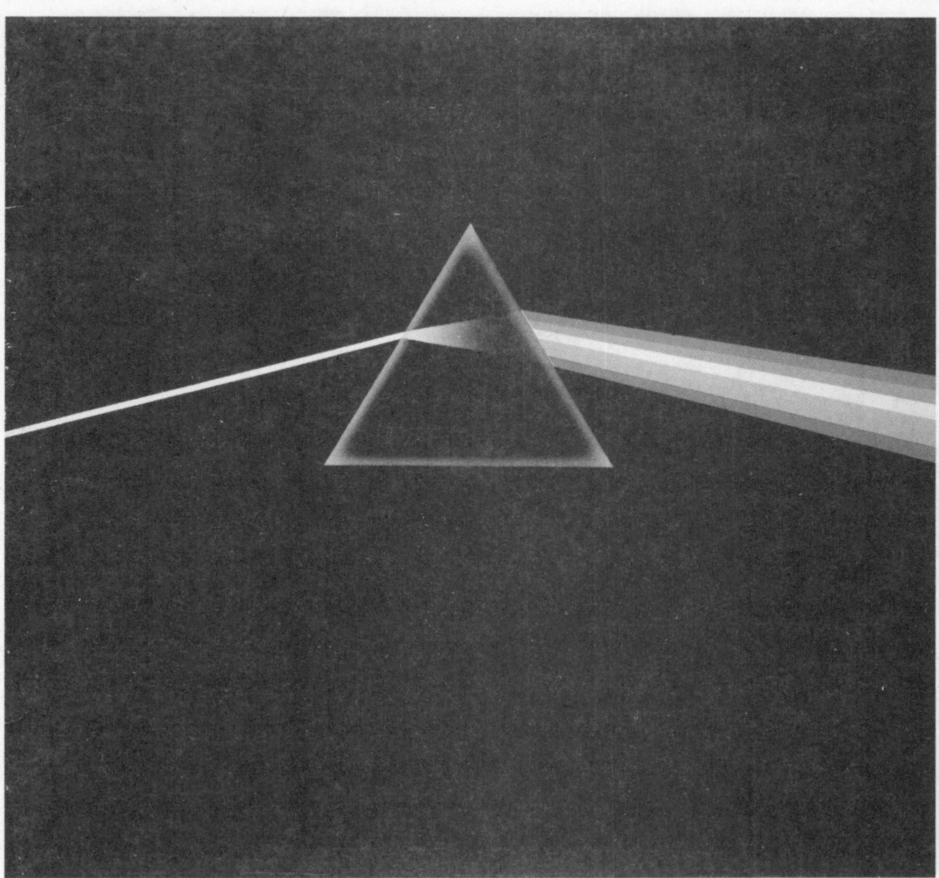

Pink Floyd, *The Dark Side of the Moon,*
Harvest SMAS-11163, 1973, original with poster and two inserts, $25.

| Number | Title (A Side/B Side) | Yr | NM |
|---|---|---|---|
| **PINETOPPERS, THE** | | | |
| CORAL | | | |
| ❑ CRL 56200 [10] | Square Dances | 195? | 40.00 |
| ❑ CRL 57048 [M] | The Pinetoppers | 195? | 30.00 |
| DECCA | | | |
| ❑ DL 8348 [M] | Saturday Night Barn Dance | 1956 | 30.00 |
| **PINK FLOYD** Also see SYD BARRETT; ROGER WATERS; RICHARD WRIGHT. | | | |
| CAPITOL | | | |
| ❑ SPRO-8116/7 [DJ] | Pink Floyd Tour '75 | 1975 | 80.00 |
| ❑ SEAX-11902 [PD] | The Dark Side of the Moon | 1978 | 30.00 |
| ❑ ST-12276 | Works | 1983 | 10.00 |
| ❑ SN-16230 | More | 1982 | 8.00 |
| *—Budget-line reissue* | | | |
| ❑ SN-16234 | Relics | 1982 | 8.00 |
| *—Budget-line reissue* | | | |
| ❑ SN-16330 | Obscured by Clouds | 1985 | 8.00 |
| *—Budget-line reissue* | | | |
| ❑ SN-16337 | Atom Heart Mother | 1985 | 8.00 |
| *—Budget-line reissue* | | | |
| COLUMBIA | | | |
| ❑ AP-1 [DJ] | Animals | 1977 | 150.00 |
| *—White cover, with the song "Pigs" edited for airplay* | | | |
| ❑ AS 736 [DJ] | Off the Wall | 1979 | 150.00 |
| *—Sampler from 2-LP set* | | | |
| ❑ AS 1636 [DJ] | The Final Cut | 1983 | 25.00 |
| *—White label, record banded for airplay* | | | |
| ❑ HC 33453 | Wish You Were Here | 1981 | 60.00 |
| *—Half-speed mastered edition (original)* | | | |
| ❑ PC 33453 | Wish You Were Here | 1975 | 12.00 |
| *—Standard copy (no blue wraparound) without bar code* | | | |
| ❑ PC 33453 | Wish You Were Here | 1975 | 25.00 |
| *—Original copies had a blue wraparound with title/artist sticker. Most buyers threw this out upon opening the LP!* | | | |
| ❑ PC 33453 [DJ] | Wish You Were Here | 1975 | 250.00 |
| *—White cover, "Special DJ Copy"; banded for airplay* | | | |
| ❑ PC 33453 [DJ] | Wish You Were Here | 1975 | 300.00 |
| *—Blue cover with photo and title on jacket; unbanded record* | | | |
| ❑ PCQ 33453 [Q] | Wish You Were Here | 1975 | 200.00 |
| ❑ JC 34474 | Animals | 1977 | 10.00 |
| ❑ JC 34474 [DJ] | Animals | 1977 | 100.00 |
| *—"Demonstration Not for Sale" on label; also has insert* | | | |
| ❑ PC2 36183 [(2)] | The Wall | 1979 | 15.00 |
| ❑ PC 37680 | A Collection of Great Dance Songs | 198? | 8.00 |
| *—Budget-line reissue* | | | |
| ❑ TC 37680 | A Collection of Great Dance Songs | 1981 | 10.00 |
| ❑ QC 38243 | The Final Cut | 1983 | 10.00 |
| ❑ OC 40599 | A Momentary Lapse of Reason | 1987 | 10.00 |
| ❑ HC 43453 | Wish You Were Here | 1982 | 40.00 |
| *—Half-speed mastered edition (reissue)* | | | |
| ❑ PC2 44484 [(2)] | Delicate Sound of Thunder | 1988 | 20.00 |
| ❑ HC2 46183 [(2)] | The Wall | 1983 | 250.00 |
| *—Half-speed mastered edition* | | | |
| ❑ HC 47680 | A Collection of Great Dance Songs | 1982 | 50.00 |
| *—Half-speed mastered edition* | | | |
| ❑ C 64200 | The Division Bell | 1994 | 150.00 |
| *—U.S. pressings on blue vinyl* | | | |
| EMI | | | |
| ❑ 32700 [(4)] | Pulse | 1995 | 80.00 |
| *—Pressed in U.K. for U.S. release; box set with 12x12 hardback book; identical to British pressings except for American bar code (67065) on shrink wrap* | | | |
| HARVEST | | | |
| ❑ SKAO-382 | Atom Heart Mother | 197? | 15.00 |
| *—With title on front cover* | | | |
| ❑ SKAO-382 | Atom Heart Mother | 1970 | 25.00 |
| *—Without title on front cover* | | | |
| ❑ SKBB-388 [(2)] | Ummagumma | 1969 | 40.00 |
| *—With the soundtrack LP from "Gigi" leaning against wall on front cover* | | | |
| ❑ SKBB-388 [(2)] | Ummagumma | 1970 | 20.00 |
| *—With white LP cover leaning against wall on front cover* | | | |
| ❑ SW-759 | Relics | 1971 | 15.00 |
| ❑ SMAS-832 | Meddle | 1971 | 15.00 |
| ❑ ST-11078 | Obscured by Clouds | 1972 | 15.00 |
| ❑ SMAS-11163 | The Dark Side of the Moon | 1973 | 12.00 |
| *—With no inserts* | | | |
| ❑ SMAS-11163 | The Dark Side of the Moon | 1973 | 25.00 |
| *—With poster and two stickers* | | | |
| ❑ ST-11198 | More | 1973 | 12.00 |
| *—Reissue of Tower 5169* | | | |
| ❑ SABB-11257 [(2)] | A Nice Pair | 1973 | 15.00 |
| MOBILE FIDELITY | | | |
| ❑ 1-017 | The Dark Side of the Moon | 1980 | 50.00 |
| *—Audiophile vinyl* | | | |
| ❑ MFQR-017 | The Dark Side of the Moon | 1982 | 300.00 |
| *—Audiophile vinyl; "Ultra High Quality Recording" in box* | | | |
| ❑ 1-190 | Meddle | 1987 | 50.00 |
| *—Audiophile vinyl* | | | |
| ❑ 1-202 | Atom Heart Mother | 1994 | 30.00 |
| *—Audiophile vinyl* | | | |

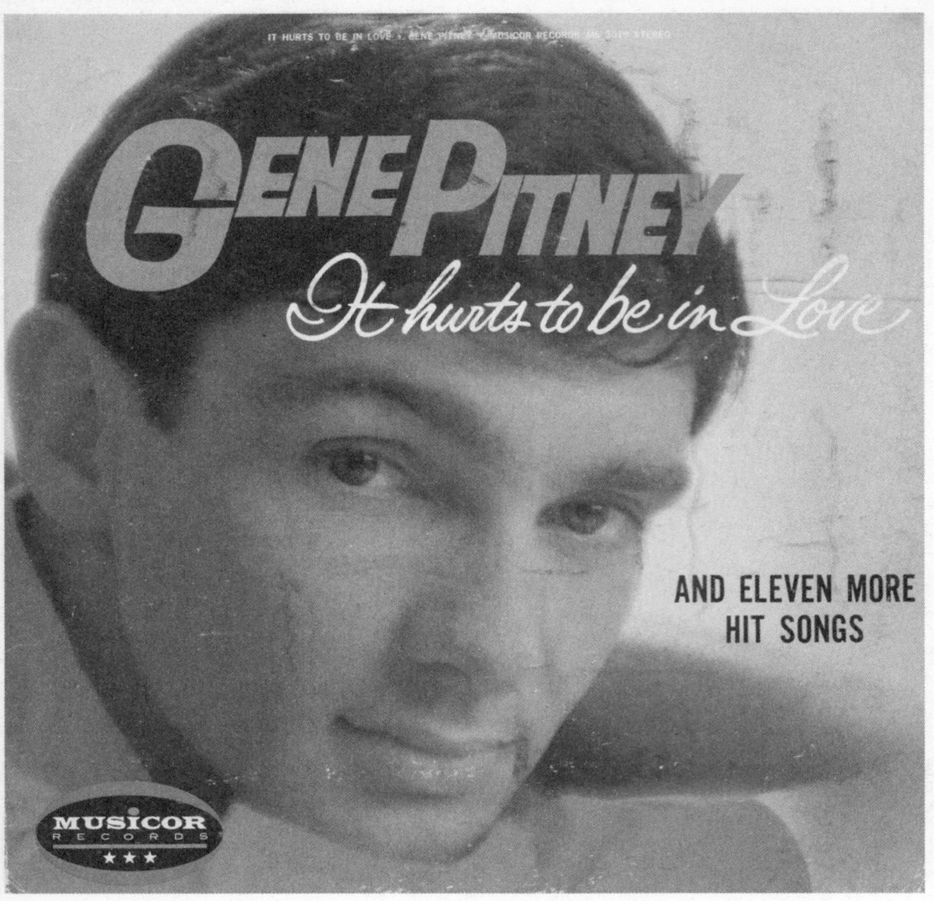

GENE PITNEY
It hurts to be in Love
AND ELEVEN MORE HIT SONGS
MUSICOR RECORDS


Gene Pitney, *It Hurts to Be in Love,* Musicor MS-3019, 1964, stereo, $30.

| Number | Title (A Side/B Side) | Yr | NM |
|---|---|---|---|
| **TOWER** | | | |
| ❑ ST 5093 [S] | Pink Floyd (The Piper at the Gates of Dawn) | 1967 | 80.00 |
| *—Orange label* | | | |
| ❑ ST 5093 [S] | Pink Floyd (The Piper at the Gates of Dawn) | 1968 | 40.00 |
| *—Multi-color striped label* | | | |
| ❑ T 5093 [M] | Pink Floyd (The Piper at the Gates of Dawn) | 1967 | 250.00 |
| ❑ ST 5131 | A Saucerful of Secrets | 1968 | 40.00 |
| *—Multi-color striped label* | | | |
| ❑ ST 5131 | A Saucerful of Secrets | 1968 | 80.00 |
| *—Orange label* | | | |
| ❑ ST 5169 | More | 1968 | 50.00 |

## PIPKINS, THE

| Number | Title (A Side/B Side) | Yr | NM |
|---|---|---|---|
| **CAPITOL** | | | |
| ❑ ST-483 | Gimme Dat Ding | 1970 | 25.00 |

## PIRANHAS, THE

| Number | Title (A Side/B Side) | Yr | NM |
|---|---|---|---|
| **CUSTOM FIDELITY** | | | |
| ❑ 1452 | Somethin' Fishy | 1969 | 150.00 |

## PISANO, JOHNNY, AND BILLY BEAN

| Number | Title (A Side/B Side) | Yr | NM |
|---|---|---|---|
| **DECCA** | | | |
| ❑ DL 9206 [M] | Makin' It | 1958 | 30.00 |
| ❑ DL 9219 [M] | Take Your Pick | 1958 | 30.00 |
| ❑ DL 79206 [S] | Makin' It | 1958 | 25.00 |
| ❑ DL 79219 [S] | Take Your Pick | 1958 | 25.00 |

## PITNEY, GENE

| Number | Title (A Side/B Side) | Yr | NM |
|---|---|---|---|
| **MUSIC DISC** | | | |
| ❑ MDS 1003 | The Man Who Shot Liberty Valance | 1969 | 12.00 |
| ❑ MDS 1005 | Town Without Pity | 1969 | 12.00 |
| ❑ MDS 1006 | America's Greatest Country Songs | 1969 | 12.00 |
| ❑ MDS 1008 | Twenty Four Hours from Tulsa | 1969 | 12.00 |
| ❑ MDS 1014 | Baby, I Need Your Lovin' | 1969 | 12.00 |
| **MUSICOR** | | | |
| ❑ MM-2001 [M] | The Many Sides of Gene Pitney | 1962 | 50.00 |
| *—Brown label* | | | |
| ❑ MM-2001 [M] | The Many Sides of Gene Pitney | 1963 | 25.00 |
| *—Black label* | | | |
| ❑ MM-2003 [M] | Only Love Can Break a Heart | 1962 | 40.00 |
| *—Brown label* | | | |
| ❑ MM-2003 [M] | Only Love Can Break a Heart | 1963 | 25.00 |
| *—Black label* | | | |
| ❑ MM-2004 [M] | Gene Pitney Sings Just for You | 1963 | 30.00 |
| ❑ MM-2005 [M] | World-Wide Winners | 1963 | 30.00 |
| ❑ MM-2006 [M] | Blue Gene | 1963 | 30.00 |
| ❑ MM-2007 [M] | Gene Pitney Meets the Fair Young Ladies of Folkland | 1964 | 30.00 |
| ❑ MM-2008 [M] | Gene Pitney's Big Sixteen | 1964 | 30.00 |
| ❑ MM-2015 [M] | Gene Italiano | 1964 | 25.00 |
| ❑ MM-2019 [M] | It Hurts to Be in Love | 1964 | 25.00 |
| ❑ MM-2043 [M] | Gene Pitney's More Big Sixteen | 1965 | 25.00 |
| ❑ MM-2056 [M] | I Must Be Seeing Things | 1965 | 25.00 |
| ❑ MM-2069 [M] | Looking Through the Eyes of Love | 1965 | 25.00 |
| ❑ MM-2072 [M] | Gene Pitney En Espanol | 1965 | 25.00 |
| ❑ MM-2085 [M] | Big Sixteen, Vol. 3 | 1966 | 20.00 |
| ❑ MM-2095 [M] | Backstage I'm Lonely | 1966 | 20.00 |
| ❑ MM-2100 [M] | Messumo Mi Puo Giudicare | 1966 | 20.00 |
| ❑ MM-2101 [M] | The Gene Pitney Show | 1966 | 20.00 |
| ❑ MM-2102 [M] | Greatest Hits of All Times | 1966 | 20.00 |
| ❑ MM-2104 [M] | The Country Side of Gene Pitney | 1967 | 20.00 |
| ❑ MM-2108 [M] | Young and Warm and Wonderful | 1967 | 20.00 |
| ❑ MM-2117 [M] | Just One Smile | 1967 | 20.00 |
| ❑ MM-2134 [M] | Golden Greats | 1967 | 25.00 |
| ❑ MS-3001 [R] | The Many Sides of Gene Pitney | 1962 | 30.00 |
| *—Brown label* | | | |
| ❑ MS-3001 [R] | The Many Sides of Gene Pitney | 1963 | 20.00 |
| *—Black label* | | | |
| ❑ MS-3003 [S] | Only Love Can Break a Heart | 1962 | 50.00 |
| *—Brown label* | | | |
| ❑ MS-3003 [S] | Only Love Can Break a Heart | 1963 | 30.00 |
| *—Black label* | | | |
| ❑ MS-3004 [S] | Gene Pitney Sings Just for You | 1963 | 40.00 |
| ❑ MS-3005 [P] | World-Wide Winners | 1963 | 40.00 |
| ❑ MS-3006 [S] | Blue Gene | 1963 | 40.00 |
| ❑ MS-3007 [S] | Gene Pitney Meets the Fair Young Ladies of Folkland | 1964 | 40.00 |
| ❑ MS-3008 [P] | Gene Pitney's Big Sixteen | 1964 | 40.00 |
| ❑ MS-3015 [S] | Gene Italiano | 1964 | 30.00 |
| ❑ MS-3019 [P] | It Hurts to Be in Love | 1964 | 30.00 |
| ❑ MS-3043 [P] | Gene Pitney's More Big Sixteen | 1965 | 30.00 |
| ❑ MS-3056 [S] | I Must Be Seeing Things | 1965 | 30.00 |
| ❑ MS-3069 [S] | Looking Through the Eyes of Love | 1965 | 30.00 |
| ❑ MS-3072 [S] | Gene Pitney En Espanol | 1965 | 30.00 |
| ❑ MS-3085 [S] | Big Sixteen, Vol. 3 | 1966 | 25.00 |
| ❑ MS-3095 [S] | Backstage I'm Lonely | 1966 | 25.00 |
| ❑ MS-3100 [S] | Messumo Mi Puo Giudicare | 1966 | 25.00 |
| ❑ MS-3101 [S] | The Gene Pitney Show | 1966 | 25.00 |
| ❑ MS-3102 [P] | Greatest Hits of All Times | 1966 | 25.00 |
| ❑ MS-3104 [S] | The Country Side of Gene Pitney | 1967 | 25.00 |
| ❑ MS-3108 [S] | Young and Warm and Wonderful | 1967 | 25.00 |
| ❑ MS-3117 [S] | Just One Smile | 1967 | 25.00 |
| ❑ MS-3134 [S] | Golden Greats | 1967 | 20.00 |
| ❑ M2-3148 [(2)M] | The Gene Pitney Story | 1968 | 40.00 |
| *—Mono is promo only* | | | |
| ❑ M2S-3148 [(2)S] | The Gene Pitney Story | 1968 | 25.00 |
| *—Add 40% if bonus photo is enclosed* | | | |
| ❑ MS-3161 | Gene Pitney Sings Burt Bacharach | 1968 | 20.00 |
| ❑ MS-3164 | She's a Heartbreaker | 1968 | 20.00 |
| ❑ MS-3174 | The Greatest Hits of Gene Pitney | 1969 | 20.00 |
| ❑ MS-3183 | Gene Pitney Sings the Platters' Golden Platters | 1970 | 15.00 |
| ❑ MS-3193 | Gene Pitney Super Star | 1971 | 15.00 |
| ❑ MS-3206 | Ten Years After | 1971 | 15.00 |
| ❑ MS-3233 | Golden Hour | 1972 | 15.00 |
| ❑ MUX-4600 [(2)] | The Best of Gene Pitney (Double Gold Series) | 1977 | 15.00 |
| **RHINO** | | | |
| ❑ RNDA-1102 [(2)] | Anthology (1961-1968) | 1984 | 12.00 |
| **SPRINGBOARD** | | | |
| ❑ SPB-4057 | Gene Pitney | 1975 | 10.00 |

## PITNEY, GENE, AND GEORGE JONES

| Number | Title (A Side/B Side) | Yr | NM |
|---|---|---|---|
| **MUSICOR** | | | |
| ❑ MM-2044 [M] | For the First Time! Two Great Singers Together: George Jones and Gene Pitney | 1965 | 25.00 |
| ❑ MM-2065 [M] | It's Country Time Again | 1965 | 25.00 |
| ❑ MS-3044 [S] | For the First Time! Two Great Singers Together: George Jones and Gene Pitney | 1965 | 30.00 |
| ❑ MS-3065 [S] | It's Country Time Again | 1965 | 30.00 |

## PITNEY, GENE, AND MELBA MONTGOMERY

| Number | Title (A Side/B Side) | Yr | NM |
|---|---|---|---|
| **MUSICOR** | | | |
| ❑ MM-2077 [M] | Being Together | 1966 | 25.00 |
| ❑ MS-3077 [S] | Being Together | 1966 | 30.00 |

## PIXIES

| Number | Title (A Side/B Side) | Yr | NM |
|---|---|---|---|
| **ELEKTRA** | | | |
| ❑ PR-8127 [DJ] | Live | 1989 | 50.00 |
| *—Promo-only seven-song live collection of mostly songs from their pre-Elektra days* | | | |
| ❑ 60856 | Doolittle | 1989 | 10.00 |
| ❑ 60856 [DJ] | Doolittle | 1989 | 12.00 |
| *—Promo-only on audiophile vinyl* | | | |
| ❑ 60963 | Bossanova | 1990 | 10.00 |
| **ROUGH TRADE** | | | |
| ❑ ROUGH US 38 | Surfer Rosa | 1988 | 20.00 |

## PIXIES THREE, THE

| Number | Title (A Side/B Side) | Yr | NM |
|---|---|---|---|
| **MERCURY** | | | |
| ❑ MG-20912 [M] | Party with the Pixies Three | 1964 | 150.00 |
| ❑ SR-60912 [S] | Party with the Pixies Three | 1964 | 200.00 |

## PIZZARELLI, BUCKY, AND VINNIE BURKE

| Number | Title (A Side/B Side) | Yr | NM |
|---|---|---|---|
| **SAVOY** | | | |
| ❑ MG-12158 [M] | Music Minus Many Men | 1960 | 30.00 |

## PLAIN JANE

| Number | Title (A Side/B Side) | Yr | NM |
|---|---|---|---|
| **HOBBIT** | | | |
| ❑ 5000 | Plain Jane | 1969 | 25.00 |

## PLANET P

| Number | Title (A Side/B Side) | Yr | NM |
|---|---|---|---|
| **GEFFEN** | | | |
| ❑ GHS 4000 | Planet P | 1983 | 12.00 |
| **MCA** | | | |
| ❑ L33-1227 [EP] | Pink World | 1984 | 12.00 |
| *—Promo-only pink vinyl EP* | | | |
| ❑ 8019 [(2)] | Pink World | 1984 | 20.00 |
| *—As "Planet P Project"* | | | |

## PLANT, ROBERT Also see LED ZEPPELIN.

| Number | Title (A Side/B Side) | Yr | NM |
|---|---|---|---|
| **ES PARANZA** | | | |
| ❑ PR 2244 [(2)DJ] | Non-Stop Go | 1988 | 50.00 |
| *—Promo-only interview album* | | | |
| ❑ 90101 | The Principle of Moments | 1983 | 8.00 |
| ❑ 90265 | Shaken 'n' Stirred | 1985 | 8.00 |
| ❑ 90485 [EP] | Little by Little Collector's Edition | 1985 | 8.00 |
| ❑ 90863 | Now and Zen | 1988 | 8.00 |
| ❑ 91336 | Manic Nirvana | 1990 | 15.00 |
| **SWAN SONG** | | | |
| ❑ SS 8512 | Pictures at Eleven | 1982 | 10.00 |

## PLANT & SEE

| Number | Title (A Side/B Side) | Yr | NM |
|---|---|---|---|
| **WHITE WHALE** | | | |
| ❑ WWS-7120 | Plant & See | 1969 | 25.00 |

| Number | Title (A Side/B Side) | Yr | NM |
|---|---|---|---|
| **PLASMATICS** | | | |
| CAPITOL | | | |
| ❑ ST-12237 | Coup d'Etat | 1982 | 15.00 |
| PVC | | | |
| ❑ 6908 | Metal Priestess | 1983 | 15.00 |
| *—Reissue of Stiff WOW-666* | | | |
| ❑ 8929 | Beyond the Valley of 1984 | 1983 | 15.00 |
| *—Reissue of Stiff USE-11* | | | |
| STIFF | | | |
| ❑ USE-9 | New Hope for the Wretched | 1980 | 25.00 |
| ❑ USE-11 | Beyond the Valley of 1984 | 1981 | 25.00 |
| ❑ WOW-666 [EP] | Metal Priestess | 1981 | 25.00 |
| VICE SQUAD | | | |
| ❑ VS 105/106 [EP] | Meet the Plasmatics | 1979 | 50.00 |
| **PLASTER CASTERS, THE** | | | |
| BLUESTIME | | | |
| ❑ BTS-9001 | The Plaster Casters Blues Band | 1969 | 50.00 |
| **PLASTIC COW, THE** | | | |
| DOT | | | |
| ❑ DLP 25961 | The Plastic Cow Goes Moooooog | 1969 | 20.00 |
| **PLASTIC ONO BAND** See JOHN LENNON; YOKO ONO. | | | |
| **PLATTERS, THE** More than one group has used this name over the years, but all are related. Also see TONY WILLIAMS. | | | |
| CANDELITE MUSIC | | | |
| ❑ CMI 1000 [(5)] | The 50 Golden Hits of the Platters | 197? | 40.00 |
| COLUMBIA SPECIAL PRODUCTS | | | |
| ❑ P 11834 [S] | Christmas with the Platters | 1973 | 15.00 |
| *—Reissue of Mercury SR-60841 with fewer tracks* | | | |
| FEDERAL | | | |
| ❑ 549 [M] | The Platters | 1957 | 1600. |
| *—Records on Federal 651 are bootlegs from the 1970s* | | | |
| KING | | | |
| ❑ 651 [M] | The Platters | 1959 | 800.00 |
| *—Records on Federal 651 are bootlegs from the 1970s* | | | |
| ❑ KLP-651 [M] | The Platters | 1987 | 10.00 |
| *—Reissue with "Highland Records" on label* | | | |
| ❑ 5002 | 19 Hits of the Platters | 197? | 12.00 |
| MERCURY | | | |
| ❑ SRM-1-4050 | Platterama | 1982 | 10.00 |
| ❑ MG-20146 [M] | The Platters | 1956 | 100.00 |
| ❑ MG-20216 [M] | The Platters, Volume Two | 1956 | 100.00 |
| ❑ MG-20298 [M] | The Flying Platters | 1957 | 100.00 |
| ❑ MG-20366 [M] | The Flying Platters Around the World | 1958 | 30.00 |
| ❑ MG-20410 [M] | Remember When? | 1959 | 30.00 |
| ❑ MG-20472 [M] | Encore of Golden Hits | 1960 | 30.00 |
| ❑ MG-20481 [M] | Reflections | 1960 | 25.00 |
| ❑ MG-20589 [M] | Life Is Just a Bowl of Cherries | 1960 | 25.00 |
| ❑ MG-20591 [M] | More Encore of Golden Hits | 1960 | 25.00 |
| ❑ MG-20613 [M] | Encore of Broadway Golden Hits | 1961 | 20.00 |
| ❑ MG-20669 [M] | Song for the Lonely | 1962 | 20.00 |
| ❑ MG-20759 [M] | Moonlight Memories | 1963 | 20.00 |
| ❑ MG-20782 [M] | The Platters Present All-Time Movie Hits | 1963 | 20.00 |
| ❑ MG-20808 [M] | The Platters Sing Latino | 1963 | 20.00 |
| ❑ MG-20841 [M] | Christmas with the Platters | 1963 | 30.00 |
| ❑ MG-20893 [M] | Encore of Golden Hits of the Groups | 1964 | 20.00 |
| ❑ MG-20933 [M] | 10th Anniversary Album | 1964 | 20.00 |
| ❑ MG-20983 [M] | The New Soul of the Platters | 1965 | 15.00 |
| ❑ SR-60043 [S] | The Flying Platters Around the World | 1959 | 50.00 |
| ❑ SR-60087 [S] | Remember When? | 1959 | 50.00 |
| ❑ SR-60160 [S] | Reflections | 1960 | 30.00 |
| ❑ SR-60243 [P] | Encore of Golden Hits | 1960 | 40.00 |
| *—Original: Black label, silver print; 12 songs on LP* | | | |
| ❑ SR-60243 [P] | Encore of Golden Hits | 1965 | 25.00 |
| *—Second edition: Red label, "MERCURY" in white across top; may or may not have "Gold Record Award" insignia on back cover; 12 songs on LP* | | | |
| ❑ SR-60243 [P] | Encore of Golden Hits | 1975 | 12.00 |
| *—Chicago skyline label; album has 10 songs* | | | |
| ❑ SR-60245 [S] | Life Is Just a Bowl of Cherries | 1960 | 30.00 |
| ❑ SR-60252 [S] | More Encore of Golden Hits | 1960 | 30.00 |
| ❑ SR-60613 [S] | Encore of Broadway Golden Hits | 1961 | 25.00 |
| ❑ SR-60669 [S] | Song for the Lonely | 1962 | 25.00 |
| ❑ SR-60759 [S] | Moonlight Memories | 1963 | 25.00 |
| ❑ SR-60782 [S] | The Platters Present All-Time Movie Hits | 1963 | 25.00 |
| ❑ SR-60808 [S] | The Platters Sing Latino | 1963 | 25.00 |
| ❑ SR-60841 [S] | Christmas with the Platters | 1963 | 40.00 |
| *—Same as above, but in stereo* | | | |
| ❑ SR-60893 [S] | Encore of Golden Hits of the Groups | 1964 | 25.00 |
| ❑ SR-60933 [S] | 10th Anniversary Album | 1964 | 25.00 |
| ❑ SR-60983 [S] | The New Soul of the Platters | 1965 | 20.00 |

| Number | Title (A Side/B Side) | Yr | NM |
|---|---|---|---|
| ❑ 828246-1 | More Encore of Golden Hits | 198? | 8.00 |
| *—Reissue* | | | |
| ❑ 828254-1 | Encore of Golden Hits | 198? | 8.00 |
| *—Reissue* | | | |
| MUSIC DISC | | | |
| ❑ MDS-1002 | Only You | 1969 | 12.00 |
| MUSICOR | | | |
| ❑ MM-2091 [M] | I Love You 1,000 Times | 1966 | 15.00 |
| ❑ MM-2111 [M] | The Platters Have the Magic Touch | 1966 | 15.00 |
| ❑ MM-2125 [M] | Going Back to Detroit | 1967 | 15.00 |
| ❑ MM-2141 [M] | New Golden Hits of the Platters | 1967 | 20.00 |
| ❑ MS-3091 [S] | I Love You 1,000 Times | 1966 | 20.00 |
| ❑ MS-3111 [S] | The Platters Have the Magic Touch | 1966 | 20.00 |
| ❑ MS-3125 [S] | Going Back to Detroit | 1967 | 15.00 |
| ❑ MS-3141 [S] | New Golden Hits of the Platters | 1967 | 15.00 |
| ❑ MS-3156 | Sweet, Sweet Lovin' | 1968 | 15.00 |
| ❑ MS-3171 | I Get the Sweetest Feeling | 1968 | 15.00 |
| ❑ MS-3185 | Singing the Great Hits Our Way | 1969 | 15.00 |
| ❑ MS-3231 | Golden Hour | 1973 | 12.00 |
| ❑ MS-3254 | The Golden Hits of the Platters | 1973 | 12.00 |
| PICKWICK | | | |
| ❑ PTP-2083 [(2)] | Only You | 1973 | 12.00 |
| ❑ SPC-3236 | Super Hits | 197? | 10.00 |
| RHINO | | | |
| ❑ RNFP-71495 [(2)] | Anthology (1955-1967) | 1986 | 12.00 |
| SPRINGBOARD | | | |
| ❑ SPB-4059 | The Platters | 197? | 10.00 |
| WING | | | |
| ❑ MGW-12112 [M] | Encores! | 1959 | 30.00 |
| *—With liner notes on back cover* | | | |
| ❑ MGW-12112 [M] | Encores! | 196? | 15.00 |
| *—With photos of other Wing LPs on back cover* | | | |
| ❑ MGW-12226 [M] | Flying Platters | 1963 | 12.00 |
| ❑ MGW-12272 [M] | Reflections | 1964 | 12.00 |
| ❑ MGW-12346 [M] | 10th Anniversary Album | 196? | 12.00 |
| ❑ SRW-16112 [R] | Encores! | 196? | 12.00 |
| ❑ SRW-16226 [S] | Flying Platters | 1963 | 12.00 |
| ❑ SRW-16272 [S] | Reflections | 1964 | 12.00 |
| ❑ SRW-16346 [S] | 10th Anniversary Album | 196? | 12.00 |
| **PLAYERS, THE** | | | |
| MINIT | | | |
| ❑ LP-24006 [S] | He'll Be Back | 1966 | 30.00 |
| ❑ LP-40006 [M] | He'll Be Back | 1966 | 25.00 |
| **PLAYMATES, THE** | | | |
| FORUM | | | |
| ❑ F-9012 [M] | At Play with the Playmates | 196? | 12.00 |
| ❑ SF-9012 [S] | At Play with the Playmates | 196? | 15.00 |
| ❑ F-9021 [M] | Broadway Show Stoppers | 196? | 12.00 |
| ❑ SF-9021 [S] | Broadway Show Stoppers | 196? | 15.00 |
| ❑ F-16001 [M] | The Playmates Visit West of the Indies | 1960 | 15.00 |
| ❑ SF-16001 [S] | The Playmates Visit West of the Indies | 1960 | 20.00 |
| ROULETTE | | | |
| ❑ R-25001 [M] | Calypso | 1957 | 25.00 |
| ❑ R-25043 [M] | At Play with the Playmates | 1958 | 25.00 |
| ❑ SR-25043 [S] | At Play with the Playmates | 1958 | 30.00 |
| ❑ R-25059 [M] | Rock and Roll Record Hop | 1959 | 20.00 |
| ❑ SR-25059 [S] | Rock and Roll Record Hop | 1959 | 25.00 |
| ❑ R-25068 [M] | Cuttin' Capers | 1960 | 20.00 |
| ❑ SR-25068 [S] | Cuttin' Capers | 1960 | 25.00 |
| ❑ R-25084 [M] | Broadway Show Stoppers | 1961 | 20.00 |
| ❑ SR-25084 [S] | Broadway Show Stoppers | 1961 | 25.00 |
| **PLEASURE FAIR, THE** With Robb Royer, later of BREAD. | | | |
| UNI | | | |
| ❑ 3008 [M] | The Pleasure Fair | 1967 | 20.00 |
| ❑ 73008 [S] | The Pleasure Fair | 1967 | 20.00 |
| **PLIMSOULS, THE** | | | |
| BEAT | | | |
| ❑ BE-1001 [EP] | Zero Hour | 1980 | 25.00 |
| GEFFEN | | | |
| ❑ GHS 4002 | Everywhere at Once | 1983 | 12.00 |
| PLANET | | | |
| ❑ 13 | The Plimsouls | 1981 | 20.00 |
| **PLONSKY, JOHN** | | | |
| GOLDEN CREST | | | |
| ❑ GC-3014 [M] | Cool Man, Cool | 1958 | 30.00 |
| **PLUGZ** | | | |
| FATIMA | | | |
| ❑ 80 | Better Luck | 1981 | 25.00 |
| PLUG/REAL LIFE | | | |
| ❑ 001 | Electrify Me | 1979 | 60.00 |
| **PLUM NELLY** | | | |
| CAPITOL | | | |
| ❑ ST-692 | Deceptive Lines | 1971 | 20.00 |

| Number | Title (A Side/B Side) | Yr | NM |
|---|---|---|---|
| **PLUMMER, BILL** | | | |
| ABC IMPULSE! | | | |
| ❑ A-9164 [M] | Bill Plummer and the Cosmic Brotherhood | 1968 | 40.00 |
| ❑ AS-9164 [S] | Bill Plummer and the Cosmic Brotherhood | 1968 | 20.00 |
| **PO' BOYS, THE** | | | |
| DECCA | | | |
| ❑ DL 4725 [M] | Bill Anderson Presents the Po' Boys | 1966 | 20.00 |
| ❑ DL 4884 [M] | The Po' Boys Pick Again | 1967 | 25.00 |
| ❑ DL 74725 [S] | Bill Anderson Presents the Po' Boys | 1966 | 25.00 |
| ❑ DL 74884 [S] | The Po' Boys Pick Again | 1967 | 20.00 |
| MCA | | | |
| ❑ 337 | The Rich Sounds of Bill Anderson's Po' Boys | 1973 | 15.00 |
| **POCO** | | | |
| ABC | | | |
| ❑ D-890 | Head Over Heels | 1975 | 10.00 |
| ❑ D-946 | Rose of Cimarron | 1976 | 10.00 |
| ❑ D-989 | Indian Summer | 1977 | 10.00 |
| ❑ AA-1099 | Legend | 1978 | 12.00 |
| ATLANTIC | | | |
| ❑ 80008 | Ghost Town | 1982 | 10.00 |
| ❑ 80148 | Inamorata | 1984 | 10.00 |
| EPIC | | | |
| ❑ BN 26460 | Pickin' Up the Pieces | 1969 | 15.00 |
| *—Yellow label* | | | |
| ❑ BN 26460 | Pickin' Up the Pieces | 1973 | 10.00 |
| *—Orange label* | | | |
| ❑ BN 26522 | Poco | 1970 | 15.00 |
| *—Yellow label* | | | |
| ❑ BN 26522 | Poco | 1973 | 10.00 |
| *—Orange label* | | | |
| ❑ EQ 30209 [Q] | Deliverin' | 1972 | 20.00 |
| ❑ KE 30209 | Deliverin' | 1971 | 15.00 |
| *—Yellow label* | | | |
| ❑ KE 30209 | Deliverin' | 1973 | 10.00 |
| *—Orange label* | | | |
| ❑ E 30753 | From the Inside | 1973 | 10.00 |
| *—Reissue with new prefix* | | | |
| ❑ KE 30753 | From the Inside | 1971 | 15.00 |
| *—Yellow label* | | | |
| ❑ KE 30753 | From the Inside | 1973 | 10.00 |
| *—Orange label* | | | |
| ❑ KE 31601 | A Good Feelin' to Know | 1972 | 15.00 |
| *—Yellow label* | | | |
| ❑ KE 31601 | A Good Feelin' to Know | 1973 | 10.00 |
| *—Orange label* | | | |
| ❑ PE 31601 | A Good Feelin' to Know | 198? | 8.00 |
| *—Budget-line reissue* | | | |
| ❑ EQ 32354 [Q] | Crazy Eyes | 1973 | 20.00 |
| ❑ KE 32354 | Crazy Eyes | 1973 | 12.00 |
| *—Orange label* | | | |
| ❑ PE 32354 | Crazy Eyes | 1979 | 8.00 |
| *—Blue label* | | | |
| ❑ EQ 32895 [Q] | Seven | 1974 | 20.00 |
| ❑ KE 32895 | Seven | 1974 | 12.00 |
| *—Orange label* | | | |
| ❑ PCQ 33192 [Q] | Cantamos | 1974 | 20.00 |
| ❑ PE 33192 | Cantamos | 1974 | 12.00 |
| *—Orange label* | | | |
| ❑ PE 33336 | Live | 1976 | 12.00 |
| *—Orange label* | | | |
| ❑ PEG 33537 [(2)] | The Very Best of Poco | 1975 | 15.00 |
| *—Orange labels* | | | |
| ❑ JE 36210 | The Songs of Paul Cotton | 1980 | 10.00 |
| ❑ JE 36211 | The Songs of Richie Furay | 1980 | 10.00 |
| MCA | | | |
| ❑ AA-1099 | Legend | 1979 | 10.00 |
| *—Reissue of ABC 1099* | | | |
| ❑ 5132 | Under the Gun | 1980 | 10.00 |
| ❑ 5227 | Blue and Gray | 1981 | 10.00 |
| ❑ 5288 | Cowboys & Englishmen | 1982 | 10.00 |
| ❑ 5363 | Backtracks | 1983 | 10.00 |
| ❑ 37009 | Head Over Heels | 1980 | 8.00 |
| *—Budget-line reissue* | | | |
| ❑ 37010 | Rose of Cimarron | 1980 | 8.00 |
| *—Budget-line reissue* | | | |
| ❑ 37011 | Indian Summer | 1980 | 8.00 |
| *—Budget-line reissue* | | | |
| ❑ 37117 | Legend | 1981 | 8.00 |
| *—Budget-line reissue* | | | |
| ❑ 37160 | Under the Gun | 198? | 8.00 |
| *—Budget-line reissue* | | | |
| MOBILE FIDELITY | | | |
| ❑ 1-020 | Legend | 1979 | 20.00 |
| *—Audiophile vinyl* | | | |
| RCA | | | |
| ❑ 9694-1-R | Legacy | 1989 | 10.00 |
| **POGUES, THE** | | | |
| ENIGMA | | | |
| ❑ ST-73225 | Red Roses for Me | 1986 | 25.00 |

Number | Title (A Side/B Side) | Yr | NM

ISLAND
❑ 90872 If I Should Fall from Grace With God 1988 12.00

STIFF/MCA
❑ 5744 Rum, Sodomy and the Lash 1985 20.00
❑ 36015 [EP] Poguetry in Motion 1986 20.00

## POI DOG PONDERING

COLUMBIA
❑ CAS 1856 [DJ] Interchords 1989 20.00
*—Promo-only interview and music*
❑ CAS 2219 [EP] Untitled (Fruitless) 1990 15.00
*—Promo-only six-song sampler*
❑ C 45403 Wishing Like a Mountain and Thinking Like the Sea 1990 12.00

TEXAS HOTEL
❑ 11 [EP] Poi Dog Pondering 1988 8.00
❑ 16 [EP] Circle Around the Sun 198? 8.00

## POINDEXTER, PONY

EPIC
❑ LA-16035 [M] Pony's Express 1962 60.00
❑ BA-17035 [S] Pony's Express 1962 80.00

NEW JAZZ
❑ NJLP-8285 [M] Pony Poindexter Plays the Big Ones 1962 80.00
*—Purple label*
❑ NJLP-8285 [M] Pony Poindexter Plays the Big Ones 1965 25.00
*—Blue label, trident logo at right*

## POISON

CAPITOL
❑ C1-598046 [(2)]Swallow This Live 1991 40.00
*—Vinyl version available only from Columbia House*

CAPITOL/ENIGMA
❑ ST-12523 Look What the Cat Dragged In 1986 8.00
❑ C1-48493 Open Up and Say...Ahh! 1988 8.00
*—With cropped front cover photo (woman's tongue is cut off; large black bars at top and bottom of cover)*
❑ C1-48493 Open Up and Say...Ahh! 1988 12.00
*—With uncropped front cover photo (woman's tongue is fully visible)*
❑ SPRO 79319/22 [(2)]Open Up and Say...Ahh! World Premiere Weekend 1988 25.00
*—Special radio-only version to promote the LP's release*
❑ C1-91813 Flesh & Blood 1990 12.00
*—With blood airbrushed out of front cover photo*
❑ C1-91813 Flesh & Blood 1990 12.00
*—With blood dripping from letters "Flesh & Blood"*
❑ R 144402 Look What the Cat Dragged In 1986 10.00
*—BMG Direct Marketing club edition*
❑ ST-512523 Look What the Cat Dragged In 1986 10.00
*—Columbia House club edition*
❑ C1-591813 Flesh & Blood 1990 12.00
*—Columbia House club edition*

## POITIER, SIDNEY

WARNER BROS.
❑ W 1561 [M] Poitier Meets Plato 1965 25.00
❑ WS 1561 [S] Poitier Meets Plato 1965 30.00

## POLICE, THE Also see KLARK KENT; STING; ANDY SUMMERS.

A&M
❑ SP-3311 Outlandos d'Amour 198? 8.00
*—Reissue*
❑ SP-3312 Reggatta de Blanc 198? 8.00
*—Reissue*
❑ SP-3713 [(2)10]Reggatta de Blanc 1979 40.00
*—Two 10" records with poster*
❑ SP-3720 Zenyatta Mondatta 1980 10.00
❑ SP-3730 Ghost in the Machine 1981 10.00
❑ SP-3730 [DJ] Ghost in the Machine 1981 1000.
*—Special prototype picture disc that lights up when placed on a turntable*
❑ SP-3735 Synchronicity 1983 10.00
*—With blue, yellow and red color bands; 93 versions of this cover exist, none more valuable than any other*
❑ SP-3735 Synchronicity 1983 40.00
*—With gold, silver and bronze color bands on cover; used on audiophile pressings*
❑ SP-3735 Synchronicity 1983 80.00
*—Black & white cover*
❑ SP-3902 Every Breath You Take — The Singles 1986 10.00
❑ SP-4753 Outlandos d'Amour 1979 12.00
❑ SP-4792 Reggatta de Blanc 1979 12.00
❑ SP-6018 [(2)10]Reggatta de Blanc 1980 30.00
*—Reissue of SP-3713*
❑ R 123571 Ghost in the Machine 1981 12.00
*—RCA Music Service edition*
❑ R 124159 Outlandos d'Amour 1979 12.00
*—RCA Music Service edition*
❑ R 130108 Zenyatta Mondatta 1980 12.00
*—RCA Music Service edition*
❑ R 134070 Synchronicity 1983 12.00
*—RCA Music Service edition*
❑ R 153349 Reggatta de Blanc 1979 12.00
*—RCA Music Service edition*
❑ R 173924 Every Breath You Take — The Singles 1986 12.00
*—BMG Direct Marketing edition*

NAUTILUS
❑ NR-19 Zenyatta Mondatta 1981 40.00
*—Audiophile vinyl*
❑ NR-40 Ghost in the Machine 1982 40.00
*—Audiophile vinyl*

## POLK, LUCY ANN

INTERLUDE
❑ MO-504 [M] Easy Livin' 1959 100.00
❑ ST-1004 [S] Easy Livin' 1959 80.00

MODE
❑ LP-115 [M] Lucky Lucy Ann 1957 150.00

TREND
❑ TL-1008 [10] Lucy Ann Polk with Dave Pell 1954 150.00

## POLL WINNERS, THE

CONTEMPORARY
❑ C-3535 [M] The Poll Winners 1957 50.00
❑ C-3556 [M] The Poll Winners Ride Again 1958 50.00
❑ M-3576 [M] Poll Winners Three 1960 40.00
❑ M-3581 [M] Exploring the Scene 1960 40.00
❑ S-7535 [S] The Poll Winners 1959 40.00
❑ S-7556 [S] The Poll Winners Ride Again 1959 40.00
❑ S-7576 [S] Poll Winners Three 1960 30.00
❑ S-7581 [S] Exploring the Scene 1960 30.00

STEREO RECORDS
❑ S-7010 [S] The Poll Winners 1958 50.00
❑ S-7029 [S] The Poll Winners Ride Again 1958 50.00

## POLLACK, BEN

BRUNSWICK
❑ BL 58025 [10] Ben Pollack 1951 60.00

SAVOY
❑ MG-12090 [M] Pick a Rib Boys 1956 50.00
❑ MG-12207 [M] Dixieland Strut 196? 20.00

"X"
❑ LX-3003 [10] Ben Pollack and His Orchestra Featuring Benny Goodman 1954 60.00

## POLLARD, TERRY

BETHLEHEM
❑ BCP-1015 [10] Terry Pollard 1954 100.00

## POLLARD, TERRY/BOBBY SCOTT

BETHLEHEM
❑ BCP-1 [M] Young Moderns 1957 50.00

## POLLUTION

CAPITOL
❑ ST-205 Heir: Pollution 1969 20.00

PROPHECY
❑ SD 6051 Pollution 1971 20.00
❑ SD 6067 Pollution II 1972 20.00

## POMEROY, HERB

ROULETTE
❑ R-52001 [M] Life Is A Many Splendored Gig 1958 120.00
❑ SR-52001 [S] Life Is A Many Splendored Gig 1958 100.00

TRANSITION
❑ TRLP-1 [M] Jazz in a Stable 1956 400.00
*—Deduct 25 percent if booklet is missing*

UNITED ARTISTS
❑ UAL-4015 [M] Band in Boston 1959 150.00
❑ UAS-5015 [S] Band in Boston 1959 120.00

## PONCE, PONCIE

WARNER BROS.
❑ W 1453 [M] Poncie Ponce Sings 1962 20.00
❑ WS 1453 [S] Poncie Ponce Sings 1962 25.00

## PONTY, JEAN-LUC

DIRECT DISC
❑ SD-16603 Cosmic Messenger 1980 30.00
*—Audiophile vinyl*

WORLD PACIFIC
❑ ST-20156 Electric Connection 1969 25.00

WORLD PACIFIC JAZZ
❑ ST-20172 King Kong — Jean-Luc Ponty Plays the Music of Frank Zappa 1970 40.00

## POOBAH

A.E.I.
❑ A-LP-1 U.S. Rock 1976 250.00

PEPPERMINT
❑ PP-1180 Steamroller 1979 150.00

RITE
❑ (no #) Let Me In 1972 600.00

## POOLE, BILLIE

RIVERSIDE
❑ RLP-425 [M] Sermonette 1962 30.00
❑ RLP-458 [M] Confessin' the Blues 1963 30.00
❑ RS-9425 [S] Sermonette 1962 40.00
❑ RS-9458 [S] Confessin' the Blues 1963 40.00

## POOLE, BRIAN, AND THE TREMELOES

AUDIO FIDELITY
❑ AFLP 2151 [M] Brian Poole Is Here 1966 50.00
❑ AFSD 2151 [R] Brian Poole Is Here 1966 40.00
❑ AFLP 2177 [M] The Tremeloes Are Here 1967 40.00
*—Reissue of above album with new title*
❑ AFSD 2177 [R] The Tremeloes Are Here 1967 30.00
*—Reissue of above album with new title*

## POP WILL EAT ITSELF

NOTHING
❑ 95887 Amalgamation 1994 10.00

RCA
❑ 9742-1-R This Is the Day...This Is the Hour...This Is This! 1989 25.00

ROUGH TRADE
❑ ROUGH 22 Now for a Feast 198? 25.00
❑ ROUGH 33 Box Frenzy! 1988 25.00

## POPCORN BLIZZARD, THE

DE-LITE
❑ DE-2004 Explode! 1969 40.00

## POPPIES, THE

EPIC
❑ LN 24200 [M] Lullaby of Love 1966 40.00
❑ BN 26200 [S] Lullaby of Love 1966 50.00

## PORCELAIN BEARMEAT

DILL PICKLE
❑ 3468 Free Love, Free Sex, Free Music 1971 20.00

## PORT OF HARLEM JAZZMEN, THE

MOSAIC
❑ MR1-108 The Complete Recordings of the Port of Harlem Jazzmen 198? 20.00

## PORTER, DAVID

ENTERPRISE
❑ ENS-1009 Gritty, Groovy, & Gettin' It 1970 20.00
❑ ENS-1012 David Porter…Into a Real Thing 1971 20.00
❑ ENS-1019 Victim of the Joke? 1972 20.00
❑ ENS-1026 Sweat and Love 1973 20.00

## PORTER, JERRY

MIRROR
❑ SWB-123 [M] Don't Bother Me! 1966 100.00

## PORTER, NOLAN

ABC
❑ ABCX-766 Nolan 1973 120.00

LIZARD
❑ A-20102 No Apologies 1971 30.00
*—As "Nolan"*

## PORTER, PEPPER

FIRST AMERICAN
❑ FA-7756 Invasion 1980 25.00

## POSEY, SANDY

COLUMBIA
❑ KC 31594 Why Don't We Go Somewhere and Love 1972 12.00

MGM
❑ GAS-125 Sandy Posey (Golden Archive Series) 1970 15.00
❑ E-4418 [M] Born a Woman 1966 15.00
❑ SE-4418 [S] Born a Woman 1966 20.00
❑ E-4455 [M] Single Girl 1967 20.00
❑ SE-4455 [S] Single Girl 1967 20.00
❑ E-4480 [M] I Take It Back 1967 20.00
❑ SE-4480 [S] I Take It Back 1967 20.00
❑ E-4509 [M] The Best of Sandy Posey 1967 25.00
❑ SE-4509 [S] The Best of Sandy Posey 1967 20.00
❑ E-4525 [M] Looking at You 1968 25.00
❑ SE-4525 [S] Looking at You 1968 15.00
❑ ST-91110 Single Girl 1967 25.00
*—Capitol Record Club issue*

## POSSUM HUNTERS, THE

TAKOMA
❑ C-1010 Death on Lee Highway 1970 20.00

## POTTER, CURTIS

DOT
❑ DLP-25988 Here Comes Curtis Potter 1971 20.00

| Number | Title (A Side/B Side) | Yr | NM |
|---|---|---|---|
| **STEP ONE** | | | |
| ❑ 0004 | Down in Texas Today | 1984 | 20.00 |
| ❑ 0020 | All I Need Is Time | 1987 | 20.00 |

**POTTER, TOMMY**

| Number | Title (A Side/B Side) | Yr | NM |
|---|---|---|---|
| **EASTWEST** | | | |
| ❑ 4001 [M] | Tommy Potter's Hard Funk | 1958 | 50.00 |

**POTTS, BILL**

| Number | Title (A Side/B Side) | Yr | NM |
|---|---|---|---|
| **COLPIX** | | | |
| ❑ CP-451 [M] | Bye Bye Birdie | 1963 | 30.00 |
| ❑ SCP-451 [S] | Bye Bye Birdie | 1963 | 40.00 |
| **UNITED ARTISTS** | | | |
| ❑ UAL-4032 [M] | The Jazz Soul of Porgy and Bess | 1959 | 30.00 |
| ❑ UAS-5032 [S] | The Jazz Soul of Porgy and Bess | 1959 | 40.00 |

**POWELL, ANDREW, AND THE PHILHARMONIA ORCHESTRA**

| Number | Title (A Side/B Side) | Yr | NM |
|---|---|---|---|
| **MOBILE FIDELITY** | | | |
| ❑ 1-175 | The Best of the Alan Parsons Project | 1986 | 25.00 |
| *—Audiophile vinyl* | | | |

**POWELL, BADEN**

| Number | Title (A Side/B Side) | Yr | NM |
|---|---|---|---|
| **BASF** | | | |
| ❑ 25155 [(2)] | Canto on Guitar | 197? | 20.00 |

**POWELL, BUD**

| Number | Title (A Side/B Side) | Yr | NM |
|---|---|---|---|
| **BLUE NOTE** | | | |
| ❑ BLP-1503 [M] | The Amazing Bud Powell, Vol. 1 | 1955 | 400.00 |
| *—"Deep groove" version; Lexington Ave. address on label* | | | |
| ❑ BLP-1503 [M] | The Amazing Bud Powell, Vol. 1 | 1958 | 250.00 |
| *—"Deep groove" version, W. 63rd St. address on label* | | | |
| ❑ BLP-1503 [M] | The Amazing Bud Powell, Vol. 1 | 1963 | 40.00 |
| *—With "New York, USA" address on label* | | | |
| ❑ BLP-1504 [M] | The Amazing Bud Powell, Vol. 2 | 1955 | 500.00 |
| *—"Deep groove" version; Lexington Ave. address on label* | | | |
| ❑ BLP-1504 [M] | The Amazing Bud Powell, Vol. 2 | 1958 | 250.00 |
| *—"Deep groove" version, W. 63rd St. address on label* | | | |
| ❑ BLP-1504 [M] | The Amazing Bud Powell, Vol. 2 | 1963 | 40.00 |
| *—With "New York, USA" address on label* | | | |
| ❑ BLP-1571 [M] | Bud! | 1957 | 200.00 |
| *—Regular version, W. 63rd St. address on label* | | | |
| ❑ BLP-1571 [M] | Bud! | 1957 | 300.00 |
| *—"Deep groove" version; W. 63rd St. address on label* | | | |
| ❑ BLP-1571 [M] | Bud! | 1963 | 40.00 |
| *—With "New York, USA" address on label* | | | |
| ❑ BST-1571 [S] | Bud! | 1959 | 150.00 |
| *—Regular version, W. 63rd St. address on label* | | | |
| ❑ BST-1571 [S] | Bud! | 1959 | 200.00 |
| *—"Deep groove" version; W. 63rd St. address on label* | | | |
| ❑ BST-1571 [S] | Bud! | 1963 | 40.00 |
| *—With "New York, USA" address on label* | | | |
| ❑ BLP-1598 [M] | The Time Waits | 1959 | 250.00 |
| *—Regular version, W. 63rd St. address on label* | | | |
| ❑ BLP-1598 [M] | The Time Waits | 1959 | 400.00 |
| *—"Deep groove" version; W. 63rd St. address on label* | | | |
| ❑ BLP-1598 [M] | The Time Waits | 1963 | 40.00 |
| *—With "New York, USA" address on label* | | | |
| ❑ BST-1598 [S] | The Time Waits | 1959 | 150.00 |
| *—Regular version, W. 63rd St. address on label* | | | |
| ❑ BST-1598 [S] | The Time Waits | 1959 | 250.00 |
| *—"Deep groove" version; W. 63rd St. address on label* | | | |
| ❑ BST-1598 [S] | The Time Waits | 1963 | 40.00 |
| *—With "New York, USA" address on label* | | | |
| ❑ BLP-4009 [M] | The Scene Changes | 1959 | 200.00 |
| *—Regular version, W. 63rd St. address on label* | | | |
| ❑ BLP-4009 [M] | The Scene Changes | 1959 | 400.00 |
| *—"Deep groove" version; W. 63rd St. address on label* | | | |
| ❑ BLP-4009 [M] | The Scene Changes | 1963 | 40.00 |
| *—With "New York, USA" address on label* | | | |
| ❑ BST-4009 [S] | The Scene Changes | 1959 | 150.00 |
| *—Regular version, W. 63rd St. address on label* | | | |
| ❑ BST-4009 [S] | The Scene Changes | 1959 | 250.00 |
| *—"Deep groove" version; W. 63rd St. address on label* | | | |
| ❑ BST-4009 [S] | The Scene Changes | 1963 | 40.00 |
| *—With "New York, USA" address on label* | | | |
| ❑ BLP-5003 [10] | The Amazing Bud Powell, Vol. 1 | 1951 | 1000. |
| ❑ BLP-5041 [10] | The Amazing Bud Powell, Vol. 2 | 1954 | 1000. |
| **CLEF** | | | |
| ❑ MGC-502 [10] | Bud Powell Piano Solos | 1954 | 400.00 |
| ❑ MGC-507 [10] | Bud Powell Piano Solos, No. 2 | 1954 | 400.00 |
| ❑ MGC-610 [M] | Bud Powell's Moods | 1954 | 300.00 |
| ❑ MGC-739 [M] | The Genius of Bud Powell | 1956 | 250.00 |
| **COLUMBIA** | | | |
| ❑ CL 2292 [M] | A Portrait of Thelonious | 1965 | 40.00 |
| ❑ CS 9092 [S] | A Portrait of Thelonious | 1965 | 50.00 |
| *—Red label with "360 Sound Stereo"* | | | |
| **DEBUT** | | | |
| ❑ DLP-3 [10] | Jazz at Massey Hall, Volume 2 | 1953 | 800.00 |
| **DELMARK** | | | |
| ❑ DL-406 [M] | Bouncing with Bud | 1966 | 40.00 |
| ❑ DS-9406 [S] | Bouncing with Bud | 1966 | 50.00 |
| **ESP-DISK'** | | | |
| ❑ 1066 [S] | Bud Powell at the Blue Note Café, Paris | 1968 | 30.00 |
| **FANTASY** | | | |
| ❑ 6006 [M] | Bud Powell Trio | 1962 | 40.00 |
| *—Black vinyl* | | | |
| ❑ 6006 [M] | Bud Powell Trio | 1962 | 80.00 |
| *—Red vinyl* | | | |
| ❑ 86006 [R] | Bud Powell Trio | 1962 | 20.00 |
| *—Black vinyl* | | | |
| ❑ 86006 [R] | Bud Powell Trio | 1962 | 40.00 |
| *—Blue vinyl* | | | |
| **MERCURY** | | | |
| ❑ MGC-102 [10] | Bud Powell Piano | 1950 | 500.00 |
| ❑ MGC-502 [10] | Bud Powell Piano Solos | 1951 | 500.00 |
| ❑ MGC-507 [10] | Bud Powell Piano Solos, No. 2 | 1951 | 500.00 |
| ❑ MGC-610 [M] | Bud Powell's Moods | 1953 | 400.00 |
| ❑ MG-35012 [10] | Bud Powell Piano | 1950 | 600.00 |
| **MOSAIC** | | | |
| ❑ MR5-116 [(5)] | The Complete Bud Powell Blue Note Recordings (1949-1958) | 199? | 250.00 |
| **NORGRAN** | | | |
| ❑ MGN-23 [10] | Bud Powell Trio | 1954 | 500.00 |
| ❑ MGN-1017 [M] | Jazz Original | 1955 | 200.00 |
| ❑ MGN-1063 [M] | Jazz Giant | 1956 | 200.00 |
| ❑ MGN-1064 [M] | Bud Powell's Moods | 1956 | 200.00 |
| ❑ MGN-1077 [M] | Piano Interpretations by Bud Powell | 1956 | 200.00 |
| ❑ MGN-1098 [M] | Bud Powell '57 | 1957 | 200.00 |
| **RCA VICTOR** | | | |
| ❑ LPM-1423 [M] | Strictly Powell | 1957 | 150.00 |
| *—Reproductions exist* | | | |
| ❑ LPM-1507 [M] | Swingin' with Bud | 1957 | 120.00 |
| *—Reproductions exist* | | | |
| **REPRISE** | | | |
| ❑ R-6098 [M] | Bud Powell in Paris | 1964 | 40.00 |
| ❑ R9-6098 [S] | Bud Powell in Paris | 1964 | 60.00 |
| **ROOST** | | | |
| ❑ LP-401 [10] | Bud Powell Trio | 1950 | 600.00 |
| ❑ LP-412 [10] | Bud Powell Trio | 1953 | 500.00 |
| ❑ LP-2224 [M] | Bud Powell Trio | 1957 | 150.00 |
| **ROULETTE** | | | |
| ❑ R-52115 [M] | The Return of Bud Powell—His First New Recordings Since 1958 | 1965 | 30.00 |
| ❑ SR-52115 [S] | The Return of Bud Powell—His First New Recordings Since 1958 | 1965 | 40.00 |
| **VERVE** | | | |
| ❑ VSP-34 [M] | The Jazz Legacy of Bud Powell | 1966 | 20.00 |
| ❑ VSP-37 [M] | This Was Bud Powell | 1966 | 20.00 |
| ❑ MGV-8115 [M] | The Genius of Bud Powell | 1957 | 50.00 |
| ❑ V-8115 [M] | The Genius of Bud Powell | 1961 | 25.00 |
| ❑ MGV-8153 [M] | Jazz Giant | 1957 | 60.00 |
| ❑ V-8153 [M] | Jazz Giant | 1961 | 25.00 |
| ❑ MGV-8154 [M] | Bud Powell's Moods | 1957 | 60.00 |
| ❑ V-8154 [M] | Bud Powell's Moods | 1961 | 25.00 |
| ❑ MGV-8167 [M] | Piano Interpretations by Bud Powell | 1957 | 60.00 |
| ❑ V-8167 [M] | Piano Interpretations by Bud Powell | 1961 | 25.00 |
| ❑ MGV-8185 [M] | Bud Powell '57 | 1957 | 50.00 |
| ❑ V-8185 [M] | Bud Powell '57 | 1961 | 25.00 |
| ❑ MGV-8218 [M] | Blues in the Closet | 1958 | 50.00 |
| ❑ V-8218 [M] | Blues in the Closet | 1961 | 25.00 |
| ❑ MGV-8301 [M] | The Lonely One... | 1959 | 50.00 |
| ❑ V-8301 [M] | The Lonely One... | 1961 | 25.00 |

**POWELL, DICK**

| Number | Title (A Side/B Side) | Yr | NM |
|---|---|---|---|
| **DECCA** | | | |
| ❑ DL 8837 [M] | Song Book | 1959 | 40.00 |
| **RPC** | | | |
| ❑ 105 [M] | The Wonderful Teens | 1962 | 25.00 |

**POWELL, JANE**

| Number | Title (A Side/B Side) | Yr | NM |
|---|---|---|---|
| **COLUMBIA MASTERWORKS** | | | |
| ❑ ML 2034 [10] | Romance | 1949 | 80.00 |
| ❑ ML 2045 [10] | A Date with Jane Powell | 1949 | 80.00 |
| **LION** | | | |
| ❑ L-70111 [M] | Jane Powell Sings | 1960 | 20.00 |
| **MGM** | | | |
| ❑ E-3451 [M] | Something Wonderful | 1957 | 40.00 |
| **VERVE** | | | |
| ❑ MGV-2023 [M] | Can't We Be Friends? | 1957 | 40.00 |

**POWELL, LOVEY**

| Number | Title (A Side/B Side) | Yr | NM |
|---|---|---|---|
| **TRANSITION** | | | |
| ❑ TRLP-1 [M] | Lovelady | 1956 | 100.00 |
| *—Deduct 25 percent if booklet is missing* | | | |

**POWELL, MEL**

| Number | Title (A Side/B Side) | Yr | NM |
|---|---|---|---|
| **CAPITOL** | | | |
| ❑ T 615 [M] | Classics in Jazz | 1955 | 40.00 |
| **VANGUARD** | | | |
| ❑ VRS-8004 [10] | Mel Powell Septet | 1953 | 80.00 |
| ❑ VRS-8015 [10] | Bandstand | 1954 | 80.00 |
| ❑ VRS-8501 [M] | Borderline | 1954 | 50.00 |
| ❑ VRS-8502 [M] | Thigamagig | 1954 | 50.00 |
| ❑ VRS-8506 [M] | Out on a Limb | 1955 | 50.00 |
| ❑ VRS-8519 [M] | Easy Swing | 1955 | 50.00 |

**POWELL, SELDON**

| Number | Title (A Side/B Side) | Yr | NM |
|---|---|---|---|
| **ROOST** | | | |
| ❑ LP-2205 [M] | Seldon Powell Plays | 1956 | 50.00 |
| ❑ LP-2220 [M] | Seldon Powell Sextet | 1956 | 50.00 |

**POWELL, SPECS**

| Number | Title (A Side/B Side) | Yr | NM |
|---|---|---|---|
| **ROULETTE** | | | |
| ❑ R-52004 [M] | Movin' In | 1958 | 30.00 |
| ❑ SR-52004 [S] | Movin' In | 1958 | 25.00 |
| **STRAND** | | | |
| ❑ SL-1027 [M] | Specs Powell Presents Big Band Jazz | 1961 | 20.00 |
| ❑ SLS-1027 [S] | Specs Powell Presents Big Band Jazz | 1961 | 25.00 |

**POWERS, JOEY**

| Number | Title (A Side/B Side) | Yr | NM |
|---|---|---|---|
| **AMY** | | | |
| ❑ 8001 [M] | Midnight Mary | 1964 | 30.00 |

**POWERS OF BLUE, THE**

| Number | Title (A Side/B Side) | Yr | NM |
|---|---|---|---|
| **MTA** | | | |
| ❑ 1002 [M] | Flipout | 1967 | 30.00 |
| ❑ 5002 [S] | Flipout | 1967 | 30.00 |

**POZAR, ROBERT**

| Number | Title (A Side/B Side) | Yr | NM |
|---|---|---|---|
| **SAVOY** | | | |
| ❑ MG-12189 [M] | Good Golly, Miss Nancy | 1967 | 20.00 |

**POZO-SECO SINGERS, THE** DON WILLIAMS was in this group.

| Number | Title (A Side/B Side) | Yr | NM |
|---|---|---|---|
| **CERTRON** | | | |
| ❑ CS-7007 | Spend Some Time with Me | 1970 | 15.00 |
| **COLUMBIA** | | | |
| ❑ CL 2515 [M] | Time/I'll Be Gone | 1966 | 15.00 |
| ❑ CL 2600 [M] | I Can Make It with You | 1967 | 20.00 |
| ❑ CS 9315 [S] | Time/I'll Be Gone | 1966 | 20.00 |
| ❑ CS 9400 [S] | I Can Make It with You | 1967 | 15.00 |
| ❑ CS 9656 | Shades of Time | 1968 | 15.00 |
| **POWER PAK** | | | |
| ❑ 285 | The Pozo-Seco Singers with Don Williams | 198? | 10.00 |

**PRADO, PEREZ**

| Number | Title (A Side/B Side) | Yr | NM |
|---|---|---|---|
| **RCA CAMDEN** | | | |
| ❑ CAL-409 [M] | Mambo Happy! | 1957 | 20.00 |
| ❑ CAL-547 [M] | Latino! | 1960 | 20.00 |
| **RCA VICTOR** | | | |
| ❑ LPM-21 [10] | Perez Prado Plays Mucho Mambo for Dancing | 1951 | 60.00 |
| ❑ LPM-1075 [M] | Mambo Mania | 1955 | 40.00 |
| ❑ LPM-1101 [M] | Voodoo Suite (and Six All-Time Greats) | 1955 | 40.00 |
| ❑ LPM-1196 [M] | Mambo by the King | 1956 | 40.00 |
| ❑ LPM-1257 [M] | Havana 3 A.M. | 1956 | 40.00 |
| ❑ LPM-1459 [M] | Latin Satin | 1957 | 40.00 |
| ❑ LPM-1556 [M] | "Prez" | 1958 | 30.00 |
| ❑ LSP-1556 [S] | "Prez" | 1959 | 40.00 |
| ❑ LPM-1883 [M] | Dilo (Ugh!) | 1958 | 30.00 |
| ❑ LSP-1883 [S] | Dilo (Ugh!) | 1959 | 40.00 |
| ❑ ANL1-1941 | Pure Gold | 1975 | 10.00 |
| ❑ LPM-2028 [M] | Pops and Prado | 1959 | 30.00 |
| ❑ LSP-2028 [S] | Pops and Prado | 1959 | 40.00 |
| ❑ LPM-2104 [M] | Big Hits by Prado | 1959 | 30.00 |
| ❑ LSP-2104 [S] | Big Hits by Prado | 1959 | 40.00 |
| ❑ LPM-2133 [M] | A Touch of Tabasco | 1960 | 20.00 |
| ❑ LSP-2133 [S] | A Touch of Tabasco | 1960 | 30.00 |
| ❑ LPM-2308 [M] | Rockambo | 1961 | 20.00 |
| ❑ LSP-2308 [S] | Rockambo | 1961 | 30.00 |
| ❑ LPM-2379 [M] | The New Dance La Chunga | 1961 | 20.00 |
| ❑ LSP-2379 [S] | The New Dance La Chunga | 1961 | 30.00 |
| ❑ LPM-2524 [M] | The Twist Goes Latin | 1962 | 20.00 |
| ❑ LSP-2524 [S] | The Twist Goes Latin | 1962 | 30.00 |
| ❑ LPM-2571 [M] | Exotic Suite | 1962 | 20.00 |
| ❑ LSP-2571 [S] | Exotic Suite | 1962 | 30.00 |
| ❑ LPM-2610 [M] | Our Man in Latin America | 1963 | 20.00 |
| ❑ LSP-2610 [S] | Our Man in Latin America | 1963 | 30.00 |
| ❑ LPM-3108 [10] | Mambo by the King | 1953 | 60.00 |
| ❑ LPM-3330 [M] | Dance Latino | 1965 | 15.00 |
| ❑ LSP-3330 [S] | Dance Latino | 1965 | 20.00 |
| ❑ LPM-3732 [M] | The Best of Perez Prado | 1967 | 20.00 |
| ❑ LSP-3732 [S] | The Best of Perez Prado | 1967 | 15.00 |
| ❑ VPS-6066 [(2)] | This Is Perez Prado | 1972 | 15.00 |
| **UNITED ARTISTS** | | | |
| ❑ LS-61032 | Estas Si Viven (The Living End) | 196? | 15.00 |

**PREACHER ROLLO**

| Number | Title (A Side/B Side) | Yr | NM |
|---|---|---|---|
| **KING** | | | |
| ❑ 295-101 [10] | Dixieland | 195? | 120.00 |
| **MGM** | | | |
| ❑ E-95 [10] | Preacher Rollo and the Five Saints | 1951 | 80.00 |
| ❑ E-217 [10] | Preacher Rollo at the Jazz Band Ball | 1953 | 80.00 |

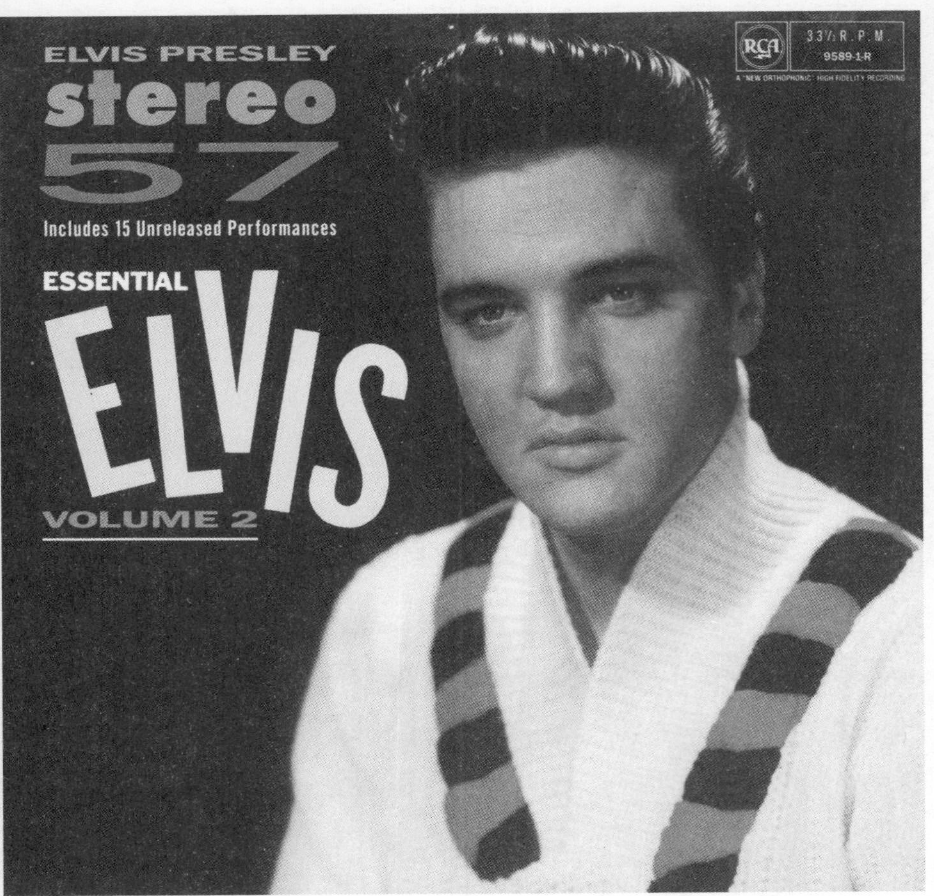


Elvis Presley, *Stereo '57: Essential Elvis Volume 2,* RCA 9589-1-R, 1989, $25.

| Number | Title (A Side/B Side) | Yr | NM |
|---|---|---|---|
| ❑ E-3259 [M] | Dixieland Favorites | 1955 | 50.00 |
| ❑ E-3403 [M] | Swanee River Jazz | 1956 | 50.00 |

## PREMIERS, THE (1)

### WARNER BROS.

| Number | Title (A Side/B Side) | Yr | NM |
|---|---|---|---|
| ❑ W 1565 [M] | Farmer John | 1964 | 40.00 |
| ❑ WS 1565 [S] | Farmer John | 1964 | 50.00 |

## PRESIDENTS, THE (1)

### SUSSEX

| Number | Title (A Side/B Side) | Yr | NM |
|---|---|---|---|
| ❑ SXBX-7005 | 5-10-15-20 (25-30 Years of Love) | 1970 | 25.00 |

## PRESLEY, ELVIS

### BMG/SUN

| Number | Title (A Side/B Side) | Yr | NM |
|---|---|---|---|
| ❑ 82876-61205-1 | Elvis at Sun | 2004 | 15.00 |

### BOXCAR

| Number | Title (A Side/B Side) | Yr | NM |
|---|---|---|---|
| ❑ (no #) | Having Fun with Elvis on Stage | 1974 | 150.00 |

*—All-talking record sold at Elvis concerts in 1974*

### COLLECTABLES

| Number | Title (A Side/B Side) | Yr | NM |
|---|---|---|---|
| ❑ COL-0165 [(6)] | Elvis Top Album Collection, Volume 1 | 2003 | 100.00 |

*—Contains reproductions, on red vinyl, of five RCA albums (LPM-1254, LPM-1382, LSP-2370, LSP-2426 and APL2-2587) using facsimiles of original labels, covers, inner sleeves and inserts; with poster and all in wooden box*

| Number | Title (A Side/B Side) | Yr | NM |
|---|---|---|---|
| ❑ COL-0166 [(6)] | Elvis Top Album Collection, Volume 2 | 2003 | 100.00 |

*—Contains reproductions, on red vinyl, of five RCA albums (LPM-1515, LOC-1035, LSP-2256, LSP-2999 and CPL2-2642) using facsimiles of original labels, covers, inner sleeves and inserts; with poster and all in wooden box*

### DCC COMPACT CLASSICS

| Number | Title (A Side/B Side) | Yr | NM |
|---|---|---|---|
| ❑ LPZ-2037 [S] | Elvis Is Back! | 1997 | 120.00 |

*—Audiophile vinyl*

| Number | Title (A Side/B Side) | Yr | NM |
|---|---|---|---|
| ❑ LPZ-2040 [(2)] | 24 Karat Hits! | 1997 | 120.00 |

*—Audiophile vinyl*

### FOTOPLAY

| Number | Title (A Side/B Side) | Yr | NM |
|---|---|---|---|
| ❑ FSP-1001 [PD] | To Elvis: Love Still Burning | 1978 | 15.00 |

*—In black cardboard cover with white printing*

| Number | Title (A Side/B Side) | Yr | NM |
|---|---|---|---|
| ❑ FSP-1001 [PD] | To Elvis: Love Still Burning | 1978 | 25.00 |

*—Tribute-song picture disc of Elvis; in plastic bag with 11x11 insert*

| Number | Title (A Side/B Side) | Yr | NM |
|---|---|---|---|
| ❑ FSP-1001 [PD] | To Elvis: Love Still Burning | 1978 | 30.00 |

*—In white cardboard cover with black printing*

### GOLDEN EDITIONS

| Number | Title (A Side/B Side) | Yr | NM |
|---|---|---|---|
| ❑ KING-1 | The First Year (Elvis, Scotty and Bill) | 1979 | 15.00 |
| ❑ GEL-101 | The First Year (Elvis, Scotty and Bill) | 1979 | 20.00 |

### GREAT NORTHWEST

| Number | Title (A Side/B Side) | Yr | NM |
|---|---|---|---|
| ❑ GV-2004 | The King Speaks (February 1961, Memphis, Tennessee) | 1977 | 10.00 |

*—Label says this is on "Green Valley" while sleeve says "Great Northwest"*

| Number | Title (A Side/B Side) | Yr | NM |
|---|---|---|---|
| ❑ GNW-4005 | The Elvis Tapes | 1977 | 12.00 |
| ❑ GNW-4006 | The King Speaks (February 1961, Memphis, Tennessee) | 1977 | 8.00 |

*—Both label and sleeve say this is on "Great Northwest"*

### GREEN VALLEY

| Number | Title (A Side/B Side) | Yr | NM |
|---|---|---|---|
| ❑ GV-2001 | Elvis Exclusive Live Press Conference (Memphis, Tennessee, February 1961) | 1977 | 40.00 |

*—Issued with two slightly different covers*

| Number | Title (A Side/B Side) | Yr | NM |
|---|---|---|---|
| ❑ GV-2001/3 [(2)] | Elvis (Speaks to You) | 1978 | 30.00 |

*—Elvis interviews plus tracks by the Jordanaires*

### GUSTO

| Number | Title (A Side/B Side) | Yr | NM |
|---|---|---|---|
| ❑ SD-995 | Interviews with Elvis (Canada 1957) | 1978 | 40.00 |

*—Reissue of Great Northwest album*

### HALW

| Number | Title (A Side/B Side) | Yr | NM |
|---|---|---|---|
| ❑ HALW-0001 | The First Years | 1978 | 20.00 |

*—Without limited edition number*

| Number | Title (A Side/B Side) | Yr | NM |
|---|---|---|---|
| ❑ HALW-0001 | The First Years | 1978 | 30.00 |

*—With stamped, limited edition number*

### K-TEL

| Number | Title (A Side/B Side) | Yr | NM |
|---|---|---|---|
| ❑ NU 9900 | Love Songs | 1981 | 20.00 |

### LOUISIANA HAYRIDE

| Number | Title (A Side/B Side) | Yr | NM |
|---|---|---|---|
| ❑ LH-3061 | Beginning Years | 1984 | 20.00 |

*—With booklet and facsimile contract*

### MARVENCO

| Number | Title (A Side/B Side) | Yr | NM |
|---|---|---|---|
| ❑ 101 | Beginning (1954-1955) | 1988 | 15.00 |

*—Pink vinyl with booklet and facsimile contract*

### MOBILE FIDELITY

| Number | Title (A Side/B Side) | Yr | NM |
|---|---|---|---|
| ❑ 1-059 | From Elvis in Memphis | 1982 | 50.00 |

*—Audiophile vinyl*

### MUSIC WORKS

| Number | Title (A Side/B Side) | Yr | NM |
|---|---|---|---|
| ❑ PB-3601 | The First Live Recordings | 1984 | 15.00 |
| ❑ PB-3602 | The Hillbilly Cat | 1984 | 15.00 |

### OAK

| Number | Title (A Side/B Side) | Yr | NM |
|---|---|---|---|
| ❑ 1003 | Vintage 1955 Elvis | 1990 | 60.00 |

### PAIR

| Number | Title (A Side/B Side) | Yr | NM |
|---|---|---|---|
| ❑ PDL2-1010 [(2)] | Double Dynamite | 1982 | 20.00 |
| ❑ PDL2-1037 [(2)] | Remembering | 1983 | 30.00 |
| ❑ PDL2-1185 [(2)] | Elvis Aron Presley Forever | 1988 | 20.00 |

### PICKWICK

| Number | Title (A Side/B Side) | Yr | NM |
|---|---|---|---|
| ❑ (no #) [(7)] | The Pickwick Pack (unofficial title) | 1978 | 60.00 |

*—Seven Pickwick albums in special package and cardboard wrapper; one of the LPs is Elvis' Christmas Album*

| Number | Title (A Side/B Side) | Yr | NM |
|---|---|---|---|
| ❑ (no #) [(7)] | The Pickwick Pack (unofficial title) | 1979 | 60.00 |

*—Seven Pickwick albums in special package and cardboard wrapper; one of the LPs is Frankie and Johnny*

| Number | Title (A Side/B Side) | Yr | NM |
|---|---|---|---|
| ❑ CAS-2304 | Elvis Sings Flaming Star | 1976 | 10.00 |
| ❑ CAS-2408 | Let's Be Friends | 1975 | 10.00 |
| ❑ CAS-2428 [M] | Elvis' Christmas Album | 1975 | 12.00 |

*—Same contents as RCA Camden LP; no Christmas trim on border; despite the "CAS" catalog number, this album is mono*

| Number | Title (A Side/B Side) | Yr | NM |
|---|---|---|---|
| ❑ CAS-2428 [M] | Elvis' Christmas Album | 1976 | 10.00 |

*—Same as above, but with Christmas trim on cover border; despite the "CAS" catalog number, this album is mono*

| Number | Title (A Side/B Side) | Yr | NM |
|---|---|---|---|
| ❑ CAS-2440 | Almost in Love | 1975 | 10.00 |
| ❑ CAL-2472 | You'll Never Walk Alone | 1975 | 10.00 |
| ❑ CAL-2518 | C'mon Everybody | 1975 | 10.00 |
| ❑ CAS-2533 | I Got Lucky | 1975 | 10.00 |
| ❑ CAS-2567 | Elvis Sings Hits from His Movies, Volume 1 | 1975 | 10.00 |
| ❑ CAS-2595 | Burning Love And Hits from His Movies, Vol. 2 | 1975 | 12.00 |

*—First cover contains a notice about the upcoming "Aloha from Hawaii" show*

| Number | Title (A Side/B Side) | Yr | NM |
|---|---|---|---|
| ❑ CAS-2595 | Burning Love And Hits from His Movies, Vol. 2 | 1976 | 8.00 |

*—Reissue deletes the "Aloha from Hawaii" notice*

| Number | Title (A Side/B Side) | Yr | NM |
|---|---|---|---|
| ❑ CAS-2611 | Separate Ways | 1975 | 10.00 |
| ❑ DL2-5001 [(2)] | Double Dynamite | 1975 | 25.00 |
| ❑ ACL-7007 | Frankie and Johnny | 1976 | 10.00 |
| ❑ ACL-7064 | Mahalo from Elvis | 1978 | 20.00 |

### PREMORE

| Number | Title (A Side/B Side) | Yr | NM |
|---|---|---|---|
| ❑ PL-589 | Early Elvis (1954-1956 Live at the Louisiana Hayride) | 1989 | 30.00 |

### RCA

| Number | Title (A Side/B Side) | Yr | NM |
|---|---|---|---|
| ❑ 2023-1-R | The Million Dollar Quartet | 1990 | 12.00 |

*—With Jerry Lee Lewis, Carl Perkins, and perhaps Johnny Cash*

| Number | Title (A Side/B Side) | Yr | NM |
|---|---|---|---|
| ❑ 2227-1-R | The Great Performances | 1990 | 40.00 |
| ❑ 3114-1-R [(3)] | Collectors Gold | 1991 | 200.00 |
| ❑ 5600-1-R | Return of the Rocker | 1986 | 20.00 |
| ❑ 6221-1-R [(2)] | The Memphis Record | 1987 | 30.00 |
| ❑ 6313-1-R | Elvis Talks! | 1987 | 30.00 |
| ❑ 6382-1-R | The Number One Hits | 1987 | 30.00 |
| ❑ 6383-1-R [(2)] | The Top Ten Hits | 1987 | 30.00 |
| ❑ 6414-1-R [(2)] | The Complete Sun Sessions | 1987 | 30.00 |
| ❑ 6738-1-R | Essential Elvis: The First Movies | 1988 | 25.00 |
| ❑ 6985-1-R | The Alternate Aloha | 1988 | 20.00 |
| ❑ 8468-1-R | Elvis in Nashville (1956-1971) | 1988 | 40.00 |
| ❑ 9586-1-R | Elvis Gospel 1957-1971 (Known Only to Him) | 1989 | 40.00 |
| ❑ 9589-1-R | Essential Elvis, Vol. 2 (Stereo '57) | 1989 | 25.00 |
| ❑ 82876-51108-1 [(2)] | 2nd to None | 2003 | 20.00 |
| ❑ 07863-67642-1 | Elvis' Golden Records | 1997 | 30.00 |

*—Reissue for the Tower Records chain with 6 bonus tracks*

| Number | Title (A Side/B Side) | Yr | NM |
|---|---|---|---|
| ❑ 07863-67643-1 | Elvis' Gold Records Volume 2 — 50,000,000 Elvis Fans Can't Be Wrong | 1997 | 30.00 |

*—Reissue for the Tower Records chain with 10 bonus tracks*

| Number | Title (A Side/B Side) | Yr | NM |
|---|---|---|---|
| ❑ 07863-68079-1 [(2)] | 30 #1 Hits | 2002 | 20.00 |

### RCA CAMDEN

| Number | Title (A Side/B Side) | Yr | NM |
|---|---|---|---|
| ❑ CAS-2304 | Elvis Sings Flaming Star | 1969 | 30.00 |
| ❑ CAS-2408 | Let's Be Friends | 1970 | 30.00 |
| ❑ CAL-2428 [M] | Elvis' Christmas Album | 1970 | 30.00 |

*—Blue label, non-flexible vinyl*

| Number | Title (A Side/B Side) | Yr | NM |
|---|---|---|---|
| ❑ CAL-2428 [M] | Elvis' Christmas Album | 1971 | 12.00 |

*—Blue label, flexible vinyl*

| Number | Title (A Side/B Side) | Yr | NM |
|---|---|---|---|
| ❑ CAS-2440 | Almost in Love | 1970 | 40.00 |

*—Last song on Side 2 is "Stay Away, Joe"*

| Number | Title (A Side/B Side) | Yr | NM |
|---|---|---|---|
| ❑ CAS-2440 | Almost in Love | 1973 | 25.00 |

*—Last song on Side 2 is "Stay Away"*

| Number | Title (A Side/B Side) | Yr | NM |
|---|---|---|---|
| ❑ CAL-2472 | You'll Never Walk Alone | 1974 | 30.00 |
| ❑ CALX-2472 | You'll Never Walk Alone | 1971 | 15.00 |
| ❑ CAL-2518 | C'mon Everybody | 1971 | 20.00 |
| ❑ CAL-2533 | I Got Lucky | 1971 | 25.00 |
| ❑ CAS-2567 | Elvis Sings Hits from His Movies, Volume 1 | 1972 | 20.00 |
| ❑ CAS-2595 | Burning Love And Hits from His Movies, Vol. 2 | 1972 | 10.00 |

*—No star on cover, no bonus photo*

| Number | Title (A Side/B Side) | Yr | NM |
|---|---|---|---|
| ❑ CAS-2595 | Burning Love And Hits from His Movies, Vol. 2 | 1972 | 25.00 |

*—With star on front cover advertising a bonus photo, the presence of which doubles the value of this LP*

| Number | Title (A Side/B Side) | Yr | NM |
|---|---|---|---|
| ❑ CAS-2611 | Separate Ways | 1973 | 30.00 |

### RCA SPECIAL PRODUCTS

| Number | Title (A Side/B Side) | Yr | NM |
|---|---|---|---|
| ❑ DPL2-0056(e) [(2)] | Elvis | 1973 | 25.00 |

*—Blue labels*

| Number | Title (A Side/B Side) | Yr | NM |
|---|---|---|---|
| ❑ DPL2-0056(e) [(2)] | Elvis | 1973 | 50.00 |

*—Mustard labels*

| Number | Title (A Side/B Side) | Yr | NM |
|---|---|---|---|
| ❑ DPL2-0056(e) [(2)] | Elvis Commemorative Album | 1978 | 80.00 |
| —Reissue of "Elvis" (same number) with new title and gold vinyl | | | |
| ❑ DPL2-0168 [(2)] | Elvis in Hollywood | 1976 | 60.00 |
| —Blue labels; with 20-page booklet | | | |
| ❑ DML5-0263 [(5)] | The Elvis Story | 1977 | 60.00 |
| —Available through Candelite Music via mail order | | | |
| ❑ DML1-0264 | His Songs of Inspiration | 1977 | 15.00 |
| ❑ DPL5-0347 [(5)] | Memories of Elvis (A Lasting Tribute to the King of Rock 'N' Roll) | 1978 | 80.00 |
| ❑ DML1-0348 | The Greatest Show on Earth | 1978 | 15.00 |
| ❑ DML6-0412 [(6)] | The Legendary Recordings of Elvis Presley | 1979 | 100.00 |
| ❑ DML1-0413 | The Greatest Moments in Music | 1980 | 15.00 |
| ❑ DML1-0437 | Rock 'N Roll Forever | 1981 | 15.00 |
| ❑ DVL1-0461 | The Legendary Magic of Elvis Presley | 1980 | 15.00 |
| ❑ DML3-0632 [(3)] | The Elvis Presley Collection | 1984 | 80.00 |
| —Available through Candelite Music via mail order | | | |
| ❑ DPL1-0647 | Elvis Country | 1984 | 30.00 |
| ❑ DVM1-0704 | Elvis (One Night with You) | 1984 | 60.00 |
| —With poster (deduct 25% if missing) | | | |
| ❑ SVL3-0710 [(3)] | 50 Years — 50 Hits | 1985 | 30.00 |
| ❑ DVL2-0728 [(2)] | His Songs of Faith and Inspiration | 1986 | 50.00 |
| ❑ SVL2-0824 [(2)] | Good Rockin' Tonight | 1988 | 20.00 |
| ❑ CAL-2428 [M] | Elvis' Christmas Album | 1986 | 30.00 |
| —Reissue for The Special Music Company | | | |

RCA VICTOR

| Number | Title (A Side/B Side) | Yr | NM |
|---|---|---|---|
| ❑ (no #) | International Hotel, Las Vegas Nevada, Presents Elvis, 1969 | 1969 | 2500. |
| —Gift box to guests at Elvis' July 31-Aug, 1, 1969 shows. Includes LPM-4088 and LSP-4155; press release; 1969 catalog; three photos; and thank-you note from Elvis and the Colonel. Most of the value is for the box; VG value 1250; VG+ value 1875 | | | |
| ❑ (no #) | International Hotel, Las Vegas Nevada, Presents Elvis, 1970 | 1970 | 2500. |
| —Gift box to guests at Elvis' Jan. 28, 1970 show. Includes LSP-6020 and 47-9791; press release; 1970 catalog; photo; booklet; and dinner menu. Most of the value is for the box; VG value 1250; VG+ value 1875 | | | |
| ❑ PRS-279 | Singer Presents Elvis Singing Flaming Star and Others | 1968 | 100.00 |
| —Sold only at Singer sewing machine dealers; reissued on RCA Camden 2304 | | | |
| ❑ APL1-0283 | Elvis | 1973 | 50.00 |
| ❑ CPL1-0341 | A Legendary Performer, Volume 1 | 1974 | 25.00 |
| —Includes booklet (deduct 40% if missing); with die-cut hole in front cover | | | |
| ❑ CPL1-0341 | A Legendary Performer, Volume 1 | 1986 | 15.00 |
| —No die-cut hole in cover and no booklet | | | |
| ❑ APL1-0388 | Raised on Rock/For Ol' Times Sake | 1973 | 30.00 |
| —Orange label | | | |
| ❑ APL1-0388 | Raised on Rock/For Ol' Times Sake | 1975 | 30.00 |
| —Tan label | | | |
| ❑ APL1-0388 | Raised on Rock/For Ol' Times Sake | 1977 | 12.00 |
| —Black label, dog near top | | | |
| ❑ SP-33-461 [DJ] | Special Palm Sunday Programming | 1967 | 700.00 |
| —White label promo. Add 25% for cue sheet. | | | |
| ❑ AFL1-0475 | Good Times | 1977 | 12.00 |
| —Black label, dog near top; includes copies with sticker wrapped around spine with new number | | | |
| ❑ CPL1-0475 | Good Times | 1974 | 50.00 |
| —Orange label | | | |
| ❑ CPL1-0475 | Good Times | 1976 | 12.00 |
| —Black label, dog near top | | | |
| ❑ SPS-33-571 [DJ] | Elvis As Recorded at Madison Square Garden | 1972 | 300.00 |
| —"Radio Station Banded Special Version"; came in plain white cover with stickers | | | |
| ❑ AFL1-0606 | Elvis Recorded Live on Stage in Memphis | 1977 | 12.00 |
| —Black label, dog near top; includes copies with sticker wrapped around spine with new number | | | |
| ❑ APD1-0606 [Q] | Elvis Recorded Live on Stage in Memphis | 1974 | 200.00 |
| —"RCA QuadraDisc" labels | | | |
| ❑ CPL1-0606 | Elvis Recorded Live on Stage in Memphis | 1974 | 25.00 |
| —Orange label | | | |
| ❑ CPL1-0606 | Elvis Recorded Live on Stage in Memphis | 1975 | 25.00 |
| —Tan label | | | |
| ❑ DJL1-0606 [DJ] | Elvis Recorded Live on Stage in Memphis | 1974 | 300.00 |
| —Special banded version for radio airplay | | | |
| ❑ AFM1-0818 | Having Fun with Elvis on Stage | 1977 | 25.00 |
| —Black label, dog near top | | | |
| ❑ CPM1-0818 | Having Fun with Elvis on Stage | 1974 | 30.00 |
| —Commercial issue of Boxcar LP; orange label | | | |
| ❑ CPM1-0818 | Having Fun with Elvis on Stage | 1975 | 20.00 |
| —Tan label | | | |
| ❑ DJM1-0835 [DJ] | Elvis Presley Interview Record: An Audio Self-Portrait | 1984 | 80.00 |
| —Promotional item for "50th Anniversary" series; later issued as RCA 6313-1-R | | | |

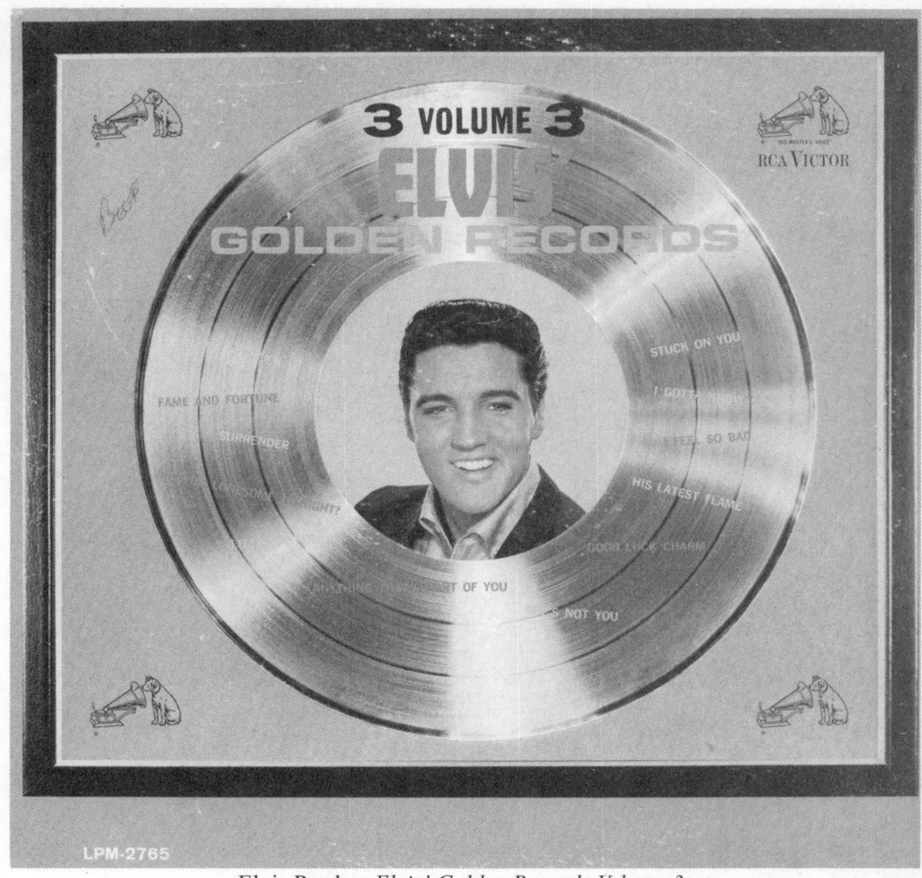


Elvis Presley, *Elvis' Golden Records Volume 3,* RCA Victor LPM-2765, 1963, mono, "Mono" on label, $100.

| Number | Title (A Side/B Side) | Yr | NM |
|---|---|---|---|
| ❑ AFL1-0873 | Promised Land | 1977 | 15.00 |
| —Black label, dog near top | | | |
| ❑ APD1-0873 [Q] | Promised Land | 1975 | 200.00 |
| —"RCA QuadraDisc" label | | | |
| ❑ APD1-0873 [Q] | Promised Land | 1977 | 120.00 |
| —Black label, dog near top; quadraphonic reissue | | | |
| ❑ APL1-0873 | Promised Land | 1975 | 20.00 |
| —Tan label | | | |
| ❑ APL1-0873 | Promised Land | 1975 | 60.00 |
| —Orange label | | | |
| ❑ ANL1-0971(e) | Pure Gold | 1975 | 15.00 |
| —Orange label | | | |
| ❑ ANL1-0971(e) | Pure Gold | 1976 | 12.00 |
| —Yellow label | | | |
| ❑ LOC-1035 [M] | Elvis' Christmas Album Sticker | 1957 | 150.00 |
| —Gold sticker with "To_______" and "From_________" blanks | | | |
| ❑ LOC-1035 [M] | Elvis' Christmas Album | 1957 | 500.00 |
| —Gatefold cover; title printed in gold on LP spine; includes bound-in booklet but not sticker | | | |
| ❑ LOC-1035 [M] | Elvis' Christmas Album | 1957 | 500.00 |
| —Gatefold cover; title printed in silver on LP spine; includes bound-in booklet but not sticker | | | |
| ❑ LOC-1035 [M] | Elvis' Christmas Album | 1957 | 15000. |
| —Red vinyl; unique; VG value 7500; VG+ value 11250 | | | |
| ❑ LOC-1035 [M] | Elvis' Christmas Album | 2003 | 20.00 |
| —Red vinyl; not to be mistaken for the unique 1957 version, as this has "DRL 13265" number in trail-off wax and BMG Special Products logo and "This is a replica of the original packaging" on back cover; from box "Elvis Top Album Collection Volume 2" | | | |
| ❑ AFL1-1039 | Elvis Today | 1977 | 12.00 |
| —Black label, dog near top; includes copies with sticker wrapped around spine with new number | | | |
| ❑ APD1-1039 [Q] | Elvis Today | 1975 | 200.00 |
| —"RCA QuadraDisc" labels | | | |
| ❑ APD1-1039 [Q] | Elvis Today | 1977 | 150.00 |
| —Black label, dog near top; quadraphonic reissue | | | |
| ❑ APL1-1039 | Elvis Today | 1975 | 30.00 |
| —Tan label | | | |
| ❑ APL1-1039 | Elvis Today | 1975 | 60.00 |
| —Orange label | | | |
| ❑ AFL1-1254(e) [R] | Elvis Presley | 1977 | 12.00 |
| —Black label, dog near top; includes copies with sticker wrapped around spine with new number | | | |
| ❑ LPM-1254 [M] | Elvis Presley | 1956 | 250.00 |
| —Version 3: "Long Play" on label; "Elvis" in pale pink, "Presley" in neon green on cover; black logo box in upper right front cover | | | |
| ❑ LPM-1254 [M] | Elvis Presley | 1956 | 400.00 |
| —Version 2: "Long Play" on label; "Elvis" in pale pink, "Presley" in neon green on cover; neon green logo box in upper right front cover | | | |
| ❑ LPM-1254 [M] | Elvis Presley | 1956 | 500.00 |
| —Version 1: "Long Play" on label; "Elvis" in pale pink, "Presley" in pale green on cover; pale green logo box in upper right front cover | | | |
| ❑ LPM-1254 [M] | Elvis Presley | 1958 | 200.00 |
| —Version 4: "Long Play" on label; "Elvis" in neon pink, almost red, "Presley" in neon green on cover; black logo box in upper right front cover | | | |
| ❑ LPM-1254 [M] | Elvis Presley | 1963 | 120.00 |
| —"Mono" on label; cover photo is slightly left of center, otherwise same as Version 4 above | | | |
| ❑ LPM-1254 [M] | Elvis Presley | 1964 | 60.00 |
| —"Monaural" on label | | | |
| ❑ LPM-1254 [M] | Elvis Presley | 2003 | 20.00 |
| —Red vinyl; "DRL 13272" in trail-off wax; "BMG Special Products" logo on back cover; from box "Elvis Top Album Collection Volume 1" | | | |
| ❑ LSP-1254(e) [R] | Elvis Presley | 1962 | 200.00 |
| —"Stereo Electronically Reprocessed" and silver "RCA Victor" on label | | | |
| ❑ LSP-1254(e) [R] | Elvis Presley | 1965 | 40.00 |
| —"Stereo Electronically Reprocessed" and white "RCA Victor" on label | | | |
| ❑ LSP-1254(e) [R] | Elvis Presley | 1968 | 30.00 |
| —Orange label, non-flexible vinyl | | | |
| ❑ LSP-1254(e) [R] | Elvis Presley | 1975 | 15.00 |
| —Tan label | | | |
| ❑ LSP-1254(e) [R] | Elvis Presley | 1976 | 12.00 |
| —Black label, dog near top | | | |
| ❑ ANL1-1319 [S] | His Hand in Mine | 1976 | 15.00 |
| —Reissue with more tightly cropped photo of Elvis on front cover | | | |
| ❑ CPL1-1349 | A Legendary Performer, Volume 2 | 1976 | 30.00 |
| —Includes booklet (deduct 40% if missing); with die-cut hole in front cover | | | |
| ❑ CPL1-1349 | A Legendary Performer, Volume 2 | 1976 | 60.00 |
| —Without false starts and outtakes of "Such a Night" and "Cane and a High Starched Collar," which are supposed to be there. End of matrix number may be "31." | | | |
| ❑ CPL1-1349 | A Legendary Performer, Volume 2 | 1986 | 15.00 |
| —No die-cut hole in cover and no booklet | | | |
| ❑ AFL1-1382(e) [R] | Elvis | 1977 | 12.00 |
| —Black label, dog near top; includes copies with sticker wrapped around spine with new number | | | |
| ❑ LPM-1382 [M] | Elvis | 1956 | 300.00 |
| —Back cover has ads for other albums. At least 11 different variations of this are known, all of equal value. | | | |

Elvis Presley, *Love Letters from Elvis,*
RCA Victor LSP-4530, 1970, title in three lines, orange label, $30.

| Number | Title (A Side/B Side) | Yr | NM |
|---|---|---|---|
| ❑ LPM-1382 [M] | Elvis | 1956 | 300.00 |
| *—Back cover has no ads for other albums. "Long Play" on label.* | | | |
| ❑ LPM-1382 [M] | Elvis | 1956 | 400.00 |
| *—With tracks listed on labels as "Band 1" through "Band 6"* | | | |
| ❑ LPM-1382 [M] | Elvis | 1956 | 800.00 |
| *—With alternate take of "Old Shep" on side 2. Matrix number on the "Old Shep" side ends in "15S," "17S" or "19S," but should be played for positive ID. On alternate take, Elvis sings "he grew old AND his eyes were growing dim" (no AND on standard press)* | | | |
| ❑ LPM-1382 [M] | Elvis | 1963 | 80.00 |
| *—"Mono" on label* | | | |
| ❑ LPM-1382 [M] | Elvis | 1965 | 60.00 |
| *—"Monaural" on label* | | | |
| ❑ LPM-1382 [M] | Elvis | 2003 | 20.00 |
| *—Red vinyl; "DRC 13271" in trail-off wax; "BMG Special Products" logo on back cover; from box "Elvis Top Album Collection Volume 1"* | | | |
| ❑ LSP-1382(e) [R] | Elvis | 1962 | 200.00 |
| *—"Stereo Electronically Reprocessed" and silver "RCA Victor" on label* | | | |
| ❑ LSP-1382(e) [R] | Elvis | 1964 | 50.00 |
| *—"Stereo Electronically Reprocessed" and white "RCA Victor" on label* | | | |
| ❑ LSP-1382(e) [R] | Elvis | 1968 | 30.00 |
| *—Orange label, non-flexible vinyl* | | | |
| ❑ LSP-1382(e) [R] | Elvis | 1971 | 20.00 |
| *—Orange label, flexible vinyl* | | | |
| ❑ LSP-1382(e) [R] | Elvis | 1975 | 15.00 |
| *—Tan label* | | | |
| ❑ LSP-1382(e) [R] | Elvis | 1976 | 12.00 |
| *—Black label, dog near top* | | | |
| ❑ AFL1-1506 | From Elvis Presley Boulevard, Memphis, Tennessee | 1977 | 10.00 |
| *—Black label, dog near top; new number is on cover and label* | | | |
| ❑ AFL1-1506 | From Elvis Presley Boulevard, Memphis, Tennessee | 1977 | 12.00 |
| *—Black label, dog near top; with sticker wrapped around spine with new number (old number still on label)* | | | |
| ❑ APL1-1506 | From Elvis Presley Boulevard, Memphis, Tennessee | 1976 | 30.00 |
| *—Tan label* | | | |
| ❑ AFL1-1515(e) [R] | Loving You | 1977 | 12.00 |
| *—Black label, dog near top; includes copies with sticker wrapped around spine with new number* | | | |
| ❑ LPM-1515 [M] | Loving You | 1957 | 300.00 |
| *—"Long Play" on label* | | | |
| ❑ LPM-1515 [M] | Loving You | 1963 | 100.00 |
| *—"Mono" on label* | | | |
| ❑ LPM-1515 [M] | Loving You | 1964 | 50.00 |
| *—"Monaural" on label* | | | |
| ❑ LPM-1515 [M] | Loving You | 2003 | 20.00 |
| *—Red vinyl; "DRL 13268" in trail-off wax; "BMG Special Products" logo on back cover; from box "Elvis Top Album Collection Volume 2"* | | | |
| ❑ LSP-1515(e) [R] | Loving You | 1962 | 150.00 |
| *—"Stereo Electronically Reprocessed" and silver "RCA Victor" on label* | | | |
| ❑ LSP-1515(e) [R] | Loving You | 1964 | 50.00 |
| *—"Stereo Electronically Reprocessed" and white "RCA Victor" on label* | | | |
| ❑ LSP-1515(e) [R] | Loving You | 1968 | 40.00 |
| *—Orange label, non-flexible vinyl* | | | |
| ❑ LSP-1515(e) [R] | Loving You | 1971 | 20.00 |
| *—Orange label, flexible vinyl* | | | |
| ❑ LSP-1515(e) [R] | Loving You | 1975 | 20.00 |
| *—Tan label* | | | |
| ❑ LSP-1515(e) [R] | Loving You | 1976 | 12.00 |
| *—Black label, dog near top* | | | |
| ❑ AFM1-1675 | The Sun Sessions | 1977 | 15.00 |
| *—Black label, dog near top; includes copies with sticker wrapped around spine with new number* | | | |
| ❑ APM1-1675 | The Sun Sessions | 1976 | 12.00 |
| *—Black label, dog near top* | | | |
| ❑ APM1-1675 | The Sun Sessions | 1976 | 20.00 |
| *—Tan label* | | | |
| ❑ AFL1-1707(e) [R] | Elvis' Golden Records | 1977 | 12.00 |
| *—Black label, dog near top; includes copies with sticker wrapped around spine with new number* | | | |
| ❑ AQL1-1707(e) [R] | Elvis' Golden Records | 1979 | 10.00 |
| *—Another reissue with new prefix* | | | |
| ❑ LPM-1707 [M] | Elvis' Golden Records | 1958 | 150.00 |
| *—Title on cover in light blue letters; no song titles listed on front cover; "RE" on back cover* | | | |
| ❑ LPM-1707 [M] | Elvis' Golden Records | 1958 | 250.00 |
| *—Title on cover in light blue letters; no song titles listed on front cover* | | | |
| ❑ LPM-1707 [M] | Elvis' Golden Records | 1963 | 60.00 |
| *—"Mono" on label; title on cover in white letters; song titles added to front cover* | | | |
| ❑ LPM-1707 [M] | Elvis' Golden Records | 1964 | 40.00 |
| *—"Monaural" on label; "RE2" on back cover* | | | |
| ❑ LSP-1707(e) [R] | Elvis' Golden Records | 1962 | 200.00 |
| *—"Stereo Electronically Reprocessed" and silver "RCA Victor" on label* | | | |
| ❑ LSP-1707(e) [R] | Elvis' Golden Records | 1964 | 50.00 |
| *—"Stereo Electronically Reprocessed" and white "RCA Victor" on label* | | | |
| ❑ LSP-1707(e) [R] | Elvis' Golden Records | 1968 | 30.00 |
| *—Orange label, non-flexible vinyl* | | | |
| ❑ LSP-1707(e) [R] | Elvis' Golden Records | 1971 | 20.00 |
| *—Orange label, flexible vinyl* | | | |
| ❑ LSP-1707(e) [R] | Elvis' Golden Records | 1975 | 20.00 |
| *—Tan label* | | | |
| ❑ LSP-1707(e) [R] | Elvis' Golden Records | 1976 | 12.00 |
| *—Black label, dog near top* | | | |
| ❑ AFL1-1884(e) [R] | King Creole | 1977 | 12.00 |
| *—Black label, dog near top; includes copies with sticker wrapped around spine with new number* | | | |
| ❑ LPM-1884 [M] | King Creole | 1958 | 200.00 |
| *—"Long Play" on label; contrary to some other sources, this was NOT issued with a bonus photo* | | | |
| ❑ LPM-1884 [M] | King Creole | 1963 | 80.00 |
| *—"Mono" on label* | | | |
| ❑ LPM-1884 [M] | King Creole | 1964 | 60.00 |
| *—"Monaural" on label* | | | |
| ❑ LSP-1884(e) [R] | King Creole | 1962 | 150.00 |
| *—"Stereo Electronically Reprocessed" and silver "RCA Victor" on label* | | | |
| ❑ LSP-1884(e) [R] | King Creole | 1964 | 60.00 |
| *—"Stereo Electronically Reprocessed" and white "RCA Victor" on label* | | | |
| ❑ LSP-1884(e) [R] | King Creole | 1968 | 40.00 |
| *—Orange label, non-flexible vinyl* | | | |
| ❑ LSP-1884(e) [R] | King Creole | 1971 | 20.00 |
| *—Orange label, flexible vinyl* | | | |
| ❑ LSP-1884(e) [R] | King Creole | 1975 | 20.00 |
| *—Tan label* | | | |
| ❑ LSP-1884(e) [R] | King Creole | 1976 | 12.00 |
| *—Black label, dog near top* | | | |
| ❑ ANL1-1936 | Elvis Sings the Wonderful World of Christmas | 1975 | 15.00 |
| *—New number; same contents as LSP-4579. Orange label.* | | | |
| ❑ ANL1-1936 | Elvis Sings the Wonderful World of Christmas | 1976 | 12.00 |
| *—Tan label* | | | |
| ❑ ANL1-1936 | Elvis Sings the Wonderful World of Christmas | 1977 | 10.00 |
| *—Black label, dog near top* | | | |
| ❑ LPM-1951 [M] | Elvis' Christmas Album | 1958 | 150.00 |
| *—Same contents as LOC-1035, but with non-gatefold blue cover; "Long Play" at bottom of label* | | | |
| ❑ LPM-1951 [M] | Elvis' Christmas Album | 1963 | 70.00 |
| *—"Mono" at bottom of label: "RE" on lower left front cover (photos on back were altered)* | | | |
| ❑ LPM-1951 [M] | Elvis' Christmas Album | 1964 | 40.00 |
| *—"Monaural" at bottom of label; "RE" on lower left front cover* | | | |
| ❑ LSP-1951(e) [R] | Elvis' Christmas Album | 1964 | 50.00 |
| *—Black label, dog on top; "Stereo Electronically Reprocessed" at bottom of label* | | | |
| ❑ LSP-1951(e) [R] | Elvis' Christmas Album | 1968 | 60.00 |
| *—Orange label, non-flexible vinyl* | | | |
| ❑ AFL1-1990(e) [R] | For LP Fans Only | 1977 | 12.00 |
| *—Black label, dog near top; includes copies with sticker wrapped around spine with new number* | | | |
| ❑ LPM-1990 [M] | For LP Fans Only | 1959 | 250.00 |
| *—"Long Play" on label* | | | |
| ❑ LPM-1990 [M] | For LP Fans Only | 1963 | 80.00 |
| *—"Mono" on label* | | | |
| ❑ LPM-1990 [M] | For LP Fans Only | 1964 | 50.00 |
| *—"Monaural" on label* | | | |
| ❑ LSP-1990(e) [R] | For LP Fans Only | 1965 | 50.00 |
| *—"Stereo Electronically Reprocessed" on label; normal cover with different front and back cover photos* | | | |
| ❑ LSP-1990(e) [R] | For LP Fans Only | 1965 | 300.00 |
| *—"Stereo Electronically Reprocessed" on label; error cover with same photo on both front and back* | | | |
| ❑ LSP-1990(e) [R] | For LP Fans Only | 1968 | 30.00 |
| *—Orange label, non-flexible vinyl* | | | |
| ❑ LSP-1990(e) [R] | For LP Fans Only | 1975 | 20.00 |
| *—Tan label* | | | |
| ❑ LSP-1990(e) [R] | For LP Fans Only | 1976 | 12.00 |
| *—Black label, dog near top* | | | |
| ❑ AFL1-2011(e) [R] | A Date with Elvis | 1977 | 12.00 |
| *—Black label, dog near top; includes copies with sticker wrapped around spine with new number* | | | |
| ❑ LPM-2011 [M] | A Date with Elvis | 1959 | 400.00 |
| *—"Long Play" on label; gatefold cover, no sticker on cover* | | | |
| ❑ LPM-2011 [M] | A Date with Elvis | 1959 | 500.00 |
| *—"Long Play" on label; gatefold cover, with sticker on cover* | | | |
| ❑ LPM-2011 [M] | A Date with Elvis | 1963 | 100.00 |
| *—"Mono" on label; no gatefold cover* | | | |
| ❑ LPM-2011 [M] | A Date with Elvis | 1965 | 50.00 |
| *—"Monaural" on label* | | | |
| ❑ LSP-2011(e) [R] | A Date with Elvis | 1965 | 50.00 |
| *—Black label, "Stereo Electronically Reprocessed" on label* | | | |
| ❑ LSP-2011(e) [R] | A Date with Elvis | 1968 | 30.00 |
| *—Orange label, non-flexible vinyl* | | | |
| ❑ LSP-2011(e) [R] | A Date with Elvis | 1971 | 20.00 |
| *—Orange label, flexible vinyl* | | | |
| ❑ LSP-2011(e) [R] | A Date with Elvis | 1975 | 20.00 |
| *—Tan label* | | | |
| ❑ LSP-2011(e) [R] | A Date with Elvis | 1977 | 12.00 |
| *—Black label, dog near top* | | | |
| ❑ AFL1-2075(e) [R] | Elvis' Gold Records Volume 2 — 50,000,000 Elvis Fans Can't Be Wrong | 1977 | 12.00 |
| *—Black label, dog near top; includes copies with sticker wrapped around spine with new number* | | | |

| Number | Title (A Side/B Side) | Yr | NM |
|---|---|---|---|
| ❑ LPM-2075 [M] | Elvis' Gold Records Volume 2 — 50,000,000 Elvis Fans Can't Be Wrong | 1960 | 200.00 |

—"Long Play" on label; "Magic Millions" on upper right front cover with RCA Victor logo

| Number | Title (A Side/B Side) | Yr | NM |
|---|---|---|---|
| ❑ LPM-2075 [M] | Elvis' Gold Records Volume 2 — 50,000,000 Elvis Fans Can't Be Wrong | 1963 | 80.00 |

—"Mono" on label; "RE" on lower right front cover

❑ LPM-2075 [M] Elvis' Gold Records Volume 2 — 50,000,000 Elvis Fans Can't Be Wrong 1964 50.00
—"Monaural" on label; label has words "50,000,000 Elvis Presley Fans Can't Be Wrong"
❑ LPM-2075 [M] Elvis' Gold Records Volume 2 — 50,000,000 Elvis Fans Can't Be Wrong 1964 50.00
—"Monaural" on label; label only has "Elvis' Gold Records - Vol. 2"
❑ LSP-2075(e) [R]Elvis' Gold Records Volume 2 — 50,000,000 Elvis Fans Can't Be Wrong 1962 150.00
—"Stereo Electronically Reprocessed" on label; label has words "50,000,000 Elvis Presley Fans Can't Be Wrong"
❑ LSP-2075(e) [R]Elvis' Gold Records Volume 2 — 50,000,000 Elvis Fans Can't Be Wrong 1964 50.00
—"Stereo Electronically Reprocessed" and white "RCA Victor" on label
❑ LSP-2075(e) [R]Elvis' Gold Records Volume 2 — 50,000,000 Elvis Fans Can't Be Wrong 1968 30.00
—Orange label, non-flexible vinyl
❑ LSP-2075(e) [R]Elvis' Gold Records Volume 2 — 50,000,000 Elvis Fans Can't Be Wrong 1971 20.00
—Orange label, flexible vinyl
❑ LSP-2075(e) [R]Elvis' Gold Records Volume 2 — 50,000,000 Elvis Fans Can't Be Wrong 1975 20.00
—Tan label
❑ LSP-2075(e) [R]Elvis' Gold Records Volume 2 — 50,000,000 Elvis Fans Can't Be Wrong 1976 12.00
—Black label, dog near top
❑ AFL1-2231 [S] Elvis Is Back! 1977 12.00
—Black label, dog near top; includes copies with sticker wrapped around spine with new number
❑ LPM-2231 [M] Elvis Is Back! 1960 150.00
—With sticker attached to front cover. Side 2, Song 4 is listed as "The Girl Next Door Went a-Walking."
❑ LPM-2231 [M] Elvis Is Back! 1960 150.00
—With sticker attached to front cover. Side 2, Song 4 is listed as "The Girl Next Door."
❑ LPM-2231 [M] Elvis Is Back! 1960 200.00
—With no sticker attached to front cover. Side 2, Song 4 is listed as "The Girl Next Door Went a-Walking."
❑ LPM-2231 [M] Elvis Is Back! 1960 200.00
—With no sticker attached to front cover. Side 2, Song 4 is listed as "The Girl Next Door."
❑ LPM-2231 [M] Elvis Is Back! 1963 60.00
—"Mono" on label; song titles printed on front cover
❑ LPM-2231 [M] Elvis Is Back! 1964 60.00
—"Monaural" on label
❑ LSP-2231 [S] Elvis Is Back! 1960 300.00
—"Living Stereo" on label; with no sticker attached to front cover. Side 2, Song 4 is listed as "The Girl Next Door Went a-Walking."
❑ LSP-2231 [S] Elvis Is Back! 1960 300.00
—"Living Stereo" on label; with no sticker attached to front cover. Side 2, Song 4 is listed as "The Girl Next Door."
❑ LSP-2231 [S] Elvis Is Back! 1960 300.00
—"Living Stereo" on label; with sticker attached to front cover. Side 2, Song 4 is listed as "The Girl Next Door Went a-Walking."
❑ LSP-2231 [S] Elvis Is Back! 1960 300.00
—"Living Stereo" on label; with sticker attached to front cover. Side 2, Song 4 is listed as "The Girl Next Door."
❑ LSP-2231 [S] Elvis Is Back! 1964 60.00
—"Stereo" on label; song titles printed on front cover
❑ LSP-2231 [S] Elvis Is Back! 1968 40.00
—Orange label, non-flexible vinyl
❑ LSP-2231 [S] Elvis Is Back! 1975 20.00
—Tan label
❑ LSP-2231 [S] Elvis Is Back! 1976 15.00
—Black label, dog on top
❑ AFL1-2256 [S] G.I. Blues 1977 12.00
—Black label, dog near top; includes copies with sticker wrapped around spine with new number
❑ LPM-2256 [M] G.I. Blues 1960 120.00
—"Long Play" on label; with no sticker on front cover
❑ LPM-2256 [M] G.I. Blues 1960 500.00
—"Long Play" on label; with sticker on front cover advertising the presence of "Wooden Heart"
❑ LPM-2256 [M] G.I. Blues 1963 100.00
—"Mono" on label
❑ LPM-2256 [M] G.I. Blues 1964 50.00
—"Monaural" on label
❑ LSP-2256 [S] G.I. Blues 1960 100.00
—"Living Stereo" on label; with no sticker on front cover
❑ LSP-2256 [S] G.I. Blues 1960 600.00
—"Living Stereo" on label; with sticker on front cover advertising the presence of "Wooden Heart"
❑ LSP-2256 [S] G.I. Blues 1964 50.00
—"Stereo" on black label

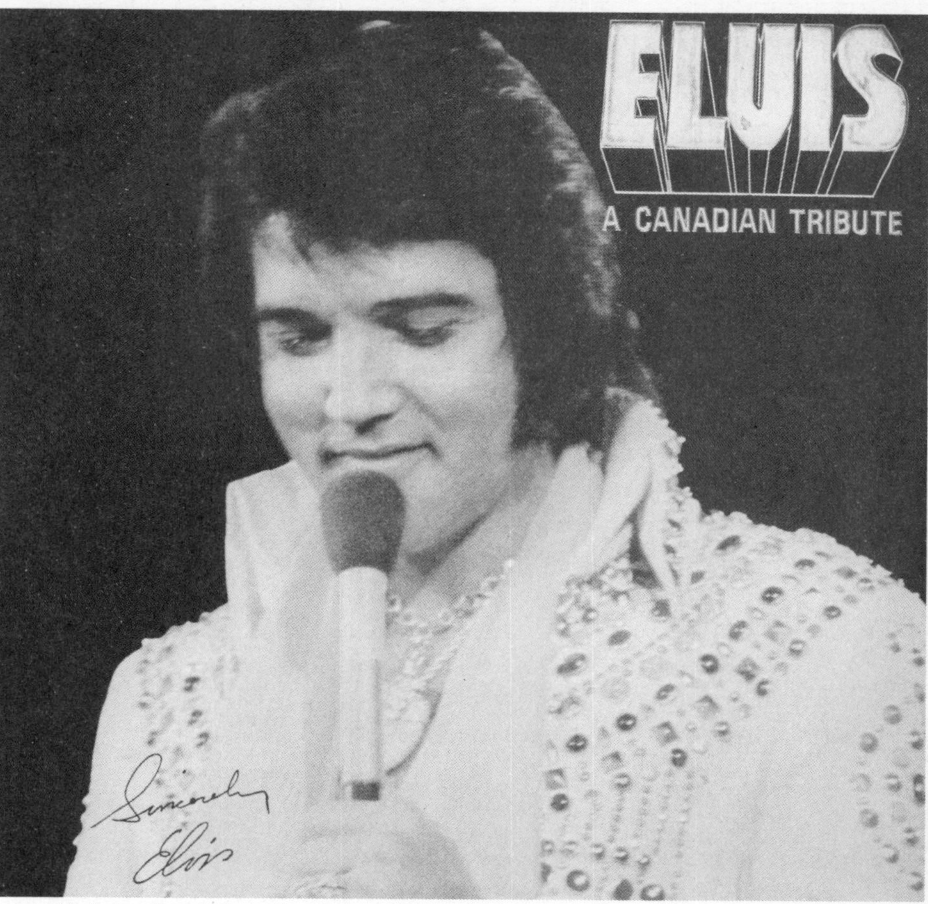


Elvis Presley, *A Canadian Tribute,* RCA Victor KKL1-7065, 1978, gold vinyl, $20.

**Number — Title (A Side/B Side) — Yr — NM**

❑ LSP-2256 [S] G.I. Blues 1968 40.00
—Orange label, non-flexible vinyl
❑ LSP-2256 [S] G.I. Blues 1971 20.00
—Orange label, flexible vinyl
❑ LSP-2256 [S] G.I. Blues 1975 25.00
—Tan label
❑ LSP-2256 [S] G.I. Blues 1976 12.00
—Black label, dog near top
❑ LSP-2256 [S] G.I. Blues 2003 20.00
—Red vinyl; "DRL 13273" in trail-off wax; "BMG Special Products" logo on back cover; from box "Elvis Top Album Collection Volume 2"
❑ AFL1-2274 Welcome to My World 1977 12.00
—Black label, dog near top; includes copies with sticker wrapped around spine with new number
❑ APL1-2274 Welcome to My World 1977 20.00
—Black label, dog near top
❑ AQL1-2274 Welcome to My World 1979 10.00
—Black label, dog near top; includes copies with sticker wrapped around spine with new number
❑ LPM-2328 [M] His Hand in Mine 1960 120.00
—"Long Play" on label
❑ LPM-2328 [M] His Hand in Mine 1963 60.00
—"Mono" on label
❑ LPM-2328 [M] His Hand in Mine 1964 50.00
—"Monaural" on label
❑ LSP-2328 [S] His Hand in Mine 1960 200.00
—"Living Stereo" on label
❑ LSP-2328 [S] His Hand in Mine 1964 100.00
—"Stereo" and white "RCA Victor" on black label
❑ LSP-2328 [S] His Hand in Mine 1964 600.00
—"Stereo" and silver "RCA Victor" on black label
❑ LSP-2328 [S] His Hand in Mine 1968 50.00
—Orange label, non-flexible vinyl
❑ LSP-2328 [S] His Hand in Mine 197? 20.00
—Orange label, flexible vinyl
❑ LSP-2328 [S] His Hand in Mine 1975 20.00
—Tan label
❑ AHL1-2347 Greatest Hits, Volume One 1981 25.00
—With embossed cover
❑ AHL1-2347 Greatest Hits, Volume One 1983 15.00
—Without embossed cover
❑ AFL1-2370 [S] Something for Everybody 1977 12.00
—Black label, dog near top; includes copies with sticker wrapped around spine with new number
❑ LPM-2370 [M] Something for Everybody 1961 120.00
—"Long Play" on label; back cover advertises RCA Compact 33 singles and doubles
❑ LPM-2370 [M] Something for Everybody 1963 80.00
—"Mono" on label; back cover advertises "Viva Las Vegas" EP

**Number — Title (A Side/B Side) — Yr — NM**

❑ LPM-2370 [M] Something for Everybody 1964 50.00
—"Monaural" on label; back cover advertises "Viva Las Vegas" EP
❑ LSP-2370 [S] Something for Everybody 1961 200.00
—"Living Stereo" on label; back cover advertises RCA Compact 33 singles and doubles
❑ LSP-2370 [S] Something for Everybody 1963 100.00
—"Stereo" and silver "RCA Victor" on black label; back cover advertises Elvis' Christmas Album and His Hand in Mine LPs and "Viva Las Vegas" EP
❑ LSP-2370 [S] Something for Everybody 1964 50.00
—"Stereo" and white "RCA Victor" on black label; back cover advertises "Viva Las Vegas" EP
❑ LSP-2370 [S] Something for Everybody 1968 40.00
—Orange label, non-flexible vinyl; final back cover change advertises Elvis (NBC-TV Special), Elvis' Christmas Album and His Hand in Mine LPs
❑ LSP-2370 [S] Something for Everybody 1971 20.00
—Orange label, flexible vinyl
❑ LSP-2370 [S] Something for Everybody 1975 20.00
—Tan label
❑ LSP-2370 [S] Something for Everybody 1976 12.00
—Black label, dog near top
❑ LSP-2370 [S] Something for Everybody 2003 20.00
—Red vinyl; "DRL 13270" in trail-off wax; "BMG Special Products" logo on back cover; from box "Elvis Top Album Collection Volume 1"
❑ AFL1-2426 [S] Blue Hawaii 1977 12.00
—Black label, dog near top; with sticker wrapped around spine with new number
❑ LPM-2426 [M] Blue Hawaii 1961 100.00
—"Long Play" on label; with sticker on cover advertising the presence of "Can't Help Falling in Love" and "Rock-a-Hula Baby"
❑ LPM-2426 [M] Blue Hawaii 1962 60.00
—"Long Play" on label; no sticker on front cover
❑ LPM-2426 [M] Blue Hawaii 1963 50.00
—"Mono" on label
❑ LPM-2426 [M] Blue Hawaii 1964 40.00
—"Monaural" on label
❑ LSP-2426 [S] Blue Hawaii 1961 150.00
—"Living Stereo" on label and upper right front cover; with sticker on cover advertising the presence of "Can't Help Falling in Love" and "Rock-a-Hula Baby"
❑ LSP-2426 [S] Blue Hawaii 1962 80.00
—"Living Stereo" on label and upper right front cover; no sticker on front cover
❑ LSP-2426 [S] Blue Hawaii 1964 50.00
—"Stereo" on label; "Victor Stereo" on upper right front cover
❑ LSP-2426 [S] Blue Hawaii 1968 40.00
—Orange label, non-flexible vinyl

**Number | Title (A Side/B Side) | Yr | NM**

❑ LSP-2426 [S] Blue Hawaii 197? 1000.
*—One-of-a-kind blue vinyl pressing with black label, dog near top*
❑ LSP-2426 [S] Blue Hawaii 1971 20.00
*—Orange label, flexible vinyl*
❑ LSP-2426 [S] Blue Hawaii 1975 20.00
*—Tan label*
❑ LSP-2426 [S] Blue Hawaii 1977 12.00
*—Black label, dog near top*
❑ LSP-2426 [S] Blue Hawaii 2003 20.00
*—Red vinyl; "DRL 13358" in trail-off wax; "BMG Special Products" logo on back cover; from box "Elvis Top Album Collection Volume 1"*
❑ AFK1-2428 Moody Blue 1977 3000.
*—Alternate cover slick (never put on an actual cover), with the words "Moody Blue" inside the large word "Elvis." See any late-1970s Elvis inner sleeve for a black and white photo of the scrapped cover; VG value 1500; VG+ value 2250*
❑ AFL1-2428 Moody Blue 1977 10.00
*—Blue vinyl*
❑ AFL1-2428 Moody Blue 1977 200.00
*—Black vinyl*
❑ AFL1-2428 [DJ]Moody Blue 1977 2000.
*—Experimental colored vinyl pressings (with no cover), any color or combination except blue or black*
❑ AQL1-2428 Moody Blue 1979 25.00
*—Reissue with new prefix*
❑ AFL1-2523 [S] Pot Luck with Elvis 1977 12.00
*—Black label, dog near top; includes copies with sticker wrapped around spine with new number*
❑ LPM-2523 [M] Pot Luck with Elvis 1962 100.00
*—"Long Play" on label*
❑ LPM-2523 [M] Pot Luck with Elvis 1964 120.00
*—"Monaural" on label*
❑ LSP-2523 [S] Pot Luck with Elvis 1962 150.00
*—"Living Stereo" on label*
❑ LSP-2523 [S] Pot Luck with Elvis 1964 60.00
*—"Stereo" on black label*
❑ LSP-2523 [S] Pot Luck with Elvis 1968 40.00
*—Orange label, non-flexible vinyl*
❑ LSP-2523 [S] Pot Luck with Elvis 1975 20.00
*—Tan label*
❑ LSP-2523 [S] Pot Luck with Elvis 1976 12.00
*—Black label, dog near top*
❑ APL1-2558 [S] Harum Scarum 1977 12.00
*—Black label, dog near top .*
❑ APL1-2560 [S] Spinout 1977 12.00
*—Black label, dog near top*
❑ APL1-2564 [S] Double Trouble 1977 12.00
*—Black label, dog near top; includes copies with sticker wrapped around spine with new number*
❑ APL1-2565 Clambake 1977 12.00
❑ APL1-2568 [S] It Happened at the World's Fair 1977 12.00
❑ AFL2-2587 [(2)]Elvis in Concert 197? 1000.
*—Both records on translucent blue vinyl; possibly an in-house demo at the RCA Indianapolis pressing plant*
❑ APL2-2587 [(2)]Elvis in Concert 1977 25.00
❑ APL2-2587 [(2)]Elvis in Concert 2003 20.00
*—Red vinyl; "DRL 13360" in trail-off wax; "This is a replica of the original packaging" on back cover and all inserts; "DRL-23360" on back cover; from box "Elvis Top Album Collection Volume 1"*
❑ CPL2-2587 [(2)]Elvis in Concert 1982 40.00
❑ AFL1-2621 [S] Girls! Girls! Girls! 1977 12.00
*—Black label, dog near top; includes copies with sticker wrapped around spine with new number*
❑ LPM-2621 [M] Girls! Girls! Girls! 1962 80.00
*—"Long Play" on label*
❑ LPM-2621 [M] Girls! Girls! Girls! 1963 60.00
*—"Mono" on label*
❑ LPM-2621 [M] Girls! Girls! Girls! 1964 40.00
*—"Monaural" on label*
❑ LPM/LSP-2621 Girls! Girls! Girls! Bonus 1963 Calendar 1962 150.00
*—With listing of other Elvis records on back*
❑ LSP-2621 [S] Girls! Girls! Girls! 1962 150.00
*—"Living Stereo" on label*
❑ LSP-2621 [S] Girls! Girls! Girls! 1964 60.00
*—"Stereo" on black label*
❑ LSP-2621 [S] Girls! Girls! Girls! 1968 40.00
*—Orange label, non-flexible vinyl*
❑ LSP-2621 [S] Girls! Girls! Girls! 1971 20.00
*—Orange label, flexible vinyl*
❑ LSP-2621 [S] Girls! Girls! Girls! 1975 25.00
*—Tan label*
❑ LSP-2621 [S] Girls! Girls! Girls! 1976 12.00
*—Black label, dog near top*
❑ CPD2-2642 [(2)Q]Aloha from Hawaii Via Satellite 1975 30.00
*—Orange labels*
❑ CPD2-2642 [(2)Q]Aloha from Hawaii Via Satellite 1977 80.00
*—Black labels, dog near top*
❑ CPL2-2642 [(2)Q]Aloha from Hawaii Via Satellite 1984 12.00
*—New prefix; single-pocket instead of gatefold jacket*
❑ CPL2-2642 [(2)S]Aloha from Hawaii Via Satellite 2003 20.00
*—Red vinyl, "DRL 13359" in trail-off wax, "DRL-23359" on back cover, "BMG Special Products" logo on back cover, from box "Elvis Top Album Collection Volume 2"*
❑ LPM-2697 [M] It Happened at the World's Fair 1963 120.00
❑ LPM/LSP-2697 It Happened at the World's Fair Photo 1963 250.00
❑ LSP-2697 [S] It Happened at the World's Fair 1963 200.00
*—"Living Stereo" and silver "RCA Victor" on black label*

**Number | Title (A Side/B Side) | Yr | NM**

❑ LSP-2697 [S] It Happened at the World's Fair 1964 80.00
*—"Stereo" and white "RCA Victor" on black label*
❑ AFL1-2756 [S] Fun in Acapulco 1977 12.00
*—Black label, dog near top; includes copies with sticker wrapped around spine with new number*
❑ LPM-2756 [M] Fun in Acapulco 1963 80.00
*—"Mono" on label*
❑ LPM-2756 [M] Fun in Acapulco 1964 50.00
*—"Monaural" on label*
❑ LSP-2756 [S] Fun in Acapulco 1963 100.00
*—"Stereo" and silver "RCA Victor" on black label*
❑ LSP-2756 [S] Fun in Acapulco 1964 60.00
*—"Stereo" and white "RCA Victor" on black label*
❑ LSP-2756 [S] Fun in Acapulco 1968 40.00
*—Orange label, non-flexible vinyl*
❑ LSP-2756 [S] Fun in Acapulco 1975 25.00
*—Tan label*
❑ LSP-2756 [S] Fun in Acapulco 1976 12.00
*—Black label, dog near top*
❑ AFL1-2765 [S] Elvis' Golden Records, Volume 3 1977 12.00
*—Black label, dog near top; includes copies with sticker wrapped around spine with new number*
❑ LPM-2765 [M] Elvis' Golden Records, Volume 3 1963 100.00
*—"Mono" on label*
❑ LPM-2765 [M] Elvis' Golden Records, Volume 3 1964 60.00
*—"Monaural" on label*
❑ LSP-2765 [S] Elvis' Golden Records, Volume 3 1963 150.00
*—"Stereo" and silver "RCA Victor" on black label*
❑ LSP-2765 [S] Elvis' Golden Records, Volume 3 1964 50.00
*—"Stereo" and white "RCA Victor" on black label*
❑ LSP-2765 [S] Elvis' Golden Records, Volume 3 1968 40.00
*—Orange label, non-flexible vinyl*
❑ LSP-2765 [S] Elvis' Golden Records, Volume 3 1975 20.00
*—Tan label*
❑ LSP-2765 [S] Elvis' Golden Records, Volume 3 1976 12.00
*—Black label, dog near top*
❑ AFL1-2772 He Walks Beside Me 1978 25.00
*—Includes 20-page photo booklet*
❑ AFL1-2894 [S] Kissin' Cousins 1977 12.00
*—Black label, dog near top; includes copies with sticker wrapped around spine with new number*
❑ LPM-2894 [M] Kissin' Cousins 1964 80.00
*—"Mono" on label; front cover has a small black and white photo of six cast members in lower right*
❑ LPM-2894 [M] Kissin' Cousins 1964 100.00
*—"Monaural" on label; front cover has a small black and white photo of six cast members in lower right*
❑ LPM-2894 [M] Kissin' Cousins 1964 200.00
*—"Monaural" on label; front cover does NOT have black and white photo in lower right*
❑ LPM-2894 [M] Kissin' Cousins 1964 200.00
*—"Mono" on label; front cover does NOT have black and white photo in lower right*
❑ LSP-2894 [S] Kissin' Cousins 1964 60.00
*—"Stereo" and white "RCA Victor" on black label; all front covers have the cast photo in lower right*
❑ LSP-2894 [S] Kissin' Cousins 1964 120.00
*—"Stereo" and silver "RCA Victor" on black label; front cover has a small black and white photo of six cast members in lower right*
❑ LSP-2894 [S] Kissin' Cousins 1964 200.00
*—"Stereo" and silver "RCA Victor" on black label; front cover does NOT have black and white photo in lower right*
❑ LSP-2894 [S] Kissin' Cousins 1968 40.00
*—Orange label, non-flexible vinyl*
❑ LSP-2894 [S] Kissin' Cousins 1971 20.00
*—Orange label, flexible vinyl*
❑ LSP-2894 [S] Kissin' Cousins 1975 25.00
*—Tan label*
❑ LSP-2894 [S] Kissin' Cousins 1976 12.00
*—Black label, dog near top*
❑ LSP-2894 [S] Kissin' Cousins 1976 1500.
*—Black label, dog near top; blue vinyl*
❑ CPL1-2901 Elvis Sings for Children and Grownups Too! 1978 10.00
*—With greeting card graphic printed on back cover, and no slits on back cover*
❑ CPL1-2901 Elvis Sings for Children and Grownups Too! 1978 20.00
*—With two slits for removable greeting card on back cover (card should be with package)*
❑ AFL1-2999 [S] Roustabout 1977 12.00
*—Black label, dog near top; includes copies with sticker wrapped around spine with new number*
❑ LPM-2999 [M] Roustabout 1964 100.00
*—"Mono" on label*
❑ LPM-2999 [M] Roustabout 1965 60.00
*—"Monaural" on label*
❑ LSP-2999 [S] Roustabout 1964 60.00
*—"Stereo" and white "RCA Victor" on black label*
❑ LSP-2999 [S] Roustabout 1964 600.00
*—"Stereo" and silver "RCA Victor" on black label*
❑ LSP-2999 [S] Roustabout 1968 40.00
*—Orange label, non-flexible vinyl*
❑ LSP-2999 [S] Roustabout 1971 20.00
*—Orange label, flexible vinyl*
❑ LSP-2999 [S] Roustabout 1975 20.00
*—Tan label*
❑ LSP-2999 [S] Roustabout 1976 12.00
*—Black label, dog near top*
❑ LSP-2999 [S] Roustabout 2003 20.00
*—Red vinyl, "DRL 13269" in trail-off wax; "BMG Special Products" logo on back cover; from box "Elvis Top Album Collection Volume 2"*

**Number | Title (A Side/B Side) | Yr | NM**

❑ CPL1-3078 [PD]A Legendary Performer, Volume 3 1978 25.00
*—Picture disc applied to blue vinyl LP; with booklet (deduct 40% if missing)*
❑ CPL1-3082 A Legendary Performer, Volume 3 1978 25.00
*—Includes booklet (deduct 40% if missing); with die-cut hole in front cover*
❑ CPL1-3082 A Legendary Performer, Volume 3 1986 8.00
*—No die-cut hole in cover and no booklet*
❑ AQL1-3279 Our Memories of Elvis 1979 20.00
❑ AFL1-3338 [S] Girl Happy 1977 12.00
*—Black label, dog near top; includes copies with sticker wrapped around spine with new number*
❑ LPM-3338 [M] Girl Happy 1965 60.00
❑ LSP-3338 [S] Girl Happy 1965 60.00
*—"Stereo" on black label*
❑ LSP-3338 [S] Girl Happy 1968 40.00
*—Orange label, non-flexible vinyl*
❑ LSP-3338 [S] Girl Happy 1971 20.00
*—Orange label, flexible vinyl*
❑ LSP-3338 [S] Girl Happy 1975 25.00
*—Tan label*
❑ LSP-3338 [S] Girl Happy 1976 12.00
*—Black label, dog near top*
❑ AQL1-3448 Our Memories of Elvis, Volume 2 1979 20.00
❑ AFL1-3450 [P] Elvis for Everyone 1977 12.00
*—Black label, dog near top; includes copies with sticker wrapped around spine with new number*
❑ LPM-3450 [M] Elvis for Everyone 1965 60.00
❑ LSP-3450 [P] Elvis for Everyone 1965 60.00
*—Black label, "Stereo" on label*
❑ LSP-3450 [P] Elvis for Everyone 1968 40.00
*—Orange label, non-flexible vinyl*
❑ LSP-3450 [P] Elvis for Everyone 1971 20.00
*—Orange label, flexible vinyl*
❑ LSP-3450 [P] Elvis for Everyone 1975 20.00
*—Tan label*
❑ LSP-3450 [P] Elvis for Everyone 1976 12.00
*—Black label, dog near top*
❑ DJL1-3455 [DJ]Pure Elvis 1979 600.00
*—Promo-only item for Our Memories of Elvis, Volume 2; contains original version of five songs on one side, "unsweetened" versions of same songs on the other*
❑ LPM-3468 [M] Harum Scarum 1965 60.00
❑ LPM/LSP-3468 Harum Scarum Bonus Photo 1965 60.00
❑ LSP-3468 [S] Harum Scarum 1965 60.00
*—"Stereo" on black label*
❑ LPM-3553 [M] Frankie and Johnny 1966 60.00
❑ LPM/LSP-3553 Frankie and Johnny Bonus Print 1966 60.00
❑ LSP-3553 [S] Frankie and Johnny 1966 60.00
*—"Stereo" on black label*
❑ AFL1-3643 [S] Paradise, Hawaiian Style 1977 12.00
*—Black label, dog near top; includes copies with sticker wrapped around spine with new number*
❑ LPM-3643 [M] Paradise, Hawaiian Style 1966 60.00
❑ LSP-3643 [S] Paradise, Hawaiian Style 1966 60.00
*—"Stereo" on black label*
❑ LSP-3643 [S] Paradise, Hawaiian Style 1968 40.00
*—Orange label, non-flexible vinyl*
❑ LSP-3643 [S] Paradise, Hawaiian Style 1971 20.00
*—Orange label, flexible vinyl*
❑ LSP-3643 [S] Paradise, Hawaiian Style 1975 15.00
*—Tan label*
❑ LSP-3643 [S] Paradise, Hawaiian Style 1976 12.00
*—Black label, dog near top*
❑ AYL1-3683 [S] Blue Hawaii 1980 10.00
*—"Best Buy Series" reissue*
❑ AYL1-3684 [S] Spinout 1980 8.00
*—"Best Buy Series" reissue*
❑ CPL8-3699 [(8)]Elvis Aron Presley 1980 100.00
*—Box set; regular issue with booklet*
❑ CPL8-3699 [(8)]Elvis Aron Presley 1980 250.00
*—Box set; "Reviewer Series" edition (will be identified as such on the cover)*
❑ LPM-3702 [M] Spinout 1966 60.00
❑ LPM/LSP-3702 Spinout Bonus Photo 1966 60.00
❑ LSP-3702 [S] Spinout 1966 60.00
*—"Stereo" on black label*
❑ DJL1-3729 [DJ]Elvis Aron Presley (Excerpts) 1980 120.00
*—Promo-only excerpts of songs from box set*
❑ AYL1-3732 Pure Gold 1980 8.00
*—"Best Buy Series" reissue*
❑ AYL1-3733 [R] King Creole 1980 8.00
*—"Best Buy Series" reissue; includes copies with sticker wrapped around spine with new number*
❑ AYL1-3734 [S] Harum Scarum 1980 8.00
*—"Best Buy Series" reissue*
❑ AYL1-3735 [S] G.I. Blues 1980 8.00
*—"Best Buy Series" reissue*
❑ AFL1-3758 [S] How Great Thou Art 1977 12.00
*—Black label, dog near top; includes copies with sticker wrapped around spine with new number*
❑ AQL1-3758 [S] How Great Thou Art 1979 10.00
*—Reissue with new prefix*
❑ LPM-3758 [M] How Great Thou Art 1967 60.00
*—"Mono Dynagroove" on label*
❑ LSP-3758 [S] How Great Thou Art 1967 60.00
*—"Stereo Dynagroove" on black label*
❑ LSP-3758 [S] How Great Thou Art 1968 40.00
*—Orange label, non-flexible vinyl*

**Except when noted otherwise, VG = 25% of NM, and VG+ = 50% of NM. (Example: VG = $2.00, VG+ = $4.00 and NM = $8.00.)**

| Number | Title (A Side/B Side) | Yr | NM |
|---|---|---|---|
| ❑ LSP-3758 [S] | How Great Thou Art | 1971 | 25.00 |
| *—Orange label, flexible vinyl* | | | |
| ❑ LSP-3758 [S] | How Great Thou Art | 1975 | 20.00 |
| *—Tan label* | | | |
| ❑ LSP-3758 [S] | How Great Thou Art | 1976 | 12.00 |
| *—Black label, dog near top* | | | |
| ❑ DJL1-3781 [DJ] | Elvis Aron Presley (Selections) | 1980 | 120.00 |
| *—Promo-only complete versions of songs from box set* | | | |
| ❑ LPM-3787 [M] | Double Trouble | 1967 | 60.00 |
| *—With bonus photo announcement on cover* | | | |
| ❑ LPM-3787 [M] | Double Trouble | 1967 | 80.00 |
| *—With no bonus photo announcement on cover* | | | |
| ❑ LPM/LSP-3787 | Double Trouble Bonus Photo | 1967 | 50.00 |
| ❑ LSP-3787 [S] | Double Trouble | 1967 | 60.00 |
| *—With bonus photo announcement on cover* | | | |
| ❑ LSP-3787 [S] | Double Trouble | 1967 | 70.00 |
| *—With no bonus photo announcement on cover; black label "Stereo"* | | | |
| ❑ LSP-3787 [S] | Double Trouble | 1968 | 40.00 |
| *—Orange label, non-flexible vinyl* | | | |
| ❑ LSP-3787 [S] | Double Trouble | 1975 | 20.00 |
| *—Tan label* | | | |
| ❑ LSP-3787 [S] | Double Trouble | 1977 | 12.00 |
| *—Black label, dog near top* | | | |
| ❑ AYL1-3892 | Elvis in Person at the International Hotel, Las Vegas, Nevada | 1981 | 8.00 |
| *—"Best Buy Series" reissue* | | | |
| ❑ AYM1-3893 | The Sun Sessions | 1981 | 8.00 |
| *—"Best Buy Series" reissue; includes copies with sticker wrapped around spine with new number* | | | |
| ❑ LPM-3893 [M] | Clambake | 1967 | 250.00 |
| ❑ LPM/LSP-3893 | Clambake Bonus Photo | 1967 | 50.00 |
| ❑ LSP-3893 [S] | Clambake | 1967 | 60.00 |
| ❑ AYM1-3894 | Elvis (NBC-TV Special) | 1981 | 8.00 |
| *—"Best Buy Series" reissue* | | | |
| ❑ AAL1-3917 | Guitar Man | 1981 | 30.00 |
| ❑ AFL1-3921 [P] | Elvis' Gold Records, Volume 4 | 1976 | 15.00 |
| *—Tan label with new prefix* | | | |
| ❑ AFL1-3921 [P] | Elvis' Gold Records, Volume 4 | 1977 | 12.00 |
| *—Black label, dog near top; includes copies with sticker wrapped around spine with new number* | | | |
| ❑ LPM-3921 [M] | Elvis' Gold Records, Volume 4 | 1968 | 2000. |
| *—"Monaural" on label* | | | |
| ❑ LSP-3921 [P] | Elvis' Gold Records, Volume 4 | 1968 | 40.00 |
| *—Orange label, non-flexible vinyl* | | | |
| ❑ LSP-3921 [P] | Elvis' Gold Records, Volume 4 | 1968 | 50.00 |
| *—"Stereo" and white "RCA Victor" on black label* | | | |
| ❑ LSP-3921 [P] | Elvis' Gold Records, Volume 4 | 197? | 20.00 |
| *—Orange label, flexible vinyl* | | | |
| ❑ LSP-3921 [P] | Elvis' Gold Records, Volume 4 | 1975 | 25.00 |
| *—Tan label* | | | |
| ❑ LSP-3921 [P] | Elvis' Gold Records, Volume 4 | 1976 | 12.00 |
| *—Black label, dog near top* | | | |
| ❑ AYL1-3935 [S] | His Hand in Mine | 1981 | 8.00 |
| *—"Best Buy Series" reissue; includes copies with sticker wrapped around spine with new number* | | | |
| ❑ AYL1-3956 | Elvis Country ("I'm 10,000 Years Old") | 1981 | 8.00 |
| *—"Best Buy Series" reissue* | | | |
| ❑ AFL1-3989 [S] | Speedway | 1977 | 12.00 |
| *—Black label, dog near top; includes copies with sticker wrapped around spine with new number* | | | |
| ❑ LPM-3989 [M] | Speedway | 1968 | 2000. |
| ❑ LPM/LSP-3989 | Speedway Bonus Photo | 1968 | 50.00 |
| ❑ LSP-3989 [S] | Speedway | 1968 | 40.00 |
| *—Orange label, non-flexible vinyl* | | | |
| ❑ LSP-3989 [S] | Speedway | 1968 | 60.00 |
| *—"Stereo" on black label* | | | |
| ❑ LSP-3989 [S] | Speedway | 1971 | 20.00 |
| *—Orange label, flexible vinyl* | | | |
| ❑ LSP-3989 [S] | Speedway | 1975 | 20.00 |
| *—Tan label* | | | |
| ❑ LSP-3989 [S] | Speedway | 1976 | 12.00 |
| *—Black label, dog near top* | | | |
| ❑ CPL2-4031 [(2)] | This Is Elvis | 1980 | 15.00 |
| ❑ AFM1-4088 | Elvis (NBC-TV Special) | 1977 | 12.00 |
| *—Black label, dog near top; includes copies with sticker wrapped around spine with new number* | | | |
| ❑ LPM-4088 | Elvis (NBC-TV Special) | 1968 | 40.00 |
| *—Orange label, non-flexible vinyl* | | | |
| ❑ LPM-4088 | Elvis (NBC-TV Special) | 1971 | 30.00 |
| *—Orange label, flexible vinyl* | | | |
| ❑ LPM-4088 | Elvis (NBC-TV Special) | 1975 | 20.00 |
| *—Tan label* | | | |
| ❑ LPM-4088 | Elvis (NBC-TV Special) | 1976 | 15.00 |
| *—Black label, dog near top* | | | |
| ❑ AYL1-4114 | That's the Way It Is | 1981 | 8.00 |
| *—"Best Buy Series" reissue; includes copies with sticker wrapped around spine with new number* | | | |
| ❑ AYL1-4115 [S] | Kissin' Cousins | 1981 | 8.00 |
| *—"Best Buy Series" reissue; includes copies with sticker wrapped around spine with new number* | | | |
| ❑ AYL1-4116 [S] | Something for Everybody | 1981 | 8.00 |
| *—"Best Buy Series" reissue; includes copies with sticker wrapped around spine with new number* | | | |
| ❑ AFL1-4155 | From Elvis in Memphis | 1977 | 12.00 |
| *—Black label, dog near top; includes copies with sticker wrapped around spine with new number* | | | |
| ❑ LSP-4155 | From Elvis in Memphis | 1969 | 40.00 |
| *—Orange label, non-flexible vinyl* | | | |
| ❑ LSP-4155 | From Elvis in Memphis Bonus Photo | 1969 | 40.00 |
| ❑ LSP-4155 | From Elvis in Memphis | 1971 | 30.00 |
| *—Orange label, flexible vinyl* | | | |
| ❑ LSP-4155 | From Elvis in Memphis | 1975 | 25.00 |
| *—Tan label* | | | |
| ❑ LSP-4155 | From Elvis in Memphis | 1976 | 15.00 |
| *—Black label, dog near top* | | | |
| ❑ AYL1-4232 [P] | Elvis for Everyone | 1982 | 8.00 |
| *—"Best Buy Series" reissue* | | | |
| ❑ AFL1-4362 | On Stage February, 1970 | 1977 | 12.00 |
| *—Black label, dog near top; includes copies with sticker wrapped around spine with new number* | | | |
| ❑ AQL1-4362 | On Stage February, 1970 | 1983 | 8.00 |
| *—Reissue with some cover changes* | | | |
| ❑ LSP-4362 | On Stage February, 1970 | 1970 | 40.00 |
| *—Orange label, non-flexible vinyl* | | | |
| ❑ LSP-4362 | On Stage February, 1970 | 1971 | 25.00 |
| *—Orange label, flexible vinyl* | | | |
| ❑ LSP-4362 | On Stage February, 1970 | 1975 | 25.00 |
| *—Tan label* | | | |
| ❑ LSP-4362 | On Stage February, 1970 | 1976 | 30.00 |
| *—Black label, dog near top* | | | |
| ❑ CPL1-4395 | Memories of Christmas | 1982 | 15.00 |
| *—With greeting card (deduct 1/3 if missing)* | | | |
| ❑ AFL1-4428 | Elvis in Person at the International Hotel, Las Vegas, Nevada | 1977 | 12.00 |
| *—Black label, dog near top; includes copies with sticker wrapped around spine with new number* | | | |
| ❑ LSP-4428 | Elvis in Person at the International Hotel, Las Vegas, Nevada | 1970 | 50.00 |
| *—Orange label, non-flexible vinyl* | | | |
| ❑ LSP-4428 | Elvis in Person at the International Hotel, Las Vegas, Nevada | 1971 | 40.00 |
| *—Orange label, flexible vinyl* | | | |
| ❑ LSP-4428 | Elvis in Person at the International Hotel, Las Vegas, Nevada | 1975 | 25.00 |
| *—Tan label* | | | |
| ❑ LSP-4428 | Elvis in Person at the International Hotel, Las Vegas, Nevada | 1976 | 15.00 |
| *—Black label, dog near top* | | | |
| ❑ AFL1-4429 | Back in Memphis | 1977 | 12.00 |
| *—Black label, dog near top; with sticker wrapped around spine with new number* | | | |
| ❑ LSP-4429 | Back in Memphis | 1970 | 40.00 |
| *—Orange label, non-flexible vinyl* | | | |
| ❑ LSP-4429 | Back in Memphis | 1971 | 30.00 |
| *—Orange label, flexible vinyl* | | | |
| ❑ LSP-4429 | Back in Memphis | 1975 | 25.00 |
| *—Tan label* | | | |
| ❑ LSP-4429 | Back in Memphis | 1977 | 15.00 |
| *—Black label, dog near top* | | | |
| ❑ AFL1-4445 | That's the Way It Is | 1977 | 12.00 |
| *—Black label, dog near top; includes copies with sticker wrapped around spine with new number* | | | |
| ❑ LSP-4445 | That's the Way It Is | 1970 | 80.00 |
| *—Orange label, non-flexible vinyl* | | | |
| ❑ LSP-4445 | That's the Way It Is | 1971 | 25.00 |
| *—Orange label, flexible vinyl* | | | |
| ❑ LSP-4445 | That's the Way It Is | 1975 | 20.00 |
| *—Tan label* | | | |
| ❑ LSP-4445 | That's the Way It Is | 1976 | 15.00 |
| *—Black label, dog near top* | | | |
| ❑ AFL1-4460 | Elvis Country ("I'm 10,000 Years Old") | 1977 | 12.00 |
| *—Black label, dog near top; includes copies with sticker wrapped around spine with new number* | | | |
| ❑ LSP-4460 | Elvis Country ("I'm 10,000 Years Old") | 197? | 2000. |
| *—Green vinyl; black label, dog near top* | | | |
| ❑ LSP-4460 | Elvis Country ("I'm 10,000 Years Old") Bonus Photo | 1971 | 15.00 |
| *—Available in either orange-label pressing* | | | |
| ❑ LSP-4460 | Elvis Country ("I'm 10,000 Years Old") | 1971 | 25.00 |
| *—Orange label, flexible vinyl* | | | |
| ❑ LSP-4460 | Elvis Country ("I'm 10,000 Years Old") | 1971 | 40.00 |
| *—Orange label, non-flexible vinyl* | | | |
| ❑ LSP-4460 | Elvis Country ("I'm 10,000 Years Old") | 1975 | 25.00 |
| *—Tan label* | | | |
| ❑ LSP-4460 | Elvis Country ("I'm 10,000 Years Old") | 1976 | 15.00 |
| *—Black label, dog near top* | | | |
| ❑ AFL1-4530 | Love Letters from Elvis | 1977 | 12.00 |
| *—Black label, dog near top; includes copies with sticker wrapped around spine with new number* | | | |
| ❑ AHL1-4530 | The Elvis Medley | 1982 | 12.00 |
| ❑ LSP-4530 | Love Letters from Elvis | 1971 | 30.00 |
| *—Orange label; "Love Letters" on one line of cover; "from" on a second line, "Elvis" on a third line* | | | |
| ❑ LSP-4530 | Love Letters from Elvis | 1971 | 40.00 |
| *—Orange label; "Love Letters from" on one line of cover, "Elvis" on a second line* | | | |
| ❑ LSP-4530 | Love Letters from Elvis | 1975 | 25.00 |
| *—Tan label; "Love Letters" on one line of cover; "from" on a second line, "Elvis" on a third line* | | | |
| ❑ LSP-4530 | Love Letters from Elvis | 1975 | 30.00 |
| *—Tan label; "Love Letters from" on one line of cover, "Elvis" on a second line* | | | |
| ❑ LSP-4530 | Love Letters from Elvis | 1976 | 20.00 |
| *—Black label, dog near top* | | | |
| ❑ LSP-4579 | Elvis Sings the Wonderful World of Christmas Postcard | 1971 | 20.00 |
| ❑ LSP-4579 | Elvis Sings the Wonderful World of Christmas | 1971 | 30.00 |
| *—Orange label. Bonus postcard is priced separately* | | | |
| ❑ AFL1-4671 | Elvis Now | 1977 | 12.00 |
| *—Black label, dog near top; includes copies with sticker wrapped around spine with new number* | | | |
| ❑ LSP-4671 | Elvis Now | 1972 | 30.00 |
| *—Orange label* | | | |
| ❑ LSP-4671 | Elvis Now | 1975 | 25.00 |
| *—Tan label* | | | |
| ❑ LSP-4671 | Elvis Now | 1976 | 15.00 |
| *—Black label, dog near top* | | | |
| ❑ LSP-4671 [DJ] | Elvis Now | 1972 | 100.00 |
| *—Orange label; with white timing sticker on front cover* | | | |
| ❑ AHL1-4678 | I Was the One | 1983 | 10.00 |
| ❑ AFL1-4690 | He Touched Me | 1977 | 12.00 |
| *—Black label, dog near top; includes copies with sticker wrapped around spine with new number* | | | |
| ❑ LSP-4690 | He Touched Me | 1972 | 40.00 |
| *—Orange label* | | | |
| ❑ LSP-4690 | He Touched Me | 1975 | 20.00 |
| *—Tan label* | | | |
| ❑ LSP-4690 | He Touched Me | 1976 | 15.00 |
| *—Black label, dog near top* | | | |
| ❑ LSP-4690 [DJ] | He Touched Me | 1972 | 100.00 |
| *—Orange label; with white timing sticker on front cover* | | | |
| ❑ AFL1-4776 | Elvis As Recorded at Madison Square Garden | 1977 | 12.00 |
| *—Black label, dog near top; includes copies with sticker wrapped around spine with new number* | | | |
| ❑ AQL1-4776 | Elvis As Recorded at Madison Square Garden | 1980 | 8.00 |
| *—Another reissue with new prefix* | | | |
| ❑ LSP-4776 | Elvis As Recorded at Madison Square Garden | 1972 | 30.00 |
| *—Orange label* | | | |
| ❑ LSP-4776 | Elvis As Recorded at Madison Square Garden | 1975 | 20.00 |
| *—Tan label* | | | |
| ❑ LSP-4776 | Elvis As Recorded at Madison Square Garden | 1976 | 15.00 |
| *—Black label, dog near top* | | | |
| ❑ LSP-4776 [DJ] | Elvis As Recorded at Madison Square Garden | 1972 | 100.00 |
| *—Orange label; with white timing sticker on front cover* | | | |
| ❑ CPL1-4848 | A Legendary Performer, Volume 4 | 1983 | 30.00 |
| *—Includes booklet (deduct 40% if missing); with die-cut hole in front cover* | | | |
| ❑ CPL1-4848 | A Legendary Performer, Volume 4 | 1986 | 20.00 |
| *—No die-cut hole in cover* | | | |
| ❑ AFL1-4941 | Elvis' Gold Records, Volume 5 | 1984 | 10.00 |
| ❑ CPM6-5172 [(6)] | A Golden Celebration | 1984 | 100.00 |
| ❑ AFM1-5182 | Rocker | 1984 | 20.00 |
| ❑ AFM1-5196 [M] | Elvis' Golden Records | 1984 | 20.00 |
| *—50th Anniversary reissue in mono with banner* | | | |
| ❑ AFM1-5197 [M] | Elvis' Gold Records Volume 2 — 50,000,000 Elvis Fans Can't Be Wrong | 1984 | 20.00 |
| *—50th Anniversary reissue in mono with banner* | | | |
| ❑ AFM1-5198 [M] | Elvis Presley | 1984 | 20.00 |
| *—50th Anniversary reissue in mono with banner* | | | |
| ❑ AFM1-5199 [M] | Elvis | 1984 | 20.00 |
| *—50th Anniversary reissue in mono with banner* | | | |
| ❑ AFL1-5353 | A Valentine Gift for You | 1985 | 10.00 |
| *—Black vinyl* | | | |
| ❑ AFL1-5353 | A Valentine Gift for You | 1985 | 20.00 |
| *—Red vinyl* | | | |
| ❑ AFL1-5418 | Reconsider Baby | 1985 | 20.00 |
| *—All copies on blue vinyl* | | | |
| ❑ AFL1-5430 | Always on My Mind | 1985 | 20.00 |
| *—All copies on purple vinyl* | | | |
| ❑ AFM1-5486 [M] | Elvis' Christmas Album | 1985 | 15.00 |
| *—Same as LOC-1035; black vinyl with booklet* | | | |
| ❑ AFM1-5486 [M] | Elvis' Christmas Album | 1985 | 20.00 |
| *—Same as LOC-1035; green vinyl with booklet* | | | |
| ❑ UNRM-5697/8 [DJ] | Special Christmas Programming | 1967 | 1200. |
| *—White label promo. Add 25% for script.* | | | |
| ❑ LSP-6020 | From Memphis to Vegas/From Vegas to Memphis Bonus Photos | 1969 | 50.00 |
| *—Four different photos came with LP, but no more than two per set. Value is for any two different of the four photos.* | | | |
| ❑ LSP-6020 [(2)] | From Memphis to Vegas/From Vegas to Memphis | 1969 | 100.00 |
| *—Orange labels, non-flexible vinyl; with composers of "Words" correctly listed as Barry, Robin and Maurice Gibb* | | | |
| ❑ LSP-6020 [(2)] | From Memphis to Vegas/From Vegas to Memphis | 1969 | 150.00 |
| *—Orange labels, non-flexible vinyl; with composers of "Words" incorrectly listed as Tommy Boyce and Bobby Hart* | | | |
| ❑ LSP-6020 [(2)] | From Memphis to Vegas/From Vegas to Memphis | 1971 | 40.00 |
| *—Orange labels, flexible vinyl* | | | |
| ❑ LSP-6020 [(2)] | From Memphis to Vegas/From Vegas to Memphis Bonus Photos | 1975 | 30.00 |
| *—Tan labels* | | | |

Number | Title (A Side/B Side) | Yr | NM

❑ LSP-6020 [(2)] From Memphis to Vegas/From Vegas to Memphis Bonus Photos 1976 20.00
*—Black label, dog near top*
❑ VPSX-6089 [(2)DJ]Aloha from Hawaii Via Satellite 1973 2000.
*—Orange or dark orange label; with white timing sticker on front cover*
❑ VPSX-6089 [(2)Q]Aloha from Hawaii Via Satellite 1973 40.00
*—Lighter orange labels, "RCA" on side*
❑ VPSX-6089 [(2)Q]Aloha from Hawaii Via Satellite 1973 100.00
*—Dark orange labels, "QuadraDisc" on top, "RCA" on bottom*
❑ VPSX-6089 [(2)Q]Aloha from Hawaii Via Satellite 1973 5000.
*—Stokely-Van Camp employee version with Saturn-shaped sticker on front cover with "Chicken of the Sea" and mermaid (beware: this has been counterfeited); VG value 2500; VG+ value 3750*
❑ LPM-6401 Worldwide 50 Gold Award Hits, Vol. 1 Photo Book 1970 40.00
*—Two different books have been found in this LP box; price is for either*
❑ LPM-6401 [(4)] Worldwide 50 Gold Award Hits, Vol. 1 1970 80.00
*—Orange labels, non-flexible vinyl; with blurb for photo book on cover*
❑ LPM-6401 [(4)] Worldwide 50 Gold Award Hits, Vol. 1 1970 80.00
*—Orange labels, flexible vinyl; with blurb for photo book on cover*
❑ LPM-6401 [(4)] Worldwide 50 Gold Award Hits, Vol. 1 1975 40.00
*—Tan labels*
❑ LPM-6401 [(4)] Worldwide 50 Gold Award Hits, Vol. 1 1977 30.00
*—Black labels, dog near top*
❑ LPM-6402 The Other Sides: Worldwide 50 Gold Award Hits, Vol. 2 Poster 1971 25.00
❑ LPM-6402 The Other Sides: Worldwide 50 Gold Award Hits, Vol. 2 Swatch and Envelope 1971 25.00
❑ LPM-6402 [(4)] The Other Sides: Worldwide 50 Gold Award Hits, Vol. 2 1971 70.00
*—Orange labels, flexible vinyl; with blurb for inserts on cover*
❑ LPM-6402 [(4)] The Other Sides: Worldwide 50 Gold Award Hits, Vol. 2 1975 30.00
*—Tan labels*
❑ LPM-6402 [(4)] The Other Sides: Worldwide 50 Gold Award Hits, Vol. 2 1977 20.00
*—Black labels, dog near top*
❑ KKL1-7065 A Canadian Tribute 1978 20.00
*—Gold vinyl, embossed cover*
❑ R 213690 [(2)] Worldwide Gold Award Hits, Parts 1 & 2 1974 40.00
*—RCA Record Club version; tan labels*
❑ R 213690 [(2)] Worldwide Gold Award Hits, Parts 1 & 2 1974 120.00
*—RCA Record Club version; one label is orange, the other is tan (orange label on both records is unknown)*
❑ R 213690 [(2)] Worldwide Gold Award Hits, Parts 1 & 2 1977 25.00
*—RCA Record Club version; black labels, dog near top*
❑ R 213736 [(2)S]Aloha from Hawaii Via Satellite 1973 70.00
*—RCA Record Club edition in stereo instead of quadraphonic; orange labels*
❑ R 213736 [(2)S]Aloha from Hawaii Via Satellite 1975 60.00
*—RCA Record Club edition in stereo instead of quadraphonic; tan labels*
❑ R 213736 [(2)S]Aloha from Hawaii Via Satellite 1977 30.00
*—RCA Record Club edition in stereo instead of quadraphonic; black labels, dog near top*
❑ R 214657 [(2)] Worldwide Gold Award Hits, Parts 3 & 4 1978 20.00
*—RCA Record Club version; black labels, dog near top*
❑ R 233299(e) [(2)]Country Classics 1980 40.00
*—RCA Music Service exclusive*
❑ R 234340 [(2)] From Elvis with Love 1978 40.00
*—RCA Music Service exclusive*
❑ R 244047 [(2)] The Legendary Concert Performances 1978 40.00
*—RCA Music Service exclusive*
❑ R 244069 [(2)] Country Memories 1978 40.00
*—RCA Music Service exclusive*

READER'S DIGEST
❑ 010/A [(7)] His Greatest Hits 1983 60.00
*—Yellow box*
❑ 010/A [(7)] His Greatest Hits 1990 40.00
*—White box*
❑ RD-10/A [(8)] His Greatest Hits 1979 400.00
*—White box*
❑ RBA-072/D Great Hits of 1956-57 1987 20.00
❑ RD4A-181/D Elvis Sings Inspirational Favorites 1983 20.00
❑ RB4-191/A [(7)]The Legend Lives On 1986 60.00
❑ RDA-242/D Elvis Sings Country Favorites 1984 60.00

SHOW-LAND
❑ LP-2001 The First of Elvis 1979 100.00

SILHOUETTE
❑ 10001/2 [(2)] Personally Elvis 1979 30.00
*—Interview records; no music*

Number | Title (A Side/B Side) | Yr | NM

SUN
❑ 1001 The Sun Years — Interviews and Memories 1977 8.00
*—With "Nashville, U.S.A." on label; white cover with brown print*
❑ 1001 The Sun Years — Interviews and Memories 1977 15.00
*—With "Nashville, U.S.A." on label; dark yellow cover with brown print*
❑ 1001 The Sun Years — Interviews and Memories 1977 25.00
*—With "Memphis, Tennessee" on label*

TIME-LIFE
❑ STL-106 [(2)] Elvis Presley: 1954-1961 1986 30.00
❑ STW-106 Country Music 1981 20.00
❑ STL-126 [(2)] Elvis the King: 1954-1965 1989 80.00

**PRESNELL, HARVE**

MGM
❑ E-4194 [M] The World's Greatest Love Songs 1964 20.00
❑ SE-4194 [S] The World's Greatest Love Songs 1964 25.00
❑ E-4266 [M] New Echoes of the Old West 1965 20.00
❑ SE-4266 [S] New Echoes of the Old West 1965 25.00

**PRESTI, IDA, AND ALEXANDRE LAGOYA**

MERCURY LIVING PRESENCE
❑ SR 90380 [S] Four Concertos for Two Guitars by Vivaldi 196? 30.00
*—Maroon label, no "Vendor: Mercury Record Corporation"*
❑ SR 90427 [S] Spanish Music for Two Guitars 196? 30.00
*—Maroon label, no "Vendor: Mercury Record Corporation"*
❑ SR 90457 [S] Baroque Music for Two Guitars 196? 40.00
*—Maroon label, with "Vendor: Mercury Record Corporation"*

**PRESTIGE BLUES SWINGERS, THE**

PRESTIGE
❑ PRLP-7145 [M]Outskirts of Town 1958 80.00

SWINGVILLE
❑ SVLP-2013 [M]Stasch 1960 25.00
*—Blue label, trident logo at right*
❑ SVLP-2013 [M]Stasch 1965 50.00
*—Purple label*

**PRESTIGE JAZZ QUARTET, THE**

PRESTIGE
❑ PRLP-7108 [M]The Prestige Jazz Quartet 1957 50.00

**PRESTON, BILLY**

A&M
❑ SP-3205 The Best of Billy Preston 1982 10.00
❑ SP-3507 I Wrote a Simple Song 1971 12.00
❑ SP-3516 Music Is My Life 1972 12.00
❑ SP-3526 Everybody Likes Some Kind of Music 1973 12.00
❑ SP-3637 Live European Tour 1974 12.00
❑ SP-3645 The Kids & Me 1974 12.00
❑ SP-4532 It's My Pleasure 1975 12.00
❑ SP-4587 Billy Preston 1976 12.00
❑ SP-4657 It's a Whole New Thing 1977 12.00

APPLE
❑ ST-3359 That's the Way God Planned It 1969 50.00
*—Cover has close-up of Billy Preston*
❑ ST-3359 That's the Way God Planned It 1972 20.00
*—Cover has multiple images of Billy Preston*
❑ ST-3370 Encouraging Words 1970 20.00

BUDDAH
❑ BDS-7502 Billy Preston 1969 15.00

CAPITOL
❑ ST 2532 [S] Wildest Organ in Town! 1966 40.00
❑ T 2532 [M] Wildest Organ in Town! 1966 30.00
❑ DT 2607 [R] Club Meetin' 1967 —
❑ T 2607 [M] Club Meetin' 1967 —
*—The above versions of Club Meetin' may not exist*

DERBY
❑ LPM-701 [M] 16 Year Old Soul 1963 250.00

EXODUS
❑ 304 [M] Early Hits of 1965 1965 25.00

GNP CRESCENDO
❑ GNPS-2071 [(2)]Soul'd Out 1973 15.00

MCA
❑ 28037 Gospel Soul 198? 8.00
*—Reissue of Peacock LP*

MOTOWN
❑ M7-925 Late at Night 1980 10.00
❑ M8-941 The Way I Am 1981 10.00
❑ M7-958 Billy Preston & Syreeta 1981 10.00
❑ 6020 ML Pressin' On 1982 10.00

MYRRH
❑ MSB-6605 Behold 1978 12.00
❑ MSB-6607 Universal Love 1979 12.00

PEACOCK
❑ 179 Gospel Soul 197? 12.00

Number | Title (A Side/B Side) | Yr | NM

PICKWICK
❑ SPC-3315 Organ Transplant 197? 10.00

VEE JAY
❑ LP-1123 [M] The Most Exciting Organ Ever 1965 30.00
❑ LPS-1123 [S] The Most Exciting Organ Ever 1965 50.00
❑ LP-1142 [M] Greatest Hits 1966 30.00
❑ LPS-1142 [S] Greatest Hits 1966 50.00

**PRESTON, JOHNNY**

MERCURY
❑ MG-20592 [M] Running Bear 1960 100.00
❑ MG-20609 [M] Come Rock with Me 1960 100.00
❑ SR-60250 [S] Running Bear 1960 150.00
*—Black label*
❑ SR-60250 [S] Running Bear 1981 12.00
*—Reissue on Chicago skyline label*
❑ SR-60609 [S] Come Rock with Me 1960 150.00

WING
❑ MGW-12246 [M]Running Bear 1963 20.00
❑ SRW-16246 [S]Running Bear 1963 25.00

**PRETENDERS**

NAUTILUS
❑ NR-38 Pretenders 1982 30.00
*—Audiophile vinyl*

SIRE
❑ MINI 3563 [EP]Extended Play 1981 10.00
❑ SRK 3572 Pretenders II 1981 10.00
❑ SRK 6083 Pretenders 1980 10.00
❑ 23980 Learning to Crawl 1983 10.00
❑ 23980 [DJ] Learning to Crawl 1983 12.00
*—Promo-only Quiex II pressing; otherwise, same as above*
❑ 25488 Get Close 1986 10.00
❑ 25664 The Singles 1987 10.00
❑ 26219 Packed! 1990 12.00
❑ R 133248 The Singles 1987 12.00
*—BMG Direct Marketing edition; otherwise, same as 25664*
❑ R 144453 Get Close 1986 12.00
*—RCA Music Service edition*

WARNER BROS.
❑ WBMS-114 [DJ]Pretenders Live 1980 40.00
*—Part of "The Warner Bros. Music Show" series; comes in red die-cut cover*
❑ WBMS-121 [DJ]Pretenders Live (Star Fleet) 1982 40.00
*—Part of "The Warner Bros. Music Show" series; comes in black cover with white sticker*
❑ WBMS-142 [DJ]Get Close Interview 1987 20.00
*—Part of "The Warner Bros. Music Show" series*

**PRETTY POISON**

SVENGALI
❑ SRPP-1 [EP] Laced 1984 20.00

VIRGIN
❑ 90885 Catch Me I'm Falling 1987 10.00
❑ R 144099 Catch Me I'm Falling 1988 12.00
*—BMG Direct Marketing edition*

**PRETTY THINGS, THE**

BIG BEAT
❑ WIK-24 Live at Heartbreak Hotel 1985 10.00

FONTANA
❑ MGF-27544 [M]The Pretty Things 1965 80.00
❑ SRF-67544 [P] The Pretty Things 1965 80.00

NORTON
❑ 282 The Pretty Things 2000 12.00
❑ 283 Get the Picture? 2000 12.00
❑ 284 Midnight to Six 2000 12.00
❑ TED-1001 [10] Defecting Grey 2000 8.00

RARE EARTH
❑ RS 506 S.F. Sorrow 1969 20.00
*—Later copies are standard in shape*
❑ RS 506 S.F. Sorrow 1969 50.00
*—Original covers are rounded at top*
❑ RS 515 Parachute 1970 20.00
❑ R 549R2 [(2)] Real Pretty 1976 15.00
*—The two prior Rare Earth albums in one package*

SIRE
❑ SASH-3713 [(2)]The Vintage Years 1976 15.00

SWAN SONG
❑ SS 8411 Silk Torpedo 1975 10.00
❑ SS 8414 Savage Eye 1976 10.00

WARNER BROS.
❑ BS 2680 Freeway Madness 1973 10.00
❑ BSK 3466 Cross Talk 1980 10.00

**PREVIN, ANDRE**

COLUMBIA
❑ CL 1530 [M] Give My Regards to Broadway 1960 20.00
*—Red and black label with six "eye" logos*
❑ CL 1569 [M] Camelot 1961 20.00
*—Red and black label with six "eye" logos*
❑ CL 1595 [M] Thinking of You 1961 20.00
*—Red and black label with six "eye" logos*
❑ CL 1649 [M] A Touch of Elegance 1961 20.00
*—Red and black label with six "eye" logos*

| Number | Title (A Side/B Side) | Yr | NM |
|---|---|---|---|
| ❑ CL 1741 [M] | Mack the Knife and Other Kurt Weill Music | 1962 | 20.00 |
| *—Red and black label with six "eye" logos* | | | |
| ❑ CL 1786 [M] | Faraway Part of Town | 1962 | 20.00 |
| *—Red and black label with six "eye" logos* | | | |
| ❑ CL 1888 [M] | The Light Fantastic | 1962 | 20.00 |
| *—Red and black label with six "eye" logos* | | | |
| ❑ CS 8233 [S] | Like Love | 1960 | 20.00 |
| *—Red and black label with six "eye" logos* | | | |
| ❑ CS 8286 [S] | Rhapsody in Blue | 1960 | 20.00 |
| *—Red and black label with six "eye" logos* | | | |
| ❑ CS 8330 [S] | Give My Regards to Broadway | 1960 | 25.00 |
| *—Red and black label with six "eye" logos* | | | |
| ❑ CS 8369 [S] | Camelot | 1961 | 25.00 |
| *—Red and black label with six "eye" logos* | | | |
| ❑ CS 8395 [S] | Thinking of You | 1961 | 25.00 |
| *—Red and black label with six "eye" logos* | | | |
| ❑ CS 8449 [S] | A Touch of Elegance | 1961 | 25.00 |
| *—Red and black label with six "eye" logos* | | | |
| ❑ CS 8541 [S] | Mack the Knife and Other Kurt Weill Music | 1962 | 25.00 |
| *—Red and black label with six "eye" logos* | | | |
| ❑ CS 8586 [S] | Faraway Part of Town | 1962 | 25.00 |
| *—Red and black label with six "eye" logos* | | | |
| ❑ CS 8688 [S] | The Light Fantastic | 1962 | 25.00 |
| *—Red and black label with six "eye" logos* | | | |
| ❑ CS 8834 [S] | Andre Previn in Hollywood | 1963 | 20.00 |
| *—Red label with "360 Sound Stereo" in black at bottom* | | | |
| ❑ CS 8914 [S] | The Soft and Swinging Music of Jimmy McHugh | 1964 | 20.00 |
| *—Red label with "360 Sound Stereo" in black at bottom* | | | |
| ❑ CS 8995 [S] | My Fair Lady | 1964 | 20.00 |
| *—Red label with "360 Sound Stereo" in black at bottom* | | | |
| ❑ CS 9094 [S] | Popular Previn | 1965 | 20.00 |
| *—Red label with "360 Sound Stereo" in black at bottom* | | | |

CONTEMPORARY

| Number | Title (A Side/B Side) | Yr | NM |
|---|---|---|---|
| ❑ C-3543 [M] | Pal Joey | 1957 | 50.00 |
| ❑ C-3548 [M] | Gigi | 1958 | 50.00 |
| ❑ M-3558 [M] | Andre Previn Plays Vernon Duke | 1959 | 50.00 |
| ❑ M-3567 [M] | Andre Previn Plays Jerome Kern | 1959 | 50.00 |
| ❑ M-3570 [M] | Jazz Trio, King Size | 1959 | 50.00 |
| ❑ M-3572 [M] | West Side Story | 1960 | 40.00 |
| ❑ M-3575 [M] | Like Previn | 1960 | 40.00 |
| ❑ M-3586 [M] | Andre Previn Plays Harold Arlen | 1960 | 40.00 |
| ❑ S-7543 [S] | Pal Joey | 1959 | 40.00 |
| ❑ S-7548 [S] | Gigi | 1959 | 40.00 |
| ❑ S-7558 [S] | Andre Previn Plays Vernon Duke | 1959 | 40.00 |
| ❑ S-7567 [S] | Andre Previn Plays Jerome Kern | 1959 | 40.00 |
| ❑ S-7570 [S] | Jazz Trio, King Size | 1959 | 40.00 |
| ❑ S-7572 [S] | West Side Story | 1960 | 30.00 |
| ❑ S-7575 [S] | Like Previn | 1960 | 30.00 |
| ❑ S-7586 [S] | Andre Previn Plays Harold Arlen | 1960 | 30.00 |

DECCA

| Number | Title (A Side/B Side) | Yr | NM |
|---|---|---|---|
| ❑ DL 8131 [M] | Let's Get Away from It All | 1955 | 40.00 |
| ❑ DL 8341 [M] | Hollywood at Midnight | 1957 | 40.00 |

MGM

| Number | Title (A Side/B Side) | Yr | NM |
|---|---|---|---|
| ❑ E-3716 [M] | Secret Songs for Young Lovers | 1959 | 20.00 |
| ❑ SE-3716 [S] | Secret Songs for Young Lovers | 1959 | 25.00 |
| ❑ E-3811 [M] | Like Blue | 1960 | 20.00 |
| ❑ SE-3811 [S] | Like Blue | 1960 | 25.00 |
| ❑ SE-4186 [S] | Andre Previn — Composer, Conductor, Arranger, Pianist | 1964 | 20.00 |

MOBILE FIDELITY

| Number | Title (A Side/B Side) | Yr | NM |
|---|---|---|---|
| ❑ 1-095 | West Side Story | 1982 | 25.00 |
| *—Audiophile vinyl* | | | |

MONARCH

| Number | Title (A Side/B Side) | Yr | NM |
|---|---|---|---|
| ❑ 203 [10] | All Star Jazz | 1952 | 80.00 |
| ❑ 204 [10] | Andre Previn Plays Duke | 1952 | 80.00 |

PRI

| Number | Title (A Side/B Side) | Yr | NM |
|---|---|---|---|
| ❑ 3026 [S] | The World's Most Honored Pianist | 1962 | 25.00 |
| *—Issued on yellow vinyl* | | | |

RCA VICTOR

| Number | Title (A Side/B Side) | Yr | NM |
|---|---|---|---|
| ❑ LPM-36 [10] | Andre Previn By Request | 1951 | 80.00 |
| ❑ LPM-1011 [M] | Gershwin | 1955 | 40.00 |
| ❑ LPM-1356 [M] | Three Little Words | 1957 | 40.00 |
| ❑ LPT-3002 [10] | Andre Previn Plays Harry Warren | 1952 | 80.00 |

STEREO RECORDS

| Number | Title (A Side/B Side) | Yr | NM |
|---|---|---|---|
| ❑ S-7004 [S] | Pal Joey | 1958 | 50.00 |
| ❑ S-7020 [S] | Gigi | 1958 | 50.00 |

STRAND

| Number | Title (A Side/B Side) | Yr | NM |
|---|---|---|---|
| ❑ SL 1074 [M] | Andre Previn Plays | 1962 | 12.00 |
| ❑ SLS 1074 [S] | Andre Previn Plays | 1962 | 15.00 |

**PREVIN, ANDRE; HERB ELLIS; SHELLY MANNE; RAY BROWN**

COLUMBIA

| Number | Title (A Side/B Side) | Yr | NM |
|---|---|---|---|
| ❑ CS 8818 [S] | Four to Go | 1963 | 25.00 |

Lloyd Price, *"Mr. Personality's" 15 Hits,* ABC-Paramount ABC-324, 1960, mono, $40.

**PREVIN, ANDRE, AND RUSS FREEMAN**

CONTEMPORARY

| Number | Title (A Side/B Side) | Yr | NM |
|---|---|---|---|
| ❑ C-3537 [M] | Double Play! | 1957 | 50.00 |
| ❑ S-7011 [S] | Double Play! | 1959 | 40.00 |

STEREO RECORDS

| Number | Title (A Side/B Side) | Yr | NM |
|---|---|---|---|
| ❑ S-7011 [S] | Double Play! | 1958 | 50.00 |

**PRICE, ALAN** Also see THE ANIMALS.

ACCORD

| Number | Title (A Side/B Side) | Yr | NM |
|---|---|---|---|
| ❑ SJA-7904 | It's Priceless | 1982 | 10.00 |

JET

| Number | Title (A Side/B Side) | Yr | NM |
|---|---|---|---|
| ❑ JT-LA809-H | Alan Price | 1977 | 10.00 |
| *—The "H" suffix is on the label, but the front and back cover, inner sleeve and spine have a "G" prefix; it's not known if any labels have a "G" prefix* | | | |
| ❑ JZ 35710 | Lucky Day | 1979 | 10.00 |
| ❑ NJZ 36510 | Rising Sun | 1980 | 10.00 |

PARROT

| Number | Title (A Side/B Side) | Yr | NM |
|---|---|---|---|
| ❑ PAS 71018 [P] | The Price Is Right | 1968 | 30.00 |

TOWNHOUSE

| Number | Title (A Side/B Side) | Yr | NM |
|---|---|---|---|
| ❑ SN-7126 | House of the Rising Sun | 1981 | 10.00 |

WARNER BROS.

| Number | Title (A Side/B Side) | Yr | NM |
|---|---|---|---|
| ❑ BS 2710 | O Lucky Man | 1973 | 12.00 |
| ❑ BS 2783 | Between Today and Yesterday | 1974 | 12.00 |

**PRICE, KENNY**

BOONE

| Number | Title (A Side/B Side) | Yr | NM |
|---|---|---|---|
| ❑ 1211 | One Hit Follows Another | 1967 | 25.00 |
| ❑ 1214 | Southern Bound | 1968 | 25.00 |

DIMENSION

| Number | Title (A Side/B Side) | Yr | NM |
|---|---|---|---|
| ❑ DLP-5000 | The Best of Both | 1980 | 12.00 |

RCA VICTOR

| Number | Title (A Side/B Side) | Yr | NM |
|---|---|---|---|
| ❑ APL1-0208 | 30 California Women | 1973 | 15.00 |
| ❑ LSP-4224 | Happy Tracks | 1969 | 20.00 |
| ❑ LSP-4225 | Walking on New Grass | 1969 | 20.00 |
| ❑ LSP-4292 | The Heavyweight | 1970 | 20.00 |
| ❑ LSP-4373 | Northeast Arkansas Mississippi County Bootlegger | 1970 | 20.00 |
| ❑ LSP-4469 | The Red Foley Songbook | 1971 | 20.00 |
| ❑ LSP-4527 | The Sheriff of Boone County | 1971 | 20.00 |
| ❑ LSP-4605 | Charlotte Fever | 1971 | 20.00 |
| ❑ LSP-4681 | Supersideman | 1972 | 20.00 |
| ❑ LSP-4763 | You Almost Slipped My Mind | 1972 | 20.00 |
| ❑ LSP-4839 | Sea of Heartbreak | 1973 | 20.00 |

**PRICE, LEONTYNE**

LONDON

| Number | Title (A Side/B Side) | Yr | NM |
|---|---|---|---|
| ❑ 5644 [M] | A Christmas Offering | 1961 | 20.00 |
| ❑ OS 25280 [S] | A Christmas Offering | 1961 | 25.00 |

RCA VICTOR RED SEAL

| Number | Title (A Side/B Side) | Yr | NM |
|---|---|---|---|
| ❑ LSC-2279 [S] | A Program of Song | 1959 | 20.00 |
| *—Original with "shaded dog" label* | | | |
| ❑ LSC-2600 [S] | Swing Low, Sweet Chariot | 1962 | 25.00 |
| *—Original with "shaded dog" label* | | | |

**PRICE, LLOYD**

ABC

| Number | Title (A Side/B Side) | Yr | NM |
|---|---|---|---|
| ❑ S-297 | Mr. Personality | 1967 | 15.00 |
| *—Reissue on revised label* | | | |
| ❑ S-324 [R] | Mr. Personality's Big 15 | 1968 | 15.00 |
| *—Reissue on revised label* | | | |
| ❑ X-763 | 16 Greatest Hits | 1972 | 15.00 |
| ❑ AC-30006 | The ABC Collection | 1976 | 15.00 |
| ❑ DW-94842 | 16 Greatest Hits | 1972 | 20.00 |
| *—Capitol Record Club edition* | | | |

ABC-PARAMOUNT

| Number | Title (A Side/B Side) | Yr | NM |
|---|---|---|---|
| ❑ ABC-277 [M] | The Exciting Lloyd Price | 1959 | 40.00 |
| ❑ ABCS-277 [S] | The Exciting Lloyd Price | 1959 | 80.00 |
| ❑ ABC-297 [M] | Mr. Personality | 1959 | 40.00 |
| ❑ ABCS-297 [S] | Mr. Personality | 1959 | 80.00 |
| ❑ ABC-315 [M] | Mr. Personality Sings the Blues | 1960 | 40.00 |
| ❑ ABCS-315 [S] | Mr. Personality Sings the Blues | 1960 | 80.00 |
| ❑ ABC-324 [M] | Mr. Personality's 15 Hits | 1960 | 40.00 |
| *—Label calls this "Mr. Personality's Big Hits"* | | | |
| ❑ ABC-346 [M] | The Fantastic Lloyd Price | 1960 | 40.00 |
| ❑ ABCS-346 [R] | The Fantastic Lloyd Price | 196? | 25.00 |
| ❑ ABC-366 [M] | Lloyd Price Sings the Million Sellers | 1961 | 40.00 |
| ❑ ABCS-366 [S] | Lloyd Price Sings the Million Sellers | 1961 | 50.00 |
| ❑ ABC-382 [M] | Cookin' with Lloyd Price | 1961 | 40.00 |
| ❑ ABCS-382 [S] | Cookin' with Lloyd Price | 1961 | 50.00 |

DOUBLE-L

| Number | Title (A Side/B Side) | Yr | NM |
|---|---|---|---|
| ❑ DL-2301 [M] | The Lloyd Price Orchestra | 1963 | 25.00 |
| ❑ DL-2303 [M] | Misty | 1963 | 25.00 |
| ❑ SDL-8301 [S] | The Lloyd Price Orchestra | 1963 | 40.00 |
| ❑ SDL-8303 [S] | Misty | 1963 | 40.00 |

| Number | Title (A Side/B Side) | Yr | NM |
|---|---|---|---|
| **GRAND PRIX** | | | |
| ❑ 422 [M] | Mr. Rhythm and Blues | 196? | 12.00 |
| ❑ S-422 [R] | Mr. Rhythm and Blues | 196? | 10.00 |
| **GUEST STAR** | | | |
| ❑ G-1910 [M] | Come to Me | 196? | 12.00 |
| ❑ GS-1910 [R] | Come to Me | 196? | 10.00 |
| **JAD** | | | |
| ❑ 1002 | Lloyd Price Now | 1969 | 25.00 |
| **LPG** | | | |
| ❑ 001 | Music...Music | 1976 | 10.00 |
| **MCA** | | | |
| ❑ 1503 | Greatest Hits | 1982 | 8.00 |
| **MONUMENT** | | | |
| ❑ MLP-8032 [M] | Lloyd Swings for Sammy | 1965 | 25.00 |
| ❑ SLP-18032 [S] | Lloyd Swings for Sammy | 1965 | 40.00 |
| **PICKWICK** | | | |
| ❑ SPC-3518 | Big Hits | 197? | 8.00 |
| **SCEPTER CITATION** | | | |
| ❑ CTN-18006 | The Best of Lloyd Price | 1972 | 10.00 |
| **SPECIALTY** | | | |
| ❑ SP-2105 | Lloyd Price | 198? | 12.00 |
| *—1980s reissue* | | | |
| ❑ SP-2105 [M] | Lloyd Price | 1959 | 180.00 |
| **TRIP** | | | |
| ❑ TOP 16-5 | 16 Greatest Hits | 1976 | 10.00 |
| **TURNTABLE** | | | |
| ❑ TTS-5001 | Lloyd Price Now | 197? | 15.00 |
| **UPFRONT** | | | |
| ❑ UPF-126 | Misty | 197? | 12.00 |

## PRICE, RAY

| Number | Title (A Side/B Side) | Yr | NM |
|---|---|---|---|
| **ABC DOT** | | | |
| ❑ DO-2037 | Say I Do | 1975 | 12.00 |
| ❑ DO-2053 | Rainbows and Tears | 1976 | 12.00 |
| ❑ DOSD-2062 | Hank 'n Me | 1976 | 12.00 |
| ❑ DO-2073 | Reunited | 1977 | 12.00 |
| **COLUMBIA** | | | |
| ❑ GP 28 [(2)] | The World of Ray Price | 1970 | 15.00 |
| ❑ CL 1015 [M] | Ray Price Sings Heart Songs | 1957 | 50.00 |
| ❑ CL 1148 [M] | Talk to Your Heart | 1958 | 40.00 |
| ❑ CL 1494 [M] | Faith | 1960 | 30.00 |
| ❑ CL 1566 [M] | Ray Price's Greatest Hits | 1961 | 30.00 |
| ❑ CL 1756 [M] | San Antonio Rose | 1962 | 20.00 |
| ❑ CL 1971 [M] | Night Life | 1963 | 15.00 |
| ❑ CL 2189 [M] | Love Life | 1964 | 15.00 |
| ❑ CL 2289 [M] | Burning Memories | 1965 | 15.00 |
| ❑ CL 2339 [M] | Western Strings | 1965 | 20.00 |
| ❑ CL 2382 [M] | The Other Woman | 1965 | 15.00 |
| ❑ CL 2528 [M] | Another Bridge to Burn | 1966 | 15.00 |
| ❑ CL 2606 [M] | Touch My Heart | 1967 | 20.00 |
| ❑ CL 2670 [M] | Ray Price's Greatest Hits, Volume 2 | 1967 | 20.00 |
| ❑ CL 2677 [M] | Danny Boy | 1967 | 20.00 |
| ❑ CL 2806 [M] | Take Me As I Am | 1968 | 30.00 |
| ❑ CS 8285 [S] | Faith | 1960 | 40.00 |
| ❑ CS 8556 [S] | San Antonio Rose | 1962 | 30.00 |
| ❑ CS 8771 [S] | Night Life | 1963 | 20.00 |
| ❑ CS 8866 [R] | Ray Price's Greatest Hits | 1964 | 12.00 |
| ❑ PC 8866 | Ray Price's Greatest Hits | 198? | 8.00 |
| *—Reissue with new prefix* | | | |
| ❑ CS 8989 [S] | Love Life | 1964 | 20.00 |
| ❑ CS 9089 [S] | Burning Memories | 1965 | 20.00 |
| ❑ CS 9139 [S] | Western Strings | 1965 | 25.00 |
| ❑ CS 9182 [S] | The Other Woman | 1965 | 20.00 |
| ❑ CS 9328 [S] | Another Bridge to Burn | 1966 | 20.00 |
| ❑ CS 9406 [S] | Touch My Heart | 1967 | 15.00 |
| ❑ CS 9470 [S] | Ray Price's Greatest Hits, Volume 2 | 1967 | 15.00 |
| ❑ CS 9477 [S] | Danny Boy | 1967 | 15.00 |
| ❑ CS 9606 [S] | Take Me As I Am | 1968 | 15.00 |
| ❑ CS 9733 | She Wears My Ring | 1968 | 15.00 |
| ❑ CS 9822 | Sweetheart of the Year | 1969 | 15.00 |
| ❑ CS 9861 | Ray Price's Christmas Album | 1969 | 15.00 |
| ❑ CS 9918 | You Wouldn't Know Love | 1970 | 15.00 |
| ❑ C 30106 | For the Good Times | 1970 | 12.00 |
| ❑ CQ 30106 [Q] | For the Good Times | 1972 | 20.00 |
| ❑ C 30510 | I Won't Mention It Again | 1971 | 12.00 |
| ❑ CG 30878 [(2)] | Welcome to My World | 1971 | 15.00 |
| ❑ KG 31364 [(2)] | Ray Price's All-Time Greatest Hits | 1972 | 15.00 |
| ❑ KC 31546 | The Lonesomest Lonesome | 1972 | 12.00 |
| ❑ KC 32033 | She's Got to Be a Saint | 1973 | 12.00 |
| ❑ PC 32033 | She's Got to Be a Saint | 197? | 8.00 |
| *—Reissue with new prefix* | | | |
| ❑ KC 32777 | You're the Best Thing That Ever Happened to Me | 1973 | 12.00 |
| ❑ PC 32777 | You're the Best Thing That Ever Happened to Me | 197? | 8.00 |
| *—Reissue with new prefix* | | | |
| ❑ PC 33560 | If You Change Your Mind | 1975 | 12.00 |
| ❑ CG 33633 [(2)] | For the Good Times/I Won't Mention It Again | 1975 | 15.00 |
| *—Reissue of two LPs in one package* | | | |
| ❑ PC 34160 | The Best of Ray Price | 1976 | 12.00 |
| ❑ PC 34710 | Help Me | 1977 | 12.00 |
| ❑ JC 37061 | A Tribute to Willie and Kris | 1982 | 10.00 |
| **COLUMBIA LIMITED EDITION** | | | |
| ❑ LE 10142 | Love Life | 197? | 10.00 |
| *—Reissue of Columbia CS 8989* | | | |
| **HARMONY** | | | |
| ❑ HL 7372 [M] | Collectors' Choice | 196? | 12.00 |
| ❑ HL 7440 [M] | Born to Lose | 1967 | 12.00 |
| ❑ HS 11172 [R] | Collectors' Choice | 196? | 12.00 |
| ❑ HS 11240 [S] | Born to Lose | 1967 | 12.00 |
| ❑ HS 11373 | I Fall to Pieces | 1969 | 10.00 |
| ❑ KH 30272 | Make the World Go Away | 1970 | 10.00 |
| **MONUMENT** | | | |
| ❑ 7633 | Always Me | 1979 | 10.00 |
| **MYRRH** | | | |
| ❑ 6532 | This Time, Lord | 1975 | 12.00 |
| **PAIR** | | | |
| ❑ PDL2-1044 [(2)] | Happens to Be the Best | 1986 | 12.00 |
| ❑ PDL2-1044 [(2)] | Ray Price Happens to Be the Best! | 1986 | 12.00 |
| ❑ PDL2-1096 [(2)] | Priceless | 1986 | 12.00 |
| **ROUNDER** | | | |
| ❑ SS-22 | The Honky Tonk Years | 1986 | 10.00 |
| **WORD** | | | |
| ❑ 8723 | Precious Memories | 197? | 12.00 |
| ❑ 8780 | How Great Thou Art | 1978 | 12.00 |

## PRICE, RUTH

| Number | Title (A Side/B Side) | Yr | NM |
|---|---|---|---|
| **AVA** | | | |
| ❑ A-54 [M] | Live and Beautiful | 1963 | 40.00 |
| ❑ AS-54 [S] | Live and Beautiful | 1963 | 50.00 |
| **CONTEMPORARY** | | | |
| ❑ M-3590 [M] | Ruth Price with Shelly Manne at the Manne-Hole | 1961 | 50.00 |
| ❑ S-7590 [S] | Ruth Price with Shelly Manne at the Manne-Hole | 1961 | 60.00 |
| **KAPP** | | | |
| ❑ KL-1006 [M] | My Name Is Ruth Price. I Sing. | 1955 | 100.00 |
| ❑ KL-1054 [M] | The Party's Over | 1957 | 100.00 |
| **ROOST** | | | |
| ❑ LP-2217 [M] | Ruth Price Sings! | 1956 | 100.00 |

## PRICE, SAMMY

| Number | Title (A Side/B Side) | Yr | NM |
|---|---|---|---|
| **CONCERT HALL JAZZ** | | | |
| ❑ 1008 [10] | Barrelhouse and Blues | 1955 | 50.00 |
| **JAZZTONE** | | | |
| ❑ J-1207 [M] | Barrelhouse and Blues | 1956 | 40.00 |
| ❑ J-1236 [M] | Les Jeunesses Musicales | 1956 | 40.00 |
| ❑ J-1260 [M] | The Price Is Right | 1957 | 40.00 |

## PRICE, VINCENT

| Number | Title (A Side/B Side) | Yr | NM |
|---|---|---|---|
| **CAEDMON** | | | |
| ❑ TC-1059 [M] | Vincent Price Reads Poems of Shelley | 196? | 30.00 |
| ❑ TC 1429 | A Graveyard of Ghost Tales | 1974 | 15.00 |
| **CAPITOL** | | | |
| ❑ SWBB-342 [(2)] | Witchcraft/Magic | 1969 | 30.00 |
| **CAPITOL CUSTOM** | | | |
| ❑ SGP-6256/7 [S] | The World Tomorrow | 1965 | 40.00 |
| *—Blue vinyl* | | | |
| ❑ SGP-6258/9 [S] | The World of the 21st Century | 1965 | 40.00 |
| *—Blue vinyl* | | | |
| **COLUMBIA MASTERWORKS** | | | |
| ❑ ML 5668 [M] | America the Beautiful | 1961 | 30.00 |
| **DOT** | | | |
| ❑ DLP-3195 [M] | Gallery | 1962 | 25.00 |
| ❑ DLP-25195 [S] | Gallery | 1962 | 30.00 |
| **NELSON INDUSTRIES** | | | |
| ❑ (# unknown) | International Cooking Course | 1977 | 40.00 |

## PRICE, VITO

| Number | Title (A Side/B Side) | Yr | NM |
|---|---|---|---|
| **ARGO** | | | |
| ❑ LP-631 [M] | Swingin' the Loop | 1958 | 40.00 |
| ❑ LPS-631 [S] | Swingin' the Loop | 1958 | 30.00 |

## PRIDE

| Number | Title (A Side/B Side) | Yr | NM |
|---|---|---|---|
| **WARNER BROS.** | | | |
| ❑ WS 1848 | Pride | 1970 | 25.00 |

## PRIDE, CHARLEY

| Number | Title (A Side/B Side) | Yr | NM |
|---|---|---|---|
| **PAIR** | | | |
| ❑ PDL2-1023 [(2)] | Country in My Soul | 1986 | 12.00 |
| **RCA CAMDEN** | | | |
| ❑ CAS-2584 | The Incomparable Charley Pride | 1972 | 15.00 |
| **RCA VICTOR** | | | |
| ❑ APD1-0217 [Q] | Sweet Country | 1973 | 25.00 |
| ❑ APL1-0217 | Sweet Country | 1973 | 15.00 |
| ❑ APL1-0315 | Charley Pride Presents the Pridesmen | 1973 | 15.00 |
| ❑ APD1-0397 [Q] | Amazing Love | 1974 | 25.00 |
| ❑ APL1-0397 | Amazing Love | 1974 | 15.00 |
| ❑ APL1-0534 | Country Feelin' | 1974 | 15.00 |
| ❑ APD1-0757 [Q] | Pride of America | 1974 | 25.00 |
| ❑ APL1-0757 | Pride of America | 1974 | 15.00 |
| ❑ ANL1-0996 | Charley Pride — In Person | 1975 | 10.00 |
| *—Reissue of LSP-4094* | | | |
| ❑ APD1-1038 [Q] | Charley | 1975 | 25.00 |
| ❑ APL1-1038 | Charley | 1975 | 15.00 |
| ❑ ANL1-1214 | I'm Just Me | 1975 | 10.00 |
| *—Reissue of LSP-4560* | | | |
| ❑ APD1-1241 [Q] | The Happiness of Having You | 1975 | 25.00 |
| ❑ APL1-1241 | The Happiness of Having You | 1975 | 15.00 |
| ❑ APD1-1359 [Q] | Sunday Morning with Charley Pride | 1976 | 25.00 |
| ❑ APL1-1359 | Sunday Morning with Charley Pride | 1976 | 15.00 |
| ❑ ANL1-1934 | Christmas in My Home Town | 1976 | 8.00 |
| *—Reissue of LSP-4406* | | | |
| ❑ APL1-2023 | The Best of Charley Pride, Vol. III | 1976 | 12.00 |
| ❑ APL1-2261 | She's Just an Old Love Turned Memory | 1977 | 12.00 |
| ❑ AHL1-2478 | Someone Loves You Honey | 1978 | 12.00 |
| ❑ AHL1-2963 | Burgers and Fries | 1978 | 12.00 |
| ❑ AHL1-3441 | You're My Jamaica | 1979 | 12.00 |
| ❑ AHL1-3548 | There's a Little Bit of Hank in Me | 1980 | 12.00 |
| ❑ LPM-3645 [M] | Country Charley Pride | 1966 | 25.00 |
| ❑ LSP-3645 [S] | Country Charley Pride | 1966 | 30.00 |
| ❑ AYL1-3676 | Someone Loves You Honey | 1980 | 8.00 |
| *—"Best Buy Series" reissue* | | | |
| ❑ AYL1-3740 | Sunday Morning with Charley Pride | 1980 | 8.00 |
| *—"Best Buy Series" reissue* | | | |
| ❑ LPM-3775 [M] | The Pride of Country Music | 1967 | 25.00 |
| ❑ LSP-3775 [S] | The Pride of Country Music | 1967 | 20.00 |
| ❑ AYL1-3874 | I'm Just Me | 1981 | 8.00 |
| *—"Best Buy Series" reissue* | | | |
| ❑ LPM-3895 [M] | The Country Way | 1967 | 25.00 |
| ❑ LSP-3895 [S] | The Country Way | 1967 | 20.00 |
| ❑ AHL1-3905 | Roll On Mississippi | 1981 | 10.00 |
| ❑ AYL1-3943 | The Happiness of Having You | 1981 | 8.00 |
| *—"Best Buy Series" reissue* | | | |
| ❑ LPM-3952 [M] | Make Mine Country | 1968 | 60.00 |
| ❑ LSP-3952 [S] | Make Mine Country | 1968 | 20.00 |
| ❑ LSP-4041 | Songs of Pride — Charley, That Is | 1968 | 20.00 |
| ❑ AYL1-4074 | Amazing Love | 1981 | 8.00 |
| *—"Best Buy Series" reissue* | | | |
| ❑ LSP-4094 | Charley Pride — In Person | 1969 | 20.00 |
| ❑ AHL1-4151 | Greatest Hits | 1981 | 10.00 |
| ❑ LSP-4153 | The Sensational Charley Pride | 1969 | 20.00 |
| ❑ AYL1-4166 | She's Just an Old Love Turned Memory | 1981 | 8.00 |
| *—"Best Buy Series" reissue* | | | |
| ❑ AHL1-4223 | The Best of Charley Pride | 198? | 10.00 |
| *—Reissue of LSP-4223* | | | |
| ❑ LSP-4223 | The Best of Charley Pride | 1969 | 20.00 |
| ❑ AYL1-4252 | Burgers and Fries | 1982 | 8.00 |
| *—"Best Buy Series" reissue* | | | |
| ❑ AHL1-4287 | Charley Pride Sings Everybody's Choice | 1982 | 10.00 |
| ❑ LSP-4290 | Just Plain Charley | 1970 | 20.00 |
| ❑ LSP-4367 | Charley Pride's 10th Album | 1970 | 20.00 |
| ❑ LSP-4406 | Christmas in My Home Town | 1970 | 20.00 |
| ❑ LSP-4468 | From Me to You | 1971 | 20.00 |
| ❑ LSP-4513 | Did You Think to Pray | 1971 | 20.00 |
| ❑ AHL1-4524 | Charley Pride Live | 1983 | 10.00 |
| ❑ LSP-4560 | I'm Just Me | 1971 | 20.00 |
| ❑ LSP-4617 | Charley Pride Sings Heart Songs | 1971 | 20.00 |
| ❑ AHL1-4662 | Country Classics | 1983 | 10.00 |
| ❑ AHL1-4682 | The Best of Charley Pride, Volume 2 | 198? | 10.00 |
| *—Reissue of LSP-4682* | | | |
| ❑ LSP-4682 | The Best of Charley Pride, Volume 2 | 1972 | 20.00 |
| ❑ LSP-4742 | A Sunshiny Day with Charley Pride | 1972 | 20.00 |
| ❑ AHL1-4822 | Night Games | 1983 | 10.00 |
| ❑ AYL1-4831 | There's a Little Bit of Hank in Me | 1983 | 8.00 |
| *—"Best Buy Series" reissue* | | | |
| ❑ LSP-4837 | Songs of Love by Charley Pride | 1973 | 15.00 |
| ❑ AHL1-5031 | The Power of Love | 1984 | 10.00 |
| ❑ AYL1-5147 | Greatest Hits | 1984 | 8.00 |
| *—"Best Buy Series" reissue* | | | |
| ❑ AYL1-5148 | The Best of Charley Pride | 1984 | 8.00 |
| *—"Best Buy Series" reissue* | | | |
| ❑ AHL1-5426 | Greatest Hits, Volume 2 | 1985 | 10.00 |
| ❑ AHL1-5851 | Back to the Country | 1986 | 10.00 |
| ❑ CPL1-7049 | Collector's Series | 1985 | 10.00 |
| ❑ AHL1-7174 | The Best There Is | 1986 | 10.00 |
| **READER'S DIGEST** | | | |
| ❑ RDA-217 [(6)] | Charley Pride's Country | 1979 | 40.00 |
| **16TH AVENUE** | | | |
| ❑ ST-70550 | After All This Time | 1987 | 12.00 |
| ❑ D1-70551 | I'm Gonna Love Her on the Radio | 1988 | 12.00 |
| ❑ D1-70554 | Moody Woman | 1989 | 12.00 |



Except when noted otherwise, VG = 25% of NM, and VG+ = 50% of NM. (Example: VG = $2.00, VG+ = $4.00 and NM = $8.00.)

| Number | Title (A Side/B Side) | Yr | NM |
|---|---|---|---|
| **TEE VEE/RCA SPECIAL PRODUCTS** | | | |
| ❑ DVL2-0208 [(2)] | Favorites | 1976 | 15.00 |
| *—Label calls this "Charley's Favorites"* | | | |
| **TIME-LIFE** | | | |
| ❑ STW-101 | Country Music | 1981 | 10.00 |

## PRIESTER, JULIAN

| Number | Title (A Side/B Side) | Yr | NM |
|---|---|---|---|
| **JAZZLAND** | | | |
| ❑ JLP-25 [M] | Spiritsville | 1960 | 50.00 |
| ❑ JLP-925 [S] | Spiritsville | 1960 | 70.00 |
| **RIVERSIDE** | | | |
| ❑ RLP 12-316 [M] | Keep Swingin' | 1960 | 80.00 |
| ❑ RLP 1163 [S] | Keep Swingin' | 1960 | 100.00 |

## PRIMA, LOUIS

| Number | Title (A Side/B Side) | Yr | NM |
|---|---|---|---|
| **BRUNSWICK** | | | |
| ❑ BL 754183 | The Prima Generation '72 | 1972 | 80.00 |
| **CAPITOL** | | | |
| ❑ T 755 [M] | The Wildest | 1956 | 50.00 |
| ❑ T 836 [M] | The Call of the Wildest | 1957 | 50.00 |
| ❑ T 908 [M] | The Wildest Show at Tahoe | 1957 | 50.00 |
| ❑ T 1010 [M] | Las Vegas Prima Style | 1958 | 50.00 |
| ❑ T 1132 [M] | Strictly Prima | 1959 | 30.00 |
| ❑ ST 1723 [S] | The Wildest Comes Home | 1962 | 30.00 |
| ❑ T 1723 [M] | The Wildest Comes Home | 1962 | 25.00 |
| ❑ ST 1797 [S] | Lake Tahoe Prima Style | 1962 | 30.00 |
| ❑ T 1797 [M] | Lake Tahoe Prima Style | 1962 | 25.00 |
| **COLUMBIA** | | | |
| ❑ CL 1206 [M] | Breakin' It Up! | 1959 | 40.00 |
| **DOT** | | | |
| ❑ DLP-3262 [M] | His Greatest Hits | 1960 | 25.00 |
| ❑ DLP-3264 [M] | Pretty Music Prima Style | 1960 | 25.00 |
| ❑ DLP-3272 [M] | The Wildest Clan | 1960 | 25.00 |
| ❑ DLP-3352 [M] | Wonderland by Night | 1960 | 25.00 |
| ❑ DLP-3385 [M] | Blue Moon | 1961 | 25.00 |
| ❑ DLP-3392 [M] | Return of the Wildest! | 1961 | 25.00 |
| ❑ DLP-3410 [M] | Doin' the Twist | 1961 | 25.00 |
| ❑ DLP-25262 [S] | His Greatest Hits | 1960 | 30.00 |
| ❑ DLP-25264 [S] | Pretty Music Prima Style | 1960 | 30.00 |
| ❑ DLP-25272 [S] | The Wildest Clan | 1960 | 30.00 |
| ❑ DLP-25352 [S] | Wonderland by Night | 1960 | 30.00 |
| ❑ DLP-25385 [S] | Blue Moon | 1961 | 30.00 |
| ❑ DLP-25392 [S] | Return of the Wildest! | 1961 | 30.00 |
| ❑ DLP-25410 [S] | Doin' the Twist | 1961 | 30.00 |
| **GOLDEN TONE** | | | |
| ❑ 326 [M] | Italian Favorites | 196? | 10.00 |
| *—Label calls this "Italian Songs"; one side is by Louis Prima, the other side by Phil Brito* | | | |
| **HANNA-BARBERA** | | | |
| ❑ HLP-8502 [M] | The Golden Hits of Louis Prima | 1966 | 30.00 |
| **MERCURY** | | | |
| ❑ MG-25142 [10] | Louis Prima Plays | 1953 | 80.00 |
| **PRIMA** | | | |
| ❑ ST 0072 | The Prima Generation | 1972 | 50.00 |
| ❑ ST 0074 | Angelina | 1973 | 25.00 |
| ❑ PM 3001 [M] | Prima Show in the Casbar | 1963 | 40.00 |
| ❑ PS 3001 [S] | Prima Show in the Casbar | 1963 | 60.00 |
| ❑ PM 3003 [M] | King of Clubs | 1964 | 70.00 |
| ❑ PS 3003 [S] | King of Clubs | 1964 | 100.00 |
| **RONDO-LETTE** | | | |
| ❑ A-9 [M] | Louis Prima in All His Moods | 1959 | 30.00 |
| ❑ A-25 [M] | Louis Prima Entertains | 1959 | 30.00 |
| **SAVOY JAZZ** | | | |
| ❑ SJL-2264 [(2)] | Play Pretty for the People | 198? | 12.00 |
| **TOPS** | | | |
| ❑ 9759 [M] | Italian Favorites | 195? | 15.00 |

## PRIMA, LOUIS, AND KEELY SMITH

| Number | Title (A Side/B Side) | Yr | NM |
|---|---|---|---|
| **CAPITOL** | | | |
| ❑ T 1160 [M] | Hey Boy! Hey Girl! | 1959 | 50.00 |
| ❑ SM-1531 | The Hits of Louis and Keely | 197? | 10.00 |
| *—Reissue with new prefix* | | | |
| ❑ ST 1531 [S] | The Hits of Louis and Keely | 1961 | 30.00 |
| ❑ T 1531 [M] | The Hits of Louis and Keely | 1961 | 25.00 |
| **CORONET** | | | |
| ❑ CX 121 [M] | Louis Prima Digs Keely Smith | 196? | 15.00 |
| **DOT** | | | |
| ❑ DLP-3210 [M] | Louis and Keely! | 1959 | 30.00 |
| ❑ DLP-3263 [M] | Together | 1960 | 25.00 |
| ❑ DLP-3266 [M] | Louis and Keely on Stage | 1960 | 25.00 |
| ❑ DLP-25210 [S] | Louis and Keely! | 1959 | 40.00 |
| ❑ DLP-25263 [S] | Together | 1960 | 30.00 |
| ❑ DLP-25266 [S] | Louis and Keely on Stage | 1960 | 30.00 |
| **FLEET** | | | |
| ❑ 101 [M] | Louis Prima Digs Keely Smith | 196? | 15.00 |
| **RHINO** | | | |
| ❑ RNLP-70225 | Zooma Zooma: The Best of Louis Prima Featuring Keely Smith | 1986 | 10.00 |
| **SPIN-O-RAMA** | | | |
| ❑ 74 [M] | Box of Oldies | 196? | 15.00 |

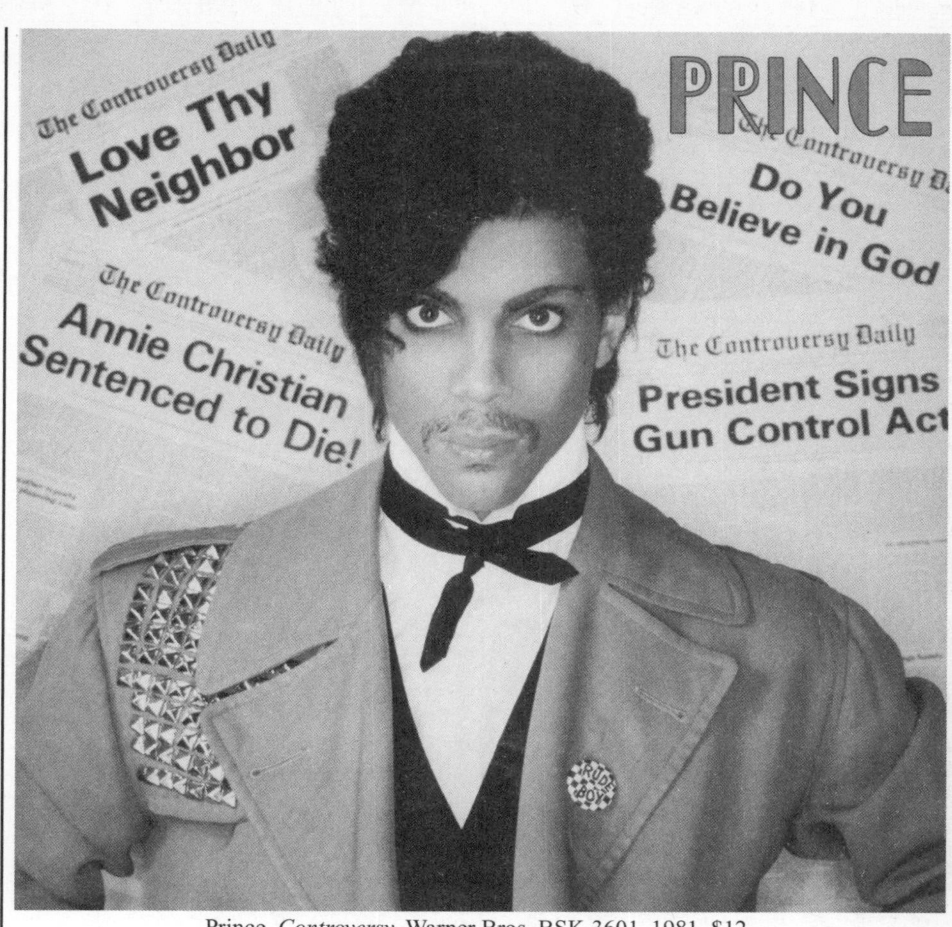


Prince, *Controversy,* Warner Bros. BSK 3601, 1981, $12.

## PRIMUS

| Number | Title (A Side/B Side) | Yr | NM |
|---|---|---|---|
| **CAROLINE** | | | |
| ❑ CAROL1619 | Frizzle Fry | 1990 | 80.00 |
| *—Red vinyl* | | | |
| ❑ CAROL1620 | Suck on This | 1990 | 60.00 |
| *—Clear vinyl* | | | |
| **INTERSCOPE** | | | |
| ❑ INT2-90126 [(2)] | Brown Album | 1997 | 50.00 |
| ❑ 92553 [(2)] | Tales from the Punchbowl | 1995 | 80.00 |
| ❑ 069-490414-01 [(2)] | Antipop | 1999 | 30.00 |
| **MOBILE FIDELITY** | | | |
| ❑ LMF45-001 [EP] | Animals Should Not Try to Act Like Humans | 2004 | 20.00 |
| *—"Original Master Recording" at top of cover; plays at 45 rpm* | | | |
| **PRAWN SONG/INTERSCOPE** | | | |
| ❑ 7-72738-1 [(2)] | Pork Soda | 1993 | 60.00 |

## PRINCE

Also see THE LEWIS CONNECTION; 94 EAST.

| Number | Title (A Side/B Side) | Yr | NM |
|---|---|---|---|
| **ARISTA** | | | |
| ❑ 14624 [(2)] | Rave Un2 the Joy Fantastic | 1999 | 12.00 |
| **NPG/BELLMARK** | | | |
| ❑ 71003 [EP] | The Beautiful Experience | 1994 | 20.00 |
| **NPG/REDLINE** | | | |
| ❑ 70004 [(2)] | The Rainbow Children | 2001 | 150.00 |
| **PAISLEY PARK** | | | |
| ❑ 25286 | Around the World in a Day | 1985 | 10.00 |
| *—Original copies have a fold-over flap (deduct 25% or more if missing)* | | | |
| ❑ 25395 | Parade | 1986 | 8.00 |
| ❑ 25577 [(2)] | Sign "O" The Times | 1987 | 15.00 |
| ❑ W1-25577 [(2)] | Sign "O" The Times | 1987 | 18.00 |
| *—Columbia House edition* | | | |
| ❑ 25677 | The Black Album | 1987 | 2000. |
| *—Withdrawn prior to release, though a few copies escaped. Numerous counterfeits exist on other labels and colored vinyl.* | | | |
| ❑ 25677-DJ [(2)] | The Black Album | 1987 | 3000. |
| *—Entire album on two 12-inch records that play at 45 RPM* | | | |
| ❑ 25720 | Lovesexy | 1988 | 12.00 |
| ❑ 25720-DJ [DJ] | Lovesexy | 1988 | 20.00 |
| *—Gold stamped and stickered cover (no UPC) with promo labels; tracks are banded* | | | |
| ❑ 27493 [(2)] | Graffiti Bridge | 1990 | 15.00 |
| *—Also includes The Time, Tevin Campbell* | | | |
| ❑ R 124370 | Around the World in a Day | 1985 | 12.00 |
| *—RCA Music Service edition* | | | |
| ❑ R 140234 | Parade | 1986 | 12.00 |
| *—RCA Music Service edition* | | | |
| ❑ R 154087 | Lovesexy | 1988 | 14.00 |
| *—BMG Direct Marketing edition* | | | |
| ❑ R 234107 [(2)] | Graffiti Bridge | 1990 | 18.00 |
| *—Also includes The Time, Tevin Campbell; BMG Direct Marketing edition* | | | |
| ❑ R 261991 [(2)] | Sign "O" The Times | 1987 | 18.00 |
| *—BMG Direct Marketing edition* | | | |
| **WARNER BROS.** | | | |
| ❑ BSK 3150 | For You | 1978 | 12.00 |
| *—White WB label* | | | |
| ❑ BSK 3150 | For You | 1978 | 20.00 |
| *—First edition on Burbank "palm trees" label* | | | |
| ❑ BSK 3366 | Prince | 1979 | 12.00 |
| ❑ BSK 3478 | Dirty Mind | 1980 | 12.00 |
| ❑ BSK 3601 | Controversy | 1981 | 12.00 |
| ❑ PRO-A-7270 [(2)DJ] | Come | 1994 | 30.00 |
| *—Promo-only vinyl* | | | |
| ❑ PRO-A-7330 [DJ] | The Black Album | 1994 | 50.00 |
| *—Promo-only vinyl* | | | |
| ❑ PRO-A-7835 [(2)DJ] | The Gold Experience | 1995 | 80.00 |
| *—Promo-only gold vinyl with numbered gold foil jacket* | | | |
| ❑ 23720 [(2)] | 1999 | 1982 | 15.00 |
| ❑ 25110 | Purple Rain | 1984 | 10.00 |
| *—With poster* | | | |
| ❑ 25110 | Purple Rain | 1984 | 50.00 |
| *—Purple vinyl; comes with poster* | | | |
| ❑ 25936 | Batman (Soundtrack) | 1989 | 10.00 |
| ❑ 45793 [DJ] | The Black Album | 1994 | 100.00 |
| *—Peach vinyl; 1,000 copies* | | | |
| ❑ 45793 [DJ] | The Black Album | 1994 | 200.00 |
| *—White vinyl; 300 copies, numbered in gold on the label (from 051 to 350)* | | | |
| ❑ 45793 [DJ] | The Black Album | 1994 | 500.00 |
| *—Gray marbled vinyl; 50 copies* | | | |
| ❑ R 160175 | Purple Rain | 1984 | 12.00 |
| *—RCA Music Service edition; includes poster* | | | |
| ❑ R 160344 | Batman (Soundtrack) | 1989 | 12.00 |
| *—BMG Direct Marketing edition* | | | |
| ❑ R 252483 [(2)] | 1999 | 1982 | 18.00 |
| *—RCA Music Service edition* | | | |

## PRINCE, BOB

| Number | Title (A Side/B Side) | Yr | NM |
|---|---|---|---|
| **RCA VICTOR** | | | |
| ❑ LPM-2435 [M] | Opus Jazz | 1961 | 20.00 |
| ❑ LSP-2435 [S] | Opus Jazz | 1961 | 25.00 |

WARNER BROS.

| Number | Title (A Side/B Side) | Yr | NM |
|---|---|---|---|
| ❑ W 1240 [M] | N.Y. Export: Op. Jazz from Ballets U.S.A.; Ballet Music from Leonard Bernstein's West Side Story | 1958 | 20.00 |
| ❑ WS 1240 [S] | N.Y. Export: Op. Jazz from Ballets U.S.A.; Ballet Music from Leonard Bernstein's West Side Story | 1958 | 25.00 |
| ❑ W 1276 [M] | Charleston 1970 | 1959 | 20.00 |
| ❑ WS 1276 [S] | Charleston 1970 | 1959 | 25.00 |

## PRINCE BUSTER

RCA VICTOR

| Number | Title (A Side/B Side) | Yr | NM |
|---|---|---|---|
| ❑ LPM-3792 [M] | Ten Commandments | 1967 | 25.00 |
| ❑ LSP-3792 [S] | Ten Commandments | 1967 | 30.00 |

## PRINZ, ROSEMARY

PHAROS

| Number | Title (A Side/B Side) | Yr | NM |
|---|---|---|---|
| ❑ MN-10001 [M] | TV's Penny Sings | 1966 | 20.00 |
| ❑ SN-30001 [S] | TV's Penny Sings | 1966 | 25.00 |

## PRITCHETT, GEORGE

KINNICKINNICK

| Number | Title (A Side/B Side) | Yr | NM |
|---|---|---|---|
| ❑ 101 | By Request | 197? | 20.00 |

## PROBY, P.J.

LIBERTY

| Number | Title (A Side/B Side) | Yr | NM |
|---|---|---|---|
| ❑ LRP-3406 [M] | Somewhere/Go Go P.J. Proby | 1965 | 20.00 |
| ❑ LRP-3421 [M] | P.J. Proby | 1965 | 20.00 |
| ❑ LRP-3497 [M] | Enigma | 1967 | 20.00 |
| ❑ LRP-3515 [M] | Phenomenon | 1967 | 20.00 |
| ❑ LST-7406 [S] | Somewhere/Go Go P.J. Proby | 1965 | 25.00 |
| ❑ LST-7421 [S] | P.J. Proby | 1965 | 25.00 |
| ❑ LST-7497 [S] | Enigma | 1967 | 25.00 |
| ❑ LST-7515 [S] | Phenomenon | 1967 | 25.00 |
| ❑ LST-7561 | What's Wrong with My World? | 1968 | 25.00 |

## PROCESSION

SMASH

| Number | Title (A Side/B Side) | Yr | NM |
|---|---|---|---|
| ❑ SRS-67122 | Procession | 1969 | 20.00 |

## PROCOL HARUM

A&M

| Number | Title (A Side/B Side) | Yr | NM |
|---|---|---|---|
| ❑ SP-3123 | A Salty Dog | 1979 | 8.00 |
| *—Reissue of 4179* | | | |
| ❑ SP-3259 | The Best of Procol Harum | 198? | 8.00 |
| *—Reissue of 4401* | | | |
| ❑ SP-4151 | Shine On Brightly | 1968 | 25.00 |
| ❑ SP-4179 | A Salty Dog | 1969 | 15.00 |
| ❑ SP-4261 | Home | 1970 | 12.00 |
| ❑ SP-4294 | Broken Barricades | 1971 | 12.00 |
| ❑ SP-4335 | Procol Harum Live in Concert with the Edmonton Symphony Orchestra | 1972 | 12.00 |
| ❑ SP-4373 | A Whiter Shade of Pale | 1972 | 12.00 |
| *—Reissue of Deram 18008 with one more track* | | | |
| ❑ SP-4401 | The Best of Procol Harum | 1973 | 12.00 |
| ❑ SP-8503 [DJ] | Procol Harum Lives | 197? | 50.00 |
| *—Interview LP alone* | | | |
| ❑ SP-8503 [DJ] | Procol Harum Lives | 197? | 300.00 |
| *—Promo-only box set with press kit, photos, keychain and interview LP* | | | |

CHRYSALIS

| Number | Title (A Side/B Side) | Yr | NM |
|---|---|---|---|
| ❑ CHR 1037 | Grand Hotel | 1973 | 12.00 |
| *—Green label with "3300 Warner Blvd." address* | | | |
| ❑ CHR 1037 | Grand Hotel | 1977 | 10.00 |
| *—Blue label with New York address* | | | |
| ❑ CHR 1058 | Exotic Birds and Fruit | 1974 | 12.00 |
| *—Green label with "3300 Warner Blvd." address* | | | |
| ❑ CHR 1058 | Exotic Birds and Fruit | 1977 | 10.00 |
| *—Blue label with New York address* | | | |
| ❑ CHR 1080 | Procol's Ninth | 1975 | 12.00 |
| *—Green label with "3300 Warner Blvd." address* | | | |
| ❑ CHR 1080 | Procol's Ninth | 1977 | 10.00 |
| *—Blue label with New York address* | | | |
| ❑ CHR 1130 | Something Magic | 1977 | 10.00 |
| ❑ PV 41037 | Grand Hotel | 1985 | 8.00 |
| ❑ PV 41058 | Exotic Birds and Fruit | 1985 | 8.00 |
| ❑ PV 41080 | Procol's Ninth | 1985 | 8.00 |

DERAM

| Number | Title (A Side/B Side) | Yr | NM |
|---|---|---|---|
| ❑ DE 16008 [M] | Procol Harum | 1967 | 80.00 |
| ❑ DE/S 16008/18008 | Procol Harum Poster | 1967 | 25.00 |
| ❑ DES 18008 [R] | Procol Harum | 1967 | 40.00 |

## PROCOPE, RUSSELL

DOT

| Number | Title (A Side/B Side) | Yr | NM |
|---|---|---|---|
| ❑ DLP 3010 [M] | The Persuasive Sax of Russell Procope | 1956 | 40.00 |

## PRODIGY

MAVERICK

| Number | Title (A Side/B Side) | Yr | NM |
|---|---|---|---|
| ❑ PRO-A-8929 [(2)DJ] | The Fat of the Land | 1997 | 25.00 |
| *—Promo-only U.S. vinyl in generic white sleeve* | | | |

## PROFESSOR LONGHAIR

ATLANTIC

| Number | Title (A Side/B Side) | Yr | NM |
|---|---|---|---|
| ❑ SD 7225 | New Orleans Piano | 1972 | 25.00 |

## PROVINE, DOROTHY

WARNER BROS.

| Number | Title (A Side/B Side) | Yr | NM |
|---|---|---|---|
| ❑ W 1394 [M] | The Roaring 20's | 1961 | 20.00 |
| ❑ WS 1394 [S] | The Roaring 20's | 1961 | 25.00 |
| ❑ W 1419 [M] | The Vamp of the Roaring 20's | 1961 | 20.00 |
| ❑ WS 1419 [S] | The Vamp of the Roaring 20's | 1961 | 25.00 |

## PRYOR, RICHARD

AUDIOFIDELITY

| Number | Title (A Side/B Side) | Yr | NM |
|---|---|---|---|
| ❑ 349 [PD] | Richard Pryor Live | 198? | 15.00 |

DOVE

| Number | Title (A Side/B Side) | Yr | NM |
|---|---|---|---|
| ❑ RS 6325 | Richard Pryor | 1968 | 20.00 |

LAFF

| Number | Title (A Side/B Side) | Yr | NM |
|---|---|---|---|
| ❑ (# unknown) | Supernigger | 198? | 8.00 |
| ❑ A 146 | Craps: After Hours | 1971 | 12.00 |
| ❑ A 170 | Pryor Goes Foxx Hunting | 197? | 12.00 |
| ❑ A 184 | Down 'N' Dirty | 197? | 12.00 |
| ❑ A 188 | Richard Pryor Meets Richard and Willie and the S.L.A. | 1976 | 12.00 |
| ❑ A 196 | Are You Serious??? | 1977 | 12.00 |
| ❑ A 198 | Who Me? I'm Not Him | 1977 | 12.00 |
| ❑ A 200 | Black Ben | 1978 | 10.00 |
| ❑ A 202 | Wizard of Comedy | 1978 | 10.00 |
| ❑ A 206 | Outrageous | 1979 | 10.00 |
| ❑ A 209 | Insane | 1980 | 10.00 |
| ❑ A 212 | Holy Smoke | 1980 | 10.00 |
| ❑ A 216 | Rev. Du Rite | 1981 | 10.00 |
| ❑ A 221 | The Very Best of Richard Pryor | 1982 | 10.00 |
| ❑ 226 | Blackjack | 198? | 8.00 |
| *—Reissue of 146* | | | |
| ❑ 227 | Show Biz | 198? | 8.00 |
| *—Reissue of 200* | | | |
| ❑ 279 | Richard Pryor Live | 198? | 8.00 |

PARTEE

| Number | Title (A Side/B Side) | Yr | NM |
|---|---|---|---|
| ❑ PBS-2404 | That Nigger's Crazy | 1974 | 15.00 |

REPRISE

| Number | Title (A Side/B Side) | Yr | NM |
|---|---|---|---|
| ❑ MS 2227 | Is It Something I Said? | 1975 | 12.00 |
| ❑ MS 2241 | That Nigger's Crazy | 197? | 12.00 |
| *—Reissue of Partee LP* | | | |
| ❑ MSK 2285 | Is It Something I Said? | 1977 | 10.00 |
| *—Reissue of 2227* | | | |
| ❑ MSK 2287 | That Nigger's Crazy | 1977 | 10.00 |
| *—Reissue of Reprise 2241* | | | |
| ❑ RS 6325 | Richard Pryor | 197? | 12.00 |
| *—Reissue of Dove LP* | | | |

TIGER LILY

| Number | Title (A Side/B Side) | Yr | NM |
|---|---|---|---|
| ❑ TL 14023 | L.A. Jail | 1977 | 12.00 |

WARNER BROS.

| Number | Title (A Side/B Side) | Yr | NM |
|---|---|---|---|
| ❑ BS 2960 | Bicentennial Nigger | 1976 | 12.00 |
| ❑ BSK 3057 | Richard Pryor's Greatest Hits | 1977 | 10.00 |
| ❑ BSK 3114 | Bicentennial Nigger | 1977 | 10.00 |
| *—Reissue of 2960* | | | |
| ❑ 2BSK 3364 [(2)] | Wanted | 1978 | 12.00 |
| ❑ BSK 3660 | Richard Pryor Live on the Sunset Strip | 1982 | 10.00 |
| ❑ 23981 | Richard Pryor: Here and Now | 1983 | 10.00 |

## PRYSOCK, ARTHUR

DECCA

| Number | Title (A Side/B Side) | Yr | NM |
|---|---|---|---|
| ❑ DL 4581 [M] | Strictly Sentimental | 1965 | 15.00 |
| ❑ DL 4628 [M] | Showcase | 1965 | 15.00 |
| ❑ DL 74581 [S] | Strictly Sentimental | 1965 | 20.00 |
| ❑ DL 74628 [S] | Showcase | 1965 | 20.00 |

KING

| Number | Title (A Side/B Side) | Yr | NM |
|---|---|---|---|
| ❑ KS-1064 | The Country Side of Arthur Prysock | 1969 | 12.00 |
| ❑ KS-1066 | Where the Soul Trees Go | 1970 | 12.00 |
| ❑ KS-1067 | The Lord Is My Shepherd | 1970 | 12.00 |
| ❑ KS-1088 | Fly My Love | 1970 | 12.00 |
| ❑ KS-1134 | Unforgettable | 1971 | 12.00 |

MCA

| Number | Title (A Side/B Side) | Yr | NM |
|---|---|---|---|
| ❑ 3061 | Here's To Good Friends | 1978 | 10.00 |

MGM

| Number | Title (A Side/B Side) | Yr | NM |
|---|---|---|---|
| ❑ GAS-134 | Arthur Prysock (Golden Archive Series) | 1970 | 12.00 |
| ❑ SE-4694 | Arthur Prysock | 1970 | 12.00 |

MILESTONE

| Number | Title (A Side/B Side) | Yr | NM |
|---|---|---|---|
| ❑ M-9139 | A Rockin' Good Way | 1986 | 10.00 |
| ❑ M-9146 | This Guy's in Love with You | 1987 | 10.00 |
| ❑ M-9157 | Today's Love Songs, Tomorrow's Blues | 1988 | 10.00 |

OLD TOWN

| Number | Title (A Side/B Side) | Yr | NM |
|---|---|---|---|
| ❑ 12-001 | Arthur Prysock '74 | 1973 | 12.00 |
| ❑ 12-002 | Love Makes It Right | 1974 | 12.00 |
| ❑ 12-004 | All My Life | 1976 | 12.00 |
| ❑ LP-102 [M] | I Worry About You | 1962 | 50.00 |
| ❑ LP-2004 [M] | Arthur Prysock Sings Only for You | 1962 | 50.00 |
| ❑ LP-2005 [M] | Coast to Coast | 1963 | 40.00 |
| ❑ LP-2006 [M] | A Portrait of Arthur Prysock | 1963 | 40.00 |
| ❑ LP-2007 [M] | Everlasting Songs for Everlasting Lovers | 1964 | 40.00 |
| ❑ LP-2008 [M] | Intimately Yours | 1964 | 40.00 |
| ❑ LP-2009 [M] | A Double Header with Arthur Prysock | 1965 | 40.00 |
| ❑ LP-2010 [M] | In a Mood | 1965 | 40.00 |
| ❑ OT 12005 | Arthur Prysock Does It Again | 1977 | 12.00 |
| ❑ ST-90604 [S] | A Portrait of Arthur Prysock | 1965 | 40.00 |
| *—Capitol Record Club edition* | | | |
| ❑ T-90604 [M] | A Portrait of Arthur Prysock | 1965 | 40.00 |
| *—Capitol Record Club edition* | | | |

POLYDOR

| Number | Title (A Side/B Side) | Yr | NM |
|---|---|---|---|
| ❑ PD-2-8901 [(2)] | Silk and Satin | 1977 | 15.00 |

VERVE

| Number | Title (A Side/B Side) | Yr | NM |
|---|---|---|---|
| ❑ V6-650 [(2)] | 24 Karat Hits | 1969 | 15.00 |
| ❑ V-5009 [M] | Art and Soul | 1966 | 12.00 |
| ❑ V6-5009 [S] | Art and Soul | 1966 | 15.00 |
| ❑ V-5011 [M] | The Best of Arthur Prysock | 1967 | 12.00 |
| ❑ V6-5011 [S] | The Best of Arthur Prysock | 1967 | 15.00 |
| ❑ V-5012 [M] | A Portrait of Arthur Prysock | 1967 | 15.00 |
| ❑ V6-5012 [S] | A Portrait of Arthur Prysock | 1967 | 15.00 |
| ❑ V-5014 [M] | Mister Prysock | 1967 | 15.00 |
| ❑ V6-5014 [S] | Mister Prysock | 1967 | 15.00 |
| ❑ V-5029 [M] | Love Me | 1968 | 15.00 |
| ❑ V6-5029 [S] | Love Me | 1968 | 12.00 |
| ❑ V-5038 [M] | The Best of Arthur Prysock, Number 2 | 1968 | 20.00 |
| *—All mono copies appear to be yellow label promos* | | | |
| ❑ V6-5038 [S] | The Best of Arthur Prysock, Number 2 | 1968 | 12.00 |
| ❑ V-5048 [M] | To Love or Not to Love | 1968 | 30.00 |
| *—May be promo only* | | | |
| ❑ V6-5048 [S] | To Love or Not to Love | 1968 | 12.00 |
| ❑ V6-5059 | I Must Be Doing Something Right | 1968 | 12.00 |
| ❑ V6-5070 | This Is My Beloved | 1969 | 12.00 |

## PRYSOCK, ARTHUR/COUNT BASIE

VERVE

| Number | Title (A Side/B Side) | Yr | NM |
|---|---|---|---|
| ❑ V-8646 [M] | Arthur Prysock/Count Basie | 1966 | 15.00 |
| ❑ V6-8646 [S] | Arthur Prysock/Count Basie | 1966 | 20.00 |
| ❑ 827011-1 | Arthur Prysock/Count Basie | 1985 | 8.00 |
| *—Reissue* | | | |

## PRYSOCK, RED

MERCURY

| Number | Title (A Side/B Side) | Yr | NM |
|---|---|---|---|
| ❑ MG-20088 [M] | Rock 'n Roll | 1955 | 200.00 |
| ❑ MG-20211 [M] | Fruit Boots | 1957 | 120.00 |
| ❑ MG-20307 [M] | The Beat | 1957 | 80.00 |
| ❑ MG-20512 [M] | Swing Softly Red | 1958 | 50.00 |
| ❑ SR-60188 [S] | Swing Softly Red | 1959 | 80.00 |

WING

| Number | Title (A Side/B Side) | Yr | NM |
|---|---|---|---|
| ❑ MGW-12007 [M] | Fruit Boots | 1959 | 40.00 |
| *—Originals have liner notes on back cover* | | | |
| ❑ MGW-12007 [M] | Fruit Boots | 196? | 20.00 |
| *—Reissues have other LPs listed on back cover* | | | |
| ❑ SRW-16007 [R] | Fruit Boots | 196? | 12.00 |

## PSYCHEDELIC FURS

COLUMBIA

| Number | Title (A Side/B Side) | Yr | NM |
|---|---|---|---|
| ❑ AS 1296 [DJ] | Interchords | 1981 | 25.00 |
| ❑ CAS 01310 [DJ] | Interchords with Richard Butler | 1988 | 20.00 |
| ❑ CAS 2719 [DJ] | Richard Butler Interview | 1987 | 15.00 |
| ❑ NFC 36791 | Psychedelic Furs | 1980 | 12.00 |
| ❑ PC 36791 | The Psychedelic Furs | 198? | 8.00 |
| *—Budget-line reissue* | | | |
| ❑ NFC 37339 | Talk Talk Talk | 1981 | 10.00 |
| ❑ PC 37339 | Talk Talk Talk | 1983 | 8.00 |
| *—Budget-line reissue* | | | |
| ❑ ARC 38261 | Forever Now | 1982 | 10.00 |
| ❑ PC 38261 | Forever Now | 198? | 8.00 |
| *—Budget-line reissue* | | | |
| ❑ BFC 39278 | Mirror Moves | 1984 | 10.00 |
| ❑ PC 39278 | Mirror Moves | 198? | 8.00 |
| *—Budget-line reissue* | | | |
| ❑ FC 40466 | Midnight to Midnight | 1987 | 10.00 |
| ❑ FC 44377 | All of This and Nothing | 1988 | 10.00 |
| ❑ FC 45412 | Book of Days | 1989 | 10.00 |

## PSYCHOTIC PINEAPPLE, THE

RICHMOND

| Number | Title (A Side/B Side) | Yr | NM |
|---|---|---|---|
| ❑ 6026 | Where's the Party | 1980 | 25.00 |

## PUCHO AND THE LATIN SOUL BROTHERS

PRESTIGE

| Number | Title (A Side/B Side) | Yr | NM |
|---|---|---|---|
| ❑ PRLP-7471 [M] | Pucho and the Latin Soul Brothers | 1967 | 40.00 |
| ❑ PRST-7471 [S] | Pucho and the Latin Soul Brothers | 1967 | 30.00 |
| ❑ PRLP-7502 [M] | Saffron and Soul | 1967 | 40.00 |
| ❑ PRST-7502 [S] | Saffron and Soul | 1967 | 30.00 |
| ❑ PRLP-7528 [M] | Shuckin' and Jivin' | 1967 | 50.00 |
| ❑ PRST-7528 [S] | Shuckin' and Jivin' | 1967 | 30.00 |
| ❑ PRST-7555 | Big Stick | 1968 | 30.00 |
| ❑ PRST-7572 | Heat! | 1968 | 30.00 |
| ❑ PRST-7616 | Dateline | 1969 | 30.00 |
| ❑ PRST-7679 | The Best of Pucho and the Latin Soul Brothers | 1969 | 25.00 |

## PUCKETT, GARY, AND THE UNION GAP

COLUMBIA

| Number | Title (A Side/B Side) | Yr | NM |
|---|---|---|---|
| ❑ CS 1042 | Gary Puckett and the Union Gap's Greatest Hits | 1970 | 20.00 |

| Number | Title (A Side/B Side) | Yr | NM |
|---|---|---|---|



❑ CL 2812 [M] Woman, Woman 1968 40.00
*—As "The Union Gap Featuring Gary Puckett"*
❑ CL 2864 [M] Young Girl 1968 50.00
*—Red label stock copy with "Mono" on label; this has been confirmed to exist*
❑ CL 2915 [M] Incredible 1968 60.00
*—Red label stock copy with "Mono" on label; this has been confirmed to exist*
❑ CS 9612 [S] Woman, Woman 1968 20.00
*—As "The Union Gap Featuring Gary Puckett"*
❑ CS 9664 [M] Young Girl 1968 40.00
*—White label promo with stereo number and "Mono" on label; "Special Mono Radio Station Copy" sticker and timing strip on front cover*
❑ CS 9664 [S] Young Girl 1968 20.00
❑ CS 9715 [S] Incredible 1968 20.00
❑ CS 9935 The New Gary Puckett and the Union Gap Album 1969 20.00
❑ C 30862 The Gary Puckett Album 1971 15.00

HARMONY
❑ KH 31184 Lady Willpower 1972 10.00

## PUENTE, TITO

DECCA
❑ DL 4910 [M] Brasilia Nueve 1967 25.00
❑ DL 74910 [S] Brasilia Nueve 1967 20.00

GNP CRESCENDO
❑ GNP-70 [M] The Exciting Tito Puente Band in Hollywood 196? 30.00

RCA VICTOR
❑ LPM-1251 [M] Cuban Carnival 1955 50.00
❑ LPM-1312 [M] Puente Goes Jazz 1956 60.00
❑ LPM-1354 [M] Mambo on Broadway 1957 40.00
❑ LPM-1392 [M] Let's Cha-Cha with Puente 1957 40.00
❑ LPM-1447 [M] Night Beat 1957 40.00
❑ LPM-1479 [M] Mucho Puente 1957 40.00
❑ LPM-1617 [M] Top Percussion 1958 30.00
❑ LSP-1617 [S] Top Percussion 1958 40.00
❑ LPM-1692 [M] Dance Mania 1958 30.00
❑ LSP-1692 [S] Dance Mania 1958 40.00
❑ LPM-1874 [M] Dancing Under Latin Skies 1958 30.00
❑ LSP-1874 [S] Dancing Under Latin Skies 1958 40.00
❑ LPM-2113 [M] Mucho Cha Cha Cha 1959 30.00
❑ LSP-2113 [S] Mucho Cha Cha Cha 1959 40.00
❑ LPM-2187 [M] Cha Cha at Grossinger's 1959 30.00
❑ LSP-2187 [S] Cha Cha at Grossinger's 1959 40.00
❑ LPM-2257 [M] Tambo 1960 30.00
❑ LSP-2257 [S] Tambo 1960 40.00
❑ LPM-2299 [M] Revolving Bandstand 1960 30.00
❑ LSP-2299 [S] Revolving Bandstand 1960 40.00
❑ LPM-2974 [M] The Best of Tito Puente 1964 25.00

ROULETTE
❑ R-25193 [M] Bossa Nova 1962 20.00
❑ SR-25193 [S] Bossa Nova 1962 25.00
❑ R-25276 [M] "My Fair Lady" Goes Latin 1964 20.00
❑ SR-25276 [S] "My Fair Lady" Goes Latin 1964 25.00

TICO
❑ LP-101 [10] Mambos, Volume 1 1951 100.00
❑ LP-103 [10] Mambos, Volume 2 1952 80.00
❑ LP-107 [10] Mambos, Volume 3 195? 80.00
❑ LP-114 [10] Mambos, Volume 4 195? 80.00
❑ LP-116 [10] Mambos, Volume 5 195? 80.00
❑ LP-120 [10] The King of the Mambo and His Orchestra 195? 80.00
❑ LP-124 [10] Tito Puente at the Vibes and His Rhythm Quartet 195? 80.00
❑ LP-128 [10] Cha Cha Cha, Volume 1 195? 80.00
❑ LP-130 [10] Cha Cha Cha, Volume 2 195? 80.00
❑ LP-131 [10] Mambos, Volume 8 195? 80.00
❑ LP-133 [10] Instrumental Mambos 195? 80.00
❑ LP-134 [10] Cha Cha Cha, Volume 3 195? 80.00
❑ LP-1001 [M] Mamborama 1955 60.00
❑ LP-1003 [M] Mambo and Me 1955 60.00
❑ LP-1006 [M] Mambos for Lovers 1955 60.00
❑ LP-1010 [M] Dance the Cha Cha Cha 195? 60.00
❑ LP-1011 [M] Puente in Percussion 1956 60.00
❑ LP-1025 [M] Cha Cha Cha at the El Morocco 1956 60.00
❑ LP-1032 [M] Basic Cha Cha Cha 1957 50.00
❑ LP-1049 [M] Tito Puente Swings/Vicentico Valdes Sings 1958 50.00
❑ LP-1058 [M] Puente in Love 1959 40.00
❑ LP-1083 [M] Pachanga Con Puente 1961 30.00
❑ SLP-1083 [S] Pachanga Con Puente 1961 40.00
❑ LP-1085 [M] Vaya Puente 1962 30.00
❑ SLP-1085 [S] Vaya Puente 1962 40.00
❑ LP-1086 [M] El Rey Tito: Bravo Puente 1962 30.00
❑ SLP-1086 [S] El Rey Tito: Bravo Puente 1962 40.00
*—This album contains the original version of "Oye Como Va," later a hit for Santana*
❑ LP-1088 [M] Tito Puente in Puerto Rico 1963 25.00
❑ SLP-1088 [S] Tito Puente in Puerto Rico 1963 30.00
❑ LP-1093 [M] Tito Puente Bailables 1963 25.00
❑ SLP-1093 [S] Tito Puente Bailables 1963 30.00
❑ LP-1106 [M] Excitente Ritmo 196? 25.00
❑ SLP-1106 [S] Excitente Ritmo 196? 30.00
❑ LP-1109 [M] El Mundo Latino de Tito Puente 196? 25.00
❑ SLP-1109 [S] El Mundo Latino de Tito Puente 196? 30.00
❑ LP-1115 [M] Mucho Puente 196? 25.00
❑ SLP-1115 [S] Mucho Puente 196? 30.00
❑ LP-1116 [M] De Mi Para Ti 196? 25.00
❑ SLP-1116 [S] De Mi Para Ti 196? 30.00
❑ LP-1121 [M] Tito Puente Swings/The Exciting Lupe Sings 196? 20.00
❑ SLP-1121 [S] Tito Puente Swings/The Exciting Lupe Sings 196? 25.00
❑ LP-1125 [M] Tu Y Yo (You 'n' Me) 196? 20.00
❑ SLP-1125 [S] Tu Y Yo (You 'n' Me) 196? 25.00
❑ LP-1127 [M] Carnival in Harlem 196? 20.00
❑ SLP-1127 [S] Carnival in Harlem 196? 25.00
❑ LP-1131 [M] Homenaje a Rafael Hernandez 196? 20.00
❑ SLP-1131 [S] Homenaje a Rafael Hernandez 196? 25.00
❑ LP-1136 [M] Cuba Y Puerto Ricon Son 196? 20.00
❑ SLP-1136 [S] Cuba Y Puerto Ricon Son 196? 25.00
❑ LP-1151 [M] 20th Anniversary 1967 25.00
❑ SLP-1151 [S] 20th Anniversary 1967 20.00
❑ LP-1154 [M] El Rey Y Yo (The King and I) 1967 25.00
❑ SLP-1154 [S] El Rey Y Yo (The King and I) 1967 20.00
❑ SLP-1172 El Rey (The King) 1968 20.00
❑ SLP-1191 Tito Puente En El Puente (On the Bridge) 1969 20.00
❑ SLP-1203 The Best of Tito Puente 1969 20.00
❑ SLP-1214 P'alante! 1970 20.00

## PUGSLEY MUNION

J&S
❑ SLP-001 Just Like You 1969 100.00

## PULLEN, DON, AND MILFORD GRAVES

PULLEN-GRAVES MUSIC
❑ (# unknown) Graves-Pullen Duo 1967 50.00

S.R.P.
❑ LP-290 Nommo 1968 40.00

## PULLEN, WHITEY

CROWN
❑ CST-332 [R] Whitey Pullen 1963 12.00
❑ CLP-5332 [M] Whitey Pullen 1963 40.00

## PULLINS, LEROY

KAPP
❑ KL-1488 [M] I'm a Nut 1966 25.00
❑ KS-3488 [S] I'm a Nut 1966 30.00
❑ KS-3557 Funny Bones and Hearts 1968 25.00

## PULSE

POISON RING
❑ 2237 Pulse 1969 25.00

## PUMA, JOE

BETHLEHEM
❑ BCP-1012 [10] East Coast Jazz 3 1954 200.00

COLUMBIA
❑ CL 1618 [M] Like Tweet 1961 30.00
❑ CS 8418 [S] Like Tweet 1961 40.00

DAWN
❑ DLP-1118 [M] Wild Kitten 1957 100.00

JUBILEE
❑ JLP-1070 [M] Joe Puma Jazz 1958 80.00

## PURDIE, BERNARD

DATE
❑ TEM 3006 [M] Soul Drums 1967 20.00
❑ TES 4006 [S] Soul Drums 1967 20.00

PRESTIGE
❑ 10013 Purdie Good 1971 15.00
❑ 10038 Shaft 1972 20.00

## PURE ENERGY

PRISM
❑ PLP-1007 Pure Energy 1980 20.00

## PURE PRAIRIE LEAGUE

CASABLANCA
❑ NBLP-7212 Firin' Up 1980 10.00
❑ NBLP-7255 Something in the Night 1981 10.00

PAIR
❑ PDL2-1034 [(2)]Home on the Range 1986 12.00

RCA VICTOR
❑ APD1-0933 [Q] Two Lane Highway 1975 20.00
❑ APL1-0933 Two Lane Highway 1975 12.00
❑ APD1-1247 [Q] If the Shoe Fits 1976 20.00
❑ APL1-1247 If the Shoe Fits 1976 12.00
❑ APL1-1924 Dance 1976 12.00
❑ CPL2-2404 [(2)]Live!! Takin' the Stage 1977 15.00
❑ AFL1-2590 Just Fly 1978 12.00
❑ AFL1-3335 Can't Hold Back 1979 12.00
❑ AYL1-3669 Two Lane Highway 1980 8.00
*—"Best Buy Series" reissue*
❑ AYL1-3717 If the Shoe Fits 1981 8.00
*—"Best Buy Series" reissue*
❑ AYL1-3718 Just Fly 1981 8.00
*—"Best Buy Series" reissue*
❑ AYL1-3719 Pure Prairie League 1981 8.00
*—"Best Buy Series" reissue*
❑ AYL1-3723 Dance 1981 8.00
*—"Best Buy Series" reissue*
❑ AFL1-4650 Pure Prairie League 1977 10.00
*—Reissue of LSP-4650*
❑ LSP-4650 Pure Prairie League 1972 12.00
❑ AYL1-4656 Bustin' Out 1984 8.00
*—"Best Buy Series" reissue*
❑ AFL1-4769 Bustin' Out 1977 10.00
*—Reissue of LSP-4769*
❑ LSP-4769 Bustin' Out 1972 12.00

## PURIFY, JAMES AND BOBBY

BELL
❑ 6003 [M] James and Bobby Purify 1966 25.00
❑ S-6003 [S] James and Bobby Purify 1966 30.00
❑ 6010 [M] The Pure Sound of the Purifys 1967 25.00
❑ S-6010 [S] The Pure Sound of the Purifys 1967 30.00

MERCURY
❑ SRM-1-1134 The Purify Brothers 1977 12.00

## PURPLE GANG, THE

SIRE
❑ SES 97006 The Purple Gang Strikes 1969 20.00

## PURPLE IMAGE

MAP CITY
❑ 3015 Purple Image 1971 50.00

## PURSELL, BILL

COLUMBIA
❑ CL 1992 [M] Our Winter Love 1963 15.00
❑ CL 2077 [M] Chasing a Dream 1964 15.00
❑ CL 2421 [M] Remembered Love 1965 15.00
❑ CS 8792 [S] Our Winter Love 1963 20.00
❑ CS 8877 [S] Chasing a Dream 1964 20.00
❑ CS 9221 [S] Remembered Love 1965 20.00

## PUSSY GALORE

BUY OUR RECORDS
❑ 10 [EP] Pussy Gold 5000 1986 50.00

CAROLINE
❑ CAROL 1337 Right Now! 1987 25.00
❑ CAROL 1369 Dial "M" for Motherfucker 1989 25.00

SHOVE
❑ 2 Groovy Hate Fuck 1986 50.00

## PUTMAN, CURLY

ABC
❑ ABC-618 [M] Lonesome 1967 25.00
❑ ABCS-618 [S] Lonesome 1967 15.00
❑ ABCS-686 World of Country Music 1969 15.00

## PUYANA, RAFAEL

MERCURY LIVING PRESENCE
❑ SR 90259 [S] Picchi: Belli d'Arpsichordo; Frescobaldi: Music for Harpsichord 196? 20.00
*—Maroon label, no "Vendor: Mercury Record Corporation"*
❑ SR 90304 [S] The Golden Age of Harpsichord Music 196? 20.00
*—Maroon label, no "Vendor: Mercury Record Corporation"*
❑ SR 90322 [S] Bachs: Harpsichord Music 196? 20.00
*—Maroon label, no "Vendor: Mercury Record Corporation"*
❑ SR 90369 [S] Bach for Harpsichord 196? 30.00
*—Maroon label, no "Vendor: Mercury Record Corporation"*
❑ SR 90369 [S] Bach for Harpsichord 196? 30.00
*—Maroon label, with "Vendor: Mercury Record Corporation"*
❑ SR 90411 [S] Baroque Masterpieces for the Harpsichord 196? 30.00
*—Maroon label, no "Vendor: Mercury Record Corporation"*
❑ SR 90459 [S] Soler: Harpsichord Music 196? 30.00
*—Maroon label, with "Vendor: Mercury Record Corporation"*

## PUZZLE

ABC
❑ ABCS-671 Puzzle 1969 20.00

## PYLE, ARTIMUS

MCA
❑ 5313 A.P.B. 1982 30.00
❑ 39003 Nightcaller 1983 30.00

## PYLE, JACK

CAMEO
❑ C-1017 [M] Listen Son...And Other Readings by Jack Pyle 1963 20.00

## PYRAMIDS, THE (1)

BEST
❑ LPM-1001 [M] The Original Penetration! And Other Favorites 1964 250.00
*—Original issue with "Walkin' the Dog"*
❑ BR 16501 [M] The Original Penetration! And Other Favorites 1964 200.00
*—Reissue with "Road Runnah"*

Queen, *The Game,* Elektra 5E-513, 1980, shiny silver cover, $15.

| Number | Title (A Side/B Side) | Yr | NM |
|---|---|---|---|
| ❑ BS 36501 [R] | The Original Penetration! And Other Favorites | 1964 | 120.00 |
| **SUNDAZED** | | | |
| ❑ LP-5012 | Penetration! The Best of the Pyramids | 1995 | 10.00 |

# Q

| Number | Title (A Side/B Side) | Yr | NM |
|---|---|---|---|
| **QUARTERMASS** | | | |
| HARVEST | | | |
| ❑ SKAO-314 | Quartermass | 1970 | 30.00 |
| **QUARTETTE TRES BIEN** | | | |
| ATLANTIC | | | |
| ❑ SD 1461 [S] | Bully! | 1966 | 15.00 |
| DECCA | | | |
| ❑ DL 4893 [M] | Here It Is | 1967 | 15.00 |
| ❑ DL 4958 [M] | Four of a Kind | 1967 | 15.00 |
| ❑ DL 74547 [S] | Boss Tres Bien | 1964 | 15.00 |
| ❑ DL 74548 [S] | Kilimanjaro | 1964 | 15.00 |
| ❑ DL 74617 [S] | Spring Into Spring | 1965 | 15.00 |
| ❑ DL 74675 [S] | Stepping Out | 1965 | 15.00 |
| ❑ DL 74715 [S] | Sky High | 1966 | 15.00 |
| ❑ DL 74791 [S] | "In" Motion | 1966 | 15.00 |
| ❑ DL 74822 [S] | Where It's At | 1966 | 15.00 |
| GNP | | | |
| ❑ GNP-102 [M] | Quartette Tres Bien | 1962 | 20.00 |
| ❑ GNPS-102 [S] | Quartette Tres Bien | 1962 | 25.00 |
| ❑ GNP-107 [M] | Kilimanjaro | 1963 | 20.00 |
| ❑ GNPS-107 [S] | Kilimanjaro | 1963 | 25.00 |
| **QUATRO, MICHAEL** | | | |
| EVOLUTION | | | |
| ❑ 3011 | Paintings | 1972 | 25.00 |
| *—As "Mike Quatro Jam Band"* | | | |
| ❑ 3021 | Look Deeply Into the Mirror | 1973 | 25.00 |
| *—As "Mike Quatro Jam Band"* | | | |
| KOALA | | | |
| ❑ KOA 14631 | Into the Mirror | 1979 | 15.00 |
| *—New version of similar 1973 album on Evolution* | | | |
| PRODIGAL | | | |
| ❑ P6-10010S1 | Dancers, Romancers, Dreamers and Schemers | 1976 | 15.00 |
| ❑ P6-10016S1 | Gettin' Ready | 1977 | 15.00 |

| Number | Title (A Side/B Side) | Yr | NM |
|---|---|---|---|
| SPECTOR | | | |
| ❑ SW-70003 | Bottom Line | 1981 | 15.00 |
| UNITED ARTISTS | | | |
| ❑ UA-LA420-G | In Collaboration with the Gods | 1975 | 20.00 |
| **QUATTLEBAUM, DOUG** | | | |
| BLUESVILLE | | | |
| ❑ BVLP-1065 [M] | Softee Man Blues | 1963 | 60.00 |
| *—Blue label, silver print* | | | |
| ❑ BVLP-1065 [M] | Softee Man Blues | 1964 | 20.00 |
| *—Blue label, trident logo at right* | | | |
| **QUEBEC, IKE** | | | |
| BLUE NOTE | | | |
| ❑ BLP-4093 [M] | Heavy Soul | 1961 | 80.00 |
| *—With 61st St. address on label* | | | |
| ❑ BLP-4093 [M] | Heavy Soul | 1962 | 25.00 |
| *—With "New York, USA" address on label* | | | |
| ❑ BLP-4098 [M] | Blue and Sentimental | 1962 | 25.00 |
| *—With "New York, USA" address on label* | | | |
| ❑ BLP-4098 [M] | Blue and Sentimental | 1962 | 80.00 |
| *—With 61st St. address on label* | | | |
| ❑ BLP-4105 [M] | It Might As Well Be Spring | 1962 | 30.00 |
| ❑ BLP-4114 [M] | Bossa Nova Soul Samba | 1962 | 30.00 |
| ❑ BST-84093 [S] | Heavy Soul | 1961 | 20.00 |
| *—With "New York, USA" address on label* | | | |
| ❑ BST-84093 [S] | Heavy Soul | 1961 | 60.00 |
| *—With 61st St. address on label* | | | |
| ❑ BST-84098 [S] | Blue and Sentimental | 1962 | 20.00 |
| *—With "New York, USA" address on label* | | | |
| ❑ BST-84098 [S] | Blue and Sentimental | 1962 | 60.00 |
| *—With 61st St. address on label* | | | |
| ❑ BST-84105 [S] | It Might As Well Be Spring | 1962 | 40.00 |
| *—With "New York, USA" address on label* | | | |
| ❑ BST-84114 | Soul Samba | 199? | 25.00 |
| *—Classic Records reissue on audiophile vinyl* | | | |
| ❑ BST-84114 [S] | Bossa Nova Soul Samba | 1962 | 40.00 |
| *—With "New York, USA" address on label* | | | |
| MOSAIC | | | |
| ❑ MR4-107 [(4)] | The Complete Blue Note Forties Recordings of Ike Quebec and John Hardee | 199? | 70.00 |
| ❑ MR3-121 [(3)] | The Complete Blue Note 45 Sessions of Ike Quebec | 199? | 60.00 |

| Number | Title (A Side/B Side) | Yr | NM |
|---|---|---|---|
| **QUEEN** | | | |
| CAPITOL | | | |
| ❑ ST-12322 | The Works | 1984 | 10.00 |
| ❑ SMAS-12476 | A Kind of Magic | 1986 | 10.00 |
| ❑ C1-92357 | The Miracle | 1989 | 15.00 |
| DCC COMPACT CLASSICS | | | |
| ❑ LPZ-2072 | A Night at the Opera | 2000 | 25.00 |
| *—Audiophile vinyl* | | | |
| ELEKTRA | | | |
| ❑ 6E-101 | A Day at the Races | 1977 | 10.00 |
| *—Butterfly, red, or red/black labels* | | | |
| ❑ 6E-112 | News of the World | 1977 | 10.00 |
| ❑ 6E-112 [DJ] | News of the World | 1977 | 150.00 |
| *—White label promo with oversize cover and press kit* | | | |
| ❑ 6E-166 | Jazz | 1978 | 8.00 |
| *—Without poster of the nude bicycle race. Some copies had a sticker on the shrink wrap with an address at which the poster was available free.* | | | |
| ❑ 6E-166 | Jazz | 1978 | 12.00 |
| *—With poster of the nude bicycle race* | | | |
| ❑ 5E-513 | The Game | 1980 | 10.00 |
| *—With dull gray cover; all copies have custom white labels* | | | |
| ❑ 5E-513 | The Game | 1980 | 15.00 |
| *—With shiny, mirrorlike cover; all copies have custom white labels* | | | |
| ❑ 5E-564 | Queen's Greatest Hits | 1981 | 12.00 |
| ❑ BB-702 [(2)] | Live Killers | 1979 | 12.00 |
| ❑ 7E-1026 | Sheer Heart Attack | 1974 | 10.00 |
| *—Butterfly, red, or red/black labels* | | | |
| ❑ 7E-1026 [DJ] | Sheer Heart Attack | 1974 | 50.00 |
| *—White label promo* | | | |
| ❑ 7E-1053 | A Night at the Opera | 1975 | 10.00 |
| *—Butterfly, red, or red/black labels* | | | |
| ❑ EQ-5064 [Q] | Queen | 1973 | 40.00 |
| ❑ 60128 | Hot Space | 1982 | 10.00 |
| ❑ EKS-75064 | Queen | 1973 | 10.00 |
| *—With "Queen" printed on the cover; butterfly, red, or red/black labels* | | | |
| ❑ EKS-75064 | Queen | 1973 | 30.00 |
| *—With "Queen" gold-embossed on the cover* | | | |
| ❑ EKS-75064 [DJ] | Queen | 1973 | 50.00 |
| *—White label promo* | | | |
| ❑ EKS-75082 | Queen II | 1974 | 10.00 |
| *—Butterfly, red, or red/black labels* | | | |
| ❑ EKS-75082 [DJ] | Queen II | 1974 | 50.00 |
| *—White label promo* | | | |
| HOLLYWOOD | | | |
| ❑ ED-62005 [PD] | Queen at the BBC | 1995 | 100.00 |
| *—Promo-only picture disc (no U.S. stock vinyl)* | | | |
| ❑ 62017 | Made in Heaven | 1996 | 20.00 |
| *—White vinyl; imported from Europe; the only distinguishing mark to make this a U.S. version is the Hollywood bar code, which was stuck to the shrink wrap* | | | |
| MOBILE FIDELITY | | | |
| ❑ 1-067 | A Night at the Opera | 1980 | 80.00 |
| *—Audiophile vinyl* | | | |
| ❑ 1-211 | The Game | 1995 | 30.00 |
| *—Audiophile vinyl* | | | |
| ❑ 1-256 | A Day at the Races | 1996 | 50.00 |
| *—Audiophile vinyl* | | | |
| **QUEEN'S NECTORINE MACHINE, THE** | | | |
| ABC | | | |
| ❑ S-666 | The Mystical Powers of Roving Tarot Gamble | 1969 | 40.00 |
| **QUEENS OF THE STONE AGE** | | | |
| IPECAC | | | |
| ❑ IPC-41 [(2)] | Songs for the Deaf | 2002 | 20.00 |
| MAN'S RUIN | | | |
| ❑ MR 151 | Queens of the Stone Age | 1998 | 120.00 |
| *—2,500 copies on black vinyl; beware of counterfeits; counterfeits lack "MR 151" in the trail-off wax* | | | |
| ❑ MR 151 | Queens of the Stone Age | 1998 | 250.00 |
| *—Approximately 200 copies on blue vinyl* | | | |
| ❑ MR 151 | Queens of the Stone Age | 1998 | 250.00 |
| *—Approximately 200 copies on green vinyl* | | | |
| ❑ MR 151 | Queens of the Stone Age | 1998 | 250.00 |
| *—Approximately 300 copies on orange-yellow vinyl* | | | |
| **QUEENSRYCHE** | | | |
| EMI | | | |
| ❑ E1-30711 | Promised Land | 1994 | 15.00 |
| ❑ E1-92806 | Empire | 1990 | 15.00 |
| EMI AMERICA | | | |
| ❑ ST-17134 | The Warning | 1984 | 10.00 |
| ❑ ST-17134 [DJ] | The Warning | 1984 | 40.00 |
| *—Promo-only "High Quality Vinyl" pressing* | | | |
| ❑ ST-17197 | Rage for Order | 1986 | 10.00 |
| *—Black circle on front cover* | | | |
| ❑ ST-17197 | Rage for Order | 1986 | 15.00 |
| *—Blue circle on front cover* | | | |
| ❑ MLP-19006 [EP] | Queensryche | 1983 | 12.00 |
| ❑ SPRO-MLP-19006 [DJ] | Queensryche | 1983 | 40.00 |
| *—White label version in film can* | | | |
| EMI MANHATTAN | | | |
| ❑ SPRO-04136/7 [PD] | Operation: Mindcrime | 1988 | 80.00 |
| *—Promo-only picture disc* | | | |

| Number | Title (A Side/B Side) | Yr | NM |
|---|---|---|---|
| ❑ SPRO-04194 [DJ] | Speak the Word | 1988 | 30.00 |
| *—Promo-only interview album* | | | |
| ❑ E1-48640 | Operation: Mindcrime | 1988 | 12.00 |
| RHINO | | | |
| ❑ R1-73306 [(2)] | Operation: Mindcrime II | 2006 | 20.00 |
| 206 RECORDS | | | |
| ❑ R-101 [EP] | Queensryche | 1983 | 100.00 |
| **QUEERS, THE** | | | |
| CLEARVIEW | | | |
| ❑ (no # ?) | Suck This | 1995 | 20.00 |
| *—Picture disc* | | | |
| HOPELESS | | | |
| ❑ HR 636 | Punk Rock Confidential | 1998 | 10.00 |
| ❑ HR 643 | Beyond the Valley of the Assfuckers | 2000 | 10.00 |
| LOOKOUT! | | | |
| ❑ LK 090 | Grow Up | 1995 | 10.00 |
| *—Reissue of rare Shakin' Street original* | | | |
| ❑ LK 114 | Move Back Home | 1995 | 10.00 |
| ❑ LK 140 | Don't Back Down | 1996 | 10.00 |
| SELFLESS | | | |
| ❑ SFLS-28 | Rocket to Russia | 1994 | 20.00 |
| *—Tour edition; 300 on pink vinyl* | | | |
| SHAKIN' STREET | | | |
| ❑ 010 | Grow Up | 1990 | 200.00 |
| *—Only 100-150 copies exist of a planned pressing of 500 (others were destroyed at the plant)* | | | |
| **? (QUESTION MARK) AND THE MYSTERIANS** | | | |
| CAMEO | | | |
| ❑ C-2004 [M] | 96 Tears | 1966 | 100.00 |
| ❑ CS-2004 [P] | 96 Tears | 1966 | 80.00 |
| *—"96 Tears," "I Need Somebody," "Up Side" and "8-Teen" are rechanneled* | | | |
| ❑ C-2006 [M] | Action | 1967 | 150.00 |
| ❑ CS-2006 [P] | Action | 1967 | 100.00 |
| *—"Don't Hold It Against Me," "Like a Rose" and "Girl (You Captivate Me)" are rechanneled* | | | |
| COLLECTABLES | | | |
| ❑ COL 2004 | Featuring 96 Tears | 1997 | 12.00 |
| *—Re-recorded tracks; orange vinyl* | | | |
| NORTON | | | |
| ❑ 262 [(2)] | Do You Feel It Baby? | 1998 | 15.00 |
| *—Live album recorded in 1997* | | | |
| **QUICKSILVER MESSENGER SERVICE** | | | |
| CAPITOL | | | |
| ❑ ST-120 | Happy Trails | 1969 | 30.00 |
| *—Black label with colorband* | | | |
| ❑ ST-120 | Happy Trails | 1973 | 12.00 |
| *—Orange label* | | | |
| ❑ SKAO-391 | Shady Grove | 1969 | 25.00 |
| *—Lime green label* | | | |
| ❑ SKAO-391 | Shady Grove | 1973 | 12.00 |
| *—Orange label* | | | |
| ❑ SM-391 | Shady Grove | 1976 | 10.00 |
| *—Reissue on yellow label and new prefix* | | | |
| ❑ SMAS-498 | Just for Love | 1970 | 25.00 |
| *—Lime green label* | | | |
| ❑ SMAS-498 | Just for Love | 1973 | 12.00 |
| *—Orange label* | | | |
| ❑ SMAS-630 | What About Me | 1970 | 25.00 |
| *—Lime green label* | | | |
| ❑ SMAS-630 | What About Me | 1973 | 12.00 |
| *—Orange label* | | | |
| ❑ SW-819 | Quicksilver | 1971 | 25.00 |
| *—Red label with stylized "C" at top* | | | |
| ❑ SW-819 | Quicksilver | 1973 | 12.00 |
| *—Orange label* | | | |
| ❑ ST 2904 | Quicksilver Messenger Service | 1968 | 40.00 |
| *—Black label with colorband; glossy black cover with red and silver foil-like printing* | | | |
| ❑ ST-2904 | Quicksilver Messenger Service | 1969 | 20.00 |
| *—Lime green or red label* | | | |
| ❑ ST-2904 | Quicksilver Messenger Service | 1973 | 12.00 |
| *—Orange label* | | | |
| ❑ SMAS-11002 | Comin' Thru | 1972 | 15.00 |
| ❑ SVBB-11165 [(2)] | Anthology | 1973 | 20.00 |
| ❑ ST-11462 | Solid Silver | 1975 | 15.00 |
| ❑ SM-11820 | Solid Silver | 1978 | 10.00 |
| *—Reissue of 11462* | | | |
| ❑ ST-12496 | Peace By Piece | 1986 | 10.00 |
| ❑ SN-16089 | Quicksilver Messenger Service | 1980 | 8.00 |
| *—Budget-line reissue* | | | |
| ❑ SN-16090 | Happy Trails | 1980 | 8.00 |
| *—Budget-line reissue* | | | |
| ❑ SN-16091 | Quicksilver | 1980 | 8.00 |
| *—Budget-line reissue* | | | |
| ❑ SN-16092 | What About Me | 1980 | 8.00 |
| *—Budget-line reissue* | | | |
| ❑ SN-16093 | Just for Love | 1980 | 8.00 |
| *—Budget-line reissue* | | | |
| ❑ SN-16094 | Shady Grove | 1980 | 8.00 |
| *—Budget-line reissue* | | | |
| **QUIGLEY, JACK** | | | |
| SAND | | | |
| ❑ C-28 [M] | Jack Quigley in Hollywood | 196? | 30.00 |
| *—Red vinyl; may or may not exist on black vinyl* | | | |

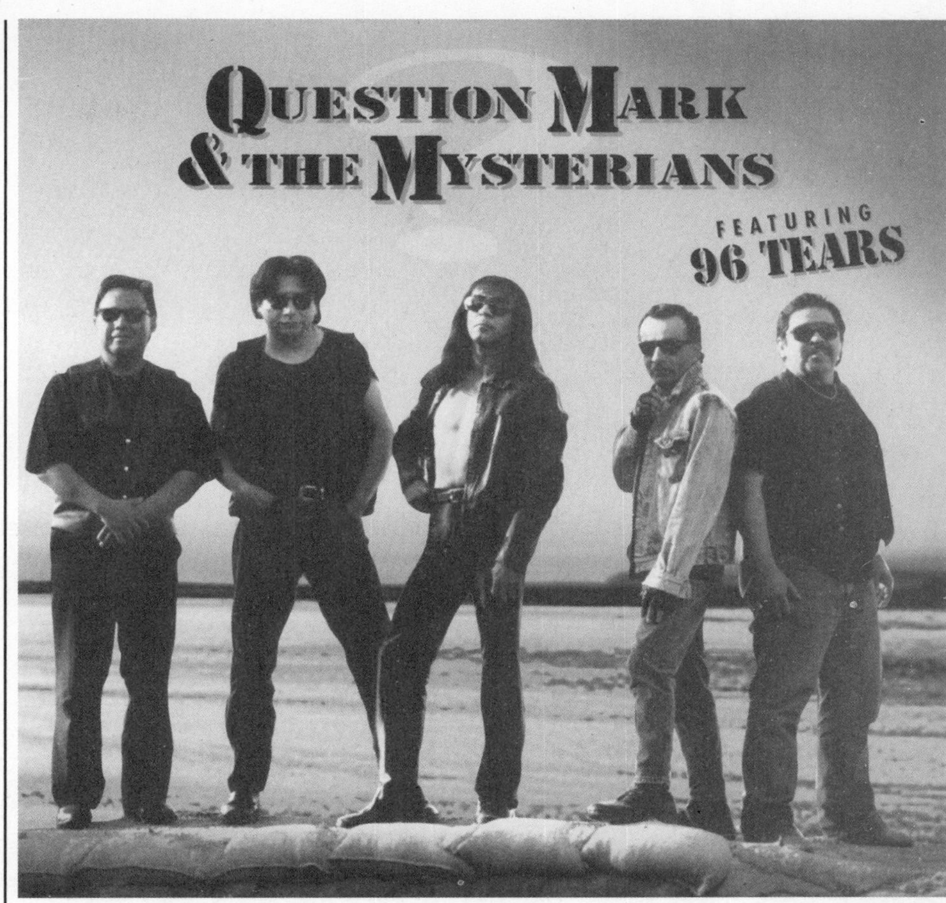


? (Question Mark) and the Mysterians, *Featuring 96 Tears,* Collectables COL-2004, 1997, $12.

| Number | Title (A Side/B Side) | Yr | NM |
|---|---|---|---|
| ❑ CS-28 [S] | Jack Quigley in Hollywood | 196? | 20.00 |
| ❑ C-30 [M] | Class In Session | 196? | 30.00 |
| *—Red vinyl; may or may not exist on black vinyl* | | | |
| ❑ CS-30 [S] | Class In Session | 196? | 20.00 |
| ❑ C-32 [M] | Listen! Quigley | 196? | 30.00 |
| *—Red vinyl; may or may not exist on black vinyl* | | | |
| ❑ CS-32 [S] | Listen! Quigley | 196? | 20.00 |
| ❑ C-38 [M] | D'Jever | 196? | 20.00 |
| ❑ CS-38 [S] | D'Jever | 196? | 25.00 |
| **QUILL** | | | |
| COTILLION | | | |
| ❑ SD 9017 | Quill | 1970 | 20.00 |
| **QUILL, GENE** | | | |
| ROOST | | | |
| ❑ LP-2229 [M] | Three Bones and a Quill | 1958 | 50.00 |
| **QUINICHETTE, PAUL** | | | |
| DAWN | | | |
| ❑ DLP-1109 [M] | The Kid from Denver | 1956 | 100.00 |
| EMARCY | | | |
| ❑ MG-26022 [10] | The Vice 'Pres' | 1954 | 250.00 |
| ❑ MG-26035 [10] | Sequel | 1954 | 250.00 |
| ❑ MG-36003 [M] | Moods | 1955 | 120.00 |
| ❑ MG-36027 [M] | The Vice 'Pres' | 1955 | 120.00 |
| PRESTIGE | | | |
| ❑ PRLP-7103 [M] | On the Sunny Side | 1957 | 150.00 |
| *—Yellow label with W. 50th St. address* | | | |
| ❑ PRLP-7127 [M] | For Basie | 1957 | 120.00 |
| *—Yellow label with W. 50th St. address* | | | |
| ❑ PRLP-7147 [M] | Basie Reunion | 1958 | 100.00 |
| STATUS | | | |
| ❑ ST-2036 [M] | For Basie | 1966 | 20.00 |
| *—Reissue of Swingville 2036* | | | |
| SWINGVILLE | | | |
| ❑ SVLP-2036 [M] | For Basie | 1962 | 50.00 |
| *—Purple label* | | | |
| ❑ SVLP-2036 [M] | For Basie | 1965 | 25.00 |
| *—Blue label, trident logo at right* | | | |
| ❑ SVLP-2037 [M] | Basie Reunion | 1962 | 50.00 |
| *—Purple label* | | | |
| ❑ SVLP-2037 [M] | Basie Reunion | 1965 | 25.00 |
| *—Blue label, trident logo at right* | | | |
| UNITED ARTISTS | | | |
| ❑ UAL-4024 [M] | Like Basie | 1959 | 50.00 |

| Number | Title (A Side/B Side) | Yr | NM |
|---|---|---|---|
| ❑ UAL-4054 [M] | Like Who? | 1959 | 40.00 |
| ❑ UAL-4077 [M] | Paul Quinichette | 1960 | 40.00 |
| ❑ UAS-5024 [S] | Like Basie | 1959 | 40.00 |
| ❑ UAS-5054 [S] | Like Who? | 1959 | 30.00 |
| ❑ UAS-5077 [S] | Paul Quinichette | 1960 | 50.00 |
| **QUINICHETTE, PAUL, AND FRANK FOSTER** | | | |
| DECCA | | | |
| ❑ DL 8058 [M] | Jazz Studio 1 | 1954 | 100.00 |
| **QUINICHETTE, PAUL/GENE ROLAND** | | | |
| DAWN | | | |
| ❑ DLP-1112 [M] | Jazzville | 1957 | 100.00 |
| **QUINN, ANTHONY** | | | |
| CAPITOL | | | |
| ❑ ST-116 | In My Own Way... I Love You | 1969 | 30.00 |
| **QUINN, CARMEL** | | | |
| COLUMBIA | | | |
| ❑ CL 629 [M] | Arthur Godfrey Presents Carmel Quinn | 1955 | 30.00 |
| **QUINTESSENCE** | | | |
| ISLAND | | | |
| ❑ SMAS-9301 | Quintessence | 1971 | 25.00 |
| ❑ SW-9305 | Dive Deep | 1971 | 25.00 |
| **QUINTET, THE** | | | |
| DEBUT | | | |
| ❑ DLP-2 [10] | Jazz at Massey Hall | 1953 | 400.00 |
| ❑ DLP-4 [10] | Jazz at Massey Hall, Volume 3 | 1953 | 400.00 |
| ❑ DEB-124 [M] | Jazz at Massey Hall | 1956 | 300.00 |
| FANTASY | | | |
| ❑ OJC-044 | Jazz at Massey Hall | 198? | 12.00 |
| ❑ 6006 [M] | Jazz at Massey Hall | 1962 | 50.00 |
| *—Red vinyl* | | | |
| ❑ 6006 [R] | Jazz at Massey Hall | 1962 | 30.00 |
| *—Black vinyl* | | | |
| ❑ 86006 [M] | Jazz at Massey Hall | 1962 | 30.00 |
| *—Blue vinyl* | | | |
| ❑ 86006 [R] | Jazz at Massey Hall | 1962 | 20.00 |
| *—Black vinyl* | | | |
| UNITED ARTISTS | | | |
| ❑ UAS-5514 | Future Tense | 1971 | 15.00 |
| ❑ UAS-5599 | The Quintet | 1972 | 15.00 |

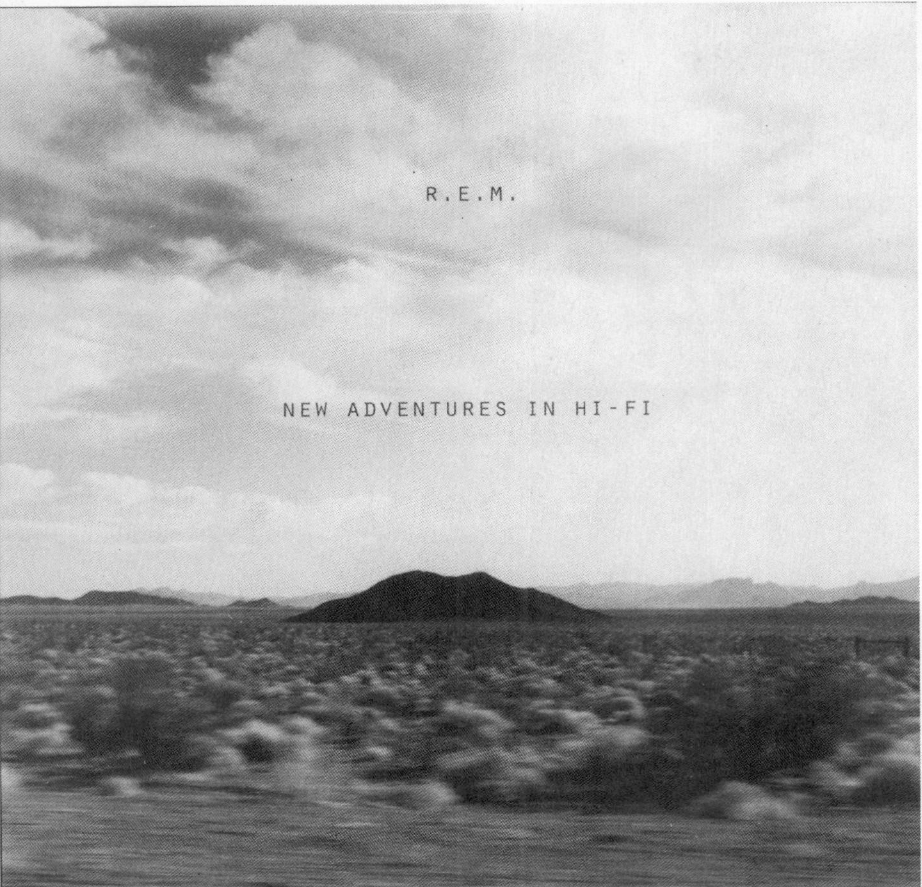


R.E.M., *New Adventures in Hi-Fi,* Warner Bros. 46320, 1996, $15.

**QUINTET OF THE HOT CLUB OF FRANCE, THE**

| Number | Title (A Side/B Side) | Yr | NM |
|---|---|---|---|
| CAPITOL | | | |
| ❑ DT 2045 [R] | Hot Club of France | 1964 | 20.00 |
| ❑ T 2045 [M] | Hot Club of France | 1964 | 30.00 |
| DIAL | | | |
| ❑ LP-214 [10] | Django Reinhardt and the Hot Club Quintet | 1951 | 300.00 |
| ❑ LP-218 [10] | Django Reinhardt and the Quintet | 1951 | 300.00 |
| LONDON | | | |
| ❑ LB-810 [10] | Hot Club Quintet | 1954 | 120.00 |
| ❑ LL 1344 [M] | Swing from Paris | 1956 | 80.00 |

# R

**R.E.M.**

| Number | Title (A Side/B Side) | Yr | NM |
|---|---|---|---|
| I.R.S. | | | |
| ❑ 5592 | Fables of the Reconstruction | 1985 | 12.00 |
| ❑ 5783 | Lifes Rich Pageant | 1986 | 12.00 |
| ❑ 6262 | Eponymous | 1988 | 10.00 |
| ❑ 42059 | Document | 1987 | 10.00 |
| ❑ SP-70014 | Murmur | 1983 | 12.00 |
| *—Reissue?* | | | |
| ❑ SP-70044 | Reckoning | 1984 | 12.00 |
| ❑ SP-70054 | Dead Letter Office | 1987 | 12.00 |
| ❑ SP-70502 [EP] | Chronic Town | 1982 | 6.00 |
| *—Later pressings have a standard I.R.S. label* | | | |
| ❑ SP-70502 [EP] | Chronic Town | 1982 | 12.00 |
| *—Original pressings have a custom gargoyle label* | | | |
| ❑ SP-70604 | Murmur | 1983 | 15.00 |
| *—Original number?* | | | |
| ❑ R 100701 | Eponymous | 1988 | 12.00 |
| *—BMG Direct Marketing edition* | | | |
| ❑ R 163503 | Document | 1987 | 12.00 |
| *—BMG Direct Marketing edition* | | | |
| ❑ R 173669 | Lifes Rich Pageant | 1986 | 14.00 |
| *—RCA Music Service edition* | | | |
| MOBILE FIDELITY | | | |
| ❑ 1-231 | Murmur | 1995 | 20.00 |
| *—Audiophile vinyl* | | | |
| ❑ 1-261 | Reckoning | 1996 | 80.00 |
| *—Audiophile vinyl* | | | |
| WARNER BROS. | | | |
| ❑ PRO-A-3377 [(2)DJ] | Should We Talk About the Weather? | 1988 | 40.00 |
| *—Promo-only interviews and music* | | | |
| ❑ 25795 | Green | 1988 | 12.00 |
| ❑ W1-25795 | Green | 1988 | 15.00 |
| *—Columbia House edition* | | | |
| ❑ 26496 | Out of Time | 1991 | 10.00 |
| ❑ 45055 | Automatic for the People | 1992 | 10.00 |
| ❑ 45740 | Monster | 1994 | 10.00 |
| ❑ 46320 [(2)] | New Adventures in Hi-Fi | 1996 | 15.00 |
| ❑ 47112 [(2)] | Up | 1998 | 15.00 |
| ❑ 47946 | Reveal | 2001 | 20.00 |
| ❑ R1-78422 [(2)] | Around the Sun | 2004 | 20.00 |
| ❑ R 100715 | Green | 1988 | 12.00 |
| *—BMG Direct Marketing edition* | | | |
| ❑ R 124762 | Out of Time | 1991 | 16.00 |
| *—BMG Direct Marketing edition; one of the last BMG vinyl releases* | | | |

**R.P.S.**

| Number | Title (A Side/B Side) | Yr | NM |
|---|---|---|---|
| MARS | | | |
| ❑ (# unknown) | R.P.S. | 197? | 80.00 |

**RABBLE, THE**

| Number | Title (A Side/B Side) | Yr | NM |
|---|---|---|---|
| ROULETTE | | | |
| ❑ SR-42010 | The Rabble | 1968 | 150.00 |

**RACKET SQUAD, THE**

| Number | Title (A Side/B Side) | Yr | NM |
|---|---|---|---|
| JUBILEE | | | |
| ❑ JGS-8015 | The Racket Squad | 1968 | 40.00 |
| ❑ JGS-8026 | Corners of Your Mind | 1969 | 40.00 |

**RADHA KRISHNA TEMPLE**

| Number | Title (A Side/B Side) | Yr | NM |
|---|---|---|---|
| APPLE | | | |
| ❑ SKAO-3376 | The Radha Krishna Temple | 1971 | 20.00 |

**RADICE, MARK**

| Number | Title (A Side/B Side) | Yr | NM |
|---|---|---|---|
| PARAMOUNT | | | |
| ❑ PAS-6033 | Mark Radice | 1972 | 40.00 |
| ROADSHOW | | | |
| ❑ RS-LA788-G | Intense | 1977 | 15.00 |
| UNITED ARTISTS | | | |
| ❑ UA-LA629-G | Ain't Nothin' But a Party | 1976 | 15.00 |

**RADIO BIRDMAN**

| Number | Title (A Side/B Side) | Yr | NM |
|---|---|---|---|
| SIRE | | | |
| ❑ SRK 6050 | Radio Appears | 1978 | 40.00 |

**RADIO CITY MUSIC HALL ORCHESTRA**

| Number | Title (A Side/B Side) | Yr | NM |
|---|---|---|---|
| RCA VICTOR | | | |
| ❑ LOP-1010 [M] | Christmas Holidays at Radio City Music Hall | 1958 | 20.00 |
| *—With gatefold and 10-page bound-in booklet with fold-open poster of the Rockettes* | | | |
| ❑ LSO-1010 [S] | Christmas Holidays at Radio City Music Hall | 1958 | 40.00 |
| *—"Living Stereo" banner on cover* | | | |

**RAE, CHARLOTTE**

| Number | Title (A Side/B Side) | Yr | NM |
|---|---|---|---|
| VANGUARD | | | |
| ❑ VRS-9004 [M] | Songs I Taught My Mother | 1956 | 40.00 |

**RAE, JOHN**

| Number | Title (A Side/B Side) | Yr | NM |
|---|---|---|---|
| SAVOY | | | |
| ❑ MG-12156 [M] | Opus De Jazz, Volume 2 | 1960 | 40.00 |

**RAEBURN, BOYD**

| Number | Title (A Side/B Side) | Yr | NM |
|---|---|---|---|
| COLUMBIA | | | |
| ❑ CL 889 [M] | Dance Spectacular | 1956 | 40.00 |
| ❑ CL 957 [M] | Fraternity Rush | 1957 | 40.00 |
| ❑ CL 1073 [M] | Teen Rock | 1958 | 50.00 |
| SAVOY | | | |
| ❑ MG-12025 [M] | Man With the Horns | 1955 | 80.00 |
| ❑ MG-12040 [M] | Boyd Meets Stravinsky | 1955 | 80.00 |
| ❑ MG-15010 [10] | Innovations by Boyd Raeburn, Volume 1 | 1951 | 150.00 |
| ❑ MG-15011 [10] | Innovations by Boyd Raeburn, Volume 2 | 1951 | 150.00 |
| ❑ MG-15012 [10] | Innovations by Boyd Raeburn, Volume 3 | 1951 | 150.00 |

**RAFF, RENEE**

| Number | Title (A Side/B Side) | Yr | NM |
|---|---|---|---|
| AUDIO FIDELITY | | | |
| ❑ AFSD-6142 [S] | Among the Stars | 1965 | 20.00 |

**RAFFERTY, GERRY**

| Number | Title (A Side/B Side) | Yr | NM |
|---|---|---|---|
| ABC/BLUE THUMB | | | |
| ❑ 6031 | Can I Have My Money Back? | 1978 | 12.00 |
| BLUE THUMB | | | |
| ❑ BTS-58 | Can I Have My Money Back? | 1973 | 20.00 |
| LIBERTY | | | |
| ❑ LO-840 | City to City | 1981 | 8.00 |
| *—Reissue of United Artists 840* | | | |
| ❑ LOO-958 | Night and Day | 1981 | 8.00 |
| *—Reissue of United Artists 958* | | | |
| ❑ LOO-1039 | Snakes and Ladders | 1981 | 8.00 |
| *—Reissue of United Artists 1039* | | | |
| ❑ LT-51132 | Sleepwalking | 1982 | 10.00 |
| MOBILE FIDELITY | | | |
| ❑ 1-058 | City to City | 1980 | 40.00 |
| *—Audiophile vinyl* | | | |
| POLYDOR | | | |
| ❑ 835449-1 | North and South | 1988 | 10.00 |
| UNITED ARTISTS | | | |
| ❑ UA-LA840-H | City to City | 1978 | 10.00 |
| ❑ UA-LA958-I | Night Owl | 1979 | 10.00 |
| ❑ LOO-1039 | Snakes and Ladders | 1980 | 10.00 |
| VISA | | | |
| ❑ 7006 | Gerry Rafferty | 1978 | 10.00 |
| *—Reissue of Blue Thumb material* | | | |

**RAHIM, EMANUEL K., AND THE KAHLIQA**

| Number | Title (A Side/B Side) | Yr | NM |
|---|---|---|---|
| COBBLESTONE | | | |
| ❑ 9014 | Total Submission | 1972 | 25.00 |

**RAIDERS, THE (3)**

| Number | Title (A Side/B Side) | Yr | NM |
|---|---|---|---|
| LIBERTY | | | |
| ❑ LRP-3225 [M] | Twistin' the Country Classics | 1962 | 25.00 |
| ❑ LST-7225 [S] | Twistin' the Country Classics | 1962 | 30.00 |

**RAIN**

| Number | Title (A Side/B Side) | Yr | NM |
|---|---|---|---|
| PROJECT 3 | | | |
| ❑ PR 5072 SD | New Rock Group | 1972 | 25.00 |
| WHAZOO | | | |
| ❑ USR-3049 | Live Christmas Night | 1969 | 150.00 |
| *—Issued with no cover* | | | |

**RAINBOW (2)**

| Number | Title (A Side/B Side) | Yr | NM |
|---|---|---|---|
| GNP CRESCENDO | | | |
| ❑ GNPS-2049 | After the Storm | 1969 | 25.00 |

**RAINBOW PRESS, THE**

| Number | Title (A Side/B Side) | Yr | NM |
|---|---|---|---|
| MR. G | | | |
| ❑ 9003 | There's a War On | 1968 | 30.00 |
| ❑ 9004 | Sunday Funnies | 1969 | 30.00 |

**RAINBOW PROMISE, THE**

| Number | Title (A Side/B Side) | Yr | NM |
|---|---|---|---|
| NEW WINE | | | |
| ❑ LPS-251-01 | The Rainbow Promise | 1970 | 300.00 |

**RAINCOATS, THE**

| Number | Title (A Side/B Side) | Yr | NM |
|---|---|---|---|
| ROUGH TRADE | | | |
| ❑ ROUGH US 13 | Odyshape | 1981 | 25.00 |
| SOUNDS LIKE | | | |
| ❑ 12 [EP] | The Raincoats | 1994 | 8.00 |



Except when noted otherwise, VG = 25% of NM, and VG+ = 50% of NM. (Example: VG = $2.00, VG+ = $4.00 and NM = $8.00.)

Number | Title (A Side/B Side) | Yr | NM

**RAINDROPS, THE (1)**

JUBILEE
❑ JGM-5023 [M] The Raindrops 1963 150.00
❑ JGS-5023 [S] The Raindrops 1963 300.00

**RAINEY, CHUCK**

COBBLESTONE
❑ 9008 Chuck Rainey Coalition 1972 20.00

**RAINEY, MA**

BIOGRAPH
❑ LP-12001 Blues the World Forgot 1968 15.00
❑ LP-12011 Oh My Babe Blues 197? 12.00
❑ LP-12032 Queen of the Blues 197? 12.00

MILESTONE
❑ 2001 Immortal Ma Rainey 1967 15.00
❑ 2008 Blame It on the Blues 196? 15.00
❑ 2017 Down in the Basement 197? 12.00
❑ 47021 [(2)] Ma Rainey 197? 15.00

RIVERSIDE
❑ RLP 12-108 [M] Ma Rainey 1955 200.00
❑ RLP 12-137 [M] Broken Hearted Blues 1956 100.00
❑ RLP-1003 [10] Ma Rainey, Vol. 1 1953 250.00
❑ RLP-1016 [10] Ma Rainey, Vol. 2 1953 250.00
❑ RLP-1045 [10] Ma Rainey, Vol. 3 1954 250.00

**RAINWATER, MARVIN**

CROWN
❑ CST-307 [R] Marvin Rainwater 196? 12.00
❑ CLP-5307 [M] Marvin Rainwater 196? 12.00

GUEST STAR
❑ GS-1435 [M] Country and Western Star 196? 12.00

MGM
❑ E-3534 [M] Songs by Marvin Rainwater 1957 150.00
❑ E-3721 [M] Marvin Rainwater Sings with a Beat 1958 120.00
❑ E-4046 [M] Gonna Find Me a Bluebird 1962 80.00
❑ SE-4046 [R] Gonna Find Me a Bluebird 1962 50.00

SPIN-O-RAMA
❑ SPM-109 [M] Golden Country Hits 196? 12.00

**RAINY DAZE, THE**

UNI
❑ 3002 [M] That Acapulco Gold 1967 20.00
❑ 73002 [S] That Acapulco Gold 1967 25.00

**RAITT, BONNIE**

CAPITOL
❑ C1-91268 Nick of Time 1989 12.00
❑ C1-96111 Luck of the Draw 1991 15.00

DCC COMPACT CLASSICS
❑ LPZ-2025 Nick of Time 1996 80.00
*—Audiophile vinyl*
❑ LPZ-2031 Luck of the Draw 1997 80.00
*—Audiophile vinyl*

WARNER BROS.
❑ WS 1953 Bonnie Raitt 1971 15.00
*—Green "WB" label*
❑ WS 1953 Bonnie Raitt 1973 12.00
*—"Burbank" palm trees label*
❑ WS 1953 Bonnie Raitt 1979 8.00
*—White or tan label*
❑ BS 2643 Give It Up 1972 15.00
*—Green "WB" label*
❑ BS 2643 Give It Up 1973 12.00
*—"Burbank" palm trees label*
❑ BS 2643 Give It Up 1979 8.00
*—White or tan label*
❑ BS 2729 Takin' My Time 1973 12.00
*—"Burbank" palm trees label*
❑ BS 2729 Takin' My Time 1979 8.00
*—White or tan label*
❑ BS 2818 Streetlights 1974 12.00
*—"Burbank" palm trees label*
❑ BS 2818 Streetlights 1979 8.00
*—White or tan label*
❑ BS 2864 Home Plate 1975 12.00
*—"Burbank" palm trees label*
❑ BS 2864 Home Plate 1979 8.00
*—White or tan label*
❑ BS 2990 Sweet Forgiveness 1977 12.00
*—"Burbank" palm trees label*
❑ BS 2990 Sweet Forgiveness 1979 8.00
*—White or tan label*
❑ HS 3369 The Glow 1979 12.00
❑ BSK 3630 Green Light 1982 12.00
❑ 25486 Nine Lives 1986 10.00

**RAITT, JOHN**

CAPITOL
❑ T 583 [M] Highlights of Broadway 1955 30.00
❑ T 714 [M] Mediterranean Magic 1956 30.00
❑ ST 1058 [S] Under Open Skies 1958 40.00
❑ T 1058 [M] Under Open Skies 1958 30.00

Bonnie Raitt, *Nick of Time,* Capitol C1-91268, 1989, $12.

Number | Title (A Side/B Side) | Yr | NM

**RALKE, DON**

CROWN
❑ CLP-5019 [M] Bongo Madness 1957 25.00

WARNER BROS.
❑ W 1321 [M] Bourbon Street Beat 1959 25.00
❑ WS 1321 [S] Bourbon Street Beat 1959 30.00
❑ W 1360 [M] But You've Never Heard Gershwin with Bongos 1960 20.00
❑ WS 1360 [S] But You've Never Heard Gershwin with Bongos 1960 25.00
❑ W 1398 [M] The Savage and Sensuous Bongos 1960 25.00
❑ WS 1398 [S] The Savage and Sensuous Bongos 1960 30.00

**RAM**

POLYDOR
❑ 24-5013 Where (In Conclusion) 1972 25.00

**RAM, BUCK**

MERCURY
❑ MG-20392 [M] The Magic Touch 1960 30.00
❑ SR-60067 [S] The Magic Touch 1960 40.00

**RAMBEAU, EDDIE**

DYNO VOICE
❑ 9001 [M] Concrete and Clay 1965 20.00
❑ DS-9001 [S] Concrete and Clay 1965 25.00

**RAMONES, THE**

RADIOACTIVE
❑ 10615 Mondo Bizarro 1992 10.00
❑ 11273 Adios Amigos! 1995 10.00

SIRE
❑ PRO-A-605 [DJ] Rock 'n' Roll High School Radio Sampler 1979 25.00
❑ PRO-A-756 [DJ] Road to Ruin Radio Sampler 1978 25.00
❑ PRO-A-996 [DJ] Pleasant Dreams Radio Sampler 1980 25.00
❑ SRK 3571 Pleasant Dreams 1981 15.00
❑ SR 6020 Ramones 1978 18.00
*—Reissue, distributed by Warner Bros.; originals have no bar code*
❑ SR 6031 Ramones Leave Home 1978 18.00
*—Third issue, distributed by Warner Bros., tracks as on second issue; originals have no bar code*

Number | Title (A Side/B Side) | Yr | NM

❑ SRK 6042 Rocket to Russia 1978 15.00
❑ SRK 6063 Road to Ruin 1979 15.00
❑ SRK 6077 End of the Century 1980 15.00
❑ SASD-7520 Ramones 1976 25.00
*—First issue, distributed by ABC*
❑ SA-7528 Ramones Leave Home 1977 25.00
*—Second issue, distributed by ABC, with "Sheena Is a Punk Rocker" replacing "Carbona Not Glue"*
❑ SA-7528 Ramones Leave Home 1977 50.00
*—First issue, distributed by ABC, with "Carbona Not Glue"*
❑ 23800 Subterranean Jungle 1983 15.00
❑ 25187 Too Tough to Die 1984 12.00
❑ 25433 Animal Boy 1986 12.00
❑ 25641 Halfway to Sanity 1987 12.00
❑ 25709 [(2)] RamonesMania 1988 15.00
❑ 25905 Brain Drain 1989 12.00

**RAMSAY, OBRAY**

PRESTIGE
❑ PRLP-13009 [M] Obray Ramsay Sings Jimmie Rodgers Favorites 1960 30.00
❑ PRLP-13020 [M] Folk Songs from the Three Laurels 1961 30.00

RIVERSIDE
❑ RLP-12-649 [M] Banjo Songs of the Blue Ridge and Great Smokies 196? 30.00

**RANDALL, TONY**

IMPERIAL
❑ LP-9090 [M] Tony Randall 1958 30.00

MERCURY
❑ MG-21108 [M] Vo, Vo, De Oh, Doe 1967 20.00
❑ MG-21128 [M] Warm and Wavery 1967 20.00
❑ SR-61108 [S] Vo, Vo, De Oh, Doe 1967 25.00
❑ SR-61128 [S] Warm and Wavery 1967 25.00

**RANDALL, TONY, AND JACK KLUGMAN**

LONDON
❑ XPS 903 The Odd Couple Sings 1973 50.00

**RANDAZZO, TEDDY**

ABC-PARAMOUNT
❑ 352 [M] Journey to Love 1961 30.00
❑ S-352 [S] Journey to Love 1961 40.00
❑ 421 [M] Teddy Randazzo Twists 1962 30.00
❑ S-421 [S] Teddy Randazzo Twists 1962 40.00

Ramones, *Adios Amigos!*, Radioactive RAR-11273, 1995, $10.

| Number | Title (A Side/B Side) | Yr | NM |
|---|---|---|---|
| **COLPIX** | | | |
| ❑ CP-445 [M] | Big Wide World | 1963 | 30.00 |
| ❑ SCP-445 [S] | Big Wide World | 1963 | 40.00 |
| **VIK** | | | |
| ❑ LX-1121 [M] | I'm Confessin' | 1958 | 200.00 |

**RANDI, DON**

| Number | Title (A Side/B Side) | Yr | NM |
|---|---|---|---|
| **CAPITOL** | | | |
| ❑ ST-287 | Love Theme from Romeo and Juliet | 1969 | 20.00 |
| **PALOMAR** | | | |
| ❑ 34002 [S] | Don Randi! | 1965 | 20.00 |
| **REPRISE** | | | |
| ❑ R-6229 [M] | Revolver Jazz | 1966 | 20.00 |
| ❑ RS-6229 [S] | Revolver Jazz | 1966 | 25.00 |
| **WORLD PACIFIC** | | | |
| ❑ ST-1297 [S] | Feelin' Like Blues | 1960 | 25.00 |
| ❑ WP-1297 [M] | Feelin' Like Blues | 1960 | 30.00 |

**RANDOLPH, BOOTS**

| Number | Title (A Side/B Side) | Yr | NM |
|---|---|---|---|
| **MONUMENT** | | | |
| ❑ DS 632 | King of Yakety | 197? | 15.00 |
| *—Manufactured by CBS Direct Marketing Services* | | | |
| ❑ 6600 | Boots Randolph's Yakety Sax | 197? | 10.00 |
| *—Reissue of 18002* | | | |
| ❑ 6601 | Hip Boots | 197? | 10.00 |
| *—Reissue of 18015* | | | |
| ❑ 6602 | Boots Randolph Plays More Yakety Sax | 197? | 10.00 |
| *—Reissue of 18037* | | | |
| ❑ 6603 | The Fantastic Boots Randolph | 197? | 10.00 |
| *—Reissue of 18042* | | | |
| ❑ 6604 | Boots with Strings | 197? | 10.00 |
| *—Reissue of 18066* | | | |
| ❑ MC 6605 | Sax-Sational | 1976 | 10.00 |
| *—Reissue of 18079* | | | |
| ❑ 6606 | Boots Randolph with the Knightsbridge Strings & Voices | 197? | 10.00 |
| *—Reissue of 18082* | | | |
| ❑ 6607 | Sunday Sax | 197? | 10.00 |
| *—Reissue of 18092* | | | |
| ❑ 6608 | The Sound of Boots | 197? | 10.00 |
| *—Reissue of 18099* | | | |
| ❑ 6609 | ...With Love/The Seductive Sax of Boots Randolph | 197? | 10.00 |
| *—Reissue of 18111* | | | |
| ❑ 6610 | Boots and Stockings | 197? | 10.00 |
| *—Reissue of 18127* | | | |
| ❑ 6611 | Yakety Revisited | 197? | 10.00 |
| *—Reissue of 18128* | | | |
| ❑ 6612 | Hit Boots 1970 | 197? | 10.00 |
| *—Reissue of 18144* | | | |
| ❑ 6613 | Boots with Brass | 197? | 10.00 |
| *—Reissue of 18147* | | | |
| ❑ 6614 | Homer Louis Randolph, III | 197? | 10.00 |
| *—Reissue of 30678* | | | |
| ❑ 6615 | Boots Randolph Plays the Great Hits of Today | 197? | 10.00 |
| *—Reissue of 31908* | | | |
| ❑ 6616 | Sentimental Journey | 197? | 10.00 |
| *—Reissue of 32292* | | | |
| ❑ 6617 | Country Boots | 197? | 10.00 |
| *—Reissue of 32912* | | | |
| ❑ 6618 | Cool Boots | 197? | 10.00 |
| *—Reissue of 33803* | | | |
| ❑ 7602 | Greatest Hits | 1977 | 10.00 |
| ❑ 7611 | Sax Appeal | 1977 | 10.00 |
| ❑ 7627 | Put a Little Sax | 1978 | 10.00 |
| ❑ MLP-8002 [M] | Boots Randolph's Yakety Sax | 1963 | 20.00 |
| ❑ MLP-8015 [M] | Hip Boots | 1964 | 15.00 |
| ❑ MLP-8029 [M] | 12 Monstrous Sax Hits | 1965 | 15.00 |
| ❑ MLP-8037 [M] | Boots Randolph Plays More Yakety Sax | 1965 | 15.00 |
| ❑ MLP-8042 [M] | The Fantastic Boots Randolph | 1966 | 15.00 |
| ❑ MLP-8066 [M] | Boots with Strings | 1966 | 15.00 |
| ❑ MLP-8079 [M] | Sax-Sational | 1967 | 20.00 |
| ❑ MLP-8082 [M] | Boots Randolph with the Knightsbridge Strings & Voices | 1967 | 20.00 |
| ❑ 8604 [(2)] | Party Boots | 197? | 12.00 |
| *—Reissue of 34082* | | | |
| ❑ SLP-18002 [S] | Boots Randolph's Yakety Sax | 1963 | 25.00 |
| ❑ SLP-18015 [S] | Hip Boots | 1964 | 20.00 |
| ❑ SLP-18029 [S] | 12 Monstrous Sax Hits | 1965 | 20.00 |
| ❑ SLP-18037 [S] | Boots Randolph Plays More Yakety Sax | 1965 | 20.00 |
| ❑ SLP-18042 [S] | The Fantastic Boots Randolph | 1966 | 20.00 |
| ❑ SLP-18066 [S] | Boots with Strings | 1966 | 20.00 |
| ❑ SLP-18079 [S] | Sax-Sational | 1967 | 15.00 |
| ❑ SLP-18082 [S] | Boots Randolph with the Knightsbridge Strings & Voices | 1967 | 15.00 |
| ❑ SLP-18092 | Sunday Sax | 1968 | 20.00 |
| ❑ SLP-18099 | The Sound of Boots | 1968 | 20.00 |
| ❑ SLP-18111 | ...With Love/The Seductive Sax of Boots Randolph | 1969 | 15.00 |
| ❑ SLP 18127 | Boots and Stockings | 1969 | 15.00 |
| ❑ SLP-18128 | Yakety Revisited | 1969 | 15.00 |
| ❑ SLP-18144 | Hit Boots 1970 | 1970 | 15.00 |
| ❑ SLP-18147 | Boots with Brass | 1970 | 15.00 |
| ❑ Z 30678 | Homer Louis Randolph, III | 1971 | 12.00 |
| ❑ ZG 30963 [(2)] | The World of Boots Randolph | 1971 | 15.00 |
| ❑ KZ 31908 | Boots Randolph Plays the Great Hits of Today | 1972 | 12.00 |
| ❑ KZ 32292 | Sentimental Journey | 1973 | 12.00 |
| ❑ KZ 32912 | Country Boots | 1974 | 12.00 |
| ❑ KZ 33298 | Boots Randolph's Yakety Sax | 1974 | 12.00 |
| ❑ KZ 33803 | Cool Boots | 1975 | 12.00 |
| ❑ BZ 33852 [(2)] | Boots with Strings | 1975 | 15.00 |
| ❑ Z2 34082 [(2)] | Party Boots | 1976 | 15.00 |
| ❑ PW 38388 | Greatest Hits | 1983 | 10.00 |
| ❑ JW 38396 | Dedication | 1983 | 10.00 |
| **RCA CAMDEN** | | | |
| ❑ CAL-825 [M] | Yakin' Sax Man | 1964 | 15.00 |
| ❑ CAS-825 [S] | Yakin' Sax Man | 1964 | 15.00 |
| ❑ CAL-865 [M] | Sweet Talk | 1965 | 15.00 |
| ❑ CAS-865 [R] | Sweet Talk | 1965 | 12.00 |
| ❑ ACL-9003 [(2)] | Yakety Sax | 1972 | 12.00 |
| **RCA VICTOR** | | | |
| ❑ LPM-2165 [M] | Yakety Sax | 1960 | 40.00 |
| ❑ LSP-2165 [S] | Yakety Sax | 1960 | 50.00 |

**RANELIN, PHIL**

| Number | Title (A Side/B Side) | Yr | NM |
|---|---|---|---|
| **TRIBE** | | | |
| ❑ PRSD-2226 | Message from the Tribe | 197? | 100.00 |
| ❑ TRCD 4006 | The Time Is Now! | 1974 | 80.00 |

**RANEY, JIMMY**

| Number | Title (A Side/B Side) | Yr | NM |
|---|---|---|---|
| **ABC-PARAMOUNT** | | | |
| ❑ ABC-129 [M] | Jimmy Raney Featuring Bob Brookmeyer | 1956 | 200.00 |
| ❑ ABC-167 [M] | Jimmy Raney in Three Attitudes | 1957 | 150.00 |
| **DAWN** | | | |
| ❑ DLP-1120 [M] | Jimmy Raney Visits Paris | 1958 | 100.00 |
| **NEW JAZZ** | | | |
| ❑ NJLP-1101 [10] | Jimmy Raney Quartet Featuring Hall Overton | 1953 | 500.00 |
| ❑ NJLP-1103 [10] | Jimmy Raney Ensemble Introducing Phil Woods | 1953 | 500.00 |
| **PRESTIGE** | | | |
| ❑ PRLP-156 [10] | Jimmy Raney Plays | 1953 | 400.00 |
| ❑ PRLP-179 [10] | Jimmy Raney in Sweden | 1954 | 400.00 |
| ❑ PRLP-199 [10] | Jimmy Raney Quintet | 1954 | 400.00 |
| ❑ PRLP-201 [10] | Jimmy Raney Quartet | 1955 | 400.00 |
| ❑ PRLP-203 [10] | Jimmy Raney Ensemble | 1955 | 400.00 |
| ❑ PRLP-7089 [M] | Jimmy Raney/A | 1957 | 300.00 |
| *—Yellow label with W. 50th St. address* | | | |

**RANEY, JIMMY/GEORGE WALLINGTON**

| Number | Title (A Side/B Side) | Yr | NM |
|---|---|---|---|
| **EMARCY** | | | |
| ❑ MG-36121 [M] | Swingin' in Sweden | 1958 | 100.00 |

**RANEY, SUE**

| Number | Title (A Side/B Side) | Yr | NM |
|---|---|---|---|
| **CAPITOL** | | | |
| ❑ ST 1335 [S] | Songs for a Raney Day | 1960 | 25.00 |
| ❑ T 1335 [M] | Songs for a Raney Day | 1960 | 20.00 |
| ❑ ST 2032 [S] | All By Myself | 1964 | 20.00 |
| **IMPERIAL** | | | |
| ❑ LP-9355 [M] | New and Now | 1967 | 25.00 |
| ❑ LP-9376 [M] | With a Little Help from My Friends | 1968 | 30.00 |
| ❑ LP-12323 [S] | Alive and In Love | 1966 | 20.00 |

**RANEY, WAYNE**

| Number | Title (A Side/B Side) | Yr | NM |
|---|---|---|---|
| **KING** | | | |
| ❑ 588 [M] | Songs from the Hills | 1958 | 100.00 |
| **NASHVILLE** | | | |
| ❑ NLP-2002 | Radio Gospel and Sacred Favorites | 196? | 15.00 |
| **STARDAY** | | | |
| ❑ SLP-124 [M] | Wayne Raney and the Raney Family | 1960 | 40.00 |
| ❑ SLP-279 [M] | Don't Try to Be What You Ain't | 1964 | 40.00 |

**RANGER, ANDY**

| Number | Title (A Side/B Side) | Yr | NM |
|---|---|---|---|
| **DOT** | | | |
| ❑ DLP-3028 [M] | The Song That Never Ends | 1956 | 60.00 |

**RARE BIRD**

| Number | Title (A Side/B Side) | Yr | NM |
|---|---|---|---|
| **ABC** | | | |
| ❑ X-715 | As Your Mind Flies | 1972 | 15.00 |
| **POLYDOR** | | | |
| ❑ PD 5530 | Epic Forest | 1973 | 15.00 |
| ❑ PD 6502 | Somebody's Watching | 1974 | 15.00 |

| Number | Title (A Side/B Side) | Yr | NM |
|---|---|---|---|
| ❑ PD 6506 | Born Again | 1974 | 15.00 |
| **PROBE** | | | |
| ❑ 4514 | Rare Bird | 1970 | 25.00 |

**RARE EARTH**

| Number | Title (A Side/B Side) | Yr | NM |
|---|---|---|---|
| **MOTOWN** | | | |
| ❑ M5-116V1 | Motown Superstar Series, Vol. 16 | 1981 | 10.00 |
| ❑ M5-202V1 | Ecology | 1981 | 8.00 |
| ❑ 5229 ML | Get Ready | 1982 | 8.00 |
| **PRODIGAL** | | | |
| ❑ P6-10019 | Rare Earth | 1977 | 10.00 |
| ❑ P7-10025 | Band Together | 1978 | 10.00 |
| ❑ P7-10027 | Grand Slam | 1979 | 10.00 |
| **RARE EARTH** | | | |
| ❑ RS 507 | Get Ready | 1969 | 30.00 |
| *—Original cover has a rounded top* | | | |
| ❑ RS 507 | Get Ready | 1970 | 12.00 |
| *—Regular square cover* | | | |
| ❑ RS 510 | Generation | 1970 | 500.00 |
| *—At least one copy of this album has been confirmed to exist* | | | |
| ❑ RS 514 | Ecology | 1970 | 15.00 |
| ❑ RS 520 | One World | 1971 | 15.00 |
| ❑ R 534 [(2)] | Rare Earth in Concert | 1971 | 15.00 |
| ❑ R 543 | Willie Remembers | 1972 | 12.00 |
| ❑ R6-546 | Ma | 1973 | 12.00 |
| ❑ R6-548 | Back to Earth | 1975 | 12.00 |
| ❑ R7-550 | Midnight Lady | 1976 | 12.00 |
| **VERVE** | | | |
| ❑ V6-5066 | Dreams/Answers | 1968 | 50.00 |

**RASCALS, THE**

| Number | Title (A Side/B Side) | Yr | NM |
|---|---|---|---|
| **ATLANTIC** | | | |
| ❑ ST-137 [DJ] | Freedom Suite Sampler | 1969 | 50.00 |
| ❑ SD 2-901 [(2)] | Freedom Suite | 1969 | 20.00 |
| ❑ 8123 [M] | The Young Rascals | 1966 | 30.00 |
| ❑ SD 8123 [S] | The Young Rascals | 1966 | 40.00 |
| *—Green and blue label* | | | |
| ❑ SD 8123 [S] | The Young Rascals | 1966 | 50.00 |
| *—Purple and green label* | | | |
| ❑ SD 8123 [S] | The Young Rascals | 1969 | 12.00 |
| *—Red and green label* | | | |
| ❑ 8134 [M] | Collections | 1967 | 25.00 |
| ❑ SD 8134 [S] | Collections | 1967 | 30.00 |
| *—Green and blue label* | | | |
| ❑ SD 8134 [S] | Collections | 1969 | 12.00 |
| *—Red and green label* | | | |
| ❑ 8148 [M] | Groovin' | 1967 | 25.00 |
| ❑ SD 8148 [S] | Groovin' | 1967 | 30.00 |
| *—Green and blue label* | | | |
| ❑ SD 8148 [S] | Groovin' | 1969 | 12.00 |
| *—Red and green label* | | | |
| ❑ 8169 [M] | Once Upon a Dream | 1968 | 40.00 |
| ❑ SD 8169 [S] | Once Upon a Dream | 1968 | 25.00 |
| *—Green and blue label* | | | |
| ❑ SD 8169 [S] | Once Upon a Dream | 1969 | 12.00 |
| *—Red and green label* | | | |
| ❑ 8190 [M] | Time Peace/The Rascals' Greatest Hits | 1968 | 50.00 |
| *—Mono is promo only* | | | |
| ❑ SD 8190 [S] | Time Peace/The Rascals' Greatest Hits | 1968 | 15.00 |
| *—Purple and gold label* | | | |
| ❑ SD 8190 [S] | Time Peace/The Rascals' Greatest Hits | 1968 | 25.00 |
| *—Green and blue label* | | | |
| ❑ SD 8190 [S] | Time Peace/The Rascals' Greatest Hits | 1969 | 12.00 |
| *—Red and green label* | | | |
| ❑ 8246 [M] | See | 1969 | 50.00 |
| *—Mono is promo only; cover has "dj copy monaural" sticker on front* | | | |
| ❑ SD 8246 [S] | See | 1969 | 15.00 |
| ❑ 8276 [M] | Search and Nearness | 1970 | 50.00 |
| *—Mono is promo only; cover has "dj copy monaural" sticker on front* | | | |
| ❑ SD 8276 [S] | Search and Nearness | 1970 | 15.00 |
| **COLUMBIA** | | | |
| ❑ G 30462 [(2)] | Peaceful World | 1971 | 15.00 |
| ❑ KC 31103 | The Island of Real | 1972 | 12.00 |
| **PAIR** | | | |
| ❑ PDL2-1106 [(2)] | Rock and Roll Treasures | 1986 | 15.00 |
| **RHINO** | | | |
| ❑ RNLP 70237 | The Young Rascals | 1988 | 10.00 |
| ❑ RNLP 70238 | Collections | 1988 | 10.00 |
| ❑ RNLP 70239 | Groovin' | 1988 | 10.00 |
| ❑ R1-70240 | Once Upon a Dream | 1988 | 10.00 |
| ❑ R1-70241 | Freedom Suite | 1988 | 10.00 |
| ❑ R1-70242 | Searching for Ecstasy: The Rest of the Rascals 1969-1972 | 1988 | 10.00 |
| **SUNDAZED** | | | |
| ❑ LP 5116 | The Young Rascals | 2002 | 12.00 |
| ❑ LP 5117 | Collections | 2002 | 12.00 |
| ❑ LP 5118 | Groovin' | 2002 | 12.00 |
| ❑ LP 5119 | Once Upon a Dream | 2002 | 12.00 |

Rare Earth, *Willie Remembers…*, Rare Earth R543L, 1972, $12.

| Number | Title (A Side/B Side) | Yr | NM |
|---|---|---|---|
| **WARNER SPECIAL PRODUCTS** | | | |
| ❑ SP-2502 [(2)] | 24 Greatest Hits | 1971 | 20.00 |
| **WES FARRELL** | | | |
| ❑ PFT-1002 [DJ] | Songs from the Rascals | 197? | 25.00 |
| *—Promo-only publisher's demo* | | | |

**RASPBERRIES**

| Number | Title (A Side/B Side) | Yr | NM |
|---|---|---|---|
| **CAPITOL** | | | |
| ❑ SK-11036 | Raspberries | 1972 | 30.00 |
| *—Originals have red labels and a "scratch 'n' sniff" cover, the smell of which fades over time* | | | |
| ❑ ST-11036 | Raspberries | 1973 | 20.00 |
| *—Orange label, "Capitol" at bottom* | | | |
| ❑ ST-11123 | Fresh | 1972 | 20.00 |
| ❑ SMAS-11220 | Side 3 | 1973 | 20.00 |
| *—With cover cut in the shape of a basket of raspberries* | | | |
| ❑ ST-11329 | Starting Over | 1974 | 20.00 |
| ❑ ST-11524 | Raspberries' Best Featuring Eric Carmen | 1976 | 15.00 |
| ❑ SN-16095 | Raspberries' Best Featuring Eric Carmen | 1979 | 10.00 |

**RATHBONE, BASIL**

| Number | Title (A Side/B Side) | Yr | NM |
|---|---|---|---|
| **CAEDMON** | | | |
| ❑ TC 1028 [M] | Basil Rathbone Reads Edgar Allan Poe | 195? | 25.00 |
| ❑ TC 1044 [M] | The Happy Prince and Other Oscar Wilde Fairy Tales | 195? | 25.00 |
| ❑ TC 1115 [M] | Basil Rathbone Reads Edgar Allan Poe, Vol. 2 | 195? | 25.00 |
| ❑ TC 1120 [M] | Stories of Hawthorne | 195? | 25.00 |
| ❑ TC 1172 [M] | Stories of Sherlock Holmes, Vol. 1 | 1963 | 25.00 |
| ❑ TC 1195 [M] | Basil Rathbone Reads Edgar Allan Poe, Vol. 3 | 196? | 25.00 |
| ❑ TC 1197 [M] | Stories of Hawthorne, Vol. 2 | 196? | 25.00 |
| ❑ TC 1208 [M] | Stories of Sherlock Holmes, Vol. 2 | 1966 | 25.00 |
| ❑ TC 1220 [M] | Stories of Sherlock Holmes, Vol. 3 | 1967 | 25.00 |
| ❑ TC 1240 [M] | Stories of Sherlock Holmes, Vol. 4 | 1967 | 25.00 |
| **CO-STAR** | | | |
| ❑ C-107 [M] | The Brothers Karamazov | 196? | 20.00 |
| ❑ CS-107 [S] | The Brothers Karamazov | 196? | 25.00 |

| Number | Title (A Side/B Side) | Yr | NM |
|---|---|---|---|
| **COLUMBIA MASTERWORKS** | | | |
| ❑ ML 4038 [10] | Peter and the Wolf; Treasure Island | 1949 | 50.00 |
| ❑ ML 4081 [10] | A Christmas Carol | 1950 | 50.00 |
| **DECCA** | | | |
| ❑ DL 9109 [M] | Selections from The Jungle Book | 1962 | 30.00 |

**RATIONALS, THE**

| Number | Title (A Side/B Side) | Yr | NM |
|---|---|---|---|
| **CREWE** | | | |
| ❑ CR-1334 | The Rationals | 1969 | 40.00 |

**RATTLES, THE**

| Number | Title (A Side/B Side) | Yr | NM |
|---|---|---|---|
| **MERCURY** | | | |
| ❑ MG 21127 [M] | The Rattles' Greatest Hits | 1967 | 80.00 |
| ❑ SR 61127 [R] | The Rattles' Greatest Hits | 1967 | 50.00 |

**RAVEN** Two different groups?

| Number | Title (A Side/B Side) | Yr | NM |
|---|---|---|---|
| **COLUMBIA** | | | |
| ❑ CS 9903 | Raven | 1969 | 20.00 |
| **DISCOVERY** | | | |
| ❑ 36133 | Live at the Inferno | 1967 | 80.00 |

**RAVEN, EDDY**

| Number | Title (A Side/B Side) | Yr | NM |
|---|---|---|---|
| **ABC DOT** | | | |
| ❑ DOSD-2031 | This Is Eddy Raven | 1975 | 15.00 |
| **DIMENSION** | | | |
| ❑ DLP-5001 | Eyes | 1980 | 15.00 |
| **ELEKTRA** | | | |
| ❑ 5E-545 | Desperate Dreams | 1981 | 12.00 |
| **LA LOUISIANNE** | | | |
| ❑ 127 | That Cajun Country Sound | 197? | 20.00 |
| **MCA** | | | |
| ❑ 910 | Thank God for Kids | 198? | 8.00 |
| **RCA** | | | |
| ❑ 5728-1-R | Right Hand Man | 1987 | 8.00 |
| ❑ 6815-1-R | The Best of Eddy Raven | 1988 | 8.00 |
| **RCA VICTOR** | | | |
| ❑ AHL1-5040 | I Could Use Another You | 1984 | 8.00 |
| ❑ AHL1-5456 | Love and Other Hard Times | 1985 | 8.00 |
| **UNIVERSAL** | | | |
| ❑ UVL-76003 | Temporary Sanity | 1989 | 10.00 |

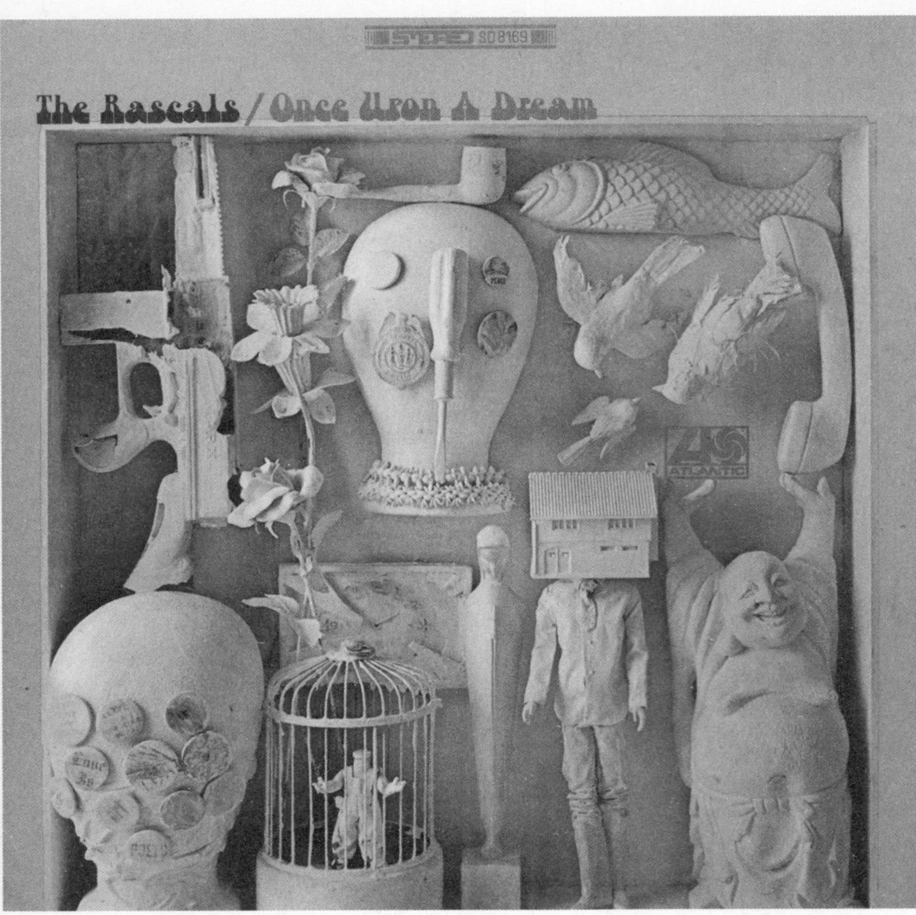


The Rascals, *Once Upon a Dream,* Atlantic SD 8169, 1968, stereo, green and blue label, $25.

| Number | Title (A Side/B Side) | Yr | NM |
|---|---|---|---|
| WARNER BROS. | | | |
| ❑ 5E-545 | Desperate Dreams | 1983 | 8.00 |
| *—Reissue of Elektra 5E-545* | | | |
| **RAVENS, THE** | | | |
| HARLEM HIT PARADE | | | |
| ❑ 1007 | The Ravens | 1975 | 10.00 |
| REGENT | | | |
| ❑ MG-6062 [M] | Write Me a Letter | 195? | 150.00 |
| *—Red label* | | | |
| ❑ MG-6062 [M] | Write Me a Letter | 1957 | 300.00 |
| *—Green label* | | | |
| SAVOY JAZZ | | | |
| ❑ SJL-2227 [(2)] | The Greatest Group of Them All | 1978 | 12.00 |
| **RAVENSCROFT, THURL** | | | |
| DOT | | | |
| ❑ DLP-3430 [M] | Great Hits | 1962 | 30.00 |
| ❑ DLP-25430 [S] | Great Hits | 1962 | 40.00 |
| **RAW** | | | |
| CORAL | | | |
| ❑ CRL 757515 | Raw Holly | 1971 | 30.00 |
| **RAW SPITT** | | | |
| UNITED ARTISTS | | | |
| ❑ UAS-6795 | Maybe You Ain't Black | 1971 | 25.00 |
| **RAWLS, LOU** | | | |
| ALLEGIANCE | | | |
| ❑ AV-5016 | Trying As Hard As I Can | 198? | 10.00 |
| BELL | | | |
| ❑ 1318 | She's Gone | 1974 | 12.00 |
| BLUE NOTE | | | |
| ❑ B1-91441 | Stormy Monday | 1990 | 12.00 |
| *—Reissue of Capitol 1714* | | | |
| ❑ B1-91937 | At Last | 1989 | 12.00 |
| ❑ B1-93841 | It's Supposed to Be Fun | 1990 | 15.00 |
| CAPITOL | | | |
| ❑ ST-122 | The Way It Was | 1969 | 15.00 |
| ❑ ST 8-0215 | The Way It Was — The Way It Is | 1969 | 20.00 |
| *—Capitol Record Club edition* | | | |
| ❑ ST-215 | The Way It Was — The Way It Is | 1969 | 15.00 |
| ❑ SWBB-261 [(2)] | Close-Up | 1969 | 20.00 |
| *—Reissue of 1824 and 2042 in one package* | | | |
| ❑ ST-325 | Your Good Thing | 1969 | 15.00 |
| ❑ ST-427 | You've Made Me So Very Happy | 1970 | 15.00 |
| ❑ ST-479 | Bring It on Home | 1970 | 15.00 |
| ❑ STBB-720 [(2)] | Down Here on the Ground/I'd Rather Drink Muddy Water | 1971 | 20.00 |
| ❑ SM-1714 | Stormy Monday | 197? | 10.00 |
| *—Reissue with new prefix* | | | |
| ❑ ST 1714 [S] | Stormy Monday | 1962 | 25.00 |
| ❑ T 1714 [M] | Stormy Monday | 1962 | 20.00 |
| ❑ ST 1824 [S] | Black and Blue | 1963 | 25.00 |
| ❑ T 1824 [M] | Black and Blue | 1963 | 20.00 |
| ❑ ST 2042 [S] | Tobacco Road | 1964 | 25.00 |
| ❑ T 2042 [M] | Tobacco Road | 1964 | 20.00 |
| ❑ ST 2273 [S] | Nobody But Lou | 1965 | 25.00 |
| ❑ T 2273 [M] | Nobody But Lou | 1965 | 20.00 |
| ❑ ST 2401 [S] | Lou Rawls and Strings | 1965 | 25.00 |
| ❑ T 2401 [M] | Lou Rawls and Strings | 1965 | 20.00 |
| ❑ SM-2459 | Lou Rawls Live! | 197? | 10.00 |
| *—Reissue with new prefix* | | | |
| ❑ ST 2459 [S] | Lou Rawls Live! | 1966 | 20.00 |
| ❑ T 2459 [M] | Lou Rawls Live! | 1966 | 15.00 |
| ❑ SM-2566 | Lou Rawls Soulin' | 197? | 10.00 |
| *—Reissue with new prefix* | | | |
| ❑ ST 2566 [S] | Lou Rawls Soulin' | 1966 | 20.00 |
| ❑ T 2566 [M] | Lou Rawls Soulin' | 1966 | 15.00 |
| ❑ ST 2632 [S] | Lou Rawls Carryin' On! | 1966 | 20.00 |
| ❑ T 2632 [M] | Lou Rawls Carryin' On! | 1966 | 15.00 |
| ❑ ST 2713 [S] | Too Much! | 1967 | 15.00 |
| ❑ T 2713 [M] | Too Much! | 1967 | 20.00 |
| ❑ ST 2756 [S] | That's Lou | 1967 | 15.00 |
| ❑ T 2756 [M] | That's Lou | 1967 | 20.00 |
| ❑ ST 2790 [S] | Merry Christmas, Ho, Ho, Ho | 1967 | 12.00 |
| ❑ T 2790 [M] | Merry Christmas, Ho, Ho, Ho | 1967 | 15.00 |
| ❑ ST 2864 [S] | Feelin' Good | 1968 | 15.00 |
| ❑ T 2864 [M] | Feelin' Good | 1968 | 30.00 |
| ❑ ST 2927 | You're Good for Me | 1968 | 15.00 |
| ❑ SKAO 2948 | The Best of Lou Rawls | 1968 | 15.00 |
| ❑ SM-2948 | The Best of Lou Rawls | 197? | 10.00 |
| *—Reissue with new prefix* | | | |
| ❑ SKBB-11585 [(2)] | The Best from Lou Rawls | 1976 | 12.00 |
| ❑ SN-16096 | The Best of Lou Rawls | 1980 | 8.00 |
| *—Budget-line reissue* | | | |
| ❑ SN-16097 | Lou Rawls Live! | 1980 | 8.00 |
| *—Budget-line reissue* | | | |
| EPIC | | | |
| ❑ FE 37448 | Now Is the Time | 1982 | 10.00 |
| ❑ FE 38553 | When the Night Comes | 1983 | 10.00 |
| ❑ FE 39403 | Close Company | 1984 | 10.00 |
| ❑ FE 40210 | Love All Your Blues Away | 1986 | 10.00 |
| MGM | | | |
| ❑ SE-4771 | Natural Man | 1971 | 12.00 |
| ❑ SE-4809 | Silk & Soul | 1972 | 12.00 |
| ❑ SE-4861 | A Man of Value | 1973 | 12.00 |
| ❑ SE-4965 | Live at the Century Plaza | 1974 | 12.00 |
| PHILADELPHIA INT'L. | | | |
| ❑ PZ 33957 | All Things in Time | 1976 | 10.00 |
| *—No bar code on cover* | | | |
| ❑ PZ 33957 | All Things in Time | 198? | 8.00 |
| *—With bar code on cover* | | | |
| ❑ PZ 34488 | Unmistakably Lou | 1977 | 10.00 |
| ❑ PZ 34488 | Unmistakably Lou | 1986 | 8.00 |
| *—Budget-line reissue* | | | |
| ❑ JZ 35036 | When You Hear Lou, You've Heard It All | 1977 | 10.00 |
| ❑ PZ2 35517 [(2)] | Lou Rawls Live | 1978 | 12.00 |
| ❑ JZ 36006 | Let Me Be Good to You | 1979 | 10.00 |
| ❑ PZ 36006 | Let Me Be Good to You | 198? | 8.00 |
| *—Budget-line reissue* | | | |
| ❑ JZ 36304 | Sit Down and Talk to Me | 1979 | 10.00 |
| ❑ PZ 36304 | Sit Down and Talk to Me | 198? | 8.00 |
| *—Budget-line reissue* | | | |
| ❑ JZ 36774 | Shades of Blue | 1980 | 10.00 |
| ❑ FZ 39285 | Classics | 1984 | 10.00 |
| PICKWICK | | | |
| ❑ SPC-3156 | Come On In, Mr. Blues | 1971 | 10.00 |
| ❑ SPC-3228 | Gee Baby | 1972 | 10.00 |
| POLYDOR | | | |
| ❑ PD-1-6086 | Naturally | 1976 | 10.00 |
| **RAY, DAVE** | | | |
| ELEKTRA | | | |
| ❑ EKL-284 [M] | Snaker's Here | 1965 | 20.00 |
| ❑ EKL-319 [M] | Fine Soft Land | 1966 | 20.00 |
| ❑ EKS-7284 [S] | Snaker's Here | 1965 | 25.00 |
| ❑ EKS-7319 [S] | Fine Soft Land | 1966 | 25.00 |
| **RAY, DIANE** | | | |
| MERCURY | | | |
| ❑ MG-20903 [M] | The Exciting Years | 1964 | 80.00 |
| ❑ SR-60903 [S] | The Exciting Years | 1964 | 100.00 |
| **RAY, JAMES** | | | |
| CAPRICE | | | |
| ❑ LP-1002 [M] | James Ray | 1962 | 80.00 |
| ❑ SLP-1002 [S] | James Ray | 1962 | 120.00 |
| **RAY, JOHNNIE** | | | |
| COLUMBIA | | | |
| ❑ CL 961 [M] | The Big Beat | 1957 | 50.00 |
| ❑ CL 1093 [M] | At the Desert Inn in Las Vegas | 1957 | 50.00 |
| ❑ CL 1225 [M] | 'Til Morning | 1958 | 40.00 |
| *—Red and black label with six "eye" logos* | | | |
| ❑ CL 1225 [M] | 'Til Morning | 1963 | 20.00 |
| *—Red label with either "Guraranteed High Fidelity" or "360 Sound Mono" at bottom* | | | |
| ❑ CL 1227 [M] | Johnnie Ray's Greatest Hits | 1958 | 40.00 |
| *—Red and black label with 6 "eye" logos* | | | |
| ❑ CL 1227 [M] | Johnnie Ray's Greatest Hits | 1962 | 25.00 |
| *—"Guaranteed High Fidelity" on label* | | | |
| ❑ CL 1227 [M] | Johnnie Ray's Greatest Hits | 1965 | 15.00 |
| *—"360 Sound" label* | | | |
| ❑ CL 1385 [M] | On the Trail | 1959 | 40.00 |
| ❑ CL 2510 [10] | I Cry for You | 1955 | 70.00 |
| *—"House Party Series" issue* | | | |
| ❑ CL 6199 [10] | Johnnie Ray | 1951 | 80.00 |
| ❑ CS 8180 [S] | On the Trail | 1959 | 50.00 |
| COLUMBIA SPECIAL PRODUCTS | | | |
| ❑ P 13086 | Greatest Hits | 197? | 10.00 |
| EPIC | | | |
| ❑ LN 1120 [10] | Johnnie Ray | 1955 | 80.00 |
| HARMONY | | | |
| ❑ H 30609 | The Best of Johnnie Ray | 1971 | 12.00 |
| LIBERTY | | | |
| ❑ LRP-3221 [M] | Johnnie Ray | 1962 | 20.00 |
| ❑ LST-7221 [S] | Johnnie Ray | 1962 | 30.00 |
| SUNSET | | | |
| ❑ SUM-1125 [M] | Mr. Cry | 196? | 12.00 |
| ❑ SUS-5125 [S] | Mr. Cry | 196? | 12.00 |
| **RAY, WADE** | | | |
| ABC-PARAMOUNT | | | |
| ❑ ABC-539 [M] | A Ray of Country Sun | 1966 | 15.00 |
| ❑ ABCS-539 [S] | A Ray of Country Sun | 1966 | 20.00 |
| RCA CAMDEN | | | |
| ❑ CAS-2107 | Walk Softly | 1969 | 15.00 |
| **RAYBURN, MARGIE** | | | |
| LIBERTY | | | |
| ❑ LRP-3126 [M] | Margie | 1959 | 25.00 |
| ❑ LST-7126 [S] | Margie | 1959 | 40.00 |



**Except when noted otherwise, VG = 25% of NM, and VG+ = 50% of NM. (Example: VG = $2.00, VG+ = $4.00 and NM = $8.00.)**

| Number | Title (A Side/B Side) | Yr | NM |
|---|---|---|---|

**RAYE, JERRY**

DEVILLE

❑ LP-101 [M] The Many Sides of Jerry Raye and Fenwyck 1967 600.00

**RAYE, MARTHA**

EPIC

❑ LG 3061 [M] Here's Martha Raye 1954 40.00

**RAYMOND, LEW**

TOPS

❑ L-1583 [M] For Men Only 1958 40.00
*—Jayne Mansfield is the cover model*
❑ L-1647 [M] Million Sellers 1960 30.00
*—Mary Tyler Moore is the cover model*

**RCA VICTOR SYMPHONY ORCHESTRA (ROBERT RUSSELL BENNETT, CONDUCTOR)**

RCA VICTOR RED SEAL

❑ LSC-2238 [S] It's Classic But It's Good 1959 20.00
*—Original with "shaded dog" label*

**RCA VICTOR SYMPHONY ORCHESTRA (KIRIL KONDRASHIN, CONDUCTOR)**

RCA VICTOR RED SEAL

❑ LSC-2323 [S] Tchaikovsky: Capriccio Italien; Rimsky-Korsakov: Capriccio Espagnole 1959 40.00
*—Original with "shaded dog" label*
❑ LSC-2323 [S] Tchaikovsky: Capriccio Italien; Rimsky-Korsakov: Capriccio Espagnole 199? 25.00
*—Classic Records reissue*
❑ LSC-2398 [S] Khachaturian: Masquerade Suite; Kabalevsky: The Comedians 1960 120.00
*—Original with "shaded dog" label*
❑ LSC-2398 [S] Khachaturian: Masquerade Suite; Kabalevsky: The Comedians 1964 100.00
*—Second edition with "white dog" label*
❑ LSC-2398 [S] Khachaturian: Masquerade Suite; Kabalevsky: The Comedians 1969 25.00
*—Third edition with no dog on label*
❑ LSC-2398 [S] Khachaturian: Masquerade Suite; Kabalevsky: The Comedians 199? 25.00
*—Classic Records reissue*

**RCA VICTOR SYMPHONY ORCHESTRA (LEOPOLD STOKOWSKI, CONDUCTOR)**

RCA VICTOR RED SEAL

❑ LSC-2471 [S] Rhapsodies 196? 40.00
*—Original with "shaded dog" label or second edition with "white dog" label*
❑ LSC-2471 [S] Rhapsodies 199? 25.00
*—Classic Records reissue*
❑ LSC-2612 [S] Handel: Royal Fireworks Music; Water Music 1962 25.00
*—Original with "shaded dog" label*
❑ LSC-2612 [S] Handel: Royal Fireworks Music; Water Music 1964 20.00
*—Second edition with "white dog" label*

**REAGAN, RONALD**

DECCA

❑ DL 4943 [M] Freedom's Finest Hour 1967 25.00
❑ DL 74943 [S] Freedom's Finest Hour 1967 30.00

KEY

❑ 690 [M] Rendezvous with Destiny 1964 25.00

"X"

❑ LVA-3051 [M] Tales from the Great Book 1956 40.00

**REALLY RED**

C.I.A.

❑ 006 Teaching You the Fear 1981 80.00

**REBECCA AND THE SUNNY BROOK FARMERS**

MUSICOR

❑ MS-3176 Rebecca and the Sunny Brook Farmers 1969 40.00

**REBIRTH**

AVANT GARDE

❑ AVS-135 Rebirth 1971 50.00

**REBS, THE**

FREDLO

❑ 6830 1968 A.D. Break Through 1968 400.00

**RED, SONNY**

BLUE NOTE

❑ BLP-4032 [M] Out of the Blue 1960 80.00
*—Regular version, W. 63rd St. address on label*

Red Hot Chili Peppers, *Mother's Milk,* EMI E1-92152, 1989, $12.

| Number | Title (A Side/B Side) | Yr | NM |
|---|---|---|---|

❑ BLP-4032 [M] Out of the Blue 1960 100.00
*—"Deep groove" version (deep indentation under label on both sides)*
❑ BLP-4032 [M] Out of the Blue 1963 25.00
*—With "New York, USA" address on label*
❑ ST-84032 [S] Out of the Blue 1960 60.00
*—With W. 63rd St. address on label*
❑ ST-84032 [S] Out of the Blue 1963 20.00
*—With "New York, USA" address on label*

JAZZLAND

❑ JLP-32 [M] Breezin' 1960 30.00
❑ JLP-59 [M] The Mode 1961 30.00
❑ JLP-74 [M] Images 1962 30.00
❑ JLP-932 [M] Breezin' 1960 40.00
❑ JLP-959 [S] The Mode 1961 40.00
❑ JLP-974 [S] Images 1962 40.00

**RED CRAYOLA, THE**

INTERNATIONAL ARTISTS

❑ 2 Parable of the Arable Land 1979 15.00
*—Reissue with "Masterfonics" in trail-off wax*
❑ 2 [M] Parable of the Arable Land 1968 100.00
❑ 2 [S] Parable of the Arable Land 1968 60.00
❑ 7 God Bless the Red Crayola 1968 60.00
❑ 7 God Bless the Red Crayola 1979 15.00
*—Reissue with "Masterfonics" in trail-off wax*

**RED HOT CHILI PEPPERS**

EMI

❑ E1-29665 Out in L.A. 1994 10.00
❑ E1-92152 Mother's Milk 1989 12.00

EMI AMERICA

❑ ST-17128 Red Hot Chili Peppers 1984 10.00
❑ ST-17168 Freaky Styley 1985 10.00
❑ E1-48036 The Uplift Mofo Party Plan 1987 10.00

EMI MANHATTAN

❑ E1-90869 [EP] The Abbey Road E.P. 1988 8.00

WARNER BROS.

❑ PRO-A-5170 [(2)DJ]Blood Sugar Sex Magik 1991 40.00
*—"Radio-ready" version of LP, this is the only U.S. vinyl release of this album*
❑ 43391-1 [(4)] Stadium Arcadium 2006 40.00
*—150-gram version; records are contained in two gatefold sleeves inside a slipcase*
❑ 47386 [(2)] Californication 1999 60.00
❑ 48140 [(2)] By the Way 2002 25.00

| Number | Title (A Side/B Side) | Yr | NM |
|---|---|---|---|

❑ 49996-1 [(4)] Stadium Arcadium 2006 80.00
*—180-gram version; box set contains records in individual sleeves plus two 12x12 booklets*

**RED ONION JAZZ BAND, THE**

RIVERSIDE

❑ RLP 12-260 [M]Dance Off Both Your Shoes In Hi-Fi 1958 40.00

**RED RIVER DAVE**

CONTINENTAL

❑ 1507 [M] Red River Dave Sings 1962 25.00

VARSITY

❑ 6962 [10] Red River Dave 1951 70.00

**REDBONE**

EPIC

❑ EGP 501 [(2)] Redbone 1970 20.00
❑ E 30109 Potlatch 1970 15.00
❑ EQ 30815 [Q] Message from a Drum 1973 20.00
❑ KE 30815 Message from a Drum 1972 15.00
❑ KE 31598 Already Here 1972 15.00
❑ KE 32462 Wovoka 1974 15.00
❑ EQ 33053 [Q] Bearded Dreams Through Turquoise Eyes 1974 20.00
❑ KE 33053 Bearded Dreams Through Turquoise Eyes 1974 15.00
❑ KEG 33456 [(2)]Come & Get Your Redbone 1975 20.00

RCA VICTOR

❑ AFL1-2352 Cycles 1977 12.00

**REDBONE, LEON**

AUGUST

❑ AS 8890 Christmas Island 1988 15.00

WARNER BROS.

❑ BS 2888 On the Track 1975 25.00
❑ BS 2971 Double Time 1977 25.00
❑ BS 3165 Champagne Charlie 1978 25.00

**REDD, FREDDIE**

BLUE NOTE

❑ BLP-4027 [M] Music From "The Connection" 1960 100.00
*—Regular version, W. 63rd St. address on label*
❑ BLP-4027 [M] Music From "The Connection" 1960 120.00
*—"Deep groove" version (deep indentation under label on both sides)*

| Number | Title (A Side/B Side) | Yr | NM |
|---|---|---|---|
| ❑ BLP-4027 [M] | Music From "The Connection" | 1963 | 25.00 |
| *—With "New York, USA" address on label* | | | |
| ❑ BLP-4045 [M] | Shades of Redd | 1960 | 100.00 |
| *—Regular version, W. 63rd St. address on label* | | | |
| ❑ BLP-4045 [M] | Shades of Redd | 1960 | 120.00 |
| *—"Deep groove" version (deep indentation under label on both sides)* | | | |
| ❑ BLP-4045 [M] | Shades of Redd | 1963 | 25.00 |
| *—With "New York, USA" address on label* | | | |
| ❑ BST-84027 [S] | Music From "The Connection" | 1960 | 100.00 |
| *—With W. 63rd St. address on label* | | | |
| ❑ BST-84027 [S] | Music From "The Connection" | 1967 | 15.00 |
| *—With "A Division of Liberty Records" on label* | | | |
| **MOSAIC** | | | |
| ❑ MR3-124 [(3)] | The Complete Blue Note Recordings of Freddie Redd | 199? | 30.00 |
| **PRESTIGE** | | | |
| ❑ PRLP-197 [10] | Introducing the Freddie Redd Trio | 1954 | 150.00 |
| **RIVERSIDE** | | | |
| ❑ RLP 12-250 [M] | San Francisco Suite For Jazz Trio | 1957 | 60.00 |

## REDD, FREDDIE, AND HAMPTON HAWES

| Number | Title (A Side/B Side) | Yr | NM |
|---|---|---|---|
| **PRESTIGE** | | | |
| ❑ PRLP-7067 [M] | Piano: East/West | 1956 | 80.00 |
| **STATUS** | | | |
| ❑ ST-8307 [M] | Movin' | 1965 | 40.00 |

## REDD, VI

| Number | Title (A Side/B Side) | Yr | NM |
|---|---|---|---|
| **ATCO** | | | |
| ❑ 33-157 [M] | Lady Soul | 1963 | 30.00 |
| ❑ SD 33-157 [S] | Lady Soul | 1963 | 40.00 |
| **UNITED ARTISTS** | | | |
| ❑ UAJ-14016 [M] | Bird Call | 1962 | 40.00 |
| ❑ UAJS-15016 [S] | Bird Call | 1962 | 50.00 |

## REDDING, GENE

| Number | Title (A Side/B Side) | Yr | NM |
|---|---|---|---|
| **HAVEN** | | | |
| ❑ ST-9200 | Blood Brother | 1974 | 20.00 |

## REDDING, OTIS

| Number | Title (A Side/B Side) | Yr | NM |
|---|---|---|---|
| **ATCO** | | | |
| ❑ 33-161 [M] | Pain in My Heart | 1964 | 250.00 |
| ❑ SD 33-161 [R] | Pain in My Heart | 1968 | 250.00 |
| ❑ 33-252 [M] | The Immortal Otis Redding | 1968 | 50.00 |
| *—Mono is white label promo only* | | | |
| ❑ SD 33-252 [S] | The Immortal Otis Redding | 1968 | 15.00 |
| ❑ SD 33-261 | History of Otis Redding | 1968 | 15.00 |
| *—Reissue of Volt 418* | | | |
| ❑ SD 33-265 | Otis Redding In Person at the Whiskey A-Go-Go | 1968 | 15.00 |
| ❑ SD 33-284 | Otis Blue/Otis Redding Sings Soul | 1969 | 15.00 |
| *—Reissue of Volt 412* | | | |
| ❑ SD 33-285 | The Soul Album | 1969 | 15.00 |
| *—Reissue of Volt 413* | | | |
| ❑ SD 33-286 | Otis Redding Live in Europe | 1969 | 15.00 |
| *—Reissue of Volt 416* | | | |
| ❑ SD 33-287 | Complete & Unbelievable...The Otis Redding Dictionary of Soul | 1969 | 15.00 |
| *—Reissue of Volt 415* | | | |
| ❑ SD 33-288 | The Dock of the Bay | 1969 | 15.00 |
| *—Reissue of Volt 419* | | | |
| ❑ SD 33-289 | Love Man | 1969 | 15.00 |
| ❑ SD 33-333 | Tell the Truth | 1970 | 15.00 |
| ❑ SD 2-801 [(2)] | The Best of Otis Redding | 1972 | 20.00 |
| **ATLANTIC** | | | |
| ❑ SD 19346 | Recorded Live | 198? | 10.00 |
| ❑ 81282 | The Best of Otis Redding | 1985 | 10.00 |
| ❑ 81762 [(4)] | The Otis Redding Story | 1987 | 30.00 |
| **4 MEN WITH BEARDS** | | | |
| ❑ 4M 105 | The Great Otis Redding Sings Soul Ballads | 2002 | 15.00 |
| *—Reissue on 180-gram vinyl* | | | |
| **PAIR** | | | |
| ❑ PDL2-1062 [(2)] | The Legend of Otis Redding | 1984 | 15.00 |
| **SUNDAZED** | | | |
| ❑ LP 5063 [M] | Complete & Unbelievable ... The Otis Redding Dictionary of Soul | 2001 | 12.00 |
| *—Reissue on 180-gram vinyl* | | | |
| ❑ LP 5064 [M] | Otis Blue/Otis Redding Sings Soul | 2001 | 12.00 |
| *—Reissue on 180-gram vinyl* | | | |
| ❑ LP 5132 [M] | The Soul Album | 2003 | 12.00 |
| *—Reissue on 180-gram vinyl* | | | |
| ❑ LP 5133 [S] | Otis Redding In Person at the Whiskey A-Go-Go | 2003 | 12.00 |
| *—Reissue on 180-gram vinyl* | | | |
| ❑ LP 5134 [S] | Otis Redding Live in Europe | 2003 | 12.00 |
| *—Reissue on 180-gram vinyl* | | | |
| ❑ LP 5172 [S] | The Dock of the Bay | 2003 | 12.00 |
| *—Reissue on 180-gram vinyl* | | | |
| **VOLT** | | | |
| ❑ 411 [M] | The Great Otis Redding Sings Soul Ballads | 1965 | 90.00 |
| ❑ S-411 [R] | The Great Otis Redding Sings Soul Ballads | 1968 | 110.00 |
| ❑ 412 [M] | Otis Blue/Otis Redding Sings Soul | 1965 | 40.00 |
| ❑ S-412 [S] | Otis Blue/Otis Redding Sings Soul | 1965 | 50.00 |
| ❑ 413 [M] | The Soul Album | 1966 | 40.00 |
| ❑ S-413 [S] | The Soul Album | 1966 | 50.00 |
| ❑ 415 [M] | Complete & Unbelievable...The Otis Redding Dictionary of Soul | 1966 | 40.00 |
| ❑ S-415 [S] | Complete & Unbelievable...The Otis Redding Dictionary of Soul | 1966 | 50.00 |
| ❑ 416 [M] | Otis Redding Live in Europe | 1967 | 30.00 |
| ❑ S-416 [S] | Otis Redding Live in Europe | 1967 | 40.00 |
| ❑ 418 [M] | History of Otis Redding | 1967 | 40.00 |
| ❑ S-418 [S] | History of Otis Redding | 1967 | 30.00 |
| ❑ S-419 | The Dock of the Bay | 1968 | 30.00 |

## REDMAN, DON

| Number | Title (A Side/B Side) | Yr | NM |
|---|---|---|---|
| **GOLDEN CREST** | | | |
| ❑ GC-3017 [M] | Park Avenue Patter | 1958 | 40.00 |
| **RCA VICTOR** | | | |
| ❑ LPV-520 [M] | Master of the Big Band | 1965 | 20.00 |
| **ROULETTE** | | | |
| ❑ R-25070 [M] | Dixieland in High Society | 1960 | 20.00 |
| ❑ SR-25070 [S] | Dixieland in High Society | 1960 | 25.00 |

## REDMAN, GEORGE

| Number | Title (A Side/B Side) | Yr | NM |
|---|---|---|---|
| **SKYLARK** | | | |
| ❑ SKLP-20 [10] | The George Redman Group | 1954 | 150.00 |

## REDMOND, EDGAR

| Number | Title (A Side/B Side) | Yr | NM |
|---|---|---|---|
| **DISQUE-PHENOMENON** | | | |
| ❑ 2696 [10] | Edgar Redmond & the Modern String Ensemble | 1965 | 30.00 |

## REDNOW, EIVETS See STEVIE WONDER.

## REDPATH, JEAN

| Number | Title (A Side/B Side) | Yr | NM |
|---|---|---|---|
| **ELEKTRA** | | | |
| ❑ EKL-214 [M] | Scottish Ballad Book | 1962 | 25.00 |
| ❑ EKL-224 [M] | Songs of Love, Lilt and Laughter | 1963 | 25.00 |
| ❑ EKL-274 [M] | Laddie Lie Near Me | 1964 | 20.00 |
| ❑ EKS-7274 [S] | Laddie Lie Near Me | 1964 | 25.00 |
| **PRESTIGE** | | | |
| ❑ PR-13041 [M] | Skipping Barefoot Through the Heather | 1962 | 30.00 |

## REECE, DIZZY

| Number | Title (A Side/B Side) | Yr | NM |
|---|---|---|---|
| **BLUE NOTE** | | | |
| ❑ BLP-4006 [M] | Blues in Trinity | 1958 | 150.00 |
| *—Regular version, W. 63rd St. address on label* | | | |
| ❑ BLP-4006 [M] | Blues in Trinity | 1958 | 300.00 |
| *—"Deep groove" version; W. 63rd St. address on label* | | | |
| ❑ BLP-4006 [M] | Blues in Trinity | 1963 | 40.00 |
| *—With "New York, USA" address on label* | | | |
| ❑ BST-4006 [S] | Blues in Trinity | 1959 | 120.00 |
| *—Regular version, W. 63rd St. address on label* | | | |
| ❑ BST-4006 [S] | Blues in Trinity | 1959 | 200.00 |
| *—"Deep groove" version; W. 63rd St. address on label* | | | |
| ❑ BST-4006 [S] | Blues in Trinity | 1963 | 30.00 |
| *—With "New York, USA" address on label* | | | |
| ❑ BLP-4023 [M] | Star Bright | 1959 | 150.00 |
| *—Regular version, W. 63rd St. address on label* | | | |
| ❑ BLP-4023 [M] | Star Bright | 1959 | 250.00 |
| *—"Deep groove" version; W. 63rd St. address on label* | | | |
| ❑ BLP-4023 [M] | Star Bright | 1963 | 40.00 |
| *—With "New York, USA" address on label* | | | |
| ❑ BLP-4023 [M] | Star Bright | 200? | 30.00 |
| *—200-gram reissue; distributed by Classic Records* | | | |
| ❑ BLP-4033 [M] | Soundin' Off | 1960 | 200.00 |
| *—Regular version, W. 63rd St. address on label* | | | |
| ❑ BLP-4033 [M] | Soundin' Off | 1960 | 400.00 |
| *—"Deep groove" version; W. 63rd St. address on label* | | | |
| ❑ BLP-4033 [M] | Soundin' Off | 1963 | 50.00 |
| *—With "New York, USA" address on label* | | | |
| ❑ BST-84023 [S] | Star Bright | 1959 | 120.00 |
| *—With W. 63rd St. address on label* | | | |
| ❑ BST-84023 [S] | Star Bright | 1963 | 40.00 |
| *—With "New York, USA" address on label* | | | |
| ❑ BST-84033 [S] | Soundin' Off | 1960 | 150.00 |
| *—With W. 63rd St. address on label* | | | |
| ❑ BST-84033 [S] | Soundin' Off | 1963 | 40.00 |
| *—With "New York, USA" address on label* | | | |
| **IMPERIAL** | | | |
| ❑ LP-9043 [M] | London Jazz | 1957 | 80.00 |
| **NEW JAZZ** | | | |
| ❑ NJLP-8274 [M] | Asia Minor | 1962 | 60.00 |
| *—Purple label* | | | |
| ❑ NJLP-8274 [M] | Asia Minor | 1965 | 25.00 |
| *—Blue label, trident logo at right* | | | |

## REECE, DIZZY, AND TUBBY HAYES

| Number | Title (A Side/B Side) | Yr | NM |
|---|---|---|---|
| **SAVOY** | | | |
| ❑ MG-12111 [M] | Changing the Jazz at Buckingham Palace | 1957 | 100.00 |

## REED, JERRY

| Number | Title (A Side/B Side) | Yr | NM |
|---|---|---|---|
| **CAPITOL** | | | |
| ❑ ST-12492 | Lookin' at You | 1986 | 8.00 |
| **HARMONY** | | | |
| ❑ H 30547 | I'm Movin' On | 1971 | 10.00 |
| **RCA CAMDEN** | | | |
| ❑ ACL1-0331 | Tupelo Mississippi Flash | 1973 | 10.00 |
| ❑ CAS-2585 | Oh What a Woman! | 1972 | 10.00 |
| **RCA VICTOR** | | | |
| ❑ APD1-0238 [Q] | Lord, Mr. Ford | 1973 | 25.00 |
| ❑ APL1-0238 | Lord, Mr. Ford | 1973 | 12.00 |
| ❑ APL1-0356 | The Uptown Poker Club | 1973 | 12.00 |
| ❑ APL1-0544 | A Good Woman's Love | 1974 | 12.00 |
| ❑ APL1-0787 | Mind Your Love | 1974 | 12.00 |
| ❑ APL1-1226 | Red Hot Picker | 1975 | 12.00 |
| ❑ ANL1-1345 | When You're Hot, You're Hot | 1975 | 10.00 |
| *—Reissue of 4506* | | | |
| ❑ APL1-1861 | Both Barrels | 1976 | 12.00 |
| ❑ ANL1-2167 | Me and Chet | 1976 | 10.00 |
| *—Reissue of 4707* | | | |
| ❑ AHL1-2346 | Jerry Reed Rides Again | 1977 | 12.00 |
| ❑ AHL1-2516 | East Bound and Down | 1977 | 12.00 |
| ❑ AHL1-2764 | Sweet Love Feelings | 1978 | 12.00 |
| ❑ AHL1-3359 | Half Singin' & Half Pickin' | 1979 | 12.00 |
| ❑ AHL1-3453 | Jerry Reed Live! | 1979 | 12.00 |
| ❑ AHL1-3604 | Jerry Reed Sings Jim Croce | 1980 | 12.00 |
| ❑ AYL1-3677 | East Bound and Down | 1980 | 8.00 |
| *—"Best Buy Series" reissue* | | | |
| ❑ LPM-3756 [M] | The Unbelievable Guitar and Voice of Jerry Reed | 1967 | 25.00 |
| ❑ LSP-3756 [S] | The Unbelievable Guitar and Voice of Jerry Reed | 1967 | 20.00 |
| ❑ AHL1-3771 | Texas Bound and Flyin' | 1980 | 12.00 |
| ❑ LPM-3978 [M] | Nashville Underground | 1968 | 50.00 |
| ❑ LSP-3978 [S] | Nashville Underground | 1968 | 20.00 |
| ❑ AHL1-4021 | Dixie Dreams | 1981 | 12.00 |
| ❑ LSP-4069 | Alabama Wild Man | 1968 | 20.00 |
| ❑ LSP-4147 | Better Things in Life | 1969 | 20.00 |
| ❑ AYL1-4167 | Jerry Reed Live! | 1982 | 8.00 |
| *—"Best Buy Series" reissue* | | | |
| ❑ LSP-4204 | Jerry Reed Explores Guitar Country | 1969 | 20.00 |
| ❑ LSP-4293 | Cookin' | 1970 | 20.00 |
| ❑ AHL1-4315 | The Man with the Golden Thumb | 1982 | 10.00 |
| ❑ LSP-4391 | Georgia Sunshine | 1970 | 20.00 |
| ❑ AYL1-4394 | Texas Bound and Flyin' | 1982 | 8.00 |
| *—"Best Buy Series" reissue* | | | |
| ❑ LSP-4506 | When You're Hot, You're Hot | 1971 | 15.00 |
| ❑ AHL1-4529 | The Bird | 1982 | 10.00 |
| ❑ LSP-4596 | Ko-Ko Joe | 1971 | 15.00 |
| ❑ LSP-4660 | Smell the Flowers | 1972 | 15.00 |
| ❑ AHL1-4692 | Ready | 1983 | 10.00 |
| ❑ LSP-4707 | Me and Chet | 1972 | 15.00 |
| *—With Chet Atkins* | | | |
| ❑ LSP-4729 | The Best of Jerry Reed | 1972 | 15.00 |
| ❑ LSP-4750 | Jerry Reed | 1972 | 15.00 |
| ❑ LSP-4838 | Hot A' Mighty! | 1973 | 15.00 |
| ❑ AYL1-5151 | The Bird | 1984 | 8.00 |
| *—"Best Buy Series" reissue* | | | |
| ❑ AHL1-5176 | Greatest Hits | 1984 | 10.00 |
| ❑ AHL1-5472 | Collector's Series | 1985 | 10.00 |

## REED, JIMMY

| Number | Title (A Side/B Side) | Yr | NM |
|---|---|---|---|
| **ANTILLES** | | | |
| ❑ 7007 | Cold Chills | 197? | 15.00 |
| **BLUESVILLE** | | | |
| ❑ BLS-6054 | I Ain't From Chicago | 1973 | 15.00 |
| ❑ BLS-6067 | The Ultimate Jimmy Reed | 1973 | 15.00 |
| ❑ BLS-6073 [(2)] | Jimmy Reed at Carnegie Hall | 1973 | 20.00 |
| **BLUESWAY** | | | |
| ❑ BL-6004 [M] | The New Jimmy Reed Album | 1967 | 20.00 |
| ❑ BLS-6004 [S] | The New Jimmy Reed Album | 1967 | 20.00 |
| ❑ BL-6009 [M] | Soulin' | 1967 | 20.00 |
| ❑ BLS-6009 [S] | Soulin' | 1967 | 20.00 |
| ❑ BLS-6015 | Big Boss Man | 1968 | 20.00 |
| ❑ BLS-6024 | Down in Virginia | 1969 | 20.00 |
| **BUDDAH** | | | |
| ❑ BDS-4003 | The Very Best of Jimmy Reed | 1969 | 15.00 |
| *—Reissue of Vee Jay 1039* | | | |
| **CHAMELEON** | | | |
| ❑ D1-74762 | Bright Lights, Big City | 1988 | 10.00 |
| **EVEREST ARCHIVE OF FOLK & JAZZ** | | | |
| ❑ 234 | Jimmy Reed | 197? | 12.00 |
| **GNP CRESCENDO** | | | |
| ❑ GNPS-10006 [(2)] | The Best of Jimmy Reed | 1974 | 15.00 |
| **SUNSET** | | | |
| ❑ SUS-5218 | Somethin' Else | 1968 | 12.00 |

| Number | Title (A Side/B Side) | Yr | NM |
|---|---|---|---|
| **TRADITION** | | | |
| ❑ 2069 | Wailin' the Blues | 1969 | 12.00 |
| **TRIP** | | | |
| ❑ 8012 [(2)] | History of Jimmy Reed | 1971 | 15.00 |
| **VEE JAY** | | | |
| ❑ LP-1004 [M] | I'm Jimmy Reed | 1958 | 220.00 |
| *—Maroon label* | | | |
| ❑ LP-1004 [M] | I'm Jimmy Reed | 1961 | 80.00 |
| *—Black label with colorband* | | | |
| ❑ VJLP-1004 | I'm Jimmy Reed | 198? | 10.00 |
| *—Reissue with glossy labels* | | | |
| ❑ LP-1008 [M] | Rockin' with Reed | 1959 | 200.00 |
| *—Maroon label* | | | |
| ❑ LP-1008 [M] | Rockin' with Reed | 1961 | 80.00 |
| *—Black label with colorband* | | | |
| ❑ VJLP-1008 | Rockin' with Reed | 198? | 10.00 |
| *—Reissue with glossy labels* | | | |
| ❑ LP-1022 [M] | Found Love | 1959 | 200.00 |
| *—Maroon label* | | | |
| ❑ LP-1022 [M] | Found Love | 1961 | 80.00 |
| *—Black label with colorband* | | | |
| ❑ LP-1025 [M] | Now Appearing | 1960 | 80.00 |
| ❑ VJLP-1025 | Now Appearing | 198? | 10.00 |
| *—Reissue with glossy labels* | | | |
| ❑ 2LP-1035 [(2)M] | Jimmy Reed at Carnegie Hall | 1961 | 50.00 |
| ❑ 2SR-1035 [(2)S] | Jimmy Reed at Carnegie Hall | 1961 | 70.00 |
| ❑ VJLP2-1035 [(2)] | Jimmy Reed at Carnegie Hall | 198? | 12.00 |
| *—Reissue with glossy labels* | | | |
| ❑ LP-1039 [M] | The Best of Jimmy Reed | 1962 | 40.00 |
| ❑ SR-1039 [S] | The Best of Jimmy Reed | 1962 | 60.00 |
| ❑ VJLP-1039 | The Best of Jimmy Reed | 198? | 10.00 |
| *—Reissue with glossy labels* | | | |
| ❑ LP-1050 [M] | Just Jimmy Reed | 1962 | 40.00 |
| ❑ SR-1050 [S] | Just Jimmy Reed | 1962 | 60.00 |
| ❑ LP-1067 [M] | T'Ain't No Big Thing...But He Is Jimmy Reed | 1963 | 40.00 |
| ❑ SR-1067 [S] | T'Ain't No Big Thing...But He Is Jimmy Reed | 1963 | 60.00 |
| ❑ LP-1072 [M] | The Best of the Blues | 1963 | 40.00 |
| ❑ LP-1073 [M] | The 12 String Guitar Blues | 1963 | 40.00 |
| ❑ SR-1073 [S] | The 12 String Guitar Blues | 1963 | 150.00 |
| ❑ LP-1080 [M] | More of the Best of Jimmy Reed | 1964 | 40.00 |
| ❑ SR-1080 [S] | More of the Best of Jimmy Reed | 1964 | 150.00 |
| ❑ LP-1095 [M] | Jimmy Reed at Soul City | 1964 | 40.00 |
| ❑ VJLP-1095 | Jimmy Reed at Soul City | 198? | 10.00 |
| *—Reissue with glossy labels* | | | |
| ❑ VJS-7303 | Blues Is My Business | 198? | 10.00 |
| ❑ LP-8501 [M] | The Legend, The Man | 1965 | 40.00 |
| ❑ VJLP-8501 | The Legend, The Man | 198? | 10.00 |
| *—Reissue with glossy labels* | | | |
| ❑ VJS-8501 [S] | The Legend, The Man | 1965 | 150.00 |

**REED, LOU** Also see THE VELVET UNDERGROUND.

| Number | Title (A Side/B Side) | Yr | NM |
|---|---|---|---|
| **ARISTA** | | | |
| ❑ AL 4100 | Rock and Roll Heart | 1976 | 15.00 |
| *—Originals on light blue labels* | | | |
| ❑ AL 4169 | Street Hassle | 1978 | 15.00 |
| ❑ AL 4229 | The Bells | 1979 | 12.00 |
| ❑ ALB6-8390 | City Lights — Classic Performances by Lou Reed | 1985 | 10.00 |
| ❑ AL11 8434 [(2)] | Rock and Roll Diary 1967-1980 | 198? | 16.00 |
| *—Reissue* | | | |
| ❑ AL 8502 [(2)] | Live! Take No Prisoners | 1978 | 18.00 |
| ❑ A2L 8603 [(2)] | Rock and Roll Diary 1967-1980 | 1980 | 18.00 |
| ❑ AL 9522 | Growing Up in Public | 1980 | 12.00 |
| ❑ R 252506 [(2)] | Rock and Roll Diary 1967-1980 | 1980 | 18.00 |
| *—RCA Music Service edition* | | | |
| **DIRECT DISK** | | | |
| ❑ (no #) [DJ] | The Blue Mask | 1982 | 150.00 |
| *—Only exists on test pressings; no stock copies made* | | | |
| **RCA VICTOR** | | | |
| ❑ APL1-0207 | Berlin | 1973 | 12.00 |
| ❑ AFL1-0472 | Rock & Roll Animal | 1977 | 8.00 |
| *—Reissue* | | | |
| ❑ APL1-0472 | Rock & Roll Animal | 1974 | 12.00 |
| ❑ AFL1-0611 | Sally Can't Dance | 1977 | 8.00 |
| *—Reissue* | | | |
| ❑ CPL1-0611 | Sally Can't Dance | 1974 | 20.00 |
| ❑ APL1-0915 | Coney Island Baby | 1976 | 16.00 |
| ❑ AFL1-0959 | Lou Reed Live | 1977 | 8.00 |
| *—Reissue* | | | |
| ❑ APL1-0959 | Lou Reed Live | 1975 | 15.00 |
| ❑ CPD2-1101 [(2)Q] | Metal Machine Music | 1975 | 150.00 |
| ❑ CPL2-1101 [(2)] | Metal Machine Music | 1975 | 50.00 |
| *—Orange or brown label* | | | |
| ❑ AFL1-2001 | Walk on the Wild Side | 1978 | 8.00 |
| *—Reissue* | | | |
| ❑ APL1-2001 | Walk on the Wild Side | 1977 | 12.00 |
| ❑ ANL1-2480 | Coney Island Baby | 1977 | 8.00 |
| *—Reissue* | | | |
| ❑ AYL1-3664 | Rock & Roll Animal | 1980 | 8.00 |
| *—Best Buy Series reissue* | | | |
| ❑ AYL1-3752 | Lou Reed Live | 1980 | 8.00 |
| *—Best Buy Series reissue* | | | |
| ❑ AYL1-3753 | Walk on the Wild Side | 1980 | 8.00 |
| *—Best Buy Series reissue* | | | |
| ❑ AYL1-3806 | Transformer | 1980 | 8.00 |
| *—Best Buy Series reissue* | | | |
| ❑ AYL1-3807 | Coney Island Baby | 1980 | 8.00 |
| *—Best Buy Series reissue* | | | |

Lou Reed, *Transformer,* RCA Victor LSP-4807, 1972, orange label, $20.

| Number | Title (A Side/B Side) | Yr | NM |
|---|---|---|---|
| ❑ AFL1-4221 | The Blue Mask | 1982 | 10.00 |
| ❑ DJL1-4266 [DJ] | Special Radio Series, Vol. XVII | 1980 | 25.00 |
| *—Promo-only with insert* | | | |
| ❑ DJL1-4267 | The Blue Mask Interview Album | 1982 | 40.00 |
| ❑ DJL1-4345 [DJ] | The Blue Mask Sampler | 1982 | 12.00 |
| *—Three-song EP released to radio* | | | |
| ❑ AYL1-4388 | Berlin | 1983 | 8.00 |
| *—Best Buy Series reissue* | | | |
| ❑ AYL1-4555 | Sally Can't Dance | 1983 | 8.00 |
| *—Best Buy Series reissue* | | | |
| ❑ AFL1-4568 | Legendary Hearts | 1983 | 10.00 |
| ❑ LSP-4701 | Lou Reed | 1972 | 20.00 |
| ❑ AYL1-4780 | The Blue Mask | 1984 | 8.00 |
| *—Best Buy Series reissue* | | | |
| ❑ AFL1-4807 | Transformer | 1977 | 8.00 |
| *—Reissue* | | | |
| ❑ LSP-4807 | Transformer | 1972 | 20.00 |
| ❑ AFL1-4998 | New Sensations | 1984 | 8.00 |
| ❑ AFL1-7190 | Mistrial | 1986 | 12.00 |
| **SIRE** | | | |
| ❑ 25829 | New York | 1989 | 10.00 |
| ❑ R 101058 | New York | 1989 | 12.00 |
| *—BMG Music Service edition* | | | |

**REED, LUCY**

| Number | Title (A Side/B Side) | Yr | NM |
|---|---|---|---|
| **FANTASY** | | | |
| ❑ 3212 [M] | The Singing Reed | 195? | 80.00 |
| *—Black vinyl* | | | |
| ❑ 3212 [M] | The Singing Reed | 1956 | 150.00 |
| *—Red vinyl* | | | |
| ❑ 3243 [M] | This Is Lucy Reed | 195? | 80.00 |
| *—Black vinyl* | | | |
| ❑ 3243 [M] | This Is Lucy Reed | 1957 | 150.00 |
| *—Red vinyl* | | | |

**REED, LULA**

| Number | Title (A Side/B Side) | Yr | NM |
|---|---|---|---|
| **KING** | | | |
| ❑ 604 [M] | Blue and Moody | 1958 | 2000. |

**REED, VIVIAN**

| Number | Title (A Side/B Side) | Yr | NM |
|---|---|---|---|
| **EPIC** | | | |
| ❑ BN 26412 | Vivian Reed | 1968 | 40.00 |
| **H&L** | | | |
| ❑ 69017 | Brown Sugar | 1976 | 20.00 |
| **UNITED ARTISTS** | | | |
| ❑ UA-LA911-H | Another Side | 1978 | 15.00 |
| ❑ UA-LA970-H | Ready and Waiting | 1979 | 15.00 |

**REESE, DELLA**

| Number | Title (A Side/B Side) | Yr | NM |
|---|---|---|---|
| **ABC** | | | |
| ❑ 569 [M] | Della Reese Live | 1966 | 15.00 |
| ❑ S-569 [S] | Della Reese Live | 1966 | 20.00 |
| ❑ 589 [M] | One More Time | 1967 | 20.00 |
| ❑ S-589 [S] | One More Time | 1967 | 15.00 |
| ❑ 612 [M] | Della on Strings of Blue | 1967 | 20.00 |
| ❑ S-612 [S] | Della on Strings of Blue | 1967 | 15.00 |
| ❑ S-636 | I Gotta Be Me...This Trip Out | 1968 | 15.00 |
| ❑ AC-30002 | The ABC Collection | 1976 | 15.00 |
| **ABC-PARAMOUNT** | | | |
| ❑ ABC-524 [M] | C'mon and Hear Della Reese | 1965 | 15.00 |
| ❑ ABCS-524 [S] | C'mon and Hear Della Reese | 1965 | 20.00 |
| ❑ ABC-540 [M] | I Like It Like Dat! | 1966 | 15.00 |
| ❑ ABCS-540 [S] | I Like It Like Dat! | 1966 | 20.00 |
| **AVCO EMBASSY** | | | |
| ❑ 33004 | Black Is Beautiful | 1969 | 15.00 |
| ❑ 33017 | Right Now | 1970 | 15.00 |
| **JAZZ A LA CARTE** | | | |
| ❑ 3 | One of a Kind | 1978 | 15.00 |
| **JUBILEE** | | | |
| ❑ JLP-1026 [M] | Melancholy Baby | 1957 | 30.00 |
| ❑ JGM-1071 [M] | A Date with Della Reese at Mr. Kelly's in Chicago | 196? | 20.00 |
| *—Black label with all-silver print* | | | |
| ❑ JGM-1071 [M] | A Date with Della Reese at Mr. Kelly's in Chicago | 1963 | 15.00 |
| *—Black label, multi-colored spokes around "jubilee"* | | | |
| ❑ JGS-1071 [S] | A Date with Della Reese at Mr. Kelly's in Chicago | 1965 | 15.00 |
| *—Black label, multi-colored spokes around "jubilee," yellow spoke goes nowhere near center hole; new prefix* | | | |
| ❑ JLP-1071 [M] | A Date with Della Reese at Mr. Kelly's in Chicago | 1959 | 25.00 |
| *—Originals have blue labels* | | | |
| ❑ SDJLP-1071 [S] | A Date with Della Reese at Mr. Kelly's in Chicago | 1959 | 25.00 |
| *—Black label with all-silver print* | | | |
| ❑ SDJLP-1071 [S] | A Date with Della Reese at Mr. Kelly's in Chicago | 1959 | 30.00 |
| *—Originals have blue labels* | | | |
| ❑ SDJLP-1071 [S] | A Date with Della Reese at Mr. Kelly's in Chicago | 1962 | 20.00 |
| *—Black label, multi-colored spokes around "jubilee," yellow spoke goes almost to center hole* | | | |

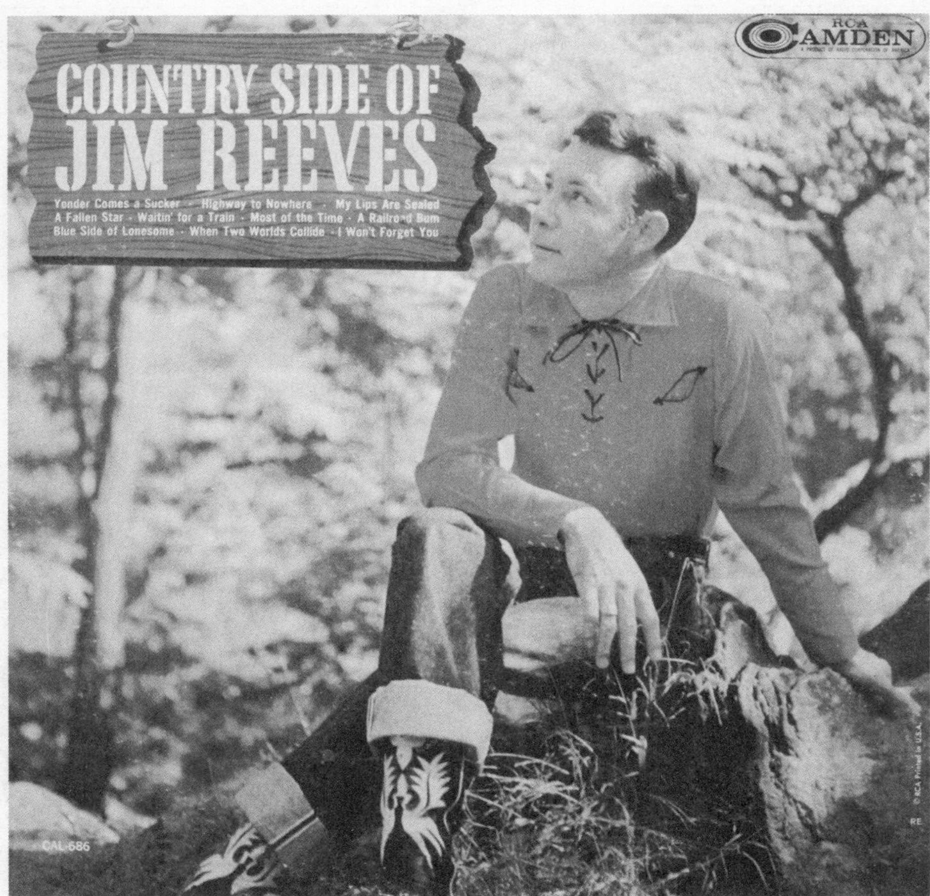


Jim Reeves, *The Country Side of Jim Reeves,* RCA Camden CAL-686, 1962, mono, $20.

| Number | Title (A Side/B Side) | Yr | NM |
|---|---|---|---|
| ❑ JLP-1083 [M] | Amen | 1959 | 25.00 |
| ❑ SDJLP-1083 [S] | Amen | 1959 | 30.00 |
| ❑ JGM-1095 [M] | The Story of the Blues | 1962 | 15.00 |
| *—Black label, multi-colored spokes around "jubilee," yellow spoke goes almost to center hole; new prefix* | | | |
| ❑ JGS-1095 [S] | The Story of the Blues | 1964 | 15.00 |
| *—Black label, multi-colored spokes around "jubilee," yellow spoke goes nowhere near center hole* | | | |
| ❑ JLP-1095 [M] | The Story of the Blues | 1960 | 20.00 |
| *—Black label, multi-colored spokes around "jubilee," yellow spoke goes almost to center hole* | | | |
| ❑ JLP-1095 [M] | The Story of the Blues | 1960 | 25.00 |
| *—Original labels are black with all-silver print* | | | |
| ❑ SDJLP-1095 [S] | The Story of the Blues | 1960 | 30.00 |
| *—Original labels are black with all-silver print* | | | |
| ❑ SDJLP-1095 [S] | The Story of the Blues | 1962 | 25.00 |
| *—Black label, multi-colored spokes around "jubilee," yellow spoke goes almost to center hole* | | | |
| ❑ JLP-1109 [M] | What Do You Know About Love | 1960 | 25.00 |
| ❑ JLP-1116 [M] | And That Reminds Me | 1960 | 25.00 |
| ❑ JGM-5002 [M] | The Best of Della Reese | 196? | 15.00 |
| ❑ JGS-5002 [S] | The Best of Della Reese | 196? | 20.00 |

PICKWICK

| Number | Title (A Side/B Side) | Yr | NM |
|---|---|---|---|
| ❑ SPC-3058 | And That Reminds Me | 196? | 12.00 |

RCA VICTOR

| Number | Title (A Side/B Side) | Yr | NM |
|---|---|---|---|
| ❑ LPM-2157 [M] | Della | 1960 | 20.00 |
| ❑ LSP-2157 [S] | Della | 1960 | 25.00 |
| ❑ LPM-2204 [M] | Della by Starlight | 1960 | 20.00 |
| ❑ LSP-2204 [S] | Della by Starlight | 1960 | 25.00 |
| ❑ LPM-2280 [M] | Della Della Cha-Cha-Cha | 1961 | 20.00 |
| ❑ LSP-2280 [S] | Della Della Cha-Cha-Cha | 1961 | 25.00 |
| ❑ LPM-2391 [M] | Special Delivery | 1961 | 20.00 |
| ❑ LSP-2391 [S] | Special Delivery | 1961 | 25.00 |
| ❑ LPM-2419 [M] | The Classic Della | 1962 | 20.00 |
| ❑ LSP-2419 [S] | The Classic Della | 1962 | 25.00 |
| ❑ LPM-2568 [M] | Della on Stage | 1962 | 20.00 |
| ❑ LSP-2568 [S] | Della on Stage | 1962 | 25.00 |
| ❑ LPM-2711 [M] | Waltz with Me, Della | 1963 | 20.00 |
| ❑ LSP-2711 [S] | Waltz with Me, Della | 1963 | 25.00 |
| ❑ LPM-2814 [M] | Moody | 1963 | 20.00 |
| ❑ LSP-2814 [S] | Moody | 1963 | 25.00 |
| ❑ LPM-2872 [M] | Della Reese at Basin Street East | 1964 | 20.00 |
| ❑ LSP-2872 [S] | Della Reese at Basin Street East | 1964 | 25.00 |
| ❑ LSP-4651 | The Best of Della Reese | 1972 | 12.00 |

## REEVES, DEL

KOALA

| Number | Title (A Side/B Side) | Yr | NM |
|---|---|---|---|
| ❑ KO 14188 | Del Reeves | 1980 | 12.00 |

PLAYBACK

| Number | Title (A Side/B Side) | Yr | NM |
|---|---|---|---|
| ❑ 12002 | Here's Del Reeves | 1988 | 15.00 |

STARDAY

| Number | Title (A Side/B Side) | Yr | NM |
|---|---|---|---|
| ❑ 998 | Greatest Hits | 197? | 10.00 |

SUNSET

| Number | Title (A Side/B Side) | Yr | NM |
|---|---|---|---|
| ❑ SUS-5230 | Wonderful World of Country Music | 1968 | 12.00 |
| ❑ SUS-5279 | Country Concert Live! | 1969 | 12.00 |
| ❑ SUS-5321 | Out in the Country | 1970 | 12.00 |

UNITED ARTISTS

| Number | Title (A Side/B Side) | Yr | NM |
|---|---|---|---|
| ❑ UA-LA044-F | Trucker's Paradise | 1973 | 15.00 |
| ❑ UA-LA204-G | Live at the Palomino Club | 1974 | 15.00 |
| ❑ UA-LA235 | The Very Best of Del Reeves | 1974 | 15.00 |
| ❑ UA-LA364-G | Del Reeves with Strings and Things | 1975 | 15.00 |
| ❑ UA-LA687-G | 10th Anniversary | 1977 | 12.00 |
| ❑ UAL-3441 [M] | Del Reeves Sings Girl on the Billboard | 1965 | 25.00 |
| ❑ UAL-3458 [M] | Doodle-Oo-Doo-Doo | 1965 | 20.00 |
| ❑ UAL-3468 [M] | Del Reeves Sings Jim Reeves | 1966 | 20.00 |
| ❑ UAL-3488 [M] | Special Delivery | 1966 | 20.00 |
| ❑ UAL-3528 [M] | Santa's Boy | 1966 | 20.00 |
| ❑ UAL-3530 [M] | Gettin' Any Feed for Your Chickens? | 1966 | 20.00 |
| ❑ UAL-3571 [M] | Struttin' My Stuff | 1967 | 25.00 |
| ❑ UAL-3595 [M] | Six of One, Half a Dozen of the Other | 1967 | 25.00 |
| ❑ UAL-3612 [M] | The Little Church in the Dell | 1967 | 30.00 |
| ❑ UAS-6441 [S] | Del Reeves Sings Girl on the Billboard | 1965 | 30.00 |
| ❑ UAS-6458 [S] | Doodle-Oo-Doo-Doo | 1965 | 25.00 |
| ❑ UAS-6468 [S] | Del Reeves Sings Jim Reeves | 1966 | 25.00 |
| ❑ UAS-6488 [S] | Special Delivery | 1966 | 25.00 |
| ❑ UAS-6528 [S] | Santa's Boy | 1966 | 25.00 |
| ❑ UAS-6530 [S] | Gettin' Any Feed for Your Chickens? | 1966 | 25.00 |
| ❑ UAS-6571 [S] | Struttin' My Stuff | 1967 | 20.00 |
| ❑ UAS-6595 [S] | Six of One, Half a Dozen of the Other | 1967 | 20.00 |
| ❑ UAS-6612 [S] | The Little Church in the Dell | 1967 | 25.00 |
| ❑ UAS-6635 | The Best of Del Reeves | 1968 | 20.00 |
| ❑ UAS-6643 | Running Wild | 1968 | 20.00 |
| ❑ UAS-6674 | Looking at the World Through a Windshield | 1968 | 20.00 |
| ❑ UAS-6705 | Down at Good Time Charlie's | 1969 | 20.00 |
| ❑ UAS-6733 | Big Daddy Del | 1970 | 20.00 |
| ❑ UAS-6758 | The Best of Del Reeves, Vol. 2 | 1970 | 20.00 |
| ❑ UAS-6789 | Friends and Neighbors | 1971 | 20.00 |
| ❑ UAS-6820 | The Del Reeves Album | 1971 | 20.00 |
| ❑ UAS-6830 | Before Goodbye | 1972 | 20.00 |

## REEVES, DEL, AND BOBBY GOLDSBORO

UNITED ARTISTS

| Number | Title (A Side/B Side) | Yr | NM |
|---|---|---|---|
| ❑ UAL 3615 [M] | Our Way of Life | 1967 | 20.00 |
| ❑ UAS 6615 [S] | Our Way of Life | 1967 | 20.00 |

## REEVES, JIM

ABBOTT

| Number | Title (A Side/B Side) | Yr | NM |
|---|---|---|---|
| ❑ LP-5001 [M] | Jim Reeves Sings | 1956 | 2000. |
| *—VG value 1000; VG+ value 1500* | | | |

COUNTRY MUSIC FOUNDATION

| Number | Title (A Side/B Side) | Yr | NM |
|---|---|---|---|
| ❑ CMF-008 | Live at the Opry | 198? | 10.00 |

PAIR

| Number | Title (A Side/B Side) | Yr | NM |
|---|---|---|---|
| ❑ PDL2-1002 [(2)] | The Country Side of Jim Reeves | 1986 | 12.00 |

RCA CAMDEN

| Number | Title (A Side/B Side) | Yr | NM |
|---|---|---|---|
| ❑ ACL1-0123 | Kimberley Jim | 1973 | 15.00 |
| ❑ CAL-583 [M] | According to My Heart | 1960 | 20.00 |
| ❑ CAS-583 [R] | According to My Heart | 1960 | 20.00 |
| ❑ CAL-686 [M] | The Country Side of Jim Reeves | 1962 | 20.00 |
| ❑ CAS-686 [S] | The Country Side of Jim Reeves | 1962 | 20.00 |
| ❑ CAL-784 [M] | Good 'N' Country | 1963 | 20.00 |
| ❑ CAS-784 [S] | Good 'N' Country | 1963 | 20.00 |
| ❑ CAL-842 [M] | Have I Told You Lately That I Love You? | 1964 | 20.00 |
| ❑ CAS-842 [S] | Have I Told You Lately That I Love You? | 1964 | 20.00 |
| ❑ CAS-2532 | Young and Country | 1971 | 15.00 |
| ❑ CAX-9001 [(2)] | Jim Reeves | 1972 | 20.00 |

RCA VICTOR

| Number | Title (A Side/B Side) | Yr | NM |
|---|---|---|---|
| ❑ APL1-0039 | Am I That Easy to Forget | 1973 | 20.00 |
| ❑ APL1-0330 | Great Moments with Jim Reeves | 1973 | 20.00 |
| ❑ APL1-0537 | I'd Fight the World | 1974 | 20.00 |
| ❑ APL1-0793 | The Best of Jim Reeves Sacred Songs | 1974 | 20.00 |
| ❑ APL1-1037 | Songs of Love | 1975 | 20.00 |
| ❑ APL1-1224 | I Love You Because | 1976 | 20.00 |
| ❑ LPM-1256 [M] | Singing Down the Lane | 1956 | 200.00 |
| ❑ LPM-1410 [M] | Bimbo | 1957 | 200.00 |
| *—Reissue of Abbott LP* | | | |
| ❑ LPM-1576 [M] | Jim Reeves | 1957 | 80.00 |
| ❑ LPM-1685 [M] | Girls I Have Known | 1958 | 60.00 |
| ❑ CPL1-1891 | A Legendary Performer | 1976 | 20.00 |
| ❑ ANL1-1927 | Twelve Songs of Christmas | 1976 | 8.00 |
| *—Reissue of LSP-2758* | | | |
| ❑ LPM-1950 [M] | God Be With You | 1958 | 40.00 |
| ❑ LSP-1950 [S] | God Be With You | 1958 | 50.00 |
| ❑ LPM-2001 [M] | Songs to Warm the Heart | 1959 | 40.00 |
| ❑ LSP-2001 [S] | Songs to Warm the Heart | 1959 | 50.00 |
| ❑ LPM-2216 [M] | The Intimate Jim Reeves | 1960 | 30.00 |
| ❑ LSP-2216 [S] | The Intimate Jim Reeves | 1960 | 40.00 |
| ❑ LPM-2223 [M] | Featuring He'll Have to Go and Other Favorites | 1960 | 30.00 |
| *—Black and white cover (original)* | | | |
| ❑ LPM-2223 [M] | Featuring He'll Have to Go and Other Favorites | 1962 | 20.00 |
| *—Color cover (reissue)* | | | |
| ❑ LSP-2223 [S] | Featuring He'll Have to Go and Other Favorites | 1960 | 40.00 |
| *—Black and white cover (original)* | | | |
| ❑ LSP-2223 [S] | Featuring He'll Have to Go and Other Favorites | 1962 | 25.00 |
| *—Color cover (reissue)* | | | |
| ❑ LPM-2284 [M] | Tall Tales and Short Tempers | 1961 | 25.00 |
| ❑ LSP-2284 [S] | Tall Tales and Short Tempers | 1961 | 30.00 |
| ❑ APL1-2309 | It's Nothin' to Me | 1977 | 15.00 |
| ❑ LPM-2339 [M] | Talkin' to Your Heart | 1961 | 25.00 |
| ❑ LSP-2339 [S] | Talkin' to Your Heart | 1961 | 30.00 |
| ❑ LPM-2487 [M] | A Touch of Velvet | 1962 | 25.00 |
| ❑ LSP-2487 [S] | A Touch of Velvet | 1962 | 30.00 |
| ❑ LPM-2552 [M] | We Thank Thee | 1962 | 25.00 |
| ❑ LSP-2552 [S] | We Thank Thee | 1962 | 30.00 |
| ❑ LPM-2605 [M] | Gentleman Jim | 1963 | 25.00 |
| ❑ LSP-2605 [S] | Gentleman Jim | 1963 | 30.00 |
| ❑ LPM-2704 [M] | The International Jim Reeves | 1963 | 25.00 |
| ❑ LSP-2704 [S] | The International Jim Reeves | 1963 | 30.00 |
| ❑ AHL1-2720 | Jim Reeves | 1978 | 15.00 |
| ❑ LPM-2758 [M] | Twelve Songs of Christmas | 1963 | 25.00 |
| ❑ LSP-2758 [S] | Twelve Songs of Christmas | 1963 | 30.00 |
| ❑ LPM-2780 [M] | Kimberley Jim | 1964 | 25.00 |
| ❑ LSP-2780 [S] | Kimberley Jim | 1964 | 30.00 |
| ❑ LPM-2854 [M] | Moonlight and Roses | 1964 | 25.00 |
| ❑ LSP-2854 [S] | Moonlight and Roses | 1964 | 30.00 |
| ❑ LPM-2890 [M] | The Best of Jim Reeves | 1964 | 20.00 |
| ❑ LSP-2890 [S] | The Best of Jim Reeves | 1964 | 25.00 |
| ❑ LPM-2968 [M] | The Jim Reeves Way | 1965 | 20.00 |

| Number | Title (A Side/B Side) | Yr | NM |
|---|---|---|---|
| ❑ LSP-2968 [S] | The Jim Reeves Way | 1965 | 25.00 |
| ❑ ANL1-3014 | Pure Gold, Volume 1 | 1978 | 12.00 |
| ❑ AHL1-3271 | The Best of Jim Reeves, Volume IV | 1979 | 15.00 |
| ❑ LPM-3427 [M] | Up Through the Years | 1965 | 20.00 |
| ❑ LSP-3427 [S] | Up Through the Years | 1965 | 25.00 |
| ❑ AHL1-3454 | Don't Let Me Cross Over | 1979 | 15.00 |
| ❑ LPM-3482 [M] | The Best of Jim Reeves, Vol. II | 1966 | 20.00 |
| ❑ LSP-3482(e) [P] | The Best of Jim Reeves, Vol. II | 1966 | 25.00 |
| *—This album is at least partially, and possibly entirely, in rechanneled stereo* | | | |
| ❑ LPM-3542 [M] | Distant Drums | 1966 | 20.00 |
| ❑ LSP-3542 [P] | Distant Drums | 1966 | 25.00 |
| *—"Overnight" and "The Gods Were Angry with Me" are rechanneled* | | | |
| ❑ AYL1-3678 | The Best of Jim Reeves | 1980 | 12.00 |
| *—"Best Buy Series" reissue* | | | |
| ❑ LPM-3709 [M] | Yours Sincerely, Jim Reeves | 1966 | 20.00 |
| ❑ LSP-3709(e) [P] | Yours Sincerely, Jim Reeves | 1966 | 25.00 |
| *—This album is at least partially, and possibly entirely, in rechanneled stereo* | | | |
| ❑ AYL1-3765 | The Best of Jim Reeves Sacred Songs | 1980 | 10.00 |
| *—"Best Buy Series" reissue* | | | |
| ❑ LPM-3793 [M] | Blue Side of Lonesome | 1967 | 25.00 |
| ❑ LSP-3793 [S] | Blue Side of Lonesome | 1967 | 20.00 |
| ❑ AHL1-3827 | There's Always Me | 1980 | 12.00 |
| ❑ LPM-3903 [M] | My Cathedral | 1967 | 30.00 |
| ❑ LSP-3903 [S] | My Cathedral | 1967 | 25.00 |
| ❑ AYL1-3936 | Pure Gold, Volume 1 | 1980 | 10.00 |
| *—"Best Buy Series" reissue* | | | |
| ❑ LPM-3987 [M] | A Touch of Sadness | 1968 | 60.00 |
| ❑ LSP-3987 [S] | A Touch of Sadness | 1968 | 20.00 |
| ❑ LSP-4062 | Jim Reeves On Stage | 1968 | 20.00 |
| ❑ AYL1-4075 | The Best of Jim Reeves, Volume IV | 1981 | 10.00 |
| *—"Best Buy Series" reissue* | | | |
| ❑ LSP-4112 | Jim Reeves and Some Friends | 1969 | 20.00 |
| ❑ AYL1-4168 | The Best of Jim Reeves, Vol. II | 1981 | 10.00 |
| *—"Best Buy Series" reissue* | | | |
| ❑ LSP-4187 | The Best of Jim Reeves Volume III | 1969 | 20.00 |
| ❑ LSP-4475 | Jim Reeves Writes You a Record | 1971 | 20.00 |
| ❑ LSP-4528 | Something Special | 1971 | 20.00 |
| ❑ AHL1-4531 | The Jim Reeves Medley | 1983 | 10.00 |
| ❑ LSP-4646 | My Friend | 1972 | 20.00 |
| ❑ LSP-4749 | Missing You | 1972 | 20.00 |
| ❑ AYL1-4833 | Don't Let Me Cross Over | 1983 | 10.00 |
| *—"Best Buy Series" reissue* | | | |
| ❑ AYL1-4835 | I Love You Because | 1983 | 10.00 |
| *—"Best Buy Series" reissue* | | | |
| ❑ AYL1-4836 | Songs of Love | 1983 | 10.00 |
| *—"Best Buy Series" reissue* | | | |
| ❑ AYL1-4838 | The Best of Jim Reeves Vol. III | 1983 | 10.00 |
| *—"Best Buy Series" reissue* | | | |
| ❑ AYL1-4839 | There's Always Me | 1983 | 10.00 |
| *—"Best Buy Series" reissue* | | | |
| ❑ AYL1-4840 | We Thank Thee | 1983 | 10.00 |
| *—"Best Buy Series" reissue* | | | |
| ❑ AHL1-4865 | A Special Collection | 1983 | 12.00 |
| ❑ CPL2-5044 [(2)] | Just for You | 1984 | 15.00 |
| ❑ AHL1-5424 | Collector's Series | 1985 | 12.00 |
| **TIME-LIFE** | | | |
| ❑ STW-113 | Country Music | 1981 | 10.00 |

### REFLECTIONS, THE (1)

| Number | Title (A Side/B Side) | Yr | NM |
|---|---|---|---|
| **GOLDEN WORLD** | | | |
| ❑ 300 [M] | (Just Like) Romeo and Juliet | 1964 | 150.00 |

### REGENT CONCERT ORCHESTRA, THE

| Number | Title (A Side/B Side) | Yr | NM |
|---|---|---|---|
| **REGENT** | | | |
| ❑ 6091 [M] | Amor | 1958 | 50.00 |
| *—Cover model is Jayne Mansfield* | | | |

### REGENTS, THE (1)

| Number | Title (A Side/B Side) | Yr | NM |
|---|---|---|---|
| **GEE** | | | |
| ❑ GLP-706 [M] | Barbara Ann | 1961 | 150.00 |
| ❑ SGLP-706 | Barbara Ann | 197? | 25.00 |
| *—Reissue by Publishers Central Bureau (clearly marked as such on cover)* | | | |
| ❑ SGLP-706 [S] | Barbara Ann | 1961 | 250.00 |

### REGENTS, THE (U)

| Number | Title (A Side/B Side) | Yr | NM |
|---|---|---|---|
| **CAPITOL** | | | |
| ❑ KAO 2153 [M] | Live at the AM-PM Discotheque | 1964 | 50.00 |
| ❑ SKAO 2153 [S] | Live at the AM-PM Discotheque | 1964 | 60.00 |

### REHAK, FRANK/ALEX SMITH

| Number | Title (A Side/B Side) | Yr | NM |
|---|---|---|---|
| **DAWN** | | | |
| ❑ DLP-1107 [M] | Jazzville, Vol. 2 | 1956 | 100.00 |

### REID, CLARENCE

| Number | Title (A Side/B Side) | Yr | NM |
|---|---|---|---|
| **ATCO** | | | |
| ❑ SD 33-307 | Dancin' with Nobody But You Babe | 1969 | 30.00 |

### REID, IRENE

| Number | Title (A Side/B Side) | Yr | NM |
|---|---|---|---|
| **MGM** | | | |
| ❑ E-4159 [M] | It's Only the Beginning for Irene Reid | 1963 | 20.00 |
| ❑ SE-4159 [S] | It's Only the Beginning for Irene Reid | 1963 | 25.00 |
| **VERVE** | | | |
| ❑ V6-8621 [S] | Room for One More | 1965 | 20.00 |

### REINER, CARL, AND MEL BROOKS

| Number | Title (A Side/B Side) | Yr | NM |
|---|---|---|---|
| **CAPITOL** | | | |
| ❑ SW 1529 [S] | 2000 Years | 1961 | 20.00 |
| ❑ W 1529 [M] | 2000 Years | 1961 | 15.00 |
| ❑ SW 1618 [S] | 2000 and One Years | 1961 | 20.00 |
| ❑ W 1618 [M] | 2000 and One Years | 1961 | 15.00 |
| ❑ SW 1815 [S] | At the Cannes Film Festival | 1962 | 20.00 |
| ❑ W 1815 [M] | At the Cannes Film Festival | 1962 | 15.00 |
| ❑ ST 2981 | The Best of the 2000 Year Old Man | 1968 | 15.00 |
| **WARNER BROS.** | | | |
| ❑ BS 2741 | 2000 and Thirteen | 1973 | 15.00 |
| ❑ 3XX 2744 [(3)] | The Incomplete Works of Reiner and Brooks | 1973 | 25.00 |
| **WORLD PACIFIC** | | | |
| ❑ WP-1401 [M] | 2000 Years | 1960 | 30.00 |

### REINHARDT, DJANGO

| Number | Title (A Side/B Side) | Yr | NM |
|---|---|---|---|
| **ANGEL** | | | |
| ❑ ANG.60003 [10] | Le Jazz Hot | 1954 | 150.00 |
| ❑ ANG.60011 [10] | Django's Guitar | 1955 | 150.00 |
| **CAPITOL** | | | |
| ❑ TBO 10226 [(2)M] | The Best of Django Reinhardt | 1960 | 50.00 |
| *—Black colorband labels, Capitol logo at left* | | | |
| **CLEF** | | | |
| ❑ MGC-516 [10] | The Great Artistry of Django Reinhardt | 1954 | 150.00 |
| **JAY** | | | |
| ❑ 3008 [10] | Django Reinhardt | 1954 | 180.00 |
| **MERCURY** | | | |
| ❑ MGC-516 [10] | The Great Artistry of Django Reinhardt | 1953 | 200.00 |
| **PERIOD** | | | |
| ❑ SPL-1100 [10] | Django Reinhardt Memorial, Volume 1 | 1954 | 120.00 |
| ❑ SPL-1101 [10] | Django Reinhardt Memorial, Volume 2 | 1954 | 120.00 |
| ❑ SPL-1102 [10] | Django Reinhardt Memorial, Volume 3 | 1954 | 120.00 |
| ❑ SPL-1201 [M] | Django Reinhardt Memorial Album, Volume 1 | 1956 | 50.00 |
| ❑ SPL-1201 [M] | Django Reinhardt Memorial Album, Volume 2 | 1956 | 50.00 |
| ❑ SPL-1203 [M] | Django Reinhardt Memorial Album, Volume 3 | 1956 | 50.00 |
| ❑ SPL-1204 [M] | The Best of Django Reinhardt | 1956 | 50.00 |
| ❑ SPL-2204 [R] | The Best of Django Reinhardt | 196? | 25.00 |
| **RCA VICTOR** | | | |
| ❑ LPM-1100 [M] | Django Reinhardt | 1955 | 100.00 |
| ❑ LPM-2319 [M] | Djangology | 1961 | 40.00 |
| ❑ LSP-2319 [R] | Djangology | 196? | 25.00 |
| **REPRISE** | | | |
| ❑ R-6075 [M] | The Immortal Django Reinhardt | 1963 | 25.00 |
| **SUTTON** | | | |
| ❑ SU-274 [M] | Django Reinhardt and His Guitar | 1966 | 20.00 |
| **SWING** | | | |
| ❑ SW-8420/7 [(7)] | Djangologie USA Volumes 1-7 | 1988 | 60.00 |

### REMAINS, THE

| Number | Title (A Side/B Side) | Yr | NM |
|---|---|---|---|
| **EPIC** | | | |
| ❑ LN 24214 [M] | The Remains | 1966 | 200.00 |
| ❑ BN 26214 [S] | The Remains | 1966 | 300.00 |
| **SPOONFED** | | | |
| ❑ SFD-3205 | The Remains | 1978 | 15.00 |
| *—Red vinyl* | | | |
| **SUNDAZED** | | | |
| ❑ SEP 10-162 [10] | The Remains | 2000 | 8.00 |
| ❑ LP 5015 | A Session with the Remains | 199? | 10.00 |
| ❑ LP 5055 | The Remains | 1999 | 12.00 |

### REMINGTON, DAVE

| Number | Title (A Side/B Side) | Yr | NM |
|---|---|---|---|
| **JUBILEE** | | | |
| ❑ JLP-1017 [M] | Chicago Jazz Reborn | 1956 | 40.00 |
| **TEMPUS** | | | |
| ❑ TL-101 [M] | Danceable Dixieland Jazz | 1958 | 40.00 |
| **VEE JAY** | | | |
| ❑ LP-3009 [M] | Dixie on the Rocks | 1960 | 25.00 |
| ❑ SR-3009 [S] | Dixie on the Rocks | 1960 | 30.00 |
| ❑ LP-3030 [M] | Dixie Chicago Style | 1962 | 20.00 |
| ❑ SR-3030 [S] | Dixie Chicago Style | 1962 | 25.00 |

### REMINGTON, HERB

| Number | Title (A Side/B Side) | Yr | NM |
|---|---|---|---|
| **D** | | | |
| ❑ 1376 | Herby Remington Plays the Steel | 197? | 12.00 |
| **HILLTOP** | | | |
| ❑ JM-6020 [M] | Herby Remington Rides Again | 196? | 15.00 |
| ❑ JS-6020 [S] | Herby Remington Rides Again | 196? | 12.00 |
| **STONEWAY** | | | |
| ❑ 138 | Pure Remington Steel | 197? | 12.00 |
| **UNITED ARTISTS** | | | |
| ❑ UAL-3167 [M] | Steel Guitar Holiday | 1961 | 25.00 |
| ❑ UAS-6167 [S] | Steel Guitar Holiday | 1961 | 30.00 |

### RENA, KID

| Number | Title (A Side/B Side) | Yr | NM |
|---|---|---|---|
| **CIRCLE** | | | |
| ❑ L-409 [10] | Kid Rena Delta Jazz Band | 1951 | 80.00 |

### RENAISSANCE

| Number | Title (A Side/B Side) | Yr | NM |
|---|---|---|---|
| **CAPITOL/SOVEREIGN** | | | |
| ❑ SMAS-11116 | Prologue | 1972 | 15.00 |
| ❑ ST-11216 | Ashes Are Burning | 1973 | 15.00 |
| ❑ SWBC-11871 [(2)] | In the Beginning | 1978 | 15.00 |
| *—Combines 11116 and 11216 in one package* | | | |
| **ELEKTRA** | | | |
| ❑ EKS-74068 | Renaissance | 1969 | 30.00 |
| **I.R.S.** | | | |
| ❑ SP-70019 | Camera Camera | 1981 | 10.00 |
| ❑ SP-70033 | Time Line | 1983 | 10.00 |
| **MOBILE FIDELITY** | | | |
| ❑ 1-099 | Scheherazade and Other Stories | 1982 | 50.00 |
| *—Audiophile vinyl* | | | |
| **SIRE** | | | |
| ❑ SASD-3902 [(2)] | Live at Carnegie Hall | 1976 | 15.00 |
| ❑ SR 6015 | Turn of the Cards | 1977 | 10.00 |
| *—Reissue of 7502* | | | |
| ❑ SR 6017 | Scheherazade and Other Stories | 1977 | 10.00 |
| *—Reissue of 7510* | | | |
| ❑ SR 6024 | Novella | 1977 | 10.00 |
| *—Reissue of 7526* | | | |
| ❑ 2XS 6029 [(2)] | Live at Carnegie Hall | 1977 | 12.00 |
| *—Reissue of 3902* | | | |
| ❑ SRK 6049 | A Song for All Seasons | 1978 | 12.00 |
| ❑ SRK 6068 | Azure d'Or | 1979 | 12.00 |
| ❑ SAS-7502 | Turn of the Cards | 1974 | 12.00 |
| ❑ SASD-7510 | Scheherazade and Other Stories | 1975 | 12.00 |
| ❑ SASD-7526 | Novella | 1977 | 12.00 |

### RENAUD, HENRI

| Number | Title (A Side/B Side) | Yr | NM |
|---|---|---|---|
| **CONTEMPORARY** | | | |
| ❑ C-2502 [10] | The Henri Renaud All-Stars | 1953 | 120.00 |
| **PERIOD** | | | |
| ❑ SPL-1211 [M] | The Birdlanders | 1954 | 80.00 |
| ❑ SPL-1212 [M] | The Birdlanders | 1954 | 80.00 |

### RENAY, DIANE

| Number | Title (A Side/B Side) | Yr | NM |
|---|---|---|---|
| **20TH CENTURY FOX** | | | |
| ❑ TF-3133 [M] | Navy Blue | 1964 | 80.00 |
| ❑ TFS-4133 [S] | Navy Blue | 1964 | 150.00 |

### RENDELL, DON

| Number | Title (A Side/B Side) | Yr | NM |
|---|---|---|---|
| **JAZZLAND** | | | |
| ❑ JLP-51 [M] | Roarin' | 1961 | 30.00 |
| ❑ JLP-951 [S] | Roarin' | 1961 | 40.00 |

### RENE, GOOGIE

| Number | Title (A Side/B Side) | Yr | NM |
|---|---|---|---|
| **CLASS** | | | |
| ❑ LP-200 [M] | Flapjacks | 1963 | 20.00 |
| ❑ LP-5001 [M] | Beautiful Weekend | 1957 | 30.00 |
| ❑ LP-5003 [M] | Googie Rene Presents Romesville | 1959 | 25.00 |
| **RENDEZVOUS** | | | |
| ❑ M-1311 [M] | Beautiful Weekend | 196? | 15.00 |
| ❑ M-1313 [M] | Romseville | 196? | 15.00 |

### RENE, HENRI

| Number | Title (A Side/B Side) | Yr | NM |
|---|---|---|---|
| **IMPERIAL** | | | |
| ❑ LP-9074 [M] | White Heat | 1959 | 20.00 |
| ❑ LP-9096 [M] | Swingin' 59 | 1960 | 20.00 |
| ❑ LP-12021 [S] | White Heat | 1959 | 30.00 |
| ❑ LP-12040 [S] | Swingin' 59 | 1960 | 30.00 |
| **RCA VICTOR** | | | |
| ❑ LPM-1033 [M] | Passion in Paint | 1955 | 80.00 |
| ❑ LPM-1046 [M] | Music for Bachelors | 1955 | 120.00 |
| *—Cover model is Jayne Mansfield* | | | |
| ❑ LPM-1583 [M] | Music for the Weaker Sex | 1957 | 25.00 |
| ❑ LPM-1947 [M] | Compulsion to Swing | 1958 | 20.00 |
| ❑ LSP-1947 [S] | Compulsion to Swing | 1958 | 30.00 |
| ❑ LPM-2002 [M] | Riot in Rhythm | 1959 | 20.00 |
| ❑ LSP-2002 [S] | Riot in Rhythm | 1959 | 30.00 |
| ❑ LSA-2396 [S] | Dynamic Dimensions | 1961 | 30.00 |
| ❑ LPM-3049 [10] | Serenade to Love | 1953 | 40.00 |
| ❑ LPM-3076 [10] | Listen to Rene | 1953 | 40.00 |

### RENO, DON, AND BILL HARRELL

| Number | Title (A Side/B Side) | Yr | NM |
|---|---|---|---|
| **JALYN** | | | |
| ❑ JLP-108 [M] | Bluegrass Favorites | 1964 | 25.00 |
| ❑ JLP-119 [M] | The Most Requested Songs | 1966 | 25.00 |

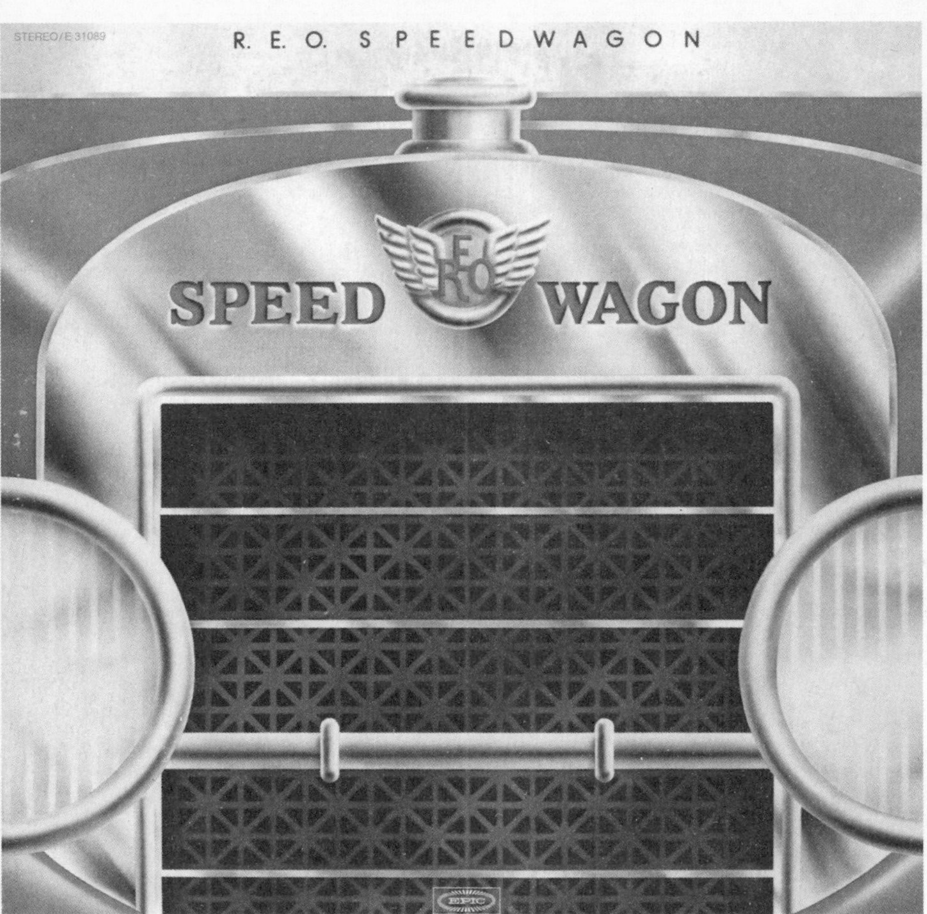


REO Speedwagon, *REO Speedwagon,* Epic E 31089, 1971, yellow label, $15.

KING

| Number | Title (A Side/B Side) | Yr | NM |
|---|---|---|---|
| ❑ KSD-1029 | A Variety of New Sacred Gospel Songs | 1968 | 20.00 |
| ❑ KSD-1033 | All the Way to Reno | 1968 | 20.00 |
| ❑ KSD-1068 | I'm Using My Bible for a Roadmap | 1969 | 20.00 |

## RENO, JACK

ATCO

| Number | Title (A Side/B Side) | Yr | NM |
|---|---|---|---|
| ❑ SD 33-251 | Meet Jack Reno | 1968 | 25.00 |

DERBYTOWN

| Number | Title (A Side/B Side) | Yr | NM |
|---|---|---|---|
| ❑ 101 | Yellow Pages | 197? | 20.00 |

DOT

| Number | Title (A Side/B Side) | Yr | NM |
|---|---|---|---|
| ❑ DLP 25921 | I Want One | 1968 | 25.00 |
| ❑ DLP 25946 | I'm a Good Man in a Bad Frame of Mind | 1969 | 25.00 |

TARGET

| Number | Title (A Side/B Side) | Yr | NM |
|---|---|---|---|
| ❑ 1313 | Hitchin' a Ride | 1972 | 20.00 |

## RENO AND SMILEY

DOT

| Number | Title (A Side/B Side) | Yr | NM |
|---|---|---|---|
| ❑ DLP-3490 [M] | Bluegrass Hits | 1963 | 25.00 |
| ❑ DLP-25490 [S] | Bluegrass Hits | 1963 | 30.00 |

KING

| Number | Title (A Side/B Side) | Yr | NM |
|---|---|---|---|
| ❑ 550 [M] | Sacred Songs | 1958 | 120.00 |
| ❑ 552 [M] | Reno and Smiley Instrumentals | 1958 | 100.00 |
| ❑ 579 [M] | Folk Ballads and Instrumentals | 1958 | 100.00 |
| ❑ 617 [M] | Someone Will Love Me in Heaven | 1959 | 100.00 |
| ❑ 621 [M] | Good Old Country Ballads | 1959 | 100.00 |
| ❑ 646 [M] | A Variety of Country Songs | 1959 | 100.00 |
| ❑ 693 [M] | Hymns Sacred and Gospel | 1959 | 100.00 |
| ❑ 701 [M] | Country Songs | 1959 | 100.00 |
| ❑ 718 [M] | Wanted | 1961 | 100.00 |
| ❑ 756 [M] | Folk Songs of the Civil War | 1961 | 100.00 |
| ❑ 776 [M] | Country Singing and Instrumentals | 1962 | 80.00 |
| ❑ 787 [M] | Banjo Special | 1962 | 80.00 |
| ❑ 816 [M] | Another Day with Reno and Smiley | 1962 | 80.00 |
| ❑ 853 [M] | The 15 Greatest Hymns of All Time | 1963 | 80.00 |
| ❑ 861 [M] | The World's Best Five String Banjo | 1963 | 80.00 |
| ❑ 874 [M] | The True Meaning of Christmas | 1963 | 80.00 |
| ❑ 874 [M] | The True Meaning of Christmas | 1963 | 100.00 |
| ❑ 911 [M] | On the Road with Reno and Smiley | 1964 | 80.00 |
| ❑ 914 [M] | A Bluegrass Tribute to Cowboy Copas | 1964 | 80.00 |
| ❑ KSD-1044 | I Know You're Married | 1969 | 25.00 |
| ❑ KSD-1091 | The Best of Reno and Smiley | 1970 | 25.00 |

## REO SPEEDWAGON

EPIC

| Number | Title (A Side/B Side) | Yr | NM |
|---|---|---|---|
| ❑ E 31089 | REO Speedwagon | 1972 | 15.00 |
| *—Yellow label original* | | | |
| ❑ KE 31089 | REO Speedwagon | 1973 | 12.00 |
| *—Orange label* | | | |
| ❑ PE 31089 | REO Speedwagon | 1979 | 8.00 |
| *—Dark blue label* | | | |
| ❑ KE 31745 | R.E.O./T.W.O. | 1972 | 15.00 |
| *—Yellow label original* | | | |
| ❑ KE 31745 | R.E.O./T.W.O. | 1973 | 12.00 |
| *—Orange label* | | | |
| ❑ PE 31745 | R.E.O./T.W.O. | 1979 | 8.00 |
| *—Dark blue label* | | | |
| ❑ KE 32378 | Ridin' the Storm Out | 1973 | 12.00 |
| *—Orange label* | | | |
| ❑ PE 32378 | Ridin' the Storm Out | 1979 | 8.00 |
| *—Dark blue label* | | | |
| ❑ PE 32948 | Lost in a Dream | 1974 | 12.00 |
| *—Orange label* | | | |
| ❑ PE 32948 | Lost in a Dream | 1979 | 8.00 |
| *—Dark blue label* | | | |
| ❑ PEQ 32948 [Q] | Lost in a Dream | 1974 | 20.00 |
| ❑ PE 33338 | This Time We Mean It | 1975 | 12.00 |
| *—Orange label* | | | |
| ❑ PE 33338 | This Time We Mean It | 1979 | 8.00 |
| *—Dark blue label* | | | |
| ❑ PEQ 33338 [Q] | This Time We Mean It | 1975 | 20.00 |
| ❑ PE 34143 | R.E.O. | 1976 | 12.00 |
| *—Orange label* | | | |
| ❑ PE 34143 | R.E.O. | 1979 | 8.00 |
| *—Dark blue label* | | | |
| ❑ PEG 34494 [(2)] | REO Speedwagon Live/You Get What You Play For | 1977 | 15.00 |
| *—Orange labels* | | | |
| ❑ PEG 34494 [(2)] | REO Speedwagon Live/You Get What You Play For | 1979 | 12.00 |
| *—Dark blue labels* | | | |
| ❑ JE 35082 | You Can Tune a Piano, But You Can't Tuna Fish | 1978 | 10.00 |
| *—Orange label; with bar code on back cover* | | | |
| ❑ JE 35082 | You Can Tune a Piano, But You Can't Tuna Fish | 1978 | 12.00 |
| *—Orange label; no bar code on back cover* | | | |
| ❑ JE 35082 | You Can Tune a Piano, But You Can't Tuna Fish | 1979 | 8.00 |
| *—Dark blue label* | | | |
| ❑ PE 35082 | You Can Tune a Piano, But You Can't Tuna Fish | 198? | 8.00 |
| ❑ FE 35988 | Nine Lives | 1979 | 10.00 |
| ❑ PE 35988 | Nine Lives | 198? | 8.00 |
| *—Budget-line reissue* | | | |
| ❑ KE2 36444 [(2)] | A Decade of Rock and Roll 1970 to 1980 | 1980 | 12.00 |
| ❑ FE 36844 | Hi Infidelity | 1980 | 8.00 |
| ❑ FE 38100 | Good Trouble | 1982 | 10.00 |
| ❑ PE 38100 | Good Trouble | 198? | 8.00 |
| *—Budget-line reissue* | | | |
| ❑ QE 39593 | Wheels Are Turnin' | 1984 | 8.00 |
| ❑ FE 40444 | Life As We Know It | 1987 | 8.00 |
| ❑ OE 44202 | The Hits | 1988 | 10.00 |
| ❑ HE 45082 | You Can Tune a Piano, But You Can't Tuna Fish | 198? | 40.00 |
| *—Half-speed mastered edition* | | | |
| ❑ E 45246 | The Earth, a Small Man, His Dog and a Chicken | 1990 | 12.00 |
| ❑ HE 46844 | Hi Infidelity | 1982 | 30.00 |
| *—Half-speed mastered edition* | | | |
| ❑ HE 48100 | Good Trouble | 1982 | 30.00 |
| *—Half-speed mastered edition* | | | |

## REPARATA AND THE DELRONS

AVCO EMBASSY

| Number | Title (A Side/B Side) | Yr | NM |
|---|---|---|---|
| ❑ AVE-33008 | Rock and Roll Revolution | 1970 | 25.00 |

WORLD ARTISTS

| Number | Title (A Side/B Side) | Yr | NM |
|---|---|---|---|
| ❑ WAM-2006 [M] | Whenever a Teenager Cries | 1965 | 50.00 |
| ❑ WAS-3006 [S] | Whenever a Teenager Cries | 1965 | 60.00 |

## REPLACEMENTS, THE

SIRE

| Number | Title (A Side/B Side) | Yr | NM |
|---|---|---|---|
| ❑ PRO-A-3633 [DJ] | Live Inconcerated | 1989 | 50.00 |
| *—Five live tracks and one studio track, each of which is repeated on the other side* | | | |
| ❑ PRO-A-4632 [DJ] | Don't Sell Or Buy...It's Crap | 1991 | 25.00 |
| *—Promo-only 5-track sampler* | | | |
| ❑ 25330 | Tim | 1985 | 12.00 |
| ❑ 25557 | Pleased to Meet Me | 1987 | 12.00 |
| ❑ 25831 | Don't Tell a Soul | 1989 | 12.00 |
| ❑ R 101024 | Don't Tell a Soul | 1989 | 15.00 |
| *—BMG Music Service edition* | | | |

TWIN/TONE

| Number | Title (A Side/B Side) | Yr | NM |
|---|---|---|---|
| ❑ TTR 8123 | Sorry, Ma, Forgot to Take Out the Trash | 1981 | 25.00 |
| ❑ TTR 8228 [EP] | The Replacements Stink | 1982 | 25.00 |
| ❑ TTR 8332 | Hootenanny | 1983 | 20.00 |
| ❑ TTR 8441 | Let It Be | 1984 | 20.00 |

WARNER BROS.

| Number | Title (A Side/B Side) | Yr | NM |
|---|---|---|---|
| ❑ WBMS-148 [DJ] | An Interview with Paul Westerberg | 1987 | 40.00 |
| *—Part of "The Warner Bros. Music Show" promotional series* | | | |

## REPRISE REPERTORY THEATRE, THE

Artists who were signed to Reprise Records at the time, including ROSEMARY CLOONEY, BING CROSBY, SAMMY DAVIS, JR., DEAN MARTIN, FRANK SINATRA and JO STAFFORD, perform new versions of famous musicals under this collective name.

REPRISE

| Number | Title (A Side/B Side) | Yr | NM |
|---|---|---|---|
| ❑ F-2015 [M] | Finian's Rainbow | 196? | 20.00 |
| *—Standard cover* | | | |
| ❑ F-2015 [M] | Finian's Rainbow | 1964 | 30.00 |
| *—Gatefold cover* | | | |
| ❑ FS-2015 [S] | Finian's Rainbow | 196? | 25.00 |
| *—Standard cover* | | | |
| ❑ FS-2015 [S] | Finian's Rainbow | 1964 | 40.00 |
| *—Gatefold cover* | | | |
| ❑ F-2016 [M] | Guys and Dolls | 196? | 20.00 |
| *—Standard cover* | | | |
| ❑ F-2016 [M] | Guys and Dolls | 1964 | 30.00 |
| *—Gatefold cover* | | | |
| ❑ FS-2016 [S] | Guys and Dolls | 196? | 25.00 |
| *—Standard cover* | | | |
| ❑ FS-2016 [S] | Guys and Dolls | 1964 | 40.00 |
| *—Gatefold cover* | | | |
| ❑ F-2017 [M] | Kiss Me, Kate | 196? | 20.00 |
| *—Standard cover* | | | |
| ❑ F-2017 [M] | Kiss Me, Kate | 1964 | 30.00 |
| *—Gatefold cover* | | | |
| ❑ FS-2017 [S] | Kiss Me, Kate | 196? | 25.00 |
| *—Standard cover* | | | |
| ❑ FS-2017 [S] | Kiss Me, Kate | 1964 | 40.00 |
| *—Gatefold cover* | | | |
| ❑ F-2018 [M] | South Pacific | 196? | 20.00 |
| *—Standard cover* | | | |
| ❑ F-2018 [M] | South Pacific | 1964 | 30.00 |
| *—Gatefold cover* | | | |
| ❑ FS-2018 [S] | South Pacific | 196? | 25.00 |
| *—Standard cover* | | | |

| Number | Title (A Side/B Side) | Yr | NM |
|---|---|---|---|
| ❑ FS-2018 [S] | South Pacific | 1964 | 40.00 |
| *—Gatefold cover* | | | |
| ❑ F-2019 [(4)M] | The Reprise Repertory Theatre | 1964 | 200.00 |
| *—Box set of all four of the above LPs in gatefold covers* | | | |
| ❑ FS-2019 [(4)S] | The Reprise Repertory Theatre | 1964 | 300.00 |
| *—Box set of all four of the above LPs in gatefold covers* | | | |

**RESIDENTS, THE**

CRYPTIC

| Number | Title (A Side/B Side) | Yr | NM |
|---|---|---|---|
| ❑ S-18335 SP-2 | For Elsie | 1987 | 100.00 |
| *—Green vinyl one-sided LP* | | | |

ENIGMA

| Number | Title (A Side/B Side) | Yr | NM |
|---|---|---|---|
| ❑ 73547 | The King & Eye | 1989 | 15.00 |

EPISODE

| Number | Title (A Side/B Side) | Yr | NM |
|---|---|---|---|
| ❑ ED 21 | The Census Taker (Soundtrack) | 1985 | 20.00 |
| ❑ ED 21 | The Census Taker (Soundtrack) | 1985 | 80.00 |
| *—Red vinyl* | | | |

RALPH

| Number | Title (A Side/B Side) | Yr | NM |
|---|---|---|---|
| ❑ Mole Show 001 | The Mole Show (The Roxy) | 1983 | 30.00 |
| ❑ C-002A | The Mole Show (The Roxy) | 1983 | 40.00 |
| *—Picture disc* | | | |
| ❑ OP-011 [DJ] | Freak Show | 1991 | 80.00 |
| *—Promo-only black vinyl pressing; 400 made* | | | |
| ❑ OP-011 [PD] | Freak Show | 1991 | 40.00 |
| *—Picture disc* | | | |
| ❑ RR 0274 | Meet the Residents | 1974 | 200.00 |
| *—First version: "Meet the Beatles" LP parody cover and "First Edition" on back cover* | | | |
| ❑ RR 0278 | Duck Stab | 1978 | 10.00 |
| *—Second version: Yellow titles box on back* | | | |
| ❑ RR 0278 | Duck Stab | 1978 | 12.00 |
| *—First version: Green titles box on back* | | | |
| ❑ RR 0677 | Meet the Residents | 1977 | 12.00 |
| *—Fourth version: same cover as second version, modified and orange back cover* | | | |
| ❑ RR 0677 | Meet the Residents | 1977 | 15.00 |
| *—Third version: same cover as second version, black "a" Ralph logo* | | | |
| ❑ RR 0677 | Meet the Residents | 1977 | 20.00 |
| *—Second version: "She Loves You" picture sleeve parody cover, split "a" Ralph logo* | | | |
| ❑ RR 1075 | The Third Reich 'N' Roll | 1976 | 10.00 |
| *—Fourth version: Gray carrot, black "a" Ralph logo* | | | |
| ❑ RR 1075 | The Third Reich 'N' Roll | 1976 | 12.00 |
| *—Third version: Orange carrot, black "a" Ralph logo* | | | |
| ❑ RR 1075 | The Third Reich 'N' Roll | 1976 | 15.00 |
| *—Second version: Gray carrot, split "a" Ralph logo* | | | |
| ❑ RR 1075 | The Third Reich 'N' Roll | 1976 | 50.00 |
| *—Censored cover with swastikas obscured, pressed in U.S. for export to Germany* | | | |
| ❑ RR 1075 | The Third Reich 'N' Roll | 1976 | 50.00 |
| *—First version of 1,000: Liner notes inside, orange carrot* | | | |
| ❑ RR 1075 | The Third Reich 'N' Roll | 1976 | 1500. |
| *—Numbered box set on marbled vinyl, silkscreened cover and lithographs inside* | | | |
| ❑ RR 1174 | Not Available | 1978 | 10.00 |
| *—Green label, address is "109 Minna"* | | | |
| ❑ RR 1174 | Not Available | 1978 | 12.00 |
| *—Green label, address is "444 Grove"* | | | |
| ❑ RR 1174 | Not Available | 1978 | 15.00 |
| *—Orange label, remastered, "Re-3" in trail-off vinyl* | | | |
| ❑ RR 1174 | Not Available | 1978 | 25.00 |
| *—Purple label, mis-mastered, "Re-1" in trail-off vinyl* | | | |
| ❑ RR 1276 | Fingerprince | 1977 | 10.00 |
| *—Third version: Color cover* | | | |
| ❑ RR 1276 | Fingerprince | 1977 | 20.00 |
| *—Second version: Lighter brown cover* | | | |
| ❑ RR 1276 | Fingerprince | 1977 | 80.00 |
| *—First version: Dark brown cover, "First Pressing" written on back cover* | | | |
| ❑ RZ 7707 [PD] | Meet the Residents | 1986 | 30.00 |
| *—Picture disc, with original cover on one side, replacement cover on other* | | | |
| ❑ DJ 7901 [DJ] | Please Do Not Steal It! | 1979 | 40.00 |
| *—Promo-only sampler* | | | |
| ❑ ESK 7906 | Eskimo | 1979 | 10.00 |
| *—Third version: Black vinyl, standard cover* | | | |
| ❑ ESK 7906 | Eskimo | 1979 | 15.00 |
| *—Second version: Black vinyl, gatefold* | | | |
| ❑ ESK 7906 | Eskimo | 1979 | 25.00 |
| *—First version: White vinyl, gatefold cover* | | | |
| ❑ RZ 7906 [PD] | Eskimo | 1979 | 30.00 |
| *—Picture disc* | | | |
| ❑ RZ 8052 | The Residents Commercial Album | 1980 | 12.00 |
| *—Third version: Green vinyl* | | | |
| ❑ RZ 8052 | The Residents Commercial Album | 1980 | 15.00 |
| *—Second version: Corrected song order, green logo* | | | |
| ❑ RZ 8052 | The Residents Commercial Album | 1980 | 20.00 |
| *—First version: Purple Ralph logo, songs listed in wrong order* | | | |
| ❑ RZ 8152 | Mark of the Mole | 1981 | 10.00 |
| ❑ RZ 8152 | Mark of the Mole | 1981 | 50.00 |
| *—Signed brown vinyl edition with lyrics* | | | |
| ❑ RZ 8202 | The Tunes of Two Cities | 1982 | 10.00 |
| *—Second edition: "109 Minna Street" address* | | | |
| ❑ RZ 8202 | The Tunes of Two Cities | 1982 | 12.00 |
| *—First edition: "444 Grove Street" address* | | | |
| ❑ RZ 8252 | Intermission | 1982 | 12.00 |

The Replacements, *Tim,* Sire 25330, 1985, $12.

| Number | Title (A Side/B Side) | Yr | NM |
|---|---|---|---|
| ❑ RZ 8252 | Intermission | 1982 | 14.00 |
| *—Red vinyl* | | | |
| ❑ RZ 8302 | Residue | 1983 | 12.00 |
| ❑ RR 8315 | Title in Limbo | 1983 | 12.00 |
| *—With Renaldo and The Loaf* | | | |
| ❑ RZ 8402 | George & James | 1984 | 10.00 |
| *—Second edition: Approved mix with "Re-5" in trail-off* | | | |
| ❑ RZ 8402 | George & James | 1984 | 30.00 |
| *—First edition: Rejected mix with "Re-1" in trail-off* | | | |
| ❑ RZ 8402 | George & James | 1984 | 50.00 |
| *—"Re-5" in trail-off, clear vinyl* | | | |
| ❑ RZ 8452 | Whatever Happened to Vileness Fats? | 1984 | 12.00 |
| ❑ RZ 8452 | Whatever Happened to Vileness Fats? | 1984 | 80.00 |
| *—Red vinyl* | | | |
| ❑ RZ 8552 | The Big Bubble | 1985 | 12.00 |
| ❑ RZ 8552 | The Big Bubble | 1985 | 80.00 |
| *—Pink vinyl* | | | |
| ❑ RZ 8602 | The Eyeball Show (The 13th Anniversary Show) Live in Japan | 1986 | 10.00 |
| ❑ RZ 8602 | The Eyeball Show (The 13th Anniversary Show) Live in Japan | 1986 | 80.00 |
| *—White vinyl* | | | |
| ❑ RZ 8652 | Stars & Hank Forever | 1986 | 10.00 |
| ❑ RZ 8652 | Stars & Hank Forever | 1986 | 40.00 |
| *—Blue vinyl* | | | |
| ❑ RR 82761 | Fingerprince | 1988 | 10.00 |
| *—New number, black vinyl* | | | |
| ❑ RR 82761 | Fingerprince | 1988 | 12.00 |
| *—New number, purple vinyl* | | | |
| ❑ RR 87521 | Duck Stab | 1988 | 10.00 |
| *—New number, black vinyl* | | | |
| ❑ RR 87521 | Duck Stab | 1988 | 12.00 |
| *—New number, red vinyl* | | | |
| ❑ RR 88521 | Meet the Residents | 1988 | 12.00 |
| *—Original "Meet the Beatles" parody cover restored, black vinyl* | | | |
| ❑ RR 88521 | Meet the Residents | 1988 | 15.00 |
| *—Original "Meet the Beatles" parody cover restored, white vinyl* | | | |

RYKO ANALOGUE

| Number | Title (A Side/B Side) | Yr | NM |
|---|---|---|---|
| ❑ RALP-0044-2 [(2)] | God in Three Persons | 1988 | 20.00 |
| *—Clear vinyl* | | | |
| ❑ RALP-0045-2 | God in Three Persons Instrumental | 1988 | 15.00 |
| *—Clear vinyl* | | | |

UWEB

| Number | Title (A Side/B Side) | Yr | NM |
|---|---|---|---|
| ❑ 0011 | Stranger Than Supper | 1990 | 25.00 |
| *—Fan club issue* | | | |

**RESTIVO, JOHNNY**

RCA VICTOR

| Number | Title (A Side/B Side) | Yr | NM |
|---|---|---|---|
| ❑ LPM-2149 [M] | Oh, Johnny! | 1959 | 60.00 |
| ❑ LSP-2149 [S] | Oh, Johnny! | 1959 | 100.00 |

**RESTUM, WILLIE**

GONE

| Number | Title (A Side/B Side) | Yr | NM |
|---|---|---|---|
| ❑ LP-5011 [M] | Willie Restum at the Dream Lounge | 1960 | 250.00 |

ROULETTE

| Number | Title (A Side/B Side) | Yr | NM |
|---|---|---|---|
| ❑ R-25152 [M] | Dream Bar | 1961 | 60.00 |

**RETURN TO FOREVER**

COLUMBIA

| Number | Title (A Side/B Side) | Yr | NM |
|---|---|---|---|
| ❑ PC 34076 | Romantic Warrior | 1976 | 12.00 |
| *—No bar code on cover* | | | |
| ❑ PC 34076 | Romantic Warrior | 198? | 8.00 |
| *—Reissue with bar code* | | | |
| ❑ PC 34682 | Musicmagic | 1977 | 12.00 |
| *—No bar code on cover* | | | |
| ❑ PC 34682 | Musicmagic | 1985 | 8.00 |
| *—Reissue with bar code* | | | |
| ❑ PCQ 34682 [Q] | Musicmagic | 1977 | 20.00 |
| ❑ JC 35281 | Return to Forever Live | 1979 | 10.00 |
| ❑ JC 36359 | The Best of Return to Forever | 1980 | 12.00 |
| ❑ PC 36359 | The Best of Return to Forever | 198? | 10.00 |
| *—Budget-line reissue with new prefix* | | | |

ECM

| Number | Title (A Side/B Side) | Yr | NM |
|---|---|---|---|
| ❑ 1022 ST | Return to Forever | 197? | 15.00 |
| *—Original issue; made in Germany?* | | | |
| ❑ ECM-1-1022 | Return to Forever | 197? | 12.00 |
| *—Distributed by Polydor* | | | |

POLYDOR

| Number | Title (A Side/B Side) | Yr | NM |
|---|---|---|---|
| ❑ PD-5525 | Light as a Feather | 1973 | 12.00 |
| ❑ PD-5536 | Hymn of the Seventh Galaxy | 1973 | 12.00 |
| ❑ PD-6509 | Where Have I Known You Before | 1974 | 12.00 |
| ❑ PD-6512 | No Mystery | 1975 | 12.00 |
| ❑ 825336-1 | Hymn of the Seventh Galaxy | 198? | 8.00 |
| *—Reissue* | | | |

| Number | Title (A Side/B Side) | Yr | NM |
|---|---|---|---|

### REVELERS, THE

**RONDO-LETTE**

| Number | Title (A Side/B Side) | Yr | NM |
|---|---|---|---|
| ❑ A-50 [M] | Jazz at the Downstairs Club | 1962 | 20.00 |
| ❑ SA-50 [S] | Jazz at the Downstairs Club | 1962 | 25.00 |

### REVELLS, THE

**REPRISE**

| Number | Title (A Side/B Side) | Yr | NM |
|---|---|---|---|
| ❑ R-6160 [M] | The Go Sound of the Slots | 1965 | 150.00 |
| ❑ RS-6160 [S] | The Go Sound of the Slots | 1965 | 200.00 |

### REVELS, THE (2)

**IMPACT**

| Number | Title (A Side/B Side) | Yr | NM |
|---|---|---|---|
| ❑ LPM-1 [M] | Revels on a Rampage | 1964 | 500.00 |

**SUNDAZED**

| Number | Title (A Side/B Side) | Yr | NM |
|---|---|---|---|
| ❑ LP 5010 | Intoxica! The Best of the Revels | 1994 | 10.00 |

### REVENGERS, THE

**METRO**

| Number | Title (A Side/B Side) | Yr | NM |
|---|---|---|---|
| ❑ M-565 [M] | Batman and Other Supermen | 1966 | 30.00 |
| ❑ MS-565 [S] | Batman and Other Supermen | 1966 | 40.00 |

### REVERE, PAUL, AND THE RAIDERS

**COLUMBIA**

| Number | Title (A Side/B Side) | Yr | NM |
|---|---|---|---|
| ❑ GP 12 [(2)] | Two All Time Great Selling LPs | 1969 | 25.00 |
| *—Combines 9395 and 9521 in one package; red labels* | | | |
| ❑ GP 12 | Two All Time Great Selling LPs | 1971 | 20.00 |
| *—Combines 9395 and 9521 in one package; orange labels* | | | |
| ❑ CL 2307 [M] | Here They Come! | 1965 | 20.00 |
| *—"360 Sound Mono" on label* | | | |
| ❑ CL 2307 [M] | Here They Come! | 1965 | 30.00 |
| *—"Guaranteed High Fidelity" on label* | | | |
| ❑ CL 2451 [M] | Just Like Us! | 1966 | 25.00 |
| ❑ CL 2508 [M] | Midnight Ride | 1966 | 25.00 |
| ❑ CL 2595 [M] | The Spirit of '67 | 1966 | 25.00 |
| ❑ KCL 2662 [M] | Greatest Hits | 1967 | 30.00 |
| *—Add 20% if booklet is included; at least some copies actually are stereo with the "XSS" prefix on the label's master numbers rather than "XLP," though we don't know if all of them are* | | | |
| ❑ CL 2721 [M] | Revolution! | 1967 | 30.00 |
| ❑ CL 2755 [M] | A Christmas Present...And Past | 1967 | 60.00 |
| ❑ CL 2805 [M] | Goin' to Memphis | 1968 | 80.00 |
| ❑ CS 9107 [S] | Here They Come! | 1965 | 25.00 |
| *—"360 Sound Stereo" in white on label* | | | |
| ❑ CS 9107 [S] | Here They Come! | 1965 | 40.00 |
| *—"360 Sound Stereo" in black on label* | | | |
| ❑ CS 9251 [S] | Just Like Us! | 1966 | 30.00 |
| ❑ CS 9308 [S] | Midnight Ride | 1966 | 30.00 |
| ❑ CS 9395 [S] | The Spirit of '67 | 1966 | 30.00 |
| ❑ KCS 9462 [P] | Greatest Hits | 1967 | 25.00 |
| *—Add 20% if booklet is included* | | | |
| ❑ CS 9521 [S] | Revolution! | 1967 | 25.00 |
| ❑ CS 9555 [S] | A Christmas Present...And Past | 1967 | 25.00 |
| ❑ CS 9605 [S] | Goin' to Memphis | 1968 | 20.00 |
| ❑ CS 9665 | Something Happening | 1968 | 20.00 |
| ❑ CS 9753 | Hard 'N' Heavy (With Marshmallow) | 1969 | 20.00 |
| *—Black and white cover* | | | |
| ❑ CS 9753 | Hard 'N' Heavy (With Marshmallow) | 1969 | 30.00 |
| *—Color cover* | | | |
| ❑ CS 9905 | Alias Pink Puzz | 1969 | 20.00 |
| ❑ CS 9964 | Collage | 1970 | 20.00 |
| ❑ C 30386 | Greatest Hits, Volume 2 | 1971 | 20.00 |
| ❑ C 30768 | Indian Reservation | 1971 | 15.00 |
| ❑ KC 31106 | Country Wine | 1972 | 15.00 |
| ❑ KG 31464 [(2)] | All-Time Greatest Hits | 1972 | 20.00 |
| ❑ PC 35593 | Greatest Hits | 1978 | 10.00 |

**COLUMBIA LIMITED EDITION**

| Number | Title (A Side/B Side) | Yr | NM |
|---|---|---|---|
| ❑ LE 10170 [S] | Midnight Ride | 197? | 15.00 |
| *—Reissue of 9308* | | | |

**COLUMBIA SPECIAL PRODUCTS**

| Number | Title (A Side/B Side) | Yr | NM |
|---|---|---|---|
| ❑ P 13512 | Goin' to Memphis | 197? | 15.00 |

**ERA**

| Number | Title (A Side/B Side) | Yr | NM |
|---|---|---|---|
| ❑ NU 5880 | The Great Raider Reunion | 1983 | 12.00 |
| *—Re-recordings* | | | |

**GARDENA**

| Number | Title (A Side/B Side) | Yr | NM |
|---|---|---|---|
| ❑ LP-G-1000 [M] | Like, Long Hair | 1961 | 600.00 |

**HARMONY**

| Number | Title (A Side/B Side) | Yr | NM |
|---|---|---|---|
| ❑ H 30089 | Paul Revere and the Raiders Featuring Mark Lindsay | 1970 | 12.00 |
| ❑ KH 30975 | Good Thing | 1971 | 12.00 |
| ❑ KH 31183 | Movin' On | 1972 | 12.00 |

**JERDEN**

| Number | Title (A Side/B Side) | Yr | NM |
|---|---|---|---|
| ❑ JRL-7004 [M] | Paul Revere and the Raiders In the Beginning | 1966 | 60.00 |
| ❑ JRS-7004 [R] | Paul Revere and the Raiders In the Beginning | 1966 | 30.00 |
| ❑ DT-90709 [R] | Paul Revere and the Raiders In the Beginning | 1966 | 50.00 |
| *—Capitol Record Club edition* | | | |
| ❑ T-90709 [M] | Paul Revere and the Raiders In the Beginning | 1966 | 70.00 |
| *—Capitol Record Club edition* | | | |

**PICKWICK**

| Number | Title (A Side/B Side) | Yr | NM |
|---|---|---|---|
| ❑ SPC-3176 [R] | Paul Revere and the Raiders | 1969 | 10.00 |

**SANDE**

| Number | Title (A Side/B Side) | Yr | NM |
|---|---|---|---|
| ❑ S-1001 [M] | Paul Revere and the Raiders | 1963 | 1200. |
| *—Original version with "Sande" and no mention of "Etiquette" in trail-off area* | | | |
| ❑ S-1001 [M] | Paul Revere and the Raiders | 1979 | 25.00 |
| *—Legitimate reissue with "Sande" and "Etiquette" in trail-off area* | | | |

**SEARS**

| Number | Title (A Side/B Side) | Yr | NM |
|---|---|---|---|
| ❑ SPS-493 | Paul Revere and the Raiders | 1969 | 25.00 |

### REXROTH, KENNETH

**FANTASY**

| Number | Title (A Side/B Side) | Yr | NM |
|---|---|---|---|
| ❑ 7008 [M] | Poetry and Jazz at the Blackhawk | 1958 | 100.00 |
| *—Black vinyl* | | | |
| ❑ 7008 [M] | Poetry and Jazz at the Blackhawk | 1958 | 200.00 |
| *—Red vinyl* | | | |

### REXROTH, KENNETH, AND LAWRENCE FERLINGHETTI

**FANTASY**

| Number | Title (A Side/B Side) | Yr | NM |
|---|---|---|---|
| ❑ 7002 [M] | Poetry Readings from the Cellar | 1957 | 100.00 |
| *—Black vinyl* | | | |
| ❑ 7002 [M] | Poetry Readings from the Cellar | 1957 | 200.00 |
| *—Red vinyl* | | | |

### REY, ALVINO

**CAPITOL**

| Number | Title (A Side/B Side) | Yr | NM |
|---|---|---|---|
| ❑ T 808 [M] | Aloha | 1957 | 30.00 |
| ❑ ST 1085 [S] | Swinging Fling | 1958 | 30.00 |
| ❑ T 1085 [M] | Swinging Fling | 1958 | 25.00 |
| ❑ ST 1262 [S] | Ping Pong! | 1959 | 25.00 |
| ❑ T 1262 [M] | Ping Pong! | 1959 | 20.00 |
| ❑ ST 1395 [S] | That Lonely Feeling | 1960 | 25.00 |
| ❑ T 1395 [M] | That Lonely Feeling | 1960 | 20.00 |

### REYNOLDS, ART, SINGERS

**CAPITOL**

| Number | Title (A Side/B Side) | Yr | NM |
|---|---|---|---|
| ❑ ST-191 | It's a Wonderful World | 1969 | 20.00 |
| ❑ ST 2534 [S] | Tellin' It Like It Is | 1966 | 25.00 |
| ❑ T 2534 [M] | Tellin' It Like It Is | 1966 | 20.00 |
| ❑ ST 2811 [S] | Long Dusty Road | 1967 | 20.00 |
| ❑ T 2811 [M] | Long Dusty Road | 1967 | 25.00 |
| ❑ ST 2900 | Soul-Gospel Sounds | 1968 | 20.00 |

### REYNOLDS, BURT

**MERCURY**

| Number | Title (A Side/B Side) | Yr | NM |
|---|---|---|---|
| ❑ MK-4 [DJ] | A Burt Reynolds Radio Special | 1973 | 25.00 |
| ❑ SRM-1-693 | Ask Me What I Am | 1973 | 15.00 |

### REYNOLDS, DEBBIE

**DOT**

| Number | Title (A Side/B Side) | Yr | NM |
|---|---|---|---|
| ❑ DLP-3191 [M] | Debbie | 1959 | 30.00 |
| ❑ DLP-3295 [M] | Am I That Easy to Forget? | 1960 | 30.00 |
| ❑ DLP-3298 [M] | Fine and Dandy | 1960 | 20.00 |
| ❑ DLP-3492 [M] | Tammy | 1963 | 20.00 |
| ❑ DLP-25191 [S] | Debbie | 1959 | 40.00 |
| ❑ DLP-25295 [S] | Am I That Easy to Forget? | 1960 | 40.00 |
| *—Black vinyl* | | | |
| ❑ DLP-25295 [S] | Am I That Easy to Forget? | 1960 | 80.00 |
| *—Blue vinyl* | | | |
| ❑ DLP-25298 [S] | Fine and Dandy | 1960 | 25.00 |
| ❑ DLP-25492 [S] | Tammy | 1963 | 25.00 |

**K-TEL**

| Number | Title (A Side/B Side) | Yr | NM |
|---|---|---|---|
| ❑ NU 9190 | Do It Debbie's Way | 1983 | 10.00 |
| *—Exercise record* | | | |

**METRO**

| Number | Title (A Side/B Side) | Yr | NM |
|---|---|---|---|
| ❑ M-535 [M] | Raise a Ruckus | 196? | 20.00 |
| ❑ MS-535 [S] | Raise a Ruckus | 196? | 20.00 |

**MGM**

| Number | Title (A Side/B Side) | Yr | NM |
|---|---|---|---|
| ❑ E-3806 [M] | From Debbie with Love | 1959 | 40.00 |

### REYNOLDS, LAWRENCE

**WARNER BROS.**

| Number | Title (A Side/B Side) | Yr | NM |
|---|---|---|---|
| ❑ WS 1825 | Jesus Is a Soul Man | 1969 | 20.00 |

### REYNOLDS, TEDDY, AND THE TWISTERS

**CROWN**

| Number | Title (A Side/B Side) | Yr | NM |
|---|---|---|---|
| ❑ CST-247 [S] | The Twist | 1962 | 40.00 |
| ❑ CLP-5247 [M] | The Twist | 1962 | 30.00 |

### REYNOLDS, TOMMY

**AUDIO LAB**

| Number | Title (A Side/B Side) | Yr | NM |
|---|---|---|---|
| ❑ AL-1509 [M] | Dixieland All-Stars | 1958 | 100.00 |

**KING**

| Number | Title (A Side/B Side) | Yr | NM |
|---|---|---|---|
| ❑ 395-510 [M] | Jazz for Happy Feet | 1956 | 80.00 |

**ROYALE**

| Number | Title (A Side/B Side) | Yr | NM |
|---|---|---|---|
| ❑ 18117 [10] | Tommy Reynolds Orchestra with Bon Bon | 195? | 80.00 |

### REYS, RITA

**COLUMBIA**

| Number | Title (A Side/B Side) | Yr | NM |
|---|---|---|---|
| ❑ CL 903 [M] | The Cool Voice of Rita Reys with Art Blakey and the Jazz Messengers | 1956 | 150.00 |

**EPIC**

| Number | Title (A Side/B Side) | Yr | NM |
|---|---|---|---|
| ❑ LN 3522 [M] | Her Name Is Rita Reys | 1957 | 80.00 |

### RHEIMS, ROBERT

**RHEIMS**

| Number | Title (A Side/B Side) | Yr | NM |
|---|---|---|---|
| ❑ LP-6006 [M] | Merry Christmas Carols | 1958 | 20.00 |
| *—Red vinyl with lyric innersleeve* | | | |
| ❑ ST-7706 [S] | Merry Christmas Carols | 1958 | 25.00 |
| *—Green vinyl with lyric innersleeve* | | | |

### RHINOCEROS

**ELEKTRA**

| Number | Title (A Side/B Side) | Yr | NM |
|---|---|---|---|
| ❑ EKS-74030 | Rhinoceros | 1968 | 25.00 |
| ❑ EKS-74056 | Satin Chickens | 1969 | 20.00 |
| ❑ EKS-74075 | Better Times Are Coming | 1970 | 20.00 |

### RHODES, EMITT

**A&M**

| Number | Title (A Side/B Side) | Yr | NM |
|---|---|---|---|
| ❑ SP-4254 | The American Dream | 1970 | 25.00 |
| *—Original album contains "You're a Very Lovely Woman" and has Rhodes in front of a paint-covered backdrop on cover* | | | |
| ❑ SP-4254 | The American Dream | 1971 | 15.00 |
| *—Reissue contains "Saturday Night" and a framed photo of Rhodes on cover* | | | |

**ABC DUNHILL**

| Number | Title (A Side/B Side) | Yr | NM |
|---|---|---|---|
| ❑ DS-50089 | Emitt Rhodes | 1970 | 12.00 |
| ❑ DS-50111 | Mirror | 1971 | 12.00 |
| ❑ DS-50122 | Farewell to Paradise | 1972 | 12.00 |

### RHODES, GEORGE

**GROOVE**

| Number | Title (A Side/B Side) | Yr | NM |
|---|---|---|---|
| ❑ LG-1005 [M] | Real George! | 1956 | 60.00 |

### RHODES, TODD

**KING**

| Number | Title (A Side/B Side) | Yr | NM |
|---|---|---|---|
| ❑ 295-88 [10] | Todd Rhodes Playing His Greatest Hits | 1954 | 1500. |
| ❑ 658 [M] | Dance Music | 1960 | 800.00 |

### RHYNE, MEL

**JAZZLAND**

| Number | Title (A Side/B Side) | Yr | NM |
|---|---|---|---|
| ❑ JLP-16 [M] | Organizing | 1960 | 30.00 |
| ❑ JLP-916 [S] | Organizing | 1960 | 40.00 |

### RHYTHM DEVILS, THE

**PASSPORT**

| Number | Title (A Side/B Side) | Yr | NM |
|---|---|---|---|
| ❑ PB-9844 | The Rhythm Devils Play River Music | 1980 | 20.00 |

### RHYTHM MASTERS, THE (1)

**ACE**

| Number | Title (A Side/B Side) | Yr | NM |
|---|---|---|---|
| ❑ LP-1010 [M] | Hymns and Spirituals | 1961 | 100.00 |

### RHYTHM ROCKERS (1)

**CHALLENGE**

| Number | Title (A Side/B Side) | Yr | NM |
|---|---|---|---|
| ❑ CHL-617 [M] | Soul Surfin' | 1963 | 90.00 |

### RHYZE

**20TH CENTURY**

| Number | Title (A Side/B Side) | Yr | NM |
|---|---|---|---|
| ❑ T-639 | Rhyze to the Top | 1981 | 30.00 |

### RICE, BOBBY G.

**AUDIOGRAPH**

| Number | Title (A Side/B Side) | Yr | NM |
|---|---|---|---|
| ❑ 6000 | Bobby G. Rice | 1982 | 10.00 |
| ❑ 7772 | Bobby's Back | 1982 | 10.00 |

**DOOR KNOB**

| Number | Title (A Side/B Side) | Yr | NM |
|---|---|---|---|
| ❑ 1008 | New Beginning | 198? | 12.00 |

**GRT**

| Number | Title (A Side/B Side) | Yr | NM |
|---|---|---|---|
| ❑ 8001 | She Sure Laid the Lonelies on Me | 1974 | 12.00 |
| ❑ 8003 | Write Me a Letter | 1975 | 12.00 |
| ❑ 8011 | Instant Rice — The Best of Bobby G. | 1976 | 12.00 |
| ❑ 8016 | With Love from Bobby G. Rice | 1977 | 12.00 |

**METROMEDIA COUNTRY**

| Number | Title (A Side/B Side) | Yr | NM |
|---|---|---|---|
| ❑ BML1-0186 | You Lay So Easy on My Mind | 1973 | 20.00 |

**ROYAL AMERICAN**

| Number | Title (A Side/B Side) | Yr | NM |
|---|---|---|---|
| ❑ 1003 | Hit After Hit | 1972 | 20.00 |

**SUNBIRD**

| Number | Title (A Side/B Side) | Yr | NM |
|---|---|---|---|
| ❑ SN-50106 | Greatest Hits | 1980 | 12.00 |

### RICH, BUDDY

**ARGO**

| Number | Title (A Side/B Side) | Yr | NM |
|---|---|---|---|
| ❑ LP-676 [M] | Playtime | 1961 | 30.00 |
| ❑ LPS-676 [S] | Playtime | 1961 | 40.00 |

**EMARCY**

| Number | Title (A Side/B Side) | Yr | NM |
|---|---|---|---|
| ❑ 66006 | Driver | 1967 | 20.00 |

**GREAT AMERICAN**

| Number | Title (A Side/B Side) | Yr | NM |
|---|---|---|---|
| ❑ 1030 | Class of '78 | 1978 | 20.00 |

*—Direct-to-disc version of Gryphon 781*

**MERCURY**

| Number | Title (A Side/B Side) | Yr | NM |
|---|---|---|---|
| ❑ MG-20451 [M] | Richcraft | 1959 | 60.00 |
| ❑ MG-20461 [M] | The Voice Is Rich | 1959 | 50.00 |
| ❑ SR-60136 [S] | Richcraft | 1959 | 70.00 |
| ❑ SR-60144 [S] | The Voice Is Rich | 1959 | 60.00 |

**NORGRAN**

| Number | Title (A Side/B Side) | Yr | NM |
|---|---|---|---|
| ❑ MGN-26 [10] | Buddy Rich Swingin' | 1954 | 120.00 |
| ❑ MGN-1031 [M] | Sing and Swing with Buddy Rich | 1955 | 80.00 |
| ❑ MGN-1052 [M] | The Swingin' Buddy Rich | 1955 | 60.00 |
| *—Reissue of 26* | | | |
| ❑ MGN-1078 [M] | The Wailing Buddy Rich | 1956 | 60.00 |
| ❑ MGN-1088 [M] | This One's for Basie | 1956 | 60.00 |

**PACIFIC JAZZ**

| Number | Title (A Side/B Side) | Yr | NM |
|---|---|---|---|
| ❑ PJ-10113 [M] | Swingin' New Big Band | 1966 | 25.00 |
| ❑ PJ-10117 [M] | Big Swing Face | 1967 | 25.00 |
| ❑ ST-20113 [S] | Swingin' New Big Band | 1966 | 20.00 |
| ❑ ST-20117 [S] | Big Swing Face | 1967 | 20.00 |
| ❑ ST-20126 | A New One | 1968 | 20.00 |

**VERVE**

| Number | Title (A Side/B Side) | Yr | NM |
|---|---|---|---|
| ❑ MGV-2009 [M] | Buddy Rich Sings Johnny Mercer | 1956 | 60.00 |
| ❑ V-2009 [M] | Buddy Rich Sings Johnny Mercer | 1961 | 20.00 |
| ❑ MGV-2075 [M] | Buddy Rich Just Sings | 1957 | 60.00 |
| ❑ V-2075 [M] | Buddy Rich Just Sings | 1961 | 20.00 |
| ❑ MGV-8142 [M] | The Swingin' Buddy Rich | 1957 | 50.00 |
| *—Reissue of Norgran 1052* | | | |
| ❑ V-8142 [M] | The Swingin' Buddy Rich | 1961 | 20.00 |
| ❑ MGV-8168 [M] | The Wailing Buddy Rich | 1957 | 50.00 |
| *—Reissue of Norgran 1078* | | | |
| ❑ V-8168 [M] | The Wailing Buddy Rich | 1961 | 20.00 |
| ❑ MGV-8176 [M] | This One's for Basie | 1957 | 50.00 |
| *—Reissue of Norgran 1086* | | | |
| ❑ V-8176 [M] | This One's for Basie | 1961 | 20.00 |
| ❑ MGV-8285 [M] | Buddy Rich in Miami | 1958 | 60.00 |
| ❑ V-8285 [M] | Buddy Rich in Miami | 1961 | 20.00 |
| ❑ V-8425 [M] | Blues Caravan | 1962 | 25.00 |
| ❑ V6-8425 [S] | Blues Caravan | 1962 | 30.00 |
| ❑ V-8471 [M] | Burnin' Beat | 1962 | 25.00 |
| ❑ V6-8471 [S] | Burnin' Beat | 1962 | 30.00 |
| ❑ V-8484 [M] | Drum Battle: Gene Krupa vs. Buddy Rich | 1962 | 25.00 |
| ❑ V6-8484 [S] | Drum Battle: Gene Krupa vs. Buddy Rich | 1962 | 30.00 |
| ❑ V-8712 [M] | Big Band Shout | 1967 | 20.00 |

## RICH, BUDDY, AND SWEETS EDISON

**NORGRAN**

| Number | Title (A Side/B Side) | Yr | NM |
|---|---|---|---|
| ❑ MGN-1038 [M] | Buddy Rich and Sweets Edison | 1955 | 80.00 |

**VERVE**

| Number | Title (A Side/B Side) | Yr | NM |
|---|---|---|---|
| ❑ MGV-8129 [M] | Buddy and Sweets | 1957 | 50.00 |
| *—Reissue of Norgran 1038* | | | |
| ❑ V-8129 [M] | Buddy and Sweets | 1961 | 20.00 |

## RICH, BUDDY, AND MAX ROACH

**MERCURY**

| Number | Title (A Side/B Side) | Yr | NM |
|---|---|---|---|
| ❑ MG-20448 [M] | Rich Versus Roach | 1959 | 60.00 |
| ❑ SR-60133 [S] | Rich Versus Roach | 1959 | 70.00 |

## RICH, CHARLIE

**BUCKBOARD**

| Number | Title (A Side/B Side) | Yr | NM |
|---|---|---|---|
| ❑ 1019 | The Entertainer | 197? | 10.00 |

**COLUMBIA SPECIAL PRODUCTS**

| Number | Title (A Side/B Side) | Yr | NM |
|---|---|---|---|
| ❑ P2 13663 [(2)] | Super Hits | 197? | 15.00 |

**ELEKTRA**

| Number | Title (A Side/B Side) | Yr | NM |
|---|---|---|---|
| ❑ 6E-301 | Once a Drifter | 1981 | 10.00 |

**EPIC**

| Number | Title (A Side/B Side) | Yr | NM |
|---|---|---|---|
| ❑ AS 50 [DJ] | Charlie Rich | 1973 | 30.00 |
| *—Promo-only compilation* | | | |
| ❑ AS 139 [DJ] | Everything You Always Wanted to Hear by Charlie Rich But Were Afraid to Ask For | 1976 | 25.00 |
| *—Promo-only sampler* | | | |
| ❑ BN 26376 | Set Me Free | 1968 | 20.00 |
| ❑ BN 26516 | The Fabulous Charlie Rich | 1970 | 20.00 |
| ❑ E 30214 | Boss Man | 1970 | 20.00 |
| ❑ CQ 31933 [Q] | The Best of Charlie Rich | 1972 | 20.00 |
| ❑ KE 31933 | The Best of Charlie Rich | 1972 | 15.00 |
| *—Yellow label; add 80 percent if bonus record AE7 1065 and its special sleeve are still there* | | | |
| ❑ KE 31933 | The Best of Charlie Rich | 1973 | 12.00 |
| *—Orange label* | | | |
| ❑ CQ 32247 [Q] | Behind Closed Doors | 1973 | 20.00 |
| ❑ KE 32247 | Behind Closed Doors | 1973 | 12.00 |
| ❑ PE 32247 | Behind Closed Doors | 197? | 8.00 |
| *—Reissue* | | | |
| ❑ PE 32531 | Very Special Love Songs | 1974 | 12.00 |
| ❑ PEQ 32531 [Q] | Very Special Love Songs | 1974 | 20.00 |
| ❑ PE 33250 | The Silver Fox | 1974 | 12.00 |
| ❑ PEQ 33250 [Q] | The Silver Fox | 1974 | 20.00 |
| ❑ PE 33455 | Every Time You Touch Me (I Get High) | 1975 | 12.00 |
| ❑ PEQ 33455 [Q] | Every Time You Touch Me (I Get High) | 1975 | 20.00 |
| ❑ PE 33545 | Silver Linings | 1976 | 10.00 |
| ❑ PE 34240 | Greatest Hits | 1976 | 10.00 |
| *—Without bar code on cover* | | | |
| ❑ PE 34240 | Greatest Hits | 1979 | 8.00 |
| *—With bar code on cover* | | | |
| ❑ PE 34444 | Take Me | 1977 | 10.00 |
| ❑ PE 34444 | Take Me | 1977 | 10.00 |
| ❑ PE 34891 | Rollin' with the Flow | 1977 | 10.00 |
| ❑ JE 35394 | Classic Rich, Vol. 1 | 1978 | 10.00 |
| ❑ JE 35624 | Classic Rich, Vol. 2 | 1978 | 10.00 |

**GROOVE**

| Number | Title (A Side/B Side) | Yr | NM |
|---|---|---|---|
| ❑ GM-1000 [M] | Charlie Rich | 1964 | 150.00 |
| ❑ GS-1000 [S] | Charlie Rich | 1964 | 300.00 |

**HARMONY**

| Number | Title (A Side/B Side) | Yr | NM |
|---|---|---|---|
| ❑ KH 32166 | I Do My Swingin' at Home | 1973 | 12.00 |

**HI**

| Number | Title (A Side/B Side) | Yr | NM |
|---|---|---|---|
| ❑ 8006 | I'm So Lonesome I Could Cry | 198? | 8.00 |
| *—Reissue of Hi 32084* | | | |
| ❑ HL 12037 [M] | Charlie Rich Sings Country and Western | 1967 | 30.00 |
| ❑ SHL 32037 [S] | Charlie Rich Sings Country and Western | 1967 | 20.00 |
| ❑ SHL 32084 | Charlie Rich Sings the Songs of Hank Williams & Others | 1974 | 12.00 |
| *—Reissue of 32037* | | | |

**HILLTOP**

| Number | Title (A Side/B Side) | Yr | NM |
|---|---|---|---|
| ❑ 6139 | Lonely Weekends | 197? | 10.00 |
| ❑ 6149 | Songs for Beautiful Girls | 1974 | 10.00 |
| ❑ 6160 | Entertainer of the Year | 197? | 10.00 |

**MERCURY**

| Number | Title (A Side/B Side) | Yr | NM |
|---|---|---|---|
| ❑ SRM-2-7505 [(2)] | Fully Realized | 1974 | 15.00 |

**PHILLIPS INTERNATIONAL**

| Number | Title (A Side/B Side) | Yr | NM |
|---|---|---|---|
| ❑ PLP-1970 [M] | Lonely Weekends | 1960 | 600.00 |

**PICKWICK**

| Number | Title (A Side/B Side) | Yr | NM |
|---|---|---|---|
| ❑ ACL-7001 | Too Many Teardrops | 1975 | 10.00 |

**POWER PAK**

| Number | Title (A Side/B Side) | Yr | NM |
|---|---|---|---|
| ❑ PO-241 | There Won't Be Anymore | 197? | 10.00 |
| ❑ PO-245 | Arkansas Traveler | 197? | 10.00 |
| ❑ PO-252 | The Silver Fox | 197? | 10.00 |

**QUICKSILVER**

| Number | Title (A Side/B Side) | Yr | NM |
|---|---|---|---|
| ❑ QS-1005 | Midnight Blue | 198? | 12.00 |

**RCA CAMDEN**

| Number | Title (A Side/B Side) | Yr | NM |
|---|---|---|---|
| ❑ CAS-2417 | The Versatile and Talented Charlie Rich | 1970 | 10.00 |

**RCA VICTOR**

| Number | Title (A Side/B Side) | Yr | NM |
|---|---|---|---|
| ❑ APL1-0258 | Tomorrow Night | 1973 | 12.00 |
| ❑ APL1-0433 | There Won't Be Anymore | 1974 | 12.00 |
| ❑ APL1-0686 | She Called Me Baby | 1974 | 12.00 |
| ❑ APL1-0857 | Greatest Hits | 1975 | 12.00 |
| ❑ APL1-1242 | Now Everybody Knows | 1975 | 12.00 |
| ❑ ANL1-1542 | Tomorrow Night | 1976 | 10.00 |
| *—Reissue* | | | |
| ❑ APL1-2260 | Big Boss Man/My Mountain Dew | 1977 | 12.00 |
| ❑ ANL1-2424 | She Called Me Baby | 1977 | 10.00 |
| *—Reissue of APL1-0686* | | | |
| ❑ LPM-3352 [M] | That's Rich | 1965 | 40.00 |
| ❑ LSP-3352 [S] | That's Rich | 1965 | 50.00 |
| ❑ LPM-3537 [M] | Big Boss Man | 1966 | 40.00 |
| ❑ LSP-3557 [S] | Big Boss Man | 1966 | 50.00 |
| ❑ AHL1-5496 | Collector's Series | 1985 | 8.00 |

**SMASH**

| Number | Title (A Side/B Side) | Yr | NM |
|---|---|---|---|
| ❑ MGS-27070 [M] | The Many New Sides of Charlie Rich | 1965 | 30.00 |
| ❑ MGS-27078 [M] | The Best Years | 1966 | 30.00 |
| ❑ SRS-67070 [S] | The Many New Sides of Charlie Rich | 1965 | 40.00 |
| ❑ SRS-67070 [S] | The Best Years | 1966 | 40.00 |

**SUN**

| Number | Title (A Side/B Side) | Yr | NM |
|---|---|---|---|
| ❑ LP 110 | Lonely Weekend | 1970 | 12.00 |
| ❑ LP 123 | A Time for Tears | 1971 | 12.00 |
| ❑ LP 132 | The Early Years | 1974 | 12.00 |
| ❑ LP 133 | The Memphis Sound of Charlie Rich | 1974 | 12.00 |
| ❑ LP 134 | Golden Treasures | 1974 | 12.00 |
| ❑ LP 135 | Sun's Best of Charlie Rich | 1974 | 12.00 |
| ❑ 1003 | 20 Golden Hits | 1979 | 10.00 |
| *—Gold vinyl* | | | |
| ❑ 1007 | The Original Charlie Rich | 1979 | 10.00 |

**SUNNYVALE**

| Number | Title (A Side/B Side) | Yr | NM |
|---|---|---|---|
| ❑ 9330 | The Sun Story Vol. 2 | 1977 | 10.00 |

**TIME-LIFE**

| Number | Title (A Side/B Side) | Yr | NM |
|---|---|---|---|
| ❑ STW-115 | Country Music | 1981 | 10.00 |

**TRIP**

| Number | Title (A Side/B Side) | Yr | NM |
|---|---|---|---|
| ❑ TLP-8502 [(2)] | The Best of Charlie Rich | 1974 | 12.00 |

**UNITED ARTISTS**

| Number | Title (A Side/B Side) | Yr | NM |
|---|---|---|---|
| ❑ UA-LA876-H | I Still Believe in Love | 1978 | 12.00 |
| ❑ UA-LA925-H | The Fool Strikes Again | 1978 | 10.00 |

**WING**

| Number | Title (A Side/B Side) | Yr | NM |
|---|---|---|---|
| ❑ SRW-16375 | A Lonely Weekend | 1969 | 12.00 |

## RICH, DAVE

**STOP**

| Number | Title (A Side/B Side) | Yr | NM |
|---|---|---|---|
| ❑ 10007 | Soul Brother | 196? | 30.00 |

## RICH, DON Also see THE BUCKAROOS.

**CAPITOL**

| Number | Title (A Side/B Side) | Yr | NM |
|---|---|---|---|
| ❑ ST-643 | That Fiddlin' Man | 1970 | 25.00 |

## RICHARD, CLIFF

**ABC-PARAMOUNT**

| Number | Title (A Side/B Side) | Yr | NM |
|---|---|---|---|
| ❑ 321 [M] | Cliff Sings | 1960 | 80.00 |
| ❑ S-321 [S] | Cliff Sings | 1960 | 100.00 |
| ❑ 391 [M] | Listen to Cliff | 1961 | 80.00 |
| ❑ S-391 [S] | Listen to Cliff | 1961 | 100.00 |

**EMI AMERICA**

| Number | Title (A Side/B Side) | Yr | NM |
|---|---|---|---|
| ❑ SN-16220 | Green Light | 1981 | 8.00 |
| ❑ SN-16221 | I'm Nearly Famous | 1981 | 8.00 |
| ❑ SN-16253 | Every Face Tells a Story | 1981 | 8.00 |
| ❑ SW-17018 | We Don't Talk Anymore | 1979 | 10.00 |
| ❑ SW-17039 | I'm No Hero | 1980 | 10.00 |
| ❑ SW-17059 | Wired for Sound | 1981 | 10.00 |
| ❑ ST-17081 | Now You See Me, Now You Don't | 1982 | 10.00 |
| ❑ ST-17105 | Give a Little Bit More | 1983 | 10.00 |

**EPIC**

| Number | Title (A Side/B Side) | Yr | NM |
|---|---|---|---|
| ❑ LN 24063 [M] | Summer Holiday | 1963 | 40.00 |
| ❑ LN 24089 [M] | It's All in the Game | 1964 | 30.00 |
| ❑ LN 24115 [M] | Cliff Richard in Spain | 1965 | 30.00 |
| ❑ BN 26063 [S] | Summer Holiday | 1963 | 50.00 |
| ❑ BN 26089 [S] | It's All in the Game | 1964 | 40.00 |
| ❑ BN 26115 [S] | Cliff Richard in Spain | 1965 | 40.00 |

**ROCKET**

| Number | Title (A Side/B Side) | Yr | NM |
|---|---|---|---|
| ❑ PIG-2210 | I'm Nearly Famous | 1976 | 12.00 |
| ❑ PIG-2268 | Every Face Tells a Story | 1977 | 12.00 |
| ❑ BXL1-2958 | Green Light | 1978 | 12.00 |

**WORD**

| Number | Title (A Side/B Side) | Yr | NM |
|---|---|---|---|
| ❑ WR-8306 | Walking in the Light | 1985 | 12.00 |

## RICHARD AND JIM

**CAPITOL**

| Number | Title (A Side/B Side) | Yr | NM |
|---|---|---|---|
| ❑ ST 2058 [S] | Folk Songs and Country Sounds | 1964 | 25.00 |
| ❑ T 2058 [M] | Folk Songs and Country Sounds | 1964 | 20.00 |
| ❑ ST 2287 [S] | Two Boys from Alabama | 1965 | 25.00 |
| ❑ T 2287 [M] | Two Boys from Alabama | 1965 | 20.00 |

## RICHARDS, ANN

**ATCO**

| Number | Title (A Side/B Side) | Yr | NM |
|---|---|---|---|
| ❑ 33-136 [M] | Ann, Man! | 1961 | 40.00 |
| ❑ SD 33-136 [S] | Ann, Man! | 1961 | 60.00 |

**CAPITOL**

| Number | Title (A Side/B Side) | Yr | NM |
|---|---|---|---|
| ❑ ST 1087 [S] | I'm Shooting High | 1959 | 60.00 |
| ❑ T 1087 [M] | I'm Shooting High | 1959 | 50.00 |
| ❑ ST 1406 [S] | The Many Moods of Ann Richards | 1960 | 80.00 |
| ❑ T 1406 [M] | The Many Moods of Ann Richards | 1960 | 60.00 |
| ❑ ST 1495 [S] | Two Much! | 1961 | 80.00 |
| ❑ T 1495 [M] | Two Much! | 1961 | 60.00 |

**VEE JAY**

| Number | Title (A Side/B Side) | Yr | NM |
|---|---|---|---|
| ❑ LP-1070 [M] | Live...At the Losers | 1963 | 40.00 |
| ❑ SR-1070 [S] | Live...At the Losers | 1963 | 50.00 |

## RICHARDS, EMIL

**ABC IMPULSE!**

| Number | Title (A Side/B Side) | Yr | NM |
|---|---|---|---|
| ❑ AS-9182 [S] | Spirit of '76 | 1968 | 20.00 |
| ❑ AS-9188 [S] | Journey to Bliss | 1969 | 20.00 |

**UNI**

| Number | Title (A Side/B Side) | Yr | NM |
|---|---|---|---|
| ❑ 3003 [M] | New Time Element | 1967 | 25.00 |
| ❑ 3008 [M] | New Sound | 1967 | 25.00 |
| ❑ 73003 [S] | New Time Element | 1967 | 20.00 |
| ❑ 73008 [S] | New Sound | 1967 | 20.00 |

## RICHARDS, JOHNNY

**BETHLEHEM**

| Number | Title (A Side/B Side) | Yr | NM |
|---|---|---|---|
| ❑ BCP-6011 [M] | Something Else by Johnny Richards | 1956 | 80.00 |

**CAPITOL**

| Number | Title (A Side/B Side) | Yr | NM |
|---|---|---|---|
| ❑ T 885 [M] | Wide Range | 1957 | 60.00 |
| *—Turquoise label* | | | |
| ❑ T 981 [M] | Experiments In Sound | 1958 | 40.00 |
| *—Turquoise label* | | | |

**CORAL**

| Number | Title (A Side/B Side) | Yr | NM |
|---|---|---|---|
| ❑ CRL 757304 [S] | Walk Softly/Run Wild | 1959 | 80.00 |

**ROULETTE**

| Number | Title (A Side/B Side) | Yr | NM |
|---|---|---|---|
| ❑ R-25351 [M] | Aqui Se Habla Espanol | 1967 | 25.00 |
| ❑ SR-25351 [S] | Aqui Se Habla Espanol | 1967 | 30.00 |
| ❑ R-52008 [M] | The Rites of Diablo | 1958 | 80.00 |
| ❑ SR-52008 [S] | The Rites of Diablo | 1958 | 60.00 |
| ❑ SR-52114 [S] | My Fair Lady, My Way | 1964 | 40.00 |

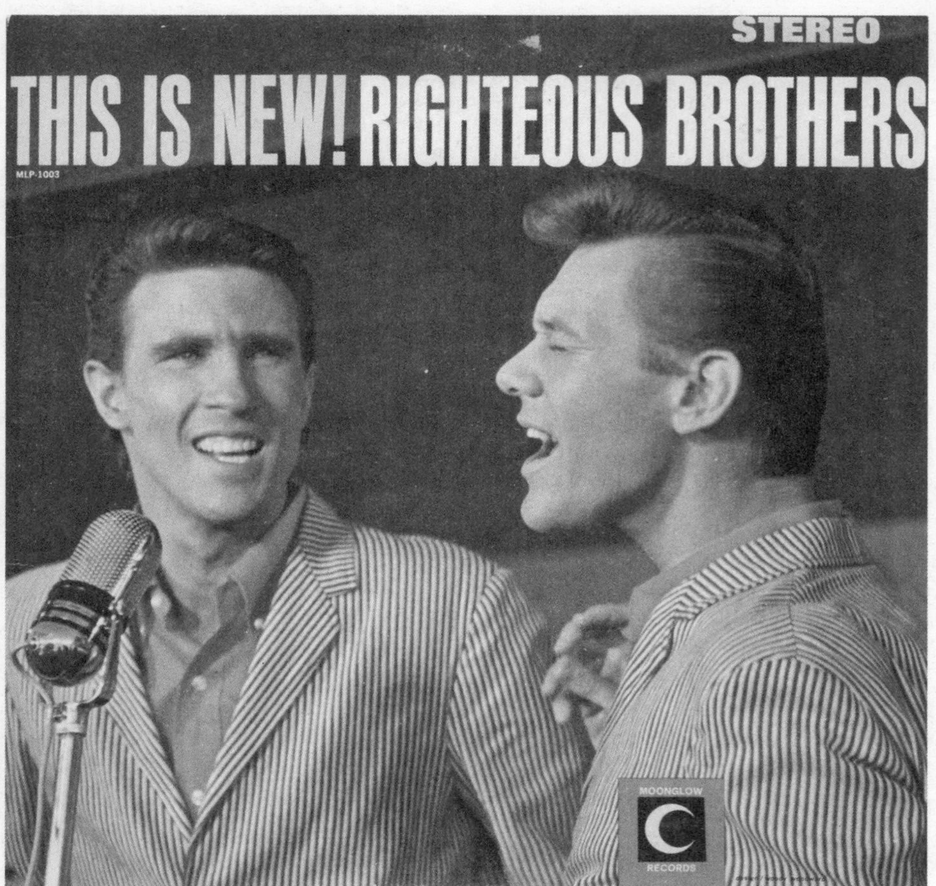


The Righteous Brothers, *This Is New!,* Moonglow 1003, 1965, stereo, $60.

| Number | Title (A Side/B Side) | Yr | NM |
|---|---|---|---|
| **RICHARDS, TRUDY** | | | |
| CAPITOL | | | |
| ❑ T 838 [M] | Crazy in Love | 1957 | 30.00 |
| **RICHARDSON, JEROME** | | | |
| NEW JAZZ | | | |
| ❑ NJLP-8205 [M] | Jerome Richardson Sextet | 1958 | 80.00 |
| *—Purple label* | | | |
| ❑ NJLP-8205 [M] | Jerome Richardson Sextet | 1965 | 25.00 |
| *—Blue label, trident logo at right* | | | |
| ❑ NJLP-8226 [M] | Roamin' with Richardson | 1959 | 80.00 |
| *—Purple label* | | | |
| ❑ NJLP-8226 [M] | Roamin' with Richardson | 1965 | 25.00 |
| *—Blue label, trident logo at right* | | | |
| UNITED ARTISTS | | | |
| ❑ UAJ-14006 [M] | Going to the Movies | 1962 | 30.00 |
| ❑ UAJS-15006 [S] | Going to the Movies | 1962 | 40.00 |
| VERVE | | | |
| ❑ V-8729 [M] | Groove Merchant | 1967 | 20.00 |
| **RICHARDSON, JIMMY** | | | |
| STARDAY | | | |
| ❑ SLP-126 [M] | Sweet with a Beat | 1960 | 30.00 |
| **RICHARDSON, WALLY** | | | |
| PRESTIGE | | | |
| ❑ PRST-7569 | Soul Guru | 1969 | 20.00 |
| **RICHARDSON, WARREN S., JR.** | | | |
| COTILLION | | | |
| ❑ SD 9013 | Warren S. Richardson, Jr. | 1970 | 30.00 |
| **RICHIE, LITTLE JOE** See LITTLE JOE. | | | |
| **RICHMAN, JONATHAN, AND THE MODERN LOVERS** | | | |
| BESERKLEY | | | |
| ❑ BZ-0048 | Jonathan Richman and the Modern Lovers | 1976 | 30.00 |
| *—Distributed by GRT* | | | |
| ❑ JBZ 0048 | Jonathan Richman and the Modern Lovers | 1976 | 25.00 |
| *—Distributed by Playboy/CBS* | | | |
| ❑ BZ-0050 | The Modern Lovers | 1976 | 30.00 |
| *—Distributed by GRT* | | | |
| ❑ JBZ 0050 | The Modern Lovers | 1978 | 25.00 |
| *—Distributed by Playboy/CBS* | | | |
| ❑ BZ-0053 | Rock 'N' Roll with the Modern Lovers | 1977 | 18.00 |
| *—Distributed by Janus/GRT* | | | |
| ❑ JBZ 0055 | Modern Lovers "Live" | 1978 | 14.00 |
| *—Distributed by Playboy/CBS* | | | |
| ❑ JBZ 0060 | Back in Your Life | 1979 | 10.00 |
| *—Distributed by Playboy/CBS* | | | |
| ❑ 10060 | Back in Your Life | 1980 | 12.00 |
| *—Reissue -- change in distributing label to Elektra* | | | |
| ❑ PZ 34800 | Rock 'N' Roll with the Modern Lovers | 1977 | 14.00 |
| *—Distributed by Playboy/CBS* | | | |
| BOMP! | | | |
| ❑ 4021 | The Original Modern Lovers | 1981 | 20.00 |
| *—Same album as Mohawk release* | | | |
| HOME OF THE HITS | | | |
| ❑ HH-1910 | The Modern Lovers | 1975 | 50.00 |
| MOHAWK | | | |
| ❑ SCALP 0002 | The Original Modern Lovers | 1981 | 25.00 |
| RHINO | | | |
| ❑ RNLP 70091 | The Modern Lovers | 1986 | 12.00 |
| *—Reissue* | | | |
| ❑ RNLP 70092 | Jonathan Richman and the Modern Lovers | 1986 | 12.00 |
| *—Reissue* | | | |
| ❑ RNLP 70093 | Rock 'N' Roll with the Modern Lovers | 1986 | 12.00 |
| *—Reissue* | | | |
| ❑ RNLP 70094 | Modern Lovers "Live" | 1986 | 12.00 |
| *—Reissue* | | | |
| ❑ RNLP 70095 | Back in Your Life | 1986 | 12.00 |
| *—Reissue* | | | |
| ROUNDER | | | |
| ❑ 9014 | Modern Lovers '88 | 1988 | 12.00 |
| ❑ 9021 | Jonathan Richman | 1989 | 12.00 |
| ❑ 9024 | Jonathan Goes Country | 1990 | 12.00 |
| SIRE | | | |
| ❑ 23939 | Jonathan Sings! | 1983 | 12.00 |
| VAPOR | | | |
| ❑ 47086 | I'm So Confused | 1998 | 15.00 |
| ❑ 48216 | Her Mystery Not of High Heels and Eye Shadow | 2001 | 15.00 |

| Number | Title (A Side/B Side) | Yr | NM |
|---|---|---|---|
| **RICHMOND, DANNIE** | | | |
| IMPULSE! | | | |
| ❑ A-98 [M] | Dannie Richmond | 1966 | 20.00 |
| ❑ AS-98 [S] | Dannie Richmond | 1966 | 25.00 |
| **RICKS, JIMMY** Also see THE RAVENS. | | | |
| JUBILEE | | | |
| ❑ JGS-8021 | Tell Her You Love Her | 1969 | 50.00 |
| MAINSTREAM | | | |
| ❑ S-6050 [S] | Vibrations | 1965 | 60.00 |
| ❑ 56050 [M] | Vibrations | 1965 | 50.00 |
| SIGNATURE | | | |
| ❑ SM-1032 [M] | Jimmy Ricks | 1961 | 200.00 |
| *—White label promo* | | | |
| ❑ SM-1032 [M] | Jimmy Ricks | 1961 | 300.00 |
| **RIDDLE, NELSON** | | | |
| ALSHIRE | | | |
| ❑ 5203 | Bridge Over Troubled Water | 197? | 10.00 |
| AVON | | | |
| ❑ 10170 | Avon Wishes You a Happy Holiday and a Joyous New Year | 1970 | 15.00 |
| *—Given to Avon salespeople* | | | |
| CAPITOL | | | |
| ❑ T 753 [M] | The Tender Touch | 1956 | 25.00 |
| ❑ T 813 [M] | Hey, Let Yourself Go | 1957 | 25.00 |
| ❑ T 893 [M] | C'mon, Get Happy | 1957 | 25.00 |
| ❑ T 915 [M] | Sea of Dreams | 1958 | 25.00 |
| ❑ ST 1148 [S] | The Joy of Living | 1959 | 25.00 |
| ❑ T 1148 [M] | The Joy of Living | 1959 | 20.00 |
| ❑ STAO 1259 [S] | Sing a Song with Riddle | 1960 | 25.00 |
| ❑ TAO 1259 [M] | Sing a Song with Riddle | 1960 | 20.00 |
| ❑ ST 1365 [S] | Can-Can | 1961 | 25.00 |
| ❑ T 1365 [M] | Can-Can | 1961 | 20.00 |
| ❑ ST 1571 [S] | Love Tide | 1961 | 25.00 |
| ❑ T 1571 [M] | Love Tide | 1961 | 20.00 |
| ❑ ST 1670 [S] | Magic Moments from "The Gay Life" | 1962 | 25.00 |
| ❑ T 1670 [M] | Magic Moments from "The Gay Life" | 1962 | 20.00 |
| ❑ ST 1771 [S] | Route 66 Theme and Other Great TV Themes | 1962 | 30.00 |
| ❑ T 1771 [M] | Route 66 Theme and Other Great TV Themes | 1962 | 25.00 |
| ❑ ST 1817 [S] | Love Is a Game of Poker | 1962 | 25.00 |
| ❑ T 1817 [M] | Love Is a Game of Poker | 1962 | 20.00 |
| ❑ ST 1869 [S] | More Hit TV Themes | 1963 | 25.00 |
| ❑ T 1869 [M] | More Hit TV Themes | 1963 | 20.00 |
| ❑ DT 1990 [P] | The Best of Nelson Riddle | 1963 | 15.00 |
| ❑ T 1990 [M] | The Best of Nelson Riddle | 1963 | 15.00 |
| ❑ SM-11764 | The Best of Nelson Riddle | 1976 | 10.00 |
| DAYBREAK | | | |
| ❑ DS 2015 | Viva Legrand! | 197? | 20.00 |
| HARMONY | | | |
| ❑ HS 11320 | Nelson Riddle and His Orchestra Play the Wonderful Nat King Cole Songs | 1969 | 12.00 |
| LIBERTY | | | |
| ❑ LRP-3508 [M] | The Bright and the Beautiful | 1967 | 15.00 |
| ❑ LST-3532 [M] | The Riddle of Today | 1967 | 20.00 |
| ❑ LST-7508 [S] | The Bright and the Beautiful | 1967 | 15.00 |
| ❑ LST-7532 [S] | The Riddle of Today | 1967 | 15.00 |
| PICKWICK | | | |
| ❑ PC 3007 [M] | Witchcraft | 1965 | 15.00 |
| ❑ SPC 3007 [R] | Witchcraft | 1965 | 12.00 |
| REPRISE | | | |
| ❑ R-6071 [M] | Come Blow Your Horn | 1963 | 15.00 |
| ❑ R9-6071 [S] | Come Blow Your Horn | 1963 | 20.00 |
| ❑ R-6120 [M] | "White on White," "Shangri-La," "Charade" and Other Hits of 1964 | 1964 | 15.00 |
| ❑ RS-6120 [S] | "White on White," "Shangri-La," "Charade" and Other Hits of 1964 | 1964 | 20.00 |
| ❑ R-6138 [M] | Great Music, Great Films, Great Sounds | 1964 | 15.00 |
| ❑ RS-6138 [S] | Great Music, Great Films, Great Sounds | 1964 | 20.00 |
| ❑ R-6162 [M] | Nat | 1965 | 15.00 |
| ❑ RS-6162 [S] | Nat | 1965 | 20.00 |
| SEARS | | | |
| ❑ SP-406 [M] | Witchcraft | 196? | 15.00 |
| ❑ SPS-406 [R] | Witchcraft | 196? | 12.00 |
| SOLID STATE | | | |
| ❑ SS-18013 | Music for Wives and Lovers | 1967 | 20.00 |
| ❑ ST-91083 | Music for Wives and Lovers | 1967 | 25.00 |
| *—Capitol Record Club edition* | | | |
| SUNSET | | | |
| ❑ SUS-5233 | The Riddle Touch | 1968 | 12.00 |
| UNITED ARTISTS | | | |
| ❑ UAS 6670 | The Contemporary Sound of Nelson Riddle | 1968 | 20.00 |

| Number | Title (A Side/B Side) | Yr | NM |
|---|---|---|---|
| ❑ ST-91566 | The Contemporary Sound of Nelson Riddle | 1968 | 25.00 |
| *—Capitol Record Club edition* | | | |
| **RIDERS OF THE PURPLE SAGE, THE** See FOY WILLING. | | | |
| **RIDLEY, LARRY** | | | |
| STRATA-EAST | | | |
| ❑ SES-19759 | Sum of the Parts | 1975 | 25.00 |
| **RIEDEL, GEORGE** | | | |
| PHILIPS | | | |
| ❑ PHS 600140 [S] | Jazz Ballet | 1964 | 20.00 |
| **RIG** | | | |
| CAPITOL | | | |
| ❑ ST-473 | Rig | 1970 | 20.00 |
| **RIGHTEOUS BROTHERS, THE** | | | |
| HAVEN | | | |
| ❑ ST-9201 | Give It to the People | 1974 | 15.00 |
| ❑ ST-9203 | Sons of Mrs. Righteous | 1975 | 15.00 |
| MGM | | | |
| ❑ GAS-102 | The Righteous Brothers (Golden Archive Series) | 1970 | 15.00 |
| ❑ SE-4885 | The History of the Righteous Brothers | 1973 | 15.00 |
| MOONGLOW | | | |
| ❑ MLP-1001 [M] | Right Now! | 1963 | 40.00 |
| ❑ MSP-1001 [S] | Right Now! | 1963 | 60.00 |
| ❑ MLP-1002 [M] | Some Blue-Eyed Soul | 1964 | 40.00 |
| ❑ MSP-1002 [S] | Some Blue-Eyed Soul | 1964 | 60.00 |
| ❑ MLP-1003 [M] | This Is New! | 1965 | 40.00 |
| ❑ MSP-1003 [S] | This Is New! | 1965 | 60.00 |
| ❑ MLP-1004 [M] | The Best of the Righteous Brothers | 1966 | 25.00 |
| ❑ MSP-1004 [S] | The Best of the Righteous Brothers | 1966 | 30.00 |
| PHILLES | | | |
| ❑ PHLP-4007 [M] | You've Lost That Lovin' Feelin' | 1964 | 25.00 |
| ❑ PHLPS-4007 [S] | You've Lost That Lovin' Feelin' | 1964 | 40.00 |
| ❑ PHLP-4008 [M] | Just Once in My Life | 1965 | 25.00 |
| ❑ PHLPS-4008 [S] | Just Once in My Life | 1965 | 40.00 |
| ❑ PHLP-4009 [M] | Back to Back | 1965 | 25.00 |
| ❑ PHLPS-4009 [S] | Back to Back | 1965 | 40.00 |
| ❑ ST-90677 [S] | Back to Back | 1965 | 40.00 |
| *—Capitol Record Club edition* | | | |
| ❑ T-90677 [M] | Back to Back | 1965 | 30.00 |
| *—Capitol Record Club edition* | | | |
| ❑ ST-90692 [S] | You've Lost That Lovin' Feelin' | 1965 | 50.00 |
| *—Capitol Record Club edition* | | | |
| ❑ T-90692 [M] | You've Lost That Lovin' Feelin' | 1965 | 50.00 |
| *—Capitol Record Club edition* | | | |
| RHINO | | | |
| ❑ R1-71488 [(2)] | Anthology | 1989 | 15.00 |
| VERVE | | | |
| ❑ V-5001 [M] | Soul and Inspiration | 1966 | 20.00 |
| ❑ V6-5001 [S] | Soul and Inspiration | 1966 | 25.00 |
| ❑ V-5004 [M] | Go Ahead and Cry | 1966 | 20.00 |
| ❑ V6-5004 [S] | Go Ahead and Cry | 1966 | 25.00 |
| ❑ V-5010 [M] | Sayin' Somethin' | 1967 | 20.00 |
| ❑ V6-5010 [S] | Sayin' Somethin' | 1967 | 25.00 |
| ❑ V-5020 [M] | Greatest Hits | 1967 | 25.00 |
| ❑ V6-5020 [S] | Greatest Hits | 1967 | 20.00 |
| ❑ V-5031 [M] | Souled Out | 1967 | 30.00 |
| ❑ V6-5031 [S] | Souled Out | 1967 | 20.00 |
| ❑ V6-5051 | Standards | 1968 | 20.00 |
| ❑ V6-5058 | One for the Road | 1968 | 20.00 |
| *—Without The Blossoms credited on the back cover* | | | |
| ❑ V6-5058 | One for the Road | 1968 | 30.00 |
| *—With The Blossoms credited on the back cover* | | | |
| ❑ V6-5071 | Greatest Hits, Vol. 2 | 1969 | 20.00 |
| ❑ V6-5076 | Re-Birth | 1970 | 20.00 |
| ❑ ST-90669 [S] | Soul and Inspiration | 1966 | 30.00 |
| *—Capitol Record Club edition* | | | |
| ❑ ST-90921 [S] | Go Ahead and Cry | 1966 | 30.00 |
| *—Capitol Record Club edition* | | | |
| ❑ ST-91057 [S] | Sayin' Somethin' | 1967 | 25.00 |
| *—Capitol Record Club edition* | | | |
| ❑ T-91057 [M] | Sayin' Somethin' | 1967 | 30.00 |
| *—Capitol Record Club edition* | | | |
| ❑ 823662-1 | Greatest Hits | 198? | 10.00 |
| **RILEY, BILLY LEE** | | | |
| GNP CRESCENDO | | | |
| ❑ GNP-2020 [M] | Billy Lee Riley | 1966 | 15.00 |
| ❑ GNPS-2020 [S] | Billy Lee Riley | 1966 | 20.00 |
| MERCURY | | | |
| ❑ MG-20958 [M] | The Whiskey A-Go-Go Presents Billy Lee Riley | 1964 | 20.00 |
| ❑ MG-20965 [M] | Big Harmonica Special | 1964 | 20.00 |
| ❑ MG-20974 [M] | Beatlemania Harmonica | 1965 | 20.00 |
| ❑ SR-60958 [S] | The Whiskey A-Go-Go Presents Billy Lee Riley | 1964 | 25.00 |
| ❑ SR-60965 [S] | Big Harmonica Special | 1964 | 25.00 |
| ❑ SR-60974 [S] | Beatlemania Harmonica | 1965 | 25.00 |

| Number | Title (A Side/B Side) | Yr | NM |
|---|---|---|---|
| **RILEY, JEANNIE C.** | | | |
| ALLEGIANCE | | | |
| ❑ AV-5026 | Tears, Joys and Memories | 198? | 10.00 |
| CAPITOL | | | |
| ❑ ST-177 | The Songs of Jeannie C. Riley | 1969 | 15.00 |
| LITTLE DARLIN' | | | |
| ❑ SLD 8011 | Sock Soul | 1968 | 20.00 |
| MGM | | | |
| ❑ SE-4805 | Give Myself a Party | 1972 | 12.00 |
| ❑ SE-4849 | Down to Earth | 1973 | 12.00 |
| ❑ SE-4891 | When Love Has Gone Away | 1973 | 12.00 |
| ❑ SE-4909 | Just Jeannie C. Riley | 1973 | 12.00 |
| PICKWICK | | | |
| ❑ 6098 | The Girl Most Likely | 197? | 10.00 |
| ❑ 6119 | The World of Country | 197? | 10.00 |
| PLANTATION | | | |
| ❑ PLM 1 [M] | Harper Valley P.T.A. | 1968 | 60.00 |
| ❑ PLP 1 [S] | Harper Valley P.T.A. | 1968 | 20.00 |
| ❑ PLP 2 | Yearbooks and Yesterdays | 1969 | 15.00 |
| ❑ PLP 3 | Things Go Better with Love | 1969 | 15.00 |
| ❑ PLP 8 | Country Girl | 1970 | 15.00 |
| ❑ PLP 11 | The Generation Gap | 1970 | 15.00 |
| ❑ PLP 13 | Jeannie C. Riley's Greatest Hits | 1971 | 15.00 |
| ❑ PLP 16 | Jeannie | 1971 | 15.00 |
| ❑ 508 | Country Queens | 197? | 12.00 |
| POWER PAK | | | |
| ❑ 250 | Country Gold | 197? | 10.00 |
| **RINCON SURFSIDE BAND, THE** | | | |
| DUNHILL | | | |
| ❑ D 50001 [M] | Surfing Songbook | 1965 | 200.00 |
| ❑ DS 50001 [S] | Surfing Songbook | 1965 | 300.00 |
| **RIOPELLE, JERRY** | | | |
| CAPITOL | | | |
| ❑ ST-732 | Jerry Riopelle | 1971 | 20.00 |
| ❑ ST-863 | Second Album | 1971 | 20.00 |
| **RIOT** | | | |
| FIRE-SIGN | | | |
| ❑ 87001 | Rock City | 1977 | 30.00 |
| **RIP CHORDS, THE** | | | |
| COLUMBIA | | | |
| ❑ CL 2151 [M] | Hey Little Cobra and Other Hot Rod Hits | 1964 | 40.00 |
| *—"Guaranteed High Fidelity" on label* | | | |
| ❑ CL 2151 [M] | Hey Little Cobra and Other Hot Rod Hits | 1966 | 25.00 |
| *—"360 Sound Mono" on label* | | | |
| ❑ CL 2216 [M] | Three Window Coupe | 1964 | 50.00 |
| ❑ CS 8951 [S] | Hey Little Cobra and Other Hot Rod Hits | 1964 | 50.00 |
| ❑ CS 9016 [S] | Three Window Coupe | 1964 | 70.00 |
| **RIPERTON, MINNIE** | | | |
| ACCORD | | | |
| ❑ SN-7205 | Wistful Memories | 1981 | 10.00 |
| CAPITOL | | | |
| ❑ SO-11936 | Minnie | 1979 | 10.00 |
| ❑ SN-12004 | Perfect Angel | 1979 | 10.00 |
| *—Reissue of Epic 32561* | | | |
| ❑ SN-12005 | Adventures in Paradise | 1979 | 10.00 |
| *—Reissue of Epic 33454* | | | |
| ❑ SN-12006 | Stay in Love | 1979 | 10.00 |
| *—Reissue of Epic 34191* | | | |
| ❑ SOO-12097 | Love Lives Forever | 1980 | 10.00 |
| ❑ ST-12189 | The Best of Minnie Riperton | 1981 | 10.00 |
| ❑ SN-16145 | Perfect Angel | 1980 | 8.00 |
| *—Budget-line reissue* | | | |
| ❑ SN-16146 | Adventures in Paradise | 1980 | 8.00 |
| *—Budget-line reissue* | | | |
| ❑ SN-16147 | Stay in Love | 1980 | 8.00 |
| *—Budget-line reissue* | | | |
| EPIC | | | |
| ❑ EQ 32561 [Q] | Perfect Angel | 1974 | 20.00 |
| ❑ KE 32561 | Perfect Angel | 1974 | 12.00 |
| ❑ PE 33454 | Adventures in Paradise | 1975 | 12.00 |
| ❑ PEQ 33454 [Q] | Adventures in Paradise | 1975 | 20.00 |
| ❑ PE 34191 | Stay in Love | 1977 | 12.00 |
| GRT | | | |
| ❑ 30001 | Come To My Garden | 1970 | 15.00 |
| JANUS | | | |
| ❑ 7011 | Come To My Garden | 1974 | 12.00 |
| *—Reissue of GRT LP* | | | |
| **RIPPY, RODNEY ALLEN** | | | |
| BELL | | | |
| ❑ 1311 | Take Life a Little Easier | 1974 | 20.00 |
| **RISERS, THE** | | | |
| IMPERIAL | | | |
| ❑ LP-9269 [M] | She's a Bad Motorcycle | 1964 | 100.00 |
| ❑ LP-12269 [S] | She's a Bad Motorcycle | 1964 | 150.00 |

| Number | Title (A Side/B Side) | Yr | NM |
|---|---|---|---|
| **RISING STORM, THE** | | | |
| ARF! ARF! | | | |
| ❑ 007 | Alive in Anover Again | 1983 | 120.00 |
| REMNANT | | | |
| ❑ BBA-3571 | Calm Before the Rising Storm | 1968 | 1200. |
| *—VG value 600; VG+ value 900* | | | |
| STANTON PARK | | | |
| ❑ 001 | Calm Before the Rising Storm | 1991 | 20.00 |
| *—Reissue of Remnant album* | | | |
| **RITENOUR, LEE** | | | |
| MOBILE FIDELITY | | | |
| ❑ 1-147 | Captain Fingers | 1985 | 25.00 |
| *—Audiophile vinyl* | | | |
| NAUTILUS | | | |
| ❑ NR-41 | Rit | 198? | 40.00 |
| *—Audiophile vinyl* | | | |
| **RITTER, TEX** Also see STAN KENTON AND TEX RITTER. | | | |
| BUCKBOARD | | | |
| ❑ BBS 1030 | Tex Ritter | 198? | 10.00 |
| CAPITOL | | | |
| ❑ ST-213 | Chuck Wagon Days | 1969 | 20.00 |
| ❑ ST-467 | Green Green Valley | 1970 | 20.00 |
| ❑ T 971 [M] | Songs from the Western Screen | 1958 | 80.00 |
| *—Turquoise or gray label* | | | |
| ❑ T 971 [M] | Songs from the Western Screen | 1959 | 40.00 |
| *—Black colorband label, logo at left* | | | |
| ❑ T 971 [M] | Songs from the Western Screen | 1962 | 25.00 |
| *—Black colorband label, logo at top* | | | |
| ❑ T 1100 [M] | Psalms | 1959 | 50.00 |
| *—Black colorband label, logo at left* | | | |
| ❑ T 1100 [M] | Psalms | 1962 | 25.00 |
| *—Black colorband label, logo at top* | | | |
| ❑ ST 1292 [S] | Blood on the Saddle | 1960 | 40.00 |
| *—Black colorband label, logo at left* | | | |
| ❑ ST 1292 [S] | Blood on the Saddle | 1962 | 25.00 |
| *—Black colorband label, logo at top* | | | |
| ❑ T 1292 [M] | Blood on the Saddle | 1960 | 30.00 |
| *—Black colorband label, logo at left* | | | |
| ❑ T 1292 [M] | Blood on the Saddle | 1962 | 20.00 |
| *—Black colorband label, logo at top* | | | |
| ❑ SW 1562 [S] | The Lincoln Hymns | 1961 | 40.00 |
| ❑ W 1562 [M] | The Lincoln Hymns | 1961 | 30.00 |
| ❑ SM-1623 | Hillbilly Heaven | 1976 | 10.00 |
| *—Reissue with new prefix* | | | |
| ❑ ST 1623 [S] | Hillbilly Heaven | 1961 | 40.00 |
| *—Black colorband label, logo at left* | | | |
| ❑ ST 1623 [S] | Hillbilly Heaven | 1962 | 25.00 |
| *—Black colorband label, logo at top* | | | |
| ❑ T 1623 [M] | Hillbilly Heaven | 1961 | 30.00 |
| *—Black colorband label, logo at left* | | | |
| ❑ T 1623 [M] | Hillbilly Heaven | 1962 | 20.00 |
| *—Black colorband label, logo at top* | | | |
| ❑ ST 1910 [S] | Border Affair | 1963 | 25.00 |
| ❑ T 1910 [M] | Border Affair | 1963 | 20.00 |
| ❑ ST 2402 [S] | The Friendly Voice of Tex Ritter | 1965 | 25.00 |
| ❑ T 2402 [M] | The Friendly Voice of Tex Ritter | 1965 | 20.00 |
| ❑ DT 2595 [R] | The Best of Tex Ritter | 1966 | 15.00 |
| ❑ T 2595 [M] | The Best of Tex Ritter | 1966 | 25.00 |
| ❑ ST 2743 [S] | Sweet Land of Liberty | 1967 | 25.00 |
| ❑ T 2743 [M] | Sweet Land of Liberty | 1967 | 30.00 |
| ❑ ST 2786 [S] | Just Beyond the Moon | 1967 | 25.00 |
| ❑ T 2786 [M] | Just Beyond the Moon | 1967 | 30.00 |
| ❑ ST 2890 [S] | Bum Tiddil Dee Bum Bum! | 1968 | 25.00 |
| ❑ T 2890 [M] | Bum Tiddil Dee Bum Bum! | 1968 | 50.00 |
| ❑ ST 2974 | Tex Ritter's Wild West | 1968 | 25.00 |
| ❑ H 4004 [10] | Cowboy Favorites | 195? | 180.00 |
| ❑ ST-11037 | Supercountrylegendary | 1972 | 15.00 |
| ❑ SKC-11241 [(3)] | An American Legend | 1973 | 30.00 |
| ❑ ST-11351 | Fall Away | 1974 | 15.00 |
| ❑ ST-11503 | Comin' After Jinny | 1976 | 15.00 |
| HILLTOP | | | |
| ❑ PTP-2020 [(2)] | My Kinda Songs | 197? | 15.00 |
| ❑ JS-6043 | Tex Ritter Sings His Hits | 196? | 12.00 |
| ❑ JS-6075 | Love You As Big As Texas | 196? | 12.00 |
| ❑ JS-6138 | High Noon | 196? | 12.00 |
| ❑ JS-6155 | Tex | 197? | 12.00 |
| LABREA | | | |
| ❑ L-8036 [M] | Jamboree, Nashville Style | 196? | 20.00 |
| ❑ LS-8036 [S] | Jamboree, Nashville Style | 196? | 25.00 |
| PREMIER | | | |
| ❑ 9023 | Tex Ritter and the Rio Grande River Boys | 196? | 12.00 |
| **RITZ, LYLE** | | | |
| VERVE | | | |
| ❑ MGV-2087 [M] | How About Uke? | 1957 | 40.00 |
| ❑ MGVS-6070 [S] | 50th State Jazz | 1960 | 40.00 |
| ❑ MGV-8333 [M] | 50th State Jazz | 1959 | 50.00 |
| ❑ V-8333 [M] | 50th State Jazz | 1961 | 25.00 |
| ❑ V6-8333 [S] | 50th State Jazz | 1961 | 20.00 |
| **RIVERA, HECTOR** | | | |
| WING | | | |
| ❑ MGW-12197 [M] | Let's Cha Cha Cha | 1960 | 20.00 |

### RIVERA, LUIS

| Number | Title (A Side/B Side) | Yr | NM |
|---|---|---|---|
| **IMPERIAL** | | | |
| ❑ LP-9139 [M] | Filet of Soul | 1961 | 30.00 |

### RIVERA, LUIS, AND DOC BAGBY

| Number | Title (A Side/B Side) | Yr | NM |
|---|---|---|---|
| **KING** | | | |
| ❑ 631 [M] | Battle of the Organs | 1959 | 100.00 |

### RIVERS, JERRY

| Number | Title (A Side/B Side) | Yr | NM |
|---|---|---|---|
| **STARDAY** | | | |
| ❑ SLP-281 [M] | Fantastic Fiddlin' and Tall Tales | 1964 | 30.00 |

### RIVERS, JOHNNY

| Number | Title (A Side/B Side) | Yr | NM |
|---|---|---|---|
| **ATLANTIC** | | | |
| ❑ SD 7301 | The Road | 1974 | 12.00 |
| **BIG TREE** | | | |
| ❑ BT 76004 | Outside Help | 1977 | 12.00 |
| **CAPITOL** | | | |
| ❑ ST 2161 [S] | The Sensational Johnny Rivers | 1964 | 25.00 |
| ❑ T 2161 [M] | The Sensational Johnny Rivers | 1964 | 20.00 |
| **COLUMBIA** | | | |
| ❑ FE 38429 | Not a Through Street | 1983 | 10.00 |
| ❑ PE 38429 | Not a Through Street | 1985 | 8.00 |
| *—Budget-line reissue* | | | |
| **EPIC** | | | |
| ❑ PE 33681 | New Lovers and Old Friends | 1975 | 12.00 |
| **IMPERIAL** | | | |
| ❑ LP-9264 [M] | Johnny Rivers at the Whiskey A-Go-Go | 1964 | 20.00 |
| *—Black label with pink and white at left* | | | |
| ❑ LP-9264 [M] | Johnny Rivers at the Whiskey A-Go-Go | 1966 | 12.00 |
| *—Black label with green and white at left* | | | |
| ❑ LP-9274 [M] | Here We A-Go-Go Again! | 1964 | 20.00 |
| *—Black label with pink and white at left* | | | |
| ❑ LP-9274 [M] | Here We A-Go-Go Again! | 1966 | 12.00 |
| *—Black label with green and white at left* | | | |
| ❑ LP-9280 [M] | Johnny Rivers In Action! | 1965 | 20.00 |
| *—Black label with pink and white at left* | | | |
| ❑ LP-9280 [M] | Johnny Rivers In Action! | 1966 | 12.00 |
| *—Black label with green and white at left* | | | |
| ❑ LP-9284 [M] | Meanwhile Back at the Whiskey a-Go-Go | 1965 | 20.00 |
| *—Black label with pink and white at left* | | | |
| ❑ LP-9284 [M] | Meanwhile Back at the Whiskey a-Go-Go | 1966 | 12.00 |
| *—Black label with green and white at left* | | | |
| ❑ LP-9293 [M] | Johnny Rivers Rocks the Folk | 1965 | 20.00 |
| *—Black label with pink and white at left* | | | |
| ❑ LP-9293 [M] | Johnny Rivers Rocks the Folk | 1966 | 12.00 |
| *—Black label with green and white at left* | | | |
| ❑ LP-9307 [M] | ...And I Know You Wanna Dance | 1966 | 12.00 |
| *—Black label with green and white at left* | | | |
| ❑ LP-9307 [M] | ...And I Know You Wanna Dance | 1966 | 20.00 |
| *—Black label with pink and white at left* | | | |
| ❑ LP-9324 [M] | Johnny Rivers' Golden Hits | 1966 | 15.00 |
| ❑ LP-9334 [M] | Changes | 1966 | 15.00 |
| ❑ LP-9341 [M] | Rewind | 1967 | 20.00 |
| ❑ LP-9372 [M] | Realization | 1968 | 40.00 |
| ❑ LP-12264 [S] | Johnny Rivers at the Whiskey A-Go-Go | 1964 | 25.00 |
| *—Black label with pink and white at left* | | | |
| ❑ LP-12264 [S] | Johnny Rivers at the Whiskey A-Go-Go | 1966 | 15.00 |
| *—Black label with green and white at left* | | | |
| ❑ LP-12274 [S] | Here We A-Go-Go Again! | 1964 | 25.00 |
| *—Black label with pink and white at left* | | | |
| ❑ LP-12274 [S] | Here We A-Go-Go Again! | 1966 | 15.00 |
| *—Black label with green and white at left* | | | |
| ❑ LP-12280 [S] | Johnny Rivers In Action! | 1965 | 25.00 |
| *—Black label with pink and white at left* | | | |
| ❑ LP-12280 [S] | Johnny Rivers In Action! | 1966 | 15.00 |
| *—Black label with green and white at left* | | | |
| ❑ LP-12284 [S] | Meanwhile Back at the Whiskey a-Go-Go | 1965 | 25.00 |
| *—Black label with pink and white at left* | | | |
| ❑ LP-12284 [S] | Meanwhile Back at the Whiskey a-Go-Go | 1966 | 15.00 |
| *—Black label with green and white at left* | | | |
| ❑ LP-12293 [S] | Johnny Rivers Rocks the Folk | 1965 | 25.00 |
| *—Black label with pink and white at left* | | | |
| ❑ LP-12293 [S] | Johnny Rivers Rocks the Folk | 1966 | 15.00 |
| *—Black label with green and white at left* | | | |
| ❑ LP-12307 [S] | ...And I Know You Wanna Dance | 1966 | 15.00 |
| *—Black label with green and white at left* | | | |
| ❑ LP-12307 [S] | ...And I Know You Wanna Dance | 1966 | 25.00 |
| *—Black label with pink and white at left* | | | |
| ❑ LP-12324 [S] | Johnny Rivers' Golden Hits | 1966 | 20.00 |
| ❑ LP-12334 [S] | Changes | 1966 | 20.00 |
| ❑ LP-12341 [S] | Rewind | 1967 | 20.00 |
| ❑ LP-12372 [S] | Realization | 1968 | 20.00 |
| ❑ LP-12427 | A Touch of Gold | 1969 | 20.00 |
| ❑ LP-16001 | Slim Slo Slider | 1970 | 20.00 |
| **LIBERTY** | | | |
| ❑ LN-10120 | The Best of Johnny Rivers | 1981 | 8.00 |
| ❑ LN-10121 | Changes | 1981 | 8.00 |
| *—Budget-line reissue* | | | |
| ❑ LN-10154 | Blue Suede Shoes | 1981 | 8.00 |
| *—Budget-line reissue* | | | |
| ❑ LO-12324 | Johnny Rivers' Golden Hits | 198? | 8.00 |
| *—Budget-line reissue* | | | |
| ❑ LW-12427 | A Touch of Gold | 198? | 8.00 |
| *—Budget-line reissue* | | | |
| **MCA** | | | |
| ❑ 917 | Greatest Hits | 1985 | 10.00 |
| **PICKWICK** | | | |
| ❑ PC-3022 [M] | Johnny Rivers | 196? | 15.00 |
| ❑ SPC-3022 [R] | Johnny Rivers | 196? | 10.00 |
| *—Later covers have "electronically enhanced for STEREO" at upper right* | | | |
| ❑ SPC-3022 [R] | Johnny Rivers | 196? | 12.00 |
| *—First pressing covers have no "electronically enhanced for STEREO" at upper right* | | | |
| ❑ SPC-3191 | If You Want It, I Got It | 196? | 12.00 |
| **RSO** | | | |
| ❑ RS-1-3082 | Borrowed Time | 1980 | 10.00 |
| **SEARS** | | | |
| ❑ SPS-417 | Mr. Teenage | 196? | 25.00 |
| ❑ SPS-487 | Groovin' | 1968 | 25.00 |
| **SOUL CITY** | | | |
| ❑ SC 1007-1 | Greatest Hits | 1998 | 20.00 |
| *—500 copies, each autographed by Johnny Rivers* | | | |
| **SUNSET** | | | |
| ❑ SUM-1157 [M] | Whiskey A-Go-Go Revisited | 1967 | 12.00 |
| ❑ SUS-5157 [S] | Whiskey A-Go-Go Revisited | 1967 | 10.00 |
| ❑ SUS-5251 | The Early Years | 1969 | 10.00 |
| **UNART** | | | |
| ❑ M-20007 [M] | The Great Johnny Rivers | 1967 | 12.00 |
| ❑ S-21007 [S] | The Great Johnny Rivers | 1967 | 12.00 |
| **UNITED ARTISTS** | | | |
| ❑ UA-LA075-F | Blue Suede Shoes | 1973 | 12.00 |
| ❑ USX-93 [(2)] | Johnny Rivers Superpak | 1971 | 20.00 |
| ❑ UA-LA253-G | The Very Best of Johnny Rivers | 1974 | 12.00 |
| ❑ UA-LA387-E | The Very Best of Johnny Rivers | 1975 | 12.00 |
| ❑ UA-LA486-G | Wild Night | 1976 | 12.00 |
| ❑ UAL-3386 [M] | Go, Johnny, Go | 1964 | 20.00 |
| ❑ UAS-5532 | Home Grown | 1971 | 15.00 |
| ❑ UAS-5650 | L.A. Reggae | 1972 | 15.00 |
| ❑ UAS-6386 [S] | Go, Johnny, Go | 1964 | 25.00 |
| ❑ ST-90813 [S] | Go, Johnny, Go | 1965 | 30.00 |
| *—Capitol Record Club edition* | | | |
| ❑ T-90813 [M] | Go, Johnny, Go | 1965 | 25.00 |
| *—Capitol Record Club edition* | | | |
| **WARNER BROS.** | | | |
| ❑ R133498 [S] | Johnny Rivers' Golden Hits | 197? | 30.00 |
| *—RCA Music Service edition of Imperial LP-12324 on "Burbank" palm trees label; why this was pressed on Warner Bros. is anyone's guess, but it doesn't appear to be an error* | | | |

### RIVERS, MAVIS

| Number | Title (A Side/B Side) | Yr | NM |
|---|---|---|---|
| **CAPITOL** | | | |
| ❑ ST 1210 [S] | Take a Number | 1959 | 40.00 |
| ❑ T 1210 [M] | Take a Number | 1959 | 30.00 |
| **REPRISE** | | | |
| ❑ R-2002 [M] | Mavis | 1961 | 30.00 |
| ❑ R9-2002 [S] | Mavis | 1961 | 40.00 |
| ❑ R-6074 [M] | Mavis Rivers Meets Shorty Rogers | 1963 | 25.00 |
| ❑ RS-6074 [S] | Mavis Rivers Meets Shorty Rogers | 1963 | 30.00 |
| **VEE JAY** | | | |
| ❑ VJ-1132 [M] | We Remember Mildred Bailey | 1964 | 25.00 |
| ❑ VJS-1132 [S] | We Remember Mildred Bailey | 1964 | 40.00 |

### RIVERS, SAM

| Number | Title (A Side/B Side) | Yr | NM |
|---|---|---|---|
| **BLUE NOTE** | | | |
| ❑ BLP-4184 [M] | Fuchsia Swing Song | 1964 | 25.00 |
| ❑ BLP-4206 [M] | Contours | 1965 | 25.00 |
| ❑ BLP-4249 [M] | A New Conception | 1966 | 25.00 |
| ❑ BST-84184 [S] | Fuchsia Swing Song | 1964 | 30.00 |
| *—With "New York, USA" address on label* | | | |
| ❑ BST-84184 [S] | Fuchsia Swing Song | 1967 | 20.00 |
| *—With "A Division of Liberty Records" on label* | | | |
| ❑ BST-84206 [S] | Contours | 1965 | 30.00 |
| *—With "New York, USA" address on label* | | | |
| ❑ BST-84206 [S] | Contours | 1967 | 20.00 |
| *—With "A Division of Liberty Records" on label* | | | |
| ❑ BST-84249 [S] | A New Conception | 1966 | 30.00 |
| *—With "New York, USA" address on label* | | | |
| ❑ BST-84249 [S] | A New Conception | 1967 | 20.00 |
| *—With "A Division of Liberty Records" on label* | | | |

### RIVERSIDE JAZZ STARS, THE

| Number | Title (A Side/B Side) | Yr | NM |
|---|---|---|---|
| **RIVERSIDE** | | | |
| ❑ RLP-397 [M] | A Jazz Version of "Kean" | 1961 | 30.00 |
| ❑ RS-9397 [S] | A Jazz Version of "Kean" | 1961 | 40.00 |

### RIVIERAS, THE (1)

| Number | Title (A Side/B Side) | Yr | NM |
|---|---|---|---|
| **POST** | | | |
| ❑ 2000 | The Rivieras Sing | 196? | 40.00 |

### RIVIERAS, THE (2)

| Number | Title (A Side/B Side) | Yr | NM |
|---|---|---|---|
| **RIVIERA** | | | |
| ❑ 701 [M] | Campus Party | 1964 | 250.00 |
| **U.S.A.** | | | |
| ❑ 102 [M] | Let's Have a Party | 1964 | 150.00 |

### RIVINGTONS, THE

| Number | Title (A Side/B Side) | Yr | NM |
|---|---|---|---|
| **LIBERTY** | | | |
| ❑ LRP-3282 [M] | Doin' the Bird | 1963 | 100.00 |
| ❑ LST-7282 [S] | Doin' the Bird | 1963 | 200.00 |

### RIZZI, TONY

| Number | Title (A Side/B Side) | Yr | NM |
|---|---|---|---|
| **STARLITE** | | | |
| ❑ 6002 [10] | Tony Rizzi Guitar | 1954 | 50.00 |

### ROACH, FREDDIE

| Number | Title (A Side/B Side) | Yr | NM |
|---|---|---|---|
| **BLUE NOTE** | | | |
| ❑ BLP-4113 [M] | Down to Earth | 1962 | 25.00 |
| ❑ BLP-4128 [M] | Mo' Greens, Please | 1963 | 25.00 |
| ❑ BLP-4158 [M] | Good Move | 1964 | 25.00 |
| ❑ BLP-4168 [M] | Brown Sugar | 1964 | 25.00 |
| ❑ BLP-4190 [M] | All That's Good | 1965 | 25.00 |
| ❑ BST-84113 [S] | Down to Earth | 1962 | 30.00 |
| *—With "New York, USA" address on label* | | | |
| ❑ BST-84128 [S] | Mo' Greens, Please | 1963 | 30.00 |
| *—With "New York, USA" address on label* | | | |
| ❑ BST-84158 [S] | Good Move | 1964 | 30.00 |
| *—With "New York, USA" address on label* | | | |
| ❑ BST-84168 [S] | Brown Sugar | 1964 | 30.00 |
| *—With "New York, USA" address on label* | | | |
| ❑ BST-84190 [S] | All That's Good | 1965 | 30.00 |
| *—With "New York, USA" address on label* | | | |
| **PRESTIGE** | | | |
| ❑ PRLP-7490 [M] | The Soul Book | 1967 | 30.00 |
| ❑ PRST-7490 [S] | The Soul Book | 1967 | 20.00 |
| ❑ PRLP-7507 [M] | Mocha Motion | 1967 | 30.00 |
| ❑ PRST-7507 [S] | Mocha Motion | 1967 | 20.00 |
| ❑ PRLP-7521 [M] | My People — Soul People | 1967 | 30.00 |
| ❑ PRST-7521 [S] | My People — Soul People | 1967 | 20.00 |

### ROACH, MAX

| Number | Title (A Side/B Side) | Yr | NM |
|---|---|---|---|
| **ABC IMPULSE!** | | | |
| ❑ AS-8 [S] | Percussion Bitter Sweet | 1968 | 20.00 |
| ❑ AS-16 [S] | It's Time | 1968 | 40.00 |
| **ARGO** | | | |
| ❑ LP-623 [M] | Max | 1958 | 50.00 |
| ❑ LPS-623 [S] | Max | 1958 | 40.00 |
| **ATLANTIC** | | | |
| ❑ 1435 [M] | Max Roach Trio Featuring the Legendary Hasaan | 1965 | 20.00 |
| ❑ SD 1435 [S] | Max Roach Trio Featuring the Legendary Hasaan | 1965 | 25.00 |
| ❑ 1467 [M] | Drums Unlimited | 1966 | 20.00 |
| ❑ SD 1467 [S] | Drums Unlimited | 1966 | 25.00 |
| ❑ SD 1510 [S] | Members Don't Get Weary | 1968 | 20.00 |
| **CANDID** | | | |
| ❑ CD-8002 [M] | We Insist — Freedom Now Suite | 1960 | 60.00 |
| ❑ CS-9002 [S] | We Insist — Freedom Now Suite | 1960 | 60.00 |
| **DEBUT** | | | |
| ❑ DLP-13 [10] | Max Roach Quartet Featuring Hank Mobley | 1954 | 400.00 |
| **EMARCY** | | | |
| ❑ MG-36098 [M] | Max Roach + 4 | 1957 | 100.00 |
| ❑ MG-36108 [M] | Jazz in 3/4 Time | 1957 | 80.00 |
| ❑ MG-36127 [M] | The Max Roach 4 Plays Charlie Parker | 1958 | 80.00 |
| ❑ MG-36132 [M] | Max Roach + 4 on the Chicago Scene | 1958 | 60.00 |
| ❑ MG-36140 [M] | Max Roach Plus Four At Newport | 1958 | 60.00 |
| ❑ MG-36144 [M] | Max Roach with the Boston Percussion Ensemble | 1958 | 60.00 |
| ❑ SR-80001 [S] | Max Roach + 4 | 1959 | 80.00 |
| ❑ SR-80002 [S] | Jazz in 3/4 Time | 1959 | 60.00 |
| ❑ SR-80010 [S] | Max Roach Plus Four At Newport | 1959 | 50.00 |
| ❑ SR-80015 [S] | Max Roach with the Boston Percussion Ensemble | 1959 | 50.00 |
| ❑ SR-80019 [S] | The Max Roach 4 Plays Charlie Parker | 1959 | 60.00 |
| **FANTASY** | | | |
| ❑ 6007 [M] | Speak Brother, Speak | 1963 | 25.00 |
| ❑ 86007 [S] | Speak Brother, Speak | 1963 | 30.00 |
| **HAT ART** | | | |
| ❑ 4026 [(4)] | The Long March | 1986 | 30.00 |
| **IMPULSE!** | | | |
| ❑ A-8 [M] | Percussion Bitter Sweet | 1961 | 30.00 |

| Number | Title (A Side/B Side) | Yr | NM |
|---|---|---|---|
| ❑ AS-8 [S] | Percussion Bitter Sweet | 1961 | 40.00 |
| ❑ A-16 [M] | It's Time | 1962 | 20.00 |
| ❑ AS-16 [S] | It's Time | 1962 | 30.00 |

JAZZLAND

| Number | Title (A Side/B Side) | Yr | NM |
|---|---|---|---|
| ❑ JLP-79 [M] | Conversation | 1962 | 30.00 |
| ❑ JLP-979 [S] | Conversation | 1962 | 25.00 |

MERCURY

| Number | Title (A Side/B Side) | Yr | NM |
|---|---|---|---|
| ❑ MG-20491 [M] | Quiet As It's Kept | 1959 | 40.00 |
| ❑ MG-20539 [M] | Moon Faced and Starry-Eyed | 1960 | 40.00 |
| ❑ MG-20760 [M] | Parisian Sketches | 1962 | 30.00 |
| ❑ MG-20911 [M] | The Many Sides of Max | 1964 | 25.00 |
| ❑ SR-60170 [S] | Quiet As It's Kept | 1959 | 50.00 |
| ❑ SR-60215 [S] | Moon Faced and Starry-Eyed | 1960 | 50.00 |
| ❑ SR-60760 [S] | Parisian Sketches | 1962 | 40.00 |
| ❑ SR-60911 [S] | The Many Sides of Max | 1964 | 30.00 |

RIVERSIDE

| Number | Title (A Side/B Side) | Yr | NM |
|---|---|---|---|
| ❑ RLP 12-280 [M] | Deeds, Not Words | 1958 | 50.00 |
| ❑ RLP-1122 [S] | Deeds, Not Words | 1959 | 40.00 |

TIME

| Number | Title (A Side/B Side) | Yr | NM |
|---|---|---|---|
| ❑ S-2087 [S] | Max Roach | 1962 | 40.00 |
| ❑ 52087 [M] | Max Roach | 1962 | 40.00 |
| ❑ ST-70003 [S] | Award Winning Drummer | 1959 | 60.00 |
| ❑ T-70003 [M] | Award Winning Drummer | 1959 | 80.00 |

## ROACH, MAX/ART BLAKEY

BLUE NOTE

| Number | Title (A Side/B Side) | Yr | NM |
|---|---|---|---|
| ❑ BLP-5010 [10] | Max Roach Quintet / Art Blakey and His Band | 1952 | 1000. |

## ROACH, MAX, AND ANTHONY BRAXTON

HAT HUT

| Number | Title (A Side/B Side) | Yr | NM |
|---|---|---|---|
| ❑ 06 [(2)] | One in Two — Two in One | 1980 | 20.00 |

## ROACH, MAX, AND CLIFFORD BROWN

See CLIFFORD BROWN.

## ROACH, MAX; SONNY CLARK; GEORGE DUVIVIER

TIME

| Number | Title (A Side/B Side) | Yr | NM |
|---|---|---|---|
| ❑ S-2101 [S] | Max Roach, Sonny Clark, George Duvivier | 1962 | 40.00 |
| ❑ 52101 [M] | Max Roach, Sonny Clark, George Duvivier | 1962 | 30.00 |

## ROACH, MAX, AND STAN LEVEY

LIBERTY

| Number | Title (A Side/B Side) | Yr | NM |
|---|---|---|---|
| ❑ LRP-3064 [M] | Drummin' the Blues | 1957 | 80.00 |

## ROACH, MAX, AND ARCHIE SHEPP

HAT HUT

| Number | Title (A Side/B Side) | Yr | NM |
|---|---|---|---|
| ❑ 13 [(2)] | The Long March | 1980 | 20.00 |

## ROAD, THE

KAMA SUTRA

| Number | Title (A Side/B Side) | Yr | NM |
|---|---|---|---|
| ❑ KSBS-2012 | The Road | 1970 | 15.00 |
| —Reissue of 8075 | | | |
| ❑ KSBS-2032 [(2)] | Cognition | 1970 | 20.00 |
| ❑ KLPS-8075 | The Road | 1969 | 20.00 |

## ROAD RUNNERS, THE

LONDON

| Number | Title (A Side/B Side) | Yr | NM |
|---|---|---|---|
| ❑ PS 381 [S] | The New Mustang (And Other Hot Rod Hits) | 1964 | 300.00 |
| ❑ LL 3381 [M] | The New Mustang (And Other Hot Rod Hits) | 1964 | 200.00 |

## ROBBINS, ADELAIDE/MARIAN MCPARTLAND/ BARBARA CARROLL

SAVOY

| Number | Title (A Side/B Side) | Yr | NM |
|---|---|---|---|
| ❑ MG-12097 [M] | Lookin' for a Boy | 1957 | 50.00 |

## ROBBINS, HARGUS "PIG"

CHART

| Number | Title (A Side/B Side) | Yr | NM |
|---|---|---|---|
| ❑ CHS-1011 | One More Time | 196? | 15.00 |

ELEKTRA

| Number | Title (A Side/B Side) | Yr | NM |
|---|---|---|---|
| ❑ 6E-129 | Pig in a Poke | 1978 | 12.00 |
| ❑ 6E-185 | Unbreakable Hearts | 1979 | 12.00 |
| ❑ 7E-1110 | Country Instrumentalist of the Year | 1977 | 12.00 |

TIME

| Number | Title (A Side/B Side) | Yr | NM |
|---|---|---|---|
| ❑ S-2107 [S] | A Bit of Country Piano | 1963 | 25.00 |
| ❑ 52107 [M] | A Bit of Country Piano | 1963 | 20.00 |

## ROBBINS, MARTY

ARTCO

| Number | Title (A Side/B Side) | Yr | NM |
|---|---|---|---|
| ❑ 110 | The Best of Marty Robbins | 1973 | 40.00 |

COLUMBIA

| Number | Title (A Side/B Side) | Yr | NM |
|---|---|---|---|
| ❑ GP 15 [(2)] | Marty's Country | 1969 | 25.00 |
| ❑ CL 976 [M] | The Song of Robbins | 1957 | 100.00 |
| —Red and black label with six "eye" logos | | | |
| ❑ CL 976 [M] | The Song of Robbins | 1963 | 20.00 |
| —Red label with "Guaranteed High Fidelity" or "360 Sound Mono" | | | |
| ❑ CL 1087 [M] | Song of the Islands | 1957 | 120.00 |
| —Red and black label with six "eye" logos | | | |
| ❑ CL 1087 [M] | Song of the Islands | 1963 | 20.00 |
| —Red label with "Guaranteed High Fidelity" or "360 Sound Mono" | | | |
| ❑ CL 1189 [M] | Marty Robbins | 1958 | 80.00 |
| —Red and black label with six "eye" logos | | | |
| ❑ CL 1189 [M] | Marty Robbins | 1963 | 20.00 |
| —Red label with "Guaranteed High Fidelity" or "360 Sound Mono" | | | |
| ❑ CL 1325 [M] | Marty's Greatest Hits | 1959 | 80.00 |
| —Red and black label with six "eye" logos | | | |
| ❑ CL 1325 [M] | Marty's Greatest Hits | 1963 | 20.00 |
| —Red label with "Guaranteed High Fidelity" or "360 Sound Mono" | | | |
| ❑ CL 1349 [M] | Gunfighter Ballads and Trail Songs | 1959 | 30.00 |
| —Red and black label with six "eye" logos | | | |
| ❑ CL 1349 [M] | Gunfighter Ballads and Trail Songs | 1963 | 15.00 |
| —Red label with "Guaranteed High Fidelity" or "360 Sound Mono" | | | |
| ❑ CL 1481 [M] | More Gunfighter Ballads and Trail Songs | 1960 | 30.00 |
| —Red and black label with six "eye" logos | | | |
| ❑ CL 1481 [M] | More Gunfighter Ballads and Trail Songs | 1963 | 15.00 |
| —Red label with "Guaranteed High Fidelity" or "360 Sound Mono" | | | |
| ❑ CL 1635 [M] | More Greatest Hits | 1961 | 25.00 |
| —Red and black label with six "eye" logos | | | |
| ❑ CL 1635 [M] | More Greatest Hits | 1963 | 15.00 |
| —Red label with "Guaranteed High Fidelity" or "360 Sound Mono" | | | |
| ❑ CL 1666 [M] | Just a Little Sentimental | 1961 | 25.00 |
| —Red and black label with six "eye" logos | | | |
| ❑ CL 1666 [M] | Just a Little Sentimental | 1963 | 15.00 |
| —Red label with "Guaranteed High Fidelity" or "360 Sound Mono" | | | |
| ❑ CL 1801 [M] | Marty After Midnight | 1962 | 20.00 |
| —Red label with "Guaranteed High Fidelity" | | | |
| ❑ CL 1801 [M] | Marty After Midnight | 1962 | 50.00 |
| —Red and black label with six "eye" logos | | | |
| ❑ CL 1801 [M] | Marty After Midnight | 1965 | 15.00 |
| —Red label with "360 Sound Mono" | | | |
| ❑ CL 1855 [M] | Portrait of Marty | 1962 | 40.00 |
| ❑ CL 1855/CS 8655 | Portrait of Marty Bonus Photo | 1962 | 30.00 |
| ❑ CL 1918 [M] | Devil Woman | 1962 | 25.00 |
| —Red label with "Guaranteed High Fidelity" | | | |
| ❑ CL 1918 [M] | Devil Woman | 1965 | 15.00 |
| —Red label with "360 Sound Mono" | | | |
| ❑ CL 2040 [M] | Hawaii's Calling Me | 1963 | 25.00 |
| —Red label with "Guaranteed High Fidelity" | | | |
| ❑ CL 2040 [M] | Hawaii's Calling Me | 1965 | 15.00 |
| —Red label with "360 Sound Mono" | | | |
| ❑ CL 2072 [M] | Return of the Gunfighter | 1963 | 20.00 |
| —Red label with "Guaranteed High Fidelity" | | | |
| ❑ CL 2072 [M] | Return of the Gunfighter | 1965 | 15.00 |
| —Red label with "360 Sound Mono" | | | |
| ❑ CL 2176 [M] | Island Woman | 1964 | 30.00 |
| —Red label with "Guaranteed High Fidelity" | | | |
| ❑ CL 2176 [M] | Island Woman | 1965 | 20.00 |
| —Red label with "360 Sound Mono" | | | |
| ❑ CL 2220 [M] | R.F.D. | 1964 | 20.00 |
| —Red label with "Guaranteed High Fidelity" | | | |
| ❑ CL 2220 [M] | R.F.D. | 1965 | 15.00 |
| —Red label with "360 Sound Mono" | | | |
| ❑ CL 2304 [M] | Turn the Lights Down Low | 1965 | 15.00 |
| —Red label with "360 Sound Mono" | | | |
| ❑ CL 2304 [M] | Turn the Lights Down Low | 1965 | 25.00 |
| —Red label with "Guaranteed High Fidelity" | | | |
| ❑ CL 2448 [M] | What God Has Done | 1966 | 15.00 |
| ❑ CL 2527 [M] | The Drifter | 1966 | 15.00 |
| ❑ CL 2601 [10] | Rock 'N Roll 'N Robbins | 1956 | 1000. |
| ❑ CL 2645 [M] | My Kind of Country | 1967 | 25.00 |
| ❑ CL 2725 [M] | Tonight Carmen | 1967 | 30.00 |
| ❑ CL 2735 [M] | Christmas with Marty Robbins | 1967 | 50.00 |
| ❑ CL 2817 [M] | By the Time I Get to Phoenix | 1968 | 60.00 |
| ❑ CS 8158 [S] | Gunfighter Ballads and Trail Songs | 1959 | 40.00 |
| —Red and black label with six "eye" logos | | | |
| ❑ CS 8158 [S] | Gunfighter Ballads and Trail Songs | 1963 | 20.00 |
| —Red label with "360 Sound Stereo" | | | |
| ❑ CS 8158 [S] | Gunfighter Ballads and Trail Songs | 1971 | 10.00 |
| —Orange label | | | |
| ❑ PC 8158 | Gunfighter Ballads and Trail Songs | 198? | 8.00 |
| —Reissue with new prefix | | | |
| ❑ CS 8272 [S] | More Gunfighter Ballads and Trail Songs | 1960 | 40.00 |
| —Red and black label with six "eye" logos | | | |
| ❑ CS 8272 [S] | More Gunfighter Ballads and Trail Songs | 1963 | 20.00 |
| —Red label with "360 Sound Stereo" | | | |
| ❑ CS 8272 [S] | More Gunfighter Ballads and Trail Songs | 1971 | 10.00 |
| —Orange label | | | |
| ❑ PC 8272 | More Gunfighter Ballads and Trail Songs❑ More | 198? | 8.00 |
| —Reissue with new prefix | | | |
| ❑ CS 8435 [S] | More Greatest Hits | 1961 | 30.00 |
| —Red and black label with six "eye" logos | | | |
| ❑ CS 8435 [S] | More Greatest Hits | 1963 | 20.00 |
| —Red label with "360 Sound Stereo" | | | |
| ❑ CS 8435 [S] | More Greatest Hits | 1971 | 10.00 |
| —Orange label | | | |
| ❑ PC 8435 | More Greatest Hits | 198? | 8.00 |
| —Reissue with new prefix | | | |
| ❑ CS 8466 [S] | Just a Little Sentimental | 1961 | 30.00 |
| —Red and black label with six "eye" logos | | | |
| ❑ CS 8466 [S] | Just a Little Sentimental | 1963 | 20.00 |
| —Red label with "360 Sound Stereo" | | | |
| ❑ CS 8601 [S] | Marty After Midnight | 1962 | 30.00 |
| —Red label with "360 Sound Stereo" in black | | | |
| ❑ CS 8601 [S] | Marty After Midnight | 1962 | 80.00 |
| —Red and black label with six "eye" logos | | | |
| ❑ CS 8601 [S] | Marty After Midnight | 1965 | 20.00 |
| —Red label with "360 Sound Stereo" in white | | | |
| ❑ CS 8639 [P] | Marty's Greatest Hits | 1962 | 30.00 |
| —Red label with "360 Sound Stereo" in black | | | |
| ❑ CS 8639 [P] | Marty's Greatest Hits | 1965 | 20.00 |
| —Red label with "360 Sound Stereo" in white | | | |
| ❑ CS 8639 [P] | Marty's Greatest Hits | 1970 | 10.00 |
| —Orange label | | | |
| ❑ PC 8639 | Marty's Greatest Hits | 198? | 8.00 |
| —Reissue with new prefix | | | |
| ❑ CS 8655 [S] | Portrait of Marty | 1962 | 50.00 |
| ❑ CS 8718 [S] | Devil Woman | 1962 | 30.00 |
| —Red label with "360 Sound Stereo" in black | | | |
| ❑ CS 8718 [S] | Devil Woman | 1965 | 20.00 |
| —Red label with "360 Sound Stereo" in white | | | |
| ❑ CS 8718 [S] | Devil Woman | 1970 | 10.00 |
| —Orange label | | | |
| ❑ CS 8840 [S] | Hawaii's Calling Me | 1963 | 30.00 |
| —Red label with "360 Sound Stereo" in black | | | |
| ❑ CS 8840 [S] | Hawaii's Calling Me | 1965 | 20.00 |
| —Red label with "360 Sound Stereo" in white | | | |
| ❑ CS 8872 [S] | Return of the Gunfighter | 1963 | 25.00 |
| —Red label with "360 Sound Stereo" in black | | | |
| ❑ CS 8872 [S] | Return of the Gunfighter | 1965 | 20.00 |
| —Red label with "360 Sound Stereo" in white | | | |
| ❑ CS 8872 [S] | Return of the Gunfighter | 1970 | 10.00 |
| —Orange label | | | |
| ❑ CS 8976 [S] | Island Woman | 1964 | 40.00 |
| —Red label with "360 Sound Stereo" in black | | | |
| ❑ CS 8976 [S] | Island Woman | 1965 | 30.00 |
| —Red label with "360 Sound Stereo" in white | | | |
| ❑ CS 9020 [S] | R.F.D. | 1964 | 25.00 |
| —Red label with "360 Sound Stereo" in black | | | |
| ❑ CS 9020 [S] | R.F.D. | 1965 | 20.00 |
| —Red label with "360 Sound Stereo" in white | | | |
| ❑ CS 9104 [S] | Turn the Lights Down Low | 1965 | 20.00 |
| —Red label with "360 Sound Stereo" in white | | | |
| ❑ CS 9104 [S] | Turn the Lights Down Low | 1965 | 30.00 |
| —Red label with "360 Sound Stereo" in black | | | |
| ❑ CS 9248 [S] | What God Has Done | 1966 | 20.00 |
| —Red "360 Sound" label | | | |
| ❑ CS 9248 [S] | What God Has Done | 1970 | 10.00 |
| —Orange label | | | |
| ❑ CS 9327 [S] | The Drifter | 1966 | 20.00 |
| —Red "360 Sound" label | | | |
| ❑ CS 9327 [S] | The Drifter | 1970 | 10.00 |
| —Orange label | | | |
| ❑ CS 9421 [R] | The Song of Robbins | 1967 | 15.00 |
| —Red "360 Sound" label | | | |
| ❑ CS 9421 [R] | The Song of Robbins | 1970 | 10.00 |
| —Orange label | | | |
| ❑ CS 9425 [R] | Song of the Islands | 1967 | 15.00 |
| ❑ CS 9445 [S] | My Kind of Country | 1967 | 20.00 |
| ❑ CS 9525 [S] | Tonight Carmen | 1967 | 20.00 |
| —Red "360 Sound" label | | | |
| ❑ CS 9525 [S] | Tonight Carmen | 1970 | 10.00 |
| —Orange label | | | |
| ❑ 3C 9535 | Christmas with Marty Robbins | 198? | 10.00 |
| —Budget-line reissue | | | |
| ❑ CS 9535 [S] | Christmas with Marty Robbins | 1967 | 30.00 |
| ❑ CS 9617 [M] | By the Time I Get to Phoenix | 1968 | 50.00 |
| —"Special Mono Radio Station Copy" with stereo number and "Mono" on white label | | | |
| ❑ CS 9617 [S] | By the Time I Get to Phoenix | 1968 | 20.00 |
| ❑ CS 9725 | I Walk Alone | 1968 | 20.00 |
| —Red "360 Sound" label | | | |
| ❑ CS 9725 | I Walk Alone | 1970 | 10.00 |
| —Orange label | | | |
| ❑ CS 9811 | It's a Sin | 1969 | 20.00 |
| —Red "360 Sound" label | | | |
| ❑ CS 9811 | It's a Sin | 1970 | 10.00 |
| —Orange label | | | |
| ❑ CS 9978 | My Woman, My Woman, My Wife | 1970 | 15.00 |
| —Orange label | | | |
| ❑ CS 9978 | My Woman, My Woman, My Wife | 1970 | 20.00 |
| —Red "360 Sound" label | | | |
| ❑ PC 30316 | El Paso | 198? | 8.00 |
| —Reissue of Harmony 30316 | | | |
| ❑ C 30571 | Marty Robbins' Greatest Hits Vol. III | 1971 | 15.00 |
| ❑ PC 30571 | Marty Robbins' Greatest Hits Vol. III | 198? | 8.00 |
| —Budget-line reissue | | | |
| ❑ C 30816 | Today | 1971 | 15.00 |
| ❑ G 30881 [(2)] | The World of Marty Robbins | 1971 | 20.00 |
| ❑ KC 31341 | Bound for Old Mexico (Great Hits from South of the Border) | 1973 | 15.00 |
| ❑ CG 31361 [(2)] | All Time Greatest Hits | 1972 | 18.00 |
| ❑ KG 31361 [(2)] | Marty Robbins' All-Time Greatest Hits | 1972 | 20.00 |
| ❑ KC 31628 | I've Got a Woman's Love | 1972 | 15.00 |
| ❑ KC 32586 | Have I Told You Lately That I Love You | 1974 | 15.00 |
| ❑ KC 33476 | No Sign of Loneliness Here | 1976 | 12.00 |

| Number | Title (A Side/B Side) | Yr | NM |
|---|---|---|---|
| ❑ CG 33630 [(2)] | Gunfighter Ballads and Trail Songs/My Woman, My Woman, My Wife | 1976 | 15.00 |
| ❑ PC 34303 | El Paso City | 1976 | 12.00 |
| *—No bar code on cover* | | | |
| ❑ PC 34303 | El Paso City | 198? | 8.00 |
| *—With bar code on cover* | | | |
| ❑ PC 34448 | Adios Amigo | 1977 | 12.00 |
| *—No bar code on cover* | | | |
| ❑ PC 34448 | Adios Amigo | 198? | 8.00 |
| *—With bar code on cover* | | | |
| ❑ KC 35040 | Don't Let Me Touch You | 1977 | 12.00 |
| ❑ JC 35446 | The Performer | 1979 | 12.00 |
| ❑ KC 35629 | Greatest Hits Vol. IV | 1978 | 12.00 |
| ❑ JC 36085 | All Around Cowboy | 1979 | 12.00 |
| ❑ PC 36085 | All Around Cowboy | 198? | 8.00 |
| *—Budget-line reissue* | | | |
| ❑ JC 36507 | With Love | 1980 | 12.00 |
| ❑ JC 36860 | Everything I've Always Wanted | 1981 | 12.00 |
| ❑ FC 37353 | Encore | 1981 | 12.00 |
| ❑ PC 37353 | Encore | 198? | 8.00 |
| *—Budget-line reissue* | | | |
| ❑ FC 37541 | The Legend | 1982 | 12.00 |
| ❑ PC 37541 | The Legend | 1985 | 8.00 |
| *—Budget-line reissue* | | | |
| ❑ FC 37995 | Come Back to Me | 1982 | 12.00 |
| ❑ PC 37995 | Come Back to Me | 198? | 8.00 |
| *—Budget-line reissue* | | | |
| ❑ FC 38309 | Biggest Hits | 1982 | 12.00 |
| ❑ FC 38603 | Some Memories Just Won't Die | 1983 | 12.00 |
| ❑ C2 38870 [(2)] | A Lifetime of Song 1951-1982 | 1983 | 15.00 |
| ❑ KC2 39575 [(2)] | Long, Long Ago | 1984 | 15.00 |
| **COLUMBIA LIMITED EDITION** | | | |
| ❑ LE 10022 | Portrait of Marty | 197? | 10.00 |
| ❑ LE 10030 | It's a Sin | 197? | 10.00 |
| ❑ LE 10033 | My Kind of Country | 197? | 10.00 |
| ❑ LE 10045 | By the Time I Get to Phoenix | 197? | 10.00 |
| ❑ LE 10046 | Today | 197? | 10.00 |
| ❑ LE 10144 | R.F.D. | 197? | 10.00 |
| ❑ LE 10145 | Turn the Lights Down Low | 197? | 10.00 |
| ❑ LE 10189 | Tonight Carmen | 197? | 10.00 |
| ❑ LE 10575 | From the Heart | 197? | 10.00 |
| ❑ LE 10576 | Streets of Laredo | 197? | 10.00 |
| ❑ LE 10577 | The Story of My Life | 197? | 10.00 |
| ❑ LE 10578 | The Song of Robbins | 197? | 10.00 |
| ❑ LE 10579 | Devil Woman | 197? | 10.00 |
| **COLUMBIA MUSICAL TREASURY** | | | |
| ❑ P5S 5812 [(5)] | Marty | 1972 | 40.00 |
| **COLUMBIA RECORD CLUB** | | | |
| ❑ DS 445 | Bend in the River | 1968 | 40.00 |
| **COLUMBIA SPECIAL PRODUCTS** | | | |
| ❑ C 10980 [S] | Christmas with Marty Robbins | 1972 | 15.00 |
| *—Stereo reissue; "Distributed by Apex Rendezvous, Inc." on back cover* | | | |
| ❑ C 11122 | Marty's Greatest Hits | 1972 | 12.00 |
| ❑ C 11311 | By the Time I Get to Phoenix | 1972 | 15.00 |
| ❑ C 11513 | By the Time I Get to Phoenix | 1973 | 15.00 |
| ❑ P 12416 | Marty Robbins' Own Favorites | 1974 | 15.00 |
| ❑ P 13358 | Christmas with Marty Robbins | 1976 | 12.00 |
| ❑ P 14035 | Legendary Music Man | 1977 | 12.00 |
| ❑ P 14613 | The Best of Marty Robbins | 1978 | 10.00 |
| ❑ P 15594 | The Number One Cowboy | 1981 | 10.00 |
| ❑ P 15812 | Marty Robbins' Best | 1982 | 10.00 |
| ❑ P 16561 | Reflections | 1982 | 10.00 |
| ❑ 3P 16578 [(3)] | Classics | 1983 | 20.00 |
| ❑ P 16914 | Country Classics | 1983 | 10.00 |
| ❑ P 17120 | Sincerely | 1983 | 10.00 |
| ❑ P 17136 | Forever Yours | 1983 | 10.00 |
| ❑ P 17137 | That Country Feeling | 1983 | 10.00 |
| ❑ P 17138 | Banquet of Songs | 1983 | 10.00 |
| ❑ P 17159 | The Great Marty Robbins | 1983 | 10.00 |
| ❑ P 17206 | The Legendary Marty Robbins | 1983 | 10.00 |
| ❑ P 17209 | Country Cowboy | 1983 | 10.00 |
| ❑ P 17367 | Song of the Islands | 1983 | 10.00 |
| **DECCA** | | | |
| ❑ DL 75389 | This Much a Man | 1972 | 15.00 |
| **HARMONY** | | | |
| ❑ HS 11338 | Singing the Blues | 1969 | 15.00 |
| ❑ HS 11409 | The Story of My Life | 1970 | 15.00 |
| ❑ KH 30316 | El Paso | 1971 | 12.00 |
| ❑ KH 31257 | Marty Robbins Favorites | 1972 | 12.00 |
| ❑ H 31258 | Songs of the Islands | 1972 | 20.00 |
| ❑ KH 32286 | Streets of Laredo | 1973 | 12.00 |
| **MCA** | | | |
| ❑ 61 | This Much a Man | 1973 | 12.00 |
| *—Reissue of Decca LP* | | | |
| ❑ 342 | Marty Robbins | 1973 | 15.00 |
| ❑ 421 | Good'n Country | 1974 | 15.00 |
| **READER'S DIGEST** | | | |
| ❑ RDA-054/A [(5)] | His Greatest Hits and Finest Performances | 1983 | 30.00 |
| **TIME-LIFE** | | | |
| ❑ STW-109 | Country Music | 1981 | 12.00 |

### ROBBINS, RONNY

| Number | Title (A Side/B Side) | Yr | NM |
|---|---|---|---|
| **COLUMBIA** | | | |
| ❑ CS 9944 | Columbia Records Presents Marty Robbins Jr. | 1970 | 25.00 |
| *—As "Marty Robbins, Jr."* | | | |

### ROBBS, THE

| Number | Title (A Side/B Side) | Yr | NM |
|---|---|---|---|
| **MERCURY** | | | |
| ❑ MG-21130 [M] | The Robbs | 1967 | 40.00 |
| ❑ SR-61130 [S] | The Robbs | 1967 | 30.00 |

### ROBERTINO

| Number | Title (A Side/B Side) | Yr | NM |
|---|---|---|---|
| **KAPP** | | | |
| ❑ KL-1252 [M] | O Sole Mio | 1962 | 15.00 |
| ❑ KL-1293 [M] | The Young Italian Singing Sensation | 1962 | 15.00 |
| ❑ KL-1338 [M] | Italia Mia | 1963 | 15.00 |
| ❑ KL-1471 [M] | The Best of Robertino | 1966 | 12.00 |
| ❑ KS-3252 [S] | O Sole Mio | 1962 | 20.00 |
| ❑ KS-3293 [S] | The Young Italian Singing Sensation | 1962 | 20.00 |
| ❑ KS-3338 [S] | Italia Mia | 1963 | 20.00 |
| ❑ KS-3471 [S] | The Best of Robertino | 1966 | 15.00 |

### ROBERTS, GEORGE

| Number | Title (A Side/B Side) | Yr | NM |
|---|---|---|---|
| **COLUMBIA** | | | |
| ❑ CL 1384 [M] | Meet Mr. Roberts — George Roberts and His Big Bass Trombone | 195? | 80.00 |

### ROBERTS, HOWARD

| Number | Title (A Side/B Side) | Yr | NM |
|---|---|---|---|
| **CAPITOL** | | | |
| ❑ ST 1887 [S] | Color Him Funky | 1963 | 30.00 |
| ❑ ST 1961 [S] | H.R. Is A Dirty Guitar Player | 1963 | 20.00 |
| ❑ ST 2214 [S] | Something's Cookin' | 1965 | 20.00 |
| ❑ ST 2400 [S] | Goodies | 1965 | 20.00 |
| ❑ ST 2478 [S] | Whatever's Fair | 1966 | 20.00 |
| ❑ ST 2609 [S] | All-Time Great Instrumental Hits | 1966 | 20.00 |
| ❑ T 2716 [M] | Jaunty — Jolly | 1967 | 25.00 |
| ❑ T 2824 [M] | Guilty | 1967 | 20.00 |
| **VERVE** | | | |
| ❑ VSP-29 [M] | The Movin' Man | 1966 | 20.00 |
| ❑ MGV-8192 [M] | Mr. Roberts Plays Guitar | 1957 | 50.00 |
| ❑ V-8192 [M] | Mr. Roberts Plays Guitar | 1961 | 25.00 |
| ❑ MGV-8305 [M] | Good Pickin's | 1959 | 50.00 |
| ❑ V-8305 [M] | Good Pickin's | 1961 | 25.00 |
| ❑ V-8662 [M] | Velvet Groove | 1966 | 20.00 |

### ROBERTS, KENNY

| Number | Title (A Side/B Side) | Yr | NM |
|---|---|---|---|
| **STARDAY** | | | |
| ❑ SLP-336 [M] | Indian Love Call | 1965 | 40.00 |
| ❑ SLP-406 [M] | The Incredible Kenny Roberts | 1967 | 30.00 |
| ❑ SLP-434 | Country Music Singing Sensation | 1969 | 20.00 |
| **VOCALION** | | | |
| ❑ VL 73770 | Kenny Roberts Sings Country Songs | 196? | 12.00 |

### ROBERTS, LUCKEY

| Number | Title (A Side/B Side) | Yr | NM |
|---|---|---|---|
| **PERIOD** | | | |
| ❑ RL-1929 [M] | Happy Go Luckey | 1956 | 40.00 |

### ROBERTS, LUCKEY, AND WILLIE "THE LION" SMITH

| Number | Title (A Side/B Side) | Yr | NM |
|---|---|---|---|
| **GOOD TIME JAZZ** | | | |
| ❑ S-10035 [S] | Harlem Piano Solos | 1958 | 30.00 |
| ❑ L-12035 [M] | Harlem Piano Solos | 1958 | 40.00 |

### ROBERTS, PERNELL

| Number | Title (A Side/B Side) | Yr | NM |
|---|---|---|---|
| **RCA VICTOR** | | | |
| ❑ LPM-2662 [M] | Come All Ye Fair and Tender Ladies | 1963 | 30.00 |
| ❑ LSP-2662 [S] | Come All Ye Fair and Tender Ladies | 1963 | 40.00 |

### ROBERTS, ROCKY, AND THE AIREDALES

| Number | Title (A Side/B Side) | Yr | NM |
|---|---|---|---|
| **BRUNSWICK** | | | |
| ❑ BL 54133 [M] | Rocky Roberts and the Airedales | 1968 | 50.00 |
| *—Mono is yellow label promo only* | | | |
| ❑ BL 754133 [S] | Rocky Roberts and the Airedales | 1968 | 20.00 |

### ROBERTSON, DALE

| Number | Title (A Side/B Side) | Yr | NM |
|---|---|---|---|
| **RCA VICTOR** | | | |
| ❑ LPM-2158 [M] | Dale Robertson Presents His Album of Western Classics | 1959 | 80.00 |
| ❑ LSP-2158 [S] | Dale Robertson Presents His Album of Western Classics | 1959 | 100.00 |

### ROBERTSON, DON

| Number | Title (A Side/B Side) | Yr | NM |
|---|---|---|---|
| **RCA VICTOR** | | | |
| ❑ LPM-3348 [M] | Heart on My Sleeve | 1965 | 20.00 |
| ❑ LSP-3348 [S] | Heart on My Sleeve | 1965 | 25.00 |

### ROBERTSON, ROBBIE

| Number | Title (A Side/B Side) | Yr | NM |
|---|---|---|---|
| **GEFFEN** | | | |
| ❑ GEF-24160 | Robbie Robertson | 1987 | 10.00 |
| ❑ GEF 24303 | Storyville | 1991 | 25.00 |

### ROBERTSON, TEXAS JIM

| Number | Title (A Side/B Side) | Yr | NM |
|---|---|---|---|
| **DESIGN** | | | |
| ❑ DLP-115 [M] | Golden Hits of Country and Western Music | 196? | 12.00 |
| ❑ DLP-132 [M] | Sacred Country & Western Songs | 196? | 12.00 |
| **GRAND PRIX** | | | |
| ❑ 185 [M] | Texas Jim Robertson Sings the Great Hits of Country & Western | 196? | 15.00 |
| **MASTERSEAL** | | | |
| ❑ (# unknown) [10] | Eight Top Western Hits | 195? | 60.00 |
| **STRAND** | | | |
| ❑ 1016 [M] | Texas Jim Robertson | 1961 | 40.00 |

### ROBESON, PAUL

| Number | Title (A Side/B Side) | Yr | NM |
|---|---|---|---|
| **COLUMBIA MASTERWORKS** | | | |
| ❑ ML 2038 [10] | Swing Low Sweet Chariot | 1949 | 80.00 |
| ❑ ML 4105 [10] | Spirituals | 1949 | 80.00 |
| **VANGUARD** | | | |
| ❑ VSD-57/58 [(2)] | Essential Paul Robeson | 197? | 20.00 |
| ❑ VRS-9037 [M] | Spirituals and Folksongs | 1959 | 40.00 |
| ❑ VRS-9051 [M] | Paul Robeson at Carnegie Hall | 1960 | 20.00 |
| ❑ VRS-9193 [M] | Ballad for Americans: Carnegie Hall Concert, Vol. 2 | 1965 | 20.00 |
| ❑ VSD-79193 [S] | Ballad for Americans: Carnegie Hall Concert, Vol. 2 | 1965 | 20.00 |

### ROBINS, THE (1)

| Number | Title (A Side/B Side) | Yr | NM |
|---|---|---|---|
| **GNP CRESCENDO** | | | |
| ❑ GNPS-9034 | The Best of the Robins | 1975 | 15.00 |
| **WHIPPET** | | | |
| ❑ WLP-703 [M] | Rock 'n' Roll with the Robins | 1958 | 800.00 |

### ROBINSON, FLOYD

| Number | Title (A Side/B Side) | Yr | NM |
|---|---|---|---|
| **RCA VICTOR** | | | |
| ❑ LPM-2162 [M] | Floyd Robinson | 1960 | 80.00 |
| ❑ LSP-2162 [S] | Floyd Robinson | 1960 | 120.00 |

### ROBINSON, JIM

| Number | Title (A Side/B Side) | Yr | NM |
|---|---|---|---|
| **RIVERSIDE** | | | |
| ❑ RLP-369 [M] | Jim Robinson's New Orleans Band | 1961 | 30.00 |
| ❑ RLP-393 [M] | Jim Robinson Plays Spirituals and Blues | 1961 | 30.00 |

### ROBINSON, JIM, AND BILLIE AND DEDE PIERCE

| Number | Title (A Side/B Side) | Yr | NM |
|---|---|---|---|
| **ATLANTIC** | | | |
| ❑ 1409 [M] | Jim Robinson and Billie & DeDe Pierce | 1963 | 20.00 |
| ❑ SD 1409 [S] | Jim Robinson and Billie & DeDe Pierce | 1963 | 25.00 |

### ROBINSON, PERRY

| Number | Title (A Side/B Side) | Yr | NM |
|---|---|---|---|
| **SAVOY** | | | |
| ❑ MG-12177 [M] | Funk Dumpling | 1962 | 25.00 |

**ROBINSON, SMOKEY, AND THE MIRACLES** See THE MIRACLES.

### ROBINSON, SUGAR CHILE

| Number | Title (A Side/B Side) | Yr | NM |
|---|---|---|---|
| **CAPITOL** | | | |
| ❑ T 589 [M] | Boogie Woogie | 1955 | 120.00 |

### ROBINSON, SUGAR RAY

| Number | Title (A Side/B Side) | Yr | NM |
|---|---|---|---|
| **CONTINENTAL** | | | |
| ❑ CLP-16009 | I'm Still Swinging | 195? | 20.00 |

### ROBISON, CARSON

| Number | Title (A Side/B Side) | Yr | NM |
|---|---|---|---|
| **COLUMBIA** | | | |
| ❑ CL 2551 [10] | Square Dance | 1955 | 80.00 |
| ❑ CL 6029 [10] | Square Dance | 1949 | 80.00 |
| **MGM** | | | |
| ❑ E-13 [M] | Call Your Own Square Dances | 195? | 60.00 |
| ❑ E-557 [10] | Square Dances with Calls | 1952 | 60.00 |
| ❑ E-3258 [M] | Square Dances | 1955 | 30.00 |
| ❑ E-3594 [M] | Life Gets Tee-Jus, Don't It | 1958 | 50.00 |
| **RCA VICTOR** | | | |
| ❑ LPM-1238 [M] | Square Dances | 1956 | 30.00 |
| ❑ LPM-3030 [10] | Square Dances | 1952 | 60.00 |

### ROCCA, ANTONIO

| Number | Title (A Side/B Side) | Yr | NM |
|---|---|---|---|
| **MGM** | | | |
| ❑ E-4183 [M] | In This Corner...The Musical World of Antonio Rocca | 1963 | 20.00 |
| ❑ SE-4183 [S] | In This Corner...The Musical World of Antonio Rocca | 1963 | 25.00 |



**Except when noted otherwise, VG = 25% of NM, and VG+ = 50% of NM. (Example: VG = $2.00, VG+ = $4.00 and NM = $8.00.)**

### ROCHE, BETTY

| Number | Title (A Side/B Side) | Yr | NM |
|---|---|---|---|
| **BETHLEHEM** | | | |
| ❑ BCP-64 [M] | Take the "A" Train | 1956 | 120.00 |
| **PRESTIGE** | | | |
| ❑ PRLP-7187 [M] | Singin' and Swingin' | 1961 | 120.00 |
| ❑ PRLP-7198 [M] | Lightly and Politely | 1961 | 120.00 |

### ROCHES, THE

| Number | Title (A Side/B Side) | Yr | NM |
|---|---|---|---|
| **MCA** | | | |
| ❑ 10020 | We Three Kings | 1990 | 20.00 |
| **RHINO** | | | |
| ❑ RNEP-70616 [EP] | No Trespassing | 1987 | 10.00 |
| **WARNER BROS.** | | | |
| ❑ BSK 3298 | The Roches | 1979 | 10.00 |
| ❑ BSK 3475 | Nurds | 1980 | 10.00 |
| ❑ 23735 | Keep On Doing | 1982 | 10.00 |
| ❑ 25321 | Another World | 1985 | 10.00 |

### ROCK ISLAND

| Number | Title (A Side/B Side) | Yr | NM |
|---|---|---|---|
| **PROJECT 3** | | | |
| ❑ PR-4005 SD | Rock Island | 1970 | 30.00 |

### ROCK-A-TEENS, THE

| Number | Title (A Side/B Side) | Yr | NM |
|---|---|---|---|
| **ROULETTE** | | | |
| ❑ R-25109 [M] | Woo-Hoo | 1960 | 150.00 |
| ❑ SR-25109 [S] | Woo-Hoo | 1960 | 250.00 |

### ROCKATS

| Number | Title (A Side/B Side) | Yr | NM |
|---|---|---|---|
| **ISLAND** | | | |
| ❑ ILPS 9626 | Live at the Ritz | 1981 | 25.00 |

### ROCKETS, THE (4)

| Number | Title (A Side/B Side) | Yr | NM |
|---|---|---|---|
| **WHITE WHALE** | | | |
| ❑ WWS-7116 | The Rockets | 1968 | 25.00 |

### ROCKIN' FOO

| Number | Title (A Side/B Side) | Yr | NM |
|---|---|---|---|
| **HOBBIT** | | | |
| ❑ HB-5001 | Rockin' Foo | 1969 | 25.00 |

### ROCKIN' REBELS, THE

| Number | Title (A Side/B Side) | Yr | NM |
|---|---|---|---|
| **SWAN** | | | |
| ❑ SLP-509 [M] | Wild Weekend | 1963 | 200.00 |

### ROCKY FELLERS, THE

| Number | Title (A Side/B Side) | Yr | NM |
|---|---|---|---|
| **SCEPTER** | | | |
| ❑ SP-512 [M] | Killer Joe | 1964 | 30.00 |
| ❑ SPS-512 [S] | Killer Joe | 1964 | 40.00 |

### RODGERS, GENE

| Number | Title (A Side/B Side) | Yr | NM |
|---|---|---|---|
| **EMARCY** | | | |
| ❑ MG-36145 [M] | Jazz Comes to the Astor | 1958 | 40.00 |

### RODGERS, IKE

| Number | Title (A Side/B Side) | Yr | NM |
|---|---|---|---|
| **RIVERSIDE** | | | |
| ❑ RLP-1013 [10] | The Trombone of Ike Rodgers | 1953 | 80.00 |

### RODGERS, JIMMIE (1)

| Number | Title (A Side/B Side) | Yr | NM |
|---|---|---|---|
| **RCA VICTOR** | | | |
| ❑ DPL2-0075 [(2)] | The Legendary Jimmie Rodgers, Vol. 1 | 1974 | 40.00 |
| *—Special-products issue for Country Music Magazine* | | | |
| ❑ ANL1-1209 | My Rough and Rowdy Ways | 1976 | 10.00 |
| ❑ LPM-1232 [M] | Never No Mo' Blues — A Memorial Album | 1955 | 150.00 |
| ❑ LPM-1640 [M] | Train Whistle Blues | 1957 | 150.00 |
| ❑ LPM-2112 [M] | My Rough and Rowdy Ways | 1960 | 80.00 |
| ❑ LPM-2213 [M] | Jimmie the Kid | 1961 | 80.00 |
| ❑ CPL1-2504 | A Legendary Performer | 1977 | 10.00 |
| ❑ LPM-2531 [M] | Country Music Hall of Fame | 1962 | 80.00 |
| ❑ LPM-2634 [M] | The Short But Brilliant Life of Jimmie Rodgers | 1963 | 80.00 |
| ❑ LPM-2865 [M] | My Time Ain't Long | 1964 | 50.00 |
| ❑ LPT-3037 [10] | Yodelingly Yours Jimmie Rodgers, Volume 1 | 1953 | 400.00 |
| ❑ LPT-3038 [10] | Yodelingly Yours Jimmie Rodgers, Volume 2 | 1953 | 400.00 |
| ❑ LPT-3039 [10] | Yodelingly Yours Jimmie Rodgers, Volume 3 | 1953 | 400.00 |
| ❑ LPM-3073 [10] | Travelin' Blues | 1952 | 400.00 |
| ❑ AHL1-3315 | The Best of the Legendary Jimmie Rodgers | 197? | 8.00 |
| *—Reissue with new prefix* | | | |
| ❑ LPM-3315 [M] | The Best of the Legendary Jimmie Rodgers | 1965 | 40.00 |
| ❑ LSP-3315 [R] | The Best of the Legendary Jimmie Rodgers | 1965 | 20.00 |
| ❑ VPS-6091(e) [(2)] | This Is Jimmie Rodgers | 1971 | 20.00 |
| **ROUNDER** | | | |
| ❑ 1056 | First Sessions 1927-1928 | 1990 | 12.00 |
| ❑ 1057 | The Early Years 1928-1929 | 1990 | 12.00 |

### RODGERS, JIMMIE (2)

| Number | Title (A Side/B Side) | Yr | NM |
|---|---|---|---|
| **A&M** | | | |
| ❑ SP-130 [M] | Child of Clay | 1967 | 25.00 |
| ❑ SP-4130 [S] | Child of Clay | 1967 | 15.00 |
| ❑ SP-4187 | Windmills of Your Mind | 1969 | 15.00 |
| ❑ SP-4242 | Troubled Times | 1970 | 15.00 |
| **ACCORD** | | | |
| ❑ SN-7198 | Honeycomb & Other Hits | 198? | 10.00 |
| **DOT** | | | |
| ❑ DLP-3453 [M] | No One Will Ever Know | 1962 | 15.00 |
| ❑ DLP-3496 [M] | Jimmie Rodgers Folk Concert | 1963 | 15.00 |
| ❑ DLP-3502 [M] | My Favorite Hymns | 1963 | 15.00 |
| ❑ DLP-3525 [M] | Honeycomb & Kisses Sweeter Than Wine | 1963 | 15.00 |
| ❑ DLP-3556 [M] | The World I Used to Know | 1964 | 15.00 |
| *—Retitled version of above* | | | |
| ❑ DLP-3556 [M] | Town and Country | 1964 | 20.00 |
| ❑ DLP-3579 [M] | 12 Great Hits | 1964 | 15.00 |
| ❑ DLP-3614 [M] | Deep Purple | 1965 | 15.00 |
| ❑ DLP 3657 [M] | Christmas with Jimmie | 1965 | 12.00 |
| ❑ DLP-3687 [M] | The Nashville Sound | 1966 | 15.00 |
| ❑ DLP-3710 [M] | Country Music 1966 | 1966 | 15.00 |
| ❑ DLP-3717 [M] | It's Over | 1966 | 15.00 |
| ❑ DLP-3780 [M] | Love Me, Please Love Me | 1967 | 15.00 |
| ❑ DLP-3815 [M] | Golden Hits/15 Hits of Jimmie Rodgers | 1967 | 20.00 |
| ❑ DLP-25453 [S] | No One Will Ever Know | 1962 | 20.00 |
| ❑ DLP-25496 [S] | Jimmie Rodgers Folk Concert | 1963 | 20.00 |
| ❑ DLP-25502 [S] | My Favorite Hymns | 1963 | 20.00 |
| ❑ DLP-25525 [S] | Honeycomb & Kisses Sweeter Than Wine | 1963 | 20.00 |
| ❑ DLP-25556 [S] | The World I Used to Know | 1964 | 20.00 |
| *—Retitled version of above* | | | |
| ❑ DLP-25556 [S] | Town and Country | 1964 | 25.00 |
| ❑ DLP-25579 [S] | 12 Great Hits | 1964 | 20.00 |
| ❑ DLP-25614 [S] | Deep Purple | 1965 | 20.00 |
| ❑ DLP 25657 [S] | Christmas with Jimmie | 1965 | 15.00 |
| ❑ DLP-25687 [S] | The Nashville Sound | 1966 | 20.00 |
| ❑ DLP-25710 [S] | Country Music 1966 | 1966 | 20.00 |
| ❑ DLP-25717 [S] | It's Over | 1966 | 20.00 |
| ❑ DLP-25780 [S] | Love Me, Please Love Me | 1967 | 20.00 |
| ❑ DLP-25815 [S] | Golden Hits/15 Hits of Jimmie Rodgers | 1967 | 15.00 |
| **FORUM** | | | |
| ❑ F-9025 [M] | At Home with Jimmie Rodgers: An Evening of Folk Songs | 196? | 12.00 |
| ❑ SF-9025 [S] | At Home with Jimmie Rodgers: An Evening of Folk Songs | 196? | 12.00 |
| ❑ F-9049 [M] | Just for You | 196? | 12.00 |
| ❑ SF-9049 [S] | Just for You | 196? | 12.00 |
| ❑ F-9059 [M] | Jimmie Rodgers Sings Folk Songs | 196? | 12.00 |
| ❑ SF-9059 [S] | Jimmie Rodgers Sings Folk Songs | 196? | 12.00 |
| **HAMILTON** | | | |
| ❑ HL-114 [M] | 6 Favorite Hymns and 6 Favorite Folk Ballads | 1964 | 12.00 |
| ❑ HL-148 [M] | 12 Immortal Songs | 196? | 12.00 |
| ❑ HS-12114 [S] | 6 Favorite Hymns and 6 Favorite Folk Ballads | 1964 | 12.00 |
| ❑ HS-12148 [S] | 12 Immortal Songs | 196? | 12.00 |
| **PARAMOUNT** | | | |
| ❑ PAS-2-1042 [(2)] | Honeycomb | 1974 | 15.00 |
| **PICKWICK** | | | |
| ❑ PC-3040 [M] | Jimmie Rodgers | 196? | 12.00 |
| ❑ SPC-3040 [S] | Jimmie Rodgers | 196? | 12.00 |
| ❑ SPC-3106 | Am I That Easy to Forget | 196? | 12.00 |
| ❑ SPC-3599 | Big Hits | 197? | 10.00 |
| **ROULETTE** | | | |
| ❑ R-25020 [M] | Jimmie Rodgers | 1957 | 50.00 |
| *—Black label* | | | |
| ❑ R-25020 [M] | Jimmie Rodgers | 1959 | 25.00 |
| *—White label with colored spokes* | | | |
| ❑ R-25033 [M] | Number One Ballads | 1958 | 50.00 |
| *—Black label* | | | |
| ❑ R-25033 [M] | Number One Ballads | 1959 | 25.00 |
| *—White label with colored spokes* | | | |
| ❑ R-25042 [M] | Jimmie Rodgers Sings Folk Songs | 1958 | 50.00 |
| *—Black label* | | | |
| ❑ R-25042 [M] | Jimmie Rodgers Sings Folk Songs | 1959 | 25.00 |
| *—White label with colored spokes* | | | |
| ❑ R-25057 [M] | His Golden Year | 1959 | 25.00 |
| ❑ R-25071 [M] | TV Favorites | 1959 | 30.00 |
| ❑ SR-25071 [S] | TV Favorites | 1959 | 50.00 |
| ❑ R-25081 [M] | Twilight on the Trail | 1959 | 30.00 |
| ❑ SR-25081 [S] | Twilight on the Trail | 1959 | 50.00 |
| ❑ R 25095 [M] | It's Christmas Once Again | 1959 | 30.00 |
| ❑ SR 25095 [S] | It's Christmas Once Again | 1959 | 50.00 |
| ❑ R-25103 [M] | When the Spirit Moves You | 1960 | 30.00 |
| ❑ SR-25103 [S] | When the Spirit Moves You | 1960 | 40.00 |
| ❑ R-25128 [M] | At Home with Jimmie Rodgers: An Evening of Folk Songs | 1960 | 30.00 |
| ❑ SR-25128 [S] | At Home with Jimmie Rodgers: An Evening of Folk Songs | 1960 | 40.00 |
| ❑ R-25150 [M] | The Folk Song World of Jimmie Rodgers | 1961 | 30.00 |
| ❑ SR-25150 [S] | The Folk Song World of Jimmie Rodgers | 1961 | 40.00 |
| ❑ R-25160 [M] | The Best of Jimmie Rodgers' Folk Tunes | 1961 | 30.00 |
| ❑ SR-25160 [S] | The Best of Jimmie Rodgers' Folk Tunes | 1961 | 40.00 |
| *—Black vinyl* | | | |
| ❑ SR-25160 [S] | The Best of Jimmie Rodgers' Folk Tunes | 1961 | 250.00 |
| *—Red vinyl* | | | |
| ❑ R-25179 [M] | 15 Million Sellers | 1962 | 25.00 |
| ❑ SR-25179 [P] | 15 Million Sellers | 1962 | 20.00 |
| *—Orange and yellow label* | | | |
| ❑ SR-25179 [P] | 15 Million Sellers | 1962 | 30.00 |
| *—White label with colored spokes* | | | |
| ❑ R-25199 [M] | Folk Songs | 1963 | 20.00 |
| ❑ SR-25199 [S] | Folk Songs | 1963 | 25.00 |
| ❑ SR-42006 | Yours Truly | 1968 | 15.00 |

### RODNEY, RED

| Number | Title (A Side/B Side) | Yr | NM |
|---|---|---|---|
| **ARGO** | | | |
| ❑ LP-643 [M] | Red Rodney Returns | 1959 | 50.00 |
| ❑ LSP-643 [S] | Red Rodney Returns | 1959 | 40.00 |
| **FANTASY** | | | |
| ❑ 3208 [M] | Modern Music from Chicago | 195? | 80.00 |
| *—Black vinyl* | | | |
| ❑ 3208 [M] | Modern Music from Chicago | 1956 | 120.00 |
| *—Red vinyl* | | | |
| **PRESTIGE** | | | |
| ❑ PRLP-122 [10] | Red Rodney | 1952 | 200.00 |
| **SAVOY** | | | |
| ❑ MG-12148 [M] | Fiery Red Rodney | 1959 | 100.00 |
| **SIGNAL** | | | |
| ❑ S-1206 [M] | Red Rodney 1957 | 1957 | 600.00 |
| ❑ S-1206 [S] | Red Rodney 1957 | 199? | 25.00 |
| *—Classic Records reissue on audiophile vinyl (in stereo)* | | | |

### RODRIGUEZ, WILLIE

| Number | Title (A Side/B Side) | Yr | NM |
|---|---|---|---|
| **RIVERSIDE** | | | |
| ❑ RLP-469 [M] | Flatjacks | 1963 | 25.00 |
| ❑ RS-9469 [S] | Flatjacks | 1963 | 30.00 |

### ROE, TOMMY

| Number | Title (A Side/B Side) | Yr | NM |
|---|---|---|---|
| **ABC** | | | |
| ❑ S-467 [R] | Something for Everybody | 1968 | 50.00 |
| *—Issued in rechanneled stereo four years after its original release* | | | |
| ❑ 594 [M] | It's Now Winters Day | 1967 | 20.00 |
| ❑ S-594 [S] | It's Now Winters Day | 1967 | 25.00 |
| ❑ 610 [M] | Phantasy | 1967 | 40.00 |
| ❑ S-610 [S] | Phantasy | 1967 | 40.00 |
| ❑ S-683 | Dizzy | 1969 | 20.00 |
| ❑ S-700 | 12 in a Roe/A Collection of Tommy Roe's Greatest Hits | 1969 | 20.00 |
| ❑ S-714 | We Can Make Music | 1970 | 15.00 |
| ❑ S-732 | Beginnings | 1971 | 15.00 |
| ❑ X-762 | 16 Greatest Hits | 1972 | 15.00 |
| ❑ ST-90883 [S] | Sweet Pea | 1966 | 40.00 |
| *—Capitol Record Club issue* | | | |
| ❑ T-90883 [M] | Sweet Pea | 1966 | 40.00 |
| *—Capitol Record Club issue* | | | |
| **ABC-PARAMOUNT** | | | |
| ❑ 432 [M] | Sheila | 1962 | 40.00 |
| ❑ S-432 [S] | Sheila | 1962 | 50.00 |
| ❑ 467 [M] | Something for Everybody | 1964 | 30.00 |
| ❑ 575 [M] | Sweet Pea | 1966 | 30.00 |
| ❑ S-575 [S] | Sweet Pea | 1966 | 40.00 |
| **ACCORD** | | | |
| ❑ SN-7155 | Sheila | 1981 | 10.00 |
| **MCA** | | | |
| ❑ 1519 | Collectibles — Greatest Hits | 1982 | 8.00 |
| **MONUMENT** | | | |
| ❑ 7604 | Energy | 1977 | 10.00 |
| *—Reissue of 34182* | | | |
| ❑ 7614 | Full Bloom | 1977 | 10.00 |
| ❑ PZ 34182 | Energy | 1976 | 12.00 |
| **PICKWICK** | | | |
| ❑ SPC-3361 | Dizzy | 197? | 10.00 |

### ROGERS, BOB

| Number | Title (A Side/B Side) | Yr | NM |
|---|---|---|---|
| **INDIGO** | | | |
| ❑ 1501 [M] | All That and This, Too | 1961 | 40.00 |

### ROGERS, DAVID

| Number | Title (A Side/B Side) | Yr | NM |
|---|---|---|---|
| **ATLANTIC** | | | |
| ❑ SD 7266 | Just Thank Me | 1973 | 15.00 |
| ❑ SD 7283 | Farewell to the Ryman | 1973 | 20.00 |
| ❑ SD 7306 | Hey There Girl | 1974 | 15.00 |
| **COLUMBIA** | | | |
| ❑ CS 1023 | A World Called You | 1970 | 15.00 |
| ❑ C 30972 | She Don't Make Me Cry | 1971 | 15.00 |
| ❑ KC 31506 | Need You | 1972 | 15.00 |
| **REPUBLIC** | | | |
| ❑ 5003 | Lovingly | 197? | 12.00 |
| ❑ 5907 | I'm Gonna Love You Right Out of This World | 1976 | 12.00 |

Number Title (A Side/B Side) Yr NM

UNITED ARTISTS
❑ UA-LA422-G A Whole Lotta Livin' in a House 1975 12.00

**ROGERS, JULIE**

MERCURY
❑ MG-20981 [M] Julie Rogers 1965 15.00
❑ SR-60981 [S] Julie Rogers 1965 20.00

**ROGERS, KENNY** Also see THE BOBBY DOYLE THREE; THE FIRST EDITION; THE NEW CHRISTY MINSTRELS.

LIBERTY
❑ LO-607 Love Lifted Me 1981 8.00
*—Reissue of United Artists 607*
❑ LO-689 Kenny Rogers 1981 8.00
*—Reissue of United Artists 689*
❑ LO-754 Daytime Friends 1981 8.00
*—Reissue of United Artists 754*
❑ LO-835 Ten Years of Gold 1981 8.00
*—Reissue of United Artists 835*
❑ LO-903 Love Or Something Like It 1981 8.00
*—Reissue of United Artists 903*
❑ LO-934 The Gambler 1981 8.00
*—Reissue of United Artists 934*
❑ LOO-979 Kenny 1981 8.00
*—Reissue of United Artists 979*
❑ LOO-1035 Gideon 1981 8.00
*—Reissue of United Artists 1035*
❑ LOO-1072 Kenny Rogers' Greatest Hits 1980 8.00
❑ LOO-1108 Share Your Love 1981 8.00
❑ LN-10207 Love Lifted Me 1984 6.00
*—Budget-line reissue*
❑ LN-10208 Kenny Rogers 1983 6.00
*—Budget-line reissue*
❑ LN-10240 Christmas 198? 8.00
*—Reissue of LOO 51115*
❑ LN-10243 Gideon 1984 6.00
*—Budget-line reissue*
❑ LN-10245 We've Got Tonight 1984 6.00
*—Budget-line reissue*
❑ LN-10246 Love Will Turn You Around 1984 6.00
*—Budget-line reissue*
❑ LN-10247 The Gambler 1984 6.00
*—Budget-line reissue*
❑ LN-10248 Kenny 1984 6.00
*—Budget-line reissue*
❑ LN-10249 Daytime Friends 1984 6.00
*—Budget-line reissue*
❑ LN-10250 Love Or Something Like It 1984 6.00
*—Budget-line reissue*
❑ LN-10254 Ten Years of Gold 1984 6.00
*—Budget-line reissue*
❑ LOO-51115 Christmas 1981 10.00
❑ LO-51124 Love Will Turn You Around 1982 8.00
❑ LO-51143 We've Got Tonight 1983 8.00
❑ LV-51152 Twenty Greatest Hits 1983 8.00
❑ LO-51154 Duets 1984 8.00
❑ LO-51157 Love Is What We Make It 1985 8.00

MOBILE FIDELITY
❑ 1-044 The Gambler 1981 20.00
*—Audiophile vinyl*
❑ 1-049 Kenny Rogers' Greatest Hits 1981 20.00
*—Audiophile vinyl*

RCA
❑ 5833-1-R They Don't Make Them Like They Used To 1986 8.00
❑ 6484-1-R I Prefer the Moonlight 1987 8.00
❑ 8371-1-R Greatest Hits 1988 8.00

RCA VICTOR
❑ AFL1-4697 Eyes That See in the Dark 1983 8.00
❑ AFL1-4697 Eyes That See in the Dark 1983 200.00
*—Picture disc on one side, regular RCA label on other; possibly an in-house demo at the RCA Indianapolis pressing plant*
❑ AJL1-5335 What About Me 1984 8.00
❑ AJL1-7023 The Heart of the Matter 1985 8.00

REPRISE
❑ 25792 Something Inside So Strong 1989 10.00
❑ 25973 Christmas in America 1989 12.00
❑ R 144593 Love Is Strange 1990 20.00
*—Only available on vinyl from BMG Direct Marketing*

UNITED ARTISTS
❑ UA-LA607-G Love Lifted Me 1976 15.00
❑ UA-LA689-G Kenny Rogers 1976 10.00
❑ UA-LA754-G Daytime Friends 1977 10.00
❑ UA-LA835-H Ten Years of Gold 1978 10.00
❑ UA-LA903-H Love Or Something Like It 1978 10.00
❑ UA-LA934-H The Gambler 1978 10.00
❑ LWAK-979 Kenny 1979 10.00
❑ LOO-1035 Gideon 1980 10.00

**ROGERS, KENNY, AND THE FIRST EDITION** See THE FIRST EDITION.

**ROGERS, ROY**

CAPITOL
❑ ST-594 The Country Side of Roy Rogers 1970 20.00
❑ ST-785 A Man from Duck Run 1971 20.00

RCA
❑ 3024-1-RRE [PD]Roy Rogers Tribute 1991 40.00
*—Picture disc; only vinyl edition of this release*

Number Title (A Side/B Side) Yr NM

RCA CAMDEN
❑ CAL-1054 [M] Pecos Bill 1964 25.00
❑ CAS-1054(e) [R]Pecos Bill 1964 15.00
❑ CAL-1074 [M] Lore of the West 1966 25.00
❑ CAS-1074(e) [R]Lore of the West 1966 15.00
❑ CAL-1097 [M] Peter Cottontail and His Friends 1968 25.00
❑ CAS-1097 [R] Peter Cottontail and His Friends 1968 15.00

RCA VICTOR
❑ LBY-1022 [M] Jesus Loves Me 1959 50.00
*—On the "Children's Bluebird Series"*
❑ LPM-3041 [M] Roy Rogers Souvenir Album 1952 300.00
❑ LPM-3168 [M] Hymns of Faith 1954 200.00

20TH CENTURY
❑ T-487 Happy Trails to You 1975 15.00

**ROGERS, ROY, AND DALE EVANS**

CAPITOL
❑ ST 1745 [S] The Bible Tells Me So 1962 50.00
❑ T 1745 [M] The Bible Tells Me So 1962 40.00
❑ ST 2818 [S] Christmas Is Always 1967 30.00
❑ T 2818 [M] Christmas Is Always 1967 30.00

GOLDEN
❑ A198-6 [M] Roy Rogers' and Dale Evans' Song Wagon 1958 80.00
*—Originals have black labels and "198" prefix*
❑ A198-7 [M] 16 Great Songs of the Old West 1958 80.00
*—Originals have black labels and "198" prefix*
❑ LP 7 [M] A Child's Introduction to the West (16 Great Songs of the Old West) 196? 40.00
*—Yellow label, "LP" prefix*
❑ A298-81 [M] Peter Cottontail 1962 60.00
*—Originals have black labels and "298" prefix*

RCA VICTOR
❑ LPM-1439 [M] Sweet Hour of Prayer 1957 80.00

**ROGERS, SHORTY**

ATLANTIC
❑ 1212 [M] The Swinging Mr. Rogers 1955 50.00
*—Black label*
❑ 1212 [M] The Swinging Mr. Rogers 1961 25.00
*—Multicolor label, white "fan" logo at right*
❑ 1212 [M] The Swinging Mr. Rogers 1963 20.00
*—Multicolor label, black "fan" logo at right*
❑ 1232 [M] Martians, Come Back 1956 50.00
*—Black label*
❑ 1232 [M] Martians, Come Back 1961 25.00
*—Multicolor label, white "fan" logo at right*
❑ 1232 [M] Martians, Come Back 1963 20.00
*—Multicolor label, black "fan" logo at right*
❑ SD 1232 [S] Martians, Come Back 1958 50.00
*—Green label*
❑ SD 1232 [S] Martians, Come Back 1961 20.00
*—Multicolor label, white "fan" logo at right*
❑ 1270 [M] Way Up There 1957 50.00
*—Black label*
❑ 1270 [M] Way Up There 1961 25.00
*—Multicolor label, white "fan" logo at right*
❑ 1270 [M] Way Up There 1963 20.00
*—Multicolor label, black "fan" logo at right*

CAPITOL
❑ H 294 [10] Modern Sounds 1952 200.00
❑ ST 1960 [S] Gospel Mission 1963 20.00
❑ T 1960 [M] Gospel Mission 1963 25.00

MGM
❑ E-3798 [M] Shorty Rogers Meets Tarzan 1960 30.00
❑ SE-3798 [S] Shorty Rogers Meets Tarzan 1960 40.00

MOSAIC
❑ MR6-125 [(6)] The Complete Atlantic and EMI Jazz Recordings of Shorty Rogers 199? 150.00
*—Limited edition of 7,500*

RCA VICTOR
❑ LJM-1004 [M] Shorty Rogers Courts the Count 1954 80.00
❑ LPM-1195 [M] Shorty Rogers and His Giants 1956 70.00
❑ LPM-1326 [M] Wherever the Five Winds Blow 1956 70.00
❑ LPM-1334 [M] Collaboration 1956 60.00
❑ LPM-1350 [M] The Big Shorty Rogers Express 1957 60.00
❑ LPM-1428 [M] Shorty Rogers Plays Richard Rogers 1957 60.00
❑ LPM-1564 [M] Portrait of Shorty 1957 60.00
❑ LPM-1696 [M] Gigi Goes Jazz 1958 50.00
❑ LSP-1696 [S] Gigi Goes Jazz 1958 60.00
❑ LPM-1763 [M] Afro-Cuban Influence 1958 40.00
❑ LSP-1763 [S] Afro-Cuban Influence 1958 50.00
❑ LPM-1975 [M] Chances Are It Swings 1959 40.00
❑ LSP-1975 [S] Chances Are It Swings 1959 50.00
❑ LPM-1997 [M] The Wizard of Oz 1959 40.00
❑ LSP-1997 [S] The Wizard of Oz 1959 50.00
❑ LPM-2110 [M] The Swingin' Nutcracker 1960 40.00
❑ LSP-2110 [S] The Swingin' Nutcracker 1960 50.00
❑ LPM-3137 [10] Shorty Rogers' Giants 1953 200.00
❑ LPM-3138 [10] Cool and Crazy 1953 200.00

Number Title (A Side/B Side) Yr NM

REPRISE
❑ R-6050 [M] Bossa Nova 1962 20.00
❑ R9-6050 [S] Bossa Nova 1962 25.00
❑ R-6060 [M] Jazz Waltz 1962 20.00
❑ R9-6060 [S] Jazz Waltz 1962 25.00

WARNER BROS.
❑ W 1443 [M] 4th Dimension Jazz 1961 25.00
❑ WS 1443 [S] 4th Dimension Jazz 1961 30.00

**ROGERS, SHORTY, AND ANDRE PREVIN**

RCA VICTOR
❑ LPM-1018 [M] Collaboration 1954 60.00

**ROGERS, TIMMIE**

PHILIPS
❑ PHM 200088 [M]If I Were President 1963 20.00
❑ PHS 600088 [S]If I Were President 1963 25.00

**ROKES, THE**

RCA VICTOR INTERNATIONAL
❑ FPM-185 [M] Che Mondo Strano 1967 80.00

**ROLAND, GENE**

BRUNSWICK
❑ BL 54114 [M] Swingin' Friends 1963 40.00
❑ BL 754114 [S] Swingin' Friends 1963 50.00

DAWN
❑ DLP-1122 [M] Jazzville, Volume 4 1958 80.00

**ROLAND, JOE**

BETHLEHEM
❑ BCP-17 [M] Joe Roland Quintet 1955 50.00

SAVOY
❑ MG-12039 [M] Joltin' Joe Roland 1955 50.00
❑ MG-15034 [10] Joe Roland Quartet 1954 120.00
❑ MG-15047 [10] Joe Roland Quartet 1954 120.00

**ROLLING STONES, THE** Also see BRIAN JONES; CHARLIE WATTS; RONNIE WOOD; BILL WYMAN.

ABKCO
❑ ANA 1 [P] Metamorphosis 1975 12.00
❑ MPD-1 [DJ] Songs of the Rolling Stones 1975 700.00
*—"Band in field" cover*
❑ MPD-1 [DJ] Songs of the Rolling Stones 1975 3000.
*—"Rock and Roll Circus" cover; VG value 1000; VG+ value 2000*
❑ DVL2-0268 [(2)P]The Rolling Stones' Greatest Hits 1977 20.00
*—RCA Special Products mail-order offer*
❑ 1218-1 [(4)] Singles Collection: The London Years 1989 50.00
❑ AB-4224 Necrophilia 1973 8000.
*—Canceled; covers exist. Value is for complete tri-fold cover.*
❑ 18771-9001-1 Big Hits (High Tide and Green Grass) 2003 20.00
*—180-gram vinyl reissue pressed in U.S. by RTI, though cover says "Made in E.U."; with loose outer bag; number on cover is "882 322-1"*
❑ 18771-9002-1 Their Satanic Majesties Request 2003 20.00
*—180-gram vinyl reissue pressed in U.S. by RTI, though cover says "Made in E.U."; with loose outer bag; cover has number "882 329-1"*
❑ 18771-9004-1 Let It Bleed 2003 20.00
*—180-gram vinyl reissue pressed in U.S. by RTI, though cover says "Made in E.U."; with loose outer bag; cover has number "882 332-1"*
❑ 18771-9005-1 Get Yer Ya-Ya's Out! 2003 20.00
*—180-gram vinyl reissue pressed in U.S. by RTI, though cover says "Made in E.U."; with loose outer bag; cover has number "882 333-1"*
❑ 18771-9006-1 Metamorphosis 2003 20.00
*—180-gram vinyl reissue pressed in U.S. by RTI, though cover says "Made in E.U."; with loose outer bag; cover has number "882 344-1"*
❑ 18771-9375-1 England's Newest Hit Makers — The Rolling Stones 2003 20.00
*—180-gram vinyl reissue pressed in U.S. by RTI, though cover says "Made in E.U."; with loose outer bag; cover has number "882 316-1"*
❑ 18771-9430-1 Out of Our Heads UK 2003 20.00
*—180-gram vinyl reissue pressed in U.S. by RTI, though cover says "Made in E.U."; with loose outer bag; cover has number "882 319-1"*
❑ 18771-9477-1 Aftermath UK 2003 20.00
*—180-gram vinyl reissue pressed in U.S. by RTI, though cover says "Made in E.U."; with loose outer bag; cover has number "882 323-1"*
❑ 18771-9500-1 Between the Buttons UK 2003 20.00
*—180-gram vinyl reissue pressed in U.S. by RTI, though cover says "Made in E.U."; with loose outer bag; cover has number "882 326-1"*
❑ 18771-9539-1 Beggars Banquet 2003 20.00
*—180-gram vinyl reissue pressed in U.S. by RTI, though cover says "Made in E.U."; with loose outer bag; cover has number "882 330-1"*
❑ 18771-9667-1 [(2)]Hot Rocks 1964-1971 2003 40.00
*—180-gram vinyl reissue pressed in U.S. by RTI, though cover says "Made in E.U."; with loose outer bag; cover has number "882 334-1"*



**Except when noted otherwise, VG = 25% of NM, and VG+ = 50% of NM. (Example: VG = $2.00, VG+ = $4.00 and NM = $8.00.)**

**Number | Title (A Side/B Side) | Yr | NM**

LONDON

❑ NP 1 [M] Big Hits (High Tide and Green Grass) 1966 40.00
*—With five lines of type on the front cover, all in capital letters*
❑ NP 1 [M] Big Hits (High Tide and Green Grass) 1966 8000.
*—With two lines of type on the front cover, all in small letters*
❑ NPS 1 [R] Big Hits (High Tide and Green Grass) 1966 10.00
❑ RSD-1 [DJ] The Rolling Stones — The Promotional Album 1969 3000.
*—Not to be confused with imports of this rare promo; VG value 1000; VG+ value 2000*
❑ NP 2 [M] Their Satanic Majesties Request 1967 250.00
❑ NPS 2 [S] Their Satanic Majesties Request 1967 40.00
*—With 3-D cover*
❑ NPS 2 [S] Their Satanic Majesties Request 197? 8.00
*—Without 3-D cover*
❑ NPS 3 [P] Through the Past, Darkly (Big Hits Vol. 2) 1969 10.00
*—With hexagonal cover*
❑ NPS 3 [P] Through the Past, Darkly (Big Hits Vol. 2) 197? 20.00
*—Reissue with regular square cover*
❑ NPS 3 [PD] Through the Past, Darkly (Big Hits Vol. 2) 1969 6000.
*—Prototype picture discs that used the cover art from "Big Hits (High Tide and Green Grass)" either on one or both sides; VG value 3000; VG+ value 4500*
❑ NPS 4 [S] Let It Bleed 1969 10.00
*—Without poster*
❑ NPS 4 [S] Let It Bleed 1969 15.00
*—With poster*
❑ NPS-4 Let It Bleed 1970 10000.
*—One-of-a-kind red/yellow/blue/green vinyl (all on the same record!); VG value 5000; VG+ value 7500*
❑ NPS 5 [S] Get Yer Ya-Ya's Out! 1970 10.00
❑ PS 375 [R] England's Newest Hit Makers — The Rolling Stones 1964 300.00
*—Dark blue label; lower left-hand corner of cover advertises a bonus photo*
❑ PS 375 [R] England's Newest Hit Makers — The Rolling Stones 1965 25.00
*—Dark blue label with "London" unboxed at top*
❑ PS 375 [R] England's Newest Hit Makers — The Rolling Stones 1966 10.00
*—Dark blue label with "London" boxed at top*
❑ PS 402 [R] 12 x 5 1964 25.00
*—Dark blue label with "London" unboxed at top*
❑ PS 402 [R] 12 x 5 1965 10.00
*—Dark blue label with "London" boxed at top*
❑ PS 420 [R] The Rolling Stones, Now! 1965 25.00
*—Dark blue label with "London" unboxed at top. Add 20% for complete liner notes (or sticker) on back cover (both columns of type about equal in length).*
❑ PS 420 [R] The Rolling Stones, Now! 1966 10.00
*—Dark blue label with "London" boxed at top. Add 20% for censored liner notes (or sticker) on back cover (second column an inch shorter than the first column; "offensive" notes were quietly restored in the 1970s).*
❑ PS 429 [R] Out of Our Heads 1965 10.00
*—Dark blue label with "London" boxed at top*
❑ PS 429 [R] Out of Our Heads 1965 25.00
*—Dark blue label with "London" unboxed at top*
❑ PS 429 [R] Out of Our Heads 1965 100.00
*—Dark blue label with "London/ffrr" in a box at top and "Made in England by the Decca Record Co. Ltd." at top edge*
❑ PS 451 [P] December's Children (and Everybody's) 1965 25.00
*—Dark blue label with "London" unboxed at top*
❑ PS 451 [P] December's Children (and Everybody's) 1966 10.00
*—Dark blue label with "London" boxed at top. "Look What You've Done" is in true stereo; all other tracks are rechanneled.*
❑ PS 476 [S] Aftermath 1966 10.00
❑ PS 493 [P] Got Live If You Want It! 1966 10.00
*—"Fortune Teller" is rechanneled (it's actually an early studio recording with overdubbed crowd noise)*
❑ PS 499 [S] Between the Buttons 1967 10.00
❑ PS 509 Back Behind and In Front 1967 5000.
*—Prototype cover slick for an unreleased LP; the same number was used for "Flowers"*
❑ PS 509 [M] Flowers 197? 8.00
*—Some later "stereo" copies of this LP are actually entirely in mono*
❑ PS 509 [P] Flowers 1967 10.00
*—"Have You Seen Your Mother, Baby, Standing in the Shadow?" and "Mother's Little Helper" are rechanneled; all others are true stereo*
❑ PS 539 Beggars Banquet 1968 10000.
*—Original "toilet graffiti" cover slick (not on a cover)*
❑ PS 539 [S] Beggars Banquet 1968 10.00
*—With "Rev. Wilkins: credited as composer of "Prodigal Son"*
❑ PS 539 [S] Beggars Banquet 1968 25.00
*—With all songs credited to "Jagger-Richard"*
❑ 2PS 606/7 [(2)P]Hot Rocks 1964-1971 1971 20.00
*—With regular versions of all tracks. All of Side 1 and "Mothers Little Helper" and "19th Nervous Breakdown" on Side 2 are rechanneled. All of Side 3 and 4 are stereo.*

The Rolling Stones, *Flowers,* London LL 3509, 1967, mono, $50.

**Number | Title (A Side/B Side) | Yr | NM**

❑ 2PS 606/7 [(2)P]Hot Rocks 1964-1971 1971 1000.
*—With alternate versions of "Brown Sugar" and "Wild Horses" unavailable elsewhere. The date "11-5-71" or "11-18-71" is in the Side 4 trail-off area.*
❑ 2PS 626/7 [(2)P]More Hot Rocks (Big Hits and Fazed Cookies) 1972 20.00
*—All of Sides 1 and 4 are rechanneled; Side 2 and 3, except "Have You Seen Your Mother, Baby, Standing in the Shadow?" are in true stereo*
❑ LL 3375 England's Newest Hit Makers — The Rolling Stones Bonus Photo 1964 200.00
❑ LL 3375 [DJ] England's Newest Hit Makers — The Rolling Stones 1964 3000.
*—White label promo*
❑ LL 3375 [M] England's Newest Hit Makers — The Rolling Stones 1964 300.00
*—Maroon label with "Full Frequency Range Recording" inside horizontal lines that go through the center hole; lower left-hand corner of cover advertises a bonus photo*
❑ LL 3375 [M] England's Newest Hit Makers — The Rolling Stones 1965 60.00
*—Maroon label with "London" unboxed at top*
❑ LL 3375 [M] England's Newest Hit Makers — The Rolling Stones 1966 40.00
*—Red or maroon label with "London" boxed at top*
❑ LL 3402 [M] 12 x 5 1964 60.00
*—Maroon label with "London" unboxed at top*
❑ LL 3402 [M] 12 x 5 1964 200.00
*—Maroon label with "London/ffrr" in a box at top*
❑ LL 3402 [M] 12 x 5 1964 10000.
*—Maroon label with "London" unboxed at top; possibly unique blue vinyl pressing; VG value 5000; VG+ value 7500*
❑ LL 3402 [M] 12 x 5 1965 40.00
*—Red or maroon label with "London" boxed at top*
❑ LL 3420 [M] The Rolling Stones, Now! 1965 60.00
*—Maroon label with "London" unboxed at top and no lines on label. Add 20% for complete liner notes (or sticker) on back cover (both columns of type about equal in length).*
❑ LL 3420 [M] The Rolling Stones, Now! 1965 200.00
*—Maroon label with "London/ffrr" in a box at top. Add 20% for complete liner notes (or sticker) on back cover (both columns of type about equal in length).*
❑ LL 3420 [M] The Rolling Stones, Now! 1965 400.00
*—Maroon label with "London" unboxed, but with "ffrr" ear above "London" and "Full Frequency Range Recording" inside horizontal lines that go through the center hole*
❑ LL 3420 [M] The Rolling Stones, Now! 1965 400.00
*—Maroon label with "London" unboxed, with horizontal lines that go through the center hole, but with NO "ffrr" ear at the top and NO "Full Frequency Range Recording" between the horizonal lines*
❑ LL 3420 [M] The Rolling Stones, Now! 1966 40.00
*—Red or maroon label with "London" boxed at top and censored liner notes (second column an inch shorter than the first column)*
❑ LL 3429 [M] Out of Our Heads 1965 40.00
*—Maroon label with "London" unboxed at top*
❑ LL 3429 [M] Out of Our Heads 1965 200.00
*—Maroon label with "London/ffrr" in a box at top*
❑ LL 3429 [M] Out of Our Heads 1966 25.00
*—Red or maroon label with "London" boxed at top*
❑ LL 3451 [M] December's Children (and Everybody's) 1965 40.00
*—Maroon label with "London" unboxed at top*
❑ LL 3451 [M] December's Children (and Everybody's) 1966 25.00
*—Maroon label with "London" boxed at top*
❑ LL 3476 [M] Aftermath 1966 40.00
❑ LL 3493 [M] Got Live If You Want It! 1966 40.00
❑ LL 3499 [M] Between the Buttons 1967 40.00
❑ LL 3509 [M] Flowers 1967 50.00

LONDON/ABKCO

❑ 62671 [(2)P] Hot Rocks 1964-1971 1986 15.00
*—"Digitally Remastered from Original Master Recording" on cover; red label; same stereo content as original*
❑ 62671 [(2)P] More Hot Rocks (Big Hits and Fazed Cookies) 1986 15.00
*—"Digitally Remastered from Original Master Recording" on cover; red label*
❑ 73751 [M] England's Newest Hit Makers — The Rolling Stones 1986 8.00
*—"Digitally Remastered from Original Master Recording" on cover; red label*
❑ 74021 [M] 12 x 5 1986 8.00
*—"Digitally Remastered from Original Master Recording" on cover; red label*
❑ 74201 [P] The Rolling Stones, Now! 1986 8.00
*—"Digitally Remastered from Original Master Recording" on cover; red label; four tracks are in true stereo*
❑ 74291 [P] Out of Our Heads 1986 8.00
*—"Digitally Remastered from Original Master Recording" on cover; red label*
❑ 74511 [M] December's Children (and Everybody's) 1986 8.00
*—"Digitally Remastered from Original Master Recording" on cover; red label*
❑ 74761 [S] Aftermath 1986 8.00
*—"Digitally Remastered from Original Master Recording" on cover; red label*

THE ROLLING STONES, NOW!
MONO LL 3420
LONDON


The Rolling Stones, *The Rolling Stones, Now!*, London LL 3420, 1965, mono, with censored liner notes, $40.

| Number | Title (A Side/B Side) | Yr | NM |
|---|---|---|---|
| ❑ 74931 [S] | Got Live If You Want It! | 1986 | 8.00 |
| *—"Digitally Remastered from Original Master Recording" on cover; red label* | | | |
| ❑ 74991 [S] | Between the Buttons | 1986 | 8.00 |
| *—"Digitally Remastered from Original Master Recording" on cover; red label* | | | |
| ❑ 75091 [S] | Flowers | 1986 | 8.00 |
| *—"Digitally Remastered from Original Master Recording" on cover; red label* | | | |
| ❑ 75391 [S] | Beggars Banquet | 1986 | 12.00 |
| *—"Digitally Remastered from Original Master Recording" on cover; red label; original banned "toilet cover" released for the first time on this reissue* | | | |
| ❑ 80011 [M] | Big Hits (High Tide and Green Grass) | 1986 | 8.00 |
| *—"Digitally Remastered from Original Master Recording" on cover; red label* | | | |
| ❑ 80021 [S] | Their Satanic Majesties Request | 1986 | 8.00 |
| *—"Digitally Remastered from Original Master Recording" on cover; red label* | | | |
| ❑ 80031 [S] | Through the Past, Darkly (Big Hits Vol. 2) | 1986 | 8.00 |
| *—"Digitally Remastered from Original Master Recording" on cover; red label* | | | |
| ❑ 80041 | Let It Bleed | 1986 | 8.00 |
| *—"Digitally Remastered from Original Master Recording" on cover; red label* | | | |
| ❑ 80051 | Get Yer Ya-Ya's Out! | 1986 | 8.00 |
| *—"Digitally Remastered from Original Master Recording" on cover; red label* | | | |
| **MOBILE FIDELITY** | | | |
| ❑ RC-1 [(11)] | The Rolling Stones | 1984 | 500.00 |
| *—London LPs pressed on audiophile vinyl in box* | | | |
| ❑ 1-060 | Sticky Fingers | 1980 | 50.00 |
| *—Audiophile vinyl* | | | |
| ❑ 1-087 | Some Girls | 1982 | 50.00 |
| *—Audiophile vinyl* | | | |
| **RADIO PULSEBEAT NEWS** | | | |
| ❑ 4 | It's Here Luv!! | 1965 | 180.00 |
| *—Ed Rudy interview album; this has been counterfeited, but originals can be identified thus: Charlie Watts' jacket should be completely black with no white marks; the label is very clear; the vinyl is all black* | | | |
| **ROLLING STONES** | | | |
| ❑ PR 164 [DJ] | Interview with Mick Jagger by Tom Donahue | 1971 | 200.00 |
| *—Yellow label* | | | |

| Number | Title (A Side/B Side) | Yr | NM |
|---|---|---|---|
| ❑ COC 2-2900 [(2)] | Exile on Main St. | 1972 | 15.00 |
| *—Original covers have Unipak design -- cover has to be opened to remove the records. Add 33% for sheet of postcards.* | | | |
| ❑ COC 2-2900 [(2)] | Exile on Main St. | 1973 | 12.00 |
| *—Reissue covers have two pockets, one for each record* | | | |
| ❑ COC 2-9001 [(2)] | Love You Live | 1977 | 12.00 |
| ❑ COC 16015 | Emotional Rescue | 1980 | 10.00 |
| *—Without poster* | | | |
| ❑ COC 16015 | Emotional Rescue | 1980 | 15.00 |
| *—Originally released with a large poster wrapped around the outside of the record jacket* | | | |
| ❑ COC 16028 | Sucking in the Seventies | 1981 | 10.00 |
| ❑ COC 16052 | Tattoo You | 1981 | 10.00 |
| ❑ COC 39100 | Jamming with Edward | 1972 | 15.00 |
| *—Not an official Stones album, this includes Jagger, Watts and Wyman with Ry Cooder and Nicky Hopkins* | | | |
| ❑ COC 39100 [DJ] | Jamming with Edward | 1972 | 175.00 |
| *—White label stereo promo* | | | |
| ❑ COC 39100 [M] | Jamming with Edward | 1972 | 250.00 |
| *—White label mono promo* | | | |
| ❑ COC 39105 | Sticky Fingers | 1977 | 8.00 |
| *—Reissue on Atlantic with photo of zipper only* | | | |
| ❑ COC 39105 | Sticky Fingers | 1977 | 10.00 |
| *—Reissue on Atlantic with working zipper* | | | |
| ❑ COC 39106 | Goats Head Soup | 1977 | 8.00 |
| *—Reissue on Atlantic* | | | |
| ❑ COC 39107 | Made in the Shade | 1977 | 8.00 |
| *—Reissue on Atlantic* | | | |
| ❑ COC 39108 | Some Girls | 1978 | 10.00 |
| *—With "cover under reconstruction." Nine different color schemes exist for the front cover.* | | | |
| ❑ COC 39108 | Some Girls | 1978 | 15.00 |
| *—With all women's faces visible. Nine different color schemes exist for the front cover.* | | | |
| ❑ COC 39113 | Still Life (American Concert 1981) | 1982 | 10.00 |
| ❑ COC 39114 [PD] | Still Life (American Concert 1981) | 1982 | 40.00 |
| ❑ OC 40250 | Dirty Work | 1986 | 8.00 |
| *—Originals came with red shrink wrap; add 50% if it is still with the package* | | | |
| ❑ FC 40488 | Sticky Fingers | 1986 | 8.00 |
| *—Reissue on CBS with photo of zipper only* | | | |
| ❑ CG2 40489 [(2)] | Exile on Main St. | 1986 | 10.00 |
| *—Reissue on CBS* | | | |
| ❑ FC 40492 | Goats Head Soup | 1986 | 8.00 |
| *—Reissue on CBS* | | | |
| ❑ FC 40493 | It's Only Rock 'n' Roll | 1986 | 8.00 |
| *—Reissue on CBS* | | | |

| Number | Title (A Side/B Side) | Yr | NM |
|---|---|---|---|
| ❑ FC 40494 | Made in the Shade | 1986 | 8.00 |
| *—Reissue on CBS* | | | |
| ❑ FC 40495 | Black and Blue | 1986 | 8.00 |
| *—Reissue on CBS* | | | |
| ❑ CG2 40496 [(2)] | Love You Live | 1986 | 10.00 |
| *—Reissue on CBS* | | | |
| ❑ FC 40499 | Some Girls | 1986 | 8.00 |
| *—Reissue on CBS* | | | |
| ❑ FC 40500 | Emotional Rescue | 1986 | 8.00 |
| *—Reissue on CBS* | | | |
| ❑ FC 40501 | Sucking in the Seventies | 1986 | 8.00 |
| *—Reissue on CBS* | | | |
| ❑ FC 40502 | Tattoo You | 1986 | 8.00 |
| *—Reissue on CBS* | | | |
| ❑ FC 40503 | Still Life (American Concert 1981) | 1986 | 8.00 |
| *—Reissue on CBS* | | | |
| ❑ FC 40504 | Undercover | 1986 | 8.00 |
| *—Reissue on CBS has no stickers on cover* | | | |
| ❑ FC 40505 | Rewind (1971-1984) | 1986 | 8.00 |
| *—Reissue on CBS* | | | |
| ❑ OC 45333 | Steel Wheels | 1989 | 10.00 |
| ❑ C 47456 | Flashpoint | 1991 | 20.00 |
| ❑ COC 59100 | Sticky Fingers | 1971 | 12.00 |
| *—With working zipper* | | | |
| ❑ COC 59100 [DJ] | Sticky Fingers | 1971 | 300.00 |
| *—White label stereo promo* | | | |
| ❑ COC 59100 [M] | Sticky Fingers | 1971 | 500.00 |
| *—White label mono promo* | | | |
| ❑ COC 59101 | Goats Head Soup | 1973 | 10.00 |
| *—Without bonus photo* | | | |
| ❑ COC 59101 | Goats Head Soup | 1973 | 15.00 |
| *—With bonus photo* | | | |
| ❑ COC 79101 | It's Only Rock 'n' Roll | 1974 | 10.00 |
| ❑ COC 79102 | Made in the Shade | 1975 | 10.00 |
| ❑ COC 79104 | Black and Blue | 1976 | 10.00 |
| ❑ 90120 | Undercover | 1983 | 8.00 |
| *—With stickers peeled off* | | | |
| ❑ 90120 | Undercover | 1983 | 12.00 |
| *—With stickers intact* | | | |
| ❑ 90176 | Rewind (1971-1984) | 1984 | 25.00 |
| **VIRGIN** | | | |
| ❑ V 2750 (8 39782 1) [(2)] | Voodoo Lounge | 1994 | 25.00 |
| *—U.S. versions pressed in U.K., but have UPC code paste-over and blue sticker "Marketed by Caroline"* | | | |
| ❑ V 2801 (8 41040 1) [(2)] | Stripped | 1995 | 15.00 |
| *—U.S. versions pressed in U.K., but have UPC code paste-over with "Marketed and Distributed by Caroline Records"* | | | |
| ❑ V 3012 [(2)] | A Bigger Bang | 2005 | 15.00 |
| *—Alternate number is "00946 3300671 3"; pressed in the EU for U.S. distribution* | | | |
| ❑ 8 44712 1 [(2)] | Bridges to Babylon | 1997 | 80.00 |
| *—U.S. versions pressed in U.K., but have "Virgin Records America Inc." on back cover* | | | |
| ❑ 8 46740 1 [(2)] | No Security | 1998 | 15.00 |
| *—U.S. versions pressed in U.K., but have "Virgin Records America Inc." on back cover* | | | |
| ❑ 47863 | Sticky Fingers | 1999 | 25.00 |
| *—Limited-edition reissue with 180-gram vinyl and original working zipper cover* | | | |
| ❑ 47864 [(2)] | Exile on Main St. | 1999 | 50.00 |
| *—Limited-edition reissue with 180-gram vinyl and all original inserts* | | | |
| ❑ 47867 | Some Girls | 1999 | 25.00 |
| *—Limited-edition reissue with 180-gram vinyl and original inserts (except it has the "cover under reconstruction" inner sleeve)* | | | |

## ROLLINI, ADRIAN

| Number | Title (A Side/B Side) | Yr | NM |
|---|---|---|---|
| **MERCURY** | | | |
| ❑ MG-20011 [M] | Chopsticks | 1953 | 50.00 |

## ROLLINS, SONNY

| Number | Title (A Side/B Side) | Yr | NM |
|---|---|---|---|
| **ANALOGUE PRODUCTIONS** | | | |
| ❑ AP 008 | Way Out West | 199? | 25.00 |
| *—180-gram audiophile vinyl* | | | |
| **BLUE NOTE** | | | |
| ❑ BLP-1542 [M] | Sonny Rollins | 1957 | 1000. |
| *—"Deep groove" version; Lexington Ave. address on label* | | | |
| ❑ BLP-1542 [M] | Sonny Rollins | 1958 | 500.00 |
| *—"Deep groove" version, W. 63rd St. address on label* | | | |
| ❑ BLP-1542 [M] | Sonny Rollins | 1963 | 80.00 |
| *—With "New York, USA" address on label* | | | |
| ❑ BLP-1558 [M] | Sonny Rollins, Volume 2 | 1957 | 400.00 |
| *—Regular version, W. 63rd St. address on label* | | | |
| ❑ BLP-1558 [M] | Sonny Rollins, Volume 2 | 1957 | 1000. |
| *—"Deep groove" version; W. 63rd St. address on label* | | | |
| ❑ BLP-1558 [M] | Sonny Rollins, Volume 2 | 1963 | 80.00 |
| *—With "New York, USA" address on label* | | | |
| ❑ BLP-1581 [M] | A Night at the Village Vanguard | 1958 | 250.00 |
| *—Regular version, W. 63rd St. address on label* | | | |
| ❑ BLP-1581 [M] | A Night at the Village Vanguard | 1958 | 400.00 |
| *—"Deep groove" version; W. 63rd St. address on label* | | | |
| ❑ BLP-1581 [M] | A Night at the Village Vanguard | 1963 | 50.00 |
| *—With "New York, USA" address on label* | | | |
| ❑ BLP-4001 [M] | Newk's Time | 1958 | 150.00 |
| *—Regular version, W. 63rd St. address on label* | | | |
| ❑ BLP-4001 [M] | Newk's Time | 1958 | 300.00 |
| *—"Deep groove" version; W. 63rd St. address on label* | | | |
| ❑ BLP-4001 [M] | Newk's Time | 1963 | 60.00 |
| *—With "New York, USA" address on label* | | | |
| ❑ BST-4001 [S] | Newk's Time | 1959 | 120.00 |
| *—Regular version, W. 63rd St. address on label* | | | |

| Number | Title (A Side/B Side) | Yr | NM |
|---|---|---|---|
| ❑ BST-4001 [S] | Newk's Time | 1959 | 250.00 |
| *—"Deep groove" version; W. 63rd St. address on label* | | | |
| ❑ BST-4001 [S] | Newk's Time | 1963 | 40.00 |
| *—With "New York, USA" address on label* | | | |
| **CONTEMPORARY** | | | |
| ❑ C-3530 [M] | Way Out West | 1957 | 250.00 |
| ❑ M-3564 [M] | Sonny Rollins and the Contemporary Leaders | 1959 | 250.00 |
| ❑ S-7530 [S] | Way Out West | 1959 | 150.00 |
| ❑ S-7564 [S] | Sonny Rollins and the Contemporary Leaders | 1959 | 200.00 |
| **DCC COMPACT CLASSICS** | | | |
| ❑ LPZ-2008 | Saxophone Colossus | 1995 | 100.00 |
| *—180-gram audiophile vinyl* | | | |
| ❑ LPZ-2022 | Tenor Madness | 1996 | 150.00 |
| *—180-gram audiophile vinyl* | | | |
| **GRP IMPULSE!** | | | |
| ❑ IMP-161 [M] | East Broadway Run Down | 199? | 20.00 |
| *—180-gram audiophile reissue* | | | |
| **IMPULSE!** | | | |
| ❑ A-91 [M] | Sonny Rollins On Impulse! | 1966 | 60.00 |
| ❑ AS-91 [S] | Sonny Rollins On Impulse! | 1966 | 80.00 |
| ❑ A-9121 [M] | East Broadway Run Down | 1967 | 80.00 |
| ❑ AS-9121 [S] | East Broadway Run Down | 1967 | 50.00 |
| **JAZZLAND** | | | |
| ❑ JLP-72 [M] | Sonny's Time | 1962 | 80.00 |
| ❑ JLP-86 [M] | Shadow Waltz | 1962 | 80.00 |
| ❑ JLP-972 [S] | Sonny's Time | 1962 | 70.00 |
| ❑ JLP-986 [S] | Shadow Waltz | 1962 | 70.00 |
| **METROJAZZ** | | | |
| ❑ E-1002 [M] | Sonny Rollins and the Big Brass | 1958 | 120.00 |
| ❑ SE-1002 [S] | Sonny Rollins and the Big Brass | 1958 | 80.00 |
| ❑ E-1011 [M] | Sonny Rollins at Music Inn | 1958 | 120.00 |
| ❑ SE-1011 [S] | Sonny Rollins at Music Inn | 1958 | 100.00 |
| **PRESTIGE** | | | |
| ❑ PRLP-137 [10] | Sonny Rollins Quartet | 1952 | 800.00 |
| ❑ PRLP-186 [10] | Sonny Rollins Quartet | 1954 | 700.00 |
| ❑ PRLP-190 [10] | Sonny Rollins | 1954 | 600.00 |
| ❑ PRLP-7020 [M] | Work Time | 1956 | 500.00 |
| *—Yellow label with W. 50th St. address* | | | |
| ❑ PRLP-7029 [M] | Sonny Rollins with the Modern Jazz Quartet | 1956 | 250.00 |
| *—Brown and yellow cover; catalog number at upper left is "Prestige Hi-Fil LP 7029"; record has yellow label with W. 50th St. address* | | | |
| ❑ PRLP-7029 [M] | Sonny Rollins with the Modern Jazz Quartet | 1956 | 300.00 |
| *—Orange cover; second edition has the correct catalog number, "Prestige LP 7029," in upper left inside an orange box* | | | |
| ❑ PRLP-7029 [M] | Sonny Rollins with the Modern Jazz Quartet | 1956 | 400.00 |
| *—Orange cover; original edition has the wrong catalog number at upper left (PR 7020), but the record has the correct number* | | | |
| ❑ PRLP-7038 [M] | Sonny Rollins Plus 4 | 1956 | 300.00 |
| *—Yellow label with W. 50th St. address* | | | |
| ❑ PRLP-7047 [M] | Tenor Madness | 1956 | 300.00 |
| *—Yellow label with W. 50th St. address* | | | |
| ❑ PRLP-7047 [M] | Tenor Madness | 1958 | 200.00 |
| *—Yellow label with Bergenfield, N.J. address* | | | |
| ❑ PRLP-7058 [M] | Moving Out | 1956 | 300.00 |
| *—Yellow label with W. 50th St. address* | | | |
| ❑ PRLP-7058 [M] | Moving Out | 1958 | 80.00 |
| *—Yellow label with Bergenfield, N.J. address* | | | |
| ❑ PRLP-7079 [M] | Saxophone Colossus | 1957 | 400.00 |
| *—Yellow label with W. 50th St. address* | | | |
| ❑ PRLP-7095 [M] | Rollins Plays for Bird | 1957 | 200.00 |
| *—Yellow label with W. 50th St. address* | | | |
| ❑ PRLP-7126 [M] | Tour de Force | 1957 | 200.00 |
| *—Yellow label with W. 50th St. address* | | | |
| ❑ PRLP-7207 [M] | Sonny Boy | 1961 | 100.00 |
| ❑ PRLP-7246 [M] | Work Time | 1962 | 80.00 |
| ❑ PRST-7246 [R] | Work Time | 1962 | 40.00 |
| ❑ PRLP-7269 [M] | Sonny and the Stars | 1963 | 80.00 |
| ❑ PRST-7269 [R] | Sonny and the Stars | 1963 | 40.00 |
| ❑ PRLP-7326 [M] | Saxophone Colossus | 1964 | 60.00 |
| ❑ PRST-7326 [R] | Saxophone Colossus | 1964 | 30.00 |
| ❑ PRLP-7433 [M] | Sonny Rollins Plays Jazz Classics | 1967 | 100.00 |
| ❑ PRST-7433 [R] | Sonny Rollins Plays Jazz Classics | 1967 | 30.00 |
| **RCA VICTOR** | | | |
| ❑ LPM-2527 [M] | The Bridge | 1962 | 40.00 |
| *—Black label, dog on top, "Long 33 1/3 Play" at bottom* | | | |
| ❑ LSP-2527 [S] | The Bridge | 1962 | 70.00 |
| *—Black label, dog on top, "Living Stereo" at bottom* | | | |
| ❑ LSP-2527 [S] | The Bridge | 199? | 30.00 |
| *—Classic Records reissue on audiophile vinyl* | | | |
| ❑ LSP-2527-45 [(4)] | The Bridge | 1999 | 60.00 |
| *—Classic Records reissue; 4 single-sided LPs that play at 45 rpm* | | | |
| ❑ LPM-2572 [M] | What's New? | 1962 | 30.00 |
| ❑ LSP-2572 [S] | What's New? | 1962 | 60.00 |
| ❑ LPM-2612 [M] | Our Man In Jazz | 1962 | 30.00 |
| ❑ LSP-2612 [S] | Our Man In Jazz | 1962 | 60.00 |
| ❑ LSP-2612 [S] | Our Man In Jazz | 199? | 25.00 |
| *—Classic Records reissue on audiophile vinyl* | | | |
| ❑ LPM-2712 [M] | Sonny Meets Hawk! | 1963 | 30.00 |

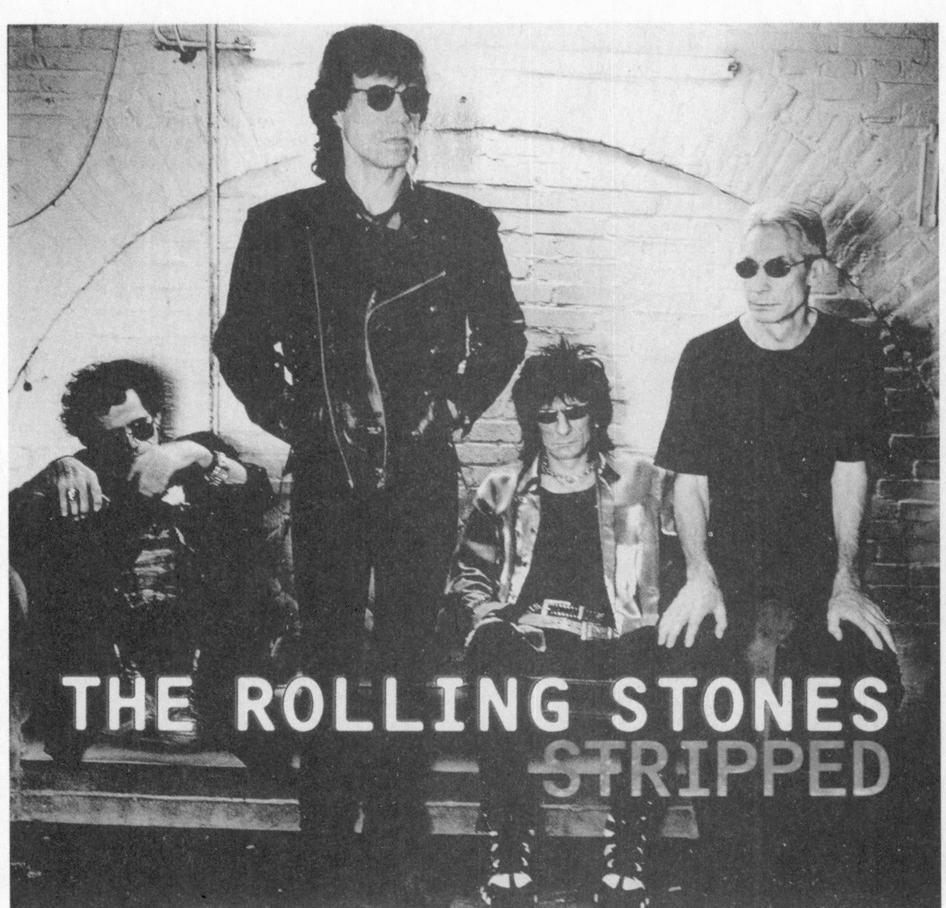


The Rolling Stones, *Stripped,* Virgin V 2801, 1995, with "Caroline" bar code sticker, $15.

| Number | Title (A Side/B Side) | Yr | NM |
|---|---|---|---|
| ❑ LSP-2712 [S] | Sonny Meets Hawk! | 1963 | 60.00 |
| ❑ LSP-2712 [S] | Sonny Meets Hawk! | 199? | 25.00 |
| *—Classic Records reissue on audiophile vinyl* | | | |
| ❑ LPM-2927 [M] | Now's the Time | 1964 | 25.00 |
| ❑ LSP-2927 [S] | Now's the Time! | 1964 | 30.00 |
| ❑ LSP-2927 [S] | Now's the Time! | 199? | 25.00 |
| *—Classic Records reissue on audiophile vinyl* | | | |
| ❑ LPM-3355 [M] | The Standard Sonny Rollins | 1965 | 25.00 |
| ❑ LSP-3355 [S] | The Standard Sonny Rollins | 1965 | 30.00 |
| **RIVERSIDE** | | | |
| ❑ RLP 12-241 [M] | The Sound of Sonny | 1957 | 400.00 |
| *—White label, blue print* | | | |
| ❑ RLP 12-241 [M] | The Sound of Sonny | 1959 | 200.00 |
| *—Blue label, microphone logo at top* | | | |
| ❑ RLP-258 [M] | Freedom Suite | 1958 | 200.00 |
| ❑ RLP-1124 [S] | The Sound of Sonny | 1959 | 200.00 |
| **STEREO RECORDS** | | | |
| ❑ S-7017 [S] | Way Out West | 1958 | 200.00 |
| **VERVE** | | | |
| ❑ V-8430 [M] | Sonny Rollins/Brass, Sonny Rollins/Trio | 1962 | 40.00 |
| ❑ V6-8430 [S] | Sonny Rollins/Brass, Sonny Rollins/Trio | 1962 | 30.00 |

### ROLLINS, SONNY; CLIFFORD BROWN; MAX ROACH

| Number | Title (A Side/B Side) | Yr | NM |
|---|---|---|---|
| **PRESTIGE** | | | |
| ❑ PRLP-7291 [M] | Three Giants | 1964 | 40.00 |
| ❑ PRST-7291 [R] | Three Giants | 1964 | 25.00 |

### ROLLINS, SONNY/JIMMY CLEVELAND

| Number | Title (A Side/B Side) | Yr | NM |
|---|---|---|---|
| **PERIOD** | | | |
| ❑ SPL-1204 [M] | Sonny Rollins Plays/Jimmy Cleveland Plays | 1956 | 100.00 |

### ROMAN NEW ORLEANS JAZZ BAND, THE

| Number | Title (A Side/B Side) | Yr | NM |
|---|---|---|---|
| **RCA VICTOR** | | | |
| ❑ LPT-3033 [10] | Around the World in Jazz — Italy | 1953 | 40.00 |

### ROMEO VOID

| Number | Title (A Side/B Side) | Yr | NM |
|---|---|---|---|
| **COLUMBIA** | | | |
| ❑ PC 38178 [EP] | Never Say Never | 1982 | 12.00 |
| *—Reissue* | | | |
| ❑ ARC 38182 | Benefactor | 1982 | 10.00 |
| ❑ PC 38182 | Benefactor | 198? | 8.00 |
| *—Reissue* | | | |
| ❑ BFC 39155 | Instincts | 1984 | 10.00 |
| ❑ PC 39155 | Instincts | 1985 | 8.00 |
| *—Reissue* | | | |
| **415 RECORDS** | | | |
| ❑ A-0004 | It's a Condition | 1981 | 15.00 |
| ❑ A-0007 [EP] | Never Say Never | 1981 | 25.00 |

### ROMEOS, THE (1)

| Number | Title (A Side/B Side) | Yr | NM |
|---|---|---|---|
| **MARK II** | | | |
| ❑ 1001 | Precious Memories | 1967 | 25.00 |

### ROMERO, CELEDONIO

| Number | Title (A Side/B Side) | Yr | NM |
|---|---|---|---|
| **MERCURY LIVING PRESENCE** | | | |
| ❑ SR 90296 [S] | Guitar Music from the Courts of Spain | 196? | 25.00 |
| *—Maroon label, no "Vendor: Mercury Record Corporation"* | | | |

### ROMERO, CELEDONIO; CELIN; PEPE; AND ANGEL

| Number | Title (A Side/B Side) | Yr | NM |
|---|---|---|---|
| **MERCURY LIVING PRESENCE** | | | |
| ❑ SR 90295 [S] | The Royal Family of the Spanish Guitar | 196? | 25.00 |
| *—Maroon label, no "Vendor: Mercury Record Corporation"* | | | |
| ❑ SR 90295 [S] | The Royal Family of the Spanish Guitar | 196? | 25.00 |
| *—Maroon label, with "Vendor: Mercury Record Corporation"* | | | |
| ❑ SR 90417 [S] | Spain's Royal Family of the Guitar | 196? | 25.00 |
| *—Maroon label, no "Vendor: Mercury Record Corporation"* | | | |
| ❑ SR 90434 [S] | An Evening of Flamenco Music | 1965 | 30.00 |
| *—Maroon label, with "Vendor: Mercury Record Corporation"* | | | |

### ROMERO, CESAR

| Number | Title (A Side/B Side) | Yr | NM |
|---|---|---|---|
| **TOPS** | | | |
| ❑ L-1631 [M] | Songs by a Latin Lover | 1958 | 30.00 |

### ROMERO, PEPE

| Number | Title (A Side/B Side) | Yr | NM |
|---|---|---|---|
| **MERCURY LIVING PRESENCE** | | | |
| ❑ SR 90297 [S] | Flamenco | 196? | 40.00 |
| *—Maroon label, no "Vendor: Mercury Record Corporation"* | | | |

### ROMNEY, HUGH
Later known as "Wavy Gravy."

| Number | Title (A Side/B Side) | Yr | NM |
|---|---|---|---|
| **WORLD PACIFIC** | | | |
| ❑ ST-1805 [S] | Third Stream Humor | 1962 | 40.00 |
| ❑ WP-1805 [M] | Third Stream Humor | 1962 | 30.00 |

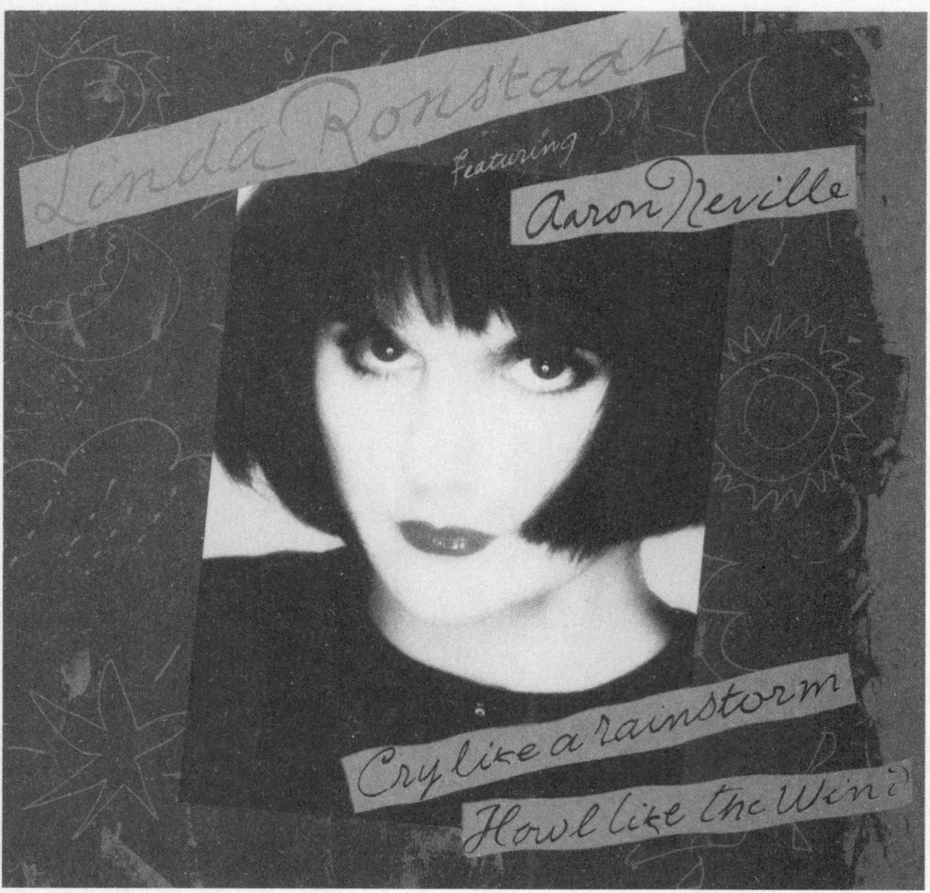


Linda Ronstadt, *Cry Like a Rainstorm, Howl Like the Wind,* Elektra 60872, 1989, $12.

| Number | Title (A Side/B Side) | Yr | NM |
|---|---|---|---|
| **RONDO, DON** | | | |
| JUBILEE | | | |
| ❑ JLP-1052 [M] | Rondo | 195? | 20.00 |
| ❑ JLP-1081 [M] | Have You Met Don Rondo | 195? | 20.00 |
| VOCALION | | | |
| ❑ VL 73897 | Two Different Worlds | 1970 | 12.00 |
| **RONETTES, THE** | | | |
| COLPIX | | | |
| ❑ CP-486 [M] | The Ronettes Featuring Veronica | 1965 | 100.00 |
| *—Blue label* | | | |
| ❑ CP-486 [M] | The Ronettes Featuring Veronica | 1965 | 200.00 |
| *—Gold label* | | | |
| ❑ SCP-486 [S] | The Ronettes Featuring Veronica | 1965 | 150.00 |
| *—Blue label* | | | |
| ❑ SCP-486 [S] | The Ronettes Featuring Veronica | 1965 | 300.00 |
| *—Gold label* | | | |
| PHILLES | | | |
| ❑ PHLP-4006 [M] | Presenting the Fabulous Ronettes Featuring Veronica | 1964 | 400.00 |
| *—Yellow and red label* | | | |
| ❑ PHLP-4006 [M] | Presenting the Fabulous Ronettes Featuring Veronica | 1964 | 800.00 |
| *—Blue and black label* | | | |
| ❑ PHLP-ST-4006 [S] | Presenting the Fabulous Ronettes Featuring Veronica | 1965 | 600.00 |
| ❑ ST-90721 [S] | Presenting the Fabulous Ronettes Featuring Veronica | 1965 | 400.00 |
| *—Capitol Record Club edition* | | | |
| ❑ T-90721 [M] | Presenting the Fabulous Ronettes Featuring Veronica | 1965 | 250.00 |
| *—Capitol Record Club edition* | | | |
| **RONNIE AND THE DEADBEATS** | | | |
| CHECK | | | |
| ❑ 103 [M] | Groovin' with Ronnie and the Deadbeats | 197? | 20.00 |
| **RONNIE AND THE POMONA CASUALS** | | | |
| DONNA | | | |
| ❑ 2113 [M] | Everybody Jerk | 1965 | 30.00 |

| Number | Title (A Side/B Side) | Yr | NM |
|---|---|---|---|
| **RONNY AND THE DAYTONAS** | | | |
| BEAT ROCKET | | | |
| ❑ BR 119 | G.T.O. | 199? | 12.00 |
| *—Reissue of Mala 4001 with four bonus tracks* | | | |
| ❑ BR 120 | Sandy | 199? | 12.00 |
| *—Reissue of Mala 4002 with three bonus tracks* | | | |
| MALA | | | |
| ❑ 4001 [M] | G.T.O. | 1964 | 120.00 |
| ❑ 4002 [M] | Sandy | 1966 | 80.00 |
| ❑ 4002S [S] | Sandy | 1966 | 100.00 |
| SUNDAZED | | | |
| ❑ LP 5050 | G.T.O. — Best of the Mala Recordings | 1997 | 10.00 |
| **RONSTADT, LINDA** Also see STONE PONEYS. | | | |
| ASYLUM | | | |
| ❑ 6E-104 | Simple Dreams | 1977 | 10.00 |
| ❑ 6E-106 | Greatest Hits | 1977 | 10.00 |
| ❑ 6E-155 | Living in the U.S.A. | 1978 | 10.00 |
| ❑ DP-401 [PD] | Living in the U.S.A. | 1978 | 18.00 |
| ❑ 5E-510 | Mad Love | 1980 | 10.00 |
| ❑ 5E-516 | Greatest Hits, Volume 2 | 1980 | 10.00 |
| ❑ 5E-540 | Keeping Out of Mischief | 1981 | — |
| *—Canceled* | | | |
| ❑ 7E-1045 | Prisoner in Disguise | 1975 | 10.00 |
| ❑ 7E-1072 | Hasten Down the Wind | 1976 | 10.00 |
| *—"Clouds" label* | | | |
| ❑ 7E-1072 | Hasten Down the Wind | 1976 | 15.00 |
| *—Solid blue label with white stylized "a" at top* | | | |
| ❑ 7E-1092 | Greatest Hits | 1976 | 12.00 |
| ❑ SD 5064 | Don't Cry Now | 1973 | 10.00 |
| ❑ 60185 | Get Closer | 1982 | 10.00 |
| ❑ 60260 | What's New | 1983 | 10.00 |
| ❑ 60387 | Lush Life | 1984 | 10.00 |
| ❑ 60474 | For Sentimental Reasons | 1987 | 10.00 |
| ❑ 60489 [(3)] | 'Round Midnight: The Nelson Riddle Sessions | 1987 | 25.00 |
| ❑ 60765 | Canciones De Mi Padre | 1988 | 12.00 |
| CAPITOL | | | |
| ❑ ST-208 | Hand Sown…Home Grown | 1969 | 20.00 |
| *—Black label with colorband* | | | |
| ❑ ST-208 | Hand Sown…Home Grown | 1970 | 15.00 |
| *—Green label* | | | |
| ❑ ST-208 | Hand Sown…Home Grown | 1971 | 12.00 |
| *—Red label* | | | |

| Number | Title (A Side/B Side) | Yr | NM |
|---|---|---|---|
| ❑ ST-407 | Silk Purse | 1970 | 15.00 |
| *—Green label* | | | |
| ❑ ST-407 | Silk Purse | 1971 | 12.00 |
| *—Red label* | | | |
| ❑ ST-8-0407 | Silk Purse | 1970 | 20.00 |
| *—Capitol Record Club edition* | | | |
| ❑ SMAS-635 | Linda Ronstadt | 1972 | 12.00 |
| ❑ ST-11269 | Different Drum | 1974 | 12.00 |
| *—Also includes Stone Poneys tracks* | | | |
| ❑ ST-11358 | Heart Like a Wheel | 1974 | 12.00 |
| ❑ SW-11358 | Heart Like a Wheel | 1975 | 10.00 |
| ❑ SKBB-11629 [(2)] | A Retrospective | 1977 | 15.00 |
| *—Also includes Stone Poneys tracks* | | | |
| ❑ SN-16130 | Hand Sown…Home Grown | 1980 | 8.00 |
| ❑ SN-16131 | Silk Purse | 1980 | 8.00 |
| ❑ SN-16132 | Linda Ronstadt | 1980 | 8.00 |
| ❑ SN-16133 | Beginnings | 1980 | 8.00 |
| ❑ SN-16299 | Different Drum | 198? | 8.00 |
| *—Budget-line reissue* | | | |
| DCC COMPACT CLASSICS | | | |
| ❑ LPZ-2048 | Greatest Hits | 1997 | 80.00 |
| *—Audiophile vinyl* | | | |
| ❑ LPZ-2065 | Greatest Hits, Volume Two | 1998 | 40.00 |
| *—Audiophile vinyl* | | | |
| ELEKTRA | | | |
| ❑ 60872 | Cry Like a Rainstorm, Howl Like the Wind | 1989 | 12.00 |
| MOBILE FIDELITY | | | |
| ❑ 1-158 | What's New | 1984 | 50.00 |
| *—Audiophile vinyl* | | | |
| NAUTILUS | | | |
| ❑ NR-26 | Simple Dreams | 1982 | 50.00 |
| *—Audiophile vinyl* | | | |
| PAIR | | | |
| ❑ PDL2-1070 [(2)] | Prime of Life | 1986 | 12.00 |
| ❑ PDL2-1125 [(2)] | Rockfile | 1986 | 12.00 |
| **ROOFTOP SINGERS, THE** | | | |
| VANGUARD | | | |
| ❑ VSD-2136 [S] | Walk Right In | 1963 | 20.00 |
| ❑ VRS-9123 [M] | Walk Right In | 1963 | 15.00 |
| ❑ VRS-9134 [M] | Good Time | 1964 | 15.00 |
| ❑ VRS-9190 [M] | Rainy River | 1965 | 15.00 |
| ❑ VSD-79134 [S] | Good Time | 1964 | 20.00 |
| ❑ VSD-79190 [S] | Rainy River | 1965 | 20.00 |
| **ROOMFUL OF BLUES** | | | |
| ANTILLES | | | |
| ❑ 7071 | Let's Have a Party! | 1980 | 20.00 |
| BLUE FLAME | | | |
| ❑ 1001 | Hot Little Mama | 197? | 25.00 |
| ISLAND | | | |
| ❑ ILPS 9474 | Roomful of Blues | 1977 | 25.00 |
| **ROONEY, MICKEY** | | | |
| RCA VICTOR | | | |
| ❑ LPM-1520 [M] | Mickey Rooney Sings George M. Cohan | 1957 | 80.00 |
| **ROSE, DAVID** | | | |
| CAPITOL | | | |
| ❑ ST-124 | Something Fresh | 1969 | 15.00 |
| ❑ ST-290 | The Little Drummer Boy | 1969 | 12.00 |
| *—Reissue of 2853* | | | |
| ❑ ST 2627 [S] | The Bible | 1966 | 15.00 |
| ❑ T 2627 [M] | The Bible | 1966 | 12.00 |
| ❑ ST 2717 [S] | Holiday for Strings | 1967 | 12.00 |
| ❑ T 2717 [M] | Holiday for Strings | 1967 | 15.00 |
| ❑ ST 2853 | Christmas Album | 1968 | 15.00 |
| DINO | | | |
| ❑ DP-3001 | Miracle | 1972 | 12.00 |
| KAPP | | | |
| ❑ K-1100-S [S] | Great Waltzes of the Fabulous Century | 1958 | 25.00 |
| ❑ KL-1100 [M] | Great Waltzes of the Fabulous Century | 1958 | 20.00 |
| ❑ KL-1205 [M] | Songs of the Fabulous Thirties, Vol. 1 | 1960 | 15.00 |
| ❑ KL-1206 [M] | Songs of the Fabulous Thirties, Vol. 2 | 1960 | 15.00 |
| ❑ KS-3010 [S] | Waltzes in Stereo | 1959 | 30.00 |
| ❑ KS-3205 [S] | Songs of the Fabulous Thirties, Vol. 1 | 1960 | 20.00 |
| ❑ KS-3206 [S] | Songs of the Fabulous Thirties, Vol. 2 | 1960 | 20.00 |
| ❑ KX-5004-S [(2)S] | Songs of the Fabulous Thirties | 1958 | 30.00 |
| ❑ KXL-5004 [(2)M] | Songs of the Fabulous Thirties | 1958 | 25.00 |
| LION | | | |
| ❑ L-70109 [M] | Magic Melodies | 1959 | 20.00 |
| METRO | | | |
| ❑ M 502 [M] | Deep Purple | 1965 | 12.00 |
| ❑ MS 502 [R] | Deep Purple | 1965 | 12.00 |
| ❑ M 585 [M] | Among the Stars | 1966 | 12.00 |

| Number | Title (A Side/B Side) | Yr | NM |
|---|---|---|---|
| ❑ MS 585 [S] | Among the Stars | 1966 | 12.00 |
| **MGM** | | | |
| ❑ E-85 [10] | David Rose and His Orchestra Play Music of George Gershwin | 1951 | 40.00 |
| ❑ GAS-129 | David Rose and His Orchestra (Golden Archive Series) | 1970 | 10.00 |
| ❑ E-196 [10] | The Magic Music Box | 1953 | 40.00 |
| ❑ E-506 [10] | Holiday for Strings | 1950 | 60.00 |
| ❑ E-515 [10] | Serenades | 1950 | 60.00 |
| ❑ E-532 [10] | A Sentimental Journey with David Rose | 1950 | 60.00 |
| ❑ E-3067 [M] | Beautiful Music to Love By | 1953 | 30.00 |
| *—Yellow label* | | | |
| ❑ E-3101 [M] | Let's Fall in Love | 1954 | 30.00 |
| *—Yellow label* | | | |
| ❑ E-3108 [M] | Fiddlin' for Fun | 1954 | 30.00 |
| *—Yellow label* | | | |
| ❑ E-3123 [M] | Love Walked In — The Music of George Gershwin | 1954 | 30.00 |
| *—Yellow label* | | | |
| ❑ E-3134 [M] | Nostalgia | 1954 | 30.00 |
| *—Yellow label* | | | |
| ❑ E-3215 [M] | Holiday for Strings | 1955 | 30.00 |
| *—Yellow label* | | | |
| ❑ E-3255 [M] | Sentimental Journey | 1955 | 30.00 |
| *—Yellow label* | | | |
| ❑ E-3289 [M] | Lover's Serenade | 1955 | 30.00 |
| *—Yellow label* | | | |
| ❑ E-3397 [M] | Music from Motion Pictures | 1956 | 30.00 |
| *—Yellow label* | | | |
| ❑ E-3469 [M] | A Merry Christmas to You | 1956 | 30.00 |
| *—Yellow label* | | | |
| ❑ E-3469 [M] | A Merry Christmas to You | 1960 | 15.00 |
| *—Black label* | | | |
| ❑ E-3481 [M] | Hi Fiddles | 1957 | 25.00 |
| *—Yellow label* | | | |
| ❑ E-3555 [M] | The Song Is You — Melodies of Jerome Kern | 1957 | 25.00 |
| *—Yellow label* | | | |
| ❑ E-3592 [M] | Autumn Leaves | 1957 | 25.00 |
| *—Yellow label* | | | |
| ❑ SE-3592 [S] | Autumn Leaves | 1959 | 30.00 |
| *—Yellow label* | | | |
| ❑ E-3603 [M] | Reflections in the Water | 1957 | 25.00 |
| *—Yellow label* | | | |
| ❑ E-3612 [M] | Music from Jamaica | 1957 | 25.00 |
| *—Yellow label* | | | |
| ❑ E-3640 [M] | David Rose Plays Music from "Gigi" | 1958 | 25.00 |
| *—Yellow label* | | | |
| ❑ SE-3640 [S] | David Rose Plays Music from "Gigi" | 1958 | 30.00 |
| *—Yellow label* | | | |
| ❑ E-3716 [M] | Secret Songs for Young Lovers | 1959 | 20.00 |
| *—With Andre Previn; yellow label* | | | |
| ❑ SE-3716 [S] | Secret Songs for Young Lovers | 1959 | 30.00 |
| *—With Andre Previn; yellow label* | | | |
| ❑ E-3746 [M] | David Rose Plays the Music from "Whoop Up!" | 1959 | 20.00 |
| *—Yellow label* | | | |
| ❑ SE-3746 [S] | David Rose Plays the Music from "Whoop Up!" | 1959 | 30.00 |
| *—Yellow label* | | | |
| ❑ E-3748 [M] | David Rose Plays David Rose | 1959 | 20.00 |
| *—Yellow label* | | | |
| ❑ SE-3748 [S] | David Rose Plays David Rose | 1959 | 20.00 |
| *—Yellow label* | | | |
| ❑ E-3852 [M] | Concert with a Beat! | 1960 | 15.00 |
| ❑ SE-3852 [S] | Concert with a Beat! | 1960 | 20.00 |
| ❑ E-3894 [M] | Box-Office Blockbusters | 1961 | 15.00 |
| ❑ SE-3894 [S] | Box-Office Blockbusters | 1961 | 20.00 |
| ❑ E-3895 [M] | Spectacular Strings | 1961 | 15.00 |
| ❑ SE-3895 [S] | Spectacular Strings | 1961 | 20.00 |
| ❑ E-3950 [M] | Exodus | 1961 | 15.00 |
| ❑ SE-3950 [S] | Exodus | 1961 | 20.00 |
| ❑ E-3952 [M] | Butterfield-8 | 1961 | 15.00 |
| ❑ SE-3952 [S] | Butterfield-8 | 1961 | 20.00 |
| ❑ E-3953 [M] | Cimarron | 1961 | 15.00 |
| ❑ SE-3953 [S] | Cimarron | 1961 | 20.00 |
| ❑ E-3960 [M] | David Rose and His Concert Orchestra Play His Dramatic Music from the NBC-TV Series "Bonanza" | 1961 | 30.00 |
| ❑ SE-3960 [S] | David Rose and His Concert Orchestra Play His Dramatic Music from the NBC-TV Series "Bonanza" | 1961 | 40.00 |
| ❑ E-4004 [M] | 21 Channel Sound | 1962 | 15.00 |
| ❑ SE-4004 [S] | 21 Channel Sound | 1962 | 20.00 |
| ❑ E-4062 [M] | The Stripper and Other Fun Songs for the Family | 1962 | 15.00 |
| *—Black label* | | | |
| ❑ SE-4062 [S] | The Stripper and Other Fun Songs for the Family | 1962 | 20.00 |
| *—Black label* | | | |
| ❑ SE-4062 [S] | The Stripper and Other Fun Songs for the Family | 1968 | 12.00 |
| *—Blue and gold label* | | | |
| ❑ E-4077 [M] | The Wonderful World of the Brothers Grimm | 1962 | 15.00 |

Diana Ross, *Diana Ross,* Motown MS 711, 1970, $15.

| Number | Title (A Side/B Side) | Yr | NM |
|---|---|---|---|
| ❑ SE-4077 [S] | The Wonderful World of the Brothers Grimm | 1962 | 20.00 |
| ❑ E-4099 [M] | More, More, More, Music of the Stripper | 1963 | 15.00 |
| ❑ SE-4099 [S] | More, More, More, Music of the Stripper | 1963 | 20.00 |
| ❑ E-4144 [M] | Love Theme from "Cleopatra" and Music from Other Great Motion Pictures | 1963 | 15.00 |
| ❑ SE-4144 [S] | Love Theme from "Cleopatra" and Music from Other Great Motion Pictures | 1963 | 20.00 |
| ❑ E-4155 [M] | The Very Best of David Rose | 1963 | 12.00 |
| ❑ SE-4155 [S] | The Very Best of David Rose | 1963 | 15.00 |
| ❑ E-4271 [M] | The Americanization of Emily and Other Great Movie Themes | 1964 | 15.00 |
| ❑ SE-4271 [S] | The Americanization of Emily and Other Great Movie Themes | 1964 | 20.00 |
| ❑ E-4285 [M] | Quick, Before It Melts and Other Selections | 1965 | 15.00 |
| ❑ SE-4285 [S] | Quick, Before It Melts and Other Selections | 1965 | 20.00 |
| ❑ E-4307 [M] | The Velvet Beat | 1965 | 12.00 |
| ❑ SE-4307 [S] | The Velvet Beat | 1965 | 15.00 |
| ❑ ST-90534 [S] | The Stripper and Other Fun Songs for the Family | 1965 | 20.00 |
| *—Capitol Record Club edition* | | | |
| ❑ T-90534 [M] | The Stripper and Other Fun Songs for the Family | 1965 | 20.00 |
| *—Capitol Record Club edition* | | | |
| ❑ ST-90754 [S] | The Velvet Beat | 1965 | 20.00 |
| *—Capitol Record Club edition* | | | |
| **ROSE, DAVID (2)** | | | |
| INNER CITY | | | |
| ❑ IC-1058 | The Distance Between Dreams | 197? | 12.00 |
| **ROSE, WALLY** | | | |
| COLUMBIA | | | |
| ❑ CL 782 [M] | Cake Walk to Lindy Hop | 1956 | 40.00 |
| ❑ CL 2535 [10] | Honky-Tonkin' | 1955 | 30.00 |
| *—"House Party Series" reissue* | | | |
| ❑ CL 6260 [10] | Wally Rose | 1953 | 50.00 |
| GOOD TIME JAZZ | | | |
| ❑ S-10034 [S] | Ragtime Classics | 1960 | 20.00 |

| Number | Title (A Side/B Side) | Yr | NM |
|---|---|---|---|
| **ROSE GARDEN, THE** | | | |
| ATCO | | | |
| ❑ 33-225 [M] | The Rose Garden | 1968 | 60.00 |
| ❑ SD 33-225 [S] | The Rose Garden | 1968 | 25.00 |
| **ROSE MARIE** | | | |
| KAPP | | | |
| ❑ KFL-4500 [M] | Songs for Single Girls | 1964 | 30.00 |
| **ROSIE AND THE ORIGINALS** | | | |
| BRUNSWICK | | | |
| ❑ BL 54102 [M] | Lonely Blue Nights with Rosie | 1961 | 150.00 |
| ❑ BL 754102 [S] | Lonely Blue Nights with Rosie | 1961 | 200.00 |
| **ROSIE O'GRADY'S GOOD TIME BAND** | | | |
| DIRECT DISK | | | |
| ❑ DD-103 | Dixieland | 1979 | 20.00 |
| *—Audiophile recording* | | | |
| **ROSOLINO, FRANK** | | | |
| BETHLEHEM | | | |
| ❑ BCP-26 [M] | I Play Trombone | 1955 | 120.00 |
| CAPITOL | | | |
| ❑ H 6507 [10] | Frank Rosolino | 1954 | 150.00 |
| ❑ T 6507 [M] | Frank Rosolino | 1955 | 100.00 |
| ❑ T 6509 [M] | Frankly Speaking | 1955 | 100.00 |
| INTERLUDE | | | |
| ❑ MO-500 [M] | The Legend of Frank Rosolino | 1959 | 80.00 |
| ❑ ST-1000 [S] | The Legend of Frank Rosolino | 1959 | 60.00 |
| MODE | | | |
| ❑ LP-107 [M] | Frank Rosolino Quintet | 1957 | 150.00 |
| REPRISE | | | |
| ❑ R-6016 [M] | Turn Me Loose | 1961 | 60.00 |
| ❑ R9-6016 [S] | Turn Me Loose | 1961 | 80.00 |
| **ROSS, ANNIE** Also see LAMBERT, HENDRICKS AND ROSS. | | | |
| DECCA | | | |
| ❑ DL 4922 [M] | Fill My Heart with Song | 1967 | 40.00 |
| ❑ DL 74922 [S] | Fill My Heart with Song | 1967 | 25.00 |
| KIMBERLY | | | |
| ❑ 2018 [M] | Annie Ross Sings A Song With Mulligan! | 1963 | 40.00 |
| ❑ 11018 [S] | Annie Ross Sings A Song With Mulligan! | 1963 | 40.00 |

| Number | Title (A Side/B Side) | Yr | NM |
|---|---|---|---|

**WORLD PACIFIC**

| Number | Title (A Side/B Side) | Yr | NM |
|---|---|---|---|
| ❑ ST-1020 [S] | Annie Ross Sings A Song With Mulligan! | 1959 | 60.00 |
| ❑ ST-1028 [S] | Gypsy | 1959 | 60.00 |
| ❑ WP-1253 [M] | Annie Ross Sings A Song With Mulligan! | 1959 | 70.00 |
| ❑ ST-1285 [S] | A Gasser! | 1960 | 60.00 |
| ❑ WP-1285 [M] | A Gasser! | 1960 | 80.00 |
| ❑ WP-1808 [M] | Gypsy | 1959 | 80.00 |

## ROSS, ANNIE; DOROTHY DUNN; SHELBY DAVIS

**SAVOY**

| Number | Title (A Side/B Side) | Yr | NM |
|---|---|---|---|
| ❑ MG-12060 [M] | Singin' 'N Swingin' | 1956 | 60.00 |

## ROSS, ARNOLD

**DISCOVERY**

| Number | Title (A Side/B Side) | Yr | NM |
|---|---|---|---|
| ❑ DL-2006 [M] | Arnold Ross | 1954 | 50.00 |

**MERCURY**

| Number | Title (A Side/B Side) | Yr | NM |
|---|---|---|---|
| ❑ MGC-134 [10] | Arnold Ross | 1952 | 150.00 |

## ROSS, DIANA

**MOTOWN**

| Number | Title (A Side/B Side) | Yr | NM |
|---|---|---|---|
| ❑ M5-135V1 | Diana Ross | 1981 | 8.00 |
| *—Reissue of 711* | | | |
| ❑ M5-155V1 | Diana! | 1981 | 8.00 |
| *—Reissue of 719* | | | |
| ❑ M5-163V1 | Touch Me in the Morning | 1981 | 8.00 |
| *—Reissue of 772* | | | |
| ❑ M5-169V1 | Diana Ross Live at Caesars Palace | 1981 | 8.00 |
| *—Reissue of 801* | | | |
| ❑ M5-198V1 | The Boss | 1981 | 8.00 |
| *—Reissue of 923* | | | |
| ❑ M5-214V1 | Duets with Diana | 1981 | 10.00 |
| ❑ MS-711 | Diana Ross | 1970 | 15.00 |
| ❑ MS-719 | Diana! | 1971 | 15.00 |
| ❑ MS-723 | Surrender | 1971 | 15.00 |
| ❑ MS-724 | Everything Is Everything | 1970 | 15.00 |
| ❑ M-758D [(2)] | Lady Sings the Blues | 1972 | 15.00 |
| *—With booklet; all but four tracks are by Diana Ross* | | | |
| ❑ M-772L | Touch Me in the Morning | 1973 | 15.00 |
| ❑ M6-801S1 | Diana Ross Live at Caesars Palace | 1974 | 12.00 |
| ❑ M7-812V1 | Last Time I Saw Him | 1974 | 12.00 |
| ❑ M6-861S1 | Diana Ross | 1976 | 12.00 |
| ❑ M6-869S1 | Diana Ross' Greatest Hits | 1976 | 12.00 |
| ❑ M7-877R2 [(2)] | An Evening with Diana Ross | 1977 | 15.00 |
| ❑ M7-890R1 | Baby It's Me | 1977 | 12.00 |
| ❑ M7-907R1 | Ross | 1978 | 12.00 |
| ❑ M8-923M1 | The Boss | 1979 | 10.00 |
| ❑ M8-936 | Diana | 1980 | 10.00 |
| ❑ M8-951M1 | To Love Again | 1981 | 10.00 |
| ❑ M13-960C2 [(2)] | All the Great Hits | 1981 | 12.00 |
| ❑ 5294 ML | Diana Ross | 1983 | 8.00 |
| *—Reissue of 861* | | | |
| ❑ 6049 ML2 [(2)] | Diana Ross Anthology | 1983 | 15.00 |
| ❑ MOT-6274 | Workin' Overtime | 1989 | 10.00 |
| ❑ 37463-6377-1 | The Remixes | 1994 | 12.00 |

**NAUTILUS**

| Number | Title (A Side/B Side) | Yr | NM |
|---|---|---|---|
| ❑ NR-37 | Diana | 1981 | 40.00 |
| *—Audiophile vinyl* | | | |

**RCA VICTOR**

| Number | Title (A Side/B Side) | Yr | NM |
|---|---|---|---|
| ❑ AFL1-4153 | Why Do Fools Fall in Love | 1981 | 10.00 |
| ❑ AFL1-4384 | Silk Electric | 1982 | 10.00 |
| ❑ AFL1-4677 | Ross | 1983 | 8.00 |
| ❑ AFL1-5009 | Swept Away | 1984 | 8.00 |
| ❑ AYL1-5162 | Why Do Fools Fall in Love | 1985 | 6.00 |
| *—"Best Buy Series" reissue* | | | |
| ❑ AFL1-5422 | Eaten Alive | 1985 | 8.00 |
| ❑ 6388-1-R | Red Hot Rhythm and Blues | 1987 | 8.00 |

## ROSS, DIANA, AND THE SUPREMES

See THE SUPREMES.

## ROSS, JACK

**DOT**

| Number | Title (A Side/B Side) | Yr | NM |
|---|---|---|---|
| ❑ DLP-3429 [M] | Cinderella | 1962 | 20.00 |
| ❑ DLP-25429 [S] | Cinderella | 1962 | 25.00 |

## ROSS, JACKIE

**CHESS**

| Number | Title (A Side/B Side) | Yr | NM |
|---|---|---|---|
| ❑ LP-1489 [M] | In Full Bloom | 1966 | 30.00 |
| ❑ LPS-1489 [S] | In Full Bloom | 1966 | 40.00 |

## ROSS, JOE E.

**ROULETTE**

| Number | Title (A Side/B Side) | Yr | NM |
|---|---|---|---|
| ❑ R-25281 [M] | Love Songs from a Cop | 1965 | 25.00 |
| ❑ SR-25281 [S] | Love Songs from a Cop | 1965 | 30.00 |

## ROSS, RONNIE

**ATLANTIC**

| Number | Title (A Side/B Side) | Yr | NM |
|---|---|---|---|
| ❑ 1333 [M] | The Jazz Makers | 1960 | 30.00 |
| ❑ SD 1333 [S] | The Jazz Makers | 1960 | 40.00 |

## ROSS, SPENCER

**COLUMBIA**

| Number | Title (A Side/B Side) | Yr | NM |
|---|---|---|---|
| ❑ CS (# unknown) [S] | Spencer Ross and His Orchestra | 1960 | 25.00 |
| ❑ CL 1525 [M] | Spencer Ross and His Orchestra | 1960 | 20.00 |

## ROSS, STAN

**DEL-FI**

| Number | Title (A Side/B Side) | Yr | NM |
|---|---|---|---|
| ❑ DFLP-1233 [M] | My Son the Copy Cat | 1963 | 30.00 |
| ❑ DFST-1233 [S] | My Son the Copy Cat | 1963 | 40.00 |

## ROTARY CONNECTION

**CADET**

| Number | Title (A Side/B Side) | Yr | NM |
|---|---|---|---|
| ❑ CS-50006 | Hey Love | 1971 | 20.00 |

**CADET CONCEPT**

| Number | Title (A Side/B Side) | Yr | NM |
|---|---|---|---|
| ❑ LP-312 [M] | Rotary Connection | 1968 | 60.00 |
| *—Mono appears to be promo only* | | | |
| ❑ LPS-312 [S] | Rotary Connection | 1968 | 25.00 |
| ❑ LPS-317 | Aladdin | 1968 | 25.00 |
| ❑ LPS 318 | Peace | 1969 | 20.00 |
| ❑ LPS-322 | Songs | 1969 | 25.00 |
| ❑ LSP-328 | Dinner Music | 1970 | 25.00 |

## ROTH, LILLIAN

**EPIC**

| Number | Title (A Side/B Side) | Yr | NM |
|---|---|---|---|
| ❑ LN 3206 [M] | I'll Cry Tomorrow | 1957 | 30.00 |

**TOPS**

| Number | Title (A Side/B Side) | Yr | NM |
|---|---|---|---|
| ❑ L-1567 [M] | Lillian Roth Sings | 1958 | 25.00 |

## ROUND, JONATHAN

**WESTBOUND**

| Number | Title (A Side/B Side) | Yr | NM |
|---|---|---|---|
| ❑ 2009 | Jonathan Round | 1971 | 30.00 |
| *—Round cover* | | | |
| ❑ 2009 | Jonathan Round | 1972 | 15.00 |
| *—Square cover* | | | |

## ROUND ROBIN

**CHALLENGE**

| Number | Title (A Side/B Side) | Yr | NM |
|---|---|---|---|
| ❑ LP-620 [M] | The Land of 1,000 Dances | 1965 | 25.00 |

**DOMAIN**

| Number | Title (A Side/B Side) | Yr | NM |
|---|---|---|---|
| ❑ 101 [M] | Greatest Dance Hits Slauson Style | 1964 | 40.00 |

## ROUSE, CHARLIE

**BLUE NOTE**

| Number | Title (A Side/B Side) | Yr | NM |
|---|---|---|---|
| ❑ BLP-4119 [M] | Bossa Nova Bacchanal | 1962 | 30.00 |
| ❑ BST-84119 [S] | Bossa Nova Bacchanal | 196? | 20.00 |
| *—With "A Division of Liberty Records" on label* | | | |
| ❑ BST-84119 [S] | Bossa Nova Bacchanal | 1962 | 40.00 |
| *—With "New York, USA" address on label* | | | |

**EPIC**

| Number | Title (A Side/B Side) | Yr | NM |
|---|---|---|---|
| ❑ LA 16012 [M] | Yeah! | 1960 | 40.00 |
| ❑ LA 16018 [M] | We Paid Our Dues | 1961 | 40.00 |
| ❑ BA 17012 [S] | Yeah! | 1960 | 50.00 |
| ❑ BA 17012 [S] | Yeah! | 199? | 25.00 |
| *—Classic Records reissue on audiophile vinyl* | | | |
| ❑ BA 17018 [S] | We Paid Our Dues | 1961 | 50.00 |

**JAZZLAND**

| Number | Title (A Side/B Side) | Yr | NM |
|---|---|---|---|
| ❑ JLP-19 [M] | Takin' Care of Business | 1960 | 40.00 |
| ❑ JLP-919 [S] | Takin' Care of Business | 1960 | 50.00 |

**STRATA-EAST**

| Number | Title (A Side/B Side) | Yr | NM |
|---|---|---|---|
| ❑ SES-19746 | Two Is One | 1974 | 25.00 |

## ROUSE, CHARLIE, AND PAUL QUINICHETTE

**BETHLEHEM**

| Number | Title (A Side/B Side) | Yr | NM |
|---|---|---|---|
| ❑ BCP-6021 [M] | The Chase Is On | 1958 | 50.00 |

## ROUTERS, THE

**WARNER BROS.**

| Number | Title (A Side/B Side) | Yr | NM |
|---|---|---|---|
| ❑ W 1490 [M] | Let's Go! with the Routers | 1963 | 25.00 |
| ❑ WS 1490 [S] | Let's Go! with the Routers | 1963 | 30.00 |
| ❑ W 1524 [M] | 1963's Great Instrumental Hits | 1964 | 30.00 |
| ❑ WS 1524 [S] | 1963's Great Instrumental Hits | 1964 | 40.00 |
| ❑ W 1559 [M] | Charge! | 1964 | 25.00 |
| ❑ WS 1559 [S] | Charge! | 1964 | 30.00 |
| ❑ W 1595 [M] | Go Go Go with the Chuck Berry Songbook | 1965 | 20.00 |
| ❑ WS 1595 [S] | Go Go Go with the Chuck Berry Songbook | 1965 | 25.00 |

## ROVA

**METALANGUAGE**

| Number | Title (A Side/B Side) | Yr | NM |
|---|---|---|---|
| ❑ (# unknown) | Daredevils | 1979 | 20.00 |
| ❑ 101 | Cinema Rovate | 1978 | 20.00 |
| ❑ 106 | The Removal of Secrecy | 1979 | 20.00 |

## ROWLES, JIMMY

**ANDEX**

| Number | Title (A Side/B Side) | Yr | NM |
|---|---|---|---|
| ❑ A-3007 [M] | Weather in a Jazz Vane | 1958 | 50.00 |
| ❑ AS-3007 [S] | Weather in a Jazz Vane | 1958 | 40.00 |

**CAPITOL**

| Number | Title (A Side/B Side) | Yr | NM |
|---|---|---|---|
| ❑ ST 1831 [S] | Kinda Groovy! | 1963 | 40.00 |

**INTERLUDE**

| Number | Title (A Side/B Side) | Yr | NM |
|---|---|---|---|
| ❑ MO-515 [M] | Upper Classmen | 1959 | 60.00 |
| ❑ ST-1015 [S] | Upper Classmen | 1959 | 40.00 |

**LIBERTY**

| Number | Title (A Side/B Side) | Yr | NM |
|---|---|---|---|
| ❑ LRP-3003 [M] | Rare — But Well Done | 1955 | 150.00 |

**SIGNATURE**

| Number | Title (A Side/B Side) | Yr | NM |
|---|---|---|---|
| ❑ SM-6011 [M] | Fiorello Uptown, Mary Sunshine Downtown | 1960 | 120.00 |
| ❑ SS-6011 [S] | Fiorello Uptown, Mary Sunshine Downtown | 1960 | 150.00 |

**TAMPA**

| Number | Title (A Side/B Side) | Yr | NM |
|---|---|---|---|
| ❑ TP-8 [M] | Let's Get Acquainted with Jazz… For People Who Hate Jazz | 1957 | 250.00 |
| *—Colored vinyl* | | | |
| ❑ TP-8 [M] | Let's Get Acquainted with Jazz… For People Who Hate Jazz | 1958 | 150.00 |
| ❑ TPS-8 [S] | Let's Get Acquainted with Jazz… For People Who Hate Jazz | 1958 | 80.00 |

## ROXETTE

**CAPITOL**

| Number | Title (A Side/B Side) | Yr | NM |
|---|---|---|---|
| ❑ MLP-15018 [EP] | Heartland | 1984 | 40.00 |

**EMI**

| Number | Title (A Side/B Side) | Yr | NM |
|---|---|---|---|
| ❑ E1-91098 | Look Sharp! | 1989 | 15.00 |

## ROXY MUSIC

**ATCO**

| Number | Title (A Side/B Side) | Yr | NM |
|---|---|---|---|
| ❑ SD 32-102 | Flesh + Blood | 1980 | 10.00 |
| ❑ SD 38-103 | Greatest Hits | 1977 | 10.00 |
| ❑ SD 36-106 | Country Life | 1975 | 25.00 |
| *—Original cover shows two semi-naked women on a grassy background* | | | |
| ❑ SD 36-106A | Country Life | 1975 | 10.00 |
| *—Revised cover deletes women, leaves only the grassy background* | | | |
| ❑ SD 38-114 | Manifesto | 1979 | 10.00 |
| ❑ SD 38-114 [PD] | Manifesto | 1979 | 30.00 |
| *—Picture disc* | | | |
| ❑ SD 36-127 | Siren | 1975 | 10.00 |
| *—Originals have yellow labels* | | | |
| ❑ SD 36-133 | The First Roxy Music Album | 1975 | 12.00 |
| *—Reissue of Reprise MS 2114; originals have yellow labels* | | | |
| ❑ SD 36-134 | For Your Pleasure | 1975 | 12.00 |
| *—Reissue of Warner Bros. BS 2696; originals have yellow labels* | | | |
| ❑ SD 36-139 | Viva! Roxy Music (Live) | 1976 | 10.00 |
| *—Originals have yellow labels* | | | |
| ❑ SD 7045 | Stranded | 1974 | 12.00 |
| ❑ 90122 | The Atlantic Years (1973-80) | 1983 | 10.00 |

**REPRISE**

| Number | Title (A Side/B Side) | Yr | NM |
|---|---|---|---|
| ❑ MS 2114 | Roxy Music | 1972 | 30.00 |
| ❑ 25857 [(2)] | Street Life: 20 Greatest Hits | 1989 | 15.00 |
| *—By "Bryan Ferry & Roxy Music"* | | | |

**WARNER BROS.**

| Number | Title (A Side/B Side) | Yr | NM |
|---|---|---|---|
| ❑ BS 2696 | For Your Pleasure | 1973 | 25.00 |
| ❑ 23686 | Avalon | 1982 | 10.00 |
| ❑ 23808 [EP] | Musique — The High Road | 1983 | 8.00 |

## ROYAL, BILLY JOE

**ATLANTIC AMERICA**

| Number | Title (A Side/B Side) | Yr | NM |
|---|---|---|---|
| ❑ 90508 | Looking Ahead | 1986 | 10.00 |
| ❑ 90658 | The Royal Treatment | 1987 | 10.00 |
| ❑ 91064 | Tell It Like It Is | 1989 | 10.00 |

**COLUMBIA**

| Number | Title (A Side/B Side) | Yr | NM |
|---|---|---|---|
| ❑ CL 2403 [M] | Down in the Boondocks | 1965 | 20.00 |
| ❑ CL 2781 [M] | Billy Joe Royal | 1967 | 25.00 |
| ❑ CS 9203 [S] | Down in the Boondocks | 1965 | 25.00 |
| ❑ CS 9581 [S] | Billy Joe Royal | 1967 | 25.00 |
| ❑ CS 9974 | Cherry Hill Park | 1969 | 25.00 |

**KAT FAMILY**

| Number | Title (A Side/B Side) | Yr | NM |
|---|---|---|---|
| ❑ JW 37342 | Billy Joe Royal | 1982 | 10.00 |

**MERCURY**

| Number | Title (A Side/B Side) | Yr | NM |
|---|---|---|---|
| ❑ SRM-1-3837 | Billy Joe Royal | 1980 | 10.00 |

## ROYAL, ERNIE

**URANIA**

| Number | Title (A Side/B Side) | Yr | NM |
|---|---|---|---|
| ❑ UJLP-1203 [M] | Accent on Trumpet | 1955 | 50.00 |

## ROYAL, MARSHALL

**EVEREST**

| Number | Title (A Side/B Side) | Yr | NM |
|---|---|---|---|
| ❑ SDBR-1087 [S] | Gordon Jenkins Presents Marshall Royal | 1960 | 30.00 |
| ❑ LPBR-5087 [M] | Gordon Jenkins Presents Marshall Royal | 1960 | 25.00 |

## ROYAL CHORAL SOCIETY, THE

**RCA VICTOR BLUEBIRD CLASSICS**

| Number | Title (A Side/B Side) | Yr | NM |
|---|---|---|---|
| ❑ LBC-1044 [M] | Yuletide Hymns and Carols | 1954 | 25.00 |

## ROYAL GUARDSMEN, THE

**HOLIDAY**

| Number | Title (A Side/B Side) | Yr | NM |
|---|---|---|---|
| ❑ HDY 1913 | Merry Snoopy's Christmas | 1980 | 10.00 |
| *—Reissue of Laurie 2042* | | | |

**LAURIE**

| Number | Title (A Side/B Side) | Yr | NM |
|---|---|---|---|
| ❑ LLP-2038 [M] | Snoopy vs. the Red Baron | 1967 | 20.00 |
| ❑ SLP-2038 [S] | Snoopy vs. the Red Baron | 1967 | 25.00 |
| ❑ LLP-2039 [M] | The Return of the Red Baron | 1967 | 20.00 |
| ❑ SLP-2039 [S] | The Return of the Red Baron | 1967 | 25.00 |



**Except when noted otherwise, VG = 25% of NM, and VG+ = 50% of NM. (Example: VG = $2.00, VG+ = $4.00 and NM = $8.00.)**

| Number | Title (A Side/B Side) | Yr | NM |
|---|---|---|---|
| ❑ LLP 2042 [M] | Snoopy and His Friends | 1967 | 15.00 |
| *—With "Merry Snoopy's Christmas" poster missing* | | | |
| ❑ LLP 2042 [M] | Snoopy and His Friends | 1967 | 25.00 |
| *—With "Merry Snoopy's Christmas" poster still attached to back cover* | | | |
| ❑ SLP 2042 [S] | Snoopy and His Friends | 1967 | 20.00 |
| *—With "Merry Snoopy's Christmas" poster missing* | | | |
| ❑ SLP 2042 [S] | Snoopy and His Friends | 1967 | 30.00 |
| *—With "Merry Snoopy's Christmas" poster still attached to back cover* | | | |
| ❑ SLP-2046 | Snoopy for President | 1968 | 25.00 |

### ROYAL MALE CHOIR OF HOLLAND, THE

**EPIC**

| Number | Title (A Side/B Side) | Yr | NM |
|---|---|---|---|
| ❑ LC 3074 | Christmas Carols | 195? | 20.00 |

### ROYAL OPERA HOUSE ORCHESTRA (ERNEST ANSERMET, CONDUCTOR)

**RCA VICTOR RED SEAL**

| Number | Title (A Side/B Side) | Yr | NM |
|---|---|---|---|
| ❑ LDS-6065 [(2)S] | The Royal Ballet Gala Performances | 195? | 1200. |
| *—Original with "shaded dog" labels* | | | |
| ❑ LDS-6065 [(2)S] | The Royal Ballet Gala Performances | 199? | 40.00 |
| *—Classic Records reissue at 33 1/3 rpm* | | | |
| ❑ LDS-6065 [(9)S] | The Royal Ballet Gala Performances | 199? | 120.00 |
| *—Classic Records reissue at 45 rpm* | | | |

### ROYAL OPERA HOUSE ORCHESTRA (ANATOLE FISTOULARI, CONDUCTOR)

**RCA VICTOR RED SEAL**

| Number | Title (A Side/B Side) | Yr | NM |
|---|---|---|---|
| ❑ LSC-2285 [S] | Walton: Facade Suite | 1959 | 200.00 |
| *—Original with "shaded dog" label* | | | |
| ❑ LSC-2285 [S] | Walton: Facade Suite | 199? | 25.00 |
| *—Classic Records reissue* | | | |

### ROYAL OPERA HOUSE ORCHESTRA (ALEXANDER GIBSON, CONDUCTOR)

**RCA VICTOR RED SEAL**

| Number | Title (A Side/B Side) | Yr | NM |
|---|---|---|---|
| ❑ LSC-2449 [S] | Gounod: Ballet Music of Faust; Bizet: Carmen | 1960 | 1000. |
| *—Original with "shaded dog" label* | | | |
| ❑ LSC-2449 [S] | Gounod: Ballet Music of Faust; Bizet: Carmen | 199? | 25.00 |
| *—Classic Records reissue* | | | |

### ROYAL OPERA HOUSE ORCHESTRA (JEAN MOREL, CONDUCTOR)

**RCA VICTOR RED SEAL**

| Number | Title (A Side/B Side) | Yr | NM |
|---|---|---|---|
| ❑ LSC-2327 [S] | Bizet: L'Arlesienne Suites | 1960 | 180.00 |
| *—Original with "shaded dog" label* | | | |
| ❑ LSC-2327 [S] | Bizet: L'Arlesienne Suites | 199? | 25.00 |
| *—Classic Records reissue* | | | |
| ❑ LSC-6094 [(2)S] | Albeniz: Iberia (Complete); Ravel: Rapsodie Espagnole | 196? | 400.00 |
| *—Original with "shaded dog" labels* | | | |
| ❑ LSC-6094 [(2)S] | Albeniz: Iberia (Complete); Ravel: Rapsodie Espagnole | 199? | 40.00 |
| *—Classic Records reissue* | | | |

### ROYAL OPERA HOUSE ORCHESTRA (HUGO RIGNOLD, CONDUCTOR)

**RCA VICTOR RED SEAL**

| Number | Title (A Side/B Side) | Yr | NM |
|---|---|---|---|
| ❑ LSC-2135 [S] | Prokofiev: Cinderella | 199? | 25.00 |
| *—Classic Records issue; this album is not known to have been issued in stereo before this.* | | | |
| ❑ LSC-2450 [S] | Schumann: Carnaval; Meyerbeer: Les Patineurs | 1960 | 60.00 |
| *—Original with "shaded dog" label* | | | |
| ❑ LSC-2450 [S] | Schumann: Carnaval; Meyerbeer: Les Patineurs | 199? | 25.00 |
| *—Classic Records reissue* | | | |

### ROYAL OPERA HOUSE ORCHESTRA (SIR GEORGE SOLTI, CONDUCTOR)

**RCA VICTOR RED SEAL**

| Number | Title (A Side/B Side) | Yr | NM |
|---|---|---|---|
| ❑ LSC-2313 [S] | Venice | 1959 | 100.00 |
| *—Original with "shaded dog" label* | | | |
| ❑ LSC-2313 [S] | Venice | 199? | 25.00 |
| *—Classic Records reissue* | | | |

### ROYAL PHILHARMONIC ORCHESTRA (RENE LEIBOWITZ, CONDUCTOR)

**RCA VICTOR RED SEAL**

| Number | Title (A Side/B Side) | Yr | NM |
|---|---|---|---|
| ❑ VCS-2659 [S] | The Power of the Orchestra | 1962 | 300.00 |
| *—Original with "shaded dog" label* | | | |

### ROYAL PLAYBOYS, THE

**WALDORF**

| Number | Title (A Side/B Side) | Yr | NM |
|---|---|---|---|
| ❑ 33-136 [10] | Rock and Roll/New Orleans Blues | 195? | 500.00 |

### ROYAL TEENS, THE

**COLLECTABLES**

| Number | Title (A Side/B Side) | Yr | NM |
|---|---|---|---|
| ❑ COL-5094 | Short Shorts: Golden Classics | 198? | 10.00 |

**MUSICOR**

| Number | Title (A Side/B Side) | Yr | NM |
|---|---|---|---|
| ❑ MS-3186 | Newies But Oldies | 1970 | 20.00 |

**TRU-GEMS**

| Number | Title (A Side/B Side) | Yr | NM |
|---|---|---|---|
| ❑ 1001 | Short Shorts & Others | 1975 | 20.00 |

### ROYALETTES, THE

**MGM**

| Number | Title (A Side/B Side) | Yr | NM |
|---|---|---|---|
| ❑ E-4332 [M] | It's Gonna Take a Miracle | 1965 | 20.00 |
| ❑ SE-4332 [S] | It's Gonna Take a Miracle | 1965 | 25.00 |
| ❑ E-4366 [M] | The Elegant Sound of the Royalettes | 1966 | 20.00 |
| ❑ SE-4366 [S] | The Elegant Sound of the Royalettes | 1966 | 25.00 |

### RUBBER BAND, THE (2)

**GRT**

| Number | Title (A Side/B Side) | Yr | NM |
|---|---|---|---|
| ❑ 10000 | Cream Songbook | 1969 | 25.00 |
| ❑ 10007 | Hendrix Songbook | 1969 | 25.00 |
| ❑ 10015 | Beatles Songbook | 1969 | 25.00 |

### RUBBER CITY REBELS

**CAPITOL**

| Number | Title (A Side/B Side) | Yr | NM |
|---|---|---|---|
| ❑ ST-12100 | Rubber City Rebels | 1980 | 40.00 |

### RUBBER MEMORY

**R.P.C.**

| Number | Title (A Side/B Side) | Yr | NM |
|---|---|---|---|
| ❑ 69401 | Welcome | 196? | 1000. |

### RUBEN AND THE JETS

**MERCURY**

| Number | Title (A Side/B Side) | Yr | NM |
|---|---|---|---|
| ❑ SRM-1-659 | For Real | 1973 | 25.00 |
| ❑ SRM-1-694 | Con Safos | 1974 | 25.00 |

### RUBENSTEIN, ARTUR

**RCA VICTOR RED SEAL**

| Number | Title (A Side/B Side) | Yr | NM |
|---|---|---|---|
| ❑ LSC-1831 [S] | Brahms: Piano Concerto No. 1 | 199? | 25.00 |
| *—With the Chicago Symphony (Fritz Reiner cond.); Classic Records issue; this album is not known to have been issued in stereo before this* | | | |
| ❑ LSC-2068 [S] | Rachmaninoff: Piano Concerto No. 2; Lizst: Piano Conceto No. 1 | 1958 | 25.00 |
| *—Original with "shaded dog" label* | | | |
| ❑ LSC-2120 [S] | Beethoven: Piano Concerto No. 1 | 1959 | 25.00 |
| *—With Josef Krips/NBC "Symphony of the Air" Orchestra; original with "shaded dog" label* | | | |
| ❑ LSC-2121 [S] | Beethoven: Piano Concerto No. 2 | 1959 | 20.00 |
| *—With Josef Krips/NBC "Symphony of the Air" Orchestra; original with "shaded dog" label* | | | |
| ❑ LSC-2122 [S] | Beethoven: Piano Concerto No. 3 | 1959 | 20.00 |
| *—With Josef Krips/NBC "Symphony of the Air" Orchestra; original with "shaded dog" label* | | | |
| ❑ LSC-2123 [S] | Beethoven: Piano Concerto No. 4 | 1959 | 20.00 |
| *—With Josef Krips/NBC "Symphony of the Air" Orchestra; original with "shaded dog" label* | | | |
| ❑ LSC-2124 [S] | Beethoven: Piano Concerto No. 5 | 1959 | 20.00 |
| *—With Josef Krips/NBC "Symphony of the Air" Orchestra; original with "shaded dog" label* | | | |
| ❑ LSC-2234 [S] | Saint-Saens: Piano Concerto No. 2 | 1959 | 20.00 |
| *—With the Symphony of the Air Orchestra (Alfred Wallenstein, conductor); original with "shaded dog" label* | | | |
| ❑ LSC-2234 [S] | Saint-Saens: Piano Concerto No. 2 | 199? | 25.00 |
| *—With the Symphony of the Air Orchestra (Alfred Wallenstein, conductor); Classic Records reissue* | | | |
| ❑ LSC-2256 [S] | Schubert: Piano Concerto in A | 1959 | 20.00 |
| *—With Josef Krips/RCA Victor Symphony Orchestra; original with "shaded dog" label* | | | |
| ❑ LSC-2265 [S] | The Rubenstein Story | 1959 | 30.00 |
| *—With Alfred Wallerstein/NBC Symphony Orchestra; original with "shaded dog" label and gatefold cover* | | | |
| ❑ LSC-2296 [S] | Brahms: Piano Concerto No. 2 | 1959 | 20.00 |
| *—With Josef Krips/RCA Victor Symphony Orchestra; original with "shaded dog" label* | | | |
| ❑ LSC-2368 [S] | Chopin: Scherzos 1-4 | 1960 | 20.00 |
| *—Original with "shaded dog" label* | | | |
| ❑ LSC-2370 [S] | Chopin: Ballades 1-4 | 1960 | 20.00 |
| *—Original with "shaded dog" label* | | | |
| ❑ LSC-2429 [S] | Grieg: Piano Concerto in A; Lizst: Piano Concerto No. 1 | 1960 | 30.00 |
| *—Original with "shaded dog" label* | | | |
| ❑ LSC-2430 [S] | Rachmaninoff: Rhapsody on a Theme of Paganini | 1960 | 20.00 |
| *—With Fritz Reiner/Chicago Symphony Orchestra; original with "shaded dog" label* | | | |
| ❑ LSC-2430 [S] | Rachmaninoff: Rhapsody on a Theme of Paganini | 199? | 25.00 |
| *—With Fritz Reiner/Chicago Symphony Orchestra; Classic Records reissue* | | | |
| ❑ LSC-2459 [S] | Brahms: Piano Sonata in F; Intermezzo; Romance | 1961 | 40.00 |
| *—Original with "shaded dog" label* | | | |
| ❑ LDS-2554 [S] | Chopin: Piano Sonatas No. 2 and 3 | 1961 | 25.00 |
| *—Original with "shaded dog" label* | | | |
| ❑ LSC-2566 [S] | Grieg: Piano Concerto | 1962 | 20.00 |
| *—Original with "shaded dog" label* | | | |
| ❑ LSC-2605 [S] | Rubenstein at Carnegie Hall | 1962 | 20.00 |
| *—Original with "shaded dog" label* | | | |
| ❑ LSC-2636 [S] | Mozart: Piano Concerto No. 17; Schubert: Impromptus | 1962 | 40.00 |
| *—Original with "shaded dog" label* | | | |

### RUBIN, STAN

**CORAL**

| Number | Title (A Side/B Side) | Yr | NM |
|---|---|---|---|
| ❑ CRL 57185 [M] | Dixieland Goes Broadway | 1959 | 25.00 |
| ❑ CRL 757185 [S] | Dixieland Goes Broadway | 1959 | 30.00 |

**JUBLIEE**

| Number | Title (A Side/B Side) | Yr | NM |
|---|---|---|---|
| ❑ JLP-4 [10] | The Tigertown Five, Vol. 1 | 1954 | 50.00 |
| ❑ JLP-5 [10] | The Tigertown Five, Vol. 2 | 1954 | 50.00 |
| ❑ JLP-6 [10] | The Tigertown Five, Vol. 3 | 1954 | 50.00 |
| ❑ JLP-1001 [M] | The College All Stars at Carnegie Hall | 1955 | 40.00 |
| ❑ JLP-1003 [M] | College Jazz Comes to Carnegie Hall | 1955 | 40.00 |
| ❑ JLP-1016 [M] | Tigertown Five | 1956 | 40.00 |
| ❑ JLP-1024 [M] | Stan Rubin in Morocco | 1956 | 40.00 |

**PRINCETON**

| Number | Title (A Side/B Side) | Yr | NM |
|---|---|---|---|
| ❑ LP-102 [10] | The Stan Rubin Tigertown Five | 1954 | 60.00 |

**RCA VICTOR**

| Number | Title (A Side/B Side) | Yr | NM |
|---|---|---|---|
| ❑ LPM-1200 [M] | Dixieland Bash | 1956 | 40.00 |
| ❑ LPM-3277 [10] | Stan Rubin's Dixieland Comes to Carnegie Hall | 1955 | 50.00 |

### RUBY AND THE ROMANTICS

**ABC**

| Number | Title (A Side/B Side) | Yr | NM |
|---|---|---|---|
| ❑ S-638 | More Than Yesterday | 1968 | 20.00 |

**KAPP**

| Number | Title (A Side/B Side) | Yr | NM |
|---|---|---|---|
| ❑ KL-1323 [M] | Our Day Will Come | 1963 | 30.00 |
| ❑ KL-1341 [M] | Till Then | 1963 | 25.00 |
| ❑ KL-1458 [M] | The Greatest Hits Album | 1966 | 20.00 |
| ❑ KL-1526 [M] | Ruby and the Romantics | 1967 | 25.00 |
| ❑ KS-3323 [S] | Our Day Will Come | 1963 | 40.00 |
| ❑ KS-3341 [S] | Till Then | 1963 | 30.00 |
| ❑ KS-3458 [S] | The Greatest Hits Album | 1966 | 25.00 |
| ❑ KS-3526 [S] | Ruby and the Romantics | 1967 | 25.00 |

**MCA**

| Number | Title (A Side/B Side) | Yr | NM |
|---|---|---|---|
| ❑ 541 | The Greatest Hits Album | 197? | 10.00 |

**PICKWICK**

| Number | Title (A Side/B Side) | Yr | NM |
|---|---|---|---|
| ❑ SPC-3519 | Makin' Out | 197? | 10.00 |

### RUDD, ROSWELL

**IMPULSE!**

| Number | Title (A Side/B Side) | Yr | NM |
|---|---|---|---|
| ❑ A-9126 [M] | Everywhere | 1967 | 30.00 |
| ❑ AS-9126 [S] | Everywhere | 1967 | 25.00 |

### RUEDEBUSCH, DICK

**JUBILEE**

| Number | Title (A Side/B Side) | Yr | NM |
|---|---|---|---|
| ❑ JGS-5008 [S] | Meet Mr. Trumpet | 1962 | 20.00 |
| ❑ JGS-5015 [S] | Dick Ruedebusch Remembers the Greats | 1962 | 20.00 |
| ❑ JGS-5021 [S] | Mr. Trumpet, Volume 2 | 1963 | 20.00 |

### RUFF, WILLIE

**COLUMBIA**

| Number | Title (A Side/B Side) | Yr | NM |
|---|---|---|---|
| ❑ CS 9603 | The Smooth Side of Willie Ruff | 1968 | 20.00 |
| *—Red "360 Sound" label* | | | |

### RUFFIN, DAVID Also see THE TEMPTATIONS.

**MOTOWN**

| Number | Title (A Side/B Side) | Yr | NM |
|---|---|---|---|
| ❑ M5-146V1 | My Whole World Ended | 1981 | 8.00 |
| *—Reissue* | | | |
| ❑ M5-211V1 | At His Best | 1981 | 8.00 |
| *—Reissue* | | | |
| ❑ MS-685 | My Whole World Ended | 1969 | 20.00 |
| ❑ MS-696 | Feelin' Good | 1969 | 15.00 |
| ❑ M 733 | David Ruffin | 1971 | — |
| *—Canceled* | | | |
| ❑ M-762 | David Ruffin | 1973 | 12.00 |
| ❑ M6-818 | Me 'N' Rock 'N' Roll Are Here to Stay | 1974 | 12.00 |
| ❑ M6-849 | Who I Am | 1975 | 12.00 |
| ❑ M6-866 | Everything's Coming Up Love | 1976 | 12.00 |
| ❑ M6-885 | In My Stride | 1977 | 12.00 |
| ❑ M7-895 | At His Best | 1978 | 12.00 |

**WARNER BROS.**

| Number | Title (A Side/B Side) | Yr | NM |
|---|---|---|---|
| ❑ BSK 3306 | So Soon We Change | 1979 | 10.00 |
| ❑ BSK 3416 | Gentleman Ruffin | 1980 | 10.00 |

### RUFFIN, JIMMY

**RSO**

| Number | Title (A Side/B Side) | Yr | NM |
|---|---|---|---|
| ❑ RS-1-3078 | Sunrise | 1980 | 10.00 |

**SOUL**

| Number | Title (A Side/B Side) | Yr | NM |
|---|---|---|---|
| ❑ 704 [M] | Top Ten | 1967 | 25.00 |
| *—Full-color cover* | | | |
| ❑ 704 [M] | Top Ten | 1967 | 50.00 |
| *—One-color cover* | | | |
| ❑ S-704 [S] | Top Ten | 1967 | 25.00 |
| ❑ S-708 | Ruff'n Ready | 1969 | 25.00 |
| ❑ SS-727 | The Groove Governor | 1970 | 20.00 |

### RUFFIN, JIMMY AND DAVID

**MOTOWN**

| Number | Title (A Side/B Side) | Yr | NM |
|---|---|---|---|
| ❑ M5-108V1 | Motown Superstar Series, Vol. 8 | 1981 | 10.00 |

| Number | Title (A Side/B Side) | Yr | NM |
|---|---|---|---|
| **SOUL** | | | |
| ❑ SS-728 | I Am My Brother's Keeper | 1970 | 20.00 |
| **RUFUS** | | | |
| **ABC** | | | |
| ❑ X-783 | Rufus | 1973 | 10.00 |
| ❑ X-809 | Rags to Rufus | 1974 | 10.00 |
| ❑ D-837 | Rufusized | 1974 | 10.00 |
| ❑ D-909 | Rufus Featuring Chaka Khan | 1975 | 10.00 |
| ❑ D-975 | Ask Rufus | 1977 | 10.00 |
| ❑ AA-1049 | Street Player | 1978 | 10.00 |
| ❑ AA-1049 [PD] | Street Player | 1978 | 25.00 |
| *—Promo-only picture disc* | | | |
| ❑ AA-1098 | Numbers | 1979 | 10.00 |
| ❑ AA-1098 [PD] | Numbers | 1979 | 20.00 |
| *—Promo-only picture disc* | | | |
| **COMMAND** | | | |
| ❑ CQD-40023 [Q] | Rufusized | 1974 | 20.00 |
| ❑ CQD-40024 [Q] | Rags to Rufus | 1974 | 20.00 |
| **MCA** | | | |
| ❑ 642 | Rufus | 1980 | 6.00 |
| *—Reissue of ABC 783* | | | |
| ❑ 5103 | Masterjam | 1979 | 10.00 |
| ❑ 5159 | Party 'Til You're Broke | 1981 | 10.00 |
| ❑ 5270 | Camouflage | 1982 | 10.00 |
| ❑ 5339 | The Very Best of Rufus | 1983 | 10.00 |
| ❑ 37034 | Rags to Rufus | 1980 | 6.00 |
| *—Reissue of ABC 809* | | | |
| ❑ 37035 | Rufusized | 1980 | 6.00 |
| *—Reissue of ABC 837* | | | |
| ❑ 37036 | Rufus Featuring Chaka Khan | 1980 | 6.00 |
| *—Reissue of ABC 909* | | | |
| ❑ 37037 | Ask Rufus | 1980 | 6.00 |
| *—Reissue of ABC 975* | | | |
| ❑ 37038 | Street Player | 1980 | 6.00 |
| *—Reissue of ABC 1049* | | | |
| ❑ 37039 | Numbers | 1980 | 6.00 |
| *—Reissue of ABC 1098* | | | |
| ❑ 37157 | Masterjam | 198? | 6.00 |
| *—Reissue of 5103* | | | |
| **WARNER BROS.** | | | |
| ❑ 23679 [(2)] | Live: Stompin' at the Savoy | 1983 | 12.00 |
| ❑ 23753 | Seal in Red | 1984 | 10.00 |
| **RUGBYS, THE** | | | |
| **AMAZON** | | | |
| ❑ 1000 | Hot Cargo | 1970 | 20.00 |
| **RUGOLO, PETE** | | | |
| **COLUMBIA** | | | |
| ❑ CL 604 [M] | Adventures in Rhythm | 1955 | 50.00 |
| *—Maroon label, gold print* | | | |
| ❑ CL 604 [M] | Adventures in Rhythm | 1956 | 40.00 |
| *—Red and black label with six "eye" logos* | | | |
| ❑ CL 635 [M] | Introducing Pete Rugolo | 1955 | 50.00 |
| *—Maroon label, gold print* | | | |
| ❑ CL 635 [M] | Introducing Pete Rugolo | 1956 | 40.00 |
| *—Red and black label with six "eye" logos* | | | |
| ❑ CL 689 [M] | Rugolomania | 1956 | 40.00 |
| *—Red and black label with six "eye" logos* | | | |
| ❑ CL 6289 [10] | Introducing Pete Rugolo | 1954 | 60.00 |
| **EMARCY** | | | |
| ❑ MG-36082 [M] | Music for Hi-Fi Bugs | 1956 | 40.00 |
| ❑ MG-36115 [M] | Out on a Limb | 1957 | 40.00 |
| ❑ MG-36122 [M] | Percussion at Work | 1958 | 40.00 |
| ❑ MG-36143 [M] | Rugolo Plays Kenton | 1958 | 40.00 |
| **MERCURY** | | | |
| ❑ MG-(# unknown) [M] | An Adventure in Sound: Reeds | 1958 | 30.00 |
| ❑ PPS-2001 [M] | 10 Trombones Like 2 Pianos | 196? | 20.00 |
| ❑ PPS-2016 [M] | 10 Trombones and 2 Guitars | 196? | 20.00 |
| ❑ PPS-2023 [M] | 10 Saxophones and 2 Basses | 196? | 20.00 |
| ❑ PPS-6001 [S] | 10 Trombones Like 2 Pianos | 196? | 25.00 |
| ❑ PPS-6016 [S] | 10 Trombones and 2 Guitars | 196? | 25.00 |
| ❑ PPS-6023 [S] | 10 Saxophones and 2 Basses | 196? | 25.00 |
| ❑ MG-20118 [M] | Music from Outer Space | 1957 | 50.00 |
| ❑ MG-20260 [M] | Reeds in Hi-Fi | 1958 | 30.00 |
| ❑ MG-20261 [M] | Brass in Hi-Fi | 1958 | 30.00 |
| ❑ SR-60039 [M] | An Adventure in Sound: Reeds | 1959 | 40.00 |
| ❑ SR-60043 [S] | Reeds in Hi-Fi | 1959 | 40.00 |
| ❑ SR-60044 [S] | Brass in Hi-Fi | 1959 | 40.00 |
| **RUMBLERS, THE** | | | |
| **DOT** | | | |
| ❑ DLP-3509 [M] | Boss! | 1963 | 50.00 |
| ❑ DLP-25509 [S] | Boss! | 1963 | 60.00 |
| **DOWNEY** | | | |
| ❑ DLP-1001 [M] | Boss! | 1963 | 180.00 |
| ❑ DLPS-1001 [S] | Boss! | 1963 | 250.00 |
| **RUMPLESTILTSKIN** | | | |
| **BELL** | | | |
| ❑ 6047 | Rumpelstiltskin | 1970 | 20.00 |
| **RUMSEY, HOWARD** | | | |
| **CONTEMPORARY** | | | |
| ❑ C-2501 [10] | Sunday Jazz a la Lighthouse | 1953 | 120.00 |
| ❑ C-2506 [10] | Howard Rumsey's Lighthouse All-Stars | 1953 | 120.00 |
| ❑ C-2510 [10] | Howard Rumsey's Lighthouse All-Stars, Volume 4 | 1954 | 120.00 |
| ❑ C-2513 [10] | Howard Rumsey's Lighthouse All-Stars, Volume 1: The Quintet | 1954 | 120.00 |
| ❑ C-2515 [10] | Howard Rumsey's Lighthouse All-Stars, Volume 2: The Octet | 1954 | 120.00 |
| ❑ C-3501 [M] | Sunday Jazz a la Lighthouse | 1955 | 80.00 |
| ❑ C-3504 [M] | Howard Rumsey's Lighthouse All-Stars, Vol. 6 | 1955 | 80.00 |
| ❑ C-3508 [M] | Howard Rumsey's Lighthouse All-Stars, Vol. 3 | 1955 | 80.00 |
| ❑ C-3509 [M] | Lighthouse at Laguna | 1955 | 80.00 |
| ❑ C-3517 [M] | In the Solo Spotlight | 1956 | 80.00 |
| ❑ C-3520 [M] | Howard Rumsey's Lighthouse All-Stars, Vol. 4: Oboe/Flute | 1956 | 80.00 |
| ❑ C-3528 [M] | Music for Lighthousekeeping | 1957 | 80.00 |
| ❑ S-7008 [S] | Music for Lighthousekeeping | 1959 | 50.00 |
| **LIBERTY** | | | |
| ❑ LRP-3045 [M] | Double or Nothin' | 1957 | 50.00 |
| ❑ LST-7014 [S] | Double or Nothin' | 1959 | 40.00 |
| **LIGHTHOUSE** | | | |
| ❑ LP-300 [M] | Jazz Rolls-Royce | 1958 | 40.00 |
| ❑ LP-301 [M] | Sunday Jazz a la Lighthouse | 1958 | 40.00 |
| *—Red vinyl* | | | |
| **OMEGA** | | | |
| ❑ OML-5 [M] | Jazz Rolls-Royce | 1960 | 30.00 |
| ❑ OSL-5 [S] | Jazz Rolls-Royce | 1960 | 30.00 |
| **PHILIPS** | | | |
| ❑ PHM 200012 [M] | Jazz Structures | 1961 | 20.00 |
| ❑ PHS 600012 [S] | Jazz Structures | 1961 | 25.00 |
| **STEREO RECORDS** | | | |
| ❑ S-7008 [S] | Music for Lighthousekeeping | 1958 | 70.00 |
| **RUNAWAYS, THE** Also see LITA FORD; JOAN JETT. | | | |
| **MARILYN** | | | |
| ❑ USM 1004 | Born to Be Bad | 1991 | 8.00 |
| **MERCURY** | | | |
| ❑ SRM-1-1090 | The Runaways | 1976 | 25.00 |
| ❑ SRM-1-1126 | Queens of Noise | 1977 | 25.00 |
| ❑ SRM-1-3705 | Waiting for the Night | 1977 | 25.00 |
| ❑ SRM-1-3740 | Live in Japan | 1978 | 50.00 |
| **RHINO** | | | |
| ❑ RNDF-250 [PD] | Little Lost Girls | 1982 | 25.00 |
| ❑ RNEP-602 [EP] | Mama Weer All Crazee Now | 1983 | 15.00 |
| ❑ RNLP-70861 | Little Lost Girls | 1987 | 12.00 |
| *—Reissue of Rhino 250 on regular vinyl* | | | |
| **RUNDGREN, TODD** Also see NAZZ (1). | | | |
| **AMPEX** | | | |
| ❑ A-10105 | Runt | 1970 | 50.00 |
| *—LP jacket and label list 10 tracks and album actually has 10* | | | |
| ❑ A-10105 | Runt | 1970 | 100.00 |
| *—LP jacket and label list 10 tracks, but the album has 11* | | | |
| ❑ A-10105 | Runt | 1970 | 150.00 |
| *—LP jacket and label list 10 tracks, but the album has 12* | | | |
| **BEARSVILLE** | | | |
| ❑ PRO 524 [DJ] | The Todd Rundgren Radio Show | 1972 | 150.00 |
| ❑ PRO 597 [DJ] | Ikon/Todd Rundgren Interview | 1974 | 120.00 |
| ❑ PRO-A-788 [DJ] | Todd Rundgren Radio Sampler | 1978 | 50.00 |
| *—Highlights of "Back to the Bars" plus interview of Todd by Patti Smith* | | | |
| ❑ BR 2046 | Runt | 1972 | 15.00 |
| *—Another reissue, after switch from Ampex to Warner Bros. distribution* | | | |
| ❑ BR 2047 | The Ballad of Todd Rundgren | 1972 | 15.00 |
| *—Reissue of 10116* | | | |
| ❑ 2BX 2066 [(2)] | Something/Anything? | 1972 | 25.00 |
| *—Regular copy with black vinyl* | | | |
| ❑ 2BX 2066 [(2)] | Something/Anything? | 1972 | 400.00 |
| *—White label with one record on red vinyl and the other on blue vinyl* | | | |
| ❑ BR 2133 | A Wizard/A True Star | 1973 | 12.00 |
| ❑ BHS 3522 | Healing | 1981 | 10.00 |
| *—Add $5 if bonus 7-inch 33 1/3 single (Time Heals/Tiny Demons) is included* | | | |
| ❑ 2BR 6952 [(2)] | Todd | 1974 | 15.00 |
| ❑ BR 6957 | Initiation | 1975 | 10.00 |
| ❑ BR 6963 | Faithful | 1976 | 10.00 |
| ❑ BRK 6981 | Hermit of Mink Hollow | 1978 | 10.00 |
| ❑ 2BRX 6986 [(2)] | Back to the Bars | 1978 | 12.00 |
| ❑ A-10105 | Runt | 1971 | 25.00 |
| *—Reissue with new label* | | | |
| ❑ A-10116 | The Ballad of Todd Rundgren | 1971 | 80.00 |
| ❑ 23732 | The Ever Popular Tortured Artist Effect | 1983 | 10.00 |
| **MOBILE FIDELITY** | | | |
| ❑ 2-225 | Something/Anything? | 1995 | 40.00 |
| *—Audiophile vinyl* | | | |
| **RHINO** | | | |
| ❑ RNLP 70862 | Runt | 1987 | 10.00 |
| ❑ RNLP 70863 | The Ballad of Todd Rundgren | 1987 | 10.00 |
| ❑ RNLP 70864 | A Wizard/A True Star | 1987 | 10.00 |
| ❑ RNLP 70866 | Initiation | 1987 | 10.00 |
| ❑ RNLP 70868 | Faithful | 1987 | 10.00 |
| ❑ RNLP 70871 | Hermit of Mink Hollow | 1988 | 10.00 |
| ❑ RNLP 70874 | Healing | 1987 | 10.00 |
| ❑ RNLP 70876 | The Ever Popular Tortured Artist Effect | 1988 | 10.00 |
| ❑ RNDA 71107 | Something/Anything? | 1987 | 12.00 |
| ❑ RNDA 71108 | Todd | 1987 | 12.00 |
| ❑ RNDA 71109 | Back to the Bars | 1987 | 12.00 |
| ❑ R1-71491 | Anthology (1968-1985) | 1989 | 20.00 |
| **WARNER BROS.** | | | |
| ❑ 25128 | A Cappella | 1985 | 10.00 |
| ❑ 25881 | Nearly Human | 1989 | 15.00 |
| **RUSH** | | | |
| **ATLANTIC** | | | |
| ❑ 82040 | Presto | 1989 | 20.00 |
| ❑ 83531 [(2)] | Vapor Trails | 2002 | 15.00 |
| ❑ 83728 | Feedback | 2004 | 12.00 |
| **MERCURY** | | | |
| ❑ MK-32 [DJ] | Everything Your Listener Ever Wanted to Hear by Rush ... But You Were Afraid to Play | 1977 | 150.00 |
| ❑ MK-185 [DJ] | Rush 'N' Roulette | 1981 | 120.00 |
| *—Promo-only six-track EP that has six grooves cut in it; the song it plays is based on where you place the stylus* | | | |
| ❑ SRM-1-1011 | Rush | 1974 | 10.00 |
| *—Based on the LP's release date, original copies theoretically have red labels, rather than the common "Chicago skyline" labels; those would be worth at least twice this price* | | | |
| ❑ SRM-1-1011 | Rush | 1983 | 8.00 |
| *—Black label* | | | |
| ❑ SRM-1-1023 | Fly by Night | 1975 | 10.00 |
| *—"Chicago skyline" label* | | | |
| ❑ SRM-1-1023 | Fly by Night | 1983 | 8.00 |
| *—Black label* | | | |
| ❑ SRM-1-1046 | Caress of Steel | 1975 | 10.00 |
| *—"Chicago skyline" label* | | | |
| ❑ SRM-1-1046 | Caress of Steel | 1983 | 8.00 |
| *—Black label* | | | |
| ❑ SRM-1-1079 | 2112 | 1976 | 10.00 |
| *—"Chicago skyline" label* | | | |
| ❑ SRM-1-1079 | 2112 | 1983 | 8.00 |
| *—Black label* | | | |
| ❑ SRM-1-1184 | A Farewell to Kings | 1977 | 10.00 |
| *—"Chicago skyline" label* | | | |
| ❑ SRM-1-1184 | A Farewell to Kings | 1983 | 8.00 |
| *—Black label* | | | |
| ❑ SRP-1-1300 [PD] | Hemispheres | 1979 | 40.00 |
| ❑ SRM-1-3743 | Hemispheres | 1978 | 10.00 |
| *—"Chicago skyline" label; with poster* | | | |
| ❑ SRM-1-3743 | Hemispheres | 1983 | 8.00 |
| *—Black label* | | | |
| ❑ SRM-1-4001 | Permanent Waves | 1980 | 10.00 |
| *—Custom label* | | | |
| ❑ SRM-1-4013 | Moving Pictures | 1981 | 10.00 |
| *—Custom label* | | | |
| ❑ SRM-1-4063 | Signals | 1982 | 10.00 |
| ❑ SRM-2-7001 [(2)] | Exit... Stage Left | 1981 | 12.00 |
| ❑ SRM-2-7508 [(2)] | All the World's a Stage | 1976 | 12.00 |
| *—"Chicago skyline" labels* | | | |
| ❑ SRM-2-7508 [(2)] | All the World's a Stage | 1983 | 10.00 |
| *—Black labels* | | | |
| ❑ SRM-3-9200 [(3)] | Archives | 1978 | 20.00 |
| *—"Chicago skyline" labels* | | | |
| ❑ SRM-3-9200 [(3)] | Archives | 1983 | 15.00 |
| *—Black labels* | | | |
| ❑ 818476-1 | Grace Under Pressure | 1984 | 10.00 |
| ❑ 822541-1 | Rush | 1985 | 8.00 |
| *—Reissue with new number* | | | |
| ❑ 822542-1 | Fly by Night | 1985 | 8.00 |
| *—Reissue with new number* | | | |
| ❑ 822543-1 | Caress of Steel | 1985 | 8.00 |
| *—Reissue with new number* | | | |
| ❑ 822545-1 | 2112 | 1985 | 8.00 |
| *—Reissue with new number* | | | |
| ❑ 822546-1 | A Farewell to Kings | 1985 | 8.00 |
| *—Reissue with new number* | | | |
| ❑ 822547-1 | Hemispheres | 1985 | 8.00 |
| *—Reissue with new number* | | | |
| ❑ 822548-1 | Permanent Waves | 1985 | 8.00 |
| *—Reissue with new number* | | | |
| ❑ 822549-1 | Moving Pictures | 1985 | 8.00 |
| *—Reissue with new number* | | | |
| ❑ 822550-1 | Signals | 1985 | 8.00 |
| *—Reissue with new number* | | | |
| ❑ 822551-1 [(2)] | Exit...Stage Left | 1985 | 10.00 |
| *—Reissue with new number* | | | |
| ❑ 822552-1 [(2)] | All the World's a Stage | 1985 | 10.00 |
| *—Reissue with new number* | | | |
| ❑ 822553-1 [(3)] | Archives | 1985 | 15.00 |
| *—Reissue with new number* | | | |
| ❑ 826098-1 | Power Windows | 1985 | 10.00 |
| ❑ 832464-1 | Hold Your Fire | 1987 | 10.00 |
| ❑ 836346-1 [(2)] | A Show of Hands | 1988 | 12.00 |

**RUSH, MERRILEE**

BELL

| Number | Title (A Side/B Side) | Yr | NM |
|---|---|---|---|
| ❑ 6020 [M] | Angel of the Morning | 1968 | 40.00 |

*—Mono is white label promo only with "Monaural" on label; sticker with "This is a monaural record for radio station play only" on cover*

| Number | Title (A Side/B Side) | Yr | NM |
|---|---|---|---|
| ❑ 6020 [S] | Angel of the Morning | 1968 | 20.00 |

LIBERTY

| Number | Title (A Side/B Side) | Yr | NM |
|---|---|---|---|
| ❑ LN-10166 | Merilee Rush | 1981 | 8.00 |

*—Budget-line reissue*

UNITED ARTISTS

| Number | Title (A Side/B Side) | Yr | NM |
|---|---|---|---|
| ❑ UA-LA735-G | Merilee Rush | 1977 | 10.00 |

**RUSH, OTIS**

BLUE HORIZON

| Number | Title (A Side/B Side) | Yr | NM |
|---|---|---|---|
| ❑ BH-4602 | Blues Masters, Volume 2 | 1968 | 25.00 |
| ❑ BH-4805 | Chicago Blues | 1970 | 25.00 |

COTILLION

| Number | Title (A Side/B Side) | Yr | NM |
|---|---|---|---|
| ❑ SD 9006 | Mourning in the Morning | 1969 | 25.00 |

**RUSH, TOM**

COLUMBIA

| Number | Title (A Side/B Side) | Yr | NM |
|---|---|---|---|
| ❑ CS 9972 | Tom Rush | 1970 | 12.00 |

*—Orange label*

| Number | Title (A Side/B Side) | Yr | NM |
|---|---|---|---|
| ❑ CS 9972 | Tom Rush | 1970 | 15.00 |

*—Red "360 Sound" label*

| Number | Title (A Side/B Side) | Yr | NM |
|---|---|---|---|
| ❑ C 30402 | Wrong End of the Rainbow | 1970 | 12.00 |
| ❑ KC 31306 | Merrimack County | 1972 | 12.00 |
| ❑ KC 33054 | Ladies Love Outlaws | 1974 | 12.00 |
| ❑ PC 33907 | The Best of Tom Rush | 1976 | 12.00 |

ELEKTRA

| Number | Title (A Side/B Side) | Yr | NM |
|---|---|---|---|
| ❑ EKL-288 [M] | Tom Rush | 1965 | 15.00 |
| ❑ EKL-308 [M] | Take a Little Walk with Me | 1966 | 15.00 |
| ❑ EKS-7288 [S] | Tom Rush | 1965 | 15.00 |
| ❑ EKS-7308 [S] | Take a Little Walk with Me | 1966 | 15.00 |
| ❑ EKS-74018 | The Circle Game | 1968 | 15.00 |
| ❑ EKS-74062 | Classic Rush | 1971 | 15.00 |

FANTASY

| Number | Title (A Side/B Side) | Yr | NM |
|---|---|---|---|
| ❑ 24709 [(2)] | Tom Rush | 1973 | 15.00 |

*—Reissue of Prestige/Folklore recordings*

FOLKLORE

| Number | Title (A Side/B Side) | Yr | NM |
|---|---|---|---|
| ❑ FRLP-14003 [M] | Got a Mind to Ramble | 1964 | 20.00 |
| ❑ FRST-14003 [S] | Got a Mind to Ramble | 1964 | 25.00 |

LY CORNU

| Number | Title (A Side/B Side) | Yr | NM |
|---|---|---|---|
| ❑ SA-70-2 | Tom Rush at the Unicorn | 1962 | 100.00 |

PRESTIGE

| Number | Title (A Side/B Side) | Yr | NM |
|---|---|---|---|
| ❑ PR-7374 [M] | Blues — Songs — Ballads | 1965 | 20.00 |
| ❑ PRST-7374 [S] | Blues — Songs — Ballads | 1965 | 25.00 |
| ❑ PRST-7536 | Got a Mind to Ramble | 1968 | 15.00 |

*—Reissue of Folklore LP*

**RUSHING, JIMMY** Also see CHAMPION JACK DUPREE AND JIMMY RUSHING.

AUDIO LAB

| Number | Title (A Side/B Side) | Yr | NM |
|---|---|---|---|
| ❑ AL-1512 [M] | Two Shades of Blue | 1959 | 120.00 |

BLUESWAY

| Number | Title (A Side/B Side) | Yr | NM |
|---|---|---|---|
| ❑ BL-6005 [M] | Everyday I Have the Blues | 1967 | 20.00 |
| ❑ BLS-6005 [S] | Everyday I Have the Blues | 1967 | 20.00 |
| ❑ BLS-6017 | Livin' the Blues | 1968 | 20.00 |
| ❑ BLS-6057 | Sent for You Yesterday | 1973 | 15.00 |

COLPIX

| Number | Title (A Side/B Side) | Yr | NM |
|---|---|---|---|
| ❑ CP-446 [M] | Five Feet of Soul | 1963 | 40.00 |
| ❑ SCP-446 [S] | Five Feet of Soul | 1963 | 60.00 |

*—The existence of this record has been confirmed*

COLUMBIA

| Number | Title (A Side/B Side) | Yr | NM |
|---|---|---|---|
| ❑ CL 963 [M] | The Jazz Odyssey of James Rushing, Esq. | 1957 | 40.00 |
| ❑ CL 1152 [M] | Little Jimmy Rushing and the Big Brass | 1958 | 40.00 |
| ❑ CL 1401 [M] | Rushing Lullabies | 1959 | 40.00 |
| ❑ CL 1605 [M] | Jimmy Rushing and the Smith Girls | 1961 | 30.00 |
| ❑ CS 8060 [S] | Little Jimmy Rushing and the Big Brass | 1958 | 50.00 |
| ❑ CS 8196 [S] | Rushing Lullabies | 1959 | 50.00 |
| ❑ CS 8405 [S] | Jimmy Rushing and the Smith Girls | 1961 | 40.00 |
| ❑ C2 36419 [(2)] | Mister Five by Five | 1979 | 12.00 |

JAZZTONE

| Number | Title (A Side/B Side) | Yr | NM |
|---|---|---|---|
| ❑ J-1244 [M] | Listen to the Blues | 195? | 40.00 |

MASTER JAZZ

| Number | Title (A Side/B Side) | Yr | NM |
|---|---|---|---|
| ❑ 8104 | Gee, Baby | 197? | 15.00 |
| ❑ 8120 | Who Was It Sang That Song? | 1971 | 15.00 |

RCA VICTOR

| Number | Title (A Side/B Side) | Yr | NM |
|---|---|---|---|
| ❑ LSP-4566 | You and Me The Used to Be | 1972 | 15.00 |

VANGUARD

| Number | Title (A Side/B Side) | Yr | NM |
|---|---|---|---|
| ❑ VRS-65/66 [(2)] | Essential Jimmy Rushing | 197? | 15.00 |
| ❑ VSD-2008 [S] | If This Ain't the Blues | 1958 | 60.00 |
| ❑ VRS-8011 [10] | Jimmy Rushing Sings the Blues | 1955 | 100.00 |
| ❑ VRS-8505 [M] | Listen to the Blues | 1955 | 50.00 |
| ❑ VRS-8513 [M] | If This Ain't the Blues | 1957 | 50.00 |

Tom Rush, *Blues – Songs – Ballads,* Prestige PR 7374, 1965, mono, $25.

| Number | Title (A Side/B Side) | Yr | NM |
|---|---|---|---|
| ❑ VRS-8518 [M] | Going to Chicago | 1957 | 50.00 |
| ❑ VSD-73007 | Listen to the Blues | 1967 | 15.00 |

**RUSHING, JIMMY; ADA MOORE; BUCK CLAYTON**

COLUMBIA

| Number | Title (A Side/B Side) | Yr | NM |
|---|---|---|---|
| ❑ CL 778 [M] | Cat Meets Chick | 1956 | 60.00 |

**RUSKIN-SPEAR, ROGER**

UNITED ARTISTS

| Number | Title (A Side/B Side) | Yr | NM |
|---|---|---|---|
| ❑ UA-LA097-F | Electric Shocks | 1973 | 25.00 |

**RUSSELL, ANNA**

COLUMBIA MASTERWORKS

| Number | Title (A Side/B Side) | Yr | NM |
|---|---|---|---|
| ❑ ML 4594 [M] | Anna Russell Sings? | 1953 | 25.00 |
| ❑ ML 4733 [M] | Anna Russell Sings! Again? | 1954 | 25.00 |
| ❑ ML 4928 [M] | Anna Russell's Guide to Concert Audiences | 1955 | 25.00 |
| ❑ ML 5036 [M] | A Square Talk on Popular Music | 1956 | 25.00 |
| ❑ ML 5195 [M] | In Darkest Africa | 1957 | 30.00 |
| ❑ ML 5295 [M] | A Practical Banana Promotion | 1959 | 50.00 |
| ❑ MG 31199 [(2)] | The Anna Russell Album? | 1972 | 20.00 |

**RUSSELL, BOBBY**

ELF

| Number | Title (A Side/B Side) | Yr | NM |
|---|---|---|---|
| ❑ 9500 [M] | Words, Music, Laughter & Tears | 1969 | 40.00 |

*—Mono copies are white label promo only and say "Monaural" on the label*

| Number | Title (A Side/B Side) | Yr | NM |
|---|---|---|---|
| ❑ 9500 [S] | Words, Music, Laughter & Tears | 1969 | 20.00 |
| ❑ 9501 | Unlimited | 1970 | 15.00 |

UNITED ARTISTS

| Number | Title (A Side/B Side) | Yr | NM |
|---|---|---|---|
| ❑ UAS-5548 | Saturday Morning Confusion | 1971 | 12.00 |

**RUSSELL, GENE**

BLACK JAZZ

| Number | Title (A Side/B Side) | Yr | NM |
|---|---|---|---|
| ❑ 1 | New Direction | 1972 | 25.00 |
| ❑ QD-10 | Talk to My Lady | 1973 | 25.00 |

**RUSSELL, GEORGE**

DECCA

| Number | Title (A Side/B Side) | Yr | NM |
|---|---|---|---|
| ❑ DL 4183 [M] | George Russell in Kansas City | 1961 | 30.00 |
| ❑ DL 9216 [M] | New York, N.Y. | 1958 | 50.00 |
| ❑ DL 9219 [M] | Jazz in the Space Age | 1958 | 50.00 |
| ❑ DL 9220 [M] | George Russell at the Five Spot | 1958 | 50.00 |
| ❑ DL 74183 [S] | George Russell in Kansas City | 1961 | 40.00 |
| ❑ DL 79216 [S] | New York, N.Y. | 1958 | 40.00 |
| ❑ DL 79219 [S] | Jazz in the Space Age | 1958 | 40.00 |
| ❑ DL 79220 [S] | George Russell at the Five Spot | 1958 | 40.00 |

FLYING DUTCHMAN

| Number | Title (A Side/B Side) | Yr | NM |
|---|---|---|---|
| ❑ FD-122 | Othello Ballet Suite/Electronic Organ Sonata No. 1 | 1970 | 20.00 |
| ❑ FD-124 | Electronic Sonata for Souls Loved by Nature | 1970 | 20.00 |

MGM

| Number | Title (A Side/B Side) | Yr | NM |
|---|---|---|---|
| ❑ E-3321 [M] | George Russell Octets | 1955 | 80.00 |

RCA VICTOR

| Number | Title (A Side/B Side) | Yr | NM |
|---|---|---|---|
| ❑ LPM-1372 [M] | Jazz Workshop | 1957 | 80.00 |
| ❑ LPM-2534 [M] | Jazz Workshop | 1962 | 30.00 |

RIVERSIDE

| Number | Title (A Side/B Side) | Yr | NM |
|---|---|---|---|
| ❑ RLP-341 [M] | Stratusphunk | 1960 | 25.00 |
| ❑ RLP-375 [M] | Ezz-thetics | 1961 | 25.00 |
| ❑ RLP-412 [M] | The Stratus Seekers | 1962 | 25.00 |
| ❑ RLP-440 [M] | The Outer View | 1963 | 25.00 |
| ❑ RS-3016 | The Outer View | 1968 | 20.00 |
| ❑ RS-9341 [S] | Stratusphunk | 1960 | 30.00 |
| ❑ RS-9375 [S] | Ezz-thetics | 1961 | 30.00 |
| ❑ RS-9412 [S] | The Stratus Seekers | 1962 | 30.00 |
| ❑ RS-9440 [S] | The Outer View | 1963 | 30.00 |

STRATA-EAST

| Number | Title (A Side/B Side) | Yr | NM |
|---|---|---|---|
| ❑ SES-19761 | Electronic Sonata for Souls Loved by Nature | 1976 | 20.00 |

**RUSSELL, HAL**

NESSA

| Number | Title (A Side/B Side) | Yr | NM |
|---|---|---|---|
| ❑ N-21 | NRG Ensemble | 1981 | 20.00 |
| ❑ N-25 | Generation | 1982 | 20.00 |

**RUSSELL, JANE**

MGM

| Number | Title (A Side/B Side) | Yr | NM |
|---|---|---|---|
| ❑ E-3715 [M] | Jane Russell | 1959 | 50.00 |
| ❑ SE-3715 [S] | Jane Russell | 1959 | 100.00 |

**RUSSELL, JIMMY**

CUCA

| Number | Title (A Side/B Side) | Yr | NM |
|---|---|---|---|
| ❑ 4100 [M] | Jimmy Russell Trio | 1965 | 25.00 |

**RUSSELL, KURT**

CAPITOL

| Number | Title (A Side/B Side) | Yr | NM |
|---|---|---|---|
| ❑ SKAO-492 | Kurt Russell | 1970 | 30.00 |

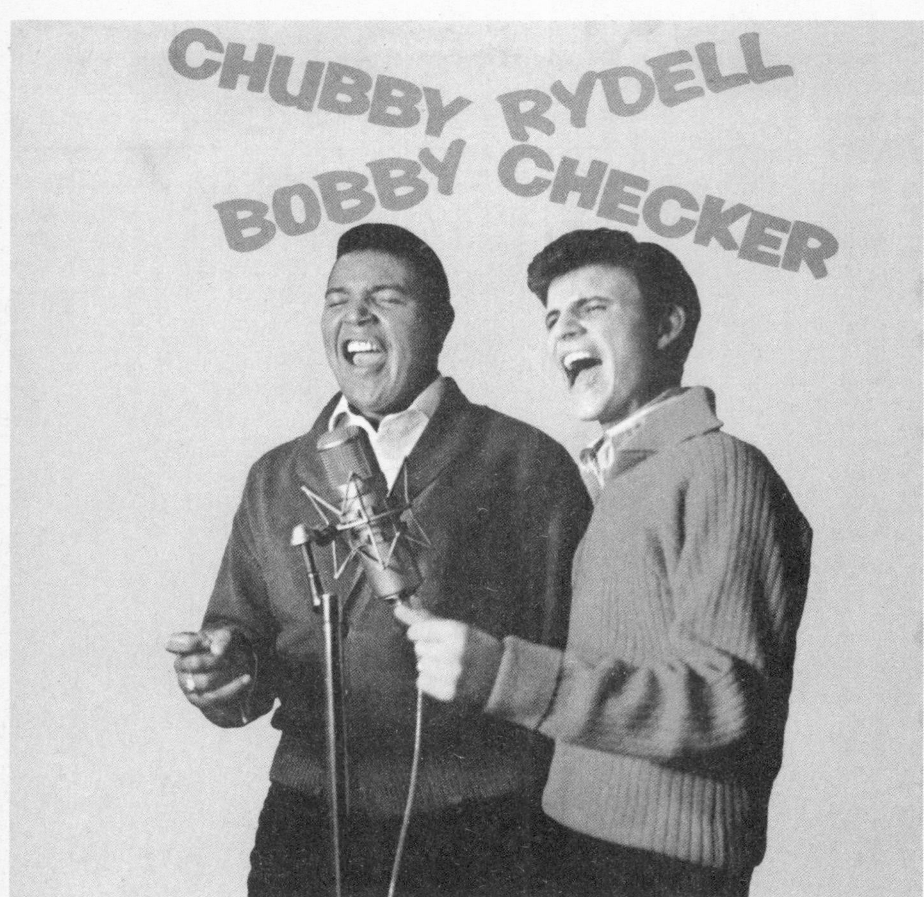


Bobby Rydell and Chubby Checker, *Bobby Rydell/Chubby Checker,* Cameo C-1013, 1961, mono, $30.

| Number | Title (A Side/B Side) | Yr | NM |
|---|---|---|---|
| **RUSSELL, LEON** | | | |
| MCA | | | |
| ❑ 682 | Leon Russell | 1979 | 8.00 |
| *—Reissue of Shelter 52007* | | | |
| ❑ 683 | Leon Russell and the Shelter People | 1979 | 8.00 |
| *—Reissue of Shelter 52008* | | | |
| ❑ 685 | Carney | 1979 | 8.00 |
| *—Reissue of Shelter 52011* | | | |
| ❑ 686 | Will O' the Wisp | 1979 | 8.00 |
| *—Reissue of Shelter 52020* | | | |
| ❑ 37114 | Best of Leon | 1980 | 8.00 |
| *—Reissue of Shelter 52004* | | | |
| PARADISE | | | |
| ❑ 0002 | Hank Wilson Vol. II | 1984 | 12.00 |
| ❑ PR 2943 | Wedding Album | 1976 | 12.00 |
| *—As "Leon and Mary Russell"* | | | |
| ❑ BSK 3066 | Make Love to the Music | 1977 | 12.00 |
| *—As "Leon and Mary Russell"* | | | |
| ❑ BSK 3172 | Americana | 1978 | 12.00 |
| ❑ BSK 3341 | Life and Love | 1979 | 12.00 |
| ❑ BSK 3532 | The Live Album | 1981 | 10.00 |
| SHELTER | | | |
| ❑ SHE-1001 | Leon Russell | 1968 | 20.00 |
| ❑ SR 2108 | Stop All That Jazz | 1974 | 15.00 |
| ❑ SR 2118 | Leon Russell | 1974 | 12.00 |
| *—Reissue of 8901* | | | |
| ❑ SR 2119 | Leon Russell and the Shelter People | 1974 | 12.00 |
| *—Reissue of 8903* | | | |
| ❑ SR 2121 | Carney | 1974 | 12.00 |
| *—Reissue of 8911* | | | |
| ❑ SR 2138 | Will O' the Wisp | 1975 | 15.00 |
| ❑ SW-8901 | Leon Russell | 1970 | 15.00 |
| *—Early reissue of 1001* | | | |
| ❑ SW-8903 | Leon Russell and the Shelter People | 1971 | 15.00 |
| ❑ SW-8911 | Carney | 1972 | 15.00 |
| ❑ STCO-8917 [(3)] | Leon Live | 1973 | 20.00 |
| ❑ SW-8923 | Hank Wilson's Back, Vol. 1 | 1973 | 15.00 |
| *—As "Hank Wilson"* | | | |
| ❑ 52004 | Best of Leon | 1976 | 10.00 |
| ❑ 52007 | Leon Russell | 1977 | 10.00 |
| *—Reissue of 2118* | | | |
| ❑ 52008 | Leon Russell and the Shelter People | 1977 | 10.00 |
| *—Reissue of 2119* | | | |
| ❑ 52011 | Carney | 1977 | 10.00 |
| *—Reissue of 2121* | | | |
| ❑ 52014 | Hank Wilson's Back, Vol. 1 | 1977 | 10.00 |
| *—Reissue of 8923* | | | |
| ❑ 52016 | Stop All That Jazz | 1977 | 10.00 |
| *—Reissue of 2108* | | | |
| ❑ 52020 | Will O' the Wisp | 1977 | 10.00 |
| *—Reissue of 2138* | | | |
| **RUSSELL, LEON, AND MARC BENNO** See ASYLUM CHOIR. | | | |
| **RUSSELL, PEE WEE** | | | |
| ATLANTIC | | | |
| ❑ ALS-126 [10] | Pee Wee Russell All Stars | 1952 | 80.00 |
| BELL | | | |
| ❑ LP-42 [M] | Pee Wee Russell Plays Pee Wee | 1961 | 25.00 |
| ❑ LPS-42 [S] | Pee Wee Russell Plays Pee Wee | 1961 | 30.00 |
| COLUMBIA | | | |
| ❑ CS 8785 [S] | New Groove | 1963 | 20.00 |
| COUNTERPOINT | | | |
| ❑ (# unknown) [M] | Portrait of Pee Wee | 1957 | 60.00 |
| DCC COMPACT CLASSICS | | | |
| ❑ LPZ-2024 | Portrait of Pee Wee | 1996 | 25.00 |
| *—Audiophile vinyl* | | | |
| DISC | | | |
| ❑ DLP-(# unknown) [10] | Jazz Ensemble | 195? | 120.00 |
| DOT | | | |
| ❑ DLP-3253 [M] | Pee Wee Russell Plays | 1960 | 25.00 |
| ❑ DLP-25253 [S] | Pee Wee Russell Plays | 1960 | 20.00 |
| ESOTERIC | | | |
| ❑ 565 [M] | Pee Wee Russell All Stars | 1959 | 40.00 |
| ❑ 5565 [S] | Pee Wee Russell All Stars | 1959 | 30.00 |
| IMPULSE! | | | |
| ❑ A-96 [M] | Ask Me Now | 1966 | 25.00 |
| ❑ AS-96 [S] | Ask Me Now | 1966 | 30.00 |
| ❑ A-9137 [M] | College Concert of Pee Wee Russell with Henry "Red" Allen | 1967 | 25.00 |
| ❑ AS-9137 [S] | College Concert of Pee Wee Russell with Henry "Red" Allen | 1967 | 20.00 |
| MAINSTREAM | | | |
| ❑ S-6026 [S] | A Legend | 1965 | 20.00 |
| RIVERSIDE | | | |
| ❑ RLP 12-141 [M] | Rhythmakers and Teagarden | 1955 | 60.00 |
| STEREO-CRAFT | | | |
| ❑ RTN-105 [M] | Pee Wee Plays Pee Wee | 196? | 20.00 |
| ❑ RTS-105 [S] | Pee Wee Plays Pee Wee | 196? | 25.00 |
| STORYVILLE | | | |
| ❑ STLP-308 [10] | Pee Wee Russell | 1954 | 80.00 |
| ❑ STLP-909 [M] | We're In the Money | 1956 | 50.00 |
| SWINGVILLE | | | |
| ❑ SVLP-2008 [M] | Swingin' with Pee Wee | 1960 | 50.00 |
| *—Purple label* | | | |
| ❑ SVLP-2008 [M] | Swingin' with Pee Wee | 1965 | 25.00 |
| *—Blue label, trident logo at right* | | | |
| **RUSSELL, PEE WEE/BILLY BANKS** | | | |
| JAZZ PANORAMA | | | |
| ❑ 1808 [10] | Pee Wee Russell / Billy Banks | 1951 | 80.00 |
| **RUSSELL, PEE WEE, AND RUBY BRAFF** | | | |
| SAVOY | | | |
| ❑ MG-12034 [M] | Jazz At Storyville, Volume 1 | 1955 | 50.00 |
| ❑ MG-12041 [M] | Jazz at Storyville, Volume 2 | 1955 | 50.00 |
| **RUSSIAN JAZZ QUARTET, THE** | | | |
| IMPULSE! | | | |
| ❑ A-80 [M] | Happiness | 1965 | 20.00 |
| ❑ AS-80 [S] | Happiness | 1965 | 25.00 |
| **RUSSIN, BABE** | | | |
| DOT | | | |
| ❑ DLP-3060 [M] | To Soothe the Savage | 1956 | 50.00 |
| **RUSSO, BILL** | | | |
| ATLANTIC | | | |
| ❑ 1241 [M] | The World of Alcina | 1956 | 80.00 |
| *—Black label* | | | |
| ❑ 1241 [M] | The World of Alcina | 1961 | 30.00 |
| *—Multicolor label, white "fan" logo at right* | | | |
| DEE GEE | | | |
| ❑ 1001 [10] | A Recital in New American Music | 1952 | 200.00 |
| FM | | | |
| ❑ 302 [M] | Stereophony | 1963 | 25.00 |
| ❑ S-302 [S] | Stereophony | 1963 | 30.00 |
| ROULETTE | | | |
| ❑ R-52045 [M] | School of Rebellion | 1960 | 25.00 |
| ❑ SR-52045 [S] | School of Rebellion | 1960 | 30.00 |
| ❑ R-52063 [M] | Seven Deadly Sins | 1960 | 25.00 |
| ❑ SR-52063 [S] | Seven Deadly Sins | 1960 | 30.00 |
| **RUSTIX** | | | |
| RARE EARTH | | | |
| ❑ RS-508 | Bedlam | 1969 | 15.00 |
| *—Regular cover* | | | |
| ❑ RS-508 | Bedlam | 1969 | 30.00 |
| *—Rounded-top cover* | | | |
| ❑ RS-513 | Come On, People | 1970 | 12.00 |
| **RUSTY AND DOUG** See RUSTY AND DOUG KERSHAW. | | | |
| **RUTLES, THE** | | | |
| WARNER BROS. | | | |
| ❑ PRO-A-723 [DJ] | The Rutles | 1978 | 25.00 |
| *—Yellow vinyl with five songs and "banana" label* | | | |
| ❑ HS 3151 | The Rutles | 1978 | 25.00 |
| *—With bound-in booklet* | | | |
| **RYAN, BUCK, AND SMITTY IRWIN** | | | |
| MONUMENT | | | |
| ❑ MLP-8031 [M] | Ballads and Bluegrass | 1965 | 20.00 |
| ❑ SLP-18031 [S] | Ballads and Bluegrass | 1965 | 25.00 |
| **RYAN, CHARLIE** | | | |
| HILLTOP | | | |
| ❑ JM-6006 [M] | Hot Rod Lincoln Drags Again | 1964 | 50.00 |
| ❑ JS-6006 [R] | Hot Rod Lincoln Drags Again | 1964 | 25.00 |
| KING | | | |
| ❑ 751 [M] | Hot Rod Lincoln | 1961 | 400.00 |
| **RYDELL, BOBBY** | | | |
| CAMEO | | | |
| ❑ C-1006 [M] | We Got Love | 1959 | 60.00 |
| ❑ C-1007 [M] | Bobby Sings | 1960 | 50.00 |
| ❑ C-1009 [M] | Bobby's Biggest Hits | 1961 | 25.00 |
| *—Standard cover* | | | |
| ❑ C-1009 [M] | Bobby's Biggest Hits | 1961 | 80.00 |
| *—Original with die-cut cover and textured inner sleeve* | | | |
| ❑ C-1010 [M] | Bobby Rydell Salutes "The Great Ones" | 1961 | 25.00 |
| ❑ SC-1010 [S] | Bobby Rydell Salutes "The Great Ones" | 1961 | 40.00 |
| ❑ C-1011 [M] | Rydell at the Copa | 1961 | 25.00 |
| ❑ SC-1011 [S] | Rydell at the Copa | 1961 | 40.00 |



Except when noted otherwise, VG = 25% of NM, and VG+ = 50% of NM. (Example: VG = $2.00, VG+ = $4.00 and NM = $8.00.)

| Number | Title (A Side/B Side) | Yr | NM |
|---|---|---|---|
| ❑ C-1019 [M] | All the Hits | 1962 | 25.00 |
| *—Black vinyl* | | | |
| ❑ C-1019 [M] | All the Hits | 1962 | 150.00 |
| *—Red vinyl* | | | |
| ❑ C-1028 [M] | Bobby Rydell's Biggest Hits, Volume 2 | 1962 | 25.00 |
| ❑ C-1040 [M] | All the Hits, Volume 2 | 1963 | 25.00 |
| ❑ SC-1040 [P] | All the Hits, Volume 2 | 1963 | 40.00 |
| ❑ C-1043 [M] | Bye Bye Birdie | 1963 | 25.00 |
| ❑ C-1055 [M] | Wild (Wood) Days | 1963 | 20.00 |
| ❑ SC-1055 [S] | Wild (Wood) Days | 1963 | 30.00 |
| ❑ C-1070 [M] | The Top Hits of 1963 | 1963 | 20.00 |
| *—Came with bonus single, also numbered 1070* | | | |
| ❑ SC-1070 [S] | The Top Hits of 1963 | 1963 | 30.00 |
| *—Came with bonus single, also numbered 1070* | | | |
| ❑ C-1080 [M] | Forget Him | 1964 | 20.00 |
| ❑ SC-1080 [R] | Forget Him | 1964 | 20.00 |
| ❑ C-2001 [M] | 16 Golden Hits | 1965 | 20.00 |
| ❑ SC-2001 [R] | 16 Golden Hits | 1965 | 20.00 |
| CAPITOL | | | |
| ❑ ST 2281 [S] | Somebody Loves You | 1965 | 20.00 |
| ❑ T 2281 [M] | Somebody Loves You | 1965 | 15.00 |
| P.I.P. | | | |
| ❑ 6818 | Born with a Smile | 1976 | 10.00 |
| SPIN-O-RAMA | | | |
| ❑ 143 [M] | Starring Bobby Rydell | 196? | 12.00 |
| ❑ S-143 [S] | Starring Bobby Rydell | 196? | 12.00 |
| STRAND | | | |
| ❑ SL-1120 [M] | Bobby Rydell Sings | 196? | 25.00 |
| ❑ SLS-1120 [R] | Bobby Rydell Sings | 196? | 20.00 |
| VENISE | | | |
| ❑ 10035 [M] | Twistin' | 1962 | 25.00 |
| *—Also includes tracks by Barry Norman and Stephen Garrick* | | | |

**RYDELL, BOBBY/CHUBBY CHECKER** Also see each artist's individual listings.

| Number | Title (A Side/B Side) | Yr | NM |
|---|---|---|---|
| CAMEO | | | |
| ❑ C 1013 [M] | Bobby Rydell/Chubby Checker | 1961 | 30.00 |
| ❑ C-1063 [M] | Chubby Checker and Bobby Rydell | 1963 | 20.00 |

**RYDER, MITCH**

| Number | Title (A Side/B Side) | Yr | NM |
|---|---|---|---|
| DYNO VOICE | | | |
| ❑ 1901 [M] | What Now My Love | 1967 | 20.00 |
| ❑ 31901 [S] | What Now My Love | 1967 | 20.00 |
| RIVA | | | |
| ❑ RV 7503 | Never Kick a Sleeping Dog | 1983 | 10.00 |
| SEEDS & STEMS | | | |
| ❑ 7801 | How I Spent My Summer Vacation | 1978 | 12.00 |
| ❑ 7804 | Naked But Not Dead | 1980 | 12.00 |

**RYDER, MITCH, AND THE DETROIT WHEELS**

| Number | Title (A Side/B Side) | Yr | NM |
|---|---|---|---|
| CREWE | | | |
| ❑ CR-1335 | All Mitch Ryder Hits! | 1969 | 15.00 |
| *—Reissue of New Voice 2004* | | | |
| NEW VOICE | | | |
| ❑ 2000 [M] | Take a Ride | 1966 | 25.00 |
| ❑ S-2000 [S] | Take a Ride | 1966 | 30.00 |
| ❑ 2002 [M] | Breakout...!!! | 1966 | 20.00 |
| *—With "Devil with a Blue Dress On/Good Golly Miss Molly"* | | | |
| ❑ 2002 [M] | Breakout...!!! | 1966 | 25.00 |
| *—Without "Devil with a Blue Dress On/Good Golly Miss Molly"* | | | |
| ❑ S-2002 [S] | Breakout...!!! | 1966 | 25.00 |
| *—With "Devil with a Blue Dress On/Good Golly Miss Molly"* | | | |
| ❑ S-2002 [S] | Breakout...!!! | 1966 | 30.00 |
| *—Without "Devil with a Blue Dress On/Good Golly Miss Molly"* | | | |
| ❑ 2003 [M] | Sock It To Me! | 1967 | 25.00 |
| ❑ S-2003 [S] | Sock It To Me! | 1967 | 30.00 |
| ❑ 2004 [M] | All Mitch Ryder Hits! | 1967 | 30.00 |
| ❑ NVS-2004 [S] | All Mitch Ryder Hits! | 1967 | 20.00 |
| ❑ S-2005 | Mitch Ryder Sings the Hits | 1968 | 20.00 |
| RHINO | | | |
| ❑ R1-70941 | Rev Up: The Best of Mitch Ryder and the Detroit Wheels | 1989 | 12.00 |
| SUNDAZED | | | |
| ❑ LP 5083 | Breakout ... !!! | 2001 | 12.00 |
| *—Reissue on 180-gram vinyl* | | | |
| VIRGO | | | |
| ❑ 12001 | The Best of Mitch Ryder and the Detroit Wheels | 1972 | 12.00 |

**RYG, JORGEN**

| Number | Title (A Side/B Side) | Yr | NM |
|---|---|---|---|
| EMARCY | | | |
| ❑ MG-36099 [M] | Jorgen Ryg Jazz Quartet | 1956 | 50.00 |

**RYLES, JOHN WESLEY**

| Number | Title (A Side/B Side) | Yr | NM |
|---|---|---|---|
| ABC | | | |
| ❑ AB-1056 | Shine on Me | 1978 | 12.00 |
| ❑ AB-1112 | Love's Sweet Pain | 1979 | 12.00 |
| ABC DOT | | | |
| ❑ DO-2089 | John Wesley Ryles | 1977 | 12.00 |

Ballads of the Green Berets
SSgt Barry Sadler
U.S.Army Special Forces
The Ballad of the Green Berets
Letter from Vietnam
I'm a Lucky One
Garet Trooper
The Soldier Has Come Home
Salute to the Nurses
I'm Watching the Raindrops Fall
Badge of Courage
Trooper's Lament
Bamiba
Saigon
Lullaby
Arranged and Conducted by
Sid Bass
RCA Victor
Dynagroove
Recording
LPM-3547


SSgt. Barry Sadler, *Ballads of the Green Berets*, RCA Victor LPM-3547, 1966, mono, $15.

| Number | Title (A Side/B Side) | Yr | NM |
|---|---|---|---|
| COLUMBIA | | | |
| ❑ CS 9768 | Kay | 1969 | 20.00 |
| MCA | | | |
| ❑ 643 | Shine on Me | 198? | 8.00 |
| *—Budget-line reissue of ABC 1056* | | | |
| ❑ 644 | John Wesley Ryles | 198? | 8.00 |
| *—Budget-line reissue of ABC Dot 2089* | | | |
| ❑ 750 | Let the Night Begin | 198? | 8.00 |
| *—Budget-line reissue* | | | |
| ❑ 798 | Love's Sweet Pain | 198? | 8.00 |
| *—Budget-line reissue of ABC 1112* | | | |
| ❑ 3183 | Let the Night Begin | 1979 | 12.00 |
| PLANTATION | | | |
| ❑ 517 | Reconsider Me | 197? | 12.00 |

# S

**SABRES, THE**

| Number | Title (A Side/B Side) | Yr | NM |
|---|---|---|---|
| RCA VICTOR | | | |
| ❑ LPM-1376 [M] | Ridin' High with the Sabres | 1956 | 60.00 |

**SABU**

| Number | Title (A Side/B Side) | Yr | NM |
|---|---|---|---|
| ALEGRE | | | |
| ❑ 802 [M] | Jazz Espagnole | 195? | 300.00 |
| BLUE NOTE | | | |
| ❑ BLP-1561 [M] | Palo Congo | 1957 | 100.00 |
| *—Regular version, W. 63rd St. address on label* | | | |
| ❑ BLP-1561 [M] | Palo Congo | 1957 | 150.00 |
| *—"Deep groove" version (deep indentation under label on both sides)* | | | |
| ❑ BLP-1561 [M] | Palo Congo | 1963 | 25.00 |
| *—With "New York, USA" address on label* | | | |

**SABU, PAUL**

| Number | Title (A Side/B Side) | Yr | NM |
|---|---|---|---|
| OCEAN/ARIOLA AMERICA | | | |
| ❑ SW-49902 | Sabu | 1979 | 25.00 |
| *—As "Sabu"* | | | |

**SACHS, AARON**

| Number | Title (A Side/B Side) | Yr | NM |
|---|---|---|---|
| BETHLEHEM | | | |
| ❑ BCP-1008 [10] | Aaron Sachs Quintet | 1954 | 120.00 |
| DAWN | | | |
| ❑ DLP-1114 [M] | Jazzville, Volume 3 | 1957 | 80.00 |
| RAMA | | | |
| ❑ LP-1004 [M] | Clarinet and Co. | 1957 | 80.00 |

**SACHS, AARON/HANK D'AMICO**

| Number | Title (A Side/B Side) | Yr | NM |
|---|---|---|---|
| BETHLEHEM | | | |
| ❑ BCP-7 [M] | We Brought Our "Axes" | 1955 | 80.00 |

**SACRED MUSHROOM, THE** Members of this group were later in POCO and PURE PRAIRIE LEAGUE.

| Number | Title (A Side/B Side) | Yr | NM |
|---|---|---|---|
| PARALLAX | | | |
| ❑ P-4001 | The Sacred Mushroom | 1969 | 150.00 |

**SADI, FATS**

| Number | Title (A Side/B Side) | Yr | NM |
|---|---|---|---|
| BLUE NOTE | | | |
| ❑ BLP-5061 [10] | The Swinging Fats Sadi Combo | 1955 | 300.00 |

**SADLER, SSGT. BARRY**

| Number | Title (A Side/B Side) | Yr | NM |
|---|---|---|---|
| RCA VICTOR | | | |
| ❑ LPM-3547 [M] | Ballads of the Green Berets | 1966 | 15.00 |
| ❑ LSP-3547 [S] | Ballads of the Green Berets | 1966 | 20.00 |
| ❑ LPM-3605 [M] | "A" Team, The | 1966 | 15.00 |
| ❑ LSP-3605 [S] | "A" Team, The | 1966 | 20.00 |
| ❑ LPM-3691 [M] | Back Home | 1967 | 20.00 |
| ❑ LSP-3691 [S] | Back Home | 1967 | 15.00 |

**SAGITTARIUS**

| Number | Title (A Side/B Side) | Yr | NM |
|---|---|---|---|
| COLUMBIA | | | |
| ❑ CS 9644 | Present Tense | 1968 | 30.00 |
| TOGETHER | | | |
| ❑ STT-1002 | The Blue Marble | 1969 | 50.00 |
| *—With two bonus photos; deduct 25 percent if missing* | | | |

**SAHL, MORT**

| Number | Title (A Side/B Side) | Yr | NM |
|---|---|---|---|
| FANTASY | | | |
| ❑ 7005 [M] | Mort Sahl at Sunset | 196? | 30.00 |
| *—Black vinyl* | | | |
| ❑ 7005 [M] | Mort Sahl at Sunset | 196? | 40.00 |
| *—Red vinyl* | | | |
| GNP CRESCENDO | | | |
| ❑ GNPS-2070 | Sing a Song of Watergate | 1973 | 15.00 |
| MERCURY | | | |
| ❑ MG-21112 [M] | Anyway...Onward | 1967 | 20.00 |
| ❑ SR-61112 [S] | Anyway...Onward | 1967 | 20.00 |
| REPRISE | | | |
| ❑ R-5002 [M] | The New Frontier | 1961 | 20.00 |

| Number | Title (A Side/B Side) | Yr | NM |
|---|---|---|---|
| ❑ R9-5002 [S] | The New Frontier | 1961 | 25.00 |
| ❑ R-5003 [M] | Mort Sahl On Relationships | 1961 | 40.00 |
| ❑ R9-5003 [S] | Mort Sahl On Relationships | 1961 | 50.00 |
| *—Joan Collins appears on the cover* | | | |
| **VERVE** | | | |
| ❑ MGV-15002 [M] | The Future Lies Ahead | 1959 | 20.00 |
| ❑ MGV-15004 [M] | 1960: Look Forward in Anger | 1959 | 20.00 |
| ❑ MGV-15006 [M] | A Way of Life | 1960 | 20.00 |
| ❑ MGV-15012 [M] | Mort Sahl at the Hungry I | 1960 | 20.00 |
| ❑ MGVS-15012 [S] | Mort Sahl at the Hungry I | 1960 | 25.00 |
| ❑ V-15021 [M] | The Next President | 1961 | 20.00 |
| ❑ V6-15021 [S] | The Next President | 1961 | 25.00 |
| ❑ V-15049 [M] | Great Moments of Comedy | 1965 | 15.00 |

## SAHM, DOUG
Also see SIR DOUGLAS QUINTET.

| Number | Title (A Side/B Side) | Yr | NM |
|---|---|---|---|
| **ABC DOT** | | | |
| ❑ DO-2057 | Texas Rock for Country Rollers | 1976 | 15.00 |
| **ANTONE'S** | | | |
| ❑ ANT-0008 | Juke Box Music | 1989 | 12.00 |
| **ATLANTIC** | | | |
| ❑ SD 7254 | Doug Sahm and Band | 1973 | 15.00 |
| **MERCURY** | | | |
| ❑ SRM-1-655 | Rough Edges | 1972 | 30.00 |
| **TAKOMA** | | | |
| ❑ TAK-7075 | Hell of a Spell | 1980 | 12.00 |
| **TEARDROP** | | | |
| ❑ TD-5000 | The West Side Sound Rolls Again | 1982 | 12.00 |
| **WARNER BROS.** | | | |
| ❑ BS 2810 | Groovers Paradise | 1974 | 20.00 |

## SAIN, OLIVER

| Number | Title (A Side/B Side) | Yr | NM |
|---|---|---|---|
| **ABAT** | | | |
| ❑ 404 | Main Man | 1973 | 20.00 |
| ❑ 406 | Bus Stop | 1974 | 20.00 |

## ST. ANTHONY'S FIRE

| Number | Title (A Side/B Side) | Yr | NM |
|---|---|---|---|
| **ZONK** | | | |
| ❑ (# unknown) | St. Anthony's Fire | 1968 | 400.00 |

## ST. CLAIRE, BETTY

| Number | Title (A Side/B Side) | Yr | NM |
|---|---|---|---|
| **JUBILEE** | | | |
| ❑ JLP-15 [10] | Hal McKusick Plays — Betty St. Clair Sings | 1955 | 150.00 |
| ❑ JLP-23 [10] | Cool and Clearer | 1955 | 100.00 |
| ❑ JLP-1011 [M] | What Is There to Say? | 1956 | 50.00 |
| **SEECO** | | | |
| ❑ SLP-456 [M] | Betty St. Claire at Basin Street | 1960 | 40.00 |
| ❑ SLP-4560 [S] | Betty St. Claire at Basin Street | 1960 | 40.00 |

## ST. CLOUD, ENDLE

| Number | Title (A Side/B Side) | Yr | NM |
|---|---|---|---|
| **INTERNATIONAL ARTISTS** | | | |
| ❑ IA-12 | Thank You All Very Much | 1970 | 60.00 |

## ST. CYR, JOHNNY

| Number | Title (A Side/B Side) | Yr | NM |
|---|---|---|---|
| **SOUTHLAND** | | | |
| ❑ 212 | Johnny St. Cyr and His Hot Five | 196? | 20.00 |

## ST. GERMAIN

| Number | Title (A Side/B Side) | Yr | NM |
|---|---|---|---|
| **BLUE NOTE** | | | |
| ❑ 25114 [(2)] | Tourist | 2000 | 30.00 |

## ST. LOUIS JIMMY

| Number | Title (A Side/B Side) | Yr | NM |
|---|---|---|---|
| **BLUESVILLE** | | | |
| ❑ BVLP-1028 [M] | Goin' Down Blues | 1961 | 120.00 |
| *—Blue label, silver print* | | | |
| ❑ BVLP-1028 [M] | Goin' Down Blues | 1964 | 25.00 |
| *—Blue label, trident logo at right* | | | |

## ST. PETER'S CHOIR

| Number | Title (A Side/B Side) | Yr | NM |
|---|---|---|---|
| **CORAL** | | | |
| ❑ CRL 56015 [10] | Hark! The Herald Angels Sing | 1950 | 40.00 |

## ST. PETERS, CRISPIAN

| Number | Title (A Side/B Side) | Yr | NM |
|---|---|---|---|
| **JAMIE** | | | |
| ❑ JLPM-3027 [M] | The Pied Piper | 1966 | 50.00 |
| ❑ JLPS-3027 [R] | The Pied Piper | 1966 | 35.00 |

## ST. SHAW, MIKE

| Number | Title (A Side/B Side) | Yr | NM |
|---|---|---|---|
| **REPRISE** | | | |
| ❑ R-6128 [M] | The Mike St. Shaw Trio | 1964 | 20.00 |
| ❑ RS-6128 [S] | The Mike St. Shaw Trio | 1964 | 25.00 |

## SAINT STEVEN

| Number | Title (A Side/B Side) | Yr | NM |
|---|---|---|---|
| **PROBE** | | | |
| ❑ CPLP-4506 | Over the Hills | 1969 | 60.00 |

## SAINTE-MARIE, BUFFY

| Number | Title (A Side/B Side) | Yr | NM |
|---|---|---|---|
| **ABC** | | | |
| ❑ D-929 | Sweet America | 1976 | 12.00 |
| **MCA** | | | |
| ❑ 405 | Buffy | 1974 | 12.00 |
| ❑ 451 | Changing Woman | 1975 | 12.00 |
| **VANGUARD** | | | |
| ❑ VSD 3/4 [(2)] | The Best of Buffy Sainte-Marie | 1970 | 20.00 |
| ❑ VSD 33/34 [(2)] | The Best of Buffy Sainte-Marie, Vol. 2 | 1974 | 15.00 |
| ❑ VRS 9142 [M] | It's My Way | 1964 | 15.00 |
| ❑ VRS 9171 [M] | Many a Mile | 1965 | 15.00 |
| ❑ VRS 9211 [M] | Little Wheel Spin and Spin | 1966 | 15.00 |
| ❑ VRS 9250 [M] | Fire & Fleet & Candlelight | 1967 | 15.00 |
| ❑ VSQ 40003 [Q] | Moon Shot | 1972 | 25.00 |
| ❑ VSQ 40020 [Q] | Quiet Places | 1973 | 25.00 |
| ❑ VMS 73113 | The Best of Buffy Sainte-Marie | 1985 | 10.00 |
| ❑ VSD 79142 [S] | It's My Way | 1964 | 20.00 |
| ❑ VSD 79171 [S] | Many a Mile | 1965 | 20.00 |
| ❑ VSD 79211 [S] | Little Wheel Spin and Spin | 1966 | 20.00 |
| ❑ VSD 79250 [S] | Fire & Fleet & Candlelight | 1967 | 20.00 |
| ❑ VSD 79280 | I'm Gonna Be a Country Girl Again | 1968 | 15.00 |
| ❑ VSD 79300 | Illuminations | 1969 | 15.00 |
| ❑ VSD 79311 | She Used to Wanna Be a Ballerina | 1971 | 15.00 |
| ❑ VSD 79312 | Moon Shot | 1972 | 15.00 |
| ❑ VSD 79330 | Quiet Places | 1973 | 12.00 |
| ❑ VSD 79340 | Native Child: Odyssey | 1974 | 12.00 |

## SAKAMOTO, KYU

| Number | Title (A Side/B Side) | Yr | NM |
|---|---|---|---|
| **CAPITOL** | | | |
| ❑ DT 10349 [R] | Sukiyaki and Other Japanese Hits | 1963 | 15.00 |
| ❑ T 10349 [M] | Sukiyaki and Other Japanese Hits | 1963 | 25.00 |

## SALEM MASS

| Number | Title (A Side/B Side) | Yr | NM |
|---|---|---|---|
| **SALEM MASS** | | | |
| ❑ SM-101 | Witch Burning | 1972 | 250.00 |

## SALES, SOUPY

| Number | Title (A Side/B Side) | Yr | NM |
|---|---|---|---|
| **ABC-PARAMOUNT** | | | |
| ❑ 503 [M] | Spy with a Pie | 1965 | 25.00 |
| ❑ S-503 [S] | Spy with a Pie | 1965 | 30.00 |
| ❑ 517 [M] | Soupy Sales Sez Do the Mouse and Other Teen Hits | 1965 | 25.00 |
| ❑ S-517 [S] | Soupy Sales Sez Do the Mouse and Other Teen Hits | 1965 | 30.00 |
| **MCA** | | | |
| ❑ 5274 | Still Soupy After All These Years | 1981 | 12.00 |
| **MOTOWN** | | | |
| ❑ MS 686 | A Bag of Soup | 1969 | 25.00 |
| **REPRISE** | | | |
| ❑ R 6010 [M] | The Soupy Sales Show | 1961 | 30.00 |
| ❑ R9 6010 [S] | The Soupy Sales Show | 1961 | 40.00 |
| ❑ R 6052 [M] | Up in the Air | 1962 | 30.00 |
| ❑ R9 6052 [S] | Up in the Air | 1962 | 40.00 |

## SALIM, A.K.

| Number | Title (A Side/B Side) | Yr | NM |
|---|---|---|---|
| **PRESTIGE** | | | |
| ❑ PRLP-7379 [M] | Afro-Soul Drum Orgy | 1966 | 25.00 |
| ❑ PRST-7379 [S] | Afro-Soul Drum Orgy | 1966 | 30.00 |
| **SAVOY** | | | |
| ❑ MG-12102 [M] | The Flute Suite | 1957 | 80.00 |
| ❑ MG-12118 [M] | Pretty for the People | 1957 | 80.00 |
| ❑ MG-12132 [M] | Blues Suite | 1958 | 50.00 |
| ❑ SST-13001 [S] | Blues Suite | 1959 | 40.00 |

## SALT CITY FIVE, THE

| Number | Title (A Side/B Side) | Yr | NM |
|---|---|---|---|
| **JUBILEE** | | | |
| ❑ JLP-13 [10] | Salt City Five | 1955 | 50.00 |
| ❑ JLP-24 [10] | Salt City Five, Volume 2 | 1955 | 50.00 |
| ❑ JLP-1012 [M] | Salt City Five | 1956 | 40.00 |

## SALT WATER TAFFY

| Number | Title (A Side/B Side) | Yr | NM |
|---|---|---|---|
| **BUDDAH** | | | |
| ❑ BDS-5021 | Finders Keepers | 1968 | 20.00 |

## SALVADOR, SAL

| Number | Title (A Side/B Side) | Yr | NM |
|---|---|---|---|
| **BETHLEHEM** | | | |
| ❑ BCP-39 [M] | Shades of Sal Salvador | 1956 | 50.00 |
| ❑ BCP-59 [M] | Frivolous Sal | 1956 | 50.00 |
| ❑ BCP-74 [M] | Tribute to the Greats | 1957 | 50.00 |
| **BLUE NOTE** | | | |
| ❑ BLP-5035 [10] | Sal Salvador Quintet | 1954 | 300.00 |
| **CAPITOL** | | | |
| ❑ H 6505 [10] | Sal Salvador | 1954 | 120.00 |
| ❑ T 6505 [M] | Sal Salvador | 1955 | 80.00 |
| **DAUNTLESS** | | | |
| ❑ DM-4307 [M] | You Ain't Heard Nothin' Yet | 1963 | 30.00 |
| ❑ DS-6307 [S] | You Ain't Heard Nothin' Yet | 1963 | 40.00 |
| **DECCA** | | | |
| ❑ DL 4026 [M] | Beat for This Generation | 1959 | 40.00 |
| ❑ DL 9210 [M] | Colors in Sound | 1958 | 50.00 |
| ❑ DL 74026 [S] | Beat for This Generation | 1959 | 50.00 |
| ❑ DL 79210 [S] | Colors in Sound | 1958 | 40.00 |
| **GOLDEN CREST** | | | |
| ❑ GC-1001 [M] | Sal Salvador Quartet | 1961 | 25.00 |
| ❑ GCS-1001 [S] | Sal Salvador Quartet | 1961 | 30.00 |
| **ROULETTE** | | | |
| ❑ R-25262 [M] | Music To Stop Smoking By | 1964 | 20.00 |
| ❑ RS-25262 [S] | Music To Stop Smoking By | 1964 | 25.00 |

## SALVATION

| Number | Title (A Side/B Side) | Yr | NM |
|---|---|---|---|
| **ABC** | | | |
| ❑ S-623 | Salvation | 1968 | 20.00 |
| ❑ S-653 | Gypsy Carnival Caravan | 1968 | 20.00 |

## SAM AND DAVE

| Number | Title (A Side/B Side) | Yr | NM |
|---|---|---|---|
| **ATLANTIC** | | | |
| ❑ SD 8205 | I Thank You | 1968 | 25.00 |
| ❑ SD 8218 | The Best of Sam and Dave | 1969 | 20.00 |
| ❑ 81279 | The Best of Sam and Dave | 1985 | 10.00 |
| ❑ 81718 | Soul Men | 1987 | 10.00 |
| *—Reissue of Stax 725* | | | |
| **GUSTO** | | | |
| ❑ 0045 | Sweet and Funky Gold | 197? | 10.00 |
| **ROULETTE** | | | |
| ❑ R-25323 [M] | Sam and Dave | 1966 | 30.00 |
| ❑ SR-25323 [S] | Sam and Dave | 1966 | 40.00 |
| **STAX** | | | |
| ❑ ST-708 [M] | Hold On, I'm Comin' | 1966 | 40.00 |
| ❑ STS-708 [S] | Hold On, I'm Comin' | 1966 | 50.00 |
| ❑ ST-712 [M] | Double Dynamite | 1966 | 30.00 |
| ❑ STS-712 [S] | Double Dynamite | 1966 | 40.00 |
| ❑ ST-725 [M] | Soul Men | 1967 | 30.00 |
| ❑ STS-725 [S] | Soul Men | 1967 | 40.00 |
| **UNITED ARTISTS** | | | |
| ❑ UA-LA524-G | Back At 'Cha! | 1975 | 12.00 |

## SAM THE SHAM AND THE PHARAOHS

| Number | Title (A Side/B Side) | Yr | NM |
|---|---|---|---|
| **ATLANTIC** | | | |
| ❑ SD 8271 | Hard and Heavy | 1971 | 15.00 |
| *—As "Sam Samudio"* | | | |
| **MGM** | | | |
| ❑ E-4297 [M] | Wooly Bully | 1965 | 30.00 |
| ❑ SE-4297 [S] | Wooly Bully | 1965 | 40.00 |
| ❑ E-4317 [M] | Their Second Album | 1965 | 25.00 |
| ❑ SE-4317 [S] | Their Second Album | 1965 | 30.00 |
| ❑ E-4347 [M] | On Tour | 1966 | 25.00 |
| ❑ SE-4347 [S] | On Tour | 1966 | 30.00 |
| ❑ E-4407 [M] | Lil' Red Riding Hood | 1966 | 25.00 |
| ❑ SE-4407 [S] | Lil' Red Riding Hood | 1966 | 30.00 |
| ❑ E-4422 [M] | The Best of Sam the Sham and the Pharoahs | 1967 | 20.00 |
| ❑ SE-4422 [S] | The Best of Sam the Sham and the Pharoahs | 1967 | 25.00 |
| ❑ E-4477 [M] | Nefertiti | 1967 | 25.00 |
| ❑ SE-4477 | The Sam The Sham Revue | 1968 | 20.00 |
| *—Retitled reissue* | | | |
| ❑ SE-4477 [S] | Nefertiti | 1967 | 25.00 |
| ❑ SE-4526 | Ten of Pentacles | 1968 | 20.00 |
| ❑ ST 90422 [S] | Wooly Bully | 1965 | 50.00 |
| *—Capitol Record Club edition* | | | |
| ❑ T 90422 [M] | Wooly Bully | 1965 | 40.00 |
| *—Capitol Record Club edition* | | | |
| **POLYDOR** | | | |
| ❑ 827917-1 | The Best of Sam the Sham and the Pharoahs | 1985 | 10.00 |
| **RHINO** | | | |
| ❑ RNLP-122 | Pharoahization: The Best of Sam the Sham and the Pharoahs (1965-1967) | 1986 | 10.00 |

## SAMHAIN
Also see THE MISFITS.

| Number | Title (A Side/B Side) | Yr | NM |
|---|---|---|---|
| **PLAN 9** | | | |
| ❑ PL9-04 | Initium | 1984 | 50.00 |
| *—Black vinyl; "8-84" scrawled in trail-off wax* | | | |
| ❑ PL9-04 | Initium | 1984 | 100.00 |
| *—500 on red vinyl* | | | |
| ❑ PL9-04 | Initium | 1984 | 300.00 |
| *—100 on white vinyl* | | | |
| ❑ PL9-04 | Initium | 1984 | 300.00 |
| *—No more than 100 on marbled black and white vinyl* | | | |
| ❑ PL9-04 | Initium | 1984 | 400.00 |
| *—Pink vinyl "error" pressing* | | | |
| ❑ PL9-05 [EP] | Unholy Passion | 1985 | 12.00 |
| *—Black vinyl, maroon cover* | | | |
| ❑ PL9-05 [EP] | Unholy Passion | 1985 | 80.00 |
| *—Black vinyl, tan cover (original)* | | | |
| ❑ PL9-05 [EP] | Unholy Passion | 1985 | 100.00 |
| *—Red vinyl, maroon cover* | | | |
| ❑ PL9-05 [EP] | Unholy Passion | 1985 | 100.00 |
| *—White vinyl, tan cover* | | | |
| ❑ PL9-07 | November Coming Fire | 1986 | 30.00 |
| *—Regular issue on black vinyl* | | | |
| ❑ PL9-07 | November Coming Fire | 1986 | 150.00 |
| *—200 on orange vinyl* | | | |

## SAMPLE, JOE

| Number | Title (A Side/B Side) | Yr | NM |
|---|---|---|---|
| **CRUSADERS** | | | |
| ❑ 16001 | Carmel | 198? | 20.00 |
| *—Audiophile vinyl* | | | |
| **MOBILE FIDELITY** | | | |
| ❑ 1-016 | Rainbow Seeker | 1979 | 20.00 |
| *—Audiophile vinyl* | | | |

## SAMPLE, JOE; RAY BROWN; SHELLY MANNE

| Number | Title (A Side/B Side) | Yr | NM |
|---|---|---|---|
| **EAST WIND** | | | |
| ❑ 10001 | The Three | 1976 | 20.00 |



Except when noted otherwise, VG = 25% of NM, and VG+ = 50% of NM. (Example: VG = $2.00, VG+ = $4.00 and NM = $8.00.)

Number | Title (A Side/B Side) | Yr | NM

## SAMPLE, JOE, AND DAVID T. WALKER

**CRUSADERS**

❑ 16004 | Swing Street Café | 198? | 20.00
*—Audiophile vinyl*

## SAMPLES, JUNIOR

**CHART**

❑ CHM-1002 [M] | The World of Junior Samples | 1967 | 20.00
❑ CHS-1002 [S] | The World of Junior Samples | 1967 | 20.00
❑ CHS-1007 | Bull Session at Bulls Gap | 1968 | 15.00
❑ CHS-1021 | That's a Hee Haw | 1969 | 15.00
❑ CHS-1045 | Best of Junior Samples | 1970 | 15.00

**HILLTOP**

❑ JS-6113 | Moonshining | 197? | 10.00

## SAMPSON, EDGAR

**CORAL**

❑ CRL 57049 [M] | Swing Softly Sweet Sampson | 1957 | 40.00

## SAN REMO GOLDEN STRINGS

**GORDY**

❑ G-923 [M] | Hungry for Love | 1967 | 25.00
❑ GS-923 [S] | Hungry for Love | 1967 | 30.00
❑ GLP-928 [M] | Swing | 1968 | 60.00
*—Mono is white label promo only; stereo cover has "Monaural Record DJ Copy" sticker on front*
❑ GS-928 [S] | Swing | 1968 | 20.00

**RIC-TIC**

❑ 901 [M] | Hungry for Love | 1966 | 50.00
❑ S-901 [S] | Hungry for Love | 1966 | 60.00

## SAN SEBASTIAN STRINGS, THE

**STANYAN**

❑ 10043 | La Mer | 1972 | 10.00

**WARNER BROS.**

❑ W 1670 [M] | The Sea | 1967 | 15.00
❑ WS 1670 [S] | The Sea | 1967 | 12.00
❑ W 1705 [M] | The Earth | 1967 | 15.00
❑ WS 1705 [S] | The Earth | 1967 | 12.00
❑ WS 1720 | The Sky | 1968 | 12.00
❑ 3WS 1730 [(3)] | The Sea, The Earth, The Sky | 1968 | 20.00
❑ WS 1764 | Home to the Sea | 1968 | 12.00
❑ WS 1795 | For Lovers | 1969 | 12.00
❑ 3WS 1827 [(3)] | The Complete Sea | 1969 | 20.00
❑ WS 1839 | The Soft Sea | 1970 | 12.00
❑ BS 2622 | Winter | 1972 | 10.00
❑ BS 2707 | Summer | 1973 | 10.00
❑ BS4-2707 [Q] | Summer | 1973 | 15.00
❑ 4WS 2754 [(4)] | Seasons | 1973 | 20.00
❑ BS 2768 | Bouquet — The Best of the San Sebastian Strings | 1974 | 10.00
❑ BS 2837 | With Love | 1975 | 10.00
❑ ST-91618 | Home to the Sea | 1968 | 15.00
*—Capitol Record Club edition*

## SANDALS, THE

**WORLD PACIFIC**

❑ ST-1818 [S] | Scrambler | 1964 | 100.00
*—As "The Sandells"; black vinyl*
❑ ST-1818 [S] | Scrambler | 1964 | 250.00
*—As "The Sandells"; red vinyl*
❑ WP-1818 [M] | Scrambler | 1964 | 80.00
*—As "The Sandells"*
❑ ST-1832 [S] | The Endless Summer | 1966 | 30.00
❑ WP-1832 [M] | The Endless Summer | 1966 | 25.00
❑ ST-21884 | The Last of the Ski Bums | 1969 | 25.00
*—With skiers' silhouettes on cover*
❑ ST-21884 | The Last of the Ski Bums | 1969 | 25.00
*—With Volkswagon bus on cover*

## SANDBERG, CARL

**COLUMBIA MASTERWORKS**

❑ ML 5539 [M] | Flat Rock Ballads | 1959 | 20.00

**DECCA**

❑ DL 5135 [10] | The People, Yes | 1950 | 50.00
❑ DL 9105 [M] | Cowboy Songs and Negro Spirituals | 1964 | 20.00

**LYRICHORD**

❑ LL-4 [10] | American Songbag | 1951 | 50.00
❑ LL-66 [M] | The Great Carl Sandburg | 1957 | 30.00

## SANDERS, ED

**REPRISE**

❑ MS 2105 | Beer Cans on the Moon | 1972 | 25.00
❑ RS-6374 | Sanders' Truckstop | 1969 | 25.00

## SANDERS, FELICIA

**COLUMBIA**

❑ CL 654 [M] | Felicia Sanders at the Blue Angel | 1955 | 30.00
❑ CL 713 [M] | Girl Meets Boy | 1955 | 30.00

**DECCA**

❑ DL 8762 [M] | That Certain Feeling | 1958 | 25.00
❑ DL 78762 [S] | That Certain Feeling | 1959 | 40.00

## SANDERS, GEORGE

**ABC-PARAMOUNT**

❑ ABC-231 [M] | The George Sanders Touch | 1958 | 30.00

## SANDERS, PHAROAH

**ABC IMPULSE!**

❑ A-9138 [M] | Tauhid | 1967 | 30.00
❑ AS-9138 [S] | Tauhid | 1967 | 20.00
❑ AS-9181 | Karma | 1969 | 20.00
❑ AS-9190 | Jewels of Thought | 1970 | 20.00
❑ AS-9199 | Summun Bukmun Umyum | 1970 | 20.00
❑ AS-9229 [(2)] | The Best of Pharoah Sanders | 1973 | 20.00

**ESP-DISK'**

❑ 1003 [M] | Pharoah's First | 1965 | 25.00
❑ S-1003 [S] | Pharoah's First | 1965 | 30.00

## SANDOLE, DENNIS

**FANTASY**

❑ 3251 [M] | Compositions and Arrangements for Guitar | 1958 | 30.00

## SANDOLE BROTHERS, THE

**FANTASY**

❑ 3209 [M] | Modern Music from Philadelphia | 1956 | 50.00
*—Red vinyl*
❑ 3209 [M] | Modern Music from Philadelphia | 1957 | 30.00
*—Black vinyl*

## SANDS, EVIE

**A&M**

❑ SP-4239 | Any Way That You Want Me | 1969 | 30.00

**HAVEN**

❑ ST-9202 | Estate of Mind | 1975 | 20.00

**RCA VICTOR**

❑ AFL1-2943 | Suspended Animation | 1979 | 15.00

## SANDS, TOMMY

**CAPITOL**

❑ T 848 [M] | Steady Date with Tommy Sands | 1957 | 60.00
❑ T 929 [M] | Sing Boy Sing | 1958 | 60.00
❑ T 1081 [M] | Sands Storm | 1959 | 50.00
❑ ST 1123 [S] | This Thing Called Love | 1959 | 40.00
❑ T 1123 [M] | This Thing Called Love | 1959 | 30.00
❑ ST 1239 [S] | When I'm Thinking of You | 1960 | 40.00
❑ T 1239 [M] | When I'm Thinking of You | 1960 | 30.00
❑ ST 1364 [S] | Sands at the Sands | 1960 | 40.00
❑ T 1364 [M] | Sands at the Sands | 1960 | 30.00
❑ ST 1426 [S] | Dream with Me | 1961 | 40.00
❑ T 1426 [M] | Dream with Me | 1961 | 30.00

**GREEN LINNET**

❑ SIF-3044 | Singing of the Times | 1989 | 12.00

## SANTA FE

**RTV**

❑ 301 | Good Earth | 197? | 30.00

## SANTAMARIA, MONGO

**BATTLE**

❑ B-6120 [M] | Watermelon Man! | 1963 | 20.00
❑ B-6129 [M] | Mongo at the Village Gate | 1964 | 20.00
❑ BS-96120 [S] | Watermelon Man! | 1963 | 25.00
❑ BS-96129 [S] | Mongo at the Village Gate | 1964 | 25.00

**COLUMBIA**

❑ CL 2298 [M] | El Pussy Cat | 1965 | 20.00
*—With "Guaranteed High Fidelity" in black at bottom of red label*
❑ CS 9098 [S] | El Pussy Cat | 1965 | 25.00
*—With "360 Sound Stereo" in black at bottom of red label*
❑ CS 9175 [S] | La Bamba | 1965 | 20.00

**FANTASY**

❑ 3267 [M] | Yambu | 1959 | 30.00
*—Black vinyl*
❑ 3267 [M] | Yambu | 1959 | 40.00
*—Red vinyl*
❑ 3291 [M] | Mongo | 1959 | 30.00
*—Black vinyl*
❑ 3291 [M] | Mongo | 1959 | 40.00
*—Red vinyl*
❑ 3302 [M] | Our Man in Havana | 1960 | 30.00
*—Black vinyl*
❑ 3302 [M] | Our Man in Havana | 1960 | 40.00
*—Red vinyl*
❑ 3311 [M] | Mongo in Havana | 1960 | 30.00
*—Black vinyl*
❑ 3311 [M] | Mongo in Havana | 1960 | 40.00
*—Red vinyl*
❑ 3314 [M] | Sabroso | 1960 | 30.00
*—Black vinyl*
❑ 3314 [M] | Sabroso | 1960 | 40.00
*—Red vinyl*
❑ 3324 [M] | Arriba! | 1961 | 30.00
*—Black vinyl*
❑ 3324 [M] | Arriba! | 1961 | 40.00
*—Red vinyl*
❑ 3328 [M] | Mas Sabroso | 1962 | 30.00
*—Black vinyl*
❑ 3328 [M] | Mas Sabroso | 1962 | 40.00
*—Red vinyl*
❑ 3335 [M] | Viva Mongo! | 1962 | 30.00
*—Black vinyl*
❑ 3335 [M] | Viva Mongo! | 1962 | 40.00
*—Red vinyl*
❑ 8012 [S] | Yambu | 1962 | 20.00
*—Black vinyl*
❑ 8012 [S] | Yambu | 1962 | 30.00
*—Blue vinyl*
❑ 8032 [S] | Mongo | 1962 | 20.00
*—Black vinyl*
❑ 8032 [S] | Mongo | 1962 | 30.00
*—Blue vinyl*
❑ 8045 [S] | Our Man in Havana | 1962 | 20.00
*—Black vinyl*
❑ 8045 [S] | Our Man in Havana | 1962 | 30.00
*—Blue vinyl*
❑ 8055 [S] | Mongo in Havana | 1962 | 20.00
*—Black vinyl*
❑ 8055 [S] | Mongo in Havana | 1962 | 30.00
*—Blue vinyl*
❑ 8058 [S] | Sabroso | 1962 | 20.00
*—Black vinyl*
❑ 8058 [S] | Sabroso | 1962 | 30.00
*—Blue vinyl*
❑ 8067 [S] | Arriba! | 1962 | 20.00
*—Black vinyl*
❑ 8067 [S] | Arriba! | 1962 | 30.00
*—Blue vinyl*
❑ 8071 [S] | Mas Sabroso | 1962 | 20.00
*—Black vinyl*
❑ 8071 [S] | Mas Sabroso | 1962 | 30.00
*—Blue vinyl*
❑ 8087 [S] | Viva Mongo! | 1962 | 20.00
*—Black vinyl*
❑ 8087 [S] | Viva Mongo! | 1962 | 30.00
*—Blue vinyl*
❑ 8351 [S] | Mighty Mongo | 1963 | 20.00

**RIVERSIDE**

❑ RLP-423 [M] | Go, Mongo! | 1962 | 25.00
❑ R-3008 [M] | Explosion | 1967 | 25.00
❑ RM-3523 [M] | Mongo Introduces La Lupe | 1963 | 20.00
❑ RM-3529 [M] | Mongo at the Village Gate | 1963 | 20.00
❑ RM-3530 [M] | Mongo Santamaria Explodes! | 1964 | 20.00
❑ RS-9423 [S] | Go, Mongo! | 1962 | 30.00
❑ RS-93523 [S] | Mongo Introduces La Lupe | 1963 | 25.00
❑ RS-93529 [S] | Mongo at the Village Gate | 1963 | 25.00
❑ RS-93530 [S] | Mongo Santamaria Explodes! | 1964 | 25.00

**TICO**

❑ LP-137 [10] | Chango | 1955 | 80.00
❑ LP-1037 [M] | Chango: Mongo Santamaria's Drums and Chants | 1957 | 60.00
❑ LP-1149 [M] | Mongo Santamaria's Drums and Chants | 1967 | 20.00

## SANTANA

**ARISTA**

❑ 19080 [(2)] | Supernatural | 2000 | 40.00
*—Classic Records audiophile vinyl issue in gatefold cover with booklet*

**CICADELIC**

❑ 1004 | Santana '68 | 1988 | 12.00

**COLUMBIA**

❑ CS 9781 | Santana | 1969 | 15.00
*—"360 Sound" on label*
❑ CS 9781 | Santana | 1970 | 10.00
*—Orange label*
❑ PC 9781 | Santana | 198? | 8.00
❑ CQ 30130 [Q] | Abraxas | 1972 | 20.00
❑ JC 30130 | Abraxas | 1977 | 8.00
❑ KC 30130 | Abraxas | 197? | 10.00
*—With no poster*
❑ KC 30130 | Abraxas | 1970 | 15.00
*—Original copies have a poster*
❑ PC 30130 | Abraxas | 1985 | 8.00
❑ CQ 30595 [Q] | Santana | 1972 | 20.00
❑ KC 30595 | Santana | 1971 | 12.00
*—Not the same album as CS 9781; this is often called "Santana III"*
❑ PC 30595 | Santana | 197? | 8.00
❑ KC 31610 | Caravanserai | 1972 | 12.00
❑ PC 31610 | Caravanserai | 197? | 8.00
❑ PCQ 31610 [Q] | Caravanserai | 1974 | 20.00
❑ PC 32455 | Welcome | 1973 | 12.00
*—No bar code on cover*
❑ PC 32455 | Welcome | 1979 | 8.00
*—With bar code on cover*
❑ PCQ 32455 [Q] | Welcome | 1974 | 20.00
❑ PCQ 32964 [Q] | Santana | 1974 | 20.00
*—Quadraphonic issue of their debut album (9781)*
❑ JC 33050 | Santana's Greatest Hits | 1977 | 8.00
❑ PC 33050 | Santana's Greatest Hits | 1974 | 12.00
*—No bar code on cover*
❑ PCQ 33050 [Q] | Santana's Greatest Hits | 1974 | 20.00
❑ PC 33135 | Borboletta | 1974 | 12.00
*—No bar code on cover*

Santana, *Abraxas,* Columbia KC 30130, 1970, with poster, $15.

| Number | Title (A Side/B Side) | Yr | NM |
|---|---|---|---|
| ❑ PC 33135 | Borboletta | 1979 | 8.00 |
| *—With bar code on cover* | | | |
| ❑ PCQ 33135 [Q] | Borboletta | 1974 | 20.00 |
| ❑ PC 33576 | Amigos | 1976 | 12.00 |
| *—No bar code on cover* | | | |
| ❑ PC 33576 | Amigos | 1979 | 8.00 |
| *—With bar code on cover* | | | |
| ❑ PCQ 33576 [Q] | Amigos | 1976 | 20.00 |
| ❑ JC 34423 | Festival | 1977 | 12.00 |
| ❑ JCQ 34423 [Q] | Festival | 1977 | 20.00 |
| ❑ PC 34423 | Festival | 198? | 8.00 |
| ❑ C2 34914 [(2)] | Moonflower | 1977 | 15.00 |
| ❑ FC 35600 | Inner Secrets | 1978 | 12.00 |
| ❑ PC 35600 | Inner Secrets | 198? | 8.00 |
| *—Budget-line reissue* | | | |
| ❑ FC 36154 | Marathon | 1979 | 12.00 |
| ❑ PC 36154 | Marathon | 198? | 8.00 |
| *—Budget-line reissue* | | | |
| ❑ C2 36590 [(2)] | Swing of Delight | 1980 | 15.00 |
| ❑ FC 37158 | Zebop! | 1981 | 12.00 |
| ❑ PC 37158 | Zebop! | 198? | 8.00 |
| *—Budget-line reissue* | | | |
| ❑ FC 38122 | Shango | 1982 | 12.00 |
| ❑ PC 38122 | Shango | 198? | 8.00 |
| *—Budget-line reissue* | | | |
| ❑ FC 39527 | Beyond Appearances | 1985 | 10.00 |
| ❑ PC 39527 | Beyond Appearances | 198? | 8.00 |
| *—Budget-line reissue* | | | |
| ❑ HC 40130 | Abraxas | 1981 | 80.00 |
| *—Half-speed mastered edition* | | | |
| ❑ FC 40272 | Freedom | 1987 | 10.00 |
| ❑ C3X 44344 [(3)] | Viva Santana | 1988 | 20.00 |
| ❑ HC 47158 | Zebop! | 1981 | 40.00 |
| *—Half-speed mastered edition* | | | |

**SANTO AND JOHNNY**

CANADIAN AMERICAN

| Number | Title (A Side/B Side) | Yr | NM |
|---|---|---|---|
| ❑ CALP-1001 [M] | Santo & Johnny | 1959 | 60.00 |
| ❑ SCALP-1001 [S] | Santo & Johnny | 1959 | 80.00 |
| ❑ CALP-1002 [M] | Encore | 1960 | 40.00 |
| ❑ SCALP-1002 [S] | Encore | 1960 | 50.00 |
| ❑ CALP-1004 [M] | Hawaii | 1961 | 40.00 |
| ❑ SCALP-1004 [S] | Hawaii | 1961 | 50.00 |
| ❑ CALP-1006 [M] | Come On In | 1962 | 30.00 |
| ❑ SCALP-1006 [S] | Come On In | 1962 | 40.00 |
| ❑ CALP-1008 [M] | Around the World with Santo and Johnny | 1962 | 30.00 |
| ❑ SCALP-1008 [S] | Around the World with Santo and Johnny | 1962 | 40.00 |
| ❑ CALP-1011 [M] | Off Shore | 1963 | 30.00 |
| ❑ SCALP-1011 [S] | Off Shore | 1963 | 40.00 |
| ❑ CALP-1014 [M] | In the Still of the Night | 1963 | 30.00 |
| ❑ SCALP-1014 [S] | In the Still of the Night | 1963 | 40.00 |
| ❑ CALP-1016 [M] | Wish You Love | 1964 | 30.00 |
| ❑ SCALP-1016 [S] | Wish You Love | 1964 | 40.00 |
| ❑ CALP-1017 [M] | The Beatles' Greatest Hits | 1965 | 40.00 |
| ❑ SCALP-1017 [S] | The Beatles' Greatest Hits | 1965 | 50.00 |
| ❑ CALP-1018 [M] | Mucho | 1965 | 30.00 |
| ❑ SCALP-1018 [S] | Mucho | 1965 | 40.00 |

IMPERIAL

| Number | Title (A Side/B Side) | Yr | NM |
|---|---|---|---|
| ❑ LP-9363 [M] | Brilliant Guitar Sounds | 1967 | 15.00 |
| ❑ LP-12363 [S] | Brilliant Guitar Sounds | 1967 | 20.00 |
| ❑ LP-12366 | Golden Guitars | 1968 | 15.00 |
| ❑ LP-12418 | On the Road Again | 1968 | 15.00 |

**SANTOS, LARRY**

CASABLANCA

| Number | Title (A Side/B Side) | Yr | NM |
|---|---|---|---|
| ❑ NBLP 7030 | You Are Everything I Need | 1976 | 12.00 |
| ❑ NBLP 7061 | Don't Let the Music Stop | 1977 | 12.00 |

EVOLUTION

| Number | Title (A Side/B Side) | Yr | NM |
|---|---|---|---|
| ❑ 2002 | Just a Man | 1969 | 20.00 |
| ❑ 2015 | Morning Sun | 1971 | 15.00 |

**SANTOS, MOACIR**

BLUE NOTE

| Number | Title (A Side/B Side) | Yr | NM |
|---|---|---|---|
| ❑ BN-LA007-F | Maestro | 1972 | 20.00 |

**SANTOS BROTHERS, THE**

METROJAZZ

| Number | Title (A Side/B Side) | Yr | NM |
|---|---|---|---|
| ❑ E-1015 [M] | Jazz For Two Trumpets | 1958 | 50.00 |
| ❑ SE-1015 [S] | Jazz For Two Trumpets | 1958 | 40.00 |

**SAPODILLA PUNCH**

PHILIPS

| Number | Title (A Side/B Side) | Yr | NM |
|---|---|---|---|
| ❑ PHS 600312 | Sapodilla Punch | 1969 | 20.00 |

**SAPPHIRE THINKERS, THE**

HOBBIT

| Number | Title (A Side/B Side) | Yr | NM |
|---|---|---|---|
| ❑ HB-5003 | From Within | 1969 | 30.00 |

**SAPPHIRES, THE (1)**

COLLECTABLES

| Number | Title (A Side/B Side) | Yr | NM |
|---|---|---|---|
| ❑ COL-5007 | Who Do You Love | 198? | 10.00 |

SWAN

| Number | Title (A Side/B Side) | Yr | NM |
|---|---|---|---|
| ❑ LP-513 [M] | Who Do You Love | 1964 | 300.00 |

**SASH, LEON**

STORYVILLE

| Number | Title (A Side/B Side) | Yr | NM |
|---|---|---|---|
| ❑ STLP-917 [M] | Leon Sash Quartet | 1956 | 50.00 |

**SATAN AND THE DISCIPLES**

GOLDBAND

| Number | Title (A Side/B Side) | Yr | NM |
|---|---|---|---|
| ❑ 7750 | Underground | 1969 | 40.00 |

**SATANS, THE**

(NO LABEL)

| Number | Title (A Side/B Side) | Yr | NM |
|---|---|---|---|
| ❑ (no #) [M] | Raisin' Hell | 1962 | 300.00 |

**SATAN'S FOUR**

B.T. PUPPY

| Number | Title (A Side/B Side) | Yr | NM |
|---|---|---|---|
| ❑ BTS-1010 | Mixed Soul | 1970 | 150.00 |
| *—With the Cinnamon Angels* | | | |

**SAUNDERS, HERM**

VOGUE

| Number | Title (A Side/B Side) | Yr | NM |
|---|---|---|---|
| ❑ 101 [10] | Music at the Bantam Cock | 1953 | 200.00 |

WARNER BROS.

| Number | Title (A Side/B Side) | Yr | NM |
|---|---|---|---|
| ❑ W 1234 [M] | The Tinkling Piano in the Next Apartment | 1958 | 20.00 |
| ❑ W 1269 [M] | That Celestial Feeling | 1959 | 20.00 |

**SAUNDERS, MERL**

CRYSTAL CLEAR

| Number | Title (A Side/B Side) | Yr | NM |
|---|---|---|---|
| ❑ 5006 | Do I Move You | 1980 | 20.00 |
| *—Direct-to-disc recording* | | | |

FANTASY

| Number | Title (A Side/B Side) | Yr | NM |
|---|---|---|---|
| ❑ 9421 | Fire Up | 1973 | 20.00 |
| *—With Jerry Garcia and Tom Fogerty* | | | |
| ❑ 79002 [(2)] | Live at the Keystone | 198? | 20.00 |

**SAUSSY, TUPPER** Also see THE NEON PHILARMONIC.

MONUMENT

| Number | Title (A Side/B Side) | Yr | NM |
|---|---|---|---|
| ❑ MLP-8004 [M] | Discover Tupper Saussy | 1964 | 20.00 |
| ❑ MLP-8027 [M] | Said I to Shostakovitch | 1965 | 20.00 |
| ❑ MLP-8034 [M] | A Swinger's Guide to "Mary Poppins" | 1965 | 20.00 |
| ❑ SLP-18004 [S] | Discover Tupper Saussy | 1964 | 25.00 |
| ❑ SLP-18027 [S] | Said I to Shostakovitch | 1965 | 25.00 |
| ❑ SLP-18034 [S] | A Swinger's Guide to "Mary Poppins" | 1965 | 25.00 |

**SAUTER-FINEGAN**

RCA VICTOR

| Number | Title (A Side/B Side) | Yr | NM |
|---|---|---|---|
| ❑ LJM-1003 [M] | Inside Sauter-Finegan | 1954 | 80.00 |
| ❑ LPM-1009 [M] | The Sound of Sauter-Finegan | 1954 | 80.00 |
| ❑ LPM-1051 [M] | Concert Jazz | 1955 | 60.00 |
| ❑ LPM-1104 [M] | Sons of Sauter-Finegan | 1955 | 60.00 |
| ❑ LPM-1227 [M] | New Directions in Music | 1956 | 60.00 |
| ❑ LPM-1240 [M] | Adventure In Time | 1956 | 60.00 |
| ❑ LPM-1341 [M] | Under Analysis | 1957 | 50.00 |
| ❑ LPM-1497 [M] | Straight Down the Middle | 1957 | 50.00 |
| ❑ LPM-1634 [M] | Memories of Goodman and Miller | 1958 | 50.00 |
| ❑ LPM-2473 [M] | Inside Sauter-Finegan Revisited | 1961 | 30.00 |
| ❑ LSP-2473 [S] | Inside Sauter-Finegan Revisited | 1961 | 40.00 |
| ❑ LPM-3115 [10] | New Directions in Music | 1953 | 120.00 |

UNITED ARTISTS

| Number | Title (A Side/B Side) | Yr | NM |
|---|---|---|---|
| ❑ WWR 3511 [M] | The Return of the Doodletown Fifers | 1959 | 40.00 |
| ❑ WWS 7511 [S] | The Return of the Doodletown Fifers | 1959 | 50.00 |

**SAUTER-FINEGAN; CHICAGO SYMPHONY ORCHESTRA (FRITZ REINER, CONDUCTOR)**

RCA VICTOR RED SEAL

| Number | Title (A Side/B Side) | Yr | NM |
|---|---|---|---|
| ❑ LM-1888 [M] | Concerto for Jazz Band and Orchestra | 1954 | 30.00 |

**SAVAGE RESURRECTION**

MERCURY

| Number | Title (A Side/B Side) | Yr | NM |
|---|---|---|---|
| ❑ MG-21156 [M] | Savage Resurrection | 1968 | 200.00 |
| ❑ SR-61156 [S] | Savage Resurrection | 1968 | 100.00 |

**SAVAGE ROSE**

POLYDOR

| Number | Title (A Side/B Side) | Yr | NM |
|---|---|---|---|
| ❑ 24-6001 | In the Plain | 1969 | 20.00 |
| *—Gatefold cover* | | | |

**SAVATAGE**

ATLANTIC

| Number | Title (A Side/B Side) | Yr | NM |
|---|---|---|---|
| ❑ 81247 | Power of the Night | 1985 | 8.00 |
| ❑ 81634 | Fight for the Rock | 1986 | 8.00 |
| ❑ 81775 | Hall of the Mountain King | 1987 | 8.00 |
| ❑ 82008 | Gutter Ballet | 1990 | 12.00 |

COMBAT

| Number | Title (A Side/B Side) | Yr | NM |
|---|---|---|---|
| ❑ MX 6016 [EP] | The Dungeons Are Calling | 1985 | 15.00 |
| ❑ 8018 | Sirens | 1986 | 12.00 |
| *—Reissue of Par LP with new cover* | | | |

| Number | Title (A Side/B Side) | Yr | NM |
|---|---|---|---|
| PAR | | | |
| ❑ PAR-1050 | Sirens | 1983 | 200.00 |
| —*Black vinyl* | | | |
| ❑ PAR-1050 | Sirens | 1983 | 400.00 |
| —*Blue vinyl* | | | |
| **SAVITT, BUDDY** | | | |
| PARKWAY | | | |
| ❑ P-7012 [M] | The Most Heard Sax in the World | 1962 | 30.00 |
| ❑ SP-7012 [S] | The Most Heard Sax in the World | 1962 | 100.00 |
| **SAVOY BROWN** | | | |
| GNP CRESCENDO | | | |
| ❑ GNPS-2193 | Make Me Sweat | 1988 | 10.00 |
| ❑ GNPS-2196 | Kings of Boogie | 1989 | 10.00 |
| LONDON | | | |
| ❑ APS 638 | Boogie Brothers | 1974 | 10.00 |
| ❑ PS 659 | Wire Fire | 1975 | 10.00 |
| ❑ PS 670 | Skin 'n' Bone | 1976 | 10.00 |
| ❑ PS 718 | Savage Return | 1978 | 10.00 |
| ❑ LC-50000 | The Best of Savoy Brown | 1977 | 10.00 |
| PARROT | | | |
| ❑ PAS 71024 | Getting to the Point | 1968 | 25.00 |
| ❑ PAS 71027 | Blue Matter | 1969 | 25.00 |
| ❑ PAS 71029 | A Step Further | 1969 | 15.00 |
| ❑ PAS 71036 | Raw Sienna | 1970 | 15.00 |
| ❑ PAS 71042 | Looking In | 1970 | 15.00 |
| ❑ PAS 71047 | Street Corner Talking | 1971 | 15.00 |
| ❑ XPAS 71052 | Hellbound Train | 1972 | 15.00 |
| ❑ XPAS 71057 | Lion's Share | 1972 | 15.00 |
| ❑ XPAS 71059 | Jack the Toad | 1973 | 15.00 |
| TOWN HOUSE | | | |
| ❑ ST-7002 | Rock 'n' Roll Warriors | 1981 | 12.00 |
| ❑ SKBK-7003 [(2)] | Greatest Hits Live in Concert | 1982 | 15.00 |
| **SAWBUCK** | | | |
| FILLMORE | | | |
| ❑ Z 31248 | Sawbuck | 1972 | 20.00 |
| **SAXON, SKY** Also see THE SEEDS. | | | |
| GNP CRESCENDO | | | |
| ❑ GNP-2040 [M] | A Full Spoon of Seedy Blues | 1967 | 40.00 |
| ❑ GNPS-2040 [S] | A Full Spoon of Seedy Blues | 1967 | 30.00 |
| **SAXONS, THE** | | | |
| MIRASONIC | | | |
| ❑ A-1017 [M] | The Saxons | 1966 | 40.00 |
| ❑ AS-1017 [S] | The Saxons | 1966 | 80.00 |
| **SAYE, JOE** | | | |
| EMARCY | | | |
| ❑ MG-36072 [M] | Scotch on the Rocks | 1956 | 40.00 |
| ❑ MG-36112 [M] | A Wee Bit of Jazz | 1957 | 40.00 |
| ❑ MG-36147 [M] | A Double Shot of Saye | 1958 | 40.00 |
| ❑ SR-80022 [S] | A Double Shot of Saye | 1958 | 30.00 |
| MERCURY | | | |
| ❑ SR-60052 [S] | A Wee Bit of Jazz | 1959 | 30.00 |
| **SCAFFOLD, THE** | | | |
| BELL | | | |
| ❑ 6018 [M] | Thank U Very Much | 1968 | 50.00 |
| —*Mono copies are promo only* | | | |
| ❑ 6018 [S] | Thank U Very Much | 1968 | 50.00 |
| **SCAGGS, BOZ** | | | |
| ATLANTIC | | | |
| ❑ SD 8239 | Boz Scaggs | 1969 | 12.00 |
| ❑ SD 19166 | Boz Scaggs | 1977 | 8.00 |
| COLUMBIA | | | |
| ❑ A2S 71 [(2)DJ] | KSAN Live Concert | 1974 | 50.00 |
| —*Promo-only set released in plain cardboard jacket* | | | |
| ❑ AS 203 [DJ] | The Boz Scaggs Sampler | 1976 | 20.00 |
| ❑ KC 30454 | Moments | 1971 | 10.00 |
| ❑ PC 30454 | Moments | 197? | 8.00 |
| ❑ KC 30976 | Boz Scaggs & Band | 1971 | 10.00 |
| ❑ PC 30976 | Boz Scaggs & Band | 197? | 8.00 |
| ❑ KC 31384 | My Time | 1972 | 10.00 |
| ❑ PC 31384 | My Time | 197? | 8.00 |
| ❑ KC 32760 | Slow Dancer | 1974 | 10.00 |
| —*Second cover has a male dancer who is not Boz Scaggs* | | | |
| ❑ KC 32760 | Slow Dancer | 1974 | 12.00 |
| —*Original cover has Boz Scaggs on a beach in only a bathing suit* | | | |
| ❑ PC 32760 | Slow Dancer | 197? | 8.00 |
| ❑ JC 33920 | Silk Degrees | 1977 | 10.00 |
| —*Early reissue with new prefix* | | | |
| ❑ PC 33920 | Silk Degrees | 1976 | 12.00 |
| —*Original edition with "PC" prefix and no bar code on back cover* | | | |
| ❑ PC 33920 | Silk Degrees | 1985 | 8.00 |
| —*Budget-line reissue; bar code on back cover* | | | |
| ❑ FC 36106 | Middle Man | 1980 | 10.00 |
| ❑ PC 36106 | Middle Man | 198? | 8.00 |
| —*Budget-line reissue* | | | |
| ❑ FC 36841 | Hits! | 1980 | 10.00 |
| ❑ PC 36841 | Hits! | 198? | 8.00 |
| —*Budget-line reissue* | | | |

| Number | Title (A Side/B Side) | Yr | NM |
|---|---|---|---|
| ❑ PC 37249 | Down Two Then Left | 198? | 8.00 |
| —*Budget-line reissue* | | | |
| ❑ JC 37429 | Down Two Then Left | 1977 | 10.00 |
| ❑ FC 40463 | Other Roads | 1988 | 10.00 |
| ❑ HC 43920 | Silk Degrees | 1981 | 30.00 |
| —*Half-speed mastered edition* | | | |
| **SCALETTA, DON** | | | |
| CAPITOL | | | |
| ❑ ST 2204 [S] | Any Time, Any Groove | 1965 | 20.00 |
| ❑ ST 2328 [S] | All in Good Time | 1965 | 20.00 |
| VERVE | | | |
| ❑ V-5027 [M] | Sunday Afternoon at the Trident | 1967 | 20.00 |
| **SCAMPS, THE** | | | |
| PROJECT | | | |
| ❑ 8002 [M] | Teen Dance and Sing Along Party | 1962 | 40.00 |
| **SCANDAL** | | | |
| COLUMBIA | | | |
| ❑ 5C 38194 [EP] | Scandal | 1983 | 10.00 |
| ❑ PC 38194 [EP] | Scandal | 198? | 6.00 |
| —*Reissue with new prefix* | | | |
| ❑ FC 39173 | Warrior | 1984 | 10.00 |
| ❑ 8C8 39905 [EP] | Scandal featuring Patty Smyth | 1985 | 20.00 |
| —*Picture disc EP with four of the group's biggest hits* | | | |
| **SCHAEFER, HAL** | | | |
| RCA VICTOR | | | |
| ❑ LPM-1106 [M] | Just Too Much | 1955 | 120.00 |
| ❑ LPM-1199 [M] | The RCA Victor Jazz Workshop | 1956 | 120.00 |
| UNITED ARTISTS | | | |
| ❑ UAL-3021 [M] | Ten Shades of Blue | 1959 | 60.00 |
| ❑ UAS-6021 [S] | Ten Shades of Blue | 1959 | 50.00 |
| **SCHAFER, KERMIT** | | | |
| JUBILEE | | | |
| ❑ BL-1 [M] | Blooperama | 196? | 20.00 |
| ❑ KS-1 [(2)M] | The Best of Bloopers | 1959 | 25.00 |
| ❑ PMB-1 [M] | Pardon My Blooper! Volume 1 | 1958 | 20.00 |
| ❑ LP-2 [10] | Pardon My Blooper! | 1954 | 40.00 |
| ❑ PMB-2 [M] | Pardon My Blooper! Volume 2 | 1958 | 20.00 |
| ❑ LP-3 [10] | Pardon My Blooper! Volume 2 | 1954 | 40.00 |
| ❑ PMB-3 [M] | Pardon My Blooper! Volume 3 | 1958 | 20.00 |
| ❑ PMB-4 [M] | Pardon My Blooper! Volume 4 | 1958 | 20.00 |
| ❑ PMB-5 [M] | Pardon My Blooper! Volume 5 | 1959 | 20.00 |
| ❑ PMB-6 [M] | Pardon My Blooper! Volume 6 | 1959 | 20.00 |
| ❑ PMB-7 [M] | Pardon My Blooper! Volume 7 | 1959 | 20.00 |
| ❑ PMB-8 [M] | Pardon My Blooper! Volume 8 | 1959 | 20.00 |
| ❑ SPMB-9 [M] | Pardon My Sports Blooper! | 196? | 20.00 |
| ❑ QPMB-10 [M] | Pardon My Quiz Blooper! | 196? | 20.00 |
| ❑ WPMB-11 [M] | Pardon My Washington Blooper! | 196? | 20.00 |
| ❑ LP-19 [10] | Pardon My Blooper! Volume 3 | 1955 | 40.00 |
| ❑ JLP-1000 [M] | Special Edition: Pardon My Blooper | 195? | 30.00 |
| ❑ JGM-2001 [M] | Comedy of Errors | 196? | 20.00 |
| ❑ JGM-2002 [M] | Slipped Disks | 196? | 20.00 |
| ❑ JGM-2003 [M] | Prize Bloopers | 196? | 20.00 |
| ❑ JGM-2004 [M] | Super Bloopers | 196? | 20.00 |
| ❑ JGM-2005 [M] | Off the Record | 196? | 20.00 |
| ❑ JGM-2006 [M] | Station Breaks | 196? | 20.00 |
| ❑ JGM-2007 [M] | Funny Boners | 196? | 20.00 |
| ❑ JGM-2008 [M] | Foot 'n Mouth Club | 196? | 20.00 |
| **SCHIFRIN, LALO** | | | |
| AUDIO FIDELITY | | | |
| ❑ AFLP-1981 [M] | Bossa Nova — New Brazilian Jazz | 1962 | 20.00 |
| ❑ AFLP-2117 [M] | Eso Es Latino Jazz | 1963 | 20.00 |
| ❑ AFSD-5981 [S] | Bossa Nova — New Brazilian Jazz | 1962 | 25.00 |
| ❑ AFSD-6117 [S] | Eso Es Latino Jazz | 1963 | 25.00 |
| COLGEMS | | | |
| ❑ COMO-5003 [M] | Murderer's Row | 1967 | 50.00 |
| ❑ COSO-5003 [S] | Murderer's Row | 1967 | 100.00 |
| DOT | | | |
| ❑ DLP-3831 [M] | Music from Mission: Impossible | 1967 | 30.00 |
| ❑ DLP-3833 [M] | Cool Hand Luke | 1968 | 50.00 |
| ❑ DLP-25831 [S] | Music from Mission: Impossible | 1967 | 40.00 |
| ❑ DLP-25833 [S] | Cool Hand Luke | 1968 | 50.00 |
| ❑ DLP-25852 | There's a Whole Lot of Schifrin Goin' On | 1968 | 20.00 |
| ENTR'ACTE | | | |
| ❑ ERS-6508 | Voyage of the Damned | 1977 | 25.00 |
| MGM | | | |
| ❑ SE-4110 [S] | Piano, Strings and Bossa Nova | 1963 | 20.00 |
| ❑ SE-4156 [S] | Between Broadway and Hollywood | 1963 | 20.00 |
| ❑ E-4313 [M] | The Cincinnati Kid | 1965 | 20.00 |
| ❑ SE-4313 [S] | The Cincinnati Kid | 1965 | 25.00 |
| ❑ E-4413 ST [M] | Liquidator | 1966 | 20.00 |
| ❑ SE-4413 ST [S] | Liquidator | 1966 | 25.00 |

| Number | Title (A Side/B Side) | Yr | NM |
|---|---|---|---|
| ❑ SE-4742 | Medical Center and Other Great Themes | 1971 | 20.00 |
| NAUTILUS | | | |
| ❑ NR-51 | Ins and Outs | 198? | 40.00 |
| —*Audiophile vinyl* | | | |
| PARAMOUNT | | | |
| ❑ PAS-5002 | More Music from Mission: Impossible | 1969 | 40.00 |
| ❑ PAS-5004 | Mannix | 1969 | 30.00 |
| ROULETTE | | | |
| ❑ R 52088 [M] | Lalo Brilliance | 1962 | 20.00 |
| ❑ SR 52088 [S] | Lalo Brilliance | 1962 | 25.00 |
| TETRAGRAMMATON | | | |
| ❑ T-5006 | Che! | 1969 | 30.00 |
| TICO | | | |
| ❑ LP-1070 [M] | Piano Espanol | 1960 | 25.00 |
| ❑ LPS-1070 [S] | Piano Espanol | 1960 | 30.00 |
| VERVE | | | |
| ❑ V6-8543 [S] | Samba Paros Dos | 1963 | 20.00 |
| —*With Bob Brookmeyer* | | | |
| ❑ V6-8601 [S] | New Fantasy | 1964 | 20.00 |
| ❑ V6-8624 [S] | Once a Thief and Other Themes | 1965 | 20.00 |
| ❑ V6-8654 [S] | The Dissection and Reconstruction of Music from the Past | 1966 | 20.00 |
| WARNER BROS. | | | |
| ❑ WS 1777 | Bullitt | 1968 | 60.00 |
| ❑ BSK 3328 | Boulevard Nights | 1979 | 10.00 |
| **SCHILLER, LAWRENCE** | | | |
| CAPITOL | | | |
| ❑ TAO 2574 [M] | LSD | 1966 | 100.00 |
| ❑ KAO 2630 [M] | Why Did Lenny Bruce Die? | 1967 | 30.00 |
| ❑ KAO 2652 [M] | Homosexuality in the American Male | 1967 | 30.00 |
| **SCHLAMME, MARTHA** | | | |
| VANGUARD | | | |
| ❑ VRS 497 [M] | Chansons de Noel | 1956 | 30.00 |
| ❑ VRS-9011 [M] | Raisins and Almonds and Other Jewish Folk Songs | 195? | 30.00 |
| ❑ VRS-9019 [M] | Folk Songs of Many Lands | 195? | 30.00 |
| **SCHORY, DICK** | | | |
| CONCERT DISC | | | |
| ❑ SC-21 [M] | Re-Percussion | 1957 | 60.00 |
| RCA VICTOR | | | |
| ❑ LPM-1866 [M] | Music for Bang, Barroom and Harp | 1958 | 60.00 |
| ❑ LSP-1866 [S] | Music for Bang, Barroom and Harp | 1958 | 200.00 |
| ❑ LPM-2125 [M] | Music to Break Any Mood | 1960 | 30.00 |
| ❑ LSP-2125 [S] | Music to Break Any Mood | 1960 | 100.00 |
| ❑ LPM-2289 [M] | Wild Percussion and Horns A-Plenty | 1960 | 30.00 |
| ❑ LSP-2289 [S] | Wild Percussion and Horns A-Plenty | 1960 | 60.00 |
| ❑ LSA-2306 [S] | Runnin' Wild | 1960 | 40.00 |
| ❑ LSA-2382 [S] | Stereo Action Goes Broadway | 1961 | 40.00 |
| ❑ LPM-2485 [M] | Holiday for Percussion | 1962 | 30.00 |
| ❑ LSA-2485 [S] | Holiday for Percussion | 1962 | 40.00 |
| ❑ LSP-2613 [S] | Supercussion | 1963 | 40.00 |
| ❑ LPM-2738 [M] | Politely Percussive | 1963 | 30.00 |
| ❑ LSP-2738 [S] | Politely Percussive | 1963 | 40.00 |
| ❑ LPM-2806 [M] | Dick Schory on Tour | 1964 | 20.00 |
| ❑ LSP-2806 [S] | Dick Schory on Tour | 1964 | 25.00 |
| ❑ LPM-2926 [M] | The Happy Hits | 1964 | 20.00 |
| ❑ LSP-2926 [S] | The Happy Hits | 1964 | 25.00 |
| **SCHULLER, GUNTHER** | | | |
| ATLANTIC | | | |
| ❑ 1368 [M] | Jazz Abstractions | 1961 | 20.00 |
| —*Multicolor label, white "fan" logo at right* | | | |
| ❑ SD 1368 [S] | Jazz Abstractions | 1961 | 25.00 |
| —*Multicolor label, white "fan" logo at right* | | | |
| **SCHUMANN, WALTER** | | | |
| CAPITOL | | | |
| ❑ H 285 [10] | Songs of the Ivy League | 195? | 40.00 |
| —*Purple label original* | | | |
| ❑ L 285 [10] | Songs of the Ivy League | 195? | 30.00 |
| —*Reissue with red label; has the same cover as the original, except the "H" has been blacked out and an "L" stamped next to it* | | | |
| ❑ H 297 [10] | The Voices of Walter Schumann | 195? | 40.00 |
| ❑ T 297 [M] | The Voices of Walter Schumann | 1955 | 25.00 |
| ❑ H 9016 [10] | Christmas in the Air! | 1951 | 40.00 |
| —*Original issue with purple label* | | | |
| ❑ L 9016 [10] | Christmas in the Air! | 1952? | 35.00 |
| —*Reissue with red label and new prefix* | | | |
| RCA VICTOR | | | |
| ❑ LPM-1025 [M] | Exploring the Unknown | 1955 | 50.00 |

Number | Title (A Side/B Side) | Yr | NM

❑ LPM-1141 [M] The Voices of Christmas 1955 20.00
*—Original cover has all-yellow lettering on front cover and eight LP/EP covers on back*
❑ LPM-1465 [M] Scrapbook: The Voices of Walter Schumann 1957 20.00
❑ LPM-1477 [M] When We Were Young 1957 20.00
❑ LSP-1558 [S] Walter Schumann Presents the Voices 1958 20.00

**SCHUUR, DIANE**

MUSIC IS MEDICINE
❑ 9057 Pilot of My Destiny 1982 20.00

**SCHWARTZ, THORNEL**

ARGO
❑ LP-704 [M] Soul Cookin' 1962 25.00
❑ LPS-704 [S] Soul Cookin' 1962 30.00

**SCIANNI, JOSEPH**

SAVOY
❑ MG-12185 [M] New Concepts 1965 30.00

**SCOBEY, BOB**

AMERICAN RECORDING SOCIETY
❑ G-408 [M] Bob Scobey's Frisco Band 1956 40.00

DOWN HOME
❑ MGD-1 [M] Bob Scobey's Frisco Band with Clancy Hayes 1954 50.00

GOOD TIME JAZZ
❑ L-14 [10] Bob Scobey's Frisco Band Vol. 2 1954 50.00
❑ L-22 [10] Bob Scobey's Frisco Band 1954 50.00
❑ L-12006 [M] Bob Scobey's Frisco Band with Clancy Hayes 1955 40.00
❑ L-12009 [M] Scobey and Clancy 1955 40.00
❑ L-12023 [M] Direct from San Francisco 1955 40.00
❑ L-12032 [M] Bob Scobey's Frisco Band, Volume 1 1957 40.00
❑ L-12033 [M] Bob Scobey's Frisco Band, Volume 2 1957 40.00

RCA VICTOR
❑ LPM-1344 [M] Beauty and the Beat 1957 40.00
❑ LPM-1448 [M] Swingin' on the Golden Gate 1957 40.00
❑ LPM-1567 [M] Between 18th and 19th on Any Street 1957 40.00
❑ LPM-1700 [M] College Classics 1958 40.00
❑ LPM-1889 [M] Something's Always Happening on the River 1958 40.00
❑ LSP-1889 [S] Something's Always Happening on the River 1958 60.00
❑ LPM-2086 [M] Rompin' and Stompin' 1959 30.00
❑ LSP-2086 [S] Rompin' and Stompin' 1959 40.00

VERVE
❑ MGV-1001 [M] Bob Scobey's Band 1956 40.00
❑ V-1001 [M] Bob Scobey's Band 1961 20.00
❑ MGV-1009 [M] Music from Bourbon Street 1956 40.00
❑ V-1009 [M] Music from Bourbon Street 1961 20.00
❑ MGV-1011 [M] The San Francisco Jazz of Bob Scobey 1957 40.00
❑ V-1011 [M] The San Francisco Jazz of Bob Scobey 1961 20.00

**SCOOBY DOO**

ZEPHYR
❑ ZMP-12002 [M] Jerry Leiber Presents Scooby Doo 1959 50.00

**SCORPION**

TOWER
❑ ST 5171 Scorpion 1969 50.00

**SCORPIONS**

BILLINGSGATE
❑ 1004 Lonesome Crow 1974 30.00

MERCURY
❑ SRM-1-3795 Lovedrive 1979 10.00
❑ SRM-1-3825 Animal Magnetism 1980 10.00
❑ SRM-1-4039 Blackout 1982 10.00
❑ 814981-1 Love at First Sting 1984 10.00
*—With man and woman on cover*
❑ 818885-1 Blackout 198? 8.00
*—Reissue of 4039*
❑ 822038-1 Love at First Sting 1984 12.00
*—Reissue with band on cover*
❑ 822555-1 Lovedrive 198? 8.00
*—Reissue of 3795*
❑ 822556-1 Animal Magnetism 198? 8.00
*—Reissue of 3825*
❑ 824344-1 [(2)] World Wide Live 1985 12.00
❑ 832963-1 Savage Amusement 1988 10.00
❑ 842002-1 Best of Rockers 'N' Ballads 1989 10.00
❑ 846908-1 Crazy World 1990 15.00

RCA VICTOR
❑ AFL1-2628 Taken by Force 1978 12.00
❑ CPL2-3039 [(2)] Toyko Tapes 1978 15.00
❑ AFL1-3516 Best of Scorpions 1979 10.00

Number | Title (A Side/B Side) | Yr | NM

❑ AYL1-3659 Virgin Killer 1980 8.00
*—"Best Buy Series" reissue*
❑ AFL1-4025 Fly to the Rainbow 1977 10.00
*—Reissue with new prefix*
❑ PPL1-4025 Fly to the Rainbow 1975 12.00
❑ AFL1-4128 In Trance 1977 10.00
*—Reissue with new prefix*
❑ PPL1-4128 In Trance 1976 12.00
❑ PPL1-4225 Virgin Killer 1977 12.00
❑ AYL1-4657 In Trance 1983 8.00
*—"Best Buy Series" reissue*
❑ AYL1-5057 Fly to the Rainbow 1984 8.00
*—"Best Buy Series" reissue*
❑ AFL1-5085 Best of Scorpions, Vol. 2 1984 10.00

**SCOT, PATRICIA**

ABC-PARAMOUNT
❑ 301 [M] Once Around the Clock 1959 20.00
❑ S-301 [S] Once Around the Clock 1959 25.00

**SCOTT, BOBBY**

ABC-PARAMOUNT
❑ ABC-102 [M] Scott Free 1956 50.00
❑ ABC-148 [M] Bobby Scott and Two Horns 1957 50.00

ATLANTIC
❑ 1341 [M] The Compleat Musician 1960 20.00
*—Multicolor label, white "fan" logo at right*
❑ SD 1341 [S] The Compleat Musician 1960 25.00
*—Multicolor label, white "fan" logo at right*
❑ 1355 [M] A Taste of Honey 1960 20.00
*—Multicolor label, white "fan" logo at right*
❑ SD 1355 [S] A Taste of Honey 1960 25.00
*—Multicolor label, white "fan" logo at right*

BETHLEHEM
❑ BCP-8 [M] The Compositions of Bobby Scott 1957 50.00
❑ BCP-1004 [10] Great Scott 1954 120.00
❑ BCP-1009 [10] The Compositions of Bobby Scott, Volume 1 1954 100.00
❑ BCP-1029 [10] The Compositions of Bobby Scott, Volume 2 1955 100.00

MERCURY
❑ MG-20701 [M] Joyful Noises 1962 20.00
❑ MG-20767 [M] When the Feeling Hits You 1963 20.00
❑ MG-20854 [M] 108 Pounds of Heartache 1963 20.00
❑ MG-20995 [M] I Had a Ball 1964 20.00
❑ SR-60701 [S] Joyful Noises 1962 25.00
❑ SR-60767 [S] When the Feeling Hits You 1963 25.00
❑ SR-60854 [S] 108 Pounds of Heartache 1963 25.00
❑ SR-60995 [S] I Had a Ball 1964 25.00

VERVE
❑ MGV-2106 [M] Bobby Scott Sings the Best of Lerner and Loewe 1958 50.00
❑ V-2106 [M] Bobby Scott Sings the Best of Lerner and Loewe 1961 25.00
❑ V6-2106 [S] Bobby Scott Sings the Best of Lerner and Loewe 1961 20.00
❑ MGVS-6030 [S] Bobby Scott Sings the Best of Lerner and Loewe 1960 40.00
❑ MGVS-6031 [S] Serenate — Bobby Scott, Pianist 1960 40.00
❑ MGVS-6065 [S] Bobby Scott Plays the Music of Leonard Bernstein 1960 40.00
❑ MGV-8297 [M] Serenate — Bobby Scott, Pianist 1959 50.00
❑ V-8297 [M] Serenate — Bobby Scott, Pianist 1961 25.00
❑ V6-8297 [S] Serenate — Bobby Scott, Pianist 1961 20.00
❑ MGV-8326 [M] Bobby Scott Plays the Music of Leonard Bernstein 1959 50.00
❑ V-8326 [M] Bobby Scott Plays the Music of Leonard Bernstein 1961 25.00
❑ V6-8326 [S] Bobby Scott Plays the Music of Leonard Bernstein 1961 20.00

**SCOTT, CALVIN**

STAX
❑ STS-2046 I'm Not Blind... I Just Can't See 1972 80.00

**SCOTT, CLIFFORD**

WORLD PACIFIC
❑ ST-1811 [S] The Big Ones 1964 30.00
*—Black vinyl*
❑ ST-1811 [S] The Big Ones 1964 80.00
*—Green vinyl*
❑ WP-1811 [M] The Big Ones 1964 20.00
*—Black vinyl*
❑ WP-1811 [M] The Big Ones 1964 60.00
*—Green vinyl*
❑ ST-1825 [S] Lavender Sax 1964 40.00
❑ WP-1825 [M] Lavender Sax 1964 30.00

**SCOTT, CLIFFORD, AND LES MCCANN**

PACIFIC JAZZ
❑ PJ-66 [M] Out Front 1963 20.00
*—Black vinyl*

Number | Title (A Side/B Side) | Yr | NM

❑ PJ-66 [M] Out Front 1963 40.00
*—Colored vinyl*
❑ ST-66 [S] Out Front 1963 25.00
*—Black vinyl*
❑ ST-66 [S] Out Front 1963 50.00
*—Colored vinyl*

**SCOTT, FREDDIE**

COLPIX
❑ CP-461 [M] Freddie Scott Sings and Sings and Sings 1964 60.00
*—Gold label*
❑ CP-461 [M] Freddie Scott Sings and Sings and Sings 1965 40.00
*—Blue label*
❑ SCP-461 [R] Freddie Scott Sings and Sings and Sings 1965 30.00
*—Blue label*
❑ SCP-461 [S] Freddie Scott Sings and Sings and Sings 1964 120.00
*—Gold label*

COLUMBIA
❑ CL 2258 [M] Everything I Have Is Yours 1964 20.00
❑ CL 2660 [M] Lonely Man 1967 20.00
❑ CS 9058 [S] Everything I Have Is Yours 1964 25.00
❑ CS 9460 [S] Lonely Man 1967 25.00

PROBE
❑ CPLP-4517 I Shall Be Released 1970 25.00

SHOUT
❑ SLP-501 [M] Are You Lonely for Me 1967 20.00
❑ SLPS-501 [S] Are You Lonely for Me 1967 25.00

**SCOTT, HAZEL**

CAPITOL
❑ H 364 [10] Late Show 1953 80.00

COLUMBIA
❑ CL 6090 [10] Great Scott 1950 80.00

CORAL
❑ CRL 56057 [10] Hazel Scott 1952 80.00

DEBUT
❑ DLP-16 [10] Relaxed Piano Moods 1955 200.00

DECCA
❑ DL 5130 [10] Swinging the Classics 1950 80.00
❑ DL 8474 [M] 'Round Midnight 1957 40.00

**SCOTT, JACK**

CAPITOL
❑ ST 2035 [S] Burning Bridges 1964 150.00
❑ ST-8-2035 Burning Bridges 196? 200.00
*—Capitol Record Club edition*
❑ T 2035 [M] Burning Bridges 1964 80.00

CARLTON
❑ LP-12-107 [M] Jack Scott 1959 150.00
❑ STLP-12-107 [S] Jack Scott 1959 200.00
*—With "Stereo" printed across the top*
❑ STLP-12-107 [S] Jack Scott 1959 300.00
*—With "Stereo" in felt letters horizontally along the top of cover*
❑ STLP-12-107 [S] Jack Scott 1959 400.00
*—With "Stereo" in felt letters vertically along the left of cover*
❑ LP-12-122 [M] What Am I Living For 1959 120.00
❑ STLP-12-122 [S] What Am I Living For 1959 320.00

JADE
❑ J33-113 Jack Is Back 198? 15.00
❑ J33-114 The Way I Rock 198? 15.00

PONIE
❑ 563 Jack Scott 1974 15.00
❑ 7055 Jack Scott 1977 15.00

TOP RANK
❑ RM-319 [M] I Remember Hank Williams 1960 150.00
❑ RM-326 [M] What in the World's Come Over You 1960 150.00
❑ RM-348 [M] The Spirit Moves Me 1961 150.00
❑ SM-619 [S] I Remember Hank Williams 1960 250.00
❑ SM-626 [S] What in the World's Come Over You 1960 250.00
❑ SM-648 [S] The Spirit Moves Me 1961 250.00

**SCOTT, JIMMY**

SAVOY
❑ MG-12027 [M] Very Truly Yours 1955 60.00
❑ MG-12150 [M] The Fabulous Little Jimmy Scott 1959 40.00
❑ MG-12181 [M] If You Only Knew 1963 40.00

TANGERINE
❑ TRCS-1501 [S] Falling in Love Is Wonderful 1963 250.00

**SCOTT, LINDA**

CANADIAN AMERICAN
❑ CALP-1005 [M] Starlight, Starbright 1961 100.00
❑ SCALP-1005 [S] Starlight, Starbright 1961 150.00
❑ CALP-1007 [M] Great Scott!! Her Greatest Hits 1962 100.00
❑ SCALP-1007 [S] Great Scott!! Her Greatest Hits 1962 150.00

CONGRESS
❑ CGL-3001 [M] Linda 1962 40.00
❑ CGS-3001 [S] Linda 1962 50.00

| Number | Title (A Side/B Side) | Yr | NM |
|---|---|---|---|
| KAPP | | | |
| ❑ KL-1424 [M] | Hey, Look at Me Now | 1965 | 40.00 |
| ❑ KS-3424 [S] | Hey, Look at Me Now | 1965 | 50.00 |

**SCOTT, LIZABETH**

| Number | Title (A Side/B Side) | Yr | NM |
|---|---|---|---|
| VIK | | | |
| ❑ LX-1130 [M] | Lizabeth | 1958 | 100.00 |

**SCOTT, PEGGY, AND JO JO BENSON**

| Number | Title (A Side/B Side) | Yr | NM |
|---|---|---|---|
| SSS INTERNATIONAL | | | |
| ❑ 1 | Soulshake | 1968 | 25.00 |
| ❑ 2 | Lover's Heaven | 1969 | 25.00 |

**SCOTT, SHIRLEY**

| Number | Title (A Side/B Side) | Yr | NM |
|---|---|---|---|
| IMPULSE! | | | |
| ❑ A-51 [M] | For Members Only | 1963 | 20.00 |
| ❑ AS-51 [S] | For Members Only | 1963 | 25.00 |
| ❑ A-67 [M] | Great Scott! | 1964 | 20.00 |
| ❑ AS-67 [S] | Great Scott! | 1964 | 25.00 |
| ❑ A-73 [M] | Everybody Loves a Lover | 1964 | 20.00 |
| ❑ AS-73 [S] | Everybody Loves a Lover | 1964 | 25.00 |
| ❑ A-81 [M] | Queen of the Organ | 1965 | 20.00 |
| ❑ AS-81 [S] | Queen of the Organ | 1965 | 25.00 |
| ❑ A-93 [M] | Latin Shadows | 1965 | 20.00 |
| ❑ AS-93 [S] | Latin Shadows | 1965 | 25.00 |
| ❑ A-9109 [M] | On a Clear Day | 1967 | 25.00 |
| ❑ AS-9109 [S] | On a Clear Day | 1967 | 20.00 |
| ❑ A-9119 [M] | Shirley Scott Plays the Big Bands | 1966 | 20.00 |
| ❑ AS-9119 [S] | Shirley Scott Plays the Big Bands | 1966 | 25.00 |
| ❑ A-9141 [M] | Girl Talk | 1967 | 30.00 |
| ❑ AS-9141 [S] | Girl Talk | 1967 | 20.00 |
| MOODSVILLE | | | |
| ❑ MVLP-5 [M] | Shirley Scott Trio | 1960 | 50.00 |
| *—Green label* | | | |
| ❑ MVLP-5 [M] | Shirley Scott Trio | 1965 | 25.00 |
| *—Blue label, trident logo at right* | | | |
| ❑ MVLP-19 [M] | Like Cozy | 1961 | 50.00 |
| *—Green label* | | | |
| ❑ MVLP-19 [M] | Like Cozy | 1965 | 25.00 |
| *—Blue label, trident logo at right* | | | |
| ❑ MVST-19 [S] | Like Cozy | 1961 | 50.00 |
| *—Green label* | | | |
| ❑ MVST-19 [S] | Like Cozy | 1965 | 25.00 |
| *—Blue label, trident logo at right* | | | |
| PRESTIGE | | | |
| ❑ PRLP-7143 [M] | Great Scott! | 1958 | 50.00 |
| ❑ PRLP-7155 [M] | Scottie | 1959 | 50.00 |
| ❑ PRLP-7163 [M] | Scottie Plays Duke | 1959 | 50.00 |
| ❑ PRLP-7173 [M] | Soul Searching | 1960 | 50.00 |
| ❑ PRLP-7182 [M] | Mucho, Mucho | 1960 | 50.00 |
| ❑ PRLP-7195 [M] | Shirley's Sounds | 1961 | 40.00 |
| ❑ PRST-7195 [S] | Shirley's Sounds | 1961 | 50.00 |
| ❑ PRLP-7205 [M] | Hip Soul | 1961 | 40.00 |
| *—Yellow label, Bergenfield, NJ address* | | | |
| ❑ PRLP-7205 [M] | Hip Soul | 1965 | 20.00 |
| *—Blue label, trident logo at right* | | | |
| ❑ PRLP-7226 [M] | Hip Twist | 1962 | 40.00 |
| *—Yellow label, Bergenfield, NJ address* | | | |
| ❑ PRLP-7226 [M] | Hip Twist | 1965 | 20.00 |
| *—Blue label, trident logo at right* | | | |
| ❑ PRST-7226 [S] | Hip Twist | 1962 | 50.00 |
| *—Silver label, Bergenfield, NJ address* | | | |
| ❑ PRST-7226 [S] | Hip Twist | 1965 | 25.00 |
| *—Blue label, trident logo at right* | | | |
| ❑ PRLP-7240 [M] | Shirley Scott Plays Horace Silver | 1962 | 40.00 |
| ❑ PRST-7240 [S] | Shirley Scott Plays Horace Silver | 1962 | 50.00 |
| ❑ PRLP-7262 [M] | Happy Talk | 1963 | 40.00 |
| ❑ PRST-7262 [S] | Happy Talk | 1963 | 50.00 |
| ❑ PRLP-7267 [M] | The Soul Is Willing | 1963 | 40.00 |
| *—Yellow label, Bergenfield, NJ address* | | | |
| ❑ PRLP-7267 [M] | The Soul Is Willing | 1965 | 20.00 |
| *—Blue label, trident logo at right* | | | |
| ❑ PRST-7267 [S] | The Soul Is Willing | 1963 | 50.00 |
| *—Silver label, Bergenfield, NJ address* | | | |
| ❑ PRST-7267 [S] | The Soul Is Willing | 1965 | 25.00 |
| *—Blue label, trident logo at right* | | | |
| ❑ PRLP-7283 [M] | Satin Doll | 1963 | 40.00 |
| ❑ PRST-7283 [S] | Satin Doll | 1963 | 50.00 |
| ❑ PRLP-7305 [M] | Drag 'Em Out | 1964 | 40.00 |
| ❑ PRST-7305 [S] | Drag 'Em Out | 1964 | 50.00 |
| ❑ PRLP-7312 [M] | Soul Shoutin' | 1964 | 40.00 |
| *—Yellow label, Bergenfield, NJ address* | | | |
| ❑ PRLP-7312 [M] | Soul Shoutin' | 1965 | 20.00 |
| *—Blue label, trident logo at right* | | | |
| ❑ PRST-7312 [S] | Soul Shoutin' | 1964 | 50.00 |
| *—Silver label, Bergenfield, NJ address* | | | |
| ❑ PRST-7312 [S] | Soul Shoutin' | 1965 | 25.00 |
| *—Blue label, trident logo at right* | | | |
| ❑ PRLP-7328 [M] | Travelin' Light | 1964 | 25.00 |
| ❑ PRST-7328 [S] | Travelin' Light | 1964 | 30.00 |
| ❑ PRLP-7338 [M] | Blue Flames | 1965 | 25.00 |
| ❑ PRST-7338 [S] | Blue Flames | 1965 | 30.00 |
| ❑ PRLP-7360 [M] | Sweet Soul | 1965 | 25.00 |
| ❑ PRST-7360 [S] | Sweet Soul | 1965 | 30.00 |
| ❑ PRLP-7376 [M] | Blue Seven | 1965 | 25.00 |
| ❑ PRST-7376 [S] | Blue Seven | 1965 | 30.00 |

Seals and Crofts, *Down Home,* T-A 5004, 1970, $25.

| Number | Title (A Side/B Side) | Yr | NM |
|---|---|---|---|
| ❑ PRLP-7392 [M] | Soul Sisters | 1965 | 25.00 |
| ❑ PRST-7392 [S] | Soul Sisters | 1965 | 30.00 |
| ❑ PRLP-7424 [M] | Workin' | 1966 | 25.00 |
| ❑ PRST-7424 [S] | Workin' | 1966 | 30.00 |
| ❑ PRLP-7440 [M] | Now's the Time | 1967 | 30.00 |
| ❑ PRST-7440 [S] | Now's the Time | 1967 | 25.00 |
| ❑ PRST-7456 [S] | Stompin' | 1968 | 25.00 |
| ❑ PRST-7707 [S] | The Best of Shirley Scott and Stanley Turrentine | 1969 | 20.00 |
| ❑ PRST-7773 | The Best for Beautiful People | 1970 | 20.00 |
| STRATA-EAST | | | |
| ❑ SES-7430 | One for Me | 197? | 20.00 |

**SCOTT, SHIRLEY, AND CLARK TERRY**

| Number | Title (A Side/B Side) | Yr | NM |
|---|---|---|---|
| IMPULSE! | | | |
| ❑ A-9133 [M] | Soul Duo | 1967 | 25.00 |
| ❑ AS-9133 [S] | Soul Duo | 1967 | 20.00 |

**SCOTT, TOM**

| Number | Title (A Side/B Side) | Yr | NM |
|---|---|---|---|
| ABC IMPULSE! | | | |
| ❑ A-9163 [M] | Honeysuckle Breeze | 1967 | 40.00 |
| ❑ AS-9163 [S] | Honeysuckle Breeze | 1967 | 25.00 |
| ❑ AS-9171 | Rural Still Life | 1968 | 25.00 |
| FLYING DUTCHMAN | | | |
| ❑ 106 | Hair | 1969 | 20.00 |
| ❑ 114 | Paint Your Wagon | 1970 | 20.00 |

**SCOTT, TONY**

| Number | Title (A Side/B Side) | Yr | NM |
|---|---|---|---|
| ABC-PARAMOUNT | | | |
| ❑ ABC-235 [M] | South Pacific | 1958 | 30.00 |
| ❑ ABCS-235 [S] | South Pacific | 1958 | 25.00 |
| BRUNSWICK | | | |
| ❑ BL 54021 [M] | Tony Scott In Hi-Fi | 1957 | 80.00 |
| ❑ BL 54056 [M] | Tony Scott Quartet | 1957 | 120.00 |
| ❑ BL 58040 [10] | Music After Midnight | 1953 | 120.00 |
| ❑ BL 58056 [10] | Tony Scott Quartet | 1954 | 120.00 |
| CORAL | | | |
| ❑ CRL 57239 [M] | 52nd Street Scene | 1958 | 50.00 |
| ❑ CRL 757239 [S] | 52nd Street Scene | 1958 | 40.00 |
| PERFECT | | | |
| ❑ PL-12010 [M] | My Kind of Jazz | 1960 | 40.00 |
| ❑ PL-14010 [S] | My Kind of Jazz | 1960 | 50.00 |
| RCA VICTOR | | | |
| ❑ LJM-1022 [M] | Scott's Fling | 1955 | 80.00 |
| ❑ LPM-1268 [M] | Both Sides of Tony Scott | 1956 | 80.00 |
| ❑ LPM-1353 [M] | A Touch of Tony Scott | 1956 | 80.00 |
| ❑ LPM-1452 [M] | The Complete Tony Scott | 1957 | 80.00 |
| SEECO | | | |
| ❑ SLP-425 [M] | The Modern Art of Jazz | 1959 | 30.00 |
| ❑ SLP-428 [M] | Hi-Fi Land of Jazz | 1959 | 30.00 |
| ❑ SLP-4250 [S] | The Modern Art of Jazz | 1959 | 40.00 |
| ❑ SLP-4280 [S] | Hi-Fi Land of Jazz | 1959 | 40.00 |
| SIGNATURE | | | |
| ❑ SM-6001 [M] | Gypsy | 1959 | 50.00 |
| ❑ SS-6001 [S] | Gypsy | 1959 | 40.00 |
| VERVE | | | |
| ❑ V6-8634 [S] | Music for Zen Meditation | 1965 | 20.00 |
| ❑ V-8742 [M] | Music for Yoga Meditation and Other Joys | 1967 | 20.00 |

**SCOTT, TONY, AND TERRY GIBBS**

| Number | Title (A Side/B Side) | Yr | NM |
|---|---|---|---|
| BRUNSWICK | | | |
| ❑ BL 58058 [10] | Hi-Fi Jazz | 1955 | 120.00 |

**SCOTT, TONY, AND JIMMY KNEPPER**

| Number | Title (A Side/B Side) | Yr | NM |
|---|---|---|---|
| CARLTON | | | |
| ❑ LP-12-113 [M] | Free Blown Jazz | 1959 | 50.00 |
| ❑ ST-12-113 [S] | Free Blown Jazz | 1959 | 50.00 |

**SCOTT, TONY, AND MAT MATTHEWS**

| Number | Title (A Side/B Side) | Yr | NM |
|---|---|---|---|
| BRUNSWICK | | | |
| ❑ BL 58057 [10] | Jazz for GI's | 1954 | 120.00 |

**SCOTT, WALTER**

| Number | Title (A Side/B Side) | Yr | NM |
|---|---|---|---|
| MUSICLAND U.S.A. | | | |
| ❑ LP-3502 [M] | Great Scott | 1967 | 20.00 |
| ❑ SLP-3502 [S] | Great Scott | 1967 | 25.00 |
| WHITE WHALE | | | |
| ❑ WWS-7131 | Walter Scott | 1970 | 20.00 |

**SCOTT-HERON, GIL**

| Number | Title (A Side/B Side) | Yr | NM |
|---|---|---|---|
| FLYING DUTCHMAN | | | |
| ❑ BLD1-0613 | The Revolution Will Not Be Televised | 1974 | 20.00 |
| ❑ FD-10143 | Pieces of a Man | 1971 | 20.00 |
| ❑ FD-10153 | Free Will | 1972 | 20.00 |
| STRATA-EAST | | | |
| ❑ SES-19742 | Winter in America | 1974 | 25.00 |

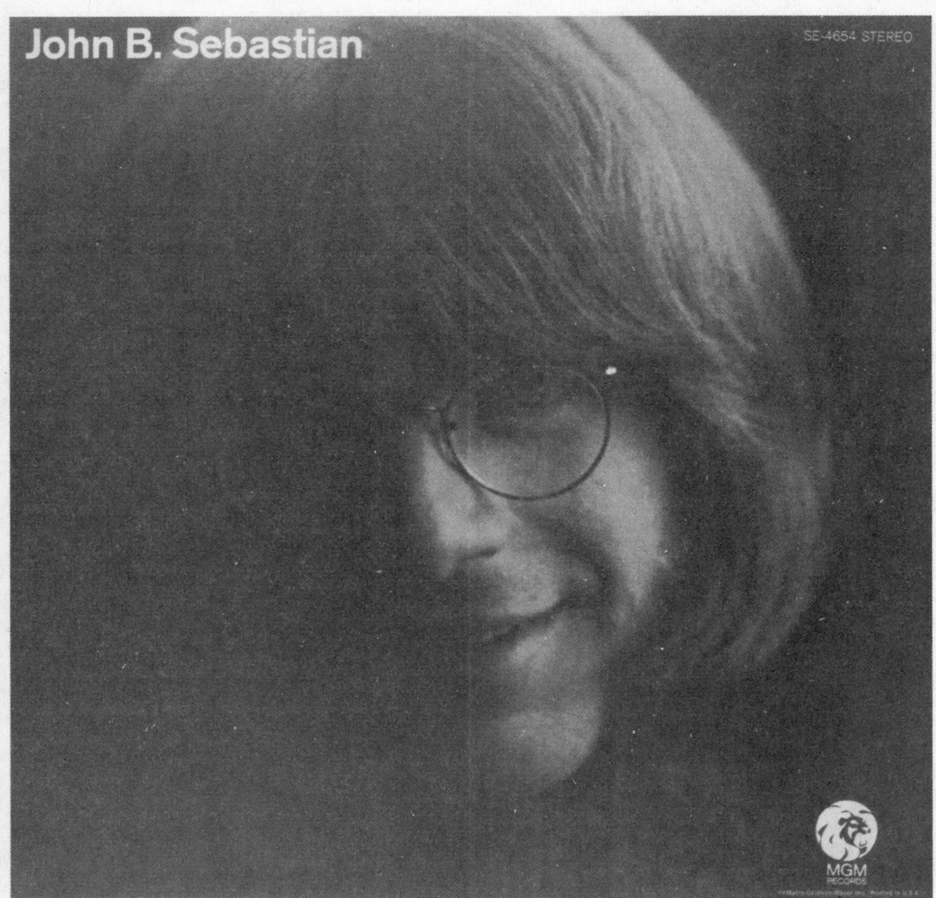


John Sebastian, *John B. Sebastian,* MGM SE-4654, 1969, $15.

**SCOTTSVILLE SQUIRREL BARKERS, THE** Chris Hillman, later of THE BYRDS, makes his first appearance on record here.

CROWN

| Number | Title (A Side/B Side) | Yr | NM |
|---|---|---|---|
| ❑ CST-346 [S] | Bluegrass Favorites | 1963 | 60.00 |
| ❑ CLP-5346 [M] | Bluegrass Favorites | 1963 | 50.00 |

**SCRAMBLERS, THE**

CROWN

| Number | Title (A Side/B Side) | Yr | NM |
|---|---|---|---|
| ❑ CST-384 [S] | Cycle Psychos | 1964 | 25.00 |
| ❑ CLP-5384 [M] | Cycle Psychos | 1964 | 20.00 |

DIPLOMAT

| Number | Title (A Side/B Side) | Yr | NM |
|---|---|---|---|
| ❑ D-2316 [M] | Motorcycle Scramble | 1964 | 20.00 |
| ❑ DS-2316 [S] | Motorcycle Scramble | 1964 | 25.00 |

WYNCOTE

| Number | Title (A Side/B Side) | Yr | NM |
|---|---|---|---|
| ❑ SW-9048 [S] | Little Honda | 1964 | 25.00 |
| ❑ W-9048 [M] | Little Honda | 1964 | 20.00 |

**SCREAMING GYPSY BANDITS**

BAR-B-Q

| Number | Title (A Side/B Side) | Yr | NM |
|---|---|---|---|
| ❑ 004 | The Dancer Inside You | 1974 | 80.00 |
| ❑ 22185 | In the Eye | 1973 | 80.00 |

**SCREAMING TREES** Also see MARK LANEGAN.

EPIC

| Number | Title (A Side/B Side) | Yr | NM |
|---|---|---|---|
| ❑ E 46800 | Uncle Anesthesia | 1991 | 12.00 |
| ❑ E 48996 | Sweet Oblivion | 1992 | 12.00 |

SST

| Number | Title (A Side/B Side) | Yr | NM |
|---|---|---|---|
| ❑ 105 [EP] | Other Worlds | 1986 | 10.00 |
| *—Reissue of Velvetone cassette-only release* | | | |
| ❑ 132 | Even If and Especially When | 1987 | 10.00 |
| ❑ 188 | Invisible Lantern | 1988 | 10.00 |
| ❑ 248 | Buzz Factory | 1989 | 10.00 |
| ❑ 260 [(2)] | Anthology | 1991 | 12.00 |

VELVETONE

| Number | Title (A Side/B Side) | Yr | NM |
|---|---|---|---|
| ❑ 86002 | Clairvoyance | 1986 | 40.00 |

**SEA, JOHNNY**

HILLTOP

| Number | Title (A Side/B Side) | Yr | NM |
|---|---|---|---|
| ❑ JM-6018 | Everybody's Favorite | 196? | 12.00 |

PHILIPS

| Number | Title (A Side/B Side) | Yr | NM |
|---|---|---|---|
| ❑ PHM 200139 [M] | World of a Country Boy | 1964 | 20.00 |
| ❑ PHM 200194 [M] | Live at the Bitter End | 1965 | 20.00 |
| ❑ PHS 600139 [S] | World of a Country Boy | 1964 | 25.00 |
| ❑ PHS 600194 [S] | Live at the Bitter End | 1965 | 25.00 |

WARNER BROS.

| Number | Title (A Side/B Side) | Yr | NM |
|---|---|---|---|
| ❑ W 1659 [M] | Day for Decision | 1966 | 15.00 |
| ❑ WS 1659 [S] | Day for Decision | 1966 | 20.00 |

**SEALS, DAN**

CAPITOL

| Number | Title (A Side/B Side) | Yr | NM |
|---|---|---|---|
| ❑ 1P 7999 | On Arrival | 1990 | 20.00 |
| *—Only available on vinyl from Columbia House* | | | |
| ❑ C1-46976 | Rage On | 1988 | 8.00 |
| ❑ CLT-48308 | The Best | 1988 | 8.00 |

EMI AMERICA

| Number | Title (A Side/B Side) | Yr | NM |
|---|---|---|---|
| ❑ ST-17131 | San Antone | 1984 | 8.00 |
| ❑ ST-17166 | Won't Be Blue Anymore | 1985 | 8.00 |
| ❑ PW-17231 | On the Front Line | 1986 | 8.00 |

LIBERTY

| Number | Title (A Side/B Side) | Yr | NM |
|---|---|---|---|
| ❑ LT-51149 | Rebel Heart | 1983 | 10.00 |

**SEALS AND CROFTS**

K-TEL

| Number | Title (A Side/B Side) | Yr | NM |
|---|---|---|---|
| ❑ NU 9610 | Collection: 16 of Their Greatest Hits | 1979 | 12.00 |

NAUTILUS

| Number | Title (A Side/B Side) | Yr | NM |
|---|---|---|---|
| ❑ NR-10 | Summer Breeze | 1980 | 30.00 |
| *—Audiophile vinyl* | | | |

T-A

| Number | Title (A Side/B Side) | Yr | NM |
|---|---|---|---|
| ❑ 5001 | Seals and Crofts | 1969 | 25.00 |
| ❑ 5004 | Down Home | 1970 | 25.00 |

WARNER BROS.

| Number | Title (A Side/B Side) | Yr | NM |
|---|---|---|---|
| ❑ BS 2568 | Year of Sunday | 1971 | 12.00 |
| *—Green "WB" label* | | | |
| ❑ BS 2568 | Year of Sunday | 1973 | 10.00 |
| *—"Burbank" palm-tree label* | | | |
| ❑ BS 2629 | Summer Breeze | 1972 | 12.00 |
| *—Green "WB" label* | | | |
| ❑ BS 2629 | Summer Breeze | 1973 | 10.00 |
| *—"Burbank" palm-tree label* | | | |
| ❑ BS 2629 | Summer Breeze | 1979 | 8.00 |
| *—White or tan label* | | | |
| ❑ BS4 2629 [Q] | Summer Breeze | 1974 | 20.00 |
| ❑ BS 2699 | Diamond Girl | 1973 | 12.00 |
| *—"Burbank" palm-tree label* | | | |
| ❑ BS 2699 | Diamond Girl | 1979 | 8.00 |
| *—White or tan label* | | | |
| ❑ BS4 2699 [Q] | Diamond Girl | 1974 | 20.00 |
| ❑ BS 2761 | Unborn Child | 1974 | 12.00 |
| ❑ BS4 2761 [Q] | Unborn Child | 1974 | 20.00 |
| ❑ 2WS 2809 [(2)] | Seals & Crofts I and II | 1974 | 15.00 |
| *—Reissue of the two T-A LPs in one package* | | | |
| ❑ BS 2848 | I'll Play for You | 1975 | 10.00 |
| ❑ BS4 2848 [Q] | I'll Play for You | 1975 | 20.00 |
| ❑ BS 2886 | Greatest Hits | 1975 | 10.00 |
| ❑ BS 2907 | Get Closer | 1976 | 10.00 |
| ❑ BS 2976 | Sudan Village | 1976 | 10.00 |
| ❑ BSK 3109 | Greatest Hits | 1977 | 8.00 |
| *—Reissue; any label variation* | | | |
| ❑ BSK 3165 | Takin' It Easy | 1978 | 10.00 |
| ❑ BSK 3365 | The Longest Road | 1980 | 10.00 |

**SEARCH PARTY, THE**

CENTURY CUSTOM

| Number | Title (A Side/B Side) | Yr | NM |
|---|---|---|---|
| ❑ 32013 | Montgomery Chapel | 1969 | 2000. |

**SEARCHERS, THE**

KAPP

| Number | Title (A Side/B Side) | Yr | NM |
|---|---|---|---|
| ❑ KL-1363 [M] | Meet the Searchers | 1964 | 25.00 |
| *—With black label* | | | |
| ❑ KL-1363 [M] | Meet the Searchers | 1964 | 40.00 |
| *—With black and blue label* | | | |
| ❑ KL-1409 [M] | This Is Us | 1964 | 25.00 |
| *—Version 2: With sticker on front cover referring to "Love Potion No. 9"* | | | |
| ❑ KL-1409 [M] | This Is Us | 1964 | 25.00 |
| *—Version 1: No sticker on front cover* | | | |
| ❑ KL-1412 [M] | The New Searchers LP | 1965 | 25.00 |
| ❑ KL-1449 [M] | The Searchers No. 4 | 1965 | 25.00 |
| ❑ KL-1477 [M] | Take Me for What I'm Worth | 1966 | 25.00 |
| ❑ KS-3363 [S] | Meet the Searchers | 1964 | 30.00 |
| *—With black label* | | | |
| ❑ KS-3363 [S] | Meet the Searchers | 1964 | 50.00 |
| *—With black and blue label* | | | |
| ❑ KS-3409 [S] | This Is Us | 1964 | 30.00 |
| *—Version 2: With sticker on front cover referring to "Love Potion No. 9"* | | | |
| ❑ KS-3409 [S] | This Is Us | 1964 | 30.00 |
| *—Version 1: No sticker on front cover* | | | |
| ❑ KS-3412 [S] | The New Searchers LP | 1965 | 30.00 |
| ❑ KS-3419 [S] | The Searchers No. 4 | 1965 | 30.00 |
| ❑ KS-3477 [S] | Take Me for What I'm Worth | 1966 | 30.00 |

MERCURY

| Number | Title (A Side/B Side) | Yr | NM |
|---|---|---|---|
| ❑ MG-20914 [M] | Hear! Hear! | 1964 | 30.00 |
| *—Version 3: With "Live from the Star Club" imprinted on cover* | | | |
| ❑ MG-20914 [M] | Hear! Hear! | 1964 | 40.00 |
| *—Version 2: With sticker "Live from the Star Club" on cover* | | | |
| ❑ MG-20914 [M] | Hear! Hear! | 1964 | 50.00 |
| *—White label promo* | | | |
| ❑ MG-20914 [M] | Hear! Hear! | 1964 | 50.00 |
| *—Version 1: With only the title on the front cover* | | | |
| ❑ MG-20994 [M] | The Searchers Meet the Rattles | 1965 | 75.00 |
| ❑ SR-60914 [S] | Hear! Hear! | 1964 | 25.00 |
| *—Version 3: With "Live from the Star Club" imprinted on cover* | | | |
| ❑ SR-60914 [S] | Hear! Hear! | 1964 | 30.00 |
| *—Version 2: With sticker "Live from the Star Club" on cover* | | | |
| ❑ SR-60914 [S] | Hear! Hear! | 1964 | 40.00 |
| *—Version 1: With only the title on the front cover* | | | |
| ❑ SR-60994 [S] | The Searchers Meet the Rattles | 1965 | 50.00 |

PYE

| Number | Title (A Side/B Side) | Yr | NM |
|---|---|---|---|
| ❑ 501 | The Searchers | 197? | 15.00 |
| *—Reissue of Kapp hits* | | | |
| ❑ 508 | The Searchers, Vol. 2 | 1976 | 15.00 |

RHINO

| Number | Title (A Side/B Side) | Yr | NM |
|---|---|---|---|
| ❑ RNLP 162 | Greatest Hits | 1985 | 10.00 |
| ❑ R1-70162 | Greatest Hits | 1988 | 8.00 |
| *—Reissue of RNLP 162* | | | |

SIRE

| Number | Title (A Side/B Side) | Yr | NM |
|---|---|---|---|
| ❑ SRK 3523 | Love's Melodies | 1981 | 10.00 |
| ❑ SRK 6082 | The Searchers | 1980 | 10.00 |

**SEARS, AL**

AUDIO LAB

| Number | Title (A Side/B Side) | Yr | NM |
|---|---|---|---|
| ❑ AL-1540 [M] | Dance Music with a Swing Beat | 1959 | 120.00 |

SWINGVILLE

| Number | Title (A Side/B Side) | Yr | NM |
|---|---|---|---|
| ❑ SVLP-2018 [M] | Swing's the Thing | 1961 | 50.00 |
| *—Purple label* | | | |
| ❑ SVLP-2018 [M] | Swing's the Thing | 1965 | 25.00 |
| *—Blue label, trident logo at right* | | | |

**SEBASTIAN, JOHN** Also see THE LOVIN' SPOONFUL.

MGM

| Number | Title (A Side/B Side) | Yr | NM |
|---|---|---|---|
| ❑ SE-4654 | John B. Sebastian | 1969 | 15.00 |
| ❑ SE-4720 | John Sebastian Live | 1970 | 15.00 |

REPRISE

| Number | Title (A Side/B Side) | Yr | NM |
|---|---|---|---|
| ❑ MS 2036 | Cheapo-Cheapo Productions Presents Real Live John Sebastian | 1971 | 12.00 |
| ❑ MS 2041 | The Four of Us | 1971 | 12.00 |
| ❑ MS 2187 | Tarzana Kid | 1974 | 12.00 |
| ❑ MS 2249 | Welcome Back | 1976 | 12.00 |
| ❑ RS 6379 | John B. Sebastian | 1969 | 20.00 |
| *—Same album as MGM 4654, but a different mix* | | | |

RHINO

| Number | Title (A Side/B Side) | Yr | NM |
|---|---|---|---|
| ❑ R1-70170 | The Best of John Sebastian (1969-1976) | 1989 | 12.00 |

| Number | Title (A Side/B Side) | Yr | NM |
|---|---|---|---|
| **SEBESKY, DON** | | | |
| MOBILE FIDELITY | | | |
| ❑ 1-503 [(2)] | Three Works for Jazz Soloists and Symphony Orchestra | 198? | 60.00 |
| *—Audiophile vinyl* | | | |
| VERVE | | | |
| ❑ V6-8756 | Don Sebesky and the Jazz-Rock Syndrome | 1968 | 20.00 |
| **SECOND TIME, THE** | | | |
| TOWER | | | |
| ❑ ST 5146 | Listen to the Music | 1968 | 20.00 |
| **SECRET OYSTER** | | | |
| PETERS INT'L. | | | |
| ❑ 9003 | Furtive Pearl | 1973 | 30.00 |
| ❑ 9009 | Sea Son | 1974 | 25.00 |
| **SEDAKA, NEIL** | | | |
| ACCORD | | | |
| ❑ SN-7152 | Singer, Songwriter, Melody Maker | 1981 | 10.00 |
| ELEKTRA | | | |
| ❑ 6E-102 | A Song | 1977 | 10.00 |
| ❑ 6E-161 | All You Need Is Music | 1978 | 10.00 |
| ❑ 6E-259 | In the Pocket | 1980 | 10.00 |
| ❑ 6E-348 | Neil Sedaka Now | 1981 | 10.00 |
| 51 WEST | | | |
| ❑ Q 16003 | I'm a Song | 1979 | 12.00 |
| INTERMEDIA | | | |
| ❑ QS 5015 | Superbird | 1982 | 10.00 |
| KIRSHNER | | | |
| ❑ KES-111 | Emergence | 1971 | 15.00 |
| ❑ KES-117 | Solitaire | 1972 | 15.00 |
| MCA | | | |
| ❑ 2357 | Sedaka's Back | 1978 | 10.00 |
| *—Reissue of Rocket 463* | | | |
| ❑ 5466 | Come See About Me | 1984 | 10.00 |
| ORBIT | | | |
| ❑ RB-17196 | Bravo! | 1983 | 10.00 |
| PICKWICK | | | |
| ❑ ACL1-7006 | Breaking Up Is Hard to Do | 197? | 8.00 |
| POLYDOR | | | |
| ❑ 831235-1 | My Friend | 1986 | 10.00 |
| RCA CAMDEN | | | |
| ❑ ACL1-7006 | Breaking Up Is Hard to Do | 197? | 10.00 |
| RCA SPECIAL PRODUCTS | | | |
| ❑ DPL2-0149 [(2)] | Original Hits | 1975 | 20.00 |
| RCA VICTOR | | | |
| ❑ ANL1-0879 | Oh! Carol | 1975 | 10.00 |
| ❑ AFL1-0928 | Neil Sedaka Sings His Greatest Hits | 1977 | 10.00 |
| *—Reissue with new prefix* | | | |
| ❑ APL1-0928 | Neil Sedaka Sings His Greatest Hits | 1975 | 12.00 |
| *—Reissue of LSP-2627* | | | |
| ❑ ANL1-1314 | Pure Gold | 1976 | 10.00 |
| ❑ VPL1-1540 | Live in Australia | 1976 | 12.00 |
| ❑ APL1-1789 | Emergence | 1976 | 12.00 |
| *—Reissue of Kirshner 111* | | | |
| ❑ APL1-1790 | Solitaire | 1976 | 12.00 |
| *—Reissue of Kirshner 117* | | | |
| ❑ LPM-2035 [M] | Neil Sedaka | 1959 | 60.00 |
| ❑ LSP-2035 [S] | Neil Sedaka | 1959 | 100.00 |
| ❑ AFL1-2254 | Sedaka — The '50s and '60s | 1977 | 10.00 |
| ❑ LPM-2317 [M] | Circulate | 1960 | 50.00 |
| ❑ LSP-2317 [S] | Circulate | 1960 | 60.00 |
| ❑ LPM-2421 [M] | "Little Devil" and His Other Hits | 1961 | 50.00 |
| ❑ LSP-2421 [S] | "Little Devil" and His Other Hits | 1961 | 60.00 |
| ❑ AFL1-2524 | The Many Sides of Neil Sedaka | 1978 | 10.00 |
| ❑ LPM-2627 [M] | Neil Sedaka Sings His Greatest Hits | 1962 | 40.00 |
| ❑ LSP-2627 [S] | Neil Sedaka Sings His Greatest Hits | 1962 | 50.00 |
| *—Black label, dog on top, "Living Stereo" at bottom* | | | |
| ❑ LSP-2627 [S] | Neil Sedaka Sings His Greatest Hits | 1969 | 20.00 |
| *—Reissue; orange label* | | | |
| ❑ ANL1-3465 | Neil Sedaka Sings His Greatest Hits | 1979 | 8.00 |
| *—Reissue of AFL1-0928* | | | |
| ❑ R 133511 | Let's Go Steady Again | 1976 | 15.00 |
| *—RCA Record Club edition* | | | |
| ROCKET | | | |
| ❑ MCA-463 | Sedaka's Back | 1974 | 12.00 |
| ❑ PIG-2157 | The Hungry Years | 1975 | 12.00 |
| ❑ PIG-2195 | Steppin' Out | 1976 | 12.00 |
| ❑ PIG-2297 | Neil Sedaka's Greatest Hits | 1977 | 12.00 |
| ROLLER SKATE | | | |
| ❑ TLA-50172 | Is Anybody Gonna Miss You | 1982 | 15.00 |
| **SEDAKA, NEIL, AND THE TOKENS WITH THE COINS** | | | |
| CROWN | | | |
| ❑ CST-366 [R] | Neil Sedaka and the Tokens and the Coins | 1963 | 20.00 |
| ❑ CLP-5366 [M] | Neil Sedaka and the Tokens and the Coins | 1963 | 30.00 |
| **SEEDS, THE** Also see SKY SAXON. | | | |
| GNP CRESCENDO | | | |
| ❑ GNP-2023 [M] | The Seeds | 1966 | 60.00 |
| ❑ GNPS-2023 [S] | The Seeds | 1966 | 40.00 |
| ❑ GNP-2033 [M] | A Web of Sound | 1967 | 60.00 |
| ❑ GNPS-2033 [S] | A Web of Sound | 1967 | 40.00 |
| ❑ GNP-2038 [M] | Future | 1967 | 40.00 |
| *—Deduct 25% if two inserts are missing* | | | |
| ❑ GNPS-2038 [S] | Future | 1967 | 30.00 |
| *—Deduct 25% if two inserts are missing* | | | |
| ❑ GNP-2040 [M] | A Full Spoon of Seedy Blues | 1968 | 60.00 |
| ❑ GNPS-2040 [S] | A Full Spoon of Seedy Blues | 1968 | 25.00 |
| ❑ GNPS-2043 | Raw and Alive | 1968 | 25.00 |
| ❑ GNPS-2107 | Fallin' Off the Edge | 1977 | 10.00 |
| ❑ ST-91224 | A Web of Sound | 1968 | 30.00 |
| *—Capitol Record Club edition* | | | |
| **SEEGER, PEGGY** | | | |
| FOLK-LYRIC | | | |
| ❑ FL 114 [M] | American Folksongs for Banjo | 196? | 30.00 |
| ❑ FL 120 [M] | Popular Ballads | 196? | 30.00 |
| FOLKLORE | | | |
| ❑ FRLP-14016 [M] | The Best of Peggy Seeger | 196? | 25.00 |
| FOLKWAYS | | | |
| ❑ FP-49 [10] | Folk Songs of Courting and Complaint | 1955 | 100.00 |
| ❑ FP-2049 [10] | Folk Songs of Courting and Complaint | 195? | 80.00 |
| ❑ FC-7551 [10] | Animal Folksongs for Children | 1957 | 100.00 |
| ❑ FW-8563 [M] | From Where I Stand | 1982 | 10.00 |
| PRESTIGE | | | |
| ❑ PRLP-13005 [M] | The Best of Peggy Seeger | 1961 | 30.00 |
| ❑ PRLP-13058 [M] | A Song for You and Me | 1962 | 30.00 |
| RIVERSIDE | | | |
| ❑ RLP-12-655 [M] | Folksongs and Ballads | 1958 | 40.00 |
| TOPIC | | | |
| ❑ 10T-9 [10] | Peggy Seeger | 1956 | 100.00 |
| **SEEGER, PEGGY, BARBARA AND PENNY** | | | |
| FOLKWAYS | | | |
| ❑ FC-7553 [10] | American Folk Songs for Christmas | 195? | 50.00 |
| SCHOLASTIC | | | |
| ❑ SC 7553 [M] | American Folk Songs for Christmas | 1966 | 20.00 |
| *—Reissue of Folkways material* | | | |
| **SEEGER, PETE** | | | |
| ARAVEL | | | |
| ❑ AB 1006 [M] | Live Hootenanny | 1963 | 15.00 |
| BROADSIDE | | | |
| ❑ 502 [(2)] | Pete Seeger Sings and Answers Questions | 1970 | 15.00 |
| BULLDOG | | | |
| ❑ BDL-2011 | 20 Golden Pieces of Pete Seeger | 198? | 10.00 |
| CAPITOL | | | |
| ❑ DW 2172 [R] | Folk Songs | 1964 | 12.00 |
| ❑ W 2172 [M] | Folk Songs | 1964 | 20.00 |
| ❑ DT 2718 [R] | Freight Train | 1967 | 12.00 |
| ❑ T 2718 [M] | Freight Train | 1967 | 20.00 |
| COLUMBIA | | | |
| ❑ CL 1668 [M] | Pete Seeger Story Songs | 1961 | 25.00 |
| ❑ CL 1916 [M] | The Bitter and the Sweet | 1962 | 25.00 |
| ❑ CL 1947 [M] | Children's Concert at Town Hall | 1963 | 25.00 |
| ❑ CL 2101 [M] | We Shall Overcome | 1963 | 15.00 |
| ❑ CL 2257 [M] | I Can See a New Day | 1965 | 15.00 |
| ❑ CL 2334 [M] | Strangers and Cousins | 1964 | 15.00 |
| ❑ CL 2432 [M] | God Bless the Grass | 1966 | 15.00 |
| ❑ CL 2503 [M] | Dangerous Songs? | 1966 | 15.00 |
| ❑ CL 2616 [M] | Pete Seeger's Greatest Hits | 1967 | 20.00 |
| ❑ CL 2705 [M] | Waist Deep in the Big Muddy | 1967 | 20.00 |
| ❑ CS 8468 [S] | Pete Seeger Story Songs | 1961 | 30.00 |
| ❑ CS 8716 [S] | The Bitter and the Sweet | 1962 | 30.00 |
| ❑ CS 8747 [S] | Children's Concert at Town Hall | 1963 | 30.00 |
| ❑ CS 8901 [S] | We Shall Overcome | 1963 | 20.00 |
| ❑ CS 9057 [S] | I Can See a New Day | 1965 | 20.00 |
| ❑ CS 9134 [S] | Strangers and Cousins | 1964 | 20.00 |
| ❑ CS 9232 [S] | God Bless the Grass | 1966 | 20.00 |
| ❑ CS 9303 [S] | Dangerous Songs? | 1966 | 20.00 |
| ❑ CS 9416 [S] | Pete Seeger's Greatest Hits | 1967 | 15.00 |
| ❑ PC 9416 | Pete Seeger's Greatest Hits | 198? | 8.00 |
| *—Reissue with new prefix* | | | |
| ❑ CS 9505 [S] | Waist Deep in the Big Muddy | 1967 | 15.00 |
| ❑ CS 9717 | Pete Seeger Now | 1968 | 15.00 |
| ❑ CS 9873 | Young vs. Old | 1969 | 15.00 |
| ❑ C 30739 | Rainbow Race | 1971 | 12.00 |
| ❑ KG 31949 [(2)] | The World of Pete Seeger | 1972 | 15.00 |
| DISC | | | |
| ❑ D-101 [M] | Sing with Seeger | 1964 | 20.00 |
| EVEREST ARCHIVE OF FOLK & JAZZ | | | |
| ❑ 201 | Pete Seeger | 1966 | 12.00 |
| FOLKWAYS | | | |
| ❑ FP-3 [10] | Darling Corey | 1950 | 100.00 |
| ❑ FP-10 [10] | Lonesome Valley | 195? | 100.00 |
| ❑ FP-43 [10] | A Pete Seeger Sampler | 195? | 100.00 |
| ❑ FP-45 [10] | Goofing Off Suite | 195? | 100.00 |
| ❑ FP-701 [10] | American Folk Songs for Children | 195? | 100.00 |
| ❑ FP-710 [10] | Birds, Beasts, Bugs and Little Fishes | 1954 | 100.00 |
| ❑ FP-911 [10] | Folk Songs of Four Continents | 195? | 100.00 |
| ❑ FA-2003 [10] | Darling Corey | 1950 | 80.00 |
| ❑ FA-2010 [10] | Lonesome Valley | 195? | 80.00 |
| ❑ FA-2043 [10] | A Pete Seeger Sampler | 1954 | 80.00 |
| ❑ FA-2045 [10] | Goofing Off Suite | 1954 | 80.00 |
| ❑ FA-2175 [10] | Frontier Ballads, Volume 1 | 1954 | 80.00 |
| ❑ FA-2176 [10] | Frontier Ballads, Volume 2 | 1954 | 80.00 |
| ❑ FA-2311 [M] | Traditional Christmas Carols | 1956 | 30.00 |
| ❑ FA-2319 [M] | American Ballads | 1957 | 30.00 |
| ❑ FA-2320 [M] | American Favorite Ballads, Vol. 1 | 1957 | 30.00 |
| ❑ FA-2321 [M] | American Favorite Ballads, Vol. 2 | 1958 | 30.00 |
| ❑ FA-2322 [M] | American Favorite Ballads, Vol. 3 | 1958 | 30.00 |
| ❑ FA-2323 [M] | American Favorite Ballads, Vol. 4 | 1961 | 20.00 |
| ❑ FA-2412 [M] | Pete Seeger and Sonny Terry | 1958 | 30.00 |
| ❑ FA-2439 [M] | Nonesuch | 196? | 20.00 |
| ❑ FA-2445 [M] | American Favorite Ballads, Vol. 5: Tunes and Songs As Sung by Pete Seeger | 1962 | 20.00 |
| ❑ FA-2450 [M] | Highlights of Pete Seeger at the Village Gate with Memphis Slim and Willie Dixon | 1960 | 30.00 |
| ❑ FA-2451 [M] | Pete Seeger at the Village Gate — Vol. 2 | 1960 | 30.00 |
| ❑ FA-2452 [M] | With Voices Together We Sing | 1956 | 25.00 |
| ❑ FA-2453 [M] | Love Songs for Friends and Foes | 1956 | 25.00 |
| ❑ FA-2454 [M] | Rainbow Quest | 1960 | 25.00 |
| ❑ FA-2455 [M] | Sing Out with Pete! | 1961 | 20.00 |
| ❑ FA-2456 [M] | Broadsides | 1964 | 20.00 |
| ❑ FA-2501 [M] | Gazette, Vol. 1 | 1958 | 25.00 |
| ❑ FA-2502 [M] | Gazette, Vol. 2 | 1962 | 20.00 |
| ❑ FN-2511 [M] | Hootenanny Tonight! | 195? | 25.00 |
| ❑ FN-2513 [M] | Sing Out! Hootenanny | 1963 | 20.00 |
| ❑ FS-3851 [M] | Indian Summer | 1960 | 25.00 |
| *—With Michael Seeger* | | | |
| ❑ 5003 [(2)] | Frontier Ballads | 1954 | 100.00 |
| ❑ FH-5210 [M] | Champlain Valley Songs | 1960 | 25.00 |
| ❑ FH-5233 [M] | Songs of Struggle and Protest 1930-50 | 1959 | 25.00 |
| ❑ FH-5251 [M] | American Industrial Ballads | 1956 | 30.00 |
| ❑ FH-5257 | Fifty Sail On Newburgh Bay | 1976 | 12.00 |
| ❑ FH-5302 [M] | Broadside Ballads, Vol. 2 | 1963 | 20.00 |
| ❑ FH-5436 [M] | Songs of the Spanish Civil War, Vol. 1 | 1961 | 20.00 |
| ❑ FH-5485 [M] | Ballads of Sacco and Vanzetti | 1963 | 20.00 |
| ❑ FH-5595 [M] | WNEW's Story of Selma | 1965 | 20.00 |
| ❑ FH-5702 [(2)] | Pete Seeger Sings and Answers Questions | 1968 | 25.00 |
| ❑ FW-6843 [10] | German Folk Songs | 1954 | 80.00 |
| ❑ FW-6911 [10] | Folk Songs of Four Continents | 1955 | 80.00 |
| ❑ FW-6912 [10] | Bantu Choral Folk Songs | 1955 | 80.00 |
| ❑ FC-7020 [10] | Songs to Grow On — Vol. 2 | 1951 | 80.00 |
| ❑ FC-7027 [10] | Songs to Grow On — Vol. 3 | 1951 | 80.00 |
| ❑ FC-7526 [M] | Song and Play Time | 195? | 50.00 |
| ❑ 7527 | Zhitkov's How I Hunted the Little Fellows | 1980 | 12.00 |
| ❑ FC-7601 [10] | American Folk Songs for Children | 1953 | 80.00 |
| ❑ FC-7610 [10] | Birds, Beasts, Bugs and Little Fishes | 1954 | 80.00 |
| ❑ FC-7611 [M] | Birds, Beasts, Bugs and Bigger Fishes | 1954 | 50.00 |
| ❑ FC-7674 [M] | American Game and Activity Songs for Children | 1962 | 20.00 |
| ❑ FI-8303 [M] | How to Play the Five String Banjo | 195? | 25.00 |
| ❑ FI-8354 [M] | Folksinger's Guitar Guide Vol. 1: An Instruction Record | 1955 | 30.00 |
| ❑ FQ-8354 [M] | The Folksinger's Guitar Gude | 1955 | 25.00 |
| ❑ FI-8371 [M] | 12-String Guitar As Played by Leadbelly | 1962 | 20.00 |
| ❑ FTS-31002 [R] | Pete Seeger Sings Woody Guthrie | 1968 | 12.00 |
| ❑ FTS-31017 [R] | American Favorite Ballads | 1968 | 12.00 |
| ❑ FTS-31018 [R] | Wimoweh and Other Songs of Freedom and Protest | 1968 | 12.00 |
| ❑ FTS-31022 [R] | Pete Seeger Sings Leadbelly | 1968 | 12.00 |
| ❑ FTS-31040 [R] | Banks of Marble and Other Songs | 1974 | 12.00 |

Bob Seger and the Silver Bullet Band, *Greatest Hits,* Capitol C1-30334, 1994, $15.

| Number | Title (A Side/B Side) | Yr | NM |
|---|---|---|---|
| ❑ FTS-32311 [R] | Traditional Christmas Carols | 1967 | 15.00 |
| ❑ FT-35001 [(2)] | The Nativity: By Sholem Asch | 1963 | 15.00 |
| ❑ FXM-36055 [(2)] | Sing Along | 1980 | 15.00 |
| ❑ 37232 | God Bless the Grass | 1982 | 12.00 |
| **HARMONY** | | | |
| ❑ HS 11337 | John Henry and Other Folk Favorites | 1969 | 12.00 |
| **ODYSSEY** | | | |
| ❑ 32160266 | 3 Saints, 4 Sinners and 6 Other People | 1968 | 15.00 |
| **OLYMPIC** | | | |
| ❑ 7102 | America's Balladeer | 1973 | 12.00 |
| **PAIR** | | | |
| ❑ PDL2-1076 [(2)] | Clearwater Classics | 1986 | 12.00 |
| **PHILIPS** | | | |
| ❑ PHM 2-300 [(2)M] | The Story of the Nativity | 1963 | 20.00 |
| ❑ PHS 2-300 [(2)S] | The Story of the Nativity | 1963 | 25.00 |
| **SMITHSONIAN FOLKWAYS** | | | |
| ❑ SF-40024 | Traditional Christmas Carols | 1989 | 12.00 |
| **STINSON** | | | |
| ❑ SLP-52 [10] | Lincoln Brigade | 1953 | 100.00 |
| ❑ SLP-57 [10] | A Pete Seeger Concert | 1953 | 100.00 |
| ❑ SLP-90 [M] | Pete | 1963 | 25.00 |
| **TRADITION** | | | |
| ❑ 2107 | Folk Music of the World | 1973 | 12.00 |
| **VANGUARD** | | | |
| ❑ VSD-97/98 [(2)] | The Essential Pete Seeger | 1978 | 15.00 |
| ❑ VSD-73111 | The Essential Pete Seeger, Vol. 1 | 198? | 8.00 |
| ❑ VSD-73112 | The Essential Pete Seeger, Vol. 2 | 198? | 8.00 |
| **VERVE FOLKWAYS** | | | |
| ❑ FV-9008 [M] | Pete Seeger and Big Bill Broonzy in Concert | 1965 | 20.00 |
| ❑ FVS-9008 [S] | Pete Seeger and Big Bill Broonzy in Concert | 1965 | 25.00 |
| ❑ FV-9009 [M] | Pete Seeger On Campus | 1965 | 20.00 |
| ❑ FVS-9009 [S] | Pete Seeger On Campus | 1965 | 25.00 |
| ❑ FV-9013 [M] | Folk Music Live at the Village Gate | 1965 | 20.00 |
| ❑ FVS-9013 [S] | Folk Music Live at the Village Gate | 1965 | 25.00 |

| Number | Title (A Side/B Side) | Yr | NM |
|---|---|---|---|
| ❑ FV-9020 [M] | Little Boxes and Other Broadsides | 1965 | 20.00 |
| ❑ FVS-9020 [S] | Little Boxes and Other Broadsides | 1965 | 25.00 |
| **WARNER BROS.** | | | |
| ❑ BSK 3329 | Circles and Seasons | 1979 | 12.00 |

## SEEGER, PETE, PENNY AND MICHAEL

| Number | Title (A Side/B Side) | Yr | NM |
|---|---|---|---|
| **PRESTIGE** | | | |
| ❑ PRLP-7375 [(2)M] | Pete, Penny and Michael Seeger | 1965 | 20.00 |
| ❑ PRST-7375 [(2)S] | Pete, Penny and Michael Seeger | 1965 | 25.00 |

## SEELY, JEANNIE

| Number | Title (A Side/B Side) | Yr | NM |
|---|---|---|---|
| **DECCA** | | | |
| ❑ DL 75093 | Jeannie Seely | 1969 | 15.00 |
| ❑ DL 75228 | Please Be My New Love | 1970 | 15.00 |
| **HARMONY** | | | |
| ❑ KH 31029 | Make the World Go Away | 1972 | 12.00 |
| **MCA** | | | |
| ❑ 385 | Can I Sleep in Your Arms/Lucky Ladies | 1973 | 12.00 |
| **MONUMENT** | | | |
| ❑ 6640 | Greatest Hits | 1977 | 12.00 |
| *—Reissue of 31911* | | | |
| ❑ MLP-8057 [M] | The Seely Style | 1966 | 15.00 |
| *—Title on label is "The Jeannie Seely Style"* | | | |
| ❑ MLP-8073 [M] | Thanks, Hank! | 1967 | 25.00 |
| ❑ SLP-18057 [S] | The Seely Style | 1966 | 20.00 |
| *—Title on label is "The Jeannie Seely Style"* | | | |
| ❑ SLP-18073 [S] | Thanks, Hank! | 1967 | 20.00 |
| ❑ SLP-18091 | I'll Love You More | 1968 | 20.00 |
| ❑ SLP-18104 | Little Things | 1968 | 20.00 |
| ❑ KZ 31911 | Greatest Hits | 1973 | 15.00 |

## SEGAL, GEORGE

| Number | Title (A Side/B Side) | Yr | NM |
|---|---|---|---|
| **PHILIPS** | | | |
| ❑ PHM 200242 [M] | The Yama-Yama Man | 1967 | 20.00 |
| ❑ PHS 600242 [S] | The Yama-Yama Man | 1967 | 20.00 |
| **SIGNATURE** | | | |
| ❑ BSL1-0654 | A Touch of Ragtime | 1976 | 15.00 |

## SEGALL, RICKY

| Number | Title (A Side/B Side) | Yr | NM |
|---|---|---|---|
| **BELL** | | | |
| ❑ 1138 | Ricky Segall and the Segalls | 1973 | 20.00 |

## SEGER, BOB

| Number | Title (A Side/B Side) | Yr | NM |
|---|---|---|---|
| **CAPITOL** | | | |
| ❑ (no #) [PD] | Night Moves | 1977 | 40.00 |
| *—Promo-only picture disc* | | | |
| ❑ SM-172 | Ramblin' Gamblin' Man | 1977 | 8.00 |
| ❑ ST-172 | Ramblin' Gamblin' Man | 1969 | 30.00 |
| *—Black label with colorband* | | | |
| ❑ ST-236 | Noah | 1969 | 80.00 |
| ❑ SKAO-499 | Mongrel | 1970 | 25.00 |
| ❑ SM-499 | Mongrel | 1977 | 8.00 |
| ❑ ST-731 | Brand New Morning | 1971 | 100.00 |
| ❑ SPRO-8433 [DJ] | Consensus Cuts Edited for Airplay from "Live Bullet" | 1976 | 25.00 |
| ❑ ST-11378 | Beautiful Loser | 1975 | 10.00 |
| *—Originals have orange labels* | | | |
| ❑ ST-11378 | Beautiful Loser | 1978 | 8.00 |
| *—Purple label with large Capitol logo* | | | |
| ❑ SKBB-11523 [(2)] | Live Bullet | 1976 | 15.00 |
| *—Originals have orange labels* | | | |
| ❑ SKBB-11523 [(2)] | Live Bullet | 1978 | 12.00 |
| *—Purple label with large Capitol logo* | | | |
| ❑ SKBB-11523 [(2)] | Live Bullet | 1983 | 12.00 |
| *—Black label, print in colorband* | | | |
| ❑ STBK-11523 [(2)] | Live Bullet | 1988 | 12.00 |
| *—Purple label with smaller Capitol logo* | | | |
| ❑ ST-11557 | Night Moves | 1976 | 10.00 |
| ❑ SW-11698 | Stranger in Town | 1978 | 10.00 |
| ❑ ST-11746 | Smokin' O.P.'s | 1978 | 10.00 |
| ❑ ST-11748 | Seven | 1978 | 10.00 |
| ❑ SEAX-11904 [PD] | Stranger in Town | 1978 | 25.00 |
| ❑ SOO-12041 | Against the Wind | 1980 | 10.00 |
| ❑ STBK-12182 [(2)] | Nine Tonight | 1981 | 15.00 |
| ❑ ST-12254 | The Distance | 1983 | 10.00 |
| ❑ PT-12398 | Like a Rock | 1986 | 10.00 |
| ❑ SN-16105 | Ramblin' Gamblin' Man | 1980 | 8.00 |
| ❑ SN-16106 | Mongrel | 1980 | 8.00 |
| ❑ SN-16107 | Smokin' O.P.'s | 1980 | 8.00 |
| ❑ SN-16108 | Seven | 1980 | 8.00 |
| ❑ SN-16315 | Beautiful Loser | 1984 | 8.00 |
| ❑ C1-30334 | Greatest Hits | 1994 | 15.00 |
| ❑ C1-91134 | The Fire Inside | 1991 | 12.00 |
| ❑ C1-99774 | It's a Mystery | 1995 | — |
| *—Canceled* | | | |
| ❑ R124284 | Ramblin' Gamblin' Man | 197? | 20.00 |
| *—Orange label, "Capitol"at bottom; RCA Music Service edition with B-side label error listing the title as "Ramblin' Bamblin' Man"* | | | |
| **MOBILE FIDELITY** | | | |
| ❑ 1-034 | Night Moves | 1980 | 40.00 |
| *—Audiophile vinyl* | | | |
| ❑ 1-127 | Against the Wind | 1983 | 40.00 |
| *—Audiophile vinyl* | | | |
| **PALLADIUM** | | | |
| ❑ P-1006 | Smokin' O.P.'s | 1972 | 25.00 |
| **REPRISE** | | | |
| ❑ MS 2109 | Smokin' O.P.'s | 1972 | 15.00 |
| ❑ MS 2126 | Back in '72 | 1973 | 60.00 |
| ❑ MS 2184 | Seven | 1974 | 20.00 |

## SEGO BROTHERS AND NAOMI, THE

| Number | Title (A Side/B Side) | Yr | NM |
|---|---|---|---|
| **GOSPEL TIME** | | | |
| ❑ 5007 | From the Soul | 196? | 25.00 |
| ❑ 5018 | Gospel Concert Special | 196? | 20.00 |
| **HARVEST** | | | |
| ❑ 1001 | Keeping It Gospel | 196? | 25.00 |
| **HEART WARMING** | | | |
| ❑ 1952 | With the Help of God | 196? | 30.00 |
| ❑ 1955 | This World Has Turned Me Down | 196? | 30.00 |
| ❑ 3056 | Happy Day | 196? | 25.00 |
| ❑ 3144 | Meetin' Time | 1972 | 25.00 |
| ❑ 3154 | Featuring Naomi | 1972 | 25.00 |
| ❑ 3186 | Sorry I Never Knew You | 1972 | 25.00 |
| ❑ 3206 | The Dearest Friend I Ever Had | 1973 | 25.00 |
| ❑ 3279 | What a Happy Time | 1974 | 25.00 |
| ❑ 3433 | It Will Be Different the Next Time | 1976 | 25.00 |
| **RUNA** | | | |
| ❑ 1941 | Gospel Singing | 196? | 30.00 |
| ❑ 1942 | Completely Gospel | 196? | 25.00 |
| **SCRIPTURE** | | | |
| ❑ 121 | The Best of the Sego Brothers and Naomi | 196? | 30.00 |
| ❑ 122 | Far Above the Starry Skies | 196? | 30.00 |
| **SILVER STAFF** | | | |
| ❑ 15003 | I Pray My Way Out of Trouble | 196? | 25.00 |
| **SIMS** | | | |
| ❑ 134 | With the Help of God | 196? | 40.00 |
| **SING** | | | |
| ❑ 9091M [M] | Sego Brothers and Naomi | 196? | 30.00 |
| ❑ 9091S [S] | Sego Brothers and Naomi | 196? | 40.00 |

| Number | Title (A Side/B Side) | Yr | NM |
|---|---|---|---|
| ❑ 9092M [M] | One Day Late | 196? | 30.00 |
| ❑ 9092S [S] | One Day Late | 196? | 40.00 |

SONGS OF FAITH

| Number | Title (A Side/B Side) | Yr | NM |
|---|---|---|---|
| ❑ 103 | Satisfied with Me | 196? | 30.00 |
| ❑ 110 | The Sego Brothers and Naomi Sing the Gospel | 1963 | 30.00 |
| ❑ 117 | From the Soul | 196? | 30.00 |
| ❑ 121 | The Award Winning Sego Brothers and Naomi | 196? | 30.00 |
| ❑ 126 | Hem of His Garment | 196? | 30.00 |
| ❑ 133 | He'll Walk By Your Side | 196? | 30.00 |
| ❑ 137 | Will the Circle Be Unbroken | 196? | 30.00 |
| ❑ 141 | Gospel Music On Stage with the Sego Brothers and Naomi | 196? | 30.00 |
| ❑ 143 | I'm Longing for Home | 196? | 30.00 |
| ❑ 145 | The Sego Brothers and Naomi Sing Weapon of Prayer | 196? | 20.00 |
| ❑ 147 | Somebody Touched Me | 196? | 30.00 |
| ❑ 150 | Daddy Sang Bass | 1969 | 25.00 |
| ❑ 156 | The Sego Brothers and Naomi Featuring W.R. Sego | 1969 | 25.00 |
| ❑ 158 | Golden Hits of the Sego Brothers and Naomi | 1970 | 25.00 |
| ❑ 168 | The Sego Brothers and Naomi at Grandfather Mountain | 197? | 25.00 |

SUPREME

| Number | Title (A Side/B Side) | Yr | NM |
|---|---|---|---|
| ❑ 33003 | I Pray My Way Out of Trouble | 196? | 30.00 |

VISTA

| Number | Title (A Side/B Side) | Yr | NM |
|---|---|---|---|
| ❑ 1224 | Old Time Singing | 196? | 30.00 |

### SELAH JUBILEE QUARTET, THE

REMINGTON

| Number | Title (A Side/B Side) | Yr | NM |
|---|---|---|---|
| ❑ 1023 [10] | Spirituals | 1951 | 200.00 |

### SELENA

CAPITOL/EMI LATIN

| Number | Title (A Side/B Side) | Yr | NM |
|---|---|---|---|
| ❑ H1-42144 | Selena Y Los Dinos | 1989 | 60.00 |
| ❑ H1-42299 | 16 Super Exitos Originales | 1990 | 60.00 |
| ❑ H1-42359 | Ven Conmingo | 1990 | 60.00 |

CBS DISCOS

| Number | Title (A Side/B Side) | Yr | NM |
|---|---|---|---|
| ❑ RRL 80323 | Personal Best | 1990 | 60.00 |

GP

| Number | Title (A Side/B Side) | Yr | NM |
|---|---|---|---|
| ❑ LP-1002 | Alpha | 1986 | 500.00 |
| ❑ LP-1005 | Menequito De Trapo | 1986 | 300.00 |
| ❑ LP-1009 | And the Winner Is... | 1987 | 200.00 |

RP

| Number | Title (A Side/B Side) | Yr | NM |
|---|---|---|---|
| ❑ LP-8801 | Preciosa | 1988 | 150.00 |
| ❑ LP-8803 | Dulce Amor | 1988 | 150.00 |

### SELLERS, BROTHER JOHN

VANGUARD

| Number | Title (A Side/B Side) | Yr | NM |
|---|---|---|---|
| ❑ VRS-8005 [10] | Brother John Sellers: Folk Songs and Blues | 1954 | 100.00 |
| ❑ VRS-9036 [M] | Blues and Folk Songs | 1957 | 80.00 |

### SELLERS, PETER

ACAPELLA

| Number | Title (A Side/B Side) | Yr | NM |
|---|---|---|---|
| ❑ 1 | Fool Brittania | 1963 | 25.00 |

*—With Joan Collins and Anthony Newley*

ANGEL

| Number | Title (A Side/B Side) | Yr | NM |
|---|---|---|---|
| ❑ 35884 [M] | The Best of Sellers | 1960 | 30.00 |
| ❑ S 35884 [S] | The Best of Sellers | 1960 | 40.00 |

EMI AMERICA

| Number | Title (A Side/B Side) | Yr | NM |
|---|---|---|---|
| ❑ SN-16396 | Songs for Swingin' Sellers | 1986 | 20.00 |

*—First American issue of 1959 U.K. LP*

### SELLERS, PETER, AND SOPHIA LOREN

ANGEL

| Number | Title (A Side/B Side) | Yr | NM |
|---|---|---|---|
| ❑ 35910 [M] | Peter Sellers and Sophia Loren | 1961 | 30.00 |
| ❑ S 35910 [S] | Peter Sellers and Sophia Loren | 1961 | 40.00 |

### SEMBELLO, MICHAEL

A&M

| Number | Title (A Side/B Side) | Yr | NM |
|---|---|---|---|
| ❑ SP-5044 | Without Walls | 1986 | 20.00 |

### SENATOR BOBBY

PARKWAY

| Number | Title (A Side/B Side) | Yr | NM |
|---|---|---|---|
| ❑ P 7057 [M] | Boston Soul with the Hardly-Worthit Players | 1967 | 20.00 |
| ❑ SP 7057 [S] | Boston Soul with the Hardly-Worthit Players | 1967 | 20.00 |

### SENOFSKY, BERL

RCA VICTOR RED SEAL

| Number | Title (A Side/B Side) | Yr | NM |
|---|---|---|---|
| ❑ LSC-2488 [S] | Debussy: Violin Sonata; Faure: Violin Sonata No. 1 in A | 1961 | 40.00 |

*—With Gary Graffman, piano; original with "shaded dog" label*

### SENSATIONS, THE

ARGO

| Number | Title (A Side/B Side) | Yr | NM |
|---|---|---|---|
| ❑ LP-4022 [M] | Let Me In/Music, Music, Music | 1963 | 500.00 |

### SENTINALS, THE

DEL-FI

| Number | Title (A Side/B Side) | Yr | NM |
|---|---|---|---|
| ❑ DFLP-1232 [M] | Big Surf! | 1963 | 100.00 |
| ❑ DFST-1232 [S] | Big Surf! | 1963 | 150.00 |
| ❑ DLF 1232 | Big Surf! | 1997 | 12.00 |
| ❑ DFLP-1241 [M] | Surfer Girl | 1963 | 70.00 |
| ❑ DFST-1241 [S] | Surfer Girl | 1963 | 100.00 |
| ❑ DLF 1241 | Surfer Girl | 1997 | 12.00 |

SUTTON

| Number | Title (A Side/B Side) | Yr | NM |
|---|---|---|---|
| ❑ SSU-338 [S] | Vegas Go-Go | 1964 | 50.00 |
| ❑ SU-338 [M] | Vegas Go-Go | 1964 | 40.00 |

### SERENDIPITY SINGERS, THE

PHILIPS

| Number | Title (A Side/B Side) | Yr | NM |
|---|---|---|---|
| ❑ PHM 200115 [M] | The Serendipity Singers | 1964 | 15.00 |
| ❑ PHM 200134 [M] | The Many Sides of the Serendipity Singers | 1964 | 15.00 |
| ❑ PHM 200151 [M] | Take Your Shoes Off with the Serendipity Singers | 1964 | 15.00 |
| ❑ PHM 200180 [M] | We Belong Together | 1965 | 15.00 |
| ❑ PHM 200190 [M] | Love, Lies and Flying Festoons | 1965 | 15.00 |
| ❑ PHS 600115 [S] | The Serendipity Singers | 1964 | 20.00 |
| ❑ PHS 600134 [S] | The Many Sides of the Serendipity Singers | 1964 | 20.00 |
| ❑ PHS 600151 [S] | Take Your Shoes Off with the Serendipity Singers | 1964 | 20.00 |
| ❑ PHS 600180 [S] | We Belong Together | 1965 | 20.00 |
| ❑ PHS 600190 [S] | Love, Lies and Flying Festoons | 1965 | 20.00 |

### SERPENT POWER

VANGUARD

| Number | Title (A Side/B Side) | Yr | NM |
|---|---|---|---|
| ❑ VRS-9252 [M] | Serpent Power | 1967 | 120.00 |
| ❑ VSD-79252 [S] | Serpent Power | 1967 | 60.00 |

### SERRANO, PAUL

RIVERSIDE

| Number | Title (A Side/B Side) | Yr | NM |
|---|---|---|---|
| ❑ RLP-359 [M] | Blues Holiday | 1961 | 25.00 |
| ❑ RS-9359 [S] | Blues Holiday | 1961 | 30.00 |

### SETE, BOLA

FANTASY

| Number | Title (A Side/B Side) | Yr | NM |
|---|---|---|---|
| ❑ 8349 [S] | Bossa Nova | 1963 | 20.00 |
| ❑ 8364 [S] | The Incomparable Bola Sete | 1965 | 20.00 |
| ❑ 8369 [S] | The Solo Guitar of Bola Sete | 1966 | 20.00 |
| ❑ 8375 [S] | Autentico! | 1966 | 20.00 |
| ❑ 8417 | Shebaba | 1971 | 12.00 |

VERVE

| Number | Title (A Side/B Side) | Yr | NM |
|---|---|---|---|
| ❑ V-8689 [M] | Bola Sete At the Monterey Jazz Festival | 1967 | 20.00 |

### SETTLE, MIKE

REPRISE

| Number | Title (A Side/B Side) | Yr | NM |
|---|---|---|---|
| ❑ R-6149 [M] | The Mike Settle Shindig | 1965 | 20.00 |
| ❑ RS-6149 [S] | The Mike Settle Shindig | 1965 | 25.00 |

### SEVEN BLENDS, THE

ROULETTE

| Number | Title (A Side/B Side) | Yr | NM |
|---|---|---|---|
| ❑ R-25172 [M] | Twistin' at the Miami Beach Peppermint Lounge | 1962 | 20.00 |
| ❑ SR-25172 [S] | Twistin' at the Miami Beach Peppermint Lounge | 1962 | 25.00 |

### SEVENTH WAVE, THE

JANUS

| Number | Title (A Side/B Side) | Yr | NM |
|---|---|---|---|
| ❑ 7008 | Things to Come | 1974 | 20.00 |
| ❑ 7021 | Psi-Fi | 1975 | 20.00 |

### SEVERINSON, DOC

COMMAND

| Number | Title (A Side/B Side) | Yr | NM |
|---|---|---|---|
| ❑ RS 819 SD [S] | Tempestuous Trumpet | 1961 | 20.00 |
| ❑ RS 837 SD [S] | The Big Band's Back in Town | 1962 | 20.00 |
| ❑ RS 859 SD [S] | Torch Songs for Trumpet | 1963 | 20.00 |
| ❑ RS 883 SD [S] | High, Wide and Wonderful | 1965 | 20.00 |

### SEVERSON, PAUL

ACADEMY

| Number | Title (A Side/B Side) | Yr | NM |
|---|---|---|---|
| ❑ MWJ-1 [M] | Midwest Jazz | 1956 | 50.00 |

### SEVILLA, JORGE

VERVE

| Number | Title (A Side/B Side) | Yr | NM |
|---|---|---|---|
| ❑ MGVS-6103 [S] | The Incredible Guitar of Jorge Sevilla | 1960 | 40.00 |
| ❑ MGV-8342 [M] | The Incredible Guitar of Jorge Sevilla | 1959 | 50.00 |
| ❑ V-8342 [M] | The Incredible Guitar of Jorge Sevilla | 1961 | 25.00 |
| ❑ V6-8342 [S] | The Incredible Guitar of Jorge Sevilla | 1961 | 20.00 |

### SEVILLE, DAVID

LIBERTY

| Number | Title (A Side/B Side) | Yr | NM |
|---|---|---|---|
| ❑ LRP-3073 [M] | The Music of David Seville | 1957 | 80.00 |
| ❑ LRP-3092 [M] | The Witch Doctor | 1958 | 100.00 |

### SEWARD, ALEC

BLUESVILLE

| Number | Title (A Side/B Side) | Yr | NM |
|---|---|---|---|
| ❑ BVLP-1076 [M] | Creepin' Blues | 1963 | 80.00 |

*—Blue label, silver print*

| Number | Title (A Side/B Side) | Yr | NM |
|---|---|---|---|
| ❑ BVLP-1076 [M] | Creepin' Blues | 1964 | 25.00 |

*—Blue label, trident logo at right*

### SEX CLARK FIVE

BLOOD MONEY

| Number | Title (A Side/B Side) | Yr | NM |
|---|---|---|---|
| ❑ ERATO 59 | Battle of Sex Clark Five | 1989 | 18.00 |

RECORDS TO RUSSIA

| Number | Title (A Side/B Side) | Yr | NM |
|---|---|---|---|
| ❑ LP 408 | Strum & Drum! | 1986 | 120.00 |

*—Test pressing with 24 tracks*

| Number | Title (A Side/B Side) | Yr | NM |
|---|---|---|---|
| ❑ LP 408 | Strum & Drum! | 1987 | 15.00 |

*—Second pressing: 20 tracks, no halftones, different back photo*

| Number | Title (A Side/B Side) | Yr | NM |
|---|---|---|---|
| ❑ LP 408 | Strum & Drum! | 1987 | 20.00 |

*—First pressing: 20 tracks, photos are halftones*

SKYCLAD

| Number | Title (A Side/B Side) | Yr | NM |
|---|---|---|---|
| ❑ (NOT) BM 131 | Antedium | 1992 | 15.00 |

### SEX PISTOLS

RESTLESS

| Number | Title (A Side/B Side) | Yr | NM |
|---|---|---|---|
| ❑ 72255 | Better Live Than Dead | 1988 | 12.00 |
| ❑ 72256 [EP] | The Mini-Album | 1988 | 8.00 |
| ❑ 72257 | The Ex-Pistols: The Swindle Continues | 1988 | 12.00 |
| ❑ 72511 | Live at Chelmsford Top Security Prison | 1990 | 10.00 |

SKYCLAD

| Number | Title (A Side/B Side) | Yr | NM |
|---|---|---|---|
| ❑ SEX 6 | We've Cum For Your Children | 1988 | 12.00 |

WARNER BROS.

| Number | Title (A Side/B Side) | Yr | NM |
|---|---|---|---|
| ❑ BSK 3147 | Never Mind the Bollocks Here's the Sex Pistols | 1978 | 10.00 |

*—With white WB label*

| Number | Title (A Side/B Side) | Yr | NM |
|---|---|---|---|
| ❑ BSK 3147 | Never Mind the Bollocks Here's the Sex Pistols | 1978 | 25.00 |

*—Any other version with custom label*

| Number | Title (A Side/B Side) | Yr | NM |
|---|---|---|---|
| ❑ BSK 3147 | Never Mind the Bollocks Here's the Sex Pistols | 1978 | 30.00 |

*—With sticker "Contains Sub-Mission"*

### SHA NA NA

ACCORD

| Number | Title (A Side/B Side) | Yr | NM |
|---|---|---|---|
| ❑ SN-7115 | Remember Then | 1981 | 10.00 |
| ❑ SN-7146 | Sh-Boom | 1981 | 10.00 |

BUDDAH

| Number | Title (A Side/B Side) | Yr | NM |
|---|---|---|---|
| ❑ BDM-5692 | Rock & Roll Is Here to Stay! | 1978 | 10.00 |
| ❑ BDM-5703 | The Best of Sha Na Na | 1978 | 10.00 |

EMUS

| Number | Title (A Side/B Side) | Yr | NM |
|---|---|---|---|
| ❑ ES-12037 | On Stage | 1978 | 10.00 |

KAMA SUTRA

| Number | Title (A Side/B Side) | Yr | NM |
|---|---|---|---|
| ❑ KSBS-2010 | Rock & Roll Is Here to Stay! | 1969 | 15.00 |
| ❑ KSBS-2034 | Sha Na Na | 1971 | 15.00 |
| ❑ KSBS-2050 | The Night Is Still Young | 1972 | 15.00 |
| ❑ KSBS-2073 [(2)] | The Golden Age of Rock 'n' Roll | 1973 | 20.00 |
| ❑ KSBS-2075 | From the Streets of New York | 1973 | 15.00 |
| ❑ KSBS-2077 | Rock & Roll Is Here to Stay! | 1974 | 15.00 |
| ❑ KSBS-2600 | Hot Sox | 1974 | 15.00 |
| ❑ KSBS-2605 | Sha Na Now | 1975 | 15.00 |
| ❑ KSBS-2609 [(2)] | The Best...Sha Na Na | 1976 | 15.00 |

NASHVILLE

| Number | Title (A Side/B Side) | Yr | NM |
|---|---|---|---|
| ❑ NR-12348-122 [(2)] | Rockin' in the 80's | 1980 | 12.00 |

REALM

| Number | Title (A Side/B Side) | Yr | NM |
|---|---|---|---|
| ❑ 2V 8058 [(2)] | All-Time Greatest Rock 'n' Roll Hits | 1977 | 15.00 |
| ❑ 1V 8059 | Rock 'n' Roll Dance Party | 1977 | 12.00 |

### SHACKLEFORDS, THE

CAPITOL

| Number | Title (A Side/B Side) | Yr | NM |
|---|---|---|---|
| ❑ ST 2450 [S] | The Shacklefords | 1966 | 25.00 |
| ❑ T 2450 [M] | The Shacklefords | 1966 | 20.00 |

MERCURY

| Number | Title (A Side/B Side) | Yr | NM |
|---|---|---|---|
| ❑ MG-20806 [M] | Until You've Heard the Shacklefords | 1963 | 20.00 |
| ❑ SR-60806 [S] | Until You've Heard the Shacklefords | 1963 | 25.00 |

### SHADES OF BLUE

IMPACT

| Number | Title (A Side/B Side) | Yr | NM |
|---|---|---|---|
| ❑ IM-101 [M] | Happiness Is the Shades of Blue | 1966 | 50.00 |
| ❑ IM-1001 [S] | Happiness Is the Shades of Blue | 1966 | 60.00 |

### SHADES OF JOY

FONTANA

| Number | Title (A Side/B Side) | Yr | NM |
|---|---|---|---|
| ❑ SRF-67592 | Shades of Joy | 1969 | 20.00 |

### SHADOWS, THE (1)

ATLANTIC

| Number | Title (A Side/B Side) | Yr | NM |
|---|---|---|---|
| ❑ 8084 [M] | Out of the Shadows | 1962 | 200.00 |

*—Canada-only release?*

| Number | Title (A Side/B Side) | Yr | NM |
|---|---|---|---|
| ❑ 8089 [M] | Surfing with the Shadows | 1963 | 150.00 |
| ❑ SD 8089 [S] | Surfing with the Shadows | 1963 | 300.00 |
| ❑ 8097 [M] | The Shadows Know | 1964 | 100.00 |
| ❑ SD 8097 [S] | The Shadows Know | 1964 | 200.00 |

### SHADOWS OF KNIGHT, THE

DUNWICH

| Number | Title (A Side/B Side) | Yr | NM |
|---|---|---|---|
| ❑ 666 [M] | Gloria | 1966 | 50.00 |

| Number | Title (A Side/B Side) | Yr | NM |
|---|---|---|---|
| ❑ S-666 [S] | Gloria | 1966 | 80.00 |
| ❑ 667 [M] | Back Door Men | 1966 | 50.00 |
| ❑ S-667 [S] | Back Door Men | 1966 | 80.00 |
| **SUNDAZED** | | | |
| ❑ LP 5006 | Raw and Live at the Cellar 1966 | 1992 | 10.00 |
| ❑ LP 5034 | Gloria | 1999 | 12.00 |
| *—Reissue on 180-gram vinyl* | | | |
| ❑ LP 5035 | Back Door Men | 1999 | 12.00 |
| *—Reissue on 180-gram vinyl* | | | |
| **SUPER K** | | | |
| ❑ SKS-6002 | The Shadows of Knight | 1969 | 50.00 |

### SHADRACK

| Number | Title (A Side/B Side) | Yr | NM |
|---|---|---|---|
| **IGL** | | | |
| ❑ 132 | Chameleon | 1971 | 300.00 |

### SHAFRAN, DANIEL

| Number | Title (A Side/B Side) | Yr | NM |
|---|---|---|---|
| **RCA VICTOR RED SEAL** | | | |
| ❑ LSC-2553 [S] | Shostakovich: Cello Sonata; Schubert: Arpeggione Sonata | 1961 | 120.00 |
| *—Original with "shaded dog" label* | | | |

### SHAGGS, THE (2)

| Number | Title (A Side/B Side) | Yr | NM |
|---|---|---|---|
| **MCM** | | | |
| ❑ 1295 | Wink | 1967 | 250.00 |
| *—No number on label -- this number is found in the trail-off wax on each side* | | | |

### SHAGGS, THE (3)

| Number | Title (A Side/B Side) | Yr | NM |
|---|---|---|---|
| **ROUNDER** | | | |
| ❑ 3032 | Philosophy of the World | 1980 | 25.00 |
| ❑ 3056 | Shaggs' Own Thing | 1982 | 25.00 |
| **THIRD WORLD** | | | |
| ❑ 3001 | Philosophy of the World | 1969 | 2000. |

### SHAKERS, THE

| Number | Title (A Side/B Side) | Yr | NM |
|---|---|---|---|
| **AUDIO FIDELITY** | | | |
| ❑ AFLP-2155 [M] | The Shakers Break It All | 1966 | 40.00 |
| ❑ AFSD-6155 [S] | The Shakers Break It All | 1966 | 50.00 |

### SHAKEY JAKE

| Number | Title (A Side/B Side) | Yr | NM |
|---|---|---|---|
| **BLUESVILLE** | | | |
| ❑ BVLP-1008 [M] | Good Times | 1960 | 120.00 |
| *—Blue label, silver print* | | | |
| ❑ BVLP-1008 [M] | Good Times | 1964 | 30.00 |
| *—Blue label, trident logo at right* | | | |
| ❑ BVLP-1027 [M] | Mouth Harp Blues | 1961 | 120.00 |
| *—Blue label, silver print* | | | |
| ❑ BVLP-1027 [M] | Mouth Harp Blues | 1964 | 30.00 |
| *—Blue label, trident logo at right* | | | |
| **WORLD PACIFIC** | | | |
| ❑ WPS-21886 | Blues Makers | 196? | 30.00 |

### SHAKEY VICK

| Number | Title (A Side/B Side) | Yr | NM |
|---|---|---|---|
| **JANUS** | | | |
| ❑ JLS-3000 | Little Woman, You're So Sweet | 1970 | 20.00 |

### SHANGRI-LAS, THE

| Number | Title (A Side/B Side) | Yr | NM |
|---|---|---|---|
| **COLLECTABLES** | | | |
| ❑ COL-5011 | Remember...Their Greatest Hits | 198? | 10.00 |
| **MERCURY** | | | |
| ❑ MG-21099 [M] | The Shangri-Las' Golden Hits | 1966 | 40.00 |
| ❑ SR-61099 [S] | The Shangri-Las' Golden Hits | 1966 | 50.00 |
| **POLYDOR** | | | |
| ❑ 824807-1 | Golden Hits of the Shangri-Las | 1985 | 10.00 |
| **POST** | | | |
| ❑ 4000 | The Shangri-Las Sing | 196? | 20.00 |
| **RED BIRD** | | | |
| ❑ 20101 [M] | Leader of the Pack | 1965 | 150.00 |
| ❑ 20104 [M] | Shangri-Las '65 | 1965 | 150.00 |
| ❑ 20104 [M] | I Can Never Go Home Anymore | 1966 | 100.00 |
| *—Retitled version with title song added and "Sophisticated Boom Boom" dropped* | | | |

### SHANK, BUD

| Number | Title (A Side/B Side) | Yr | NM |
|---|---|---|---|
| **KIMBERLY** | | | |
| ❑ 2025 [M] | The Talents of Bud Shank | 1963 | 20.00 |
| ❑ 11025 [S] | The Talents of Bud Shank | 1963 | 25.00 |
| **NOCTURNE** | | | |
| ❑ NLP-2 [10] | Compositions of Shorty Rogers | 1953 | 200.00 |
| **PACIFIC JAZZ** | | | |
| ❑ PJ-4 [M] | Bud Shank Plays Tenor | 1960 | 25.00 |
| ❑ ST-4 [S] | Bud Shank Plays Tenor | 1960 | 30.00 |
| ❑ PJLP-14 [10] | Bud Shank with Three Trombones | 1954 | 120.00 |
| ❑ PJLP-20 [10] | Bud Shank and Bob Brookmeyer | 1954 | 120.00 |
| ❑ PJ-21 [M] | New Groove | 1961 | 25.00 |
| ❑ ST-21 [S] | New Groove | 1961 | 30.00 |
| ❑ PJ-58 [M] | Bossa Nova Jazz Samba | 1962 | 25.00 |
| ❑ ST-58 [S] | Bossa Nova Jazz Samba | 1962 | 30.00 |
| ❑ PJ-64 [M] | Brassamba Bossa Nova | 1963 | 20.00 |
| ❑ ST-64 [S] | Brassamba Bossa Nova | 1963 | 25.00 |
| ❑ PJ-89 [M] | Bud Shank and His Brazilian Friends | 1965 | 20.00 |
| ❑ ST-89 [S] | Bud Shank and His Brazilian Friends | 1965 | 25.00 |
| ❑ PJM-411 [M] | The Swing's to TV | 1957 | 60.00 |
| ❑ PJ-1205 [M] | Bud Shank/Shorty Rogers | 1955 | 80.00 |
| ❑ PJ-1213 [M] | Strings and Trombones | 1956 | 80.00 |
| ❑ PJ-1215 [M] | The Bud Shank Quartet | 1956 | 80.00 |
| ❑ PJ-1219 [M] | Jazz at Cal-Tech | 1956 | 60.00 |
| ❑ PJ-1226 [M] | Flute 'n Oboe | 1957 | 60.00 |
| ❑ PJ-1230 [M] | The Bud Shank Quartet | 1957 | 60.00 |
| ❑ ST-20110 [S] | Bud Shank and the Sax Section | 1966 | 20.00 |
| ❑ ST-20157 | Windmills of Your Mind | 1969 | 15.00 |
| **WORLD PACIFIC** | | | |
| ❑ PJM-411 [M] | The Swing's to TV | 1958 | 50.00 |
| ❑ WPM-411 [M] | The Swing's to TV | 1958 | 40.00 |
| ❑ ST-1002 [S] | The Swing's to TV | 1959 | 30.00 |
| ❑ ST-1018 [S] | Holiday in Brazil | 1959 | 30.00 |
| ❑ WP-1205 [M] | Bud Shank/Shorty Rogers | 1958 | 40.00 |
| ❑ WP-1215 [M] | The Bud Shank Quartet | 1958 | 40.00 |
| ❑ WP-1219 [M] | Jazz at Cal-Tech | 1958 | 40.00 |
| ❑ WP-1226 [M] | Flute 'n Oboe | 1958 | 40.00 |
| ❑ WP-1230 [M] | The Bud Shank Quartet | 1958 | 40.00 |
| ❑ WP-1251 [M] | I'll Take Romance | 1958 | 40.00 |
| ❑ WP-1259 [M] | Holiday in Brazil | 1959 | 40.00 |
| ❑ ST-1281 [S] | Latin Contrasts | 1959 | 30.00 |
| ❑ WP-1281 [M] | Latin Contrasts | 1959 | 40.00 |
| ❑ ST-1286 [S] | Flute 'n Alto | 1960 | 40.00 |
| ❑ WP-1286 [M] | Flute 'n Alto | 1960 | 30.00 |
| ❑ ST-1299 [S] | Koto 'n Flute | 1960 | 40.00 |
| ❑ WP-1299 [M] | Koto 'n Flute | 1960 | 30.00 |
| ❑ WP-1416 [M] | Improvisations | 1961 | 25.00 |
| ❑ WP-1424 [M] | Koto 'n Flute | 1962 | 25.00 |
| ❑ WP-1853 [M] | Girl in Love | 1967 | 20.00 |
| ❑ WP-1855 [M] | Brazil! Brazil! Brazil! | 1967 | 20.00 |
| ❑ WP-1864 [M] | Bud Shank Plays Music from Today's Movies | 1967 | 20.00 |
| ❑ ST-21819 [S] | Folk 'n Flute | 1965 | 20.00 |
| ❑ ST-21827 [S] | Flute, Oboe and Strings | 1965 | 20.00 |
| ❑ ST-21840 [S] | Michelle | 1966 | 20.00 |
| ❑ ST-21845 [S] | California Dreaming | 1966 | 20.00 |

### SHANK, BUD/CHET BAKER

| Number | Title (A Side/B Side) | Yr | NM |
|---|---|---|---|
| **KIMBERLY** | | | |
| ❑ 2016 [M] | Swinging Soundtrack | 1963 | 20.00 |
| ❑ 11016 [S] | Swinging Soundtrack | 1963 | 25.00 |

### SHANKAR, ANANDA

| Number | Title (A Side/B Side) | Yr | NM |
|---|---|---|---|
| **REPRISE** | | | |
| ❑ RS-6398 | Ananda Shankar | 1970 | 20.00 |

### SHANKAR, L.

| Number | Title (A Side/B Side) | Yr | NM |
|---|---|---|---|
| **ZAPPA** | | | |
| ❑ SRZ-1-1602 | Touch Me There | 1979 | 20.00 |

### SHANKAR, RAVI

| Number | Title (A Side/B Side) | Yr | NM |
|---|---|---|---|
| **ANGEL** | | | |
| ❑ 35468 [M] | Music of India | 196? | 25.00 |
| ❑ S 36026 [S] | West Meets East, Vol. 2 | 1968 | 15.00 |
| ❑ 36418 [M] | West Meets East | 1967 | 25.00 |
| *—With Yahudi Menuhin* | | | |
| ❑ S 36418 [S] | West Meets East | 1967 | 20.00 |
| *—With Yahudi Menuhin* | | | |
| ❑ S 36806 | Concerto for Sitar and Orchestra | 1972 | 12.00 |
| ❑ DS-37920 | Raga Mishra Piloo | 1982 | 10.00 |
| ❑ DS-37935 | Raga-Mala (Sitar Concert No. 2) | 1983 | 10.00 |
| **APPLE** | | | |
| ❑ SWAO-3384 | Raga | 1971 | 25.00 |
| ❑ SVBB-3396 [(2)] | Ravi Shankar In Concert | 1973 | 40.00 |
| **BLUESVILLE** | | | |
| ❑ BVLP-1078 [M] | The Master Musician of India | 1964 | 25.00 |
| **CAPITOL** | | | |
| ❑ DT 2720 [R] | Three Ragas | 1967 | 15.00 |
| ❑ T 2720 [M] | Three Ragas | 1967 | 20.00 |
| ❑ ST 10482 [S] | Two Raga Moods | 196? | 25.00 |
| ❑ T 10482 [M] | Two Raga Moods | 196? | 20.00 |
| ❑ ST 10497 [S] | Exotic Sitar and Sarod | 196? | 25.00 |
| ❑ T 10497 [M] | Exotic Sitar and Sarod | 196? | 20.00 |
| ❑ ST 10504 | Ravi | 196? | 15.00 |
| ❑ SP-10561 | Raga Parameshwari | 1972 | 12.00 |
| **COLUMBIA** | | | |
| ❑ WL 119 [M] | The Sounds of India | 196? | 25.00 |
| ❑ CL 2496 [M] | Sounds of India | 1966 | 15.00 |
| ❑ CL 2760 [M] | The Genius of Ravi Shankar | 1967 | 20.00 |
| ❑ OS 3230 | Chappaqua | 1968 | 15.00 |
| ❑ CS 9296 [S] | Sounds of India | 1966 | 20.00 |
| ❑ CS 9560 [S] | The Genius of Ravi Shankar | 1967 | 15.00 |
| **DARK HORSE** | | | |
| ❑ SP 22002 | Shankar Family and Friends | 1974 | 12.00 |
| ❑ SP 22007 | Music Festival from India | 1975 | 12.00 |
| **DEUTCHE GRAMMOPHON** | | | |
| ❑ 2531 216 | Ragas Hameer & Gara | 198? | 10.00 |
| ❑ 2531 280 | Raga Jogeshwari | 198? | 10.00 |
| ❑ 2531 356 | Homage to Mahatma Gandhi; Homage to Baba Allauddin | 198? | 10.00 |
| ❑ 2531 381 | Pad Hasapa, for Koto; etc. | 198? | 10.00 |
| **FANTASY** | | | |
| ❑ 24714 [(2)] | Ragas | 1973 | 15.00 |
| **ORIENTAL** | | | |
| ❑ BGRP-108 | Raga Sanjh Kalyan | 198? | 10.00 |
| **PRIVATE MUSIC** | | | |
| ❑ 2016-1-P | The Shankar Project: Tana Mana | 1988 | 10.00 |
| ❑ 2044-1-P | Inside the Kremlin | 1989 | 10.00 |
| **SPARK** | | | |
| ❑ 06 | Transmigration Macabre | 1973 | 12.00 |
| **WORLD PACIFIC** | | | |
| ❑ WP-1421 [M] | Ravi Shankar In Concert | 1965 | 15.00 |
| ❑ WP-1422 [M] | India's Master Musician | 1965 | 15.00 |
| ❑ WP-1430 [M] | Ravi Shankar In London | 1966 | 15.00 |
| ❑ WP-1431 [M] | Ragas and Talas | 1966 | 15.00 |
| ❑ WP-1432 [M] | Portrait of Genius | 1966 | 15.00 |
| ❑ WP-1434 [M] | Sound of the Sitar | 1967 | 15.00 |
| ❑ WP-1438 [M] | Three Ragas | 1967 | 15.00 |
| ❑ WP-1441 [M] | Ravi Shankar in New York | 1967 | 15.00 |
| ❑ WP-1442 [M] | Ravi Shankar at the Monterey International Pop Festival | 1967 | 20.00 |
| ❑ ST-21421 [S] | Ravi Shankar In Concert | 1965 | 20.00 |
| ❑ ST-21422 [S] | India's Master Musician | 1965 | 20.00 |
| ❑ ST-21430 [S] | Ravi Shankar In London | 1966 | 20.00 |
| ❑ ST-21431 [S] | Ragas and Talas | 1966 | 20.00 |
| ❑ ST-21432 [S] | Portrait of Genius | 1966 | 20.00 |
| ❑ ST-21434 [S] | Sound of the Sitar | 1967 | 20.00 |
| ❑ ST-21438 [S] | Three Ragas | 1967 | 20.00 |
| ❑ ST-21441 [S] | Ravi Shankar in New York | 1967 | 20.00 |
| ❑ ST-21442 [S] | Ravi Shankar at the Monterey International Pop Festival | 1967 | 20.00 |
| ❑ ST-21449 | Ravi Shankar in San Francisco | 1968 | 20.00 |
| ❑ ST-21454 | Charly | 1969 | 15.00 |
| ❑ ST-21464 | Morning Raga/Evening Raga | 1970 | 15.00 |
| ❑ ST-21467 | Ravi Shankar at Woodstock | 1970 | 15.00 |
| ❑ WPS-26201 [(2)] | His Festival from India | 1968 | 20.00 |

### SHANNON, DEL

| Number | Title (A Side/B Side) | Yr | NM |
|---|---|---|---|
| **AMY** | | | |
| ❑ 8003 [M] | Handy Man | 1964 | 50.00 |
| ❑ S-8003 [S] | Handy Man | 1964 | 80.00 |
| ❑ 8004 [M] | Del Shannon Sings Hank Williams | 1965 | 50.00 |
| ❑ S-8004 [S] | Del Shannon Sings Hank Williams | 1965 | 80.00 |
| ❑ 8006 [M] | 1,661 Seconds with Del Shannon | 1965 | 50.00 |
| ❑ S-8006 [S] | 1,661 Seconds with Del Shannon | 1965 | 80.00 |
| **BIG TOP** | | | |
| ❑ 12-1303 [M] | Runaway | 1961 | 300.00 |
| ❑ 12-1303 [S] | Runaway | 1961 | 1600. |
| ❑ 12-1308 [B] | Little Town Flirt | 1963 | 1000. |
| *—One side is mono, one side is stereo; should be played to identify* | | | |
| ❑ 12-1308 [M] | Little Town Flirt | 1963 | 150.00 |
| ❑ 12-1308 [S] | Little Town Flirt | 1963 | 1500. |
| *—Stereo copies are not identified as such on either cover or label; some, but not all, copies have an "S" in the dead wax. Playing is the best way to identify.* | | | |
| **DOT** | | | |
| ❑ DLP 3824 [M] | The Best of Del Shannon | 1967 | 50.00 |
| ❑ DLP 25824 [R] | The Best of Del Shannon | 1967 | 40.00 |
| **ELEKTRA** | | | |
| ❑ 5E-568 | Drop Down and Get Me | 1981 | 10.00 |
| **LIBERTY** | | | |
| ❑ LRP-3453 [M] | This Is My Bag | 1966 | 30.00 |
| ❑ LRP-3479 [M] | Total Commitment | 1966 | 30.00 |
| ❑ LRP-3539 [M] | The Further Adventures of Charles Westover | 1967 | 50.00 |
| ❑ LST-7453 [S] | This Is My Bag | 1966 | 40.00 |
| ❑ LST-7479 [S] | Total Commitment | 1966 | 40.00 |
| ❑ LST-7539 [S] | The Further Adventures of Charles Westover | 1967 | 80.00 |
| **PICKWICK** | | | |
| ❑ SPC-3595 [R] | The Best of Del Shannon | 197? | 10.00 |
| **POST** | | | |
| ❑ 9000 [R] | Del Shannon Sings | 196? | 40.00 |
| **RHINO** | | | |
| ❑ RNLP-71056 [M] | Runaway Hits | 1986 | 10.00 |
| **SIRE** | | | |
| ❑ SASH-3708 [(2)P] | The Vintage Years | 1975 | 25.00 |
| **TWIRL** | | | |
| ❑ 5001 [M] | Del Shannon's Greatest Hits | 196? | 200.00 |
| *—LP was never issued; price is for front cover slick, which is known to exist* | | | |
| **UNITED ARTISTS** | | | |
| ❑ UA-LA151-E | Del Shannon Live in England | 1973 | 25.00 |

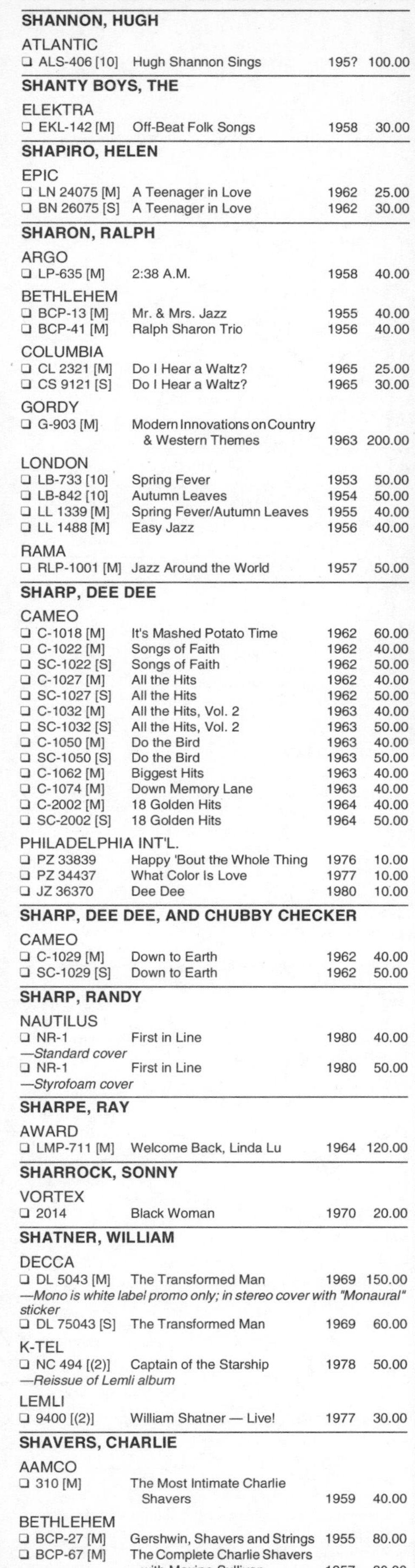

| Number | Title (A Side/B Side) | Yr | NM |
|---|---|---|---|
| **SHANNON, HUGH** | | | |
| ATLANTIC | | | |
| ❑ ALS-406 [10] | Hugh Shannon Sings | 195? | 100.00 |
| **SHANTY BOYS, THE** | | | |
| ELEKTRA | | | |
| ❑ EKL-142 [M] | Off-Beat Folk Songs | 1958 | 30.00 |
| **SHAPIRO, HELEN** | | | |
| EPIC | | | |
| ❑ LN 24075 [M] | A Teenager in Love | 1962 | 25.00 |
| ❑ BN 26075 [S] | A Teenager in Love | 1962 | 30.00 |
| **SHARON, RALPH** | | | |
| ARGO | | | |
| ❑ LP-635 [M] | 2:38 A.M. | 1958 | 40.00 |
| BETHLEHEM | | | |
| ❑ BCP-13 [M] | Mr. & Mrs. Jazz | 1955 | 40.00 |
| ❑ BCP-41 [M] | Ralph Sharon Trio | 1956 | 40.00 |
| COLUMBIA | | | |
| ❑ CL 2321 [M] | Do I Hear a Waltz? | 1965 | 25.00 |
| ❑ CS 9121 [S] | Do I Hear a Waltz? | 1965 | 30.00 |
| GORDY | | | |
| ❑ G-903 [M] | Modern Innovations on Country & Western Themes | 1963 | 200.00 |
| LONDON | | | |
| ❑ LB-733 [10] | Spring Fever | 1953 | 50.00 |
| ❑ LB-842 [10] | Autumn Leaves | 1954 | 50.00 |
| ❑ LL 1339 [M] | Spring Fever/Autumn Leaves | 1955 | 40.00 |
| ❑ LL 1488 [M] | Easy Jazz | 1956 | 40.00 |
| RAMA | | | |
| ❑ RLP-1001 [M] | Jazz Around the World | 1957 | 50.00 |
| **SHARP, DEE DEE** | | | |
| CAMEO | | | |
| ❑ C-1018 [M] | It's Mashed Potato Time | 1962 | 60.00 |
| ❑ C-1022 [M] | Songs of Faith | 1962 | 40.00 |
| ❑ SC-1022 [S] | Songs of Faith | 1962 | 50.00 |
| ❑ C-1027 [M] | All the Hits | 1962 | 40.00 |
| ❑ SC-1027 [S] | All the Hits | 1962 | 50.00 |
| ❑ C-1032 [M] | All the Hits, Vol. 2 | 1963 | 40.00 |
| ❑ SC-1032 [S] | All the Hits, Vol. 2 | 1963 | 50.00 |
| ❑ C-1050 [M] | Do the Bird | 1963 | 40.00 |
| ❑ SC-1050 [S] | Do the Bird | 1963 | 50.00 |
| ❑ C-1062 [M] | Biggest Hits | 1963 | 40.00 |
| ❑ C-1074 [M] | Down Memory Lane | 1963 | 40.00 |
| ❑ C-2002 [M] | 18 Golden Hits | 1964 | 40.00 |
| ❑ SC-2002 [S] | 18 Golden Hits | 1964 | 50.00 |
| PHILADELPHIA INT'L. | | | |
| ❑ PZ 33839 | Happy 'Bout the Whole Thing | 1976 | 10.00 |
| ❑ PZ 34437 | What Color Is Love | 1977 | 10.00 |
| ❑ JZ 36370 | Dee Dee | 1980 | 10.00 |
| **SHARP, DEE DEE, AND CHUBBY CHECKER** | | | |
| CAMEO | | | |
| ❑ C-1029 [M] | Down to Earth | 1962 | 40.00 |
| ❑ SC-1029 [S] | Down to Earth | 1962 | 50.00 |
| **SHARP, RANDY** | | | |
| NAUTILUS | | | |
| ❑ NR-1 | First in Line | 1980 | 40.00 |
| *—Standard cover* | | | |
| ❑ NR-1 | First in Line | 1980 | 50.00 |
| *—Styrofoam cover* | | | |
| **SHARPE, RAY** | | | |
| AWARD | | | |
| ❑ LMP-711 [M] | Welcome Back, Linda Lu | 1964 | 120.00 |
| **SHARROCK, SONNY** | | | |
| VORTEX | | | |
| ❑ 2014 | Black Woman | 1970 | 20.00 |
| **SHATNER, WILLIAM** | | | |
| DECCA | | | |
| ❑ DL 5043 [M] | The Transformed Man | 1969 | 150.00 |
| *—Mono is white label promo only; in stereo cover with "Monaural" sticker* | | | |
| ❑ DL 75043 [S] | The Transformed Man | 1969 | 60.00 |
| K-TEL | | | |
| ❑ NC 494 [(2)] | Captain of the Starship | 1978 | 50.00 |
| *—Reissue of Lemli album* | | | |
| LEMLI | | | |
| ❑ 9400 [(2)] | William Shatner — Live! | 1977 | 30.00 |
| **SHAVERS, CHARLIE** | | | |
| AAMCO | | | |
| ❑ 310 [M] | The Most Intimate Charlie Shavers | 1959 | 40.00 |
| BETHLEHEM | | | |
| ❑ BCP-27 [M] | Gershwin, Shavers and Strings | 1955 | 80.00 |
| ❑ BCP-67 [M] | The Complete Charlie Shavers with Maxine Sullivan | 1957 | 80.00 |

Dee Dee Sharp, *All the Hits, Volume 2,* Cameo C-1032, 1963, mono, $40.

| Number | Title (A Side/B Side) | Yr | NM |
|---|---|---|---|
| ❑ BCP-1007 [10] | Horn o' Plenty | 1954 | 100.00 |
| ❑ BCP-1021 [10] | The Most Intimate Charlie Shavers | 1955 | 100.00 |
| ❑ BCP-5002 [M] | The Most Intimate Charlie Shavers | 1958 | 80.00 |
| CAPITOL | | | |
| ❑ ST 1883 [S] | Excitement Unlimited | 1963 | 25.00 |
| ❑ T 1883 [M] | Excitement Unlimited | 1963 | 20.00 |
| EVEREST | | | |
| ❑ SDBR-1070 [S] | Girl of My Dreams | 1960 | 25.00 |
| ❑ SDBR-1108 [S] | Here Comes Charlie | 1960 | 25.00 |
| ❑ SDBR-1127 [S] | Like Charlie | 1961 | 25.00 |
| ❑ LPBR-5070 [M] | Girl of My Dreams | 1960 | 20.00 |
| ❑ LPBR-5108 [M] | Here Comes Charlie | 1960 | 20.00 |
| ❑ LPBR-5127 [M] | Like Charlie | 1961 | 20.00 |
| JAZZTONE | | | |
| ❑ J-1229 [M] | Flow Gently, Sweet Rhythm | 1956 | 40.00 |
| MGM | | | |
| ❑ E-3765 [M] | Charlie Digs Paree | 1959 | 25.00 |
| ❑ SE-3765 [S] | Charlie Digs Paree | 1959 | 30.00 |
| ❑ E-3809 [M] | Charlie Digs Dixie | 1960 | 25.00 |
| ❑ SE-3809 [S] | Charlie Digs Dixie | 1960 | 30.00 |
| PERIOD | | | |
| ❑ SPL-1113 [10] | Flow Gently, Sweet Rhythm | 1955 | 120.00 |
| **SHAW, ARTIE** | | | |
| ALLEGRO | | | |
| ❑ 1405 [M] | An Hour with Artie Shaw | 1955 | 40.00 |
| ❑ 1466 [M] | Artie Shaw Hour | 1955 | 40.00 |
| ALLEGRO EILTE | | | |
| ❑ 4023 [10] | Artie Shaw Plays | 195? | 40.00 |
| ❑ 4107 [10] | Artie Shaw Plays Cole Porter | 195? | 40.00 |
| CLEF | | | |
| ❑ MGC-159 [10] | Artie Shaw and His Gramercy Five, Volume 1 | 1954 | 60.00 |
| ❑ MGC-160 [10] | Artie Shaw and His Gramercy Five, Volume 2 | 1954 | 60.00 |
| ❑ MGC-630 [M] | Artie Shaw and His Gramercy Five, Volume 3 | 1954 | 60.00 |
| ❑ MGC-645 [M] | Artie Shaw and His Gramercy Five, Volume 4 | 1955 | 60.00 |
| COLUMBIA MASTERWORKS | | | |
| ❑ ML 4260 [M] | Modern Music for Clarinet | 1950 | 50.00 |

| Number | Title (A Side/B Side) | Yr | NM |
|---|---|---|---|
| DECCA | | | |
| ❑ DL 5286 [10] | Artie Shaw Dance Program | 195? | 50.00 |
| ❑ DL 5524 [10] | Speak to Me of Love | 195? | 50.00 |
| ❑ DL 8309 [M] | Did Someone Say Party? | 1956 | 40.00 |
| *—Black label, silver print* | | | |
| EPIC | | | |
| ❑ LG 1006 [10] | Artie Shaw with Strings | 1954 | 50.00 |
| ❑ LG 1017 [10] | Non-Stop Flight | 1954 | 50.00 |
| ❑ LG 1102 [10] | Artie Shaw | 1955 | 50.00 |
| ❑ LN 3112 [M] | Artie Shaw with Strings | 1955 | 40.00 |
| ❑ LN 3150 [M] | Artie Shaw and His Orchestra | 1955 | 40.00 |
| LION | | | |
| ❑ L-70058 [M] | Artie Shaw Plays Irving Berlin and Cole Porter | 1958 | 25.00 |
| MGM | | | |
| ❑ E-517 [10] | Artie Shaw Plays Cole Porter | 1950 | 50.00 |
| RCA CAMDEN | | | |
| ❑ CAL-465 [M] | The Great Artie Shaw | 195? | 20.00 |
| ❑ CAL-584 [M] | One Night Stand | 1959 | 20.00 |
| ❑ CAL-908 [M] | September Song and Other Favorites | 196? | 20.00 |
| RCA VICTOR | | | |
| ❑ LPT-28 [10] | Artie Shaw Favorites | 195? | 50.00 |
| ❑ LPM-30 [10] | Four Star Favorites | 1955 | 50.00 |
| ❑ LPT-1020 [M] | My Concerto | 195? | 40.00 |
| ❑ LPM-1201 [M] | Both Feet in the Groove | 1956 | 40.00 |
| ❑ LPM-1217 [M] | Back Bay Shuffle | 1956 | 40.00 |
| ❑ LPM-1241 [M] | Artie Shaw and His Gramercy Five | 1956 | 40.00 |
| ❑ LPM-1244 [M] | Moonglow | 1956 | 40.00 |
| ❑ LPM-1570 [M] | Any Old Time | 1957 | 40.00 |
| ❑ LPM-1648 [M] | A Man and His Dream | 1957 | 40.00 |
| ❑ LPT-3013 [10] | This Is Artie Shaw | 1952 | 50.00 |
| ❑ LPM-3675 [M] | The Best of Artie Shaw | 1967 | 20.00 |
| ❑ LPT-6000 [(2)M] | In the Blue Room/In the Café Rouge | 195? | 50.00 |
| *—Originals are in a box; silver labels, red print* | | | |
| ❑ VPM-6062 [(2)] | This Is Artie Shaw, Volume 2 | 1976 | 12.00 |
| *—Black labels, dog near top* | | | |
| ROYALE | | | |
| ❑ 18135 [10] | The Best in Dance Music | 195? | 30.00 |
| VERVE | | | |
| ❑ MGV-2014 [M] | I Can't Get Started | 1956 | 40.00 |
| ❑ V-2014 [M] | I Can't Get Started | 1961 | 20.00 |

Number | Title (A Side/B Side) | Yr | NM

❑ MGV-2015 [M] Sequence in Music 1956 40.00
❑ V-2015 [M] Sequence in Music 1961 20.00

## SHAW, GENE

### ARGO

❑ LP-707 [M] Breakthrough 1962 25.00
❑ LPS-707 [S] Breakthrough 1962 30.00
❑ LP-726 [M] Debut In Blues 1963 25.00
❑ LPS-726 [S] Debut In Blues 1963 30.00
❑ LP-743 [M] Carnival Sketches 1964 25.00
❑ LPS-743 [S] Carnival Sketches 1964 30.00

## SHAW, MARLENA

### CADET

❑ LPS-803 Different Bags 1968 20.00
❑ LPS-833 Spice of Life 1969 20.00

## SHAW, ROBERT, CHORALE

### RCA VICTOR RED SEAL

❑ LM-1112 [M] Christmas Hymns and Carols 1952 30.00
*—Original has 2" brown border around all four sides of front cover*
❑ LM-1112 [M] Christmas Hymns and Carols, Volume I 1954 20.00
*—Mostly pink front cover with "Enhanced Sound" at top and under dog on label*
❑ LM-1711 [M] Christmas Hymns and Carols Vol. 2 195? 20.00
*—Pink "ornaments" cover; maroon label, large dog on top*
❑ LM-1711 [M] Christmas Hymns and Carols Volume II 1954 25.00
*—Original carolers cover; red label with outline of dog*
❑ LM-2139 [M] Christmas Hymns and Carols, Volume 1 1957 20.00
*—Original cover has "LM-2139" with "RCA Victor" in box on upper right*
❑ LM-2139 [M] Christmas Hymns and Carols, Volume 1 1958 16.00
*—Second cover has "LM-2139" in lower left corner; small "RE" is on front cover*
❑ LSC-2139 [S] Christmas Hymns and Carols, Volume 1 1958 20.00
*—Original with "shaded dog" label*
❑ LSC-2199 [S] A Mighty Fortress 1959 20.00
*—Original with "shaded dog" label*
❑ LSC-2231 [S] On Stage 1959 20.00
*—Original with "shaded dog" label*
❑ LSC-2247 [S] Deep River and Other Spirituals 1959 20.00
*—Original with "shaded dog" label*
❑ LSC-2273 [S] Bach, J.S.: Cantata 4 1959 20.00
*—Original with "shaded dog" label*
❑ LSC-2295 [S] The Stephen Foster Song Book 1959 20.00
*—Original with "shaded dog" label*
❑ LSC-2402 [S] A Chorus of Love 1960 20.00
*—Original with "shaded dog" label or second edition with "white dog" label*
❑ LSC-2403 [S] What Wondrous Love 1960 20.00
*—Original with "shaded dog" label*
❑ LSC-2416 [S] Operatic Choruses 1960 20.00
*—Original with "shaded dog" label*
❑ LSC-2551 [S] Sea Shanties 1961 30.00
*—Original with "shaded dog" label*
❑ LSC-2580 [S] I'm Goin' to Sing 1962 40.00
*—Original with "shaded dog" label*
❑ LSC-2598 [S] 23 Glee Club Favorites 1962 40.00
*—Original with "shaded dog" label*
❑ LM-2684 [M] The Many Moods of Christmas 1963 12.00
❑ LSC-2684 [S] The Many Moods of Christmas 1963 15.00

## SHAW, SANDIE

### REPRISE

❑ R-6166 [M] Sandie Shaw 1965 40.00
❑ RS-6166 [R] Sandie Shaw 1965 50.00
❑ R-6191 [M] Me 1966 30.00
❑ RS-6191 [S] Me 1966 40.00

## SHAW, SERENA

### RAMA

❑ RLP-5001 [M] Cry My Love 1956 400.00

## SHAW, WOODY

### CONTEMPORARY

❑ C-7627/8 [(2)] Blackstone Legacy 1971 20.00

### MOSAIC

❑ MR4-142 [(4)] The Complete CBS Studio Recordings of Woody Shaw 199? 80.00

## SHAWN, DICK

### 20TH CENTURY FOX

❑ TFM-3124 [M] Dick Shawn Sings with His Little People 1964 20.00
❑ TFS-4124 [S] Dick Shawn Sings with His Little People 1964 25.00

## SHAY, DOROTHY

### CAPITOL

❑ H 444 [10] Park Avenue Hillbilly 195? 50.00
❑ H 517 [10] Broadway Ditties 195? 50.00

### COLUMBIA

❑ CL 6003 [10] Dorothy Shay Sings 1948 50.00
*—With envelope-like cover*
❑ CL 6089 [10] Coming 'Round the Mountain 1950 50.00

### HARMONY

❑ HL 7017 [M] Coming 'Round the Mountain 195? 25.00

## SHEA, GEORGE BEVERLY

### RCA VICTOR

❑ LPM-1062 [M] Evening Vespers 1955 20.00
❑ LPM-1187 [M] Inspirational Songs 1955 20.00
❑ LPM-1235 [M] Sacred Songs 1956 20.00
❑ LPM-1349 [M] Evening Prayer 1956 20.00
❑ LPM-1406 [M] A Billy Graham Crusade in Song 1956 20.00
❑ LPM-1564 [M] George Beverly Shea 1957 20.00
❑ LPM-1642 [M] Through the Years 1957 20.00
❑ LSP-1949 [S] The Love of God 1958 20.00
❑ LSP-1967 [S] Blessed Assurance 1959 20.00
❑ LSP-2064 [S] Christmas Hymns 1959 20.00

## SHEARING, GEORGE

### CAPITOL

❑ T 648 [M] The Shearing Spell 1956 30.00
*—Turquoise label*
❑ T 648 [M] The Shearing Spell 1959 20.00
*—Black label with colorband, logo on left*
❑ T 720 [M] Velvet Carpet 1956 30.00
*—Turquoise label*
❑ T 720 [M] Velvet Carpet 1959 20.00
*—Black label with colorband, logo on left*
❑ T 737 [M] Latin Escapade 1957 30.00
*—Turquoise label*
❑ T 737 [M] Latin Escapade 1959 20.00
*—Black label with colorband, logo on left*
❑ ST 858 [S] Black Satin 1959 20.00
*—Black label with colorband, logo on left*
❑ T 858 [M] Black Satin 1957 30.00
*—Turquoise label*
❑ T 858 [M] Black Satin 1959 20.00
*—Black label with colorband, logo on left*
❑ T 909 [M] Shearing Piano 1957 30.00
*—Turquoise label*
❑ T 909 [M] Shearing Piano 1959 20.00
*—Black label with colorband, logo on left*
❑ T 943 [M] Night Mist 1957 30.00
*—Turquoise label*
❑ ST 1038 [S] Burnished Brass 1959 25.00
*—Black label with colorband, logo on left*
❑ ST 1038 [S] Burnished Brass 1962 20.00
*—Black label with colorband, logo on top*
❑ T 1038 [M] Burnished Brass 1958 20.00
*—Black label with colorband, logo on left*
❑ ST 1082 [S] Latin Lace 1958 25.00
*—Black label with colorband, logo on left*
❑ ST 1082 [S] Latin Lace 1962 20.00
*—Black label with colorband, logo on top*
❑ T 1082 [M] Latin Lace 1958 20.00
*—Black label with colorband, logo on left*
❑ ST 1124 [S] Blue Chiffon 1959 25.00
*—Black label with colorband, logo on left*
❑ ST 1124 [S] Blue Chiffon 1962 20.00
*—Black label with colorband, logo on top*
❑ T 1124 [M] Blue Chiffon 1959 20.00
*—Black label with colorband, logo on left*
❑ ST 1187 [S] George Shearing On Stage 1959 25.00
*—Black label with colorband, logo on left*
❑ ST 1187 [S] George Shearing On Stage 1962 20.00
*—Black label with colorband, logo on top*
❑ T 1187 [M] George Shearing On Stage 1959 20.00
*—Black label with colorband, logo on left*
❑ ST 1275 [S] Latin Affair 1960 25.00
*—Black label with colorband, logo on left*
❑ ST 1275 [S] Latin Affair 1962 20.00
*—Black label with colorband, logo on top*
❑ T 1275 [M] Latin Affair 1960 20.00
*—Black label with colorband, logo on left*
❑ ST 1334 [S] White Satin 1960 25.00
*—Black label with colorband, logo on left*
❑ ST 1334 [S] White Satin 1962 20.00
*—Black label with colorband, logo on top*
❑ T 1334 [M] White Satin 1960 20.00
*—Black label with colorband, logo on left*
❑ ST 1416 [S] On the Sunny Side of the Strip 1960 25.00
*—Black label with colorband, logo on left*
❑ ST 1416 [S] On the Sunny Side of the Strip 1962 20.00
*—Black label with colorband, logo on top*
❑ T 1416 [M] On the Sunny Side of the Strip 1960 20.00
*—Black label with colorband, logo on left*
❑ ST 1472 [S] The Shearing Touch 1961 25.00
*—Black label with colorband, logo on left*
❑ ST 1472 [S] The Shearing Touch 1962 20.00
*—Black label with colorband, logo on top*
❑ T 1472 [M] The Shearing Touch 1961 20.00
*—Black label with colorband, logo on left*
❑ ST 1567 [S] Mood Latino 1961 25.00
*—Black label with colorband, logo on left*
❑ ST 1567 [S] Mood Latino 1962 20.00
*—Black label with colorband, logo on top*
❑ T 1567 [M] Mood Latino 1961 20.00
*—Black label with colorband, logo on left*
❑ ST 1628 [S] Satin Affair 1961 25.00
*—Black label with colorband, logo on left*
❑ ST 1628 [S] Satin Affair 1962 20.00
*—Black label with colorband, logo on top*
❑ T 1628 [M] Satin Affair 1961 20.00
*—Black label with colorband, logo on left*
❑ ST 1715 [S] San Francisco Scene 1962 20.00
❑ ST 1755 [S] Concerto for My Love 1962 20.00
❑ ST 1827 [S] Jazz Moments 1963 20.00
❑ ST 1873 [S] Bossa Nova 1963 20.00
❑ ST 1874 [S] Touch Me Softly 1963 20.00

### DISCOVERY

❑ DL-3002 [10] George Shearing Quintet 1950 60.00

### LONDON

❑ LL 295 [10] Souvenirs 1951 60.00
❑ LL 1343 [M] By Request 1956 30.00

### MGM

❑ E-90 [10] A Touch of Genius 1951 50.00
❑ E-155 [10] I Hear Music 1952 50.00
❑ E-226 [10] When Lights Are Low 1953 50.00
❑ E-252 [10] An Evening with George Shearing 1954 50.00
❑ E-518 [10] You're Hearing the George Shearing Quartet 1950 60.00
❑ E-3122 [M] An Evening with Shearing 1955 30.00
❑ E-3175 [M] Shearing Caravan 1955 30.00
❑ E-3216 [M] You're Hearing George Shearing 1955 30.00
❑ E-3264 [M] When Lights Are Low 1955 30.00
❑ E-3265 [M] Touch of Genius 1955 30.00
❑ E-3266 [M] I Hear Music 1955 30.00
❑ E-3293 [M] Shearing in Hi-Fi 1955 30.00

### MOSAIC

❑ MQ7-157 [(7)] The Complete Capitol Live Recordings of George Shearing 199? 120.00

### SAVOY

❑ MG-15003 [10] Piano Solo 1951 60.00

## SHEARING, GEORGE, AND THE MONTGOMERY BROTHERS

### JAZZLAND

❑ JLP-55 [M] Love Walked In 1961 30.00
*—Cover has Shearing and the brothers*
❑ JLP-55 [M] Love Walked In 1962 25.00
*—Cover has a woman*
❑ JLP-955 [S] Love Walked In 1961 40.00
*—Cover has Shearing and the brothers*
❑ JLP-955 [S] Love Walked In 1962 30.00
*—Cover has a woman*

## SHEEN, MICKEY

### HERALD

❑ HLP-0105 [M] Have Swing, Will Travel 1956 60.00

## SHELDON, JACK

### CAPITOL

❑ ST 1851 [S] Out! 1963 20.00
❑ ST 2029 [S] Play Buddy, Play! 1966 20.00

### GENE NORMAN

❑ GNP-60 [M] Jack's Groove 1961 40.00

### JAZZ WEST

❑ JWLP-1 [10] Get Out of Town 1955 400.00
❑ JWLP-2 [10] Jack Sheldon Quintet 1955 400.00
❑ JWLP-6 [M] The Quartet and the Quintet 1956 30.00

### REPRISE

❑ R-2004 [M] A Jazz Profile of Ray Charles 1961 25.00
❑ R9-2004 [S] A Jazz Profile of Ray Charles 1961 30.00

## SHELTON, RICKY VAN

### COLUMBIA

❑ B6C 40602 Wild-Eyed Dream 1987 8.00
❑ FC 44221 Loving Proof 1988 8.00
❑ C 45250 RVS III 1990 15.00
❑ FC 45269 Ricky Van Shelton Sings Christmas 1989 12.00
❑ C 46855 Backroads 1990 20.00
*—Vinyl available only through Columbia House*

## SHELTON, ROSCOE

### EXCELLO

❑ LP-8002 [M] Roscoe Shelton Sings 1961 600.00

### SOUND STAGE 7

❑ SSS-5002 [M] Soul in His Music, Music in His Soul 1966 40.00
❑ SSS-15002 [S] Soul in His Music, Music in His Soul 1966 50.00

## SHENANDOAH

### COLUMBIA

❑ BFC 40788 Shenandoah 1987 10.00
❑ FC 44468 The Road Not Taken 1989 12.00
❑ C 48885 Greatest Hits 1992 20.00
*—Vinyl available only through Columbia House*

## SHEP AND THE LIMELITES

### HULL

❑ 1001 [M] Our Anniversary 1962 1200.

### ROULETTE

❑ R-25350 [M] Our Anniversary 1967 80.00
❑ SR-25350 [R] Our Anniversary 1967 50.00

## SHEPARD, JEAN

CAPITOL

| Number | Title (A Side/B Side) | Yr | NM |
|---|---|---|---|
| ❑ ST-171 | I'll Fly Away | 1969 | 15.00 |
| ❑ ST-321 | Seven Lonely Days | 1969 | 15.00 |
| ❑ ST-441 | Best By Request | 1970 | 15.00 |
| ❑ ST-559 | A Woman's Hand | 1970 | 15.00 |
| ❑ T 728 [M] | Songs of a Love Affair | 1956 | 60.00 |
| ❑ ST-738 | Here and Now | 1971 | 15.00 |
| ❑ ST-815 | Just As Soon As I Get Over Loving You | 1971 | 15.00 |
| ❑ T 1126 [M] | Lonesome Love | 1959 | 40.00 |
| ❑ T 1253 [M] | This Is Jean Shepard | 1959 | 40.00 |
| ❑ ST 1525 [S] | Got You on My Mind | 1961 | 30.00 |
| ❑ T 1525 [M] | Got You on My Mind | 1961 | 25.00 |
| ❑ ST 1663 [S] | Heartaches and Tears | 1962 | 30.00 |
| ❑ T 1663 [M] | Heartaches and Tears | 1962 | 25.00 |
| ❑ DT 1922 [R] | The Best of Jean Shepherd | 1963 | 15.00 |
| ❑ T 1922 [M] | The Best of Jean Shepherd | 1963 | 25.00 |
| ❑ ST 2187 [S] | Lighthearted and Blue | 1964 | 20.00 |
| ❑ T 2187 [M] | Lighthearted and Blue | 1964 | 15.00 |
| ❑ ST 2416 [S] | It's a Man Every Time | 1965 | 15.00 |
| ❑ T 2416 [M] | It's a Man Every Time | 1965 | 12.00 |
| ❑ ST 2547 [S] | Many Happy Hangovers | 1966 | 15.00 |
| ❑ T 2547 [M] | Many Happy Hangovers | 1966 | 12.00 |
| ❑ ST 2690 [S] | Heart, We Did All That We Could | 1967 | 15.00 |
| ❑ T 2690 [M] | Heart, We Did All That We Could | 1967 | 15.00 |
| ❑ ST 2765 [S] | Your Forevers Don't Last Very Long | 1967 | 15.00 |
| ❑ T 2765 [M] | Your Forevers Don't Last Very Long | 1967 | 20.00 |
| ❑ ST 2871 [S] | Heart to Heart | 1968 | 15.00 |
| ❑ T 2871 [M] | Heart to Heart | 1968 | 40.00 |
| ❑ ST 2966 | A Real Good Woman | 1968 | 15.00 |
| ❑ ST-11049 | Just Like Walkin' in the Sunshine | 1972 | 12.00 |
| ❑ SM-11409 | For the Good Times | 1975 | 10.00 |

HILLTOP

| Number | Title (A Side/B Side) | Yr | NM |
|---|---|---|---|
| ❑ JS-6068 | Under Your Spell Again | 197? | 10.00 |

UNITED ARTISTS

| Number | Title (A Side/B Side) | Yr | NM |
|---|---|---|---|
| ❑ UA-LA144-F | Slippin' Away | 1973 | 12.00 |
| ❑ UA-LA307-R | I'll Do Anything It Takes | 1974 | 12.00 |
| ❑ UA-LA363-G | Poor Sweet Baby and Ten More Bill Anderson Songs | 1975 | 12.00 |
| ❑ UA-LA525-G | I'm a Believer | 1975 | 12.00 |
| ❑ UA-LA609 | Mercy, Ain't Love Good | 1976 | 12.00 |
| ❑ UA-LA685-G | Jean Shepard's Greatest Hits | 1976 | 10.00 |

## SHEPARD, JEAN, AND RAY PILLOW

CAPITOL

| Number | Title (A Side/B Side) | Yr | NM |
|---|---|---|---|
| ❑ ST 2537 [S] | I'll Take the Dog | 1966 | 20.00 |
| ❑ T 2537 [M] | I'll Take the Dog | 1966 | 15.00 |

## SHEPARD, TOMMY

CORAL

| Number | Title (A Side/B Side) | Yr | NM |
|---|---|---|---|
| ❑ CRL 57110 [M] | Shepard's Flock | 1957 | 80.00 |

## SHEPHERD, CYBILL

PARAMOUNT

| Number | Title (A Side/B Side) | Yr | NM |
|---|---|---|---|
| ❑ PAS-1018 | Cybill Does It...to Cole Porter | 1974 | 20.00 |

*—With poster*

## SHEPHERD, JEAN

ELEKTRA

| Number | Title (A Side/B Side) | Yr | NM |
|---|---|---|---|
| ❑ EKL-172 [M] | Jean Shepherd and Other Foibles | 1959 | 50.00 |

## SHEPP, ARCHIE

ABC IMPULSE!

| Number | Title (A Side/B Side) | Yr | NM |
|---|---|---|---|
| ❑ AS-9154 [S] | The Magic of Ju Ju | 1968 | 20.00 |
| ❑ AS-9162 [S] | Three for a Quarter, One for a Dime | 1968 | 20.00 |
| ❑ AS-9170 [S] | The Way Ahead | 1969 | 20.00 |
| ❑ AS-9188 | For Losers | 1970 | 20.00 |

DELMARK

| Number | Title (A Side/B Side) | Yr | NM |
|---|---|---|---|
| ❑ DL-409 [M] | Archie Shepp in Europe | 1968 | 30.00 |
| ❑ DS-9409 [S] | Archie Shepp in Europe | 1968 | 20.00 |

IMPULSE!

| Number | Title (A Side/B Side) | Yr | NM |
|---|---|---|---|
| ❑ A-71 [M] | Four for Trane | 1964 | 25.00 |
| ❑ AS-71 [S] | Four for Trane | 1964 | 30.00 |
| ❑ A-86 [M] | Fire Music | 1965 | 25.00 |
| ❑ AS-86 [S] | Fire Music | 1965 | 30.00 |
| ❑ A-97 [M] | On This Night | 1966 | 30.00 |
| ❑ AS-97 [S] | On This Night | 1966 | 25.00 |
| ❑ A-9118 [M] | Live In San Francisco | 1967 | 30.00 |
| ❑ AS-9118 [S] | Live In San Francisco | 1967 | 25.00 |
| ❑ A-9134 [M] | Mama Too Tight | 1967 | 30.00 |
| ❑ AS-9134 [S] | Mama Too Tight | 1967 | 25.00 |

## SHEPP, ARCHIE, AND BILL DIXON

SAVOY

| Number | Title (A Side/B Side) | Yr | NM |
|---|---|---|---|
| ❑ MG-12178 [M] | The Archie Shepp-Bill Dixon Quartet | 1962 | 30.00 |
| ❑ MG-12184 [M] | Archie Shepp and the New Contemporary 5/The Bill Dixon 7-Tette | 1964 | 50.00 |

*—White bordered cover*

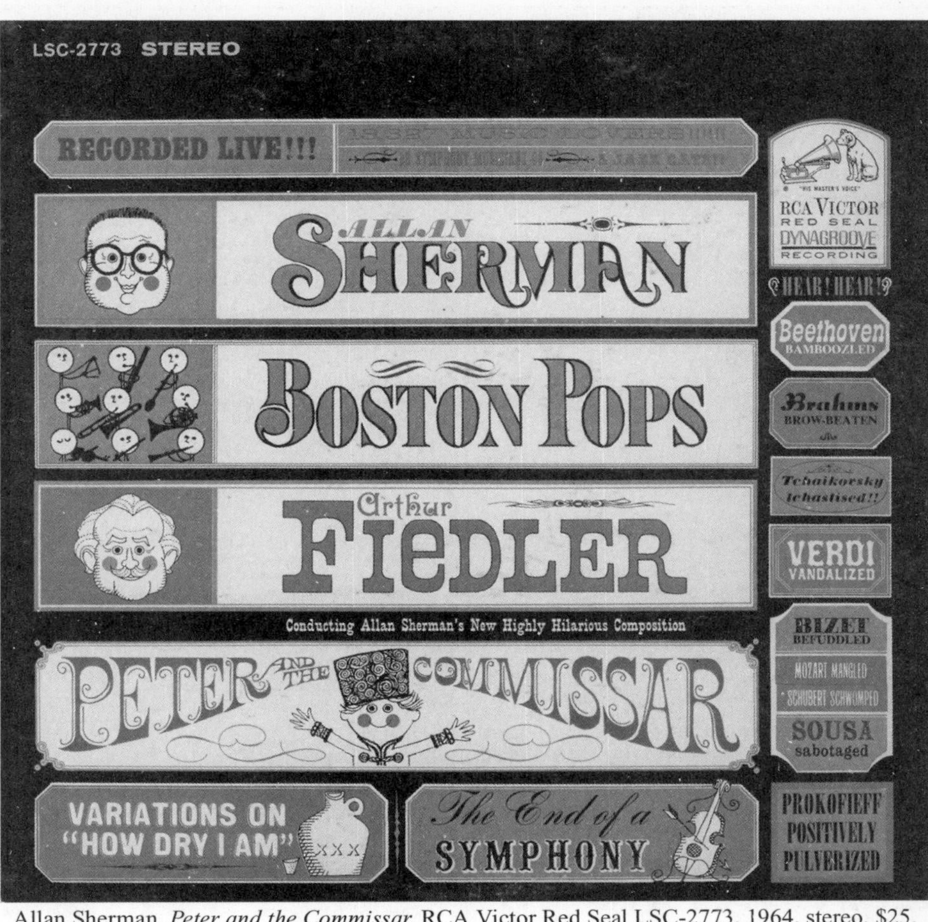


Allan Sherman, *Peter and the Commissar,* RCA Victor Red Seal LSC-2773, 1964, stereo, $25.

| Number | Title (A Side/B Side) | Yr | NM |
|---|---|---|---|
| ❑ MG-12184 [M] | Archie Shepp and the New Contemporary 5/The Bill Dixon 7-Tette | 1965 | 25.00 |

*—Purple bordered cover*

## SHEPPARDS, THE

COLLECTABLES

| Number | Title (A Side/B Side) | Yr | NM |
|---|---|---|---|
| ❑ COL-5078 | Golden Classics | 198? | 10.00 |

CONSTELLATION

| Number | Title (A Side/B Side) | Yr | NM |
|---|---|---|---|
| ❑ C-4 [M] | Collectors Showcase: The Sheppards | 1964 | 80.00 |
| ❑ CS-4 [R] | Collectors Showcase: The Sheppards | 1964 | 40.00 |

SOLID SMOKE

| Number | Title (A Side/B Side) | Yr | NM |
|---|---|---|---|
| ❑ SS-8004 | The Sheppards | 1980 | 10.00 |
| ❑ SS-8028 | 18 Dusty Diamonds | 1984 | 10.00 |

## SHERMAN, ALLAN

JUBLIEE

| Number | Title (A Side/B Side) | Yr | NM |
|---|---|---|---|
| ❑ JGM 5019 [M] | More Folk Songs by Allan Sherman | 1963 | 20.00 |

*—Two early Allan Sherman sides plus comedy bits by others*

RCA RED SEAL

| Number | Title (A Side/B Side) | Yr | NM |
|---|---|---|---|
| ❑ LM-2773 [M] | Peter and the Commissar | 1964 | 20.00 |
| ❑ LSC-2773 [S] | Peter and the Commissar | 1964 | 25.00 |

*—With Arthur Fiedler and the Boston Pops Orchestra*

RHINO

| Number | Title (A Side/B Side) | Yr | NM |
|---|---|---|---|
| ❑ RNLP-005 | The Best of Allan Sherman | 198? | 10.00 |
| ❑ RNLP 70818 | A Gift of Laughter | 1986 | 10.00 |

WARNER BROS.

| Number | Title (A Side/B Side) | Yr | NM |
|---|---|---|---|
| ❑ W 1475 [M] | My Son, the Folk Singer | 1962 | 15.00 |
| ❑ WS 1475 [S] | My Son, the Folk Singer | 1962 | 20.00 |
| *—Gold label* | | | |
| ❑ W 1487 [M] | My Son, the Celebrity | 1963 | 15.00 |
| ❑ WS 1487 [S] | My Son, the Celebrity | 1963 | 20.00 |
| *—Gold label* | | | |
| ❑ W 1501 [M] | My Son, the Nut | 1963 | 15.00 |
| ❑ WS 1501 [S] | My Son, the Nut | 1963 | 20.00 |
| *—Gold label* | | | |
| ❑ W 1539 [M] | Allan in Wonderland | 1964 | 12.00 |
| ❑ WS 1539 [S] | Allan in Wonderland | 1964 | 15.00 |
| *—Gold label* | | | |
| ❑ W 1569 [M] | For Swingin' Livers Only! | 1964 | 12.00 |
| ❑ WS 1569 [S] | For Swingin' Livers Only! | 1964 | 15.00 |
| ❑ W 1604 [M] | My Name Is Allan | 1965 | 12.00 |
| ❑ WS 1604 [S] | My Name Is Allan | 1965 | 15.00 |
| *—Gold label* | | | |
| ❑ W 1649 [M] | Allan Sherman — Live | 1966 | 12.00 |
| ❑ WS 1649 [S] | Allan Sherman — Live | 1966 | 15.00 |
| *—Gold label* | | | |
| ❑ W 1684 [M] | Togetherness | 1967 | 15.00 |
| ❑ WS 1684 [S] | Togetherness | 1967 | 20.00 |
| *—Gold label* | | | |

## SHERRILL, JOYA

COLUMBIA

| Number | Title (A Side/B Side) | Yr | NM |
|---|---|---|---|
| ❑ CL 1378 [M] | Sugar and Spice | 1959 | 25.00 |
| ❑ CS 8178 [S] | Sugar and Spice | 1960 | 30.00 |

20TH CENTURY FOX

| Number | Title (A Side/B Side) | Yr | NM |
|---|---|---|---|
| ❑ TFL-3170 [M] | Joya Sherrill Sings Duke Ellington | 196? | 25.00 |
| ❑ TFS-4170 [S] | Joya Sherrill Sings Duke Ellington | 196? | 30.00 |

## SHERRYS, THE

GUYDEN

| Number | Title (A Side/B Side) | Yr | NM |
|---|---|---|---|
| ❑ GLP 503 [M] | At the Hop with the Sherrys | 1963 | 250.00 |

## SHERWOOD, BOBBY

CAPITOL

| Number | Title (A Side/B Side) | Yr | NM |
|---|---|---|---|
| ❑ H 320 [10] | Classics in Jazz | 1952 | 60.00 |
| ❑ T 320 [M] | Classics in Jazz | 1955 | 40.00 |
| ❑ H 463 [10] | Bobby Sherwood | 1954 | 50.00 |

JUBILEE

| Number | Title (A Side/B Side) | Yr | NM |
|---|---|---|---|
| ❑ JLP-1040 [M] | I'm an Old Cowhand | 1957 | 30.00 |
| ❑ JLP-1061 [M] | Pal Joey | 1958 | 30.00 |
| ❑ SDJLP-1061 [S] | Pal Joey | 1959 | 25.00 |

## SHIGETA, JAMES

CHOREO

| Number | Title (A Side/B Side) | Yr | NM |
|---|---|---|---|
| ❑ A-7 [M] | We Speak the Same Language | 1962 | 25.00 |
| ❑ AS-7 [S] | We Speak the Same Language | 1962 | 30.00 |

## SHIHAB, SAHIB

ARGO

| Number | Title (A Side/B Side) | Yr | NM |
|---|---|---|---|
| ❑ LP-742 [M] | Summer Dawn | 1964 | 25.00 |
| ❑ LPS-742 [S] | Summer Dawn | 1964 | 30.00 |

SAVOY

| Number | Title (A Side/B Side) | Yr | NM |
|---|---|---|---|
| ❑ MG-12124 [M] | Jazz Sahib | 1957 | 50.00 |

### SHIHAB, SAHIB/HERBIE MANN

#### SAVOY

| Number | Title (A Side/B Side) | Yr | NM |
|---|---|---|---|
| ❑ MG-12112 [M] | The Jazz We Heard Last Summer | 1957 | 50.00 |

### SHILOH

#### AMOS

| Number | Title (A Side/B Side) | Yr | NM |
|---|---|---|---|
| ❑ AAS-7015 | Shiloh | 1971 | 80.00 |

### SHIP, THE

#### ELEKTRA

| Number | Title (A Side/B Side) | Yr | NM |
|---|---|---|---|
| ❑ EKS-75036 | The Ship | 1972 | 20.00 |

### SHIRELLES, THE

#### RCA VICTOR

| Number | Title (A Side/B Side) | Yr | NM |
|---|---|---|---|
| ❑ LSP-4581 | Happy and In Love | 1971 | 15.00 |
| ❑ LSP-4698 | The Shirelles | 1972 | 15.00 |

#### RHINO

| Number | Title (A Side/B Side) | Yr | NM |
|---|---|---|---|
| ❑ RNDA-1101 [(2)] | Anthology (1959-1967) | 1984 | 12.00 |

#### SCEPTER

| Number | Title (A Side/B Side) | Yr | NM |
|---|---|---|---|
| ❑ S-501 [M] | Tonight's the Night | 1961 | 200.00 |
| *—"Scepter" in scroll at top of label* | | | |
| ❑ SPM-501 [M] | Tonight's the Night | 1962 | 60.00 |
| *—"Scepter Records" at left of label* | | | |
| ❑ SPS-501 [S] | Tonight's the Night | 1965 | 100.00 |
| ❑ S-502 [M] | The Shirelles Sing to Trumpets and Strings | 1961 | 200.00 |
| *—"Scepter" in scroll at top of label* | | | |
| ❑ SPM-502 [M] | The Shirelles Sing to Trumpets and Strings | 1962 | 60.00 |
| *—"Scepter Records" at left of label* | | | |
| ❑ SPS-502 [S] | The Shirelles Sing to Trumpets and Strings | 1965 | 100.00 |
| ❑ SPM-504 [M] | Baby It's You | 1962 | 100.00 |
| ❑ SPS-504 [S] | Baby It's You | 1965 | 100.00 |
| ❑ SPM-505 [M] | A Twist Party | 1962 | 80.00 |
| ❑ SPS-505 [S] | A Twist Party | 1965 | 100.00 |
| ❑ SPM-507 [M] | The Shirelles' Greatest Hits | 1962 | 40.00 |
| ❑ SPS-507 [S] | The Shirelles' Greatest Hits | 1965 | 50.00 |
| ❑ SPM-511 [M] | Foolish Little Girl | 1963 | 50.00 |
| ❑ SPS-511 [S] | Foolish Little Girl | 1965 | 80.00 |
| ❑ SPM-514 [M] | It's a Mad, Mad, Mad, Mad World | 1963 | 40.00 |
| ❑ SPS-514 [S] | It's a Mad, Mad, Mad, Mad World | 1963 | 50.00 |
| ❑ SPM-516 [M] | The Shirelles Sing the Golden Oldies | 1964 | 40.00 |
| ❑ SPS-516 [S] | The Shirelles Sing the Golden Oldies | 1964 | 50.00 |
| ❑ SPM-560 [M] | The Shirelles' Greatest Hits, Volume 2 | 1967 | 20.00 |
| ❑ SPS-560 [S] | The Shirelles' Greatest Hits, Volume 2 | 1967 | 25.00 |
| ❑ SPM-562 [M] | Spontaneous Combustion | 1967 | 40.00 |
| ❑ SPS-562 [S] | Spontaneous Combustion | 1967 | 50.00 |
| ❑ SPS-569 | Eternally Soul | 1968 | 30.00 |
| ❑ SPS-2-599 [(2)] | Remember When | 1972 | 20.00 |

#### SPRINGBOARD

| Number | Title (A Side/B Side) | Yr | NM |
|---|---|---|---|
| ❑ 4006 | The Shirelles Sing Their Very Best | 1973 | 8.00 |

#### UNITED ARTISTS

| Number | Title (A Side/B Side) | Yr | NM |
|---|---|---|---|
| ❑ UA-LA340-E | The Very Best of the Shirelles | 1974 | 10.00 |

### SHIRLEY, DON

#### AUDIO FIDELITY

| Number | Title (A Side/B Side) | Yr | NM |
|---|---|---|---|
| ❑ AFLP-1897 [M] | Don Shirley | 1959 | 20.00 |
| ❑ AFSD-5897 [S] | Don Shirley | 1959 | 30.00 |

#### CADENCE

| Number | Title (A Side/B Side) | Yr | NM |
|---|---|---|---|
| ❑ CLP-1001 [M] | Tonal Expressions | 1955 | 40.00 |
| ❑ CLP-1004 [M] | Piano Perspectives | 1955 | 40.00 |
| ❑ CLP-1009 [M] | Orpheus in the Underworld | 1956 | 40.00 |
| ❑ CLP-1015 [M] | Don Shirley Duo | 1956 | 40.00 |
| ❑ CLP-3007 [M] | Don Shirley Solos | 1958 | 30.00 |
| ❑ CLP-3008 [M] | Don Shirley with Two Basses | 1958 | 30.00 |
| ❑ CLP-3032 [M] | Don Shirley Plays Gershwin | 1960 | 25.00 |
| ❑ CLP-3033 [M] | Don Shirley Plays Standards | 1960 | 25.00 |
| ❑ CLP-3034 [M] | Don Shirley Plays Love Songs | 1960 | 25.00 |
| ❑ CLP-3035 [M] | Don Shirley Plays Birdland Lullabies | 1960 | 25.00 |
| ❑ CLP-3036 [M] | Don Shirley Plays Showtunes | 1960 | 25.00 |
| ❑ CLP-3037 [M] | Orpheus in the Underworld | 1960 | 25.00 |
| *—Reissue of 1009* | | | |
| ❑ CLP-3046 [M] | Trio | 1961 | 20.00 |
| ❑ CLP-3048 [M] | Pianist Extraordinary | 1962 | 20.00 |
| ❑ CLP-3049 [M] | Piano Arrangements of Spirituals | 1962 | 20.00 |
| ❑ CLP-3057 [M] | Drown in My Own Tears | 1962 | 20.00 |
| ❑ CLP-25046 [S] | Trio | 1961 | 30.00 |
| ❑ CLP-25048 [S] | Pianist Extraordinary | 1962 | 30.00 |
| ❑ CLP-25049 [S] | Piano Arrangements of Spirituals | 1962 | 30.00 |
| ❑ CLP-25057 [S] | Drown in My Own Tears | 1962 | 30.00 |

#### COLUMBIA

| Number | Title (A Side/B Side) | Yr | NM |
|---|---|---|---|
| ❑ CL 2396 [M] | Water Boy | 1965 | 15.00 |
| ❑ CS 9196 [S] | Water Boy | 1965 | 20.00 |

### SHIRLEY AND LEE

#### ALADDIN

| Number | Title (A Side/B Side) | Yr | NM |
|---|---|---|---|
| ❑ 807 [M] | Let the Good Times Roll | 1956 | 1500. |

#### IMPERIAL

| Number | Title (A Side/B Side) | Yr | NM |
|---|---|---|---|
| ❑ LP-9179 [M] | Let the Good Times Roll | 1962 | 300.00 |
| *—Reissue of Aladdin LP* | | | |

#### SCORE

| Number | Title (A Side/B Side) | Yr | NM |
|---|---|---|---|
| ❑ SLP-4023 [M] | Let the Good Times Roll | 1957 | 800.00 |
| *—Reissue of Aladdin LP* | | | |

#### WARWICK

| Number | Title (A Side/B Side) | Yr | NM |
|---|---|---|---|
| ❑ W-2028 [M] | Let the Good Times Roll | 1961 | 150.00 |
| ❑ W-2028ST [S] | Let the Good Times Roll | 1961 | 300.00 |

### SHIVA'S HEADBAND

#### APE

| Number | Title (A Side/B Side) | Yr | NM |
|---|---|---|---|
| ❑ 1001 | Psychedelic Yesterday | 1981 | 20.00 |

#### ARMADILLO

| Number | Title (A Side/B Side) | Yr | NM |
|---|---|---|---|
| ❑ (no #) | Coming to a Head | 1969 | 250.00 |

#### CAPITOL

| Number | Title (A Side/B Side) | Yr | NM |
|---|---|---|---|
| ❑ ST-538 | Take Me to the Mountains | 1970 | 60.00 |

### SHOCKED, MICHELLE

#### MERCURY

| Number | Title (A Side/B Side) | Yr | NM |
|---|---|---|---|
| ❑ PRO 797 [DJ] | Live | 1990 | 20.00 |
| *—Five-song mini-LP for radio stations with custom jacket* | | | |
| ❑ 834581-1 | The Texas Campfire Tapes | 1988 | 12.00 |
| ❑ 834924-1 | Short Sharp Shocked | 1988 | 10.00 |
| ❑ 838878-1 | Captain Swing | 1989 | 10.00 |

### SHOCKING BLUE, THE

#### COLOSSUS

| Number | Title (A Side/B Side) | Yr | NM |
|---|---|---|---|
| ❑ CS-1000 | The Shocking Blue | 1970 | 25.00 |

### SHOES

#### (NO LABEL)

| Number | Title (A Side/B Side) | Yr | NM |
|---|---|---|---|
| ❑ (no #) | One in Versailles | 1976 | 120.00 |

#### BLACK VINYL

| Number | Title (A Side/B Side) | Yr | NM |
|---|---|---|---|
| ❑ 51477 | Black Vinyl Shoes | 1977 | 80.00 |

#### ELEKTRA

| Number | Title (A Side/B Side) | Yr | NM |
|---|---|---|---|
| ❑ 6E-244 | Present Tense | 1979 | 10.00 |
| ❑ 6E-303 | Tongue Twister | 1980 | 10.00 |
| ❑ AS 11570 [DJ] | Shoes on Ice — Live | 1982 | 50.00 |
| *—Promo-only 7-song live record; issued in generic jacket* | | | |
| ❑ 60146 | Boomerang | 1982 | 10.00 |

#### PVC

| Number | Title (A Side/B Side) | Yr | NM |
|---|---|---|---|
| ❑ 7904 | Black Vinyl Shoes | 1979 | 20.00 |

### SHONDELL, TROY

#### EVEREST

| Number | Title (A Side/B Side) | Yr | NM |
|---|---|---|---|
| ❑ 1206 [S] | The Many Sides of Troy Shondell | 1963 | 80.00 |
| ❑ 5206 [M] | The Many Sides of Troy Shondell | 1963 | 50.00 |

#### SUNSET

| Number | Title (A Side/B Side) | Yr | NM |
|---|---|---|---|
| ❑ SUM-1174 [M] | This Time | 1967 | 15.00 |
| ❑ SUS-5174 [S] | This Time | 1967 | 15.00 |

### SHORE, DINAH

#### BAINBRIDGE

| Number | Title (A Side/B Side) | Yr | NM |
|---|---|---|---|
| ❑ 6232 | Once Upon a Summertime | 198? | 10.00 |

#### CAPITOL

| Number | Title (A Side/B Side) | Yr | NM |
|---|---|---|---|
| ❑ ST 1247 [S] | Dinah, Yes Indeed | 1959 | 25.00 |
| ❑ T 1247 [M] | Dinah, Yes Indeed | 1959 | 20.00 |
| ❑ ST 1296 [S] | Somebody Loves Me | 1959 | 25.00 |
| ❑ T 1296 [M] | Somebody Loves Me | 1959 | 20.00 |
| ❑ ST 1354 [S] | Dinah Sings Some Blues with Red | 1960 | 30.00 |
| ❑ T 1354 [M] | Dinah Sings Some Blues with Red | 1960 | 25.00 |
| ❑ ST 1422 [S] | Dinah Sings/Previn Plays | 1960 | 25.00 |
| ❑ T 1422 [M] | Dinah Sings/Previn Plays | 1960 | 20.00 |
| ❑ ST 1655 [S] | Dinah Down Home | 1962 | 25.00 |
| ❑ T 1655 [M] | Dinah Down Home | 1962 | 20.00 |
| ❑ ST 1704 [S] | The Fabulous Hits of Dinah Shore | 1962 | 15.00 |
| *—Black label with colorband, logo at top* | | | |
| ❑ ST 1704 [S] | The Fabulous Hits of Dinah Shore | 1962 | 25.00 |
| *—Black label with colorband, logo at left* | | | |
| ❑ T 1704 [M] | The Fabulous Hits of Dinah Shore | 1962 | 12.00 |
| *—Black label with colorband, logo at top* | | | |
| ❑ T 1704 [M] | The Fabulous Hits of Dinah Shore | 1962 | 20.00 |
| *—Black label with colorband, logo at left* | | | |

#### COLUMBIA

| Number | Title (A Side/B Side) | Yr | NM |
|---|---|---|---|
| ❑ CL 6004 [10] | Dinah Shore Sings | 1949 | 50.00 |
| ❑ CL 6069 [10] | Reminiscing | 1949 | 50.00 |
| ❑ C 34395 | The Best of Dinah Shore | 1977 | 10.00 |

#### HARMONY

| Number | Title (A Side/B Side) | Yr | NM |
|---|---|---|---|
| ❑ HL 7010 [M] | Dinah Shore Sings Cole Porter and Richard Rodgers | 195? | 20.00 |
| ❑ HL 7188 [M] | Buttons and Bows | 195? | 15.00 |
| ❑ HL 7239 [M] | Lavender Blue | 1959 | 15.00 |

#### PICKWICK

| Number | Title (A Side/B Side) | Yr | NM |
|---|---|---|---|
| ❑ SPC-3524 | It's So Nice to Have a Man Around the House | 197? | 8.00 |

#### PROJECT 3

| Number | Title (A Side/B Side) | Yr | NM |
|---|---|---|---|
| ❑ PR-5018 SD | Songs for Sometime Losers | 1968 | 15.00 |

#### RCA CAMDEN

| Number | Title (A Side/B Side) | Yr | NM |
|---|---|---|---|
| ❑ CAL-477 [M] | I'm Your Girl | 1959 | 15.00 |
| ❑ CAL-572 [M] | Vivacious Dinah Shore | 1960 | 15.00 |

#### RCA VICTOR

| Number | Title (A Side/B Side) | Yr | NM |
|---|---|---|---|
| ❑ LPM-1154 [M] | Holding Hands at Midnight | 1955 | 30.00 |
| ❑ ANL1-1158 | The Best of Dinah Shore | 1976 | 10.00 |
| ❑ LPM-1214 [M] | Bouquet of Blues | 1956 | 30.00 |
| ❑ LPM-1719 [M] | Moments Like These | 1958 | 25.00 |
| ❑ LPM-3103 [10] | Dinah Shore Sings the Blues | 1953 | 40.00 |
| ❑ LPM-3214 [10] | The Dinah Shore TV Show | 1954 | 40.00 |

#### REPRISE

| Number | Title (A Side/B Side) | Yr | NM |
|---|---|---|---|
| ❑ R-6150 [M] | The Lower East Side Revisited | 1965 | 12.00 |
| ❑ RS-6150 [S] | The Lower East Side Revisited | 1965 | 15.00 |

#### SEAGULL

| Number | Title (A Side/B Side) | Yr | NM |
|---|---|---|---|
| ❑ LG-8203 | Oh Lonesome Me | 198? | 10.00 |

#### STANYAN

| Number | Title (A Side/B Side) | Yr | NM |
|---|---|---|---|
| ❑ 10071 | Dinah Sings the Blues | 197? | 10.00 |
| ❑ 10125 | Once Upon a Summertime | 197? | 10.00 |
| ❑ 10139 | For Always | 1977 | 10.00 |

### SHORT, BOBBY

#### ATLANTIC

| Number | Title (A Side/B Side) | Yr | NM |
|---|---|---|---|
| ❑ SD 2-606 [(2)] | Bobby Short Loves Cole Porter | 1972 | 20.00 |
| ❑ SD 2-607 [(2)] | Mad About Noel Coward | 1972 | 20.00 |
| ❑ 1214 [M] | Songs by Bobby Short | 1955 | 30.00 |
| *—Black label* | | | |
| ❑ 1214 [M] | Songs by Bobby Short | 1961 | 20.00 |
| *—White "fan" logo at right of label* | | | |
| ❑ 1230 [M] | Bobby Short | 1956 | 30.00 |
| *—Black label* | | | |
| ❑ 1230 [M] | Bobby Short | 1961 | 20.00 |
| *—White "fan" logo at right of label* | | | |
| ❑ 1262 [M] | Speaking of Love | 1958 | 30.00 |
| *—Black label* | | | |
| ❑ 1262 [M] | Speaking of Love | 1961 | 20.00 |
| *—White "fan" logo at right of label* | | | |
| ❑ SD 1262 [S] | Speaking of Love | 1959 | 40.00 |
| *—Green label* | | | |
| ❑ SD 1262 [S] | Speaking of Love | 1961 | 25.00 |
| *—White "fan" logo at right of label* | | | |
| ❑ 1285 [M] | Sing Me a Swing Song | 1958 | 30.00 |
| *—Black label* | | | |
| ❑ 1285 [M] | Sing Me a Swing Song | 1961 | 20.00 |
| *—White "fan" logo at right of label* | | | |
| ❑ 1302 [M] | The Mad Twenties | 1959 | 30.00 |
| *—Black label* | | | |
| ❑ 1302 [M] | The Mad Twenties | 1961 | 20.00 |
| *—White "fan" logo at right of label* | | | |
| ❑ SD 1302 [S] | The Mad Twenties | 1959 | 40.00 |
| *—Green label* | | | |
| ❑ SD 1302 [S] | The Mad Twenties | 1961 | 25.00 |
| *—White "fan" logo at right of label* | | | |
| ❑ SD 1302 [S] | The Mad Twenties | 1963 | 20.00 |
| *—Black "fan" logo at right of label* | | | |
| ❑ 1321 [M] | On the East Side | 1960 | 30.00 |
| *—Black label* | | | |
| ❑ 1321 [M] | On the East Side | 1961 | 20.00 |
| *—White "fan" logo at right of label* | | | |
| ❑ SD 1321 [S] | On the East Side | 1960 | 40.00 |
| *—Green label* | | | |
| ❑ SD 1321 [S] | On the East Side | 1961 | 25.00 |
| *—White "fan" logo at right of label* | | | |
| ❑ SD 1321 [S] | On the East Side | 1963 | 20.00 |
| *—Black "fan" logo at right of label* | | | |
| ❑ 81715 [(4)] | 50 from Bobby Short | 1987 | 30.00 |

### SHORTER, ALAN

#### VERVE

| Number | Title (A Side/B Side) | Yr | NM |
|---|---|---|---|
| ❑ V6-8769 | Orgasm | 1969 | 20.00 |

### SHORTER, WAYNE

#### BLUE NOTE

| Number | Title (A Side/B Side) | Yr | NM |
|---|---|---|---|
| ❑ BLP-4173 [M] | Night Drreamer | 1964 | 25.00 |
| ❑ BLP-4182 [M] | Juju | 1965 | 25.00 |
| ❑ BLP-4194 [M] | Speak No Evil | 1966 | 25.00 |
| ❑ BLP-4219 [M] | The All Seeing Eye | 1966 | 25.00 |
| ❑ BST-84173 [S] | Night Drreamer | 1964 | 30.00 |
| *—With New York, USA address on label* | | | |
| ❑ BST-84182 [S] | Juju | 1965 | 30.00 |
| *—With New York, USA address on label* | | | |
| ❑ BST-84194 [S] | Speak No Evil | 1966 | 30.00 |
| *—With New York, USA address on label* | | | |
| ❑ BST-84219 [S] | The All Seeing Eye | 1966 | 30.00 |
| *—With New York, USA address on label* | | | |
| ❑ BST-84232 | Adam's Apple | 1967 | 20.00 |
| ❑ BST-84297 | Schizophrenia | 1969 | 20.00 |
| ❑ BST-84332 | Super Nova | 1970 | 20.00 |

#### VEE JAY

| Number | Title (A Side/B Side) | Yr | NM |
|---|---|---|---|
| ❑ LP-3006 [M] | Introducing Wayne Shorter | 1960 | 40.00 |
| ❑ SR-3006 [S] | Introducing Wayne Shorter | 1960 | 50.00 |



**Except when noted otherwise, VG = 25% of NM, and VG+ = 50% of NM. (Example: VG = $2.00, VG+ = $4.00 and NM = $8.00.)**

Number | Title (A Side/B Side) | Yr | NM

❑ LP-3029 [M] Wayning Moments 1962 30.00
❑ SR-3029 [S] Wayning Moments 1962 40.00
❑ LP-3057 [M] Second Genesis 1963 30.00
❑ SR-3057 [S] Second Genesis 1963 40.00

**SHOTGUN LTD.**

PROPHESY
❑ 6050 Shotgun Ltd. 1971 20.00

**SHQ**

ESP-DISK'
❑ 1080 [S] The Uhu Sleeps Only During the Day 1969 30.00

**SHRINER, HERB**

COLUMBIA
❑ CL 774 [M] Herb Shriner On Stage 1957 30.00

DOT
❑ DLP-3149 [M] Polka Dot Party 1959 30.00
❑ DLP-25149 [S] Polka Dot Party 1959 40.00

**SHU, EDDIE**

BETHLEHEM
❑ BCP-1013 [10] I Only Have Eyes For Shu 1954 100.00

**SHU, EDDIE/BOB HARDAWAY**

BETHLEHEM
❑ BCP-3 [M] Jazz Practitioners 1957 80.00

**SHU, EDDIE/JOE ROLAND/"WILD" BILL DAVIS**

MERCER
❑ LP-1002 [10] New Stars, New Sounds, Volume 1 1951 150.00

**SHULMAN, JOEL**

JAMAL
❑ 5162 Peninah 197? 20.00

**SICKNICKS, THE**

AMY
❑ 2 [M] Sick #2 1961 30.00

**SIDEKICKS, THE**

RCA VICTOR
❑ LPM-3712 [M] Fifi the Flea 1966 20.00
❑ LSP-3712 [S] Fifi the Flea 1966 25.00

**SIDEWINDERS, THE**

RCA VICTOR
❑ LSP-4694 The Sidewinders 1972 20.00

**SIDRAN, BEN**

CAPITOL
❑ ST-825 Feel Your Groove 1971 50.00

**SIEGEL-SCHWALL BAND, THE**

VANGUARD
❑ VSD-6562 Siegel-Schwall '70 1970 20.00
❑ VRS-9235 [M] The Siegel-Schwall Band 1966 20.00
❑ VRS-9249 [M] Say Siegel-Schwall 1967 25.00
❑ VSD-79235 [S] The Siegel-Schwall Band 1966 25.00
❑ VSD-79249 [S] Say Siegel-Schwall 1967 20.00
❑ VSD-79289 Shake! 1968 20.00

WOODEN NICKEL
❑ BWL1-0121 953 West 1973 20.00
❑ BWL1-0288 Last Summer — Live 1974 20.00
❑ BWL1-0554 R.I.P. 1974 20.00
❑ WNS-1002 The Siegel-Schwall Band 1971 25.00
❑ WNS-1010 Sleepy Hollow 1972 25.00

**SIGLER, BUNNY**

GOLD MIND
❑ 7502 Let Me Party with You 1978 12.00
❑ 9503 I've Always Wanted to Sing... Not Just Write Songs 1979 12.00

PARKWAY
❑ P-50000 [M] Let the Good Times Roll 1967 40.00
❑ PS-50000 [S] Let the Good Times Roll 1967 40.00

PHILADELPHIA INT'L.
❑ KZ 32589 That's How Long I'll Be Loving You 1974 15.00
❑ KZ 33249 Keep Smilin' 1974 15.00
❑ PZ 34267 My Music 1976 15.00

SALSOUL
❑ SA-8531 Let It Snow 1980 12.00

**SIGNATURES, THE**

WARNER BROS.
❑ W 1250 [M] The Signatures Sing In 1958 30.00
❑ WS 1250 [S] The Signatures Sing In 1958 40.00
❑ W 1353 [M] Prepare to Flip! 1959 30.00
❑ WS 1353 [S] Prepare to Flip! 1959 40.00

WHIPPET
❑ WLP-702 [M] The Signatures — Their Voices and Instruments 1957 60.00

Number | Title (A Side/B Side) | Yr | NM

**SIGNORELLI, FRANK**

DAVIS
❑ JD-103 [M] Piano Moods 1951 50.00

**SILHOUETTES, THE**

GOODWAY
❑ GLP-100 The Silhouettes 1958-1968/ Get a Job 1968 300.00

**SILK**

ABC
❑ S-694 Smooth As Raw Silk 1969 25.00

**SILKIE, THE**

FONTANA
❑ MGF 27548 [M] You've Got to Hide Your Love Away 1965 40.00
*—With purplish, black and white cover*
❑ MGF 27548 [M] You've Got to Hide Your Love Away 1965 50.00
*—With full-color cover*
❑ SRF 67548 [R] You've Got to Hide Your Love Away 1965 30.00
*—With purplish, black and white cover*
❑ SRF 67548 [R] You've Got to Hide Your Love Away 1965 40.00
*—With full-color cover*

**SILLY SURFERS, THE**

MERCURY
❑ MG-20977 [M] The Sounds of the Silly Surfers 1965 80.00
❑ SR-60977 [S] The Sounds of the Silly Surfers 1965 100.00

**SILLY SURFERS, THE / THE WEIRD-OHS**

HAIRY
❑ 101 [M] The Sounds of the Silly Surfers/ The Sounds of the Weird-Ohs 1964 150.00

**SILVA, ALAN**

ESP-DISK'
❑ 1091 [S] Alan Silva 1969 20.00

**SILVER, HORACE**

BLUE NOTE
❑ BN-LA402-H2 [(2)] Horace Silver 1975 25.00
❑ BLP-1518 [M] Horace Silver and the Jazz Messengers 1956 300.00
*—"Deep groove" edition, W. 63rd St. address on label*
❑ BLP-1518 [M] Horace Silver and the Jazz Messengers 1956 600.00
*—"Deep groove" version; Lexington Ave. address on label*
❑ BLP-1518 [M] Horace Silver and the Jazz Messengers 1963 50.00
*—"New York, USA" address on label*
❑ BLP-1520 [M] Spotlight on Drums 1956 300.00
*—"Deep groove" edition, W. 63rd St. address on label*
❑ BLP-1520 [M] Spotlight on Drums 1956 600.00
*—"Deep groove" version; Lexington Ave. address on label*
❑ BLP-1520 [M] Spotlight on Drums 1963 50.00
*—"New York, USA" address on label*
❑ BLP-1539 [M] Six Pieces of Silver 1957 200.00
*—"Deep groove" edition, W. 63rd St. address on label*
❑ BLP-1539 [M] Six Pieces of Silver 1957 600.00
*—"Deep groove" version; Lexington Ave. address on label*
❑ BLP-1539 [M] Six Pieces of Silver 1963 50.00
*—"New York, USA" address on label*
❑ BLP-1562 [M] The Stylings of Silver 1957 120.00
*—Regular edition, W. 63rd St. address on label*
❑ BLP-1562 [M] The Stylings of Silver 1957 250.00
*—"Deep groove" version; W. 63rd St. address on label*
❑ BLP-1562 [M] The Stylings of Silver 1963 40.00
*—"New York, USA" address on label*
❑ BST-1562 [S] The Stylings of Silver 1959 100.00
*—Regular edition, W. 63rd St. address on label*
❑ BST-1562 [S] The Stylings of Silver 1959 200.00
*—"Deep groove" version; W. 63rd St. address on label*
❑ BST-1562 [S] The Stylings of Silver 1963 40.00
*—"New York, USA" address on label*
❑ BLP-1589 [M] Further Explorations 1958 120.00
*—Regular edition, W. 63rd St. address on label*
❑ BLP-1589 [M] Further Explorations 1958 200.00
*—"Deep groove" version; W. 63rd St. address on label*
❑ BLP-1589 [M] Further Explorations 1963 40.00
*—"New York, USA" address on label*
❑ BST-1589 [S] Further Explorations 1959 100.00
*—Regular edition, W. 63rd St. address on label*
❑ BST-1589 [S] Further Explorations 1959 150.00
*—"Deep groove" version; W. 63rd St. address on label*
❑ BST-1589 [S] Further Explorations 1963 40.00
*—"New York, USA" address on label*
❑ BLP-4008 [M] Finger Poppin' 1959 120.00
*—Regular edition, W. 63rd St. address on label*
❑ BLP-4008 [M] Finger Poppin' 1959 200.00
*—"Deep groove" version; W. 63rd St. address on label*
❑ BLP-4008 [M] Finger Poppin' 1963 40.00
*—"New York, USA" address on label*
❑ BST-4008 [S] Finger Poppin' 1959 100.00
*—Regular edition, W. 63rd St. address on label*
❑ BST-4008 [S] Finger Poppin' 1959 150.00
*—"Deep groove" version; W. 63rd St. address on label*

Number | Title (A Side/B Side) | Yr | NM

❑ BST-4008 [S] Finger Poppin' 1963 40.00
*—"New York, USA" address on label*
❑ BLP-4017 [M] Blowin' the Blues Away 1959 120.00
*—Regular edition, W. 63rd St. address on label*
❑ BLP-4017 [M] Blowin' the Blues Away 1959 200.00
*—"Deep groove" version; W. 63rd St. address on label*
❑ BLP-4017 [M] Blowin' the Blues Away 1963 40.00
*—"New York, USA" address on label*
❑ BLP-4042 [M] Horace-Scope 1960 120.00
*—Regular edition, W. 63rd St. address on label*
❑ BLP-4042 [M] Horace-Scope 1960 200.00
*—"Deep groove" version; W. 63rd St. address on label*
❑ BLP-4042 [M] Horace-Scope 1963 40.00
*—"New York, USA" address on label*
❑ BLP-4076 [M] Doin' the Thing at the Village Gate 1961 150.00
*—W. 63rd St. address on label*
❑ BLP-4076 [M] Doin' the Thing at the Village Gate 1963 80.00
*—"New York, USA" address on label*
❑ BLP-4110 [M] The Tokyo Blues 1962 100.00
*—"New York, USA" on label*
❑ BLP-4131 [M] Silver's Serenade 1963 100.00
*—"New York, USA" on label*
❑ BLP-4185 [M] Song for My Father (Cantiga Para Meu Pai) 1965 100.00
*—"New York, USA" on label*
❑ BLP-4220 [M] The Cape Verdean Blues 1965 100.00
❑ BLP-4250 [M] The Jody Grind 1966 80.00
*—"A Division of Liberty Records" on label*
❑ BLP-5018 [10] New Faces 1953 800.00
❑ BLP-5034 [10] Horace Silver Trio, Vol. 2 1954 800.00
❑ BLP-5058 [10] Horace Silver Quintet 1955 700.00
❑ BLP-5062 [10] Horace Silver Quintet 1955 700.00
❑ BST-84017 [S] Blowin' the Blues Away 1959 120.00
*—W. 63rd St. address on label*
❑ BST-84017 [S] Blowin' the Blues Away 1963 40.00
*—"New York, USA" address on label*
❑ BST-84042 [S] Horace-Scope 1960 120.00
*—W. 63rd St. address on label*
❑ BST-84042 [S] Horace-Scope 1963 40.00
*—"New York, USA" address on label*
❑ BST-84076 [S] Doin' the Thing at the Village Gate 1961 120.00
*—W. 63rd St. address on label*
❑ BST-84076 [S] Doin' the Thing at the Village Gate 1963 80.00
*—"New York, USA" address on label*
❑ BST-84110 [S] The Tokyo Blues 1962 80.00
*—"New York, USA" address on label*
❑ BST-84131 [S] Silver's Serenade 1963 80.00
*—"New York, USA" address on label*
❑ BST-84185 [S] Song for My Father (Cantiga Para Meu Pai) 1965 70.00
*—"New York, USA" address on label*
❑ BST-84220 [S] The Cape Verdean Blues 1965 70.00
*—"New York, USA" address on label*
❑ BST-84250 [S] The Jody Grind 1966 60.00
*—"New York, USA" address on label*

EPIC
❑ LN 3326 [M] Silver's Blue 1956 120.00
❑ LA 16006 [M] Silver's Blue 1959 60.00
*—Reissue with new cover*
❑ BA 17006 [R] Silver's Blue 196? 25.00

**SILVER APPLES**

KAPP
❑ KS-3562 Silver Apples 1968 30.00
*—Add 1/3 if poster is enclosed*
❑ KS-3584 Contact 1969 30.00

**SILVERS, PHIL**

COLUMBIA
❑ CL 1011 [M] Phil Silvers and the Swinging Brass 1957 50.00

HARMONY
❑ HL 7170 [M] Bugle Calls for Big Band 196? 25.00

**SILVERSTEIN, SHEL**

ATLANTIC
❑ 8072 [M] Inside Folk Songs 1962 30.00
❑ SD 8072 [S] Inside Folk Songs 1962 40.00

CADET
❑ LP 4052 [M] I'm So Good I Don't Have to Brag! 1965 25.00
❑ LPS 4052 [S] I'm So Good I Don't Have to Brag! 1965 30.00
❑ LP 4054 [M] Drain My Brain 1966 25.00
❑ LPS 4054 [S] Drain My Brain 1966 30.00

COLUMBIA
❑ KC 31119 Freakin' at the Freakers' Ball 1972 15.00
❑ PC 31119 Freakin' at the Freakers' Ball 1979 8.00
*—Budget-line reissue*
❑ FC 39412 Where the Sidewalk Ends 1984 10.00
❑ 9C9 39611 [PD] Where the Sidewalk Ends 1984 25.00
*—Picture disc*
❑ FC 40219 A Light in the Attic 1985 10.00

CRESTVIEW
❑ CRV 804 [M] Stag Party 1963 25.00

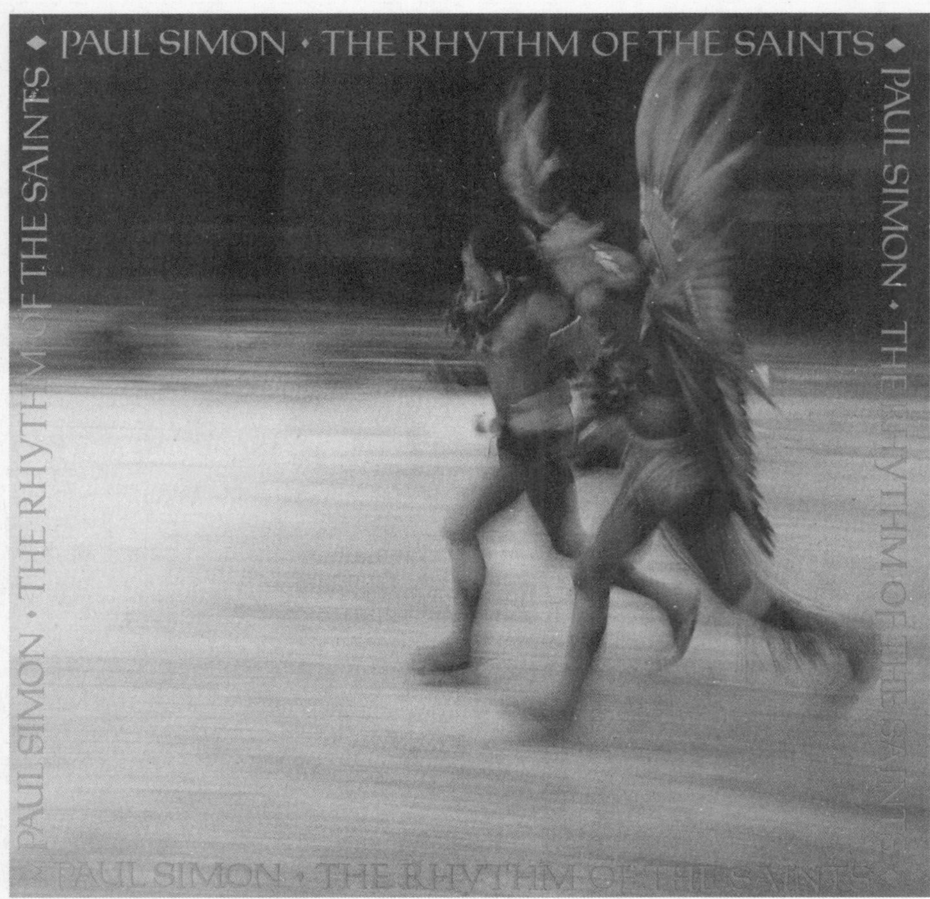


Paul Simon, *The Rhythm of the Saints,* Warner Bros. 26098, 1990, $15.

| Number | Title (A Side/B Side) | Yr | NM |
|---|---|---|---|
| ❑ CRS 7804 [S] | Stag Party | 1963 | 30.00 |
| **ELEKTRA** | | | |
| ❑ EKL-176 [M] | Hairy Jazz | 1961 | 100.00 |
| ❑ EKS-7176 [S] | Hairy Jazz | 1961 | 150.00 |
| **FLYING FISH** | | | |
| ❑ FF-211 | Conch Train Robbery | 1980 | 12.00 |
| **JANUS** | | | |
| ❑ 2JLS 3052 [(2)] | Crouching on the Outside | 1973 | 15.00 |
| **PARACHUTE** | | | |
| ❑ RRLP-9007 | Songs and Stories | 1978 | 12.00 |
| ❑ 20512 [DJ] | Selected Cuts from Songs and Stories | 1978 | 20.00 |
| *—Promo-only EP* | | | |
| **RCA VICTOR** | | | |
| ❑ LSP-4192 | A Boy Named Sue (And His Other Country Songs) | 1969 | 20.00 |

## SIMEON, OMER

| Number | Title (A Side/B Side) | Yr | NM |
|---|---|---|---|
| **CONCERT HALL JAZZ** | | | |
| ❑ 1014 [10] | Clarinet A La Creole | 195? | 50.00 |
| **DISC** | | | |
| ❑ DLP-748 [10] | Omer Simeon Trio With James P. Johnson | 195? | 200.00 |

## SIMEONE, HARRY, CHORALE

| Number | Title (A Side/B Side) | Yr | NM |
|---|---|---|---|
| **MERCURY** | | | |
| ❑ SR 60820 [S] | The Wonderful Songs of Christmas | 1963 | 20.00 |
| **20TH FOX** | | | |
| ❑ FOX-3002 [M] | Sing We Now of Christmas | 1959 | 20.00 |
| *—With "The Little Drummer Boy" mentioned at bottom of front cover* | | | |
| ❑ FOX-3002 [M] | Sing We Now of Christmas | 1959 | 25.00 |
| *—With no mention of "The Little Drummer Boy" at bottom of front cover* | | | |
| ❑ SFX-3002 [S] | Sing We Now of Christmas | 1959 | 20.00 |
| *—Sky blue label* | | | |

## SIMMONS, GENE Also see KISS.

| Number | Title (A Side/B Side) | Yr | NM |
|---|---|---|---|
| **CASABLANCA** | | | |
| ❑ NBLP 7120 | Gene Simmons | 1978 | 25.00 |
| ❑ NBPIX 7120 [PD] | Gene Simmons | 1978 | 60.00 |

## SIMMONS, JEFF

| Number | Title (A Side/B Side) | Yr | NM |
|---|---|---|---|
| **REPRISE** | | | |
| ❑ RS-6391 | Lucille Has Messed Up My Mind | 1969 | 30.00 |
| **STRAIGHT** | | | |
| ❑ STS-1057 | Lucille Has Messed Up My Mind | 1969 | 80.00 |

## SIMMONS, "JUMPIN'" GENE

| Number | Title (A Side/B Side) | Yr | NM |
|---|---|---|---|
| **HI** | | | |
| ❑ HL 2018 [M] | Jumpin' Gene Simmons | 1964 | 50.00 |
| ❑ SHL 32018 [S] | Jumpin' Gene Simmons | 1964 | 70.00 |

## SIMMONS, NORMAN

| Number | Title (A Side/B Side) | Yr | NM |
|---|---|---|---|
| **ARGO** | | | |
| ❑ LP-607 [M] | Norman Simmons Trio | 1956 | 40.00 |
| **CREATIVE** | | | |
| ❑ LP-607 [M] | Interpolations | 1956 | 80.00 |

## SIMMONS, SONNY

| Number | Title (A Side/B Side) | Yr | NM |
|---|---|---|---|
| **CONTEMPORARY** | | | |
| ❑ M-3623 [M] | Rumasuma | 1966 | 20.00 |
| ❑ S-7623 [S] | Rumasuma | 1966 | 25.00 |
| ❑ S-7625/6 [(2)] | Burning Spirits | 1970 | 20.00 |
| **ESP-DISK'** | | | |
| ❑ 1030 [M] | Sonny Simmons | 1966 | 20.00 |
| ❑ S-1030 [S] | Sonny Simmons | 1966 | 25.00 |
| ❑ 1043 [M] | Music from the Spheres | 1967 | 25.00 |
| ❑ S-1043 [S] | Music from the Spheres | 1967 | 20.00 |

## SIMON, CARLY Also see THE SIMON SISTERS.

| Number | Title (A Side/B Side) | Yr | NM |
|---|---|---|---|
| **ARISTA** | | | |
| ❑ AL-8443 | Coming Around Again | 1987 | 8.00 |
| ❑ AL-8526 | Greatest Hits Live | 1988 | 8.00 |
| ❑ AL-8582 | My Romance | 1990 | 12.00 |
| ❑ AL-8650 | Have You Seen Me Lately? | 1990 | 12.00 |
| **DIRECT DISK** | | | |
| ❑ SD-16608 | Boys in the Trees | 1980 | 50.00 |
| *—Audiophile vinyl* | | | |
| **ELEKTRA** | | | |
| ❑ 6E-109 | The Best of Carly Simon | 1977 | 8.00 |
| *—Reissue of 7E-1048* | | | |
| ❑ 6E-128 | Boys in the Trees | 1978 | 10.00 |
| ❑ 5E-506 | Spy | 1979 | 10.00 |
| ❑ 7E-1002 | Hotcakes | 1974 | 10.00 |
| ❑ EQ-1002 [Q] | Hotcakes | 1974 | 20.00 |
| ❑ 7E-1033 | Playing Possum | 1975 | 10.00 |
| ❑ EQ-1033 [Q] | Playing Possum | 1975 | 20.00 |
| ❑ 7E-1048 | The Best of Carly Simon | 1975 | 10.00 |
| ❑ EQ-1048 [Q] | The Best of Carly Simon | 1975 | 20.00 |
| ❑ 7E-1064 | Another Passenger | 1976 | 10.00 |
| ❑ EQ-1064 [Q] | Another Passenger | 1976 | — |
| *—Not released* | | | |
| ❑ EQ-4082 [Q] | Carly Simon | 1974 | 20.00 |
| ❑ EQ-5049 [Q] | No Secrets | 1974 | 20.00 |
| ❑ EKS-74082 | Carly Simon | 1971 | 12.00 |
| ❑ EKS-75016 | Anticipation | 1971 | 12.00 |
| ❑ EKS-75049 | No Secrets | 1972 | 12.00 |
| *—With lyrics on innersleeve* | | | |
| ❑ EKS-75049 | No Secrets | 1973 | 10.00 |
| *—Without lyrics on innersleeve* | | | |
| **EPIC** | | | |
| ❑ FE 39970 | Spoiled Girl | 1985 | 10.00 |
| **WARNER BROS.** | | | |
| ❑ BSK 3443 | Come Upstairs | 1980 | 10.00 |
| ❑ BSK 3592 | Torch | 1981 | 10.00 |
| ❑ 23886 | Hello Big Man | 1983 | 10.00 |

## SIMON, FRANK

| Number | Title (A Side/B Side) | Yr | NM |
|---|---|---|---|
| **AUDIO LAB** | | | |
| ❑ AL-1552 [M] | Four Star Hits | 1960 | 150.00 |

## SIMON, JOE

| Number | Title (A Side/B Side) | Yr | NM |
|---|---|---|---|
| **BUDDAH** | | | |
| ❑ BDS-7512 | Joe Simon | 1969 | 25.00 |
| **COMPLEAT** | | | |
| ❑ 671015-1 | Mr. Right | 1985 | 12.00 |
| **POSSE** | | | |
| ❑ 10002 | Glad You Came My Way | 1981 | 12.00 |
| ❑ 10003 | By Popular Demand | 1982 | 12.00 |
| **SOUND STAGE 7** | | | |
| ❑ 5000 [(2)] | The World of Joe Simon | 197? | 12.00 |
| *—Reissue of 32536* | | | |
| ❑ SSM-5003 [M] | Pure Soul | 1967 | 30.00 |
| ❑ SSS-15003 [S] | Pure Soul | 1967 | 40.00 |
| ❑ SSS-15004 | No Sad Songs | 1968 | 40.00 |
| ❑ SSS-15005 | Simon Sings | 1968 | 40.00 |
| ❑ SSS-15006 | The Chokin' Kind | 1969 | 30.00 |
| ❑ SSS-15008 | Joe Simon…Better Than Ever | 1969 | 30.00 |
| ❑ SSS-15009 | The Best of Joe Simon | 1972 | 15.00 |
| ❑ KZ 31916 | Greatest Hits | 1972 | 12.00 |
| ❑ ZG 32536 [(2)] | The World of Joe Simon | 1974 | 15.00 |
| ❑ ZG 33879 [(2)] | The Chokin' Kind/Joe Simon…Better Than Ever | 1975 | 15.00 |
| **SPRING** | | | |
| ❑ SPR-4701 | The Sounds of Simon | 1971 | 25.00 |
| ❑ SPR-5702 | Drowning in the Sea of Love | 1972 | 25.00 |
| ❑ SPR-5704 | The Power of Joe Simon | 1973 | 25.00 |
| ❑ SPR-5705 | Simon Country | 1973 | 15.00 |
| ❑ SPR-6702 | Mood, Heart and Soul | 1974 | 15.00 |
| ❑ SPR-6706 | Get Down | 1975 | 15.00 |
| ❑ SPR-6710 | Today | 1975 | 15.00 |
| ❑ SPR-6713 | Easy to Love | 1976 | 15.00 |
| ❑ SPR-6716 | Bad Case of Love | 1977 | 15.00 |
| ❑ SPR-6720 | Love Vibrations | 1979 | 15.00 |

## SIMON, PAUL Also see SIMON AND GARFUNKEL.

| Number | Title (A Side/B Side) | Yr | NM |
|---|---|---|---|
| **COLUMBIA** | | | |
| ❑ CQ 30750 [Q] | Paul Simon | 1974 | 20.00 |
| ❑ KC 30750 | Paul Simon | 1972 | 10.00 |
| ❑ CQ 32280 [Q] | There Goes Rhymin' Simon | 1974 | 20.00 |
| ❑ KC 32280 | There Goes Rhymin' Simon | 1973 | 10.00 |
| ❑ PC 32280 | There Goes Rhymin' Simon | 1980 | 8.00 |
| ❑ PC 32855 | Paul Simon in Concert — Live Rhymin' | 1974 | 10.00 |
| ❑ PC 33540 | Still Crazy After All These Years | 1975 | 10.00 |
| *—Original release has no bar code on cover* | | | |
| ❑ PC 33540 | Still Crazy After All These Years | 1980 | 8.00 |
| *—With bar code on cover* | | | |
| ❑ PCQ 33540 [Q] | Still Crazy After All These Years | 1975 | 20.00 |
| ❑ JC 35032 | Greatest Hits, Etc. | 1977 | 10.00 |
| ❑ C5X 37581 [(5)] | Collected Works | 1981 | 40.00 |
| *—Contains his first four post-S&G solo albums plus the elusive "Paul Simon Songbook," otherwise unavailable in U.S.* | | | |
| ❑ HC 43540 | Still Crazy After All These Years | 1981 | 40.00 |
| *—Half-speed mastered edition* | | | |
| ❑ HC 45032 | Greatest Hits, Etc. | 1981 | 40.00 |
| *—Half-speed mastered edition* | | | |
| **DCC COMPACT CLASSICS** | | | |
| ❑ LPZ-2060 | Paul Simon | 1998 | 30.00 |
| *—Audiophile vinyl* | | | |
| ❑ LPZ-2062 | There Goes Rhymin' Simon | 1998 | 30.00 |
| *—Audiophile vinyl* | | | |
| **WARNER BROS.** | | | |
| ❑ WBMS-140 [(2)DJ] | The Paul Simon Interview Show | 1986 | 50.00 |
| *—Promo-only "Graceland"-era program in the "Warner Bros. Music Show" series* | | | |
| ❑ HS 3472 | One-Trick Pony | 1980 | 10.00 |



Except when noted otherwise, VG = 25% of NM, and VG+ = 50% of NM. (Example: VG = $2.00, VG+ = $4.00 and NM = $8.00.)

| Number | Title (A Side/B Side) | Yr | NM |
|---|---|---|---|
| ❑ 23942 | Hearts and Bones | 1983 | 10.00 |
| ❑ 23942 [DJ] | Hearts and Bones | 1983 | 20.00 |
| *—Promo only on Quiex II vinyl* | | | |
| ❑ 25447 | Graceland | 1986 | 10.00 |
| ❑ 25588 | Paul Simon | 1988 | 12.00 |
| ❑ 25589 | There Goes Rhymin' Simon | 1988 | 12.00 |
| ❑ 25590 | Paul Simon in Concert — Live Rhymin' | 1988 | 12.00 |
| ❑ 25591 | Still Crazy After All These Years | 1988 | 12.00 |
| ❑ 25789 [(2)] | Negotiations and Love Songs | 1988 | 15.00 |
| ❑ 26098 | The Rhythm of the Saints | 1990 | 15.00 |
| ❑ 46814 | Songs from The Capeman | 1997 | 80.00 |
| ❑ 49982-1 | Surprise | 2006 | 15.00 |

**SIMON AND GARFUNKEL** Also see ART GARFUNKEL; PAUL SIMON.

CBS

| Number | Title (A Side/B Side) | Yr | NM |
|---|---|---|---|
| ❑ KCS 9914 | Bridge Over Troubled Water | 1970 | 15.00 |
| *—"360 Sound Stereo" on label; pressed in U.S. for export* | | | |

COLUMBIA

| Number | Title (A Side/B Side) | Yr | NM |
|---|---|---|---|
| ❑ CL 2249 [M] | Wednesday Morning, 3 A.M. | 1964 | 25.00 |
| *—"Guaranteed High Fidelity" on label* | | | |
| ❑ CL 2249 [M] | Wednesday Morning, 3 A.M. | 1965 | 15.00 |
| *—"Mono" on label* | | | |
| ❑ CL 2469 [M] | Sounds of Silence | 1966 | 15.00 |
| *—With "Simon and Garfunkel" and "Sounds of Silence" in large upper and lowercase letters on front cover with all song titles listed; "Tiger Beat" magazines on back cover are airbrushed out* | | | |
| ❑ CL 2469 [M] | Sounds of Silence | 1966 | 20.00 |
| *—With "Simon and Garfunkel" and "Sounds of Silence" in large upper and lowercase letters on front cover with all song titles listed; "Tiger Beat" magazine is pictured twice on back cover* | | | |
| ❑ CL 2469 [M] | Sounds of Silence | 1966 | 30.00 |
| *—With "Simon and Garfunkel" and "Sounds of Silence" in all capital letters on front cover with no list of songs* | | | |
| ❑ CL 2563 [M] | Parsley, Sage, Rosemary and Thyme | 1966 | 20.00 |
| ❑ KCL 2729 [M] | Bookends | 1968 | 100.00 |
| *—Red label, "Mono" at bottom* | | | |
| ❑ CS 9049 [S] | Wednesday Morning, 3 A.M. | 1964 | 25.00 |
| *—"360 Sound Stereo" in black on label* | | | |
| ❑ CS 9049 [S] | Wednesday Morning, 3 A.M. | 1965 | 15.00 |
| *—"360 Sound Stereo" in white on label* | | | |
| ❑ CS 9049 [S] | Wednesday Morning, 3 A.M. | 1970 | 10.00 |
| *—Orange label* | | | |
| ❑ PC 9049 [S] | Wednesday Morning, 3 A.M. | 197? | 8.00 |
| *—Budget-line reissue* | | | |
| ❑ CS 9269 [S] | Sounds of Silence | 1966 | 12.00 |
| *—With "Simon and Garfunkel" and "Sounds of Silence" in large upper and lowercase letters on front cover with all song titles listed; "Tiger Beat" magazines on back cover are airbrushed out* | | | |
| ❑ CS 9269 [S] | Sounds of Silence | 1966 | 20.00 |
| *—With "Simon and Garfunkel" and "Sounds of Silence" in large upper and lowercase letters on front cover with all song titles listed; "Tiger Beat" magazine is pictured twice on back cover* | | | |
| ❑ CS 9269 [S] | Sounds of Silence | 1966 | 30.00 |
| *—With "Simon and Garfunkel" and "Sounds of Silence" in all capital letters on front cover with no list of songs* | | | |
| ❑ CS 9269 [S] | Sounds of Silence | 1970 | 10.00 |
| *—Orange label* | | | |
| ❑ JC 9269 | Sounds of Silence | 197? | 8.00 |
| *—Reissue with new prefix* | | | |
| ❑ PC 9269 [S] | Sounds of Silence | 198? | 8.00 |
| *—Budget-line reissue* | | | |
| ❑ CS 9363 [S] | Parsley, Sage, Rosemary and Thyme | 1966 | 15.00 |
| *—"360 Sound Stereo" on label* | | | |
| ❑ CS 9363 [S] | Parsley, Sage, Rosemary and Thyme | 1970 | 10.00 |
| *—Orange label* | | | |
| ❑ PC 9363 [S] | Parsley, Sage, Rosemary and Thyme | 197? | 8.00 |
| *—Budget-line reissue* | | | |
| ❑ KCS 9529 [M] | Bookends | 1968 | 30.00 |
| *—White label "Special Mono Radio Station Copy"* | | | |
| ❑ KCS 9529 [S] | Bookends | 1968 | 12.00 |
| *—"360 Sound Stereo" on label; add 25% for poster* | | | |
| ❑ KCS 9529 [S] | Bookends | 1970 | 10.00 |
| *—Orange label* | | | |
| ❑ PC 9529 [S] | Bookends | 197? | 8.00 |
| *—Budget-line reissue* | | | |
| ❑ JC 9914 | Bridge Over Troubled Water | 197? | 8.00 |
| *—Reissue with new prefix* | | | |
| ❑ KCS 9914 | Bridge Over Troubled Water | 1970 | 10.00 |
| *—Orange label* | | | |
| ❑ KCS 9914 | Bridge Over Troubled Water | 1970 | 12.00 |
| *—"360 Sound Stereo" on label* | | | |
| ❑ KCS 9914 | Bridge Over Troubled Water | 2000 | 25.00 |
| *—Classic Records reissue on audiophile vinyl* | | | |
| ❑ PC 9914 | Bridge Over Troubled Water | 198? | 8.00 |
| *—Budget-line reissue* | | | |
| ❑ CQ 30995 [Q] | Bridge Over Troubled Water | 1971 | 25.00 |
| ❑ PCQ 30995 [Q] | Bridge Over Troubled Water | 1974 | 20.00 |
| *—Reissue with new prefix; possibly the only difference between this and the original is a sticker on the cover with the new number* | | | |
| ❑ JC 31350 | Simon and Garfunkel's Greatest Hits | 197? | 8.00 |
| *—Reissue with new prefix* | | | |
| ❑ KC 31350 | Simon and Garfunkel's Greatest Hits | 1972 | 12.00 |
| *—Original covers are slightly oversized* | | | |
| ❑ C5X 37587 [(5)] | Collected Works | 1981 | 40.00 |

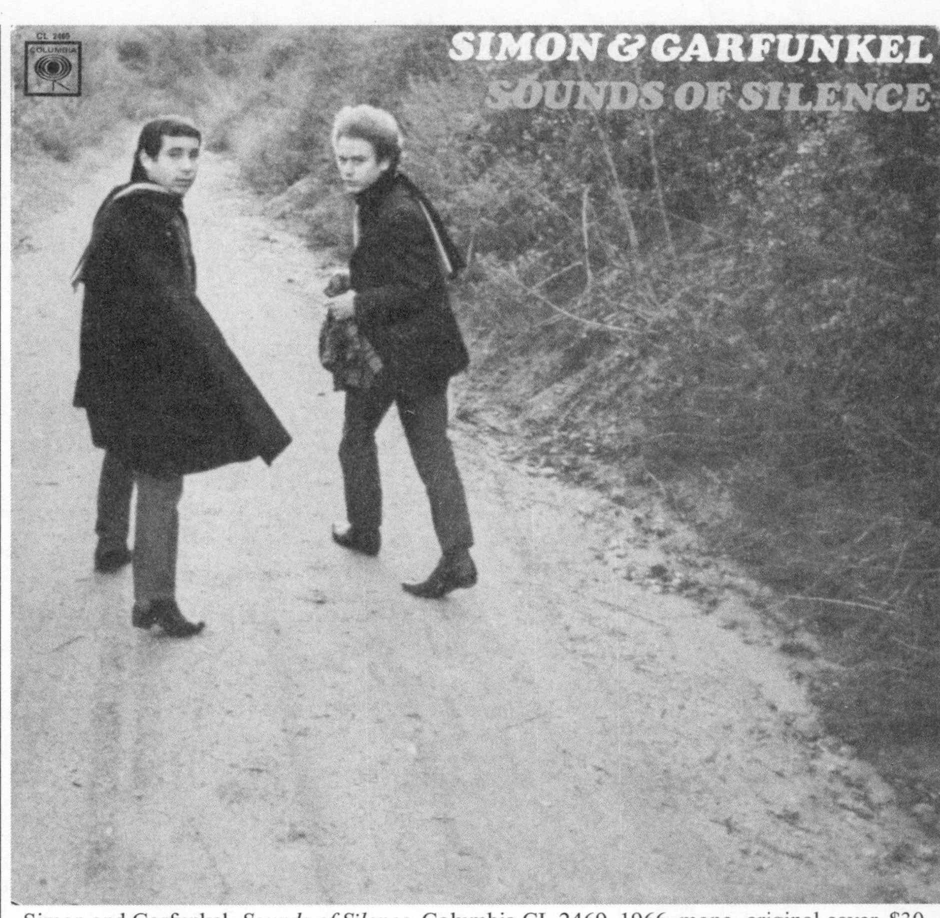


Simon and Garfunkel, *Sounds of Silence,* Columbia CL 2469, 1966, mono, original cover, $30.

| Number | Title (A Side/B Side) | Yr | NM |
|---|---|---|---|
| ❑ HC 41350 | Simon and Garfunkel's Greatest Hits | 1982 | 30.00 |
| *—Half-speed mastered edition* | | | |
| ❑ HC 49914 | Bridge Over Troubled Water | 1982 | 30.00 |
| *—Half-speed mastered edition* | | | |

MOBILE FIDELITY

| Number | Title (A Side/B Side) | Yr | NM |
|---|---|---|---|
| ❑ 1-173 | Bridge Over Troubled Water | 198? | 40.00 |
| *—Audiophile vinyl* | | | |

PICKWICK

| Number | Title (A Side/B Side) | Yr | NM |
|---|---|---|---|
| ❑ PC-3059 [M] | The Hit Sounds of Simon and Garfunkel | 1966 | 60.00 |
| ❑ SPC-3059 [R] | The Hit Sounds of Simon and Garfunkel | 1966 | 30.00 |

SEARS

| Number | Title (A Side/B Side) | Yr | NM |
|---|---|---|---|
| ❑ SPS-435 | Simon and Garfunkel | 196? | 30.00 |

TEE VEE

| Number | Title (A Side/B Side) | Yr | NM |
|---|---|---|---|
| ❑ TV-2002 [(5)] | The Complete Collection | 1980 | 50.00 |
| *—Alternate number is Columbia Special Products P5-15333; also contains solo material by both Paul Simon and Art Garfunkel, plus a rare true stereo mix of "You Don't Know Where Your Interest Lies"* | | | |

WARNER BROS.

| Number | Title (A Side/B Side) | Yr | NM |
|---|---|---|---|
| ❑ 2BSK 3654 [(2)] | The Concert in Central Park | 1982 | 12.00 |

**SIMON SISTERS, THE** CARLY SIMON and her sister Lucy.

COLUMBIA

| Number | Title (A Side/B Side) | Yr | NM |
|---|---|---|---|
| ❑ CR 21525 | The Lobster Quadrille | 1969 | 15.00 |
| ❑ CR 21539 | The Simon Sisters Sing for Children | 1972 | 15.00 |
| ❑ CC 24506 | The Lobster Quadrille | 1969 | 20.00 |
| *—Special edition with booklet* | | | |

KAPP

| Number | Title (A Side/B Side) | Yr | NM |
|---|---|---|---|
| ❑ KL-1359 [M] | Winkin', Blinkin' and Nod | 1964 | 30.00 |
| ❑ KL-1397 [M] | Cuddlebug | 1964 | 40.00 |
| ❑ KS-3359 [S] | Winkin', Blinkin' and Nod | 1964 | 40.00 |
| ❑ KS-3397 [S] | Cuddlebug | 1964 | 50.00 |

**SIMONE, NINA**

BETHLEHEM

| Number | Title (A Side/B Side) | Yr | NM |
|---|---|---|---|
| ❑ BCP-6028 [M] | Jazz As Played in an Exclusive Side Street Club | 1959 | 80.00 |
| ❑ BCP-6028 [M] | The Original Nina Simone | 1961 | 30.00 |
| *—Retitled reissue* | | | |
| ❑ SBCP-6028 [S] | Jazz As Played in an Exclusive Side Street Club | 1959 | 100.00 |
| ❑ SBCP-6028 [S] | The Original Nina Simone | 1961 | 40.00 |
| *—Retitled reissue* | | | |
| ❑ BCP-6041 [M] | Nina Simone and Her Friends | 1960 | 40.00 |
| ❑ SBCP-6041 [S] | Nina Simone and Her Friends | 1960 | 50.00 |
| *—With Carmen McRae and Chris Connor* | | | |

COLPIX

| Number | Title (A Side/B Side) | Yr | NM |
|---|---|---|---|
| ❑ CP-407 [M] | The Amazing Nina Simone | 1959 | 25.00 |
| ❑ SCP-407 [S] | The Amazing Nina Simone | 1959 | 30.00 |
| ❑ CP-409 [M] | Nina at Town Hall | 1960 | 25.00 |
| ❑ SCP-409 [S] | Nina at Town Hall | 1960 | 30.00 |
| ❑ CP-412 [M] | Nina at Newport | 1960 | 25.00 |
| ❑ SCP-412 [S] | Nina at Newport | 1960 | 30.00 |
| ❑ CP-419 [M] | Forbidden Fruit | 1961 | 25.00 |
| ❑ SCP-419 [S] | Forbidden Fruit | 1961 | 30.00 |
| ❑ CP-421 [M] | Nina Simone at the Village Gate | 1961 | 25.00 |
| ❑ SCP-421 [S] | Nina Simone at the Village Gate | 1961 | 30.00 |
| ❑ CP-425 [M] | Nina Sings Ellington | 1962 | 25.00 |
| ❑ SCP-425 [S] | Nina Sings Ellington | 1962 | 30.00 |
| ❑ CP-443 [M] | Nina's Choice | 1963 | 25.00 |
| ❑ SCP-443 [S] | Nina's Choice | 1963 | 30.00 |
| ❑ CP-455 [M] | Nina Simone at Carnegie Hall | 1963 | 25.00 |
| ❑ SCP-455 [S] | Nina Simone at Carnegie Hall | 1963 | 30.00 |
| ❑ CP-465 [M] | Folksy Nina | 1964 | 25.00 |
| ❑ SCP-465 [S] | Folksy Nina | 1964 | 30.00 |
| ❑ CP-496 [M] | Nina with Strings | 1966 | 25.00 |
| ❑ SCP-496 [S] | Nina with Strings | 1966 | 30.00 |

PHILIPS

| Number | Title (A Side/B Side) | Yr | NM |
|---|---|---|---|
| ❑ PHS 600135 [S] | Nina Simone In Concert | 1964 | 20.00 |
| ❑ PHS 600148 [S] | Broadway...Blues...Ballads | 1964 | 20.00 |
| ❑ PHS 600172 [S] | I Put a Spell on You | 1965 | 20.00 |
| ❑ PHS 600187 [S] | Pastel Blues | 1965 | 20.00 |
| ❑ PHS 600202 [S] | Let It All Out | 1966 | 20.00 |
| ❑ PHS 600207 [S] | Wild Is the Wind | 1966 | 20.00 |
| ❑ PHS 600219 [S] | The High Priestess of Soul | 1967 | 20.00 |
| ❑ PHS 600298 | The Best of Nina Simone | 1969 | 20.00 |

RCA VICTOR

| Number | Title (A Side/B Side) | Yr | NM |
|---|---|---|---|
| ❑ LPM-3789 [M] | Nina Simone Sings the Blues | 1967 | 25.00 |
| ❑ LPM-3837 [M] | Silk and Soul | 1967 | 25.00 |

**SIMPLE MINDS**

A&M

| Number | Title (A Side/B Side) | Yr | NM |
|---|---|---|---|
| ❑ SP-3927 | Street Fighting Years | 1989 | 10.00 |
| ❑ SP-6-4928 | New Gold Dream (81-82-83-84) | 1982 | 12.00 |
| *—Originals have gold and purple marbled vinyl* | | | |
| ❑ SP-6-4981 | Sparkle in the Rain | 1984 | 10.00 |

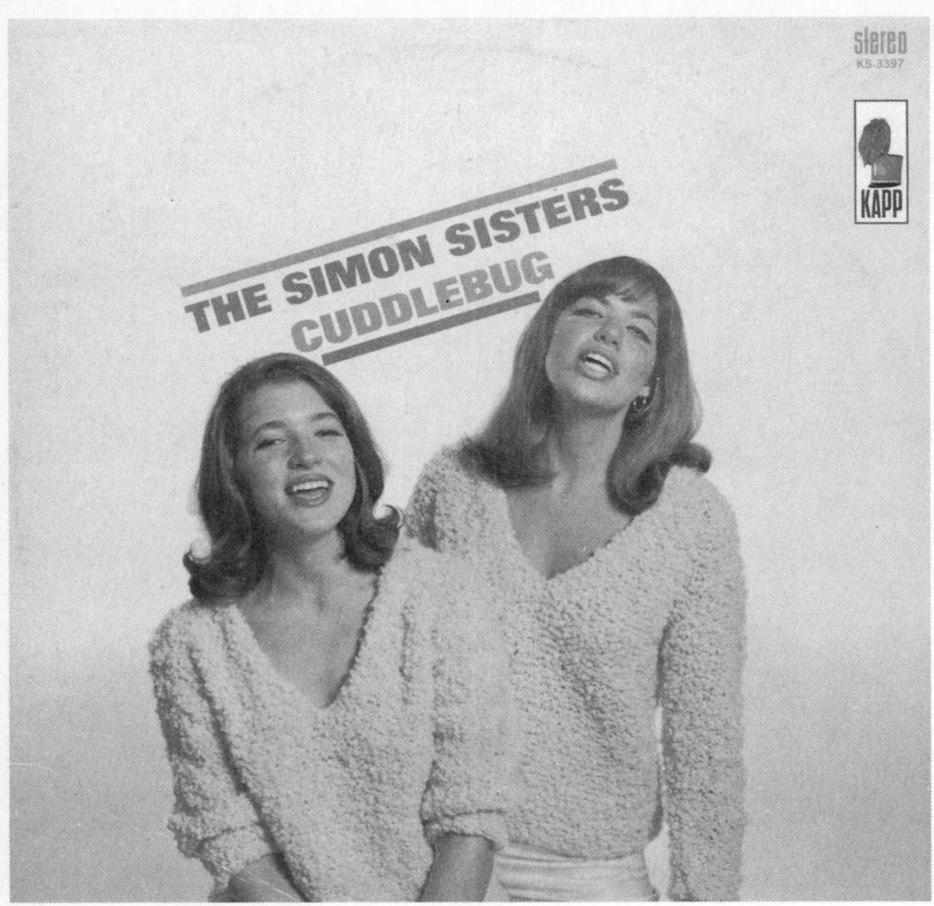


The Simon Sisters, *Cuddlebug,* Kapp KS-3397, 1964, stereo, $50.

**Number — Title (A Side/B Side) — Yr — NM**

❑ SP-5092 Once Upon a Time 1985 8.00
❑ SP-6850 [(2)] Live in the City of Light 1987 15.00
❑ R 101142 Street Fighting Years 1989 12.00
*—BMG Direct Marketing edition*
❑ R 142320 Once Upon a Time 1985 12.00
*—RCA Music Service edition; has front and back covers reversed*
❑ R 209526 [(2)] Live in the City of Light 1987 20.00
*—BMG Direct Marketing edition*

PVC
❑ 7910 Life in a Day 1979 20.00

STIFF
❑ TEES-102 Themes for Great Cities 1982 15.00

VIRGIN
❑ 90610 Sister Feelings Call 1987 10.00
*—First U.S. issue of LP originally released in 1981*
❑ 90858 Life in a Day 1988 10.00
*—Reissue of PVC 7910*
❑ 90859 Real to Real Cacophony 1988 10.00
*—First U.S. edition of early LP*

**SIMPLY RED**

ELEKTRA
❑ ED 5236 [DJ] Simply Red Billboard Interview 1989 40.00
*—Nelson George interviews Mick Hucknall and Lamont Dozier; promo-only*
❑ 60452 Picture Book 1985 8.00
❑ 60727 Men and Women 1987 8.00
❑ 60828 A New Flame 1989 10.00
❑ R 101012 A New Flame 1989 12.00
*—BMG Direct Marketing edition*
❑ R 152858 Men and Women 1987 10.00
*—RCA Music Service edition*
❑ R 153936 Picture Book 1985 10.00
*—RCA Music Service edition*

**SIMPSON, CAROLE**

CAPITOL
❑ T 878 [M] All About Carole 1957 80.00

TOPS
❑ L-1732 [M] Singin' and Swingin' 1960 25.00

**SIMPSON, CASS**

ABC-PARAMOUNT
❑ ABC-103 [M] Cass Simpson 1956 40.00

**Number — Title (A Side/B Side) — Yr — NM**

**SIMPSON, RED**

CAPITOL
❑ ST-881 I'm a Truck 1972 15.00
❑ ST 2468 [S] Roll, Truck, Roll 1966 20.00
❑ T 2468 [M] Roll, Truck, Roll 1966 15.00
❑ ST 2569 [S] The Man Behind the Badge 1966 20.00
❑ T 2569 [M] The Man Behind the Badge 1966 15.00
❑ ST 2691 [S] Truck Drivin' Fool 1967 20.00
❑ T 2691 [M] Truck Drivin' Fool 1967 20.00
❑ ST 2829 [S] A Bakersfield Dozen 1967 20.00
❑ T 2829 [M] A Bakersfield Dozen 1967 25.00
❑ ST-11093 The Very Real Red Simpson 1973 15.00
❑ ST-11231 A Trucker's Christmas 1973 15.00

PORTLAND
❑ 1005 [M] Hello, I'm a Truck 1965 80.00

SEA SHELL
❑ 16253 Ramblin' Road 198? 12.00

**SIMPSONS, THE**

GEFFEN
❑ GHS 24308 The Simpsons Sing the Blues 1990 25.00

**SIMS, FRANKIE LEE**

SPECIALTY
❑ SPS-2124 Lucy Mae Blues 1970 40.00

**SIMS, ZOOT**

ABC IMPULSE!
❑ AS-9131 [S] The Waiting Game 1968 25.00
*—Black label with red ring*

ABC-PARAMOUNT
❑ ABC-155 [M] Zoot Sims Plays Alto, Tenor and Baritone 1957 80.00
❑ ABC-198 [M] Zoot Sims Plays Four Altos 1957 80.00

ARGO
❑ LP-608 [M] Zoot 1956 120.00
*—Color cover*
❑ LP-608 [M] Zoot 1957 80.00
*—Black and white cover*

BETHLEHEM
❑ BCP-6051 [M] Down Home 1960 200.00
❑ SBCP-6051 [S] Down Home 1960 150.00

**Number — Title (A Side/B Side) — Yr — NM**

COLPIX
❑ CP-435 [M] New Beat Bossa Nova 1962 40.00
❑ SCP-435 [S] New Beat Bossa Nova 1962 50.00
❑ CP-437 [M] New Beat Bossa Nova, Volume 2 1962 40.00
❑ SCP-437 [S] New Beat Bossa Nova, Volume 2 1962 50.00

DAWN
❑ DLP-1102 [M] The Modern Art of Jazz 1956 120.00
❑ DLP-1115 [M] Zoot Sims Goes to Jazzville 1957 120.00

DISCOVERY
❑ DL-3015 [10] The Zoot Sims Quartet In Paris 1951 250.00

IMPULSE!
❑ A-9131 [M] The Waiting Game 1967 50.00

JAZZLAND
❑ JLP-2 [M] Zoot Sims Quintet 1960 40.00
❑ JLP-92 [S] Zoot Sims Quintet 1960 30.00

NEW JAZZ
❑ NJLP-1102 [10] Zoot Sims in Hollywood 1954 300.00
❑ NJLP-8280 [M] Good Old Zoot 1962 50.00

PACIFIC JAZZ
❑ PJ-20 [M] Choice 1961 40.00

PRESTIGE
❑ PRLP-117 [10] Swingin' with Zoot Sims 1951 300.00
❑ PRLP-118 [10] Tenor Sax Favorites 1951 300.00
❑ PRLP-138 [10] Zoot Sims All Stars 1953 300.00
❑ PRLP-202 [10] Zoot Sims Quintet 1955 250.00
❑ PRLP-7026 [M] Zoot Sims Quartets 1956 200.00
*—Yellow label with W. 50th St. address*
❑ PRLP-16009 [M] Trotting 1963 60.00

RIVERSIDE
❑ RLP 12-228 [M] Zoot! 1957 100.00

SEECO
❑ CELP-452 [M] The Modern Art of Jazz 1960 40.00
❑ CELP-4520 [S] The Modern Art of Jazz 1960 40.00

STATUS
❑ ST-8280 [M] Good Old Zoot 1965 40.00
❑ ST-8309 [M] Koo Koo 1965 40.00

UNITED ARTISTS
❑ UAL-4040 [M] A Night at the Half Note 1959 40.00
❑ UAS-5040 [S] A Night at the Half Note 1959 50.00
❑ UAJ-14013 [M] Zoot Sims in Paris 1962 40.00
❑ UAJS-15013 [S] Zoot Sims in Paris 1962 50.00

**SIMS, ZOOT; JIMMY RANEY; JIM HALL**

MAINSTREAM
❑ S-6013 [S] Two Jims and Zoot 1965 25.00
❑ 56013 [M] Two Jims and Zoot 1965 20.00

**SIMS, ZOOT; TONY SCOTT; AL COHN**

JAZZLAND
❑ JLP-11 [M] East Coast Sounds 1960 40.00
❑ JLP-911 [S] East Coast Sounds 1960 40.00

**SIN SAY SHUNS, THE**

VENETT
❑ V-940 [M] I'll Be There 1966 40.00
❑ VS-940 [S] I'll Be There 1966 50.00

**SINATRA, FRANK**

ARTANIS
❑ ARZ 101 [(2)] Sinatra '57 In Concert 1999 —
*—Canceled*

BOOK-OF-THE-MONTH
❑ (# unknown) [(6)] Tommy Dorsey/Frank Sinatra: The Complete Sessions 1983 100.00

CAPITOL
❑ DWBB-254 [(2)R] Close-Up 1969 20.00
*—Reissue in one package of "This Is Sinatra" and "This Is Sinatra, Volume Two"*
❑ DKAO-374 [R] Frank Sinatra's Greatest Hits 1969 12.00
❑ H 488 [10] Songs for Young Lovers 1954 60.00
❑ H 528 [10] Swing Easy 1954 60.00
❑ STBB-529 [(2)] What Is This Thing Called Love?/The Night We Called It a Day 1970 15.00
❑ DW 581 [R] In the Wee Small Hours 196? 12.00
❑ H1-581 [10] In the Wee Small Hours, Part 1 1955 100.00
❑ H2-581 [10] In the Wee Small Hours, Part 2 1955 100.00
❑ SM-581 In the Wee Small Hours 197? 8.00
❑ W 581 [M] In the Wee Small Hours 1955 40.00
*—Gray label original*
❑ W 581 [M] In the Wee Small Hours 1959 25.00
*—Black label with colorband*
❑ W 587 [M] Swing Easy/Songs for Young Lovers 1955 40.00
*—Gray label original; 12-inch version of two 10-inch LPs*
❑ W 587 [M] Swing Easy/Songs for Young Lovers 1959 25.00
*—Black label with colorband*
❑ DW 653 [R] Songs for Swingin' Lovers! 196? 12.00
❑ SM-653 Songs for Swingin' Lovers! 197? 8.00

| Number | Title (A Side/B Side) | Yr | NM |
|---|---|---|---|
| ❑ W 653 [M] | Songs for Swingin' Lovers! | 1956 | 40.00 |
| *—Gray label; cover has Sinatra facing toward the embracing couple* | | | |
| ❑ W 653 [M] | Songs for Swingin' Lovers! | 1956 | 50.00 |
| *—Gray label; cover has Sinatra facing away from the embracing couple* | | | |
| ❑ W 653 [M] | Songs for Swingin' Lovers! | 1959 | 25.00 |
| *—Black label with colorband* | | | |
| ❑ STBB-724 [(2)] | My One and Only Love/ Sentimental Journey | 1971 | 15.00 |
| ❑ T 735 [M] | Frank Sinatra Conducts Tone Poems of Color | 1956 | 60.00 |
| *—Turquoise label* | | | |
| ❑ T 735 [M] | Frank Sinatra Conducts Tone Poems of Color | 1959 | 40.00 |
| *—Black label with colorband* | | | |
| ❑ DT 768 [R] | This Is Sinatra! | 196? | 12.00 |
| ❑ T 768 [M] | This Is Sinatra! | 1956 | 30.00 |
| *—Turquoise label* | | | |
| ❑ T 768 [M] | This Is Sinatra! | 196? | 15.00 |
| *—Gold "Starline" label* | | | |
| ❑ T 768 [M] | This Is Sinatra! | 196? | 20.00 |
| *—Black "Starline" label* | | | |
| ❑ DW 789 [R] | Close to You | 196? | 12.00 |
| ❑ W 789 [M] | Close to You | 1957 | 30.00 |
| *—Gray label* | | | |
| ❑ W 789 [M] | Close to You | 1959 | 20.00 |
| *—Black label with colorband* | | | |
| ❑ DW 803 [R] | A Swingin' Affair! | 196? | 12.00 |
| ❑ W 803 [M] | A Swingin' Affair! | 1957 | 20.00 |
| *—Black label with colorband* | | | |
| ❑ W 803 [M] | A Swingin' Affair! | 1957 | 30.00 |
| *—Gray label* | | | |
| ❑ SW 855 [S] | Where Are You? | 1959 | 40.00 |
| *—Originals do not include "I Cover the Waterfront"* | | | |
| ❑ SW 855 [S] | Where Are You? | 196? | 30.00 |
| *—Later releases restore "I Cover the Waterfront"* | | | |
| ❑ W 855 [M] | Where Are You? | 1957 | 30.00 |
| *—Gray label* | | | |
| ❑ W 855 [M] | Where Are You? | 1959 | 20.00 |
| *—Black label with colorband* | | | |
| ❑ DT 894 [R] | The Sinatra Christmas Album | 196? | 10.00 |
| *—Rechanneled reissue of A Jolly Christmas with Frank Sinatra with same contents; some copies have this cover and "A Jolly Christmas" labels* | | | |
| ❑ SM-894 [R] | The Sinatra Christmas Album | 197? | 8.00 |
| *—Reissue in rechanneled stereo; any color label* | | | |
| ❑ T 894 [M] | The Sinatra Christmas Album | 196? | 20.00 |
| *—Reissue of A Jolly Christmas with Frank Sinatra with same contents; some copies have this cover and "A Jolly Christmas" labels* | | | |
| ❑ W 894 [M] | A Jolly Christmas from Frank Sinatra | 1957 | 40.00 |
| *—Original mono with gray label* | | | |
| ❑ W 894 [M] | A Jolly Christmas from Frank Sinatra | 1958 | 30.00 |
| *—Black colorband label, logo at left* | | | |
| ❑ SM-920 | Come Fly with Me | 197? | 8.00 |
| ❑ SW 920 [S] | Come Fly with Me | 1959 | 30.00 |
| ❑ W 920 [M] | Come Fly with Me | 1958 | 40.00 |
| *—Gray label* | | | |
| ❑ W 920 [M] | Come Fly with Me | 1959 | 20.00 |
| *—Black label with colorband* | | | |
| ❑ DW 982 [R] | This Is Sinatra, Volume Two | 196? | 12.00 |
| ❑ W 982 [M] | This Is Sinatra, Volume Two | 1958 | 40.00 |
| *—Gray label* | | | |
| ❑ W 982 [M] | This Is Sinatra, Volume Two | 1959 | 20.00 |
| *—Black label with colorband, logo at left* | | | |
| ❑ W 982 [M] | This Is Sinatra, Volume Two | 1963 | 15.00 |
| *—Black label with colorband, logo at top* | | | |
| ❑ SW 1053 [S] | Frank Sinatra Sings for Only the Lonely | 1959 | 30.00 |
| *—Originals do not include "It's a Lonesome Old Town" and "Spring Is Here"* | | | |
| ❑ SW 1053 [S] | Frank Sinatra Sings for Only the Lonely | 196? | 25.00 |
| *—Later releases restore "It's a Lonesome Old Town" and "Spring Is Here"* | | | |
| ❑ W 1053 [M] | Frank Sinatra Sings for Only the Lonely | 1958 | 40.00 |
| *—Gray label* | | | |
| ❑ W 1053 [M] | Frank Sinatra Sings for Only the Lonely | 1959 | 20.00 |
| *—Black label with colorband* | | | |
| ❑ SW 1069 [S] | Come Dance with Me! | 1959 | 30.00 |
| ❑ W 1069 [M] | Come Dance with Me! | 1959 | 20.00 |
| ❑ DW 1164 [R] | Look to Your Heart | 196? | 12.00 |
| ❑ W 1164 [M] | Look to Your Heart | 1959 | 30.00 |
| ❑ SM-1221 | No One Cares | 197? | 8.00 |
| ❑ SW 1221 [S] | No One Cares | 1959 | 30.00 |
| ❑ W 1221 [M] | No One Cares | 1959 | 20.00 |
| ❑ SW 1417 [S] | Nice 'N' Easy | 1960 | 25.00 |
| ❑ W 1417 [M] | Nice 'N' Easy | 1960 | 20.00 |
| ❑ DW 1429 [R] | Swing Easy | 1960 | 12.00 |
| ❑ W 1429 [M] | Swing Easy | 1960 | 20.00 |
| ❑ DW 1432 [R] | Songs for Young Lovers | 1960 | 12.00 |
| ❑ W 1432 [M] | Songs for Young Lovers | 1960 | 20.00 |
| ❑ SM-1491 | Sinatra's Swingin' Session!!! | 197? | 8.00 |
| ❑ SW 1491 [S] | Sinatra's Swingin' Session!!! | 1961 | 25.00 |
| ❑ W 1491 [M] | Sinatra's Swingin' Session!!! | 1961 | 20.00 |
| ❑ SW 1538 [S] | All the Way | 1961 | 25.00 |
| ❑ W 1538 [M] | All the Way | 1961 | 20.00 |
| ❑ SW 1594 [S] | Come Swing with Me! | 1961 | 25.00 |

Frank Sinatra, *The Voice,* Columbia CL 743, 1956, mono, $25.

| Number | Title (A Side/B Side) | Yr | NM |
|---|---|---|---|
| ❑ W 1594 [M] | Come Swing with Me! | 1961 | 20.00 |
| ❑ SM-1676 | Point of No Return | 197? | 8.00 |
| ❑ SW 1676 [S] | Point of No Return | 1962 | 25.00 |
| ❑ W 1676 [M] | Point of No Return | 1962 | 20.00 |
| ❑ SW 1729 [P] | Sinatra Sings…Of Love and Things | 1962 | 20.00 |
| ❑ W 1729 [M] | Sinatra Sings…Of Love and Things | 1962 | 20.00 |
| ❑ SWCO 1762 [(3)P] | Sinatra, The Great Years | 1962 | 40.00 |
| ❑ WCO 1762 [(3)M] | Sinatra, The Great Years | 1962 | 30.00 |
| ❑ DW 1825 [R] | Sinatra Sings Rodgers and Hart | 1963 | 12.00 |
| ❑ W 1825 [M] | Sinatra Sings Rodgers and Hart | 1963 | 20.00 |
| ❑ DT 1919 [R] | Tell Her You Love Her | 1963 | 12.00 |
| ❑ T 1919 [M] | Tell Her You Love Her | 1963 | 20.00 |
| ❑ DW 1994 [R] | Sinatra Sings the Select Johnny Mercer | 1963 | 12.00 |
| ❑ W 1994 [M] | Sinatra Sings the Select Johnny Mercer | 1963 | 20.00 |
| ❑ DT 2036 [R] | The Greatest Hits of Frank Sinatra | 1964 | 12.00 |
| ❑ T 2036 [M] | The Greatest Hits of Frank Sinatra | 1964 | 20.00 |
| ❑ T 2123 [M] | Sinatra Sings the Select Harold Arlen | 1964 | 100.00 |
| *—Only released in Canada, Australia and the UK* | | | |
| ❑ PRO-2163/4/5/6 [(2)DJ] | Selections from Sinatra, The Great Years | 1962 | 40.00 |
| ❑ DW 2301 [R] | Sinatra Sings the Select Cole Porter | 1965 | 12.00 |
| ❑ W 2301 [M] | Sinatra Sings the Select Cole Porter | 1965 | 20.00 |
| ❑ DT 2602 [R] | Forever Frank | 1966 | 12.00 |
| ❑ T 2602 [M] | Forever Frank | 1966 | 20.00 |
| ❑ DT 2700 [R] | The Movie Songs | 1967 | 12.00 |
| ❑ T 2700 [M] | The Movie Songs | 1967 | 20.00 |
| ❑ STFL 2814 [(6)P] | The Frank Sinatra Deluxe Set | 1968 | 60.00 |
| ❑ TFL 2814 [(6)M] | The Frank Sinatra Deluxe Set | 1968 | 100.00 |
| ❑ DKAO 2900 [R] | The Best of Frank Sinatra | 1968 | 15.00 |
| ❑ PRO-2974/5 [DJ] | Frank Sinatra Minute Masters | 1965 | 40.00 |
| *—Edited version of 20 songs* | | | |
| ❑ SY-4528 [S] | Come Fly with Me | 197? | 10.00 |
| *—Reissue of SW 920 with orange label and "Capitol" at bottom* | | | |
| ❑ SY-4533 [S] | Frank Sinatra Sings for Only the Lonely | 197? | 10.00 |
| *—Reissue of SW-1053 on orange label with "Capitol" at bottom* | | | |
| ❑ DNFR 7630 [(6)P] | The Sinatra Touch | 19?? | 60.00 |
| ❑ ST-11309 | One More for the Road | 1973 | 10.00 |
| ❑ SABB-11367 [(2)P] | Round #1 | 1974 | 15.00 |
| ❑ SM-11502 | A Swingin' Affair! | 1976 | 10.00 |
| ❑ SM-11801 | Come Swing with Me | 1978 | 10.00 |
| ❑ M-11883 | This Is Sinatra! | 1979 | 10.00 |
| ❑ SN-16109 | The Best of Frank Sinatra | 198? | 8.00 |
| *—Budget-line reissue* | | | |
| ❑ DN-16110 | What Is This Thing Called Love | 198? | 8.00 |
| *—Budget-line reissue* | | | |
| ❑ SN-16111 | The Night We Called It a Day | 198? | 8.00 |
| *—Budget-line reissue* | | | |
| ❑ N-16112 | My One and Only Love | 198? | 8.00 |
| *—Budget-line reissue* | | | |
| ❑ SN-16113 | Sentimental Journey | 198? | 8.00 |
| *—Budget-line reissue* | | | |
| ❑ N-16148 | Look to Your Heart | 198? | 8.00 |
| *—Budget-line reissue* | | | |
| ❑ SN-16149 | Sinatra Sings…Of Love and Things | 198? | 8.00 |
| *—Budget-line reissue* | | | |
| ❑ SN-16202 | Frank Sinatra Sings for Only the Lonely | 198? | 8.00 |
| *—Budget-line reissue* | | | |
| ❑ SN-16203 | Come Dance with Me! | 198? | 8.00 |
| *—Budget-line reissue* | | | |
| ❑ SN-16204 | Nice 'N' Easy | 198? | 8.00 |
| *—Budget-line reissue* | | | |
| ❑ SN-16205 | All the Way | 198? | 8.00 |
| *—Budget-line reissue* | | | |
| ❑ SN-16267 | Where Are You | 198? | 8.00 |
| *—Budget-line reissue* | | | |
| ❑ DN-16268 | This Is Sinatra, Volume Two | 198? | 8.00 |
| *—Budget-line reissue* | | | |
| ❑ C1-89611 | Duets | 1993 | 20.00 |
| ❑ DW 90986 [R] | Sentimental Journey | 1966 | 15.00 |
| *—Capitol Record Club issue* | | | |
| ❑ W 90986 [M] | Sentimental Journey | 1966 | 25.00 |
| *—Capitol Record Club issue* | | | |
| ❑ DQBO 91261 [(2)R] | Songs for the Young at Heart | 196? | 30.00 |
| *—Capitol Record Club issue* | | | |
| ❑ C1-94777 [(5)] | The Capitol Years | 1990 | 100.00 |
| *—With book and wraparound banner. Only 5,000 were pressed* | | | |
| ❑ STBB-95191 [(2)] | Sinatra Sings the Great Ones | 1973 | 20.00 |
| *—Longines Symphonette (formerly Capitol) Record Club issue* | | | |
| ❑ STBB-500724 [(2)] | My One and Only Love/ Sentimental Journey | 197? | 15.00 |
| *—Columbia Record Club edition of STBB-724* | | | |

Frank Sinatra, *I Remember Tommy,* Reprise R-1003, 1961, mono, $20.

| Number | Title (A Side/B Side) | Yr | NM |
|---|---|---|---|
| **CAPITOL PICKWICK SERIES** | | | |
| ❑ PC-3450 [M] | The Nearness of You | 196? | 12.00 |
| ❑ SPC-3450 [R] | The Nearness of You | 196? | 10.00 |
| ❑ PC-3452 [M] | Try a Little Tenderness | 196? | 12.00 |
| ❑ SPC-3452 [R] | Try a Little Tenderness | 196? | 10.00 |
| ❑ PC-3456 [M] | Nevertheless | 196? | 12.00 |
| ❑ SPC-3456 [R] | Nevertheless | 196? | 10.00 |
| ❑ PC-3457 [M] | Just One of Those Things | 196? | 12.00 |
| ❑ SPC-3457 [R] | Just One of Those Things | 196? | 10.00 |
| ❑ PC-3458 [M] | This Love of Mine | 196? | 12.00 |
| ❑ SPC-3458 [R] | This Love of Mine | 196? | 10.00 |
| ❑ PC-3463 [M] | My Cole Porter | 196? | 12.00 |
| ❑ SPC-3463 [R] | My Cole Porter | 196? | 10.00 |
| **COLUMBIA** | | | |
| ❑ C2L 6 [(2)M] | The Frank Sinatra Story | 1958 | 30.00 |
| ❑ S3L 42 [(3)M] | The Essential Frank Sinatra | 1966 | 100.00 |
| ❑ S3S 42 [(3)R] | The Essential Frank Sinatra | 1966 | 50.00 |
| ❑ CL 606 [M] | Frankie | 1955 | 25.00 |
| *—Cover has Frank with Debbie Reynolds* | | | |
| ❑ CL 606 [M] | Frankie | 1955 | 30.00 |
| *—Cover has drawing of Frank Sinatra wearing a hat* | | | |
| ❑ CL 743 [M] | The Voice | 1956 | 25.00 |
| ❑ CL 743 [M] | The Voice | 1999 | 25.00 |
| *—Classic Records reissue on audiophile vinyl* | | | |
| ❑ CL 884 [M] | Frank Sinatra Conducts Music of Alec Wilder | 1956 | 40.00 |
| *—Reissue of Columbia Masterworks ML 4271* | | | |
| ❑ CL 902 [M] | That Old Feeling | 1956 | 25.00 |
| ❑ CL 953 [M] | Adventures of the Heart | 1957 | 25.00 |
| ❑ CL 1032 [M] | Christmas Dreaming | 1957 | 80.00 |
| ❑ CL 1136 [M] | Put Your Dreams Away | 1958 | 25.00 |
| ❑ CL 1241 [M] | Love Is a Kick | 1958 | 25.00 |
| ❑ CL 1297 [M] | The Broadway Kick | 1958 | 25.00 |
| ❑ CL 1359 [M] | Come Back to Sorrento | 1959 | 25.00 |
| ❑ CL 1448 [M] | Reflections | 1959 | 60.00 |
| ❑ CL 2474 [M] | Greatest Hits, The Early Years, Vol. 1 | 1966 | 15.00 |
| ❑ CAS 2475 [DJ] | The Voice: The Columbia Years Sampler | 1986 | 40.00 |
| ❑ CL 2521 [10] | Get Happy | 1955 | 60.00 |
| *—"House Party Series" release* | | | |
| ❑ CL 2539 [10] | I've Got a Crush on You | 1955 | 60.00 |
| *—"House Party Series" release; different contents from CL 6290* | | | |
| ❑ CL 2542 [10] | Christmas with Sinatra | 1955 | 60.00 |
| *—"House Party Series" release* | | | |
| ❑ CL 2572 [M] | Greatest Hits, The Early Years, Vol. 2 | 1966 | 15.00 |
| ❑ CL 2739 [M] | The Essential Frank Sinatra, Volume 1 | 1967 | 25.00 |
| ❑ CL 2740 [M] | The Essential Frank Sinatra, Volume 2 | 1967 | 25.00 |
| ❑ CL 2741 [M] | The Essential Frank Sinatra, Volume 3 | 1967 | 25.00 |
| ❑ CL 2913 [M] | Frank Sinatra in Hollywood | 1968 | 80.00 |
| ❑ CL 6001 [10] | The Voice of Frank Sinatra | 1949 | 70.00 |
| *—Original in pink paper cover* | | | |
| ❑ CL 6001 [10] | The Voice of Frank Sinatra | 1950 | 60.00 |
| *—Blue cardboard cover* | | | |
| ❑ CL 6019 [10] | Christmas Songs by Sinatra | 1948 | 100.00 |
| *—With "gingerbread man" cover* | | | |
| ❑ CL 6019 [10] | Christmas Songs by Sinatra | 1949 | 80.00 |
| *—With green vinylite cover* | | | |
| ❑ CL 6059 [10] | Frankly Sentimental | 1951 | 60.00 |
| ❑ CL 6087 [10] | Songs by Sinatra, Volume 1 | 1952 | 60.00 |
| ❑ CL 6096 [10] | Dedicated to You | 1952 | 100.00 |
| *—Three of the tracks on this LP are alternate takes unavailable on vinyl anywhere else* | | | |
| ❑ CL 6143 [10] | Sing and Dance with Frank Sinatra | 1953 | 60.00 |
| ❑ CL 6290 [10] | I've Got a Crush on You | 1954 | 60.00 |
| ❑ CS 9274 [R] | Greatest Hits, The Early Years, Vol. 1 | 1966 | 10.00 |
| ❑ PC 9274 | Greatest Hits, The Early Years, Vol. 1 | 197? | 8.00 |
| ❑ CS 9372 [R] | Greatest Hits, The Early Years, Vol. 2 | 1966 | 10.00 |
| ❑ PC 9372 | Greatest Hits, The Early Years, Vol. 2 | 197? | 8.00 |
| ❑ CS 9539 [R] | The Essential Frank Sinatra, Volume 1 | 1967 | 12.00 |
| ❑ CS 9540 [R] | The Essential Frank Sinatra, Volume 2 | 1967 | 12.00 |
| ❑ CS 9541 [R] | The Essential Frank Sinatra, Volume 3 | 1967 | 12.00 |
| ❑ CS 9713 [R] | Frank Sinatra in Hollywood | 1968 | 12.00 |
| ❑ KG 31358 [(2)] | In the Beginning | 1971 | 40.00 |
| *—Original edition; titles of songs at left on front cover* | | | |
| ❑ PG 31358 [(2)] | In the Beginning | 197? | 12.00 |
| *—Revised version; titles of songs at right on front cover* | | | |
| ❑ C6X 40343 [(6)] | The Voice: The Columbia Years 1943-1952 | 1986 | 80.00 |
| ❑ PC 40707 | Christmas Dreaming | 1987 | 30.00 |
| *—Reissue of CL 1032 with an extra track* | | | |
| ❑ C2X 40897 [(2)] | Hello Young Lovers | 1988 | 30.00 |
| ❑ PC 44238 [M] | Sinatra Rarities | 1989 | 40.00 |

| Number | Title (A Side/B Side) | Yr | NM |
|---|---|---|---|
| **COLUMBIA MASTERWORKS** | | | |
| ❑ ML 4271 [M] | Frank Sinatra Conducts Music of Alec Wilder | 1955 | 100.00 |
| **HARMONY** | | | |
| ❑ HL 7400 [M] | Have Yourself a Merry Little Christmas | 1967 | 30.00 |
| ❑ HL 7405 [M] | Romantic Scenes from the Early Years | 1967 | 30.00 |
| ❑ HS 11200 [R] | Have Yourself a Merry Little Christmas | 1967 | 20.00 |
| *—At least two different cover designs exist* | | | |
| ❑ HS 11205 [R] | Romantic Scenes from the Early Years | 1967 | 12.00 |
| ❑ HS 11277 [R] | Someone to Watch Over Me | 1968 | 15.00 |
| ❑ HS 11390 [R] | Frank Sinatra | 1969 | 15.00 |
| ❑ KH 30318 [R] | Greatest Hits, Early Years | 1971 | 15.00 |
| **LONGINES SYMPHONETTE** | | | |
| ❑ LS-308A [(10)] | Sinatra: The Works | 1972 | 75.00 |
| ❑ LS-309A [(6)] | Sinatra: The Works | 1973 | 40.00 |
| *—Abridged version of LS-308A* | | | |
| ❑ SYS-5637 | Sinatra Like Never Before | 1972 | 25.00 |
| *—Bonus LP with purchase of LS-308A* | | | |
| **MOBILE FIDELITY** | | | |
| ❑ SC-1 [(16)] | Sinatra | 1983 | 600.00 |
| *—Audiophile vinyl; only two of the 16 records in this box were released individually* | | | |
| ❑ 1-086 | Nice 'N' Easy | 1981 | 40.00 |
| *—Audiophile vinyl* | | | |
| ❑ 1-135 [M] | A Jolly Christmas from Frank Sinatra | 1984 | 40.00 |
| *—Audiophile vinyl using the original title* | | | |
| **PAIR** | | | |
| ❑ PDL2-1027 [(2)] | All-Time Classics | 1986 | 12.00 |
| ❑ PDL2-1028 [(2)] | Timeless | 1986 | 12.00 |
| ❑ PDL2-1122 [(2)] | Classic Performances | 1986 | 12.00 |
| **QWEST** | | | |
| ❑ 25145 | L.A. Is My Lady | 1984 | 12.00 |
| **RCA VICTOR** | | | |
| ❑ APL1-0497 [R] | What'll I Do | 1974 | 12.00 |
| ❑ LPV-583 [M] | This Love of Mine | 1971 | 40.00 |
| ❑ ANL1-1050 [R] | What'll I Do | 1976 | 10.00 |
| ❑ LPM-1569 [M] | Tommy Plays, Frankie Sings | 1957 | 40.00 |
| *—Second issue with new title* | | | |
| ❑ LPM-1569 [M] | Frankie and Tommy | 1957 | 60.00 |
| *—First issue of this LP* | | | |
| ❑ LPM-1632 [M] | We Three | 1958 | 40.00 |
| *—Second issue, "RE" on cover* | | | |
| ❑ LPM-1632 [M] | We Three | 1958 | 60.00 |
| *—First issue* | | | |
| ❑ LPT-3063 [10] | Fabulous Frankie | 1953 | 60.00 |
| ❑ CPL2-4334 [(2)] | The Sinatra/Dorsey Sessions, Vol. 1 | 1982 | 25.00 |
| ❑ CPL2-4335 [(2)] | The Sinatra/Dorsey Sessions, Vol. 2 | 1982 | 25.00 |
| ❑ CPL2-4336 [(2)] | The Sinatra/Dorsey Sessions, Vol. 3 | 1982 | 25.00 |
| ❑ AFL1-4741 [R] | Radio Years (Sinatra/Dorsey/Stordahl) | 1983 | 15.00 |
| **REPRISE** | | | |
| ❑ F 1001 [M] | Ring-a-Ding-Ding! | 1961 | 20.00 |
| ❑ R9 1001 [S] | Ring-a-Ding-Ding! | 1961 | 25.00 |
| ❑ F 1002 [M] | Sinatra Swings | 1961 | 20.00 |
| *—Retitled version of "Swing Along with Me"; Capitol threatened legal action because of its "Come Swing With Me!" collection* | | | |
| ❑ F 1002 [M] | Swing Along with Me | 1961 | 40.00 |
| *—Original title* | | | |
| ❑ R9 1002 [S] | Sinatra Swings | 1961 | 25.00 |
| *—Retitled version of "Swing Along with Me"; Capitol threatened legal action because of its "Come Swing With Me!" collection* | | | |
| ❑ R9 1002 [S] | Swing Along with Me | 1961 | 50.00 |
| *—Original title* | | | |
| ❑ F 1003 [M] | I Remember Tommy | 1961 | 20.00 |
| ❑ R9 1003 [S] | I Remember Tommy | 1961 | 25.00 |
| ❑ F 1004 [M] | Sinatra & Strings | 1962 | 15.00 |
| ❑ R9 1004 [S] | Sinatra & Strings | 1962 | 20.00 |
| ❑ F 1005 [M] | Sinatra and Swingin' Brass | 1962 | 15.00 |
| ❑ R9 1005 [S] | Sinatra and Swingin' Brass | 1962 | 20.00 |
| ❑ F 1006 [M] | Great Songs from Great Britain | 1962 | 80.00 |
| *—Only released in the UK* | | | |
| ❑ R9 1006 [S] | Great Songs from Great Britain | 1962 | 100.00 |
| *—Only released in the UK* | | | |
| ❑ F 1007 [M] | All Alone | 1962 | 15.00 |
| ❑ R9 1007 [S] | All Alone | 1962 | 20.00 |
| ❑ F 1008 [M] | Sinatra-Basie | 1963 | 15.00 |
| ❑ R9 1008 [S] | Sinatra-Basie | 1963 | 20.00 |
| ❑ F 1009 [M] | The Concert Sinatra | 1963 | 15.00 |
| ❑ R9 1009 [S] | The Concert Sinatra | 196? | 20.00 |
| *—Without cover reference to "35mm Stereo"* | | | |
| ❑ R9 1009 [S] | The Concert Sinatra | 1963 | 25.00 |
| *—Original pressings declare this was recorded in "35mm Stereo"* | | | |
| ❑ R-1010 [M] | Sinatra's Sinatra | 1963 | 15.00 |
| *—Gatefold jacket; some copies have eight photos of previous Frank Sinatra Reprise LPs at the right side of the inside gatefold; we don't yet know the relative rarity of these variations, or which came first, or whether they also exist on stereo copies* | | | |
| ❑ R-1010 [M] | Sinatra's Sinatra | 1963 | 15.00 |
| *—Gatefold jacket; some copies have a large photo of Sinatra holding a pack of Lucky Strikes at the right side of the inside gatefold; we don't yet know the relative rarity of these variations, or which came first, or whether they also exist on stereo copies* | | | |

| Number | Title (A Side/B Side) | Yr | NM |
|---|---|---|---|
| ❑ R9 1010 [S] | Sinatra's Sinatra | 1963 | 20.00 |
| ❑ F 1011 [M] | Days of Wine and Roses, Moon River, and Other Academy Award Winners | 1964 | 15.00 |
| ❑ FS 1011 [S] | Days of Wine and Roses, Moon River, and Other Academy Award Winners | 1964 | 20.00 |
| ❑ F 1012 [M] | It Might As Well Be Swing | 1964 | 15.00 |
| ❑ FS 1012 [S] | It Might As Well Be Swing | 1964 | 20.00 |
| ❑ F 1013 [M] | Softly, As I Leave You | 1964 | 15.00 |
| ❑ FS 1013 [S] | Softly, As I Leave You | 1964 | 20.00 |
| ❑ F 1014 [M] | September of My Years | 1965 | 15.00 |
| ❑ FS 1014 [S] | September of My Years | 1965 | 20.00 |
| ❑ F 1015 [M] | My Kind of Broadway | 1965 | 15.00 |
| ❑ FS 1015 [S] | My Kind of Broadway | 1965 | 20.00 |
| ❑ 2F 1016 [(2)M] | A Man and His Music | 1965 | 20.00 |
| ❑ 2F/2FS 1016 | A Man and His Music Special Box | 1965 | 200.00 |
| *—Blue slipcase with embossed silver front, raised letters, plus 4-page booklet and a signed card (deduct 50% if card missing). Add this to LP value.* | | | |
| ❑ 2FS 1016 [(2)S] | A Man and His Music | 1965 | 25.00 |
| ❑ F 1017 [M] | Strangers in the Night | 1966 | 12.00 |
| ❑ FS 1017 [S] | Strangers in the Night | 1966 | 15.00 |
| ❑ F 1018 [M] | Moonlight Sinatra | 1966 | 15.00 |
| ❑ FS 1018 [S] | Moonlight Sinatra | 1966 | 20.00 |
| ❑ 2F 1019 [(2)M] | Sinatra at the Sands | 1966 | 20.00 |
| ❑ 2FS 1019 [(2)S] | Sinatra at the Sands | 1966 | 25.00 |
| ❑ F 1020 [M] | That's Life | 1966 | 12.00 |
| ❑ FS 1020 [S] | That's Life | 1966 | 15.00 |
| ❑ F 1021 [M] | Francis Albert Sinatra & Antonio Carlos Jobim | 1967 | 12.00 |
| ❑ FS 1021 [S] | Francis Albert Sinatra & Antonio Carlos Jobim | 1967 | 15.00 |
| ❑ F 1022 [M] | Frank Sinatra (The World We Knew) | 1967 | 15.00 |
| ❑ FS 1022 [S] | Frank Sinatra (The World We Knew) | 1967 | 15.00 |
| ❑ FS 1023 | The Sinatra Christmas Album | 1967 | 100.00 |
| *—Album never released; value is for cover slick* | | | |
| ❑ FS 1024 | Francis A. and Edward K. | 1968 | 20.00 |
| ❑ FS 1025 | Frank Sinatra's Greatest Hits | 1968 | 15.00 |
| ❑ FS 1027 | Cycles | 1969 | 15.00 |
| ❑ FS 1028 | SinatraJobim | 1969 | 4000. |
| *—Unreleased; test pressings exist (value is for one of these). 8-track tapes also exist and are 10% of this value; VG value 1000; VG+ value 1000* | | | |
| ❑ FS 1029 | My Way | 1969 | 15.00 |
| ❑ FS4 1029 [Q] | My Way | 1974 | 25.00 |
| ❑ FS 1030 | A Man Alone & Other Songs of Rod McKuen | 1969 | 15.00 |
| ❑ FS 1030 | A Man Alone & Other Songs of Rod McKuen | 1969 | 400.00 |
| *—Signed copies with gatefold cover and hardbound book; 400 made* | | | |
| ❑ FS 1031 | Watertown | 1970 | 25.00 |
| *—With gatefold and poster* | | | |
| ❑ FS 1032 | Frank Sinatra's Greatest Hits, Vol. 2 | 1970 | — |
| *—Canceled?* | | | |
| ❑ FS 1033 | Sinatra and Company | 1971 | 15.00 |
| ❑ FS 1034 | Frank Sinatra's Greatest Hits, Vol. 2 | 1972 | 15.00 |
| ❑ FS4-1034 [Q] | Frank Sinatra's Greatest Hits, Vol. 2 | 1974 | 25.00 |
| ❑ FS 2155 | Ol' Blue Eyes Is Back | 1973 | 12.00 |
| ❑ FS4 2155 [Q] | Ol' Blue Eyes Is Back | 1974 | 25.00 |
| ❑ FS4 2194 [Q] | Some Nice Things I've Missed | 1974 | 25.00 |
| ❑ FS 2195 | Some Nice Things I've Missed | 1974 | 12.00 |
| ❑ FS 2207 | Sinatra — The Main Event Live | 1974 | 12.00 |
| ❑ 3FS 2300 [(3)] | Trilogy: Past, Present, Future | 1980 | 20.00 |
| ❑ FS 2305 | She Shot Me Down | 1981 | 12.00 |
| ❑ 5004 [DJ] | A Man and His Music, Part II | 1966 | 300.00 |
| *—Promotional album for use by Budweiser* | | | |
| ❑ 5230 [DJ] | Songbook, Vol. 1 | 1971 | 50.00 |
| ❑ 5267 [(2)DJ] | Songbook, Vol. 2 | 1972 | 100.00 |
| ❑ 5409 [DJ] | I Sing the Songs | 1976 | 50.00 |
| ❑ F 6045 [M] | Sinatra Conducts Music from Pictures and Plays | 1962 | 30.00 |
| ❑ R9 6045 [S] | Sinatra Conducts Music from Pictures and Plays | 1962 | 40.00 |
| ❑ R 6167 [M] | Sinatra '65 | 1965 | 15.00 |
| ❑ RS 6167 [S] | Sinatra '65 | 1965 | 20.00 |
| ❑ R1 73798 [S] | Francis Albert Sinatra & Antonio Carlos Jobim | 2004 | 15.00 |
| *—180-gram reissue* | | | |
| ❑ R1 73799 [S] | September of My Years | 2004 | 15.00 |
| *—180-gram reissue* | | | |
| ❑ SMAS-92081 | A Man Alone & Other Songs of Rod McKuen | 1969 | 20.00 |
| *—Capitol Record Club edition* | | | |
| ❑ SMAS-93119 | Watertown | 1970 | 25.00 |
| *—Capitol Record Club edition; does not contain poster* | | | |
| **TIME-LIFE** | | | |
| ❑ SLGD-02 [(2)] | Legendary Singers: Frank Sinatra | 1985 | 25.00 |

### SINATRA, FRANK; DEAN MARTIN; SAMMY DAVIS, JR.

| Number | Title (A Side/B Side) | Yr | NM |
|---|---|---|---|
| **ARTANIS** | | | |
| ❑ ARZ 102 [(2)] | The Summit | 1999 | — |
| *—Canceled* | | | |

### SINATRA, NANCY

| Number | Title (A Side/B Side) | Yr | NM |
|---|---|---|---|
| **RCA VICTOR** | | | |
| ❑ LSP-4645 | Nancy and Lee Again | 1972 | 30.00 |
| *—With Lee Hazlewood* | | | |
| ❑ LSP-4774 | Woman | 1973 | 25.00 |
| ❑ VPS-6078 [(2)] | This Is Nancy Sinatra | 1972 | 50.00 |
| **REPRISE** | | | |
| ❑ R-6202 [M] | Boots | 1966 | 25.00 |
| ❑ RS-6202 [S] | Boots | 1966 | 30.00 |
| ❑ R-6207 [M] | How Does That Grab You? | 1966 | 20.00 |
| ❑ RS-6207 [S] | How Does That Grab You? | 1966 | 25.00 |
| ❑ R-6221 [M] | Nancy in London | 1966 | 20.00 |
| ❑ RS-6221 [S] | Nancy in London | 1966 | 25.00 |
| ❑ R-6239 [M] | Sugar | 1967 | 25.00 |
| ❑ RS-6239 [S] | Sugar | 1967 | 20.00 |
| ❑ R-6251 [M] | Country, My Way | 1967 | 25.00 |
| ❑ RS-6251 [S] | Country, My Way | 1967 | 20.00 |
| ❑ RS-6273 | Nancy and Lee | 1968 | 20.00 |
| *—With Lee Hazlewood* | | | |
| ❑ R-6277 [M] | Movin' with Nancy | 1967 | 25.00 |
| ❑ RS-6277 [S] | Movin' with Nancy | 1967 | 20.00 |
| ❑ RS-6333 | Nancy | 1969 | 20.00 |
| ❑ RS-6409 | Nancy's Greatest Hits | 1970 | 20.00 |
| ❑ ST-91341 [S] | Boots | 1967 | 40.00 |
| *—Capitol Record Club edition* | | | |
| ❑ ST-91349 [S] | Movin' with Nancy | 1967 | 30.00 |
| *—Capitol Record Club edition* | | | |
| **RHINO** | | | |
| ❑ R1-70166 | Fairy Tales and Fantasies: The Best of Nancy and Lee | 1989 | 10.00 |
| *—With Lee Hazlewood* | | | |
| ❑ RNLP-70227 | Boots: Nancy Sinatra's All-Time Hits (1966-1970) | 1987 | 10.00 |

### SING A SONG WITH THE BEATLES

| Number | Title (A Side/B Side) | Yr | NM |
|---|---|---|---|
| **TOWER** | | | |
| ❑ DKAO 5000 [R] | Sing a Song with the Beatles | 1965 | 200.00 |
| ❑ KAO 5000 [M] | Sing a Song with the Beatles | 1965 | 150.00 |
| *—No artist listed on label* | | | |

### SINGER, HAL, AND CHARLIE SHAVERS

| Number | Title (A Side/B Side) | Yr | NM |
|---|---|---|---|
| **PRESTIGE** | | | |
| ❑ PRLP-7153 [M] | Blue Stompin' | 1959 | 80.00 |
| **SWINGVILLE** | | | |
| ❑ SVLP-2023 [M] | Blue Stompin' | 1961 | 50.00 |
| *—Purple label* | | | |
| ❑ SVLP-2023 [M] | Blue Stompin' | 1965 | 25.00 |
| *—Blue label, trident logo at right* | | | |

### SINGER ORCHESTRA, THE

| Number | Title (A Side/B Side) | Yr | NM |
|---|---|---|---|
| **SINGER** | | | |
| ❑ HE-M-1 [M] | Favorite Christmas Songs from Singer | 1964 | 15.00 |
| *—Cover photo of the cast of "The Donna Reed Show"* | | | |
| ❑ HE-S-1 [S] | Favorite Christmas Songs from Singer | 1964 | 20.00 |
| *—Cover photo of the cast of "The Donna Reed Show"* | | | |

### SINGLETON, CHARLIE

| Number | Title (A Side/B Side) | Yr | NM |
|---|---|---|---|
| **RCA CAMDEN** | | | |
| ❑ CAL-713 [M] | Big Twist Hits | 1962 | 20.00 |
| ❑ CAS-713 [S] | Big Twist Hits | 1962 | 25.00 |

### SINGLETON, MARGIE

| Number | Title (A Side/B Side) | Yr | NM |
|---|---|---|---|
| **ASHLEY** | | | |
| ❑ 3003 | Margie Singleton Sings Country Music with Soul | 1968 | 15.00 |
| **PICKWICK** | | | |
| ❑ SPC-3133 | Harper Valley P.T.A. | 197? | 10.00 |
| **UNITED ARTISTS** | | | |
| ❑ UAL-3459 [M] | Crying Time | 1965 | 15.00 |
| ❑ UAS-6459 [S] | Crying Time | 1965 | 20.00 |

### SINGLETON, ZUTTY/ART TATUM

| Number | Title (A Side/B Side) | Yr | NM |
|---|---|---|---|
| **BRUNSWICK** | | | |
| ❑ BL 58038 [10] | Battle of Jazz, Vol. 2 | 1953 | 50.00 |

### SIOUXSIE AND THE BANSHEES

| Number | Title (A Side/B Side) | Yr | NM |
|---|---|---|---|
| **GEFFEN** | | | |
| ❑ GHS 24030 | Hyaena | 1984 | 10.00 |
| ❑ GHS 24046 | The Scream | 1984 | 10.00 |
| *—Reissue of Polydor PD1-6207* | | | |
| ❑ GHS 24047 | Join Hands | 1984 | 10.00 |
| *—Apparently, this 1979 album's first U.S. release* | | | |
| ❑ GHS 24048 | Kaleidoscope | 1984 | 10.00 |
| *—Reissue of PVC 7921* | | | |
| ❑ GHS 24049 | A Kiss in the Dream House | 1984 | 10.00 |
| *—Apparently, this 1982 album's first U.S. release* | | | |
| ❑ GHS 24050 | Juju | 1984 | 10.00 |
| *—Reissue of PVC 8903* | | | |
| ❑ GHS 24051 | Once Upon a Time: The Singles | 1984 | 10.00 |
| *—Reissue of PVC 8906* | | | |
| ❑ GHS 24052 [(2)] | Nocturne | 1984 | 10.00 |
| ❑ GHS 24092 | Tinderbox | 1986 | 10.00 |
| ❑ GHS 24134 | Through the Looking Glass | 1987 | 10.00 |
| ❑ GHS 24205 | Peepshow | 1988 | 10.00 |
| ❑ GEF 24387 | Superstition | 1991 | 12.00 |
| ❑ GEF 24630 | The Rapture | 1995 | 12.00 |
| **POLYDOR** | | | |
| ❑ PD1-6207 | The Scream | 1978 | 30.00 |
| **PVC** | | | |
| ❑ 7921 | Kaleidoscope | 1980 | 25.00 |
| ❑ 8903 | Ju Ju | 1981 | 25.00 |
| *—Original copies include bonus single "Israel"/"Red Over White"* | | | |
| ❑ 8906 | Once Upon a Time: The Singles | 1981 | 20.00 |
| *—With poster and inner sleeve* | | | |
| **WARNER BROS.** | | | |
| ❑ WBMS-138 [DJ] | The Tinderbox Interview | 1986 | 25.00 |
| *—Part of "The Warner Bros. Music Show"* | | | |

### SIR DOUGLAS QUINTET Also see DOUG SAHM.

| Number | Title (A Side/B Side) | Yr | NM |
|---|---|---|---|
| **ABC DOT** | | | |
| ❑ DO-2057 | Texas Rock for Country Rollers | 1976 | 15.00 |
| *—As "Sir Doug and the Texas Tornadoes"* | | | |
| **ATLANTIC** | | | |
| ❑ SD 7287 | Texas Tornado | 1974 | 15.00 |
| *—As "Sir Douglas Band"* | | | |
| **BEAT ROCKET** | | | |
| ❑ BR 123 | The Best of the Sir Douglas Quintet | 2000 | 12.00 |
| *—Reissue of Tribe LP on 180-gram vinyl* | | | |
| ❑ BR 124 | The Sir Douglas Quintet Is Back! | 2000 | 12.00 |
| *—New compilation of Tribe material on 180-gram vinyl* | | | |
| **PHILIPS** | | | |
| ❑ PHS 600344 | 1 + 1 + 1 = 4 | 1970 | 25.00 |
| ❑ PHS 600353 | The Return of Doug Saldana | 1971 | 25.00 |
| **R&M** | | | |
| ❑ UDL-2343 | The Tracker | 1981 | 20.00 |
| **SMASH** | | | |
| ❑ SRS-67108 | Sir Douglas Quintet + 2 = Honkey Blues | 1968 | 30.00 |
| ❑ SRS-67115 | Mendocino | 1969 | 25.00 |
| ❑ SRS-67130 | Together After Five | 1970 | 25.00 |
| **TAKOMA** | | | |
| ❑ TAK-7086 | The Best of the Sir Douglas Quintet | 1980 | 12.00 |
| ❑ TAK-7088 | Border Wave | 1981 | 12.00 |
| ❑ TAK-7095 | Sir Douglas Quintet Live | 1985 | 12.00 |
| **TRIBE** | | | |
| ❑ TR 37001 [M] | The Best of the Sir Douglas Quintet | 1966 | 70.00 |
| ❑ TRS 47001 [R] | The Best of the Sir Douglas Quintet | 1966 | 50.00 |
| **VARRICK** | | | |
| ❑ 004 | Quintessence | 1983 | 12.00 |

### SIR LANCELOT

| Number | Title (A Side/B Side) | Yr | NM |
|---|---|---|---|
| **MERCURY** | | | |
| ❑ MG-25159 [10] | Calypso | 1952 | 50.00 |

### SIR LORD BALTIMORE

| Number | Title (A Side/B Side) | Yr | NM |
|---|---|---|---|
| **MERCURY** | | | |
| ❑ SRM-1-613 | Sir Lord Baltimore | 1971 | 25.00 |
| ❑ SR-61328 | Kingdom Come | 1970 | 25.00 |

### SIRAVO, GEORGE

| Number | Title (A Side/B Side) | Yr | NM |
|---|---|---|---|
| **AD-LIB** | | | |
| ❑ S-226 [S] | Out on a Limb | 196? | 20.00 |
| **COLUMBIA** | | | |
| ❑ CL 6146 [10] | Your Dance Date with George Siravo | 1951 | 40.00 |
| **EPIC** | | | |
| ❑ BN 607 [S] | Everything Goes | 1961 | 20.00 |
| **KAPP** | | | |
| ❑ KL-1016 [M] | Polite Jazz | 1956 | 30.00 |
| **MERCURY** | | | |
| ❑ MG-20327 [M] | Darling, Please Forgive Me | 1958 | 30.00 |
| **RCA CAMDEN** | | | |
| ❑ CAS-505 [S] | Siravo Swing Session | 1959 | 20.00 |
| **RCA VICTOR** | | | |
| ❑ LPM-1970 [M] | Swingin' in Hi-Fi in Studio A | 1959 | 25.00 |
| ❑ LSP-1970 [S] | Swingin' in Hi-Fi in Studio A | 1959 | 30.00 |
| **TIME** | | | |
| ❑ S-2019 [S] | Seductive Strings | 196? | 20.00 |
| ❑ S-2115 [S] | And Then I Wrote Richard Rodgers | 196? | 20.00 |
| **VIK** | | | |
| ❑ LX-1091 [M] | Old But New | 1957 | 30.00 |
| ❑ LX-1125 [M] | Swing Hi, Swing Fi | 1958 | 30.00 |

### SIREN

| Number | Title (A Side/B Side) | Yr | NM |
|---|---|---|---|
| **ELEKTRA** | | | |
| ❑ EKS-74087 | Strange Locomotion | 1971 | 20.00 |

### SISTER DOUBLE HAPPINESS

REPRISE

❑ PRO-A-5010 [DJ] Heart and Mind 1991 40.00
—*Vinyl is promo only*

SST

❑ 162 Sister Double Happiness 1988 10.00

### SISTER SLEDGE

ATCO

❑ SD 36-105 Circle of Love 1975 20.00

ATLANTIC

❑ 81255 When the Boys Meet the Girls 1985 10.00

COTILLION

❑ SD 5209 We Are Family 1979 10.00
❑ SD 5231 The Sisters 1982 10.00
❑ SD 9919 Together 1976 20.00
❑ SD 16012 Love Somebody Today 1980 10.00
❑ SD 16027 All American Girls 1981 10.00
❑ 90069 Bet Cha Say That to All the Girls 1983 10.00

### SIX, THE

BETHLEHEM

❑ BCP-28 [M] The Six 1955 80.00
❑ BCP-57 [M] The View From Jazzbo's Head 1956 100.00

### SIX AND SEVEN-EIGHTHS STRING BAND, THE

FOLKWAYS

❑ FP-671 [M] The Six and Seven-Eighths String Band 1951 50.00
❑ FP-2671 [M] The Six and Seven-Eighths String Band 195? 40.00

### SIZEMORE, ARTHUR

DECCA

❑ DL 4785 [M] Mountain Ballads and Old Hymns 1966 30.00
❑ DL 74785 [S] Mountain Ballads and Old Hymns 1966 40.00

### SKAGGS, RICKY

ATLANTIC

❑ 82834 Solid Ground 1995 15.00

EPIC

❑ EAS 2022 [DJ] The Ricky Skaggs Story 1990 30.00
—*Promo-only interview record*
❑ FE 37193 Waitin' for the Sun to Shine 1981 10.00
❑ FE 37996 Highways and Heartaches 1982 10.00
❑ FE 39409 Favorite Country Songs 1985 10.00
❑ FE 39410 Country Boy 1984 10.00
❑ FE 40103 Live in London 1985 10.00
❑ FE 40309 Love's Gonna Get Ya! 1986 8.00
❑ FE 40623 Comin' Home to Stay 1988 8.00
❑ FE 45027 Kentucky Thunder 1989 10.00

ROUNDER

❑ 0151 Family and Friends 1982 12.00

SUGAR HILL

❑ SH-3706 Sweet Temptation 1979 12.00
❑ SH-3711 Skaggs and Rice 1980 12.00

SUGAR HILL/EPIC

❑ FE 38954 Don't Cheat in Our Hometown 1983 10.00

### SKAGGS, RICKY, AND KEITH WHITLEY

REBEL

❑ 1504 Second Generation Bluegrass 1972 20.00
❑ 1550 That's It 1975 20.00

### SKELTON, RED

LIBERTY

❑ LRP-3425 [M] Red Skelton Conducts 1966 20.00
❑ LRP-3477 [M] Music from the Heart 1966 20.00
❑ LST-7425 [S] Red Skelton Conducts 1966 25.00
❑ LST-7477 [S] Music from the Heart 1966 25.00

### SKID ROW Two different groups.

ATLANTIC

❑ 1P-8136 Slave to the Grind 1991 30.00
—*U.S. vinyl version available only from Columbia House; all copies are the censored version with "Beggars Day"*
❑ 81936 Skid Row 1989 10.00

EPIC

❑ E 30404 Skid Row 1971 20.00
❑ E 30913 34 Hours 1971 25.00

### SKIN ALLEY

STAX

❑ STS-3013 Two Quid Deal 1973 20.00
—*With poster*

### SKINNER, CORNELIA AND OTIS

RCA CAMDEN

❑ CAL-190 [M] Cornelia Skinner with Otis Skinner 1955 30.00

### SKINNER, JIMMIE

DECCA

❑ DL 4132 [M] Country Singer 1961 40.00

MERCURY

❑ MG-20352 [M] Songs That Make the Jukebox Play 1957 80.00
❑ MG-20700 [M] Jimmie Skinner Sings Jimmie Rodgers 1962 25.00
❑ SR-60700 [S] Jimmie Skinner Sings Jimmie Rodgers 1962 30.00

STARDAY

❑ SLP-240 [M] Jimmie Skinner 1963 40.00

VETCO

❑ 3001 Jimmie Skinner Sings Bluegrass 1976 15.00

WING

❑ MGW-12277 [M] Country Blues 1964 25.00
❑ SRW-16277 [R] Country Blues 1964 15.00

### SKIP AND THE CREATIONS

JUSTICE

❑ (# unknown) Mobam 196? 400.00

### SKUNKS, THE

TEEN TOWN

❑ TTLP-101 Getting Started 1968 50.00

### SKYLINERS, THE

CALICO

❑ LP-3000 [M] The Skyliners 1959 600.00
—*Yellow and blue label*
❑ LP-3000 [M] The Skyliners 196? 200.00
—*Blue label*

KAMA SUTRA

❑ KSBS-2026 Once Upon a Time 1971 25.00

ORIGINAL SOUND

❑ OS-5010 [M] Since I Don't Have You 1963 50.00
❑ OSS-8873 [S] Since I Don't Have You 1963 70.00
❑ OSS-8873 [S] Since I Don't Have You 197? 15.00
—*Reissue on thinner vinyl*

### SLACK, FREDDIE

EMARCY

❑ MG-36094 [M] Boogie-Woogie on the 88 1956 40.00

### SLADE

CBS ASSOCIATED

❑ FZ 39336 Keep Your Hands Off My Power Supply 1984 10.00
❑ PZ 39336 Keep Your Hands Off My Power Supply 1985 8.00
—*Budget-line reissue*
❑ FZ 39976 Rogues Gallery 1985 12.00
❑ BFZ 40908 You Boyz Make Big Noize 1986 12.00

COTILLION

❑ SD 9035 Play It Loud 1970 50.00

FONTANA

❑ SRF-67598 Ballzy 1969 150.00
❑ SRF-67598 [DJ] Ballzy 1969 100.00
—*White label promo*

POLYDOR

❑ PD-5508 Slade Alive! 1972 15.00
❑ PD-5524 Slayed? 1973 15.00

REPRISE

❑ MS 2173 Sladest 1973 15.00

WARNER BROS.

❑ BS 2770 Stomp Your Hands, Clap Your Feet 1974 15.00
❑ BS 2865 Slade in Flame 1975 15.00
❑ BS 2936 Nobody's Fools 1976 20.00

### SLATKIN, FELIX

LIBERTY

❑ LRP-3150 [M] Fantastic Percussion 1960 15.00
❑ LRP-3287 [M] Our Winter Love 1963 12.00
❑ LST-7150 [S] Fantastic Percussion 1960 20.00
❑ LST-7287 [S] Our Winter Love 1963 15.00
❑ LMM-13001 [M] Paradise Found 1960 15.00
❑ LMM-13008 [M] Street Scene 1961 15.00
❑ LMM-13011 [M] Many Splendored Themes 1962 15.00
❑ LMM-13019 [M] Inspired Themes from the Inspired Films 1962 15.00
❑ LMM-13021 [M] Fantastic Strings Play Fantastic Themes 1962 15.00
❑ LMM-13024 [M] Hoedown 1963 15.00
❑ LMM-13027 [M] The Ballad of New Orleans 1963 15.00
❑ LSS-14001 [S] Paradise Found 1960 18.00
❑ LSS-14008 [S] Street Scene 1961 18.00
❑ LSS-14011 [S] Many Splendored Themes 1962 18.00
❑ LSS-14019 [S] Inspired Themes from the Inspired Films 1962 18.00
❑ LSS-14021 [S] Fantastic Strings Play Fantastic Themes 1962 18.00
❑ LSS-14024 [S] Hoedown 1963 18.00
❑ LSS-14027 [S] The Ballad of New Orleans 1963 18.00

SUNSET

❑ SUM-1106 [M] Love Strings 196? 12.00
❑ SUM-1141 [M] Seasons Greetings 196? 12.00
❑ SUM-1170 [M] Tender Strings 196? 12.00
❑ SUS-5106 [S] Love Strings 196? 12.00
❑ SUS-5141 [S] Seasons Greetings 196? 12.00
❑ SUS-5170 [S] Tender Strings 196? 12.00

UNITED ARTISTS

❑ UAS-6818 Classic Country 1971 10.00

### SLAUGHTER

CHRYSALIS

❑ F1-21702 [DJ] Stick It To Ya 1990 30.00
—*Black generic sleeve with hole; numbered edition of 500 with sticker that says "Limited Edition Special Vinyl Pressing Metal Radio Only"*
❑ F1-21911 The Wild Life 1992 20.00
—*Vinyl version available only through Columbia House*
❑ R 120666 [EP] Stick It Live 1990 20.00
—*Vinyl version available only through BMG Direct Marketing*

### SLAYER

AMERICAN

❑ C2 69192 [(2)] Diabolus in Musica 1998 20.00

COMBAT

❑ MX 8020 Hell Awaits 1985 15.00

DEF AMERICAN

❑ DFS 24307 Seasons in the Abyss 1990 20.00

DEF JAM

❑ GHS 24131 Reign in Blood 1986 8.00
❑ GHS 24203 South of Heaven 1988 8.00

METAL BLADE

❑ E 1034 Show No Mercy 1983 20.00
❑ MBR 1037 [PD] Live Undead 1984 30.00
—*Limited edition picture disc*
❑ 71034 Show No Mercy 198? 15.00
—*Early reissue of 1034*
❑ 72214 [PD] Show No Mercy 1987 25.00
—*Picture disc in plastic sleeve*
❑ 72217 [EP] Live Undead 1987 10.00
❑ 72297 Hell Awaits 1988 10.00
—*Reissue of Combat LP*

### SLEDGE, PERCY

ATLANTIC

❑ 8125 [M] When a Man Loves a Woman 1966 50.00
❑ SD 8125 [R] When a Man Loves a Woman 1966 30.00
❑ 8132 [M] Warm and Tender Soul 1966 50.00
❑ SD 8132 [R] Warm and Tender Soul 1966 30.00
❑ 8146 [M] The Percy Sledge Way 1967 50.00
❑ SD 8146 [S] The Percy Sledge Way 1967 50.00
❑ SD 8180 Take Time to Know Her 1968 50.00
❑ SD 8210 The Best of Percy Sledge 1969 25.00
❑ 80212 The Ultimate Collection: When a Man Loves a Woman 1983 12.00

CAPRICORN

❑ CP 0147 I'll Be Your Everything 1974 15.00

MONUMENT

❑ FW 38532 Percy! 1983 12.00

### SLEET, DON

JAZZLAND

❑ JLP-45 [M] All Members 1961 25.00
❑ JLP-945 [S] All Members 1961 30.00

### SLICK, GRACE Also see THE GREAT SOCIETY; JEFFERSON AIRPLANE; JEFFERSON STARSHIP.

GRUNT

❑ BFL1-0347 Manhole 1974 12.00
❑ AYL1-3736 Manhole 1981 8.00
—*"Best Buy Series" reissue*

RCA VICTOR

❑ AFL1-3544 Dreams 1980 10.00
❑ AQL1-3851 Welcome to the Wrecking Ball 1981 10.00
❑ DJL1-3922 [DJ] Welcome to the Wrecking Ball Interview 1981 20.00
❑ DJL1-3923 [DJ] RCA Special Radio Series 1981 20.00

### SLICKEE BOYS

DACOIT

❑ 1001 Separated Vegetables 1977 80.00
—*Limited edition of 100 copies*

GIANT

❑ GR 16037-1 Live at Last 1989 10.00

LIMP

❑ 1003 Separated Vegetables 1980 25.00
—*Limited edition of 300 copies; reissue with new cover*

TWIN/TONE

❑ TTR 8337 Cybernetic Dreams of Pi 1983 15.00
❑ TTR 8544 Uh Oh, No Breaks 1985 12.00

### SLIM JIM

SOMA

❑ MG 1225 [M] Slim Jim Sings 1958 40.00

### SLITS, THE

ANTILLES

❑ AN-7077 Cut 1979 40.00



**Except when noted otherwise, VG = 25% of NM, and VG+ = 50% of NM. (Example: VG = $2.00, VG+ = $4.00 and NM = $8.00.)**

### SLOAN, P.F.

| Number | Title (A Side/B Side) | Yr | NM |
|---|---|---|---|
| **ATCO** | | | |
| ❑ SD 33-268 | Measure of Pleasure | 1968 | 25.00 |
| **DUNHILL** | | | |
| ❑ D-50004 [M] | Songs of Our Times | 1965 | 25.00 |
| ❑ DS-50004 [S] | Songs of Our Times | 1965 | 30.00 |
| ❑ D-50007 [M] | Twelve More Times | 1966 | 25.00 |
| ❑ DS-50007 [S] | Twelve More Times | 1966 | 30.00 |
| **MUMS** | | | |
| ❑ KZ 31260 | Raised on Records | 1972 | 20.00 |
| **RHINO** | | | |
| ❑ RNLP-70133 | Precious Times: The Best of P.F. Sloan | 1986 | 10.00 |

### SLOANE, CAROL

| Number | Title (A Side/B Side) | Yr | NM |
|---|---|---|---|
| **COLUMBIA** | | | |
| ❑ CL 1766 [M] | Out of the Blue | 1962 | 60.00 |
| ❑ CL 1923 [M] | Carol Sloane Live at 30th Street | 1963 | 60.00 |
| ❑ CS 8566 [S] | Out of the Blue | 1962 | 80.00 |
| ❑ CS 8723 [S] | Carol Sloane Live at 30th Street | 1963 | 80.00 |

### SLY AND THE FAMILY STONE

| Number | Title (A Side/B Side) | Yr | NM |
|---|---|---|---|
| **EPIC** | | | |
| ❑ AS 264 [DJ] | Everything You Always Wanted to Hear by Sly and the Family Stone But Were Afraid to Ask For | 1976 | 25.00 |
| *—Promo-only compilation* | | | |
| ❑ LN 24324 [M] | A Whole New Thing | 1967 | 20.00 |
| ❑ LN 24371 [M] | Dance to the Music | 1968 | 40.00 |
| ❑ BN 26324 [S] | A Whole New Thing | 1967 | 20.00 |
| ❑ BN 26371 [S] | Dance to the Music | 1968 | 15.00 |
| ❑ BN 26397 | Life | 1968 | 15.00 |
| ❑ BN 26456 | Stand! | 1969 | 15.00 |
| ❑ PE 26456 | Stand! | 1986 | 8.00 |
| *—Budget-line reissue* | | | |
| ❑ EQ 30325 [Q] | Sly and the Family Stone's Greatest Hits | 1971 | 100.00 |
| *—Has alternate mixes of "Hot Fun in the Summertime," "Thank You" and "Everybody Is a Star," which are not rechanneled stereo as they are on other LPs* | | | |
| ❑ KE 30325 | Sly and the Family Stone's Greatest Hits | 1970 | 12.00 |
| *—Yellow label, gatefold cover* | | | |
| ❑ PE 30325 | Sly and the Family Stone's Greatest Hits | 1979 | 8.00 |
| *—Budget-line reissue* | | | |
| ❑ E 30333 | Life | 1971 | 12.00 |
| *—Reissue of 26397* | | | |
| ❑ E 30334 | Dance to the Music | 1971 | 12.00 |
| *—Reissue of 26371* | | | |
| ❑ E 30335 | A Whole New Thing | 1971 | 12.00 |
| *—Reissue of 26324* | | | |
| ❑ KE 30986 | There's a Riot Goin' On | 1971 | 12.00 |
| *—Yellow label, gatefold cover* | | | |
| ❑ KE 32134 | Fresh | 1973 | 10.00 |
| *—Orange label* | | | |
| ❑ PE 32930 | Small Talk | 1974 | 10.00 |
| *—Orange label* | | | |
| ❑ PEQ 32930 [Q] | Small Talk | 1974 | 25.00 |
| ❑ PE 33835 | High on You | 1975 | 10.00 |
| *—Orange label* | | | |
| ❑ PEQ 33835 [Q] | High on You | 1975 | 25.00 |
| ❑ PE 34348 | Heard Ya Missed Me, Well I'm Back | 1976 | 10.00 |
| *—Orange label* | | | |
| ❑ JE 35974 | Ten Years Too Soon | 1979 | 10.00 |
| ❑ E2 37071 [(2)] | Anthology | 1981 | 15.00 |
| **WARNER BROS.** | | | |
| ❑ BSK 3303 | Back on the Right Track | 1979 | 10.00 |
| ❑ 23700 | Ain't But the Right Way | 1983 | 10.00 |

### SMACK, THE

| Number | Title (A Side/B Side) | Yr | NM |
|---|---|---|---|
| **AUDIO HOUSE** | | | |
| ❑ (# unknown) | The Smack | 1968 | 2000. |

### SMALL, DANNY

| Number | Title (A Side/B Side) | Yr | NM |
|---|---|---|---|
| **UNITED ARTISTS** | | | |
| ❑ UAJ-14004 [M] | Woman She Was Born for Sorrow | 1962 | 20.00 |
| ❑ UAJS-15004 [S] | Woman She Was Born for Sorrow | 1962 | 25.00 |

### SMALL, MILLIE

| Number | Title (A Side/B Side) | Yr | NM |
|---|---|---|---|
| **SMASH** | | | |
| ❑ MGS-27055 [M] | My Boy Lollipop | 1964 | 50.00 |
| ❑ SRS-67055 [R] | My Boy Lollipop | 1964 | 40.00 |

### SMALL FACES Also see FACES.

| Number | Title (A Side/B Side) | Yr | NM |
|---|---|---|---|
| **ACCORD** | | | |
| ❑ AN-7157 | By Appointment | 1982 | 10.00 |
| **ATLANTIC** | | | |
| ❑ SD 19113 | Playmates | 1977 | 10.00 |
| ❑ SD 19171 | 78 in the Shade | 1978 | 10.00 |
| **COMPLEAT** | | | |
| ❑ 67-2004 [(2)] | Big Music | 1985 | 12.00 |
| ❑ 67-5003 | Ogden's Nut Gone Flake | 1985 | 10.00 |
| *—Reissue* | | | |
| **IMMEDIATE** | | | |
| ❑ 4225 | Ogden's Nut Gone Flake | 1973 | 15.00 |
| *—Reissue has a standard square cover* | | | |
| ❑ Z12 52002 [S] | There Are But Four Small Faces | 1967 | 50.00 |
| *—Color cover (counterfeits have either black and white or black and green covers)* | | | |
| ❑ Z12 52008 [S] | Ogden's Nut Gone Flake | 1968 | 50.00 |
| *—Originals have a round cover* | | | |
| **MGM** | | | |
| ❑ M3F-4955 | Archetypes | 1974 | 12.00 |
| **PRIDE** | | | |
| ❑ PRD 0001 [R] | Early Faces | 1972 | 15.00 |
| ❑ PRD 0014 [P] | The History of the Small Faces | 1973 | 12.00 |
| **SIRE** | | | |
| ❑ SASH-3709 [(2)] | The Vintage Years | 1976 | 15.00 |

### SMART SET, THE

| Number | Title (A Side/B Side) | Yr | NM |
|---|---|---|---|
| **WARNER BROS.** | | | |
| ❑ W-1203 [M] | A New Experience in Vocal Styles | 1958 | 30.00 |
| ❑ WS-1203 [S] | A New Experience in Vocal Styles | 1958 | 40.00 |

### SMASHING PUMPKINS

| Number | Title (A Side/B Side) | Yr | NM |
|---|---|---|---|
| **CAROLINE** | | | |
| ❑ 1705 | Gish | 199? | 15.00 |
| *—With "Remastered" under the bar code* | | | |
| ❑ 1705 | Gish | 1991 | 60.00 |
| *—Originals do not have the word "Remastered" under the bar code* | | | |
| ❑ 1740 [(2)] | Siamese Dream | 199? | 50.00 |
| *—Pink marbled vinyl* | | | |
| ❑ 1740 [(2)] | Siamese Dream | 1993 | 80.00 |
| *—Originals have dark red vinyl* | | | |
| ❑ 1767 | Pisces Iscariot | 1994 | 100.00 |
| *—Regular pressing on colored vinyl, not numbered, no bonus 7-inch single* | | | |
| ❑ 1767 | Pisces Iscariot | 1994 | 300.00 |
| *—First 2,000 copies, hand-numbered on back cover, came with a bonus 7-inch single* | | | |
| ❑ 45879 [(2)] | Adore | 1998 | 30.00 |
| *—Different cover than CD version, and the entire LP was remixed into mono* | | | |
| ❑ 48936 [(2)] | Machina/The Machines of God | 2000 | 30.00 |
| *—With bound-in booklet* | | | |
| **CONSTANTINOPLE** | | | |
| ❑ CR 01-04 [(5)] | Machina II/The Friends and Enemies of Modern Music | 2000 | 3000. |
| *—Exactly 25 copies were pressed as two 12-inch and three 10-inch records, with the presumption that at least some of them would be bootlegged onto CDs and into downloadable files via the Internet. (This has indeed happened, so many fans have heard the music.) It's not known whether any of the 25 copies have left the hands of their original recipients, so the price above is highly speculative and probably conservative; VG value 1000; VG+ value 2000* | | | |

### SMECK, ROY

| Number | Title (A Side/B Side) | Yr | NM |
|---|---|---|---|
| **ABC-PARAMOUNT** | | | |
| ❑ ABC-119 [M] | South Seas Serenade | 1956 | 40.00 |
| ❑ ABC-174 [M] | Melodies with Memories | 1957 | 40.00 |
| ❑ ABC-234 [M] | Hi-Fi Paradise | 1958 | 40.00 |
| ❑ ABC-279 [M] | The Magic Ukulele | 1959 | 30.00 |
| ❑ ABCS-279 [S] | The Magic Ukulele | 1959 | 40.00 |
| ❑ ABC-309 [M] | The Happy Banjo | 1959 | 30.00 |
| ❑ ABCS-309 [S] | The Happy Banjo | 1959 | 40.00 |
| ❑ ABC-329 [M] | Adventures in Paradise | 1960 | 30.00 |
| ❑ ABCS-329 [S] | Adventures in Paradise | 1960 | 40.00 |
| ❑ ABC-330 [M] | The Haunting Hawaiian Guitar | 1960 | 25.00 |
| ❑ ABCS-330 [S] | The Haunting Hawaiian Guitar | 1960 | 30.00 |
| ❑ ABC-358 [M] | Adventures in Paradise, Volume 2 | 1961 | 25.00 |
| ❑ ABCS-358 [S] | Adventures in Paradise, Volume 2 | 1961 | 30.00 |
| ❑ ABC-379 [M] | Roy Smeck, His Singing Guitar and Paradise Serenaders | 1961 | 25.00 |
| ❑ ABCS-379 [S] | Roy Smeck, His Singing Guitar and Paradise Serenaders | 1961 | 30.00 |
| ❑ ABC-412 [M] | Stringing Along | 1962 | 25.00 |
| ❑ ABCS-412 [S] | Stringing Along | 1962 | 30.00 |
| ❑ ABC-414 [M] | Adventures in Paradise, Volume 3 | 1962 | 25.00 |
| ❑ ABCS-414 [S] | Adventures in Paradise, Volume 3 | 1962 | 30.00 |
| ❑ ABC-452 [M] | The Many Guitar Moods of Roy Smeck | 1963 | 25.00 |
| ❑ ABCS-452 [S] | The Many Guitar Moods of Roy Smeck | 1963 | 30.00 |
| ❑ ABC-462 [M] | Adventures in Paradise, Volume 4 | 1963 | 25.00 |
| ❑ ABCS-462 [S] | Adventures in Paradise, Volume 4 | 1963 | 30.00 |
| ❑ ABC-484 [M] | I Love to Hear a Banjo | 1964 | 25.00 |
| ❑ ABCS-484 [S] | I Love to Hear a Banjo | 1964 | 30.00 |
| **CORAL** | | | |
| ❑ CRL 56013 [10] | Drifting and Dreaming | 195? | 120.00 |
| **DECCA** | | | |
| ❑ DL 5458 [10] | Memory Lane | 1953 | 100.00 |
| ❑ DL 5473 [10] | Songs of the Range | 1953 | 100.00 |
| ❑ DL 8674 [M] | Memories of You | 1958 | 40.00 |
| *—Black label, silver print* | | | |
| **"X"** | | | |
| ❑ LPX-3012 [10] | South of the Border | 1954 | 120.00 |
| **"X"** | | | |
| ❑ LPA-3016 [10] | Christmas in Hawaii | 195? | 120.00 |

### SMILE (1)

| Number | Title (A Side/B Side) | Yr | NM |
|---|---|---|---|
| **PICKWICK** | | | |
| ❑ SPC-3288 | Smile | 1973 | 30.00 |

### SMITH, AL

| Number | Title (A Side/B Side) | Yr | NM |
|---|---|---|---|
| **BLUESVILLE** | | | |
| ❑ BVLP-1001 [M] | Hear My Blues | 1960 | 80.00 |
| *—Blue label, silver print* | | | |
| ❑ BVLP-1001 [M] | Hear My Blues | 1964 | 25.00 |
| *—Blue label, trident logo at right* | | | |
| ❑ BVLP-1014 [M] | Midnight Special | 1961 | 80.00 |
| *—Blue label, silver print* | | | |
| ❑ BVLP-1014 [M] | Midnight Special | 1964 | 25.00 |
| *—Blue label, trident logo at right* | | | |
| ❑ BVLP-1069 [M] | Blues Shout | 196? | 20.00 |

### SMITH, ARTHUR "GUITAR BOOGIE"

| Number | Title (A Side/B Side) | Yr | NM |
|---|---|---|---|
| **ABC-PARAMOUNT** | | | |
| ❑ ABC-441 [M] | Arthur "Guitar" Smith and Voices | 1963 | 20.00 |
| ❑ ABCS-441 [S] | Arthur "Guitar" Smith and Voices | 1963 | 25.00 |
| **DOT** | | | |
| ❑ DLP-3600 [M] | Original Guitar Boogie | 1964 | 20.00 |
| ❑ DLP-3636 [M] | Great Country and Western Hits | 1965 | 15.00 |
| ❑ DLP-3642 [M] | Singing on the Mountain with the Crossroads Quartet | 1965 | 20.00 |
| ❑ DLP-3769 [M] | A Tribute to Jim Reeves | 1966 | 15.00 |
| ❑ DLP-25600 [S] | Original Guitar Boogie | 1964 | 25.00 |
| ❑ DLP-25636 [S] | Great Country and Western Hits | 1965 | 20.00 |
| ❑ DLP-25642 [S] | Singing on the Mountain with the Crossroads Quartet | 1965 | 25.00 |
| ❑ DLP-25769 [S] | A Tribute to Jim Reeves | 1966 | 20.00 |
| **MGM** | | | |
| ❑ E-236 [10] | Foolish Questions | 1954 | 120.00 |
| ❑ E-533 [10] | Fingers on Fire | 1955 | 100.00 |
| ❑ E-3301 [M] | Specials | 1955 | 80.00 |
| ❑ E-3525 [M] | Fingers on Fire | 1957 | 80.00 |
| **MONUMENT** | | | |
| ❑ Z 32259 | Battling Banjos | 1973 | 12.00 |
| **STARDAY** | | | |
| ❑ SLP-173 [M] | Mister Guitar | 1962 | 30.00 |
| ❑ SLP-186 [M] | Arthur Smith and the Crossroads Quartet | 1962 | 40.00 |
| ❑ SLP-216 [M] | Arthur "Guitar Boogie" Smith Goes to Town | 1963 | 30.00 |
| ❑ SLP-241 [M] | In Person | 1963 | 30.00 |
| ❑ SLP-266 [M] | Down Home | 1964 | 30.00 |

### SMITH, "FIDDLIN' " ARTHUR

| Number | Title (A Side/B Side) | Yr | NM |
|---|---|---|---|
| **STARDAY** | | | |
| ❑ SLP-202 [M] | Rare Old Time Fiddle Tunes | 1962 | 30.00 |

### SMITH, BESSIE

| Number | Title (A Side/B Side) | Yr | NM |
|---|---|---|---|
| **COLUMBIA** | | | |
| ❑ GP 33 [(2)] | The World's Greatest Blues Singer | 1970 | 20.00 |
| ❑ GL 503 [M] | The Bessie Smith Story, Volume 1 | 1951 | 50.00 |
| *—Maroon label, gold print* | | | |
| ❑ GL 504 [M] | The Bessie Smith Story, Volume 2 | 1951 | 50.00 |
| *—Maroon label, gold print* | | | |
| ❑ GL 505 [M] | The Bessie Smith Story, Volume 3 | 1951 | 50.00 |
| *—Maroon label, gold print* | | | |
| ❑ GL 506 [M] | The Bessie Smith Story, Volume 4 | 1951 | 50.00 |
| *—Maroon label, gold print* | | | |
| ❑ CL 855 [M] | The Bessie Smith Story, Volume 1 | 1956 | 25.00 |
| *—Red and black label with six "eye" logos* | | | |
| ❑ CL 856 [M] | The Bessie Smith Story, Volume 2 | 1956 | 25.00 |
| *—Red and black label with six "eye" logos* | | | |
| ❑ CL 857 [M] | The Bessie Smith Story, Volume 3 | 1956 | 25.00 |
| *—Red and black label with six "eye" logos* | | | |
| ❑ CL 858 [M] | The Bessie Smith Story, Volume 4 | 1956 | 25.00 |
| *—Red and black label with six "eye" logos* | | | |
| ❑ C2 47091 [(2)] | The Complete Recordings Volume 1: Empress of the Blues | 1991 | 20.00 |
| *—Box set; none of the subsequent volumes came out on vinyl* | | | |

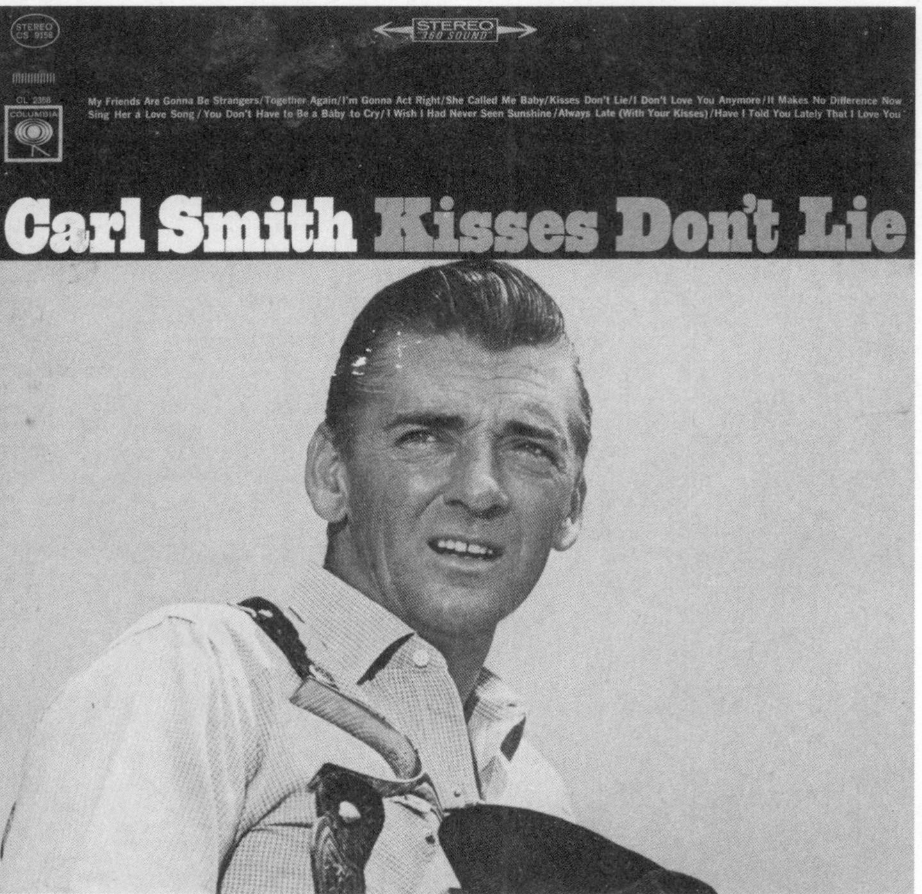


Carl Smith, *Kisses Don't Lie,* Columbia CS 9158, 1965, stereo, $25.

| Number | Title (A Side/B Side) | Yr | NM |
|---|---|---|---|
| **COLUMBIA MASTERWORKS** | | | |
| ❑ ML 4801 [M] | The Bessie Smith Story, Volume 1 | 1954 | 30.00 |
| ❑ ML 4802 [M] | The Bessie Smith Story, Volume 2 | 1954 | 30.00 |
| ❑ ML 4809 [M] | The Bessie Smith Story, Volume 3 | 1954 | 30.00 |
| ❑ ML 4810 [M] | The Bessie Smith Story, Volume 4 | 1954 | 30.00 |

**SMITH, BILL**

| Number | Title (A Side/B Side) | Yr | NM |
|---|---|---|---|
| **CONTEMPORARY** | | | |
| ❑ M-3591 [M] | Folk Jazz | 1961 | 20.00 |
| ❑ S-7591 [S] | Folk Jazz | 1961 | 25.00 |

**SMITH, BOB**

| Number | Title (A Side/B Side) | Yr | NM |
|---|---|---|---|
| **KENT** | | | |
| ❑ KST-551 [(2)] | The Visit | 1970 | 100.00 |
| *—Deduct 25 percent if poster is missing* | | | |

**SMITH, BUSTER**

| Number | Title (A Side/B Side) | Yr | NM |
|---|---|---|---|
| **ATLANTIC** | | | |
| ❑ 1323 [M] | The Legendary Buster Smith | 1960 | 50.00 |
| *—Black label* | | | |
| ❑ 1323 [M] | The Legendary Buster Smith | 1961 | 20.00 |
| *—Multi-color label, white "fan" logo* | | | |
| ❑ SD 1323 [S] | The Legendary Buster Smith | 1960 | 50.00 |
| *—Green label* | | | |
| ❑ SD 1323 [S] | The Legendary Buster Smith | 1961 | 20.00 |
| *—Multi-color label, white "fan" logo* | | | |

**SMITH, CAL**

| Number | Title (A Side/B Side) | Yr | NM |
|---|---|---|---|
| **DECCA** | | | |
| ❑ DL 75369 | I've Found Someone of My Own | 1972 | 15.00 |
| **KAPP** | | | |
| ❑ KL-1504 [M] | All the World Is Lonely Now | 1966 | 25.00 |
| ❑ KL-1537 [M] | Goin' to Cal's Place | 1967 | 25.00 |
| ❑ KL-1544 [M] | Travelin' Man | 1968 | 40.00 |
| *—White label promo only; in stereo cover with "Mono" sticker* | | | |
| ❑ KS-3504 [S] | All the World Is Lonely Now | 1966 | 20.00 |
| ❑ KS-3537 [S] | Goin' to Cal's Place | 1967 | 20.00 |
| ❑ KS-3544 [S] | Travelin' Man | 1968 | 20.00 |
| ❑ KS-3585 | Drinking Champagne | 1968 | 20.00 |
| ❑ KS-3608 | Cal Smith Sings It Takes Me All Night Long | 1969 | 20.00 |
| ❑ KS-3642 | The Best of Cal Smith | 1969 | 15.00 |
| **MCA** | | | |
| ❑ 70 | The Best of Cal Smith | 1973 | 10.00 |
| *—Reissue of Kapp 3642* | | | |
| ❑ 344 | Cal Smith | 1973 | 10.00 |
| *—Reissue of Decca LP* | | | |
| ❑ 424 | Country Bumpkin | 1974 | 10.00 |
| ❑ 467 | It's Time to Pay the Fiddler | 1975 | 10.00 |
| ❑ 485 | My Kind of Country | 1975 | 10.00 |
| ❑ 2172 | Jason's Farm | 1976 | 10.00 |
| ❑ 2266 | I Just Came Home to Count the Memories | 1977 | 10.00 |

**SMITH, CARL**

| Number | Title (A Side/B Side) | Yr | NM |
|---|---|---|---|
| **ABC HICKORY** | | | |
| ❑ HB-44005 | This Lady Loves Me | 1977 | 12.00 |
| ❑ HB-44015 | The Silver-Tongued Cowboy | 1978 | 12.00 |
| **COLUMBIA** | | | |
| ❑ GP 31 [(2)] | The Carl Smith Anniversary Album/20 Years of Hits | 1970 | 25.00 |
| ❑ CL 959 [M] | Sunday Down South | 1957 | 50.00 |
| ❑ CL 1022 [M] | Smith's the Name | 1957 | 50.00 |
| ❑ CL 1172 [M] | Let's Live a Little | 1958 | 50.00 |
| ❑ CL 1532 [M] | The Carl Smith Touch | 1960 | 25.00 |
| ❑ CL 1740 [M] | Easy to Please | 1961 | 25.00 |
| ❑ CL 1937 [M] | Carl Smith's Greatest Hits | 1962 | 20.00 |
| ❑ CL 2091 [M] | The Tall, Tall Gentleman | 1963 | 20.00 |
| ❑ CL 2173 [M] | There Stands the Glass | 1964 | 20.00 |
| ❑ CL 2293 [M] | I Want to Live and Love | 1965 | 20.00 |
| ❑ CL 2358 [M] | Kisses Don't Lie | 1965 | 20.00 |
| ❑ CL 2501 [M] | Man with a Plan | 1966 | 20.00 |
| ❑ CL 2579 [10] | Carl Smith | 1955 | 100.00 |
| ❑ CL 2610 [M] | The Country Gentleman | 1967 | 20.00 |
| ❑ CL 2687 [M] | The Country Gentleman Sings His Favorites | 1967 | 25.00 |
| ❑ CL 2822 [M] | Deep Water | 1968 | 30.00 |
| ❑ CL 2888 [M] | Country on My Mind | 1968 | 50.00 |
| ❑ CS 8352 [S] | The Carl Smith Touch | 1960 | 30.00 |
| ❑ CS 8540 [S] | Easy to Please | 1961 | 30.00 |
| ❑ CS 8737 [S] | Carl Smith's Greatest Hits | 1962 | 25.00 |
| ❑ CS 8891 [S] | The Tall, Tall Gentleman | 1963 | 25.00 |
| ❑ CS 8973 [S] | There Stands the Glass | 1964 | 25.00 |
| ❑ CL 9023 [10] | Sentimental Songs | 195? | 100.00 |
| ❑ CL 9026 [10] | Softly and Tenderly | 195? | 80.00 |
| ❑ CS 9093 [S] | I Want to Live and Love | 1965 | 25.00 |
| ❑ CS 9158 [S] | Kisses Don't Lie | 1965 | 25.00 |
| ❑ CS 9301 [S] | Man with a Plan | 1966 | 25.00 |
| ❑ CS 9410 [S] | The Country Gentleman | 1967 | 25.00 |
| ❑ CS 9487 [S] | The Country Gentleman Sings His Favorites | 1967 | 20.00 |
| ❑ CS 9622 [S] | Deep Water | 1968 | 20.00 |
| ❑ CS 9688 [S] | Country on My Mind | 1968 | 20.00 |
| ❑ CS 9786 | Faded Love and Winter Roses | 1969 | 20.00 |
| ❑ CS 9807 | Carl Smith's Greatest Hits, Vol. 2 | 1969 | 20.00 |
| ❑ CS 9870 | Carl Smith Sings a Tribute to Roy Acuff | 1969 | 20.00 |
| ❑ CS 9898 | I Love You Because | 1970 | 20.00 |
| ❑ C 30215 | Carl Smith with the Tunesmiths | 1970 | 20.00 |
| ❑ C 30548 | Bluegrass | 1971 | 20.00 |
| ❑ C 31277 | Don't Say You're Mine | 1972 | 20.00 |
| ❑ KC 31606 | If This Is Goodbye | 1972 | 20.00 |
| ❑ FC 38906 | Carl Smith | 198? | 10.00 |
| **HICKORY/MGM** | | | |
| ❑ H3G 4518 | The Way I Lose My Mind | 1975 | 12.00 |
| ❑ H3G 4522 | The Girl I Love | 1975 | 12.00 |
| **ROUNDER** | | | |
| ❑ SS-25 | Old Lonesome Times | 1988 | 10.00 |

**SMITH, CARL; LEFTY FRIZZELL; MARTY ROBBINS**

| Number | Title (A Side/B Side) | Yr | NM |
|---|---|---|---|
| **COLUMBIA** | | | |
| ❑ CL 2544 [10] | Carl, Lefty and Marty | 1955 | 400.00 |

**SMITH, CONNIE**

| Number | Title (A Side/B Side) | Yr | NM |
|---|---|---|---|
| **COLUMBIA** | | | |
| ❑ KC 32185 | A Lady Named Smith | 1973 | 12.00 |
| ❑ KC 32492 | God Is Abundant | 1973 | 12.00 |
| ❑ KC 32581 | That's the Way Love Goes | 1974 | 12.00 |
| ❑ KC 33055 | I Never Knew (What That Song Meant Before) | 1974 | 12.00 |
| ❑ KC 33375 | I Got a Lot of Hurtin' Done Today/I've Got My Baby on My Mind | 1975 | 12.00 |
| ❑ KC 33414 | Connie Smith Sings Hank Williams Gospel | 1975 | 12.00 |
| ❑ KC 33918 | The Song We Fell in Love To | 1976 | 12.00 |
| ❑ KC 34270 | I Don't Want to Talk It Over Anymore | 1976 | 12.00 |
| ❑ KC 34877 | The Best of Connie Smith | 1977 | 12.00 |
| **MONUMENT** | | | |
| ❑ 7609 | Pure Connie Smith | 1977 | 12.00 |
| ❑ 7624 | New Horizons | 1978 | 12.00 |
| **RCA CAMDEN** | | | |
| ❑ ACL1-0250 | Even the Bad Times Are Good | 1973 | 10.00 |
| *—With Nat Stuckey* | | | |
| ❑ CAL-2120 [M] | Connie in the Country | 1967 | 15.00 |
| ❑ CAS-2120 [S] | Connie in the Country | 1967 | 12.00 |
| ❑ CAS-2495 | My Heart Has a Mind of Its Own | 1971 | 10.00 |
| ❑ CAS-2550 | City Lights — Country Favorites | 1972 | 10.00 |
| **RCA VICTOR** | | | |
| ❑ APL1-0188 | Dream Painter | 1973 | 12.00 |
| ❑ APL1-0275 | Connie Smith's Greatest Hits, Volume 1 | 1973 | 12.00 |
| ❑ APL1-0607 | Now | 1974 | 12.00 |
| ❑ LPM-3341 [M] | Connie Smith | 1965 | 20.00 |
| ❑ LSP-3341 [S] | Connie Smith | 1965 | 25.00 |
| ❑ LPM-3444 [M] | Cute 'n' Country | 1965 | 20.00 |
| ❑ LSP-3444 [S] | Cute 'n' Country | 1965 | 25.00 |
| ❑ LPM-3520 [M] | Miss Smith Goes to Nashville | 1966 | 20.00 |
| ❑ LSP-3520 [S] | Miss Smith Goes to Nashville | 1966 | 25.00 |
| ❑ LPM-3589 [M] | Connie Smith Sings Great Sacred Songs | 1966 | 20.00 |
| ❑ LSP-3589 [S] | Connie Smith Sings Great Sacred Songs | 1966 | 25.00 |
| ❑ LPM-3628 [M] | Born to Sing | 1966 | 20.00 |
| ❑ LSP-3628 [S] | Born to Sing | 1966 | 25.00 |
| ❑ LPM-3725 [M] | Downtown Country | 1967 | 25.00 |
| ❑ LSP-3725 [S] | Downtown Country | 1967 | 20.00 |
| ❑ LPM-3768 [M] | Connie Smith Sings Bill Anderson | 1967 | 25.00 |
| ❑ LSP-3768 [S] | Connie Smith Sings Bill Anderson | 1967 | 20.00 |
| ❑ LPM-3848 [M] | The Best of Connie Smith | 1967 | 25.00 |
| ❑ LSP-3848 [S] | The Best of Connie Smith | 1967 | 20.00 |
| *—Black label, dog on top, "Stereo Dynagroove" at bottom* | | | |
| ❑ LSP-3848 [S] | The Best of Connie Smith | 1969 | 12.00 |
| *—Orange label* | | | |
| ❑ LPM-3889 [M] | Soul of Country Music | 1968 | 50.00 |
| ❑ LSP-3889 [S] | Soul of Country Music | 1968 | 20.00 |
| ❑ LPM-4002 [M] | I Love Charley Brown | 1968 | 80.00 |
| ❑ LSP-4002 [S] | I Love Charley Brown | 1968 | 20.00 |
| ❑ LSP-4077 | Sunshine and Rain | 1968 | 20.00 |
| ❑ LSP-4132 | Connie's Country | 1969 | 20.00 |
| ❑ LSP-4229 | Back in Baby's Arms | 1969 | 20.00 |
| ❑ LSP-4324 | The Best of Connie Smith Volume II | 1970 | 20.00 |
| ❑ LSP-4394 | I Never Once Stopped Loving You | 1970 | 20.00 |
| ❑ LSP-4474 | Where's My Castle | 1971 | 15.00 |
| ❑ LSP-4537 | Just One Time | 1971 | 15.00 |
| ❑ LSP-4598 | Come Along and Walk with Me | 1971 | 20.00 |
| ❑ LSP-4694 | Ain't We Having a Good Time | 1972 | 15.00 |
| ❑ LSP-4748 | "If It Ain't Love" And Other Great Dallas Frazier Songs | 1972 | 15.00 |
| ❑ LSP-4840 | Love Is the Look You're Looking For | 1973 | 15.00 |

## SMITH, CONNIE, AND NAT STUCKEY

**RCA VICTOR**

| Number | Title (A Side/B Side) | Yr | NM |
|---|---|---|---|
| ❑ LSP-4190 | Young Love | 1969 | 20.00 |
| ❑ LSP-4300 | Sunday Morning | 1970 | 15.00 |

## SMITH, DARDEN

**COLUMBIA**

| Number | Title (A Side/B Side) | Yr | NM |
|---|---|---|---|
| ❑ CAS 3034 [DJ] | Interchords | 1988 | 15.00 |
| *—Promo-only interview record* | | | |

**EPIC**

| Number | Title (A Side/B Side) | Yr | NM |
|---|---|---|---|
| ❑ EAS 1282 [EP] | Live Tracks: Darden Smith | 1988 | 15.00 |
| *—Promo-only three-song live EP* | | | |
| ❑ E 40938 | Darden Smith | 1988 | 10.00 |

**REDI MIX**

| Number | Title (A Side/B Side) | Yr | NM |
|---|---|---|---|
| ❑ RM 001 | Native Soil | 1986 | 20.00 |

## SMITH, EFFIE

**JUBILEE**

| Number | Title (A Side/B Side) | Yr | NM |
|---|---|---|---|
| ❑ JGM-2057 [M] | Dial That Telephone | 1966 | 25.00 |

## SMITH, ETHEL

**DECCA**

| Number | Title (A Side/B Side) | Yr | NM |
|---|---|---|---|
| ❑ DL 8187 [M] | Christmas Music | 1955 | 20.00 |
| *—Black label, silver print* | | | |

## SMITH, HUEY "PIANO"

**ACE**

| Number | Title (A Side/B Side) | Yr | NM |
|---|---|---|---|
| ❑ LP-1004 [M] | Having a Good Time | 1959 | 400.00 |
| ❑ LP-1015 [M] | For Dancing | 1961 | 250.00 |
| ❑ LP-1027 [M] | 'Twas the Night Before Christmas | 1962 | 250.00 |
| ❑ LP-1027 [M] | 'Twas the Night Before Christmas | 198? | 15.00 |
| *—Reissue with "Dr. John Band" credited on front cover and label* | | | |
| ❑ LP-2021 | Rock 'N' Roll Revival | 197? | 30.00 |
| ❑ 2038 | Good Old Rock & Roll | 198? | 15.00 |

**GRAND PRIX**

| Number | Title (A Side/B Side) | Yr | NM |
|---|---|---|---|
| ❑ K-418 [M] | Huey "Piano" Smith | 196? | 20.00 |
| ❑ KS-418 [R] | Huey "Piano" Smith | 196? | 12.00 |

**RHINO**

| Number | Title (A Side/B Side) | Yr | NM |
|---|---|---|---|
| ❑ RNLP-70222 | Serious Clownin': The History of Huey "Piano" Smith and the Clowns | 1986 | 12.00 |

## SMITH, JACK

**BEL CANTO**

| Number | Title (A Side/B Side) | Yr | NM |
|---|---|---|---|
| ❑ BCM-37 [M] | You Asked for It: Jack Smith Sings | 1959 | 25.00 |
| ❑ SR-1015 [S] | You Asked for It: Jack Smith Sings | 1959 | 30.00 |

## SMITH, JENNIE

**CANADIAN AMERICAN**

| Number | Title (A Side/B Side) | Yr | NM |
|---|---|---|---|
| ❑ CALP-1010 [M] | Nightly Yours on the Steve Allen Show | 1963 | 25.00 |

**COLUMBIA**

| Number | Title (A Side/B Side) | Yr | NM |
|---|---|---|---|
| ❑ CL 1242 [M] | Love Among the Young | 1959 | 30.00 |
| ❑ CS 8028 [S] | Love Among the Young | 1959 | 40.00 |

**DOT**

| Number | Title (A Side/B Side) | Yr | NM |
|---|---|---|---|
| ❑ DLP-3586 [M] | Jennie | 1964 | 15.00 |
| ❑ DLP-25586 [S] | Jennie | 1964 | 20.00 |

**RCA VICTOR**

| Number | Title (A Side/B Side) | Yr | NM |
|---|---|---|---|
| ❑ LPM-1523 [M] | Jennie | 1957 | 40.00 |

## SMITH, JIMMY

**BLUE NOTE**

| Number | Title (A Side/B Side) | Yr | NM |
|---|---|---|---|
| ❑ BLP-1512 [M] | Jimmy Smith at the Organ, Vol. 1 | 1956 | 100.00 |
| *—Regular edition, Lexington Ave. address on label* | | | |
| ❑ BLP-1512 [M] | Jimmy Smith at the Organ, Vol. 1 | 1956 | 150.00 |
| *—"Deep groove" version (deep indentation under label on both sides)* | | | |
| ❑ BLP-1512 [M] | Jimmy Smith at the Organ, Vol. 1 | 1963 | 25.00 |
| *—With New York, USA address on label* | | | |
| ❑ BLP-1514 [M] | Jimmy Smith at the Organ, Vol. 2 | 1956 | 100.00 |
| *—Regular edition, Lexington Ave. address on label* | | | |
| ❑ BLP-1514 [M] | Jimmy Smith at the Organ, Vol. 2 | 1956 | 150.00 |
| *—"Deep groove" version (deep indentation under label on both sides)* | | | |
| ❑ BLP-1514 [M] | Jimmy Smith at the Organ, Vol. 2 | 1963 | 25.00 |
| *—With New York, USA address on label* | | | |
| ❑ BLP-1525 [M] | The Incredible Jimmy Smith at the Organ, Vol. 3 | 1956 | 100.00 |
| *—Regular edition, Lexington Ave. address on label* | | | |
| ❑ BLP-1525 [M] | The Incredible Jimmy Smith at the Organ, Vol. 3 | 1956 | 150.00 |
| *—"Deep groove" version (deep indentation under label on both sides)* | | | |
| ❑ BLP-1525 [M] | The Incredible Jimmy Smith at the Organ, Vol. 3 | 1963 | 25.00 |
| *—With New York, USA address on label* | | | |
| ❑ BLP-1528 [M] | The Incredible Jimmy Smith at Club Baby Grand, Wilmington, Delaware, Vol. 1 | 1956 | 100.00 |
| *—Regular edition, Lexington Ave. address on label* | | | |
| ❑ BLP-1528 [M] | The Incredible Jimmy Smith at Club Baby Grand, Wilmington, Delaware, Vol. 1 | 1956 | 150.00 |
| *—"Deep groove" version (deep indentation under label on both sides)* | | | |
| ❑ BLP-1528 [M] | The Incredible Jimmy Smith at Club Baby Grand, Wilmington, Delaware, Vol. 1 | 1963 | 25.00 |
| *—With New York, USA address on label* | | | |
| ❑ BLP-1529 [M] | The Incredible Jimmy Smith at Club Baby Grand, Wilmington, Delaware, Vol. 2 | 1956 | 100.00 |
| *—Regular edition, Lexington Ave. address on label* | | | |
| ❑ BLP-1529 [M] | The Incredible Jimmy Smith at Club Baby Grand, Wilmington, Delaware, Vol. 2 | 1956 | 150.00 |
| *—"Deep groove" version (deep indentation under label on both sides)* | | | |
| ❑ BLP-1529 [M] | The Incredible Jimmy Smith at Club Baby Grand, Wilmington, Delaware, Vol. 2 | 1963 | 25.00 |
| *—With New York, USA address on label* | | | |
| ❑ BLP-1547 [M] | A Date with Jimmy Smith, Vol. 1 | 1957 | 80.00 |
| *—Regular edition, W. 63rd St. address on label* | | | |
| ❑ BLP-1547 [M] | A Date with Jimmy Smith, Vol. 1 | 1957 | 120.00 |
| *—"Deep groove" version (deep indentation under label on both sides)* | | | |
| ❑ BLP-1547 [M] | A Date with Jimmy Smith, Vol. 1 | 1963 | 25.00 |
| *—With New York, USA address on label* | | | |
| ❑ BLP-1548 [M] | A Date with Jimmy Smith, Vol. 2 | 1957 | 80.00 |
| *—Regular edition, W. 63rd St. address on label* | | | |
| ❑ BLP-1548 [M] | A Date with Jimmy Smith, Vol. 2 | 1957 | 120.00 |
| *—"Deep groove" version (deep indentation under label on both sides)* | | | |
| ❑ BLP-1548 [M] | A Date with Jimmy Smith, Vol. 2 | 1963 | 25.00 |
| *—With New York, USA address on label* | | | |
| ❑ BLP-1551 [M] | Jimmy Smith at the Organ, Vol. 1 | 1957 | 80.00 |
| *—Regular edition, W. 63rd St. address on label* | | | |
| ❑ BLP-1551 [M] | Jimmy Smith at the Organ, Vol. 1 | 1957 | 120.00 |
| *—"Deep groove" version (deep indentation under label on both sides)* | | | |
| ❑ BLP-1551 [M] | Jimmy Smith at the Organ, Vol. 1 | 1963 | 25.00 |
| *—With New York, USA address on label* | | | |
| ❑ BLP-1552 [M] | Jimmy Smith at the Organ, Vol. 2 | 1957 | 80.00 |
| *—Regular edition, W. 63rd St. address on label* | | | |
| ❑ BLP-1552 [M] | Jimmy Smith at the Organ, Vol. 2 | 1957 | 120.00 |
| *—"Deep groove" version (deep indentation under label on both sides)* | | | |
| ❑ BLP-1552 [M] | Jimmy Smith at the Organ, Vol. 2 | 1963 | 25.00 |
| *—With New York, USA address on label* | | | |
| ❑ BLP-1556 [M] | The Sounds of Jimmy Smith | 1957 | 80.00 |
| *—Regular edition, W. 63rd St. address on label* | | | |
| ❑ BLP-1556 [M] | The Sounds of Jimmy Smith | 1957 | 120.00 |
| *—"Deep groove" version (deep indentation under label on both sides)* | | | |
| ❑ BLP-1556 [M] | The Sounds of Jimmy Smith | 1963 | 25.00 |
| *—With New York, USA address on label* | | | |
| ❑ BLP-1563 [M] | Jimmy Smith Plays Pretty Just for You | 1957 | 80.00 |
| *—Regular edition, W. 63rd St. address on label* | | | |
| ❑ BLP-1563 [M] | Jimmy Smith Plays Pretty Just for You | 1957 | 120.00 |
| *—"Deep groove" version (deep indentation under label on both sides)* | | | |
| ❑ BLP-1563 [M] | Jimmy Smith Plays Pretty Just for You | 1963 | 25.00 |
| *—With New York, USA address on label* | | | |
| ❑ BST-1563 [S] | Jimmy Smith Plays Pretty Just for You | 1959 | 50.00 |
| *—Regular edition, W. 63rd St. address on label* | | | |
| ❑ BST-1563 [S] | Jimmy Smith Plays Pretty Just for You | 1959 | 80.00 |
| *—"Deep groove" version (deep indentation under label on both sides)* | | | |
| ❑ BST-1563 [S] | Jimmy Smith Plays Pretty Just for You | 1963 | 20.00 |
| *—With New York, USA address on label* | | | |
| ❑ BLP-1585 [M] | Groovin' at Small's Paradise, Vol. 1 | 1958 | 80.00 |
| *—Regular edition, W. 63rd St. address on label* | | | |
| ❑ BLP-1585 [M] | Groovin' at Small's Paradise, Vol. 1 | 1958 | 120.00 |
| *—"Deep groove" version (deep indentation under label on both sides)* | | | |
| ❑ BLP-1585 [M] | Groovin' at Small's Paradise, Vol. 1 | 1963 | 25.00 |
| *—With New York, USA address on label* | | | |
| ❑ BST-1585 [S] | Groovin' at Small's Paradise, Vol. 1 | 1959 | 50.00 |
| *—Regular edition, W. 63rd St. address on label* | | | |
| ❑ BST-1585 [S] | Groovin' at Small's Paradise, Vol. 1 | 1959 | 80.00 |
| *—"Deep groove" version (deep indentation under label on both sides)* | | | |
| ❑ BST-1585 [S] | Groovin' at Small's Paradise, Vol. 1 | 1963 | 20.00 |
| *—With New York, USA address on label* | | | |
| ❑ BLP-1586 [M] | Groovin' at Small's Paradise, Vol. 2 | 1958 | 80.00 |
| *—Regular edition, W. 63rd St. address on label* | | | |
| ❑ BLP-1586 [M] | Groovin' at Small's Paradise, Vol. 2 | 1958 | 120.00 |
| *—"Deep groove" version (deep indentation under label on both sides)* | | | |
| ❑ BLP-1586 [M] | Groovin' at Small's Paradise, Vol. 2 | 1963 | 25.00 |
| *—With New York, USA address on label* | | | |
| ❑ BST-1586 [S] | Groovin' at Small's Paradise, Vol. 2 | 1959 | 50.00 |
| *—Regular edition, W. 63rd St. address on label* | | | |
| ❑ BST-1586 [S] | Groovin' at Small's Paradise, Vol. 2 | 1959 | 80.00 |
| *—"Deep groove" version (deep indentation under label on both sides)* | | | |
| ❑ BST-1586 [S] | Groovin' at Small's Paradise, Vol. 2 | 1963 | 20.00 |
| *—With New York, USA address on label* | | | |
| ❑ BLP-4002 [M] | House Party | 1959 | 80.00 |
| *—Regular edition, W. 63rd St. address on label* | | | |
| ❑ BLP-4002 [M] | House Party | 1959 | 120.00 |
| *—"Deep groove" version (deep indentation under label on both sides)* | | | |
| ❑ BLP-4002 [M] | House Party | 1963 | 25.00 |
| *—With New York, USA address on label* | | | |
| ❑ BST-4002 [S] | House Party | 1959 | 50.00 |
| *—Regular edition, W. 63rd St. address on label* | | | |
| ❑ BST-4002 [S] | House Party | 1959 | 80.00 |
| *—"Deep groove" version (deep indentation under label on both sides)* | | | |
| ❑ BST-4002 [S] | House Party | 1963 | 20.00 |
| *—With New York, USA address on label* | | | |
| ❑ BLP-4011 [M] | The Sermon | 1959 | 80.00 |
| *—Regular edition, W. 63rd St. address on label* | | | |
| ❑ BLP-4011 [M] | The Sermon | 1959 | 120.00 |
| *—"Deep groove" version (deep indentation under label on both sides)* | | | |
| ❑ BLP-4011 [M] | The Sermon | 1963 | 25.00 |
| *—With New York, USA address on label* | | | |
| ❑ BST-4011 [S] | The Sermon | 1959 | 50.00 |
| *—Regular edition, W. 63rd St. address on label* | | | |
| ❑ BST-4011 [S] | The Sermon | 1959 | 80.00 |
| *—"Deep groove" version (deep indentation under label on both sides)* | | | |
| ❑ BST-4011 [S] | The Sermon | 1963 | 20.00 |
| *—With New York, USA address on label* | | | |
| ❑ BLP-4030 [M] | Crazy Baby | 1960 | 80.00 |
| *—Regular edition, W. 63rd St. address on label* | | | |
| ❑ BLP-4030 [M] | Crazy Baby | 1960 | 120.00 |
| *—"Deep groove" version (deep indentation under label on both sides)* | | | |
| ❑ BLP-4030 [M] | Crazy Baby | 1963 | 25.00 |
| *—With New York, USA address on label* | | | |
| ❑ BLP-4050 [M] | Home Cookin' | 1961 | 50.00 |
| *—With W. 63rd St. address on label* | | | |
| ❑ BLP-4050 [M] | Home Cookin' | 1963 | 20.00 |
| *—With New York, USA address on label* | | | |
| ❑ BLP-4078 [M] | Midnight Special | 1961 | 50.00 |
| *—With 61st St. address on label* | | | |
| ❑ BLP-4078 [M] | Midnight Special | 1963 | 20.00 |
| *—With New York, USA address on label* | | | |
| ❑ BLP-4100 [M] | Jimmy Smith Plays Fats Waller | 1962 | 50.00 |
| *—With 61st St. address on label* | | | |
| ❑ BLP-4100 [M] | Jimmy Smith Plays Fats Waller | 1963 | 20.00 |
| *—With New York, USA address on label* | | | |
| ❑ BLP-4117 [M] | Back at the Chicken Shack | 1963 | 25.00 |
| ❑ BLP-4141 [M] | Rockin' the Boat | 1963 | 25.00 |
| ❑ BLP-4164 [M] | Prayer Meetin' | 1964 | 25.00 |
| ❑ BLP-4200 [M] | Softly as a Summer Breeze | 1965 | 25.00 |
| ❑ BLP-4235 [M] | Bucket! | 1966 | 25.00 |
| ❑ BLP-4255 [M] | I'm Movin' On | 1967 | 30.00 |
| ❑ BST-84030 [S] | Crazy Baby | 1960 | 50.00 |
| *—With W. 63rd St. address on label* | | | |
| ❑ BST-84030 [S] | Crazy Baby | 1963 | 20.00 |
| *—With New York, USA address on label* | | | |
| ❑ BST-84050 [S] | Home Cookin' | 1961 | 50.00 |
| *—With W. 63rd St. address on label* | | | |
| ❑ BST-84050 [S] | Home Cookin' | 1963 | 20.00 |
| *—With New York, USA address on label* | | | |
| ❑ BST-84078 [S] | Midnight Special | 1961 | 50.00 |
| *—With 61st St. address on label* | | | |
| ❑ BST-84078 [S] | Midnight Special | 1963 | 20.00 |
| *—With New York, USA address on label* | | | |
| ❑ BST-84100 [S] | Jimmy Smith Plays Fats Waller | 1962 | 50.00 |
| *—With 61st St. address on label* | | | |
| ❑ BST-84100 [S] | Jimmy Smith Plays Fats Waller | 1963 | 20.00 |
| *—With New York, USA address on label* | | | |
| ❑ BST-84117 [S] | Back at the Chicken Shack | 1963 | 30.00 |
| *—With New York, USA address on label* | | | |
| ❑ BST-84141 [S] | Rockin' the Boat | 1963 | 30.00 |
| *—With New York, USA address on label* | | | |
| ❑ BST-84164 [S] | Prayer Meetin' | 1964 | 30.00 |
| *—With New York, USA address on label* | | | |
| ❑ BST-84200 [S] | Softly as a Summer Breeze | 1965 | 30.00 |
| *—With New York, USA address on label* | | | |
| ❑ BST-84235 [S] | Bucket! | 1966 | 30.00 |
| *—With New York, USA address on label* | | | |
| ❑ BST-84255 [S] | I'm Movin' On | 1967 | 20.00 |
| ❑ BST-84269 | Open House | 1968 | 20.00 |
| ❑ BST-84296 | Plain Talk | 1969 | 20.00 |
| ❑ BST-89901 [(2)] | Jimmy Smith's Greatest Hits! | 1969 | 25.00 |

**MOSAIC**

| Number | Title (A Side/B Side) | Yr | NM |
|---|---|---|---|
| ❑ MQ5-154 [(5)] | The Complete February 1957 Jimmy Smith Blue Note Sessions | 199? | 80.00 |

**VERVE**

| Number | Title (A Side/B Side) | Yr | NM |
|---|---|---|---|
| ❑ V-8474 [M] | Bashin' | 1962 | 20.00 |
| ❑ V6-8474 [S] | Bashin' | 1962 | 25.00 |

| Number | Title (A Side/B Side) | Yr | NM |
|---|---|---|---|
| ❑ V-8544 [M] | Hobo Flats | 1963 | 20.00 |
| ❑ V6-8544 [S] | Hobo Flats | 1963 | 25.00 |
| ❑ V-8552 [M] | Any Number Can Win | 1963 | 20.00 |
| ❑ V6-8552 [S] | Any Number Can Win | 1963 | 25.00 |
| ❑ V-8583 [M] | Who's Afraid of Virginia Woolf? | 1964 | 20.00 |
| ❑ V6-8583 [S] | Who's Afraid of Virginia Woolf? | 1964 | 25.00 |
| ❑ V-8587 [M] | The Cat | 1964 | 20.00 |
| ❑ V6-8587 [S] | The Cat | 1964 | 25.00 |
| ❑ V-8604 [M] | Christmas '64 | 1964 | 20.00 |
| ❑ V6-8604 [S] | Christmas '64 | 1964 | 25.00 |
| ❑ V6-8618 [S] | The Monster | 1965 | 20.00 |
| ❑ V6-8628 [S] | Organ Grinder Swing | 1965 | 20.00 |
| ❑ V6-8641 [S] | Got My Mojo Workin' | 1966 | 20.00 |
| ❑ V-8652 [M] | Peter and the Wolf | 1966 | 20.00 |
| ❑ V6-8652 [S] | Peter and the Wolf | 1966 | 25.00 |
| ❑ V-8666 [M] | Christmas Cookin' | 1966 | 20.00 |
| ❑ V6-8666 [S] | Christmas Cookin' | 1966 | 25.00 |
| ❑ V6-8667 [S] | Hoochie Coochie Man | 1966 | 20.00 |
| ❑ V-8705 [M] | Respect | 1967 | 20.00 |
| ❑ V-8721 [M] | The Best of Jimmy Smith | 1967 | 20.00 |
| ❑ SMAS-90643 [S] | The Monster | 1965 | 25.00 |
| *—Capitol Record Club edition* | | | |

### SMITH, JIMMY, AND WES MONTGOMERY

**VERVE**

| Number | Title (A Side/B Side) | Yr | NM |
|---|---|---|---|
| ❑ V-8678 [M] | Jimmy and Wes, The Dynamic Duo | 1967 | 20.00 |

### SMITH, JOHNNY

**LEGENDE**

| Number | Title (A Side/B Side) | Yr | NM |
|---|---|---|---|
| ❑ 1401 [10] | Annotations of the Muses | 1955 | 100.00 |

**ROOST**

| Number | Title (A Side/B Side) | Yr | NM |
|---|---|---|---|
| ❑ R-410 [10] | A Three-Dimension Sound Recording of Jazz at NBC with the Johnny Smith Quintet | 1953 | 150.00 |
| ❑ R-413 [10] | Johnny Smith Quintet | 1953 | 120.00 |
| ❑ R-421 [10] | In a Mellow Mood | 1954 | 100.00 |
| ❑ R-424 [10] | In a Sentimental Mood | 1954 | 100.00 |
| ❑ LP-2201 [M] | Johnny Smith Plays Jimmy Van Heusen | 1955 | 80.00 |
| ❑ LP-2203 [M] | Johnny Smith Quartet | 1955 | 80.00 |
| ❑ LP-2211 [M] | Moonlight in Vermont | 1956 | 80.00 |
| ❑ LP-2215 [M] | Moods | 1956 | 60.00 |
| ❑ LP-2216 [M] | New Quartet | 1956 | 60.00 |
| ❑ LP-2223 [M] | Johnny Smith Foursome, Volume 1 | 1956 | 50.00 |
| ❑ LP-2228 [M] | Johnny Smith Foursome, Volume 2 | 1957 | 50.00 |
| ❑ LP-2231 [M] | Flower Drum Song | 1958 | 40.00 |
| ❑ SLP-2231 [S] | Flower Drum Song | 1958 | 30.00 |
| ❑ LP-2233 [M] | Easy Listening | 1959 | 40.00 |
| ❑ SLP-2233 [S] | Easy Listening | 1959 | 30.00 |
| ❑ LP-2237 [M] | Favorites | 1959 | 40.00 |
| ❑ SLP-2237 [S] | Favorites | 1959 | 30.00 |
| ❑ LP-2238 [M] | Designed for You | 1960 | 30.00 |
| ❑ SLP-2238 [S] | Designed for You | 1960 | 40.00 |
| ❑ LP-2239 [M] | Dear Little Sweetheart | 1960 | 30.00 |
| ❑ SLP-2239 [S] | Dear Little Sweetheart | 1960 | 40.00 |
| ❑ LP-2242 [M] | Guitar and Strings | 1960 | 30.00 |
| ❑ SLP-2242 [S] | Guitar and Strings | 1960 | 40.00 |
| ❑ LP-2243 [M] | Johnny Smith Plus the Trio | 1960 | 30.00 |
| ❑ SLP-2243 [S] | Johnny Smith Plus the Trio | 1960 | 40.00 |
| ❑ LP-2246 [M] | The Sound of the Johnny Smith Guitar | 1961 | 30.00 |
| ❑ SLP-2246 [S] | The Sound of the Johnny Smith Guitar | 1961 | 40.00 |
| ❑ LP-2248 [M] | Man with the Blue Guitar | 1962 | 30.00 |
| ❑ SLP-2248 [S] | Man with the Blue Guitar | 1962 | 40.00 |
| ❑ LP-2250 [M] | Johnny Smith Plays Jimmy Van Heusen | 1963 | 25.00 |
| ❑ SLP-2250 [S] | Johnny Smith Plays Jimmy Van Heusen | 1963 | 30.00 |
| ❑ LP-2254 [M] | Guitar World | 1963 | 25.00 |
| ❑ SLP-2254 [S] | Guitar World | 1963 | 30.00 |
| ❑ LP-2259 [M] | Reminiscing | 1965 | 25.00 |
| ❑ SLP-2259 [S] | Reminiscing | 1965 | 30.00 |

**VERVE**

| Number | Title (A Side/B Side) | Yr | NM |
|---|---|---|---|
| ❑ V-8692 [M] | Johnny Smith | 1967 | 30.00 |
| ❑ V6-8692 [S] | Johnny Smith | 1967 | 20.00 |
| ❑ V-8737 [M] | Johnny Smith's Kaleidoscope | 1968 | 30.00 |
| ❑ V6-8737 [S] | Johnny Smith's Kaleidoscope | 1968 | 20.00 |
| ❑ V6-8767 [S] | Phase II | 1969 | 20.00 |

### SMITH, JOHNNY "HAMMOND" See JOHNNY HAMMOND.

### SMITH, KEELY Also see LOUIS PRIMA AND KEELY SMITH.

**CAPITOL**

| Number | Title (A Side/B Side) | Yr | NM |
|---|---|---|---|
| ❑ SW 914 [S] | I Wish You Love | 1959 | 30.00 |
| *—Black label with colorband, Capitol logo at left* | | | |
| ❑ SW 914 [S] | I Wish You Love | 1962 | 15.00 |
| *—Black label with colorband, Capitol logo at top* | | | |
| ❑ W 914 [M] | I Wish You Love | 1957 | 50.00 |
| *—Turquoise label* | | | |
| ❑ W 914 [M] | I Wish You Love | 1959 | 30.00 |
| *—Black label with colorband, Capitol logo at left* | | | |
| ❑ W 914 [M] | I Wish You Love | 1962 | 15.00 |
| *—Black label with colorband, Capitol logo at top* | | | |
| ❑ ST 1073 [S] | Politely! | 1959 | 50.00 |
| *—Black label with colorband, Capitol logo at left* | | | |
| ❑ ST 1073 [S] | Politely! | 1962 | 20.00 |
| *—Black label with colorband, Capitol logo at top* | | | |
| ❑ T 1073 [M] | Politely! | 1958 | 40.00 |
| *—Black label with colorband, Capitol logo at left* | | | |
| ❑ T 1073 [M] | Politely! | 1962 | 15.00 |
| *—Black label with colorband, Capitol logo at top* | | | |
| ❑ ST 1145 [S] | Swingin' Pretty | 1959 | 50.00 |
| *—Black label with colorband, Capitol logo at left* | | | |
| ❑ ST 1145 [S] | Swingin' Pretty | 1962 | 20.00 |
| *—Black label with colorband, Capitol logo at top* | | | |
| ❑ T 1145 [M] | Swingin' Pretty | 1959 | 40.00 |
| *—Black label with colorband, Capitol logo at left* | | | |
| ❑ T 1145 [M] | Swingin' Pretty | 1962 | 15.00 |
| *—Black label with colorband, Capitol logo at top* | | | |

**DOT**

| Number | Title (A Side/B Side) | Yr | NM |
|---|---|---|---|
| ❑ DLP-3241 [M] | Be My Love | 1959 | 25.00 |
| ❑ DLP-3265 [M] | Swing, You Lovers | 1960 | 25.00 |
| ❑ DLP-3287 [M] | Dearly Beloved | 1961 | 25.00 |
| ❑ DLP-3345 [M] | A Keely Christmas | 1961 | 25.00 |
| ❑ DLP-3415 [M] | Because You're Mine | 1962 | 25.00 |
| ❑ DLP-3423 [M] | Twist with Keely Smith | 1962 | 25.00 |
| ❑ DLP-3460 [M] | Cherokeely Swings | 1962 | 25.00 |
| ❑ DLP-3461 [M] | What Kind of Fool Am I | 1962 | 25.00 |
| ❑ DLP-25241 [S] | Be My Love | 1959 | 30.00 |
| ❑ DLP-25265 [S] | Swing, You Lovers | 1960 | 30.00 |
| ❑ DLP-25287 [S] | Dearly Beloved | 1961 | 30.00 |
| ❑ DLP-25345 [S] | A Keely Christmas | 1961 | 30.00 |
| ❑ DLP-25415 [S] | Because You're Mine | 1962 | 30.00 |
| ❑ DLP-25423 [S] | Twist with Keely Smith | 1962 | 30.00 |
| ❑ DLP-25460 [S] | Cherokeely Swings | 1962 | 30.00 |
| ❑ DLP-25461 [S] | What Kind of Fool Am I | 1962 | 30.00 |

**HARMONY**

| Number | Title (A Side/B Side) | Yr | NM |
|---|---|---|---|
| ❑ HS 11333 | That Old Black Magic | 1968 | 12.00 |

**REPRISE**

| Number | Title (A Side/B Side) | Yr | NM |
|---|---|---|---|
| ❑ R-6086 [M] | Little Girl Blue, Little Girl New | 1963 | 20.00 |
| ❑ R9-6086 [S] | Little Girl Blue, Little Girl New | 1963 | 25.00 |
| ❑ R-6132 [M] | The Intimate Keely Smith | 1964 | 20.00 |
| ❑ RS-6132 [S] | The Intimate Keely Smith | 1964 | 25.00 |
| ❑ R-6142 [M] | Keely Smith Sings the John Lennon/Paul McCartney Songbook | 1964 | 25.00 |
| ❑ RS-6142 [S] | Keely Smith Sings the John Lennon/Paul McCartney Songbook | 1964 | 30.00 |
| ❑ R-6175 [M] | That Old Black Magic | 1965 | 20.00 |
| ❑ RS-6175 [S] | That Old Black Magic | 1965 | 25.00 |

### SMITH, LAVERGNE

**COOK**

| Number | Title (A Side/B Side) | Yr | NM |
|---|---|---|---|
| ❑ LP-1081 [10] | Angel in the Absinthe House | 1955 | 150.00 |

**SAVOY**

| Number | Title (A Side/B Side) | Yr | NM |
|---|---|---|---|
| ❑ MG-12031 [M] | New Orleans Nightingale | 1955 | 50.00 |

**VIK**

| Number | Title (A Side/B Side) | Yr | NM |
|---|---|---|---|
| ❑ LX-1056 [M] | La Vergne Smith | 1956 | 50.00 |

### SMITH, LONNIE

**BLUE NOTE**

| Number | Title (A Side/B Side) | Yr | NM |
|---|---|---|---|
| ❑ BST-84290 | Think! | 1968 | 20.00 |
| ❑ BST-84313 | Turning Point | 1969 | 20.00 |

**COLUMBIA**

| Number | Title (A Side/B Side) | Yr | NM |
|---|---|---|---|
| ❑ CL 2696 [M] | Finger-Lickin' Good Soul Organ | 1967 | 25.00 |
| ❑ CS 9496 [S] | Finger-Lickin' Good Soul Organ | 1967 | 20.00 |

### SMITH, LOUIS

**BLUE NOTE**

| Number | Title (A Side/B Side) | Yr | NM |
|---|---|---|---|
| ❑ BLP-1584 [M] | Here Comes Louis Smith | 1958 | 120.00 |
| *—Regular version, W. 63rd St. address on label* | | | |
| ❑ BLP-1584 [M] | Here Comes Louis Smith | 1958 | 150.00 |
| *—"Deep groove" version (deep indentation under label on both sides)* | | | |
| ❑ BST-1584 [S] | Here Comes Louis Smith | 1959 | 80.00 |
| *—Regular version, W. 63rd St. address on label* | | | |
| ❑ BST-1584 [S] | Here Comes Louis Smith | 1959 | 100.00 |
| *—"Deep groove" version (deep indentation under label on both sides)* | | | |
| ❑ BLP-1594 [M] | Smithville | 1958 | 80.00 |
| *—Regular version, W. 63rd St. address on label* | | | |
| ❑ BLP-1594 [M] | Smithville | 1958 | 100.00 |
| *—"Deep groove" version (deep indentation under label on both sides)* | | | |
| ❑ BST-1594 [S] | Smithville | 1959 | 60.00 |
| *—Regular version, W. 63rd St. address on label* | | | |
| ❑ BST-1594 [S] | Smithville | 1959 | 80.00 |
| *—"Deep groove" version (deep indentation under label on both sides)* | | | |

### SMITH, O.C.

**CARIBOU**

| Number | Title (A Side/B Side) | Yr | NM |
|---|---|---|---|
| ❑ PZ 34471 | Together | 1977 | 25.00 |

**COLUMBIA**

| Number | Title (A Side/B Side) | Yr | NM |
|---|---|---|---|
| ❑ CL 2714 [M] | The Dynamic O.C. Smith | 1967 | 50.00 |
| ❑ CS 9514 [S] | The Dynamic O.C. Smith | 1967 | 30.00 |
| ❑ CS 9680 [M] | Hickory Holler Revisited | 1968 | 25.00 |
| *—White label promo "Special Mono Radio Station Copy" with stereo number* | | | |
| ❑ CS 9680 [S] | Hickory Holler Revisited | 1968 | 12.00 |
| ❑ CS 9756 | For Once in My Life | 1969 | 12.00 |
| ❑ CS 9908 | O.C. Smith at Home | 1969 | 12.00 |
| ❑ C 30227 | O.C. Smith's Greatest Hits | 1970 | 12.00 |
| ❑ C 30664 | Help Me Make It Through the Night | 1971 | 20.00 |
| ❑ KC 33247 | La La Peace Song | 1974 | 20.00 |

**FAMILY**

| Number | Title (A Side/B Side) | Yr | NM |
|---|---|---|---|
| ❑ 1000 | Dreams Come True | 1980 | 15.00 |

**HARMONY**

| Number | Title (A Side/B Side) | Yr | NM |
|---|---|---|---|
| ❑ KH 30317 | O.C. Smith | 1971 | 10.00 |

**MOTOWN**

| Number | Title (A Side/B Side) | Yr | NM |
|---|---|---|---|
| ❑ 6019 ML | Love Changes | 1982 | 25.00 |

**RENDEZVOUS**

| Number | Title (A Side/B Side) | Yr | NM |
|---|---|---|---|
| ❑ 50006 | What'cha Gonna Do | 1986 | 15.00 |

**SHADY BROOK**

| Number | Title (A Side/B Side) | Yr | NM |
|---|---|---|---|
| ❑ SB-012 | Love Is Forever | 1978 | 12.00 |

**SOUTH BAY**

| Number | Title (A Side/B Side) | Yr | NM |
|---|---|---|---|
| ❑ SB 1001 | Love Changes | 1982 | 30.00 |

### SMITH, OSBORNE

**ARGO**

| Number | Title (A Side/B Side) | Yr | NM |
|---|---|---|---|
| ❑ LP-4000 [M] | Eyes of Love | 1960 | 30.00 |
| ❑ LPS-4000 [S] | Eyes of Love | 1960 | 40.00 |

### SMITH, PAUL

**CAPITOL**

| Number | Title (A Side/B Side) | Yr | NM |
|---|---|---|---|
| ❑ H 493 [10] | Liquid Sounds | 1954 | 80.00 |
| ❑ T 665 [M] | Cascades | 1955 | 40.00 |
| ❑ T 757 [M] | Cool and Sparkling | 1956 | 40.00 |
| ❑ T 829 [M] | Softly, Baby | 1957 | 40.00 |
| ❑ ST 1017 [S] | Delicate Jazz | 1958 | 25.00 |
| ❑ T 1017 [M] | Delicate Jazz | 1958 | 30.00 |

**DISCOVERY**

| Number | Title (A Side/B Side) | Yr | NM |
|---|---|---|---|
| ❑ DL-3009 [10] | Paul Smith | 1950 | 100.00 |
| ❑ DL-3017 [10] | Paul Smith Trio | 1952 | 80.00 |

**MGM**

| Number | Title (A Side/B Side) | Yr | NM |
|---|---|---|---|
| ❑ E-4057 [M] | Memories of Paris | 1962 | 20.00 |
| ❑ SE-4057 [S] | Memories of Paris | 1962 | 25.00 |

**SAVOY**

| Number | Title (A Side/B Side) | Yr | NM |
|---|---|---|---|
| ❑ MG-12094 [M] | By the Fireside | 1956 | 50.00 |

**SKYLARK**

| Number | Title (A Side/B Side) | Yr | NM |
|---|---|---|---|
| ❑ SKLP-13 [10] | Paul Smith Quartet | 1954 | 120.00 |

**TAMPA**

| Number | Title (A Side/B Side) | Yr | NM |
|---|---|---|---|
| ❑ TP-9 [M] | Fine, Sweet and Tasty | 1957 | 100.00 |
| *—Colored vinyl* | | | |
| ❑ TP-9 [M] | Fine, Sweet and Tasty | 1958 | 50.00 |
| *—Black vinyl* | | | |

**VERVE**

| Number | Title (A Side/B Side) | Yr | NM |
|---|---|---|---|
| ❑ MGV-2128 [M] | The Sound of Music | 1960 | 40.00 |
| ❑ V-2128 [M] | The Sound of Music | 1961 | 20.00 |
| ❑ MGV-2130 [M] | The Big Men | 1960 | 40.00 |
| ❑ V-2130 [M] | The Big Men | 1961 | 20.00 |
| ❑ MGV-2148 [M] | Latin Keyboards and Percussion | 1960 | 40.00 |
| ❑ V-2148 [M] | Latin Keyboards and Percussion | 1961 | 20.00 |
| ❑ MGV-4051 [M] | Carnival! In Percussion | 1961 | 30.00 |
| ❑ V-4051 [M] | Carnival! In Percussion | 1961 | 20.00 |
| ❑ V6-4051 [S] | Carnival! In Percussion | 1961 | 25.00 |
| ❑ MGVS-6128 [S] | The Sound of Music | 1960 | 30.00 |
| ❑ MGVS-6135 [S] | The Big Men | 1960 | 30.00 |

### SMITH, PAUL; RAY BROWN; LOUIS BELLSON

**DISCWASHER**

| Number | Title (A Side/B Side) | Yr | NM |
|---|---|---|---|
| ❑ 001 | Intensive Care | 1979 | 20.00 |

### SMITH, PINE TOP

**BRUNSWICK**

| Number | Title (A Side/B Side) | Yr | NM |
|---|---|---|---|
| ❑ BL 58003 [10] | Pine Top Smith | 1950 | 120.00 |

### SMITH, RAY

**COLUMBIA**

| Number | Title (A Side/B Side) | Yr | NM |
|---|---|---|---|
| ❑ CL 1937 [M] | Ray Smith's Greatest Hits | 1963 | 25.00 |
| ❑ CS 8737 [S] | Ray Smith's Greatest Hits | 1963 | 30.00 |

**JUDD**

| Number | Title (A Side/B Side) | Yr | NM |
|---|---|---|---|
| ❑ JLPA-701 [M] | Travelin' with Ray | 1960 | 700.00 |

**STOMP OFF**

| Number | Title (A Side/B Side) | Yr | NM |
|---|---|---|---|
| ❑ SOS-1012 | Jungle Blues | 198? | 12.00 |

**"T"**

| Number | Title (A Side/B Side) | Yr | NM |
|---|---|---|---|
| ❑ 56062 [M] | The Best of Ray Smith | 196? | 100.00 |

**WIX**

| Number | Title (A Side/B Side) | Yr | NM |
|---|---|---|---|
| ❑ 1000 | I'm Gonna Rock Some More | 197? | 15.00 |

### SMITH, ROBERT CURTIS

**BLUESVILLE**

| Number | Title (A Side/B Side) | Yr | NM |
|---|---|---|---|
| ❑ BVLP-1064 [M] | Clarksdale Blues | 1963 | 80.00 |
| *—Blue label, silver print* | | | |
| ❑ BVLP-1064 [M] | Clarksdale Blues | 1964 | 25.00 |
| *—Blue label, trident logo at right* | | | |

| Number | Title (A Side/B Side) | Yr | NM |
|---|---|---|---|

### SMITH, ROGER

| Number | Title (A Side/B Side) | Yr | NM |
|---|---|---|---|
| **WARNER BROS.** | | | |
| ❑ W 1305 [M] | Beach Romance | 1960 | 40.00 |
| ❑ WS 1305 [S] | Beach Romance | 1960 | 50.00 |

### SMITH, SOMETHIN', AND THE REDHEADS

| Number | Title (A Side/B Side) | Yr | NM |
|---|---|---|---|
| **EPIC** | | | |
| ❑ LN 3138 [M] | Somethin' Smith and the Redheads | 1959 | 30.00 |
| ❑ LN 3373 [M] | Put the Blame on Mame | 196? | 25.00 |
| **MGM** | | | |
| ❑ E-3941 [M] | Ain't We Got Fun Kinda Songs | 1961 | 20.00 |
| ❑ SE-3941 [S] | Ain't We Got Fun Kinda Songs | 1961 | 25.00 |

### SMITH, STUFF

| Number | Title (A Side/B Side) | Yr | NM |
|---|---|---|---|
| **20TH FOX** | | | |
| ❑ FTM-3008 [M] | Sweet Singin' Stuff | 1959 | 30.00 |
| ❑ FTS-3008 [S] | Sweet Singin' Stuff | 1959 | 25.00 |
| **VERVE** | | | |
| ❑ MGVS-6097 [S] | Cat on a Hot Fiddle | 1960 | 40.00 |
| ❑ MGV-8206 [M] | Soft Winds | 1958 | 50.00 |
| ❑ V-8206 [M] | Soft Winds | 1961 | 20.00 |
| ❑ MGV-8282 [M] | Have Violin, Will Swing | 1958 | 50.00 |
| ❑ V-8282 [M] | Have Violin, Will Swing | 1961 | 20.00 |
| ❑ MGV-8339 [M] | Cat on a Hot Fiddle | 1959 | 50.00 |
| ❑ V-8339 [M] | Cat on a Hot Fiddle | 1961 | 20.00 |

### SMITH, TAB

| Number | Title (A Side/B Side) | Yr | NM |
|---|---|---|---|
| **CHECKER** | | | |
| ❑ LP-2971 [M] | Tab Smith | 1960 | 100.00 |
| *—Regular issue* | | | |
| ❑ LP-2971 [M] | Tab Smith | 1960 | 600.00 |
| *—White label promo with multi-color vinyl* | | | |
| **UNITED** | | | |
| ❑ LP-001 [10] | Music Styled by Tab Smith | 1955 | 200.00 |
| ❑ LP-003 [10] | Red, Hot and Cool Blues | 1955 | 200.00 |

### SMITH, WHISTLING JACK

| Number | Title (A Side/B Side) | Yr | NM |
|---|---|---|---|
| **DERAM** | | | |
| ❑ DE 16006 [M] | I Was Kaiser Bill's Batman | 1967 | 25.00 |
| ❑ DES 18006 [S] | I Was Kaiser Bill's Batman | 1967 | 20.00 |

### SMITH, WILLIE

| Number | Title (A Side/B Side) | Yr | NM |
|---|---|---|---|
| **EMARCY** | | | |
| ❑ MG-26000 [10] | Relaxin' After Hours | 1954 | 100.00 |
| **MERCURY** | | | |
| ❑ MG-25075 [10] | Alto Sax Artistry | 1950 | 120.00 |

### SMITH, WILLIE "THE LION"

| Number | Title (A Side/B Side) | Yr | NM |
|---|---|---|---|
| **BLUE CIRCLE** | | | |
| ❑ 1500-33 [10] | Willie "The Lion" Smith | 1952 | 80.00 |
| **COMMODORE** | | | |
| ❑ DL-30004 [M] | The Lion of the Piano | 1951 | 100.00 |
| **DIAL** | | | |
| ❑ LP-305 [10] | Harlem Memories | 1953 | 250.00 |
| **DOT** | | | |
| ❑ DLP-3094 [M] | The Lion Roars | 1958 | 50.00 |
| **GRAND AWARD** | | | |
| ❑ GA-33-368 [M] | The Legend of Willie Smith | 1956 | 50.00 |
| **MAINSTREAM** | | | |
| ❑ 56027 [M] | A Legend | 1965 | 25.00 |
| **RCA VICTOR** | | | |
| ❑ LSP-6016 [(2)] | Memoirs | 1968 | 20.00 |
| **URANIA** | | | |
| ❑ UJLP-1207 [M] | Accent On Piano | 1955 | 60.00 |

### SMITH-GLAMANN QUINTET

| Number | Title (A Side/B Side) | Yr | NM |
|---|---|---|---|
| **BETHLEHEM** | | | |
| ❑ BCP-22 [M] | Smith-Glamann Quintet | 1955 | 50.00 |

### SMITHEREENS, THE

| Number | Title (A Side/B Side) | Yr | NM |
|---|---|---|---|
| **CAPITOL** | | | |
| ❑ C1-91194 | 11 | 1989 | 12.00 |
| **CAPITOL/ENIGMA** | | | |
| ❑ C1-48375 | Green Thoughts | 1988 | 10.00 |
| ❑ R 130120 | Green Thoughts | 1988 | 12.00 |
| *—BMG Direct Marketing edition* | | | |
| **ENIGMA** | | | |
| ❑ (no #) [DJ] | Live at the Roxy — Special Forces Radio Concert | 1986 | 40.00 |
| ❑ ST-73208 | Especially for You | 1986 | 10.00 |
| ❑ 73220 [EP] | Beauty and Sadness | 1988 | 8.00 |
| *—Remixed version of Little Ricky 103 with one track deleted* | | | |
| ❑ SEAX-73258 [PD] | Especially for You | 1986 | 20.00 |
| *—Picture disc in plastic sleeve, sticker on sleeve* | | | |
| ❑ R 164050 | Especially for You | 1987 | 12.00 |
| *—BMG Direct Marketing edition* | | | |
| **LITTLE RICKY** | | | |
| ❑ 103 [EP] | Beauty and Sadness | 1983 | 40.00 |

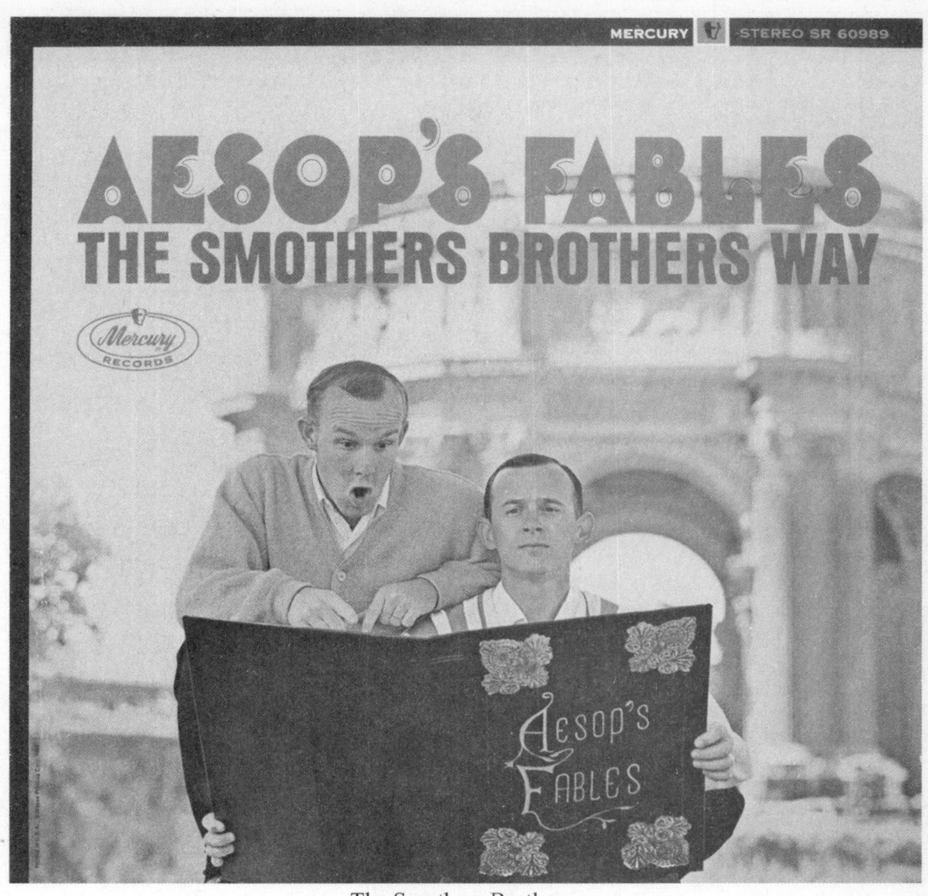


The Smothers Brothers,
*Aesop's Fables the Smothers Brothers Way,* Mercury SR-60989, 1965, stereo, $20.

### SMITHS, THE

| Number | Title (A Side/B Side) | Yr | NM |
|---|---|---|---|
| **SIRE** | | | |
| ❑ 25065 | The Smiths | 1984 | 10.00 |
| ❑ 25269 | Meat Is Murder | 1985 | 10.00 |
| ❑ 25426 | The Queen Is Dead | 1986 | 10.00 |
| ❑ 25649 | Strangeways, Here We Come | 1987 | 10.00 |
| ❑ 25669 [(2)] | Louder Than Bombs | 1987 | 15.00 |
| ❑ 25786 | "Rank" | 1988 | 10.00 |
| **WARNER BROS.** | | | |
| ❑ WBMS-130 [DJ] | Music and Interviews | 1985 | 40.00 |
| *—Part of "The Warner Bros. Music Show" series; one side is The Smiths; the other side is The Blasters* | | | |

### SMOKE, THE (1)

California group. Jimmy Greenspoon, later a member of THREE DOG NIGHT, appears on the LP cover, but not on the record itself.

| Number | Title (A Side/B Side) | Yr | NM |
|---|---|---|---|
| **SIDEWALK** | | | |
| ❑ ST 5912 | The Smoke | 1968 | 40.00 |

### SMOKE, THE (2)

Houston-based group.

| Number | Title (A Side/B Side) | Yr | NM |
|---|---|---|---|
| **UNI** | | | |
| ❑ 73052 | The Smoke | 1969 | 25.00 |
| ❑ 73065 | The Smoke at George's Coffee Shop | 1970 | 25.00 |

### SMOKE RISE, THE

| Number | Title (A Side/B Side) | Yr | NM |
|---|---|---|---|
| **PARAMOUNT** | | | |
| ❑ PAS-9000 [(2)] | The Survival of St. Joan | 1971 | 20.00 |
| *—With booklet* | | | |

### SMOKESTACK LIGHTNIN'

| Number | Title (A Side/B Side) | Yr | NM |
|---|---|---|---|
| **BELL** | | | |
| ❑ 6026 | Off the Wall | 1969 | 20.00 |

### SMOKY BABE

| Number | Title (A Side/B Side) | Yr | NM |
|---|---|---|---|
| **BLUESVILLE** | | | |
| ❑ BVLP-1063 [M] | Hottest Brand Going | 1963 | 80.00 |
| *—Blue label, silver print* | | | |
| ❑ BVLP-1063 [M] | Hottest Brand Going | 1964 | 25.00 |
| *—Blue label, trident logo at right* | | | |
| **FOLK-LYRIC** | | | |
| ❑ FL-108 [M] | Smokey Babe | 196? | 100.00 |

### SMOTHERS, SMOKEY

| Number | Title (A Side/B Side) | Yr | NM |
|---|---|---|---|
| **KING** | | | |
| ❑ 779 [M] | The Backporch Blues | 1962 | 1000. |

### SMOTHERS BROTHERS, THE

| Number | Title (A Side/B Side) | Yr | NM |
|---|---|---|---|
| **MERCURY** | | | |
| ❑ MGDJ-20 [DJ] | Best of the Smothers Brothers | 1964 | 40.00 |
| ❑ MGDJ-25 [DJ] | It's Brothers Smothers Month | 1964 | 40.00 |
| ❑ MG-20611 [M] | The Songs and Comedy of the Smothers Brothers! | 1962 | 15.00 |
| ❑ MG-20675 [M] | The Two Sides of the Smothers Brothers | 1962 | 15.00 |
| ❑ MG-20777 [M] | (Think Ethnic!) | 1963 | 15.00 |
| ❑ MG-20862 [M] | Curb Your Tongue, Knave! | 1963 | 15.00 |
| ❑ MG-20904 [M] | It Must Have Been Something I Said! | 1964 | 15.00 |
| ❑ MG-20948 [M] | Tour De Farce American History and Other Unrelated Subjects | 1964 | 15.00 |
| ❑ MG-20989 [M] | Aesop's Fables the Smothers Brothers Way | 1965 | 15.00 |
| ❑ MG-21051 [M] | Mom Always Liked You Best! | 1965 | 15.00 |
| ❑ MG-21064 [M] | The Smothers Brothers Play It Straight | 1966 | 15.00 |
| ❑ MG-21089 [M] | Golden Hits of the Smothers Brothers, Vol. 2 | 1966 | 15.00 |
| ❑ SR-60611 [S] | The Songs and Comedy of the Smothers Brothers! | 1962 | 20.00 |
| ❑ SR-60675 [S] | The Two Sides of the Smothers Brothers | 1962 | 20.00 |
| ❑ SR-60777 [S] | (Think Ethnic!) | 1963 | 20.00 |
| ❑ SR-60862 [S] | Curb Your Tongue, Knave! | 1963 | 20.00 |
| ❑ SR-60904 [S] | It Must Have Been Something I Said! | 1964 | 20.00 |
| ❑ SR-60948 [S] | Tour De Farce American History and Other Unrelated Subjects | 1964 | 20.00 |
| ❑ SR-60989 [S] | Aesop's Fables the Smothers Brothers Way | 1965 | 20.00 |
| ❑ SR-61051 [S] | Mom Always Liked You Best! | 1965 | 20.00 |
| ❑ SR-61064 [S] | The Smothers Brothers Play It Straight | 1966 | 20.00 |
| ❑ SR-61089 [S] | Golden Hits of the Smothers Brothers, Vol. 2 | 1966 | 20.00 |
| ❑ SR-61193 | Smothers Comedy Brothers Hour | 1968 | 20.00 |
| **RHINO** | | | |
| ❑ R1-70188 | Sibling Revelry: The Best of the Smothers Brothers | 1988 | 10.00 |

Hank Snow and Anita Carter, *Together Again,* RCA Victor LPM-2580, 1962, mono, $30.

| Number | Title (A Side/B Side) | Yr | NM |
|---|---|---|---|
| **SNEAKY PETE** | | | |
| SHILO | | | |
| ❑ 4086 | Sneaky Pete | 1979 | 30.00 |
| **SNELL, TONY** | | | |
| ESP-DISK' | | | |
| ❑ 3004 | Medieval and Latter Day Lays | 197? | 20.00 |
| **SNOOP DOGG** Also includes records credited to "Snoop Doggy Dogg." | | | |
| DEATH ROW/INTERSCOPE | | | |
| ❑ INT2-90038 [(2)] | Tha Doggfather | 1996 | 50.00 |
| *—As "Snoop Doggy Dogg"* | | | |
| ❑ 92279 | Doggystyle | 1993 | 50.00 |
| *—As "Snoop Doggy Dogg"* | | | |
| GEFFEN | | | |
| ❑ B0003763-01 [(2)] | R&G (Rhythm & Gangsta): The Masterpiece | 2004 | 15.00 |
| NO LIMIT | | | |
| ❑ 50006 [(2)] | Da Game Is to Be Sold, Not to Be Told | 1998 | 25.00 |
| ❑ 50062 [(2)] | No Limit Top Dogg | 1999 | 30.00 |
| PRIORITY | | | |
| ❑ P1 23225 [(2)] | Tha Last Meal | 2000 | 25.00 |
| ❑ 39157 [(3)] | Paid Tha Cost to Be Tha Bo$$ | 2002 | 25.00 |
| **SNOW** | | | |
| EPIC | | | |
| ❑ BN 26435 | Snow | 1969 | 20.00 |
| **SNOW, HANK** | | | |
| PAIR | | | |
| ❑ PDL2-1004 [(2)] | I'm Movin' On | 1986 | 12.00 |
| RCA CAMDEN | | | |
| ❑ ACL1-0124 | Snowbird | 1973 | 10.00 |
| ❑ ACL2-0337 [(2)] | When My Blue Moon Turns to Gold Again | 197? | 15.00 |
| ❑ CAL-514 [M] | The Singing Ranger | 1959 | 20.00 |
| ❑ CAS-514 [R] | The Singing Ranger | 196? | 12.00 |
| ❑ ACL1-0540 | I'm Movin' On | 1974 | 10.00 |
| ❑ CAL-680 [M] | The Southern Cannonball | 1961 | 20.00 |
| ❑ CAS-680 [R] | The Southern Cannonball | 196? | 12.00 |
| ❑ CAL-722 [M] | The One and Only Hank Snow | 1962 | 20.00 |
| ❑ CAS-722 [R] | The One and Only Hank Snow | 1962 | 12.00 |
| ❑ CAL-782 [M] | The Last Ride | 1963 | 20.00 |
| ❑ CAS-782 [R] | The Last Ride | 1963 | 12.00 |
| ❑ CAL-836 [M] | Old and Great Songs | 1964 | 15.00 |
| ❑ CAS-836 [S] | Old and Great Songs | 1964 | 12.00 |
| ❑ CAL-910 [M] | The Highest Bidder | 1965 | 12.00 |
| ❑ CAS-910 [S] | The Highest Bidder | 1965 | 15.00 |
| ❑ CAL-964 [M] | Travelin' Blues | 1966 | 12.00 |
| ❑ CAS-964 [S] | Travelin' Blues | 1966 | 15.00 |
| ❑ CAL-2160 [M] | My Early Favorites | 1967 | 15.00 |
| ❑ CAS-2160 [S] | My Early Favorites | 1967 | 12.00 |
| ❑ CAS-2235 | Somewhere Along Life's Highway | 1968 | 12.00 |
| ❑ CAS-2257 | My Nova Scotia Home | 1968 | 12.00 |
| ❑ CAS-2348 | I Went to Your Wedding | 1969 | 12.00 |
| ❑ CAS-2443 | Memories Are Made of This | 1970 | 12.00 |
| ❑ CAS-2513 | Lonesome Whistle | 1972 | 12.00 |
| ❑ CAS-2560 | The Legend of Old Doc Brown | 1972 | 12.00 |
| ❑ CXS-9009 [(2)] | The Wreck of the 97 | 197? | 15.00 |
| RCA VICTOR | | | |
| ❑ DPL2-0134 [(2)] | The Living Legend | 197? | 100.00 |
| *—RCA Special Products release* | | | |
| ❑ APL1-0162 | Grand Ole Opry Favorites | 1973 | 15.00 |
| ❑ APL1-0441 | Hello Love | 1974 | 15.00 |
| ❑ APL1-0608 | That's You and Me | 1974 | 15.00 |
| ❑ APL1-0908 | You're Easy to Love | 1975 | 15.00 |
| ❑ LPM-1113 [M] | Just Keep a-Movin' | 1955 | 100.00 |
| ❑ LPM-1156 [M] | Old Doc Brown and Other Narrations | 1955 | 100.00 |
| ❑ ANL1-1207 | Grand Ole Opry Favorites | 1975 | 10.00 |
| *—Reissue of APL1-0162* | | | |
| ❑ LPM-1233 [M] | Country Classics | 1956 | 80.00 |
| ❑ APL1-1361 | Live from Evangel Temple | 1976 | 12.00 |
| *—With Jimmy Snow* | | | |
| ❑ LPM-1419 [M] | Country and Western Jamboree | 1957 | 80.00 |
| ❑ LPM-1435 [M] | Hank Snow's Country Guitar | 1957 | 80.00 |
| ❑ LPM-1638 [M] | Hank Snow Sings Sacred Songs | 1958 | 60.00 |
| ❑ LPM-2043 [M] | Hank Snow Sings Jimmie Rodgers Songs | 1959 | 50.00 |
| ❑ LSP-2043 [S] | Hank Snow Sings Jimmie Rodgers Songs | 1959 | 80.00 |
| ❑ ANL1-2194 | The Jimmie Rodgers Story | 1977 | 10.00 |
| *—Reissue of 4708* | | | |
| ❑ LPM-2285 [M] | Hank Snow Souvenirs | 1961 | 30.00 |
| ❑ LSP-2285 [S] | Hank Snow Souvenirs | 1961 | 40.00 |
| ❑ APL1-2400 | #104 — Still Movin' On | 1977 | 12.00 |
| ❑ LPM-2458 [M] | Big Country Hits | 1961 | 30.00 |
| ❑ LSP-2458 [S] | Big Country Hits | 1961 | 40.00 |
| ❑ LPM-2675 [M] | I've Been Everywhere | 1963 | 30.00 |
| ❑ LSP-2675 [S] | I've Been Everywhere | 1963 | 40.00 |
| ❑ LPM-2705 [M] | Railroad Man | 1963 | 30.00 |
| ❑ LSP-2705 [S] | Railroad Man | 1963 | 40.00 |
| ❑ LPM-2812 [M] | More Hank Snow Souvenirs | 1964 | 25.00 |
| ❑ LSP-2812 [S] | More Hank Snow Souvenirs | 1964 | 30.00 |
| ❑ LPM-2901 [M] | Songs of Tragedy | 1964 | 25.00 |
| ❑ LSP-2901 [S] | Songs of Tragedy | 1964 | 30.00 |
| ❑ LPM-3026 [10] | Country Classics | 1952 | 200.00 |
| ❑ LPM-3070 [10] | Hank Snow Sings | 1952 | 180.00 |
| ❑ LPM-3131 [10] | Hank Snow Salutes Jimmie Rodgers | 1953 | 180.00 |
| ❑ AHL1-3208 | Mysterious Lady | 1979 | 12.00 |
| ❑ LPM-3267 [10] | Hank Snow's Country Guitar | 1954 | 180.00 |
| ❑ LPM-3317 [M] | Your Favorite Country Hits | 1965 | 25.00 |
| ❑ LSP-3317 [S] | Your Favorite Country Hits | 1965 | 30.00 |
| ❑ LPM-3378 [M] | Gloryland March | 1965 | 25.00 |
| ❑ LSP-3378 [S] | Gloryland March | 1965 | 30.00 |
| ❑ ANL1-3470 | The Best of Hank Snow | 1980 | 8.00 |
| ❑ LPM-3471 [M] | Heartbreak Trail - A Tribute to the Sons of the Pioneers | 1966 | 25.00 |
| ❑ LSP-3471 [S] | Heartbreak Trail - A Tribute to the Sons of the Pioneers | 1966 | 30.00 |
| ❑ LPM-3478 [M] | The Best of Hank Snow | 1966 | 20.00 |
| ❑ LSP-3478 [S] | The Best of Hank Snow | 1966 | 25.00 |
| ❑ AHL1-3511 | Instrumentally Yours | 1980 | 12.00 |
| ❑ LPM-3548 [M] | Guitar Stylings of Hank Snow | 1966 | 25.00 |
| ❑ LSP-3548 [S] | Guitar Stylings of Hank Snow | 1966 | 30.00 |
| ❑ LPM-3595 [M] | Gospel Train | 1966 | 30.00 |
| ❑ LSP-3595 [S] | Gospel Train | 1966 | 40.00 |
| ❑ LPM-3737 [M] | Snow in Hawaii | 1967 | 30.00 |
| ❑ LSP-3737 [S] | Snow in Hawaii | 1967 | 25.00 |
| ❑ LPM-3826 [M] | Christmas with Hank Snow | 1967 | 30.00 |
| ❑ LSP-3826 [S] | Christmas with Hank Snow | 1967 | 25.00 |
| ❑ LPM-3857 [M] | Spanish Fire Ball and Other Great Hank Snow Stylings | 1967 | 30.00 |
| ❑ LSP-3857 [S] | Spanish Fire Ball and Other Great Hank Snow Stylings | 1967 | 25.00 |
| ❑ LPM-3965 [M] | Hits, Hits and More Hits | 1968 | 100.00 |
| ❑ LSP-3965 [S] | Hits, Hits and More Hits | 1968 | 25.00 |
| ❑ LSP-4032 | Tales of the Yukon | 1968 | 25.00 |
| ❑ LSP-4122 | Snow in All Seasons | 1969 | 25.00 |
| ❑ LSP-4306 | Hank Snow Sings in Memory of Jimmie Rodgers | 1970 | 20.00 |
| ❑ LSP-4379 | Cure for the Blues | 1970 | 20.00 |
| ❑ LSP-4501 | Tracks and Trains | 1971 | 20.00 |
| ❑ LSP-4601 | Award Winners | 1971 | 20.00 |
| ❑ LSP-4708 | The Jimmie Rodgers Story | 1972 | 15.00 |
| ❑ LSP-4798 | The Best of Hank Snow, Vol. 2 | 1972 | 15.00 |
| ❑ AHL1-5497 | Collector's Series | 1986 | 10.00 |
| ❑ LPM-6014 [(2)M] | This Is My Story | 1966 | 40.00 |
| ❑ LSP-6014 [(2)S] | This Is My Story | 1966 | 50.00 |
| READER'S DIGEST | | | |
| ❑ RDA-216 [(6)] | I'm Movin' On | 197? | 120.00 |
| SCHOOL OF MUSIC | | | |
| ❑ 1149 [M] | The Guitar | 1958 | 250.00 |
| *—Deduct 20 percent if instruction book is missing* | | | |
| **SNOW, HANK, AND CHET ATKINS** | | | |
| RCA VICTOR | | | |
| ❑ LPM-2952 [M] | Reminiscing | 1964 | 25.00 |
| ❑ LSP-2952 [S] | Reminiscing | 1964 | 30.00 |
| ❑ LSP-4254 | By Special Request - C.B. Atkins and C.E. Snow | 1970 | 20.00 |
| **SNOW, HANK, AND ANITA CARTER** | | | |
| RCA VICTOR | | | |
| ❑ LPM-2580 [M] | Together Again | 1962 | 30.00 |
| ❑ LSP-2580 [S] | Together Again | 1962 | 40.00 |
| **SNOW, HANK; PORTER WAGONER; HANK LOCKLIN** | | | |
| RCA VICTOR | | | |
| ❑ LPM-2723 [M] | Three Country Gentlemen | 1963 | 30.00 |
| ❑ LSP-2723 [S] | Three Country Gentlemen | 1963 | 40.00 |
| **SNOW, PHOEBE** | | | |
| COLUMBIA | | | |
| ❑ PC 33952 | Second Childhood | 1976 | 10.00 |
| *—Original with no bar code* | | | |
| ❑ PC 33952 | Second Childhood | 198? | 8.00 |
| *—Budget-line reissue with bar code* | | | |
| ❑ PCQ 33952 [Q] | Second Childhood | 1976 | 15.00 |
| ❑ PC 34387 | It Looks Like Snow | 1976 | 10.00 |
| *—Original with no bar code* | | | |
| ❑ PC 34387 | It Looks Like Snow | 198? | 8.00 |
| *—Budget-line reissue with bar code* | | | |
| ❑ JC 34875 | Never Letting Go | 1977 | 10.00 |
| ❑ JC 35456 | Against the Grain | 1978 | 10.00 |
| ❑ JC 37091 | The Best of Phoebe Snow | 1981 | 10.00 |
| ❑ PC 37091 | The Best of Phoebe Snow | 1981 | 8.00 |
| *—Budget-line reissue* | | | |
| DCC COMPACT CLASSICS | | | |
| ❑ LPZ-2027 | Phoebe Snow | 1996 | 30.00 |
| *—Audiophile vinyl* | | | |



**Except when noted otherwise, VG = 25% of NM, and VG+ = 50% of NM. (Example: VG = $2.00, VG+ = $4.00 and NM = $8.00.)**

| Number | Title (A Side/B Side) | Yr | NM |
|---|---|---|---|
| **ELEKTRA** | | | |
| ❑ 60852 | Something Real | 1989 | 10.00 |
| **MCA** | | | |
| ❑ 37119 | Phoebe Snow | 198? | 8.00 |
| *—Budget-line reissue of Shelter LP* | | | |
| **MIRAGE** | | | |
| ❑ SD 19297 | Rock Away | 1981 | 10.00 |
| **SHELTER** | | | |
| ❑ 2109 | Phoebe Snow | 1974 | 10.00 |
| ❑ 52017 | Phoebe Snow | 1977 | 8.00 |
| *—Reissue with ABC distribution* | | | |
| **SNOWDEN, ELMER** | | | |
| **RIVERSIDE** | | | |
| ❑ RLP-348 [M] | Harlem Banjo | 1960 | 20.00 |
| ❑ RS-9348 [S] | Harlem Banjo | 1960 | 25.00 |
| **SNYDER, TERRY, AND THE ALL-STARS** See ENOCH LIGHT. | | | |
| **SOCIAL DISTORTION** | | | |
| **EPIC** | | | |
| ❑ E 46055 | Social Distortion | 1990 | 20.00 |
| ❑ E 47948 | Somewhere Between Heaven and Hell | 1992 | 20.00 |
| **EPIC/550 MUSIC** | | | |
| ❑ E 64380 | White Light, White Heat, White Trash | 1996 | 12.00 |
| **RESTLESS** | | | |
| ❑ 72251 | Prison Bound | 1988 | 20.00 |
| **13TH FLOOR** | | | |
| ❑ SD 1301 | Mommy's Little Monster | 1983 | 40.00 |
| *—Standard cover with lyric sheet* | | | |
| ❑ SD 1301 | Mommy's Little Monster | 1983 | 60.00 |
| *—Gatefold cover* | | | |
| **TIME BOMB** | | | |
| ❑ 43500 | Mommy's Little Monster | 1995 | 10.00 |
| ❑ 43501 | Prison Bound | 1995 | 10.00 |
| ❑ 43502 | Mainliner (Wreckage from the Past) | 1995 | 10.00 |
| ❑ 43516 [(2)] | Live at the Roxy | 1998 | 12.00 |
| **TRIPLE X** | | | |
| ❑ 51019 | Mommy's Little Monster | 1989 | 20.00 |
| *—Clear vinyl* | | | |
| **SOCIAL UNREST** | | | |
| **LIBERTINE** | | | |
| ❑ LSU 1 [EP] | Rat in a Maze | 1982 | 25.00 |
| ❑ LSU 2461 | SU-2000 | 1985 | 20.00 |
| **SOCIETY OF SEVEN** | | | |
| **SILVER SWORD** | | | |
| ❑ 7012 | How Has Your Love Life Been? | 1970 | 20.00 |
| **SOCOLOW, FRANK** | | | |
| **BETHLEHEM** | | | |
| ❑ BCP-70 [M] | Sounds By Socolow | 1957 | 80.00 |
| **SOFT MACHINE, THE** | | | |
| **ACCORD** | | | |
| ❑ SN-7178 | Memories | 1981 | 10.00 |
| **COLUMBIA** | | | |
| ❑ G 30339 [(2)] | Third | 1970 | 15.00 |
| ❑ C 30754 | Fourth | 1971 | 12.00 |
| ❑ KC 31604 | 5 | 1972 | 12.00 |
| ❑ KG 32260 [(2)] | Six | 1973 | 15.00 |
| ❑ KC 32716 | Seven | 1974 | 12.00 |
| **COMMAND** | | | |
| ❑ 964 SD [(2)] | Soft Machine | 1973 | 15.00 |
| *—Reissue of Probe LPs in one package* | | | |
| **PROBE** | | | |
| ❑ CPLP-4500 | The Soft Machine | 1968 | 40.00 |
| *—Cover with moving parts* | | | |
| ❑ CPLP-4500 | The Soft Machine | 1969 | 20.00 |
| *—Regular cover* | | | |
| ❑ CPLP-4505 | The Soft Machine, Vol. 2 | 1969 | 25.00 |
| **SOFTWARE** | | | |
| **INNOVATIVE COMMUNICATION** | | | |
| ❑ KS 80.055 [(2)] | Electronic Universe | 1987 | 20.00 |
| **SOLAL, MARTIAL** | | | |
| **CAPITOL** | | | |
| ❑ ST 10261 [S] | Martial Solal | 1960 | 30.00 |
| ❑ T 10261 [M] | Martial Solal | 1960 | 25.00 |
| ❑ ST 10354 [S] | Vive La France! Viva La Jazz! Vive Solal! | 1961 | 25.00 |
| ❑ T 10354 [M] | Vive La France! Viva La Jazz! Vive Solal! | 1961 | 20.00 |
| **CONTEMPORARY** | | | |
| ❑ C-2512 [10] | French Modern Sounds | 1954 | 80.00 |
| **LIBERTY** | | | |
| ❑ LST-7335 [S] | Martial Solal in Concert | 1963 | 20.00 |

| Number | Title (A Side/B Side) | Yr | NM |
|---|---|---|---|
| **MILESTONE** | | | |
| ❑ MLP-1001 [M] | Solal! | 1967 | 25.00 |
| **RCA VICTOR** | | | |
| ❑ LSP-2777 [S] | Martial Solal at Newport '63 | 1963 | 20.00 |
| **SOMERSET STRINGS, THE** | | | |
| **EPIC** | | | |
| ❑ LN 3159 [M] | Music for Christmas at Home | 1955 | 20.00 |
| **SOMMER, ELKE** | | | |
| **MGM** | | | |
| ❑ E-4321 [M] | Love in Any Language | 1965 | 25.00 |
| ❑ SE-4321 [S] | Love in Any Language | 1965 | 30.00 |
| **SOMMERS, JOANIE** | | | |
| **COLUMBIA** | | | |
| ❑ CL 2495 [M] | Come Alive | 1966 | 20.00 |
| ❑ CS 9295 [S] | Come Alive | 1966 | 25.00 |
| **DISCOVERY** | | | |
| ❑ DS-883 | Dream | 1983 | 12.00 |
| *—With Bob Florence* | | | |
| **WARNER BROS.** | | | |
| ❑ W 1346 [M] | Positively the Most | 1960 | 30.00 |
| ❑ WS 1346 [S] | Positively the Most | 1960 | 40.00 |
| ❑ B 1348 [M] | Behind Closed Doors at a Recording Session | 1960 | 150.00 |
| *—Record comes in a box with a booklet included* | | | |
| ❑ W 1412 [M] | Joanie Sommers | 1961 | 30.00 |
| ❑ WS 1412 [S] | Joanie Sommers | 1961 | 40.00 |
| ❑ W 1436 [M] | For Those Who Think Young | 1962 | 30.00 |
| ❑ WS 1436 [S] | For Those Who Think Young | 1962 | 40.00 |
| ❑ W 1470 [M] | Johnny Get Angry | 1962 | 40.00 |
| ❑ WS 1470 [S] | Johnny Get Angry | 1962 | 50.00 |
| ❑ W 1474 [M] | Let's Talk About Love | 1962 | 30.00 |
| ❑ WS 1474 [S] | Let's Talk About Love | 1962 | 40.00 |
| ❑ W 1504 [M] | Sommers' Seasons | 1963 | 25.00 |
| ❑ WS 1504 [S] | Sommers' Seasons | 1963 | 30.00 |
| ❑ W 1575 [M] | Softly, The Brazilian Sound | 1964 | 25.00 |
| ❑ WS 1575 [S] | Softly, The Brazilian Sound | 1964 | 30.00 |
| **SONDHEIM, ALAN** | | | |
| **ESP-DISK'** | | | |
| ❑ 1048 [S] | Ritual-All-7-70 | 1969 | 20.00 |
| ❑ 1082 [S] | T'Other Little Tune | 1969 | 20.00 |
| **SONIC YOUTH** | | | |
| **DGC** | | | |
| ❑ 24297 | Goo | 1990 | 30.00 |
| ❑ 24485 | Dirty | 1992 | 25.00 |
| ❑ 24632 | Experimental Jet Set, Trash and No Star | 1994 | 40.00 |
| ❑ 24825 [(2)] | Washing Machine | 1995 | 40.00 |
| **ENIGMA** | | | |
| ❑ 75403 [(2)] | Daydream Nation | 1988 | 30.00 |
| **GEFFEN** | | | |
| ❑ 490650-1 | NYC Ghosts and Flowers | 2000 | 15.00 |
| **GOOFIN'** | | | |
| ❑ GOO 04 | Murray Street | 2002 | 12.00 |
| ❑ GOO 05 [(4)] | Dirty (Deluxe Edition) | 2003 | 30.00 |
| ❑ GOO 06 [(2)] | Sonic Nurse | 2004 | 15.00 |
| ❑ GOO 07 [(4)] | Goo (Deluxe Edition) | 2005 | 30.00 |
| ❑ GOO 08 [(2)] | Sonic Youth | 2006 | 20.00 |
| *—Reissue of 1982 debut album with a second record of bonus tracks* | | | |
| ❑ GOO 11 | Rather Ripped | 2006 | 12.00 |
| **HOMESTEAD** | | | |
| ❑ HMS 016 | Bad Moon Rising | 1985 | 25.00 |
| ❑ HMS 021 [EP] | Death Valley '69 | 1985 | 25.00 |
| *—With Lydia Lunch* | | | |
| **KONKURRENT** | | | |
| ❑ FISH-9 | In the Fishtank | 2002 | 15.00 |
| *—With I.C.P. and The Ex; U.S. editions are distributed by Touch and Go Records* | | | |
| **MOBILE FIDELITY** | | | |
| ❑ 1-257 | Goo | 1996 | 100.00 |
| *—Audiophile vinyl* | | | |
| **MY SO-CALLED RECORDS** | | | |
| ❑ 3 [(2)] | A Thousand Leaves | 1998 | 15.00 |
| **NEUTRAL** | | | |
| ❑ 001 [EP] | Sonic Youth | 1982 | 80.00 |
| ❑ N-1 [EP] | Sonic Youth | 1982 | 80.00 |
| ❑ 9 | Confusion Is Sex | 1983 | 70.00 |
| **RHINO** | | | |
| ❑ R1 71591 | Made in U.S.A. (Soundtrack) | 1995 | 15.00 |
| *—Clear vinyl record and sleeve; music recorded in 1986* | | | |
| **SST** | | | |
| ❑ 059 | Evol | 1986 | 40.00 |
| ❑ 080 [EP] | Starpower | 1986 | 30.00 |
| ❑ 096 | Confusion Is Sex | 1987 | 40.00 |
| *—Reissue of Neutral 9* | | | |
| ❑ 097 [EP] | Sonic Youth | 1987 | 25.00 |
| ❑ 134 | Sister | 1987 | 25.00 |
| ❑ 155 [EP] | Master Dik | 1988 | 25.00 |

| Number | Title (A Side/B Side) | Yr | NM |
|---|---|---|---|
| **SYR** | | | |
| ❑ 1 | Anagrama | 1997 | 10.00 |
| *—Red vinyl* | | | |
| ❑ 2 | Slaapkamers Met Slagroom | 1997 | 10.00 |
| *—Teal vinyl* | | | |
| ❑ 3 | Invito Al Cielo | 1998 | 10.00 |
| *—With Jim O'Rourke; clear vinyl* | | | |
| ❑ 4 [(2)] | Goodbye 20th Century | 1999 | 15.00 |
| ❑ 5 [(2)] | Kim Gordon - DJ Olive - Ikue Mori | 2000 | 12.00 |
| **SONICS, THE (2)** | | | |
| **BEAT ROCKET** | | | |
| ❑ BR 114 | Introducing the Sonics | 199? | 12.00 |
| **BOMP!** | | | |
| ❑ 4011 | Sinderella | 1980 | 15.00 |
| **BUCKSHOT** | | | |
| ❑ 001 | Explosives | 1973 | 200.00 |
| **ETIQUETTE** | | | |
| ❑ ETALB-024 [M] | Here Are the Sonics!!! | 1965 | 200.00 |
| *—Purple label* | | | |
| ❑ ETALB-024 [M] | Here Are the Sonics!!! | 1965 | 250.00 |
| *—Red label* | | | |
| ❑ ETLPS-024 | Here Are the Sonics!!! | 1984 | 10.00 |
| *—Purple label, flimsier vinyl, with date on back cover* | | | |
| ❑ ETLPS-024 [S] | Here Are the Sonics!!! | 1965 | 300.00 |
| *—Purple label* | | | |
| ❑ ETLPS-024 [S] | Here Are the Sonics!!! | 1965 | 400.00 |
| *—Red label* | | | |
| ❑ ETALB-027 [M] | The Sonics Boom | 1966 | 300.00 |
| ❑ ETLPS-027 | The Sonics Boom | 1984 | 10.00 |
| *—Flimsier vinyl, with date on back cover* | | | |
| ❑ ETLPS-027 [R] | The Sonics Boom | 1966 | 200.00 |
| **FIRST AMERICAN** | | | |
| ❑ FA-7715 | Original Northwest Punk | 1978 | 20.00 |
| ❑ FA-7719 | Unreleased | 1980 | 20.00 |
| ❑ FA-7779 | Fire and Ice | 1983 | 20.00 |
| **JERDEN** | | | |
| ❑ JRL-7007 [M] | Introducing the Sonics | 1967 | 200.00 |
| ❑ JRS-7007 [R] | Introducing the Sonics | 1967 | 150.00 |
| **SONICS, THE (2); THE WAILERS; THE GALAXIES** | | | |
| **ETIQUETTE** | | | |
| ❑ ETALB-025 | Merry Christmas | 1984 | 10.00 |
| *—Flimsier vinyl, with date on back cover* | | | |
| ❑ ETALB-025 [M] | Merry Christmas | 1965 | 500.00 |
| **SONN, LARRY** | | | |
| **CORAL** | | | |
| ❑ CRL 57057 [M] | The Sound of Sonn | 1956 | 40.00 |
| **DOT** | | | |
| ❑ DLP-9005 [M] | Jazz Band Having a Ball | 1958 | 25.00 |
| ❑ DLP-29005 [S] | Jazz Band Having a Ball | 1958 | 30.00 |
| **SONNY** | | | |
| **ATCO** | | | |
| ❑ 33-229 [M] | Inner Views | 1967 | 20.00 |
| ❑ SD 33-229 [S] | Inner Views | 1967 | 20.00 |
| **SONNY AND CHER** | | | |
| **ATCO** | | | |
| ❑ 33-177 [M] | Look At Us | 1965 | 15.00 |
| *—With white box that says "Includes Their Big Hit 'I Got You Babe'" (second edition)* | | | |
| ❑ 33-177 [M] | Look At Us | 1965 | 20.00 |
| *—Without white box that says "Includes Their Big Hit 'I Got You Babe'" (original)* | | | |
| ❑ SD 33-177 [S] | Look At Us | 1965 | 15.00 |
| *—With white box that says "Includes Their Big Hit 'I Got You Babe'" (second edition)* | | | |
| ❑ SD 33-177 [S] | Look At Us | 1965 | 25.00 |
| *—Without white box that says "Includes Their Big Hit 'I Got You Babe'" (original)* | | | |
| ❑ 33-183 [M] | The Wondrous World of Sonny and Cher | 1966 | 15.00 |
| ❑ SD 33-183 [S] | The Wondrous World of Sonny and Cher | 1966 | 20.00 |
| ❑ 33-203 [M] | In Case You're in Love | 1967 | 15.00 |
| ❑ SD 33-203 [S] | In Case You're in Love | 1967 | 20.00 |
| ❑ 33-214 [M] | Good Times | 1967 | 15.00 |
| ❑ SD 33-214 [S] | Good Times | 1967 | 20.00 |
| ❑ 33-219 [M] | The Best of Sonny and Cher | 1967 | 15.00 |
| ❑ SD 33-219 [P] | The Best of Sonny and Cher | 1967 | 20.00 |
| *—"What Now My Love," "A Beautiful Story," "But You're Mine" and "Laugh at Me" are rechanneled* | | | |
| ❑ SD 2-804 [(2)] | The Two of Us | 1972 | 20.00 |
| *—Combines "Look at Us" and "In Case You're in Love"* | | | |
| ❑ A2M 5177 [(2)M] | Sonny & Cher's Greatest Hits | 1967 | 30.00 |
| *—Columbia Record Club exclusive* | | | |
| ❑ A2S 5178 [(2)S] | Sonny & Cher's Greatest Hits | 1967 | 30.00 |
| *—Columbia Record Club exclusive* | | | |
| ❑ SD 11000 | The Beat Goes On | 1975 | 15.00 |
| **KAPP** | | | |
| ❑ KS-3654 | Sonny & Cher Live | 1971 | 15.00 |
| ❑ KS-3660 | All I Ever Need Is You | 1972 | 15.00 |
| *—Orange and red swirl label* | | | |

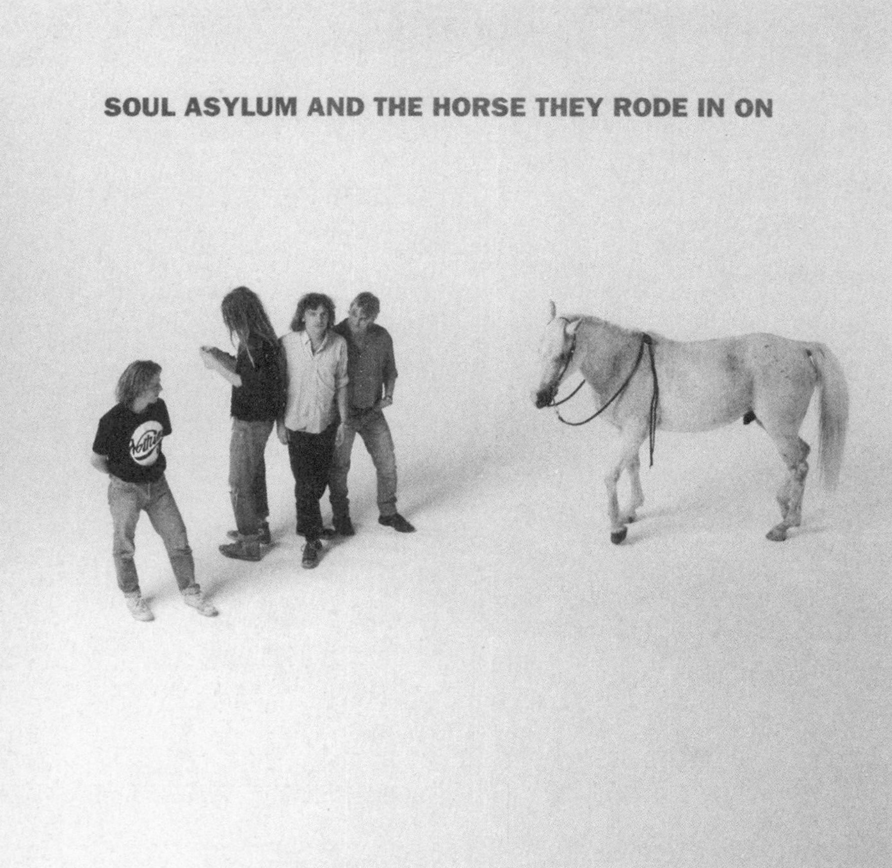


Soul Asylum, *And the Horse They Rode In On,* A&M 75021 5318 1, 1990, $20.

| Number | Title (A Side/B Side) | Yr | NM |
|---|---|---|---|
| ❑ KS-3660 | All I Ever Need Is You | 1972 | 20.00 |
| *—Black label with red "Kapp" cap at top* | | | |
| ❑ KS-3660 | All I Ever Need Is You | 1972 | 30.00 |
| *—Red label with red "Kapp" cap at top* | | | |
| ❑ KRS-5560 | All I Ever Need Is You | 1972 | 12.00 |
| *—Reissue; orange and red swirl label; some of these have a sticker on the front cover with the new number with no difference in value* | | | |
| ❑ ST-94312 | All I Ever Need Is You | 1972 | 20.00 |
| *—Capitol Record Club edition* | | | |

MCA

| Number | Title (A Side/B Side) | Yr | NM |
|---|---|---|---|
| ❑ 2009 | Sonny & Cher Live | 1973 | 12.00 |
| *—Reissue of Kapp 3654* | | | |
| ❑ 2021 | All I Ever Need Is You | 1973 | 12.00 |
| *—Reissue of Kapp 3660* | | | |
| ❑ 2101 | Mama Was a Rock & Roll Singer Papa Used to Write All Her Songs | 1973 | 12.00 |
| ❑ 2117 | Greatest Hits | 1974 | 12.00 |
| ❑ 2-8004 [(2)] | Sonny & Cher Live in Las Vegas, Vol. 2 | 1973 | 15.00 |

PAIR

| Number | Title (A Side/B Side) | Yr | NM |
|---|---|---|---|
| ❑ PDL2-1140 [(2)] | Sonny & Cher At Their Best | 1986 | 12.00 |

REPRISE

| Number | Title (A Side/B Side) | Yr | NM |
|---|---|---|---|
| ❑ R 6177 [M] | Baby Don't Go | 1965 | 30.00 |
| ❑ RS 6177 [P] | Baby Don't Go | 1965 | 30.00 |
| *—By "Sonny & Cher & Friends" (also includes The Lettermen, Bill Medley and The Blendells)* | | | |

TVP

| Number | Title (A Side/B Side) | Yr | NM |
|---|---|---|---|
| ❑ TVP-1021 | The Hits of Sonny & Cher | 1977 | 12.00 |

**SONNY AND THE DEMONS**

UNITED ARTISTS

| Number | Title (A Side/B Side) | Yr | NM |
|---|---|---|---|
| ❑ UAL-3316 [M] | Drag Kings | 1964 | 50.00 |
| ❑ UAS-6316 [S] | Drag Kings | 1964 | 60.00 |

**SONS OF CHAMPLIN, THE**

ARIOLA AMERICA

| Number | Title (A Side/B Side) | Yr | NM |
|---|---|---|---|
| ❑ SW-50002 | The Sons of Champlin | 1975 | 10.00 |
| ❑ ST-50007 | A Circle Filled with Love | 1976 | 10.00 |
| ❑ SW-50017 | Loving Is Why | 1977 | 10.00 |

CAPITOL

| Number | Title (A Side/B Side) | Yr | NM |
|---|---|---|---|
| ❑ SWBB-200 [(2)] | Loosen Up Naturally | 1969 | 20.00 |
| *—With the F-word airbrushed off the cover artwork* | | | |
| ❑ SWBB-200 [(2)] | Loosen Up Naturally | 1969 | 25.00 |
| *—With the F-word scratched off the cover artwork* | | | |
| ❑ SWBB-200 [(2)] | Loosen Up Naturally | 1969 | 50.00 |
| *—With the F-word clearly visible as part of the cover artwork* | | | |
| ❑ SKAO-322 | The Sons | 1969 | 25.00 |
| ❑ ST-675 | Follow Your Heart | 1971 | 20.00 |

COLUMBIA

| Number | Title (A Side/B Side) | Yr | NM |
|---|---|---|---|
| ❑ KC 32341 | Welcome to the Dance | 1973 | 15.00 |

GOLDMINE

| Number | Title (A Side/B Side) | Yr | NM |
|---|---|---|---|
| ❑ GM 94930 | The Sons of Champlin | 1975 | 20.00 |

SONS OF CHAMPLIN

| Number | Title (A Side/B Side) | Yr | NM |
|---|---|---|---|
| ❑ (no #) | Minus Seeds and Stems | 1969 | 500.00 |

**SONS OF HEROES**

MCA

| Number | Title (A Side/B Side) | Yr | NM |
|---|---|---|---|
| ❑ 39010 | Sons of Heroes | 1983 | 20.00 |

**SONS OF THE PIONEERS**

COLUMBIA

| Number | Title (A Side/B Side) | Yr | NM |
|---|---|---|---|
| ❑ FC 37439 | The Sons of the Pioneers: Columbia Historical Edition | 1981 | 10.00 |

MCA

| Number | Title (A Side/B Side) | Yr | NM |
|---|---|---|---|
| ❑ 730 | Tumbleweed Trails | 198? | 10.00 |

RCA CAMDEN

| Number | Title (A Side/B Side) | Yr | NM |
|---|---|---|---|
| ❑ CAL-413 [M] | Wagons West | 1958 | 20.00 |
| ❑ CAS-413 [R] | Wagons West | 1963 | 12.00 |
| ❑ CAL-587 [M] | Room Full of Roses | 1960 | 20.00 |

RCA VICTOR

| Number | Title (A Side/B Side) | Yr | NM |
|---|---|---|---|
| ❑ PRM-104 [M] | Westward Ho! | 1961 | 25.00 |
| *—Special-products issue* | | | |
| ❑ LPM-1130 [M] | Favorite Cowboy Songs | 1955 | 50.00 |
| ❑ LPM-1431 [M] | How Great Thou Art | 1957 | 50.00 |
| ❑ LPM-1483 [M] | One Man's Songs | 1957 | 50.00 |
| ❑ LPM-2118 [M] | Cool Water | 1960 | 25.00 |
| ❑ LSP-2118 [S] | Cool Water | 1960 | 30.00 |
| ❑ ANL1-2332 | A Country-Western Songbook | 1977 | 15.00 |
| ❑ LPM-2356 [M] | Lure of the West | 1961 | 25.00 |
| ❑ LSP-2356 [S] | Lure of the West | 1961 | 30.00 |
| ❑ LPM-2456 [M] | Tumbleweed Trails | 1962 | 25.00 |
| ❑ LSP-2456 [S] | Tumbleweed Trails | 1962 | 30.00 |
| ❑ LPM-2603 [M] | Our Men Out West | 1963 | 20.00 |
| ❑ LSP-2603 [S] | Our Men Out West | 1963 | 25.00 |
| ❑ LPM-2652 [M] | Hymns of the Cowboy | 1963 | 20.00 |
| ❑ LSP-2652 [S] | Hymns of the Cowboy | 1963 | 25.00 |
| ❑ LPM-2737 [M] | Trail Dust | 1963 | 20.00 |
| ❑ LSP-2737 [S] | Trail Dust | 1963 | 25.00 |
| ❑ LPM-2855 [M] | Country Fare | 1964 | 20.00 |
| ❑ LSP-2855 [S] | Country Fare | 1964 | 25.00 |
| ❑ LPM-2957 [M] | Down Memory Trail | 1964 | 20.00 |
| ❑ LSP-2957 [S] | Down Memory Trail | 1964 | 25.00 |
| ❑ LPM-3032 [10] | Cowboy Classics | 1952 | 100.00 |
| ❑ LPM-3095 [10] | Cowboy Hymns and Spirituals | 1952 | 100.00 |
| ❑ LPM-3162 [10] | Western Classics | 1953 | 100.00 |
| ❑ LPM-3351 [M] | Legends of the West | 1965 | 15.00 |
| ❑ LSP-3351 [S] | Legends of the West | 1965 | 20.00 |
| ❑ ANL1-3468 | The Best of the Sons of the Pioneers | 1980 | 10.00 |
| ❑ LPM-3476 [M] | The Best of Sons of the Pioneers | 1966 | 15.00 |
| ❑ LSP-3476 [S] | The Best of Sons of the Pioneers | 1966 | 20.00 |
| ❑ LPM-3554 [M] | The Songs of Bob Nolan | 1966 | 15.00 |
| ❑ LSP-3554 [S] | The Songs of Bob Nolan | 1966 | 20.00 |
| ❑ AYL1-3679 | Cool Water | 1980 | 10.00 |
| ❑ LPM-3714 [M] | Campfire Favorites | 1967 | 25.00 |
| ❑ LSP-3714 [S] | Campfire Favorites | 1967 | 20.00 |
| ❑ LPM-3964 [M] | South of the Border | 1968 | 80.00 |
| ❑ LSP-3964 [S] | South of the Border | 1968 | 20.00 |
| ❑ AYM1-4092 | Let's Go West Again | 1981 | 10.00 |

READER'S DIGEST

| Number | Title (A Side/B Side) | Yr | NM |
|---|---|---|---|
| ❑ RBA-135-A [(7)] | Down Memory Trail with the Sons of the Pioneers | 1981 | 60.00 |

SILVER SPUR

| Number | Title (A Side/B Side) | Yr | NM |
|---|---|---|---|
| ❑ S 581 [(2)] | Celebration: Commemorating 50 Years of the Sons of the Pioneers | 1982 | 15.00 |

**SONS OF THE PURPLE SAGE**

TOPS

| Number | Title (A Side/B Side) | Yr | NM |
|---|---|---|---|
| ❑ L-1588 [M] | Western Favorites | 1959 | 20.00 |

WALDORF

| Number | Title (A Side/B Side) | Yr | NM |
|---|---|---|---|
| ❑ 143 [10] | Songs of the Golden West | 1955 | 50.00 |

**SOPHOMORES, THE (1)**

SEECO

| Number | Title (A Side/B Side) | Yr | NM |
|---|---|---|---|
| ❑ CELP-451 [M] | The Sophomores | 1958 | 200.00 |

**SOPWITH "CAMEL," THE**

KAMA SUTRA

| Number | Title (A Side/B Side) | Yr | NM |
|---|---|---|---|
| ❑ KSBS-2063 | Hello Hello | 1973 | 20.00 |
| ❑ KLP-8060 [M] | The Sopwith Camel | 1967 | 30.00 |
| ❑ KLPS-8060 [S] | The Sopwith Camel | 1967 | 30.00 |

REPRISE

| Number | Title (A Side/B Side) | Yr | NM |
|---|---|---|---|
| ❑ MS 2108 | The Miraculous Hump Returns | 1973 | 25.00 |

**SOTHERN, ANN**

CRAFTSMAN

| Number | Title (A Side/B Side) | Yr | NM |
|---|---|---|---|
| ❑ C-8061 [M] | It's Ann Sothern Time | 1961 | 20.00 |

TOPS

| Number | Title (A Side/B Side) | Yr | NM |
|---|---|---|---|
| ❑ L-1611 [M] | Sothern Exposure | 1959 | 25.00 |

**SOUL, JIMMY**

SPQR

| Number | Title (A Side/B Side) | Yr | NM |
|---|---|---|---|
| ❑ E 16001 | If You Wanna Be Happy | 1963 | 150.00 |

**SOUL ASYLUM**

A&M

| Number | Title (A Side/B Side) | Yr | NM |
|---|---|---|---|
| ❑ SP-5197 | Hang Time | 1988 | 15.00 |
| ❑ 75031 5318 1 | ...And the Horse They Rode In On | 1990 | 20.00 |
| *—Blue vinyl* | | | |

COLUMBIA

| Number | Title (A Side/B Side) | Yr | NM |
|---|---|---|---|
| ❑ C 48898 | Grave Dancers Union | 1993 | 20.00 |
| ❑ C 57616 | Let Your Dim Light Shine | 1995 | 12.00 |
| ❑ C 67618 | Candy From a Stranger | 1998 | 12.00 |

TWIN/TONE

| Number | Title (A Side/B Side) | Yr | NM |
|---|---|---|---|
| ❑ TTR 8439 | Say What You Will, Clarence...Karl Sold the Truck | 1984 | 20.00 |
| ❑ TTR 8666 | Made to Be Broken | 1986 | 15.00 |
| ❑ TTR 8691 | While You Were Out | 1986 | 15.00 |
| ❑ TTR 88144 [EP] | Clam Dip & Other Delights | 1988 | 20.00 |

**SOUL CHILDREN, THE**

EPIC

| Number | Title (A Side/B Side) | Yr | NM |
|---|---|---|---|
| ❑ PE 33902 | Finders Keepers | 1976 | 15.00 |
| ❑ PE 34455 | Where Is Your Woman Tonight | 1977 | 15.00 |

STAX

| Number | Title (A Side/B Side) | Yr | NM |
|---|---|---|---|
| ❑ STS-2018 | Soul Children | 1969 | 30.00 |
| ❑ STS-2043 | The Best of Two Worlds | 1971 | 30.00 |
| ❑ STS-3003 | Genesis | 1972 | 30.00 |
| ❑ STX-4105 | Open Door Policy | 1978 | 15.00 |
| ❑ STX-4120 | Chronicle | 1979 | 12.00 |
| ❑ STS-5507 | Friction | 1974 | 30.00 |

**SOUL FINDERS, THE**

RCA CAMDEN

| Number | Title (A Side/B Side) | Yr | NM |
|---|---|---|---|
| ❑ CAL-2170 [M] | Sweet Soul Music | 1967 | 30.00 |

| Number | Title (A Side/B Side) | Yr | NM |
|---|---|---|---|
| ❑ CAS-2170 [S] | Sweet Soul Music | 1967 | 30.00 |
| ❑ CAL-2239 [M] | An Explosive Album of Soul | 1968 | 30.00 |
| ❑ CAS-2239 [S] | An Explosive Album of Soul | 1968 | 30.00 |

**SOUL FLUTES**

A&M

| Number | Title (A Side/B Side) | Yr | NM |
|---|---|---|---|
| ❑ SP-3009 | Trust in Me | 1968 | 20.00 |

**SOUL GENERATION, THE**

EBONY SOUNDS

| Number | Title (A Side/B Side) | Yr | NM |
|---|---|---|---|
| ❑ 2000 | Beyond Body and Soul | 1972 | 20.00 |

**SOUL SET, THE**

JOHNSON

| Number | Title (A Side/B Side) | Yr | NM |
|---|---|---|---|
| ❑ 1001 | The Soul Set | 196? | 25.00 |

**SOUL SISTERS, THE**

SUE

| Number | Title (A Side/B Side) | Yr | NM |
|---|---|---|---|
| ❑ LP-1022 [M] | I Can't Stand It | 1964 | 200.00 |
| ❑ STLP-1022 [S] | I Can't Stand It | 1964 | 400.00 |

**SOUL SOCIETY, THE**

DOT

| Number | Title (A Side/B Side) | Yr | NM |
|---|---|---|---|
| ❑ DLP-25842 | Satisfaction | 1969 | 25.00 |

**SOUL STIRRERS, THE**

SPECIALTY

| Number | Title (A Side/B Side) | Yr | NM |
|---|---|---|---|
| ❑ SP-2106 [M] | The Soul Stirrers Featuring Sam Cooke | 1959 | 50.00 |

**SOUL SURVIVORS**

ATCO

| Number | Title (A Side/B Side) | Yr | NM |
|---|---|---|---|
| ❑ SD 33-277 | Take Another Look | 1969 | 25.00 |

CRIMSON

| Number | Title (A Side/B Side) | Yr | NM |
|---|---|---|---|
| ❑ CR-502 [M] | When the Whistle Blows Anything Goes | 1967 | 50.00 |
| ❑ CR-502 S [S] | When the Whistle Blows Anything Goes | 1967 | 30.00 |

TSOP

| Number | Title (A Side/B Side) | Yr | NM |
|---|---|---|---|
| ❑ KZ 33186 | The Soul Survivors | 1975 | 12.00 |

**SOUND FOUNDATION**

SMOBRO

| Number | Title (A Side/B Side) | Yr | NM |
|---|---|---|---|
| ❑ 9001 | Sound Foundation | 1971 | 25.00 |

**SOUND OF FEELING**

LIMELIGHT

| Number | Title (A Side/B Side) | Yr | NM |
|---|---|---|---|
| ❑ LS-86063 | Spleen | 1969 | 20.00 |

**SOUND SYMPOSIUM, THE**

DOT

| Number | Title (A Side/B Side) | Yr | NM |
|---|---|---|---|
| ❑ DLP-3871 [M] | Paul Simon Interpreted | 1968 | 30.00 |
| *—Stereo cover with white "Monaural" sticker; label is regular stock copy* | | | |
| ❑ DLP-25871 [S] | Paul Simon Interpreted | 1968 | 20.00 |
| ❑ DLP-25952 | Bob Dylan Interpreted | 1969 | 20.00 |

**SOUNDGARDEN**

A&M

| Number | Title (A Side/B Side) | Yr | NM |
|---|---|---|---|
| ❑ 31454 0198 1 [(2)] | Superunknown | 1994 | 30.00 |
| *—Blue vinyl* | | | |
| ❑ 31454 0198 1 [(2)] | Superunknown | 1994 | 30.00 |
| *—Clear vinyl* | | | |
| ❑ 31454 0198 1 [(2)] | Superunknown | 1994 | 30.00 |
| *—Gold vinyl* | | | |
| ❑ 31454 0526-1 [(2)] | Down on the Upside | 1996 | 20.00 |
| ❑ SP-5252 | Louder Than Love | 1989 | 20.00 |
| *—Black vinyl* | | | |
| ❑ SP-5252 | Louder Than Love | 1989 | 40.00 |
| *—Red vinyl* | | | |
| ❑ SP-5252 | Louder Than Love | 1989 | 60.00 |
| *—Green vinyl* | | | |
| ❑ 75021 5374 1 | Badmotorfinger | 1991 | 40.00 |
| *—Limited edition on yellow vinyl* | | | |
| ❑ SP-17951 [DJ] | Louder Than Live | 1990 | 80.00 |
| *—Promo-only live album on blue vinyl* | | | |

SST

| Number | Title (A Side/B Side) | Yr | NM |
|---|---|---|---|
| ❑ 201 | Ultramega OK | 1988 | 20.00 |
| ❑ 231 [EP] | Flower | 1988 | 15.00 |
| ❑ 911 [10] | Flower | 1988 | 10.00 |

SUB POP

| Number | Title (A Side/B Side) | Yr | NM |
|---|---|---|---|
| ❑ 12 [EP] | Screaming Life | 1987 | 150.00 |
| *—First 500 copies on orange vinyl* | | | |
| ❑ 12 [EP] | Screaming Life | 1987 | 15.00 |
| *—Reissues on any color vinyl except black or orange* | | | |
| ❑ 12 [EP] | Screaming Life | 1987 | 20.00 |
| *—Black vinyl* | | | |
| ❑ 17 [EP] | Fopp | 1988 | 50.00 |

**SOUNDS OF OUR TIMES, THE**

CAPITOL

| Number | Title (A Side/B Side) | Yr | NM |
|---|---|---|---|
| ❑ ST-117 | Hey Jude | 1969 | 12.00 |
| ❑ ST-8-0117 | Hey Jude | 1969 | 15.00 |
| *—Capitol Record Club edition* | | | |
| ❑ ST-182 | Galveston | 1969 | 12.00 |
| ❑ ST 2817 [S] | Music of the Flower Children | 1968 | 12.00 |
| ❑ T 2817 [M] | Music of the Flower Children | 1968 | 20.00 |

Sounds Orchestral, *Cast Your Fate to the Wind,* Parkway P-7046, 1965, mono, $15.

| Number | Title (A Side/B Side) | Yr | NM |
|---|---|---|---|
| ❑ ST 2892 [S] | The Sounds of Our Time Play "Love Is Blue" | 1968 | 12.00 |
| ❑ T 2892 [M] | The Sounds of Our Time Play "Love Is Blue" | 1968 | 25.00 |

**SOUNDS ORCHESTRAL**

JANUS

| Number | Title (A Side/B Side) | Yr | NM |
|---|---|---|---|
| ❑ JLS-3014 | One More Time | 197? | 15.00 |

PARKWAY

| Number | Title (A Side/B Side) | Yr | NM |
|---|---|---|---|
| ❑ P 7046 [M] | Cast Your Fate to the Wind | 1965 | 15.00 |
| ❑ SP 7046 [S] | Cast Your Fate to the Wind | 1965 | 20.00 |
| ❑ P 7047 [M] | The Soul of Sounds Orchestral | 1965 | 15.00 |
| ❑ SP 7047 [S] | The Soul of Sounds Orchestral | 1965 | 20.00 |
| ❑ P 7050 [M] | Impressions of James Bond | 1966 | 20.00 |
| ❑ SP 7050 [S] | Impressions of James Bond | 1966 | 30.00 |

**SOUNDSTAGE ALL-STARS, THE**

DOT

| Number | Title (A Side/B Side) | Yr | NM |
|---|---|---|---|
| ❑ DLP-3204 [M] | More "Peter Gunn" | 1959 | 25.00 |
| ❑ DLP-25204 [S] | More "Peter Gunn" | 1959 | 30.00 |

**SOUP**

ARF ARM

| Number | Title (A Side/B Side) | Yr | NM |
|---|---|---|---|
| ❑ 1 | Soup | 1970 | 120.00 |

BIG TREE

| Number | Title (A Side/B Side) | Yr | NM |
|---|---|---|---|
| ❑ BTS 2007 | The Album Soup | 1971 | 25.00 |

**SOUTH, EDDIE**

MERCURY

| Number | Title (A Side/B Side) | Yr | NM |
|---|---|---|---|
| ❑ MG-20401 [M] | The Distinguished Violin of Eddie South | 1959 | 30.00 |
| ❑ SR-60070 [S] | The Distinguished Violin of Eddie South | 1959 | 25.00 |

**SOUTH, JOE**

ACCORD

| Number | Title (A Side/B Side) | Yr | NM |
|---|---|---|---|
| ❑ SN-7119 | Party People | 1981 | 10.00 |

CAPITOL

| Number | Title (A Side/B Side) | Yr | NM |
|---|---|---|---|
| ❑ ST-108 | Introspect | 1968 | 20.00 |
| ❑ ST-235 | Games People Play | 1969 | 15.00 |
| ❑ ST-392 | Don't It Make You Want to Go Home | 1969 | 15.00 |
| ❑ SM-450 | Joe South's Greatest Hits | 1977 | 8.00 |
| *—Reissue with new prefix* | | | |
| ❑ ST-450 | Joe South's Greatest Hits | 1970 | 15.00 |
| ❑ ST-637 | So the Seeds Are Growing | 1971 | 12.00 |
| ❑ ST-845 | Joe South | 1972 | 12.00 |
| ❑ ST-11074 | A Look Inside | 1972 | 12.00 |

ISLAND

| Number | Title (A Side/B Side) | Yr | NM |
|---|---|---|---|
| ❑ ILPS-9328 | Midnight Rainbows | 1975 | 10.00 |

MINE

| Number | Title (A Side/B Side) | Yr | NM |
|---|---|---|---|
| ❑ MSG-1100 | Walkin' Shoes | 1971 | 12.00 |
| *—Reissue with new title* | | | |
| ❑ MSG-1100 | The Joe South Story | 1971 | 15.00 |

NASHVILLE

| Number | Title (A Side/B Side) | Yr | NM |
|---|---|---|---|
| ❑ 2092 | You're the Reason | 1970 | 12.00 |

PICKWICK

| Number | Title (A Side/B Side) | Yr | NM |
|---|---|---|---|
| ❑ SPC-3314 | Games People Play | 197? | 10.00 |

**SOUTH 40**

METROBEAT

| Number | Title (A Side/B Side) | Yr | NM |
|---|---|---|---|
| ❑ MBS-1000 | Live at the Someplace Else | 1968 | 25.00 |

**SOUTH CENTRAL AVENUE MUNICIPAL BLUES BAND**

BLUESWAY

| Number | Title (A Side/B Side) | Yr | NM |
|---|---|---|---|
| ❑ BL-6018 | The Soul of Bonnie and Clyde | 1968 | 25.00 |

**SOUTHERN, HAL**

SAGE & SAND

| Number | Title (A Side/B Side) | Yr | NM |
|---|---|---|---|
| ❑ 46 | You Got a Man on Your Hands | 1967 | 25.00 |

**SOUTHERN, JERI**

CAPITOL

| Number | Title (A Side/B Side) | Yr | NM |
|---|---|---|---|
| ❑ ST 1173 [S] | Jeri Southern Meets Cole Porter | 1959 | 40.00 |
| *—Black colorband label, Capitol logo at left* | | | |
| ❑ ST 1173 [S] | Jeri Southern Meets Cole Porter | 1963 | 20.00 |
| *—Black colorband label, Capitol logo at top* | | | |
| ❑ T 1173 [M] | Jeri Southern Meets Cole Porter | 1959 | 30.00 |
| *—Black colorband label, Capitol logo at left* | | | |
| ❑ ST 1278 [S] | Jeri Southern at the Crescendo | 1960 | 40.00 |
| *—Black colorband label, Capitol logo at left* | | | |
| ❑ ST 1278 [S] | Jeri Southern at the Crescendo | 1963 | 20.00 |
| *—Black colorband label, Capitol logo at top* | | | |
| ❑ T 1278 [M] | Jeri Southern at the Crescendo | 1960 | 30.00 |
| *—Black colorband label, Capitol logo at left* | | | |

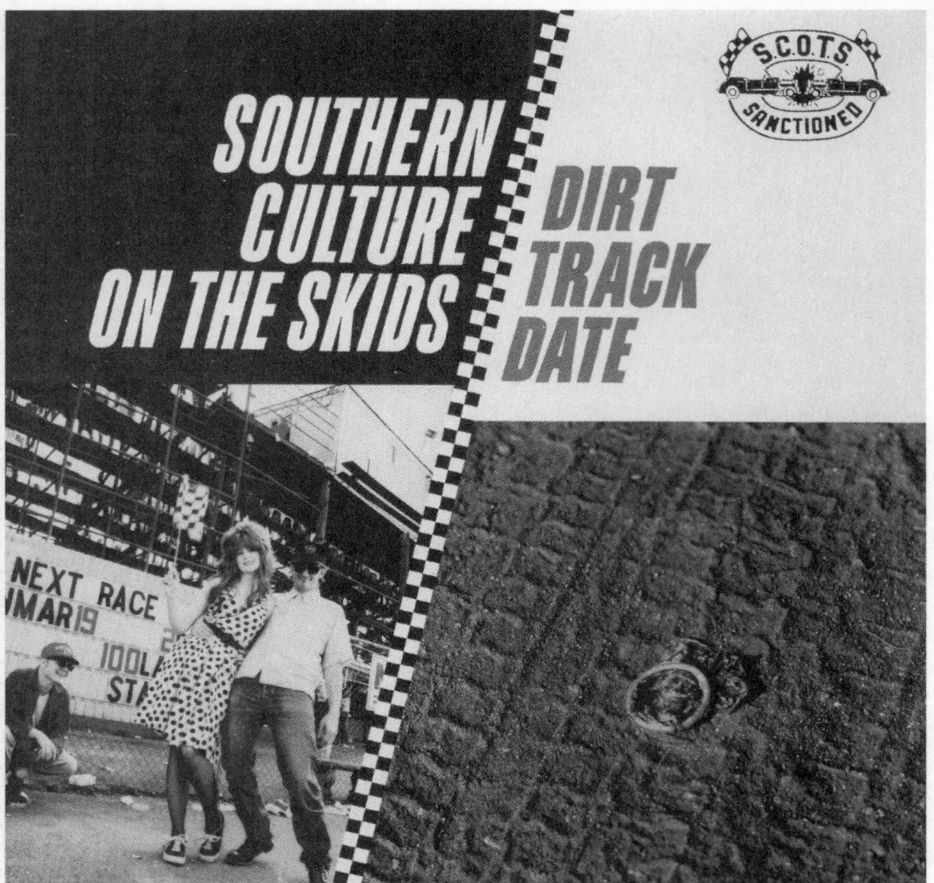


Southern Culture on the Skids, *Dirt Track Date,* Telstar TR 020, 1995, $40.

| Number | Title (A Side/B Side) | Yr | NM |
|---|---|---|---|
| **DECCA** | | | |
| ❑ DL 5531 [10] | Intimate Songs | 1954 | 80.00 |
| ❑ DL 8055 [M] | Southern Style | 1955 | 50.00 |
| ❑ DL 8214 [M] | You Better Go Now | 1956 | 50.00 |
| ❑ DL 8394 [M] | When Your Heart's on Fire | 1956 | 50.00 |
| ❑ DL 8472 [M] | Jeri Southern Gently Jumps | 1957 | 50.00 |
| ❑ DL 8745 [M] | Prelude to a Kiss | 1958 | 50.00 |
| ❑ DL 8761 [M] | Southern Hospitality | 1958 | 50.00 |
| **ROULETTE** | | | |
| ❑ R-25039 [M] | Coffee, Cigarettes and Memories | 1958 | 40.00 |
| ❑ R-52010 [M] | Southern Breeze | 1958 | 40.00 |
| ❑ RS-52010 [S] | Southern Breeze | 1958 | 50.00 |
| ❑ R-52016 [M] | Jeri Southern Meets Johnny Smith | 1958 | 40.00 |
| ❑ RS-52016 [S] | Jeri Southern Meets Johnny Smith | 1958 | 50.00 |

### SOUTHERN CULTURE ON THE SKIDS

| Number | Title (A Side/B Side) | Yr | NM |
|---|---|---|---|
| **LLOYD STREET** | | | |
| ❑ SO 17737 | Southern Culture on the Skids | 1985 | 80.00 |
| **SAFEHOUSE** | | | |
| ❑ SH-2114-1 [PD] | Ditch Diggin' | 1994 | 30.00 |
| *—Picture disc* | | | |
| **TELSTAR** | | | |
| ❑ 20 | Dirt Track Date | 1995 | 40.00 |
| ❑ TR 30 | Plastic Seat Sweat | 1997 | 12.00 |
| ❑ TR-40 | Liquored Up and Lacquered Down | 2000 | 10.00 |
| **YEP ROC** | | | |
| ❑ 2063 | Mojo Box | 2004 | 15.00 |
| ❑ LP-YEP-2120 [(2)] | Double Wide and Live | 2006 | 20.00 |

### SOUTHSIDE JOHNNY AND THE ASBURY JUKES

| Number | Title (A Side/B Side) | Yr | NM |
|---|---|---|---|
| **ATLANTIC** | | | |
| ❑ 81654 | At Least We Got Shoes | 1986 | 8.00 |
| **CYPRESS** | | | |
| ❑ YL-0115 | Slow Dance | 1988 | 10.00 |
| **EPIC** | | | |
| ❑ AS 275 [DJ] | Jukes Live at the Bottom Line | 1976 | 30.00 |
| ❑ PE 34180 | I Don't Want to Go Home | 1976 | 10.00 |
| *—Orange label, no bar code* | | | |
| ❑ PE 34180 | I Don't Want to Go Home | 1979 | 8.00 |
| *—Dark blue label, most have bar codes on back cover* | | | |
| ❑ PE 34668 | This Time It's for Real | 1977 | 10.00 |
| *—Orange label, no bar code* | | | |
| ❑ PE 34668 | This Time It's for Real | 198? | 8.00 |
| *—Dark blue label, bar code on back cover* | | | |
| ❑ JE 35488 | Hearts of Stone | 1978 | 10.00 |
| *—Orange label, no bar code* | | | |
| ❑ PE 35488 | Hearts of Stone | 198? | 8.00 |
| *—Dark blue label, bar code on back cover* | | | |
| ❑ JE 36246 | Havin' a Party with Southside Johnny | 1979 | 10.00 |
| ❑ PE 36246 | Havin' a Party with Southside Johnny | 198? | 8.00 |
| *—Budget-line reissue with new prefix* | | | |
| **MERCURY** | | | |
| ❑ SRM-1-3793 | The Jukes | 1979 | 10.00 |
| ❑ SRM-1-3836 | Love Is a Sacrifice | 1980 | 10.00 |
| ❑ SRM-2-8602 [(2)] | Live — Reach Out and Touch the Sky | 1981 | 12.00 |
| ❑ 826285-1 [(2)] | Live — Reach Out and Touch the Sky | 198? | 10.00 |
| *—Reissue of 8602* | | | |
| **MIRAGE** | | | |
| ❑ 90113 | Trash It Up! | 1983 | 10.00 |
| ❑ 90186 | In the Heat | 1984 | 10.00 |

### SOUTHWEST F.O.B.

| Number | Title (A Side/B Side) | Yr | NM |
|---|---|---|---|
| **HIP** | | | |
| ❑ 7001 | Smell of Incense | 1969 | 30.00 |

### SOVINE, RED

| Number | Title (A Side/B Side) | Yr | NM |
|---|---|---|---|
| **CHART** | | | |
| ❑ 1052 | The Greatest Grand Ol' Opry | 1972 | 15.00 |
| ❑ 2056 | It'll Come Back | 1974 | 15.00 |
| **DECCA** | | | |
| ❑ DL 4445 [M] | Red Sovine | 1963 | 30.00 |
| ❑ DL 4736 [M] | Country Music Time | 1966 | 30.00 |
| ❑ DL 74445 [R] | Red Sovine | 1963 | 20.00 |
| ❑ DL 74736 [R] | Country Music Time | 1966 | 20.00 |
| **GUSTO** | | | |
| ❑ 3010 | 16 All-Time Favorites | 1978 | 12.00 |
| **MGM** | | | |
| ❑ E-3465 [M] | Red Sovine | 1957 | 60.00 |
| **NASHVILLE** | | | |
| ❑ 2033 | Giddy-Up Go | 196? | 12.00 |
| ❑ 2044 | A Dear John Letter | 196? | 12.00 |
| ❑ 2056 | Anytime | 196? | 12.00 |
| ❑ 2083 | Don't Take Your Love to Town | 1969 | 12.00 |
| **POWER PAK** | | | |
| ❑ 270 | Phantom 309 | 197? | 10.00 |
| **STARDAY** | | | |
| ❑ SLP-132 [M] | The One and Only Red Sovine | 1961 | 40.00 |
| ❑ SLP-197 [M] | Golden Country Ballads of the 1960s | 1962 | 40.00 |
| ❑ SLP-341 [M] | Little Rosa | 1965 | 25.00 |
| ❑ SLP-357 | That's Truckdrivin' | 196? | 20.00 |
| ❑ SLP-363 [M] | Giddy-Up Go | 1966 | 20.00 |
| ❑ SLP-383 [M] | Town and Country Action | 1966 | 20.00 |
| ❑ SLP-396 [M] | The Nashville Sound of Red Sovine | 1967 | 20.00 |
| ❑ SLP-405 [M] | I Didn't Jump the Fence | 1967 | 20.00 |
| ❑ SLP-414 [M] | Phantom 309 | 1967 | 20.00 |
| ❑ SLP-420 | Tell Maude I Slipped | 1968 | 20.00 |
| ❑ SLP-427 | Sunday with Sovine | 1968 | 20.00 |
| ❑ SLP-436 | Classic Narrations | 1968 | 20.00 |
| ❑ SLP-441 | Closing Time 'Til Dawn | 1969 | 20.00 |
| ❑ SLP-445 | Who Am I | 1969 | 20.00 |
| ❑ SLP-459 | I Know You're Married But I Love You Still | 1970 | 20.00 |
| ❑ 952 | The Best of Red Sovine | 197? | 15.00 |
| ❑ 968 | Teddy Bear | 1976 | 15.00 |
| ❑ 970 | Woodrow Wilson Sovine | 1977 | 15.00 |
| ❑ 991 | Red Sovine's 16 Greatest Hits | 1977 | 15.00 |
| ❑ ST-90712 [S] | Giddy-Up Go | 1966 | 30.00 |
| *—Capitol Record Club edition* | | | |
| ❑ T-90712 [M] | Giddy-Up Go | 1966 | 25.00 |
| *—Capitol Record Club edition* | | | |
| **VOCALION** | | | |
| ❑ VL 3829 [M] | The Country Way | 196? | 15.00 |
| ❑ VL 73829 [R] | The Country Way | 196? | 12.00 |

### SPACE

| Number | Title (A Side/B Side) | Yr | NM |
|---|---|---|---|
| **HAND** | | | |
| ❑ 5167 | Space | 1969 | 25.00 |

### SPACEMEN, THE

| Number | Title (A Side/B Side) | Yr | NM |
|---|---|---|---|
| **ROULETTE** | | | |
| ❑ R-25275 [M] | Rockin' in the 25th Century | 1964 | 30.00 |
| ❑ SR-25275 [S] | Rockin' in the 25th Century | 1964 | 40.00 |
| ❑ R-25322 [M] | Music for Batman and Robin | 1966 | 40.00 |
| ❑ SR-25322 [S] | Music for Batman and Robin | 1966 | 50.00 |

### SPANDAU BALLET

| Number | Title (A Side/B Side) | Yr | NM |
|---|---|---|---|
| **CHRYSALIS** | | | |
| ❑ CHR 1331 | Journeys to Glory | 1981 | 12.00 |
| ❑ CHR 1353 | Diamond | 1982 | 10.00 |
| ❑ FV 41331 | Journeys to Glory | 1983 | 8.00 |
| *—Reissue* | | | |
| ❑ FV 41353 | Diamond | 1983 | 8.00 |
| *—Reissue of CHR 1353* | | | |
| ❑ PV 41353 | Diamond | 1986 | 8.00 |
| *—Reissue of FV 41353 with new prefix* | | | |
| ❑ B6V 41403 | True | 1983 | 12.00 |
| *—Original prefix* | | | |
| ❑ FV 41403 | True | 1983 | 8.00 |
| *—Reissue with new prefix* | | | |
| ❑ FV 41473 | Parade | 1984 | 10.00 |
| ❑ FV 41498 | The Singles Collection | 1985 | 10.00 |
| **EPIC** | | | |
| ❑ FE 40642 | Through the Barricades | 1987 | 12.00 |
| **MOBILE FIDELITY** | | | |
| ❑ 1-152 | True | 1984 | 20.00 |
| *—Audiophile vinyl* | | | |

### SPANIELS, THE

| Number | Title (A Side/B Side) | Yr | NM |
|---|---|---|---|
| **LOST-NITE** | | | |
| ❑ LLP-19 [10] | The Spaniels | 1981 | 12.00 |
| *—Red vinyl* | | | |
| **VEE JAY** | | | |
| ❑ LP-1002 [M] | Goodnite, It's Time to Go | 1958 | 600.00 |
| *—Maroon label; group pictured on cover* | | | |
| ❑ LP-1002 [M] | Goodnite, It's Time to Go | 1961 | 200.00 |
| *—Black label; dogs on cover* | | | |
| ❑ VJLP-1002 [M] | Goodnite, It's Time to Go | 198? | 12.00 |
| *—Legitimate reissue on flimsier vinyl than originals* | | | |
| ❑ LP-1024 [M] | The Spaniels | 1960 | 300.00 |

### SPANIER, MUGGSY

| Number | Title (A Side/B Side) | Yr | NM |
|---|---|---|---|
| **COMMODORE** | | | |
| ❑ FL-20009 [10] | Spanier's Ragtimers | 1950 | 100.00 |
| ❑ FL-30016 [M] | Chicago Jazz | 1957 | 50.00 |
| **DECCA** | | | |
| ❑ DL 5552 [10] | Hot Horn | 1955 | 60.00 |
| **EMARCY** | | | |
| ❑ MG-26011 [10] | Muggsy Spanier and His Dixieland Band | 1954 | 100.00 |
| **LONDON** | | | |
| ❑ AL-3503 [S] | Muggsy, Tesch and the Chicagoans | 195? | 30.00 |

| Number | Title (A Side/B Side) | Yr | NM |
|---|---|---|---|
| ❑ LL 3528 [M] | Muggsy Spanier and the Bucktown Five | 1959 | 40.00 |
| MERCURY | | | |
| ❑ MG-20171 [M] | Muggsy Spanier and His Dixieland Band | 1956 | 50.00 |
| ❑ MG-25095 [10] | Muggsy Spanier and His Dixieland Band | 1953 | 120.00 |
| RCA VICTOR | | | |
| ❑ LPM-1295 [M] | The Great 16 | 1956 | 50.00 |
| ❑ LPM-3043 [10] | Ragtime Favorites | 195? | 120.00 |
| RIVERSIDE | | | |
| ❑ RLP 12-107 [M] | Classic Early Recordings | 1955 | 60.00 |
| ❑ RLP-1004 [10] | Muggsy Spanier and Frank Teschemacher | 1953 | 120.00 |
| ❑ RLP-1035 [10] | Muggsy Spanier and His Bucktown Five | 1954 | 120.00 |
| RKO | | | |
| ❑ ULP 130 [M] | Chicago Jazz | 195? | 20.00 |
| STINSON | | | |
| ❑ SLP 30 [M] | Muggsy Spanier's Ragtimers, Vol. 1 | 1962 | 25.00 |
| *—Black vinyl* | | | |
| ❑ SLP 30 [M] | Muggsy Spanier's Ragtimers, Vol. 1 | 1962 | 50.00 |
| *—Red vinyl* | | | |
| ❑ SLP 31 [M] | Muggsy Spanier's Ragtimers, Vol. 2 | 1962 | 25.00 |
| *—Black vinyl* | | | |
| ❑ SLP 31 [M] | Muggsy Spanier's Ragtimers, Vol. 2 | 1962 | 50.00 |
| *—Red vinyl* | | | |
| WEATHERS INDUSTRIES | | | |
| ❑ W-5401 [M] | Dynamic Dixie | 1954 | 60.00 |
| ZEE GEE | | | |
| ❑ 101 [10] | Muggsy Spanier's Ragtimers, Vol. 1 | 195? | 120.00 |
| ❑ 102 [10] | Muggsy Spanier's Ragtimers, Vol. 2 | 195? | 120.00 |
| **SPANKY AND OUR GANG** | | | |
| EPIC | | | |
| ❑ PE 33580 | Change | 1975 | 12.00 |
| MERCURY | | | |
| ❑ MG-21124 [M] | Spanky and Our Gang | 1967 | 30.00 |
| ❑ SR-61124 [S] | Spanky and Our Gang | 1967 | 20.00 |
| ❑ SR-61161 | Like to Get to Know You | 1968 | 20.00 |
| ❑ SR-61183 | Anything You Choose/Without Rhyme or Reason | 1969 | 20.00 |
| ❑ SR-61227 | Spanky's Greatest Hit(s) | 1969 | 20.00 |
| ❑ SR-61326 | Live | 1971 | 15.00 |
| RHINO | | | |
| ❑ RNLP-70131 | The Best of Spanky and Our Gang (1967-1969) | 1986 | 12.00 |
| **SPANN, LES** | | | |
| JAZZLAND | | | |
| ❑ JLP-35 [M] | Gemini | 1961 | 25.00 |
| ❑ JLP-935 [S] | Gemini | 1961 | 30.00 |
| **SPANN, LUCILLE** | | | |
| BLUESWAY | | | |
| ❑ BLS-6070 | Cry Before I Go | 1974 | 25.00 |
| **SPANN, OTIS** | | | |
| BARNABY | | | |
| ❑ Z 30246 | Otis Spann Is the Blues | 1970 | 20.00 |
| ❑ KZ 31290 | Walking the Blues | 1972 | 20.00 |
| BLUE HORIZON | | | |
| ❑ BH 4802 | The Biggest Thing Since Colossus | 1970 | 25.00 |
| BLUES TIME | | | |
| ❑ 9006 | Sweet Giant of the Blues | 1970 | 20.00 |
| BLUESWAY | | | |
| ❑ BL-6003 [M] | The Blues Is Where It's At | 1967 | 25.00 |
| ❑ BLS-6003 [S] | The Blues Is Where It's At | 1967 | 25.00 |
| ❑ BLS-6013 | The Bottom of the Blues | 1968 | 25.00 |
| ❑ BLS-6063 | Heart Loaded with Trouble | 1973 | 20.00 |
| CANDID | | | |
| ❑ CM-8001 [M] | Otis Spann Is the Blues | 1966 | 150.00 |
| ❑ CS-9001 [S] | Otis Spann Is the Blues | 1966 | 200.00 |
| LONDON | | | |
| ❑ PS 543 | Raw Blues | 1968 | 30.00 |
| ❑ PS 551 | Cracked Spanner Head | 1969 | 30.00 |
| PRESTIGE | | | |
| ❑ PRST-7719 | The Blues Will Never Die | 1969 | 20.00 |
| TESTAMENT | | | |
| ❑ T-2211 | Otis Spann's Chicago Blues | 1966 | 40.00 |
| VANGUARD | | | |
| ❑ VSD-6514 | Cryin' Time | 1970 | 20.00 |

Spanky and Our Gang, *Spanky's Greatest Hit(s),* Mercury SR-61227, 1969, $20.

| Number | Title (A Side/B Side) | Yr | NM |
|---|---|---|---|
| **SPARKS** | | | |
| ANTILLES | | | |
| ❑ ANT-7044 | Kimono My House | 198? | 10.00 |
| *—Reissue of Island 9272* | | | |
| ATLANTIC | | | |
| ❑ SD 19347 | Angst in My Pants | 1982 | 10.00 |
| ❑ 80055 | Sparks in Outer Space | 1983 | 10.00 |
| ❑ 80160 | Pulling Rabbits Out of a Hat | 1984 | 10.00 |
| BEARSVILLE | | | |
| ❑ BV 2048 | Halfnelson | 1971 | 25.00 |
| *—Original issue of "Sparks" as "Halfnelson"* | | | |
| ❑ BV 2048 | Sparks | 1972 | 12.00 |
| *—Reissue under the group's new name* | | | |
| ❑ BR 2110 | A Woofer in Tweeter's Clothing | 1973 | 12.00 |
| COLUMBIA | | | |
| ❑ PC 34359 | Big Beat | 1976 | 10.00 |
| *—Originals have no bar code* | | | |
| ❑ PC 34901 | Introducing Sparks | 1977 | 10.00 |
| *—Originals have no bar code* | | | |
| ELEKTRA | | | |
| ❑ 6E-186 | No. 1 in Heaven | 1979 | 10.00 |
| IN THE RED | | | |
| ❑ ITR 131 | Hello Young Lovers | 2006 | 12.00 |
| ISLAND | | | |
| ❑ ILPS-9272 | Kimono My House | 1974 | 12.00 |
| *—Originals have multicolor island-scene label* | | | |
| ❑ ILPS-9312 | Propaganda | 1975 | 12.00 |
| *—Originals have multicolor island-scene label* | | | |
| ❑ ILPS-9345 | Indiscreet | 1975 | 12.00 |
| *—Originals have black label and no Warner Bros. distribution* | | | |
| MCA CURB | | | |
| ❑ 5780 | Music That You Can Dance To | 1986 | 10.00 |
| RCA VICTOR | | | |
| ❑ AFL1-4091 | Whomp That Sucker | 1981 | 10.00 |
| RHINO | | | |
| ❑ R1-70841 | Interior Design | 1988 | 10.00 |
| **SPARKS, MELVIN** | | | |
| PRESTIGE | | | |
| ❑ 10001 | Sparks! | 1971 | 20.00 |
| ❑ 10016 | Spark Plug | 1972 | 20.00 |
| ❑ 10039 | Akilah! | 1973 | 20.00 |
| WESTBOUND | | | |
| ❑ 204 | Melvin Sparks '75 | 1975 | 20.00 |

| Number | Title (A Side/B Side) | Yr | NM |
|---|---|---|---|
| **SPARKS, RANDY** | | | |
| VERVE | | | |
| ❑ MGV-2103 [M] | Randy Sparks | 1959 | 30.00 |
| ❑ MGV-2126 [M] | Walkin' the Low Road | 1960 | 30.00 |
| ❑ MGV-2143 [M] | Randy Sparks Three | 1960 | 30.00 |
| **SPARROW, THE** | | | |
| COLUMBIA | | | |
| ❑ CS 9758 | John Kay and Sparrow | 1969 | 40.00 |
| *—Red "360 Sound" label* | | | |
| **SPARROWS, THE** | | | |
| ELKAY | | | |
| ❑ 3009 [M] | That Mersey Sound | 1964 | 40.00 |
| **SPATS, THE** | | | |
| ABC-PARAMOUNT | | | |
| ❑ 502 [M] | Cookin' with the Spats | 1965 | 20.00 |
| ❑ S-502 [S] | Cookin' with the Spats | 1965 | 30.00 |
| **SPEARS, BILLIE JO** | | | |
| CAPITOL | | | |
| ❑ ST-114 | The Voice of Billie Jo Spears | 1969 | 20.00 |
| ❑ ST-224 | Mr. Walker, It's All Over! | 1969 | 15.00 |
| ❑ ST-397 | Miss Sincerity | 1969 | 15.00 |
| ❑ ST-454 | With Love | 1970 | 15.00 |
| ❑ ST-560 | Country Girl | 1970 | 15.00 |
| ❑ ST-688 | Just Singin' | 1971 | 15.00 |
| ❑ SM-11887 | The Best of Billie Jo Spears | 1979 | 10.00 |
| LIBERTY | | | |
| ❑ LT-1074 | Only the Hits | 1981 | 8.00 |
| ❑ LN-10018 | Blanket on the Ground | 1980 | 8.00 |
| ❑ LN-10019 | Love Ain't Gonna Wait for Us | 1980 | 8.00 |
| ❑ LN-10020 | I Will Survive | 1980 | 8.00 |
| ❑ LN-10021 | If You Want Me | 1980 | 8.00 |
| UNITED ARTISTS | | | |
| ❑ UA-LA390-G | Blanket on the Ground | 1975 | 10.00 |
| ❑ UA-LA508-G | Billie Jo | 1975 | 10.00 |
| ❑ UA-LA608-G | What I've Got in Mind | 1976 | 10.00 |
| ❑ UA-LA684-G | I'm Not Easy | 1976 | 10.00 |
| ❑ UA-LA748-G | If You Want Me | 1977 | 10.00 |
| ❑ UA-LA859-G | Lonely Hearts Club | 1977 | 10.00 |
| ❑ UA-LA921-H | Love Ain't Gonna Wait for Us | 1978 | 10.00 |
| ❑ LT-983 | The Singles Album | 1979 | 10.00 |
| ❑ LT-1018 | Standing Tall | 1980 | 10.00 |

| Number | Title (A Side/B Side) | Yr | NM |
|---|---|---|---|

**SPELLBINDERS, THE**

COLUMBIA

❑ CL 2514 [M] The Magic of the Spellbinders 1966 20.00
❑ CS 9314 [S] The Magic of the Spellbinders 1966 25.00

**SPENCE, ALEXANDER "SKIP"** Also see MOBY GRAPE.

COLUMBIA

❑ CS 9831 Oar 1969 60.00

SUNDAZED

❑ LP 5030 Oar 2000 12.00
*—Reissue on 180-gram vinyl*

**SPENCER, JON, BLUES EXPLOSION**

MATADOR

❑ (# unknown) [DJ]Controversial Negro 1997 30.00
*—Promo-only vinyl issue of a Japanese live CD*
❑ OLE 52-1 Extra Width 1993 12.00
❑ OLE 105-1 Orange 1994 10.00
❑ OLE 193-1 Now I Got Worry 1996 10.00
❑ OLE 322-1 Acme 1998 10.00
❑ OLE 376-1 [(2)]Xtra-Acme USA 1999 15.00

**SPENCER, LEON, JR.**

PRESTIGE

❑ 10011 Sneak Preview! 1971 20.00
❑ 10033 Louisiana Slim 1972 20.00
❑ 10042 Bad Walking Woman 1973 20.00

**SPIDER-MAN**

LIFESONG

❑ LS 6001 Rock Reflections of a Superhero 1976 25.00

**SPIDERS, THE (1)**

IMPERIAL

❑ LP-9142 [M] I Didn't Wanna Do It 1961 600.00

**SPINNERS**

ATLANTIC

❑ SD 2-910 [(2)] Spinners Live! 1975 15.00
❑ QD 7256 [Q] Spinners 1974 20.00
❑ SD 7256 Spinners 1973 12.00
❑ SD 7296 Mighty Love 1974 12.00
❑ SD 16032 Labor of Love 1981 10.00
❑ QD 18118 [Q] New and Improved 1974 20.00
❑ SD 18118 New and Improved 1974 12.00
❑ QD 18141 [Q] Pick of the Litter 1975 20.00
❑ SD 18141 Pick of the Litter 1975 12.00
❑ SD 18181 Happiness is Being with the Spinners 1976 12.00
❑ SD 19100 Yesterday, Today & Tomorrow 1977 12.00
❑ SD 19146 Spinners/8 1977 12.00
❑ SD 19179 The Best of the Spinners 1978 12.00
❑ SD 19219 From Here to Eternally 1979 12.00
❑ SD 19256 Dancin' and Lovin' 1980 10.00
❑ SD 19270 Love Trippin' 1980 10.00
❑ SD 19318 Can't Shake This Feelin' 1981 10.00
❑ 80020 Grand Slam 1982 10.00

MIRAGE

❑ 90456 Lovin' Feelings 1985 10.00

MOTOWN

❑ M5-109V1 Motown Superstar Series, Vol. 9 1982 8.00
❑ M5-132V1 The Original Spinners 1981 12.00
*—Reissue of Motown 639*
❑ M5-199V1 The Best of the Spinners 1981 12.00
*—Reissue of Motown 769*
❑ M 639 [M] The Original Spinners 1967 25.00
❑ MS 639 [P] The Original Spinners 1967 30.00
❑ M 769 The Best of the Spinners 1973 15.00

V.I.P.

❑ 405 2nd Time Around 1970 40.00

VOLT

❑ V-3403 Down to Business 1989 12.00

**SPINNERS, THE**

TIME

❑ S-2092 [S] Party — My Pad After Surfin' 1963 30.00
❑ 52092 [M] Party — My Pad After Surfin' 1963 25.00

**SPIRAL STARECASE**

COLUMBIA

❑ CS 9852 More Today Than Yesterday 1969 25.00
*—"360 Sound" label*

**SPIRIT**

EPIC

❑ E 30267 Twelve Dreams of Dr. Sardonicus 1970 20.00
*—Yellow label*
❑ KE 30267 Twelve Dreams of Dr. Sardonicus 1973 10.00
*—Orange label*
❑ PE 30267 Twelve Dreams of Dr. Sardonicus 197? 8.00
*—Orange or dark blue label, with or without bar code*
❑ KE 31175 Feedback 1972 20.00
*—Yellow label*
❑ KE 31175 Feedback 1973 10.00
*—Orange label*
❑ KEG 31457 [(2)]Spirit 1972 15.00
*—Reissue of Ode 44004 and 44016 in one package; yellow labels*
❑ PEG 31457 [(2)]Spirit 197? 12.00
*—Reissue with new prefix and orange labels*
❑ KE 31461 The Family That Plays Together 1972 12.00
*—Reissue of Ode 44014 with slightly different cover; yellow label*
❑ KE 31461 The Family That Plays Together 1973 10.00
*—Orange label*
❑ KE 32271 The Best of Spirit 1973 12.00
❑ PE 32271 The Best of Spirit 1979 8.00
*—Dark blue label; bar code on cover*
❑ BG 33761 [(2)] The Family That Plays Together/Feedback 1976 12.00

I.R.S.

❑ 82007 Rapture in the Chambers 1989 12.00

MERCURY

❑ SRM-2-804 [(2)]Spirit of '76 1975 15.00
❑ SRM-1-1053 Son of Spirit 1975 12.00
❑ SRM-1-1094 Farther Along 1976 12.00
❑ SRM-1-1122 Future Games 1977 12.00
❑ 818514-1 Spirit of '84 1984 10.00

ODE

❑ Z12 44003 [M] Spirit 1968 40.00
❑ Z12 44004 [S] Spirit 1968 25.00
❑ Z12 44014 The Family That Plays Together 1968 25.00
❑ Z12 44016 Clear Spirit 1969 25.00

POTATO

❑ 2001 Live 1978 10.00

RHINO

❑ RNSP-303 Potatoland 1981 10.00

SUNDAZED

❑ LP 5067 Now or Anywhere 2000 12.00
❑ LP 5068 Eventide 2000 12.00
❑ LP 5082 Clear 2001 12.00
❑ LP 5085 The Family That Plays Together 2001 12.00

**SPIRITS AND WORM**

A&M

❑ SP-4229 Spirits and Worm 1969 800.00

**SPIVEY, VICTORIA**

SPIVEY

❑ LP-1001 [M] Basket of Blues 1962 25.00
❑ LP-1002 [M] Victoria and Her Blues 1963 25.00
❑ LP-1004 [M] Three Kings and a Queen 196? 30.00
*—"Historic Tracks, Bob Dylan Appears with Big Joe Williams" blurb on cover*
❑ LP-1004 [M] Three Kings and a Queen 1964 50.00
*—Bob Dylan plays on this LP; no blurb on cover*
❑ LP-1006 [M] The Queen and Her Knights 1964 25.00
❑ LP-1008 [M] The Bluesmen of the Muddy Waters Band 1964 25.00
❑ LP-1009 [M] Encore for the Chicago Blues 1964 25.00
❑ LP-1010 [M] The Bluesmen of the Muddy Waters Band, Volume Two 1964 25.00
❑ LP-1012 [M] Spivey's Blues Parade 196? 25.00
❑ LP-1014 [M] Three Kings and a Queen, Volume Two 196? 25.00
❑ LP-1015 [M] Spivey's Blues Cavalcade 196? 25.00
❑ LP-1017 [M] Spivey's Blues Showcase 196? 25.00
❑ LP-2001 [M] Recorded Legacy of the Blues 196? 25.00

**SPLINTER**

DARK HORSE

❑ DH 3073 Two Man Band 1977 25.00
❑ SP-22001 The Place I Love 1974 20.00
❑ SP-22006 Harder to Live 1975 20.00

**SPOELSTRA, MARK**

ELEKTRA

❑ EKL-283 [M] Five and Twenty Questions 1965 20.00
❑ EKL-307 [M] State of Mind 1966 20.00
❑ EKS-7283 [S] Five and Twenty Questions 1965 25.00
❑ EKS-7307 [S] State of Mind 1966 25.00

VERVE FOLKWAYS

❑ FV-9018 [M] The Times I've Had 196? 20.00
❑ FVS-9018 [S] The Times I've Had 196? 25.00

**SPOKESMEN, THE**

DECCA

❑ DL 4712 [M] The Dawn of Correction 1965 25.00
❑ DL 74712 [S] The Dawn of Correction 1965 30.00

**SPONTANEOUS COMBUSTION**

CAPITOL

❑ ST-11021 Spontaneous Combustion 1972 20.00

FLYING DUTCHMAN

❑ 102 Spontaneous Combustion 1969 25.00

HARVEST

❑ SW-11095 Triad 1972 20.00

**SPONTANEOUS MUSIC ENSEMBLE, THE**

EMANEM

❑ 303 Face to Face 1974 20.00

**SPOOKY TOOTH**

A&M

❑ SP-3124 Spooky Two 198? 8.00
*—Budget-line reissue*
❑ SP-4194 Spooky Two 1969 15.00
❑ SP-4225 Ceremony 1970 15.00
❑ SP-4266 The Last Puff 1970 15.00
❑ SP-4300 Tobacco Road 1971 15.00
*—Reissue of Bell LP*
❑ SP-4385 You Broke My Heart So I Busted Your Jaw 1973 15.00

ACCORD

❑ SN-7168 Hell or High Water 1982 10.00

BELL

❑ 6019 [M] Spooky Tooth 1968 60.00
*—Mono is white label promo only; record in stereo cover*
❑ 6019 [S] Spooky Tooth 1968 25.00

ISLAND

❑ SW-9255 Witness 1973 12.00
❑ SW-9292 The Mirror 1974 12.00
❑ ILPS-9337 Witness 1974 10.00

**SPRING**

UNITED ARTISTS

❑ UAS-5571 Spring 1972 25.00
❑ UAS-5571 [DJ] Spring 1972 100.00
*—Special promo package in 12x12 folder; includes LP, press kit and a packet of seeds*

**SPRING STREET STOMPERS, THE**

JUBILEE

❑ JLP-1002 [M] The Spring Street Stompers at Carnegie Hall 1955 40.00
❑ JLP-1004 [M] I Go, Hook, Line and Sinker 1955 40.00

**SPRINGFIELD, DUSTY**

ABC DUNHILL

❑ DSX-50128 Cameo 1973 15.00
❑ DSX-50186 Longings 1974 —
*—Unreleased*

ATLANTIC

❑ SD 8214 Dusty in Memphis 1969 15.00
*—Second pressings have green and red labels*
❑ SD 8214 Dusty in Memphis 1969 30.00
*—Originals have purple and brown labels*
❑ 8249 [DJ] A Brand New Me 1970 40.00
*—Mono white label promo*
❑ SD 8249 A Brand New Me 1970 15.00

CASABLANCA

❑ NBLP-7271 White Heat 1982 12.00

4 MEN WITH BEARDS

❑ 4M 112 Dusty in Memphis 2002 15.00
*—Reissue on 180-gram vinyl*

LIBERTY

❑ LN-10024 It Begins Again 1980 8.00
*—Budget-line reissue of United Artists LP of same name*
❑ LN-10026 Living Without Your Love 1980 8.00
*—Budget-line reissue of United Artists LP of same name*

PHILIPS

❑ PHM-200133 [M]Stay Awhile 1964 30.00
❑ PHM-200156 [M]Dusty 1964 30.00
❑ PHM-200174 [M]Oooooo Weeeee! 1965 40.00
❑ PHM-200210 [M]You Don't Have to Say You Love Me 1966 30.00
❑ PHM-200220 [M]Dusty Springfield's Golden Hits 1966 25.00
*—With "Goin' Back"*
❑ PHM-200220 [M]Dusty Springfield's Golden Hits 1967 20.00
*—Without "Goin' Back"*
❑ PHM-200256 [M]The Look of Love 1967 25.00
❑ PHM-200303 [M]Everything's Coming Up Dusty 1967 25.00
❑ PHS-600133 [P]Stay Awhile 1964 40.00
❑ PHS-600156 [P]Dusty 1964 40.00
❑ PHS-600174 [S]Oooooo Weeeee! 1965 50.00
❑ PHS-600210 [S]You Don't Have to Say You Love Me 1966 40.00
❑ PHS-600220 [P]Dusty Springfield's Golden Hits 1966 35.00
*—With "Goin' Back"*
❑ PHS-600220 [P]Dusty Springfield's Golden Hits 1967 25.00
*—Without "Goin' Back"*
❑ PHS-600256 [S]The Look of Love 1967 30.00
❑ PHS-600303 [S]Everything's Coming Up Dusty 1967 30.00

POLYDOR

❑ 824467-1 Dusty Springfield's Golden Hits 1985 10.00

UNITED ARTISTS

❑ UA-LA791 It Begins Again 1978 15.00
❑ UA-LA936 Living Without Your Love 1979 15.00

| Number | Title (A Side/B Side) | Yr | NM |
|---|---|---|---|
| **WING** | | | |
| ❑ PKW-2-120 [(2)] | Something Special | 196? | 20.00 |
| ❑ SRW-16380 | Just Dusty | 196? | 12.00 |

**SPRINGFIELD, RICK**

| Number | Title (A Side/B Side) | Yr | NM |
|---|---|---|---|
| **CAPITOL** | | | |
| ❑ SMAS-11047 | Beginnings | 1972 | 20.00 |
| ❑ SMAS-11206 | Comic Book Heroes | 1973 | 40.00 |
| *—Withdrawn and reissued on Columbia* | | | |
| ❑ SN-16251 | Beginnings | 1981 | 8.00 |
| *—Budget-line reissue* | | | |
| **CHELSEA** | | | |
| ❑ 515 | Wait for Night | 1976 | 15.00 |
| **COLUMBIA** | | | |
| ❑ KC 32704 | Comic Book Heroes | 1973 | 15.00 |
| ❑ PC 32704 | Comic Book Heroes | 1981 | 8.00 |
| *—Budget-line reissue* | | | |
| **MERCURY** | | | |
| ❑ 824107-1 | Beautiful Feelings | 1984 | 10.00 |
| **RCA** | | | |
| ❑ 6620-1-R | Rock of Life | 1988 | 8.00 |
| ❑ 9817-1-R | Rick Springfield's Greatest Hits | 1989 | 12.00 |
| **RCA VICTOR** | | | |
| ❑ ARL1-3697 | Working Class Dog | 1981 | 10.00 |
| ❑ AFL1-4125 | Success Hasn't Spoiled Me Yet | 1982 | 10.00 |
| ❑ AFL1-4235 | Wait for Night | 1982 | 10.00 |
| *—Reissue of Chelsea LP* | | | |
| ❑ AFL1-4660 | Living in Oz | 1983 | 10.00 |
| ❑ AYL1-4766 | Working Class Dog | 1983 | 8.00 |
| *—"Best Buy Series" reissue* | | | |
| ❑ AYL1-4767 | Success Hasn't Spoiled Me Yet | 1983 | 8.00 |
| *—"Best Buy Series" reissue* | | | |
| ❑ ABL1-4935 | Hard to Hold | 1984 | 10.00 |
| ❑ AJL1-5370 | Tao | 1985 | 10.00 |

**SPRINGFIELD RIFLE, THE**

| Number | Title (A Side/B Side) | Yr | NM |
|---|---|---|---|
| **BURDETTE** | | | |
| ❑ ST-5159 | The Springfield Rifle | 1969 | 25.00 |

**SPRINGFIELDS, THE**

| Number | Title (A Side/B Side) | Yr | NM |
|---|---|---|---|
| **PHILIPS** | | | |
| ❑ PHM 200052 [M] | Silver Threads and Golden Needles | 1962 | 30.00 |
| ❑ PHM 200076 [M] | Folksongs from the Hills | 1963 | 30.00 |
| ❑ PHS 600052 [S] | Silver Threads and Golden Needles | 1962 | 40.00 |
| ❑ PHS 600076 [S] | Folksongs from the Hills | 1963 | 40.00 |

**SPRINGSTEEN, BRUCE**

| Number | Title (A Side/B Side) | Yr | NM |
|---|---|---|---|
| **COLUMBIA** | | | |
| ❑ (# unknown) [PD] | Darkness on the Edge of Town | 1978 | 150.00 |
| *—Promo-only picture disc* | | | |
| ❑ AS 978 [DJ] | As Requested Around the World | 1981 | 50.00 |
| ❑ AS 1957 [DJ] | Bruce Springsteen | 1985 | 30.00 |
| *—Five-song mini-LP with five B-sides of singles from Born in the U.S.A.* | | | |
| ❑ AS 1957 [DJ] | Bruce Springsteen | 1987 | 20.00 |
| *—Five-song mini-LP with five B-sides of singles from Born in the U.S.A.; second pressings say so on the label* | | | |
| ❑ CAS 2543 [DJ] | Bruce Springsteen and the E Street Band: Live 1975-1985 | 1986 | 30.00 |
| *—Sampler from 5-LP live set* | | | |
| ❑ JC 31903 | Greetings from Asbury Park, N.J. | 1977 | 8.00 |
| *—Reissue of the first PC-prefix version* | | | |
| ❑ KC 31903 | Greetings from Asbury Park, N.J. | 1973 | 20.00 |
| ❑ KC 31903 [DJ] | Greetings from Asbury Park, N.J. | 1973 | 200.00 |
| *—Promotional copy with timing strip and "Bruce Springsteen Fact Sheet" attached to back cover. Authentic fact sheets are on glossy stock* | | | |
| ❑ PC 31903 | Greetings from Asbury Park, N.J. | 1975 | 10.00 |
| *—Without bar code on cover* | | | |
| ❑ PC 31903 | Greetings from Asbury Park, N.J. | 1979 | 8.00 |
| *—With bar code on cover* | | | |
| ❑ JC 32432 | The Wild, the Innocent & the E Street Shuffle | 1977 | 8.00 |
| *—Reissue of the first PC-prefix version* | | | |
| ❑ KC 32432 | The Wild, the Innocent & the E Street Shuffle | 1973 | 20.00 |
| ❑ PC 32432 | The Wild, the Innocent & the E Street Shuffle | 1975 | 10.00 |
| *—Without bar code on cover* | | | |
| ❑ PC 32432 | The Wild, the Innocent & the E Street Shuffle | 1979 | 8.00 |
| *—With bar code on cover* | | | |
| ❑ HC 33795 | Born to Run | 1981 | 50.00 |
| *—Half-speed mastered edition (original)* | | | |
| ❑ JC 33795 | Born to Run | 1977 | 8.00 |
| ❑ PC 33795 | Born to Run | 1975 | 10.00 |
| *—Jon Landau's name is correct on the back cover* | | | |

Bruce Springsteen, *The Ghost of Tom Joad,* Columbia C 67484, 1995, $12.

| Number | Title (A Side/B Side) | Yr | NM |
|---|---|---|---|
| ❑ PC 33795 | Born to Run | 1975 | 15.00 |
| *—Sticker with the correct spelling of Jon Landau is on the back cover* | | | |
| ❑ PC 33795 | Born to Run | 1975 | 25.00 |
| *—Jon Landau's name is misspelled "John" on the back cover* | | | |
| ❑ PC 33795 | Born to Run | 1999 | 25.00 |
| *—Classic Records reissue, identified as such on back cover; corrected pressing with gatefold* | | | |
| ❑ PC 33795 | Born to Run | 1999 | 40.00 |
| *—Classic Records reissue, identified as such on back cover; "error" first pressing with no gatefold* | | | |
| ❑ PC 33795 [DJ] | Born to Run | 1975 | 100.00 |
| *—White label promo* | | | |
| ❑ PC 33795 [DJ] | Born to Run | 1975 | 1200. |
| *—Test pressing with "Bruce Springsteen -- Born to Run" in script print. Also includes mailing envelope, letter from CBS and orange patch; VG value 400; VG+ value 800* | | | |
| ❑ JC 35318 | Darkness on the Edge of Town | 1978 | 10.00 |
| *—Original pressings have thick paper innersleeves and small titles on back cover* | | | |
| ❑ JC 35318 | Darkness on the Edge of Town | 198? | 8.00 |
| *—Later pressings have thin paper innersleeves and larger titles on back cover* | | | |
| ❑ JC 35318 [DJ] | Darkness on the Edge of Town | 1978 | 100.00 |
| *—White label promo* | | | |
| ❑ PC2 36854 [(2)] | The River | 1980 | 12.00 |
| ❑ PC2 36854 [(2)DJ] | The River | 1980 | 40.00 |
| *—White label promo, without letter* | | | |
| ❑ PC2 36854 [(2)DJ] | The River | 1980 | 75.00 |
| *—White label promo, with photocopied letter from CBS* | | | |
| ❑ TC 38358 | Nebraska | 1982 | 10.00 |
| ❑ QC 38653 | Born in the U.S.A. | 1984 | 10.00 |
| ❑ C5X 40558 [(5)] | Bruce Springsteen and the E Street Band: Live 1975-1985 | 1986 | 40.00 |
| ❑ OC 40999 | Tunnel of Love | 1987 | 10.00 |
| ❑ HC 43795 | Born to Run | 1982 | 40.00 |
| *—Half-speed mastered edition (reissue)* | | | |
| ❑ 3C 44445 [EP] | Chimes of Freedom | 1988 | 10.00 |
| ❑ HC 45318 | Darkness on the Edge of Town | 1981 | 40.00 |
| *—Half-speed mastered edition* | | | |
| ❑ C 53000 | Human Touch | 1992 | 12.00 |
| ❑ C 53001 | Lucky Town | 1992 | 12.00 |
| ❑ C2 67060 [(2)] | Greatest Hits | 1995 | 15.00 |
| ❑ C 67484 | The Ghost of Tom Joad | 1995 | 12.00 |
| ❑ C2 69746 [(2)] | 18 Tracks | 1999 | 15.00 |
| ❑ C3 85490 [(3)] | Live in New York City | 2001 | 20.00 |
| *—As of press date, all known copies contain "Born to Run," but the song is not listed on either the record jacket or label* | | | |
| ❑ C2 86600 [(2)] | The Rising | 2002 | 15.00 |
| ❑ C2 93900 [(2)] | Devils and Dust | 2005 | 15.00 |

**SPUR**

| Number | Title (A Side/B Side) | Yr | NM |
|---|---|---|---|
| **CINEMA** | | | |
| ❑ CSLP-1500 | Spur of the Moment | 196? | 80.00 |

**SPYRO GYRA**

| Number | Title (A Side/B Side) | Yr | NM |
|---|---|---|---|
| **MCA** | | | |
| ❑ 16010 | Catching the Sun | 1982 | 40.00 |
| *—Audiophile vinyl* | | | |
| **NAUTILUS** | | | |
| ❑ NR-9 | Morning Dance | 1979 | 40.00 |
| *—Audiophile vinyl* | | | |

**SQUEEZE**

| Number | Title (A Side/B Side) | Yr | NM |
|---|---|---|---|
| **A&M** | | | |
| ❑ SP-3185 | U.K. Squeeze | 198? | 8.00 |
| *—Reissue* | | | |
| ❑ SP-3231 | Cool for Cats | 198? | 8.00 |
| *—Reissue* | | | |
| ❑ SP-3232 | Argybargy | 198? | 8.00 |
| *—Reissue* | | | |
| ❑ SP-3253 | East Side Story | 198? | 8.00 |
| *—Reissue* | | | |
| ❑ SP-3254 | Sweets from a Stranger | 198? | 8.00 |
| *—Reissue; none of these have 2-inch flap* | | | |
| ❑ SP-3413 [EP] | Six Squeeze Songs Crammed Into One 10-Inch Record | 1979 | 10.00 |
| *—10-inch EP in 12-inch "squeezed" jacket* | | | |
| ❑ SP-4687 | U.K. Squeeze | 1978 | 12.00 |
| *—Later pressings on black vinyl* | | | |
| ❑ SP-4687 | U.K. Squeeze | 1978 | 20.00 |
| *—First pressing on red vinyl* | | | |
| ❑ SP-4759 | Cool for Cats | 1979 | 12.00 |
| ❑ SP-4802 | Argybargy | 1980 | 12.00 |
| ❑ SP-4854 | East Side Story | 1981 | 10.00 |
| ❑ SP-4899 | Sweets from a Stranger | 1982 | 10.00 |
| *—With flap removed or never there* | | | |
| ❑ SP-4899 | Sweets from a Stranger | 1982 | 12.00 |
| *—Original pressings have a 2-inch flap on the right side of the front cover with critics' raves* | | | |
| ❑ SP-4922 | Singles 45's and Under | 1983 | 10.00 |
| ❑ SP-5085 | Cosi Fan Tutti Frutti | 1985 | 10.00 |
| ❑ SP-5161 | Babylon and On | 1987 | 10.00 |
| ❑ SP-5278 | Frank | 1989 | 10.00 |
| ❑ R 124200 | Frank | 1989 | 12.00 |
| *—BMG Music Service edition* | | | |

Squeeze, *U.K. Squeeze,* A&M SP-3185, 1980s, reissue, $8.

| Number | Title (A Side/B Side) | Yr | NM |
|---|---|---|---|
| **SRC** | | | |
| CAPITOL | | | |
| ❑ ST-134 | Milestones | 1969 | 40.00 |
| ❑ SKAO-273 | Travellers Tale | 1970 | 40.00 |
| ❑ ST 2991 | SRC | 1968 | 60.00 |
| **STACKRIDGE** | | | |
| DECCA | | | |
| ❑ DL 75317 | Stackridge | 1971 | 25.00 |
| MCA | | | |
| ❑ 308 | Friendliness | 1973 | 10.00 |
| SIRE | | | |
| ❑ SASD-7503 | Pinafore Days | 1974 | 10.00 |
| ❑ SASD-7509 | Extravaganza | 1975 | 10.00 |
| **STACY, JESS** | | | |
| ATLANTIC | | | |
| ❑ 1225 [M] | A Tribute to Benny Goodman | 1956 | 50.00 |
| *—Black label* | | | |
| BRUNSWICK | | | |
| ❑ BL 54017 [M] | Piano Solos | 1956 | 50.00 |
| ❑ BL 58029 [10] | Piano Solos | 1951 | 80.00 |
| COLUMBIA | | | |
| ❑ CL 6147 [10] | Piano Moods | 1950 | 100.00 |
| HANOVER | | | |
| ❑ HS-8010 [S] | The Return of Jess Stacy | 1964 | 20.00 |
| **STAETER, TED** | | | |
| ATLANTIC | | | |
| ❑ 1218 [M] | Ted Staeter's New York | 1955 | 25.00 |
| *—Multicolor label, white "fan" logo at right* | | | |
| ❑ 1218 [M] | Ted Staeter's New York | 1961 | 50.00 |
| *—Black label* | | | |
| **STAFFORD, JO** | | | |
| BAINBRIDGE | | | |
| ❑ 6234 | Look at Me Now | 1982 | 10.00 |
| CAPITOL | | | |
| ❑ H 75 [10] | American Folk Songs | 1950 | 60.00 |
| ❑ H 197 [10] | Autumn in New York | 195? | 60.00 |
| ❑ T 197 [M] | Autumn in New York | 1955 | 50.00 |
| *—Turquoise or gray label* | | | |
| ❑ T 197 [M] | Autumn in New York | 1959 | 30.00 |
| *—Black colorband label, Capitol logo at left* | | | |
| ❑ H 247 [10] | Songs for Sunday Evening | 195? | 60.00 |
| ❑ T 423 [M] | Memory Songs | 1955 | 50.00 |
| *—Turquoise or gray label* | | | |
| ❑ T 423 [M] | Memory Songs | 1959 | 30.00 |
| *—Black colorband label, Capitol logo at left* | | | |
| ❑ H 435 [10] | Starring Jo Stafford | 1953 | 60.00 |
| ❑ T 435 [M] | Starring Jo Stafford | 1955 | 50.00 |
| *—Turquoise or gray label* | | | |
| ❑ T 435 [M] | Starring Jo Stafford | 1959 | 30.00 |
| *—Black colorband label, Capitol logo at left* | | | |
| ❑ ST 1653 [S] | American Folk Songs | 1962 | 25.00 |
| ❑ T 1653 [M] | American Folk Songs | 1962 | 20.00 |
| ❑ SM-1696 | Whispering Hope | 1977 | 10.00 |
| *—Reissue with new prefix* | | | |
| ❑ ST 1921 [S] | The Hits of Jo Stafford | 1963 | 25.00 |
| ❑ T 1921 [M] | The Hits of Jo Stafford | 1963 | 20.00 |
| ❑ ST 2069 [S] | Sweet Hour of Prayer | 1964 | 25.00 |
| ❑ T 2069 [M] | Sweet Hour of Prayer | 1964 | 20.00 |
| ❑ ST 2166 [S] | The Joyful Season | 1964 | 25.00 |
| ❑ T 2166 [M] | The Joyful Season | 1964 | 20.00 |
| ❑ H 9014 [10] | Songs of Faith | 1950 | 60.00 |
| ❑ SM-11889 | The Hits of Jo Stafford | 1979 | 10.00 |
| COLUMBIA | | | |
| ❑ CL 578 [M] | New Orleans | 1954 | 40.00 |
| *—Maroon label, gold print* | | | |
| ❑ CL 578 [M] | New Orleans | 1955 | 30.00 |
| *—Red and black label with six "eye" logos* | | | |
| ❑ CL 584 [M] | Jo Stafford Sings Broadway's Best | 1954 | 40.00 |
| *—Maroon label, gold print* | | | |
| ❑ CL 584 [M] | Jo Stafford Sings Broadway's Best | 1955 | 30.00 |
| *—Red and black label with six "eye" logos* | | | |
| ❑ CL 691 [M] | Happy Holiday | 1955 | 60.00 |
| ❑ CL 910 [M] | Ski Trails | 1956 | 40.00 |
| ❑ CL 968 [M] | Once Over Lightly | 1957 | 40.00 |
| ❑ CL 1043 [M] | Songs of Scotland | 1957 | 40.00 |
| ❑ CL 1124 [M] | Swingin' Down Broadway | 1958 | 40.00 |
| ❑ CL 1228 [M] | Jo Stafford's Greatest Hits | 1958 | 40.00 |
| *—Red and black label with six "eye" logos* | | | |
| ❑ CL 1228 [M] | Jo Stafford's Greatest Hits | 1963 | 20.00 |
| *—Red label with "Guaranteed High Fidelity" in black* | | | |
| ❑ CL 1228 [M] | Jo Stafford's Greatest Hits | 1965 | 15.00 |
| *—Red label with "360 Sound Mono" in white* | | | |
| ❑ CL 1262 [M] | I'll Be Seeing You | 1959 | 30.00 |
| ❑ CL 1339 [M] | Ballad of the Blues | 1959 | 30.00 |
| ❑ CL 1561 [M] | Jo + Jazz | 1960 | 40.00 |
| ❑ CL 2501 [10] | Soft and Sentimental | 1955 | 40.00 |
| ❑ CL 2591 [10] | A Gal Named Jo | 1955 | 40.00 |
| ❑ CL 6210 [10] | As You Desire Me | 1952 | 50.00 |
| ❑ CL 6238 [10] | Jo Stafford Sings Broadway's Best | 1953 | 50.00 |
| ❑ CL 6268 [10] | New Orleans | 1954 | 50.00 |
| ❑ CL 6274 [10] | My Heart's in the Highland | 1954 | 50.00 |
| ❑ CL 6286 [10] | Garden of Prayer | 1954 | 50.00 |
| ❑ CS 8080 [S] | I'll Be Seeing You | 1959 | 40.00 |
| ❑ CS 8139 [S] | Ballad of the Blues | 1959 | 40.00 |
| ❑ CS 8361 [S] | Jo + Jazz | 1960 | 60.00 |
| CORINTHIAN | | | |
| ❑ COR-105 | G.I. Jo | 1977 | 10.00 |
| ❑ COR-106 | Greatest Hits | 1977 | 10.00 |
| ❑ COR-108 | Jo + Jazz | 197? | 10.00 |
| ❑ COR-110 | Jo Stafford Sings American Folk Songs | 197? | 10.00 |
| ❑ COR-111 | Songs of Faith, Hope and Love | 197? | 10.00 |
| ❑ COR-112 | Jo + Broadway | 197? | 10.00 |
| ❑ COR-113 | Ski Trails | 197? | 10.00 |
| ❑ COR-114 | Jo + Blues | 197? | 10.00 |
| ❑ COR-115 | International Hits | 197? | 10.00 |
| ❑ COR-118 | Broadway Revisited | 198? | 10.00 |
| ❑ COR-119 | By Request | 198? | 10.00 |
| ❑ COR-123 | Music of My Life | 1986 | 10.00 |
| DECCA | | | |
| ❑ DL 74973 | Jo Stafford's Greatest Hits | 1968 | 15.00 |
| DOT | | | |
| ❑ DLP-3673 [M] | Do I Hear a Waltz? | 1966 | 15.00 |
| ❑ DLP-3745 [M] | This Is Jo Stafford | 1967 | 15.00 |
| ❑ DLP-25673 [S] | Do I Hear a Waltz? | 1966 | 20.00 |
| ❑ DLP-25745 [S] | This Is Jo Stafford | 1967 | 20.00 |
| REPRISE | | | |
| ❑ R-6090 [M] | Getting Sentimental Over Tommy Dorsey | 1963 | 20.00 |
| ❑ R9-6090 [S] | Getting Sentimental Over Tommy Dorsey | 1963 | 25.00 |
| STANYAN | | | |
| ❑ 10073 | Look at Me Now | 197? | 12.00 |
| TIME-LIFE | | | |
| ❑ SLGD-14 [(2)] | Legendary Singers: Jo Stafford | 1986 | 15.00 |
| VOCALION | | | |
| ❑ VL 73856 [R] | Happy Holidays | 1968 | 12.00 |
| ❑ VL 73866 [R] | Sweet Singer of Songs | 1969 | 12.00 |
| ❑ VL 73892 | In the Mood for Love | 1970 | 12.00 |
| **STAFFORD, JO, AND GORDON MACRAE** | | | |
| CAPITOL | | | |
| ❑ H 247 [10] | Sunday Evening Songs | 1952 | 60.00 |
| ❑ T 423 [M] | Memory Songs | 1955 | 50.00 |
| ❑ ST 1696 [S] | Whispering Hope | 1962 | 25.00 |
| ❑ T 1696 [M] | Whispering Hope | 1962 | 20.00 |
| ❑ ST 1916 [S] | There's Peace in the Valley | 1963 | 25.00 |
| ❑ T 1916 [M] | There's Peace in the Valley | 1963 | 20.00 |
| ❑ SM-11890 | There's Peace in the Valley | 1978 | 10.00 |
| *—Reissue* | | | |
| **STAFFORD, TERRY** | | | |
| ATLANTIC | | | |
| ❑ SD 7282 | Say, Has Anybody Seen My Sweet Gypsy Rose | 1974 | 12.00 |
| CRUSADER | | | |
| ❑ CLP-1001 [M] | Suspicion! | 1964 | 40.00 |
| ❑ CLP-1001S [S] | Suspicion! | 1964 | 60.00 |
| **STAINED GLASS** | | | |
| CAPITOL | | | |
| ❑ ST-154 | Crazy Horse Roads | 1969 | 30.00 |
| ❑ ST-242 | Aurora | 1969 | 30.00 |
| **STALLINGS, MARY, AND CAL TJADER** | | | |
| FANTASY | | | |
| ❑ 3325 [M] | Cal Tjader Plays, Mary Stallings Sings | 1962 | 30.00 |
| *—Black vinyl* | | | |
| ❑ 3325 [M] | Cal Tjader Plays, Mary Stallings Sings | 1962 | 50.00 |
| *—Red vinyl* | | | |
| ❑ 8068 [S] | Cal Tjader Plays, Mary Stallings Sings | 1962 | 20.00 |
| *—Black vinyl* | | | |
| ❑ 8068 [S] | Cal Tjader Plays, Mary Stallings Sings | 1962 | 40.00 |
| *—Blue vinyl* | | | |
| **STAMM, MARVIN** | | | |
| VERVE | | | |
| ❑ V6-8759 | Machinations | 1968 | 20.00 |
| **STANDELLS, THE** | | | |
| LIBERTY | | | |
| ❑ LRP-3384 [M] | The Standells In Person at P.J.'s | 1964 | 80.00 |
| ❑ LST-7384 [S] | The Standells In Person at P.J.'s | 1964 | 100.00 |



Except when noted otherwise, VG = 25% of NM, and VG+ = 50% of NM. (Example: VG = $2.00, VG+ = $4.00 and NM = $8.00.)

| Number | Title (A Side/B Side) | Yr | NM |
|---|---|---|---|
| **RHINO** | | | |
| ❑ RNLP-107 | The Best of the Standells | 1983 | 10.00 |
| ❑ RNLP-115 | Rarities | 1983 | 10.00 |
| ❑ RNLP-70176 | The Best of the Standells (Golden Archive Series) | 1987 | 10.00 |
| **SUNSET** | | | |
| ❑ SUM-1136 [M] | Live and Out of Sight | 1966 | 25.00 |
| ❑ SUS-5136 [S] | Live and Out of Sight | 1966 | 30.00 |
| **TOWER** | | | |
| ❑ ST 5027 [R] | Dirty Water | 1966 | 50.00 |
| ❑ T 5027 [M] | Dirty Water | 1966 | 60.00 |
| ❑ ST 5044 [S] | Why Pick on Me | 1966 | 60.00 |
| ❑ T 5044 [M] | Why Pick on Me | 1966 | 50.00 |
| ❑ ST 5049 [S] | The Hot Ones | 1966 | 60.00 |
| ❑ T 5049 [M] | The Hot Ones | 1966 | 50.00 |
| ❑ ST 5098 [S] | Try It | 1967 | 60.00 |
| ❑ T 5098 [M] | Try It | 1967 | 50.00 |

## STANLEY, MICHAEL, BAND

| Number | Title (A Side/B Side) | Yr | NM |
|---|---|---|---|
| **ARISTA** | | | |
| ❑ AL 4182 | Cabin Fever | 1978 | 10.00 |
| ❑ AL 4236 | Greatest Hints | 1979 | 10.00 |
| **EMI AMERICA** | | | |
| ❑ SN-16352 | Heartland | 1985 | 8.00 |
| *—Budget-line reissue* | | | |
| ❑ SN-16353 | You Can't Fight Fashion | 1985 | 8.00 |
| *—Budget-line reissue* | | | |
| ❑ SN-16392 | MSB | 1986 | 8.00 |
| *—Budget-line reissue* | | | |
| ❑ SW-17040 | Heartland | 1980 | 10.00 |
| ❑ SW-17056 | North Coast | 1981 | 10.00 |
| ❑ ST-17071 | MSB | 1982 | 10.00 |
| ❑ ST-17100 | You Can't Fight Fashion | 1983 | 10.00 |
| **EPIC** | | | |
| ❑ PE 33492 | You Break It...You Bought It! | 1975 | 12.00 |
| *—Original with orange label and no bar code* | | | |
| ❑ PE 33492 | You Break It...You Bought It! | 198? | 8.00 |
| *—Reissue with dark blue label and bar code* | | | |
| ❑ PE 33917 | Ladies' Choice | 1976 | 12.00 |
| *—Original with orange label and no bar code* | | | |
| ❑ PE 33917 | Ladies' Choice | 198? | 8.00 |
| *—Reissue with dark blue label and bar code* | | | |
| ❑ PEG 34661 [(2)] | Stagepass | 1977 | 15.00 |
| **MCA** | | | |
| ❑ 372 | Friends and Legends | 1973 | 12.00 |
| **TUMBLEWEED** | | | |
| ❑ TWS 106 | Michael Stanley | 1972 | 20.00 |
| *—Blue textured cover* | | | |

## STANLEY, PAUL Also see KISS.

| Number | Title (A Side/B Side) | Yr | NM |
|---|---|---|---|
| **CASABLANCA** | | | |
| ❑ NBLP-7123 | Paul Stanley | 1978 | 25.00 |
| ❑ NBPIX-7123 [PD] | Paul Stanley | 1978 | 60.00 |

## STANLEY, RALPH

| Number | Title (A Side/B Side) | Yr | NM |
|---|---|---|---|
| **JALYN** | | | |
| ❑ JLP-118 [M] | Old Time Music | 1966 | 25.00 |
| ❑ JLP-120 [M] | The Bluegrass Sound of Ralph Stanley | 1966 | 25.00 |
| ❑ JLP-129 [M] | Ralph Stanley and the Clinch Mountain Boys | 196? | 25.00 |
| **KING** | | | |
| ❑ KSD-1028 | Brand New Country Songs by Ralph Stanley | 1968 | 20.00 |
| ❑ KSD-1032 | Over the Sunset Hill | 1968 | 20.00 |
| ❑ KSD-1046 | How Far to Little Rock? | 1969 | 20.00 |
| ❑ KSD-1069 | The Hills of Home | 1969 | 20.00 |

## STANLEY BROTHERS, THE

| Number | Title (A Side/B Side) | Yr | NM |
|---|---|---|---|
| **CABIN CREEK** | | | |
| ❑ LP-203 [M] | Bluegrass Gospel Favorites | 1966 | 60.00 |
| **HARMONY** | | | |
| ❑ HL 7291 [M] | The Stanley Brothers | 1961 | 25.00 |
| **KING** | | | |
| ❑ 615 [M] | The Stanley Brothers | 1959 | 100.00 |
| ❑ 645 [M] | Hymns and Sacred Songs | 1960 | 80.00 |
| ❑ 690 [M] | Everybody's Country Favorites | 1961 | 80.00 |
| ❑ KS-690 [S] | Everybody's Country Favorites | 1961 | 100.00 |
| ❑ 698 [M] | For the Good People | 1961 | 80.00 |
| ❑ 719 [M] | The Stanleys In Person | 1961 | 80.00 |
| ❑ KS-719 [S] | The Stanleys In Person | 1961 | 100.00 |
| ❑ 750 [M] | Old Time Camp Meeting | 1962 | 80.00 |
| ❑ 772 [M] | The Stanley Brothers and the Clinch Mountain Boys Sing the Songs They Like Best | 1962 | 80.00 |
| ❑ 791 [M] | Award Winners | 1962 | 80.00 |
| ❑ KS-791 [S] | Award Winners | 1962 | 100.00 |
| ❑ 805 [M] | Good Old Camp Meeting Songs | 1963 | 80.00 |
| ❑ KS-805 [S] | Good Old Camp Meeting Songs | 1963 | 100.00 |
| ❑ 834 [M] | Just Because | 1964 | 50.00 |
| ❑ 864 [M] | Country Folk Music Spotlight | 1964 | 50.00 |
| ❑ 872 [M] | Five String Banjo Hootenanny | 1964 | 50.00 |
| ❑ 918 [M] | Hymns of the Cross | 1964 | 50.00 |
| ❑ 924 [M] | The Remarkable Stanley Brothers Play and Sing Bluegrass Songs for You | 1965 | 50.00 |
| ❑ 953 [M] | The Best of the Stanley Brothers | 1966 | 25.00 |
| ❑ 963 [M] | A Collection of Gospel and Sacred Songs | 1966 | 25.00 |
| ❑ 1013 [M] | The Stanley Brothers Sing the Best-Loved Sacred Songs of the Carter Family | 1967 | 25.00 |
| ❑ KS-1013 [S] | The Stanley Brothers Sing the Best-Loved Sacred Songs of the Carter Family | 1967 | 30.00 |
| **MERCURY** | | | |
| ❑ MG-20349 [M] | Country Pickin' and Singin' | 1958 | 80.00 |
| ❑ MG-20884 [M] | Hard Times | 1963 | 25.00 |
| ❑ SR-60884 [S] | Hard Times | 1963 | 30.00 |
| **STARDAY** | | | |
| ❑ SLP-106 [M] | Mountain Song Favorites | 1959 | 50.00 |
| ❑ SLP-122 [M] | Sacred Songs from the Hills | 1960 | 50.00 |
| ❑ SLP-201 [M] | The Mountain Music Sound of the Stanley Brothers | 1962 | 40.00 |
| ❑ SLP-384 [M] | Jacob's Vision | 1966 | 30.00 |
| **VINTAGE** | | | |
| ❑ ZK-002 [M] | The Stanley Brothers Live at Antioch College | 1961 | 70.00 |

## STAPLE SINGERS, THE

| Number | Title (A Side/B Side) | Yr | NM |
|---|---|---|---|
| **ARCHIVE OF GOSPEL MUSIC** | | | |
| ❑ 62 | The Staple Singers | 1968 | 12.00 |
| ❑ 72 | The Staple Singers, Vol. 2 | 1969 | 12.00 |
| **BUDDAH** | | | |
| ❑ BDS-2009 | The Best of the Staple Singers | 1969 | 20.00 |
| ❑ BDS-7508 | Will the Circle Be Unbroken | 1969 | 20.00 |
| **CURTOM** | | | |
| ❑ CU 5005 | Let's Do It Again | 1975 | 12.00 |
| **EPIC** | | | |
| ❑ LN 24132 [M] | Amen | 1965 | 20.00 |
| ❑ LN 24163 [M] | Freedom Highway | 1965 | 20.00 |
| ❑ LN 24196 [M] | Why | 1966 | 20.00 |
| ❑ LN 24237 [M] | Pray On | 1967 | 25.00 |
| ❑ LN 24332 [M] | For What It's Worth | 1967 | 25.00 |
| ❑ BN 26132 [S] | Amen | 1965 | 25.00 |
| ❑ BN 26163 [S] | Freedom Highway | 1965 | 25.00 |
| ❑ BN 26196 [S] | Why | 1966 | 25.00 |
| ❑ BN 26237 [S] | Pray On | 1967 | 20.00 |
| ❑ BN 26332 [S] | For What It's Worth | 1967 | 20.00 |
| ❑ BN 26373 | What the World Needs Now Is Love | 1968 | 20.00 |
| ❑ EG 30635 [(2)] | The Staple Singers Make You Happy | 1971 | 20.00 |
| **FANTASY** | | | |
| ❑ 9423 | Use What You Got | 1973 | 15.00 |
| ❑ 9442 | The 25th Day of December | 1973 | 15.00 |
| **HARMONY** | | | |
| ❑ KH 31775 | Tell It Like It Is | 1972 | 12.00 |
| **MILESTONE** | | | |
| ❑ 47028 [(2)] | A Great Day | 197? | 15.00 |
| **PICKWICK** | | | |
| ❑ 7001 | The Staple Singers | 197? | 10.00 |
| **PRIVATE I** | | | |
| ❑ FZ 39460 | The Turning Point | 1984 | 10.00 |
| ❑ BFZ 40109 | The Staple Singers | 1985 | 10.00 |
| **STAX** | | | |
| ❑ STS-2004 | Soul Folk in Action | 1968 | 25.00 |
| ❑ STS-2016 | We'll Get Over | 1969 | 20.00 |
| ❑ STS-2034 | The Staple Swingers | 1971 | 20.00 |
| ❑ STS-3002 | Be Altitude: Respect Yourself | 1972 | 15.00 |
| ❑ STS-3015 | Be What You Are | 1973 | 15.00 |
| ❑ STX-4116 | Be Altitude: Respect Yourself | 198? | 10.00 |
| *—Reissue of 3002* | | | |
| ❑ STX-4119 | Chronicle | 198? | 10.00 |
| ❑ STS-5515 | City in the Sky | 1974 | 15.00 |
| ❑ STS-5523 | The Best of the Staple Singers | 1975 | 15.00 |
| ❑ MPS-8511 | This Time Around | 198? | 10.00 |
| ❑ MPS-8532 | We'll Get Over | 198? | 10.00 |
| *—Reissue of 2016* | | | |
| ❑ MPS-8553 | Be What You Are | 1990 | 12.00 |
| *—Reissue of 3015* | | | |
| **TRIP** | | | |
| ❑ 7000 | Uncloudy Day | 197? | 10.00 |
| ❑ 7014 | Swing Low | 197? | 10.00 |
| ❑ 7019 | The Best of the Staple Singers | 197? | 10.00 |
| ❑ 8014 | The Other Side of the Staple Singers | 1972 | 10.00 |
| **20TH CENTURY** | | | |
| ❑ T-636 | Hold On to Your Dream | 1981 | 10.00 |
| **VEE JAY** | | | |
| ❑ LP-5000 [M] | Uncloudy Day | 1959 | 30.00 |
| ❑ LP-5008 [M] | Will the Circle Be Unbroken | 1960 | 30.00 |
| ❑ LP-5014 [M] | Swing Low | 1961 | 30.00 |
| ❑ LP-5019 [M] | Best of the Staple Singers | 1962 | 30.00 |
| ❑ LP-5030 [M] | Swing Low Sweet Chariot | 1963 | 30.00 |
| **VEE JAY/CHAMELEON** | | | |
| ❑ D1-74782 [(2)] | The Best of the Staple Singers | 1988 | 15.00 |
| **WARNER BROS.** | | | |
| ❑ BS 2945 | Pass It On | 1976 | 12.00 |
| *—As "The Staples"* | | | |
| ❑ BS 3084 | Family Tree | 1977 | 12.00 |
| *—As "The Staples"* | | | |
| ❑ BSK 3192 | Unlock Your Mind | 1978 | 12.00 |
| *—As "The Staples"* | | | |

## STAPLES, MAVIS

| Number | Title (A Side/B Side) | Yr | NM |
|---|---|---|---|
| **CURTOM** | | | |
| ❑ CU 5019 | A Piece of the Action | 1977 | 12.00 |
| **PAISLEY PARK** | | | |
| ❑ 25798 | Time Waits for No One | 1989 | 12.00 |
| **STAX** | | | |
| ❑ STX-4118 | Mavis Staples | 198? | 10.00 |
| *—Reissue of Volt 6007* | | | |
| ❑ MPS-8539 | Only for the Lonely | 1987 | 10.00 |
| *—Reissue of Volt 6010* | | | |
| **VOLT** | | | |
| ❑ VOS-6007 | Mavis Staples | 1969 | 20.00 |
| ❑ VOS-6010 | Only for the Lonely | 1970 | 20.00 |
| **WARNER BROS.** | | | |
| ❑ BSK 3319 | Oh What a Feeling | 1979 | 12.00 |

## STARCASTLE

| Number | Title (A Side/B Side) | Yr | NM |
|---|---|---|---|
| **EPIC** | | | |
| ❑ AS 296 [DJ] | Fountains of Light Banded for Airplay | 1977 | 40.00 |
| *—White label, promo-only version with separations between tracks* | | | |
| ❑ PE 33914 | Starcastle | 1976 | 10.00 |
| *—Orange label* | | | |
| ❑ PE 34375 | Fountains of Light | 1977 | 10.00 |
| *—Orange label* | | | |
| ❑ 34935 [PD] | Citadel | 1978 | 50.00 |
| *—Picture disc, possibly promo only* | | | |
| ❑ PE 34935 | Citadel | 1977 | 10.00 |
| *—Orange label* | | | |
| ❑ JE 35441 | Real to Reel | 1978 | 10.00 |
| *—Orange label* | | | |

## STARCHER, BUDDY

| Number | Title (A Side/B Side) | Yr | NM |
|---|---|---|---|
| **DECCA** | | | |
| ❑ DL 4796 [M] | History Repeats Itself | 1966 | 20.00 |
| ❑ DL 74796 [S] | History Repeats Itself | 1966 | 25.00 |
| **STARDAY** | | | |
| ❑ SLP-211 [M] | Buddy Starcher and His Mountain Guitar | 1962 | 30.00 |
| ❑ SLP-382 [M] | History Repeats Itself | 1966 | 30.00 |

## STARFIRES, THE (4)

| Number | Title (A Side/B Side) | Yr | NM |
|---|---|---|---|
| **OHIO RECORDING SERVICE** | | | |
| ❑ 34 [M] | The Starfires Play | 1964 | 50.00 |

## STARFIRES, THE (5)

| Number | Title (A Side/B Side) | Yr | NM |
|---|---|---|---|
| **LABREA** | | | |
| ❑ LS-8018 [M] | Teenbeat A-Go-Go | 1965 | 50.00 |

## STARK NAKED

| Number | Title (A Side/B Side) | Yr | NM |
|---|---|---|---|
| **RCA VICTOR** | | | |
| ❑ LSP-4592 | Stark Naked | 1971 | 25.00 |

## STARKER, JANOS

| Number | Title (A Side/B Side) | Yr | NM |
|---|---|---|---|
| **MERCURY LIVING PRESENCE** | | | |
| ❑ SR 90303 [S] | Dvorak: Cello Concerto; Bruch: Kol Nidre | 196? | 40.00 |
| *—With Antal Dorati/London Symphony Orchestra; third edition (dark red, not maroon, label)* | | | |
| ❑ SR 90303 [S] | Dvorak: Cello Concerto; Bruch: Kol Nidre | 196? | 70.00 |
| *—With Antal Dorati/London Symphony Orchestra; maroon label, with "Vendor: Mercury Record Corporation"* | | | |
| ❑ SR 90303 [S] | Dvorak: Cello Concerto; Bruch: Kol Nidre | 196? | 120.00 |
| *—With Antal Dorati/London Symphony Orchestra; maroon label, no "Vendor: Mercury Record Corporation"* | | | |
| ❑ SR 90320 [S] | Mendelssohn: Cello Sonata; Chopin: Cello Sonata in G | 196? | 60.00 |
| *—Maroon label, with "Vendor: Mercury Record Corporation"* | | | |
| ❑ SR 90320 [S] | Mendelssohn: Cello Sonata; Chopin: Cello Sonata in G | 196? | 100.00 |
| *—Maroon label, no "Vendor: Mercury Record Corporation"* | | | |
| ❑ SR 90347 [S] | Schumann: Cello Concerto; Lalo: Cello Concerto | 196? | 40.00 |
| *—With Stanislaw Skrowaczewski/London Symphony Orchestra; maroon label, with "Vendor: Mercury Record Corporation"* | | | |
| ❑ SR 90347 [S] | Schumann: Cello Concerto; Lalo: Cello Concerto | 196? | 120.00 |
| *—With Stanislaw Skrowaczewski/London Symphony Orchestra; maroon label, no "Vendor: Mercury Record Corporation"* | | | |
| ❑ SR 90370 [S] | Bach: Suites 2 and 5 for Solo Violin | 196? | 40.00 |
| *—Third edition: Dark red (not maroon) label* | | | |
| ❑ SR 90370 [S] | Bach: Suites 2 and 5 for Solo Violin | 196? | 60.00 |
| *—Maroon label, with "Vendor: Mercury Record Corporation"* | | | |

Ringo Starr, *Stop and Smell the Roses,* Boardwalk NB1-33246, 1981, $10.

| Number | Title (A Side/B Side) | Yr | NM |
|---|---|---|---|
| ❑ SR 90370 [S] | Bach: Suites 2 and 5 for Solo Violin | 196? | 80.00 |
| *—Maroon label, no "Vendor: Mercury Record Corporation"* | | | |
| ❑ SR 90392 [S] | Brahms: Cello Sonatas No. 1 and 2 | 196? | 50.00 |
| *—Maroon label, with "Vendor: Mercury Record Corporation"* | | | |
| ❑ SR 90392 [S] | Brahms: Cello Sonatas No. 1 and 2 | 196? | 150.00 |
| *—Maroon label, no "Vendor: Mercury Record Corporation"* | | | |
| ❑ SR 90405 [S] | Bartok: First Rhapsody; Mendelssohn: Various Concertantes; Martinu: Rossini Variations; et al. | 196? | 40.00 |
| *—Third edition: Dark red (not maroon) label* | | | |
| ❑ SR 90405 [S] | Bartok: First Rhapsody; Mendelssohn: Various Concertantes; Martinu: Rossini Variations; et al. | 196? | 60.00 |
| *—Maroon label, with "Vendor: Mercury Record Corporation"* | | | |
| ❑ SR 90405 [S] | Bartok: First Rhapsody; Mendelssohn: Various Concertantes; Martinu: Rossini Variations; et al. | 196? | 120.00 |
| *—Maroon label, no "Vendor: Mercury Record Corporation"* | | | |
| ❑ SR 90480 [S] | Bach, J.S.: Three Sonatas | 196? | 200.00 |
| *—Maroon label, with "Vendor: Mercury Record Corporation"* | | | |

**STARR, EDWIN**

| Number | Title (A Side/B Side) | Yr | NM |
|---|---|---|---|
| GORDY | | | |
| ❑ GS-931 | Soul Master | 1968 | 25.00 |
| ❑ GS-940 | 25 Miles | 1969 | 25.00 |
| ❑ GS-945 | Just We Two | 1969 | 20.00 |
| *—With Blinky* | | | |
| ❑ GS-948 | War & Peace | 1970 | 20.00 |
| ❑ GS-956 | Involved | 1971 | 20.00 |
| GRANITE | | | |
| ❑ 1005 | Free to Be Myself | 1975 | 12.00 |
| MOTOWN | | | |
| ❑ M5-103V1 | Superstar Series, Vol. 3 | 1981 | 10.00 |
| ❑ M5-170V1 | War & Peace | 1981 | 10.00 |
| PICKWICK | | | |
| ❑ SPC-3387 | 25 Miles | 197? | 10.00 |
| 20TH CENTURY | | | |
| ❑ T-538 | Edwin Starr | 1977 | 10.00 |
| ❑ T-559 | Clean | 1978 | 10.00 |
| ❑ T-591 | Happy Radio | 1979 | 10.00 |
| ❑ T-615 | Stronger Than You | 1980 | 10.00 |
| ❑ T-634 | The Best of Edwin Starr | 1981 | 10.00 |

**STARR, KAY**

| Number | Title (A Side/B Side) | Yr | NM |
|---|---|---|---|
| ABC | | | |
| ❑ S-631 | When the Lights Go On Again | 1968 | 12.00 |
| CAPITOL | | | |
| ❑ H 211 [10] | Songs by Starr | 1950 | 70.00 |
| ❑ T 211 [M] | Songs by Starr | 1955 | 50.00 |
| ❑ H 363 [10] | The Kay Starr Style | 1953 | 70.00 |
| ❑ T 363 [M] | The Kay Starr Style | 1955 | 50.00 |
| ❑ DT 415 [R] | The Hits of Kay Starr | 196? | 12.00 |
| ❑ H 415 [10] | The Hits of Kay Starr | 1953 | 70.00 |
| ❑ T 415 [M] | The Hits of Kay Starr | 1955 | 50.00 |
| *—Turquoise or gray label* | | | |
| ❑ T 415 [M] | The Hits of Kay Starr | 1958 | 30.00 |
| *—Black label with colorband, Capitol logo at left* | | | |
| ❑ T 415 [M] | The Hits of Kay Starr | 1962 | 20.00 |
| *—Black label with colorband, Capitol logo at top* | | | |
| ❑ T 580 [M] | In a Blue Mood | 1955 | 50.00 |
| ❑ ST 1254 [S] | Movin' | 1959 | 30.00 |
| ❑ T 1254 [M] | Movin' | 1959 | 25.00 |
| ❑ ST 1303 [S] | Losers Weepers | 1960 | 30.00 |
| ❑ T 1303 [M] | Losers Weepers | 1960 | 25.00 |
| ❑ ST 1358 [S] | One More Time | 1960 | 30.00 |
| ❑ T 1358 [M] | One More Time | 1960 | 25.00 |
| ❑ ST 1374 [S] | Movin' on Broadway | 1960 | 30.00 |
| ❑ T 1374 [M] | Movin' on Broadway | 1960 | 25.00 |
| ❑ ST 1438 [S] | Kay Starr, Jazz Singer | 1960 | 40.00 |
| ❑ T 1438 [M] | Kay Starr, Jazz Singer | 1960 | 30.00 |
| ❑ ST 1468 [S] | All Starr Hits | 1961 | 30.00 |
| ❑ T 1468 [M] | All Starr Hits | 1961 | 25.00 |
| ❑ ST 1681 [S] | I Cry by Night | 1962 | 25.00 |
| ❑ T 1681 [M] | I Cry by Night | 1962 | 20.00 |
| ❑ ST 1795 [S] | Just Plain Country | 1962 | 25.00 |
| ❑ ST-8-1795 [S] | Just Plain Country | 196? | 30.00 |
| *—Capitol Record Club edition* | | | |
| ❑ T 1795 [M] | Just Plain Country | 1962 | 20.00 |
| ❑ ST 2106 [S] | The Fabulous Favorites | 1964 | 15.00 |
| ❑ T 2106 [M] | The Fabulous Favorites | 1964 | 12.00 |
| ❑ ST 2550 [S] | Tears and Heartaches/Old Records | 1966 | 15.00 |
| ❑ T 2550 [M] | Tears and Heartaches/Old Records | 1966 | 12.00 |
| ❑ SM-11323 | Kay Starrs Again | 1977 | 8.00 |
| *—Reissue with new prefix* | | | |
| ❑ ST-11323 | Kay Starrs Again | 1974 | 10.00 |
| ❑ SM-11880 | Movin' | 1979 | 10.00 |
| CORONET | | | |
| ❑ CX-106 [M] | Kay Starr Sings | 196? | 12.00 |
| ❑ CXS-106 [S] | Kay Starr Sings | 196? | 12.00 |
| GNP CRESCENDO | | | |
| ❑ GNPS-2083 | Country | 1974 | 10.00 |
| ❑ GNPS-2090 | Back to the Roots | 1975 | 10.00 |
| HINDSIGHT | | | |
| ❑ HSR-214 | Kay Starr 1947 | 1985 | 10.00 |
| LIBERTY | | | |
| ❑ LRP-3280 [M] | Swingin' with the Starr | 1963 | 25.00 |
| *—Reissue of 9001* | | | |
| ❑ LRP-9001 [M] | Swingin' with the Starr | 1956 | 50.00 |
| PARAMOUNT | | | |
| ❑ PAS-5001 | How About This | 1969 | 12.00 |
| RCA CAMDEN | | | |
| ❑ CAL-567 [M] | Kay Starr | 196? | 12.00 |
| RCA VICTOR | | | |
| ❑ LPM-1149 [M] | The One and Only Kay Starr | 1955 | 30.00 |
| ❑ ANL1-1311 | Pure Gold | 1976 | 8.00 |
| ❑ LPM-1549 [M] | Blue Starr | 1957 | 30.00 |
| ❑ LPM-1720 [M] | Rockin' with Kay | 1958 | 50.00 |
| ❑ LPM-2055 [M] | I Hear the Word | 1959 | 25.00 |
| ❑ LSP-2055 [S] | I Hear the Word | 1959 | 30.00 |
| RONDO-LETTE | | | |
| ❑ A-3 [M] | Them There Eyes | 1958 | 25.00 |
| SUNSET | | | |
| ❑ SUM-1126 [M] | Portrait of a Starr | 196? | 15.00 |
| ❑ SUS-5126 [R] | Portrait of a Starr | 196? | 10.00 |

**STARR, KAY/ERROLL GARNER**

| Number | Title (A Side/B Side) | Yr | NM |
|---|---|---|---|
| CROWN | | | |
| ❑ CLP-5003 [M] | Singin' Kay Starr, Swingin' Erroll Garner | 1957 | 30.00 |
| MODERN | | | |
| ❑ MLP-1203 [M] | Singin' Kay Starr, Swingin' Erroll Garner | 1956 | 80.00 |

**STARR, LUCILLE**

| Number | Title (A Side/B Side) | Yr | NM |
|---|---|---|---|
| A&M | | | |
| ❑ LP-107 [M] | French Song | 1966 | 30.00 |
| EPIC | | | |
| ❑ BN 26436 | Lonely Street | 1969 | 30.00 |

**STARR, RINGO** Also see THE BEATLES; GEORGE HARRISON AND FRIENDS.

| Number | Title (A Side/B Side) | Yr | NM |
|---|---|---|---|
| APPLE | | | |
| ❑ SW-3365 | Sentimental Journey | 1970 | 20.00 |
| ❑ SMAS-3368 | Beaucoups of Blues | 1970 | 20.00 |
| ❑ SWAL-3413 | Ringo | 1973 | 20.00 |
| *—Standard issue with booklet; Side 1, Song 2 identified on cover as "Hold On"* | | | |
| ❑ SWAL-3413 | Ringo | 1973 | 400.00 |
| *—With a 5:26 version of "Six O'Clock." On later copies, the song is shortened to 4:05 though the label still says 5:26. All known copies have a promo punch-hole in top corner of jacket; on Side 2 record, "Six O'Clock" will be the widest track.* | | | |
| ❑ SWAL-3413 | Ringo | 1974 | 25.00 |
| *—Later issue with booklet; Side 1, Song 2 identified on cover as "Have You Seen My Baby"* | | | |
| ❑ SW-3417 | Goodnight Vienna | 1974 | 12.00 |
| ❑ SW-3422 | Blast from Your Past | 1975 | 15.00 |
| ATLANTIC | | | |
| ❑ SD 18193 | Ringo's Rotogravure | 1976 | 15.00 |
| *—Deduct 2/3 for cut-outs* | | | |
| ❑ SD 18193 [DJ] | Ringo's Rotogravure | 1976 | 30.00 |
| *—With "DJ Only" scrawled into trail-off area* | | | |
| ❑ SD 19108 | Ringo the 4th | 1977 | 15.00 |
| *—Deduct 1/2 for cut-outs* | | | |
| ❑ SD 19108 [DJ] | Ringo the 4th | 1977 | 30.00 |
| *—With "DJ Only" scrawled into trail-off area* | | | |
| BOARDWALK | | | |
| ❑ NB1-33246 | Stop and Smell the Roses | 1981 | 10.00 |
| *—Deduct 1/2 for cut-outs* | | | |
| CAPITOL | | | |
| ❑ SW-3365 | Sentimental Journey | 197? | 40.00 |
| *—Purple label, large Capitol logo* | | | |
| ❑ SN-16114 | Ringo | 198? | 15.00 |
| *—Green label budget-line reissue with all errors corrected* | | | |
| ❑ SN-16218 | Sentimental Journey | 198? | 25.00 |
| *—Green label budget-line reissue* | | | |
| ❑ SN-16219 | Goodnight Vienna | 198? | 25.00 |
| *—Green label budget-line reissue* | | | |
| ❑ SN-16235 | Beaucoups of Blues | 198? | 20.00 |
| *—Green label budget-line reissue* | | | |
| ❑ SN-16236 | Blast from Your Past | 198? | 15.00 |
| *—Green label budget-line reissue* | | | |
| PORTRAIT | | | |
| ❑ JR 35378 | Bad Boy | 1978 | 15.00 |
| *—Deduct 1/3 for cut-outs* | | | |
| ❑ JR 35378 [DJ] | Bad Boy | 1978 | 30.00 |
| *—Regular white-label promo in standard jacket* | | | |

| Number | Title (A Side/B Side) | Yr | NM |
|---|---|---|---|
| ❑ JR 35378 [DJ] | Bad Boy | 1978 | 100.00 |
| *—White label promo with "Advance Promotion" on label; in plain white cover* | | | |
| **RHINO** | | | |
| ❑ R1 70199 | Starr Struck: Ringo's Best 1976-1983 | 1989 | 25.00 |
| **RYKODISC** | | | |
| ❑ RALP 0190 | Ringo Starr and His All-Starr Band | 1990 | 30.00 |
| *—With limited, numbered obi (deduct $5 if missing)* | | | |

**STARR, SALLY**

| Number | Title (A Side/B Side) | Yr | NM |
|---|---|---|---|
| **ARCADE** | | | |
| ❑ 1001 [M] | Our Gal Sal | 1960 | 80.00 |
| **CLYMAX** | | | |
| ❑ 1001 [M] | Our Gal Sal | 1959 | 200.00 |

**STARZ**

| Number | Title (A Side/B Side) | Yr | NM |
|---|---|---|---|
| **CAPITOL** | | | |
| ❑ SPRO-8657/8 [DJ] | Live at Municipal Auditorium, Louisville, March 30, 1978 | 1978 | 30.00 |
| *—Promo-only "Superstars Radio Network Presents" album* | | | |
| ❑ ST-11539 | Starz | 1976 | 10.00 |
| ❑ SW-11617 | Violation | 1977 | 10.00 |
| *—Black vinyl* | | | |
| ❑ SW-11617 | Violation | 1977 | 20.00 |
| *—Gold vinyl* | | | |
| ❑ ST-11730 | Attention Shoppers! | 1978 | 10.00 |
| ❑ ST-11861 | Coliseum Rock | 1978 | 10.00 |
| **METAL BLADE** | | | |
| ❑ 73430 | Live in Action | 1989 | 12.00 |
| **VIOLATION** | | | |
| ❑ 0001 | Live in America | 1983 | 15.00 |

**STATLER BROTHERS, THE**

| Number | Title (A Side/B Side) | Yr | NM |
|---|---|---|---|
| **COLUMBIA** | | | |
| ❑ CL 2449 [M] | Flowers on the Wall | 1966 | 25.00 |
| ❑ CL 2719 [M] | The Big Hits | 1967 | 30.00 |
| ❑ CS 9249 [S] | Flowers on the Wall | 1966 | 30.00 |
| ❑ PC 9249 | Flowers on the Wall | 198? | 8.00 |
| *—Reissue with new prefix* | | | |
| ❑ CS 9519 [S] | The Big Hits | 1967 | 25.00 |
| ❑ PC 9519 | The Big Hits | 198? | 8.00 |
| *—Reissue with new prefix* | | | |
| ❑ CS 9878 | Oh Happy Day | 1969 | 25.00 |
| ❑ PC 9878 | Oh Happy Day | 198? | 8.00 |
| *—Reissue with new prefix* | | | |
| ❑ CG 31557 [(2)] | The World of the Statler Brothers | 198? | 12.00 |
| *—Reissue with new prefix* | | | |
| ❑ KG 31557 [(2)] | The World of the Statler Brothers | 1972 | 20.00 |
| ❑ C 31560 | How Great Thou Art | 197? | 10.00 |
| *—Reissue of Harmony 31560* | | | |
| **HARMONY** | | | |
| ❑ H 30610 | Big Country Hits | 1971 | 12.00 |
| ❑ KH 31560 | How Great Thou Art | 1972 | 12.00 |
| ❑ KH 32256 | Do You Love Me Tonight | 1973 | 12.00 |
| **MERCURY** | | | |
| ❑ SRM-2-101 [(2)] | Holy Bible/The Old and New Testaments | 1978 | 20.00 |
| *—Reissue of 1051 and 1052 in one package* | | | |
| ❑ SRM-1-676 | Carry Me Back | 1973 | 15.00 |
| ❑ SRM-1-707 | Thank You World | 1974 | 15.00 |
| ❑ SRM-1-1019 | Sons of the Motherland | 1975 | 15.00 |
| ❑ SRM-1-1037 | The Best of the Statler Brothers | 1975 | 12.00 |
| ❑ SRM-1-1051 | Holy Bible: Old Testament | 1975 | 15.00 |
| ❑ SRM-1-1052 | Holy Bible: New Testament | 1975 | 15.00 |
| ❑ SRM-1-1077 | Harold, Lew, Phil & Don | 1976 | 15.00 |
| ❑ SRM-1-1125 | The Country America Loves | 1977 | 15.00 |
| ❑ SRM-1-4048 | The Legend Goes On | 1982 | 12.00 |
| ❑ SRM-1-5001 | Short Stories | 1977 | 12.00 |
| ❑ SRM-1-5007 | Entertainers...On and Off the Record | 1978 | 12.00 |
| ❑ SRM-1-5012 | Christmas Card | 1978 | 10.00 |
| ❑ SRM-1-5016 | The Originals | 1979 | 12.00 |
| ❑ SRM-1-5024 | The Best of the Statler Brothers Rides Again, Volume II | 1980 | 12.00 |
| ❑ SRM-1-5027 | 10th Anniversary | 1980 | 12.00 |
| ❑ SRM-1-6002 | Years Ago | 1981 | 12.00 |
| ❑ SR-61317 | Bed of Rose's | 1970 | 15.00 |
| ❑ SR-61349 | Pictures of Moments to Remember | 1971 | 15.00 |
| ❑ SR-61358 | Innerview | 1972 | 15.00 |
| ❑ SR-61367 | Country Music "Then and Now" | 1972 | 15.00 |
| ❑ SR-61374 | The Statler Brothers Sing Country Symphonies in E Major | 1973 | 15.00 |
| ❑ 812184-1 | Today | 1983 | 10.00 |
| ❑ 812282-1 | 10th Anniversary | 1983 | 8.00 |
| ❑ 812283-1 | Entertainers...On and Off the Record | 1983 | 8.00 |
| ❑ 812284-1 | Carry Me Back | 1983 | 8.00 |
| ❑ 818652-1 | Atlanta Blue | 1984 | 10.00 |
| ❑ 822524-1 | The Best of the Statler Brothers | 1984 | 8.00 |

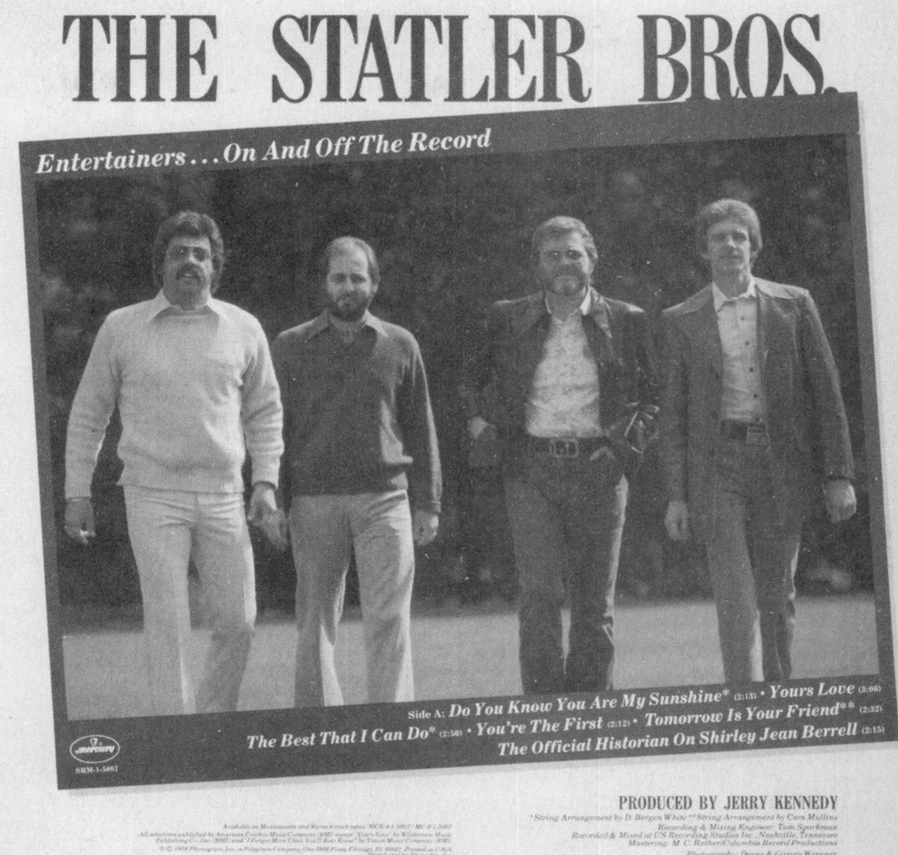


The Statler Brothers, *Entertainers... On and Off the Record,* Mercury SRM-1-5007, 1978, $12.

| Number | Title (A Side/B Side) | Yr | NM |
|---|---|---|---|
| ❑ 822525-1 | The Best of the Statler Brothers Rides Again, Volume II | 1984 | 8.00 |
| ❑ 822743-1 | Christmas Card | 1985 | 8.00 |
| ❑ 824420-1 | Pardners in Rhyme | 1985 | 10.00 |
| ❑ 824785-1 | Christmas Present | 1985 | 10.00 |
| ❑ 826247-1 | Bed of Rose's | 1986 | 8.00 |
| ❑ 826259-1 | Innerview | 1986 | 8.00 |
| ❑ 826260-1 | Country Music "Then and Now" | 1986 | 8.00 |
| ❑ 826264-1 [(2)] | Holy Bible/The Old and New Testaments | 1986 | 10.00 |
| ❑ 826267-1 | Holy Bible: Old Testament | 1986 | 8.00 |
| ❑ 826268-1 | Holy Bible: New Testament | 1986 | 8.00 |
| ❑ 826269-1 | Harold, Lew, Phil & Don | 1986 | 8.00 |
| ❑ 826275-1 | The Country America Loves | 1986 | 8.00 |
| ❑ 826278-1 | The Legend Goes On | 1986 | 8.00 |
| ❑ 826280-1 | Short Stories | 1986 | 8.00 |
| ❑ 826281-1 | The Originals | 1986 | 8.00 |
| ❑ 826710-1 | Radio Gospel Favorites | 1986 | 10.00 |
| ❑ 826782-1 | Four for the Show | 1986 | 10.00 |
| ❑ 832404-1 | Maple Street Memories | 1987 | 10.00 |
| ❑ 834626-1 | The Statlers Greatest Hits | 1988 | 10.00 |
| ❑ 838231-1 | Statler Brothers Live — Sold Out | 1989 | 15.00 |
| **PRIORITY** | | | |
| ❑ PU 37709 | Country Gospel | 1982 | 10.00 |
| **REALM** | | | |
| ❑ 2V 8077 [(2)] | The Very Best of the Statler Brothers | 1977 | 15.00 |
| **TIME-LIFE** | | | |
| ❑ STW-105 | Country Music | 1981 | 10.00 |

**STATON, CANDI**

| Number | Title (A Side/B Side) | Yr | NM |
|---|---|---|---|
| **FAME** | | | |
| ❑ 1800 | Candi Staton | 1972 | 20.00 |
| ❑ ST-4201 | I'm a Prisoner | 1970 | 20.00 |
| ❑ ST-4202 | Stand By Your Man | 1971 | 20.00 |
| **WARNER BROS.** | | | |
| ❑ BS 2830 | Candi | 1974 | 12.00 |
| ❑ BS 2948 | Young Hearts Run Free | 1976 | 12.00 |
| ❑ BS 3040 | Music Speaks Louder Than Words | 1977 | 12.00 |
| ❑ BSK 3207 | House of Love | 1978 | 12.00 |
| ❑ BSK 3333 | Chance | 1979 | 12.00 |
| ❑ BSK 3428 | Candi Staton | 1980 | 12.00 |

**STATON, DAKOTA**

| Number | Title (A Side/B Side) | Yr | NM |
|---|---|---|---|
| **CAPITOL** | | | |
| ❑ T 876 [M] | The Late, Late Show | 1957 | 50.00 |
| *—Turquoise or gray label* | | | |
| ❑ T 876 [M] | The Late, Late Show | 1959 | 30.00 |
| *—Black label with colorband, Capitol logo at left* | | | |
| ❑ T 1003 [M] | In the Night | 1958 | 50.00 |
| *—Turquoise or gray label* | | | |
| ❑ T 1003 [M] | In the Night | 1959 | 30.00 |
| *—Black label with colorband, Capitol logo at left* | | | |
| ❑ ST 1054 [S] | Dynamic! | 1959 | 40.00 |
| *—Black label with colorband, Capitol logo at left* | | | |
| ❑ ST 1054 [S] | Dynamic! | 1962 | 20.00 |
| *—Black label with colorband, Capitol logo at top* | | | |
| ❑ T 1054 [M] | Dynamic! | 1958 | 30.00 |
| *—Black label with colorband, Capitol logo at left* | | | |
| ❑ ST 1170 [S] | Crazy He Calls Me | 1959 | 40.00 |
| *—Black label with colorband, Capitol logo at left* | | | |
| ❑ ST 1170 [S] | Crazy He Calls Me | 1962 | 20.00 |
| *—Black label with colorband, Capitol logo at top* | | | |
| ❑ T 1170 [M] | Crazy He Calls Me | 1959 | 30.00 |
| *—Black label with colorband, Capitol logo at left* | | | |
| ❑ ST 1241 [S] | Time to Swing | 1959 | 40.00 |
| *—Black label with colorband, Capitol logo at left* | | | |
| ❑ ST 1241 [S] | Time to Swing | 1962 | 20.00 |
| *—Black label with colorband, Capitol logo at top* | | | |
| ❑ T 1241 [M] | Time to Swing | 1959 | 30.00 |
| *—Black label with colorband, Capitol logo at left* | | | |
| ❑ ST 1325 [S] | More Than the Most | 1960 | 40.00 |
| *—Black label with colorband, Capitol logo at left* | | | |
| ❑ ST 1325 [S] | More Than the Most | 1962 | 20.00 |
| *—Black label with colorband, Capitol logo at top* | | | |
| ❑ T 1325 [M] | More Than the Most | 1960 | 30.00 |
| *—Black label with colorband, Capitol logo at left* | | | |
| ❑ ST 1387 [S] | Ballads and the Blues | 1962 | 20.00 |
| *—Black label with colorband, Capitol logo at top* | | | |
| ❑ T 1387 [M] | Ballads and the Blues | 1960 | 30.00 |
| *—Black label with colorband, Capitol logo at left* | | | |
| ❑ T 1387 [M] | Ballads and the Blues | 1962 | 15.00 |
| *—Black label with colorband, Capitol logo at top* | | | |
| ❑ ST 1427 [S] | Softly | 1961 | 40.00 |
| *—Black label with colorband, Capitol logo at left* | | | |
| ❑ ST 1427 [S] | Softly | 1962 | 20.00 |
| *—Black label with colorband, Capitol logo at top* | | | |
| ❑ T 1427 [M] | Softly | 1961 | 30.00 |
| *—Black label with colorband, Capitol logo at left* | | | |
| ❑ ST 1490 [S] | Dakota | 1961 | 40.00 |
| *—Black label with colorband, Capitol logo at left* | | | |

| Number | Title (A Side/B Side) | Yr | NM |
|---|---|---|---|
| ❑ ST 1490 [S] | Dakota | 1962 | 20.00 |
| *—Black label with colorband, Capitol logo at top* | | | |
| ❑ T 1490 [M] | Dakota | 1961 | 30.00 |
| *—Black label with colorband, Capitol logo at left* | | | |
| ❑ ST 1597 [S] | 'Round Midnight | 1961 | 40.00 |
| *—Black label with colorband, Capitol logo at left* | | | |
| ❑ ST 1597 [S] | 'Round Midnight | 1962 | 20.00 |
| *—Black label with colorband, Capitol logo at top* | | | |
| ❑ T 1597 [M] | 'Round Midnight | 1961 | 30.00 |
| *—Black label with colorband, Capitol logo at left* | | | |
| ❑ ST 1649 [S] | Dakota at Storyville | 1962 | 25.00 |
| ❑ T 1649 [M] | Dakota at Storyville | 1962 | 20.00 |
| LONDON | | | |
| ❑ LL 3495 [M] | Dakota '67 | 1967 | 20.00 |
| UNITED ARTISTS | | | |
| ❑ UAL-3292 [M] | From Dakota with Love | 1963 | 20.00 |
| ❑ UAL-3312 [M] | Live and Swinging | 1963 | 20.00 |
| ❑ UAL-3355 [M] | Dakota Staton with Strings | 1964 | 20.00 |
| ❑ UAS-6292 [S] | From Dakota with Love | 1963 | 25.00 |
| ❑ UAS-6316 [S] | Live and Swinging | 1963 | 25.00 |
| ❑ UAS-6355 [S] | Dakota Staton with Strings | 1964 | 25.00 |
| **STATUS CYMBAL, THE** | | | |
| RCA VICTOR | | | |
| ❑ LPM-3993 [M] | In the Morning | 1968 | 40.00 |
| ❑ LSP-3993 [S] | In the Morning | 1968 | 20.00 |
| **STATUS QUO** | | | |
| A&M | | | |
| ❑ SP-3615 | Hello! | 1974 | 12.00 |
| ❑ SP-3649 | Quo | 1974 | 12.00 |
| ❑ SP-4381 | Piledriver | 1973 | 12.00 |
| CADET CONCEPT | | | |
| ❑ LPS-315 | Messages from the Status Quo | 1968 | 50.00 |
| CAPITOL | | | |
| ❑ ST-11381 | On the Level | 1975 | 10.00 |
| ❑ ST-11509 | Status Quo | 1976 | 10.00 |
| ❑ SKBB-11623 [(2)] | Status Quo Live | 1977 | 12.00 |
| ❑ ST-11749 | Rockin' All Over the World | 1978 | 10.00 |
| JANUS | | | |
| ❑ JLS-3018 | Ma Kelly's Greasy Spoon | 1970 | 15.00 |
| MERCURY | | | |
| ❑ 836651-1 | Status Quo | 1989 | 12.00 |
| PYE | | | |
| ❑ 3301 | Dog of Two Head | 1971 | 15.00 |
| RIVA | | | |
| ❑ 7402 | Now Here This | 1980 | 10.00 |
| **STEAGALL, RED** | | | |
| ABC | | | |
| ❑ AB-1051 | Hang On Feelin' | 1978 | 12.00 |
| ABC DOT | | | |
| ❑ DOSD-2055 | Lone Star Beer and Bob Wills Music | 1976 | 15.00 |
| ❑ DOSD-2068 | Texas Red | 1976 | 12.00 |
| ❑ DO-2078 | For All Our Cowboy Friends | 1977 | 12.00 |
| CAPITOL | | | |
| ❑ ST-11056 | Party Dolls and Wine | 1972 | 20.00 |
| ❑ ST-11162 | Somewhere My Love | 1973 | 12.00 |
| ❑ ST-11228 | If You've Got the Time, I've Got the Song | 1973 | 12.00 |
| ❑ ST-11321 | Finer Things in Life | 1974 | 12.00 |
| MCA | | | |
| ❑ 680 | For All Our Cowboy Friends | 198? | 8.00 |
| *—Reissue of ABC Dot 2078* | | | |
| ❑ 681 | Hang On Feelin' | 198? | 8.00 |
| *—Reissue of ABC 1051* | | | |
| ❑ 985 | Lone Star Beer and Bob Wills Music | 1986 | 10.00 |
| *—Reissue of ABC Dot 2055* | | | |
| **STEAM** | | | |
| MERCURY | | | |
| ❑ SR 61254 | Steam | 1969 | 20.00 |
| **STEAMHAMMER** | | | |
| EPIC | | | |
| ❑ BN 26490 | Reflection | 1969 | 30.00 |
| ❑ BN 26552 | Steamhammer | 1970 | 30.00 |
| **STEARNS, JUNE** | | | |
| COLUMBIA | | | |
| ❑ CS 9783 | River of Regret | 1969 | 20.00 |
| **STEEL** | | | |
| EPIC | | | |
| ❑ E 30875 | Steel | 1971 | 20.00 |
| **STEELE, TOMMY** | | | |
| LIBERTY | | | |
| ❑ LRP-3426 [M] | Everything's Coming Up Broadway | 1965 | 20.00 |
| ❑ LRP-3566 [M] | Sixpenny Millionaire | 1968 | 30.00 |
| *—Stereo cover with "Audition Mono LP Not for Sale" sticker attached; label is stock* | | | |

| Number | Title (A Side/B Side) | Yr | NM |
|---|---|---|---|
| ❑ LST-7426 [S] | Everything's Coming Up Broadway | 1965 | 25.00 |
| ❑ LST-7566 [S] | Sixpenny Millionaire | 1968 | 15.00 |
| LONDON | | | |
| ❑ LL 1770 [M] | Rock Around the World | 195? | 50.00 |
| **STEELEYE SPAN** | | | |
| BIG TREE | | | |
| ❑ BTS 2004 | Please to See the King | 1971 | 30.00 |
| CHRYSALIS | | | |
| ❑ CHR 1008 | Below the Salt | 1972 | 15.00 |
| *—Green label, "3300 Warner Blvd." address* | | | |
| ❑ CHR 1008 | Below the Salt | 1977 | 12.00 |
| *—Blue label, New York address* | | | |
| ❑ CHR 1046 | Parcel of Rogues | 1973 | 15.00 |
| *—Green label, "3300 Warner Blvd." address* | | | |
| ❑ CHR 1046 | Parcel of Rogues | 1977 | 12.00 |
| *—Blue label, New York address* | | | |
| ❑ CHR 1053 | Now We Are Six | 1974 | 15.00 |
| *—Green label, "3300 Warner Blvd." address* | | | |
| ❑ CHR 1053 | Now We Are Six | 1977 | 12.00 |
| *—Blue label, New York address* | | | |
| ❑ CHR 1071 | Commoners Crown | 1975 | 15.00 |
| *—Green label, "3300 Warner Blvd." address* | | | |
| ❑ CHR 1071 | Commoners Crown | 1977 | 12.00 |
| *—Blue label, New York address* | | | |
| ❑ CHR 1091 | All Around My Hat | 1975 | 15.00 |
| *—Green label, "3300 Warner Blvd." address* | | | |
| ❑ CHR 1091 | All Around My Hat | 1977 | 12.00 |
| *—Blue label, New York address* | | | |
| ❑ CHR 1119 | Please to See the King | 1976 | 15.00 |
| *—Reissue of Big Tree LP; green label, "3300 Warner Blvd." address* | | | |
| ❑ CHR 1119 | Please to See the King | 1977 | 12.00 |
| *—Blue label, New York address* | | | |
| ❑ CHR 1120 | Hark the Village Wait | 1976 | 15.00 |
| *—First US issue of debut LP; green label, "3300 Warner Blvd." address* | | | |
| ❑ CHR 1120 | Hark the Village Wait | 1977 | 12.00 |
| *—Blue label, New York address* | | | |
| ❑ CHR 1121 | Ten Man Mop | 1976 | 15.00 |
| *—First US issue of third UK LP; green label, "3300 Warner Blvd." address* | | | |
| ❑ CHR 1121 | Ten Man Mop | 1977 | 12.00 |
| *—Blue label, New York address* | | | |
| ❑ CHR 1123 | Rocket Cottage | 1976 | 15.00 |
| *—Green label, "3300 Warner Blvd." address* | | | |
| ❑ CHR 1123 | Rocket Cottage | 1977 | 12.00 |
| *—Blue label, New York address* | | | |
| ❑ CHR2 1136 [(2)] | The Steeleye Span Story: Original Masters | 1977 | 15.00 |
| ❑ CHR 1151 | Storm Force Ten | 1978 | 12.00 |
| ❑ CHR 1199 | Live at Last | 1978 | 12.00 |
| ❑ V2X 41136 [(2)] | The Steeleye Span Story: Original Masters | 1984 | 12.00 |
| *—Reissue of 1136* | | | |
| MOBILE FIDELITY | | | |
| ❑ 1-027 | All Around My Hat | 1980 | 25.00 |
| *—Audiophile vinyl* | | | |
| PAIR | | | |
| ❑ CRPDL-2-1021 [(2)] | Dogs and Ferrets | 1983 | 15.00 |
| SHANACHIE | | | |
| ❑ 64020 | Tempted and Tried | 1989 | 12.00 |
| ❑ 79039 | Below the Salt | 1989 | 12.00 |
| ❑ 79045 | Parcel of Rogues | 1989 | 12.00 |
| ❑ 79049 | Ten Man Mop | 1989 | 12.00 |
| ❑ 79052 | Hark the Village Wait | 1989 | 12.00 |
| ❑ 79059 | All Around My Hat | 1989 | 12.00 |
| ❑ 79060 | Now We Are Six | 1989 | 12.00 |
| ❑ 79063 | Back in Line | 1989 | 12.00 |
| ❑ 79071/2 [(2)] | Portfolio | 1990 | 20.00 |
| TAKOMA | | | |
| ❑ TAK-7097 | Sails of Silver | 1981 | 10.00 |
| **STEELY DAN** | | | |
| ABC | | | |
| ❑ 758 | Can't Buy a Thrill | 1972 | 12.00 |
| *—Black label* | | | |
| ❑ 758 | Can't Buy a Thrill | 1974 | 10.00 |
| *—Multicolor label* | | | |
| ❑ 779 | Countdown to Ecstasy | 1973 | 12.00 |
| *—Black label* | | | |
| ❑ 779 | Countdown to Ecstasy | 1974 | 10.00 |
| *—Multicolor label* | | | |
| ❑ 806 | Pretzel Logic | 1974 | 10.00 |
| *—Multicolor label* | | | |
| ❑ 806 | Pretzel Logic | 1974 | 12.00 |
| *—Black label* | | | |
| ❑ 846 | Katy Lied | 1975 | 12.00 |
| ❑ 931 | The Royal Scam | 1976 | 12.00 |
| ❑ AA-1006 | Aja | 1977 | 12.00 |
| ❑ 2022-1107 [(2)] | Greatest Hits | 1978 | 20.00 |
| *—Canadian import on gold vinyl, widely available in U.S.* | | | |
| ❑ AK-1107 [(2)] | Greatest Hits | 1978 | 15.00 |
| ABC DUNHILL | | | |
| ❑ SMAS-94976 | Can't Buy a Thrill | 1973 | 25.00 |
| *—Capitol Record Club edition pressed on the wrong label* | | | |
| COMMAND | | | |
| ❑ QD-40009 [Q] | Can't Buy a Thrill | 1974 | 20.00 |
| *—Second issue with no border around the cover* | | | |

| Number | Title (A Side/B Side) | Yr | NM |
|---|---|---|---|
| ❑ QD-40009 [Q] | Can't Buy a Thrill | 1974 | 25.00 |
| *—First issue with wide border around outside of cover* | | | |
| ❑ QD-40010 [Q] | Countdown to Ecstasy | 1974 | 20.00 |
| ❑ QD-40015 [Q] | Pretzel Logic | 1974 | 20.00 |
| MCA | | | |
| ❑ AA-1006 | Aja | 1980 | 10.00 |
| ❑ 1591 | Can't Buy a Thrill | 1987 | 6.00 |
| ❑ 1592 | Countdown to Ecstasy | 1987 | 6.00 |
| ❑ 1593 | Pretzel Logic | 1987 | 6.00 |
| ❑ 1594 | Katy Lied | 1987 | 6.00 |
| ❑ 1595 | The Royal Scam | 1987 | 6.00 |
| ❑ 1688 | Aja | 1987 | 6.00 |
| ❑ 1693 | Gaucho | 1987 | 6.00 |
| *—Many in the 1500 and 1600 series have a gold stamp with the new number on the cover* | | | |
| ❑ 5324 | Gold | 1982 | 10.00 |
| ❑ 2-6008 [(2)] | Greatest Hits | 1980 | 12.00 |
| ❑ 6102 | Gaucho | 1980 | 10.00 |
| ❑ 16009 | Gaucho | 1981 | 50.00 |
| *—Audiophile pressing* | | | |
| ❑ 16016 | Gold | 1982 | 50.00 |
| *—Audiophile pressing* | | | |
| ❑ 37040 | Can't Buy a Thrill | 1980 | 8.00 |
| ❑ 37041 | Countdown to Ecstasy | 1980 | 8.00 |
| ❑ 37042 | Pretzel Logic | 1980 | 8.00 |
| ❑ 37043 | Katy Lied | 1980 | 8.00 |
| ❑ 37044 | The Royal Scam | 1980 | 8.00 |
| ❑ 37243 | Gold | 1984 | 8.00 |
| MOBILE FIDELITY | | | |
| ❑ 1-007 | Katy Lied | 1979 | 80.00 |
| *—Audiophile vinyl* | | | |
| ❑ 1-033 | Aja | 1980 | 50.00 |
| *—Audiophile vinyl* | | | |
| **STEIG, JEREMY** | | | |
| BLUE NOTE | | | |
| ❑ BST-84354 | Wayfaring Stranger | 1970 | 20.00 |
| **STEIN, HAL, AND WARREN FITZGERALD** | | | |
| PROGRESSIVE | | | |
| ❑ PLP-1002 [M] | Hal Stein-Warren Fitzgerald Quintet | 1955 | 500.00 |
| **STEIN, LOU** | | | |
| AUDIOPHILE | | | |
| ❑ AP-198 | Solo Piano | 1984 | 10.00 |
| BRUNSWICK | | | |
| ❑ BL 58053 [10] | Lou Stein | 1953 | 50.00 |
| CHIAROSCURO | | | |
| ❑ 140 | Tribute to Tatum | 197? | 12.00 |
| ❑ CR-2027 | Temple of the Gods | 1979 | 15.00 |
| CORAL | | | |
| ❑ CRL 57003 [M] | Sweet and Lovely | 195? | 25.00 |
| ❑ CRL 57201 [M] | Sing Around the Piano | 1958 | 20.00 |
| DREAMSTREET | | | |
| ❑ DR-106 | Lou Stein Trio Live at the Dome | 1986 | 10.00 |
| EPIC | | | |
| ❑ LG 3101 [M] | House Top | 1955 | 40.00 |
| ❑ LN 3148 [M] | Three, Four and Five | 1955 | 40.00 |
| ❑ LN 3186 [M] | From Broadway to Paris | 1955 | 40.00 |
| JUBILEE | | | |
| ❑ JLP-8 [10] | Six for Kicks | 1954 | 50.00 |
| ❑ JLP-1019 [M] | Eight for Kicks, Four for Laughs | 1956 | 40.00 |
| MASTERSEAL | | | |
| ❑ MS33-1812 [M] | Mood Music for Beer and Pretzels | 1957 | 15.00 |
| MERCURY | | | |
| ❑ MG-20159 [M] | Honky Tonk Piano | 195? | 20.00 |
| ❑ MG-20271 [M] | Saloon Favorites | 195? | 15.00 |
| ❑ MG-20364 [M] | Honky Tonk Piano | 195? | 15.00 |
| ❑ MG-20469 [M] | Honky Tonk Piano and a Hot Banjo | 1960 | 12.00 |
| ❑ SR-60054 [S] | Honky Tonk Piano | 1959 | 20.00 |
| ❑ SR-60151 [S] | Honky Tonk Piano and a Hot Banjo | 1960 | 15.00 |
| MUSICOR | | | |
| ❑ MM-2057 [M] | Hey Louie! Play Melancholy Baby! | 1967 | 15.00 |
| ❑ MS-3057 [S] | Hey Louie! Play Melancholy Baby! | 1967 | 12.00 |
| WING | | | |
| ❑ MGW-12219 [M] | The Lou Stein-Way of Piano Pleasure | 196? | 12.00 |
| ❑ SRW-16219 [S] | The Lou Stein-Way of Piano Pleasure | 196? | 15.00 |
| WORLD JAZZ | | | |
| ❑ WJLPS-17 | Lou Stein and Friends | 1980 | 12.00 |
| **STEPHENS, LEIGH** | | | |
| PHILIPS | | | |
| ❑ PHS 600294 | Red Weather | 1969 | 80.00 |

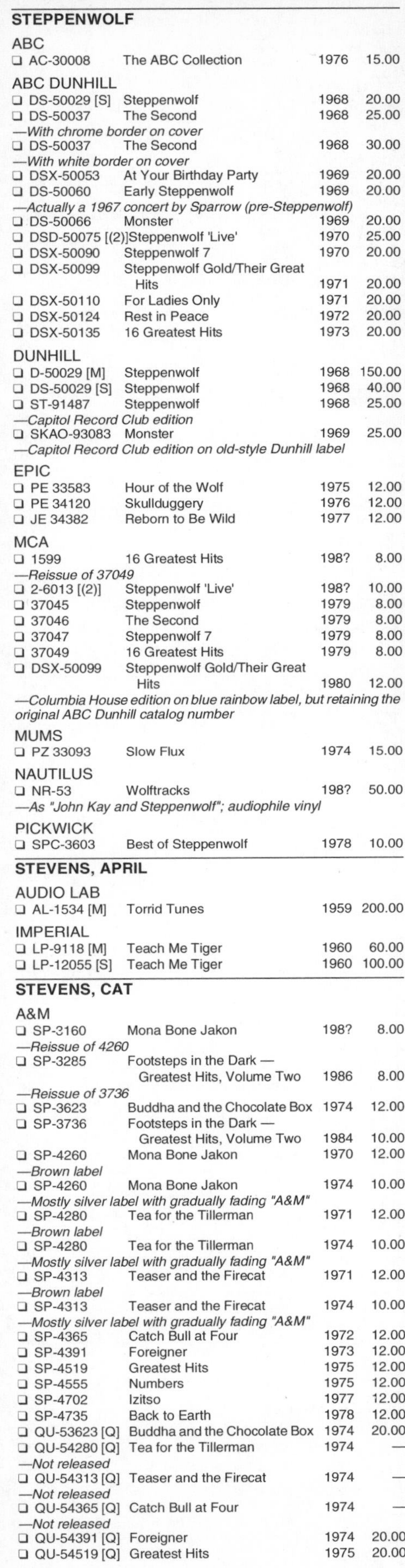

| Number | Title (A Side/B Side) | Yr | NM |
|---|---|---|---|
| **STEPPENWOLF** | | | |
| ABC | | | |
| ❑ AC-30008 | The ABC Collection | 1976 | 15.00 |
| ABC DUNHILL | | | |
| ❑ DS-50029 [S] | Steppenwolf | 1968 | 20.00 |
| ❑ DS-50037 | The Second | 1968 | 25.00 |
| *—With chrome border on cover* | | | |
| ❑ DS-50037 | The Second | 1968 | 30.00 |
| *—With white border on cover* | | | |
| ❑ DSX-50053 | At Your Birthday Party | 1969 | 20.00 |
| ❑ DS-50060 | Early Steppenwolf | 1969 | 20.00 |
| *—Actually a 1967 concert by Sparrow (pre-Steppenwolf)* | | | |
| ❑ DS-50066 | Monster | 1969 | 20.00 |
| ❑ DSD-50075 [(2)] | Steppenwolf 'Live' | 1970 | 25.00 |
| ❑ DSX-50090 | Steppenwolf 7 | 1970 | 20.00 |
| ❑ DSX-50099 | Steppenwolf Gold/Their Great Hits | 1971 | 20.00 |
| ❑ DSX-50110 | For Ladies Only | 1971 | 20.00 |
| ❑ DSX-50124 | Rest in Peace | 1972 | 20.00 |
| ❑ DSX-50135 | 16 Greatest Hits | 1973 | 20.00 |
| DUNHILL | | | |
| ❑ D-50029 [M] | Steppenwolf | 1968 | 150.00 |
| ❑ DS-50029 [S] | Steppenwolf | 1968 | 40.00 |
| ❑ ST-91487 | Steppenwolf | 1968 | 25.00 |
| *—Capitol Record Club edition* | | | |
| ❑ SKAO-93083 | Monster | 1969 | 25.00 |
| *—Capitol Record Club edition on old-style Dunhill label* | | | |
| EPIC | | | |
| ❑ PE 33583 | Hour of the Wolf | 1975 | 12.00 |
| ❑ PE 34120 | Skullduggery | 1976 | 12.00 |
| ❑ JE 34382 | Reborn to Be Wild | 1977 | 12.00 |
| MCA | | | |
| ❑ 1599 | 16 Greatest Hits | 198? | 8.00 |
| *—Reissue of 37049* | | | |
| ❑ 2-6013 [(2)] | Steppenwolf 'Live' | 198? | 10.00 |
| ❑ 37045 | Steppenwolf | 1979 | 8.00 |
| ❑ 37046 | The Second | 1979 | 8.00 |
| ❑ 37047 | Steppenwolf 7 | 1979 | 8.00 |
| ❑ 37049 | 16 Greatest Hits | 1979 | 8.00 |
| ❑ DSX-50099 | Steppenwolf Gold/Their Great Hits | 1980 | 12.00 |
| *—Columbia House edition on blue rainbow label, but retaining the original ABC Dunhill catalog number* | | | |
| MUMS | | | |
| ❑ PZ 33093 | Slow Flux | 1974 | 15.00 |
| NAUTILUS | | | |
| ❑ NR-53 | Wolftracks | 198? | 50.00 |
| *—As "John Kay and Steppenwolf"; audiophile vinyl* | | | |
| PICKWICK | | | |
| ❑ SPC-3603 | Best of Steppenwolf | 1978 | 10.00 |
| **STEVENS, APRIL** | | | |
| AUDIO LAB | | | |
| ❑ AL-1534 [M] | Torrid Tunes | 1959 | 200.00 |
| IMPERIAL | | | |
| ❑ LP-9118 [M] | Teach Me Tiger | 1960 | 60.00 |
| ❑ LP-12055 [S] | Teach Me Tiger | 1960 | 100.00 |
| **STEVENS, CAT** | | | |
| A&M | | | |
| ❑ SP-3160 | Mona Bone Jakon | 198? | 8.00 |
| *—Reissue of 4260* | | | |
| ❑ SP-3285 | Footsteps in the Dark — Greatest Hits, Volume Two | 1986 | 8.00 |
| *—Reissue of 3736* | | | |
| ❑ SP-3623 | Buddha and the Chocolate Box | 1974 | 12.00 |
| ❑ SP-3736 | Footsteps in the Dark — Greatest Hits, Volume Two | 1984 | 10.00 |
| ❑ SP-4260 | Mona Bone Jakon | 1970 | 12.00 |
| *—Brown label* | | | |
| ❑ SP-4260 | Mona Bone Jakon | 1974 | 10.00 |
| *—Mostly silver label with gradually fading "A&M"* | | | |
| ❑ SP-4280 | Tea for the Tillerman | 1971 | 12.00 |
| *—Brown label* | | | |
| ❑ SP-4280 | Tea for the Tillerman | 1974 | 10.00 |
| *—Mostly silver label with gradually fading "A&M"* | | | |
| ❑ SP-4313 | Teaser and the Firecat | 1971 | 12.00 |
| *—Brown label* | | | |
| ❑ SP-4313 | Teaser and the Firecat | 1974 | 10.00 |
| *—Mostly silver label with gradually fading "A&M"* | | | |
| ❑ SP-4365 | Catch Bull at Four | 1972 | 12.00 |
| ❑ SP-4391 | Foreigner | 1973 | 12.00 |
| ❑ SP-4519 | Greatest Hits | 1975 | 12.00 |
| ❑ SP-4555 | Numbers | 1975 | 12.00 |
| ❑ SP-4702 | Izitso | 1977 | 12.00 |
| ❑ SP-4735 | Back to Earth | 1978 | 12.00 |
| ❑ QU-53623 [Q] | Buddha and the Chocolate Box | 1974 | 20.00 |
| ❑ QU-54280 [Q] | Tea for the Tillerman | 1974 | — |
| *—Not released* | | | |
| ❑ QU-54313 [Q] | Teaser and the Firecat | 1974 | — |
| *—Not released* | | | |
| ❑ QU-54365 [Q] | Catch Bull at Four | 1974 | — |
| *—Not released* | | | |
| ❑ QU-54391 [Q] | Foreigner | 1974 | 20.00 |
| ❑ QU-54519 [Q] | Greatest Hits | 1975 | 20.00 |

Steppenwolf, *Steppenwolf the Second,* ABC-Dunhill DS-50037, 1969, chrome-colored border, $25.

| Number | Title (A Side/B Side) | Yr | NM |
|---|---|---|---|
| DERAM | | | |
| ❑ DE 16005 [M] | Matthew and Son | 1967 | 20.00 |
| ❑ DES 18005 [P] | Matthew and Son | 1967 | 15.00 |
| ❑ DES 18005/10 [(2)P] | Matthew and Son/New Masters | 1971 | 15.00 |
| ❑ DES 18010 [S] | New Masters | 1968 | 15.00 |
| ❑ DES 18061 [P] | Very Young and Early Songs | 1972 | 12.00 |
| LONDON | | | |
| ❑ LC-50010 | Cat's Cradle | 1977 | 12.00 |
| ❑ 820321-1 | Cat's Cradle | 1985 | 8.00 |
| MOBILE FIDELITY | | | |
| ❑ 1-035 | Tea for the Tillerman | 1979 | 40.00 |
| *—Audiophile vinyl* | | | |
| ❑ MFQR-035 | Tea for the Tillerman | 1984 | 120.00 |
| *—Ultra High Quality Recording in a box* | | | |
| ❑ 1-244 | Teaser and the Firecat | 1996 | 40.00 |
| *—Audiophile vinyl* | | | |
| ❑ 1-254 | Izitso | 1996 | 25.00 |
| *—Audiophile vinyl* | | | |
| **STEVENS, CONNIE** | | | |
| HARMONY | | | |
| ❑ HS 11312 | The Hank Williams Songbook | 1969 | 15.00 |
| WARNER BROS. | | | |
| ❑ W 1208 [M] | Conchetta | 1958 | 50.00 |
| ❑ WS 1208 [S] | Conchetta | 1958 | 60.00 |
| ❑ W 1382 [M] | Connie Stevens from "Hawaiian Eye" | 1960 | 30.00 |
| ❑ WS 1382 [S] | Connie Stevens from "Hawaiian Eye" | 1960 | 40.00 |
| ❑ W 1431 [M] | From Me to You | 1962 | 30.00 |
| ❑ WS 1431 [S] | From Me to You | 1962 | 40.00 |
| ❑ W 1432 [M] | Connie | 1962 | 30.00 |
| ❑ WS 1432 [S] | Connie | 1962 | 40.00 |
| ❑ W 1460 [M] | The Hank Williams Songbook | 1962 | 30.00 |
| ❑ WS 1460 [S] | The Hank Williams Songbook | 1962 | 40.00 |
| **STEVENS, DODIE** | | | |
| DOT | | | |
| ❑ DLP-3212 [M] | Dodie Stevens | 1960 | 30.00 |
| ❑ DLP-3323 [M] | Over the Rainbow | 1960 | 30.00 |
| ❑ DLP-3371 [M] | Pink Shoelaces | 1961 | 30.00 |
| ❑ DLP-25212 [S] | Dodie Stevens | 1960 | 40.00 |
| ❑ DLP-25323 [S] | Over the Rainbow | 1960 | 40.00 |
| ❑ DLP-25371 [S] | Pink Shoelaces | 1961 | 40.00 |

| Number | Title (A Side/B Side) | Yr | NM |
|---|---|---|---|
| **STEVENS, LEITH** | | | |
| CORAL | | | |
| ❑ CRL 57283 [M] | Jazz Themes for Cops and Robbers | 1958 | 50.00 |
| DECCA | | | |
| ❑ DL 5515 [10] | Jazz Themes in "The Wild One" | 1954 | 80.00 |
| **STEVENS, RAY** | | | |
| BARNABY | | | |
| ❑ 5004 | Ray Stevens' Greatest Hits | 1974 | 10.00 |
| *—Reissue of 30770* | | | |
| ❑ 5005 | Nashville | 1974 | 10.00 |
| *—Reissue of 15007* | | | |
| ❑ 6003 | Boogity Boogity | 1974 | 12.00 |
| ❑ 6012 | Misty | 1975 | 12.00 |
| ❑ 6018 | The Very Best of Ray Stevens | 1975 | 12.00 |
| ❑ BR 15007 | Nashville | 1973 | 12.00 |
| ❑ Z 30092 | Ray Stevens...Unreal!!! | 1970 | 12.00 |
| ❑ Z 30770 | Ray Stevens' Greatest Hits | 1971 | 12.00 |
| ❑ ZQ 30770 [Q] | Ray Stevens' Greatest Hits | 1971 | 20.00 |
| ❑ Z 30809 | Turn Your Radio On | 1972 | 12.00 |
| ❑ ZQ 30809 [Q] | Turn Your Radio On | 1972 | 20.00 |
| ❑ KZ 32139 | Losin' Streak | 1972 | 12.00 |
| ❑ Z12 35005 | Everything Is Beautiful | 1970 | 15.00 |
| MCA | | | |
| ❑ 5517 | He Thinks He's Ray Stevens | 1984 | 10.00 |
| ❑ 5635 | I Have Returned | 1985 | 10.00 |
| ❑ 5795 | Surely You Joust | 1986 | 10.00 |
| ❑ 5918 | Greatest Hits | 1987 | 10.00 |
| ❑ 42020 | Crackin' Up! | 1987 | 10.00 |
| ❑ 42062 | Greatest Hits, Volume 2 | 1987 | 10.00 |
| ❑ 42172 | I Never Made a Record I Didn't Like | 1988 | 10.00 |
| ❑ 42303 | Beside Myself | 1989 | 10.00 |
| MERCURY | | | |
| ❑ MG-20732 [M] | 1,837 Seconds of Humor | 1962 | 40.00 |
| ❑ MG-20828 [M] | This Is Ray Stevens | 1963 | 25.00 |
| ❑ SR-60732 [S] | 1,837 Seconds of Humor | 1962 | 50.00 |
| ❑ SR-60828 [S] | This Is Ray Stevens | 1963 | 30.00 |
| ❑ SR-61272 | The Best of Ray Stevens | 1968 | 15.00 |
| ❑ 812780-1 | Me | 1984 | 10.00 |
| MONUMENT | | | |
| ❑ SLP-18102 | Even Stevens | 1968 | 15.00 |
| ❑ SLP-18115 | Gitarzan | 1969 | 15.00 |

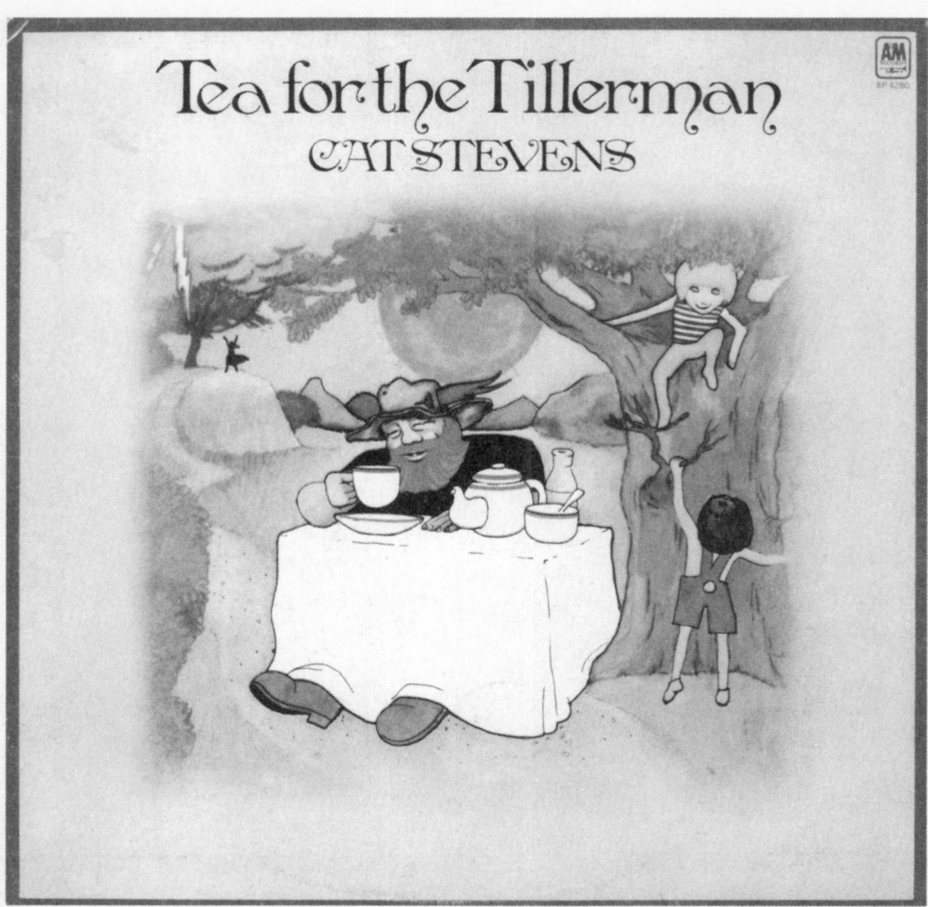


Cat Stevens, *Tea for the Tillerman*, A&M SP-4280, 1971, brown label, $12.

| Number | Title (A Side/B Side) | Yr | NM |
|---|---|---|---|
| ❑ SLP-18134 | Have a Little Talk with Myself | 1970 | 15.00 |
| **PICKWICK** | | | |
| ❑ SPC-3266 | Rock and Roll Show | 1971 | 10.00 |
| **PRIORITY** | | | |
| ❑ PU 38075 | Turn Your Radio On | 1982 | 10.00 |
| *—Reissue of Barnaby 30809* | | | |
| **RCA VICTOR** | | | |
| ❑ AHL1-3574 | Shriner's Convention | 1980 | 10.00 |
| ❑ AHL1-3841 | One More Last Chance | 1981 | 10.00 |
| ❑ AYL1-4253 | Shriner's Convention | 1982 | 8.00 |
| *—"Best Buy Series" reissue* | | | |
| ❑ AHL1-4288 | Don't Laugh Now | 1982 | 10.00 |
| ❑ AHL1-4727 | Greatest Hits | 1983 | 10.00 |
| ❑ AYL1-5153 | Greatest Hits | 1985 | 8.00 |
| *—"Best Buy Series" reissue* | | | |
| ❑ CPL1-7161 | Collector's Series | 1986 | 10.00 |
| **WARNER BROS.** | | | |
| ❑ BS 2914 | Just for the Record | 1976 | 10.00 |
| ❑ BS 2997 | Feel the Music | 1977 | 10.00 |
| ❑ BS 3098 | There Is Something... | 1977 | 10.00 |
| ❑ BS 3195 | Be Your Own Best Friend | 1978 | 10.00 |
| ❑ BSK 3332 | The Feeling's Not Right Again | 1979 | 10.00 |

### STEVENS, TERRI

| Number | Title (A Side/B Side) | Yr | NM |
|---|---|---|---|
| **EVEREST** | | | |
| ❑ SDBR-1088 [S] | It's Been a Long, Long Time | 1960 | 25.00 |
| ❑ LPBR-5088 [M] | It's Been a Long, Long Time | 1960 | 20.00 |

### STEWARD, ALEC

| Number | Title (A Side/B Side) | Yr | NM |
|---|---|---|---|
| **BLUESVILLE** | | | |
| ❑ BVLP-1076 [M] | Creepin' Blues | 1963 | 80.00 |
| *—Blue label, silver print* | | | |
| ❑ BVLP-1076 [M] | Creepin' Blues | 1964 | 25.00 |
| *—Blue label, trident logo at right* | | | |

### STEWARD, HERB

| Number | Title (A Side/B Side) | Yr | NM |
|---|---|---|---|
| **AVA** | | | |
| ❑ A-9 [M] | So Pretty | 1962 | 25.00 |
| ❑ AS-9 [S] | So Pretty | 1962 | 30.00 |

### STEWART, AL

| Number | Title (A Side/B Side) | Yr | NM |
|---|---|---|---|
| **ARISTA** | | | |
| ❑ AL 4190 | Time Passages | 1978 | 10.00 |
| ❑ AL6-8326 | Year of the Cat | 198? | 8.00 |
| *—Reissue of Arista 9503* | | | |
| ❑ AL6-8342 | Time Passages | 198? | 8.00 |
| *—Reissue of 4190* | | | |
| ❑ AL6-8359 | Past, Present and Future | 198? | 8.00 |
| *—Reissue of Arista 9524* | | | |
| ❑ A2L 8607 [(2)] | Live/Indian Summer | 1981 | 12.00 |
| ❑ AL 9503 | Year of the Cat | 1979 | 10.00 |
| *—Reissue of Janus 7022* | | | |
| ❑ AL 9520 | 24 Carrots | 1980 | 10.00 |
| ❑ AL 9524 | Past, Present and Future | 1980 | 10.00 |
| *—Reissue of Janus 3063* | | | |
| ❑ AL 9525 | Modern Times | 1980 | 10.00 |
| *—Reissue of Janus 7012* | | | |
| **ENIGMA** | | | |
| ❑ D1-73316 | Last Days of the Century | 1988 | 12.00 |
| **EPIC** | | | |
| ❑ BN 26564 | Love Chronicles | 1970 | 20.00 |
| **JANUS** | | | |
| ❑ 3063 | Past, Present and Future | 1974 | 15.00 |
| ❑ 7012 | Modern Times | 1975 | 12.00 |
| ❑ 7022 | Year of the Cat | 1976 | 12.00 |
| ❑ 7026 [(2)] | The Early Years | 1977 | 15.00 |
| ❑ 7026 [DJ] | The Early Years | 1977 | 30.00 |
| *—Promo-only condensation of 2-LP set with rubber-stamp cover* | | | |
| **MOBILE FIDELITY** | | | |
| ❑ 1-009 | Year of the Cat | 1979 | 40.00 |
| *—Audiophile vinyl* | | | |
| ❑ 1-082 | Time Passages | 1981 | 30.00 |
| *—Audiophile vinyl* | | | |
| **NAUTILUS** | | | |
| ❑ NR-34 | 24 Carrots | 198? | 30.00 |
| *—Audiophile vinyl* | | | |
| **PASSPORT** | | | |
| ❑ PB-6042 | Russians and Americans | 1986 | 12.00 |

### STEWART, ANDY

| Number | Title (A Side/B Side) | Yr | NM |
|---|---|---|---|
| **CAPITOL** | | | |
| ❑ ST 10320 [S] | Andy Stewart's Scotland | 196? | 20.00 |
| ❑ T 10320 [M] | Andy Stewart's Scotland | 196? | 15.00 |
| **EPIC** | | | |
| ❑ LF 18027 [M] | A Scottish Soldier | 196? | 12.00 |
| ❑ LF 18031 [M] | Tunes of Glory | 196? | 12.00 |
| ❑ LF 18048 [M] | I'm Off to Bonnie Scotland | 196? | 12.00 |
| ❑ BF 19027 [S] | A Scottish Soldier | 196? | 15.00 |
| ❑ BF 19031 [S] | Tunes of Glory | 196? | 15.00 |
| ❑ BF 19048 [S] | I'm Off to Bonnie Scotland | 196? | 15.00 |
| **WARWICK** | | | |
| ❑ W 3043 [M] | A Scottish Soldier | 1961 | 20.00 |
| ❑ WST 3043 [S] | A Scottish Soldier | 1961 | 30.00 |

### STEWART, BILLY

| Number | Title (A Side/B Side) | Yr | NM |
|---|---|---|---|
| **CHESS** | | | |
| ❑ LP-1496 [M] | I Do Love You | 196? | 30.00 |
| *—Green "woman" cover* | | | |
| ❑ LP-1496 [M] | I Do Love You | 1965 | 80.00 |
| *—Red cover, black "wheel"* | | | |
| ❑ LPS-1496 [S] | I Do Love You | 196? | 40.00 |
| *—Green "woman" cover* | | | |
| ❑ LPS-1496 [S] | I Do Love You | 1965 | 100.00 |
| *—Red cover, black "wheel"* | | | |
| ❑ LP-1499 [M] | Unbelievable | 1966 | 30.00 |
| ❑ LPS-1499 [S] | Unbelievable | 1966 | 40.00 |
| ❑ LP-1513 [M] | Billy Stewart Teaches Old Standards New Tricks | 1967 | 30.00 |
| ❑ LPS-1513 [S] | Billy Stewart Teaches Old Standards New Tricks | 1967 | 40.00 |
| ❑ LPS-1547 | Billy Stewart Remembered | 1970 | 25.00 |
| ❑ CH-9104 | The Greatest Sides | 198? | 10.00 |
| ❑ CH-50059 | Cross My Heart | 1974 | 15.00 |

### STEWART, BOB

| Number | Title (A Side/B Side) | Yr | NM |
|---|---|---|---|
| **DAWN** | | | |
| ❑ DLP-1103 [M] | Let's Talk About Love | 1956 | 50.00 |

### STEWART, HELYNE

| Number | Title (A Side/B Side) | Yr | NM |
|---|---|---|---|
| **CONTEMPORARY** | | | |
| ❑ M-3601 [M] | Love Moods | 1962 | 30.00 |
| ❑ S-7601 [S] | Love Moods | 1962 | 40.00 |

### STEWART, JOHN Also see THE KINGSTON TRIO.

| Number | Title (A Side/B Side) | Yr | NM |
|---|---|---|---|
| **AFFORDABLE DREAMS** | | | |
| ❑ AD-01 | Trancas | 1984 | 10.00 |
| **ALLEGIANCE** | | | |
| ❑ AV-431 | Blondes | 1982 | 10.00 |
| **CAPITOL** | | | |
| ❑ ST-203 | California Bloodlines | 1969 | 15.00 |
| ❑ ST-540 | Willard | 1970 | 15.00 |
| ❑ SM-2975 | Signals Through the Glass | 1977 | 10.00 |
| *—Reissue with new prefix* | | | |
| ❑ ST 2975 | Signals Through the Glass | 1968 | 20.00 |
| ❑ SN-16150 | California Bloodlines | 198? | 8.00 |
| *—Budget-line reissue* | | | |
| ❑ SN-16151 | Willard | 198? | 8.00 |
| *—Budget-line reissue* | | | |
| **CYPRESS** | | | |
| ❑ 661117-1 | Punch the Big Guy | 1987 | 10.00 |
| **HOMECOMING** | | | |
| ❑ HC-0200 | Centennial | 1984 | 10.00 |
| ❑ HC-0300 | The Last Campaign | 1985 | 10.00 |
| ❑ HC-0500 | The Trio Years | 1986 | 10.00 |
| **RCA VICTOR** | | | |
| ❑ CPL2-0265 [(2)] | The Phoenix Concerts — Live | 1974 | 15.00 |
| ❑ APL1-0816 | Wingless Angels | 1975 | 12.00 |
| ❑ AFL1-3513 | John Stewart in Concert | 1980 | 10.00 |
| ❑ AYL1-3731 | Cannons in the Rain | 1981 | 8.00 |
| *—"Best Buy Series" reissue* | | | |
| ❑ LSP-4827 | Cannons in the Rain | 1973 | 12.00 |
| **RSO** | | | |
| ❑ RS-1-3027 | Fire in the Wind | 1977 | 10.00 |
| ❑ RS-1-3051 | Bombs Away Dream Babies | 1979 | 10.00 |
| ❑ RS-1-3074 | Dream Babies Go Hollywood | 1980 | 10.00 |
| **WARNER BROS.** | | | |
| ❑ WS 1948 | The Lonesome Picker Rides Again | 1971 | 12.00 |
| ❑ BS 2611 | Sunstorm | 1972 | 12.00 |

### STEWART, REDD

| Number | Title (A Side/B Side) | Yr | NM |
|---|---|---|---|
| **AUDIO LAB** | | | |
| ❑ AL-1528 [M] | Redd Stewart Sings Favorite Old Time Tunes | 1959 | 200.00 |
| **HICKORY/MGM** | | | |
| ❑ H3G-4512 | I Remember | 1974 | 15.00 |

### STEWART, REX

| Number | Title (A Side/B Side) | Yr | NM |
|---|---|---|---|
| **AMERICAN RECORDING SOCIETY** | | | |
| ❑ G-448 [M] | The Big Challenge | 1958 | 40.00 |
| **ATLANTIC** | | | |
| ❑ 1209 [M] | Big Jazz | 1956 | 50.00 |
| **CONCERT HALL JAZZ** | | | |
| ❑ 1202 [M] | Dixieland On Location | 1954 | 80.00 |
| **DIAL** | | | |
| ❑ LP-215 [10] | Ellingtonia | 1951 | 250.00 |
| **FELSTED** | | | |
| ❑ 2001 [S] | Rendezvous with Rex | 1958 | 30.00 |
| ❑ 7001 [M] | Rendezvous with Rex | 1958 | 40.00 |
| **GRAND AWARD** | | | |
| ❑ GA 33-414 [M] | Just for Kicks | 195? | 40.00 |

| Number | Title (A Side/B Side) | Yr | NM |
|---|---|---|---|
| **JAZZTONE** | | | |
| ❑ J-1202 [M] | Dixieland Free-for-All | 1956 | 40.00 |
| ❑ J-1268 [M] | The Big Challenge | 1957 | 40.00 |
| ❑ J-1285 [M] | The Big Reunion | 1957 | 40.00 |
| **SWINGVILLE** | | | |
| ❑ SVLP-2006 [M] | The Happy Jazz of Rex Stewart | 1960 | 50.00 |
| *—Purple label* | | | |
| ❑ SVLP-2006 [M] | The Happy Jazz of Rex Stewart | 1965 | 25.00 |
| *—Blue label, trident logo at right* | | | |
| **UNITED ARTISTS** | | | |
| ❑ UAL-4009 [M] | Henderson Homecoming | 1959 | 40.00 |
| ❑ UAS-5009 [S] | Henderson Homecoming | 1959 | 30.00 |
| **URANIA** | | | |
| ❑ UJLP-2012 [M] | Cool Fever | 1955 | 60.00 |
| **WARNER BROS.** | | | |
| ❑ W 1260 [M] | Porgy and Bess Revisited | 1958 | 40.00 |
| ❑ WS 1260 [S] | Porgy and Bess Revisited | 1958 | 30.00 |
| **"X"** | | | |
| ❑ LX-3001 [10] | Rex Stewart and His Orchestra | 1954 | 100.00 |

### STEWART, REX/PEANUTS HUCKO

| Number | Title (A Side/B Side) | Yr | NM |
|---|---|---|---|
| **JAZZTONE** | | | |
| ❑ J-1250 [M] | Dedicated Jazz | 1957 | 40.00 |

### STEWART, REX/ILLINOIS JACQUET

| Number | Title (A Side/B Side) | Yr | NM |
|---|---|---|---|
| **GRAND AWARD** | | | |
| ❑ GA 33-315 [M] | Rex Stewart Plays Duke/ Uptown Jazz | 1955 | 40.00 |

### STEWART, REX, AND DICKIE WELLS

| Number | Title (A Side/B Side) | Yr | NM |
|---|---|---|---|
| **RCA VICTOR** | | | |
| ❑ LPM-2024 [M] | Chatter Jazz | 1959 | 25.00 |
| ❑ LSP-2024 [S] | Chatter Jazz | 1959 | 30.00 |

### STEWART, ROD Also see JEFF BECK; FACES.

| Number | Title (A Side/B Side) | Yr | NM |
|---|---|---|---|
| **ACCORD** | | | |
| ❑ SN-7142 | Rod the Mod | 1981 | 12.00 |
| **DCC COMPACT CLASSICS** | | | |
| ❑ LPZ-2010 | Never a Dull Moment | 1995 | 30.00 |
| *—Audiophile vinyl* | | | |
| **J** | | | |
| ❑ 55710 | As Time Goes By... The Great American Songbook Vol. 2 | 2003 | 15.00 |
| ❑ 62182 | Stardust... The Great American Songbook Volume III | 2004 | 15.00 |
| **MERCURY** | | | |
| ❑ SRM-1-609 | Every Picture Tells a Story | 1971 | 10.00 |
| *—With poster missing; red label* | | | |
| ❑ SRM-1-609 | Every Picture Tells a Story | 1971 | 15.00 |
| *—Original cover has an attached, perforated poster* | | | |
| ❑ SRM-1-646 | Never a Dull Moment | 1972 | 12.00 |
| *—Red label* | | | |
| ❑ SRM-1-680 | Sing It Again Rod | 1973 | 12.00 |
| *—Red label* | | | |
| ❑ SRM-1-697 | Rod Stewart/Faces Live: Coast to Coast Overtures and Beginners | 1973 | 15.00 |
| *—By "Rod Stewart/Faces"* | | | |
| ❑ SRM-1-1017 | Smiler | 1974 | 12.00 |
| *—Chicago skyline label* | | | |
| ❑ SRM-2-7507 [(2)] | The Best of Rod Stewart | 1976 | 15.00 |
| ❑ SRM-2-7509 [(2)] | The Best of Rod Stewart, Volume 2 | 1977 | 15.00 |
| ❑ SR-61237 | The Rod Stewart Album | 1969 | 25.00 |
| *—Cover is yellow with no black border* | | | |
| ❑ SR-61237 | The Rod Stewart Album | 1971 | 15.00 |
| *—Cover is yellow with black border; red label* | | | |
| ❑ SR-61264 | Gasoline Alley | 1970 | 20.00 |
| *—Cover is textured, most noticeably on the pebbles* | | | |
| ❑ SR-61264 | Gasoline Alley | 1971 | 15.00 |
| *—Cover is not textured; red label* | | | |
| ❑ 822385-1 | Every Picture Tells a Story | 1984 | 8.00 |
| ❑ 822791-1 [(2)] | The Best of Rod Stewart, Volume 2 | 1985 | 12.00 |
| ❑ 824881-1 | Gasoline Alley | 1985 | 8.00 |
| ❑ 824882-1 | Sing It Again Rod | 1985 | 8.00 |
| ❑ 826287-1 [(2)] | The Best of Rod Stewart | 1985 | 12.00 |
| **MOBILE FIDELITY** | | | |
| ❑ 1-054 | Blondes Have More Fun | 1980 | 25.00 |
| *—Audiophile vinyl* | | | |
| **PRIVATE STOCK** | | | |
| ❑ PS-2021 | A Shot of Rhythm and Blues | 1976 | 15.00 |
| **SPRINGBOARD** | | | |
| ❑ SPB-4030 | Rod Stewart and The Faces | 197? | 12.00 |
| ❑ SPB-4063 | Rod Stewart and Steampacket | 197? | 12.00 |
| **TRIP** | | | |
| ❑ TOP-16-31 | Looking Back/16 Early Hits | 1974 | 12.00 |
| **UNITED DISTRIBUTORS** | | | |
| ❑ UDL-2391 | The Day Will Come | 1981 | 20.00 |
| **WARNER BROS.** | | | |
| ❑ BS 2875 | Atlantic Crossing | 1975 | 10.00 |
| ❑ BS 2938 | A Night on the Town | 1976 | 10.00 |
| ❑ BSK 3092 | Foot Loose and Fancy Free | 1977 | 10.00 |

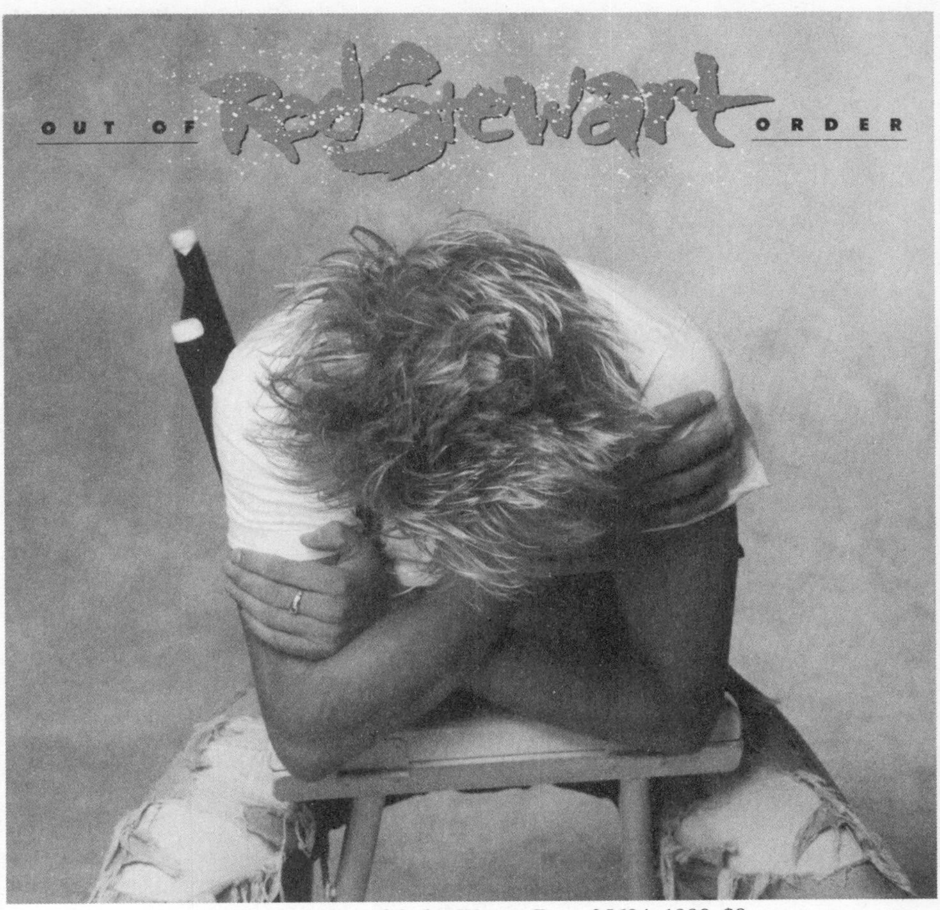


Rod Stewart, *Out of Order,* Warner Bros. 25684, 1988, $8.

| Number | Title (A Side/B Side) | Yr | NM |
|---|---|---|---|
| ❑ BSK 3108 | Atlantic Crossing | 1977 | 8.00 |
| *—Reissue of 2875* | | | |
| ❑ BSK 3116 | A Night on the Town | 1977 | 8.00 |
| *—Reissue of 2938* | | | |
| ❑ BSK 3261 | Blondes Have More Fun | 1978 | 10.00 |
| ❑ BSP 3276 [PD] | Blondes Have More Fun | 1978 | 20.00 |
| ❑ HS 3373 | Rod Stewart Greatest Hits | 1979 | 10.00 |
| ❑ HS 3485 | Foolish Behaviour | 1980 | 10.00 |
| ❑ BSK 3602 | Tonight I'm Yours | 1981 | 10.00 |
| ❑ 23743 [(2)] | Absolutely Live | 1982 | 12.00 |
| ❑ 23743 [(2)DJ] | Absolutely Live | 1982 | 25.00 |
| *—Promo only on Quiex II vinyl* | | | |
| ❑ 23877 | Body Wishes | 1983 | 8.00 |
| ❑ 23877 [DJ] | Body Wishes | 1983 | 15.00 |
| *—Promo only on Quiex II vinyl* | | | |
| ❑ 25095 | Camouflage | 1984 | 8.00 |
| *—Issued with 16 different back covers, all of equal value, that, when assembled, form a giant poster* | | | |
| ❑ 25446 | Rod Stewart | 1986 | 8.00 |
| ❑ 25884 | Out of Order | 1988 | 8.00 |
| ❑ 26158 | Downtown Train: Selections from the Storyteller Anthology | 1990 | 12.00 |

### STEWART, SANDY

| Number | Title (A Side/B Side) | Yr | NM |
|---|---|---|---|
| **AUDIOPHILE** | | | |
| ❑ AP-205 | Sandy Stewart Sings Songs of Jerome Kern | 1985 | 10.00 |
| *—Accompanied by Dick Hyman on piano* | | | |
| **COLPIX** | | | |
| ❑ CP-441 [M] | My Coloring Book | 1963 | 25.00 |
| ❑ SCP-441 [S] | My Coloring Book | 1963 | 30.00 |

### STEWART, SLAM

| Number | Title (A Side/B Side) | Yr | NM |
|---|---|---|---|
| **SAVOY** | | | |
| ❑ MG-12067 [M] | Bowin' Singin' Slam | 1956 | 40.00 |

### STEWART, SLY

| Number | Title (A Side/B Side) | Yr | NM |
|---|---|---|---|
| **SCULPTURE** | | | |
| ❑ SCP-2001 | San Francisco Recordings 1964-1967 | 197? | 20.00 |
| *—As "Sly Stone"* | | | |

### STEWART, TOM

| Number | Title (A Side/B Side) | Yr | NM |
|---|---|---|---|
| **ABC-PARAMOUNT** | | | |
| ❑ ABC-117 [M] | Tom Stewart Sextette/Quintet | 1956 | 50.00 |

### STEWART, WYNN

| Number | Title (A Side/B Side) | Yr | NM |
|---|---|---|---|
| **CAPITOL** | | | |
| ❑ ST-113 | In Love | 1969 | 20.00 |
| ❑ ST-214 | Let the Whole World Sing It with Me | 1969 | 20.00 |
| ❑ ST-324 | Yours Forever | 1969 | 20.00 |
| ❑ ST 2332 [S] | The Songs of Wynn Stewart | 1965 | 25.00 |
| ❑ T 2332 [M] | The Songs of Wynn Stewart | 1965 | 20.00 |
| ❑ ST 2737 [S] | It's Such a Pretty World Today | 1967 | 25.00 |
| ❑ T 2737 [M] | It's Such a Pretty World Today | 1967 | 20.00 |
| ❑ ST 2849 [S] | Love's Gonna Happen to Me | 1968 | 20.00 |
| ❑ T 2849 [M] | Love's Gonna Happen to Me | 1968 | 30.00 |
| ❑ ST 2921 | Something Pretty | 1968 | 20.00 |
| **HILLTOP** | | | |
| ❑ JM-6050 [M] | Above and Beyond the Call of Love | 1967 | 15.00 |
| ❑ JS-6050 [S] | Above and Beyond the Call of Love | 1967 | 12.00 |
| **PLAYBOY** | | | |
| ❑ PB 416 | After the Storm | 1976 | 10.00 |
| **WRANGLER** | | | |
| ❑ W-1006 [M] | Wynn Stewart | 1962 | 30.00 |
| ❑ W-31006 [S] | Wynn Stewart | 1962 | 40.00 |

### STEWART, WYNN, AND JAN HOWARD

| Number | Title (A Side/B Side) | Yr | NM |
|---|---|---|---|
| **CHALLENGE** | | | |
| ❑ CHL-611 [M] | Sweethearts of Country Music | 1961 | 50.00 |
| **STARDAY** | | | |
| ❑ SLP-421 | Wynn Stewart and Jan Howard Sing Their Hits | 1968 | 25.00 |

### STEWART FAMILY, THE

| Number | Title (A Side/B Side) | Yr | NM |
|---|---|---|---|
| **KING** | | | |
| ❑ 687 [M] | Country Sacred Songs | 1960 | 30.00 |
| ❑ 695 [M] | Golden Country Favorites | 1960 | 30.00 |

### STIDHAM, ARBEE

| Number | Title (A Side/B Side) | Yr | NM |
|---|---|---|---|
| **BLUESVILLE** | | | |
| ❑ BVLP-1021 [M] | Tired of Wandering | 1964 | 25.00 |
| *—Blue label, trident logo at right* | | | |
| **FOLKWAYS** | | | |
| ❑ F-31033 | There's Always Tomorrow | 1973 | 20.00 |

Sting, *The Soul Cages,* A&M 75021 6405 1, 1991, $12.

| Number | Title (A Side/B Side) | Yr | NM |
|---|---|---|---|
| **STIFF LITTLE FINGERS** | | | |
| CAROLINE | | | |
| ❑ 1377 | See You Up There | 1990 | 12.00 |
| CHRYSALIS | | | |
| ❑ CHR 1270 | Nobody's Heroes | 1980 | 20.00 |
| ❑ CHR 1300 | Hanx | 1980 | 20.00 |
| ❑ CHR 1339 | Go For It | 1981 | 20.00 |
| ROUGH TRADE | | | |
| ❑ ROUGH US 5 | Inflammable Material | 1980 | 25.00 |
| *—Released in U.K. in 1979* | | | |
| **STILLS, STEPHEN** | | | |
| ATLANTIC | | | |
| ❑ SD 2-903 [(2)] | Manassas | 1972 | 15.00 |
| ❑ SD 7202 | Stephen Stills | 1970 | 12.00 |
| ❑ SD 7206 | Stephen Stills 2 | 1971 | 12.00 |
| ❑ SD 7250 | Down the Road | 1973 | 12.00 |
| ❑ SD 18156 | Stephen Stills Live | 1975 | 12.00 |
| ❑ SD 18201 | Still Stills — The Best of Stephen Stills | 1976 | 10.00 |
| ❑ 80177 | Right By You | 1984 | 8.00 |
| COLUMBIA | | | |
| ❑ PC 33575 | Stills | 1975 | 10.00 |
| *—No bar code on cover* | | | |
| ❑ PC 33575 | Stills | 198? | 8.00 |
| *—Bar code on cover* | | | |
| ❑ PCQ 33575 [Q] | Stills | 1975 | 20.00 |
| ❑ PC 34348 | Illegal Stills | 1976 | 10.00 |
| ❑ JC 35380 | Thoroughfare Gap | 1978 | 10.00 |
| **STING** Also see THE POLICE. | | | |
| A&M | | | |
| ❑ SP-3295 [EP] | ...Nada Como El Sol | 1988 | 20.00 |
| *—Spanish versions of songs from "...Nothing Like the Sun"* | | | |
| ❑ SP-3750 | The Dream of the Blue Turtles | 1985 | 10.00 |
| ❑ SP-6402 [(2)] | ...Nothing Like the Sun | 1987 | 12.00 |
| ❑ 75021 6405-1 | The Soul Cages | 1991 | 12.00 |
| ❑ R 150266 | The Dream of the Blue Turtles | 1985 | 12.00 |
| *—RCA Music Service edition* | | | |
| ❑ R 273965 [(2)] | ...Nothing Like the Sun | 1987 | 14.00 |
| *—BMG Direct Marketing edition* | | | |
| MOBILE FIDELITY | | | |
| ❑ 1-185 | The Dream of the Blue Turtles | 1985 | 20.00 |
| *—Audiophile vinyl* | | | |

| Number | Title (A Side/B Side) | Yr | NM |
|---|---|---|---|
| **STINGERS, THE** | | | |
| CROWN | | | |
| ❑ CST-476 [S] | Guitars A Go Go | 196? | 40.00 |
| ❑ CLP-5476 [M] | Guitars A Go Go | 196? | 30.00 |
| **STINSON BROTHERS, THE** | | | |
| CANADIAN AMERICAN | | | |
| ❑ CALP-1012 [M] | The Stinson Brothers in Las Vegas | 196? | 20.00 |
| ❑ SCALP-1012 [S] | The Stinson Brothers in Las Vegas | 196? | 25.00 |
| **STITES, GARY** | | | |
| CARLTON | | | |
| ❑ LP-120 [M] | Lonely for You | 1960 | 80.00 |
| ❑ STLP-120 [S] | Lonely for You | 1960 | 120.00 |
| **STITT, SONNY** | | | |
| ARGO | | | |
| ❑ LP-629 [M] | Sonny Stitt | 1958 | 50.00 |
| ❑ LP-661 [M] | Burnin' | 1960 | 40.00 |
| ❑ LPS-661 [S] | Burnin' | 1960 | 50.00 |
| ❑ LP-683 [M] | Sonny Stitt at the D.J. Lounge | 1961 | 40.00 |
| ❑ LPS-683 [S] | Sonny Stitt at the D.J. Lounge | 1961 | 50.00 |
| ❑ LP-709 [M] | Rearin' Back | 1962 | 40.00 |
| ❑ LPS-709 [S] | Rearin' Back | 1962 | 50.00 |
| ❑ LP-730 [M] | Move On Over | 1964 | 40.00 |
| ❑ LPS-730 [S] | Move On Over | 1964 | 50.00 |
| ❑ LP-744 [M] | My Main Man | 1965 | 40.00 |
| ❑ LPS-744 [S] | My Main Man | 1965 | 50.00 |
| ATLANTIC | | | |
| ❑ 1395 [M] | Sonny Stitt and the Top Brass | 1962 | 25.00 |
| ❑ SD 1395 [S] | Sonny Stitt and the Top Brass | 1962 | 30.00 |
| ❑ 1418 [M] | Stitt Plays Bird | 1964 | 30.00 |
| ❑ SD 1418 [S] | Stitt Plays Bird | 1964 | 40.00 |
| CADET | | | |
| ❑ CA-629 [R] | Sonny Stitt | 197? | 10.00 |
| *—Yellow and pink label* | | | |
| ❑ CA-661 | Burnin' | 197? | 12.00 |
| *—Yellow and pink label* | | | |
| ❑ CA-683 | Sonny Stitt at the D.J. Lounge | 197? | 12.00 |
| *—Yellow and pink label* | | | |
| ❑ CA-709 | Rearin' Back | 197? | 12.00 |
| *—Yellow and pink label* | | | |

| Number | Title (A Side/B Side) | Yr | NM |
|---|---|---|---|
| ❑ LPS-760 [S] | Inter-Action | 1966 | 40.00 |
| *—Fading blue label* | | | |
| ❑ LPS-770 [S] | Soul In the Night | 1966 | 40.00 |
| *—Fading blue label* | | | |
| COLPIX | | | |
| ❑ CP-499 [M] | Broadway Soul | 1964 | 30.00 |
| ❑ SCP-499 [S] | Broadway Soul | 1964 | 40.00 |
| IMPULSE! | | | |
| ❑ A-43 [M] | Sonny Stitt Now! | 1963 | 50.00 |
| ❑ AS-43 [S] | Sonny Stitt Now! | 1963 | 60.00 |
| ❑ A-52 [M] | Salt and Pepper | 1964 | 40.00 |
| ❑ AS-52 [S] | Salt and Pepper | 1964 | 50.00 |
| *—With Paul Gonsalves* | | | |
| JAZZLAND | | | |
| ❑ JLP-71 [M] | Low Flame | 1962 | 40.00 |
| ❑ JLP-971 [S] | Low Flame | 1962 | 50.00 |
| JAZZTONE | | | |
| ❑ J-1231 [M] | Early Modern | 1956 | 80.00 |
| ❑ J-1263 [M] | Early Modern | 1957 | 60.00 |
| NEW JAZZ | | | |
| ❑ NJLP-103 [10] | Sonny Stitt and Bud Powell | 1950 | 500.00 |
| PACIFIC JAZZ | | | |
| ❑ PJ-71 [M] | My Mother's Eyes | 1963 | 80.00 |
| ❑ ST-71 [S] | My Mother's Eyes | 1963 | 80.00 |
| PRESTIGE | | | |
| ❑ PRLP-103 [10] | Sonny Stitt Plays | 1951 | 400.00 |
| ❑ PRLP-111 [10] | Mr. Saxophone | 1951 | 400.00 |
| ❑ PRLP-126 [10] | Favorites, Volume 1 | 1952 | 400.00 |
| ❑ PRLP-148 [10] | Favorites, Volume 2 | 1953 | 400.00 |
| ❑ PRLP-7024 [M] | Sonny Stitt with Bud Powell and J.J. Johnson | 1956 | 150.00 |
| ❑ PRLP-7077 [M] | Kaleidoscope | 1957 | 120.00 |
| *—Yellow label with W. 50th St address* | | | |
| ❑ PRLP-7133 [M] | Stitt's Bits | 1958 | 120.00 |
| ❑ PRLP-7244 [M] | Stitt Meets Brother Jack | 1962 | 80.00 |
| *—Yellow label with Bergenfield, N.J. address* | | | |
| ❑ PRLP-7244 [M] | Stitt Meets Brother Jack | 1964 | 40.00 |
| *—Blue label with trident logo* | | | |
| ❑ PRST-7244 [S] | Stitt Meets Brother Jack | 1962 | 70.00 |
| ❑ PRLP-7248 [M] | All God's Chillun Got Rhythm | 1962 | 80.00 |
| *—Yellow label with Bergenfield, N.J. address* | | | |
| ❑ PRLP-7248 [M] | All God's Chillun Got Rhythm | 1964 | 40.00 |
| *—Blue label with trident logo* | | | |
| ❑ PRST-7248 [R] | All God's Chillun Got Rhythm | 1962 | 30.00 |
| ❑ PRLP-7297 [M] | Soul Shack | 1964 | 80.00 |
| *—Yellow label with Bergenfield, N.J. address* | | | |
| ❑ PRLP-7297 [M] | Soul Shack | 1965 | 40.00 |
| *—Blue label with trident logo* | | | |
| ❑ PRST-7297 [S] | Soul Shack | 1964 | 70.00 |
| *—Silver label with Bergenfield, N.J. address* | | | |
| ❑ PRST-7297 [S] | Soul Shack | 1965 | 40.00 |
| *—Blue label with trident logo* | | | |
| ❑ PRLP-7302 [M] | Primitive Soul! | 1964 | 80.00 |
| *—Yellow label with Bergenfield, N.J. address* | | | |
| ❑ PRLP-7302 [M] | Primitive Soul! | 1965 | 40.00 |
| *—Blue label with trident logo* | | | |
| ❑ PRST-7302 [S] | Primitive Soul! | 1964 | 70.00 |
| *—Silver label* | | | |
| ❑ PRST-7302 [S] | Primitive Soul! | 1965 | 40.00 |
| *—Blue label with trident logo* | | | |
| ❑ PRLP-7332 [M] | Shangri-La | 1964 | 40.00 |
| *—Blue label, trident logo at right* | | | |
| ❑ PRST-7332 [S] | Shangri-La | 1964 | 50.00 |
| *—Blue label, trident logo at right* | | | |
| ❑ PRLP-7372 [M] | Soul People | 1965 | 40.00 |
| *—Blue label, trident logo at right* | | | |
| ❑ PRST-7372 [S] | Soul People | 1965 | 50.00 |
| *—Blue label, trident logo at right* | | | |
| ❑ PRST-7372 [S] | Soul People | 197? | 25.00 |
| *—Green label* | | | |
| ❑ PRLP-7436 [M] | Night Crawler | 1966 | 40.00 |
| *—Blue label, trident logo at right* | | | |
| ❑ PRST-7436 [S] | Night Crawler | 1966 | 50.00 |
| *—Blue label, trident logo at right* | | | |
| ❑ PRLP-7452 [M] | 'Nuther Fu'ther | 1966 | 40.00 |
| *—Blue label, trident logo at right* | | | |
| ❑ PRST-7452 [S] | 'Nuther Fu'ther | 1966 | 50.00 |
| *—Blue label, trident logo at right* | | | |
| ❑ PRST-7452 [S] | 'Nuther Fu'ther | 197? | 25.00 |
| *—Green label* | | | |
| ❑ PRLP-7459 [M] | Pow! | 1967 | 50.00 |
| *—Blue label, trident logo at right* | | | |
| ❑ PRST-7459 [S] | Pow! | 1967 | 40.00 |
| *—Blue label, trident logo at right* | | | |
| ROOST | | | |
| ❑ LP-415 [10] | Sonny Stitt Plays Arrangements from the Pen of Johnny Richards | 1952 | 400.00 |
| ❑ LP-418 [10] | Jazz at the Hi-Hat | 1954 | 400.00 |
| ❑ LP-1203 [M] | Battle of Birdland | 1955 | 120.00 |
| ❑ LP-1208 [M] | Sonny Stitt | 1956 | 120.00 |
| ❑ LP-2204 [M] | Sonny Stitt Plays Arrangements of Quincy Jones | 1957 | 150.00 |
| ❑ LP-2208 [M] | Sonny Stitt | 1957 | 120.00 |
| ❑ LP-2219 [M] | 37 Minutes and 48 Seconds with Sonny Stitt | 1957 | 80.00 |
| ❑ LP-2226 [M] | Sonny Stitt with the New Yorkers | 1958 | 80.00 |

| Number | Title (A Side/B Side) | Yr | NM |
|---|---|---|---|
| ❑ LP-2230 [M] | The Saxophone of Sonny Stitt | 1959 | 70.00 |
| ❑ SLP-2230 [S] | The Saxophone of Sonny Stitt | 1959 | 60.00 |
| ❑ LP-2235 [M] | A Little Bit of Stitt | 1959 | 70.00 |
| ❑ SLP-2235 [S] | A Little Bit of Stitt | 1959 | 60.00 |
| ❑ LP-2240 [M] | The Sonny Side of Stitt | 1960 | 70.00 |
| ❑ SLP-2240 [S] | The Sonny Side of Stitt | 1960 | 60.00 |
| ❑ LP-2244 [M] | Stittsville | 1960 | 70.00 |
| ❑ SLP-2244 [S] | Stittsville | 1960 | 80.00 |
| ❑ LP-2245 [M] | Sonny Side Up | 1960 | 80.00 |
| ❑ SLP-2245 [S] | Sonny Side Up | 1960 | 80.00 |
| ❑ LP-2247 [M] | Feelin's | 1962 | 60.00 |
| ❑ SLP-2247 [S] | Feelin's | 1962 | 60.00 |
| ❑ LP-2252 [M] | Sonny Stitt in Orbit | 1963 | 50.00 |
| ❑ SLP-2252 [S] | Sonny Stitt in Orbit | 1963 | 50.00 |
| ❑ LP-2253 [M] | Sonny Stitt Goes Latin | 1963 | 50.00 |
| ❑ SLP-2253 [S] | Sonny Stitt Goes Latin | 1963 | 50.00 |

ROULETTE

| Number | Title (A Side/B Side) | Yr | NM |
|---|---|---|---|
| ❑ R-25339 [M] | The Matadors Meet the Bull | 1965 | 40.00 |
| ❑ SR-25339 [S] | The Matadors Meet the Bull | 1965 | 50.00 |
| ❑ R-25343 [M] | What's New? | 1966 | 30.00 |
| ❑ SR-25343 [S] | What's New? | 1966 | 40.00 |
| ❑ R-25348 [M] | I Keep Comin' Back | 1967 | 40.00 |
| ❑ SR-25348 [S] | I Keep Comin' Back | 1967 | 30.00 |

SAVOY

| Number | Title (A Side/B Side) | Yr | NM |
|---|---|---|---|
| ❑ MG-9006 [10] | All Star Series: Sonny Stitt | 1953 | 300.00 |
| ❑ MG-9012 [10] | New Sounds in Modern Music | 1953 | 300.00 |
| ❑ MG-9014 [10] | New Trends Of Jazz | 1953 | 300.00 |

VERVE

| Number | Title (A Side/B Side) | Yr | NM |
|---|---|---|---|
| ❑ MGVS-6038 [S] | The Hard Swing | 1960 | 40.00 |
| ❑ MGVS-6041 [S] | Sonny Stitt Plays Jimmy Giuffre Arrangements | 1960 | 40.00 |
| ❑ MGVS-6108 [S] | Sonny Stitt Sits In with the Oscar Peterson Trio | 1960 | 40.00 |
| ❑ MGVS-6149 | Sonny Stitt Blows the Blues | 1996 | 40.00 |
| *—Audiophile reissue by Classic Records* | | | |
| ❑ MGVS-6149 [S] | Sonny Stitt Blows the Blues | 1960 | 40.00 |
| ❑ MGVS-6149-45 [(4)] | Sonny Stitt Blows the Blues | 1999 | 40.00 |
| *—Audiophile reissue by Classic Records; plays at 45 rpm* | | | |
| ❑ MGV-8219 [M] | New York Jazz | 1957 | 50.00 |
| ❑ V-8219 [M] | New York Jazz | 1961 | 25.00 |
| ❑ MGV-8250 [M] | Only the Blues | 1958 | 50.00 |
| ❑ V-8250 [M] | Only the Blues | 1961 | 25.00 |
| ❑ MGV-8262 [M] | Sonny Side Up | 1958 | 60.00 |
| ❑ V-8262 [M] | Sonny Side Up | 1961 | 30.00 |
| ❑ MGV-8306 [M] | The Hard Swing | 1959 | 50.00 |
| ❑ V-8306 [M] | The Hard Swing | 1961 | 25.00 |
| ❑ V6-8306 [S] | The Hard Swing | 1961 | 20.00 |
| ❑ MGV-8309 [M] | Sonny Stitt Plays Jimmy Giuffre Arrangements | 1959 | 50.00 |
| ❑ V-8309 [M] | Sonny Stitt Plays Jimmy Giuffre Arrangements | 1961 | 25.00 |
| ❑ V6-8309 [S] | Sonny Stitt Plays Jimmy Giuffre Arrangements | 1961 | 20.00 |
| ❑ MGV-8324 [M] | Personal Appearance | 1959 | 50.00 |
| ❑ V-8324 [M] | Personal Appearance | 1961 | 25.00 |
| ❑ MGV-8344 [M] | Sonny Stitt Sits In with the Oscar Peterson Trio | 1959 | 50.00 |
| ❑ V-8344 [M] | Sonny Stitt Sits In with the Oscar Peterson Trio | 1961 | 25.00 |
| ❑ V6-8344 [S] | Sonny Stitt Sits In with the Oscar Peterson Trio | 1961 | 20.00 |
| ❑ MGV-8374 [M] | Sonny Stitt Blows the Blues | 1960 | 50.00 |
| ❑ V-8374 [M] | Sonny Stitt Blows the Blues | 1961 | 25.00 |
| ❑ V6-8374 [S] | Sonny Stitt Blows the Blues | 1961 | 20.00 |
| ❑ MGV-8377 [M] | Saxophone Supremacy | 1960 | 50.00 |
| ❑ V-8377 [M] | Saxophone Supremacy | 1961 | 25.00 |
| ❑ MGV-8380 [M] | Sonny Stitt Swings the Most | 1960 | 50.00 |
| ❑ V-8380 [M] | Sommy Stitt Swings the Most | 1961 | 25.00 |
| ❑ V-8451 [M] | The Sensual Sound of Sonny Stitt | 1962 | 20.00 |
| ❑ V6-8451 [S] | The Sensual Sound of Sonny Stitt | 1962 | 25.00 |

**STITT, SONNY, AND GENE AMMONS** See GENE AMMONS AND SONNY STITT.

**STOECKLEIN, VAL**

DOT

| Number | Title (A Side/B Side) | Yr | NM |
|---|---|---|---|
| ❑ DLP-3904 [M] | Grey Life | 1968 | 100.00 |
| *—Label is black, as if stock copy, but record is found inside stereo (25904) cover with "Monaural Promotion Not for Sale" sticker on front* | | | |
| ❑ DLP-25904 [S] | Grey Life | 1968 | 40.00 |

**STOKOWSKI, LEOPOLD**

RCA VICTOR RED SEAL

| Number | Title (A Side/B Side) | Yr | NM |
|---|---|---|---|
| ❑ LSC-2593 [S] | Inspiration | 1962 | 20.00 |
| *—Original with "shaded dog" label* | | | |

**STOLOFF, MORRIS**

DECCA

| Number | Title (A Side/B Side) | Yr | NM |
|---|---|---|---|
| ❑ DL 8574 [M] | This Is Kim | 1957 | 60.00 |
| *—Black label, silver print; Kim Novak is the cover model* | | | |

**STONE, ANGIE**

J

| Number | Title (A Side/B Side) | Yr | NM |
|---|---|---|---|
| ❑ 80813-20013-1 [(2)] | Mahogany Soul | 2001 | 30.00 |
| ❑ 82876-56215-1 [(2)] | Stone Love | 2004 | 15.00 |

**STONE, CLIFFIE**

CAPITOL

| Number | Title (A Side/B Side) | Yr | NM |
|---|---|---|---|
| ❑ T 1080 [M] | The Party's on Me | 1958 | 40.00 |
| ❑ ST 1230 [S] | Cool Cowboy | 1959 | 40.00 |
| ❑ T 1230 [M] | Cool Cowboy | 1959 | 30.00 |
| ❑ ST 1286 [S] | Square Dance Promenade | 1960 | 40.00 |
| ❑ T 1286 [M] | Square Dance Promenade | 1960 | 30.00 |
| ❑ KAO 1555 [M] | Original Cowboy Sing-A-Long | 1961 | 30.00 |
| ❑ SKAO 1555 [S] | Original Cowboy Sing-A-Long | 1961 | 40.00 |
| ❑ ST 1685 [S] | It's Fun to Square Dance | 1962 | 25.00 |
| ❑ T 1685 [M] | It's Fun to Square Dance | 1962 | 20.00 |
| ❑ H 4009 [10] | Square Dances | 195? | 60.00 |

TOWER

| Number | Title (A Side/B Side) | Yr | NM |
|---|---|---|---|
| ❑ ST 5073 [S] | Together Again | 1967 | 30.00 |
| ❑ T 5073 [M] | Together Again | 1967 | 25.00 |

**STONE, KIRBY, FOUR**

CADENCE

| Number | Title (A Side/B Side) | Yr | NM |
|---|---|---|---|
| ❑ CLP 1023 [M] | Man I Flipped | 1958 | 25.00 |

COLUMBIA

| Number | Title (A Side/B Side) | Yr | NM |
|---|---|---|---|
| ❑ CL 1211 [M] | Baubles, Bangles and Beads | 1959 | 20.00 |
| ❑ CL 1290 [M] | The "Go" Sound of the Kirby Stone Four | 1959 | 20.00 |
| ❑ CL 1356 [M] | The Kirby Stone Touch | 1959 | 20.00 |
| ❑ CL 1646 [M] | The Kirby Stone Four at the Playboy Club | 1960 | 20.00 |
| ❑ CL 1714 [M] | Guys and Dolls | 1961 | 20.00 |
| ❑ CS 8014 [S] | Baubles, Bangles and Beads | 1959 | 25.00 |
| ❑ CS 8130 [S] | The "Go" Sound of the Kirby Stone Four | 1959 | 25.00 |
| ❑ CS 8164 [S] | The Kirby Stone Touch | 1959 | 25.00 |
| ❑ CS 8446 [S] | The Kirby Stone Four at the Playboy Club | 1960 | 25.00 |
| ❑ CS 8514 [S] | Guys and Dolls | 1961 | 25.00 |

TOPS

| Number | Title (A Side/B Side) | Yr | NM |
|---|---|---|---|
| ❑ L-1582 [M] | The Kirby Stone Four | 1957 | 30.00 |

**STONE, ROLAND**

ACE

| Number | Title (A Side/B Side) | Yr | NM |
|---|---|---|---|
| ❑ LP-1018 [M] | Just a Moment | 1961 | 150.00 |

**STONE CIRCUS, THE**

MAINSTREAM

| Number | Title (A Side/B Side) | Yr | NM |
|---|---|---|---|
| ❑ S-6119 | The Stone Circus | 1969 | 80.00 |

**STONE COUNTRY**

RCA VICTOR

| Number | Title (A Side/B Side) | Yr | NM |
|---|---|---|---|
| ❑ LSP-3958 | Stone Country | 1968 | 20.00 |

**STONE HARBOUR**

STONE HARBOUR

| Number | Title (A Side/B Side) | Yr | NM |
|---|---|---|---|
| ❑ 398 | Stone Harbour Emerges | 197? | 500.00 |

**STONE PONEYS** Also see LINDA RONSTADT.

CAPITOL

| Number | Title (A Side/B Side) | Yr | NM |
|---|---|---|---|
| ❑ ST 2666 [S] | The Stone Poneys | 1967 | 30.00 |
| ❑ T 2666 [M] | The Stone Poneys | 1967 | 25.00 |
| ❑ ST 2763 [S] | Evergreen, Vol. 2 | 1967 | 30.00 |
| ❑ T 2763 [M] | Evergreen, Vol. 2 | 1967 | 40.00 |
| ❑ ST 2863 | Linda Ronstadt/Stone Poneys and Friends Vol. III | 1968 | 50.00 |
| ❑ ST-11383 | The Stone Poneys Featuring Linda Ronstadt | 1974 | 10.00 |

PICKWICK

| Number | Title (A Side/B Side) | Yr | NM |
|---|---|---|---|
| ❑ SPC-3298 | Stoney End | 1976 | 12.00 |

**STONE TEMPLE PILOTS** Also see VELVET REVOLVER.

ATLANTIC

| Number | Title (A Side/B Side) | Yr | NM |
|---|---|---|---|
| ❑ 82607 | Purple | 1994 | 15.00 |
| ❑ 82871 | Tiny Music — Music from the Vatican Gift Shop | 1996 | 20.00 |

**STONE THE CROWS**

POLYDOR

| Number | Title (A Side/B Side) | Yr | NM |
|---|---|---|---|
| ❑ 24-4019 | Stone the Crows | 1970 | 20.00 |
| ❑ PD-5020 | Teenage Licks | 1972 | 20.00 |
| ❑ PD-5037 | Continuous Performance | 1972 | 20.00 |

**STONEGROUND**

WARNER BROS.

| Number | Title (A Side/B Side) | Yr | NM |
|---|---|---|---|
| ❑ WS 1895 | Stoneground | 1971 | 15.00 |
| ❑ 2WS 1956 [(2)] | Family Album | 1971 | 20.00 |
| ❑ BS 2645 | Stoneground 3 | 1972 | 15.00 |

**STONEHILL, RANDY**

ONE WAY

| Number | Title (A Side/B Side) | Yr | NM |
|---|---|---|---|
| ❑ JC-31252 | Born Twice | 1972 | 60.00 |

**STONEMANS, THE**

MGM

| Number | Title (A Side/B Side) | Yr | NM |
|---|---|---|---|
| ❑ GAS-124 | The Stonemans (Golden Archive Series) | 1970 | 15.00 |
| ❑ E-4363 [M] | Those Singin' Swingin' Stompin' Sensational Stonemans | 1966 | 20.00 |
| ❑ SE-4363 [S] | Those Singin' Swingin' Stompin' Sensational Stonemans | 1966 | 25.00 |
| ❑ E-4453 [M] | Stoneman's Country | 1967 | 20.00 |
| ❑ SE-4453 [S] | Stoneman's Country | 1967 | 25.00 |
| ❑ E-4511 [M] | All in the Family | 1968 | 25.00 |
| ❑ SE-4511 [S] | All in the Family | 1968 | 20.00 |
| ❑ SE-4578 | The Great Stonemans | 1968 | 20.00 |
| ❑ SE-4613 | A Stoneman Christmas | 1968 | 20.00 |

RCA VICTOR

| Number | Title (A Side/B Side) | Yr | NM |
|---|---|---|---|
| ❑ LSP-4264 | Dawn of the Stonemans' Age | 1970 | 15.00 |
| ❑ LSP-4343 | In All Honesty | 1970 | 15.00 |
| ❑ LSP-4431 | California Blues | 1970 | 15.00 |

STARDAY

| Number | Title (A Side/B Side) | Yr | NM |
|---|---|---|---|
| ❑ SLP-393 [M] | White Lightning | 1965 | 40.00 |

WORLD PACIFIC

| Number | Title (A Side/B Side) | Yr | NM |
|---|---|---|---|
| ❑ ST-1828 [S] | Big Ball in Monterey | 1964 | 40.00 |
| ❑ WP-1828 [M] | Big Ball in Monterey | 1964 | 30.00 |

**STONEY AND MEATLOAF** Also see MEAT LOAF.

PRODIGAL

| Number | Title (A Side/B Side) | Yr | NM |
|---|---|---|---|
| ❑ 10 | Stoney and Meatloaf | 1978 | 12.00 |

RARE EARTH

| Number | Title (A Side/B Side) | Yr | NM |
|---|---|---|---|
| ❑ R 528 | Stoney and Meatloaf | 1971 | 20.00 |

**STOOGES, THE** See IGGY AND THE STOOGES.

**STORIES**

KAMA SUTRA

| Number | Title (A Side/B Side) | Yr | NM |
|---|---|---|---|
| ❑ KSBS-2051 | Stories | 1972 | 12.00 |
| ❑ KSBS-2068 | About Us | 1973 | 12.00 |
| *—Regular cover; "Brother Louie" added as the last song on side 2* | | | |
| ❑ KSBS-2068 | About Us | 1973 | 15.00 |
| *—Gatefold cover; "Brother Louie" added as the last song on side 2* | | | |
| ❑ KSBS-2068 | About Us | 1973 | 30.00 |
| *—Gatefold; does NOT contain "Brother Louie"* | | | |
| ❑ KSBS-2078 | Traveling Underground | 1974 | 12.00 |

**STORM, BILLY**

BUENA VISTA

| Number | Title (A Side/B Side) | Yr | NM |
|---|---|---|---|
| ❑ BV-3315 [M] | Billy Storm | 1963 | 100.00 |
| ❑ STER-3315 [S] | Billy Storm | 1963 | 120.00 |

FAMOUS

| Number | Title (A Side/B Side) | Yr | NM |
|---|---|---|---|
| ❑ F-504 | This Is the Night | 1969 | 100.00 |

**STORM, GALE**

DOT

| Number | Title (A Side/B Side) | Yr | NM |
|---|---|---|---|
| ❑ DLP-3011 [M] | Gale Storm | 1956 | 50.00 |
| ❑ DLP-3017 [M] | Sentimental Me | 1956 | 50.00 |
| ❑ DLP-3098 [M] | Gale Storm Hits | 1958 | 40.00 |
| ❑ DLP-3197 [M] | Softly and Tenderly | 1959 | 30.00 |
| ❑ DLP-3209 [M] | Gale Storm Sings | 1959 | 30.00 |
| ❑ DLP-25197 [S] | Softly and Tenderly | 1959 | 40.00 |
| ❑ DLP-25209 [S] | Gale Storm Sings | 1959 | 40.00 |

HAMILTON

| Number | Title (A Side/B Side) | Yr | NM |
|---|---|---|---|
| ❑ HLP-171 [M] | I Don't Want to Walk | 1966 | 12.00 |
| ❑ HLP-12171 [S] | I Don't Want to Walk | 1966 | 15.00 |

MCA

| Number | Title (A Side/B Side) | Yr | NM |
|---|---|---|---|
| ❑ 1504 | Gale Storm | 198? | 10.00 |

**STORY, CARL**

MERCURY

| Number | Title (A Side/B Side) | Yr | NM |
|---|---|---|---|
| ❑ MG-20323 [M] | Gospel Quartet Favorites | 1958 | 40.00 |
| ❑ MG-20584 [M] | More Gospel Quartet Favorites | 1961 | 30.00 |
| ❑ SR-60584 [S] | More Gospel Quartet Favorites | 1961 | 40.00 |

STARDAY

| Number | Title (A Side/B Side) | Yr | NM |
|---|---|---|---|
| ❑ SLP-107 [M] | America's Favorite Country Gospel Artist | 1959 | 50.00 |
| ❑ SLP-127 [M] | Gospel Revival | 1961 | 40.00 |
| ❑ SLP-137 [M] | All Day Singing with Dinner on the Ground | 1961 | 40.00 |
| ❑ SLP-152 [M] | Get Religion | 1962 | 40.00 |
| ❑ SLP-219 [M] | Mighty Close to Heaven | 1963 | 40.00 |
| ❑ SLP-278 [M] | All Day Sacred Singing | 1964 | 40.00 |
| ❑ SLP-315 [M] | Sacred Songs of Life and the Hereafter | 1965 | 40.00 |
| ❑ SLP-348 [M] | There's Nothing on Earth (That Heaven Can't Cure) | 1965 | 40.00 |
| ❑ SLP-411 [M] | My Lord Keeps a Record | 1968 | 30.00 |

**STORYVILLE STOMPERS, THE**

TROPICANA

| Number | Title (A Side/B Side) | Yr | NM |
|---|---|---|---|
| ❑ 1204 [M] | New Orleans Jazz | 195? | 40.00 |

**STOVER, SMOKEY**

ARGO

| Number | Title (A Side/B Side) | Yr | NM |
|---|---|---|---|
| ❑ LP-652 [DJ] | Smokey Stover's Original Firemen | 1960 | 60.00 |
| *—White label, multi-color vinyl* | | | |
| ❑ LP-652 [M] | Smokey Stover's Original Firemen | 1960 | 25.00 |
| ❑ LPS-652 [S] | Smokey Stover's Original Firemen | 1960 | 30.00 |

**STOWAWAYS, THE**

JUSTICE

| Number | Title (A Side/B Side) | Yr | NM |
|---|---|---|---|
| ❑ JLP-148 | The Stowaways | 1968 | 500.00 |

Strawberry Alarm Clock, *The World in a Sea Shell,* Uni 73035, 1968, $40.

| Number | Title (A Side/B Side) | Yr | NM |
|---|---|---|---|
| **STRADIVARI STRINGS, THE** | | | |
| SPIN-O-RAMA | | | |
| ❑ 590 [M] | String Along with Me | 196? | 30.00 |
| ❑ S-590 [S] | String Along with Me | 196? | 40.00 |
| *—Cover model on the above LP is Jayne Mansfield* | | | |
| **STRAIT, GEORGE** | | | |
| HEARTLAND | | | |
| ❑ HL 1172/3 [(2)] | The Very Best of George Strait | 1991 | 15.00 |
| MCA | | | |
| ❑ 5248 | Strait Country | 1981 | 10.00 |
| ❑ 5320 | Strait from the Heart | 1982 | 10.00 |
| ❑ 5450 | Right or Wrong | 1983 | 10.00 |
| ❑ 5518 | Does Fort Worth Ever Cross Your Mind | 1984 | 10.00 |
| ❑ 5567 | Greatest Hits | 1985 | 10.00 |
| ❑ 5605 | Something Special | 1985 | 10.00 |
| ❑ 5750 | #7 | 1986 | 10.00 |
| ❑ 5800 | Merry Christmas Strait to You | 1986 | 10.00 |
| ❑ 5913 | Ocean Front Property | 1987 | 10.00 |
| ❑ 6415 | Livin' It Up | 1990 | 12.00 |
| ❑ 10450 | Ten Strait Hits | 1992 | 20.00 |
| *—Only available on vinyl through Columbia House* | | | |
| ❑ 10532 | Holding My Own | 1992 | 20.00 |
| *—Only available on vinyl through Columbia House* | | | |
| ❑ 27092 | Strait Country | 1984 | 8.00 |
| *—Reissue of 5248* | | | |
| ❑ 42035 | Greatest Hits, Volume Two | 1987 | 8.00 |
| ❑ 42114 | If You Ain't Lovin' You Ain't Livin' | 1988 | 8.00 |
| ❑ 42266 | Beyond the Blue Neon | 1989 | 8.00 |
| ❑ R 134172 | Merry Christmas Strait to You | 1986 | 12.00 |
| *—BMG Direct Marketing version* | | | |
| ❑ R 153641 | Chill of an Early Fall | 1991 | 20.00 |
| *—Only released on vinyl through BMG Direct Marketing* | | | |
| **STRAND, LES** | | | |
| FANTASY | | | |
| ❑ 3231 [M] | Les Strand on the Baldwin Organ | 195? | 20.00 |
| *—Black vinyl* | | | |
| ❑ 3231 [M] | Les Strand on the Baldwin Organ | 1956 | 50.00 |
| *—Red vinyl* | | | |
| ❑ 3242 [M] | Jazz Classics on the Baldwin Organ | 195? | 20.00 |
| *—Black vinyl* | | | |
| ❑ 3242 [M] | Jazz Classics on the Baldwin Organ | 1956 | 50.00 |
| *—Red vinyl* | | | |
| **STRANGE** | | | |
| OUTER GALAXIE | | | |
| ❑ 1000 | Translucent World | 1973 | 100.00 |
| ❑ 1001 | Raw Power | 1976 | 100.00 |
| **STRANGE, BILLY** | | | |
| CHESS | | | |
| ❑ CH2-6027 [(2)] | One More Time | 1988 | 12.00 |
| COLISEUM | | | |
| ❑ CM-1001 [M] | Limbo Rock | 1962 | 40.00 |
| GNP CRESCENDO | | | |
| ❑ GNP-94 [M] | Twelve String Guitar | 1963 | 12.00 |
| ❑ GNPS-94 [S] | Twelve String Guitar | 1963 | 15.00 |
| ❑ GNP-97 [M] | Mr. Guitar | 1963 | 12.00 |
| ❑ GNPS-97 [S] | Mr. Guitar | 1963 | 15.00 |
| ❑ GNP-98 [M] | Five String Banjo | 1964 | 12.00 |
| ❑ GNPS-98 [S] | Five String Banjo | 1964 | 15.00 |
| ❑ GNP-2004 [M] | The James Bond Theme | 1964 | 12.00 |
| ❑ GNPS-2004 [S] | The James Bond Theme | 1964 | 15.00 |
| ❑ GNP-2006 [M] | Goldfinger | 1965 | 12.00 |
| ❑ GNPS-2006 [S] | Goldfinger | 1965 | 15.00 |
| ❑ GNP-2009 [M] | English Hits of '65 | 1965 | 12.00 |
| ❑ GNPS-2009 [S] | English Hits of '65 | 1965 | 15.00 |
| ❑ GNP-2012 [M] | Billy Strange Plays the Hits | 1965 | 12.00 |
| ❑ GNPS-2012 [S] | Billy Strange Plays the Hits | 1965 | 15.00 |
| ❑ GNP-2016 [M] | Folk Rock Hits | 1965 | 12.00 |
| ❑ GNPS-2016 [S] | Folk Rock Hits | 1965 | 15.00 |
| ❑ GNP-2019 [M] | Secret Agent File | 1966 | 12.00 |
| ❑ GNPS-2019 [S] | Secret Agent File | 1966 | 15.00 |
| ❑ GNP-2022 [M] | In the Mexican Bag | 1966 | 12.00 |
| ❑ GNPS-2022 [S] | In the Mexican Bag | 1966 | 15.00 |
| ❑ GNP-2024 [M] | Billy Strange Plays Roger Miller Hits | 1966 | 12.00 |
| ❑ GNPS-2024 [S] | Billy Strange Plays Roger Miller Hits | 1966 | 15.00 |
| ❑ GNP-2030 [M] | Billy Strange with the Challengers | 1966 | 15.00 |
| ❑ GNPS-2030 [S] | Billy Strange with the Challengers | 1966 | 20.00 |
| ❑ GNP-2037 [M] | The Best of Billy Strange | 1967 | 12.00 |
| ❑ GNPS-2037 [S] | The Best of Billy Strange | 1967 | 12.00 |
| ❑ GNPS-2039 | A James Bond Double Feature | 1967 | 12.00 |
| ❑ GNPS-2041 | Railroad Man | 1968 | 12.00 |
| ❑ GNPS-2046 | Great Western Themes | 1969 | 12.00 |
| ❑ GNPS-2094 | Dyn-o-mite Guitar | 197? | 10.00 |
| SUNSET | | | |
| ❑ SUS-5209 | Mr. Guitar | 1968 | 10.00 |
| SURREY | | | |
| ❑ SS-1002 | The Best of Billy Strange | 1965 | 15.00 |
| TRADITION | | | |
| ❑ 2080 | Strange Country | 1969 | 10.00 |
| **STRANGEBREW** | | | |
| ABC | | | |
| ❑ ABCS-672 | Very Strangebrew | 1969 | 20.00 |
| **STRANGELOVES, THE** | | | |
| BANG | | | |
| ❑ BLP-211 [M] | I Want Candy | 1965 | 80.00 |
| ❑ BLPS-211 [S] | I Want Candy | 1965 | 100.00 |
| **STRANGERS, THE** | | | |
| CAPITOL | | | |
| ❑ ST-169 | Instrumental Sounds of Merle Haggard's Strangers | 1969 | 20.00 |
| ❑ ST-445 | Introducing My Friends the Strangers | 1970 | 20.00 |
| ❑ ST-590 | Getting to Know Merle Haggard's Strangers | 1970 | 20.00 |
| ❑ ST-796 | Honky Tonkin' | 1971 | 20.00 |
| ❑ ST-11141 | Totally Instrumental with One Exception... | 1973 | 15.00 |
| **STRATAVARIOUS** | | | |
| ROULETTE | | | |
| ❑ RS 3019 | Stratavarious | 1976 | 25.00 |
| **STRATTON, DON** | | | |
| ABC-PARAMOUNT | | | |
| ❑ ABC-118 [M] | Modern Jazz with Dixieland Roots | 1956 | 40.00 |
| **STRAWBERRY ALARM CLOCK** | | | |
| UNI | | | |
| ❑ 3014 [M] | Incense and Peppermints | 1967 | 50.00 |
| ❑ 73014 [S] | Incense and Peppermints | 1967 | 40.00 |
| ❑ 73025 | Wake Up It's Tomorrow | 1968 | 40.00 |
| ❑ 73035 | The World in a Sea Shell | 1968 | 40.00 |
| ❑ 73054 | Good Morning Starshine | 1969 | 40.00 |
| ❑ 73074 | The Best of the Strawberry Alarm Clock | 1970 | 40.00 |
| VOCALION | | | |
| ❑ VL 73915 | Changes | 1971 | 50.00 |
| **STRAYHORN, BILLY** | | | |
| FELSTED | | | |
| ❑ 2008 [S] | Billy Strayhorn Septet | 1958 | 60.00 |
| ❑ 7008 [M] | Billy Strayhorn Septet | 1958 | 80.00 |
| MERCER | | | |
| ❑ LP-1001 [10] | Billy Strayhorn Trio | 1951 | 200.00 |
| ❑ LP-1005 [10] | Billy Strayhorn and All-Stars | 1951 | 200.00 |
| ROULETTE | | | |
| ❑ R-52119 [M] | Live! | 1965 | 20.00 |
| ❑ SR-52119 [S] | Live! | 1965 | 25.00 |
| UNITED ARTISTS | | | |
| ❑ UAJ-14010 [M] | The Peaceful Side of Billy Strayhorn | 1962 | 40.00 |
| ❑ UAJS-15010 [S] | The Peaceful Side of Billy Strayhorn | 1962 | 50.00 |
| **STRAZZERI, FRANK** | | | |
| REVELATION | | | |
| ❑ REV-10 | That's Him and This Is New | 1969 | 25.00 |
| **STREET NOISE** | | | |
| EVOLUTION | | | |
| ❑ 2010 | Street Noise | 1970 | 20.00 |
| **STREET PEOPLE** | | | |
| MUSICOR | | | |
| ❑ MS-3189 | Jennifer Tomkins | 1970 | 20.00 |
| **STREET PLAYERS** | | | |
| ARIOLA AMERICA | | | |
| ❑ SW-50071 | Dancin' Fever | 1979 | 20.00 |
| **STREISAND, BARBRA** | | | |
| COLUMBIA | | | |
| ❑ A2S 1779 [(2)DJ] | The Legend of Barbra Streisand | 1983 | 80.00 |
| *—Promo-only interview LP for "Yentl"* | | | |
| ❑ CL 2007 [M] | The Barbra Streisand Album | 1963 | 20.00 |
| *—"Guaranteed High Fidelity" on label* | | | |

| Number | Title (A Side/B Side) | Yr | NM |
|---|---|---|---|
| ❑ CL 2007 [M] | The Barbra Streisand Album | 1966 | 12.00 |
| *—"360 Sound Mono" on label* | | | |
| ❑ CL 2054 [M] | The Second Barbra Streisand Album | 1963 | 20.00 |
| *—"Guaranteed High Fidelity" on label* | | | |
| ❑ CL 2054 [M] | The Second Barbra Streisand Album | 1963 | 200.00 |
| *—Promo only on blue vinyl (white label)* | | | |
| ❑ CL 2054 [M] | The Second Barbra Streisand Album | 1966 | 12.00 |
| *—"360 Sound Mono" on label* | | | |
| ❑ CL 2154 [M] | The Third Album | 1964 | 20.00 |
| *—"Guaranteed High Fidelity" on label* | | | |
| ❑ CL 2154 [M] | The Third Album | 1966 | 12.00 |
| *—"360 Sound Mono" on label* | | | |
| ❑ CL 2215 [M] | People | 1964 | 20.00 |
| *—"Guaranteed High Fidelity" on label* | | | |
| ❑ CL 2215 [M] | People | 1966 | 12.00 |
| *—"360 Sound Mono" on label* | | | |
| ❑ CL 2336 [M] | My Name Is Barbra | 1965 | 20.00 |
| *—"Guaranteed High Fidelity" on label* | | | |
| ❑ CL 2336 [M] | My Name Is Barbra | 1966 | 12.00 |
| *—"360 Sound Mono" on label* | | | |
| ❑ CL 2409 [M] | My Name Is Barbra, Two | 1965 | 15.00 |
| ❑ CL 2478 [M] | Color Me Barbra | 1966 | 15.00 |
| ❑ CL 2478 [M] | Color Me Barbra | 1966 | 200.00 |
| *—Promo only on red vinyl (white label)* | | | |
| ❑ CL 2547 [M] | Je M'Appelle Barbra | 1966 | 15.00 |
| ❑ CL 2682 [M] | Simply Streisand | 1967 | 30.00 |
| ❑ CL 2757 [M] | A Christmas Album | 1967 | 25.00 |
| ❑ CS 8807 [S] | The Barbra Streisand Album | 1963 | 25.00 |
| *—"360 Sound Stereo" in black on label* | | | |
| ❑ CS 8807 [S] | The Barbra Streisand Album | 1966 | 15.00 |
| *—"360 Sound Stereo" in white on label* | | | |
| ❑ CS 8807 [S] | The Barbra Streisand Album | 1970 | 10.00 |
| *—Orange label* | | | |
| ❑ PC 8807 | The Barbra Streisand Album | 197? | 8.00 |
| *—Reissue with new prefix* | | | |
| ❑ CS 8854 [S] | The Second Barbra Streisand Album | 1963 | 25.00 |
| *—"360 Sound Stereo" in black on label* | | | |
| ❑ CS 8854 [S] | The Second Barbra Streisand Album | 1963 | 200.00 |
| *—Promo only on blue vinyl (white label)* | | | |
| ❑ CS 8854 [S] | The Second Barbra Streisand Album | 1966 | 15.00 |
| *—"360 Sound Stereo" in white on label* | | | |
| ❑ CS 8854 [S] | The Second Barbra Streisand Album | 1970 | 10.00 |
| *—Orange label* | | | |
| ❑ PC 8854 | The Second Barbra Streisand Album | 197? | 8.00 |
| *—Reissue with new prefix* | | | |
| ❑ CS 8954 [S] | The Third Album | 1964 | 25.00 |
| *—"360 Sound Stereo" in black on label* | | | |
| ❑ CS 8954 [S] | The Third Album | 1966 | 15.00 |
| *—"360 Sound Stereo" in white on label* | | | |
| ❑ CS 8954 [S] | The Third Album | 1970 | 10.00 |
| *—Orange label* | | | |
| ❑ PC 8954 | The Third Album | 197? | 8.00 |
| *—Reissue with new prefix* | | | |
| ❑ CS 9015 [S] | People | 1964 | 25.00 |
| *—"360 Sound Stereo" in black on label* | | | |
| ❑ CS 9015 [S] | People | 1966 | 15.00 |
| *—"360 Sound Stereo" in white on label* | | | |
| ❑ CS 9015 [S] | People | 1970 | 10.00 |
| *—Orange label* | | | |
| ❑ PC 9015 | People | 197? | 8.00 |
| *—Reissue with new prefix* | | | |
| ❑ CS 9136 [S] | My Name Is Barbra | 1965 | 25.00 |
| *—"360 Sound Stereo" in black on label* | | | |
| ❑ CS 9136 [S] | My Name Is Barbra | 1966 | 15.00 |
| *—"360 Sound Stereo" in white on label* | | | |
| ❑ CS 9136 [S] | My Name Is Barbra | 1970 | 10.00 |
| *—Orange label* | | | |
| ❑ PC 9136 | My Name Is Barbra | 197? | 8.00 |
| *—Reissue with new prefix* | | | |
| ❑ CS 9209 [S] | My Name Is Barbra, Two | 1965 | 20.00 |
| *—Red "360 Sound Stereo" label* | | | |
| ❑ CS 9209 [S] | My Name Is Barbra, Two | 1970 | 10.00 |
| *—Orange label* | | | |
| ❑ PC 9209 | My Name Is Barbra, Two | 197? | 8.00 |
| *—Reissue with new prefix* | | | |
| ❑ CS 9278 [S] | Color Me Barbra | 1966 | 20.00 |
| *—Red "360 Sound Stereo" label* | | | |
| ❑ CS 9278 [S] | Color Me Barbra | 1966 | 200.00 |
| *—Promo only on red vinyl (white label)* | | | |
| ❑ CS 9278 [S] | Color Me Barbra | 1970 | 10.00 |
| *—Orange label* | | | |
| ❑ PC 9278 | Color Me Barbra | 197? | 8.00 |
| *—Reissue with new prefix* | | | |
| ❑ CS 9347 [S] | Je M'Appelle Barbra | 1966 | 20.00 |
| *—Red "360 Sound Stereo" label* | | | |
| ❑ CS 9347 [S] | Je M'Appelle Barbra | 1970 | 10.00 |
| *—Orange label* | | | |
| ❑ PC 9347 | Je M'Appelle Barbra | 197? | 8.00 |
| *—Reissue with new prefix* | | | |
| ❑ CS 9482 [S] | Simply Streisand | 1967 | 20.00 |
| *—Red "360 Sound Stereo" label* | | | |
| ❑ CS 9482 [S] | Simply Streisand | 1970 | 10.00 |
| *—Orange label* | | | |
| ❑ PC 9482 | Simply Streisand | 197? | 8.00 |
| *—Reissue with new prefix* | | | |

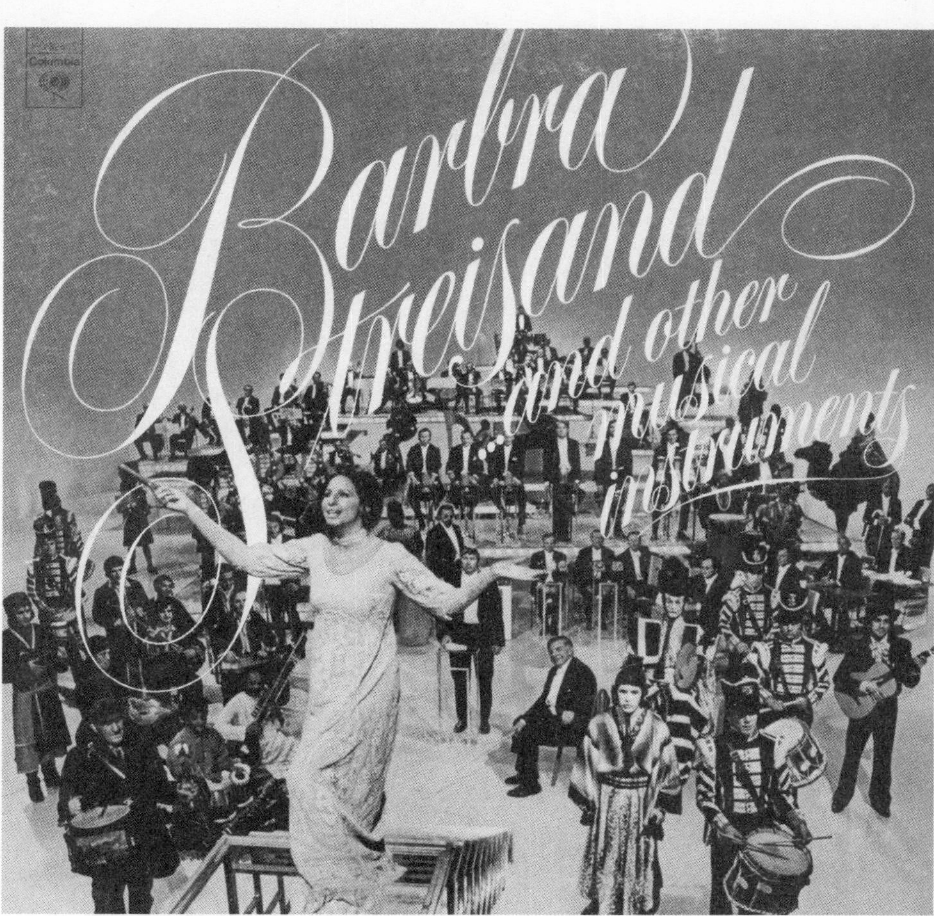


Barbra Streisand, *Barbra Streisand and Other Musical Instruments,* Columbia KC 32655, 1973, $12.

| Number | Title (A Side/B Side) | Yr | NM |
|---|---|---|---|
| ❑ CS 9557 [S] | A Christmas Album | 1967 | 20.00 |
| *—Red "360 Sound Stereo" label* | | | |
| ❑ CS 9557 [S] | A Christmas Album | 1970 | 8.00 |
| *—Orange label* | | | |
| ❑ PC 9557 | A Christmas Album | 198? | 6.00 |
| *—Reissue with new prefix and bar code* | | | |
| ❑ CS 9710 | A Happening in Central Park | 1968 | 15.00 |
| *—Red "360 Sound Stereo" label* | | | |
| ❑ CS 9710 | A Happening in Central Park | 1970 | 10.00 |
| *—Orange label* | | | |
| ❑ PC 9710 | A Happening in Central Park | 197? | 8.00 |
| *—Reissue with new prefix* | | | |
| ❑ CS 9816 | What About Today? | 1969 | 15.00 |
| *—Red "360 Sound Stereo" label* | | | |
| ❑ CS 9816 | What About Today? | 1970 | 10.00 |
| *—Orange label* | | | |
| ❑ PC 9816 | What About Today? | 197? | 8.00 |
| *—Reissue with new prefix* | | | |
| ❑ JC 9968 | Barbra Streisand's Greatest Hits | 197? | 6.00 |
| *—Another reissue with a new prefix (postdates PC)* | | | |
| ❑ KCS 9968 | Barbra Streisand's Greatest Hits | 1970 | 10.00 |
| *—Orange label* | | | |
| ❑ KCS 9968 | Barbra Streisand's Greatest Hits | 1970 | 15.00 |
| *—Red "360 Sound Stereo" label* | | | |
| ❑ PC 9968 | Barbra Streisand's Greatest Hits | 197? | 8.00 |
| *—Reissue with new prefix* | | | |
| ❑ CQ 30378 [Q] | Stoney End | 1972 | 25.00 |
| ❑ KC 30378 | Stoney End | 1971 | 15.00 |
| ❑ PC 30378 | Stoney End | 197? | 8.00 |
| *—Reissue with new prefix* | | | |
| ❑ CQ 30792 [Q] | Barbra Joan Streisand | 1972 | 25.00 |
| ❑ KC 30792 | Barbra Joan Streisand | 1971 | 15.00 |
| ❑ PC 30792 | Barbra Joan Streisand | 197? | 8.00 |
| *—Reissue with new prefix* | | | |
| ❑ CQ 31760 [Q] | Live Concert at the Forum | 1972 | 25.00 |
| ❑ KC 31760 | Live Concert at the Forum | 1972 | 15.00 |
| ❑ PC 31760 | Live Concert at the Forum | 197? | 8.00 |
| *—Reissue with new prefix* | | | |
| ❑ KC 32655 | Barbra Streisand...And Other Musical Instruments | 1973 | 12.00 |
| ❑ PC 32655 | Barbra Streisand...And Other Musical Instruments | 197? | 8.00 |
| *—Reissue with new prefix* | | | |
| ❑ JC 32801 | The Way We Were | 197? | 8.00 |
| *—Reissue with new prefix* | | | |

| Number | Title (A Side/B Side) | Yr | NM |
|---|---|---|---|
| ❑ PC 32801 | The Way We Were | 1974 | 12.00 |
| *—Revised version; has this title on spine, label and front cover* | | | |
| ❑ PC 32801 | Barbra Streisand Featuring The Way We Were and All In Love Is Fair | 1974 | 20.00 |
| *—Original version with this title on spine and label, and no title on front cover* | | | |
| ❑ PCQ 32801 [Q] | The Way We Were | 1974 | 25.00 |
| ❑ PC 33095 | Butterfly | 1974 | 12.00 |
| *—Original with no bar code* | | | |
| ❑ PC 33095 | Butterfly | 198? | 8.00 |
| *—Reissue with bar code* | | | |
| ❑ PCQ 33095 [Q] | Butterfly | 1974 | 20.00 |
| ❑ PC 33815 | Lazy Afternoon | 1975 | 12.00 |
| *—Original with no bar code* | | | |
| ❑ PC 33815 | Lazy Afternoon | 198? | 8.00 |
| *—Reissue with bar code* | | | |
| ❑ PCQ 33815 [Q] | Lazy Afternoon | 1975 | 25.00 |
| ❑ JS 34403 | A Star Is Born | 1976 | 12.00 |
| *—With Kris Kristofferson* | | | |
| ❑ JC 34830 | Streisand Superman | 1977 | 12.00 |
| ❑ PC 34830 | Streisand Superman | 198? | 8.00 |
| *—Budget-line reissue* | | | |
| ❑ PC 35275 | Songbird | 198? | 8.00 |
| *—Budget-line reissue* | | | |
| ❑ JC 35375 | Songbird | 1978 | 12.00 |
| ❑ FC 35679 | Barbra Streisand's Greatest Hits, Volume 2 | 1978 | 12.00 |
| ❑ FC 36258 | Wet | 1979 | 10.00 |
| ❑ FC 36750 | Guilty | 1980 | 10.00 |
| ❑ TC 37678 | Memories | 1981 | 10.00 |
| ❑ JS 39152 | Yentl | 1983 | 10.00 |
| ❑ QC 39480 | Emotion | 1984 | 10.00 |
| ❑ OC 40092 | The Broadway Album | 1985 | 10.00 |
| ❑ OC 40788 | One Voice | 1987 | 10.00 |
| ❑ OC 40880 | Till I Loved You | 1988 | 10.00 |
| ❑ HC 42801 | The Way We Were | 1982 | 30.00 |
| *—Half-speed mastered edition* | | | |
| ❑ OC 45369 | A Collection: Greatest Hits.. And More | 1989 | 15.00 |
| ❑ HC 45679 | Barbra Streisand's Greatest Hits, Volume 2 | 1980 | 30.00 |
| *—Half-speed mastered edition* | | | |
| ❑ HC 46750 | Guilty | 1982 | 30.00 |
| *—Half-speed mastered edition* | | | |
| ❑ HC 47678 | Memories | 1982 | 30.00 |
| *—Half-speed mastered edition* | | | |

COLUMBIA MASTERWORKS

| Number | Title (A Side/B Side) | Yr | NM |
|---|---|---|---|
| ❑ M 33452 | Classical Barbra | 1976 | 12.00 |

Styx, *Styx II,* Wooden Nickel WNS-1012, 1973, die-cut front cover, $20.

| Number | Title (A Side/B Side) | Yr | NM |
|---|---|---|---|
| **STRENGTH, "TEXAS" BILL** | | | |
| RE-CAR | | | |
| ❑ 2022 | Greatest Hits | 1967 | 25.00 |
| **STRIDER** | | | |
| WARNER BROS. | | | |
| ❑ BS 2722 | Exposed | 1973 | 20.00 |
| **STRING CHEESE** | | | |
| WOODEN NICKEL | | | |
| ❑ WNS-1001 | String Cheese | 1971 | 20.00 |
| **STRING-A-LONGS, THE** | | | |
| ATCO | | | |
| ❑ 33-241 [M] | Wide World Hits | 1969 | 50.00 |
| *—Mono is white label promo only* | | | |
| ❑ SD 33-241 [S] | Wide World Hits | 1969 | 25.00 |
| DOT | | | |
| ❑ DLP-3463 [M] | Matilda | 1962 | 25.00 |
| ❑ DLP-3723 [M] | Great Instrumental Hits | 1966 | 20.00 |
| ❑ DLP-25463 [S] | Matilda | 1962 | 30.00 |
| ❑ DLP-25723 [S] | Great Instrumental Hits | 1966 | 25.00 |
| WARWICK | | | |
| ❑ W-2036 [M] | Pick-A-Hit Featuring "Wheels" | 1961 | 50.00 |
| ❑ W-2036ST [S] | Pick-A-Hit Featuring "Wheels" | 1961 | 80.00 |
| **STRINGBEAN** | | | |
| STARDAY | | | |
| ❑ SLP-142 [M] | Old Time Pickin' and Singin' with Stringbean | 1961 | 60.00 |
| ❑ SLP-179 [M] | Stringbean | 1962 | 50.00 |
| ❑ SLP-215 [M] | A Salute to Uncle Dave Macon | 1963 | 50.00 |
| ❑ SLP-260 [M] | Way Back in the Hills of Old Kentucky | 1964 | 50.00 |
| **STRONG, NOLAN, AND THE DIABLOS** | | | |
| FORTUNE | | | |
| ❑ LP-8010 [M] | Fortune of Hits | 196? | 50.00 |
| *—Yellow label* | | | |
| ❑ LP-8010 [M] | Fortune of Hits | 1961 | 220.00 |
| *—Purple label, thick vinyl* | | | |
| ❑ LP-8010 [M] | Fortune of Hits | 197? | 15.00 |
| *—Purple label, thinner, more flexible vinyl* | | | |
| ❑ LP-8012 [M] | Fortune of Hits, Vol. 2 | 196? | 50.00 |
| *—Yellow label* | | | |

| Number | Title (A Side/B Side) | Yr | NM |
|---|---|---|---|
| ❑ LP-8012 [M] | Fortune of Hits, Vol. 2 | 1962 | 220.00 |
| *—Purple label, thick vinyl* | | | |
| ❑ LP-8012 [M] | Fortune of Hits, Vol. 2 | 197? | 15.00 |
| *—Purple label, thinner, more flexible vinyl* | | | |
| ❑ LP-8015 [M] | Mind Over Matter | 196? | 60.00 |
| *—Yellow label* | | | |
| ❑ LP-8015 [M] | Mind Over Matter | 1963 | 250.00 |
| *—Purple label, thick vinyl* | | | |
| ❑ LP-8015 [M] | Mind Over Matter | 197? | 20.00 |
| *—Purple label, thinner, more flexible vinyl* | | | |
| **STROZIER, FRANK** | | | |
| JAZZLAND | | | |
| ❑ JLP-56 [M] | Long Night | 1961 | 25.00 |
| ❑ JLP-70 [M] | March of the Siamese Children | 1962 | 25.00 |
| ❑ JLP-956 [S] | Long Night | 1961 | 30.00 |
| ❑ JLP-970 [S] | March of the Siamese Children | 1962 | 30.00 |
| VEE JAY | | | |
| ❑ LP-3005 [M] | Fantastic Frank Strozier | 1960 | 30.00 |
| ❑ SR-3005 [S] | Fantastic Frank Strozier | 1960 | 40.00 |
| **STRYPER** | | | |
| ENIGMA | | | |
| ❑ E-1064 | The Yellow and Black Attack | 1984 | 40.00 |
| *—Original with six tracks; yellow vinyl* | | | |
| ❑ 71064 | The Yellow and Black Attack | 1984 | 20.00 |
| *—Original with six tracks; black vinyl* | | | |
| ❑ 72077 | Soldiers Under Command | 1985 | 12.00 |
| *—Black vinyl* | | | |
| ❑ 72077 | Soldiers Under Command | 1985 | 20.00 |
| *—White vinyl* | | | |
| ❑ ST-73207 | The Yellow and Black Attack | 1985 | 10.00 |
| *—Reissue with eight tracks; black vinyl, square sleeve* | | | |
| ❑ ST-73207 | The Yellow and Black Attack | 1985 | 20.00 |
| *—Reissue with eight tracks; blue vinyl, round sleeve* | | | |
| ❑ ST-73217 | Soldiers Under Command | 1985 | 10.00 |
| *—Reissue with new number* | | | |
| ❑ PJAS-73237 | To Hell with the Devil | 1986 | 10.00 |
| *—Cover is black* | | | |
| ❑ PJAS-73237 | To Hell with the Devil | 1986 | 20.00 |
| *—Cover has band as winged angels in battle* | | | |
| ❑ SEAX-73277 | To Hell with the Devil | 1986 | 25.00 |
| *—Picture disc in plastic sleeve* | | | |
| ❑ D1-73317 | In God We Trust | 1988 | 10.00 |
| **STUART, MARTY** | | | |
| COLUMBIA | | | |
| ❑ B6C 40302 | Marty Stuart | 1986 | 30.00 |

| Number | Title (A Side/B Side) | Yr | NM |
|---|---|---|---|
| MCA | | | |
| ❑ 42312 | Hillbilly Rock | 1989 | 15.00 |
| ❑ R 170076 | Tempted | 1990 | 25.00 |
| *—Vinyl version available only through BMG Direct Marketing* | | | |
| RIDGE RUNNER | | | |
| ❑ RRR 0013 | Marty | 1978 | 30.00 |
| SUGAR HILL | | | |
| ❑ 3726 | Busy Bee Café | 1981 | 30.00 |
| **STUART, MARY** | | | |
| BELL | | | |
| ❑ 1133 | Mary Stuart | 1973 | 20.00 |
| COLUMBIA | | | |
| ❑ CL 6333 [10] | Joanne Sings | 1954 | 40.00 |
| **STUCKEY, NAT** | | | |
| MCA | | | |
| ❑ 2184 | Independence | 1976 | 12.00 |
| PAULA | | | |
| ❑ LP-2192 [M] | Nat Stuckey Sings | 1966 | 20.00 |
| ❑ LPS-2192 [S] | Nat Stuckey Sings | 1966 | 25.00 |
| ❑ LP-2196 [M] | All My Tomorrows | 1967 | 20.00 |
| ❑ LPS-2196 [S] | All My Tomorrows | 1967 | 25.00 |
| ❑ LPS-2203 | Country Favorites | 1968 | 25.00 |
| RCA CAMDEN | | | |
| ❑ ACL1-0780 | In the Ghetto | 1974 | 10.00 |
| RCA VICTOR | | | |
| ❑ APD1-0080 [Q] | Take Time to Love Her/I Used It All on You | 1973 | 25.00 |
| *—"QuadraDisc"; may not exist in regular stereo* | | | |
| ❑ APL1-0541 | The Best of Nat Stuckey | 1974 | 15.00 |
| ❑ LSP-4090 | Nat Stuckey Sings | 1968 | 20.00 |
| ❑ LSP-4123 | Keep 'Em Country | 1969 | 20.00 |
| ❑ LSP-4226 | New Country Roads | 1969 | 20.00 |
| ❑ LSP-4330 | Old Man Willie | 1970 | 15.00 |
| ❑ LSP-4389 | Country Fever | 1970 | 15.00 |
| ❑ LSP-4477 | She Wakes Me with a Kiss Every Morning | 1971 | 15.00 |
| ❑ LSP-4559 | Only a Woman Like You | 1971 | 15.00 |
| ❑ LSP-4635 | Forgive Me for Calling You Darling | 1972 | 15.00 |
| ❑ LSP-4743 | Is It Any Wonder That I Love You | 1972 | 15.00 |
| **STUFFY AND HIS FROZEN PARACHUTE BAND** | | | |
| PARAMOUNT | | | |
| ❑ PAS-6070 | Stuffy and His Frozen Parachute Band | 1974 | 25.00 |
| *—Reissue of Water Street 1002* | | | |
| WATER STREET | | | |
| ❑ WST 1002 | Stuffy and His Frozen Parachute Band | 1974 | 50.00 |
| **STUTTGART BAROQUE ENSEMBLE (MARCEL COURAND, CONDUCTOR)** | | | |
| MERCURY LIVING PRESENCE | | | |
| ❑ SR 90402 [S] | Couperin: Les Nations (selections); Rameau: Concerts en Sextuor Nos. 1, 4, 5 and 6 | 196? | 50.00 |
| *—Maroon label, no "Vendor: Mercury Record Corporation"* | | | |
| **STYLISTICS, THE** | | | |
| AMHERST | | | |
| ❑ AMH-743 | The Best of the Stylistics | 1986 | 10.00 |
| ❑ AMH-744 | All-Time Classics | 1986 | 10.00 |
| ❑ AMH-745 | The Best of the Stylistics, Vol. 2 | 1986 | 10.00 |
| ❑ AMH-746 | Greatest Love Hits | 1986 | 10.00 |
| AVCO | | | |
| ❑ 11006 | Round 2: The Stylistics | 1972 | 20.00 |
| ❑ 11010 | Rockin' Roll Baby | 1973 | 20.00 |
| ❑ AV-33023 | The Stylistics | 1971 | 20.00 |
| ❑ AV-69001 | Let's Put It All Together | 1974 | 15.00 |
| ❑ AV-69004 | Heavy | 1974 | 15.00 |
| ❑ AV-69005 | The Best of the Stylistics | 1975 | 15.00 |
| ❑ 69008 | Thank You Baby | 1975 | 15.00 |
| ❑ 69010 | You Are Beautiful | 1975 | 15.00 |
| H&L | | | |
| ❑ 69013 | Fabulous | 1976 | 12.00 |
| ❑ 69032 | Wonder Woman | 1978 | 12.00 |
| MERCURY | | | |
| ❑ SRM-1-3727 | In Fashion | 1978 | 12.00 |
| ❑ SRM-1-3753 | Love Spell | 1979 | 12.00 |
| PHILADELPHIA INT'L. | | | |
| ❑ FZ 37955 | 1982 | 1982 | 10.00 |
| TSOP | | | |
| ❑ JZ 36470 | Hurry Up This Way Again | 1980 | 10.00 |
| ❑ FZ 37458 | Closer Than Close | 1981 | 10.00 |
| **STYX** | | | |
| A&M | | | |
| ❑ SP-3217 | Equinox | 1984 | 8.00 |
| ❑ SP-3218 | Crystal Ball | 1984 | 8.00 |
| ❑ SP-3223 | The Grand Illusion | 1984 | 8.00 |
| ❑ SP-3224 | Pieces of Eight | 1984 | 8.00 |

| Number | Title (A Side/B Side) | Yr | NM |
|---|---|---|---|
| ❑ SP-3239 | Cornerstone | 1984 | 8.00 |
| ❑ SP-3240 | Paradise Theater | 1984 | 8.00 |
| *—3200 series LPs are reissues* | | | |
| ❑ SP-3711 | Cornerstone | 1979 | 10.00 |
| ❑ SP-3711 | Cornerstone | 1979 | 30.00 |
| *—Silver vinyl pressing, reportedly for fan club members* | | | |
| ❑ SP-3719 | Paradise Theater | 1981 | 10.00 |
| ❑ SP-3734 | Kilroy Was Here | 1983 | 10.00 |
| ❑ SP-4559 | Equinox | 1975 | 10.00 |
| ❑ SP-4604 | Crystal Ball | 1976 | 10.00 |
| ❑ SP-4637 | The Grand Illusion | 1977 | 10.00 |
| ❑ PR-4724 [PD] | Pieces of Eight | 1978 | 25.00 |
| ❑ SP-4724 | Pieces of Eight | 1978 | 10.00 |
| ❑ 75021 5327 1 | Edge of the Century | 1990 | 20.00 |
| ❑ SP-6514 [(2)] | Caught in the Act | 1984 | 12.00 |
| ❑ SP-8431 [(2)DJ] | The Styx Radio Special | 1977 | 25.00 |
| *—Promo only; green cover* | | | |
| ❑ SP-17053 [(3)DJ] | Styx Radio Special | 1978 | 40.00 |
| *—Promo-only box set* | | | |
| ❑ SP-17222 [(2)DJ] | Radio Sampler and Interview Album | 1983 | 25.00 |
| *—Promo only; with "Kilroy Was Here" album graphic on cover* | | | |

MOBILE FIDELITY

| Number | Title (A Side/B Side) | Yr | NM |
|---|---|---|---|
| ❑ 1-026 | The Grand Illusion | 1979 | 30.00 |
| *—Audiophile vinyl* | | | |

NAUTILUS

| Number | Title (A Side/B Side) | Yr | NM |
|---|---|---|---|
| ❑ NR-15 | Pieces of Eight | 1981 | 25.00 |
| *—Audiophile vinyl* | | | |
| ❑ NR-27 | Cornerstone | 1982 | 20.00 |
| *—Audiophile vinyl* | | | |
| ❑ NR-45 | Paradise Theater | 198? | 30.00 |
| *—Audiophile vinyl* | | | |

RCA VICTOR

| Number | Title (A Side/B Side) | Yr | NM |
|---|---|---|---|
| ❑ AFL1-3593 | Styx | 1979 | 10.00 |
| ❑ AFL1-3594 | Lady | 1979 | 10.00 |
| *—Retitled version of "Styx II"* | | | |
| ❑ AFL1-3595 | Serpent | 1979 | 10.00 |
| *—Retitled version of "The Serpent Is Rising"* | | | |
| ❑ AFL1-3596 | Miracles | 1979 | 10.00 |
| *—Retitled version of "Man of Miracles"* | | | |
| ❑ AFL1-3597 | Best of Styx | 1979 | 10.00 |
| ❑ AYL1-3888 | Styx | 1980 | 8.00 |
| ❑ AYL1-4233 | Lady | 1981 | 8.00 |
| *—Retitled version of "Styx II"* | | | |
| ❑ AYL1-4756 | Best of Styx | 1982 | 8.00 |

WOODEN NICKEL

| Number | Title (A Side/B Side) | Yr | NM |
|---|---|---|---|
| ❑ BWL1-0287 | The Serpent Is Rising | 1974 | 20.00 |
| ❑ BWL1-0638 | Man of Miracles | 1974 | 20.00 |
| *—Second version contains "Best Thing"* | | | |
| ❑ BWL1-0638 | Man of Miracles | 1974 | 30.00 |
| *—Original version contains "Lies"* | | | |
| ❑ BWL1-1008 | Styx | 1975 | 15.00 |
| ❑ WNS-1008 | Styx | 1972 | 20.00 |
| ❑ BWL1-1012 | Styx II | 1975 | 15.00 |
| ❑ WNS-1012 | Styx II | 1973 | 20.00 |
| *—With die-cut cover* | | | |
| ❑ BWL1-2250 | Best of Styx | 1977 | 12.00 |

**SUB-ZERO BAND, THE**

SUB-ZERO

| Number | Title (A Side/B Side) | Yr | NM |
|---|---|---|---|
| ❑ 1172 | The Sub-Zero Band | 197? | 200.00 |

**SUBRAMANIAM, DR. L.**

CRUSADERS

| Number | Title (A Side/B Side) | Yr | NM |
|---|---|---|---|
| ❑ 16003 | Blossom | 198? | 20.00 |
| *—Audiophile vinyl* | | | |

**SUGAR BEARS, THE** KIM CARNES was in this group.

BIG TREE

| Number | Title (A Side/B Side) | Yr | NM |
|---|---|---|---|
| ❑ BTS-2009 | Introducing the Sugar Bears | 1972 | 20.00 |

**SUGAR CREEK**

METROMEDIA

| Number | Title (A Side/B Side) | Yr | NM |
|---|---|---|---|
| ❑ MD 1020 | Please Tell a Friend | 1969 | 60.00 |

**SUGARLOAF**

BRUT

| Number | Title (A Side/B Side) | Yr | NM |
|---|---|---|---|
| ❑ 6006 | I Got a Song | 1973 | 15.00 |

CLARIDGE

| Number | Title (A Side/B Side) | Yr | NM |
|---|---|---|---|
| ❑ 1000 | Don't Call Us, We'll Call You | 1975 | 12.00 |

LIBERTY

| Number | Title (A Side/B Side) | Yr | NM |
|---|---|---|---|
| ❑ LST-7640 | Sugarloaf | 1970 | 20.00 |
| ❑ LST-11010 | Spaceship Earth | 1971 | 20.00 |

**SUICIDE COMMANDOS**

BLANK

| Number | Title (A Side/B Side) | Yr | NM |
|---|---|---|---|
| ❑ 002 | The Suicide Commandos Make a Record | 1977 | 25.00 |

TWIN/TONE

| Number | Title (A Side/B Side) | Yr | NM |
|---|---|---|---|
| ❑ TTR 7906 | The Commandos Commit Suicide Dance Concert | 1979 | 75.00 |
| *—Limited edition of 1,000 copies* | | | |

**SUKMAN, HARRY**

LIBERTY

| Number | Title (A Side/B Side) | Yr | NM |
|---|---|---|---|
| ❑ LRP-3005 [M] | Nightfall | 1955 | 20.00 |
| ❑ LRP-3135 [M] | Command Performance | 1959 | 20.00 |
| ❑ LRP-3151 [M] | The Franz Liszt Story | 1960 | 20.00 |
| ❑ LST-7135 [S] | Command Performance | 1959 | 25.00 |
| ❑ LST-7151 [S] | The Franz Liszt Story | 1960 | 25.00 |

Donna Summer, *Another Place and Time,* Atlantic 81987, 1989, $12.

**SULIEMAN, IDREES**

NEW JAZZ

| Number | Title (A Side/B Side) | Yr | NM |
|---|---|---|---|
| ❑ NJLP-8202 [M] | Roots | 1958 | 60.00 |
| *—Purple label* | | | |
| ❑ NJLP-8202 [M] | Roots | 1958 | 100.00 |
| *—Yellow label* | | | |
| ❑ NJLP-8202 [M] | Roots | 1965 | 25.00 |
| *—Blue label, trident logo at right* | | | |

**SULLIVAN, IRA**

ATLANTIC

| Number | Title (A Side/B Side) | Yr | NM |
|---|---|---|---|
| ❑ 1476 [M] | Horizons | 1967 | 25.00 |

DELMARK

| Number | Title (A Side/B Side) | Yr | NM |
|---|---|---|---|
| ❑ DL-402 [M] | Blue Stroll | 1961 | 30.00 |
| ❑ DS-402 [S] | Blue Stroll | 1961 | 40.00 |

VEE JAY

| Number | Title (A Side/B Side) | Yr | NM |
|---|---|---|---|
| ❑ LP-3003 [M] | Bird Lives! | 1960 | 50.00 |
| ❑ SR-3003 [S] | Bird Lives! | 1960 | 60.00 |

**SULLIVAN, JIM**

MERCURY

| Number | Title (A Side/B Side) | Yr | NM |
|---|---|---|---|
| ❑ MG-21137 [M] | Sitar Beat | 1967 | 20.00 |
| ❑ SR-61137 [S] | Sitar Beat | 1967 | 20.00 |

**SULLIVAN, JOE**

CAPITOL

| Number | Title (A Side/B Side) | Yr | NM |
|---|---|---|---|
| ❑ T 636 [M] | Classics in Jazz | 1955 | 40.00 |

DOWN HOME

| Number | Title (A Side/B Side) | Yr | NM |
|---|---|---|---|
| ❑ MGD-2 [M] | Mr. Piano Man: The Music of Joe Sullivan | 1956 | 50.00 |

EPIC

| Number | Title (A Side/B Side) | Yr | NM |
|---|---|---|---|
| ❑ LG 1003 [10] | Joe Sullivan Plays Fats Waller Compositions | 1954 | 80.00 |

RIVERSIDE

| Number | Title (A Side/B Side) | Yr | NM |
|---|---|---|---|
| ❑ RLP 12-202 [M] | New Solos by an Old Master | 1955 | 60.00 |

VERVE

| Number | Title (A Side/B Side) | Yr | NM |
|---|---|---|---|
| ❑ MGV-1002 [M] | Mr. Piano Man: The Music of Joe Sullivan | 1957 | 40.00 |
| ❑ V-1002 [M] | Mr. Piano Man: The Music of Joe Sullivan | 1961 | 20.00 |

**SULLIVAN, MAXINE**

PERIOD

| Number | Title (A Side/B Side) | Yr | NM |
|---|---|---|---|
| ❑ SPL-1207 [M] | Maxine Sullivan, Volume 2 | 1956 | 50.00 |
| ❑ RL-1909 [M] | Maxine Sullivan 1956 | 1956 | 50.00 |

**SUMAC, YMA**

CAPITOL

| Number | Title (A Side/B Side) | Yr | NM |
|---|---|---|---|
| ❑ H 244 [10] | Voice of the Xtabay | 1952 | 100.00 |
| ❑ L 299 [10] | Legend of the Sun Virgin | 1952 | 120.00 |
| ❑ SM-299 [M] | Legend of the Sun Virgin | 197? | 12.00 |
| ❑ T 299 [M] | Legend of the Sun Virgin | 1955 | 50.00 |
| ❑ L 423 [10] | Inca Taqui | 1953 | 100.00 |
| ❑ H 564 [10] | Mambo! | 1954 | 100.00 |
| ❑ T 564 [M] | Mambo! | 1955 | 50.00 |
| ❑ DW 684 [R] | Voice of the Xtabay and Inca Taqui | 1963 | 15.00 |
| ❑ SM-684 | Voice of the Xtabay and Inca Taqui | 197? | 12.00 |
| *—On this reissue, Side 1 is in mono* | | | |
| ❑ W 684 [M] | Voice of the Xtabay and Inca Taqui | 1955 | 50.00 |
| *—Gray label* | | | |
| ❑ W 684 [M] | Voice of the Xtabay and Inca Taqui | 1963 | 20.00 |
| *—Black colorband label, "Capitol" at top* | | | |
| ❑ T 770 [M] | Legend of the Jivaro | 1956 | 50.00 |
| *—Turquoise label* | | | |
| ❑ T 770 [M] | Legend of the Jivaro | 1963 | 20.00 |
| *—Black colorband label, "Capitol" at top* | | | |
| ❑ ST 1169 [S] | Fuego del Andes | 1959 | 50.00 |
| ❑ T 1169 [M] | Fuego del Andes | 1959 | 40.00 |
| ❑ M-11892 | Mambo! | 1979 | 12.00 |

CORAL

| Number | Title (A Side/B Side) | Yr | NM |
|---|---|---|---|
| ❑ CRL 56058 [10] | Presenting Yma Sumac | 1952 | 120.00 |

LONDON

| Number | Title (A Side/B Side) | Yr | NM |
|---|---|---|---|
| ❑ XPS 608 | Miracles | 1972 | 20.00 |

**SUMMER, DONNA**

ATLANTIC

| Number | Title (A Side/B Side) | Yr | NM |
|---|---|---|---|
| ❑ 81987 | Another Place and Time | 1989 | 12.00 |

CASABLANCA

| Number | Title (A Side/B Side) | Yr | NM |
|---|---|---|---|
| ❑ NBLP 7038 | Four Seasons of Love | 1976 | 10.00 |
| ❑ NBLP 7056 | I Remember Yesterday | 1977 | 10.00 |

| Number | Title (A Side/B Side) | Yr | NM |
|---|---|---|---|
| ❑ NBLP 7078 [(2)] | Once Upon a Time... | 1977 | 12.00 |
| ❑ NBLP 7119 [(2)] | Live and More | 1978 | 12.00 |
| ❑ NBPIX 7119 [PD] | The Best of Live and More | 1979 | 20.00 |
| ❑ NBLP 7150 [(2)] | Bad Girls | 1979 | 12.00 |
| ❑ NBLP 7191 [(2)] | On the Radio — Greatest Hits Vols. 1 and 2 | 1979 | 12.00 |
| ❑ NBLP 7201 | Greatest Hits, Vol. 1 | 1979 | 8.00 |
| ❑ NBLP 7202 | Greatest Hits, Vol. 2 | 1979 | 8.00 |
| ❑ NBLP 7244 | Walk Away — Collector's Edition (The Best of 1977-1980) | 1980 | 10.00 |
| ❑ 811123-1 [(2)] | Live and More | 1985 | 10.00 |
| ❑ 822557-1 [(2)] | Bad Girls | 1984 | 10.00 |
| ❑ 822558-1 [(2)] | On the Radio — Greatest Hits Vols. 1 and 2 | 1984 | 10.00 |
| ❑ 822559-1 | Greatest Hits, Vol. 2 | 1984 | 8.00 |
| ❑ 822560-1 | Walk Away | 1984 | 8.00 |
| EPIC | | | |
| ❑ E2 69910 [(2)] | Live and More Encore | 1999 | 15.00 |
| GEFFEN | | | |
| ❑ GHS 2000 | The Wanderer | 1980 | 10.00 |
| ❑ GHS 2005 | Donna Summer | 1982 | 10.00 |
| ❑ GHS 24040 | Cats Without Claws | 1984 | 10.00 |
| ❑ GHS 24040 [DJ] | Cats Without Claws | 1984 | 15.00 |
| | *—Promo only on Quiex II vinyl* | | |
| ❑ GHS 24102 | All Systems Go | 1987 | 10.00 |
| MERCURY | | | |
| ❑ 812265-1 | She Works Hard for the Money | 1983 | 10.00 |
| ❑ 826144-1 | The Summer Collection | 1985 | 10.00 |
| OASIS | | | |
| ❑ OCLP 5003 | Love to Love You Baby | 1975 | 12.00 |
| | *—Add 50% if poster is included* | | |
| ❑ OCLP 5004 | A Love Trilogy | 1976 | 12.00 |
| ❑ 822792-1 | Love to Love You Baby | 1985 | 8.00 |

### SUMMER SOUNDS, THE

| Number | Title (A Side/B Side) | Yr | NM |
|---|---|---|---|
| LAUREL | | | |
| ❑ 90973 | Up Down | 196? | 1000. |

### SUMMERHILL

| Number | Title (A Side/B Side) | Yr | NM |
|---|---|---|---|
| TETRAGRAMMATON | | | |
| ❑ T-114 | Summerhill | 1969 | 30.00 |

### SUMMERLIN, ED

| Number | Title (A Side/B Side) | Yr | NM |
|---|---|---|---|
| ECCLESIA | | | |
| ❑ ER-101 [M] | Liturgical Jazz | 1959 | 60.00 |

### SUMMERS, ANDREW ROWAN

| Number | Title (A Side/B Side) | Yr | NM |
|---|---|---|---|
| FOLKWAYS | | | |
| ❑ FP-21 [10] | Seeds of Love | 1951 | 50.00 |
| ❑ FP-41 [10] | The Lady Gay | 1954 | 50.00 |
| ❑ FP-44 [10] | The Faulse Lady | 1954 | 50.00 |
| ❑ FA-2002 [10] | Christmas Carols | 195? | 50.00 |
| ❑ FA-2021 [10] | Seeds of Love | 1951 | 50.00 |
| ❑ FA-2041 [10] | The Lady Gay | 1954 | 50.00 |
| ❑ FA-2044 [10] | The Faulse Lady | 1954 | 50.00 |
| ❑ FA-2348 [M] | Andrew Rowan Summers | 1957 | 30.00 |
| ❑ FA-2361 [M] | Hymns and Carols | 195? | 30.00 |
| ❑ FA-2364 [M] | The Unquiet Grave and Other American Tragic Ballads | 195? | 30.00 |
| ❑ FC 7502 [M] | Christmas Carols | 196? | 15.00 |

### SUMMERS, ANDY, AND ROBERT FRIPP

| Number | Title (A Side/B Side) | Yr | NM |
|---|---|---|---|
| A&M | | | |
| ❑ SP-4913 | I Advance Masked | 1982 | 10.00 |
| ❑ SP9-5011 | Bewitched | 1984 | 10.00 |
| ❑ SP-17299 [DJ] | Speak Out Interview | 1982 | 25.00 |
| | *—Issued in generic cover with sticker* | | |

### SUN RA

| Number | Title (A Side/B Side) | Yr | NM |
|---|---|---|---|
| ABC IMPULSE! | | | |
| ❑ 1974 | Welcome to Saturn | 1974 | 60.00 |
| ❑ AS-9239 | Atlantis | 1973 | 40.00 |
| ❑ AS-9242 | The Nubians of Plutonia | 1974 | 50.00 |
| ❑ AS-9243 | The Magic City | 1973 | 50.00 |
| ❑ AS-9245 | Angels and Demons at Play | 1974 | 40.00 |
| ❑ AS-9255 | Astro Black | 1973 | 60.00 |
| ❑ ASD-9265 | Jazz in Silhouette | 1974 | 50.00 |
| ❑ AS-9270 | Fate in a Pleasant Mood | 1974 | 50.00 |
| ❑ AS-9271 | Super Sonic Sounds | 1974 | 50.00 |
| ❑ ASD-9276 | The Bad and the Beautiful | 1974 | 40.00 |
| ❑ ASD-9298 | Pathways to Unknown Worlds | 1975 | 60.00 |
| AFFINITY | | | |
| ❑ AFF 10 | The Solar-Myth Approach Volume I | 1978 | 40.00 |
| ❑ AFF 76 | The Solar-Myth Approach Volume II | 1978 | 40.00 |
| BASF | | | |
| ❑ 20748 | It's After the End of the World | 1971 | 50.00 |
| BLACK LION | | | |
| ❑ 106 | Pictures of Infinity | 197? | 40.00 |
| BLUE THUMB | | | |
| ❑ BTS-41 [Q] | Space Is the Place | 1973 | 100.00 |
| | *—All copies are quad* | | |
| DELMARK | | | |
| ❑ DL-411 [M] | Sun Song | 1967 | 30.00 |
| DIW | | | |
| ❑ DIWP-2 [PD] | Cosmo Omnibus Imaginable Illusion: Live at Pit-Inn | 1988 | 120.00 |
| | *—Picture disc; limited to under 1,000 copies* | | |
| ESP-DISK' | | | |
| ❑ 1014 [M] | The Heliocentric Worlds of Sun Ra, Volume 1 | 1966 | 60.00 |
| ❑ S-1014 [S] | The Heliocentric Worlds of Sun Ra, Volume 1 | 1966 | 80.00 |
| | *—Reproductions exist of this LP* | | |
| ❑ 1017 [M] | The Heliocentric Worlds of Sun Ra, Volume 2 | 1966 | 60.00 |
| | *—Without voices overdubbed on "The Sun Myth"* | | |
| ❑ S-1017 [S] | The Heliocentric Worlds of Sun Ra, Volume 2 | 1966 | 100.00 |
| | *—Without voices overdubbed on "The Sun Myth"* | | |
| ❑ S-1045 [S] | Nothing Is | 1969 | 30.00 |
| HAT HUT | | | |
| ❑ 17 [(2)] | Sunrise in Different Directions | 1980 | 60.00 |
| HORO | | | |
| ❑ HDP-19/20 [(2)] | Unity | 1978 | 150.00 |
| ❑ HDP-23/24 [(2)] | Other Voices, Other Blues | 1978 | 150.00 |
| ❑ HDP-25/26 [(2)] | New Steps | 1978 | 200.00 |
| INNER CITY | | | |
| ❑ IC-1039 [(2)] | Live at Montreux | 1978 | 40.00 |
| JIHAD | | | |
| ❑ 1968 [S] | A Black Mass | 1968 | 200.00 |
| | *—Color cover* | | |
| ❑ 1968 [S] | A Black Mass | 1968 | 300.00 |
| | *—Black and white cover* | | |
| MELTDOWN | | | |
| ❑ MPA-1 | John Cage Meets Sun Ra | 1987 | 200.00 |
| PHILLY JAZZ | | | |
| ❑ PJ-666 | Lanquidity | 1978 | 250.00 |
| | *—Reproductions exist* | | |
| ❑ PJ-1007 | Of Mythic Worlds | 1980 | 250.00 |
| PRAXIS | | | |
| ❑ CM 106 | Sun Ra Arkestra Meets Salah Ragab in Egypt | 1983 | 60.00 |
| ❑ CM 108 | Live at Praxis Volume 1 | 1984 | 70.00 |
| ❑ CM 109 | Live at Praxis Volume 2 | 1985 | 80.00 |
| ❑ CM 110 | Live at Praxis 84 Volume 3 | 1985 | 80.00 |
| RECOMMENDED | | | |
| ❑ RR-11 | Nuits de la Fondation Maeght Volume I | 1981 | 50.00 |
| | *—Reissue of Shandar 10.001; plays at 45 rpm* | | |
| SATURN | | | |
| ❑ CMIJ 78 | Disco 3000 | 1978 | 150.00 |
| ❑ IHNY-165 | Sun Ra and His Arkestra Featuring Pharoah Sanders and Black Harold | 1976 | 150.00 |
| ❑ LP-200 | Universe in Blue | 197? | 150.00 |
| ❑ LP-202 [M] | Fate in a Pleasant Mood | 196? | 100.00 |
| | *—Chicago address on label* | | |
| ❑ LP-203 [M] | Interstellar Low Ways | 1969 | 50.00 |
| | *—Chicago address on label; reproductions exist* | | |
| ❑ LP-204 [M] | Super-Sonic Sounds | 1968 | 80.00 |
| | *—Blue or green cover; Chicago address on label* | | |
| ❑ LP-205 [M] | Jazz in Silhouette | 1967 | 80.00 |
| | *—Green label* | | |
| ❑ LP-205 [M] | Jazz in Silhouette | 1967 | 100.00 |
| | *—Red label* | | |
| ❑ LP-206 [M] | Other Planes of There | 1967 | 100.00 |
| | *—Chicago address on label* | | |
| ❑ LP-207 [M] | Sun Ra Visits Planet Earth | 196? | 80.00 |
| | *—"El Saturn" label* | | |
| ❑ LP-207 [M] | Sun Ra Visits Planet Earth | 1968 | 100.00 |
| | *—Minneapolis address on label* | | |
| ❑ LP-208 [M] | Secrets of the Sun | 196? | 100.00 |
| | *—Chicago address on label* | | |
| ❑ SRLP-0216 [M] | Super-Sonic Jazz | 1957 | 300.00 |
| | *—Blank cover* | | |
| ❑ SRLP-0216 [M] | Super-Sonic Jazz | 1957 | 600.00 |
| | *—Silk-screened cover* | | |
| ❑ SRLP-0216 [M] | Super-Sonic Jazz | 1958 | 250.00 |
| | *—Purple "keyboard" cover* | | |
| ❑ SRLP-0216 [M] | Super-Sonic Jazz | 1965 | 80.00 |
| | *—Blue or green cover* | | |
| ❑ LP-402 | When Sun Comes Out | 196? | 40.00 |
| ❑ LP-403 [M] | The Magic City | 196? | 60.00 |
| | *—Chicago address on label* | | |
| ❑ LP-404 [M] | Art Forms of Dimensions Tomorrow | 1969 | 40.00 |
| | *—Chicago address on label; reproductions exist* | | |
| ❑ LP-405 | When Angels Speak of Love | 196? | 40.00 |
| ❑ LP-406 [M] | The Nubians of Plutonia | 1969 | 100.00 |
| | *—Chicago address on label; reproductions exist* | | |
| ❑ LP-407 [M] | Angels and Demons at Play | 196? | 40.00 |
| | *—Chicago address on label; reproductions exist* | | |
| ❑ LP-408 [S] | Cosmic Tones for Mental Therapy | 1967 | 200.00 |
| | *—Red label; Sun Ra art on cover; reproductions exist* | | |
| ❑ LP-409 [M] | We Travel the Spaceways | 196? | 60.00 |
| | *—"El Saturn" label; reproductions exist* | | |
| ❑ LP-485 | Deep Purple | 1973 | 150.00 |
| ❑ LP-487 | Song of the Stargazers | 1979 | 150.00 |
| ❑ LP-502 [S] | Strange Strings | 1967 | 100.00 |
| | *—Red label; reproductions exist* | | |
| ❑ ESR-507 [S] | Atlantis | 1969 | 80.00 |
| | *—"El Saturn" label* | | |
| ❑ ESR-508 [S] | Holiday for Soul-Dance | 1969 | 60.00 |
| | *—"El Saturn" label; reproductions exist* | | |
| ❑ LP-509 [M] | Monorails and Satellites | 1968 | 100.00 |
| | *—"El Saturn" label; reproductions exist* | | |
| ❑ LP-512 | Sound Sun Pleasure!! | 1970 | 60.00 |
| | *—Reproductions exist* | | |
| ❑ LP-519 [S] | Monorails and Satellites, Vol. II | 1969 | 80.00 |
| | *—"El Saturn" label* | | |
| ❑ ESR-520 | Continuation | 1969 | 80.00 |
| ❑ LP-520 | Continuation | 1970 | 50.00 |
| ❑ ESR-521 | My Brother the Wind | 1970 | 100.00 |
| | *—Reproductions exist* | | |
| ❑ LP-521 | My Brother the Wind | 197? | 50.00 |
| ❑ LP-522 | The Night of the Purple Moon | 197? | 100.00 |
| | *—Reproductions exist* | | |
| ❑ ESR-523 | My Brother the Wind, Volume II | 1971 | 100.00 |
| | *—Reproductions exist* | | |
| ❑ LP-527 | Space Probe | 197? | 150.00 |
| ❑ LP-529 | The Invisible Shield | 1974 | 150.00 |
| | *—Philadelphia address on label* | | |
| ❑ LP-529 | The Invisible Shield | 1974 | 200.00 |
| | *—Chicago address on label* | | |
| ❑ LP-530 | Outer Spaceways Incorporated | 1974 | 150.00 |
| | *—Philadelphia address on label* | | |
| ❑ LP-530 | Outer Spaceways Incorporated | 1974 | 200.00 |
| | *—Chicago address on label* | | |
| ❑ ESR-532 | The Bad and the Beautiful | 196? | 50.00 |
| | *—Chicago address on label; reproductions exist* | | |
| ❑ LP-538 | Discipline 27-II | 1973 | 150.00 |
| ❑ LP-539 | What's New? | 197? | 150.00 |
| ❑ LPB-711 [M] | The Magic City | 1966 | 80.00 |
| | *—Red label; reproductions exist* | | |
| ❑ LP-747 | Some Blues But Not the Kind That's Blue | 1977 | 150.00 |
| ❑ 752 | What's New? | 197? | 100.00 |
| ❑ LP-771 | The Soul Vibrations of Man | 1977 | 200.00 |
| ❑ LP-772 | Taking a Chance on Chances | 1977 | 150.00 |
| ❑ LP-849 | Horizon | 1974 | 150.00 |
| ❑ 1272 | Live in Egypt 1 | 1973 | 80.00 |
| ❑ LP-1966 [M] | When Angels Speak of Love | 1966 | 500.00 |
| | *—Red cover with a "sideways" image of Sun Ra* | | |
| ❑ ESR-1970 | My Brother the Wind | 1970 | 150.00 |
| ❑ 1978 | Media Dream | 1978 | 150.00 |
| ❑ 1981 | Dance of Innocent Passion | 1981 | 150.00 |
| ❑ 1982 | Nuclear War | 1982 | 150.00 |
| ❑ IX/1983-220 | Ra to the Rescue | 1983 | 150.00 |
| ❑ 1984A/B | Just Friends | 1984 | 150.00 |
| ❑ A/B-1984SG-9 | A Fireside Chat with Lucifer | 1984 | 150.00 |
| ❑ C/D-1984SG-9 | Celestial Love | 1984 | 150.00 |
| ❑ SRA-2000 | My Brother the Wind, Volume II | 1971 | 150.00 |
| ❑ LP-2066 [M] | When Sun Comes Out | 1963 | 400.00 |
| | *—Blank cover* | | |
| ❑ LP-2066 [M] | When Sun Comes Out | 1963 | 500.00 |
| | *—Black ameboid figure on cover* | | |
| ❑ LP-2066 [M] | When Sun Comes Out | 1963 | 500.00 |
| | *—Green cover with yellow sun* | | |
| ❑ LP-2066 [M] | When Sun Comes Out | 1967 | 300.00 |
| | *—Spaceman at piano cover; reproductions exist* | | |
| ❑ KH-2772 [S] | Cosmic Tones for Mental Therapy | 196? | 80.00 |
| | *—Blue cover; Chicago address on label* | | |
| ❑ ESR-5000 | Universe in Blue | 1972 | 150.00 |
| ❑ HK-5445 [M] | We Travel the Spaceways | 1966 | 120.00 |
| | *—Red label* | | |
| ❑ LP-5786 [M] | Jazz in Silhouette | 1958 | 150.00 |
| | *—Yellow label* | | |
| ❑ 6161 | Song of the Stargazers | 1979 | 200.00 |
| ❑ 6680 | I, Pharaoh | 1980 | 150.00 |
| | *—"El Saturn" label* | | |
| ❑ 7771 | Nidhamu | 197? | 150.00 |
| ❑ 7877 | Somewhere Over the Rainbow | 1977 | 150.00 |
| ❑ GH-9954-E/F [M] | Secrets of the Sun | 1965 | 250.00 |
| | *—Red label* | | |
| ❑ SR-9956 [M] | Art Forms of Dimensions Tomorrow | 1965 | 50.00 |
| | *—Red label; reproductions exist* | | |
| ❑ SR-9956-11A/B [M] | Sun Ra Visits Planet Earth | 1966 | 80.00 |
| | *—Red label; reproductions exist* | | |
| ❑ SR-9956-11E/F [M] | The Lady with the Golden Stockings | 1966 | 600.00 |
| | *—Cover is generic and says "Tonal Views of Times Tomorrow"* | | |
| ❑ SR-9956-2-M/N [M] | Rocket #9 Take Off For the Planet Venus | 1966 | 500.00 |
| | *—Cover has "burning candle" logo* | | |
| ❑ SR-9956-2/A/B [M] | Fate in a Pleasant Mood | 1965 | 80.00 |
| | *—Red label; reproductions exist* | | |
| ❑ SR-9956-2/O/P [M] | Angels and Demons at Play | 1965 | 80.00 |
| | *—Red label; metallic gold cover* | | |
| ❑ 10480 | Aurora Borealis | 1980 | 80.00 |
| ❑ 11179 | Sleeping Beauty | 1979 | 80.00 |
| ❑ 13088A/12988B | Hidden Fire 2 | 1988 | 80.00 |
| ❑ 13188III/12988II | Hidden Fire 1 | 1988 | 80.00 |
| ❑ 14200-A/B | Space Probe | 197? | 80.00 |
| ❑ 19782 | Sound Mirror | 1978 | 150.00 |
| ❑ 19783 | Media Dream | 1978 | 150.00 |
| ❑ 19841 | A Fireside Chat with Lucifer | 1984 | 150.00 |

| Number | Title (A Side/B Side) | Yr | NM |
|---|---|---|---|
| ❑ 19842 | Celestial Love | 1984 | 150.00 |
| ❑ 52375 | What's New? | 1975 | 120.00 |
| ❑ 61674 | Out Beyond the Kingdom Of | 1974 | 150.00 |
| ❑ 72579 | God Is More Than Love Can Ever Be | 1979 | 200.00 |
| ❑ IX SR 72881 | Oblique Parallax | 1981 | 200.00 |
| ❑ 77771 | Nidhamu | 197? | 250.00 |
| ❑ 81774 | The Antique Blacks | 1974 | 200.00 |
| ❑ MS 87976 [(2)] | Live at Montreux | 1976 | 150.00 |
| ❑ 91379 | Omniverse | 1979 | 150.00 |
| ❑ 91780 | Voice of the Eternal Tomorrow | 1980 | 150.00 |
| ❑ 92074 | Sub Underground | 1974 | 200.00 |
| ❑ KH-98766 [M] | Other Planes of There | 1966 | 100.00 |
| *—Red label; reproductions exist* | | | |
| ❑ 101185 | Hiroshima | 1985 | 150.00 |
| ❑ 101477 | Some Blues But Not the Kind That's Blue | 1977 | 150.00 |
| ❑ 101485 | When Spaceships Appear | 1985 | 150.00 |
| ❑ 101679 | On Jupiter | 1979 | 150.00 |
| *—"El Saturn" label* | | | |
| ❑ 123180 | Beyond the Purple Star Zone | 1981 | 200.00 |
| ❑ 144000 | Invisible Shield | 197? | 200.00 |
| ❑ 1014077 | Some Blues But Not the Kind That's Blue | 1977 | 150.00 |
| ❑ 1217718 | Horizon | 1974 | 150.00 |
| ❑ 9121385 | Outer Reach Intensity-Energy | 1985 | 200.00 |

SATURN/RECOMMENDED

| Number | Title (A Side/B Side) | Yr | NM |
|---|---|---|---|
| ❑ SRRD-1 | Cosmo Sun Connection | 1985 | 40.00 |

SAVOY

| Number | Title (A Side/B Side) | Yr | NM |
|---|---|---|---|
| ❑ MG-12169 [M] | The Futuristic Sounds of Sun Ra | 1961 | 100.00 |

SHANDAR

| Number | Title (A Side/B Side) | Yr | NM |
|---|---|---|---|
| ❑ SR 10.001 | Nuits de la Fondation Maeght Volume I | 1971 | 50.00 |
| ❑ SR 10.003 | Nuits de la Fondation Maeght Volume II | 1971 | 50.00 |

SWEET EARTH

| Number | Title (A Side/B Side) | Yr | NM |
|---|---|---|---|
| ❑ SER 1003 | The Other Side of the Sun | 1979 | 150.00 |
| *—Reproductions exist* | | | |

THOTH INTERGALACTIC

| Number | Title (A Side/B Side) | Yr | NM |
|---|---|---|---|
| ❑ LPB-711 [M] | The Magic City | 1969 | 60.00 |
| ❑ KH-1272 | Live in Egypt 1 | 1973 | 60.00 |
| ❑ IR-1972 | The Night of the Purple Moon | 1970 | 60.00 |
| ❑ KH-2772 [S] | Cosmic Tones for Mental Therapy | 1969 | 60.00 |
| ❑ KH-5472 [M] | Strange Strings | 196? | 80.00 |
| ❑ 7771 | Nidhamu | 197? | 60.00 |
| ❑ KH-98766 [M] | Other Planes of There | 1969 | 60.00 |

TRANSITION

| Number | Title (A Side/B Side) | Yr | NM |
|---|---|---|---|
| ❑ TLP-10 [M] | Jazz by Sun Ra | 1957 | 500.00 |
| *—With booklet (deduct 1/5 if missing)* | | | |

## SUNDOWNERS, THE

LIBERTY

| Number | Title (A Side/B Side) | Yr | NM |
|---|---|---|---|
| ❑ LRP-3269 [M] | Folk Songs for the Rich | 1962 | 20.00 |
| ❑ LST-7269 [S] | Folk Songs for the Rich | 1962 | 25.00 |

## SUNGLOWS, THE
See SUNNY AND THE SUNLINERS.

## SUNKEL, PHIL

ABC-PARAMOUNT

| Number | Title (A Side/B Side) | Yr | NM |
|---|---|---|---|
| ❑ ABC-136 [M] | Jazz Band | 1956 | 80.00 |
| ❑ ABC-225 [M] | Gerry Mulligan and Bob Brookmeyer Play Phil Sunkel's Jazz Concerto Grosso | 1958 | 60.00 |
| ❑ ABCS-225 [S] | Gerry Mulligan and Bob Brookmeyer Play Phil Sunkel's Jazz Concerto Grosso | 1958 | 50.00 |

## SUNNA

ASTRALWERKS

| Number | Title (A Side/B Side) | Yr | NM |
|---|---|---|---|
| ❑ ASW 49708-1 | One Minute Science | 2000 | 30.00 |

## SUNNY AND THE SUNLINERS

KEY-LOC

| Number | Title (A Side/B Side) | Yr | NM |
|---|---|---|---|
| ❑ 3001 [M] | Smile Now, Cry Later | 196? | 25.00 |
| ❑ 3002 [M] | No Te Chifles | 196? | 25.00 |
| ❑ 3003 [M] | Sunny and the Sunliners Live in Hollywood | 196? | 25.00 |
| ❑ 3004 [M] | Canta Sunny | 196? | 25.00 |
| ❑ 3005 [M] | A Little Brown-Eyed Soul | 196? | 25.00 |
| ❑ 3006 [M] | This Is My Band | 196? | 25.00 |
| ❑ 3007 [M] | Versatile | 196? | 25.00 |
| ❑ 3008 [M] | Adelante | 196? | 25.00 |
| ❑ 3009 [M] | Sky High | 196? | 25.00 |
| ❑ 3010 [M] | The Missing Link | 196? | 25.00 |

SUNGLOW

| Number | Title (A Side/B Side) | Yr | NM |
|---|---|---|---|
| ❑ SLP-101 [M] | Sunny Ozuna and the Sunglows | 1963 | 100.00 |
| *—As "The Sunglows"* | | | |
| ❑ SLP-102 [M] | The Fabulous Sunglows | 1964 | 100.00 |
| *—As "The Sunglows"* | | | |
| ❑ SLP-103 [M] | The Original Peanuts | 1965 | 80.00 |
| *—As "The Sunglows"* | | | |
| ❑ SLP-103S [S] | The Original Peanuts | 1965 | 100.00 |
| *—As "The Sunglows"* | | | |

TEAR DROP

| Number | Title (A Side/B Side) | Yr | NM |
|---|---|---|---|
| ❑ LPM-2000 [M] | Talk to Me | 1963 | 100.00 |
| ❑ LPM-2001 [M] | Las Vegas Welcomes Sunny and the Sunliners | 1964 | 40.00 |
| ❑ LPM-2008 [M] | Teardrop Presents Sunny and the Sunliners | 196? | 40.00 |

## SUNNY DAY REAL ESTATE

SUB POP

| Number | Title (A Side/B Side) | Yr | NM |
|---|---|---|---|
| ❑ SP-246 | Diary | 1994 | 20.00 |
| *—Black vinyl* | | | |
| ❑ SP-246 | Diary | 1994 | 40.00 |
| *—Aqua vinyl* | | | |
| ❑ SP-316 | Sunny Day Real Estate | 1995 | 20.00 |
| ❑ SP-409 | How It Feels to Be Something On | 1997 | 25.00 |
| ❑ SP-485 [(2)] | Sunny Day Real Estate Live | 1999 | 25.00 |

TIME BOMB

| Number | Title (A Side/B Side) | Yr | NM |
|---|---|---|---|
| ❑ 42541-1 [(2)] | The Rising Tide | 2000 | 40.00 |

## SUNNYLAND SLIM

BLUESVILLE

| Number | Title (A Side/B Side) | Yr | NM |
|---|---|---|---|
| ❑ BVLP-1016 [M] | Slim's Shout | 1961 | 120.00 |
| *—Blue label, silver print* | | | |
| ❑ BVLP-1016 [M] | Slim's Shout | 1964 | 30.00 |
| *—Blue label, trident logo at right* | | | |

PRESTIGE

| Number | Title (A Side/B Side) | Yr | NM |
|---|---|---|---|
| ❑ PRST-7723 | Slim's Shout | 1969 | 20.00 |

WORLD PACIFIC

| Number | Title (A Side/B Side) | Yr | NM |
|---|---|---|---|
| ❑ WPS-21890 | Slim's Got His Thing Goin' On | 1969 | 20.00 |

## SUNRAYS, THE

TOWER

| Number | Title (A Side/B Side) | Yr | NM |
|---|---|---|---|
| ❑ ST 5017 [S] | Andrea | 1966 | 60.00 |
| ❑ T 5017 [M] | Andrea | 1966 | 50.00 |

## SUNSET DRAGSTERS, THE

PALACE

| Number | Title (A Side/B Side) | Yr | NM |
|---|---|---|---|
| ❑ M-775 [M] | Hot Rod Rally | 196? | 60.00 |
| ❑ PST-775 [S] | Hot Rod Rally | 196? | 80.00 |

## SUNSETS, THE (1)

PALACE

| Number | Title (A Side/B Side) | Yr | NM |
|---|---|---|---|
| ❑ M-752 [M] | Surfing with the Sunsets | 1963 | 40.00 |
| ❑ PST-752 [S] | Surfing with the Sunsets | 1963 | 50.00 |

## SUNSHINE BOYS, THE

DOT

| Number | Title (A Side/B Side) | Yr | NM |
|---|---|---|---|
| ❑ DLP-3189 [M] | Sing Unto Him | 1959 | 30.00 |
| ❑ DLP-25189 [S] | Sing Unto Him | 1959 | 40.00 |

STARDAY

| Number | Title (A Side/B Side) | Yr | NM |
|---|---|---|---|
| ❑ SLP-113 [M] | America's Number One Gospel Group | 1960 | 40.00 |
| ❑ SLP-166 [M] | More Country Music Sing-Along | 1962 | 30.00 |
| ❑ SLP-349 [M] | A Happy Home Up There | 1965 | 30.00 |

## SUNSHINE COMPANY, THE

IMPERIAL

| Number | Title (A Side/B Side) | Yr | NM |
|---|---|---|---|
| ❑ LP-9359 [M] | Happy Is the Sunshine Company | 1967 | 20.00 |
| ❑ LP-9368 [M] | The Sunshine Company | 1968 | 25.00 |
| *—Mono copies are promo only* | | | |
| ❑ LP-12359 [S] | Happy Is the Sunshine Company | 1967 | 20.00 |
| ❑ LP-12368 [S] | The Sunshine Company | 1968 | 20.00 |
| ❑ LP-12399 | Sunshine and Shadows | 1969 | 20.00 |

## SUPER STOCKS, THE

CAPITOL

| Number | Title (A Side/B Side) | Yr | NM |
|---|---|---|---|
| ❑ ST 1997 [S] | Hot Rod Rally | 1963 | 70.00 |
| ❑ T 1997 [M] | Hot Rod Rally | 1963 | 50.00 |
| ❑ (S)T 2060 | Thunder Road Bonus Poster | 1964 | 50.00 |
| ❑ ST 2060 [S] | Thunder Road | 1964 | 125.00 |
| ❑ T 2060 [M] | Thunder Road | 1964 | 100.00 |
| ❑ ST 2113 [S] | Surf Route 101 | 1964 | 125.00 |
| *—Without bonus single* | | | |
| ❑ ST 2113 [S] | Surf Route 101 | 1964 | 150.00 |
| *—With bonus single, "Doin' the Surfink"/"Finksville, U.S.A." by Mr. Gasser and the Weirdos, in special pocket on front cover* | | | |
| ❑ T 2113 [M] | Surf Route 101 | 1964 | 100.00 |
| *—Without bonus single* | | | |
| ❑ T 2113 [M] | Surf Route 101 | 1964 | 125.00 |
| *—With bonus single, "Doin' the Surfink"/"Finksville, U.S.A." by Mr. Gasser and the Weirdos, in special pocket on front cover* | | | |
| ❑ ST 2190 [S] | School Is a Drag | 1964 | 120.00 |
| ❑ T 2190 [M] | School Is a Drag | 1964 | 100.00 |

## SUPERFINE DANDELION, THE

MAINSTREAM

| Number | Title (A Side/B Side) | Yr | NM |
|---|---|---|---|
| ❑ S-6102 [S] | The Superfine Dandelion | 1967 | 40.00 |
| ❑ 56102 [M] | The Superfine Dandelion | 1967 | 40.00 |

## SUPERSAX

MOBILE FIDELITY

| Number | Title (A Side/B Side) | Yr | NM |
|---|---|---|---|
| ❑ 1-511 | Supersax Plays Bird | 1981 | 40.00 |
| *—Audiophile vinyl* | | | |

## SUPERSISTER

DWARF

| Number | Title (A Side/B Side) | Yr | NM |
|---|---|---|---|
| ❑ PDLP-2001 | Supersister | 197? | 30.00 |

## SUPERTRAMP

A&M

| Number | Title (A Side/B Side) | Yr | NM |
|---|---|---|---|
| ❑ SP-3129 | Indelibly Stamped | 198? | 8.00 |
| *—Budget-line reissue* | | | |
| ❑ SP-3149 | Supertramp | 198? | 8.00 |
| *—Budget-line reissue* | | | |
| ❑ SP-3214 | Crisis? What Crisis? | 1982 | 8.00 |
| *—Budget-line reissue* | | | |
| ❑ SP-3215 | Even in the Quietest Moments | 1982 | 8.00 |
| *—Budget-line reissue* | | | |
| ❑ SP-3284 | …Famous Last Words… | 1986 | 8.00 |
| *—Budget-line reissue* | | | |
| ❑ SP-3647 | Crime of the Century | 1974 | 12.00 |
| ❑ SP-3708 | Breakfast in America | 1979 | 10.00 |
| ❑ SP-3730 [PD] | Breakfast in America | 1979 | 500.00 |
| *—In-house picture discs featuring A&M staff members posing with the cover model* | | | |
| ❑ SP-3732 | …Famous Last Words… | 1982 | 10.00 |
| ❑ SP-4274 | Supertramp | 197? | 10.00 |
| *—Second edition with silverish label* | | | |
| ❑ SP-4274 | Supertramp | 1970 | 20.00 |
| *—First edition with brown label* | | | |
| ❑ SP-4311 | Indelibly Stamped | 197? | 10.00 |
| *—Second edition with silverish label* | | | |
| ❑ SP-4311 | Indelibly Stamped | 1971 | 20.00 |
| *—First edition with brown label* | | | |
| ❑ SP-4560 | Crisis? What Crisis? | 1975 | 12.00 |
| ❑ SP-4634 | Even in the Quietest Moments… | 1977 | 12.00 |
| ❑ SP-4665 | Supertramp | 1978 | 12.00 |
| *—Reissue of 4274* | | | |
| ❑ SP-5013 | Brother Where You Bound | 1985 | 10.00 |
| ❑ SP-5181 | Free as a Bird | 1987 | 10.00 |
| ❑ SP-6702 [(2)] | Paris | 1980 | 12.00 |

MOBILE FIDELITY

| Number | Title (A Side/B Side) | Yr | NM |
|---|---|---|---|
| ❑ 1-005 | Crime of the Century | 1979 | 40.00 |
| *—Audiophile vinyl* | | | |
| ❑ MFQR-005 | Crime of the Century | 1983 | 120.00 |
| *—Ultra High Quality Recording; in box* | | | |
| ❑ 1-045 | Breakfast in America | 1980 | 50.00 |
| *—Audiophile vinyl* | | | |

SWEET THUNDER

| Number | Title (A Side/B Side) | Yr | NM |
|---|---|---|---|
| ❑ 5 | Even in the Quietest Moments… | 198? | 40.00 |
| *—Audiophile vinyl* | | | |

## SUPREMES, THE

DORAL

| Number | Title (A Side/B Side) | Yr | NM |
|---|---|---|---|
| ❑ DRL 104 | Doral Presents Diana Ross and the Supremes | 1971 | 50.00 |
| *—Available through Doral cigarettes* | | | |

MOTOWN

| Number | Title (A Side/B Side) | Yr | NM |
|---|---|---|---|
| ❑ M5-101V1 | Superstar Series, Vol. 1 | 1981 | 12.00 |
| *—By "Diana Ross and the Supremes"* | | | |
| ❑ PR-102 [DJ] | Touch Interview | 1971 | 25.00 |
| ❑ M5-138V1 | The Supremes A' Go-Go | 1981 | 12.00 |
| *—Reissue of Motown 649* | | | |
| ❑ M5-147V1 | I Hear a Symphony | 1981 | 12.00 |
| *—Reissue of Motown 643* | | | |
| ❑ M5-158V1 | The Supremes Sing Country Western and Pop | 1981 | 8.00 |
| *—Reissue of Motown 625* | | | |
| ❑ M5-162V1 | The Supremes at the Copa | 1981 | 12.00 |
| *—Reissue of Motown 636* | | | |
| ❑ M5-182V1 | The Supremes Sing Holland-Dozier-Holland | 1981 | 12.00 |
| *—Reissue of Motown 650* | | | |
| ❑ M5-203V1 | Diana Ross and the Supremes Greatest Hits, Volume 3 | 1981 | 12.00 |
| *—Reissue of Motown 702* | | | |
| ❑ M5-223V1 | Meet the Supremes | 1982 | 8.00 |
| *—Reissue of Motown 606* | | | |
| ❑ M5-237V1 | Greatest Hits | 1982 | 10.00 |
| *—Reissue (unknown if it's the complete 2-record set or an edited version)* | | | |
| ❑ M 606 [M] | Meet the Supremes | 1963 | 30.00 |
| *—With close-up of group's faces* | | | |
| ❑ M 606 [M] | Meet the Supremes | 1963 | 900.00 |
| *—With group sitting on stools* | | | |
| ❑ MS 606 [S] | Meet the Supremes | 1964 | 40.00 |
| *—With close-up of group's faces* | | | |
| ❑ MT/MS 610 | The Supremes Sing Ballads and Blues | 1963 | — |
| *—Unreleased* | | | |
| ❑ M 621 [M] | Where Did Our Love Go | 1964 | 30.00 |
| ❑ MS 621 [S] | Where Did Our Love Go | 1964 | 40.00 |
| ❑ M 623 [M] | A Bit of Liverpool | 1964 | 40.00 |
| ❑ MS 623 [S] | A Bit of Liverpool | 1964 | 50.00 |
| ❑ MS 625 [S] | The Supremes Sing Country, Western & Pop | 1965 | 30.00 |
| ❑ MT-625 [M] | The Supremes Sing Country, Western & Pop | 1965 | 25.00 |
| ❑ MT/MS 626 | The Supremes Live! Live! Live! | 1965 | — |
| *—Unreleased* | | | |
| ❑ M 627 [M] | More Hits by the Supremes | 1965 | 25.00 |
| ❑ MS 627 [S] | More Hits by the Supremes | 1965 | 30.00 |

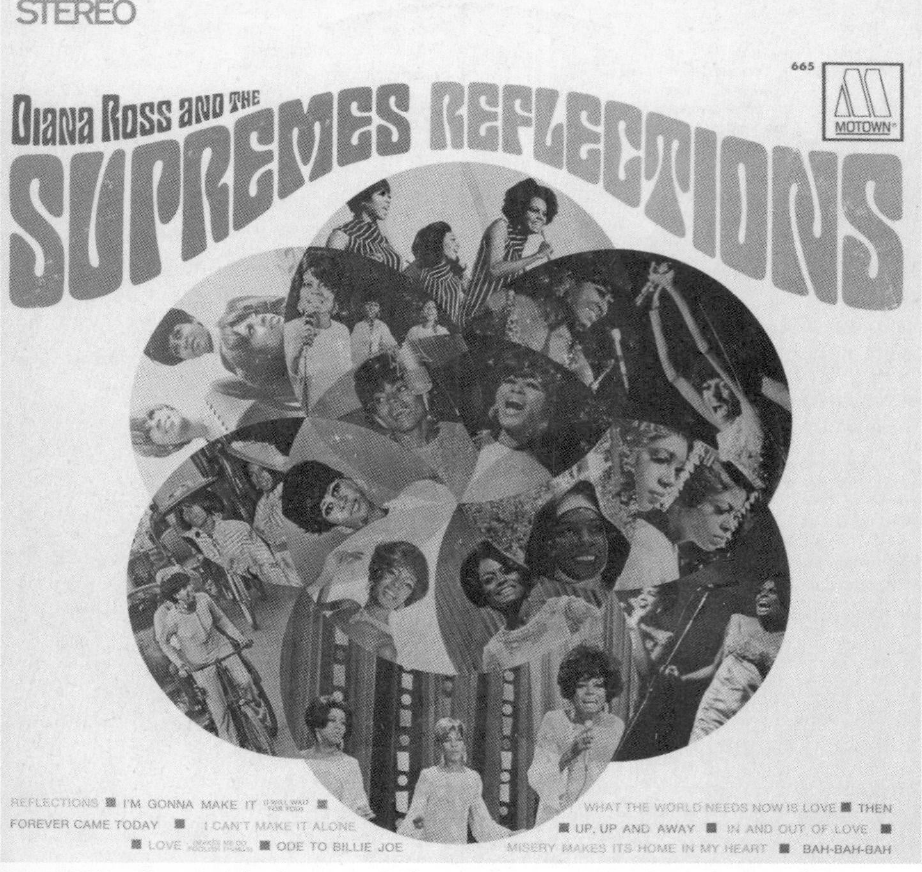

STEREO
665
MOTOWN
Diana Ross and the
SUPREMES REFLECTIONS
REFLECTIONS ■ I'M GONNA MAKE IT (I WILL WAIT FOR YOU) ■ FOREVER CAME TODAY ■ I CAN'T MAKE IT ALONE ■ LOVE ■ ODE TO BILLIE JOE
WHAT THE WORLD NEEDS NOW IS LOVE ■ THEN ■ UP, UP AND AWAY ■ IN AND OUT OF LOVE ■ MISERY MAKES ITS HOME IN MY HEART ■ BAH-BAH-BAH


Diana Ross and the Supremes, *Reflections,* Motown MS 665, 1968, stereo, $20.

| Number | Title (A Side/B Side) | Yr | NM |
|---|---|---|---|
| ❑ MT/MS 628 | There's a Place for Us | 1965 | — |
| *—Unreleased* | | | |
| ❑ M 629 [M] | We Remember Sam Cooke | 1965 | 25.00 |
| ❑ MS 629 [S] | We Remember Sam Cooke | 1965 | 30.00 |
| *—The above LP came out before Motown 627* | | | |
| ❑ M 636 [M] | The Supremes at the Copa | 1965 | 25.00 |
| ❑ MS 636 [S] | The Supremes at the Copa | 1965 | 30.00 |
| ❑ MT/MS 637 | A Tribute to the Girls | 1965 | — |
| *—Unreleased* | | | |
| ❑ MS 638 [S] | Merry Christmas | 1965 | 40.00 |
| *—Same as above, but in stereo* | | | |
| ❑ MT 638 [M] | Merry Christmas | 1965 | 30.00 |
| ❑ M 643 [M] | I Hear a Symphony | 1966 | 25.00 |
| ❑ MS 643 [S] | I Hear a Symphony | 1966 | 30.00 |
| ❑ MTMS 648 | Pure Gold | 1966 | — |
| *—Unreleased* | | | |
| ❑ M 649 [M] | The Supremes A' Go-Go | 1966 | 25.00 |
| ❑ MS 649 [S] | The Supremes A' Go-Go | 1966 | 30.00 |
| ❑ M 650 [M] | The Supremes Sing Holland-Dozier-Holland | 1967 | 25.00 |
| ❑ MS 650 [S] | The Supremes Sing Holland-Dozier-Holland | 1967 | 30.00 |
| ❑ M 659 [M] | The Supremes Sing Rodgers & Hart | 1967 | 25.00 |
| ❑ MS 659 [S] | The Supremes Sing Rodgers & Hart | 1967 | 30.00 |
| ❑ M 663 [(2)M] | Diana Ross and the Supremes Greatest Hits | 1967 | 30.00 |
| ❑ MS 663 [(2)S] | Diana Ross and the Supremes Greatest Hits | 1967 | 40.00 |
| ❑ MT/MS 663 | Diana Ross and the Supremes Greatest Hits Poster | 1967 | 10.00 |
| ❑ M 665 [M] | Reflections | 1968 | 30.00 |
| ❑ MS 665 [S] | Reflections | 1968 | 20.00 |
| ❑ MS 670 | Love Child | 1968 | 20.00 |
| ❑ M 672 [M] | Funny Girl | 1968 | 30.00 |
| *—Mono appears to be promo only* | | | |
| ❑ MS 672 [S] | Funny Girl | 1968 | 20.00 |
| *—The above LP came out before Motown 670* | | | |
| ❑ M 676 [M] | Live at London's Talk of the Town | 1968 | 30.00 |
| *—Mono is promo only* | | | |
| ❑ MS 676 [S] | Live at London's Talk of the Town | 1968 | 20.00 |
| *—The above LP came out before Motown 670 and 672* | | | |
| ❑ MS 689 | Let the Sunshine In | 1969 | 20.00 |
| ❑ MS 694 | Cream of the Crop | 1969 | 20.00 |
| ❑ MS 702 | Diana Ross and the Supremes Greatest Hits, Volume 3 | 1970 | 20.00 |

| Number | Title (A Side/B Side) | Yr | NM |
|---|---|---|---|
| ❑ MS 705 | Right On | 1970 | 15.00 |
| *—By "The Supremes"; the first LP after Diana Ross left* | | | |
| ❑ MS 708 [(2)] | Farewell | 1970 | 25.00 |
| *—By "Diana Ross and the Supremes"* | | | |
| ❑ MS 720 | New Ways But Love Stays | 1970 | 15.00 |
| ❑ MS 737 | Touch | 1971 | 15.00 |
| ❑ MS 746 | Promises Kept | 1972 | — |
| *—Unreleased* | | | |
| ❑ M 751L | Floy Joy | 1972 | 15.00 |
| ❑ M 756L | The Supremes | 1972 | 15.00 |
| ❑ M9-794L3 [(3)] | Anthology (1962-1969) | 1974 | 25.00 |
| *—By "Diana Ross and the Supremes"* | | | |
| ❑ M6-828 | The Supremes | 1975 | 15.00 |
| ❑ M6-863S1 | High Energy | 1976 | 15.00 |
| ❑ M6-873S1 | Mary, Scherrie and Susaye | 1976 | 15.00 |
| ❑ M7-904R1 | The Supremes at Their Best | 1978 | 15.00 |
| ❑ 5245 ML | Love Child | 1982 | 8.00 |
| *—Reissue of MS 670* | | | |
| ❑ 5252 ML | Merry Christmas | 1982 | 10.00 |
| *—Reissue of MS 638* | | | |
| ❑ 5270 ML | Where Did Our Love Go | 1982 | 8.00 |
| *—Reissue of MS 621* | | | |
| ❑ 5278 ML | Captured Live on Stage | 1982 | 8.00 |
| *—Reissue?* | | | |
| ❑ 5305 ML | Let the Sunshine In | 1983 | 8.00 |
| *—Reissue of MS 689* | | | |
| ❑ 5313 ML | Great Songs and Performances That Inspired the Motown 25th Anniversary TV Special | 1983 | 10.00 |
| ❑ 5361 ML | Motown Legends | 1985 | 10.00 |
| ❑ 5371 ML | Diana Ross and the Supremes Sing Motown | 1985 | 10.00 |
| ❑ 5381 ML3 [(3)] | 25th Anniversary | 1986 | 20.00 |
| *—By "Diana Ross and the Supremes"* | | | |
| **NATURAL RESOURCES** | | | |
| ❑ NR 4006T1 | Where Did Our Love Go | 1978 | 12.00 |
| *—Reissue of Motown 621* | | | |
| ❑ NR 4010 | Merry Christmas | 1978 | 12.00 |
| *—Reissue of Motown 638* | | | |
| **PICKWICK** | | | |
| ❑ SPC-3383 | Baby Love | 197? | 12.00 |
| *—Edited reissue of Motown 621* | | | |

| Number | Title (A Side/B Side) | Yr | NM |
|---|---|---|---|

### SUPREMES, THE, AND THE FOUR TOPS
Also see each artist's individual listings.

| Number | Title (A Side/B Side) | Yr | NM |
|---|---|---|---|
| **MOTOWN** | | | |
| ❑ M5-123V1A | The Magnificent Seven | 1981 | 12.00 |
| *—Reissue of Motown 717* | | | |
| ❑ MS 717 | The Magnificent Seven | 1970 | 15.00 |
| ❑ MS 736 | The Return of the Magnificent Seven | 1971 | 15.00 |
| ❑ MS 745 | Dynamite | 1971 | 15.00 |

### SUPREMES, THE, DIANA ROSS AND, AND THE TEMPTATIONS
Also see each artist's individual listings.

| Number | Title (A Side/B Side) | Yr | NM |
|---|---|---|---|
| **MOTOWN** | | | |
| ❑ M5-139V1 | Diana Ross and the Supremes Join the Temptations | 1981 | 12.00 |
| *—Reissue of Motown 679* | | | |
| ❑ M5-171V1 | TCB | 1981 | 12.00 |
| *—Reissue of Motown 682* | | | |
| ❑ M 679 [M] | Diana Ross and the Supremes Join the Temptations | 1968 | 30.00 |
| ❑ MS 679 [S] | Diana Ross and the Supremes Join the Temptations | 1968 | 20.00 |
| ❑ MS 682 | TCB | 1968 | 20.00 |
| ❑ MS 692 | Together | 1969 | 20.00 |
| ❑ MS 699 | On Broadway | 1969 | 20.00 |

### SURF STOMPERS, THE

| Number | Title (A Side/B Side) | Yr | NM |
|---|---|---|---|
| **DEL-FI** | | | |
| ❑ DFLP-1236 [M] | The Original Surfer Stomp | 1963 | 60.00 |
| ❑ DFST-1236 [S] | The Original Surfer Stomp | 1963 | 80.00 |
| ❑ DLF-1236 | The Original Surfer Stomp | 1997 | 12.00 |

### SURF TEENS, THE

| Number | Title (A Side/B Side) | Yr | NM |
|---|---|---|---|
| **SUTTON** | | | |
| ❑ SSU-339 [S] | Surf Mania | 1963 | 60.00 |
| ❑ SU-339 [M] | Surf Mania | 1963 | 50.00 |

### SURFARIS, THE (1)

| Number | Title (A Side/B Side) | Yr | NM |
|---|---|---|---|
| **DECCA** | | | |
| ❑ DL 4470 [M] | The Surfaris Play Wipe Out | 1963 | 25.00 |
| ❑ DL 4487 [M] | Hit City '64 | 1964 | 40.00 |
| ❑ DL 4560 [M] | Fun City, U.S.A. | 1964 | 40.00 |
| ❑ DL 4614 [M] | Hit City '65 | 1965 | 40.00 |
| ❑ DL 4663 [M] | It Ain't Me, Babe | 1965 | 40.00 |
| ❑ DL 74470 [S] | The Surfaris Play Wipe Out | 1963 | 30.00 |
| ❑ DL 74487 [S] | Hit City '64 | 1964 | 50.00 |
| ❑ DL 74560 [S] | Fun City, U.S.A. | 1964 | 50.00 |
| ❑ DL 74614 [S] | Hit City '65 | 1965 | 50.00 |
| ❑ DL 74663 [S] | It Ain't Me, Babe | 1965 | 50.00 |
| **DOT** | | | |
| ❑ DLP-3535 [M] | Wipe Out | 1963 | 30.00 |
| *—With no back cover photo of the Surfaris* | | | |
| ❑ DLP-3535 [M] | Wipe Out | 1963 | 40.00 |
| *—With back cover photo featuring four Surfaris* | | | |
| ❑ DLP-3535 [M] | Wipe Out | 1963 | 50.00 |
| *—With back cover photo featuring five Surfaris* | | | |
| ❑ DLP-25535 [S] | Wipe Out | 1963 | 40.00 |
| *—With no back cover photo of the Surfaris* | | | |
| ❑ DLP-25535 [S] | Wipe Out | 1963 | 50.00 |
| *—With back cover photo featuring four Surfaris* | | | |
| ❑ DLP-25535 [S] | Wipe Out | 1963 | 80.00 |
| *—With back cover photo featuring five Surfaris* | | | |
| **PICKWICK** | | | |
| ❑ SPC-3636 | Wipe Out and Surfer Joe | 1978 | 15.00 |

### SURFARIS, THE (2)

| Number | Title (A Side/B Side) | Yr | NM |
|---|---|---|---|
| **DIPLOMAT** | | | |
| ❑ D-2309 [M] | Wheels-Shorts-Hot Rods | 1963 | 25.00 |
| *—As "The Original Surfaris"* | | | |
| ❑ DS-2309 [S] | Wheels-Shorts-Hot Rods | 1963 | 30.00 |
| *—As "The Original Surfaris"* | | | |
| **SUNDAZED** | | | |
| ❑ LP-5014 | Bombora! | 199? | 10.00 |
| *—As "The Original Surfaris"* | | | |

### SURFERS, THE

| Number | Title (A Side/B Side) | Yr | NM |
|---|---|---|---|
| **HIFI** | | | |
| ❑ R-408 [M] | On the Rocks | 1959 | 120.00 |
| ❑ SR-408 [S] | On the Rocks | 1959 | 150.00 |

### SURFRIDERS, THE

| Number | Title (A Side/B Side) | Yr | NM |
|---|---|---|---|
| **VAULT** | | | |
| ❑ LP-105 [M] | Surfbeat, Volume 2 | 1963 | 30.00 |
| ❑ VS-105 [S] | Surfbeat, Volume 2 | 1963 | 40.00 |

### SURFSIDERS, THE

| Number | Title (A Side/B Side) | Yr | NM |
|---|---|---|---|
| **DESIGN** | | | |
| ❑ DLP-208 [M] | The Beach Boys Songbook | 1965 | 15.00 |
| ❑ DLPS-208 [S] | The Beach Boys Songbook | 1965 | 20.00 |

### SURPRISE PACKAGE

| Number | Title (A Side/B Side) | Yr | NM |
|---|---|---|---|
| **LHI** | | | |
| ❑ S-12005 | Free Up | 1968 | 40.00 |

### SURRATT, CECIL, AND SMITTY SMITH

| Number | Title (A Side/B Side) | Yr | NM |
|---|---|---|---|
| **AUDIO LAB** | | | |
| ❑ AL-1565 [M] | Songs Everybody Knows | 1961 | 100.00 |



**Except when noted otherwise, VG = 25% of NM, and VG+ = 50% of NM. (Example: VG = $2.00, VG+ = $4.00 and NM = $8.00.)**

| Number | Title (A Side/B Side) | Yr | NM |
|---|---|---|---|
| KING | | | |
| ❑ 860 [M] | Country Music from the Heart of the Country | 1963 | 50.00 |
| ❑ 966 [M] | Good Country Singin' and Pickin' | 1966 | 40.00 |
| **SUTCH, SCREAMING LORD** | | | |
| COTILLION | | | |
| ❑ SD 9015 | Lord Sutch and Heavy Friends | 1970 | 30.00 |
| *—With Jimmy Page, John Bonham and Jeff Beck* | | | |
| ❑ SD 9049 | Hands of Jack the Ripper | 1972 | 30.00 |
| **SUTTON, DICK** | | | |
| JAGUAR | | | |
| ❑ JP-802 [10] | Jazz Idiom | 1954 | 80.00 |
| ❑ JP-804 [10] | Progressive Dixieland | 1954 | 80.00 |
| **SUTTON, RALPH** | | | |
| ANALOGUE PRODUCTIONS | | | |
| ❑ AP 018 | Partners in Crime | 199? | 25.00 |
| *—Audiophile vinyl* | | | |
| CIRCLE | | | |
| ❑ L-413 [10] | Ralph Sutton | 1951 | 80.00 |
| COLUMBIA | | | |
| ❑ CL 6140 [10] | Piano Moods | 1950 | 80.00 |
| COMMODORE | | | |
| ❑ FL-30001 [M] | Ralph Sutton | 1951 | 80.00 |
| DECCA | | | |
| ❑ DL 5498 [10] | I Got Rhythm | 1953 | 80.00 |
| DOWN HOME | | | |
| ❑ MGD-4 [M] | Backroom Piano: The Ragtime Piano of Ralph Sutton | 1955 | 60.00 |
| ❑ DH-1003 [10] | Ragtime Piano Solos | 1953 | 80.00 |
| HARMONY | | | |
| ❑ HL 7109 [M] | Tribute to Fats | 1958 | 20.00 |
| OMEGA | | | |
| ❑ OSL-51 [S] | Jazz At the Olympics | 196? | 20.00 |
| RIVERSIDE | | | |
| ❑ RLP 12-212 [M] | Classic Jazz Piano | 1956 | 60.00 |
| ROULETTE | | | |
| ❑ SR-25232 [S] | Ragtime, U.S.A. | 1963 | 20.00 |
| VERVE | | | |
| ❑ MGV-1004 [M] | Backroom Piano: The Ragtime Piano of Ralph Sutton | 1956 | 50.00 |
| **SUZUKI, PAT** | | | |
| RCA VICTOR | | | |
| ❑ LPM-1965 [M] | Broadway '59 | 1959 | 20.00 |
| ❑ LSP-1965 [S] | Broadway '59 | 1959 | 25.00 |
| ❑ LPM-2030 [M] | Pat Suzuki | 1959 | 20.00 |
| ❑ LSP-2030 [S] | Pat Suzuki | 1959 | 25.00 |
| ❑ LPM-2186 [M] | Looking at You | 1960 | 20.00 |
| ❑ LSP-2186 [S] | Looking at You | 1960 | 25.00 |
| VIK | | | |
| ❑ LX-1127 [M] | The Many Sides of Pat Suzuki | 1958 | 30.00 |
| ❑ LX-1147 [M] | Pat Suzuki | 1958 | 30.00 |
| **SVENSSON, REINHOLD** | | | |
| PRESTIGE | | | |
| ❑ PRLP-106 [10] | Reinhold Svensson Piano | 1951 | 200.00 |
| ❑ PRLP-129 [10] | Reinhold Svensson, Volume 2: Favorites | 1952 | 200.00 |
| ❑ PRLP-155 [10] | New Sounds from Sweden, Volume 8 | 1953 | 200.00 |
| **SVENSSON, REINHOLD/BENGT HALLBERG** | | | |
| PRESTIGE | | | |
| ❑ PRLP-174 [10] | Piano Moderns | 1953 | 200.00 |
| **SWAGGART, JIMMY** | | | |
| JIM | | | |
| ❑ 24-141 [(2)] | Silver Jubilee Album: The Very Best of Jimmy Swaggart | 1981 | 20.00 |
| *—One of the two records is a picture disc* | | | |
| **SWAGMEN, THE** | | | |
| PARKWAY | | | |
| ❑ P-7015 [M] | Meet the Swagmen | 1962 | 40.00 |
| ❑ SP-7015 [S] | Meet the Swagmen | 1962 | 50.00 |
| **SWAMP DOGG** | | | |
| CANYON | | | |
| ❑ LP-7706 | Total Destruction to Your Mind | 1970 | 30.00 |
| ELEKTRA | | | |
| ❑ EKS-74089 | Rat On | 1971 | 20.00 |
| **SWAN SILVERTONES, THE** | | | |
| SPECIALTY | | | |
| ❑ SPS-2122 | Love Lifted Me | 1970 | 20.00 |
| ❑ SPS-2148 | My Rock | 1971 | 20.00 |

The Surfaris, *Surfer Joe and Wipe Out,* Dot DLP-3535, 1963, mono, $30 to $50 depending on the back cover photo (see listings).

| Number | Title (A Side/B Side) | Yr | NM |
|---|---|---|---|
| UPFRONT | | | |
| ❑ UPF-112 | The Lord's Prayer | 1968 | 20.00 |
| VEE JAY | | | |
| ❑ LP-5003 [M] | The Swan Silvertones | 1959 | 40.00 |
| ❑ LP-5006 [M] | Singing in My Soul | 1960 | 30.00 |
| ❑ LP-5013 [M] | Savior Pass Me Not | 1962 | 30.00 |
| ❑ LP-5034 [M] | Blessed Assurance | 1963 | 30.00 |
| ❑ LP-5052 [M] | The Best of the Swan Silvertones | 1963 | 30.00 |
| ❑ LP-5059 [M] | Let's Go to Church Together | 1964 | 25.00 |
| ❑ SR-5059 [S] | Let's Go to Church Together | 1964 | 30.00 |
| ❑ VJS-18008 | Pray for Me | 1975 | 20.00 |
| **SWANN, BETTYE** | | | |
| ABET | | | |
| ❑ LP 405 | Make Me Yours | 197? | 20.00 |
| CAPITOL | | | |
| ❑ ST-190 | The Soul View Now! | 1969 | 100.00 |
| ❑ ST-270 | Don't You Ever Get Tired of Hurting Me | 1969 | 50.00 |
| COLLECTABLES | | | |
| ❑ COL-5177 | Make Me Yours | 198? | 10.00 |
| MONEY | | | |
| ❑ 1103 [M] | Make Me Yours | 1967 | 25.00 |
| ❑ S-1103 [S] | Make Me Yours | 1967 | 25.00 |
| **SWEDES FROM JAZZVILLE** | | | |
| EPIC | | | |
| ❑ LN 3309 [M] | Swedes from Jazzville | 195? | 50.00 |
| **SWEENEY TODD** | | | |
| LONDON | | | |
| ❑ PS 694 | If Wishes Were Horses | 1977 | 60.00 |
| *—Possibly a Canadian import only* | | | |
| **SWEET, MATTHEW** | | | |
| A&M | | | |
| ❑ SP-5233 | Earth | 1989 | 15.00 |
| COLUMBIA | | | |
| ❑ BFC 40417 | Inside | 1986 | 15.00 |
| ZOO | | | |
| ❑ 31130 | Blue Sky on Mars | 1997 | 15.00 |
| *—All copies autographed by Matthew Steel on the label* | | | |

| Number | Title (A Side/B Side) | Yr | NM |
|---|---|---|---|
| ZOO/CLASSIC | | | |
| ❑ 11015 | Girlfriend | 1995 | 50.00 |
| *—Audiophile vinyl pressing; released on CD in 1991* | | | |
| ❑ 11050 | Altered Beast | 1995 | 20.00 |
| *—Audiophile vinyl pressing; released on CD in 1993* | | | |
| ❑ 11081 | 100% Fun | 1995 | 20.00 |
| **SWEET, THE (1)** | | | |
| BEAT ROCKET | | | |
| ❑ BR 125 | Hell Raisers! | 2000 | 12.00 |
| BELL | | | |
| ❑ 1125 | The Sweet | 1973 | 25.00 |
| CAPITOL | | | |
| ❑ SPRO-8371/2 [DJ] | For A.O.R. Radio Only | 1976 | 25.00 |
| ❑ SPRO-8849 [DJ] | Short and Sweet | 1978 | 30.00 |
| ❑ ST-11395 | Desolation Boulevard | 1975 | 12.00 |
| ❑ ST-11496 | Give Us a Wink | 1976 | 12.00 |
| ❑ STAO-11636 | Off the Record | 1977 | 12.00 |
| ❑ SKAO-11744 | Level Headed | 1978 | 12.00 |
| ❑ PRO-11929 [DJ] | Cut Above the Rest | 1979 | 50.00 |
| *—Special promo box contains record, cassette, 8-track, photo, bio* | | | |
| ❑ ST-11929 | Cut Above the Rest | 1979 | 12.00 |
| ❑ ST-12106 | Sweet VI | 1980 | 12.00 |
| ❑ SN-16115 | Give Us a Wink | 1980 | 8.00 |
| *—Budget-line reissue* | | | |
| ❑ SN-16116 | Off the Record | 1980 | 8.00 |
| *—Budget-line reissue* | | | |
| ❑ SN-16117 | Level Headed | 1980 | 8.00 |
| *—Budget-line reissue* | | | |
| ❑ SN-16118 | Cut Above the Rest | 1980 | 8.00 |
| *—Budget-line reissue* | | | |
| ❑ SN-16287 | Desolation Boulevard | 1981 | 8.00 |
| *—Budget-line reissue* | | | |
| KORY | | | |
| ❑ 3009 | The Sweet | 1977 | 10.00 |
| *—Reissue of Bell LP* | | | |
| **SWEET INSPIRATIONS, THE** | | | |
| ATLANTIC | | | |
| ❑ SD 8155 | The Sweet Inspirations | 1968 | 20.00 |
| ❑ SD 8182 | Songs of Faith and Inspiration | 1968 | 20.00 |
| ❑ 8201 [M] | What the World Needs Now Is Love | 1969 | 50.00 |
| *—Mono is white label promo only; "d/j copy monaural" sticker on stereo cover* | | | |

❑ SD 8201 [S] What the World Needs Now Is Love 1969 20.00
❑ SD 8225 Sweets for My Sweet 1969 20.00
❑ SD 8253 Sweet, Sweet Soul 1970 20.00

RSO
❑ RS-1-3058 Hot Butterfly 1979 10.00

STAX
❑ STS-3017 Estelle, Myrna and Sylvia 1973 20.00

**SWEET PANTS**

BARKLEY
❑ 1141 Fat Peter Presents Sweet Pants 1969 200.00

**SWEET THURSDAY**

TETRAGRAMMATON
❑ T-112 Sweet Thursday 1969 20.00

**SWEET TOOTHE**

DOMINION
❑ NR-7360 Testing 1974 300.00

**SWENSON, INGA**

LIBERTY
❑ LRP-3379 [M] I'm Old Fashioned 1964 25.00
❑ LST-7379 [S] I'm Old Fashioned 1964 30.00

**SWINGIN' MEDALLIONS**

SMASH
❑ MGS-27083 [M] Double Shot (Of My Baby's Love) 1966 30.00
*—Later pressings contain a "censored" version of the title song*
❑ MGS-27083 [M] Double Shot (Of My Baby's Love) 1966 40.00
*—First pressing contains the original 45 version of the title song*
❑ SRS-67083 [S] Double Shot (Of My Baby's Love) 1966 40.00
*—Later pressings contain a "censored" version of the title song*
❑ SRS-67083 [S] Double Shot (Of My Baby's Love) 1966 50.00
*—First pressing contains the original 45 version of the title song*

**SWINGING BLUE JEANS, THE**

IMPERIAL
❑ LP-9261 [M] Hippy Hippy Shake 1964 80.00
❑ LP-12261 [R] Hippy Hippy Shake 1964 80.00

**SWINGING SWEDES, THE**

TELEFUNKEN
❑ LGX-66050 [M] The Swinging Swedes 195? 50.00

**SWINGING SWEDES, THE/THE COOL BRITONS**

BLUE NOTE
❑ BLP-5019 [10] New Sounds from the Olde World 1951 300.00

**SWITTEL, JIMMY**

DECCA
❑ DL 8618 [M] Hymns to the Blessed Virgin Mary 1957 20.00

**SYKES, ROOSEVELT**

BLUESVILLE
❑ BVLP-1006 [M] The Return of Roosevelt Sykes 1960 100.00
*—Blue label, silver print*
❑ BVLP-1006 [M] The Return of Roosevelt Sykes 1964 30.00
*—Blue label, trident logo at right*
❑ BVLP-1014 [M] The Honeydripper 1961 100.00
*—Blue label, silver print*
❑ BVLP-1014 [M] The Honeydripper 1964 30.00
*—Blue label, trident logo at right*

CROWN
❑ CST-287 [S] Roosevelt Sykes Sings the Blues 1962 50.00
❑ CLP-5287 [M] Roosevelt Sykes Sings the Blues 1962 50.00

DELMARK
❑ DL-607 The Hard Driving Blues of Roosevelt Sykes 1963 50.00

**SYLVAIN SYLVAIN**

RCA VICTOR
❑ AFL1-3475 Sylvain Sylvain 1980 12.00
❑ AFL1-3913 Syl Sylvain and the Teardrops 1982 12.00
❑ DJL1-4062 [DJ] RCA Special Radio Series XII 1981 20.00
*—Promo-only interviews and music*

**SYLVERN, HANK**

ABC-PARAMOUNT
❑ 146 [M] Christmas in Hi-Fi 1956 25.00

**SYLVIA (1)**

STANG
❑ 1010 Sylvia 197? 20.00

SUGAR HILL
❑ 258 Sylvia I 1981 10.00

VIBRATION
❑ 126 Pillow Talk 1973 15.00
❑ 131 Lay It On Me 1977 12.00
❑ 143 Brand New Funk 197? 12.00

**SYLVIAN, DAVID**

VIRGIN
❑ 2167 [DJ] Ink in the Well — A Conversation 1987 20.00
*—Promo-only interview album*
❑ 90677 Secrets of the Beehive 1987 10.00
❑ 90904 Plight and Premonition 1988 10.00
*—With Holger Czukay*

**SYMS, SYLVIA**

ATLANTIC
❑ ALS-137 [10] Songs by Sylvia Syms 1952 100.00
❑ 1243 [M] Songs by Sylvia Syms 1956 50.00
*—Black label*
❑ 1243 [M] Songs by Sylvia Syms 1960 25.00
*—Multicolor label, white "fan" logo at right*

COLUMBIA
❑ CL 1447 [M] Torch Song 1960 30.00
*—Red and black label with six "eye" logos*
❑ CS 8243 [S] Torch Song 1960 40.00
*—Red and black label with six "eye" logos*

DECCA
❑ DL 8188 [M] Sylvia Syms Sings 1955 50.00
*—Black label, silver print*
❑ DL 8639 [M] Songs of Love 1958 40.00
*—Black label, silver print*

KAPP
❑ KL-1236 [M] That Man — Love Songs to Frank Sinatra 1961 30.00
❑ KS-3236 [S] That Man — Love Songs to Frank Sinatra 1961 40.00

MOVIETONE
❑ 2022 [M] In a Sentimental Mood 1967 20.00

PRESTIGE
❑ PRLP-7439 [M] Sylvia Is! 1965 20.00
❑ PRST-7439 [S] Sylvia Is! 1965 25.00
❑ PRLP-7489 [M] For Once in My Life 1967 25.00
❑ PRST-7489 [S] For Once in My Life 1967 20.00

20TH CENTURY FOX
❑ TFM-4123 [M] The Fabulous Sylvia Syms 1963 25.00
❑ TFS-4123 [S] The Fabulous Sylvia Syms 1963 30.00

VERSION
❑ VLP-103 [10] After Dark 1954 80.00

**SYNDICATE OF SOUND**

BELL
❑ 6001 [M] Little Girl 1966 50.00
❑ S-6001 [S] Little Girl 1966 80.00

SUNDAZED
❑ LP 5051 Little Girl 2001 12.00
*—Reissue on 180-gram vinyl*

**SZABO, GABOR**

IMPULSE!
❑ A-9105 [M] Gypsy 66 1966 20.00
❑ AS-9105 [S] Gypsy 66 1966 25.00
❑ A-9123 [M] Spellbinder 1966 20.00
❑ AS-9123 [S] Spellbinder 1966 25.00
❑ A-9128 [M] Jazz Raga 1967 25.00
❑ AS-9128 [S] Jazz Raga 1967 20.00
❑ A-9146 [M] The Sorcerer 1967 25.00
❑ AS-9146 [S] The Sorcerer 1967 20.00
❑ AS-9151 Wind, Sky and Diamonds 1968 25.00
*—This exists on the pre-ABC Impulse! label, though theoretically it shouldn't. Other titles may exist on that label also.*

**SZERYNG, HENRYK**

MERCURY LIVING PRESENCE
❑ SR 90308 [S] Brahms: Violin Concerto in D 196? 30.00
*—With Antal Dorati/London Symphony Orchestra; maroon label, with "Vendor: Mercury Record Corporation"*
❑ SR 90308 [S] Brahms: Violin Concerto in D 196? 80.00
*—With Antal Dorati/London Symphony Orchestra; maroon label, no "Vendor: Mercury Record Corporation"*
❑ SR 90348 [S] Kreisler: Caprice Viennois and 12 Others 196? 30.00
*—Maroon label, no "Vendor: Mercury Record Corporation"*
❑ SR 90367 [S] Treasures 196? 25.00
*—Maroon label, no "Vendor: Mercury Record Corporation"*
❑ SR 90393 [S] Khachaturian: Violin Concerto 196? 20.00
*—With Antal Dorati/London Symphony Orchestra; third edition (dark red, not maroon, label)*
❑ SR 90393 [S] Khachaturian: Violin Concerto 196? 40.00
*—With Antal Dorati/London Symphony Orchestra; maroon label, with "Vendor: Mercury Record Corporation"*
❑ SR 90393 [S] Khachaturian: Violin Concerto 196? 50.00
*—With Antal Dorati/London Symphony Orchestra; maroon label, no "Vendor: Mercury Record Corporation"*
❑ SR 90406 [S] Mendelssohn: Violin Concerto in E; Schumann: Violin Concerto in D 196? 25.00
*—With Antal Dorati/London Symphony Orchestra; maroon label, no "Vendor: Mercury Record Corporation"*
❑ SR 90466 [S] Bach: Violin Concertos in A and E; Double Concerto in D 196? 70.00
*—Maroon label, with "Vendor: Mercury Record Corporation"*

RCA VICTOR RED SEAL
❑ LSC-2281 [S] Brahms: Violin Concerto 1959 150.00
*—With Pierre Monteux/London Symphony Orchestra; original with "shaded dog" label*
❑ LSC-2363 [S] Tchaikovsky: Violin Concerto in D 1960 80.00
*—With Charles Munch/Boston Symphony Orchestra; original with "shaded dog" label*
❑ LSC-2421 [S] In Recital 1960 50.00
*—Original with "shaded dog" label*
❑ LSC-2456 [S] Lalo: Symphonie Espagnole 1961 200.00
*—With Walter Hendl/Chicago Symphony Orch.; original with "shaded dog" label*

**SZERYNG, HENRYK / ARTUR RUBENSTEIN**

RCA VICTOR RED SEAL
❑ LSC-2377 [S] Beethoven: Kreutzer and Spring Sonatas 1960 40.00
*—Original with "shaded dog" label*
❑ LSC-2619 [S] Brahms: Violin Concertos 2 and 3 1962 50.00
*—Original with "shaded dog" label*
❑ LSC-2620 [S] Beethoven: Violin Sonata No. 8; Brahms: Violin Sonata No. 1 1962 50.00
*—Original with "shaded dog" label*

**SZIGETI, JOSEF**

MERCURY LIVING PRESENCE
❑ SR 90225 [S] Brahms: Violin Concerto in D 196? 180.00
*—Maroon label, no "Vendor: Mercury Record Corporation"*
❑ SR 90319 [S] Prokofiev: Violin Sonatas No. 1 and 2 196? 100.00
*—Maroon label, no "Vendor: Mercury Record Corporation"*
❑ SR 90358 [S] Beethoven: Violin Concerto in D 196? 100.00
*—With Antal Dorati/London Symphony Orchestra; maroon label, no "Vendor: Mercury Record Corporation"*
❑ SR 90419 [S] Prokofiev: Violin Concerto No. 1; Stravinsky: Duo Concertante 196? 30.00
*—Maroon label, no "Vendor: Mercury Record Corporation"*
❑ SR 90419 [S] Prokofiev: Violin Concerto No. 1; Stravinsky: Duo Concertante 196? 50.00
*—Maroon label, with "Vendor: Mercury Record Corporation" (second edition is more sought after than the first)*
❑ SR 90442 [S] Violin Sonatas 1965 50.00
*—Maroon label, with "Vendor: Mercury Record Corporation"*

**SZIGETI, JOSEF; MIECZYSLAW HORSZOWSKI; JOHN BARROWS**

MERCURY LIVING PRESENCE
❑ SR 90210 [S] Brahms: Horn Trio; Violin Sonata No. 2 196? 70.00
*—Maroon label, with "Vendor: Mercury Record Corporation"*
❑ SR 90210 [S] Brahms: Horn Trio; Violin Sonata No. 2 196? 180.00
*—Maroon label, no "Vendor: Mercury Record Corporation"*

# T

**T.C. ATLANTIC**

DOVE
❑ LP-4459 T.C. Atlantic 1966 100.00

**T.I.M.E.**

LIBERTY
❑ LST-7558 T.I.M.E. 1968 25.00
❑ LST-7605 Smooth Ball 1969 25.00

**T. REX**

A&M
❑ SP-3514 [(2)] Tyrannosaurus Rex (A Beginning) 1972 15.00
*—Compilation of early LPs Prophets, Seers & Sages and My People Were Fair and Had Sky in Their Hair But Now They're Content to Wear Stars on Their Brows*

BLUE THUMB
❑ BTS 7 Unicorn 1969 20.00
❑ BTS 18 A Beard of Stars 1970 20.00
*—Add $5 for bonus single SP-6115/6, "Ride a White Swan"/"Is It Love." For reasons unknown, the single seems to be much more readily available than the LP*

CASABLANCA
❑ NBLP 7005 Light of Love 1974 12.00
*—Reissue of 9006*
❑ NB 9006 Light of Love 1974 15.00
*—Original, distributed by Warner Bros.*

MARC ON WAX/RELATIVITY
❑ 8249 Bolan's Zip Gun 198? 10.00
❑ 8250 Zinc Alloy & The Hidden Riders of Tomorrow 198? 10.00
❑ 8251 Dandy in the Underworld 198? 10.00
❑ 8252 Futuristic Dragon 198? 10.00
❑ 8253 The Slider 198? 10.00
❑ 8254 Tanx 198? 10.00

| Number | Title (A Side/B Side) | Yr | NM |
|---|---|---|---|
| **REPRISE** | | | |
| ❑ PRO 511 [DJ] | An Interview with Marc Bolan | 1971 | 100.00 |
| ❑ MS 2095 | The Slider | 1972 | 12.00 |
| ❑ MS 2132 | Tanx | 1973 | 12.00 |
| ❑ RS 6440 | T. Rex | 1971 | 12.00 |
| ❑ RS 6466 | Electric Warrior | 1971 | 12.00 |
| **RHINO** | | | |
| ❑ R1-76111 | Electric Warrior | 2003 | 15.00 |
| *—Reissue on 180-gram vinyl* | | | |
| **WARNER BROS.** | | | |
| ❑ 25333 | T. Rextasy: The Best of T. Rex, 1970-1973 | 1985 | 10.00 |

### T2

| Number | Title (A Side/B Side) | Yr | NM |
|---|---|---|---|
| **LONDON** | | | |
| ❑ PS 583 | It'll All Work Out in Boomland | 1971 | 80.00 |

### T.V. AND THE TRIBESMEN

| Number | Title (A Side/B Side) | Yr | NM |
|---|---|---|---|
| **HANNA-BARBERA** | | | |
| ❑ HLP-9507 [S] | Barefootin' | 1966 | 25.00 |

### T-BONES, THE

Members of this group later formed HAMILTON, JOE FRANK AND REYNOLDS.

| Number | Title (A Side/B Side) | Yr | NM |
|---|---|---|---|
| **LIBERTY** | | | |
| ❑ LRP-3346 [M] | Boss Drag | 1963 | 60.00 |
| ❑ LRP-3363 [M] | Boss Drag at the Beach | 1964 | 60.00 |
| ❑ LRP-3404 [M] | Doin' the Jerk | 1965 | 40.00 |
| ❑ LRP-3439 [M] | No Matter What Shape (Your Stomach's In) | 1966 | 20.00 |
| ❑ LRP-3446 [M] | Sippin' and Chippin' | 1966 | 20.00 |
| ❑ LRP-3471 [M] | Everyone's Gone to the Moon | 1966 | 20.00 |
| ❑ LST-7346 [S] | Boss Drag | 1963 | 100.00 |
| ❑ LST-7363 [S] | Boss Drag at the Beach | 1964 | 100.00 |
| ❑ LST-7404 [S] | Doin' the Jerk | 1965 | 60.00 |
| ❑ LST-7439 [S] | No Matter What Shape (Your Stomach's In) | 1966 | 25.00 |
| ❑ LST-7446 [S] | Sippin' and Chippin' | 1966 | 25.00 |
| ❑ LST-7471 [S] | Everyone's Gone to the Moon | 1966 | 25.00 |
| **SUNSET** | | | |
| ❑ SUM-1119 [M] | Shapin' Things Up | 196? | 12.00 |
| ❑ SUS-5119 [S] | Shapin' Things Up | 196? | 15.00 |

### TABOR, ERON

| Number | Title (A Side/B Side) | Yr | NM |
|---|---|---|---|
| **STUDIO ONE** | | | |
| ❑ S-104 | Eron Tabor | 196? | 20.00 |

### TAD

| Number | Title (A Side/B Side) | Yr | NM |
|---|---|---|---|
| **SUB POP** | | | |
| ❑ 27 | God's Balls | 1989 | 10.00 |
| *—Others in standard cover* | | | |
| ❑ 27 | God's Balls | 1989 | 15.00 |
| *—Next 500 with "Manzine"* | | | |
| ❑ 27 | God's Balls | 1989 | 20.00 |
| *—First 2,000 with gatefold cover* | | | |
| ❑ 49 [EP] | Salt Lick | 1990 | 8.00 |
| ❑ 89 | 8-Way Santa | 1991 | 10.00 |

### TALBERT, THOMAS

| Number | Title (A Side/B Side) | Yr | NM |
|---|---|---|---|
| **ATLANTIC** | | | |
| ❑ 1250 [M] | Bix Fats Duke Interpreted by Thomas Talbert | 1957 | 40.00 |
| *—Black label* | | | |
| ❑ 1250 [M] | Bix Fats Duke Interpreted by Thomas Talbert | 1961 | 20.00 |
| *—Multicolor label, white "fan" logo at right* | | | |
| ❑ SD 1250 [S] | Bix Fats Duke Interpreted by Thomas Talbert | 1958 | 40.00 |
| *—Green label* | | | |
| ❑ SD 1250 [S] | Bix Fats Duke Interpreted by Thomas Talbert | 1961 | 20.00 |
| *—Multicolor label, white "fan" logo at right* | | | |

### TALISMEN, THE

| Number | Title (A Side/B Side) | Yr | NM |
|---|---|---|---|
| **BLUE STAR** | | | |
| ❑ M-6323 [M] | Treasury of American Railroad Songs and Ballads | 1964 | 20.00 |
| ❑ MS-6323 [S] | Treasury of American Railroad Songs and Ballads | 1964 | 25.00 |
| **PRESTIGE** | | | |
| ❑ PRLP-7406 [M] | Folk Swingers Extraordinaire | 1965 | 20.00 |
| ❑ PRST-7406 [S] | Folk Swingers Extraordinaire | 1965 | 25.00 |

### TALKING HEADS

| Number | Title (A Side/B Side) | Yr | NM |
|---|---|---|---|
| **RHINO VINYL** | | | |
| ❑ R1-70802 | Remain in Light | 2006 | 15.00 |
| *—Reissue on 180-gram vinyl* | | | |
| **SIRE** | | | |
| ❑ PRO-A-930 [DJ] | Talking Heads | 1980 | 15.00 |
| *—Promo-only 4-song sampler from "Remain in Light"* | | | |
| ❑ PRO-A-1033 [DJ] | The Name of This Band Is Talking Heads Sampler | 1982 | 15.00 |
| *—Promo only* | | | |
| ❑ 2SR 3590 [(2)] | The Name of This Band Is Talking Heads | 1982 | 20.00 |
| ❑ SR 6036 | Talking Heads '77 | 1977 | 12.00 |
| ❑ SR 6058 | More Songs About Buildings and Food | 1978 | 12.00 |

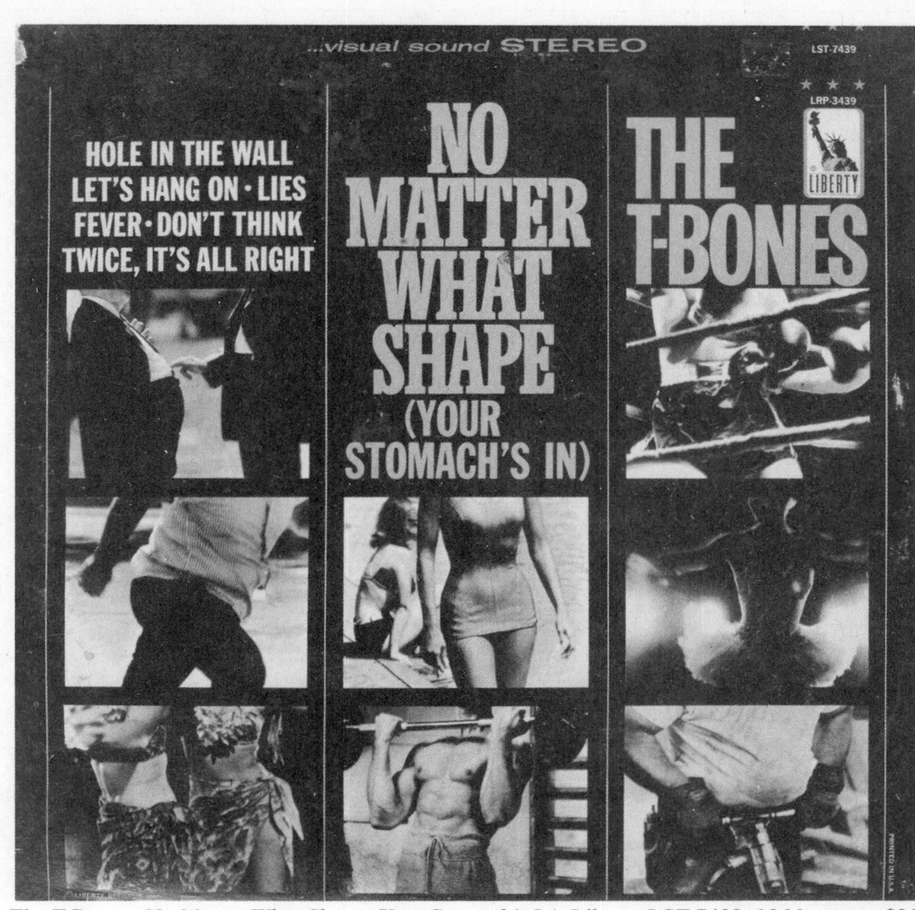


The T-Bones, *No Matter What Shape (Your Stomach's In),* Liberty LST-7439, 1966, stereo, $25.

| Number | Title (A Side/B Side) | Yr | NM |
|---|---|---|---|
| ❑ SRK 6058 | More Songs About Buildings and Food | 1979 | 8.00 |
| *—Reissue with new prefix* | | | |
| ❑ SRK 6076 | Fear of Music | 1979 | 10.00 |
| ❑ SRK 6095 | Remain in Light | 1981 | 10.00 |
| ❑ 23771 | Speaking in Tongues | 1983 | 20.00 |
| *—Clear vinyl in oversize plastic container with Robert Rauschenberg artwork* | | | |
| ❑ 23883 | Speaking in Tongues | 1983 | 10.00 |
| *—Standard issue* | | | |
| ❑ 25121 | Stop Making Sense (Soundtrack) | 1984 | 15.00 |
| *—First issue with booklet and black & white cover* | | | |
| ❑ 25186 | Stop Making Sense (Soundtrack) | 1984 | 10.00 |
| *—Second issue: No booklet, color cover* | | | |
| ❑ 25305 | Little Creatures | 1985 | 10.00 |
| ❑ 25512 | True Stories | 1986 | 10.00 |
| ❑ 25654 | Naked | 1988 | 10.00 |
| ❑ R 124560 | Stop Making Sense | 1984 | 12.00 |
| *—RCA Music Service edition* | | | |
| ❑ R 150102 | Speaking in Tongues | 1983 | 12.00 |
| *—BMG Direct Marketing edition* | | | |
| ❑ R 153810 | Naked | 1988 | 12.00 |
| *—BMG Direct Marketing edition* | | | |
| ❑ R 153839 | Little Creatures | 1985 | 12.00 |
| *—RCA Music Service edition* | | | |
| **WARNER BROS.** | | | |
| ❑ WBMS-104 [DJ] | Talking Heads Live on Tour | 1979 | 25.00 |
| *—Part of "The Warner Bros. Music Show" series (has been counterfeited)* | | | |

### TAMBA 4, THE

| Number | Title (A Side/B Side) | Yr | NM |
|---|---|---|---|
| **A&M** | | | |
| ❑ SP-3004 | We and the Sea | 1968 | 25.00 |
| ❑ SP-3013 | Samba Blim | 1969 | 30.00 |

### TAMPA RED

| Number | Title (A Side/B Side) | Yr | NM |
|---|---|---|---|
| **BLUEBIRD** | | | |
| ❑ AXM2-5501 [(2)] | Guitar Wizard | 1975 | 15.00 |
| **BLUES CLASSICS** | | | |
| ❑ 25 | Guitar Wizard (1935-53) | 197? | 12.00 |
| **BLUESVILLE** | | | |
| ❑ BVLP-1030 [M] | Don't Tampa with the Blues | 1961 | 120.00 |
| *—Blue label, silver print* | | | |
| ❑ BVLP-1030 [M] | Don't Tampa with the Blues | 1963 | 30.00 |
| *—Blue label, trident logo at right* | | | |
| ❑ BVLP-1043 [M] | Don't Jive Me | 1962 | 120.00 |
| *—Blue label, silver print* | | | |
| ❑ BVLP-1043 [M] | Don't Jive Me | 1963 | 30.00 |
| *—Blue label, trident logo at right* | | | |
| **FANTASY** | | | |
| ❑ OBC-516 | Don't Tampa with the Blues | 198? | 10.00 |
| **YAZOO** | | | |
| ❑ 1039 | Bottleneck Guitar | 197? | 12.00 |

### TAMS, THE

| Number | Title (A Side/B Side) | Yr | NM |
|---|---|---|---|
| **ABC** | | | |
| ❑ ABCS-481 [R] | Presenting the Tams | 1968 | 20.00 |
| *—Reissue of ABC-Paramount 481* | | | |
| ❑ ABCS-499 [S] | Hey Girl, Don't Bother Me | 1964 | 20.00 |
| *—Reissue of ABC-Paramount 499* | | | |
| ❑ ABC-596 [M] | Time for the Tams | 1967 | 30.00 |
| ❑ ABCS-596 [S] | Time for the Tams | 1967 | 30.00 |
| ❑ ABCS-627 | A Little More Soul | 1968 | 25.00 |
| ❑ ABCS-673 | A Portrait of the Tams | 1969 | 25.00 |
| **ABC-PARAMOUNT** | | | |
| ❑ ABC-481 [M] | Presenting the Tams | 1964 | 50.00 |
| ❑ ABCS-481 [R] | Presenting the Tams | 1964 | 30.00 |
| ❑ ABC-499 [M] | Hey Girl, Don't Bother Me | 1964 | 30.00 |
| ❑ ABCS-499 [S] | Hey Girl, Don't Bother Me | 1964 | 40.00 |
| **CAPITOL** | | | |
| ❑ SM-11839 | The Best of the Tams | 1979 | 12.00 |
| **COMPLEAT** | | | |
| ❑ CMLP-5001 [EP] | Beach Music from the Tams | 198? | 8.00 |
| **1-2-3** | | | |
| ❑ ST-567 | The Best of the Tams | 1970 | 20.00 |
| **SOUNDS SOUTH** | | | |
| ❑ SO-16010 | The Mighty, Mighty Tams | 1977 | 15.00 |

### TANEGA, NORMA

| Number | Title (A Side/B Side) | Yr | NM |
|---|---|---|---|
| **NEW VOICE** | | | |
| ❑ NV-2001 [M] | Walkin' My Cat Named Dog | 1966 | 40.00 |
| ❑ NVS-2001 [S] | Walkin' My Cat Named Dog | 1966 | 80.00 |

### TANGERINE DREAM

| Number | Title (A Side/B Side) | Yr | NM |
|---|---|---|---|
| **CAROLINE** | | | |
| ❑ CAROL 1349 | Livemiles | 1988 | 12.00 |

Talking Heads, *Talking Heads: 77,* Sire SR 6036, 1977, $12.

| Number | Title (A Side/B Side) | Yr | NM |
|---|---|---|---|
| **ELEKTRA** | | | |
| ❑ 5E-521 | Thief | 1981 | 10.00 |
| ❑ 5E-557 | Exit | 1981 | 10.00 |
| **EMI AMERICA** | | | |
| ❑ ST-17141 | Flashpoint | 1984 | 10.00 |
| **MCA** | | | |
| ❑ 2277 | Sorcerer | 1977 | 12.00 |
| ❑ 6165 | Legend | 1986 | 8.00 |
| **PRIVATE MUSIC** | | | |
| ❑ 2042-1-P | Optical Race | 1988 | 15.00 |
| ❑ 2047-1-P | Miracle Mile | 1989 | 15.00 |
| ❑ 2057-1-P | Lily on the Beach | 1989 | 15.00 |
| **RELATIVITY** | | | |
| ❑ EMC 8043 | Le Parc | 198? | 12.00 |
| ❑ EMC 8045 [(2)] | Poland | 198? | 15.00 |
| ❑ 86561 8068 | Electronic Meditation | 1986 | 12.00 |
| ❑ 86561 8069 | Alpha Centauri | 1986 | 12.00 |
| ❑ 86561 8070 [(2)] | Zeit | 1986 | 15.00 |
| ❑ 86561 8071 | Atam | 1986 | 12.00 |
| ❑ 86561 8072 | Green Desert | 1986 | 12.00 |
| ❑ 86561 8113 | Underwater Sunlight | 1986 | 12.00 |
| **VIRGIN** | | | |
| ❑ VR 13-108 | Phaedra | 1974 | 15.00 |
| ❑ VR 13-116 | Rubycon | 1975 | 15.00 |
| ❑ PZ 34427 | Stratosfear | 1976 | 15.00 |
| ❑ PZG 35014 [(2)] | Encore | 1977 | 20.00 |
| **VIRGIN INTERNATIONAL** | | | |
| ❑ VI 2010 | Phaedra | 1979 | 10.00 |
| *—Reissue* | | | |
| ❑ VI 2025 | Rubycon | 1979 | 10.00 |
| *—Reissue* | | | |
| ❑ VI 2044 | Ricochet | 1975 | 15.00 |
| ❑ VI 2068 | Stratosfear | 1979 | 12.00 |
| *—Reissue of 34427* | | | |
| ❑ VI 2097 | Cyclone | 1979 | 10.00 |
| *—Reissue* | | | |
| ❑ VI 2111 | Force Majeure | 1979 | 12.00 |
| **TANGERINE ZOO, THE** | | | |
| **MAINSTREAM** | | | |
| ❑ S-6107 | Tangerine Zoo | 1968 | 50.00 |
| ❑ S-6118 | Outside Looking In | 1969 | 70.00 |

| Number | Title (A Side/B Side) | Yr | NM |
|---|---|---|---|
| **TAPSCOTT, HORACE** | | | |
| **FLYING DUTCHMAN** | | | |
| ❑ FDS-107 | The Giant Is Awakened | 1969 | 20.00 |
| **TARANTULA** | | | |
| **A&M** | | | |
| ❑ SP-4202 | Tarantula | 1969 | 20.00 |
| **TARRIERS, THE** | | | |
| **ATLANTIC** | | | |
| ❑ 8042 [M] | Tell the World | 1960 | 30.00 |
| ❑ SD 8042 [S] | Tell the World | 1960 | 40.00 |
| **DECCA** | | | |
| ❑ DL 4342 [M] | The Tarriers | 1962 | 25.00 |
| ❑ DL 4538 [M] | Gather 'Round | 1964 | 25.00 |
| ❑ DL 74342 [S] | The Tarriers | 1962 | 30.00 |
| ❑ DL 74538 [S] | Gather 'Round | 1964 | 30.00 |
| **GLORY** | | | |
| ❑ PG-1200 [M] | The Tarriers | 1958 | 60.00 |
| **KAPP** | | | |
| ❑ KL 1349 [M] | The Original Tarriers | 1963 | 25.00 |
| ❑ KS 3349 [S] | The Original Tarriers | 1963 | 30.00 |
| **UNITED ARTISTS** | | | |
| ❑ UAL-4033 [M] | Hard Travelin' | 1959 | 30.00 |
| ❑ UAS-5033 [S] | Hard Travelin' | 1959 | 40.00 |
| **TASTE** | | | |
| **ATCO** | | | |
| ❑ SD 33-296 | Taste | 1969 | 25.00 |
| ❑ SD 33-322 | On the Boards | 1970 | 25.00 |
| **TATE, BABY** | | | |
| **BLUESVILLE** | | | |
| ❑ BVLP-1072 [M] | What You Done | 1963 | 25.00 |
| *—Blue label, trident logo at right* | | | |
| ❑ BVLP-1072 [M] | What You Done | 1963 | 80.00 |
| *—Blue label, silver print* | | | |
| **TATE, BUDDY** | | | |
| **FELSTED** | | | |
| ❑ 2004 [S] | Swinging Like Tate | 1958 | 80.00 |
| ❑ 7004 [M] | Swinging Like Tate | 1958 | 80.00 |

| Number | Title (A Side/B Side) | Yr | NM |
|---|---|---|---|
| **SWINGVILLE** | | | |
| ❑ SVLP-2003 [M] | Tate's Date | 1960 | 50.00 |
| *—Purple label* | | | |
| ❑ SVLP-2003 [M] | Tate's Date | 1965 | 25.00 |
| *—Blue label, trident logo at right* | | | |
| ❑ SVLP-2014 [M] | Tate-A-Tate | 1960 | 50.00 |
| *—Purple label* | | | |
| ❑ SVLP-2014 [M] | Tate-A-Tate | 1965 | 25.00 |
| *—Blue label, trident logo at right* | | | |
| ❑ SVLP-2029 [M] | Groovin' with Buddy Tate | 1961 | 50.00 |
| *—Purple label* | | | |
| ❑ SVLP-2029 [M] | Groovin' with Buddy Tate | 1965 | 25.00 |
| *—Blue label, trident logo at right* | | | |
| **TATE, GRADY** | | | |
| **SKYE** | | | |
| ❑ SK-4 | Windmills of My Mind | 1969 | 20.00 |
| **TATRO, DUANE** | | | |
| **CONTEMPORARY** | | | |
| ❑ C-3514 [M] | Jazz for Moderns | 1956 | 80.00 |
| **TATUM, ART** | | | |
| **ASCH** | | | |
| ❑ ALP-356 [10] | Art Tatum | 1950 | 150.00 |
| **BOOK-OF-THE-MONTH** | | | |
| ❑ 51-5400 [(4)] | The One and Only | 1980 | 30.00 |
| **BRUNSWICK** | | | |
| ❑ BL 54004 [M] | Here's Art Tatum | 1955 | 120.00 |
| ❑ BL 58013 [10] | Art Tatum Trio | 1950 | 100.00 |
| ❑ BL 58023 [10] | Art Tatum Piano Solos | 1950 | 100.00 |
| **CAPITOL** | | | |
| ❑ H 216 [10] | Art Tatum | 1950 | 100.00 |
| ❑ T 216 [M] | Art Tatum | 1955 | 80.00 |
| *—Turquoise label* | | | |
| ❑ T 216 [M] | Art Tatum | 1959 | 40.00 |
| *—Black colorband label, logo at left* | | | |
| ❑ T 216 [M] | Art Tatum | 196? | 20.00 |
| *—Black colorband label, logo at top* | | | |
| ❑ H 269 [10] | Art Tatum Encores | 1951 | 100.00 |
| ❑ H 408 [10] | Art Tatum Trio | 1953 | 100.00 |
| **CLEF** | | | |
| ❑ (no #) [(4)M] | Art Tatum | 1954 | 300.00 |
| *—Boxed set with volumes 2, 3, 4 and 5 of The Genius of Art Tatum* | | | |
| ❑ MGC-612 [M] | The Genius of Art Tatum #1 | 1954 | 80.00 |
| ❑ MGC-613 [M] | The Genius of Art Tatum #2 | 1954 | 80.00 |
| ❑ MGC-614 [M] | The Genius of Art Tatum #3 | 1954 | 80.00 |
| ❑ MGC-615 [M] | The Genius of Art Tatum #4 | 1954 | 80.00 |
| ❑ MGC-618 [M] | The Genius of Art Tatum #5 | 1954 | 80.00 |
| ❑ MGC-657 [M] | The Genius of Art Tatum #6 | 1955 | 80.00 |
| ❑ MGC-658 [M] | The Genius of Art Tatum #7 | 1955 | 80.00 |
| ❑ MGC-659 [M] | The Genius of Art Tatum #8 | 1955 | 80.00 |
| ❑ MGC-660 [M] | The Genius of Art Tatum #9 | 1955 | 80.00 |
| ❑ MGC-661 [M] | The Genius of Art Tatum #10 | 1955 | 80.00 |
| ❑ MGC-712 [M] | The Genius of Art Tatum #11 | 1956 | 80.00 |
| **COLUMBIA** | | | |
| ❑ GL 101 [10] | Gene Norman Concert at Shrine Auditorium, May 1949 | 1952 | 150.00 |
| ❑ CL 2565 [10] | The Tatum Touch | 1956 | 50.00 |
| ❑ CL 6301 [10] | An Art Tatum Concert | 1954 | 80.00 |
| ❑ CS 9655 [M] | Piano Starts Here | 1968 | 40.00 |
| *—Mono is white label promo only with stereo number; "Special Mono Radio Station Copy" sticker on cover* | | | |
| ❑ CS 9655 [S] | Piano Starts Here | 1968 | 20.00 |
| *—Red "360 Sound" label* | | | |
| **DECCA** | | | |
| ❑ DL 5086 [10] | Art Tatum Piano Solos | 1950 | 120.00 |
| ❑ DL 8715 [M] | The Art of Tatum | 1958 | 50.00 |
| **DIAL** | | | |
| ❑ LP-206 [10] | Art Tatum Trio | 1950 | 250.00 |
| **FOLKWAYS** | | | |
| ❑ FL-33 [10] | Art Tatum Trio | 1951 | 80.00 |
| **HARMONY** | | | |
| ❑ HL 7006 [M] | An Art Tatum Concert | 1957 | 25.00 |
| **PABLO** | | | |
| ❑ 2625703 [(13)] | The Tatum Solo Masterpieces | 1974 | 150.00 |
| *—Box set with all 13 volumes included* | | | |
| ❑ 2625706 [(8)] | The Tatum Group Masterpieces | 197? | 60.00 |
| *—Boxed set with eight volumes (except 2310 775) included* | | | |
| **REM HOLLYWOOD** | | | |
| ❑ LP-3 [10] | Piano Virtuoso | 1950 | 120.00 |
| *—The number "2" is on the front cover, but "LP-3" appears on the label* | | | |
| **STINSON** | | | |
| ❑ SLP-40 [10] | Art Tatum Trio | 1950 | 150.00 |
| ❑ SLP-40 [M] | Art Tatum Solos and Trio | 195? | 40.00 |
| **20TH FOX** | | | |
| ❑ FTM-102-2 [(2)M] | Piano Discoveries | 1961 | 30.00 |
| ❑ FTS-102-2 [(2)R] | Piano Discoveries | 1961 | 20.00 |
| ❑ FTM-3029 [M] | Piano Discoveries Vol. I | 1960 | 20.00 |
| ❑ FTM-3033 [M] | Piano Discoveries Vol. II | 1960 | 20.00 |

| Number | Title (A Side/B Side) | Yr | NM |
|---|---|---|---|

VERVE

| Number | Title (A Side/B Side) | Yr | NM |
|---|---|---|---|
| ❑ MGV-8036 [M] | The Genius of Art Tatum #1 | 1957 | 50.00 |
| ❑ V-8036 [M] | The Genius of Art Tatum #1 | 1961 | 20.00 |
| ❑ MGV-8037 [M] | The Genius of Art Tatum #2 | 1957 | 50.00 |
| ❑ V-8037 [M] | The Genius of Art Tatum #2 | 1961 | 20.00 |
| ❑ MGV-8038 [M] | The Genius of Art Tatum #3 | 1957 | 50.00 |
| ❑ V-8038 [M] | The Genius of Art Tatum #3 | 1961 | 20.00 |
| ❑ MGV-8039 [M] | The Genius of Art Tatum #4 | 1957 | 50.00 |
| ❑ V-8039 [M] | The Genius of Art Tatum #4 | 1961 | 20.00 |
| ❑ MGV-8040 [M] | The Genius of Art Tatum #5 | 1957 | 50.00 |
| ❑ V-8040 [M] | The Genius of Art Tatum #5 | 1961 | 20.00 |
| ❑ MGV-8055 [M] | The Genius of Art Tatum #6 | 1957 | 50.00 |
| ❑ V-8055 [M] | The Genius of Art Tatum #6 | 1961 | 20.00 |
| ❑ MGV-8056 [M] | The Genius of Art Tatum #7 | 1957 | 50.00 |
| ❑ V-8056 [M] | The Genius of Art Tatum #7 | 1961 | 20.00 |
| ❑ MGV-8057 [M] | The Genius of Art Tatum #8 | 1957 | 50.00 |
| ❑ V-8057 [M] | The Genius of Art Tatum #8 | 1961 | 20.00 |
| ❑ MGV-8058 [M] | The Genius of Art Tatum #9 | 1957 | 50.00 |
| ❑ V-8058 [M] | The Genius of Art Tatum #9 | 1961 | 20.00 |
| ❑ MGV-8059 [M] | The Genius of Art Tatum #10 | 1957 | 50.00 |
| ❑ V-8059 [M] | The Genius of Art Tatum #10 | 1961 | 20.00 |
| ❑ MGV-8095 [M] | The Genius of Art Tatum #11 | 1957 | 50.00 |
| ❑ V-8095 [M] | The Genius of Art Tatum #11 | 1961 | 20.00 |
| ❑ MGV-8101-5 [(5)M] | Art Tatum, Volume 1 | 1957 | 200.00 |
| *—Boxed set with volumes 1-5 of The Genius of Art Tatum* | | | |
| ❑ MGV-8102-5 [(5)M] | Art Tatum, Volume 2 | 1957 | 200.00 |
| *—Boxed set with volumes 6-10 of The Genius of Art Tatum* | | | |
| ❑ MGV-8118 [M] | Presenting the Art Tatum Trio | 1957 | 50.00 |
| ❑ V-8118 [M] | Presenting the Art Tatum Trio | 1961 | 20.00 |
| ❑ MGV-8220 [M] | The Art Tatum-Ben Webster Quartet | 1958 | 50.00 |
| ❑ V-8220 [M] | The Art Tatum-Ben Webster Quartet | 1961 | 20.00 |
| ❑ MGV-8323 [M] | The Greatest Piano of Them All | 1959 | 50.00 |
| ❑ V-8323 [M] | The Greatest Piano of Them All | 1961 | 20.00 |
| ❑ MGV-8332 [M] | The Incomparable Music of Art Tatum | 1959 | 50.00 |
| ❑ V-8332 [M] | The Incomparable Music of Art Tatum | 1961 | 20.00 |
| ❑ MGV-8347 [M] | More of the Greatest Piano of Them All | 1959 | 50.00 |
| ❑ V-8347 [M] | More of the Greatest Piano of Them All | 1961 | 20.00 |
| ❑ MGV-8360 [M] | Still More of the Greatest Piano of Them All | 1960 | 50.00 |
| ❑ V-8360 [M] | Still More of the Greatest Piano of Them All | 1961 | 20.00 |
| ❑ V-8433 [M] | The Essential Art Tatum | 1962 | 20.00 |

**TATUM, ART; BENNY CARTER; LOUIS BELLSON**

CLEF

| Number | Title (A Side/B Side) | Yr | NM |
|---|---|---|---|
| ❑ MGC-643 [M] | Tatum-Carter-Bellson | 1955 | 80.00 |

VERVE

| Number | Title (A Side/B Side) | Yr | NM |
|---|---|---|---|
| ❑ MGV-8013 [M] | The Three Giants | 1957 | 50.00 |
| ❑ V-8013 [M] | The Three Giants | 1961 | 20.00 |
| ❑ MGV-8227 [M] | Makin' Whoopee | 1958 | 50.00 |
| ❑ V-8227 [M] | Makin' Whoopee | 1961 | 20.00 |

**TATUM, ART, AND BUDDY DEFRANCO**

AMERICAN RECORDING SOCIETY

| Number | Title (A Side/B Side) | Yr | NM |
|---|---|---|---|
| ❑ G-412 [M] | The Art Tatum-Buddy DeFranco Quartet | 1956 | 40.00 |

VERVE

| Number | Title (A Side/B Side) | Yr | NM |
|---|---|---|---|
| ❑ MGV-8229 [M] | The Art Tatum-Buddy DeFranco Quartet | 1958 | 50.00 |
| ❑ V-8229 [M] | The Art Tatum-Buddy DeFranco Quartet | 1961 | 20.00 |

**TATUM, ART; ROY ELDRIDGE; ALVIN STOLLER; JOHN SIMMONS**

CLEF

| Number | Title (A Side/B Side) | Yr | NM |
|---|---|---|---|
| ❑ MGC-679 [M] | The Art Tatum-Roy Eldridge-Alvin Stoller-John Simmons Quartet | 1955 | 120.00 |

VERVE

| Number | Title (A Side/B Side) | Yr | NM |
|---|---|---|---|
| ❑ MGV-8064 [M] | The Art Tatum-Roy Eldridge-Alvin Stoller-John Simmons Quartet | 1957 | 80.00 |
| ❑ V-8064 [M] | The Art Tatum-Roy Eldridge-Alvin Stoller-John Simmons Quartet | 1961 | 25.00 |

**TATUM, ART/ERROLL GARNER**

JAZZTONE

| Number | Title (A Side/B Side) | Yr | NM |
|---|---|---|---|
| ❑ J-1203 [M] | Kings of the Keyboard | 1956 | 40.00 |

ROOST

| Number | Title (A Side/B Side) | Yr | NM |
|---|---|---|---|
| ❑ LP-2213 [M] | Giants of the Piano | 1956 | 50.00 |

**TAUPIN, BERNIE** ELTON JOHN's songwriting partner.

ASYLUM

| Number | Title (A Side/B Side) | Yr | NM |
|---|---|---|---|
| ❑ 6E-263 | He Who Rides the Tiger | 1980 | 12.00 |

ELEKTRA

| Number | Title (A Side/B Side) | Yr | NM |
|---|---|---|---|
| ❑ EKS-75020 | Bernie Taupin | 1972 | 15.00 |

RCA

| Number | Title (A Side/B Side) | Yr | NM |
|---|---|---|---|
| ❑ 5922-1-R | Tribe | 1987 | 10.00 |
| ❑ 6420-1-RAB [(2)DJ] | Interview Album | 1987 | 20.00 |

**TAVENER, JOHN**

APPLE

| Number | Title (A Side/B Side) | Yr | NM |
|---|---|---|---|
| ❑ SMAS-3369 | The Whale | 1972 | 20.00 |

**TAX FREE**

POLYDOR

| Number | Title (A Side/B Side) | Yr | NM |
|---|---|---|---|
| ❑ 24-4053 | Tax Free | 1971 | 20.00 |

**TAXXI**

FANTASY

| Number | Title (A Side/B Side) | Yr | NM |
|---|---|---|---|
| ❑ F-9603 | Day for Night | 1980 | 15.00 |
| ❑ F-9617 | States of Emergency | 1982 | 20.00 |
| ❑ F-9628 | Foreign Tongue | 1983 | 15.00 |

MCA

| Number | Title (A Side/B Side) | Yr | NM |
|---|---|---|---|
| ❑ 5580 | Expose | 1985 | 10.00 |

**TAYLES, THE**

CINEVISTA

| Number | Title (A Side/B Side) | Yr | NM |
|---|---|---|---|
| ❑ US 1001 | Who Are These Guys — Live at the Nitty Gritty | 1972 | 80.00 |

**TAYLOR, ART**

BLUE NOTE

| Number | Title (A Side/B Side) | Yr | NM |
|---|---|---|---|
| ❑ BLP-4047 [M] | A.T.'s Delight | 1960 | 80.00 |
| *—Regular version, W. 63rd St. address on label* | | | |
| ❑ BLP-4047 [M] | A.T.'s Delight | 1960 | 120.00 |
| *—"Deep groove" version (deep indentation under label on both sides)* | | | |
| ❑ BST-84047 [S] | A.T.'s Delight | 1960 | 60.00 |
| *—W. 63rd St. address on label* | | | |

NEW JAZZ

| Number | Title (A Side/B Side) | Yr | NM |
|---|---|---|---|
| ❑ NJLP-8219 [M] | Taylor's Tenors | 1959 | 50.00 |
| *—Purple label* | | | |
| ❑ NJLP-8219 [M] | Taylor's Tenors | 1965 | 25.00 |
| *—Blue label, trident logo at right* | | | |

PRESTIGE

| Number | Title (A Side/B Side) | Yr | NM |
|---|---|---|---|
| ❑ PRLP-7117 [M] | Taylor's Wailers | 1957 | 100.00 |

**TAYLOR, BILLY**

ABC-PARAMOUNT

| Number | Title (A Side/B Side) | Yr | NM |
|---|---|---|---|
| ❑ ABC-112 [M] | Evergreens | 1956 | 50.00 |
| ❑ ABC-134 [M] | Billy Taylor At the London House | 1956 | 50.00 |
| ❑ ABC-162 [M] | Billy Taylor Introduces Ira Sullivan | 1957 | 50.00 |
| ❑ ABC-177 [M] | My Fair Lady Loves Jazz | 1957 | 50.00 |
| ❑ ABC-226 [M] | The New Trio | 1958 | 50.00 |
| ❑ ABCS-226 [S] | The New Trio | 1958 | 40.00 |

ARGO

| Number | Title (A Side/B Side) | Yr | NM |
|---|---|---|---|
| ❑ LP-650 [M] | Taylor Made Flute | 1959 | 50.00 |
| ❑ LPS-650 [S] | Taylor Made Flute | 1959 | 40.00 |

ATLANTIC

| Number | Title (A Side/B Side) | Yr | NM |
|---|---|---|---|
| ❑ ALR-113 [10] | Piano Panorama | 1951 | 150.00 |
| ❑ 1277 [M] | The Billy Taylor Touch | 1958 | 50.00 |
| *—Black label* | | | |
| ❑ 1277 [M] | The Billy Taylor Touch | 1961 | 25.00 |
| *—Multicolor label, white "fan" logo at right* | | | |
| ❑ 1329 [M] | One for Fun | 1960 | 50.00 |
| *—Black label* | | | |
| ❑ SD 1329 [S] | One for Fun | 1960 | 50.00 |
| *—Green label* | | | |

CAPITOL

| Number | Title (A Side/B Side) | Yr | NM |
|---|---|---|---|
| ❑ ST 2039 [S] | Right Here, Right Now | 1963 | 25.00 |
| ❑ T 2039 [M] | Right Here, Right Now | 1963 | 20.00 |
| ❑ ST 2302 [S] | Midnight Piano | 1965 | 25.00 |
| ❑ T 2302 [M] | Midnight Piano | 1965 | 20.00 |

IMPULSE!

| Number | Title (A Side/B Side) | Yr | NM |
|---|---|---|---|
| ❑ A-71 [M] | My Fair Lady Loves Jazz | 1965 | 20.00 |
| ❑ AS-71 [S] | My Fair Lady Loves Jazz | 1965 | 25.00 |

MERCURY

| Number | Title (A Side/B Side) | Yr | NM |
|---|---|---|---|
| ❑ MG-20722 [M] | Impromptu | 1962 | 20.00 |
| ❑ SR-60722 [S] | Impromptu | 1962 | 25.00 |

MOODSVILLE

| Number | Title (A Side/B Side) | Yr | NM |
|---|---|---|---|
| ❑ MVLP-16 [M] | Interlude | 1961 | 50.00 |
| *—Green label* | | | |
| ❑ MVLP-16 [M] | Interlude | 1965 | 25.00 |
| *—Blue label, trident logo at right* | | | |

PRESTIGE

| Number | Title (A Side/B Side) | Yr | NM |
|---|---|---|---|
| ❑ 16-2 [M] | Let's Get Away from It All | 1957 | 500.00 |
| *—This album plays at 16 2/3 rpm and is marked as such; white label* | | | |
| ❑ PRLP-139 [10] | Billy Taylor Trio, Volume 1 | 1953 | 220.00 |
| ❑ PRLP-165 [10] | Billy Taylor Trio, Volume 2 | 1953 | 250.00 |
| ❑ PRLP-168 [10] | Billy Taylor Trio, Volume 3 | 1953 | 220.00 |
| ❑ PRLP-184 [10] | Billy Taylor Trio | 1954 | 200.00 |
| ❑ PRLP-188 [10] | Billy Taylor Trio | 1954 | 200.00 |
| ❑ PRLP-194 [10] | Billy Taylor Trio In Concert at Town Hall, December 17, 1954 | 1955 | 200.00 |
| ❑ PRLP-7001 [M] | A Touch of Taylor | 1955 | 80.00 |
| ❑ PRLP-7015 [M] | Billy Taylor Trio, Volume 1 | 1956 | 80.00 |
| ❑ PRLP-7016 [M] | Billy Taylor Trio, Volume 2 | 1956 | 100.00 |
| ❑ PRLP-7051 [M] | The Billy Taylor Trio with Candido | 1956 | 80.00 |
| ❑ PRLP-7071 [M] | Cross Section | 1956 | 80.00 |
| ❑ PRLP-7093 [M] | Billy Taylor Trio at Town Hall | 1957 | 80.00 |

RIVERSIDE

| Number | Title (A Side/B Side) | Yr | NM |
|---|---|---|---|
| ❑ RLP 12-306 [M] | Billy Taylor with Four Flutes | 1959 | 50.00 |
| ❑ RLP 12-319 [M] | Billy Taylor Trio Uptown | 1960 | 50.00 |
| ❑ RLP 12-339 [M] | Warming Up | 1960 | 50.00 |
| ❑ RLP-1151 [S] | Billy Taylor with Four Flutes | 1959 | 40.00 |
| ❑ RLP-1168 [S] | Billy Taylor Trio Uptown | 1960 | 40.00 |
| ❑ RLP-1195 [S] | Warming Up | 1960 | 40.00 |

ROOST

| Number | Title (A Side/B Side) | Yr | NM |
|---|---|---|---|
| ❑ R-406 [10] | Jazz at Storyville | 1952 | 120.00 |
| ❑ R-409 [10] | Taylor Made Jazz | 1952 | 120.00 |

SAVOY

| Number | Title (A Side/B Side) | Yr | NM |
|---|---|---|---|
| ❑ MG-9035 [10] | Billy Taylor Piano | 1953 | 120.00 |

SESAC

| Number | Title (A Side/B Side) | Yr | NM |
|---|---|---|---|
| ❑ N-3001 [M] | Custom Taylored | 1959 | 60.00 |
| ❑ SN-3001 [S] | Custom Taylored | 1959 | 50.00 |

STATUS

| Number | Title (A Side/B Side) | Yr | NM |
|---|---|---|---|
| ❑ ST-8313 [M] | Live! At Town Hall | 1965 | 40.00 |

SURREY

| Number | Title (A Side/B Side) | Yr | NM |
|---|---|---|---|
| ❑ S-1033 [M] | Easy Life | 1966 | 25.00 |
| ❑ SS-1033 [S] | Easy Life | 1966 | 30.00 |

TOWER

| Number | Title (A Side/B Side) | Yr | NM |
|---|---|---|---|
| ❑ ST-5111 [S] | I Wish I Knew | 1968 | 25.00 |

**TAYLOR, BOBBY, AND THE VANCOUVERS**

GORDY

| Number | Title (A Side/B Side) | Yr | NM |
|---|---|---|---|
| ❑ G-930 [M] | Bobby Taylor and the Vancouvers | 1968 | 80.00 |
| *—Mono is promo only* | | | |
| ❑ GS-930 [S] | Bobby Taylor and the Vancouvers | 1968 | 60.00 |
| ❑ GS-942 | Taylor Made Soul | 1969 | 60.00 |

**TAYLOR, BUCK**

JPL

| Number | Title (A Side/B Side) | Yr | NM |
|---|---|---|---|
| ❑ 14098 | That Man from Gunsmoke | 197? | 40.00 |

**TAYLOR, CATHIE**

CAPITOL

| Number | Title (A Side/B Side) | Yr | NM |
|---|---|---|---|
| ❑ ST 1359 [S] | A Little Bit of Sweetness | 1960 | 25.00 |
| ❑ T 1359 [M] | A Little Bit of Sweetness | 1960 | 20.00 |
| ❑ ST 1448 [S] | The Tree Near My House | 1961 | 25.00 |
| ❑ T 1448 [M] | The Tree Near My House | 1961 | 20.00 |

**TAYLOR, CECIL**

AMERICAN RECORDING SOCIETY

| Number | Title (A Side/B Side) | Yr | NM |
|---|---|---|---|
| ❑ G-437 [M] | Modern Jazz | 195? | 40.00 |

BLUE NOTE

| Number | Title (A Side/B Side) | Yr | NM |
|---|---|---|---|
| ❑ BLP-4237 [M] | Unit Structures | 1966 | 25.00 |
| ❑ BLP-4260 [M] | Conquistador | 1967 | 30.00 |
| ❑ BST-84237 [S] | Unit Structures | 1966 | 30.00 |
| *—With "New York, USA" on label* | | | |
| ❑ BST-84260 [S] | Conquistador | 1967 | 25.00 |
| *—With "A Division of Liberty Records" on label* | | | |
| ❑ BST-84260 [S] | Conquistador | 197? | 15.00 |
| *—Reissue with newer label; with "A Division of United Artists Records" on label* | | | |

CANDID

| Number | Title (A Side/B Side) | Yr | NM |
|---|---|---|---|
| ❑ CD-8006 [M] | The World of Cecil Taylor | 1960 | 50.00 |
| ❑ CS-9006 [S] | The World of Cecil Taylor | 1960 | 40.00 |

CONTEMPORARY

| Number | Title (A Side/B Side) | Yr | NM |
|---|---|---|---|
| ❑ C-3562 [M] | Looking Ahead! | 1959 | 50.00 |
| ❑ S-7562 [S] | Looking Ahead! | 1959 | 40.00 |

FANTASY

| Number | Title (A Side/B Side) | Yr | NM |
|---|---|---|---|
| ❑ 6014 [M] | Live At the Café Montmarte | 1964 | 20.00 |
| ❑ 86014 [S] | Live At the Café Montmarte | 1964 | 25.00 |

HAT ART

| Number | Title (A Side/B Side) | Yr | NM |
|---|---|---|---|
| ❑ 3011 [(3)] | One Too Many Salty Swift & Not Goodbye | 1986 | 20.00 |
| *—Reissue of Hat Hut 02* | | | |

HAT HUT

| Number | Title (A Side/B Side) | Yr | NM |
|---|---|---|---|
| ❑ 02 [(3)] | One Too Many Salty Swift & Not Goodbye | 197? | 25.00 |
| ❑ 1993/4 [(2)] | Garden | 198? | 20.00 |

MOSAIC

| Number | Title (A Side/B Side) | Yr | NM |
|---|---|---|---|
| ❑ MR6-127 [(6)] | The Complete Candid Recordings of Cecil Taylor and Buell Neidlinger | 199? | 100.00 |

PRESTIGE

| Number | Title (A Side/B Side) | Yr | NM |
|---|---|---|---|
| ❑ 34003 [(3)] | Great Concert | 197? | 20.00 |

TRANSITION

| Number | Title (A Side/B Side) | Yr | NM |
|---|---|---|---|
| ❑ TRLP-19 [M] | Jazz Advance | 1956 | 200.00 |
| *—With booklet (deduct 1/4 if missing)* | | | |

UNIT CORE

| Number | Title (A Side/B Side) | Yr | NM |
|---|---|---|---|
| ❑ 30551 | Spring of Two Blue-J's | 197? | 20.00 |

UNITED ARTISTS

| Number | Title (A Side/B Side) | Yr | NM |
|---|---|---|---|
| ❑ UAL-4014 [M] | Hard Driving Jazz | 1959 | 50.00 |
| ❑ UAL-4046 [M] | Love for Sale | 1959 | 50.00 |
| ❑ UAS-5014 [S] | Stereo Drive | 1959 | 40.00 |
| ❑ UAS-5046 [S] | Love for Sale | 1959 | 40.00 |

James Taylor, *Sweet Baby James,* Warner Bros. WS 1843, 1970, no titles on front cover, with green "W7" label $25, with green "WB" label $15.

### TAYLOR, CREED

**ABC-PARAMOUNT**

| Number | Title (A Side/B Side) | Yr | NM |
|---|---|---|---|
| ❑ ABC-259 [M] | Shock Music in Hi-Fi | 1958 | 40.00 |
| ❑ ABCS-259 [S] | Shock Music in Hi-Fi | 1958 | 60.00 |
| ❑ ABC-308 [M] | Lonelyville "The Nervous Beat" | 1960 | 25.00 |
| ❑ ABCS-308 [S] | Lonelyville "The Nervous Beat" | 1960 | 30.00 |
| ❑ ABC-317 [M] | The Best of the Barracks Ballads | 1960 | 25.00 |
| ❑ ABCS-317 [S] | The Best of the Barracks Ballads | 1960 | 30.00 |

### TAYLOR, DICK

**SKYLARK**

| Number | Title (A Side/B Side) | Yr | NM |
|---|---|---|---|
| ❑ SKLP-18 [10] | Blue Moon | 1954 | 80.00 |

### TAYLOR, EARL

**CAPITOL**

| Number | Title (A Side/B Side) | Yr | NM |
|---|---|---|---|
| ❑ ST 2090 [S] | Bluegrass Taylor-Made | 1963 | 50.00 |
| ❑ T 2090 [M] | Bluegrass Taylor-Made | 1963 | 40.00 |

**UNITED ARTISTS**

| Number | Title (A Side/B Side) | Yr | NM |
|---|---|---|---|
| ❑ UAL-3049 [M] | Folk Songs from the Bluegrass | 1960 | 25.00 |
| ❑ UAS-6049 [S] | Folk Songs from the Bluegrass | 1960 | 30.00 |

### TAYLOR, HOUND DOG

**ALLIGATOR**

| Number | Title (A Side/B Side) | Yr | NM |
|---|---|---|---|
| ❑ 4701 | Hound Dog Taylor | 1971 | 25.00 |
| ❑ 4704 | Natural Boogie | 1974 | 20.00 |

### TAYLOR, JAMES

**APPLE**

| Number | Title (A Side/B Side) | Yr | NM |
|---|---|---|---|
| ❑ SKAO 3352 | James Taylor | 1969 | 25.00 |
| *—With title in black print* | | | |
| ❑ SKAO 3352 | James Taylor | 1970 | 20.00 |
| *—With title in orange print* | | | |

**COLUMBIA**

| Number | Title (A Side/B Side) | Yr | NM |
|---|---|---|---|
| ❑ JC 34811 | JT | 1977 | 10.00 |
| ❑ PC 34811 | JT | 198? | 8.00 |
| ❑ FC 36058 | Flag | 1979 | 10.00 |
| ❑ PC 36058 | Flag | 198? | 8.00 |
| ❑ PC 37009 | Dad Loves His Work | 198? | 8.00 |
| ❑ TC 37009 | Dad Loves His Work | 1981 | 10.00 |
| ❑ FC 40052 | That's Why I'm Here | 1985 | 10.00 |
| ❑ FC 40851 | Never Die Young | 1988 | 10.00 |
| ❑ HC 47009 | Dad Loves His Work | 1983 | 40.00 |
| *—Half-speed mastered edition* | | | |

**EUPHORIA**

| Number | Title (A Side/B Side) | Yr | NM |
|---|---|---|---|
| ❑ EST-2 | James Taylor and the Original Flying Machine 1967 | 1971 | 12.00 |

**NAUTILUS**

| Number | Title (A Side/B Side) | Yr | NM |
|---|---|---|---|
| ❑ NR-29 | Gorilla | 1981 | 40.00 |
| *—Audiophile pressing* | | | |

**TRIP**

| Number | Title (A Side/B Side) | Yr | NM |
|---|---|---|---|
| ❑ TLP-9513 | Rainy Day Man | 197? | 10.00 |
| *—Reissue of Euphoria album* | | | |

**WARNER BROS.**

| Number | Title (A Side/B Side) | Yr | NM |
|---|---|---|---|
| ❑ WS 1843 | Sweet Baby James | 1970 | 10.00 |
| *—Green "WB" label with "Contains Fire and Rain and Country Road" added to front cover* | | | |
| ❑ WS 1843 | Sweet Baby James | 1970 | 15.00 |
| *—Green "WB" label with no reference to other songs on front cover* | | | |
| ❑ WS 1843 | Sweet Baby James | 1970 | 25.00 |
| *—Very early pressings have green label with "W7" logo* | | | |
| ❑ WS 1843 | Sweet Baby James | 1973 | 8.00 |
| *—"Burbank" label or cream label* | | | |
| ❑ BS 2561 | Mud Slide Slim and the Blue Horizon | 1971 | 10.00 |
| *—Green "WB" label* | | | |
| ❑ BS 2561 | Mud Slide Slim and the Blue Horizon | 1973 | 8.00 |
| *—"Burbank" label or cream label* | | | |
| ❑ BS 2660 | One Man Dog | 1972 | 10.00 |
| *—Green "WB" label* | | | |
| ❑ BS 2660 | One Man Dog | 1973 | 8.00 |
| *—"Burbank" label or cream label* | | | |
| ❑ BS4 2660 [Q] | One Man Dog | 1975 | 15.00 |
| ❑ BS 2794 | Walking Man | 1973 | 10.00 |
| *—"Burbank" label* | | | |
| ❑ BS 2794 | Walking Man | 1979 | 8.00 |
| *—Cream label* | | | |
| ❑ BS 2866 | Gorilla | 1975 | 10.00 |
| *—"Burbank" label* | | | |
| ❑ BS 2866 | Gorilla | 1979 | 8.00 |
| *—Cream label* | | | |
| ❑ BS4 2866 [Q] | Gorilla | 1975 | 15.00 |
| ❑ BS 2912 | In the Pocket | 1976 | 10.00 |
| *—"Burbank" label* | | | |
| ❑ BS 2912 | In the Pocket | 1979 | 8.00 |
| *—Cream label* | | | |
| ❑ BS 2979 | Greatest Hits | 1976 | 12.00 |
| *—This and other variations of this title have re-recorded versions of "Carolina in My Mind" and "Something in the Way She Moves."* | | | |
| ❑ BSK 3113 | Greatest Hits | 1977 | 10.00 |
| *—"Burbank" label* | | | |
| ❑ BSK 3113 | Greatest Hits | 1979 | 8.00 |
| *—Cream label* | | | |
| ❑ ST-93138 | Sweet Baby James | 1970 | 20.00 |
| *—Capitol Record Club edition* | | | |

### TAYLOR, JOHNNIE

**BEVERLY GLEN**

| Number | Title (A Side/B Side) | Yr | NM |
|---|---|---|---|
| ❑ 10001 | Just Ain't Good Enough | 1982 | 12.00 |

**COLUMBIA**

| Number | Title (A Side/B Side) | Yr | NM |
|---|---|---|---|
| ❑ PC 33951 | Eargasm | 1976 | 12.00 |
| *—Originals have no bar code* | | | |
| ❑ PC 33951 | Eargasm | 1986 | 8.00 |
| *—Budget-line reissue with bar code* | | | |
| ❑ PCQ 33951 [Q] | Eargasm | 1976 | 20.00 |
| ❑ PC 34401 | Rated Extraordinaire | 1977 | 12.00 |
| ❑ PCQ 34401 [Q] | Rated Extraordinaire | 1977 | 20.00 |
| ❑ JC 35340 | Ever Ready | 1978 | 12.00 |
| ❑ JC 36061 | She's Killing Me | 1979 | 12.00 |
| ❑ JC 36548 | A New Day | 1980 | 12.00 |
| ❑ JC 37127 | The Best of Johnnie Taylor | 1981 | 12.00 |

**ICHIBAN**

| Number | Title (A Side/B Side) | Yr | NM |
|---|---|---|---|
| ❑ ICH-1022 | Stuck in the Mud | 198? | 10.00 |
| ❑ ICH-1042 | Ugly Man | 198? | 10.00 |

**MALACO**

| Number | Title (A Side/B Side) | Yr | NM |
|---|---|---|---|
| ❑ MAL-7421 | This Is Your Night | 198? | 10.00 |
| ❑ MAL-7431 | Wall to Wall | 198? | 10.00 |
| ❑ MAL-7440 | Lover Boy | 198? | 10.00 |
| ❑ MAL-7446 | In Control | 198? | 10.00 |
| ❑ MAL-7452 | Crazy 'Bout You | 1989 | 10.00 |
| ❑ MAL-7460 | Just Can't Do Right | 1991 | 10.00 |
| ❑ MAL-7463 | The Best of Johnnie Taylor on Malaco, Vol. 1 | 1992 | 10.00 |

**STAX**

| Number | Title (A Side/B Side) | Yr | NM |
|---|---|---|---|
| ❑ ST-715 [M] | Wanted: One Soul Singer | 1967 | 50.00 |
| ❑ STS-715 [S] | Wanted: One Soul Singer | 1967 | 60.00 |
| ❑ STS-2005 | Who's Making Love | 1968 | 40.00 |
| ❑ STS-2008 | Raw Blues | 1969 | 25.00 |
| ❑ STS-2012 | Rare Stamps | 1969 | 25.00 |
| ❑ STS-2023 | The Johnnie Taylor Philosophy Continues | 1969 | 25.00 |
| ❑ STS-2030 | One Step Beyond | 1971 | 25.00 |
| ❑ STS-2032 | Johnnie Taylor's Greatest Hits | 1970 | 25.00 |
| ❑ STS-3014 | Taylored in Silk | 1973 | 20.00 |
| ❑ STX-4115 | Who's Making Love | 198? | 10.00 |
| *—Reissue of 2005* | | | |
| ❑ STS-5509 | Super Taylor | 1974 | 20.00 |
| ❑ STS-5521 | The Best of Johnnie Taylor | 1975 | 20.00 |
| ❑ MPS-8508 | Raw Blues | 1982 | 10.00 |
| ❑ MPS-8520 | Super Hits | 1983 | 10.00 |
| ❑ MPS-8537 | Taylored in Silk | 1987 | 10.00 |
| *—Reissue of 3014* | | | |
| ❑ MPS-8558 | Little Bluebird | 1988 | 10.00 |
| ❑ 88001 [(2)] | Chronicle | 1977 | 20.00 |

### TAYLOR, KINGSIZE, AND THE DOMINOES

**MIDNIGHT**

| Number | Title (A Side/B Side) | Yr | NM |
|---|---|---|---|
| ❑ HLP-2101 [M] | Real Gonk Man | 1965 | 50.00 |
| ❑ HST-2101 [S] | Real Gonk Man | 1965 | 100.00 |

### TAYLOR, KOKO

**ALLIGATOR**

| Number | Title (A Side/B Side) | Yr | NM |
|---|---|---|---|
| ❑ AL 4706 | I Got What It Takes | 1976 | 12.00 |
| ❑ AL 4711 | The Earthshaker | 1978 | 12.00 |
| ❑ AL 4724 | From the Heart of a Woman | 1981 | 10.00 |
| ❑ AL 4740 | Queen of the Blues | 1985 | 10.00 |
| ❑ AL 4754 | An Audience with the Queen | 1987 | 10.00 |
| ❑ AL 4784 | Junp for Joy | 1990 | 15.00 |

**CHESS**

| Number | Title (A Side/B Side) | Yr | NM |
|---|---|---|---|
| ❑ LPS-1532 | Koko Taylor | 1969 | 30.00 |
| ❑ CH-9263 | Koko Taylor | 1987 | 12.00 |
| *—Reissue of 1532* | | | |
| ❑ CH-50018 | Basic Soul | 1972 | 30.00 |

### TAYLOR, LAURA

**GOOD SOUNDS**

| Number | Title (A Side/B Side) | Yr | NM |
|---|---|---|---|
| ❑ GS-105 | Dancin' in My Feet | 1979 | 30.00 |

### TAYLOR, LITTLE JOHNNY

**FANTASY**

| Number | Title (A Side/B Side) | Yr | NM |
|---|---|---|---|
| ❑ MPF-4510 | Little Johnny Taylor's Greatest Hits | 1982 | 10.00 |

**GALAXY**

| Number | Title (A Side/B Side) | Yr | NM |
|---|---|---|---|
| ❑ 203 [M] | Little Johnny Taylor | 1963 | 100.00 |
| ❑ 207 [M] | Little Johnny Taylor's Greatest Hits | 1964 | 100.00 |
| ❑ 8203 [S] | Little Johnny Taylor | 1963 | 150.00 |
| ❑ 8207 [S] | Little Johnny Taylor's Greatest Hits | 1964 | 150.00 |

**RONN**

| Number | Title (A Side/B Side) | Yr | NM |
|---|---|---|---|
| ❑ LPS-7530 | Everybody Knows About My Good Thing | 1972 | 25.00 |
| ❑ LSP-7532 | Open House at My House | 1973 | 25.00 |
| ❑ LSP-7535 | L.J.T. | 1975 | 20.00 |



**Except when noted otherwise, VG = 25% of NM, and VG+ = 50% of NM. (Example: VG = $2.00, VG+ = $4.00 and NM = $8.00.)**

### TAYLOR, LITTLE JOHNNY, AND TED TAYLOR

**RONN**

| Number | Title (A Side/B Side) | Yr | NM |
|---|---|---|---|
| ❑ LSP-7533 | The Super Taylors | 1973 | 20.00 |

### TAYLOR, LYNN

**GRAND AWARD**

| Number | Title (A Side/B Side) | Yr | NM |
|---|---|---|---|
| ❑ GA-33-(# unk) [M] | Lynn Taylor Sings | 195? | 300.00 |

### TAYLOR, MEL

**WARNER BROS.**

| Number | Title (A Side/B Side) | Yr | NM |
|---|---|---|---|
| ❑ W 1624 [M] | Mel Taylor in Action | 1966 | 30.00 |
| ❑ WS 1624 [S] | Mel Taylor in Action | 1966 | 40.00 |

### TAYLOR, SAM "THE MAN"

**DECCA**

| Number | Title (A Side/B Side) | Yr | NM |
|---|---|---|---|
| ❑ DL 74302 [S] | Misty Mood | 1962 | 20.00 |
| ❑ DL 74417 [S] | It's a Blue World | 1963 | 20.00 |
| ❑ DL 74573 [S] | Somewhere in the Night | 1964 | 20.00 |

**LION**

| Number | Title (A Side/B Side) | Yr | NM |
|---|---|---|---|
| ❑ L-70054 [M] | Sam "The Man" Taylor | 1958 | 25.00 |

**METROJAZZ**

| Number | Title (A Side/B Side) | Yr | NM |
|---|---|---|---|
| ❑ E-1008 [M] | Jazz for Commuters | 1958 | 50.00 |
| ❑ SE-1008 [S] | Jazz for Commuters | 1958 | 40.00 |

**MGM**

| Number | Title (A Side/B Side) | Yr | NM |
|---|---|---|---|
| ❑ E-293 [10] | Music with the Big Beat | 195? | 100.00 |
| ❑ E-3292 [M] | Blue Mist | 1955 | 60.00 |
| *—Yellow label* | | | |
| ❑ E-3380 [M] | Out of This World | 1956 | 60.00 |
| *—Yellow label* | | | |
| ❑ E-3473 [M] | Music with the Big Beat | 1956 | 80.00 |
| *—Yellow label* | | | |
| ❑ E-3482 [M] | Music for Melancholy Babies | 1957 | 60.00 |
| *—Yellow label* | | | |
| ❑ E-3553 [M] | Rockin' Sax and Rollin' Organ | 1957 | 60.00 |
| *—Yellow label* | | | |
| ❑ E-3573 [M] | Prelude to Blues | 1957 | 60.00 |
| *—Yellow label* | | | |
| ❑ E-3783 [M] | More Blue Mist | 1959 | 30.00 |
| ❑ SE-3783 [S] | More Blue Mist | 1959 | 40.00 |
| ❑ E-3967 [M] | Sam "The Man" Taylor Plays Hollywood | 1960 | 30.00 |
| ❑ SE-3967 [S] | Sam "The Man" Taylor Plays Hollywood | 1960 | 40.00 |
| ❑ E-3973 [M] | Blue Mist | 1961 | 30.00 |
| ❑ SE-3973 [S] | Blue Mist | 1961 | 25.00 |
| *—Possibly a re-recording of 3292* | | | |

**MOODSVILLE**

| Number | Title (A Side/B Side) | Yr | NM |
|---|---|---|---|
| ❑ MVLP-24 [M] | The Bad and the Beautiful | 1962 | 50.00 |
| *—Green label* | | | |
| ❑ MVLP-24 [M] | The Bad and the Beautiful | 1965 | 25.00 |
| *—Blue label, trident logo at right* | | | |

### TAYLOR, TED

**ALARM**

| Number | Title (A Side/B Side) | Yr | NM |
|---|---|---|---|
| ❑ 1000 | 1976 | 1976 | 30.00 |

**OKEH**

| Number | Title (A Side/B Side) | Yr | NM |
|---|---|---|---|
| ❑ OKM-12104 [M] | Be Ever Wonderful | 1963 | 30.00 |
| ❑ OKM-12109 [M] | Blues and Soul | 1965 | 30.00 |
| ❑ OKM-12113 [M] | Ted Taylor's Greatest Hits | 1966 | 25.00 |
| ❑ OKS-14104 [S] | Be Ever Wonderful | 1963 | 40.00 |
| ❑ OKS-14109 [S] | Blues and Soul | 1965 | 40.00 |
| ❑ OKS-14113 [S] | Ted Taylor's Greatest Hits | 1966 | 30.00 |

**RONN**

| Number | Title (A Side/B Side) | Yr | NM |
|---|---|---|---|
| ❑ LPS-7528 | Shades of Blue | 1969 | 12.00 |
| ❑ LPS-7529 | You Can Dig It! | 197? | 12.00 |
| ❑ LPS-7531 | Taylor Made | 1972 | 12.00 |
| ❑ LP-8003 | Be Ever Wonderful | 198? | 10.00 |
| ❑ LP-8004 | Steal Away | 198? | 10.00 |

**SOLPUGIDS**

| Number | Title (A Side/B Side) | Yr | NM |
|---|---|---|---|
| ❑ 1001 | Be Ever Wonderful | 198? | 15.00 |
| ❑ 1002 | Taylor Made for You | 198? | 15.00 |

### TAYLOR, TUT

**WORLD PACIFIC**

| Number | Title (A Side/B Side) | Yr | NM |
|---|---|---|---|
| ❑ ST-1816 [S] | 12 String Dobro | 1964 | 30.00 |
| *—Black vinyl* | | | |
| ❑ ST-1816 [S] | 12 String Dobro | 1964 | 80.00 |
| *—Red vinyl* | | | |
| ❑ WP-1816 [M] | 12 String Dobro | 1964 | 25.00 |
| ❑ ST-1829 [S] | Dobro Country | 1964 | 30.00 |
| ❑ WP-1829 [M] | Dobro Country | 1964 | 25.00 |

### TCHAIKOVSKY, ANDRE

**RCA VICTOR RED SEAL**

| Number | Title (A Side/B Side) | Yr | NM |
|---|---|---|---|
| ❑ LSC-2287 [S] | Mozart: Piano Concerto No. 25 | 1959 | 100.00 |
| *—With Fritz Reiner/Chicago Symphony Orchestra; original with "shaded dog" label* | | | |
| ❑ LSC-2354 [S] | Mozart: Fantasia in C; Sonata in C, K. 457; Sonata in C, K. 330 | 1960 | 70.00 |
| *—Original with "shaded dog" label* | | | |
| ❑ LSC-2360 [S] | Chopin: Preludes; Barcarolle: Mazurkas, Etudes, Ballade 3 | 1960 | 60.00 |
| *—Original with "shaded dog" label* | | | |

### TEA COMPANY, THE

**SMASH**

| Number | Title (A Side/B Side) | Yr | NM |
|---|---|---|---|
| ❑ SRS-67105 | Come and Have Some Tea | 1968 | 50.00 |

### TEAGARDEN, JACK

**BETHLEHEM**

| Number | Title (A Side/B Side) | Yr | NM |
|---|---|---|---|
| ❑ BCP-32 [M] | Jazz Great | 1955 | 50.00 |

**CAPITOL**

| Number | Title (A Side/B Side) | Yr | NM |
|---|---|---|---|
| ❑ T 721 [M] | This Is Teagarden | 1956 | 40.00 |
| ❑ T 820 [M] | Swing Low Sweet Spiritual | 1957 | 40.00 |
| ❑ ST 1095 [S] | Big T's Dixieland Band | 1959 | 25.00 |
| ❑ T 1095 [M] | Big T's Dixieland Band | 1959 | 20.00 |
| ❑ ST 1143 [S] | Shades of Night | 1959 | 25.00 |
| ❑ T 1143 [M] | Shades of Night | 1959 | 20.00 |

**COLUMBIA SPECIAL PRODUCTS**

| Number | Title (A Side/B Side) | Yr | NM |
|---|---|---|---|
| ❑ JSN 6044 [(3)M] | King of the Blues Trombone | 197? | 25.00 |

**COMMODORE**

| Number | Title (A Side/B Side) | Yr | NM |
|---|---|---|---|
| ❑ 20015 [10] | Big T | 195? | 80.00 |

**DECCA**

| Number | Title (A Side/B Side) | Yr | NM |
|---|---|---|---|
| ❑ DL 8304 [M] | Big T's Jazz | 1956 | 40.00 |

**EPIC**

| Number | Title (A Side/B Side) | Yr | NM |
|---|---|---|---|
| ❑ SN 6044 [(3)M] | King of the Blues Trombone | 1963 | 80.00 |
| ❑ LN 24045 [M] | King of the Blues Trombone, Vol. 1 | 1963 | 25.00 |
| ❑ LN 24046 [M] | King of the Blues Trombone, Vol. 2 | 1963 | 25.00 |
| ❑ LN 24047 [M] | King of the Blues Trombone, Vol. 3 | 1963 | 25.00 |

**JAZZTONE**

| Number | Title (A Side/B Side) | Yr | NM |
|---|---|---|---|
| ❑ J-1222 [M] | Big T | 195? | 30.00 |
| *—Reissue of Period material* | | | |

**JOLLY ROGER**

| Number | Title (A Side/B Side) | Yr | NM |
|---|---|---|---|
| ❑ 5026 [10] | Jack Teagarden | 1955 | 50.00 |

**MOSAIC**

| Number | Title (A Side/B Side) | Yr | NM |
|---|---|---|---|
| ❑ MQ6-168 [(6)] | The Complete Capitol Fifties Jack Teagarden Sessions | 199? | 100.00 |

**PERIOD**

| Number | Title (A Side/B Side) | Yr | NM |
|---|---|---|---|
| ❑ SLP-1106 [10] | Meet Me Where They Play the Blues | 1955 | 80.00 |
| ❑ SLP-1110 [10] | Original Dixieland | 1955 | 80.00 |

**RCA VICTOR**

| Number | Title (A Side/B Side) | Yr | NM |
|---|---|---|---|
| ❑ LPV-528 [M] | Jack Teagarden | 1965 | 20.00 |

**RONDO-LETTE**

| Number | Title (A Side/B Side) | Yr | NM |
|---|---|---|---|
| ❑ A-18 [M] | The Blues and Dixie | 1958 | 25.00 |

**ROULETTE**

| Number | Title (A Side/B Side) | Yr | NM |
|---|---|---|---|
| ❑ SR-25091 [S] | Jack Teagarden at the Round Table | 1960 | 20.00 |
| ❑ SR-25119 [S] | Jazz Maverick | 1961 | 20.00 |
| ❑ SR-25177 [S] | Dixie Sound | 1962 | 20.00 |
| ❑ SR-25243 [S] | Portrait of Mr. T | 1963 | 20.00 |

**ROYALE**

| Number | Title (A Side/B Side) | Yr | NM |
|---|---|---|---|
| ❑ 18156 [10] | The Blues | 195? | 80.00 |

**URANIA**

| Number | Title (A Side/B Side) | Yr | NM |
|---|---|---|---|
| ❑ UJLP-1001 [10] | Meet the New Jack Teagarden | 1954 | 100.00 |
| ❑ UJLP-1002 [10] | Jack Teagarden Sings and Plays | 1954 | 100.00 |

**VERVE**

| Number | Title (A Side/B Side) | Yr | NM |
|---|---|---|---|
| ❑ V6-8416 [S] | Mis'ry and the Blues | 1961 | 20.00 |
| ❑ V6-8465 [S] | Think Well of Me | 1962 | 20.00 |
| ❑ V6-8495 [S] | Jack Teagarden!! | 1962 | 20.00 |

### TEAGARDEN, JACK/BOBBY HACKETT

**COMMODORE**

| Number | Title (A Side/B Side) | Yr | NM |
|---|---|---|---|
| ❑ FL-30012 [M] | Jack Teagarden and Bobby Hackett | 1959 | 30.00 |

### TEAGARDEN, JACK/JONAH JONES

**AAMCO**

| Number | Title (A Side/B Side) | Yr | NM |
|---|---|---|---|
| ❑ ALP-309 [M] | Two Boys from Dixieland | 196? | 25.00 |
| *—Reissue of Bethlehem material* | | | |

**BETHLEHEM**

| Number | Title (A Side/B Side) | Yr | NM |
|---|---|---|---|
| ❑ BCP-6042 [M] | Dixieland | 1959 | 40.00 |

### TEAGARDEN, JACK/PEE WEE RUSSELL

**RIVERSIDE**

| Number | Title (A Side/B Side) | Yr | NM |
|---|---|---|---|
| ❑ RLP 12-141 | Jack Teagarden's Big Eight / Pee Wee Russell's Rhythmakers | 1956 | 60.00 |

### TEARDROPS, THE (U)

**20TH CENTURY FOX**

| Number | Title (A Side/B Side) | Yr | NM |
|---|---|---|---|
| ❑ FXG-5011 [M] | The Teardrops at Trinchi's | 1963 | 25.00 |

### TECHNOTRONIC

**SBK**

| Number | Title (A Side/B Side) | Yr | NM |
|---|---|---|---|
| ❑ K1-93422 | Pump Up the Jam — The Album | 1989 | 20.00 |
| ❑ K1-95028 | Trip On This — The Remixes | 1990 | 20.00 |

### TEDDY AND THE PANDAS

**TOWER**

| Number | Title (A Side/B Side) | Yr | NM |
|---|---|---|---|
| ❑ ST-5125 | Basic Magnetism | 1968 | 25.00 |

### TEDDY BEARS, THE

**IMPERIAL**

| Number | Title (A Side/B Side) | Yr | NM |
|---|---|---|---|
| ❑ LP-9067 [M] | The Teddy Bears Sing! | 1959 | 300.00 |
| ❑ LP-12010 [S] | The Teddy Bears Sing! | 1959 | 1200. |

### TEDESCO, TOMMY

**DISCOVERY**

| Number | Title (A Side/B Side) | Yr | NM |
|---|---|---|---|
| ❑ 789 | When Do We Start | 1978 | 12.00 |
| ❑ 851 | My Desiree | 1982 | 10.00 |
| ❑ 928 | Hollywood Gypsy | 1986 | 10.00 |

**IMPERIAL**

| Number | Title (A Side/B Side) | Yr | NM |
|---|---|---|---|
| ❑ LP-9263 [M] | The Electric 12 String Guitar of Tommy Tedesco | 1964 | 15.00 |
| ❑ LP-9295 [M] | Guitars | 1965 | 15.00 |
| ❑ LP-9321 [M] | Calypso Soul | 1966 | 15.00 |
| ❑ LP-12263 [S] | The Electric 12 String Guitar of Tommy Tedesco | 1964 | 20.00 |
| ❑ LP-12295 [S] | Guitars | 1965 | 20.00 |
| ❑ LP-12321 [S] | Calypso Soul | 1966 | 20.00 |

**TREND**

| Number | Title (A Side/B Side) | Yr | NM |
|---|---|---|---|
| ❑ TR-514 | Autumn | 1978 | 20.00 |
| *—Direct-to-disc recording* | | | |
| ❑ TR-517 | Alone at Last | 1979 | 20.00 |
| *—Direct-to-disc recording* | | | |
| ❑ TR-534 | Carnival Time | 1983 | 12.00 |

### TEEMATES, THE

**AUDIO FIDELITY**

| Number | Title (A Side/B Side) | Yr | NM |
|---|---|---|---|
| ❑ AFLP-3042 [M] | Jet Set Dance Discotheque | 1964 | 40.00 |
| ❑ AFSD-7042 [S] | Jet Set Dance Discotheque | 1964 | 50.00 |

### TEEN QUEENS, THE

**CROWN**

| Number | Title (A Side/B Side) | Yr | NM |
|---|---|---|---|
| ❑ CST-373 [R] | The Teen Queens | 1963 | 30.00 |
| ❑ CLP-5022 [M] | Eddie My Love | 1956 | 250.00 |
| *—Black label, all silver print* | | | |
| ❑ CLP-5022 [M] | Eddie My Love | 196? | 100.00 |
| *—Black label, "CROWN" in alternating colored letters* | | | |
| ❑ CLP-5373 [M] | The Teen Queens | 1963 | 50.00 |

**RPM**

| Number | Title (A Side/B Side) | Yr | NM |
|---|---|---|---|
| ❑ LRP-3007 [M] | Eddie My Love | 1956 | — |
| *—Canceled* | | | |

### TEENAGE JESUS AND THE JERKS

**MIGRANE/LUST UNLUST**

| Number | Title (A Side/B Side) | Yr | NM |
|---|---|---|---|
| ❑ CC-336 [EP] | Teenage Jesus and the Jerks | 1979 | 30.00 |
| *—Black vinyl* | | | |
| ❑ CC-336 [EP] | Teenage Jesus and the Jerks | 1979 | 40.00 |
| *—Pink vinyl* | | | |

### TEENAGERS, THE

See FRANKIE LYMON AND THE TEENAGERS.

### TELEVISION

**CAPITOL**

| Number | Title (A Side/B Side) | Yr | NM |
|---|---|---|---|
| ❑ SPRO-79456 [DJ] | Television | 1992 | 20.00 |
| *—Vinyl is promo only* | | | |

**ELEKTRA**

| Number | Title (A Side/B Side) | Yr | NM |
|---|---|---|---|
| ❑ 6E-133 | Adventure | 1978 | 10.00 |
| ❑ 7E-1098 | Marquee Moon | 1977 | 15.00 |

### TEMPEST

**WARNER BROS.**

| Number | Title (A Side/B Side) | Yr | NM |
|---|---|---|---|
| ❑ BS 2682 | Tempest | 1973 | 25.00 |

### TEMPESTS, THE

**SMASH**

| Number | Title (A Side/B Side) | Yr | NM |
|---|---|---|---|
| ❑ MGS-27098 [M] | Would You Believe? | 1966 | 25.00 |
| ❑ SRS-67098 [S] | Would You Believe? | 1966 | 30.00 |

### TEMPLE, PICK

**PRESTIGE INT'L.**

| Number | Title (A Side/B Side) | Yr | NM |
|---|---|---|---|
| ❑ PRLP-13008 [M] | Pick of the Crop | 196? | 30.00 |

**"X"**

| Number | Title (A Side/B Side) | Yr | NM |
|---|---|---|---|
| ❑ LXA-3022 [10] | Folk Songs of the People | 1954 | 50.00 |

### TEMPLE, SHIRLEY

**MOVIETONE**

| Number | Title (A Side/B Side) | Yr | NM |
|---|---|---|---|
| ❑ MTM-71001 [M] | On the Good Ship Lollipop | 1966 | 20.00 |
| ❑ MTM-71012 [M] | Curtain Call | 1966 | 20.00 |

**20TH CENTURY FOX**

| Number | Title (A Side/B Side) | Yr | NM |
|---|---|---|---|
| ❑ TFM-3102 [M] | The Best of Shirley Temple | 1963 | 25.00 |
| ❑ TFM-3172 [M] | The Best of Shirley Temple, Vol. 2 | 1965 | 25.00 |

**20TH FOX**

| Number | Title (A Side/B Side) | Yr | NM |
|---|---|---|---|
| ❑ TCF-103 [(2)M] | The Shirley Temple Songbook | 1961 | 50.00 |
| ❑ FOX-3006 [M] | Little Miss Wonderful | 1959 | 40.00 |
| *—Shirley Temple pictured as an adult on cover* | | | |
| ❑ FOX-3006 [M] | Little Miss Wonderful | 196? | 40.00 |
| *—Shirley Temple pictured as a child on cover* | | | |
| ❑ FOX-3045 [M] | More Little Miss Wonderful | 1961 | 40.00 |

### TEMPLETON, ALEC

**ATLANTIC**

| Number | Title (A Side/B Side) | Yr | NM |
|---|---|---|---|
| ❑ 1222 [M] | The Magic Piano | 1956 | 40.00 |
| *—Black label* | | | |
| ❑ 1222 [M] | The Magic Piano | 1961 | 20.00 |
| *—Multicolor label, white "fan" logo at right* | | | |

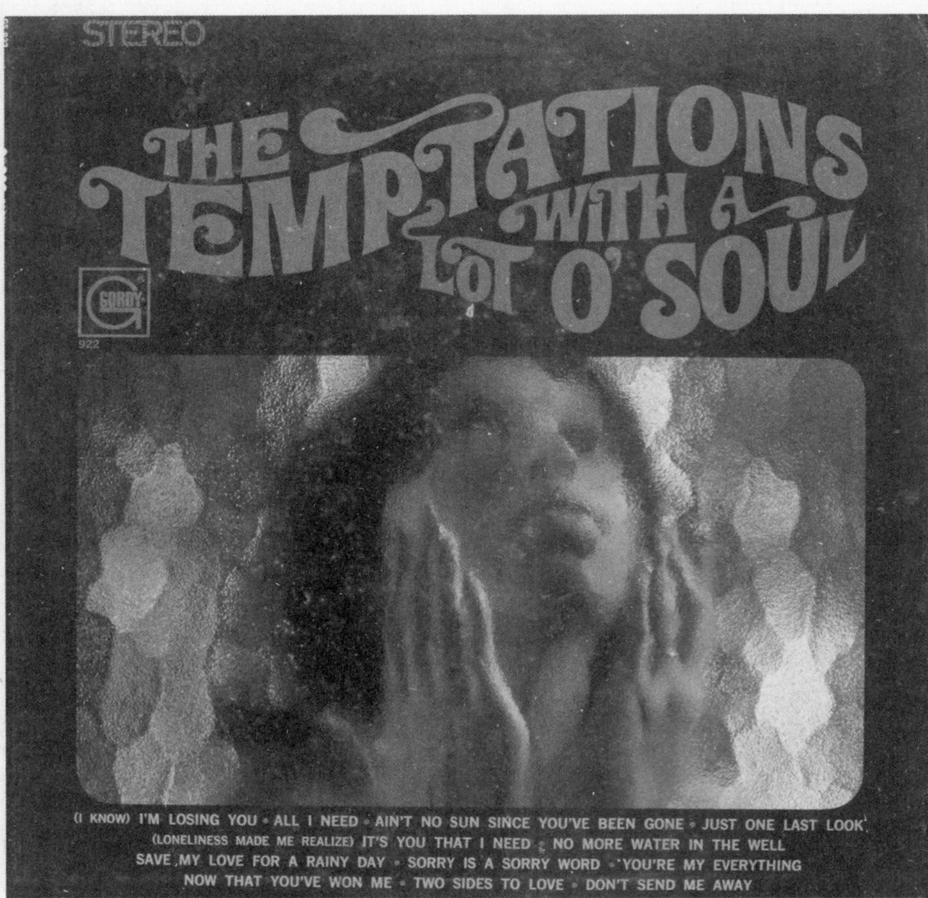


The Temptations, *With a Lot o' Soul,* Gordy GS-922, 196, stereo, $20.

## TEMPO, NINO

### A&M

| Number | Title (A Side/B Side) | Yr | NM |
|---|---|---|---|
| ❑ SP-3629 | Come See Me 'Round Midnight | 1974 | 30.00 |

### LIBERTY

| Number | Title (A Side/B Side) | Yr | NM |
|---|---|---|---|
| ❑ LRP-3023 [M] | Rock 'n' Roll Beach Party | 1958 | 120.00 |

## TEMPO, NINO, AND APRIL STEVENS

Also see each artist's individual listings.

### ATCO

| Number | Title (A Side/B Side) | Yr | NM |
|---|---|---|---|
| ❑ 33-156 [M] | Deep Purple | 1963 | 40.00 |
| ❑ SD 33-156 [S] | Deep Purple | 1963 | 50.00 |
| ❑ 33-162 [M] | Nino and April Sing the Great Songs | 1964 | 30.00 |
| ❑ SD 33-162 [S] | Nino and April Sing the Great Songs | 1964 | 40.00 |
| ❑ 33-180 [M] | Hey Baby | 1966 | 30.00 |
| ❑ SD 33-180 [S] | Hey Baby | 1966 | 40.00 |

### RCA CAMDEN

| Number | Title (A Side/B Side) | Yr | NM |
|---|---|---|---|
| ❑ CAL-824 [M] | A Nino Tempo/April Stevens Program | 1964 | 12.00 |
| *—Actually contains solo recordings by each, packaged together to capitalize on the success of "Deep Purple"* | | | |

### WHITE WHALE

| Number | Title (A Side/B Side) | Yr | NM |
|---|---|---|---|
| ❑ WW-113 [M] | All Strung Out | 1967 | 20.00 |
| ❑ WWS-7113 [S] | All Strung Out | 1967 | 25.00 |

## TEMPOS, THE

### JUSTICE

| Number | Title (A Side/B Side) | Yr | NM |
|---|---|---|---|
| ❑ JLP-104 | Speaking of the Tempos | 1966 | 500.00 |

## TEMPREES

### WE PRODUCE

| Number | Title (A Side/B Side) | Yr | NM |
|---|---|---|---|
| ❑ 1901 | Love Men | 1972 | 60.00 |
| ❑ 1903 | Love Maze | 1973 | 60.00 |
| ❑ 1905 | Temprees 3 | 1974 | 60.00 |

## TEMPTATIONS, THE

Also see DAVID RUFFIN.

### ATLANTIC

| Number | Title (A Side/B Side) | Yr | NM |
|---|---|---|---|
| ❑ SD 19143 | Hear to Tempt You | 1977 | 12.00 |
| ❑ SD 19188 | Bare Back | 1978 | 12.00 |

### GORDY

| Number | Title (A Side/B Side) | Yr | NM |
|---|---|---|---|
| ❑ G 911 [M] | Meet the Temptations | 1964 | 30.00 |
| ❑ GS 911 [S] | Meet the Temptations | 1964 | 40.00 |
| *—Script "Gordy" at top of label* | | | |
| ❑ GS 911 [S] | Meet the Temptations | 1967 | 20.00 |
| *—Block "GORDY" inside "G" on left of label* | | | |
| ❑ G 912 [M] | The Temptations Sing Smokey | 1965 | 30.00 |
| ❑ GS 912 [S] | The Temptations Sing Smokey | 1965 | 40.00 |
| *—Script "Gordy" at top of label* | | | |
| ❑ GS 912 [S] | The Temptations Sing Smokey | 1967 | 20.00 |
| *—Block "GORDY" inside "G" on left of label* | | | |
| ❑ G 914 [M] | Temptin' Temptations | 1965 | 25.00 |
| ❑ GS 914 [S] | Temptin' Temptations | 1965 | 30.00 |
| *—Script "Gordy" at top of label* | | | |
| ❑ GS 914 [S] | Temptin' Temptations | 1967 | 20.00 |
| *—Block "GORDY" inside "G" on left of label* | | | |
| ❑ G 918 [M] | Gettin' Ready | 1966 | 25.00 |
| ❑ GS 918 [S] | Gettin' Ready | 1966 | 30.00 |
| *—Script "Gordy" at top of label* | | | |
| ❑ GS 918 [S] | Gettin' Ready | 1967 | 20.00 |
| *—Block "GORDY" inside "G" on left of label* | | | |
| ❑ G 919 [M] | The Temptations' Greatest Hits | 1966 | 25.00 |
| ❑ GS 919 [S] | The Temptations' Greatest Hits | 1966 | 30.00 |
| *—Script "Gordy" at top of label* | | | |
| ❑ GS 919 [S] | The Temptations' Greatest Hits | 1967 | 20.00 |
| *—Block "GORDY" inside "G" on left of label* | | | |
| ❑ G 921 [M] | Temptations Live! | 1967 | 25.00 |
| ❑ GS 921 [S] | Temptations Live! | 1967 | 20.00 |
| *—Block "GORDY" inside "G" on left of label* | | | |
| ❑ GS 921 [S] | Temptations Live! | 1967 | 30.00 |
| *—Script "Gordy" at top of label* | | | |
| ❑ G 922 [M] | With a Lot o' Soul | 1967 | 25.00 |
| ❑ GS 922 [S] | With a Lot o' Soul | 1967 | 20.00 |
| *—Block "GORDY" inside "G" on left of label* | | | |
| ❑ GS 922 [S] | With a Lot o' Soul | 1967 | 25.00 |
| *—Script "Gordy" at top of label* | | | |
| ❑ G 924 [M] | The Temptations in a Mellow Mood | 1967 | 25.00 |
| ❑ GS 924 [S] | The Temptations in a Mellow Mood | 1967 | 25.00 |
| ❑ G 927 [M] | The Temptations Wish It Would Rain | 1968 | 40.00 |
| *—Mono is white-label promo only* | | | |
| ❑ GS 927 [S] | The Temptations Wish It Would Rain | 1968 | 20.00 |
| ❑ GS 933 | The Temptations Show | 1969 | 20.00 |
| ❑ GS 938 | Live at the Copa | 1968 | 20.00 |
| ❑ GS 939 | Cloud Nine | 1969 | 20.00 |
| ❑ GS 947 | Psychedelic Shack | 1970 | 20.00 |
| ❑ GS 949 | Puzzle People | 1969 | 20.00 |
| ❑ GS 951 | The Temptations' Christmas Card | 1969 | 25.00 |
| ❑ GS 953 | Live at London's Talk of the Town | 1970 | 20.00 |
| ❑ GS 954 | Temptations Greatest Hits II | 1970 | 20.00 |
| ❑ GS 957 | Sky's the Limit | 1971 | 20.00 |
| ❑ G 961L | Solid Rock | 1972 | 20.00 |
| ❑ G 962L | All Directions | 1972 | 20.00 |
| ❑ G 965L | Masterpiece | 1973 | 20.00 |
| ❑ G 966V1 | 1990 | 1973 | 15.00 |
| ❑ G6-969S1 | A Song for You | 1975 | 15.00 |
| ❑ G6-971S1 | Wings of Love | 1976 | 15.00 |
| ❑ G6-973S1 | House Party | 1975 | 15.00 |
| ❑ G7-975S1 | The Temptations Do the Temptations | 1976 | 15.00 |
| ❑ G8-994M1 | Power | 1980 | 12.00 |
| ❑ G8-998M1 | Give Love at Christmas | 1980 | 15.00 |
| ❑ G8-1006M1 | The Temptations | 1981 | 12.00 |
| ❑ 6008 GL | Reunion | 1982 | 12.00 |
| ❑ 6032 GL | Surface Thrills | 1983 | 12.00 |
| ❑ 6085 GL | Back to Basics | 1984 | 12.00 |
| ❑ 6119 GL | Truly for You | 1984 | 12.00 |
| ❑ 6164 GL | Touch Me | 1986 | 12.00 |
| ❑ 6207 GL | To Be Continued | 1986 | 12.00 |

### MOTOWN

| Number | Title (A Side/B Side) | Yr | NM |
|---|---|---|---|
| ❑ M5-140V1 | Meet the Temptations | 1981 | 12.00 |
| *—Reissue of Gordy 911* | | | |
| ❑ M5-144V1 | Masterpiece | 1981 | 12.00 |
| *—Reissue of Gordy 965* | | | |
| ❑ M5-159V1 | Cloud Nine | 1981 | 12.00 |
| *—Reissue of Gordy 939* | | | |
| ❑ M5-164V1 | Psychedelic Shack | 1981 | 12.00 |
| *—Reissue of Gordy 947* | | | |
| ❑ M5-172V1 | Puzzle People | 1981 | 12.00 |
| *—Reissue of Gordy 949* | | | |
| ❑ M5-205V1 | The Temptations Sing Smokey | 1981 | 12.00 |
| *—Reissue of Gordy 912* | | | |
| ❑ M5-212V1 | All the Million Sellers | 1982 | 12.00 |
| ❑ M 782 [(3)] | Anthology | 1973 | 25.00 |
| ❑ 5251 ML | The Temptations Christmas Card | 1982 | 10.00 |
| *—Reissue of Gordy 951* | | | |
| ❑ 5279 ML | Give Love at Christmas | 1983 | 10.00 |
| *—Reissue of Gordy 998* | | | |
| ❑ 5389 ML [(2)] | 25th Anniversary | 1986 | 15.00 |
| ❑ 6246 ML | Together Again | 1987 | 12.00 |
| ❑ MOT-6275 | Special | 1989 | 12.00 |

### NATURAL RESOURCES

| Number | Title (A Side/B Side) | Yr | NM |
|---|---|---|---|
| ❑ NR 4005T1 | The Temptations in a Mellow Mood | 1978 | 12.00 |
| *—Reissue of Gordy 924* | | | |

### PICKWICK

| Number | Title (A Side/B Side) | Yr | NM |
|---|---|---|---|
| ❑ SPC-3540 | Psychedelic Shack | 197? | 12.00 |
| *—Reissue of Gordy 947* | | | |

## 10,000 MANIACS

### CHRISTIAN BURIAL

| Number | Title (A Side/B Side) | Yr | NM |
|---|---|---|---|
| ❑ P-2010 [EP] | Human Conflict #5 | 1983 | 80.00 |
| ❑ P-3001 | Secrets of the I Ching | 1984 | 120.00 |

### ELEKTRA

| Number | Title (A Side/B Side) | Yr | NM |
|---|---|---|---|
| ❑ ED 5270 [DJ] | Interview | 1987 | 30.00 |
| *—Lenny Kaye interviews Natalie Merchant; promo only* | | | |
| ❑ 60428 | The Wishing Chair | 1985 | 12.00 |
| ❑ 60738 | In My Tribe | 1987 | 10.00 |
| ❑ 60738 [DJ] | In My Tribe | 1987 | 15.00 |
| *—Promo-only audiophile pressing* | | | |
| ❑ 60815 | Blind Man's Zoo | 1989 | 12.00 |
| ❑ 60815 [DJ] | Blind Man's Zoo | 1989 | 15.00 |
| *—Promo-only audiophile pressing (white labels)* | | | |
| ❑ R 100481 | In My Tribe | 1987 | 12.00 |
| *—BMG Direct Marketing edition* | | | |
| ❑ R 130236 | Blind Man's Zoo | 1989 | 12.00 |
| *—BMG Direct Marketing edition* | | | |

## TEN YEARS AFTER

### CHRYSALIS

| Number | Title (A Side/B Side) | Yr | NM |
|---|---|---|---|
| ❑ CHS 1083 | Ssssh | 1975 | 10.00 |
| ❑ CHS 1084 | Cricklewood Green | 1975 | 10.00 |
| ❑ CHS 1085 | Watt | 1975 | 10.00 |
| ❑ F1-21001 | A Space in Time | 1989 | 8.00 |
| ❑ F1-21009 | Rock and Roll Music to the World | 1989 | 8.00 |
| ❑ F1-21083 | Ssssh | 1989 | 8.00 |
| ❑ F1-21084 | Cricklewood Green | 1989 | 8.00 |
| ❑ F1-21085 | Watt | 1989 | 8.00 |
| ❑ F1-21573 | Positive Vibrations | 1989 | 8.00 |
| ❑ F1-21580 | Universal | 1989 | 8.00 |
| ❑ F1-21722 | About Time | 1989 | 12.00 |
| ❑ PV 41001 | A Space in Time | 1987 | 8.00 |
| ❑ PV 41009 | Rock and Roll Music to the World | 1987 | 8.00 |
| ❑ FV 41049 [(2)] | Recorded Live | 1987 | 10.00 |
| ❑ PV 41083 | Ssssh | 1983 | 8.00 |
| ❑ PV 41084 | Cricklewood Green | 1983 | 8.00 |
| ❑ PV 41085 | Watt | 1983 | 8.00 |
| ❑ PV 41573 | Positive Vibrations | 1987 | 8.00 |
| ❑ FV 41580 | Universal | 1988 | 10.00 |

COLUMBIA

| Number | Title (A Side/B Side) | Yr | NM |
|---|---|---|---|
| ❑ CQ 30801 [Q] | A Space in Time | 1973 | 16.00 |
| ❑ KC 30801 | A Space in Time | 1971 | 12.00 |
| ❑ PC 30801 | A Space in Time | 1979 | 8.00 |
| ❑ C 31779 | Rock and Roll Music to the World | 197? | 10.00 |
| *—Reissue with new prefix* | | | |
| ❑ KC 31779 | Rock and Roll Music to the World | 1972 | 12.00 |
| ❑ C2X 32288 [(2)] | Recorded Live | 1973 | 15.00 |
| ❑ PC 32851 | Positive Vibrations | 1974 | 10.00 |
| ❑ PC 34366 | Classic Performances of Ten Years After | 1976 | 10.00 |

DERAM

| Number | Title (A Side/B Side) | Yr | NM |
|---|---|---|---|
| ❑ DE 16009 [M] | Ten Years After | 1968 | 50.00 |
| ❑ DES 18009 [S] | Ten Years After | 1968 | 20.00 |
| ❑ DES 18016 | Undead | 1968 | 15.00 |
| ❑ DES 18021 | Stonedhenge | 1969 | 15.00 |
| ❑ DES 18029 | Ssssh | 1969 | 15.00 |
| ❑ DES 18038 | Cricklewood Green | 1970 | 15.00 |
| ❑ XDES 18050 | Watt | 1970 | 15.00 |
| *—With large "DERAM" on top half of label* | | | |
| ❑ XDES 18050 | Watt | 1970 | 25.00 |
| *—With "LONDON" under smaller "DERAM" at top of label* | | | |
| ❑ XDES 18064 | Alvin Lee and Company | 1972 | 12.00 |
| ❑ DES 18072 | Goin' Home! Their Greatest Hits | 1975 | 12.00 |
| ❑ SMAS-93428 | Watt | 1970 | 20.00 |
| *—Capitol Record Club edition* | | | |

LONDON

| Number | Title (A Side/B Side) | Yr | NM |
|---|---|---|---|
| ❑ LC 50008 | Greatest Hits | 1977 | 10.00 |
| ❑ 820324-1 | Greatest Hits | 1986 | 8.00 |

### TERRACE, PETE

FANTASY

| Number | Title (A Side/B Side) | Yr | NM |
|---|---|---|---|
| ❑ 3203 [M] | Going Loco | 195? | 25.00 |
| ❑ 3203 [M] | Going Loco | 1956 | 60.00 |
| *—Red vinyl* | | | |
| ❑ 3215 [M] | Invitation to the Mambo | 195? | 25.00 |
| ❑ 3215 [M] | Invitation to the Mambo | 1956 | 60.00 |
| *—Red vinyl* | | | |
| ❑ 3234 [M] | The Pete Terrace Quintet | 195? | 25.00 |
| ❑ 3234 [M] | The Pete Terrace Quintet | 1957 | 60.00 |
| *—Red vinyl* | | | |

TICO

| Number | Title (A Side/B Side) | Yr | NM |
|---|---|---|---|
| ❑ LP-1023 [M] | A Night in Mambo Jazzland | 1956 | 40.00 |
| ❑ LP-1028 [M] | The Nearness of You | 1956 | 40.00 |
| ❑ LP-1036 [M] | Cha Cha Cha in New York | 1957 | 40.00 |
| ❑ LP-1050 [M] | Pete with a Latin Beat | 1958 | 30.00 |
| ❑ LP-1057 [M] | My One and Only Love | 1959 | 30.00 |
| ❑ LP-1063 [M] | Cole Porter in Latin America | 1959 | 30.00 |
| ❑ LP-1082 [M] | Bella Pachanga | 1961 | 25.00 |
| ❑ SLP-1082 [S] | Bella Pachanga | 1961 | 30.00 |

### TERRACE, RAY

TOWER

| Number | Title (A Side/B Side) | Yr | NM |
|---|---|---|---|
| ❑ ST-5105 | The Home of Boogaloo | 1968 | 20.00 |

### TERRELL, TAMMI

MOTOWN

| Number | Title (A Side/B Side) | Yr | NM |
|---|---|---|---|
| ❑ M5-231V1 | Irresistible Tammi | 1982 | 10.00 |
| ❑ MS-652 | Irresistible Tammi | 1969 | 50.00 |

### TERRY, BUDDY

PRESTIGE

| Number | Title (A Side/B Side) | Yr | NM |
|---|---|---|---|
| ❑ PRLP-7525 [M] | Electric Soul | 1967 | 30.00 |
| ❑ PRST-7525 [S] | Electric Soul | 1967 | 25.00 |
| ❑ PRLP-7541 [M] | Natural Soul | 1967 | 30.00 |
| ❑ PRST-7541 [S] | Natural Soul | 1967 | 25.00 |

### TERRY, CLARK

ABC IMPULSE!

| Number | Title (A Side/B Side) | Yr | NM |
|---|---|---|---|
| ❑ AS-9157 [S] | It's What's Happenin' | 1968 | 20.00 |

ARGO

| Number | Title (A Side/B Side) | Yr | NM |
|---|---|---|---|
| ❑ LP-620 [M] | Out on a Limb | 1957 | 60.00 |

CAMEO

| Number | Title (A Side/B Side) | Yr | NM |
|---|---|---|---|
| ❑ C-1064 [M] | More | 1964 | 30.00 |
| ❑ CS-1064 [S] | More | 1964 | 40.00 |
| ❑ C-1071 [M] | Tread Ye Lightly | 1964 | 30.00 |
| ❑ CS-1071 [S] | Tread Ye Lightly | 1964 | 40.00 |

CANDID

| Number | Title (A Side/B Side) | Yr | NM |
|---|---|---|---|
| ❑ CD-8009 [M] | Color Changes | 1960 | 50.00 |
| ❑ CS-9009 [S] | Color Changes | 1960 | 40.00 |

EMARCY

| Number | Title (A Side/B Side) | Yr | NM |
|---|---|---|---|
| ❑ MG-36007 [M] | Clark Terry | 1955 | 80.00 |
| ❑ MG-36093 [M] | The Jazz School | 1956 | 60.00 |

ETOILE

| Number | Title (A Side/B Side) | Yr | NM |
|---|---|---|---|
| ❑ CPR-1 | Clark Terry's Big Bad Band | 197? | 20.00 |

IMPULSE!

| Number | Title (A Side/B Side) | Yr | NM |
|---|---|---|---|
| ❑ A-64 [M] | The Happy Horn of Clark Terry | 1964 | 25.00 |
| ❑ AS-64 [S] | The Happy Horn of Clark Terry | 1964 | 30.00 |
| ❑ A-9127 [M] | Spanish Rice | 1966 | 25.00 |
| ❑ AS-9127 [S] | Spanish Rice | 1966 | 30.00 |

MAINSTREAM

| Number | Title (A Side/B Side) | Yr | NM |
|---|---|---|---|
| ❑ MRL-803 [(2)] | What'd He Say | 197? | 20.00 |

Ten Years After, *Watt,* Deram XDES-18050, 1970, large "Deram" at top of label, $15.

| Number | Title (A Side/B Side) | Yr | NM |
|---|---|---|---|
| ❑ S-6043 [S] | Clark Terry Tonight | 1965 | 25.00 |
| ❑ S-6054 [S] | The Power of Positive Swinging | 1965 | 25.00 |
| ❑ S-6066 [S] | Mumbles | 1966 | 25.00 |
| ❑ S-6086 | Clark Terry with Bob Brookmeyer | 196? | 20.00 |
| ❑ 56043 [M] | Clark Terry Tonight | 1965 | 20.00 |
| ❑ 56054 [M] | The Power of Positive Swinging | 1965 | 20.00 |
| ❑ 56066 [M] | Mumbles | 1966 | 20.00 |

MOODSVILLE

| Number | Title (A Side/B Side) | Yr | NM |
|---|---|---|---|
| ❑ MVLP-20 [M] | Everything's Mellow | 1961 | 50.00 |
| *—Green label* | | | |
| ❑ MVLP-20 [M] | Everything's Mellow | 1965 | 25.00 |
| *—Blue label, trident logo at right* | | | |
| ❑ MVLP-26 [M] | The Jazz Version of "All American" | 1962 | 50.00 |
| *—Green label* | | | |
| ❑ MVLP-26 [M] | The Jazz Version of "All American" | 1965 | 25.00 |
| *—Blue label, trident logo at right* | | | |

RIVERSIDE

| Number | Title (A Side/B Side) | Yr | NM |
|---|---|---|---|
| ❑ RLP 12-237 [M] | Serenade to a Bus Seat | 1957 | 100.00 |
| *—Blue label, microphone logo at top* | | | |
| ❑ RLP 12-237 [M] | Serenade to a Bus Seat | 1957 | 300.00 |
| *—White label, blue print* | | | |
| ❑ RLP 12-246 [M] | Duke with a Difference | 1957 | 100.00 |
| ❑ RLP 12-271 [M] | In Orbit | 1958 | 100.00 |
| ❑ RLP 12-295 [M] | Top and Bottom Brass | 1959 | 100.00 |
| ❑ RLP-1108 [S] | Duke with a Difference | 1959 | 80.00 |
| ❑ RLP-1137 [S] | Top and Bottom Brass | 1959 | 80.00 |
| ❑ RM-3009 [M] | C.T. Meets Monk | 1967 | 25.00 |
| ❑ RS-3009 [S] | C.T. Meets Monk | 1967 | 20.00 |

20TH CENTURY FOX

| Number | Title (A Side/B Side) | Yr | NM |
|---|---|---|---|
| ❑ TFM-3137 [M] | What Makes Sammy Swing | 1963 | 20.00 |
| ❑ TFS-4137 [S] | What Makes Sammy Swing | 1963 | 25.00 |

WING

| Number | Title (A Side/B Side) | Yr | NM |
|---|---|---|---|
| ❑ MGW-60002 [M] | The Jazz School | 1955 | 80.00 |

### TERRY, CLARK/COLEMAN HAWKINS

COLPIX

| Number | Title (A Side/B Side) | Yr | NM |
|---|---|---|---|
| ❑ CP-450 [M] | Eddie Costa Memorial Concert | 1963 | 40.00 |
| ❑ SCP-450 [S] | Eddie Costa Memorial Concert | 1963 | 50.00 |

### TERRY, DON

COLUMBIA

| Number | Title (A Side/B Side) | Yr | NM |
|---|---|---|---|
| ❑ CL 6288 [10] | Teen-Age Dance Session | 1955 | 50.00 |

### TERRY, GORDON

LIBERTY

| Number | Title (A Side/B Side) | Yr | NM |
|---|---|---|---|
| ❑ LRP-3218 [M] | Liberty Square Dance Club | 1962 | 20.00 |
| *—With calls* | | | |
| ❑ LRP-3219 [M] | Liberty Square Dance Club | 1962 | 20.00 |
| *—Without calls* | | | |

PLANTATION

| Number | Title (A Side/B Side) | Yr | NM |
|---|---|---|---|
| ❑ 514 | Disco Country | 1977 | 12.00 |

### TERRY, RON

WING

| Number | Title (A Side/B Side) | Yr | NM |
|---|---|---|---|
| ❑ MGW-12108 [M] | Polkas and Waltzes | 1959 | 15.00 |
| ❑ SRW-16108 [S] | Polkas and Waltzes | 1959 | 20.00 |

### TERRY, SONNY

ALLIGATOR

| Number | Title (A Side/B Side) | Yr | NM |
|---|---|---|---|
| ❑ AL-4734 | Whoopin' | 198? | 12.00 |
| *—With Johnny Winter, Willie Dixon and others* | | | |

BLUE LABOR

| Number | Title (A Side/B Side) | Yr | NM |
|---|---|---|---|
| ❑ 101 | Robbin' the Grave | 197? | 12.00 |

BLUESVILLE

| Number | Title (A Side/B Side) | Yr | NM |
|---|---|---|---|
| ❑ BVLP-1025 [M] | Sonny's Story | 1961 | 80.00 |
| *—Bright blue label, no trident logo* | | | |
| ❑ BVLP-1025 [M] | Sonny's Story | 1964 | 25.00 |
| *—Blue label with trident logo on right* | | | |
| ❑ BVLP-1069 [M] | Sonny Is King | 1963 | 80.00 |
| *—Bright blue label, no trident logo* | | | |
| ❑ BVLP-1069 [M] | Sonny Is King | 1964 | 25.00 |
| *—Blue label with trident logo on right* | | | |

COLLECTABLES

| Number | Title (A Side/B Side) | Yr | NM |
|---|---|---|---|
| ❑ COL-5195 | Chain Gang Blues | 198? | 10.00 |
| ❑ COL-5307 | Sonny Terry | 198? | 10.00 |

ELEKTRA

| Number | Title (A Side/B Side) | Yr | NM |
|---|---|---|---|
| ❑ EKL-14 [10] | Folk Blues | 1954 | 150.00 |
| ❑ EKL-15 [10] | City Blues | 1954 | 150.00 |
| *—With Alec Stewart* | | | |

FANTASY

| Number | Title (A Side/B Side) | Yr | NM |
|---|---|---|---|
| ❑ OBC-521 | Sonny Is King | 198? | 10.00 |

FOLKWAYS

| Number | Title (A Side/B Side) | Yr | NM |
|---|---|---|---|
| ❑ FP-35 [10] | Harmonica and Vocal Solos | 1952 | 150.00 |
| ❑ FA-2006 [10] | Sonny Terry's Washboard Band | 195? | 100.00 |
| *—Black and white cover (reissue)* | | | |

| Number | Title (A Side/B Side) | Yr | NM |
|---|---|---|---|
| ❑ FP-2006 [10] | Sonny Terry's Washboard Band | 1950 | 150.00 |
| *—Blue and white cover* | | | |
| ❑ FA-2035 [10] | Harmonica and Vocal Solos | 1952 | 100.00 |
| ❑ FS-2369 | On the Road | 196? | 15.00 |
| ❑ 3821 | A New Sound | 198? | 12.00 |
| **PRESTIGE** | | | |
| ❑ PRST-7802 | Sonny Is King | 1970 | 15.00 |
| **RIVERSIDE** | | | |
| ❑ RLP-644 [M] | Sonny Terry and His Mouth Harp | 195? | 80.00 |
| **STINSON** | | | |
| ❑ 55 | Sonny Terry and His Mouth Harp | 197? | 12.00 |
| *—Reissue of 10-inch LP* | | | |
| ❑ SLP-55 [10] | Sonny Terry and His Mouth Harp | 1950 | 150.00 |

### TERRY, SONNY, AND BROWNIE MCGHEE

| Number | Title (A Side/B Side) | Yr | NM |
|---|---|---|---|
| **A&M** | | | |
| ❑ SP-4379 | Sonny & Brownie | 1973 | 12.00 |
| **ARCHIVE OF FOLK MUSIC** | | | |
| ❑ 242 | Brownie & Sonny | 198? | 12.00 |
| **BLUESVILLE** | | | |
| ❑ BVLP-1002 [M] | Down Home Blues | 1960 | 80.00 |
| *—Bright blue label, no trident logo* | | | |
| ❑ BVLP-1002 [M] | Down Home Blues | 1964 | 25.00 |
| *—Blue label with trident logo on right* | | | |
| ❑ BVLP-1005 [M] | Blues and Folk | 1960 | 80.00 |
| *—Bright blue label, no trident logo* | | | |
| ❑ BVLP-1005 [M] | Blues and Folk | 1964 | 25.00 |
| *—Blue label with trident logo on right* | | | |
| ❑ BVLP-1020 [M] | Blues All Around My Head | 1961 | 80.00 |
| *—Bright blue label, no trident logo* | | | |
| ❑ BVLP-1020 [M] | Blues All Around My Head | 1964 | 25.00 |
| *—Blue label with trident logo on right* | | | |
| ❑ BVLP-1033 [M] | Blues in My Soul | 1961 | 80.00 |
| *—Bright blue label, no trident logo* | | | |
| ❑ BVLP-1033 [M] | Blues in My Soul | 1964 | 25.00 |
| *—Blue label with trident logo on right* | | | |
| ❑ BVLP-1058 [M] | Live at the Second Fret | 1962 | 80.00 |
| *—Bright blue label, no trident logo* | | | |
| ❑ BVLP-1058 [M] | Live at the Second Fret | 1964 | 25.00 |
| *—Blue label with trident logo on right* | | | |
| **BLUESWAY** | | | |
| ❑ BLS-6028 | Long Way from Home | 1969 | 15.00 |
| ❑ BLS-6059 | Couldn't Believe My Eyes | 1970 | 15.00 |
| **COLLECTABLES** | | | |
| ❑ COL-5198 | Golden Classics: Blowin' the Fuses | 198? | 10.00 |
| **EVEREST** | | | |
| ❑ 206 | Sonny Terry | 1968 | 25.00 |
| ❑ 242 | Brownie McGhee and Sonny Terry | 1969 | 25.00 |
| **FANTASY** | | | |
| ❑ OBC-503 | Sonny's Story | 1984 | 10.00 |
| ❑ OBC-505 | Brownie's Blues | 1984 | 10.00 |
| ❑ F-3254 [M] | Sonny Terry & Brownie McGhee | 1961 | 40.00 |
| *—Black vinyl* | | | |
| ❑ F-3254 [M] | Sonny Terry & Brownie McGhee | 1961 | 150.00 |
| *—Red vinyl* | | | |
| ❑ F-3296 [M] | Just a Closer Walk with Thee | 1962 | 40.00 |
| *—Black vinyl* | | | |
| ❑ F-3296 [M] | Just a Closer Walk with Thee | 1962 | 150.00 |
| *—Red vinyl* | | | |
| ❑ F-3317 [M] | Blues and Shouts | 1962 | 40.00 |
| *—Black vinyl* | | | |
| ❑ F-3317 [M] | Blues and Shouts | 1962 | 150.00 |
| *—Red vinyl* | | | |
| ❑ F-3340 [M] | Sonny and Brownie at Sugar Hill | 1962 | 40.00 |
| *—Black vinyl* | | | |
| ❑ F-3340 [M] | Sonny and Brownie at Sugar Hill | 1962 | 150.00 |
| *—Red vinyl* | | | |
| ❑ FS-8091 [S] | Sonny and Brownie at Sugar Hill | 1962 | 40.00 |
| *—Black vinyl* | | | |
| ❑ FS-8091 [S] | Sonny and Brownie at Sugar Hill | 1962 | 150.00 |
| *—Blue vinyl* | | | |
| ❑ 24708 [(2)] | Back to New Orleans | 1972 | 15.00 |
| ❑ 24721 [(2)] | Midnight Special | 1977 | 15.00 |
| ❑ 24723 [(2)] | California Blues | 1981 | 15.00 |
| **FOLKLORE** | | | |
| ❑ FRLP-14013 [M] | Down Home Blues | 1964 | 40.00 |
| ❑ FRST-14013 [S] | Down Home Blues | 1964 | 50.00 |
| **FOLKWAYS** | | | |
| ❑ FA-2327 [M] | Blues and Folk Songs | 1960 | 30.00 |
| ❑ F-2421 [M] | Traditional Blues, Volume 1 | 1961 | 30.00 |
| ❑ FS-2421 [S] | Traditional Blues, Volume 1 | 1961 | 40.00 |
| ❑ F-2422 [M] | Traditional Blues, Volume 2 | 1961 | 30.00 |
| ❑ FS-2422 [S] | Traditional Blues, Volume 2 | 1961 | 40.00 |
| **FONTANA** | | | |
| ❑ SGF-67599 | Where the Blues Begin | 1969 | 25.00 |
| **KIMBERLEY** | | | |
| ❑ 2017 [M] | Southern Meetin' | 1963 | 20.00 |
| ❑ 11017 [S] | Southern Meetin' | 1963 | 25.00 |
| **MAINSTREAM** | | | |
| ❑ M-6049 [M] | Hometown Blues | 1966 | 20.00 |
| ❑ MS-6049 [S] | Hometown Blues | 1966 | 25.00 |
| **MOBILE FIDELITY** | | | |
| ❑ 1-233 | Sonny and Brownie | 1996 | 20.00 |
| *—Audiophile vinyl* | | | |
| **MUSE** | | | |
| ❑ 5117 | Hootin' | 198? | 12.00 |
| ❑ 5131 | You Hear Me Talkin' | 198? | 12.00 |
| **OLYMPIC** | | | |
| ❑ 7108 | Hootin' & Hollerin' | 1972 | 12.00 |
| **PRESTIGE** | | | |
| ❑ PRLP-7715 | Best of Sonny Terry and Brownie McGhee | 1969 | 15.00 |
| ❑ PRLP-7803 | Live at the Second Fret | 1970 | 15.00 |
| **ROULETTE** | | | |
| ❑ R-25074 [M] | The Folk Songs of Sonny & Brownie | 1959 | 50.00 |
| ❑ RS-25074 [S] | The Folk Songs of Sonny & Brownie | 1959 | 80.00 |
| **SAVOY** | | | |
| ❑ SJL-1137 | Climbin' Up | 1984 | 10.00 |
| ❑ 12218 | Down Home Blues | 1973 | 12.00 |
| **SHARP** | | | |
| ❑ 2003 [M] | Down Home Blues | 195? | 150.00 |
| **SMASH** | | | |
| ❑ MGS-27067 [M] | Brownie McGhee at the Bunkhouse | 1965 | 30.00 |
| ❑ SRS-67067 [S] | Brownie McGhee at the Bunkhouse | 1965 | 40.00 |
| **SMITHSONIAN/FOLKWAYS** | | | |
| ❑ SF-40011 | Sing | 198? | 10.00 |
| **STORYVILLE** | | | |
| ❑ 4007 | Brownie & Sonny | 1972 | 12.00 |
| **TOPIC** | | | |
| ❑ T-29 [M] | Songs | 1958 | 50.00 |
| **VEE JAY** | | | |
| ❑ VJLP-1138 | Coffee House Blues | 198? | 10.00 |
| *—With Lightnin' Hopkins* | | | |
| **VERVE** | | | |
| ❑ MGV 3008 [M] | Blues Is My Companion | 1961 | 80.00 |
| **VERVE FOLKWAYS** | | | |
| ❑ FV 9010 [M] | Get Together | 1965 | 25.00 |
| ❑ FVS 9010 [S] | Get Together | 1965 | 30.00 |
| ❑ FV 9019 [M] | Guitar Highway | 1965 | 25.00 |
| ❑ FVS 9019 [S] | Guitar Highway | 1965 | 30.00 |
| **WASHINGTON** | | | |
| ❑ W-702 [M] | Talkin' 'Bout the Blues | 1961 | 50.00 |
| **WORLD PACIFIC** | | | |
| ❑ ST-1294 [S] | Blues Is a Story | 1960 | 80.00 |
| ❑ WP-1294 [M] | Blues Is a Story | 1960 | 50.00 |
| ❑ ST-1296 [S] | Down South Summit Meetin' | 1960 | 80.00 |
| ❑ WP-1296 [M] | Down South Summit Meetin' | 1960 | 50.00 |

### TESCHEMACHER, FRANK

| Number | Title (A Side/B Side) | Yr | NM |
|---|---|---|---|
| **BRUNSWICK** | | | |
| ❑ BL 58017 [10] | Tesch Plays Jazz Classics | 1950 | 80.00 |
| **TIME-LIFE** | | | |
| ❑ STL-J23 [(3)] | Giants of Jazz | 1982 | 20.00 |

### TEX, JOE

| Number | Title (A Side/B Side) | Yr | NM |
|---|---|---|---|
| **ACCORD** | | | |
| ❑ SN-7174 | J.T.'s Funk | 1982 | 10.00 |
| **ATLANTIC** | | | |
| ❑ 8106 [M] | Hold What You've Got | 1965 | 40.00 |
| ❑ SD 8106 [P] | Hold What You've Got | 1965 | 50.00 |
| ❑ 8115 [M] | The New Boss | 1965 | 40.00 |
| ❑ SD 8115 [S] | The New Boss | 1965 | 50.00 |
| ❑ 8124 [M] | The Love You Save | 1966 | 40.00 |
| ❑ SD 8124 [S] | The Love You Save | 1966 | 50.00 |
| ❑ 8133 [M] | I've Got to Do a Little Better | 1966 | 40.00 |
| ❑ SD 8133 [S] | I've Got to Do a Little Better | 1966 | 50.00 |
| ❑ 8144 [M] | The Best of Joe Tex | 1967 | 20.00 |
| ❑ SD 8144 [P] | The Best of Joe Tex | 1967 | 25.00 |
| ❑ SD 8156 | Live and Lively | 1968 | 20.00 |
| ❑ 8187 [M] | Soul Country | 1968 | 40.00 |
| *—Mono is white label promo only; "d/j copy monaural" sticker on cover* | | | |
| ❑ SD 8187 [S] | Soul Country | 1968 | 20.00 |
| ❑ SD 8211 | Happy Soul | 1969 | 20.00 |
| ❑ SD 8231 | Buying a Book | 1969 | 20.00 |
| ❑ SD 8254 | Joe Tex Sings with Strings and Things | 1970 | 15.00 |
| ❑ SD 8292 | From the Roots Came the Rapper | 1972 | 15.00 |
| ❑ 81278 | The Best of Joe Tex | 1985 | 10.00 |
| **CHECKER** | | | |
| ❑ LP-2993 [M] | Hold On | 1965 | 150.00 |
| **DIAL** | | | |
| ❑ DL 6002 | I Gotcha | 1972 | 15.00 |
| ❑ DL 6004 | Joe Tex Spills the Beans | 1973 | 15.00 |
| ❑ DL 6100 | He Who Is Without Funk Cast the First Stone | 1979 | 10.00 |
| **EPIC** | | | |
| ❑ PE 34666 | Bumps and Bruises | 1977 | 12.00 |
| **KING** | | | |
| ❑ 935 [M] | The Best of Joe Tex | 1965 | 100.00 |
| ❑ KS-935 [R] | The Best of Joe Tex | 1965 | 75.00 |
| **LONDON** | | | |
| ❑ LC-50017 | Super Soul | 1977 | 10.00 |
| **PARROT** | | | |
| ❑ PA 61002 [M] | The Best of Joe Tex | 1965 | 50.00 |
| ❑ PAS 71002 [R] | The Best of Joe Tex | 1965 | 30.00 |
| **PRIDE** | | | |
| ❑ PRD-0020 | The History of Joe Tex | 1973 | 10.00 |
| **RHINO** | | | |
| ❑ RNLP-70191 | I Believe I'm Gonna Make It: The Best of Joe Tex 1964-1972 | 1988 | 10.00 |

### TEXAS RANGERS, THE

| Number | Title (A Side/B Side) | Yr | NM |
|---|---|---|---|
| **CUMBERLAND** | | | |
| ❑ MGC-29507 [M] | The Best of Western Swing | 1963 | 20.00 |
| ❑ SRC-69505 [S] | The Best of Western Swing | 1963 | 25.00 |

### TEXAS RUBY

| Number | Title (A Side/B Side) | Yr | NM |
|---|---|---|---|
| **KING** | | | |
| ❑ 840 [M] | Texas Ruby Sings His Favorite Songs | 1963 | 50.00 |

### TEXAS TROUBADOURS, THE

| Number | Title (A Side/B Side) | Yr | NM |
|---|---|---|---|
| **DECCA** | | | |
| ❑ DL 4459 [M] | The Texas Troubadours | 1964 | 25.00 |
| ❑ DL 4644 [M] | Country Dance Time | 1965 | 20.00 |
| ❑ DL 4745 [M] | Ernest Tubb's Fabulous Texas Troubadours | 1966 | 20.00 |
| ❑ DL 74459 [S] | The Texas Troubadours | 1964 | 30.00 |
| ❑ DL 74644 [S] | Country Dance Time | 1965 | 25.00 |
| ❑ DL 74745 [S] | Ernest Tubb's Fabulous Texas Troubadours | 1966 | 25.00 |
| ❑ DL 75017 | The Terrific Texas Troubadours and Guests | 1968 | 20.00 |

### THAXTON, LLOYD

| Number | Title (A Side/B Side) | Yr | NM |
|---|---|---|---|
| **DECCA** | | | |
| ❑ DL 4594 [M] | Lloyd Thaxton Presents | 1964 | 20.00 |
| ❑ DL 74594 [S] | Lloyd Thaxton Presents | 1964 | 25.00 |

### THEE MIDNITERS

| Number | Title (A Side/B Side) | Yr | NM |
|---|---|---|---|
| **CHATTAHOOCHIE** | | | |
| ❑ C-1001 [M] | Thee Midniters | 1965 | 60.00 |
| ❑ CS-1001 [S] | Thee Midniters | 1965 | 80.00 |
| **WHITTIER** | | | |
| ❑ W-5000 [M] | Bring You Love Special Delivery | 1966 | 40.00 |
| ❑ WS-5000 [S] | Bring You Love Special Delivery | 1966 | 50.00 |
| ❑ W-5001 [M] | Unlimited | 1966 | 40.00 |
| ❑ WS-5001 [S] | Unlimited | 1966 | 50.00 |
| ❑ W-5002 [M] | Giants | 1967 | 40.00 |
| ❑ WS-5002 [S] | Giants | 1967 | 50.00 |
| **ZYANYA/RHINO** | | | |
| ❑ RNLP-063 | The Best of Thee Midniters | 1983 | 12.00 |

### THEE MUFFINS

| Number | Title (A Side/B Side) | Yr | NM |
|---|---|---|---|
| **(NO LABEL)** | | | |
| ❑ (no #) | Thee Muffins Pop Up! | 1967 | 200.00 |

### THEE PROPHETS

| Number | Title (A Side/B Side) | Yr | NM |
|---|---|---|---|
| **KAPP** | | | |
| ❑ KS-3596 | Playgirl | 1969 | 20.00 |

### THEM Also see VAN MORRISON.

| Number | Title (A Side/B Side) | Yr | NM |
|---|---|---|---|
| **HAPPY TIGER** | | | |
| ❑ HT-1004 | Them | 1969 | 50.00 |
| ❑ HT-1012 | Them In Reality | 1971 | 120.00 |
| **LONDON** | | | |
| ❑ PS 639 [P] | Backtrackin' | 1974 | 10.00 |
| ❑ LC-50001 [R] | The Story of Them | 1977 | 10.00 |
| ❑ 820326-1 | Them Featuring Van Morrison | 1985 | 10.00 |
| **PARROT** | | | |
| ❑ PA 61005 [M] | Them Featuring "Here Comes the Night" | 1965 | 80.00 |
| ❑ PA 61005 [M] | Them Featuring "Gloria" | 1966 | 50.00 |
| *—Same album as above, but with slightly different title* | | | |
| ❑ PA 61008 [M] | Them Again | 1966 | 80.00 |
| ❑ PAS 71005 [R] | Them Featuring "Here Comes the Night" | 1965 | 70.00 |
| ❑ PAS 71005 [R] | Them Featuring "Gloria" | 1966 | 40.00 |
| *—Same album as above, but with slightly different title* | | | |

| Number | Title (A Side/B Side) | Yr | NM |
|---|---|---|---|
| ❑ PAS 71008 [R] | Them Again | 1966 | 50.00 |
| ❑ BP 71053 [(2)P] | Them Featuring Van Morrison | 1972 | 12.00 |

*—"Gloria," "Here Comes the Night," "If You and I Could Be as Two," "One More Time" and "One Two Brown Eyes" are true stereo.*

TOWER

| Number | Title (A Side/B Side) | Yr | NM |
|---|---|---|---|
| ❑ ST 5104 [S] | Now and Them | 1967 | 80.00 |
| ❑ T 5104 [M] | Now and Them | 1967 | 50.00 |
| ❑ ST 5116 [S] | Time Out! Time In for Them | 1968 | 100.00 |

### THEODORE

CORAL

| Number | Title (A Side/B Side) | Yr | NM |
|---|---|---|---|
| ❑ CRL 757322 [S] | Coral Records Presents Theodore in Stereo | 1959 | 100.00 |

### THESE TRAILS

SINERGIA

| Number | Title (A Side/B Side) | Yr | NM |
|---|---|---|---|
| ❑ (# unknown) | These Trails | 1973 | 120.00 |

### THESELIUS, GOSTA

BALLY

| Number | Title (A Side/B Side) | Yr | NM |
|---|---|---|---|
| ❑ BAL-12002 [M] | Swedish Jazz | 1956 | 50.00 |

### THEY MIGHT BE GIANTS

BAR NONE

| Number | Title (A Side/B Side) | Yr | NM |
|---|---|---|---|
| ❑ A-HAON 005 [EP] | (She Was a) Hotel Detective | 1988 | 20.00 |

BAR NONE/RESTLESS

| Number | Title (A Side/B Side) | Yr | NM |
|---|---|---|---|
| ❑ A-HAON 002 | They Might Be Giants | 1988 | 15.00 |
| *—With mention of Restless Records* | | | |
| ❑ 72605 [EP] | Don't Let's Start | 1988 | 15.00 |
| *—Reissue of A-HAON 004* | | | |

### THIELEMANS, TOOTS

ABC-PARAMOUNT

| Number | Title (A Side/B Side) | Yr | NM |
|---|---|---|---|
| ❑ ABC-482 [M] | The Whistler and His Guitar | 1965 | 25.00 |
| ❑ ABCS-482 [S] | The Whistler and His Guitar | 1965 | 30.00 |

COLUMBIA

| Number | Title (A Side/B Side) | Yr | NM |
|---|---|---|---|
| ❑ CL 658 [M] | The Sound | 1955 | 50.00 |

COMMAND

| Number | Title (A Side/B Side) | Yr | NM |
|---|---|---|---|
| ❑ RS 33-906 [M] | Contrasts | 1967 | 20.00 |
| ❑ RS 33-918 [M] | Guitars and Strings... And Things | 1967 | 20.00 |

DECCA

| Number | Title (A Side/B Side) | Yr | NM |
|---|---|---|---|
| ❑ DL 9204 [M] | Time Out for Toots | 1958 | 50.00 |
| ❑ DL 79204 [S] | Time Out for Toots | 1958 | 40.00 |

RIVERSIDE

| Number | Title (A Side/B Side) | Yr | NM |
|---|---|---|---|
| ❑ RLP 12-257 [M] | Man Bites Harmonica | 1958 | 100.00 |

SIGNATURE

| Number | Title (A Side/B Side) | Yr | NM |
|---|---|---|---|
| ❑ SM-6006 [M] | The Soul of Toots Thielmans | 1960 | 80.00 |
| ❑ SS-6006 [S] | The Soul of Toots Thielmans | 1960 | 60.00 |

### THIGPEN, ED

VERVE

| Number | Title (A Side/B Side) | Yr | NM |
|---|---|---|---|
| ❑ V-8663 [M] | Out of the Storm | 1966 | 20.00 |
| ❑ V6-8663 [S] | Out of the Storm | 1966 | 25.00 |

### THIN LIZZY

LONDON

| Number | Title (A Side/B Side) | Yr | NM |
|---|---|---|---|
| ❑ PS 594 | Thin Lizzy | 1971 | 40.00 |
| ❑ PS 636 | Vagabonds of the Western World | 1973 | 30.00 |
| ❑ LC-50004 | The Rocker (1971-1974) | 1977 | 12.00 |

MERCURY

| Number | Title (A Side/B Side) | Yr | NM |
|---|---|---|---|
| ❑ SRM-1-1081 | Jailbreak | 1976 | 12.00 |
| ❑ SRM-1-1107 | Night Life | 1976 | 12.00 |
| *—Reissue of Vertigo 2002* | | | |
| ❑ SRM-1-1108 | Fighting | 1976 | 12.00 |
| *—Reissue of Vertigo 2005* | | | |
| ■ SRM-1-1119 | Johnny the Fox | 1976 | 12.00 |
| ■ SRM-1-1186 | Bad Reputation | 1977 | 12.00 |

VERTIGO

| Number | Title (A Side/B Side) | Yr | NM |
|---|---|---|---|
| ❑ VEL-2002 | Night Life | 1974 | 15.00 |
| ❑ VEL-2005 | Fighting | 1975 | 15.00 |

WARNER BROS.

| Number | Title (A Side/B Side) | Yr | NM |
|---|---|---|---|
| ■ BS2 3213 [(2)] | Live and Dangerous | 1978 | 12.00 |
| ❑ BSK 3338 | Black Rose/A Rock Legend | 1979 | 10.00 |
| ❑ BSK 3496 | Chinatown | 1980 | 10.00 |
| ❑ BSK 3622 | Renegade | 1982 | 10.00 |
| ❑ 23831 | Thunder and Lightning | 1983 | 10.00 |
| ❑ 23986 [(2)] | "Life" — Live | 1984 | 12.00 |

### THIRD ESTATE, THE

THIRD ESTATE

| Number | Title (A Side/B Side) | Yr | NM |
|---|---|---|---|
| ❑ LP-1000 | Years Before the Wine | 1976 | 200.00 |

### THIRD EYE BLIND

ELEKTRA

| Number | Title (A Side/B Side) | Yr | NM |
|---|---|---|---|
| ❑ 62012-1 [(2)] | Third Eye Blind | 1997 | 40.00 |
| ❑ 62415-1 [(2)] | Blue | 1999 | 60.00 |

### THIRD POWER

VANGUARD

| Number | Title (A Side/B Side) | Yr | NM |
|---|---|---|---|
| ❑ VSD-6554 | Believe | 1970 | 30.00 |

### THIRD RAIL, THE

EPIC

| Number | Title (A Side/B Side) | Yr | NM |
|---|---|---|---|
| ❑ LN 24327 [M] | Id Music | 1967 | 30.00 |
| ❑ BN 26327 [S] | Id Music | 1967 | 40.00 |

### THIRTEENTH FLOOR ELEVATORS, THE

INTERNATIONAL ARTISTS

| Number | Title (A Side/B Side) | Yr | NM |
|---|---|---|---|
| ❑ 1 [M] | Psychedelic Sounds | 1967 | 250.00 |
| *—Green and yellow label* | | | |
| ❑ 1 [M] | Psychedelic Sounds | 1968 | 150.00 |
| *—All-yellow label* | | | |
| ❑ 1 [S] | Psychedelic Sounds | 1968 | 150.00 |
| *—All-yellow label* | | | |
| ❑ 1 [S] | Psychedelic Sounds | 1968 | 200.00 |
| *—Aqua-blue label* | | | |
| ❑ 1 [S] | Psychedelic Sounds | 1979 | 30.00 |
| *—Repressing with "Masterfonics" in dead wax* | | | |
| ❑ 5 [M] | Easter Everywhere | 1968 | 400.00 |
| *—Mono is promo only* | | | |
| ❑ 5 [S] | Easter Everywhere | 1968 | 150.00 |
| *—With custom inner sleeve* | | | |
| ❑ 5 [S] | Easter Everywhere | 1968 | 150.00 |
| *—Without custom inner sleeve* | | | |
| ❑ 5 [S] | Easter Everywhere | 1979 | 30.00 |
| *—Repressing with "Masterfonics" in dead wax* | | | |
| ❑ 8 | 13th Floor Elevators Live | 1968 | 100.00 |
| ❑ 8 | 13th Floor Elevators Live | 1979 | 25.00 |
| *—Repressing with "Masterfonics" in dead wax* | | | |
| ❑ 9 | Bull of the Woods | 1968 | 80.00 |
| ❑ 9 | Bull of the Woods | 1979 | 25.00 |
| *—Repressing with "Masterfonics" in dead wax* | | | |

### 31ST OF FEBRUARY, THE

VANGUARD

| Number | Title (A Side/B Side) | Yr | NM |
|---|---|---|---|
| ❑ VSD-6503 | The 31st of February | 1969 | 40.00 |

### 31 FLAVORS, THE

CROWN

| Number | Title (A Side/B Side) | Yr | NM |
|---|---|---|---|
| ❑ CST-592 | Hair | 1968 | 50.00 |

### THOMAS, B.J.

ABC

| Number | Title (A Side/B Side) | Yr | NM |
|---|---|---|---|
| ❑ ABDP-858 | Reunion | 1975 | 10.00 |
| ❑ ABCD-912 | Help Me Make It to My Rockin' Chair | 1976 | 10.00 |

ACCORD

| Number | Title (A Side/B Side) | Yr | NM |
|---|---|---|---|
| ❑ SN-7106 | Lovin' You | 198? | 10.00 |

BUCKBOARD

| Number | Title (A Side/B Side) | Yr | NM |
|---|---|---|---|
| ❑ 1023 | B.J. Thomas Sings Hank Williams and Other Favorites | 198? | 10.00 |

CLEVELAND INT'L.

| Number | Title (A Side/B Side) | Yr | NM |
|---|---|---|---|
| ❑ FC 38561 | New Looks | 1983 | 10.00 |
| ❑ PC 38561 | New Looks | 1984 | 8.00 |
| *—Budget-line reissue* | | | |
| ❑ FC 39111 | The Great American Dream | 1983 | 10.00 |
| ❑ PC 39111 | The Great American Dream | 1984 | 8.00 |
| *—Budget-line reissue* | | | |
| ❑ FC 39337 | Shining | 1984 | 10.00 |
| ❑ FC 40157 | Throwing Rocks at the Moon | 1985 | 10.00 |

COLUMBIA

| Number | Title (A Side/B Side) | Yr | NM |
|---|---|---|---|
| ❑ PC 38400 | Love Shines | 1984 | 8.00 |
| *—Reissue of Priority 38400* | | | |
| ❑ PC 40148 | All Is Calm, All Is Bright... | 1985 | 10.00 |
| ❑ FC 40496 | Night Life | 1986 | 10.00 |

DORAL

| Number | Title (A Side/B Side) | Yr | NM |
|---|---|---|---|
| ❑ (# unknown) | Doral Presents B.J. Thomas | 1971 | 20.00 |
| *—Mail-order promotion from Doral cigarettes* | | | |

EVEREST

| Number | Title (A Side/B Side) | Yr | NM |
|---|---|---|---|
| ❑ 4104 | Golden Greats | 1981 | 10.00 |

HICKORY

| Number | Title (A Side/B Side) | Yr | NM |
|---|---|---|---|
| ❑ LPM-133 [M] | The Very Best of B.J. Thomas | 1966 | 20.00 |
| ❑ LPS-133 [S] | The Very Best of B.J. Thomas | 1966 | 25.00 |
| ❑ ST 90956 [S] | The Very Best of B.J. Thomas | 1966 | 30.00 |
| *—Capitol Record Club edition* | | | |
| ❑ T 90956 [M] | The Very Best of B.J. Thomas | 1966 | 25.00 |
| *—Capitol Record Club edition* | | | |

MCA

| Number | Title (A Side/B Side) | Yr | NM |
|---|---|---|---|
| ❑ 746 | Everybody Loves a Rain Song | 1980 | 8.00 |
| *—Budget-line reissue* | | | |
| ❑ 2286 | B.J. Thomas | 1977 | 10.00 |
| ❑ 3035 | Everybody Loves a Rain Song | 1978 | 10.00 |
| ❑ 3231 | For the Best | 1979 | 10.00 |
| ❑ 5155 | In Concert | 1980 | 10.00 |
| ❑ 5195 | Some Love Songs Never Die | 1980 | 10.00 |
| ❑ 5296 | As We Know Him | 1982 | 10.00 |
| ❑ 27032 | In Concert | 198? | 8.00 |
| *—Reissue of MCA 5155* | | | |

MYRRH

| Number | Title (A Side/B Side) | Yr | NM |
|---|---|---|---|
| ❑ MSB-6574 | Home Where I Belong | 1978 | 10.00 |
| ❑ MSB-6593 | A Happy Man | 1979 | 10.00 |
| ❑ MSB-6633 | You Gave Me Love | 1979 | 10.00 |
| ❑ MSB-6653 | The Best of B.J. Thomas | 1980 | 10.00 |
| ❑ MSB-6675 | Amazing Grace | 1981 | 10.00 |
| ❑ MSB-6705 | Miracle | 1983 | 10.00 |
| ❑ MSB-6710 | Peace in the Valley | 1983 | 10.00 |
| ❑ MSB-6725 | The Best of B.J. Thomas, Volume 2 | 1984 | 10.00 |
| ❑ WR-8153 | Peace in the Valley | 1985 | 10.00 |
| *—Reissue of 6710* | | | |
| ❑ WR-8200 | Amazing Grace | 1985 | 8.00 |
| *—Reissue of 6675* | | | |

PACEMAKER

| Number | Title (A Side/B Side) | Yr | NM |
|---|---|---|---|
| ❑ PLP-3001 [M] | B.J. Thomas and the Triumphs | 1965 | 200.00 |

PAIR

| Number | Title (A Side/B Side) | Yr | NM |
|---|---|---|---|
| ❑ PDL2-1099 [(2)] | Greatest Hits | 1986 | 12.00 |

PARAMOUNT

| Number | Title (A Side/B Side) | Yr | NM |
|---|---|---|---|
| ❑ PAS 1020 | Longhorns & Londonbridges | 1974 | 12.00 |
| ❑ PAS-6052 | B.J. Thomas Songs | 1973 | 12.00 |

PICKWICK

| Number | Title (A Side/B Side) | Yr | NM |
|---|---|---|---|
| ❑ SPC-3623 | The Best of B.J. Thomas | 197? | 10.00 |

PRIORITY

| Number | Title (A Side/B Side) | Yr | NM |
|---|---|---|---|
| ❑ JU 38400 | Love Shines | 1982 | 10.00 |

REPRISE

| Number | Title (A Side/B Side) | Yr | NM |
|---|---|---|---|
| ❑ 25898 | Midnight Minute | 1989 | 12.00 |

SCEPTER

| Number | Title (A Side/B Side) | Yr | NM |
|---|---|---|---|
| ❑ SPS-535 [S] | I'm So Lonesome I Could Cry | 1966 | 25.00 |
| ❑ SRM-535 [M] | I'm So Lonesome I Could Cry | 1966 | 20.00 |
| ❑ SPS-556 [S] | Tomorrow Never Comes | 1966 | 20.00 |
| ❑ SRM-556 [M] | Tomorrow Never Comes | 1966 | 15.00 |
| ❑ SPS-561 [S] | For Lovers and Losers | 1967 | 15.00 |
| ❑ SRM-561 [M] | For Lovers and Losers | 1967 | 20.00 |
| ❑ SPS-570 [S] | On My Way | 1968 | 15.00 |
| ❑ SRM-570 [M] | On My Way | 1968 | 30.00 |
| *—Mono appears to be white label promo only; in stereo cover with "Promotional DJ Copy Monaural Not for Sale" sticker on front* | | | |
| ❑ SPS-576 | Young and In Love | 1969 | 15.00 |
| ❑ SPS-578 | Greatest Hits, Volume 1 | 1969 | 12.00 |
| ❑ SPS-580 | Raindrops Keep Fallin' on My Head | 1970 | 12.00 |
| *—Remixed version; trail-off wax number on Side 1 is "SPS-580-A-1C" or "SPS-580-A-1D" and on Side 2 is "SPS-580-B-1C"* | | | |
| ❑ SPS-580 | Raindrops Keep Fallin' on My Head | 1970 | 15.00 |
| *—Original "muddy mix"; trail-off wax number on Side 1 is "SPS-580-A-1B" and on Side 2 is "SPS-580-B-1A"* | | | |
| ❑ SPS-582 | Everybody's Out of Town | 1970 | 12.00 |
| ❑ SPS-586 | Most of All | 1970 | 12.00 |
| ❑ SPS-597 | Greatest Hits, Volume Two | 1971 | 12.00 |
| ❑ 5101 | Billy Joe Thomas | 1972 | 12.00 |
| ❑ 5108 | B.J. Thomas Country | 1972 | 12.00 |
| ❑ 5112 [(2)] | Greatest All-Time Hits | 1973 | 15.00 |

STARDAY

| Number | Title (A Side/B Side) | Yr | NM |
|---|---|---|---|
| ❑ 992 | The Best of B.J. Thomas | 197? | 10.00 |

UNITED ARTISTS

| Number | Title (A Side/B Side) | Yr | NM |
|---|---|---|---|
| ❑ UA-LA389-E | The Very Best of B.J. Thomas | 1974 | 12.00 |

### THOMAS, CARLA

Also see OTIS AND CARLA; RUFUS AND CARLA.

ATLANTIC

| Number | Title (A Side/B Side) | Yr | NM |
|---|---|---|---|
| ❑ 8057 [M] | Gee Whiz | 1961 | 100.00 |
| *—With white "fan" logo* | | | |
| ❑ 8057 [M] | Gee Whiz | 1963 | 40.00 |
| *—With black "fan" logo* | | | |
| ❑ SD 8057 [S] | Gee Whiz | 1961 | 150.00 |
| *—With white "fan" logo* | | | |
| ❑ SD 8057 [S] | Gee Whiz | 1963 | 50.00 |
| *—With black "fan" logo* | | | |
| ❑ SD 8232 | The Best of Carla Thomas | 1969 | 25.00 |

STAX

| Number | Title (A Side/B Side) | Yr | NM |
|---|---|---|---|
| ❑ 706 [M] | Comfort Me | 1966 | 35.00 |
| ❑ 706 [P] | Comfort Me | 1966 | 50.00 |
| ❑ 709 [M] | Carla | 1966 | 35.00 |
| ❑ 709 [S] | Carla | 1966 | 50.00 |
| ❑ 718 [M] | The Queen Alone | 1967 | 35.00 |
| ❑ 718 [S] | The Queen Alone | 1967 | 50.00 |
| ❑ STS-2019 | Memphis Queen | 1969 | 35.00 |
| ❑ STS-2044 | Love Means Carla Thomas | 1971 | 35.00 |
| ❑ MPS-8538 | Memphis Queen | 1987 | 10.00 |
| *—Budget-line reissue* | | | |

### THOMAS, CARLA, AND RUFUS THOMAS

See RUFUS AND CARLA.

### THOMAS, DANNY

COLUMBIA

| Number | Title (A Side/B Side) | Yr | NM |
|---|---|---|---|
| ❑ XTV 60818/9 [M] | An Evening with Danny Thomas | 1960 | 25.00 |
| *—Made for Post Cereals* | | | |

MGM

| Number | Title (A Side/B Side) | Yr | NM |
|---|---|---|---|
| ❑ E-201 [10] | An Evening with Danny Thomas | 1954 | 100.00 |

MYRRH

| Number | Title (A Side/B Side) | Yr | NM |
|---|---|---|---|
| ❑ MST-6520 | Tomorrow Belongs to You | 1973 | 10.00 |
| ❑ MST-6522 | I'll Still Be Loving You | 197? | 10.00 |
| ❑ MSA-6539 | Jesus Is My Kind of People | 197? | 10.00 |

### THOMAS, DYLAN

CAEDMON

| Number | Title (A Side/B Side) | Yr | NM |
|---|---|---|---|
| ❑ TC 1002 [M] | A Child's Christmas in Wales and Five Poems (Dylan Thomas, Volume 1) | 1957 | 20.00 |
| *—Number stamped into dead wax; "New York, 1, New York" address on label and cover* | | | |

| Number | Title (A Side/B Side) | Yr | NM |
|---|---|---|---|
| **THOMAS, IRMA** | | | |
| BANDY | | | |
| ❑ 70003 | Irma Thomas Sings | 197? | 30.00 |
| FUNGUS | | | |
| ❑ FB-25150 | In Between Tears | 1973 | 40.00 |
| IMPERIAL | | | |
| ❑ LP-9266 [M] | Wish Someone Would Care | 1964 | 50.00 |
| ❑ LP-9302 [M] | Take a Look | 1966 | 50.00 |
| ❑ LP-12266 [S] | Wish Someone Would Care | 1964 | 60.00 |
| ❑ LP-12302 [S] | Take a Look | 1966 | 60.00 |
| RCS | | | |
| ❑ 1004 | Safe with Me | 1980 | 30.00 |
| **THOMAS, JEANNIE** | | | |
| STRAND | | | |
| ❑ SL-1030 [M] | Jeannie Thomas Sings for the Boys | 1961 | 40.00 |
| ❑ SLS-1030 [S] | Jeannie Thomas Sings for the Boys | 1961 | 50.00 |
| **THOMAS, JOE (3), AND BILL ELLIOTT** | | | |
| SUE | | | |
| ❑ LP-1025 [M] | Speak Your Piece | 1964 | 50.00 |
| **THOMAS, JON** | | | |
| ABC-PARAMOUNT | | | |
| ❑ 351 [M] | Heartbreak | 1960 | 30.00 |
| ❑ S-351 [S] | Heartbreak | 1960 | 40.00 |
| WING | | | |
| ❑ MGW-12258 [M] | The Big Beat on the Organ | 1963 | 20.00 |
| ❑ SRW-16258 [R] | The Big Beat on the Organ | 1963 | 12.00 |
| **THOMAS, LEON** | | | |
| FLYING DUTCHMAN | | | |
| ❑ FD-10115 | Spirits Known and Unknown | 1969 | 20.00 |
| ❑ FD-10132 | The Leon Thomas Album | 197? | 20.00 |
| MEGA | | | |
| ❑ M51-5003 | Gold Sunrise on Magic Mountain | 197? | 20.00 |
| **THOMAS, PAT** | | | |
| MGM | | | |
| ❑ E-4103 [M] | Desafinado | 1962 | 15.00 |
| ❑ SE-4103 [S] | Desafinado | 1962 | 20.00 |
| ❑ E-4206 [M] | Moody's Mood | 1964 | 20.00 |
| ❑ SE-4206 [S] | Moody's Mood | 1964 | 25.00 |
| STRAND | | | |
| ❑ SL-1015 [M] | Jazz Patterns | 1961 | 40.00 |
| ❑ SLS-1015 [S] | Jazz Patterns | 1961 | 50.00 |
| **THOMAS, RAY** Also see THE MOODY BLUES. | | | |
| THRESHOLD | | | |
| ❑ THS 16 | From Mighty Oaks | 1975 | 15.00 |
| ❑ THS 17 | Hopes Wishes & Dreams | 1976 | 15.00 |
| ❑ THSX-102 [DJ] | Ray Thomas Discusses The Recording of His First Solo Album From Mighty Oaks | 1975 | 50.00 |
| **THOMAS, RENE** | | | |
| JAZZLAND | | | |
| ❑ JLP-27 [M] | Guitar Groove | 1960 | 30.00 |
| ❑ JLP-927 [S] | Guitar Groove | 1960 | 40.00 |
| **THOMAS, RUFUS** | | | |
| A.V.I. | | | |
| ❑ 6015 | If There Were No Music | 1977 | 15.00 |
| ❑ 6046 | I Ain't Gettin' Older, I'm Gettin' Better | 1978 | 15.00 |
| ALLIGATOR | | | |
| ❑ AV-4769 | That Woman Is Poison | 1988 | 10.00 |
| GUSTO | | | |
| ❑ 0064 | Rufus Thomas | 1980 | 10.00 |
| STAX | | | |
| ❑ ST-704 [M] | Walking the Dog | 1963 | 150.00 |
| ❑ STS-2028 | Do the Funky Chicken | 1970 | 25.00 |
| ❑ STS-2039 | Rufus Thomas Live/Doing the Push and Pull at P.J.'s | 1971 | 25.00 |
| ❑ STS-3004 | Did You Hear Me | 1972 | 25.00 |
| ❑ STS-3008 | Crown Prince of Dance | 1973 | 25.00 |
| **THOMPSON, BOB** | | | |
| RAINBOW | | | |
| ❑ 2010 | 7 In, 7 Out | 1986 | 20.00 |
| **THOMPSON, CHESTER** | | | |
| BLACK JAZZ | | | |
| ❑ 6 | Powerhouse | 197? | 25.00 |
| **THOMPSON, HANK** | | | |
| ABC | | | |
| ❑ AB-1095 | Brand New Hank | 1978 | 12.00 |
| ABC DOT | | | |
| ❑ DOSD-2003 | Moving On | 1974 | 12.00 |
| ❑ DOSD-2032 | Hank Thompson Sings Nat King Cole | 1975 | 12.00 |
| ❑ DOSD-2060 | Back in the Swing of Things | 1976 | 12.00 |
| ❑ DOSD-2069 | The Thompson Touch | 1977 | 12.00 |
| ❑ DO-2091 | Doin' My Thing | 1977 | 12.00 |
| CAPITOL | | | |
| ❑ H 418 [10] | Songs of the Brazos Valley | 1953 | 120.00 |
| ❑ T 418 [M] | Songs of the Brazos Valley | 1956 | 80.00 |
| *—Turquoise or gray label* | | | |
| ❑ T 418 [M] | Songs of the Brazos Valley | 1959 | 30.00 |
| *—Black colorband label, logo at left* | | | |
| ❑ T 418 [M] | Songs of the Brazos Valley | 1962 | 20.00 |
| *—Black colorband label, logo at top* | | | |
| ❑ H 618 [10] | North of the Rio Grande | 1953 | 120.00 |
| ❑ T 618 [M] | North of the Rio Grande | 1956 | 80.00 |
| *—Turquoise or gray label* | | | |
| ❑ H 729 [10] | New Recordings of Hank's All-Time Hits | 195? | 120.00 |
| ❑ T 729 [M] | New Recordings of Hank's All-Time Hits | 1956 | 80.00 |
| *—Turquoise or gray label* | | | |
| ❑ T 729 [M] | New Recordings of Hank's All-Time Hits | 1959 | 30.00 |
| *—Black colorband label, logo at left* | | | |
| ❑ T 729 [M] | New Recordings of Hank's All-Time Hits | 1962 | 20.00 |
| *—Black colorband label, logo at top* | | | |
| ❑ T 826 [M] | Hank! | 1957 | 80.00 |
| *—Turquoise or gray label* | | | |
| ❑ T 826 [M] | Hank! | 1959 | 30.00 |
| *—Black colorband label, logo at left* | | | |
| ❑ T 826 [M] | Hank! | 1962 | 20.00 |
| *—Black colorband label, logo at top* | | | |
| ❑ T 911 [M] | Hank Thompson Favorites | 1957 | 80.00 |
| *—Turquoise or gray label* | | | |
| ❑ T 975 [M] | Hank Thompson's Dance Ranch | 1958 | 80.00 |
| *—Turquoise or gray label* | | | |
| ❑ T 975 [M] | Hank Thompson's Dance Ranch | 1959 | 30.00 |
| *—Black colorband label, logo at left* | | | |
| ❑ T 975 [M] | Hank Thompson's Dance Ranch | 1962 | 20.00 |
| *—Black colorband label, logo at top* | | | |
| ❑ T 1111 [M] | Favorite Waltzes | 1959 | 80.00 |
| *—Black colorband label, logo at left* | | | |
| ❑ T 1111 [M] | Favorite Waltzes | 1962 | 20.00 |
| *—Black colorband label, logo at top* | | | |
| ❑ ST 1246 [S] | Songs for Rounders | 1959 | 40.00 |
| ❑ T 1246 [M] | Songs for Rounders | 1959 | 30.00 |
| ❑ ST 1360 [S] | Most of All | 1960 | 40.00 |
| *—Black colorband label, logo at left* | | | |
| ❑ ST 1360 [S] | Most of All | 1962 | 25.00 |
| *—Black colorband label, logo at top* | | | |
| ❑ T 1360 [M] | Most of All | 1960 | 30.00 |
| *—Black colorband label, logo at left* | | | |
| ❑ T 1360 [M] | Most of All | 1962 | 20.00 |
| *—Black colorband label, logo at top* | | | |
| ❑ ST 1469 [S] | This Broken Heart of Mine | 1960 | 40.00 |
| *—Black colorband label, logo at left* | | | |
| ❑ ST 1469 [S] | This Broken Heart of Mine | 1962 | 25.00 |
| *—Black colorband label, logo at top* | | | |
| ❑ T 1469 [M] | This Broken Heart of Mine | 1960 | 30.00 |
| *—Black colorband label, logo at left* | | | |
| ❑ T 1469 [M] | This Broken Heart of Mine | 1962 | 20.00 |
| *—Black colorband label, logo at top* | | | |
| ❑ ST 1544 [S] | An Old Love Affair | 1961 | 30.00 |
| *—Black colorband label, logo at left* | | | |
| ❑ ST 1544 [S] | An Old Love Affair | 1962 | 20.00 |
| *—Black colorband label, logo at top* | | | |
| ❑ T 1544 [M] | An Old Love Affair | 1961 | 25.00 |
| *—Black colorband label, logo at left* | | | |
| ❑ T 1544 [M] | An Old Love Affair | 1962 | 15.00 |
| *—Black colorband label, logo at top* | | | |
| ❑ ST 1632 [S] | Hank Thompson at the Golden Nugget | 1961 | 30.00 |
| *—Black colorband label, logo at left* | | | |
| ❑ ST 1632 [S] | Hank Thompson at the Golden Nugget | 1962 | 20.00 |
| *—Black colorband label, logo at top* | | | |
| ❑ T 1632 [M] | Hank Thompson at the Golden Nugget | 1961 | 25.00 |
| *—Black colorband label, logo at left* | | | |
| ❑ T 1632 [M] | Hank Thompson at the Golden Nugget | 1962 | 15.00 |
| *—Black colorband label, logo at top* | | | |
| ❑ DT 1741 [R] | The #1 Country and Western Band | 1962 | 12.00 |
| *—Black colorband label, logo at top* | | | |
| ❑ DT 1741 [R] | The #1 Country and Western Band | 1962 | 20.00 |
| *—Black colorband label, logo at left* | | | |
| ❑ T 1741 [M] | The #1 Country and Western Band | 1962 | 20.00 |
| *—Black colorband label, logo at top* | | | |
| ❑ T 1741 [M] | The #1 Country and Western Band | 1962 | 30.00 |
| *—Black colorband label, logo at left* | | | |
| ❑ ST 1775 [S] | Cheyenne Frontier Days | 1962 | 25.00 |
| ❑ T 1775 [M] | Cheyenne Frontier Days | 1962 | 20.00 |
| ❑ ST 1878 [S] | The Best of Hank Thompson | 1963 | 25.00 |
| ❑ T 1878 [M] | The Best of Hank Thompson | 1963 | 20.00 |
| ❑ ST 1955 [S] | Hank Thompson at the State Fair of Texas | 1963 | 25.00 |
| ❑ T 1955 [M] | Hank Thompson at the State Fair of Texas | 1963 | 20.00 |
| ❑ ST 2089 [S] | Golden Country Hits | 1964 | 25.00 |
| ❑ T 2089 [M] | Golden Country Hits | 1964 | 20.00 |
| ❑ ST 2154 [S] | It's Christmas Time | 1963 | 25.00 |
| ❑ T 2154 [M] | It's Christmas Time | 1963 | 20.00 |
| ❑ ST 2274 [S] | Breakin' In Another Heart | 1965 | 25.00 |
| ❑ T 2274 [M] | Breakin' In Another Heart | 1965 | 20.00 |
| ❑ ST 2342 [S] | Luckiest Heartache in Town | 1965 | 25.00 |
| ❑ T 2342 [M] | Luckiest Heartache in Town | 1965 | 20.00 |
| ❑ ST 2460 [S] | A Six Pack to Go | 1966 | 25.00 |
| ❑ T 2460 [M] | A Six Pack to Go | 1966 | 20.00 |
| ❑ ST 2575 [S] | Breakin' the Rules | 1966 | 25.00 |
| ❑ T 2575 [M] | Breakin' the Rules | 1966 | 20.00 |
| ❑ ST 2661 [S] | The Best of Hank Thompson Vol. 2 | 1967 | 20.00 |
| ❑ T 2661 [M] | The Best of Hank Thompson Vol. 2 | 1967 | 25.00 |
| ❑ ST 2826 [S] | Just an Old Flame | 1967 | 20.00 |
| ❑ T 2826 [M] | Just an Old Flame | 1967 | 25.00 |
| DOT | | | |
| ❑ DOS 2-2000 [(2)] | Hank Thompson's 25th Anniversary Album | 1971 | 20.00 |
| ❑ DLP-25864 | Hank Thompson Sings the Gold Standards | 1968 | 15.00 |
| ❑ DLP-25894 | On Tap, In the Can, or In the Bottle | 1968 | 15.00 |
| ❑ DLP-25932 | Smoky the Bar | 1969 | 15.00 |
| ❑ DLP-25971 | Hank Thompson Salutes Oklahoma | 1969 | 15.00 |
| ❑ DLP-25991 | Next Time I Fall in Love (I Won't) | 1971 | 15.00 |
| ❑ DOS-25996 | Cab Driver (A Salute to the Mills Brothers) | 1972 | 15.00 |
| ❑ DOS-26004 | Hank Thompson's Greatest Hits Vol. 1 | 1972 | 15.00 |
| ❑ DOS-26015 | Kindly Keep It Country | 1973 | 15.00 |
| HILLTOP | | | |
| ❑ JS-6085 [S] | You Always Hurt the One You Love | 196? | 12.00 |
| *—Five tracks are rechanneled, five are true stereo* | | | |
| MCA | | | |
| ❑ 689 | Brand New Hank | 198? | 8.00 |
| ❑ 3250 | Take Me Back to Tulsa | 1980 | 10.00 |
| WARNER BROS. | | | |
| ❑ W 1664 [M] | Where Is the Circus and Other Heart Breakin' Hits | 1966 | 15.00 |
| ❑ WS 1664 [S] | Where Is the Circus and Other Heart Breakin' Hits | 1966 | 20.00 |
| ❑ W 1679 [M] | The Countrypolitan Sound of Hank Thompson | 1967 | 15.00 |
| ❑ WS 1679 [S] | The Countrypolitan Sound of Hank Thompson | 1967 | 20.00 |
| ❑ W 1686 [M] | The Gold Standard Collection of Hank Thompson | 1967 | 15.00 |
| ❑ WS 1686 [S] | The Gold Standard Collection of Hank Thompson | 1967 | 20.00 |
| **THOMPSON, HAYDEN** | | | |
| KAPP | | | |
| ❑ KL-1507 [M] | Here's Hayden Thompson | 1966 | 30.00 |
| ❑ KS-3507 [S] | Here's Hayden Thompson | 1966 | 40.00 |
| **THOMPSON, KAY** | | | |
| MGM | | | |
| ❑ E-3146 [M] | Kay Thompson Sings | 1955 | 30.00 |
| SIGNATURE | | | |
| ❑ SM-1017 [M] | Let's Talk About Russia | 1959 | 25.00 |
| **THOMPSON, LES** | | | |
| RCA VICTOR | | | |
| ❑ LPT-3102 [10] | Gene Norman Presents "Just Jazz" | 1952 | 150.00 |
| **THOMPSON, LUCKY** | | | |
| ABC IMPULSE! | | | |
| ❑ ASH-9307-2 [(2)] | Dancing Sunbeam | 1975 | 30.00 |
| ABC-PARAMOUNT | | | |
| ❑ ABC-111 [M] | Lucky Thompson Featuring Oscar Pettiford, Volume 1 | 1956 | 120.00 |
| ❑ ABC-171 [M] | Lucky Thompson Featuring Oscar Pettiford, Volume 2 | 1957 | 120.00 |
| DAWN | | | |
| ❑ DLP-1113 [M] | Lucky Thompson | 1957 | 100.00 |
| GROOVE MERCHANT | | | |
| ❑ GM-4411 [(2)] | Illuminations | 197? | 30.00 |
| LONDON | | | |
| ❑ D-93098 [10] | Recorded in Paris '56 | 1956 | 100.00 |
| MOODSVILLE | | | |
| ❑ MVLP-39 [M] | Lucky Thompson Plays Jerome Kern and No More | 1963 | 60.00 |
| *—Green label* | | | |



**Except when noted otherwise, VG = 25% of NM, and VG+ = 50% of NM. (Example: VG = $2.00, VG+ = $4.00 and NM = $8.00.)**

| Number | Title (A Side/B Side) | Yr | NM |
|---|---|---|---|
| ❑ MVLP-39 [M] | Lucky Thompson Plays Jerome Kern and No More | 1965 | 25.00 |
| *—Blue label, trident logo at right* | | | |
| ❑ MVST-39 [S] | Lucky Thompson Plays Jerome Kern and No More | 1963 | 80.00 |
| *—Green label* | | | |
| ❑ MVST-39 [S] | Lucky Thompson Plays Jerome Kern and No More | 1965 | 40.00 |
| *—Blue label, trident logo at right* | | | |
| **PRESTIGE** | | | |
| ❑ PRLP-7365 [M] | Lucky Strikes | 1965 | 50.00 |
| *—Blue label, trident logo at right* | | | |
| ❑ PRST-7365 [S] | Lucky Strikes | 1965 | 60.00 |
| *—Blue label, trident logo at right* | | | |
| ❑ PRLP-7394 [M] | Happy Days Are Here Again | 1965 | 50.00 |
| *—Blue label, trident logo at right* | | | |
| ❑ PRST-7394 [S] | Happy Days Are Here Again | 1965 | 60.00 |
| *—Blue label, trident logo at right* | | | |
| **RIVOLI** | | | |
| ❑ 40 [M] | Lucky Is Back! | 1965 | 100.00 |
| ❑ S-40 [S] | Lucky Is Back! | 1965 | 120.00 |
| ❑ 44 [M] | Kinfolk's Corner | 1965 | 100.00 |
| ❑ S-44 [S] | Kinfolk's Corner | 1965 | 120.00 |
| **TOPS** | | | |
| ❑ L-928 [10] | Jazz at the Auditorium | 1954 | 150.00 |
| **TRANSITION** | | | |
| ❑ TRLP-21 [M] | Lucky Strikes | 1956 | 500.00 |
| *—With booklet (deduct 1/5 if missing)* | | | |
| **URANIA** | | | |
| ❑ UJLP-1206 [M] | Accent on Tenor Sax | 1955 | 120.00 |

### THOMPSON, MAYO

| Number | Title (A Side/B Side) | Yr | NM |
|---|---|---|---|
| **TEXAS REVOLUTION** | | | |
| ❑ 2270 | Corky's Debt to His Father | 1969 | 80.00 |

### THOMPSON, RICHARD

Also see FAIRPORT CONVENTION; RICHARD AND LINDA THOMPSON.

| Number | Title (A Side/B Side) | Yr | NM |
|---|---|---|---|
| **BONG LOAD** | | | |
| ❑ BL 44 [(2)] | Mock Tudor | 1999 | 15.00 |
| ❑ BL 52 [(2)] | Action Packed | 2001 | 15.00 |
| *—1,000 copies pressed on "Coke-bottle green" vinyl* | | | |
| **CAPITOL** | | | |
| ❑ C1-48845 | Amnesia | 1988 | 8.00 |
| ❑ C1-95713 | Rumor & Sigh | 1991 | 12.00 |
| **CARTHAGE** | | | |
| ❑ CGLP-4405 | Henry the Human Fly | 1983 | 8.00 |
| *—Reissue of Reprise LP* | | | |
| ❑ CGLP-4409 | Strict Tempo | 1983 | 8.00 |
| ❑ CGLP-4413 [(2)] | Richard Thompson (Guitar/Vocal) | 1983 | 10.00 |
| *—Reissue of Island 9421 with original UK title* | | | |
| **DIVERSE** | | | |
| ❑ DIV 009 | Front Parlour Ballads | 2005 | 25.00 |
| **HANNIBAL** | | | |
| ❑ HNLP-1313 | Heart of Kindness | 1983 | 10.00 |
| ❑ HNLP-1316 | Small Town Romance | 1984 | 10.00 |
| **POLYDOR** | | | |
| ❑ 825421-1 | Across a Crowded Room | 1985 | 8.00 |
| ❑ 829728-1 | Daring Adventures | 1986 | 8.00 |
| **REPRISE** | | | |
| ❑ MS 2112 | Henry the Human Fly | 1972 | 20.00 |

### THOMPSON, RICHARD AND LINDA

| Number | Title (A Side/B Side) | Yr | NM |
|---|---|---|---|
| **CARTHAGE** | | | |
| ❑ CGLP-4403 | Sunnyvista | 1983 | 10.00 |
| *—First U.S. issue of this LP* | | | |
| ❑ CGLP-4404 | Pour Down Like Silver | 1983 | 8.00 |
| *—Reissue of Island 9348* | | | |
| ❑ CGLP-4407 | I Want to See the Bright Lights Tonight | 1983 | 10.00 |
| *—Reissue of Island 9266 (UK)* | | | |
| ❑ CGLP-4408 | Hokey Pokey | 1983 | 8.00 |
| *—Reissue of Island 9305* | | | |
| ❑ CGLP-4412 | First Light | 1983 | 8.00 |
| *—Reissue of Chrysalis 1177* | | | |
| **CHRYSALIS** | | | |
| ❑ CHR 1177 | First Light | 1978 | 15.00 |
| ❑ CHR 1247 | Sunnyvista | 1979 | — |
| *—Unreleased in U.S.* | | | |
| **HANNIBAL** | | | |
| ❑ HNBL 1303 | Shoot Out the Lights | 1982 | 10.00 |
| **ISLAND** | | | |
| ❑ ILPS 9266 | I Want to See the Bright Lights Tonight | 1974 | — |
| *—Unreleased in U.S. on this number* | | | |
| ❑ ILPS 9305 | Hokey Pokey | 1974 | 15.00 |
| ❑ ILPS 9348 | Pour Down Like Silver | 1975 | 15.00 |
| ❑ ISLA 9421 [(2)] | Bright Lights and Live! More or Less | 1977 | 20.00 |
| *—First U.S. issue of "I Want to See the Bright Lights Tonight" plus an LP of unreleased material* | | | |

### THOMPSON, SIR CHARLES

| Number | Title (A Side/B Side) | Yr | NM |
|---|---|---|---|
| **AMERICAN RECORDING SOCIETY** | | | |
| ❑ G-447 [M] | Basically Swing | 1957 | 30.00 |
| **APOLLO** | | | |
| ❑ 103 [10] | Sir Charles Thompson and His All Stars | 1951 | 400.00 |
| **COLUMBIA** | | | |
| ❑ CL 1364 [M] | Sir Charles Thompson and the Swing Organ | 1959 | 25.00 |
| ❑ CL 1663 [M] | Rockin' Rhythm | 1961 | 25.00 |
| ❑ CS 8205 [S] | Sir Charles Thompson and the Swing Organ | 1959 | 30.00 |
| ❑ CS 8463 [S] | Rockin' Rhythm | 1961 | 30.00 |
| **VANGUARD** | | | |
| ❑ VRS-8003 [10] | Sir Charles Thompson Sextet | 1953 | 100.00 |
| ❑ VRS-8006 [10] | Sir Charles Thompson Quartet | 1954 | 100.00 |
| ❑ VRS-8009 [10] | Sir Charles Thompson and His Band | 1954 | 150.00 |
| ❑ VRS-8018 [10] | Sir Charles Thompson Trio | 1955 | 100.00 |

### THOMPSON, SONNY

| Number | Title (A Side/B Side) | Yr | NM |
|---|---|---|---|
| **KING** | | | |
| ❑ 568 [M] | Moody Blues | 1956 | 500.00 |
| ❑ 655 [M] | Mellow Blues | 1959 | 250.00 |

### THOMPSON, SUE

| Number | Title (A Side/B Side) | Yr | NM |
|---|---|---|---|
| **HICKORY** | | | |
| ❑ LPM-104 [M] | Meet Sue Thompson | 1962 | 50.00 |
| ❑ LPS-104 [S] | Meet Sue Thompson | 1962 | 80.00 |
| ❑ LPM-107 [M] | Two of a Kind | 1962 | 30.00 |
| ❑ LPS-107 [S] | Two of a Kind | 1962 | 40.00 |
| ❑ LPM-111 [M] | Sue Thompson's Golden Hits | 1963 | 30.00 |
| ❑ LPS-111 [S] | Sue Thompson's Golden Hits | 1963 | 40.00 |
| ❑ LPM-121 [M] | Paper Tiger | 1965 | 30.00 |
| ❑ LPS-121 [S] | Paper Tiger | 1965 | 40.00 |
| ❑ LPM-130 [M] | Sue Thompson with Strings Attached | 1966 | 30.00 |
| ❑ LPS-130 [S] | Sue Thompson with Strings Attached | 1966 | 40.00 |
| ❑ LPS-148 | This Is Sue Thompson Country | 1969 | 20.00 |
| ❑ H3F-4511 | Sweet Memories | 1974 | 15.00 |
| ❑ H3G-4515 | ...And Love Me | 1974 | 15.00 |
| **WING** | | | |
| ❑ MGW-12317 [M] | The Country Side of Sue Thompson | 1965 | 20.00 |
| ❑ SRW-16317 [R] | The Country Side of Sue Thompson | 1965 | 15.00 |

### THOMPSON TWINS

| Number | Title (A Side/B Side) | Yr | NM |
|---|---|---|---|
| **ARISTA** | | | |
| ❑ SP-137 [EP] | Extra Special Tuneful Twosome! | 1982 | 12.00 |
| *—Promo-only remixes; Side 1 is "Identical Twin Side" and Side 2 is "Fraternal Twin Side"* | | | |
| ❑ AL 6601 | In the Name of Love | 1982 | 12.00 |
| ❑ AL 6607 | Side Kicks | 1983 | 12.00 |
| ❑ AL8-8002 | Side Kicks | 1984 | 8.00 |
| *—Reissue of 9624* | | | |
| ❑ AL8-8200 | Into the Gap | 1984 | 10.00 |
| ❑ AL8-8244 | In the Name of Love | 1984 | 10.00 |
| *—Reissue of AL 6601* | | | |
| ❑ AL8-8276 | Here's to Future Days | 1985 | 10.00 |
| ❑ ALB6-8309 | In the Name of Love | 1985 | 8.00 |
| *—Reissue of AL8-8244* | | | |
| ❑ ALB6-8310 | Side Kicks | 1985 | 8.00 |
| *—Reissue of AL8-8002* | | | |
| ❑ AL-8449 | Close to the Bone | 1987 | 10.00 |
| ❑ AL 8542 | Best of the Thompson Twins: Greatest Mixes | 1988 | 12.00 |
| ❑ ADP 9586 [DJ] | Interview Sampler | 1987 | 20.00 |
| *—One side of interviews, the other of music; promo only* | | | |
| ❑ AL 9624 | Side Kicks | 1983 | 10.00 |
| *—Reissue of 6607* | | | |
| ❑ R 124567 | Into the Gap | 1984 | 12.00 |
| *—RCA Music Service edition* | | | |
| ❑ R 144367 | Here's to Future Days | 1985 | 12.00 |
| *—RCA Music Service edition* | | | |
| ❑ R 154307 | Close to the Bone | 1987 | 12.00 |
| *—BMG Direct Marketing edition* | | | |
| ❑ R 154479 | Best of the Thompson Twins: Greatest Mixes | 1988 | 12.00 |
| *—BMG Direct Marketing edition* | | | |
| **WARNER BROS.** | | | |
| ❑ 25921 | Big Trash | 1989 | 10.00 |

### THORINSHIELD

| Number | Title (A Side/B Side) | Yr | NM |
|---|---|---|---|
| **PHILIPS** | | | |
| ❑ PHS 600251 | Thorinshield | 1968 | 20.00 |

### THORNE, FRAN

| Number | Title (A Side/B Side) | Yr | NM |
|---|---|---|---|
| **TRANSITION** | | | |
| ❑ TRLP-27 [M] | Piano Reflections | 1956 | 200.00 |
| *—With booklet (deduct 1/4 if missing)* | | | |

### THORNHILL, CLAUDE

| Number | Title (A Side/B Side) | Yr | NM |
|---|---|---|---|
| **COLUMBIA** | | | |
| ❑ CL 709 [M] | Dancing After Midnight | 1955 | 40.00 |
| ❑ CL 6035 [10] | Piano Reflections | 1949 | 80.00 |
| ❑ CL 6050 [10] | Dance Parade | 1949 | 80.00 |
| ❑ CL 6164 [10] | Claude Thornhill Encores | 1951 | 80.00 |
| **DECCA** | | | |
| ❑ DL 8722 [M] | Claude on a Cloud | 1958 | 25.00 |
| ❑ DL 8878 [M] | Dance to the Sound of Claude Thornhill | 1958 | 25.00 |
| ❑ DL 78722 [S] | Claude on a Cloud | 1958 | 30.00 |
| ❑ DL 78878 [S] | Dance to the Sound of Claude Thornhill | 1958 | 30.00 |
| **HARMONY** | | | |
| ❑ HL 7088 [M] | The Thornhill Sound | 1957 | 25.00 |
| **KAPP** | | | |
| ❑ KL-1058 [M] | Two Sides of Claude Thornhill | 1958 | 30.00 |
| ❑ KS-3058 [S] | Two Sides of Claude Thornhill | 1958 | 25.00 |
| **RCA CAMDEN** | | | |
| ❑ CAL-307 [M] | Dinner for Two | 1958 | 25.00 |
| **TREND** | | | |
| ❑ TL-1001 [10] | Dream Stuff | 1953 | 120.00 |
| ❑ TL-1002 [10] | Claude Thornhill Plays the Great Jazz Arrangements of Gerry Mulligan and Ralph Aldrich | 1953 | 120.00 |

### THORNTON, BIG MAMA

| Number | Title (A Side/B Side) | Yr | NM |
|---|---|---|---|
| **ARHOOLIE** | | | |
| ❑ F-1028 [M] | Big Mama Thornton in Europe | 1966 | 30.00 |
| ❑ F-1032 [M] | Chicago Blues: The Queen at Monterey | 1967 | 30.00 |
| ❑ F-1039 [M] | Ball and Chain | 1968 | 30.00 |
| **BACK BEAT** | | | |
| ❑ BLP-68 | She's Back | 1970 | 25.00 |
| **MERCURY** | | | |
| ❑ SR-61225 | Stronger Than Dirt | 1969 | 25.00 |
| ❑ SR-61249 | The Way It Is | 1970 | 25.00 |
| **PENTAGRAM** | | | |
| ❑ PE-10005 | Saved | 1971 | 20.00 |
| **VANGUARD** | | | |
| ❑ VSD-79351 | Jail | 1974 | 15.00 |
| ❑ VSD-79354 | Sassy Mama | 1975 | 15.00 |

### THORNTON, CLIFFORD

| Number | Title (A Side/B Side) | Yr | NM |
|---|---|---|---|
| **THIRD WORLD** | | | |
| ❑ 9636 [S] | Freedom and Unity | 1969 | 25.00 |

### THORNTON, TERI

| Number | Title (A Side/B Side) | Yr | NM |
|---|---|---|---|
| **COLUMBIA** | | | |
| ❑ CL 2094 [M] | Open Highway | 1963 | 30.00 |
| ❑ CS 8894 [S] | Open Highway | 1963 | 40.00 |
| **DAUNTLESS** | | | |
| ❑ DM-4306 [M] | Somewhere in the Night | 1963 | 25.00 |
| ❑ DS-6306 [S] | Somewhere in the Night | 1963 | 30.00 |
| **RIVERSIDE** | | | |
| ❑ RLP-352 [M] | Devil May Care | 1961 | 40.00 |
| ❑ RM-3525 [M] | Lullabye of the Leaves | 1964 | 25.00 |
| ❑ RS-9352 [S] | Devil May Care | 1961 | 30.00 |
| ❑ RS-93525 [S] | Lullabye of the Leaves | 1964 | 30.00 |

### THORPE, BILLY

| Number | Title (A Side/B Side) | Yr | NM |
|---|---|---|---|
| **CAPRICORN** | | | |
| ❑ CPN 0221 | Children of the Sun | 1979 | 20.00 |
| **ELEKTRA** | | | |
| ❑ 6E-294 | 21st Century Man | 1980 | 10.00 |
| **PASHA** | | | |
| ❑ ARZ 37499 | Stimulation | 1981 | 10.00 |
| ❑ FZ 38179 | East of Eden's Gate | 1982 | 10.00 |
| ❑ BFZ 40682 | Children of the Sun... Revisited | 1987 | 10.00 |
| **POLYDOR** | | | |
| ❑ PD-1-6228 | Children of the Sun | 1979 | 12.00 |

### THREE CHUCKLES, THE

| Number | Title (A Side/B Side) | Yr | NM |
|---|---|---|---|
| **VIK** | | | |
| ❑ LX-1067 [M] | The Three Chuckles | 1956 | 250.00 |

### THREE D'S, THE (2)

| Number | Title (A Side/B Side) | Yr | NM |
|---|---|---|---|
| **CAPITOL** | | | |
| ❑ ST 2171 [S] | New Dimensions in Folk Songs | 1964 | 25.00 |
| ❑ T 2171 [M] | New Dimensions in Folk Songs | 1964 | 20.00 |
| ❑ ST 2314 [S] | I Won't Be Worried Long | 1965 | 25.00 |
| ❑ T 2314 [M] | I Won't Be Worried Long | 1965 | 20.00 |

### THREE DEGREES, THE

| Number | Title (A Side/B Side) | Yr | NM |
|---|---|---|---|
| **ARIOLA AMERICA** | | | |
| ❑ OL 1501 | Three D | 1980 | 10.00 |
| ❑ SW-50044 | New Dimensions | 1978 | 10.00 |
| **EPIC** | | | |
| ❑ PE 34385 | Standing Up for Love | 1977 | 12.00 |
| **ICHIBAN** | | | |
| ❑ ICH-1041 | Three Degrees...And Holding | 198? | 10.00 |
| **PHILADELPHIA INT'L.** | | | |
| ❑ KZ 32406 | The Three Degrees | 1974 | 12.00 |
| ❑ KZ 33162 | International | 1975 | 12.00 |
| ❑ PZ 33840 | The Three Degrees Live | 1975 | 12.00 |

Three Dog Night, *Seven Separate Fools,*
ABC-Dunhill DSD-50118, 1972, with oversize playing cards, $12.

| Number | Title (A Side/B Side) | Yr | NM |
|---|---|---|---|
| **ROULETTE** | | | |
| ❑ 3015 | So Much Love | 1975 | 10.00 |
| ❑ SR-42050 | Maybe | 1970 | 40.00 |

### THREE DOG NIGHT

| Number | Title (A Side/B Side) | Yr | NM |
|---|---|---|---|
| **ABC** | | | |
| ❑ 888 | Coming Down Your Way | 1975 | 10.00 |
| ❑ 928 | American Pastime | 1976 | 10.00 |
| **ABC COMMAND** | | | |
| ❑ CQD-40014 [Q] | Hard Labor | 1974 | 20.00 |
| ❑ CQD-40018 [Q] | Coming Down Your Way | 1975 | 20.00 |
| **ABC DUNHILL** | | | |
| ❑ DS-50048 | Three Dog Night | 1968 | 15.00 |
| ❑ DS-50048 | Three Dog Night "One" | 1969 | 12.00 |
| *—Same album as above, but with revised title on cover* | | | |
| ❑ DS-50058 | Suitable for Framing | 1969 | 12.00 |
| ❑ DS-50068 | Three Dog Night Was Captured Live at the Forum | 1969 | 12.00 |
| ❑ DS-50078 | It Ain't Easy | 1970 | 12.00 |
| *—Regular front cover with gatefold* | | | |
| ❑ DS-50078 | It Ain't Easy | 1970 | 100.00 |
| *—Original cover with band members in the nude* | | | |
| ❑ DSX-50088 | Naturally | 1970 | 12.00 |
| *—With detachable cardboard poster intact* | | | |
| ❑ DSX-50098 | Golden Bisquits | 1971 | 12.00 |
| *—With detachable cardboard poster intact; interestingly, the label spells the LP title "Golden Biscuits"* | | | |
| ❑ DSX-50108 | Harmony | 1971 | 12.00 |
| ❑ DSD-50118 | Seven Separate Fools | 1972 | 12.00 |
| *—With seven oversize playing cards included* | | | |
| ❑ DSY-50138 [(2)] | Around the World with Three Dog Night | 1973 | 15.00 |
| ❑ DSX-50158 | Cyan | 1973 | 12.00 |
| ❑ DSD-50168 | Hard Labor | 1974 | 10.00 |
| *—With huge Band-Aid as part of the LP artwork* | | | |
| ❑ DSD-50168 | Hard Labor | 1974 | 15.00 |
| *—With huge Band-Aid attached to jacket, covering the "childbirth"* | | | |
| ❑ DSD-50168 | Hard Labor | 1974 | 30.00 |
| *—With uncensored "childbirth" front cover* | | | |
| ❑ DSD-50178 | Joy to the World: Their Greatest Hits | 1974 | 12.00 |
| *—With gatefold cover* | | | |
| ❑ DSD-50178 | Joy to the World: Their Greatest Hits | 1975 | 10.00 |
| *—With standard cover* | | | |
| ❑ SKAO-92057 | Suitable for Framing | 1969 | 15.00 |
| *—Capitol Record Club edition* | | | |
| ❑ SKAO-93211 | It Ain't Easy | 1970 | 15.00 |
| *—Capitol Record Club edition* | | | |
| ❑ SMAS-93422 | Naturally | 1970 | 15.00 |
| *—Capitol Record Club edition* | | | |
| ❑ SVAS-94772 | Seven Separate Fools | 1972 | 15.00 |
| *—Capitol Record Club edition* | | | |
| **AT EASE** | | | |
| ❑ MD 11109 | Three Dog Night: Their Greatest Recordings | 1978 | 20.00 |
| *—"This Album Compiled Exclusively for Military Personnel" by ABC* | | | |
| **COLUMBIA SPECIAL PRODUCTS** | | | |
| ❑ P 14769 | Three Dog Night | 1978 | 15.00 |
| **MCA** | | | |
| ❑ 6018 [(2)] | The Best of Three Dog Night | 1982 | 12.00 |
| ❑ 37120 | Joy to the World: Their Greatest Hits | 1980 | 8.00 |
| **PASSPORT** | | | |
| ❑ PB 5001 [EP] | It's a Jungle | 1983 | 8.00 |
| **PICKWICK** | | | |
| ❑ SPC-3664 | Golden Greats of Three Dog Night | 1979 | 10.00 |
| **SESSIONS** | | | |
| ❑ ARI-1004 [(2)] | Sessions Presents Three Dog Night | 1977 | 12.00 |

### THREE FACES WEST

| Number | Title (A Side/B Side) | Yr | NM |
|---|---|---|---|
| **OUTPOST** | | | |
| ❑ 1000 | Three Faces West | 197? | 20.00 |

### THREE FLAMES, THE

| Number | Title (A Side/B Side) | Yr | NM |
|---|---|---|---|
| **MERCURY** | | | |
| ❑ MG-20239 [M] | At the Ben Soir | 1957 | 50.00 |

### THREE MAN ARMY, THE

| Number | Title (A Side/B Side) | Yr | NM |
|---|---|---|---|
| **KAMA SUTRA** | | | |
| ❑ KSBS-2044 | A Third of a Lifetime | 1971 | 30.00 |
| *—Pink label, gatefold cover* | | | |
| **REPRISE** | | | |
| ❑ MS 2150 | Three Man Army | 1973 | 20.00 |
| ❑ MS 2182 | Three Man Army Two | 1974 | 20.00 |

### THREE SOULS, THE

| Number | Title (A Side/B Side) | Yr | NM |
|---|---|---|---|
| **ARGO** | | | |
| ❑ LP-4005 [M] | Almost Like Being In Love | 1960 | — |
| *—Canceled* | | | |
| ❑ LPS-4005 [S] | Almost Like Being In Love | 1960 | — |
| *—Canceled* | | | |
| ❑ LP-4036 [M] | Dangerous Dan Express | 1964 | 20.00 |
| ❑ LPS-4036 [S] | Dangerous Dan Express | 1964 | 25.00 |
| ❑ LP-4044 [M] | Soul Sounds | 1965 | 20.00 |
| ❑ LPS-4044 [S] | Soul Sounds | 1965 | 25.00 |

### THREE SOUNDS, THE

| Number | Title (A Side/B Side) | Yr | NM |
|---|---|---|---|
| **BLUE NOTE** | | | |
| ❑ BLP-1600 [M] | Introducing the Three Sounds | 1958 | 80.00 |
| *—Regular version, W. 63rd St. address on label* | | | |
| ❑ BLP-1600 [M] | Introducing the Three Sounds | 1958 | 120.00 |
| *—"Deep groove" version (deep indentation under label on both sides)* | | | |
| ❑ BLP-1600 [M] | Introducing the Three Sounds | 1963 | 25.00 |
| *—With "New York, USA" address on label* | | | |
| ❑ BST-1600 [S] | Introducing the Three Sounds | 1959 | 60.00 |
| *—Regular version, W. 63rd St. address on label* | | | |
| ❑ BST-1600 [S] | Introducing the Three Sounds | 1959 | 80.00 |
| *—"Deep groove" version (deep indentation under label on both sides)* | | | |
| ❑ BST-1600 [S] | Introducing the Three Sounds | 1963 | 20.00 |
| *—With "New York, USA" address on label* | | | |
| ❑ BLP-4014 [M] | Bottoms Up | 1959 | 80.00 |
| *—Regular version, W. 63rd St. address on label* | | | |
| ❑ BLP-4014 [M] | Bottoms Up | 1959 | 120.00 |
| *—"Deep groove" version (deep indentation under label on both sides)* | | | |
| ❑ BLP-4014 [M] | Bottoms Up | 1963 | 25.00 |
| *—With "New York, USA" address on label* | | | |
| ❑ BST-4014 [S] | Bottoms Up | 1959 | 60.00 |
| *—Regular version, W. 63rd St. address on label* | | | |
| ❑ BST-4014 [S] | Bottoms Up | 1959 | 80.00 |
| *—"Deep groove" version (deep indentation under label on both sides)* | | | |
| ❑ BST-4014 [S] | Bottoms Up | 1963 | 20.00 |
| *—With "New York, USA" address on label* | | | |
| ❑ BLP-4020 [M] | Good Deal | 1959 | 80.00 |
| *—Regular version, W. 63rd St. address on label* | | | |
| ❑ BLP-4020 [M] | Good Deal | 1959 | 120.00 |
| *—"Deep groove" version (deep indentation under label on both sides)* | | | |
| ❑ BLP-4020 [M] | Good Deal | 1963 | 25.00 |
| *—With "New York, USA" address on label* | | | |
| ❑ BLP-4044 [M] | Moods | 1960 | 80.00 |
| *—Regular version, W. 63rd St. address on label* | | | |
| ❑ BLP-4044 [M] | Moods | 1960 | 120.00 |
| *—"Deep groove" version (deep indentation under label on both sides)* | | | |
| ❑ BLP-4044 [M] | Moods | 1963 | 25.00 |
| *—With "New York, USA" address on label* | | | |
| ❑ BLP-4072 [M] | Feelin' Good | 1961 | 80.00 |
| *—With W. 63rd St. address on label* | | | |
| ❑ BLP-4072 [M] | Feelin' Good | 1963 | 25.00 |
| *—With "New York, USA" address on label* | | | |
| ❑ BLP-4088 [M] | Here We Come | 1961 | 80.00 |
| *—With 61st St. address on label* | | | |
| ❑ BLP-4088 [M] | Here We Come | 1963 | 25.00 |
| *—With "New York, USA" address on label* | | | |
| ❑ BLP-4102 [M] | Hey! There | 1962 | 30.00 |
| ❑ BLP-4120 [M] | It Just Got To Be | 1963 | 30.00 |
| ❑ BLP-4155 [M] | Black Orchid | 1963 | 30.00 |
| ❑ BLP-4197 [M] | Out of This World | 1965 | 30.00 |
| ❑ BLP-4248 [M] | Vibrations | 1966 | 30.00 |
| ❑ BLP-4265 [M] | Live at the Lighthouse | 1967 | 30.00 |
| ❑ BST-84020 [S] | Good Deal | 1959 | 50.00 |
| *—With W. 63rd St. address on label* | | | |
| ❑ BST-84020 [S] | Good Deal | 1963 | 20.00 |
| *—With "New York, USA" address on label* | | | |
| ❑ BST-84044 [S] | Moods | 1960 | 50.00 |
| *—With W. 63rd St. address on label* | | | |
| ❑ BST-84044 [S] | Moods | 1963 | 20.00 |
| *—With "New York, USA" address on label* | | | |
| ❑ BST-84072 [S] | Feelin' Good | 1961 | 50.00 |
| *—With W. 63rd St. address on label* | | | |
| ❑ BST-84072 [S] | Feelin' Good | 1963 | 20.00 |
| *—With "New York, USA" address on label* | | | |
| ❑ BST-84088 [S] | Here We Come | 1961 | 50.00 |
| *—With 61st St. address on label* | | | |
| ❑ BST-84088 [S] | Here We Come | 1963 | 20.00 |
| *—With "New York, USA" address on label* | | | |
| ❑ BST-84102 [S] | Hey! There | 1962 | 30.00 |
| *—With "New York, USA" address on label* | | | |
| ❑ BST-84120 [S] | It Just Got To Be | 1963 | 30.00 |
| *—With "New York, USA" address on label* | | | |
| ❑ BST-84155 [S] | Black Orchid | 1963 | 30.00 |
| *—With "New York, USA" address on label* | | | |
| ❑ BST-84197 [S] | Out of This World | 1965 | 30.00 |
| *—With "New York, USA" address on label* | | | |
| ❑ BST-84248 [S] | Vibrations | 1966 | 30.00 |
| *—With "New York, USA" address on label* | | | |
| ❑ BST-84265 [S] | Live at the Lighthouse | 1967 | 20.00 |
| *—With "A Division of Liberty Records" on label* | | | |
| ❑ BST-84285 [S] | Coldwater Flat | 1968 | 20.00 |
| *—With "A Division of Liberty Records" on label* | | | |
| ❑ BST-84301 [S] | Elegant Soul | 1968 | 20.00 |
| *—With "A Division of Liberty Records" on label* | | | |
| ❑ BST-84341 [S] | Soul Symphony | 1969 | 20.00 |
| *—With "A Division of Liberty Records" on label* | | | |

Number | Title (A Side/B Side) | Yr | NM

**LIMELIGHT**
❑ LM-82014 [M] Three Moods 1965 20.00
❑ LM-82026 [M] Beautiful Friendship 1965 20.00
❑ LS-86014 [S] Three Moods 1965 25.00
❑ LS-86026 [S] Beautiful Friendship 1965 25.00

**MERCURY**
❑ MG-20776 [M] Jazz On Broadway 1963 25.00
❑ MG-20839 [M] Some Like It Modern 1963 25.00
❑ MG-20921 [M] Live at the Living Room 1963 25.00
❑ SR-60776 [S] Jazz On Broadway 1963 30.00
❑ SR-60839 [S] Some Like It Modern 1963 30.00
❑ SR-60921 [S] Live at the Living Room 1963 30.00

**VERVE**
❑ V-8513 [M] Blue Genes 1963 25.00
❑ V6-8513 [S] Blue Genes 1963 30.00

## THREE STOOGES, THE

**CORAL**
❑ CRL 57289 [M] Nonsense Song Book 1959 80.00
❑ CRL 757289 [S] Nonsense Song Book 1959 100.00

**GOLDEN**
❑ GLP-43 [M] Madcap Musical Nonsense 1962 80.00

**PETER PAN**
❑ 8098 The Three Stooges 1970 25.00

**VOCALION**
❑ VL 3823 [M] The Three Stooges Sing for Kids 196? 20.00
❑ VL 73823 [S] The Three Stooges Sing for Kids 196? 25.00

## THREE SUNS, THE

**GOLDEN TONE**
❑ 14094 In Orbit 195? 12.00

**PICKWICK**
❑ SPC-3037 Twilight Time 197? 10.00

**RCA CAMDEN**
❑ CAL-633 [M] The Sound of Christmas 1964 12.00
❑ CAS-633(e) [R] The Sound of Christmas 1964 12.00

**RCA VICTOR**
❑ LPM-3 [10] Three-Quarter Time 1951 50.00
❑ LPM-28 [10] Hands Across the Table 1951 50.00
❑ LPM-52 [10] Christmas Favorites 1951 50.00
❑ LPM-1041 [M] Soft and Sweet 1955 30.00
❑ LPM-1132 [M] Sounds of Christmas 1955 30.00
❑ LPM-1171 [M] Twilight Time 1956 30.00
❑ LPM-1173 [M] My Reverie 1956 30.00
❑ LPM-1219 [M] Slumber Time 1956 30.00
❑ LPM-1220 [M] Malaguena 1956 30.00
❑ LPM-1249 [M] High Fi and Wide 1956 30.00
❑ LPM-1316 [M] Easy Listening 1956 30.00
❑ LPM-1333 [M] Midnight for Two 1957 30.00
❑ LPM-1543 [M] The Things in Love in Hi-Fi 1958 20.00
❑ LSP-1543 [S] The Things in Love in Hi-Fi 1958 30.00
❑ LPM-1578 [M] Let's Dance with the Three Suns 1958 20.00
❑ LSP-1578 [S] Let's Dance with the Three Suns 1958 30.00
❑ LPM-1669 [M] Love in the Afternoon 1959 20.00
❑ LSP-1669 [S] Love in the Afternoon 1959 30.00
❑ LPM-1734 [M] Having a Ball with the Three Suns 1959 20.00
❑ LSP-1734 [S] Having a Ball with the Three Suns 1959 30.00
❑ ANL1-1779(e) Pure Gold 1974 10.00
❑ LPM-1964 [M] Swingin' on a Star 1959 20.00
❑ LSP-1964 [S] Swingin' on a Star 1959 30.00
❑ LPM-2054 [M] A Ding Dong Dandy Christmas! 1959 20.00
❑ LSP-2054 [S] A Ding Dong Dandy Christmas! 1959 30.00
❑ LPM-2120 [M] Twilight Memories 1960 20.00
❑ LSP-2120 [S] Twilight Memories 1960 25.00
❑ LPM-2235 [M] On a Magic Carpet 1960 20.00
❑ LSP-2235 [S] On a Magic Carpet 1960 25.00
❑ LPM-2307 [M] Dancing on a Cloud 1961 20.00
❑ LSP-2307 [S] Dancing on a Cloud 1961 25.00
❑ LPM-2310 [M] Fever and Smoke 1961 20.00
❑ LSP-2310 [S] Fever and Smoke 1961 25.00
❑ LPM-2437 [M] Fun in the Sun 1961 20.00
❑ LSP-2437 [S] Fun in the Sun 1961 25.00
❑ LPM-2532 [M] Movin' 'N' Groovin' 1962 20.00
❑ LSP-2532 [S] Movin' 'N' Groovin' 1962 25.00
❑ LPM-2617 [M] Warm and Tender 1962 20.00
❑ LSP-2617 [S] Warm and Tender 1962 25.00
❑ LPM-2715 [M] Everything Under the Sun 1963 15.00
❑ LSP-2715 [S] Everything Under the Sun 1963 20.00
❑ LPM-2904 [M] One Enchanted Evening 1964 15.00
❑ LSP-2904 [S] One Enchanted Evening 1964 20.00
❑ LPM-2963 [M] A Swingin' Thing 1964 15.00
❑ LSP-2963 [S] A Swingin' Thing 1964 20.00
❑ LPM-3012 [10] Twilight Moods 1952 50.00
❑ LPM-3034 [10] The Three Suns Present 1952 50.00
❑ LPM-3040 [10] Busy Fingers 1952 50.00
❑ LPM-3056 [10] Christmas Party 1952 50.00
❑ LPM-3075 [10] Slumbertime 1953 50.00
❑ LPM-3113 [10] Pops Concert Favorites 1953 50.00
❑ LPM-3125 [10] Mods 1953 50.00

Number | Title (A Side/B Side) | Yr | NM

❑ LPM-3130 [10] Top Pops 1953 50.00
❑ LPM-3146 [10] Polka Time 1954 50.00
❑ LPM-3174 [10] Sacred Hymns 1954 50.00
❑ LPM-3354 [M] Country Music Shindig 1965 15.00
❑ LSP-3354 [S] Country Music Shindig 1965 20.00
❑ LPM-3447 [M] The Best of the Three Suns 1965 15.00
❑ LSP-3447 [S] The Best of the Three Suns 1965 20.00
❑ VPS-6075 [(2)] This Is the Three Suns 1972 15.00

**ROYALE**
❑ 1 [10] Twilight Time 1951 50.00
❑ 29 [10] Midnight Time 1951 50.00

**SEARS**
❑ SPS-437 Twilight Time 1969 12.00

**VARSITY**
❑ VLP-6001 [10] Twilight Time 1950 50.00
❑ VLP-6048 [10] Midnight Time 1950 50.00

## THRILLINGTON, PERCY "THRILLS"
See PAUL McCARTNEY.

## THUDPUCKER, JIMMY
Fictional singing star from Garry Trudeau's "Doonesbury" comic strip.

**WINDSONG**
❑ BXL1-2589 Greatest Hits 1977 20.00

## THUNDER, JOHNNY

**DIAMOND**
❑ D-5001 [M] Loop De Loop 1963 100.00
❑ DS-5001 [S] Loop De Loop 1963 150.00

**REAL**
❑ RR-1 So Alone 196? 15.00

## THUNDER AND ROSES

**UNITED ARTISTS**
❑ UAS-6709 King of the Black Sunrise 1969 30.00

## THUNDERBIRDS, THE

**RED FEATHER**
❑ TH-1 [M] Meet the Fabulous Thunderbirds 1964 200.00

## THUNDERCLAP NEWMAN

**MCA**
❑ 354 Hollywood Dream 1974 10.00
*—Reissue of Track 354*

**TRACK**
❑ 354 Hollywood Dream 1973 12.00
*—Reissue of Track 8264*
❑ SD 8264 Hollywood Dream 1970 25.00

## THUNDERPUSSY

**M.R.T.**
❑ 31748 Documents of Captivity 1973 150.00

## THUNDERTREE

**ROULETTE**
❑ SR-42038 Thundertree 1970 30.00

## TIDE, THE

**MOUTH**
❑ 7237 Almost Live 1971 50.00

## TIDES, THE

**MERCURY**
❑ MG-20714 [M] Limbo Rock 1962 15.00
❑ SR-60714 [S] Limbo Rock 1962 20.00

**WING**
❑ MGW-12248 [M] The Best of Bossa Nova 1963 15.00
❑ MGW-12265 [M] Surf City and Other Surfin' Favorites 1963 25.00
❑ SRW-16248 [S] The Best of Bossa Nova 1963 20.00
❑ SRW-16265 [S] Surf City and Other Surfin' Favorites 1963 30.00

## TIEKEN, FREDDIE, AND THE ROCKERS

**I.T.**
❑ 2301 [M] By Popular Demand 1957 50.00
❑ 2304 [M] Freddie Tieken and the Rockers 1958 50.00

## TIFFANY SHADE, THE

**MAINSTREAM**
❑ S-6105 The Tiffany Shade 1968 100.00

## TIKIS, THE
Probably two different groups.

**MINARET**
❑ TLP-7001 [M] The Tikis 196? 100.00

**PHILIPS**
❑ PHM 200043 [M] The Tikis 1962 25.00
❑ PHS 600043 [S] The Tikis 1962 30.00

## TIL, SONNY
Also see THE ORIOLES.

**DOBRE**
❑ 1026 Back to the Chapel 1978 12.00

Number | Title (A Side/B Side) | Yr | NM

**RCA VICTOR**
❑ LSP-4451 Sonny Til Returns 1970 20.00
❑ LSP-4538 Old Gold/New Gold 1971 15.00

## TILLIS, MEL

**COLUMBIA**
❑ CL 1724 [M] Heart Over Mind and Other Big Country Hits 1962 30.00
❑ CS 8524 [S] Heart Over Mind and Other Big Country Hits 1962 40.00
❑ C 30253 Heart Over Mind 1970 12.00

**ELEKTRA**
❑ 6E-236 Me and Pepper 1979 10.00
❑ 6E-271 Your Body Is an Outlaw 1980 10.00
❑ 6E-310 Southern Rain 1980 10.00
❑ 60016 It's a Long Way to Daytona 1982 10.00
❑ 60192 Mel Tillis' Greatest Hits 1982 10.00

**HARMONY**
❑ HL 7370 [M] The Great Mel Tillis Sings Walk On, Boy and Other Great Country Hits 196? 15.00
❑ HS 11170 [S] The Great Mel Tillis Sings Walk On, Boy and Other Great Country Hits 196? 12.00
❑ KH 31952 Mel 1972 12.00

**HILLTOP**
❑ JS-6153 Detroit City 197? 10.00

**KAPP**
❑ KL-1493 [M] Stateside 1966 15.00
❑ KL-1514 [M] Life Turned Her That Way 1967 15.00
❑ KL-1535 [M] Mr. Mel 1967 20.00
❑ KS-3493 [S] Stateside 1966 20.00
❑ KS-3514 [S] Life Turned Her That Way 1967 20.00
❑ KS-3535 [S] Mr. Mel 1967 15.00
❑ KS-3543 Let Me Talk to You 1968 15.00
❑ KS-3570 Something Special 1968 15.00
❑ KS-3589 Mel Tillis' Greatest Hits 1969 15.00
❑ KS-3594 Who's Julie 1969 15.00
❑ KS-3609 Mel Tillis Sings Old Faithful 1969 15.00
❑ KS-3630 She'll Be Hanging 'Round Somewhere 1970 15.00
❑ KS-3639 Mel Tillis In Person 1970 15.00

**MCA**
❑ 66 Mel Tillis' Greatest Hits 1973 12.00
*—Reissue of Kapp 3589*
❑ 550 Mel Tillis In Person 197? 10.00
*—Reissue of Kapp 3639*
❑ 649 Love Revival 198? 8.00
*—Reissue of 2204*
❑ 650 Heart Healer 198? 8.00
*—Reissue of 2252*
❑ 651 Love's Troubled Waters 198? 8.00
*—Reissue of 2288*
❑ 652 I Believe in You 198? 8.00
*—Reissue of 2364*
❑ 653 Are You Sincere 198? 8.00
*—Reissue of 3077*
❑ 789 M-M-Mel Live 198? 8.00
*—Reissue of 3208*
❑ 2204 Love Revival 1976 12.00
❑ 2252 Heart Healer 1977 12.00
❑ 2288 Love's Troubled Waters 1977 12.00
❑ 2364 I Believe in You 1978 12.00
❑ 3077 Are You Sincere 1979 12.00
❑ 3167 Mr. Entertainer 1979 12.00
❑ 3208 M-M-Mel Live 1980 12.00
❑ 3274 The Very Best of Mel Tillis 1980 10.00
❑ 4091 [(2)] The Best of Mel Tillis 1975 15.00
❑ 5378 After All This Time 1983 8.00
❑ 5472 New Patches 1984 8.00
❑ 37121 Mr. Entertainer 198? 8.00
*—Reissue of 3167*

**MERCURY**
❑ 835310-1 Brand New Mister Me 1988 8.00

**MGM**
❑ SE-4681 One More Time 1970 15.00
❑ SE-4757 The Arms of a Fool/Commercial Affection 1971 15.00
❑ SE-4788 Recorded Live at the Sam Houston Coliseum, Houston, Texas 1971 15.00
❑ SE-4806 The Very Best of Mel Tillis and the Statesiders 1972 15.00
❑ SE-4841 Would You Want Your World to End 1972 15.00
❑ SE-4870 I Ain't Never/Neon Rose 1972 15.00
❑ SE-4889 Mel Tillis and the Statesiders On Stage at the Birmingham Municipal Auditorium 1973 15.00
❑ SE-4907 Sawmill 1973 15.00
❑ M3F-4960 Stomp Them Grapes 1974 12.00
❑ M3G-4970 Mel Tillis' Greatest Hits 1974 12.00
❑ M3G-4981 Mel Tillis Time 1975 —
*—Canceled*
❑ M3G-4987 Mel Tillis and the Statesiders 1975 12.00
❑ MG-1-5002 M-M-Mel 1975 12.00

| Number | Title (A Side/B Side) | Yr | NM |
|---|---|---|---|
| ❑ MG-1-5021 | The Best of Mel Tillis and the Statesiders | 1976 | 12.00 |
| ❑ MG-1-5022 | Welcome to Mel Tillis Country | 1976 | 12.00 |
| ❑ MG-2-5402 [(2)] | 24 Great Hits | 1977 | 15.00 |
| ❑ MG-2-5404 [(2)] | Live at the Sam Houston Coliseum & Birmingham Municipal Auditorium | 1978 | 15.00 |
| *—Combines 4788 and 4889 in one package* | | | |
| **POWER PAK** | | | |
| ❑ PO-295 | Mel Tillis & Friends | 197? | 10.00 |
| **RCA VICTOR** | | | |
| ❑ AHL1-5483 | California Road | 1985 | 8.00 |
| **STARDAY** | | | |
| ❑ SLP-471 | Stateside | 1972 | 12.00 |
| **TIME-LIFE** | | | |
| ❑ STW- 111 | Country Music | 1981 | 10.00 |
| **VOCALION** | | | |
| ❑ VL 73914 | Big 'n' Country | 1970 | 12.00 |
| **TILLIS, PAM** | | | |
| **WARNER BROS.** | | | |
| ❑ 23871 | Above and Beyond the Doll of Cutey | 1983 | 25.00 |
| **TILLMAN, FLOYD** | | | |
| **CIMARRON** | | | |
| ❑ C-2003 [M] | Let's Make Memories | 1962 | 50.00 |
| **HARMONY** | | | |
| ❑ HL 7316 [M] | Floyd Tillman's Best | 1964 | 25.00 |
| ❑ HS 11297 | I'll Still Be Lovin' You | 1969 | 25.00 |
| **HILLTOP** | | | |
| ❑ JM-6017 [M] | Floyd Tillman Sings His Greatest Hits of Lovin' | 196? | 15.00 |
| **MUSICOR** | | | |
| ❑ MM-2136 [M] | Floyd Tillman's Country | 1967 | 20.00 |
| ❑ MS-3136 [S] | Floyd Tillman's Country | 1967 | 25.00 |
| ❑ MS-3157 | Dream On | 1968 | 20.00 |
| **RCA VICTOR** | | | |
| ❑ LPM-1686 [M] | Floyd Tillman's Greatest | 1958 | 60.00 |
| **STARDAY** | | | |
| ❑ SLP-310 [M] | Let's Make Memories | 1965 | 30.00 |
| **TILLOTSON, JOHNNY** | | | |
| **ACCORD** | | | |
| ❑ SN-7194 | Scrapbook | 1982 | 10.00 |
| **AMOS** | | | |
| ❑ AAS 7006 | Tears on My Pillow | 1969 | 20.00 |
| **BARNABY** | | | |
| ❑ BR-4007 | Johnny Tillotson's Greatest | 1977 | 12.00 |
| **BUDDAH** | | | |
| ❑ BDS-5112 | Johnny Tillotson | 1972 | 15.00 |
| **CADENCE** | | | |
| ❑ CLP-3052 [M] | Johnny Tillotson's Best | 1961 | 40.00 |
| *—Maroon and silver label* | | | |
| ❑ CLP-3052 [M] | Johnny Tillotson's Best | 1962 | 25.00 |
| *—Red and black label* | | | |
| ❑ CLP-3058 [M] | It Keeps Right On a-Hurtin' | 1962 | 30.00 |
| ❑ CLP-3067 [M] | You Can Never Stop Me Loving You | 1963 | 30.00 |
| ❑ CLP-25052 [P] | Johnny Tillotson's Best | 1961 | 50.00 |
| *—Maroon and silver label* | | | |
| ❑ CLP-25052 [P] | Johnny Tillotson's Best | 1962 | 30.00 |
| *—Red and black label* | | | |
| ❑ CLP-25058 [S] | It Keeps Right On a-Hurtin' | 1962 | 40.00 |
| ❑ CLP-25067 [P] | You Can Never Stop Me Loving You | 1963 | 40.00 |
| **EVEREST** | | | |
| ❑ 4113 | Johnny Tillotson's Greatest Hits | 1982 | 10.00 |
| **METRO** | | | |
| ❑ M-561 [M] | Johnny Tillotson Sings Tillotson | 1967 | 15.00 |
| ❑ MS-561 [S] | Johnny Tillotson Sings Tillotson | 1967 | 20.00 |
| **MGM** | | | |
| ❑ E-4188 [M] | Talk Back Trembling Lips | 1964 | 20.00 |
| ❑ SE-4188 [S] | Talk Back Trembling Lips | 1964 | 25.00 |
| ❑ E-4224 [M] | The Tillotson Touch | 1964 | 20.00 |
| ❑ SE-4224 [S] | The Tillotson Touch | 1964 | 25.00 |
| ❑ E-4270 [M] | She Understands Me | 1965 | 20.00 |
| ❑ SE-4270 [S] | She Understands Me | 1965 | 25.00 |
| ❑ E-4302 [M] | That's My Style | 1965 | 20.00 |
| ❑ SE-4302 [S] | That's My Style | 1965 | 25.00 |
| ❑ E-4328 [M] | Our World | 1965 | 20.00 |
| ❑ SE-4328 [S] | Our World | 1965 | 25.00 |
| ❑ E-4395 [M] | No Love at All | 1966 | 20.00 |
| ❑ SE-4395 [S] | No Love at All | 1966 | 25.00 |
| ❑ E-4402 [M] | The Christmas Touch | 1966 | 20.00 |
| ❑ SE-4402 [S] | The Christmas Touch | 1966 | 25.00 |
| ❑ E-4452 [M] | Here I Am | 1967 | 20.00 |
| ❑ SE-4452 [S] | Here I Am | 1967 | 25.00 |
| ❑ E-4532 [M] | The Best of Johnny Tillotson | 1968 | 30.00 |
| *—May be promo only (yellow label)* | | | |
| ❑ SE-4532 [S] | The Best of Johnny Tillotson | 1968 | 20.00 |
| ❑ SE-4814 | The Very Best of Johnny Tillotson | 1971 | 12.00 |
| ❑ ST 90410 [S] | The Tillotson Touch | 1965 | 30.00 |
| *—Capitol Record Club edition* | | | |
| ❑ T 90410 [M] | The Tillotson Touch | 1965 | 30.00 |
| *—Capitol Record Club edition* | | | |
| **UNITED ARTISTS** | | | |
| ❑ UA-LA759-G | Johnny Tillotson | 1977 | 10.00 |
| **TIMBER CREEK** | | | |
| **RENEGADE** | | | |
| ❑ 95014 | Hellbound Highway | 1975 | 150.00 |
| **TIMBERLAKE, JUSTIN** | | | |
| **JIVE** | | | |
| ❑ 01241-41823-1 [(2)] | Justified | 2002 | 20.00 |
| ❑ 82876-88062-1 [(2)] | Futuresex/Lovesounds | 2006 | 20.00 |
| **TIMMENS, JIM, AND HIS JAZZ ALL-STARS** | | | |
| **WARNER BROS.** | | | |
| ❑ W 1278 [M] | Gilbert and Sullivan Revisited | 1958 | 20.00 |
| ❑ WS 1278 [S] | Gilbert and Sullivan Revisited | 1958 | 25.00 |
| **TIMMONS, BOBBY** | | | |
| **MILESTONE** | | | |
| ❑ MSP-9011 | Got to Get It | 1969 | 20.00 |
| ❑ MSP-9020 | Do You Know the Way | 1969 | 20.00 |
| **PRESTIGE** | | | |
| ❑ PRLP-7335 [M] | Little Barefoot Soul | 1964 | 25.00 |
| ❑ PRST-7335 [S] | Little Barefoot Soul | 1964 | 30.00 |
| ❑ PRLP-7351 [M] | Chun-King | 1965 | 25.00 |
| ❑ PRST-7351 [S] | Chun-King | 1965 | 30.00 |
| ❑ PRLP-7387 [M] | Workin' Out | 1966 | 25.00 |
| ❑ PRST-7387 [S] | Workin' Out | 1966 | 30.00 |
| ❑ PRLP-7414 [M] | Holiday Soul | 1966 | 30.00 |
| ❑ PRST-7414 [S] | Holiday Soul | 1966 | 40.00 |
| ❑ PRLP-7429 [M] | Chicken and Dumplin's | 1966 | 25.00 |
| ❑ PRST-7429 [S] | Chicken and Dumplin's | 1966 | 30.00 |
| ❑ PRLP-7465 [M] | Soul Man | 1967 | 60.00 |
| ❑ PRST-7465 [S] | Soul Man | 1967 | 50.00 |
| ❑ PRLP-7483 [M] | Soul Food | 1967 | 60.00 |
| ❑ PRST-7483 [S] | Soul Food | 1967 | 50.00 |
| **RIVERSIDE** | | | |
| ❑ RLP 12-317 [M] | This Here Is Bobby Timmons | 1960 | 150.00 |
| ❑ RLP-334 [M] | Soul Time | 1960 | 80.00 |
| ❑ RLP-363 [M] | Easy Does It | 1961 | 80.00 |
| ❑ RLP-391 [M] | The Bobby Timmons Trio In Person — Recorded "Live" at the Village Vanguard | 1961 | 120.00 |
| ❑ RLP-422 [M] | Sweet and Soulful Sounds | 1962 | 50.00 |
| ❑ RLP-468 [M] | Born to Be Blue! | 1963 | 50.00 |
| ❑ RLP-1164 [S] | This Here Is Bobby Timmons | 1960 | 120.00 |
| ❑ RS-9334 [S] | Soul Time | 1960 | 60.00 |
| ❑ RS-9363 [S] | Easy Does It | 1961 | 60.00 |
| ❑ RS-9391 [S] | The Bobby Timmons Trio In Person — Recorded "Live" at the Village Vanguard | 1961 | 80.00 |
| ❑ RS-9422 [S] | Sweet and Soulful Sounds | 1962 | 40.00 |
| ❑ RS-9468 [S] | Born to Be Blue! | 1963 | 40.00 |
| **TIMMOTHY** | | | |
| **PEAR** | | | |
| ❑ (# unknown) | Strange But True | 1972 | 200.00 |
| **TIN HOUSE** | | | |
| **EPIC** | | | |
| ❑ E 30511 | Tin House | 1971 | 20.00 |
| **TINGLING MOTHER'S CIRCUS** | | | |
| **MUSICOR** | | | |
| ❑ MS-3167 | Circus of the Mind | 1968 | 25.00 |
| **TINO AND THE REVLONS** | | | |
| **DEARBORN** | | | |
| ❑ 1004 | By Request at the Sway-Zee | 1966 | 200.00 |
| **TIPTON, CARL** | | | |
| **SIMS** | | | |
| ❑ LP-143 [M] | The Carl Tipton Show | 196? | 40.00 |
| **TITANS, THE** | | | |
| **MGM** | | | |
| ❑ E-3992 [M] | Today's Teen Beat | 1961 | 30.00 |
| ❑ SE-3992 [S] | Today's Teen Beat | 1961 | 40.00 |
| **TITUS GROAN** | | | |
| **JANUS** | | | |
| ❑ JLS-3024 | Titus Groan | 1971 | 30.00 |
| **TITUS OATES** | | | |
| **LIPS** | | | |
| ❑ (no #) | Jungle Lady | 1974 | 200.00 |
| **TJADER, CAL** | | | |
| **CRYSTAL CLEAR** | | | |
| ❑ 8003 | Huracan | 1978 | 25.00 |
| *—Direct-to-disc recording* | | | |
| **FANTASY** | | | |
| ❑ 3-9 [10] | The Cal Tjader Trio | 1953 | 100.00 |
| *—Black vinyl* | | | |
| ❑ 3-9 [10] | The Cal Tjader Trio | 1953 | 150.00 |
| *—Any of various non-black vinyl pressings* | | | |
| ❑ 3-17 [10] | Ritmo Caliente | 1954 | 100.00 |
| *—Black vinyl* | | | |
| ❑ 3-17 [10] | Ritmo Caliente | 1954 | 150.00 |
| *—Any of various non-black vinyl pressings* | | | |
| ❑ 3-18 [10] | Tjader Plays Mambo | 1954 | 150.00 |
| *—Red vinyl* | | | |
| ❑ 3202 [M] | Mambo with Tjader | 1955 | 100.00 |
| *—Red vinyl* | | | |
| ❑ 3202 [M] | Mambo with Tjader | 1956 | 50.00 |
| *—Black vinyl, red label, non-flexible vinyl* | | | |
| ❑ 3202 [M] | Mambo with Tjader | 196? | 25.00 |
| *—Black vinyl, red label, flexible vinyl* | | | |
| ❑ 3211 [M] | Tjader Plays Tjazz | 1956 | 50.00 |
| *—Black vinyl, red label, non-flexible vinyl* | | | |
| ❑ 3211 [M] | Tjader Plays Tjazz | 1956 | 100.00 |
| *—Red vinyl* | | | |
| ❑ 3216 [M] | Ritmo Caliente | 1956 | 50.00 |
| *—Black vinyl, red label, non-flexible vinyl* | | | |
| ❑ 3216 [M] | Ritmo Caliente | 1956 | 100.00 |
| *—Red vinyl* | | | |
| ❑ 3216 [M] | Ritmo Caliente | 196? | 25.00 |
| *—Black vinyl, red label, flexible vinyl* | | | |
| ❑ 3221 [M] | Tjader Plays Mambo | 1956 | 50.00 |
| *—Black vinyl, red label, non-flexible vinyl* | | | |
| ❑ 3221 [M] | Tjader Plays Mambo | 1956 | 100.00 |
| *—Red vinyl* | | | |
| ❑ 3221 [M] | Tjader Plays Mambo | 196? | 25.00 |
| *—Black vinyl, red label, flexible vinyl* | | | |
| ❑ 3227 [M] | Cal Tjader Quartet | 1956 | 100.00 |
| *—Red vinyl* | | | |
| ❑ 3232 [M] | The Cal Tjader Quintet | 1956 | 50.00 |
| *—Black vinyl, red label, non-flexible vinyl* | | | |
| ❑ 3232 [M] | The Cal Tjader Quintet | 1956 | 100.00 |
| *—Red vinyl* | | | |
| ❑ 3232 [M] | The Cal Tjader Quintet | 196? | 25.00 |
| *—Black vinyl, red label, flexible vinyl* | | | |
| ❑ 3241 [M] | Jazz at the Blackhawk | 1957 | 30.00 |
| *—Black vinyl, red label, non-flexible vinyl* | | | |
| ❑ 3241 [M] | Jazz at the Blackhawk | 1957 | 50.00 |
| *—Red vinyl* | | | |
| ❑ 3250 [M] | Latin Kick | 1957 | 30.00 |
| *—Black vinyl, red label, non-flexible vinyl* | | | |
| ❑ 3250 [M] | Latin Kick | 1957 | 50.00 |
| *—Red vinyl* | | | |
| ❑ 3253 [M] | Cal Tjader | 1958 | 40.00 |
| *—Black vinyl, non-flexible vinyl* | | | |
| ❑ 3253 [M] | Cal Tjader | 1958 | 60.00 |
| *—Red vinyl* | | | |
| ❑ 3262 [M] | Mas Ritmo Caliente | 1958 | 30.00 |
| *—Black vinyl, red label, non-flexible vinyl* | | | |
| ❑ 3262 [M] | Mas Ritmo Caliente | 1958 | 50.00 |
| *—Red vinyl* | | | |
| ❑ 3271 [M] | San Francisco Moods | 1958 | 30.00 |
| *—Black vinyl, red label, non-flexible vinyl* | | | |
| ❑ 3271 [M] | San Francisco Moods | 1958 | 50.00 |
| *—Red vinyl* | | | |
| ❑ 3275 [M] | Cal Tjader's Latin Concert | 1958 | 30.00 |
| *—Black vinyl, red label, non-flexible vinyl* | | | |
| ❑ 3275 [M] | Cal Tjader's Latin Concert | 1958 | 50.00 |
| *—Red vinyl* | | | |
| ❑ 3278 [M] | Tjader Plays Tjazz | 1958 | 30.00 |
| *—Black vinyl, red label, non-flexible vinyl* | | | |
| ❑ 3278 [M] | Tjader Plays Tjazz | 1958 | 50.00 |
| *—Red vinyl; reissue of 3211* | | | |
| ❑ 3279 [M] | Latin for Lovers | 1958 | 30.00 |
| *—Black vinyl, red label, non-flexible vinyl* | | | |
| ❑ 3279 [M] | Latin for Lovers | 1958 | 50.00 |
| *—Red vinyl* | | | |
| ❑ 3283 [M] | A Night at the Blackhawk | 1959 | 30.00 |
| *—Black vinyl, red label, non-flexible vinyl* | | | |
| ❑ 3283 [M] | A Night at the Blackhawk | 1959 | 50.00 |
| *—Red vinyl* | | | |
| ❑ 3289 [M] | Tjader Goes Latin | 1959 | 30.00 |
| *—Black vinyl, red label, non-flexible vinyl* | | | |
| ❑ 3289 [M] | Tjader Goes Latin | 1959 | 50.00 |
| *—Red vinyl* | | | |
| ❑ 3295 [M] | Concert by the Sea | 1959 | 30.00 |
| *—Black vinyl, red label, non-flexible vinyl* | | | |
| ❑ 3295 [M] | Concert by the Sea | 1959 | 50.00 |
| *—Red vinyl* | | | |
| ❑ 3299 [M] | Concert on the Campus | 1960 | 25.00 |
| *—Black vinyl, red label, non-flexible vinyl* | | | |
| ❑ 3299 [M] | Concert on the Campus | 1960 | 40.00 |
| *—Red vinyl* | | | |
| ❑ 3307 [M] | Cal Tjader Quartet | 1960 | 25.00 |
| *—Black vinyl, red label, non-flexible vinyl* | | | |
| ❑ 3307 [M] | Cal Tjader Quartet | 1960 | 40.00 |
| *—Red vinyl* | | | |
| ❑ 3309 [M] | Demasiado Caliente | 1960 | 25.00 |
| *—Black vinyl, red label, non-flexible vinyl* | | | |
| ❑ 3309 [M] | Demasiado Caliente | 1960 | 40.00 |
| *—Red vinyl* | | | |
| ❑ 3310 [M] | West Side Story | 1960 | 25.00 |
| *—Black vinyl, red label, non-flexible vinyl* | | | |

| Number | Title (A Side/B Side) | Yr | NM |
|---|---|---|---|
| ❑ 3310 [M] | West Side Story | 1960 | 40.00 |
| *—Red vinyl* | | | |
| ❑ 3313 [M] | Cal Tjader Quintet | 1961 | 25.00 |
| *—Black vinyl, red label, non-flexible vinyl* | | | |
| ❑ 3313 [M] | Cal Tjader Quintet | 1961 | 40.00 |
| *—Red vinyl; evidently a different album than 3232* | | | |
| ❑ 3315 [M] | Cal Tjader Live and Direct | 1961 | 25.00 |
| *—Black vinyl, red label, non-flexible vinyl* | | | |
| ❑ 3315 [M] | Cal Tjader Live and Direct | 1961 | 40.00 |
| *—Red vinyl* | | | |
| ❑ 3326 [M] | Mambo | 1961 | 25.00 |
| *—Black vinyl, red label, non-flexible vinyl* | | | |
| ❑ 3326 [M] | Mambo | 1961 | 40.00 |
| *—Red vinyl* | | | |
| ❑ 3330 [M] | Cal Tjader Plays the Harold Arlen Songbook | 1961 | 25.00 |
| *—Black vinyl, red label, non-flexible vinyl* | | | |
| ❑ 3330 [M] | Cal Tjader Plays the Harold Arlen Songbook | 1961 | 40.00 |
| *—Red vinyl* | | | |
| ❑ 3339 [M] | Latino | 1962 | 25.00 |
| *—Black vinyl, red label, non-flexible vinyl* | | | |
| ❑ 3339 [M] | Latino | 1962 | 40.00 |
| *—Red vinyl* | | | |
| ❑ 3341 [M] | Concert by the Sea, Volume 2 | 1962 | 25.00 |
| *—Black vinyl, red label, non-flexible vinyl* | | | |
| ❑ 3341 [M] | Concert by the Sea, Volume 2 | 1962 | 40.00 |
| *—Red vinyl* | | | |
| ❑ 8003 [S] | Mas Ritmo Caliente | 196? | 20.00 |
| *—Black vinyl, blue label, non-flexible vinyl* | | | |
| ❑ 8003 [S] | Mas Ritmo Caliente | 196? | 30.00 |
| *—Blue vinyl* | | | |
| ❑ 8014 [S] | Cal Tjader's Latin Concert | 196? | 20.00 |
| *—Black vinyl, blue label, non-flexible vinyl* | | | |
| ❑ 8014 [S] | Cal Tjader's Latin Concert | 196? | 30.00 |
| *—Blue vinyl* | | | |
| ❑ 8016 [S] | Latin for Lovers | 196? | 20.00 |
| *—Black vinyl, blue label, non-flexible vinyl* | | | |
| ❑ 8016 [S] | Latin for Lovers | 196? | 30.00 |
| *—Blue vinyl* | | | |
| ❑ 8017 [S] | San Francisco Moods | 196? | 20.00 |
| *—Black vinyl, blue label, non-flexible vinyl* | | | |
| ❑ 8017 [S] | San Francisco Moods | 196? | 30.00 |
| *—Blue vinyl* | | | |
| ❑ 8019 [S] | Latin for Dancers | 196? | 100.00 |
| *—Blue vinyl; the existence of this has been confirmed. Black vinyl copies of 8019 are unknown.* | | | |
| ❑ 8019 [S] | Latin for Dancers | 196? | 120.00 |
| *—A red vinyl copy with this number is known to exist also, probably pressed in error* | | | |
| ❑ 8026 [S] | A Night at the Blackhawk | 196? | 20.00 |
| *—Black vinyl, blue label, non-flexible vinyl* | | | |
| ❑ 8026 [S] | A Night at the Blackhawk | 196? | 30.00 |
| *—Blue vinyl* | | | |
| ❑ 8030 [S] | Tjader Goes Latin | 196? | 20.00 |
| *—Black vinyl, blue label, non-flexible vinyl* | | | |
| ❑ 8030 [S] | Tjader Goes Latin | 196? | 30.00 |
| *—Blue vinyl* | | | |
| ❑ 8033 [S] | Latin Kick | 196? | 20.00 |
| *—Black vinyl, blue label, non-flexible vinyl* | | | |
| ❑ 8033 [S] | Latin Kick | 196? | 30.00 |
| *—Blue vinyl* | | | |
| ❑ 8038 [S] | Concert by the Sea | 196? | 20.00 |
| *—Black vinyl, blue label, non-flexible vinyl* | | | |
| ❑ 8038 [S] | Concert by the Sea | 196? | 30.00 |
| *—Blue vinyl* | | | |
| ❑ 8044 [S] | Concert on the Campus | 196? | 20.00 |
| *—Black vinyl, blue label, non-flexible vinyl* | | | |
| ❑ 8044 [S] | Concert on the Campus | 196? | 30.00 |
| *—Blue vinyl* | | | |
| ❑ 8053 [S] | Demasiado Caliente | 196? | 20.00 |
| *—Black vinyl, blue label, non-flexible vinyl* | | | |
| ❑ 8053 [S] | Demasiado Caliente | 196? | 30.00 |
| *—Blue vinyl* | | | |
| ❑ 8054 [S] | West Side Story | 196? | 20.00 |
| *—Black vinyl, blue label, non-flexible vinyl* | | | |
| ❑ 8054 [S] | West Side Story | 196? | 30.00 |
| *—Blue vinyl* | | | |
| ❑ 8057 [S] | Mambo | 1962 | 20.00 |
| *—Black vinyl, blue label, non-flexible vinyl* | | | |
| ❑ 8057 [S] | Mambo | 1962 | 30.00 |
| *—Blue vinyl* | | | |
| ❑ 8059 [S] | Cal Tjader Live and Direct | 1962 | 20.00 |
| *—Black vinyl, blue label, non-flexible vinyl* | | | |
| ❑ 8059 [S] | Cal Tjader Live and Direct | 1962 | 30.00 |
| *—Blue vinyl* | | | |
| ❑ 8072 [S] | Cal Tjader Plays the Harold Arlen Songbook | 1962 | 20.00 |
| *—Black vinyl, blue label, non-flexible vinyl* | | | |
| ❑ 8072 [S] | Cal Tjader Plays the Harold Arlen Songbook | 1962 | 30.00 |
| *—Blue vinyl* | | | |
| ❑ 8077 [R] | Ritmo Caliente | 1962 | 20.00 |
| *—Black vinyl, blue label, non-flexible vinyl* | | | |
| ❑ 8077 [R] | Ritmo Caliente | 1962 | 30.00 |
| *—Blue vinyl* | | | |
| ❑ 8079 [S] | Latino | 1962 | 20.00 |
| *—Black vinyl, blue label, non-flexible vinyl* | | | |
| ❑ 8079 [S] | Latino | 1962 | 30.00 |
| *—Blue vinyl* | | | |
| ❑ 8083 [R] | Cal Tjader Quartet | 1962 | 20.00 |
| *—Black vinyl, blue label, non-flexible vinyl* | | | |
| ❑ 8083 [R] | Cal Tjader Quartet | 1962 | 30.00 |
| *—Blue vinyl* | | | |
| ❑ 8084 [S] | Cal Tjader Quintet | 1962 | 20.00 |
| *—Black vinyl, blue label, non-flexible vinyl* | | | |
| ❑ 8084 [S] | Cal Tjader Quintet | 1962 | 30.00 |
| *—Blue vinyl; stereo version of 3313* | | | |
| ❑ 8085 [R] | The Cal Tjader Quintet | 196? | 20.00 |
| *—Black vinyl, blue label, non-flexible vinyl* | | | |
| ❑ 8085 [R] | The Cal Tjader Quintet | 196? | 30.00 |
| *—Blue vinyl; stereo version of 3232* | | | |
| ❑ 8096 [R] | Jazz at the Blackhawk | 1962 | 20.00 |
| *—Black vinyl, blue label, non-flexible vinyl* | | | |
| ❑ 8096 [R] | Jazz at the Blackhawk | 1962 | 30.00 |
| *—Blue vinyl* | | | |
| ❑ 8097 [R] | Tjader Plays Tjazz | 1962 | 20.00 |
| *—Black vinyl, blue label, non-flexible vinyl* | | | |
| ❑ 8097 [R] | Tjader Plays Tjazz | 1962 | 30.00 |
| *—Blue vinyl* | | | |
| ❑ 8098 [S] | Concert by the Sea, Volume 2 | 1962 | 20.00 |
| *—Black vinyl, blue label, non-flexible vinyl* | | | |
| ❑ 8098 [S] | Concert by the Sea, Volume 2 | 1962 | 30.00 |
| *—Blue vinyl* | | | |
| **SAVOY** | | | |
| ❑ MG-9036 [10] | Cal Tjader — Vibist | 1954 | 100.00 |
| **SKYE** | | | |
| ❑ SK-1 | Solar Heat | 1968 | 20.00 |
| ❑ SK-10 | Cal Tjader Plugs In | 1969 | 20.00 |
| **VERVE** | | | |
| ❑ V-8419 [M] | In a Latin Bag | 1961 | 20.00 |
| ❑ V6-8419 [S] | In a Latin Bag | 1961 | 25.00 |
| ❑ V-8459 [M] | Saturday Night…Sunday Night at the Blackhawk | 1962 | 20.00 |
| ❑ V6-8459 [S] | Saturday Night…Sunday Night at the Blackhawk | 1962 | 25.00 |
| ❑ V-8470 [M] | The Contemporary Music of Mexico and Brazil | 1962 | 20.00 |
| ❑ V6-8470 [S] | The Contemporary Music of Mexico and Brazil | 1962 | 25.00 |
| ❑ V-8507 [M] | Several Shades of Jade | 1963 | 20.00 |
| ❑ V6-8507 [S] | Several Shades of Jade | 1963 | 25.00 |
| ❑ V-8531 [M] | Sona Libre | 1963 | 20.00 |
| ❑ V6-8531 [S] | Sona Libre | 1963 | 25.00 |
| ❑ V-8575 [M] | Breeze from the East | 1964 | 20.00 |
| ❑ V6-8575 [S] | Breeze from the East | 1964 | 25.00 |
| ❑ V-8585 [M] | Warm Wave | 1964 | 20.00 |
| ❑ V6-8585 [S] | Warm Wave | 1964 | 25.00 |
| ❑ V-8614 [M] | Soul Sauce | 1965 | 20.00 |
| ❑ V6-8614 [S] | Soul Sauce | 1965 | 25.00 |
| ❑ V-8626 [M] | Soul Bird: Whippenpoof | 1965 | 20.00 |
| ❑ V6-8626 [S] | Soul Bird: Whippenpoof | 1965 | 25.00 |
| ❑ V-8637 [M] | Soul Burst | 1965 | 20.00 |
| ❑ V6-8637 [S] | Soul Burst | 1965 | 25.00 |
| ❑ V6-8651 [S] | El Soni Do Nuevo — The New Soul Sound | 1966 | 20.00 |
| ❑ V6-8671 [S] | Along Comes Cal | 1966 | 20.00 |
| ❑ V6-8725 [S] | The Best of Cal Tjader | 1967 | 20.00 |
| ❑ V-8730 [M] | Hip Vibrations | 1967 | 20.00 |

## TJADER, CAL/DON ELLIOTT

| Number | Title (A Side/B Side) | Yr | NM |
|---|---|---|---|
| **SAVOY** | | | |
| ❑ MG-12054 [M] | Vib-Rations | 1956 | 40.00 |
| *—Reissue of 9036 and 9033* | | | |

## TJADER, CAL, AND STAN GETZ

Also see each artist's individual listings.

| Number | Title (A Side/B Side) | Yr | NM |
|---|---|---|---|
| **FANTASY** | | | |
| ❑ 3266 [M] | Cal Tjader-Stan Getz Sextet | 1958 | 30.00 |
| *—Black vinyl, red label, non-flexible vinyl* | | | |
| ❑ 3266 [M] | Cal Tjader-Stan Getz Sextet | 1958 | 50.00 |
| *—Red vinyl* | | | |
| ❑ 8005 [S] | Cal Tjader-Stan Getz Sextet | 196? | 20.00 |
| *—Black vinyl, blue label, non-flexible vinyl* | | | |
| ❑ 8005 [S] | Cal Tjader-Stan Getz Sextet | 196? | 30.00 |
| *—Blue vinyl* | | | |

## TOAD HALL

| Number | Title (A Side/B Side) | Yr | NM |
|---|---|---|---|
| **LIBERTY** | | | |
| ❑ LST-7580 | Toad Hall | 1968 | 25.00 |

## TOAD THE WET SPROCKET

| Number | Title (A Side/B Side) | Yr | NM |
|---|---|---|---|
| **COLUMBIA** | | | |
| ❑ FC 45326 | Bread and Circus | 1989 | 12.00 |
| ❑ C 46060 | Pale | 1990 | 30.00 |
| *—Marbled white (almost greenish) vinyl* | | | |
| ❑ C 47309 | Fear | 1991 | 20.00 |

## TOADS, THE

| Number | Title (A Side/B Side) | Yr | NM |
|---|---|---|---|
| **WIGGINS** | | | |
| ❑ 64021 [M] | The Toads | 1964 | 300.00 |

## TODD, ART AND DOTTY

| Number | Title (A Side/B Side) | Yr | NM |
|---|---|---|---|
| **DART** | | | |
| ❑ D-444 [M] | Black Velvet Eyes | 1959 | 40.00 |
| **DOT** | | | |
| ❑ DLP-3742 [M] | Chanson d'Amour (Song of Love) | 1966 | 25.00 |
| ❑ DLP-25742 [S] | Chanson d'Amour (Song of Love) | 1966 | 30.00 |

## TOE FAT

| Number | Title (A Side/B Side) | Yr | NM |
|---|---|---|---|
| **RARE EARTH** | | | |
| ❑ RS-511 | Toe Fat | 1970 | 25.00 |
| ❑ RS-525 | Toe Fat Two | 1971 | 25.00 |

## TOGAWA, PAUL

| Number | Title (A Side/B Side) | Yr | NM |
|---|---|---|---|
| **MODE** | | | |
| ❑ LP-104 [M] | Paul Togawa Quartet | 1957 | 80.00 |

## TOKENS, THE

| Number | Title (A Side/B Side) | Yr | NM |
|---|---|---|---|
| **B.T. PUPPY** | | | |
| ❑ BTP-1000 [M] | I Hear Trumpets Blow | 1966 | 20.00 |
| ❑ BTPS-1000 [P] | I Hear Trumpets Blow | 1966 | 25.00 |
| ❑ BTPS-1006 | Tokens of Gold | 1969 | 25.00 |
| ❑ BTPS-1012 | Greatest Moments | 1970 | 25.00 |
| ❑ BTPS-1014 | December 5th | 1971 | 200.00 |
| ❑ BTPS-1027 | Intercourse | 1971 | 600.00 |
| **BUDDAH** | | | |
| ❑ BDS-5059 | Both Sides Now | 1971 | 15.00 |
| **DIPLOMAT** | | | |
| ❑ D-2308 [M] | Kings of the Hot Rods | 196? | 25.00 |
| ❑ DS-2308 [S] | Kings of the Hot Rods | 196? | 30.00 |
| **RCA** | | | |
| ❑ 8534-1-R | Re-Doo-Wopp | 1988 | 10.00 |
| **RCA VICTOR** | | | |
| ❑ LPM-2514 [M] | The Lion Sleeps Tonight | 1961 | 80.00 |
| ❑ LSP-2514 [S] | The Lion Sleeps Tonight | 1961 | 150.00 |
| ❑ LPM-2631 [M] | We, The Tokens, Sing Folk | 1962 | 40.00 |
| ❑ LSP-2631 [S] | We, The Tokens, Sing Folk | 1962 | 50.00 |
| ❑ LPM-2886 [M] | Wheels | 1964 | 80.00 |
| ❑ LSP-2886 [S] | Wheels | 1964 | 100.00 |
| ❑ LPM-3685 [M] | The Tokens Again | 1966 | 40.00 |
| ❑ LSP-3685 [S] | The Tokens Again | 1966 | 50.00 |
| **WARNER BROS.** | | | |
| ❑ W 1685 [M] | It's a Happening World | 1967 | 25.00 |
| ❑ WS 1685 [S] | It's a Happening World | 1967 | 20.00 |

## TOKENS, THE AND THE HAPPENINGS

Also see each artist's individual listings.

| Number | Title (A Side/B Side) | Yr | NM |
|---|---|---|---|
| **B.T. PUPPY** | | | |
| ❑ BTP-1002 [M] | Back to Back | 1967 | 20.00 |
| *—Half this LP is by the Tokens, the other half by the Happenings* | | | |
| ❑ BTPS-1002 [S] | Back to Back | 1967 | 25.00 |

## TOLBERT, ISRAEL

| Number | Title (A Side/B Side) | Yr | NM |
|---|---|---|---|
| **WARREN/STAX** | | | |
| ❑ STS-2038 | Popper Stopper | 1971 | 30.00 |
| *—Cover says "Warren Records Distributed by Stax," label is Stax* | | | |

## TOLKIEN, J.R.R.

| Number | Title (A Side/B Side) | Yr | NM |
|---|---|---|---|
| **CAEDMON** | | | |
| ❑ TC 1478 | J.R.R. Tolkien Reads and Sings His "The Lord of the Rings" | 1975 | 20.00 |

## TOLLIVER, CHARLES

| Number | Title (A Side/B Side) | Yr | NM |
|---|---|---|---|
| **STRATA-EAST** | | | |
| ❑ SES-1971 | Music Inc. | 1971 | 20.00 |
| ❑ SES-1972 | Live at Slugs' | 1972 | 20.00 |
| ❑ SES-19720 | Live at Slugs', Vol. 2 | 1972 | 20.00 |
| ❑ SES-19740/1 [(2)] | Live at the Loosdrecht Jazz Festival | 1974 | 25.00 |
| ❑ SES-19745 | Live in Tokyo | 1974 | 20.00 |

## TOM AND JERRY (2)

Tommy Tomlinson and JERRY KENNEDY, a country instrumental duo.

| Number | Title (A Side/B Side) | Yr | NM |
|---|---|---|---|
| **MERCURY** | | | |
| ❑ MG-20626 [M] | Guitar's Greatest Hits | 1961 | 30.00 |
| ❑ MG-20671 [M] | Guitars Play the Sound of Ray Charles | 1962 | 30.00 |
| ❑ MG-20756 [M] | Guitar's Greatest Hits, Vol. 2 | 1962 | 30.00 |
| ❑ MG-20842 [M] | Surfin' Hootenanny | 1963 | 40.00 |
| ❑ SR-60626 [S] | Guitar's Greatest Hits | 1961 | 40.00 |
| ❑ SR-60671 [S] | Guitars Play the Sound of Ray Charles | 1962 | 40.00 |
| ❑ SR-60756 [S] | Guitar's Greatest Hits, Vol. 2 | 1962 | 40.00 |
| ❑ SR-60842 [S] | Surfin' Hootenanny | 1963 | 50.00 |

## TOM TOM CLUB

| Number | Title (A Side/B Side) | Yr | NM |
|---|---|---|---|
| **SIRE** | | | |
| ❑ SRK 3628 | Tom Tom Club | 1981 | 10.00 |
| ❑ 23916 | Close to the Bone | 1983 | 10.00 |
| ❑ 25888 | Boom Boom Chi Boom Boom | 1989 | 10.00 |
| **WARNER BROS.** | | | |
| ❑ WBMS-120 [DJ] | Wordy Rapping with the Tom Tom Club | 1986 | 20.00 |
| *—Part of "The Warner Bros. Music Show"; promo only* | | | |

## TOMMY AND THE TWISTERS

| Number | Title (A Side/B Side) | Yr | NM |
|---|---|---|---|
| **REGENT** | | | |
| ❑ MG-6104 [M] | Let's All Do the Twist | 1961 | 40.00 |

## TOMORROW

| Number | Title (A Side/B Side) | Yr | NM |
|---|---|---|---|
| **SIRE** | | | |
| ❑ SES-97912 | Tomorrow | 1968 | 60.00 |

## TOMPALL AND THE GLASER BROTHERS

| Number | Title (A Side/B Side) | Yr | NM |
|---|---|---|---|
| **DECCA** | | | |
| ❑ DL 4041 [M] | This Land Folk Songs | 1960 | 30.00 |
| ❑ DL 74041 [S] | This Land Folk Songs | 1960 | 40.00 |

| Number | Title (A Side/B Side) | Yr | NM |
|---|---|---|---|
| **ELEKTRA** | | | |
| ❑ 5E-542 | Lovin' Her Was Easier | 1981 | 10.00 |
| ❑ 60148 | After All These Years | 1982 | 10.00 |
| **MGM** | | | |
| ❑ E-4465 [M] | Tompall & the Glaser Brothers | 1967 | 25.00 |
| ❑ SE-4465 [S] | Tompall & the Glaser Brothers | 1967 | 20.00 |
| ❑ SE-4510 | Through the Eyes of Love | 1968 | 15.00 |
| ❑ SE-4620 | Now Country | 1969 | 15.00 |
| ❑ SE-4775 | Award Winners | 1971 | 15.00 |
| ❑ SE-4812 | Rings and Things | 1972 | 15.00 |
| ❑ SE-4888 | Great Hits from Two Decades | 1973 | 15.00 |
| ❑ SE-4976 | Vocal Group of the Decade | 1974 | 15.00 |
| **TONE LOC** | | | |
| **DELICIOUS VINYL** | | | |
| ❑ DV 3000 | Loc-ed After Dark | 1989 | 25.00 |
| **TONEY, OSCAR, JR.** | | | |
| **BELL** | | | |
| ❑ 6006 [M] | For Your Precious Love | 1967 | 25.00 |
| ❑ S-6006 [S] | For Your Precious Love | 1967 | 30.00 |
| **TONGUE** | | | |
| **HEMISPHERE** | | | |
| ❑ HIS-101 | Tongue | 1970 | 30.00 |
| **TONGUE AND GROOVE** | | | |
| **FONTANA** | | | |
| ❑ SRF-67593 | Tongue and Groove | 1968 | 20.00 |
| **TONTO'S EXPANDING HEAD BAND** | | | |
| **EMBRYO** | | | |
| ❑ SD 732 | Zero Time | 1971 | 20.00 |
| **TOO MUCH JOY** | | | |
| **ALIAS** | | | |
| ❑ A-003 | Son of Sam I Am | 1988 | 10.00 |
| **GIANT** | | | |
| ❑ PRO-A-5054 [DJ] | Besides | 1991 | 12.00 |
| *—Promo-only collection* | | | |
| **STONEGARDEN** | | | |
| ❑ SGN-901 | Green Eggs and Crack | 1987 | 200.00 |
| **TOOL** | | | |
| **VOLCANO** | | | |
| ❑ 31160-1 [(2)] | Lateralus | 2005 | 40.00 |
| *—Two picture discs; CD version issued in 2001* | | | |
| **ZOO** | | | |
| ❑ 11027-1 | Opiate | 1992 | 12.00 |
| ❑ 11052-1 RE | Undertow | 1993 | 12.00 |
| ❑ 11087-1 [(2)] | Aenima | 1996 | 250.00 |
| **TOP DRAWER** | | | |
| **WISH BONE** | | | |
| ❑ 721207 | Solid Oak | 1969 | 400.00 |
| **TOPSIDERS, THE** | | | |
| **JOSIE** | | | |
| ❑ JOZ-4000 [M] | Rock Goes Folk | 1963 | 25.00 |
| **TORME, MEL** | | | |
| **ALLEGRO ELITE** | | | |
| ❑ 4117 [10] | Mel Torme Sings | 195? | 30.00 |
| **ATLANTIC** | | | |
| ❑ 8066 [M] | Mel Torme at the Red Hill Inn | 1962 | 30.00 |
| ❑ SD 8066 [S] | Mel Torme at the Red Hill Inn | 1962 | 40.00 |
| ❑ 8069 [M] | Comin' Home Baby | 1962 | 30.00 |
| ❑ SD 8069 [S] | Comin' Home Baby | 1962 | 40.00 |
| ❑ 8091 [M] | Sunday in New York | 1963 | 30.00 |
| ❑ SD 8091 [S] | Sunday in New York | 1963 | 40.00 |
| **AUDIOPHILE** | | | |
| ❑ 67 | Mel Torme Sings About Love | 198? | 20.00 |
| **BETHLEHEM** | | | |
| ❑ BCP-34 [M] | It's a Blue World | 1956 | 50.00 |
| ❑ BCP-52 [M] | Mel Torme and the Marty Paich Dektette | 1956 | 50.00 |
| ❑ BCP 6013 [M] | Mel Torme Sings Fred Astaire | 1957 | 50.00 |
| ❑ BCP 6016 [M] | California Suite | 1957 | 50.00 |
| ❑ BCP 6020 [M] | Mel Torme Live at the Crescendo | 1958 | 50.00 |
| ❑ BCP 6031 [M] | Songs for Any Taste | 1959 | 50.00 |
| ❑ BCP 6042 | The Torme Touch | 1978 | 12.00 |
| *—Reissue of BCP 52* | | | |
| **CAPITOL** | | | |
| ❑ P 200 [M] | California Suite | 1950 | 100.00 |
| ❑ ST-313 | A Time for Us | 1969 | 12.00 |
| ❑ ST-430 | Raindrops Keep Falling on My Head | 1970 | 12.00 |
| **COLUMBIA** | | | |
| ❑ CS 9118 [S] | That's All — A Lush Romantic Album | 1965 | 20.00 |
| **CORAL** | | | |
| ❑ CRL 57012 [M] | Gene Norman Presents Mel Torme "Live" at the Crescendo | 1955 | 50.00 |
| ❑ CRL 57044 [M] | Musical Sounds Are the Best Songs | 1956 | 50.00 |
| **LIBERTY** | | | |
| ❑ LRP-3560 [M] | A Day in the Life of Bonnie and Clyde | 1968 | 40.00 |
| *—Stock copy mono inside stereo cover with "Audition Mono LP Not for Sale" sticker* | | | |
| ❑ LST-7560 [S] | A Day in the Life of Bonnie and Clyde | 1968 | 20.00 |
| **MGM** | | | |
| ❑ E 552 [10] | Mel Torme Sings | 1952 | 100.00 |
| **STRAND** | | | |
| ❑ SL-1076 [M] | Mel Torme Sings | 1960 | 20.00 |
| ❑ SLS-1076 [S] | Mel Torme Sings | 1960 | 25.00 |
| **VENISE** | | | |
| ❑ 10021 [M] | The Touch of Your Lips | 196? | 20.00 |
| *—Yellow vinyl; reissue of Tops L-1615 without patter in between songs* | | | |
| **VERVE** | | | |
| ❑ MGV 2105 [M] | Torme | 1958 | 50.00 |
| ❑ V-2105 [M] | Torme | 1961 | 20.00 |
| *—Reissue* | | | |
| ❑ V6-2105 [S] | Torme | 1961 | 25.00 |
| *—Reissue* | | | |
| ❑ MGV 2117 [M] | Ole Torme! Mel Torme Goes South of the Border with Billy May | 1959 | 50.00 |
| ❑ V-2117 [M] | Ole Torme! Mel Torme Goes South of the Border with Billy May | 1961 | 20.00 |
| *—Reissue* | | | |
| ❑ V6-2117 [S] | Ole Torme! Mel Torme Goes South of the Border with Billy May | 1961 | 25.00 |
| *—Reissue* | | | |
| ❑ MGV 2120 [M] | Back in Town | 1959 | 50.00 |
| ❑ V-2120 [M] | Back in Town | 1961 | 20.00 |
| *—Reissue* | | | |
| ❑ V6-2120 [S] | Back in Town | 1961 | 25.00 |
| *—Reissue* | | | |
| ❑ MGV 2132 [M] | Mel Torme Swings Schubert Alley | 1960 | 50.00 |
| ❑ V-2132 [M] | Mel Torme Swings Shubert Alley | 1961 | 20.00 |
| *—Reissue* | | | |
| ❑ V6-2132 [S] | Mel Torme Swings Shubert Alley | 196? | 25.00 |
| *—Reissue of 62132* | | | |
| ❑ MGV 2144 [M] | Swingin' on the Moon | 1960 | 50.00 |
| ❑ V-2144 [M] | Swingin' on the Moon | 1961 | 20.00 |
| *—Reissue* | | | |
| ❑ V6-2144 [S] | Swingin' on the Moon | 1961 | 25.00 |
| *—Reissue of 62144* | | | |
| ❑ MGV 2146 [M] | Broadway, Right Now | 1961 | 50.00 |
| ❑ V-2146 [M] | Broadway, Right Now | 1961 | 20.00 |
| *—Reissue* | | | |
| ❑ V6-2146 [S] | Broadway, Right Now | 1961 | 25.00 |
| ❑ MGVS 6015 [S] | Torme | 1960 | 50.00 |
| ❑ MGVS 6058 [S] | Ole Torme! Mel Torme Goes South of the Border with Billy May | 1960 | 50.00 |
| ❑ MGVS 6063 [S] | Back in Town | 1960 | 50.00 |
| ❑ MGVS 6146 [S] | Mel Torme Swings Shubert Alley | 1960 | 50.00 |
| ❑ V-8440 [M] | My Kind of Music | 1962 | 25.00 |
| ❑ V6-8440 [S] | My Kind of Music | 1962 | 30.00 |
| ❑ V-8491 [M] | I Dig the Duke! I Dig the Count! | 1962 | 25.00 |
| ❑ V6-8491 [S] | I Dig the Duke! I Dig the Count! | 1962 | 30.00 |
| ❑ MGVS 62132 [S] | Mel Torme Swings Shubert Alley | 196? | 40.00 |
| *—Early reissue of 6146* | | | |
| ❑ MGVS 62144 [S] | Swingin' on the Moon | 1960 | 60.00 |
| **TORME, MEL, AND BUDDY RICH** | | | |
| **CENTURY** | | | |
| ❑ 1100 | Together Again — For the First Time | 1978 | 25.00 |
| *—Direct-to-disc recording* | | | |
| **TORMENTORS, THE** | | | |
| **ROYAL** | | | |
| ❑ RLP-111 [M] | Hanging Around | 1967 | 200.00 |
| **TORNADOES, THE (1)** | | | |
| **LONDON** | | | |
| ❑ LL 3279 [M] | Telstar | 1963 | 200.00 |
| ❑ LL 3293 [M] | The Sounds of the Tornadoes | 1963 | 200.00 |
| *—Basically the same album as above, but with a new cover, one different track and the song order shuffled.* | | | |
| **TORNADOES, THE (2)** | | | |
| **JOSIE** | | | |
| ❑ J-4005 [M] | Bustin' Surfboards | 1963 | 200.00 |
| ❑ JS-4005 [S] | Bustin' Surfboards | 1963 | 300.00 |
| **SUNDAZED** | | | |
| ❑ LP-5024 | Bustin' Surfboards | 1996 | 10.00 |
| **TOROK, MITCHELL** | | | |
| **GUYDEN** | | | |
| ❑ GLP-502 [M] | Caribbean | 1960 | 40.00 |
| ❑ ST-502 [S] | Caribbean | 1960 | 50.00 |
| **REPRISE** | | | |
| ❑ R 6223 [M] | Guitar Course | 1966 | 20.00 |
| ❑ RS 6223 [S] | Guitar Course | 1966 | 25.00 |
| **TORQUES, THE** | | | |
| **LEMCO** | | | |
| ❑ 604 | The Torques Live | 1966 | 200.00 |
| **WIGGINS** | | | |
| ❑ 64010 | Zoom! | 1967 | 200.00 |
| **TOTO** | | | |
| **COLUMBIA** | | | |
| ❑ AS 577 [DJ] | Special Radio Interview | 1979 | 20.00 |
| ❑ JC 35317 | Toto | 1978 | 10.00 |
| ❑ PC 35317 | Toto | 198? | 8.00 |
| *—Budget-line reissue with new prefix* | | | |
| ❑ FC 36229 | Hydra | 1979 | 10.00 |
| ❑ PC 36229 | Hydra | 198? | 8.00 |
| *—Budget-line reissue with new prefix* | | | |
| ❑ FC 36813 | Turn Back | 1981 | 10.00 |
| ❑ PC 36813 | Turn Back | 1984 | 8.00 |
| *—Budget-line reissue with new prefix* | | | |
| ❑ PD 36813 [PD] | Turn Back | 1981 | 25.00 |
| *—Promo-only picture disc* | | | |
| ❑ FC 37728 | Toto IV | 1982 | 10.00 |
| ❑ 8C8 38685 [EP] | Africa/Rosanna | 1983 | 20.00 |
| *—Africa-shaped picture disc; numbered like an LP although it has only these two songs on it and is (approximately) 7 inches* | | | |
| ❑ QC 38962 | Isolation | 1984 | 10.00 |
| ❑ 9C9 39911 [PD] | Isolation | 1984 | 20.00 |
| ❑ FC 40273 | Fahrenheit | 1986 | 10.00 |
| ❑ FC 40873 | The Seventh One | 1988 | 10.00 |
| ❑ C 45369 | Past to Present 1977-1990 | 1990 | 25.00 |
| *—Vinyl available only from Columbia House* | | | |
| ❑ HC 47728 | Toto IV | 198? | 40.00 |
| *—Half-speed mastered edition* | | | |
| **MOBILE FIDELITY** | | | |
| ❑ 1-250 | Toto IV | 1996 | 40.00 |
| *—Audiophile vinyl* | | | |
| **TOUCH** | | | |
| **GEAR FAB** | | | |
| ❑ GF 105 [(2)] | Street Suite | 1999 | 25.00 |
| *—Reissue of rare album plus bonus tracks* | | | |
| **MAINLINE** | | | |
| ❑ 2001 | Street Suite | 1969 | 2000. |
| *—VG value 1000; VG+ value 1500* | | | |
| **TOUCH, THE** | | | |
| **COLISEUM** | | | |
| ❑ DS-51004 | The Touch | 1968 | 25.00 |
| **TOUCHSTONE** | | | |
| **UNITED ARTISTS** | | | |
| ❑ UAS-5563 | Tarot | 1972 | 30.00 |
| **TOUFF, CY** | | | |
| **ARGO** | | | |
| ❑ LP-606 [M] | Doorway To Dixie | 1956 | 40.00 |
| ❑ LP-641 [M] | Touff Assignment | 1959 | 30.00 |
| ❑ LPS-641 [S] | Touff Assignment | 1959 | 25.00 |
| **PACIFIC JAZZ** | | | |
| ❑ PJ-42 [M] | Keester Parade | 1962 | 60.00 |
| ❑ PJ-1211 [M] | Cy Touff, His Octet and Quintet | 1956 | 150.00 |
| **WORLD PACIFIC** | | | |
| ❑ PJM-410 [M] | Havin' A Ball | 1958 | 100.00 |
| **TOUSSAINT, ALLEN** | | | |
| **RCA VICTOR** | | | |
| ❑ LPM-1767 [M] | The Wild Sounds of New Orleans | 1958 | 300.00 |
| *—As "Al Tousan"* | | | |
| **REPRISE** | | | |
| ❑ MS 2062 | Life, Love and Faith | 1972 | 25.00 |
| **SCEPTER** | | | |
| ❑ 24003 | Toussaint | 1971 | 25.00 |
| **WARNER BROS.** | | | |
| ❑ BSK 3142 | Motion | 1978 | 12.00 |
| **TOWER OF POWER** | | | |
| **COLUMBIA** | | | |
| ❑ PC 34302 | Ain't Nothin' Stoppin' Us Now | 1976 | 10.00 |
| *—No bar code on cover* | | | |
| ❑ PC 34302 | Ain't Nothin' Stoppin' Us Now | 198? | 8.00 |
| *—Budget-line reissue with bar code* | | | |
| ❑ PCQ 34302 [Q] | Ain't Nothin' Stoppin' Us Now | 1976 | 15.00 |
| ❑ JC 34906 | We Came to Play! | 1978 | 10.00 |
| ❑ JC 35784 | Back on the Streets | 1979 | 10.00 |



**Except when noted otherwise, VG = 25% of NM, and VG+ = 50% of NM. (Example: VG = $2.00, VG+ = $4.00 and NM = $8.00.)**

| Number | Title (A Side/B Side) | Yr | NM |
|---|---|---|---|
| DIRECT DISC | | | |
| ❑ SD 16601 | Back to Oakland | 1980 | 25.00 |
| *—Audiophile vinyl* | | | |
| SAN FRANCISCO | | | |
| ❑ SD 204 | East Bay Grease | 1971 | 50.00 |
| SHEFFIELD LABS | | | |
| ❑ 17 | Direct | 1982 | 25.00 |
| *—Direct-to-disc recording* | | | |
| WARNER BROS. | | | |
| ❑ BS 2616 | Bump City | 1972 | 15.00 |
| *—Green "WB" label* | | | |
| ❑ BS 2681 | Tower of Power | 1973 | 12.00 |
| *—"Burbank" palm trees label* | | | |
| ❑ BS 2681 | Tower of Power | 1973 | 15.00 |
| *—Green "WB" label* | | | |
| ❑ BS 2681 | Tower of Power | 1979 | 8.00 |
| *—White or tan label* | | | |
| ❑ BS 2749 | Back to Oakland | 1974 | 15.00 |
| *—"Burbank" palm trees label* | | | |
| ❑ BS 2749 | Back to Oakland | 1979 | 8.00 |
| *—White or tan label* | | | |
| ❑ BS 2834 | Urban Renewal | 1975 | 15.00 |
| *—"Burbank" palm trees label* | | | |
| ❑ BS 2880 | In the Slot | 1975 | 15.00 |
| *—"Burbank" palm trees label* | | | |
| ❑ BS 2924 | Live and In Living Color | 1976 | 15.00 |
| *—"Burbank" palm trees label* | | | |
| ❑ BS 2924 | Live and In Living Color | 1979 | 8.00 |
| *—White or tan label* | | | |

**TOWNSEND, ED**

| Number | Title (A Side/B Side) | Yr | NM |
|---|---|---|---|
| CAPITOL | | | |
| ❑ ST 1140 [S] | New in Town | 1959 | 30.00 |
| ❑ T 1140 [M] | New in Town | 1959 | 25.00 |
| ❑ ST 1214 [S] | Glad to Be Here | 1959 | 30.00 |
| ❑ T 1214 [M] | Glad to Be Here | 1959 | 25.00 |
| CURTOM | | | |
| ❑ 5006 | Ed Townsend Now | 1976 | 12.00 |

**TOWNSEND, HENRY**

| Number | Title (A Side/B Side) | Yr | NM |
|---|---|---|---|
| BLUESVILLE | | | |
| ❑ BVLP-1041 [M] | Tired Bein' Mistreated | 1962 | 120.00 |
| *—Blue label, silver print* | | | |
| ❑ BVLP-1041 [M] | Tired Bein' Mistreated | 1964 | 30.00 |
| *—Blue label, trident logo at side* | | | |

**TOWNSHEND, PETE** Also see THE WHO.

| Number | Title (A Side/B Side) | Yr | NM |
|---|---|---|---|
| ATCO | | | |
| ❑ SD 32-100 | Empty Glass | 1980 | 10.00 |
| ❑ SD 38-149 | All the Best Cowboys Have Chinese Eyes | 1982 | 10.00 |
| ❑ PR 940 [EP] | Deep End Sampler | 1986 | 20.00 |
| *—Promo-only sampler from Deep End Live* | | | |
| ❑ 90063 [(2)] | Scoop | 1983 | 12.00 |
| ❑ 90473 | White City — A Novel | 1985 | 10.00 |
| ❑ 90539 [(2)] | Another Scoop | 1987 | 12.00 |
| ❑ 90553 | Pete Townshend's Deep End Live! | 1986 | 10.00 |
| ATLANTIC | | | |
| ❑ 81996 | The Iron Man: The Musical by Pete Townshend | 1989 | 10.00 |
| *—Also includes tracks by John Lee Hooker, Simon Townshend, Nina Simone, The Who* | | | |
| DECCA | | | |
| ❑ 79189 | Who Came First | 1972 | 20.00 |
| *—With poster (deduct 50% if missing). Evidently a near-simultaneous release with Track 79189* | | | |
| EEL PIE | | | |
| ❑ EPR-0007 [(2)] | Another Scoop | 2002 | 40.00 |
| *—Classic Records edition on "Quiex SV" vinyl* | | | |
| ❑ EPR-0013 [(3)] | Scoop 3 | 2001 | 50.00 |
| *—Classic Records edition on "Quiex SV" vinyl* | | | |
| MCA | | | |
| ❑ 2026 | Who Came First | 1973 | 12.00 |
| *—Reissue of 79189* | | | |
| TRACK | | | |
| ❑ PR-A-160 [DJ] | Pete Townshend Talks To and About Thunderclap Newman | 1970 | 100.00 |
| *—One-sided promo-only interview record* | | | |
| ❑ 79189 | Who Came First | 1972 | 20.00 |
| *—With poster (deduct 50% if missing)* | | | |

**TOYS, THE**

| Number | Title (A Side/B Side) | Yr | NM |
|---|---|---|---|
| DYNOVOICE | | | |
| ❑ 9002 [M] | The Toys Sing "A Lover's Concerto" and "Attack!" | 1966 | 40.00 |
| ❑ S-9002 [P] | The Toys Sing "A Lover's Concerto" and "Attack!" | 1966 | 50.00 |

**TRACEY, STAN**

| Number | Title (A Side/B Side) | Yr | NM |
|---|---|---|---|
| LONDON | | | |
| ❑ LL 3107 [M] | Showcase | 195? | 40.00 |

**TRADE WINDS, THE**

| Number | Title (A Side/B Side) | Yr | NM |
|---|---|---|---|
| KAMA SUTRA | | | |
| ❑ KLP-8057 [M] | Excursions | 1967 | 25.00 |
| ❑ KLPS-8057 [S] | Excursions | 1967 | 30.00 |

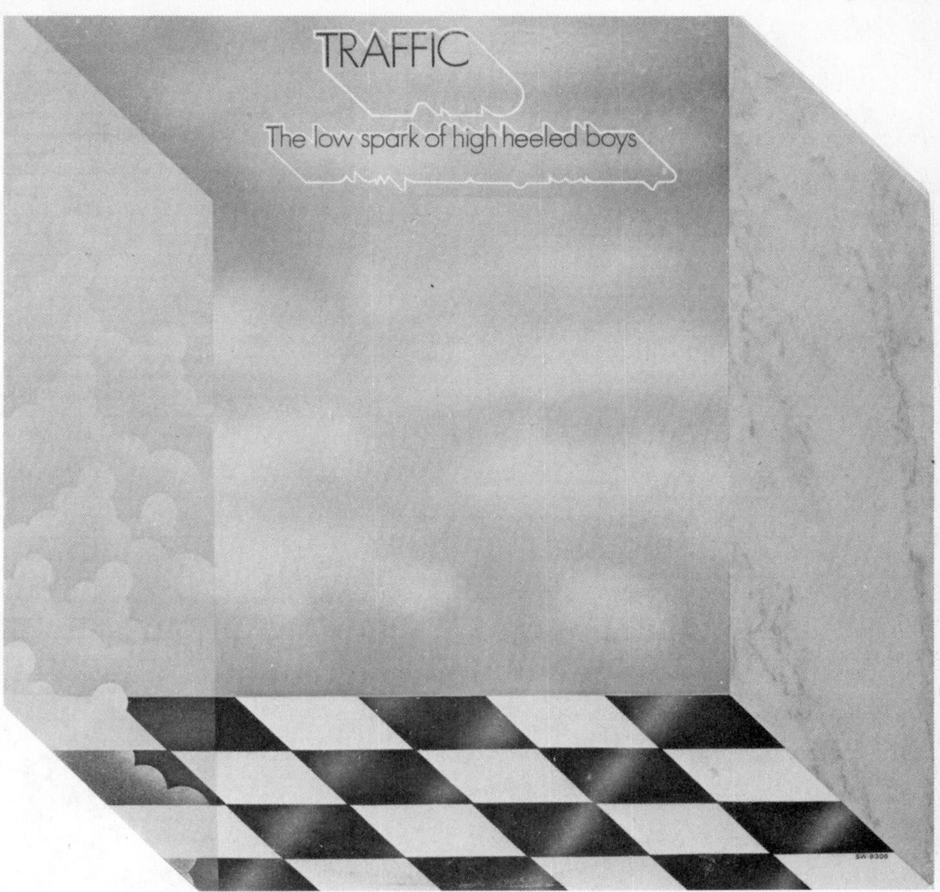


Traffic, *The Low Spark of High Heeled Boys,* Island SW-9306, 1971, $15.

**TRADER HORNE**

| Number | Title (A Side/B Side) | Yr | NM |
|---|---|---|---|
| JANUS | | | |
| ❑ JLS-3012 | Morning Way | 1970 | 30.00 |

**TRAFFIC** Also see DAVE MASON; STEVE WINWOOD.

| Number | Title (A Side/B Side) | Yr | NM |
|---|---|---|---|
| ASYLUM | | | |
| ❑ 7E-1020 | When the Eagle Flies | 1974 | 12.00 |
| ISLAND | | | |
| ❑ ILSD 2 [(2)] | Traffic — On the Road | 197? | 15.00 |
| *—Reissue* | | | |
| ❑ ILPS 9180 | The Low Spark of High Heeled Boys | 197? | 12.00 |
| *—Reissue* | | | |
| ❑ ILPS 9224 | Shoot Out at the Fantasy Factory | 197? | 12.00 |
| *—Reissue* | | | |
| ❑ SW-9306 | The Low Spark of High Heeled Boys | 1971 | 15.00 |
| ❑ SW-9323 | Shoot Out at the Fantasy Factory | 1973 | 15.00 |
| ❑ SMAS-9336 [(2)] | Traffic — On the Road | 1973 | 20.00 |
| ❑ 90026 | The Low Spark of High Heeled Boys | 1983 | 8.00 |
| *—Reissue* | | | |
| ❑ 90027 | Shoot Out at the Fantasy Factory | 1983 | 8.00 |
| *—Reissue* | | | |
| ❑ 90028 [(2)] | Traffic — On the Road | 1983 | 12.00 |
| *—Reissue* | | | |
| ❑ 90058 | John Barleycorn Must Die | 1983 | 8.00 |
| *—Reissue* | | | |
| ❑ 90059 | Traffic | 1983 | 8.00 |
| *—Reissue* | | | |
| ❑ 90060 | Mr. Fantasy | 1983 | 8.00 |
| *—Reissue* | | | |
| MOBILE FIDELITY | | | |
| ❑ 1-209 | The Low Spark of High Heeled Boys | 1994 | 25.00 |
| *—Audiophile vinyl* | | | |
| UNITED ARTISTS | | | |
| ❑ UA-LA421-G | Heavy Traffic | 1975 | 15.00 |
| ❑ UA-LA526-G | More Heavy Traffic | 1975 | 15.00 |
| ❑ UAL-3651 [M] | Heaven Is In Your Mind | 1967 | 60.00 |
| ❑ UAS-5500 | Best of Traffic | 1969 | 20.00 |
| *—Originals have pink and orange labels* | | | |
| ❑ UAS-5504 | John Barleycorn Must Die | 1970 | 20.00 |
| *—Originals have black and orange labels* | | | |
| ❑ UAS-5550 | Welcome to the Canteen | 1971 | 15.00 |
| ❑ UAS-6651 [S] | Heaven Is In Your Mind | 1967 | 50.00 |
| ❑ UAS-6651 [S] | Mr. Fantasy | 1968 | 25.00 |
| *—Retitled version of "Heaven Is In Your Mind" with green strip across top of back with song titles* | | | |
| ❑ UAS-6651 [S] | Mr. Fantasy | 1968 | 35.00 |
| *—Retitled version of "Heaven Is In Your Mind" with old title still on back cover* | | | |
| ❑ UAS-6676 | Traffic | 1968 | 20.00 |
| *—Originals have purple and orange labels* | | | |
| ❑ UAS-6702 | Last Exit | 1969 | 20.00 |
| *—Originals have purple and orange labels* | | | |
| ❑ ST-92018 | Last Exit | 1969 | 30.00 |
| *—Capitol Record Club edition; label is the old-style black with circles at the top!* | | | |

**TRAILER, REX, AND THE PLAYBOYS**

| Number | Title (A Side/B Side) | Yr | NM |
|---|---|---|---|
| CROWN | | | |
| ❑ CLP-5158 [M] | Country & Western | 1958 | 25.00 |

**TRAMLINE**

| Number | Title (A Side/B Side) | Yr | NM |
|---|---|---|---|
| A&M | | | |
| ❑ SP-4208 | Somewhere Down the Line | 1969 | 20.00 |

**TRAMMELL, BOBBY LEE**

| Number | Title (A Side/B Side) | Yr | NM |
|---|---|---|---|
| ATLANTA | | | |
| ❑ 1503 [M] | Arkansas Twist | 1962 | 1000. |
| SOUNCOT | | | |
| ❑ SC-1102 | I Dare America to Be Great | 1971 | 20.00 |
| ❑ SC-1141 | Love Isn't Love Till You Give It Away | 1972 | 15.00 |

**TRAPEZE**

| Number | Title (A Side/B Side) | Yr | NM |
|---|---|---|---|
| THRESHOLD | | | |
| ❑ THS 2 | Trapeze | 1970 | 40.00 |
| ❑ THS 4 | Medusa | 1971 | 80.00 |
| ❑ THS 8 | You Are the Music, We're Just the Band | 1972 | 40.00 |
| ❑ THS 11 | The Final Swing | 1974 | 40.00 |
| WARNER BROS. | | | |
| ❑ BS 2828 | Hot Wire | 1974 | 12.00 |
| ❑ BS 2887 | Trapeze | 1975 | 12.00 |

The Tremeloes, *Suddenly You Love Me,* Epic LN 24363, 1968, mono, $30.

| Number | Title (A Side/B Side) | Yr | NM |
|---|---|---|---|
| **TRAPP FAMILY SINGERS, THE** | | | |
| RCA CAMDEN | | | |
| ❑ CAL-209 [M] | The Trapp Family Singers Present Christmas and Folk Songs | 195? | 20.00 |
| **TRASHMEN, THE** | | | |
| BEAT ROCKET | | | |
| ❑ BR 107 | Surfin' Bird | 1999 | 12.00 |
| *—Reissue on 180-gram vinyl* | | | |
| GARRETT | | | |
| ❑ GA-200 [M] | Surfin' Bird | 1964 | 220.00 |
| ❑ GAS-200 [R] | Surfin' Bird | 1964 | 350.00 |
| SUNDAZED | | | |
| ❑ LP 5002 | Live Bird '65-'67 | 1991 | 10.00 |
| ❑ LP 5003 | Great Lost Album | 1991 | 10.00 |
| **TRASK, DIANA** | | | |
| ABC | | | |
| ❑ ABDP-948 | Believe Me Now or Believe Me Later | 1976 | 12.00 |
| ❑ AC-30030 | The ABC Collection | 1976 | 12.00 |
| ABC DOT | | | |
| ❑ DOSD-2007 | Diana Trask's Greatest Hits | 1974 | 12.00 |
| ❑ DOSD-2024 | The Mood I'm In | 1975 | 12.00 |
| COLUMBIA | | | |
| ❑ CL 1601 [M] | Diana Trask | 1961 | 25.00 |
| ❑ CL 1705 [M] | Diana Trask on TV | 1961 | 25.00 |
| ❑ CS 8401 [S] | Diana Trask | 1961 | 30.00 |
| ❑ CS 8505 [S] | Diana Trask on TV | 1961 | 30.00 |
| DOT | | | |
| ❑ DLP-25920 | Miss Country Soul | 1969 | 15.00 |
| ❑ DLP-25957 | From the Heart | 1969 | 15.00 |
| ❑ DOS-25989 | Diana's Country | 1971 | 15.00 |
| ❑ DOS-25999 | Diana Trask Sings About Loving | 1972 | 15.00 |
| ❑ DOS-26016 | It's a Man's World | 1973 | 15.00 |
| ❑ DOS-26022 | Lean It All on Me | 1974 | 15.00 |
| PICKWICK/HILLTOP | | | |
| ❑ 6188 | Miss Country Soul | 197? | 10.00 |
| **TRAVEL AGENCY, THE** | | | |
| VIVA | | | |
| ❑ V-36017 | The Travel Agency | 1968 | 25.00 |
| **TRAVELERS 3, THE** | | | |
| ELEKTRA | | | |
| ❑ EKL-216 [M] | The Travelers 3 | 1963 | 25.00 |
| ❑ EKL-226 [M] | Open House | 1963 | 25.00 |
| ❑ EKL-236 [M] | Live! Live! Live! | 1963 | 25.00 |
| **TRAVELING WILBURYS** Also see BOB DYLAN; GEORGE HARRISON; ROY ORBISON; TOM PETTY AND THE HEARTBREAKERS. | | | |
| WILBURY | | | |
| ❑ 25796 | Traveling Wilburys (Volume One) | 1988 | 20.00 |
| ❑ 26324 | Traveling Wilburys, Vol. 3 | 1990 | 20.00 |
| **TRAVELLERS, THE** | | | |
| KAPP | | | |
| ❑ KL-1157 [M] | Journey with the Travellers | 1960 | 25.00 |
| ❑ KS-3051 [S] | Journey with the Travellers | 1960 | 30.00 |
| **TRAVIS, MERLE** | | | |
| CAPITOL | | | |
| ❑ T 650 [M] | The Merle Travis Guitar | 1956 | 120.00 |
| *—Turquoise or gray label* | | | |
| ❑ T 650 [M] | The Merle Travis Guitar | 1959 | 30.00 |
| *—Black colorband label, logo at left* | | | |
| ❑ T 650 [M] | The Merle Travis Guitar | 1962 | 20.00 |
| *—Black colorband label, logo at top* | | | |
| ❑ T 891 [M] | Back Home | 1957 | 100.00 |
| *—Turquoise or gray label* | | | |
| ❑ T 891 [M] | Back Home | 1959 | 30.00 |
| *—Black colorband label, logo at left* | | | |
| ❑ T 891 [M] | Back Home | 1962 | 20.00 |
| *—Black colorband label, logo at top* | | | |
| ❑ T 1391 [M] | Walkin' the Strings | 1960 | 80.00 |
| *—Black colorband label, logo at left* | | | |
| ❑ T 1391 [M] | Walkin' the Strings | 1962 | 20.00 |
| *—Black colorband label, logo at top* | | | |
| ❑ ST 1664 [S] | Travis | 1962 | 25.00 |
| *—Black colorband label, logo at top* | | | |
| ❑ ST 1664 [S] | Travis | 1962 | 50.00 |
| *—Black colorband label, logo at left* | | | |
| ❑ T 1664 [M] | Travis | 1962 | 20.00 |
| *—Black colorband label, logo at top* | | | |
| ❑ T 1664 [M] | Travis | 1962 | 40.00 |
| *—Black colorband label, logo at left* | | | |
| ❑ ST 1956 [S] | Songs of the Coal Mines | 1963 | 50.00 |
| ❑ T 1956 [M] | Songs of the Coal Mines | 1963 | 40.00 |
| ❑ DT 2662 [R] | The Best of Merle Travis | 1967 | 20.00 |
| ❑ T 2662 [M] | The Best of Merle Travis | 1967 | 30.00 |
| ❑ ST 2938 | Strictly Guitar | 1968 | 25.00 |
| **TRAVIS, MERLE, AND JOE MAPHIS** | | | |
| CAPITOL | | | |
| ❑ ST 2102 [S] | Merle Travis and Joe Maphis | 1964 | 50.00 |
| ❑ T 2102 [M] | Merle Travis and Joe Maphis | 1964 | 40.00 |
| **TRAVIS, NICK** | | | |
| RCA VICTOR | | | |
| ❑ LJM-1010 [M] | The Panic Is On | 1954 | 120.00 |
| **TRAVIS, RANDY** | | | |
| MUSIC VALLEY | | | |
| ❑ (# unknown) | Randy Ray Live at the Nashville Palace | 1982 | 300.00 |
| *—With no "Randy Travis" sticker on front cover* | | | |
| ❑ (# unknown) | Randy Ray Live at the Nashville Palace | 1986 | 200.00 |
| *—With "Randy Travis" sticker on front cover; the records are the same as the first edition* | | | |
| WARNER BROS. | | | |
| ❑ 25435 | Storms of Life | 1986 | 10.00 |
| ❑ 25568 | Always & Forever | 1987 | 10.00 |
| ❑ 25738 | Old 8x10 | 1988 | 10.00 |
| ❑ 25972 | An Old-Fashioned Christmas | 1989 | 12.00 |
| ❑ 25988 | No Holdin' Back | 1989 | 12.00 |
| ❑ R 174597 | Heroes and Friends | 1990 | 20.00 |
| *—Only released on vinyl through BMG Direct Marketing* | | | |
| **TREE** | | | |
| GOAT FARM | | | |
| ❑ 580 | Tree | 1970 | 70.00 |
| **TREMELOES, THE** | | | |
| DJM | | | |
| ❑ 2 | Shiner | 1974 | 12.00 |
| EPIC | | | |
| ❑ LN 24310 [M] | Here Comes My Baby | 1967 | 30.00 |
| ❑ LN 24326 [M] | Even the Bad Times Are Good | 1967 | 25.00 |
| ❑ LN 24363 [M] | Suddenly You Love Me | 1968 | 30.00 |
| ❑ LN 24388 [M] | World Explosion '58/'68 | 1968 | 60.00 |
| *—White label promo only* | | | |
| ❑ BN 26310 [R] | Here Comes My Baby | 1967 | 20.00 |
| ❑ BN 26326 [P] | Even the Bad Times Are Good | 1967 | 30.00 |
| ❑ BN 26363 [R] | Suddenly You Love Me | 1968 | 20.00 |
| ❑ BN 26388 [S] | World Explosion '58/'68 | 1968 | 30.00 |
| **TRENIERS, THE** | | | |
| DOT | | | |
| ❑ DLP-3257 [M] | Souvenir Album | 1960 | 100.00 |
| EPIC | | | |
| ❑ LG 3125 [M] | The Treniers on TV | 1955 | 200.00 |
| **TRENT, BUCK** | | | |
| ABC DOT | | | |
| ❑ DOSD-2058 | Bionic Banjo | 1976 | 10.00 |
| ❑ DO-2077 | Oh Yeah! | 1977 | 10.00 |
| BOONE | | | |
| ❑ 1212 | Give Me Five | 1967 | 20.00 |
| RCA VICTOR | | | |
| ❑ LSP-4705 | Sounds of Now and Beyond | 1972 | 12.00 |
| SMASH | | | |
| ❑ MGS-27002 [M] | The Sound of a Bluegrass Banjo | 1962 | 20.00 |
| *—Smash LPs as "Charles Trent"* | | | |
| ❑ MGS-27017 [M] | The Sound of a Five String Banjo | 1962 | 20.00 |
| ❑ SRS-67002 [S] | The Sound of a Bluegrass Banjo | 1962 | 25.00 |
| ❑ SRS-67017 [S] | The Sound of a Five String Banjo | 1962 | 25.00 |
| **TREVOR, JEANNIE** | | | |
| MAINSTREAM | | | |
| ❑ S-6075 [S] | Jeannie Trevor Sings!! | 1965 | 30.00 |
| ❑ 56075 [M] | Jeannie Trevor Sings!! | 1965 | 25.00 |
| **TREVOR, VAN** | | | |
| BAND BOX | | | |
| ❑ (# unknown) | Come On Over to Our Side | 1967 | 20.00 |
| DATE | | | |
| ❑ DES-4008 | You've Been So Good to Me | 1967 | 15.00 |
| ROYAL AMERICAN | | | |
| ❑ 2800 | Funny Familiar Forgotten Feelings | 1969 | 15.00 |
| **TRIANGLE, THE** | | | |
| AMARET | | | |
| ❑ 5000 | How Now Brown Cow | 1969 | 25.00 |
| **TRICHT, EVERT VAN** | | | |
| MERCURY LIVING PRESENCE | | | |
| ❑ SR 90403 [S] | Oboe Concerti | 196? | 30.00 |
| *—With Kurt Redel/Vienna Symphony Orchestra and Pro Arte Orchestra of Munich; maroon label, no "Vendor: Mercury Record Corporation"* | | | |

| Number | Title (A Side/B Side) | Yr | NM |
|---|---|---|---|
| **TRICYCLE** | | | |
| ABC | | | |
| ❑ S-674 | Tricycle | 1969 | 20.00 |
| **TRIGGER, VIC** | | | |
| SANCTUARY | | | |
| ❑ 12103 | Electronic Wizard | 1977 | 100.00 |
| **TRIMBLE, BOBB** | | | |
| (NO LABEL) | | | |
| ❑ (no #) | Harvest of Dreams | 1982 | 150.00 |
| VENGEANCE | | | |
| ❑ BT-8458 | Iron Curtain Dream | 1980 | 800.00 |
| **TRIO** | | | |
| MERCURY | | | |
| ❑ MX-1-509 [EP] | Trio (Contains the Hit Da Da Da) | 1982 | 15.00 |
| ❑ 814320-1 | Trio and Error | 1983 | 20.00 |
| **TRIO, THE** | | | |
| SAVOY | | | |
| ❑ MG-12023 [M] | The Trio | 1955 | 100.00 |
| **TRIPSICHORD MUSIC BOX, THE** | | | |
| JANUS | | | |
| ❑ JLS-3016 | The Tripsichord Music Box | 1971 | 200.00 |
| **TRISTANO, LENNIE** | | | |
| ATLANTIC | | | |
| ❑ 1224 [M] | Lennie Tristano | 1955 | 80.00 |
| *—Black label* | | | |
| ❑ 1224 [M] | Lennie Tristano | 1960 | 25.00 |
| *—Multicolor label, white "fan" logo at right* | | | |
| ❑ 1357 [M] | The New Tristano | 1960 | 50.00 |
| *—Multicolor label, white "fan" logo at right* | | | |
| MOSAIC | | | |
| ❑ MQ10-174 [(10)] | The Complete Atlantic Recordings of Lennie Tristano, Lee Konitz and Warne Marsh | 199? | 300.00 |
| NEW JAZZ | | | |
| ❑ NJLP-101 [10] | Lennie Tristano with Lee Konitz | 1950 | 600.00 |
| PRESTIGE | | | |
| ❑ PRLP-101 [10] | Lennie Tristano with Lee Konitz | 1951 | 500.00 |
| **TRISTANO, LENNIE; JO BUSHKIN; BOBBY SCOTT; MARIAN MCPARTLAND** | | | |
| SAVOY | | | |
| ❑ MG-12043 [M] | The Jazz Keyboards of Lennie Tristano, Joe Bushkin, Bobby Scott & Marian McPartland | 1955 | 80.00 |
| **TRISTANO, LENNIE/ARNOLD ROSS** | | | |
| EMARCY | | | |
| ❑ MG-26029 [10] | Holiday in Piano | 1953 | 400.00 |
| **TRITT, TRAVIS** | | | |
| WARNER BROS. | | | |
| ❑ W1-26589 | It's All About to Change | 1991 | 20.00 |
| *—Vinyl available only from Columbia House* | | | |
| **TRIZO 50** | | | |
| CAVERN | | | |
| ❑ 740142 | Trizo 50 | 197? | 300.00 |
| **TROGGS, THE** | | | |
| ATCO | | | |
| ❑ 33-193 [M] | Wild Thing | 1966 | 50.00 |
| ❑ SD 33-193 [R] | Wild Thing | 1966 | 40.00 |
| FONTANA | | | |
| ❑ MGF 27556 [M] | Wild Thing/With a Girl Like You | 1966 | 40.00 |
| *—Contents identical to the Atco LP; two slightly different cover variations are known; record has mono number and plays mono; number "27556" in trail-off* | | | |
| ❑ MGF 27556 [R] | Wild Thing/With a Girl Like You | 1966 | 30.00 |
| *—Contents identical to the Atco LP; two slightly different cover variations are known; record has mono number but plays in rechanneled stereo; number "2/67556" in trail-off* | | | |
| ❑ SRF 67556 [R] | Wild Thing/With a Girl Like You | 1966 | 30.00 |
| *—Contents identical to the Atco LP; two slightly different cover variations are known* | | | |
| ❑ SRF 67576 [R] | Love Is All Around | 1968 | 30.00 |
| MKC | | | |
| ❑ 214 | Live at Max's Kansas City | 1980 | 12.00 |
| PRIVATE STOCK | | | |
| ❑ PS-2008 | The Troggs Tapes | 1976 | 12.00 |
| PYE | | | |
| ❑ 12112 | The Troggs | 1975 | 12.00 |
| RHINO | | | |
| ❑ RNLP-118 | The Best of the Troggs | 1985 | 10.00 |
| ❑ R1 70118 | The Best of the Troggs | 1988 | 8.00 |

| Number | Title (A Side/B Side) | Yr | NM |
|---|---|---|---|
| SIRE | | | |
| ❑ SASH-3714 [(2)] | The Vintage Years | 1976 | 15.00 |
| **TROLL, THE** | | | |
| SMASH | | | |
| ❑ SRS-67114 | Animated Music | 1969 | 50.00 |
| **TROMBONES, INC., THE** | | | |
| WARNER BROS. | | | |
| ❑ W 1272 [M] | They Met at the Continental Divide | 1959 | 50.00 |
| ❑ WS 1272 [S] | They Met at the Continental Divide | 1959 | 60.00 |
| **TROMBONES UNLIMITED** | | | |
| LIBERTY | | | |
| ❑ LRP-3449 [M] | These Bones are Made for Walking | 1966 | 15.00 |
| ❑ LRP-3472 [M] | You're Gonna Hear From Me | 1966 | 15.00 |
| ❑ LRP-3494 [M] | Big Boss Bones | 1967 | 20.00 |
| ❑ LRP-3527 [M] | Holiday for Trombones | 1967 | 20.00 |
| ❑ LRP-3549 [M] | One of Those Songs | 1968 | 25.00 |
| ❑ LST-7449 [S] | These Bones are Made for Walking | 1966 | 20.00 |
| ❑ LST-7472 [S] | You're Gonna Hear From Me | 1966 | 20.00 |
| ❑ LST-7494 [S] | Big Boss Bones | 1967 | 15.00 |
| ❑ LST-7527 [S] | Holiday for Trombones | 1967 | 15.00 |
| ❑ LST-7549 [S] | One of Those Songs | 1968 | 15.00 |
| ❑ LST-7592 | Grazing in the Grass | 1968 | 15.00 |
| **TROUP, BOBBY** | | | |
| BETHLEHEM | | | |
| ❑ BCP-19 [M] | Bobby Troup Sings Johnny Mercer | 1955 | 50.00 |
| ❑ BCP-35 [M] | The Distinctive Style of Bobby Troup | 1955 | 50.00 |
| ❑ BCP-1030 [10] | Bobby Troup | 1955 | 60.00 |
| CAPITOL | | | |
| ❑ H 484 [10] | Bobby | 1953 | 80.00 |
| ❑ T 484 [M] | Bobby | 1955 | 50.00 |
| INTERLUDE | | | |
| ❑ MO-501 [M] | Cool | 1959 | 40.00 |
| ❑ ST-1001 [S] | Cool | 1959 | 40.00 |
| LIBERTY | | | |
| ❑ LRP-3002 [M] | Bobby Troup and His Trio | 1955 | 50.00 |
| ❑ LRP-3026 [M] | Do Re Mi | 1957 | 50.00 |
| ❑ LRP-3078 [M] | Here's to My Lady | 1958 | 50.00 |
| MODE | | | |
| ❑ LP-111 [M] | Bobby Swings Tenderly | 1957 | 100.00 |
| RCA VICTOR | | | |
| ❑ LPM-1959 [M] | Bobby Troup and His Jazz All-Stars | 1959 | 40.00 |
| ❑ LSP-1959 [S] | Bobby Troup and His Jazz All-Stars | 1959 | 50.00 |
| **TROY, DORIS** | | | |
| APPLE | | | |
| ❑ ST-3371 | Doris Troy | 1970 | 25.00 |
| ATLANTIC | | | |
| ❑ 8088 [M] | Just One Look | 1964 | 30.00 |
| ❑ SD 8088 [P] | Just One Look | 1964 | 50.00 |
| *—The title song is rechanneled* | | | |
| **TROYKA** | | | |
| COTILLION | | | |
| ❑ SD 9020 | Troyka | 1970 | 30.00 |
| **TRUMAN, MARGARET** | | | |
| RCA VICTOR | | | |
| ❑ LM-57 [10] | American Songs | 1951 | 80.00 |
| ❑ LM-145 [10] | A Margaret Truman Program | 1952 | 80.00 |
| **TRUMPETEERS, THE (1)** | | | |
| GRAND | | | |
| ❑ 7701 [M] | The Last Supper | 195? | 100.00 |
| SCORE | | | |
| ❑ SLP-4021 [M] | Milky White Way | 1956 | 300.00 |
| **TUBB, ERNEST** | | | |
| CACHET | | | |
| ❑ 33001 | Ernest Tubb: The Legend and the Legacy, Volume One | 1979 | 12.00 |
| DECCA | | | |
| ❑ DXA 159 [(2)M] | The Ernest Tubb Story | 1959 | 80.00 |
| *—Deduct 25 percent if book is missing* | | | |
| ❑ DL 4046 [M] | All Time Hits | 1961 | 30.00 |
| ❑ DL 4064 [M] | The Ernest Tubb Record Shop | 1960 | 40.00 |
| ❑ DL 4118 [M] | Ernest Tubb's Golden Favorites | 1961 | 30.00 |
| ❑ DL 4321 [M] | On Tour | 1962 | 25.00 |
| ❑ DL 4385 [M] | Just Call Me Lonesome | 1962 | 25.00 |
| ❑ DL 4397 [M] | The Family Bible | 1963 | 25.00 |
| ❑ DL 4514 [M] | Thanks a Lot | 1964 | 25.00 |
| ❑ DL 4518 [M] | Blue Christmas | 1963 | 25.00 |

| Number | Title (A Side/B Side) | Yr | NM |
|---|---|---|---|
| ❑ DL 4640 [M] | My Pick of the Hits | 1965 | 25.00 |
| ❑ DL 4681 [M] | Hittin' the Road | 1965 | 25.00 |
| ❑ DL 4746 [M] | By Request | 1966 | 25.00 |
| ❑ DL 4772 [M] | Ernest Tubb Sings Country Hits Old & New | 1966 | 25.00 |
| ❑ DL 4867 [M] | Another Story | 1967 | 30.00 |
| ❑ DL 4957 [M] | Ernest Tubb Sings Hank Williams | 1968 | 50.00 |
| ❑ DL 5006 [M] | Ernest Tubb's Greatest Hits | 1968 | 80.00 |
| *—White label promo only* | | | |
| ❑ DL 5301 [10] | Ernest Tubb Favorites | 1951 | 150.00 |
| ❑ DL 5334 [10] | The Old Rugged Cross | 1951 | 150.00 |
| ❑ DL 5336 [10] | Jimmie Rodgers Songs Sung by Ernest Tubb | 1951 | 150.00 |
| ❑ DL 5497 [10] | Sing a Song of Christmas | 1954 | 150.00 |
| ❑ DXSA 7159 [(2)R] | The Ernest Tubb Story | 196? | 30.00 |
| *—Deduct 25 percent if book is missing* | | | |
| ❑ DL 8291 [M] | Ernest Tubb Favorites | 1955 | 70.00 |
| ❑ DL 8553 [M] | The Daddy of 'Em All | 1956 | 70.00 |
| ❑ DL 8834 [M] | The Importance of Being Ernest | 1959 | 50.00 |
| ❑ DL 74046 [S] | All Time Hits | 1961 | 40.00 |
| ❑ DL 74064 [S] | The Ernest Tubb Record Shop | 1960 | 50.00 |
| ❑ DL 74118 [S] | Ernest Tubb's Golden Favorites | 1961 | 40.00 |
| ❑ DL 74321 [S] | On Tour | 1962 | 30.00 |
| ❑ DL 74385 [S] | Just Call Me Lonesome | 1962 | 30.00 |
| ❑ DL 74397 [S] | The Family Bible | 1963 | 30.00 |
| ❑ DL 74514 [S] | Thanks a Lot | 1964 | 30.00 |
| ❑ DL 74518 [S] | Blue Christmas | 1963 | 30.00 |
| ❑ DL 74640 [S] | My Pick of the Hits | 1965 | 30.00 |
| ❑ DL 74681 [S] | Hittin' the Road | 1965 | 30.00 |
| ❑ DL 74746 [S] | By Request | 1966 | 30.00 |
| ❑ DL 74772 [S] | Ernest Tubb Sings Country Hits Old & New | 1966 | 30.00 |
| ❑ DL 74867 [S] | Another Story | 1967 | 25.00 |
| ❑ DL 74957 [S] | Ernest Tubb Sings Hank Williams | 1968 | 25.00 |
| ❑ DL 75006 [S] | Ernest Tubb's Greatest Hits | 1968 | 25.00 |
| ❑ DL 75072 | Country Hit Time | 1968 | 20.00 |
| ❑ DL 75114 | Let's Turn Back the Years | 1969 | 15.00 |
| ❑ DL 75122 | Saturday Satan, Sunday Saint | 1969 | 20.00 |
| ❑ DL 75222 | A Great Year for the Wine | 1970 | 20.00 |
| ❑ DL 75252 | Ernest Tubb's Greatest Hits, Vol. 2 | 1970 | 20.00 |
| ❑ DL 75301 | One Sweet Hello | 1971 | 20.00 |
| ❑ DL 75345 | Say Something Nice to Sarah | 1972 | 20.00 |
| ❑ DL 75388 | Baby, It's So Hard to Be Good | 1972 | 20.00 |
| ❑ DL 78834 [S] | The Importance of Being Ernest | 1959 | 60.00 |
| FIRST GENERATION | | | |
| ❑ LP-0002 [(2)] | The Legend and the Legacy | 1979 | 40.00 |
| *—With ad for Ernest Tubb Record Shop on back cover* | | | |
| ❑ LP-0002 [(2)] | The Legend and the Legacy | 1979 | 50.00 |
| *—No ads on back cover* | | | |
| ❑ TV-1033 [(2)] | The Legend and the Legacy | 1979 | 25.00 |
| *—Mail-order version* | | | |
| MCA | | | |
| ❑ 16 | Ernest Tubb's Greatest Hits | 1973 | 12.00 |
| *—Reissue of Decca 75006* | | | |
| ❑ 24 | Ernest Tubb's Greatest Hits, Vol. 2 | 1973 | 12.00 |
| *—Reissue of Decca 75252* | | | |
| ❑ 84 | Ernest Tubb's Golden Favorites | 1973 | 12.00 |
| *—Reissue of Decca 74118* | | | |
| ❑ 341 | I've Got All the Heartaches I Can Handle | 1973 | 12.00 |
| ❑ 496 | Ernest Tubb | 1975 | 12.00 |
| ❑ 512 | Baby, It's So Hard to Be Good | 197? | 12.00 |
| *—Reissue of Decca 75388* | | | |
| ❑ 4040 [(2)] | The Ernest Tubb Story | 197? | 15.00 |
| *—Reissue of Decca DXSA 7159* | | | |
| VOCALION | | | |
| ❑ VL 3684 [M] | Ernest Tubb and His Texas Troubadours | 196? | 15.00 |
| ❑ VL 73684 [R] | Ernest Tubb and His Texas Troubadours | 196? | 10.00 |
| **TUBB, ERNEST, AND LORETTA LYNN** | | | |
| DECCA | | | |
| ❑ DL 4639 [M] | Mr. and Mrs. Used to Be | 1965 | 30.00 |
| ❑ DL 4872 [M] | Singin' Again | 1967 | 30.00 |
| ❑ DL 74639 [S] | Mr. and Mrs. Used to Be | 1965 | 40.00 |
| ❑ DL 74872 [S] | Singin' Again | 1967 | 25.00 |
| ❑ DL 75115 | If We Put Our Heads Together | 1969 | 25.00 |
| MCA | | | |
| ❑ 4000 | The Ernest Tubb/Loretta Lynn Story | 1973 | 15.00 |
| **TUBB, JUSTIN** | | | |
| CUTLASS | | | |
| ❑ 123 | Travelin' Singin' Man | 1972 | 30.00 |
| DECCA | | | |
| ❑ DL 8644 [M] | Country Boy in Love | 1957 | 60.00 |
| DOT | | | |
| ❑ DLP-3922 [M] | Things I Still Remember Very Well | 1969 | 50.00 |
| *—Record is black label stock copy; "Mounaural" sticker appears on stereo cover* | | | |

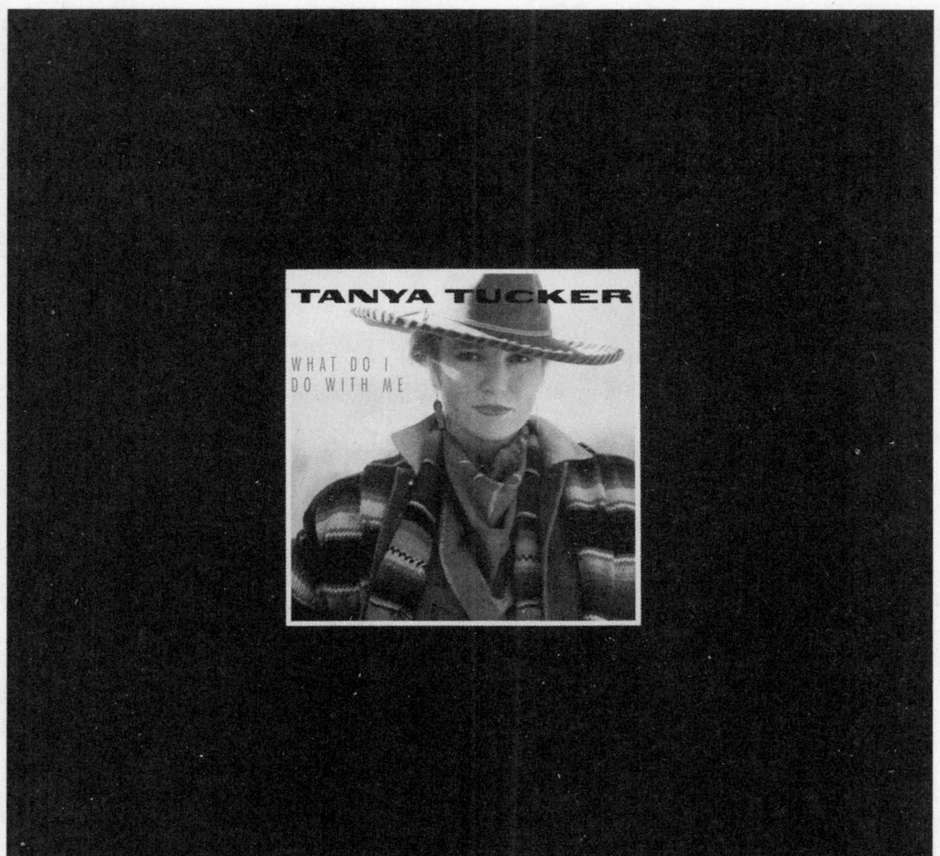


Tanya Tucker, *What Do I Do with Me,* Capitol Nashville 1P-8140, 1991, Columbia House exclusive, $20.

| Number | Title (A Side/B Side) | Yr | NM |
|---|---|---|---|
| DLP-25922 [S] | Things I Still Remember Very Well | 1969 | 15.00 |
| **FIRST GENERATION** | | | |
| 1 | What's Wrong with the Way We're Doing It Now | 1979 | 12.00 |
| **PHONORAMA** | | | |
| 5565 | What's Wrong with the Way We're Doing It Now | 1983 | 8.00 |
| **RCA VICTOR** | | | |
| LPM-3339 [M] | Where You're Concerned | 1965 | 20.00 |
| LSP-3339 [S] | Where You're Concerned | 1965 | 25.00 |
| **STARDAY** | | | |
| SLP-160 [M] | Star of the Grand Ole Opry | 1962 | 40.00 |
| SLP-198 [M] | The Modern Country Sound of Justin Tubb | 1962 | 40.00 |
| SLP-334 [M] | The Best of Justin Tubb | 1965 | 25.00 |
| **VOCALION** | | | |
| VL 73802 | That Country Style | 196? | 12.00 |

## TUBB, JUSTIN, AND LORENE MANN

| Number | Title (A Side/B Side) | Yr | NM |
|---|---|---|---|
| **RCA VICTOR** | | | |
| LPM-3591 [M] | Together and Alone | 1966 | 30.00 |
| LSP-3591 [S] | Together and Alone | 1966 | 40.00 |

## TUBES, THE

| Number | Title (A Side/B Side) | Yr | NM |
|---|---|---|---|
| **A&M** | | | |
| SP-3161 | The Tubes | 198? | 8.00 |
| *—Reissue of SP-4534* | | | |
| SP-3222 | Young and Rich | 198? | 8.00 |
| *—Reissue of SP-4580* | | | |
| SP-3242 | Remote Control | 198? | 8.00 |
| *—Reissue of SP-4751* | | | |
| SP-3243 | Now | 198? | 10.00 |
| *—Reissue of SP-4632* | | | |
| SP-3244 | T.R.A.S.H. (Tubes Rarities And Smash Hits) | 198? | 8.00 |
| *—Reissue of SP-4870* | | | |
| SP-4534 | The Tubes | 1975 | 12.00 |
| SP-4580 | Young and Rich | 1976 | 12.00 |
| SP-4632 | Now | 1977 | 12.00 |
| SP-4751 | Remote Control | 1979 | 12.00 |
| SP-4870 | T.R.A.S.H. (Tubes Rarities And Smash Hits) | 1981 | 10.00 |
| SP-6003 [(2)] | What Do You Want From Live! | 1978 | 15.00 |
| SP-17012 [DJ] | Tubes Live/Edited for Trouble-Free Airplay (The First "Clean" Tubes Album) | 1978 | 20.00 |
| *—Generic cover with sticker; promo only* | | | |
| **CAPITOL** | | | |
| SOO-12151 | The Completion Backward Principle | 1981 | 10.00 |
| ST-12260 | Outside/Inside | 1983 | 10.00 |
| ST-12381 | Love Bomb | 1985 | 10.00 |
| SN-16360 | Outside/Inside | 1985 | 8.00 |
| *—Reissue of ST-12260* | | | |
| SN-16378 | The Completion Backward Principle | 1986 | 8.00 |
| *—Reissue of SOO-12151* | | | |
| SN-16446 | Love Bomb | 1987 | 8.00 |
| *—Reissue of ST-12381* | | | |

## TUCKER, FAYE

| Number | Title (A Side/B Side) | Yr | NM |
|---|---|---|---|
| **TIME** | | | |
| S-2018 [S] | Country & Western Soul | 1963 | 25.00 |
| 52108 [M] | Country & Western Soul | 1963 | 20.00 |

## TUCKER, MAUREEN Also see THE VELVET UNDERGROUND.

| Number | Title (A Side/B Side) | Yr | NM |
|---|---|---|---|
| **50 SKIDILLION WATTS** | | | |
| MOE 1 [EP] | Moejadkatebarry | 1987 | 14.00 |
| MOE 7 | Life in Exile After Abdication | 1989 | 12.00 |
| **TRASH** | | | |
| TLP-1001 | Playin' Possum | 1981 | 30.00 |

## TUCKER, TANYA

| Number | Title (A Side/B Side) | Yr | NM |
|---|---|---|---|
| **ARISTA** | | | |
| AL 8381 | Changes | 1984 | 8.00 |
| *—Reissue of 9596* | | | |
| AL 9596 | Changes | 1982 | 10.00 |
| **CAPITOL** | | | |
| ST-12474 | Girls Like Me | 1986 | 10.00 |
| CLT-46870 | Love Me Like You Used To | 1987 | 10.00 |
| C1-48865 | Strong Enough to Bend | 1988 | 10.00 |
| C1-91814 | Greatest Hits | 1989 | 12.00 |
| **CAPITOL NASHVILLE** | | | |
| 1P 8140 | What Do I Do with Me | 1991 | 20.00 |
| *—Only available on vinyl through Columbia House* | | | |
| **COLUMBIA** | | | |
| KC 31742 | Delta Dawn | 1972 | 15.00 |
| PC 31742 | Delta Dawn | 198? | 8.00 |
| KC 32272 | What's Your Mama's Name | 1973 | 15.00 |
| KC 32744 | Would You Lay with Me (In a Field of Stone) | 1974 | 12.00 |
| PC 32744 | Would You Lay with Me (In a Field of Stone) | 197? | 8.00 |
| KC 33355 | Greatest Hits | 1975 | 12.00 |
| *—No bar code on cover* | | | |
| PC 33355 | Greatest Hits | 197? | 8.00 |
| *—With bar code on cover* | | | |
| PC 34733 | You Are So Beautiful | 197? | 8.00 |
| *—With bar code on cover* | | | |
| PC 34733 | You Are So Beautiful | 1977 | 12.00 |
| *—No bar code on cover* | | | |
| **COLUMBIA SPECIAL PRODUCTS** | | | |
| P 15770 | The Best of Tanya Tucker | 1981 | 12.00 |
| **MCA** | | | |
| 654 | Tanya Tucker | 1980 | 8.00 |
| *—Reissue of 2141* | | | |
| 655 | Lovin' and Learnin' | 1980 | 8.00 |
| *—Reissue of 2167* | | | |
| 656 | Here's Some Love | 1980 | 8.00 |
| *—Reissue of 2213* | | | |
| 657 | Ridin' Rainbows | 1980 | 8.00 |
| *—Reissue of 2253* | | | |
| 2141 | Tanya Tucker | 1975 | 12.00 |
| 2167 | Lovin' and Learnin' | 1976 | 12.00 |
| 2213 | Here's Some Love | 1976 | 12.00 |
| 2253 | Ridin' Rainbows | 1977 | 12.00 |
| 3032 | Tanya Tucker's Greatest Hits | 1978 | 12.00 |
| 3066 | TNT | 1978 | 12.00 |
| *—Original gatefold cover* | | | |
| 5106 | Tear Me Apart | 1979 | 10.00 |
| 5140 | Dreamlovers | 1980 | 10.00 |
| 5228 | Should I Do It | 1981 | 10.00 |
| 5299 | Tanya Tucker Live | 1982 | 10.00 |
| 5357 | The Best of Tanya Tucker | 1983 | 10.00 |
| 27030 | Dreamlovers | 198? | 8.00 |
| *—Reissue of 5140* | | | |
| 37075 | TNT | 1981 | 8.00 |
| *—Reissue of 3066; gatefold removed* | | | |
| 37158 | Tear Me Apart | 1981 | 8.00 |
| *—Reissue of 5106* | | | |
| 37225 | Greatest Hits | 1984 | 8.00 |
| *—Reissue of 3032* | | | |
| 37242 | Tanya Tucker Live | 1984 | 8.00 |
| *—Reissue of 5299* | | | |

## TUCKER, TOMMY

| Number | Title (A Side/B Side) | Yr | NM |
|---|---|---|---|
| **CHECKER** | | | |
| LP-2990 [M] | Hi-Heel Sneakers | 1964 | 250.00 |
| *—Black label* | | | |
| LP-2990 [M] | Hi-Heel Sneakers | 1965 | 120.00 |
| *—Blue label with checkers* | | | |

## TURBANS, THE

| Number | Title (A Side/B Side) | Yr | NM |
|---|---|---|---|
| **HERALD** | | | |
| 5009 | Presenting the Turbans | 197? | 20.00 |
| *—No such album was released in the 1950s; this is a bootleg that has some collector value.* | | | |
| **LOST-NITE** | | | |
| LLP-25 [10] | The Turbans | 1981 | 10.00 |
| *—Red vinyl* | | | |
| **RELIC** | | | |
| 5009 | The Turbans' Greatest Hits | 198? | 12.00 |

## TURNER, HANK

| Number | Title (A Side/B Side) | Yr | NM |
|---|---|---|---|
| **COLUMBIA** | | | |
| CL 1958 [M] | Golden Country and Western Hits | 1963 | 20.00 |
| CS 8758 [S] | Golden Country and Western Hits | 1963 | 25.00 |

## TURNER, IKE Also see IKE AND TINA TURNER.

| Number | Title (A Side/B Side) | Yr | NM |
|---|---|---|---|
| **CROWN** | | | |
| CST-367 [R] | Ike Turner Rocks the Blues | 1963 | 100.00 |
| CLP-5367 [M] | Ike Turner Rocks the Blues | 1963 | 200.00 |
| **FANTASY** | | | |
| F-9597 | The Edge | 1980 | 10.00 |
| **POMPEII** | | | |
| SD 6003 | A Black Man's Soul | 1969 | 15.00 |
| **UNITED ARTISTS** | | | |
| UA-LA087-F | Bad Dreams | 1973 | 15.00 |
| UAS-5576 | Blues Roots | 1972 | 15.00 |

## TURNER, IKE AND TINA Also see IKE TURNER; TINA TURNER.

| Number | Title (A Side/B Side) | Yr | NM |
|---|---|---|---|
| **A&M** | | | |
| SP-3179 | River Deep — Mountain High | 1982 | 10.00 |
| *—Budget-line reissue* | | | |
| SP-4178 | River Deep — Mountain High | 1969 | 25.00 |
| *—Official release of Philles 4011* | | | |
| **ABC** | | | |
| 4014 | 16 Great Performances | 1975 | 12.00 |

**Number | Title (A Side/B Side) | Yr | NM**

ACCORD
❑ SN-7147 | Hot and Sassy | 1981 | 10.00

BLUE THUMB
❑ BTS 5 | Outta Season | 1968 | 15.00
❑ BTS 11 | The Hunter | 1969 | 15.00
❑ BTS 49 | The Best of Ike & Tina Turner | 1973 | 12.00
❑ BTS-8805 | Outta Season | 1971 | 12.00
*—Early reissue of Blue Thumb 5*

CAPITOL
❑ ST-571 | Her Man, His Woman | 1971 | 15.00

COLLECTABLES
❑ COL-5107 | Golden Classics | 198? | 10.00
❑ COL-5137 | It's Gonna Work Out Fine | 198? | 10.00

EMI AMERICA
❑ ST-17212 | It's Gonna Work Out Fine | 1986 | 10.00
❑ SQ-17216 | Workin' Together | 1986 | 10.00

HARMONY
❑ HS 11360 | Ooh Poo Pah Doo | 1969 | 15.00
❑ H 30567 | Something's Got a Hold on Me | 1971 | 15.00

KENT
❑ KST-514 [S] | The Ike and Tina Turner Revue Live | 1964 | 40.00
❑ KST-519 [S] | The Soul of Ike and Tina | 1966 | 40.00
❑ KST-538 | Festival of Live Performances | 1969 | 30.00
❑ KST-550 | Please Please Please | 1971 | 30.00
❑ K-5014 [M] | The Ike and Tina Turner Revue Live | 1964 | 30.00
❑ K-5019 [M] | The Soul of Ike and Tina | 1966 | 30.00

LIBERTY
❑ LT-917 | Airwaves | 1981 | 8.00
❑ LST-7637 | Come Together | 1970 | 15.00
❑ LST-7650 | Workin' Together | 1970 | 15.00
❑ LO-51156 | Get Back! | 1985 | 10.00

LOMA
❑ L 5904 [M] | Live! The Ike & Tina Turner Show Vol. 2 | 1966 | 25.00
❑ LS 5904 [S] | Live! The Ike & Tina Turner Show, Vol. 2 | 1966 | 30.00
*—Reissue of Warner Bros. 1579?*

MINIT
❑ 24018 | In Person | 1969 | 20.00

PHILLES
❑ PHLP 4011 [M] | River Deep — Mountain High | 1967 | 8000.
*—Value is for record alone; covers were not printed*

PICKWICK
❑ SPC-3284 | Too Hot to Hold | 197? | 10.00

POMPEII
❑ 6000 [M] | So Fine | 1968 | 60.00
*—Mono is white label promo only; fromt cover has "d/j copy monaural" sticker on it*
❑ SD 6000 [S] | So Fine | 1968 | 25.00
❑ SD 6004 | Cussin', Cryin' and Carryin' On | 1969 | 25.00
❑ SD 6006 | Get It Together | 1969 | 25.00

STRIPED HORSE
❑ SHL-2001 | Golden Empire | 1986 | 10.00

SUE
❑ LP 1038 [M] | The Greatest Hits of Ike and Tina Turner | 1965 | 300.00
❑ LP 2001 [M] | The Soul of Ike and Tina Turner | 1961 | 400.00
❑ LP 2003 [M] | Ike and Tina Turner's Kings of Rhythm Dance | 1962 | 400.00
*—Despite the title, this is an all-instrumental album (Tina's vocals do not appear)*
❑ LP 2004 [M] | Dynamite | 1963 | 400.00
❑ LP 2005 [M] | Don't Play Me Cheap | 1963 | 400.00
❑ LP 2007 [M] | It's Gonna Work Out Fine | 1963 | 400.00

SUNSET
❑ SUS-5265 | The Fantastic Ike & Tina Turner | 1969 | 15.00
❑ SUS-5286 | Ike & Tima Turner's Greatest Hits | 1969 | 15.00

UNART
❑ S 21021 | Greatest Hits | 197? | 10.00

UNITED ARTISTS
❑ UA-LA064-G [(2)] | The World of Ike & Tina Live | 1973 | 15.00
❑ UA-LA180-F | Nutbush City Limits | 1973 | 12.00
❑ UA-LA203-G | The Gospel According to Ike & Tina Turner | 1974 | 12.00
❑ UA-LA312-G | Sweet Rhode Island Red | 1974 | 12.00
❑ UA-LA592-G | Greatest Hits | 1976 | 12.00
❑ UA-LA707-G | Delilah's Power | 1977 | 12.00
❑ UA-LA917-H | Airwaves | 1978 | 12.00
❑ UAS-5530 | 'Nuff Said | 1971 | 12.00
❑ UAS-5598 | Feel Good | 1972 | 12.00
❑ UAS-5660 | Let Me Touch Your Mind | 1972 | 12.00
❑ UAS-5667 | Ike & Tina Turner's Greatest Hits | 1972 | 12.00
❑ UAS-9953 [(2)] | Live at Carnegie Hall/What You Hear Is What You Get | 1971 | 15.00

WARNER BROS.
❑ W 1579 [M] | Live! The Ike & Tina Turner Show | 1965 | 30.00
❑ WS 1579 [S] | Live! The Ike & Tina Turner Show | 1965 | 40.00
❑ WS 1810 | Ike & Tina Turner's Greatest Hits | 1969 | 25.00

**TURNER, JOE**

ARHOOLIE
❑ 2004 [M] | Jumpin' the Blues | 1962 | 20.00

ATLANTIC
❑ 1234 [M] | The Boss of the Blues | 1956 | 120.00
*—Black label*
❑ 1234 [M] | The Boss of the Blues | 1960 | 100.00
*—White "bullseye" label*
❑ 1234 [M] | The Boss of the Blues | 1961 | 40.00
*—White "fan" logo on label*
❑ SD 1234 [S] | The Boss of the Blues | 1959 | 180.00
*—Green label*
❑ SD 1234 [S] | The Boss of the Blues | 1960 | 150.00
*—White "bullseye" label*
❑ SD 1234 [S] | The Boss of the Blues | 1961 | 50.00
*—White "fan" logo on label*
❑ SD 1234 [S] | The Boss of the Blues | 1963 | 20.00
*—Black "fan" logo on label*
❑ 1332 [M] | Big Joe Rides Again | 1959 | 150.00
*—Black label*
❑ 1332 [M] | Big Joe Rides Again | 1960 | 40.00
*—White "fan" logo on label*
❑ SD 1332 [S] | Big Joe Rides Again | 1959 | 200.00
*—Green label*
❑ SD 1332 [S] | Big Joe Rides Again | 1960 | 50.00
*—White "fan" logo on label*
❑ SD 1332 [S] | Big Joe Rides Again | 1963 | 20.00
*—Black "fan" logo on label*
❑ 8005 [M] | Joe Turner | 1957 | 150.00
*—Black label*
❑ 8005 [M] | Joe Turner | 1961 | 40.00
*—White "fan" logo on label*
❑ 8023 [M] | Rockin' the Blues | 1958 | 120.00
*—Black label*
❑ 8023 [M] | Rockin' the Blues | 1960 | 40.00
*—White "fan" logo on label*
❑ 8033 [M] | Big Joe Is Here | 1959 | 120.00
*—Black label*
❑ 8033 [M] | Big Joe Is Here | 1960 | 40.00
*—White "fan" logo on label*
❑ 8033 [M] | Big Joe Is Here | 1960 | 100.00
*—White "bullseye" label*
❑ 8081 [M] | The Best of Joe Turner | 1963 | 50.00

BLUESTIME
❑ 9002 [M] | The Real Boss of the Blues | 196? | 40.00
❑ 29002 [S] | The Real Boss of the Blues | 196? | 30.00

BLUESWAY
❑ BL 6006 [M] | Singing the Blues | 1967 | 20.00
❑ BLS-6006 [S] | Singing the Blues | 1967 | 25.00

DECCA
❑ DL 8044 [M] | Joe Turner Sings Kansas City Jazz | 1953 | 250.00

SAVOY
❑ MG-14012 [M] | Blues'll Make You Happy | 1958 | 150.00
❑ MG-14106 [M] | Careless Love | 1963 | 80.00

**TURNER, JOE, AND PETE JOHNSON**

EMARCY
❑ MG-36014 [M] | Joe Turner and Pete Johnson | 1955 | 200.00

**TURNER, RAY**

CAPITOL
❑ H 306 [10] | Kitten on the Keys | 1952 | 50.00

**TURNER, SAMMY**

BIG TOP
❑ 12-1301 [M] | Lavender Blue Moods | 1959 | 300.00
*—May not exist in stereo*

**TURNER, SPYDER**

MGM
❑ E-4450 [M] | Stand By Me | 1967 | 25.00
❑ SE-4450 [S] | Stand By Me | 1967 | 30.00

WHITFIELD
❑ BSK 3124 | Music Web | 1978 | 10.00
❑ BSK 3397 | Only Love | 1979 | 10.00

**TURNER, TINA** Also see IKE AND TINA TURNER.

CAPITOL
❑ 1P 8192 [(2)] | Simply the Best | 1991 | 20.00
*—Columbia House edition (only US vinyl version)*
❑ ST-12330 | Private Dancer | 1984 | 8.00
❑ PJ-12530 | Break Every Rule | 1986 | 8.00
❑ C1-90126 [(2)] | Tina Live in Europe | 1988 | 12.00
❑ C1-91873 | Foreign Affair | 1989 | 8.00

FANTASY
❑ MFP-4520 [EP] | Mini | 1984 | 8.00

SPRINGBOARD
❑ SPB-4033 | The Queen | 1972 | 10.00

UNITED ARTISTS
❑ UA-LA200-F | Tina Turns the Country On | 1973 | 15.00
❑ UA-LA495-G | Acid Queen | 1975 | 12.00
❑ UA-LA919-G | Rough | 1978 | 12.00

WAGNER
❑ 14108 | Good Hearted Woman | 1979 | 12.00

**TURNER, TITUS**

JAMIE
❑ JLP-3018 [M] | Sound Off | 1961 | 20.00
❑ JLPS-3018 [S] | Sound Off | 1961 | 30.00

**TURNER, VELVERT, GROUP**

FAMILY PRODUCTIONS
❑ FPS-2704 | Velvert Turner Group | 1972 | 50.00

**TURNER, ZEB**

AUDIO LAB
❑ AL-1537 [M] | Country Music in the Turner Style | 1959 | 150.00

**TURNQUIST REMEDY**

PENTAGRAM
❑ PE-10004 | Turnquist Remedy | 1970 | 25.00

**TURRENTINE, STANLEY**

BLUE NOTE
❑ BLP-4039 [M] | Look Out! | 1960 | 150.00
*—Regular version with W. 63rd St. address on label*
❑ BLP-4039 [M] | Look Out! | 1960 | 200.00
*—"Deep groove" version; W. 63rd St. address on label*
❑ BLP-4039 [M] | Look Out! | 1963 | 40.00
*—With New York, USA address on label*
❑ BLP-4057 [M] | Blue Hour | 1961 | 150.00
*—With W. 63rd St. addresss on label*
❑ BLP-4057 [M] | Blue Hour | 1963 | 40.00
*—With New York, USA address on label*
❑ BLP-4069 [M] | Up at Minton's, Volume 1 | 1961 | 120.00
*—With W. 63rd St. addresss on label*
❑ BLP-4069 [M] | Up at Minton's, Volume 1 | 1963 | 40.00
*—With New York, USA address on label*
❑ BLP-4070 [M] | Up at Minton's, Volume 2 | 1961 | 120.00
*—With W. 63rd St. addresss on label*
❑ BLP-4070 [M] | Up at Minton's, Volume 2 | 1963 | 40.00
*—With New York, USA address on label*
❑ BLP-4081 [M] | Dearly Beloved | 1961 | 120.00
*—With W. 63rd St. address on label*
❑ BLP-4081 [M] | Dearly Beloved | 1963 | 40.00
*—With New York, USA address on label*
❑ BLP-4096 [M] | That's Where It's At | 1962 | 120.00
*—With W. 63rd St. address on label*
❑ BLP-4096 [M] | That's Where It's At | 1963 | 60.00
*—With New York, USA address on label*
❑ BLP-4129 [M] | Never Let Me Go | 1963 | 60.00
❑ BLP-4150 [M] | A Chip Off the Old Block | 1963 | 60.00
❑ BLP-4162 [M] | Hustlin' | 1964 | 60.00
❑ BLP-4201 [M] | Joyride | 1965 | 50.00
❑ BLP-4240 [M] | Rough 'n Tumble | 1966 | 50.00
❑ BLP-4256 [M] | The Spoiler | 1967 | 80.00
*—"A Division of Liberty Records" on label*
❑ BLP-4268 [M] | Easy Walker | 1967 | 100.00
*—"A Division of Liberty Records" on label*
❑ BST-84039 [S] | Look Out! | 1960 | 60.00
*—With W. 63rd St. address on label*
❑ BST-84039 [S] | Look Out! | 1963 | 40.00
*—With New York, USA address on label*
❑ BST-84057 [S] | Blue Hour | 1961 | 120.00
*—With W. 63rd St. addresss on label*
❑ BST-84057 [S] | Blue Hour | 1963 | 40.00
*—With New York, USA address on label*
❑ BST-84069 [S] | Up at Minton's, Volume 1 | 1961 | 120.00
*—With W. 63rd St. addresss on label*
❑ BST-84069 [S] | Up at Minton's, Volume 1 | 1963 | 40.00
*—With New York, USA address on label*
❑ BST-84070 [S] | Up at Minton's, Volume 2 | 1961 | 120.00
*—With W. 63rd St. addresss on label*
❑ BST-84070 [S] | Up at Minton's, Volume 2 | 1963 | 40.00
*—With New York, USA address on label*
❑ BST-84081 [S] | Dearly Beloved | 1961 | 120.00
*—With W. 63rd St. address on label*
❑ BST-84081 [S] | Dearly Beloved | 1963 | 50.00
*—With New York, USA address on label*
❑ BST-84096 [S] | That's Where It's At | 1962 | 120.00
*—With W. 63rd St. address on label*
❑ BST-84096 [S] | That's Where It's At | 1963 | 50.00
*—With New York, USA address on label*
❑ BST-84129 [S] | Never Let Me Go | 1963 | 60.00
*—With New York, USA address on label*
❑ BST-84150 [S] | A Chip Off the Old Block | 1963 | 60.00
*—With New York, USA address on label*
❑ BST-84162 [S] | Hustlin' | 1964 | 60.00
*—With New York, USA address on label*
❑ BST-84201 [S] | Joyride | 1964 | 60.00
*—With New York, USA address on label*
❑ BST-84240 [S] | Rough 'n Tumble | 1966 | 50.00
*—With New York, USA address on label*
❑ BST-84256 [S] | The Spoiler | 1967 | 40.00
*—"A Division of Liberty Records" on label*
❑ BST-84268 [S] | Easy Walker | 1967 | 50.00
*—"A Division of Liberty Records" on label*
❑ BST-84286 | The Look of Love | 1968 | 30.00
*—With "A Division of Liberty Records" on label*
❑ BST-84298 | Always Something There | 1968 | 40.00
*—"A Division of Liberty Records" on label*
❑ BST-84315 | Common Touch! | 1969 | 30.00
*—"A Division of Liberty Records" on label*
❑ BST-84336 | Another Story | 1969 | 40.00
*—"A Division of Liberty Records" on label*

| Number | Title (A Side/B Side) | Yr | NM |
|---|---|---|---|
| **FANTASY** | | | |
| ❑ FPM-4002 [Q] | Pieces of Dreams | 1974 | 25.00 |
| **IMPULSE!** | | | |
| ❑ AS-9115 | Let It Go | 1967 | 25.00 |
| **MAINSTREAM** | | | |
| ❑ S-6041 [S] | Tiger Tail | 1965 | 50.00 |
| ❑ 56041 [M] | Tiger Tail | 1965 | 40.00 |
| **TIME** | | | |
| ❑ S-2086 [S] | Stan the Man | 1962 | 120.00 |
| ❑ 52086 [M] | Stan the Man | 1962 | 100.00 |

## TURRENTINE, TOMMY

| Number | Title (A Side/B Side) | Yr | NM |
|---|---|---|---|
| **TIME** | | | |
| ❑ ST-70008 [S] | Tommy Turrentine | 1960 | 100.00 |
| ❑ T-70008 [M] | Tommy Turrentine | 1960 | 80.00 |
| *—Reproductions exist* | | | |

## TURTLES, THE Also see FLO AND EDDIE.

| Number | Title (A Side/B Side) | Yr | NM |
|---|---|---|---|
| **RHINO** | | | |
| ❑ RNLP 151 | It Ain't Me Babe | 1983 | 10.00 |
| ❑ RNLP 152 | Happy Together | 1983 | 10.00 |
| ❑ RNLP 153 | You Baby | 1983 | 10.00 |
| ❑ RNLP 154 | Wooden Head | 1983 | 10.00 |
| ❑ RNLP 160 | Greatest Hits | 1983 | 10.00 |
| ❑ RNDF 280 [EP] | Turtle-Sized | 1984 | 12.00 |
| *—Green vinyl turtle-shaped EP* | | | |
| ❑ RNPD 900 | 1968 | 1984 | 8.00 |
| ❑ RNPD 901 [PD] | 1968 | 1984 | 12.00 |
| ❑ RNLP 70155 | Chalon Road | 1986 | 10.00 |
| ❑ RNLP 70156 | The Turtles Present the Battle of the Bands | 1986 | 10.00 |
| ❑ RNLP 70157 | Turtle Soup | 1986 | 10.00 |
| ❑ RNLP 70158 | Shell Shock | 1986 | 10.00 |
| ❑ RNLP 70159 | Turtle Wax: The Best of the Turtles, Vol. 2 | 1988 | 10.00 |
| ❑ RNLP 70177 | The Best of the Turtles (Golden Archives Series) | 1987 | 10.00 |
| **SIRE** | | | |
| ❑ SASH-3703 [(2)] | The Turtles' Greatest Hits/ Happy Together Again | 1974 | 20.00 |
| **WHITE WHALE** | | | |
| ❑ WW 111 [M] | It Ain't Me Babe | 1965 | 30.00 |
| ❑ WW 112 [M] | You Baby | 1966 | 30.00 |
| ❑ WW 114 [M] | Happy Together | 1967 | 20.00 |
| ❑ WW 115 [M] | The Turtles! Golden Hits | 1967 | 25.00 |
| ❑ WWS 7111 [S] | It Ain't Me Babe | 1965 | 40.00 |
| ❑ WWS 7112 [S] | You Baby | 1966 | 40.00 |
| ❑ WWS 7114 [S] | Happy Together | 1967 | 25.00 |
| ❑ WWS 7115 [S] | The Turtles! Golden Hits | 1967 | 20.00 |
| ❑ WWS 7118 | The Turtles Present the Battle of the Bands | 1968 | 25.00 |
| ❑ WW 7124 | Turtle Soup | 1969 | 25.00 |
| ❑ WW 7127 | The Turtles! More Golden Hits | 1970 | 20.00 |
| ❑ WW 7133 | Wooden Head | 1970 | 20.00 |

## TUXEDOMOON

| Number | Title (A Side/B Side) | Yr | NM |
|---|---|---|---|
| **RALPH** | | | |
| ❑ TX 8004-L | Half-Mute | 1980 | 12.00 |
| ❑ TX 8104 | Desire | 1981 | 12.00 |
| ❑ TX 8354 | A Thousand Lives by Picture | 1983 | 12.00 |
| **TUXEDOMOON** | | | |
| ❑ EP 45 [EP] | Tuxedomoon | 1978 | 20.00 |
| ❑ EP 79 [EP] | Scream with a View | 1979 | 20.00 |

## TWARDZIK, RICHARD

| Number | Title (A Side/B Side) | Yr | NM |
|---|---|---|---|
| **PACIFIC JAZZ** | | | |
| ❑ PJ-37 [M] | The Last Set | 1962 | 60.00 |

## TWENTIETH CENTURY ZOO, THE

| Number | Title (A Side/B Side) | Yr | NM |
|---|---|---|---|
| **VAULT** | | | |
| ❑ LPS-122 | Thunder on a Clear Day | 1968 | 60.00 |

## 21ST CENTURY, THE

| Number | Title (A Side/B Side) | Yr | NM |
|---|---|---|---|
| **RCA VICTOR** | | | |
| ❑ APL1-1189 | Ahead of Our Time | 1975 | 30.00 |

## $27 SNAP-ON FACE

| Number | Title (A Side/B Side) | Yr | NM |
|---|---|---|---|
| **HETERODYNE** | | | |
| ❑ 0001 | $27 Snap-On Face | 1977 | 100.00 |
| *—Blue vinyl; with lyric sheet* | | | |

## TWINK

| Number | Title (A Side/B Side) | Yr | NM |
|---|---|---|---|
| **SIRE** | | | |
| ❑ SES-97022 | Think Pink | 1970 | 100.00 |

## TWINS, THE

| Number | Title (A Side/B Side) | Yr | NM |
|---|---|---|---|
| **RCA VICTOR** | | | |
| ❑ LPM-1708 [M] | Teenagers Love the Twins | 1958 | 50.00 |

## TWISTERS, THE

| Number | Title (A Side/B Side) | Yr | NM |
|---|---|---|---|
| **TREASURE** | | | |
| ❑ TLP-890 [M] | Doin' the Twist | 1962 | 30.00 |

## TWISTIN' KINGS

| Number | Title (A Side/B Side) | Yr | NM |
|---|---|---|---|
| **MOTOWN** | | | |
| ❑ M-601 [M] | Twistin' the World Around | 1961 | 300.00 |

## TWITTY, CONWAY

| Number | Title (A Side/B Side) | Yr | NM |
|---|---|---|---|
| **ACCORD** | | | |
| ❑ SN-7169 | Early Favorites | 1982 | 12.00 |
| **ALLEGIANCE** | | | |
| ❑ AV-5012 | You Made Me What I Am | 1983 | 15.00 |
| **DECCA** | | | |
| ❑ DL 4724 [M] | Conway Twitty Sings | 1965 | 25.00 |
| ❑ DL 4828 [M] | Look Into My Teardrops | 1966 | 25.00 |
| ❑ DL 4913 [M] | Conway Twitty Country | 1967 | 30.00 |
| ❑ DL 4990 [M] | Here's Conway Twitty | 1968 | 50.00 |
| ❑ DL 74724 [S] | Conway Twitty Sings | 1965 | 30.00 |
| ❑ DL 74828 [S] | Look Into My Teardrops | 1966 | 30.00 |
| ❑ DL 74913 [S] | Conway Twitty Country | 1967 | 30.00 |
| ❑ DL 74990 [S] | Here's Conway Twitty | 1968 | 30.00 |
| ❑ DL 75062 | Next in Line | 1968 | 25.00 |
| ❑ DL 75105 | Darling, You Know I Wouldn't Lie | 1968 | 20.00 |
| ❑ DL 75131 | I Love You More Today | 1969 | 20.00 |
| ❑ DL 75172 | To See My Angel Cry | 1970 | 20.00 |
| ❑ DL 75209 | Hello Darlin' | 1970 | 20.00 |
| ❑ DL 75248 | Fifteen Years Ago | 1970 | 20.00 |
| ❑ DL 75276 | How Much More Can She Stand | 1971 | 20.00 |
| ❑ DL 75292 | I Wonder What She'll Think About Me Leaving | 1971 | 20.00 |
| ❑ DL 75335 | I Can't See Me Without You | 1972 | 20.00 |
| ❑ DL 75352 | Conway Twitty's Greatest Hits Vol. I | 1972 | 20.00 |
| ❑ DL 75361 | I Can't Stop Loving You/Last Date | 1972 | 20.00 |
| ❑ ST-93776 | How Much More Can She Stand | 1971 | 25.00 |
| *—Capitol Record Club edition* | | | |
| **ELEKTRA** | | | |
| ❑ 60005 | Southern Confort | 1982 | 10.00 |
| ❑ 60115 | #1 Classics, Volume 1 | 1982 | 10.00 |
| ❑ 60182 | Dream Maker | 1982 | 10.00 |
| ❑ 60209 | #1 Classics, Volume 2 | 1982 | 10.00 |
| **HEARTLAND** | | | |
| ❑ HL-1088/9 [(2)] | The Very Best of Conway Twitty | 1989 | 20.00 |
| **MCA** | | | |
| ❑ 18 | To See My Angel Cry | 1973 | 12.00 |
| *—Reissue of Decca 75172* | | | |
| ❑ 19 | Hello Darlin' | 1973 | 12.00 |
| *—Reissue of Decca 75209* | | | |
| ❑ 52 | Conway Twitty's Greatest Hits | 1973 | 12.00 |
| *—Reissue of Decca 75352* | | | |
| ❑ 53 | I Can't Stop Loving You/Last Date | 1973 | 12.00 |
| *—Reissue of Decca 75361* | | | |
| ❑ 303 | She Needs Someone to Hold Her (When She Cries) | 1973 | 15.00 |
| ❑ 359 | You've Never Been This Far Before/Baby's Gone | 1973 | 15.00 |
| ❑ 376 | Clinging to a Saving Hand | 1973 | 60.00 |
| ❑ 406 | Honky Tonk Angel | 1974 | 15.00 |
| ❑ 441 | I'm Not Through Loving You Yet | 1974 | 15.00 |
| ❑ 469 | Linda on My Mind | 1975 | 15.00 |
| ❑ 625 | High Priest of Country | 197? | 10.00 |
| *—Reissue of MCA 2144* | | | |
| ❑ 702 | Conway | 197? | 10.00 |
| *—Reissue of MCA 3063* | | | |
| ❑ 2144 | High Priest of Country Music | 1975 | 15.00 |
| ❑ 2176 | Twitty (This Time I've Hurt Her More Than She Loves Me) | 1975 | 15.00 |
| ❑ 2206 | Now and Then | 1976 | 15.00 |
| ❑ 2235 | Conway Twitty's Greatest Hits, Vol. 2 | 1976 | 15.00 |
| ❑ 2262 | Play Guitar Play | 1977 | 12.00 |
| ❑ 2293 | I've Already Loved You in My Mind | 1977 | 12.00 |
| ❑ 2328 | Georgia Keeps Pullin' on My Ring | 1978 | 12.00 |
| ❑ 2345 | Conway Twitty's Greatest Hits, Vol. 1 | 1978 | 12.00 |
| *—Reissue of Decca 75352* | | | |
| ❑ 3043 | The Very Best of Conway Twitty | 1978 | 12.00 |
| ❑ 3063 | Conway | 1978 | 12.00 |
| ❑ 3086 | Cross Winds | 1979 | 12.00 |
| ❑ 3210 | Heart and Soul | 1980 | 12.00 |
| ❑ 5138 | Rest Your Love on Me | 1980 | 12.00 |
| ❑ 5204 | Mr. T. | 1981 | 12.00 |
| ❑ 5318 | Number Ones | 1982 | 12.00 |
| ❑ 5424 | Classic Conway | 1983 | 10.00 |
| ❑ 5700 | Songwriter | 1986 | 8.00 |
| ❑ 5817 | A Night with Conway Twitty | 1986 | 8.00 |
| ❑ 5969 | Borderline | 1987 | 8.00 |
| ❑ 37081 | Georgia Keeps Pullin' on My Ring | 198? | 8.00 |
| *—Budget-line reissue* | | | |
| ❑ 37163 | Cross Winds | 198? | 8.00 |
| *—Budget-line reissue* | | | |
| ❑ 37227 | Heart and Soul | 1983 | 8.00 |
| *—Budget-line reissue* | | | |
| ❑ 37228 | Rest Your Love on Me | 1983 | 8.00 |
| *—Budget-line reissue* | | | |
| ❑ 37229 | Conway Twitty's Greatest Hits, Vol. 1 | 1983 | 8.00 |
| *—Budget-line reissue* | | | |
| ❑ 42115 | Still in Your Dreams | 1988 | 8.00 |
| ❑ 42297 | House on Old Lonesome Road | 1989 | 12.00 |
| **MCA CORAL** | | | |
| ❑ CB-20000 | I'm So Used to Loving You | 1973 | 12.00 |
| **METRO** | | | |
| ❑ M-512 [M] | It's Only Make Believe | 1966 | 15.00 |
| ❑ MS-512 [S] | It's Only Make Believe | 1966 | 20.00 |
| **MGM** | | | |
| ❑ GAS-110 | Conway Twitty (Golden Archive Series) | 1970 | 20.00 |
| ❑ E-3744 [M] | Conway Twitty Sings | 1959 | 100.00 |
| *—Yellow label* | | | |
| ❑ E-3744 [M] | Conway Twitty Sings | 196? | 300.00 |
| *—Reissue with orange cover and a clean-cut photo of Conway* | | | |
| ❑ E-3744 [M] | Conway Twitty Sings | 1960 | 40.00 |
| *—Black label* | | | |
| ❑ SE-3744 [S] | Conway Twitty Sings | 1959 | 150.00 |
| *—Yellow label* | | | |
| ❑ SE-3744 [S] | Conway Twitty Sings | 196? | 300.00 |
| *—Reissue with orange cover and a clean-cut photo of Conway* | | | |
| ❑ SE-3744 [S] | Conway Twitty Sings | 1960 | 50.00 |
| *—Black label* | | | |
| ❑ E-3786 [M] | Saturday Night with Conway Twitty | 1960 | 70.00 |
| ❑ SE-3786 [S] | Saturday Night with Conway Twitty | 1960 | 100.00 |
| ❑ E-3818 [M] | Lonely Blue Boy | 1960 | 70.00 |
| ❑ SE-3818 [S] | Lonely Blue Boy | 1960 | 100.00 |
| ❑ E-3849 [M] | Conway Twitty's Greatest Hits | 1960 | 40.00 |
| *—Without poster* | | | |
| ❑ E-3849 [M] | Conway Twitty's Greatest Hits | 1960 | 70.00 |
| *—With poster* | | | |
| ❑ SE-3849 [P] | Conway Twitty's Greatest Hits | 1960 | 50.00 |
| *—Without poster* | | | |
| ❑ SE-3849 [P] | Conway Twitty's Greatest Hits | 1960 | 80.00 |
| *—With poster* | | | |
| ❑ E-3907 [M] | The Rock and Roll Story | 1961 | 50.00 |
| ❑ SE-3907 [S] | The Rock and Roll Story | 1961 | 80.00 |
| ❑ E-3943 [M] | The Conway Twitty Touch | 1961 | 50.00 |
| ❑ SE-3943 [S] | The Conway Twitty Touch | 1961 | 80.00 |
| ❑ E-4019 [M] | Portrait of a Fool and Others | 1962 | 40.00 |
| ❑ SE-4019 [S] | Portrait of a Fool and Others | 1962 | 50.00 |
| ❑ E-4089 [M] | R & B '63 | 1963 | 40.00 |
| ❑ SE-4089 [S] | R & B '63 | 1963 | 50.00 |
| ❑ E-4217 [M] | Hit the Road | 1964 | 25.00 |
| ❑ SE-4217 [S] | Hit the Road | 1964 | 30.00 |
| ❑ SE-4650 | You Can't Take the Country Out of Conway | 1969 | 15.00 |
| ❑ SE-4799 | Conway Twitty Hits | 1971 | 15.00 |
| ❑ SE-4837 | Conway Twitty Sings the Blues | 1972 | 15.00 |
| ❑ SES-4844 [(2)] | 20 Great Hits by Conway Twitty | 1973 | 18.00 |
| **PICKWICK** | | | |
| ❑ SPC-3360 | Shake It Up | 1973 | 12.00 |
| **TEE VEE** | | | |
| ❑ TV-1009 | 20 Certified #1 Hits | 1978 | 15.00 |
| *—Alternate number is MCA Special Markets MSM-35003* | | | |
| **WARNER BROS.** | | | |
| ❑ 23869 | Lost in the Feeling | 1983 | 10.00 |
| ❑ 23971 | Merry Twismas | 1983 | 20.00 |
| ❑ 25078 | By Heart | 1984 | 10.00 |
| ❑ 25170 | Conway's Latest Greatest Hits | 1984 | 10.00 |
| ❑ 25207 | Don't Call Him a Cowboy | 1985 | 10.00 |
| ❑ 25294 | Chasin' Rainbows | 1985 | 10.00 |
| ❑ 25406 | Fallin' for You for Years | 1986 | 10.00 |
| ❑ 25777 | #1's — The Warner Bros. Years | 1988 | 8.00 |
| ❑ 60115 | #1 Classics, Volume 1 | 1983 | 8.00 |
| *—Reissue of Elektra LP* | | | |
| ❑ 60182 | Dream Maker | 1983 | 8.00 |
| *—Reissue of Elektra LP* | | | |
| ❑ 60209 | #1 Classics, Volume 2 | 1983 | 8.00 |
| *—Reissue of Elektra LP* | | | |

## TWITTY, CONWAY, AND LORETTA LYNN Also see each artist's individual listings.

| Number | Title (A Side/B Side) | Yr | NM |
|---|---|---|---|
| **DECCA** | | | |
| ❑ DL 75251 | We Only Make Believe | 1971 | 20.00 |
| ❑ DL 75326 | Lead Me On | 1972 | 20.00 |
| **HEARTLAND** | | | |
| ❑ HL-1059/60 [(2)] | The Best of Conway and Loretta | 1987 | 20.00 |
| **MCA** | | | |
| ❑ 8 | We Only Make Believe | 1973 | 12.00 |
| *—Reissue of Decca 75251* | | | |
| ❑ 9 | Lead Me On | 1973 | 12.00 |
| *—Reissue of Decca 75326* | | | |
| ❑ 335 | Louisiana Woman, Mississippi Man | 1973 | 15.00 |
| ❑ 427 | Country Partners | 1974 | 15.00 |
| ❑ 629 | United Talent | 198? | 10.00 |
| *—Reissue of MCA 2209* | | | |

| Number | Title (A Side/B Side) | Yr | NM |
|---|---|---|---|
| ❑ 722 | Honky Tonk Heroes | 198? | 10.00 |
| *—Reissue of MCA 2372* | | | |
| ❑ 723 | Diamond Duet | 198? | 10.00 |
| *—Reissue of MCA 3190* | | | |
| ❑ 2143 | Feelins' | 1975 | 15.00 |
| ❑ 2209 | United Talent | 1976 | 15.00 |
| ❑ 2278 | Dynamic Duo | 1977 | 12.00 |
| ❑ 2354 | Country Partners | 1978 | 10.00 |
| *—Reissue of MCA 427* | | | |
| ❑ 2372 | Honky Tonk Heroes | 1978 | 12.00 |
| ❑ 3164 | The Very Best of Loretta and Conway | 1979 | 12.00 |
| ❑ 3190 | Diamond Duet | 1979 | 12.00 |
| ❑ 5178 | Two's a Party | 1981 | 12.00 |
| ❑ 37237 | The Very Best of Loretta and Conway | 1983 | 8.00 |
| *—Budget-line reissue* | | | |
| ❑ 42216 | Making Believe | 1988 | 8.00 |
| MCA CORAL | | | |
| ❑ CDL-8006 | Never Ending Song of Love | 1973 | 12.00 |
| **2 LIVE CREW, THE** | | | |
| EFFECT | | | |
| ❑ E 3003 | Live in Concert | 1990 | 10.00 |
| LIL' JOE | | | |
| ❑ XR-215 [(2)] | Shake a Lil' Somethin' | 1996 | 15.00 |
| ❑ XR-227 [(2)] | The 2 Live Crew Goes to the Movies — A Decade of Hits | 1997 | 12.00 |
| ❑ XR-231 [(2)] | The Real One | 1998 | 12.00 |
| ❑ XR-238 [(2)] | Greatest Hits Vol. 2 | 1999 | 15.00 |
| ❑ XR- 239 [(2)] | Greatest Hits Vol. 2/Edit | 1999 | 15.00 |
| ❑ 264 [(2)] | Private Personal Parts | 2000 | 12.00 |
| ❑ 286 [(2)] | Essential DJ 12" and Mega Mixes | 2002 | 10.00 |
| LUKE | | | |
| ❑ 122 [(2)] | Greatest Hits | 1992 | 20.00 |
| ❑ 123 [(2)] | Greatest Hits/Edit | 1992 | 20.00 |
| ❑ 207 [(2)] | Back at Your Ass for the Nine-4 | 1994 | 20.00 |
| *—As "The New 2 Live Crew"* | | | |
| ❑ 208 [(2)] | Back At You for '94 | 1994 | 20.00 |
| *—As "The New 2 Live Crew"; edited version* | | | |
| ❑ DMD 1760 [(2)] | Sports Weekend (As Nasty As They Wanna Be Part II) | 1991 | 15.00 |
| *—Promo-only vinyl issue in generic black cardboard sleeve* | | | |
| ❑ 91424 | Banned in the U.S.A. | 1990 | 15.00 |
| *—As "Luke Featuring The 2 Live Crew"* | | | |
| LUKE SKYYWALKER | | | |
| ❑ XR-100 | The 2 Live Crew "Is What We Are" | 1987 | 15.00 |
| ❑ XR-101 | Move Somethin' | 1988 | 12.00 |
| ❑ XR-107 [(2)] | As Nasty As They Wanna Be | 1989 | 15.00 |
| ❑ XR- 108 | As Clean As They Wanna Be | 1989 | 15.00 |
| **2PAC** Includes records as "Makaveli." | | | |
| AMARU/JIVE | | | |
| ❑ 41628 [(3)] | R U Still Down? (Remember Me) | 1997 | 25.00 |
| DEATH ROW | | | |
| ❑ 63008 [(4)] | All Eyez on Me | 2001 | 20.00 |
| *—Reissue* | | | |
| ❑ 63012 [(2)] | The Don Killuminati — The 7 Day Theory | 2001 | 15.00 |
| *—As "Makaveli"; reissue* | | | |
| DEATH ROW/INTERSCOPE | | | |
| ❑ INT2-90039 [(2)] | The Don Killuminati — The 7 Day Theory | 1996 | 15.00 |
| *—As "Makaveli"* | | | |
| ❑ INT4-90301 [(4)] | Greatest Hits | 1998 | 30.00 |
| ❑ 490413-1 [(2)] | Still I Rise | 1999 | 15.00 |
| *—As "2Pac + Outlawz"* | | | |
| ❑ 490840-1 [(4)] | Until the End of Time | 2001 | 30.00 |
| ❑ 524204-1 [(4)] | All Eyez on Me | 1996 | 30.00 |
| INTERSCOPE | | | |
| ❑ 91767 | 2Pacalypse Now | 1991 | 15.00 |
| ❑ 92399 [(2)] | Me Against the World | 1995 | 20.00 |
| RESTLESS | | | |
| ❑ 72737 [(2)] | Strictly 4 My N.I.G.G.A.Z. | 1998 | 15.00 |
| *—Vinyl reissue of 1993 album (we can't prove or disprove the existence of the original Interscope edition on vinyl)* | | | |
| **TYLE, TEDDY** | | | |
| GOLDEN CREST | | | |
| ❑ GC-3060 [M] | Moon Shot | 1959 | 40.00 |
| **TYLER, ALVIN "RED"** | | | |
| ACE | | | |
| ❑ LP-1006 [M] | Rockin' and Rollin' | 1960 | 150.00 |
| ❑ LP-1021 [M] | Twistin' with Mr. Sax | 1962 | 120.00 |
| **TYLER, CHARLES** | | | |
| ESP-DISK' | | | |
| ❑ 1029 [M] | The Charles Tyler Ensemble | 1966 | 20.00 |
| ❑ S-1029 [S] | The Charles Tyler Ensemble | 1966 | 25.00 |
| ❑ S-1059 [S] | Eastern Man Alone | 1968 | 20.00 |

Loretta Lynn & Conway Twitty, *We Only Make Believe,* Decca DL 75251, 1971, $20.

| Number | Title (A Side/B Side) | Yr | NM |
|---|---|---|---|
| **TYLER, T. TEXAS** | | | |
| CAPITOL | | | |
| ❑ ST 1662 [S] | Salvation | 1962 | 30.00 |
| ❑ T 1662 [M] | Salvation | 1962 | 25.00 |
| ❑ ST 2344 [S] | The Hits of T. Texas Tyler | 1965 | 25.00 |
| ❑ T 2344 [M] | The Hits of T. Texas Tyler | 1965 | 20.00 |
| KING | | | |
| ❑ 664 [M] | T. Texas Tyler | 1959 | 120.00 |
| ❑ 689 [M] | The Great Texan | 1960 | 120.00 |
| ❑ 721 [M] | T. Texas Tyler | 1961 | 80.00 |
| ❑ 734 [M] | Songs Along the Way | 1962 | 80.00 |
| SOUND | | | |
| ❑ 607 [M] | Deck of Cards | 1958 | 80.00 |
| STARDAY | | | |
| ❑ SLP-379 [M] | The Man with a Million Friends | 1966 | 25.00 |
| WRANGLER | | | |
| ❑ W-1002 [M] | T. Texas Tyler | 1962 | 40.00 |
| ❑ W-31002 [S] | T. Texas Tyler | 1962 | 50.00 |
| **TYLER, WILLIE, AND LESTER** | | | |
| TAMLA | | | |
| ❑ TM-265 [M] | Hello Dummy | 1965 | 200.00 |
| **TYMES, THE** | | | |
| ABKCO | | | |
| ❑ 4228 | The Best of Tymes | 1973 | 12.00 |
| COLUMBIA | | | |
| ❑ CS 9778 | People | 1969 | 15.00 |
| PARKWAY | | | |
| ❑ P 7032 [M] | So Much in Love | 1963 | 40.00 |
| *—With group standing in front-cover photo* | | | |
| ❑ P 7032 [M] | So Much in Love | 1963 | 200.00 |
| *—With head-and-shoulders group photo on front cover* | | | |
| ❑ P 7038 [M] | The Sound of the Wonderful Tymes | 1963 | 40.00 |
| ❑ SP 7038 [S] | The Sound of the Wonderful Tymes | 1963 | 50.00 |
| ❑ P 7039 [M] | Somewhere | 1964 | 50.00 |
| *—Includes bonus single 7039 (deduct 20 percent if missing)* | | | |
| ❑ P 7049 [M] | 18 Greatest Hits | 1964 | 40.00 |
| RCA VICTOR | | | |
| ❑ APL1-0727 | Trustmaker | 1974 | 12.00 |

| Number | Title (A Side/B Side) | Yr | NM |
|---|---|---|---|
| ❑ APL1-1835 | Turning Point | 1976 | 12.00 |
| ❑ APL1-2406 | Diggin' Their Roots | 1977 | 12.00 |
| **TYNER, MCCOY** | | | |
| BLUE NOTE | | | |
| ❑ BLP-4264 [M] | The Real McCoy | 1967 | 25.00 |
| ❑ BST-84264 [S] | The Real McCoy | 1967 | 20.00 |
| *—With "A Division of Liberty Records" on label* | | | |
| ❑ BST-84275 | Tender Moments | 1968 | 20.00 |
| *—With "A Division of Liberty Records" on label* | | | |
| ❑ BST-84307 | Time for Tyner | 1969 | 20.00 |
| *—With "A Division of Liberty Records" on label* | | | |
| ❑ BST-84338 | Expansions | 1969 | 20.00 |
| *—With "A Division of Liberty Records" on label* | | | |
| GRP/IMPULSE! | | | |
| ❑ 216 | McCoy Tyner Plays Duke Ellington | 1997 | 20.00 |
| *—Reissue on audiophile vinyl* | | | |
| ❑ 220 | Inception | 1997 | 20.00 |
| *—Reissue on audiophile vinyl* | | | |
| ❑ 221 | Nights of Ballads and Blues | 1997 | 20.00 |
| *—Reissue on audiophile vinyl* | | | |
| IMPULSE! | | | |
| ❑ A-18 [M] | Inception | 1962 | 25.00 |
| ❑ AS-18 [S] | Inception | 1962 | 25.00 |
| ❑ A-33 [M] | Reaching Fourth | 1963 | 25.00 |
| ❑ AS-33 [S] | Reaching Fourth | 1963 | 25.00 |
| ❑ A-39 [M] | Nights of Ballads and Blues | 1963 | 25.00 |
| ❑ AS-39 [S] | Nights of Ballads and Blues | 1963 | 25.00 |
| ❑ A-48 [M] | McCoy Tyner Live at Newport | 1963 | 25.00 |
| ❑ AS-48 [S] | McCoy Tyner Live at Newport | 1963 | 25.00 |
| ❑ A-63 [M] | Today and Tomorrow | 1964 | 25.00 |
| ❑ AS-63 [S] | Today and Tomorrow | 1964 | 25.00 |
| ❑ A-79 [M] | McCoy Tyner Plays Duke Ellington | 1965 | 25.00 |
| ❑ AS-79 [S] | McCoy Tyner Plays Duke Ellington | 1965 | 25.00 |
| MILESTONE | | | |
| ❑ FPM-4006 [Q] | Song of the New World | 197? | 20.00 |
| **TYRANNOSAURUS REX** See T. REX. | | | |

U2, *Pop,* Island 314-524 334-1, 1997, 2 records, $20.

**Number — Title (A Side/B Side) — Yr — NM**

# U

## U2

### ISLAND

❑ PR 2049 [DJ] The Joshua Tree Interview...Their Words and Music 1987 40.00
❑ PR12 7545-1 [(2)]PopMart Sampler 1997 50.00
*—Promo-only 8-song collection of old and new U2 material*
❑ ILPS 9646 Boy 1980 15.00
❑ ILPS 9680 October 1981 12.00
*—Back cover has engineering credits, etc., in upper left*
❑ ILPS 9680 October 1981 15.00
*—Back cover is blank (no engineering credits, etc.) in upper left*
❑ 90040 Boy 1983 8.00
*—Third pressings have black labels*
❑ 90040 Boy 1983 10.00
*—Second pressings have light blue labels*
❑ 90040 Boy 1983 12.00
*—Reissue; first pressings have dark purple labels*
❑ 90067 War 1983 8.00
*—Third pressings have black labels*
❑ 90067 War 1983 10.00
*—Second pressings have light blue labels*
❑ 90067 War 1983 12.00
*—Original pressings have dark purple labels*
❑ 90092 October 1983 8.00
*—Third pressings have black labels*
❑ 90092 October 1983 10.00
*—Second pressings have light blue labels*
❑ 90092 October 1983 10.00
*—Reissue; first pressings have dark purple labels*
❑ 90127-1-B [EP]Under a Blood Red Sky 1983 10.00
*—White labels with "Mini LP" logo; edited version of "The Electric Co."*
❑ 90127-1-B [EP]Under a Blood Red Sky 1983 15.00
*—White labels with "Mini LP" logo; with version of "The Electric Co." in which Bono sings snippets of "A-Me-Ri-Ca" from West Side Story and "Send In The Clowns" during the instrumental break.*
❑ 90231 The Unforgettable Fire 1984 10.00
❑ 90279-1-A [EP]Wide Awake in America 1985 10.00
❑ 90581 The Joshua Tree 1987 10.00
*—With lyric sheet*
❑ 91003 [(2)] Rattle and Hum 1988 15.00
❑ R 114632 October 1983 12.00
*—RCA Music Service edition*
❑ R 124619 War 1983 12.00
*—BMG Direct Marketing edition*
❑ R 140642 [EP] Wide Awake in America 1985 12.00
*—RCA Music Service edition*
❑ R 144636 Boy 1983 12.00
*—RCA Music Service edition*
❑ R 153501 The Joshua Tree 1987 12.00
*—RCA Music Service edition; no lyric sheet*
❑ R 153598 [EP] Under a Blood Red Sky 1983 10.00
*—BMG Direct Marketing edition*
❑ R 154515 The Unforgettable Fire 1985 12.00
*—RCA Music Service edition*
❑ R 200596 [(2)] Rattle and Hum 1988 15.00
*—BMG Direct Marketing edition*
❑ 510347-1 Achtung Baby 1991 40.00
*—U.S. LP covers are uncensored (Adam Clayton appears naked without any "X" or shamrock over his appendage)*
❑ 518047-1 Zooropa 1993 25.00
*—All "U.S." copies actually are British imports*
❑ 524334-1 [(2)] Pop 1997 20.00
❑ 811148-1 War 1990 8.00
*—Reissue; sticker with new number placed over bar code of leftover 90067 pressings*
❑ 818008-1 [EP] Under a Blood Red Sky 1990 8.00
*—Reissue; sticker with new number placed over bar code of leftover 90127 pressings*
❑ 822898-1 The Unforgettable Fire 1990 8.00
*—Reissue; new sticker placed on leftover Island/Atco pressings*
❑ 842296-1 Boy 1990 8.00
*—Reissue; sticker with new number placed over bar code of leftover 90040 pressings*
❑ 842297-1 October 1990 8.00
*—Reissue; sticker with new number placed over bar code of leftover 90092 pressings*
❑ 842298-1 The Joshua Tree 1990 8.00
*—Reissue; sticker with new number placed over bar code of leftover 90581 pressings*
❑ 842299-1 [(2)] Rattle and Hum 1990 12.00
*—Reissue; sticker with new number placed over bar code of leftover 91003 pressings*
❑ 842479-1 [EP] Wide Awake in America 1990 8.00
*—Reissue; sticker with new number placed over bar code of leftover 90279 pressings*

### MOBILE FIDELITY

❑ 1-207 The Unforgettable Fire 1994 25.00
*—Audiophile vinyl*

### WARNER BROS.

❑ WBMS-117 [DJ]Two Sides Live 1981 120.00
*—Promo only, part of "The Warner Bros. Music Show"; legitimate copies are on black vinyl*

## UFO

### CHRYSALIS

❑ CHR 1059 Phenomenon 1974 15.00
*—Green label*
❑ CHR 1059 Phenomenon 1977 12.00
*—Fading blue label*
❑ CHR 1074 Force It 1975 12.00
❑ CHR 1103 No Heavy Petting 1976 12.00
❑ CHR 1127 Lights Out 1977 12.00
❑ CHR 1182 Obsession 1978 12.00
❑ CHR 1209 [(2)] Strangers in the Night 1979 15.00
❑ CHR 1239 No Place to Run 1980 12.00
❑ CHR 1307 The Wild, the Willing and the Innocent 1981 12.00
❑ CHR 1360 Mechanix 1982 12.00
❑ PV 41059 Phenomenon 1983 8.00
❑ PV 41074 Force It 1983 8.00
❑ PV 41103 No Heavy Petting 1983 8.00
❑ FV 41127 Lights Out 1983 8.00
❑ PV 41127 Lights Out 1986 8.00
*—Reissue of FV 41127*
❑ PV 41182 Obsession 1983 8.00
❑ V2X 41209 [(2)]Strangers in the Night 1983 10.00
❑ PV 41239 No Place to Run 1983 8.00
❑ PV 41307 The Wild, the Willing and the Innocent 1983 8.00
❑ PV 41360 Mechanix 1983 8.00
❑ FV 41402 Making Contact 1983 10.00
❑ PV 41402 Making Contact 1986 8.00
*—Reissue of FV 41402*
❑ BFV 41518 Misdemeanor 1986 10.00
❑ FV 41644 The Best of the Rest 1988 10.00

### METAL BLADE/ENIGMA

❑ 7 73404 1 [EP] Ain't Misbehavin' 1989 12.00

### RARE EARTH

❑ RS 624 UFO 1 1971 25.00

## UGGAMS, LESLIE

### ATLANTIC

❑ 8128 [M] Time to Love 1967 15.00
❑ SD 8128 [S] Time to Love 1967 20.00
❑ 8196 [M] What's an Uggams? 1968 40.00
*—Mono is white label promo only; cover has "d/j copy monaural" sticker on front*
❑ SD 8196 [S] What's an Uggams? 1968 15.00
❑ SD 8241 Just to Satisfy You 1969 15.00

### COLUMBIA

❑ CL 1706 [M] Leslie Uggams on TV 1962 15.00
❑ CL 1865 [M] More Leslie Uggams on TV 1963 15.00
❑ CL 2071 [M] So in Love 1963 15.00
❑ CS 8506 [S] Leslie Uggams on TV 1962 20.00
❑ CS 8665 [S] More Leslie Uggams on TV 1963 20.00
❑ CS 8871 [S] So in Love 1963 20.00
❑ CS 9936 Leslie 1970 12.00

### MOTOWN

❑ M6-846 Leslie Uggams 1975 12.00

### SONDAY

❑ 8000 Try to See It My Way 1972 12.00

## ULANO, SAM Drummer.

### LANE

❑ LP-140 [M] Sam Ulano 195? 50.00
❑ LP-151 [M] Sam Ulano Is Mr. Rhythm 195? 50.00

## ULMER, JAMES "BLOOD"

### ARTISTS HOUSE

❑ 13 Are You Glad to Be in America? 1980 20.00
❑ AH 9407 Tales of Captain Black 1979 20.00

### COLUMBIA

❑ ARC 37493 Free Lancing 1981 20.00
❑ ARC 38285 Black Rock 1982 20.00

## ULTIMATE SPINACH

### MGM

❑ E-4518 [M] Ultimate Spinach 1968 30.00
❑ SE-4518 [S] Ultimate Spinach 1968 25.00
❑ E-4570 [M] Behold & See 1968 50.00
*—Mono is promo only (yellow label)*
❑ SE-4570 [S] Behold & See 1968 25.00
❑ SE-4600 Ultimate Spinach 1969 25.00

## ULTRA VIOLET

### CAPITOL

❑ ST-11244 Ultra Violet 1973 25.00

## UMEKI, MIYOSHI

### MERCURY

❑ MG-20568 [M] Miyoshi 1958 20.00
❑ SR-60228 [S] Miyoshi 1959 25.00

### UNBEATABLES, THE

**DAWN**

| Number | Title (A Side/B Side) | Yr | NM |
|---|---|---|---|
| ❑ 5050 [M] | Live at Palisades Park | 1964 | 150.00 |

### UNCLE DOG

**MCA**

| Number | Title (A Side/B Side) | Yr | NM |
|---|---|---|---|
| ❑ 302 | Old Hat | 1973 | 20.00 |

### UNCLE JOSH AND COUSIN JAKE

**COTTON TOWN**

| Number | Title (A Side/B Side) | Yr | NM |
|---|---|---|---|
| ❑ 101 [M] | Just Joshing | 1958 | 100.00 |

### UNCLE KRACKER

**ATLANTIC**

| Number | Title (A Side/B Side) | Yr | NM |
|---|---|---|---|
| ❑ 83279-1 [(2)] | Double Wide | 2000 | 20.00 |
| ❑ 83542-1 [(2)] | No Stranger to Shame | 2002 | 15.00 |

### UNCLE LAR' AND LIL' TOMMY

**WLS**

| Number | Title (A Side/B Side) | Yr | NM |
|---|---|---|---|
| ❑ WLS-890 | Animal Stories | 1981 | 20.00 |
| ❑ WLS-947 | Animal Stories Volume Three | 1983 | 20.00 |
| ❑ WLS-1000 | Animal Stories Volume Two | 1982 | 20.00 |

### UNCLE TUPELO Also see WILCO.

**ROCKVILLE**

| Number | Title (A Side/B Side) | Yr | NM |
|---|---|---|---|
| ❑ 6050-1 | No Depression | 1990 | 60.00 |
| ❑ 6110-1 [(2)] | Still Feel Gone/March 16-20, 1992 | 1992 | 150.00 |

**SUNDAZED**

| Number | Title (A Side/B Side) | Yr | NM |
|---|---|---|---|
| ❑ LP-5153 [(2)] | 89/93: An Anthology | 2002 | 25.00 |

### UNDERGROUND, THE

**WING**

| Number | Title (A Side/B Side) | Yr | NM |
|---|---|---|---|
| ❑ MGW-12337 [M] | Psychedelic Visions | 1967 | 80.00 |
| ❑ SRW-16337 [S] | Psychedelic Visions | 1967 | 100.00 |

### UNDERGROUND SUNSHINE

**INTREPID**

| Number | Title (A Side/B Side) | Yr | NM |
|---|---|---|---|
| ❑ IT-74003 | Let There Be Light | 1969 | 30.00 |

### UNDISPUTED TRUTH, THE

**GORDY**

| Number | Title (A Side/B Side) | Yr | NM |
|---|---|---|---|
| ❑ G 955L | The Undisputed Truth | 1971 | 25.00 |
| ❑ G5-959 | Face to Face with the Truth | 1972 | 20.00 |
| ❑ G5-963 | Law of the Land | 1973 | 20.00 |
| ❑ G6-968 | Down to Earth | 1974 | 20.00 |
| ❑ G6-970 | Cosmic Truth | 1975 | 20.00 |
| ❑ G6-972 | Higher Than High | 1975 | 20.00 |

**WHITFIELD**

| Number | Title (A Side/B Side) | Yr | NM |
|---|---|---|---|
| ❑ BS 2967 | Method to the Madness | 1977 | 20.00 |
| ❑ BSK 3202 | Smokin' | 1979 | 15.00 |

### UNFOLDING

**AUDIO FIDELITY**

| Number | Title (A Side/B Side) | Yr | NM |
|---|---|---|---|
| ❑ AFLP-2184 [M] | How to Blow Your Mind and Have a Freak-Out Party | 1967 | 70.00 |
| ❑ AFSD-6184 [S] | How to Blow Your Mind and Have a Freak-Out Party | 1967 | 100.00 |

### UNIFICS, THE

**KAPP**

| Number | Title (A Side/B Side) | Yr | NM |
|---|---|---|---|
| ❑ KS-3582 | Sittin' In at the Court of Love | 1968 | 25.00 |

### UNIQUES, THE (1)

**PAULA**

| Number | Title (A Side/B Side) | Yr | NM |
|---|---|---|---|
| ❑ LP-2190 [M] | Uniquely Yours | 1966 | 25.00 |
| ❑ LPS-2190 [S] | Uniquely Yours | 1966 | 30.00 |
| ❑ LP-2194 [M] | Happening Now | 1967 | 25.00 |
| ❑ LPS-2194 [S] | Happening Now | 1967 | 30.00 |
| ❑ LP-2199 [M] | Playtime | 1968 | 25.00 |
| ❑ LPS-2199 [S] | Playtime | 1968 | 25.00 |
| ❑ LPS-2204 | The Uniques | 1969 | 25.00 |
| ❑ LPS-2208 | Golden Hits | 1970 | 25.00 |

### UNIT FOUR PLUS TWO

**LONDON**

| Number | Title (A Side/B Side) | Yr | NM |
|---|---|---|---|
| ❑ PS 427 [P] | Unit Four Plus Two #1 | 1965 | 50.00 |
| ❑ LL 3427 [M] | Unit Four Plus Two #1 | 1965 | 40.00 |

### UNITED STATES DOUBLE QUARTET

**B.T. PUPPY**

| Number | Title (A Side/B Side) | Yr | NM |
|---|---|---|---|
| ❑ BTS-1005 | Life Is Groovy | 1969 | 50.00 |

### UNITED STATES OF AMERICA, THE

**COLUMBIA**

| Number | Title (A Side/B Side) | Yr | NM |
|---|---|---|---|
| ❑ CL 2814 [M] | The United States of America | 1968 | 100.00 |
| *—Mono is promo only* | | | |
| ❑ CS 9614 [S] | The United States of America | 1968 | 40.00 |
| *—Without outer bag* | | | |
| ❑ CS 9614 [S] | The United States of America | 1968 | 80.00 |
| *—With outer bag* | | | |

### UNSPOKEN WORD, THE

**ASCOT**

| Number | Title (A Side/B Side) | Yr | NM |
|---|---|---|---|
| ❑ AS 16028 | Tuesday, April 19th | 1968 | 20.00 |

### UNUSUAL WE

**PULSAR**

| Number | Title (A Side/B Side) | Yr | NM |
|---|---|---|---|
| ❑ 10608 | Unusual We | 1969 | 30.00 |

### UPCHURCH, PHIL

**BLUE THUMB**

| Number | Title (A Side/B Side) | Yr | NM |
|---|---|---|---|
| ❑ BTS-59 | Lovin' Feelin' | 1973 | 12.00 |
| ❑ BTS-6005 [(2)] | Darkness, Darkness | 1971 | 20.00 |

**BOYD**

| Number | Title (A Side/B Side) | Yr | NM |
|---|---|---|---|
| ❑ B-398 [M] | You Can't Sit Down | 1961 | 80.00 |
| ❑ BS-398 [S] | You Can't Sit Down | 1961 | 100.00 |

**CADET**

| Number | Title (A Side/B Side) | Yr | NM |
|---|---|---|---|
| ❑ LPS-826 | Upchurch | 1969 | 15.00 |
| ❑ LPS-840 | The Way I Feel | 1970 | 15.00 |

**JAM**

| Number | Title (A Side/B Side) | Yr | NM |
|---|---|---|---|
| ❑ 007 | Free and Easy | 198? | 12.00 |

**KUDU**

| Number | Title (A Side/B Side) | Yr | NM |
|---|---|---|---|
| ❑ 22 | Phil Upchurch and Tennyson Stevens | 1975 | 12.00 |

**MARLIN**

| Number | Title (A Side/B Side) | Yr | NM |
|---|---|---|---|
| ❑ 2209 | Phil Upchurch | 1978 | 12.00 |

**MILESTONE**

| Number | Title (A Side/B Side) | Yr | NM |
|---|---|---|---|
| ❑ MSP-9010 | Feeling Blue | 1968 | 15.00 |

**UNITED ARTISTS**

| Number | Title (A Side/B Side) | Yr | NM |
|---|---|---|---|
| ❑ UAL-3162 [M] | You Can't Sit Down, Part 2 | 1961 | 30.00 |
| ❑ UAL-3175 [M] | Big Hit Dances | 1962 | 25.00 |
| ❑ UAS-6162 [S] | You Can't Sit Down, Part 2 | 1961 | 40.00 |
| ❑ UAS-6175 [S] | Big Hit Dances | 1962 | 30.00 |

### URGE OVERKILL

**GEFFEN**

| Number | Title (A Side/B Side) | Yr | NM |
|---|---|---|---|
| ❑ GEF-24529 | Saturation | 1993 | 12.00 |
| *—All copies on orange vinyl* | | | |
| ❑ GEF-24818 [(2)] | Exit the Dragon | 1995 | 15.00 |

**TOUCH & GO**

| Number | Title (A Side/B Side) | Yr | NM |
|---|---|---|---|
| ❑ 37 | Jesus Urge Superstar | 1989 | 12.00 |
| ❑ 52 | Americruiser | 1990 | 12.00 |
| ❑ 70 | The Supersonic Storybook | 1991 | 12.00 |
| ❑ 86 [10] | Stull | 1992 | 10.00 |
| *—Black vinyl* | | | |
| ❑ 86 [10] | Stull | 1992 | 40.00 |
| *—Whitish vinyl original* | | | |

### URSO, PHIL

**REGENT**

| Number | Title (A Side/B Side) | Yr | NM |
|---|---|---|---|
| ❑ MG-6003 [M] | Sentimental Journey | 1956 | 50.00 |

**SAVOY**

| Number | Title (A Side/B Side) | Yr | NM |
|---|---|---|---|
| ❑ MG-12056 [M] | The Philosophy of Urso | 1956 | 50.00 |
| ❑ MG-15041 [10] | Bob Brookmeyer with Phil Urso | 1954 | 150.00 |

### USSELTON, BILLY

**KAPP**

| Number | Title (A Side/B Side) | Yr | NM |
|---|---|---|---|
| ❑ KL-1051 [M] | Bill Usselton — His First Album | 1957 | 50.00 |

# V

### VAGABONDS, THE

**UNIQUE**

| Number | Title (A Side/B Side) | Yr | NM |
|---|---|---|---|
| ❑ LP-112 [M] | The Vagabonds | 1957 | 25.00 |

### VAGRANTS, THE

**ARISTA**

| Number | Title (A Side/B Side) | Yr | NM |
|---|---|---|---|
| ❑ AL-8459 | The Great Lost Vagrants Album | 1987 | 20.00 |

### VALE, JERRY

**COLUMBIA**

| Number | Title (A Side/B Side) | Yr | NM |
|---|---|---|---|
| ❑ GP 16 [(2)] | With Love, Jerry Vale | 1969 | 15.00 |
| ❑ CS 1021 | Let It Be | 1970 | 12.00 |
| ❑ CL 1114 [M] | I Remember Buddy | 1958 | 15.00 |
| ❑ CL 1164 [M] | I Remember Russ | 1958 | 15.00 |
| ❑ CL 1380 [M] | The Same Old Moon | 1959 | 15.00 |
| ❑ CL 1529 [M] | Jerry Vale's Greatest Hits | 1961 | 15.00 |
| ❑ CL 1797 [M] | I Have But One Heart | 1962 | 12.00 |
| ❑ CL 1955 [M] | Arrivederci, Roma | 1963 | 12.00 |
| ❑ CL 2043 [M] | The Language of Love | 1963 | 12.00 |
| ❑ CL 2116 [M] | Till the End of Time | 1964 | 12.00 |
| ❑ CL 2181 [M] | Be My Love | 1964 | 12.00 |
| ❑ CL 2225 [M] | Christmas Greetings from Jerry Vale | 1964 | 12.00 |
| ❑ CL 2273 [M] | Standing Ovation! | 1965 | 12.00 |
| ❑ CL 2313 [M] | Have You Looked Into Your Heart | 1965 | 12.00 |
| ❑ CL 2371 [M] | Moonlight Becomes You | 1965 | 12.00 |
| ❑ CL 2387 [M] | There Goes My Heart | 1965 | 12.00 |
| ❑ CL 2444 [M] | It's Magic | 1966 | 12.00 |
| ❑ CL 2489 [M] | Great Moments on Broadway | 1966 | 12.00 |
| ❑ CL 2530 [M] | Everybody Loves Somebody | 1966 | 12.00 |
| ❑ CL 2583 [M] | The Impossible Dream | 1967 | 12.00 |
| ❑ CL 2659 [M] | More Jerry Vale's Greatest Hits | 1967 | 15.00 |
| ❑ CL 2684 [M] | Time Alone Will Tell | 1967 | 12.00 |
| ❑ CL 2774 [M] | You Don't Have to Say You Love Me | 1968 | 15.00 |
| ❑ CS 8016 [S] | I Remember Russ | 1958 | 20.00 |
| *—Originals have red and black "6 eye" labels* | | | |
| ❑ CS 8069 [S] | I Remember Buddy | 1959 | 20.00 |
| *—Originals have red and black "6 eye" labels* | | | |
| ❑ CS 8175 [S] | The Same Old Moon | 1960 | 15.00 |
| ❑ CS 8597 [S] | I Have But One Heart | 1962 | 15.00 |
| ❑ CS 8755 [S] | Arrivederci, Roma | 1963 | 15.00 |
| ❑ CS 8778 [R] | Jerry Vale's Greatest Hits | 1963 | 12.00 |
| ❑ CS 8843 [S] | The Language of Love | 1963 | 15.00 |
| ❑ CS 8916 [S] | Till the End of Time | 1964 | 15.00 |
| ❑ CS 8981 [S] | Be My Love | 1964 | 15.00 |
| ❑ CS 9025 [S] | Christmas Greetings from Jerry Vale | 1964 | 15.00 |
| ❑ CS 9073 [S] | Standing Ovation! | 1965 | 15.00 |
| ❑ CS 9113 [S] | Have You Looked Into Your Heart | 1965 | 15.00 |
| ❑ CS 9171 [S] | Moonlight Becomes You | 1965 | 15.00 |
| ❑ CS 9187 [S] | There Goes My Heart | 1965 | 15.00 |
| ❑ CS 9244 [S] | It's Magic | 1966 | 15.00 |
| ❑ CS 9289 [S] | Great Moments on Broadway | 1966 | 15.00 |
| ❑ CS 9383 [S] | The Impossible Dream | 1967 | 15.00 |
| ❑ CS 9459 [S] | More Jerry Vale's Greatest Hits | 1967 | 12.00 |
| ❑ CS 9484 [S] | Time Alone Will Tell | 1967 | 15.00 |
| ❑ CS 9574 [S] | You Don't Have to Say You Love Me | 1968 | 15.00 |
| ❑ CS 9634 | I Hear a Rhapsody | 1968 | 15.00 |
| ❑ CS 9694 | This Guy's in Love with You | 1968 | 15.00 |
| ❑ CS 9757 | Till | 1969 | 15.00 |
| ❑ CS 9838 | Where's the Playground Susie? | 1969 | 15.00 |
| ❑ CS 9982 | Jerry Vale Sings 16 Greatest Hits of the 60's | 1970 | 12.00 |
| ❑ C 30104 | We've Only Just Begun | 1971 | 10.00 |
| ❑ C 30389 | The Italian Album | 1970 | 10.00 |
| ❑ C 30799 | I Don't Know How to Love Her | 1971 | 10.00 |
| ❑ C 31147 | Jerry Vale Sings the Great Hits of Nat King Cole | 1972 | 12.00 |
| ❑ KG 31543 [(2)] | All-Time Greatest Hits | 1972 | 12.00 |
| ❑ KC 31716 | Alone Again (Naturally) | 1972 | 10.00 |
| ❑ KG 31938 [(2)] | Great Italian Hits | 1973 | 12.00 |
| ❑ KG 32083 [(2)] | Jerry Vale Sings the Great Love Songs | 1973 | 12.00 |
| ❑ C 32238 | Love Is a Many-Splendored Thing | 1973 | 10.00 |
| ❑ KC 32454 | Jerry Vale's World | 1973 | 10.00 |
| ❑ KC 32829 | Free As the Wind | 1974 | 10.00 |
| ❑ CG 33615 [(2)] | The Italian Album/Arrivederci, Roma | 1974 | 12.00 |

**COLUMBIA LIMITED EDITION**

| Number | Title (A Side/B Side) | Yr | NM |
|---|---|---|---|
| ❑ LE 10058 | Till | 197? | 10.00 |
| *—Reissue of 9757* | | | |
| ❑ LE 10164 | Christmas Greetings from Jerry Vale | 197? | 10.00 |
| *—Reissue* | | | |

**HARMONY**

| Number | Title (A Side/B Side) | Yr | NM |
|---|---|---|---|
| ❑ HS 11298 | As Long As She Needs Me | 1969 | 10.00 |
| ❑ HS 11376 | Hey Look Me Over | 1970 | 10.00 |
| ❑ KH 30345 | Born Free | 1971 | 10.00 |
| ❑ KH 30759 | More | 1971 | 10.00 |
| ❑ KH 32478 | What a Wonderful World | 1973 | 10.00 |

### VALE, RICKY, AND THE SURFERS

**STRAND**

| Number | Title (A Side/B Side) | Yr | NM |
|---|---|---|---|
| ❑ SL-1104 [M] | Everybody's Surfin' | 1963 | 40.00 |
| ❑ SLS-1104 [S] | Everybody's Surfin' | 1963 | 50.00 |

### VALENS, RITCHIE

**DEL-FI**

| Number | Title (A Side/B Side) | Yr | NM |
|---|---|---|---|
| ❑ DFLP 1201 [M] | Ritchie Valens | 1959 | 150.00 |
| *—Black label with "diamonds" border* | | | |
| ❑ DFLP 1201 [M] | Ritchie Valens | 1959 | 250.00 |
| *—Blue label with black border* | | | |
| ❑ DFLP 1206 [M] | Ritchie | 1959 | 150.00 |
| ❑ DFLP 1214 [M] | In Concert at Pacoima Jr. High | 1960 | 250.00 |
| ❑ DFLP 1225 [M] | His Greatest Hits | 1963 | 150.00 |
| *—White cover* | | | |
| ❑ DFLP 1225 [M] | His Greatest Hits | 1963 | 350.00 |
| *—Black cover* | | | |
| ❑ DFLP 1247 [M] | His Greatest Hits, Volume 2 | 1965 | 150.00 |

**GUEST STAR**

| Number | Title (A Side/B Side) | Yr | NM |
|---|---|---|---|
| ❑ GS-1469 [M] | The Original Ritchie Valens | 1963 | 30.00 |
| ❑ GSS-1469 [R] | The Original Ritchie Valens | 1963 | 20.00 |
| ❑ GS-1484 [M] | The Original La Bamba | 1963 | 30.00 |
| ❑ GSS-1484 [R] | The Original La Bamba | 1963 | 20.00 |

**MGM**

| Number | Title (A Side/B Side) | Yr | NM |
|---|---|---|---|
| ❑ GAS-117 | Ritchie Valens (Golden Archive Series) | 1970 | 30.00 |

**RHINO**

| Number | Title (A Side/B Side) | Yr | NM |
|---|---|---|---|
| ❑ RNDF-200 | The Best of Ritchie Valens | 1981 | 12.00 |
| ❑ RNBC-2798 [(3)] | The History of Ritchie Valens | 198? | 25.00 |
| ❑ RNLP-70178 | The Best of Ritchie Valens (Golden Archive Series) | 1987 | 10.00 |
| ❑ RNLP-70231 | Ritchie Valens | 1987 | 10.00 |
| ❑ RNLP-70232 | Ritchie | 1987 | 10.00 |
| ❑ RNLP-70233 | In Concert at Pacoima Jr. High | 1987 | 10.00 |

Number | Title (A Side/B Side) | Yr | NM

**VALENS, RITCHIE / JERRY KOLE**

CROWN
❑ CLP-5336 [M] Ritchie Valens and Jerry Kole 1963 30.00

**VALENTE, CATERINA**

DECCA
❑ DL 4035 [M] More Schlagerparade 1959 25.00
❑ DL 4050 [M] Caterina A La Carte 1959 25.00
❑ DL 4051 [M] Arriba 1959 25.00
❑ DL 4052 [M] Catarina: The Greatest in Any Language 1959 25.00
❑ DL 4504 [M] Golden Favorites 1964 20.00
❑ DL 8203 [M] The Hi-Fi Nightingale 1956 25.00
❑ DL 8436 [M] Ole Caterina 1957 25.00
❑ DL 8440 [M] Plenty Valente! 1957 25.00
❑ DL 8755 [M] A Toast to the Girls 1958 25.00
❑ DL 8852 [M] Schlagerparade 1958 20.00
❑ DL 74504 [R] Golden Favorites 1964 12.00

LONDON
❑ PS 275 [S] I Wish You Love 196? 15.00
*—With Stanley Black*
❑ PS 307 [S] Strictly U.S.A. 196? 15.00
❑ PS 355 [S] Songs I've Sung on the Perry Como Show 196? 15.00
❑ PS 362 [S] I Happen to Like New York 196? 15.00
❑ PS 363 [S] Valente and Violins 196? 15.00
❑ PS 441 [S] Caterina Valente's Greatest Hits 1965 15.00
❑ PS 471 [S] Go Latin! 196? 15.00
*—With Silvio Francesco*
❑ PS 473 [S] Intimate Valente 196? 15.00
❑ PS 536 Sweet Beat 1969 15.00
❑ LL 3275 [M] I Wish You Love 196? 12.00
*—With Stanley Black*
❑ LL 3307 [M] Strictly U.S.A. 196? 12.00
❑ LL 3355 [M] Songs I've Sung on the Perry Como Show 196? 12.00
❑ LL 3362 [M] I Happen to Like New York 196? 12.00
❑ LL 3363 [M] Valente and Violins 196? 12.00
❑ LL 3441 [M] Caterina Valente's Greatest Hits 1965 12.00
❑ LL 3471 [M] Go Latin! 196? 12.00
*—With Silvio Francesco*
❑ LL 3473 [M] Intimate Valente 196? 12.00
❑ TW 91198 [M] Continental Favorites 196? 15.00
❑ TW 91253 [M] Fire and Frenzy 196? 15.00
*—With Edmundo Ros*
❑ TW 91260 [M] Miss Personality 196? 15.00
❑ TW 91267 [M] German Evergreens 196? 15.00
*—With Silvio Francesco*
❑ TW 91292 [M] South of the Border 196? 15.00
❑ ST-93108 [S] Caterina Valente's Greatest Hits 196? 20.00
*—Capitol Record Club edition*
❑ SW 99019 [S] Fire and Frenzy 196? 20.00
*—With Edmundo Ros*
❑ SW 99025 [S] German Evergreens 196? 20.00
*—With Silvio Francesco*
❑ SW 99292 [S] South of the Border 196? 20.00

LONDON PHASE 4
❑ SP-44125 Silk and Latin 197? 25.00
❑ SP-44181 Love 197? 25.00

PETERS INT'L.
❑ PLD-7021 Golden Days 197? 12.00
❑ PLD-7046 Caterina Valente 197? 12.00

RCA VICTOR
❑ LPM-2119 [M] Classics with a Chaser 1960 20.00
❑ LSP-2119 [S] Classics with a Chaser 1960 25.00
❑ LPM-2241 [M] Superfonics 1961 20.00
❑ LSP-2241 [S] Superfonics 1961 25.00

**VALENTI, DINO**

EPIC
❑ LN 24335 [M] Dino Valenti 1967 20.00
❑ BN 26335 [S] Dino Valenti 1967 20.00

**VALENTINE, HILTON** Former member of THE ANIMALS.

CAPITOL
❑ ST-330 All in Your Head 1969 30.00

**VALENTINE, JIMMIE**

JUBILEE
❑ LP-9 [10] Music to Beat By 1954 40.00

**VALENTINO, MARK**

SWAN
❑ SLP-508 [M] Mark Valentino 1963 50.00

**VALENTYNE, RUDY**

ROULETTE
❑ R-25299 [M] And Now... Rudy Valentyne 1965 20.00
❑ SR-25299 [S] And Now... Rudy Valentyne 1965 25.00

**VALHALLA**

UNITED ARTISTS
❑ UAS-6730 Valhalla 1969 25.00

Number | Title (A Side/B Side) | Yr | NM

**VALIDS, THE**

AMBER
❑ 802 [M] Accapella 1966 25.00

**VALJEAN**

CARLTON
❑ LP-143 [M] The Theme from Ben Casey 1962 20.00
❑ STLP-143 [S] The Theme from Ben Casey 1962 25.00
❑ LP-146 [M] Mashin' the Classics 1963 20.00
❑ STLP-146 [S] Mashin' the Classics 1963 25.00

**VALLEE, RUDY**

RCA VICTOR
❑ LPM-2507 [M] Young Rudy Vallee 1961 30.00
❑ LSP-2507 [R] Young Rudy Vallee 196? 20.00

**VALLEY, JIM**

FIRST AMERICAN
❑ 7710 Dance Inside Your Head 1977 15.00

LIGHT
❑ LS-5564 Family 197? 15.00

PANORAMA
❑ 104-S Jim "Harpo" Valley 1968 40.00

**VALLI, FRANKIE** Also see THE FOUR SEASONS.

MCA
❑ 743 Heaven Above Me 1982 8.00
*—Reissue of 5134*
❑ 756 The Very Best of Frankie Valli 1982 8.00
*—Reissue of 3198*
❑ 3198 The Very Best of Frankie Valli 1980 10.00
❑ 5134 Heaven Above Me 1979 10.00

MOTOWN
❑ M5-104V1 Motown Superstar Series, Vol. 4 1981 10.00
❑ M6-852 Inside You 1975 15.00

PHILIPS
❑ PHM 200247 [M] Frankie Valli — Solo 1967 40.00
❑ PHS 600247 [S] Frankie Valli — Solo 1967 30.00
❑ PHS 600274 Timeless 1968 25.00

PRIVATE STOCK
❑ PS-2000 Closeup 1975 12.00
❑ PS-2001 Frankie Valli Gold 1975 12.00
❑ PS-2006 Our Day Will Come 1975 12.00
❑ PS-2017 Valli 1976 12.00
❑ PS-7002 Lady Put the Light Out 1977 12.00
❑ PS-7012 Hits 1978 12.00

WARNER BROS.
❑ BSK 3233 Frankie Valli...Is the Word 1978 10.00

**VALLI, FRANKIE, AND THE FOUR SEASONS** See THE FOUR SEASONS.

**VALLI, JUNE**

AUDIO FIDELITY
❑ AFSD-6214 [S] June Valli Today 1969 20.00

MERCURY
❑ MG-20463 [M] Do-It-Yourself Wedding Album 1959 20.00
❑ SR-60145 [S] Do-It-Yourself Wedding Album 1959 25.00

RCA VICTOR
❑ LPM-1120 [M] The Torch 1955 40.00

**VAMPIRES, THE**

UNITED ARTISTS
❑ UAL-3378 [M] The Vampires at the Monster Ball 1964 25.00
❑ UAS-6378 [S] The Vampires at the Monster Ball 1964 30.00

**VAN DAMME, ART**

BASF
❑ 25113 [(2)] The Many Moods of Art Van Damme 197? 20.00
❑ 25257 [(2)] Star Spangled Rhythm 197? 20.00

CAPITOL
❑ H 178 [10] Cocktail Capers 1950 50.00
❑ T 178 [M] Cocktail Capers 1954 40.00
❑ L 300 [10] More Cocktail Capers 1952 50.00
❑ T 300 [M] More Cocktail Capers 1954 40.00

COLUMBIA
❑ C2L 7 [(2)M] They're Playing Our Song 1958 40.00
❑ CL 544 [M] The Van Damme Sound 1955 30.00
❑ CL 630 [M] Martini Time 1955 30.00
❑ CL 801 [M] Manhattan Time 1956 30.00
❑ CL 876 [M] The Art of Van Damme 1956 30.00
❑ CL 1382 [M] Everything's Coming Up Music 1959 25.00
❑ CL 1563 [M] Accordion A La Mode 1960 25.00
❑ CL 2585 [10] The Art Van Damme Quintet 1956 40.00
❑ CL 6265 [10] Martini Time 1953 40.00
❑ CS 8177 [S] Everything's Coming Up Music 1959 30.00
❑ CS 8363 [S] Accordion A La Mode 1960 30.00
❑ CS 8594 [M] Art Van Damme Swings Sweetly 1962 20.00

Number | Title (A Side/B Side) | Yr | NM

❑ CS 8813 [S] A Perfect Match 1963 20.00

**VAN DER GRAAF GENERATOR**

ABC DUNHILL
❑ DS 50097 H to He Who Am the Only One 1971 15.00

CHARISMA
❑ CAS-1051 Pawn Hearts 1971 15.00

MERCURY
❑ SRM-1-1069 Godbluff 1975 12.00
❑ SRM-1-1096 Still Life 1976 12.00
❑ SRM-1-1116 World Record 1976 12.00
❑ SR-61238 The Aerosol Grey Machine 1969 100.00

PROBE
❑ CPLP-4515 The Least We Can Do Is Wave to Each Other 1970 30.00

PVC
❑ 9901 [(2)] Vital 1979 15.00

**VAN DERBUR, MARILYN**

DECCA
❑ DL 8770 [M] Miss America 1958 40.00

**VAN DYKE, DICK**

COMMAND
❑ RS 860 SD [S] Songs I Like 1963 30.00
❑ RS 33-860 [M] Songs I Like 1963 25.00

**VAN DYKE, EARL, AND THE SOUL BROTHERS**

MOTOWN
❑ M-631 [M] The Motown Sound 1965 40.00
❑ MS-631 [S] The Motown Sound 1965 50.00

SOUL
❑ SS-715 The Earl of Funk 1970 40.00

**VAN DYKE, LEROY**

DOT
❑ DLP 3693 [M] Auctioneer 1966 20.00

HARMONY
❑ HS 11308 I've Never Been Loved 196? 12.00

KAPP
❑ KS-3571 Lonesome Is 1968 15.00
❑ KS-3605 Greatest Hits 1969 15.00
❑ KS-3607 Just a Closer Walk with Thee 1969 15.00

MCA
❑ 145 Greatest Hits 1973 12.00

MERCURY
❑ MG-20682 [M] Walk On By 1962 20.00
❑ MG-20716 [M] Movin' Van Dyke 1963 20.00
❑ MG-20802 [M] The Great Hits of Leroy Van Dyke 1963 20.00
❑ MG-20922 [M] Songs for Mom and Dad 1964 20.00
❑ MG-20950 [M] Leroy Van Dyke at the Tradewinds 1964 10.00
❑ SR-60682 [S] Walk On By 1962 25.00
❑ SR-60716 [S] Movin' Van Dyke 1963 25.00
❑ SR-60802 [S] The Great Hits of Leroy Van Dyke 1963 25.00
❑ SR-60922 [S] Songs for Mom and Dad 1964 25.00
❑ SR-60950 [S] Leroy Van Dyke at the Tradewinds 1964 25.00

PLANTATION
❑ 516 Gospel Greats 1977 12.00

SUN
❑ 131 Golden Hits 1974 12.00

WARNER BROS.
❑ W 1618 [M] The Leroy Van Dyke Show 1965 15.00
❑ WS 1618 [S] The Leroy Van Dyke Show 1965 20.00
❑ W 1652 [M] Country Hits 1966 15.00
❑ WS 1652 [S] Country Hits 1966 20.00

WING
❑ MGW-12302 [M] Out of Love 196? 12.00
❑ MGW-12322 [M] Movin' 196? 12.00
❑ SRW-16302 [S] Out of Love 196? 15.00
❑ SRW-16322 [S] Movin' 196? 15.00

**VAN DYKES, THE (2)**

BELL
❑ 6004 [M] Tellin' It Like It Is 1967 50.00
❑ S-6004 [S] Tellin' It Like It Is 1967 60.00

**VAN EPS, GEORGE**

CAPITOL
❑ ST 2533 [S] My Guitar 1966 20.00

COLUMBIA
❑ CL 929 [M] Mellow Guitar 1956 40.00

**VAN HALEN**

DCC COMPACT CLASSICS
❑ LPZ-2066 Van Halen 1998 40.00
*—Audiophile vinyl*

| Number | Title (A Side/B Side) | Yr | NM |
|---|---|---|---|
| **WARNER BROS.** | | | |
| ❑ PRO 705 [DJ] | Looney Tunes | 1978 | 60.00 |
| *—Promo-only EP on red vinyl* | | | |
| ❑ BSK 3075 | Van Halen | 1978 | 12.00 |
| *—Early pressings have "Burbank" labels* | | | |
| ❑ BSK 3075 | Van Halen | 1979 | 10.00 |
| *—White/cream labels* | | | |
| ❑ HS 3312 | Van Halen II | 1979 | 10.00 |
| ❑ HS 3415 | Women and Children First | 1980 | 10.00 |
| ❑ HS 3540 | Fair Warning | 1981 | 10.00 |
| ❑ BSK 3677 | Diver Down | 1982 | 10.00 |
| ❑ 23985 | 1984 | 1984 | 10.00 |
| ❑ 23985 [DJ] | 1984 | 1984 | 25.00 |
| *—Promo on Quiex II vinyl* | | | |
| ❑ 25394 | 5150 | 1986 | 10.00 |
| ❑ 25732 | OU812 | 1988 | 10.00 |
| ❑ W1-26594 | For Unlawful Carnal Knowledge | 1991 | 20.00 |
| *—The only U.S. vinyl version was released through Columbia House* | | | |
| ❑ 45760 | Balance | 1995 | 12.00 |

### VAN HEUSEN, JIMMY

| Number | Title (A Side/B Side) | Yr | NM |
|---|---|---|---|
| **UNITED ARTISTS** | | | |
| ❑ UAL-3494 [M] | Van Heusen Plays Van Heusen | 1966 | 20.00 |
| ❑ UAS-6494 [S] | Van Heusen Plays Van Heusen | 1966 | 25.00 |

### VAN RONK, DAVE

| Number | Title (A Side/B Side) | Yr | NM |
|---|---|---|---|
| **CADET** | | | |
| ❑ CA-50044 | Songs for Aging Children | 1973 | 20.00 |
| **FANTASY** | | | |
| ❑ 24710 [(2)] | Dave Van Ronk | 1972 | 20.00 |
| **FOLKLORE** | | | |
| ❑ FRLP-14001 [M] | In the Tradition | 1963 | 30.00 |
| ❑ FRST-14001 [S] | In the Tradition | 1963 | 40.00 |
| ❑ FRLP-14012 [M] | Dave Van Ronk, Folksinger | 1963 | 30.00 |
| ❑ FRST-14012 [S] | Dave Van Ronk, Folksinger | 1963 | 40.00 |
| ❑ FRLP-14025 [M] | Inside Dave Van Ronk | 1964 | 30.00 |
| ❑ FRST-14025 [S] | Inside Dave Van Ronk | 1964 | 40.00 |
| **FOLKWAYS** | | | |
| ❑ FA-2383 [M] | Dave Van Ronk Sings Earthy Ballads and Blues | 1961 | 40.00 |
| ❑ FS-3818 [M] | Dave Van Ronk Sings Ballads, Blues and Spirituals | 1959 | 40.00 |
| ❑ FTS 31020 | Black Mountain Blues | 1968 | 25.00 |
| **MERCURY** | | | |
| ❑ MG-20864 [M] | Dave Van Ronk and the Ragtime Jug Stompers | 1964 | 25.00 |
| ❑ MG-20908 [M] | Just Dave Van Ronk | 1964 | 25.00 |
| ❑ SR-60864 [S] | Dave Van Ronk and the Ragtime Jug Stompers | 1964 | 30.00 |
| ❑ SR-60908 [S] | Just Dave Van Ronk | 1964 | 30.00 |
| **POLYDOR** | | | |
| ❑ 24-4052 | Van Ronk | 1972 | 20.00 |
| **VERVE FOLKWAYS** | | | |
| ❑ FV-9006 [M] | Dave Van Ronk Sings the Blues | 1965 | 25.00 |
| ❑ FVS-9006 [S] | Dave Van Ronk Sings the Blues | 1965 | 30.00 |
| ❑ FV-9017 [M] | Gambler's Blues | 1965 | 25.00 |
| ❑ FVS-9017 [S] | Gambler's Blues | 1965 | 30.00 |
| **VERVE FORECAST** | | | |
| ❑ FT-3009 [M] | No Dirty Names | 1967 | 25.00 |
| ❑ FTS-3009 [S] | No Dirty Names | 1967 | 30.00 |
| ❑ FTS-3041 [M] | Dave Van Ronk and the Hudson Dusters | 1968 | 25.00 |

### VAN VOOREN, MONIQUE

| Number | Title (A Side/B Side) | Yr | NM |
|---|---|---|---|
| **RCA VICTOR** | | | |
| ❑ LPM-1553 [M] | Mink in Hi-Fi | 1958 | 25.00 |

### VAN ZANDT, TOWNES

| Number | Title (A Side/B Side) | Yr | NM |
|---|---|---|---|
| **POPPY** | | | |
| ❑ PP-LA004-F | The Late Great Townes Van Zandt | 1973 | 15.00 |
| ❑ PYS-5700 | High, Low and In Between | 1972 | 15.00 |
| ❑ PYS-40001 | For the Sake of a Song | 1968 | 25.00 |
| ❑ PYS-40004 | Our Mother, The Mountain | 1969 | 15.00 |
| ❑ PYS-40007 | Townes Van Zandt | 1969 | 15.00 |
| ❑ PYS-40012 | Delta Momma Blues | 1970 | 15.00 |
| **SUGAR HILL** | | | |
| ❑ SH-1020 | At My Window | 1987 | 10.00 |
| ❑ SH-1026 | Live and Obscure | 1989 | 10.00 |
| **TOMATO** | | | |
| ❑ 7001 [(2)] | Live at the Old Quarter, Houston, Texas | 1977 | 15.00 |
| ❑ 7011 | The Late Great Townes Van Zandt | 1978 | 12.00 |
| *—Reissue of Poppy 004* | | | |
| ❑ 7012 | High, Low and In Between | 1978 | 12.00 |
| *—Reissue of Poppy 5700* | | | |
| ❑ 7013 | Delta Momma Blues | 1978 | 12.00 |
| *—Reissue of Poppy 40012* | | | |
| ❑ 7014 | Townes Van Zandt | 1978 | 12.00 |
| *—Reissue of Poppy 40007* | | | |
| ❑ 7015 | Our Mother, The Mountain | 1978 | 12.00 |
| *—Reissue of Poppy 40004* | | | |

Vanilla Fudge, *Renaissance,* Atco SD 33-244, 1968, purple and brown label, $20.

| Number | Title (A Side/B Side) | Yr | NM |
|---|---|---|---|
| ❑ 7017 | Flyin' Shoes | 1978 | 12.00 |

### VANCE, PAUL

| Number | Title (A Side/B Side) | Yr | NM |
|---|---|---|---|
| **SCEPTER** | | | |
| ❑ SPS-557 [S] | Ma Vie (My Life) | 1966 | 20.00 |
| ❑ SRM-557 [M] | Ma Vie (My Life) | 1966 | 15.00 |

### VANDROSS, LUTHER

| Number | Title (A Side/B Side) | Yr | NM |
|---|---|---|---|
| **EPIC** | | | |
| ❑ FE 37451 | Never Too Much | 1981 | 10.00 |
| ❑ FE 38235 | Forever, For Always, For Love | 1982 | 10.00 |
| ❑ FE 39196 | Busy Body | 1983 | 10.00 |
| ❑ FE 39882 | The Night I Fell in Love | 1985 | 8.00 |
| ❑ FE 40415 | Give Me the Reason | 1986 | 8.00 |
| ❑ FE 44308 | Any Love | 1988 | 8.00 |
| ❑ E2 45320 [(2)] | The Best of Luther Vandross... The Best of Love | 1989 | 12.00 |
| ❑ E 46789 | Power of Love | 1991 | 12.00 |
| ❑ HE 47451 | Never Too Much | 198? | 30.00 |
| *—Half-speed mastered edition* | | | |
| ❑ E 57775 | Songs | 1994 | 15.00 |
| ❑ E 57795 | This Is Christmas | 1995 | 12.00 |
| ❑ E 67553 | Your Secret Love | 1996 | 12.00 |

### VANILLA FUDGE

| Number | Title (A Side/B Side) | Yr | NM |
|---|---|---|---|
| **ATCO** | | | |
| ❑ 33-224 [M] | Vanilla Fudge | 1967 | 25.00 |
| ❑ SD 33-224 | Vanilla Fudge | 197? | 8.00 |
| *—Any later label* | | | |
| ❑ SD 33-224 [S] | Vanilla Fudge | 1967 | 20.00 |
| *—Purple and brown label* | | | |
| ❑ SD 33-224 [S] | Vanilla Fudge | 1969 | 12.00 |
| *—Yellow label* | | | |
| ❑ 33-237 [M] | The Beat Goes On | 1968 | 40.00 |
| ❑ SD 33-237 | The Beat Goes On | 1968 | 20.00 |
| *—Purple and brown label* | | | |
| ❑ SD 33-237 | The Beat Goes On | 1969 | 12.00 |
| *—Yellow label* | | | |
| ❑ SD 33-244 | Renaissance | 1968 | 20.00 |
| *—Purple and brown label* | | | |
| ❑ SD 33-244 | Renaissance | 1969 | 12.00 |
| *—Yellow label* | | | |
| ❑ SD 33-278 | Near the Beginning | 1969 | 15.00 |
| ❑ SD 33-303 | Rock 'N' Roll | 1969 | 15.00 |
| ❑ 90006 | The Best of Vanilla Fudge | 1982 | 10.00 |
| ❑ 90149 | Mystery | 1984 | 12.00 |
| **SUNDAZED** | | | |
| ❑ LP 5168 [M] | Vanilla Fudge | 2004 | 12.00 |
| *—Reissue on 180-gram vinyl* | | | |

### VANILLA ICE

| Number | Title (A Side/B Side) | Yr | NM |
|---|---|---|---|
| **ULTRA** | | | |
| ❑ ULT 4019 | Hooked | 1990 | 40.00 |
| *—Basically the same album as "To the Extreme," which was not issued on vinyl in the United States* | | | |

### VANITY FARE

| Number | Title (A Side/B Side) | Yr | NM |
|---|---|---|---|
| **PAGE ONE** | | | |
| ❑ 2502 | Early in the Morning | 1970 | 20.00 |

### VANNELLI, GINO

| Number | Title (A Side/B Side) | Yr | NM |
|---|---|---|---|
| **A&M** | | | |
| ❑ SP-3112 | The Gist of the Gemini | 1981 | 8.00 |
| *—Reissue of 4596* | | | |
| ❑ SP-3120 | Powerful People | 1981 | 8.00 |
| *—Reissue of 3630* | | | |
| ❑ SP-3139 | Crazy Life | 1981 | 8.00 |
| *—Reissue of 4395* | | | |
| ❑ SP-3170 | Brother to Brother | 1981 | 8.00 |
| *—Reissue of 4722* | | | |
| ❑ SP-3260 | The Best of Gino Vannelli | 1982 | 8.00 |
| *—Reissue of 3729* | | | |
| ❑ SP-3630 | Powerful People | 1974 | 10.00 |
| ❑ SP-3729 | The Best of Gino Vannelli | 1981 | 10.00 |
| ❑ SP-4395 | Crazy Life | 1973 | 12.00 |
| ❑ SP-4533 | Storm at Sunup | 1975 | 10.00 |
| ❑ SP-4596 | The Gist of the Gemini | 1976 | 10.00 |
| ❑ SP-4664 | A Pauper in Paradise | 1977 | 10.00 |
| ❑ SP-4722 | Brother to Brother | 1978 | 10.00 |
| **ARISTA** | | | |
| ❑ AB 9539 | Nightwalker | 1981 | 10.00 |
| **CBS ASSOCIATED** | | | |
| ❑ BFZ 40337 | Big Dreamers Never Sleep | 1987 | 10.00 |
| **HME** | | | |
| ❑ FZ 40077 | Black Cars | 1985 | 10.00 |
| **MOBILE FIDELITY** | | | |
| ❑ 1-041 | Powerful People | 1980 | 20.00 |
| *—Audiophile vinyl* | | | |
| **NAUTILUS** | | | |
| ❑ NR-35 | Brother to Brother | 198? | 25.00 |
| *—Audiophile vinyl* | | | |

## VARIATIONS, THE

### JUSTICE
❑ JLP-212 Dig 'Em Up 196? 400.00

## VAUGHAN, DENNY

### BEVERLY HILLS
❑ BHS-19 Aberga-Denny 1969 15.00

### CORAL
❑ CRL 56038 [10] Moonlight and Roses 1951 50.00

## VAUGHAN, FRANKIE

### PHILIPS
❑ PHM 200006 [M] Singin' Happy 1962 20.00
❑ PHS 600006 [S] Singin' Happy 1962 25.00

## VAUGHAN, SARAH

### ACCORD
❑ SN-7195 Simply Divine 1981 10.00

### ALLEGRO
❑ 1592 [M] Sarah Vaughan 1955 50.00
❑ 1608 [M] Sarah Vaughan 1955 50.00
❑ 3080 [10] Early Sarah 195? 80.00

### ALLEGRO ELITE
❑ 4106 [10] Sarah Vaughan Sings 195? 30.00

### ATLANTIC
❑ SD 16037 Songs of the Beatles 1981 12.00

### BRYLEN
❑ BN 4411 Desires 198? 10.00
*—Last name is misspelled "Vaughn"*

### CBS MASTERWORKS
❑ FM 37277 Gershwin Live! 1982 10.00
*—With the Los Angeles Philharmonic Orchestra*
❑ FM 42519 Brazilian Romance 1987 10.00

### COLUMBIA
❑ CL 660 [M] After Hours with Sarah Vaughan 1955 50.00
❑ CL 745 [M] Sarah Vaughan in Hi-Fi 1956 50.00
❑ CL 914 [M] Linger Awhile 1956 50.00
❑ CL 6133 [10] Sarah Vaughan 1950 120.00

### COLUMBIA SPECIAL PRODUCTS
❑ P 13084 Sarah Vaughan in Hi-Fi 1976 10.00
*—Reissue of Columbia 745*
❑ P 14364 Linger Awhile 1978 10.00
*—Reissue of Columbia 914*

### CONCORD
❑ 3018 [M] Sarah Vaughan Concert 1957 30.00

### CORONET
❑ 277 Sarah Vaughan Belts the Hits 196? 15.00

### EMARCY
❑ EMS-2-412 [(2)] Sarah Vaughan Live 197? 12.00
❑ MG-26005 [10] Images 1954 80.00
❑ MG-36004 [M] Sarah Vaughan 1955 80.00
❑ MG-36058 [M] In the Land of Hi-Fi 1956 80.00
❑ MG-36089 [M] Sassy 1956 50.00
❑ MG-36109 [M] Swingin' Easy 1957 50.00
❑ 814187-1 [(2)] The George Gershwin Songbook 1983 12.00
❑ 824864-1 The Rodgers & Hart Songbook 1985 10.00
❑ 826454-1 In the Land of Hi-Fi 1986 10.00
*—Reissue of 36058*

### EVEREST ARCHIVE OF FOLK & JAZZ
❑ 250 Sarah Vaughan 197? 10.00
❑ 271 Sarah Vaughan, Volume 2 1973 10.00
❑ 325 Sarah Vaughan, Volume 3 197? 10.00

### FORUM
❑ F-9034 [M] Dreamy 196? 12.00
❑ SF-9034 [S] Dreamy 196? 15.00

### HARMONY
❑ HL 7158 [M] The Great Sarah Vaughan 196? 12.00

### LION
❑ L 70052 [M] Tenderly 1958 25.00

### MAINSTREAM
❑ MRL 340 Time in My Life 1972 15.00
❑ MRL 361 Sarah Vaughan/Michel Legrand 1972 15.00
❑ MRL 379 Feelin' Good 1973 15.00
❑ MRL 404 Sarah Vaughan and the Jimmy Rowles Quintet 1974 15.00
❑ MRL 412 Send In the Clowns 1974 15.00
❑ MRL 419 More Sarah Vaughan from Japan 1974 15.00
❑ MRL 2401 [(2)] Sarah Vaughan "Live" In Japan 1973 20.00

### MASTERSEAL
❑ MS-55 [M] Sarah Vaughan Sings 195? 25.00

### MERCURY
❑ MGP-2-100 [(2)M] Great Songs from Hit Shows 1957 60.00
❑ MGP-2-101 [(2)M] Sarah Vaughan Sings George Gershwin 1957 60.00
❑ MG-20094 [M] Sarah Vaughan at the Blue Note 1956 40.00
❑ MG-20219 [M] Wonderful Sarah 1957 40.00
❑ MG-20223 [M] In a Romantic Mood 1957 40.00
❑ MG-20244 [M] Great Songs from Hit Shows, Vol. 1 1958 30.00
❑ MG-20245 [M] Great Songs from Hit Shows, Vol. 2 1958 30.00
❑ MG-20310 [M] Sarah Vaughan Sings George Gershwin, Vol. 1 1958 30.00
❑ MG-20311 [M] Sarah Vaughan Sings George Gershwin, Vol. 2 1958 30.00
❑ MG-20326 [M] Sarah Vaughan and Her Trio at Mr. Kelly's 1958 40.00
❑ MG-20370 [M] Vaughan and Violins 1958 40.00
❑ MG-20383 [M] After Hours at the London House 1958 40.00
❑ MG-20438 [M] The Magic of Sarah Vaughan 1959 30.00
❑ MG-20441 [M] No 'Count Sarah 1959 30.00
❑ MG-20540 [M] The Divine Sarah Vaughan 1960 25.00
❑ MG-20580 [M] Close to You 1960 25.00
❑ MG-20617 [M] My Heart Sings 1961 25.00
❑ MG-20645 [M] Sarah Vaughan's Golden Hits 1961 20.00
❑ MG-20831 [M] Sassy Swings the Tivoli 1962 20.00
❑ MG-20882 [M] Vaughan with Voices 1963 20.00
❑ MG-20941 [M] Viva Vaughan 1964 15.00
❑ MG-21009 [M] Sarah Vaughan Sings the Mancini Songbook 1965 15.00
❑ MG-21069 [M] Pop Artistry 1966 15.00
❑ MG-21079 [M] The New Scene 1966 15.00
❑ MG-21116 [M] Sassy Swings Again 1967 15.00
❑ MG-21122 [M] It's a Man's World 1967 15.00
❑ MG-25188 [10] Divine Sarah 1955 100.00
❑ MG-25213 [10] The Divine Sarah Sings 1955 100.00
❑ SR-60020 [S] After Hours at the London House 1959 40.00
❑ SR-60038 [S] Vaughan and Violins 1959 40.00
❑ SR-60041 [S] Great Songs from Hit Shows, Vol. 1 1959 40.00
❑ SR-60045 [S] Sarah Vaughan Sings George Gershwin, Vol. 1 1959 40.00
❑ SR-60046 [S] Sarah Vaughan Sings George Gershwin, Vol. 2 1959 40.00
❑ SR-60078 [S] Great Songs from Hit Shows, Vol. 2 1959 40.00
❑ SR-60110 [S] The Magic of Sarah Vaughan 1959 40.00
❑ SR-60116 [S] No 'Count Sarah 1959 40.00
❑ SR-60240 [S] Close to You 1960 30.00
❑ SR-60255 [S] The Divine Sarah Vaughan 1960 30.00
❑ SR-60617 [S] My Heart Sings 1961 30.00
❑ SR-60645 [S] Sarah Vaughan's Golden Hits 1961 25.00
*—Original black label version*
❑ SR-60645 [S] Sarah Vaughan's Golden Hits 1965 15.00
*—Red label version with white "MERCURY" alone at top*
❑ SR-60645 [S] Sarah Vaughan's Golden Hits 1968 12.00
*—Red label with multiple Mercury logos along the label edge*
❑ SR-60831 [S] Sassy Swings the Tivoli 1962 25.00
❑ SR-60882 [S] Vaughan with Voices 1963 25.00
❑ SR-60941 [S] Viva Vaughan 1964 20.00
❑ SR-61009 [S] Sarah Vaughan Sings the Mancini Songbook 1965 20.00
❑ SR-61069 [S] Pop Artistry 1966 20.00
❑ SR-61079 [S] The New Scene 1966 20.00
❑ SR-61116 [S] Sassy Swings Again 1967 20.00
❑ SR-61122 [S] It's a Man's World 1967 20.00
❑ 826320-1 [(6)] The Complete Sarah Vaughan on Mercury Vol. 1: Great Jazz years (1954-56) 1986 40.00
❑ 826327-1 [(5)] The Complete Sarah Vaughan on Mercury Vol. 2: Great American Songs (1956-57) 1986 40.00
❑ 826333-1 [(6)] The Complete Sarah Vaughan on Mercury Vol. 3: Great Show on Stage (1954-56) 1986 40.00
❑ 830721-1 [(4)] The Complete Sarah Vaughan on Mercury Vol. 4 Part 1: Live in Europe (1963-64) 1987 40.00
❑ 830726-1 [(5)] The Complete Sarah Vaughan on Mercury Vol. 4 Part 2: Sassy Swings Again 1987 40.00

### METRO
❑ M-539 [M] Tenderly 1965 12.00
❑ MS-539 [S] Tenderly 1965 15.00

### MGM
❑ E-165 [10] Tenderly 1950 120.00
❑ E-544 [10] Sarah Vaughan Sings 1951 120.00
❑ E-3274 [M] My Kinda Love 1955 50.00
*—Combination of two 10-inch LPs on one 12-inch LP*

### MUSICRAFT
❑ 504 Divine Sarah 197? 10.00
❑ MVS-2002 The Man I Love 1986 10.00
❑ MVS-2006 Lover Man 1986 10.00

### PABLO
❑ 2310821 How Long 1978 10.00
❑ 2310885 The Best of Sarah Vaughan 1983 10.00
❑ 2312101 I Love Brazil 1978 10.00
❑ 2312111 The Duke Ellington Songbook One 1979 10.00
❑ 2312116 The Duke Ellington Songbook Two 1980 10.00
❑ 2312125 Copacabana 1981 10.00
❑ 2405416 The Best of Sarah Vaughan 1990 10.00

### PABLO TODAY
❑ 2312137 Crazy and Mixed Up 1982 10.00

### PALACE
❑ 5191 [M] Sarah Vaughan Sings 195? 25.00

### PICKWICK
❑ PCS-3035 Fabulous Sarah Vaughan 197? 10.00

### REMINGTON
❑ RLP-1024 [10] Hot Jazz 1953 200.00

### RIVERSIDE
❑ RLP 2511 [10] Sarah Vaughan Sings with John Kirby 1955 100.00

### RONDO-LETTE
❑ A-35 [M] Songs of Broadway 1958 25.00
❑ A-53 [M] Sarah Vaughan Sings 1959 25.00

### ROULETTE
❑ RE-103 [(2)] Echoes of an Era: The Sarah Vaughan Years 197? 15.00
❑ K-105 [(2)M] The Sarah Vaughan Years 196? 20.00
❑ SK-105 [(2)S] The Sarah Vaughan Years 196? 30.00
❑ R 52046 [M] Dreamy 1960 30.00
❑ SR 52046 [S] Dreamy 1960 40.00
❑ R 52060 [M] Divine One 1960 25.00
❑ SR 52060 [S] Divine One 1960 30.00
❑ R 52070 [M] After Hours 1961 25.00
❑ SR 52070 [S] After Hours 1961 30.00
❑ R 52082 [M] You're Mine 1962 25.00
❑ SR 52082 [S] You're Mine 1962 30.00
*—Black vinyl*
❑ SR 52082 [S] You're Mine 1962 60.00
*—Red vinyl*
❑ R 52091 [M] Snowbound 1962 20.00
❑ SR 52091 [S] Snowbound 1962 25.00
❑ R 52092 [M] The Explosive Side of Sarah 1962 20.00
❑ SR 52092 [S] The Explosive Side of Sarah 1962 25.00
❑ R 52100 [M] Star Eyes 1963 15.00
❑ SR 52100 [S] Star Eyes 1963 20.00
❑ R 52104 [M] Lonely Hours 1963 15.00
❑ SR 52104 [S] Lonely Hours 1963 20.00
❑ R 52109 [M] The World of Sarah Vaughan 1964 15.00
❑ SR 52109 [S] The World of Sarah Vaughan 1964 20.00
❑ R 52112 [M] Sweet 'N Sassy 1964 15.00
❑ SR 52112 [S] Sweet 'N Sassy 1964 20.00
❑ R 52116 [M] Sarah Sings Soulfully 1965 15.00
❑ SR 52116 [S] Sarah Sings Soulfully 1965 20.00
❑ R 52118 [M] Sarah Plus Two 1965 15.00
❑ SR 52118 [S] Sarah Plus Two 1965 20.00
❑ R 52123 [M] Sarah Slightly Classical 1966 15.00
❑ SR 52123 [S] Sarah Slightly Classical 1966 20.00

### ROYALE
❑ 18129 [10] Sarah Vaughan and Orchestra 195? 30.00
❑ 18149 [10] Sarah Vaughan and Orchestra 195? 30.00
*—Includes recordings made on the Musicraft label in the 1940s*

### SCEPTER CITATION
❑ CTN-18029 The Best of Sarah Vaughan 1972 12.00

### SPIN-O-RAMA
❑ 73 [M] Sweet, Sultry and Swinging 196? 40.00
❑ S-73 [S] Sweet, Sultry and Swinging 196? 50.00
❑ 114 [M] The Divine Sarah Vaughan 196? 40.00
❑ S-114 [S] The Divine Sarah Vaughan 196? 50.00

### TIME-LIFE
❑ SLGD-09 [(2)] Legendary Singers: Sarah Vaughan 1985 15.00

### TRIP
❑ 5501 Sarah Vaughan 197? 10.00
❑ 5517 Sassy 197? 10.00
❑ 5523 In the Land of Hi-Fi 197? 10.00
❑ 5551 Swingin' Easy 197? 10.00

### WING
❑ MGW-12123 [M] All Time Favorites 1963 12.00
❑ MGW-12280 [M] The Magic of Sarah Vaughan 1964 12.00
❑ SRW-16123 [S] All Time Favorites 1963 15.00
❑ SRW-16280 [S] The Magic of Sarah Vaughan 1964 15.00

## VAUGHAN, SARAH, AND COUNT BASIE
Also see each artist's individual listings.

### PABLO
❑ 2312130 Send In the Clowns 1980 10.00

### ROULETTE
❑ SR 42018 Count Basie and Sarah Vaughan 1968 15.00
❑ R 52061 [M] Count Basie and Sarah Vaughan 1960 25.00
❑ SR 52061 [S] Count Basie and Sarah Vaughan 1960 30.00

## VAUGHAN, SARAH, AND BILLY ECKSTINE
Also see each artist's individual listings.

### EMARCY
❑ 822526-1 The Irving Berlin Songbook 1984 10.00

LION

| Number | Title (A Side/B Side) | Yr | NM |
|---|---|---|---|
| L-70088 [M] | Billy and Sarah | 195? | 25.00 |

MERCURY

| Number | Title (A Side/B Side) | Yr | NM |
|---|---|---|---|
| MG-20316 [M] | Sarah Vaughan and Billy Eckstine Sing the Best of Irving Berlin | 1959 | 30.00 |
| SR-60002 [S] | Sarah Vaughan and Billy Eckstine Sing the Best of Irving Berlin | 1959 | 40.00 |

### VAUGHAN, SARAH; DINAH WASHINGTON; JOE WILLIAMS

ROULETTE

| Number | Title (A Side/B Side) | Yr | NM |
|---|---|---|---|
| R 52108 [M] | We Three | 1964 | 15.00 |
| SR 52108 [S] | We Three | 1964 | 20.00 |

### VAUGHAN, STEVIE RAY

EPIC

| Number | Title (A Side/B Side) | Yr | NM |
|---|---|---|---|
| BFE 38734 | Texas Flood | 1983 | 10.00 |
| FE 39304 | Couldn't Stand the Weather | 1984 | 10.00 |
| 8E8 39609 [PD] | Couldn't Stand the Weather | 1984 | 150.00 |
| FE 40036 | Soul to Soul | 1985 | 10.00 |
| E2 40511 [(2)] | Live Alive | 1986 | 12.00 |
| FE 45024 | In Step | 1989 | 10.00 |
| E 47390 | The Sky Is Crying | 1991 | 30.00 |
| E 66217 | Greatest Hits | 1995 | 10.00 |

### VAUGHAN BROTHERS, THE

CBS ASSOCIATED

| Number | Title (A Side/B Side) | Yr | NM |
|---|---|---|---|
| Z 46625 | Family Style | 1990 | 20.00 |

### VAUGHN, BILLY

ABC

| Number | Title (A Side/B Side) | Yr | NM |
|---|---|---|---|
| 4005 | 16 Great Performances | 1974 | 10.00 |

DOT

| Number | Title (A Side/B Side) | Yr | NM |
|---|---|---|---|
| DLP 3001 [M] | Sweet Music and Memories | 1955 | 25.00 |
| *—Maroon label* | | | |
| DLP 3001 [M] | Sweet Music and Memories | 1957 | 15.00 |
| *—Black label* | | | |
| DLP 3016 [M] | The Golden Instrumentals | 1956 | 25.00 |
| *—Maroon label* | | | |
| DLP 3016 [M] | The Golden Instrumentals | 1957 | 15.00 |
| *—Black label* | | | |
| DLP 3045 [M] | Instrumental Souvenirs | 1957 | 15.00 |
| DLP 3064 [M] | Melodies in Gold | 1957 | 15.00 |
| DLP 3086 [M] | Music for the Golden Hours | 1958 | 15.00 |
| DLP 3100 [M] | Sail Along Silv'ry Moon | 1958 | 15.00 |
| DLP 3119 [M] | Billy Vaughn Plays the Million Sellers | 1958 | 15.00 |
| DLP 3140 [M] | La Paloma | 1959 | 15.00 |
| DLP 3148 [M] | Christmas Carols | 1958 | 15.00 |
| DLP 3156 [M] | Billy Vaughn Plays | 1959 | 15.00 |
| DLP 3165 [M] | Blue Hawaii | 1959 | 15.00 |
| DLP 3201 [M] | Golden Hits | 1959 | 15.00 |
| DLP 3205 [M] | Golden Saxophones | 1959 | 15.00 |
| DLP 3260 [M] | Billy Vaughn Plays Stephen Foster | 1960 | 15.00 |
| DLP 3275 [M] | Linger Awhile | 1960 | 15.00 |
| DLP 3276 [M] | Theme from A Summer Place | 1960 | 15.00 |
| DLP 3280 [M] | Golden Waltzes | 1961 | 15.00 |
| DLP 3288 [M] | Great Golden Hits | 1960 | 15.00 |
| DLP 3322 [M] | Look for a Star | 1960 | 15.00 |
| DLP 3349 [M] | Theme from The Sundowners | 1960 | 15.00 |
| DLP 3366 [M] | Orange Blossom Special and Wheels | 1961 | 15.00 |
| DLP 3396 [M] | Berlin Melody | 1961 | 15.00 |
| DLP 3409 [M] | Greatest String Band Hits | 1962 | 15.00 |
| DLP 3424 [M] | Chapel by the Sea | 1962 | 15.00 |
| DLP 3442 [M] | The Shifting, Whispering Sands | 1962 | 15.00 |
| DLP 3458 [M] | A Swingin' Safari | 1962 | 15.00 |
| DLP 3497 [M] | 1962's Greatest Hits | 1963 | 12.00 |
| DLP 3523 [M] | Sukiyaki and 11 Hawaiian Hits | 1963 | 12.00 |
| DLP 3540 [M] | Number One Hits, Vol. #1 | 1963 | 12.00 |
| DLP 3558 [M] | Greatest Boogie Woogie Hits | 1963 | 12.00 |
| DLP 3559 [M] | Blue Velvet & 1963's Great Hits | 1964 | 12.00 |
| DLP 3578 [M] | Forever | 1964 | 12.00 |
| DLP 3593 [M] | Another Hit Album! | 1964 | 12.00 |
| DLP 3605 [M] | Pearly Shells | 1965 | 12.00 |
| DLP 3625 [M] | 12 Golden Hits from Latin America | 1965 | 12.00 |
| DLP 3628 [M] | Mexican Pearls | 1965 | 12.00 |
| DLP 3654 [M] | Moon Over Naples | 1965 | 12.00 |
| DLP 3679 [M] | Michelle | 1966 | 12.00 |
| DLP 3698 [M] | Great Country Hits | 1966 | 12.00 |
| DLP 3751 [M] | Alfie | 1966 | 12.00 |
| DLP 3782 [M] | Sweet Maria | 1967 | 12.00 |
| DLP 3788 [M] | That's Life & Pineapple Market | 1967 | 12.00 |
| DLP 3796 [M] | Josephine | 1967 | 12.00 |
| DLP 3800 [M] | Billy Vaughn Presents Friends from Rio Playing "Something Stupid" | 1967 | 12.00 |
| DLP 3811 [M] | Golden Hits/The Best of Billy Vaughn | 1967 | 12.00 |
| DLP 3813 [M] | I Love You | 1967 | 12.00 |
| DLP 3828 [M] | Ode to Billy Joe | 1967 | 12.00 |
| DLP 5857 | Quietly Wild | 1968 | 10.00 |
| DLP 25001 [R] | Sweet Music and Memories | 196? | 10.00 |
| DLP 25016 [R] | The Golden Instrumentals | 196? | 10.00 |
| DLP 25064 [R] | Melodies in Gold | 196? | 10.00 |
| DLP 25086 [R] | Music for the Golden Hours | 196? | 10.00 |
| DLP 25100 [S] | Sail Along Silv'ry Moon | 1959 | 20.00 |
| DLP 25119 [S] | Billy Vaughn Plays the Million Sellers | 1959 | 20.00 |
| DLP 25140 [S] | La Paloma | 1959 | 20.00 |
| DLP 25156 [S] | Billy Vaughn Plays | 1959 | 20.00 |
| DLP 25165 [S] | Blue Hawaii | 1959 | 20.00 |
| DLP 25201 [S] | Golden Hits | 1959 | 20.00 |
| DLP 25205 [S] | Golden Saxophones | 1959 | 20.00 |
| DLP 25260 [S] | Billy Vaughn Plays Stephen Foster | 1960 | 20.00 |
| DLP 25275 [S] | Linger Awhile | 1960 | 20.00 |
| DLP 25276 [S] | Theme from A Summer Place | 1960 | 20.00 |
| DLP 25280 [S] | Golden Waltzes | 1961 | 20.00 |
| DLP 25288 [S] | Great Golden Hits | 1960 | 20.00 |
| DLP 25322 [S] | Look for a Star | 1960 | 20.00 |
| DLP 25349 [S] | Theme from The Sundowners | 1960 | 20.00 |
| DLP 25366 [S] | Orange Blossom Special and Wheels | 1961 | 20.00 |
| DLP 25396 [S] | Berlin Melody | 1961 | 20.00 |
| DLP 25409 [S] | Greatest String Band Hits | 1962 | 20.00 |
| DLP 25424 [S] | Chapel by the Sea | 1962 | 20.00 |
| DLP 25442 [S] | The Shifting, Whispering Sands | 1962 | 20.00 |
| DLP 25458 [S] | A Swingin' Safari | 1962 | 20.00 |
| DLP 25497 [S] | 1962's Greatest Hits | 1963 | 15.00 |
| DLP 25523 [S] | Sukiyaki and 11 Hawaiian Hits | 1963 | 15.00 |
| DLP 25540 [S] | Number One Hits, Vol. #1 | 1963 | 15.00 |
| DLP 25558 [S] | Greatest Boogie Woogie Hits | 1963 | 15.00 |
| DLP 25559 [S] | Blue Velvet & 1963's Great Hits | 1964 | 15.00 |
| DLP 25578 [S] | Forever | 1964 | 15.00 |
| DLP 25593 [S] | Another Hit Album! | 1964 | 15.00 |
| DLP 25605 [S] | Pearly Shells | 1965 | 15.00 |
| DLP 25625 [S] | 12 Golden Hits from Latin America | 1965 | 15.00 |
| DLP 25628 [S] | Mexican Pearls | 1965 | 15.00 |
| DLP 25654 [S] | Moon Over Naples | 1965 | 15.00 |
| DLP 25679 [S] | Michelle | 1966 | 15.00 |
| DLP 25698 [S] | Great Country Hits | 1966 | 15.00 |
| DLP 25751 [S] | Alfie | 1966 | 15.00 |
| DLP 25782 [S] | Sweet Maria | 1967 | 10.00 |
| DLP 25788 [S] | That's Life & Pineapple Market | 1967 | 10.00 |
| DLP 25796 [S] | Josephine | 1967 | 10.00 |
| DLP 25800 [S] | Billy Vaughn Presents Friends from Rio Playing "Something Stupid" | 1967 | 10.00 |
| DLP 25811 [S] | Golden Hits/The Best of Billy Vaughn | 1967 | 10.00 |
| DLP 25813 [S] | I Love You | 1967 | 10.00 |
| DLP 25828 [S] | Ode to Billy Joe | 1967 | 10.00 |
| DLP 25837 | Pretty Country | 1968 | 10.00 |
| DLP 25841 | As Requested | 1968 | 10.00 |
| DLP 25882 | A Current Set of Standards | 1968 | 10.00 |
| DLP-25897 | Alone with Today | 1968 | 10.00 |
| DLP 25899 | Have Yourself a Merry Merry Christmas | 1968 | 12.00 |
| DLP 25911 | Nashville Saxophones | 1969 | 10.00 |
| DLP 25937 | The Windmills of Your Mind | 1969 | 10.00 |
| DLP 25969 | True Grit | 1969 | 10.00 |
| DLP 25975 | Winter World of Love | 1970 | 10.00 |
| DLP 25985 | Everything Is Beautiful | 1970 | 10.00 |

HAMILTON

| Number | Title (A Side/B Side) | Yr | NM |
|---|---|---|---|
| HLP 113 [M] | Golden Gems | 196? | 12.00 |
| HLP 147 [M] | Strauss Waltz Concert | 196? | 12.00 |
| HLP 162 [M] | Songs I Wrote | 196? | 12.00 |
| HLP 12113 [S] | Golden Gems | 196? | 12.00 |
| HLP 12147 [S] | Strauss Waltz Concert | 196? | 12.00 |
| HLP 12162 [S] | Songs I Wrote | 196? | 12.00 |

MCA

| Number | Title (A Side/B Side) | Yr | NM |
|---|---|---|---|
| 801 | La Paloma | 198? | 8.00 |
| *—Budget-line reissue* | | | |
| 4164 [(2)] | The Best of Billy Vaughn | 198? | 12.00 |
| 27018 | Blue Hawaii | 198? | 8.00 |
| *—Budget-line reissue* | | | |

PARAMOUNT

| Number | Title (A Side/B Side) | Yr | NM |
|---|---|---|---|
| PAS-1031 [(2)] | Billy Vaughn Plays His Greatest Hits | 1974 | 12.00 |
| PAS-1033 | Electrified | 1974 | 10.00 |
| PAS-5032 | Theme from Love Story | 1971 | 10.00 |
| PAS-5037 | I Don't Know How to Love Him | 1971 | 10.00 |
| PAS-6025 | An Old Fashioned Love Song | 1972 | 10.00 |
| PAS-6035 | Soundstage! | 1972 | 10.00 |
| PAS-6044 | Country's Greatest Hits | 1973 | 10.00 |

PICKWICK

| Number | Title (A Side/B Side) | Yr | NM |
|---|---|---|---|
| SPC-3093 | Embraceable You | 197? | 10.00 |
| SPC-3146 | Up, Up and Away | 197? | 10.00 |
| SPC-3213 | Moon River | 197? | 10.00 |

RANWOOD

| Number | Title (A Side/B Side) | Yr | NM |
|---|---|---|---|
| 7025 [(2)] | Billy Vaughn and His Orchestra Play 22 Greatest Hits | 1982 | 12.00 |

### VAUGHN, FATHER TOM

RCA VICTOR

| Number | Title (A Side/B Side) | Yr | NM |
|---|---|---|---|
| LSP-3577 [S] | Jazz In Concert at the Village Gate | 1966 | 20.00 |
| LPM-3708 [M] | Cornbread (Meat Loaf, Greens and Deviled Eggs) | 1967 | 20.00 |
| LPM-3845 [M] | Motor City Soul | 1967 | 20.00 |

### VAUGHN, ROBERT

MGM

| Number | Title (A Side/B Side) | Yr | NM |
|---|---|---|---|
| E-4488 [M] | Readings from Hamlet | 1962 | 25.00 |
| SE-4488 [S] | Readings from Hamlet | 1962 | 30.00 |

### VAUGHT, BOB, AND THE RENEGADES

GNP CRESCENDO

| Number | Title (A Side/B Side) | Yr | NM |
|---|---|---|---|
| GNP-83 [M] | Surf Crazy | 1963 | 30.00 |
| GNPS-83 [S] | Surf Crazy | 1963 | 40.00 |

### VEE, BOBBY

LIBERTY

| Number | Title (A Side/B Side) | Yr | NM |
|---|---|---|---|
| LRP-3165 [M] | Bobby Vee Sings Your Favorites | 1960 | 50.00 |
| LRP-3181 [M] | Bobby Vee | 1961 | 40.00 |
| LRP-3186 [M] | Bobby Vee With Strings and Things | 1961 | 40.00 |
| LRP-3205 [M] | Bobby Vee Sings Hits of the Rockin' 50's | 1961 | 40.00 |
| LRP-3211 [M] | Take Good Care of My Baby | 1962 | 30.00 |
| LRP-3228 [M] | Bobby Vee Meets the Crickets | 1962 | 40.00 |
| LRP-3232 [M] | A Bobby Vee Recording Session | 1962 | 30.00 |
| LRP-3245 [M] | Bobby Vee's Golden Greats | 1962 | 30.00 |
| LRP-3267 [M] | Merry Christmas from Bobby Vee | 1962 | 30.00 |
| LRP-3285 [M] | The Night Has a Thousand Eyes | 1963 | 30.00 |
| LRP-3289 [M] | Bobby Vee Meets the Ventures | 1963 | 40.00 |
| LRP-3336 [M] | I Remember Buddy Holly | 1963 | 40.00 |
| LRP-3352 [M] | Bobby Vee Sings the New Sound from England! | 1964 | 25.00 |
| LRP-3385 [M] | 30 Big Hits From the 60's | 1964 | 25.00 |
| LRP-3393 [M] | Bobby Vee Live on Tour | 1965 | 25.00 |
| LRP-3448 [M] | 30 Big Hits From the 60's, Volume 2 | 1966 | 25.00 |
| LRP-3464 [M] | Bobby Vee's Golden Greats, Volume 2 | 1966 | 20.00 |
| LRP-3480 [M] | Look at Me Girl | 1966 | 20.00 |
| LRP-3534 [M] | Come Back When You Grow Up | 1967 | 20.00 |
| LST-3554 [M] | Just Today | 1968 | 40.00 |
| *—Cover is stereo with "Audition Mono Not for Sale" sticker, but the label is regular stock mono* | | | |
| LST-7165 [S] | Bobby Vee Sings Your Favorites | 1960 | 80.00 |
| LST-7181 [S] | Bobby Vee | 1961 | 50.00 |
| LST-7186 [S] | Bobby Vee With Strings and Things | 1961 | 50.00 |
| LST-7205 [S] | Bobby Vee Sings Hits of the Rockin' 50's | 1961 | 50.00 |
| LST-7211 [S] | Take Good Care of My Baby | 1962 | 40.00 |
| LST-7228 [S] | Bobby Vee Meets the Crickets | 1962 | 50.00 |
| LST-7232 [S] | A Bobby Vee Recording Session | 1962 | 40.00 |
| LST-7245 [S] | Bobby Vee's Golden Greats | 1962 | 40.00 |
| LST-7267 [S] | Merry Christmas from Bobby Vee | 1962 | 40.00 |
| LST-7285 [S] | The Night Has a Thousand Eyes | 1963 | 40.00 |
| LST-7289 [S] | Bobby Vee Meets the Ventures | 1963 | 50.00 |
| LST-7336 [S] | I Remember Buddy Holly | 1963 | 50.00 |
| LST-7352 [S] | Bobby Vee Sings the New Sound from England! | 1964 | 30.00 |
| LST-7385 [S] | 30 Big Hits From the 60's | 1964 | 30.00 |
| LST-7393 [S] | Bobby Vee Live on Tour | 1965 | 30.00 |
| LST-7448 [S] | 30 Big Hits From the 60's, Volume 2 | 1966 | 30.00 |
| LST-7464 [S] | Bobby Vee's Golden Greats, Volume 2 | 1966 | 25.00 |
| LST-7480 [S] | Look at Me Girl | 1966 | 25.00 |
| LST-7534 [S] | Come Back When You Grow Up | 1967 | 25.00 |
| LST-7554 [S] | Just Today | 1968 | 25.00 |
| LST-7592 | Do What You Gotta Do | 1968 | 30.00 |
| LST-7612 | Gates, Grills and Railings | 1969 | 30.00 |
| LN-10223 | I Remember Buddy Holly | 198? | 8.00 |
| LM-51008 | Bobby Vee's Golden Greats | 198? | 8.00 |

SUNSET

| Number | Title (A Side/B Side) | Yr | NM |
|---|---|---|---|
| SUM-1111 [M] | Bobby Vee | 1966 | 10.00 |
| SUM-1162 [M] | A Forever Kind of Love | 1967 | 10.00 |
| SUM-1186 [M] | The Christmas Album | 1967 | 12.00 |
| *—Reissue of Liberty album with two fewer tracks* | | | |
| SUS-5111 [S] | Bobby Vee | 1966 | 12.00 |
| SUS-5162 [S] | A Forever Kind of Love | 1967 | 12.00 |
| SUS-5186 [S] | The Christmas Album | 1967 | 12.00 |

UNITED ARTISTS

| Number | Title (A Side/B Side) | Yr | NM |
|---|---|---|---|
| UA-LA025-G2 [(2)] | Legendary Masters Series | 1973 | 300.00 |
| *—Withdrawn before release, but a few copies survived* | | | |
| UA-LA085-G | Robert Thomas Velline | 1973 | 20.00 |
| UA-LA332-E | The Very Best of Bobby Vee | 1975 | 12.00 |
| LT-1008 | Bobby Vee's Golden Greats | 1980 | 10.00 |
| UAS-5656 | Nothin' Like a Sunny Day | 1972 | 12.00 |

### VEGA, AL

PRESTIGE

| Number | Title (A Side/B Side) | Yr | NM |
|---|---|---|---|
| PRLP-152 [10] | Al Vega Piano Solos With Bongos | 1953 | 150.00 |

The Velvet Underground, *The Velvet Underground,*
MGM SE-4617, 1969, stock copy, $40-$50 (see listings).

| Number | Title (A Side/B Side) | Yr | NM |
|---|---|---|---|
| **VEGA, TATA** | | | |
| TAMLA | | | |
| ❑ T6-347S1 | Full Speed Ahead | 1976 | 15.00 |
| ❑ T6-353S1 | Totally Tata | 1977 | 15.00 |
| ❑ T7-360R1 | Try My Love | 1978 | 15.00 |
| ❑ T8-370M1 | Givin' All My Love | 1980 | 25.00 |
| **VEGAS, PAT AND LOLLY** Also see REDBONE. | | | |
| MERCURY | | | |
| ❑ MG-21059 [M] | At the Haunted House | 1966 | 30.00 |
| ❑ SR-61059 [S] | At the Haunted House | 1966 | 40.00 |
| **VELASCO, VI** | | | |
| VEE JAY | | | |
| ❑ VJ-1135 [M] | The Vi Velasco Album | 1965 | 20.00 |
| **VELEZ, MARTHA** | | | |
| POLYDOR | | | |
| ❑ PD 5034 | Hypnotized | 1972 | 15.00 |
| SIRE | | | |
| ❑ SR 6040 | American Heartbeat | 1977 | 10.00 |
| ❑ SES-7409 | Matinee Weepers | 1973 | 15.00 |
| ❑ SASD-7515 | Escape from Babylon | 1976 | 10.00 |
| *—Produced by Bob Marley* | | | |
| ❑ SES-97008 | Fiends and Angels | 1969 | 30.00 |
| **VELVET NIGHT** | | | |
| METROMEDIA | | | |
| ❑ MD-1028 | Velvet Night | 1970 | 30.00 |
| **VELVET REVOLVER** Consists of members of GUNS N' ROSES and STONE TEMPLE PILOTS. | | | |
| RCA | | | |
| ❑ 59794-1 [(2)] | Contraband | 2004 | 20.00 |
| **VELVET UNDERGROUND, THE** Also see JOHN CALE; LOU REED; MAUREEN TUCKER. | | | |
| COTILLION | | | |
| ❑ 9034 [M] | Loaded | 1970 | 250.00 |
| *—Mono is white label promo only; "d/j copy monaural" sticker on front cover; no "SD" prefix on label* | | | |
| ❑ SD 9034 [S] | Loaded | 197? | 15.00 |
| *—Reissue with purplish label* | | | |
| ❑ SD 9034 [S] | Loaded | 1970 | 150.00 |
| *—White label promo; not the monaural version, this one has no sticker on the cover and has the "SD" prefix on the label* | | | |

| Number | Title (A Side/B Side) | Yr | NM |
|---|---|---|---|
| ❑ SD 9034 [S] | Loaded | 1970 | 20.00 |
| *—Original pressing has a light blue label* | | | |
| ❑ SD 9034 [S] | Loaded | 198? | 12.00 |
| *—Reissue with purplish label and bar code on back cover* | | | |
| ❑ SD 9034 [S] | Loaded | 2001 | 10.00 |
| *—Rhino/Scorpio reissue; purplish label* | | | |
| ❑ SD 9500 | Live at Max's Kansas City | 197? | 15.00 |
| *—Reissue with purplish label* | | | |
| ❑ SD 9500 | Live at Max's Kansas City | 1972 | 20.00 |
| *—Original pressing has a light blue label* | | | |
| ❑ SD 9500 | Live at Max's Kansas City | 198? | 12.00 |
| *—Reissue with purplish label and bar code on back cover* | | | |
| ❑ SD 9500 | Live at Max's Kansas City | 2001 | 10.00 |
| *—Rhino/Scorpio reissue; light blue label* | | | |
| ❑ SD 9500 [DJ] | Live at Max's Kansas City | 1972 | 75.00 |
| *—White label promo with "d/j copy monaural" sticker on front cover, which in this case is odd because all copies are mono!* | | | |
| MERCURY | | | |
| ❑ SRM-2-7504 [(2)] | 1969 (Live) | 1974 | 15.00 |
| *—Reissues with Chicago skyline labels* | | | |
| ❑ SRM-2-7504 [(2)] | 1969 (Live) | 1974 | 50.00 |
| *—Originals with red labels* | | | |
| ❑ SRM-2-7504 [(2)] | 1969 (Live) | 1983 | 20.00 |
| *—Reissue with black labels; non-gatefold cover; no bar code on back* | | | |
| ❑ SRM-2-7504 [(2)DJ] | 1969 (Live) | 1974 | 100.00 |
| *—White label promo* | | | |
| MGM | | | |
| ❑ GAS-131 | The Velvet Underground (Golden Archive Series) | 1970 | 40.00 |
| *—Blue and gold label stock copy* | | | |
| ❑ GAS-131 [DJ] | The Velvet Underground (Golden Archive Series) | 1970 | 100.00 |
| *—White label promo* | | | |
| ❑ GAS-131 [DJ] | The Velvet Underground (Golden Archive Series) | 1970 | 100.00 |
| *—Yellow label promo* | | | |
| ❑ SE-4617 | The Velvet Underground | 1969 | 50.00 |
| *—With "BMI" publishing credit* | | | |
| ❑ SE-4617 | The Velvet Underground | 1971 | 40.00 |
| *—With "ASCAP" publishing credit* | | | |
| ❑ SE-4617 [DJ] | The Velvet Underground | 1969 | 250.00 |
| *—White label promo* | | | |
| ❑ SE-4617 [DJ] | The Velvet Underground | 1969 | 250.00 |
| *—Yellow label promo* | | | |
| ❑ M3G 4950 | Archetypes | 1974 | 20.00 |
| ❑ M3G 4950 [DJ] | Archetypes | 1974 | 40.00 |
| *—White label promo* | | | |

| Number | Title (A Side/B Side) | Yr | NM |
|---|---|---|---|
| ❑ SW-95722 | Archetypes | 1974 | 30.00 |
| *—Longines Symphonette edition* | | | |
| PRIDE | | | |
| ❑ 0022 | Lou Reed and the Velvet Underground | 1973 | 15.00 |
| *—Tan label; label calls this "That's the Story of My Life"* | | | |
| ❑ 0022 [DJ] | Lou Reed and the Velvet Underground | 1973 | 50.00 |
| *—White label; label calls this "That's the Story of My Life"* | | | |
| VERVE | | | |
| ❑ V-5008 [M] | The Velvet Underground and Nico | 1967 | 200.00 |
| *—Version 3: With peel-off banana peel, torso is airbrushed off the cover (deduct 50% if banana sticker removed)* | | | |
| ❑ V-5008 [M] | The Velvet Underground and Nico | 1967 | 300.00 |
| *—Version 1: With peel-off banana peel, photo of band framed by a male torso (deduct 50% if banana sticker is gone)* | | | |
| ❑ V-5008 [M] | The Velvet Underground and Nico | 1967 | 300.00 |
| *—Version 2: With peel-off banana peel, photo of torso obscured by a large black sticker (deduct 50% if stickers removed)* | | | |
| ❑ V-5008 [M] | The Velvet Underground and Nico | 1967 | 400.00 |
| *—Promo copy; white label* | | | |
| ❑ V-5008 [M] | The Velvet Underground and Nico | 1967 | 400.00 |
| *—Promo copy; yellow label* | | | |
| ❑ V6-5008 [S] | The Velvet Underground and Nico | 1967 | 150.00 |
| *—Version 3: With peel-off banana peel, torso is airbrushed off the cover, publishing on label is credited to "Three Prong Music" (deduct 50% if banana sticker removed)* | | | |
| ❑ V6-5008 [S] | The Velvet Underground and Nico | 1967 | 200.00 |
| *—Version 1: With peel-off banana peel, photo of band framed by a male torso (deduct 50% if banana sticker is gone)* | | | |
| ❑ V6-5008 [S] | The Velvet Underground and Nico | 1967 | 200.00 |
| *—Version 2: With peel-off banana peel, photo of torso obscured by a sticker (deduct 50% if stickers removed)* | | | |
| ❑ V6-5008 [S] | The Velvet Underground and Nico | 1968 | 100.00 |
| *—Version 4: With peel-off banana peel, torso is airbrushed off the cover, publishing on label is credited to "Oakfield Avenue Music," Side 2 trail-off wax has an "RE-1" (deduct 50% if banana sticker removed)* | | | |
| ❑ V6-5008 [S] | The Velvet Underground and Nico | 1970 | 80.00 |
| *—Version 5: With unpeelable banana; blue label with silver "T" shape on it; publishing on the label is credited to "Oakfield Avenue Music"* | | | |
| ❑ V6-5008 [S] | The Velvet Underground and Nico | 1973 | 70.00 |
| *—Version 6: Same as Version 5 except the label is now white with "MGM" at left and "Verve" at right* | | | |
| ❑ V6-5008 [S] | The Velvet Underground and Nico | 1975 | 50.00 |
| *—Version 7: Same as Version 5, but the label is now black with silver T-shape* | | | |
| ❑ V6-5008 [S] | The Velvet Underground and Nico | 1978 | 25.00 |
| *—Version 8; The cover is no longer a gatefold* | | | |
| ❑ V-5046 [M] | White Light/White Heat | 1967 | 300.00 |
| *—White label promo* | | | |
| ❑ V-5046 [M] | White Light/White Heat | 1967 | 300.00 |
| *—Yellow label promo* | | | |
| ❑ V-5046 [M] | White Light/White Heat | 1967 | 700.00 |
| *—Version 2: No "skeleton" on cover* | | | |
| ❑ V-5046 [M] | White Light/White Heat | 1967 | 800.00 |
| *—Version 1: "Skeleton" cover -- a black-on-black skeleton is visible when cover is viewed at an angle* | | | |
| ❑ V6-5046 [S] | White Light/White Heat | 1967 | 40.00 |
| *—Version 2: No "skeleton" on cover; publishing on label is credited to "Three Prong Music"* | | | |
| ❑ V6-5046 [S] | White Light/White Heat | 1967 | 80.00 |
| *—Version 1: "Skeleton" cover -- a black-on-black skeleton is visible when cover is viewed at an angle* | | | |
| ❑ V6-5046 [S] | White Light/White Heat | 1967 | 250.00 |
| *—Yellow label promo* | | | |
| ❑ V6-5046 [S] | White Light/White Heat | 1968 | 30.00 |
| *—Version 3: No "skeleton" on cover; publishing on label is credited to "Oakfield Avenue Music"* | | | |
| ❑ 815454-1 | The Velvet Underground | 1985 | 12.00 |
| *—Reissue of MGM SE-4617* | | | |
| ❑ 823290-1 | The Velvet Underground and Nico | 1985 | 12.00 |
| *—Reissue of Verve V6-5008* | | | |
| ❑ 823721-1 | VU | 1985 | 12.00 |
| ❑ 825119-1 | White Light/White Heat | 1985 | 12.00 |
| *—Reissue of Verve V6-5046* | | | |
| ❑ 826284-1 [(2)] | 1969 (Live) | 1985 | 12.00 |
| *—Reissue of Mercury SRM-2-7504* | | | |
| ❑ 829405-1 | Another View | 1986 | 12.00 |
| **VENTURA, CAROL** | | | |
| PRESTIGE | | | |
| ❑ PRLP-7358 [M] | Carol! | 1965 | 25.00 |
| ❑ PRST-7358 [S] | Carol! | 1965 | 30.00 |
| ❑ PRLP-7405 [M] | I Love to Sing! | 1965 | 25.00 |
| ❑ PRST-7405 [S] | I Love to Sing! | 1965 | 30.00 |

| Number | Title (A Side/B Side) | Yr | NM |
|---|---|---|---|
| **VENTURA, CHARLIE** | | | |
| BATON | | | |
| ❑ 1202 [M] | New Charlie Ventura in Hi-Fi | 1957 | 50.00 |
| BRUNSWICK | | | |
| ❑ BL 54025 [M] | Here's Charlie | 1957 | 80.00 |
| CLEF | | | |
| ❑ MGC-117 [10] | Charlie Ventura Collates | 1953 | 250.00 |
| CORAL | | | |
| ❑ CRL 56067 [10] | Open House | 1952 | 150.00 |
| CRAFTSMAN | | | |
| ❑ 8039 [M] | Charlie Ventura Plays for the People | 1960 | 25.00 |
| CRYSTALETTE | | | |
| ❑ 5000 [10] | Stomping With the Sax | 1950 | 200.00 |
| DECCA | | | |
| ❑ DL 8046 [M] | Charlie Ventura Concert | 1954 | 100.00 |
| EMARCY | | | |
| ❑ MG-26028 [10] | F.Y.I. Ventura | 1954 | 120.00 |
| ❑ MG-36015 [M] | Jumping with Ventura | 1955 | 80.00 |
| GENE NORMAN | | | |
| ❑ GNP-1 [M] | Charlie Ventura In Concert | 1954 | 100.00 |
| IMPERIAL | | | |
| ❑ IM-3002 [10] | Charlie Ventura and His Sextet | 1953 | 200.00 |
| KING | | | |
| ❑ 543 [M] | Adventure with Charlie Ventura | 1958 | 80.00 |
| MERCURY | | | |
| ❑ MGC-117 [10] | Charlie Ventura Collates | 1952 | 250.00 |
| MOSAIC | | | |
| ❑ MQ9-182 [(9)] | The Complete Verve/Clef Charlie Ventura/Flip Phillips Studio Sessions | 199? | 150.00 |
| NORGRAN | | | |
| ❑ MGN-8 [10] | Charlie Ventura Quartet | 1953 | 250.00 |
| ❑ MGN-1041 [M] | Charlie Ventura's Carnegie Hall Concert | 1955 | 120.00 |
| ❑ MGN-1073 [M] | Charlie Ventura in a Jazz Mood | 1956 | 120.00 |
| ❑ MGN-1075 [M] | Blue Saxophone | 1956 | 120.00 |
| ❑ MGN-1103 [M] | Charley's Parley | 1956 | 120.00 |
| RCA VICTOR | | | |
| ❑ LPM-1135 [M] | It's All Bop to Me | 1955 | 120.00 |
| REGENT | | | |
| ❑ MG-6064 [M] | East of Suez | 1958 | 50.00 |
| TOPS | | | |
| ❑ L-1528 [M] | Charlie Ventura Plays Hi-Fi Jazz | 1958 | 25.00 |
| VERVE | | | |
| ❑ MGV-8132 [M] | Charlie Ventura's Carnegie Hall Concert | 1957 | 80.00 |
| ❑ V-8132 [M] | Charlie Ventura'a Carnegie Hall Concert | 1961 | 25.00 |
| ❑ MGV-8163 [M] | Charlie Ventura in a Jazz Mood | 1957 | 60.00 |
| ❑ V-8163 [M] | Charlie Ventura in a Jazz Mood | 1961 | 25.00 |
| ❑ MGV-8165 [M] | Blue Saxophone | 1957 | 60.00 |
| ❑ V-8165 [M] | Blue Saxophone | 1961 | 25.00 |
| **VENTURA, CHARLIE/CHARLIE KENNEDY** | | | |
| REGENT | | | |
| ❑ MG-6047 [M] | Crazy Rhythms | 1957 | 60.00 |
| **VENTURA, CHARLIE, AND MARY ANN MCCALL** | | | |
| NORGRAN | | | |
| ❑ MGN-20 [10] | An Evening with Mary Ann McCall and Charlie Ventura | 1954 | 200.00 |
| ❑ MGN-1013 [M] | Another Evening with Charlie Ventura and Mary Ann McCall | 1954 | 120.00 |
| ❑ MGN-1053 [M] | An Evening with Mary Ann McCall and Charlie Ventura | 1955 | 100.00 |
| VERVE | | | |
| ❑ MGV-8143 [M] | An Evening with Mary Ann McCall and Charlie Ventura | 1957 | 80.00 |
| ❑ V-8143 [M] | An Evening with Mary Ann McCall and Charlie Ventura | 1961 | 25.00 |
| **VENTURA, RAY** | | | |
| ATLANTIC | | | |
| ❑ 8011 [M] | Hi-Fi Music for Young Parisians | 1956 | 50.00 |
| *—Black label* | | | |
| DOT | | | |
| ❑ DLP-3120 [M] | La Belle Bardot | 1958 | 50.00 |
| *—Brigitte Bardot is the cover model* | | | |
| **VENTURAS, THE** | | | |
| DRUM BOY | | | |
| ❑ DBM-1003 [M] | Here They Are | 1964 | 200.00 |
| ❑ DBS-1003 [S] | Here They Are | 1964 | 300.00 |

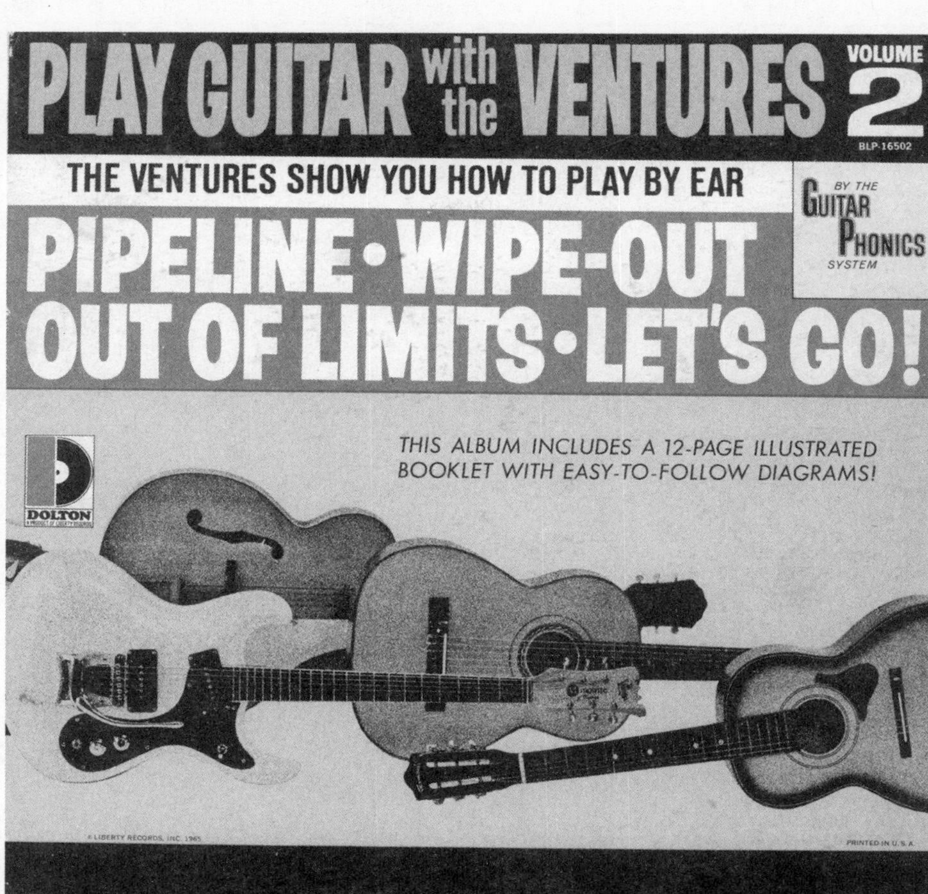


The Ventures, *Play Guitar with the Ventures, Volume 2,* Dolton BLP-16502, 1960s, mono, $25.

| Number | Title (A Side/B Side) | Yr | NM |
|---|---|---|---|
| **VENTURES, THE** | | | |
| COMPLEAT | | | |
| ❑ 672013-1 | The Best of the Ventures | 1986 | 10.00 |
| DOLTON | | | |
| ❑ BLP 2003 [M] | Walk Don't Run | 1960 | 50.00 |
| *—Pale blue label with dolphins on top* | | | |
| ❑ BLP 2003 [M] | Walk Don't Run | 1963 | 20.00 |
| *—Dark label, logo on left* | | | |
| ❑ BLP 2004 [M] | The Ventures | 1961 | 50.00 |
| *—Pale blue label with dolphins on top* | | | |
| ❑ BLP 2004 [M] | The Ventures | 1963 | 20.00 |
| *—Dark label, logo on left* | | | |
| ❑ BLP 2006 [M] | Another Smash!!! | 1961 | 50.00 |
| *—Pale blue label with dolphins on top* | | | |
| ❑ BLP 2006 [M] | Another Smash!!! | 1963 | 20.00 |
| *—Dark label, logo on left* | | | |
| ❑ BLP 2008 [M] | The Colorful Ventures | 1961 | 50.00 |
| *—Pale blue label with dolphins on top* | | | |
| ❑ BLP 2008 [M] | The Colorful Ventures | 1963 | 20.00 |
| *—Dark label, logo on left* | | | |
| ❑ BLP 2010 [M] | Twist with the Ventures | 1962 | 50.00 |
| *—Pale blue label with dolphins on top* | | | |
| ❑ BLP 2010 [M] | Dance! | 1963 | 20.00 |
| *—Dark label, logo on left; retitled version of "Twist with the Ventures"* | | | |
| ❑ BLP 2014 [M] | The Ventures' Twist Party, Vol. 2 | 1962 | 50.00 |
| *—Pale blue label with dolphins on top* | | | |
| ❑ BLP 2014 [M] | Dance with the Ventures | 1963 | 20.00 |
| *—Dark label, logo on left' retitled version of "The Ventures' Twist Party, Vol. 2"* | | | |
| ❑ BLP 2016 [M] | Mashed Potatoes and Gravy | 1962 | 30.00 |
| ❑ BLP 2016 [M] | Beach Party | 1963 | 20.00 |
| *—Retitled version of "Mashed Potatoes and Gravy"* | | | |
| ❑ BLP 2017 [M] | Going to the Ventures Dance Party! | 1962 | 30.00 |
| ❑ BLP 2019 [M] | The Ventures Play Telstar, The Lonely Bull | 1962 | 30.00 |
| ❑ BLP 2022 [M] | Surfing | 1963 | 25.00 |
| ❑ BLP 2023 [M] | The Ventures Play the Country Classics | 1963 | 25.00 |
| ❑ BLP 2024 [M] | Let's Go! | 1963 | 25.00 |
| ❑ BLP 2027 [M] | (The) Ventures in Space | 1964 | 40.00 |
| ❑ BLP 2029 [M] | The Fabulous Ventures | 1964 | 25.00 |
| ❑ BLP 2031 [M] | Walk, Don't Run, Vol. 2 | 1964 | 25.00 |
| ❑ BLP 2033 [M] | The Ventures Knock Me Out! | 1965 | 25.00 |
| ❑ BLP 2035 [M] | The Ventures on Stage | 1965 | 25.00 |
| ❑ BLP 2037 [M] | The Ventures A-Go-Go | 1965 | 25.00 |
| ❑ BLP-2038 [M] | The Ventures' Christmas Album | 1965 | 30.00 |
| ❑ BLP 2040 [M] | Where the Action Is | 1966 | 20.00 |
| ❑ BLP 2042 [M] | The Ventures/Batman Theme | 1966 | 30.00 |
| ❑ BLP 2045 [M] | Go with the Ventures! | 1966 | 20.00 |
| ❑ BLP 2047 [M] | Wild Things! | 1966 | 20.00 |
| ❑ BLP 2050 [M] | Guitar Freakout | 1967 | 20.00 |
| ❑ BST 8003 [S] | Walk Don't Run | 1960 | 60.00 |
| *—Pale blue label with dolphins on top* | | | |
| ❑ BST 8003 [S] | Walk Don't Run | 1963 | 25.00 |
| *—Dark label, logo on left* | | | |
| ❑ BST 8004 [S] | The Ventures | 1961 | 60.00 |
| *—Pale blue label with dolphins on top* | | | |
| ❑ BST 8004 [S] | The Ventures | 1963 | 25.00 |
| *—Dark label, logo on left* | | | |
| ❑ BST 8006 [S] | Another Smash!!! | 1961 | 60.00 |
| *—Pale blue label with dolphins on top* | | | |
| ❑ BST 8006 [S] | Another Smash!!! | 1963 | 25.00 |
| *—Dark label, logo on left* | | | |
| ❑ BST 8008 [S] | The Colorful Ventures | 1961 | 60.00 |
| *—Pale blue label with dolphins on top* | | | |
| ❑ BST 8008 [S] | The Colorful Ventures | 1963 | 25.00 |
| *—Dark label, logo on left* | | | |
| ❑ BST 8010 [S] | Twist with the Ventures | 1962 | 60.00 |
| *—Pale blue label with dolphins on top* | | | |
| ❑ BST 8010 [S] | Dance! | 1963 | 25.00 |
| *—Dark label, logo on left; retitled version of "Twist with the Ventures"* | | | |
| ❑ BST 8014 [S] | The Ventures' Twist Party, Vol. 2 | 1962 | 60.00 |
| *—Pale blue label with dolphins on top* | | | |
| ❑ BST 8014 [S] | Dance with the Ventures | 1963 | 25.00 |
| *—Dark label, logo on left' retitled version of "The Ventures' Twist Party, Vol. 2"* | | | |
| ❑ BST 8016 [S] | Mashed Potatoes and Gravy | 1962 | 40.00 |
| ❑ BST 8016 [S] | Beach Party | 1963 | 25.00 |
| *—Retitled version of "Mashed Potatoes and Gravy"* | | | |
| ❑ BST 8017 [S] | Going to the Ventures Dance Party! | 1962 | 40.00 |
| ❑ BST 8019 [S] | The Ventures Play Telstar, The Lonely Bull | 1962 | 40.00 |
| ❑ BST 8022 [S] | Surfing | 1963 | 30.00 |
| ❑ BST 8023 [S] | The Ventures Play the Country Classics | 1963 | 30.00 |
| ❑ BST 8024 [S] | Let's Go! | 1963 | 30.00 |
| ❑ BST 8027 [S] | (The) Ventures in Space | 1964 | 50.00 |
| ❑ BST 8029 [S] | The Fabulous Ventures | 1964 | 30.00 |

| Number | Title (A Side/B Side) | Yr | NM |
|---|---|---|---|
| ❑ BST 8031 [S] | Walk, Don't Run, Vol. 2 | 1964 | 30.00 |
| ❑ BST 8033 [S] | The Ventures Knock Me Out! | 1965 | 30.00 |
| ❑ BST 8035 [S] | The Ventures on Stage | 1965 | 30.00 |
| ❑ BST 8037 [S] | The Ventures A-Go-Go | 1965 | 30.00 |
| ❑ BST-8038 [S] | The Ventures' Christmas Album | 1965 | 20.00 |
| ❑ BST 8040 [S] | Where the Action Is | 1966 | 25.00 |
| ❑ BST 8042 [S] | The Ventures/Batman Theme | 1966 | 40.00 |
| ❑ BST 8045 [S] | Go with the Ventures! | 1966 | 25.00 |
| ❑ BST 8047 [S] | Wild Things! | 1966 | 25.00 |
| ❑ BST 8050 [S] | Guitar Freakout | 1967 | 25.00 |
| ❑ BLP 16501 [M] | Play Guitar with the Ventures | 1965 | 25.00 |
| ❑ BLP 16502 [M] | Play Guitar with the Ventures, Vol. 2 | 196? | 25.00 |
| ❑ BLP 16503 [M] | Play Guitar with the Ventures, Vol. 3 | 196? | 25.00 |
| ❑ BLP 16504 [M] | Play Guitar with the Ventures, Vol. 4 | 196? | 25.00 |
| ❑ BST 16504 [S] | Play Guitar with the Ventures, Vol. 4 | 196? | 30.00 |
| ❑ BST 17501 [S] | Play Guitar with the Ventures | 1965 | 30.00 |
| ❑ BST 17502 [S] | Play Guitar with the Ventures, Vol. 2 | 196? | 30.00 |
| ❑ BST 17503 [S] | Play Guitar with the Ventures, Vol. 3 | 196? | 30.00 |

**LIBERTY**

| Number | Title (A Side/B Side) | Yr | NM |
|---|---|---|---|
| ❑ LRP-2052 [M] | Super Psychedelics | 1967 | 20.00 |
| ❑ LRP-2053 [M] | Golden Greats by the Ventures | 1967 | 20.00 |
| ❑ LRP-2054 [M] | $1,000,000.00 Weekend | 1967 | 20.00 |
| ❑ LRP-2055 [M] | Flights of Fancy | 1968 | 30.00 |
| ❑ LST-8003 | Walk Don't Run | 1970 | 15.00 |
| *—Reissue of Dolton 8003 with new front cover, original back cover* | | | |
| ❑ LST-8003 | Walk Don't Run | 1970 | 20.00 |
| *—Reissue of Dolton 8003 with new front and back covers* | | | |
| ❑ LT-8003 | Walk Don't Run | 1981 | 8.00 |
| ❑ LST-8023 | I Walk the Line and Other Giant Hits | 1970 | 20.00 |
| *—Reissue of "The Ventures Play the Country Classics"* | | | |
| ❑ LST-8031 | Walk, Don't Run, Vol. 2 | 1970 | 25.00 |
| *—Reissue of Dolton 8031 with new cover* | | | |
| ❑ LST-8050 | Revolving Sounds | 1970 | 30.00 |
| *—Reissue of "Guitar Freakout"* | | | |
| ❑ LST-8052 [S] | Super Psychedelics | 1967 | 25.00 |
| ❑ LST-8052 [S] | Changing Times | 1970 | 40.00 |
| *—Reissue of "Super Psychedelics"* | | | |
| ❑ LST-8053 [S] | Golden Greats by the Ventures | 1967 | 20.00 |
| ❑ LTAO-8053 | Golden Greats by the Ventures | 1981 | 8.00 |
| ❑ LST-8054 [S] | $1,000,000.00 Weekend | 1967 | 20.00 |
| ❑ LST-8055 [S] | Flights of Fancy | 1968 | 20.00 |
| ❑ LST-8057 | The Horse | 1968 | 20.00 |
| ❑ LST-8057 | On the Scene | 1970 | 15.00 |
| *—Reissue of "The Horse"* | | | |
| ❑ LST-8059 | Underground Fire | 1969 | 20.00 |
| ❑ LST-8060 | More Golden Greats | 1970 | 15.00 |
| ❑ LST-8061 | Hawaii Five-O | 1969 | 15.00 |
| ❑ LST-8062 | Swamp Rock | 1969 | 15.00 |
| ❑ LN-10122 | The Very Best of the Ventures | 1981 | 8.00 |
| ❑ LN-10155 | The Ventures Play Telstar, The Lonely Bull | 1981 | 8.00 |
| ❑ LN-10156 | The Ventures Play the Country Classics | 1981 | 8.00 |
| ❑ LN-10188 | Walk, Don't Run, Vol. 2 | 1984 | 8.00 |
| ❑ LN-10190 | (The) Ventures in Space | 1984 | 8.00 |
| ❑ LN-10203 | The Ventures | 1984 | 8.00 |
| ❑ LN-10224 | TV Themes | 1984 | 8.00 |
| ❑ LST-35000 [(2)] | The Ventures 10th Anniversary Album | 1970 | 20.00 |

**SUNSET**

| Number | Title (A Side/B Side) | Yr | NM |
|---|---|---|---|
| ❑ SUM-1160 [M] | The Guitar Genius of the Ventures | 1967 | 12.00 |
| ❑ SUS-5160 [S] | The Guitar Genius of the Ventures | 1967 | 15.00 |
| ❑ SUS-5270 | Super Group | 1969 | 12.00 |

**UNITED ARTISTS**

| Number | Title (A Side/B Side) | Yr | NM |
|---|---|---|---|
| ❑ UXS-80 [(2)] | The Ventures | 1971 | 15.00 |
| ❑ UA-LA147-G [(2)] | Only Hits | 1973 | 15.00 |
| ❑ UA-LA217-E | The Jim Croce Songbook | 1973 | 12.00 |
| ❑ UA-LA331-E | The Very Best of the Ventures | 1974 | 12.00 |
| ❑ UA-LA586-F | Rocky Road | 1976 | 12.00 |
| ❑ UA-LA717-F | TV Themes | 1977 | 25.00 |
| ❑ UAS-5547 | Theme from Shaft | 1971 | 12.00 |
| ❑ UAS-5575 | Joy/The Ventures Play the Classics | 1972 | 12.00 |
| ❑ UAS-5649 | Rock and Roll Forever | 1972 | 12.00 |
| ❑ UAS-6796 | New Testament | 1971 | 12.00 |

### VENUTA, BENAY

**MERCURY**

| Number | Title (A Side/B Side) | Yr | NM |
|---|---|---|---|
| ❑ MG-25006 [10] | Old Time Favorites | 1949 | 70.00 |

### VENUTI, JOE

**GOLDEN CREST**

| Number | Title (A Side/B Side) | Yr | NM |
|---|---|---|---|
| ❑ GC-3100 [M] | Joe Venuti Plays Gershwin | 1959 | 30.00 |
| ❑ GC-3101 [M] | Joe Venuti Plays Jerome Kern | 1959 | 30.00 |

**GRAND AWARD**

| Number | Title (A Side/B Side) | Yr | NM |
|---|---|---|---|
| ❑ GA-33-351 [M] | Fiddle on Fire | 1956 | 40.00 |

**TOPS**

| Number | Title (A Side/B Side) | Yr | NM |
|---|---|---|---|
| ❑ L 923 [10] | Twilight on the Trail | 195? | 30.00 |

### VENUTI, JOE/EDDIE LANG

**COLUMBIA**

| Number | Title (A Side/B Side) | Yr | NM |
|---|---|---|---|
| ❑ C2L 24 [(2)M] | Swinging the Blues | 1963 | 25.00 |
| *—"Guaranteed High Fidelity" on labels* | | | |
| ❑ C2L 24 [(2)M] | Swinging the Blues | 1965 | 20.00 |
| *—Red labels with "360 Sound Mono" on labels* | | | |

**"X"**

| Number | Title (A Side/B Side) | Yr | NM |
|---|---|---|---|
| ❑ LVA-3036 [M] | Joe Venuti and Eddie Lang | 1955 | 40.00 |

### VENUTI, JOE, AND LOUIS PRIMA

**DESIGN**

| Number | Title (A Side/B Side) | Yr | NM |
|---|---|---|---|
| ❑ DLP-54 [M] | Hi-Fi Lootin' | 195? | 20.00 |

### VER PLANCK, BILLY

**SAVOY**

| Number | Title (A Side/B Side) | Yr | NM |
|---|---|---|---|
| ❑ MG-12101 [M] | Dancing Jazz | 1957 | 40.00 |
| ❑ MG-12121 [M] | Jazz for Playgirls | 1957 | 40.00 |

### VER PLANCK, MARLENE

**SAVOY**

| Number | Title (A Side/B Side) | Yr | NM |
|---|---|---|---|
| ❑ MG-12058 [M] | I Think of You with Every Breath I Take | 1956 | 50.00 |
| *—As "Marlene"* | | | |

### VERA, BILLY

**ALFA**

| Number | Title (A Side/B Side) | Yr | NM |
|---|---|---|---|
| ❑ 10001 | Billy and the Beaters | 1981 | 15.00 |
| ❑ 10012 | Billy Vera | 1982 | 12.00 |

**ATLANTIC**

| Number | Title (A Side/B Side) | Yr | NM |
|---|---|---|---|
| ❑ 8197 [M] | With Pen in Hand | 1968 | 40.00 |
| ❑ SD 8197 [S] | With Pen in Hand | 1968 | 25.00 |

**CAPITOL**

| Number | Title (A Side/B Side) | Yr | NM |
|---|---|---|---|
| ❑ C1-46948 | Retro Nuevo | 1988 | 10.00 |

**MACOLA**

| Number | Title (A Side/B Side) | Yr | NM |
|---|---|---|---|
| ❑ 0961 | The Billy Vera Album | 1987 | 10.00 |
| *—Reissue of Midsong Int'l. LP* | | | |

**MIDSONG INT'L.**

| Number | Title (A Side/B Side) | Yr | NM |
|---|---|---|---|
| ❑ BKL1-2219 | Out of the Darkness | 1977 | 12.00 |

**RHINO**

| Number | Title (A Side/B Side) | Yr | NM |
|---|---|---|---|
| ❑ RNLP 70185 | The Atlantic Years | 1987 | 10.00 |
| ❑ RNLP 70858 | By Request — The Best of Billy Vera and the Beaters | 1986 | 12.00 |

**THUNDER**

| Number | Title (A Side/B Side) | Yr | NM |
|---|---|---|---|
| ❑ TVLP 0018 | The Hollywood Sessions | 1987 | 10.00 |

### VERA, BILLY, AND JUDY CLAY

**ATLANTIC**

| Number | Title (A Side/B Side) | Yr | NM |
|---|---|---|---|
| ❑ 8174 [M] | Storybook Children | 1967 | 25.00 |
| ❑ SD 8174 [S] | Storybook Children | 1967 | 30.00 |

### VERDON, GWEN

**RCA VICTOR**

| Number | Title (A Side/B Side) | Yr | NM |
|---|---|---|---|
| ❑ LPM-1152 [M] | The Girl I Left Home For | 1956 | 40.00 |

### VERITY, JOHN, BAND

**ABC DUNHILL**

| Number | Title (A Side/B Side) | Yr | NM |
|---|---|---|---|
| ❑ DSX-50170 | The John Verity Band | 1974 | 20.00 |

### VERNE, LARRY

**ERA**

| Number | Title (A Side/B Side) | Yr | NM |
|---|---|---|---|
| ❑ 104 [M] | Mister Larry Verne | 1961 | 60.00 |

### VERNON, MILLI

**AUDIOPHILE**

| Number | Title (A Side/B Side) | Yr | NM |
|---|---|---|---|
| ❑ AP-178 | Old Shoes | 1989 | 10.00 |
| *—As "Millie Vernon"* | | | |

### VERSATONES, THE

**RCA VICTOR**

| Number | Title (A Side/B Side) | Yr | NM |
|---|---|---|---|
| ❑ LPM-1538 [M] | The Versatones | 1957 | 100.00 |

### VERY SPECIAL ENVOY

**ROULETTE**

| Number | Title (A Side/B Side) | Yr | NM |
|---|---|---|---|
| ❑ SR-42003 | Very Special Envoy | 1968 | 20.00 |

### VETTES, THE

**MGM**

| Number | Title (A Side/B Side) | Yr | NM |
|---|---|---|---|
| ❑ E-4193 [M] | Rev-Up | 1963 | 100.00 |
| ❑ SE-4193 [S] | Rev-Up | 1963 | 120.00 |

### VIBRATIONS, THE

**CHECKER**

| Number | Title (A Side/B Side) | Yr | NM |
|---|---|---|---|
| ❑ LP-2978 [M] | The Watusi | 1961 | 200.00 |

**MANDALA**

| Number | Title (A Side/B Side) | Yr | NM |
|---|---|---|---|
| ❑ 3006 | Taking a New Step | 1972 | 20.00 |

**OKEH**

| Number | Title (A Side/B Side) | Yr | NM |
|---|---|---|---|
| ❑ OKM-12111 [M] | Shout | 1965 | 30.00 |
| ❑ OKM-12112 [M] | Misty | 1966 | 30.00 |
| ❑ OKM-12114 [M] | New Vibrations | 1967 | 30.00 |
| ❑ OKS-14111 [S] | Shout | 1965 | 40.00 |
| ❑ OKS-14112 [S] | Misty | 1966 | 40.00 |
| ❑ OKS-14114 [S] | New Vibrations | 1967 | 40.00 |
| ❑ OKS-14129 | The Vibrations' Greatest Hits | 1969 | 30.00 |

### VICEROYS, THE (3)

**BOLO**

| Number | Title (A Side/B Side) | Yr | NM |
|---|---|---|---|
| ❑ BLP-8000 [M] | The Viceroys at Granny's Pad | 1963 | 40.00 |

### VICK, HAROLD

**BLUE NOTE**

| Number | Title (A Side/B Side) | Yr | NM |
|---|---|---|---|
| ❑ BLP-4138 [M] | Steppin' Out | 1963 | 40.00 |
| ❑ BST-84138 [S] | Steppin' Out | 1963 | 50.00 |
| *—With "New York, USA" address on label* | | | |

**RCA VICTOR**

| Number | Title (A Side/B Side) | Yr | NM |
|---|---|---|---|
| ❑ LSP-3677 [S] | The Caribbean Suite | 1966 | 20.00 |
| ❑ LPM-3761 [M] | Straight Up | 1967 | 20.00 |

**STRATA-EAST**

| Number | Title (A Side/B Side) | Yr | NM |
|---|---|---|---|
| ❑ SES-7431 | Don't Look Back | 197? | 20.00 |

### VICTIMS OF CHANCE, THE

**CRESTVIEW**

| Number | Title (A Side/B Side) | Yr | NM |
|---|---|---|---|
| ❑ CRS-3052 | The Victims of Chance | 197? | 60.00 |

### VIDEO ALL STARS, THE

**SOMERSET**

| Number | Title (A Side/B Side) | Yr | NM |
|---|---|---|---|
| ❑ SF-8800 [M] | The Video All Stars Play TV Jazz Themes | 1956 | 120.00 |

### VIENNA ART ORCHESTRA

**HAT HUT**

| Number | Title (A Side/B Side) | Yr | NM |
|---|---|---|---|
| ❑ 1980/1 [(2)] | Concerto Piccolo | 1980 | 20.00 |
| ❑ 1991/2 [(2)] | Suite for the Green Eighties | 1981 | 20.00 |
| ❑ 1999/2000 [(2)] | From No Time to Rag Time | 1982 | 20.00 |

### VIENNA PHILHARMONIC ORCHESTRA (WILHELM FURTWANGLER, CONDUCTOR)

**URANIA**

| Number | Title (A Side/B Side) | Yr | NM |
|---|---|---|---|
| ❑ URLP-7095 [M] | Beethoven: Symphony No. 3 | 195? | 600.00 |
| *—Withdrawn from the market when it was discovered that the record had been mastered slightly fast* | | | |

### VIENNA PHILHARMONIC ORCHESTRA (PIERRE MONTEUX, CONDUCTOR)

**RCA VICTOR RED SEAL**

| Number | Title (A Side/B Side) | Yr | NM |
|---|---|---|---|
| ❑ LSC-2316 [S] | Beethoven: Symphony No. 6 | 1959 | 50.00 |
| *—Original with "shaded dog" label* | | | |
| ❑ LSC-2362 [S] | Berlioz: Symphonie Fantastique | 1960 | 40.00 |
| *—Original with "shaded dog" label* | | | |
| ❑ LSC-2394 [S] | Haydn: Symphonies No. 94 and 101 | 1960 | 25.00 |
| *—Original with "shaded dog" label* | | | |
| ❑ LSC-2491 [S] | Beethoven: Symphonies No. 1 and 8 | 1961 | 40.00 |
| *—Original with "shaded dog" label* | | | |

### VIENNA PHILHARMONIC ORCHESTRA (FRITZ REINER, CONDUCTOR)

**RCA VICTOR RED SEAL**

| Number | Title (A Side/B Side) | Yr | NM |
|---|---|---|---|
| ❑ LSC-2077 [S] | Strauss: Till Eulenspiegel | 1959 | 100.00 |
| *—Original with "shaded dog" label* | | | |
| ❑ LSC-2077 [S] | Strauss: Till Eulenspiegel | 199? | 25.00 |
| *—Classic Records reissue* | | | |

### VIG, TOMMY

**MILESTONE**

| Number | Title (A Side/B Side) | Yr | NM |
|---|---|---|---|
| ❑ MSP-9007 | Sounds of the Seventies | 1968 | 20.00 |

### VILLA, PEPE

**KING**

| Number | Title (A Side/B Side) | Yr | NM |
|---|---|---|---|
| ❑ 660 [M] | Music of Mexico | 1959 | 30.00 |

### VILLAGE PEOPLE

**CASABLANCA**

| Number | Title (A Side/B Side) | Yr | NM |
|---|---|---|---|
| ❑ NBLP-7064 | Village People | 1977 | 10.00 |
| ❑ NBPIX-7064 [PD] | Village People | 1978 | 20.00 |
| ❑ NBLP-7096 | Macho Man | 1978 | 10.00 |
| ❑ NBPIX-7096 [PD] | Macho Man | 1978 | 20.00 |
| ❑ NBLP-7118 | Cruisin' | 1978 | 10.00 |
| ❑ NBPIX-7118 [PD] | Cruisin' | 1978 | 20.00 |
| ❑ NBLP-7144 | Go West | 1979 | 10.00 |
| ❑ NBLP-7183 [(2)] | Live and Sleazy | 1979 | 12.00 |
| ❑ NBLP-7220 | Can't Stop the Music (Soundtrack) | 1980 | 10.00 |
| *—Also includes one song by the Ritchie Family and one song by David London* | | | |

**RCA VICTOR**

| Number | Title (A Side/B Side) | Yr | NM |
|---|---|---|---|
| ❑ AFL1-4105 | Renaissance | 1981 | 10.00 |

**RHINO**

| Number | Title (A Side/B Side) | Yr | NM |
|---|---|---|---|
| ❑ R1-70167 | Greatest Hits | 1988 | 10.00 |

### VILLAGE STOMPERS, THE

**EPIC**

| Number | Title (A Side/B Side) | Yr | NM |
|---|---|---|---|
| ❑ LN 24078 [M] | Washington Square | 1963 | 15.00 |
| ❑ LN 24090 [M] | More Sounds of Washington Square | 1964 | 15.00 |

| Number | Title (A Side/B Side) | Yr | NM |
|---|---|---|---|
| ❑ LN 24109 [M] | Around the World with the Village Stompers | 1964 | 12.00 |
| ❑ LN 24129 [M] | New Beat on Broadway! | 1964 | 12.00 |
| ❑ LN 24161 [M] | Some Folk, a Bit of Country and a Whole Lot of Dixie | 1965 | 12.00 |
| ❑ LN 24180 [M] | A Taste of Honey | 1965 | 12.00 |
| ❑ LN 24235 [M] | One More Time | 1966 | 12.00 |
| ❑ LN 24318 [M] | The Village Stompers' Greatest Hits | 1967 | 12.00 |
| ❑ BN 26078 [S] | Washington Square | 1963 | 20.00 |
| ❑ BN 26090 [S] | More Sounds of Washington Square | 1964 | 20.00 |
| ❑ BN 26109 [S] | Around the World with the Village Stompers | 1964 | 15.00 |
| ❑ BN 26129 [S] | New Beat on Broadway! | 1964 | 15.00 |
| ❑ BN 26161 [S] | Some Folk, a Bit of Country and a Whole Lot of Dixie | 1965 | 15.00 |
| ❑ BN 26180 [S] | A Taste of Honey | 1965 | 15.00 |
| ❑ BN 26235 [S] | One More Time | 1966 | 15.00 |
| ❑ BN 26318 [S] | The Village Stompers' Greatest Hits | 1967 | 15.00 |

## VILLEGAS

### COLUMBIA

| Number | Title (A Side/B Side) | Yr | NM |
|---|---|---|---|
| ❑ CL 787 [M] | Introducing Villegas | 1956 | 30.00 |
| ❑ CL 877 [M] | Very, Very Villegas | 1956 | 30.00 |

## VINCENT, GENE

### CAPITOL

| Number | Title (A Side/B Side) | Yr | NM |
|---|---|---|---|
| ❑ DKAO-380 [R] | Gene Vincent's Greatest | 1969 | 50.00 |
| ❑ SM-380 [R] | Gene Vincent's Greatest | 197? | 15.00 |
| *—Abridged reissue of DKAO-380* | | | |
| ❑ T 764 [M] | Bluejean Bop! | 1957 | 400.00 |
| *—Turquoise label stock copy* | | | |
| ❑ T 764 [M] | Bluejean Bop! | 1957 | 1000. |
| *—Black label promo* | | | |
| ❑ T 764 [M] | Bluejean Bop! | 1957 | 1000. |
| *—Yellow label promo* | | | |
| ❑ T 811 [M] | Gene Vincent and the Blue Caps | 1957 | 400.00 |
| *—Turquoise label stock copy* | | | |
| ❑ T 811 [M] | Gene Vincent and the Blue Caps | 1957 | 1000. |
| *—Black label promo* | | | |
| ❑ T 811 [M] | Gene Vincent and the Blue Caps | 1957 | 1000. |
| *—Yellow label promo* | | | |
| ❑ T 970 [M] | Gene Vincent Rocks! And the Blue Caps Roll | 1958 | 400.00 |
| *—Turquoise label stock copy* | | | |
| ❑ T 970 [M] | Gene Vincent Rocks! And the Blue Caps Roll | 1958 | 1000. |
| *—Black label promo* | | | |
| ❑ T 970 [M] | Gene Vincent Rocks! And the Blue Caps Roll | 1958 | 1000. |
| *—Yellow label promo* | | | |
| ❑ T 1059 [M] | A Gene Vincent Record Date | 1958 | 400.00 |
| *—Turquoise label stock copy* | | | |
| ❑ T 1059 [M] | A Gene Vincent Record Date | 1958 | 1000. |
| *—Black label promo* | | | |
| ❑ T 1059 [M] | A Gene Vincent Record Date | 1958 | 1000. |
| *—Yellow label promo* | | | |
| ❑ T 1207 [M] | Sounds Like Gene Vincent | 1959 | 300.00 |
| *—Black label with colorband, Capitol logo at left* | | | |
| ❑ ST 1342 [S] | Crazy Times | 1960 | 500.00 |
| *—Black label with colorband, Capitol logo at left* | | | |
| ❑ T 1342 [M] | Crazy Times | 1960 | 300.00 |
| *—Black label with colorband, Capitol logo at left* | | | |
| ❑ SM-11287 | The Bop That Just Won't Stop | 1974 | 15.00 |
| ❑ N-16208 | Gene Vincent's Greatest | 198? | 12.00 |
| *—Budget-line reissue* | | | |
| ❑ N-16209 | The Bop That Just Won't Stop | 198? | 12.00 |
| *—Budget-line reissue* | | | |

### DANDELION

| Number | Title (A Side/B Side) | Yr | NM |
|---|---|---|---|
| ❑ 9-102 | I'm Back and I'm Proud | 1970 | 50.00 |

### INTERMEDIA

| Number | Title (A Side/B Side) | Yr | NM |
|---|---|---|---|
| ❑ QS-5074 | Rockabilly Fever | 198? | 12.00 |

### KAMA SUTRA

| Number | Title (A Side/B Side) | Yr | NM |
|---|---|---|---|
| ❑ KSBS 2019 | Gene Vincent | 1970 | 50.00 |
| ❑ KSBS 2027 | The Day the World Turned Blue | 1971 | 50.00 |

### ROLLIN' ROCK

| Number | Title (A Side/B Side) | Yr | NM |
|---|---|---|---|
| ❑ 022 | Forever | 1981 | 15.00 |

## VINNEGAR, LEROY

### CONTEMPORARY

| Number | Title (A Side/B Side) | Yr | NM |
|---|---|---|---|
| ❑ C-3542 [M] | Leroy Walks! | 1957 | 80.00 |
| ❑ M-3608 [M] | Leroy Walks Again! | 1962 | 30.00 |
| ❑ S-7003 [S] | Leroy Walks! | 1959 | 50.00 |
| ❑ S-7608 [S] | Leroy Walks Again! | 1962 | 40.00 |

### STEREO RECORDS

| Number | Title (A Side/B Side) | Yr | NM |
|---|---|---|---|
| ❑ S-7003 [S] | Leroy Walks! | 1958 | 60.00 |

### VEE JAY

| Number | Title (A Side/B Side) | Yr | NM |
|---|---|---|---|
| ❑ LP-2502 [M] | Jazz's Great Walker | 1964 | 30.00 |
| ❑ LPS-2502 [S] | Jazz's Great Walker | 1964 | 30.00 |

## VINSON, EDDIE "CLEANHEAD"

### AAMCO

| Number | Title (A Side/B Side) | Yr | NM |
|---|---|---|---|
| ❑ 312 [M] | Cleanhead's Back in Town | 196? | 40.00 |

### BETHLEHEM

| Number | Title (A Side/B Side) | Yr | NM |
|---|---|---|---|
| ❑ BCP-5005 [M] | Eddie "Cleanhead" Vinson Sings | 1957 | 100.00 |

### BLUESWAY

| Number | Title (A Side/B Side) | Yr | NM |
|---|---|---|---|
| ❑ BL-6007 [M] | Cherry Red | 1967 | 25.00 |
| ❑ BLS-6007 [S] | Cherry Red | 1967 | 25.00 |

### KING

| Number | Title (A Side/B Side) | Yr | NM |
|---|---|---|---|
| ❑ KS-1087 | Cherry Red | 1969 | 25.00 |

### RIVERSIDE

| Number | Title (A Side/B Side) | Yr | NM |
|---|---|---|---|
| ❑ RLP-502 [M] | Back Door Blues | 1965 | 40.00 |
| ❑ RLS-9502 [S] | Back Door Blues | 1965 | 40.00 |

## VINSON, EDDIE "CLEANHEAD"/JIMMY WITHERSPOON

### KING

| Number | Title (A Side/B Side) | Yr | NM |
|---|---|---|---|
| ❑ 634 [M] | Battle of the Blues, Volume 3 | 1960 | 1500. |

## VINTON, BOBBY

### ABC

| Number | Title (A Side/B Side) | Yr | NM |
|---|---|---|---|
| ❑ X-851 | Melodies of Love | 1974 | 10.00 |
| ❑ D-891 | Heart of Hearts | 1975 | 10.00 |
| ❑ D-924 | The Bobby Vinton Show | 1975 | 10.00 |
| ❑ D-957 | Serenades of Love | 1976 | 10.00 |
| ❑ AB-981 | The Name Is Love | 1977 | 10.00 |

### COLUMBIA LIMITED EDITION

| Number | Title (A Side/B Side) | Yr | NM |
|---|---|---|---|
| ❑ LE 10016 | Big Ones | 197? | 10.00 |
| ❑ LE 10052 | Please Love Me Forever | 197? | 10.00 |
| ❑ LE 10139 | Roses Are Red | 197? | 10.00 |
| ❑ LE 10140 | Blue Velvet | 197? | 10.00 |
| *—Reissue of Epic 26068* | | | |

### COLUMBIA MUSICAL TREASURY

| Number | Title (A Side/B Side) | Yr | NM |
|---|---|---|---|
| ❑ 6P 6035 [(6)] | The Bobby Vinton Treasury | 197? | 30.00 |
| *—"Columbia House" logo on upper right back cover* | | | |

### EPIC

| Number | Title (A Side/B Side) | Yr | NM |
|---|---|---|---|
| ❑ BN 579 [S] | Dancing at the Hop | 1961 | 50.00 |
| ❑ BN 597 [S] | Young Man with a Big Band | 1961 | 50.00 |
| ❑ LN 3727 [M] | Dancing at the Hop | 1961 | 30.00 |
| ❑ LN 3780 [M] | Young Man with a Big Band | 1961 | 30.00 |
| ❑ LN 24020 [M] | Roses Are Red | 1962 | 15.00 |
| ❑ LN 24035 [M] | Bobby Vinton Sings the Big Ones | 1962 | 15.00 |
| ❑ LN 24049 [M] | The Greatest Hits of the Greatest Groups | 1963 | 15.00 |
| ❑ LN 24068 [M] | Blue Velvet | 1963 | 15.00 |
| *—Retitled version of "Blue On Blue"* | | | |
| ❑ LN 24068 [M] | Blue On Blue | 1963 | 25.00 |
| *—Stock copy on black vinyl* | | | |
| ❑ LN 24068 [M] | Blue On Blue | 1963 | 150.00 |
| *—Promo only on blue vinyl* | | | |
| ❑ LN 24081 [M] | There! I've Said It Again | 1964 | 15.00 |
| ❑ LN 24098 [M] | Bobby Vinton's Greatest Hits | 1964 | 12.00 |
| *—Despite lower number, this came out after "Tell Me Why"* | | | |
| ❑ LN 24113 [M] | Tell Me Why | 1964 | 12.00 |
| ❑ LN 24122 [M] | A Very Merry Christmas | 1964 | 12.00 |
| ❑ LN 24136 [M] | Mr. Lonely | 1965 | 12.00 |
| ❑ LN 24154 [M] | Bobby Vinton Sings for Lonely Nights | 1965 | 12.00 |
| ❑ LN 24170 [M] | Drive-In Movie Time | 1965 | 12.00 |
| ❑ LN 24182 [M] | Satin Pillows and Careless | 1966 | 12.00 |
| ❑ LN 24187 [M] | More of Bobby Vinton's Greatest Hits | 1966 | 12.00 |
| ❑ LN 24188 [M] | Country Boy | 1966 | 12.00 |
| ❑ LN 24203 [M] | Live at the Copa | 1967 | 12.00 |
| ❑ LN 24245 [M] | Bobby Vinton's Newest Hits | 1967 | 12.00 |
| ❑ LN 24341 [M] | Please Love Me Forever | 1967 | 15.00 |
| ❑ BN 26020 [S] | Roses Are Red | 1962 | 20.00 |
| ❑ BN 26035 [S] | Bobby Vinton Sings the Big Ones | 1962 | 20.00 |
| ❑ BN 26049 [S] | The Greatest Hits of the Greatest Groups | 1963 | 20.00 |
| ❑ BN 26068 [S] | Blue Velvet | 1963 | 20.00 |
| *—Retitled version of "Blue On Blue"* | | | |
| ❑ BN 26068 [S] | Blue On Blue | 1963 | 30.00 |
| ❑ BN 26081 [S] | There! I've Said It Again | 1964 | 20.00 |
| ❑ BN 26098 [S] | Bobby Vinton's Greatest Hits | 1964 | 15.00 |
| *—Despite lower number, this came out after "Tell Me Why"* | | | |
| ❑ PE 26098 | Bobby Vinton's Greatest Hits | 198? | 8.00 |
| *—Budget-line reissue* | | | |
| ❑ BN 26113 [S] | Tell Me Why | 1964 | 15.00 |
| ❑ BN 26122 [S] | A Very Merry Christmas | 1964 | 15.00 |
| ❑ BN 26136 [S] | Mr. Lonely | 1965 | 15.00 |
| ❑ BN 26154 [S] | Bobby Vinton Sings for Lonely Nights | 1965 | 15.00 |
| ❑ BN 26170 [S] | Drive-In Movie Time | 1965 | 15.00 |
| ❑ BN 26182 [S] | Satin Pillows and Careless | 1966 | 15.00 |
| ❑ BN 26187 [S] | More of Bobby Vinton's Greatest Hits | 1966 | 15.00 |
| ❑ BN 26188 [S] | Country Boy | 1966 | 15.00 |
| ❑ BN 26203 [S] | Live at the Copa | 1967 | 15.00 |
| ❑ BN 26245 [S] | Bobby Vinton's Newest Hits | 1967 | 15.00 |
| ❑ BN 26341 [S] | Please Love Me Forever | 1967 | 15.00 |
| ❑ BN 26382 | Take Good Care of My Baby | 1968 | 15.00 |
| ❑ BN 26437 | I Love How You Love Me | 1968 | 15.00 |
| ❑ BN 26471 | Vinton | 1969 | 15.00 |
| ❑ BN 26517 | Bobby Vinton's Greatest Hits of Love | 1970 | 15.00 |
| ❑ BN 26540 | My Elusive Dreams | 1970 | 15.00 |
| ❑ KE 31286 | Ev'ry Day of My Life | 1972 | 12.00 |
| ❑ KEG 31487 [(2)] | Bobby Vinton's All-Time Greatest Hits | 1972 | 15.00 |
| ❑ PEG 31487 [(2)] | Bobby Vinton's All-Time Greatest Hits | 197? | 12.00 |
| *—Reissue* | | | |
| ❑ KE 31642 | Sealed with a Kiss | 1972 | 12.00 |
| ❑ PE 32921 | With Love | 1974 | 10.00 |
| ❑ KEG 33468 [(2)] | Bobby Vinton Sings the Golden Decade of Love | 1975 | 12.00 |
| ❑ KEG 33767 [(2)] | Greatest Hits/Greatest Hits of Love | 1976 | 12.00 |
| ❑ JE 35605 | Autumn Memories | 1979 | 10.00 |
| ❑ JE 35998 | Spring Sensations | 1979 | 10.00 |
| ❑ JE 35999 | Summer Serenade | 1979 | 10.00 |

### HARMONY

| Number | Title (A Side/B Side) | Yr | NM |
|---|---|---|---|
| ❑ KH 11402 | Vinton Sings Vinton | 197? | 10.00 |

### PICKWICK

| Number | Title (A Side/B Side) | Yr | NM |
|---|---|---|---|
| ❑ SPC-3353 | Melodies of Love | 197? | 8.00 |

### TAPESTRY

| Number | Title (A Side/B Side) | Yr | NM |
|---|---|---|---|
| ❑ TRS-1001 [EP] | Santa Must Be Polish | 1987 | 10.00 |

## VIOLA, AL

### MODE

| Number | Title (A Side/B Side) | Yr | NM |
|---|---|---|---|
| ❑ LP-121 [M] | Solo Guitar | 1957 | 80.00 |

## VIOLENT FEMMES

### RHINO

| Number | Title (A Side/B Side) | Yr | NM |
|---|---|---|---|
| ❑ R1-79951 | Violent Femmes | 2003 | 15.00 |
| *—Reissue on 180-gram vinyl* | | | |

### SLASH

| Number | Title (A Side/B Side) | Yr | NM |
|---|---|---|---|
| ❑ 23845 | Violent Femmes | 1983 | 15.00 |
| ❑ 25094 | Hallowed Ground | 1984 | 12.00 |
| ❑ 25340 | The Blind Leading the Naked | 1986 | 10.00 |
| ❑ 25819 | 3 | 1988 | 10.00 |

### WARNER BROS.

| Number | Title (A Side/B Side) | Yr | NM |
|---|---|---|---|
| ❑ PRO-A-3519 [DJ] | 3 On 3 | 1989 | 25.00 |
| *—Promo-only interviews and music* | | | |

## VIOLINAIRES, THE

### CHECKER

| Number | Title (A Side/B Side) | Yr | NM |
|---|---|---|---|
| ❑ LP-10011 [M] | Stand By Me | 1965 | 25.00 |
| ❑ LP-10017 [M] | The Fantastic Violinaires | 1966 | 25.00 |
| ❑ LP-10020 [M] | I'm Going to Serve the Lord | 196? | 20.00 |
| ❑ LPS-10020 [S] | I'm Going to Serve the Lord | 196? | 25.00 |
| ❑ LP-10030 [M] | Move On Up | 196? | 20.00 |
| ❑ LPS-10030 [S] | Move On Up | 196? | 25.00 |
| ❑ LP-10040 [M] | Shout! | 196? | 20.00 |
| ❑ LPS-10040 [S] | Shout! | 196? | 25.00 |
| ❑ LP-10045 [M] | Live the Right Way | 196? | 25.00 |
| ❑ LPS-10045 [S] | Live the Right Way | 196? | 25.00 |
| ❑ LPS-10053 | The Violinaires in Concert | 1968 | 20.00 |
| ❑ LPS-10057 | God's Creation | 1969 | 20.00 |
| ❑ LP-10060 | At His Command | 1970 | 20.00 |
| ❑ 2CK-10065 [(2)] | Please Answer This Prayer | 197? | 25.00 |
| ❑ CK-10067 | Groovin' with Jesus | 197? | 20.00 |

## VIRGIN INSANITY

### FUNKY

| Number | Title (A Side/B Side) | Yr | NM |
|---|---|---|---|
| ❑ 71411 | Illusions of the Maintenance Man | 1970 | 200.00 |

## VIRGINIANS, THE

### MONUMENT

| Number | Title (A Side/B Side) | Yr | NM |
|---|---|---|---|
| ❑ MLP-8031 [M] | Ballads and Bluegrass | 1965 | 20.00 |
| ❑ SLP-18031 [S] | Ballads and Bluegrass | 1965 | 25.00 |

### UNITED ARTISTS

| Number | Title (A Side/B Side) | Yr | NM |
|---|---|---|---|
| ❑ UAL-3293 [M] | The Wonderful World of Bluegrass Music | 1963 | 20.00 |
| ❑ UAS-6293 [S] | The Wonderful World of Bluegrass Music | 1963 | 25.00 |

## VIRTUES, THE

### FAYETTE

| Number | Title (A Side/B Side) | Yr | NM |
|---|---|---|---|
| ❑ 1816 [M] | Frank Virtue and the Virtues | 1964 | 40.00 |
| *—White cover* | | | |
| ❑ 1816 [M] | Frank Virtue and the Virtues | 1964 | 60.00 |
| *—Blue cover* | | | |

### STRAND

| Number | Title (A Side/B Side) | Yr | NM |
|---|---|---|---|
| ❑ L-1061 [M] | Guitar Boogie Shuffle | 1960 | 30.00 |
| ❑ SL-1061 [S] | Guitar Boogie Shuffle | 1960 | 40.00 |

### WYNNE

| Number | Title (A Side/B Side) | Yr | NM |
|---|---|---|---|
| ❑ WLP-111 [M] | Guitar Boogie Shuffle | 1960 | 120.00 |
| ❑ WLP-711 [S] | Guitar Boogie Shuffle | 1960 | 180.00 |

## VISCOUNTS, THE (1)

### AMY

| Number | Title (A Side/B Side) | Yr | NM |
|---|---|---|---|
| ❑ 8008 [M] | Harlem Nocturne | 1965 | 40.00 |
| ❑ S-8008 [S] | Harlem Nocturne | 1965 | 50.00 |

### MADISON

| Number | Title (A Side/B Side) | Yr | NM |
|---|---|---|---|
| ❑ 1001 [M] | The Viscounts | 1960 | 200.00 |

| Number | Title (A Side/B Side) | Yr | NM |
|---|---|---|---|

### VISION OF SUNSHINE

AVCO EMBASSY

| Number | Title (A Side/B Side) | Yr | NM |
|---|---|---|---|
| ❑ 33007 | Vision of Sunshine | 1970 | 30.00 |

### VISITORS, THE

COBBLESTONE

| Number | Title (A Side/B Side) | Yr | NM |
|---|---|---|---|
| ❑ 9010 | Neptune | 197? | 20.00 |

### VOGUES, THE

CO & CE

| Number | Title (A Side/B Side) | Yr | NM |
|---|---|---|---|
| ❑ LP-1229 [M] | Meet the Vogues | 1965 | 50.00 |
| ❑ LP-1230 [M] | Five O'Clock World | 1966 | 50.00 |

*—Stereo pressings of these two albums are not known to exist!*

PICKWICK

| Number | Title (A Side/B Side) | Yr | NM |
|---|---|---|---|
| ❑ SPC-3188 [R] | Five O'Clock World | 1971 | 10.00 |
| ❑ SPC-3214 [R] | A Lover's Concerto | 1971 | 10.00 |

REPRISE

| Number | Title (A Side/B Side) | Yr | NM |
|---|---|---|---|
| ❑ RS 6314 | Turn Around, Look at Me | 1968 | 15.00 |
| *—With "W7" and "r:" logos on two-tone orange label* | | | |
| ❑ RS 6326 | Till | 1969 | 15.00 |
| *—With "W7" and "r:" logos on two-tone orange label* | | | |
| ❑ RS 6347 | Memories | 1969 | 15.00 |
| *—With "W7" and "r:" logos on two-tone orange label* | | | |
| ❑ RS 6371 | The Vogues' Greatest Hits | 1969 | 15.00 |
| *—With "W7" and "r:" logos on two-tone orange label* | | | |
| ❑ RS 6395 | The Vogues Sing the Good Old Songs | 1970 | 12.00 |
| ❑ ST-91559 | Turn Around, Look at Me | 1968 | 20.00 |
| *—Capitol Record Club edition* | | | |
| ❑ SW-93040 | The Vogues' Greatest Hits | 1970 | 20.00 |
| *—Capitol Record Club edition* | | | |

SSS INTERNATIONAL

| Number | Title (A Side/B Side) | Yr | NM |
|---|---|---|---|
| ❑ 34 | The Vogues' Greatest Hits | 1977 | 10.00 |

### VOICE OF THE BEEHIVE

LONDON

| Number | Title (A Side/B Side) | Yr | NM |
|---|---|---|---|
| ❑ 828100-1 | Let It Bee | 1988 | 15.00 |

### VOLTAGE BROTHERS, THE

LIFESONG

| Number | Title (A Side/B Side) | Yr | NM |
|---|---|---|---|
| ❑ JZ 35042 | The Voltage Brothers | 1978 | 20.00 |
| ❑ JZ 35653 | Throw Down | 1978 | 20.00 |

### VON SCHMIDT, ERIC

FOLKLORE

| Number | Title (A Side/B Side) | Yr | NM |
|---|---|---|---|
| ❑ FRLP-14005 [M] | Folk Blues | 1964 | 30.00 |
| ❑ FRST-14005 [S] | Folk Blues | 1964 | 40.00 |

PRESTIGE

| Number | Title (A Side/B Side) | Yr | NM |
|---|---|---|---|
| ❑ PRLP-7384 [M] | Eric Sings Von Schmidt | 1966 | 20.00 |
| ❑ PRST-7384 [S] | Eric Sings Von Schmidt | 1966 | 25.00 |

SMASH

| Number | Title (A Side/B Side) | Yr | NM |
|---|---|---|---|
| ❑ SRS-67124 | Who Knocked the Brains Out of the Sky? | 1969 | 20.00 |

### VRONSKY AND BABIN

RCA VICTOR RED SEAL

| Number | Title (A Side/B Side) | Yr | NM |
|---|---|---|---|
| ❑ LSC-2417 [S] | 178 Keys | 1960 | 25.00 |

*—Original with "shaded dog" label*

# W

### WACKER, FRED

DOLPHIN

| Number | Title (A Side/B Side) | Yr | NM |
|---|---|---|---|
| ❑ 9 [M] | Freddy Wacker and His Windy City Seven | 195? | 50.00 |

### WADE, ADAM

COED

| Number | Title (A Side/B Side) | Yr | NM |
|---|---|---|---|
| ❑ LPC-902 [M] | And Then Came Adam | 1960 | 50.00 |
| ❑ LPCS-902 [S] | And Then Came Adam | 1960 | 60.00 |
| ❑ LPC-903 [M] | Adam and Evening | 1961 | 50.00 |
| ❑ LPCS-903 [S] | Adam and Evening | 1961 | 60.00 |

EPIC

| Number | Title (A Side/B Side) | Yr | NM |
|---|---|---|---|
| ❑ LN 24019 [M] | Adam Wade's Greatest Hits | 1962 | 25.00 |
| ❑ LN 24026 [M] | One Is a Lonely Number | 1962 | 25.00 |
| ❑ LN 24044 [M] | What Kind of Fool Am I? | 1963 | 25.00 |
| ❑ LN 24056 [M] | A Very Good Year for Girls | 1963 | 25.00 |
| ❑ BN 26019 [S] | Adam Wade's Greatest Hits | 1962 | 30.00 |
| ❑ BN 26026 [S] | One Is a Lonely Number | 1962 | 30.00 |
| ❑ BN 26044 [S] | What Kind of Fool Am I? | 1963 | 30.00 |
| ❑ BN 26056 [S] | A Very Good Year for Girls | 1963 | 30.00 |

KIRSHNER

| Number | Title (A Side/B Side) | Yr | NM |
|---|---|---|---|
| ❑ PZ 34919 | Adam Wade | 1977 | 12.00 |

### WADSWORTH MANSION

SUSSEX

| Number | Title (A Side/B Side) | Yr | NM |
|---|---|---|---|
| ❑ SXBS-7008 | Wadsworth Mansion | 1971 | 20.00 |
| ❑ SXBS-7008 | Wadsworth Manison | 1971 | 25.00 |

*—Some copies of this LP have the above typographical error*

### WAGNER, LARRY

A44

| Number | Title (A Side/B Side) | Yr | NM |
|---|---|---|---|
| ❑ AP-501 [10] | Larry Wagner | 1954 | 60.00 |

### WAGNER, ROGER, CHORALE

CAPITOL

| Number | Title (A Side/B Side) | Yr | NM |
|---|---|---|---|
| ❑ P 8267 [M] | Songs of Stephen Foster | 195? | 30.00 |
| ❑ P 8324 [M] | Folk Songs of the New World | 195? | 30.00 |
| ❑ P 8332 [M] | Folk Songs of the Frontier | 195? | 30.00 |
| ❑ PBR 8345 [(2)M] | Folk Songs of the Old World | 195? | 40.00 |
| ❑ SP 8353 [S] | Joy to the World! | 195? | 25.00 |
| ❑ P 8387 [M] | Folk Songs of the World | 195? | 20.00 |

### WAGONER, PORTER

ACCORD

| Number | Title (A Side/B Side) | Yr | NM |
|---|---|---|---|
| ❑ SN-7179 | Down Home Country | 1982 | 12.00 |

DOT/MCA

| Number | Title (A Side/B Side) | Yr | NM |
|---|---|---|---|
| ❑ 39053 | Porter Wagoner | 1986 | 10.00 |

RCA CAMDEN

| Number | Title (A Side/B Side) | Yr | NM |
|---|---|---|---|
| ❑ CAL-769 [M] | A Satisfied Mind | 1963 | 12.00 |
| ❑ CAS-769(e) [R] | A Satisfied Mind | 1963 | 10.00 |
| ❑ CAL-861 [M] | An Old Log Cabin for Sale | 1965 | 12.00 |
| ❑ CAS-861 [S] | An Old Log Cabin for Sale | 1965 | 12.00 |
| ❑ CAL-942 [M] | "Your Old Love Letters" And Other Country Hits | 1966 | 12.00 |
| ❑ CAS-942 [S] | "Your Old Love Letters" And Other Country Hits | 1966 | 12.00 |
| ❑ CAL-2116 [M] | I'm Day Dreamin' Tonight | 1967 | 12.00 |
| ❑ CAS-2116 [S] | I'm Day Dreamin' Tonight | 1967 | 12.00 |
| ❑ CAL-2191 [M] | Green, Green Grass of Home | 1967 | 12.00 |
| ❑ CAS-2191 [S] | Green, Green Grass of Home | 1967 | 12.00 |
| ❑ CAS-2321 | Country Feeling | 1968 | 12.00 |
| ❑ CAS-2409 | Howdy Neighbor | 1970 | 12.00 |
| ❑ CAS-2478 | Porter Wagoner Country | 1971 | 12.00 |
| ❑ CAS-2588 | The Silent Kind | 1972 | 12.00 |
| ❑ CXS-9010 [(2)] | Blue Moon of Kentucky | 1971 | 15.00 |

RCA VICTOR

| Number | Title (A Side/B Side) | Yr | NM |
|---|---|---|---|
| ❑ APL1-0142 | I'll Keep on Lovin' You | 1973 | 15.00 |
| ❑ APL1-0346 | The Farmer | 1974 | 15.00 |
| ❑ APL1-0496 | Tore Down | 1974 | 15.00 |
| ❑ APL1-0713 | Highway Headin' South | 1974 | 15.00 |
| ❑ APL1-1056 | Sing Love | 1975 | 15.00 |
| ❑ ANL1-1213 | The Best of Porter Wagoner | 1975 | 12.00 |
| ❑ LPM-1358 [M] | A Satisfied Mind | 1956 | 200.00 |
| ❑ AHL1-2432 | Porter | 1977 | 12.00 |
| ❑ LPM-2447 [M] | A Slice of Life — Songs Happy 'N' Sad | 1962 | 25.00 |
| ❑ LSP-2447 [S] | A Slice of Life — Songs Happy 'N' Sad | 1962 | 30.00 |
| ❑ LPM-2650 [M] | The Porter Wagoner Show | 1963 | 25.00 |
| ❑ LSP-2650 [S] | The Porter Wagoner Show | 1963 | 30.00 |
| ❑ LPM-2706 [M] | Y'All Come | 1963 | 25.00 |
| ❑ LSP-2706 [S] | Y'All Come | 1963 | 30.00 |
| ❑ LPM-2840 [M] | In Person | 1964 | 25.00 |
| ❑ LSP-2840 [S] | In Person | 1964 | 30.00 |
| ❑ LPM-2960 [M] | The Bluegrass Story | 1964 | 20.00 |
| ❑ LSP-2960 [S] | The Bluegrass Story | 1964 | 25.00 |
| ❑ LPM-3389 [M] | The Thin Man from West Plains | 1965 | 20.00 |
| ❑ LSP-3389 [S] | The Thin Man from West Plains | 1965 | 25.00 |
| ❑ LPM-3488 [M] | Grand Old Gospel | 1966 | 20.00 |
| ❑ LSP-3488 [S] | Grand Old Gospel | 1966 | 25.00 |
| ❑ LPM-3509 [M] | On the Road | 1966 | 20.00 |
| ❑ LSP-3509 [S] | On the Road | 1966 | 25.00 |
| ❑ LPM-3560 [M] | The Best of Porter Wagoner | 1966 | 20.00 |
| ❑ LSP-3560 [S] | The Best of Porter Wagoner | 1966 | 25.00 |
| ❑ LPM-3593 [M] | Confessions of a Broken Man | 1966 | 20.00 |
| ❑ LSP-3593 [S] | Confessions of a Broken Man | 1966 | 25.00 |
| ❑ LPM-3683 [M] | Soul of a Convict | 1967 | 25.00 |
| ❑ LSP-3683 [S] | Soul of a Convict | 1967 | 20.00 |
| ❑ LPM-3797 [M] | The Cold Hard Facts of Life | 1967 | 25.00 |
| ❑ LSP-3797 [S] | The Cold Hard Facts of Life | 1967 | 20.00 |
| ❑ LPM-3855 [M] | More Grand Old Gospel | 1967 | 25.00 |
| ❑ LSP-3855 [S] | More Grand Old Gospel | 1967 | 20.00 |
| ❑ LPM-3968 [M] | The Bottom of the Bottle | 1968 | 100.00 |
| ❑ LSP-3968 [S] | The Bottom of the Bottle | 1968 | 20.00 |
| ❑ LSP-4034 | Gospel Country | 1968 | 20.00 |
| ❑ LSP-4116 | The Carroll County Accident | 1969 | 20.00 |
| ❑ LSP-4181 | Me and My Boys | 1969 | 20.00 |
| ❑ LSP-4286 | You Got-ta Have a License | 1970 | 20.00 |
| ❑ LSP-4321 | The Best of Porter Wagoner, Volume 2 | 1970 | 20.00 |
| ❑ LSP-4386 | Down in the Alley | 1970 | 20.00 |
| ❑ LSP-4508 | Simple As I Am | 1971 | 20.00 |
| ❑ LSP-4586 | Porter Wagoner Sings His Own | 1971 | 15.00 |
| ❑ LSP-4661 | What Ain't to Be | 1972 | 15.00 |
| ❑ LSP-4734 | Ballads of Love | 1972 | 15.00 |
| ❑ LSP-4810 | The Porter Wagoner Experience | 1973 | 15.00 |
| ❑ AHL1-7000 | Collector's Series | 1985 | 10.00 |

WARNER BROS.

| Number | Title (A Side/B Side) | Yr | NM |
|---|---|---|---|
| ❑ 23783 | Viva Porter Wagoner! | 1983 | 10.00 |

### WAGONER, PORTER, AND SKEETER DAVIS

Also see each artist's individual listings.

RCA VICTOR

| Number | Title (A Side/B Side) | Yr | NM |
|---|---|---|---|
| ❑ LPM-2529 [M] | Porter Wagoner and Skeeter Davis Sing Duets | 1962 | 25.00 |
| ❑ LSP-2529 [S] | Porter Wagoner and Skeeter Davis Sing Duets | 1962 | 30.00 |

### WAGONER, PORTER, AND DOLLY PARTON

Also see each artist's individual listings.

PAIR

| Number | Title (A Side/B Side) | Yr | NM |
|---|---|---|---|
| ❑ PDL1-1013 [(2)] | Sweet Harmony | 1986 | 12.00 |

RCA VICTOR

| Number | Title (A Side/B Side) | Yr | NM |
|---|---|---|---|
| ❑ APL1-0248 | Love and Music | 1973 | 15.00 |
| ❑ APL1-0646 | Porter 'N' Dolly | 1974 | 15.00 |
| ❑ APL1-1116 | Say Forever | 1975 | 15.00 |
| ❑ AHL1-3700 | Porter Wagoner and Dolly Parton | 1980 | 12.00 |
| ❑ LPM-3926 [M] | Just Between You and Me | 1968 | 100.00 |
| ❑ LSP-3926 [S] | Just Between You and Me | 1968 | 20.00 |
| ❑ LSP-4039 | Just the Two of Us | 1968 | 20.00 |
| ❑ LSP-4186 | Always, Always | 1969 | 20.00 |
| ❑ AYL1-4251 | Porter Wagoner and Dolly Parton | 1982 | 8.00 |
| *—"Best Buy Series" reissue* | | | |
| ❑ LSP-4305 | Porter Wayne and Dolly Rebecca | 1970 | 20.00 |
| ❑ LSP-4388 | Once More | 1970 | 20.00 |
| ❑ LSP-4490 | Two of a Kind | 1971 | 20.00 |
| ❑ AHL1-4556 | The Best of Porter Wagoner and Dolly Parton | 1983 | 10.00 |
| ❑ LSP-4556 | The Best of Porter Wagoner and Dolly Parton | 1971 | 20.00 |
| ❑ LSP-4628 | The Right Combination/ Burning the Midnight Oil | 1972 | 15.00 |
| ❑ LSP-4761 | Together Always | 1972 | 15.00 |
| ❑ LSP-4841 | We Found It | 1973 | 15.00 |

### WAIKIKIS, THE

KAPP

| Number | Title (A Side/B Side) | Yr | NM |
|---|---|---|---|
| ❑ KL-1366 [M] | Hawaii Tattoo | 1964 | 15.00 |
| ❑ KL-1432 [M] | Hawaii Honeymoon | 1965 | 15.00 |
| ❑ KL-1437 [M] | Beach Party | 1965 | 15.00 |
| ❑ KL-1473 [M] | Lollipops and Roses | 1966 | 15.00 |
| ❑ KL-1484 [M] | A Taste of Hawaii | 1966 | 15.00 |
| ❑ KL-1555 [M] | Pearly Shells from Hawaii | 1968 | 30.00 |
| *—White label promo in stereo cover, "Mono" sticker on front* | | | |
| ❑ KS-3366 [S] | Hawaii Tattoo | 1964 | 20.00 |
| ❑ KS-3432 [S] | Hawaii Honeymoon | 1965 | 20.00 |
| ❑ KS-3437 [S] | Beach Party | 1965 | 20.00 |
| ❑ KS-3473 [S] | Lollipops and Roses | 1966 | 20.00 |
| ❑ KS-3484 [S] | A Taste of Hawaii | 1966 | 20.00 |
| ❑ KS-3555 [S] | Pearly Shells from Hawaii | 1968 | 15.00 |
| ❑ KS-3575 | Midnight Luau | 1969 | 15.00 |
| ❑ KS-3593 | Moonlight on Diamond Head | 1969 | 15.00 |
| ❑ KS-3612 | Greatest Hits | 1970 | 12.00 |

MCA

| Number | Title (A Side/B Side) | Yr | NM |
|---|---|---|---|
| ❑ 544 | Pearly Shells from Hawaii | 197? | 10.00 |
| ❑ 547 | Greatest Hits | 197? | 10.00 |

### WAILERS, THE

ETIQUETTE

| Number | Title (A Side/B Side) | Yr | NM |
|---|---|---|---|
| ❑ ALB-01 [M] | The Fabulous Wailers at the Castle | 196? | 100.00 |
| ❑ ALB-022 [M] | The Wailers and Company | 196? | 80.00 |
| ❑ ALB-023 [M] | Wailers, Wailers, Everywhere | 196? | 100.00 |
| ❑ ALB-026 [M] | Out of Our Tree | 1966 | 100.00 |
| ❑ 22296/7 [(2)] | The Wailers and Their Greatest Hits | 1979 | 25.00 |

GOLDEN CREST

| Number | Title (A Side/B Side) | Yr | NM |
|---|---|---|---|
| ❑ CR-3075 [M] | Fabulous Wailers | 1959 | 250.00 |
| *—Full-color photo on cover* | | | |
| ❑ CR-3075 [M] | Fabulous Wailers | 196? | 50.00 |
| *—Title, no photo, on cover* | | | |
| ❑ CR-3075 [M] | Fabulous Wailers | 1962 | 100.00 |
| *—Black and white photo on cover* | | | |

IMPERIAL

| Number | Title (A Side/B Side) | Yr | NM |
|---|---|---|---|
| ❑ LP-9262 [M] | Tall Cool One | 1964 | 50.00 |
| ❑ LP-12262 [S] | Tall Cool One | 1964 | 80.00 |

UNITED ARTISTS

| Number | Title (A Side/B Side) | Yr | NM |
|---|---|---|---|
| ❑ UAL-3557 [M] | Outburst! | 1966 | 50.00 |
| ❑ UAS-6557 [S] | Outburst! | 1966 | 80.00 |

### WAINWRIGHT, LOUDON, III

ARISTA

| Number | Title (A Side/B Side) | Yr | NM |
|---|---|---|---|
| ❑ AL 4063 | T Shirt | 1976 | 12.00 |
| ❑ AB 4173 | Final Exam | 1978 | 12.00 |

ATLANTIC

| Number | Title (A Side/B Side) | Yr | NM |
|---|---|---|---|
| ❑ SD 8260 | Loudon Wainwright III | 1970 | 20.00 |
| ❑ SD 8291 | Album II | 1971 | 20.00 |

COLUMBIA

| Number | Title (A Side/B Side) | Yr | NM |
|---|---|---|---|
| ❑ KC 31462 | Album III | 1972 | 15.00 |
| ❑ PC 31462 | Album III | 198? | 8.00 |
| *—Budget-line reissue* | | | |
| ❑ KC 32710 | Attempted Mustache | 1973 | 15.00 |
| ❑ PC 32710 | Attempted Mustache | 198? | 8.00 |
| *—Budget-line reissue* | | | |
| ❑ PC 33369 | Unrequited | 1975 | 12.00 |
| *—No bar code on cover* | | | |
| ❑ PC 33369 | Unrequited | 198? | 8.00 |
| *—Budget-line reissue with bar code* | | | |

ROUNDER

| Number | Title (A Side/B Side) | Yr | NM |
|---|---|---|---|
| ❑ 3050 | A Live One | 1979 | 12.00 |
| ❑ 3076 | Fame and Wealth | 1983 | 12.00 |
| ❑ 3096 | I'm Alright | 1986 | 10.00 |
| ❑ 3106 | More Love Songs | 1987 | 10.00 |

SILVERTONE

| Number | Title (A Side/B Side) | Yr | NM |
|---|---|---|---|
| ❑ 1203-1-J | Therapy | 1989 | 12.00 |



**Except when noted otherwise, VG = 25% of NM, and VG+ = 50% of NM. (Example: VG = $2.00, VG+ = $4.00 and NM = $8.00.)**

### WAITE, GENEVIEVE

| Number | Title (A Side/B Side) | Yr | NM |
|---|---|---|---|
| **PARAMOUR** | | | |
| ❑ 5088 | Romance Is on the Rise | 1974 | 25.00 |

### WAITRESSES, THE

| Number | Title (A Side/B Side) | Yr | NM |
|---|---|---|---|
| **POLYDOR** | | | |
| ❑ PX-1-507 [EP] | I Could Rule the World If I Could Only Get the Parts | 1982 | 10.00 |
| ❑ PD-1-6346 | Wasn't Tomorrow Wonderful? | 1982 | 10.00 |
| ❑ 810980-1 | Bruiseology | 1983 | 10.00 |
| ❑ 810980-1 [DJ] | Bruiseology | 1983 | 25.00 |
| *—Promo only on purpleish vinyl* | | | |

### WAKEFIELD SUN

| Number | Title (A Side/B Side) | Yr | NM |
|---|---|---|---|
| **MGM** | | | |
| ❑ SE-4626 | Wakefield Sun | 1969 | 25.00 |

### WAKELY, JIMMY

| Number | Title (A Side/B Side) | Yr | NM |
|---|---|---|---|
| **CAPITOL** | | | |
| ❑ H 4008 [10] | Songs of the West | 195? | 120.00 |
| ❑ H-9004 [10] | Christmas on the Range | 1950 | 150.00 |
| **DECCA** | | | |
| ❑ DL 8409 [M] | Santa Fe Trail | 1956 | 80.00 |
| ❑ DL 8680 [M] | Enter and Rest and Pray | 1957 | 60.00 |
| ❑ DL 75077 | Heartaches | 1969 | 15.00 |
| ❑ DL 75192 | Now and Then | 1970 | 15.00 |
| **DOT** | | | |
| ❑ DLP-3711 [M] | Slippin' Around | 1966 | 20.00 |
| ❑ DLP-3754 [M] | Christmas with Jimmy Wakely | 1966 | 20.00 |
| ❑ DLP-25711 [S] | Slippin' Around | 1966 | 25.00 |
| ❑ DLP-25734 [S] | Christmas with Jimmy Wakely | 1966 | 25.00 |
| **MCA CORAL** | | | |
| ❑ 20033 | Blue Shadows | 1973 | 10.00 |
| **MCR** | | | |
| ❑ 1250 | Jimmy Wakely Sings a Tribute to Bob Wills | 1974 | 15.00 |
| ❑ 1254 | Jimmy Wakely Revisits Country Western Swing with the Big Band Sound | 1974 | 15.00 |
| **SHASTA** | | | |
| ❑ 501 | Country Million Sellers | 195? | 15.00 |
| ❑ 502 | Merry Christmas | 1959 | 15.00 |
| ❑ 505 | Jimmy Wakely Sings | 196? | 15.00 |
| ❑ 512 | The Jimmy Wakely Family Show | 196? | 15.00 |
| ❑ 528 | J.W. Country | 196? | 15.00 |
| **TOPS** | | | |
| ❑ L-1601 [M] | A Cowboy Serenade | 195? | 25.00 |
| **VOCALION** | | | |
| ❑ VL 73857 | Here's Jimmy Wakely | 1968 | 12.00 |
| ❑ VL 73904 | Big Country Songs | 1970 | 12.00 |

### WAKEMAN, RICK Also see YES.

| Number | Title (A Side/B Side) | Yr | NM |
|---|---|---|---|
| **A&M** | | | |
| ❑ SP-3156 | Journey to the Centre of the Earth | 198? | 8.00 |
| *—Budget-line reissue of 3621* | | | |
| ❑ SP-3229 | The Six Wives of Henry VIII | 1984 | 8.00 |
| *—Budget-line reissue of 4361* | | | |
| ❑ SP-3230 | The Myths and Legends of King Arthur and the Knights of the Round Table | 1984 | 8.00 |
| *—Budget-line reissue of 4515* | | | |
| ❑ SP-3621 | Journey to the Centre of the Earth | 1974 | 12.00 |
| ❑ SP-4361 | The Six Wives of Henry VIII | 1973 | 12.00 |
| *—Originals have brown labels* | | | |
| ❑ SP-4361 | The Six Wives of Henry VIII | 1974 | 10.00 |
| *—Silver label with "fading" A&M logo* | | | |
| ❑ SP-4515 | The Myths and Legends of King Arthur and the Knights of the Round Table | 1975 | 12.00 |
| ❑ SP-4583 | No Earthly Connection | 1976 | 12.00 |
| ❑ SP-4614 | White Rock | 1977 | 12.00 |
| ❑ SP-4660 | Rick Wakeman's Criminal Record | 1977 | 12.00 |
| ❑ SP-6501 [(2)] | Rhapsodies | 1979 | 15.00 |
| ❑ QU-53621 [Q] | Journey to the Centre of the Earth | 1974 | 25.00 |
| ❑ QU-54361 [Q] | The Six Wives of Henry VIII | 1974 | 25.00 |
| ❑ QU-54515 [Q] | The Myths and Legends of King Arthur and the Knights of the Round Table | 1975 | 25.00 |
| **MOBILE FIDELITY** | | | |
| ❑ 1-230 | Journey to the Centre of the Earth | 1995 | 20.00 |
| *—Audiophile vinyl* | | | |
| **SWEET THUNDER** | | | |
| ❑ 1 | Journey to the Centre of the Earth | 1981 | 50.00 |
| *—Audiophile vinyl* | | | |
| **VARESE SARABANDE** | | | |
| ❑ STV-81162 | The Burning (Soundtrack) | 1982 | 20.00 |

### WALD, JERRY

| Number | Title (A Side/B Side) | Yr | NM |
|---|---|---|---|
| **KAPP** | | | |
| ❑ KL-1043 [M] | Listen to the Music of Jerry Wald | 1956 | 40.00 |
| **LION** | | | |
| ❑ L-70014 [M] | Tops in Pops — Designed for Dancing | 1958 | 25.00 |

### WALDRON, MAL

| Number | Title (A Side/B Side) | Yr | NM |
|---|---|---|---|
| **BETHLEHEM** | | | |
| ❑ BCP-6045 [M] | Left Alone | 1960 | 40.00 |
| ❑ SBCP-6045 [S] | Left Alone | 1960 | 40.00 |
| **MUSIC MINUS ONE** | | | |
| ❑ 175 [M] | Fun With Brushes | 1960 | 20.00 |
| ❑ 1012 [M] | Moonglow and Stardust | 1960 | 20.00 |
| ❑ 1015 [M] | Music of Duke Ellington | 1960 | 20.00 |
| ❑ 1016 [M] | Music of McHugh | 1960 | 20.00 |
| ❑ 1017 [M] | Mal Waldron | 1960 | 20.00 |
| ❑ 1018 [M] | For Singers 'N Singer | 1960 | 20.00 |
| ❑ 4005 [M] | Blue Drums | 1961 | 20.00 |
| ❑ 4007 [M] | For Pianists Only | 1961 | 20.00 |
| ❑ 4008 [M] | They Laughed When I Sat Down to Play | 1961 | 20.00 |
| **NEW JAZZ** | | | |
| ❑ NJLP-8201 [M] | Mal/3: Sounds | 1958 | 50.00 |
| *—Purple label* | | | |
| ❑ NJLP-8201 [M] | Mal/3: Sounds | 1958 | 100.00 |
| *—Yellow label* | | | |
| ❑ NJLP-8201 [M] | Mal/3: Sounds | 1965 | 25.00 |
| *—Blue label, trident logo at right* | | | |
| ❑ NJLP-8208 [M] | Mal/4: Trio | 1958 | 50.00 |
| *—Purple label* | | | |
| ❑ NJLP-8208 [M] | Mal/4: Trio | 1965 | 25.00 |
| *—Blue label, trident logo at right* | | | |
| ❑ NJLP-8242 [M] | Impressions | 1960 | 50.00 |
| *—Purple label* | | | |
| ❑ NJLP-8242 [M] | Impressions | 1965 | 25.00 |
| *—Blue label, trident logo at right* | | | |
| ❑ NJLP-8269 [M] | The Quest | 1962 | 50.00 |
| *—Purple label* | | | |
| ❑ NJLP-8269 [M] | The Quest | 1965 | 25.00 |
| *—Blue label, trident logo at right* | | | |
| **PRESTIGE** | | | |
| ❑ PRLP-7090 [M] | Mal/1 | 1957 | 80.00 |
| ❑ PRLP-7111 [M] | Mal/2 | 1957 | 80.00 |
| ❑ PRST-7579 [S] | The Quest | 1969 | 20.00 |
| **STATUS** | | | |
| ❑ ST-8316 [M] | The Dealers | 1965 | 40.00 |

### WALES, HOWARD, AND JERRY GARCIA

| Number | Title (A Side/B Side) | Yr | NM |
|---|---|---|---|
| **DOUGLAS** | | | |
| ❑ Z 30589 | Hooteroll | 1971 | 40.00 |

### WALI AND THE AFRO-CARAVAN

| Number | Title (A Side/B Side) | Yr | NM |
|---|---|---|---|
| **SOLID STATE** | | | |
| ❑ SS-18065 | Home Lost and Found | 1969 | 20.00 |

### WALKER, BILLY

| Number | Title (A Side/B Side) | Yr | NM |
|---|---|---|---|
| **COLUMBIA** | | | |
| ❑ CL 1624 [M] | Everybody's Hits But Mine | 1961 | 20.00 |
| ❑ CL 1935 [M] | Billy Walker's Greatest Hits | 1963 | 15.00 |
| ❑ CL 2206 [M] | Thank You for Calling | 1964 | 15.00 |
| ❑ CL 2331 [M] | The Gun, the Gold and the Girl/Cross the Brazos at Waco | 1965 | 15.00 |
| ❑ CS 8424 [S] | Everybody's Hits But Mine | 1961 | 30.00 |
| ❑ CS 8735 [S] | Billy Walker's Greatest Hits | 1963 | 20.00 |
| ❑ CS 9006 [S] | Thank You for Calling | 1964 | 20.00 |
| ❑ CS 9131 [S] | The Gun, the Gold and the Girl/Cross the Brazos at Waco | 1965 | 20.00 |
| ❑ CS 9798 | Billy Walker's Greatest Hits, Volume 2 | 1969 | 15.00 |
| ❑ C 30226 | Goodnight | 1971 | 12.00 |
| **HARMONY** | | | |
| ❑ HL 7306 [M] | Anything Your Heart Desires | 1964 | 15.00 |
| ❑ HL 7410 [M] | Big Country Hits | 1967 | 15.00 |
| ❑ HS 11210 [S] | Big Country Hits | 1967 | 12.00 |
| ❑ HS 11414 | Charlie's Shoes | 1970 | 12.00 |
| ❑ H 31177 | There May Be No Tomorrow | 1972 | 10.00 |
| **MGM** | | | |
| ❑ SE-4682 | When a Man Loves a Woman (The Way That I Love You) | 1970 | 15.00 |
| ❑ SE-4756 | I'm Gonna Keep On Lovin' You/She Goes Walking Through My Mind | 1971 | 15.00 |
| ❑ SE-4789 | Live! | 1972 | 15.00 |
| ❑ SE-4863 | The Billy Walker Show | 1973 | 12.00 |
| ❑ SE-4887 | Billy Walker's All Time Greatest Hits | 1972 | 12.00 |
| ❑ SE-4938 | Too Many Memories | 1974 | 12.00 |
| **MONUMENT** | | | |
| ❑ 6641 | Billy Walker's Greatest Hits | 1976 | 10.00 |
| ❑ MLP-8047 [M] | A Million and One | 1966 | 12.00 |
| ❑ MLP-8072 [M] | The Walker Way | 1967 | 20.00 |
| ❑ SLP-18047 [S] | A Million and One | 1966 | 15.00 |
| ❑ SLP-18072 [S] | The Walker Way | 1967 | 15.00 |
| ❑ SLP-18090 | I Taught Her Everything She Knows | 1968 | 15.00 |
| ❑ SLP-18101 | Billy Walker Salutes the Country Music Hall of Fame | 1969 | 15.00 |
| ❑ SLP-18116 | Portrait of Billy | 1969 | 15.00 |
| ❑ SLP-18143 | Darling Days | 1970 | 15.00 |
| ❑ KZ 31912 | Billy Walker's Greatest Hits | 1972 | 12.00 |
| **RCA VICTOR** | | | |
| ❑ APL1-1160 | Lovin' and Losin' | 1975 | 12.00 |
| ❑ APL1-1489 | Alone Again | 1976 | 12.00 |

### WALKER, CHARLIE

| Number | Title (A Side/B Side) | Yr | NM |
|---|---|---|---|
| **COLUMBIA** | | | |
| ❑ CL 1691 [M] | Charlie Walker's Greatest Hits | 1961 | 20.00 |
| ❑ CS 8491 [S] | Charlie Walker's Greatest Hits | 1961 | 30.00 |
| **EPIC** | | | |
| ❑ LN 24137 [M] | Close All the Honky Tonks | 1965 | 15.00 |
| ❑ LN 24153 [M] | Born to Lose | 1965 | 15.00 |
| ❑ LN 24209 [M] | Wine, Women and Walker | 1966 | 15.00 |
| ❑ LN 24328 [M] | Don't Squeeze My Sharmon | 1967 | 25.00 |
| ❑ LN 24343 [M] | Charlie Walker's Greatest Hits | 1968 | 40.00 |
| ❑ BN 26137 [S] | Close All the Honky Tonks | 1965 | 20.00 |
| ❑ BN 26153 [S] | Born to Lose | 1965 | 20.00 |
| ❑ BN 26209 [S] | Wine, Women and Walker | 1966 | 20.00 |
| ❑ BN 26328 [S] | Don't Squeeze My Sharmon | 1967 | 20.00 |
| ❑ BN 26343 [S] | Charlie Walker's Greatest Hits | 1968 | 15.00 |
| ❑ BN 26424 | He Is My Everything | 1969 | 15.00 |
| ❑ BN 26483 | Recorded Live in Dallas | 1969 | 15.00 |
| ❑ E 30660 | Honky Tonkin' | 1971 | 15.00 |
| **HARMONY** | | | |
| ❑ HL 7415 [M] | Golden Hits | 1967 | 15.00 |
| ❑ HS 11215 [S] | Golden Hits | 1967 | 12.00 |
| **PLANTATION** | | | |
| ❑ 535 | Golden Hits | 1978 | 10.00 |
| **RCA VICTOR** | | | |
| ❑ APL1-0181 | Break Out the Bottle | 1973 | 12.00 |
| ❑ LSP-4737 | Charlie Walker | 1972 | 15.00 |
| **VOCALION** | | | |
| ❑ VL 73814 | The Style of Charlie Walker | 1968 | 12.00 |

### WALKER, CINDY

| Number | Title (A Side/B Side) | Yr | NM |
|---|---|---|---|
| **MONUMENT** | | | |
| ❑ MLP-8020 [M] | Words and Music by Cindy Walker | 1964 | 20.00 |
| ❑ SLP-18020 [S] | Words and Music by Cindy Walker | 1964 | 25.00 |

### WALKER, CLINT

| Number | Title (A Side/B Side) | Yr | NM |
|---|---|---|---|
| **WARNER BROS.** | | | |
| ❑ W 1343 [M] | Inspiration | 1959 | 30.00 |
| ❑ WS 1343 [S] | Inspiration | 1959 | 40.00 |

### WALKER, JERRY JEFF Also see CIRCUS MAXIMUS.

| Number | Title (A Side/B Side) | Yr | NM |
|---|---|---|---|
| **ATCO** | | | |
| ❑ SD 33-259 | Mr. Bojangles | 1968 | 25.00 |
| ❑ SD 33-297 | Five Years Gone | 1969 | 30.00 |
| ❑ SD 33-336 | Bein' Free | 1970 | 20.00 |
| **BAINBRIDGE** | | | |
| ❑ 6222 | Mr. Bojangles | 198? | 10.00 |
| **DECCA** | | | |
| ❑ DL 75384 | Jerry Jeff Walker | 1972 | 15.00 |
| **ELEKTRA** | | | |
| ❑ 6E-163 | Jerry Jeff | 1978 | 10.00 |
| ❑ 6E-239 | Too Old to Change | 1980 | 10.00 |
| **MCA** | | | |
| ❑ 382 | Viva Terlingua! | 1973 | 10.00 |
| ❑ 450 | Walker's Collectibles | 1974 | 10.00 |
| ❑ 510 | Jerry Jeff Walker | 1975 | 10.00 |
| *—Reissue of Decca LP* | | | |
| ❑ 2156 | Ridin' High | 1975 | 10.00 |
| ❑ 2202 | It's a Good Night for Singin' | 1976 | 10.00 |
| ❑ 2350 | Viva Terlingua! | 1977 | 8.00 |
| *—Reissue of MCA 382* | | | |
| ❑ 2355 | Walker's Collectibles | 1977 | 8.00 |
| *—Reissue of MCA 450* | | | |
| ❑ 2358 | Jerry Jeff Walker | 1977 | 8.00 |
| *—Reissue of MCA 510* | | | |
| ❑ 3041 | Contrary to Ordinary | 1978 | 10.00 |
| ❑ 5128 | The Best of Jerry Jeff Walker | 1980 | 10.00 |
| ❑ 5355 | Cowjazz | 1983 | 10.00 |
| ❑ 6003 [(2)] | A Man Must Carry On | 198? | 10.00 |
| *—Budget-line reissue* | | | |
| ❑ 8013 [(2)] | A Man Must Carry On | 1977 | 12.00 |
| ❑ 27026 | It's a Good Night for Singin' | 198? | 8.00 |
| *—Budget-line reissue* | | | |
| ❑ 27027 | Walker's Collectibles | 198? | 6.00 |
| *—Budget-line reissue* | | | |
| ❑ 37004 | Jerry Jeff Walker | 198? | 6.00 |
| *—Budget-line reissue* | | | |
| ❑ 37005 | Viva Terlingua! | 198? | 6.00 |
| *—Budget-line reissue* | | | |
| ❑ 37006 | Ridin' High | 198? | 8.00 |
| *—Budget-line reissue* | | | |

| Number | Title (A Side/B Side) | Yr | NM |
|---|---|---|---|
| ❑ 37162 | Contrary to Ordinary | 198? | 8.00 |
| *—Budget-line reissue* | | | |
| **SOUTHCOAST** | | | |
| ❑ 5199 | Reunion | 1981 | 10.00 |
| **VANGUARD** | | | |
| ❑ VSD-6521 | Driftin' Way of Life | 1969 | 20.00 |
| ❑ VMS-73124 | Driftin' Way of Life | 1985 | 8.00 |
| *—Reissue of 6521* | | | |

### WALKER, JR., AND THE ALL STARS

| Number | Title (A Side/B Side) | Yr | NM |
|---|---|---|---|
| **MOTOWN** | | | |
| ❑ M5-105V1 | Motown Superstar Series, Vol. 5 | 1981 | 10.00 |
| ❑ M5-141V1 | Shotgun | 1981 | 10.00 |
| *—Reissue of Soul 701* | | | |
| ❑ M5-208V1 | Greatest Hits | 1981 | 10.00 |
| *—Reissue of Soul 718* | | | |
| ❑ M7-786 [(2)] | Anthology | 1974 | 20.00 |
| ❑ 5297 ML | All the Great Hits of Jr. Walker and the All Stars | 1984 | 10.00 |
| ❑ 6053 ML | Blow the House Down | 1983 | 10.00 |
| **PICKWICK** | | | |
| ❑ SPC-3391 | Shotgun | 197? | 12.00 |
| **SOUL** | | | |
| ❑ 701 [M] | Shotgun | 1965 | 20.00 |
| *—Purple swirl label with "Soul" at top* | | | |
| ❑ 701 [M] | Shotgun | 1965 | 60.00 |
| *—Mostly white label with vertical "Soul" at left* | | | |
| ❑ SS-701 [S] | Shotgun | 1965 | 30.00 |
| ❑ 702 [M] | Soul Session | 1966 | 20.00 |
| *—Purple swirl label with "Soul" at top* | | | |
| ❑ 702 [M] | Soul Session | 1966 | 60.00 |
| *—Mostly white label with vertical "Soul" at left* | | | |
| ❑ SS-702 [S] | Soul Session | 1966 | 30.00 |
| ❑ 703 [M] | Road Runner | 1966 | 20.00 |
| ❑ SS-703 [S] | Road Runner | 1966 | 30.00 |
| ❑ 705 [M] | "Live" | 1967 | 20.00 |
| ❑ SS-705 [S] | "Live" | 1967 | 30.00 |
| ❑ SS-710 | Home Cookin' | 1969 | 20.00 |
| ❑ SS-718 | Greatest Hits | 1969 | 20.00 |
| ❑ SS-721 | Gotta Hold on to This Feeling | 1969 | 25.00 |
| ❑ SS-721 | What Does It Take to Win Your Love | 1970 | 20.00 |
| *—Retitled version of above* | | | |
| ❑ SS-726 | A Gasssss | 1970 | 15.00 |
| ❑ S-732L | Rainbow Funk | 1971 | 15.00 |
| ❑ SS-733 | Moody Jr. | 1971 | 15.00 |
| ❑ SS-738 | Peace and Understanding Is Hard to Find | 1973 | 15.00 |
| ❑ S6-742 | Jr. Walker and the All Stars | 1973 | — |
| *—Canceled* | | | |
| ❑ S6-745 | Hot Shot | 1976 | 15.00 |
| ❑ S6-747 | Sax Appeal | 1976 | 15.00 |
| ❑ S6-748 | Whopper Bopper Show Stopper | 1977 | 15.00 |
| ❑ S7-750 | Smooth | 1978 | 15.00 |
| **WHITFIELD** | | | |
| ❑ WHK 3331 | Back Street Boogie | 1980 | 12.00 |

### WALKER, MARTIN

| Number | Title (A Side/B Side) | Yr | NM |
|---|---|---|---|
| **ABC-PARAMOUNT** | | | |
| ❑ ABC-483 [M] | From Scotland with Love | 1964 | 15.00 |
| ❑ ABCS-483 [S] | From Scotland with Love | 1964 | 20.00 |

### WALKER, NANCY

| Number | Title (A Side/B Side) | Yr | NM |
|---|---|---|---|
| **RCA CAMDEN** | | | |
| ❑ CAL-561 [M] | I Hate Men | 1960 | 25.00 |
| ❑ CAS-561 [S] | I Hate Men | 1960 | 30.00 |

### WALKER, PETER

| Number | Title (A Side/B Side) | Yr | NM |
|---|---|---|---|
| **VANGUARD** | | | |
| ❑ VSD-79282 | Second Poem to Karmela | 1968 | 20.00 |

### WALKER, SCOTT Also see THE WALKER BROTHERS.

| Number | Title (A Side/B Side) | Yr | NM |
|---|---|---|---|
| **SMASH** | | | |
| ❑ SRS-67099 | Aloner | 1968 | 20.00 |
| ❑ SRS-67106 | Scott, Volume 2 | 1968 | 20.00 |
| ❑ SRS-67121 | Scott Walker 3 | 1969 | 20.00 |

### WALKER, T-BONE

| Number | Title (A Side/B Side) | Yr | NM |
|---|---|---|---|
| **ATLANTIC** | | | |
| ❑ 8020 [M] | T-Bone Blues | 1959 | 220.00 |
| *—Black label* | | | |
| ❑ 8020 [M] | T-Bone Blues | 1960 | 70.00 |
| *—Red and purple label* | | | |
| ❑ SD 8256 | T-Bone Blues | 1970 | 20.00 |
| **BLUE NOTE** | | | |
| ❑ BN-LA533-H2 [(2)] | Classics | 1975 | 20.00 |
| **BLUESTIME** | | | |
| ❑ 29004 | Everyday I Have the Blues | 1968 | 30.00 |
| ❑ 29010 | Blue Rocks | 1969 | 30.00 |
| **BLUESWAY** | | | |
| ❑ BLS-6008 | Stormy Monday Blues | 1968 | 30.00 |
| *—Reissue of Wet Soul LP?* | | | |
| ❑ BLS-6014 | Funky Town | 1968 | 30.00 |
| ❑ BLS-6058 | Dirty Mistreater | 1973 | 15.00 |
| **BRUNSWICK** | | | |
| ❑ BL 754126 | The Truth | 1968 | 30.00 |
| **CAPITOL** | | | |
| ❑ H 370 [10] | Classics in Jazz | 1953 | 1000. |
| ❑ T 370 [M] | Classics in Jazz | 1953 | 300.00 |
| ❑ T 1958 [M] | Great Blues Vocal and Guitar | 1963 | 150.00 |
| *—Black "The Star Line" label (existence of black colorband label not confirmed)* | | | |
| **DELMARK** | | | |
| ❑ D-633 [M] | I Want a Little Girl | 1967 | 40.00 |
| ❑ DS-633 [S] | I Want a Little Girl | 1967 | 50.00 |
| **IMPERIAL** | | | |
| ❑ LP-9098 [M] | T-Bone Walker Sings the Blues | 1959 | 300.00 |
| ❑ LP-9116 [M] | Singing the Blues | 1960 | 250.00 |
| ❑ LP-9146 [M] | I Get So Weary | 1961 | 300.00 |
| **MOSAIC** | | | |
| ❑ MR9-130 [(9)] | The Complete Recordings of T-Bone Walker 1940-1954 | 199? | 300.00 |
| *—Limited edition of 7,500* | | | |
| **POLYDOR** | | | |
| ❑ 24-4502 | Good Feelin' | 1972 | 15.00 |
| ❑ PD-5521 | Fly Walker Airlines | 1973 | 15.00 |
| **REPRISE** | | | |
| ❑ 2RS 6483 [(2)] | Very Rare | 1973 | 20.00 |
| **WET SOUL** | | | |
| ❑ 1002 | Stormy Monday Blues | 1967 | 50.00 |

### WALKER BROTHERS, THE

| Number | Title (A Side/B Side) | Yr | NM |
|---|---|---|---|
| **SMASH** | | | |
| ❑ MGS-27076 [M] | Introducing the Walker Brothers | 1965 | 50.00 |
| ❑ MGS-27082 [M] | The Sun Ain't Gonna Shine (Anymore) | 1966 | 40.00 |
| ❑ SRS-67076 [R] | Introducing the Walker Brothers | 1965 | 40.00 |
| ❑ SRS-67082 [P] | The Sun Ain't Gonna Shine (Anymore) | 1966 | 50.00 |
| *—"The Sun Ain't Gonna Shine (Anymore)" and "When the Lights Go Out" are rechanneled.* | | | |
| **TOWER** | | | |
| ❑ ST 5026 [S] | I Only Came to Dance with You | 1966 | 20.00 |
| *—As "Scott Engel and John Stewart"* | | | |
| ❑ T 5026 [M] | I Only Came to Dance with You | 1966 | 15.00 |
| *—As "Scott Engel and John Stewart"* | | | |

### WALLACE, GEORGE, JR.

| Number | Title (A Side/B Side) | Yr | NM |
|---|---|---|---|
| **PORTRAIT** | | | |
| ❑ JR 36579 | Heroes Like You and Me | 1981 | 25.00 |

### WALLACE, JERRY

| Number | Title (A Side/B Side) | Yr | NM |
|---|---|---|---|
| **CHALLENGE** | | | |
| ❑ CHL 606 [M] | Just Jerry | 1959 | 60.00 |
| ❑ CH 612 [M] | There She Goes | 1961 | 30.00 |
| ❑ CHS 612 [S] | There She Goes | 1961 | 40.00 |
| ❑ CH 616 [M] | Shutters and Boards | 1962 | 30.00 |
| ❑ CHS 616 [S] | Shutters and Boards | 1962 | 40.00 |
| ❑ CH 619 [M] | In the Misty Moonlight | 1964 | 20.00 |
| ❑ CHS 619 [S] | In the Misty Moonlight | 1964 | 25.00 |
| ❑ 2002 | Greatest Hits | 1969 | 15.00 |
| **DECCA** | | | |
| ❑ DL 75294 | This Is Jerry Wallace | 1971 | 15.00 |
| ❑ DL 75349 | To Get to You | 1972 | 15.00 |
| **LIBERTY** | | | |
| ❑ LRP-3545 [M] | This One's on the House | 1967 | 40.00 |
| *—Stock copy inside stereo cover; "Audition Mono LP Not for Sale" sticker on front* | | | |
| ❑ LST-7545 [S] | This One's on the House | 1967 | 20.00 |
| ❑ LST-7564 | Another Time, Another World | 1968 | 20.00 |
| ❑ LST-7597 | Sweet Child of Sunshine | 1968 | 20.00 |
| **MCA** | | | |
| ❑ 301 | Do You Know What It's Like to Be Lonesome? | 1973 | 12.00 |
| ❑ 366 | Primrose Lane/Don't Give Up on Me | 1973 | 12.00 |
| ❑ 408 | For Wives and Lovers | 1974 | 12.00 |
| ❑ 462 | I Wonder Whose Baby (You Are Now)/Make Hay While the Sun Shines | 1975 | 12.00 |
| **MERCURY** | | | |
| ❑ MG-21072 [M] | The Best of Jerry Wallace | 1966 | 15.00 |
| ❑ SR-61072 [S] | The Best of Jerry Wallace | 1966 | 20.00 |
| **MGM** | | | |
| ❑ M3G-4990 | Greatest Hits | 1975 | 10.00 |
| ❑ M3G-4995 | Comin' Home to You | 1976 | 12.00 |
| ❑ M3G-5007 | Jerry Wallace | 1976 | 10.00 |
| **SUNSET** | | | |
| ❑ SUS-5294 | Primrose Lane | 1969 | 12.00 |
| **UNITED ARTISTS** | | | |
| ❑ UXS-95 [(2)] | Jerry Wallace Superpak | 1972 | 20.00 |

### WALLACE BROTHERS, THE

| Number | Title (A Side/B Side) | Yr | NM |
|---|---|---|---|
| **SIMS** | | | |
| ❑ LP-128 [M] | Soul, Soul and More Soul | 1965 | 200.00 |
| ❑ LPS-128 [S] | Soul, Soul and More Soul | 1965 | 250.00 |

### WALLER, FATS

| Number | Title (A Side/B Side) | Yr | NM |
|---|---|---|---|
| **BLUEBIRD** | | | |
| ❑ 9983-1-RB [(4)] | The Last Years: Fats Waller and His Rhythm, 1940-1943 | 198? | 30.00 |
| **RCA VICTOR** | | | |
| ❑ LPT-8 [10] | Fats Waller 1934-42 | 1951 | 150.00 |
| ❑ LPT-14 [10] | Fats Waller Favoites | 1951 | 150.00 |
| ❑ LPV-473 [M] | The Real Fats Waller | 1965 | 25.00 |
| ❑ LPV-516 [M] | Fats Waller '34/'35 | 1965 | 20.00 |
| ❑ LPV-525 [M] | Valentine Stomp | 1966 | 20.00 |
| ❑ LPV-550 [M] | Smashing Thirds | 1968 | 20.00 |
| ❑ LPV-562 [M] | African Ripples | 1969 | 20.00 |
| ❑ LPT-1001 [M] | Fats Waller Plays and Sings | 1954 | 80.00 |
| ❑ LPM-1246 [M] | Ain't Misbehavin' | 1956 | 50.00 |
| ❑ LPM-1502 [M] | Handful of Keys | 1957 | 50.00 |
| ❑ LPM-1503 [M] | One Never Knows, Do One? | 1959 | 50.00 |
| ❑ LPT-3040 [10] | Swingin' the Organ | 1953 | 120.00 |
| ❑ LPM-6000 [(2)M] | Fats | 1960 | 80.00 |
| ❑ LPT-6001 [(2)M] | Fats Waller Radio Transcriptions | 1954 | 120.00 |
| *—Boxed set with booklet* | | | |
| **RIVERSIDE** | | | |
| ❑ RLP 12-103 [M] | The Young Fats Waller | 1955 | 60.00 |
| ❑ RLP 12-109 [M] | The Amazing Mr. Waller | 1955 | 60.00 |
| ❑ RLP-1010 [10] | Rediscovered Fats Waller Piano Solos | 1953 | 150.00 |
| ❑ RLP-1021 [10] | Fats Waller at the Organ | 1953 | 150.00 |
| ❑ RLP-1022 [10] | The Amazing Mr. Waller Vol. 2: Jivin' with Fats | 1953 | 150.00 |
| *—Black vinyl* | | | |
| ❑ RLP-1022 [10] | The Amazing Mr. Waller Vol. 2: Jivin' with Fats | 1953 | 250.00 |
| *—Red vinyl* | | | |
| **"X"** | | | |
| ❑ LVA-3035 [10] | The Young Fats Waller | 1955 | 150.00 |

### WALLER, GORDON

| Number | Title (A Side/B Side) | Yr | NM |
|---|---|---|---|
| **ABC** | | | |
| ❑ X-749 | And Gordon | 1972 | 15.00 |

### WALLER, JIM, AND THE DELTAS

| Number | Title (A Side/B Side) | Yr | NM |
|---|---|---|---|
| **ARVEE** | | | |
| ❑ A-432 [M] | Surfin' Wild | 1963 | 80.00 |
| ❑ AS-432 [S] | Surfin' Wild | 1963 | 100.00 |

### WALLINGTON, GEORGE

| Number | Title (A Side/B Side) | Yr | NM |
|---|---|---|---|
| **ATLANTIC** | | | |
| ❑ 1275 [M] | Knight Music | 1958 | 80.00 |
| *—Black label* | | | |
| ❑ 1275 [M] | Knight Music | 1961 | 25.00 |
| *—Multicolor label, white "fan" logo at right* | | | |
| ❑ SD 1275 [S] | Knight Music | 1958 | 80.00 |
| *—Green label* | | | |
| ❑ SD 1275 [S] | Knight Music | 1961 | 20.00 |
| *—Multicolor label, white "fan" logo at right* | | | |
| **BLUE NOTE** | | | |
| ❑ BLP-5045 [10] | George Wallington and His All-Star Band | 1954 | 1000. |
| **EAST-WEST** | | | |
| ❑ 4004 [M] | The Prestidigitator | 1958 | 250.00 |
| **NEW JAZZ** | | | |
| ❑ NJLP-8207 [M] | The New York Scene | 1958 | 250.00 |
| *—Purple label* | | | |
| ❑ NJLP-8207 [M] | The New York Scene | 1965 | 60.00 |
| *—Blue label, trident logo at right* | | | |
| **NORGRAN** | | | |
| ❑ MGN-24 [10] | The Workshop of the George Wallington Trio | 1954 | 200.00 |
| ❑ MGN-1010 [M] | George Wallington with Strings | 1954 | 120.00 |
| **PRESTIGE** | | | |
| ❑ PRLP-136 [10] | The George Wallington Trio | 1952 | 500.00 |
| ❑ PRLP-158 [10] | The George Wallington Trio, Volume 2 | 1953 | 500.00 |
| ❑ PRLP-7032 [M] | Jazz for the Carriage Trade | 1956 | 800.00 |
| ❑ PRST-7587 [R] | The George Wallington Trios | 1968 | 30.00 |
| **PROGRESSIVE** | | | |
| ❑ PLP-1001 [M] | George Wallington Quintet at the Bohemia | 1955 | 1500. |
| ❑ PLP-3001 [10] | The George Wallington Trio | 1952 | 500.00 |
| **SAVOY** | | | |
| ❑ MG-12081 [M] | The George Wallington Trio | 1956 | 100.00 |
| ❑ MG-12122 [M] | Jazz at Hotchkiss | 1957 | 100.00 |
| ❑ MG-15037 [10] | The George Wallington Trio | 1954 | 150.00 |
| **VERVE** | | | |
| ❑ MGV-2017 [M] | Variations | 1956 | 80.00 |

### WALLIS, RUTH

| Number | Title (A Side/B Side) | Yr | NM |
|---|---|---|---|
| **JUBILEE** | | | |
| ❑ JGM-2050 [M] | Ruth Wallis Sings The Spice Is Right | 1963 | 20.00 |
| **KING** | | | |
| ❑ 265-6 [10] | Rhumba Party | 1952 | 120.00 |

| Number | Title (A Side/B Side) | Yr | NM |
|---|---|---|---|
| ❑ 265-9 [10] | House Party | 1952 | 120.00 |
| ❑ 395-507 [M] | House Party | 1956 | 100.00 |
| ❑ 904 [M] | Saucy Hit Parade | 1964 | 30.00 |
| ❑ 986 [M] | Here's Looking Up Your Hatch | 1966 | 30.00 |
| ❑ 987 [M] | Davy's Little Dinghy | 1966 | 30.00 |
| ❑ 988 [M] | Marry Go Round | 1966 | 30.00 |
| ❑ 989 [M] | Red Lights | 1966 | 30.00 |
| ❑ 990 [M] | Ubangi Me | 1966 | 30.00 |
| ❑ 991 [M] | Oil Man from Texas | 1966 | 30.00 |
| ❑ 992 [M] | He Wants a Little...Pizza | 1966 | 30.00 |
| ❑ 993 [M] | Bahama Mama | 1966 | 30.00 |
| MERCURY | | | |
| ❑ SR-61210 | How to Stay Sexy Tho' Married | 1969 | 20.00 |
| WALLIS ORIGINAL | | | |
| ❑ W-1 [10] | Ruth Wallis' Old Party Favorites | 195? | 40.00 |
| ❑ W-2 [M] | Ruth Wallis | 195? | 40.00 |
| ❑ W-3 [10] | Cafe Party | 195? | 40.00 |
| ❑ W-4 [10] | Senorita Ruth Wallis and Her Latin Party Rhythms | 195? | 40.00 |
| ❑ W-5 [10] | Holiday Party | 195? | 40.00 |
| *—Black vinyl* | | | |
| ❑ W-5 [10] | Holiday Party | 195? | 60.00 |
| *—Red vinyl* | | | |
| ❑ W-6 [10] | Life of the Party | 195? | 40.00 |
| ❑ W-9 [M] | Men and Memories | 195? | 40.00 |
| ❑ WLP-10 [M] | Wallis on the Party Line | 195? | 30.00 |
| ❑ WLP-11 [M] | Saucy Hit Parade | 195? | 30.00 |
| ❑ WLP-12 [M] | That Saucy Redhead | 195? | 30.00 |
| ❑ WLP-13 [M] | For Sophisticates Only | 195? | 30.00 |
| ❑ WLP-14 [M] | French Postcards Set to Music | 195? | 30.00 |
| ❑ WLP-15 [M] | Cruise Party | 195? | 30.00 |
| ❑ WLP-16 [M] | Salty Songs for Underwater Listening | 195? | 30.00 |
| ❑ WLP-17 [M] | Love Is for the Birds | 195? | 30.00 |
| ❑ WLP-18 [M] | Hot Songs for Cool Knights | 195? | 30.00 |
| **WALSH, JOE** Also see EAGLES; THE JAMES GANG (1). | | | |
| ABC | | | |
| ❑ ABCD-932 | You Can't Argue with a Sick Mind | 1976 | 10.00 |
| ❑ AA-1083 | The Best of Joe Walsh | 1978 | 10.00 |
| *—Also contains two James Gang tracks* | | | |
| ABC COMMAND | | | |
| ❑ QD-40016 [Q] | The Smoker You Drink, the Player You Get | 1974 | 20.00 |
| ❑ QD-40017 [Q] | So What | 1975 | — |
| *—Not released* | | | |
| ABC DUNHILL | | | |
| ❑ DS-50130 | Barnstorm | 1972 | 10.00 |
| *—Of the James Gang and the Eagles* | | | |
| ❑ DS-50140 | The Smoker You Drink, the Player You Get | 1973 | 10.00 |
| ❑ DS-51071 | So What | 1974 | 10.00 |
| ASYLUM | | | |
| ❑ 6E-141 | But Seriously, Folks... | 1978 | 10.00 |
| ❑ 5E-523 | There Goes the Neighborhood | 1981 | 8.00 |
| MCA | | | |
| ❑ 37051 | You Can't Argue with a Sick Mind | 1979 | 8.00 |
| *—Reissue of ABC 932* | | | |
| ❑ 37052 | The Best of Joe Walsh | 1979 | 8.00 |
| *—Reissue of ABC 1083* | | | |
| ❑ 37053 | Barnstorm | 1979 | 8.00 |
| *—Reissue of ABC Dunhill 50130* | | | |
| ❑ 37054 | The Smoker You Drink, the Player You Get | 1979 | 8.00 |
| *—Reissue of ABC Dunhill 50140* | | | |
| ❑ 37055 | So What | 1979 | 8.00 |
| *—Reissue of ABC Dunhill 50171* | | | |
| WARNER BROS. | | | |
| ❑ 23884 | You Bought It — You Name It | 1983 | 8.00 |
| ❑ 25281 | The Confessor | 1985 | 8.00 |
| ❑ 25281 [DJ] | The Confessor | 1985 | 15.00 |
| *—Promo only on Quiex II vinyl* | | | |
| ❑ 25606 | Got Any Gum? | 1987 | 8.00 |
| **WALSTON, RAY** | | | |
| VEE JAY | | | |
| ❑ LP-1110 [M] | My Favorite Songs from "Mary Poppins" and Other Songs to Delight | 1965 | 25.00 |
| ❑ SR-1110 [S] | My Favorite Songs from "Mary Poppins" and Other Songs to Delight | 1965 | 30.00 |
| **WALT, SHERMAN** | | | |
| RCA VICTOR RED SEAL | | | |
| ❑ LSC-2353 [S] | Vivaldi: The Four Seasons Concertos | 1960 | 25.00 |
| *—Original with "shaded dog" label* | | | |
| **WALTER, CY** | | | |
| ATLANTIC | | | |
| ❑ 1236 [M] | Rodgers Revisited | 1956 | 40.00 |
| *—Black label* | | | |

| Number | Title (A Side/B Side) | Yr | NM |
|---|---|---|---|
| ❑ 1236 [M] | Rodgers Revisited | 1961 | 20.00 |
| *—Multicolor label, white "fan" logo at right* | | | |
| WESTMINSTER | | | |
| ❑ WP-6120 [M] | Dry Martini, Please | 195? | 25.00 |
| ❑ WST-15054 [S] | Dry Martini, Please | 195? | 30.00 |
| **WALTON, CEDAR** | | | |
| PRESTIGE | | | |
| ❑ PRLP-7519 [M] | Cedar! | 1967 | 25.00 |
| ❑ PRST-7519 [S] | Cedar! | 1967 | 20.00 |
| ❑ PRST-7591 | Spectrum | 1968 | 20.00 |
| ❑ PRST-7618 | The Electric Boogaloo Song | 1969 | 20.00 |
| ❑ PRST-7693 | Soul Cycle | 1970 | 20.00 |
| RCA VICTOR | | | |
| ❑ APL1-1009 | Mobius | 1975 | 20.00 |
| ❑ APL1-1435 | Beyond Mobius | 1976 | 20.00 |
| **WALTON, MERCY DEE** See MERCY DEE. | | | |
| **WALTON, WADE** | | | |
| BLUESVILLE | | | |
| ❑ BVLP-1060 [M] | Shake 'Em on Down | 1963 | 100.00 |
| *—Blue label, silver print* | | | |
| ❑ BVLP-1060 [M] | Shake 'Em on Down | 1964 | 30.00 |
| *—Blue label, trident logo at right* | | | |
| **WALTONS, THE** See VARIOUS ARTISTS COMPILATIONS in back. | | | |
| **WANDERERS THREE, THE** | | | |
| DOLTON | | | |
| ❑ BLP 2021 [M] | We Sing Folk Songs | 1963 | 20.00 |
| ❑ BST 8021 [S] | We Sing Folk Songs | 1963 | 25.00 |
| **WANDERLEY, WALTER** | | | |
| MGM LATINO SERIES | | | |
| ❑ LAT 10010 [S] | Cheganca | 197? | 15.00 |
| *—Reissue of Verve V6-8676* | | | |
| VERVE | | | |
| ❑ V6-8658 [S] | Rain Forest | 1966 | 20.00 |
| ❑ V6-8676 [S] | Cheganca | 1966 | 20.00 |
| ❑ V-8706 [M] | Batucada | 1967 | 20.00 |
| ❑ V-8739 [M] | Kee-Ka-Roo | 1967 | 20.00 |
| WORLD PACIFIC | | | |
| ❑ WP-1856 [M] | Samba So! | 1967 | 20.00 |
| ❑ WP-1866 [M] | Quarteto Bossamba | 1967 | 25.00 |
| **WAR** Also see ERIC BURDON AND WAR. | | | |
| AVENUE | | | |
| ❑ R1 71706 | Peace Sign | 1994 | 15.00 |
| BLUE NOTE | | | |
| ❑ BN-LA690-G [(2)] | Platinum Jazz | 1977 | 12.00 |
| LAX | | | |
| ❑ PW 37111 | All Day Music | 1981 | 10.00 |
| *—Reissue of United Artists 5546* | | | |
| ❑ PW 37112 | The World Is a Ghetto | 1981 | 10.00 |
| *—Reissue of United Artists 5652* | | | |
| ❑ PW 37113 | Why Can't We Be Friends? | 1981 | 10.00 |
| *—Reissue of United Artists 441* | | | |
| MCA | | | |
| ❑ 745 | Galaxy | 1983 | 8.00 |
| *—Reissue of MCA 3030* | | | |
| ❑ 747 | The Music Band | 1983 | 8.00 |
| *—Reissue of MCA 3085* | | | |
| ❑ 751 | The Music Band 2 | 1983 | 8.00 |
| *—Reissue of MCA 3193* | | | |
| ❑ 3030 | Galaxy | 1977 | 10.00 |
| ❑ 3085 | The Music Band | 1979 | 10.00 |
| ❑ 3193 | The Music Band 2 | 1979 | 10.00 |
| ❑ 5156 | The Music Band Live | 1980 | 10.00 |
| ❑ 5362 | Best of the Music Band | 1982 | 10.00 |
| ❑ 5411 | Music Band Jazz | 1983 | 10.00 |
| PRIORITY | | | |
| ❑ SL 9467 | The Best of War...And More | 1987 | 10.00 |
| RCA VICTOR | | | |
| ❑ AFL1-4208 | Outlaw | 1982 | 10.00 |
| ❑ AFL1-4598 | Life (Is So Strange) | 1983 | 10.00 |
| UNITED ARTISTS | | | |
| ❑ SP-103 [DJ] | Radio Free War | 1974 | 25.00 |
| *—Promo only on blue vinyl* | | | |
| ❑ UA-LA128-F | Deliver the Word | 1973 | 12.00 |
| ❑ UA-LA193-J [(2)] | War Live! | 1974 | 15.00 |
| ❑ UA-LA441-G | Why Can't We Be Friends? | 1975 | 10.00 |
| ❑ UA-LA648-G | Greatest Hits | 1976 | 10.00 |
| ❑ UAS-5508 | War | 1971 | 15.00 |
| ❑ UAS-5546 | All Day Music | 1971 | 15.00 |
| ❑ UAS-5652 | The World Is a Ghetto | 1972 | 12.00 |
| **WARD, ALAN** | | | |
| RCA VICTOR RED SEAL | | | |
| ❑ LSC-2302 [S] | Gilbert and Sullivan Overtures | 1959 | 20.00 |
| *—Original with "shaded dog" label* | | | |
| **WARD, BILLY, AND THE DOMINOES** | | | |
| DECCA | | | |
| ❑ DL 8621 [M] | Billy Ward and the Dominoes | 1958 | 200.00 |

| Number | Title (A Side/B Side) | Yr | NM |
|---|---|---|---|
| FEDERAL | | | |
| ❑ 295-94 [10] | Billy Ward and His Dominoes | 1955 | 13000. |
| *—VG value 6000; VG+ value 9500* | | | |
| ❑ 548 [M] | Billy Ward and His Dominoes | 1958 | 1500. |
| ❑ 559 [M] | Clyde McPhatter with Billy Ward and His Dominoes | 1958 | 1200. |
| KING | | | |
| ❑ 548 [M] | Billy Ward and His Dominoes | 1958 | — |
| *—Unknown* | | | |
| ❑ 559 [M] | Clyde McPhatter with Billy Ward and His Dominoes | 1958 | 600.00 |
| *—Yellow cover* | | | |
| ❑ 559 [M] | Clyde McPhatter with Billy Ward and His Dominoes | 196? | 300.00 |
| *—Pink cover* | | | |
| ❑ 733 [M] | Billy Ward and His Dominoes Featuring Clyde McPhatter and Jackie Wilson | 1961 | 600.00 |
| ❑ 952 [M] | 24 Songs | 1966 | 50.00 |
| ❑ 5005 | 14 Hits | 197? | 12.00 |
| ❑ 5008 | 21 Hits | 197? | 12.00 |
| LIBERTY | | | |
| ❑ LRP-3056 [M] | Sea of Glass | 1957 | 60.00 |
| ❑ LRP-3083 [M] | Yours Forever | 1958 | 60.00 |
| ❑ LRP-3113 [M] | Pagan Love Song | 1959 | 60.00 |
| ❑ LST-7113 [S] | Pagan Love Song | 1959 | 100.00 |
| **WARD, HELEN** | | | |
| COLUMBIA | | | |
| ❑ CL-6271 [10] | It's Been So Long | 1954 | 50.00 |
| PAX | | | |
| ❑ 6004 [10] | Wild Bill Davison with Helen Ward | 1954 | 60.00 |
| RCA VICTOR | | | |
| ❑ LPM-1464 [M] | With a Little Bit of Swing | 1957 | 40.00 |
| **WARD, ROBIN** | | | |
| DOT | | | |
| ❑ DLP 3555 [M] | Wonderful Summer | 1963 | 200.00 |
| ❑ DLP 25555 [S] | Wonderful Summer | 1963 | 300.00 |
| **WARDELL, ROOSEVELT** | | | |
| RIVERSIDE | | | |
| ❑ RLP-350 [M] | The Revelation | 1960 | 25.00 |
| ❑ RS-9350 [S] | The Revelation | 1960 | 30.00 |
| **WARE, WILBUR** | | | |
| RIVERSIDE | | | |
| ❑ RLP 12-252 [M] | The Chicago Sound | 1957 | 80.00 |
| **WARFIELD, WILLIAM** | | | |
| COLUMBIA MASTERWORKS | | | |
| ❑ ML 2206 [M] | Old American Songs and Five Sea Chanties | 195? | 50.00 |
| **WARINER, STEVE** | | | |
| ARISTA | | | |
| ❑ AL 8691 | I Am Ready | 1992 | 20.00 |
| *—Vinyl version available only from Columbia House* | | | |
| MCA | | | |
| ❑ 5545 | One Good Night Deserves Another | 1985 | 8.00 |
| ❑ 5672 | Life's Highway | 1985 | 8.00 |
| ❑ 5926 | It's a Crazy World | 1987 | 8.00 |
| ❑ 42032 | Greatest Hits | 1987 | 8.00 |
| ❑ 42130 | I Should Be with You | 1988 | 8.00 |
| ❑ 42272 | I Got Dreams | 1989 | 10.00 |
| RCA VICTOR | | | |
| ❑ AHL1-4154 | Steve Wariner | 1982 | 10.00 |
| ❑ AHL1-4859 | Midnight Fire | 1983 | 10.00 |
| ❑ AHL1-5326 | Greatest Hits | 1985 | 8.00 |
| ❑ AYL1-5440 | Steve Wariner | 1985 | 8.00 |
| *—"Best Buy Series" reissue* | | | |
| ❑ AHL1-7164 | Down in Tennessee | 1986 | 8.00 |
| **WARING, FRED, AND THE PENNSYLVANIANS** | | | |
| CAPITOL | | | |
| ❑ STBB-347 [(2)] | Christmas Magic | 1969 | 15.00 |
| *—Collects ST 1260 and ST 1610 in one package (abridged); green label original* | | | |
| ❑ STBB-347 [(2)] | Christmas Magic | 1972 | 12.00 |
| *—Orange label reissue* | | | |
| ❑ ST 896 [S] | Now Is the Caroling Season | 1959 | 15.00 |
| *—Black colorband label, logo at left* | | | |
| ❑ ST 896 [S] | Now Is the Caroling Season | 1962 | 12.00 |
| *—Black colorband label, logo at top* | | | |
| ❑ T 896 [M] | Now Is the Caroling Season | 1957 | 20.00 |
| *—Originals have turquoise labels* | | | |
| ❑ T 896 [M] | Now Is the Caroling Season | 1959 | 15.00 |
| *—Black colorband label, logo at left* | | | |
| ❑ T 896 [M] | Now Is the Caroling Season | 1962 | 12.00 |
| *—Black colorband label, logo at top* | | | |
| ❑ ST 936 [S] | All Through the Night | 1958 | 20.00 |
| ❑ T 936 [M] | All Through the Night | 1958 | 20.00 |
| *—Black colorband label, logo at left* | | | |

| Number | Title (A Side/B Side) | Yr | NM |
|---|---|---|---|
| ❑ ST 1260 [S] | The Sounds of Christmas | 1959 | 20.00 |
| *—Originals have black label with colorband and "Capitol" logo at 9 o'clock* | | | |
| ❑ T 1260 [M] | The Sounds of Christmas | 1959 | 15.00 |
| *—Black colorband label, logo at left* | | | |
| ❑ SM-1610 | The Meaning of Christmas | 197? | 8.00 |
| *—Reissue of ST 1610 with same contents* | | | |
| ❑ ST 1610 [S] | The Meaning of Christmas | 1961 | 20.00 |
| ❑ T 1610 [M] | The Meaning of Christmas | 1961 | 15.00 |
| ❑ ST 2054 [S] | This I Believe | 1964 | 15.00 |
| ❑ T 2054 [M] | This I Believe | 1964 | 12.00 |
| ❑ ST 2625 [S] | The Best of Fred Waring and the Pennsylvanians | 1967 | 15.00 |
| ❑ T 2625 [M] | The Best of Fred Waring and the Pennsylvanians | 1967 | 12.00 |

### CAPITOL CREATIVE PRODUCTS

| Number | Title (A Side/B Side) | Yr | NM |
|---|---|---|---|
| ❑ L-6550 [M] | Fred Waring and the Pennsylvanians Sing of Faith, Home and Christmas | 1967 | 15.00 |
| *—Compiled for the E.F. MacDonald Company, Dayton, Ohio* | | | |

### CAPITOL PICKWICK SERIES

| Number | Title (A Side/B Side) | Yr | NM |
|---|---|---|---|
| ❑ PC-3451 [M] | The Romantic Sound | 196? | 10.00 |
| ❑ SPC-3451 [S] | The Romantic Sound | 196? | 12.00 |
| ❑ PC-3454 [M] | Some Enchanted Evening | 196? | 10.00 |
| ❑ SPC-3454 [S] | Some Enchanted Evening | 196? | 12.00 |

### DECCA

| Number | Title (A Side/B Side) | Yr | NM |
|---|---|---|---|
| ❑ DBX 186 [(2)M] | The Best of Fred Waring | 1965 | 15.00 |
| ❑ DL 4158 [M] | This Is My Country | 1961 | 12.00 |
| ❑ DL 4234 [M] | Songs of Faith | 1962 | 12.00 |
| ❑ DL 4345 [M] | God's Trombones | 1962 | 12.00 |
| ❑ DL 4511 [M] | Song of Easter | 1965 | 10.00 |
| ❑ DL 4753 [M] | Fred Waring Showcase | 1966 | 10.00 |
| ❑ DL 4759 [M] | Magic Music | 1966 | 10.00 |
| ❑ DL 4809 [M] | A-Caroling We Go | 1966 | 12.00 |
| ❑ DL 4875 [M] | Barbershop Sing | 1967 | 12.00 |
| ❑ DLP 5004 [10] | Jerome Kern Songs | 1950 | 50.00 |
| ❑ DLP 5005 [10] | Cole Porter Songs | 1950 | 50.00 |
| ❑ DLP 5009 [10] | Selections from Miss Liberty | 1950 | 50.00 |
| ❑ DLP 5021 [10] | 'Twas the Night Before Christmas | 1950 | 50.00 |
| ❑ DLP 5036 [10] | Pleasure Time | 1951 | 40.00 |
| ❑ DL 5061 [10] | Songs of Devotion, Vol. 1 | 1950 | 40.00 |
| ❑ DL 5062 [10] | Songs of Devotion, Vol. 2 | 1950 | 40.00 |
| ❑ DL 5141 [10] | This Is My Country | 1950 | 40.00 |
| ❑ DL 5202 [10] | Columbia, the Gem of the Ocean (Patriotic and Service Songs) | 1950 | 40.00 |
| ❑ DL 5292 [10] | Richard Rodgers and Oscar Hammerstein II Songs, Vol. 1 | 1950 | 40.00 |
| ❑ DL 5293 [10] | Richard Rodgers and Oscar Hammerstein II Songs, Vol. 2 | 1950 | 40.00 |
| ❑ DL 5295 [10] | Christmas Time | 1950 | 40.00 |
| ❑ DXSB 7186 [(2)S] | The Best of Fred Waring | 1965 | 15.00 |
| ❑ DL 8005 [M] | Listening Time | 1950 | 40.00 |
| ❑ DL 8026 [M] | Program Time | 1950 | 30.00 |
| ❑ DL 8033 [M] | Song of America | 195? | 40.00 |
| ❑ DL 8039 [M] | Songs of Faith, Vols. 1 and 2 | 195? | 30.00 |
| ❑ DL 8047 [M] | God's Trombones and Other Spirituals | 195? | 30.00 |
| ❑ DL 8082 [M] | For Listening Only | 1954 | 25.00 |
| ❑ DL 8084 [M] | Song of Christmas | 1954 | 25.00 |
| ❑ DL 8110 [M] | Lullaby Time | 1955 | 20.00 |
| ❑ DL 8111 [M] | Songs in Reverence | 1955 | 20.00 |
| ❑ DL 8171 [M] | 'Twas the Night Before Christmas | 1955 | 20.00 |
| ❑ DL 8172 [M] | Christmas Time | 1955 | 20.00 |
| ❑ DL 8222 [M] | College Memories | 1956 | 15.00 |
| ❑ DL 8335 [M] | Harmonizin' the Old Songs | 1956 | 15.00 |
| ❑ DL 8670 [M] | Songs of Devotion | 1958 | 15.00 |
| ❑ DL 8708 [M] | Excerpts from Carousel and Oklahoma | 1958 | 15.00 |
| ❑ DL 8709 [M] | Songs of Inspiration | 1958 | 15.00 |
| ❑ DL 8710 [M] | Stars and Stripes Forever | 1958 | 15.00 |
| ❑ DL 8829 | Memorable Moments from Broadway Musicals | 1959 | 15.00 |
| ❑ DL 9031 [M] | Hear, Hear | 195? | 15.00 |
| ❑ DL 74158 [S] | This Is My Country | 1961 | 15.00 |
| ❑ DL 74234 [S] | Songs of Faith | 1962 | 15.00 |
| ❑ DL 74345 [S] | God's Trombones | 1962 | 15.00 |
| ❑ DL 74511 [S] | Song of Easter | 1965 | 12.00 |
| ❑ DL 74753 [S] | Fred Waring Showcase | 1966 | 12.00 |
| ❑ DL 74759 [S] | Magic Music | 1966 | 12.00 |
| ❑ DL 74809 [S] | A-Caroling We Go | 1966 | 15.00 |
| ❑ DL 74875 [S] | Barbershop Sing | 1967 | 12.00 |
| ❑ DL 75007 | Two Sides of Fred Waring and the Pennsylvanians | 1968 | 12.00 |
| ❑ DL 78171 [R] | 'Twas the Night Before Christmas | 196? | 12.00 |
| ❑ DL 78172 [R] | Christmas Time | 196? | 12.00 |

### HARMONY

| Number | Title (A Side/B Side) | Yr | NM |
|---|---|---|---|
| ❑ HS 11363 | In Concert | 1970 | 10.00 |

### MCA

| Number | Title (A Side/B Side) | Yr | NM |
|---|---|---|---|
| ❑ 193 | This Is My Country | 1973 | 8.00 |
| *—Reissue of Decca 74158* | | | |
| ❑ 207 | God's Trombones | 1973 | 8.00 |
| *—Reissue of Decca 74345* | | | |
| ❑ 4008 [(2)] | The Best of Fred Waring and the Pennsylvanians | 1973 | 12.00 |
| *—Reissue of Decca 7186; black labels with rainbow* | | | |
| ❑ 15009 | A-Caroling We Go | 1973 | 10.00 |
| *—Reissue of DL 74809; black label with rainbow* | | | |
| ❑ 15009 | A-Caroling We Go | 1980 | 8.00 |
| *—Blue label with rainbow* | | | |
| ❑ 15011 | Christmas Time | 1973 | 10.00 |
| *—Reissue of DL 78172; black label with rainbow* | | | |
| ❑ 15011 | Christmas Time | 1980 | 8.00 |
| *—Blue label with rainbow* | | | |
| ❑ 15016 | 'Twas the Night Before Christmas | 1973 | 10.00 |
| *—Reissue of DL 78171; black label with rainbow* | | | |
| ❑ 15016 | 'Twas the Night Before Christmas | 1980 | 8.00 |
| *—Blue label with rainbow* | | | |

### MEGA

| Number | Title (A Side/B Side) | Yr | NM |
|---|---|---|---|
| ❑ 31-1005 | Nashville | 1971 | 10.00 |

### REPRISE

| Number | Title (A Side/B Side) | Yr | NM |
|---|---|---|---|
| ❑ R 6137 [M] | To You...Forever | 1964 | 12.00 |
| ❑ RS 6137 [S] | To You...Forever | 1964 | 15.00 |
| ❑ R 6148 [M] | Fred Waring and the Pennsylvanians in Concert | 1964 | 12.00 |
| ❑ RS 6148 [S] | Fred Waring and the Pennsylvanians in Concert | 1964 | 15.00 |

### STASH

| Number | Title (A Side/B Side) | Yr | NM |
|---|---|---|---|
| ❑ 126 | Memorial Album | 1985 | 10.00 |

## WARNES, JENNIFER Includes records as "Jennifer."

### ARISTA

| Number | Title (A Side/B Side) | Yr | NM |
|---|---|---|---|
| ❑ AL 4062 | Jennifer Warnes | 1977 | 10.00 |
| ❑ AB 4217 | Shot Through the Heart | 1979 | 10.00 |
| ❑ AL 9560 | The Best of Jennifer Warnes | 1982 | 8.00 |

### CYPRESS

| Number | Title (A Side/B Side) | Yr | NM |
|---|---|---|---|
| ❑ 661111-1 | Famous Blue Raincoat | 1987 | 30.00 |

### PARROT

| Number | Title (A Side/B Side) | Yr | NM |
|---|---|---|---|
| ❑ PAS-71020 | I Can Remember Anything | 1968 | 20.00 |
| *—As "Jennifer"* | | | |
| ❑ PAS-71034 | See Me | 1970 | 20.00 |
| *—As "Jennifer"* | | | |

### ROCK THE HOUSE

| Number | Title (A Side/B Side) | Yr | NM |
|---|---|---|---|
| ❑ RTH 5052 | Famous Blue Raincoat | 1996 | 50.00 |
| *—Classic Records reissue* | | | |

## WARREN, FRAN

### AUDIO FIDELITY

| Number | Title (A Side/B Side) | Yr | NM |
|---|---|---|---|
| ❑ AFSD-6207 | Come Into My World | 1968 | 25.00 |

### MGM

| Number | Title (A Side/B Side) | Yr | NM |
|---|---|---|---|
| ❑ E-3394 [M] | Mood Indigo | 1956 | 50.00 |
| *—Yellow label* | | | |

### TOPS

| Number | Title (A Side/B Side) | Yr | NM |
|---|---|---|---|
| ❑ L-1585 [M] | Hey There | 195? | 20.00 |

### VENISE

| Number | Title (A Side/B Side) | Yr | NM |
|---|---|---|---|
| ❑ 7019 [M] | Come Rain or Come Shine | 195? | 25.00 |
| ❑ 10019 [S] | Come Rain or Come Shine | 195? | 50.00 |
| *—Yellow vinyl* | | | |

### WARWICK

| Number | Title (A Side/B Side) | Yr | NM |
|---|---|---|---|
| ❑ W-2012 [M] | Something's Coming | 1960 | 25.00 |

## WARREN, RUSTY

### GNP CRESCENDO

| Number | Title (A Side/B Side) | Yr | NM |
|---|---|---|---|
| ❑ 2079 [(2)] | Knockers Up!/Songs for Sinners | 1975 | 15.00 |
| ❑ 2080 [(2)] | Rusty Warren Bounces Back/Sin-Sational | 1975 | 15.00 |
| ❑ 2081 | Rusty Warren Lays It on the Line | 1975 | 12.00 |
| ❑ 2088 | Knockers Up! '76 | 1976 | 12.00 |
| ❑ 2103 | Bottoms Up! | 1976 | 12.00 |
| ❑ 2114 | Sexplosion | 1977 | 12.00 |

### JUBILEE

| Number | Title (A Side/B Side) | Yr | NM |
|---|---|---|---|
| ❑ JLP 2024 [M] | Songs for Sinners | 1960 | 25.00 |
| ❑ JLP 2029 [M] | Knockers Up! | 1960 | 25.00 |
| ❑ JLP 2034 [M] | Sin-Sational | 1961 | 25.00 |
| ❑ JGM 2039 [M] | Rusty Warren Bounces Back | 1961 | 25.00 |
| ❑ JGM 2044 [M] | Rusty Warren in Orbit | 1962 | 25.00 |
| ❑ JLP 2049 [M] | Banned in Boston? | 1963 | 25.00 |
| ❑ JLP 2054 [M] | Sex-X-Ponent | 1964 | 25.00 |
| ❑ JLP 2059 [M] | More Knockers Up! | 1965 | 25.00 |
| ❑ JLP 2064 [M] | Rusty Rides Again | 1966 | 25.00 |
| ❑ JGM 2069 [M] | Bottoms Up! | 1967 | 20.00 |
| ❑ JGS 2069 [S] | Bottoms Up! | 1967 | 20.00 |
| ❑ JGM 2074 | Look What I've Got for You | 1967 | 20.00 |
| ❑ JLP 5025 [M] | Portrait of Life | 196? | 20.00 |
| ❑ JLPS 5025 [S] | Portrait of Life | 196? | 20.00 |

## WARWICK, DEE DEE

### ATCO

| Number | Title (A Side/B Side) | Yr | NM |
|---|---|---|---|
| ❑ SD 33-337 | Turnin' Around | 1970 | 25.00 |

### MERCURY

| Number | Title (A Side/B Side) | Yr | NM |
|---|---|---|---|
| ❑ MG-21100 [M] | I Want to Be with You | 1967 | 25.00 |
| ❑ SR-61100 [S] | I Want to Be with You | 1967 | 25.00 |
| ❑ SR-61221 | Foolish Fool | 1968 | 25.00 |

## WARWICK, DIONNE

### ARISTA

| Number | Title (A Side/B Side) | Yr | NM |
|---|---|---|---|
| ❑ AB 4230 | Dionne | 1979 | 10.00 |
| ❑ AL 8104 | How Many Times Can We Say Goodbye | 1983 | 10.00 |
| ❑ A2L 8111 [(2)] | Hot! Live and Otherwise | 1983 | 10.00 |
| *—Budget-line reissue* | | | |
| ❑ AL 8262 | Finder of Lost Loves | 1985 | 10.00 |
| ❑ AL 8295 | Dionne | 1985 | 8.00 |
| *—Budget-line reissue* | | | |
| ❑ AL 8338 | Heartbreaker | 1985 | 8.00 |
| *—Budget-line reissue* | | | |
| ❑ AL 8358 | Friends in Love | 1985 | 8.00 |
| *—Budget-line reissue* | | | |
| ❑ AL 8398 | Friends | 1985 | 10.00 |
| ❑ AL 8446 | Reservations for Two | 1987 | 10.00 |
| ❑ AL 8540 | Greatest Hits 1979-1990 | 1989 | 12.00 |
| ❑ AL 8573 | Dionne Warwick Sings Cole Porter | 1990 | 12.00 |
| ❑ A2L 8605 [(2)] | Hot! Live and Otherwise | 1981 | 12.00 |
| ❑ AL 9526 | No Night So Long | 1980 | 10.00 |
| ❑ AL 9585 | Friends in Love | 1982 | 10.00 |
| ❑ AL 9609 | Heartbreaker | 1982 | 10.00 |

### EVEREST

| Number | Title (A Side/B Side) | Yr | NM |
|---|---|---|---|
| ❑ 4103 | Dionne Warwick | 1981 | 10.00 |

### MOBILE FIDELITY

| Number | Title (A Side/B Side) | Yr | NM |
|---|---|---|---|
| ❑ 2-098 [(2)] | Hot! Live and Otherwise | 1982 | 30.00 |
| *—Audiophile vinyl* | | | |

### MUSICOR

| Number | Title (A Side/B Side) | Yr | NM |
|---|---|---|---|
| ❑ 2501 | Only Love Can Break a Heart | 1977 | 12.00 |

### PAIR

| Number | Title (A Side/B Side) | Yr | NM |
|---|---|---|---|
| ❑ PDL2-1043 [(2)] | The Dynamic Dionne Warwick | 1986 | 12.00 |
| ❑ PDL2-1098 [(2)] | Masterpieces | 1986 | 12.00 |

### PICKWICK

| Number | Title (A Side/B Side) | Yr | NM |
|---|---|---|---|
| ❑ PTP-2056 [(2)] | Alfie | 1973 | 12.00 |
| *—As "Dionne Warwicke"* | | | |

### RHINO

| Number | Title (A Side/B Side) | Yr | NM |
|---|---|---|---|
| ❑ RNDA-1100 [(2)] | Anthology 1962-1971 | 1985 | 15.00 |

### SCEPTER

| Number | Title (A Side/B Side) | Yr | NM |
|---|---|---|---|
| ❑ S-508 [M] | Presenting Dionne Warwick | 1963 | 15.00 |
| ❑ SS-508 [S] | Presenting Dionne Warwick | 1963 | 20.00 |
| ❑ S-517 [M] | Anyone Who Had a Heart | 1964 | 15.00 |
| ❑ SS-517 [S] | Anyone Who Had a Heart | 1964 | 20.00 |
| ❑ LP-523 [M] | Make Way for Dionne Warwick | 1964 | 15.00 |
| ❑ SPS-523 [S] | Make Way for Dionne Warwick | 1964 | 20.00 |
| ❑ LP-528 [M] | The Sensitive Sound of Dionne Warwick | 1965 | 15.00 |
| ❑ SPS-528 [S] | The Sensitive Sound of Dionne Warwick | 1965 | 20.00 |
| ❑ SPS-531 [S] | Here I Am | 1965 | 20.00 |
| ❑ SRM-531 [M] | Here I Am | 1965 | 15.00 |
| ❑ SPS-534 [S] | Dionne Warwick in Paris | 1966 | 15.00 |
| ❑ SRM-534 [M] | Dionne Warwick in Paris | 1966 | 12.00 |
| ❑ SPS-555 [S] | Here Where There Is Love | 1966 | 15.00 |
| ❑ SRM-555 [M] | Here Where There Is Love | 1966 | 12.00 |
| ❑ SPS-559 [S] | On Stage and in the Movies | 1967 | 15.00 |
| ❑ SRM-559 [M] | On Stage and in the Movies | 1967 | 12.00 |
| ❑ SPS-563 [S] | The Windows of the World | 1967 | 15.00 |
| ❑ SRM-563 [M] | The Windows of the World | 1967 | 12.00 |
| ❑ SPS-565 [S] | Dionne Warwick's Golden Hits, Part One | 1967 | 15.00 |
| ❑ SRM-565 [M] | Dionne Warwick's Golden Hits, Part One | 1967 | 20.00 |
| ❑ SPS-567 [S] | The Magic of Believing | 1968 | 20.00 |
| ❑ SRM-567 [M] | The Magic of Believing | 1968 | 30.00 |
| ❑ SPS-568 [S] | Valley of the Dolls | 1968 | 15.00 |
| ❑ SRM-568 [M] | Valley of the Dolls | 1968 | 50.00 |
| *—May only exist as a white label promo* | | | |
| ❑ SPS-571 | Promises, Promises | 1968 | 15.00 |
| ❑ SPS-573 | Soulful | 1969 | 15.00 |
| ❑ SPS-575 | Dionne Warwick's Greatest Motion Picture Hits | 1969 | 15.00 |
| ❑ SPS-577 | Dionne Warwick's Golden Hits, Part 2 | 1969 | 15.00 |
| ❑ SPS-581 | I'll Never Fall in Love Again | 1970 | 15.00 |
| ❑ SPS-587 | Very Dionne | 1970 | 15.00 |
| ❑ SPS 2-596 [(2)] | The Dionne Warwicke Story | 1971 | 20.00 |
| *—As "Dionne Warwicke"* | | | |
| ❑ SPS-598 [(2)] | From Within | 1972 | 20.00 |
| *—As "Dionne Warwicke"* | | | |
| ❑ P2M 5139 [(2)M] | Dionne! | 1967 | 20.00 |
| *—Columbia Record Club exclusive* | | | |
| ❑ P2S 5140 [(2)S] | Dionne! | 1967 | 20.00 |
| *—Columbia Record Club exclusive* | | | |
| ❑ ST-91010 [S] | Here Where There Is Love | 1966 | 20.00 |
| *—Capitol Record Club edition* | | | |
| ❑ ST-91099 [S] | On Stage and in the Movies | 1967 | 20.00 |
| *—Capitol Record Club edition* | | | |

### SPRINGBOARD

| Number | Title (A Side/B Side) | Yr | NM |
|---|---|---|---|
| ❑ SPS-4001 | The Golden Voice of Dionne Warwicke | 1972 | 10.00 |
| *—As "Dionne Warwicke"* | | | |
| ❑ SPS-4002 | Dionne Warwicke Sings Her Very Best | 1972 | 10.00 |
| *—As "Dionne Warwicke"* | | | |

| Number | Title (A Side/B Side) | Yr | NM |
|---|---|---|---|
| ❑ SPS-4003 | One Hit After Another | 1972 | 10.00 |
| *—As "Dionne Warwicke"* | | | |
| ❑ SPS-4032 | Greatest Hits, Vol. 2 | 197? | 10.00 |

TIME-LIFE

| Number | Title (A Side/B Side) | Yr | NM |
|---|---|---|---|
| ❑ SLGD-18 [(2)] | Legendary Singers: Dionne Warwick | 1987 | 15.00 |

UNITED ARTISTS

| Number | Title (A Side/B Side) | Yr | NM |
|---|---|---|---|
| ❑ UA-LA337-G | The Very Best of Dionne Warwicke | 1974 | 12.00 |
| *—As "Dionne Warwicke"* | | | |

WARNER BROS.

| Number | Title (A Side/B Side) | Yr | NM |
|---|---|---|---|
| ❑ BS 2585 | Dionne | 1971 | 12.00 |
| *—As "Dionne Warwicke"* | | | |
| ❑ BS 2658 | Just Being Myself | 1973 | 12.00 |
| *—As "Dionne Warwicke"* | | | |
| ❑ BS 2846 | Then Came You | 1975 | 12.00 |
| *—As "Dionne Warwicke"* | | | |
| ❑ BS4 2846 [Q] | Then Came You | 1975 | 20.00 |
| *—As "Dionne Warwicke"* | | | |
| ❑ BS 2893 | Track of the Cat | 1975 | 12.00 |
| ❑ BS 3119 | Love at First Sight | 1976 | 12.00 |

## WASHBOARD SAM

RCA VICTOR

| Number | Title (A Side/B Side) | Yr | NM |
|---|---|---|---|
| ❑ LPV-577 [M] | Feeling Lowdown | 196? | 25.00 |

## WASHINGTON, BABY

AVI

| Number | Title (A Side/B Side) | Yr | NM |
|---|---|---|---|
| ❑ AV-6038 | I Wanna Dance | 1978 | 10.00 |

COLLECTABLES

| Number | Title (A Side/B Side) | Yr | NM |
|---|---|---|---|
| ❑ COL-5040 | The Best of Baby Washington | 198? | 10.00 |
| ❑ COL-5108 | Only Those in Love | 198? | 10.00 |
| ❑ COL-5124 | That's How Heartaches Are Made | 198? | 10.00 |

SUE

| Number | Title (A Side/B Side) | Yr | NM |
|---|---|---|---|
| ❑ LP-1014 [M] | That's How Heartaches Are Made | 1963 | 150.00 |
| ❑ LP-1042 [M] | Only Those in Love | 1965 | 150.00 |
| ❑ LPS-1042 [S] | Only Those in Love | 1965 | 300.00 |

TRIP

| Number | Title (A Side/B Side) | Yr | NM |
|---|---|---|---|
| ❑ 8009 | The One and Only Baby Washington | 1971 | 15.00 |

VEEP

| Number | Title (A Side/B Side) | Yr | NM |
|---|---|---|---|
| ❑ VPS-16528 | With You in Mind | 1968 | 25.00 |

## WASHINGTON, DINAH

ACCORD

| Number | Title (A Side/B Side) | Yr | NM |
|---|---|---|---|
| ❑ SN-7207 | Retrospective | 1982 | 10.00 |

COLLECTABLES

| Number | Title (A Side/B Side) | Yr | NM |
|---|---|---|---|
| ❑ COL-5200 | Golden Classics | 1989 | 10.00 |

DELMARK

| Number | Title (A Side/B Side) | Yr | NM |
|---|---|---|---|
| ❑ DL-451 | Mellow Mama | 1992 | 20.00 |

EMARCY

| Number | Title (A Side/B Side) | Yr | NM |
|---|---|---|---|
| ❑ EMS-2-401 [(2)] | Jazz Sides | 197? | 15.00 |
| ❑ MG-26032 [10] | After Hours with Miss D | 1954 | 150.00 |
| ❑ MG-36000 [M] | Dinah Jams | 1955 | 80.00 |
| ❑ MG-36011 [M] | For Those in Love | 1955 | 70.00 |
| ❑ MG-36028 [M] | After Hours with Miss D | 1955 | 70.00 |
| *—Reissue of 26032* | | | |
| ❑ MG-36065 [M] | Dinah | 1956 | 70.00 |
| ❑ MG-36073 [M] | In the Land of Hi-Fi | 1956 | 60.00 |
| ❑ MG-36104 [M] | The Swingin' Miss "D" | 1956 | 60.00 |
| ❑ MG-36119 [M] | Dinah Washington Sings Fats Waller | 1957 | 60.00 |
| ❑ MG-36130 [M] | Dinah Washington Sings Bessie Smith | 1957 | 60.00 |
| ❑ MG-36141 [M] | Newport '58 | 1958 | 50.00 |
| ❑ 814184-1 [(2)] | Slick Chick (On the Mellow Side) | 1983 | 12.00 |
| ❑ 824883-1 [(2)] | Jazz Sides | 198? | 12.00 |
| *—Reissue of 401* | | | |
| ❑ 826453-1 | In the Land of Hi-Fi | 1986 | 10.00 |

EVEREST ARCHIVE OF FOLK & JAZZ

| Number | Title (A Side/B Side) | Yr | NM |
|---|---|---|---|
| ❑ FS-297 | Dinah Washington | 197? | 12.00 |

GRAND AWARD

| Number | Title (A Side/B Side) | Yr | NM |
|---|---|---|---|
| ❑ GA 33-318 [M] | Dinah Washington Sings the Blues | 1955 | 50.00 |
| *—Add 50% if removable wrap-around cover is still there* | | | |

HARLEM HIT PARADE

| Number | Title (A Side/B Side) | Yr | NM |
|---|---|---|---|
| ❑ 8002 | Finer Dinah | 197? | 10.00 |

MERCURY

| Number | Title (A Side/B Side) | Yr | NM |
|---|---|---|---|
| ❑ MGP-2-103 [(2)M] | This Is My Story | 1963 | 25.00 |
| *—Combines 20788 and 20789 in one package* | | | |
| ❑ MGP-2-603 [(2)S] | This Is My Story | 1963 | 30.00 |
| *—Combines 60788 and 60789 in one package* | | | |
| ❑ MG-20119 [M] | Music for a First Love | 1957 | 50.00 |
| ❑ MG-20120 [M] | Music for Late Hours | 1957 | 50.00 |
| ❑ MG-20247 [M] | The Best in Blues | 1958 | 50.00 |
| ❑ MG-20439 [M] | The Queen | 1959 | 30.00 |
| ❑ MG-20479 [M] | What a Diff'rence a Day Makes! | 1960 | 30.00 |
| ❑ MG-20523 [M] | Newport '58 | 1960 | 30.00 |
| *—Reissue of EmArcy 36141* | | | |
| ❑ MG-20525 [M] | Dinah Washington Sings Fats Waller | 1960 | 30.00 |
| *—Reissue of EmArcy 36119* | | | |
| ❑ MG-20572 [M] | Unforgettable | 1961 | 25.00 |
| ❑ MG-20604 [M] | I Concentrate on You | 1961 | 25.00 |
| ❑ MG-20614 [M] | For Lonely Lovers | 1961 | 25.00 |
| ❑ MG-20638 [M] | September in the Rain | 1961 | 25.00 |
| ❑ MG-20661 [M] | Tears and Laughter | 1962 | 25.00 |
| ❑ MG-20729 [M] | I Wanna Be Loved | 1962 | 25.00 |
| ❑ MG-20788 [M] | This Is My Story — Dinah Washington's Golden Hits, Volume 1 | 1963 | 15.00 |
| ❑ MG-20789 [M] | This Is My Story — Dinah Washington's Golden Hits, Volume 2 | 1963 | 15.00 |
| ❑ MG-20829 [M] | The Good Old Days | 1963 | 15.00 |
| ❑ MG-20928 [M] | The Queen and Quincy | 1965 | 15.00 |
| ❑ MG-21119 [M] | Dinah Discovered | 1967 | 20.00 |
| ❑ MG-25060 [10] | Dinah Washington | 1950 | 150.00 |
| ❑ MG-25138 [10] | Dynamic Dinah | 1952 | 150.00 |
| ❑ MG-25140 [10] | Blazing Ballads | 1952 | 150.00 |
| ❑ SR-60111 [S] | The Queen | 1959 | 40.00 |
| ❑ SR-60158 [S] | What a Diff'rence a Day Makes! | 1960 | 40.00 |
| ❑ SR-60200 [S] | Newport '58 | 1960 | 40.00 |
| ❑ SR-60202 [S] | Dinah Washington Sings Fats Waller | 1960 | 40.00 |
| ❑ SR-60232 [S] | Unforgettable | 1961 | 30.00 |
| ❑ SR-60604 [S] | I Concentrate on You | 1961 | 30.00 |
| ❑ SR-60614 [S] | For Lonely Lovers | 1961 | 30.00 |
| ❑ SR-60638 [S] | September in the Rain | 1961 | 30.00 |
| ❑ SR-60661 [S] | Tears and Laughter | 1962 | 30.00 |
| ❑ SR-60729 [S] | I Wanna Be Loved | 1962 | 30.00 |
| ❑ SR-60788 [S] | This Is My Story — Dinah Washington's Golden Hits, Volume 1 | 1963 | 20.00 |
| ❑ SR-60789 [S] | This Is My Story — Dinah Washington's Golden Hits, Volume 2 | 1963 | 20.00 |
| ❑ SR-60829 [S] | The Good Old Days | 1963 | 20.00 |
| ❑ SR-60928 [S] | The Queen and Quincy | 1965 | 20.00 |
| ❑ SR-61119 [S] | Dinah Discovered | 1967 | 15.00 |
| ❑ 818815-1 | What a Diff'rence a Day Makes! | 198? | 8.00 |
| *—Reissue* | | | |
| ❑ 822867-1 | This Is My Story — Dinah Washington's Golden Hits, Volume 1 | 1985 | 8.00 |
| *—Reissue* | | | |

PICKWICK

| Number | Title (A Side/B Side) | Yr | NM |
|---|---|---|---|
| ❑ SPC-3043 | Dinah Washington | 196? | 10.00 |
| ❑ SPC-3230 | I Don't Hurt Anymore | 197? | 10.00 |
| ❑ SPC-3536 | Greatest Hits | 197? | 10.00 |

ROULETTE

| Number | Title (A Side/B Side) | Yr | NM |
|---|---|---|---|
| ❑ RE 104 [(2)] | Echoes of an Era | 196? | 15.00 |
| ❑ RE 117 [(2)] | Queen of the Blues | 1971 | 15.00 |
| ❑ RE 125 [(2)] | The Immortal Dinah Washington | 1973 | 15.00 |
| ❑ R 25170 [M] | Dinah '62 | 1962 | 15.00 |
| ❑ SR 25170 [S] | Dinah '62 | 1962 | 20.00 |
| ❑ R 25180 [M] | In Love | 1962 | 15.00 |
| ❑ SR 25180 [S] | In Love | 1962 | 20.00 |
| ❑ R 25183 [M] | Drinking Again | 1962 | 15.00 |
| ❑ SR 25183 [S] | Drinking Again | 1962 | 20.00 |
| ❑ R 25189 [M] | Back to the Blues | 1963 | 15.00 |
| ❑ SR 25189 [S] | Back to the Blues | 1963 | 20.00 |
| ❑ R 25220 [M] | Dinah '63 | 1963 | 15.00 |
| ❑ SR 25220 [S] | Dinah '63 | 1963 | 20.00 |
| ❑ R 25244 [M] | In Tribute | 1963 | 15.00 |
| ❑ SR 25244 [S] | In Tribute | 1963 | 20.00 |
| ❑ R 25253 [M] | A Stranger on Earth | 1964 | 15.00 |
| ❑ SR 25253 [S] | A Stranger on Earth | 1964 | 20.00 |
| ❑ R 25269 [M] | Dinah Washington | 1964 | 15.00 |
| ❑ SR 25269 [S] | Dinah Washington | 1964 | 20.00 |
| ❑ R 25289 [M] | The Best of Dinah Washington | 1965 | 15.00 |
| ❑ SR 25289 [S] | The Best of Dinah Washington | 1965 | 20.00 |
| ❑ 42014 | The Best of Dinah Washington | 1968 | 12.00 |
| *—Reissue of 25289* | | | |

TRIP

| Number | Title (A Side/B Side) | Yr | NM |
|---|---|---|---|
| ❑ 5500 | Dinah Jams | 1973 | 10.00 |
| ❑ 5516 | After Hours | 1973 | 10.00 |
| ❑ 5524 | Tears and Laughter | 1974 | 10.00 |
| ❑ 5556 | Dinah Washington Sings Bessie Smith | 197? | 10.00 |
| ❑ 5565 | The Swingin' Miss D | 197? | 10.00 |
| ❑ TLX 9505 [(2)] | Sad Songs — Blue Songs | 197? | 12.00 |

VERVE

| Number | Title (A Side/B Side) | Yr | NM |
|---|---|---|---|
| ❑ 818930-1 | The Fats Waller Songbook | 1984 | 10.00 |

WING

| Number | Title (A Side/B Side) | Yr | NM |
|---|---|---|---|
| ❑ PKW-2-121 [(2)] | The Original Queen of Soul | 1969 | 20.00 |
| ❑ MGW-12140 [M] | The Late Late Show | 1963 | 12.00 |
| ❑ MGW-12271 [M] | Dinah Washington Sings Fats Waller | 1964 | 12.00 |
| ❑ SRW-16140 [S] | The Late Late Show | 1963 | 12.00 |
| ❑ SRW-16271 [S] | Dinah Washington Sings Fats Waller | 1964 | 12.00 |
| ❑ SRW-16386 | The Original Soul Sister | 196? | 12.00 |

## WASHINGTON, DINAH, AND BROOK BENTON

MERCURY

| Number | Title (A Side/B Side) | Yr | NM |
|---|---|---|---|
| ❑ MG-20588 [M] | The Two of Us | 1960 | 25.00 |
| ❑ SR-60244 [S] | The Two of Us | 1960 | 30.00 |
| ❑ 824823-1 | The Two of Us | 1985 | 8.00 |
| *—Reissue* | | | |

## WASHINGTON, EARL

JAZZ WORKSHOP

| Number | Title (A Side/B Side) | Yr | NM |
|---|---|---|---|
| ❑ JWS-202 [M] | All Star Jazz | 1963 | 60.00 |
| ❑ JWS-213 [M] | Reflections | 1963 | 60.00 |

## WASHINGTON, ERNESTINE

DISC

| Number | Title (A Side/B Side) | Yr | NM |
|---|---|---|---|
| ❑ DLP-712 [10] | Ernestine Washington with Bunk Johnson | 195? | 200.00 |

## WASHINGTON, GINO

ATAC

| Number | Title (A Side/B Side) | Yr | NM |
|---|---|---|---|
| ❑ 2730 | Gino Washington's Golden Hits | 1969 | 30.00 |

KAPP

| Number | Title (A Side/B Side) | Yr | NM |
|---|---|---|---|
| ❑ KL-1415 [M] | Gino Washington's Ram Jam Band | 1967 | 20.00 |
| ❑ KS-3415 [S] | Gino Washington's Ram Jam Band | 1967 | 25.00 |

## WASHINGTON, GROVER, JR.

COLUMBIA

| Number | Title (A Side/B Side) | Yr | NM |
|---|---|---|---|
| ❑ FC 40510 | Strawberry Moon | 1987 | 10.00 |
| ❑ OC 44256 | Then and Now | 1988 | 10.00 |
| ❑ OC 45253 | Time Out of Mind | 1989 | 10.00 |
| ❑ C 48530 | Next Exit | 1992 | 20.00 |

ELEKTRA

| Number | Title (A Side/B Side) | Yr | NM |
|---|---|---|---|
| ❑ 6E-182 | Paradise | 1979 | 10.00 |
| ❑ 6E-305 | Winelight | 1980 | 10.00 |
| ❑ 5E-562 | Come Morning | 1981 | 10.00 |
| ❑ 60215 | The Best Is Yet to Come | 1982 | 10.00 |
| ❑ 60318 | Inside Moves | 1984 | 10.00 |
| ❑ 60415 | Anthology of Grover Washington, Jr. | 1985 | 10.00 |

KUDU

| Number | Title (A Side/B Side) | Yr | NM |
|---|---|---|---|
| ❑ KU-03 | Inner City Blues | 1971 | 12.00 |
| ❑ KU-07 | All the King's Horses | 1972 | 12.00 |
| ❑ KU-12 | Soul Box, Vol. 1 | 1973 | 12.00 |
| ❑ KU-13 | Soul Box, Vol. 2 | 1973 | 12.00 |
| ❑ KU-20 | Mister Magic | 1975 | 12.00 |
| ❑ KU-24 | Feels So Good | 1975 | 12.00 |
| ❑ KU-32 | A Secret Place | 1976 | 12.00 |
| ❑ KSQX-1213 [(2)Q] | Soul Box | 1973 | 25.00 |
| ❑ KUX-1213 [(2)] | Soul Box | 1973 | 15.00 |
| *—The two records also were issued separately* | | | |
| ❑ KUX-3637 [(2)] | Live at the Bijou | 1977 | 15.00 |

MOTOWN

| Number | Title (A Side/B Side) | Yr | NM |
|---|---|---|---|
| ❑ M5-165V1 | A Secret Place | 1981 | 8.00 |
| *—Reissue of Kudu 32* | | | |
| ❑ M5-175V1 | Mister Magic | 1981 | 8.00 |
| *—Reissue of Kudu 20* | | | |
| ❑ M5-177V1 | Feels So Good | 1981 | 8.00 |
| *—Reissue of Kudu 24* | | | |
| ❑ M5-184V1 | Soul Box, Vol. 1 | 1981 | 8.00 |
| *—Reissue of half of Kudu 1213* | | | |
| ❑ M5-186V1 | All the King's Horses | 1981 | 8.00 |
| *—Reissue of Kudu 07* | | | |
| ❑ M5-187V1 | Soul Box, Vol. 2 | 1981 | 8.00 |
| *—Reissue of half of Kudu 1213* | | | |
| ❑ M5-189V1 | Inner City Blues | 1981 | 8.00 |
| *—Reissue of Kudu 03* | | | |
| ❑ M8-239 [(2)] | Live at the Bijou | 1982 | 12.00 |
| *—Reissue* | | | |
| ❑ M7-910 | Reed Seed | 1978 | 10.00 |
| ❑ M7-933 | Skylarkin' | 1980 | 10.00 |
| ❑ M9-940 [(2)] | Baddest | 1980 | 15.00 |
| ❑ M9-961A2 [(2)] | Anthology | 1981 | 15.00 |
| ❑ 5232 ML | Skylarkin' | 1982 | 8.00 |
| *—Reissue of 933* | | | |
| ❑ 5236 ML | Reed Seed | 1982 | 8.00 |
| *—Reissue of 910* | | | |
| ❑ 5307 ML | Greatest Performances | 1983 | 10.00 |
| ❑ 6126 ML | Grover Washington Jr. at His Best | 198? | 10.00 |

NAUTILUS

| Number | Title (A Side/B Side) | Yr | NM |
|---|---|---|---|
| ❑ NR-39 | Winelight | 1981 | 50.00 |
| *—Audiophile vinyl* | | | |

## WASHINGTON, TYRONE

BLUE LABOR

| Number | Title (A Side/B Side) | Yr | NM |
|---|---|---|---|
| ❑ 102 | Do Right | 197? | 20.00 |

BLUE NOTE

| Number | Title (A Side/B Side) | Yr | NM |
|---|---|---|---|
| ❑ BST-84274 | Natural Essence | 1968 | 25.00 |

## WATERS, ETHEL

MERCURY

| Number | Title (A Side/B Side) | Yr | NM |
|---|---|---|---|
| ❑ MG-20051 [M] | Ethel Waters | 1954 | 50.00 |

REMINGTON

| Number | Title (A Side/B Side) | Yr | NM |
|---|---|---|---|
| ❑ RLP-1025 [10] | Ethel Waters | 1950 | 50.00 |

"X"

| Number | Title (A Side/B Side) | Yr | NM |
|---|---|---|---|
| ❑ LVA-1009 [M] | Ethel Waters | 1955 | 50.00 |

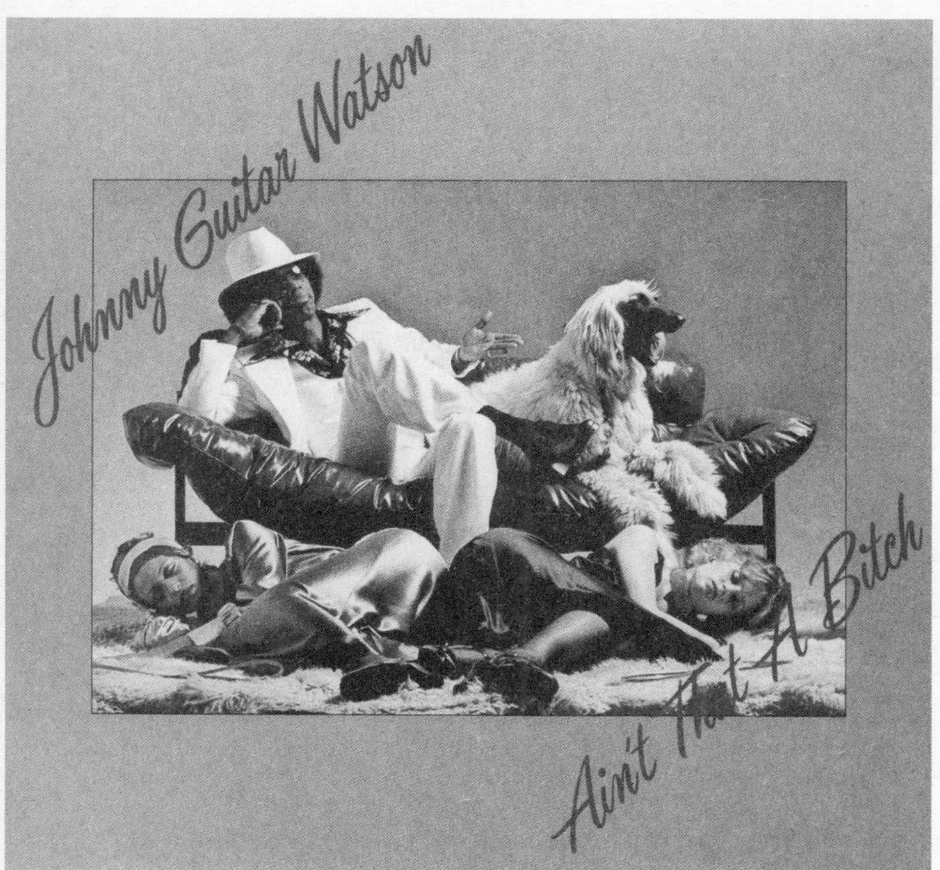


Johnny "Guitar" Watson, *Ain't That a Bitch,* DJM 3, 1976, $10.

| Number | Title (A Side/B Side) | Yr | NM |
|---|---|---|---|
| **WATERS, MUDDY** | | | |
| BLUE SKY | | | |
| ❑ PZ 34449 | Hard Again | 1977 | 12.00 |
| *—No bar code on cover* | | | |
| ❑ PZ 34449 | Hard Again | 198? | 8.00 |
| *—Budget-line reissue with bar code* | | | |
| ❑ JZ 34928 | I'm Ready | 1978 | 12.00 |
| ❑ PZ 34928 | I'm Ready | 198? | 8.00 |
| *—Budget-line reissue* | | | |
| ❑ JZ 35712 | Muddy "Missisiippi" Waters Live | 1980 | 12.00 |
| ❑ PZ 35712 | Muddy "Missisiippi" Waters Live | 198? | 8.00 |
| *—Budget-line reissue* | | | |
| ❑ JZ 37064 | King Bee | 1981 | 12.00 |
| ❑ PZ 37064 | King Bee | 198? | 8.00 |
| *—Budget-line reissue* | | | |
| CADET CONCEPT | | | |
| ❑ CS-314 | Electric Mud | 1968 | 25.00 |
| ❑ CS-320 | After the Rain | 1969 | 25.00 |
| CHESS | | | |
| ❑ 127 [(2)] | Fathers and Sons | 1969 | 25.00 |
| ❑ LP-1427 [DJ] | The Best of Muddy Waters | 1957 | 1500. |
| *—White label promo; VG value 500; VG+ value 1000* | | | |
| ❑ LP-1427 [M] | The Best of Muddy Waters | 1957 | 500.00 |
| *—Black label* | | | |
| ❑ LPS-1427 [R] | The Best of Muddy Waters | 196? | 12.00 |
| *—Black label* | | | |
| ❑ LP-1444 [DJ] | Muddy Waters Sings Big Bill | 1960 | 1000. |
| *—White label promo* | | | |
| ❑ LP-1444 [M] | Muddy Waters Sings Big Bill | 1960 | 300.00 |
| ❑ LPS-1444 [R] | Muddy Waters Sings Big Bill | 196? | 15.00 |
| *—Rechanneled stereo reissue* | | | |
| ❑ LP-1449 [M] | Muddy Waters at Newport | 1962 | 120.00 |
| ❑ LP-1483 [M] | Folk Singer | 1964 | 120.00 |
| ❑ LP-1501 [M] | The Real Folk Blues of Muddy Waters | 1965 | 60.00 |
| ❑ LP-1507 [M] | Muddy, Brass and Blues | 1966 | 40.00 |
| ❑ LPS-1507 [S] | Muddy, Brass and Blues | 1966 | 50.00 |
| ❑ LP-1511 [M] | More Real Folk Blues | 1967 | 50.00 |
| ❑ LPS-1511 [S] | More Real Folk Blues | 1967 | 40.00 |
| ❑ LP-1533 [M] | Blues from Big Bill's Copacabana | 1968 | 50.00 |
| ❑ LPS-1539 | Sail On | 1969 | 25.00 |
| ❑ LPS-1553 | They Call Me Muddy Waters | 1971 | 20.00 |
| ❑ CH-9101 | Rolling Stone | 1985 | 12.00 |
| ❑ CH-9180 | Rare and Unissued | 1986 | 12.00 |
| ❑ CH-9197 | Muddy Waters Sings Big Bill | 1986 | 10.00 |
| *—Reissue of 1444* | | | |
| ❑ CH-9198 | Muddy Waters at Newport | 1986 | 10.00 |
| *—Reissue of 1449* | | | |
| ❑ CH-9255 | The Best of Muddy Waters | 1987 | 10.00 |
| *—Reissue of 1427* | | | |
| ❑ CH-9261 | Folk Singer | 1987 | 10.00 |
| *—Reissue of 1483* | | | |
| ❑ CH-9274 | The Real Folk Blues of Muddy Waters | 1987 | 10.00 |
| *—Reissue of 1501* | | | |
| ❑ CH-9278 | More Real Folk Blues | 1988 | 10.00 |
| *—Reissue of 1511* | | | |
| ❑ CH-9286 | Muddy, Brass and the Blues | 1989 | 10.00 |
| *—Reissue of 1507* | | | |
| ❑ CH-9291 | Trouble No More: Singles 1955-1959 | 1989 | 12.00 |
| ❑ CH-9298 | The London Muddy Waters Sessions | 1989 | 10.00 |
| *—Reissue of 60013* | | | |
| ❑ CH-9299 | They Call Me Muddy Waters | 1989 | 10.00 |
| *—Reissue of 1553* | | | |
| ❑ CH-9319 | Can't Get No Grindin' | 1990 | 10.00 |
| *—Reissue of 50023* | | | |
| ❑ CH-50012 | Muddy Waters Live | 1972 | 20.00 |
| ❑ CH-50023 | Can't Get No Grindin' | 1973 | 20.00 |
| ❑ 2CH-50033 [(2)] | Fathers and Sons | 1974 | 20.00 |
| *—Reissue of 127* | | | |
| ❑ CH-50035 | The Muddy Waters Woodstock Album | 1976 | 15.00 |
| ❑ 2CH-60006 [(2)] | McKinley Morganfield, A.K.A. Muddy Waters | 1971 | 25.00 |
| ❑ CH-60013 | The London Muddy Waters Sessions | 1972 | 20.00 |
| ❑ CH-60026 | London Revisited | 1974 | 15.00 |
| ❑ CH-60031 | "Unk" in Funk | 1975 | 15.00 |
| ❑ CH6-80002 [(6)] | The Chess Box | 1990 | 50.00 |
| INTERMEDIA | | | |
| ❑ QS-5071 | Sweet Home Chicago | 198? | 10.00 |
| MOBILE FIDELITY | | | |
| ❑ 1-201 | Folk Singer | 1994 | 25.00 |
| *—Audiophile vinyl* | | | |
| MUSE | | | |
| ❑ MR-5008 | Mud in Your Ear | 198? | 12.00 |
| TESTAMENT | | | |
| ❑ 2210 | Stovall's Plantation | 197? | 12.00 |
| **WATERS, MUDDY, AND HOWLIN' WOLF** | | | |
| CHESS | | | |
| ❑ CH-9100 | Muddy and The Wolf | 1985 | 12.00 |
| **WATERS, PATTY** | | | |
| ESP-DISK' | | | |
| ❑ 1025 [M] | Patty Waters Sings | 1966 | 25.00 |
| ❑ S-1025 [S] | Patty Waters Sings | 1966 | 30.00 |
| ❑ 1055 [S] | Patty Waters College Tour | 1968 | 60.00 |
| **WATERS, ROGER** Also see PINK FLOYD. | | | |
| COLUMBIA | | | |
| ❑ FC 39290 | The Pros and Cons of Hitch Hiking | 1984 | 10.00 |
| *—Revised cover with black rectangle over woman's naked rear end* | | | |
| ❑ FC 39290 | The Pros and Cons of Hitch Hiking | 1984 | 20.00 |
| *—Original nude cover* | | | |
| ❑ PC 39290 | The Pros and Cons of Hitch Hiking | 1986 | 8.00 |
| *—Budget-line reissue with new prefix* | | | |
| ❑ FC 40795 | Radio K.A.O.S. | 1987 | 8.00 |
| MERCURY | | | |
| ❑ R 209833 [(2)] | The Wall — Live in Berlin | 1990 | 20.00 |
| *—BMG Direct Marketing version* | | | |
| ❑ 846611-1 [(2)] | The Wall — Live in Berlin | 1990 | 20.00 |
| **WATKINS, DOUG** | | | |
| NEW JAZZ | | | |
| ❑ NJLP-8238 [M] | Soulnik | 1960 | 60.00 |
| *—Purple label* | | | |
| ❑ NJLP-8238 [M] | Soulnik | 1965 | 25.00 |
| *—Blue label, trident logo at right* | | | |
| PHILIPS | | | |
| ❑ PHM 200001 [M] | French Horns for My Lady | 1962 | 20.00 |
| ❑ PHS 600001 [S] | French Horns for My Lady | 1962 | 25.00 |
| TRANSITION | | | |
| ❑ TRLP-20 [M] | Watkins at Large | 1956 | 1200. |
| *—Deduct 1/10 if booklet is missing* | | | |
| **WATKINS, JULIUS** | | | |
| BLUE NOTE | | | |
| ❑ BLP-5053 [10] | Julius Watkins Sextet | 1954 | 400.00 |
| ❑ BLP-5064 [10] | Julius Watkins Sextet, Volume 2 | 1955 | 400.00 |
| **WATKINS, LOVELACE** | | | |
| MGM | | | |
| ❑ E-3831 [M] | The Voice of Lovelace Watkins | 1960 | 25.00 |
| ❑ SE-3831 [S] | The Voice of Lovelace Watkins | 1960 | 40.00 |
| **WATSON, DOC** Includes records by the father-son duo of "Doc and Merle Watson." | | | |
| FLYING FISH | | | |
| ❑ FF-252 | Red Rocking Chair | 1981 | 12.00 |
| ❑ FF-301 | Guitar Album | 1983 | 12.00 |
| ❑ FF-352 | Pickin' the Blues | 1985 | 10.00 |
| FOLKWAYS | | | |
| ❑ FA-2366 [M] | Doc Watson and Family | 1963 | 25.00 |
| ❑ FA-31021 [S] | Doc Watson and Family | 196? | 15.00 |
| INTERMEDIA | | | |
| ❑ QS-5031 | Out in the Country | 198? | 10.00 |
| LIBERTY | | | |
| ❑ LWB-423 | Memories | 1981 | 12.00 |
| *—Reissue of United Artists 423* | | | |
| ❑ LW-601 | Doc and the Boys | 1981 | 10.00 |
| *—Reissue of United Artists 601* | | | |
| ❑ LT-887 | Look Away! | 1981 | 10.00 |
| *—Reissue of United Artists 887* | | | |
| ❑ LT-943 | Live and Pickin' | 1981 | 10.00 |
| *—Reissue of United Artists 943* | | | |
| ❑ LN-10027 | Lonesome Road | 1981 | 8.00 |
| *—Budget-line reissue* | | | |
| POPPY | | | |
| ❑ PP-LA022-F | Then and Now | 1973 | 15.00 |
| ❑ PP-LA210-G | Two Days in November | 1974 | 15.00 |
| ❑ PYS-5703 | The Elementary Doc Watson | 1972 | 15.00 |
| SMITHSONIAN/FOLKWAYS | | | |
| ❑ SF-40012 | The Doc Watson Family | 1990 | 12.00 |
| *—Reissue of Folkways LP* | | | |
| SUGAR HILL | | | |
| ❑ SH-3742 | Down South | 1985 | 10.00 |
| ❑ SH-3752 | Riding the Midnight Train | 1986 | 10.00 |
| ❑ SH-3759 | Portrait | 1987 | 10.00 |
| UNITED ARTISTS | | | |
| ❑ UA-LA423-G [(2)] | Memories | 1975 | 15.00 |
| ❑ UA-LA601-G | Doc and the Boys | 1976 | 12.00 |
| ❑ UA-LA725-G | Lonesome Road | 1977 | 12.00 |
| ❑ UA-LA887-H | Look Away! | 1978 | 12.00 |
| ❑ UA-LA943-H | Live and Pickin' | 1979 | 12.00 |

**Number — Title (A Side/B Side) — Yr — NM**

**Number — Title (A Side/B Side) — Yr — NM**

**Number — Title (A Side/B Side) — Yr — NM**

VANGUARD
- ❑ VSD-9/10 [(2)] Doc Watson on Stage 1970 20.00
- ❑ VSD 45/46 [(2)]The Essential Doc Watson 1973 20.00
- ❑ VSD 107/8 [(2)]Old Timey Concert 1977 20.00
- ❑ VSD-6576 Ballads from Deep Gap 1971 15.00
- ❑ VRS-9152 [M] Doc Watson 1964 20.00
- ❑ VRS-9170 [M] Doc Watson and Son 1965 20.00
- ❑ VRS-9213 [M] Southbound 1966 15.00
- ❑ VRS-9239 [M] Home Again 1967 15.00
- ❑ VMS-73108 The Essential Doc Watson, Vol. 1 1985 10.00
- ❑ VMS-73121 The Essential Doc Watson, Vol. 2 1985 10.00
- ❑ VSD-79152 [S] Doc Watson 1964 25.00
- ❑ VSD-79170 [S] Doc Watson and Son 1965 25.00
- ❑ VSD-79213 [S] Southbound 1966 20.00
- ❑ VSD-79239 [S] Home Again 1967 20.00
- ❑ VSD-79276 Good Deal 1968 15.00

### WATSON, JOHNNY "GUITAR"

A&M
- ❑ SP-4880 That's What Time It Is 1981 10.00

CADET
- ❑ LP-4056 [M] I Cried for You 1967 25.00
- ❑ LPS-4056 [S] I Cried for You 1967 30.00

CHESS
- ❑ LP-1490 [M] Blues Soul 1965 70.00
- ❑ LPS-1490 [S] Blues Soul 1965 80.00

DJM
- ❑ 3 Ain't That a Bitch 1976 10.00
- ❑ 7 A Real Mother for Ya 1977 10.00
- ❑ 13 Master Funk 1978 10.00
  *—As "Watsonian Institute"*
- ❑ 19 Giant 1978 10.00
- ❑ 24 What the Hell Is This? 1979 10.00
- ❑ 27 E.D.P. Extra Disco Perception 1979 10.00
  *—As "Watsonian Institute"*
- ❑ 31 Love Jones 1980 10.00
- ❑ 501 Johnny "Guitar" Watson and the Family Clone 1981 10.00
- ❑ 714 Funk Beyond the Call of Duty 1977 10.00

FANTASY
- ❑ MPF-4503 Greatest Hits 1981 10.00
- ❑ 9437 Listen 1973 12.00
- ❑ 9484 I Don't Want to Be Alone Stranger 1975 12.00

KING
- ❑ 857 [M] Johnny Guitar Watson 1963 400.00

MCA
- ❑ 5273 The Very Best of Johnny "Guitar" Watson 1981 10.00

OKEH
- ❑ OKM 12118 [M]Bad 1967 30.00
- ❑ OKM 12124 [M]In the Fats Bag 1967 30.00
- ❑ OKS 14118 [S] Bad 1967 40.00
- ❑ OKS 14124 [S] In the Fats Bag 1967 40.00

POWER PAK
- ❑ 306 Gangster of Love 1978 10.00

### WATSON, JOHNNY "GUITAR", AND LARRY WILLIAMS

OKEH
- ❑ OKM 12122 [M]Two for the Price of One 1967 40.00
- ❑ OKS 14122 [S] Two for the Price of One 1967 60.00

### WATSONIAN INSTITUTE See JOHNNY "GUITAR" WATSON.

### WATT, TOMMY

BETHLEHEM
- ❑ BCP-6052 [M] Watts Cooking 1961 30.00

### WATTERS, LU

CLEF
- ❑ MGC-503 [10] Lu Watters Jazz 1954 100.00

DOWN HOME
- ❑ MGD-5 [10] Lu Watters and His Yerba Buena Jazz Band 1955 60.00

GOOD TIME JAZZ
- ❑ L-A [(3)M] San Francisco Style 195? 60.00
- ❑ L-8 [10] Lu Watters and His Yerba Buena Jazz Band 1952 50.00
- ❑ L-12001 [M] Dawn Club Favorites 1954 40.00
- ❑ L-12002 [M] Originals and Ragtime 1954 40.00
- ❑ L-12003 [M] Stomps, Etc. and the Blues 1954 40.00
- ❑ L-12007 [M] 1942 Series 1955 40.00

MERCURY
- ❑ MGC-103 [10] Lu Watters and the Yerba Buena Jazz Band 1950 120.00
- ❑ MGC-503 [10] Lu Watters Jazz 1951 120.00
- ❑ MGC-510 [10] Lu Watters and His Yerba Buena Jazz Band 1952 120.00
- ❑ MG-35013 [10] Lu Watters and the Yerba Buena Jazz Band 1950 150.00

RIVERSIDE
- ❑ RLP 12-213 [M]San Francisco Style 1956 60.00
- ❑ RLP-2513 [10] Lu Watters 1947 1955 120.00

VERVE
- ❑ MGV-1005 [M] Lu Watters and His Yerba Buena Jazz Band 1956 50.00
- ❑ V-1005 [M] Lu Watters and His Yerba Buena Jazz Band 1961 20.00

### WATTERS, LU/SANTO PECORA

VERVE
- ❑ MGV-1008 [M] Dixieland Jamboree 1956 50.00
- ❑ V-1008 [M] Dixieland Jamboree 1961 25.00

### WATTS, ALAN

ASCENSION
- ❑ (# unknown) Dhyana: of the Art of Meditation, Vol. 1 1970 30.00
- ❑ (# unknown) Dhyana: of the Art of Meditation, Vol. 2 1970 30.00

MEA
- ❑ LP-1001 [M] Haiku Poems 1962 50.00
- ❑ LP-1002 [M] Zen and Senryu 1962 50.00
- ❑ LP-1007 [M] This Is It 1962 60.00

TOGETHER
- ❑ 1025 Why Not Now 1970 25.00

WARNER BROS.
- ❑ W 1923 The Sounds of Hinduism 1968 25.00

### WATTS, CHARLIE Also see THE ROLLING STONES.

COLUMBIA
- ❑ FC 40570 The Charlie Watts Orchestra Live Fulham Town Hall 1986 15.00

CONTINUUM
- ❑ 19308 From One Charlie 1990 25.00
  *—Box set with LP, book ("Ode to a High Flying Bird") and photo of Charlie Parker*

### WATTS, ERNIE

PACIFIC JAZZ
- ❑ PJ-20155 Planet Love 1969 30.00

VAULT
- ❑ LP-9011 Wonderbag 1968 20.00

### WATTS, MARZETTE

ESP-DISK'
- ❑ 1044 [S] Marzette Watts and Company 1971 20.00

SAVOY
- ❑ MG-12193 [M] The Marzette Watts Ensemble 1968 20.00

### WATTS 103RD STREET RHYTHM BAND, THE See CHARLES WRIGHT AND THE WATTS 103RD STREET RHYTHM BAND.

### WAVE CRESTS, THE

VIKING
- ❑ VKL-6606 [M] Surftime U.S.A. 1963 60.00
- ❑ VKS-6606 [S] Surftime U.S.A. 1963 100.00

### WAYFARERS, THE

RCA VICTOR
- ❑ LPM-1213 [M] The Wayfarers 1956 50.00
- ❑ LPM-2666 [M] Come Along with the Wayfarers 1963 25.00
- ❑ LSP-2666 [S] Come Along with the Wayfarers 1963 30.00
- ❑ LPM-2735 [M] The Wayfarers at the Hungry I 1963 25.00
- ❑ LSP-2735 [S] The Wayfarers at the Hungry I 1963 30.00
- ❑ LPM-2946 [M] The Wayfarers at the World's Fair 1964 30.00
- ❑ LSP-2946 [S] The Wayfarers at the World's Fair 1964 40.00

### WAYLON AND WILLIE For convenience's sake, we've listed all the variations of their credits here, including "Willie Nelson and Waylon Jennings." Also see WAYLON JENNINGS; WILLIE NELSON.

COLUMBIA
- ❑ FC 38562 Take It to the Limit 1983 10.00

RCA VICTOR
- ❑ AAL1-2686 Waylon and Willie 198? 8.00
  *—Reissue with new prefix*
- ❑ AFL1-2686 Waylon and Willie 1978 10.00
- ❑ AFL1-2686 [DJ]Waylon and Willie 1978 25.00
  *—Promo only on gold vinyl*
- ❑ AHL1-4455 WW II 1982 10.00
- ❑ AYL1-5134 Waylon and Willie 198? 8.00
  *—"Best Buy Series" reissue*
- ❑ AYL1-5138 WW II 198? 8.00
  *—"Best Buy Series" reissue*

### WAYNE, CHUCK

FOCUS
- ❑ FL-333 [M] Tapestry 1964 25.00
- ❑ FS-333 [M] Tapestry 1964 30.00

PRESTIGE
- ❑ PRLP-7367 [M]Morning Mist 1965 20.00
- ❑ PRST-7367 [S]Morning Mist 1965 25.00

PROGRESSIVE
- ❑ 3003 [10] The Chuck Wayne Quintet 1953 200.00

SAVOY
- ❑ MG-12077 [M] The Jazz Guitarist 1956 50.00

VIK
- ❑ LX-1098 [M] String Fever 1957 50.00

### WAYNE, FRANCES

ATLANTIC
- ❑ 1263 [M] The Warm Sound 1957 50.00
  *—Black label*
- ❑ 1263 [M] The Warm Sound 1961 20.00
  *—White "fan" logo at right of label*

BRUNSWICK
- ❑ BL 54022 [M] Frances Wayne 1958 40.00

CORAL
- ❑ CRL 56019 [10]Salute to Ethel Waters 195? 60.00

EPIC
- ❑ LN 3222 [M] Songs for My Man 1956 50.00

### WAYNE, JOHN

RCA VICTOR
- ❑ AFL1-3484 America, Why I Love Her 1979 10.00
  *—Reissue of 4828*
- ❑ AYL1-3959 America, Why I Love Her 1981 8.00
  *—"Best Buy Series" reissue*
- ❑ LSP-4828 America, Why I Love Her 1973 25.00

### WAYNE, WEE WILLIE

IMPERIAL
- ❑ LP-9144 [M] Travelin' Mood 1961 500.00

### WAZOO

ZIG ZAG
- ❑ 217 Wazoo 197? 30.00

### WE FIVE

A&M
- ❑ SP-111 [M] You Were On My Mind 1965 15.00
- ❑ SP-138 [M] Make Someone Happy 1967 20.00
- ❑ SP-4111 [S] You Were On My Mind 1965 20.00
- ❑ SP-4138 [S] Make Someone Happy 1967 15.00
- ❑ SP-4168 The Return of We Five 1969 15.00

VAULT
- ❑ 136 Catch the Wind 1970 15.00

### WEASELS, THE

WING
- ❑ MGW-12282 [M]The Liverpool Beat 1964 25.00
- ❑ SRW-16282 [S]The Liverpool Beat 1964 30.00

### WEATHER REPORT

ARC
- ❑ HC 47616 Weather Report 1982 40.00
  *—"Half Speed Mastered" on cover*

COLUMBIA
- ❑ CQ 32494 [Q] Mysterious Traveller 1974 30.00
- ❑ PCQ 33417 [Q]Tale Spinnin' 1975 30.00
- ❑ HC 44418 Heavy Weather 198? 40.00
  *—"Half-Speed Mastered" on cover*

### WEAVER, CHARLIE

COLUMBIA
- ❑ CL 1345 [M] Charlie Weaver Sings for His People 1959 30.00

STARLITE
- ❑ 6003 [10] Charlie Weaver Sings 1954 50.00

### WEAVERS, THE

ANALOGUE PRODUCTIONS
- ❑ 005 Reunion at Carnegie Hall, 1963 199? 30.00
  *—Audiophile vinyl*

DECCA
- ❑ DXB 173 [(2)M]The Best of the Weavers 1965 25.00
- ❑ DL 4277 [M] Weavers' Gold 1962 20.00
- ❑ DL 5285 [10] Folk Songs of America and Other Lands 1951 100.00
- ❑ DL-5373 [10] We Wish You a Merry Christmas 1952 100.00
- ❑ DXSB 7173 [(2)R]The Best of the Weavers 1965 20.00
- ❑ DL 8893 [M] The Best of the Weavers 1959 40.00
  *—Black label, silver print*
- ❑ DL 8893 [M] Folk Songs Made Famous by the Weavers 196? 20.00
- ❑ DL 8909 [M] Folk Songs Around the World 1959 40.00
- ❑ DL 74277 [R] Weavers' Gold 1962 15.00
- ❑ DL 75169 [R] The Weavers' Greatest Hits 1971 12.00
- ❑ DL 78893 [R] Folk Songs Made Famous by the Weavers 196? 15.00

| Number | Title (A Side/B Side) | Yr | NM |
|---|---|---|---|
| **MCA** | | | |
| ❑ 4052 [(2)] | The Best of the Weavers | 197? | 15.00 |
| *—Reissue of Decca 7173; black rainbow labels* | | | |
| ❑ 4052 [(2)] | The Best of the Weavers | 1980 | 12.00 |
| *—Blue rainbow labels* | | | |
| **VANGUARD** | | | |
| ❑ VSD-15/16 [(2)] | The Weavers' Greatest Hits | 1971 | 15.00 |
| ❑ VSD 2022 [S] | Travelling on with the Weavers | 1959 | 40.00 |
| ❑ VSD 2030 [S] | The Weavers at Home | 1959 | 40.00 |
| ❑ VSD 2069 [S] | The Weavers at Carnegie Hall, Vol. 2 | 1960 | 40.00 |
| ❑ VSD 2101 [S] | Almanac | 1961 | 40.00 |
| ❑ VSD 2150 [S] | Reunion at Carnegie Hall, 1963 | 1963 | 30.00 |
| ❑ SRV-3001 [(2)M] | The Weavers Song Bag | 1967 | 20.00 |
| ❑ VRS-6533 [R] | The Weavers at Carnegie Hall | 1970 | 12.00 |
| ❑ VRS-6537 [R] | The Weavers on Tour | 1970 | 12.00 |
| ❑ VRS 9010 [M] | The Weavers at Carnegie Hall | 1957 | 40.00 |
| ❑ VRS 9013 [M] | The Weavers on Tour | 1957 | 40.00 |
| ❑ VRS 9024 [M] | The Weavers at Home | 1959 | 30.00 |
| ❑ VRS 9043 [M] | Travelling on with the Weavers | 1959 | 30.00 |
| ❑ VRS 9075 [M] | The Weavers at Carnegie Hall, Vol. 2 | 1960 | 30.00 |
| ❑ VRS 9100 [M] | Almanac | 1961 | 30.00 |
| ❑ VRS 9130 [M] | Reunion at Carnegie Hall, 1963 | 1963 | 20.00 |
| ❑ VRS 9161 [M] | Reunion at Carnegie Hall, Part 2 | 1965 | 20.00 |
| ❑ SRV-73001 [(2)S] | The Weavers Song Bag | 1967 | 25.00 |
| ❑ VMS-73101 | The Weavers at Carnegie Hall | 1984 | 8.00 |
| *—Reissue of 6533* | | | |
| ❑ VMS-73116 | The Weavers on Tour | 1985 | 8.00 |
| *—Reissue of 6537* | | | |
| ❑ VMS-73122 | Classics | 1985 | 10.00 |
| ❑ VSD 79161 [S] | Reunion at Carnegie Hall, Part 2 | 1965 | 30.00 |

## WEB, THE

| Number | Title (A Side/B Side) | Yr | NM |
|---|---|---|---|
| **DERAM** | | | |
| ❑ DES 18018 | Fully Interlocking | 1968 | 25.00 |

## WEBB, CHICK

| Number | Title (A Side/B Side) | Yr | NM |
|---|---|---|---|
| **COLUMBIA** | | | |
| ❑ CL 2639 [M] | The Immortal Chick Webb | 1967 | 25.00 |
| **DECCA** | | | |
| ❑ DL 9223 [M] | Chick Webb 1937-39 | 1958 | 40.00 |
| ❑ DL 79223 [R] | Chick Webb 1937-39 | 1958 | 25.00 |

## WEBB, JACK

| Number | Title (A Side/B Side) | Yr | NM |
|---|---|---|---|
| **RCA VICTOR** | | | |
| ❑ LPM-1126 [M] | Pete Kelly's Blues | 1955 | 50.00 |
| *—Webb narrates; jazz combo plays* | | | |
| ❑ LPM-2053 [M] | Pete Kelly's Blues | 1959 | 30.00 |
| *—Reissue of 1126* | | | |
| ❑ LSP-2053(e) [R] | Pete Kelly's Blues | 1959 | 20.00 |
| ❑ LPM-3199 [10] | Dragnet — The Christmas Story | 1954 | 150.00 |
| **WARNER BROS.** | | | |
| ❑ W 1207 [M] | You're My Girl | 1958 | 30.00 |
| ❑ WS 1207 [S] | You're My Girl | 1958 | 40.00 |
| ❑ WS 1207 [S] | You're My Girl | 1958 | 40.00 |

## WEBB, JAY LEE

| Number | Title (A Side/B Side) | Yr | NM |
|---|---|---|---|
| **DECCA** | | | |
| ❑ DL 4933 [M] | I Come Home a-Drinkin' | 1967 | 25.00 |
| ❑ DL 74933 [S] | I Come Home a-Drinkin' | 1967 | 20.00 |
| ❑ DL 75121 | She's Looking Better by the Minute | 1969 | 20.00 |

## WEBB, JIMMY

| Number | Title (A Side/B Side) | Yr | NM |
|---|---|---|---|
| **ASYLUM** | | | |
| ❑ SD 5070 | Land's End | 1974 | 15.00 |
| **ATLANTIC** | | | |
| ❑ SD 18218 | El Mirage | 1977 | 12.00 |
| **EPIC** | | | |
| ❑ BN 26401 | Jim Webb Sings Jim Webb | 1968 | 20.00 |
| **LORIMAR** | | | |
| ❑ FC 37695 | Angel Heart | 1982 | 12.00 |
| **REPRISE** | | | |
| ❑ MS 2055 | Letters | 1972 | 15.00 |
| ❑ RS 6421 | Words and Music | 1970 | 15.00 |
| ❑ RS 6448 | And So: On | 1971 | 15.00 |

## WEBB, ROGER

| Number | Title (A Side/B Side) | Yr | NM |
|---|---|---|---|
| **SWAN** | | | |
| ❑ SLP-516 [M] | John, Paul and All That Jazz | 1964 | 30.00 |

## WEBSTER, BEN

| Number | Title (A Side/B Side) | Yr | NM |
|---|---|---|---|
| **ANALOGUE PRODUCTIONS** | | | |
| ❑ AP 011 | Ben Webster at the Renaissance | 199? | 25.00 |
| **BRUNSWICK** | | | |
| ❑ BL 58031 [10] | Tenor Sax Stylings | 1952 | 600.00 |
| **EMARCY** | | | |
| ❑ MG-26006 [10] | The Big Tenor | 1954 | 300.00 |
| **IMPULSE!** | | | |
| ❑ A-65 [M] | See You at the Fair | 1964 | 25.00 |
| ❑ AS-65 [S] | See You at the Fair | 1964 | 30.00 |
| **NESSA** | | | |
| ❑ N-8 | Did You Call? | 197? | 20.00 |
| **NORGRAN** | | | |
| ❑ MGN-1001 [M] | The Consummate Artistry of Ben Webster | 1954 | 150.00 |
| ❑ MGN-1018 [M] | Music for Loving | 1955 | 200.00 |
| ❑ MGN-1039 [M] | Ben Webster Plays Music with Feeling | 1955 | 200.00 |
| ❑ MGN-1089 [M] | King of the Tenors | 1956 | 120.00 |
| **REPRISE** | | | |
| ❑ R-2001 [M] | The Warm Moods of Ben Webster | 1961 | 25.00 |
| ❑ R9-2001 [S] | The Warm Moods of Ben Webster | 1961 | 30.00 |
| **VERVE** | | | |
| ❑ MGV-2026 [M] | Sophisticated Lady — Ben Webster with Strings | 1956 | 50.00 |
| ❑ V-2026 [M] | Sophisticated Lady — Ben Webster with Strings | 1961 | 25.00 |
| ❑ MGVS-6056 [S] | Ben Webster and Associates | 1959 | 40.00 |
| ❑ MGVS-6114 [S] | Ben Webster Meets Oscar Peterson | 1960 | 40.00 |
| ❑ MGV-8020 [M] | King of the Tenors | 1957 | 50.00 |
| ❑ V-8020 [M] | King of the Tenors | 1961 | 25.00 |
| ❑ MGV-8130 [M] | Music with Feeling — Ben Webster with Strings | 1957 | 50.00 |
| ❑ V-8130 [M] | Music with Feeling — Ben Webster with Strings | 1961 | 25.00 |
| ❑ MGV-8274 [M] | Soulville | 1958 | 50.00 |
| ❑ V-8274 [M] | Soulville | 1961 | 25.00 |
| ❑ MGV-8318 [M] | Ben Webster and Associates | 1959 | 50.00 |
| ❑ V-8318 [M] | Ben Webster and Associates | 1961 | 25.00 |
| ❑ V6-8318 [S] | Ben Webster and Associates | 1961 | 20.00 |
| ❑ MGV-8349 [M] | Ben Webster Meets Oscar Peterson | 1959 | 50.00 |
| ❑ V-8349 [M] | Ben Webster Meets Oscar Peterson | 1961 | 25.00 |
| ❑ V6-8349 [S] | Ben Webster Meets Oscar Peterson | 1961 | 20.00 |
| ❑ MGV-8359 [M] | The Soul of Ben Webster | 1960 | 50.00 |
| ❑ V-8359 [M] | The Soul of Ben Webster | 1961 | 25.00 |

## WEBSTER, BEN, AND HARRY "SWEETS" EDISON

| Number | Title (A Side/B Side) | Yr | NM |
|---|---|---|---|
| **COLUMBIA** | | | |
| ❑ CL 1891 [M] | Ben Webster-Sweets Edison | 1962 | 25.00 |
| ❑ CS 8691 [S] | Ben Webster-Sweets Edison | 1962 | 30.00 |

## WEBSTER, BEN, AND JOE ZAWINUL

| Number | Title (A Side/B Side) | Yr | NM |
|---|---|---|---|
| **RIVERSIDE** | | | |
| ❑ RLP-476 [M] | Soulmates | 1964 | 25.00 |
| ❑ RS-9476 [S] | Soulmates | 1964 | 30.00 |

## WEBSTER, MAMIE

| Number | Title (A Side/B Side) | Yr | NM |
|---|---|---|---|
| **CUB** | | | |
| ❑ 8002 [M] | The Blues | 1959 | 150.00 |

## WECHTER, JULIUS

| Number | Title (A Side/B Side) | Yr | NM |
|---|---|---|---|
| **JAZZ: WEST** | | | |
| ❑ LP-9 [M] | Linear Sketches | 1956 | 200.00 |

## WEDGES, THE

| Number | Title (A Side/B Side) | Yr | NM |
|---|---|---|---|
| **TIME** | | | |
| ❑ S-2090 [S] | Hang Ten (For Surfers Only) | 1963 | 70.00 |
| ❑ 52090 [M] | Hang Ten (For Surfers Only) | 1963 | 50.00 |

## WEED, BUDDY

| Number | Title (A Side/B Side) | Yr | NM |
|---|---|---|---|
| **COLUMBIA** | | | |
| ❑ CL 6160 [10] | Piano Moods | 1951 | 50.00 |
| **CORAL** | | | |
| ❑ CRL 57087 [M] | Piano Solos with Rhythm Accompaniment | 1957 | 40.00 |

## WEEKS, ANSON

| Number | Title (A Side/B Side) | Yr | NM |
|---|---|---|---|
| **FANTASY** | | | |
| ❑ 3258 [M] | Dancin' with Anson | 1958 | 30.00 |
| *—Red vinyl* | | | |
| ❑ 3269 [M] | Memories | 1958 | 30.00 |
| *—Red vinyl* | | | |
| ❑ 3297 [M] | More Dancin' with Anson | 1959 | 30.00 |
| *—Red vinyl* | | | |
| ❑ 3306 [M] | Cruisin' with Anson | 1960 | 30.00 |
| *—Red vinyl* | | | |
| ❑ 3333 [M] | Dancin' at Anson's | 1961 | 12.00 |
| *—Black vinyl* | | | |
| ❑ 3338 [M] | Old Favorites and New | 1962 | 25.00 |
| *—Red vinyl* | | | |
| ❑ 8001 [S] | Dancin' with Anson | 1960 | 25.00 |
| *—Blue vinyl* | | | |
| ❑ 8001 [S] | Dancin' with Anson | 1960 | 30.00 |
| *—Red vinyl (error pressing?)* | | | |
| ❑ 8006 [S] | Memories | 1960 | 25.00 |
| *—Blue vinyl* | | | |
| ❑ 8043 [S] | More Dancin' with Anson | 1960 | 25.00 |
| *—Blue vinyl* | | | |
| ❑ 8051 [S] | Cruisin' with Anson | 1960 | 25.00 |
| *—Blue vinyl* | | | |
| ❑ 8076 [S] | Dancin' at Anson's | 1961 | 15.00 |
| *—Black vinyl* | | | |
| ❑ 8090 [S] | Old Favorites and New | 1962 | 30.00 |
| *—Blue vinyl* | | | |

## WEEZER

| Number | Title (A Side/B Side) | Yr | NM |
|---|---|---|---|
| **DGC** | | | |
| ❑ DGC-25007 | Pinkerton | 1996 | 25.00 |
| **GEFFEN** | | | |
| ❑ B0004520-01 | Make Believe | 2005 | 12.00 |
| ❑ 069-493045-1 | Weezer | 2001 | 12.00 |
| *—Black vinyl* | | | |
| ❑ 069-493045-1 | Weezer | 2001 | 15.00 |
| *—Green vinyl* | | | |
| ❑ 069-493241-1 | Maladroit | 2002 | 12.00 |

## WEIN, GEORGE

| Number | Title (A Side/B Side) | Yr | NM |
|---|---|---|---|
| **ATLANTIC** | | | |
| ❑ 1221 [M] | Wein, Women and Song | 1955 | 50.00 |
| *—Black label* | | | |
| ❑ 1221 [M] | Wein, Women and Song | 1961 | 25.00 |
| *—Multicolor label, white "fan" logo at right* | | | |
| **BETHLEHEM** | | | |
| ❑ BCP-6050 [M] | George Wein and the Storyville Sextet — Jazz at the Modern | 1960 | 40.00 |
| ❑ SBCP-6050 [S] | George Wein and the Storyville Sextet — Jazz at the Modern | 1960 | 40.00 |
| **IMPULSE!** | | | |
| ❑ A-31 [M] | George Wein and the Newport All-Stars | 1963 | 20.00 |
| ❑ AS-31 [S] | George Wein and the Newport All-Stars | 1963 | 25.00 |
| **RCA VICTOR** | | | |
| ❑ LPM-1332 [M] | The Magic Horn of George Wein | 1956 | 40.00 |

## WEIR, BOB Also see THE GRATEFUL DEAD.

| Number | Title (A Side/B Side) | Yr | NM |
|---|---|---|---|
| **ARISTA** | | | |
| ❑ AL 4155 | Heaven Help the Fool | 1978 | 10.00 |
| ❑ AL 8366 | Heaven Help the Fool | 1985 | 8.00 |
| *—Budget-line reissue* | | | |
| ❑ AL 8367 | Bobby and the Midnites | 1985 | 8.00 |
| *—Budget-line reissue* | | | |
| ❑ AL 9568 | Bobby and the Midnites | 1981 | 10.00 |
| **WARNER BROS.** | | | |
| ❑ BS 2627 | Ace | 1972 | 30.00 |
| *—Black and white photo on back cover* | | | |
| ❑ BS 2627 | Ace | 1972 | 40.00 |
| *—Color photo on back cover* | | | |

## WEIRD-OHS, THE

| Number | Title (A Side/B Side) | Yr | NM |
|---|---|---|---|
| **MERCURY** | | | |
| ❑ MG-20976 [M] | The Sounds of the Weird-Ohs | 1964 | 150.00 |
| ❑ SR-60976 [S] | The Sounds of the Weird-Ohs | 1964 | 200.00 |

## WEIRDOS

| Number | Title (A Side/B Side) | Yr | NM |
|---|---|---|---|
| **BOMP!** | | | |
| ❑ 4007 [EP] | Who? What? When? Where? Why? | 1979 | 15.00 |
| **FRONTIER** | | | |
| ❑ 4623-1-L | Condor | 1990 | 12.00 |
| ❑ 4630-1-L | Weird World | 1991 | 12.00 |
| **OUT OF DARKNESS** | | | |
| ❑ OTD 001 [DJ] | Message from the Underworld | 198? | 40.00 |
| *—Promo-only release* | | | |
| **RHINO** | | | |
| ❑ RNEP 508 [EP] | Action Design | 1980 | 20.00 |

## WEISBERG, TIM

| Number | Title (A Side/B Side) | Yr | NM |
|---|---|---|---|
| **NAUTILUS** | | | |
| ❑ NR-7 | Tip of the Weisberg | 1980 | 30.00 |
| *—Audiophile vinyl* | | | |

## WEISSBERG, ERIC, AND MARSHALL BRICKMAN

| Number | Title (A Side/B Side) | Yr | NM |
|---|---|---|---|
| **ELEKTRA** | | | |
| ❑ EKL-238 [M] | New Dimensions in Banjo and Bluegrass | 1963 | 20.00 |
| ❑ EKS-7238 [S] | New Dimensions in Banjo and Bluegrass | 1963 | 25.00 |
| *—Mandolin-player label* | | | |
| ❑ EKS-7238 [S] | New Dimensions in Banjo and Bluegrass | 1967 | 20.00 |
| *—Tan label with large stylized "E" at top* | | | |
| ❑ EKS-7238 [S] | New Dimensions in Banjo and Bluegrass | 1969 | 15.00 |
| *—Red label with large stylized "E" at top* | | | |
| ❑ EKS-7238 [S] | New Dimensions in Banjo and Bluegrass | 1971 | 12.00 |
| *—Butterfly label* | | | |
| ❑ EKS-7238 [S] | New Dimensions in Banjo and Bluegrass | 1980 | 10.00 |
| *—Red label with Warner Communications logo in lower right* | | | |

## WELCH, LENNY

### CADENCE

| Number | Title (A Side/B Side) | Yr | NM |
|---|---|---|---|
| ❑ CLP 3068 [M] | Since I Fell for You | 1963 | 30.00 |
| ❑ CLP 25068 [S] | Since I Fell for You | 1963 | 50.00 |

### COLUMBIA

| Number | Title (A Side/B Side) | Yr | NM |
|---|---|---|---|
| ❑ CL 2430 [M] | Since I Fell for You | 1965 | 20.00 |
| *—Reissue of Cadence 3068* | | | |
| ❑ CS 9230 [S] | Since I Fell for You | 1965 | 30.00 |
| *—Reissue of Cadence 25068* | | | |

### KAPP

| Number | Title (A Side/B Side) | Yr | NM |
|---|---|---|---|
| ❑ KL-1457 [M] | Two Different Worlds | 1965 | 15.00 |
| ❑ KL-1481 [M] | Rags to Riches | 1966 | 15.00 |
| ❑ KL-1517 [M] | Lenny | 1967 | 15.00 |
| ❑ KS-3457 [S] | Two Different Worlds | 1965 | 20.00 |
| ❑ KS-3481 [S] | Rags to Riches | 1966 | 20.00 |
| ❑ KS-3517 [S] | Lenny | 1967 | 20.00 |

## WELCH CHORALE, THE

### VANGUARD

| Number | Title (A Side/B Side) | Yr | NM |
|---|---|---|---|
| ❑ VRS 428 [M] | A Music Box of Christmas Carols | 1954 | 20.00 |
| *—With Music Boxes from the Bornand Collection* | | | |

## WELK, LAWRENCE

### CORAL

| Number | Title (A Side/B Side) | Yr | NM |
|---|---|---|---|
| ❑ 7CXSB 5 [(2)S] | The Best of Lawrence Welk | 196? | 15.00 |
| ❑ CXB 5 [(2)M] | The Best of Lawrence Welk | 196? | 20.00 |
| ❑ CRL 56043 [10] | On Moonlight Bay | 195? | 30.00 |
| ❑ CRL 56045 [10] | Songs About My Extraordinary Gal and Her Friends | 195? | 30.00 |
| ❑ CRL 56088 [10] | Souvenir Album | 195? | 30.00 |
| ❑ CRL 56101 [10] | Nimble Fingers | 195? | 30.00 |
| ❑ CRL 56120 [10] | Viennese Waltzes for Dancing | 1954 | 30.00 |
| ❑ CRL 57011 [M] | Lawrence Welk and His Sparkling Strings | 1955 | 20.00 |
| ❑ CRL 57023 [M] | Lawrence Welk Introduces the Girl Friends | 1955 | 25.00 |
| ❑ CRL 57025 [M] | TV Favorites | 1955 | 20.00 |
| ❑ CRL 57036 [M] | Shamrocks and Champagne | 1955 | 20.00 |
| ❑ CRL 57038 [M] | Bubbles in the Wine | 1956 | 20.00 |
| ❑ CRL 57041 [M] | Say It With Music | 1956 | 20.00 |
| ❑ CRL 57066 [M] | Lawrence Welk at Madison Square Garden | 1956 | 20.00 |
| ❑ CRL 57067 [M] | Pick-A-Polka! | 1956 | 20.00 |
| ❑ CRL 57068 [M] | Moments to Remember | 1956 | 20.00 |
| ❑ CRL 57078 [M] | Champagne Pops Parade | 1956 | 20.00 |
| ❑ CRL 57093 [M] | Merry Christmas from Lawrence Welk | 1956 | 20.00 |
| ❑ CRL 57111 [M] | Show Time | 1957 | 20.00 |
| ❑ CRL 57113 [M] | The World's Finest Music | 1957 | 20.00 |
| ❑ CRL 57119 [M] | Waltz with Lawrence Welk | 1957 | 20.00 |
| ❑ CRL 57146 [M] | Lawrence Welk Plays Dixieland | 1957 | 20.00 |
| ❑ CRL 57178 [M] | Nimble Fingers | 1957 | 20.00 |
| ❑ CRL 57186 [M] | Jingle Bells | 1957 | 20.00 |
| ❑ CRL 57191 [M] | Songs of Faith | 1958 | 15.00 |
| ❑ CRL 57214 [M] | Lawrence Welk Presents Keyboard Kapers | 1958 | 15.00 |
| ❑ CRL 57226 [M] | Champagne Dancing Party | 1958 | 15.00 |
| ❑ CRL 57260 [M] | Lawrence Welk Featuring the Lennon Sisters | 1959 | 15.00 |
| ❑ CRL 57262 [M] | Lawrence Welk Featuring Larry Hooper | 1959 | 15.00 |
| ❑ CRL 57267 [M] | TV Western Theme Songs | 1959 | 15.00 |
| ❑ CRL 57353 [M] | My Golden Favorites | 1961 | 12.00 |
| ❑ CRL 57383 [M] | Lawrence Welk Showcase | 1962 | 12.00 |
| ❑ CRL 57439 [M] | Songs Everybody Knows | 1964 | 12.00 |
| ❑ CRL 757036 [R] | Shamrocks and Champagne | 196? | 12.00 |
| ❑ CRL 757041 [R] | Say It With Music | 196? | 12.00 |
| ❑ CRL 757067 [R] | Pick-A-Polka! | 1959 | 12.00 |
| ❑ CRL 757093 [R] | Merry Christmas from Lawrence Welk | 196? | 12.00 |
| ❑ CRL 757113 [R] | The World's Finest Music | 196? | 12.00 |
| ❑ CRL 757186 [R] | Jingle Bells | 196? | 12.00 |
| ❑ CRL 757226 [S] | Champagne Dancing Party | 1958 | 20.00 |
| ❑ CRL 757267 [S] | TV Western Theme Songs | 1959 | 20.00 |
| ❑ CRL 757353 [S] | My Golden Favorites | 1961 | 12.00 |
| ❑ CRL 757383 [S] | Lawrence Welk Showcase | 1962 | 12.00 |
| ❑ CRL 757439 [S] | Songs Everybody Knows | 1964 | 12.00 |

### CORONET

| Number | Title (A Side/B Side) | Yr | NM |
|---|---|---|---|
| ❑ 275 | Lawrence Welk and His Orchestra | 196? | 10.00 |

### DECCA

| Number | Title (A Side/B Side) | Yr | NM |
|---|---|---|---|
| ❑ DL 8213 [M] | Lawrence Welk's Polka Party | 1956 | 15.00 |
| ❑ DL 8323 [M] | Around We Go | 1956 | 15.00 |
| ❑ DL 8324 [M] | Welktime | 1956 | 15.00 |

### DESIGN

| Number | Title (A Side/B Side) | Yr | NM |
|---|---|---|---|
| ❑ 200 | Champagne Time | 196? | 10.00 |
| ❑ 912 | Three of a Kind | 196? | 10.00 |

### DOT

| Number | Title (A Side/B Side) | Yr | NM |
|---|---|---|---|
| ❑ DLP 3164 [M] | Mr. Music Maker | 1959 | 12.00 |
| ❑ DLP 3200 [M] | The Voices and Strings of Lawrence Welk | 1959 | 12.00 |
| ❑ DLP 3218 [M] | The Lawrence Welk Glee Club | 1959 | 12.00 |
| ❑ DLP 3224 [M] | Dance with Lawrence Welk | 1959 | 12.00 |
| ❑ DLP 3238 [M] | Lawrence Welk Presents Great American Composers | 1960 | 10.00 |
| ❑ DLP 3247 [M] | Lawrence Welk Presents Great Overtures in Dance Time | 1960 | 10.00 |
| ❑ DLP 3248 [M] | I'm Forever Blowing Bubbles | 1960 | 10.00 |
| ❑ DLP 3251 [M] | Songs of the Islands | 1960 | 10.00 |
| ❑ DLP 3274 [M] | Strictly for Dancing | 1960 | 10.00 |
| ❑ DLP 3284 [M] | To Mother | 1960 | 10.00 |
| ❑ DLP 3296 [M] | Sweet and Lovely | 1960 | 10.00 |
| ❑ DLP 3302 [M] | Polkas | 1960 | 10.00 |
| ❑ DLP 3317 [M] | Lawrence in Dixieland | 1960 | 10.00 |
| ❑ DLP 3318 [M] | Double Shuffle | 1960 | 10.00 |
| ❑ DLP 3342 [M] | The Champagne Music of Lawrence Welk | 1960 | 10.00 |
| ❑ DLP 3350 [M] | Last Date | 1960 | 10.00 |
| ❑ DLP 3359 [M] | Calcutta! | 1961 | 10.00 |
| ❑ DLP 3389 [M] | Yellow Bird | 1961 | 10.00 |
| ❑ DLP 3395 [M] | Diamond Jubilee | 1961 | 10.00 |
| ❑ DLP 3397 [M] | Silent Night and 13 Other Best-Loved Christmas Songs | 1961 | 12.00 |
| ❑ DLP 3412 [M] | Moon River | 1961 | 10.00 |
| ❑ DLP 3428 [M] | Young World | 1962 | 10.00 |
| ❑ DLP 3432 [M] | Sing-a-Long Party | 1962 | 10.00 |
| ❑ DLP 3457 [M] | Baby Elephant Walk and Theme from The Brothers Grimm | 1962 | 10.00 |
| ❑ DLP 3489 [M] | Bubbles in the Wine | 1962 | 10.00 |
| ❑ DLP 3499 [M] | Waltz Time | 1963 | 10.00 |
| ❑ DLP 3510 [M] | 1963's Early Hits | 1963 | 10.00 |
| ❑ DLP 3528 [M] | Scarlett O'Hara | 1963 | 10.00 |
| ❑ DLP 3544 [M] | A Tribute to the All-Time Greats | 1963 | 10.00 |
| ❑ DLP 3552 [M] | Wonderful! Wonderful! | 1963 | 10.00 |
| ❑ DLP 3572 [M] | Early Hits of 1964 | 1964 | 10.00 |
| ❑ DLP 3591 [M] | The Lawrence Welk Television Show 10th Anniversary | 1964 | 10.00 |
| ❑ DLP 3611 [M] | The Golden Millions | 1964 | 10.00 |
| ❑ DLP 3616 [M] | My First of 1965 | 1965 | 10.00 |
| ❑ DLP 3629 [M] | Apples and Bananas | 1965 | 10.00 |
| ❑ DLP 3653 [M] | The Happy Wanderer | 1966 | 10.00 |
| ❑ DLP 3663 [M] | Today's Great Hits | 1966 | 10.00 |
| ❑ DLP 3688 [M] | Champagne on Broadway | 1966 | 10.00 |
| ❑ DLP 3774 [M] | Winchester Cathedral | 1966 | 10.00 |
| ❑ DLP 3779 [M] | Hymns We Love | 1967 | 10.00 |
| ❑ DLP 3790 [M] | Lawrence Welk's "Hits of Our Time" | 1967 | 10.00 |
| ❑ DLP 3812 [M] | Golden Hits/The Best of Lawrence Welk | 1967 | 12.00 |
| ❑ DLP 25164 [S] | Mr. Music Maker | 1959 | 15.00 |
| ❑ DLP 25200 [S] | Voices and Strings | 1959 | 15.00 |
| ❑ DLP 25218 [S] | The Lawrence Welk Glee Club | 1959 | 15.00 |
| ❑ DLP 25224 [S] | Dance with Lawrence Welk | 1959 | 15.00 |
| ❑ DLP 25238 [S] | Lawrence Welk Presents Great American Composers | 1960 | 12.00 |
| ❑ DLP 25247 [S] | Lawrence Welk Presents Great Overtures in Dance Time | 1960 | 12.00 |
| ❑ DLP 25248 [S] | I'm Forever Blowing Bubbles | 1960 | 12.00 |
| ❑ DLP 25251 [S] | Songs of the Islands | 1960 | 12.00 |
| ❑ DLP 25274 [S] | Strictly for Dancing | 1960 | 12.00 |
| ❑ DLP 25284 [S] | To Mother | 1960 | 12.00 |
| ❑ DLP 25296 [S] | Sweet and Lovely | 1960 | 12.00 |
| ❑ DLP 25302 [S] | Polkas | 1960 | 12.00 |
| ❑ DLP 25317 [S] | Lawrence in Dixieland | 1960 | 12.00 |
| ❑ DLP 25318 [S] | Double Shuffle | 1960 | 12.00 |
| ❑ DLP 25342 [S] | The Champagne Music of Lawrence Welk | 1960 | 12.00 |
| ❑ DLP 25350 [S] | Last Date | 1960 | 12.00 |
| ❑ DLP 25359 [S] | Calcutta! | 1961 | 12.00 |
| ❑ DLP 25389 [S] | Yellow Bird | 1961 | 12.00 |
| ❑ DLP 25395 [S] | Diamond Jubilee | 1961 | 12.00 |
| ❑ DLP 25397 [S] | Silent Night and 13 Other Best-Loved Christmas Songs | 1961 | 15.00 |
| ❑ DLP 25412 [S] | Moon River | 1961 | 12.00 |
| ❑ DLP 25428 [S] | Young World | 1962 | 12.00 |
| ❑ DLP 25432 [S] | Sing-a-Long Party | 1962 | 12.00 |
| ❑ DLP 25457 [S] | Baby Elephant Walk and Theme from The Brothers Grimm | 1962 | 12.00 |
| ❑ DLP 25489 [S] | Bubbles in the Wine | 1962 | 12.00 |
| ❑ DLP 25499 [S] | Waltz Time | 1963 | 12.00 |
| ❑ DLP 25510 [S] | 1963's Early Hits | 1963 | 12.00 |
| ❑ DLP 25528 [S] | Scarlett O'Hara | 1963 | 12.00 |
| ❑ DLP 25544 [S] | A Tribute to the All-Time Greats | 1963 | 12.00 |
| ❑ DLP 25552 [S] | Wonderful! Wonderful! | 1963 | 12.00 |
| ❑ DLP 25572 [S] | Early Hits of 1964 | 1964 | 12.00 |
| ❑ DLP 25591 [S] | The Lawrence Welk Television Show 10th Anniversary | 1964 | 12.00 |
| ❑ DLP 25611 [S] | The Golden Millions | 1964 | 12.00 |
| ❑ DLP 25616 [S] | My First of 1965 | 1965 | 12.00 |
| ❑ DLP 25629 [S] | Apples and Bananas | 1965 | 12.00 |
| ❑ DLP 25653 [S] | The Happy Wanderer | 1966 | 12.00 |
| ❑ DLP 25663 [S] | Today's Great Hits | 1966 | 12.00 |
| ❑ DLP 25688 [S] | Champagne on Broadway | 1966 | 12.00 |
| ❑ DLP 25774 [S] | Winchester Cathedral | 1966 | 12.00 |
| ❑ DLP 25779 [S] | Hymns We Love | 1967 | 12.00 |
| ❑ DLP 25790 [S] | Lawrence Welk's "Hits of Our Time" | 1967 | 12.00 |
| ❑ DLP 25812 [S] | Golden Hits/The Best of Lawrence Welk | 1967 | 10.00 |

### HAMILTON

| Number | Title (A Side/B Side) | Yr | NM |
|---|---|---|---|
| ❑ HLP 152 [M] | Mary Poppins | 1965 | 10.00 |
| ❑ HLP 12152 [S] | Mary Poppins | 1965 | 12.00 |

### HARMONY

| Number | Title (A Side/B Side) | Yr | NM |
|---|---|---|---|
| ❑ HL 7394 [M] | Vintage Champagne | 1966 | 12.00 |
| ❑ HS 11194 [S] | Vintage Champagne | 1966 | 12.00 |
| ❑ HS 11301 | Champagne Dance Party | 1969 | 10.00 |

### HEARTLAND

| Number | Title (A Side/B Side) | Yr | NM |
|---|---|---|---|
| ❑ 1006 | Musical Family Reunion | 198? | 10.00 |

### MCA

| Number | Title (A Side/B Side) | Yr | NM |
|---|---|---|---|
| ❑ 733 | Polka and Waltz Time | 197? | 8.00 |
| *—Reissue of Vocalion 73670* | | | |
| ❑ 4026 [(2)] | The Best of Lawrence Welk, Volume 2 | 197? | 12.00 |
| ❑ 4044 [(2)] | The Best of Lawrence Welk | 197? | 12.00 |
| ❑ 4104 [(2)] | The Best Polkas | 197? | 12.00 |

### MCA CORAL

| Number | Title (A Side/B Side) | Yr | NM |
|---|---|---|---|
| ❑ 20100 | Champagne Music | 197? | 8.00 |

### MERCURY

| Number | Title (A Side/B Side) | Yr | NM |
|---|---|---|---|
| ❑ MG-20092 [M] | Dance Party | 1956 | 15.00 |

### MISTLETOE

| Number | Title (A Side/B Side) | Yr | NM |
|---|---|---|---|
| ❑ MLP-1215 | Christmas with Lawrence Welk | 197? | 10.00 |

### PICKWICK

| Number | Title (A Side/B Side) | Yr | NM |
|---|---|---|---|
| ❑ SPC-1019 | The Christmas Song | 197? | 10.00 |
| *—Reissue of Coral LP "Jingle Bells" with shuffled running order* | | | |
| ❑ SPC-3070 | Save the Last Dance for Me | 196? | 10.00 |
| ❑ SPC-3092 | I'll See You Again | 196? | 10.00 |
| ❑ SPC-3116 | You'll Never Walk Alone | 196? | 10.00 |
| ❑ SPC-3143 | If You Were the Only One | 196? | 10.00 |
| ❑ SPC-3157 | As Time Goes By | 196? | 10.00 |
| ❑ SPC-3196 | Love Is a Many-Splendored Thing | 197? | 10.00 |
| ❑ SPC-3212 | Blue Hawaii | 197? | 10.00 |
| ❑ SPC-3252 | Polkas! | 197? | 10.00 |

### PREMIER

| Number | Title (A Side/B Side) | Yr | NM |
|---|---|---|---|
| ❑ 9043 | Lawrence Welk | 196? | 10.00 |

### RANWOOD

| Number | Title (A Side/B Side) | Yr | NM |
|---|---|---|---|
| ❑ 2000 | Merry Christmas | 197? | 10.00 |
| ❑ 2004 | Polkas | 197? | 8.00 |
| *—With Myron Floren* | | | |
| ❑ 2005 | Moon River | 197? | 6.00 |
| *—Reissue of Ranwood 8016* | | | |
| ❑ 2006 | Yellow Bird | 197? | 6.00 |
| *—Reissue of Ranwood 8021* | | | |
| ❑ 2007 | Songs of the Islands | 197? | 6.00 |
| *—Reissue of Ranwood 8022* | | | |
| ❑ 2008 | Waltz Time | 197? | 6.00 |
| *—Reissue of Ranwood 8025* | | | |
| ❑ 2009 | Hymns We Love | 197? | 6.00 |
| *—Reissue of Ranwood 8042* | | | |
| ❑ 2010 | Memories | 197? | 6.00 |
| *—Reissue of Ranwood 8044* | | | |
| ❑ 4100 | On Tour, Volume 1 | 198? | 8.00 |
| ❑ 4101 | On Tour, Volume 2 | 198? | 8.00 |
| ❑ 5001 [(2)] | Reminiscing | 1972 | 12.00 |
| ❑ 5005 [(2)] | 24 of the World's Greatest Polkas | 197? | 12.00 |
| *—With Myron Floren* | | | |
| ❑ 6001 [(2)] | Lawrence Welk and His Musical Family in Concert | 1973 | 12.00 |
| ❑ 6002 | Lawrence Welk and His Musical Family Celebrate 50 Years in Music | 1974 | 10.00 |
| ❑ 7002 [(2)] | 200 Years of American Music | 1976 | 12.00 |
| ❑ 7004 [(2)] | 22 Great Waltzes | 1977 | 12.00 |
| ❑ 7009 [(2)] | 22 Great Songs for Dancing | 1978 | 12.00 |
| ❑ 7016 [(2)] | 22 Great Songs for Easy Listening | 198? | 12.00 |
| ❑ 7023 [(2)] | 22 All-Time Big Band Favorites | 1983 | 12.00 |
| ❑ 7028 [(2)] | 22 All-Time Favorite Waltzes | 198? | 12.00 |
| ❑ 7029 [(2)] | 22 Merry Christmas Favorites | 198? | 12.00 |
| ❑ 8003 | Love Is Blue | 1968 | 10.00 |
| ❑ 8016 | Moon River | 1968 | 8.00 |
| *—Reissue of Dot 25412* | | | |
| ❑ 8017 | Winchester Cathedral | 1968 | 8.00 |
| *—Reissue of Dot 25774* | | | |
| ❑ 8020 | Silent Night and 13 Other Best-Loved Christmas Songs | 1968 | 8.00 |
| *—Reissue of Dot 25397* | | | |
| ❑ 8021 | Yellow Bird | 1968 | 8.00 |
| *—Reissue of Dot 25389* | | | |
| ❑ 8022 | Songs of the Islands | 1968 | 8.00 |
| *—Reissue of Dot 25251* | | | |
| ❑ 8023 | The Champagne Music of Lawrence Welk | 1968 | 8.00 |
| *—Reissue of Dot 25342* | | | |
| ❑ 8024 | Calcutta! | 1968 | 8.00 |
| *—Reissue of Dot 25359* | | | |
| ❑ 8025 | Waltz Time | 1968 | 8.00 |
| *—Reissue of Dot 25499* | | | |
| ❑ 8026 | The Lawrence Welk Television Show | 1968 | 8.00 |
| *—Reissue of Dot 25591* | | | |
| ❑ 8027 | Country Music's Great Hits | 1968 | 10.00 |

| Number | Title (A Side/B Side) | Yr | NM |
|---|---|---|---|
| ❑ 8028 | Golden Hits/The Best of Lawrence Welk | 1968 | 8.00 |
| *—Reissue of Dot 25812* | | | |
| ❑ 8030 | To America with Love | 1968 | 10.00 |
| ❑ 8034 | The Lawrence Welk Singers and Orchestra | 1968 | 10.00 |
| ❑ 8042 | Hymns We Love | 1968 | 8.00 |
| *—Reissue of Dot 25779* | | | |
| ❑ 8044 | Memories | 1969 | 10.00 |
| ❑ 8049 | Galveston | 1969 | 10.00 |
| ❑ 8053 | Lawrence Welk Plays I Love You Truly and Other Songs of Love | 1969 | 10.00 |
| ❑ 8060 | Jean | 1969 | 10.00 |
| ❑ 8068 | The Golden 60's | 1970 | 10.00 |
| ❑ 8077 | The Big Band Sound | 1970 | 10.00 |
| ❑ 8079 | Champagne Strings | 1970 | 10.00 |
| ❑ 8083 | Candida | 1970 | 10.00 |
| ❑ 8087 | No, No, Nanette | 1971 | 10.00 |
| ❑ 8091 | Go Away Little Girl | 1971 | 10.00 |
| ❑ 8109 | (More of) The Big Band Sound | 1972 | 10.00 |
| ❑ 8114 | The Good Life | 1973 | 10.00 |
| ❑ 8130 | Lawrence Welk Plays From That's Entertainment | 1974 | 10.00 |
| ❑ 8140 | Most Requested TV Favorites | 1974 | 10.00 |
| ❑ 8145 | 25 Years on Television | 1975 | 10.00 |
| ❑ 8162 | The Best of Lawrence Welk: 20 Great Hits | 1976 | 10.00 |
| ❑ 8165 | Nadia's Theme | 1976 | 10.00 |
| ❑ 8183 | My Personal Favorites | 1978 | 10.00 |
| ❑ 8184 | Hallelujah! | 1978 | 10.00 |
| ❑ 8191 | Remembering the Sweet and Swing Band Era, Vol. 1 | 1979 | 10.00 |
| ❑ 8192 | Remembering the Sweet and Swing Band Era, Vol. 2 | 1979 | 10.00 |
| ❑ 8194 | Lawrence Welk Plays Dixieland | 1980 | 10.00 |
| ❑ 8195 [(2)] | Reminiscing, Vol. 2 | 1980 | 12.00 |
| ❑ 8201 | Lawrence Welk Presents Anacani | 1982 | 10.00 |
| ❑ 8210 | Musical Memories with Lawrence Welk | 1984 | 8.00 |
| ❑ 8211 | Come Waltz with Me | 1984 | 8.00 |
| ❑ 10001 [(2)] | Live at Lake Tahoe | 1978 | 12.00 |
| ❑ 10002 [(2)] | The Sweet and Swing Band Era | 1979 | 12.00 |

### READER'S DIGEST

| Number | Title (A Side/B Side) | Yr | NM |
|---|---|---|---|
| ❑ RDA-07-A [(4)] | Merry Christmas from Lawrence Welk and His Champagne Music Makers | 1970 | 25.00 |
| ❑ RDA 95 [(6)] | Champagne Music Varieties | 196? | 25.00 |
| ❑ RDA 156 | Champagne Dance Time with Lawrence Welk | 196? | 10.00 |

### SUNNYVALE

| Number | Title (A Side/B Side) | Yr | NM |
|---|---|---|---|
| ❑ SVL-1015 | Silent Night and 13 Other Best-Loved Christmas Songs | 1978 | 8.00 |
| *—Same contents as Dot 25397* | | | |

### THOMAS

| Number | Title (A Side/B Side) | Yr | NM |
|---|---|---|---|
| ❑ 20052 | The Magic of Color-Glo | 196? | 12.00 |

### VOCALION

| Number | Title (A Side/B Side) | Yr | NM |
|---|---|---|---|
| ❑ VL 3670 [M] | Polka and Waltz Time | 196? | 10.00 |
| ❑ VL 3671 [M] | Lawrence Welk and His Champagne Music | 196? | 10.00 |
| ❑ VL 3783 [M] | Lawrence Welk and His Champagne Music Makers Play for You | 1967 | 12.00 |
| ❑ VL 73670 [R] | Polka and Waltz Time | 196? | 10.00 |
| ❑ VL 73671 [R] | Lawrence Welk and His Champagne Music | 196? | 10.00 |
| ❑ VL 73783 [R] | Lawrence Welk and His Champagne Music Makers Play for You | 1967 | 10.00 |
| ❑ VL 73865 | Champagne Polkas | 1969 | 10.00 |
| ❑ VL 73888 | Til the End of Time | 1969 | 10.00 |
| ❑ VL 73921 | Wonderful Music | 1970 | 10.00 |

### WING

| Number | Title (A Side/B Side) | Yr | NM |
|---|---|---|---|
| ❑ PKW-2-114 [(2)] | With a-One and a-Two | 1969 | 15.00 |
| ❑ MGW-12119 [M] | Dance Party | 196? | 12.00 |
| ❑ MGW-12210 [M] | Music for Polka Lovers | 196? | 12.00 |
| ❑ MGW-12214 [M] | Aragon Trianon Memories | 196? | 12.00 |
| ❑ SRW-16210 [S] | Music for Polka Lovers | 196? | 10.00 |
| ❑ SRW-16214 [R] | Aragon Trianon Memories | 196? | 10.00 |
| ❑ SRW-16379 | The Best of Welk | 196? | 10.00 |

## WELLS, DICKY

### FELSTED

| Number | Title (A Side/B Side) | Yr | NM |
|---|---|---|---|
| ❑ SJA-2006 [S] | Bones for the King | 1958 | 40.00 |
| ❑ SJA-2009 [S] | Trombone Four in Hand | 1958 | 40.00 |
| ❑ FAJ-7006 [M] | Bones for the King | 1958 | 40.00 |
| ❑ FAJ-7009 [M] | Trombone Four in Hand | 1958 | 40.00 |

### PRESTIGE

| Number | Title (A Side/B Side) | Yr | NM |
|---|---|---|---|
| ❑ PRST-7593 [R] | Dicky Wells in Pais 1937 | 1968 | 25.00 |

## WELLS, JUNIOR

### BLUE ROCK

| Number | Title (A Side/B Side) | Yr | NM |
|---|---|---|---|
| ❑ 64002 | You're Tuff Enough | 1968 | 30.00 |
| ❑ 64003 | Live at the Golden Bear | 1969 | 30.00 |

### DELMARK

| Number | Title (A Side/B Side) | Yr | NM |
|---|---|---|---|
| ❑ DL-612 [M] | Hoodoo Man Blues | 1966 | 40.00 |
| ❑ DS-612 [S] | Hoodoo Man Blues | 1966 | 50.00 |
| ❑ DS-628 | Southside Blues Jam | 1967 | 25.00 |
| ❑ DS-640 | Blues Hit the Big Town | 1969 | 25.00 |
| ❑ DS-640 | Blue Hit Big Towns | 1969 | 30.00 |

### VANGUARD

| Number | Title (A Side/B Side) | Yr | NM |
|---|---|---|---|
| ❑ VRS-9231 [M] | It's My Life Baby | 1966 | 30.00 |
| ❑ VSD-79231 [S] | It's My Life Baby | 1966 | 40.00 |
| ❑ VSD-79262 | Comin' At You | 1968 | 25.00 |

## WELLS, KITTY

### DECCA

| Number | Title (A Side/B Side) | Yr | NM |
|---|---|---|---|
| ❑ DXB 174 [(2)M] | The Kitty Wells Story | 1963 | 30.00 |
| ❑ DL 4075 [M] | Seasons of My Heart | 1961 | 30.00 |
| ❑ DL 4108 [M] | Kitty Wells' Golden Favorites | 1961 | 30.00 |
| ❑ DL 4141 [M] | Heartbreak U.S.A. | 1961 | 30.00 |
| ❑ DL 4197 [M] | Queen of Country Music | 1962 | 30.00 |
| ❑ DL 4270 [M] | Singing on Sunday | 1962 | 30.00 |
| ❑ DL 4349 [M] | Christmas Day with Kitty Wells | 1962 | 25.00 |
| ❑ DL 4493 [M] | Especially for You | 1964 | 25.00 |
| ❑ DL 4554 [M] | Country Music Time | 1964 | 25.00 |
| ❑ DL 4612 [M] | Burning Memories | 1965 | 25.00 |
| ❑ DL 4658 [M] | Lonesome Sad and Blue | 1965 | 25.00 |
| ❑ DL 4679 [M] | Family Gospel Sing | 1965 | 25.00 |
| ❑ DL 4741 [M] | Kitty Wells Sings Songs Made Famous by Jim Reeves | 1966 | 25.00 |
| ❑ DL 4776 [M] | Country All the Way | 1966 | 25.00 |
| ❑ DL 4831 [M] | The Kitty Wells Show | 1966 | 25.00 |
| ❑ DL 4857 [M] | Love Makes the World Go Around | 1967 | 30.00 |
| ❑ DL 4929 [M] | Queen of Honky Tonk Street | 1967 | 40.00 |
| ❑ DL 5001 [M] | Kitty Wells' Greatest Hits | 1968 | 50.00 |
| *—White label promo only* | | | |
| ❑ DXSB 7174 [(2)P] | The Kitty Wells Story | 1963 | 40.00 |
| ❑ DL 8293 [M] | Kitty Wells' Country Hit Parade | 1956 | 60.00 |
| *—Black label, silver print* | | | |
| ❑ DL 8293 [M] | Kitty Wells' Country Hit Parade | 1961 | 30.00 |
| *—Black label with color bars* | | | |
| ❑ DL 8552 [M] | Winner of Your Heart | 1957 | 60.00 |
| *—Black label, silver print* | | | |
| ❑ DL 8552 [M] | Winner of Your Heart | 1961 | 30.00 |
| *—Black label with color bars* | | | |
| ❑ DL 8732 [M] | Lonely Street | 1958 | 60.00 |
| *—Black label, silver print* | | | |
| ❑ DL 8732 [M] | Lonely Street | 1961 | 30.00 |
| *—Black label with color bars* | | | |
| ❑ DL 8858 [M] | Dust on the Bible | 1959 | 60.00 |
| *—Black label, silver print* | | | |
| ❑ DL 8858 [M] | Dust on the Bible | 1961 | 30.00 |
| *—Black label with color bars* | | | |
| ❑ DL 8888 [M] | After Dark | 1959 | 60.00 |
| *—Black label, silver print* | | | |
| ❑ DL 8888 [M] | After Dark | 1961 | 30.00 |
| *—Black label with color bars* | | | |
| ❑ DL 8979 [M] | Kitty's Choice | 1960 | 50.00 |
| *—Black label, silver print* | | | |
| ❑ DL 8979 [M] | Kitty's Choice | 1961 | 25.00 |
| *—Black label with color bars* | | | |
| ❑ DL 74075 [S] | Seasons of My Heart | 1961 | 40.00 |
| ❑ DL 74108 [R] | Kitty Wells' Golden Favorites | 196? | 20.00 |
| ❑ DL 74141 [S] | Heartbreak U.S.A. | 1961 | 40.00 |
| ❑ DL 74197 [S] | Queen of Country Music | 1962 | 40.00 |
| ❑ DL 74270 [S] | Singing on Sunday | 1962 | 40.00 |
| ❑ DL 74349 [S] | Christmas Day with Kitty Wells | 1962 | 30.00 |
| ❑ DL 74493 [S] | Especially for You | 1964 | 30.00 |
| ❑ DL 74554 [S] | Country Music Time | 1964 | 30.00 |
| ❑ DL 74612 [S] | Burning Memories | 1965 | 30.00 |
| ❑ DL 74658 [S] | Lonesome Sad and Blue | 1965 | 30.00 |
| ❑ DL 74679 [S] | Family Gospel Sing | 1965 | 30.00 |
| ❑ DL 74741 [S] | Kitty Wells Sings Songs Made Famous by Jim Reeves | 1966 | 30.00 |
| ❑ DL 74776 [S] | Country All the Way | 1966 | 30.00 |
| ❑ DL 74831 [S] | The Kitty Wells Show | 1966 | 30.00 |
| ❑ DL 74857 [S] | Love Makes the World Go Around | 1967 | 30.00 |
| ❑ DL 74929 [S] | Queen of Honky Tonk Street | 1967 | 25.00 |
| ❑ DL 74961 | Kitty Wells Showcase | 1968 | 25.00 |
| ❑ DL 75001 [S] | Kitty Wells' Greatest Hits | 1968 | 25.00 |
| ❑ DL 75067 | Cream of Country Hits | 1968 | 25.00 |
| ❑ DL 75098 | Guilty Street | 1969 | 25.00 |
| ❑ DL 75164 | Bouquet of Country Hits | 1969 | 20.00 |
| ❑ DL 75221 | Singin' 'Em Country | 1970 | 20.00 |
| ❑ DL 75245 | Your Love Is the Way | 1970 | 20.00 |
| ❑ DL 75277 | They're Stepping All Over My Heart | 1971 | 20.00 |
| ❑ DL 75313 | Pledging My Love | 1971 | 20.00 |
| ❑ DL 75325 | Heartwarming Gospel Songs | 1972 | 20.00 |
| ❑ DL 75350 | Sincerely | 1972 | 20.00 |
| ❑ DL 75382 | I've Got Yesterday | 1972 | 20.00 |
| ❑ DL 78293 [R] | Kitty Wells' Country Hit Parade | 196? | 20.00 |
| ❑ DL 78552 [R] | Winner of Your Heart | 196? | 20.00 |
| ❑ DL 78732 [R] | Lonely Street | 196? | 20.00 |
| ❑ DL 78858 [R] | Dust on the Bible | 196? | 20.00 |
| ❑ DL 78979 [S] | Kitty's Choice | 1960 | 60.00 |
| *—Maroon label, silver print* | | | |
| ❑ DL 78979 [S] | Kitty's Choice | 1961 | 30.00 |
| *—Black label with color bars* | | | |
| ❑ SW-94491 | Sincerely | 1972 | 25.00 |
| *—Capitol Record Club edition* | | | |

## WELLS, KITTY, AND RED FOLEY

Also see each artist's individual listings.

### DECCA

| Number | Title (A Side/B Side) | Yr | NM |
|---|---|---|---|
| ❑ DL 4109 [M] | Golden Favorites | 1961 | 30.00 |
| ❑ DL 4906 [M] | Together Again | 1967 | 30.00 |
| ❑ DL 74109 [S] | Golden Favorites | 1961 | 40.00 |
| ❑ DL 74906 [S] | Together Again | 1967 | 25.00 |

## WELLS, KITTY, AND JOHNNY WRIGHT

### DECCA

| Number | Title (A Side/B Side) | Yr | NM |
|---|---|---|---|
| ❑ DL 5028 [M] | We'll Stick Together | 1968 | 50.00 |
| *—Mono appears to be white label promo only* | | | |
| ❑ DL 75028 [S] | We'll Stick Together | 1968 | 25.00 |

## WELLS, MARY

### ALLEGIANCE

| Number | Title (A Side/B Side) | Yr | NM |
|---|---|---|---|
| ❑ AV-444 | The Old, the New, and the Best of Mary Wells | 1984 | 10.00 |

### ATCO

| Number | Title (A Side/B Side) | Yr | NM |
|---|---|---|---|
| ❑ 33-199 [M] | Two Sides of Mary Wells | 1966 | 25.00 |
| ❑ SD 33-199 [S] | Two Sides of Mary Wells | 1966 | 30.00 |

### EPIC

| Number | Title (A Side/B Side) | Yr | NM |
|---|---|---|---|
| ❑ ARE 37540 | In and Out of Love | 1981 | 15.00 |

### JUBILEE

| Number | Title (A Side/B Side) | Yr | NM |
|---|---|---|---|
| ❑ JGS-8018 | Servin' Up Some Soul | 1968 | 25.00 |

### MOTOWN

| Number | Title (A Side/B Side) | Yr | NM |
|---|---|---|---|
| ❑ M5-161V1 | Bye Bye Baby/I Don't Want to Take a Chance | 1981 | 10.00 |
| ❑ M5-167V1 | Mary Wells Sings My Guy | 1981 | 10.00 |
| ❑ M5-221V1 | Two Lovers | 1981 | 10.00 |
| ❑ MLP-600 [M] | Bye Bye Baby/I Don't Want to Take a Chance | 1961 | 300.00 |
| *—White label stock copy* | | | |
| ❑ MLP-600 [M] | Bye Bye Baby/I Don't Want to Take a Chance | 1962 | 250.00 |
| *—With map; label address above the center hole* | | | |
| ❑ M 605 [M] | The One Who Really Loves You | 1962 | 160.00 |
| *—With map; label address above the center hole* | | | |
| ❑ M 605 [M] | The One Who Really Loves You | 1964 | 40.00 |
| *—With map; label address around lower part of label* | | | |
| ❑ M 607 [M] | Two Lovers and Other Great Hits | 1963 | 120.00 |
| *—With map; label address above the center hole* | | | |
| ❑ M 607 [M] | Two Lovers and Other Great Hits | 1964 | 40.00 |
| *—With map; label address around lower part of label* | | | |
| ❑ M 611 [M] | Recorded Live on Stage | 1963 | 120.00 |
| *—With map; label address above the center hole* | | | |
| ❑ M 611 [M] | Recorded Live on Stage | 1964 | 40.00 |
| *—With map; label address around lower part of label* | | | |
| ❑ M 612 | Second Time Around | 1963 | — |
| *—Canceled* | | | |
| ❑ M 616 [M] | Greatest Hits | 1964 | 40.00 |
| ❑ MS 616 [S] | Greatest Hits | 1964 | 40.00 |
| ❑ M 617 [M] | Mary Wells Sings My Guy | 1964 | 50.00 |
| ❑ M 653 [M] | Vintage Stock | 1967 | 50.00 |
| ❑ MS 653 [S] | Vintage Stock | 1967 | 50.00 |
| ❑ 5233 ML | Greatest Hits | 1982 | 10.00 |

### MOVIETONE

| Number | Title (A Side/B Side) | Yr | NM |
|---|---|---|---|
| ❑ 71010 [M] | Ooh | 1966 | 25.00 |
| ❑ 72010 [S] | Ooh | 1966 | 30.00 |

### 20TH FOX

| Number | Title (A Side/B Side) | Yr | NM |
|---|---|---|---|
| ❑ TFM 3171 [M] | Mary Wells | 1965 | 40.00 |
| ❑ TFM 3178 [M] | Love Songs to the Beatles | 1965 | 80.00 |
| ❑ TFS 4171 [S] | Mary Wells | 1965 | 60.00 |
| ❑ TFS 4178 [S] | Love Songs to the Beatles | 1965 | 100.00 |
| ❑ ST-90790 [S] | Love Songs to the Beatles | 1965 | 150.00 |
| *—Capitol Record Club edition* | | | |

## WELLSTOOD, DICK

### RIVERSIDE

| Number | Title (A Side/B Side) | Yr | NM |
|---|---|---|---|
| ❑ RLP-2506 [10] | Dick Wellstood | 1955 | 100.00 |

## WELLSTOOD, DICK, AND CLIFF JACKSON

### SWINGVILLE

| Number | Title (A Side/B Side) | Yr | NM |
|---|---|---|---|
| ❑ SVLP-2026 [M] | Uptown and Downtown | 1961 | 50.00 |
| *—Purple label* | | | |
| ❑ SVLP-2026 [M] | Uptown and Downtown | 1965 | 25.00 |
| *—Blue label, trident logo at right* | | | |

## WESLEY, FRED

### ATLANTIC

| Number | Title (A Side/B Side) | Yr | NM |
|---|---|---|---|
| ❑ SD 18214 | A Blow for Me, A Toot to You | 1977 | 12.00 |
| ❑ SD 19254 | Say Blow by Blow Backwards | 1979 | 12.00 |

### PEOPLE

| Number | Title (A Side/B Side) | Yr | NM |
|---|---|---|---|
| ❑ PE-5601 | Food for Thought | 1972 | 80.00 |
| ❑ PE-5603 | Doing It to Death | 1973 | 80.00 |
| ❑ PE-6602 | Damn Right I Am Somebody | 1974 | 20.00 |
| ❑ PE-6604 | Breakin' Bread | 1974 | 20.00 |

## WESS, FRANK

### COMMODORE

| Number | Title (A Side/B Side) | Yr | NM |
|---|---|---|---|
| ❑ FL-20031 [10] | Frank Wess Quintet | 1952 | 120.00 |

| Number | Title (A Side/B Side) | Yr | NM |
|---|---|---|---|
| ❑ FL-20032 [10] | Frank Wess | 1952 | 120.00 |

**MAINSTREAM**

| Number | Title (A Side/B Side) | Yr | NM |
|---|---|---|---|
| ❑ 56033 [M] | Award Winner | 1965 | 25.00 |

**MOODSVILLE**

| Number | Title (A Side/B Side) | Yr | NM |
|---|---|---|---|
| ❑ MVLP-8 [M] | Frank Wess Quartet | 1960 | 50.00 |

*—Green label*

| Number | Title (A Side/B Side) | Yr | NM |
|---|---|---|---|
| ❑ MVLP-8 [M] | Frank Wess Quartet | 1965 | 25.00 |

*—Blue label, trident logo at right*

**PRESTIGE**

| Number | Title (A Side/B Side) | Yr | NM |
|---|---|---|---|
| ❑ PRLP-7231 [M] | Southern Comfort | 1962 | 40.00 |
| ❑ PRST-7231 [S] | Southern Comfort | 1962 | 50.00 |
| ❑ PRLP-7266 [M] | Yo Ho! Poor You, Little Me | 1963 | 40.00 |
| ❑ PRST-7266 [S] | Yo Ho! Poor You, Little Me | 1963 | 50.00 |

**SAVOY**

| Number | Title (A Side/B Side) | Yr | NM |
|---|---|---|---|
| ❑ MG-12022 [M] | Flutes and Reeds | 1955 | 80.00 |
| ❑ MG-12072 [M] | North, South, East, Wess | 1956 | 80.00 |
| ❑ MG-12095 [M] | Jazz for Playboys | 1956 | 80.00 |

**STATUS**

| Number | Title (A Side/B Side) | Yr | NM |
|---|---|---|---|
| ❑ ST-7266 [S] | Yo Ho! Poor You, Little Me | 1965 | 20.00 |

### WESS, FRANK, AND KENNY BURRELL

**PRESTIGE**

| Number | Title (A Side/B Side) | Yr | NM |
|---|---|---|---|
| ❑ PRLP-7278 [M] | Steamin' | 1963 | 40.00 |
| ❑ PRST-7278 [R] | Steamin' | 1963 | 25.00 |

### WESS, FRANK, AND THAD JONES

**STATUS**

| Number | Title (A Side/B Side) | Yr | NM |
|---|---|---|---|
| ❑ ST-8310 [M] | Touche | 1965 | 40.00 |

### WEST

**EPIC**

| Number | Title (A Side/B Side) | Yr | NM |
|---|---|---|---|
| ❑ BN 26380 | West | 1968 | 20.00 |
| ❑ BN 26433 | Bridges | 1969 | 20.00 |

### WEST, ALVY

**COLUMBIA**

| Number | Title (A Side/B Side) | Yr | NM |
|---|---|---|---|
| ❑ CL 6062 [10] | Alvy West and His Little Band | 1949 | 60.00 |

### WEST, DOTTIE

**LIBERTY**

| Number | Title (A Side/B Side) | Yr | NM |
|---|---|---|---|
| ❑ LT-740 | When It's Just You and Me | 1981 | 8.00 |

*—Reissue of United Artists 740*

| Number | Title (A Side/B Side) | Yr | NM |
|---|---|---|---|
| ❑ LT-860 | Dottie | 1981 | 8.00 |

*—Reissue of United Artists 860*

| Number | Title (A Side/B Side) | Yr | NM |
|---|---|---|---|
| ❑ LT-1000 | Special Delivery | 1981 | 8.00 |

*—Reissue of United Artists 1000*

| Number | Title (A Side/B Side) | Yr | NM |
|---|---|---|---|
| ❑ LT-1062 | Wild West | 1981 | 10.00 |
| ❑ LT-51114 | High Times | 1982 | 10.00 |
| ❑ LT-51129 | Full Circle | 1982 | 10.00 |
| ❑ LT-51145 | New Horizons | 1983 | 10.00 |
| ❑ LT-51155 | Greatest Hits | 1984 | 10.00 |

**POWER PAK**

| Number | Title (A Side/B Side) | Yr | NM |
|---|---|---|---|
| ❑ 274 | Country Girl Singing Sensation | 197? | 10.00 |

**RCA CAMDEN**

| Number | Title (A Side/B Side) | Yr | NM |
|---|---|---|---|
| ❑ ACL1-0125 | Would You Hold It Against Me | 1973 | 10.00 |
| ❑ ACL1-0482 | Loving You | 1974 | 10.00 |
| ❑ CAL-2155 [M] | The Sound of Country Music | 1967 | 15.00 |
| ❑ CAS-2155 [S] | The Sound of Country Music | 1967 | 12.00 |
| ❑ CAS-2454 | A Legend in My Time | 1971 | 12.00 |

**RCA VICTOR**

| Number | Title (A Side/B Side) | Yr | NM |
|---|---|---|---|
| ❑ APD1-0151 [Q] | If It's All Right with You/Just What I've Been Looking For | 1973 | 20.00 |
| ❑ APL1-0151 | If It's All Right with You/Just What I've Been Looking For | 1973 | 12.00 |
| ❑ APL1-0344 | Country Sunshine | 1973 | 12.00 |
| ❑ APL1-0543 | House of Love | 1974 | 12.00 |
| ❑ APL1-1041 | Carolina Cousins | 1975 | 12.00 |
| ❑ ANL1-2327 | Country Sunshine | 1977 | 10.00 |

*—Reissue of APL1-0344*

| Number | Title (A Side/B Side) | Yr | NM |
|---|---|---|---|
| ❑ LPM-3368 [M] | Here Comes My Baby | 1965 | 25.00 |
| ❑ LSP-3368 [S] | Here Comes My Baby | 1965 | 30.00 |
| ❑ LPM-3490 [M] | Dottie West Sings | 1966 | 25.00 |
| ❑ LSP-3490 [S] | Dottie West Sings | 1966 | 30.00 |
| ❑ LPM-3587 [M] | Suffer Time | 1966 | 25.00 |
| ❑ LSP-3587 [S] | Suffer Time | 1966 | 30.00 |
| ❑ LPM-3693 [M] | With All My Heart and Soul | 1967 | 30.00 |
| ❑ LSP-3693 [S] | With All My Heart and Soul | 1967 | 25.00 |
| ❑ LPM-3784 [M] | Dottie West Sings Sacred Ballads | 1967 | 30.00 |
| ❑ LSP-3784 [S] | Dottie West Sings Sacred Ballads | 1967 | 25.00 |
| ❑ LPM-3830 [M] | I'll Help You Forget Her | 1967 | 30.00 |
| ❑ LSP-3830 [S] | I'll Help You Forget Her | 1967 | 25.00 |
| ❑ LPM-3932 [M] | What I'm Cut Out to Be | 1968 | 50.00 |
| ❑ LSP-3932 [S] | What I'm Cut Out to Be | 1968 | 25.00 |
| ❑ LSP-4004 | Country Girl | 1968 | 25.00 |
| ❑ LSP-4095 | Feminine Fancy | 1969 | 20.00 |
| ❑ AHL1-4117 | Once You Were Mine | 1981 | 10.00 |
| ❑ LSP-4154 | Dottie Sings Eddy | 1969 | 20.00 |
| ❑ LSP-4276 | Makin' Memories | 1970 | 20.00 |
| ❑ AYL1-4302 | Once You Were Mine | 1982 | 8.00 |
| ❑ LSP-4332 | Country and West | 1970 | 20.00 |
| ❑ LSP-4433 | Forever Yours | 1970 | 20.00 |
| ❑ LSP-4482 | Careless Hands | 1971 | 15.00 |
| ❑ LSP-4606 | Have You Heard | 1971 | 15.00 |
| ❑ LSP-4704 | I'm Only a Woman | 1972 | 15.00 |
| ❑ LSP-4811 | The Best of Dottie West | 1973 | 15.00 |
| ❑ CPL1-7047 | Collector's Series | 1985 | 10.00 |

**STARDAY**

| Number | Title (A Side/B Side) | Yr | NM |
|---|---|---|---|
| ❑ SLP-302 [M] | Country Girl Singing Sensation | 1964 | 40.00 |

**UNITED ARTISTS**

| Number | Title (A Side/B Side) | Yr | NM |
|---|---|---|---|
| ❑ UA-LA740-G | When It's Just You and Me | 1977 | 10.00 |
| ❑ UA-LA860-G | Dottie | 1978 | 10.00 |
| ❑ LT-1000 | Special Delivery | 1980 | 10.00 |

### WEST, DOTTIE, AND DON GIBSON

**RCA VICTOR**

| Number | Title (A Side/B Side) | Yr | NM |
|---|---|---|---|
| ❑ LSP-4131 | Dottie and Don | 1969 | 20.00 |

### WEST, HEDY

**VANGUARD**

| Number | Title (A Side/B Side) | Yr | NM |
|---|---|---|---|
| ❑ VSD-2124 [S] | Hedy West Accompanying Herself on the 5-String Banjo | 1963 | 25.00 |
| ❑ VSD-2126 [S] | Hedy West, Volume 2 | 1963 | 25.00 |
| ❑ VRS-9124 [M] | Hedy West Accompanying Herself on the 5-String Banjo | 1963 | 20.00 |
| ❑ VRS-9126 [M] | Hedy West, Volume 2 | 1963 | 20.00 |

### WEST, LUCRETIA

**WESTMINSTER**

| Number | Title (A Side/B Side) | Yr | NM |
|---|---|---|---|
| ❑ WP-6063 [M] | Spirituals | 1957 | 40.00 |

### WEST, MAE

**DAGONET**

| Number | Title (A Side/B Side) | Yr | NM |
|---|---|---|---|
| ❑ DG-4 [M] | Wild Christmas | 1966 | 30.00 |
| ❑ DGS-4 [S] | Wild Christmas | 1966 | 40.00 |

**DECCA**

| Number | Title (A Side/B Side) | Yr | NM |
|---|---|---|---|
| ❑ DL 9016 [M] | The Fabulous Mae West | 1955 | 60.00 |

*—All-black label with silver print*

| Number | Title (A Side/B Side) | Yr | NM |
|---|---|---|---|
| ❑ DL 9016 [M] | The Fabulous Mae West | 1960 | 30.00 |

*—Black label with colorband*

| Number | Title (A Side/B Side) | Yr | NM |
|---|---|---|---|
| ❑ DL 79016 [R] | The Fabulous Mae West | 1960 | 15.00 |
| ❑ DL 79176 | The Original Voice Tracks from Her Greatest Movies | 1970 | 15.00 |

**MCA**

| Number | Title (A Side/B Side) | Yr | NM |
|---|---|---|---|
| ❑ 2053 | The Fabulous Mae West | 1974 | 12.00 |

*—Reissue of Decca LP*

**MEZZOTONE**

| Number | Title (A Side/B Side) | Yr | NM |
|---|---|---|---|
| ❑ 1 [10] | Mae West Songs, Vol. 1 | 1952 | 100.00 |
| ❑ 2 [10] | Mae West Songs, Vol. 2 | 1952 | 100.00 |

**MGM**

| Number | Title (A Side/B Side) | Yr | NM |
|---|---|---|---|
| ❑ SE-4869 | Great Balls of Fire | 1972 | 20.00 |

**ROUND**

| Number | Title (A Side/B Side) | Yr | NM |
|---|---|---|---|
| ❑ RS-100 | Under the Mistletoe with Mae West | 1977 | 20.00 |

**TOWER**

| Number | Title (A Side/B Side) | Yr | NM |
|---|---|---|---|
| ❑ ST 5028 [S] | Way Out West | 1966 | 40.00 |
| ❑ T 5028 [M] | Way Out West | 1966 | 30.00 |

### WEST, SPEEDY

**CAPITOL**

| Number | Title (A Side/B Side) | Yr | NM |
|---|---|---|---|
| ❑ T 956 [M] | West of Hawaii | 1958 | 80.00 |
| ❑ ST 1341 [S] | Steel Guitar | 1960 | 60.00 |
| ❑ T 1341 [M] | Steel Guitar | 1960 | 40.00 |
| ❑ ST 1835 [S] | Guitar Spectacular | 1962 | 40.00 |
| ❑ T 1835 [M] | Guitar Spectacular | 1962 | 30.00 |

### WEST, SPEEDY, AND JIMMY BRYANT

**CAPITOL**

| Number | Title (A Side/B Side) | Yr | NM |
|---|---|---|---|
| ❑ H 520 [10] | Two Guitars Country Style | 1954 | 200.00 |
| ❑ T 520 [M] | Two Guitars Country Style | 1954 | 120.00 |

### WEST, BRUCE & LAING

**WINDFALL**

| Number | Title (A Side/B Side) | Yr | NM |
|---|---|---|---|
| ❑ CQ 31929 [Q] | Why Dontcha | 1972 | 20.00 |
| ❑ KC 31929 | Why Dontcha | 1972 | 12.00 |
| ❑ CQ 32216 [Q] | Whatever Turns You On | 1973 | 20.00 |
| ❑ KC 32216 | Whatever Turns You On | 1973 | 12.00 |
| ❑ KC 32899 | Live 'N' Kickin' | 1974 | 12.00 |

### WEST COAST POP ART EXPERIMENTAL BAND, THE

**AMOS**

| Number | Title (A Side/B Side) | Yr | NM |
|---|---|---|---|
| ❑ AAS-7004 | Where's My Daddy | 1969 | 50.00 |

**FIFO**

| Number | Title (A Side/B Side) | Yr | NM |
|---|---|---|---|
| ❑ M 101 | West Coast Pop Art Experimental Band | 1966 | 500.00 |

*—With plain cardboard cover*

| Number | Title (A Side/B Side) | Yr | NM |
|---|---|---|---|
| ❑ M 101 | West Coast Pop Art Experimental Band | 1966 | 2000. |

*—With regular cover; VG value 1000; VG+ value 1500*

**RAZZBERRY SAWFLY**

| Number | Title (A Side/B Side) | Yr | NM |
|---|---|---|---|
| ❑ 800 | West Coast Pop Art Experimental Band | 1980 | 100.00 |

*—Reissue of Fifo LP*

**REPRISE**

| Number | Title (A Side/B Side) | Yr | NM |
|---|---|---|---|
| ❑ R 6247 [M] | The West Coast Pop Art Experimental Band, Part One | 1967 | 80.00 |
| ❑ RS 6247 [S] | The West Coast Pop Art Experimental Band, Part One | 1967 | 100.00 |
| ❑ R 6270 [M] | The West Coast Pop Art Experimental Band, Vol. 2 | 1967 | 80.00 |
| ❑ RS 6270 [S] | The West Coast Pop Art Experimental Band, Vol. 2 | 1967 | 100.00 |
| ❑ R 6298 [M] | Vol. 3: A Child's Guide to Good and Evil | 1968 | 200.00 |

*—May exist only as a white label promo*

| Number | Title (A Side/B Side) | Yr | NM |
|---|---|---|---|
| ❑ RS 6298 [S] | Vol. 3: A Child's Guide to Good and Evil | 1968 | 100.00 |

**SUNDAZED**

| Number | Title (A Side/B Side) | Yr | NM |
|---|---|---|---|
| ❑ LP 5036 [(2)] | West Coast Pop Art Experimental Band, Volume One | 1997 | 15.00 |

### WESTCHESTER WORKSHOP, THE

**UNIQUE**

| Number | Title (A Side/B Side) | Yr | NM |
|---|---|---|---|
| ❑ LP-103 [M] | Unique Jazz | 1957 | 50.00 |

### WESTERN, JOHNNY

**COLUMBIA**

| Number | Title (A Side/B Side) | Yr | NM |
|---|---|---|---|
| ❑ CL 1788 [M] | Have Gun, Will Travel | 1962 | 40.00 |
| ❑ CS 8588 [S] | Have Gun, Will Travel | 1962 | 50.00 |

### WESTON, KIM

**MGM**

| Number | Title (A Side/B Side) | Yr | NM |
|---|---|---|---|
| ❑ E-4477 [M] | For the First Time | 1967 | 30.00 |
| ❑ SE-4477 [S] | For the First Time | 1967 | 40.00 |
| ❑ SE-4561 | This Is America | 1968 | 40.00 |

**VOLT**

| Number | Title (A Side/B Side) | Yr | NM |
|---|---|---|---|
| ❑ VOS-6014 | Kim, Kim, Kim | 1971 | 25.00 |

### WESTON, PAUL

**CAPITOL**

| Number | Title (A Side/B Side) | Yr | NM |
|---|---|---|---|
| ❑ H 222 [10] | Music for Dreaming | 195? | 40.00 |
| ❑ T 1153 [M] | Floatin' Like a Feather | 1959 | 12.00 |
| ❑ ST 1154 [S] | Music for Dreaming | 1959 | 15.00 |
| ❑ T 1154 [M] | Music for Dreaming | 1959 | 12.00 |
| ❑ ST 1192 [S] | Music for the Fireside | 1959 | 15.00 |
| ❑ T 1192 [M] | Music for the Fireside | 1959 | 12.00 |
| ❑ ST 1222 [S] | Music for Memories | 1959 | 15.00 |
| ❑ T 1222 [M] | Music for Memories | 1959 | 12.00 |
| ❑ ST 1563 [S] | Music for My Love | 1961 | 15.00 |
| ❑ T 1563 [M] | Music for My Love | 1961 | 12.00 |
| ❑ ST-91212 | Romantic Reflections | 196? | 15.00 |

*—Capitol Record Club exclusive*

**COLUMBIA**

| Number | Title (A Side/B Side) | Yr | NM |
|---|---|---|---|
| ❑ CL 572 [M] | Caribbean Cruise | 1955 | 15.00 |
| ❑ CL 693 [M] | Mood for 12 | 1955 | 15.00 |
| ❑ CL 794 [M] | Love Music from Hollywood | 1956 | 15.00 |
| ❑ CL 879 [M] | Solo Mood | 1956 | 15.00 |
| ❑ CL 909 [M] | Moonlight Becomes You | 1956 | 15.00 |
| ❑ CL 977 [M] | Crescent City | 1956 | 15.00 |
| ❑ CL 1112 [M] | Hollywood | 1958 | 15.00 |
| ❑ CL 6232 [10] | Whispers in the Dark | 195? | 40.00 |

**CORINTHIAN**

| Number | Title (A Side/B Side) | Yr | NM |
|---|---|---|---|
| ❑ 107 | Cinema Cameos | 198? | 8.00 |
| ❑ 109 | Easy Jazz | 198? | 8.00 |
| ❑ 116 | Crescent City | 198? | 8.00 |

**HARMONY**

| Number | Title (A Side/B Side) | Yr | NM |
|---|---|---|---|
| ❑ KH 31578 | Paul Weston Plays Jerome Kern | 1972 | 10.00 |
| ❑ KH 31603 | Paul Weston Plays Jerome Kern, Vol. 2 | 1972 | 10.00 |

### WESTON, RANDY

**COLPIX**

| Number | Title (A Side/B Side) | Yr | NM |
|---|---|---|---|
| ❑ CP-456 [M] | Highlight | 1963 | 30.00 |
| ❑ SCP-456 [S] | Highlight | 1963 | 60.00 |

**DAWN**

| Number | Title (A Side/B Side) | Yr | NM |
|---|---|---|---|
| ❑ DLP-1116 [M] | The Modern Art of Jazz | 1957 | 80.00 |

**JAZZLAND**

| Number | Title (A Side/B Side) | Yr | NM |
|---|---|---|---|
| ❑ JLP-4 [M] | Zulu! | 1960 | 40.00 |

**JUBILEE**

| Number | Title (A Side/B Side) | Yr | NM |
|---|---|---|---|
| ❑ JLP-1060 [M] | Piano A La Mode | 1957 | 40.00 |

**RIVERSIDE**

| Number | Title (A Side/B Side) | Yr | NM |
|---|---|---|---|
| ❑ RLP 12-203 [M] | Get Happy | 1956 | 60.00 |
| ❑ RLP 12-214 [M] | With These Hands... | 1956 | 60.00 |
| ❑ RLP 12-227 [M] | Randy Weston Trio and Solo | 1957 | 60.00 |
| ❑ RLP 12-232 [M] | Jazz A La Bohemia | 1957 | 60.00 |
| ❑ RLP-2508 [10] | Cole Porter in a Modern Mood | 1954 | 120.00 |
| ❑ RLP-2515 [10] | Randy Weston Trio | 1955 | 120.00 |

**ROULETTE**

| Number | Title (A Side/B Side) | Yr | NM |
|---|---|---|---|
| ❑ R-65001 [M] | Uhuru Afrika | 1960 | 100.00 |
| ❑ RS-65001 [S] | Uhuru Afrika | 1960 | 120.00 |

**UNITED ARTISTS**

| Number | Title (A Side/B Side) | Yr | NM |
|---|---|---|---|
| ❑ UAL-4011 [M] | Little Niles | 1959 | 40.00 |
| ❑ UAL-4045 [M] | Destry Rides Again | 1959 | 40.00 |
| ❑ UAL-4066 [M] | Live at the Five Spot | 1959 | 40.00 |
| ❑ UAS-5011 [S] | Little Niles | 1959 | 50.00 |
| ❑ UAS-5045 [S] | Destry Rides Again | 1959 | 50.00 |
| ❑ UAS-5066 [S] | Live at the Five Spot | 1959 | 50.00 |

Number | Title (A Side/B Side) | Yr | NM

**WESTON, RANDY, AND CECIL PAYNE**

JAZZLAND
❑ JLP-13 [M] Greenwich Village Jazz 1960 40.00

**WESTON, RANDY/LEM WINCHESTER**

METROJAZZ
❑ E-1005 [M] New Faces at Newport 1958 50.00
❑ SE-1005 [S] New Faces at Newport 1958 40.00

**WETMORE, DICK**

BETHLEHEM
❑ BCP-1035 [10] Dick Wetmore 1955 250.00

**WETTLING, GEORGE**

COLUMBIA
❑ CL 2559 [10] George Wettling's Jazz Band 1956 50.00
*—"House Party Series" issue*
❑ CL 6189 [10] George Wettling's Jazz Band 1951 80.00
*—Original issue*

HARMONY
❑ HL 7080 [M] Dixieland in Hi-Fi 1957 20.00

KAPP
❑ KL-1005 [M] Ragtime Duo 1955 40.00
❑ KL-1028 [M] Jazz Trios 1956 40.00

WEATHERS INDUSTRIES
❑ 5501 [M] High Fidelity Rhythms 1955 40.00

**WHALEFEATHERS, THE**

NASCO
❑ 9003 The Whalefeathers Declare 1969 100.00
❑ 9005 The Whalefeathers 1970 100.00

**WHAM!**

COLUMBIA
❑ BFC 38911 Fantastic 1983 15.00
*—Cover and label list artist as "Wham! U.K."*
❑ FC 38911 Fantastic 1985 10.00
*—Reissue; cover and label list artist as "Wham!"*
❑ FC 39595 Make It Big 1984 10.00
❑ 9C9 40062 [PD] Make It Big 1985 25.00
*—Picture disc*
❑ OC 40285 Music from the Edge of Heaven 1986 10.00
*—With "removable sticker" list of song titles still on front cover*

**WHATNAUTS, THE**

STANG
❑ 1005 The Whatnauts 1970 20.00

**WHEELER, BILLY EDD**

FLYING FISH
❑ FF-085 Wild Mountain Flowers 1979 12.00

FOLKWAYS
❑ 31014 When Kentucky Had No Union Men 196? 20.00

KAPP
❑ KL-1351 [M] A New Bag of Songs Written and Sung by Billy Edd Wheeler 1964 15.00
❑ KL-1425 [M] Memories of America/Ode to the Little Brown Shack Out Back 1965 15.00
❑ KL-1443 [M] Wheeler Man 1965 15.00
❑ KL-1479 [M] Goin' Town and Country 1966 15.00
❑ KL-1533 [M] Paper Birds 1967 20.00
❑ KS-3351 [S] A New Bag of Songs Written and Sung by Billy Edd Wheeler 1964 20.00
❑ KS-3425 [S] Memories of America/Ode to the Little Brown Shack Out Back 1965 20.00
❑ KS-3443 [S] Wheeler Man 1965 20.00
❑ KS-3479 [S] Goin' Town and Country 1966 20.00
❑ KS-3533 [S] Paper Birds 1967 15.00
❑ KS-3567 I Ain't the Worryin' Kind 1968 15.00

MONITOR
❑ MF-354 [M] Billy Edd U.S.A. 1961 30.00
❑ MF-367 [M] Billy Edd and Bluegrass 1962 30.00

RCA VICTOR
❑ LSP-4491 Love 1971 15.00

UNITED ARTISTS
❑ UAS-6711 Nashville Zodiac 1969 15.00

**WHEELER, CLARENCE**

ATLANTIC
❑ SD 1551 Doin' What We Wanna 197? 40.00
❑ SD 1585 The Love I've Been Looking For 197? 20.00

**WHEELS, BURT, AND THE SPEEDSTERS**

CORONET
❑ CX-216 [M] Sounds of the Big Racers 196? 25.00
❑ CXS-216 [S] Sounds of the Big Racers 196? 30.00

**WHEELS, THE**

MONTGOMERY WARD
❑ 010 Sounds of the Hot Rods 196? 120.00

**WHISPERS, THE**

ACCORD
❑ SN-7100 I Can Remember 1981 10.00

ALLEGIANCE
❑ AV-5004 Excellence 1985 10.00

CAPITOL
❑ C1-92957 More of the Night 1990 12.00

DORE
❑ 338 Shhh 197? 12.00

INTERMEDIA
❑ QS-5075 Doctor Love 198? 10.00

JANUS
❑ JLS-3041 The Whispers' Love Story 1972 50.00
❑ JLS-3046 Life and Breath 1973 40.00
❑ 7006 Bingo 1974 40.00
❑ 7013 Greatest Hits 1975 30.00

SOLAR
❑ S-27 Love Is Where You Find It 1982 10.00
❑ BXL1-2270 Open Up Your Love 1978 12.00
*—Reissue of Soul Train 2270*
❑ BXL1-2774 Headlights 1978 12.00
❑ BXL1-3105 Whisper in Your Ear 1979 12.00
❑ BXL1-3521 The Whspers 1979 12.00
❑ BXL1-3578 Imagination 1980 12.00
❑ AYL1-3839 Open Up Your Love 1981 8.00
*—"Best Buy Series" reissue*
❑ BXL1-3976 This Kind of Lovin' 1981 12.00
❑ BXL1-4242 The Best of the Whispers 1982 12.00
❑ 60216 Love for Love 1983 10.00
❑ 60356 So Good 1984 10.00
❑ 60451 Happy Holidays to You 1985 12.00
❑ ST-72554 Just Gets Better with Time 1987 10.00
❑ PZ 75306 Vintage Whispers 1989 12.00

SOUL CLOCK
❑ 22001 Planets of Life 1969 100.00

SOUL TRAIN
❑ BVL1-1450 One for the Money 1976 15.00
❑ BVL1-2270 Open Up Your Love 1977 15.00

**WHITCOMB, IAN**

AUDIOPHILE
❑ AP-115 Treasures of Tin Pan Alley 197? 12.00
❑ AP-147 At the Ragtime Ball 1983 12.00

FIRST AMERICAN
❑ 7704 Crooner Tunes 1979 10.00
❑ 7725 Red Hot "Blue Heaven" 1980 10.00
❑ 7729 The Rock and Roll Years 1981 10.00
❑ 7751 Instrumentals 1981 10.00
❑ 7789 In Hollywood 1982 10.00

RHINO
❑ RNLP-127 The Best of Ian Whitcomb (1964-1968) 1986 8.00

SIERRA
❑ 8708 Pianomelt 1980 10.00

TOWER
❑ DT 5004 [R] You Turn Me On 1965 20.00
❑ T 5004 [M] You Turn Me On 1965 25.00
❑ ST 5042 [S] Mod, Mod Music Hall 1966 20.00
❑ T 5042 [M] Mod, Mod Music Hall 1966 15.00
❑ ST 5071 [S] Yellow Underground 1967 20.00
❑ T 5071 [M] Yellow Underground 1967 15.00
❑ ST 5100 Sock Me Some Rock 1968 20.00

UNITED ARTISTS
❑ UA-LA021-F Under the Ragtime Moon 1972 10.00

**WHITE, ANDREW** Also see THE J.F.K. QUINTET.

ANDREW'S MUSIC
❑ AM-1 Andrew Nathaniel White III 197? 20.00
❑ AM-2 [(2)] Live at the "New Thing" 197? 25.00
❑ AM-3 Live in Bucharest 197? 20.00
❑ AM-4 Who Got Da Funk? 197? 20.00
❑ AM-5 Passion Flower 197? 20.00
❑ AM-6 Songs for a French Lady 197? 20.00
❑ AM-7 Theme 1975 20.00

**WHITE, BUKKA**

ARHOOLIE
❑ 1019 [M] Sky Songs, Volume 1 1966 30.00
❑ 1020 [M] Sky Songs, Volume 2 1966 30.00

BLUE HORIZON
❑ 4604 Blues Masters, Volume 4 1970 25.00

HERWIN
❑ 201 Sic 'em Dogs 196? 25.00

TAKOMA
❑ C-1001 [M] Mississippi Blues 196? 30.00

**WHITE, DANNY**

GRAND PRIX
❑ 101 Danny White Sings Country 1983 25.00

**WHITE, JOSH**

ABC-PARAMOUNT
❑ ABC-124 [M] Josh White Stories, Vol. 1 1956 60.00
❑ ABC-166 [M] Josh White Stories, Vol. 2 1957 60.00
❑ ABC-407 [M] Josh White — Live! 1962 30.00
❑ ABCS-407 [S] Josh White — Live! 1962 40.00
❑ T-90190 [M] Josh White — Live! 1964 30.00
*—Capitol Record Club edition*

DECCA
❑ DL 5062 [10] Ballads and Blues 1949 150.00
❑ DL 5247 [10] Ballads and Blues, Vol. 2 195? 120.00
❑ DL 8665 [M] Josh White 1958 40.00
*—Black label, silver print*

ELEKTRA
❑ EKL-102 [M] Josh at Midnight 1956 40.00
❑ EKL-114 [M] Josh, Ballads and Blues 1957 40.00
❑ EKL-123 [M] 25th Anniversary Album 1957 40.00
❑ EKL-158 [M] Chain Gang Songs 1958 80.00
❑ EKL-193 [M] Spirituals and Blues 1960 30.00
❑ EKL-203 [M] The House I Live In 1961 30.00
❑ EKL-211 [M] Empty Bed Blues 1962 25.00
❑ EKL-701 [(2)10] The Story of John Henry/Ballads, Blues and Other Songs 1955 50.00
❑ EKS-7158 [S] Chain Gang Songs 195? 100.00
❑ EKS-7193 [S] Spirituals and Blues 1960 40.00
❑ EKS-7203 [S] The House I Live In 1961 40.00
❑ EKS-7211 [S] Empty Bed Blues 1962 30.00

EMARCY
❑ MG-26010 [10] Strange Fruit 1954 120.00

LONDON
❑ LPB-338 [10] A Josh White Program 195? 120.00
❑ LPB-341 [10] A Josh White Program, Vol. 2 195? 120.00
❑ LL 1147 [M] A Josh White Program 1956 50.00
❑ LL 1341 [M] A Josh White Program, Vol. 2 195? 50.00

MERCURY
❑ MG-20203 [M] Josh White's Blues 1957 60.00
❑ MG-20821 [M] The Beginning 1963 30.00
❑ MG-21022 [M] I'm on My Own Way 1963 30.00
❑ MG-25014 [10] Josh White Sings Blues 1949 150.00
❑ SR-60821 [R] The Beginning 1963 20.00
❑ SR-61022 [R] I'm on My Own Way 1963 20.00

PERIOD
❑ SLP-1115 [10] Josh White Comes a-Visiting 1956 60.00

STINSON
❑ SLP-14 [10] Josh White Sings the Blues 1950 120.00
❑ SLP-15 [10] Josh White Sings Folk Songs 1950 120.00

**WHITE, KITTY**

EMARCY
❑ MG-36020 [M] A New Voice in Jazz 1955 50.00
❑ MG-36068 [M] Kitty White 1955 50.00

PACIFICA
❑ PL-802 [10] Kitty White 1955 100.00

**WHITE, MIKE**

SEECO
❑ SLP-442 [M] Dixieland Jazz 1960 20.00
❑ SLP-4420 [S] Dixieland Jazz 1960 25.00

**WHITE, STEVE**

LIBERTY
❑ LJH-6006 [M] Jazz Mad—The Unpredictable Steve White 1955 50.00

**WHITE BOY**

TRADEWIND
❑ MM-11761 The Average Rat Band 1976 150.00

**WHITE LIGHT**

CENTURY
❑ 39955 White Light 1968 300.00

**WHITE LIGHTNIN'**

ABC
❑ S-690 File Under Rock 1969 20.00

**WHITE TIGER** With Mark St. John, who was briefly a member of KISS.

E.M.C.
❑ EMC-3653 White Tiger 1986 20.00

**WHITE WITCH**

CAPRICORN
❑ CP 0107 White Witch 1973 25.00
❑ CP 0129 A Spiritual Greeting 1974 25.00



Except when noted otherwise, VG = 25% of NM, and VG+ = 50% of NM. (Example: VG = $2.00, VG+ = $4.00 and NM = $8.00.)

## WHITE ZOMBIE

#### CAROLINE

| Number | Title (A Side/B Side) | Yr | NM |
|---|---|---|---|
| ❑ 1350 | Soul Crusher | 1988 | 20.00 |
| ❑ 1362 | Make Them Die Slowly | 1989 | 20.00 |

#### GEFFEN

| Number | Title (A Side/B Side) | Yr | NM |
|---|---|---|---|
| ❑ GEF 24806 | Astro-Creep: 2000 | 1995 | 15.00 |

#### SILENT EXPLOSION

| Number | Title (A Side/B Side) | Yr | NM |
|---|---|---|---|
| ❑ (# unknown) [EP] | Psycho-Head Blowout | 1986 | 60.00 |
| ❑ SE 002 | Soul Crusher | 1987 | 60.00 |

## WHITEMAN, PAUL

#### CAPITOL

| Number | Title (A Side/B Side) | Yr | NM |
|---|---|---|---|
| ❑ T 622 [M] | Classics in Jazz | 1955 | 50.00 |

#### CORAL

| Number | Title (A Side/B Side) | Yr | NM |
|---|---|---|---|
| ❑ CRL 57021 [M] | The Great Gershwin | 1955 | 20.00 |

#### GRAND AWARD

| Number | Title (A Side/B Side) | Yr | NM |
|---|---|---|---|
| ❑ GA-208 SD [S] | Hawaiian Magic | 1958 | 30.00 |
| ❑ GA-241 SD [S] | The Night I Played at 666 Fifth Ave. | 1960 | 30.00 |
| ❑ GA-244 SD [S] | Cavalcade of Music | 1960 | 30.00 |
| ❑ GA-33-351 [M] | Fiddle on Fire | 195? | 30.00 |
| ❑ GA-33-356 [M] | Hawaiian Magic | 1958 | 20.00 |
| ❑ GA-33-409 [M] | The Night I Played at 666 Fifth Ave. | 1960 | 20.00 |
| ❑ GA-33-412 [M] | Cavalcade of Music | 1960 | 20.00 |
| ❑ GA-33-502 [M] | Great Whiteman Hits | 195? | 30.00 |
| ❑ GA-33-503 [M] | The Greatest Stars of My Life | 195? | 50.00 |
| *—In red velvet jacket* | | | |
| ❑ GA-33-901 [(2)M] | Paul Whiteman/50th Anniversary | 1956 | 50.00 |

#### "X"

| Number | Title (A Side/B Side) | Yr | NM |
|---|---|---|---|
| ❑ LVA-3040 [10] | Paul Whiteman's Orchestra Featuring Bix Beiderbecke | 1955 | 80.00 |

## WHITING, MARGARET

#### AUDIOPHILE

| Number | Title (A Side/B Side) | Yr | NM |
|---|---|---|---|
| ❑ AP-152 | Too Marvelous for Words | 198? | 10.00 |
| ❑ AP-173 | Come a Little Closer | 198? | 10.00 |
| ❑ AP-207 | This Lady's in Love with You | 1986 | 10.00 |

#### CAPITOL

| Number | Title (A Side/B Side) | Yr | NM |
|---|---|---|---|
| ❑ H 163 [10] | South Pacific | 1950 | 50.00 |
| ❑ H 209 [10] | Margaret Whiting Sings Rodgers and Hart | 1950 | 50.00 |
| ❑ H 234 [10] | Songs | 1950 | 50.00 |
| ❑ T 410 [M] | Love Songs | 1954 | 40.00 |
| ❑ T 685 [M] | For the Starry-Eyed | 1955 | 40.00 |

#### DOT

| Number | Title (A Side/B Side) | Yr | NM |
|---|---|---|---|
| ❑ DLP 3072 [M] | Goin' Places | 1957 | 25.00 |
| ❑ DLP 3113 [M] | Margaret | 1958 | 15.00 |
| ❑ DLP 3176 [M] | Margaret Whiting's Great Hits | 1959 | 15.00 |
| ❑ DLP 3235 [M] | Ten Top Hits | 1960 | 15.00 |
| ❑ DLP 3337 [M] | Just a Dream | 1960 | 15.00 |
| ❑ DLP 25113 [S] | Margaret | 1958 | 20.00 |
| ❑ DLP 25176 [S] | Margaret Whiting's Great Hits | 1959 | 20.00 |
| ❑ DLP 25235 [S] | Ten Top Hits | 1960 | 20.00 |
| ❑ DLP 25337 [S] | Just a Dream | 1960 | 20.00 |

#### HAMILTON

| Number | Title (A Side/B Side) | Yr | NM |
|---|---|---|---|
| ❑ HLP 143 [M] | My Ideal | 196? | 12.00 |
| ❑ HLP 12143 [S] | My Ideal | 196? | 15.00 |

#### LONDON

| Number | Title (A Side/B Side) | Yr | NM |
|---|---|---|---|
| ❑ PS 497 [S] | The Wheel of Hurt | 1967 | 15.00 |
| ❑ PS 510 [S] | Maggie Isn't Margaret Anymore | 1967 | 15.00 |
| ❑ PS 527 | Pop Country | 1968 | 15.00 |
| ❑ LL 3497 [M] | The Wheel of Hurt | 1967 | 20.00 |
| ❑ LL 3510 [M] | Maggie Isn't Margaret Anymore | 1967 | 20.00 |

#### MGM

| Number | Title (A Side/B Side) | Yr | NM |
|---|---|---|---|
| ❑ E-4006 [M] | Past Midnight | 1961 | 15.00 |
| ❑ SE-4006 [S] | Past Midnight | 1961 | 20.00 |

#### VERVE

| Number | Title (A Side/B Side) | Yr | NM |
|---|---|---|---|
| ❑ V-4038 [M] | The Jerome Kern Song Book | 1960 | 15.00 |
| ❑ V6-4038 [S] | The Jerome Kern Song Book | 1960 | 20.00 |

## WHITMAN, SLIM

#### CLEVELAND INT'L.

| Number | Title (A Side/B Side) | Yr | NM |
|---|---|---|---|
| ❑ AS99-875 [DJ] | Songs I Love to Sing | 1980 | 30.00 |
| *—Promo-only picture disc* | | | |
| ❑ JE 36768 | Songs I Love to Sing | 1980 | 10.00 |
| ❑ JE 36847 | Christmas with Slim Whitman | 1980 | 12.00 |
| ❑ FE 37403 | Mr. Songman | 1982 | 10.00 |

#### COLUMBIA SPECIAL PRODUCTS

| Number | Title (A Side/B Side) | Yr | NM |
|---|---|---|---|
| ❑ P 16323 | Christmas with Slim Whitman | 1981 | 10.00 |

#### EPIC

| Number | Title (A Side/B Side) | Yr | NM |
|---|---|---|---|
| ❑ PE 36768 | Songs I Love to Sing | 198? | 8.00 |
| *—Reissue of Cleveland Int'l. JE 36768* | | | |
| ❑ PE 36847 | Christmas with Slim Whitman | 1981 | 8.00 |
| *—Reissue of Cleveland Int'l. JE 36847* | | | |

#### IMPERIAL

| Number | Title (A Side/B Side) | Yr | NM |
|---|---|---|---|
| ❑ LP-3004 [10] | America's Favorite Folk Artist | 1954 | 600.00 |
| ❑ LP-9003 [M] | Favorites | 1956 | 50.00 |
| *—Maroon label* | | | |
| ❑ LP-9003 [M] | Favorites | 1958 | 30.00 |
| *—Black label with stars on top* | | | |
| ❑ LP-9003 [M] | Favorites | 1964 | 20.00 |
| *—Black and pink label* | | | |
| ❑ LP-9003 [M] | Favorites | 1966 | 15.00 |
| *—Black and green label* | | | |
| ❑ LP-9026 [M] | Slim Whitman Sings | 1957 | 50.00 |
| *—Maroon label* | | | |
| ❑ LP-9026 [M] | Slim Whitman Sings | 1958 | 30.00 |
| *—Black label with stars on top* | | | |
| ❑ LP-9026 [M] | Slim Whitman Sings | 1964 | 20.00 |
| *—Black and pink label* | | | |
| ❑ LP-9026 [M] | Slim Whitman Sings | 1966 | 15.00 |
| *—Black and green label* | | | |
| ❑ LP-9056 [M] | Slim Whitman Sings | 1958 | 30.00 |
| *—Black label with stars on top* | | | |
| ❑ LP-9056 [M] | Slim Whitman Sings | 1958 | 50.00 |
| *—Maroon label* | | | |
| ❑ LP-9056 [M] | Slim Whitman Sings | 1964 | 20.00 |
| *—Black and pink label* | | | |
| ❑ LP-9056 [M] | Slim Whitman Sings | 1966 | 15.00 |
| *—Black and green label* | | | |
| ❑ LP-9064 [M] | Slim Whitman Sings | 1959 | 30.00 |
| *—Black label with stars on top* | | | |
| ❑ LP-9064 [M] | Slim Whitman Sings | 1964 | 20.00 |
| *—Black and pink label* | | | |
| ❑ LP-9064 [M] | Slim Whitman Sings | 1966 | 15.00 |
| *—Black and green label* | | | |
| ❑ LP-9088 [M] | I'll Walk with God | 1960 | 30.00 |
| *—Black label with stars on top* | | | |
| ❑ LP-9088 [M] | I'll Walk with God | 1964 | 20.00 |
| *—Black and pink label* | | | |
| ❑ LP-9088 [M] | I'll Walk with God | 1966 | 15.00 |
| *—Black and green label* | | | |
| ❑ LP-9102 [M] | Million Record Hits | 1960 | 30.00 |
| *—Black label with stars on top* | | | |
| ❑ LP-9102 [M] | Song of the Old Waterwheel | 1964 | 20.00 |
| *—Black and pink label; title changed* | | | |
| ❑ LP-9102 [M] | Song of the Old Waterwheel | 1966 | 15.00 |
| *—Black and green label* | | | |
| ❑ LP-9135 [M] | Slim Whitman's First Visit to Britain | 1960 | 25.00 |
| *—Black label with stars on top* | | | |
| ❑ LP-9135 [M] | Slim Whitman's First Visit to Britain | 1964 | 15.00 |
| *—Black and pink label* | | | |
| ❑ LP-9135 [M] | Slim Whitman's First Visit to Britain | 1966 | 12.00 |
| *—Black and green label* | | | |
| ❑ LP-9137 [M] | Just Call Me Lonesome | 1961 | 25.00 |
| *—Black label with stars on top* | | | |
| ❑ LP-9137 [M] | Just Call Me Lonesome | 1964 | 15.00 |
| *—Black and pink label* | | | |
| ❑ LP-9137 [M] | Just Call Me Lonesome | 1966 | 12.00 |
| *—Black and green label* | | | |
| ❑ LP-9156 [M] | Once in a Lifetime | 1961 | 25.00 |
| *—Black label with stars on top* | | | |
| ❑ LP-9156 [M] | Once in a Lifetime | 1964 | 15.00 |
| *—Black and pink label* | | | |
| ❑ LP-9156 [M] | Once in a Lifetime | 1966 | 12.00 |
| *—Black and green label* | | | |
| ❑ LP-9163 [M] | Slim Whitman Sings Annie Laurie | 1961 | 25.00 |
| *—Black label with stars on top* | | | |
| ❑ LP-9163 [M] | Slim Whitman Sings Annie Laurie | 1964 | 15.00 |
| *—Black and pink label* | | | |
| ❑ LP-9163 [M] | Slim Whitman Sings Annie Laurie | 1966 | 12.00 |
| *—Black and green label* | | | |
| ❑ LP-9171 [M] | Forever | 1961 | 25.00 |
| *—Black label with stars on top* | | | |
| ❑ LP-9171 [M] | Forever | 1964 | 15.00 |
| *—Black and pink label* | | | |
| ❑ LP-9171 [M] | Forever | 1966 | 12.00 |
| *—Black and green label* | | | |
| ❑ LP-9194 [M] | Slim Whitman Sings | 1962 | 25.00 |
| *—Black label with stars on top* | | | |
| ❑ LP-9194 [M] | Slim Whitman Sings | 1964 | 15.00 |
| *—Black and pink label* | | | |
| ❑ LP-9194 [M] | Slim Whitman Sings | 1966 | 12.00 |
| *—Black and green label* | | | |
| ❑ LP-9209 [M] | Heart Songs and Love Songs | 1962 | 25.00 |
| *—Black label with stars on top* | | | |
| ❑ LP-9209 [M] | Heart Songs and Love Songs | 1964 | 15.00 |
| *—Black and pink label* | | | |
| ❑ LP-9209 [M] | Heart Songs and Love Songs | 1966 | 12.00 |
| *—Black and green label* | | | |
| ❑ LP-9226 [M] | I'm a Lonely Wanderer | 1963 | 25.00 |
| *—Black label with stars on top* | | | |
| ❑ LP-9226 [M] | I'm a Lonely Wanderer | 1964 | 15.00 |
| *—Black and pink label* | | | |
| ❑ LP-9226 [M] | I'm a Lonely Wanderer | 1966 | 12.00 |
| *—Black and green label* | | | |
| ❑ LP-9235 [M] | Yodeling | 1963 | 25.00 |
| *—Black label with stars on top* | | | |
| ❑ LP-9235 [M] | Yodeling | 1964 | 15.00 |
| *—Black and pink label* | | | |
| ❑ LP-9235 [M] | Yodeling | 1966 | 12.00 |
| *—Black and green label* | | | |
| ❑ LP-9245 [M] | Irish Songs The Whitman Way | 1963 | 25.00 |
| *—Black label with stars on top* | | | |
| ❑ LP-9245 [M] | Irish Songs The Whitman Way | 1964 | 15.00 |
| *—Black and pink label* | | | |
| ❑ LP-9245 [M] | Irish Songs The Whitman Way | 1966 | 12.00 |
| *—Black and green label* | | | |
| ❑ LP-9252 [M] | All-Time Favorites | 1964 | 15.00 |
| *—Black and pink label* | | | |
| ❑ LP-9252 [M] | All-Time Favorites | 1964 | 30.00 |
| *—Black label with stars on top* | | | |
| ❑ LP-9252 [M] | All-Time Favorites | 1966 | 12.00 |
| *—Black and green label* | | | |
| ❑ LP-9268 [M] | Country Songs/City Hits | 1964 | 15.00 |
| *—Black and pink label* | | | |
| ❑ LP-9268 [M] | Country Songs/City Hits | 1966 | 12.00 |
| *—Black and green label* | | | |
| ❑ LP-9277 [M] | Love Song of the Waterfall | 1964 | 15.00 |
| *—Black and pink label* | | | |
| ❑ LP-9277 [M] | Love Song of the Waterfall | 1966 | 12.00 |
| *—Black and green label* | | | |
| ❑ LP-9288 [M] | Reminiscing | 1965 | 15.00 |
| *—Black and pink label* | | | |
| ❑ LP-9288 [M] | Reminiscing | 1966 | 12.00 |
| *—Black and green label* | | | |
| ❑ LP-9303 [M] | More Than Yesterday | 1965 | 15.00 |
| *—Black and pink label* | | | |
| ❑ LP-9303 [M] | More Than Yesterday | 1966 | 12.00 |
| *—Black and green label* | | | |
| ❑ LP-9308 [M] | God's Hand in Mine | 1966 | 12.00 |
| ❑ LP-9313 [M] | A Travelin' Man | 1966 | 12.00 |
| ❑ LP-9333 [M] | A Time for Love | 1966 | 12.00 |
| ❑ LP-9342 [M] | 15th Anniversary | 1967 | 15.00 |
| ❑ LP-9356 [M] | Country Memories | 1967 | 15.00 |
| ❑ LP-12032 [S] | I'll Walk with God | 1959 | 40.00 |
| *—Black label with silver top* | | | |
| ❑ LP-12032 [S] | I'll Walk with God | 1964 | 25.00 |
| *—Black and pink label* | | | |
| ❑ LP-12032 [S] | I'll Walk with God | 1966 | 20.00 |
| *—Black and green label* | | | |
| ❑ LP-12077 [S] | Slim Whitman Sings Annie Laurie | 1961 | 30.00 |
| *—Black label with silver top* | | | |
| ❑ LP-12077 [S] | Slim Whitman Sings Annie Laurie | 1964 | 20.00 |
| *—Black and pink label* | | | |
| ❑ LP-12077 [S] | Slim Whitman Sings Annie Laurie | 1966 | 15.00 |
| *—Black and green label* | | | |
| ❑ LP-12100 [R] | Slim Whitman | 1964 | 15.00 |
| *—Black and pink label* | | | |
| ❑ LP-12100 [R] | Slim Whitman | 1966 | 12.00 |
| *—Black and green label* | | | |
| ❑ LP-12102 [R] | Song of the Old Waterwheel | 1964 | 15.00 |
| *—Black and pink label* | | | |
| ❑ LP-12102 [R] | Song of the Old Waterwheel | 1966 | 12.00 |
| *—Black and green label* | | | |
| ❑ LP-12194 [S] | Slim Whitman Sings | 1962 | 30.00 |
| *—Black label with silver top* | | | |
| ❑ LP-12194 [S] | Slim Whitman Sings | 1964 | 20.00 |
| *—Black and pink label* | | | |
| ❑ LP-12194 [S] | Slim Whitman Sings | 1966 | 15.00 |
| *—Black and green label* | | | |
| ❑ LP-12268 [S] | Country Songs/City Hits | 1964 | 20.00 |
| *—Black and pink label* | | | |
| ❑ LP-12268 [S] | Country Songs/City Hits | 1966 | 15.00 |
| *—Black and green label* | | | |
| ❑ LP-12277 [S] | Love Song of the Waterfall | 1964 | 20.00 |
| *—Black and pink label* | | | |
| ❑ LP-12277 [S] | Love Song of the Waterfall | 1966 | 15.00 |
| *—Black and green label* | | | |
| ❑ LP-12288 [S] | Reminiscing | 1965 | 20.00 |
| *—Black and pink label* | | | |
| ❑ LP-12288 [S] | Reminiscing | 1966 | 15.00 |
| *—Black and green label* | | | |
| ❑ LP-12303 [S] | More Than Yesterday | 1965 | 20.00 |
| *—Black and pink label* | | | |
| ❑ LP-12303 [S] | More Than Yesterday | 1966 | 15.00 |
| *—Black and green label* | | | |
| ❑ LP-12313 [S] | A Travelin' Man | 1966 | 15.00 |
| ❑ LP-12333 [S] | A Time for Love | 1966 | 15.00 |
| ❑ LP-12342 [S] | 15th Anniversary | 1967 | 12.00 |
| ❑ LP-12356 [S] | Country Memories | 1967 | 12.00 |
| ❑ LP-12375 | In Love, The Whitman Way | 1968 | 12.00 |
| ❑ LP-12411 | Happy Street | 1969 | 12.00 |
| ❑ LP-12436 | Slim | 1969 | 12.00 |
| ❑ LP-12448 | The Slim Whitman Christmas Album | 1969 | 15.00 |

#### LIBERTY

| Number | Title (A Side/B Side) | Yr | NM |
|---|---|---|---|
| ❑ LM-1005 | The Very Best of Slim Whitman | 1981 | 8.00 |
| *—Reissue of United Artists 1005* | | | |
| ❑ LM-1067 | The Slim Whitman Christmas Album | 1980 | 8.00 |
| *—Abridged reissue of Imperial 12448* | | | |
| ❑ SL-8128 | All My Best | 1981 | 12.00 |
| *—Mail-order album* | | | |
| ❑ LN-10033 | Red River Valley | 1981 | 8.00 |
| *—Budget-line reissue* | | | |
| ❑ LN-10123 | Till We Meet Again | 1981 | 8.00 |
| *—Budget-line reissue* | | | |
| ❑ LN-10124 | Ghost Riders in the Sky | 1981 | 8.00 |
| *—Budget-line reissue* | | | |
| ❑ LN-10125 | The Best of Slim Whitman, Vol. 2 | 1981 | 8.00 |
| *—Budget-line reissue* | | | |
| ❑ LN-10152 | God's Hand in Mine | 1981 | 8.00 |
| *—Budget-line reissue* | | | |

The Who, *Who Are You,* MCA L33-1987, 1978, white label promo edited for airplay, $25.

| Number | Title (A Side/B Side) | Yr | NM |
|---|---|---|---|
| ❑ LN-10153 | Country Songs/City Hits | 1981 | 8.00 |

*—Budget-line reissue*

PAIR

| Number | Title (A Side/B Side) | Yr | NM |
|---|---|---|---|
| ❑ PDL2-1085 [(2)] | One of a Kind | 1986 | 12.00 |

PICKWICK

| Number | Title (A Side/B Side) | Yr | NM |
|---|---|---|---|
| ❑ SPC-3590 | Happy Anniversary | 1978 | 10.00 |

RCA CAMDEN

| Number | Title (A Side/B Side) | Yr | NM |
|---|---|---|---|
| ❑ CAL-954 [M] | Birmingham Jail | 1966 | 20.00 |
| ❑ CAS-954(e) [R] | Birmingham Jail | 1966 | 12.00 |

RCA VICTOR

| Number | Title (A Side/B Side) | Yr | NM |
|---|---|---|---|
| ❑ LPM-3217 [10] | Slim Whitman Sings and Yodels | 1954 | 300.00 |
| ❑ AYL1-3774 | Birmingham Jail | 1980 | 8.00 |

*—"Best Buy Series" reissue*

SUNSET

| Number | Title (A Side/B Side) | Yr | NM |
|---|---|---|---|
| ❑ SUM-1112 [M] | Unchain Your Heart | 1966 | 12.00 |
| ❑ SUM-1167 [M] | Lonesome Heart | 1967 | 12.00 |
| ❑ SUS-5112 [R] | Unchain Your Heart | 1966 | 12.00 |
| ❑ SUS-5167 [R] | Lonesome Heart | 1967 | 12.00 |
| ❑ SUS-5267 | Slim Whitman | 1969 | 12.00 |
| ❑ SUS-5320 | Ramblin' Rose | 1970 | 10.00 |

UNITED ARTISTS

| Number | Title (A Side/B Side) | Yr | NM |
|---|---|---|---|
| ❑ UA-LA046-F | I'll See You When I Get There | 1973 | 10.00 |
| ❑ UA-LA245-G | The Very Best of Slim Whitman | 1974 | 10.00 |
| ❑ UA-LA319-G | Happy Anniversary | 1974 | 10.00 |
| ❑ UA-LA386-E | The Very Best of Slim Whitman | 1974 | 10.00 |
| ❑ UA-LA513-G | Everything Leads Back to You | 1975 | 10.00 |
| ❑ UA-LA752-G | Red River Valley | 1977 | 10.00 |
| ❑ UA-LA787-G | Home on the Range | 1978 | 10.00 |
| ❑ LM-1005 | The Very Best of Slim Whitman | 1980 | 10.00 |
| ❑ UAS-6763 | Tomorrow Never Comes | 1970 | 12.00 |
| ❑ UAS-6783 | Guess Who | 1970 | 12.00 |
| ❑ UAS-6819 | It's a Sin to Tell a Lie | 1971 | 12.00 |
| ❑ UAS-6832 | The Best of Slim Whitman | 1972 | 12.00 |

**WHITNEY, MARVA**

KING

| Number | Title (A Side/B Side) | Yr | NM |
|---|---|---|---|
| ❑ KS-1053 | I Sing Soul | 1969 | 120.00 |
| ❑ KS-1062 | It's My Thing | 1969 | 120.00 |
| ❑ KS-1079 | Live and Lowdown at the Apollo | 1970 | 200.00 |

**WHITNEY SUNDAY**

DECCA

| Number | Title (A Side/B Side) | Yr | NM |
|---|---|---|---|
| ❑ DL 75239 | Whitney Sunday | 1970 | 20.00 |

**WHO, THE** Also see ROGER DALTREY; JOHN ENTWISTLE; KEITH MOON; PETE TOWNSHEND.

DECCA

| Number | Title (A Side/B Side) | Yr | NM |
|---|---|---|---|
| ❑ DL 4664 [M] | The Who Sing My Generation | 1966 | 100.00 |
| ❑ DL 4664 [M] | The Who Sing My Generation | 1966 | 200.00 |

*—White label promo*

| Number | Title (A Side/B Side) | Yr | NM |
|---|---|---|---|
| ❑ DL 4892 [M] | Happy Jack | 1967 | 50.00 |
| ❑ DL 4892 [M] | Happy Jack | 1967 | 150.00 |

*—White label promo*

| Number | Title (A Side/B Side) | Yr | NM |
|---|---|---|---|
| ❑ DL 4950 [M] | The Who Sell Out | 1967 | 100.00 |
| ❑ DL 4950 [M] | The Who Sell Out | 1967 | 200.00 |

*—White label promo with songs in the same order as the stock copy*

| Number | Title (A Side/B Side) | Yr | NM |
|---|---|---|---|
| ❑ DL 4950 [M] | The Who Sell Out | 1967 | 300.00 |

*—White label promo with side 1 banded for airplay and all the commercials on one side*

| Number | Title (A Side/B Side) | Yr | NM |
|---|---|---|---|
| ❑ DL 5064 [M] | Magic Bus — The Who on Tour | 1968 | 200.00 |

*—White label promo; no stock copies were released in mono*

| Number | Title (A Side/B Side) | Yr | NM |
|---|---|---|---|
| ❑ DXSW 7205 [(2)] | Tommy | 1969 | 40.00 |

*—With booklet*

| Number | Title (A Side/B Side) | Yr | NM |
|---|---|---|---|
| ❑ DXSW 7205 [(2)DJ] | Tommy | 1969 | 200.00 |

*—White label promo*

| Number | Title (A Side/B Side) | Yr | NM |
|---|---|---|---|
| ❑ DL 74664 [R] | The Who Sing My Generation | 1966 | 60.00 |
| ❑ DL 74664 [R] | The Who Sing My Generation | 1966 | 200.00 |

*—White label promo*

| Number | Title (A Side/B Side) | Yr | NM |
|---|---|---|---|
| ❑ DL 74892 [P] | Happy Jack | 1967 | 50.00 |

*—All stereo except that "Happy Jack" and "Don't Look Away" are rechanneled*

| Number | Title (A Side/B Side) | Yr | NM |
|---|---|---|---|
| ❑ DL 74892 [P] | Happy Jack | 1967 | 150.00 |

*—White label promo*

| Number | Title (A Side/B Side) | Yr | NM |
|---|---|---|---|
| ❑ DL 74950 [S] | The Who Sell Out | 1967 | 50.00 |
| ❑ DL 74950 [S] | The Who Sell Out | 1967 | 250.00 |

*—White label promo with songs in the same order as the stock copy*

| Number | Title (A Side/B Side) | Yr | NM |
|---|---|---|---|
| ❑ DL 74950 [S] | The Who Sell Out | 1967 | 400.00 |

*—White label promo with side 1 banded for airplay and all the commercials on one side*

| Number | Title (A Side/B Side) | Yr | NM |
|---|---|---|---|
| ❑ DL 75064 [P] | Magic Bus — The Who on Tour | 1968 | 50.00 |

*—All rechanneled except "Magic Bus" and "I Can't Reach You," which are true stereo.*

| Number | Title (A Side/B Side) | Yr | NM |
|---|---|---|---|
| ❑ DL 75064 [P] | Magic Bus — The Who on Tour | 1968 | 150.00 |

*—White label promo*

| Number | Title (A Side/B Side) | Yr | NM |
|---|---|---|---|
| ❑ DL 79175 | Live at Leeds | 1970 | 40.00 |

*—With gatefold cover and numerous inserts*

| Number | Title (A Side/B Side) | Yr | NM |
|---|---|---|---|
| ❑ DL 79182 | Who's Next | 1971 | 25.00 |
| ❑ DL 79184 | Meaty Beaty Big and Bouncy | 1971 | 30.00 |

*—With poster (deduct 1/3 if missing)*

| Number | Title (A Side/B Side) | Yr | NM |
|---|---|---|---|
| ❑ DL 734586 | The Who/The Strawberry Alarm Clock | 1969 | 100.00 |

*—Special Products release for Philco. One side has Who songs, the other, Strawberry Alarm Clock songs*

DIRECT DISC

| Number | Title (A Side/B Side) | Yr | NM |
|---|---|---|---|
| ❑ SD 16610 | Who Are You | 1980 | 30.00 |

*—Audiophile vinyl*

LIFE

| Number | Title (A Side/B Side) | Yr | NM |
|---|---|---|---|
| ❑ DL 74664 [R] | The Who Sing My Generation | 1967 | 150.00 |

MCA

| Number | Title (A Side/B Side) | Yr | NM |
|---|---|---|---|
| ❑ 1496 | Who's Greatest Hits | 1987 | 8.00 |
| ❑ 1577 | Live at Leeds | 1988 | 8.00 |
| ❑ 1578 | Meaty Beaty Big and Bouncy | 1988 | 8.00 |
| ❑ 1579 | The Who By Numbers | 1988 | 8.00 |
| ❑ 1580 | Who Are You | 1988 | 8.00 |
| ❑ L33-1987 [DJ] | Who Are You | 1978 | 25.00 |

*—White label promo with sticker "Who Are You Edited for Broadcast" on cover -- the line "Who the fuck are you?" is deleted twice.*

| Number | Title (A Side/B Side) | Yr | NM |
|---|---|---|---|
| ❑ 2022 | Live at Leeds | 1973 | 12.00 |
| ❑ 2023 | Who's Next | 1973 | 12.00 |
| ❑ 2025 | Meaty Beaty Big and Bouncy | 1973 | 12.00 |
| ❑ 2044 [R] | The Who Sing My Generation | 1974 | 50.00 |
| ❑ 2045 [P] | Happy Jack | 1974 | 50.00 |
| ❑ 2161 | The Who By Numbers | 1975 | 12.00 |
| ❑ 3023 | Live at Leeds | 1977 | 10.00 |
| ❑ 3024 | Who's Next | 1977 | 10.00 |
| ❑ 3025 | Meaty Beaty Big and Bouncy | 1977 | 10.00 |
| ❑ 3026 | The Who By Numbers | 1977 | 10.00 |
| ❑ 3050 | Who Are You | 1978 | 10.00 |
| ❑ 2-4067 [(2)P] | A Quick One/The Who Sell Out | 1976 | 20.00 |

*—Black labels with rainbow*

| Number | Title (A Side/B Side) | Yr | NM |
|---|---|---|---|
| ❑ 2-4067 [(2)P] | A Quick One/The Who Sell Out | 1978 | 15.00 |

*—Tan labels*

| Number | Title (A Side/B Side) | Yr | NM |
|---|---|---|---|
| ❑ 2-4067 [(2)P] | A Quick One/The Who Sell Out | 1980 | 12.00 |

*—Blue labels with rainbow*

| Number | Title (A Side/B Side) | Yr | NM |
|---|---|---|---|
| ❑ 2-4068 [(2)P] | Magic Bus/The Who Sing My Generation | 1976 | 20.00 |

*—Black labels with rainbow*

| Number | Title (A Side/B Side) | Yr | NM |
|---|---|---|---|
| ❑ 2-4068 [(2)P] | Magic Bus/The Who Sing My Generation | 1978 | 15.00 |

*—Tan labels*

| Number | Title (A Side/B Side) | Yr | NM |
|---|---|---|---|
| ❑ 2-4068 [(2)P] | Magic Bus/The Who Sing My Generation | 1980 | 12.00 |

*—Blue labels with rainbow*

| Number | Title (A Side/B Side) | Yr | NM |
|---|---|---|---|
| ❑ 5220 | Who's Next | 1979 | 8.00 |
| ❑ 5408 | Who's Greatest Hits | 1983 | 8.00 |
| ❑ 5641 | Who's Missing | 1986 | 10.00 |
| ❑ 5712 | Two's Missing | 1987 | 10.00 |
| ❑ 6895 [(2)] | Quadrophenia | 1980 | 10.00 |
| ❑ 6899 [(2)] | The Kids Are Alright | 1980 | 10.00 |

*—Early versions have number stamped in gold on cover with 11005 records. No difference in value.*

| Number | Title (A Side/B Side) | Yr | NM |
|---|---|---|---|
| ❑ 8018 [(2)] | Who's Last | 1984 | 10.00 |
| ❑ 8031 [(2)] | Who's Better, Who's Best | 1989 | 15.00 |
| ❑ 2-10004 [(2)] | Quadrophenia | 1973 | 15.00 |

*—Black labels with rainbow*

| Number | Title (A Side/B Side) | Yr | NM |
|---|---|---|---|
| ❑ 2-10004 [(2)] | Quadrophenia | 1978 | 12.00 |

*—Tan labels*

| Number | Title (A Side/B Side) | Yr | NM |
|---|---|---|---|
| ❑ 2-10005 [(2)] | Tommy | 1973 | 15.00 |

*—Black labels with rainbow*

| Number | Title (A Side/B Side) | Yr | NM |
|---|---|---|---|
| ❑ 2-10005 [(2)] | Tommy | 1978 | 12.00 |

*—Tan labels*

| Number | Title (A Side/B Side) | Yr | NM |
|---|---|---|---|
| ❑ 2-10005 [(2)] | Tommy | 1980 | 10.00 |

*—Blue labels with rainbow*

| Number | Title (A Side/B Side) | Yr | NM |
|---|---|---|---|
| ❑ 2-11005 [(2)] | The Kids Are Alright | 1979 | 12.00 |
| ❑ 11164 | Who's Next | 1995 | 25.00 |

*—"Heavy Vinyl" reissue on 180-gram vinyl with gatefold cover*

| Number | Title (A Side/B Side) | Yr | NM |
|---|---|---|---|
| ❑ 2-12001 [(2)] | Hooligans | 1981 | 10.00 |
| ❑ 14950 [PD] | Who Are You | 1978 | 15.00 |

*—Picture disc*

| Number | Title (A Side/B Side) | Yr | NM |
|---|---|---|---|
| ❑ 3-19501 [(3)] | Join Together | 1990 | 20.00 |

*—Box set with booklet*

| Number | Title (A Side/B Side) | Yr | NM |
|---|---|---|---|
| ❑ 25986 | It's Hard | 1989 | 8.00 |
| ❑ 25987 | Face Dances | 1989 | 8.00 |
| ❑ 37000 | Live at Leeds | 1979 | 8.00 |
| ❑ 37001 | Meaty Beaty Big and Bouncy | 1979 | 8.00 |
| ❑ 37002 | The Who By Numbers | 1979 | 8.00 |
| ❑ 37003 | Who Are You | 1979 | 8.00 |
| ❑ 37169 | Odds and Sods | 1980 | 8.00 |

MOBILE FIDELITY

| Number | Title (A Side/B Side) | Yr | NM |
|---|---|---|---|
| ❑ 1-115 | Face Dances | 1984 | 25.00 |

*—Audiophile vinyl*

TRACK

| Number | Title (A Side/B Side) | Yr | NM |
|---|---|---|---|
| ❑ 2126 | Odds and Sods | 1974 | 25.00 |
| ❑ 2-4067 [(2)P] | A Quick One/The Who Sell Out | 1974 | 25.00 |
| ❑ 2-4068 [(2)P] | Magic Bus/The Who Sing My Generation | 1974 | 25.00 |
| ❑ 2-10004 [(2)] | Quadrophenia | 1973 | 20.00 |

WARNER BROS.

| Number | Title (A Side/B Side) | Yr | NM |
|---|---|---|---|
| ❑ WBMS-116 [DJ] | Filling In the Gaps | 1981 | 50.00 |

*—With generic "Warner Bros. Music Show" cover*

| Number | Title (A Side/B Side) | Yr | NM |
|---|---|---|---|
| ❑ WBMS-116 [DJ] | Filling In the Gaps | 1981 | 80.00 |

*—With drawing on cover*

| Number | Title (A Side/B Side) | Yr | NM |
|---|---|---|---|
| ❑ HS 3516 | Face Dances | 1981 | 8.00 |
| ❑ 23731 | It's Hard | 1982 | 8.00 |
| ❑ 23731 [DJ] | It's Hard | 1982 | 30.00 |

*—Promo version on Quiex II vinyl*



**Except when noted otherwise, VG = 25% of NM, and VG+ = 50% of NM. (Example: VG = $2.00, VG+ = $4.00 and NM = $8.00.)**

| Number | Title (A Side/B Side) | Yr | NM |
|---|---|---|---|
| **WICHITA TRAIN WHISTLE, THE** | | | |
| DOT | | | |
| ❑ DLP-25861 | Mike Nesmith Presents/The Wichita Train Whistle Sings | 1968 | 30.00 |
| **WIGGINS, GERALD** | | | |
| CHALLENGE | | | |
| ❑ CHP-604 [M] | The King and I | 1957 | 60.00 |
| CONTEMPORARY | | | |
| ❑ M-3595 [M] | Relax and Enjoy It | 1961 | 30.00 |
| ❑ S-7595 [S] | Relax and Enjoy It | 1961 | 40.00 |
| DIG | | | |
| ❑ LP-102 [M] | Gerald Wiggins Trio | 1956 | 60.00 |
| DISCOVERY | | | |
| ❑ DL-2003 [10] | Gerald Wiggins Trio | 1953 | 120.00 |
| HIFI | | | |
| ❑ J-618 [M] | Wiggin' Out | 1961 | 30.00 |
| ❑ JS-618 [S] | Wiggin' Out | 1961 | 40.00 |
| MOTIF | | | |
| ❑ 504 [M] | Reminiscin' with Wig | 1956 | 60.00 |
| SPECIALTY | | | |
| ❑ SP-2101 [S] | Around the World | 1969 | 20.00 |
| TAMPA | | | |
| ❑ TP-1 [M] | The Loveliness of You | 1957 | 100.00 |
| *—Colored vinyl* | | | |
| ❑ TP-1 [M] | The Loveliness of You | 1958 | 50.00 |
| *—Black vinyl* | | | |
| ❑ TP-33 [M] | Gerald Wiggins Trio | 1957 | 100.00 |
| *—Colored vinyl* | | | |
| ❑ TP-33 [M] | Gerald Wiggins Trio | 1958 | 50.00 |
| *—Black vinyl* | | | |
| **WIGGINS, ROY** | | | |
| DIPLOMAT | | | |
| ❑ DPL 2615 [M] | Songs I Played for Eddy Arnold | 196? | 15.00 |
| STARDAY | | | |
| ❑ SLP-188 [M] | Mister Steel Guitar | 1962 | 30.00 |
| ❑ SLP-259 [M] | The Fabulous Steel Guitar Artistry of Roy Wiggins | 1963 | 30.00 |
| ❑ SLP-392 [M] | Nashville Steel Guitar | 1965 | 25.00 |
| **WIGGS, JOHNNY** | | | |
| PARAMOUNT | | | |
| ❑ CJS 107 [10] | Johnny Wiggs' New Orleanians Playing Jazz Favorites and Featuring Ray Burke | 195? | 60.00 |
| SOUTHLAND | | | |
| ❑ LP-200 [10] | Johnny Wiggs | 1954 | 50.00 |
| ❑ LP-200 [M] | Johnny Wiggs | 195? | 30.00 |
| **WIGGS, JOHNNY, AND RAYMOND BURKE** | | | |
| S/D | | | |
| ❑ LP-1001 [10] | Chamber Jazz | 1955 | 50.00 |
| **WIGWAM** | | | |
| VERVE FORECAST | | | |
| ❑ FTS-3089 | Tombstone Valentine | 1970 | 20.00 |
| **WILBER, BOB** | | | |
| CIRCLE | | | |
| ❑ L-406 [10] | Bob Wilbur Jazz Band | 1951 | 50.00 |
| RIVERSIDE | | | |
| ❑ RLP-2501 [10] | Young Men With Horns | 1952 | 80.00 |
| **WILBURN BROTHERS, THE** | | | |
| DECCA | | | |
| ❑ DL 4058 [M] | The Big Heartbreak | 1960 | 30.00 |
| ❑ DL 4142 [M] | The Wilburn Brothers Sing | 1961 | 30.00 |
| ❑ DL 4211 [M] | City Limits | 1961 | 30.00 |
| ❑ DL 4225 [M] | Folk Songs | 1962 | 20.00 |
| ❑ DL 4391 [M] | Trouble's Back in Town | 1963 | 20.00 |
| ❑ DL 4464 [M] | Take Up Thy Cross | 1964 | 20.00 |
| ❑ DL 4544 [M] | Never Alone | 1964 | 20.00 |
| ❑ DL 4615 [M] | Country Gold | 1965 | 20.00 |
| ❑ DL 4645 [M] | I'm Gonna Tie One on Tonight | 1965 | 20.00 |
| ❑ DL 4721 [M] | The Wilburn Brothers Show | 1966 | 60.00 |
| *—With guests Loretta Lynn, Ernest Tubb, Harold Morrison* | | | |
| ❑ DL 4764 [M] | Let's Go Country | 1966 | 20.00 |
| ❑ DL 4824 [M] | Two for the Show | 1967 | 25.00 |
| ❑ DL 4871 [M] | Cool | 1967 | 30.00 |
| ❑ DL 4954 [M] | It's Another World | 1968 | 40.00 |
| ❑ DL 8576 [M] | The Wilburn Brothers | 1957 | 40.00 |
| ❑ DL 8774 [M] | Side by Side | 1958 | 40.00 |
| ❑ DL 8959 [M] | Livin' in God's Country | 1959 | 40.00 |
| ❑ DL 74058 [S] | The Big Heartbreak | 1960 | 40.00 |
| ❑ DL 74142 [S] | The Wilburn Brothers Sing | 1961 | 40.00 |
| ❑ DL 74211 [S] | City Limits | 1961 | 40.00 |
| ❑ DL 74225 [S] | Folk Songs | 1962 | 30.00 |
| ❑ DL 74391 [S] | Trouble's Back in Town | 1963 | 30.00 |
| ❑ DL 74464 [S] | Take Up Thy Cross | 1964 | 25.00 |
| ❑ DL 74544 [S] | Never Alone | 1964 | 25.00 |
| ❑ DL 74615 [S] | Country Gold | 1965 | 25.00 |
| ❑ DL 74645 [S] | I'm Gonna Tie One on Tonight | 1965 | 25.00 |
| ❑ DL 74721 [S] | The Wilburn Brothers Show | 1966 | 80.00 |
| *—With guests Loretta Lynn, Ernest Tubb, Harold Morrison* | | | |
| ❑ DL 74764 [S] | Let's Go Country | 1966 | 25.00 |
| ❑ DL 74824 [S] | Two for the Show | 1967 | 20.00 |
| ❑ DL 74871 [S] | Cool | 1967 | 20.00 |
| ❑ DL 74954 [S] | It's Another World | 1968 | 20.00 |
| ❑ DL 75173 | Little Johnny from Down the Street | 1970 | 20.00 |
| ❑ DL 75214 | Sing Your Heart Out Country Boy | 1971 | 20.00 |
| ❑ DL 75291 | That She's Leaving Feeling | 1972 | 20.00 |
| ❑ DL 78774 [S] | Side by Side | 1959 | 60.00 |
| ❑ DL 78959 [S] | Livin' in God's Country | 1959 | 60.00 |
| KING | | | |
| ❑ 746 [M] | The Wonderful Wilburn Brothers | 1961 | 100.00 |
| MCA | | | |
| ❑ 4011 [(2)] | Portrait | 197? | 15.00 |
| MCA CORAL | | | |
| ❑ 20058 | That Country Feeling | 1973 | 10.00 |
| VOCALION | | | |
| ❑ VL 3691 [M] | Carefree Moments | 1962 | 15.00 |
| ❑ VL 73691 [S] | Carefree Moments | 1962 | 15.00 |
| ❑ VL 73876 | That Country Feeling | 197? | 12.00 |
| ❑ VL 73889 | I Walk the Line | 197? | 12.00 |
| **WILCO** Also see UNCLE TUPELO. | | | |
| REPRISE | | | |
| ❑ 46236-1 [(2)] | Being There | 1996 | 20.00 |
| RHINO VINYL | | | |
| ❑ RI-76492 [(2)] | A Ghost is Born | 2005 | 25.00 |
| SIRE | | | |
| ❑ 45857 | A.M. | 1995 | 80.00 |
| *—Red vinyl in generic plastic sleeve with sticker in upper left corner* | | | |
| SUNDAZED | | | |
| ❑ LP 5161 [(2)] | Yankee Hotel Foxtrot | 2002 | 25.00 |
| **WILCOX, LARRY** | | | |
| COLUMBIA | | | |
| ❑ CL 2147 [M] | Hot Rod Jazz | 1964 | 30.00 |
| ❑ CS 8947 [S] | Hot Rod Jazz | 1964 | 40.00 |
| COLUMBIA SPECIAL PRODUCTS | | | |
| ❑ CSRP 8947 [M] | Hot Rod Jazz | 196? | 20.00 |
| **WILCOX THREE, THE** | | | |
| RCA CAMDEN | | | |
| ❑ CAL-669 [M] | The Greatest Folk Songs Ever Sung | 1961 | 20.00 |
| **WILD, EARL** See BOSTON POPS ORCHESTRA (ARTHUR FIEDLER, CONDUCTOR) | | | |
| **WILD, JACK** | | | |
| BUDDAH | | | |
| ❑ BDS-5083 | Everything's Coming Up Roses | 1971 | 25.00 |
| ❑ BDS-5110 | A Beautiful World | 1972 | 25.00 |
| CAPITOL | | | |
| ❑ SKAO-545 | The Jack Wild Album | 1970 | 25.00 |
| **WILD BUTTER** | | | |
| UNITED ARTISTS | | | |
| ❑ UAS-6766 | Wild Butter | 1970 | 25.00 |
| **WILD-CATS, THE** | | | |
| UNITED ARTISTS | | | |
| ❑ UAL-3031 [M] | Bandstand Record Hop | 1958 | 50.00 |
| **WILD COUNTRY** See ALABAMA. | | | |
| **WILD MAN STEVE** | | | |
| DEALER'S CHOICE | | | |
| ❑ 777 | Is It Good Baby | 198? | 15.00 |
| ❑ 780 | Did He Really Say That | 198? | 15.00 |
| DICK-ER | | | |
| ❑ D 70 | Do Not Disturb | 1972 | 20.00 |
| LAFF | | | |
| ❑ 181 | Eatin' Ain't Cheatin' | 1973 | 12.00 |
| ❑ 191 | When You're Hot You're Hot | 1976 | 12.00 |
| RAW | | | |
| ❑ 7000 | My Man! Wild Man! | 1969 | 15.00 |
| ❑ 7001 | Wild! Wild! Wild! Wild! | 1970 | 15.00 |
| ❑ 7002 | King of Them All | 1971 | 15.00 |
| **WILD ONES, THE (1)** | | | |
| UNITED ARTISTS | | | |
| ❑ UAL-3450 [M] | The Arthur Sound | 1965 | 25.00 |
| ❑ UAS-6450 [S] | The Arthur Sound | 1965 | 30.00 |
| **WILDE, MARTY** | | | |
| EPIC | | | |
| ❑ BN 575 [S] | Wilde About Marty | 1960 | 100.00 |
| ❑ LN 3686 [M] | Bad Boy | 1960 | 80.00 |
| ❑ LN 3711 [M] | Wilde About Marty | 1960 | 80.00 |
| **WILDER, ALEC** | | | |
| COLUMBIA | | | |
| ❑ CL 6181 [10] | Alec Wilder Octet | 1951 | 60.00 |
| MERCURY | | | |
| ❑ MG 25008 [10] | Alec Wilder and His Octet | 1949 | 60.00 |
| **WILDER, JOE** | | | |
| COLUMBIA | | | |
| ❑ CL 1319 [M] | Jazz from "Peter Gunn" | 1959 | 40.00 |
| *—Red and black label with six "eye" logos* | | | |
| ❑ CL 1372 [M] | The Pretty Sound of Joe Wilder | 1959 | 50.00 |
| *—Red and black label with six "eye" logos* | | | |
| ❑ CS 8121 [S] | Jazz from "Peter Gunn" | 1959 | 60.00 |
| *—Red and black label with six "eye" logos* | | | |
| ❑ CS 8173 [S] | The Pretty Sound of Joe Wilder | 1959 | 100.00 |
| *—Red and black label with six "eye" logos* | | | |
| SAVOY | | | |
| ❑ MG-12063 [M] | 'N' Wilder... | 1956 | 50.00 |
| **WILDERNESS ROAD** | | | |
| COLUMBIA | | | |
| ❑ C 31118 | Wilderness Road | 1972 | 20.00 |
| REPRISE | | | |
| ❑ MS 2125 | Sold for the Prevention of Disease Only | 1973 | 20.00 |
| **WILDWEEDS, THE** | | | |
| VANGUARD | | | |
| ❑ VSD-6552 | The Wildweeds | 1970 | 25.00 |
| **WILEY, LEE** | | | |
| ALLEGRO ELITE | | | |
| ❑ 4019 [10] | Lee Wiley Sings — Lennie Tristano Plays | 195? | 100.00 |
| COLUMBIA | | | |
| ❑ CL 656 [M] | Night in Manhattan | 1955 | 80.00 |
| ❑ CL 6169 [10] | Night in Manhattan | 1951 | 120.00 |
| ❑ CL 6215 [10] | Lee Wiley Sings Vincent Youmans | 1952 | 100.00 |
| ❑ CL 6216 [10] | Lee Wiley Sings Irving Berlin | 1952 | 100.00 |
| JAZZTONE | | | |
| ❑ J-1248 [M] | The Songs of Rodgers and Hart — Intimate Jazz | 1956 | 50.00 |
| JJC | | | |
| ❑ M-2002 [M] | The One and Only Lee Wiley | 195? | 50.00 |
| ❑ M-2003 [M] | The Classic Interpretations of the Immortal Cole Porter | 195? | 50.00 |
| LIBERTY MUSIC SHOP | | | |
| ❑ 1003 [10] | Cole Porter Songs by Lee Wiley | 195? | 300.00 |
| ❑ 1004 [10] | George Gershwin Songs by Lee Wiley | 195? | 300.00 |
| RCA VICTOR | | | |
| ❑ LPM-1408 [M] | West of the Moon | 1957 | 80.00 |
| ❑ LPM-1566 [M] | Touch of the Blues | 1957 | 60.00 |
| RIC | | | |
| ❑ M-2002 [M] | The One and Only Lee Wiley | 1964 | 20.00 |
| ❑ S-2002 [S] | The One and Only Lee Wiley | 1964 | 25.00 |
| STORYVILLE | | | |
| ❑ STLP-312 [10] | Lee Wiley Sings Rodgers and Hart | 1954 | 200.00 |
| **WILKERSON, DON** | | | |
| BLUE NOTE | | | |
| ❑ BLP-4107 [M] | Preach, Brother! | 1962 | 30.00 |
| ❑ BLP-4121 [M] | Elder Don | 1963 | 30.00 |
| ❑ BLP-4145 [M] | Shoutin' | 1963 | 30.00 |
| ❑ BST-84107 [S] | Preach, Brother! | 1962 | 40.00 |
| *—With "New York, USA" address on label* | | | |
| ❑ BST-84107 [S] | Preach, Brother! | 1967 | 20.00 |
| *—With "A Division of Liberty Records" on label* | | | |
| ❑ BST-84121 [S] | Elder Don | 1963 | 40.00 |
| *—With "New York, USA" address on label* | | | |
| ❑ BST-84121 [S] | Elder Don | 1967 | 20.00 |
| *—With "A Division of Liberty Records" on label* | | | |
| ❑ BST-84145 [S] | Shoutin' | 1963 | 40.00 |
| *—With "New York, USA" address on label* | | | |
| ❑ BST-84145 [S] | Shoutin' | 1967 | 20.00 |
| *—With "A Division of Liberty Records" on label* | | | |
| RIVERSIDE | | | |
| ❑ RLP-332 [M] | Texas Twister | 1960 | 40.00 |
| ❑ RLP-1186 [S] | Texas Twister | 1960 | 40.00 |
| **WILKINS, ERNIE** | | | |
| EVEREST | | | |
| ❑ SDBR-1077 [S] | Here Comes the Swingin' Mr. Wilkins | 1959 | 30.00 |
| ❑ SDBR-1104 [S] | The Big New Band of the '60s | 1960 | 30.00 |
| ❑ LPBR-5077 [M] | Here Comes the Swingin' Mr. Wilkins | 1959 | 25.00 |
| ❑ LPBR-5104 [M] | The Big New Band of the '60s | 1960 | 25.00 |
| SAVOY | | | |
| ❑ MG-12044 [M] | Top Brass Featuring 5 Trumpets | 1955 | 60.00 |

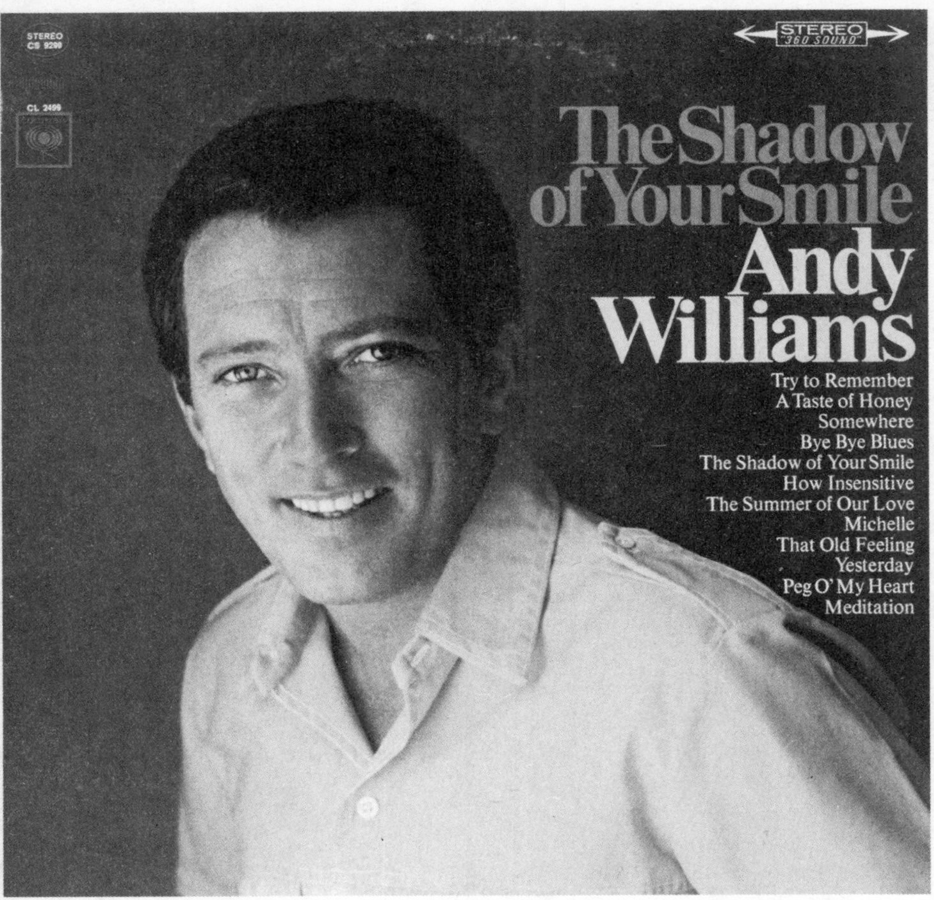


Andy Williams, *The Shadow of Your Smile,* Columbia CS 9299, 1966, stereo, $15.

| Number | Title (A Side/B Side) | Yr | NM |
|---|---|---|---|
| **WILKINSON TRI-CYCLE** | | | |
| DATE | | | |
| ❑ TES 4016 | Wilkinson Tri-Cycle | 1969 | 40.00 |
| **WILLET, SLIM** | | | |
| AUDIO LAB | | | |
| ❑ AL-1542 [M] | Slim Willet | 1959 | 100.00 |
| **WILLETTE, BABY FACE** | | | |
| ARGO | | | |
| ❑ LP-739 [M] | No Rock | 1964 | 25.00 |
| ❑ LPS-739 [S] | No Rock | 1964 | 30.00 |
| ❑ LP-749 [M] | Behind the 8-Ball | 1965 | 25.00 |
| ❑ LPS-749 [S] | Behind the 8-Ball | 1965 | 30.00 |
| BLUE NOTE | | | |
| ❑ BLP-4068 [M] | Face to Face | 1961 | 150.00 |
| *—With W. 63rd St. address on label* | | | |
| ❑ BLP-4068 [M] | Face to Face | 1963 | 25.00 |
| *—With "New York, USA" address on label* | | | |
| ❑ BLP-4084 [M] | Stop and Listen | 1962 | 120.00 |
| *—With 61st St. address on label* | | | |
| ❑ BLP-4084 [M] | Stop and Listen | 1963 | 25.00 |
| *—With "New York, USA" address on label* | | | |
| ❑ BST-84068 [S] | Face to Face | 1961 | 120.00 |
| *—With W. 63rd St. address on label* | | | |
| ❑ BST-84068 [S] | Face to Face | 1963 | 20.00 |
| *—With "New York, USA" address on label* | | | |
| ❑ BST-84084 [S] | Stop and Listen | 1962 | 100.00 |
| *—With 61st St. address on label* | | | |
| ❑ BST-84084 [S] | Stop and Listen | 1963 | 20.00 |
| *—With "New York, USA" address on label* | | | |
| **WILLIAMS, ANDY** | | | |
| ATCO | | | |
| ❑ 90561 | Close Enough for Love | 1987 | 10.00 |
| CADENCE | | | |
| ❑ CLP 1018 [M] | Andy Williams | 1957 | 50.00 |
| ❑ CLP 3002 [M] | Andy Williams | 1958 | 50.00 |
| *—Cover depicts Andy standing* | | | |
| ❑ CLP 3002 [M] | Andy Williams | 1960 | 20.00 |
| *—Cover depicts Andy reclining* | | | |
| ❑ CLP 3005 [M] | Andy Williams Sings Rodgers and Hammerstein | 1958 | 40.00 |
| *—Cover depicts a cafÈ scene* | | | |
| ❑ CLP 3005 [M] | Andy Williams Sings Rodgers and Hammerstein | 1960 | 20.00 |
| *—Cover depicts a close-up of Andy's face* | | | |
| ❑ CLP 3026 [M] | Two Time Winners | 1959 | 20.00 |
| ❑ CLP 3027 [M] | Andy Williams Sings…Steve Allen | 1959 | 20.00 |
| ❑ CLP 3029 [M] | To You Sweetheart, Aloha | 1959 | 20.00 |
| ❑ CLP 3030 [M] | Lonely Street | 1960 | 20.00 |
| ❑ CLP 3038 [M] | The Village of St. Bernadette | 1960 | 20.00 |
| ❑ CLP 3047 [M] | Under Paris Skies | 1961 | 20.00 |
| ❑ CLP 3054 [M] | Andy Williams' Best | 1962 | 20.00 |
| ❑ CLP 3061 [M] | Million Seller Songs | 1962 | 20.00 |
| ❑ CLP 25026 [S] | Two Time Winners | 1959 | 30.00 |
| *—Black vinyl* | | | |
| ❑ CLP 25026 [S] | Two Time Winners | 1959 | 80.00 |
| *—Red vinyl* | | | |
| ❑ CLP 25027 [R] | Andy Williams Sings…Steve Allen | 1959 | 15.00 |
| ❑ CLP 25029 [S] | To You Sweetheart, Aloha | 1959 | 30.00 |
| ❑ CLP 25030 [S] | Lonely Street | 1960 | 30.00 |
| ❑ CLP 25038 [S] | The Village of St. Bernadette | 1960 | 30.00 |
| ❑ CLP 25047 [S] | Under Paris Skies | 1961 | 30.00 |
| ❑ CLP 25054 [S] | Andy Williams' Best | 1962 | 25.00 |
| ❑ CLP 25061 [S] | Million Seller Songs | 1962 | 25.00 |
| CAPITOL | | | |
| ❑ ST-12387 | Greatest Love Classics | 1984 | 10.00 |
| COLUMBIA | | | |
| ❑ GP 5 [(2)] | The Andy Williams Sound of Music | 1969 | 20.00 |
| ❑ CL 1751 [M] | Danny Boy And Other Songs I Love to Sing | 1962 | 15.00 |
| ❑ CL 1809 [M] | Moon River and Other Great Movie Themes | 1962 | 12.00 |
| ❑ CL 1879 [M] | Warm and Willing | 1962 | 12.00 |
| ❑ CL 2015 [M] | Days of Wine and Roses | 1963 | 12.00 |
| ❑ CL 2087 [M] | The Andy Williams Christmas Album | 1963 | 12.00 |
| ❑ CL 2137 [M] | The Wonderful World of Andy Williams | 1964 | 12.00 |
| ❑ CL 2171 [M] | The Academy Award Winning "Call Me Irresponsible" and Other Hits Songs from the Movies | 1964 | 12.00 |
| ❑ CL 2205 [M] | The Great Songs from "My Fair Lady" and Other Broadway Hits | 1964 | 12.00 |
| ❑ CL 2323 [M] | Hawaiian Wedding Song | 1965 | 12.00 |
| *—Reissue of Cadence 3029* | | | |
| ❑ CL 2324 [M] | Canadian Sunset | 1965 | 12.00 |
| *—Reissue of Cadence 3054* | | | |
| ❑ CL 2338 [M] | Dear Heart | 1965 | 12.00 |
| ❑ CL 2383 [M] | Andy Williams' Newest Hits | 1966 | 12.00 |
| ❑ CL 2420 [M] | Merry Christmas | 1965 | 12.00 |
| ❑ CL 2499 [M] | The Shadow of Your Smile | 1966 | 12.00 |
| ❑ CL 2533 [M] | In the Arms of Love | 1967 | 12.00 |
| ❑ CL 2680 [M] | Born Free | 1967 | 12.00 |
| ❑ CL 2766 [M] | Love, Andy | 1967 | 15.00 |
| ❑ CS 2862 [M] | Honey | 1968 | 20.00 |
| ❑ CS 8551 [S] | Danny Boy And Other Songs I Love to Sing | 1962 | 20.00 |
| ❑ CS 8609 [S] | Moon River and Other Great Movie Themes | 1962 | 15.00 |
| ❑ CS 8679 [S] | Warm and Willing | 1962 | 15.00 |
| ❑ CS 8815 [S] | Days of Wine and Roses | 1963 | 15.00 |
| ❑ CS 8887 [S] | The Andy Williams Christmas Album | 1963 | 12.00 |
| ❑ CS 8937 [S] | The Wonderful World of Andy Williams | 1964 | 15.00 |
| ❑ CS 8971 [S] | The Academy Award Winning "Call Me Irresponsible" and Other Hits Songs from the Movies | 1964 | 15.00 |
| ❑ CS 9005 [S] | The Great Songs from "My Fair Lady" and Other Broadway Hits | 1964 | 15.00 |
| ❑ CS 9123 [S] | Hawaiian Wedding Song | 1965 | 15.00 |
| *—Reissue of Cadence 25029* | | | |
| ❑ CS 9124 [S] | Canadian Sunset | 1965 | 15.00 |
| *—Reissue of Cadence 25054* | | | |
| ❑ CS 9138 [S] | Dear Heart | 1965 | 15.00 |
| ❑ CS 9183 [S] | Andy Williams' Newest Hits | 1966 | 15.00 |
| ❑ CS 9220 [S] | Merry Christmas | 1965 | 12.00 |
| ❑ CS 9299 [S] | The Shadow of Your Smile | 1966 | 15.00 |
| ❑ CS 9333 [S] | In the Arms of Love | 1967 | 15.00 |
| ❑ CS 9480 [S] | Born Free | 1967 | 15.00 |
| ❑ CS 9566 [S] | Love, Andy | 1967 | 12.00 |
| ❑ CS 9662 [S] | Honey | 1968 | 12.00 |
| ❑ CS 9844 | Happy Heart | 1969 | 12.00 |
| ❑ CS 9896 | Raindrops Keep Fallin' on My Head | 1970 | 12.00 |
| ❑ CS 9922 | Get Together with Andy Williams | 1969 | 15.00 |
| *—The Osmonds appear on three tracks* | | | |
| ❑ KCS 9979 | Andy Williams' Greatest Hits | 1970 | 12.00 |
| ❑ KC 30105 | The Andy Williams Show | 1970 | 10.00 |
| ❑ CQ 30497 [Q] | Love Story | 1972 | 15.00 |
| ❑ KC 30497 | Love Story | 1971 | 10.00 |
| ❑ CQ 30797 [Q] | You've Got a Friend | 1971 | 15.00 |
| ❑ KC 30797 | You've Got a Friend | 1971 | 10.00 |
| ❑ CG 31064 [(2)] | The Impossible Dream | 1971 | 15.00 |
| ❑ CQ 31303 [Q] | Love Theme from "The Godfather" | 1972 | 15.00 |
| ❑ KC 31303 | Love Theme from "The Godfather" | 1972 | 10.00 |
| ❑ CQ 31625 [Q] | Alone Again (Naturally) | 1972 | 15.00 |
| ❑ KC 31625 | Alone Again (Naturally) | 1972 | 10.00 |
| ❑ KC 32383 | Solitaire | 1973 | 10.00 |
| ❑ KC 32384 | Andy Williams' Greatest Hits, Vol. 2 | 1973 | 10.00 |
| ❑ KC 32949 | The Way We Were | 1974 | 10.00 |
| ❑ C 33191 | Christmas Present | 1974 | 10.00 |
| ❑ KC 33234 | You Lay So Easy on My Mind | 1974 | 10.00 |
| ❑ PC 33563 | The Other Side of Me | 1975 | 10.00 |
| ❑ CG 33597 [(2)] | Love Story/Born Free | 1975 | 12.00 |
| ❑ CG 33600 [(2)] | Moon River/Days of Wine and Roses | 1975 | 12.00 |
| ❑ PC 34299 | Andy | 1976 | 10.00 |
| ❑ PCQ 34299 [Q] | Andy | 1976 | 15.00 |
| COLUMBIA SPECIAL PRODUCTS | | | |
| ❑ CSS 966 | Andy... & Company | 1969 | 12.00 |
| *—Side 1 is Andy Williams; Side 2 has tracks by the Williams Brothers, Claudine Longet and the Osmond Brothers; sold only at Woolworth's* | | | |
| HARMONY | | | |
| ❑ KH 30133 | Andy Williams | 1970 | 10.00 |
| PAIR | | | |
| ❑ PDL2-1103 [(2)] | The Best of Andy Williams | 1986 | 12.00 |
| TIME-LIFE | | | |
| ❑ SLGD-11 [(2)] | Legendary Singers: Andy Williams | 1986 | 15.00 |
| **WILLIAMS, ANN** | | | |
| CHARLIE PARKER | | | |
| ❑ PLP-807 [M] | First Time Out | 1963 | 40.00 |
| ❑ PLP-807S [S] | First Time Out | 1963 | 40.00 |
| **WILLIAMS, BETTY VAIDEN** | | | |
| VANGUARD | | | |
| ❑ VRS-9028 [M] | Folk Songs and Ballads of North Carolina | 195? | 30.00 |
| **WILLIAMS, BIG JOE** | | | |
| BLUESVILLE | | | |
| ❑ BVLP-1056 [M] | Blues for 9 Strings | 1962 | 100.00 |
| *—Blue label, silver print* | | | |



**Except when noted otherwise, VG = 25% of NM, and VG+ = 50% of NM. (Example: VG = $2.00, VG+ = $4.00 and NM = $8.00.)**

| Number | Title (A Side/B Side) | Yr | NM |
|---|---|---|---|
| ❑ BVLP-1056 [M] | Blues for 9 Strings | 1964 | 25.00 |
| *—Blue label with trident logo* | | | |
| ❑ BVLP-1067 [M] | Big Joe Williams at Folk City | 1963 | 100.00 |
| *—Blue label, silver print* | | | |
| ❑ BVLP-1067 [M] | Big Joe Williams at Folk City | 1964 | 25.00 |
| *—Blue label with trident logo* | | | |
| ❑ BVLP-1083 [M] | Studio Blues | 1964 | 25.00 |
| *—Blue label with trident logo* | | | |
| ❑ BVLP-1083 [M] | Studio Blues | 1964 | 100.00 |
| *—Blue label, silver print* | | | |
| DELMARK | | | |
| ❑ DL-604 [M] | Blues on Highway 49 | 1962 | 60.00 |
| ❑ DL-609 [M] | Starvin' Chain Blues | 1966 | 25.00 |
| FOLKWAYS | | | |
| ❑ FA-3820 [M] | Mississippi's Big Joe Williams | 1962 | 30.00 |
| ❑ FAS-3820 [R] | Mississippi's Big Joe Williams | 1962 | 20.00 |
| MILESTONE | | | |
| ❑ 3001 [M] | Classic Delta Blues | 1966 | 25.00 |
| **WILLIAMS, BILLY** | | | |
| CORAL | | | |
| ❑ CRL 57184 [M] | Billy Williams | 1957 | 60.00 |
| ❑ CRL 57251 [M] | Half Sweet, Half Beat | 1959 | 50.00 |
| ❑ CRL 57343 [M] | The Billy Williams Revue | 1960 | 50.00 |
| ❑ CRL 757251 [S] | Half Sweet, Half Beat | 1959 | 80.00 |
| ❑ CRL 757343 [S] | The Billy Williams Revue | 1960 | 60.00 |
| MERCURY | | | |
| ❑ MG 20317 [M] | Oh Yeah! | 1958 | 60.00 |
| MGM | | | |
| ❑ E-3400 [M] | The Billy Williams Quartet | 1957 | 60.00 |
| WING | | | |
| ❑ MGW-12131 [M] | Vote for Billy Williams | 1959 | 40.00 |
| **WILLIAMS, BILLY DEE** | | | |
| PRESTIGE LIVELY ARTS | | | |
| ❑ 30001 [M] | Let's Misbehave | 1962 | 40.00 |
| **WILLIAMS, CAMILLA** | | | |
| MGM | | | |
| ❑ E-156 [10] | Spirituals | 1952 | 100.00 |
| **WILLIAMS, CLARENCE** | | | |
| RIVERSIDE | | | |
| ❑ RLP-1033 [10] | Clarence Williams and Orchestra | 1954 | 60.00 |
| **WILLIAMS, COOTIE** | | | |
| JARO | | | |
| ❑ JAM-5001 [M] | Around Midnight | 1959 | 100.00 |
| ❑ JAS-8001 [S] | Around Midnight | 1959 | 80.00 |
| MOODSVILLE | | | |
| ❑ MVLP-27 [M] | The Solid Trumpet of Cootie Williams | 1962 | 50.00 |
| *—Green label* | | | |
| ❑ MVLP-27 [M] | The Solid Trumpet of Cootie Williams | 1965 | 25.00 |
| *—Blue label, trident logo at right* | | | |
| RCA VICTOR | | | |
| ❑ LPM-1718 [M] | Cootie Williams in Hi-Fi | 1958 | 80.00 |
| ❑ LSP-1718 [S] | Cootie Williams in Stereo | 1958 | 150.00 |
| WARWICK | | | |
| ❑ W-2027 [M] | Do Nothing Till You Hear From Me | 1960 | 40.00 |
| ❑ W-2027ST [S] | Do Nothing Till You Hear From Me | 1960 | 60.00 |
| **WILLIAMS, COOTIE/JIMMY PRESTON** | | | |
| ALLEGRO ELITE | | | |
| ❑ 4109 [10] | Rock 'N' Roll | 195? | 50.00 |
| **WILLIAMS, DANNY** | | | |
| UNITED ARTISTS | | | |
| ❑ UAL-3297 [M] | The Exciting Danny Williams | 1963 | 15.00 |
| ❑ UAL-3359 [M] | White on White | 1964 | 15.00 |
| ❑ UAL-3380 [M] | With You in Mind | 1964 | 15.00 |
| ❑ UAL-3493 [M] | Magic Town | 1966 | 15.00 |
| ❑ UAS-6297 [S] | The Exciting Danny Williams | 1963 | 20.00 |
| ❑ UAS-6359 [S] | White on White | 1964 | 20.00 |
| ❑ UAS-6380 [S] | With You in Mind | 1964 | 20.00 |
| ❑ UAS-6493 [S] | Magic Town | 1966 | 20.00 |
| **WILLIAMS, DENIECE** | | | |
| ARC | | | |
| ❑ AS 1432 [DJ] | Niecy | 1982 | 25.00 |
| *—Promo-only picture disc* | | | |
| ❑ JC 35568 | When Love Comes Calling | 1979 | 12.00 |
| ❑ FC 37048 | My Melody | 1981 | 10.00 |
| ❑ PC 37048 | My Melody | 198? | 8.00 |
| *—Budget-line reissue* | | | |
| ❑ FC 37952 | Niecy | 1982 | 10.00 |
| ❑ PC 37952 | Niecy | 198? | 8.00 |
| *—Budget-line reissue* | | | |
| ❑ HC 47952 | Niecy | 1983 | 50.00 |
| *—Half-speed mastered edition* | | | |

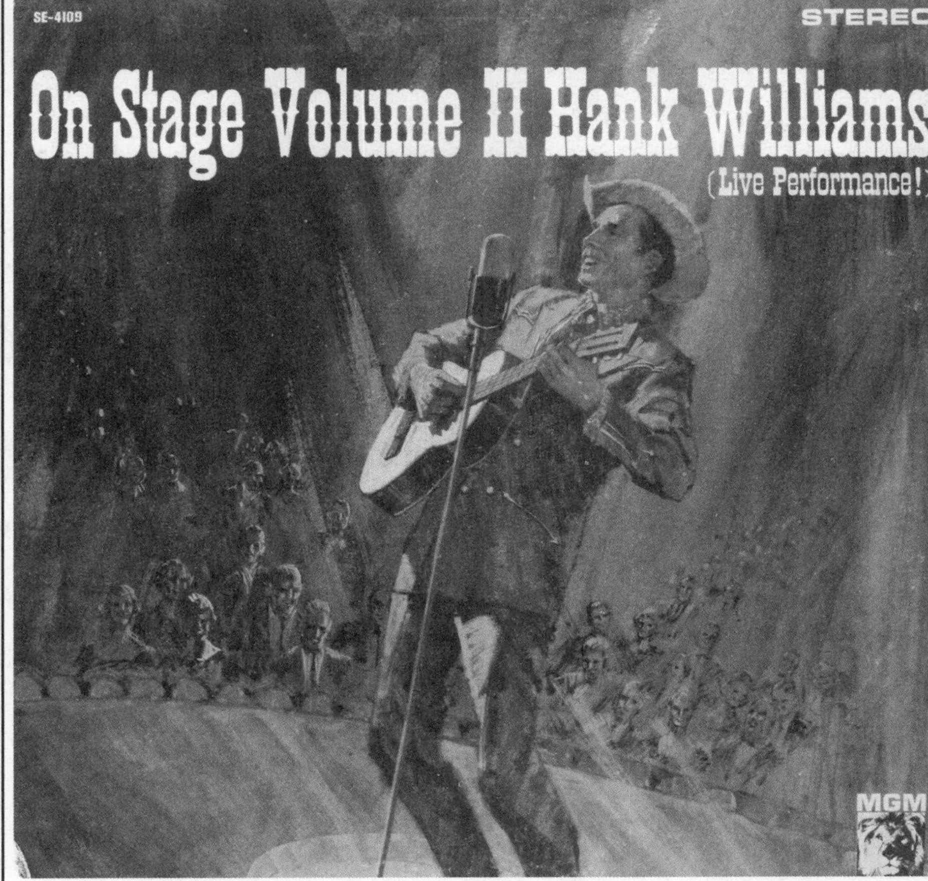


Hank Williams, *On Stage Volume II,* MGM SE-4109, 1963, stereo, black label, $20.

| Number | Title (A Side/B Side) | Yr | NM |
|---|---|---|---|
| COLUMBIA | | | |
| ❑ PC 34242 | This Is Niecy | 1976 | 12.00 |
| *—No bar code on cover* | | | |
| ❑ PC 34242 | This Is Niecy | 198? | 8.00 |
| *—Reissue with bar code on cover* | | | |
| ❑ JC 34911 | Song Bird | 1977 | 10.00 |
| ❑ PC 34911 | Song Bird | 198? | 8.00 |
| *—Budget-line reissue* | | | |
| ❑ FC 38622 | I'm So Proud | 1983 | 10.00 |
| ❑ PC 38622 | I'm So Proud | 198? | 8.00 |
| *—Budget-line reissue* | | | |
| ❑ FC 39366 | Let's Hear It for the Boy | 1984 | 10.00 |
| ❑ FC 40084 | Hot on the Trail | 1986 | 10.00 |
| ❑ FC 40486 | Water Under the Bridge | 1987 | 10.00 |
| ❑ FC 44322 | As Good As It Gets | 1989 | 10.00 |
| MCA | | | |
| ❑ 6338 | Special Love | 1989 | 10.00 |
| SPARROW | | | |
| ❑ SPR-1121 | So Glad I Know | 1986 | 12.00 |
| ❑ SPR-1174 | Special Love | 1989 | 12.00 |
| ❑ SPR-1256 | From the Beginning | 1990 | 15.00 |
| ❑ ST-41039 | So Glad I Know | 198? | 12.00 |
| *—Reissue of 1121?* | | | |
| **WILLIAMS, DON** Also see THE POZO-SECO SINGERS. | | | |
| ABC | | | |
| ❑ AA-1069 | Expressions | 1978 | 12.00 |
| ABC/DOT | | | |
| ❑ DOSD-2004 | Don Williams, Vol. III | 1974 | 12.00 |
| ❑ DOSD-2014 | Don Williams, Volume One | 1974 | 12.00 |
| *—Reissue of JMI 4004* | | | |
| ❑ DOSD-2018 | Don Williams, Vol. 2 | 1974 | 12.00 |
| *—Reissue of JMI 4006* | | | |
| ❑ DOSD-2021 | You're My Best Friend | 1975 | 12.00 |
| ❑ DO-2035 | Greatest Hits | 1975 | 12.00 |
| ❑ DO-2049 | Harmony | 1976 | 12.00 |
| ❑ DO-2064 | Visions | 1976 | 12.00 |
| ❑ DO-2088 | I'm Just a Country Boy | 1977 | 12.00 |
| CAPITOL | | | |
| ❑ ST-12440 | New Moves | 1987 | 8.00 |
| ❑ CLT-48034 | Traces | 1988 | 8.00 |
| ❑ C1-91444 | Prime Cuts | 1989 | 8.00 |
| JMI | | | |
| ❑ 4004 | Don Williams, Volume One | 1973 | 25.00 |
| ❑ 4006 | Don Williams, Volume 2 | 1974 | 20.00 |

| Number | Title (A Side/B Side) | Yr | NM |
|---|---|---|---|
| MCA | | | |
| ❑ 1442 | The Best of Don Williams, Vol. 3 | 1985 | 8.00 |
| *—Budget-line reissue* | | | |
| ❑ 3096 | The Best of Don Williams, Vol. 2 | 1979 | 10.00 |
| ❑ 3192 | Portrait | 1980 | 10.00 |
| ❑ 3279 | Expressions | 1980 | 8.00 |
| *—Reissue of ABC 1069* | | | |
| ❑ 5133 | I Believe in You | 1980 | 10.00 |
| ❑ 5210 | Especially for You | 1981 | 10.00 |
| ❑ 5306 | Listen to the Radio | 1982 | 10.00 |
| ❑ 5407 | Yellow Moon | 1983 | 10.00 |
| ❑ 5465 | The Best of Don Williams, Vol. 3 | 1984 | 10.00 |
| ❑ 5493 | Café Carolina | 1984 | 10.00 |
| ❑ 5671 | The Best of Don Williams, Vol. 4 | 1985 | 10.00 |
| ❑ 5697 | Don Williams Sings Bob McDill | 1986 | 10.00 |
| ❑ 5803 | Lovers and Best Friends | 1986 | 10.00 |
| ❑ 37135 | Greatest Hits | 198? | 8.00 |
| *—Budget-line reissue* | | | |
| ❑ 37155 | The Best of Don Williams, Vol. 2 | 198? | 8.00 |
| *—Budget-line reissue* | | | |
| ❑ 37230 | Visions | 198? | 8.00 |
| *—Budget-line reissue* | | | |
| ❑ 37231 | Portrait | 198? | 8.00 |
| *—Budget-line reissue* | | | |
| ❑ 37232 | I'm Just a Country Boy | 198? | 8.00 |
| *—Budget-line reissue* | | | |
| ❑ 37233 | Especially for You | 198? | 8.00 |
| *—Budget-line reissue* | | | |
| ❑ 37234 | I Believe in You | 198? | 8.00 |
| *—Budget-line reissue* | | | |
| RCA | | | |
| ❑ 9656-1-R | One Good Well | 1989 | 10.00 |
| ❑ R 124814 | True Love | 1990 | 15.00 |
| *—BMG Music Service pressing; only US vinyl edition* | | | |
| **WILLIAMS, GEORGE** | | | |
| BRUNSWICK | | | |
| ❑ BL 54020 [M] | The Fox | 1957 | 50.00 |
| RCA VICTOR | | | |
| ❑ LPM-1205 [M] | We Could Make Such Beautiful Music | 1956 | 40.00 |
| ❑ LPM-1301 [M] | Rhythm Was His Business | 1956 | 40.00 |
| **WILLIAMS, HANK** | | | |
| COUNTRY MUSIC FOUNDATION | | | |
| ❑ CMF-006 | Just Me and My Guitar | 198? | 10.00 |
| ❑ CMF-007 | The First Recordings | 198? | 10.00 |

| Number | Title (A Side/B Side) | Yr | NM |
|---|---|---|---|
| **METRO** | | | |
| ❑ M-509 [M] | Hank Williams | 1966 | 20.00 |
| ❑ MS-509 [R] | Hank Williams | 1966 | 12.00 |
| ❑ M-547 [M] | Mr. and Mrs. Hank Williams | 1966 | 20.00 |
| ❑ MS-547 [R] | Mr. and Mrs. Hank Williams | 1966 | 12.00 |
| ❑ M-602 [M] | The Immortal Hank Williams | 1967 | 20.00 |
| ❑ MS-602 [R] | The Immortal Hank Williams | 1967 | 12.00 |
| **MGM** | | | |
| ❑ 3E-2 [(3)M] | 36 of His Greatest Hits | 1957 | 200.00 |
| *—Yellow labels* | | | |
| ❑ 3E-2 [(3)M] | 36 of His Greatest Hits | 1960 | 100.00 |
| *—Black labels* | | | |
| ❑ 3E-4 [(3)M] | Hank Williams Sings 36 More of His Greatest Hits | 1958 | 200.00 |
| *—Yellow labels* | | | |
| ❑ 3E-4 [(3)M] | Hank Williams Sings 36 More of His Greatest Hits | 1960 | 100.00 |
| *—Black labels* | | | |
| ❑ E-107 [10] | Hank Williams Sings | 1952 | 400.00 |
| ❑ E-168 [10] | Moanin' the Blues | 1952 | 400.00 |
| ❑ E-202 [10] | Memorial Album | 1953 | 400.00 |
| ❑ E-203 [10] | Hank Williams as Luke the Drifter | 1953 | 400.00 |
| ❑ SE 240-2 [(2)] | 24 Karat Hits | 1969 | 25.00 |
| ❑ E-242 [10] | Honky Tonkin' | 1954 | 400.00 |
| ❑ E-243 [10] | I Saw the Light | 1954 | 400.00 |
| ❑ E-291 [10] | Ramblin' Man | 1954 | 400.00 |
| ❑ PRO-912 [(3)DJ] | Reflections of Those Who Loved Him | 1975 | 250.00 |
| *—Promo-only box set* | | | |
| ❑ E-3219 [M] | Ramblin' Man | 1955 | 100.00 |
| *—Yellow label* | | | |
| ❑ E-3219 [M] | Ramblin' Man | 1960 | 40.00 |
| *—Black label* | | | |
| ❑ E-3267 [M] | Hank Williams as Luke the Drifter | 1955 | 100.00 |
| *—Yellow label* | | | |
| ❑ E-3267 [M] | Hank Williams as Luke the Drifter | 1960 | 40.00 |
| *—Black label* | | | |
| ❑ E-3272 [M] | Memorial Album | 1955 | 100.00 |
| *—Yellow label* | | | |
| ❑ E-3272 [M] | Memorial Album | 1960 | 40.00 |
| *—Black label* | | | |
| ❑ E-3272 [M] | Memorial Album | 1968 | 20.00 |
| *—Blue and gold label* | | | |
| ❑ E-3330 [M] | Moanin' the Blues | 1956 | 100.00 |
| *—Yellow label* | | | |
| ❑ E-3330 [M] | Moanin' the Blues | 1960 | 40.00 |
| *—Black label* | | | |
| ❑ E-3331 [M] | I Saw the Light | 1956 | 200.00 |
| *—Yellow label; green cover* | | | |
| ❑ E-3331 [M] | I Saw the Light | 1959 | 100.00 |
| *—Yellow label; church on cover* | | | |
| ❑ E-3331 [M] | I Saw the Light | 1960 | 40.00 |
| *—Black label* | | | |
| ❑ SE-3331 [R] | I Saw the Light | 1968 | 12.00 |
| *—Blue and gold label* | | | |
| ❑ E-3412 [M] | Honky Tonkin' | 1957 | 100.00 |
| *—Yellow label* | | | |
| ❑ E-3412 [M] | Honky Tonkin' | 1960 | 40.00 |
| *—Black label* | | | |
| ❑ E-3560 [M] | Sing Me a Blue Song | 1957 | 100.00 |
| *—Yellow label* | | | |
| ❑ E-3560 [M] | Sing Me a Blue Song | 1960 | 40.00 |
| *—Black label* | | | |
| ❑ E-3605 [M] | The Immortal Hank Williams | 1958 | 100.00 |
| *—Yellow label* | | | |
| ❑ E-3605 [M] | The Immortal Hank Williams | 1960 | 40.00 |
| *—Black label* | | | |
| ❑ E-3733 [M] | The Unforgettable Hank Williams | 1959 | 100.00 |
| *—Yellow label* | | | |
| ❑ E-3733 [M] | The Unforgettable Hank Williams | 1960 | 40.00 |
| *—Black label* | | | |
| ❑ SE-3733 [R] | The Unforgettable Hank Williams | 1968 | 12.00 |
| *—Blue and gold label* | | | |
| ❑ E-3803 [M] | The Lonesome Sound of Hank Williams | 1960 | 40.00 |
| ❑ E-3850 [M] | Wait for the Light to Shine | 1960 | 40.00 |
| ❑ SE-3850 [R] | Wait for the Light to Shine | 1968 | 12.00 |
| *—Blue and gold label* | | | |
| ❑ E-3918 [M] | Hank Williams' Greatest Hits | 1961 | 40.00 |
| ❑ SE-3918 [R] | Hank Williams' Greatest Hits | 1963 | 20.00 |
| *—Black label* | | | |
| ❑ SE-3918 [R] | Hank Williams' Greatest Hits | 1968 | 12.00 |
| *—Blue and gold label* | | | |
| ❑ E-3923 [M] | Hank Williams Lives Again | 1961 | 40.00 |
| *—Reissue of E-3272 with new title* | | | |
| ❑ SE-3923 [R] | Hank Williams Lives Again | 1968 | 12.00 |
| *—Blue and gold label* | | | |
| ❑ E-3924 [M] | Let Me Sing a Blue Song | 1961 | 40.00 |
| *—Reissue of E-3560* | | | |
| ❑ SE-3924 [R] | Let Me Sing a Blue Song | 1968 | 12.00 |
| *—Blue and gold label* | | | |
| ❑ E-3925 [M] | Wanderin' Around | 1961 | 40.00 |
| *—Reissue of E-3219* | | | |
| ❑ SE-3925 [R] | Wanderin' Around | 1968 | 12.00 |
| *—Blue and gold label* | | | |
| ❑ E-3926 [M] | I'm Blue Inside | 1961 | 40.00 |
| *—Reissue of E-3330* | | | |
| ❑ SE-3926 [R] | I'm Blue Inside | 1968 | 12.00 |
| *—Blue and gold label* | | | |
| ❑ E-3927 [M] | Hank Williams as Luke the Drifter | 1961 | 40.00 |
| *—Reissue of E-3267* | | | |
| ❑ SE-3927 [R] | Hank Williams as Luke the Drifter | 1968 | 12.00 |
| *—Blue and gold label* | | | |
| ❑ E-3928 [M] | First, Last and Always | 1961 | 40.00 |
| *—Reissue of E-3605* | | | |
| ❑ SE-3928 [R] | First, Last and Always | 1968 | 12.00 |
| *—Blue and gold label* | | | |
| ❑ E-3955 [M] | The Spirit of Hank Williams | 1961 | 40.00 |
| ❑ SE-3955 [R] | The Spirit of Hank Williams | 1968 | 12.00 |
| *—Blue and gold label* | | | |
| ❑ E-3999 [M] | Hank Williams on Stage Recorded Live | 1962 | 40.00 |
| *—Note revised title* | | | |
| ❑ E-3999 [M] | On Stage! Hank Williams Recorded Live | 1962 | 60.00 |
| ❑ SE-3999 [R] | On Stage! Hank Williams Recorded Live | 196? | 20.00 |
| *—Black label* | | | |
| ❑ SE-3999 [R] | Hank Williams on Stage Recorded Live | 1968 | 12.00 |
| *—Blue and gold label* | | | |
| ❑ E-4040 [M] | 14 More of Hank Williams' Greatest Hits — Vol. II | 1962 | 40.00 |
| ❑ SE-4040 [R] | 14 More of Hank Williams' Greatest Hits — Vol. II | 1963 | 15.00 |
| *—Black label* | | | |
| ❑ SE-4040 [R] | Hank Williams' Greatest Hits, Volume 2 | 1968 | 12.00 |
| *—Blue and gold label* | | | |
| ❑ E-4109 [M] | On Stage Volume II/Hank Williams | 1963 | 40.00 |
| ❑ SE-4109 [R] | On Stage Volume II/Hank Williams | 1963 | 20.00 |
| *—Black label* | | | |
| ❑ SE-4109 [R] | On Stage Volume II/Hank Williams | 1968 | 12.00 |
| *—Blue and gold label* | | | |
| ❑ E-4138 [M] | Beyond the Sunset | 1963 | 30.00 |
| ❑ SE-4138 [R] | Beyond the Sunset | 1963 | 15.00 |
| *—Black label* | | | |
| ❑ E-4140 [M] | 14 More of Hank Williams' Greatest Hits (Volume 3) | 1963 | 30.00 |
| ❑ SE-4140 [R] | 14 More of Hank Williams' Greatest Hits (Volume 3) | 1963 | 15.00 |
| *—Black label* | | | |
| ❑ SE-4140 [R] | 14 More of Hank Williams' Greatest Hits (Volume 3) | 1968 | 12.00 |
| *—Blue and gold label* | | | |
| ❑ E-4168 [M] | The Very Best of Hank Williams | 1963 | 30.00 |
| ❑ SE-4168 [R] | The Very Best of Hank Williams | 1963 | 15.00 |
| *—Black label* | | | |
| ❑ SE-4168 [R] | The Very Best of Hank Williams | 1968 | 12.00 |
| *—Blue and gold label* | | | |
| ❑ E-4227 [M] | The Very Best of Hank Williams, Volume 2 | 1964 | 30.00 |
| ❑ SE-4227 [R] | The Very Best of Hank Williams, Volume 2 | 1964 | 15.00 |
| *—Black label* | | | |
| ❑ SE-4227 [R] | The Very Best of Hank Williams, Volume 2 | 1968 | 12.00 |
| *—Blue and gold label* | | | |
| ❑ E-4254 [M] | Lost Highway (and Other Folk Ballads) | 1964 | 40.00 |
| ❑ SE-4254 [R] | Lost Highway (and Other Folk Ballads) | 1964 | 20.00 |
| *—Black label* | | | |
| ❑ SE-4254 [R] | Lost Highway (and Other Folk Ballads) | 1968 | 12.00 |
| *—Blue and gold label* | | | |
| ❑ E-4267-4 [(4)M] | The Hank Williams Story | 1965 | 60.00 |
| ❑ E-4300 [M] | Kaw-Liga and Other Humorous Songs | 1965 | 30.00 |
| ❑ SE-4300 [R] | Kaw-Liga and Other Humorous Songs | 1965 | 15.00 |
| *—Black label* | | | |
| ❑ SE-4300 [R] | Kaw-Liga and Other Humorous Songs | 1968 | 12.00 |
| *—Blue and gold label* | | | |
| ❑ E-4377 [M] | The Legend Lives Anew — Hank Williams with Strings | 1966 | 20.00 |
| ❑ SE-4377 [S] | The Legend Lives Anew — Hank Williams with Strings | 1966 | 25.00 |
| *—Black label* | | | |
| ❑ SE-4377 [S] | The Legend Lives Anew — Hank Williams with Strings | 1968 | 15.00 |
| *—Blue and gold label* | | | |
| ❑ E-4380 [M] | Movin' on — Luke the Drifter | 1966 | 30.00 |
| ❑ SE-4380 [R] | Movin' on — Luke the Drifter | 1968 | 12.00 |
| *—Blue and gold label* | | | |
| ❑ E-4429 [M] | More Hank Williams and Strings | 1966 | 20.00 |
| ❑ SE-4429 [S] | More Hank Williams and Strings | 1966 | 25.00 |
| *—Black label* | | | |
| ❑ SE-4429 [S] | More Hank Williams and Strings | 1968 | 15.00 |
| *—Blue and gold label* | | | |
| ❑ E-4481 [M] | I Won't Be Home No More | 1967 | 30.00 |
| ❑ SE-4481 [S] | I Won't Be Home No More | 1967 | 20.00 |
| *—Black label* | | | |
| ❑ SE-4481 [S] | I Won't Be Home No More | 1968 | 15.00 |
| *—Blue and gold label* | | | |
| ❑ E-4529 [M] | Hank Williams and Strings, Volume 3 | 1968 | 40.00 |
| ❑ SE-4529 [S] | Hank Williams and Strings, Volume 3 | 1968 | 20.00 |
| ❑ E-4576 [M] | Hank Williams in the Beginning | 1968 | 40.00 |
| ❑ SE-4576 [R] | Hank Williams in the Beginning | 1968 | 15.00 |
| ❑ SE-4651 | Essential Hank Williams | 1969 | 12.00 |
| ❑ SE-4680 | Life to Legend | 1970 | 12.00 |
| ❑ SE-4755-2 [(2)] | 24 Greatest Hits | 1971 | 15.00 |
| ❑ M3G-4954 | Archetypes | 1974 | 12.00 |
| ❑ MG-1-5019 | Hank Williams, Sr., Live at the Grand Old Opry | 1976 | 12.00 |
| ❑ MG-2-5401 [(2)] | 24 Greatest Hits, Volume 2 | 197? | 15.00 |
| ❑ ST-90511 [R] | The Very Best of Hank Williams | 1965 | 20.00 |
| *—Capitol Record Club edition* | | | |
| ❑ T-90511 [M] | The Very Best of Hank Williams | 1965 | 40.00 |
| *—Capitol Record Club edition* | | | |
| ❑ ST-90884 [R] | Movin' on — Luke the Drifter | 1968 | 15.00 |
| *—Capitol Record Club edition; blue and gold label* | | | |
| ❑ ST-91115 [S] | The Legend Lives Anew — Hank Williams with Strings | 1968 | 20.00 |
| *—Capitol Record Club edition; blue and gold label* | | | |
| **POLYDOR** | | | |
| ❑ SE-4168 | The Very Best of Hank Williams | 1976 | 8.00 |
| *—Reissue of MGM SE-4168* | | | |
| ❑ 821233-1 [(2)] | 40 Greatest Hits | 1984 | 15.00 |
| ❑ 823291-1 | Hank Williams' Greatest Hits | 1984 | 8.00 |
| ❑ 823292-1 | The Very Best of Hank Williams | 1984 | 8.00 |
| ❑ 823293-1 [(2)] | 24 Greatest Hits | 1984 | 12.00 |
| ❑ 823294-1 [(2)] | 24 Greatest Hits, Volume 2 | 1984 | 12.00 |
| ❑ 823695-1 | Rare Takes and Radio Cuts | 1984 | 10.00 |
| ❑ 825531-1 | On the Air | 1985 | 10.00 |
| ❑ 825548-1 | I Ain't Got Nothin' But Time | 1985 | 10.00 |
| ❑ 825551-1 | Lovesick Blues | 1985 | 10.00 |
| ❑ 825554-1 | Lost Highway | 1986 | 10.00 |
| ❑ 825557-1 | I'm So Lonesome I Could Cry | 1986 | 10.00 |
| ❑ 831574-1 | Beyond the Sunset | 1987 | 10.00 |
| ❑ 831633-1 | Long Gone Lonesome Blues | 1987 | 10.00 |
| ❑ 831634-1 | Hey, Good Lookin' | 1987 | 10.00 |
| ❑ 833749-1 | Let's Turn Back the Years | 1988 | 10.00 |
| ❑ 833752-1 | I Won't Be Home No More | 1988 | 10.00 |
| **TIME-LIFE** | | | |
| ❑ TLCW-01 [(3)] | Country and Western Classics | 1981 | 25.00 |
| ❑ STW-118 | Country Music | 1981 | 10.00 |

## WILLIAMS, HANK /ROY ACUFF

| Number | Title (A Side/B Side) | Yr | NM |
|---|---|---|---|
| **LAMB AND LION** | | | |
| ❑ LL-706 [(3)] | Hank Williams, Sr./Roy Acuff "Collector's Item!" | 197? | 40.00 |
| *—Sides 1-4 are reissues of Hank Williams; side 5-6 are Roy Acuff* | | | |

## WILLIAMS, HANK, AND HANK WILLIAMS, JR.

Also see each artist's individual listings.

| Number | Title (A Side/B Side) | Yr | NM |
|---|---|---|---|
| **MGM** | | | |
| ❑ E-4276 [M] | Father and Son | 1965 | 20.00 |
| ❑ SE-4276 [S] | Father and Son | 1965 | 25.00 |
| ❑ E-4378 [M] | Again | 1966 | 20.00 |
| ❑ SE-4378 [S] | Again | 1966 | 25.00 |
| ❑ 2SES-4865 [(2)] | Hank Williams: The Legend in Story and Song | 1973 | 15.00 |
| ❑ M3HB 4975 [(2)] | Insights Into Hank Williams in Song and Story | 1974 | 15.00 |

## WILLIAMS, HANK, JR.

| Number | Title (A Side/B Side) | Yr | NM |
|---|---|---|---|
| **CAPRICORN** | | | |
| ❑ W1-26806 | Maverick | 1992 | 20.00 |
| *—Columbia House edition (only U.S. vinyl release)* | | | |
| **ELEKTRA** | | | |
| ❑ 6E-194 | Family Tradition | 1979 | 12.00 |
| ❑ 6E-237 | Whiskey Bent and Hell Bound | 1979 | 10.00 |
| ❑ 6E-278 | Habits Old and New | 1980 | 10.00 |
| ❑ 6E-330 | Rowdy | 1981 | 10.00 |
| ❑ 5E-535 | The Pressure Is On | 1981 | 10.00 |
| ❑ 5E-538 | One Night Stands | 1982 | 10.00 |
| *—Reissue* | | | |
| ❑ 5E-539 | The New South | 1982 | 10.00 |
| *—Reissue* | | | |
| ❑ 60100 | High Notes | 1982 | 10.00 |
| ❑ 60193 | Hank Williams, Jr.'s, Greatest Hits | 1982 | 10.00 |
| ❑ 60223 | Strong Stuff | 1983 | 15.00 |
| **MGM** | | | |
| ❑ GAS-119 | Hank Williams, Jr. (Golden Archive Series) | 1970 | 15.00 |
| ❑ E-4213 [M] | Sings the Songs of Hank Williams | 1964 | 20.00 |
| ❑ SE-4213 [S] | Sings the Songs of Hank Williams | 1964 | 25.00 |
| ❑ E-4260 [M] | Your Cheatin' Heart | 1964 | 20.00 |
| ❑ SE-4260 [S] | Your Cheatin' Heart | 1964 | 25.00 |

| Number | Title (A Side/B Side) | Yr | NM |
|---|---|---|---|
| E-4316 [M] | Ballads of the Hills and Plains | 1965 | 20.00 |
| SE-4316 [S] | Ballads of the Hills and Plains | 1965 | 25.00 |
| E-4344 [M] | Blues My Name | 1966 | 20.00 |
| SE-4344 [S] | Blues My Name | 1966 | 25.00 |
| E-4391 [M] | Country Shadows | 1966 | 20.00 |
| SE-4391 [S] | Country Shadows | 1966 | 25.00 |
| E-4428 [M] | My Own Way | 1967 | 20.00 |
| SE-4428 [S] | My Own Way | 1967 | 25.00 |
| E-4513 [M] | The Best of Hank Williams, Jr. | 1967 | 20.00 |
| SE-4513 [S] | The Best of Hank Williams, Jr. | 1967 | 25.00 |
| E-4527 [M] | My Songs | 1968 | 40.00 |
| SE-4527 [S] | My Songs | 1968 | 25.00 |
| SE-4540 | A Time to Sing | 1968 | 25.00 |
| SE-4559 | Luke the Drifter, Jr. | 1969 | 20.00 |
| SE-4621 | Songs My Father Left Me | 1969 | 20.00 |
| SE-4632 | Luke the Drifter, Jr. (Vol. 2) | 1969 | 20.00 |
| SE-4644 | Live at Cobo Hall, Detroit | 1969 | 20.00 |
| SE-4656 | Hank Williams, Jr.'s Greatest Hits | 1970 | 15.00 |
| SE-4657 | Sunday Morning | 1970 | 15.00 |
| SE-4673 | Luke the Drifter, Jr. (Vol. 3) | 1970 | 15.00 |
| SE-4675 | Hank Williams, Jr., Singing My Songs (Johnny Cash) | 1970 | 15.00 |
| SE-4774 | I've Got a Right to Cry/They All Used to Belong to Me | 1971 | 15.00 |
| SE-4798 | Sweet Dreams | 1972 | 12.00 |
| *—With the Mike Curb Congregation* | | | |
| SE-4822 | Hank Williams, Jr.'s Greatest Hits, Volume 2 | 1972 | 12.00 |
| SE-4843 | Eleven Roses | 1972 | 12.00 |
| SE-4862 | After You/Pride's Not Hard to Swallow | 1973 | 12.00 |
| SE-4906 | Just Pickin' — No Singin' | 1973 | 12.00 |
| SE-4936 | The Last Love Song | 1973 | 12.00 |
| M3G-4971 | Living Proof | 1974 | 12.00 |
| M3G-4988 | Bocephus | 1974 | 12.00 |
| MG-1-5009 | Hank Williams, Jr., and Friends | 1975 | 40.00 |
| MG-1-5020 | 14 Greatest Hits | 1976 | 12.00 |
| ST-90695 [S] | Blues My Name | 1966 | 30.00 |
| *—Capitol Record Club edition* | | | |
| T-90695 [M] | Blues My Name | 1966 | 25.00 |
| *—Capitol Record Club edition* | | | |
| T-90925 [M] | Country Shadows | 1966 | 25.00 |
| *—Capitol Record Club edition* | | | |

PAIR

| Number | Title (A Side/B Side) | Yr | NM |
|---|---|---|---|
| PDL2-1164 [(2)] | I'm Walkin' | 1987 | 12.00 |

POLYDOR

| Number | Title (A Side/B Side) | Yr | NM |
|---|---|---|---|
| 811902-1 | Live at Cobo Hall, Detroit | 1983 | 8.00 |
| *—Reissue* | | | |
| 811903-1 | Hank Williams, Jr.'s Greatest Hits | 1983 | 8.00 |
| 811906-1 | Hank Williams, Jr.'s Greatest Hits, Volume 2 | 1983 | 8.00 |
| 825091-1 | 14 Greatest Hits | 1985 | 8.00 |
| 831575-1 | Hank Williams, Jr., and Friends | 1987 | 12.00 |
| 833069-1 | Blues My Name | 1987 | 8.00 |
| 833070-1 | Eleven Roses | 1987 | 8.00 |
| 835132-1 | Standing in the Shadows | 1988 | 8.00 |

WARNER BROS.

| Number | Title (A Side/B Side) | Yr | NM |
|---|---|---|---|
| 6E-194 | Family Tradition | 1983 | 8.00 |
| 6E-237 | Whiskey Bent and Hell Bound | 1983 | 8.00 |
| 6E-278 | Habits Old and New | 1983 | 8.00 |
| 6E-330 | Rowdy | 1983 | 8.00 |
| 5E-535 | The Pressure Is On | 1983 | 8.00 |
| 5E-538 | One Night Stands | 1983 | 8.00 |
| 5E-539 | The New South | 1983 | 8.00 |
| PRO-A-2092 [DJ] | The Hank Williams, Jr., Interview | 1983 | 25.00 |
| BS 2988 | One Night Stands | 1977 | 12.00 |
| BS 3127 | The New South | 1977 | 12.00 |
| 23924 | Man of Steel | 1983 | 10.00 |
| 25088 | Major Moves | 1984 | 10.00 |
| 25267 | Five-O | 1985 | 10.00 |
| 25328 | Greatest Hits — Volume 2 | 1985 | 8.00 |
| 25412 | Montana Café | 1986 | 8.00 |
| 25514 [(2)] | The Early Years | 1984 | 12.00 |
| 25538 | Hank "Live" | 1987 | 8.00 |
| 25593 | Born to Boogie | 1987 | 8.00 |
| 25725 | Wild Streak | 1988 | 8.00 |
| 25834 | Greatest Hits III | 1989 | 8.00 |
| 26090 | Lone Wolf | 1990 | 12.00 |
| 60100 | High Notes | 1983 | 8.00 |
| 60193 | Hank Williams, Jr.'s, Greatest Hits | 1983 | 8.00 |
| 60223 | Strong Stuff | 1983 | 10.00 |
| R 120612 | America (The Way I See It) | 1990 | 20.00 |
| *—BMG Music Service edition (no regular vinyl release)* | | | |
| R 160351 | Pure Hank | 1991 | 20.00 |
| *—BMG Music Service edition (no regular vinyl release)* | | | |

### WILLIAMS, HANK, JR., AND LOIS JOHNSON

MGM

| Number | Title (A Side/B Side) | Yr | NM |
|---|---|---|---|
| SE-4721 | Removing the Shadow | 1971 | 15.00 |
| *—The label has the word "Shadows" instead of "Shadow"* | | | |
| SE-4750 | All for the Love of Sunshine | 1971 | 20.00 |
| SE-4857 | Send Me Some Lovin'/Whole Lotta Lovin' | 1972 | 20.00 |

### WILLIAMS, HERBIE

WORKSHOP JAZZ

| Number | Title (A Side/B Side) | Yr | NM |
|---|---|---|---|
| WSJ-216 [M] | The Soul and Sound of Herbie Williams | 1963 | 60.00 |

### WILLIAMS, JOE

RCA VICTOR

| Number | Title (A Side/B Side) | Yr | NM |
|---|---|---|---|
| LPM-2713 [M] | Jump for Joy | 1963 | 25.00 |
| LSP-2713 [S] | Jump for Joy | 1963 | 30.00 |
| LPM-2762 [M] | Joe Williams at Newport '63 | 1963 | 25.00 |
| LSP-2762 [S] | Joe Williams at Newport '63 | 1963 | 30.00 |
| LPM-2879 [M] | Me and the Blues | 1964 | 25.00 |
| LSP-2879 [S] | Me and the Blues | 1964 | 30.00 |
| LPM-3433 [M] | The Song Is You | 1965 | 20.00 |
| LSP-3433 [S] | The Song Is You | 1965 | 25.00 |
| LPM-3461 [M] | The Exciting Joe Williams | 1965 | 20.00 |
| LSP-3461 [S] | The Exciting Joe Williams | 1965 | 25.00 |

REGENT

| Number | Title (A Side/B Side) | Yr | NM |
|---|---|---|---|
| MG-6002 [M] | Everyday | 1956 | 50.00 |

ROULETTE

| Number | Title (A Side/B Side) | Yr | NM |
|---|---|---|---|
| R-52005 [M] | A Man Ain't Supposed to Cry | 1958 | 30.00 |
| SR-52005 [S] | A Man Ain't Supposed to Cry | 1958 | 40.00 |
| R-52030 [M] | Joe Williams Sings About You! | 1959 | 30.00 |
| SR-52030 [S] | Joe Williams Sings About You! | 1959 | 40.00 |
| R-52039 [M] | That Kind of Woman | 1960 | 30.00 |
| SR-52039 [S] | That Kind of Woman | 1960 | 40.00 |
| R-52066 [M] | Sentimental and Melancholy | 1961 | 30.00 |
| SR-52066 [S] | Sentimental and Melancholy | 1961 | 40.00 |
| R-52069 [M] | Together | 1961 | 30.00 |
| SR-52069 [S] | Together | 1961 | 40.00 |
| *—With Harry "Sweets" Edison* | | | |
| R-52071 [M] | Have a Good Time with Joe Williams | 1961 | 30.00 |
| SR-52071 [S] | Have a Good Time with Joe Williams | 1961 | 40.00 |
| R-52085 [M] | Swingin' Night at Birdland | 1962 | 25.00 |
| SR-52085 [S] | Swingin' Night at Birdland | 1962 | 30.00 |
| R-52102 [M] | One Is a Lonesome Number | 1963 | 25.00 |
| SR-52102 [S] | One Is a Lonesome Number | 1963 | 30.00 |
| R-52105 [M] | New Kind of Love | 1964 | 25.00 |
| SR-52105 [S] | New Kind of Love | 1964 | 30.00 |

SOLID STATE

| Number | Title (A Side/B Side) | Yr | NM |
|---|---|---|---|
| SM-17008 [M] | Presenting Joe Williams and the Jazz Orchestra | 1967 | 25.00 |
| SS-18008 [S] | Presenting Joe Williams and the Jazz Orchestra | 1967 | 20.00 |
| SS-18015 [S] | Something Old, New and Blue | 1968 | 20.00 |

### WILLIAMS, JOHN

EMARCY

| Number | Title (A Side/B Side) | Yr | NM |
|---|---|---|---|
| MG-26047 [10] | John Williams | 1955 | 100.00 |
| MG-36061 [M] | John Williams Trio | 1956 | 50.00 |

### WILLIAMS, JOHN TOWNER

BETHLEHEM

| Number | Title (A Side/B Side) | Yr | NM |
|---|---|---|---|
| BCP-6025 [M] | World on a String | 1958 | 50.00 |

### WILLIAMS, KEITH

EDISON INTERNATIONAL

| Number | Title (A Side/B Side) | Yr | NM |
|---|---|---|---|
| 501 [M] | Big Band Jazz Themes | 1960 | 20.00 |
| SDP-501 [S] | Big Band Jazz Themes | 1960 | 25.00 |

LIBERTY

| Number | Title (A Side/B Side) | Yr | NM |
|---|---|---|---|
| LRP-3040 [M] | The Dazzling Sound | 1957 | 25.00 |

### WILLIAMS, LARRY

CHESS

| Number | Title (A Side/B Side) | Yr | NM |
|---|---|---|---|
| LP-1457 [M] | Larry Williams | 1961 | 200.00 |

OKEH

| Number | Title (A Side/B Side) | Yr | NM |
|---|---|---|---|
| OKM-12123 [M] | Larry Williams' Greatest Hits | 1967 | 30.00 |
| OKS-14123 [S] | Larry Williams' Greatest Hits | 1967 | 40.00 |

SPECIALTY

| Number | Title (A Side/B Side) | Yr | NM |
|---|---|---|---|
| SP-2109 [M] | Here's Larry Williams | 1959 | 200.00 |
| *—Original pressing on thick vinyl with no copyright information on back cover* | | | |
| SP-2109 [M] | Here's Larry Williams | 198? | 10.00 |
| *—Reissue with thinner vinyl and copyright information on back* | | | |
| SP-7002 [(2)] | Bad Boy | 1990 | 20.00 |

### WILLIAMS, LAWTON

MEGA

| Number | Title (A Side/B Side) | Yr | NM |
|---|---|---|---|
| 1004 | Between Truck Stops | 1971 | 12.00 |

### WILLIAMS, LOIS

STARDAY

| Number | Title (A Side/B Side) | Yr | NM |
|---|---|---|---|
| SLP-448 | A Girl Named Sam | 1970 | 20.00 |

### WILLIAMS, LUCINDA

FOLKWAYS

| Number | Title (A Side/B Side) | Yr | NM |
|---|---|---|---|
| 31066 | Ramblin' on My Mind | 1979 | 200.00 |
| *—As "Lucinda"* | | | |
| 31067 | Happy Woman Blues | 1980 | 150.00 |
| *—As "Lucinda"* | | | |

LOST HIGHWAY

| Number | Title (A Side/B Side) | Yr | NM |
|---|---|---|---|
| B0002368-01 [(3)] | Live @ the Fillmore | 2005 | 20.00 |
| B0006398-01 [(2)] | West | 2007 | 15.00 |
| 088 170255-1 | World Without Tears | 2003 | 15.00 |

ROUGH TRADE

| Number | Title (A Side/B Side) | Yr | NM |
|---|---|---|---|
| 66 [EP] | Passionate Kisses | 1989 | 10.00 |

SMITHSONIAN/FOLKWAYS

| Number | Title (A Side/B Side) | Yr | NM |
|---|---|---|---|
| 40003 | Happy Woman Blues | 1990 | 12.00 |
| *—Reissue* | | | |

### WILLIAMS, MARY LOU

ASCH

| Number | Title (A Side/B Side) | Yr | NM |
|---|---|---|---|
| ALP-345 [10] | Mary Lou Williams Trio | 1950 | 200.00 |

ATLANTIC

| Number | Title (A Side/B Side) | Yr | NM |
|---|---|---|---|
| ALR-114 [10] | Piano Panorama, Volume 2 | 1951 | 120.00 |

CIRCLE

| Number | Title (A Side/B Side) | Yr | NM |
|---|---|---|---|
| 412 [10] | Piano Contempo | 1951 | 120.00 |

CONCERT HALL JAZZ

| Number | Title (A Side/B Side) | Yr | NM |
|---|---|---|---|
| 1007 [10] | A Keyboard History | 1955 | 50.00 |

CONTEMPORARY

| Number | Title (A Side/B Side) | Yr | NM |
|---|---|---|---|
| C-2507 [10] | Piano '53 | 1953 | 100.00 |

EMARCY

| Number | Title (A Side/B Side) | Yr | NM |
|---|---|---|---|
| MG-26033 [10] | Mary Lou | 1954 | 100.00 |

FOLKWAYS

| Number | Title (A Side/B Side) | Yr | NM |
|---|---|---|---|
| FP-32 [10] | Rehearsal — Jazz Session/ Footnotes to Jazz, Vol. 3 | 1951 | 100.00 |

JAZZTONE

| Number | Title (A Side/B Side) | Yr | NM |
|---|---|---|---|
| J-1206 [M] | A Keyboard History | 1955 | 40.00 |

KING

| Number | Title (A Side/B Side) | Yr | NM |
|---|---|---|---|
| 295-85 [10] | Progressive Piano Stylings | 1953 | 150.00 |

MARY

| Number | Title (A Side/B Side) | Yr | NM |
|---|---|---|---|
| 32843 [M] | Black Christ of the Andes | 1964 | 25.00 |
| 32843 [S] | Black Christ of the Andes | 1964 | 30.00 |
| 282489 [M] | Music for Peace | 1964 | 25.00 |
| 282489 [S] | Music for Peace | 1964 | 30.00 |

STINSON

| Number | Title (A Side/B Side) | Yr | NM |
|---|---|---|---|
| SLP-24 [10] | Mary Lou Williams | 1950 | 150.00 |
| SLP-24 [M] | Mary Lou Williams | 195? | 30.00 |
| SLP-29 [10] | Jazz Variation | 1950 | 150.00 |

### WILLIAMS, MARY LOU/RALPH BURNS

JAZZTONE

| Number | Title (A Side/B Side) | Yr | NM |
|---|---|---|---|
| J-1255 [M] | Composers — Pianists | 1956 | 40.00 |

### WILLIAMS, MARY LOU, AND DON BYAS/BUCK CLAYTON AND ALIX COMBELLE

STORYVILLE

| Number | Title (A Side/B Side) | Yr | NM |
|---|---|---|---|
| STLP-906 [M] | Messin' 'Round in Montmarte | 1956 | 50.00 |

### WILLIAMS, MASON

AMERICAN GRAMAPHONE

| Number | Title (A Side/B Side) | Yr | NM |
|---|---|---|---|
| AG-800 | Classical Gas | 1987 | 10.00 |
| *—With Mannheim Steamroller* | | | |

EVEREST

| Number | Title (A Side/B Side) | Yr | NM |
|---|---|---|---|
| 3265 | Listening Matter | 1969 | 12.00 |

FLYING FISH

| Number | Title (A Side/B Side) | Yr | NM |
|---|---|---|---|
| FF-059 | Fresh Fish | 1978 | 10.00 |

VEE JAY

| Number | Title (A Side/B Side) | Yr | NM |
|---|---|---|---|
| VJ-1103 [M] | Them Poems and Things | 1964 | 20.00 |
| VJS-1103 [S] | Them Poems and Things | 1964 | 25.00 |

WARNER BROS.

| Number | Title (A Side/B Side) | Yr | NM |
|---|---|---|---|
| W 1729 [M] | The Mason Williams Phonograph Record | 1968 | 25.00 |
| *—Mono is white label promo only* | | | |
| WS 1729 | The Mason Williams Phonograph Record | 1970 | 10.00 |
| *—Green label with "WB" logo* | | | |
| WS 1729 | The Mason Williams Phonograph Record | 1973 | 8.00 |
| *—"Burbank" palm trees label* | | | |
| WS 1729 | The Mason Williams Phonograph Record | 1979 | 6.00 |
| *—White or tan label* | | | |
| WS 1729 [S] | The Mason Williams Phonograph Record | 1968 | 12.00 |
| *—Green label with "W7" logo* | | | |
| WS 1776 | The Mason Williams Ear Show | 1968 | 12.00 |
| WS 1788 | Music by Mason Williams | 1969 | 12.00 |
| WS 1838 | Hand Made | 1970 | 12.00 |
| WS 1941 | Sharepickers | 1971 | 12.00 |

### WILLIAMS, MAURICE, AND THE ZODIACS

COLLECTABLES

| Number | Title (A Side/B Side) | Yr | NM |
|---|---|---|---|
| COL-5021 | The Best of Maurice Williams and the Zodiacs | 198? | 10.00 |

HERALD

| Number | Title (A Side/B Side) | Yr | NM |
|---|---|---|---|
| HLP-1014 [M] | Stay | 1961 | 500.00 |

RELIC

| Number | Title (A Side/B Side) | Yr | NM |
|---|---|---|---|
| 5017 | Greatest Hits | 197? | 15.00 |

SNYDER

| Number | Title (A Side/B Side) | Yr | NM |
|---|---|---|---|
| 5586 [M] | At the Beach | 196? | 100.00 |

| Number | Title (A Side/B Side) | Yr | NM |
|---|---|---|---|
| **SPHERE SOUND** | | | |
| ❑ SR-7007 [M] | Stay | 1965 | 120.00 |
| ❑ SSR-7007 [R] | Stay | 1965 | 80.00 |

## WILLIAMS, MEL

| Number | Title (A Side/B Side) | Yr | NM |
|---|---|---|---|
| **DIG** | | | |
| ❑ LP-103 [M] | All Thru the Night | 1956 | 600.00 |

## WILLIAMS, OTIS, AND HIS CHARMS

| Number | Title (A Side/B Side) | Yr | NM |
|---|---|---|---|
| **DELUXE** | | | |
| ❑ 570 [M] | Their All Time Hits | 1957 | 1000. |
| **KING** | | | |
| ❑ 570 [M] | Their All Time Hits | 1957 | 600.00 |
| ❑ 614 [M] | This Is Otis Williams and His Charms | 1959 | 400.00 |
| **STOP** | | | |
| ❑ STLP-1022 | Otis Williams and the Midnight Cowboys | 1971 | 25.00 |

## WILLIAMS, RICHARD

| Number | Title (A Side/B Side) | Yr | NM |
|---|---|---|---|
| **CANDID** | | | |
| ❑ CD-8003 [M] | New Horn in Town | 1960 | 40.00 |
| ❑ CS-9003 [S] | New Horn in Town | 1960 | 50.00 |

## WILLIAMS, ROBERT PETE

| Number | Title (A Side/B Side) | Yr | NM |
|---|---|---|---|
| **BLUESVILLE** | | | |
| ❑ BVLP-1026 [M] | Free Again | 1961 | 100.00 |
| *—Blue label, silver print* | | | |
| ❑ BVLP-1026 [M] | Free Again | 1964 | 30.00 |
| *—Blue label with trident logo* | | | |
| **FOLK/LYRIC** | | | |
| ❑ FL-109 [M] | Prison Blues | 1960 | 100.00 |

## WILLIAMS, ROGER

| Number | Title (A Side/B Side) | Yr | NM |
|---|---|---|---|
| **BAINBRIDGE** | | | |
| ❑ 6265 | Somewhere in Time | 1986 | 10.00 |
| ❑ 8002 [(2)] | Ivory Impact | 1982 | 12.00 |
| **HOLIDAY** | | | |
| ❑ HDY 1927 | Golden Christmas | 1981 | 8.00 |
| **KAPP** | | | |
| ❑ KLE-1 [(3)M] | 10th Anniversary/Limited Edition | 1964 | 20.00 |
| *—Reissue of Kapp 1088, 1130 and 1172 in one package* | | | |
| ❑ SKLE-1 [(3)S] | 10th Anniversary/Limited Edition | 1964 | 25.00 |
| ❑ KL-3 [M] | By Special Request | 196? | 12.00 |
| *—Columbia Record Club exclusive* | | | |
| ❑ KL-4 [M] | By Special Request, Vol. 2 | 196? | 12.00 |
| *—Columbia Record Club exclusive* | | | |
| ❑ KW-900 [M] | Roger Williams Showcase | 196? | 12.00 |
| ❑ SKW-900 [S] | Roger Williams Showcase | 196? | 15.00 |
| ❑ KL-1003 [M] | The Boy Next Door | 1955 | 25.00 |
| *—Maroon and silver (or blue and silver) labels* | | | |
| ❑ KL-1003 [M] | The Boy Next Door | 1962 | 12.00 |
| *—Any later label variation* | | | |
| ❑ KL-1008 [M] | It's a Big, Wide, Wonderful World | 1955 | 25.00 |
| *—Maroon and silver (or blue and silver) labels* | | | |
| ❑ KL-1008 [M] | It's a Big, Wide, Wonderful World | 1962 | 12.00 |
| *—Any later label variation* | | | |
| ❑ KL-1012 [M] | Autumn Leaves | 1956 | 20.00 |
| *—Retitled version of above; maroon and silver (or blue and silver) label* | | | |
| ❑ KL-1012 [M] | Roger Williams | 1956 | 25.00 |
| ❑ KL-1012 [M] | Autumn Leaves | 1962 | 12.00 |
| *—Any later label variation* | | | |
| ❑ KL-1031 [M] | Daydreams | 1956 | 15.00 |
| *—Maroon and silver (or blue and silver) label* | | | |
| ❑ KL-1031 [M] | Daydreams | 1962 | 12.00 |
| *—Any later label variation* | | | |
| ❑ KL-1040 [M] | Roger Williams Plays the Wonderful Music of the Masters | 1956 | 15.00 |
| *—Maroon and silver (or blue and silver) label* | | | |
| ❑ KL-1040 [M] | Roger Williams Plays the Wonderful Music of the Masters | 1962 | 12.00 |
| *—Any later label variation* | | | |
| ❑ KL-1042 [M] | Roger Williams Plays Christmas Songs | 1956 | 15.00 |
| *—Maroon and silver label; unbanded* | | | |
| ❑ KL-1062 [M] | Roger Williams Plays Beautiful Waltzes | 1957 | 15.00 |
| *—Maroon and silver (or blue and silver) label* | | | |
| ❑ KL-1062 [M] | Roger Williams Plays Beautiful Waltzes | 1962 | 12.00 |
| *—Any later label variation* | | | |
| ❑ KL-1063 [M] | Almost Paradise | 1957 | 15.00 |
| *—Maroon and silver (or blue and silver) label* | | | |
| ❑ KL-1063 [M] | Almost Paradise | 1962 | 12.00 |
| *—Any later label variation* | | | |
| ❑ K-1081-S [S] | Till | 1959 | 20.00 |
| *—Maroon and silver (or blue and silver) labels* | | | |
| ❑ KL-1081 [M] | Till | 1958 | 15.00 |
| *—Maroon and silver (or blue and silver) label* | | | |
| ❑ KL-1081 [M] | Till | 1962 | 12.00 |
| *—Any later label variation* | | | |
| ❑ KS-1081 [S] | Till | 1962 | 15.00 |
| *—Any later label variation* | | | |
| ❑ KL-1088 [M] | Roger Williams Plays Gershwin | 1958 | 15.00 |
| *—Maroon and silver (or blue and silver) labels* | | | |
| ❑ KL-1088 [M] | Roger Williams Plays Gershwin | 1962 | 12.00 |
| *—Any later label variation* | | | |
| ❑ KL-1112 [M] | Near You | 1959 | 15.00 |
| *—Maroon and silver (or blue and silver) labels* | | | |
| ❑ KL-1112 [M] | Near You | 1962 | 12.00 |
| *—Any later label variation* | | | |
| ❑ KS-1112 [S] | Near You | 1959 | 20.00 |
| *—Maroon and silver (or blue and silver) labels* | | | |
| ❑ KS-1112 [S] | Near You | 1962 | 15.00 |
| *—Any later label variation* | | | |
| ❑ KL-1130 [M] | More Songs of the Fabulous Fifties | 1959 | 15.00 |
| *—Maroon and silver (or blue and silver) labels* | | | |
| ❑ KL-1130 [M] | More Songs of the Fabulous Fifties | 1962 | 12.00 |
| *—Any later label variation* | | | |
| ❑ KL-1147 [M] | With These Hands | 1959 | 15.00 |
| *—Maroon and silver (or blue and silver) labels* | | | |
| ❑ KL-1147 [M] | With These Hands | 1962 | 12.00 |
| *—Any later label variation* | | | |
| ❑ KL-1164 [M] | Christmas Time | 1959 | 15.00 |
| *—"Merry Christmas" silver, red and green label* | | | |
| ❑ KL-1164 [M] | Christmas Time | 1962 | 12.00 |
| *—Any later label variation* | | | |
| ❑ KL-1172 [M] | Always | 1960 | 15.00 |
| *—Maroon and silver (or blue and silver) labels* | | | |
| ❑ KL-1172 [M] | Always | 1962 | 12.00 |
| *—Any later label variation* | | | |
| ❑ KL-1207 [M] | Songs of the Fabulous Forties, Volume 1 | 1960 | 12.00 |
| ❑ KL-1208 [M] | Songs of the Fabulous Forties, Volume 2 | 1960 | 12.00 |
| ❑ KL-1209 [M] | Songs of the Fabulous Fifties, Volume 1 | 1960 | 12.00 |
| ❑ KL-1210 [M] | Songs of the Fabulous Fifties, Volume 2 | 1960 | 12.00 |
| ❑ KL-1211 [M] | Songs of the Fabulous Century, Volume 1 | 1960 | 12.00 |
| ❑ KL-1212 [M] | Songs of the Fabulous Century, Volume 2 | 1960 | 12.00 |
| ❑ KL-1217 [M] | Temptation | 1960 | 15.00 |
| *—Maroon and silver (or blue and silver) labels* | | | |
| ❑ KL-1217 [M] | Temptation | 1962 | 12.00 |
| *—Any later label variation* | | | |
| ❑ KL-1222 [M] | Roger Williams Invites You to Dance | 1961 | 15.00 |
| ❑ KL-1244 [M] | Yellow Bird | 1961 | 15.00 |
| ❑ KL-1251 [M] | Songs of the Soaring '60s | 1961 | 15.00 |
| ❑ KL-1260 [M] | Greatest Hits | 1962 | 12.00 |
| ❑ KL-1266 [M] | Maria | 1962 | 12.00 |
| ❑ KL-1290 [M] | Mr. Piano | 1962 | 12.00 |
| ❑ KL-1305 [M] | Country Style | 1963 | 12.00 |
| ❑ KL-1336 [M] | For You | 1963 | 12.00 |
| ❑ KL-1354 [M] | The Solid Gold Steinway | 1964 | 12.00 |
| ❑ KL-1395 [M] | Family Album of Hymns | 1964 | 10.00 |
| ❑ KL-1406 [M] | Academy Award Winners | 1964 | 10.00 |
| ❑ KL-1414 [M] | Roger Williams Plays the Hits | 1965 | 10.00 |
| ❑ KL-1434 [M] | Summer Wind | 1965 | 10.00 |
| ❑ KL-1452 [M] | Autumn Leaves — 1965 | 1965 | 10.00 |
| ❑ KL-1470 [M] | I'll Remember You | 1966 | 10.00 |
| ❑ KL-1483 [M] | Academy Award Winners, Vol. 2 | 1966 | 10.00 |
| ❑ KL-1501 [M] | Born Free | 1966 | 10.00 |
| ❑ KL-1512 [M] | Roger! | 1967 | 10.00 |
| ❑ KL-1530 [M] | Roger Williams/Golden Hits | 1967 | 12.00 |
| ❑ KS-3000 [S] | Waltzes in Stereo | 1959 | 20.00 |
| *—Maroon and silver (or blue and silver) labels* | | | |
| ❑ KS-3000 [S] | Waltzes in Stereo | 1962 | 15.00 |
| *—Any later label variation* | | | |
| ❑ KS-3013 [S] | More Songs of the Fabulous Fifties | 1959 | 20.00 |
| *—Maroon and silver (or blue and silver) labels* | | | |
| ❑ KS-3013 [S] | More Songs of the Fabulous Fifties | 1962 | 15.00 |
| *—Any later label variation* | | | |
| ❑ KS-3030 [S] | With These Hands | 1959 | 20.00 |
| *—Maroon and silver (or blue and silver) labels* | | | |
| ❑ KS-3030 [S] | With These Hands | 1962 | 15.00 |
| *—Any later label variation* | | | |
| ❑ KS-3048 [S] | Christmas Time | 1959 | 20.00 |
| ❑ KS-3056 [S] | Always | 1960 | 20.00 |
| *—Maroon and silver (or blue and silver) labels* | | | |
| ❑ KS-3056 [S] | Always | 1962 | 15.00 |
| *—Any later label variation* | | | |
| ❑ KS-3164 [S] | Christmas Time | 196? | 12.00 |
| *—Reissue of KS-3048 (new cover, no gatefold)* | | | |
| ❑ KS-3207 [S] | Songs of the Fabulous Forties, Volume 1 | 1960 | 15.00 |
| ❑ KS-3208 [S] | Songs of the Fabulous Forties, Volume 2 | 1960 | 15.00 |
| ❑ KS-3209 [S] | Songs of the Fabulous Fifties, Volume 1 | 1960 | 15.00 |
| ❑ KS-3210 [S] | Songs of the Fabulous Fifties, Volume 2 | 1960 | 15.00 |
| ❑ KS-3211 [S] | Songs of the Fabulous Century, Volume 1 | 1960 | 15.00 |
| ❑ KS-3212 [S] | Songs of the Fabulous Century, Volume 2 | 1960 | 15.00 |
| ❑ KS-3217 [S] | Temptation | 1960 | 20.00 |
| ❑ KS-3222 [S] | Roger Williams Invites You to Dance | 1961 | 20.00 |
| ❑ KS-3244 [S] | Yellow Bird | 1961 | 20.00 |
| ❑ KS-3251 [S] | Songs of the Soaring '60s | 1961 | 20.00 |
| ❑ KS-3260 [S] | Greatest Hits | 1962 | 15.00 |
| ❑ KS-3266 [S] | Maria | 1962 | 15.00 |
| ❑ KS-3290 [S] | Mr. Piano | 1962 | 15.00 |
| ❑ KS-3305 [S] | Country Style | 1963 | 15.00 |
| ❑ KS-3336 [S] | For You | 1963 | 15.00 |
| ❑ KS-3354 [S] | The Solid Gold Steinway | 1964 | 15.00 |
| ❑ KS-3395 [S] | Family Album of Hymns | 1964 | 12.00 |
| ❑ KS-3406 [S] | Academy Award Winners | 1964 | 12.00 |
| ❑ KS-3414 [S] | Roger Williams Plays the Hits | 1965 | 12.00 |
| ❑ KS-3434 [S] | Summer Wind | 1965 | 12.00 |
| ❑ KS-3452 [S] | Autumn Leaves — 1965 | 1965 | 12.00 |
| ❑ KS-3470 [S] | I'll Remember You | 1966 | 12.00 |
| ❑ KS-3483 [S] | Academy Award Winners, Vol. 2 | 1966 | 12.00 |
| ❑ KS-3501 [S] | Born Free | 1966 | 12.00 |
| ❑ KS-3512 [S] | Roger! | 1967 | 12.00 |
| ❑ KS-3530 [S] | Roger Williams/Golden Hits | 1967 | 12.00 |
| ❑ KS-3549 | Amore | 1968 | 12.00 |
| ❑ KS-3550 | More Than a Miracle | 1968 | 12.00 |
| ❑ KS-3565 | Only for Lovers | 1969 | 12.00 |
| ❑ KS-3595 | Happy Heart | 1969 | 12.00 |
| ❑ KS-3610 | Love Theme from "Romeo and Juliet" | 1969 | 12.00 |
| ❑ KS-3629 | Themes from Great Movies | 1970 | 12.00 |
| ❑ KS-3638 | Roger Williams/Golden Hits, Volume 2 | 1970 | 12.00 |
| ❑ KS-3645 | Love Story | 1971 | 10.00 |
| ❑ KS-3650 | Summer of '42 | 1971 | 10.00 |
| ❑ KS-3665 | Love Theme from "The Godfather" | 1972 | 10.00 |
| ❑ KS-3671 | Play Me | 1972 | 10.00 |
| ❑ KXL-5000 [(2)M] | Songs of the Fabulous Fifties | 1957 | 20.00 |
| *—Maroon and silver (or blue and silver) labels* | | | |
| ❑ KXL-5000 [(2)M] | Songs of the Fabulous Fifties | 1962 | 15.00 |
| *—Any later label variation* | | | |
| ❑ KXS-5000 [(2)S] | Songs of the Fabulous Fifties | 1959 | 25.00 |
| *—Maroon and silver (or blue and silver) labels* | | | |
| ❑ KXS-5000 [(2)S] | Songs of the Fabulous Fifties | 1962 | 20.00 |
| *—Any later label variation* | | | |
| ❑ KXL-5003 [(2)M] | Songs of the Fabulous Forties | 1957 | 20.00 |
| *—Maroon and silver (or blue and silver) labels* | | | |
| ❑ KXL-5003 [(2)M] | Songs of the Fabulous Forties | 1962 | 15.00 |
| *—Any later label variation* | | | |
| ❑ KXS-5003 [(2)S] | Songs of the Fabulous Forties | 1959 | 25.00 |
| *—Maroon and silver (or blue and silver) labels* | | | |
| ❑ KXS-5003 [(2)S] | Songs of the Fabulous Forties | 1962 | 20.00 |
| *—Any later label variation* | | | |
| ❑ KXL-5005 [(2)M] | Songs of the Fabulous Century | 195? | 20.00 |
| *—Maroon and silver (or blue and silver) labels* | | | |
| ❑ KXL-5005 [(2)M] | Songs of the Fabulous Century | 1962 | 15.00 |
| *—Any later label variation* | | | |
| ❑ KXS-5005 [(2)S] | Songs of the Fabulous Century | 1959 | 25.00 |
| *—Maroon and silver (or blue and silver) labels* | | | |
| ❑ KXS-5005 [(2)S] | Songs of the Fabulous Century | 1962 | 20.00 |
| *—Any later label variation* | | | |
| ❑ KXL-5008 [(2)M] | Tonight! Roger Williams at Town Hall | 196? | 20.00 |
| ❑ KXS-5008 [(2)S] | Tonight! Roger Williams at Town Hall | 196? | 25.00 |
| **MCA** | | | |
| ❑ 63 | Greatest Hits | 1973 | 8.00 |
| *—Reissue of Kapp 3260* | | | |
| ❑ 64 | Roger Williams/Golden Hits | 1973 | 8.00 |
| *—Reissue of Kapp 3530* | | | |
| ❑ 68 | Roger Williams/Golden Hits, Volume 2 | 1973 | 8.00 |
| *—Reissue of Kapp 3638* | | | |
| ❑ 71 | Somewhere My Love | 1973 | 8.00 |
| *—Retitled reissue of unknown Kapp LP* | | | |
| ❑ 76 | Play Me | 1973 | 8.00 |
| *—Reissue of Kapp 3671* | | | |
| ❑ 324 | Last Tango in Paris | 1973 | 10.00 |
| ❑ 378 | Live | 1973 | 10.00 |
| ❑ 403 | The Way We Were | 1974 | 10.00 |
| ❑ 438 | I Honestly Love You | 1974 | 10.00 |
| ❑ 539 | Family Album of Hymns | 1975 | 8.00 |
| *—Reissue of Kapp 3395* | | | |
| ❑ 542 | Somewhere My Love | 1975 | 6.00 |
| *—Reissue of MCA 71* | | | |
| ❑ 2175 | Virtuoso | 1975 | 10.00 |
| ❑ 2237 | Nadia's Theme | 1976 | 10.00 |
| ❑ 2279 | Evergreen | 1977 | 10.00 |
| ❑ 4106 [(2)] | The Best of Roger Williams | 197? | 12.00 |
| ❑ 5574 | To Amadeus With Love | 1985 | 10.00 |
| ❑ 15005 | Christmas Time | 197? | 8.00 |
| *—Reissue of Kapp material* | | | |
| ❑ 20202 | Autumn Leaves | 198? | 8.00 |
| *—Reissue of Kapp material* | | | |
| **PICKWICK** | | | |
| ❑ PTP-2086 [(2)] | Roger Williams at the Piano | 197? | 12.00 |
| ❑ SPC-3367 | Spanish Eyes | 197? | 8.00 |

| Number | Title (A Side/B Side) | Yr | NM |
|---|---|---|---|
| ❑ SPC-3511 | Sunrise, Sunset | 197? | 8.00 |
| **VOCALION** | | | |
| ❑ VL 73918 | Moments to Remember | 1970 | 10.00 |

### WILLIAMS, TEX

| Number | Title (A Side/B Side) | Yr | NM |
|---|---|---|---|
| **BOONE** | | | |
| ❑ LP-1210 [M] | The Two Sides of Tex Williams | 1966 | 20.00 |
| ❑ LSP-1210 [S] | The Two Sides of Tex Williams | 1966 | 25.00 |
| **CAPITOL** | | | |
| ❑ ST 1463 [S] | Smoke! Smoke! Smoke! | 1960 | 40.00 |
| ❑ T 1463 [M] | Smoke! Smoke! Smoke! | 1960 | 30.00 |
| **DECCA** | | | |
| ❑ DL 4295 [M] | Country Music Time | 1962 | 20.00 |
| ❑ DL 5565 [10] | Dance-O-Rama #5 | 1955 | 300.00 |
| ❑ DL 74295 [S] | Country Music Time | 1962 | 30.00 |
| **IMPERIAL** | | | |
| ❑ LP-9309 [M] | The Voice of Authority | 1966 | 20.00 |
| ❑ LP-12309 [S] | The Voice of Authority | 1966 | 25.00 |
| **LIBERTY** | | | |
| ❑ LRP-3304 [M] | Tex Williams in Las Vegas | 1963 | 20.00 |
| ❑ LST-7304 [S] | Tex Williams in Las Vegas | 1963 | 30.00 |
| **MONUMENT** | | | |
| ❑ Z 30909 | A Man Called Tex | 1971 | 20.00 |
| **RCA CAMDEN** | | | |
| ❑ CAL-363 [M] | Tex Williams' Best | 1958 | 25.00 |

### WILLIAMS, TONY

Lead singer of THE PLATTERS when they were having their biggest hits in the 1950s.

| Number | Title (A Side/B Side) | Yr | NM |
|---|---|---|---|
| **MERCURY** | | | |
| ❑ MG-20454 [M] | A Girl Is a Girl Is a Girl | 1959 | 40.00 |
| ❑ SR-60138 [S] | A Girl Is a Girl Is a Girl | 1959 | 50.00 |
| **PHILIPS** | | | |
| ❑ PHM 200051 [M] | The Magic Touch of Tony | 1962 | 25.00 |
| ❑ PHS 600051 [S] | The Magic Touch of Tony | 1962 | 30.00 |
| **REPRISE** | | | |
| ❑ R-6006 [M] | His Greatest Hits | 1961 | 25.00 |
| ❑ R9-6006 [S] | His Greatest Hits | 1961 | 30.00 |

### WILLIAMS, TONY (2)

Jazz drummer.

| Number | Title (A Side/B Side) | Yr | NM |
|---|---|---|---|
| **BLUE NOTE** | | | |
| ❑ BLP-4180 [M] | Life Time | 1964 | 25.00 |
| ❑ BLP-4216 [M] | Spring | 1965 | 25.00 |
| ❑ BST-84180 [S] | Life Time | 1964 | 30.00 |
| *—With "New York, USA" address on label* | | | |
| ❑ BST-84216 [S] | Spring | 1965 | 30.00 |
| *—With "New York, USA" address on label* | | | |
| **COLUMBIA** | | | |
| ❑ HC 45705 | Joy of Flying | 198? | 50.00 |
| *—Half-speed mastered edition* | | | |

### WILLIAMS, VALDO

| Number | Title (A Side/B Side) | Yr | NM |
|---|---|---|---|
| **SAVOY** | | | |
| ❑ MG-12188 [M] | New Advanced Jazz | 1967 | 30.00 |

### WILLIAMSON, CLAUDE

| Number | Title (A Side/B Side) | Yr | NM |
|---|---|---|---|
| **BETHLEHEM** | | | |
| ❑ BCP-54 [M] | Claude Williamson | 1956 | 80.00 |
| ❑ BCP-69 [M] | 'Round Midnight | 1957 | 80.00 |
| **CAPITOL** | | | |
| ❑ H 6502 [10] | Claude Williamson | 1954 | 120.00 |
| ❑ H 6511 [10] | Keys West | 1955 | 120.00 |
| ❑ T 6511 [M] | Keys West | 1956 | 100.00 |
| *—Turquoise label* | | | |
| **CONTRACT** | | | |
| ❑ 15001 [M] | The Fabulous Claude Williamson Trio | 196? | 30.00 |
| ❑ 15003 [M] | Theatre Party | 196? | 30.00 |
| **CRITERION** | | | |
| ❑ 601 [M] | Claude Williamson Mulls the Mulligan Scene | 1958 | 80.00 |

### WILLIAMSON, SONNY BOY (1)

| Number | Title (A Side/B Side) | Yr | NM |
|---|---|---|---|
| **BLUES CLASSICS** | | | |
| ❑ 3 | Blues Classics by Sonny Boy Williamson | 196? | 25.00 |
| ❑ 20 | Blues Classics by Sonny Boy Williamson, Vol. 2 | 196? | 25.00 |
| ❑ BC 24 | Blues Classics by Sonny Boy Williamson, Volume 3 | 196? | 25.00 |

### WILLIAMSON, SONNY BOY (2)

| Number | Title (A Side/B Side) | Yr | NM |
|---|---|---|---|
| **ALLIGATOR** | | | |
| ❑ AL-4787 | Keep It To Ourselves | 1990 | 12.00 |
| **ARHOOLIE** | | | |
| ❑ 2020 | King Biscuit Time | 197? | 12.00 |
| **CHECKER** | | | |
| ❑ LP-1437 [M] | Down and Out Blues | 1959 | 320.00 |
| **CHESS** | | | |
| ❑ 2ACMB-206 [(2)] | Sonny Boy Williamson | 1976 | 20.00 |
| *—Reissue of 50027* | | | |
| ❑ CHV-417 | One Way Out | 1975 | 15.00 |
| ❑ LP-1503 [M] | The Real Folk Blues | 1966 | 80.00 |
| ❑ LP-1509 [M] | More Real Folk Blues | 1966 | 80.00 |
| ❑ LPS-1536 | Bummer Road | 1969 | 25.00 |
| ❑ CH-9116 | One Way Out | 198? | 10.00 |
| ❑ CH-9257 | Down and Out Blues | 1988 | 10.00 |
| ❑ CH-9272 | The Real Folk Blues | 1988 | 10.00 |
| ❑ CH-9277 | More Real Folk Blues | 1988 | 10.00 |
| ❑ 2CH-50027 [(2)] | This Is My Story | 1972 | 25.00 |
| **GNP CRESCENDO** | | | |
| ❑ GNPS-10003 | Sonny Boy Williamson in Chicago | 198? | 10.00 |
| **STORYVILLE** | | | |
| ❑ 4016 | A Portrait in Blues | 197? | 12.00 |
| ❑ 4062 | The Blues of Sonny Boy Williamson | 197? | 12.00 |

### WILLIAMSON, SONNY BOY (2), AND THE YARDBIRDS

| Number | Title (A Side/B Side) | Yr | NM |
|---|---|---|---|
| **MERCURY** | | | |
| ❑ MG-21071 [M] | Sonny Boy Williamson and the Yardbirds | 1965 | 80.00 |
| ❑ SR-61071 [R] | Sonny Boy Williamson and the Yardbirds | 196? | 25.00 |
| *—Later cover with cartoon artwork on the cover* | | | |
| ❑ SR-61071 [R] | Sonny Boy Williamson and the Yardbirds | 1965 | 50.00 |
| *—First cover with a picture of the bluesman and the band* | | | |
| ❑ SR-61271 [R] | Eric Clapton and the Yardbirds Live with Sonny Boy Williamson | 1970 | 20.00 |
| *—Reissue* | | | |

### WILLIAMSON, STU

| Number | Title (A Side/B Side) | Yr | NM |
|---|---|---|---|
| **BETHLEHEM** | | | |
| ❑ BCP-31 [M] | Stu Williamson Plays | 1955 | 120.00 |
| ❑ BCP-55 [M] | Stu Williamson | 1956 | 120.00 |
| ❑ BCP-1024 [10] | Stu Williamson Plays | 1955 | 250.00 |

### WILLING, FOY, AND THE RIDERS OF THE PURPLE SAGE

| Number | Title (A Side/B Side) | Yr | NM |
|---|---|---|---|
| **CROWN** | | | |
| ❑ CST-582 | Country & Western Favorites | 196? | 10.00 |
| ❑ CLP-5306 [M] | Cool Water | 196? | 12.00 |
| **CUSTOM** | | | |
| ❑ CS 1017 | Cool, Cool Water | 197? | 10.00 |
| **JUBILEE** | | | |
| ❑ JL-5028 [M] | The New Sound of American Folk | 1962 | 20.00 |
| ❑ JLS-5028 [S] | The New Sound of American Folk | 1962 | 25.00 |
| **ROULETTE** | | | |
| ❑ R-25035 [M] | Cowboy | 1958 | 40.00 |
| **ROYALE** | | | |
| ❑ 6032 [10] | The Riders of the Purple Sage | 1952 | 100.00 |
| **VARSITY** | | | |
| ❑ 6032 [10] | The Riders of the Purple Sage | 1950 | 120.00 |

### WILLIS, CHUCK

| Number | Title (A Side/B Side) | Yr | NM |
|---|---|---|---|
| **ATLANTIC** | | | |
| ❑ 8018 [M] | The King of the Stroll | 1958 | 300.00 |
| *—Black label* | | | |
| ❑ 8018 [M] | The King of the Stroll | 1960 | 150.00 |
| *—Purple and orange label* | | | |
| ❑ 8079 [M] | I Remember Chuck Willis | 1963 | 150.00 |
| ❑ SD 8079 [P] | I Remember Chuck Willis | 1963 | 200.00 |
| **EPIC** | | | |
| ❑ LN 3425 [M] | Chuck Willis Wails the Blues | 1958 | 500.00 |
| ❑ LN 3728 [M] | A Tribute to Chuck Willis | 1960 | 300.00 |

### WILLIS BROTHERS, THE

| Number | Title (A Side/B Side) | Yr | NM |
|---|---|---|---|
| **STARDAY** | | | |
| ❑ SLP-163 [M] | The Willis Brothers in Action | 1962 | 60.00 |
| ❑ SLP-229 [M] | Code of the West | 1963 | 50.00 |
| ❑ SLP-306 [M] | Let's Hit the Road | 1965 | 40.00 |
| ❑ SLP-323 [M] | Give Me 40 Acres | 1965 | 40.00 |
| ❑ SLP-353 [M] | Road Stop Juke Box Hits | 1966 | 30.00 |
| ❑ SLP-369 [M] | The Wild Side of Life | 1966 | 30.00 |
| ❑ SLP-387 [M] | Goin' to Town | 1966 | 30.00 |
| ❑ SLP-403 [M] | Bob | 1967 | 25.00 |
| ❑ SLP-428 | Hey, Mister Truck Driver | 1968 | 25.00 |
| ❑ SLP-442 | Bummin' Around | 1969 | 25.00 |
| ❑ SLP-466 | The Best of the Willis Brothers | 1970 | 20.00 |
| ❑ SLP-472 | For the Good Times | 1971 | 20.00 |

### WILLS, BOB

| Number | Title (A Side/B Side) | Yr | NM |
|---|---|---|---|
| **ANTONES** | | | |
| ❑ 6000 [10] | Old Time Favorites | 195? | 500.00 |
| *—Fan club release* | | | |
| ❑ 6010 [10] | Old Time Favorites | 195? | 500.00 |
| *—Fan club release* | | | |
| **CAPITOL** | | | |
| ❑ SKBB-11550 [(2)] | Bob Wills and His Texas Playboys in Concert | 1976 | 20.00 |
| **COLUMBIA** | | | |
| ❑ CL 9003 [10] | Bob Wills Round-Up | 1949 | 300.00 |
| ❑ KG 32416 [(2)] | Anthology | 1973 | 20.00 |
| **DECCA** | | | |
| ❑ DL 5562 [10] | Dance-O-Rama #2 | 1955 | 300.00 |
| ❑ DL 8727 [M] | Bob Wills and His Texas Playboys | 1957 | 100.00 |
| *—Black label, silver print* | | | |
| ❑ DL 8727 [M] | Bob Wills and His Texas Playboys | 1961 | 40.00 |
| *—Black label with color bars* | | | |
| ❑ DL 78727 [R] | Bob Wills and His Texas Playboys | 196? | 20.00 |
| **DELTA** | | | |
| ❑ DLP-1149 | Bob Wills and His Texas Playboys On Stage | 1982 | 10.00 |
| **HARMONY** | | | |
| ❑ HL 7036 [M] | Bob Wills Special | 1957 | 40.00 |
| *—Maroon label* | | | |
| ❑ HL 7036 [M] | Bob Wills Special | 196? | 20.00 |
| *—Black label* | | | |
| ❑ HL 7304 [M] | The Best of Bob Wills | 1963 | 25.00 |
| ❑ HL 7345 [M] | The Great Bob Wills | 1965 | 20.00 |
| **KAPP** | | | |
| ❑ KL-1506 [M] | From the Heart of Texas | 1966 | 20.00 |
| ❑ KL-1523 [M] | King of Western Swing | 1967 | 25.00 |
| ❑ KL-1542 [M] | Here's That Man Again | 1968 | 50.00 |
| *—Mono is white label promo only; in stereo cover with "Mono" sticker* | | | |
| ❑ KS-3506 [S] | From the Heart of Texas | 1966 | 25.00 |
| ❑ KS-3523 [S] | King of Western Swing | 1967 | 25.00 |
| ❑ KS-3542 [S] | Here's That Man Again | 1968 | 25.00 |
| ❑ KS-3569 | Time Changes Everything | 1969 | 20.00 |
| ❑ KS-3587 | The Living Legend | 1969 | 20.00 |
| ❑ KS-3601 | The Greatest String Band Hits | 1969 | 20.00 |
| ❑ KS-3639 | Bob Wills in Person | 1970 | 20.00 |
| ❑ KS-3641 | The Best of Bob Wills | 1971 | 20.00 |
| **LIBERTY** | | | |
| ❑ LRP-3173 [M] | Together Again | 1960 | 30.00 |
| ❑ LRP-3182 [M] | Living Legend | 1961 | 30.00 |
| ❑ LRP-3194 [M] | Mr. Words and Mr. Music | 1961 | 30.00 |
| ❑ LRP-3303 [M] | Bob Wills Sings and Plays | 1963 | 30.00 |
| ❑ LST-7173 [S] | Together Again | 1960 | 40.00 |
| ❑ LST-7182 [S] | Living Legend | 1961 | 40.00 |
| ❑ LST-7194 [S] | Mr. Words and Mr. Music | 1961 | 40.00 |
| ❑ LST-7303 [S] | Bob Wills Sings and Plays | 1963 | 40.00 |
| **LONGHORN** | | | |
| ❑ LP-001 [M] | My Keepsake Album | 1965 | 80.00 |
| **MGM** | | | |
| ❑ E-91 [10] | Ranch House Favorites | 1951 | 300.00 |
| ❑ GAS-141 | A Tribute (Golden Archive Series) | 1971 | 25.00 |
| ❑ E-3352 [M] | Ranch House Favorites | 1956 | 150.00 |
| **STARDAY** | | | |
| ❑ SLP-375 [M] | San Antonio Rose | 1965 | 40.00 |
| **TIME-LIFE** | | | |
| ❑ STW-119 | Country Music | 1981 | 10.00 |
| **UNITED ARTISTS** | | | |
| ❑ UA-LA216-J [(2)] | For the Last Time | 1974 | 40.00 |
| *—Box set with booklet* | | | |
| ❑ LST-7303 [S] | Bob Wills Sings and Plays | 1978 | 15.00 |
| *—Reissue of Liberty 7303 on "sunrise" label; tan label variations may exist but are unconfirmed* | | | |
| ❑ UAS-9962 [(2)] | Legendary Masters | 1971 | 25.00 |
| **VOCALION** | | | |
| ❑ VL 3735 [M] | Western Swing Band | 1965 | 20.00 |

### WILLS, JOHNNIE LEE

| Number | Title (A Side/B Side) | Yr | NM |
|---|---|---|---|
| **FLYING FISH** | | | |
| ❑ FF-069 | Reunion | 1978 | 12.00 |
| **ROUNDER** | | | |
| ❑ 1027 | Tulsa Swing | 1978 | 12.00 |
| **SIMS** | | | |
| ❑ LP-101 [M] | Where There's a Wills, There's a Way | 1962 | 40.00 |
| ❑ LPS-101 [S] | Where There's a Wills, There's a Way | 1962 | 60.00 |
| ❑ LP-108 [M] | Johnny Lee Wills at the Tulsa Stampede | 1963 | 30.00 |
| ❑ LPS-108 [S] | Johnny Lee Wills at the Tulsa Stampede | 1963 | 50.00 |

### WILMER AND THE DUKES

| Number | Title (A Side/B Side) | Yr | NM |
|---|---|---|---|
| **APHRODISIAC** | | | |
| ❑ 6001 | Wilmer and the Dukes | 1969 | 20.00 |

### WILSON, AL

| Number | Title (A Side/B Side) | Yr | NM |
|---|---|---|---|
| **PLAYBOY** | | | |
| ❑ PB 410 | I've Got a Feeling | 1976 | 12.00 |
| ❑ JZ 34744 | I've Got a Feeling | 1977 | 10.00 |
| *—Reissue of 410* | | | |

**Except when noted otherwise, VG = 25% of NM, and VG+ = 50% of NM. (Example: VG = $2.00, VG+ = $4.00 and NM = $8.00.)**

| Number | Title (A Side/B Side) | Yr | NM |
|---|---|---|---|
| **ROCKY ROAD** | | | |
| ❑ RR-3600 | Weighing In | 1973 | 15.00 |
| ❑ RR-3601 | Show and Tell | 1973 | 15.00 |
| ❑ 3700 | La La Peace Song | 1974 | 15.00 |
| **SOUL CITY** | | | |
| ❑ SCS-92006 | Searching for the Dolphins | 1969 | 25.00 |

### WILSON, BRIAN Also see THE BEACH BOYS.

| Number | Title (A Side/B Side) | Yr | NM |
|---|---|---|---|
| **ARISTA** | | | |
| ❑ 82876-70300-1 | What I Really Want for Christmas | 2005 | 12.00 |
| **RHINO** | | | |
| ❑ RI-76471 [(2)] | Gettin' In Over My Head | 2004 | 20.00 |
| ❑ RI-76582 [(2)] | Brian Wilson Presents Smile | 2004 | 25.00 |
| **SIRE** | | | |
| ❑ PRO-A-3248 [DJ] | Words and Music | 1988 | 25.00 |
| *—Promo-only music and interview* | | | |
| ❑ 25669 | Brian Wilson | 1988 | 10.00 |

### WILSON, CARL Also see THE BEACH BOYS.

| Number | Title (A Side/B Side) | Yr | NM |
|---|---|---|---|
| **CARIBOU** | | | |
| ❑ NJZ 37010 | Carl Wilson | 1981 | 20.00 |
| ❑ ARZ 37970 | Youngblood | 1982 | 20.00 |

### WILSON, DENNIS Also see THE BEACH BOYS.

| Number | Title (A Side/B Side) | Yr | NM |
|---|---|---|---|
| **CARIBOU** | | | |
| ❑ PZ 34354 | Pacific Ocean Blue | 1977 | 30.00 |

### WILSON, FLIP

| Number | Title (A Side/B Side) | Yr | NM |
|---|---|---|---|
| **ATLANTIC** | | | |
| ❑ 8149 [M] | Cowboys and Colored People | 1967 | 25.00 |
| ❑ SD 8149 [S] | Cowboys and Colored People | 1967 | 15.00 |
| *—Green and blue label* | | | |
| ❑ SD 8149 [S] | Cowboys and Colored People | 1969 | 12.00 |
| *—Red and green label* | | | |
| ❑ SD 8179 | You Devil You | 1968 | 15.00 |
| *—Green and blue label* | | | |
| ❑ SD 8179 | You Devil You | 1969 | 12.00 |
| *—Red and green label* | | | |
| **IMPERIAL** | | | |
| ❑ LP-9155 [M] | Flippin' | 1961 | 25.00 |
| **LITTLE DAVID** | | | |
| ❑ LD 1000 | The Devil Made Me Buy This Dress | 1970 | 12.00 |
| ❑ LD 1001 [M] | Geraldine/Don't Fight the Feeling | 1972 | 25.00 |
| *—White label promo only; sticker on cover says "Promotional DJ Copy Monaural Not for Sale"* | | | |
| ❑ LD 1001 [S] | Geraldine/Don't Fight the Feeling | 1972 | 12.00 |
| ❑ LD 2000 | The Flip Wilson Show | 1970 | 12.00 |
| **MINIT** | | | |
| ❑ 24012 | Flippin' | 1968 | 15.00 |
| *—Reissue of Imperial LP* | | | |
| **SCEPTER** | | | |
| ❑ S-520 | Flip Wilson's Pot Luck | 1964 | 20.00 |
| **SPRINGBOARD** | | | |
| ❑ SPB-4004 | Funny and Live at the Village Gate | 1972 | 12.00 |
| *—Reissue of Scepter LP* | | | |
| **SUNSET** | | | |
| ❑ SUS-5297 | Flipped Out | 1970 | 12.00 |
| *—Reissue of Minit LP* | | | |

### WILSON, GERALD

| Number | Title (A Side/B Side) | Yr | NM |
|---|---|---|---|
| **AUDIO LAB** | | | |
| ❑ AL-1538 [M] | Big Band Modern | 1959 | 150.00 |
| **FEDERAL** | | | |
| ❑ 295-93 [10] | Gerald Wilson | 1953 | 300.00 |
| **PACIFIC JAZZ** | | | |
| ❑ PJ-34 [M] | You Better Believe It | 1961 | 25.00 |
| ❑ ST-34 [S] | You Better Believe It | 1961 | 30.00 |
| ❑ PJ-61 [M] | Moment of Truth | 1962 | 25.00 |
| ❑ ST-61 [S] | Moment of Truth | 1962 | 30.00 |
| ❑ PJ-80 [M] | Portraits | 1964 | 25.00 |
| ❑ ST-80 [S] | Portraits | 1964 | 30.00 |
| ❑ PJ-88 [M] | Gerald Wilson on Stage | 1964 | 25.00 |
| ❑ ST-88 [S] | Gerald Wilson on Stage | 1964 | 30.00 |
| ❑ PJ-10118 [M] | Live and Swinging | 1967 | 20.00 |
| ❑ ST-20099 [S] | Feelin' Kinda Blue | 1966 | 20.00 |
| ❑ ST-20111 [S] | Golden Sword | 1966 | 20.00 |

### WILSON, J. FRANK, AND THE CAVALIERS

| Number | Title (A Side/B Side) | Yr | NM |
|---|---|---|---|
| **JOSIE** | | | |
| ❑ JM-4006 [M] | Last Kiss | 1964 | 75.00 |
| ❑ JS-4006 [S] | Last Kiss | 1964 | 100.00 |

### WILSON, JACK

| Number | Title (A Side/B Side) | Yr | NM |
|---|---|---|---|
| **ATLANTIC** | | | |
| ❑ 1406 [M] | Jack Wilson Quartet | 1963 | 30.00 |
| ❑ SD 1406 [S] | Jack Wilson Quartet | 1963 | 40.00 |
| ❑ 1427 [M] | The Two Sides of Jack Wilson | 1964 | 30.00 |
| ❑ SD 1427 [S] | The Two Sides of Jack Wilson | 1964 | 40.00 |
| **BLUE NOTE** | | | |
| ❑ BLP-4251 [M] | Something Personal | 1967 | 40.00 |
| ❑ BST-84251 [S] | Something Personal | 1967 | 20.00 |
| *—With "A Division of Liberty Records" on label* | | | |
| ❑ BST-84251 [S] | Something Personal | 1967 | 30.00 |
| *—With "New York, USA" address on label* | | | |
| ❑ BST-84270 [S] | Easterly Winds | 1968 | 20.00 |
| *—With "A Division of Liberty Records" on label* | | | |
| ❑ BST-84328 [S] | Song for My Daughter | 1969 | 20.00 |
| *—With "A Division of Liberty Records" on label* | | | |
| **VAULT** | | | |
| ❑ LP-9001 [M] | Brazilian Mancini | 1964 | 25.00 |
| ❑ LPS-9001 [S] | Brazilian Mancini | 1964 | 30.00 |
| ❑ LP-9002 [M] | Ramblin' | 1964 | 25.00 |
| ❑ LPS-9002 [S] | Ramblin' | 1964 | 30.00 |
| ❑ LP-9008 [M] | Jazz Organs | 1965 | 25.00 |
| ❑ LPS-9008 [S] | Jazz Organs | 1965 | 30.00 |

### WILSON, JACKIE

| Number | Title (A Side/B Side) | Yr | NM |
|---|---|---|---|
| **BRUNSWICK** | | | |
| ❑ BL 54042 [M] | He's So Fine | 1959 | 120.00 |
| *—All-black label* | | | |
| ❑ BL 54042 [M] | He's So Fine | 1964 | 25.00 |
| *—Black label with color bars* | | | |
| ❑ BL 54045 [M] | Lonely Teardrops | 1959 | 150.00 |
| *—All-black label* | | | |
| ❑ BL 54045 [M] | Lonely Teardrops | 1964 | 25.00 |
| *—Black label with color bars* | | | |
| ❑ BL 54050 [M] | So Much | 1960 | 100.00 |
| *—All-black label* | | | |
| ❑ BL 54050 [M] | So Much | 1964 | 20.00 |
| *—Black label with color bars* | | | |
| ❑ BL 54055 [M] | Jackie Sings the Blues | 1960 | 150.00 |
| *—All-black label* | | | |
| ❑ BL 54055 [M] | Jackie Sings the Blues | 1964 | 20.00 |
| *—Black label with color bars* | | | |
| ❑ BL 54058 [M] | My Golden Favorites | 1960 | 60.00 |
| *—All-black label* | | | |
| ❑ BL 54058 [M] | My Golden Favorites | 1964 | 25.00 |
| *—Black label with color bars* | | | |
| ❑ BL 54059 [M] | A Woman, a Lover, a Friend | 1961 | 50.00 |
| *—All-black label* | | | |
| ❑ BL 54059 [M] | A Woman, a Lover, a Friend | 1964 | 20.00 |
| *—Black label with color bars* | | | |
| ❑ BL 54100 [M] | You Ain't Heard Nothin' Yet | 1961 | 50.00 |
| *—All-black label* | | | |
| ❑ BL 54100 [M] | You Ain't Heard Nothin' Yet | 1964 | 20.00 |
| *—Black label with color bars* | | | |
| ❑ BL 54101 [M] | By Special Request | 1961 | 50.00 |
| *—All-black label* | | | |
| ❑ BL 54101 [M] | By Special Request | 1964 | 20.00 |
| *—Black label with color bars* | | | |
| ❑ BL 54105 [M] | Body and Soul | 1962 | 50.00 |
| *—All-black label* | | | |
| ❑ BL 54105 [M] | Body and Soul | 1964 | 20.00 |
| *—Black label with color bars* | | | |
| ❑ BL 54106 [M] | The World's Greatest Melodies | 1962 | 50.00 |
| *—All-black label* | | | |
| ❑ BL 54106 [M] | The World's Greatest Melodies | 1964 | 20.00 |
| *—Black label with color bars* | | | |
| ❑ BL 54108 [M] | Jackie Wilson at the Copa | 1962 | 50.00 |
| *—All-black label* | | | |
| ❑ BL 54108 [M] | Jackie Wilson at the Copa | 1964 | 20.00 |
| *—Black label with color bars* | | | |
| ❑ BL 54110 [M] | Baby Workout | 1963 | 20.00 |
| *—Black label with color bars* | | | |
| ❑ BL 54110 [M] | Baby Workout | 1963 | 50.00 |
| *—All-black label* | | | |
| ❑ BL 54112 [M] | Merry Christmas from Jackie Wilson | 1963 | 30.00 |
| ❑ BL 54113 [M] | Shake a Hand | 1964 | 25.00 |
| ❑ BL 54115 [M] | My Golden Favorites, Volume 2 | 1964 | 25.00 |
| ❑ BL 54117 [M] | Somethin' Else | 1964 | 25.00 |
| ❑ BL 54118 [M] | Soul Time | 1965 | 25.00 |
| ❑ BL 54119 [M] | Spotlight on Jackie | 1965 | 25.00 |
| ❑ BL 54120 [M] | Soul Galore | 1966 | 25.00 |
| ❑ BL 54122 [M] | Whispers | 1966 | 25.00 |
| ❑ BL 54130 [M] | Higher and Higher | 1967 | 25.00 |
| ❑ BL 54134 [M] | Manufacturers of Soul | 1968 | 50.00 |
| *—With Count Basie* | | | |
| ❑ BL 54138 [M] | I Get the Sweetest Feeling | 1968 | 100.00 |
| *—Yellow label promo only; "Monaural" sticker over the word "Stereo" on cover* | | | |
| ❑ BL 754050 [S] | So Much | 1960 | 150.00 |
| *—All-black label* | | | |
| ❑ BL 754050 [S] | So Much | 1964 | 25.00 |
| *—Black label with color bars* | | | |
| ❑ BL 754055 [S] | Jackie Sings the Blues | 1960 | 200.00 |
| *—All-black label* | | | |
| ❑ BL 754055 [S] | Jackie Sings the Blues | 1964 | 25.00 |
| *—Black label with color bars* | | | |
| ❑ BL 754059 [S] | A Woman, a Lover, a Friend | 1961 | 80.00 |
| *—All-black label* | | | |
| ❑ BL 754059 [S] | A Woman, a Lover, a Friend | 1964 | 25.00 |
| *—Black label with color bars* | | | |
| ❑ BL 754100 [S] | You Ain't Heard Nothin' Yet | 1961 | 80.00 |
| *—All-black label* | | | |
| ❑ BL 754100 [S] | You Ain't Heard Nothin' Yet | 1964 | 25.00 |
| *—Black label with color bars* | | | |
| ❑ BL 754101 [S] | By Special Request | 1961 | 80.00 |
| *—All-black label* | | | |
| ❑ BL 754101 [S] | By Special Request | 1964 | 25.00 |
| *—Black label with color bars* | | | |
| ❑ BL 754105 [S] | Body and Soul | 1962 | 80.00 |
| *—All-black label* | | | |
| ❑ BL 754105 [S] | Body and Soul | 1964 | 25.00 |
| *—Black label with color bars* | | | |
| ❑ BL 754106 [S] | The World's Greatest Melodies | 1962 | 80.00 |
| *—All-black label* | | | |
| ❑ BL 754106 [S] | The World's Greatest Melodies | 1964 | 25.00 |
| *—Black label with color bars* | | | |
| ❑ BL 754108 [S] | Jackie Wilson at the Copa | 1962 | 80.00 |
| *—All-black label* | | | |
| ❑ BL 754108 [S] | Jackie Wilson at the Copa | 1964 | 25.00 |
| *—Black label with color bars* | | | |
| ❑ BL 754110 [S] | Baby Workout | 1963 | 25.00 |
| *—Black label with color bars* | | | |
| ❑ BL 754110 [S] | Baby Workout | 1963 | 80.00 |
| *—All-black label* | | | |
| ❑ BL 754112 [S] | Merry Christmas from Jackie Wilson | 1963 | 40.00 |
| ❑ BL 754113 [S] | Shake a Hand | 1964 | 30.00 |
| ❑ BL 754115 [S] | My Golden Favorites, Volume 2 | 1964 | 30.00 |
| ❑ BL 754117 [S] | Somethin' Else | 1964 | 30.00 |
| ❑ BL 754118 [S] | Soul Time | 1965 | 30.00 |
| ❑ BL 754119 [S] | Spotlight on Jackie | 1965 | 30.00 |
| ❑ BL 754120 [S] | Soul Galore | 1966 | 30.00 |
| ❑ BL 754122 [S] | Whispers | 1966 | 30.00 |
| ❑ BL 754130 [S] | Higher and Higher | 1967 | 30.00 |
| ❑ BL 754134 [S] | Manufacturers of Soul | 1968 | 20.00 |
| *—With Count Basie* | | | |
| ❑ BL 754138 [S] | I Get the Sweetest Feeling | 1968 | 20.00 |
| ❑ BL 754140 | Jackie Wilson's Greatest Hits | 1969 | 20.00 |
| ❑ BL 754154 | Do Your Thing | 1969 | 20.00 |
| ❑ BL 754158 | It's All a Part of Love | 1970 | 20.00 |
| ❑ BL 754167 | This Love Is Real | 1971 | 20.00 |
| ❑ BL 754172 | You Got Me Walking | 1971 | 20.00 |
| ❑ BL 754185 | Beautiful Day | 1972 | 15.00 |
| ❑ BL 754199 | Nowstalgia | 1974 | 15.00 |
| ❑ BL 754212 | Nobody But You | 1977 | 15.00 |
| **COLUMBIA** | | | |
| ❑ FC 40866 | Reet Petite: The Best of Jackie Wilson | 1987 | 12.00 |
| **EPIC** | | | |
| ❑ EG 38623 [(2)] | The Jackie Wilson Story | 1983 | 20.00 |
| ❑ FE 39408 | The Jackie Wilson Story, Vol. 2 | 1985 | 12.00 |
| ❑ PE 39408 | The Jackie Wilson Story, Vol. 2 | 198? | 8.00 |
| *—Budget-line reissue* | | | |
| **RHINO** | | | |
| ❑ RNLP-70230 | Through the Years: A Collection of Rare Album Tracks and Single Sides | 1987 | 12.00 |

### WILSON, JULIE

| Number | Title (A Side/B Side) | Yr | NM |
|---|---|---|---|
| **ARDEN** | | | |
| ❑ B&S-1 | Julie Wilson at Brothers and Sisters, Vol. 1 | 1976 | 20.00 |
| ❑ B&S-2 | Julie Wilson at Brothers and Sisters, Vol. 2 | 1976 | 20.00 |
| **CAMEO** | | | |
| ❑ C-1021 [M] | Meet Julie Wilson | 1962 | 30.00 |
| **DOLPHIN** | | | |
| ❑ 6 [M] | Love | 1956 | 50.00 |
| **VIK** | | | |
| ❑ LX-1095 [M] | My Old Flame | 1957 | 30.00 |
| ❑ LX-1118 [M] | Julie Wilson at the St. Regis | 1958 | 30.00 |

### WILSON, LONNIE

| Number | Title (A Side/B Side) | Yr | NM |
|---|---|---|---|
| **STARDAY** | | | |
| ❑ SLP-217 [M] | The Playboy Farmer | 196? | 30.00 |

### WILSON, MARIE

| Number | Title (A Side/B Side) | Yr | NM |
|---|---|---|---|
| **DESIGN** | | | |
| ❑ DLP-76 [M] | Gentlemen Prefer Marie Wilson | 1959 | 40.00 |

### WILSON, MARTY

| Number | Title (A Side/B Side) | Yr | NM |
|---|---|---|---|
| **20TH CENTURY FOX** | | | |
| ❑ TF-3101 [M] | Young America Dances to Golden Goodies | 1963 | 20.00 |
| ❑ TFS-4101 [S] | Young America Dances to Golden Goodies | 1963 | 25.00 |

### WILSON, MURRY Father of Brian, Carl and Dennis Wilson of the Beach Boys.

| Number | Title (A Side/B Side) | Yr | NM |
|---|---|---|---|
| **CAPITOL** | | | |
| ❑ ST 2819 [S] | The Many Moods of Murry Wilson | 1967 | 50.00 |
| ❑ T 2819 [M] | The Many Moods of Murry Wilson | 1967 | 60.00 |

### WILSON, NANCY

| Number | Title (A Side/B Side) | Yr | NM |
|---|---|---|---|
| **CAPITOL** | | | |
| ❑ ST-148 | Nancy | 1969 | 15.00 |
| ❑ ST-234 | Son of a Preacher Man | 1969 | 15.00 |
| ❑ SWBB-256 [(2)] | Close-Up | 1969 | 20.00 |
| *—Combines 1828 and 1934 into one package* | | | |
| ❑ ST-353 | Hurt So Bad | 1969 | 15.00 |
| ❑ ST-429 | Can't Take My Eyes Off You | 1970 | 15.00 |

| Number | Title (A Side/B Side) | Yr | NM |
|---|---|---|---|
| ❑ ST-541 | Now I'm a Woman | 1970 | 15.00 |
| ❑ STBB-727 [(2)] | For Once in My Life/Who Can I Turn To | 1971 | 20.00 |
| ❑ ST-763 | The Right to Love | 1971 | 15.00 |
| *—Retitled reissue of 2757* | | | |
| ❑ SM-798 | But Beautiful | 197? | 10.00 |
| *—Reissue* | | | |
| ❑ ST-798 | But Beautiful | 1971 | 15.00 |
| ❑ ST-842 | Kaleidoscope | 1971 | 15.00 |
| ❑ ST 1319 [S] | Like in Love | 1960 | 20.00 |
| *—Black label with colorband, Capitol logo on top* | | | |
| ❑ ST 1319 [S] | Like in Love | 1960 | 30.00 |
| *—Black label with colorband, Capitol logo on left* | | | |
| ❑ T 1319 [M] | Like in Love | 1960 | 15.00 |
| *—Black label with colorband, Capitol logo on top* | | | |
| ❑ T 1319 [M] | Like in Love | 1960 | 25.00 |
| *—Black label with colorband, Capitol logo on left* | | | |
| ❑ ST 1440 [S] | Something Wonderful | 1960 | 20.00 |
| *—Black label with colorband, Capitol logo on top* | | | |
| ❑ ST 1440 [S] | Something Wonderful | 1960 | 30.00 |
| *—Black label with colorband, Capitol logo on left* | | | |
| ❑ T 1440 [M] | Something Wonderful | 1960 | 15.00 |
| *—Black label with colorband, Capitol logo on top* | | | |
| ❑ T 1440 [M] | Something Wonderful | 1960 | 25.00 |
| *—Black label with colorband, Capitol logo on left* | | | |
| ❑ SM-1524 [S] | The Swingin's Mutual | 1976 | 10.00 |
| *—With George Shearing; reissue* | | | |
| ❑ ST 1524 [S] | The Swingin's Mutual | 1961 | 20.00 |
| *—Black label with colorband, Capitol logo on top* | | | |
| ❑ ST 1524 [S] | The Swingin's Mutual | 1961 | 30.00 |
| *—Black label with colorband, Capitol logo on left* | | | |
| ❑ T 1524 [M] | The Swingin's Mutual | 1961 | 15.00 |
| *—Black label with colorband, Capitol logo on top* | | | |
| ❑ T 1524 [M] | The Swingin's Mutual | 1961 | 25.00 |
| *—Black label with colorband, Capitol logo on left* | | | |
| ❑ ST 1767 [S] | Hello Young Lovers | 1962 | 25.00 |
| ❑ T 1767 [M] | Hello Young Lovers | 1962 | 20.00 |
| ❑ SM-1828 | Broadway My Way | 197? | 10.00 |
| *—Reissue* | | | |
| ❑ ST 1828 [S] | Broadway My Way | 1963 | 20.00 |
| ❑ T 1828 [M] | Broadway My Way | 1963 | 15.00 |
| ❑ SM-1934 | Hollywood My Way | 197? | 10.00 |
| *—Reissue* | | | |
| ❑ ST 1934 [S] | Hollywood My Way | 1963 | 20.00 |
| ❑ T 1934 [M] | Hollywood My Way | 1963 | 15.00 |
| ❑ ST 2012 [S] | Yesterday's Love Songs/ Today's Blues | 1964 | 20.00 |
| ❑ T 2012 [M] | Yesterday's Love Songs/ Today's Blues | 1964 | 15.00 |
| ❑ ST 2082 [S] | Today, Tomorrow, Forever | 1964 | 20.00 |
| ❑ T 2082 [M] | Today, Tomorrow, Forever | 1964 | 15.00 |
| ❑ KAO 2136 [M] | The Nancy Wilson Show! | 1965 | 15.00 |
| ❑ SKAO 2136 [S] | The Nancy Wilson Show! | 1965 | 20.00 |
| ❑ ST 2155 [S] | How Glad I Am | 1964 | 20.00 |
| ❑ T 2155 [M] | How Glad I Am | 1964 | 15.00 |
| ❑ ST 2321 [S] | Today — My Way | 1965 | 20.00 |
| ❑ T 2321 [M] | Today — My Way | 1965 | 15.00 |
| ❑ ST 2351 [S] | Gentle Is My Love | 1965 | 20.00 |
| ❑ T 2351 [M] | Gentle Is My Love | 1965 | 15.00 |
| ❑ ST 2433 [S] | From Broadway with Love | 1966 | 20.00 |
| ❑ T 2433 [M] | From Broadway with Love | 1966 | 15.00 |
| ❑ SM-2495 | A Touch of Today | 197? | 10.00 |
| *—Reissue* | | | |
| ❑ ST 2495 [S] | A Touch of Today | 1966 | 20.00 |
| ❑ T 2495 [M] | A Touch of Today | 1966 | 15.00 |
| ❑ ST 2555 [S] | Tender Loving Care | 1966 | 20.00 |
| ❑ T 2555 [M] | Tender Loving Care | 1966 | 15.00 |
| ❑ ST 2634 [S] | Nancy — Naturally | 1967 | 20.00 |
| ❑ T 2634 [M] | Nancy — Naturally | 1967 | 15.00 |
| ❑ ST 2712 [S] | Just for Now | 1967 | 20.00 |
| ❑ T 2712 [M] | Just for Now | 1967 | 15.00 |
| ❑ ST 2757 [S] | Lush Life | 1967 | 15.00 |
| ❑ T 2757 [M] | Lush Life | 1967 | 20.00 |
| ❑ ST 2844 [S] | Welcome to My Love | 1968 | 15.00 |
| ❑ T 2844 [M] | Welcome to My Love | 1968 | 25.00 |
| ❑ ST 2909 | Easy | 1968 | 15.00 |
| ❑ SKAO 2947 | The Best of Nancy Wilson | 1968 | 15.00 |
| ❑ ST 2970 | The Sound of Nancy Wilson | 1968 | 15.00 |
| ❑ SY-4575 | Broadway My Way | 197? | 10.00 |
| *—Odd reissue* | | | |
| ❑ ST-11131 | I Know I Love Him | 1972 | 12.00 |
| ❑ ST-11317 | All in Love Is Fair | 1974 | 12.00 |
| ❑ ST-11386 | Come Get to This | 1975 | 12.00 |
| ❑ ST-11518 | This Mother's Daughter | 1976 | 12.00 |
| ❑ ST-11659 | I've Never Been to Me | 1977 | 12.00 |
| ❑ SM-11767 | How Glad I Am | 1978 | 10.00 |
| *—Reissue of 2155* | | | |
| ❑ SMAS-11786 | Music on My Mind | 1978 | 12.00 |
| ❑ SM-11802 | Easy | 1978 | 10.00 |
| *—Reissue of 2909* | | | |
| ❑ SM-11819 | Come Get to This | 1978 | 10.00 |
| *—Reissue of 11386* | | | |
| ❑ SM-11884 | Nancy — Naturally | 1979 | 10.00 |
| *—Reissue of 2634* | | | |
| ❑ ST-11943 | Life, Love and Happiness | 1979 | 12.00 |
| ❑ SM-12031 | Can't Take My Eyes Off You | 1980 | 10.00 |
| *—Reissue of 429* | | | |
| ❑ ST-12055 | Take My Love | 1980 | 12.00 |
| ❑ SN-16128 | The Best of Nancy Wilson | 198? | 8.00 |
| *—Budget-line reissue* | | | |

### COLUMBIA

| Number | Title (A Side/B Side) | Yr | NM |
|---|---|---|---|
| ❑ FC 40330 | Keep You Satisfied | 1986 | 10.00 |
| ❑ FC 40787 | Forbidden Lover | 1987 | 10.00 |
| ❑ FC 44464 | Nancy Now! | 1989 | 10.00 |

### PAUSA

| Number | Title (A Side/B Side) | Yr | NM |
|---|---|---|---|
| ❑ PR-9041 | Nancy — Naturally | 1985 | 10.00 |

### PICKWICK

| Number | Title (A Side/B Side) | Yr | NM |
|---|---|---|---|
| ❑ SPC-3273 | Goin' Out of My Head | 197? | 10.00 |
| ❑ SPC-3348 | The Good Life | 197? | 10.00 |

## WILSON, NANCY, AND CANNONBALL ADDERLEY

### CAPITOL

| Number | Title (A Side/B Side) | Yr | NM |
|---|---|---|---|
| ❑ SM-1657 | Nancy Wilson/Cannonball Adderley | 197? | 10.00 |
| *—Reissue* | | | |
| ❑ ST 1657 [S] | Nancy Wilson/Cannonball Adderley | 1962 | 20.00 |
| *—Black label with colorband, Capitol logo on top* | | | |
| ❑ ST 1657 [S] | Nancy Wilson/Cannonball Adderley | 1962 | 30.00 |
| *—Black label with colorband, Capitol logo on left* | | | |
| ❑ T 1657 [M] | Nancy Wilson/Cannonball Adderley | 1962 | 15.00 |
| *—Black label with colorband, Capitol logo on top* | | | |
| ❑ T 1657 [M] | Nancy Wilson/Cannonball Adderley | 1962 | 25.00 |
| *—Black label with colorband, Capitol logo on left* | | | |

## WILSON, REG

### HERALD

| Number | Title (A Side/B Side) | Yr | NM |
|---|---|---|---|
| ❑ HLP-0104 [M] | All By Himself | 1956 | 50.00 |

## WILSON, REUBEN

### BLUE NOTE

| Number | Title (A Side/B Side) | Yr | NM |
|---|---|---|---|
| ❑ BST-84295 | On Broadway | 1968 | 25.00 |
| *—With "A Division of Liberty Records" on label* | | | |
| ❑ BST-84317 | Love Bug | 1969 | 25.00 |
| *—With "A Division of Liberty Records" on label* | | | |
| ❑ BST-84343 | Blue Mode | 1970 | 25.00 |
| ❑ BST-84365 | Groovy Situation | 1971 | 25.00 |
| ❑ BST-84377 | Set Us Free | 1972 | 25.00 |

### GROOVE MERCHANT

| Number | Title (A Side/B Side) | Yr | NM |
|---|---|---|---|
| ❑ 511 | Sweet Life | 1973 | 20.00 |
| ❑ 4404 [(2)] | Bad Stuff | 197? | 20.00 |

## WILSON, TEDDY

### ALLEGRO

| Number | Title (A Side/B Side) | Yr | NM |
|---|---|---|---|
| ❑ 4024 [10] | All Star Sextet | 1954 | 100.00 |
| ❑ 4031 [10] | All Star Sextet | 1954 | 100.00 |

### CAMEO

| Number | Title (A Side/B Side) | Yr | NM |
|---|---|---|---|
| ❑ C-1059 [M] | Teddy Wilson 1964 | 1964 | 30.00 |
| ❑ SC-1059 [S] | Teddy Wilson 1964 | 1964 | 30.00 |

### CLEF

| Number | Title (A Side/B Side) | Yr | NM |
|---|---|---|---|
| ❑ MGC-140 [10] | The Didactic Mr. Wilson | 1953 | 200.00 |
| ❑ MGC-156 [10] | Soft Moods with Teddy Wilson | 1954 | 200.00 |

### COLUMBIA

| Number | Title (A Side/B Side) | Yr | NM |
|---|---|---|---|
| ❑ CL 748 [M] | Mr. Wilson | 1956 | 60.00 |
| ❑ CL 1318 [M] | Mr. Wilson and Mr. Gershwin | 1959 | 40.00 |
| ❑ CL 1352 [M] | Gypsy in Jazz | 1959 | 30.00 |
| ❑ CL 1442 [M] | And Then They Wrote | 1960 | 30.00 |
| ❑ CL 6040 [10] | Teddy Wilson Featuring Billie Holiday | 1949 | 400.00 |
| ❑ CL 6098 [10] | Teddy Wilson and His Piano | 1950 | 250.00 |
| ❑ CL 6153 [10] | Piano Moods | 1950 | 120.00 |
| ❑ CS 8160 [S] | Gypsy | 1959 | 40.00 |
| ❑ CS 8242 [S] | And Then They Wrote | 1960 | 40.00 |

### COMMODORE

| Number | Title (A Side/B Side) | Yr | NM |
|---|---|---|---|
| ❑ FL-20029 [10] | Town Hall Concert | 1952 | 200.00 |

### DIAL

| Number | Title (A Side/B Side) | Yr | NM |
|---|---|---|---|
| ❑ LP-213 [10] | Teddy Wilson All Stars | 1950 | 300.00 |

### MERCURY

| Number | Title (A Side/B Side) | Yr | NM |
|---|---|---|---|
| ❑ MG-25172 [10] | Piano Pastries | 1953 | 120.00 |

### MGM

| Number | Title (A Side/B Side) | Yr | NM |
|---|---|---|---|
| ❑ E-129 [10] | Runnin' Wild | 1951 | 200.00 |

### MOSAIC

| Number | Title (A Side/B Side) | Yr | NM |
|---|---|---|---|
| ❑ MQ8-173 [(8)] | The Complete Verve Recordings of the Teddy Wilson Trio | 199? | 150.00 |

### NORGRAN

| Number | Title (A Side/B Side) | Yr | NM |
|---|---|---|---|
| ❑ MGN-1019 [M] | The Creative Teddy Wilson | 1955 | 100.00 |

### ROYALE

| Number | Title (A Side/B Side) | Yr | NM |
|---|---|---|---|
| ❑ 18169 [10] | Teddy Wilson and His All Stars | 195? | 100.00 |

### VERVE

| Number | Title (A Side/B Side) | Yr | NM |
|---|---|---|---|
| ❑ MGV-2011 [M] | Intimate Listening | 1956 | 50.00 |
| ❑ V-2011 [M] | Intimate Listening | 1961 | 20.00 |
| ❑ MGV-2029 [M] | For Quiet Lovers | 1956 | 60.00 |
| ❑ V-2029 [M] | For Quiet Lovers | 1961 | 25.00 |
| ❑ MGV-2073 [M] | I Got Rhythm | 1957 | 50.00 |
| ❑ V-2073 [M] | I Got Rhythm | 1961 | 20.00 |
| ❑ MGV-8272 [M] | The Impeccable Mr. Teddy Wilson | 1958 | 50.00 |
| ❑ V-8272 [M] | The Impeccable Mr. Teddy Wilson | 1961 | 20.00 |
| ❑ MGV-8299 [M] | These Tunes Remind Me of You | 1959 | 50.00 |
| ❑ V-8299 [M] | These Tunes Remind Me of You | 1961 | 20.00 |
| ❑ MGV-8330 [M] | The Touch of Teddy Wilson | 1959 | 50.00 |
| ❑ V-8330 [M] | The Touch of Teddy Wilson | 1961 | 20.00 |

## WILSON, TEDDY/GERRY MULLIGAN

### VERVE

| Number | Title (A Side/B Side) | Yr | NM |
|---|---|---|---|
| ❑ MGV-8235 [M] | The Teddy Wilson Trio and the Gerry Mulligan Quartet at Newport | 1958 | 50.00 |
| ❑ V-8235 [M] | The Teddy Wilson Trio and the Gerry Mulligan Quartet at Newport | 1961 | 20.00 |

## WILSON PHILLIPS

### SBK

| Number | Title (A Side/B Side) | Yr | NM |
|---|---|---|---|
| ❑ 1P-8219 | Shadows and Light | 1992 | 60.00 |
| *—Only U.S. vinyl release was through Columbia House* | | | |
| ❑ K1-93745 | Wilson Phillips | 1990 | 12.00 |

## WINCHESTER, JESSE

### AMPEX

| Number | Title (A Side/B Side) | Yr | NM |
|---|---|---|---|
| ❑ A 10104 | Jesse Winchester | 1970 | 20.00 |

### BEARSVILLE

| Number | Title (A Side/B Side) | Yr | NM |
|---|---|---|---|
| ❑ PRO 560 [DJ] | The Jesse Winchester Radio Show | 1976 | 40.00 |
| ❑ PRO-A-693 [(2)DJ] | Live at the Bijou Café Plus a Live Interview at Media College in Montreal | 1977 | 40.00 |
| ❑ BR 2045 | Jesse Winchester | 1971 | 15.00 |
| *—Reissue of Ampex LP* | | | |
| ❑ BR 2102 | Third Down, 110 to Go | 1972 | 15.00 |
| ❑ BR 6953 | Learn to Love It | 1974 | 12.00 |
| ❑ BR 6964 | Let the Rough Side Drag | 1976 | 12.00 |
| ❑ BR 6968 | Nothing But a Breeze | 1977 | 10.00 |
| ❑ BRK 6984 | A Touch on the Rainy Side | 1978 | 10.00 |
| ❑ BRK 6989 | Talk Memphis | 1981 | 10.00 |

### RHINO

| Number | Title (A Side/B Side) | Yr | NM |
|---|---|---|---|
| ❑ R1-70085 | The Best of Jesse Winchester | 1989 | 10.00 |
| ❑ RNLP-70885 | Jesse Winchester | 1988 | 10.00 |
| ❑ RNLP-70886 | Third Down, 110 to Go | 1988 | 10.00 |

### SUGAR HILL

| Number | Title (A Side/B Side) | Yr | NM |
|---|---|---|---|
| ❑ SH-1023 | Humour Me | 1988 | 12.00 |

## WINCHESTER, LEM

### ARGO

| Number | Title (A Side/B Side) | Yr | NM |
|---|---|---|---|
| ❑ LP-642 [M] | Lem Winchester with the Ramsey Lewis Trio | 1959 | 50.00 |
| ❑ LPS-642 [S] | Lem Winchester with the Ramsey Lewis Trio | 1959 | 40.00 |

### METROJAZZ

| Number | Title (A Side/B Side) | Yr | NM |
|---|---|---|---|
| ❑ E-1005 [M] | New Faces at Newport | 1958 | 50.00 |

### MOODSVILLE

| Number | Title (A Side/B Side) | Yr | NM |
|---|---|---|---|
| ❑ MVLP-11 [M] | Lem Winchester with Feeling | 1960 | 50.00 |
| *—Green label* | | | |
| ❑ MVLP-11 [M] | Lem Winchester with Feeling | 1965 | 25.00 |
| *—Blue label, trident logo at right* | | | |

### NEW JAZZ

| Number | Title (A Side/B Side) | Yr | NM |
|---|---|---|---|
| ❑ NJLP-8223 [M] | Winchester Special | 1959 | 80.00 |
| *—Purple label* | | | |
| ❑ NJLP-8223 [M] | Winchester Special | 1965 | 25.00 |
| *—Blue label, trident logo at right* | | | |
| ❑ NJLP-8239 [M] | Lem's Beat | 1960 | 50.00 |
| *—Purple label* | | | |
| ❑ NJLP-8239 [M] | Lem's Beat | 1965 | 25.00 |
| *—Blue label, trident logo at right* | | | |
| ❑ NJLP-8244 [M] | Another Opus | 1960 | 50.00 |
| *—Purple label* | | | |
| ❑ NJLP-8244 [M] | Another Opus | 1965 | 25.00 |
| *—Blue label, trident logo at right* | | | |

## WIND
TONY ORLANDO was in this group.

### LIFE

| Number | Title (A Side/B Side) | Yr | NM |
|---|---|---|---|
| ❑ LLPS-2000 | Make Believe | 1969 | 20.00 |

## WIND HARP, THE

### UNITED ARTISTS

| Number | Title (A Side/B Side) | Yr | NM |
|---|---|---|---|
| ❑ UAS-9963 [(2)] | Song from the Hill | 1972 | 20.00 |

## WIND IN THE WILLOWS, THE
With Debbie Harry, later of BLONDIE.

### CAPITOL

| Number | Title (A Side/B Side) | Yr | NM |
|---|---|---|---|
| ❑ SKAO 2956 | The Wind in the Willows | 1968 | 50.00 |

## WINDHURST, JOHNNY

### TRANSITION

| Number | Title (A Side/B Side) | Yr | NM |
|---|---|---|---|
| ❑ TRLP-2 [M] | Jazz at Columbus Ave. | 1956 | 200.00 |
| *—Deduct 1/4 if booklet is missing* | | | |

## WINDING, KAI

### COLUMBIA

| Number | Title (A Side/B Side) | Yr | NM |
|---|---|---|---|
| ❑ CL 936 [M] | Trombone Sound | 1956 | 50.00 |

| Number | Title (A Side/B Side) | Yr | NM |
|---|---|---|---|
| ❑ CL 999 [M] | Trombone Panorama | 1957 | 50.00 |
| ❑ CL 1264 [M] | Swingin' State | 1958 | 50.00 |
| ❑ CL 1329 [M] | Dance to the City Beat | 1959 | 40.00 |
| ❑ CS 8062 [S] | Swingin' State | 1958 | 40.00 |
| ❑ CS 8136 [S] | Dance to the City Beat | 1959 | 30.00 |
| **IMPULSE!** | | | |
| ❑ A 3 [M] | The Incredible Kai Winding Trombones | 1960 | 30.00 |
| ❑ AS 3 [S] | The Incredible Kai Winding Trombones | 1960 | 25.00 |
| *—Orange and black label* | | | |
| **ROOST** | | | |
| ❑ LP 408 [10] | Kai Winding All Stars | 1952 | 120.00 |
| **SAVOY** | | | |
| ❑ MG-9017 [10] | New Trends Of Jazz | 1952 | 120.00 |
| **VERVE** | | | |
| ❑ V-8427 [M] | Kai Ole | 1962 | 25.00 |
| ❑ V6-8427 [S] | Kai Ole | 1962 | 25.00 |
| ❑ V-8493 [M] | Suspense Themes in Jazz | 1962 | 25.00 |
| ❑ V6-8493 [S] | Suspense Themes in Jazz | 1962 | 25.00 |
| ❑ V-8525 [M] | Kai Winding Solo | 1963 | 25.00 |
| ❑ V6-8525 [S] | Kai Winding Solo | 1963 | 25.00 |
| ❑ V-8551 [M] | More!!! | 1963 | 25.00 |
| ❑ V6-8551 [S] | More!!! | 1963 | 25.00 |
| ❑ V-8556 [M] | The Lonely One | 1963 | 25.00 |
| ❑ V6-8556 [S] | The Lonely One | 1963 | 25.00 |
| ❑ V-8573 [M] | Mondo Cane #2 | 1964 | 25.00 |
| ❑ V6-8573 [S] | Mondo Cane #2 | 1964 | 30.00 |
| ❑ V6-8602 [S] | Modern Country | 1964 | 20.00 |
| ❑ V6-8620 [S] | Rainy Day | 1965 | 20.00 |
| ❑ V6-8639 [S] | The "In" Instrumentals | 1965 | 20.00 |

## WINDOWS

| Number | Title (A Side/B Side) | Yr | NM |
|---|---|---|---|
| **(LABEL UNKNOWN)** | | | |
| ❑ (# unknown) | Windows | 1985 | 20.00 |

**WINGS** See PAUL McCARTNEY.

## WINNERS, THE

| Number | Title (A Side/B Side) | Yr | NM |
|---|---|---|---|
| **CROWN** | | | |
| ❑ CST-394 [S] | Checkered Flag | 1963 | 30.00 |
| ❑ CLP-5394 [M] | Checkered Flag | 1963 | 25.00 |

## WINSTONS, THE

| Number | Title (A Side/B Side) | Yr | NM |
|---|---|---|---|
| **METROMEDIA** | | | |
| ❑ MD-1010 | Color Him Father | 1969 | 50.00 |

## WINTER, EDGAR

| Number | Title (A Side/B Side) | Yr | NM |
|---|---|---|---|
| **BLUE SKY** | | | |
| ❑ PZ 33483 | Jasmine Nightdreams | 1975 | 12.00 |
| ❑ PZQ 33483 [Q] | Jasmine Nightdreams | 1975 | 20.00 |
| ❑ PZ 33798 | The Edgar Winter Group with Rick Derringer | 1975 | 12.00 |
| ❑ PZQ 33798 [Q] | The Edgar Winter Group with Rick Derringer | 1975 | 20.00 |
| ❑ PZ 34858 | Re-Cycled | 1977 | 12.00 |
| ❑ JZ 35989 | The Edger Winter Album | 1979 | 12.00 |
| ❑ JZ 36494 | Standing on Rock | 1981 | 12.00 |
| **EPIC** | | | |
| ❑ BN 26503 | Entrance | 1970 | 15.00 |
| *—Yellow label* | | | |
| ❑ BN 26503 | Entrance | 1973 | 12.00 |
| *—Orange label* | | | |
| ❑ E 30512 | Edgar Winter's White Trash | 1971 | 15.00 |
| *—Yellow label* | | | |
| ❑ KE 30512 | Edgar Winter's White Trash | 1973 | 12.00 |
| *—Orange label* | | | |
| ❑ PE 30512 | Edger Winter's White Trash | 1985 | 8.00 |
| *—Budget-line reissue; dark blue label* | | | |
| ❑ EG 31249 [(2)] | Roadwork | 1987 | 10.00 |
| *—Budget-line reissue; dark blue labels* | | | |
| ❑ KEG 31249 [(2)] | Roadwork | 1972 | 20.00 |
| *—Yellow labels* | | | |
| ❑ KEG 31249 [(2)] | Roadwork | 1973 | 15.00 |
| *—Orange labels* | | | |
| ❑ EQ 31584 [Q] | They Only Come Out at Night | 1973 | 25.00 |
| ❑ KE 31584 | They Only Come Out at Night | 1972 | 15.00 |
| *—Yellow label* | | | |
| ❑ KE 31584 | They Only Come Out at Night | 1973 | 12.00 |
| *—Orange label* | | | |
| ❑ PE 31584 | They Only Come Out at Night | 197? | 10.00 |
| *—Reissue with new prefix; orange label* | | | |
| ❑ PE 31584 | They Only Come Out at Night | 1979 | 8.00 |
| *—Budget-line reissue; dark blue label* | | | |
| ❑ PE 32461 | Shock Treatment | 1974 | 15.00 |
| *—Orange label* | | | |
| ❑ PE 32461 | Shock Treatment | 1985 | 8.00 |
| *—Budget-line reissue; dark blue label* | | | |
| ❑ PEQ 32461 [Q] | Shock Treatment | 1974 | 25.00 |
| ❑ BG 33770 [(2)] | Entrance/White Trash | 1975 | 15.00 |
| *—Combines 26503 and 30512 into one package* | | | |
| **RHINO** | | | |
| ❑ R1-70709 | Mission Earth | 1989 | 12.00 |
| ❑ R1-70895 | The Edger Winter Collection | 1989 | 10.00 |

## WINTER, JOHNNY

| Number | Title (A Side/B Side) | Yr | NM |
|---|---|---|---|
| **ACCORD** | | | |
| ❑ SN-7135 | Ready for Winter | 1981 | 10.00 |
| **ALLIGATOR** | | | |
| ❑ 4735 | Guitar Slinger | 1984 | 10.00 |
| ❑ 4742 | Serious Business | 1985 | 10.00 |
| ❑ 4748 | Third Degree | 1986 | 10.00 |
| **BLUE SKY** | | | |
| ❑ PZ 33292 | John Dawson Winter III | 1974 | 12.00 |
| ❑ PZQ 33292 [Q] | John Dawson Winter III | 1974 | 20.00 |
| ❑ PZ 33944 | Captured Live! | 1976 | 12.00 |
| *—No bar code on cover* | | | |
| ❑ PZ 33944 | Captured Live | 198? | 8.00 |
| *—Budget-line reissue with bar code on cover* | | | |
| ❑ PZ 34813 | Nothin' But the Blues | 1977 | 12.00 |
| *—No bar code on cover* | | | |
| ❑ PZ 34813 | Nothin' But the Blues | 198? | 8.00 |
| *—Budget-line reissue with bar code on cover* | | | |
| ❑ JZ 35475 | White, Hot and Blue | 1978 | 12.00 |
| ❑ JZ 36343 | Raisin' Cain | 1980 | 12.00 |
| **BUDDAH** | | | |
| ❑ BDS-7513 | First Winter | 1969 | 20.00 |
| **COLUMBIA** | | | |
| ❑ CS 9826 | Johnny Winter | 1969 | 20.00 |
| *—"360 Sound" label* | | | |
| ❑ CS 9826 | Johnny Winter | 1970 | 12.00 |
| *—Orange label* | | | |
| ❑ PC 9826 | Johnny Winter | 198? | 8.00 |
| *—Budget-line reissue* | | | |
| ❑ KCS 9947 [(2)] | Second Winter | 1969 | 25.00 |
| *—"360 Sound" labels; record 2 has music on only one side (other side is blank)* | | | |
| ❑ KCS 9947 [(2)] | Second Winter | 1970 | 15.00 |
| *—Orange labels* | | | |
| ❑ PC 9947 [(2)] | Second Winter | 198? | 10.00 |
| *—Budget-line reissue* | | | |
| ❑ C 30221 | Johnny Winter And | 1970 | 12.00 |
| *—Orange labels* | | | |
| ❑ C 30221 | Johnny Winter And | 1970 | 20.00 |
| *—"360 Sound" label* | | | |
| ❑ PC 30221 | Johnny Winter And | 198? | 8.00 |
| *—Budget-line reissue* | | | |
| ❑ C 30475 | Live/Johnny Winter And | 1971 | 15.00 |
| ❑ PC 30475 | Live/Johnny Winter And | 198? | 8.00 |
| *—Budget-line reissue* | | | |
| ❑ CQ 32188 [Q] | Still Alive and Well | 1973 | 25.00 |
| ❑ KC 32188 | Still Alive and Well | 1973 | 15.00 |
| ❑ PC 32188 | Still Alive and Well | 198? | 8.00 |
| *—Budget-line reissue* | | | |
| ❑ CQ 32715 [Q] | Saints and Sinners | 1974 | 25.00 |
| ❑ KC 32715 | Saints and Sinners | 1974 | 15.00 |
| ❑ PC 32715 | Saints and Sinners | 197? | 8.00 |
| *—Budget-line reissue* | | | |
| ❑ CG 33651 [(2)] | Johnny Winter And//Live/ Johnny Winter And | 1975 | 15.00 |
| **GRT** | | | |
| ❑ 10010 | The Johnny Winter Story | 1969 | 20.00 |
| **IMPERIAL** | | | |
| ❑ LP-12431 | The Progressive Blues Experiment | 1969 | 50.00 |
| **JANUS** | | | |
| ❑ 3008 | About Blues | 1970 | 20.00 |
| ❑ 3023 | Early Times | 1970 | 25.00 |
| ❑ 3056 [(2)] | Before the Storm | 197? | 20.00 |
| **LIBERTY** | | | |
| ❑ LN-10294 | The Progressive Blues Experiment | 1986 | 10.00 |
| *—Reissue of Imperial LP* | | | |
| **MCA/VOYAGER** | | | |
| ❑ 42241 | The Winter of '88 | 1988 | 10.00 |
| **SONOBEAT** | | | |
| ❑ RS-1002 | The Progressive Blues Experiment | 1968 | 300.00 |
| *—Released in plain white cardboard jacket* | | | |
| **UNITED ARTISTS** | | | |
| ❑ UA-LA139-F | Austin, Tex. | 1974 | 15.00 |

## WINTER, JOHNNY AND EDGAR

Also see each artist's individual listings.

| Number | Title (A Side/B Side) | Yr | NM |
|---|---|---|---|
| **BLUE SKY** | | | |
| ❑ ASZ 242 [DJ] | Johnny and Edgar Winter Discuss Together | 1976 | 25.00 |
| *—Promo-only interview album* | | | |
| ❑ PZ 34033 | Together | 1976 | 12.00 |

## WINTER, PAUL

| Number | Title (A Side/B Side) | Yr | NM |
|---|---|---|---|
| **COLUMBIA** | | | |
| ❑ CS 8725 [S] | Jazz Meets the Bossa Nova | 1962 | 20.00 |
| ❑ CS 8797 [S] | Jazz Premiere: Washington | 1963 | 20.00 |
| ❑ CS 8864 [S] | New Jazz on Campus | 1963 | 20.00 |
| ❑ CS 8955 [S] | Jazz Meets the Folk Song | 1964 | 20.00 |
| ❑ CS 9072 [S] | The Sound of Ipanema | 1965 | 20.00 |
| ❑ CS 9115 [S] | Rio | 1965 | 20.00 |
| **LIVING MUSIC** | | | |
| ❑ LMR-1 [(2)] | Callings | 1980 | 20.00 |
| *—With 20-page booklet* | | | |
| ❑ LMR-2 [(2)] | Missa Gaia/Earth Mass | 1983 | 20.00 |

## WINTERHALTER, HUGO

| Number | Title (A Side/B Side) | Yr | NM |
|---|---|---|---|
| **ABC-PARAMOUNT** | | | |
| ❑ ABC-447 [M] | Season for My Beloved | 1963 | 12.00 |
| ❑ ABCS-447 [S] | Season for My Beloved | 1963 | 15.00 |
| **HARMONY** | | | |
| ❑ HL 7078 [M] | Music, Music, Music | 195? | 15.00 |
| **KAPP** | | | |
| ❑ KL 1407 [M] | Best of '64, The | 1964 | 12.00 |
| ❑ KL-1426 [M] | Semi-Classical Favorites | 196? | 12.00 |
| ❑ KL 1429 [M] | Big Hits of 1965 | 1965 | 12.00 |
| ❑ KS 3407 [S] | Best of '64, The | 1964 | 15.00 |
| ❑ KS-3426 [S] | Semi-Classical Favorites | 196? | 15.00 |
| ❑ KS 3429 [S] | Big Hits of 1965 | 1965 | 15.00 |
| **MUSICOR** | | | |
| ❑ MDS-1013 | Pop Parade | 197? | 12.00 |
| ❑ MDS-1029 | Midnight Cowboy | 197? | 12.00 |
| ❑ MDS-1036 | Airport Love Theme | 197? | 10.00 |
| ❑ MDS-1042 | Best of the Motion Picture Hits | 197? | 12.00 |
| ❑ M2S 3160 [(2)] | All Time Movie Greats | 196? | 15.00 |
| ❑ M2S 3168 [(2)] | Romanceable and Danceable | 196? | 15.00 |
| ❑ MS-3170 | Classical Gas | 1970 | 10.00 |
| ❑ M2S 3178 [(2)] | Your Favorite Motion Picture Music | 197? | 15.00 |
| ❑ MS-3184 | My Favorite Broadway and Hollywood Music | 197? | 10.00 |
| ❑ MS 3190 | Applause | 1971 | 12.00 |
| ❑ MS-3196 | Love Story | 1971 | 10.00 |
| **PICKWICK** | | | |
| ❑ CAS-2309 | Hawaiian Wedding Song | 197? | 8.00 |
| *—Black label, multi-color "P" logo* | | | |
| **RCA CAMDEN** | | | |
| ❑ CAL-379 [M] | Magic Touch | 195? | 15.00 |
| ❑ CAL-443 [M] | Big and Sweet with a Beat | 1958 | 15.00 |
| ❑ CAL-449 [M] | Christmas Magic | 1958 | 15.00 |
| *—Reissue of RCA Victor 3132 with two extra tracks* | | | |
| ❑ CAS-2309 | Hawaiian Wedding Song | 1969 | 10.00 |
| ❑ CAS-2546 | Latin Gold | 1972 | 10.00 |
| **RCA VICTOR** | | | |
| ❑ LPM-1020 [M] | Great Music Themes of TV | 1954 | 25.00 |
| ❑ LPM-1179 [M] | Always | 1955 | 20.00 |
| ❑ LPM-1185 [M] | Music by Starlight | 1955 | 20.00 |
| ❑ LPM-1338 [M] | The Eyes of Love | 1956 | 20.00 |
| ❑ LPM-1400 [M] | Happy Hunting | 1956 | 20.00 |
| ❑ LPM-1677 [M] | Hugo Winterhalter Goes...Latin | 1957 | 20.00 |
| ❑ LSP-1677 [S] | Hugo Winterhalter Goes...Latin | 1958 | 25.00 |
| ❑ LPM-1904 [M] | Wish You Were Here | 1958 | 20.00 |
| ❑ LSP-1904 [S] | Wish You Were Here | 1958 | 25.00 |
| ❑ LPM-1905 [M] | Two Sides of Hugo Winterhalter | 1958 | 20.00 |
| ❑ LSP-1905 [S] | Two Sides of Hugo Winterhalter | 1958 | 30.00 |
| ❑ LPM-2167 [M] | Hugo Winterhalter Goes...Gypsy | 1960 | 15.00 |
| ❑ LSP-2167 [S] | Hugo Winterhalter Goes...Gypsy | 1960 | 20.00 |
| ❑ LPM-2271 [M] | Hugo Winterhalter Goes...South of the Border | 1960 | 15.00 |
| ❑ LSP-2271 [S] | Hugo Winterhalter Goes...South of the Border | 1960 | 20.00 |
| ❑ LPM-2417 [M] | Hugo Winterhalter Goes...Hawaiian | 1961 | 15.00 |
| ❑ LSP-2417 [S] | Hugo Winterhalter Goes...Hawaiian | 1961 | 20.00 |
| ❑ LPM-2482 [M] | Hugo Winterhalter Goes...Continental | 1961 | 15.00 |
| ❑ LSP-2482 [S] | Hugo Winterhalter Goes...Continental | 1961 | 20.00 |
| ❑ ANL1-2483 | Pure Gold | 1977 | 10.00 |
| ❑ LPM-2645 [M] | I Only Have Eyes for You | 1964 | 12.00 |
| ❑ LSP-2645 [S] | I Only Have Eyes for You | 1964 | 15.00 |
| ❑ LPM-3050 [10] | Reminiscing | 195? | 30.00 |
| ❑ LPM-3051 [10] | Music by Starlight | 195? | 30.00 |
| ❑ LPM-3100 [10] | Winterhalter Magic | 195? | 30.00 |
| ❑ LPM-3101 [10] | Song Hits from "Peter Pan" and "Hans Christian Andersen" | 195? | 30.00 |
| ❑ LPM-3132 [10] | Christmas Magic | 1954 | 30.00 |
| ❑ LPM-3379 [M] | The Best of Hugo Winterhalter | 1965 | 12.00 |
| ❑ LSP-3379 [S] | The Best of Hugo Winterhalter | 1965 | 15.00 |

## WINTERS, JERRI

| Number | Title (A Side/B Side) | Yr | NM |
|---|---|---|---|
| **BETHLEHEM** | | | |
| ❑ BCP-76 [M] | Somebody Loves Me | 1957 | 50.00 |
| **FRATERNITY** | | | |
| ❑ F-1001 [M] | Winter's Here | 1955 | 60.00 |

## WINTERS, JONATHAN

| Number | Title (A Side/B Side) | Yr | NM |
|---|---|---|---|
| **COLUMBIA** | | | |
| ❑ CL 2811 [M] | Jonathan Winters Wings It! | 1968 | 25.00 |
| ❑ CS 9611 [S] | Jonathan Winters Wings It! | 1968 | 15.00 |
| ❑ CS 9799 | Stuff 'N' Nonsense | 1969 | 15.00 |
| ❑ KG 31985 [(2)] | Jonathan Winters Laughs Live | 1972 | 20.00 |
| *—Reissue of 9611 and 9799 in one package* | | | |

| Number | Title (A Side/B Side) | Yr | NM |
|---|---|---|---|
| ❑ PG 31985 [(2)] | Jonathan Winters Laughs Live | 197? | 12.00 |

*—Reissue with new prefix*

VERVE

| Number | Title (A Side/B Side) | Yr | NM |
|---|---|---|---|
| ❑ MGVS-6099 [S] | The Wonderful World of Jonathan Winters | 1960 | 25.00 |
| ❑ MGVS-6155 [S] | Down to Earth | 1960 | 25.00 |
| ❑ MGV-15009 [M] | The Wonderful World of Jonathan Winters | 1960 | 25.00 |
| ❑ V-15009 [M] | The Wonderful World of Jonathan Winters | 1961 | 20.00 |
| ❑ V6-15009 [S] | The Wonderful World of Jonathan Winters | 1961 | 20.00 |

*—Reissue of 6099*

| Number | Title (A Side/B Side) | Yr | NM |
|---|---|---|---|
| ❑ MGV-15011 [M] | Down to Earth | 1960 | 25.00 |
| ❑ V-15011 [M] | Down to Earth | 1961 | 20.00 |
| ❑ V6-15011 [S] | Down to Earth | 1961 | 20.00 |

*—Reissue of 6155*

| Number | Title (A Side/B Side) | Yr | NM |
|---|---|---|---|
| ❑ V-15025 [M] | Here's Jonathan | 1961 | 25.00 |
| ❑ V6-15025 [S] | Here's Jonathan | 1961 | 25.00 |
| ❑ V-15032 [M] | Another Day, Another World | 1962 | 25.00 |
| ❑ V6-15032 [R] | Another Day, Another World | 196? | 12.00 |
| ❑ V-15035 [M] | Humor As Seen Through the Eyes of Jonathan Winters | 1963 | 25.00 |
| ❑ V6-15035 [S] | Humor As Seen Through the Eyes of Jonathan Winters | 1963 | 25.00 |
| ❑ V-15037 [M] | Whistle Stopping with Jonathan Winters | 1964 | 20.00 |
| ❑ V6-15037 [R] | Whistle Stopping with Jonathan Winters | 196? | 12.00 |
| ❑ V-15041 [M] | Jonathan Winters' Mad, Mad, Mad, Mad World | 1964 | 20.00 |
| ❑ V6-15041 [R] | Jonathan Winters' Mad, Mad, Mad, Mad World | 196? | 12.00 |
| ❑ V-15047 [M] | Great Moments in Comedy | 1965 | 20.00 |
| ❑ V6-15047 [R] | Great Moments in Comedy | 196? | 12.00 |
| ❑ V-15052 [M] | The Best of Frickert and Suggins | 1966 | 20.00 |
| ❑ V6-15052 [R] | The Best of Frickert and Suggins | 196? | 12.00 |
| ❑ V-15057 [M] | Movies Are Better Than Ever | 1967 | 20.00 |
| ❑ V6-15057 [R] | Movies Are Better Than Ever | 196? | 12.00 |

## WINTERS, PINKY

ARGO

| Number | Title (A Side/B Side) | Yr | NM |
|---|---|---|---|
| ❑ LP-604 [M] | Lonely One | 1956 | 40.00 |

CREATIVE

| Number | Title (A Side/B Side) | Yr | NM |
|---|---|---|---|
| ❑ LP-604 [M] | Lonely One | 1956 | 60.00 |

VANTAGE

| Number | Title (A Side/B Side) | Yr | NM |
|---|---|---|---|
| ❑ VLP-3 [10] | Pinky Winters | 1954 | 1000. |

## WINTERS, SMILEY

ARHOOLIE

| Number | Title (A Side/B Side) | Yr | NM |
|---|---|---|---|
| ❑ 8004/5 [(2)] | Smiley Etc. | 1969 | 20.00 |

## WINWOOD, STEVE

Also see BLIND FAITH; THE SPENCER DAVIS GROUP; TRAFFIC.

ISLAND

| Number | Title (A Side/B Side) | Yr | NM |
|---|---|---|---|
| ❑ ILPS 9387 | Go | 1976 | 12.00 |

*—With Stomo Yamahita and Michael Shrieve*

| Number | Title (A Side/B Side) | Yr | NM |
|---|---|---|---|
| ❑ ILPS 9494 | Steve Winwood | 1977 | 10.00 |
| ❑ ILPS 9576 | Arc of a Diver | 1981 | 10.00 |
| ❑ ILPS 9777 | Talking Back to the Night | 1982 | 10.00 |
| ❑ 25448 | Back in the High Life | 1986 | 8.00 |
| ❑ 25660 | Chronicles | 1987 | 8.00 |

SPRINGBOARD

| Number | Title (A Side/B Side) | Yr | NM |
|---|---|---|---|
| ❑ SPB-4040 | Winwood & Friends | 197? | 15.00 |

*—Budget release with Winwood material on Side 1 and a collection of Jeff Beck, Yardbirds, Long John Baldry and Jack Bruce/Ginger Baker material on Side 2*

UNITED ARTISTS

| Number | Title (A Side/B Side) | Yr | NM |
|---|---|---|---|
| ❑ UAS-9950 [(2)] | Winwood | 1971 | 15.00 |

*—Collection of tracks Winwood recorded with the Spencer Davis Group, Traffic and Blind Faith; without booklet*

| Number | Title (A Side/B Side) | Yr | NM |
|---|---|---|---|
| ❑ UAS-9950 [(2)] | Winwood | 1971 | 25.00 |

*—Collection of tracks Winwood recorded with the Spencer Davis Group, Traffic and Blind Faith; with booklet*

VIRGIN

| Number | Title (A Side/B Side) | Yr | NM |
|---|---|---|---|
| ❑ 90946 | Roll With It | 1988 | 8.00 |
| ❑ 91405 | Refugees of the Heart | 1990 | 15.00 |
| ❑ R 154633 | Roll With It | 1988 | 10.00 |

*—BMG Direct Marketing edition*

## WIPERS, THE

PARK AVE.

| Number | Title (A Side/B Side) | Yr | NM |
|---|---|---|---|
| ❑ (# unknown) | Is This Real? | 1980 | 50.00 |
| ❑ 82802 | Youth of America | 1981 | 50.00 |

RESTLESS

| Number | Title (A Side/B Side) | Yr | NM |
|---|---|---|---|
| ❑ 72026 | Wipers Live | 1985 | 12.00 |
| ❑ 72094 | Land of the Lost | 1986 | 12.00 |
| ❑ 72187 | Over the Edge | 1987 | 12.00 |

*—Reissue*

| Number | Title (A Side/B Side) | Yr | NM |
|---|---|---|---|
| ❑ 72194 | Follow Blind | 1987 | 12.00 |

TIM/KERR

| Number | Title (A Side/B Side) | Yr | NM |
|---|---|---|---|
| ❑ 31 | Silver Sail | 1993 | 12.00 |

## WISE, CHUBBY

STARDAY

| Number | Title (A Side/B Side) | Yr | NM |
|---|---|---|---|
| ❑ SLP-154 [M] | The Tennessee Fiddler | 1961 | 50.00 |

## WISE, CHUBBY, AND MAC WISEMAN

GILLEY'S

| Number | Title (A Side/B Side) | Yr | NM |
|---|---|---|---|
| ❑ 500 | Give Me My Smokies and The Tennessee Waltz | 197? | 20.00 |

## WISEMAN, MAC

ABC

| Number | Title (A Side/B Side) | Yr | NM |
|---|---|---|---|
| ❑ 4009 | 16 Great Performances | 1974 | 12.00 |
| ❑ AC-30033 | The ABC Collection | 1976 | 12.00 |

CAPITOL

| Number | Title (A Side/B Side) | Yr | NM |
|---|---|---|---|
| ❑ ST 1800 [S] | Bluegrass Favorites | 1962 | 40.00 |
| ❑ T 1800 [M] | Bluegrass Favorites | 1962 | 30.00 |

CMH

| Number | Title (A Side/B Side) | Yr | NM |
|---|---|---|---|
| ❑ 4502 | Greatest Bluegrass Hits | 198? | 10.00 |
| ❑ 6202 | Country Memories | 197? | 12.00 |
| ❑ 6217 | Mac Wiseman Sings Gordon Lightfoot | 197? | 12.00 |
| ❑ 9001 [(2)] | The Mac Wiseman Story | 197? | 15.00 |
| ❑ 9021 [(2)] | Songs That Made the Juke Box Play | 197? | 15.00 |

DOT

| Number | Title (A Side/B Side) | Yr | NM |
|---|---|---|---|
| ❑ DLP-3084 [M] | Tis Sweet to Be Remembered | 1958 | 50.00 |
| ❑ DLP-3135 [M] | Beside the Still Waters | 1959 | 30.00 |
| ❑ DLP-3213 [M] | Great Folk Ballads | 1959 | 30.00 |
| ❑ DLP-3313 [M] | 12 Great Hits | 1960 | 30.00 |
| ❑ DLP-3336 [M] | Keep on the Sunny Side | 1960 | 40.00 |
| ❑ DLP-3373 [M] | Best Loved Gospel Hymns | 1961 | 30.00 |
| ❑ DLP-3408 [M] | Fireball Mail | 1961 | 40.00 |
| ❑ DLP-3697 [M] | This Is Mac Wiseman | 1966 | 20.00 |
| ❑ DLP-3730 [M] | A Master at Work | 1966 | 20.00 |
| ❑ DLP-3731 [M] | Bluegrass | 1966 | 20.00 |
| ❑ DLP-25084 [R] | Tis Sweet to Be Remembered | 196? | 20.00 |
| ❑ DLP-25135 [S] | Beside the Still Waters | 1959 | 40.00 |
| ❑ DLP-25213 [S] | Great Folk Ballads | 1959 | 40.00 |
| ❑ DLP-25313 [S] | 12 Great Hits | 1960 | 40.00 |
| ❑ DLP-25336 [R] | Keep on the Sunny Side | 196? | 20.00 |
| ❑ DLP-25373 [S] | Best Loved Gospel Hymns | 1961 | 40.00 |
| ❑ DLP-25408 [R] | Fireball Mail | 196? | 20.00 |
| ❑ DLP-25697 [S] | This Is Mac Wiseman | 1966 | 25.00 |
| ❑ DLP-25730 [S] | A Master at Work | 1966 | 25.00 |
| ❑ DLP-25731 [S] | Bluegrass | 1966 | 25.00 |
| ❑ DLP-25896 | Golden Hits of Mac Wiseman | 1968 | 20.00 |

HAMILTON

| Number | Title (A Side/B Side) | Yr | NM |
|---|---|---|---|
| ❑ HLP-12130 [M] | Sincerely | 1964 | 20.00 |
| ❑ HLP-12167 [M] | Songs of the Dear Old Days | 1965 | 20.00 |

HILLTOP

| Number | Title (A Side/B Side) | Yr | NM |
|---|---|---|---|
| ❑ JM-6047 [M] | Mac Wiseman | 1967 | 15.00 |
| ❑ JS-6047 [R] | Mac Wiseman | 1967 | 12.00 |

MCA

| Number | Title (A Side/B Side) | Yr | NM |
|---|---|---|---|
| ❑ 4009 | 16 Great Performances | 198? | 8.00 |

*—Reissue of ABC 4009*

RCA VICTOR

| Number | Title (A Side/B Side) | Yr | NM |
|---|---|---|---|
| ❑ ANL1-1208 | Concert Favorites | 1975 | 10.00 |

*—Reissue of 4845*

| Number | Title (A Side/B Side) | Yr | NM |
|---|---|---|---|
| ❑ LSP-4336 | Johnny's Cash and Charley's Pride | 1970 | 15.00 |
| ❑ LSP-4845 | Concert Favorites | 1972 | 15.00 |

VETCO

| Number | Title (A Side/B Side) | Yr | NM |
|---|---|---|---|
| ❑ 508 | New Traditions, Vol. 1 | 197? | 15.00 |
| ❑ 509 | New Traditions, Vol. 2 | 197? | 15.00 |

## WISNER, JIMMY

CHANCELLOR

| Number | Title (A Side/B Side) | Yr | NM |
|---|---|---|---|
| ❑ CHJ-5014 [M] | Aper-Sepshun | 1960 | 25.00 |
| ❑ CHJS-5014 [S] | Aper-Sepshun | 1960 | 30.00 |

COLUMBIA

| Number | Title (A Side/B Side) | Yr | NM |
|---|---|---|---|
| ❑ CS 9837 | Love Theme from "Romeo and Juliet" | 1969 | 10.00 |

FELSTED

| Number | Title (A Side/B Side) | Yr | NM |
|---|---|---|---|
| ❑ FL-2509 [S] | Blues for Harvey | 1962 | 25.00 |
| ❑ FL-7509 [M] | Blues for Harvey | 1962 | 30.00 |

WYNCOTE

| Number | Title (A Side/B Side) | Yr | NM |
|---|---|---|---|
| ❑ SW-9103 [S] | Cast Your Fate to the Wind | 1965 | 12.00 |
| ❑ W-9103 [M] | Cast Your Fate to the Wind | 1965 | 10.00 |

## WITHERS, BILL

COLUMBIA

| Number | Title (A Side/B Side) | Yr | NM |
|---|---|---|---|
| ❑ PC 33704 | Making Music | 1975 | 10.00 |
| ❑ PC 34327 | Naked and Warm | 1976 | 10.00 |
| ❑ JC 34903 | Menagerie | 1977 | 10.00 |
| ❑ JC 35596 | 'Bout Love | 1979 | 10.00 |
| ❑ JC 36877 | The Best of Bill Withers | 1981 | — |

*—Canceled?*

| Number | Title (A Side/B Side) | Yr | NM |
|---|---|---|---|
| ❑ FC 37199 | Bill Withers' Greatest Hits | 1981 | 10.00 |

*—Re-release of 36877 with "Just the Two of Us" added*

| Number | Title (A Side/B Side) | Yr | NM |
|---|---|---|---|
| ❑ FC 39887 | Watching You Watching Me | 1985 | 10.00 |
| ❑ PC 40177 | Still Bill | 1985 | 8.00 |

*—Reissue of Sussex 7014*

| Number | Title (A Side/B Side) | Yr | NM |
|---|---|---|---|
| ❑ PC 40178 | Just As I Am | 1985 | 8.00 |

*—Reissue of Sussex 7006*

SUSSEX

| Number | Title (A Side/B Side) | Yr | NM |
|---|---|---|---|
| ❑ SXBS-7006 | Just As I Am | 1971 | 20.00 |
| ❑ SXBS-7014 | Still Bill | 1972 | 20.00 |
| ❑ SXBS-7025-2 [(2)] | Bill Withers Live at Carnegie Hall | 1973 | 20.00 |
| ❑ SUX-8032 | +'Justments | 1974 | 15.00 |
| ❑ SUX-8037 | The Best of Bill Withers | 1975 | 15.00 |

## WITHERSPOON, JIMMY

ABC

| Number | Title (A Side/B Side) | Yr | NM |
|---|---|---|---|
| ❑ 717 | Handbags and Gladrags | 1970 | 25.00 |

ANALOGUE PRODUCTIONS

| Number | Title (A Side/B Side) | Yr | NM |
|---|---|---|---|
| ❑ APR 3008 | Evenin' Blues | 199? | 15.00 |

BLUE NOTE

| Number | Title (A Side/B Side) | Yr | NM |
|---|---|---|---|
| ❑ BN-LA534-G | Spoonful | 1976 | 12.00 |

BLUESWAY

| Number | Title (A Side/B Side) | Yr | NM |
|---|---|---|---|
| ❑ BLS-6026 | Blues Singer | 1969 | 25.00 |
| ❑ BLS-6040 | Hunh | 1970 | 25.00 |
| ❑ BLS-6051 | The Best of Jimmy Witherspoon | 1970 | 25.00 |

CAPITOL

| Number | Title (A Side/B Side) | Yr | NM |
|---|---|---|---|
| ❑ ST-11360 | Love Is a Five Letter Word | 1975 | 12.00 |

CHESS

| Number | Title (A Side/B Side) | Yr | NM |
|---|---|---|---|
| ❑ CH-93003 | Spoon So Easy: The Chess Years | 1990 | 12.00 |

CONSTELLATION

| Number | Title (A Side/B Side) | Yr | NM |
|---|---|---|---|
| ❑ CM 1422 [M] | Take This Hammer | 1964 | 50.00 |
| ❑ CMS 1422 [R] | Take This Hammer | 1964 | 30.00 |

CROWN

| Number | Title (A Side/B Side) | Yr | NM |
|---|---|---|---|
| ❑ CST-215 [S] | Jimmy Witherspoon Sings the Blues | 1961 | 100.00 |

*—Black vinyl; this value assumes that this is in true stereo, as the red vinyl version is, but this has not been confirmed*

| Number | Title (A Side/B Side) | Yr | NM |
|---|---|---|---|
| ❑ CST-215 [S] | Jimmy Witherspoon Sings the Blues | 1961 | 150.00 |

*—Red vinyl; contrary to prior reports, this album -- at least the red vinyl version -- is in true stereo!*

| Number | Title (A Side/B Side) | Yr | NM |
|---|---|---|---|
| ❑ CLP-5156 [M] | Jimmy Witherspoon | 1959 | 80.00 |

*—Black label, silver print*

| Number | Title (A Side/B Side) | Yr | NM |
|---|---|---|---|
| ❑ CLP-5156 [M] | Jimmy Witherspoon | 1961 | 25.00 |

*—Gray label, black print*

| Number | Title (A Side/B Side) | Yr | NM |
|---|---|---|---|
| ❑ CLP-5192 [M] | Jimmy Witherspoon Sings the Blues | 1959 | 80.00 |

*—Black label, silver print*

| Number | Title (A Side/B Side) | Yr | NM |
|---|---|---|---|
| ❑ CLP-5192 [M] | Jimmy Witherspoon Sings the Blues | 1961 | 25.00 |

*—Gray label, black print*

FANTASY

| Number | Title (A Side/B Side) | Yr | NM |
|---|---|---|---|
| ❑ OBC-511 | Evenin' Blues | 1988 | 12.00 |

*—Reissue of Prestige 7300*

| Number | Title (A Side/B Side) | Yr | NM |
|---|---|---|---|
| ❑ OBC-527 | Baby, Baby, Baby | 1990 | 12.00 |

*—Reissue of Prestige 7290*

| Number | Title (A Side/B Side) | Yr | NM |
|---|---|---|---|
| ❑ 9660 | Rockin' L.A. | 1989 | 12.00 |
| ❑ 24701 [(2)] | The 'Spoon Concerts | 1972 | 20.00 |

HIFI

| Number | Title (A Side/B Side) | Yr | NM |
|---|---|---|---|
| ❑ R-421 [M] | At the Monterey Jazz Festival | 1959 | 100.00 |
| ❑ SR-421 [S] | At the Monterey Jazz Festival | 1959 | 60.00 |
| ❑ R-422 [M] | Feelin' the Spirit | 1959 | 100.00 |
| ❑ SR-422 [S] | Feelin' the Spirit | 1959 | 60.00 |
| ❑ R-426 [M] | Jimmy Witherspoon at the Renaissance | 1959 | 100.00 |
| ❑ SR-426 [S] | Jimmy Witherspoon at the Renaissance | 1959 | 60.00 |

JAZZ MAN

| Number | Title (A Side/B Side) | Yr | NM |
|---|---|---|---|
| ❑ 5013 | Jimmy Witherspoon Sings the Blues | 1980 | 12.00 |

LAX

| Number | Title (A Side/B Side) | Yr | NM |
|---|---|---|---|
| ❑ PW 37115 | Love Is a Five Letter Word | 1981 | 10.00 |

*—Reissue of Capitol LP*

MUSE

| Number | Title (A Side/B Side) | Yr | NM |
|---|---|---|---|
| ❑ MR-5288 | Jimmy Witherspoon Sings the Blues | 1983 | 10.00 |
| ❑ MR-5327 | Midnight Lady Called the Blues | 1986 | 10.00 |

PRESTIGE

| Number | Title (A Side/B Side) | Yr | NM |
|---|---|---|---|
| ❑ PRLP-7290 [M] | Baby, Baby, Baby | 1963 | 40.00 |
| ❑ PRST-7290 [S] | Baby, Baby, Baby | 1963 | 40.00 |
| ❑ PRLP-7300 [M] | Evenin' Blues | 1964 | 40.00 |
| ❑ PRST-7300 [S] | Evenin' Blues | 1964 | 40.00 |
| ❑ PRLP-7314 [M] | Blues Around the Clock | 1964 | 40.00 |
| ❑ PRST-7314 [S] | Blues Around the Clock | 1964 | 40.00 |
| ❑ PRLP-7327 [M] | Blue Spoon | 1964 | 40.00 |
| ❑ PRST-7327 [S] | Blue Spoon | 1964 | 40.00 |
| ❑ PRLP-7356 [M] | Some of My Best Friends Are the Blues | 1965 | 25.00 |
| ❑ PRST-7356 [S] | Some of My Best Friends Are the Blues | 1965 | 25.00 |
| ❑ PRLP-7418 [M] | Spoon in London | 1966 | 25.00 |
| ❑ PRST-7418 [S] | Spoon in London | 1966 | 25.00 |
| ❑ PRLP-7475 [M] | Blues for Easy Livers | 1967 | 25.00 |
| ❑ PRST-7475 [S] | Blues for Easy Livers | 1967 | 20.00 |

Stevie Wonder, *Looking Back,* Motown M-804LP3, 1977, 3-record set, $25.

| Number | Title (A Side/B Side) | Yr | NM |
|---|---|---|---|
| ❑ PRST-7713 | The Best of Jimmy Witherspoon | 1969 | 20.00 |
| ❑ 7855 | Mean Old Frisco | 1974 | 15.00 |
| RCA VICTOR | | | |
| ❑ ANL1-1048 | Goin' to Kansas City Blues | 1976 | 10.00 |
| *—Reissue* | | | |
| ❑ LPM-1639 [M] | Goin' to Kansas City Blues | 1957 | 100.00 |
| REPRISE | | | |
| ❑ R-2008 [M] | Spoon | 1961 | 40.00 |
| ❑ R9-2008 [S] | Spoon | 1961 | 60.00 |
| ❑ R-6012 [M] | Hey, Mrs. Jones | 1961 | 40.00 |
| ❑ R9-6012 [S] | Hey, Mrs. Jones | 1961 | 60.00 |
| ❑ R-6059 [M] | Roots | 1962 | 40.00 |
| ❑ R9-6059 [S] | Roots | 1962 | 60.00 |
| UNITED | | | |
| ❑ 7715 | A Spoonful of Blues | 197? | 12.00 |
| VERVE | | | |
| ❑ V-5007 [M] | Blue Point of View | 1966 | 20.00 |
| ❑ V6-5007 [S] | Blue Point of View | 1966 | 25.00 |
| ❑ V-5030 [M] | Blues Is Now | 1967 | 25.00 |
| ❑ V6-5030 [S] | Blues Is Now | 1967 | 20.00 |
| ❑ V-5050 [M] | A Spoonful of Soul | 1968 | 30.00 |
| ❑ V6-5050 [S] | A Spoonful of Soul | 1968 | 20.00 |
| WORLD PACIFIC | | | |
| ❑ WP-1267 [M] | Singin' the Blues | 1959 | 100.00 |
| ❑ WP-1402 [M] | There's Good Rockin' Tonight | 1961 | 60.00 |
| *—Reissue of 1267* | | | |

**WITHERSPOON, JIMMY, AND RICHARD "GROOVE" HOLMES**

| Number | Title (A Side/B Side) | Yr | NM |
|---|---|---|---|
| OLYMPIC GOLD MEDAL | | | |
| ❑ 7107 | Groovin' and Spoonin' | 1974 | 12.00 |
| SURREY | | | |
| ❑ S-1106 [M] | Blues for Spoon and Groove | 1965 | 25.00 |
| ❑ SS-1106 [S] | Blues for Spoon and Groove | 1965 | 30.00 |

**WITHERSPOON, JIMMY, AND GERRY MULLIGAN**

| Number | Title (A Side/B Side) | Yr | NM |
|---|---|---|---|
| EVEREST ARCHIVE OF FOLK & JAZZ | | | |
| ❑ 264 | Jimmy Witherspoon and Gerry Mulligan | 197? | 12.00 |

**WITHERSPOON, JIMMY, AND BEN WEBSTER**

| Number | Title (A Side/B Side) | Yr | NM |
|---|---|---|---|
| VERVE | | | |
| ❑ V6-8835 | Previously Unreleased Recordings | 197? | 15.00 |

**WITTWER, JOHNNY**

| Number | Title (A Side/B Side) | Yr | NM |
|---|---|---|---|
| STINSON | | | |
| ❑ SLP-58 | Piano Rags | 195? | 20.00 |

**WIZARD**

| Number | Title (A Side/B Side) | Yr | NM |
|---|---|---|---|
| PEON | | | |
| ❑ 1069 | Original Wizard | 1971 | 200.00 |

**WIZARDS FROM KANSAS, THE**

| Number | Title (A Side/B Side) | Yr | NM |
|---|---|---|---|
| MERCURY | | | |
| ❑ SR-61309 | The Wizards from Kansas | 1970 | 200.00 |

**WOFFORD, MIKE**

| Number | Title (A Side/B Side) | Yr | NM |
|---|---|---|---|
| EPIC | | | |
| ❑ LN 24225 [M] | Strawberry Wine | 1967 | 20.00 |
| MILESTONE | | | |
| ❑ MPS-9012 | Summer Night | 1968 | 20.00 |

**WOLFE, NEIL**

| Number | Title (A Side/B Side) | Yr | NM |
|---|---|---|---|
| IMPERIAL | | | |
| ❑ LP-12084 [S] | Neil Swings Nicely | 1962 | 20.00 |
| ❑ LP-12192 [S] | One Order of Blues | 1962 | 20.00 |

**WOLFMAN JACK**

| Number | Title (A Side/B Side) | Yr | NM |
|---|---|---|---|
| BREAD | | | |
| ❑ 0170 | Wolfman Jack and the Wolf Pack | 1965 | 400.00 |
| WOODEN NICKEL | | | |
| ❑ BWS1-0119 | Fun and Romance Through the Ages | 1974 | 25.00 |
| ❑ WNS-1009 | Wolfman Jack | 1972 | 30.00 |

**WOMACK, BOBBY**

| Number | Title (A Side/B Side) | Yr | NM |
|---|---|---|---|
| ARISTA | | | |
| ❑ AB 4222 | Roads of Life | 1979 | 10.00 |
| BEVERLY GLEN | | | |
| ❑ 10000 | The Poet | 1981 | 10.00 |
| ❑ 10003 | The Poet II | 1984 | 10.00 |
| COLUMBIA | | | |
| ❑ PC 34384 | Home Is Where the Heart Is | 1977 | 10.00 |
| ❑ JC 35083 | Pieces | 1978 | 10.00 |
| LIBERTY | | | |
| ❑ LST-7645 | The Womack "Live" | 1971 | 12.00 |
| ❑ LN-10171 | Bobby Womack's Greatest Hits | 198? | 8.00 |
| *—Budget-line reissue of United Artists 346* | | | |
| MCA | | | |
| ❑ 5617 | So Many Rivers | 1985 | 8.00 |
| MINIT | | | |
| ❑ 24014 | Fly Me to the Moon | 1968 | 30.00 |
| ❑ 24027 | My Prescription | 1969 | 30.00 |
| UNITED ARTISTS | | | |
| ❑ UA-LA043-F | Facts of Life | 1973 | 12.00 |
| ❑ UA-LA199-G | Lookin' for a Love Again | 1974 | 12.00 |
| ❑ UA-LA346-G | Bobby Womack's Greatest Hits | 1974 | 12.00 |
| ❑ UA-LA353-G | I Don't Know What the World Is Coming To | 1975 | 12.00 |
| ❑ UA-LA544-G | Safety Zone | 1975 | 12.00 |
| ❑ UA-LA638-G | B.W. Goes C and W | 1976 | 12.00 |
| ❑ LM-1002 | Understanding | 1980 | 8.00 |
| *—Reissue of 5577* | | | |
| ❑ UAS-5225 | Across 110th Street | 1972 | 12.00 |
| ❑ UAS-5539 | Communication | 1971 | 12.00 |
| ❑ UAS-5577 | Understanding | 1972 | 12.00 |

**WOMB**

| Number | Title (A Side/B Side) | Yr | NM |
|---|---|---|---|
| DOT | | | |
| ❑ DLP-25933 | Womb | 1969 | 20.00 |
| ❑ DLP-25959 | Overdub | 1969 | 20.00 |

**WONDER, STEVIE**

| Number | Title (A Side/B Side) | Yr | NM |
|---|---|---|---|
| GORDY | | | |
| ❑ GS 932 | Eivets Rednow | 1968 | 30.00 |
| *—As "Eivets Rednow"* | | | |
| JOBETE | | | |
| ❑ JSA-6253 [DJ] | The Wonder of Stevie | 1988 | 20.00 |
| *—Publisher's demo with excerpts of 105 (!) Stevie Wonder songs* | | | |
| MOTOWN | | | |
| ❑ M5-131V1 | Recorded Live/Little Stevie Wonder/The 12 Year Old Genius | 1981 | 12.00 |
| *—Reissue of Tamla 240* | | | |
| ❑ M5-150V1 | With a Song in My Heart | 1981 | 12.00 |
| *—Reissue of Tamla 250* | | | |
| ❑ M5-166V1 | Down to Earth | 1981 | 12.00 |
| *—Reissue of Tamla 272* | | | |
| ❑ M5-173V1 | Tribute to Uncle Ray | 1981 | 12.00 |
| *—Reissue of Tamla 232* | | | |
| ❑ M5-176V1 | Signed, Sealed and Delivered | 1981 | 12.00 |
| *—Reissue of Tamla 304* | | | |
| ❑ M5-179V1 | My Cherie Amour | 1981 | 12.00 |
| *—Reissue of Tamla 296* | | | |
| ❑ M5-183V1 | Up-Tight Everything's Alright | 1981 | 12.00 |
| *—Reissue of Tamla 268* | | | |
| ❑ M5-219V1 | The Jazz Soul of Little Stevie | 1981 | 12.00 |
| *—Reissue of Tamla 233* | | | |
| ❑ 31453 0238-1 [(2)DJ] | Conversation Peace | 1995 | 25.00 |
| *—Vinyl is promo only; white cover with custom sticker* | | | |
| ❑ M9-804A3 [(3)] | Looking Back | 1977 | 25.00 |
| *—Withdrawn after Stevie Wonder objected to its release* | | | |
| ❑ 5255 ML | Someday at Christmas | 1982 | 10.00 |
| *—Reissue of Tamla 281* | | | |
| ❑ 6108 ML | The Woman in Red | 1984 | 10.00 |
| *—With sticker at top proclaiming "New Stevie Wonder Album"* | | | |
| ❑ 6108 ML | The Woman in Red | 1984 | 12.00 |
| *—With no sticker proclaiming "New Stevie Wonder Album"* | | | |
| ❑ 6248 ML | Characters | 1987 | 10.00 |
| ❑ 6291 ML | Music from the Movie Jungle Fever | 1991 | 20.00 |
| TAMLA | | | |
| ❑ T 232 [M] | Tribute to Uncle Ray | 1962 | 150.00 |
| ❑ T 233 [M] | The Jazz Soul of Little Stevie | 1962 | 150.00 |
| ❑ T 240 [M] | Recorded Live/Little Stevie Wonder/The 12 Year Old Genius | 1963 | 120.00 |
| *—The above three LPs as "Little Stevie Wonder"* | | | |
| ❑ T 248 [M] | Workout Stevie, Workout | 1963 | 1000. |
| *—Canceled; test pressings or acetates may exist* | | | |
| ❑ T 250 [M] | With a Song in My Heart | 1964 | 80.00 |
| ❑ T 255 [M] | Stevie at the Beach | 1964 | 80.00 |
| ❑ T 268 [M] | Up-Tight Everything's Alright | 1966 | 25.00 |
| ❑ TS 268 [S] | Up-Tight Everything's Alright | 1966 | 30.00 |
| ❑ T 272 [M] | Down to Earth | 1966 | 20.00 |
| ❑ TS 272 [S] | Down to Earth | 1966 | 25.00 |
| ❑ T 279 [M] | I Was Made to Love Her | 1967 | 20.00 |
| ❑ TS 279 [S] | I Was Made to Love Her | 1967 | 25.00 |
| ❑ T 281 [M] | Someday at Christmas | 1967 | 30.00 |
| ❑ TS 281 [S] | Someday at Christmas | 1967 | 40.00 |
| ❑ T 282 [M] | Greatest Hits | 1968 | 30.00 |
| ❑ TS 282 [S] | Greatest Hits | 1968 | 20.00 |
| ❑ TS 291 | For Once in My Life | 1968 | 20.00 |
| ❑ TS 296 | My Cherie Amour | 1969 | 20.00 |
| ❑ TS 298 | Stevie Wonder Live | 1970 | 20.00 |
| ❑ TS 304 | Signed Sealed and Delivered | 1970 | 20.00 |
| ❑ TS 308 | Where I'm Coming From | 1971 | 20.00 |
| ❑ T 313L | Stevie Wonder's Greatest Hits Vol. 2 | 1971 | 20.00 |
| *—Some, if not all, LP covers have the title mis-punctuated as "Stevie Wonders' Greatest Hits Vol. 2"* | | | |
| ❑ T 314L | Music of My Mind | 1972 | 20.00 |
| ❑ T 319L | Talking Book | 1972 | 15.00 |
| *—Original pressings have a braille note on cover* | | | |



Except when noted otherwise, VG = 25% of NM, and VG+ = 50% of NM. (Example: VG = $2.00, VG+ = $4.00 and NM = $8.00.)

| Number | Title (A Side/B Side) | Yr | NM |
|---|---|---|---|
| ❑ T 319L | Talking Book | 1973 | 10.00 |

*—No braille note on cover*

❑ T 326L Innervisions 1973 15.00
❑ T6-332S1 Fulfillingness' First Finale 1974 15.00
❑ T13-340C2 [(2)]Songs in the Key of Life 1976 20.00
*—With booklet and bonus 7-inch EP (deduct 25% if missing)*
❑ T7-362R1 Someday at Christmas 1978 20.00
*—Unusual reissue of 281*
❑ T13-371C2 [(2)]Journey Through the Secret Life of Plants 1979 15.00
❑ T8-373S1 Hotter Than July 1980 12.00
❑ 6002 TL2 [(2)] Stevie Wonder's Original Musiquarium I 1982 15.00
❑ 6134 TL In Square Circle 1985 10.00

### WOOD, BOBBY
JOY
❑ JL 1001 [M] Bobby Wood 1964 40.00

### WOOD, BRENTON
BRENT
❑ S-100 [S] Introducing Brenton Wood! Boogaloo 1967 60.00
*—Four tracks by Brenton Wood, six by other artists*
❑ 5100 [M] Introducing Brenton Wood! Boogaloo 1967 40.00
CREAM
❑ 1006 Come Softly 1977 15.00
DOUBLE SHOT
❑ 1002 [M] Oogum Boogum 1967 25.00
❑ 1003 [M] Baby You Got It 1967 25.00
❑ 5002 [S] Oogum Boogum 1967 30.00
❑ 5003 [S] Baby You Got It 1967 30.00
*—Black vinyl*
❑ 5003 [S] Baby You Got It 1967 200.00
*—Multi-color vinyl*
RHINO
❑ RNLP-70223 The Best of Brenton Wood 1986 10.00

### WOOD, DEL
COLUMBIA
❑ CL 2539 [M] Upright, Low Down and Honky Tonk 1966 12.00
❑ CS 9339 [S] Upright, Low Down and Honky Tonk 1966 15.00
LAMB & LION
❑ 1009 Rag Time Glory Special 197? 12.00
MERCURY
❑ MG-20678 [M] Ragtime Goes South of the Border 1962 12.00
❑ MG-20713 [M] Ragtime Goes International 1962 12.00
❑ MG-20804 [M] Piano Roll Blues 1963 12.00
❑ MG-20978 [M] Roll Out the Piano 1964 12.00
❑ SR-60678 [S] Ragtime Goes South of the Border 1962 15.00
❑ SR-60713 [S] Ragtime Goes International 1962 15.00
❑ SR-60804 [S] Piano Roll Blues 1963 15.00
❑ SR-60978 [S] Roll Out the Piano 1964 15.00
RCA CAMDEN
❑ CAL-684 [M] Honky Tonk Piano 1962 12.00
❑ CAS-684 [R] Honky Tonk Piano 1962 10.00
❑ CAL-796 [M] It's Honky Tonk Time 1964 12.00
❑ CAS-796 [R] It's Honky Tonk Time 1964 10.00
RCA VICTOR
❑ LPM-1129 [M] Down Yonder 1955 20.00
❑ LPM-1437 [M] Hot, Happy and Honky 1957 20.00
❑ LPM-1633 [M] Rags to Riches 1958 15.00
❑ LSP-1633 [S] Rags to Riches 1958 20.00
❑ LPM-2091 [M] Mississippi Show Boat 1959 15.00
❑ LSP-2091 [S] Mississippi Show Boat 1959 20.00
❑ LPM-2203 [M] Flivvers, Flappers and Fox Trots 1960 15.00
❑ LSP-2203 [S] Flivvers, Flappers and Fox Trots 1960 20.00
❑ LPM-2240 [M] Buggies, Bustles and Barrelhouse 1960 15.00
❑ LSP-2240 [S] Buggies, Bustles and Barrelhouse 1960 20.00
❑ LPM-3907 [M] The Best of Del Wood 1968 25.00
❑ LSP-3907 [S] The Best of Del Wood 1968 12.00
VOCALION
❑ VL 3609 [M] There's a Tavern in the Town 196? 12.00

### WOOD, HALLY
ELEKTRA
❑ EKL-10 [10] O Lovely Appearance of Death 1953 50.00

### WOOD, RONNIE
Also see FACES; THE ROLLING STONES.
COLUMBIA
❑ JC 35702 Gimme Some Neck 1979 15.00
❑ PC 35702 Gimme Some Neck 198? 8.00
*—Budget-line reissue*
❑ FC 37473 1234 1981 15.00
WARNER BROS.
❑ BS 2819 I've Got My Own Album to Do 1974 20.00
❑ BS 2872 Now Look 1975 15.00

### WOOD, ROY
Also see ELECTRIC LIGHT ORCHESTRA; THE MOVE.
TOWNHOUSE
❑ SN-7127 One Man Band 1981 12.00
UNITED ARTISTS
❑ (# unknown) [DJ]Boulders Folder 1973 40.00
*—Promo version of 168 in 13x13 folder with press kit and postcards*
❑ UA-LA042-F Wizzard's Brew 1973 10.00
❑ UA-LA168-F Boulders 1973 10.00
❑ UA-LA219-G Introducing Eddy and the Falcons 1974 10.00
❑ UA-LA575-G Mustard 1976 10.00
WARNER BROS.
❑ BS 3065 Super Active Wizzo 1977 10.00
❑ BSK 3247 On the Road Again 1979 10.00

### WOODBURY, WOODY
STEREODDITIES
❑ BITOA Booze Is the Only Answer 1961 40.00
*—With record, paperback book and smaller booklets*
❑ MW 1 Woody Woodbury Looks at Love and Life 1960 25.00
❑ MW 2 Woody Woodbury's Laughing Room 1960 25.00
❑ MW 3 Woody Woodbury's Concert in Comedy 1961 25.00
❑ MW 4 Woody Woodbury's Saloonatics 1961 25.00
❑ MW 5 The Spice Is Right 1962 25.00
❑ MW 6 The Best of Woody Woodbury 1963 20.00
❑ MW 7 Through the Keyhole 1964 20.00

### WOODS, BILL
COUNTRY TOWN
❑ CTR-24803 [M]Bill Woods from Bakersfield 196? 120.00

### WOODS, JIMMY
CAPITOL
❑ ST-654 Essence 1971 15.00
CONTEMPORARY
❑ M-3605 [M] Awakening 1962 25.00
❑ M-3612 [M] Conflict 1963 25.00
❑ S-7605 [S] Awakening 1962 30.00
❑ S-7612 [S] Conflict 1963 30.00

### WOODS, MACEO
VEE JAY
❑ LP-5001 [M] Amazing Grace 1959 30.00
*—Maroon label*
❑ LP-5001 [M] Amazing Grace 1961 20.00
*—Black colorband label*
❑ LP-5010 [M] The Lord Will Make a Way 1960 30.00
*—Maroon label*
❑ LP-5010 [M] The Lord Will Make a Way 1961 20.00
*—Black colorband label*
❑ LP-5053 [M] Garden of Prayer 1963 20.00
❑ SR-5053 [S] Garden of Prayer 1963 30.00
❑ VJS-18002 Seeking Salvation 1975 15.00
VOLT
❑ VOS-6009 Hello Sunshine 1970 20.00
❑ VOS-6013 Step to Jesus 1971 20.00

### WOODS, PHIL
CANDID
❑ CD-8016 [M] Rights of Swing 1960 40.00
❑ CS-9016 [S] Rights of Swing 1960 50.00
CENTURY
❑ 1050 Songs for Sisyphus 197? 20.00
EPIC
❑ LN 3436 [M] Warm Woods 1958 50.00
IMPULSE!
❑ A-9143 [M] Greek Cooking 1967 30.00
❑ AS-9143 [S] Greek Cooking 1967 25.00
MOSAIC
❑ MQ7-159 [(7)] The Phil Woods Quartet/ Quintet 20th Anniversary Set 199? 120.00
NEW JAZZ
❑ NJLP-1104 [10]Phil Woods New Jazz Quintet 1954 500.00
❑ NJLP-8291 [M] Pot Pie 1962 100.00
*—Purple label*
❑ NJLP-8291 [M] Pot Pie 1965 40.00
*—Blue label, trident logo at right*
PRESTIGE
❑ PRLP-191 [10] Phil Woods New Jazz Quartet 1954 400.00
❑ PRLP-204 [10] Phil Woods New Jazz Quintet 1955 400.00
❑ PRLP-7018 [M]Woodlore 1956 150.00
*—Yellow label with W. 50th St. address*
❑ PRLP-7046 [M]Paring Off 1956 100.00
❑ PRLP-7080 [M]The Young Bloods 1957 100.00
STATUS
❑ ST-8304 [M] Sugan 1965 40.00

### WOODS, PHIL, AND GENE QUILL
EPIC
❑ BN 554 [S] Phil Talks with Quill 1959 40.00
❑ BN 554 [S] Phil Talks with Quill 199? 25.00
*—Classic Records reissue on audiophile vinyl*
❑ LN 3521 [M] Phil Talks with Quill 1959 50.00
PRESTIGE
❑ PRLP-7115 [M]Phil and Quill with Prestige 1957 80.00
RCA VICTOR
❑ LPM-1284 [M] The Woods-Quill Sextet 1956 80.00

### WOODS, PHIL, AND GENE QUILL/JACKIE MCLEAN AND JOHN JENKINS/HAL MCKUSICK
NEW JAZZ
❑ NJLP-8204 [M] Bird Feathers 1958 150.00
*—Yellow Prestige label*
❑ NJLP-8204 [M] Bird Feathers 1959 80.00
*—Purple label*
❑ NJLP-8204 [M] Bird Feathers 1965 40.00
*—Blue label, trident logo at right*

### WOODY'S TRUCK STOP
SMASH
❑ SRS-67111 Woody's Truck Stop 1969 25.00

### WOOFERS, THE
WYNCOTE
❑ SW 9011 [S] Dragsville 1964 50.00
❑ W 9011 [M] Dragsville 1964 40.00

### WOOLEY, SHEB
Includes records by his comedic alter ego, "Ben Colder."
GUSTO
❑ GTV-110 Greatest Hits of Sheb Wooley Or Do You Say Ben Colder 1979 12.00
MGM
❑ GAS-139 Ben Colder (Golden Archive Series) 1970 15.00
*—As "Ben Colder"*
❑ E-3299 [M] Sheb Wooley 1956 150.00
❑ E-3904 [M] Songs from the Days of Rawhide 1961 40.00
❑ SE-3904 [S] Songs from the Days of Rawhide 1961 50.00
❑ E-4026 [M] That's My Ma and That's My Pa 1962 30.00
❑ SE-4026 [S] That's My Ma and That's My Pa 1962 40.00
❑ E-4117 [M] Spoofing the Big Ones 1961 40.00
❑ SE-4117 [S] Spoofing the Big Ones 1961 50.00
*—MGM 4117 as "Ben Colder"*
❑ E-4136 [M] Tales of How the West Was Won 1963 30.00
❑ SE-4136 [S] Tales of How the West Was Won 1963 40.00
❑ E-4173 [M] Ben Colder 1963 30.00
❑ SE-4173 [S] Ben Colder 1963 40.00
*—MGM 4173 as "Ben Colder"*
❑ E-4275 [M] The Very Best of Sheb Wooley 1965 20.00
❑ SE-4275 [S] The Very Best of Sheb Wooley 1965 25.00
❑ E-4325 [M] It's a Big Land 1965 20.00
❑ SE-4325 [S] It's a Big Land 1965 25.00
❑ E-4421 [M] Big Ben Strikes Again 1967 20.00
❑ SE-4421 [S] Big Ben Strikes Again 1967 20.00
*—MGM 4421 as "Ben Colder"*
❑ E-4482 [M] Wine, Women and Song 1967 20.00
❑ SE-4482 [S] Wine, Women and Song 1967 20.00
*—MGM 4482 as "Ben Colder"*
❑ SE-4530 The Best of Ben Colder 1968 20.00
*—As "Ben Colder"*
❑ SE-4614 Harper Valley P.T.A. 1968 20.00
*—As "Ben Colder"*
❑ SE-4615 Warm and Wooley 1969 20.00
❑ SE-4629 Have One On 1969 15.00
*—As "Ben Colder"*
❑ SE-4674 Wild Again 1970 15.00
*—As "Ben Colder"*
❑ SE-4758 Live and Loaded 1971 15.00
*—As "Ben Colder"*
❑ SE-4807 Warming Up to Colder 1972 15.00
*—As "Ben Colder"*
❑ SE-4876 The Wacky World of Ben Colder 1973 15.00
*—As "Ben Colder"*

### WOOLIES, THE
SPIRIT
❑ 9645-2001 Basic Rock 1971 40.00
❑ 9645-2005 Live at Lizards 1973 40.00

### WORLD OF OZ, THE
DERAM
❑ DES 18022 The World of Oz 1969 50.00

### WORTH, MARION
COLUMBIA
❑ CL 2011 [M] Marion Worth's Greatest Hits 1963 20.00
❑ CL 2287 [M] Marion Worth Sings Marty Robbins 1964 20.00

| Number | Title (A Side/B Side) | Yr | NM |
|---|---|---|---|
| ❑ CS 8811 [S] | Marion Worth's Greatest Hits | 1963 | 25.00 |
| ❑ CS 9087 [S] | Marion Worth Sings Marty Robbins | 1964 | 25.00 |

DECCA

| Number | Title (A Side/B Side) | Yr | NM |
|---|---|---|---|
| ❑ DL 4936 [M] | A Woman Needs Love | 1967 | 25.00 |
| ❑ DL 74936 [S] | A Woman Needs Love | 1967 | 20.00 |

## WORTH, MARION, AND GEORGE MORGAN
Also see each artist's individual listings.

COLUMBIA

| Number | Title (A Side/B Side) | Yr | NM |
|---|---|---|---|
| ❑ CL 2197 [M] | Slippin' Around | 1964 | 20.00 |
| ❑ CS 8997 [S] | Slippin' Around | 1964 | 25.00 |

## WOULD

PERCEPTION

| Number | Title (A Side/B Side) | Yr | NM |
|---|---|---|---|
| ❑ 24 | Would | 1972 | 30.00 |

## WRAY, LINK

EPIC

| Number | Title (A Side/B Side) | Yr | NM |
|---|---|---|---|
| ❑ LN 3661 [M] | Link Wray and the Wraymen | 1960 | 250.00 |

NORTON

| Number | Title (A Side/B Side) | Yr | NM |
|---|---|---|---|
| ❑ 210 | Hillbilly Wolf (Missing Links Vol. 1) | 199? | 10.00 |
| ❑ 211 | Big City After Dark (Missing Links Vol. 2) | 199? | 10.00 |
| ❑ 212 | Some Kinda Nut (Missing Links Vol. 3) | 199? | 10.00 |
| ❑ 253 | Streets of Chicago (Missing Links Vol. 4) | 1995 | 10.00 |

POLYDOR

| Number | Title (A Side/B Side) | Yr | NM |
|---|---|---|---|
| ❑ 24-4064 | Link Wray | 1971 | 20.00 |
| ❑ PD-5047 | Be What You Want To | 1972 | 20.00 |
| ❑ PD-6025 | The Link Wray Rumble | 1974 | 20.00 |

RECORD FACTORY

| Number | Title (A Side/B Side) | Yr | NM |
|---|---|---|---|
| ❑ 1929 | Yesterday and Today | 1969 | 80.00 |

SWAN

| Number | Title (A Side/B Side) | Yr | NM |
|---|---|---|---|
| ❑ SLP-510 [M] | Jack the Ripper | 1963 | 150.00 |

VERMILLION

| Number | Title (A Side/B Side) | Yr | NM |
|---|---|---|---|
| ❑ 1924 [M] | Great Guitar Hits | 196? | 80.00 |
| ❑ 1925 [M] | Link Wray Sings and Plays Guitar | 196? | 80.00 |

VISA

| Number | Title (A Side/B Side) | Yr | NM |
|---|---|---|---|
| ❑ 7009 | Bullshot | 1979 | 12.00 |
| ❑ 7010 | Live at the Paradiso | 1980 | 12.00 |

## WRAY, VERNON

VERMILLION

| Number | Title (A Side/B Side) | Yr | NM |
|---|---|---|---|
| ❑ 1972 | Wasted | 1972 | 100.00 |

## WRICE, LARRY "WILD"

PACIFIC JAZZ

| Number | Title (A Side/B Side) | Yr | NM |
|---|---|---|---|
| ❑ PJ-24 [M] | Wild! | 1961 | 25.00 |
| ❑ ST-24 [S] | Wild! | 1961 | 30.00 |

## WRIGHT, BETTY

ALSTON

| Number | Title (A Side/B Side) | Yr | NM |
|---|---|---|---|
| ❑ SD 33-388 | I Love the Way You Love | 1972 | 15.00 |
| ❑ 4400 | Danger High Voltage | 1974 | 12.00 |
| ❑ 4406 | This Time for Real | 1977 | 12.00 |
| ❑ 4408 | Betty Wright Live | 1978 | 12.00 |
| ❑ 4410 | Betty Travelin' in the Wright Circle | 1979 | 12.00 |
| ❑ SD 7026 | Hard to Stop | 1973 | 15.00 |

ATCO

| Number | Title (A Side/B Side) | Yr | NM |
|---|---|---|---|
| ❑ SD 33-260 | My First Time Around | 1968 | 25.00 |

COLLECTABLES

| Number | Title (A Side/B Side) | Yr | NM |
|---|---|---|---|
| ❑ COL-5118 | Golden Classics | 198? | 10.00 |

EPIC

| Number | Title (A Side/B Side) | Yr | NM |
|---|---|---|---|
| ❑ JE 36879 | Betty Wright | 1981 | 10.00 |
| ❑ FE 38558 | Wright Back at You | 1983 | 10.00 |

FANTASY

| Number | Title (A Side/B Side) | Yr | NM |
|---|---|---|---|
| ❑ 9644 | Sevens | 1986 | 10.00 |

MS. B.

| Number | Title (A Side/B Side) | Yr | NM |
|---|---|---|---|
| ❑ 3301 | Mother Wit | 1988 | 10.00 |
| ❑ 3318 | Passion and Compassion | 198? | 15.00 |

## WRIGHT, BOBBY

ABC

| Number | Title (A Side/B Side) | Yr | NM |
|---|---|---|---|
| ❑ ABCD-842 | Seasons of Love | 1974 | 12.00 |

DECCA

| Number | Title (A Side/B Side) | Yr | NM |
|---|---|---|---|
| ❑ DL 75319 | Here I Go Again | 1971 | 15.00 |

## WRIGHT, CHARLES, AND THE WATTS 103RD STREET RHYTHM BAND

ABC

| Number | Title (A Side/B Side) | Yr | NM |
|---|---|---|---|
| ❑ D-887 | Lil' Encouragement | 1975 | 12.00 |

ABC DUNHILL

| Number | Title (A Side/B Side) | Yr | NM |
|---|---|---|---|
| ❑ DS-50162 [(2)] | Doin' What Comes Naturally | 1973 | 15.00 |
| ❑ DS-50187 | Ninety Day Cycle People | 1974 | 12.00 |

WARNER BROS.

| Number | Title (A Side/B Side) | Yr | NM |
|---|---|---|---|
| ❑ WS 1741 | The Watts 103rd Street Rhythm Band | 1968 | 20.00 |
| *—Green label with "W7" logo* | | | |
| ❑ WS 1761 | Together | 1969 | 20.00 |
| *—Green label with "W7" logo* | | | |
| ❑ WS 1761 | Together | 1970 | 15.00 |
| *—Green label with "WB" logo* | | | |
| ❑ WS 1801 | In the Jungle, Babe | 1969 | 20.00 |
| *—Green label with "W7" logo* | | | |
| ❑ WS 1801 | In the Jungle, Babe | 1970 | 15.00 |
| *—Green label with "WB" logo* | | | |
| ❑ WS 1864 | Express Yourself | 1970 | 15.00 |
| ❑ WS 1904 | You're So Beautiful | 1971 | 15.00 |
| ❑ BS 2620 | Rhythm and Poetry | 1972 | 15.00 |
| *—Green label with "WB" logo* | | | |
| ❑ BS 2620 | Rhythm and Poetry | 1973 | 12.00 |
| *—"Burbank" palm-trees logo* | | | |

## WRIGHT, DEMPSEY

ANDEX

| Number | Title (A Side/B Side) | Yr | NM |
|---|---|---|---|
| ❑ A-3006 [M] | The Wright Approach | 1958 | 60.00 |
| ❑ AS-3006 [S] | The Wright Approach | 1958 | 50.00 |

## WRIGHT, FRANK

ESP-DISK'

| Number | Title (A Side/B Side) | Yr | NM |
|---|---|---|---|
| ❑ 1023 [M] | Frank Wright Trio | 1966 | 25.00 |
| ❑ S-1023 [S] | Frank Wright Trio | 1966 | 20.00 |
| ❑ 1053 [S] | Your Prayer | 1968 | 20.00 |

## WRIGHT, JOHN

PRESTIGE

| Number | Title (A Side/B Side) | Yr | NM |
|---|---|---|---|
| ❑ PRLP-7190 [M] | South Side Soul | 1960 | 100.00 |
| ❑ PRLP-7197 [M] | Nice 'N' Nasty | 1961 | 80.00 |
| ❑ PRLP-7212 [M] | Makin' Out | 1961 | 80.00 |
| ❑ PRLP-7233 [M] | Mr. Soul | 1962 | 80.00 |
| ❑ PRST-7233 [S] | Mr. Soul | 1962 | 60.00 |

STATUS

| Number | Title (A Side/B Side) | Yr | NM |
|---|---|---|---|
| ❑ ST-8322 [M] | The Last Amen | 1965 | 80.00 |

## WRIGHT, JOHNNY

DECCA

| Number | Title (A Side/B Side) | Yr | NM |
|---|---|---|---|
| ❑ DL 4698 [M] | Hello Vietnam | 1965 | 25.00 |
| ❑ DL 4770 [M] | Country Music Special | 1966 | 25.00 |
| ❑ DL 4846 [M] | Country the Wright Way | 1967 | 25.00 |
| ❑ DL 74698 [S] | Hello Vietnam | 1965 | 30.00 |
| ❑ DL 74770 [S] | Country Music Special | 1966 | 30.00 |
| ❑ DL 74846 [S] | Country the Wright Way | 1967 | 20.00 |
| ❑ DL 75019 | Johnny Wright Sings Country Favorites | 1968 | 20.00 |

## WRIGHT, LEO

ATLANTIC

| Number | Title (A Side/B Side) | Yr | NM |
|---|---|---|---|
| ❑ 1358 [M] | Blues Shout | 1960 | 25.00 |
| *—Multicolor label, white "fan" logo at right* | | | |
| ❑ SD 1358 [S] | Blues Shout | 196? | 20.00 |
| *—Multicolor label, black "fan" logo at right* | | | |
| ❑ SD 1358 [S] | Blues Shout | 1960 | 30.00 |
| *—Multicolor label, white "fan" logo at right* | | | |
| ❑ 1393 [M] | Suddenly the Blues | 1962 | 25.00 |
| *—Multicolor label, black "fan" logo at right* | | | |
| ❑ SD 1393 [S] | Suddenly the Blues | 1962 | 30.00 |
| *—Multicolor label, black "fan" logo at right* | | | |

VORTEX

| Number | Title (A Side/B Side) | Yr | NM |
|---|---|---|---|
| ❑ 2011 | Soul Talk | 197? | 20.00 |

## WRIGHT, MARVIN "LEFTY"

"X"

| Number | Title (A Side/B Side) | Yr | NM |
|---|---|---|---|
| ❑ LXA-3028 [10] | Boogie Woogie Piano | 1954 | 60.00 |

## WRIGHT, NAT

WARWICK

| Number | Title (A Side/B Side) | Yr | NM |
|---|---|---|---|
| ❑ W-2040 [M] | The Biggest Voice in Jazz | 1961 | 50.00 |
| ❑ W-2040ST [S] | The Biggest Voice in Jazz | 1961 | 80.00 |

## WRIGHT, O.V.

BACK BEAT

| Number | Title (A Side/B Side) | Yr | NM |
|---|---|---|---|
| ❑ 61 [M] | If It's Only for Tonight | 1965 | 100.00 |
| ❑ S-61 [S] | If It's Only for Tonight | 1965 | 150.00 |
| ❑ 66 | Eight Men, Four Women | 1968 | 60.00 |
| ❑ 67 | Nucleus of Soul | 1969 | 60.00 |
| ❑ 70 | A Nickel and a Nail and Ace of Spade | 1971 | 60.00 |
| ❑ 72 | Memphis Unlimited | 1973 | 50.00 |

HI

| Number | Title (A Side/B Side) | Yr | NM |
|---|---|---|---|
| ❑ 6001 | Into Something | 1977 | 25.00 |
| ❑ 6008 | Bottom Line | 1978 | 25.00 |
| ❑ 6011 | We're Still Together | 1979 | 25.00 |

## WRIGHT, RICHARD
Also see PINK FLOYD.

COLUMBIA

| Number | Title (A Side/B Side) | Yr | NM |
|---|---|---|---|
| ❑ JC 35559 | Wet Dream | 1978 | 20.00 |

## WRIGHT, SONNY (2)

KAPP

| Number | Title (A Side/B Side) | Yr | NM |
|---|---|---|---|
| ❑ KS-3614 | I Love You, Loretta Lynn | 1968 | 20.00 |

## WRIGHT, WILLIE

ARGO

| Number | Title (A Side/B Side) | Yr | NM |
|---|---|---|---|
| ❑ LP-4024 [M] | I'm on My Way | 1963 | 20.00 |
| ❑ LPS-4024 [S] | I'm on My Way | 1963 | 25.00 |

CONCERT DISC

| Number | Title (A Side/B Side) | Yr | NM |
|---|---|---|---|
| ❑ 45 [S] | I Sing Folk Songs | 1960 | 40.00 |
| ❑ 1045 [M] | I Sing Folk Songs | 1960 | 30.00 |

## WYLER, GRETCHEN

JUBILEE

| Number | Title (A Side/B Side) | Yr | NM |
|---|---|---|---|
| ❑ JLP-1100 [M] | Wild, Wyler, Wildest | 1959 | 25.00 |
| ❑ SDJLP-1100 [S] | Wild, Wyler, Wildest | 1959 | 30.00 |

## WYLIE, RICHARD "POPCORN"

ABC

| Number | Title (A Side/B Side) | Yr | NM |
|---|---|---|---|
| ❑ ABCD-834 | E.S.P. | 1974 | 60.00 |

## WYMAN, BILL
Also see THE ROLLING STONES.

ROLLING STONES

| Number | Title (A Side/B Side) | Yr | NM |
|---|---|---|---|
| ❑ COC 59102 | Monkey Grip | 1974 | 15.00 |
| ❑ COC 79100 | Monkey Grip | 1974 | 12.00 |
| *—Reissue of 59102* | | | |
| ❑ QD 79100 [Q] | Monkey Grip | 1974 | 20.00 |
| ❑ COC 79103 | Stone Alone | 1976 | 12.00 |
| ❑ QD 79103 [Q] | Stone Alone | 1976 | 20.00 |

## WYNETTE, TAMMY
Also see DAVID HOUSTON AND TAMMY WYNETTE; GEORGE JONES AND TAMMY WYNETTE.

COLUMBIA LIMITED EDITION

| Number | Title (A Side/B Side) | Yr | NM |
|---|---|---|---|
| ❑ LE 10049 | The First Lady | 197? | 12.00 |
| ❑ LE 10193 | The Ways to Love a Man | 197? | 12.00 |
| ❑ LE 10194 | Tammy's Touch | 197? | 12.00 |
| ❑ LE 10195 | We Sure Can Love Each Other | 197? | 12.00 |

COLUMBIA SPECIAL PRODUCTS

| Number | Title (A Side/B Side) | Yr | NM |
|---|---|---|---|
| ❑ P 11228 | Take Me to Your World | 1973 | 12.00 |
| ❑ P 11519 | Your Good Girl's Gonna Go Bad | 1973 | 12.00 |
| ❑ P 13256 | The Ways to Love a Man | 1976 | 12.00 |
| ❑ P 13259 | My Man | 1976 | 12.00 |
| ❑ P 13261 | Bedtime Story | 1976 | 12.00 |
| ❑ P 13611 | Twenty Big Hits of Tammy Wynette | 197? | 15.00 |

EPIC

| Number | Title (A Side/B Side) | Yr | NM |
|---|---|---|---|
| ❑ EGP 503 [(2)] | The World of Tammy Wynette | 1970 | 25.00 |
| ❑ LN 24305 [M] | Your Good Girl's Gonna Go Bad | 1967 | 30.00 |
| ❑ LN 24353 [M] | Take Me to Your World/I Don't Wanna Play House | 1968 | 40.00 |
| *—May exist only as a white label promo* | | | |
| ❑ LN 24392 [M] | D-I-V-O-R-C-E | 1968 | 50.00 |
| *—This has been confirmed to exist on yellow label stock copies* | | | |
| ❑ BN 26305 [S] | Your Good Girl's Gonna Go Bad | 1967 | 20.00 |
| ❑ BN 26353 [S] | Take Me to Your World/I Don't Wanna Play House | 1968 | 20.00 |
| ❑ BN 26392 [S] | D-I-V-O-R-C-E | 1968 | 20.00 |
| ❑ BN 26423 | Inspiration | 1969 | 20.00 |
| ❑ BN 26451 | Stand By Your Man | 1969 | 20.00 |
| ❑ BN 26486 | Tammy's Greatest Hits | 1969 | 20.00 |
| ❑ PE 26486 | Tammy's Greatest Hits | 198? | 8.00 |
| *—Budget-line reissue* | | | |
| ❑ BN 26519 | The Ways to Love a Man | 1970 | 20.00 |
| ❑ BN 26549 | Tammy's Touch | 1970 | 20.00 |
| ❑ E 30213 | The First Lady | 1970 | 20.00 |
| ❑ E 30343 | Christmas with Tammy | 1970 | 20.00 |
| ❑ KEG 30358 [(2)] | The First Songs of the First Lady | 1970 | 20.00 |
| ❑ E 30658 | We Sure Can Love Each Other | 1971 | 20.00 |
| ❑ EQ 30658 [Q] | We Sure Can Love Each Other | 1972 | 30.00 |
| ❑ E 30733 | Tammy's Greatest Hits, Volume II | 1971 | 20.00 |
| ❑ PE 30733 | Tammy's Greatest Hits, Volume II | 198? | 8.00 |
| *—Budget-line reissue* | | | |
| ❑ KE 31285 | Bedtime Story | 1972 | 15.00 |
| ❑ KE 31717 | My Man | 1972 | 15.00 |
| ❑ KE 31937 | Kids Say the Darndest Things | 1973 | 15.00 |
| ❑ KE 32745 | Another Lonely Song | 1974 | 12.00 |
| ❑ KE 33246 | Woman to Woman | 1975 | 12.00 |
| ❑ KE 33396 | Tammy's Greatest Hits, Volume III | 1975 | 12.00 |
| ❑ PE 33396 | Tammy's Greatest Hits, Volume III | 198? | 8.00 |
| *—Budget-line reissue* | | | |
| ❑ KE 33582 | I Still Believe in Fairy Tales | 1975 | 12.00 |
| ❑ BG 33773 [(2)] | Stand By Your Man/Bedtime Story | 1976 | 15.00 |
| ❑ PE 34075 | 'Til I Can Make It on My Own | 1976 | 12.00 |
| ❑ PE 34289 | You and Me | 1976 | 12.00 |
| ❑ PE 34694 | Let's Get Together One Last Time | 1977 | 12.00 |
| ❑ KE 35044 | One of a Kind | 1977 | 12.00 |
| ❑ KE 35442 | Womanhood | 1978 | 12.00 |
| ❑ KE 35630 | Tammy's Greatest Hits, Volume IV | 1978 | 12.00 |
| ❑ KE 36013 | Just Tammy | 1979 | 12.00 |

| Number | Title (A Side/B Side) | Yr | NM |
|---|---|---|---|
| ❑ JE 36485 | Only Lonely Sometimes | 1980 | 10.00 |
| ❑ FE 37104 | You Brought Me Back | 1981 | 10.00 |
| ❑ FE 37344 | Encore | 1981 | 10.00 |
| ❑ PE 37344 | Encore | 198? | 8.00 |
| *—Budget-line reissue* | | | |
| ❑ FE 37980 | Soft Touch | 1982 | 10.00 |
| ❑ FE 38312 | Biggest Hits | 1984 | 10.00 |
| ❑ FE 38372 | Good Love and Heartbreak | 1983 | 10.00 |
| ❑ FE 38744 | Even the Strong Get Lonely | 1983 | 10.00 |
| ❑ FE 39971 | Sometimes When We Touch | 1985 | 10.00 |
| ❑ EG 40625 [(2)] | Anniversary: 20 Years of Hits | 1987 | 15.00 |
| ❑ FE 40832 | Higher Ground | 1987 | 10.00 |
| ❑ FE 44498 | Next to You | 1989 | 12.00 |

HARMONY

| Number | Title (A Side/B Side) | Yr | NM |
|---|---|---|---|
| ❑ KH 30096 | Send Me No Roses | 1970 | 12.00 |
| ❑ KH 30914 | Just a Matter of Time | 1971 | 12.00 |

PAIR

| Number | Title (A Side/B Side) | Yr | NM |
|---|---|---|---|
| ❑ PDL2-1073 [(2)] | From the Bottom of My Heart | 1986 | 12.00 |

REALM

| Number | Title (A Side/B Side) | Yr | NM |
|---|---|---|---|
| ❑ 2V 8047 [(2)] | The Queen Volume 1 | 1976 | 15.00 |
| ❑ 1V 8048 | The Queen Volume 2 | 1976 | 10.00 |

TIME-LIFE

| Number | Title (A Side/B Side) | Yr | NM |
|---|---|---|---|
| ❑ STW-116 | Country Music | 1981 | 12.00 |

**WYNN, ALBERT**

RIVERSIDE

| Number | Title (A Side/B Side) | Yr | NM |
|---|---|---|---|
| ❑ RLP-426 [M] | Albert Wynn and His Gutbucket Seven | 1962 | 30.00 |
| ❑ RS-9426 [R] | Albert Wynn and His Gutbucket Seven | 1962 | 20.00 |

**WYNONNA** See WYNONNA JUDD.

**WYNTERS, GAIL**

HICKORY

| Number | Title (A Side/B Side) | Yr | NM |
|---|---|---|---|
| ❑ LPM-138 [M] | A Girl for All Seasons | 1967 | 20.00 |
| ❑ LPS-138 [S] | A Girl for All Seasons | 1967 | 15.00 |

RCA VICTOR

| Number | Title (A Side/B Side) | Yr | NM |
|---|---|---|---|
| ❑ APL1-2285 | Let the Lady Sing | 1977 | 20.00 |

# X

**X**

ELEKTRA

| Number | Title (A Side/B Side) | Yr | NM |
|---|---|---|---|
| ❑ 60150 | Under the Big Black Sun | 1982 | 12.00 |
| ❑ 60283 | More Fun in the New World | 1983 | 10.00 |
| ❑ 60430 | Ain't Love Grand | 1985 | 10.00 |
| ❑ 60492 | See How We Are | 1987 | 10.00 |
| ❑ 60788 [(2)] | Live at the Whiskey A-Go-Go on the Fabulous Sunset Strip | 1988 | 12.00 |

RHINO

| Number | Title (A Side/B Side) | Yr | NM |
|---|---|---|---|
| ❑ R1-74370 | Los Angeles | 2003 | 15.00 |
| *—Reissue on 180-gram vinyl* | | | |

SLASH

| Number | Title (A Side/B Side) | Yr | NM |
|---|---|---|---|
| ❑ SR-104 | Los Angeles | 1980 | 25.00 |
| ❑ SR-107 | Wild Gift | 1981 | 20.00 |
| ❑ 23930 | Los Angeles | 1983 | 10.00 |
| *—Reissue of Slash 104* | | | |
| ❑ 23931 | Wild Gift | 1983 | 10.00 |
| *—Reissue of Slash 107* | | | |

**XIT**

CANYON

| Number | Title (A Side/B Side) | Yr | NM |
|---|---|---|---|
| ❑ 7114 | Entrance | 197? | 50.00 |
| ❑ C-7121 | Relocation | 1977 | 40.00 |

RARE EARTH

| Number | Title (A Side/B Side) | Yr | NM |
|---|---|---|---|
| ❑ R-536 | Plight of the Redman | 1972 | 30.00 |
| ❑ R-545 | Silent Warrior | 1973 | 30.00 |

WARRIOR

| Number | Title (A Side/B Side) | Yr | NM |
|---|---|---|---|
| ❑ WAR 49 | Plight of the Redman | 1981 | 15.00 |
| *—Reissue of Rare Earth 536* | | | |

**XTC**

GEFFEN

| Number | Title (A Side/B Side) | Yr | NM |
|---|---|---|---|
| ❑ GHS 4027 | Mummer | 1983 | 10.00 |
| ❑ GHS 4032 | White Music | 1984 | 10.00 |
| *—Reissue of Virgin/Epic 38153* | | | |
| ❑ GHS 4033 | Go2 | 1984 | 10.00 |
| *—Reissue of Virgin/Epic 38152* | | | |
| ❑ GHS 4034 | Drums and Wires | 1984 | 10.00 |
| *—Reissue of Virgin/Epic 38151* | | | |
| ❑ GHS 4035 | Black Sea | 1984 | 10.00 |
| *—Reissue of Virgin/Epic 38150* | | | |
| ❑ GHS 4036 [(2)] | English Settlement | 1984 | 15.00 |
| *—First release of British version of this album in U.S.* | | | |
| ❑ GHS 4037 | Waxworks (Some Singles, 1977-82) | 1984 | 12.00 |
| ❑ GHS 24054 | The Big Express | 1984 | 10.00 |
| ❑ GHS 24117 | Skylarking | 1986 | 10.00 |
| *—Second pressing, with "Dear God" and without "Mermaid Smiled"* | | | |
| ❑ GHS 24117 | Skylarking | 1986 | 15.00 |
| *—First pressing, with "Mermaid Smiled" and without "Dear God"* | | | |
| ❑ GHS 24218 [(2)] | Oranges and Lemons | 1989 | 15.00 |

XTC, *English Settlement,* Virgin/Epic ARE 37943, 1982, $10.

| Number | Title (A Side/B Side) | Yr | NM |
|---|---|---|---|
| ❑ R 201086 [(2)] | Oranges and Lemons | 1989 | 15.00 |
| *—BMG Direct Marketing edition* | | | |

VIRGIN

| Number | Title (A Side/B Side) | Yr | NM |
|---|---|---|---|
| ❑ VA 13134 | Drums and Wires | 1979 | 20.00 |
| *—With bonus 7-inch record (PR 344) enclosed -- deduct 40 percent if missing* | | | |
| ❑ VA 13147 | Black Sea | 1980 | 30.00 |
| *—Promo only; label, jacket and innersleeve ALL must have this number* | | | |

VIRGIN INTERNATIONAL

| Number | Title (A Side/B Side) | Yr | NM |
|---|---|---|---|
| ❑ VI-2095 | White Music | 1979 | 15.00 |
| ❑ VI-2108 | Go2 | 1979 | 15.00 |

VIRGIN/EPIC

| Number | Title (A Side/B Side) | Yr | NM |
|---|---|---|---|
| ❑ ARE 37943 | English Settlement | 1982 | 10.00 |
| *—Drastically edited version of U.K. original, which was a 2-record set* | | | |
| ❑ PE 38150 | Black Sea | 1982 | 10.00 |
| *—Reissue of Virgin/RSO 1001* | | | |
| ❑ PE 38151 | Drums and Wires | 1982 | 10.00 |
| *—Reissue of Virgin 13134* | | | |
| ❑ PE 38152 | Go2 | 1982 | 10.00 |
| *—Reissue of Virgin International VI-2108* | | | |
| ❑ PE 38153 | White Music | 1982 | 10.00 |
| *—Reissue of Virgin International VI-2095* | | | |

VIRGIN/RSO

| Number | Title (A Side/B Side) | Yr | NM |
|---|---|---|---|
| ❑ VR-1-1000 | Black Sea | 1980 | 12.00 |
| *—Without green outer bag; innersleeves may or may not have "VA 13147" reference* | | | |
| ❑ VR-1-1000 | Black Sea | 1980 | 20.00 |
| *—With green outer bag and "VA 13147" on innersleeve* | | | |

WARNER BROS.

| Number | Title (A Side/B Side) | Yr | NM |
|---|---|---|---|
| ❑ WBMS-146 [DJ] | Skylarking Interview with Andy Partridge | 1986 | 25.00 |
| *—Part of "The Warner Bros. Music Show" series* | | | |

# Y

**Y KANT TORI READ** Lead singer: Tori Amos.

ATLANTIC

| Number | Title (A Side/B Side) | Yr | NM |
|---|---|---|---|
| ❑ 81845 | Y Kant Tori Read | 1989 | 200.00 |
| *—Deduct 20% for albums with a gold promo stamp and cut-out mark. Also, any picture disc of this album is a bootleg, no matter what it claims to be* | | | |

**YA HO WA 13**

HIGHER KEY

| Number | Title (A Side/B Side) | Yr | NM |
|---|---|---|---|
| ❑ 3301 | Kohoutek | 1973 | 300.00 |
| ❑ 3302 | Contraction | 1974 | 500.00 |
| ❑ 3303 | Expansion | 1974 | 500.00 |
| ❑ 3304 | All or Nothing at All | 1974 | 400.00 |
| *—Above 4 as "Father Yod and the Spirit of '76"* | | | |
| ❑ 3305 | Ya Ho Wa 13 | 1974 | 500.00 |
| ❑ 3306 | The Savage Sons of Ya Ho Wa | 1974 | 400.00 |
| ❑ 3307 | Penetration: An Aquarian Symphony | 1974 | 400.00 |
| ❑ 3308 [(2)] | I'm Gonna Take You Home | 1975 | 800.00 |
| ❑ 3309 | To the Principles for the Children | 1975 | 800.00 |

**YACHTSMEN, THE**

BUENA VISTA

| Number | Title (A Side/B Side) | Yr | NM |
|---|---|---|---|
| ❑ BV-3310 [M] | High and Dry with the Yachtsmen | 1961 | 25.00 |

**YAGED, SOL**

HERALD

| Number | Title (A Side/B Side) | Yr | NM |
|---|---|---|---|
| ❑ HLP-0103 [M] | It Might As Well Be Swing | 1956 | 50.00 |

LANE

| Number | Title (A Side/B Side) | Yr | NM |
|---|---|---|---|
| ❑ LP-149 [M] | Live at the Gaslight Club | 195? | 50.00 |
| ❑ LP-154 [M] | One More Time | 195? | 50.00 |
| ❑ LPS-154 [S] | One More Time | 195? | 50.00 |
| ❑ LP-155 [M] | Sol Yaged at the Gaslight Club | 195? | 50.00 |
| ❑ LPS-155 [S] | Sol Yaged at the Gaslight Club | 195? | 50.00 |

PHILIPS

| Number | Title (A Side/B Side) | Yr | NM |
|---|---|---|---|
| ❑ PHS 600002 [S] | Jazz at the Metropole | 1961 | 20.00 |

**YALE DIXIELAND BAND, THE**

COLUMBIA

| Number | Title (A Side/B Side) | Yr | NM |
|---|---|---|---|
| ❑ CL 736 [M] | Eli's Chosen Six | 1955 | 40.00 |

**YAMA AND THE KARMA DUSTERS**

MANHOLE

| Number | Title (A Side/B Side) | Yr | NM |
|---|---|---|---|
| ❑ 1 | Up from the Sewers | 1970 | 200.00 |

**YAMAMOTO, TSUYOSHI**

THREE BLIND MICE

| Number | Title (A Side/B Side) | Yr | NM |
|---|---|---|---|
| ❑ TBM-23 | Midnight Sugar | 1995 | 30.00 |
| *—Audiophile vinyl* | | | |

Yes, *Drama,* Atlantic SD 16019, 1980, $10.

| Number | Title (A Side/B Side) | Yr | NM |
|---|---|---|---|
| ❑ TBM-30 | Misty | 199? | 30.00 |
| *—Audiophile vinyl* | | | |

**YANCEY, JIMMY**

ATLANTIC

| Number | Title (A Side/B Side) | Yr | NM |
|---|---|---|---|
| ❑ ALS-103 [10] | Yancey Special | 1950 | 100.00 |
| ❑ ALS-130 [10] | Yancey Special | 1952 | 80.00 |
| ❑ ALS-134 [10] | Piano Solos | 1952 | 80.00 |
| ❑ 1283 [M] | Pure Blues | 1958 | 50.00 |
| *—Black label* | | | |
| ❑ 1283 [M] | Pure Blues | 1961 | 20.00 |
| *—Multicolor label, white "fan" logo at right* | | | |

PARAMOUNT

| Number | Title (A Side/B Side) | Yr | NM |
|---|---|---|---|
| ❑ CJS-101 [10] | Yancey Special | 1951 | 100.00 |

PAX

| Number | Title (A Side/B Side) | Yr | NM |
|---|---|---|---|
| ❑ LP-6011 [10] | 1943 Mixture | 1954 | 80.00 |
| ❑ LP-6012 [10] | Evening With the Yanceys | 1954 | 80.00 |

RIVERSIDE

| Number | Title (A Side/B Side) | Yr | NM |
|---|---|---|---|
| ❑ RLP 12-124 [M] | Yancey's Getaway | 1956 | 60.00 |
| ❑ RLP-1028 [10] | Lost Recording Date | 1954 | 100.00 |

"X"

| Number | Title (A Side/B Side) | Yr | NM |
|---|---|---|---|
| ❑ LX-3000 [10] | Blues and Boogie | 1954 | 100.00 |

**YANCEY, MAMA, AND ART HODES**

VERVE FOLKWAYS

| Number | Title (A Side/B Side) | Yr | NM |
|---|---|---|---|
| ❑ FV-9015 [M] | Blues | 1965 | 20.00 |
| ❑ FVS-9015 [S] | Blues | 1965 | 25.00 |

**YANCY DERRINGER**

HEMISPHERE

| Number | Title (A Side/B Side) | Yr | NM |
|---|---|---|---|
| ❑ H-15104 | Openers | 1975 | 50.00 |

**YANKEE DOLLAR, THE**

DOT

| Number | Title (A Side/B Side) | Yr | NM |
|---|---|---|---|
| ❑ DLP-25874 | The Yankee Dollar | 1968 | 120.00 |

**YANOVSKY, ZALMAN** Also see THE LOVIN' SPOONFUL.

BUDDAH

| Number | Title (A Side/B Side) | Yr | NM |
|---|---|---|---|
| ❑ BDS-5019 | Alive and Well in Argentina | 1968 | 40.00 |

KAMA SUTRA

| Number | Title (A Side/B Side) | Yr | NM |
|---|---|---|---|
| ❑ KSBS-2030 | Alive and Well in Argentina | 1971 | 20.00 |

**YARBROUGH, GLENN**

ELEKTRA

| Number | Title (A Side/B Side) | Yr | NM |
|---|---|---|---|
| ❑ EKL-135 [M] | Here We Go, Baby | 1957 | 40.00 |

FIRST AMERICAN

| Number | Title (A Side/B Side) | Yr | NM |
|---|---|---|---|
| ❑ 7766 | Just a Little Love | 1981 | 10.00 |

RCA VICTOR

| Number | Title (A Side/B Side) | Yr | NM |
|---|---|---|---|
| ❑ ANL1-2138 | Baby the Rain Must Fall | 1977 | 10.00 |
| *—Reissue of LSP-3422* | | | |
| ❑ LPM-2836 [M] | Time to Move On | 1964 | 15.00 |
| ❑ LSP-2836 [S] | Time to Move On | 1964 | 20.00 |
| ❑ LPM-2905 [M] | One More Round | 1964 | 15.00 |
| ❑ LSP-2905 [S] | One More Round | 1964 | 20.00 |
| ❑ LPM-3301 [M] | Come Share My Life | 1965 | 15.00 |
| ❑ LSP-3301 [S] | Come Share My Life | 1965 | 20.00 |
| ❑ LPM-3422 [M] | Baby the Rain Must Fall | 1965 | 12.00 |
| ❑ LSP-3422 [S] | Baby the Rain Must Fall | 1965 | 15.00 |
| ❑ LPM-3472 [M] | It's Gonna Be Fine | 1965 | 12.00 |
| ❑ LSP-3472 [S] | It's Gonna Be Fine | 1965 | 15.00 |
| ❑ LPM-3539 [M] | The Lonely Things | 1966 | 12.00 |
| ❑ LSP-3539 [S] | The Lonely Things | 1966 | 15.00 |
| ❑ LPM-3661 [M] | Live at the Hungry I | 1966 | 12.00 |
| ❑ LSP-3661 [S] | Live at the Hungry I | 1966 | 15.00 |
| ❑ LPM-3801 [M] | For Emily, Whenever I May Find Her | 1967 | 15.00 |
| ❑ LSP-3801 [S] | For Emily, Whenever I May Find Her | 1967 | 15.00 |
| ❑ LPM-3860 [M] | Honey and Wine | 1967 | 20.00 |
| ❑ LSP-3860 [S] | Honey and Wine | 1967 | 15.00 |
| ❑ LPM-3951 [M] | The Bitter and the Sweet | 1968 | 30.00 |
| ❑ LSP-3951 [S] | The Bitter and the Sweet | 1968 | 15.00 |
| ❑ LSP-4047 | We Survived the Madness | 1968 | 15.00 |
| ❑ LSP-4349 | The Best of Glenn Yarbrough | 1970 | 12.00 |
| ❑ VPS-6018 [(2)] | Glenn Yarbrough Sings the Rod McKuen Songbook | 1969 | 15.00 |

STAX

| Number | Title (A Side/B Side) | Yr | NM |
|---|---|---|---|
| ❑ STX-5506 | My Sweet Lady | 1975 | 10.00 |

TRADITION

| Number | Title (A Side/B Side) | Yr | NM |
|---|---|---|---|
| ❑ 1019 [M] | Come Sit By My Side | 195? | 20.00 |
| ❑ 2054 | The Best of Glenn Yarbrough | 1967 | 15.00 |
| ❑ 2095 | Looking Back | 1970 | 12.00 |

WARNER BROS.

| Number | Title (A Side/B Side) | Yr | NM |
|---|---|---|---|
| ❑ WS 1736 | Each of Us Alone: Glenn Yarbrough Sings the Words and Music of Rod McKuen | 1968 | 12.00 |
| ❑ WS 1782 | Somehow, Someway | 1969 | 12.00 |
| ❑ WS 1817 | Yarbrough Country | 1969 | 12.00 |
| ❑ WS 1832 | Let Me Choose Life | 1969 | 12.00 |
| ❑ WS 1876 | Jubilee | 1970 | 12.00 |
| ❑ WS 1911 | Bend Down and Touch Me | 1971 | 12.00 |

**YARDBIRDS, THE** Also see JEFF BECK; ERIC CLAPTON; JIMMY PAGE; KEITH RELF; SONNY BOY WILLIAMSON (2). Ex-members of the group formed LED ZEPPELIN and RENAISSANCE.

ACCORD

| Number | Title (A Side/B Side) | Yr | NM |
|---|---|---|---|
| ❑ SN-7143 [S] | For Your Love | 1981 | 8.00 |
| ❑ SN-7237 [R] | Having a Rave Up with the Yardbirds | 1981 | 8.00 |

COLUMBIA SPECIAL PRODUCTS

| Number | Title (A Side/B Side) | Yr | NM |
|---|---|---|---|
| ❑ P 13311 [S] | Live Yardbirds Featuring Jimmy Page | 1976 | 80.00 |

COMPLEAT

| Number | Title (A Side/B Side) | Yr | NM |
|---|---|---|---|
| ❑ CPL-2-2002 [(2)] | A Compleat Collection | 1984 | 12.00 |

EPIC

| Number | Title (A Side/B Side) | Yr | NM |
|---|---|---|---|
| ❑ LN 24167 [DJ] | For Your Love | 1965 | 400.00 |
| *—White label promo* | | | |
| ❑ LN 24167 [M] | For Your Love | 1965 | 300.00 |
| ❑ LN 24177 [DJ] | Having a Rave Up with the Yardbirds | 1965 | 400.00 |
| *—White label promo* | | | |
| ❑ LN 24177 [M] | Having a Rave Up with the Yardbirds | 1965 | 80.00 |
| ❑ LN 24210 [DJ] | Over Under Sideways Down | 1966 | 400.00 |
| *—White label promo* | | | |
| ❑ LN 24210 [M] | Over Under Sideways Down | 1966 | 60.00 |
| ❑ LN 24246 [DJ] | The Yardbirds' Greatest Hits | 1966 | 300.00 |
| *—White label promo* | | | |
| ❑ LN 24246 [M] | The Yardbirds' Greatest Hits | 1966 | 50.00 |
| ❑ LN 24313 [DJ] | Little Games | 1967 | 300.00 |
| ❑ LN 24313 [M] | Little Games | 1967 | 80.00 |
| *—Some copies with this number are stereo; look for the "XSB" prefix before the master number* | | | |
| ❑ BN 26167 [P] | For Your Love | 1965 | 200.00 |
| *—The album is in true stereo except for "Sweet Music"* | | | |
| ❑ BN 26177 [R] | Having a Rave Up with the Yardbirds | 1965 | 50.00 |
| ❑ BN 26177 [R] | Having a Rave Up with the Yardbirds | 1973 | 30.00 |
| *—Reissue with orange label* | | | |
| ❑ BN 26210 [P] | Over Under Sideways Down | 1966 | 80.00 |
| *—"Over Under Sideways Down" is rechanneled* | | | |
| ❑ BN 26246 [P] | The Yardbirds' Greatest Hits | 1966 | 30.00 |
| ❑ BN 26313 [S] | Little Games | 1967 | 50.00 |
| ❑ EG 30135 [(2)] | The Yardbirds Featuring Performances by Jeff Beck, Eric Clapton, Jimmy Page | 1970 | 50.00 |
| ❑ E 30615 [S] | Live Yardbirds Featuring Jimmy Page | 1971 | 80.00 |
| ❑ PE 34490 [P] | Yardbirds Favorites | 1977 | 10.00 |
| ❑ PE 34491 [P] | Great Hits | 1977 | 10.00 |
| ❑ FE 38455 | Yardbirds (Roger the Engineer) | 1982 | 30.00 |
| ❑ HE 48455 | Yardbirds (Roger the Engineer) | 1982 | 250.00 |
| *—"Half-Speed Mastered" edition* | | | |

PAIR

| Number | Title (A Side/B Side) | Yr | NM |
|---|---|---|---|
| ❑ PDL2-1151 [(2)] | Best of British Rock | 1988 | 12.00 |

RHINO

| Number | Title (A Side/B Side) | Yr | NM |
|---|---|---|---|
| ❑ RNDF 253 [PD] | Afternoon Tea | 1982 | 15.00 |
| ❑ RNLP 70128 [M] | Greatest Hits, Volume 1: 1964-1966 | 1986 | 8.00 |
| ❑ RNLP 70189 [M] | Five Live Yardbirds | 1986 | 8.00 |

SPRINGBOARD

| Number | Title (A Side/B Side) | Yr | NM |
|---|---|---|---|
| ❑ SPB-4036 [R] | Eric Clapton and the Yardbirds | 1972 | 10.00 |
| ❑ SPB-4039 [R] | Shapes of Things | 1972 | 10.00 |

SUNDAZED

| Number | Title (A Side/B Side) | Yr | NM |
|---|---|---|---|
| ❑ LP 5181 | Live! Blueswailing July '64 | 2004 | 12.00 |

**YAZ**

SIRE

| Number | Title (A Side/B Side) | Yr | NM |
|---|---|---|---|
| ❑ 23737 | Upstairs at Eric's | 1982 | 10.00 |
| *—As "Yaz"* | | | |
| ❑ 23737 | Upstairs at Eric's | 1982 | 20.00 |
| *—As "Yazoo"* | | | |
| ❑ 23903 | You and Me Both | 1983 | 10.00 |

**YEARWOOD, TRISHA**

MCA

| Number | Title (A Side/B Side) | Yr | NM |
|---|---|---|---|
| ❑ 1P-8161 | Trisha Yearwood | 1991 | 25.00 |
| *—Vinyl edition available only from Columbia House* | | | |

**YELL CHASERS, THE**

REALTIME

| Number | Title (A Side/B Side) | Yr | NM |
|---|---|---|---|
| ❑ 822 | I've Got My Fingers | 197? | 20.00 |
| *—Direct-to-disc recording; plays at 45 rpm* | | | |

## YELLO

### ELEKTRA

| Number | Title (A Side/B Side) | Yr | NM |
|---|---|---|---|
| ❑ 60271 | You Gotta Say Yes to Another Excess | 1983 | 12.00 |
| ❑ 60401 | Stella | 1985 | 12.00 |

### MERCURY

| Number | Title (A Side/B Side) | Yr | NM |
|---|---|---|---|
| ❑ 812166-1 | You Gotta Say Yes to Another Excess | 1988 | 8.00 |
| *—Reissue* | | | |
| ❑ 818339-1 | Solid Pleasure | 1988 | 8.00 |
| *—Reissue* | | | |
| ❑ 818340-1 | Claro Que Si | 1988 | 8.00 |
| *—Reissue* | | | |
| ❑ 822820-1 | Stella | 1988 | 8.00 |
| *—Reissue* | | | |
| ❑ 832675-1 | One Second | 1987 | 12.00 |
| ❑ 836426-1 | Flag | 1989 | 12.00 |

### RALPH

| Number | Title (A Side/B Side) | Yr | NM |
|---|---|---|---|
| ❑ YL 8059-L | Solid Pleasure | 1980 | 20.00 |
| ❑ YL 8159 | Claro Que Si | 1981 | 20.00 |

## YELLOW BALLOON, THE

### CANTERBURY

| Number | Title (A Side/B Side) | Yr | NM |
|---|---|---|---|
| ❑ CLPM-1502 [M] | The Yellow Balloon | 1967 | 25.00 |
| ❑ CLPS-1502 [S] | The Yellow Balloon | 1967 | 30.00 |

## YELLOW PAYGES, THE

### UNI

| Number | Title (A Side/B Side) | Yr | NM |
|---|---|---|---|
| ❑ 73045 | The Yellow Payges, Volume 1 | 1969 | 30.00 |

## YES Also see RICK WAKEMAN.

### ARISTA

| Number | Title (A Side/B Side) | Yr | NM |
|---|---|---|---|
| ❑ AL 8643 | Union | 1991 | 20.00 |
| *—U.S. vinyl available only through Columbia House* | | | |

### ATCO

| Number | Title (A Side/B Side) | Yr | NM |
|---|---|---|---|
| ❑ 90125 | 90125 | 1983 | 8.00 |
| ❑ 90474 | 9012Live: The Solos | 1985 | 8.00 |
| ❑ 90522 | Big Generator | 1987 | 8.00 |

### ATLANTIC

| Number | Title (A Side/B Side) | Yr | NM |
|---|---|---|---|
| ❑ SD 3-100 [(3)] | Yessongs | 1973 | 18.00 |
| ❑ PR 260 [DJ] | Yes Solo LP Sampler | 1976 | 25.00 |
| ❑ PR 285 [DJ] | Yes Music: An Evening with Jon Anderson | 1977 | 50.00 |
| ❑ SD 2-510 [(2)] | Yesshows | 1980 | 12.00 |
| ❑ SD 2-908 [(2)] | Tales from Topographic Oceans | 1974 | 15.00 |
| ❑ SD 2-908 [(2)DJ] | Tales from Topographic Oceans | 1974 | 30.00 |
| *—Promo copies banded for airplay* | | | |
| ❑ SD 7211 | Fragile | 1972 | 12.00 |
| ❑ 7244 [DJ] | Close to the Edge | 1972 | 50.00 |
| *—White label mono copies banded for airplay* | | | |
| ❑ SD 7244 | Close to the Edge | 1972 | 12.00 |
| ❑ SD 8243 | Yes | 1969 | 12.00 |
| ❑ SD 8273 | Time and a Word | 1970 | 12.00 |
| ❑ 8283 [M] | The Yes Album | 1971 | 40.00 |
| *—White label promo only; "DJ Copy Monaural" sticker on cover* | | | |
| ❑ SD 8283 | The Yes Album | 1971 | 12.00 |
| ❑ SD 16019 | Drama | 1980 | 10.00 |
| ❑ SD 18103 | Yesterdays | 1975 | 10.00 |
| ❑ SD 18122 | Relayer | 1974 | 10.00 |
| ❑ SD 18122 [DJ] | Relayer | 1974 | 20.00 |
| *—Promo copies banded for airplay* | | | |
| ❑ SD 19106 | Going for the One | 1977 | 10.00 |
| ❑ SD 19131 | The Yes Album | 1977 | 8.00 |
| ❑ SD 19132 | Fragile | 1977 | 8.00 |
| ❑ SD 19133 | Close to the Edge | 1977 | 8.00 |
| ❑ SD 19134 | Yesterdays | 1977 | 8.00 |
| ❑ SD 19135 | Relayer | 1977 | 8.00 |
| ❑ SD 19202 | Tormato | 1978 | 10.00 |
| ❑ SD 19320 | Classic Yes | 1982 | 10.00 |
| *—With bonus single missing* | | | |
| ❑ SD 19320 | Classic Yes | 1982 | 15.00 |
| *—Original copies include a bonus 7-inch promo single* | | | |

### MOBILE FIDELITY

| Number | Title (A Side/B Side) | Yr | NM |
|---|---|---|---|
| ❑ 1-077 | Close to the Edge | 1982 | 60.00 |
| *—Audiophile vinyl* | | | |

### RHINO

| Number | Title (A Side/B Side) | Yr | NM |
|---|---|---|---|
| ❑ R1-73788 | The Yes Album | 2003 | 15.00 |
| *—Reissue on 180-gram vinyl* | | | |

## YESTERDAY'S CHILDREN

### MAP CITY

| Number | Title (A Side/B Side) | Yr | NM |
|---|---|---|---|
| ❑ 3012 | Yesterday's Children | 197? | 60.00 |

## YESTERDAY'S FOLK

### BUDDAH

| Number | Title (A Side/B Side) | Yr | NM |
|---|---|---|---|
| ❑ BDS-5035 | U.S. 69 | 1969 | 20.00 |

## YETTI-MEN, THE / THE UPPA TRIO

### KAL

| Number | Title (A Side/B Side) | Yr | NM |
|---|---|---|---|
| ❑ KB-4348 | The Yetti-Men/The Uppa Trio | 1967 | 600.00 |

## YOAKAM, DWIGHT

### OAK

| Number | Title (A Side/B Side) | Yr | NM |
|---|---|---|---|
| ❑ OR 2356 [EP] | Guitars, Cadillacs, Etc., Etc. | 1984 | 80.00 |
| *—Six-song EP; cover is in black and white; the song "Guitars, Cadillacs" does NOT appear on this release* | | | |

### REPRISE

| Number | Title (A Side/B Side) | Yr | NM |
|---|---|---|---|
| ❑ 25372 | Guitars, Cadillacs, Etc., Etc. | 1986 | 10.00 |
| *—LP has 10 songs rather than the six on the Oak EP; front cover has color on it* | | | |
| ❑ W1-25372 | Guitars, Cadillacs, Etc., Etc. | 1986 | 12.00 |
| *—Columbia House edition* | | | |
| ❑ 25567 | Hillbilly Deluxe | 1987 | 10.00 |
| ❑ W1-25567 | Hillbilly Deluxe | 1987 | 12.00 |
| *—Columbia House edition* | | | |
| ❑ 25749 | Buenas Noches from a Lonely Room | 1988 | 10.00 |
| ❑ W1-25749 | Buenas Noches from a Lonely Room | 1988 | 12.00 |
| *—Columbia House edition* | | | |
| ❑ 25989 | Just Lookin' for a Hit | 1989 | 10.00 |
| ❑ W1-25989 | Just Lookin' for a Hit | 1989 | 12.00 |
| *—Columbia House edition* | | | |
| ❑ R 100009 | Buenas Noches from a Lonely Room | 1988 | 12.00 |
| *—BMG Direct Marketing edition* | | | |
| ❑ R 150223 | Guitars, Cadillacs, Etc., Etc. | 1986 | 12.00 |
| *—RCA Music Service edition* | | | |
| ❑ R 164146 | Hillbilly Deluxe | 1987 | 12.00 |
| *—BMG Direct Marketing edition* | | | |
| ❑ R 164310 | If There Was a Way | 1990 | 20.00 |
| *—BMG Direct Marketing edition; only U.S. vinyl version* | | | |
| ❑ R 174052 | Just Lookin' for a Hit | 1989 | 12.00 |
| *—BMG Direct Marketing edition* | | | |

## YORK BROTHERS, THE

### KING

| Number | Title (A Side/B Side) | Yr | NM |
|---|---|---|---|
| ❑ 581 [M] | The York Brothers | 1958 | 100.00 |
| ❑ 586 [M] | The York Brothers, Volume 2 | 1958 | 100.00 |
| ❑ 820 [M] | 16 Great Country and Western Hits | 1963 | 80.00 |

## YOST, PHIL

### TAKOMA

| Number | Title (A Side/B Side) | Yr | NM |
|---|---|---|---|
| ❑ C-1016 | Bent City | 196? | 20.00 |
| ❑ C-1021 | Fog-Hat Ramble | 196? | 20.00 |

## YOU KNOW WHO GROUP, THE

### INTERNATIONAL ALLIED

| Number | Title (A Side/B Side) | Yr | NM |
|---|---|---|---|
| ❑ 420 [M] | The "You Know Who" Group | 1965 | 50.00 |

## YOUNG, BARRY

### DOT

| Number | Title (A Side/B Side) | Yr | NM |
|---|---|---|---|
| ❑ DLP 3672 [M] | One Has My Name | 1965 | 20.00 |
| ❑ DLP 25672 [S] | One Has My Name | 1965 | 25.00 |

## YOUNG, CATHY

### MAINSTREAM

| Number | Title (A Side/B Side) | Yr | NM |
|---|---|---|---|
| ❑ S-6121 | A Spoonful of Cathy Young | 1968 | 40.00 |

## YOUNG, CECIL

### AUDIO LAB

| Number | Title (A Side/B Side) | Yr | NM |
|---|---|---|---|
| ❑ AL-1516 [M] | Jazz on the Rocks | 1959 | 80.00 |

### KING

| Number | Title (A Side/B Side) | Yr | NM |
|---|---|---|---|
| ❑ 295-1 [10] | A Concert of Cool Jazz | 1952 | 100.00 |

## YOUNG, ELDEE

### ARGO

| Number | Title (A Side/B Side) | Yr | NM |
|---|---|---|---|
| ❑ LPS-699 [S] | Just for Kicks | 1962 | 20.00 |
| ❑ LP-1003 [M] | Eldee Young and Company | 1962 | 20.00 |
| ❑ LPS-1003 [S] | Eldee Young and Company | 1962 | 25.00 |

## YOUNG, FARON

### ALLEGIANCE

| Number | Title (A Side/B Side) | Yr | NM |
|---|---|---|---|
| ❑ AV-5008 | The Sheriff | 198? | 10.00 |

### CAPITOL

| Number | Title (A Side/B Side) | Yr | NM |
|---|---|---|---|
| ❑ T 778 [M] | Sweethearts or Strangers | 1957 | 60.00 |
| *—Turquoise or gray label* | | | |
| ❑ T 778 [M] | Sweethearts or Strangers | 1959 | 25.00 |
| *—Black colorband label, logo at left* | | | |
| ❑ T 1004 [M] | The Object of My Affection | 1958 | 50.00 |
| ❑ T 1096 [M] | This Is Faron Young | 1959 | 50.00 |
| ❑ T 1185 [M] | My Garden of Prayer | 1959 | 40.00 |
| ❑ ST 1245 [S] | Talk About Hits | 1959 | 40.00 |
| ❑ T 1245 [M] | Talk About Hits | 1959 | 30.00 |
| ❑ ST 1450 [S] | The Best of Faron Young | 1960 | 40.00 |
| ❑ T 1450 [M] | The Best of Faron Young | 1960 | 30.00 |
| ❑ ST 1528 [S] | Hello Walls | 1961 | 40.00 |
| ❑ T 1528 [M] | Hello Walls | 1961 | 30.00 |
| ❑ ST 1634 [S] | The Young Approach | 1961 | 40.00 |
| ❑ T 1634 [M] | The Young Approach | 1961 | 30.00 |
| ❑ DT 1876 [P] | The All-Time Great Hits of Faron Young | 1963 | 20.00 |
| ❑ T 1876 [M] | The All-Time Great Hits of Faron Young | 1963 | 25.00 |
| ❑ DT 2037 [R] | Faron Young's Memory Lane | 1964 | 20.00 |
| ❑ T 2037 [M] | Faron Young's Memory Lane | 1964 | 25.00 |
| ❑ ST 2307 [S] | Falling in Love | 1965 | 25.00 |
| ❑ T 2307 [M] | Falling in Love | 1965 | 20.00 |
| ❑ DT 2536 [R] | If You Ain't Lovin' You Ain't Livin' | 1966 | 20.00 |
| ❑ T 2536 [M] | If You Ain't Lovin' You Ain't Livin' | 1966 | 25.00 |

### HILLTOP

| Number | Title (A Side/B Side) | Yr | NM |
|---|---|---|---|
| ❑ JM-6037 [M] | Faron Young | 1966 | 15.00 |
| ❑ JS-6037 [S] | Faron Young | 1966 | 12.00 |
| ❑ JS-6073 | I'll Be Yours | 1968 | 12.00 |

### MARY CARTER

| Number | Title (A Side/B Side) | Yr | NM |
|---|---|---|---|
| ❑ MC 1000 [M] | Faron Young Sings on Stage for Mary Carter Paints | 196? | 60.00 |
| *—Promotional item for sponsor of The Faron Young Show* | | | |

### MCA

| Number | Title (A Side/B Side) | Yr | NM |
|---|---|---|---|
| ❑ 757 | Chapter Two | 198? | 8.00 |
| *—Budget-line reissue of 3092* | | | |
| ❑ 3092 | Chapter Two | 1979 | 12.00 |
| ❑ 3212 | Free and Easy | 1980 | 12.00 |

### MERCURY

| Number | Title (A Side/B Side) | Yr | NM |
|---|---|---|---|
| ❑ SRM-1-674 | Just What I Had in Mind | 1973 | 15.00 |
| ❑ SRM-1-698 | Faron Young Sings "Some Kind of a Woman" | 1974 | 15.00 |
| ❑ SRM-1-1016 | A Man and His Music | 1974 | 12.00 |
| ❑ SRM-1-1075 | I'd Just Be Fool Enough | 1976 | 12.00 |
| ❑ SRM-1-1130 | The Best of Faron Young, Vol. 2 | 1977 | 12.00 |
| ❑ SRM-1-5005 | Young Feelin' | 1978 | 12.00 |
| ❑ MG 20785 [M] | This Is Faron | 1963 | 20.00 |
| ❑ MG 20840 [M] | Faron Young Aims at the West | 1963 | 20.00 |
| ❑ MG 20896 [M] | Story Songs for Country Folks | 1964 | 20.00 |
| ❑ MG 20931 [M] | Country Dance Favorites | 1964 | 20.00 |
| ❑ MG 20971 [M] | Story Songs of Mountains and Valleys | 1965 | 20.00 |
| ❑ MG 21007 [M] | Pen and Paper | 1965 | 20.00 |
| ❑ MG 21047 [M] | Faron Young's Greatest Hits | 1965 | 20.00 |
| ❑ MG 21058 [M] | Faron Young Sings the Best of Jim Reeves | 1966 | 20.00 |
| ❑ MG 21110 [M] | Unmitigated Gall | 1967 | 25.00 |
| ❑ SR 60785 [S] | This Is Faron | 1963 | 25.00 |
| ❑ SR 60840 [S] | Faron Young Aims at the West | 1963 | 25.00 |
| ❑ SR 60896 [S] | Story Songs for Country Folks | 1964 | 25.00 |
| ❑ SR 60931 [S] | Country Dance Favorites | 1964 | 25.00 |
| ❑ SR 60971 [S] | Story Songs of Mountains and Valleys | 1965 | 25.00 |
| ❑ SR 61007 [S] | Pen and Paper | 1965 | 25.00 |
| ❑ SR 61047 [S] | Faron Young's Greatest Hits | 1965 | 25.00 |
| ❑ SR 61058 [S] | Faron Young Sings the Best of Jim Reeves | 1966 | 25.00 |
| ❑ SR 61110 [S] | Unmitigated Gall | 1967 | 20.00 |
| ❑ SR 61143 | Greatest Hits Vol. 2 | 1968 | 20.00 |
| ❑ SR 61174 | Here's Faron Young | 1968 | 20.00 |
| ❑ SR 61212 | I've Got Precious Memories | 1969 | 20.00 |
| ❑ SR 61241 | Wine Me Up | 1969 | 20.00 |
| ❑ SR 61267 | The Best of Faron Young | 1970 | 20.00 |
| ❑ SR 61275 | Faron Young Sings "Occasional Wife" and "If I Ever Fall in Love with a Honky Tonk Girl" | 1970 | 20.00 |
| ❑ SR 61337 | Step Aside | 1971 | 20.00 |
| ❑ SR 61354 | Faron Young Sings "Leavin' and Sayin' Goodbye" | 1971 | 15.00 |
| ❑ SR 61359 | It's Four in the Morning | 1972 | 15.00 |
| *—Revised title to reflect the hit?* | | | |
| ❑ SR 61359 | Evening | 1972 | 20.00 |
| *—Original title?* | | | |
| ❑ SR 61364 | Faron Young Sings This Little Girl of Mine | 1972 | 15.00 |
| ❑ SR 61376 | This Time the Hurtin's on Me | 1973 | 15.00 |

### PICCADILLY

| Number | Title (A Side/B Side) | Yr | NM |
|---|---|---|---|
| ❑ 3547 | Hello Walls | 198? | 10.00 |

### SEARS

| Number | Title (A Side/B Side) | Yr | NM |
|---|---|---|---|
| ❑ SPS-124 | Candy Kisses | 1969 | 25.00 |

### SESAC

| Number | Title (A Side/B Side) | Yr | NM |
|---|---|---|---|
| ❑ (# unknown) [DJ] | Church Songs | 196? | 80.00 |

### TOWER

| Number | Title (A Side/B Side) | Yr | NM |
|---|---|---|---|
| ❑ DT 5022 [R] | It's a Great Life | 1966 | 12.00 |
| ❑ T 5022 [M] | It's a Great Life | 1966 | 20.00 |
| ❑ DT 5121 | The World of Faron Young | 1968 | 15.00 |

## YOUNG, JESSE COLIN Also see THE YOUNGBLOODS.

### CAPITOL

| Number | Title (A Side/B Side) | Yr | NM |
|---|---|---|---|
| ❑ T 2070 [M] | The Soul of a City Boy | 1964 | 50.00 |
| ❑ ST-11267 | The Soul of a City Boy | 1974 | 12.00 |
| *—Reissue of 2070* | | | |
| ❑ N-16129 | The Soul of a City Boy | 1981 | 8.00 |
| *—Budget-line reissue* | | | |

### CYPRESS

| Number | Title (A Side/B Side) | Yr | NM |
|---|---|---|---|
| ❑ 0103 | The Highway Is for Heroes | 1987 | 10.00 |

### ELEKTRA

| Number | Title (A Side/B Side) | Yr | NM |
|---|---|---|---|
| ❑ 6E-157 | American Dreams | 1978 | 10.00 |

### MERCURY

| Number | Title (A Side/B Side) | Yr | NM |
|---|---|---|---|
| ❑ MG 21005 [M] | Young Blood | 1965 | 30.00 |
| ❑ SR 61005 [S] | Young Blood | 1965 | 40.00 |

Number | Title (A Side/B Side) | Yr | NM

RACCOON
❑ BS 2588 Together 1972 12.00
WARNER BROS.
❑ BS 2734 Song for Juli 1973 10.00
❑ BS 2790 Light Shine 1974 10.00
❑ BS 2845 Songbird 1975 10.00
❑ BS 2913 On the Road 1976 10.00
❑ BS 3033 Love on the Wing 1977 10.00

**YOUNG, JOHN**
ARGO
❑ LP-612 [M] Young John Young 1957 40.00
❑ LP-692 [M] Themes and Things 1962 25.00
❑ LPS-692 [S] Themes and Things 1962 30.00
❑ LP-713 [M] A Touch of Pepper 1962 25.00
❑ LPS-713 [S] A Touch of Pepper 1962 30.00
DELMARK
❑ DL-403 [M] The John Young Trio 1961 30.00
❑ DS-403 [S] The John Young Trio 1961 40.00
VEE JAY
❑ VJS-3060 Opus de Funk 1974 20.00

**YOUNG, JOHNNY**
ARHOOLIE
❑ F-1029 Johnny Williams and His Chicago Blues Band 1965 25.00
❑ F-1037 Chicago Blues 1966 25.00
BLUE HORIZON
❑ BH-4609 Blues Masters, Volume 9 1969 20.00

**YOUNG, KATHY, AND THE INNOCENTS**
INDIGO
❑ LP-504 [M] The Sound of Kathy Young 1961 300.00

**YOUNG, LARRY**
BLUE NOTE
❑ BLP-4187 [M] Into Somethin' 1964 30.00
❑ BLP-4221 [M] Unity 1966 30.00
❑ BLP-4242 [M] Of Love and Peace 1966 30.00
❑ BLP-4266 [S] Contrasts 1967 40.00
❑ BST-84187 [S] Into Somethin' 1964 40.00
*—With "New York, USA" address on label*
❑ BST-84187 [S] Into Somethin' 1967 20.00
*—With "A Division of Liberty Records" on label*
❑ BST-84221 [S] Unity 1966 40.00
*—With "New York, USA" address on label*
❑ BST-84221 [S] Unity 1967 20.00
*—With "A Division of Liberty Records" on label*
❑ BST-84242 [S] Of Love and Peace 1966 40.00
*—With "New York, USA" address on label*
❑ BST-84242 [S] Of Love and Peace 1967 20.00
*—With "A Division of Liberty Records" on label*
❑ BST-84266 [S] Contrasts 1967 30.00
*—With "A Division of Liberty Records" on label*
❑ BST-84304 [S] Heaven on Earth 1968 30.00
*—With "A Division of Liberty Records" on label*
MOSAIC
❑ MR9-137 [(9)] The Complete Blue Note Recordings of Larry Young 199? 200.00
NEW JAZZ
❑ NJLP-8249 [M] Testifying 1960 50.00
*—Purple label*
❑ NJLP-8249 [M] Testifying 1965 25.00
*—Blue label, trident logo at right*
❑ NJLP-8264 [M] Young Blues 1961 50.00
*—Purple label*
❑ NJLP-8264 [M] Young Blues 1965 25.00
*—Blue label, trident logo at right*
PRESTIGE
❑ PRLP-7237 [M] Groove Street 1962 40.00
❑ PRST-7237 [S] Groove Street 1962 40.00

**YOUNG, LEON**
ATCO
❑ 33-163 [M] Liverpool Sound for Strings 1964 25.00
❑ SD 33-163 [S] Liverpool Sound for Strings 1964 30.00

**YOUNG, LESTER**
ALADDIN
❑ LP-705 [10] Lester Young Trio 1953 300.00
❑ LP-706 [10] Easy Does It 1954 300.00
❑ LP-801 [M] Lester Young and His Tenor Sax, Volume 1 1956 120.00
❑ LP-802 [M] Lester Young and His Tenor Sax, Volume 2 1956 120.00
AMERICAN RECORDING SOCIETY
❑ G-417 [M] Pres and Teddy 1957 50.00
CHARLIE PARKER
❑ CLP-402 [M] Pres 1961 50.00
❑ CLP-405 [M] Pres Is Blue 1961 50.00
CLEF
❑ MGC-104 [10] The Lester Young Trio 1953 250.00
❑ MGC-108 [10] Lester Young Collates 1953 250.00
❑ MGC-124 [10] Lester Young Collates No. 2 1953 250.00
*—Some copies of this have Mercury covers; no difference in value*
❑ MGC-135 [10] The Lester Young Trio No. 2 1953 250.00
COMMODORE
❑ FL-20021 [10] Kansas City Style 1952 300.00
❑ FL-30014 [M] Kansas City Style 1959 100.00
CROWN
❑ CLP-5305 [M] Nat "King" Cole Meets Lester Young 196? 25.00
EPIC
❑ LN 3107 [M] Lester Leaps In 1956 100.00
❑ LN 3168 [M] Let's Go to Pres 1956 100.00
❑ LN 3576 [M] Lester Young Memorial Album, Volume 1 1959 50.00
❑ LN 3577 [M] Lester Young Memorial Album, Volume 2 1959 50.00
❑ SN 6031 [(2)M] Lester Young Memorial Album 1959 150.00
IMPERIAL
❑ LP-9181-A [M] The Immortal Lester Young 1962 50.00
❑ LP-9187-A [M] The Great Lester Young, Volume 2 1962 50.00
❑ LP-12181-A [R] The Immortal Lester Young 196? 20.00
❑ LP-12187-A [R] The Great Lester Young, Volume 2 196? 20.00
INTRO
❑ LP-602 [M] Swinging Lester Young 1957 100.00
❑ LP-603 [M] The Greatest 1957 100.00
MAINSTREAM
❑ 56002 [M] The Influence of Five 1965 25.00
❑ 56004 [M] Town Hall Concert 1965 25.00
❑ 56008 [M] Chairman of the Board 1965 25.00
❑ 56009 [M] 52nd Street 1965 25.00
❑ 56012 [M] Prez 1965 25.00
MERCURY
❑ MGC-104 [10] The Lester Young Trio 1951 300.00
❑ MGC-108 [10] Lester Young Collates 1951 300.00
NORGRAN
❑ MGN-5 [10] Lester Young with the Oscar Peterson Trio No. 1 1954 200.00
❑ MGN-6 [10] Lester Young with the Oscar Peterson Trio No. 2 1954 200.00
❑ MGN-1005 [M] The President 1954 200.00
❑ MGN-1022 [M] Lester Young 1955 200.00
❑ MGN-1043 [M] Pres and Sweets 1955 200.00
❑ MGN-1054 [M] The President Plays with the Oscar Peterson Trio 1955 100.00
❑ MGN-1071 [M] Lester's Here 1956 100.00
❑ MGN-1072 [M] Pres 1956 100.00
❑ MGN-1074 [M] Lester Young and the Buddy Rich Trio 1956 100.00
❑ MGN-1093 [M] Lester Swings Again 1956 100.00
❑ MGN-1100 [M] Lester Young 1956 100.00
SAVOY
❑ MG-9002 [10] Lester Young (All Star Be Bop) 1951 300.00
❑ MG-12068 [M] Blue Lester 1956 80.00
❑ MG-12071 [M] The Master's Touch 1956 80.00
❑ MG-12155 [M] The Immortal Lester Young 1959 60.00
SCORE
❑ SLP-4019 [M] Lester Young / The King Cole Trio 1958 80.00
❑ SLP-4028 [M] Swinging Lester Young 1958 80.00
❑ SLP-4029 [M] The Great Lester Young 1958 80.00
VERVE
❑ VSP-27 [M] Pres and His Cabinet 1966 25.00
❑ VSP-30 [M] Giants 3 1966 25.00
*—With Buddy Rich and Nat King Cole*
❑ MGV-8134 [M] Pres and Sweets 1957 60.00
❑ V-8134 [M] Pres and Sweets 1961 25.00
❑ MGV-8144 [M] The President Plays with the Oscar Peterson Trio 1957 60.00
❑ V-8144 [M] The President Plays with the Oscar Peterson Trio 1961 25.00
❑ MGV-8161 [M] Lester's Here 1957 60.00
❑ V-8161 [M] Lester's Here 1961 25.00
❑ MGV-8162 [M] Pres 1957 60.00
❑ V-8162 [M] Pres 1961 25.00
❑ MGV-8164 [M] Lester Young and the Buddy Rich Trio 1957 60.00
❑ V-8164 [M] Lester Young and the Buddy Rich Trio 1961 25.00
❑ MGV-8181 [M] Lester Swings Again 1957 60.00
❑ V-8181 [M] Lester Swings Again 1961 25.00
❑ MGV-8187 [M] It Don't Mean a Thing (If It Ain't Got That Swing) 1957 60.00
❑ V-8187 [M] It Don't Mean a Thing (If It Ain't Got That Swing) 1961 25.00
❑ MGV-8205 [M] Pres and Teddy 1957 60.00
❑ V-8205 [M] Pres and Teddy 1961 25.00
❑ MGV-8308 [M] The Lester Young Story 1959 60.00
❑ V-8308 [M] The Lester Young Story 1961 25.00
❑ MGV-8378 [M] Lester Young in Paris 1960 60.00
❑ V-8378 [M] Lester Young in Paris 1961 25.00
❑ MGV-8398 [M] The Essential Lester Young 1961 60.00
❑ V-8398 [M] The Essential Lester Young 1961 25.00

**YOUNG, LESTER/COUNT BASIE**
MERCURY
❑ MG-25015 [10] Lester Young Quartet/Count Basie Seven 1950 250.00

**YOUNG, LESTER/CHU BERRY**
JAZZTONE
❑ J-1218 [M] Tops on Tenor: Pres and Chu 1956 70.00

**YOUNG, LESTER; ROY ELDRIDGE; HARRY "SWEETS" EDISON**
VERVE
❑ MGVS-6054 [S] Laughin' to Keep from Cryin' 1960 70.00
❑ MGVS-6054 [S] Laughin' to Keep from Cryin' 199? 25.00
*—Classic Records reissue on audiophile vinyl*
❑ MGV-8298 [M] Going for Myself 1959 60.00
❑ V-8298 [M] Going for Myself 1961 25.00
❑ MGV-8316 [M] Laughin' to Keep from Cryin' 1960 60.00
❑ V-8316 [M] Laughin' to Keep from Cryin' 1961 25.00
❑ V6-8316 [S] Laughin' to Keep from Cryin' 1961 30.00

**YOUNG, LESTER, AND PAUL QUINICHETTE**
EMARCY
❑ MG-26021 [10] Pres Meets Vice-Pres 1954 250.00

**YOUNG, NEIL** Also see BUFFALO SPRINGFIELD; CROSBY, STILLS, NASH AND YOUNG.
GEFFEN
❑ GHS 2018 Trans 1982 10.00
*—Later pressings have neither sticker nor title of absent song*
❑ GHS 2018 Trans 1982 15.00
*—First pressings have a sticker on rear cover explaining the absence of "If You've Got Love"*
❑ GHS 2018 [DJ] Trans 1982 20.00
*—Promo on Quiex II audiophile vinyl*
❑ GHS 4013 Everybody's Rockin' 1983 10.00
❑ GHS 4013 Everybody's Rockin' 1983 20.00
*—Promo on Quiex II audiophile vinyl*
❑ GHS 24068 Old Ways 1985 12.00
❑ GHS 24109 Landing on Water 1986 12.00
❑ GHS 24154 Life 1987 12.00
❑ R 134125 Landing on Water 1986 15.00
*—RCA Music Service edition*
❑ R 144439 Life 1987 15.00
*—BMG Direct Marketing edition*
❑ R 163233 Old Ways 1985 15.00
*—RCA Music Service edition*
MOBILE FIDELITY
❑ 1-252 Old Ways 1996 20.00
*—Audiophile vinyl*
NAUTILUS
❑ NR-44 Harvest 1982 150.00
*—Audiophile vinyl*
REPRISE
❑ MS 2032 Harvest 1972 10.00
❑ MS 2032 Harvest 1972 15.00
*—First pressings have textured cover and lyric insert*
❑ M 2151 [M] Time Fades Away 1973 100.00
*—Special mono pressing for radio stations only*
❑ MS 2151 Time Fades Away 1973 10.00
❑ MS 2151 [S] Time Fades Away 1973 200.00
*—With a cardboard inner sleeve, withdrawn after the earliest pressing*
❑ R 2180 On the Beach 1974 20.00
❑ MS 2221 Tonight's the Night 1975 10.00
❑ MS 2242 Zuma 1975 10.00
❑ 3RS 2257 [(3)] Decade 1977 20.00
❑ 3RS 2257 [(3)DJ] Decade 1977 500.00
*—Test pressing; "Campaigner" contains extra verse deleted from the final version*
❑ MSK 2261 American Stars 'N' Bars 1977 10.00
❑ MSK 2266 Comes A Time 1978 10.00
*—With "Peace of Mind" as the last song on side 1. Covers can list either "Lotta Love" or "Peace of Mind."*
❑ MSK 2266 Comes A Time 1978 75.00
*—With "Lotta Love" listed and playing as the last song on side 1*
❑ MSK 2266 [DJ] Give to the Wind 1978 1000.
*—Test pressing; plain white jacket with inserts and STOCK COPY LABEL. Title changed to "Comes A Time" for commercial release.*
❑ MSK 2277 Harvest 1978 8.00
*—Brown "Reprise" label; new number*
❑ MSK 2282 Everybody Knows This Is Nowhere 1978 8.00
*—Brown "Reprise" label; new number*
❑ MSK 2283 After the Gold Rush 1978 40.00
*—Contains remixed extended version of "When You Dance I Can Really Love." Title on cover in red, "RE 2" in trail-off vinyl*
❑ HS 2295 Rust Never Sleeps 1979 10.00
❑ 2RX 2296 [(2)] Live Rust 1979 15.00
❑ HS 2297 Hawks and Doves 1980 10.00
❑ HS 2304 Re-Ac-Tor 1981 10.00
❑ RS 6317 Neil Young 1968 200.00
*—Brown and orange "Reprise/W7" label, no name on front cover, no "RE-1" in trail-off wax*
❑ RS 6317 Neil Young 1969 60.00
*—Re-release: Brown and orange "Reprise/W7" label, no name on front cover, four tracks remixed ("RE 1" in trail-off wax)*

| Number | Title (A Side/B Side) | Yr | NM |
|---|---|---|---|
| ❑ RS 6317 | Neil Young | 1970 | 15.00 |
| *—Reissue: Brown "Reprise" label, Neil Young's name is now on front cover* | | | |
| ❑ RS 6349 | Everybody Knows This Is Nowhere | 1969 | 30.00 |
| *—Brown and orange "Reprise/W7" label* | | | |
| ❑ RS 6349 | Everybody Knows This Is Nowhere | 1970 | 15.00 |
| *—Brown "Reprise" label* | | | |
| ❑ RS 6349 [DJ] | Everybody Knows This Is Nowhere | 1969 | 75.00 |
| *—White label promo* | | | |
| ❑ RS 6383 | After the Gold Rush | 1970 | 10.00 |
| *—Brown "Reprise" label* | | | |
| ❑ RS 6383 | After the Gold Rush | 1970 | 15.00 |
| *—Brown and orange label; all photos correct* | | | |
| ❑ RS 6383 | After the Gold Rush | 1970 | 35.00 |
| *—Brown and orange label; photo of Neil Young appears erroneously printed upside down in gatefold* | | | |
| ❑ RS 6383 | After the Gold Rush | 1970 | 40.00 |
| *—Brown and orange label; photo of Marc Bolan (of T. Rex) appears erroneously in gatefold* | | | |
| ❑ 2XS 6480 [(2)] | Journey Through the Past (Soundtrack) | 1972 | 20.00 |
| ❑ 25719 | This Note's for You | 1988 | 12.00 |
| ❑ 25899 | Freedom | 1989 | 15.00 |
| ❑ 26315 | Ragged Glory | 1990 | 20.00 |
| ❑ 44335-1 | Living with War | 2006 | 25.00 |
| *—Distributed by Classic Records; 200-gram vinyl* | | | |
| ❑ 45749 [(2)] | Sleeps with Angels | 1994 | 25.00 |
| ❑ 45934 [(2)] | Mirror Ball | 1995 | 15.00 |
| *—With Pearl Jam (uncredited)* | | | |
| ❑ 46291 [(2)] | Broken Arrow | 1996 | 40.00 |
| ❑ 46652 [(2)] | Year of the Horse | 1997 | 40.00 |
| ❑ 48935-1 [(2)] | Greatest Hits | 2005 | 40.00 |
| *—Distributed by Classic Records; 200-gram vinyl; with poster; also includes a bonus 7-inch single of "The Loner"/"Sugar Mountain" on either red, white or blue vinyl (not marked on packaging which color is inside; no difference in value)* | | | |
| ❑ 49593-1 [(2)] | Prairie Wind | 2005 | 40.00 |
| *—Distributed by Classic Records; 200-gram vinyl* | | | |
| ❑ SMAS-94285 | Harvest | 1972 | 25.00 |
| *—Capitol Record Club edition* | | | |
| ❑ R 113998 | Harvest | 1972 | 12.00 |
| *—RCA Music Service edition* | | | |
| ❑ R 154182 | This Note's for You | 1987 | 12.00 |
| *—BMG Direct Marketing edition* | | | |
| VAPOR | | | |
| ❑ VAP-1001 [(3)] | Greendale | 2005 | 50.00 |
| *—Distributed by Classic Records; 140-gram vinyl with bonus 7-inch single, book, bumper sticker and stage bill* | | | |
| ❑ VAP-1001 [(3)] | Greendale | 2005 | 80.00 |
| *—Distributed by Classic Records; 200-gram vinyl with bonus 7-inch single, book, bumper sticker and stage bill* | | | |
| ❑ 46171 [(2)] | Dead Man (Soundtrack) | 1996 | 12.00 |
| ❑ 48111 [(2)] | Are You Passionate? | 2002 | 25.00 |
| WARNER BROS. | | | |
| ❑ WBMS-107 [DJ] | The Warner Bros. Music Show | 1979 | 50.00 |
| *—Promo-only interview album* | | | |

**YOUNG, WEBSTER**

| Number | Title (A Side/B Side) | Yr | NM |
|---|---|---|---|
| PRESTIGE | | | |
| ❑ PRLP-7106 [M] | For Lady | 1957 | 100.00 |

**YOUNG HEARTS, THE**

| Number | Title (A Side/B Side) | Yr | NM |
|---|---|---|---|
| MINIT | | | |
| ❑ LP-24016 [S] | Sweet Soul Shakin'! | 1968 | 25.00 |
| ❑ LP-40016 [M] | Sweet Soul Shakin'! | 1968 | 25.00 |

**YOUNG-HOLT UNLIMITED**

| Number | Title (A Side/B Side) | Yr | NM |
|---|---|---|---|
| ATLANTIC | | | |
| ❑ SD 1634 | Oh Girl | 1973 | 12.00 |
| BRUNSWICK | | | |
| ❑ BL 54121 [M] | Wack-Wack | 1966 | 20.00 |
| *—As "Young-Holt Trio"* | | | |
| ❑ BL 54125 [M] | On Stage | 1967 | 20.00 |
| *—As "Young-Holt Trio"* | | | |
| ❑ BL 54128 [M] | The Beat Goes On | 1967 | 30.00 |
| ❑ BL 754121 [S] | Wack-Wack | 1966 | 20.00 |
| *—As "Young-Holt Trio"* | | | |
| ❑ BL 754125 [S] | On Stage | 1967 | 20.00 |
| *—As "Young-Holt Trio"* | | | |
| ❑ BL 754128 [S] | The Beat Goes On | 1967 | 20.00 |
| ❑ BL 754141 | Funky But! | 1968 | 20.00 |
| ❑ BL 754144 | Soulful Strut | 1968 | 15.00 |
| ❑ BL 754150 | Just a Melody | 1969 | 15.00 |
| CADET | | | |
| ❑ LP-791 [M] | Feature Spot | 1967 | 30.00 |
| ❑ LPS-791 [S] | Feature Spot | 1967 | 20.00 |
| *—As "Eldee Young and Red Holt (of the Ramsey Lewis Trio)"* | | | |
| COTILLION | | | |
| ❑ SD 18001 | Mellow Dreamin' | 1971 | 12.00 |
| ❑ SD 18004 | Born Again | 1972 | 12.00 |
| PAULA | | | |
| ❑ LPS-4002 | Super Fly | 1973 | 20.00 |

**YOUNG LIONS, THE (1)**

| Number | Title (A Side/B Side) | Yr | NM |
|---|---|---|---|
| VEE JAY | | | |
| ❑ LP-3013 [M] | The Young Lions | 1960 | 40.00 |

Neil Young, *Everybody Knows This Is Nowhere,* Reprise RS 6349, 1969, "Reprise/W7" logos on two-tone orange label $30, "Reprise" on one-tone orange label $15.

| Number | Title (A Side/B Side) | Yr | NM |
|---|---|---|---|
| ❑ SR-3013 [S] | The Young Lions | 1960 | 50.00 |

**YOUNG MEN FROM MEMPHIS**

| Number | Title (A Side/B Side) | Yr | NM |
|---|---|---|---|
| UNITED ARTISTS | | | |
| ❑ UAL-4029 [M] | Down Home Reunion | 1959 | 50.00 |
| ❑ UAS-5029 [S] | Down Home Reunion | 1959 | 40.00 |

**YOUNG RASCALS, THE** See THE RASCALS.

**YOUNG TUXEDO BRASS BAND, THE**

| Number | Title (A Side/B Side) | Yr | NM |
|---|---|---|---|
| ATLANTIC | | | |
| ❑ 1297 [M] | Jazz Begins | 1958 | 40.00 |
| *—Black label* | | | |
| ❑ 1297 [M] | Jazz Begins | 1961 | 20.00 |
| *—Multicolor label, white "fan" logo at right* | | | |
| ❑ SD-1297 [M] | Jazz Begins | 1958 | 50.00 |
| *—Green label* | | | |

**YOUNGBLOOD, LONNIE**

| Number | Title (A Side/B Side) | Yr | NM |
|---|---|---|---|
| RADIO | | | |
| ❑ RR 16045 | Lonnie Youngblood | 1981 | 15.00 |
| TURBO | | | |
| ❑ TU 7011 | Sweet Sweet Tootie | 1972 | 50.00 |
| ❑ TU 7019 | Lonnie Youngblood | 1977 | 20.00 |

**YOUNGBLOODS, THE** Also see JESSE COLIN YOUNG.

| Number | Title (A Side/B Side) | Yr | NM |
|---|---|---|---|
| MERCURY | | | |
| ❑ SR-61273 | Two Trips | 1970 | 25.00 |
| *—Gold border on cover* | | | |
| ❑ SR-61273 | Two Trips | 1971 | 20.00 |
| *—Red border on cover* | | | |
| RACCOON | | | |
| ❑ WS 1878 | Rock Festival | 1970 | 12.00 |
| ❑ BS 2563 | Ride the Wind | 1971 | 12.00 |
| ❑ BS 2566 | Good and Dusty | 1971 | 12.00 |
| ❑ BS 2653 | High on a Ridge Top | 1972 | 12.00 |
| RCA VICTOR | | | |
| ❑ AYL1-3680 | The Best of the Youngbloods | 1980 | 8.00 |
| *—"Best Buy Series" reissue* | | | |
| ❑ LPM-3724 [M] | The Youngbloods | 1967 | 40.00 |
| ❑ LSP-3724 | Get Together | 1969 | 15.00 |
| *—Retitled version of "The Youngbloods"* | | | |
| ❑ LSP-3724 [S] | The Youngbloods | 1967 | 25.00 |
| ❑ LPM-3865 [M] | Earth Music | 1968 | 50.00 |
| ❑ LSP-3865 [S] | Earth Music | 1968 | 25.00 |
| ❑ AFL1-4150 | Elephant Mountain | 1977 | 10.00 |
| *—Reissue of LSP-4150* | | | |
| ❑ LSP-4150 | Elephant Mountain | 1969 | 15.00 |
| *—Orange label* | | | |
| ❑ LSP-4150 | Elephant Mountain | 1975 | 12.00 |
| *—Tan label* | | | |
| ❑ AFL1-4399 | The Best of the Youngbloods | 1977 | 10.00 |
| *—Reissue of LSP-4399* | | | |
| ❑ LSP-4399 | The Best of the Youngbloods | 1970 | 15.00 |
| ❑ LSP-4561 | Sunlight | 1971 | 12.00 |
| ❑ VPS-6051 [(2)] | This Is the Youngbloods | 1972 | 15.00 |

**YOUNGMAN, HENNY**

| Number | Title (A Side/B Side) | Yr | NM |
|---|---|---|---|
| URANIA | | | |
| ❑ UR-9014 [M] | The Horse and Auto Race Game | 195? | 50.00 |

**YUM YUM KIDS, THE**

| Number | Title (A Side/B Side) | Yr | NM |
|---|---|---|---|
| MGM | | | |
| ❑ E-4396 [M] | Yummy in Your Tummy | 1966 | 15.00 |
| ❑ SE-4396 [S] | Yummy in Your Tummy | 1966 | 20.00 |

**YURO, TIMI**

| Number | Title (A Side/B Side) | Yr | NM |
|---|---|---|---|
| LIBERTY | | | |
| ❑ LRP-3208 [M] | Hurt | 1961 | 40.00 |
| ❑ LRP-3212 [M] | Soul | 1962 | 15.00 |
| ❑ LRP-3234 [M] | Let Me Call You Sweetheart | 1962 | 15.00 |
| ❑ LRP-3263 [M] | What's a Matter Baby? | 1963 | 15.00 |
| ❑ LRP-3286 [M] | The Best of Timi Yuro | 1963 | 15.00 |
| ❑ LRP-3319 [M] | Make the World Go Away | 1963 | 15.00 |
| ❑ LST-7208 [S] | Hurt | 1961 | 50.00 |
| ❑ LST-7212 [S] | Soul | 1962 | 20.00 |
| ❑ LST-7234 [S] | Let Me Call You Sweetheart | 1962 | 20.00 |
| ❑ LST-7263 [S] | What's a Matter Baby? | 1963 | 20.00 |
| ❑ LST-7286 [S] | The Best of Timi Yuro | 1963 | 20.00 |
| ❑ LST-7319 [S] | Make the World Go Away | 1963 | 20.00 |
| ❑ LST-7594 | Something Bad on My Mind | 1968 | 12.00 |
| MERCURY | | | |
| ❑ MG-20963 [M] | The Amazing Timi Yuro | 1964 | 12.00 |
| ❑ SR-60963 [S] | The Amazing Timi Yuro | 1964 | 15.00 |
| SUNSET | | | |
| ❑ SUM-1107 [M] | Timi Yuro | 1966 | 10.00 |
| ❑ SUS-5107 [S] | Timi Yuro | 1966 | 12.00 |
| UNITED ARTISTS | | | |
| ❑ UA-LA429-E | The Very Best of Timi Yuro | 1974 | 12.00 |

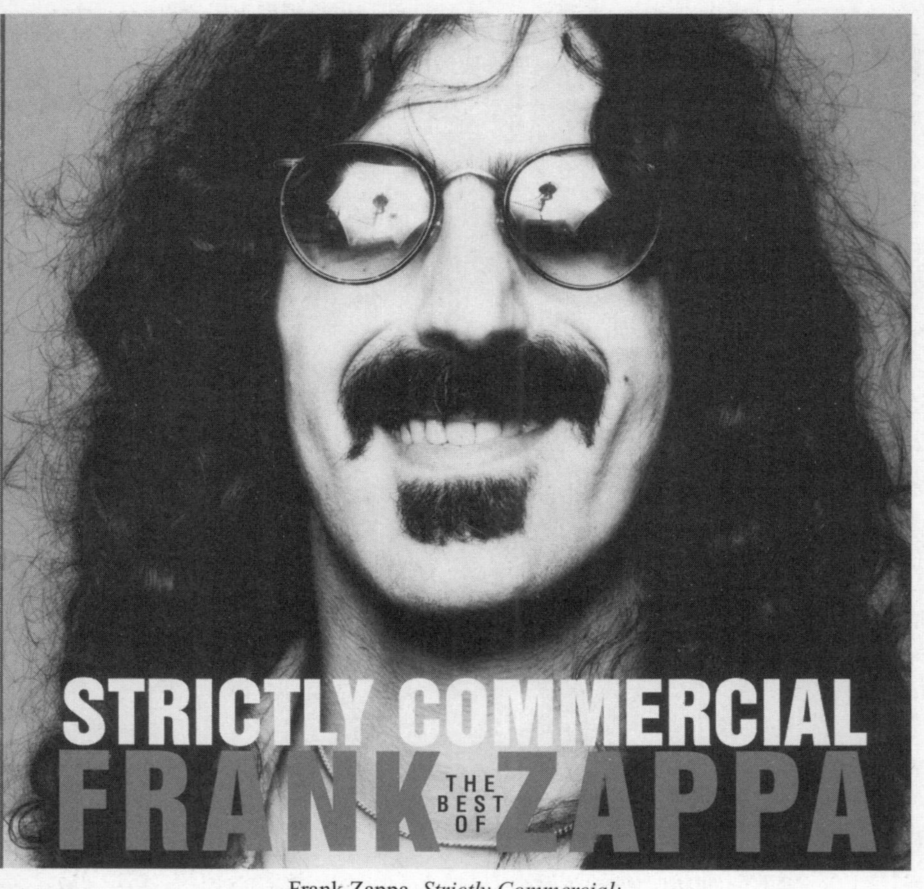


Frank Zappa, *Strictly Commercial: The Best of Frank Zappa*, Ryko Analogue RALP 40500, 1995, 2 records, $20.

# Z

## ZABACH, FLORIAN

### DECCA

| Number | Title (A Side/B Side) | Yr | NM |
|---|---|---|---|
| ❑ DL 4425 [M] | The Hot Canary | 196? | 15.00 |
| ❑ DL 5367 [10] | The Hot Canary | 1951 | 50.00 |
| ❑ DL 8086 [M] | Hour of Love | 195? | 25.00 |
| *—Black label, silver print* | | | |
| ❑ DL 8158 [M] | Dream of Romance | 195? | 25.00 |
| *—Black label, silver print* | | | |
| ❑ DL 8239 [M] | Hi-Fi Fiddle | 195? | 25.00 |
| *—Black label, silver print* | | | |

### MERCURY

| Number | Title (A Side/B Side) | Yr | NM |
|---|---|---|---|
| ❑ MG 20305 [M] | Till the End of Time | 1958 | 15.00 |
| ❑ MG 20436 [M] | It's Easy to Dance with Florian Zabach | 1959 | 20.00 |
| ❑ MG 20463 [M] | Do-It-Yourself Wedding Album | 1959 | 20.00 |
| ❑ SR 60084 [S] | Till the End of Time | 1958 | 20.00 |
| ❑ SR 60107 [S] | It's Easy to Dance with Florian Zabach | 1959 | 25.00 |
| ❑ SR 60145 [S] | Do-It-Yourself Wedding Album | 1959 | 25.00 |

### VOCALION

| Number | Title (A Side/B Side) | Yr | NM |
|---|---|---|---|
| ❑ VL 3701 [M] | String Along | 196? | 12.00 |

### WING

| Number | Title (A Side/B Side) | Yr | NM |
|---|---|---|---|
| ❑ MGW 12172 [M] | Golden Strings | 196? | 12.00 |
| ❑ MGW 12245 [M] | Till the End of Time | 196? | 12.00 |
| ❑ SRW 16172 [S] | Golden Strings | 196? | 15.00 |
| ❑ SRW 16245 [S] | Till the End of Time | 196? | 15.00 |

## ZACHERLE, JOHN

### CRESTVIEW

| Number | Title (A Side/B Side) | Yr | NM |
|---|---|---|---|
| ❑ CR 803 [M] | Zacherle's Monster Gallery | 1963 | 40.00 |
| ❑ CRS 7803 [S] | Zacherle's Monster Gallery | 1963 | 50.00 |

### ELEKTRA

| Number | Title (A Side/B Side) | Yr | NM |
|---|---|---|---|
| ❑ EKL-190 [M] | Spook Along with Zacherle | 1960 | 60.00 |
| ❑ EKS-7190 [S] | Spook Along with Zacherle | 1960 | 80.00 |

### PARKWAY

| Number | Title (A Side/B Side) | Yr | NM |
|---|---|---|---|
| ❑ P 7018 [M] | Monster Mash | 1962 | 60.00 |
| ❑ P 7023 [M] | Scary Tales | 1963 | 60.00 |

## ZACK, GEORGE

### COMMODORE

| Number | Title (A Side/B Side) | Yr | NM |
|---|---|---|---|
| ❑ FL-20001 [10] | Party Piano of the Roaring '20s | 1950 | 50.00 |

## ZAGER AND EVANS

### RCA VICTOR

| Number | Title (A Side/B Side) | Yr | NM |
|---|---|---|---|
| ❑ ANL1-1077 | 2525 (Exordium and Terminus) | 1975 | 10.00 |
| *—Reissue of 4214* | | | |
| ❑ LSP-4214 | 2525 (Exordium and Terminus) | 1969 | 20.00 |
| ❑ LSP-4302 | Zager and Evans | 1970 | 20.00 |

### VANGUARD

| Number | Title (A Side/B Side) | Yr | NM |
|---|---|---|---|
| ❑ VSD-6568 | Food for the Mind | 1971 | 15.00 |

### WHITE WHALE

| Number | Title (A Side/B Side) | Yr | NM |
|---|---|---|---|
| ❑ WWS-7123 | The Early Writings of Zager and Evans (And Others) | 1969 | 20.00 |
| *—Actually doesn't contain any music by Zager or Evans, but only songs they wrote; it remains here as it's usually considered a "Zager and Evans" LP* | | | |

## ZANIES, THE

### DORE

| Number | Title (A Side/B Side) | Yr | NM |
|---|---|---|---|
| ❑ 321 | The Zanies | 1969 | 30.00 |
| ❑ 337 | The Zanies | 1979 | 15.00 |

## ZAPPA, FRANK

Includes his work with The Mothers of Invention.

### ANGEL

| Number | Title (A Side/B Side) | Yr | NM |
|---|---|---|---|
| ❑ DS-38170 | Boulez Conducts Zappa: The Perfect Stranger | 1983 | 12.00 |

### BARKING PUMPKIN

| Number | Title (A Side/B Side) | Yr | NM |
|---|---|---|---|
| ❑ 7X4-1 | The Old Masters Sampler | 1984 | 25.00 |
| ❑ AS 995 [DJ] | Tinsel Town Rebellion | 1981 | 20.00 |
| *—Promo-only sampler* | | | |
| ❑ BPR-1111 | Shut Up 'N' Play Yer Guitar | 1981 | 20.00 |
| *—Mail-order item only* | | | |
| ❑ BPR-1112 | Shut Up 'N' Play Yer Guitar Some More | 1981 | 20.00 |
| *—Mail-order item only* | | | |
| ❑ BPR-1113 | Return of the Son of Shut Up 'N' Play Yer Guitar | 1981 | 20.00 |
| *—Mail-order item only* | | | |
| ❑ BPRP-1114 [PD] | Zappa | 1982 | 15.00 |
| *—Picture disc with two songs* | | | |
| ❑ BPRP-1115 [PD] | Baby Snakes | 1983 | 15.00 |
| *—Picture disc* | | | |
| ❑ AS 1294 [DJ] | You Are What You Is Special Clean Cuts Edition | 1981 | 20.00 |
| ❑ 7777 [(8)] | The Old Masters, Box 1 | 1984 | 60.00 |
| *—Boxed set* | | | |
| ❑ 8888 [(8)] | The Old Masters, Box 2 | 1986 | 60.00 |
| *—Another boxed set* | | | |
| ❑ 8888X | The Old Masters Sampler 2 | 1986 | 25.00 |
| ❑ 9999 [(8)] | The Old Masters, Box 3 | 1987 | 60.00 |
| *—Still another boxed set* | | | |
| ❑ PW2 37336 [(2)] | Tinsel Town Rebellion | 1981 | 20.00 |
| ❑ PW2 37537 [(2)] | You Are What You Is | 1981 | 20.00 |
| ❑ FW 38066 | Ship Arriving Too Late to Save a Drowning Witch | 1982 | 12.00 |
| ❑ W3X-38289 [(3)] | Shut Up 'N' Play Yer Guitar | 1982 | 25.00 |
| *—Box set containing all three "Shut Up 'N' Play Yer Guitar" albums* | | | |
| ❑ FW 38403 | Man from Utopia | 1983 | 12.00 |
| ❑ FW 38820 | London Symphony Orchestra | 1983 | 12.00 |
| ❑ SVBO-74200 [(2)] | Them Or Us | 1984 | 15.00 |
| ❑ SWCO-74201 [(3)] | Thing-Fish | 1984 | 20.00 |
| ❑ ST-74202 | Francesco Zappa | 1985 | 10.00 |
| ❑ ST-74203 | Frank Zappa Meets the Mothers of Prevention | 1985 | 10.00 |
| ❑ ST-74205 | Jazz from Hell | 1986 | 10.00 |
| ❑ 74206 [(3)] | Joe's Garage, Acts 1, 2 and 3 | 1986 | 50.00 |
| *—Box set, two gatefolds, with insert* | | | |
| ❑ SJ-74207 | London Symphony Orchestra, Volume 2 | 1987 | 10.00 |
| ❑ D1-74212 [(2)] | Guitar | 1988 | 10.00 |
| ❑ D1-74213 [(3)] | You Can't Do That on Stage Anymore Sampler | 1988 | 10.00 |
| ❑ R1 74213 | You Can't Do That on Stage Anymore Sampler | 1988 | 12.00 |
| ❑ D1-74217 [(3)] | You Can't Do That on Stage Anymore Vol. 2 | 1988 | 10.00 |
| ❑ D1-74218 | Broadway the Hard Way | 1988 | 10.00 |

### BIZARRE

| Number | Title (A Side/B Side) | Yr | NM |
|---|---|---|---|
| ❑ MS-2024 [(2)] | Uncle Meat | 1969 | 35.00 |
| *—Originals come with a booklet; blue label* | | | |
| ❑ MS-2024 [(2)] | Uncle Meat | 1973 | 20.00 |
| *—Reissue with brown Reprise label* | | | |
| ❑ MS-2028 | Weasels Ripped My Flesh | 1970 | 25.00 |
| *—Blue label original* | | | |
| ❑ MS-2028 | Weasels Ripped My Flesh | 1973 | 15.00 |
| *—Reissue with brown Reprise label* | | | |
| ❑ MS 2030 [DJ] | Chunga's Revenge | 1970 | 50.00 |
| *—White label promo* | | | |
| ❑ MS-2030 | Chunga's Revenge | 1970 | 25.00 |
| *—Blue label original* | | | |
| ❑ MS-2030 | Chunga's Revenge | 1973 | 15.00 |
| *—Reissue with brown Reprise label* | | | |
| ❑ MS-2042 | Fillmore East, June 1971 | 1971 | 25.00 |
| *—Blue label original* | | | |
| ❑ MS-2042 | Fillmore East, June 1971 | 1973 | 15.00 |
| *—Reissue with brown Reprise label* | | | |
| ❑ MS 2075 | Just Another Band from L.A. | 1972 | 25.00 |
| *—Blue label original* | | | |
| ❑ MS 2075 | Just Another Band from L.A. | 1973 | 15.00 |
| *—Reissue with brown Reprise label* | | | |
| ❑ MS 2093 | The Grand Wazoo | 1972 | 25.00 |
| *—Blue label original* | | | |
| ❑ MS 2093 | The Grand Wazoo | 1973 | 15.00 |
| *—Reissue with brown Reprise label* | | | |
| ❑ MS 2094 | Waka/Jawaka | 1972 | 25.00 |
| *—Blue label original* | | | |
| ❑ MS 2094 | Waka/Jawaka | 1973 | 15.00 |
| *—Reissue with brown Reprise label* | | | |
| ❑ RS-6356 | Hot Rats | 1969 | 50.00 |
| *—Blue label original* | | | |
| ❑ RS-6356 | Hot Rats | 1973 | 15.00 |
| *—Reissue with brown Reprise label* | | | |
| ❑ RS-6370 | Burnt Weenie Sandwich | 1970 | 25.00 |
| *—Blue label original; with booklet* | | | |
| ❑ RS-6370 | Burnt Weenie Sandwich | 1973 | 15.00 |
| *—Reissue with brown Reprise label* | | | |

### COLUMBIA

| Number | Title (A Side/B Side) | Yr | NM |
|---|---|---|---|
| ❑ (no #) [(4)DJ] | Lather | 1977 | 750.00 |
| *—Test pressing only; parts of this LP are on DSK 2291, 2292 and 2294; released as a whole only after Zappa's death, with vinyl only coming out in Japan* | | | |

### DISCREET

| Number | Title (A Side/B Side) | Yr | NM |
|---|---|---|---|
| ❑ MS 2149 | Over-Nite Sensation | 1973 | 20.00 |
| ❑ MS4 2149 [Q] | Over-Nite Sensation | 1973 | 40.00 |
| ❑ DS 2175 | Apostrophe (') | 1974 | 15.00 |
| ❑ DS 2175 | Apostrophe (') | 1974 | 50.00 |
| *—White label promo* | | | |
| ❑ DS4 2175 [Q] | Apostrophe (') | 1974 | 35.00 |
| ❑ 2DS 2202 [(2)] | Roxy and Elsewhere | 1974 | 25.00 |
| ❑ DS 2216 | One Size Fits All | 1975 | 15.00 |
| ❑ DS 2234 | Bongo Fury | 1975 | 15.00 |
| ❑ DSK 2288 | Over-Nite Sensation | 1977 | 12.00 |
| *—Reissue of DiscReet 2149 with new number* | | | |
| ❑ DSK 2289 | Apostrophe (') | 1977 | 12.00 |
| *—Reissue with new number* | | | |
| ❑ 2D 2290 [(2)] | Zappa in New York | 1978 | 20.00 |
| ❑ 2D 2290 [(2)] | Zappa in New York | 1978 | 250.00 |
| *—Stock copy with "Punky's Whips" erroneously listed on jacket* | | | |
| ❑ 2D 2290 [(2)DJ] | Zappa in New York | 1978 | 400.00 |
| *—Test pressing with "Punky's Whips"* | | | |
| ❑ DSK 2291 | Studio Tan | 1978 | 15.00 |
| ❑ DSK 2292 | Sleep Dirt | 1978 | 15.00 |
| ❑ DSK 2294 | Orchestral Favorites | 1978 | 15.00 |

| Number | Title (A Side/B Side) | Yr | NM |
|---|---|---|---|
| **FOO-EEE** | | | |
| ❑ R1-70372 [(11)] | Beat the Boots #2 | 1992 | 100.00 |
| *—Legitimate box-set release by Rhino of 11 bootlegged concerts* | | | |
| ❑ R1-70907 [(10)] | Beat the Boots | 1991 | 100.00 |
| *—Legitimate box-set release by Rhino of eight bootlegged concerts* | | | |
| **MCA** | | | |
| ❑ 4183 [(2)] | 200 Motels (movie soundtrack) | 1986 | 15.00 |
| *—Reissue* | | | |
| **MGM** | | | |
| ❑ GAS-112 | The Mothers of Invention | 1970 | 50.00 |
| ❑ GAS-112 [DJ] | The Mothers of Invention | 1970 | 100.00 |
| *—Yellow label promo* | | | |
| ❑ SE-4754 | The Worst of the Mothers | 1971 | 50.00 |
| ❑ SE-4754 [DJ] | The Worst of the Mothers | 1971 | 150.00 |
| *—Yellow label promo* | | | |
| **RHINO/DEL-FI** | | | |
| ❑ RNEP-604 | Rare Meat: The Early Productions of Frank Zappa | 1984 | 40.00 |
| *—With original cover* | | | |
| **RYKO ANALOGUE** | | | |
| ❑ RALP 10503 | We're Only in It for the Money | 1995 | 12.00 |
| *—Vinyl reissue; Frank Zappa/The Mothers of Invention* | | | |
| ❑ RALP 40500 [(2)] | Strictly Commercial: The Best of Frank Zappa | 1995 | 20.00 |
| *—Issued with obi* | | | |
| **UNITED ARTISTS** | | | |
| ❑ UAS-9956 [(2)] | 200 Motels (movie soundtrack) | 1971 | 50.00 |
| **VERVE** | | | |
| ❑ V-5005-2 [(2)M] | Freak Out! | 1966 | 150.00 |
| *—Cover version 2: Has no blurb inside on getting a map of "freak-out hot spots"* | | | |
| ❑ V-5005-2 [(2)M] | Freak Out! | 1966 | 200.00 |
| *—Cover version 1: Has blurb on inside gatefold on how to get a map of "freak-out hot spots" in L.A.* | | | |
| ❑ V-5005-2 [(2)M] | Freak Out! | 1966 | 400.00 |
| *—White label promo* | | | |
| ❑ V6-5005-2 [(2)S] | Freak Out! | 1966 | 60.00 |
| *—Cover version 2: Has no blurb inside on getting a map of "freak-out hot spots"* | | | |
| ❑ V6-5005-2 [(2)S] | Freak Out! | 1966 | 80.00 |
| *—Cover version 1: Has blurb on inside gatefold on how to get a map of "freak-out hot spots" in L.A.* | | | |
| ❑ V6-5005-2 [(2)S] | Freak Out! | 1966 | 300.00 |
| *—Yellow label promo* | | | |
| ❑ V-5013 [M] | Absolutely Free | 1967 | 120.00 |
| ❑ V-5013 [M] | Absolutely Free | 1967 | 200.00 |
| *—White label promo* | | | |
| ❑ V6-5013 [S] | Absolutely Free | 1967 | 60.00 |
| ❑ V-5045 [M] | We're Only in It for the Money | 1968 | 150.00 |
| *—With sheet of cut-outs a la "Sgt. Pepper's Lonely Hearts Club Band"* | | | |
| ❑ V-5045 [M] | We're Only in It for the Money | 1968 | 300.00 |
| *—White label promo* | | | |
| ❑ V6-5045 [S] | We're Only in It for the Money | 1968 | 60.00 |
| *—Un-censored version, with cut-outs* | | | |
| ❑ V6-5045 [S] | We're Only in It for the Money | 1968 | 150.00 |
| *—Censored version: the songs "Who Needs the Peace Corps?" and "Let's Make the Water Turn Black" have lines deleted* | | | |
| ❑ V6-5055 | Cruising with Ruben and the Jets | 1968 | 60.00 |
| ❑ V6-5055 [DJ] | Cruising with Ruben and the Jets | 1968 | 150.00 |
| *—Yellow label promo* | | | |
| ❑ V6-5068 | Mothermania — The Best of the Mothers | 1969 | 75.00 |
| ❑ V6-5068 [DJ] | Mothermania — The Best of the Mothers | 1969 | 150.00 |
| *—Yellow label promo* | | | |
| ❑ V6-5074 | The XXXX of the Mothers | 1969 | 50.00 |
| ❑ V6-5074 [DJ] | The XXXX of the Mothers | 1969 | 150.00 |
| *—Yellow label promo* | | | |
| ❑ V-8741 [M] | Lumpy Gravy | 1968 | 300.00 |
| *—Yellow label promo; no stock copies were issued in mono* | | | |
| ❑ V6-8741 | Lumpy Gravy | 1968 | 50.00 |
| ❑ V6-8741 [DJ] | Lumpy Gravy | 1968 | 200.00 |
| *—Yellow label promo* | | | |
| **WARNER BROS.** | | | |
| ❑ BS-2970 | Zoot Allures | 1976 | 15.00 |
| **ZAPPA** | | | |
| ❑ MK-78 [DJ] | Sheik Yerbouti Clean Cuts | 1979 | 35.00 |
| ❑ MK-129 [DJ] | Joe's Garage Acts I, II and III Sampler | 1980 | 35.00 |
| ❑ SRZ-2-1501 [(2)] | Sheik Yerbouti | 1979 | 20.00 |
| ❑ SRZ-2-1502 [(2)] | Joe's Garage, Acts II and III | 1980 | 20.00 |
| ❑ SRZ-1-1603 | Joe's Garage, Act I | 1979 | 15.00 |

## ZAWINUL, JOE

| Number | Title (A Side/B Side) | Yr | NM |
|---|---|---|---|
| **ATLANTIC** | | | |
| ❑ SD 1579 | Zawinul | 1970 | 20.00 |
| ❑ 3004 [M] | Money in the Pocket | 1966 | 20.00 |
| ❑ SD 3004 [S] | Money in the Pocket | 1966 | 25.00 |
| **VORTEX** | | | |
| ❑ 2002 [S] | The Rise and Fall of the 3rd Stream | 1968 | 20.00 |

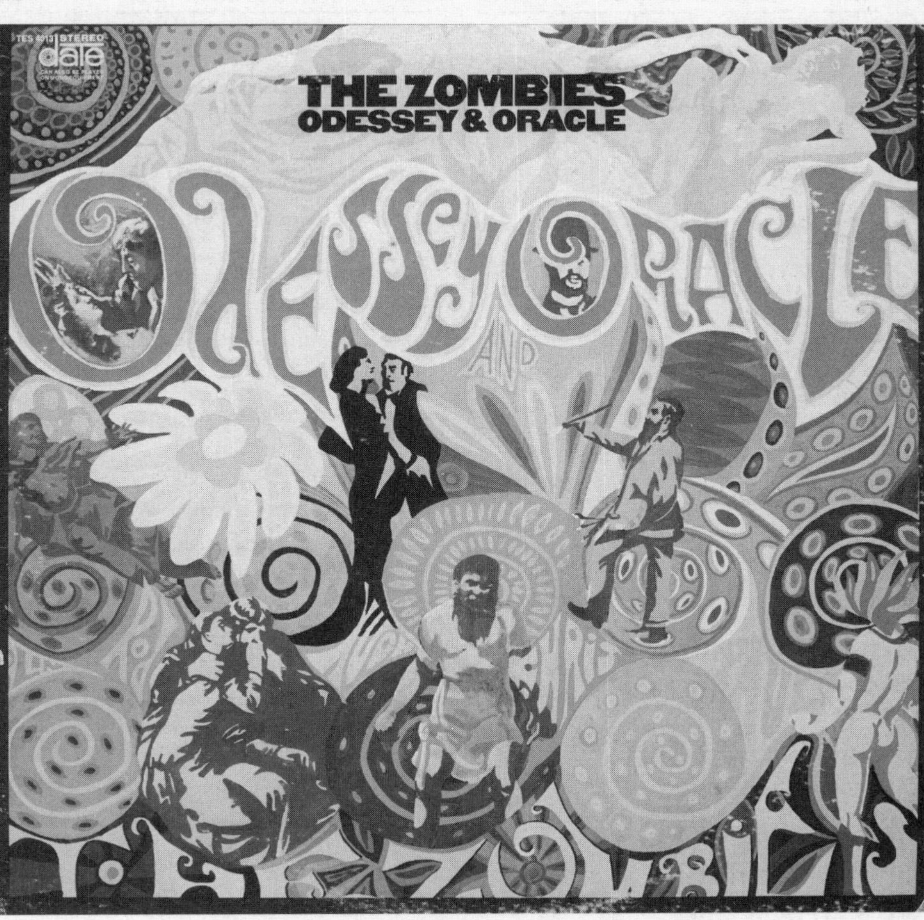


The Zombies, *Odessey & Oracle,* Date TES 4013, 1968, $30.

## ZAZU

| Number | Title (A Side/B Side) | Yr | NM |
|---|---|---|---|
| **WOODEN NICKEL** | | | |
| ❑ BWL1-0791 | Zazu | 1975 | 20.00 |

## ZEITLIN, DENNY

| Number | Title (A Side/B Side) | Yr | NM |
|---|---|---|---|
| **COLUMBIA** | | | |
| ❑ CL 2182 [M] | Cathexis | 1964 | 20.00 |
| ❑ CL 2340 [M] | Carnival | 1965 | 20.00 |
| ❑ CS 8982 [S] | Cathexis | 1964 | 25.00 |
| ❑ CS 9140 [S] | Carnival | 1965 | 25.00 |
| ❑ CS 9263 [S] | My Shining Hour | 1966 | 20.00 |
| ❑ CS 9548 [S] | Zeitgeist | 1966 | 20.00 |

## ZENITHS, THE

| Number | Title (A Side/B Side) | Yr | NM |
|---|---|---|---|
| **ATLANTIC** | | | |
| ❑ 8043 [M] | Makin' the Scene | 1960 | 100.00 |
| ❑ SD 8043 [S] | Makin' the Scene | 1960 | 150.00 |

## ZENTNER, SI

| Number | Title (A Side/B Side) | Yr | NM |
|---|---|---|---|
| **LIBERTY** | | | |
| ❑ LRP-3197 [M] | Big Band Plays the Big Hits | 1961 | 12.00 |
| ❑ LRP-3216 [M] | Up a Lazy River (Big Band Plays the Big Hits: Vol. 2) | 1962 | 12.00 |
| ❑ LRP-3247 [M] | The Stripper and Other Big Band Hits | 1962 | 12.00 |
| ❑ LRP-3273 [M] | Desafinado | 1963 | 12.00 |
| ❑ LRP-3284 [M] | Waltz in Jazz Time | 1963 | 12.00 |
| ❑ LRP-3326 [M] | More | 1963 | 12.00 |
| ❑ LRP-3350 [M] | Big Big Band Hits | 1964 | 12.00 |
| ❑ LRP-3353 [M] | From Russia with Love | 1964 | 12.00 |
| ❑ LRP-3457 [M] | The Best of Si Zentner | 1966 | 12.00 |
| ❑ LST-7197 [S] | Big Band Plays the Big Hits | 1961 | 15.00 |
| ❑ LST-7216 [S] | Up a Lazy River (Big Band Plays the Big Hits: Vol. 2) | 1962 | 15.00 |
| ❑ LST-7247 [S] | The Stripper and Other Big Band Hits | 1962 | 15.00 |
| ❑ LST-7273 [S] | Desafinado | 1963 | 15.00 |
| ❑ LST-7284 [S] | Waltz in Jazz Time | 1963 | 15.00 |
| ❑ LST-7326 [S] | More | 1963 | 15.00 |
| ❑ LST-7350 [S] | Big Big Band Hits | 1964 | 15.00 |
| ❑ LST-7353 [S] | From Russia with Love | 1964 | 15.00 |
| ❑ LST-7457 [S] | The Best of Si Zentner | 1966 | 12.00 |
| ❑ LMM-13009 [M] | A Great Band with Great Voices | 1961 | 12.00 |
| ❑ LMM-13017 [M] | A Great Band with Great Voices Swing the Great Voices of the Great Bands | 1962 | 12.00 |
| ❑ LSS-14009 [S] | A Great Band with Great Voices | 1961 | 15.00 |
| ❑ LSS-14017 [S] | A Great Band with Great Voices Swing the Great Voices of the Great Bands | 1962 | 15.00 |
| **SMASH** | | | |
| ❑ MGS-27007 [M] | Presenting Si Zentner | 1961 | 15.00 |
| ❑ MGS-27013 [M] | Swing Fever | 1962 | 15.00 |
| ❑ SRS-67007 [S] | Presenting Si Zentner | 1961 | 20.00 |
| ❑ SRS-67013 [S] | Swing Fever | 1962 | 20.00 |
| **SUNSET** | | | |
| ❑ SUM-1110 [M] | Big Band Brilliance | 196? | 10.00 |
| ❑ SUS-5110 [S] | Big Band Brilliance | 196? | 12.00 |

## ZENTNER, SI AND MARTIN DENNY

| Number | Title (A Side/B Side) | Yr | NM |
|---|---|---|---|
| **LIBERTY** | | | |
| ❑ LMM-13020 [M] | Exotica Suite | 1962 | 15.00 |
| ❑ LSS-14020 [S] | Exotica Suite | 1962 | 20.00 |

## ZEPHYR

| Number | Title (A Side/B Side) | Yr | NM |
|---|---|---|---|
| **PROBE** | | | |
| ❑ 4510 | Zephyr | 1969 | 50.00 |
| **WARNER BROS.** | | | |
| ❑ WS 1897 | Goin' Back to Colorado | 1971 | 40.00 |
| ❑ BS 2603 | Sunset Ride | 1972 | 20.00 |

## ZERFAS

| Number | Title (A Side/B Side) | Yr | NM |
|---|---|---|---|
| **700 WEST** | | | |
| ❑ 730710 | Zerfas | 1973 | 800.00 |

## ZERO BOYS

| Number | Title (A Side/B Side) | Yr | NM |
|---|---|---|---|
| **NIMROD** | | | |
| ❑ 1 | Vicious Circle | 1982 | 100.00 |
| **TOXIC SHOCK** | | | |
| ❑ TXLP 11 | Vicious Circle | 1987 | 30.00 |
| *—Reissue of Nimrod release* | | | |

## ZEVON, WARREN

| Number | Title (A Side/B Side) | Yr | NM |
|---|---|---|---|
| **ARTEMIS** | | | |
| ❑ 51156 | The Wind | 2004 | 20.00 |
| *—180-gram version; CD was issued in 2003* | | | |

| Number | Title (A Side/B Side) | Yr | NM |
|---|---|---|---|
| **ASYLUM** | | | |
| ❑ 6E-118 | Excitable Boy | 1978 | 10.00 |
| ❑ 5E-509 | Bad Luck Streak in Dancing School | 1980 | 10.00 |
| ❑ 5E-519 | Stand in the Fire | 1980 | 10.00 |
| ❑ 7E-1060 | Warren Zevon | 1976 | 10.00 |
| ❑ 60159 | The Envoy | 1982 | 10.00 |
| ❑ 60503 | A Quiet Normal Life: The Best of Warren Zevon | 1987 | 10.00 |
| **IMPERIAL** | | | |
| ❑ LP-12456 | Wanted Dead or Alive | 1970 | 50.00 |
| *—As "Zevon"* | | | |
| **PICKWICK** | | | |
| ❑ SPC-3715 | Wanted Dead or Alive | 1979 | 15.00 |
| *—Reissue of Imperial album* | | | |
| **VIRGIN** | | | |
| ❑ 90603 | Sentimental Hygiene | 1987 | 10.00 |
| ❑ 91068 | Transverse City | 1989 | 10.00 |

**ZIG ZAG PEOPLE, THE**

| Number | Title (A Side/B Side) | Yr | NM |
|---|---|---|---|
| **DECCA** | | | |
| ❑ DL 75110 | The Zig Zag People Take Bubble Gum Music Underground | 1969 | 25.00 |

**ZIP CODES, THE**

| Number | Title (A Side/B Side) | Yr | NM |
|---|---|---|---|
| **LIBERTY** | | | |
| ❑ LRP-3367 [M] | Mustang | 1964 | 150.00 |
| ❑ LST-7367 [S] | Mustang | 1964 | 200.00 |

**ZIPPERS, THE**

| Number | Title (A Side/B Side) | Yr | NM |
|---|---|---|---|
| **RHINO** | | | |
| ❑ RNEP 601 [EP] | Six Song Mini Album | 1981 | 30.00 |

**ZIRCONS, THE**

| Number | Title (A Side/B Side) | Yr | NM |
|---|---|---|---|
| **SNOWFLAKE** | | | |
| ❑ 1003 | The Crown Kings of Acappella | 196? | 60.00 |

**ZITO, PHIL**

| Number | Title (A Side/B Side) | Yr | NM |
|---|---|---|---|
| **COLUMBIA** | | | |
| ❑ CL 6110 [10] | International City Dixielanders | 1950 | 50.00 |

**ZITRO, JAMES**

| Number | Title (A Side/B Side) | Yr | NM |
|---|---|---|---|
| **ESP-DISK'** | | | |
| ❑ 1052 [S] | Zitro | 1968 | 25.00 |

**ZOLLER, ATTILA**

| Number | Title (A Side/B Side) | Yr | NM |
|---|---|---|---|
| **EMBRYO** | | | |
| ❑ SD 523 | Gypsy Cry | 1970 | 20.00 |
| **INNER CITY** | | | |
| ❑ IC-3008 | Dream Bells | 1976 | 15.00 |

**ZOMBIE, ROB**

| Number | Title (A Side/B Side) | Yr | NM |
|---|---|---|---|
| **1500 RECORDS** | | | |
| ❑ 497201-1 [EP] | Remix-A-Go-Go | 2000 | 8.00 |
| *—Five-song remix EP in generic black sleeve with sticker* | | | |
| **GEFFEN** | | | |
| ❑ GEF 25212 | Hellbilly Deluxe | 1998 | 40.00 |
| *—Picture disc in plastic sleeve with sticker* | | | |
| ❑ 069490349-1 [(2)] | American Made Music to Strip By | 1999 | 50.00 |
| ❑ 069 493147 1 [(2)] | The Sinister Urge | 2001 | 50.00 |

**ZOMBIES, THE**

| Number | Title (A Side/B Side) | Yr | NM |
|---|---|---|---|
| **DATE** | | | |
| ❑ TES-4013 | Odessey and Oracle | 1968 | 30.00 |
| *—With no mention of "Time of the Season" on front cover* | | | |
| ❑ TES-4013 | Odessey and Oracle | 1969 | 20.00 |
| *—With "Time of the Season" mentioned on front cover* | | | |
| **EPIC** | | | |
| ❑ KEG 32861 [(2)B] | Time of the Zombies | 1974 | 20.00 |
| *—Record 1 is mono; Record 2 is stereo; orange labels* | | | |
| ❑ PEG 32861 [(2)B] | Time of the Zombies | 1979 | 15.00 |
| *—Later edition with blue labels* | | | |
| **LONDON** | | | |
| ❑ PS 557 [P] | Early Days | 1969 | 20.00 |
| *—All tracks in true stereo except "Tell Her No"* | | | |
| **PARROT** | | | |
| ❑ PA 61001 [M] | The Zombies | 1965 | 60.00 |
| ❑ PAS 71001 [R] | The Zombies | 1965 | 40.00 |
| **RHINO** | | | |
| ❑ RNLP-120 | Live on the BBC, 1965-67 | 1985 | 10.00 |
| ❑ RNLP 70186 [S] | Odessy and Oracle | 1986 | 8.00 |

**ZOO, THE (1)**

| Number | Title (A Side/B Side) | Yr | NM |
|---|---|---|---|
| **MERCURY** | | | |
| ❑ SR-61300 | The Zoo | 1970 | 20.00 |
| **SUNBURST** | | | |
| ❑ 7500 | The Zoo Presents the Chocolate Moose | 1968 | 50.00 |

**ZURKE, BOB**

| Number | Title (A Side/B Side) | Yr | NM |
|---|---|---|---|
| **RCA VICTOR** | | | |
| ❑ LPM-1013 [M] | The Tom Cat on the Keys | 1955 | 80.00 |

**ZZ TOP**

| Number | Title (A Side/B Side) | Yr | NM |
|---|---|---|---|
| **LONDON** | | | |
| ❑ PS 584 | ZZ Top's First Album | 1971 | 12.00 |
| ❑ PS 612 | Rio Grande Mud | 1972 | 12.00 |
| ❑ XPS 631 | Tres Hombres | 1973 | 12.00 |
| ❑ PS 656 | Fandango! | 1975 | 12.00 |
| ❑ PS 680 | Tejas | 1977 | 12.00 |
| ❑ PS 706 | The Best of ZZ Top | 1977 | 12.00 |
| ❑ PS-X-1001 [DJ] | Takin' Texas to the People | 1976 | 50.00 |
| **WARNER BROS.** | | | |
| ❑ BSK 3268 | ZZ Top's First Album | 1979 | 8.00 |
| ❑ BSK 3269 | Rio Grande Mud | 1979 | 8.00 |
| ❑ BSK 3270 | Tres Hombres | 1979 | 8.00 |
| ❑ BSK 3271 | Fandango! | 1979 | 8.00 |
| ❑ BSK 3272 | Tejas | 1979 | 8.00 |
| ❑ BSK 3273 | The Best of ZZ Top | 1979 | 8.00 |
| ❑ HS 3361 | Deguello | 1979 | 10.00 |
| ❑ BSK 3593 | El Loco | 1981 | 10.00 |
| ❑ 23774 | Eliminator | 1983 | 8.00 |
| ❑ 25342 | Afterburner | 1985 | 8.00 |
| ❑ 26265 | Recycler | 1990 | 15.00 |
| ❑ 26846 | Greatest Hits | 1992 | 20.00 |
| *—U.S. vinyl available only through Columbia House* | | | |

# ORIGINAL CAST RECORDINGS

| Number | Title (A Side/B Side) | Yr | NM |
|---|---|---|---|
| **ALL AMERICAN** | | | |
| ❑ Columbia Masterworks KOS 2160 [S] | | 1962 | 30.00 |
| ❑ Columbia Masterworks KOL 5760 [M] | | 1962 | 25.00 |
| **ALL NIGHT STRUT!** | | | |
| ❑ Playhouse Square PHS-CLE 1S-1001 | | 1976 | 80.00 |
| **ANKLES AWEIGHT** | | | |
| ❑ Decca DL 9025 [M] | | 1955 | 40.00 |
| **ANNIE GET YOUR GUN** | | | |
| ❑ Decca DL 8001 [M] | | 1949 | 50.00 |
| *—Original LP issue of the Broadway cast* | | | |
| ❑ Decca DL 9018 [M] | | 1955 | 40.00 |
| *—Early reissue of DL 8001; black label with silver print* | | | |
| ❑ Decca DL 79018 [R] | | 196? | 12.00 |
| ❑ RCA Victor LOC-1124 [M] | | 1966 | 12.00 |
| ❑ RCA Victor LSO-1124 [S] | | 1966 | 15.00 |
| *—Revival cast; black label, dog on top, "Stereo Dynagroove" at bottom* | | | |
| ❑ RCA Victor LSO-1124 [S] | | 1969 | 10.00 |
| *—Revival cast; orange, tan or black "dog near top" label* | | | |
| **ANYA** | | | |
| ❑ United Artists UAL-4133 [M] | | 1965 | 20.00 |
| ❑ United Artists UAS-5133 [S] | | 1965 | 50.00 |
| **APPLAUSE** | | | |
| ❑ ABC ABCS-OC-11 | | 1970 | 20.00 |
| **THE APPLE TREE** | | | |
| ❑ Columbia Masterworks KOS 3020 [S] | | 1966 | 25.00 |
| ❑ Columbia Masterworks KOL 6620 [M] | | 1966 | 20.00 |
| **ARABIAN NIGHTS** | | | |
| ❑ Decca DL 9013 [M] | | 1954 | 80.00 |
| **THE ATHENIAN TOUCH** | | | |
| ❑ Broadway East OCM-101 [M] | | 1964 | 150.00 |
| ❑ Broadway East OCS-101 [S] | | 1964 | 200.00 |
| **BAJOUR** | | | |
| ❑ Columbia Masterworks KOS 2700 [S] | | 1964 | 30.00 |
| ❑ Columbia Masterworks KOL 6300 [M] | | 1964 | 25.00 |
| **BAKER STREET (A MUSICAL ADVENTURE OF SHERLOCK HOLMES)** | | | |
| ❑ MGM E-7000 [M] | | 1965 | 25.00 |
| ❑ MGM SE-7000 [S] | | 1965 | 30.00 |
| **A BALLAD FOR BIMSHIRE** | | | |
| ❑ London AM 48002 [M] | | 1963 | 40.00 |
| ❑ London AMS 78002 [S] | | 1963 | 80.00 |
| **THE BALLAD OF BABY DOE** | | | |
| ❑ MGM 3GC-1 [(3)M] | | 1958 | 150.00 |
| *—Box set* | | | |
| **THE BAND WAGON** | | | |
| ❑ "X" LVA-1001 [M] | | 1955 | 70.00 |
| **BELLS ARE RINGING** | | | |
| ❑ Columbia Masterworks OS 2006 [S] | | 1959 | 25.00 |
| *—Re-recording in stereo of OL 5170* | | | |
| ❑ Columbia Masterworks OL 5170 [M] | | 1957 | 30.00 |
| *—Gray and black label with six "eye" logos* | | | |
| **BEN FRANKLIN IN PARIS** | | | |
| ❑ Capitol SVAS 2191 [S] | | 1964 | 30.00 |
| ❑ Capitol VAS 2191 [M] | | 1964 | 25.00 |
| **BEST FOOT FORWARD** | | | |
| ❑ Cadence CLP-4012 [M] | | 1963 | 20.00 |
| ❑ Cadence CLP-24012 [S] | | 1963 | 30.00 |
| *—1963 revival of 1941 play* | | | |
| **BEYOND THE FRINGE** | | | |
| ❑ Capitol SW 1792 [S] | | 1962 | 30.00 |
| ❑ Capitol W 1792 [M] | | 1962 | 25.00 |
| **BEYOND THE FRINGE '64** | | | |
| ❑ Capitol SW 2072 [S] | | 1964 | 25.00 |
| ❑ Capitol W 2072 [M] | | 1964 | 20.00 |
| **THE BOY FRIEND** | | | |
| ❑ RCA Victor LOC-1018 [M] | | 1954 | 30.00 |
| *—Originals have green labels* | | | |
| **THE BOYS IN THE BAND** | | | |
| ❑ A&M SP-6001 [(2)] | | 1969 | 25.00 |
| **BRAVO, GIOVANNI** | | | |
| ❑ Columbia Masterworks KOS 2200 [S] | | 1962 | 20.00 |
| ❑ Columbia Masterworks KOL 5800 [M] | | 1962 | 15.00 |
| **BRIGADOON** | | | |
| ❑ RCA Victor LOC-1001 [M] | | 195? | 20.00 |
| *—Photos of kilted dancers on front cover; black "Long Play" label* | | | |
| ❑ RCA Victor LOC-1001 [M] | | 1951 | 30.00 |
| *—Green front cover; green label* | | | |
| ❑ RCA Victor LOC-1001 [M] | | 1963 | 15.00 |
| *—Drawing of kilted dancers on front cover; black "Mono" label* | | | |
| ❑ RCA Victor LSO-1001(e) [R] | | 1963 | 12.00 |
| *—Black label, dog on top* | | | |
| **BY JUPITER** | | | |
| ❑ RCA Victor LOC-1137 [M] | | 1967 | 40.00 |
| ❑ RCA Victor LSO-1137 [S] | | 1967 | 75.00 |
| *—Above is by a revival cast* | | | |
| **BY THE BEAUTIFUL SEA** | | | |
| ❑ Capitol S 531 [M] | | 1954 | 70.00 |
| **BYE BYE BIRDIE** | | | |
| ❑ Columbia Masterworks KOS 2025 [S] | | 1960 | 30.00 |
| *—Gray and black label with six "eye" logos; with gatefold cover* | | | |
| ❑ Columbia Masterworks OS 2025 [S] | | 196? | 25.00 |
| *—Gray and black label with six "eye" logos; with regular cover* | | | |
| ❑ Columbia Masterworks KOL 5510 [M] | | 1960 | 25.00 |
| *—Gray and black label with six "eye" logos; with gatefold cover* | | | |

**Number Title (A Side/B Side) Yr NM**

❑ Columbia Masterworks OL 5510 [M] 196? 20.00
*—Gray and black label with six "eye" logos; with regular cover*

CABARET
❑ Columbia Masterworks KOS 3040 [S] 1966 20.00
❑ Columbia Masterworks KOL 6640 [M] 1966 15.00

CABIN IN THE SKY
❑ Capitol SW 2073 [S] 1964 50.00
*—Above is by a revival cast*
❑ Capitol W 2073 [M] 1964 30.00

CALL ME MADAM
❑ RCA Victor LOC-1000 [M] 1950 80.00
*—Dinah Shore sings Ethel Merman's part for contractual reasons, otherwise it's by the entire original cast*

CAMELOT
❑ Columbia Masterworks KOS 2031 [S] 1960 25.00
*—Gray and black label with six "eye" logos; gatefold cover*
❑ Columbia Masterworks KOL 5620 [M] 1960 20.00
*—Gray and black label with six "eye" logos*

CAN-CAN
❑ Capitol DW 452 [R] 196? 12.00
❑ Capitol S 452 [M] 1953 25.00
*—Originals have red labels with Capitol logo at top*
❑ Capitol W 452 [M] 195? 15.00

CANTERBURY TALES
❑ Capitol SW-229 1969 25.00

CAPTAIN JINKS OF THE HORSE MARINES
❑ RCA Victor ARL2-1727 [(2)] 1975 30.00
*—Box set*

CARMEN JONES
❑ Decca DL 8014 [M] 1949 40.00
*—Black label, gold print*
❑ Decca DL 9021 [M] 1955 20.00
*—Reissue of 8014; black label, silver print*

CARNIVAL
❑ MGM E-3946 [M] 1961 20.00
❑ MGM SE-3946 [S] 1961 25.00
*—Black label*
❑ MGM SE-3946 [S] 1968 10.00
*—Blue and gold label*

CAROUSEL
❑ Command RS 33-843 [M] 1962 15.00
*—Studio cast*
❑ Command RS-843 SD [M] 1962 20.00
*—Studio cast witrh Alfred Drake and Roberta Peters, and Enoch Light's orchestra*
❑ Decca DL 8003 [M] 1949 40.00
*—Original LP issue of the Broadway cast*
❑ Decca DL 9020 [M] 1955 30.00
*—Early reissue of DL 8003; black label with silver print*
❑ Decca DL 79020 [R] 196? 10.00
❑ MCA 1627 [R] 198? 8.00
*—Reissue of MCA 37093*
❑ MCA 2033 [R] 1973 8.00
*—Reissue of Decca 79020; black label with rainbow*
❑ MCA 37093 [R] 1980 8.00
*—Reissue of MCA 2033*

A CHORUS LINE
❑ Columbia JS 33581 197? 10.00
*—Second issue with new prefix; no bar code*
❑ Columbia JS 33581 1981 8.00
*—Third edition; bar code added to back cover*
❑ Columbia PS 33581 1975 12.00
*—Original edition; no bar code on back cover*
❑ Columbia PSQ 33581 [Q] 1976 20.00

CHRISTINE
❑ Columbia Masterworks OS 2026 [S] 1960 100.00
❑ Columbia Masterworks OL 5520 [M] 1960 60.00

CINDY
❑ ABC-Paramount ABC-OC-2 [M] 1964 30.00
❑ ABC-Paramount ABC-OCS-2 [S] 1964 50.00

CLARA (BEG, BORROW OR STEAL)
❑ Commentary CYN-02 [M] 1960 60.00

CLOWNAROUND
❑ RCA Victor LSP-4741 1972 250.00

CLUB 15
❑ Decca DL 5155 [10] 1949 60.00

THE COACH WITH THE SIX INSIDES
❑ ESP-Disk' 1019 [M] 1967 25.00

COCO
❑ Paramount PMS-1002 1969 25.00

THE COMMITTEE
❑ Reprise F-2023 [M] 1964 30.00
❑ Reprise FS-2023 [S] 1964 40.00

COMPANY
❑ Columbia Masterworks OS 3550 1970 12.00
❑ Columbia Masterworks SQ 30993 [Q] 1971 30.00
*—Quadraphonic version has substantially different mixes than the original stereo LP*

THE CRADLE WILL ROCK
❑ MGM E-4289-2 [(2)M] 1964 25.00
❑ MGM SE-4289-2 [(2)S] 1964 30.00
*—The above is by a revival cast*

THE CRITIC
❑ Decca DL 9154 [M] 1967 20.00
❑ Decca DL 79154 [S] 1967 20.00

CRY FOR US ALL
❑ Project 3 TS-1000 SD 1970 40.00

DAMES AT SEA
❑ Columbia Masterworks OS 3550 1969 20.00

Original cast, *Bye Bye Birdie,*
Columbia Masterworks KOL 5510, 1960, gatefold cover, "6 eye" label, $25.

**Number Title (A Side/B Side) Yr NM**

DAMN YANKEES
❑ RCA Victor LOC-1021 [M] 195? 20.00
*—Orange cover*
❑ RCA Victor LOC-1021 [M] 1955 30.00
*—Green cover*
❑ RCA Victor LSO-1021(e) [R] 1965 15.00
*—Black label, dog on top, "Stereo Electronically Reprocessed" at bottom*
❑ RCA Victor AYL1-3948 1980 8.00
*—"Best Buy Series" reissue*

THE DANCERS OF BALI
❑ Columbia Masterworks ML 4618 [M] 1952 40.00

DARLING OF THE DAY
❑ RCA Victor LOC-1149 [M] 1968 40.00
❑ RCA Victor LSO-1149 [S] 1968 60.00

DEAR WORLD
❑ Columbia Masterworks BOS 3260 1969 20.00

DEATH OF A SALESMAN
❑ Decca DX 102 [(2)M] 1951 40.00
*—Two-record boxed set with contents of 9007 and 9008*

DEATH OF A SALESMAN (PART 1)
❑ Decca DL 9006 [M] 1951 25.00
*—Black label, gold print*

DEATH OF A SALESMAN (PART 2)
❑ Decca DL 9007 [M] 1951 25.00
*—Black label, gold print*

DESTRY RIDES AGAIN
❑ Decca DL 9075 [M] 1959 30.00
❑ Decca DL 79075 [S] 1959 40.00

DO I HEAR A WALTZ?
❑ Columbia Masterworks KOS 2770 [S] 1965 20.00
❑ Columbia Masterworks KOL 6370 [M] 1965 15.00

DO RE MI
❑ RCA Victor LOC-1105 [M] 1965 15.00
*—Reissue of 2002 with standard red cover*
❑ RCA Victor LSO-1105 [S] 1965 20.00
*—Reissue of 2002 with standard red cover*
❑ RCA Victor LOCD-2002 [M] 1961 30.00
*—In black box with orange sleeve*
❑ RCA Victor LSOD-2002 [S] 1961 40.00
*—In black box with orange sleeve*

DOCTOR SELAVY'S MAGIC THEATRE
❑ United Artists UA-LA196-G 1974 30.00

DONNYBROOK!
❑ Kapp KD-8500-S [S] 1961 25.00
❑ Kapp KDL-8500 [M] 1961 20.00

**Number Title (A Side/B Side) Yr NM**

DRESSED TO THE NINES
❑ MGM E-3914 [M] 1960 25.00
❑ MGM SE-3914 [S] 1960 40.00

THE EARL OF RUSTON
❑ Capitol ST-465 1971 40.00

ERNEST IN LOVE
❑ Columbia Masterworks OS 2027 [S] 1960 100.00
❑ Columbia Masterworks OL 5530 [M] 1960 60.00

AN EVENING WITH RICHARD NIXON
❑ Ode SP-77015 1972 30.00

EVITA
❑ MCA 2-11003 [(2)] 1976 20.00
*—London cast; white cover; with booklet*
❑ MCA 2-11007 [(2)] 1979 15.00
*—New York cast; mostly black cover; with booklet*

FADE OUT-FADE IN
❑ ABC-Paramount ABC-OC-3 [M] 1964 25.00
❑ ABC-Paramount ABCS-OC-3 [S] 1964 30.00

A FAMILY AFFAIR
❑ United Artists UAL-4099 [M] 1962 30.00
❑ United Artists UAS-5099 [S] 1962 50.00

FANNY
❑ RCA Victor LOC-1015 [M] 1954 25.00
*—"Long Play" on label*
❑ RCA Victor LOC-1015 [M] 196? 15.00
*—"Mono" on label*
❑ RCA Victor LSO-1015(e) [R] 196? 12.00
*—"Stereo Electronically Reprocessed" on label*

THE FANTASTICKS
❑ MGM E-3872 [M] 196? 10.00
*—White gatefold cover*
❑ MGM E-3872 [M] 1963 20.00
*—Original non-gatefold cover*
❑ MGM SE-3872 [S] 196? 10.00
*—Black gatefold cover*
❑ MGM SE-3872 [S] 196? 12.00
*—White gatefold cover*
❑ MGM SE-3872 [S] 1963 25.00
*—Original non-gatefold cover*

FIDDLER ON THE ROOF
❑ RCA Victor LOC-1093 [M] 1964 15.00
❑ RCA Victor LSO-1093 [S] 1964 20.00
*—Black label, dog on top*

FINIAN'S RAINBOW
❑ Columbia Masterworks OS 2080 [R] 1963 12.00
❑ Columbia Masterworks ML 4062 [M] 1948 30.00
*—Original cover with no photo; green label*

**Except when noted otherwise, VG = 25% of NM, and VG+ = 50% of NM. (Example: VG = $2.00, VG+ = $4.00 and NM = $8.00.)**

Original cast, *Funny Girl,* Capitol SVAS 2059, 1964, gatefold cover, stereo, $20.

| Number | Title (A Side/B Side) | Yr | NM |
|---|---|---|---|
| ❑ Columbia Masterworks OL 4062 [M] | | 196? | 12.00 |
| *—Reissue cover, either pink or green; gray label* | | | |
| ❑ RCA Victor LOC-1057 [M] | | 1960 | 10.00 |
| *—Revival cast; cover shows co-stars hiding in the trees* | | | |
| ❑ RCA Victor LOC-1057 [M] | | 1960 | 12.00 |
| *—Revival cast; "pot of gold" cover* | | | |
| ❑ RCA Victor LSO-1057 [S] | | 1960 | 12.00 |
| *—Revival cast; cover shows co-stars hiding in the trees* | | | |
| ❑ RCA Victor LSO-1057 [S] | | 1960 | 15.00 |
| *—Revival cast; "pot of gold" cover* | | | |
| FIORELLO! | | | |
| ❑ Capitol SWAO 1321 [S] | | 1959 | 25.00 |
| ❑ Capitol WAO 1321 [M] | | 1959 | 20.00 |
| FIRST IMPRESSIONS | | | |
| ❑ Columbia Masterworks OS 2014 [S] | | 1959 | 60.00 |
| ❑ Columbia Masterworks OL 5400 [M] | | 1959 | 30.00 |
| FLAHOOLEY | | | |
| ❑ Capitol S 284 [M] | | 1951 | 150.00 |
| ❑ Capitol T-11649 [M] | | 1977 | 15.00 |
| FLORA, THE RED MENACE | | | |
| ❑ RCA Victor LOC-1111 [M] | | 1965 | 25.00 |
| ❑ RCA Victor LSO-1111 [S] | | 1965 | 30.00 |
| FLOWER DRUM SONG | | | |
| ❑ Columbia Masterworks OS 2009 [S] | | 1958 | 25.00 |
| *—Gray and black label with six "eye" logos* | | | |
| ❑ Columbia Masterworks OL 5350 [M] | | 1958 | 20.00 |
| *—Gray and black label with six "eye" logos* | | | |
| FLY BLACKBIRD | | | |
| ❑ Mercury OCM-2206 [M] | | 1962 | 30.00 |
| ❑ Mercury OCS-6206 [S] | | 1962 | 60.00 |
| FUNNY GIRL | | | |
| ❑ Capitol STAO 2059 [S] | | 196? | 12.00 |
| *—Only Barbra Streisand is pictured on the back cover* | | | |
| ❑ Capitol SVAS 2059 [S] | | 1964 | 20.00 |
| *—Both Barbra Streisand and Sydney Chaplin are pictured on the back cover* | | | |
| ❑ Capitol VAS 2059 [M] | | 1964 | 15.00 |
| A FUNNY THING HAPPENED ON THE WAY TO THE FORUM | | | |
| ❑ Capitol SWAO 1717 [S] | | 1962 | 20.00 |
| *—Gatefold cover* | | | |
| ❑ Capitol WAO 1717 [M] | | 1962 | 15.00 |
| *—Gatefold cover* | | | |
| THE GAY LIFE | | | |
| ❑ Capitol SWAO 1560 [S] | | 1961 | 50.00 |
| ❑ Capitol WAO 1560 [M] | | 1961 | 25.00 |

| Number | Title (A Side/B Side) | Yr | NM |
|---|---|---|---|
| GENTLEMEN PREFER BLONDES | | | |
| ❑ Columbia Masterworks OS 2310 [R] | | 1963 | 10.00 |
| *—Gray label* | | | |
| ❑ Columbia Masterworks ML 4290 [M] | | 1949 | 25.00 |
| *—Original with green label* | | | |
| ❑ Columbia Masterworks OL 4290 [M] | | 196? | 15.00 |
| *—Reissue with new prefix and various gray labels* | | | |
| ❑ Columbia Masterworks S 32610 [R] | | 1973 | 8.00 |
| GEORGE M! | | | |
| ❑ Columbia Masterworks KOS 3200 [S] | | 1968 | 20.00 |
| ❑ Columbia Masterworks KOL 6800 [M] | | 1968 | 30.00 |
| THE GIRL IN PINK TIGHTS | | | |
| ❑ Columbia Masterworks ML 4890 [M] | | 1954 | 60.00 |
| THE GIRL WHO CAME TO SUPPER | | | |
| ❑ Columbia Masterworks KOS 2420 [S] | | 1963 | 30.00 |
| ❑ Columbia Masterworks KOL 6020 [M] | | 1963 | 25.00 |
| GIVE 'EM HELL, HARRY! | | | |
| ❑ United Artists UA-LA540-H2 [(2)] | | 1975 | 20.00 |
| THE GOLDEN APPLE | | | |
| ❑ RCA Victor LOC-1014 [M] | | 1954 | 100.00 |
| GOLDEN BOY | | | |
| ❑ Capitol SVAS 2124 [S] | | 1964 | 30.00 |
| ❑ Capitol VAS 2124 [M] | | 1964 | 25.00 |
| GOLDILOCKS | | | |
| ❑ Columbia Masterworks OS 2007 [S] | | 1958 | 60.00 |
| ❑ Columbia Masterworks OL 5340 [M] | | 1958 | 25.00 |
| GOODTIME CHARLEY | | | |
| ❑ RCA Victor ARL1-1011 | | 1975 | 30.00 |
| THE GREAT WALTZ | | | |
| ❑ Capitol SVAS 2426 [S] | | 1965 | 25.00 |
| ❑ Capitol VAS 2426 [M] | | 1965 | 20.00 |
| GREENWICH VILLAGE U.S.A. | | | |
| ❑ 20th Fox TCF-105-2 [(2)M] | | 1960 | 60.00 |
| *—With complete show* | | | |
| ❑ 20th Fox TCF-105-2S [(2)S] | | 1960 | 100.00 |
| *—With complete show* | | | |
| ❑ 20th Fox FOX-4005 [M] | | 1960 | 40.00 |
| *—With excerpts from the show* | | | |
| ❑ 20th Fox SFX-4005 [S] | | 1960 | 50.00 |
| *—With excerpts from the show* | | | |
| GREENWILLOW | | | |
| ❑ RCA Victor LOC-2001 [M] | | 1960 | 20.00 |
| ❑ RCA Victor LSO-2001 [S] | | 1960 | 50.00 |
| GUYS AND DOLLS | | | |
| ❑ Decca DL 8036 [M] | | 1950 | 30.00 |
| ❑ Decca DL 9023 [M] | | 1955 | 20.00 |
| *—Reissue of 8036* | | | |

| Number | Title (A Side/B Side) | Yr | NM |
|---|---|---|---|
| ❑ Decca DL 79023 [R] | | 196? | 12.00 |
| ❑ MCA 1628 | | 198? | 6.00 |
| *—Reissue of 37094* | | | |
| ❑ MCA 2034 | | 1973 | 10.00 |
| *—Reissue of 79023* | | | |
| ❑ MCA 37094 | | 198? | 8.00 |
| *—Reissue of 2034* | | | |
| GYPSY | | | |
| ❑ Columbia Masterworks OS 2017 [S] | | 1959 | 25.00 |
| *—Original covers are white with drawings* | | | |
| ❑ Columbia Masterworks OS 2017 [S] | | 1962 | 15.00 |
| *—Reissue covers are brown with show photos* | | | |
| ❑ Columbia Masterworks OL 5420 [M] | | 1959 | 20.00 |
| *—Original covers are white with drawings* | | | |
| ❑ Columbia Masterworks OL 5420 [M] | | 1962 | 12.00 |
| *—Reissue covers are brown with show photos* | | | |
| HAIR | | | |
| ❑ Atco SD 7002 | | 1969 | 25.00 |
| *—Original London cast* | | | |
| ❑ Philips PHS 600329 | | 1969 | 25.00 |
| *—Original French cast* | | | |
| ❑ RCA Victor ABD1-0245 [Q] | | 1973 | 20.00 |
| *—Broadway cast; quadraphonic remix* | | | |
| ❑ RCA Victor ANL1-0986 | | 1974 | 10.00 |
| *—Off-Broadway cast; reissue with new number* | | | |
| ❑ RCA Victor LOC-1143 [M] | | 1967 | 15.00 |
| *—Off-Broadway cast* | | | |
| ❑ RCA Victor LSO-1143 [S] | | 1967 | 12.00 |
| *—Off-Broadway cast; black label, dog at top, "Stereo" at bottom* | | | |
| ❑ RCA Victor LOC-1150 [M] | | 1968 | 30.00 |
| *—Broadway cast* | | | |
| ❑ RCA Victor LSO-1150 [S] | | 1968 | 10.00 |
| *—Broadway cast; orange label* | | | |
| ❑ RCA Victor LSO-1150 [S] | | 1968 | 20.00 |
| *—Broadway cast; black label, dog on top, "Stereo" at bottom* | | | |
| HALF A SIXPENCE | | | |
| ❑ RCA Victor LOC-1110 [M] | | 1965 | 20.00 |
| ❑ RCA Victor LSO-1110 [S] | | 1965 | 25.00 |
| HALF PAST WEDNESDAY | | | |
| ❑ Columbia CL 1917 [M] | | 1962 | 30.00 |
| ❑ Columbia CS 8717 [S] | | 1962 | 40.00 |
| HAMLET | | | |
| ❑ Columbia Masterworks DOL 302 [(4)M] | | 1964 | 25.00 |
| *—Boxed set with entire play (Broadway revival)* | | | |
| ❑ Columbia Masterworks DOS 702 [(4)S] | | 1964 | 25.00 |
| *—Boxed set with entire play (Broadway revival)* | | | |
| ❑ Columbia Masterworks OS 2620 [S] | | 1964 | 15.00 |
| *—Highlights from the box set* | | | |
| ❑ Columbia Masterworks OL 6220 [M] | | 1964 | 15.00 |
| *—Highlights from the box set* | | | |
| THE HAPPIEST GIRL IN THE WORLD | | | |
| ❑ Columbia Masterworks KOS 2050 [S] | | 1961 | 40.00 |
| *—Second covers are white* | | | |
| ❑ Columbia Masterworks KOS 2050 [S] | | 1961 | 60.00 |
| *—Original covers are yellow* | | | |
| ❑ Columbia Masterworks KOL 5650 [M] | | 1961 | 30.00 |
| *—Second covers are white* | | | |
| ❑ Columbia Masterworks KOL 5650 [M] | | 1961 | 40.00 |
| *—Original covers are yellow* | | | |
| HAPPY HUNTING | | | |
| ❑ RCA Victor LOC-1026 [M] | | 1956 | 40.00 |
| HEAR! HEAR! | | | |
| ❑ Decca DL 9031 [M] | | 1955 | 50.00 |
| HELLO, DOLLY! | | | |
| ❑ RCA Victor LOCD-1087 [M] | | 1964 | 15.00 |
| *—New back cover is in color and has a photo of Carol Channing; "RE" is on cover* | | | |
| ❑ RCA Victor LOCD-1087 [M] | | 1964 | 25.00 |
| *—Original cover is black and white on back and spotlights "Come and Be My Butterfly"; this song was deleted from the show, so the cover was changed* | | | |
| ❑ RCA Victor LSOD-1087 [S] | | 1964 | 20.00 |
| *—New back cover is in color and has a photo of Carol Channing; "RE" is on cover; black label, dog on top* | | | |
| ❑ RCA Victor LSOD-1087 [S] | | 1964 | 30.00 |
| *—Original cover is black and white on back and spotlights "Come and Be My Butterfly"; this song was deleted from the show, so the cover was changed* | | | |
| ❑ RCA Victor LSOD-1087 [S] | | 1969 | 10.00 |
| *—Orange or tan label* | | | |
| HENRY, SWEET HENRY | | | |
| ❑ ABC ABC-OC-4 [M] | | 1967 | 30.00 |
| ❑ ABC ABCS-OC-4 [S] | | 1967 | 50.00 |
| HERE'S LOVE | | | |
| ❑ Columbia Masterworks KOS 2400 [S] | | 1963 | 40.00 |
| ❑ Columbia Masterworks KOL 6000 [M] | | 1963 | 30.00 |
| HIGH BUTTON SHOES | | | |
| ❑ RCA Camden CAL-457 [M] | | 1958 | 30.00 |
| ❑ RCA Victor LOC-1107 [M] | | 1964 | 40.00 |
| ❑ RCA Victor LSO-1107 [R] | | 1964 | 30.00 |
| HIGH SPIRITS | | | |
| ❑ ABC-Paramount ABC-OC-1 [M] | | 1964 | 25.00 |
| ❑ ABC-Paramount ABCS-OC-1 [S] | | 1964 | 30.00 |
| HOUSE OF FLOWERS | | | |
| ❑ Columbia Masterworks ML 4969 [M] | | 1954 | 40.00 |
| *—Blue label original* | | | |
| ❑ United Artists UAS-5180 | | 1968 | 40.00 |
| *—Revival cast* | | | |
| HOW NOW, DOW JONES | | | |
| ❑ RCA Victor LOC-1142 [M] | | 1967 | 25.00 |
| ❑ RCA Victor LSO-1142 [S] | | 1967 | 30.00 |

| Number | Title (A Side/B Side) | Yr | NM |
|---|---|---|---|
| HOW TO SUCCEED IN BUSINESS WITHOUT REALLY TRYING | | | |
| ❑ RCA Victor LOC-1066 [M] | | 1961 | 20.00 |
| ❑ RCA Victor LSO-1066 [S] | | 1961 | 25.00 |
| *—Black label, dog on top* | | | |
| ❑ RCA Victor LSO-1066 [S] | | 1969 | 10.00 |
| *—Orange or tan label* | | | |
| HUGHIE | | | |
| ❑ Columbia Masterworks OS 2760 [S] | | 1965 | 30.00 |
| ❑ Columbia Masterworks OL 6260 [M] | | 1965 | 25.00 |
| I CAN GET IT FOR YOU WHOLESALE | | | |
| ❑ Columbia Masterworks KOS 2180 [S] | | 1962 | 30.00 |
| ❑ Columbia Masterworks KOL 5780 [M] | | 1962 | 25.00 |
| I DO! I DO! | | | |
| ❑ RCA Victor LOC-1128 [M] | | 1966 | 15.00 |
| ❑ RCA Victor LSO-1128 [S] | | 1966 | 20.00 |
| *—Black label, dog on top* | | | |
| I HAD A BALL | | | |
| ❑ Mercury OCM-2210 [M] | | 1964 | 20.00 |
| ❑ Mercury OCM-2210 [(2)M] | | 1964 | 40.00 |
| *—Promo-only two-record set with bonus interview record MGD-2-24* | | | |
| ❑ Mercury OCS-6210 [S] | | 1964 | 25.00 |
| ICE FOLLIES | | | |
| ❑ Dot DLP-3757 [M] | | 1967 | 25.00 |
| ❑ Dot DLP-25757 [S] | | 1967 | 30.00 |
| ILLYA DARLING | | | |
| ❑ United Artists UAL-8901 [M] | | 1967 | 20.00 |
| ❑ United Artists UAS-9901 [S] | | 1967 | 20.00 |
| INTO THE WOODS | | | |
| ❑ RCA 6796-1-RC | | 1988 | 20.00 |
| IRMA LA DOUCE | | | |
| ❑ Columbia Masterworks OS 2029 [S] | | 1960 | 25.00 |
| ❑ Columbia Masterworks OL 5560 [M] | | 1960 | 20.00 |
| J.B. | | | |
| ❑ RCA Victor LD-6075 [(2)M] | | 1959 | 60.00 |
| ❑ RCA Victor LDS-6075 [(2)S] | | 1959 | 70.00 |
| JACQUES BREL IS ALIVE AND WELL AND LIVING IN PARIS | | | |
| ❑ Columbia Masterworks D2S 779 [(2)] | | 1968 | 20.00 |
| *—Box set; gray "360 Sound" labels* | | | |
| JENNIE | | | |
| ❑ RCA Victor LOC-1083 [M] | | 1963 | 25.00 |
| ❑ RCA Victor LSO-1083 [S] | | 1963 | 50.00 |
| JESUS CHRIST SUPERSTAR | | | |
| ❑ Decca DL 71503 | | 1971 | 20.00 |
| *—From the Broadway production; also see listings for this title in the VARIOUS ARTISTS COLLECTIONS sections.* | | | |
| ❑ MCA 5000 | | 1973 | 12.00 |
| *—From the Broadway production; reissue* | | | |
| JOSEPH AND THE AMAZING TECHNICOLOR DREAMCOAT | | | |
| ❑ Scepter SPS-588X | | 1968 | 20.00 |
| *—With gatefold cover and libretto* | | | |
| ❑ Scepter SMAS-93738 | | 197? | 25.00 |
| *—Capitol Record Club edition* | | | |
| JOY | | | |
| ❑ RCA Victor LSO-1166 | | 1970 | 20.00 |
| JUNO | | | |
| ❑ Columbia Masterworks OS 2013 [S] | | 1959 | 70.00 |
| ❑ Columbia Masterworks OL 5380 [M] | | 1959 | 40.00 |
| KEAN | | | |
| ❑ Columbia Masterworks KSO 2120 [S] | | 1961 | 40.00 |
| ❑ Columbia Masterworks KOL 5720 [M] | | 1961 | 30.00 |
| THE KING AND I | | | |
| ❑ Decca DL 9008 [M] | | 195? | 12.00 |
| *—Drawing of Gertrude Lawrence and Yul Brynner on cover, with title on two lines* | | | |
| ❑ Decca DL 9008 [M] | | 195? | 40.00 |
| *—Drawing of Gertrude Lawrence and Yul Brynner on cover, with title on three lines* | | | |
| ❑ Decca DL 9008 [M] | | 1951 | 25.00 |
| *—Black label, gold print* | | | |
| ❑ Decca DL 79008 [R] | | 196? | 10.00 |
| KWAMINA | | | |
| ❑ Capitol SW 1645 [S] | | 1962 | 50.00 |
| ❑ Capitol W 1645 [M] | | 1962 | 30.00 |
| THE LADY'S NOT FOR BURNING | | | |
| ❑ Decca DL 9508 /9 [(2)M] | | 1951 | 50.00 |
| *—Oversize box set* | | | |
| LAGINAPPE '59 PRESENTS BE MY GUEST | | | |
| ❑ (no label) XCTV-10303 [M] | | 1959 | 250.00 |
| *—Custom pressing for New Trier High School, Illinois. Collectible because the future Ann-Margret sings one track on the LP!* | | | |
| LEGS DIAMOND | | | |
| ❑ RCA 7983-1-RC | | 1989 | 25.00 |
| LES MISERABLES | | | |
| ❑ Geffen GHS 24151 [(2)] | | 1987 | 15.00 |
| *—Original Broadway cast recording* | | | |
| ❑ Relativity 88561-8140-1 [(2)] | | 1985 | 20.00 |
| *—Original London cast recording* | | | |
| LET IT RIDE | | | |
| ❑ RCA Victor LOC-1064 [M] | | 1961 | 20.00 |
| ❑ RCA Victor LSO-1064 [S] | | 1961 | 40.00 |
| LI'L ABNER | | | |
| ❑ Columbia Masterworks OL 5150 [M] | | 1956 | 30.00 |
| LITTLE ME | | | |
| ❑ RCA Victor LOC-1078 [M] | | 1962 | 20.00 |
| ❑ RCA Victor LSO-1078 [S] | | 1962 | 25.00 |

Original cast, *Lost in the Stars,* Decca DL 8028, 1949, mono, $50.

| Number | Title (A Side/B Side) | Yr | NM |
|---|---|---|---|
| LITTLE SHOP OF HORRORS | | | |
| ❑ Geffen GHSP-2020 | | 1982 | 25.00 |
| LOOK MA, I'M DANCIN'! | | | |
| ❑ Decca DL 5231 [M] | | 1950 | 100.00 |
| LORELEI | | | |
| ❑ MGM M3G-55 | | 1974 | 30.00 |
| *—Second version, recorded with Broadway cast* | | | |
| ❑ Verve MV-5097-OC | | 1974 | 25.00 |
| *—First version, recorded before the show hit Broadway* | | | |
| LOST IN THE STARS | | | |
| ❑ Decca DL 8028 [M] | | 1949 | 50.00 |
| ❑ Decca DL 9120 [M] | | 1965 | 15.00 |
| *—Reissue of 8028* | | | |
| THE MAD SHOW | | | |
| ❑ Columbia Masterworks OS 2930 [S] | | 1965 | 100.00 |
| ❑ Columbia Masterworks OL 6530 [M] | | 1965 | 50.00 |
| MAGGIE FLYNN | | | |
| ❑ RCA Victor LSOD-2009 | | 1968 | 20.00 |
| ❑ RCA Victor LSOD-2009 | | 1968 | 25.00 |
| THE MAGIC SHOW | | | |
| ❑ Bell 9003 | | 1974 | 20.00 |
| MAKE A WISH | | | |
| ❑ RCA Victor LOC-1002 [M] | | 1951 | 150.00 |
| MAME | | | |
| ❑ Columbia Masterworks KOS 3000 [S] | | 1966 | 20.00 |
| *—Gray label with "360 Sound Stereo"* | | | |
| ❑ Columbia Masterworks KOS 3000 [S] | | 1970 | 12.00 |
| *—Olive label with orange "Columbia" around outside* | | | |
| ❑ Columbia Masterworks KOL 6600 [M] | | 1966 | 15.00 |
| MAN OF LA MANCHA | | | |
| ❑ Kapp KRL-4505 [M] | | 1965 | 15.00 |
| ❑ Kapp KRS-4505 [S] | | 1965 | 20.00 |
| MARK TWAIN TONIGHT! | | | |
| ❑ Columbia Masterworks OS 2019 [S] | | 1959 | 15.00 |
| ❑ Columbia Masterworks OL 5440 [M] | | 1959 | 12.00 |
| ME AND JULIET | | | |
| ❑ RCA Victor LOC-1012 [M] | | 1953 | 70.00 |
| MEDEA | | | |
| ❑ Decca DLP 9000 [M] | | 1949 | 30.00 |
| MEGILLA OF ITZIG MANGER | | | |
| ❑ Columbia Masterworks OS 3270 | | 1968 | 40.00 |
| MERRILY WE ROLL ALONG | | | |
| ❑ RCA Victor CBL1-4197 | | 1981 | 30.00 |
| THE MERRY WIDOW | | | |
| ❑ RCA Victor LOC-1094 [M] | | 1964 | 20.00 |
| ❑ RCA Victor LSO-1094 [S] | | 1964 | 25.00 |

| Number | Title (A Side/B Side) | Yr | NM |
|---|---|---|---|
| MEXICAN HAYRIDE | | | |
| ❑ Decca DL 5232 [10] | | 1950 | 120.00 |
| MILK AND HONEY | | | |
| ❑ RCA Victor LOC-1065 [M] | | 1961 | 20.00 |
| *—With picture of Tommy Rall and two dancers on front cover* | | | |
| ❑ RCA Victor LOC-1065 [M] | | 1961 | 25.00 |
| *—With only credits (no picture) on front cover* | | | |
| ❑ RCA Victor LSO-1065 [S] | | 1961 | 25.00 |
| *—With picture of Tommy Rall and two dancers on front cover* | | | |
| ❑ RCA Victor LSO-1065 [S] | | 1961 | 30.00 |
| *—With only credits (no picture) on front cover* | | | |
| MISS LIBERTY | | | |
| ❑ Columbia Masterworks ML 4220 [M] | | 1949 | 30.00 |
| *—Originals have green labels* | | | |
| MISS SAIGON | | | |
| ❑ Geffen GHS 24271 [(2)] | | 1990 | 20.00 |
| THE MOST HAPPY FELLA | | | |
| ❑ Columbia Masterworks O3L 240 [(3)M] | | 1956 | 50.00 |
| *—Box set with entire show* | | | |
| ❑ Columbia Masterworks OS 2330 [R] | | 196? | 15.00 |
| ❑ Columbia Masterworks OL 5118 [M] | | 1956 | 30.00 |
| *—Gray and black label with six "eye" logos* | | | |
| MR. PRESIDENT | | | |
| ❑ Columbia Masterworks KOS 2270 [S] | | 1962 | 30.00 |
| *—Gatefold with shiny silver cover* | | | |
| ❑ Columbia Masterworks KOL 5870 [M] | | 1962 | 20.00 |
| *—Gatefold with shiny silver cover* | | | |
| MR. WONDERFUL | | | |
| ❑ Decca DL 9032 [M] | | 1956 | 50.00 |
| MRS. PATTERSON | | | |
| ❑ RCA Victor LOC-1017 [M] | | 1954 | 150.00 |
| THE MUSIC MAN | | | |
| ❑ Capitol SW 990 [S] | | 196? | 15.00 |
| *—Regular cover with photo of Robert Preston as Harold Hill* | | | |
| ❑ Capitol SWAO 990 [S] | | 1957 | 25.00 |
| *—Gatefold cover, white with credits and drawing on front; gray label* | | | |
| ❑ Capitol W 990 [M] | | 196? | 12.00 |
| *—Regular cover with photo of Robert Preston as Harold Hill* | | | |
| ❑ Capitol WAO 990 [M] | | 1957 | 20.00 |
| *—Gatefold cover, white with credits and drawing on front; gray label* | | | |
| MY FAIR LADY | | | |
| ❑ Columbia Masterworks OS 2015 [S] | | 1959 | 12.00 |
| *—Gray label, "Stereo" at bottom; original London cast* | | | |
| ❑ Columbia Masterworks OS 2015 [S] | | 1959 | 20.00 |
| *—Gray and black label with six "eye" logos; original London cast* | | | |

| Number Title (A Side/B Side) | Yr | NM |
|---|---|---|
| ❑ Columbia Masterworks PS 2015 [S] | 198? | 6.00 |
| *—Budget-line reissue with new prefix* | | |
| ❑ Columbia Masterworks OL 5090 [M] | 1956 | 10.00 |
| *—Gray label, "Mono" at bottom* | | |
| ❑ Columbia Masterworks OL 5090 [M] | 1956 | 25.00 |
| *—Gray and black label with six "eye" logos* | | |
| ❑ Columbia Masterworks OL 5090 [M] | 1963 | 15.00 |
| *—Gray label with "Guaranteed High Fidelity" at bottom* | | |
| ❑ Columbia Masterworks PS 34197 | 1976 | 10.00 |
| *—Revival cast* | | |
| MY PEOPLE | | |
| ❑ Contact C-1 [M] | 1966 | 20.00 |
| ❑ Contact CS-1 [S] | 1966 | 25.00 |
| THE NERVOUS SET | | |
| ❑ Columbia Masterworks OS 2018 [S] | 1959 | 60.00 |
| ❑ Columbia Masterworks OL 5430 [M] | 1959 | 30.00 |
| NEW FACES OF 1952 | | |
| ❑ RCA Victor LOC-1008 [M] | 1952 | 25.00 |
| NEW FACES OF 1956 | | |
| ❑ RCA Victor LOC-1025 [M] | 1956 | 50.00 |
| NEW FACES OF 1968 | | |
| ❑ Warner Bros. BS 2551 | 1968 | 30.00 |
| THE NEW GIRL IN TOWN | | |
| ❑ RCA Victor LOC-1027 [M] | 1957 | 20.00 |
| ❑ RCA Victor LSO-1027 [S] | 1958 | 50.00 |
| ❑ RCA Victor LOC-1106 [M] | 1965 | 20.00 |
| ❑ RCA Victor LSC-1106 [S] | 1965 | 30.00 |
| THE NINA, THE PINTA AND THE SANTA MARIA | | |
| ❑ Dot DLP-9009 [M] | 1960 | 40.00 |
| ❑ Dot DLP-29009 [S] | 1960 | 50.00 |
| NO STRINGS | | |
| ❑ Capitol O 1695 [M] | 1962 | 20.00 |
| ❑ Capitol SO 1695 [S] | 1962 | 40.00 |
| OF THEE I SING | | |
| ❑ Capitol S 350 [M] | 1952 | 150.00 |
| OH, KAY! | | |
| ❑ 20th Fox FOX-4003 [M] | 1960 | 25.00 |
| ❑ 20th Fox SFX-4003 [S] | 1960 | 50.00 |
| OKLAHOMA! | | |
| ❑ Decca DLP 8000 [M] | 1949 | 30.00 |
| *—Black label, gold print; the first 12-inch LP on Decca* | | |
| ❑ Decca DL 9017 [M] | 1955 | 20.00 |
| *—Reissue of 8000* | | |
| ❑ Decca DL 9017 [M] | 196? | 20.00 |
| *—Reissue with new cover art* | | |
| ❑ Decca DL 79017 [R] | 196? | 15.00 |
| ❑ Decca DL 79017 [R] | 1968 | 20.00 |
| *—Special 25th Anniversary edition; cover has yellow drawing, inner sleeve has liner notes* | | |
| ❑ MCA 2030 | 1973 | 8.00 |
| *—Reissue of 79017; black label with rainbow* | | |
| ❑ MCA 37096 | 198? | 8.00 |
| *—Reissue of 2030* | | |
| OLIVER! | | |
| ❑ RCA Victor LOCD-2004 [M] | 1962 | 15.00 |
| ❑ RCA Victor LSOD-2004 [S] | 1962 | 20.00 |
| ON A CLEAR DAY YOU CAN SEE FOREVER | | |
| ❑ RCA Victor LOCD-2006 [M] | 1965 | 20.00 |
| ❑ RCA Victor LSOD-2006 [S] | 1965 | 25.00 |
| ON YOUR TOES | | |
| ❑ Decca DL 9015 [M] | 1954 | 75.00 |
| ONCE UPON A MATTRESS | | |
| ❑ Kapp KDL-7004 [M] | 1959 | 25.00 |
| ❑ Kapp KDL-7004-S [S] | 1959 | 30.00 |
| 110 IN THE SHADE | | |
| ❑ RCA Victor LOC-1085 [M] | 1963 | 25.00 |
| ❑ RCA Victor LSO-1085 [S] | 1963 | 40.00 |
| ONE TOUCH OF VENUS | | |
| ❑ Decca DL 9122 [M] | 1965 | 25.00 |
| ❑ Decca DL 79122 [R] | 1965 | 25.00 |
| OVER HERE! | | |
| ❑ Columbia Masterworks KS 32961 | 1974 | 20.00 |
| ❑ Columbia Masterworks SQ 32961 [Q] | 1974 | 30.00 |
| PAINT YOUR WAGON | | |
| ❑ RCA Victor LOC-1006 [M] | 1951 | 25.00 |
| *—Green label* | | |
| ❑ RCA Victor LOC-1006 [M] | 1955 | 20.00 |
| *—Black label, dog on top, "Long Play" at bottom* | | |
| ❑ RCA Victor LOC-1006 [M] | 1965 | 15.00 |
| *—Black label, dog on top, "Mono" at bottom* | | |
| ❑ RCA Victor LSO-1006 [R] | 1965 | 12.00 |
| *—Black label, dog on top* | | |
| ❑ RCA Victor LSO-1006 [R] | 1969 | 10.00 |
| *—Orange or tan label* | | |
| PARADE | | |
| ❑ Kapp KDL-7005 [M] | 1960 | 200.00 |
| ❑ Kapp KDS-7005 [S] | 1960 | 250.00 |
| PARIS '90 | | |
| ❑ Columbia Masterworks ML 4619 [M] | 1952 | 150.00 |
| PEACE | | |
| ❑ Metromedia MP-33001 | 1969 | 30.00 |
| PETER PAN | | |
| ❑ RCA Victor LOC-1019 [M] | 1954 | 40.00 |
| ❑ RCA Victor LSO-1019 [R] | 196? | 12.00 |
| ❑ RCA Victor AYL1-3762 [R] | 1980 | 8.00 |
| THE PHANTOM OF THE OPERA | | |
| ❑ Polydor 831273-1 [(2)] | 1987 | 20.00 |
| *—With libretto* | | |
| ❑ Polydor 831563-1 | 1987 | 10.00 |
| *—One-record "highlights" release* | | |
| PIPE DREAM | | |
| ❑ RCA Victor LOC-1023 [M] | 1955 | 50.00 |
| *—Without "Special Advance Edition" sticker on cover* | | |
| ❑ RCA Victor LOC-1023 [M] | 1955 | 70.00 |
| *—With "Special Advance Edition" sticker on cover* | | |
| PLAIN AND FANCY | | |
| ❑ Capitol S 603 [M] | 1955 | 25.00 |
| *—Red label* | | |
| PLAYGIRLS | | |
| ❑ Warner Bros. W 1530 [M] | 1964 | 25.00 |
| ❑ Warner Bros. WS 1530 [S] | 1964 | 30.00 |
| PORGY AND BESS | | |
| ❑ Decca DL 7006 [10] | 1950 | 30.00 |
| *—Reissue of material first released on 78s* | | |
| ❑ Decca DL 8042 [M] | 1950 | 30.00 |
| ❑ Decca DL 9024 [M] | 1955 | 25.00 |
| *—Reissue of 8042; drawing of Catfish Row on cover* | | |
| ❑ Decca DL 9024 [M] | 196? | 15.00 |
| *—Photo of cast members on cover* | | |
| ❑ Decca DL 79024 [R] | 196? | 10.00 |
| *—Photo of cast members on cover* | | |
| ❑ MCA 1631 [R] | 198? | 6.00 |
| *—Reissue of 2035* | | |
| ❑ MCA 2035 [R] | 1973 | 8.00 |
| *—Reissue of 79024; black label with rainbow* | | |
| THE PREMISE | | |
| ❑ Vanguard VRS-9092 [M] | 1960 | 40.00 |
| PURLIE | | |
| ❑ Ampex A-40101 | 1970 | 30.00 |
| RASHOMON | | |
| ❑ Carlton LPX-5000 [M] | 1959 | 25.00 |
| ❑ Carlton STLPX-5000 [S] | 1959 | 30.00 |
| *—Not actually the original cast recording, but the play's incidental music* | | |
| REDHEAD | | |
| ❑ RCA Victor LOC-1048 [M] | 1959 | 20.00 |
| ❑ RCA Victor LSO-1048 [S] | 1959 | 50.00 |
| *—Without "Essie's Vision"* | | |
| ❑ RCA Victor LOC-1104 [M] | 1959 | 15.00 |
| *—Reissue of 1048* | | |
| ❑ RCA Victor LSO-1104 [S] | 1965 | 25.00 |
| *—Reissue adds "Essie's Vision" to stereo version* | | |
| THE RIVER WIND | | |
| ❑ London AM-48001 [M] | 1962 | 40.00 |
| ❑ London AMS-78001 [S] | 1962 | 80.00 |
| THE ROAR OF THE GREASEPAINT — THE SMELL OF THE CROWD | | |
| ❑ RCA Victor LOC-1109 [M] | 1965 | 15.00 |
| ❑ RCA Victor LSO-1109 [S] | 1965 | 20.00 |
| THE ROTHSCHILDS | | |
| ❑ Columbia Masterworks S 30337 | 1970 | 25.00 |
| SAIL AWAY | | |
| ❑ Capitol SWAO 1643 [S] | 1961 | 30.00 |
| ❑ Capitol WAO 1643 [M] | 1961 | 20.00 |
| SARATOGA | | |
| ❑ RCA Victor LOC-1051 [M] | 1959 | 25.00 |
| ❑ RCA Victor LSO-1051 [S] | 1959 | 50.00 |
| SAY, DARLING | | |
| ❑ RCA Victor LOC-1045 [M] | 1958 | 40.00 |
| ❑ RCA Victor LSO-1045 [S] | 1958 | 60.00 |
| SELMA | | |
| ❑ Cotillion SD 2-110 [(2)] | 1976 | 20.00 |
| SEVENTEEN | | |
| ❑ RCA Victor LOC-1003 [M] | 1951 | 150.00 |
| 1776 | | |
| ❑ Columbia Masterworks BOS 3310 | 1969 | 12.00 |
| *—Revised (correct) edition has Rex Everhart shown as Ben Franklin in credits and synopsis* | | |
| ❑ Columbia Masterworks BOS 3310 | 1969 | 30.00 |
| *—The first edition has Howard DaSilva shown as Ben Franklin in credits and synopsis, though he does not appear on the LP* | | |
| SEVENTH HEAVEN | | |
| ❑ Decca DL 9001 [M] | 1955 | 150.00 |
| 70 GIRLS, 70 | | |
| ❑ Columbia Masterworks S 30589 | 1971 | 50.00 |
| SHE LOVES ME | | |
| ❑ MGM E 4118OC-2 [(2)M] | 1963 | 40.00 |
| ❑ MGM SE 4118OC-2 [(2)S] | 1963 | 50.00 |
| SHOW BIZ (FROM VAUDE TO VIDEO) | | |
| ❑ RCA Victor LOC-1011 [M] | 1954 | 40.00 |
| SHOW BOAT | | |
| ❑ Columbia Masterworks ML 4058 [M] | 1948 | 25.00 |
| *—From the 1946 revival; paper envelope jacket with its opening on top* | | |
| ❑ Columbia Masterworks OL 4058 [M] | 195? | 20.00 |
| *—From the 1946 revival; reissue of ML 4058* | | |
| SHOW GIRL | | |
| ❑ Roulette R-80001 [M] | 1961 | 20.00 |
| ❑ Roulette SR-80001 [S] | 1961 | 25.00 |
| SIDE BY SIDE BY SONDHEIM | | |
| ❑ RCA Victor CBL2-1851 [(2)] | 1976 | 20.00 |
| SILK STOCKINGS | | |
| ❑ RCA Victor LOC-1016 [M] | 1955 | 40.00 |
| ❑ RCA Victor LOC-1102 [M] | 1965 | 20.00 |
| *—Reissue; regular cover* | | |
| ❑ RCA Victor LSO-1102 [R] | 1965 | 20.00 |
| SIMPLY HEAVENLY | | |
| ❑ Columbia Masterworks OL 5240 [M] | 1957 | 25.00 |
| SING OUT, SWEET LAND! | | |
| ❑ Decca DL 4304 [M] | 1963 | 20.00 |
| ❑ Decca DL 8023 [M] | 1950 | 50.00 |
| ❑ Decca DL 74304 [R] | 1963 | 20.00 |
| SKYSCRAPER | | |
| ❑ Capitol SVAS 2422 [S] | 1965 | 25.00 |
| ❑ Capitol VAS 2422 [M] | 1965 | 20.00 |
| SNOW WHITE AND THE SEVEN DWARFS | | |
| ❑ Buena Vista STER-5009 | 1979 | 30.00 |
| SONDHEIM: A MUSICAL TRIBUTE | | |
| ❑ Warner Bros. 2WS 2705 [(2)] | 1973 | 20.00 |
| SONG OF NORWAY | | |
| ❑ Columbia CL 1328 [M] | 1959 | 20.00 |
| *—1958 revival cast* | | |
| ❑ Columbia CS 8135 [S] | 1959 | 50.00 |
| *—1958 revival cast* | | |
| ❑ Decca DL 8002 [M] | 1949 | 30.00 |
| ❑ Decca DL 9019 [M] | 1955 | 20.00 |
| ❑ Decca DL 79019 [R] | 196? | 12.00 |
| ❑ MCA 2032 [R] | 1973 | 10.00 |
| *—Reissue of 79019; black label with rainbow* | | |
| THE SOUND OF MUSIC | | |
| ❑ Capitol DT 91034 [R] | 1966 | 12.00 |
| *—Original London cast; Capitol Record Club exclusive* | | |
| ❑ Columbia Masterworks KOS 2020 [S] | 1959 | 12.00 |
| *—Gray label with "360 Sound Stereo" at bottom* | | |
| ❑ Columbia Masterworks KOS 2020 [S] | 1959 | 25.00 |
| *—Gray and black label with six "eye" logos* | | |
| ❑ Columbia Masterworks KOL 5450 [M] | 1959 | 20.00 |
| *—Gray and black label with six "eye" logos* | | |
| ❑ Columbia Masterworks KOL 5450 [M] | 1963 | 12.00 |
| *—Gray label with "Guaranteed High Fidelity" or "360 Sound Mono" on label* | | |
| ❑ Columbia Masterworks S 32601 [S] | 1973 | 10.00 |
| *—Reissue of 2020* | | |
| SOUTH PACIFIC | | |
| ❑ Columbia Masterworks OS 2040 [R] | 196? | 10.00 |
| *—Gray label with "360 Sound Stereo"* | | |
| ❑ Columbia Masterworks ML 4180 [M] | 1949 | 25.00 |
| *—Green or blue label; large anchor on front cover* | | |
| ❑ Columbia Masterworks OL 4180 [M] | 195? | 12.00 |
| *—Gray and black label with six "eye" logos; glossy gatefold cover with Ezio Pinza and Mary Martin pictured* | | |
| ❑ Columbia Masterworks OL 4180 [M] | 195? | 15.00 |
| *—Gray and black label with six "eye" logos; large anchor on front cover* | | |
| ❑ Columbia Masterworks OL 4180 [M] | 1963 | 10.00 |
| *—Gray label with "Guaranteed High Fidelity" or "360 Sound Mono"* | | |
| ❑ Columbia Masterworks S 32604 [R] | 1973 | 8.00 |
| *—Reissue of 2040* | | |
| ST. LOUIS WOMAN | | |
| ❑ Capitol L 355 [10] | 1952 | 80.00 |
| STOP THE WORLD-I WANT TO GET OFF | | |
| ❑ London AM 58001 [M] | 1962 | 15.00 |
| ❑ London AMS 88001 [S] | 1962 | 20.00 |
| STREET SCENE | | |
| ❑ Columbia Masterworks ML 4139 [M] | 1949 | 30.00 |
| *—Paper envelope jacket with its opening on top* | | |
| THE SUBJECT WAS ROSES | | |
| ❑ Columbia Masterworks DOL 308 [(3)M] | 1964 | 20.00 |
| ❑ Columbia Masterworks DOS 708 [(3)S] | 1964 | 30.00 |
| SUBWAYS ARE FOR SLEEPING | | |
| ❑ Columbia Masterworks KOS 2130 [S] | 1962 | 40.00 |
| ❑ Columbia Masterworks KOL 5730 [M] | 1962 | 25.00 |
| THE SURVIVAL OF ST. JOAN | | |
| ❑ Paramount PAS-9000 [(2)] | 1971 | 25.00 |
| SWEENEY TODD-THE DEMON BARBER OF FLEET STREET | | |
| ❑ RCA Victor CBL2-3379 [(2)] | 1979 | 20.00 |
| SWEET CHARITY | | |
| ❑ Columbia Masterworks KOS 2900 [S] | 1966 | 20.00 |
| ❑ Columbia Masterworks KOL 6500 [M] | 1966 | 15.00 |
| TAKE ME ALONG | | |
| ❑ RCA Victor LOC-1050 [M] | 1959 | 15.00 |
| ❑ RCA Victor LSO-1050 [S] | 1959 | 20.00 |
| *—Black label* | | |
| TAMALPAIS EXCHANGE | | |
| ❑ Atlantic SD 8263 | 1970 | 30.00 |
| TAROT | | |
| ❑ United Artists UAS-5563 | 1970 | 20.00 |
| TENDERLOIN | | |
| ❑ Capitol SWAO 1492 [S] | 1960 | 40.00 |
| *—With program* | | |
| ❑ Capitol WAO 1492 [M] | 1960 | 25.00 |
| *—With program* | | |
| TEVYA AND HIS DAUGHTERS | | |
| ❑ Columbia Masterworks OL 5225 [M] | 1957 | 30.00 |
| TEXAS, LI'L DARLIN' | | |
| ❑ Decca DL 5188 [10] | 1950 | 80.00 |
| THIS IS THE ARMY | | |
| ❑ Decca DL 5108 [10] | 1950 | 100.00 |
| THIS WAS BURLESQUE | | |
| ❑ Roulette R-25185 [M] | 1962 | 25.00 |
| ❑ Roulette SR-25186 [S] | 1962 | 30.00 |
| THREE TO MAKE MUSIC | | |
| ❑ RCA Victor LPM-2012 [M] | 1958 | 25.00 |
| ❑ RCA Victor LSP-2012 [S] | 1958 | 30.00 |
| THREE WISHES FOR JAMIE | | |
| ❑ Capitol S 317 [M] | 1952 | 120.00 |

| Number Title (A Side/B Side) | Yr | NM |
|---|---|---|
| THE THREEPENNY OPERA | | |
| ❑ Columbia Masterworks PS 34326 | 1976 | 20.00 |
| *—Another revival cast* | | |
| ❑ MGM E-3121 [M] | 1954 | 25.00 |
| *—Revival cast; yellow label* | | |
| ❑ MGM E-3121 [M] | 1959 | 15.00 |
| *—Revival cast; black label* | | |
| ❑ MGM SE-3121 [R] | 196? | 12.00 |
| *—Revival cast; rechanneled stereo* | | |
| ❑ Polydor 820260-1 | 198? | 8.00 |
| *—Revival cast; reissue* | | |
| TIME CHANGES | | |
| ❑ ABC ABCS-681 | 1969 | 30.00 |
| A TIME FOR SINGING | | |
| ❑ Warner Bros. W 1639 [M] | 1966 | 40.00 |
| ❑ Warner Bros. WS 1639 [S] | 1966 | 60.00 |
| A TIME REMEMBERED | | |
| ❑ Mercury MG-20380 [M] | 1957 | 25.00 |
| ❑ Mercury SR-60023 [S] | 1957 | 40.00 |
| *—Music from the dramatic play* | | |
| TO BROADWAY WITH LOVE | | |
| ❑ Columbia Masterworks OS 2630 [S] | 1964 | 50.00 |
| ❑ Columbia Masterworks OL 6030 [M] | 1964 | 25.00 |
| TOP BANANA | | |
| ❑ Capitol S 308 [M] | 1952 | 100.00 |
| TOVARICH | | |
| ❑ Capitol STAO 1940 [S] | 1963 | 30.00 |
| ❑ Capitol TAO 1940 [M] | 1963 | 20.00 |
| A TREE GROWS IN BROOKLYN | | |
| ❑ Columbia Masterworks ML 4405 [M] | 1951 | 30.00 |
| *—Blue label* | | |
| TWO BY TWO | | |
| ❑ Columbia Masterworks S 30338 | 1970 | 20.00 |
| TWO ON THE AISLE | | |
| ❑ Decca DL 8040 [M] | 1951 | 100.00 |
| *—Black label, gold print* | | |
| ❑ Decca DL 8040 [M] | 1955 | 60.00 |
| *—Black label, silver print* | | |
| ❑ Decca DL 8040 [M] | 196? | 60.00 |
| *—Black label with color bars* | | |
| TWO'S COMPANY | | |
| ❑ RCA Victor LOC-1009 [M] | 1952 | 100.00 |
| THE UNSINKABLE MOLLY BROWN | | |
| ❑ Capitol SWAO 1509 [S] | 1960 | 25.00 |
| ❑ Capitol WAO 1509 [M] | 1960 | 20.00 |
| UP IN CENTRAL PARK | | |
| ❑ Decca DL 8016 [M] | 1950 | 40.00 |
| *—Black label, gold print* | | |
| ❑ Decca DL 8016 [M] | 1955 | 30.00 |
| *—Black label, silver print* | | |
| WAITING FOR GODOT | | |
| ❑ Columbia Masterworks O2L 238 [(2)M] | 1956 | 30.00 |
| WEST SIDE STORY | | |
| ❑ Columbia Masterworks OS 2001 [S] | 1958 | 30.00 |
| *—Gray and black label with six "eye" logos* | | |
| ❑ Columbia Masterworks OS 2001 [S] | 1963 | 15.00 |
| *—Gray label with "360 Sound Stereo"* | | |
| ❑ Columbia Masterworks OL 5230 [M] | 1958 | 25.00 |
| *—Gray and black label with six "eye" logos* | | |
| ❑ Columbia Masterworks OL 5230 [M] | 1963 | 12.00 |
| *—Gray label with "Guaranteed High Fidelity" or "360 Sound Mono"* | | |
| ❑ Columbia Masterworks S 32603 [S] | 1973 | 10.00 |
| *—Reissue with new number* | | |
| WHAT MAKES SAMMY RUN? | | |
| ❑ Columbia Masterworks KSO 2440 [S] | 1964 | 40.00 |
| ❑ Columbia Masterworks KOL 6040 [M] | 1964 | 30.00 |
| WILDCAT | | |
| ❑ RCA Victor LOC-1060 [M] | 1961 | 25.00 |
| ❑ RCA Victor LSO-1060 [S] | 1961 | 40.00 |
| WISH YOU WERE HERE | | |
| ❑ RCA Victor LOC-1007 [M] | 1952 | 60.00 |
| WONDERFUL TOWN | | |
| ❑ Decca DL 9010 [M] | 1953 | 30.00 |
| *—Black label, gold print* | | |
| WORDS AND MUSIC | | |
| ❑ RCA Victor LRL1-5079 | 1974 | 20.00 |
| YOU'RE A GOOD MAN, CHARLIE BROWN | | |
| ❑ MGM 1E-9 [M] | 1967 | 20.00 |
| ❑ MGM S1E-9 [S] | 1967 | 20.00 |
| YOUR OWN THING | | |
| ❑ RCA Victor LOC-1148 [M] | 1968 | 25.00 |
| ❑ RCA Victor LSO-1148 [S] | 1968 | 20.00 |
| ZORBA | | |
| ❑ Capitol SO-118 | 1969 | 20.00 |

## SOUNDTRACKS

| Number Title (A Side/B Side) | Yr | NM |
|---|---|---|
| AARON SLICK FROM PUNKIN CRICK | | |
| ❑ RCA Victor LPM-3006 [10] | 1952 | 150.00 |
| ADVENTURES IN PARADISE | | |
| ❑ ABC-Paramount ABC-329 [M] | 1960 | 30.00 |
| ❑ ABC-Paramount ABCS-329 [S] | 1960 | 40.00 |
| ADVISE AND CONSENT | | |
| ❑ RCA Victor LOC-1068 [M] | 1962 | 30.00 |
| ❑ RCA Victor LSO-1068 [S] | 1962 | 60.00 |
| AN AFFAIR TO REMEMBER | | |
| ❑ Columbia CL 1013 [M] | 1957 | 40.00 |

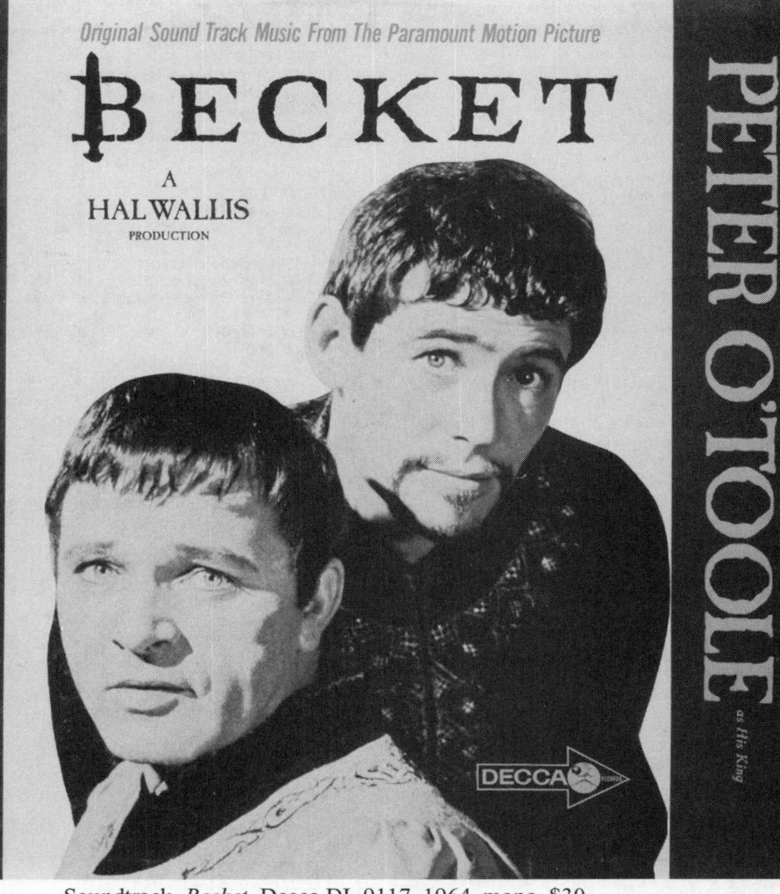


Soundtrack, *Becket,* Decca DL 9117, 1964, mono, $30.

| Number Title (A Side/B Side) | Yr | NM |
|---|---|---|
| AFRICA ADDIO | | |
| ❑ United Artists UAL-4141 [M] | 1966 | 20.00 |
| ❑ United Artists UAS-5141 [S] | 1966 | 25.00 |
| THE AGONY AND THE ECSTASY | | |
| ❑ Capitol MAS 2427 [M] | 1965 | 60.00 |
| ❑ Capitol SMAS 2427 [S] | 1965 | 80.00 |
| AIRPORT | | |
| ❑ Decca DL 79173 | 1970 | 25.00 |
| ALAKAZAM THE GREAT | | |
| ❑ Vee Jay LP-6000 [M] | 1961 | 80.00 |
| THE ALAMO | | |
| ❑ Columbia CL 1558 [M] | 1960 | 20.00 |
| ❑ Columbia CS 8358 [S] | 1960 | 25.00 |
| ALBERT PECKINPAW'S REVENGE | | |
| ❑ Sidewalk ST 5907 [S] | 1967 | 30.00 |
| ❑ Sidewalk T 5907 [M] | 1967 | 30.00 |
| ALEXANDER THE GREAT | | |
| ❑ Mercury MG-20148 [M] | 1956 | 250.00 |
| ALFIE | | |
| ❑ ABC Impulse! AS-9111 [S] | 1968 | 15.00 |
| ❑ Impulse! A-9111 [M] | 1966 | 30.00 |
| ❑ Impulse! AS-9111 [S] | 1966 | 30.00 |
| ALIEN | | |
| ❑ 20th Century T-593 | 1979 | 25.00 |
| ALIENS | | |
| ❑ Varese Sarabande STV-81283 | 1986 | 25.00 |
| ALIKI, MY LOVE | | |
| ❑ Fontana MGF-27523 [M] | 1963 | 25.00 |
| ❑ Fontana SRF-67523 [S] | 1963 | 30.00 |
| ALL NIGHT LONG | | |
| ❑ Epic LA 16032 [M] | 1962 | 40.00 |
| ❑ Epic BA 17032 [S] | 1962 | 50.00 |
| ALL THE LOVING COUPLES | | |
| ❑ GNP Crescendo GNPS-2051 | 1969 | 40.00 |
| ALL THE RIGHT NOISES | | |
| ❑ Buddah BDS-5132 | 1971 | 30.00 |
| ALL THIS AND WORLD WAR II | | |
| ❑ 20th Century 2T-522 [(2)] | 1976 | 25.00 |
| *—Box set with booklet and flyer* | | |
| THE ALLNIGHTER | | |
| ❑ Chameleon CHPD 9601 [PD] | 1987 | 30.00 |
| *—Picture disc* | | |
| ❑ Chameleon CHST 9601 | 1987 | 15.00 |

| Number Title (A Side/B Side) | Yr | NM |
|---|---|---|
| ALMOST FAMOUS | | |
| ❑ Dreamworks RTH-2001 [(2)] | 2001 | 40.00 |
| *—Album is called "Untitled"; contains five songs by Stillwater not on the CD version; 180-gram vinyl; with poster* | | |
| ALMOST SUMMER | | |
| ❑ MCA 3037 | 1978 | 25.00 |
| AMERICA, AMERICA | | |
| ❑ Warner Bros. W 1527 [M] | 1963 | 20.00 |
| ❑ Warner Bros. WS 1527 [S] | 1963 | 25.00 |
| AMERICAN HOT WAX | | |
| ❑ A&M SP-6500 [(2)] | 1978 | 20.00 |
| AN AMERICAN IN PARIS | | |
| ❑ MGM E-93 [10] | 1951 | 40.00 |
| AMERICAN POP | | |
| ❑ MCA 5201 | 1981 | 30.00 |
| THE AMOROUS ADVENTURES OF MOLL FLANDERS | | |
| ❑ RCA Victor LOC-1113 [M] | 1965 | 40.00 |
| ❑ RCA Victor LSO-1113 [S] | 1965 | 80.00 |
| ANASTASIA | | |
| ❑ Decca DL 8460 [M] | 1956 | 30.00 |
| ANATOMY OF A MURDER | | |
| ❑ Columbia CL 1360 [M] | 1959 | 40.00 |
| ❑ Columbia CS 8166 [S] | 1959 | 50.00 |
| AND GOD CREATED WOMAN | | |
| ❑ Decca DL 8685 [M] | 1957 | 120.00 |
| THE ANDROMEDA STRAIN | | |
| ❑ Kapp KRS-5513 | 1971 | 40.00 |
| *—Regular cover* | | |
| ❑ Kapp KRS-5513 | 1971 | 100.00 |
| *—Hexagonal cover glued onto silver cardboard* | | |
| ANGEL, ANGEL, DOWN WE GO | | |
| ❑ Tower ST-5161 | 1970 | 25.00 |
| ANGELS DIE HARD | | |
| ❑ Uni 73091 | 1971 | 30.00 |
| ANGELS FROM HELL | | |
| ❑ Tower ST 5128 | 1968 | 60.00 |
| THE ANONYMOUS VENETIAN | | |
| ❑ United Artists UAS-5218 | 1971 | 30.00 |
| ANOTHER TIME, ANOTHER PLACE | | |
| ❑ Columbia CL 1180 [M] | 1958 | 40.00 |
| ANY WEDNESDAY | | |
| ❑ Warner Bros. W 1669 [M] | 1966 | 25.00 |
| ❑ Warner Bros. WS 1669 [S] | 1966 | 40.00 |
| THE APARTMENT | | |
| ❑ United Artists UAL-3105 [M] | 1960 | 30.00 |
| ❑ United Artists UAS-6105 [S] | 1960 | 40.00 |

| Number | Title (A Side/B Side) | Yr | NM |
|---|---|---|---|
| **APOCALYPSE NOW** | | | |
| ❑ Elektra DP-90001 [(2)] | | 1979 | 30.00 |
| **THE APPLE** | | | |
| ❑ Cannon 1001 | | 1980 | 70.00 |
| **APRIL LOVE** | | | |
| ❑ Dot DLP-9000 [M] | | 1957 | 20.00 |
| **ARMS AND THE GIRL** | | | |
| ❑ Decca DL 5200 [10] | | 1950 | 100.00 |
| **AROUND THE WORLD IN 80 DAYS** | | | |
| ❑ Decca DL 9046 [M] | | 1957 | 25.00 |
| *—Black label, silver print* | | | |
| ❑ Decca DL 79046 [S] | | 1959 | 40.00 |
| *—Maroon label, silver print; cover has "Full Stereo" banner* | | | |
| ❑ Decca DL 79046 [S] | | 196? | 12.00 |
| *—Black label with color bars* | | | |
| ❑ Decca SW-94840 [S] | | 1972 | 15.00 |
| *—Capitol Record Club edition* | | | |
| ❑ MCA 2062 [S] | | 1973 | 10.00 |
| *—Reissue of 79046; black label with rainbow* | | | |
| ❑ MCA 37086 [S] | | 198? | 8.00 |
| *—Reissue of 2062* | | | |
| **AROUND THE WORLD UNDER THE SEA** | | | |
| ❑ Monument MLP-8050 [M] | | 1966 | 30.00 |
| ❑ Monument SLP-18050 [S] | | 1966 | 50.00 |
| **ARRIVIDERCI, BABY!** | | | |
| ❑ RCA Victor LOC-1132 [M] | | 1966 | 20.00 |
| ❑ RCA Victor LSO-1132 [S] | | 1966 | 40.00 |
| **AT LONG LAST LOVE** | | | |
| ❑ RCA Victor ABL2-0967 [(2)] | | 1975 | 20.00 |
| **ATHENA** | | | |
| ❑ Mercury MG-25202 [10] | | 1954 | 150.00 |
| **AVIATOR** | | | |
| ❑ Varese Sarabande STV-81240 | | 1985 | 20.00 |
| **BABES IN TOYLAND** | | | |
| ❑ Buena Vista BV-4022 [M] | | 1961 | 30.00 |
| ❑ Buena Vista STER-4022 [S] | | 1961 | 40.00 |
| **BABY DOLL** | | | |
| ❑ Columbia CL 958 [M] | | 195? | 50.00 |
| *—No ads for LPs on back cover* | | | |
| ❑ Columbia CL 958 [M] | | 1956 | 60.00 |
| *—Ads for other Columbia LPs on back cover* | | | |
| **BABY FACE NELSON** | | | |
| ❑ Jubilee JLP-2021 [M] | | 1957 | 120.00 |
| **BABY, THE RAIN MUST FALL** | | | |
| ❑ Ava A-53 [M] | | 1965 | 40.00 |
| ❑ Ava AS-53 [S] | | 1965 | 50.00 |
| ❑ Mainstream S-6056 [S] | | 1965 | 40.00 |
| *—Reissue of Ava AS-53* | | | |
| ❑ Mainstream 56056 [M] | | 1965 | 30.00 |
| *—Reissue of Ava A-53* | | | |
| **BACK STREET** | | | |
| ❑ Decca DL 9097 [M] | | 1961 | 40.00 |
| ❑ Decca DL 79097 [S] | | 1961 | 80.00 |
| **THE BAD SEED** | | | |
| ❑ RCA Victor LPM-1395 [M] | | 1956 | 300.00 |
| **BAND OF ANGELS** | | | |
| ❑ RCA Victor LPM-1557 [M] | | 1957 | 100.00 |
| **THE BAND WAGON** | | | |
| ❑ MGM E-3051 [M] | | 1953 | 30.00 |
| *—Yellow label* | | | |
| ❑ MGM E-3051 [M] | | 1960 | 20.00 |
| *—Black label* | | | |
| **THE BANJOMAN** | | | |
| ❑ Sire SA-7527 | | 1977 | 20.00 |
| **BARABBAS** | | | |
| ❑ Colpix CP 510 [M] | | 1962 | 40.00 |
| ❑ Colpix SCP 510 [S] | | 1962 | 80.00 |
| **BARBARELLA** | | | |
| ❑ Dyno Voice DV-31908 | | 1968 | 50.00 |
| **THE BARBARIAN AND THE GEISHA** | | | |
| ❑ 20th Fox FOX-3004 [M] | | 1958 | 250.00 |
| **BAREFOOT ADVENTURE** | | | |
| ❑ Pacific Jazz PJ-35 [M] | | 1961 | 40.00 |
| ❑ Pacific Jazz ST-35 [S] | | 1961 | 60.00 |
| **BAREFOOT IN THE PARK** | | | |
| ❑ Dot DLP-3803 [M] | | 1967 | 20.00 |
| ❑ Dot DLP-25803 [S] | | 1967 | 30.00 |
| **THE BARKLEYS OF BROADWAY** | | | |
| ❑ MGM E-503 [10] | | 1949 | 80.00 |
| **BATMAN** | | | |
| ❑ Warner Bros. 25977 | | 1989 | 20.00 |
| *—Music composed and conducted by Danny Elfman* | | | |
| **BATMAN FOREVER** | | | |
| ❑ Atlantic PR 6339 [(2)DJ] | | 1995 | 25.00 |
| *—Promo only; generic white cover with sticker* | | | |
| **BATTLE OF THE BULGE** | | | |
| ❑ Warner Bros. W 1617 [M] | | 1965 | 40.00 |
| ❑ Warner Bros. WS 1617 [S] | | 1965 | 40.00 |
| **BEACH BLANKET BINGO** | | | |
| ❑ Capitol ST 2323 [S] | | 1965 | 60.00 |
| ❑ Capitol T 2323 [M] | | 1965 | 30.00 |
| **BEAU JAMES** | | | |
| ❑ Imperial LP-9041 [M] | | 1957 | 40.00 |
| **BECKET** | | | |
| ❑ Decca DL 9117 [M] | | 1964 | 30.00 |
| ❑ Decca DL 79117 [S] | | 1964 | 50.00 |
| **BEDAZZLED** | | | |
| ❑ London MS-82009 | | 1967 | 80.00 |
| **BEHOLD A PALE HORSE** | | | |
| ❑ Colpix CP 519 [M] | | 1964 | 50.00 |
| ❑ Colpix SCP 519 [S] | | 1964 | 70.00 |
| **THE BELIEVERS** | | | |
| ❑ Varese Sarabande STV-81328 | | 1987 | 20.00 |
| **BELL, BOOK AND CANDLE** | | | |
| ❑ Colpix CP 502 [M] | | 1959 | 60.00 |
| **BELLS ARE RINGING** | | | |
| ❑ Capitol SW 1435 [S] | | 1960 | 30.00 |
| ❑ Capitol W 1435 [M] | | 1960 | 25.00 |
| **BEN-HUR** | | | |
| ❑ MGM 1E1 [M] | | 1959 | 40.00 |
| *—Boxed edition with hardcover book* | | | |
| ❑ MGM 1E1 [M] | | 196? | 12.00 |
| *—Gatefold cover, no book* | | | |
| ❑ MGM S-1E1 [S] | | 1959 | 50.00 |
| *—Boxed edition with hardcover book* | | | |
| ❑ MGM S-1E1 [S] | | 196? | 10.00 |
| *—Gatefold cover, no book; blue and gold label* | | | |
| ❑ MGM S-1E1 [S] | | 196? | 15.00 |
| *—Gatefold cover, no book; black label* | | | |
| **BEST OF THE BEST** | | | |
| ❑ Relativity 88561 034 1 | | 1989 | 20.00 |
| **BETRAYED** | | | |
| ❑ Varese Sarabande 704.700 | | 1988 | 30.00 |
| **BEYOND THE GREAT WALL** | | | |
| ❑ Capitol T 10401 [M] | | 1965 | 50.00 |
| **BEYOND THE VALLEY OF THE DOLLS** | | | |
| ❑ 20th Century Fox TFS-4211 | | 1970 | 200.00 |
| **THE BIBLE** | | | |
| ❑ 20th Century Fox TF-3184 [M] | | 1966 | 20.00 |
| ❑ 20th Century Fox TFS-4184 [S] | | 1966 | 30.00 |
| **THE BIG COUNTRY** | | | |
| ❑ United Artists UAL-4004 [M] | | 1958 | 25.00 |
| ❑ United Artists UAS-5004 [S] | | 1958 | 50.00 |
| **THE BIG GUNDOWN** | | | |
| ❑ United Artists UAS-5190 | | 1967 | 40.00 |
| **THE BIGGEST BUNDLE OF THEM ALL** | | | |
| ❑ MGM E-4446 [M] | | 1967 | 20.00 |
| ❑ MGM SE-4446 [S] | | 1967 | 25.00 |
| **BILLIE** | | | |
| ❑ United Artists UAL-4131 [M] | | 1965 | 20.00 |
| ❑ United Artists UAS-5131 [S] | | 1965 | 25.00 |
| **THE BILLION DOLLAR BRAIN** | | | |
| ❑ United Artists UAL-4174 [M] | | 1967 | 15.00 |
| ❑ United Artists UAS-5174 [S] | | 1967 | 20.00 |
| **BILLY JACK** | | | |
| ❑ Warner Bros. BJS-1001 | | 1973 | 15.00 |
| *—Reissue; "Burbank" palm trees label* | | | |
| ❑ Warner Bros. WS 1926 | | 1971 | 25.00 |
| *—Original; green "WB" label* | | | |
| **THE BIRD WITH THE CRYSTAL PLUMAGE** | | | |
| ❑ Capitol ST-642 | | 1970 | 100.00 |
| **BLACK AND WHITE IN COLOR** | | | |
| ❑ Buddah BDS-5698 | | 1977 | 40.00 |
| **BLACK GIRL** | | | |
| ❑ Fantasy F-9420 | | 1973 | 70.00 |
| **THE BLACK HOLE** | | | |
| ❑ Buena Vista STER-5008 | | 1979 | 50.00 |
| **THE BLACK ORCHID** | | | |
| ❑ Dot DLP-3178 [M] | | 1959 | 40.00 |
| ❑ Dot SLP-25178 [S] | | 1959 | 50.00 |
| **BLACK ORPHEUS** | | | |
| ❑ Epic LN 3672 [M] | | 1959 | 40.00 |
| ❑ Fontana MGF-27520 [M] | | 1963 | 20.00 |
| ❑ Fontana SRF-67520 [R] | | 1963 | 15.00 |
| **BLACKBIRDS OF 1928** | | | |
| ❑ Columbia Masterworks OL 6770 [M] | | 1968 | 15.00 |
| ❑ Revue 1 [M] | | 196? | 30.00 |
| ❑ Sutton SSU-270 [R] | | 196? | 12.00 |
| ❑ Sutton SU-270 [M] | | 196? | 20.00 |
| **BLACULA** | | | |
| ❑ RCA Victor LSP-4806 | | 1972 | 60.00 |
| **BLADE RUNNER** | | | |
| ❑ Full Moon/Warner Bros. 23748 | | 1982 | 20.00 |
| **BLESS THE BEASTS AND CHILDREN** | | | |
| ❑ A&M SP-4322 | | 1971 | 25.00 |
| **BLOOD AND SAND** | | | |
| ❑ Decca DL 5380 [10] | | 1952 | 80.00 |
| **BLOOMER GIRL** | | | |
| ❑ Decca DL 8015 [M] | | 1950 | 30.00 |
| **BLOW-UP** | | | |
| ❑ MGM E-4447 [M] | | 1967 | 40.00 |
| ❑ MGM SE-4447 [S] | | 1967 | 50.00 |
| **THE BLUE MAX** | | | |
| ❑ Mainstream S-6081 [S] | | 1966 | 80.00 |
| ❑ Mainstream 56081 [M] | | 1966 | 40.00 |
| **BLUE VELVET** | | | |
| ❑ Varese Sarabande STV-81292 | | 1986 | 25.00 |
| **BOBO** | | | |
| ❑ Warner Bros. W 1711 [M] | | 1967 | 20.00 |
| ❑ Warner Bros. WS 1711 [S] | | 1967 | 20.00 |
| **BODY HEAT** | | | |
| ❑ Label X LXSE-1-002 | | 1983 | 120.00 |
| **BOEING, BOEING** | | | |
| ❑ RCA Victor LOC-1121 [M] | | 1965 | 25.00 |
| ❑ RCA Victor LSO-1121 [S] | | 1965 | 30.00 |
| **BONNIE AND CLYDE** | | | |
| ❑ Warner Bros. W 1742 [M] | | 1968 | 40.00 |
| ❑ Warner Bros. WS 1742 [S] | | 1968 | 25.00 |
| *—Originals have green labels with "W7" logo in a square at top* | | | |
| ❑ Warner Bros. ST-91414 [S] | | 1968 | 30.00 |
| *—Capitol Record Club issue* | | | |
| **BORA, BORA** | | | |
| ❑ American Int'l. STA-1029 | | 1970 | 30.00 |
| **BORN FREE** | | | |
| ❑ MGM E-4368 [M] | | 1966 | 15.00 |
| ❑ MGM SE-4368 [S] | | 1966 | 20.00 |
| **BORSALINO** | | | |
| ❑ Paramount PAS-5019 | | 1970 | 30.00 |
| **THE BOY FRIEND** | | | |
| ❑ MGM 1SE-32 | | 1971 | 20.00 |
| **A BOY NAMED CHARLIE BROWN** | | | |
| ❑ Columbia Masterworks OS 3500 | | 1970 | 20.00 |
| **BOY ON A DOLPHIN** | | | |
| ❑ Decca DL 8580 [M] | | 1957 | 60.00 |
| *—Black label with silver print, or pink label with black print (promo)* | | | |
| ❑ Decca DL 8580 [M] | | 196? | 20.00 |
| *—Black label with color bars* | | | |
| **THE BOY WHO COULD FLY** | | | |
| ❑ Varese Sarabande STV-81299 | | 1986 | 20.00 |
| **THE BOYS FROM SYRACUSE** | | | |
| ❑ Capitol STAO 1933 [S] | | 1963 | 30.00 |
| ❑ Capitol TAO 1933 [M] | | 1963 | 25.00 |
| **BOYZ 'N THE HOOD** | | | |
| ❑ Warner Bros. PRO-A-4996 [DJ] | | 1991 | 20.00 |
| *—Promo-only vinyl release* | | | |
| **THE BRAVE ONE** | | | |
| ❑ Decca DL 8344 [M] | | 1956 | 40.00 |
| **BROTHER ON THE RUN** | | | |
| ❑ Perception PLP-45 | | 1973 | 40.00 |
| **THE BROTHERS** | | | |
| ❑ Warner Bros. 48058-1 [(2)] | | 2001 | 20.00 |
| **BUCCANEER** | | | |
| ❑ Columbia CL 1278 [M] | | 1958 | 25.00 |
| ❑ Columbia CS 8096 [S] | | 1958 | 40.00 |
| **BULLITT** | | | |
| ❑ Warner Bros. WS 1777 | | 1968 | 60.00 |
| **BUNDLE OF JOY** | | | |
| ❑ RCA Victor LPM-1399 [M] | | 1956 | 40.00 |
| **BUNNY LAKE IS MISSING** | | | |
| ❑ RCA Victor LOC-1115 [M] | | 1965 | 40.00 |
| ❑ RCA Victor LSO-1115 [S] | | 1965 | 70.00 |
| **BUNNY O'HARE** | | | |
| ❑ American Int'l. STA-1041 | | 1971 | 20.00 |
| **BUONA SERA, MRS. CAMPBELL** | | | |
| ❑ United Artists UAS-5192 | | 1969 | 30.00 |
| **THE BURGLARS** | | | |
| ❑ Bell 1105 | | 1971 | 40.00 |
| **BUTTERFIELD-8** | | | |
| ❑ MGM SE-3952 [S] | | 1960 | 25.00 |
| **BYE BYE BIRDIE** | | | |
| ❑ RCA Victor LOC-1081 [M] | | 196? | 20.00 |
| *—Second cover with Ann-Margret on front, but with no credits underneath* | | | |
| ❑ RCA Victor LOC-1081 [M] | | 1963 | 25.00 |
| *—First cover without Ann-Margret on the front* | | | |
| ❑ RCA Victor LSO-1081 [S] | | 196? | 20.00 |
| *—Third cover with Ann-Margret on front and with credits underneath* | | | |
| ❑ RCA Victor LSO-1081 [S] | | 196? | 25.00 |
| *—Second cover with Ann-Margret on front, but with no credits underneath* | | | |
| ❑ RCA Victor LSO-1081 [S] | | 1963 | 30.00 |
| *—First cover without Ann-Margret on the front* | | | |
| ❑ RCA Victor AYL1-3947 [S] | | 1980 | 8.00 |
| *—"Best Buy Series" reissue* | | | |
| **C'MON, LET'S LIVE A LITTLE** | | | |
| ❑ Liberty LRP-3430 [M] | | 1966 | 25.00 |
| ❑ Liberty LST-7430 [S] | | 1966 | 30.00 |
| **CABARET** | | | |
| ❑ ABC ABCD-752 | | 1972 | 20.00 |
| ❑ MCA 37125 | | 198? | 8.00 |
| *—Reissue; blue label with rainbow* | | | |
| **THE CAINE MUTINY** | | | |
| ❑ RCA Victor LOC-1013 [M] | | 1993 | 200.00 |
| *—Very limited edition (100 copies) reproduction of the original LP* | | | |
| ❑ RCA Victor LOC-1013 [M] | | 1954 | 10000. |
| *—VG value 4000; VG+ value 7000* | | | |
| **CALL ME MADAM** | | | |
| ❑ Decca DL 5465 [10] | | 1953 | 50.00 |
| **CALL ME MISTER** | | | |
| ❑ Decca DLP 7005 [10] | | 1950 | 100.00 |
| **CAMELOT** | | | |
| ❑ Warner Bros. B 1712 [M] | | 1967 | 25.00 |
| ❑ Warner Bros. BS 1712 [S] | | 1967 | 20.00 |
| *—Gold label original* | | | |
| ❑ Warner Bros. BS 1712 [S] | | 1968 | 15.00 |
| *—Green label, "W7" box logo at top* | | | |
| ❑ Warner Bros. BS 1712 [S] | | 1970 | 12.00 |
| *—Green label, "WB" shield logo at top* | | | |
| ❑ Warner Bros. BS 1712 [S] | | 1973 | 10.00 |
| *—"Burbank" palm trees label* | | | |
| ❑ Warner Bros. BSK 3102 [S] | | 1977 | 8.00 |
| *—Reissue with new number* | | | |



**Except when noted otherwise, VG = 25% of NM, and VG+ = 50% of NM. (Example: VG = $2.00, VG+ = $4.00 and NM = $8.00.)**

| Number | Title (A Side/B Side) | Yr | NM |
|---|---|---|---|
| ❑ Warner Bros. SW-91347 | | 1968 | 25.00 |
| *—Capitol Record Club edition* | | | |
| CAN-CAN | | | |
| ❑ Capitol SW 1301 [S] | | 1960 | 30.00 |
| ❑ Capitol W 1301 [M] | | 1960 | 20.00 |
| CANDY | | | |
| ❑ ABC ABCS-OC-9 | | 1968 | 30.00 |
| THE CARDINAL | | | |
| ❑ RCA Victor LOC-1084 [M] | | 1963 | 40.00 |
| ❑ RCA Victor LSO-1084 [S] | | 1963 | 60.00 |
| THE CARE BEARS MOVIE | | | |
| ❑ Kid Stuff 3901 | | 1985 | 20.00 |
| THE CARETAKERS | | | |
| ❑ Ava A-31 [M] | | 1963 | 20.00 |
| ❑ Ava AS-31 [S] | | 1963 | 25.00 |
| CAROUSEL | | | |
| ❑ Capitol SW 694 [S] | | 1962 | 20.00 |
| *—Black colorband label* | | | |
| ❑ Capitol SW 694 [S] | | 1969 | 15.00 |
| *—Lime green label* | | | |
| ❑ Capitol SW 694 [S] | | 1973 | 12.00 |
| *—Orange label* | | | |
| ❑ Capitol W 694 [M] | | 1956 | 30.00 |
| *—Gray label* | | | |
| ❑ Capitol W 694 [M] | | 1959 | 20.00 |
| *—Black colorband label, logo at left* | | | |
| ❑ Capitol W 694 [M] | | 1962 | 15.00 |
| *—Black colorband label, logo at top* | | | |
| THE CARPETBAGGERS | | | |
| ❑ Ava A-45 [M] | | 1964 | 30.00 |
| ❑ Ava AS-45 [S] | | 1964 | 40.00 |
| CARRY IT ON | | | |
| ❑ Vanguard VSD-79313 | | 1971 | 25.00 |
| CASINO ROYALE | | | |
| ❑ Colgems COMO-5005 [M] | | 1967 | 30.00 |
| ❑ Colgems COSO-5005 [S] | | 1967 | 100.00 |
| ❑ Colgems COSO-5005 [S] | | 1999 | 25.00 |
| *—Classic Records reissue on audiophile vinyl* | | | |
| ❑ Colgems COSO-5005-45 [(4)] | | 199? | 40.00 |
| *—Classic Records reissue on four 12-inch 45 rpm records* | | | |
| CAT PEOPLE | | | |
| ❑ Backstreet BSR 6107 | | 1982 | 20.00 |
| A CERTAIN SMILE | | | |
| ❑ Columbia CL 1194 [M] | | 1958 | 40.00 |
| ❑ Columbia CS 8068 [S] | | 1958 | 80.00 |
| THE CHAIRMAN | | | |
| ❑ Tetragrammaton T-5007 | | 1969 | 30.00 |
| CHARLOTTE'S WEB | | | |
| ❑ Paramount PAS-1008 | | 1973 | 30.00 |
| THE CHASE | | | |
| ❑ Columbia Masterworks OS 2960 [S] | | 1966 | 60.00 |
| ❑ Columbia Masterworks OL 6560 [M] | | 1966 | 40.00 |
| CHINATOWN | | | |
| ❑ ABC ABDP-848 | | 1974 | 40.00 |
| CHITTY CHITTY BANG BANG | | | |
| ❑ United Artists UAS-5188 | | 1968 | 25.00 |
| THE CHRISTMAS THAT ALMOST WASN'T | | | |
| ❑ RCA Camden CAL-1086 [M] | | 1966 | 25.00 |
| ❑ RCA Camden CAS-1086 [S] | | 1966 | 40.00 |
| CINDERELLA | | | |
| ❑ Disneyland DQ-1207 [M] | | 1959 | 40.00 |
| *—Second issue, white back cover with ads for nine other LPs* | | | |
| ❑ Disneyland DQ-1207 [M] | | 1963 | 30.00 |
| *—Third issue, pink back cover* | | | |
| ❑ Disneyland DQ-1207 [M] | | 1987 | 25.00 |
| *—Fifth issue, high gloss cover with prince putting slipper on Cinderella's foot* | | | |
| ❑ Disneyland 3107 [PD] | | 1981 | 30.00 |
| *—Fourth issue, picture disc* | | | |
| ❑ Disneyland WDL-4007 [M] | | 1957 | 200.00 |
| *—Original issue, gatefold cover* | | | |
| CINDERFELLA | | | |
| ❑ Dot DLP-8001 [M] | | 1960 | 60.00 |
| ❑ Dot SLP-38001 [S] | | 1960 | 100.00 |
| *—Gatefold cover with many extras including game board, spinner, booklet, music stand.* | | | |
| CLEOPATRA | | | |
| ❑ 20th Century Fox FXG-5008 [M] | | 1963 | 30.00 |
| ❑ 20th Century Fox SXG-5008 [S] | | 1963 | 40.00 |
| CLEOPATRA JONES | | | |
| ❑ Warner Bros. BS 2719 | | 1973 | 30.00 |
| CLOSE ENCOUNTERS OF THE THIRD KIND | | | |
| ❑ Arista AL 9500 [(2)] | | 1977 | 25.00 |
| *—Includes one 12-inch record and one 7-inch record. Deduct 50 percent if the 7-inch record is missing.* | | | |
| THE CLOWNS | | | |
| ❑ Columbia S 30772 | | 1971 | 40.00 |
| COFFY | | | |
| ❑ Polydor PD-5048 | | 1973 | 100.00 |
| THE COLLECTOR | | | |
| ❑ Mainstream S-6053 [S] | | 1965 | 50.00 |
| ❑ Mainstream 56053 [M] | | 1965 | 30.00 |
| COLLEGE CONFIDENTIAL | | | |
| ❑ Chancellor CHL-5016 [M] | | 1960 | 40.00 |
| ❑ Chancellor CHLS-5016 [S] | | 1960 | 50.00 |
| THE COLOR PURPLE | | | |
| ❑ Qwest 25289 [(2)] | | 1985 | 25.00 |
| *—Box set "limited edition" on purple vinyl with booklet* | | | |

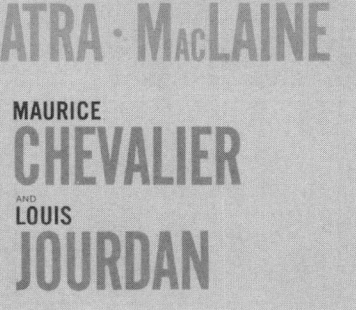

Soundtrack, *Can-Can,* Capitol SW 1301, 1960, stereo, Capitol logo at left on label, $30.

| Number | Title (A Side/B Side) | Yr | NM |
|---|---|---|---|
| ❑ Qwest 25336 [(2)] | | 1985 | 20.00 |
| *—Regular gatefold edition; records are still on purple vinyl* | | | |
| COMANCHE | | | |
| ❑ Coral CRL 57046 [M] | | 1956 | 400.00 |
| COME BACK CHARLESTON BLUE | | | |
| ❑ Atco SD 7010 | | 1972 | 30.00 |
| COME BLOW YOUR HORN | | | |
| ❑ Reprise R-6071 [M] | | 1963 | 30.00 |
| ❑ Reprise R9-6071 [S] | | 1963 | 50.00 |
| COMETOGETHER | | | |
| ❑ Apple SW-3377 | | 1971 | 20.00 |
| THE CONNECTION | | | |
| ❑ Felsted 2512 [S] | | 1960 | 300.00 |
| ❑ Felsted 7512 [M] | | 1960 | 200.00 |
| COOLEY HIGH | | | |
| ❑ Motown M7-840 R2 [(2)] | | 1975 | 20.00 |
| THE CORRUPT ONES | | | |
| ❑ United Artists UAL-4158 [M] | | 1967 | 40.00 |
| ❑ United Artists UAS-5158 [S] | | 1967 | 40.00 |
| COTTON COMES TO HARLEM | | | |
| ❑ United Artists UAS-5211 | | 1970 | 30.00 |
| THE COURT JESTER | | | |
| ❑ Decca DL 8212 [M] | | 1956 | 70.00 |
| *—Black label, silver print, or pink label, black print promo copy* | | | |
| ❑ Decca DL 8212 [M] | | 196? | 30.00 |
| *—Black label with color bars* | | | |
| THE COWBOY | | | |
| ❑ Decca DL 8684 [M] | | 1958 | 60.00 |
| *—Black label, silver print, or pink label, black print promo copy* | | | |
| ❑ Decca DL 8684 [M] | | 196? | 20.00 |
| *—Black label with color bars* | | | |
| CRADLE 2 THE GRAVE | | | |
| ❑ Def Jam 440 63615-1 [(2)] | | 2002 | 20.00 |
| CRIME IN THE STREETS | | | |
| ❑ Decca DL 8376 [M] | | 1956 | 60.00 |
| *—Black label, silver print, or pink label, black print promo copy* | | | |
| ❑ Decca DL 8376 [S] | | 196? | 30.00 |
| *—Black label with color bars* | | | |
| THE CROSS AND THE SWITCHBLADE | | | |
| ❑ Light LS-5550 | | 1970 | 30.00 |
| CRUISING | | | |
| ❑ Columbia JS 36410 | | 1980 | 40.00 |
| CUSTER OF THE WEST | | | |
| ❑ ABC ABC-OC-5 [M] | | 1968 | 80.00 |
| ❑ ABC ABCS-OC-5 [S] | | 1968 | 100.00 |

| Number | Title (A Side/B Side) | Yr | NM |
|---|---|---|---|
| CYCLE SAVAGES | | | |
| ❑ American Int'l. STA-1033 | | 1970 | 30.00 |
| CYRANO DE BERGERAC | | | |
| ❑ Capitol S 283 [M] | | 1951 | 30.00 |
| *—Originals have red labels with Capitol logo at top* | | | |
| D.O.A. | | | |
| ❑ Varese Sarabande 704.610 | | 1988 | 40.00 |
| DAKTARI | | | |
| ❑ Leo the Lion CH-1043 [M] | | 1967 | 20.00 |
| ❑ MGM CH-1043 [M] | | 1967 | 20.00 |
| DAMN THE DEFIANT! | | | |
| ❑ Colpix CP 511 [M] | | 1962 | 30.00 |
| ❑ Colpix SCP 511 [S] | | 1962 | 60.00 |
| DAMN YANKEES | | | |
| ❑ RCA Victor LOC-1047 [M] | | 1958 | 40.00 |
| *—Original pressing with "Long Play" on label* | | | |
| THE DAMNED | | | |
| ❑ Warner Bros. WS 1829 | | 1969 | 30.00 |
| THE DARK OF THE SUN | | | |
| ❑ MGM SE-4544 | | 1968 | 40.00 |
| DARLING LILI | | | |
| ❑ RCA Victor LSPX-1000 | | 1969 | 20.00 |
| DAWN OF THE DEAD | | | |
| ❑ Varese Sarabande VC-81106 | | 1979 | 30.00 |
| DAY OF ANGER | | | |
| ❑ RCA Victor LSO-1165 | | 1969 | 20.00 |
| THE DAY OF THE DOLPHIN | | | |
| ❑ Avco AV-11014 | | 1973 | 25.00 |
| THE DAY THE FISH CAME OUT | | | |
| ❑ 20th Century Fox TF-3194 [M] | | 1967 | 30.00 |
| ❑ 20th Century Fox TFS-4194 [S] | | 1967 | 40.00 |
| DAYDREAMER | | | |
| ❑ Columbia Masterworks OS 2940 [S] | | 1966 | 40.00 |
| ❑ Columbia Masterworks OL 6540 [M] | | 1966 | 30.00 |
| DAYS OF HEAVEN | | | |
| ❑ Pacific Arts PAC8-128 | | 1978 | 40.00 |
| DAYS OF THUNDER | | | |
| ❑ DGC 24294 | | 1990 | 20.00 |
| DE SADE | | | |
| ❑ Tower ST-5170 | | 1969 | 30.00 |
| DEAD MAN WALKING | | | |
| ❑ Columbia C3 67989 [(3)] | | 1997 | 200.00 |
| DEADFALL | | | |
| ❑ 20th Century Fox S-4203 | | 1968 | 60.00 |

Soundtrack, *Days of Heaven,* Pacific Arts PAC8-128, 1978, $40.

| Number | Title (A Side/B Side) | Yr | NM |
|---|---|---|---|
| THE DEADLY AFFAIR | | | |
| ❑ Verve V-8679 [M] | | 1966 | 25.00 |
| ❑ Verve V6-8679 [S] | | 1966 | 30.00 |
| DEAR JOHN | | | |
| ❑ Dunhill OCD-55001 [M] | | 1966 | 20.00 |
| ❑ Dunhill OCDS-55001 [S] | | 1966 | 25.00 |
| THE DECLINE OF WESTERN CIVILIZATION | | | |
| ❑ Slash 105 | | 1981 | 20.00 |
| DEEP IN MY HEART | | | |
| ❑ MGM E-3153 [M] | | 1955 | 40.00 |
| ❑ MGM E-3153 [M] | | 1955 | 50.00 |
| DESIRE UNDER THE ELMS | | | |
| ❑ Dot DLP-3095 [M] | | 1958 | 100.00 |
| DESTINATION MOON | | | |
| ❑ Columbia CL 6151 [10] | | 1950 | 120.00 |
| ❑ Omega OL-3 [M] | | 1959 | 40.00 |
| ❑ Omega OSL-3 [S] | | 196? | 80.00 |
| THE DEVIL AT 4 O'CLOCK | | | |
| ❑ Colpix CP 509 [M] | | 1962 | 40.00 |
| ❑ Colpix SCP 509 [S] | | 1962 | 70.00 |
| THE DEVIL IN MISS JONES | | | |
| ❑ Janus JLS-3059 | | 1973 | 25.00 |
| THE DEVIL'S BRIGADE | | | |
| ❑ United Artists UAS-6654 | | 1968 | 20.00 |
| DIAMOND HEAD | | | |
| ❑ Colpix CP-440 [M] | | 1963 | 30.00 |
| ❑ Colpix SCP 440 [S] | | 1963 | 60.00 |
| DIAMONDS ARE FOREVER | | | |
| ❑ United Artists UA-LA301-G | | 1974 | 12.00 |
| *—Reissue of 5520* | | | |
| ❑ United Artists UAS-5520 | | 1971 | 20.00 |
| THE DIARY OF ANNE FRANK | | | |
| ❑ 20th Fox FOX-3012 [M] | | 1959 | 50.00 |
| ❑ 20th Fox SFX-3012 [S] | | 1959 | 80.00 |
| DIRTY GAME | | | |
| ❑ Laurie LLP-2034 [M] | | 1966 | 25.00 |
| ❑ Laurie SLP-2034 [S] | | 1966 | 30.00 |
| DIVORCE AMERICAN STYLE | | | |
| ❑ United Artists UAL-4163 [M] | | 1967 | 20.00 |
| ❑ United Artists UAS-5163 [S] | | 1967 | 20.00 |
| DIVORCE ITALIAN STYLE | | | |
| ❑ United Artists UAL-4106 [M] | | 1962 | 40.00 |
| ❑ United Artists UAS-5106 [S] | | 1962 | 50.00 |
| DOCTOR DOLITTLE | | | |
| ❑ 20th Century Fox TCF-5101 [M] | | 1967 | 20.00 |
| ❑ 20th Century Fox TCS-5101 [S] | | 1967 | 20.00 |

| Number | Title (A Side/B Side) | Yr | NM |
|---|---|---|---|
| DOCTOR GOLDFOOT AND THE GIRL BOMBS | | | |
| ❑ Tower DT 5053 [R] | | 1966 | 25.00 |
| ❑ Tower T 5053 [M] | | 1966 | 20.00 |
| DOCTOR ZHIVAGO | | | |
| ❑ MCA 39042 | | 198? | 8.00 |
| *—Reissue* | | | |
| ❑ MGM 1E-6 [M] | | 1965 | 15.00 |
| ❑ MGM S1E-6 ST [S] | | 1965 | 20.00 |
| ❑ MGM SWAE-90620 [S] | | 1965 | 20.00 |
| *—Capitol Record Club issue* | | | |
| A DOG OF FLANDERS | | | |
| ❑ 20th Fox FOX-3026 [M] | | 1959 | 80.00 |
| ❑ 20th Fox SFX-3026 [S] | | 1959 | 300.00 |
| $ (DOLLARS) | | | |
| ❑ Reprise MS 2051 | | 1971 | 20.00 |
| DON'T MAKE WAVES | | | |
| ❑ MGM E-4483 [M] | | 1967 | 30.00 |
| ❑ MGM SE-4483 [S] | | 1967 | 30.00 |
| THE DOORS | | | |
| ❑ Elektra E1-61047 | | 1991 | 100.00 |
| *—Only vinyl edition in US released through Columbia House* | | | |
| DR. NO | | | |
| ❑ Liberty LT-50275 | | 1981 | 8.00 |
| *—Reissue of United Artists 275* | | | |
| ❑ United Artists UA-LA275-G | | 1974 | 10.00 |
| *—Reissue of 5108* | | | |
| ❑ United Artists UAL-4108 [M] | | 1963 | 40.00 |
| ❑ United Artists UAS-5108 [S] | | 1963 | 50.00 |
| DR. PHIBES | | | |
| ❑ American Int'l. A-1040 | | 1971 | 60.00 |
| DRANGO | | | |
| ❑ Liberty LRP-3036 [M] | | 1957 | 150.00 |
| A DREAM OF KINGS | | | |
| ❑ National General NG-1000 | | 1969 | 30.00 |
| DUCK, YOU SUCKER | | | |
| ❑ United Artists UAS-5221 | | 1972 | 40.00 |
| DUEL AT DIABLO | | | |
| ❑ United Artists UAL-4139 [M] | | 1966 | 25.00 |
| ❑ United Artists UAS-5139 [S] | | 1966 | 30.00 |
| DUMBO | | | |
| ❑ Disneyland 1204 [M] | | 197? | 10.00 |
| *—Fourth issue, yellow rainbow label, flying Dumbo on back cover* | | | |
| ❑ Disneyland DQ-1204 [M] | | 1959 | 25.00 |
| *—Second issue, back cover has ads for nine other LPs* | | | |
| ❑ Disneyland DQ-1204 [M] | | 1963 | 15.00 |
| *—Third issue, four black & white photos on back cover* | | | |

| Number | Title (A Side/B Side) | Yr | NM |
|---|---|---|---|
| ❑ Disneyland WDL-4013 [M] | | 1957 | 200.00 |
| *—Original issue, gatefold cover* | | | |
| ❑ Disneyland ST-4904 [M] | | 1963 | 200.00 |
| *—Special issue with pop-up figures in gatefold* | | | |
| DUNE | | | |
| ❑ Polydor 823770-1 | | 1984 | 30.00 |
| THE DUNWICH HORROR | | | |
| ❑ American Int'l. STA-1028 | | 1970 | 40.00 |
| E.T. THE EXTRA-TERRESTRIAL | | | |
| ❑ MCA 6109 | | 1982 | 10.00 |
| ❑ MCA 6113 [PD] | | 1982 | 25.00 |
| *—Picture disc in plastic envelope* | | | |
| ❑ MCA 16014 | | 1982 | 40.00 |
| *—Audiophile edition* | | | |
| ❑ MCA 70000 | | 1982 | 80.00 |
| *—Boxed version with booklet; story narrated by Michael Jackson* | | | |
| EAST SIDE, WEST SIDE | | | |
| ❑ Columbia CL 2123 [M] | | 1963 | 30.00 |
| ❑ Columbia CS 8923 [S] | | 1963 | 40.00 |
| EASTER PARADE | | | |
| ❑ MGM E-502 [10] | | 1950 | 80.00 |
| EASY RIDER | | | |
| ❑ ABC Dunhill DSX-50063 | | 1969 | 25.00 |
| ECCO | | | |
| ❑ Warner Bros. W 1600 [M] | | 1965 | 25.00 |
| ❑ Warner Bros. WS 1600 [S] | | 1965 | 30.00 |
| THE EDDY DUCHIN STORY | | | |
| ❑ Decca DL 8289 [M] | | 1956 | 40.00 |
| *—Original cover with Tyrone Power and Kim Novak at a piano* | | | |
| ❑ Decca DL 8289 [M] | | 1959 | 20.00 |
| *—Reissue cover with Tyrone Power and Kim Novak kissing* | | | |
| ❑ Decca DL 9121 [M] | | 196? | 12.00 |
| *—Reissue of 8289* | | | |
| ❑ Decca DL 78289 [S] | | 1959 | 25.00 |
| *—Maroon label, silver print, "Full Stereo" on front cover* | | | |
| ❑ Decca DL 79121 [S] | | 196? | 15.00 |
| *—Reissue of 78289* | | | |
| ❑ MCA 2041 | | 1973 | 10.00 |
| *—Reissue of 79121; black label with rainbow* | | | |
| ❑ MCA 37088 | | 198? | 8.00 |
| *—Reissue of 2041* | | | |
| THE EDUCATION OF SONNY CARSON | | | |
| ❑ Paramount PAS-1045 | | 1974 | 20.00 |
| THE EGYPTIAN | | | |
| ❑ Decca DL 9014 [M] | | 1954 | 60.00 |
| ❑ Decca DL 79014 [R] | | 196? | 20.00 |
| EIGHT MEN OUT | | | |
| ❑ Varese Sarabande 704.600 | | 1988 | 25.00 |
| 8 MILE, MORE MUSIC FROM | | | |
| ❑ Shady/Interscope 004 450979-1 | | 2002 | 25.00 |
| *—U.S. edition comes in generic black sleeve with center hole and sticker across top of cover* | | | |
| EL CID | | | |
| ❑ MGM E-3977 [M] | | 1962 | 40.00 |
| ❑ MGM SE-3977 [S] | | 1962 | 50.00 |
| EL DORADO | | | |
| ❑ Epic FLM-13114 [M] | | 1967 | 50.00 |
| ❑ Epic LFS-15114 [S] | | 1967 | 70.00 |
| EL TOPO | | | |
| ❑ Apple SWAO-3388 | | 1972 | 40.00 |
| ELECTRA GLIDE IN BLUE | | | |
| ❑ United Artists UA-LA062-H [(2)] | | 1973 | 40.00 |
| *—With booklet and two posters* | | | |
| ELEPHANT STEPS | | | |
| ❑ Columbia Masterwords M2X 33044 [(2)] | | 1975 | 20.00 |
| ELMER GANTRY | | | |
| ❑ United Artists UAL-4069 [M] | | 1960 | 40.00 |
| ❑ United Artists UAS-5069 [S] | | 1960 | 50.00 |
| THE EMPIRE STRIKES BACK | | | |
| ❑ RSO RS-2-4201 [(2)] | | 1980 | 20.00 |
| *—With booklet* | | | |
| ENTER THE DRAGON | | | |
| ❑ Warner Bros. BS 2727 | | 1973 | 60.00 |
| EVERYTHING I HAVE IS YOURS | | | |
| ❑ MGM E-187 [10] | | 1953 | 40.00 |
| EVIL DEAD | | | |
| ❑ Varese Sarabande STV-81199 | | 1984 | 20.00 |
| EXODUS | | | |
| ❑ RCA Victor LOC-1058 [M] | | 1960 | 20.00 |
| *—"Long Play" on label* | | | |
| ❑ RCA Victor LSO-1058 [S] | | 1960 | 25.00 |
| *—"Living Stereo" on label* | | | |
| THE EXORCIST | | | |
| ❑ Warner Bros. W 2774 | | 1974 | 30.00 |
| A FACE IN THE CROWD | | | |
| ❑ Capitol W 872 [M] | | 1957 | 50.00 |
| THE FALL OF THE ROMAN EMPIRE | | | |
| ❑ Columbia Masterworks OS 2460 [S] | | 1964 | 60.00 |
| ❑ Columbia Masterworks OL 6060 [M] | | 1964 | 40.00 |
| THE FAMILY WAY | | | |
| ❑ London M 76007 [M] | | 1967 | 100.00 |
| *—No promo sticker on front cover (deduct 20 percent for promo)* | | | |
| ❑ London ST 82007 [S] | | 1967 | 120.00 |
| *—No promo sticker on front cover (deduct 20 percent for promo)* | | | |
| FANNY | | | |
| ❑ Warner Bros. W 1416 [M] | | 1961 | 25.00 |
| ❑ Warner Bros. WS 1416 [S] | | 1961 | 30.00 |



**Except when noted otherwise, VG = 25% of NM, and VG+ = 50% of NM. (Example: VG = $2.00, VG+ = $4.00 and NM = $8.00.)**

| Number | Title (A Side/B Side) | Yr | NM |
|---|---|---|---|
| | FANTASIA | | |
| ❑ Buena Vista 101 [(2)S] | | 1982 | 20.00 |
| *—Stereo reissue, two records, no booklet* | | | |
| ❑ Buena Vista STER-101 [(3)S] | | 1961 | 40.00 |
| *—First stereo issue, black and yellow rainbow labels, includes 24-page booklet* | | | |
| ❑ Buena Vista WDX-101 [(3)M] | | 1961 | 30.00 |
| *—Second issue, blue labels, includes 24-page booklet* | | | |
| ❑ Buena Vista V-104 [(2)] | | 1982 | 25.00 |
| *—Digitally re-recorded music track, Mickey Mouse as The Sorcerer on cover* | | | |
| ❑ Disneyland WDX-101 [(3)] | | 1957 | 60.00 |
| *—Original issue, maroon/red labels, includes 24-page booklet* | | | |
| | FANTASIA: NIGHT ON BALD MOUNTAIN; PASTORAL SYMPHONY; AVE MARIA | | |
| ❑ Disneyland STER-4101C [S] | | 1958 | 30.00 |
| ❑ Disneyland WDL-4101C [M] | | 1958 | 20.00 |
| | FANTASIA: RITE OF SPRING; TOCCATA AND FUGUE | | |
| ❑ Disneyland STER-4101A [S] | | 1959 | 30.00 |
| ❑ Disneyland WDL-4101A [M] | | 1958 | 20.00 |
| | FANTASIA: THE NUTCRACKER SUITE; DANCE OF THE HOURS | | |
| ❑ Disneyland STER-4101B [S] | | 1959 | 30.00 |
| ❑ Disneyland WDL-4101B [M] | | 1958 | 20.00 |
| | THE FANTASTIC PLASTIC MACHINE | | |
| ❑ Epic BN 26469 | | 1969 | 25.00 |
| | FAR FROM THE MADDING CROWD | | |
| ❑ MGM 1E-11 [M] | | 1967 | 15.00 |
| ❑ MGM S1E-11 [S] | | 1967 | 25.00 |
| | A FAREWELL TO ARMS | | |
| ❑ Capitol W 918 [M] | | 1957 | 50.00 |
| | THE FASTEST GUITAR ALIVE | | |
| ❑ MGM SE-4475 | | 1968 | 30.00 |
| | FATHOM | | |
| ❑ 20th Century Fox TFM-4195 [M] | | 1967 | 40.00 |
| ❑ 20th Century Fox TFS-4195 [S] | | 1967 | 50.00 |
| | FELLINI SATYRICON | | |
| ❑ United Artists UAS-5208 | | 1969 | 30.00 |
| | FELLINI'S ROMA | | |
| ❑ United Artists UA-LA052-F | | 1972 | 30.00 |
| | THE FEMALE PRISONER | | |
| ❑ Columbia Masterworks OS 3320 | | 1969 | 30.00 |
| | FIDDLER ON THE ROOF | | |
| ❑ United Artists UAS-10900 [(2)] | | 1971 | 20.00 |
| *—With booklet* | | | |
| | 55 DAYS AT PEKING | | |
| ❑ Columbia CL 2028 [M] | | 1963 | 40.00 |
| ❑ Columbia CS 8828 [S] | | 1963 | 70.00 |
| | THE FIGHTER | | |
| ❑ Decca DL 5414 [10] | | 1952 | 80.00 |
| | THE FINAL COUNTDOWN | | |
| ❑ Casablanca NBLP-7232 | | 1980 | 40.00 |
| | FINIAN'S RAINBOW | | |
| ❑ Warner Bros. BS 2550 | | 1968 | 20.00 |
| | FIRE DOWN BELOW | | |
| ❑ Decca DL 8597 [M] | | 1957 | 70.00 |
| | A FISTFUL OF DOLLARS | | |
| ❑ RCA Victor LOC-1135 [M] | | 1967 | 20.00 |
| ❑ RCA Victor LSO-1135 [S] | | 1967 | 30.00 |
| *—Black label, dog on top* | | | |
| ❑ RCA Victor LSO-1135 [S] | | 1969 | 12.00 |
| *—Orange label, tan label, or black label with dog at 1 o'clock* | | | |
| | FITZWILLY | | |
| ❑ United Artists UAL-4173 [M] | | 1967 | 20.00 |
| ❑ United Artists UAS-5173 [S] | | 1967 | 25.00 |
| | FIVE EASY PIECES | | |
| ❑ Epic KE 30456 | | 1971 | 25.00 |
| | THE FIVE PENNIES | | |
| ❑ Dot DLP-9500 [M] | | 1959 | 25.00 |
| ❑ Dot DLP-29500 [S] | | 1959 | 50.00 |
| | THE FLAMINGO KID | | |
| ❑ Motown 6131ML | | 1984 | 10.00 |
| *—Commonly distributed issue* | | | |
| ❑ Varese Sarabande STV-81232 | | 1984 | 40.00 |
| *—Original issue* | | | |
| | A FLEA IN HER EAR | | |
| ❑ 20th Century Fox TFS-4200 | | 1968 | 30.00 |
| | FLOWER DRUM SONG | | |
| ❑ Decca DL 9098 [M] | | 1961 | 20.00 |
| ❑ Decca DL 79098 [S] | | 1961 | 25.00 |
| ❑ MCA 2069 | | 1973 | 10.00 |
| *—Reissue; black label with rainbow* | | | |
| | THE FOG | | |
| ❑ Varese Sarabande STV-81191 | | 1980 | 25.00 |
| | FOLIES BERGERE | | |
| ❑ Decca DL 8571 [M] | | 1958 | 25.00 |
| | FOLLOW ME | | |
| ❑ Uni 73056 | | 1969 | 30.00 |
| | FOOTLOOSE | | |
| ❑ Columbia JS 39242 | | 1984 | 10.00 |
| ❑ Columbia 9C9 39404 [PD] | | 1984 | 20.00 |
| *—Picture disc version* | | | |
| | FOR A FEW DOLLARS MORE | | |
| ❑ United Artists UAL-3608 [M] | | 1967 | 20.00 |
| ❑ United Artists UAS-6608 [S] | | 1967 | 25.00 |
| | FOR LOVE OF IVY | | |
| ❑ ABC SOC-7 | | 1968 | 25.00 |

Soundtrack, *Easy Rider,* ABC-Dunhill DSX-50063, 1969, $25.

| Number | Title (A Side/B Side) | Yr | NM |
|---|---|---|---|
| | FOR THE FIRST TIME | | |
| ❑ RCA Victor Red Seal LM-2338 [M] | | 1959 | 15.00 |
| ❑ RCA Victor Red Seal LSC-2338 [S] | | 1959 | 20.00 |
| *—"Shaded dog" and smaller "RCA Victor" lettering* | | | |
| ❑ RCA Victor Red Seal LSC-2338 [S] | | 1965 | 15.00 |
| *—"White dog" and larger "RCA Victor" lettering* | | | |
| ❑ RCA Victor Red Seal LSC-2338 [S] | | 1969 | 12.00 |
| *—Red label, no dog* | | | |
| | FOR YOUR EYES ONLY | | |
| ❑ Liberty LOO-1109 | | 1981 | 30.00 |
| | 40 POUNDS OF TROUBLE | | |
| ❑ Mercury MG-20784 [M] | | 1963 | 30.00 |
| ❑ Mercury SR-60784 [S] | | 1963 | 40.00 |
| | THE FOUR HORSEMEN OF THE APOCALYPSE | | |
| ❑ MGM E-3993 [M] | | 1962 | 20.00 |
| ❑ MGM SE-3993 [S] | | 1962 | 25.00 |
| | FOUR IN THE MORNING | | |
| ❑ Roulette OS 805 [M] | | 1966 | 40.00 |
| ❑ Roulette OSS 805 [S] | | 1966 | 50.00 |
| | THE FOX | | |
| ❑ Warner Bros. W 1738 [M] | | 1968 | 40.00 |
| ❑ Warner Bros. WS 1738 [S] | | 1968 | 25.00 |
| | THE FOX AND THE HOUND | | |
| ❑ Disneyland 3106 [PD] | | 1981 | 30.00 |
| *—"Disney Picture Disc" series* | | | |
| ❑ Disneyland ST-3823 | | 1981 | 20.00 |
| *—Non-picture disc version* | | | |
| | FOXY BROWN | | |
| ❑ Motown M7-811 | | 1974 | 20.00 |
| | FRANCIS OF ASSISI | | |
| ❑ 20th Fox FOX-3053 [M] | | 1961 | 200.00 |
| ❑ 20th Fox SFX-3053 [S] | | 1961 | 250.00 |
| | THE FRENCH LINE | | |
| ❑ Mercury MG-25182 [10] | | 1954 | 80.00 |
| | FRIENDLY PERSUASION | | |
| ❑ RKO Unique LP-110 [M] | | 1956 | 75.00 |
| | FRITZ THE CAT | | |
| ❑ Fantasy F-9406 | | 1972 | 30.00 |
| | FROM RUSSIA WITH LOVE | | |
| ❑ United Artists UAL-4114 [M] | | 1964 | 20.00 |
| ❑ United Artists UAS-5114 [S] | | 1964 | 25.00 |
| | THE FUGITIVE KIND | | |
| ❑ United Artists UAL-4065 [M] | | 1959 | 50.00 |
| ❑ United Artists UAS-5065 [S] | | 1959 | 70.00 |
| | FUNERAL IN BERLIN | | |
| ❑ RCA Victor LOC-1136 [M] | | 1966 | 30.00 |

| Number | Title (A Side/B Side) | Yr | NM |
|---|---|---|---|
| ❑ RCA Victor LSO-1136 [S] | | 1966 | 50.00 |
| | FUNNY GIRL | | |
| ❑ Columbia Masterworks BOS 3220 | | 1968 | 12.00 |
| *—Gray "360 Sound" label; record is removed from inside the gatefold; liner notes on a tan background* | | | |
| ❑ Columbia Masterworks BOS 3220 | | 1968 | 15.00 |
| *—Gray "360 Sound" label; record is removed from inside the gatefold; liner notes on a black background* | | | |
| ❑ Columbia Masterworks BOS 3220 | | 1970 | 10.00 |
| *—Olive label with "Columbia" encircling the edge* | | | |
| ❑ Columbia Masterworks SQ 30992 [Q] | | 1971 | 40.00 |
| | A FUNNY THING HAPPENED ON THE WAY TO THE FORUM | | |
| ❑ United Artists UA-LA284-G | | 1974 | 10.00 |
| *—Reissue of 5144* | | | |
| ❑ United Artists UAL-4144 [M] | | 1966 | 12.00 |
| ❑ United Artists UAS-5144 [S] | | 1966 | 15.00 |
| | GAILY, GAILY | | |
| ❑ United Artists UAS 5202 | | 1969 | 25.00 |
| | THE GAME IS OVER | | |
| ❑ Atco 33-205 [M] | | 1967 | 20.00 |
| ❑ Atco SD 33-205 [S] | | 1967 | 25.00 |
| | THE GAMES | | |
| ❑ Viking LPS-105 | | 1970 | 200.00 |
| | GAY PURR-EE | | |
| ❑ Warner Bros. B 1479 [M] | | 1963 | 20.00 |
| ❑ Warner Bros. BS 1479 [S] | | 1963 | 30.00 |
| | GEISHA BOY | | |
| ❑ Jubilee JGS-1096 [S] | | 1959 | 80.00 |
| ❑ Jubilee JLP-1096 [M] | | 1958 | 50.00 |
| | THE GENE KRUPA STORY | | |
| ❑ Verve MGVS-6105 [S] | | 1959 | 100.00 |
| *—Original issue* | | | |
| ❑ Verve MGV-15010 [M] | | 1959 | 50.00 |
| ❑ Verve V-15010 [M] | | 1961 | 20.00 |
| ❑ Verve V6-15010 [S] | | 1963 | 80.00 |
| *—Early reissue* | | | |
| | GENGHIS KHAN | | |
| ❑ Liberty LRP-3412 [M] | | 1965 | 40.00 |
| ❑ Liberty LST-7412 [S] | | 1965 | 60.00 |
| | THE GENTLE RAIN | | |
| ❑ Mercury MG-21016 [M] | | 1966 | 20.00 |
| ❑ Mercury SR-61016 [S] | | 1966 | 25.00 |
| | GENTLEMEN MARRY BRUNETTES | | |
| ❑ Coral CRL 57013 [M] | | 1955 | 70.00 |
| | GENTLEMEN PREFER BLONDES | | |
| ❑ MGM E-208 [M] | | 1953 | 120.00 |

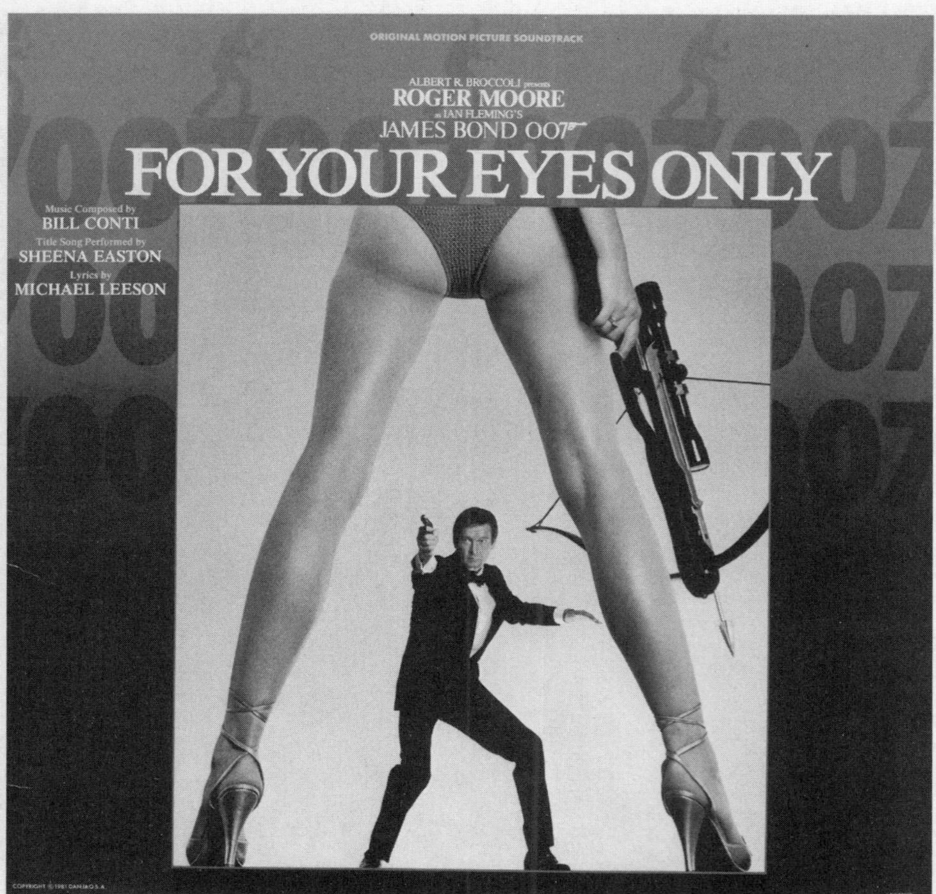


Soundtrack, *For Your Eyes Only,* Liberty LOO-51109, 1981, $30.

| Number | Title (A Side/B Side) | Yr | NM |
|---|---|---|---|
| | GET YOURSELF A COLLEGE GIRL | | |
| ❑ MGM E-4273 [M] | | 1965 | 20.00 |
| ❑ MGM SE-4273 [S] | | 1965 | 40.00 |
| | GETTING STRAIGHT | | |
| ❑ Colgems COSO-5010 | | 1970 | 30.00 |
| | GIANT | | |
| ❑ Capitol DW 773 [R] | | 196? | 12.00 |
| ❑ Capitol W 773 [M] | | 1956 | 40.00 |
| *—Turquoise or gray label* | | | |
| ❑ Capitol W 773 [M] | | 1959 | 25.00 |
| *—Black colorband label, logo at left* | | | |
| ❑ Capitol W 773 [M] | | 1962 | 15.00 |
| *—Black colorband label, logo at top* | | | |
| | GIGI | | |
| ❑ MCA 39045 | | 1986 | 8.00 |
| *—Reissue* | | | |
| ❑ MGM E-3641 [M] | | 1958 | 20.00 |
| *—Yellow label* | | | |
| ❑ MGM E-3641 [M] | | 1960 | 12.00 |
| *—Black label* | | | |
| ❑ MGM SE-3641 [S] | | 1959 | 25.00 |
| *—Yellow label* | | | |
| ❑ MGM SE-3641 [S] | | 1960 | 15.00 |
| *—Black label* | | | |
| ❑ MGM SE-3641 [S] | | 1968 | 12.00 |
| *—Blue and gold label* | | | |
| ❑ MGM SW 90523 [S] | | 1965 | 15.00 |
| ❑ MGM W 90523 [M] | | 1965 | 12.00 |
| *—Capitol Record Club edition* | | | |
| | GIGOT | | |
| ❑ Capitol SW 1754 [S] | | 1962 | 40.00 |
| ❑ Capitol W 1754 [M] | | 1962 | 30.00 |
| | THE GIRL IN THE BIKINI | | |
| ❑ Poplar PLP 33-1002 [M] | | 1952 | 400.00 |
| | THE GIRL MOST LIKELY | | |
| ❑ Capitol W 930 [M] | | 1957 | 60.00 |
| | GIRL ON A MOTORCYCLE | | |
| ❑ Tetragrammaton T-5000 | | 1969 | 30.00 |
| | THE GLENN MILLER STORY | | |
| ❑ Decca DL 5519 [10] | | 1954 | 40.00 |
| ❑ Decca DL 8226 [M] | | 1956 | 30.00 |
| ❑ Decca DL 9123 [M] | | 196? | 20.00 |
| *—Reissue of 8226* | | | |
| ❑ Decca DL 79123 [R] | | 196? | 15.00 |
| ❑ MCA 1624 | | 198? | 15.00 |
| *—This reissue is a bit more desirable because it was issued in true stereo* | | | |
| ❑ MCA 2036 | | 1973 | 10.00 |

| Number | Title (A Side/B Side) | Yr | NM |
|---|---|---|---|
| | GLORY | | |
| ❑ Virgin 91329 | | 1989 | 30.00 |
| ❑ Virgin 91329 | | 1998 | 20.00 |
| *—Classic Records edition; audiophile reissue; cover is noticeably less sharp than the originals* | | | |
| | THE GLORY STOMPERS | | |
| ❑ Sidewalk DT 5910 [R] | | 1968 | 50.00 |
| | GO, GO, GO WORLD | | |
| ❑ Musicor MM-2059 [M] | | 1965 | 40.00 |
| ❑ Musicor MS-3059 [S] | | 1965 | 60.00 |
| | GO, JOHNNY, GO! | | |
| ❑ (no label) (no number) [DJ] | | 1959 | 1000. |
| *—Only exists as a promo* | | | |
| | GOD'S LITTLE ACRE | | |
| ❑ United Artists UAL-4002 [M] | | 1958 | 150.00 |
| | THE GODFATHER | | |
| ❑ Paramount PAS-1003 | | 1972 | 20.00 |
| *—Original cover with triple gatefold* | | | |
| | THE GODFATHER PART II | | |
| ❑ ABC ABDP-856 | | 1975 | 20.00 |
| | THE GODFATHER PART III | | |
| ❑ Columbia C 47078 | | 1990 | 20.00 |
| | GOLD | | |
| ❑ ABC ABCD-855 | | 1975 | 30.00 |
| | GOLDEN BOY | | |
| ❑ Colpix CP-478 [M] | | 1964 | 20.00 |
| ❑ Colpix SCP-478 [S] | | 1964 | 25.00 |
| | THE GOLDEN BREED | | |
| ❑ Capitol ST 2886 | | 1967 | 30.00 |
| | THE GOLDEN SCREW | | |
| ❑ Atco 33-208 [M] | | 1967 | 30.00 |
| ❑ Atco SD 33-208 [S] | | 1967 | 40.00 |
| | GOLDFINGER | | |
| ❑ United Artists UAL-4117 [M] | | 1964 | 15.00 |
| ❑ United Artists UAS-5117 [S] | | 1964 | 20.00 |
| | GOLIATH AND THE BARBARIANS | | |
| ❑ American Int'l. 1001-M [M] | | 1960 | 40.00 |
| ❑ American Int'l. 1001-S [S] | | 1960 | 70.00 |
| | GONE WITH THE WAVE | | |
| ❑ Colpix CP-492 [M] | | 1965 | 40.00 |
| ❑ Colpix SCP-492 [S] | | 1965 | 60.00 |
| | GONE WITH THE WIND | | |
| ❑ MGM 1E-10 [M] | | 1967 | 20.00 |
| *—Gatefold edition with 32-page booklet* | | | |
| ❑ MGM S1E-10 [S] | | 1967 | 20.00 |
| *—Gatefold edition with 32-page booklet* | | | |

| Number | Title (A Side/B Side) | Yr | NM |
|---|---|---|---|
| | GOOD NEWS | | |
| ❑ MGM E-504 [10] | | 1950 | 50.00 |
| | GOODBYE AGAIN | | |
| ❑ United Artists UAL-4091 [M] | | 1961 | 30.00 |
| ❑ United Artists UAS-5091 [S] | | 1961 | 40.00 |
| | GOODBYE, CHARLIE | | |
| ❑ 20th Century Fox TFM-3165 [M] | | 1964 | 25.00 |
| ❑ 20th Century Fox TFS-4165 [S] | | 1964 | 30.00 |
| | GOODBYE, MR. CHIPS | | |
| ❑ MCA 39006 | | 1986 | 8.00 |
| *—Reissue* | | | |
| ❑ MGM 1SE-19 | | 1969 | 20.00 |
| | GORDON'S WAR | | |
| ❑ Buddah BDS-5137 | | 1973 | 40.00 |
| | THE GOSPEL ACCORDING TO ST. MATTHEW | | |
| ❑ Mainstream S-4000 [S] | | 1966 | 100.00 |
| ❑ Mainstream 54000 [M] | | 1966 | 25.00 |
| | GOTHIC | | |
| ❑ Virgin 90607 | | 1987 | 20.00 |
| | GOYA | | |
| ❑ Decca DL 8236 [M] | | 1959 | 150.00 |
| | THE GRADUATE | | |
| ❑ CBS Masterworks JS 3180 [S] | | 198? | 8.00 |
| *—"CBS Masterworks" replaces "Columbia" along outer edge of label* | | | |
| ❑ Columbia Masterworks JS 3180 [S] | | 197? | 8.00 |
| *—Reissue with new prefix* | | | |
| ❑ Columbia Masterworks OS 3180 [S] | | 1968 | 12.00 |
| *—Original stereo edition: Gray label, "360 Sound Stereo" in white* | | | |
| ❑ Columbia Masterworks OS 3180 [S] | | 1971 | 10.00 |
| *—Olive label, "Columbia" along outer edge* | | | |
| ❑ Columbia Masterworks OL 6780 [M] | | 1968 | 50.00 |
| *—"Mono" on label* | | | |
| | GRAND PRIX | | |
| ❑ MGM 1E-8 [M] | | 1967 | 20.00 |
| ❑ MGM 1SE-8 [S] | | 1967 | 25.00 |
| | THE GREAT ESCAPE | | |
| ❑ United Artists UAL-4107 [M] | | 1963 | 25.00 |
| ❑ United Artists UAS-5107 [S] | | 1963 | 30.00 |
| | THE GREAT GATSBY | | |
| ❑ Paramount 2-3001 [(2)] | | 1974 | 20.00 |
| | THE GREATEST SHOW ON EARTH | | |
| ❑ RCA Victor LPM-3018 [10] | | 1952 | 200.00 |
| | THE GREATEST STORY EVER TOLD | | |
| ❑ United Artists UAL-4120 [M] | | 1965 | 25.00 |
| ❑ United Artists UAS-5120 [S] | | 1965 | 30.00 |
| | GROUNDS FOR MARRIAGE | | |
| ❑ MGM E-536 [M] | | 1950 | 80.00 |
| | GUESS WHO'S COMING TO DINNER | | |
| ❑ Colgems COM-108 [M] | | 1968 | 30.00 |
| ❑ Colgems COS-108 [S] | | 1968 | 30.00 |
| | GULLIVER'S TRAVELS BEYOND THE MOON | | |
| ❑ Mainstream S-4001 [S] | | 1965 | 40.00 |
| ❑ Mainstream 54001 [M] | | 1965 | 30.00 |
| | GUNS FOR SAN SEBASTIAN | | |
| ❑ MGM SE-4565 | | 1968 | 60.00 |
| | THE GUNS OF NAVARONE | | |
| ❑ Columbia CL 1655 [M] | | 1961 | 20.00 |
| ❑ Columbia CS 8455 [S] | | 1961 | 50.00 |
| | GURU | | |
| ❑ RCA Victor LSO-1158 | | 1969 | 20.00 |
| | GYPSY | | |
| ❑ Warner Bros. B 1480 [M] | | 1962 | 20.00 |
| ❑ Warner Bros. BS 1480 [S] | | 1962 | 30.00 |
| | GYPSY GIRL | | |
| ❑ Mainstream S-6090 [S] | | 1966 | 40.00 |
| ❑ Mainstream 56090 [M] | | 1966 | 30.00 |
| | HALLELUJAH THE HILLS | | |
| ❑ Fontana MGF-27524 [M] | | 1964 | 25.00 |
| ❑ Fontana SRF-67524 [S] | | 1964 | 30.00 |
| | THE HALLELUJAH TRAIL | | |
| ❑ United Artists UAL-4127 [M] | | 1965 | 20.00 |
| ❑ United Artists UAS-5127 [S] | | 1965 | 25.00 |
| | HAMMERHEAD | | |
| ❑ Colgems COS-110 | | 1968 | 40.00 |
| | HAMMERSMITH IS OUT | | |
| ❑ Capitol SW-861 | | 1972 | 30.00 |
| | HANG 'EM HIGH | | |
| ❑ United Artists UAS-5179 | | 1968 | 25.00 |
| | THE HAPPENING | | |
| ❑ Colgems COMO-5006 [M] | | 1967 | 30.00 |
| ❑ Colgems COSO-5006 [S] | | 1967 | 50.00 |
| | THE HAPPIEST MILLIONAIRE | | |
| ❑ Buena Vista BV-5001 [M] | | 1967 | 15.00 |
| ❑ Buena Vista STER-5001 [S] | | 1967 | 20.00 |
| | THE HARD RIDE | | |
| ❑ Paramount PAS-6005 | | 1971 | 30.00 |
| | HARPER | | |
| ❑ Mainstream S-6078 [S] | | 1966 | 25.00 |
| ❑ Mainstream 56078 [M] | | 1966 | 20.00 |
| | THE HARRAD EXPERIMENT | | |
| ❑ Capitol ST-11182 | | 1973 | 25.00 |
| | HARRAD SUMMER | | |
| ❑ Capitol ST-11338 | | 1974 | 25.00 |
| | HAWAII | | |
| ❑ United Artists UAL-4143 [M] | | 1966 | 20.00 |
| ❑ United Artists UAS-5143 [S] | | 1966 | 25.00 |

| Number | Title (A Side/B Side) | Yr | NM |
|---|---|---|---|
| ❑ United Artists SW-90935 [S] | | 1966 | 30.00 |
| *—Capitol Record Club issue* | | | |
| THE HEART IS A LONELY HUNTER | | | |
| ❑ Warner Bros. WS 1759 | | 1968 | 30.00 |
| HEART OF DIXIE | | | |
| ❑ A&M SP-3930 | | 1989 | 20.00 |
| HEAVY METAL | | | |
| ❑ Full Moon/Asylum DP-90004 [(2)] | | 1981 | 20.00 |
| *—Contains two LPs of pop/rock music* | | | |
| HEAVY METAL, THE SCORE | | | |
| ❑ Full Moon/Asylum 5E-547 | | 1981 | 50.00 |
| *—Contains Elmer Bernstein's instrumental music* | | | |
| HEAVY TRAFFIC | | | |
| ❑ Fantasy F-9436 | | 1973 | 25.00 |
| HEIDI'S SONG | | | |
| ❑ K-Tel NU 5310 | | 1982 | 20.00 |
| THE HELEN MORGAN STORY | | | |
| ❑ RCA Victor LOC-1030 [M] | | 1957 | 60.00 |
| HELL TO ETERNITY | | | |
| ❑ Warwick W 2030 [M] | | 1960 | 120.00 |
| ❑ Warwick WST 2030 [S] | | 1960 | 200.00 |
| HELL UP IN HARLEM | | | |
| ❑ Motown M 802V1 | | 1974 | 30.00 |
| HELL'S ANGELS '69 | | | |
| ❑ Capitol SKAO-303 | | 1969 | 25.00 |
| HELL'S ANGELS ON WHEELS | | | |
| ❑ Smash MGS-27094 [M] | | 1967 | 25.00 |
| ❑ Smash SRS-67094 [S] | | 1967 | 30.00 |
| HELL'S BELLS | | | |
| ❑ Sidewalk ST 5919 | | 1969 | 30.00 |
| HELLCATS | | | |
| ❑ Tower ST 5124 | | 1968 | 30.00 |
| HELLO-GOODBYE | | | |
| ❑ 20th Century Fox S-4210 | | 1970 | 40.00 |
| HEMINGWAY'S ADVENTURES OF A YOUNG MAN | | | |
| ❑ RCA Victor LOC-1074 [M] | | 1962 | 40.00 |
| ❑ RCA Victor LSO-1074 [S] | | 1962 | 70.00 |
| HERCULES | | | |
| ❑ Varese Sarabande STV-81187 | | 1983 | 20.00 |
| THE HERO | | | |
| ❑ Capitol SW-11098 | | 1972 | 20.00 |
| A HERO AIN'T NOTHIN' BUT A SANDWICH | | | |
| ❑ Columbia PS 35046 | | 1978 | 20.00 |
| HEROES OF TELEMARK | | | |
| ❑ Mainstream S-6064 [S] | | 1965 | 30.00 |
| ❑ Mainstream 56064 [M] | | 1965 | 20.00 |
| HEY THERE, IT'S YOGI BEAR! | | | |
| ❑ Colpix CP-472 [M] | | 1964 | 50.00 |
| ❑ Colpix SCP-472 [S] | | 1964 | 80.00 |
| HEY, LET'S TWIST | | | |
| ❑ Roulette R-25168 [M] | | 1962 | 25.00 |
| ❑ Roulette SR-25168 [S] | | 1962 | 30.00 |
| HIGH SOCIETY | | | |
| ❑ Capitol SW 750 [S] | | 1959 | 30.00 |
| *—Black colorband label, logo at left* | | | |
| ❑ Capitol SW 750 [S] | | 1962 | 20.00 |
| *—Black colorband label, logo at top* | | | |
| ❑ Capitol W 750 [M] | | 1956 | 30.00 |
| *—Gray label original* | | | |
| ❑ Capitol W 750 [M] | | 1959 | 20.00 |
| *—Black colorband label, logo at left* | | | |
| ❑ Capitol W 750 [M] | | 1962 | 15.00 |
| *—Black colorband label, logo at top* | | | |
| THE HOBBIT | | | |
| ❑ Buena Vista 103 [(2)] | | 1977 | 30.00 |
| ❑ Buena Vista 103A [(2)] | | 1977 | 40.00 |
| *—Special edition sold at Sears stores, with four decals and poster* | | | |
| ❑ Disneyland ST-3819 | | 1978 | 30.00 |
| HOLIDAY INN | | | |
| ❑ Decca DL 4256 | | 1962 | 25.00 |
| ❑ MCA 25205 | | 1987 | 8.00 |
| *—Reissue of Decca LP* | | | |
| HOMER AND EDDIE | | | |
| ❑ Apache D1-71654 | | 1989 | 25.00 |
| HOOSIERS | | | |
| ❑ Polydor 831475-1 | | 1987 | 30.00 |
| HOOTENANNY HOOT | | | |
| ❑ MGM E-4172 [M] | | 1963 | 20.00 |
| ❑ MGM SE-4172 [S] | | 1963 | 25.00 |
| THE HORSE SOLDIERS | | | |
| ❑ United Artists UAL-4035 [M] | | 1959 | 60.00 |
| ❑ United Artists UAS-5035 [S] | | 1959 | 150.00 |
| THE HORSEMEN | | | |
| ❑ Sunflower SNF-5007 | | 1971 | 40.00 |
| THE HOT ROCK | | | |
| ❑ Prophesy SD 8055 | | 1972 | 20.00 |
| HOT ROD RUMBLE | | | |
| ❑ Liberty LRP-3048 [M] | | 1957 | 150.00 |
| HOTEL PARADISO | | | |
| ❑ MGM E-4419 [M] | | 1966 | 20.00 |
| ❑ MGM SE-4419 [S] | | 1966 | 25.00 |
| THE HOUR OF THE GUN | | | |
| ❑ United Artists UAL-4166 [M] | | 1967 | 40.00 |
| ❑ United Artists UAS-5166 [S] | | 1967 | 70.00 |
| A HOUSE IS NOT A HOME | | | |
| ❑ Ava A-50 [M] | | 1964 | 25.00 |
| ❑ Ava AS-50 [S] | | 1964 | 30.00 |

Soundtrack, *The Great Escape,* United Artists UAS 5107, 1963, stereo, $30.

| Number | Title (A Side/B Side) | Yr | NM |
|---|---|---|---|
| HOUSEBOAT | | | |
| ❑ Columbia CL 1222 [M] | | 1958 | 50.00 |
| HOW SWEET IT IS | | | |
| ❑ RCA Victor LSP-4037 | | 1968 | 20.00 |
| HOW THE WEST WAS WON | | | |
| ❑ MCA 39043 | | 1986 | 8.00 |
| *—Reissue* | | | |
| ❑ MGM 1E-5 [M] | | 1963 | 15.00 |
| ❑ MGM 1SE-5 [S] | | 1963 | 20.00 |
| HOW TO MURDER YOUR WIFE | | | |
| ❑ United Artists UAL-4119 [M] | | 1965 | 15.00 |
| ❑ United Artists UAS-5119 [S] | | 1965 | 20.00 |
| HOW TO SAVE A MARRIAGE AND RUIN YOUR LIFE | | | |
| ❑ Columbia Masterworks OS 3140 | | 1968 | 20.00 |
| HOW TO STEAL A MILLION | | | |
| ❑ 20th Century Fox TFM-3183 [M] | | 1966 | 40.00 |
| ❑ 20th Century Fox TFS-4183 [S] | | 1966 | 50.00 |
| HOW TO STUFF A WILD BIKINI | | | |
| ❑ Wand 671 [M] | | 1965 | 30.00 |
| ❑ Wand S-671 [S] | | 1965 | 40.00 |
| HOW TO SUCCEED IN BUSINESS WITHOUT REALLY TRYING | | | |
| ❑ United Artists UAL-4151 [M] | | 1967 | 20.00 |
| ❑ United Artists UAS-5151 [S] | | 1967 | 25.00 |
| HOWARD THE DUCK | | | |
| ❑ MCA 6173 | | 1986 | 20.00 |
| HUGO THE HIPPO | | | |
| ❑ United Artists UA-LA637-G | | 1976 | 20.00 |
| I LOVE MELVIN | | | |
| ❑ MGM E-190 [10] | | 1953 | 50.00 |
| I NEVER SANG FOR MY FATHER | | | |
| ❑ Bell 1204 | | 1970 | 40.00 |
| I WANT TO LIVE | | | |
| ❑ United Artists UXL 1 [(2)M] | | 1958 | 60.00 |
| *—Combines 4005 and 4006 into one package* | | | |
| ❑ United Artists UXS 51 [(2)S] | | 1958 | 80.00 |
| *—Combines 5005 and 5006 into one package* | | | |
| ❑ United Artists UAL-4005 [M] | | 1958 | 25.00 |
| *—Orchestral music by Johnny Mandel* | | | |
| ❑ United Artists UAS-4005 [S] | | 1958 | 40.00 |
| *—Orchestral music by Johnny Mandel* | | | |
| ❑ United Artists UAL-4006 [M] | | 1958 | 30.00 |
| *—Jazz music by Gerry Mulligan, Shelly Manne and Art Farmer* | | | |
| ❑ United Artists UAS-4006 [S] | | 1958 | 40.00 |
| *—Jazz music by Gerry Mulligan, Shelly Mann and Art Farmer* | | | |
| I'LL NEVER FORGET WHAT'S 'IS NAME | | | |
| ❑ Decca DL 9163 [M] | | 1967 | 25.00 |

| Number | Title (A Side/B Side) | Yr | NM |
|---|---|---|---|
| ❑ Decca DL 79163 [S] | | 1967 | 30.00 |
| ICE STATION ZEBRA | | | |
| ❑ MGM S1E-14 ST | | 1968 | 40.00 |
| ICEMAN | | | |
| ❑ Southern Cross SCRS-1006 | | 1983 | 20.00 |
| IF HE HOLLERS, LET HIM GO | | | |
| ❑ Tower ST 5152 | | 1968 | 40.00 |
| IMITATION OF LIFE | | | |
| ❑ Decca DL 8879 [M] | | 1959 | 50.00 |
| ❑ Decca DL 78879 [S] | | 1959 | 80.00 |
| IN A SHALLOW GRAVE | | | |
| ❑ Varese Sarabande STV-81359 | | 1988 | 40.00 |
| IN HARM'S WAY | | | |
| ❑ RCA Victor LOC-1100 [M] | | 1965 | 40.00 |
| ❑ RCA Victor LSO-1100 [S] | | 1965 | 80.00 |
| IN LIKE FLINT | | | |
| ❑ 20th Century Fox 4193 [M] | | 1967 | 40.00 |
| ❑ 20th Century Fox S-4193 [S] | | 1967 | 80.00 |
| IN SEARCH OF THE CASTAWAYS | | | |
| ❑ Disneyland ST-3916 [M] | | 1962 | 70.00 |
| IN THE GOOD OLD SUMMERTIME | | | |
| ❑ MGM E-169 [10] | | 1949 | 100.00 |
| IN THE HEAT OF THE NIGHT | | | |
| ❑ United Artists UAL-4160 [M] | | 1967 | 15.00 |
| ❑ United Artists UAS-5160 [S] | | 1967 | 20.00 |
| INCHON | | | |
| ❑ Regency RI-8502 | | 1982 | 30.00 |
| INDIANA JONES AND THE TEMPLE OF DOOM | | | |
| ❑ Polydor 821592-1 | | 1984 | 20.00 |
| THE INDISCRETION OF AN AMERICAN WIFE | | | |
| ❑ Columbia CL 6277 [10] | | 1954 | 80.00 |
| THE INN OF THE SIXTH HAPPINESS | | | |
| ❑ 20th Century Fox FOX-3011 [M] | | 1958 | 50.00 |
| ❑ 20th Century Fox SFX-3011 [S] | | 1958 | 70.00 |
| INSIDE DAISY CLOVER | | | |
| ❑ Warner Bros. W 1616 [M] | | 1965 | 20.00 |
| ❑ Warner Bros. WS 1616 [S] | | 1965 | 30.00 |
| INSPECTOR CLOUSEAU | | | |
| ❑ MCA 25107 | | 1986 | 8.00 |
| *—Reissue* | | | |
| ❑ United Artists UAS-5186 | | 1968 | 30.00 |
| INTERLUDE | | | |
| ❑ Colgems COSO-5007 | | 1968 | 40.00 |
| THE INTERNS | | | |
| ❑ Colpix CP 427 [M] | | 1962 | 30.00 |

SOUNDTRACKS

Soundtrack, *Light Fantastic,* 20th Century Fox FXG 5016, 1963, mono, $20.

| Number | Title (A Side/B Side) | Yr | NM |
|---|---|---|---|
| ❑ Colpix SCP 427 [S] | | 1962 | 40.00 |
| INVITATION TO THE DANCE | | | |
| ❑ MGM E-3207 [M] | | 1956 | 50.00 |
| THE IPCRESS FILE | | | |
| ❑ Decca DL 9124 [M] | | 1965 | 30.00 |
| ❑ Decca DL 79124 [S] | | 1965 | 40.00 |
| IRMA LA DOUCE | | | |
| ❑ United Artists UAL-4109 [M] | | 1963 | 20.00 |
| ❑ United Artists UAS-5109 [S] | | 1963 | 25.00 |
| IS PARIS BURNING? | | | |
| ❑ Columbia Masterworks OS 3030 [S] | | 1966 | 40.00 |
| ❑ Columbia Masterworks OL 6630 [M] | | 1966 | 30.00 |
| THE ISLAND | | | |
| ❑ Varese Sarabande VC-81147 | | 1979 | 20.00 |
| THE ISLAND AT THE TOP OF THE WORLD | | | |
| ❑ Disneyland ST-3814 | | 1974 | 25.00 |
| ISLAND IN THE SKY | | | |
| ❑ Decca DL 7029 [10] | | 1953 | 300.00 |
| IT STARTED IN NAPLES | | | |
| ❑ Dot DLP-3324 [M] | | 1960 | 60.00 |
| ❑ Dot DLP-25324 [S] | | 1960 | 100.00 |
| ❑ Varese Sarabande STV-81122 | | 1982 | 15.00 |
| *—Reissue of Dot 25324* | | | |
| IT'S A MAD, MAD, MAD, MAD WORLD | | | |
| ❑ MCA 39076 | | 198? | 8.00 |
| *—Reissue of United Artists 276* | | | |
| ❑ United Artists UA-LA276-G | | 1974 | 10.00 |
| *—Reissue of 5110* | | | |
| ❑ United Artists UAL-4110 [M] | | 1963 | 20.00 |
| ❑ United Artists UAS-5110 [S] | | 1963 | 25.00 |
| IT'S ALWAYS FAIR WEATHER | | | |
| ❑ MCA 25018 | | 1986 | 10.00 |
| *—Reissue* | | | |
| ❑ MGM E-3241 [M] | | 1955 | 50.00 |
| THE ITALIAN JOB | | | |
| ❑ Paramount PAS-5007 | | 1969 | 40.00 |
| JACK THE RIPPER | | | |
| ❑ RCA Victor LPM-2199 [M] | | 1960 | 30.00 |
| ❑ RCA Victor LSP-2199 [S] | | 1960 | 50.00 |
| JAMBOREE! | | | |
| ❑ Warner Bros. (no #) [M] | | 1957 | 1200. |
| *—Album has been counterfeited. Originals have front cover slicks and back cover notes printed on the cardboard, and the records have "Jam 1" and "Jam 2" stamped (not etched) in the dead wax.* | | | |

| Number | Title (A Side/B Side) | Yr | NM |
|---|---|---|---|
| THE JAMES DEAN STORY | | | |
| ❑ Capitol W 881 [M] | | 1957 | 60.00 |
| ❑ Kimberly 2016 [M] | | 1960 | 40.00 |
| ❑ Kimberly 11016 [S] | | 1960 | 50.00 |
| *—Reissue of World Pacific 2005* | | | |
| ❑ World Pacific P-2005 [M] | | 1958 | 100.00 |
| JAWS | | | |
| ❑ MCA 1660 | | 198? | 8.00 |
| *—Reissue of 2087* | | | |
| ❑ MCA 2087 | | 1975 | 20.00 |
| JEAN DE FLORETTE | | | |
| ❑ TVT 3004 | | 1986 | 20.00 |
| JEREMIAH JOHNSON | | | |
| ❑ Warner Bros. BS 2902 | | 1972 | 20.00 |
| *—Green label* | | | |
| JESSICA | | | |
| ❑ United Artists UAL-4096 [M] | | 1962 | 20.00 |
| ❑ United Artists UAS-5096 [S] | | 1962 | 25.00 |
| THE JOE LOUIS STORY | | | |
| ❑ MGM E-221 [10] | | 1953 | 80.00 |
| JOHN PAUL JONES | | | |
| ❑ Varese Sarabande STV- 81146 | | 1981 | 15.00 |
| *—Reissue of Warner Bros. WS 1293* | | | |
| ❑ Warner Bros. W 1293 [M] | | 1959 | 60.00 |
| ❑ Warner Bros. WS 1293 [S] | | 1959 | 120.00 |
| JOHNNY COOL | | | |
| ❑ United Artists UAL-4111 [M] | | 1963 | 20.00 |
| ❑ United Artists UAS-5111 [S] | | 1963 | 25.00 |
| JOHNNY TREMAIN | | | |
| ❑ Disneyland WDL-4014 [M] | | 1957 | 50.00 |
| JUD | | | |
| ❑ Ampex A-50101 | | 1971 | 20.00 |
| JUDGMENT AT NUREMBERG | | | |
| ❑ MCA 39055 | | 198? | 10.00 |
| *—Reissue of United Artists 5095* | | | |
| ❑ United Artists UAL-4095 [M] | | 1961 | 20.00 |
| ❑ United Artists UAS-5095 [S] | | 1961 | 50.00 |
| JUDITH | | | |
| ❑ RCA Victor LOC-1119 [M] | | 1966 | 15.00 |
| ❑ RCA Victor LSO-1119 [S] | | 1966 | 30.00 |
| JULIET OF THE SPIRITS | | | |
| ❑ Mainstream S-6062 [S] | | 1965 | 60.00 |
| ❑ Mainstream 56062 [M] | | 1965 | 25.00 |
| JULIUS CAESAR | | | |
| ❑ MGM E-3033 [M] | | 1953 | 40.00 |

| Number | Title (A Side/B Side) | Yr | NM |
|---|---|---|---|
| JUMBO (BILLY ROSE'S) | | | |
| ❑ Columbia Masterworks OS 2260 [S] | | 1962 | 30.00 |
| ❑ Columbia Masterworks OL 5860 [M] | | 1962 | 20.00 |
| THE JUNGLE BOOK | | | |
| ❑ Buena Vista BV-4041 [M] | | 1967 | 15.00 |
| ❑ Buena Vista STER-4041 [S] | | 1967 | 25.00 |
| ❑ Disneyland 3105 [PD] | | 1981 | 30.00 |
| *—"Disney Picture Disc" series* | | | |
| JURASSIC PARK | | | |
| ❑ MCA/BMG (no #) [PD] | | 1993 | 1500. |
| *—Custom-made picture disc; promo only* | | | |
| JUSTINE | | | |
| ❑ Monument SLP-18123 | | 1969 | 30.00 |
| KALEIDOSCOPE | | | |
| ❑ Warner Bros. W 1663 [M] | | 1966 | 20.00 |
| ❑ Warner Bros. WS 1663 [S] | | 1966 | 25.00 |
| KELLY'S HEROES | | | |
| ❑ MGM S1E-23 | | 1970 | 30.00 |
| THE KEY | | | |
| ❑ Columbia CL 1185 [M] | | 1958 | 80.00 |
| KILLERS THREE | | | |
| ❑ Tower ST-5141 | | 1968 | 20.00 |
| THE KING AND I | | | |
| ❑ Capitol SW 740 [S] | | 1959 | 20.00 |
| *—Black colorband label, logo at left* | | | |
| ❑ Capitol SW 740 [S] | | 1962 | 15.00 |
| *—Black colorband label, logo at top* | | | |
| ❑ Capitol SW 740 [S] | | 1969 | 12.00 |
| *—Lime green label* | | | |
| ❑ Capitol SW 740 [S] | | 1973 | 10.00 |
| *—Orange label* | | | |
| ❑ Capitol SW 740 [S] | | 1978 | 8.00 |
| *—Purple label* | | | |
| ❑ Capitol W 740 [M] | | 1956 | 25.00 |
| *—Gray label* | | | |
| ❑ Capitol W 740 [M] | | 1959 | 15.00 |
| *—Black colorband label, logo at left* | | | |
| ❑ Capitol W 740 [M] | | 1962 | 12.00 |
| *—Black colorband label, logo at top* | | | |
| KING KONG | | | |
| ❑ Reprise MS 2260 | | 1976 | 20.00 |
| KING KONG LIVES | | | |
| ❑ MCA 6203 | | 1987 | 25.00 |
| KING OF KINGS | | | |
| ❑ MCA 39056 | | 198? | 8.00 |
| *—Reissue of MGM S1E-2* | | | |
| ❑ MGM 1E-2 [M] | | 1961 | 15.00 |
| *—Standard cover* | | | |
| ❑ MGM 1E-2 [M] | | 1961 | 30.00 |
| *—Boxed version with hardbound book and four 8x10 photos* | | | |
| ❑ MGM S1E-2 [S] | | 1961 | 20.00 |
| *—Standard cover* | | | |
| ❑ MGM S1E-2 [S] | | 1961 | 40.00 |
| *—Boxed version with hardbound book and four 8x10 photos* | | | |
| KING RAT | | | |
| ❑ Mainstream S-6061 [S] | | 1965 | 50.00 |
| ❑ Mainstream 56061 [M] | | 1965 | 30.00 |
| KING SOLOMON'S MINES | | | |
| ❑ Restless 72106 | | 1985 | 20.00 |
| KINGS GO FORTH | | | |
| ❑ Capitol W 1063 [M] | | 1958 | 150.00 |
| KISMET | | | |
| ❑ MCA 1424 | | 198? | 8.00 |
| *—Reissue of MGM 3281* | | | |
| ❑ Metro M-526 [M] | | 1965 | 12.00 |
| *—Reissue of MGM E-3281 with one fewer track* | | | |
| ❑ Metro MS-526 [R] | | 1955 | 10.00 |
| *—Rechanneled reissue of MGM E-3281 with one fewer track* | | | |
| ❑ MGM E-3281 [M] | | 1955 | 20.00 |
| *—Yellow label* | | | |
| ❑ MGM E-3281 [M] | | 1960 | 15.00 |
| *—Black label* | | | |
| KISS ME, KATE | | | |
| ❑ MCA 25003 | | 1986 | 10.00 |
| *—Reissue of MGM 3077* | | | |
| ❑ Metro M-525 [M] | | 1965 | 12.00 |
| *—Reissue of MGM 3077, but with only 10 songs* | | | |
| ❑ Metro MS-525 [R] | | 1965 | 10.00 |
| *—Rechanneled reissue of MGM 3077, but with only 10 songs* | | | |
| ❑ MGM E-3077 [M] | | 1953 | 20.00 |
| *—Yellow label* | | | |
| ❑ MGM E-3077 [M] | | 1959 | 15.00 |
| *—Black label* | | | |
| KRULL | | | |
| ❑ Southern Cross SCRS-1004 | | 1983 | 20.00 |
| KWAMINA | | | |
| ❑ Mercury MG-20654 [M] | | 1961 | 25.00 |
| ❑ Mercury SR-60654 [S] | | 1961 | 30.00 |
| LADY AND THE TRAMP | | | |
| ❑ Decca DL 5557 [10] | | 1955 | 60.00 |
| ❑ Decca DL 8462 [M] | | 1957 | 70.00 |
| ❑ Disneyland 3103 [PD] | | 1981 | 30.00 |
| *—"Disney Picture Disc" edition* | | | |
| LADYHAWKE | | | |
| ❑ Atlantic 81248 | | 1985 | 20.00 |
| THE LANDLORD | | | |
| ❑ United Artists UAS-5209 | | 1970 | 20.00 |
| THE LAST AMERICAN VIRGIN | | | |
| ❑ Columbia JS 38279 | | 1982 | 40.00 |



**Except when noted otherwise, VG = 25% of NM, and VG+ = 50% of NM. (Example: VG = $2.00, VG+ = $4.00 and NM = $8.00.)**

Number Title (A Side/B Side) Yr NM

THE LAST EMBRACE
❑ Varese Sarabande STV-81166 1983 20.00
THE LAST OF THE SECRET AGENTS
❑ Dot DLP-3714 [M] 1966 20.00
❑ Dot DLP-25714 [S] 1966 25.00
THE LAST RUN
❑ MCA 25116 1986 8.00
*—Reissue of MGM 1SE-30*
❑ MGM 1SE-30 1971 25.00
THE LAST STARFIGHTER
❑ Southern Cross SCRS-1007 1984 25.00
LAST SUMMER
❑ Warner Bros. WS 1791 1969 20.00
THE LAST VALLEY
❑ ABC-Dunhill DSX-50102 1971 40.00
LAWRENCE OF ARABIA
❑ Arista ABM-4009 1975 10.00
*—Reissue of Bell 1205*
❑ Bell 1205 1971 10.00
*—Reissue of Colgems COSO-5004*
❑ Colgems COMO-5004 [M] 1967 12.00
*—Reissue of Colpix CP-514*
❑ Colgems COSO-5004 [S] 1967 15.00
*—Reissue of Colpix SCP-514*
❑ Colpix CP-514 [M] 1962 20.00
❑ Colpix SCP-514 [S] 1962 30.00
LENNY
❑ United Artists UA-LA359-H [(2)] 1974 20.00
THE LEOPARD
❑ 20th Century Fox FXG-5015 [M] 1963 30.00
❑ 20th Century Fox SXG-5015 [S] 1963 40.00
❑ Varese Sarabande STV-81190 1982 15.00
*—Reissue of 20th Century Fox SXG-5015*
LES LIAISONS DANGEREUSES
❑ Charlie Parker PLP-813 [M] 1962 25.00
❑ Charlie Parker PLP-813S [S] 1962 30.00
❑ Epic LA 16022 [M] 1961 40.00
❑ Epic BA 17022 [S] 1961 30.00
❑ Fontana MGF-27539 [M] 1965 20.00
LET THE GOOD TIMES ROLL
❑ Bell 9002 [(2)] 1973 25.00
LET'S MAKE LOVE
❑ Columbia CL 1527 [M] 1960 30.00
❑ Columbia CS 8327 [S] 1960 50.00
LEVIATHAN
❑ Varese Sarabande VS-5226 1989 20.00
LI'L ABNER
❑ Columbia Masterworks OS 2021 [S] 1959 40.00
*—Credits within photo*
❑ Columbia Masterworks OS 2021 [S] 196? 25.00
*—Credits in red strip at bottom of photo*
❑ Columbia Masterworks OL 5460 [M] 1959 30.00
*—Credits within photo*
❑ Columbia Masterworks OL 5460 [M] 196? 20.00
*—Credits in red strip at bottom of photo*
THE LIFE AND TIMES OF JUDGE ROY BEAN
❑ Columbia Masterworks S 31948 1972 25.00
LIFEFORCE
❑ Varese Sarabande STV-81249 1985 25.00
LIGHT FANTASTIC
❑ 20th Century Fox FXG-5016 [M] 1963 20.00
❑ 20th Century Fox SXG-5016 [S] 1963 25.00
LILIES OF THE FIELD
❑ Epic LN 24094 [M] 1964 20.00
❑ Epic BN 26094 [S] 1964 30.00
THE LION
❑ London M-76001 [M] 1962 400.00
THE LION IN WINTER
❑ Columbia Masterworks OS 3250 1969 20.00
LIONHEART
❑ Varese Sarabande STV-81304 1987 20.00
LIONHEART (MORE MUSIC FROM THE FILM)
❑ Varese Sarabande STV-81311 1987 50.00
LITTLE BIG MAN
❑ Columbia Masterworks S 30545 1970 20.00
LITTLE SHOP OF HORRORS
❑ Geffen GHS-24125 1986 20.00
LIVE AND LET DIE
❑ Liberty LMAS-100 1981 12.00
*—Gray label; reissue of United Artists 100 with gatefold cover*
❑ Liberty LT-50100 1982 12.00
*—Gray label; reissue of Liberty 100 with standard cover*
❑ United Artists LMAS-100 1979 10.00
*—"Sunrise" label with this number on label (jacket still has UA-LA100-G)*
❑ United Artists UA-LA100-G 1973 10.00
*—Tan label; cover corner is clipped*
❑ United Artists UA-LA100-G 1973 20.00
*—Tan label; cover corner is not clipped off*
❑ United Artists UA-LA100-G 1977 10.00
*—"Sunrise" label with this number on both jacket and label*
❑ United Artists SWAO-95120 1973 30.00
*—Longines (formerly Capitol) Record Club edition*
LIVE FOR LIFE
❑ United Artists UAL-4165 [M] 1967 20.00
❑ United Artists UAS-5165 [S] 1967 20.00
THE LIVELY SET
❑ Decca DL 9119 [M] 1964 30.00
❑ Decca DL 79119 [S] 1964 40.00

Number Title (A Side/B Side) Yr NM

LOGAN'S RUN
❑ MGM MG-1-5302 1976 30.00
LOLITA
❑ MCA 39067 198? 8.00
*—Reissue of MGM SE-4050*
❑ MGM E-4050 [M] 1962 20.00
❑ MGM SE-4050 [S] 1962 30.00
THE LOLLIPOP COVER
❑ Mainstream S-6067 [S] 1966 30.00
❑ Mainstream 56067 [M] 1966 20.00
THE LONG HOT SUMMER
❑ Roulette R-25026 [M] 1958 75.00
LONG JOHN SILVER
❑ RCA Victor LPM-3279 [10] 1954 300.00
THE LONG SHIPS
❑ Colpix CP-517 [M] 1964 50.00
❑ Colpix SCP-517 [S] 1964 60.00
THE LONGEST DAY
❑ 20th Century Fox FXG-5007 [M] 1962 20.00
❑ 20th Century Fox SXG-5007 [S] 1962 25.00
LORD JIM
❑ Colpix CP-521 [M] 1965 25.00
❑ Colpix SCP-521 [S] 1965 40.00
LORD LOVE A DUCK
❑ United Artists UAL-4137 [M] 1966 20.00
❑ United Artists UAS-5137 [S] 1966 25.00
THE LORD OF THE RINGS
❑ Fantasy LOR-1 [(2)] 1978 20.00
❑ Fantasy LOR-PD2 [(2)] 1978 30.00
*—Two picture discs*
THE LORDS OF FLATBUSH
❑ ABC ABCD-828 1974 30.00
A LOSS OF INNOCENCE
❑ Colpix CP-508 [M] 1961 40.00
THE LOST CONTINENT
❑ MGM E-3635 [M] 1957 200.00
LOVE IN 4 DIMENSIONS
❑ Request RLP-8090 [M] 1966 25.00
❑ Request SRLP-8090 [S] 1966 30.00
LOVE LIFE
❑ Heritage 600 [M] 195? 60.00
LOVERS AND OTHER STRANGERS
❑ ABC ABCS-OC-15 1970 20.00
❑ ABC SW-93479 1971 25.00
*—Capitol Record Club edition*
M*A*S*H
❑ Columbia Masterworks OS 3520 1970 20.00
*—Original copies do not have the theme song done by Ahmad Jamal*
❑ Columbia Masterworks S 32753 1973 10.00
*—Reissue with the movie's theme performed by Ahmad Jamal*
MACARTHUR
❑ MCA 2287 1977 20.00
THE MAD ADVENTURES OF RABBI JACOB
❑ London PS 652 1974 10.00
*—Cover has cut-out markings (usually a hole punch or a cut-off corner)*
❑ London PS 652 1974 20.00
*—Cover is intact with no cut-out markings*
MADAME BOVARY
❑ MGM E-3507 [M] 195? 150.00
THE MAGIC CHRISTIAN
❑ Commonwealth United CU-6004 1970 25.00
MAGNIFICENT OBSESSION
❑ Decca DL 8078 [M] 1954 60.00
*—Black label, gold print*
❑ Decca DL 8078 [M] 1955 50.00
*—Black label, silver print*
❑ Decca DL 8078 [M] 196? 30.00
*—Black label with color bars*
❑ Varese Sarabande STV-81118 1981 12.00
*—Reissue of Decca 8078*
MAJOR DUNDEE
❑ Columbia Masterworks OS 2780 [S] 1965 30.00
❑ Columbia Masterworks OL 6380 [M] 1965 20.00
MALAMONDO
❑ Epic LN 24126 [M] 1964 30.00
❑ Epic BN 26126 [S] 1964 40.00
MAME
❑ Warner Bros. PRO 580 [DJ] 1973 50.00
*—Promo-only gatefold edition with Lucille Ball in Christmas hat on the cover*
❑ Warner Bros. W 2773 1974 15.00
A MAN AND A WOMAN (UN HOMME ET UNE FEMME)
❑ United Artists UAL-4147 [M] 1966 15.00
❑ United Artists UAS-5147 [S] 1966 20.00
❑ United Artists SW-91032 [S] 1967 25.00
*—Capitol Record Club edition*
A MAN CALLED ADAM
❑ Reprise R 6180 [M] 1966 15.00
❑ Reprise RS 6180 [S] 1966 20.00
A MAN CALLED DAGGER
❑ MGM E-4516 [M] 1967 15.00
❑ MGM SE-4516 [S] 1967 20.00
A MAN COULD GET KILLED
❑ Decca DL 4750 [M] 1966 15.00
❑ Decca DL 74750 [S] 1966 20.00

Number Title (A Side/B Side) Yr NM

A MAN FOR ALL SEASONS
❑ RCA Victor VDM-116 [(2)M] 1966 30.00
MAN FROM SHAFT
❑ MGM SE-4836 1972 30.00
MAN IN THE MIDDLE
❑ 20th Century Fox TFM-3128 [M] 1965 30.00
❑ 20th Century Fox TFS-4128 [S] 1965 50.00
THE MAN OF A THOUSAND FACES
❑ Decca DL 8623 [M] 1957 50.00
*—Black label, silver print, or pink label, black print promos*
❑ Decca DL 8623 [M] 196? 30.00
*—Black label with color bars*
❑ Varese Sarabande STV- 81121 1981 12.00
*—Reissue of Decca 8623*
MAN OF LA MANCHA
❑ United Artists UAS-9906 1972 10.00
*—Cover has cut-out marking such as a cut-off corner*
❑ United Artists UAS-9906 1972 20.00
*—Cover is intact with no cut corners*
THE MAN WHO WOULD BE KING
❑ Capitol SW-11474 1975 20.00
THE MAN WITH THE GOLDEN ARM
❑ Decca DL 8257 [M] 1956 40.00
❑ Decca DL 78257 [R] 196? 20.00
❑ MCA 1528 198? 8.00
*—Reissue of MCA 2043*
❑ MCA 2043 [R] 1973 10.00
*—Reissue of Decca 78257; black label with rainbow*
THE MAN WITH THE GOLDEN GUN
❑ United Artists UA-LA358-G 1974 20.00
MANIAC
❑ Varese Sarabande STV-81143 1980 20.00
MARACAIBO
❑ Decca DL 8756 [M] 1958 40.00
*—Black label, silver print, or pink label, black print promos*
❑ Decca DL 8756 [M] 196? 20.00
*—Black label with color bars*
MARCO THE MAGNIFICENT
❑ Columbia Masterworks OS 2870 [S] 1966 40.00
❑ Columbia Masterworks OL 6470 [M] 1966 25.00
MARIE WARD
❑ Varese Sarabande STV-81268 1985 50.00
MARJORIE MORNINGSTAR
❑ RCA Victor LOC-1044 [M] 1958 40.00
*—"RE" next to label number*
❑ RCA Victor LOC-1044 [M] 1958 60.00
*—"An Original Soundtrack Recording" on spine*
MARRY ME, MARRY ME
❑ RCA Victor LSO-1160 1969 20.00
MARY POPPINS
❑ Buena Vista BV-4026 [M] 1964 12.00
*—Originals have gatefold covers*
❑ Buena Vista STER-4026 [S] 1964 15.00
*—Originals have gatefold covers*
❑ Buena Vista STER-5005 [S] 1973 10.00
*—Reissue with new number and no gatefold*
❑ RCA Victor COP-111 [M] 1964 15.00
*—With gatefold; RCA Record Club edition*
❑ RCA Victor CSO-111 [S] 1964 20.00
*—With gatefold; RCA Record Club edition*
MARY, QUEEN OF SCOTS
❑ Decca DL 79186 1972 30.00
THE MASK
❑ Chaos 6455 [DJ] 1994 20.00
*—Generic cover; no other U.S. vinyl*
MASKED AND ANONYMOUS
❑ Columbia CSK 90618-1 [(2)] 2006 30.00
*—Classic Records issue on 140-gram vinyl; CD issued in 2003*
MASTER OF THE WORLD
❑ Varese Sarabande VC-81070 1978 15.00
*—Reissue of Vee Jay 4000*
❑ Vee Jay LP-4000 [M] 1961 25.00
❑ Vee Jay SR-4000 [S] 1961 40.00
MASTERS OF THE UNIVERSE
❑ Varese Sarabande STV-81333 1987 20.00
MCLINTOCK!
❑ United Artists UAL-4112 [M] 1963 60.00
❑ United Artists UAS-5112 [S] 1963 80.00
ME AND THE COLONEL
❑ RCA Victor LOC-1046 [M] 1958 50.00
MEDITERRANEAN HOLIDAY
❑ London M-76003 [M] 1964 50.00
❑ London MS-82003 [S] 1964 80.00
MEET ME IN ST. LOUIS
❑ AEI 3101 1978 12.00
*—Reissue of Decca LP*
❑ Decca DL 8498 [M] 1957 30.00
*—LP reissue of 78 rpm album from 1944; B-side of LP is "The Harvey Girls."*
MEMORIES AUX BRUXELLES
❑ Carlton LP-112 [M] 1959 25.00
❑ Carlton LP-12112 [S] 1959 40.00
MEN IN WAR
❑ Imperial LP-9032 W [M] 1957 150.00
MENACE II SOCIETY
❑ Jive 41522 [(2)DJ] 1993 20.00
*—Vinyl is promo only*
MERRY ANDREW
❑ Capitol T 1016 [M] 1958 50.00

| Number | Title (A Side/B Side) | Yr | NM |
|---|---|---|---|
| MICKEY ONE | | | |
| ❑ MGM E-4312 [M] | | 1965 | 20.00 |
| ❑ MGM SE-4312 [S] | | 1965 | 25.00 |
| MIDNIGHT COWBOY | | | |
| ❑ United Artists UAS-5198 | | 1969 | 20.00 |
| MIDNIGHT EXPRESS | | | |
| ❑ Casablanca NBLP-7114 | | 1978 | 20.00 |
| A MILANESE STORY | | | |
| ❑ Atlantic 1388 [M] | | 1962 | 20.00 |
| ❑ Atlantic SD 1388 [S] | | 1962 | 25.00 |
| THE MINX | | | |
| ❑ Amsterdam 12007 | | 1970 | 120.00 |
| THE MISFITS | | | |
| ❑ United Artists UA-LA273-G [S] | | 1974 | 12.00 |
| *—Reissue of 5087* | | | |
| ❑ United Artists UAL-4087 [M] | | 1961 | 50.00 |
| ❑ United Artists UAS-5087 [S] | | 1961 | 100.00 |
| MISS SADIE THOMPSON | | | |
| ❑ Mercury MG-20123 [M] | | 1956 | 150.00 |
| ❑ Mercury MG-25181 [10] | | 1954 | 75.00 |
| THE MISSOURI BREAKS | | | |
| ❑ MCA 25113 | | 1986 | 10.00 |
| *—Reissue of United Artists UA-LA623-G* | | | |
| ❑ United Artists UA-LA623-G | | 1976 | 30.00 |
| MOBY DICK | | | |
| ❑ RCA Victor LPM-1247 [M] | | 1956 | 120.00 |
| MODERN TIMES | | | |
| ❑ United Artists UAL-4049 [M] | | 1959 | 25.00 |
| ❑ United Artists UAS-5049 [R] | | 196? | 20.00 |
| MODESTY BLAISE | | | |
| ❑ 20th Century Fox TFM-3182 [M] | | 1966 | 30.00 |
| ❑ 20th Century Fox TFS-4182 [S] | | 1966 | 50.00 |
| MOHAMMAD, MESSENGER OF GOD | | | |
| ❑ Namara 79001 | | 1977 | 25.00 |
| MONDO CANE | | | |
| ❑ United Artists UAS-5105 [S] | | 1963 | 20.00 |
| MONDO CANE NO. 2 | | | |
| ❑ 20th Century Fox TFM-3147 [M] | | 1964 | 30.00 |
| ❑ 20th Century Fox TFS-4147 [S] | | 1964 | 40.00 |
| MOON OVER PARADOR | | | |
| ❑ MCA 6249 | | 1988 | 25.00 |
| THE MOON SPINNERS | | | |
| ❑ Buena Vista BV-3323 [M] | | 1964 | 40.00 |
| MORE AMERICAN GRAFFITI | | | |
| ❑ MCA MCA2-11006 [(2)] | | 1979 | 20.00 |
| *—Tan labels* | | | |
| MR. BUDWING | | | |
| ❑ Verve V6-8638 [S] | | 1965 | 25.00 |
| MR. MAGOO: 1001 ARABIAN NIGHTS | | | |
| ❑ Colpix CP-410 [M] | | 1959 | 50.00 |
| ❑ Colpix SCP-410 [S] | | 1959 | 150.00 |
| MURDER INC. | | | |
| ❑ Canadian American CALP-1003 [M] | | 1960 | 100.00 |
| MUSCLE BEACH PARTY PLUS MERLIN JONES AND THE SCRAMBLED EGGHEAD | | | |
| ❑ Buena Vista BV-3314 [M] | | 1964 | 60.00 |
| ❑ Buena Vista STER-3314 [S] | | 1964 | 120.00 |
| THE MUSIC MAN | | | |
| ❑ Warner Bros. BS 1459 [S] | | 1962 | 20.00 |
| *—Gold label originals* | | | |
| ❑ Warner Bros. BS 1459 [S] | | 1968 | 12.00 |
| *—Green label with "W7" box logo at top* | | | |
| ❑ Warner Bros. BS 1459 [S] | | 1970 | 10.00 |
| *—Green label with "WB" shield logo at top* | | | |
| ❑ Warner Bros. BS 1459 [S] | | 1973 | 8.00 |
| *—"Burbank" palm trees label or later white label* | | | |
| MUTINY ON THE BOUNTY | | | |
| ❑ MCA 25007 | | 1986 | 8.00 |
| *—Reissue of MGM 1SE-4* | | | |
| ❑ MGM 1E-4 [M] | | 196? | 12.00 |
| *—Standard cover* | | | |
| ❑ MGM 1E-4 [M] | | 1962 | 30.00 |
| *—Boxed set with book and painting* | | | |
| ❑ MGM S1E-4 [S] | | 196? | 15.00 |
| *—Standard cover* | | | |
| ❑ MGM S1E-4 [S] | | 1962 | 40.00 |
| *—Boxed set with book and painting* | | | |
| MY GEISHA | | | |
| ❑ RCA Victor LOC-1070 [M] | | 1962 | 50.00 |
| ❑ RCA Victor LSO-1070 [S] | | 1962 | 100.00 |
| MY SIDE OF THE MOUNTAIN | | | |
| ❑ Capitol ST-245 | | 1969 | 25.00 |
| MY WILD IRISH ROSE | | | |
| ❑ RCA Victor LPM-3036 [10] | | 1952 | 40.00 |
| NAKED ANGELS | | | |
| ❑ Straight STS-1056 | | 1969 | 25.00 |
| THE NAKED MAJA | | | |
| ❑ United Artists UAL-4031 [M] | | 1959 | 30.00 |
| ❑ United Artists UAS-5031 [S] | | 1959 | 40.00 |
| NANCY GOES TO RIO | | | |
| ❑ MGM E-508 [10] | | 1950 | 60.00 |
| NASHVILLE | | | |
| ❑ ABC ABCD-893 | | 1975 | 20.00 |
| NATIVE SON | | | |
| ❑ MCA 6198 | | 1986 | 20.00 |
| NAVAJO JOE | | | |
| ❑ United Artists UA-LA292-G | | 1974 | 25.00 |

| Number | Title (A Side/B Side) | Yr | NM |
|---|---|---|---|
| NED KELLY | | | |
| ❑ United Artists UA-LA300-G | | 1974 | 12.00 |
| *—Reissue of 5213* | | | |
| ❑ United Artists UAS-5213 | | 1970 | 25.00 |
| NEVADA SMITH | | | |
| ❑ Dot DLP-3718 [M] | | 1966 | 25.00 |
| ❑ Dot DLP-25718 [S] | | 1966 | 40.00 |
| THE NEVER ENDING STORY | | | |
| ❑ EMI America ST-17139 | | 1984 | 20.00 |
| NEVER ON SUNDAY | | | |
| ❑ United Artists UAL-4070 [M] | | 1960 | 15.00 |
| ❑ United Artists UAS-5070 [S] | | 1960 | 20.00 |
| ❑ United Artists SW-90834 [S] | | 196? | 20.00 |
| *—Capitol Record Club edition* | | | |
| THE NEW INTERNS | | | |
| ❑ Colpix CP-473 [M] | | 1964 | 30.00 |
| ❑ Colpix SCP-473 [S] | | 1964 | 40.00 |
| A NEW KIND OF LOVE | | | |
| ❑ Mercury SR-60859 [S] | | 1963 | 20.00 |
| THE NEW MESSIAH | | | |
| ❑ Columbia KC 31713 | | 1972 | 20.00 |
| NICHOLAS AND ALEXANDRA | | | |
| ❑ Bell 1103 | | 1971 | 25.00 |
| NIGHT OF THE GENERALS | | | |
| ❑ Colgems COMO-5002 [M] | | 1967 | 40.00 |
| ❑ Colgems COSO-5002 [S] | | 1967 | 70.00 |
| THE NIGHT OF THE HUNTER | | | |
| ❑ RCA Victor LPM-1136 [M] | | 1955 | 250.00 |
| NINE HOURS TO RAMA | | | |
| ❑ London M-76002 [M] | | 1963 | 300.00 |
| NO WAY TO TREAT A LADY | | | |
| ❑ Dot DLP-25846 | | 1968 | 25.00 |
| NOT WITH MY WIFE, YOU DON'T | | | |
| ❑ Warner Bros. W 1668 [M] | | 1966 | 15.00 |
| ❑ Warner Bros. WS 1668 [S] | | 1966 | 20.00 |
| NOTHING BUT THE BEST | | | |
| ❑ Colpix CP-477 [M] | | 1964 | 20.00 |
| ❑ Colpix SCP-477 [S] | | 1964 | 25.00 |
| A NUN'S STORY | | | |
| ❑ Warner Bros. B 1306 [M] | | 1959 | 60.00 |
| ❑ Warner Bros. BS 1306 [S] | | 1959 | 100.00 |
| O BROTHER, WHERE ART THOU? | | | |
| ❑ Lost Highway 088 170069-1 [(2)] | | 2003 | 20.00 |
| OBSESSION | | | |
| ❑ London Phase 4 SPC-21160 | | 1976 | 25.00 |
| OCTOPUSSY | | | |
| ❑ A&M SP-4967 | | 1983 | 20.00 |
| THE ODD COUPLE | | | |
| ❑ Dot DLP-25862 | | 1968 | 20.00 |
| ODDS AGAINST TOMORROW | | | |
| ❑ United Artists UAL-4061 [M] | | 1959 | 30.00 |
| ❑ United Artists UAS-5061 [S] | | 1959 | 50.00 |
| OF LOVE AND DESIRE | | | |
| ❑ 20th Century Fox FXG-5014 [M] | | 1963 | 25.00 |
| ❑ 20th Century Fox SXG-5014 [S] | | 1963 | 30.00 |
| OH DAD, POOR DAD, MAMMA'S HUNG YOU IN THE CLOSET AND I'M FEELIN' SO SAD | | | |
| ❑ RCA Victor LPM-3750 [M] | | 1967 | 20.00 |
| ❑ RCA Victor LSP-3750 [S] | | 1967 | 25.00 |
| OH, ROSALINDA! | | | |
| ❑ Mercury MG-20145 [M] | | 1957 | 50.00 |
| OIL TOWN, U.S.A. | | | |
| ❑ RCA Victor LFM-2000 [10] | | 1953 | 60.00 |
| OKLAHOMA! | | | |
| ❑ Capitol SWAO 595 [S] | | 1959 | 20.00 |
| *—Black colorband label, logo at left* | | | |
| ❑ Capitol SWAO 595 [S] | | 1962 | 15.00 |
| *—Black colorband label, logo at top* | | | |
| ❑ Capitol SWAO 595 [S] | | 1969 | 12.00 |
| *—Lime green label* | | | |
| ❑ Capitol SWAO 595 [S] | | 1973 | 10.00 |
| *—Orange label* | | | |
| ❑ Capitol WAO 595 [M] | | 1955 | 25.00 |
| *—Purple or dark red label* | | | |
| ❑ Capitol WAO 595 [M] | | 1956 | 20.00 |
| *—Gray label* | | | |
| ❑ Capitol WAO 595 [M] | | 1959 | 15.00 |
| *—Black colorband label, logo at left* | | | |
| ❑ Capitol WAO 595 [M] | | 1962 | 12.00 |
| *—Black colorband label, logo at top* | | | |
| OLD BOYFRIENDS | | | |
| ❑ Columbia Masterworks JS 36072 | | 1979 | 50.00 |
| THE OLD MAN AND THE SEA | | | |
| ❑ Columbia CL 1183 [M] | | 1958 | 30.00 |
| ❑ Columbia CS 8013 [S] | | 1958 | 60.00 |
| OLD YELLER | | | |
| ❑ Disneyland 1024 [M] | | 1974 | 25.00 |
| *—Reissue with no prefix* | | | |
| ❑ Disneyland WDL-1024 [M] | | 1960 | 40.00 |
| *—Second edition* | | | |
| ❑ Disneyland WDL-3024 [M] | | 1957 | 50.00 |
| *—First edition* | | | |
| OLIVER AND COMPANY | | | |
| ❑ Disney 64101 | | 1988 | 25.00 |
| ON HER MAJESTY'S SECRET SERVICE | | | |
| ❑ United Artists UA-LA299-G | | 1974 | 12.00 |
| *—Reissue of 5204* | | | |
| ❑ United Artists UAS-5204 | | 1969 | 20.00 |

| Number | Title (A Side/B Side) | Yr | NM |
|---|---|---|---|
| ON THE BEACH | | | |
| ❑ Roulette R-25098 [M] | | 1959 | 80.00 |
| ❑ Roulette SR-25098 [S] | | 1959 | 150.00 |
| ONCE UPON A TIME IN THE WEST | | | |
| ❑ RCA Victor LSP-4736 | | 1969 | 30.00 |
| THE ONE AND ONLY, GENUINE, ORIGINAL FAMILY BAND | | | |
| ❑ Buena Vista BV-5002 [M] | | 1968 | 15.00 |
| ❑ Buena Vista STER-5002 [S] | | 1968 | 20.00 |
| ONE FLEW OVER THE CUCKOO'S NEST | | | |
| ❑ Fantasy MPF-4531 | | 198? | 10.00 |
| *—Budget-line reissue of 9500* | | | |
| ❑ Fantasy F-9500 | | 1975 | 20.00 |
| 101 DALMATIONS | | | |
| ❑ Disneyland DQ-1308 [M] | | 1966 | 20.00 |
| ❑ Disneyland ST-1908 [M] | | 1960 | 25.00 |
| ❑ Disneyland ST-3931 [M] | | 1965 | 40.00 |
| ❑ Disneyland ST-4903 [M] | | 1963 | 150.00 |
| *—Gatefold cover with pop-up scene in center* | | | |
| THE ONE-EYED JACKS | | | |
| ❑ Liberty LOM-16001 [M] | | 1961 | 30.00 |
| ❑ Liberty LOS-17001 [S] | | 1961 | 50.00 |
| THE OPTIMISTS | | | |
| ❑ Paramount PAS-1015 | | 1973 | 30.00 |
| ORCHESTRA WIVES | | | |
| ❑ RCA Victor LPT-3065 [10] | | 1954 | 60.00 |
| THE OSCAR | | | |
| ❑ Columbia Masterworks OS 2950 [S] | | 1966 | 25.00 |
| ❑ Columbia Masterworks OL 6550 [M] | | 1966 | 20.00 |
| OTLEY | | | |
| ❑ Colgems COS-112 | | 1969 | 30.00 |
| OUR MAN FLINT | | | |
| ❑ 20th Century Fox TFM-3179 [M] | | 1966 | 40.00 |
| ❑ 20th Century Fox TFS-4179 [S] | | 1966 | 60.00 |
| OUT OF AFRICA | | | |
| ❑ MCA 6158 | | 1985 | 20.00 |
| ❑ MCA 11327 | | 1995 | 20.00 |
| *—Limited edition on "Heavy Vinyl"* | | | |
| OUT OF SIGHT | | | |
| ❑ Decca DL 4751 [M] | | 1966 | 20.00 |
| ❑ Decca DL 74751 [S] | | 1966 | 25.00 |
| OUTLAND | | | |
| ❑ Warner Bros. HS 3551 | | 1981 | 25.00 |
| THE OUTLAW JOSEY WALES | | | |
| ❑ Warner Bros. BS 2956 | | 1976 | 25.00 |
| THE OUTLAW RIDERS | | | |
| ❑ MGM 1SE-26 | | 1970 | 20.00 |
| PAGAN LOVE SONG | | | |
| ❑ MGM E-534 [M] | | 1950 | 40.00 |
| PAINT YOUR WAGON | | | |
| ❑ MCA 37099 | | 198? | 8.00 |
| *—Reissue of Paramount 1001* | | | |
| ❑ Paramount PMS-1001 | | 1969 | 20.00 |
| *—With booklet* | | | |
| THE PAJAMA GAME | | | |
| ❑ Columbia Masterworks OL 5210 [M] | | 1957 | 30.00 |
| *—Gray and black label with six "eye" logos* | | | |
| PAL JOEY | | | |
| ❑ Capitol DW 912 [R] | | 196? | 10.00 |
| *—Black colorband label* | | | |
| ❑ Capitol SM-912 [R] | | 1977 | 8.00 |
| *—Reissue with new prefix* | | | |
| ❑ Capitol W 912 [M] | | 1957 | 20.00 |
| *—Gray label* | | | |
| ❑ Capitol W 912 [M] | | 1959 | 15.00 |
| *—Black colorband label, logo at left* | | | |
| ❑ Capitol W 912 [M] | | 1962 | 12.00 |
| *—Black colorband label, logo on top* | | | |
| PANIC BUTTON | | | |
| ❑ Musicor MM-2026 [M] | | 1964 | 80.00 |
| ❑ Musicor MS-3026 [S] | | 1964 | 120.00 |
| PAPER MOON | | | |
| ❑ Paramount PAS-1012 | | 1973 | 20.00 |
| PAPER TIGER | | | |
| ❑ Capitol SW-11475 | | 1975 | 20.00 |
| PAPILLON | | | |
| ❑ Capitol ST-11260 | | 1973 | 20.00 |
| THE PARENT TRAP! | | | |
| ❑ Buena Vista BV-3309 [M] | | 1961 | 40.00 |
| ❑ Buena Vista STER-3309 [S] | | 1961 | 60.00 |
| *—B-side of the above two: Camerata Conducts Themes from Great Motion Pictures* | | | |
| PARIS BLUES | | | |
| ❑ United Artists UAL-4092 [M] | | 1961 | 25.00 |
| ❑ United Artists UAS-5092 [S] | | 1961 | 30.00 |
| PARIS HOLIDAY | | | |
| ❑ United Artists UAL-4001 [M] | | 1958 | 50.00 |
| PARIS WHEN IT SIZZLES | | | |
| ❑ Reprise R 6113 [M] | | 1964 | 25.00 |
| ❑ Reprise RS 6113 [S] | | 1964 | 40.00 |
| PARRISH | | | |
| ❑ Warner Bros. W 1413 [M] | | 1961 | 30.00 |
| ❑ Warner Bros. WS 1413 [S] | | 1961 | 80.00 |
| *—B-side of the above two: Popular Piano Concertos by George Greeley* | | | |
| A PATCH OF BLUE | | | |
| ❑ Mainstream S-6068 [S] | | 1965 | 25.00 |
| ❑ Mainstream 56068 [M] | | 1965 | 20.00 |



**Except when noted otherwise, VG = 25% of NM, and VG+ = 50% of NM. (Example: VG = $2.00, VG+ = $4.00 and NM = $8.00.)**

| Number | Title (A Side/B Side) | Yr | NM |
|---|---|---|---|
| ❑ Mainstream ST-90805 [S] | | 1965 | 30.00 |
| *—Capitol Record Club edition* | | | |
| PATTON | | | |
| ❑ 20th Century Fox S-4208 | | 1970 | 20.00 |
| PATTY | | | |
| ❑ Stang 1026 | | 1976 | 20.00 |
| PENELOPE | | | |
| ❑ MGM E-4426 [M] | | 1966 | 20.00 |
| ❑ MGM SE-4426 [S] | | 1966 | 30.00 |
| PENTHOUSE | | | |
| ❑ United Artists UAL-4170 [M] | | 1967 | 20.00 |
| ❑ United Artists UAS-5170 [S] | | 1967 | 20.00 |
| THE PEOPLE NEXT DOOR | | | |
| ❑ Avco AV-11002 | | 1970 | 25.00 |
| PEPE | | | |
| ❑ Colpix CP-507 [M] | | 1960 | 20.00 |
| ❑ Colpix SCP-507 [S] | | 1960 | 25.00 |
| PERFORMANCE | | | |
| ❑ Warner Bros. WS 1846 | | 1970 | 1500. |
| *—Original issue; has a completely different cover to the more common 2554* | | | |
| ❑ Warner Bros. BS 2554 | | 1970 | 20.00 |
| *—Second issue* | | | |
| PETE KELLY'S BLUES | | | |
| ❑ Columbia CL 690 [M] | | 1955 | 40.00 |
| ❑ Decca DL 8166 [M] | | 1955 | 50.00 |
| *—Black label, silver print* | | | |
| PETE'S DRAGON | | | |
| ❑ Capitol SW-11704 | | 1977 | 20.00 |
| PETULIA | | | |
| ❑ Warner Bros. WS 1755 | | 1968 | 25.00 |
| PEYTON PLACE | | | |
| ❑ RCA Victor LOC-1042 [M] | | 1958 | 30.00 |
| *—"Long Play" at bottom of label* | | | |
| ❑ RCA Victor LOC-1042 [M] | | 1965 | 25.00 |
| *—"Monaural" at bottom of label* | | | |
| ❑ RCA Victor LSO-1042 [S] | | 1958 | 100.00 |
| *—"Living Stereo" at bottom of label* | | | |
| ❑ RCA Victor LSO-1042 [S] | | 1965 | 60.00 |
| *—"Stereo" at bottom of label* | | | |
| PHAEDRA | | | |
| ❑ United Artists UAL-4102 [M] | | 1962 | 20.00 |
| ❑ United Artists UAS-5102 [S] | | 1962 | 30.00 |
| THE PHILADELPHIA EXPERIMENT | | | |
| ❑ Rhino RNSP-306 | | 1984 | 25.00 |
| PICNIC | | | |
| ❑ Decca DL 8320 [M] | | 1956 | 30.00 |
| *—Black label, silver print* | | | |
| ❑ Decca DL 8320 [M] | | 196? | 15.00 |
| *—Black label with color bars* | | | |
| ❑ Decca DL 78320 [S] | | 1959 | 30.00 |
| *—Maroon or all-black label* | | | |
| ❑ Decca DL 78320 [S] | | 196? | 15.00 |
| *—Black label with color bars* | | | |
| ❑ MCA 1527 | | 198? | 8.00 |
| *—Reissue of 2049* | | | |
| ❑ MCA 2049 | | 1973 | 10.00 |
| *—Reissue of Decca 78320; black label with rainbow* | | | |
| A PIECE OF THE ACTION | | | |
| ❑ Curtom CU 5019 | | 1977 | 20.00 |
| PINOCCHIO | | | |
| ❑ Disneyland DQ-1202 [M] | | 1959 | 30.00 |
| *—Second edition* | | | |
| ❑ Disneyland DQ-1202MO [M] | | 1963 | 20.00 |
| *—Third edition* | | | |
| ❑ Disneyland 3102 [PD] | | 1981 | 30.00 |
| *—"Disney Picture Disc" edition* | | | |
| ❑ Disneyland WDL-4002 [M] | | 1956 | 250.00 |
| *—Original edition* | | | |
| ❑ Disneyland ST-4905 [M] | | 1963 | 150.00 |
| *—Gatefold cover with pop-up center graphics* | | | |
| PIRANHA | | | |
| ❑ Varese Sarabande STV-81126 | | 1979 | 20.00 |
| THE PIRATE | | | |
| ❑ MGM E-21 [10] | | 1951 | 70.00 |
| PLANET OF THE APES | | | |
| ❑ Project 3 PR-5023 SD | | 1968 | 20.00 |
| *—Regular cover* | | | |
| ❑ Project 3 PR-5023 SD | | 1968 | 30.00 |
| *—Gatefold cover* | | | |
| THE PLEASURE SEEKERS | | | |
| ❑ RCA Victor LOC-1101 [M] | | 1964 | 50.00 |
| ❑ RCA Victor LSO-1101 [S] | | 1964 | 100.00 |
| POLLYANNA | | | |
| ❑ Disneyland DQ-1307 [M] | | 1967 | 25.00 |
| ❑ Disneyland ST-1906 [M] | | 1960 | 50.00 |
| POLTERGEIST | | | |
| ❑ MGM MG-1-5408 | | 1982 | 40.00 |
| POLTERGEIST III | | | |
| ❑ Varese Sarabande 704.620 | | 1988 | 80.00 |
| PORGY AND BESS | | | |
| ❑ Columbia Masterworks OS 2016 [S] | | 1959 | 20.00 |
| ❑ Columbia Masterworks OL 5410 [M] | | 1959 | 15.00 |
| THE POWER | | | |
| ❑ Cerberus CST-0211 | | 1984 | 20.00 |
| PRET-A-PORTER | | | |
| ❑ Miramax CAS 6700 [DJ] | | 1994 | 25.00 |
| *—Promo only vinyl* | | | |

Soundtrack, *The Producers,* RCA Victor LSP-4008, 1968, stereo, $30.

| Number | Title (A Side/B Side) | Yr | NM |
|---|---|---|---|
| PRETTY BOY FLOYD | | | |
| ❑ Audio Fidelity AFLP-1936 [M] | | 1960 | 60.00 |
| ❑ Audio Fidelity AFSD-5936 [S] | | 1960 | 80.00 |
| THE PRIDE AND THE PASSION | | | |
| ❑ Capitol W 873 [M] | | 1957 | 60.00 |
| THE PRINCESS BRIDE | | | |
| ❑ Warner Bros. 25610 | | 1987 | 20.00 |
| THE PRISONER OF ZENDA | | | |
| ❑ United Artists UA-LA374-G | | 1974 | 20.00 |
| PRIVATE HELL 36 | | | |
| ❑ Coral CRL 56122 [10] | | 1954 | 100.00 |
| THE PRODUCERS | | | |
| ❑ RCA Victor ANL1-1132 | | 1975 | 10.00 |
| *—Reissue of LSP-4008* | | | |
| ❑ RCA Victor LPM-4008 [M] | | 1968 | 50.00 |
| ❑ RCA Victor LSP-4008 [S] | | 1968 | 30.00 |
| THE PROFESSIONALS | | | |
| ❑ Colgems COMO-5001 [M] | | 1966 | 60.00 |
| ❑ Colgems COSO-5001 [S] | | 1966 | 150.00 |
| A PROMISE AT DAWN | | | |
| ❑ Polydor 24-5502 | | 1970 | 30.00 |
| THE PROPER TIME | | | |
| ❑ Contemporary M-3587 [M] | | 1960 | 30.00 |
| ❑ Contemporary S-7587 [S] | | 1960 | 40.00 |
| PROVIDENCE | | | |
| ❑ DRG SL-9502 | | 1977 | 20.00 |
| PRUDENCE AND THE PILL | | | |
| ❑ 20th Century Fox S-4199 | | 1968 | 20.00 |
| PSYCHO II | | | |
| ❑ MCA 6119 | | 1983 | 20.00 |
| Q THE WINGED SERPENT | | | |
| ❑ Cerberus CST-0206 | | 1983 | 20.00 |
| QUEST FOR FIRE | | | |
| ❑ RCA Victor ABL1-4274 | | 1982 | 20.00 |
| THE QUIET MAN | | | |
| ❑ Decca DL 5411 [10] | | 1952 | 120.00 |
| THE QUILLER MEMORANDUM | | | |
| ❑ Columbia Masterworks OS 3060 [S] | | 1966 | 60.00 |
| ❑ Columbia Masterworks OL 6660 [M] | | 1966 | 30.00 |
| QUO VADIS? | | | |
| ❑ MCA 39075 | | 198? | 8.00 |
| *—Reissue of MGM 3524* | | | |
| ❑ MGM E-103 [10] | | 1951 | 40.00 |
| *—Music soundtrack only* | | | |
| ❑ MGM E-134 [(2)10] | | 1951 | 60.00 |
| *—Box set of two discs; includes dialogue* | | | |

| Number | Title (A Side/B Side) | Yr | NM |
|---|---|---|---|
| ❑ MGM E-3524 [M] | | 1957 | 25.00 |
| *—Yellow label; has both music and dialogue* | | | |
| RAGTIME | | | |
| ❑ Elektra 5E-565 | | 1981 | 20.00 |
| RAIDERS OF THE LOST ARK | | | |
| ❑ Columbia JS 37373 | | 1981 | 12.00 |
| *—Original issue; music only* | | | |
| ❑ Columbia JS 37696 | | 1981 | 12.00 |
| *—Music and dialogue* | | | |
| ❑ DCC Compact Classics LPZ 2-2009 [(2)] | | 1995 | 30.00 |
| *—Audiophile edition; includes music not on other releases of the soundtrack* | | | |
| ❑ Polydor 821583-1 | | 1984 | 10.00 |
| *—Reissue* | | | |
| THE RAILWAY CHILDREN | | | |
| ❑ Capitol SW-871 | | 1972 | 20.00 |
| THE RAINMAKER | | | |
| ❑ RCA Victor LPM-1434 [M] | | 1956 | 100.00 |
| RAINTREE COUNTY | | | |
| ❑ RCA Victor LOC-1038 [M] | | 1958 | 30.00 |
| ❑ RCA Victor LSO-1038 [S] | | 1958 | 50.00 |
| ❑ RCA Victor LOC-6000 [(2)M] | | 1957 | 120.00 |
| RAN | | | |
| ❑ Fantasy FSP-21004 | | 1985 | 20.00 |
| THE RAT RACE | | | |
| ❑ Dot DLP-3306 [M] | | 1960 | 40.00 |
| ❑ Dot DLP-25306 [S] | | 1960 | 50.00 |
| RED DAWN | | | |
| ❑ Intrada RVF-6001 | | 1985 | 40.00 |
| RED GARTERS | | | |
| ❑ Columbia CL 6282 [10] | | 1954 | 50.00 |
| RED HEAT | | | |
| ❑ Virgin Movie Music 90891 | | 1988 | 25.00 |
| THE RED PONY | | | |
| ❑ Columbia Masterworks ML 5983 [M] | | 196? | 25.00 |
| ❑ Columbia Masterworks MS 6583 [R] | | 196? | 25.00 |
| ❑ Varese Sarabande STV-81259 | | 1986 | 25.00 |
| THE RED TENT | | | |
| ❑ Paramount PAS-6019 | | 1971 | 25.00 |
| REDS | | | |
| ❑ Columbia Masterworks BJS 37960 | | 1981 | 20.00 |
| RENT-A-COP | | | |
| ❑ Intrada MAS-7002 | | 1988 | 20.00 |
| THE REPORTER | | | |
| ❑ Columbia CL 2269 [M] | | 1963 | 30.00 |
| ❑ Columbia CS 9069 [S] | | 1963 | 40.00 |

Soundtrack, *Quo Vadis,* MGM E-103, 1951, 10-inch LP, $40.

| Number | Title (A Side/B Side) | Yr | NM |
|---|---|---|---|
| THE RESCUERS | | | |
| ❑ Disneyland ST-3816 | | 1977 | 20.00 |
| RETURN TO PARADISE | | | |
| ❑ Decca DL 5489 [10] | | 1953 | 200.00 |
| THE REVOLUTION | | | |
| ❑ United Artists UA-LA296-G | | 1974 | 12.00 |
| *—Reissue of 5185* | | | |
| ❑ United Artists UAS-5185 | | 1968 | 25.00 |
| RHAPSODY OF STEEL | | | |
| ❑ U.S. Steel JB-502/3 | | 1958 | 100.00 |
| RICH, YOUNG AND PRETTY | | | |
| ❑ MGM E-86 [10] | | 1951 | 40.00 |
| RIDER ON THE RAIN | | | |
| ❑ Capitol ST-584 | | 1970 | 25.00 |
| RIOT ON SUNSET STRIP | | | |
| ❑ Tower DT 5065 [R] | | 1967 | 25.00 |
| ❑ Tower T 5065 [M] | | 1967 | 20.00 |
| ROAD TO HONG KONG | | | |
| ❑ Liberty LOM-16002 [M] | | 1962 | 20.00 |
| ❑ Liberty LOS-17002 [S] | | 1962 | 40.00 |
| THE ROBE | | | |
| ❑ Decca DL 9012 [M] | | 1953 | 30.00 |
| *—Maroon label* | | | |
| ❑ Decca DL 79012 [R] | | 196? | 12.00 |
| ❑ MCA 1529 | | 198? | 8.00 |
| *—Reissue of MCA 2052* | | | |
| ❑ MCA 2052 | | 1973 | 10.00 |
| *—Reissue of Decca 79012; black label with rainbow* | | | |
| ROBIN AND THE SEVEN HOODS | | | |
| ❑ Reprise F 2021 [M] | | 1964 | 50.00 |
| ❑ Reprise FS 2021 [S] | | 1964 | 60.00 |
| ROBIN HOOD | | | |
| ❑ Disneyland ST-3810 | | 1973 | 25.00 |
| ROCK ALL NIGHT | | | |
| ❑ Mercury MG-20293 [M] | | 1957 | 100.00 |
| ROCK, PRETTY BABY | | | |
| ❑ Decca DL 8429 [M] | | 1957 | 120.00 |
| *—Black label, silver print; also includes pink label promo* | | | |
| ❑ Decca DL 8429 [M] | | 196? | 30.00 |
| *—Black label with color bars* | | | |
| ROCK, ROCK, ROCK | | | |
| ❑ (no label) (no #) [M] | | 1958 | 1500. |
| *—Demo version, 20 tracks* | | | |
| ❑ Chess LP-1425 [M] | | 1958 | 200.00 |
| ROMANCE OF A HORSETHIEF | | | |
| ❑ Allied Artists AAS-110-100 | | 1971 | 50.00 |

| Number | Title (A Side/B Side) | Yr | NM |
|---|---|---|---|
| ROME ADVENTURE | | | |
| ❑ Warner Bros. W 1458 [M] | | 1962 | 20.00 |
| ❑ Warner Bros. WS 1458 [S] | | 1962 | 25.00 |
| ROMEO AND JULIET | | | |
| ❑ Capitol SWDR-289 [(4)] | | 1969 | 30.00 |
| *—From the 1968 Franco Zeffirelli remake; contains dialogue and music* | | | |
| ❑ Capitol ST-400 | | 1970 | 15.00 |
| *—From the 1968 Franco Zeffirelli remake; edited version of 289* | | | |
| ❑ Capitol ST-2993 | | 1968 | 12.00 |
| *—From the 1968 Franco Zeffirelli remake; contains the music; black label with colorband* | | | |
| ❑ Epic LC 3126 [M] | | 1954 | 60.00 |
| ❑ Epic FLM 13104 [M] | | 1966 | 30.00 |
| *—Reissue of 3126* | | | |
| ❑ Epic FLS 15104 [R] | | 1966 | 25.00 |
| ROOTS OF HEAVEN | | | |
| ❑ 20th Fox FOX-3005 [M] | | 1958 | 300.00 |
| ROSE MARIE | | | |
| ❑ MGM E-229 [10] | | 1954 | 40.00 |
| THE ROSE TATTOO | | | |
| ❑ Columbia CL 727 [M] | | 1955 | 50.00 |
| ROSEMARY'S BABY | | | |
| ❑ Dot DLP-25875 | | 1968 | 20.00 |
| THE ROYAL WEDDING | | | |
| ❑ MGM E-543 [10] | | 1951 | 50.00 |
| THE RULING CLASS | | | |
| ❑ Avco AV-11003 | | 1972 | 25.00 |
| THE RUN OF THE ARROW | | | |
| ❑ Decca DL 8620 [M] | | 1957 | 60.00 |
| *—Black label, silver print, or pink label, black print promo* | | | |
| ❑ Decca DL 8620 [M] | | 196? | 30.00 |
| *—Black label with color bars* | | | |
| RUN WILD, RUN FREE | | | |
| ❑ SGC SD 5003 | | 1969 | 20.00 |
| RUN, ANGEL, RUN | | | |
| ❑ Epic BN 26474 | | 1969 | 20.00 |
| RYAN'S DAUGHTER | | | |
| ❑ MGM 1SE-27 | | 1970 | 25.00 |
| SACCO AND VANZETTI | | | |
| ❑ RCA Victor LSP-4612 | | 1971 | 20.00 |
| THE SACRED IDOL | | | |
| ❑ Capitol ST 1293 [S] | | 1960 | 30.00 |
| ❑ Capitol T 1293 [M] | | 1960 | 25.00 |
| THE SAINT | | | |
| ❑ Virgin SPRO-12261 [(2)DJ] | | 1997 | 25.00 |

| Number | Title (A Side/B Side) | Yr | NM |
|---|---|---|---|
| SAINT JOAN | | | |
| ❑ Capitol W 865 [M] | | 1957 | 30.00 |
| SALLAH | | | |
| ❑ Philips PHM 200177 [M] | | 1965 | 20.00 |
| ❑ Philips PHS 600177 [S] | | 1965 | 25.00 |
| SALOME | | | |
| ❑ Decca DL 6026 [10] | | 1953 | 120.00 |
| SAMSON AND DELILAH | | | |
| ❑ Decca DL 6007 [10] | | 1952 | 60.00 |
| THE SAND CASTLE | | | |
| ❑ Columbia CL 1455 [M] | | 1961 | 15.00 |
| ❑ Columbia CS 8249 [S] | | 1961 | 20.00 |
| THE SAND PEBBLES | | | |
| ❑ 20th Century Fox 3189 [M] | | 1966 | 30.00 |
| ❑ 20th Century Fox S-4189 [S] | | 1966 | 50.00 |
| THE SANDPIPER | | | |
| ❑ Mercury MG-21032 [M] | | 1965 | 25.00 |
| ❑ Mercury SR-61032 [S] | | 1965 | 30.00 |
| SANTA AND THE 3 BEARS | | | |
| ❑ Mr. Pickwick SPC 1501 | | 196? | 20.00 |
| *—With "Santa" cutout intact* | | | |
| SATAN IN HIGH HEELS | | | |
| ❑ Charlie Parker PLP-406 [M] | | 1962 | 30.00 |
| *—Standard cover* | | | |
| ❑ Charlie Parker PLP-406 [M] | | 1962 | 50.00 |
| *—Gatefold cover* | | | |
| ❑ Charlie Parker PLP-406S [S] | | 1962 | 40.00 |
| *—Standard cover* | | | |
| ❑ Charlie Parker PLP-406S [S] | | 1962 | 60.00 |
| *—Gatefold cover* | | | |
| SATAN'S SADISTS | | | |
| ❑ Smash SRS-67127 | | 1969 | 30.00 |
| SATURDAY NIGHT FEVER | | | |
| ❑ RSO RS-2-4001 [(2)] | | 1977 | 15.00 |
| *—First editions have the studio version of "Jive Talkin'" by the Bee Gees on side 3* | | | |
| ❑ RSO RS-2-4001 [(2)] | | 1978 | 12.00 |
| *—Later editions have a live version of "Jive Talkin'" by the Bee Gees on side 3 ("REV" is in the Side 3 trail-off wax)* | | | |
| ❑ RSO 825389-1 [(2)] | | 198? | 10.00 |
| *—Reissue with new number* | | | |
| SATURDAY NIGHT FEVER/GREASE | | | |
| ❑ RSO RPO 1011 [DJ] | | 1978 | 25.00 |
| *—Side 1 has "The Best of Saturday Night Fever" (side 1 of original LP); Side 2 has "The Best of Grease" (side 1 of original LP)* | | | |
| THE SAVAGE SEVEN | | | |
| ❑ Atco 33-245 [M] | | 1968 | 30.00 |
| ❑ Atco SD 33-245 [S] | | 1968 | 30.00 |
| SAVAGE WILD | | | |
| ❑ American Int'l. STA-1032 | | 1970 | 20.00 |
| SAY ONE FOR ME | | | |
| ❑ Columbia CL 1337 [M] | | 1959 | 40.00 |
| ❑ Columbia CS 8147 [S] | | 1959 | 80.00 |
| SAYONARA | | | |
| ❑ RCA Victor LOC-1041 [M] | | 1957 | 50.00 |
| ❑ RCA Victor LSO-1041 [S] | | 1957 | 70.00 |
| THE SCALPHUNTERS | | | |
| ❑ MCA 25042 | | 1986 | 10.00 |
| *—Reissue of United Artists 5176* | | | |
| ❑ United Artists UAL-4176 [M] | | 1968 | 30.00 |
| ❑ United Artists UAS-5176 [S] | | 1968 | 40.00 |
| SCARFACE | | | |
| ❑ MCA 6126 | | 1984 | 20.00 |
| THE SCARLET AND THE BLACK | | | |
| ❑ Cerberus CEM-0120 | | 1983 | 25.00 |
| SCENT OF MYSTERY | | | |
| ❑ Ramrod ST-6001 [S] | | 1960 | 100.00 |
| ❑ Ramrod T-6001 [M] | | 1960 | 50.00 |
| SCROOGE | | | |
| ❑ Columbia Masterworks S 30258 | | 1970 | 30.00 |
| ❑ Columbia Special Products P 14077 | | 1977 | 12.00 |
| *—Special Products reissue* | | | |
| SEARCH FOR PARADISE | | | |
| ❑ RCA Victor LOC-1034 [M] | | 1957 | 40.00 |
| SEASIDE SWINGERS | | | |
| ❑ Mercury MG-21031 [M] | | 1965 | 20.00 |
| ❑ Mercury SR-61031 [S] | | 1965 | 25.00 |
| SEBASTIAN | | | |
| ❑ Dot DLP-3845 [M] | | 1968 | 50.00 |
| ❑ Dot DLP-25845 [S] | | 1968 | 20.00 |
| THE SECRET OF SANTA VITTORIA | | | |
| ❑ MCA 25034 | | 1986 | 10.00 |
| *—Reissue of United Artists 5200* | | | |
| ❑ United Artists UAS-5200 | | 1969 | 30.00 |
| SERGEANTS 3 | | | |
| ❑ Reprise R-2013 [M] | | 1962 | 30.00 |
| ❑ Reprise RS-2013 [S] | | 1962 | 50.00 |
| THE SERPENT AND THE RAINBOW | | | |
| ❑ Varese Sarabande STV-81362 | | 1988 | 40.00 |
| SERPICO | | | |
| ❑ Paramount PAS-1016 | | 1973 | 25.00 |
| SEVEN BRIDES FOR SEVEN BROTHERS | | | |
| ❑ MGM E-244 [10] | | 1954 | 40.00 |
| SEVEN GOLDEN MEN | | | |
| ❑ United Artists UAS-5193 | | 1969 | 25.00 |
| THE SEVEN LITTLE FOYS | | | |
| ❑ RCA Victor LPM-3275 [10] | | 1955 | 70.00 |



Except when noted otherwise, VG = 25% of NM, and VG+ = 50% of NM. (Example: VG = $2.00, VG+ = $4.00 and NM = $8.00.)

| Number | Title (A Side/B Side) | Yr | NM |
|---|---|---|---|
| 1776 | | | |
| ❑ Columbia S 31741 | | 1972 | 20.00 |
| THE 7TH DAWN | | | |
| ❑ United Artists UAL-4115 [M] | | 1964 | 30.00 |
| THE SEVENTH DAWN | | | |
| ❑ United Artists UAL-4115 [M] | | 1964 | 30.00 |
| THE 7TH DAWN | | | |
| ❑ United Artists UAS-5115 [S] | | 1964 | 40.00 |
| THE SEVENTH DAWN | | | |
| ❑ United Artists UAS-5115 [S] | | 1964 | 40.00 |
| THE 7TH VOYAGE OF SINBAD | | | |
| ❑ Colpix CP-504 [M] | | 1958 | 200.00 |
| ❑ Varese Sarabande STV-81135 | | 1983 | 20.00 |
| SEX AND THE SINGLE GIRL | | | |
| ❑ Warner Bros. W 1572 [M] | | 1964 | 15.00 |
| ❑ Warner Bros. WS 1572 [S] | | 1964 | 20.00 |
| SHAFT IN AFRICA | | | |
| ❑ ABC ABCX-793 | | 1973 | 30.00 |
| SHAFT'S BIG SCORE | | | |
| ❑ MGM 1SE-36 | | 1972 | 30.00 |
| SHAKE HANDS WITH THE DEVIL | | | |
| ❑ United Artists UAL-4043 [M] | | 1959 | 30.00 |
| ❑ United Artists UAS-5043 [S] | | 1959 | 50.00 |
| SHALAKO | | | |
| ❑ Philips PHS 600286 | | 1968 | 30.00 |
| SHE-DEVIL | | | |
| ❑ Polydor 841583-1 | | 1989 | 30.00 |
| SHEBA BABY | | | |
| ❑ Buddah BDS-5634 | | 1975 | 30.00 |
| SHENANDOAH | | | |
| ❑ Decca DL 9125 [M] | | 1965 | 30.00 |
| ❑ Decca DL 79125 [S] | | 1965 | 40.00 |
| THE SHINING | | | |
| ❑ Warner Bros. HS 3449 | | 1980 | 20.00 |
| THE SHOP ON MAIN STREET | | | |
| ❑ Mainstream S-6082 [S] | | 1966 | 40.00 |
| ❑ Mainstream 56082 [M] | | 1966 | 25.00 |
| SHORT EYES | | | |
| ❑ Curtom CU 5017 | | 1977 | 25.00 |
| SHOW BOAT | | | |
| ❑ MGM E-559 [10] | | 1951 | 30.00 |
| THE SICILIAN CLAN | | | |
| ❑ 20th Century Fox S-4209 | | 1970 | 50.00 |
| THE SIDEHACKERS | | | |
| ❑ Amaret ST-5004 | | 1969 | 20.00 |
| THE SILENCERS | | | |
| ❑ RCA Victor LOC-1120 [M] | | 1966 | 30.00 |
| ❑ RCA Victor LSO-1120 [S] | | 1966 | 50.00 |
| SILENT RUNNING | | | |
| ❑ Decca DL 79188 | | 1972 | 40.00 |
| ❑ Varese Sarabande STV- 81072 | | 1980 | 15.00 |
| *—Reissue* | | | |
| SILK STOCKINGS | | | |
| ❑ MCA 39074 | | 198? | 10.00 |
| *—Reissue* | | | |
| ❑ MGM E-3542 [M] | | 1957 | 30.00 |
| SILVERADO | | | |
| ❑ Geffen GHS 24080 | | 1985 | 20.00 |
| SINGIN' IN THE RAIN | | | |
| ❑ MCA 39044 | | 198? | 10.00 |
| ❑ Metro M-599 [M] | | 1966 | 15.00 |
| *—Reissue of MGM LP* | | | |
| ❑ Metro MS-599 [R] | | 1966 | 12.00 |
| ❑ MGM E-113 [10] | | 1952 | 30.00 |
| SINGLE ROOM FURNISHED | | | |
| ❑ Sidewalk ST-5917 | | 1968 | 40.00 |
| THE 633 SQUADRON | | | |
| ❑ United Artists UA-LA305-G | | 1974 | 25.00 |
| SKATEDANCER | | | |
| ❑ Mira LP-3004 [M] | | 1966 | 20.00 |
| ❑ Mira LPS-3004 [S] | | 1966 | 25.00 |
| SKI ON THE WILD SIDE | | | |
| ❑ MGM E-4439 [M] | | 1967 | 30.00 |
| ❑ MGM SE-4439 [S] | | 1967 | 50.00 |
| SLAUGHTER ON 10TH AVENUE | | | |
| ❑ Decca DL 8657 [M] | | 1957 | 25.00 |
| *—Black label, silver print* | | | |
| ❑ Decca DL 8657 [M] | | 1960 | 12.00 |
| *—Black label with color bars* | | | |
| ❑ Decca DL 78657 [S] | | 1957 | 30.00 |
| *—Black label, silver print* | | | |
| ❑ Decca DL 78657 [S] | | 1960 | 15.00 |
| *—Black label with color bars* | | | |
| SLAUGHTERHOUSE-FIVE | | | |
| ❑ Columbia Masterworks S 31333 | | 1972 | 25.00 |
| THE SLAVE TRADE IN THE WORLD TODAY | | | |
| ❑ London M-76006 [M] | | 1964 | 200.00 |
| SLAVES | | | |
| ❑ Skye SK-11 | | 1969 | 30.00 |
| SLEEPING BEAUTY | | | |
| ❑ Disneyland STER-4018 [S] | | 1959 | 40.00 |
| ❑ Disneyland WDL-4018 [M] | | 1959 | 30.00 |
| ❑ Disneyland STER-4036 [S] | | 1970 | 20.00 |
| *—Reissue of STER-4018* | | | |
| SLEUTH | | | |
| ❑ Columbia Masterworks S 32154 | | 1973 | 20.00 |

| Number | Title (A Side/B Side) | Yr | NM |
|---|---|---|---|
| SLIPPERY WHEN WET | | | |
| ❑ World Pacific WP-1265 [M] | | 1959 | 50.00 |
| SLUMBER PARTY '57 | | | |
| ❑ Mercury SRM-1-1097 | | 1976 | 25.00 |
| A SMASHING TIME | | | |
| ❑ ABC ABC-OC-6 [M] | | 1967 | 20.00 |
| ❑ ABC ABCS-OC-6 [S] | | 1967 | 25.00 |
| ❑ ABC SW-91399 [S] | | 1967 | 25.00 |
| *—Capitol Record Club edition* | | | |
| SNOOPY COME HOME | | | |
| ❑ Columbia Masterworks S 31451 | | 1972 | 20.00 |
| THE SNOW QUEEN | | | |
| ❑ Decca DL 8977 [M] | | 1959 | 40.00 |
| ❑ Decca DL 78977 [S] | | 1959 | 60.00 |
| SNOW WHITE AND THE SEVEN DWARFS | | | |
| ❑ Buena Vista 102 [(3)] | | 1975 | 50.00 |
| *—Entire movie on three LPs; TV mail-order item* | | | |
| ❑ Disneyland DQ-1201 [M] | | 1959 | 50.00 |
| *—Reissue of 4005; whirlpool-like designs on cover* | | | |
| ❑ Disneyland DQ-1201 [M] | | 1968 | 25.00 |
| *—Reissue; with same cover as 4005, but no gatefold* | | | |
| ❑ Disneyland DQ-1201 [M] | | 1987 | 30.00 |
| *—Reissue; high-gloss cover with cel photos on back* | | | |
| ❑ Disneyland 3101 [PD] | | 1981 | 30.00 |
| *—"Disney Picture Disc" edition* | | | |
| ❑ Disneyland WDL-4005 [M] | | 1956 | 200.00 |
| *—Gatefold cover* | | | |
| SNOW WHITE AND THE THREE STOOGES | | | |
| ❑ Columbia CL 1650 [M] | | 1961 | 60.00 |
| ❑ Columbia CS 8450 [S] | | 1961 | 100.00 |
| SO THIS IS LOVE | | | |
| ❑ RCA Victor LOC-3000 [10] | | 1953 | 80.00 |
| SO THIS IS PARIS | | | |
| ❑ Decca DL 5553 [10] | | 1955 | 50.00 |
| SODOM AND GOMORRAH | | | |
| ❑ RCA Victor LOC-1076 [M] | | 1963 | 80.00 |
| ❑ RCA Victor LSO-1076 [S] | | 1963 | 100.00 |
| SOL MADRID | | | |
| ❑ MGM SE-4541 ST | | 1968 | 30.00 |
| SOLOMON AND SHEBA | | | |
| ❑ MCA 1425 | | 198? | 8.00 |
| *—Reissue* | | | |
| ❑ United Artists UAL-4051 [M] | | 1959 | 25.00 |
| *—Second, regular cover* | | | |
| ❑ United Artists UAL-4051 [M] | | 1959 | 50.00 |
| *—First cover with silky finish* | | | |
| ❑ United Artists UAS-5051 [S] | | 1959 | 60.00 |
| *—Second, regular cover* | | | |
| ❑ United Artists UAS-5051 [S] | | 1959 | 120.00 |
| *—First cover with silky finish* | | | |
| SOME CAME RUNNING | | | |
| ❑ Capitol SW 1109 [S] | | 1958 | 80.00 |
| ❑ Capitol W 1109 [M] | | 1958 | 30.00 |
| SOME LIKE IT HOT | | | |
| ❑ United Artists UA-LA272-G | | 1974 | 12.00 |
| *—Reissue of 5030* | | | |
| ❑ United Artists UAL-4030 [M] | | 1959 | 50.00 |
| ❑ United Artists UAS-5030 [S] | | 1959 | 75.00 |
| SOMEBODY LOVES ME | | | |
| ❑ RCA Victor LPM-3097 [10] | | 1952 | 50.00 |
| SOMEWHERE IN TIME | | | |
| ❑ MCA 5154 | | 1980 | 20.00 |
| SONG OF THE SOUTH | | | |
| ❑ Disneyland WDL-4001 [M] | | 1956 | 300.00 |
| *—Yellow label (first pressing)* | | | |
| ❑ Disneyland WDL-4001 [M] | | 1957 | 200.00 |
| *—Red/maroon label (second pressing)* | | | |
| SONG OF THE SOUTH (UNCLE REMUS) | | | |
| ❑ Disneyland DQ-1205 [M] | | 1959 | 25.00 |
| SONG WITHOUT END | | | |
| ❑ Colpix CP-506 [M] | | 1960 | 20.00 |
| ❑ Colpix SCP-506 [S] | | 1960 | 25.00 |
| THE SONS OF KATIE ELDER | | | |
| ❑ Columbia Masterworks OS 2820 [S] | | 1965 | 100.00 |
| ❑ Columbia Masterworks OL 6420 [M] | | 1965 | 50.00 |
| THE SOUL OF NIGGER CHARLEY | | | |
| ❑ MGM 1SE-46 | | 1973 | 20.00 |
| THE SOUND AND THE FURY | | | |
| ❑ Decca DL 8885 [M] | | 1959 | 30.00 |
| ❑ Decca DL 78885 [S] | | 1959 | 70.00 |
| THE SOUND OF MUSIC | | | |
| ❑ RCA Victor LOCD-2005 [M] | | 1965 | 12.00 |
| *—With booklet; back cover lists "I Have Confidence" correctly* | | | |
| ❑ RCA Victor LOCD-2005 [M] | | 1965 | 15.00 |
| *—With booklet; back cover lists "I Have Confidence" as "I Have Confidence in Me"* | | | |
| ❑ RCA Victor LSOD-2005 [S] | | 1965 | 15.00 |
| *—With booklet; back cover lists "I Have Confidence" correctly* | | | |
| ❑ RCA Victor LSOD-2005 [S] | | 1965 | 20.00 |
| *—With booklet; back cover lists "I Have Confidence" as "I Have Confidence in Me"* | | | |
| ❑ RCA Victor LSOD-2005 [S] | | 1969 | 12.00 |
| *—No booklet; gatefold cover, record comes out from inside; orange or tan label* | | | |
| ❑ RCA Victor LSOD-2005 [S] | | 1977 | 10.00 |
| *—Gatefold cover, record comes out from outside; black label with dog at 1 o'clock* | | | |
| SOUTH CENTRAL | | | |
| ❑ Hollywood 61403 [DJ] | | 1992 | 20.00 |
| *—Vinyl is promo only* | | | |

| Number | Title (A Side/B Side) | Yr | NM |
|---|---|---|---|
| SOUTH PACIFIC | | | |
| ❑ RCA Victor LOC-1032 [M] | | 1958 | 20.00 |
| *—"Long Play" on label; no "Academy Award Winner" on front cover* | | | |
| ❑ RCA Victor LOC-1032 [M] | | 196? | 12.00 |
| *—"Long Play" or "Mono" on label; with "Academy Award Winner" on front cover* | | | |
| ❑ RCA Victor LSO-1032 [S] | | 1958 | 12.00 |
| *—Orange label* | | | |
| ❑ RCA Victor LSO-1032 [S] | | 1958 | 25.00 |
| *—"Living Stereo" on label; no "Academy Award Winner" on front cover* | | | |
| ❑ RCA Victor LSO-1032 [S] | | 196? | 15.00 |
| *—"Living Stereo" or "Stereo" on black label; with "Academy Award Winner" on front cover* | | | |
| ❑ RCA Victor LOCD-2000 [M] | | 1958 | 40.00 |
| *—Gatefold cover with photos inside* | | | |
| ❑ RCA Victor AYL1-3681 | | 1981 | 8.00 |
| *—"Best Buy Series" reissue* | | | |
| SOUTHERN STAR | | | |
| ❑ Colgems COSO-5009 | | 1969 | 60.00 |
| SPACECAMP | | | |
| ❑ RCA Victor ABL1-5856 | | 1986 | 40.00 |
| A SPANISH AFFAIR | | | |
| ❑ Dot DLP-3078 [M] | | 1958 | 100.00 |
| SPARKLE | | | |
| ❑ Atlantic SD 18176 | | 1976 | 20.00 |
| SPARTACUS | | | |
| ❑ Decca DL 9092 [M] | | 1960 | 20.00 |
| *—Black label, silver print* | | | |
| ❑ Decca DL 9092 [M] | | 1961 | 12.00 |
| *—Black label with color bars* | | | |
| ❑ Decca DL 79092 [S] | | 1960 | 25.00 |
| *—Maroon label, silver print* | | | |
| ❑ Decca DL 79092 [S] | | 1961 | 15.00 |
| *—Black label with color bars* | | | |
| ❑ MCA 1534 | | 198? | 10.00 |
| *—Reissue of 2068* | | | |
| ❑ MCA 2068 | | 1973 | 12.00 |
| *—Reissue of 79092; black label with rainbow* | | | |
| THE SPIRIT OF ST. LOUIS | | | |
| ❑ RCA Victor LPM-1472 [M] | | 1957 | 50.00 |
| SPLASH | | | |
| ❑ Cherry Lane 00301 | | 1984 | 25.00 |
| *—With poster of Daryl Hannah* | | | |
| THE SPY WHO CAME IN FROM THE COLD | | | |
| ❑ RCA Victor LOC-1118 [M] | | 1965 | 20.00 |
| ❑ RCA Victor LSO-1118 [S] | | 1965 | 40.00 |
| THE SPY WITH A COLD NOSE | | | |
| ❑ Columbia Masterworks OS 3070 [S] | | 1966 | 30.00 |
| ❑ Columbia Masterworks OL 6670 [M] | | 1966 | 20.00 |
| ST. LOUIS BLUES | | | |
| ❑ Capitol W 993 [M] | | 1958 | 50.00 |
| *—Turquoise or gray label* | | | |
| ❑ Capitol W 993 [M] | | 1959 | 25.00 |
| *—Black colorband label, logo at left* | | | |
| ❑ Capitol W 993 [M] | | 196? | 20.00 |
| *—Black colorband label, logo at top* | | | |
| ST. LOUIS WOMAN | | | |
| ❑ Capitol L 355 [10] | | 1955 | 80.00 |
| STAGECOACH | | | |
| ❑ Mainstream S-6077 [S] | | 1966 | 30.00 |
| ❑ Mainstream 56077 [M] | | 1966 | 20.00 |
| ❑ Mainstream ST-90802 [S] | | 1966 | 30.00 |
| *—Capitol Record Club edition* | | | |
| ❑ Mainstream T-90802 [M] | | 1966 | 25.00 |
| *—Capitol Record Club edition* | | | |
| STAR TREK — THE MOTION PICTURE | | | |
| ❑ Columbia JS 36334 | | 1979 | 20.00 |
| STAR! | | | |
| ❑ 20th Century Fox DTCS-5102 | | 1968 | 20.00 |
| THE STARS AND STRIPES FOREVER | | | |
| ❑ MGM E-176 [10] | | 1952 | 30.00 |
| STATE FAIR | | | |
| ❑ Dot DLP-9011 [M] | | 1962 | 25.00 |
| ❑ Dot DLP-29011 [S] | | 1962 | 30.00 |
| THE STERILE CUCKOO | | | |
| ❑ Paramount PAS-5009 | | 1970 | 20.00 |
| STILETTO | | | |
| ❑ Columbia Masterworks OS 3360 | | 1969 | 20.00 |
| THE STRANGE ONE | | | |
| ❑ Coral CRL 57132 [M] | | 1957 | 70.00 |
| THE STRAWBERRY STATEMENT | | | |
| ❑ MGM 2SE-14 [(2)] | | 1970 | 25.00 |
| A STREETCAR NAMED DESIRE | | | |
| ❑ Capitol L 289 [10] | | 1951 | 50.00 |
| A STUDY IN TERROR | | | |
| ❑ Roulette OS-801 [M] | | 1965 | 40.00 |
| ❑ Roulette OSS-801 [S] | | 1965 | 80.00 |
| THE STUNT MAN | | | |
| ❑ 20th Century T-626 | | 1980 | 25.00 |
| THE SUBTERRANEANS | | | |
| ❑ MGM E-3812 ST [M] | | 1960 | 40.00 |
| ❑ MGM SE-3812 ST [S] | | 1960 | 80.00 |
| SUMMER AND SMOKE | | | |
| ❑ RCA Victor LOC-1067 [M] | | 1961 | 50.00 |
| ❑ RCA Victor LSO-1067 [S] | | 1961 | 70.00 |
| SUMMER HOLIDAY | | | |
| ❑ Epic LN 24063 [M] | | 1963 | 25.00 |
| ❑ Epic BN 26063 [S] | | 1963 | 30.00 |

| Number | Title (A Side/B Side) | Yr | NM |
|---|---|---|---|
| SUMMER LOVE | | | |
| ❑ Decca DL 8714 [M] | | 1958 | 60.00 |
| *—Black label, silver print, or pink label, black print promo* | | | |
| ❑ Decca DL 8714 [M] | | 196? | 30.00 |
| *—Black label with color bars* | | | |
| SUMMER MAGIC | | | |
| ❑ Buena Vista BV-4025 [M] | | 1963 | 40.00 |
| ❑ Buena Vista STER-4025 [S] | | 1963 | 60.00 |
| SUMMER STOCK | | | |
| ❑ MGM E-519 [10] | | 1950 | 40.00 |
| THE SUN ALSO RISES | | | |
| ❑ Kapp KDL-7001 [M] | | 1957 | 60.00 |
| SUN VALLEY SERENADE | | | |
| ❑ RCA Victor LPT-3064 [10] | | 1954 | 60.00 |
| THE SUNNY SIDE OF THE STREET | | | |
| ❑ Mercury MG-25100 [10] | | 1951 | 60.00 |
| SURF PARTY | | | |
| ❑ 20th Century Fox TFM-3131 [M] | | 1964 | 25.00 |
| ❑ 20th Century Fox TFS-4131 [S] | | 1964 | 30.00 |
| SURFER GIRLS | | | |
| ❑ Oakwood SUS-1001 | | 1978 | 100.00 |
| THE SWAN | | | |
| ❑ MCA 25086 | | 1986 | 10.00 |
| *—Reissue of MGM 3399* | | | |
| ❑ MGM E-3399 [M] | | 1956 | 70.00 |
| THE SWARM | | | |
| ❑ Warner Bros. BSK 3208 | | 1978 | 30.00 |
| SWEDISH HEAVEN AND HELL | | | |
| ❑ Ariel ARS-15000 | | 1969 | 25.00 |
| SWEET CHARITY | | | |
| ❑ Decca DL 71502 | | 1969 | 20.00 |
| SWEET LOVE, BITTER | | | |
| ❑ ABC Impulse! AS-9141 [S] | | 1968 | 15.00 |
| ❑ Impulse! A-9141 [M] | | 1967 | 40.00 |
| ❑ Impulse! AS-9141 [S] | | 1967 | 30.00 |
| THE SWEET RIDE | | | |
| ❑ 20th Century Fox S-4198 | | 1968 | 20.00 |
| THE SWEET SMELL OF SUCCESS | | | |
| ❑ Decca DL 8610 [M] | | 1957 | 60.00 |
| SWEET SWEETBACK'S BADASSSSSS SONG | | | |
| ❑ Stax STS-3001 | | 1971 | 30.00 |
| SWEPT AWAY | | | |
| ❑ Peters International PLD 1005 | | 1957 | 40.00 |
| THE SWIMMER | | | |
| ❑ Columbia Masterworks OS 3210 | | 1968 | 25.00 |
| SWINGER'S PARADISE | | | |
| ❑ Epic LN 24145 [M] | | 1965 | 20.00 |
| ❑ Epic BN 26145 [S] | | 1965 | 25.00 |
| A SWINGIN' SUMMER | | | |
| ❑ Hanna-Barbera HLP-8500 [M] | | 1966 | 25.00 |
| ❑ Hanna-Barbera HST-9500 [S] | | 1966 | 30.00 |
| SYLVIA | | | |
| ❑ Mercury MG-21004 [M] | | 1965 | 20.00 |
| ❑ Mercury SR-61004 [S] | | 1965 | 30.00 |
| TARAS BULBA | | | |
| ❑ United Artists UAL-4100 [M] | | 1962 | 30.00 |
| ❑ United Artists UAS-5100 [S] | | 1962 | 50.00 |
| TAXI DRIVER | | | |
| ❑ Arista AL 4079 | | 1976 | 20.00 |
| ❑ Arista AL 8179 | | 198? | 15.00 |
| *—Reissue of 4079* | | | |
| TEENAGE REBELLION | | | |
| ❑ Sidewalk ST-5903 [S] | | 1967 | 25.00 |
| ❑ Sidewalk T-5903 [M] | | 1967 | 20.00 |
| TELL ME THAT YOU LOVE ME, JUNIE MOON | | | |
| ❑ Columbia Masterworks OS 3540 | | 1970 | 20.00 |
| THE TEN COMMANDMENTS | | | |
| ❑ Dot DLP-3054 [M] | | 1956 | 40.00 |
| ❑ Dot DLP-25054 [S] | | 1959 | 25.00 |
| *—Re-recording of the original soundtrack in stereo* | | | |
| ❑ MCA 4159 [(2)] | | 198? | 15.00 |
| *—Reissue of Paramount set* | | | |
| ❑ Paramount PAS-1006 [(2)] | | 1973 | 20.00 |
| *—Reissue of Dot 25054* | | | |
| TENDER IS THE NIGHT | | | |
| ❑ 20th Century Fox FOX-3054 [M] | | 1962 | 150.00 |
| ❑ 20th Century Fox SFX-3054 [S] | | 1962 | 200.00 |
| THE TENTH VICTIM | | | |
| ❑ Mainstream S-6071 [S] | | 1965 | 50.00 |
| ❑ Mainstream 56071 [M] | | 1965 | 40.00 |
| THANK GOD IT'S FRIDAY | | | |
| ❑ Casablanca NBLP-7099-3 [(3)] | | 1978 | 20.00 |
| *—Two full-length LPs plus a bonus 12-inch single by Donna Summer with blank B-side* | | | |
| THAT DARN CAT | | | |
| ❑ Buena Vista BV-3334 [M] | | 1965 | 20.00 |
| ❑ Buena Vista STER-3334 [S] | | 1965 | 25.00 |
| THAT MAN IN ISTANBUL | | | |
| ❑ Mainstream S-6072 [S] | | 1966 | 25.00 |
| ❑ Mainstream 56072 [M] | | 1966 | 20.00 |
| THAT'S ENTERTAINMENT! | | | |
| ❑ MCA 11002 [(2)] | | 1974 | 20.00 |
| *—Film credits in small print on back cover, and list of songs omits "That's Entertainment"* | | | |
| ❑ MCA 11002 [(2)] | | 1976 | 15.00 |
| *—Film credits in larger print on back cover, and list of songs includes "That's Entertainment"* | | | |
| THERE'S NO BUSINESS LIKE SHOW BUSINESS | | | |
| ❑ Decca DL 8091 [M] | | 1954 | 30.00 |
| *—Black label with silver print* | | | |
| ❑ Decca DL 8091 [M] | | 196? | 20.00 |
| *—Black label with color bars* | | | |
| THEY SHOOT HORSES, DON'T THEY? | | | |
| ❑ ABC ABCS-OC-10 | | 1969 | 20.00 |
| THIEF OF HEARTS | | | |
| ❑ Casablanca 822942-1 | | 1984 | 20.00 |
| THE THIN BLUE LINE | | | |
| ❑ Nonesuch 79209-1 | | 1988 | 20.00 |
| THIS COULD BE THE NIGHT | | | |
| ❑ MGM E-3530 [M] | | 1957 | 50.00 |
| THIS EARTH IS MINE | | | |
| ❑ Decca DL 8915 [M] | | 1959 | 80.00 |
| ❑ Decca DL 78915 [S] | | 1959 | 100.00 |
| ❑ Varese Sarabande VC-81076 | | 1979 | 15.00 |
| *—Reissue of Decca 78915* | | | |
| THIS PROPERTY IS CONDEMNED | | | |
| ❑ Verve V-8664 [M] | | 1966 | 20.00 |
| ❑ Verve V6-8664 [S] | | 1966 | 30.00 |
| THE THOMAS CROWN AFFAIR | | | |
| ❑ United Artists UA-LA295-G | | 1974 | 12.00 |
| *—Reissue of 5182* | | | |
| ❑ United Artists UAS-5182 | | 1968 | 20.00 |
| THOROUGHLY MODERN MILLIE | | | |
| ❑ Decca DL 1500 [M] | | 1967 | 20.00 |
| *—With bound-in booklet* | | | |
| ❑ Decca DL 71500 [S] | | 1967 | 20.00 |
| *—With bound-in booklet* | | | |
| THOSE GLORIOUS MGM MUSICALS: DEEP IN MY HEART/WORDS AND MUSIC | | | |
| ❑ MGM 2-SES-54-ST [(2)] | | 1973 | 20.00 |
| THOSE GLORIOUS MGM MUSICALS: EVERYTHING I HAVE IS YOURS/SUMMER STOCK/I LOVE MELVIN | | | |
| ❑ MGM 2-SES-52-ST [(2)] | | 1973 | 20.00 |
| THOSE GLORIOUS MGM MUSICALS: GOOD NEWS/IN THE GOOD OLD SUMMERTIME/TWO WEEKS WITH LOVE | | | |
| ❑ MGM 2-SES-49-ST [(2)] | | 1973 | 20.00 |
| THOSE GLORIOUS MGM MUSICALS: LOVELY TO LOOK AT/BRIGADOON | | | |
| ❑ MGM 2-SES-50-ST [(2)] | | 1973 | 20.00 |
| THOSE GLORIOUS MGM MUSICALS: NANCY GOES TO RIO/RICH, YOUNG AND PRETTY/ROYAL WEDDING | | | |
| ❑ MGM 2-SES-53-ST [(2)] | | 1973 | 20.00 |
| THOSE GLORIOUS MGM MUSICALS: ROSE MARIE/ SEVN BRIDES FOR SEVEN BROTHERS | | | |
| ❑ MGM 2-SES-41-ST [(2)] | | 1973 | 20.00 |
| THOSE GLORIOUS MGM MUSICALS: SHOW BOAT/ ANNIE GET YOUR GUN | | | |
| ❑ MGM 2-SES-42-ST [(2)] | | 1973 | 20.00 |
| THOSE GLORIOUS MGM MUSICALS: SINGIN' IN THE RAIN/EASTER PARADE | | | |
| ❑ MGM 2-SES-40-ST [(2)] | | 1973 | 20.00 |
| THOSE GLORIOUS MGM MUSICALS: THE BAND WAGON/KISS ME, KATE | | | |
| ❑ MGM 2-SES-44-ST [(2)] | | 1973 | 20.00 |
| THOSE GLORIOUS MGM MUSICALS: THE BARKLEYS OF BROADWAY/LES GIRLS | | | |
| ❑ MGM 2-SES-51-ST [(2)] | | 1973 | 20.00 |
| THOSE GLORIOUS MGM MUSICALS: THE PIRATE/ PAGAN LOVE SONG/HIT THE DECK | | | |
| ❑ MGM 2-SES-43-ST [(2)] | | 1973 | 40.00 |
| THOSE GLORIOUS MGM MUSICALS: TILL THE CLOUDS ROLL BY/THREE LITTLE WORDS | | | |
| ❑ MGM 2-SES-45-ST [(2)] | | 1973 | 20.00 |
| THREE BITES OF THE APPLE | | | |
| ❑ MCA 25010 | | 198? | 8.00 |
| *—Reissue of MGM SE-4444* | | | |
| ❑ MGM E-4444 [M] | | 1967 | 25.00 |
| ❑ MGM SE-4444 [S] | | 1967 | 20.00 |
| THREE FOR THE SHOW | | | |
| ❑ Mercury MG-25204 [M] | | 1955 | 60.00 |
| THREE IN THE ATTIC | | | |
| ❑ Sidewalk ST-5918 | | 1968 | 30.00 |
| THREE LITTLE WORDS | | | |
| ❑ MGM E-516 [10] | | 1959 | 60.00 |
| THE THREE WORLDS OF GULLIVER | | | |
| ❑ Colpix CP-414 [M] | | 1960 | 60.00 |
| THE THREEPENNY OPERA | | | |
| ❑ RCA Victor LOC-1086 [M] | | 1964 | 15.00 |
| *—Reissue cover: White background, orange drawing, Sammy Davis Jr. in foreground, "RE" at bottom* | | | |
| ❑ RCA Victor LOC-1086 [M] | | 1964 | 150.00 |
| *—With rare original cover: White background, pink and black drawing, characters underneath* | | | |
| ❑ RCA Victor LSO-1086 [S] | | 1964 | 20.00 |
| *—Reissue cover: White background, orange drawing, Sammy Davis Jr. in foreground, "RE" at bottom* | | | |
| ❑ RCA Victor LSO-1086 [S] | | 1964 | 200.00 |
| *—With rare original cover: White background, pink and black drawing, characters underneath* | | | |
| THUNDER ALLEY | | | |
| ❑ Sidewalk ST-5902 [S] | | 1967 | 25.00 |
| ❑ Sidewalk T-5902 [M] | | 1967 | 20.00 |
| THUNDERBALL | | | |
| ❑ United Artists UAL-4132 [M] | | 1965 | 20.00 |
| ❑ United Artists UAS-5132 [S] | | 1965 | 30.00 |
| ❑ United Artists SW-90820 [S] | | 1965 | 40.00 |
| *—Capitol Record Club edition* | | | |
| TICK...TICK...TICK | | | |
| ❑ MGM SE-4667 [M] | | 1970 | 25.00 |
| TILL THE CLOUDS ROLL BY | | | |
| ❑ MCA 25000 | | 1986 | 10.00 |
| ❑ Metro M-578 [M] | | 1966 | 12.00 |
| *—Reissue of MGM 501* | | | |
| ❑ Metro MS-578 [R] | | 1966 | 10.00 |
| ❑ MGM E-501 [10] | | 1950 | 50.00 |
| A TIME TO LOVE AND A TIME TO DIE | | | |
| ❑ Decca DL 8778 [M] | | 1958 | 100.00 |
| ❑ Varese Sarabande VC- 81075 | | 1979 | 15.00 |
| *—Reissue of Decca 8778* | | | |
| TO BED... OR NOT TO BED | | | |
| ❑ London M-76005 [M] | | 1963 | 40.00 |
| TO KILL A MOCKINGBIRD | | | |
| ❑ Ava A-20 [M] | | 1962 | 25.00 |
| ❑ Ava AS-20 [S] | | 1962 | 30.00 |
| TOKYO OLYMPIAD | | | |
| ❑ Monument MLP-8046 [M] | | 1966 | 15.00 |
| ❑ Monument SLP-18046 [S] | | 1966 | 20.00 |
| TOM JONES | | | |
| ❑ United Artists UAL-4113 [M] | | 1963 | 20.00 |
| ❑ United Artists UAS-5113 [S] | | 1963 | 25.00 |
| TOM SAWYER | | | |
| ❑ United Artists UA-LA057-F | | 1973 | 20.00 |
| TOMMY | | | |
| ❑ Polydor PD 2-9502 [(2)] | | 1975 | 20.00 |
| TOO MUCH TOO SOON | | | |
| ❑ Mercury MG-20381 [M] | | 1958 | 30.00 |
| ❑ Mercury SR-60019 [S] | | 1958 | 80.00 |
| TOPKAPI | | | |
| ❑ MCA 25118 | | 1986 | 10.00 |
| ❑ United Artists UAL-4118 [M] | | 1964 | 20.00 |
| ❑ United Artists UAS-5118 [S] | | 1964 | 30.00 |
| THE TOUCHABLES | | | |
| ❑ 20th Century Fox S-4206 | | 1969 | 20.00 |
| THE TRAIN | | | |
| ❑ United Artists UAL-4122 [M] | | 1965 | 20.00 |
| ❑ United Artists UAS-5122 [S] | | 1965 | 40.00 |
| TRANSYLVANIA 6-5000 | | | |
| ❑ Varese Sarabande STV-81267 | | 1985 | 20.00 |
| THE TRAP | | | |
| ❑ Atco 33-204 [M] | | 1966 | 40.00 |
| ❑ Atco SD 33-204 [S] | | 1966 | 70.00 |
| TRAPEZE | | | |
| ❑ Columbia CL 870 [M] | | 1956 | 25.00 |
| THE TRAPP FAMILY | | | |
| ❑ 20th Fox FOX-3044 [M] | | 1961 | 25.00 |
| ❑ 20th Fox STX-3044 [S] | | 1961 | 40.00 |
| THE TREASURE OF SAN GENNARO | | | |
| ❑ Buddah BDS-5011 | | 1968 | 40.00 |
| THE TRIP | | | |
| ❑ Sidewalk ST-5908 [S] | | 1967 | 40.00 |
| ❑ Sidewalk T-5908 [M] | | 1967 | 30.00 |
| TRIPLE CROSS | | | |
| ❑ United Artists UAL-4162 [M] | | 1967 | 20.00 |
| ❑ United Artists UAS-5162 [S] | | 1967 | 30.00 |
| THE TROUBLE WITH ANGELS | | | |
| ❑ Mainstream S-6073 [S] | | 1966 | 80.00 |
| ❑ Mainstream 56073 [M] | | 1966 | 40.00 |
| TRUE GRIT | | | |
| ❑ Capitol ST-263 | | 1969 | 30.00 |
| ❑ Capitol ST-8-0263 | | 1969 | 40.00 |
| *—Capitol Record Club edition* | | | |
| TRUE LIFE ADVENTURES | | | |
| ❑ Disneyland WDL-4011 [M] | | 1957 | 70.00 |
| THE TRUE STORY OF THE CIVIL WAR | | | |
| ❑ Coral CRL 59100 [M] | | 1958 | 80.00 |
| TWO MULES FOR SISTER SARA | | | |
| ❑ Kapp KRS-5512 | | 1970 | 25.00 |
| TWO WEEKS WITH LOVE | | | |
| ❑ MGM E-530 [10] | | 1950 | 40.00 |
| ULYSSES | | | |
| ❑ RCA Victor LOC-1138 [M] | | 1967 | 25.00 |
| ❑ RCA Victor LSO-1138 [S] | | 1967 | 30.00 |
| THE UMBRELLAS OF CHERBOURG (LES PARAPLUIES DE CHERBOURG) | | | |
| ❑ Philips PCC 216 [M] | | 1965 | 20.00 |
| ❑ Philips PCC 616 [S] | | 1965 | 30.00 |
| THE UNBEARABLE LIGHTNESS OF BEING | | | |
| ❑ Fantasy FSP-21006 | | 1988 | 20.00 |
| UNCLE TOM'S CABIN | | | |
| ❑ Philips PHS 600272 | | 1968 | 40.00 |
| THE UNFORGIVEN | | | |
| ❑ United Artists UAL-4068 [M] | | 1960 | 40.00 |
| ❑ United Artists UAS-5068 [S] | | 1960 | 70.00 |
| THE UNSINKABLE MOLLY BROWN | | | |
| ❑ MCA 25011 | | 1986 | 10.00 |
| *—Reissue of MGM 4232* | | | |
| ❑ MGM E-4232 [M] | | 1964 | 15.00 |
| ❑ MGM SE-4232 [S] | | 1964 | 20.00 |



**Except when noted otherwise, VG = 25% of NM, and VG+ = 50% of NM. (Example: VG = $2.00, VG+ = $4.00 and NM = $8.00.)**

| Number | Title (A Side/B Side) | Yr | NM |
|---|---|---|---|
| ❑ MGM SW-90048 [S] | | 1964 | 15.00 |
| *—Capitol Record Club edition* | | | |
| ❑ MGM W-90048 [M] | | 1964 | 12.00 |
| *—Capitol Record Club edition* | | | |
| UP IN THE CELLAR | | | |
| ❑ American Int'l. A-1036 | | 1970 | 20.00 |
| UP THE DOWN STAIRCASE | | | |
| ❑ United Artists UAL-4169 [M] | | 1967 | 20.00 |
| ❑ United Artists UAS-5169 [S] | | 1967 | 40.00 |
| UP THE JUNCTION | | | |
| ❑ Mercury SR-61159 | | 1968 | 25.00 |
| THE V.I.P.S | | | |
| ❑ MGM E-4184 [M] | | 1963 | 20.00 |
| ❑ MGM SE-4184 [S] | | 1963 | 25.00 |
| *—Music by Bill Evans* | | | |
| VALENTINO | | | |
| ❑ United Artists UA-LA810-H | | 1977 | 25.00 |
| VALLEY GIRL | | | |
| ❑ Epic FE 38623 | | 1983 | 80.00 |
| ❑ Roadshow RS-101 | | 1983 | 120.00 |
| VALLEY OF THE DOLLS | | | |
| ❑ 20th Century Fox TF-4196 [M] | | 1968 | 30.00 |
| ❑ 20th Century Fox TFS-4196 [S] | | 1968 | 30.00 |
| ❑ 20th Century Fox SW-91374 [S] | | 1968 | 30.00 |
| *—Capitol Record Club edition* | | | |
| VANILLA SKY | | | |
| ❑ Reprise RTH-2002 [(2)] | | 2002 | 40.00 |
| *—Classic Records edition on 180-gram vinyl ; contains a packet with a piece of film from the movie* | | | |
| THE VANISHING POINT | | | |
| ❑ Amos AAS-8002 | | 1971 | 20.00 |
| THE VANISHING PRAIRIE | | | |
| ❑ Columbia CL 6332 [10] | | 1954 | 80.00 |
| VERTIGO | | | |
| ❑ Mercury MG-20384 [M] | | 1958 | 150.00 |
| VICTOR/VICTORIA | | | |
| ❑ MGM MG-1-5407 | | 1982 | 30.00 |
| ❑ Polydor MG-1-5407 | | 198? | 10.00 |
| *—Reissue of MGM release* | | | |
| THE VICTORS | | | |
| ❑ Colpix CP-516 [M] | | 1963 | 20.00 |
| ❑ Colpix SCP-516 [S] | | 1963 | 30.00 |
| A VIEW TO A KILL | | | |
| ❑ Capitol SJ-12413 | | 1985 | 20.00 |
| THE VIKINGS | | | |
| ❑ United Artists UAL-4003 [M] | | 1958 | 30.00 |
| ❑ United Artists UAS-5003 [S] | | 1958 | 40.00 |
| VILLA RIDES! | | | |
| ❑ Dot DLP-25870 | | 1968 | 40.00 |
| VIVA MARIA! | | | |
| ❑ United Artists UAL-4135 [M] | | 1965 | 20.00 |
| ❑ United Artists UAS-5135 [S] | | 1965 | 30.00 |
| VIVA MAX! | | | |
| ❑ RCA Victor LSP-4275 | | 1969 | 20.00 |
| THE VIXEN | | | |
| ❑ Beverly Hills BHS-22 | | 1968 | 50.00 |
| VOYAGE EN BALLON | | | |
| ❑ Philips PHM 200029 [M] | | 1960 | 30.00 |
| ❑ Philips PHS 600029 [S] | | 1960 | 40.00 |
| W.W. AND THE DIXIE DANCEKINGS | | | |
| ❑ 20th Century ST-103 | | 1975 | 25.00 |
| WALK DON'T RUN | | | |
| ❑ Mainstream S-6080 [S] | | 1966 | 40.00 |
| ❑ Mainstream 56080 [M] | | 1966 | 20.00 |
| WALK ON THE WILD SIDE | | | |
| ❑ Ava A-4-ST [M] | | 1962 | 20.00 |
| ❑ Ava AS-4-ST [S] | | 1962 | 40.00 |
| ❑ Choreo A-4-ST [M] | | 1962 | 30.00 |
| ❑ Choreo AS-4-ST [S] | | 1962 | 50.00 |
| A WALK WITH LOVE AND DEATH | | | |
| ❑ Citadel CT-6025 | | 1969 | 80.00 |
| THE WANDERERS | | | |
| ❑ Warner Bros. BSK 3359 | | 1979 | 30.00 |
| WAR AND PEACE | | | |
| ❑ Columbia CL 930 [M] | | 1956 | 25.00 |
| ❑ Melodiya/Capitol SWAO 2918 | | 1968 | 40.00 |
| THE WAR LORD | | | |
| ❑ Decca DL 9149 [M] | | 1965 | 25.00 |
| ❑ Decca DL 79149 [S] | | 1965 | 50.00 |
| THE WARLOCK | | | |
| ❑ Intrada MAF-7003 | | 1990 | 20.00 |
| WARNING SHOT | | | |
| ❑ Liberty LRP-3498 [M] | | 1967 | 30.00 |
| ❑ Liberty LST-7498 [S] | | 1967 | 40.00 |
| WATERLOO | | | |
| ❑ Paramount PAS-6003 | | 1971 | 30.00 |
| ❑ Paramount SW-93729 | | 1971 | 30.00 |
| *—Capitol Record Club edition* | | | |
| WATERMELON MAN | | | |
| ❑ Beverly Hills BHS-26 | | 1970 | 30.00 |
| WATERSHIP DOWN | | | |
| ❑ Columbia JS 35707 | | 1978 | 25.00 |
| WAY...WAY OUT | | | |
| ❑ 20th Century Fox 3192 [M] | | 1966 | 30.00 |
| ❑ 20th Century Fox S-4192 [S] | | 1966 | 40.00 |
| WEDDING IN MONACO | | | |
| ❑ Mercury MG-20149 [M] | | 1956 | 250.00 |

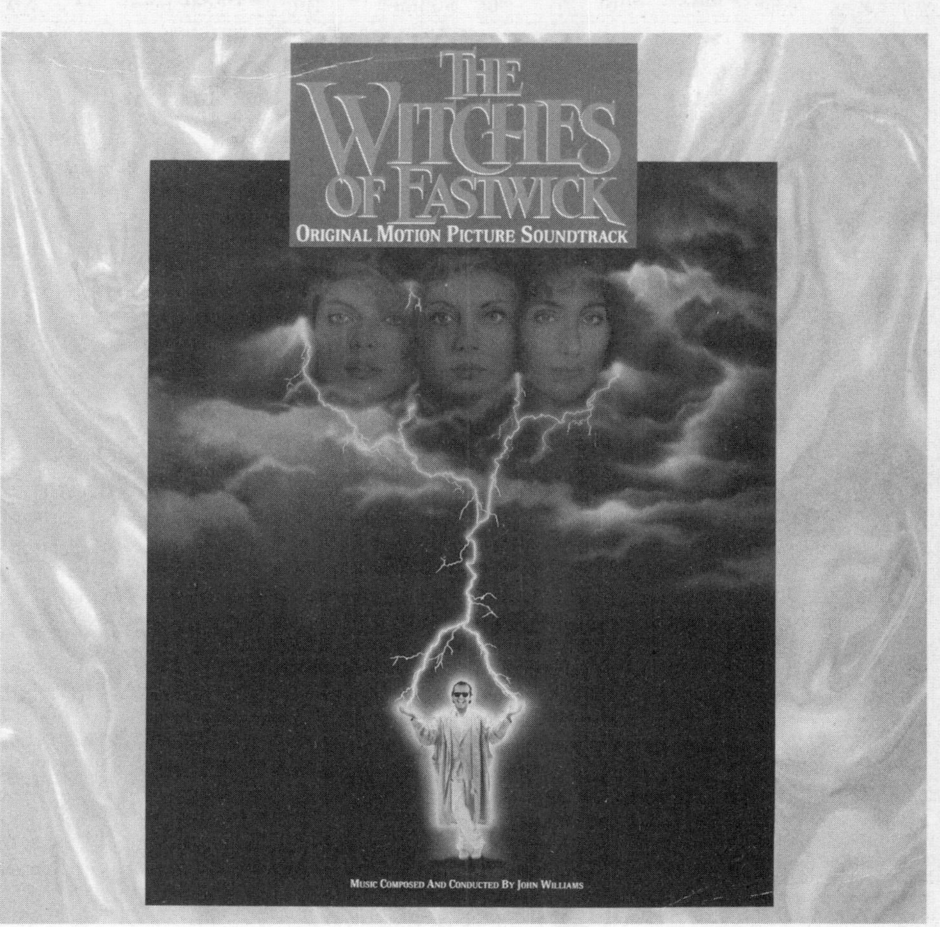


Soundtrack, *The Witches of Eastwick,* Warner Bros. 25607, 1987, $30.

| Number | Title (A Side/B Side) | Yr | NM |
|---|---|---|---|
| WEST SIDE STORY | | | |
| ❑ Columbia Masterworks OS 2070 [S] | | 196? | 12.00 |
| *—Regular cover; gray "360 Sound Stereo" label* | | | |
| ❑ Columbia Masterworks OS 2070 [S] | | 1961 | 25.00 |
| *—Originals have gatefold covers and gray and black labels with six "eye" logos* | | | |
| ❑ Columbia Masterworks OS 2070 [S] | | 1963 | 15.00 |
| *—Gatefold cover; gray "360 Sound Stereo" label* | | | |
| ❑ Columbia Masterworks OS 2070 [S] | | 1971 | 10.00 |
| *—Regular cover; olive label with "Columbia" continuously around edge* | | | |
| ❑ Columbia Masterworks OL 5670 [M] | | 196? | 10.00 |
| *—Regular cover; gray "360 Sound Stereo" label* | | | |
| ❑ Columbia Masterworks OL 5670 [M] | | 1961 | 20.00 |
| *—Originals have gatefold covers and gray and black labels with six "eye" logos* | | | |
| ❑ Columbia Masterworks OL 5670 [M] | | 1963 | 12.00 |
| *—Gatefold cover; gray "360 Sound Stereo" label* | | | |
| WHAT A WAY TO GO! | | | |
| ❑ 20th Century Fox TFM-3143 [M] | | 1964 | 20.00 |
| ❑ 20th Century Fox TFS-4143 [S] | | 1964 | 40.00 |
| WHAT'S NEW PUSSYCAT? | | | |
| ❑ United Artists UA-LA278-G | | 1974 | 12.00 |
| *—Reissue of 5128* | | | |
| ❑ United Artists UAL-4128 [M] | | 1965 | 20.00 |
| ❑ United Artists UAS-5128 [S] | | 1965 | 25.00 |
| WHEN THE BOYS MEET THE GIRLS | | | |
| ❑ MCA 25013 | | 1986 | 10.00 |
| *—Reissue of MGM 4334* | | | |
| ❑ MGM E-4334 [M] | | 1965 | 15.00 |
| ❑ MGM SE-4334 [S] | | 1965 | 30.00 |
| WHERE EAGLES DARE | | | |
| ❑ MCA 25082 | | 1986 | 10.00 |
| *—Reissue of MGM S1E-16* | | | |
| ❑ MGM S1E-16 ST | | 1969 | 30.00 |
| WHERE'S JACK? | | | |
| ❑ Paramount PAS-5005 | | 1969 | 25.00 |
| WHERE'S POPPA? | | | |
| ❑ United Artists UAS-5216 | | 1970 | 25.00 |
| THE WHISPERERS | | | |
| ❑ MCA 25041 | | 1986 | 10.00 |
| *—Reissue of United Artists 5161* | | | |
| ❑ United Artists UAL-4161 [M] | | 1967 | 20.00 |
| ❑ United Artists UAS-5161 [S] | | 1967 | 30.00 |
| WHITE CHRISTMAS | | | |
| ❑ Decca DL 8083 | | 1954 | 50.00 |
| WHO FRAMED ROGER RABBIT? | | | |
| ❑ Buena Vista 64100 | | 1988 | 20.00 |

| Number | Title (A Side/B Side) | Yr | NM |
|---|---|---|---|
| WHO'S AFRAID OF VIRGINIA WOOLF? | | | |
| ❑ Warner Bros. B 1656 [M] | | 1966 | 25.00 |
| ❑ Warner Bros. BS 1656 [S] | | 1966 | 30.00 |
| ❑ Warner Bros. 2B 1657 [(2)M] | | 1966 | 40.00 |
| *—Above (1657) is the complete film, not just the music and some dialogue* | | | |
| THE WILD BUNCH | | | |
| ❑ Varese Sarabande STV-81145 | | 1981 | 15.00 |
| *—Reissue of Warner Bros. 1814* | | | |
| ❑ Warner Bros. WS 1814 | | 1969 | 100.00 |
| THE WILD EYE | | | |
| ❑ RCA Victor LSP-4003 | | 1968 | 25.00 |
| WILD GEESE | | | |
| ❑ A&M SP-4730 | | 1978 | 20.00 |
| WILD IN THE STREETS | | | |
| ❑ Tower SKAO 5099 | | 1968 | 30.00 |
| WILD IS THE WIND | | | |
| ❑ Columbia CL 1090 [M] | | 1957 | 25.00 |
| WILD ON THE BEACH | | | |
| ❑ RCA Victor LPM-3441 [M] | | 1965 | 25.00 |
| ❑ RCA Victor LSP-3441 [S] | | 1965 | 40.00 |
| THE WILD ONE | | | |
| ❑ Decca DL 5515 [10] | | 1954 | 80.00 |
| ❑ Decca DL 8349 [M] | | 1956 | 40.00 |
| THE WILD RACERS | | | |
| ❑ Sidewalk ST-5914 | | 1968 | 25.00 |
| WILD WHEELS | | | |
| ❑ RCA Victor LSO-1156 | | 1969 | 20.00 |
| WILD, WILD WINTER | | | |
| ❑ Decca DL 4699 [M] | | 1966 | 20.00 |
| ❑ Decca DL 74699 [S] | | 1966 | 30.00 |
| WILLIE DYNAMITE | | | |
| ❑ MCA 393 | | 1974 | 20.00 |
| WILLOW | | | |
| ❑ Virgin Movie Music 90939 | | 1988 | 25.00 |
| WILLY WONKA AND THE CHOCOLATE FACTORY | | | |
| ❑ MCA 37124 | | 198? | 10.00 |
| *—Reissue of Paramount 6012* | | | |
| ❑ Paramount PAS-6012 | | 1971 | 40.00 |
| THE WITCHES OF EASTWICK | | | |
| ❑ Warner Bros. 25607 | | 1987 | 30.00 |
| WITH A SONG IN MY HEART | | | |
| ❑ Capitol L 309 [10] | | 1952 | 40.00 |
| ❑ Capitol T 309 [M] | | 195? | 25.00 |

| Number | Title (A Side/B Side) | Yr | NM |
|---|---|---|---|
| THE WIZARD OF OZ | | | |
| ❑ MCA 39046 | | 198? | 10.00 |
| *—Reissue of MGM 3996* | | | |
| ❑ MGM E-3464 [M] | | 1956 | 50.00 |
| *—Yellow label* | | | |
| ❑ MGM E-3996 [M] | | 1962 | 15.00 |
| *—Gatefold cover, black label* | | | |
| ❑ MGM SE-3996 [R] | | 196? | 15.00 |
| *—Gatefold cover, black label* | | | |
| WOMEN OF THE WORLD | | | |
| ❑ Decca DL 9112 [M] | | 1963 | 20.00 |
| ❑ Decca DL 79112 [S] | | 1963 | 30.00 |
| WONDERFUL COUNTRY | | | |
| ❑ United Artists UAL-4050 [M] | | 1959 | 50.00 |
| ❑ United Artists UAS-5050 [S] | | 1959 | 100.00 |
| WONDERFUL TO BE YOUNG | | | |
| ❑ Dot DLP-3474 [M] | | 1962 | 25.00 |
| ❑ Dot DLP-25474 [S] | | 1962 | 40.00 |
| THE WONDERFUL WORLD OF THE BROTHERS GRIMM | | | |
| ❑ MGM 1E-3 [M] | | 1962 | 25.00 |
| *—With box and hardback book* | | | |
| ❑ MGM S1E-3 [S] | | 1962 | 40.00 |
| *—With box and hardback book* | | | |
| WORDS AND MUSIC | | | |
| ❑ MCA 25029 | | 1986 | 12.00 |
| *—Reissue of MGM 505 with the addition of "Slaughter on Tenth Avenue," which does not appear on either the 10-inch LP or the budget-line Metro reissues* | | | |
| ❑ Metro M-580 [M] | | 1966 | 12.00 |
| ❑ Metro MS-580 [R] | | 1966 | 10.00 |
| ❑ MGM E-505 [10] | | 1950 | 50.00 |
| THE WORLD OF SUZIE WONG | | | |
| ❑ RCA Victor LOC-1059 [M] | | 1960 | 20.00 |
| ❑ RCA Victor LSO-1059 [S] | | 1960 | 50.00 |
| WRITTEN ON THE WIND | | | |
| ❑ Decca DL 8424 [M] | | 1956 | 40.00 |
| *—Black label, silver print, or pink label, black print promo* | | | |
| ❑ Decca DL 8424 [M] | | 196? | 20.00 |
| *—Black label with color bars* | | | |
| ❑ Varese Sarabande VC-81074 | | 1979 | 12.00 |
| *—Reissue of Decca 8424* | | | |
| THE WRONG BOX | | | |
| ❑ Mainstream S-6088 [S] | | 1966 | 150.00 |
| ❑ Mainstream 56088 [M] | | 1966 | 100.00 |
| WUTHERING HEIGHTS | | | |
| ❑ American Int'l. A-1039 | | 1971 | 30.00 |
| THE YELLOW CANARY | | | |
| ❑ Verve V-8548 [M] | | 1963 | 20.00 |
| ❑ Verve V6-8548 [S] | | 1963 | 25.00 |
| THE YELLOW ROLLS-ROYCE | | | |
| ❑ MGM E-4292 [M] | | 1965 | 20.00 |
| ❑ MGM SE-4292 [S] | | 1965 | 30.00 |
| ❑ MGM ST 90424 [S] | | 1965 | 15.00 |
| *—Capitol Record Club edition* | | | |
| ❑ MGM T 90424 [M] | | 1965 | 15.00 |
| *—Capitol Record Club edition* | | | |
| YESTERDAY, TODAY AND TOMORROW | | | |
| ❑ Warner Bros. W 1552 [M] | | 1964 | 40.00 |
| ❑ Warner Bros. WS 1552 [S] | | 1964 | 50.00 |
| YOJIMBO | | | |
| ❑ MGM E-4096 [M] | | 1962 | 100.00 |
| ❑ MGM SE-4096 [S] | | 1962 | 150.00 |
| YOU ARE WHAT YOU EAT | | | |
| ❑ Columbia Masterworks OS 3240 | | 1968 | 20.00 |
| YOU ONLY LIVE TWICE | | | |
| ❑ United Artists UA-LA289-G | | 1974 | 12.00 |
| *—Reissue of 5155* | | | |
| ❑ United Artists UAL-4155 [M] | | 1967 | 20.00 |
| ❑ United Artists UAS-5155 [S] | | 1967 | 25.00 |
| YOUNG BILLY YOUNG | | | |
| ❑ MCA 25031 | | 1986 | 10.00 |
| *—Reissue of United Artists 5199* | | | |
| ❑ United Artists UAS-5199 | | 1969 | 25.00 |
| YOUNG DOCTORS IN LOVE | | | |
| ❑ Regency RI-8501 | | 1982 | 20.00 |
| YOUNG FRANKENSTEIN | | | |
| ❑ ABC ABCD-870 | | 1975 | 20.00 |
| THE YOUNG GIRLS OF ROCHEFORT | | | |
| ❑ Philips PCC 2-226 [(2)M] | | 1968 | 20.00 |
| ❑ Philips PCC 2-626 [(2)S] | | 1968 | 30.00 |
| THE YOUNG LIONS | | | |
| ❑ Decca DL 8719 [M] | | 1958 | 30.00 |
| ❑ Decca DL 78719 [S] | | 1958 | 80.00 |
| ❑ Varese Sarabande STV-81115 | | 1981 | 15.00 |
| *—Reissue of Decca 78719* | | | |
| YOUNG LOVERS | | | |
| ❑ Columbia Masterworks OS 2510 [S] | | 1964 | 25.00 |
| ❑ Columbia Masterworks OL 7010 [M] | | 1964 | 20.00 |
| YOUNG MAN WITH A HORN | | | |
| ❑ Columbia CL 582 [M] | | 1950 | 40.00 |
| ❑ Columbia CL 6106 [10] | | 1950 | 100.00 |
| THE YOUNG SAVAGES | | | |
| ❑ Columbia CL 1672 [M] | | 1961 | 30.00 |
| ❑ Columbia CS 8472 [S] | | 1961 | 100.00 |
| YOUNG WINSTON | | | |
| ❑ Angel SFO-36901 | | 1972 | 25.00 |
| YOURS, MINE AND OURS | | | |
| ❑ MCA 1434 | | 198? | 8.00 |
| *—Reissue of United Artists 5181* | | | |
| ❑ United Artists UAS-5181 | | 1968 | 20.00 |

| Number | Title (A Side/B Side) | Yr | NM |
|---|---|---|---|
| Z | | | |
| ❑ Columbia Masterworks OS 3370 | | 1970 | 20.00 |
| ZABRISKIE POINT | | | |
| ❑ MCA 25032 | | 1986 | 10.00 |
| *—Reissue of MGM 4468* | | | |
| ❑ MGM SE-4468 | | 1970 | 20.00 |
| ZACHARIAH | | | |
| ❑ ABC ABCS-OC-13 | | 1970 | 25.00 |
| ZOOT SUIT | | | |
| ❑ MCA 5267 | | 1981 | 20.00 |
| ZORBA THE GREEK | | | |
| ❑ Casablanca 826245-1 | | 198? | 8.00 |
| *—Reissue of 20th Century 903* | | | |
| ❑ 20th Century T-903 | | 1973 | 12.00 |
| *—Reissue of 20th Century Fox 4167* | | | |
| ❑ 20th Century Fox TFM-3167 [M] | | 1965 | 20.00 |
| ❑ 20th Century Fox TFS-4167 [S] | | 1965 | 25.00 |
| ZULU | | | |
| ❑ United Artists UAL-4116 [M] | | 1964 | 40.00 |
| ❑ United Artists UAS-5116 [S] | | 1964 | 70.00 |

# TELEVISION RECORDS

| Number | Title (A Side/B Side) | Yr | NM |
|---|---|---|---|
| THE ADDAMS FAMILY | | | |
| ❑ RCA Victor LPM-3421 [M] | | 1965 | 80.00 |
| ❑ RCA Victor LSP-3421 [S] | | 1965 | 150.00 |
| AFRICA | | | |
| ❑ MGM E-4462 [M] | | 1967 | 50.00 |
| ❑ MGM SE-4462 [S] | | 1967 | 60.00 |
| THE AGE OF TELEVISION — A CHRONICLE OF THE FIRST 25 YEARS | | | |
| ❑ RCA Victor LL-8 | | 1972 | 20.00 |
| *—With booklet* | | | |
| ❑ Warner Bros. BS 2670 | | 1972 | 30.00 |
| *—With booklet; this version seems to be much rarer than the RCA issue* | | | |
| ALADDIN | | | |
| ❑ Columbia CL 1117 [M] | | 1958 | 50.00 |
| ALICE THROUGH THE LOOKING GLASS | | | |
| ❑ RCA Victor LOC-1130 [M] | | 1966 | 25.00 |
| ❑ RCA Victor LSO-1130 [S] | | 1966 | 30.00 |
| AMAHL AND THE NIGHT VISITORS | | | |
| ❑ RCA Red Seal LM-1701 [10] | | 1952 | 50.00 |
| *—Soundtrack of the 1951 NBC-TV production* | | | |
| ❑ RCA Red Seal LM-1701 [M] | | 1952 | 40.00 |
| *—Soundtrack of the 1951 NBC-TV production; 12-inch record in box with booklet* | | | |
| ❑ RCA Red Seal LM-2762 [M] | | 1964 | 15.00 |
| *—Soundtrack of the 1963 NBC Opera Company TV production* | | | |
| ❑ RCA Red Seal LSC-2762 [S] | | 1964 | 15.00 |
| *—Large "RCA Victor" and dog at top of label* | | | |
| ❑ RCA Red Seal LSC-2762 [S] | | 1969 | 12.00 |
| *—Stereo reissue on red label without dog; no bar code on back cover* | | | |
| ❑ RCA Red Seal LSC-2762 [S] | | 198? | 10.00 |
| *—Stereo reissue on red label without dog; with bar code on back cover* | | | |
| ANDROCLES AND THE LION | | | |
| ❑ RCA Victor LOC-1141 [M] | | 1967 | 25.00 |
| ❑ RCA Victor LSO-1141 [S] | | 1967 | 25.00 |
| ANNIE GET YOUR GUN | | | |
| ❑ Capitol W 913 [M] | | 1957 | 30.00 |
| *—Los Angeles/San Francisco production aired on NBC-TV* | | | |
| AT HOME WITH THE MUNSTERS | | | |
| ❑ Golden LP-139 [M] | | 1964 | 200.00 |
| ATOM ANT IN MUSCLE MAGIC | | | |
| ❑ Hanna-Barbera HLP-2041 [M] | | 1966 | 150.00 |
| THE AVENGERS | | | |
| ❑ Hanna-Barbera HLP-8506 [M] | | 1966 | 60.00 |
| ❑ Hanna-Barbera HST-9506 [S] | | 1966 | 80.00 |
| BATMAN | | | |
| ❑ 20th Century Fox TFM-3180 [M] | | 1966 | 60.00 |
| ❑ 20th Century Fox TFS-4180 [S] | | 1966 | 100.00 |
| THE BEVERLY HILLBILLIES | | | |
| ❑ Columbia CL 2402 [M] | | 1965 | 40.00 |
| ❑ Columbia CS 9202 [S] | | 1965 | 60.00 |
| THE BIG VALLEY | | | |
| ❑ ABC-Paramount ABC-527 [M] | | 1965 | 40.00 |
| ❑ ABC-Paramount ABCS-527 [S] | | 1965 | 50.00 |
| THE BORN LOSERS | | | |
| ❑ Tower DT 5082 [R] | | 1967 | 20.00 |
| ❑ Tower T 5082 [M] | | 1967 | 25.00 |
| THE BORROWERS | | | |
| ❑ Stanyan SRQ-4014 [Q] | | 1973 | 50.00 |
| BOURBON STREET BEAT | | | |
| ❑ Warner Bros. W 1321 [M] | | 1960 | 25.00 |
| ❑ Warner Bros. WS 1321 [S] | | 1960 | 30.00 |
| BRIGADOON | | | |
| ❑ Columbia Special Products CSM 385 | | 1968 | 20.00 |
| *—Sold through the mail by broadcast sponsor Armstrong* | | | |
| BURKE'S LAW | | | |
| ❑ Liberty LRP-3374 [M] | | 1964 | 60.00 |
| ❑ Liberty LST-7374 [S] | | 1964 | 80.00 |
| CAROUSEL | | | |
| ❑ Columbia Special Products CSM 479 | | 1969 | 20.00 |
| *—Sold through the mail by broadcast sponsor Armstrong* | | | |

| Number | Title (A Side/B Side) | Yr | NM |
|---|---|---|---|
| A CHARLIE BROWN CHRISTMAS | | | |
| ❑ Charlie Brown 3701 | | 1977 | 20.00 |
| *—Complete soundtrack with dialogue, plus music by Vince Guaraldi; includes 12-page bound-in booklet with script and illustrations* | | | |
| CHECKMATE | | | |
| ❑ Columbia CL 1591 [M] | | 1960 | 40.00 |
| ❑ Columbia CS 8391 [S] | | 1960 | 60.00 |
| CINDERELLA | | | |
| ❑ Columbia Masterworks OS 2005 [S] | | 1959 | 40.00 |
| *—Stage presentation for TV starring Julie Andrews* | | | |
| ❑ Columbia Masterworks OS 2730 [S] | | 1965 | 30.00 |
| *—Stage presentation for TV starring Lesley-Ann Warren* | | | |
| ❑ Columbia Masterworks OL 5190 [M] | | 1957 | 30.00 |
| ❑ Columbia Masterworks OL 6330 [M] | | 1965 | 25.00 |
| THE COMING OF CHRIST | | | |
| ❑ Decca DL 9093 [M] | | 1960 | 40.00 |
| ❑ Decca DL 79093 [S] | | 1960 | 50.00 |
| THE CRICKET ON THE HEARTH | | | |
| ❑ RCA Victor LOC-1140 [M] | | 1967 | 20.00 |
| ❑ RCA Victor LSO-1140 [S] | | 1967 | 30.00 |
| DANGER | | | |
| ❑ MGM E-111 [10] | | 1951 | 120.00 |
| THE DANGEROUS CHRISTMAS OF RED RIDING HOOD | | | |
| ❑ ABC-Paramount ABC-536 [M] | | 1965 | 15.00 |
| ❑ ABC-Paramount ABCS-536 [S] | | 1965 | 25.00 |
| DARK SHADOWS | | | |
| ❑ Philips PHS 600314 | | 1969 | 30.00 |
| *—With poster* | | | |
| DAVID COPPERFIELD | | | |
| ❑ GRT 10008 | | 1970 | 150.00 |
| DENNIS THE MENACE SONGS | | | |
| ❑ Golden LP-59 [M] | | 1960 | 80.00 |
| *—Black label original* | | | |
| DOGGIE DADDY TELLS AUGGY DOGGIE THE STORY OF PINOCCHIO | | | |
| ❑ Hanna-Barbera HLP-2028 [M] | | 1965 | 100.00 |
| EAST SIDE, WEST SIDE | | | |
| ❑ Columbia CL 2123 [M] | | 1963 | 30.00 |
| ❑ Columbia CS 8923 [S] | | 1963 | 40.00 |
| ELEVEN AGAINST THE ICE | | | |
| ❑ RCA Victor LPM-1618 [M] | | 1958 | 60.00 |
| ELIZABETH TAYLOR IN LONDON | | | |
| ❑ Colpix CP 459 [M] | | 1963 | 30.00 |
| ❑ Colpix SCP 459 [S] | | 1963 | 50.00 |
| THE EWOK ADVENTURE | | | |
| ❑ Varese Sarabande STV-81281 | | 198? | 50.00 |
| EXCITING HONG KONG | | | |
| ❑ ABC-Paramount ABC-367 [M] | | 1961 | 40.00 |
| ❑ ABC-Paramount ABCS-367 [S] | | 1961 | 50.00 |
| FAWLTY TOWERS | | | |
| ❑ BBC 22377 | | 1980 | 20.00 |
| *—Excerpts from two episodes of the series; pressed by Columbia, possibly for exclusive use by the record club* | | | |
| FAWTLY TOWERS — SECOND SITTING | | | |
| ❑ BBC 22405 | | 1981 | 20.00 |
| *—More excerpts from the series; again, pressed by Columbia possibly for exclusive record club use* | | | |
| FELIX THE CAT | | | |
| ❑ Cricket CR-28 [M] | | 1958 | 100.00 |
| FENWICK | | | |
| ❑ Fenwick FLP-621 | | 1968 | 20.00 |
| *—Soundtrack to TV special; packaged in oversize (13 1/2 x 13 1/2) sleeve with color cartoon booklet; made especially for Motorola* | | | |
| THE FLINTSTONES | | | |
| ❑ Colpix CP-302 [M] | | 1961 | 200.00 |
| THE FLINTSTONES AND JOSE JIMENEZ IN THE TIME MACHINE | | | |
| ❑ Hanna-Barbera HLP-2052 [M] | | 1966 | 80.00 |
| THE FLINTSTONES IN S.A.S.F.A.T.P.O.G.O.B.S.O.A.L.T. | | | |
| ❑ Hanna-Barbera HLP-2047 [M] | | 1966 | 100.00 |
| THE FLINTSTONES' FLIP FABLES: GOLDI-ROCKS AND THE THREE BEAROSAURUSES | | | |
| ❑ Hanna-Barbera HLP-2021 [M] | | 1965 | 100.00 |
| THE FORD 50TH ANNIVERSARY TELEVISION SHOW | | | |
| ❑ Decca DL 7027 [10] | | 1953 | 40.00 |
| FOUR ADVENTURES OF ZORRO | | | |
| ❑ Disneyland WDA-3601 [M] | | 1958 | 80.00 |
| *—Gatefold with booklet* | | | |
| FRED FLINTSTONE AND BARNEY RUBBLE SING SONGS FROM MARY POPPINS | | | |
| ❑ Hanna-Barbera HLP-2035 [M] | | 1965 | 100.00 |
| FROSTY THE SNOWMAN | | | |
| ❑ MGM SE-4733 | | 1970 | 60.00 |
| FROSTY'S WINTER WONDERLAND | | | |
| ❑ Disneyland 1368 | | 1976 | 20.00 |
| GENERAL ELECTRIC THEATER | | | |
| ❑ Columbia CL 1395 [M] | | 1959 | 40.00 |
| ❑ Columbia CS 8190 [S] | | 1959 | 50.00 |
| GENERAL MOTORS' 50TH ANNIVERSARY SHOW | | | |
| ❑ RCA Victor LOC-1037 [M] | | 1958 | 100.00 |
| GET SMART | | | |
| ❑ United Artists UAL-3533 [M] | | 1965 | 40.00 |
| ❑ United Artists UAS-6566 [S] | | 1965 | 60.00 |
| THE GIFT OF LOVE | | | |
| ❑ Columbia CL 1113 [M] | | 1958 | 30.00 |

| Number | Title (A Side/B Side) | Yr | NM |
|---|---|---|---|
| THE GIFT OF THE MAGI | | | |
| ❑ United Artists UAL-4013 [M] | | 1959 | 40.00 |
| ❑ United Artists UAS-5103 [S] | | 1959 | 50.00 |
| THE GIRL FROM U.N.C.L.E. | | | |
| ❑ MGM E-4410 [M] | | 1966 | 40.00 |
| ❑ MGM SE-4410 [S] | | 1966 | 60.00 |
| GOOFY'S TV SPECTACULAR | | | |
| ❑ Disneyland DQ-1252 [M] | | 1964 | 20.00 |
| THE GREEN HORNET | | | |
| ❑ 20th Century Fox S-3186 [S] | | 1966 | 250.00 |
| ❑ 20th Century Fox TF-3186 [M] | | 1966 | 200.00 |
| HANS BRINKER | | | |
| ❑ Dot DLP-9001 [M] | | 1958 | 40.00 |
| HANSEL AND GRETEL STARRING THE FLINTSTONES | | | |
| ❑ Hanna-Barbera HLP-2038 [M] | | 1965 | 100.00 |
| HAWAII FIVE-O | | | |
| ❑ Capitol ST-410 | | 1969 | 40.00 |
| HAWAIIAN EYE | | | |
| ❑ Warner Bros. W 1355 [M] | | 1959 | 30.00 |
| ❑ Warner Bros. WS 1355 [S] | | 1959 | 40.00 |
| HECTOR, THE STOWAWAY PUP | | | |
| ❑ Disneyland ST-1921 [M] | | 1964 | 30.00 |
| HEIDI | | | |
| ❑ Capitol SKAO 2995 | | 1968 | 40.00 |
| HENNESSEY | | | |
| ❑ Signature 1049 [M] | | 1959 | 60.00 |
| ❑ Signature SS-1049 [S] | | 1959 | 80.00 |
| HERE COMES HUCKLEBERRY HOUND | | | |
| ❑ Colpix CP-207 [M] | | 1961 | 180.00 |
| HERE'S JOHNNY! MAGIC MOMENTS FROM THE TONIGHT SHOW | | | |
| ❑ Casablanca SPNB-1296 [(2)] | | 1976 | 20.00 |
| *—Price for intact copies with poster; cut-outs go for 50-75 percent of this* | | | |
| HEY THERE, IT'S YOGI BEAR | | | |
| ❑ Golden LP-124 [M] | | 1964 | 40.00 |
| HIGH TOR | | | |
| ❑ Decca DL 8272 [M] | | 1956 | 400.00 |
| THE HILLBILLY BEARS IN HILLBILLY SHINDIG | | | |
| ❑ Hanna-Barbera HLP-2044 [M] | | 1966 | 150.00 |
| HOGAN'S HEROES SING THE BEST OF WWII | | | |
| ❑ Sunset SUM-1137 [M] | | 1967 | 30.00 |
| ❑ Sunset SUS-5137 [S] | | 1967 | 40.00 |
| HOLOCAUST | | | |
| ❑ RCA Victor ARL1-2785 | | 1978 | 25.00 |
| HONEY WEST | | | |
| ❑ ABC-Paramount ABC-532 [M] | | 1965 | 40.00 |
| ❑ ABC-Paramount ABCS-532 [S] | | 1965 | 50.00 |
| HOW THE GRINCH STOLE CHRISTMAS | | | |
| ❑ Leo LE-901 [M] | | 1966 | 50.00 |
| ❑ Leo LES-901 [S] | | 1966 | 70.00 |
| ❑ Mercury Nashville 528439-1 | | 1995 | 20.00 |
| *—Picture disc* | | | |
| HOWL ALONG WITH HUCKLEBERRY HOUND AND YOGI BEAR | | | |
| ❑ Golden LP-55 [M] | | 1959 | 150.00 |
| *—Black label original* | | | |
| HUCKLEBERRY HOUND AND THE GHOST SHIP | | | |
| ❑ Colpix CP-210 [M] | | 1962 | 100.00 |
| HUCKLEBERRY HOUND FOR PRESIDENT | | | |
| ❑ Golden LP-60 [M] | | 1960 | 100.00 |
| *—Black label original* | | | |
| HUCKLEBERRY HOUND TELLS STORIES OF UNCLE REMUS | | | |
| ❑ Hanna-Barbera HLP-2022 [M] | | 1965 | 100.00 |
| HUCKLEBERRY HOUND, THE GREAT KELLOGG'S TV SHOW | | | |
| ❑ Colpix CP-202 [M] | | 1959 | 200.00 |
| I SPY | | | |
| ❑ Warner Bros. W 1637 [M] | | 1965 | 30.00 |
| ❑ Warner Bros. WS 1637 [S] | | 1965 | 40.00 |
| I SPY, VOLUME 2 | | | |
| ❑ Capitol ST 2839 | | 1968 | 30.00 |
| IT'S HOWDY DOODY TIME | | | |
| ❑ RCA Victor LSP-4546 | | 1971 | 25.00 |
| THE JACKSONS: AN AMERICAN DREAM | | | |
| ❑ Motown 37463 6356-1 [DJ] | | 1992 | 20.00 |
| *—Promo only vinyl* | | | |
| JAMES BOMB STARRING SUPER SNOOPER AND BLABBER MOUSE | | | |
| ❑ Hanna-Barbera HLP-2036 [M] | | 1965 | 100.00 |
| JANE EYRE | | | |
| ❑ Capitol SW-749 | | 1971 | 30.00 |
| THE JETSONS | | | |
| ❑ Colpix CP-213 [M] | | 1962 | 250.00 |
| ❑ Golden LP-98 [M] | | 1963 | 200.00 |
| *—Red cover original* | | | |
| ❑ Golden LP-98 [M] | | 1964 | 120.00 |
| *—Blue cover reissue* | | | |
| THE JETSONS IN FIRST FAMILY ON THE MOON | | | |
| ❑ Hanna-Barbera HLP-2037 [M] | | 1965 | 150.00 |
| THE JIMMY DURANTE TV SHOW | | | |
| ❑ Royale 1812 [10] | | 1955 | 100.00 |
| JONNY QUEST IN 20,000 LEAGUES UNDER THE SEA | | | |
| ❑ Hanna-Barbera HLP-2030 [M] | | 1965 | 150.00 |

Television soundtrack, *The Dangerous Christmas of Red Riding Hood,* ABC-Paramount ABCS-536, 1965, stereo, $25.

| Number | Title (A Side/B Side) | Yr | NM |
|---|---|---|---|
| JOURNEY BACK TO OZ | | | |
| ❑ Filmation (no #) | | 1980 | 50.00 |
| KENT STATE | | | |
| ❑ RCA Victor ABL1-3928 | | 1981 | 20.00 |
| KING KONG | | | |
| ❑ Golden LP-151 [M] | | 1965 | 40.00 |
| KISS ME, KATE | | | |
| ❑ Columbia Special Products CSS 645 | | 1968 | 25.00 |
| *—Sold through the mail by broadcast sponsor Armstrong* | | | |
| A LOOK AT MONACO | | | |
| ❑ Columbia CL 2019 [M] | | 1963 | 50.00 |
| ❑ Columbia CS 8819 [R] | | 1963 | 50.00 |
| LOVE, AMERICAN STYLE | | | |
| ❑ Capitol ST-11250 | | 1973 | 40.00 |
| MAGILLA GORILLA AND HIS PALS | | | |
| ❑ Golden LP-120 [M] | | 1964 | 50.00 |
| MAGILLA GORILLA TELLS OGEE THE STORY OF ALICE IN WONDERLAND | | | |
| ❑ Hanna-Barbera HLP-2024 [M] | | 1965 | 100.00 |
| THE MAN FROM INTERPOL | | | |
| ❑ Top Rank RM-327 [M] | | 1962 | 50.00 |
| ❑ Top Rank RS-627 [S] | | 1962 | 60.00 |
| THE MAN FROM U.N.C.L.E. | | | |
| ❑ RCA Victor LPM-3475 [M] | | 1965 | 60.00 |
| ❑ RCA Victor LSP-3475 [S] | | 1965 | 80.00 |
| THE MAN FROM U.N.C.L.E. VOLUME 2 | | | |
| ❑ RCA Victor LPM-3574 [M] | | 1966 | 40.00 |
| ❑ RCA Victor LSP-3574 [S] | | 1966 | 50.00 |
| MARK TWAIN TONIGHT! | | | |
| ❑ Columbia Masterworks OS 3080 [S] | | 1967 | 20.00 |
| ❑ Columbia Masterworks OL 6680 [M] | | 1967 | 15.00 |
| MASADA | | | |
| ❑ MCA 5168 | | 1981 | 20.00 |
| MERRY CHRISTMAS FROM KUKLA, FRAN AND OLLIE | | | |
| ❑ Decca DL 8192 [M] | | 1955 | 80.00 |
| MICKEY MOUSE CLUB — ALL NEW FROM 1977 — ORIGINAL TV CAST | | | |
| ❑ Buena Vista 62501 | | 1979 | 20.00 |
| MICKEY MOUSE CLUB MOUSEKEDANCES AND OTHER MOUSEKETEER FAVORITES | | | |
| ❑ Disneyland DQ-1362 [M] | | 1974 | 20.00 |
| *—With booklet* | | | |
| ❑ Disneyland STER-1362 [S] | | 1974 | 25.00 |
| *—With booklet* | | | |

| Number | Title (A Side/B Side) | Yr | NM |
|---|---|---|---|
| MICKEY MOUSE CLUB SONG HITS | | | |
| ❑ Disneyland ST-3815 | | 1975 | 40.00 |
| *—With 16-page photo album* | | | |
| MICKEY MOUSE CLUB: 27 NEW SONGS FROM THE MICKEY MOUSE CLUB TV SHOW | | | |
| ❑ Mickey Mouse Club MM-14 | | 1958 | 50.00 |
| MICKEY MOUSE CLUB: A WALT DISNEY SONG FEST | | | |
| ❑ Mickey Mouse Club MM-20 | | 1958 | 40.00 |
| MICKEY MOUSE CLUB: FUN WITH MUSIC — 30 FAVORITE DISNEY SONGS | | | |
| ❑ Disneyland DQ-1209 [M] | | 1959 | 25.00 |
| MICKEY MOUSE CLUB: HOLIDAYS WITH THE MOUSEKETEERS (A SONG FOR EVERY HOLIDAY) | | | |
| ❑ Mickey Mouse Club MM-22 | | 1958 | 40.00 |
| MICKEY MOUSE CLUB: HOW TO BE A MOUSEKETEER | | | |
| ❑ Disneyland ST-3918 | | 1962 | 40.00 |
| MICKEY MOUSE CLUB: MOUSEKETEERS TALENT ROUNDUP | | | |
| ❑ Mickey Mouse Club MM-16 | | 1958 | 40.00 |
| MICKEY MOUSE CLUB: MUSICAL HIGHLIGHTS FROM THE MICKEY MOUSE CLUB | | | |
| ❑ Disneyland DQ-1227 [M] | | 1962 | 30.00 |
| MICKEY MOUSE CLUB: MUSICAL HIGHLIGHTS FROM THE MICKEY MOUSE CLUB TV SHOW | | | |
| ❑ Mickey Mouse Club MM-12 | | 1958 | 80.00 |
| MICKEY MOUSE CLUB: SONGS FROM ANNETTE AND OTHER WALT DISNEY SERIALS | | | |
| ❑ Mickey Mouse Club MM-24 | | 1958 | 120.00 |
| MICKEY MOUSE CLUB: SONGS FROM THE MICKEY MOUSE CLUB SERIALS | | | |
| ❑ Disneyland DQ-1229 [M] | | 1962 | 40.00 |
| MICKEY MOUSE CLUB: THE ALL NEW MICKEY MOUSE CLUB | | | |
| ❑ Disneyland 2501 | | 1977 | 20.00 |
| MICKEY MOUSE CLUB: WE'RE THE MOUSEKETEERS | | | |
| ❑ Mickey Mouse Club MM-18 | | 1957 | 40.00 |
| THE MIGHTY HERCULES | | | |
| ❑ Golden LP-109 [M] | | 1963 | 200.00 |
| MIKADO | | | |
| ❑ Columbia Masterworks OS 2022 [S] | | 1960 | 100.00 |
| ❑ Columbia Masterworks OL 5480 [M] | | 1960 | 30.00 |
| THE MISADVENTURES OF DENNIS THE MENACE | | | |
| ❑ Colpix CP-204 [M] | | 1960 | 200.00 |
| MR. BROADWAY | | | |
| ❑ RCA Victor LPM-1520 [M] | | 1957 | 30.00 |

MR. ED, THE TALKING HORSE
❑ Colpix CP-209 [M] 1962 300.00
MR. ED: STRAIGHT FROM THE HORSE'S MOUTH
❑ Golden LP-88 [M] 1962 200.00
MR. JINKS, PIXIE AND DIXIE
❑ Colpix CP-208 [M] 1961 100.00
THE MUNSTERS
❑ Decca DL 4588 [M] 1964 60.00
❑ Decca DL 74588 [S] 1964 100.00
THE MUSIC FROM M SQUAD
❑ RCA Victor LPM-2062 [M] 1959 30.00
❑ RCA Victor LSP-2062 [S] 1959 40.00
THE MUSIC FROM MARLBORO COUNTRY
❑ United Artists SP-107 1967 50.00
MUSIC FROM SHUBERT ALLEY
❑ Sinclair OSS-2250 [M] 1959 40.00
*—From the NBC TV program, November 13, 1959*
NAKED CITY — A MUSICAL PORTRAIT
❑ Colpix CP-505 [M] 1958 40.00
❑ Colpix SCP-505 [S] 1959 60.00
OF THEE I SING
❑ Columbia S 31763 1972 20.00
THE OFFICIAL ALBUM OF NBC'S BAT MASTERSON
❑ Sea Horse/Chancellor CSH-7002 [M] 1960 80.00
ON THE FLIP SIDE
❑ Decca DL 4836 1966 25.00
❑ Decca DL 74836 [S] 1966 30.00
ONE STEP BEYOND
❑ Decca DL 8970 [M] 1960 30.00
❑ Decca DL 78970 [S] 1960 40.00
ORIGINAL AMATEUR HOUR 25TH ANNIVERSARY ALBUM
❑ United Artists UXL 2 [(2)M] 1960 40.00
THE ORIGINAL TV ADVENTURES OF KING KONG
❑ Epic LN 24231 [M] 1966 25.00
❑ Epic BN 26231 [S] 1966 30.00
THE OTHER WORLD OF WINSTON CHURCHILL
❑ Mercury MG-21033 [M] 1965 30.00
❑ Mercury SR-61033 [S] 1965 40.00
OZZIE AND HARRIET
❑ Imperial LP-9049 [M] 1957 200.00
PEYTON PLACE
❑ Epic LN 24147 [M] 1965 30.00
❑ Epic BN 26147 [S] 1965 40.00
THE PIED PIPER OF HAMELIN
❑ RCA Victor LPM-1563 [M] 1957 50.00
PINOCCHIO
❑ Columbia CL 1055 [M] 1957 40.00
PIXIE AND DIXIE WITH MR. JINKS TELL THE STORY OF CINDERELLA
❑ Hanna-Barbera HLP-2025 [M] 1965 100.00
PRECIOUS PUPP IN HOT ROD GRANNY
❑ Hanna-Barbera HLP-2045 [M] 1966 150.00
QUICK DRAW MCGRAW
❑ Colpix CP-203 [M] 1960 80.00
QUICK DRAW MCGRAW AND HUCKLEBERRY HOUND
❑ Golden LP-51 [M] 1959 150.00
*—Black label original*
QUICK DRAW MCGRAW: THE TREASURE OF SARAH'S MATTRESS
❑ Colpix CP-211 [M] 1962 120.00
THE REPORTER
❑ Columbia CL 2269 [M] 1964 30.00
❑ Columbia CS 9069 [S] 1964 40.00
RICH MAN, POOR MAN
❑ MCA 2095 1976 25.00
RICHARD DIAMOND
❑ EmArcy MG-36162 [M] 1959 50.00
❑ EmArcy SR-80045 [S] 1959 80.00
THE RISE AND FALL OF THE THIRD REICH
❑ MGM 1SE-12 1968 30.00
ROBIN HOOD STARRING TOP CAT
❑ Hanna-Barbera HLP-2031 [M] 1965 100.00
ROCKY AND HIS FRIENDS
❑ Golden LP-64 [M] 1961 200.00
*—Gold label original*
THE ROGUES
❑ RCA Victor LPM-2976 [M] 1964 20.00
❑ RCA Victor LSP-2976 [S] 1964 30.00
ROOTS
❑ Warner Bros. 3WS 3048 [(3)] 1978 25.00
RUDOLPH THE RED-NOSED REINDEER
❑ Decca DL 4815 [M] 1964 60.00
❑ Decca DL 34327 [M] 1965 40.00
*—Same as DL 4815; custom products reissue*
❑ Decca DL 74815 [S] 1964 80.00
❑ MCA 15003 1973 20.00
*—Reissue; black rainbow label*
❑ MCA 15003 198? 12.00
*—Reissue; blue rainbow label*
RUFF AND READY ADVENTURES IN SPACE
❑ Colpix CP-201 [M] 1959 200.00
RUGGLES OF RED GAP
❑ Verve MGV-15000 [M] 1957 50.00
THE SAINT
❑ RCA Victor LPM-3631 [M] 1966 120.00
❑ RCA Victor LSP-3631 [S] 1966 200.00
SANTA CLAUS IS COMIN' TO TOWN
❑ MGM SE-4732 1970 60.00
SATINS AND SPURS
❑ Capitol L 547 [10] 1954 70.00
SECRET AGENT
❑ RCA Victor LPM-3630 [M] 1966 250.00
❑ RCA Victor LSP-3630 [S] 1966 250.00
*—With incorrect title, "Danger Man," on label*
❑ RCA Victor LSP-3630 [S] 1966 300.00
*—With correct title on label*
SECRET AGENT MEETS THE SAINT
❑ RCA Victor LPM-3467 [M] 1965 200.00
❑ RCA Victor LSP-3467 [S] 1965 220.00
*—Music from both TV shows; pre-dates the individual albums*
SECRET SQUIRREL AND MOROCCO MOLE IN SUPER SPY
❑ Hanna-Barbera HLP-2046 [M] 1966 150.00
77 SUNSET STRIP
❑ Warner Bros. W 1289 [M] 1959 30.00
❑ Warner Bros. WS 1289 [S] 1959 40.00
SHOGUN
❑ RSO RX-1-3088 1981 20.00
SHOTGUN SLADE
❑ Mercury MG-20575 [M] 1960 40.00
❑ Mercury SR-60235 [S] 1960 60.00
SINBAD JR. IN TREASURE ISLAND
❑ Hanna-Barbera HLP-2039 [M] 1965 120.00
67 MELODY LANE
❑ Columbia CL 724 [M] 1955 30.00
SNAGGLEPUSS TELLS THE STORY OF THE WIZARD OF OZ
❑ Hanna-Barbera HLP-2026 [M] 1965 100.00
SONGS OF THE FLINTSTONES
❑ Golden LP-66 [M] 1961 250.00
*—Gold label original*
SONGS OF YOGI BEAR AND HIS PALS
❑ Golden LP-70 [M] 1961 80.00
*—Gold label original*
THE SOUND OF JAZZ
❑ Columbia CL 1098 [M] 1958 25.00
❑ Columbia CS 8040 [S] 1958 40.00
SPACE: 1999
❑ RCA Victor ABL1-1422 1975 20.00
SQUIDDLEY DIDDLEY IN SURFIN' SAFARI
❑ Hanna-Barbera HLP-2043 [M] 1966 150.00
STACCATO (MUSIC FROM JOHNNY STACCATO)
❑ Capitol ST 1287 [S] 1959 50.00
❑ Capitol T 1287 [M] 1959 30.00
THE STINGIEST MAN IN TOWN
❑ Columbia CL 950 1956 20.00
*—Music from a television play first aired on The Alcoa Hour*
❑ Columbia Special Products P 12637 1975 10.00
*—Reissue of Columbia LP; same contents*
SUPER SNOOPER AND BLABBER MOUSE IN MONSTER SHINDIG
❑ Hanna-Barbera HLP-2020 [M] 1965 100.00
THRILLER
❑ Time S-2034 [S] 1960 40.00
❑ Time 52034 [M] 1960 30.00
TOM SAWYER
❑ Decca DL 8432 [M] 1957 40.00
*—First aired on the U.S. Steel Hour, starring Jimmy Boyd*
TOP CAT
❑ Colpix CP-212 [M] 1963 300.00
TOUCHE TURTLE AND DUM-DUM IN THE RELUCTANT DRAGON
❑ Hanna-Barbera HLP-2029 [M] 1965 100.00
'TWAS THE NIGHT BEFORE CHRISTMAS
❑ Disneyland 1367 1976 20.00
THE UNTOUCHABLES
❑ Capitol ST 1430 [S] 1960 50.00
❑ Capitol T 1430 [M] 1960 40.00
UP WITH PEOPLE!
❑ Pace 1101 1965 20.00
*—Among the many people on this LP is a young Glenn Close (first name misspelled "Gleen")*
THE VALIANT YEARS
❑ ABC-Paramount ABC-387 [M] 1962 30.00
❑ ABC-Paramount ABCS-387 [S] 1962 40.00
VICTORY AT SEA
❑ Mobile Fidelity 3-150 [(3)] 1984 100.00
*—Audiophile vinyl*
❑ RCA Victor LM-1779 [M] 1954 25.00
*—Original recording*
❑ RCA Victor LM-2335 [M] 1959 20.00
*—Re-recording of 1779*
❑ RCA Victor LSC-2335 [S] 1959 20.00
*—Re-recording of 1779 in stereo*
VICTORY AT SEA, VOL. 2
❑ RCA Victor LM-2226 [M] 1958 20.00
❑ RCA Victor LSC-2226 [S] 1958 25.00
*—Original with "shaded dog" label*
VICTORY AT SEA, VOL. 3
❑ RCA Victor LM-2523 [M] 1961 20.00
❑ RCA Victor LSC-2523 [S] 1961 25.00
WAGON TRAIN
❑ Mercury MG-20502 [M] 1959 50.00
❑ Mercury SR-60179 [S] 1959 80.00
WALT DISNEY'S WONDERFUL WORLD OF COLOR
❑ Disneyland DQ-1245 [M] 1963 30.00
WASHINGTON: BEHIND CLOSED DOORS
❑ ABC AB-1044 1977 25.00
WIDE, WIDE WORLD
❑ RCA Victor LPM-1280 [M] 1956 40.00
WILMA FLINTSTONE TELLS THE STORY OF BAMBI
❑ Hanna-Barbera HLP-2027 [M] 1965 100.00
THE WINDS OF WAR
❑ Varese Sarabande STV-81180 1983 20.00
WINSOME WITCH IN IT'S MAGIC
❑ Hanna-Barbera HLP-2042 [M] 1966 150.00
WONDERFUL TOWN
❑ Columbia Masterworks OS 2008 [S] 1958 25.00
❑ Columbia Masterworks OL 5360 [M] 1958 20.00
YOGI BEAR AND BOO-BOO
❑ Colpix CP-205 [M] 1961 120.00
YOGI BEAR AND BOO-BOO TELL STORIES OF LITTLE RED RIDING HOOD AND JACK AND THE BEANSTALK
❑ Hanna-Barbera HLP-2023 [M] 1965 100.00
YOGI BEAR AND THE THREE STOOGES IN THE MAD, MAD, DR. NO-NO
❑ Hanna-Barbera HLP-2050 [M] 1966 100.00
YOGI BEAR: HOW TO BE A BETTER THAN AVERAGE CHILD
❑ Golden LP-90 [M] 1962 80.00

# VARIOUS ARTISTS COLLECTIONS

A LA CARTE
❑ Warner Bros. PRO-A-794 [(2)] 1978 20.00
ACCENT ON PIANO
❑ Urania UJLP-1207 [M] 1955 —
*—See WILLIE "THE LION" SMITH.*
ACCENT ON TROMBONE
❑ Urania UJLP-1205 [M] 1955 30.00
ADD-A-PART JAZZ
❑ Columbia CL 908 [M] 1956 25.00
THE ADVANCE GUARD OF THE '40S
❑ EmArcy MG-36016 [M] 1955 50.00
AFRO SUMMIT
❑ BASF 20675 197? 20.00
AFRO-COOL
❑ GNP Crescendo GNP-48 [M] 1959 20.00
AFTER HOUR JAZZ
❑ Epic LN (# unk) [M] 1955 30.00
AFTER HOURS
❑ King 395-528 [M] 1956 500.00
❑ King KLP-528 1987 12.00
*—With "Highland Music" on label*
AIN'T THAT GOOD NEWS
❑ Specialty SPS-2115 1969 20.00
ALAN FREED'S GOLDEN PICS
❑ End LP-313 [M] 1961 60.00
ALAN FREED'S MEMORY LANE
❑ End LP-314 [M] 1962 60.00
ALAN FREED'S TOP 15
❑ End LP-315 [M] 1962 60.00
❑ Roulette SR 42042 [R] 1970 15.00
*—Reissue of End LP-315*
ALL DAY LONG
❑ Prestige PRLP-7081 [M] 1957 100.00
*—Reissued as Prestige 7277; see KENNY BURRELL.*
ALL DAY THUMB SUCKER REVISITED
❑ Blue Thumb BT3-7002 [(3)] 1995 20.00
*—Boxed set*
ALL GIRL MILLION SELLERS
❑ Ascot AM-13007 [M] 1964 40.00
❑ Ascot AS-16007 [P] 1964 40.00
ALL MEAT
❑ Warner Bros. PRO 604 [(2)] 1975 20.00
ALL NIGHT LONG
❑ Prestige PRLP-7073 [M] 1957 100.00
*—Reissued as Prestige 7289; see KENNY BURRELL.*
ALL SINGING — ALL TALKING — ALL ROCKING
❑ Warner Bros. PRO 573 [(2)] 1973 25.00
ALL STAR JAZZ
❑ Halo 50223 [M] 195? 30.00
ALL STAR ROCK AND ROLL REVUE
❑ King 395-513 [M] 1956 400.00
❑ King 638 [M] 1959 200.00
*—Reissue of King 395-513*
ALL STAR ROCK, VOLUME 1
❑ Original Sound Recordings OSR-1 1972 10.00
ALL STAR ROCK, VOLUME 10
❑ Original Sound Recordings OSR-10 1972 10.00
ALL STAR ROCK, VOLUME 11
❑ Original Sound Recordings OSR-11 1972 40.00
*—This volume has an Elvis track on it, thus the higher price*
ALL STAR ROCK, VOLUME 2
❑ Original Sound Recordings OSR-2 1972 10.00

| Number Title (A Side/B Side) | Yr | NM |
|---|---|---|
| **ALL STAR ROCK, VOLUME 3** | | |
| ❑ Original Sound Recordings OSR-3 | 1972 | 10.00 |
| **ALL STAR ROCK, VOLUME 4** | | |
| ❑ Original Sound Recordings OSR-4 | 1972 | 10.00 |
| **ALL STAR ROCK, VOLUME 5** | | |
| ❑ Original Sound Recordings OSR-5 | 1972 | 10.00 |
| **ALL STAR ROCK, VOLUME 6** | | |
| ❑ Original Sound Recordings OSR-6 | 1972 | 10.00 |
| **ALL STAR ROCK, VOLUME 7** | | |
| ❑ Original Sound Recordings OSR-7 | 1972 | 10.00 |
| **ALL STAR ROCK, VOLUME 8** | | |
| ❑ Original Sound Recordings OSR-8 | 1972 | 10.00 |
| **ALL STAR ROCK, VOLUME 9** | | |
| ❑ Original Sound Recordings OSR-9 | 1972 | 10.00 |
| **ALL STAR TRIBUTE TO TATUM** | | |
| ❑ American Recording Society G-424 [M] | 1957 | 30.00 |
| **ALL THE HITS BY ALL THE STARS** | | |
| ❑ Parkway P 7013 [M] | 1962 | 40.00 |
| **ALL THE HITS BY ALL THE STARS, VOL. 2** | | |
| ❑ Parkway P 7016 [M] | 1963 | 30.00 |
| **ALL THE STARS' BIGGEST HITS** | | |
| ❑ Parkway P-7033 [M] | 1963 | 50.00 |
| *—With "pull-off pix" still intact on cover* | | |
| **ALL THE STARS' BIGGEST HITS, VOLUME 2** | | |
| ❑ Parkway P-7034 [M] | 1963 | 50.00 |
| *—With "pull-off pix" still intact on cover* | | |
| **ALL THESE THINGS** | | |
| ❑ Instant LP-71000 | 1969 | 30.00 |
| **ALL-TIME ALL-STAR COUNTRY HITS: 48 HISTORIC PERFORMANCES** | | |
| ❑ RCA Victor CWS 0002 [(4)] | 196? | 30.00 |
| *—Box set* | | |
| **ALL TIME COUNTRY AND WESTERN** | | |
| ❑ Decca DL 4010 [M] | 1960 | 30.00 |
| ❑ Decca DL 74010 [R] | 196? | 20.00 |
| **ALL TIME COUNTRY AND WESTERN HITS** | | |
| ❑ King 537 [M] | 1956 | 150.00 |
| ❑ King 710 [M] | 1961 | 100.00 |
| *—Not a reissue of King 537, but a different collection* | | |
| **ALL TIME COUNTRY AND WESTERN, VOL. 2** | | |
| ❑ Decca DL 4090 [M] | 1961 | 25.00 |
| ❑ Decca DL 74090 [R] | 196? | 15.00 |
| **ALL TIME COUNTRY AND WESTERN, VOL. 3** | | |
| ❑ Decca DL 4134 [M] | 1961 | 25.00 |
| ❑ Decca DL 74134 [R] | 196? | 15.00 |
| **ALL TIME COUNTRY AND WESTERN, VOL. 4** | | |
| ❑ Decca DL 4359 [M] | 1963 | 25.00 |
| ❑ Decca DL 74359 [R] | 196? | 15.00 |
| **ALL TIME COUNTRY AND WESTERN, VOL. 5** | | |
| ❑ Decca DL 4549 [M] | 1964 | 25.00 |
| ❑ Decca DL 74549 [R] | 1964 | 15.00 |
| **ALL TIME COUNTRY AND WESTERN, VOL. 6** | | |
| ❑ Decca DL 4657 [M] | 1965 | 20.00 |
| ❑ Decca DL 74657 [R] | 1965 | 12.00 |
| **ALL TIME COUNTRY AND WESTERN, VOL. 7** | | |
| ❑ Decca DL 4775 [M] | 1966 | 20.00 |
| ❑ Decca DL 74775 [R] | 1966 | 12.00 |
| **ALL TIME COUNTRY AND WESTERN, VOL. 8** | | |
| ❑ Decca DL 4881 [M] | 1967 | 20.00 |
| ❑ Decca DL 74881 [S] | 1967 | 20.00 |
| **ALL TIME COUNTRY AND WESTERN, VOL. 9** | | |
| ❑ Decca DL 5025 [M] | 1968 | 50.00 |
| *—Mono is white label promo only; cover is stereo with "Monaural" sticker* | | |
| ❑ Decca DL 75025 [S] | 1968 | 20.00 |
| **ALL TIME HIT SACRED AND GOSPEL SONGS** | | |
| ❑ King 1023 [M] | 1967 | 30.00 |
| **ALL-STAR DATES** | | |
| ❑ RCA Victor LPT-21 [10] | 1951 | 50.00 |
| **ALL-STAR STOMPERS** | | |
| ❑ Circle L-402 [M] | 1951 | 40.00 |
| **ALTO ALTITUDE** | | |
| ❑ EmArcy MG-36018 [M] | 1955 | 50.00 |
| **ALTO SAXES** | | |
| ❑ Norgran MGN-1035 [M] | 1955 | 80.00 |
| ❑ Verve MGV-8126 [M] | 1957 | 30.00 |
| ❑ Verve V-8126 [M] | 1961 | 20.00 |
| **THE AMAZING METS** | | |
| ❑ Buddah 1969 | 1969 | 25.00 |
| **AMERICA'S GREATEST JAZZMEN PLAY COLE PORTER** | | |
| ❑ Moodsville MVLP-34 [M] | 1963 | 40.00 |
| *—Green label* | | |
| ❑ Moodsville MVLP-34 [M] | 1965 | 20.00 |
| *—Blue label, trident logo at right* | | |
| ❑ Moodsville MVST-34 [S] | 1963 | 40.00 |
| *—Green label* | | |
| ❑ Moodsville MVST-34 [S] | 1965 | 20.00 |
| *—Blue label, trident logo at right* | | |
| **AMERICA'S GREATEST JAZZMEN PLAY GEORGE GERSHWIN** | | |
| ❑ Moodsville MVLP-33 [M] | 1963 | 40.00 |
| *—Green label* | | |
| ❑ Moodsville MVLP-33 [M] | 1965 | 20.00 |
| *—Blue label, trident logo at right* | | |
| ❑ Moodsville MVST-33 [S] | 1963 | 40.00 |
| *—Green label* | | |
| ❑ Moodsville MVST-33 [S] | 1965 | 20.00 |
| *—Blue label, trident logo at right* | | |
| **AMERICA'S GREATEST JAZZMEN PLAY RICHARD RODGERS** | | |
| ❑ Moodsville MVLP-35 [M] | 1963 | 40.00 |
| *—Green label* | | |
| ❑ Moodsville MVLP-35 [M] | 1965 | 20.00 |
| *—Blue label, trident logo at right* | | |
| ❑ Moodsville MVST-35 [S] | 1963 | 40.00 |
| *—Green label* | | |
| ❑ Moodsville MVST-35 [S] | 1965 | 20.00 |
| *—Blue label, trident logo at right* | | |
| **AMERICA'S GREATEST JAZZMEN PLAY THE BROADWAY SCENE** | | |
| ❑ Moodsville MVLP-38 [M] | 1963 | 40.00 |
| *—Green label* | | |
| ❑ Moodsville MVLP-38 [M] | 1965 | 20.00 |
| *—Blue label, trident logo at right* | | |
| ❑ Moodsville MVST-38 [S] | 1963 | 40.00 |
| *—Green label* | | |
| ❑ Moodsville MVST-38 [S] | 1965 | 20.00 |
| *—Blue label, trident logo at right* | | |
| **AMERICAN FOLK BLUES FESTIVAL** | | |
| ❑ Excello LPS-8029 | 1972 | 20.00 |
| ❑ Exodus EX-302 [M] | 1966 | 20.00 |
| ❑ Exodus EXS-302 [S] | 1966 | 25.00 |
| **AMERICANS ABROAD, VOL. 1** | | |
| ❑ Pax LP-6009 [10] | 1955 | 40.00 |
| **AMERICANS ABROAD, VOL. 2** | | |
| ❑ Pax LP-6015 [10] | 1955 | 40.00 |
| **AMERICANS IN EUROPE, VOL. 1** | | |
| ❑ ABC Impulse! AS-36 [S] | 1968 | 12.00 |
| ❑ Impulse! A-36 [M] | 1963 | 20.00 |
| ❑ Impulse! AS-36 [S] | 1963 | 25.00 |
| **AMERICANS IN EUROPE, VOL. 2** | | |
| ❑ ABC Impulse! AS-37 [S] | 1968 | 12.00 |
| ❑ Impulse! A-37 [M] | 1963 | 20.00 |
| ❑ Impulse! AS-37 [S] | 1963 | 25.00 |
| **THE ANATOMY OF IMPROVISATION** | | |
| ❑ Verve MGV-8230 [M] | 1958 | 30.00 |
| ❑ Verve V-8230 [M] | 1961 | 20.00 |
| **ANOTHER MONDAY NIGHT AT BIRDLAND** | | |
| ❑ Roulette R 52022 [M] | 1959 | 30.00 |
| ❑ Roulette SR 52022 [S] | 1959 | 30.00 |
| **AN ANTHOLOGY OF BRITISH BLUES, VOL. 1** | | |
| ❑ Immediate Z12 52006 | 1968 | 30.00 |
| **AN ANTHOLOGY OF BRITISH BLUES, VOL. 2** | | |
| ❑ Immediate Z12 52014 | 1968 | 30.00 |
| **AN ANTHOLOGY OF CALIFORNIA MUSIC** | | |
| ❑ Jazz: West Coast JWC-500 [M] | 1955 | 150.00 |
| **AN ANTHOLOGY OF CALIFORNIA MUSIC, VOL. 2** | | |
| ❑ Jazz: West Coast JWC-501 [M] | 1956 | 150.00 |
| **APOLLO SATURDAY NIGHT** | | |
| ❑ Atco 33-159 [M] | 1964 | 40.00 |
| ❑ Atco SD 33-159 [S] | 1964 | 50.00 |
| **APPETIZERS** | | |
| ❑ Warner Bros. PRO 569 [(2)] | 1973 | 25.00 |
| **APPROVED BY 10,000,000** | | |
| ❑ Teem LP-5004 [M] | 196? | 30.00 |
| **ARISTA AOR SAMPLER** | | |
| ❑ Arista ALS 06 [(2)DJ] | 1978 | 20.00 |
| **ARISTA'S GREATEST HITS: PORTRAIT OF A DECADE 1975-1985** | | |
| ❑ Arista/Silver Eagle SE 10383 [(3)] | 1985 | 20.00 |
| **THE ART OF JAZZ PIANO** | | |
| ❑ Epic LN 3295 [M] | 1956 | 30.00 |
| **THE ART OF THE JAM SESSION: MONTREUX '77** | | |
| ❑ Pablo Live 2620106 [(8)] | 1978 | 70.00 |
| **THE ARTISTS AND MUSIC THAT STARTED IT ALL** | | |
| ❑ Motown PR-84 [(6)DJ] | 1981 | 200.00 |
| *—Promo-only box set; five of the records appeared as "The Motown Story: The First Twenty-Five Years" two years later* | | |
| **ASSORTED FLAVORS OF PACIFIC JAZZ** | | |
| ❑ Pacific Jazz HFS-1 [M] | 1956 | 50.00 |
| **ATLANTIC BLUES** | | |
| ❑ Atlantic 81713 [(8)] | 1987 | 50.00 |
| *—Boxed set; also available as four 2-LP sets* | | |
| **ATLANTIC JAZZ** | | |
| ❑ Atlantic 81712 [(15)] | 1987 | 250.00 |
| *—Boxed set with 12 volumes in 15 records, liner notes and credits* | | |
| **THE ATLANTIC NEW ORLEANS JAZZ SESSIONS** | | |
| ❑ Mosaic MQ6-179 [(6)] | 199? | 120.00 |
| **ATLANTIC RECORDS: CLASSIC ROCK** | | |
| ❑ Atlantic 81908 [(4)] | 1989 | 30.00 |
| *—Boxed set* | | |
| **ATLANTIC RECORDS: GREAT MOMENTS IN JAZZ** | | |
| ❑ Atlantic 81907 [(3)] | 1989 | 25.00 |
| **ATLANTIC RHYTHM AND BLUES** | | |
| ❑ Atlantic 81620 [(14)] | 1986 | 100.00 |
| *—Boxed set; also available as seven 2-LP sets* | | |
| **AUTOBIOGRAPHY IN JAZZ** | | |
| ❑ Debut DEB-198 [M] | 1955 | 150.00 |
| ❑ Fantasy OJC-115 | 198? | 10.00 |
| **AWARD ALBUM JAZZ VOCALS** | | |
| ❑ Bethlehem BCP-6060 [M] | 1961 | 25.00 |
| **BACKGROUNDS OF JAZZ, VOL. 1: THE JUG BANDS** | | |
| ❑ "X" LX-3009 [10] | 1954 | 80.00 |
| **BACKGROUNDS OF JAZZ, VOL. 2: COUNTRY & URBAN BLUES** | | |
| ❑ "X" LVA-3016 [10] | 1954 | 80.00 |
| **BACKGROUNDS OF JAZZ, VOL. 3: KINGS OF THE BLUES** | | |
| ❑ "X" LVA-3032 [10] | 1955 | 80.00 |
| **BACKWOOD BLUES** | | |
| ❑ Riverside RLP-1039 [10] | 1954 | 80.00 |
| **BALLADS AND BREAKDOWNS OF THE GOLDEN ERA** | | |
| ❑ Columbia CS 9660 | 1968 | 20.00 |
| **BALLROOM BANDSTAND** | | |
| ❑ Columbia CL 611 [M] | 1955 | 25.00 |
| **BANG AND SHOUT SUPER HITS** | | |
| ❑ Bang BLPS-220 [P] | 1969 | 20.00 |
| **BANJO COUNTRY STYLE** | | |
| ❑ Audio Lab AL-1569 [M] | 1962 | 80.00 |
| **BARGAIN DAY** | | |
| ❑ EmArcy MG-36087 [M] | 1956 | 40.00 |
| **BARREL HOUSE PIANO** | | |
| ❑ Brunswick BL 58022 [10] | 1951 | 60.00 |
| **A BARREL OF OLDIES** | | |
| ❑ Del-Fi DFLP-1219 [M] | 1961 | 50.00 |
| **BARRY MANN AND CYNTHIA WEIL: SOLID GOLD** | | |
| ❑ Screen Gems/Columbia CPL-712 [DJ] | 1975 | 20.00 |
| *—Promo-only compilation of oldies sent to radio to spur airplay on songs owned by this publishing house* | | |
| **THE BASS** | | |
| ❑ ABC Impulse! AS-9284 [(3)] | 197? | 20.00 |
| **BATTLE OF BANDS** | | |
| ❑ Capitol H 235 [10] | 1950 | 50.00 |
| **BATTLE OF JAZZ, VOL. 3** | | |
| ❑ Brunswick BL 58039 [10] | 1953 | 50.00 |
| **BATTLE OF THE BIG BANDS** | | |
| ❑ Capitol T 667 [M] | 1956 | 30.00 |
| **BATTLE OF THE GROUPS** | | |
| ❑ End LP-305 [M] | 1960 | 60.00 |
| **BATTLE OF THE GROUPS, VOLUME 2** | | |
| ❑ End LP-309 [M] | 1960 | 60.00 |
| **BATTLE OF THE SAXES** | | |
| ❑ Aladdin LP-701 [10] | 1950 | — |
| *—See LESTER YOUNG AND ILLINOIS JACQUET.* | | |
| **BATTLE OF THE SAXES-TENOR ALL STARS** | | |
| ❑ EmArcy MG-36023 [M] | 1955 | 50.00 |
| **BE OUR GUEST** | | |
| ❑ Gene Norman GNP-20 [M] | 1955 | 25.00 |
| **THE BE-BOP ERA** | | |
| ❑ RCA Victor LPV-519 | 1965 | 20.00 |
| **THE BEAT: SOUND WAVE OF THE 80'S** | | |
| ❑ K-Tel TU 5040 | 1982 | 20.00 |
| **THE BELLS OF CHRISTMAS** | | |
| ❑ Book-of-the-Month Club 90-5677 [(3)] | 1973 | 20.00 |
| *—Sold through Book-of-the-Month Records; secondary number is "P3 11972"* | | |
| **BEST COAST JAZZ** | | |
| ❑ EmArcy MG-36039 [M] | 1955 | 80.00 |
| **BEST FROM THE WEST: MODERN SOUNDS FROM CALIFORNIA, VOL. 1** | | |
| ❑ Blue Note BLP-5059 [10] | 1955 | 200.00 |
| **BEST FROM THE WEST: MODERN SOUNDS FROM CALIFORNIA, VOL. 2** | | |
| ❑ Blue Note BLP-5060 [10] | 1955 | 200.00 |
| **THE BEST OF ARGO JAZZ** | | |
| ❑ Argo ALPS-1 [M] | 1961 | 30.00 |
| **THE BEST OF BLUE NOTE, VOL. 1** | | |
| ❑ Blue Note BST-84429 [(2)] | 197? | 20.00 |
| **THE BEST OF BLUE NOTE, VOL. 2** | | |
| ❑ Blue Note BST-84433 [(2)] | 197? | 20.00 |
| **THE BEST OF BOMP! VOLUME ONE** | | |
| ❑ Bomp! 4002 | 1978 | 20.00 |
| *—First pressings on white vinyl.* | | |
| **THE BEST OF CHRISTMAS** | | |
| ❑ Capitol STBB 2979 [(2)] | 1968 | 20.00 |
| **THE BEST OF DISNEY VOL. I** | | |
| ❑ Disneyland 2502 | 1978 | 25.00 |
| **THE BEST OF DISNEY VOL. II** | | |
| ❑ Disneyland 2503 | 1978 | 25.00 |
| **BEST OF DIXIELAND** | | |
| ❑ RCA Victor ANL1-1431 | 1976 | 10.00 |
| **THE BEST OF DIXIELAND** | | |
| ❑ RCA Victor LPM-2982 [M] | 1965 | 20.00 |
| ❑ RCA Victor LSP-2982 [R] | 1965 | 12.00 |
| **BEST OF LIMP, REST OF LIMP** | | |
| ❑ Limp 1004 | 1980 | 40.00 |
| *—Numbered edition of 1,000* | | |
| **BEST OF RALPH** | | |
| ❑ Ralph RR 8251-2 [(2)] | 1982 | 20.00 |
| **BEST OF RHYTHM AND BLUES** | | |
| ❑ Jubilee JLP-1014 [M] | 1956 | 150.00 |
| *—Blue label, black vinyl* | | |
| ❑ Jubilee JLP-1014 [M] | 1956 | 200.00 |
| *—Pink label, black vinyl* | | |
| ❑ Jubilee JLP-1014 [M] | 1956 | 500.00 |
| *—Pink label, red vinyl* | | |
| **THE BEST OF RHYTHM AND BLUES** | | |
| ❑ Warwick W 2026 [M] | 1961 | 80.00 |

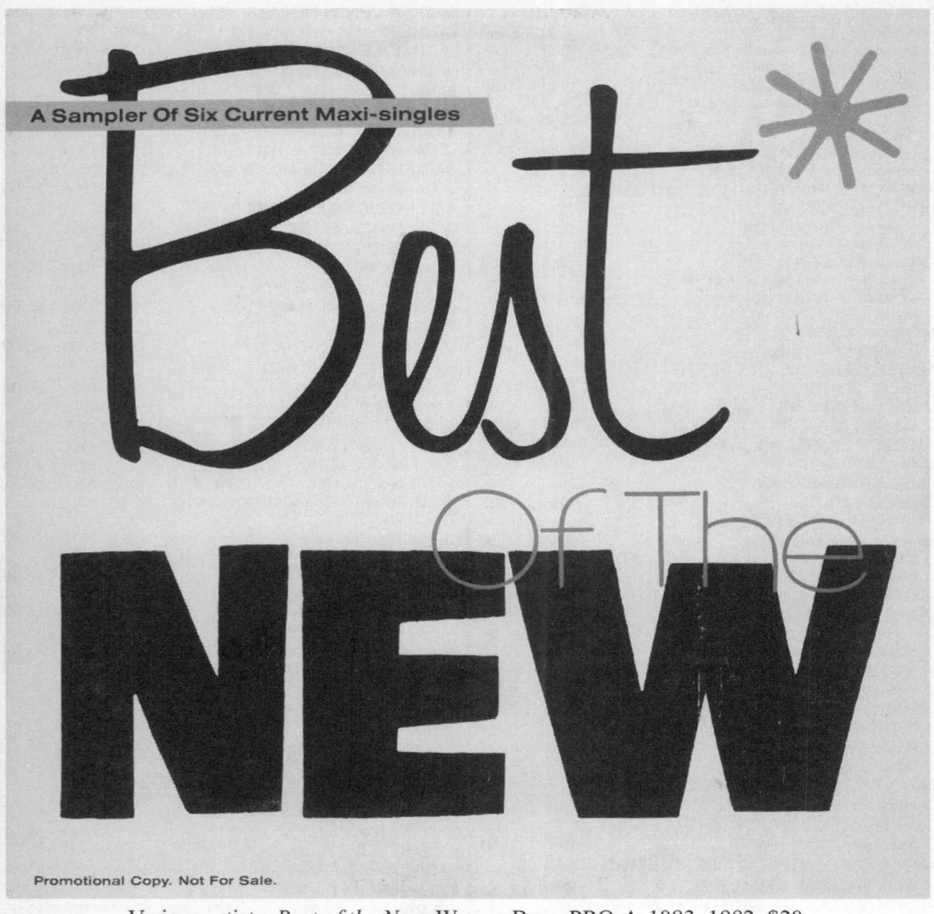

A Sampler Of Six Current Maxi-singles
Best
Of The
NEW
Promotional Copy. Not For Sale.


Various artists, *Best of the New,* Warner Bros. PRO-A-1083, 1982, $20.

| Number | Title (A Side/B Side) | Yr | NM |
|---|---|---|---|
| BEST OF THE BIG NAME BANDS | | | |
| ❑ RCA Camden CAL-368 [M] | | 1958 | 25.00 |
| BEST OF THE BLUES, VOLUME 1 | | | |
| ❑ Imperial LP-9257 [M] | | 1964 | 25.00 |
| ❑ Imperial LP-12257 [R] | | 1964 | 20.00 |
| BEST OF THE BLUES, VOLUME 2 | | | |
| ❑ Imperial LP-9259 [M] | | 1964 | 25.00 |
| ❑ Imperial LP-12259 [R] | | 1964 | 20.00 |
| THE BEST OF THE KING BISCUIT FLOWER HOUR | | | |
| ❑ Silver Eagle SE 10674 [(3)] | | 1988 | 25.00 |
| BEST OF THE NEW | | | |
| ❑ Warner Bros. PRO-A-1083 [DJ] | | 1982 | 20.00 |
| *—Promo-only collection of mixes from 12-inch singles; this was the first album to include a song by Madonna, the 12-inch version of "Everybody," before her debut LP was issued* | | | |
| THE BEST OF THE R AND B GROUPS | | | |
| ❑ Warwick W 2025 [M] | | 1961 | 100.00 |
| BEST OF THE SOUNDTRACKS | | | |
| ❑ Tower ST-5148 | | 1969 | 25.00 |
| THE BEST VOCAL GROUPS IN ROCK 'N' ROLL | | | |
| ❑ Dooto DL-224 [M] | | 1957 | 100.00 |
| *—Yellow label* | | | |
| ❑ Dooto DL-224 [M] | | 196? | 30.00 |
| *—Multi-color label* | | | |
| BETHLEHEM'S BEST | | | |
| ❑ Bethlehem EXLP-6 [(3)M] | | 1958 | 70.00 |
| *—Box set of 82, 83, and 84* | | | |
| BETHLEHEM'S BEST, VOLUME 1 | | | |
| ❑ Bethlehem BCP-82 [M] | | 1958 | 30.00 |
| BETHLEHEM'S BEST, VOLUME 2 | | | |
| ❑ Bethlehem BCP-83 [M] | | 1958 | 30.00 |
| BETHLEHEM'S BEST, VOLUME 3 | | | |
| ❑ Bethlehem BCP-84 [M] | | 1958 | 30.00 |
| BETHLEHEM'S GRAB BAG | | | |
| ❑ Bethlehem EXLP-2 [M] | | 1958 | 40.00 |
| THE BIG 18 — LIVE ECHOES OF THE SWINGING BANDS | | | |
| ❑ RCA Victor LPM-1921 [M] | | 1959 | 40.00 |
| ❑ RCA Victor LSP-1921 [S] | | 1959 | 50.00 |
| THE BIG BALL | | | |
| ❑ Warner Bros. PRO 358 [(2)] | | 1970 | 25.00 |
| *—Originals have green labels* | | | |
| BIG BAND CONTRAST | | | |
| ❑ Bethlehem BCP-6037 [M] | | 1960 | 30.00 |
| BIG BAND JAZZ | | | |
| ❑ Brunswick BL 58050 [10] | | 1953 | 50.00 |
| BIG BAND STEREO | | | |
| ❑ Capitol SW 1055 [S] | | 1959 | 25.00 |
| BIG BANDS | | | |
| ❑ Capitol STFL-293 [(6)] | | 1969 | 30.00 |
| *—One album each by Les Brown, Glen Gray, Duke Ellington, Benny Goodman, Harry James and Woody Herman* | | | |
| BIG BANDS' GREATEST HITS | | | |
| ❑ Columbia CG 30009 [(2)] | | 197? | 12.00 |
| *—"CG" prefix is a reissue of "G"* | | | |
| ❑ Columbia G 30009 [(2)] | | 1970 | 15.00 |
| *—Orange labels* | | | |
| ❑ Columbia G 30009 [(2)] | | 1970 | 20.00 |
| *—Red "360 Sound" labels* | | | |
| BIG COUNTRY HITS | | | |
| ❑ Pickwick JS-6166 | | 1975 | 30.00 |
| BIG COUNTRY HITS, VOL. 1 | | | |
| ❑ RCA Victor LPM-3606 [M] | | 1966 | 15.00 |
| ❑ RCA Victor LSP-3606 [S] | | 1966 | 20.00 |
| THE BIG HITS | | | |
| ❑ Columbia CL 1353 [M] | | 1959 | 30.00 |
| ❑ Columbia CS 8161 [S] | | 1959 | 40.00 |
| THE BIG HITS OF MID-AMERICA | | | |
| ❑ Soma MG-1245 [M] | | 1965 | 80.00 |
| BIG HITS OF MID-AMERICA VOLUME THREE | | | |
| ❑ Twin/Tone TTTR 7907/8 [(2)] | | 1979 | 20.00 |
| THE BIG HITS OF MID-AMERICA, VOLUME 2 | | | |
| ❑ Soma MG-1246 [M] | | 1965 | 80.00 |
| BIG NAME DIXIE | | | |
| ❑ Score SLP-4024 [M] | | 1958 | 50.00 |
| THE BIG ONES FROM DUKE AND PEACOCK RECORDS | | | |
| ❑ Peacock PLP-2000 [M] | | 1967 | 20.00 |
| THE BIG SOUNDS OF THE DRAGS! | | | |
| ❑ Capitol ST 2001 [S] | | 1963 | 25.00 |
| ❑ Capitol T 2001 [M] | | 1963 | 20.00 |
| BIG SUR FESTIVAL/ONE HAND CLAPPING | | | |
| ❑ Columbia KC 31138 | | 1972 | 20.00 |
| BIG SURF HITS | | | |
| ❑ Del-Fi DFLP-1249 [M] | | 1964 | 50.00 |
| ❑ Del-Fi DFST-1249 [S] | | 1964 | 75.00 |
| BIRD'S NIGHT — THE MUSIC OF CHARLIE PARKER | | | |
| ❑ Savoy MG-12138 [M] | | 1958 | 50.00 |
| THE BIRDLAND STARS ON TOUR, VOL. 1 | | | |
| ❑ RCA Victor LPM-1327 [M] | | 1956 | 40.00 |
| THE BIRDLAND STARS ON TOUR, VOL. 2 | | | |
| ❑ RCA Victor LPM-1328 [M] | | 1956 | 40.00 |
| THE BIRDLAND STORY | | | |
| ❑ Roulette RB-2 [(2)M] | | 1961 | 40.00 |
| ❑ Roulette SRB-2 [(2)S] | | 1961 | 40.00 |
| THE BIRTH OF BOP, VOL. 1 | | | |
| ❑ Savoy MG-9022 [10] | | 1953 | 150.00 |
| THE BIRTH OF BOP, VOL. 2 | | | |
| ❑ Savoy MG-9023 [10] | | 1953 | 150.00 |
| THE BIRTH OF BOP, VOL. 3 | | | |
| ❑ Savoy MG-9024 [10] | | 1953 | 150.00 |
| THE BIRTH OF BOP, VOL. 4 | | | |
| ❑ Savoy MG-9025 [10] | | 1953 | 150.00 |
| THE BIRTH OF BOP, VOL. 5 | | | |
| ❑ Savoy MG-9026 [10] | | 1953 | 150.00 |
| BLEECKER AND MACDOUGAL: THE FOLK SCENE OF THE 1960S | | | |
| ❑ Elektra 60381 [(3)] | | 1984 | 20.00 |
| BLOWIN' SESSIONS | | | |
| ❑ Blue Note BN-LA521-H2 [(2)] | | 1975 | 20.00 |
| BLOWOUT AT MARDI GRAS | | | |
| ❑ Cook LP-1084 [M] | | 1955 | 40.00 |
| BLUE CHRISTMAS | | | |
| ❑ Welk Music Group WM-3002 [DJ] | | 1984 | 80.00 |
| *—Promo only; compiled by the publisher of "Blue Christmas" and other holiday tunes for radio use* | | | |
| BLUE RIBBON COUNTRY | | | |
| ❑ Capitol STBB 2969 [(2)] | | 1968 | 25.00 |
| BLUE RIBBON COUNTRY, VOL. 2 | | | |
| ❑ Capitol STBB-217 [(2)] | | 1969 | 25.00 |
| BLUEGRASS OLDIES BUT GOODIES | | | |
| ❑ Smash MGS-27028 [M] | | 1963 | 20.00 |
| ❑ Smash SRS-67028 [S] | | 1963 | 20.00 |
| BLUEGRASS SPECTACULAR | | | |
| ❑ Starday SLP-232 [M] | | 1963 | 25.00 |
| THE BLUES | | | |
| ❑ Vee Jay VJS-2-1007 [(2)] | | 1974 | 20.00 |
| ❑ Vee Jay LP-1020 [M] | | 1960 | 40.00 |
| BLUES 'N' FOLK | | | |
| ❑ Bethlehem BCP-6071 [M] | | 1963 | 60.00 |
| BLUES FOR TOMORROW | | | |
| ❑ Fantasy OJC-030 | | 1982 | 10.00 |
| ❑ Riverside RLP 12-243 [M] | | 1957 | 40.00 |
| BLUES FROM BIG BILL'S COPACABANA | | | |
| ❑ Chess LP 1533 [M] | | 1969 | 25.00 |
| *—Possibly a reissue of "Folk Festival of the Blues," Argo 4031* | | | |
| BLUES IN CONCERT | | | |
| ❑ Groove Merchant 4405 [(2)] | | 197? | 20.00 |
| THE BLUES IN MODERN JAZZ | | | |
| ❑ Atlantic 1337 [M] | | 1961 | 20.00 |
| *—Multicolor label, white "fan" logo at right* | | | |
| ❑ Atlantic 1337 [M] | | 1963 | 15.00 |
| *—Multicolor label, black "fan" logo at right* | | | |
| ❑ Atlantic SD 1337 [R] | | 1969 | 12.00 |
| THE BLUES IN STEREO | | | |
| ❑ World Pacific ST-1021 [S] | | 1959 | 30.00 |
| BLUES LIVE IN BATON ROUGE | | | |
| ❑ Excello LPS-8021 | | 1971 | 25.00 |
| THE BLUES PROJECT | | | |
| ❑ Elektra EKL-264 [M] | | 1964 | 25.00 |
| ❑ Elektra EKS-7264 [S] | | 1964 | 30.00 |
| *—No relation to the band of the same name; on one track, Bob Dylan plays piano under the name "Bob Landy"* | | | |
| BLUES THAT GAVE AMERICA SOUL | | | |
| ❑ ABC Duke DLPX-82 [S] | | 1974 | 15.00 |
| ❑ Duke DLP-82 [M] | | 1966 | 20.00 |
| ❑ Duke DLPS-82 [S] | | 1966 | 25.00 |
| BLUES UPTOWN: URBAN BLUES, VOLUME 1 | | | |
| ❑ Imperial LP-94002 | | 1968 | 20.00 |
| THE BLUES, VOL. 2 | | | |
| ❑ Pacific Jazz JWC-502 [M] | | 1956 | 50.00 |
| ❑ World Pacific JWC-502 [M] | | 1958 | 40.00 |
| THE BLUES, VOL. 2: HAVE BLUES, WILL TRAVEL | | | |
| ❑ World Pacific JWC-509 [M] | | 1958 | 40.00 |
| THE BLUES, VOL. 3: BLOWIN' THE BLUES | | | |
| ❑ World Pacific JWC-512 [M] | | 1958 | 40.00 |
| ❑ World Pacific ST-1029 [S] | | 1959 | 30.00 |
| THE BLUES, VOLUME 1 | | | |
| ❑ Argo LP-4026 [M] | | 1963 | 25.00 |
| THE BLUES, VOLUME 2 | | | |
| ❑ Argo LP-4027 [M] | | 1963 | 25.00 |
| THE BLUES, VOLUME 3 | | | |
| ❑ Argo LP-4034 [M] | | 1964 | 25.00 |
| THE BLUES, VOLUME 4 | | | |
| ❑ Argo LP-4042 [M] | | 1964 | 25.00 |
| THE BLUES, VOLUME 5 | | | |
| ❑ Cadet LP-4051 [M] | | 1966 | 25.00 |
| BLUESVILLE | | | |
| ❑ Bethlehem BCP-6038 [M] | | 1960 | 30.00 |
| BODY AND SOUL | | | |
| ❑ RCA Victor LPV-501 | | 1964 | 20.00 |
| BONING UP ON 'BONES | | | |
| ❑ EmArcy MG-36038 [M] | | 1955 | 50.00 |
| BOOGIE WOOGIE | | | |
| ❑ Decca DL 5248 [10] | | 1950 | 50.00 |
| BOOGIE WOOGIE KINGS AND QUEENS | | | |
| ❑ Decca DL 5249 [10] | | 1950 | 50.00 |



Except when noted otherwise, VG = 25% of NM, and VG+ = 50% of NM. (Example: VG = $2.00, VG+ = $4.00 and NM = $8.00.)

| Number Title (A Side/B Side) | Yr | NM |
|---|---|---|
| BOOGIE WOOGIE PIANO | | |
| ❑ Brunswick BL 58018 [10] | 1950 | 60.00 |
| BOPPIN' | | |
| ❑ Jubilee JGM-1118 [M] | 1960 | 150.00 |
| BOSS GOLDIES — SOUNDS FROM THE GROOVEYARD | | |
| ❑ Columbia CL 2559 [M] | 1966 | 20.00 |
| ❑ Columbia CS 9339 [S] | 1966 | 25.00 |
| BOY MEETS GIRL | | |
| ❑ Stax STS 2-2024 [(2)] | 1969 | 20.00 |
| BREAKING THE RULES | | |
| ❑ Columbia A2S 881 [(2)DJ] | 1980 | 20.00 |
| THE BRIDGE SCHOOL CONCERTS, VOL. ONE | | |
| ❑ Reprise 46824-1 [(2)] | 1997 | 20.00 |
| BRIGHT LIGHTS AND HONKY TONKS | | |
| ❑ Starday SLP-239 [M] | 1963 | 25.00 |
| THE BRIGHTEST STARS OF CHRISTMAS | | |
| ❑ RCA Special Products DPL1-0086 | 1974 | 20.00 |
| *—Sold only at JCPenney department stores* | | |
| BRITISH FESTIVAL OF JAZZ CONCERT | | |
| ❑ Decca DL 5422 [10] | 1952 | 50.00 |
| BRITISH GOLD | | |
| ❑ Sire R 224095 [(2)] | 1978 | 20.00 |
| *—RCA Music Service edition* | | |
| BRITISH JAZZ FESTIVAL | | |
| ❑ Decca DL 5424 [10] | 1952 | 50.00 |
| BRITISH ROCK CLASSICS | | |
| ❑ Sire R 234021 [(2)] | 1978 | 20.00 |
| *—RCA Music Service edition* | | |
| BRITISH STERLING | | |
| ❑ Lakefront LSM 811 | 1981 | 25.00 |
| BRUNSWICK'S GREATEST HITS | | |
| ❑ Brunswick BL 754186 | 1973 | 20.00 |
| BUBBLE GUM MUSIC IS THE NAKED TRUTH, VOLUME 1 | | |
| ❑ Buddah BDA 5032 | 1969 | 25.00 |
| BUDDAH'S 360 DEGREE DIAL-A-HIT | | |
| ❑ Buddah BDA 5039 | 1969 | 30.00 |
| *—With rotating wheel under the front LP cover* | | |
| A BUMPER CROP OF ALL STARS | | |
| ❑ King 753 [M] | 1961 | 100.00 |
| BUNCH OF GOODIES | | |
| ❑ Chess LP 1441 [DJ] | 1960 | 600.00 |
| *—Multi-color splash vinyl* | | |
| ❑ Chess LP 1441 [M] | 1960 | 120.00 |
| *—Black vinyl* | | |
| BURBANK | | |
| ❑ Warner Bros. PRO 529 [(2)] | 1972 | 25.00 |
| *—Originals have green labels* | | |
| BURBANK'S GREATEST HITS | | |
| ❑ Warner Bros. PRO 548 | 1973 | 20.00 |
| BUSHKIN-SAFRANSKI-WILSON GROUPS | | |
| ❑ Allegro 1590 [10] | 1955 | 50.00 |
| BYE BYE BIRDIE | | |
| ❑ Colpix CP-454 [M] | 1963 | 80.00 |
| ❑ Colpix SCP-454 [S] | 1963 | 100.00 |
| *—Studio version performed by Paul Petersen, Shelley Fabares, James Darren, the Marcels and others* | | |
| CALIFORNIA JAM 2 | | |
| ❑ Columbia PC2 35389 [(2)] | 1978 | 20.00 |
| CAN YOU HEAR ME? MUSIC FROM THE DEAF CLUB | | |
| ❑ Optional/Walking Dead 001 | 1980 | 25.00 |
| ❑ PVC 7920 | 1980 | 20.00 |
| CARLOAD O' HITS | | |
| ❑ Muse M-500 [M] | 1959 | 200.00 |
| A CARNIVAL OF SONGS | | |
| ❑ King 819 [M] | 1963 | 100.00 |
| THE CATS | | |
| ❑ Fantasy OJC-079 | 198? | 10.00 |
| ❑ New Jazz NJLP-8217 [M] | 1959 | 80.00 |
| *—Purple label* | | |
| ❑ New Jazz NJLP-8217 [M] | 1965 | 30.00 |
| *—Blue label, trident logo at right* | | |
| CATS AND JAMMER KIDS | | |
| ❑ Angel ANG-60007 [10] | 1955 | 50.00 |
| CATS VS. CHICKS | | |
| ❑ MGM E-255 [10] | 1954 | 50.00 |
| CBS TWO-FERS ARE GREAT MUSICAL VALUES! | | |
| ❑ CBS A2S 143/4 [(2)DJ] | 1975 | 20.00 |
| CELEBRATE THE SEASON WITH TUPPERWARE | | |
| ❑ RCA Special Products DPL1-0803 | 1987 | 20.00 |
| *—Sold only at Tupperware parties* | | |
| CHARLIE PARKER MEMORIAL CONCERT | | |
| ❑ Cadet 2CA-60002 [(2)] | 1971 | 20.00 |
| ❑ Chess CH-92510 | 198? | 12.00 |
| CHART BUSTERS '62 | | |
| ❑ Capitol ST 1837 [S] | 1963 | 40.00 |
| ❑ Capitol T 1837 [M] | 1963 | 30.00 |
| CHARTBUSTERS, VOL. 2 | | |
| ❑ Capitol ST 1945 [S] | 1963 | 40.00 |
| ❑ Capitol T 1945 [M] | 1963 | 30.00 |
| CHARTBUSTERS, VOL. 3 | | |
| ❑ Capitol ST 2006 [S] | 1963 | 40.00 |
| ❑ Capitol T 2006 [M] | 1963 | 30.00 |
| CHARTBUSTERS, VOL. 4 | | |
| ❑ Capitol ST 2094 [S] | 1964 | 60.00 |
| ❑ Capitol T 2094 [M] | 1964 | 40.00 |

| Number Title (A Side/B Side) | Yr | NM |
|---|---|---|
| CHESS IS BACK! | | |
| ❑ Chess CH-333 [DJ] | 1982 | 20.00 |
| *—Promo only, distributed by Sugar Hill* | | |
| CHICAGO / AUSTIN HIGH SCHOOL | | |
| ❑ RCA Victor LPM-1508 [M] | 1957 | 30.00 |
| CHICAGO AND ALL THAT JAZZ! | | |
| ❑ Verve V-8441 [M] | 1961 | 25.00 |
| ❑ Verve V6-8441 [S] | 1962 | 30.00 |
| CHICAGO BLUES ANTHOLOGY | | |
| ❑ Chess 2CH-60012 [(2)] | 1972 | 20.00 |
| CHICAGO JAZZ ALBUM | | |
| ❑ Decca DL 8029 [M] | 1954 | 40.00 |
| CHICAGO STYLE JAZZ | | |
| ❑ Columbia CL 632 [M] | 1955 | — |
| *—See EDDIE CONDON.* | | |
| CHICAGO: THE LIVING LEGENDS, VOL. 1 | | |
| ❑ Riverside RLP-389 [M] | 196? | 20.00 |
| ❑ Riverside RS-9389 [R] | 196? | 12.00 |
| CHICAGO: THE LIVING LEGENDS, VOL. 2 | | |
| ❑ Riverside RLP-390 [M] | 196? | 20.00 |
| ❑ Riverside RS-9390 [R] | 196? | 12.00 |
| A CHRISTMAS CAROL/MUSIC OF CHRISTMAS | | |
| ❑ MGM E3222 [M] | 1955 | 30.00 |
| *—Expanded version of 10-inch LP. Also see LIONEL BARRYMORE.* | | |
| CHRISTMAS CLASSICS | | |
| ❑ WCI UN-540 [(4)] | 1985 | 20.00 |
| *—Records individually numbered: 1. Capitol Special Markets SL-9309; 2. CBS Special Products P-18335; 3. CBS Special Products P-18334; 4. Capitol Special Markets SL-9308* | | |
| CHRISTMAS CLASSICS 1963 | | |
| ❑ E.F. MacDonald EFMX-63 | 1963 | 20.00 |
| *—Special album done by the E.F. MacDonald Company, Dayton, Ohio* | | |
| CHRISTMAS DAY WITH COLONEL SANDERS | | |
| ❑ RCA Victor PRS-274 | 1968 | 20.00 |
| *—Sold only at Kentucky Fried Chicken restaurants* | | |
| CHRISTMAS EVE WITH COLONEL SANDERS | | |
| ❑ RCA Victor PRS-256 | 1967 | 20.00 |
| *—Sold only at Kentucky Fried Chicken restaurants* | | |
| CHRISTMAS GIFT 'RAP | | |
| ❑ Motown MS-725 | 1970 | 20.00 |
| *—Reissue of "Merry Christmas from Motown," MS-681* | | |
| A CHRISTMAS GIFT FOR YOU FROM PHIL SPECTOR | | |
| ❑ Phil Spector/Abkco D1-4005 [M] | 1989 | 20.00 |
| *—Eighth edition of this group of songs* | | |
| ❑ Phil Spector/Rhino RNLP 70235 [M] | 1987 | 12.00 |
| *—Seventh edition of this group of songs; title and cover design restored to one similar to the original, with the typo on "Marshmallow World" corrected* | | |
| A CHRISTMAS GIFT FOR YOU FROM PHILLES RECORDS | | |
| ❑ Philles PHLP-4005 [M] | 1963 | 150.00 |
| *—First edition of this group of songs; blue and black labels* | | |
| ❑ Philles PHLP-4005 [M] | 1964 | 80.00 |
| *—Second edition of this group of songs; yellow and red labels; both first and second editions have "Marshmellow [sic] World" typo on front cover; also see PHIL SPECTOR'S CHRISTMAS ALBUM* | | |
| CHRISTMAS HITS FROM WARNER BROS. | | |
| ❑ Warner Bros. 8467/8 [DJ] | 1959 | 50.00 |
| CHRISTMAS PROGRAMMING FROM RCA VICTOR | | |
| ❑ RCA Victor SP-33-66 [DJ] | 1959 | 1000. |
| *—Promo-only collection; has been counterfeited, but originals have color covers* | | |
| A CHRISTMAS RECORD | | |
| ❑ Ze/Passport PB 6020 | 1982 | 20.00 |
| CHRISTMAS THROUGH THE YEARS | | |
| ❑ Reader's Digest RDA-143 [(5)] | 1984 | 20.00 |
| *—Available only through Reader's Digest magazine by mail order* | | |
| CHRISTMAS WITH COLONEL SANDERS | | |
| ❑ RCA Victor PRS-291 | 1969 | 20.00 |
| *—Sold only at Kentucky Fried Chicken restaurants* | | |
| CHRISTMASTIME IN CAROL AND SONG | | |
| ❑ RCA Victor PRM-271 [M] | 1968 | 20.00 |
| ❑ RCA Victor PRS-271 [S] | 1968 | 12.00 |
| CLAMBAKE ON BOURBON STREET | | |
| ❑ Cook LP-1085 [10] | 1955 | 50.00 |
| CLASSIC BLUES ACCOMPANISTS | | |
| ❑ Riverside RLP-1052 [10] | 1955 | 80.00 |
| CLASSIC CAPITOL JAZZ SESSIONS | | |
| ❑ Mosaic MQ19-170 [(19)] | 199? | 400.00 |
| CLASSIC COUNTRY MUSIC | | |
| ❑ Columbia Special Products P8 15640 [(8)] | 1981 | 50.00 |
| *—Boxed set; sold only by the Smithsonian; original version* | | |
| ❑ RCA Special Products DML6-0914 [(6)] | 1990 | 50.00 |
| *—Boxed set; sold only by the Smithsonian; revised version* | | |
| CLASSIC JAZZ PIANO STYLES | | |
| ❑ RCA Victor LPV-544 [M] | 1967 | 20.00 |
| CLASSICS IN JAZZ | | |
| ❑ Capitol T 320 [M] | 1954 | 40.00 |
| CLASSICS IN JAZZ: COOL AND QUIET | | |
| ❑ Capitol H 371 [10] | 1953 | 50.00 |
| CLASSICS IN JAZZ: DIXIELAND STYLISTS | | |
| ❑ Capitol H 321 [10] | 1952 | 50.00 |
| CLASSICS IN JAZZ: SMALL COMBOS | | |
| ❑ Capitol H 322 [10] | 1952 | 50.00 |

| Number Title (A Side/B Side) | Yr | NM |
|---|---|---|
| CLAY COLE PRESENTS BLASTS FROM THE PAST | | |
| ❑ Blast BLP 6803 [M] | 196? | 50.00 |
| CLAY COLE'S BIN OF ORIGINAL GOLDEN OLDIES | | |
| ❑ Jubilee JGM-5026 [M] | 1964 | 100.00 |
| A COLLECTION OF 16 ORIGINAL BIG HITS, VOLUME 10 | | |
| ❑ Motown MS 684 | 1969 | 20.00 |
| A COLLECTION OF 16 ORIGINAL BIG HITS, VOLUME 11 | | |
| ❑ Motown MS 693 | 1969 | 20.00 |
| A COLLECTION OF 16 ORIGINAL BIG HITS, VOLUME 3 | | |
| ❑ Motown MS 624 [S] | 1966 | 25.00 |
| A COLLECTION OF 16 ORIGINAL BIG HITS, VOLUME 5 | | |
| ❑ Motown MS 651 [S] | 1966 | 20.00 |
| A COLLECTION OF 16 ORIGINAL BIG HITS, VOLUME 6 | | |
| ❑ Motown MS 655 [S] | 1967 | 20.00 |
| ❑ Motown MT 655 [M] | 1967 | 20.00 |
| A COLLECTION OF 16 ORIGINAL BIG HITS, VOLUME 7 | | |
| ❑ Motown M 661 [M] | 1967 | 20.00 |
| ❑ Motown MS 661 [S] | 1967 | 20.00 |
| A COLLECTION OF 16 ORIGINAL BIG HITS, VOLUME 8 | | |
| ❑ Motown MS 666 [S] | 1967 | 20.00 |
| ❑ Motown MT 666 [M] | 1967 | 20.00 |
| A COLLECTION OF 16 ORIGINAL BIG HITS, VOLUME 9 | | |
| ❑ Motown MS 668 [S] | 1968 | 20.00 |
| ❑ Motown MT 668 [M] | 1968 | 50.00 |
| *—Mono is white label promo only; "Monaural Record DJ Copy" sticker on stereo cover* | | |
| COLLECTOR'S SERIES SAMPLER RECORD | | |
| ❑ London LCX 1004 [DJ] | 1977 | 20.00 |
| COLLECTORS ITEMS, VOL. 2 | | |
| ❑ Riverside RLP-1040 [10] | 1954 | 80.00 |
| COLLECTUS INTERRUPTUS | | |
| ❑ Warner Bros. PRO 726 [(2)] | 1977 | 20.00 |
| COLLEGE JAZZ: DIXIELAND | | |
| ❑ Columbia CL 736 [M] | 1956 | 20.00 |
| COLOR ME OBG: STATION WDRC | | |
| ❑ Roulette R 25347 [M] | 1967 | 20.00 |
| COLORADO JAZZ PARTY | | |
| ❑ BASF 25099 [(2)] | 197? | 20.00 |
| COLUMBIA JAZZ FESTIVAL | | |
| ❑ Columbia JJ-1 [M] | 1959 | 25.00 |
| COLUMBIA'S 24 HITS IN THE TOP 20 FOR 1982! | | |
| ❑ Columbia A2S 1588 [(2)DJ] | 1982 | 25.00 |
| COMBO JAZZ | | |
| ❑ Jazztone J-1221 [M] | 1956 | 30.00 |
| COME CLOSER TO GOD | | |
| ❑ Vee Jay LP-5061 [M] | 1964 | 30.00 |
| COME TOGETHER: AMERICA SALUTES THE BEATLES | | |
| ❑ Liberty 31712 | 1995 | 20.00 |
| COMPARATIVE BLUES | | |
| ❑ Jazztone J-1258 [M] | 1957 | 30.00 |
| THE COMPLETE COMMODORE JAZZ RECORDINGS, VOLUME I | | |
| ❑ Mosaic M23-123 [(23)] | 199? | 400.00 |
| THE COMPLETE COMMODORE JAZZ RECORDINGS, VOLUME II | | |
| ❑ Mosaic M23-128 [(23)] | 199? | 400.00 |
| THE COMPLETE COMMODORE JAZZ RECORDINGS, VOLUME III | | |
| ❑ Mosaic M20-134 [(20)] | 199? | 300.00 |
| THE COMPLETE KEYNOTE COLLECTION | | |
| ❑ Keynote 830121-1 [(21)] | 1986 | 250.00 |
| THE COMPLETE MASTER JAZZ PIANO SERIES | | |
| ❑ Mosaic M6-140 [(6)] | 199? | 100.00 |
| COMPOSERS AT PLAY: HAROLD ARLEN AND COLE PORTER | | |
| ❑ "X" LVA-1003 [M] | 1955 | 40.00 |
| THE COMPOSITIONS OF BENNY GOLSON | | |
| ❑ Riverside RLP-3505 [M] | 1962 | 15.00 |
| ❑ Riverside RS-93505 [S] | 1962 | 20.00 |
| THE COMPOSITIONS OF BOBBY TIMMONS | | |
| ❑ Riverside RLP-3512 [M] | 1962 | 15.00 |
| ❑ Riverside RS-93512 [S] | 1962 | 20.00 |
| THE COMPOSITIONS OF CHARLIE PARKER | | |
| ❑ Riverside RLP-3506 [M] | 1962 | 15.00 |
| ❑ Riverside RS-93506 [S] | 1962 | 20.00 |
| THE COMPOSITIONS OF COLE PORTER | | |
| ❑ Riverside RM-3515 [M] | 1963 | 15.00 |
| ❑ Riverside RS-93515 [S] | 1963 | 20.00 |
| THE COMPOSITIONS OF DIZZY GILLESPIE | | |
| ❑ Riverside RLP-3508 [M] | 1962 | 15.00 |
| ❑ Riverside RS-93508 [S] | 1962 | 20.00 |
| THE COMPOSITIONS OF DUKE ELLINGTON | | |
| ❑ Riverside RLP-3507 [M] | 1962 | 15.00 |
| ❑ Riverside RS-93507 [S] | 1962 | 20.00 |
| THE COMPOSITIONS OF DUKE ELLINGTON, VOL. 2 | | |
| ❑ Riverside RLP-3510 [M] | 1962 | 15.00 |
| ❑ Riverside RS-93510 [S] | 1962 | 20.00 |
| THE COMPOSITIONS OF GEORGE GERSHWIN | | |
| ❑ Riverside RM-3517 [M] | 1963 | 15.00 |
| ❑ Riverside RS-93517 [S] | 1963 | 20.00 |
| THE COMPOSITIONS OF HAROLD ARLEN | | |
| ❑ Riverside RM-3518 [M] | 1963 | 15.00 |
| ❑ Riverside RS-93518 [S] | 1963 | 20.00 |
| THE COMPOSITIONS OF HORACE SILVER | | |
| ❑ Riverside RLP-3509 [M] | 1962 | 15.00 |

| Number / Title (A Side/B Side) | Yr | NM |
|---|---|---|
| ❑ Riverside RS-93509 [S] | 1962 | 20.00 |
| THE COMPOSITIONS OF IRVING BERLIN | | |
| ❑ Riverside RM-3519 [M] | 1963 | 15.00 |
| ❑ Riverside RS-93519 [S] | 1963 | 20.00 |
| THE COMPOSITIONS OF JEROME KERN | | |
| ❑ Riverside RM-3516 [M] | 1963 | 15.00 |
| ❑ Riverside RS-93516 [S] | 1963 | 20.00 |
| COMPOSITIONS OF LIONEL HAMPTON | | |
| ❑ Crown CLP-5107 [M] | 195? | 25.00 |
| THE COMPOSITIONS OF MILES DAVIS | | |
| ❑ Riverside RLP-3504 [M] | 1962 | 15.00 |
| ❑ Riverside RS-93504 [S] | 1962 | 20.00 |
| THE COMPOSITIONS OF RICHARD RODGERS | | |
| ❑ Riverside RM-3514 [M] | 1963 | 15.00 |
| ❑ Riverside RS-93514 [S] | 1963 | 20.00 |
| THE COMPOSITIONS OF TADD DAMERON | | |
| ❑ Riverside RLP-3511 [M] | 1962 | 15.00 |
| ❑ Riverside RS-93511 [S] | 1962 | 20.00 |
| THE COMPOSITIONS OF THELONIOUS MONK | | |
| ❑ Riverside RLP-3503 [M] | 1962 | 15.00 |
| ❑ Riverside RS-93503 [S] | 1962 | 20.00 |
| CONCEPTION | | |
| ❑ Prestige PRLP-7013 [M] | 1956 | 100.00 |
| CONCERT IN JAZZ | | |
| ❑ Tops L-1532 [M] | 1958 | 20.00 |
| CONCERT JAZZ | | |
| ❑ Brunswick BL 54027 [M] | 1956 | 30.00 |
| CONCERTS FOR THE PEOPLE OF KAMPUCHEA | | |
| ❑ Atlantic SD 2-7005 [(2)] | 1981 | 20.00 |
| CONNECTED | | |
| ❑ Limp 1005 | 1981 | 20.00 |
| COOK BOOK | | |
| ❑ Warner Bros. PRO 660 [(2)] | 1976 | 20.00 |
| COOL EUROPE | | |
| ❑ MGM E-3157 [M] | 1955 | 30.00 |
| COOL GABRIELS | | |
| ❑ Groove LG-1003 [M] | 1956 | 60.00 |
| COOL JAZZ | | |
| ❑ Seeco CELP-465 [M] | 1960 | 20.00 |
| COOL JAZZ FROM HOLLAND | | |
| ❑ Epic LN 1126 [10] | 1955 | 40.00 |
| COOLIN' | | |
| ❑ New Jazz NJLP-8216 [M] | 1959 | 60.00 |
| *—Purple label* | | |
| ❑ New Jazz NJLP-8216 [M] | 1965 | 30.00 |
| *—Blue label, trident logo at right* | | |
| COUNTRY & WESTERN CLASSICS 1955 | | |
| ❑ Economic Consultants 1955 | 1973 | 20.00 |
| COUNTRY & WESTERN CLASSICS 1956 | | |
| ❑ Economic Consultants 1956 | 1973 | 20.00 |
| COUNTRY & WESTERN CLASSICS 1957 | | |
| ❑ Economic Consultants 1957 | 1973 | 20.00 |
| COUNTRY & WESTERN CLASSICS 1958 | | |
| ❑ Economic Consultants 1958 | 1973 | 20.00 |
| COUNTRY AND WESTERN AWARD WINNERS 1964 | | |
| ❑ Decca DL 4622 [M] | 1965 | 20.00 |
| ❑ Decca DL 74622 [S] | 1965 | 25.00 |
| COUNTRY AND WESTERN AWARD WINNERS 1966 | | |
| ❑ Decca DL 4837 [M] | 1967 | 20.00 |
| ❑ Decca DL 74837 [S] | 1967 | 15.00 |
| COUNTRY AND WESTERN JAMBOREE | | |
| ❑ King 697 [M] | 1961 | 150.00 |
| COUNTRY BOY — COUNTRY GIRL | | |
| ❑ Decca DL 4201 [M] | 1962 | 25.00 |
| ❑ Decca DL 74201 [S] | 1962 | 30.00 |
| COUNTRY CHRISTMAS | | |
| ❑ King 811 [M] | 1962 | 100.00 |
| ❑ Monument SLP-18125 | 1969 | 20.00 |
| ❑ Time-Life STL-109 [(3)] | 1988 | 20.00 |
| *—Available from Time-Life by mail order only; boxed set* | | |
| COUNTRY CLASSICS | | |
| ❑ RCA Victor LPM-2313 [M] | 1961 | 25.00 |
| ❑ RCA Victor LSP-2313(e) [R] | 1962 | 20.00 |
| COUNTRY EXPRESS | | |
| ❑ Starday SLP-109 [M] | 1959 | 40.00 |
| COUNTRY FAIR | | |
| ❑ Capitol SWBB-562 [(2)] | 1970 | 25.00 |
| COUNTRY GOLD | | |
| ❑ RCA Special Products DPL1-0561 | 1980 | 20.00 |
| COUNTRY HIT PARADE | | |
| ❑ Starday SLP-110 [M] | 1959 | 40.00 |
| COUNTRY HITS BY COUNTRY STARS | | |
| ❑ Capitol ST 1912 [S] | 1963 | 25.00 |
| ❑ Capitol T 1912 [M] | 1963 | 20.00 |
| COUNTRY HITS PARADE | | |
| ❑ RCA Victor LPM-3452 [M] | 1966 | 15.00 |
| ❑ RCA Victor LSP-3452 [S] | 1966 | 20.00 |
| COUNTRY JUBILEE | | |
| ❑ Decca DL 4172 [M] | 1961 | 30.00 |
| COUNTRY MEMORIES | | |
| ❑ Reader's Digest RBA-066-A [(7)] | 1989 | 50.00 |
| COUNTRY MUSIC BY THE WAYSIDE | | |
| ❑ Wayside 1013 | 1968 | 20.00 |
| COUNTRY MUSIC HALL OF FAME | | |
| ❑ Starday SLP-164 [(2)M] | 1962 | 30.00 |
| COUNTRY MUSIC HALL OF FAME, VOL. 2 | | |
| ❑ Starday SLP-190 [(2)M] | 1963 | 30.00 |
| COUNTRY MUSIC HALL OF FAME, VOL. 3 | | |
| ❑ Starday SLP-256 [(2)M] | 1963 | 30.00 |
| COUNTRY MUSIC HALL OF FAME, VOL. 4 | | |
| ❑ Starday SLP-295 [(2)M] | 1964 | 30.00 |
| COUNTRY MUSIC HALL OF FAME, VOL. 5 | | |
| ❑ Starday SLP-360 [M] | 1966 | 25.00 |
| COUNTRY MUSIC HALL OF FAME, VOL. 6 | | |
| ❑ Starday SLP-390 | 1967 | 25.00 |
| COUNTRY MUSIC HALL OF FAME, VOL. 7 | | |
| ❑ Starday SLP-409 | 1969 | 20.00 |
| COUNTRY MUSIC HALL OF FAME, VOL. 8 | | |
| ❑ Starday SLP-430 | 1969 | 20.00 |
| COUNTRY MUSIC HALL OF FAME, VOL. 9 | | |
| ❑ Starday SLP-449 | 1970 | 20.00 |
| COUNTRY MUSIC HITS BY COUNTRY MUSIC STARS | | |
| ❑ RCA Camden CAL-689 [M] | 1962 | 20.00 |
| ❑ RCA Camden CAS-689 [R] | 196? | 15.00 |
| COUNTRY MUSIC HOOTENANNY | | |
| ❑ Capitol ST 2009 [S] | 1963 | 30.00 |
| ❑ Capitol T 2009 [M] | 1963 | 25.00 |
| COUNTRY MUSIC JAMBOREE | | |
| ❑ Mercury MG-20350 [M] | 1958 | 40.00 |
| COUNTRY MUSIC SPECTACULAR | | |
| ❑ Starday SLP-117 [M] | 1961 | 40.00 |
| COUNTRY MUSIC STAR SPECTACULAR | | |
| ❑ Hickory LPM-116 [M] | 1963 | 25.00 |
| COUNTRY MUSIC WHO'S WHO | | |
| ❑ Starday SLP-304 [M] | 1964 | 20.00 |
| *—Without booklet* | | |
| ❑ Starday SLP-304 [M] | 1964 | 30.00 |
| *—With 52-page booklet* | | |
| COUNTRY OLDIES BUT GOODIES | | |
| ❑ Smash MGS-27016 [M] | 1962 | 20.00 |
| ❑ Smash SRS-67016 [S] | 1962 | 20.00 |
| A COUNTRY SALUTE TO HANK WILLIAMS | | |
| ❑ Harmony HL 7265 [M] | 1960 | 20.00 |
| COUNTRY SOFT AND MELLOW | | |
| ❑ Reader's Digest RB4-200 [(7)] | 1989 | 50.00 |
| COUNTRY SPECIAL | | |
| ❑ Capitol STBB-402 [(2)] | 1969 | 25.00 |
| COUNTRY SPECTACULAR | | |
| ❑ Columbia CL 894 [M] | 1956 | 50.00 |
| COUNTRY STARS, COUNTRY HITS | | |
| ❑ RCA Camden CAL-793 [M] | 1964 | 20.00 |
| ❑ RCA Camden CAS-793 [S] | 1964 | 20.00 |
| COUNTRY USA: 1950 | | |
| ❑ Time-Life CTR-23 [(2)] | 1991 | 20.00 |
| COUNTRY USA: 1951 | | |
| ❑ Time-Life CTR-22 [(2)] | 1991 | 20.00 |
| COUNTRY USA: 1952 | | |
| ❑ Time-Life CTR-16 [(2)] | 1990 | 15.00 |
| COUNTRY USA: 1953 | | |
| ❑ Time-Life CTR-20 [(2)] | 1990 | 15.00 |
| COUNTRY USA: 1954 | | |
| ❑ Time-Life CTR-15 [(2)] | 1990 | 20.00 |
| COUNTRY USA: 1955 | | |
| ❑ Time-Life CTR-19 [(2)] | 1990 | 20.00 |
| COUNTRY USA: 1956 | | |
| ❑ Time-Life CTR-13 [(2)] | 1990 | 20.00 |
| COUNTRY USA: 1957 | | |
| ❑ Time-Life CTR-02 [(2)] | 1988 | 15.00 |
| COUNTRY USA: 1958 | | |
| ❑ Time-Life CTR-07 [(2)] | 1989 | 20.00 |
| COUNTRY USA: 1959 | | |
| ❑ Time-Life CTR-09 [(2)] | 1989 | 15.00 |
| COUNTRY USA: 1960 | | |
| ❑ Time-Life CTR-12 [(2)] | 1989 | 15.00 |
| COUNTRY USA: 1961 | | |
| ❑ Time-Life CTR-01 [(2)] | 1988 | 15.00 |
| COUNTRY USA: 1962 | | |
| ❑ Time-Life CTR-03 [(2)] | 1988 | 15.00 |
| COUNTRY USA: 1963 | | |
| ❑ Time-Life CTR-11 [(2)] | 1989 | 15.00 |
| COUNTRY USA: 1964 | | |
| ❑ Time-Life CTR-14 [(2)] | 1990 | 15.00 |
| COUNTRY USA: 1965 | | |
| ❑ Time-Life CTR-10 [(2)] | 1989 | 15.00 |
| COUNTRY USA: 1966 | | |
| ❑ Time-Life CTR-21 [(2)] | 1991 | 20.00 |
| COUNTRY USA: 1967 | | |
| ❑ Time-Life CTR-17 [(2)] | 1990 | 15.00 |
| COUNTRY USA: 1968 | | |
| ❑ Time-Life CTR-06 [(2)] | 1989 | 15.00 |
| COUNTRY USA: 1969 | | |
| ❑ Time-Life CTR-08 [(2)] | 1989 | 20.00 |
| COUNTRY USA: 1970 | | |
| ❑ Time-Life CTR-04 [(2)] | 1988 | 15.00 |
| COUNTRY USA: 1971 | | |
| ❑ Time-Life CTR-05 [(2)] | 1989 | 15.00 |
| COUNTRY USA: 1972 | | |
| ❑ Time-Life CTR-18 [(2)] | 1990 | 15.00 |
| THE COUNTRY'S BEST | | |
| ❑ Capitol T 1179 [M] | 1959 | 30.00 |
| CRITICS' CHOICE | | |
| ❑ Dawn DLP-1123 [M] | 1958 | 80.00 |
| CROSSROADS: WHITE BLUES IN THE 1960S | | |
| ❑ Elektra 60383 [(3)] | 1984 | 20.00 |
| CRUISIN' | | |
| ❑ Jazzland JLP-7 [M] | 1960 | 25.00 |
| ❑ Jazzland JLP-97 [S] | 1960 | 30.00 |
| CURTAIN UP! AMERICAN DANCE FAVORITES | | |
| ❑ Mercury Living Presence SR 90326 [S] | 196? | 40.00 |
| *—Maroon label, no "Vendor: Mercury Record Corporation"* | | |
| CURTAIN UP! FAVORITE CONCERT OVERTURES | | |
| ❑ Mercury Living Presence SR 90323 | 196? | 60.00 |
| *—Maroon label, no "Vendor: Mercury Record Corporation"* | | |
| CURTAIN UP! OPERA BALLET FAVORITES | | |
| ❑ Mercury Living Presence SR 90327 [S] | 196? | 30.00 |
| *—Maroon label, no "Vendor: Mercury Record Corporation"* | | |
| D'OES CRAZY OLDIES | | |
| ❑ Oldies 33 OL-8007 [M] | 1964 | 25.00 |
| THE D.I.Y. ALBUM | | |
| ❑ D.I.Y./JW Productions DIY-0001 | 1982 | 50.00 |
| *—Band copies on black vinyl* | | |
| ❑ D.I.Y./JW Productions DIY-0001A | 1982 | 30.00 |
| *—Store copies on clear vinyl (3-D pressing was planned but never done)* | | |
| DANCE BAND HITS | | |
| ❑ RCA Victor LPT-2 [10] | 1951 | 40.00 |
| DANCE DISCOTHEQUE | | |
| ❑ Decca DL 4556 [M] | 1964 | 15.00 |
| ❑ Decca DL 74556 [S] | 1964 | 20.00 |
| DANCE ON THE WILD SIDE | | |
| ❑ Chancellor CHL-5028 [M] | 1962 | 25.00 |
| ❑ Chancellor CHLS-5028 [S] | 1962 | 30.00 |
| DANCE RHYTHM 'N' ROCK NEW MUSIC SEMINAR MIXER | | |
| ❑ Warner Bros. PRO-A-2061 [DJ] | 1983 | 80.00 |
| DANCE THE ROCK & ROLL | | |
| ❑ Atlantic 8013 [M] | 1957 | 80.00 |
| DANCE TO THE BANDS | | |
| ❑ Capitol TBO 727 [(2)M] | 1956 | 40.00 |
| ❑ Capitol T 977 [M] | 1958 | 20.00 |
| DANCE TUNES FROM THE VAULT, VOLUME 2 | | |
| ❑ Chess LP 1476 [M] | 1962 | 40.00 |
| DANCE, BE HAPPY! | | |
| ❑ Columbia CL 967 [M] | 1957 | 20.00 |
| DANCING WITH THE STARS | | |
| ❑ Epic LN 3136 [M] | 1955 | 30.00 |
| DARK MUDDY BOTTOM BLUES | | |
| ❑ Specialty SPS-2149 | 1971 | 20.00 |
| DAS IS JAZZ! | | |
| ❑ Decca DL 8229 [M] | 1956 | 30.00 |
| A DATE WITH GREATNESS | | |
| ❑ Imperial LP-9188A [M] | 1962 | 50.00 |
| *—Features Aladdin tracks by Coleman Hawkins, Howard McGhee and Lester Young* | | |
| ❑ Imperial LP-12188A [R] | 1962 | 25.00 |
| A DATE WITH RIVERSIDE | | |
| ❑ Riverside S-4 [M] | 195? | 40.00 |
| A DAY IN THE COUNTRY | | |
| ❑ Audio Lab AL-1519 [M] | 1959 | 80.00 |
| DAYS OF WINE AND VINYL | | |
| ❑ Warner Bros. PRO 540 [(2)] | 1973 | 30.00 |
| DEEP EAR | | |
| ❑ Warner Bros. PRO 591 [(2)] | 1974 | 25.00 |
| DEEP SIX | | |
| ❑ C/Z CZ 001 | 1985 | 50.00 |
| DEF JAM RECORDINGS — RETAIL TRACKS | | |
| ❑ Def Jam CAS 2715 [DJ] | 1987 | 20.00 |
| THE DEFINITIVE JAZZ SCENE, VOL. 1 | | |
| ❑ ABC Impulse! AS-99 [S] | 1968 | 12.00 |
| ❑ Impulse! A-99 [M] | 1966 | 15.00 |
| ❑ Impulse! AS-99 [S] | 1966 | 20.00 |
| THE DEFINITIVE JAZZ SCENE, VOL. 2 | | |
| ❑ ABC Impulse! AS-100 [S] | 1968 | 12.00 |
| ❑ Impulse! A-100 [M] | 1966 | 15.00 |
| ❑ Impulse! AS-100 [S] | 1966 | 20.00 |
| THE DEFINITIVE JAZZ SCENE, VOL. 3 | | |
| ❑ ABC Impulse! AS-9101 [S] | 1968 | 12.00 |
| ❑ Impulse! A-9101 [M] | 1966 | 15.00 |
| ❑ Impulse! AS-9101 [S] | 1966 | 20.00 |
| DEL-FI ALBUM SAMPLER | | |
| ❑ Del-Fi (no #) [DJ] | 1959 | 500.00 |
| *—Green vinyl, promo only, with paper sleeve* | | |
| DEL-FI RECORD HOP | | |
| ❑ Del-Fi DFLP-1210 [M] | 1959 | 80.00 |
| DEMAND PERFORMANCES | | |
| ❑ Monument MLP-8010 [M] | 1963 | 25.00 |
| ❑ Monument SLP-18010 [S] | 1963 | 40.00 |
| DEMONSTRATION RECORD — DISC JOCKEYS — JAN.-FEB. 1955 | | |
| ❑ Capitol PRO-213 [DJ] | 1955 | 40.00 |
| DESTINATION STEREO | | |
| ❑ RCA Victor Red Seal LSC-2307 [S] | 1959 | 30.00 |
| DIAL A HIT | | |
| ❑ Bell 6030 | 1969 | 20.00 |

| Number | Title (A Side/B Side) | Yr | NM |
|---|---|---|---|
| A DIAMOND HIDDEN IN THE MOUTH OF A CORPSE | | | |
| ❑ Giorno Poetry Systems 035 | | 1985 | 30.00 |
| DICK CLARK ALL TIME HITS | | | |
| ❑ Click Corp. B-100/101 [Picture Sleeve] | | 1958 | 20.00 |
| DICK CLARK: 20 YEARS OF ROCK N' ROLL | | | |
| ❑ Buddah BDS 5133 [(2)] | | 1973 | 20.00 |
| *—Gatefold cover with booklet and bonus 7-inch cardboard record* | | | |
| ❑ Buddah BDS 5133 [(2)] | | 1974 | 10.00 |
| *—With none of the extras* | | | |
| DIESEL SMOKE, DANGEROUS CURVES AND OTHER TRUCK DRIVERS FAVORITES | | | |
| ❑ Starday SLP-250 [M] | | 1963 | 30.00 |
| DISCO-TEEN '66 | | | |
| ❑ Columbia Record Club D 155 [M] | | 1966 | 20.00 |
| ❑ Columbia Record Club DS 155 [S] | | 1966 | 50.00 |
| *—Sought-after for its otherwise unavailable extended stereo mix of Bob Dylan's "Positively 4th Street"* | | | |
| DISPLAY CASE #10 | | | |
| ❑ Warner Bros. PRO 542 [(3)] | | 1973 | 30.00 |
| DISPLAY CASE #8 | | | |
| ❑ Warner Bros. PRO 532 [(2)] | | 1972 | 30.00 |
| DISPLAY CASE #9 | | | |
| ❑ Warner Bros. PRO 538 [(2)] | | 1972 | 30.00 |
| DIXIE, LONDON STYLE | | | |
| ❑ London LL 1337 [M] | | 1956 | 20.00 |
| DIXIELAND — NEW ORLEANS | | | |
| ❑ Mainstream S-6003 [R] | | 1965 | 12.00 |
| ❑ Mainstream 56003 [M] | | 1965 | 25.00 |
| DIXIELAND AT CARNEGIE HALL | | | |
| ❑ Forum F-9011 [M] | | 196? | 20.00 |
| ❑ Forum SF-9011 [S] | | 196? | 25.00 |
| ❑ Roulette R 25038 [M] | | 1958 | 30.00 |
| *—Originals have a black label* | | | |
| ❑ Roulette R 25038 [M] | | 1959 | 20.00 |
| *—Second pressings have a white label with colored spokes* | | | |
| DIXIELAND AT JAZZ, LTD. | | | |
| ❑ Atlantic 1261 [M] | | 1957 | 40.00 |
| *—Black label* | | | |
| ❑ Atlantic 1261 [M] | | 1961 | 25.00 |
| *—Multicolor label, white "fan" logo at right* | | | |
| DIXIELAND AT JAZZ, LTD., VOL. 1 | | | |
| ❑ Atlantic ALS-139 [10] | | 1952 | 60.00 |
| DIXIELAND AT JAZZ, LTD., VOL. 2 | | | |
| ❑ Atlantic ALS-140 [10] | | 1952 | 60.00 |
| DIXIELAND CLASSICS | | | |
| ❑ Jazztone J-1216 [M] | | 1956 | 30.00 |
| DIXIELAND CONTRASTS | | | |
| ❑ Jazzman LJ-334 [M] | | 1954 | 30.00 |
| DIXIELAND DETOUR | | | |
| ❑ Capitol H 312 [10] | | 1952 | — |
| *—See PEE WEE HUNT.* | | | |
| DIXIELAND FESTIVAL, VOL. 1 | | | |
| ❑ Vik LX-1057 [M] | | 1956 | 30.00 |
| DIXIELAND HITS | | | |
| ❑ Swingville SVLP-2040 [M] | | 1962 | 40.00 |
| *—Purple label* | | | |
| ❑ Swingville SVLP-2040 [M] | | 1965 | 20.00 |
| *—Blue label, trident logo at right* | | | |
| DIXIELAND IN OLD NEW ORLEANS | | | |
| ❑ Golden Crest GC-3021 [M] | | 1958 | 20.00 |
| DIXIELAND JAZZ | | | |
| ❑ Audiophile XL-325 [M] | | 1954 | 30.00 |
| ❑ Audiophile XL-330 [M] | | 1954 | 30.00 |
| ❑ Grand Award GA 33-310 [M] | | 1955 | 25.00 |
| *—Without wrap-around outer cover* | | | |
| ❑ Grand Award GA 33-310 [M] | | 1955 | 60.00 |
| *—With wrap-around outer cover* | | | |
| DIXIELAND JAZZ GEMS | | | |
| ❑ Commodore FL-20010 [10] | | 1950 | 50.00 |
| DIXIELAND MAIN STREAM | | | |
| ❑ Savoy MG-12213 [M] | | 196? | 20.00 |
| DIXIELAND RHYTHM KINGS | | | |
| ❑ Paradox LP-6002 [10] | | 1951 | 50.00 |
| DIXIELAND SERIES, VOL. 1 | | | |
| ❑ Savoy MG-15005 [10] | | 1952 | 80.00 |
| DIXIELAND SERIES, VOL. 2 | | | |
| ❑ Savoy MG-15009 [10] | | 1952 | 80.00 |
| DIXIELAND VS. BIRDLAND | | | |
| ❑ MGM E-231 [10] | | 1954 | 80.00 |
| DIZZY ATMOSPHERE | | | |
| ❑ Specialty LP-2110 [M] | | 1957 | 40.00 |
| *—Original edition, heavier vinyl* | | | |
| DO IT NOW - 20 GIANT HITS | | | |
| ❑ Ronco LP-1001 | | 1971 | 20.00 |
| DOCTOR DEATH'S VOLUME 1 | | | |
| ❑ C'est La Mort 001 | | 1986 | 30.00 |
| DOO WOP | | | |
| ❑ Specialty SPS-2114 | | 1969 | 20.00 |
| DOUBLE BARREL JAZZ | | | |
| ❑ Bethlehem BCP-87 [M] | | 1958 | 30.00 |
| DOWN BEAT JAZZ CONCERT | | | |
| ❑ Dot DLP-9003 [M] | | 1958 | 30.00 |
| ❑ Dot DLP-29003 [S] | | 1958 | 25.00 |
| DOWN BEAT JAZZ CONCERT, VOL. 2 | | | |
| ❑ Dot DLP-3188 [M] | | 1959 | 30.00 |
| ❑ Dot DLP-25188 [S] | | 1959 | 25.00 |

Various artists, *Elektra New Folk Sampler,* Elektra SMP-2, 1956, mono, $30.

| Number | Title (A Side/B Side) | Yr | NM |
|---|---|---|---|
| DOWN BEAT'S HALL OF FAME, VOL. 1 | | | |
| ❑ Verve MGV-8320 [M] | | 1959 | 50.00 |
| ❑ Verve V-8320 [M] | | 1961 | 20.00 |
| DOWN HOME STOMP: RURAL BLUES, VOLUME 3 | | | |
| ❑ Imperial LP-94006 | | 1968 | 20.00 |
| THE DRUMS | | | |
| ❑ ABC Impulse! AS-9272 [(3)] | | 197? | 20.00 |
| DRUMS ON FIRE | | | |
| ❑ World Pacific WP-1247 [M] | | 1958 | 40.00 |
| THE DUTCH EXPLOSION | | | |
| ❑ White Whale WWS-7130 | | 1970 | 30.00 |
| THE EARLY '60S: THESE WERE OUR SONGS | | | |
| ❑ Reader's Digest RC4-100 [(7)] | | 1989 | 50.00 |
| EARLY AND RARE: CLASSIC JAZZ "COLLECTORS ITEMS" | | | |
| ❑ Riverside RLP 12-134 [M] | | 1957 | 40.00 |
| EARLY JAZZ GREATS, VOL. 1 | | | |
| ❑ Jazztone J-1249 [M] | | 1957 | 30.00 |
| EARLY JAZZ GREATS, VOL. 2 | | | |
| ❑ Jazztone J-1252 [M] | | 1957 | 30.00 |
| EARTHY! | | | |
| ❑ Prestige PRLP-7102 [M] | | 1957 | 100.00 |
| THE EAST COAST JAZZ SCENE, VOL. 1 | | | |
| ❑ Coral CRL 57035 [M] | | 1956 | 50.00 |
| EASY LISTENING | | | |
| ❑ Audiophile AP-27 [M] | | 1953 | 30.00 |
| ❑ Audiophile AP-38 [M] | | 1953 | 30.00 |
| ❑ Audiophile XL-327 [M] | | 1954 | 30.00 |
| EASY LISTENING HITS OF THE '60S AND '70S | | | |
| ❑ Reader's Digest RBA-040A [(7)] | | 1989 | 50.00 |
| ECLIPSE | | | |
| ❑ Warner Bros. PRO-A-828 [(2)] | | 1978 | 20.00 |
| EIGHT WAYS TO JAZZ | | | |
| ❑ Riverside RLP 12-272 [M] | | 1958 | 30.00 |
| 18 ALL TIME COUNTRY AND WESTERN HITS | | | |
| ❑ King 1027 [M] | | 1968 | 30.00 |
| 18 ALL TIME RHYTHM 'N' BLUES HITS | | | |
| ❑ King 1026 [M] | | 1968 | 30.00 |
| 18 KING-SIZE COUNTRY HITS | | | |
| ❑ Columbia CL 2668 [M] | | 1967 | 20.00 |
| ❑ Columbia CS 9468 [R] | | 1967 | 20.00 |
| 18 KING-SIZE RHYTHM AND BLUES HITS | | | |
| ❑ Columbia CL 2667 [M] | | 1967 | 30.00 |
| ❑ Columbia CS 9467 [R] | | 1967 | 20.00 |

| Number | Title (A Side/B Side) | Yr | NM |
|---|---|---|---|
| ELEKTRA NEW FOLK SAMPLER | | | |
| ❑ Elektra SMP 2 [M] | | 1956 | 30.00 |
| ELEKTRA'S BEST, VOLUME 1: 1966-1968 | | | |
| ❑ Elektra EB-1 [(2)] | | 1969 | 25.00 |
| *—Promo only, red labels* | | | |
| ELEKTROCK: THE SIXTIES | | | |
| ❑ Elektra 60403 [(4)] | | 1985 | 30.00 |
| ENCYCLOPEDIA OF JAZZ IN THE '60'S, VOL. 1 | | | |
| ❑ Verve V-8677 [M] | | 1966 | 15.00 |
| ❑ Verve V6-8677 [S] | | 1966 | 20.00 |
| THE ENCYCLOPEDIA OF JAZZ ON RECORDS | | | |
| ❑ Decca DXF 140 [(4)M] | | 1957 | 100.00 |
| *—Box set; individually issued as Decca 8398, 8399, 8400 and 8401* | | | |
| THE ENCYCLOPEDIA OF JAZZ ON RECORDS, VOL. 1 AND 2: JAZZ OF THE TWENTIES/JAZZ OF THE THIRTIES | | | |
| ❑ MCA 4061 [(2)] | | 197? | 15.00 |
| THE ENCYCLOPEDIA OF JAZZ ON RECORDS, VOL. 1: JAZZ OF THE TWENTIES | | | |
| ❑ Decca DL 8398 [M] | | 1957 | 20.00 |
| THE ENCYCLOPEDIA OF JAZZ ON RECORDS, VOL. 2: JAZZ OF THE THIRTIES | | | |
| ❑ Decca DL 8399 [M] | | 1957 | 20.00 |
| THE ENCYCLOPEDIA OF JAZZ ON RECORDS, VOL. 3 AND 4: JAZZ OF THE FORTIES/JAZZ OF THE FIFTIES | | | |
| ❑ MCA 4062 [(2)] | | 197? | 15.00 |
| THE ENCYCLOPEDIA OF JAZZ ON RECORDS, VOL. 3: JAZZ OF THE FORTIES | | | |
| ❑ Decca DL 8400 [M] | | 1957 | 20.00 |
| THE ENCYCLOPEDIA OF JAZZ ON RECORDS, VOL. 4: JAZZ OF THE FIFTIES | | | |
| ❑ Decca DL 8401 [M] | | 1957 | 20.00 |
| THE ENCYCLOPEDIA OF JAZZ ON RECORDS, VOL. 5: JAZZ OF THE SIXTIES | | | |
| ❑ MCA 4063 [(2)] | | 197? | 15.00 |
| END OF AN ERA: RHYTHM 'N' BLUES, VOLUME 1 | | | |
| ❑ Imperial LP-94003 | | 1968 | 20.00 |
| ENERGY ESSENTIALS | | | |
| ❑ ABC Impulse! ASD-9228 [(3)] | | 197? | 20.00 |
| ENGLAND'S GREATEST HIT MAKERS | | | |
| ❑ London PS 430 [R] | | 1965 | 20.00 |
| ❑ London LL 3430 [M] | | 1965 | 25.00 |
| ENGLAND'S GREATEST HITS | | | |
| ❑ Fontana MGF 27570 [M] | | 1967 | 40.00 |
| *—Without poster* | | | |

Various artists, *50 Years of Film,* Warner Bros. 3XX 2737, 1973, 3 records, $25.

| Number | Title (A Side/B Side) | Yr | NM |
|---|---|---|---|
| ❑ Fontana MGF 27570 [M] | | 1967 | 50.00 |
| *—With poster* | | | |
| ❑ Fontana SRF 67570 [R] | | 1967 | 20.00 |
| *—Without poster* | | | |
| ❑ Fontana SRF 67570 [R] | | 1967 | 30.00 |
| *—With poster* | | | |
| ERA OF THE CLARINET | | | |
| ❑ Mainstream S-6011 [R] | | 1965 | 12.00 |
| ❑ Mainstream 56011 [M] | | 1965 | 25.00 |
| ESCAPADE REVIEWS THE JAZZ SCENE | | | |
| ❑ Liberty SL-9005 [M] | | 1957 | 30.00 |
| ESCAPE | | | |
| ❑ Gene Norman GNP-27 [M] | | 1958 | 25.00 |
| ESQUIRE'S ALL-AMERICAN HOT JAZZ | | | |
| ❑ RCA Victor LPV-544 [M] | | 1967 | 20.00 |
| ESQUIRE'S WORLD OF JAZZ | | | |
| ❑ Capitol STBO 1970 [(2)S] | | 1963 | 20.00 |
| ❑ Capitol TBO 1970 [(2)M] | | 1963 | 20.00 |
| THE ESSENTIAL JAZZ VOCALS | | | |
| ❑ Verve V-8505 [M] | | 1963 | 20.00 |
| ❑ Verve V6-8505 [R] | | 1963 | 12.00 |
| AN EVENING OF JAZZ | | | |
| ❑ Norgran MGN-1065 [M] | | 1956 | 80.00 |
| ❑ Verve MGV-8155 [M] | | 1957 | 30.00 |
| ❑ Verve V-8155 [M] | | 1961 | 20.00 |
| EVERYBODY ROCKS! | | | |
| ❑ Capitol T 1025 [M] | | 1957 | 40.00 |
| *—Turquoise label* | | | |
| EVERYBODY'S FAVORITE BLUES | | | |
| ❑ King 875 [M] | | 1963 | 70.00 |
| EVERYBODY'S GONE SURFIN' | | | |
| ❑ Parkway P-7035 [M] | | 1963 | 50.00 |
| THE EXCELLO STORY | | | |
| ❑ Excello LPS-8025 [(2)] | | 1972 | 25.00 |
| THE EXCITING NEW LIVERPOOL SOUND | | | |
| ❑ Columbia CL 2172 [M] | | 1964 | 30.00 |
| EXPLOSIVE! | | | |
| ❑ Liberty MM-412 [DJ] | | 1962 | 50.00 |
| *—Promo-only release* | | | |
| FABULOUS FAVORITES OF OUR TIME | | | |
| ❑ Liberty LRP-3223 [M] | | 1962 | 20.00 |
| ❑ Liberty LST-7223 [S] | | 1962 | 25.00 |
| THE FAMILY CHRISTMAS COLLECTION | | | |
| ❑ Time-Life STL-131 [(5)] | | 1990 | 30.00 |
| *—Available from Time-Life by mail order only* | | | |

| Number | Title (A Side/B Side) | Yr | NM |
|---|---|---|---|
| FAMILY PORTRAIT | | | |
| ❑ A&M SP-19002 | | 1968 | 20.00 |
| FANFARE OF HITS | | | |
| ❑ Argo LP-656 [M] | | 1960 | 25.00 |
| FANTASY SAMPLER | | | |
| ❑ Fantasy FS-654 [M] | | 195? | 20.00 |
| *—Red vinyl* | | | |
| FAVORITE SACRED SONGS | | | |
| ❑ King 556 [M] | | 1956 | 150.00 |
| THE FEMININE TOUCH | | | |
| ❑ Decca DL 5486 [10] | | 1953 | 50.00 |
| ❑ Decca DL 8316 [M] | | 1956 | 30.00 |
| FIDDLER'S HALL OF FAME | | | |
| ❑ Starday SLP-209 [M] | | 1963 | 30.00 |
| FIDDLIN' COUNTRY STYLE | | | |
| ❑ Nashville NLP-2015 [M] | | 1965 | 20.00 |
| ❑ Power Pak PO-296 | | 197? | 10.00 |
| ❑ Starday SLP-114 [M] | | 1960 | 40.00 |
| 15 FAVORITES | | | |
| ❑ Hickory LPM-105 [M] | | 1962 | 25.00 |
| 15 GOLDEN HITS | | | |
| ❑ United Artists UAL-3192 [M] | | 1962 | 25.00 |
| ❑ United Artists UAS-6192 [S] | | 1962 | 30.00 |
| 15 HITS: THE ORIGINAL RECORDINGS (THE ORIGINAL HITS, VOLUME 5) | | | |
| ❑ Liberty LRP-3235 [M] | | 1962 | 20.00 |
| FIFTEEN STAR SAXOPHONES | | | |
| ❑ Bethlehem BCP-6035 [M] | | 1959 | 30.00 |
| 50 BELOVED SONGS OF FAITH | | | |
| ❑ Reader's Digest BMR3-100 [(3)] | | 1990 | 25.00 |
| 50 YEARS OF FILM | | | |
| ❑ Warner Bros. 3XX 2737 [(3)] | | 1973 | 25.00 |
| *—Box set with 60-page booklet* | | | |
| 50 YEARS OF FILM MUSIC | | | |
| ❑ Warner Bros. 3XX 2736 [(3)] | | 1973 | 25.00 |
| *—Box set with 28-page booklet* | | | |
| 50 YEARS OF JAZZ GREATS | | | |
| ❑ Columbia Musical Treasury P3S 5932 [(3)] | | 197? | 20.00 |
| 52ND STREET JAZZ | | | |
| ❑ Waldorf Music Hall MH 33-148 [10] | | 195? | 100.00 |
| FILLET OF SOUL | | | |
| ❑ Stax STS 3021 | | 1972 | 20.00 |
| FILLMORE: THE LAST DAYS | | | |
| ❑ Fillmore Z3X 31390 [(3)] | | 1972 | 50.00 |
| *—With booklet and bonus 7-inch single* | | | |

| Number | Title (A Side/B Side) | Yr | NM |
|---|---|---|---|
| FILM MUSIC FROM FRANCE | | | |
| ❑ Philips PHM 200071 [M] | | 1962 | 20.00 |
| ❑ Philips PHS 600071 [S] | | 1962 | 30.00 |
| THE FINEST OF FOLK BLUESMEN | | | |
| ❑ Bethlehem BCP-6017 | | 197? | 20.00 |
| *—Despite lower number, this is a reissue of Bethlehem 6071, distributed by RCA* | | | |
| FINK ALONG WITH MAD | | | |
| ❑ Big Top 12-1306 [M] | | 1962 | 100.00 |
| FIRE ON THE STRINGS | | | |
| ❑ Starday SLP-221 [M] | | 1963 | 30.00 |
| FIRST ALBUM OF JAZZ | | | |
| ❑ Folkways FP-712 [10] | | 1951 | 50.00 |
| FIRST DECADE | | | |
| ❑ WEA 10 [(3)DJ] | | 1981 | 150.00 |
| *—Only 1,000 were made paying tribute to WEA's 10th anniversary* | | | |
| THE FIRST GREAT ROCK FESTIVALS OF THE SEVENTIES: ISLE OF WIGHT/ATLANTA POP FESTIVAL | | | |
| ❑ Columbia G3X 30805 [(3)] | | 1971 | 25.00 |
| FIRST OF THE FAMOUS | | | |
| ❑ Capitol T 2275 [M] | | 1965 | 25.00 |
| FIVE FEET OF SWING | | | |
| ❑ Decca DL 8045 [M] | | 1954 | 40.00 |
| 5-STRING BANJO PICKIN' AND SINGIN' | | | |
| ❑ King 994 [M] | | 1966 | 40.00 |
| FLEX YOUR HEAD | | | |
| ❑ Dischord 7 | | 1982 | 50.00 |
| THE FOLK BOX | | | |
| ❑ Elektra EKL-9001 [(4)] | | 1964 | 50.00 |
| FOLK FESTIVAL OF THE BLUES | | | |
| ❑ Argo LP-4031 [M] | | 1964 | 40.00 |
| FOLK POPS 'N JAZZ SAMPLER | | | |
| ❑ Elektra SMP 3 [M] | | 1957 | 25.00 |
| FOLK SAMPLER FIVE | | | |
| ❑ Elektra SMP 5 [M] | | 196? | 25.00 |
| THE FOLK SCENE | | | |
| ❑ Elektra SMP 6 [M] | | 196? | 25.00 |
| FOLKSONG '65 | | | |
| ❑ Elektra SMP 8 [M] | | 1965 | 20.00 |
| ❑ Elektra S 78 [S] | | 1965 | 25.00 |
| FOOTNOTES TO JAZZ, VOL. 2: ANATOMY OF A JAZZ COMPOSITION | | | |
| ❑ Folkways FP-31 [10] | | 1951 | 50.00 |
| FOOTPRINTS IN TIME | | | |
| ❑ White Whale WWS-7125 | | 1970 | 25.00 |
| FOR CHRISTMAS SEALS…A MATTER OF LIFE AND BREATH | | | |
| ❑ Decca Custom Style E [DJ] | | 1968 | 20.00 |
| *—Promo-only album for Christmas Seals* | | | |
| ❑ Decca Custom Style F [DJ] | | 1968 | 25.00 |
| *—Promo-only album for Christmas Seals; four five-minute programs* | | | |
| FOR DANCERS ONLY | | | |
| ❑ Epic LN 3120 [M] | | 1955 | 30.00 |
| FOR JAZZ LOVERS | | | |
| ❑ EmArcy MG-36086 [M] | | 1956 | 40.00 |
| FOR TWISTERS ONLY | | | |
| ❑ Ace LP-1020 [M] | | 1962 | 70.00 |
| THE FORCE | | | |
| ❑ Warner Bros. PRO 593 | | 1974 | 20.00 |
| ❑ Warner Bros. PRO 596 [(2)] | | 1974 | 25.00 |
| FORD HOOTENANNY | | | |
| ❑ RCA Victor PRM-152 [M] | | 1964 | 20.00 |
| *—Sold only at Ford dealers* | | | |
| FOREPLAY #45 | | | |
| ❑ A&M SP-17162 [DJ] | | 1981 | 25.00 |
| *—Includes 20-minute collage of music from "Urgh! A Music War"* | | | |
| FORGOTTEN MILLION SELLERS | | | |
| ❑ King 792 [M] | | 1962 | 100.00 |
| FORTY GOSPEL GREATS | | | |
| ❑ Vee Jay VJS-2-19000 [(2)] | | 1975 | 25.00 |
| FOUR ALTOS | | | |
| ❑ Prestige PRLP-7116 [M] | | 1957 | 100.00 |
| FOUR FRENCH HORNS | | | |
| ❑ Savoy MG-12173 [M] | | 1961 | 50.00 |
| THE FOUR MOST GUITARS | | | |
| ❑ ABC-Paramount ABC-109 [M] | | 1956 | 30.00 |
| ❑ Paramount LP-109 [10] | | 1954 | 60.00 |
| FOUR TO GO | | | |
| ❑ Columbia CL 2018 [M] | | 1963 | 20.00 |
| 14 GOLDEN RECORDINGS FROM THE HISTORIC VAULTS OF DUKE-PEACOCK RECORDS | | | |
| ❑ ABC ABCX-784 | | 1973 | 20.00 |
| 14 GOLDEN RECORDINGS FROM THE HISTORIC VAULTS OF DUKE-PEACOCK RECORDS, VOLUME 2 | | | |
| ❑ ABC ABCX-789 | | 1973 | 20.00 |
| 14 GREAT ALL TIME C&W WALTZES | | | |
| ❑ King 890 [M] | | 1964 | 70.00 |
| 14 HIT FLASHBACKS FROM THE GOLDEN GROUP ERA | | | |
| ❑ King 893 [M] | | 1964 | 70.00 |
| 14 MORE NEWIES BUT GOODIES | | | |
| ❑ Mercury MG-20493 [M] | | 1960 | 30.00 |
| ❑ Mercury SR-60241 [S] | | 1960 | 40.00 |
| 14 NEWIES BUT GOODIES | | | |
| ❑ Mercury MG-20493 [M] | | 1960 | 30.00 |

**Number Title (A Side/B Side) Yr NM**

❑ Mercury SR-60172 [S] 1960 40.00
FRANK BULL AND GENE NORMAN PRESENT DIXIELAND JUBILEE
❑ Decca DL 7022 [10] 1952 50.00
FRANK JOHNSON'S FAVORITES
❑ Ralph 8110 1981 20.00
FRENCH TOAST
❑ Angel ANG-60009 [10] 1956 50.00
FUNKY BLUES NO. 2
❑ American Recording Society G-404 [M] 1956 30.00
THE FUTURE LOOKS BRIGHT
❑ SST/Posh Boy PBS 120 [DJ] 1981 30.00
*—Vinyl is promo only*
GALA FAVORITES
❑ Mercury Living Presence SR 90339 [S] 196? 25.00
*—Maroon label, no "Vendor: Mercury Record Corporation"*
GARDEN OF DELIGHTS
❑ Elektra S3 10 [(3)] 1971 20.00
*—Butterfly labels, possibly promo only*
GARY MOORE PRESENTS "MY KIND OF MUSIC"
❑ Columbia CL 717 [M] 1956 25.00
GEMS OF JAZZ, VOL. 1
❑ Decca DL 5133 [10] 1950 50.00
❑ Decca DL 8039 [M] 1954 40.00
GEMS OF JAZZ, VOL. 2
❑ Decca DL 5134 [10] 1950 50.00
❑ Decca DL 8040 [M] 1954 40.00
GEMS OF JAZZ, VOL. 3
❑ Decca DL 5383 [10] 1952 50.00
❑ Decca DL 8041 [M] 1954 40.00
GEMS OF JAZZ, VOL. 4
❑ Decca DL 5384 [10] 1952 50.00
❑ Decca DL 8042 [M] 1954 40.00
GEMS OF JAZZ, VOL. 5
❑ Decca DL 8043 [M] 1954 40.00
GENE NORMAN PRESENTS JUST JAZZ
❑ RCA Victor LPT-3102 [10] 1952 —
*—See LES THOMPSON.*
GERRY GOFFIN AND CAROLE KING: SOLID GOLD
❑ Screen Gems/Columbia CPL-713 [DJ] 1975 20.00
*—Promo-only compilation of oldies sent to radio to spur airplay on songs owned by this publishing house*
GIANTS OF BOOGIE WOOGIE
❑ Riverside RLP 12-106 [M] 1956 40.00
GIANTS OF JAZZ
❑ American Recording Society G-401 [M] 1956 30.00
THE GIANTS OF JAZZ
❑ Columbia CL 1970 [M] 1963 30.00
GIANTS OF JAZZ ORGAN
❑ King 837 [M] 1963 120.00
GIANTS OF JAZZ VOL. 2
❑ American Recording Society G-444 [M] 1957 30.00
GIANTS OF SMALL BAND SWING, VOL. 1
❑ Fantasy OJC-1723 1990 10.00
❑ Riverside RLP 12-143 [M] 1957 40.00
GIANTS OF SMALL BAND SWING, VOL. 2
❑ Fantasy OJC-1724 1990 10.00
❑ Riverside RLP 12-145 [M] 1957 40.00
THE GIRLS SING
❑ Savoy MG-12220 [M] 196? 20.00
GOIN' UP THE COUNTRY: RURAL BLUES, VOLUME 1
❑ Imperial LP-94000 1968 20.00
GOLD HITS
❑ Warwick W 2008 [M] 1959 80.00
*—Reissue of "Goodies But Oldies, Volume 2"; this title still appears on the label*
GOLD SOUL
❑ Stax STS 2031 1970 20.00
GOLDEN AGE OF COUNTRY MUSIC 1940-1970
❑ Reader's Digest RBA-005-A [(7)] 1987 40.00
THE GOLDEN AGE OF RHYTHM AND BLUES
❑ Chess 2CH-50030 [(2)] 1972 25.00
GOLDEN COUNTRY GROUPS
❑ Reader's Digest RBA-201-A [(7)] 1988 40.00
GOLDEN COUNTRY HITS
❑ United Artists UAL-3327 [M] 1964 15.00
❑ United Artists UAS-6327 [S] 1964 20.00
THE GOLDEN DAYS OF BRITISH ROCK
❑ Sire V 6046 [(4)] 1976 40.00
GOLDEN ECHOES
❑ Arvee A-433 [M] 1962 25.00
❑ Arvee SA-433 [S] 1962 30.00
GOLDEN ENCORES
❑ Cadence CLP-3043 [M] 1960 40.00
THE GOLDEN ERA OF JAZZ, VOL. 1
❑ Savoy MG-15015 [10] 1952 80.00
THE GOLDEN ERA OF JAZZ, VOL. 2
❑ Savoy MG-15018 [10] 1952 80.00
GOLDEN GASSERS
❑ Chess LP 1458 USA [M] 1961 120.00
*—National version; see listings in this section under "KYA," "Murray the K" and "WAMO" for regional releases*
GOLDEN GOODIES OF 1963, VOL. 18
❑ Roulette R 25247 [M] 1964 20.00
GOLDEN GOODIES, VOL. 1
❑ Roulette R 25207 [M] 1963 25.00

Various artists, *Golden Treasure Chest,* United Artists UAL 3314, 1963, mono, $25.

**Number Title (A Side/B Side) Yr NM**

GOLDEN GOODIES, VOL. 2
❑ Roulette R 25210 [M] 1963 25.00
GOLDEN GOODIES, VOL. 3
❑ Roulette R 25218 [M] 1963 25.00
GOLDEN GOODIES, VOL. 4: GOODIES FOR A DANCE PARTY
❑ Roulette R 25209 [M] 1963 25.00
GOLDEN GOODIES, VOL. 5
❑ Roulette R 25215 [M] 1963 25.00
GOLDEN GOODIES, VOL. 6
❑ Roulette R 25216 [M] 1963 25.00
GOLDEN GOODIES, VOL. 7
❑ Roulette R 25212 [M] 1963 25.00
GOLDEN GOODIES, VOL. 8
❑ Roulette R 25214 [M] 1963 25.00
GOLDEN GOODIES, VOL. 9
❑ Roulette R 25213 [M] 1963 25.00
GOLDEN GOODIES, VOL. 10
❑ Roulette R 25217 [M] 1963 25.00
GOLDEN GOODIES, VOL. 11
❑ Roulette R 25219 [M] 1963 25.00
GOLDEN GOODIES, VOL. 12
❑ Roulette R 25211 [M] 1963 25.00
GOLDEN GOODIES, VOL. 14
❑ Roulette R 25239 [M] 1964 20.00
GOLDEN GOODIES, VOL. 15
❑ Roulette R 25240 [M] 1964 20.00
GOLDEN GOODIES, VOL. 16
❑ Roulette R 25241 [M] 1964 20.00
GOLDEN GOODIES, VOL. 17
❑ Roulette R 25242 [M] 1964 20.00
GOLDEN GREATS
❑ Liberty LRP-3500 [M] 1967 15.00
❑ Liberty LST-7500 [P] 1967 20.00
THE GOLDEN GROUPS
❑ Specialty SPS-2155 1972 20.00
GOLDEN HITS FROM THE GANG AT BANG
❑ Bang BLP-215 [M] 1967 20.00
❑ Bang BLPS-215 [P] 1967 25.00
GOLDEN INSTRUMENTALS
❑ Dot DLP-3820 [M] 1967 25.00
❑ Dot DLP-25820 [S] 1967 25.00
GOLDEN INSTRUMENTALS COUNTRY STYLE
❑ Wing MGW-12261 [M] 1964 20.00
❑ Wing SRW-16261 [S] 1964 20.00

**Number Title (A Side/B Side) Yr NM**

GOLDEN JAZZ INTRSUMENTALS
❑ Bethlehem BCP-6065 [M] 1962 25.00
GOLDEN MOMENTS IN COUNTRY AND WESTERN MUSIC
❑ Capitol SQBO-90985 [(2)S] 196? 20.00
*—Capitol Record Club exclusive*
GOLDEN SOUVENIRS
❑ United Artists UAL-3317 [M] 1963 25.00
❑ United Artists UAS-6317 [S] 1963 30.00
GOLDEN TEEN HITS
❑ Liberty L-5505 [M] 1962 40.00
GOLDEN TREASURE CHEST
❑ United Artists UAL-3314 [M] 1963 25.00
❑ United Artists UAS-6314 [S] 1963 30.00
GONE BUT NOT FORGOTTEN
❑ Class LP-5004 [M] 1959 100.00
❑ Rendezvous M-1314 [M] 196? 40.00
*—Reissue of Class 5004*
GOOD GUY JACK SPECTOR PRESENTS 22 ORIGINAL WINNERS
❑ Roulette R 25254 [M] 1964 20.00
THE GOOD OLD 50'S
❑ Atco 33-118 [M] 1960 60.00
GOODIES BUT OLDIES VOLUME 2
❑ Warwick W 2008 [M] 1959 120.00
*—Original title of LP appears on both cover and label; reissued as "Gold Hits" -- and there was no Volume 1!*
GOSPEL HOOTENANNY
❑ Imperial LP-9240 [M] 1963 20.00
❑ Imperial LP-12240 [S] 1963 25.00
GOSPEL STARS IN CONCERT
❑ Specialty SPS-2153 1971 20.00
GRAFFITI GOLD
❑ Vee Jay VJS-2-9000 [(2)] 1974 20.00
GRAND OLE OPRY HITS
❑ RCA Camden CAL-737 [M] 1963 20.00
❑ RCA Camden CAS-737 [R] 1966 15.00
GRAND OLE OPRY SPECTACULAR
❑ Starday SLP-242 [(2)M] 1963 30.00
THE GREAT BANDS
❑ Columbia Musical Treasury P2M 5267 [(2)] 1968 20.00
GREAT BLUES
❑ Riverside RLP-1074 [10] 1955 80.00
GREAT BLUES SINGERS
❑ Riverside RLP 12-121 [M] 1957 40.00

| Number | Title (A Side/B Side) | Yr | NM |
|---|---|---|---|
| THE GREAT BLUES SINGERS | | | |
| ❑ Riverside RLP-1032 [10] | | 1954 | 80.00 |
| GREAT COUNTRY AND WESTERN STARS | | | |
| ❑ Wing MGW-12268 [M] | | 1964 | 20.00 |
| ❑ Wing SRW-16268 [S] | | 1964 | 20.00 |
| GREAT COUNTRY FAVORITES | | | |
| ❑ MGM E-4211 [M] | | 1964 | 20.00 |
| ❑ MGM SE-4211 [S] | | 1964 | 25.00 |
| GREAT COUNTRY HITS | | | |
| ❑ United Artists UAL-3159 [M] | | 1961 | 25.00 |
| THE GREAT GROUP GOODIES | | | |
| ❑ Atco 33-143 [M] | | 1962 | 80.00 |
| GREAT GROUP OLDIES | | | |
| ❑ Oldies 33 OL-8003 [M] | | 1963 | 25.00 |
| GREAT GROUP OLDIES, VOL. 2 | | | |
| ❑ Oldies 33 OL-8006 [M] | | 1964 | 25.00 |
| GREAT GROUPS, GREAT RECORDS | | | |
| ❑ Laurie LLP-2010 [M] | | 1961 | 30.00 |
| THE GREAT HITS OF 1964 AND SOME GOLDEN OLDIES | | | |
| ❑ Vee Jay LP-1112 [M] | | 1965 | 30.00 |
| *—Not known to exist in stereo* | | | |
| GREAT INSTRUMENTAL R&B HITS | | | |
| ❑ Imperial LP-9271 [M] | | 1964 | 25.00 |
| ❑ Imperial LP-12271 [R] | | 1964 | 20.00 |
| GREAT JAZZ | | | |
| ❑ Rondo-lette A-31 [M] | | 195? | 25.00 |
| GREAT JAZZ BRASS | | | |
| ❑ RCA Camden CAL-383 [M] | | 1958 | 25.00 |
| GREAT JAZZ PIANISTS | | | |
| ❑ RCA Camden CAL-328 [M] | | 1958 | 25.00 |
| GREAT JAZZ REEDS | | | |
| ❑ RCA Camden CAL-339 [M] | | 1958 | 25.00 |
| GREAT MOMENTS AT THE GRAND OLE OPRY | | | |
| ❑ RCA Victor CPL2-1904 [(2)] | | 1977 | 20.00 |
| GREAT MOTION PICTURE THEMES | | | |
| ❑ United Artists UAL-3122 [M] | | 1960 | 15.00 |
| ❑ United Artists UAS-6122 [S] | | 1960 | 20.00 |
| GREAT MOTION PICTURE THEMES (MORE ORIGINAL SOUND TRACKS AND HIT MUSIC) | | | |
| ❑ United Artists UAL-3158 [M] | | 1961 | 15.00 |
| ❑ United Artists UAS-6158 [S] | | 1961 | 20.00 |
| THE GREAT ONES | | | |
| ❑ Capitol ST 1718 [S] | | 1962 | 30.00 |
| ❑ Capitol T 1718 [M] | | 1962 | 25.00 |
| THE GREAT SOUL HITS | | | |
| ❑ Brunswick BL 54129 [M] | | 1968 | 25.00 |
| ❑ Brunswick BL 754129 [S] | | 1968 | 15.00 |
| THE GREAT SWING BANDS | | | |
| ❑ Jazztone J-1245 [M] | | 1957 | 30.00 |
| GREAT SWING BANDS OF THE FORTIES | | | |
| ❑ Audio Lab AL-1530 [M] | | 1959 | 80.00 |
| THE GREAT TENOR JAZZMEN | | | |
| ❑ Allegro 1634 [M] | | 195? | 40.00 |
| GREAT TRUMPET ARTISTS | | | |
| ❑ RCA Victor LPT-26 [10] | | 1951 | 50.00 |
| ❑ RCA Victor LPT-35 [10] | | 1952 | 50.00 |
| THE GREATEST 15 HITS ON ACE RECORDS | | | |
| ❑ Ace LP-1012 [M] | | 1960 | 70.00 |
| GREATEST COUNTRY AND WESTERN HITS NO. 3 | | | |
| ❑ Columbia CL 1816 [M] | | 1962 | 20.00 |
| ❑ Columbia CS 8616 [S] | | 1962 | 25.00 |
| GREATEST COUNTRY AND WESTERN HITS NO. 4 | | | |
| ❑ Columbia CL 2081 [M] | | 1963 | 20.00 |
| ❑ Columbia CS 8881 [S] | | 1963 | 25.00 |
| THE GREATEST GOLDEN GOODIES | | | |
| ❑ Laurie LLP-2014 [M] | | 1962 | 30.00 |
| ❑ Laurie SLP-2014 [R] | | 196? | 15.00 |
| GREATEST GOSPEL SONGS OF OUR TIMES | | | |
| ❑ Vee Jay LP-5043 [M] | | 1963 | 30.00 |
| GREATEST GOSPEL SONGS, VOLUME 1 | | | |
| ❑ Specialty SPS-2144 | | 1970 | 20.00 |
| GREATEST GOSPEL SONGS, VOLUME 2 | | | |
| ❑ Specialty SPS-2145 | | 1970 | 20.00 |
| THE GREATEST HITS FROM ENGLAND | | | |
| ❑ Parrot PA 61010 [M] | | 1967 | 25.00 |
| ❑ Parrot PAS 71010 [R] | | 1967 | 20.00 |
| THE GREATEST HITS FROM ENGLAND, VOLUME 2 | | | |
| ❑ Parrot PA 61017 [M] | | 1968 | 25.00 |
| ❑ Parrot PAS 71017 [R] | | 1968 | 20.00 |
| THE GREATEST JAZZ CONCERT IN THE WORLD | | | |
| ❑ Pablo 2625704 [(4)] | | 197? | 30.00 |
| THE GREATEST NAMES IN JAZZ | | | |
| ❑ Verve PR2-3 [(3)] | | 196? | 20.00 |
| *—Box set* | | | |
| GREATEST RAP HITS, VOL. 1 | | | |
| ❑ Sugar Hill 9132 | | 1984 | 20.00 |
| THE GREATEST ROCK & ROLL | | | |
| ❑ Atlantic 8001 [M] | | 1956 | 120.00 |
| THE GREATEST TEENAGE HITS OF ALL TIME! | | | |
| ❑ Teem LP-5003 [M] | | 196? | 30.00 |
| GREATEST WESTERN HITS | | | |
| ❑ Columbia CL 1257 [M] | | 1959 | 30.00 |
| ❑ Columbia CS 8776 [R] | | 1963 | 20.00 |
| GREATEST WESTERN HITS NO. 2 | | | |
| ❑ Columbia CL 1408 [M] | | 1960 | 30.00 |
| ❑ Columbia CS 8777 [R] | | 1963 | 20.00 |

| Number | Title (A Side/B Side) | Yr | NM |
|---|---|---|---|
| GRETSCH DRUM NIGHT AT BIRDLAND | | | |
| ❑ Roulette R 52049 [M] | | 1960 | 30.00 |
| ❑ Roulette SR 52049 [S] | | 1960 | 30.00 |
| GRETSCH DRUM NIGHT, VOLUME 2 | | | |
| ❑ Roulette R 52067 [M] | | 1961 | 30.00 |
| ❑ Roulette SR 52067 [S] | | 1961 | 30.00 |
| GROOVY GOODIES | | | |
| ❑ Colpix CP-466 [M] | | 1964 | 80.00 |
| ❑ Colpix SCP-466 [S] | | 1964 | 100.00 |
| GROUP OF GOODIES | | | |
| ❑ Chess LP 1478 [M] | | 1963 | 50.00 |
| ❑ Chess LPS 1478 [R] | | 196? | 20.00 |
| GROUP OF GOODIES, VOLUME 2 | | | |
| ❑ Chess LP 1491 [M] | | 1965 | 50.00 |
| GUARANTEED TO PLEASE | | | |
| ❑ Teem LP-5002 [M] | | 196? | 30.00 |
| GUIDE TO JAZZ | | | |
| ❑ RCA Victor LPM-1393 [M] | | 1956 | 30.00 |
| HANDFUL OF COOL JAZZ | | | |
| ❑ Bethlehem BCP-90 [M] | | 1959 | 30.00 |
| HAPPY HOLIDAYS VOL. 25 | | | |
| ❑ RCA Special Products DPL2-0936 [(2)] | | 1990 | 25.00 |
| *—Sold only at True Value Hardware stores; the last one on vinyl LP -- and it contains an Elvis track among its 25 selections* | | | |
| HAPPY JAZZ | | | |
| ❑ Jazztone J-1215 [M] | | 1956 | 30.00 |
| HARD GOODS | | | |
| ❑ Warner Bros. PRO 583 [(2)] | | 1974 | 25.00 |
| THE HARD SWING | | | |
| ❑ Pacific Jazz JWC-508 [M] | | 1957 | 50.00 |
| ❑ World Pacific JWC-508 [M] | | 1958 | 40.00 |
| HARD TO BELIEVE — A KISS COVERS COMPILATION | | | |
| ❑ C/Z CZ 024 | | 1990 | 30.00 |
| HARLEM JAZZ 1930 | | | |
| ❑ Brunswick BL 58024 [10] | | 1951 | 50.00 |
| HAVE YOURSELF A MERRY LITTLE CHRISTMAS | | | |
| ❑ Reprise 50001 [M] | | 1963 | 25.00 |
| *—Red and green cover with ornaments at top; titled on back cover "Top Hollywood Stars Want You to..."* | | | |
| ❑ Reprise R 50001 [M] | | 1963 | 25.00 |
| *—Christmas tree cover; titled "Frank Sinatra and His Friends Want You to..."* | | | |
| ❑ Reprise R 50001 [M] | | 1963 | 25.00 |
| *—Wreath cover; titled on back cover "Top Hollywood Stars Want You to..."* | | | |
| ❑ Reprise R9-50001 [S] | | 1963 | 30.00 |
| *—Christmas tree cover; titled "Frank Sinatra and His Friends Want You to..."; stereo version of above* | | | |
| HAVING A BALL | | | |
| ❑ End LP-302 [M] | | 1958 | 500.00 |
| *—Original cover with groups pictured on a record* | | | |
| HEAD START — BOB THIELE EMERGENCY | | | |
| ❑ Flying Dutchman FDS-104 [(2)] | | 1969 | 25.00 |
| HEAVY HEADS | | | |
| ❑ Chess LP 1522 [M] | | 1967 | 25.00 |
| ❑ Chess LPS 1522 [P] | | 1967 | 25.00 |
| HEAVY HEADS, VOYAGE 2 | | | |
| ❑ Chess LP 1528 [M] | | 1969 | 20.00 |
| HEAVY METAL (SUPERSTARS OF THE 70S, VOLUME 2) | | | |
| ❑ Warner Special Products SP-2001 | | 1974 | 20.00 |
| HERALD THE BEAT | | | |
| ❑ Herald HLP-0110 [M] | | 195? | 150.00 |
| *—Yellow label* | | | |
| ❑ Herald HLP-0110 [M] | | 1957 | 300.00 |
| *—Black label* | | | |
| HERE ARE THE HITS! | | | |
| ❑ Fire FLP-100 [M] | | 1959 | 400.00 |
| *—Reissued as "Memory Lane, Hits by the Original Groups" with the same label and number* | | | |
| HERE COME THE GIRLS | | | |
| ❑ Verve MGV-2036 [M] | | 1956 | 40.00 |
| ❑ Verve V-2036 [M] | | 1961 | 20.00 |
| HERE COME THE SWINGING BANDS | | | |
| ❑ Verve MGV-8207 [M] | | 1957 | 30.00 |
| ❑ Verve V-8207 [M] | | 1961 | 20.00 |
| HI-FI JAZZ | | | |
| ❑ Brunswick BL 58058 [10] | | 1954 | 50.00 |
| HI-FI JAZZ SESSION | | | |
| ❑ Masterseal MSLP 5013 [M] | | 1957 | 25.00 |
| A HI-FI SALUTE TO THE GREAT ONES | | | |
| ❑ MGM E-3325 [M] | | 1956 | 30.00 |
| A HI-FI SALUTE TO THE GREAT ONES, VOL. 2 | | | |
| ❑ MGM E-3354 [M] | | 1956 | 30.00 |
| HILLBILLY HIT PARADE | | | |
| ❑ Mercury MG-20282 [M] | | 1957 | 50.00 |
| ❑ Starday SLP-102 [M] | | 1956 | 100.00 |
| HILLBILLY HOUSE PARTY | | | |
| ❑ Imperial LP-9214 [M] | | 1963 | 25.00 |
| ❑ Imperial LP-12214 [R] | | 1963 | 20.00 |
| HISTORIC JAZZ CONCERT AT MUSIC INN | | | |
| ❑ Atlantic 1298 [M] | | 1958 | 40.00 |
| *—Black label* | | | |
| ❑ Atlantic 1298 [M] | | 1961 | 25.00 |
| *—Multicolor label, white "fan" logo at right* | | | |
| ❑ Atlantic 1298 [M] | | 1963 | 20.00 |
| *—Multicolor label, black "fan" logo at right* | | | |
| HISTORY OF BRITISH BLUES, VOLUME 1 | | | |
| ❑ Sire SASH-3701 [(2)] | | 1973 | 20.00 |

| Number | Title (A Side/B Side) | Yr | NM |
|---|---|---|---|
| HISTORY OF BRITISH ROCK | | | |
| ❑ Sire SASH-3702 [(2)] | | 1974 | 20.00 |
| ❑ Sire 2P 6547 [(2)] | | 1975 | 20.00 |
| *—Columbia House edition* | | | |
| HISTORY OF BRITISH ROCK, VOLUME 2 | | | |
| ❑ Sire SASH-3705 [(2)] | | 1974 | 20.00 |
| HISTORY OF BRITISH ROCK, VOLUME 3 | | | |
| ❑ Sire SASH-3712 [(2)] | | 1975 | 20.00 |
| HISTORY OF CLASSIC JAZZ | | | |
| ❑ Riverside SDP-11 [(5)M] | | 1956 | 300.00 |
| *—Five-record set in leatherette album with booklet; records were available separately as Riverside 112, 113, 114, 115 and 116.* | | | |
| HISTORY OF CLASSIC JAZZ, VOL. 1 | | | |
| ❑ Riverside RLP 12-112 [M] | | 1957 | 40.00 |
| HISTORY OF CLASSIC JAZZ, VOL. 2 | | | |
| ❑ Riverside RLP 12-113 [M] | | 1957 | 40.00 |
| HISTORY OF CLASSIC JAZZ, VOL. 3 | | | |
| ❑ Riverside RLP 12-114 [M] | | 1957 | 40.00 |
| HISTORY OF CLASSIC JAZZ, VOL. 4 | | | |
| ❑ Riverside RLP 12-115 [M] | | 1957 | 40.00 |
| HISTORY OF CLASSIC JAZZ, VOL. 5 | | | |
| ❑ Riverside RLP 12-116 [M] | | 1957 | 40.00 |
| HISTORY OF JAZZ, VOL. 1: NEW ORLEANS ORIGINS | | | |
| ❑ Capitol T 793 [M] | | 1956 | 25.00 |
| HISTORY OF JAZZ, VOL. 1: THE SOLID SOUTH | | | |
| ❑ Capitol H 239 [10] | | 1950 | 50.00 |
| HISTORY OF JAZZ, VOL. 2: THE GOLDEN ERA | | | |
| ❑ Capitol H 240 [10] | | 1950 | 50.00 |
| HISTORY OF JAZZ, VOL. 2: THE TURBULENT '20S | | | |
| ❑ Capitol T 794 [M] | | 1956 | 25.00 |
| HISTORY OF JAZZ, VOL. 3: EVERYBODY SWINGS | | | |
| ❑ Capitol T 795 [M] | | 1956 | 25.00 |
| HISTORY OF JAZZ, VOL. 3: THEN CAME SWING | | | |
| ❑ Capitol H 241 [10] | | 1950 | 50.00 |
| HISTORY OF JAZZ, VOL. 4: ENTER THE COOL | | | |
| ❑ Capitol H 242 [10] | | 1950 | 50.00 |
| ❑ Capitol T 796 [M] | | 1956 | 25.00 |
| THE HISTORY OF NEW ORLEANS ROCK 'N' ROLL VOLUME I | | | |
| ❑ Ace 7184 | | 1984 | 20.00 |
| *—Sold only at the Louisiana World's Fair in New Orleans, May 12-Nov. 11, 1984* | | | |
| THE HISTORY OF NEW ORLEANS ROCK 'N' ROLL VOLUME II | | | |
| ❑ Ace 7284 | | 1984 | 20.00 |
| *—Sold only at the Louisiana World's Fair in New Orleans, May 12-Nov. 11, 1984* | | | |
| THE HISTORY OF NEW ORLEANS ROCK 'N' ROLL VOLUME III | | | |
| ❑ Ace 7384 | | 1984 | 20.00 |
| *—Sold only at the Louisiana World's Fair in New Orleans, May 12-Nov. 11, 1984* | | | |
| THE HISTORY OF NEW ORLEANS ROCK 'N' ROLL VOLUME IV | | | |
| ❑ Ace 7484 | | 1984 | 20.00 |
| *—Sold only at the Louisiana World's Fair in New Orleans, May 12-Nov. 11, 1984* | | | |
| HISTORY OF RHYTHM & BLUES, VOLUME 1/THE ROOTS 1947-52 | | | |
| ❑ Atlantic SD 8161 | | 1968 | 20.00 |
| HISTORY OF RHYTHM & BLUES, VOLUME 2/THE GOLDEN YEARS 1953-55 | | | |
| ❑ Atlantic 8162 [M] | | 1968 | 40.00 |
| ❑ Atlantic SD 8162 [S] | | 1968 | 20.00 |
| HISTORY OF RHYTHM & BLUES, VOLUME 3/ROCK & ROLL 1956-57 | | | |
| ❑ Atlantic SD 8163 | | 1968 | 20.00 |
| HISTORY OF RHYTHM & BLUES, VOLUME 4/THE BIG BEAT 1958-60 | | | |
| ❑ Atlantic SD 8164 | | 1968 | 20.00 |
| HISTORY OF RHYTHM & BLUES, VOLUME 5/THE BEAT GOES ON, 1961-62 | | | |
| ❑ Atlantic 8193 [M] | | 1968 | 40.00 |
| *—Mono is promo only; "DJ Copy Monaural" sticker on front cover* | | | |
| ❑ Atlantic SD 8193 [S] | | 1968 | 20.00 |
| THE HIT MAKERS AND THEIR RECORD BREAKERS | | | |
| ❑ King 737 [M] | | 1961 | 100.00 |
| HIT PARADE OF COUNTRY MUSIC | | | |
| ❑ Starday SLP-184 [M] | | 1962 | 30.00 |
| HIT SOUNDS OF MERRIE MELODIES | | | |
| ❑ Warner Bros. PRO 550 [(2)] | | 1973 | 25.00 |
| HITCHHIKER 2 | | | |
| ❑ Columbia CAS 1826 [DJ] | | 1989 | 25.00 |
| THE HITCHHIKER COLLEGE RADIO HOUR | | | |
| ❑ Columbia CAS 1598 [DJ] | | 1989 | 25.00 |
| THE HITS ARE ON VERVE | | | |
| ❑ Verve V6-201 [S] | | 1964 | 20.00 |
| HITS FROM THE SOUTH PRESENTED BY NICK CHARLES | | | |
| ❑ Stax 702 [M] | | 1962 | 100.00 |
| *—Has the same number as "Walk Right In" by Gus Cannon, but this LP doesn't have any mention of Atlantic distribution* | | | |
| HITS I FORGOT TO BUY | | | |
| ❑ Swan SLP-512 [M] | | 1963 | 50.00 |
| HITS OF THE HOPS | | | |
| ❑ Warner Bros. W 1448 [M] | | 1962 | 30.00 |



**Except when noted otherwise, VG = 25% of NM, and VG+ = 50% of NM. (Example: VG = $2.00, VG+ = $4.00 and NM = $8.00.)**

| Number / Title (A Side/B Side) | Yr | NM |
|---|---|---|
| ❑ Warner Bros. WS 1448 [S] | 1962 | 40.00 |
| HITS THAT JUMPED | | |
| ❑ Checker LP 2975 [M] | 1959 | 120.00 |
| HITSVILLE | | |
| ❑ Coral CRL 57269 [M] | 1959 | 80.00 |
| ❑ Coral CRL 757269 [S] | 1959 | 100.00 |
| HITSVILLE U.S.A. | | |
| ❑ Imperial LP-9084 [M] | 1959 | 40.00 |
| HITSVILLE U.S.A., VOLUME 2 | | |
| ❑ Imperial LP-9099 [M] | 1960 | 40.00 |
| HOLIDAY IN SAX | | |
| ❑ EmArcy MG-26019 [10] | 1954 | 80.00 |
| HOLIDAY IN TRUMPET | | |
| ❑ EmArcy MG-26015 [10] | 1954 | 80.00 |
| HOLLAND-DOZIER-HOLLAND: YESTERDAY, TODAY AND FOREVER | | |
| ❑ Jobete PRO-9 [(3)DJ] | 1977 | 50.00 |
| *—Promo-only publisher's demo* | | |
| HOME FOR CHRISTMAS: A JOYOUS EVENING OF YULETIDE MUSIC | | |
| ❑ RCA Victor CPM-109 [M] | 1964 | 15.00 |
| *—Label reads "RCA Victor Club Recording Selected by the Editors of Reader's Digest Music Guide"* | | |
| ❑ RCA Victor CSP-109 [S] | 1964 | 20.00 |
| HOME OF THE BLUES | | |
| ❑ Minit LP-0001 [M] | 1961 | 50.00 |
| HOME OF THE BLUES, VOLUME 2 | | |
| ❑ Minit LP-0004 [M] | 1963 | 50.00 |
| ❑ Minit LP-24004 [R] | 1964 | 20.00 |
| ❑ Minit LP-40004 [M] | 1964 | 25.00 |
| *—Reissue of 0004* | | |
| HOMESPUN HUMOR | | |
| ❑ King 726 [M] | 1961 | 100.00 |
| HONEST TO GOODNESS COUNTRY MUSIC HITS | | |
| ❑ RCA Victor LPM-2564 [M] | 1962 | 20.00 |
| ❑ RCA Victor LSP-2564 [S] | 1962 | 25.00 |
| THE HONEST-TO-GOODNESS COUNTRY MUSIC HITS!!!! VOLUME 2 | | |
| ❑ RCA Victor LPM-2633 [M] | 1963 | 20.00 |
| ❑ RCA Victor LSP-2633(e) [R] | 1963 | 15.00 |
| HOT CANARIES | | |
| ❑ Columbia CL 2534 [10] | 1954 | 30.00 |
| THE HOT ONES | | |
| ❑ Columbia Special Products CSP-107 [M] | 1963 | 20.00 |
| *—Available only from Johnson Sea Horse boat dealers* | | |
| HOT PLATTERS | | |
| ❑ Warner Bros. PRO 474 [(2)] | 1971 | 25.00 |
| *—Originals have green labels* | | |
| HOT VS. COOL: A BATTLE OF JAZZ | | |
| ❑ MGM E-211 [10] | 1953 | 50.00 |
| HOUSE RENT PARTY | | |
| ❑ Savoy MG-12199 [M] | 1961 | 50.00 |
| HOW HIGH THE MOON | | |
| ❑ Clef MGC-Vol. 1 [M] | 1955 | 50.00 |
| *—Reissue of 608* | | |
| ❑ Clef MGC-608 [M] | 1955 | 40.00 |
| *—Reissue of Mercury 608* | | |
| ❑ Mercury MGC-Vol. 1 [10] | 1951 | 60.00 |
| *—Reissue of 35001* | | |
| ❑ Mercury MGC-608 [M] | 1953 | 80.00 |
| *—Reissue of Vol. 1* | | |
| ❑ Mercury MG-35001 [10] | 1950 | 80.00 |
| ❑ Verve MGV-Vol. 1 [M] | 1957 | 30.00 |
| *—Reissue of 12-inch Clef Vol. 1* | | |
| HYMNS OF FAITH | | |
| ❑ Colpix CP-408 [M] | 1959 | 30.00 |
| I DIDN'T KNOW THEY STILL MADE RECORDS LIKE THIS | | |
| ❑ Warner Bros. PRO 608 [(2)] | 1975 | 20.00 |
| I DIG ROCK AND ROLL | | |
| ❑ Score SLP-4002 [M] | 1957 | 200.00 |
| *—Reissue of "Rock & Roll with Rhythm & Blues," Aladdin 710* | | |
| I LIKE JAZZ! | | |
| ❑ Columbia JZ 1 [M] | 1955 | 30.00 |
| IMPERIAL MOVES | | |
| ❑ Imperial MM-428 [DJ] | 1966 | 40.00 |
| IMPERIAL SAMPLER | | |
| ❑ Imperial DJLP-1 [10] | 195? | 100.00 |
| *—Promo-only item* | | |
| THE IMPOSSIBLE DREAM — THE STORY OF THE 1967 BOSTON RED SOX | | |
| ❑ Fleetwood FCLP 3024 | 1967 | 20.00 |
| IN LOVING MEMORY | | |
| ❑ Motown M 642 [DJ] | 1969 | 500.00 |
| *—With custom silver cover; Loucye Gordy Wakefield Scholarship Fund benefit giveaway* | | |
| ❑ Motown M 642 [M] | 1968 | 150.00 |
| *—With song titles on cover* | | |
| ❑ Motown M 642 [M] | 1968 | 250.00 |
| *—Without song titles on cover* | | |
| ❑ Motown MS 642 [S] | 1968 | 150.00 |
| *—With song titles on cover* | | |
| ❑ Motown MS 642 [S] | 1968 | 250.00 |
| *—Without song titles on cover* | | |
| INCENSE AND OLDIES | | |
| ❑ Buddah BDS 5014 | 1969 | 20.00 |
| INFORMAL SESSION AT SQUIRREL'S BY THE SONS OF BIX | | |
| ❑ Paramount LP-104 [(2)10] | 1954 | 80.00 |
| INSTRUMENTAL GOLDEN GOODIES, VOL. 13 | | |
| ❑ Roulette R 25238 [M] | 1964 | 20.00 |
| INTERCOLLEGIATE MUSIC FESTIVAL, VOL. 1 | | |
| ❑ ABC Impulse! AS-9145 [S] | 1968 | 12.00 |
| ❑ Impulse! A-9145 [M] | 1967 | 20.00 |
| ❑ Impulse! AS-9145 [S] | 1967 | 15.00 |
| INTERNATIONAL JAZZ WORKSHOP | | |
| ❑ EmArcy MGE-26002 [M] | 1964 | 25.00 |
| ❑ EmArcy SRE-66002 [S] | 1964 | 30.00 |
| INTERPLAY FOR TWO TRUMPETS AND TWO TENORS | | |
| ❑ Prestige PRLP-7112 [M] | 1957 | 100.00 |
| INTRODUCTION TO RARE EARTH RECORDS | | |
| ❑ Rare Earth RS-505 to 509 [(5)DJ] | 1969 | 200.00 |
| *—Promo-only box set with rounded top; contains the first five LPs on the Rare Earth label* | | |
| THE ISLAND STORY | | |
| ❑ Island 90684 [(2)] | 1988 | 18.00 |
| ❑ Island R 243395 [(2)] | 1988 | 20.00 |
| *—BMG Direct Marketing edition* | | |
| ISLES OF JAZZ | | |
| ❑ Discovery DL-2010 [10] | 1954 | 50.00 |
| IT'S DANCE TIME | | |
| ❑ Cameo C-1068 [M] | 1964 | 30.00 |
| ITALIAN JAZZ STARS | | |
| ❑ Angel ANG-60001 [10] | 1955 | 50.00 |
| IVY LEAGUE JAZZ | | |
| ❑ Decca DL 8282 [M] | 1956 | 30.00 |
| ❑ Golden Crest GC-3039 [M] | 1958 | 20.00 |
| JACKPOT OF HITS | | |
| ❑ Apollo LP-490 [M] | 1959 | 150.00 |
| JAM SESSION | | |
| ❑ Clef MGC-4001/7 [(7)M] | 1953 | 300.00 |
| *—Boxed set containing 4001-4007* | | |
| ❑ EmArcy MG-36002 [M] | 1954 | 50.00 |
| JAM SESSION #1 | | |
| ❑ Clef MGC-601 [M] | 1954 | 40.00 |
| ❑ Clef MGC-651 [M] | 1955 | 40.00 |
| *—Reissue of 4001* | | |
| ❑ Clef MGC-4001 [M] | 1953 | 50.00 |
| ❑ Mercury MGC-601 [M] | 1953 | 80.00 |
| ❑ Verve MGV-8049 [M] | 1956 | 30.00 |
| *—Reissue of Clef 651* | | |
| JAM SESSION #2 | | |
| ❑ Clef MGC-602 [M] | 1954 | 40.00 |
| ❑ Clef MGC-652 [M] | 1955 | 40.00 |
| *—Reissue of 4002* | | |
| ❑ Clef MGC-4002 [M] | 1953 | 50.00 |
| ❑ Mercury MGC-602 [M] | 1953 | 80.00 |
| ❑ Verve MGV-8050 [M] | 1956 | 30.00 |
| *—Reissue of Clef 652* | | |
| JAM SESSION #3 | | |
| ❑ Clef MGC-653 [M] | 1955 | 40.00 |
| *—Reissue of 4003* | | |
| ❑ Clef MGC-4003 [M] | 1953 | 50.00 |
| ❑ Verve MGV-8051 [M] | 1956 | 30.00 |
| *—Reissue of Clef 653* | | |
| JAM SESSION #4 | | |
| ❑ Clef MGC-654 [M] | 1955 | 40.00 |
| *—Reissue of 4004* | | |
| ❑ Clef MGC-4004 [M] | 1953 | 50.00 |
| ❑ Verve MGV-8052 [M] | 1956 | 30.00 |
| *—Reissue of Clef 654* | | |
| JAM SESSION #5 | | |
| ❑ Clef MGC-655 [M] | 1955 | 40.00 |
| *—Reissue of 4005* | | |
| ❑ Clef MGC-4005 [M] | 1953 | 50.00 |
| ❑ Verve MGV-8053 [M] | 1956 | 30.00 |
| *—Reissue of Clef 655* | | |
| JAM SESSION #6 | | |
| ❑ Clef MGC-656 [M] | 1955 | 40.00 |
| *—Reissue of 4006* | | |
| ❑ Clef MGC-4006 [M] | 1953 | 50.00 |
| ❑ Verve MGV-8054 [M] | 1956 | 30.00 |
| *—Reissue of Clef 656* | | |
| JAM SESSION #7 | | |
| ❑ Clef MGC-677 [M] | 1955 | 40.00 |
| ❑ Verve MGV-8062 [M] | 1957 | 30.00 |
| *—Reissue of Clef 677* | | |
| JAM SESSION #8 | | |
| ❑ Clef MGC-711 [M] | 1955 | 40.00 |
| ❑ Verve MGV-8094 [M] | 1957 | 30.00 |
| *—Reissue of Clef 711* | | |
| JAM SESSION #9 | | |
| ❑ Verve MGV-8196 [M] | 1957 | 30.00 |
| JAM SESSION AT CARNEGIE HALL | | |
| ❑ Columbia CL 557 [M] | 1954 | 30.00 |
| JAM SESSION AT COMMODORE | | |
| ❑ Commodore FL-30006 [M] | 1951 | 40.00 |
| JAM SESSION COAST TO COAST | | |
| ❑ Columbia CL 547 [M] | 1954 | 30.00 |
| JAM SESSION, VOL. 2 | | |
| ❑ Skylark SKLP-12 [10] | 1954 | 250.00 |
| JAMES BOND — 10TH ANNIVERSARY | | |
| ❑ United Artists UXS-91 [(2)] | 1972 | 30.00 |
| JAMMING AT RUDI'S, VOL. 1 | | |
| ❑ Circle L-407 [M] | 1951 | 40.00 |
| JAMMING AT RUDI'S, VOL. 2 | | |
| ❑ Circle L-410 [M] | 1951 | 40.00 |
| THE JATP ALL-STARS AT THE OPERA HOUSE | | |
| ❑ Verve MGVS-6029 [S] | 1960 | 30.00 |
| ❑ Verve MGV-8267 [M] | 1958 | 40.00 |
| ❑ Verve V-8267 [M] | 1961 | 20.00 |
| ❑ Verve V-8489 [M] | 1962 | 25.00 |
| ❑ Verve V6-8489 [S] | 1962 | 30.00 |
| THE JATP ALL-STARS: FUNKY BLUES | | |
| ❑ Verve V-8486 [M] | 1962 | 25.00 |
| ❑ Verve V6-8486 [S] | 1962 | 30.00 |
| JAZZ | | |
| ❑ Royale 1883 [10] | 195? | 30.00 |
| JAZZ — WEST COAST VOL. III | | |
| ❑ Jazztone J-1274 [M] | 195? | 30.00 |
| JAZZ A LA MIDNIGHT | | |
| ❑ Hall of Fame 608 | 197? | 10.00 |
| ❑ Jazztone J-1282 [M] | 1957 | 30.00 |
| JAZZ A LA MOOD | | |
| ❑ Jazztone J-1254 [M] | 1957 | 30.00 |
| JAZZ AMERICANA | | |
| ❑ Tampa TP-11 [M] | 1957 | 100.00 |
| *—Colored vinyl* | | |
| ❑ Tampa TP-11 [M] | 1958 | 40.00 |
| *—Black vinyl* | | |
| JAZZ AND POPS FROM THE SOVIET UNION | | |
| ❑ Colosseum CRLP-171 [M] | 1955 | 30.00 |
| JAZZ ANTHOLOGY OF WEST COAST JAZZ | | |
| ❑ Jazztone J-1243 [M] | 1957 | 30.00 |
| JAZZ AT CARNEGIE HALL | | |
| ❑ Arco AL-4 [10] | 1950 | 80.00 |
| ❑ Mercury MG-35002 [10] | 1950 | 80.00 |
| *—Reissue of Arco 4* | | |
| JAZZ AT CARNEGIE HALL, VOLUME 2 | | |
| ❑ Arco AL-8 [10] | 195? | 80.00 |
| JAZZ AT COLUMBIA — COLLECTORS ITEMS | | |
| ❑ Columbia CB-16 [M] | 195? | 20.00 |
| *—Columbia Record Club "bonus record" in generic sleeve with die-cut circle in middle* | | |
| JAZZ AT COLUMBIA — DIXIELAND | | |
| ❑ Columbia CB-8 [M] | 195? | 20.00 |
| *—Columbia Record Club "bonus record" in generic sleeve with die-cut circle in middle* | | |
| JAZZ AT JAZZ LTD. | | |
| ❑ Atlantic 1338 [M] | 1961 | 25.00 |
| *—Multicolor label, white "fan" logo at right* | | |
| JAZZ AT STORYVILLE | | |
| ❑ Paradox LP-6003 [10] | 1951 | 50.00 |
| ❑ Savoy MG-15001 [10] | 1952 | 80.00 |
| ❑ Savoy MG-15014 [10] | 1952 | 80.00 |
| ❑ Storyville STLP-319 [10] | 1955 | 80.00 |
| JAZZ AT STORYVILLE, VOL. 2 | | |
| ❑ Savoy MG-15016 [10] | 1952 | 80.00 |
| JAZZ AT STORYVILLE, VOL. 3 | | |
| ❑ Savoy MG-15019 [10] | 1953 | 80.00 |
| JAZZ AT STORYVILLE, VOL. 4 | | |
| ❑ Savoy MG-15020 [10] | 1953 | 80.00 |
| JAZZ AT THE BOSTON ARTS FESTIVAL | | |
| ❑ Storyville STLP-311 [10] | 1954 | 80.00 |
| JAZZ AT THE HOLLYWOOD BOWL | | |
| ❑ Verve MGV-8231-2 [(2)M] | 1958 | 50.00 |
| ❑ Verve V-8231-2 [(2)M] | 1961 | 25.00 |
| JAZZ AT THE PHILHARMONIC | | |
| ❑ Stinson SLP-23 [10] | 195? | 80.00 |
| *—Black vinyl* | | |
| ❑ Stinson SLP-23 [10] | 195? | 80.00 |
| *—Opaque red vinyl* | | |
| ❑ Stinson SLP-23 [10] | 1950 | 120.00 |
| *—See-through red vinyl; the first pressing of the first volume to be issued* | | |
| ❑ Stinson SLP-23 [M] | 195? | 20.00 |
| JAZZ AT THE PHILHARMONIC ALL STARS | | |
| ❑ American Recording Society G-416 [M] | 1957 | 30.00 |
| JAZZ AT THE PHILHARMONIC IN EUROPE | | |
| ❑ Verve V6-8823 [(2)] | 197? | 20.00 |
| JAZZ AT THE PHILHARMONIC IN EUROPE, VOL. 1 | | |
| ❑ Verve V-8539 [M] | 1963 | 20.00 |
| ❑ Verve V6-8539 [S] | 1963 | 25.00 |
| JAZZ AT THE PHILHARMONIC IN EUROPE, VOL. 2 | | |
| ❑ Verve V-8540 [M] | 1963 | 20.00 |
| ❑ Verve V6-8540 [S] | 1963 | 25.00 |
| JAZZ AT THE PHILHARMONIC IN EUROPE, VOL. 3 | | |
| ❑ Verve V-8541 [M] | 1963 | 20.00 |
| ❑ Verve V6-8541 [S] | 1963 | 25.00 |
| JAZZ AT THE PHILHARMONIC IN EUROPE, VOL. 4 | | |
| ❑ Verve V-8542 [M] | 1963 | 20.00 |
| ❑ Verve V6-8542 [S] | 1963 | 25.00 |
| JAZZ AT THE PHILHARMONIC IN TOKYO | | |
| ❑ Pablo Live 2620104 [(3)] | 198? | 25.00 |
| JAZZ AT THE PHILHARMONIC, NEW VOLUME 2 | | |
| ❑ Clef MGC-Vol. 2 [M] | 1955 | 50.00 |
| *—Side 1 is the 10-inch Vol. 2; Side 2 is the 10-inch Vol. 3* | | |
| JAZZ AT THE PHILHARMONIC, NEW VOLUME 3 | | |
| ❑ Clef MGC-Vol. 3 [M] | 1955 | 50.00 |
| *—Side 1 is the 10-inch Vol. 4; Side 2 is the 10-inch Vol. 5* | | |
| JAZZ AT THE PHILHARMONIC, NEW VOLUME 4 | | |
| ❑ Clef MGC-Vol. 4 [M] | 1955 | 50.00 |
| *—Combines the 10-inch Vol. 6 and Vol. 14 on one record* | | |

| Number | Title (A Side/B Side) | Yr | NM |
|---|---|---|---|
| JAZZ AT THE PHILHARMONIC, NEW VOLUME 5 | | | |
| ❑ Clef MGC-Vol. 5 [M] | | 1955 | 50.00 |
| *—Combines the 10-inch Vol. 7, 10 and 11 on one record* | | | |
| JAZZ AT THE PHILHARMONIC, NEW VOLUME 6 | | | |
| ❑ Clef MGC-Vol. 6 [M] | | 1955 | 50.00 |
| *—Combines the 10-inch Vol. 8 and Vol. 9 on one record* | | | |
| JAZZ AT THE PHILHARMONIC, NEW VOLUME 7 | | | |
| ❑ Clef MGC-Vol. 7 [M] | | 1955 | 50.00 |
| *—Combines the 10-inch Vol. 12 and 13 on one record* | | | |
| JAZZ AT THE PHILHARMONIC, VOL. 10 | | | |
| ❑ Verve MGV-Vol. 10 [(3)M] | | 1957 | 60.00 |
| *—Reissue of Clef Vol. 17* | | | |
| JAZZ AT THE PHILHARMONIC, VOL. 11 | | | |
| ❑ Verve MGV-Vol. 11 [(3)M] | | 1957 | 60.00 |
| *—Reissue of Clef Vol. 18* | | | |
| JAZZ AT THE PHILHARMONIC, VOL. 2 | | | |
| ❑ Verve MGV-Vol. 2 [M] | | 1957 | 30.00 |
| *—Reissue of 12-inch Clef Vol. 2* | | | |
| JAZZ AT THE PHILHARMONIC, VOL. 3 | | | |
| ❑ Verve MGV-Vol. 3 [M] | | 1957 | 30.00 |
| *—Reissue of 12-inch Clef Vol. 3* | | | |
| JAZZ AT THE PHILHARMONIC, VOL. 4 | | | |
| ❑ Verve MGV-Vol. 4 [M] | | 1957 | 30.00 |
| *—Reissue of 12-inch Clef Vol. 4* | | | |
| JAZZ AT THE PHILHARMONIC, VOL. 5 | | | |
| ❑ Verve MGV-Vol. 5 [M] | | 1957 | 30.00 |
| *—Reissue of 12-inch Clef Vol. 5* | | | |
| JAZZ AT THE PHILHARMONIC, VOL. 6 | | | |
| ❑ Verve MGV-Vol. 6 [M] | | 1957 | 30.00 |
| *—Reissue of 12-inch Clef Vol. 6* | | | |
| JAZZ AT THE PHILHARMONIC, VOL. 7 | | | |
| ❑ Verve MGV-Vol. 7 [M] | | 1957 | 30.00 |
| *—Reissue of 12-inch Clef Vol. 7* | | | |
| JAZZ AT THE PHILHARMONIC, VOL. 8 | | | |
| ❑ Verve MGV-Vol. 8 [(3)M] | | 1957 | 60.00 |
| *—Reissue of Clef Vol. 15* | | | |
| JAZZ AT THE PHILHARMONIC, VOL. 9 | | | |
| ❑ Verve MGV-Vol. 9 [(3)M] | | 1957 | 60.00 |
| *—Reissue of Clef Vol. 16* | | | |
| JAZZ AT THE PHILHARMONIC, VOLUME 10 | | | |
| ❑ Clef MGC-Vol. 10 [10] | | 1953 | 60.00 |
| *—Reissue of Mercury Vol. 10* | | | |
| ❑ Mercury MGC-Vol. 10 [10] | | 1951 | 60.00 |
| *—Reissue of 35010* | | | |
| ❑ Mercury MG-35010 [10] | | 1950 | 100.00 |
| JAZZ AT THE PHILHARMONIC, VOLUME 11 | | | |
| ❑ Clef MGC-Vol. 11 [10] | | 1953 | 60.00 |
| *—Reissue of Mercury Vol. 11* | | | |
| ❑ Mercury MGC-Vol. 11 [10] | | 1951 | 60.00 |
| *—Reissue of 35011* | | | |
| ❑ Mercury MG-35011 [10] | | 1950 | 80.00 |
| JAZZ AT THE PHILHARMONIC, VOLUME 12 | | | |
| ❑ Clef MGC-Vol. 12 [10] | | 1953 | 60.00 |
| *—Reissue of Mercury Vol. 12* | | | |
| ❑ Mercury MGC-Vol. 12 [10] | | 1951 | 60.00 |
| JAZZ AT THE PHILHARMONIC, VOLUME 13 | | | |
| ❑ Clef MGC-Vol. 13 [10] | | 1953 | 60.00 |
| *—Reissue of Mercury Vol. 13* | | | |
| ❑ Mercury MGC-Vol. 13 [10] | | 1951 | 60.00 |
| JAZZ AT THE PHILHARMONIC, VOLUME 14 | | | |
| ❑ Clef MGC-Vol. 14 [10] | | 1953 | 60.00 |
| *—Reissue of Mercury Vol. 14* | | | |
| ❑ Mercury MGC-Vol. 14 [10] | | 1951 | 60.00 |
| JAZZ AT THE PHILHARMONIC, VOLUME 15 | | | |
| ❑ Clef MGC-Vol. 15 [10] | | 1953 | 60.00 |
| *—Reissue of Mercury Vol. 15* | | | |
| ❑ Clef MGC-Vol. 15 [(3)M] | | 1954 | 80.00 |
| *—Boxed set of new material with program* | | | |
| ❑ Mercury MGC-Vol. 15 [10] | | 1951 | 60.00 |
| JAZZ AT THE PHILHARMONIC, VOLUME 16 | | | |
| ❑ Clef MGC-Vol. 16 [(3)M] | | 1954 | 80.00 |
| *—Boxed set of new material with program* | | | |
| JAZZ AT THE PHILHARMONIC, VOLUME 17 | | | |
| ❑ Clef MGC-Vol. 17 [(3)M] | | 1955 | 80.00 |
| *—Boxed set of new material with photo booklet* | | | |
| JAZZ AT THE PHILHARMONIC, VOLUME 18 | | | |
| ❑ Clef MGC-Vol. 18 [(3)M] | | 1955 | 80.00 |
| *—Boxed set of new material with booklet* | | | |
| JAZZ AT THE PHILHARMONIC, VOLUME 2 | | | |
| ❑ Arco AL-1 [10] | | 1950 | 80.00 |
| ❑ Clef MGC-Vol. 2 [10] | | 1953 | 60.00 |
| *—Reissue of Mercury Vol. 2* | | | |
| ❑ Mercury MGC-Vol. 2 [10] | | 1951 | 60.00 |
| *—Reissue of 35003* | | | |
| ❑ Mercury MG-35003 [10] | | 1950 | 80.00 |
| *—Reissue of Arco 1* | | | |
| JAZZ AT THE PHILHARMONIC, VOLUME 3 | | | |
| ❑ Arco AL-2 [10] | | 1950 | 80.00 |
| ❑ Clef MGC-Vol. 3 [10] | | 1953 | 60.00 |
| *—Reissue of Mercury Vol. 3* | | | |
| ❑ Mercury MGC-Vol. 3 [10] | | 1951 | 60.00 |
| *—Reissue of 35004* | | | |
| ❑ Mercury MG-35004 [10] | | 1950 | 80.00 |
| *—Reissue of Arco 2* | | | |
| JAZZ AT THE PHILHARMONIC, VOLUME 4 | | | |
| ❑ Clef MGC-Vol. 4 [10] | | 1953 | 60.00 |
| *—Reissue of Mercury Vol. 4* | | | |
| ❑ Mercury MGC-Vol. 4 [10] | | 1951 | 60.00 |
| *—Reissue of 35005* | | | |
| ❑ Mercury MG-35005 [10] | | 1950 | 80.00 |
| JAZZ AT THE PHILHARMONIC, VOLUME 5 | | | |
| ❑ Clef MGC-Vol. 5 [10] | | 1953 | 60.00 |
| *—Reissue of Mercury Vol. 5* | | | |
| ❑ Mercury MGC-Vol. 5 [10] | | 1951 | 60.00 |
| *—Reissue of 35006* | | | |
| ❑ Mercury MG-35006 [10] | | 1950 | 80.00 |
| JAZZ AT THE PHILHARMONIC, VOLUME 6 | | | |
| ❑ Clef MGC-Vol. 6 [10] | | 1953 | 60.00 |
| *—Reissue of Mercury Vol. 6* | | | |
| ❑ Mercury MGC-Vol. 6 [10] | | 1951 | 60.00 |
| *—Reissue of 35007* | | | |
| ❑ Mercury MG-35007 [10] | | 1950 | 80.00 |
| JAZZ AT THE PHILHARMONIC, VOLUME 7 | | | |
| ❑ Clef MGC-Vol. 7 [10] | | 1953 | 60.00 |
| *—Reissue of Mercury Vol. 7* | | | |
| ❑ Mercury MGC-Vol. 7 [10] | | 1951 | 60.00 |
| *—Reissue of 35008* | | | |
| ❑ Mercury MG-35008 [10] | | 1950 | 80.00 |
| JAZZ AT THE PHILHARMONIC, VOLUME 8 | | | |
| ❑ Clef MGC-Vol. 8 [10] | | 1953 | 60.00 |
| *—Reissue of Mercury Vol. 8* | | | |
| ❑ Mercury MGC-Vol. 8 [10] | | 1951 | 60.00 |
| *—Reissue of 35000* | | | |
| ❑ Mercury MG-35000 [10] | | 1950 | 80.00 |
| JAZZ AT THE PHILHARMONIC, VOLUME 9 | | | |
| ❑ Clef MGC-Vol. 9 [10] | | 1953 | 60.00 |
| *—Reissue of Mercury Vol. 9* | | | |
| ❑ Mercury MGC-Vol. 9 [10] | | 1951 | 60.00 |
| *—Reissue of 35009* | | | |
| ❑ Mercury MG-35009 [10] | | 1950 | 80.00 |
| JAZZ AT THE PHILHARMONIC: IN TOKYO 1983 | | | |
| ❑ Pablo Live 2620117 [(3)] | | 1984 | 20.00 |
| JAZZ AT THE PHILHARMONIC: THE 1940S | | | |
| ❑ Verve UMV-9070/2 [(3)] | | 197? | 25.00 |
| JAZZ AT THE SANTA MONICA CIVIC '72 | | | |
| ❑ Pablo 2625701 [(3)] | | 197? | 25.00 |
| JAZZ BAND BALL | | | |
| ❑ Good Time Jazz L-12005 [M] | | 1954 | 20.00 |
| JAZZ CITY PRESENTS | | | |
| ❑ Bethlehem BCP-80 [M] | | 1957 | 30.00 |
| JAZZ COMMITTEE FOR LATIN AMERICAN AFFAIRS | | | |
| ❑ FM LP-303 [M] | | 1963 | 50.00 |
| ❑ Vee-Jay LP-303 [S] | | 196? | 20.00 |
| *—All-black label with Vee Jay "brackets" logo and "STEREO" on label; most likely a reissue* | | | |
| JAZZ CONCERT | | | |
| ❑ Jazztone J-1219 [M] | | 1956 | 30.00 |
| ❑ Mercury MGJC-1 [(2)M] | | 1953 | 120.00 |
| *—Combines 601 and 602 in a box* | | | |
| ❑ Norgran MGN-3501-2 [(2)M] | | 1956 | 120.00 |
| *—Reissue of Mercury MGJC-1* | | | |
| JAZZ CONCERT WEST COAST | | | |
| ❑ Savoy MG-12012 [M] | | 1955 | 80.00 |
| ❑ Savoy MG-12196 [M] | | 1961 | 50.00 |
| JAZZ CONFIDENTIAL | | | |
| ❑ Crown CLP-5056 [M] | | 1959 | 20.00 |
| JAZZ CORNUCOPIA | | | |
| ❑ Coral CRL 57149 [M] | | 1958 | 30.00 |
| JAZZ CRITICS' CHOICE: GREAT JAZZ CRITICS CHOOSE HISTORIC PERFORMANCES | | | |
| ❑ Columbia CL 2126 [M] | | 1964 | 12.00 |
| JAZZ DANCE | | | |
| ❑ Jaguar JP-801 [10] | | 1954 | 50.00 |
| JAZZ DUPLEX | | | |
| ❑ Pax LP-6006 [10] | | 1954 | 30.00 |
| JAZZ FESTIVAL | | | |
| ❑ Imperial LP-9233 [M] | | 1963 | 20.00 |
| ❑ Imperial LP-12233 [S] | | 1963 | 25.00 |
| ❑ Kapp KS-1 [M] | | 1956 | 20.00 |
| JAZZ FESTIVAL IN HI-FI: NEAR IN AND FAR OUT | | | |
| ❑ Warner Bros. W 1281 [M] | | 1959 | 25.00 |
| JAZZ FESTIVAL IN STEREO: NEAR IN AND FAR OUT | | | |
| ❑ Warner Bros. WS 1281 [S] | | 1959 | 30.00 |
| JAZZ FESTIVAL, VOLUME 2 | | | |
| ❑ Imperial LP-9238 [M] | | 1963 | 20.00 |
| ❑ Imperial LP-12238 [S] | | 1963 | 25.00 |
| JAZZ FOR ART'S SAKE | | | |
| ❑ Dotted Eighth 101 [M] | | 195? | 40.00 |
| JAZZ FOR HI-FI LOVERS | | | |
| ❑ Dawn DLP-1124 [M] | | 1958 | 80.00 |
| JAZZ FOR LOVERS | | | |
| ❑ Riverside RLP 12-244 [M] | | 1957 | 40.00 |
| JAZZ FOR PEOPLE WHO HATE JAZZ | | | |
| ❑ RCA Victor LJM-1008 [M] | | 1954 | 50.00 |
| JAZZ FOR SURF-NIKS | | | |
| ❑ Bethlehem BCP-6073 [M] | | 1961 | 30.00 |
| JAZZ FROM DOWN UNDER | | | |
| ❑ Jaguar JP-803 [10] | | 1954 | 50.00 |
| JAZZ FROM SWEDEN | | | |
| ❑ Discovery DL-2002 [10] | | 1953 | 50.00 |
| THE JAZZ GIANTS | | | |
| ❑ Norgran MGN-1056 [M] | | 1956 | 80.00 |
| JAZZ GIANTS '56 | | | |
| ❑ Verve UMV-2511 | | 197? | 12.00 |
| THE JAZZ GIANTS '56 | | | |
| ❑ Verve MGV-8146 [M] | | 1957 | 30.00 |
| ❑ Verve V-8146 [M] | | 1961 | 20.00 |
| JAZZ GIANTS '58 | | | |
| ❑ Verve MGV-8248 [M] | | 1958 | 50.00 |
| ❑ Verve V-8248 [M] | | 1961 | 25.00 |
| JAZZ GIANTS, VOL. 1 | | | |
| ❑ EmArcy MG-36048 [M] | | 1955 | 40.00 |
| JAZZ GIANTS, VOL. 2: THE PIANO PLAYERS | | | |
| ❑ EmArcy MG-36049 [M] | | 1955 | 40.00 |
| JAZZ GIANTS, VOL. 3: REEDS, PART 1 | | | |
| ❑ EmArcy MG-36050 [M] | | 1955 | 40.00 |
| JAZZ GIANTS, VOL. 3: REEDS, PART 2 | | | |
| ❑ EmArcy MG-36051 [M] | | 1955 | 40.00 |
| JAZZ GIANTS, VOL. 4: FOLK BLUES | | | |
| ❑ EmArcy MG-36052 [M] | | 1955 | 40.00 |
| JAZZ GIANTS, VOL. 5: BRASS | | | |
| ❑ EmArcy MG-36053 [M] | | 1955 | 40.00 |
| JAZZ GIANTS, VOL. 6: MODERN SWEDES | | | |
| ❑ EmArcy MG-36054 [M] | | 1955 | 40.00 |
| JAZZ GIANTS, VOL. 7: DIXIELAND | | | |
| ❑ EmArcy MG-36055 [M] | | 1955 | 40.00 |
| JAZZ GIANTS, VOL. 8: DRUM ROLE | | | |
| ❑ EmArcy MG-36071 [M] | | 1956 | 40.00 |
| JAZZ GOES TO BROADWAY | | | |
| ❑ Kapp KL-1007 [M] | | 1956 | 20.00 |
| JAZZ GREATS | | | |
| ❑ Tops L-1508 [M] | | 1958 | 20.00 |
| JAZZ GREATS! | | | |
| ❑ Allegro 737 [M] | | 1958 | 30.00 |
| JAZZ HALL OF FAME, VOL. 2 | | | |
| ❑ Design DLP-113 [M] | | 196? | 20.00 |
| THE JAZZ HOUR | | | |
| ❑ Savoy MG-12126 [M] | | 1957 | 50.00 |
| JAZZ IN HOLLYWOOD | | | |
| ❑ Liberty LJH-6001 [M] | | 1955 | 30.00 |
| JAZZ IN TRANSITION | | | |
| ❑ Transition TRLP-30 [M] | | 1956 | 200.00 |
| *—With booklet (deduct 1/4 if missing)* | | | |
| JAZZ INTERPLAY | | | |
| ❑ Prestige PRLP-7341 [(2)M] | | 1964 | 40.00 |
| ❑ Prestige PRLP-7341 [(2)R] | | 1964 | 25.00 |
| JAZZ IS BUSTING OUT ALL OVER | | | |
| ❑ Savoy MG-12123 [M] | | 1957 | 50.00 |
| ❑ Savoy Jazz SJC-408 | | 198? | 10.00 |
| JAZZ JAMBOREE | | | |
| ❑ Halo 50229 [M] | | 1957 | 20.00 |
| JAZZ LAB | | | |
| ❑ Starlite ST-7003 [M] | | 1955 | 50.00 |
| THE JAZZ LIFE | | | |
| ❑ Candid CD-8019 [M] | | 1960 | 40.00 |
| ❑ Candid CS-9019 [S] | | 1960 | 30.00 |
| JAZZ LTD. | | | |
| ❑ Regal LP-11 [10] | | 1951 | 50.00 |
| THE JAZZ MAKERS | | | |
| ❑ Columbia CL 1036 [M] | | 1957 | 20.00 |
| JAZZ MONTAGE | | | |
| ❑ Liberty LRP-3292 [M] | | 1963 | 15.00 |
| ❑ Liberty LST-7292 [S] | | 1963 | 20.00 |
| JAZZ MUSIC FOR BIRDS | | | |
| ❑ Bethlehem BCP-6039 [M] | | 1959 | 30.00 |
| JAZZ MUSIC FOR PEOPLE WHO DON'T CARE ABOUT MONEY | | | |
| ❑ Bethlehem BCP-88 [M] | | 1958 | 30.00 |
| JAZZ ODYSSEY: THE SOUND OF CHICAGO | | | |
| ❑ Columbia C3L 32 [(3)M] | | 1964 | 40.00 |
| JAZZ ODYSSEY: THE SOUND OF HARLEM | | | |
| ❑ Columbia C3L 33 [(3)M] | | 1964 | 40.00 |
| JAZZ ODYSSEY: THE SOUND OF NEW ORLEANS | | | |
| ❑ Columbia C3L 30 [(3)M] | | 1964 | 40.00 |
| JAZZ OF THE ROARING 20'S | | | |
| ❑ Riverside RLP 12-801 [M] | | 195? | 50.00 |
| JAZZ OF THE ROARING TWENTIES: DANCE MUSIC OF THE CHARLESTON ERA | | | |
| ❑ Riverside RLP 12-108 [M] | | 1956 | 40.00 |
| JAZZ OF THE SIXTIES | | | |
| ❑ Vee Jay VJS-2-1008 [(2)] | | 1974 | 20.00 |
| JAZZ OF TWO DECADES | | | |
| ❑ EmArcy DEM-2 [M] | | 1956 | 40.00 |
| JAZZ OFF THE AIR, VOL. 1 | | | |
| ❑ Esoteric ESJ-2 [10] | | 1952 | 80.00 |
| JAZZ OFF THE AIR, VOL. 2 | | | |
| ❑ Esoteric ESJ-3 [10] | | 1952 | 80.00 |
| JAZZ OMNIBUS | | | |
| ❑ Columbia CL 1020 [M] | | 1957 | 20.00 |
| JAZZ ON THE AIR | | | |
| ❑ Brunswick BL 58048 [10] | | 1953 | 50.00 |
| JAZZ ON THE SCREEN | | | |
| ❑ Fontana MGF-27532 [M] | | 1965 | 40.00 |
| ❑ Fontana SRF-67532 [S] | | 1965 | 40.00 |
| JAZZ PIANISTS GALORE | | | |
| ❑ Jazz: West Coast JWC-506 [M] | | 1956 | 150.00 |
| THE JAZZ PIANO | | | |
| ❑ RCA Victor LPM-3499 [M] | | 1966 | 20.00 |
| ❑ RCA Victor LSP-3499 [S] | | 1966 | 25.00 |
| JAZZ POLL WINNERS | | | |
| ❑ Columbia CL 1610 [M] | | 1960 | 20.00 |

| Number Title (A Side/B Side) | Yr | NM |
|---|---|---|
| JAZZ POTPOURRI | | |
| ❑ Audiophile AP-24 [M] | 1953 | 30.00 |
| A JAZZ SALUTE TO FREEDOM | | |
| ❑ Core 100 [(2)M] | 196? | 25.00 |
| THE JAZZ SCENE | | |
| ❑ American Recording Society G-419 [M] | 1957 | 30.00 |
| ❑ Clef MGC-674 [M] | 1955 | 40.00 |
| *—Reissue of 4007* | | |
| ❑ Clef MGC-4007 [M] | 1953 | 50.00 |
| ❑ Clef Special Edition (no #) [(2)10] | 1953 | 100.00 |
| *—Two 10-inch LPs in box. Buyers had the option of purchasing a collection of photos that had been used in the original 78 rpm album; add another 50 percent if these photos are included* | | |
| ❑ Verve MGV-8060 [M] | 1957 | 30.00 |
| *—Reissue of Clef 674* | | |
| ❑ Verve V-8060 [M] | 1961 | 20.00 |
| JAZZ SET | | |
| ❑ Columbia Special Products CSP-217S [S] | 1965 | 10.00 |
| *—Special item for Zenith* | | |
| JAZZ SOUL OF "CLEOPATRA" | | |
| ❑ New Jazz NJLP-8292 [M] | 1962 | 40.00 |
| *—Purple label* | | |
| ❑ New Jazz NJLP-8292 [M] | 1965 | 20.00 |
| *—Blue label, trident logo at right* | | |
| JAZZ SOUTH PACIFIC | | |
| ❑ Regent MG-6001 [M] | 1956 | — |
| *—See J.J. JOHNSON.* | | |
| THE JAZZ STORY | | |
| ❑ Coral CJE-100 [(3)M] | 195? | 100.00 |
| *—Box set; narrated by Steve Allen* | | |
| JAZZ SUPER HITS | | |
| ❑ Atlantic SD 1528 | 1969 | 25.00 |
| JAZZ SUPER HITS, VOL. 2 | | |
| ❑ Atlantic SD 1559 | 1970 | 20.00 |
| JAZZ SURPRISE | | |
| ❑ Crown CLP-5008 [M] | 1957 | 20.00 |
| JAZZ SWINGS BROADWAY | | |
| ❑ Pacific Jazz PJM-404 [M] | 1956 | 50.00 |
| ❑ World Pacific PJM-404 [M] | 1958 | 40.00 |
| JAZZ TIME U.S.A. — VOLUME 1 | | |
| ❑ Brunswick BL 54000 [M] | 1952 | 30.00 |
| JAZZ TIME U.S.A. — VOLUME 2 | | |
| ❑ Brunswick BL 54001 [M] | 1953 | 30.00 |
| JAZZ TIME U.S.A. — VOLUME 3 | | |
| ❑ Brunswick BL 54002 [M] | 1954 | 30.00 |
| JAZZ VARIATIONS, VOL. 1 | | |
| ❑ Stinson SLP-20 [10] | 195? | 60.00 |
| ❑ Stinson SLP-20 [M] | 196? | 25.00 |
| JAZZ VARIATIONS, VOL. 2 | | |
| ❑ Stinson SLP-29 [M] | 196? | 25.00 |
| JAZZ VOCALS AWARD ALBUM | | |
| ❑ Bethlehem BCP-6068 [M] | 1963 | 25.00 |
| JAZZ WEST COAST, VOL. 1 | | |
| ❑ Pacific Jazz JWC-500 [M] | 1956 | 50.00 |
| ❑ World Pacific JWC-500 [M] | 1958 | 40.00 |
| JAZZ WEST COAST, VOL. 2 | | |
| ❑ Pacific Jazz JWC-501 [M] | 1956 | 50.00 |
| ❑ World Pacific JWC-501 [M] | 1958 | 40.00 |
| JAZZ WEST COAST, VOL. 3 | | |
| ❑ Pacific Jazz JWC-507 [M] | 1957 | 50.00 |
| ❑ World Pacific JWC-507 [M] | 1958 | 40.00 |
| JAZZ WEST COAST, VOL. 4 | | |
| ❑ World Pacific JWC-510 [M] | 1958 | 40.00 |
| ❑ World Pacific ST-1009 [S] | 1959 | 30.00 |
| JAZZ WEST COAST, VOL. 5 | | |
| ❑ World Pacific JWC-511 [M] | 1958 | 40.00 |
| JAZZ, VOL. 1: THE SOUTH | | |
| ❑ Folkways FP-53/4 [M] | 1951 | 25.00 |
| JAZZ, VOL. 10: BOOGIE WOOGIE, JUMP, KANSAS CITY | | |
| ❑ Folkways FP-73/4 [M] | 1951 | 25.00 |
| JAZZ, VOL. 11: ADDENDA | | |
| ❑ Folkways FP-75/6 [M] | 1951 | 25.00 |
| JAZZ, VOL. 2: THE BLUES | | |
| ❑ Folkways FP-55/6 [M] | 1951 | 25.00 |
| JAZZ, VOL. 3: NEW ORLEANS | | |
| ❑ Folkways FP-57/8 [M] | 1951 | 25.00 |
| JAZZ, VOL. 4: JAZZ SINGERS | | |
| ❑ Folkways FP-59/60 [M] | 1951 | 25.00 |
| JAZZ, VOL. 5: CHICAGO | | |
| ❑ Folkways FP-63/4 [M] | 1951 | 25.00 |
| JAZZ, VOL. 6: CHICAGO #2 | | |
| ❑ Folkways FP-65/6 [M] | 1951 | 25.00 |
| JAZZ, VOL. 7: NEW YORK 1922-1934 | | |
| ❑ Folkways FP-67/8 [M] | 1951 | 25.00 |
| JAZZ, VOL. 8: BIG BANDS BEFORE 1938 | | |
| ❑ Folkways FP-69/70 [M] | 1951 | 25.00 |
| JAZZ, VOL. 9: PIANO | | |
| ❑ Folkways FP-71/2 [M] | 1951 | 25.00 |
| JAZZMEN — DETROIT | | |
| ❑ Savoy MG-12083 [M] | 1956 | 80.00 |
| JAZZTONE SAMPLER | | |
| ❑ Jazztone J-SPEC-100 [10] | 1955 | 50.00 |
| *—With booklet* | | |
| JAZZVILLE, VOL. 1 | | |
| ❑ Dawn DLP-1101 [M] | 1956 | 80.00 |
| JESUS CHRIST SUPERSTAR | | |
| ❑ Decca DXA 7206 [(2)] | 1970 | 30.00 |
| *—Box set with booklet* | | |
| ❑ Decca DXSA 7206 [(2)] | 1970 | 25.00 |
| *—Gatefold cover with booklet* | | |
| ❑ Decca MCA 2-10000 [(2)] | 1973 | 12.00 |
| *—Gatefold cover with booklet; reissue; same custom labels as Decca issue* | | |
| ❑ MCA 10000 [(2)] | 197? | 12.00 |
| *—Gatefold cover with booklet; reissue; generic MCA labels* | | |
| JINGLE BELL JAZZ | | |
| ❑ Columbia CL 1893 [M] | 1962 | 20.00 |
| ❑ Columbia CS 8693 [S] | 1962 | 15.00 |
| ❑ Columbia PC 36803 | 1980 | 10.00 |
| *—Reissue of Harmony KH 32529 on the "Jazz Odyssey" series* | | |
| ❑ Harmony KH 32529 | 1973 | 12.00 |
| *—Reissue of CS 8693 with one track changed* | | |
| JINGLE BELL ROCK | | |
| ❑ Time-Life SRNR-XM [(2)] | 1987 | 20.00 |
| *—Available from Time-Life by mail order only; boxed set* | | |
| JOHN COLTRANE IN THE WINNER'S CIRCLE | | |
| ❑ Bethlehem BCP-6066 [M] | 1961 | 25.00 |
| *—Reissue of 6024 with new title* | | |
| JOHN HAMMOND PRESENTS "FROM SPIRITUALS TO SWING" AT CARNEGIE HALL 1938 | | |
| ❑ Vanguard VRS-8523 [M] | 1959 | 40.00 |
| JOHN HAMMOND PRESENTS "FROM SPIRITUALS TO SWING" AT CARNEGIE HALL 1939 | | |
| ❑ Vanguard VRS-8524 [M] | 1959 | 40.00 |
| JOY TO THE WORLD (30 CLASSIC CHRISTMAS MELODIES) | | |
| ❑ Columbia Special Products P3 14654 [(3)] | 1978 | 20.00 |
| *—Box set; produced for Murray Hill Records* | | |
| THE JOYFUL SOUND OF CHRISTMAS | | |
| ❑ RCA Record Club CSP-0601 [(2)] | 1969 | 20.00 |
| *—Available only through the RCA Record Club* | | |
| JOYOUS MUSIC FOR CHRISTMAS TIME | | |
| ❑ Reader's Digest RD 45-M [(4)M] | 1963 | 20.00 |
| ❑ Reader's Digest RD 45-S [(4)S] | 1963 | 20.00 |
| *—Available only through Reader's Digest magazine by mail order* | | |
| JOYOUS NOEL | | |
| ❑ Reader's Digest RDA-57A [(4)] | 1966 | 20.00 |
| *—Available only through Reader's Digest magazine by mail order* | | |
| JUBILEE MONAURAL SAMPLER: VOCALS AND INSTRUMENTALS | | |
| ❑ Jubilee MSJLP-803 [M] | 1959 | 30.00 |
| JUBILEE STEREOSONIC VOCAL SAMPLER, VOLUME 2 | | |
| ❑ Jubilee SSJLP-802 [S] | 1959 | 40.00 |
| JUBILEE SURPRISE PARTY | | |
| ❑ Jubilee JGM-1107 [M] | 1959 | 150.00 |
| ❑ Jubilee JGS-1107 [S] | 1959 | 200.00 |
| JUST JAZZ | | |
| ❑ Imperial LP-9246 [M] | 1963 | 20.00 |
| ❑ Imperial LP-12246 [S] | 1963 | 25.00 |
| K-BOX DUSTY DISCS | | |
| ❑ Roulette R 25338 [M] | 1966 | 20.00 |
| KANSAS CITY IN THE '30S | | |
| ❑ Capitol T 1057 [M] | 1958 | 25.00 |
| KANSAS CITY JAZZ | | |
| ❑ Decca DL 8044 [M] | 1954 | 40.00 |
| KANSAS CITY PIANO | | |
| ❑ Decca DL 9226 [M] | 1967 | 30.00 |
| KATS KARAVAN (OLD FAVORITES WITH JIM LOWE) | | |
| ❑ Vee Jay LP-100 [M] | 1957 | 50.00 |
| *—Gold label, black print* | | |
| KBIG CHOICES | | |
| ❑ World Pacific KBIG-1 [S] | 1964 | 25.00 |
| KEATS RIDES A HARLEY | | |
| ❑ Happy Squid HS 002 | 1981 | 20.00 |
| KEYBOARD KINGS | | |
| ❑ MGM E-100 [10] | 1951 | 50.00 |
| KEYBOARD KINGS OF JAZZ | | |
| ❑ RCA Victor LPT-4 [10] | 1951 | 40.00 |
| KGFJ SOUNDS OF SUCCESS | | |
| ❑ Roulette R 25349 [M] | 1967 | 20.00 |
| KINGS OF CLASSIC JAZZ | | |
| ❑ Riverside RLP 12-131 [M] | 1957 | 40.00 |
| KINGS OF THE KEYBOARD | | |
| ❑ American Recording Society G-406 [M] | 1956 | 30.00 |
| THE KINGS SING THE BLUES | | |
| ❑ Teem LP-5005 [M] | 196? | 30.00 |
| KISS MY ASS — CLASSIC KISS REGROOVED | | |
| ❑ Mercury 522123-1 | 1994 | 40.00 |
| *—All copies on red vinyl* | | |
| KNOW YOUR JAZZ | | |
| ❑ ABC-Paramount ABC-115 [M] | 1956 | 30.00 |
| KPOI'S BATTLE OF THE SURFING BANDS | | |
| ❑ Del-Fi DFLP-1235 [M] | 1964 | 60.00 |
| ❑ Del-Fi DFST-1235 [S] | 1964 | 100.00 |
| *—Honolulu version of the above LP* | | |
| KTLA'S BATTLE OF THE SURFING BANDS | | |
| ❑ Del-Fi DFLP-1235 [M] | 1964 | 50.00 |
| ❑ Del-Fi DFST-1235 [S] | 1964 | 80.00 |
| *—Los Angeles version of the above LP* | | |
| KYA GOLDEN GATE GREATS | | |
| ❑ Chess LP 1458 SF [M] | 1961 | 150.00 |
| *—San Francisco version of "Golden Gassers," Chess 1458* | | |
| KYA'S BATTLE OF THE SURFING BANDS | | |
| ❑ Del-Fi DFLP-1235 [M] | 1964 | 50.00 |
| ❑ Del-Fi DFST-1235 [S] | 1964 | 80.00 |
| *—San Francisco version of the above LP, with slightly different contents* | | |
| KYA'S MEMORIES OF THE COW PALACE | | |
| ❑ Autumn LP 101 [M] | 1963 | 70.00 |
| THE LAST RECORD ALBUM | | |
| ❑ A&M (# unknown) | 1989 | 40.00 |
| LATE MUSIC, VOLUME I | | |
| ❑ Columbia CL 541 [M] | 1954 | 25.00 |
| LATE MUSIC, VOLUME II | | |
| ❑ Columbia CL 542 [M] | 1954 | 25.00 |
| LATE MUSIC, VOLUME III | | |
| ❑ Columbia CL 543 [M] | 1954 | 25.00 |
| THE LAUGHTOUR | | |
| ❑ Sire PRO-A-3931 [EP] | 1990 | 20.00 |
| *—Promo-only sampler* | | |
| LAURIE GOLDEN GOODIES | | |
| ❑ Laurie LLP-2041 [M] | 1967 | 15.00 |
| ❑ Laurie SLLP-2041 [P] | 1967 | 25.00 |
| LENNY TRISTANO MEMORIAL CONCERT | | |
| ❑ Jazz Records JR-3 [(5)] | 198? | 40.00 |
| LEONARD FEATHER'S ENCYCLOPEDIA OF JAZZ | | |
| ❑ Vee Jay VJSP-400 [(2)] | 1977 | 25.00 |
| LEONARD FEATHER'S ENCYCLOPEDIA OF JAZZ OF THE '60S: BLUES BAG | | |
| ❑ Vee Jay LP-2506 [M] | 1964 | 20.00 |
| LEONARD FEATHER'S ENCYCLOPEDIA OF JAZZ, VOLUME ONE: GIANTS OF THE SAXOPHONE | | |
| ❑ Vee Jay LP-2501 [M] | 1964 | 20.00 |
| ❑ Vee Jay VJS-2501 [S] | 1964 | 25.00 |
| LET THEM EAT JELLYBEANS | | |
| ❑ Alternative Tentacles VIRUS 4 | 1982 | 25.00 |
| LET'S HAVE A DANCE PARTY | | |
| ❑ Ace LP-1019 [M] | 1961 | 70.00 |
| LET'S SING ABOUT FREEDOM | | |
| ❑ Vee Jay LP-5044 [M] | 1963 | 30.00 |
| LIBERTY PREMIER SERIES SPECTACULAR | | |
| ❑ Liberty L-5504 [M] | 1962 | 20.00 |
| ❑ Liberty S-6604 [S] | 1962 | 30.00 |
| LIBERTY PROUDLY PRESENTS STEREO — THE VISUAL SOUND | | |
| ❑ Liberty LST-100 [S] | 1959 | 40.00 |
| LIFE IS BEAUTIFUL, SO WHY NOT EAT HEALTH FOOD? | | |
| ❑ New Underground 44 | 1981 | 20.00 |
| LIFE IS UGLY, SO WHY NOT KILL YOURSELF? | | |
| ❑ New Underground 11 | 1981 | 20.00 |
| THE LIFE TREASURY OF CHRISTMAS MUSIC | | |
| ❑ Project/Capitol TL 100 [M] | 1963 | 20.00 |
| *—Designed as a supplement to the Life Book of Christmas; selections performed by anonymous chorus and orchestra and Boy Choristers from the Church of the Transfiguration (NY)* | | |
| LIGHTS OUT SAN FRANCISCO | | |
| ❑ Blue Thumb BT 6004 | 1970 | 25.00 |
| LIKE 'ER RED HOT | | |
| ❑ Duke DLP-73 [M] | 196? | 30.00 |
| *—Green label, "Distributed by ABC-Dunhill"* | | |
| ❑ Duke DLP-73 [M] | 196? | 50.00 |
| *—Orange label* | | |
| ❑ Duke DLP-73 [M] | 1960 | 120.00 |
| *—Purple and yellow label* | | |
| LIMO | | |
| ❑ Warner Bros. PRO 691 [(2)] | 1977 | 20.00 |
| LISTEN TO OUR STORY | | |
| ❑ Brunswick BL 59001 [10] | 1950 | 60.00 |
| A LITTLE ROCK AND ROLL FOR EVERYBODY | | |
| ❑ Audio Lab AL-1567 [M] | 1960 | 200.00 |
| LIVE AT CBGB'S | | |
| ❑ Atlantic SD2-508 [(2)] | 1976 | 20.00 |
| *—Same album as CBGB/Omfug release* | | |
| ❑ CBGB/Omfug 315 [(2)] | 1976 | 30.00 |
| LIVE AT TARGET | | |
| ❑ Subterranean 3 | 1980 | 25.00 |
| LIVE AT THE WHISKEY A-GO-GO | | |
| ❑ Vee Jay LP-1100 [M] | 1964 | 30.00 |
| *—Not known to exist in stereo* | | |
| THE LIVELY SOUND OF UNIVERSITY | | |
| ❑ Capitol Custom (no #) [M] | 1966 | 20.00 |
| *—"Mustang Sweepstakes Prize Winner" on front cover* | | |
| LOADED | | |
| ❑ Savoy MG-12074 [M] | 1956 | 50.00 |
| LONDON BROIL | | |
| ❑ Angel ANG-60004 [10] | 1955 | 50.00 |
| A LOOK AT YESTERDAY | | |
| ❑ Mainstream 56025 [M] | 1965 | 25.00 |
| LOOK WHO'S SURFIN' NOW! | | |
| ❑ King 882 [M] | 1964 | 150.00 |
| LOONEY TUNES AND MERRIE MELODIES | | |
| ❑ Warner Bros. PRO 423 [(3)] | 1970 | 100.00 |
| *—Box set with booklet of liner notes; originals have green labels* | | |
| A LOT OF YARN BUT A WELL-KNITTED JAZZ ALBUM | | |
| ❑ Bethlehem BCP-91 [M] | 1958 | 30.00 |
| LOVE ME TENDER | | |
| ❑ Time-Life STL-133 [(2)] | 1991 | 25.00 |

| Number | Title (A Side/B Side) | Yr | NM |
|---|---|---|---|
| LOVE THOSE GOODIES | | | |
| ❑ Checker LP 2973 [DJ] | | 1959 | 500.00 |
| *—White label, multi-color splash vinyl* | | | |
| ❑ Checker LP 2973 [M] | | 1959 | 120.00 |
| LULLABY OF BIRDLAND | | | |
| ❑ RCA Victor LPM-1146 [M] | | 1955 | 50.00 |
| LUSTY MOODS | | | |
| ❑ Moodsville MVLP-37 [M] | | 1963 | 40.00 |
| *—Green label* | | | |
| ❑ Moodsville MVLP-37 [M] | | 1965 | 20.00 |
| *—Blue label, trident logo at right* | | | |
| ❑ Moodsville MVST-37 [S] | | 1963 | 40.00 |
| *—Green label* | | | |
| ❑ Moodsville MVST-37 [S] | | 1965 | 20.00 |
| *—Blue label, trident logo at right* | | | |
| ❑ Status ST-8319 [M] | | 1965 | 30.00 |
| MAD "TWISTS" ROCK 'N' ROLL | | | |
| ❑ Big Top 12-1305 [M] | | 1962 | 100.00 |
| THE MAGIC HORN | | | |
| ❑ RCA Victor LPM-1332 [M] | | 1956 | 40.00 |
| THE MAGIC OF CHRISTMAS | | | |
| ❑ Columbia Musical Treasury P3S 5806 [(3)] | | 1972 | 20.00 |
| THE MAGICAL MUSIC OF WALT DISNEY | | | |
| ❑ Ovation OV-5000 [(4)] | | 1978 | 60.00 |
| *—Box set* | | | |
| MAGNAVOX ALBUM OF CHRISTMAS MUSIC | | | |
| ❑ Columbia Special Products CSQ 11093 [Q] | | 1972 | 20.00 |
| *—Sold only at Magnavox dealers; yes, this is in quadraphonic!* | | | |
| MAMBO JAZZ | | | |
| ❑ Prestige PRLP-135 [10] | | 1952 | 150.00 |
| THE MAN WITH A HORN | | | |
| ❑ Decca DL 5191 [10] | | 1950 | 50.00 |
| THE MANY FACES OF THE BLUES | | | |
| ❑ Savoy MG-12125 [M] | | 1957 | 50.00 |
| MAX'S KANSAS CITY 1976 | | | |
| ❑ Ram 1213 | | 1976 | 20.00 |
| MAX'S KANSAS CITY PRESENTS NEW WAVE HITS FOR THE '80S | | | |
| ❑ Max's Kansas City 19801 | | 1981 | 20.00 |
| *—Compilation of first two Max's Kansas City albums plus new tracks* | | | |
| MAX'S KANSAS CITY VOL. 2, 1977 | | | |
| ❑ Ram 2213 | | 1977 | 12.00 |
| THE MELLOW MOODS | | | |
| ❑ RCA Victor LPM-1365 [M] | | 1956 | 40.00 |
| MELLOW THE MOOD/JAZZ IN A MELLOW MOOD | | | |
| ❑ Blue Note BLP-5001 [10] | | 1951 | 200.00 |
| MEMORABLE SESSIONS IN JAZZ | | | |
| ❑ Blue Note BLP-5026 [10] | | 1953 | 200.00 |
| MEMORIES ARE MADE OF HITS | | | |
| ❑ Liberty LRP-3200 [M] | | 1961 | 25.00 |
| *—Reissued as "The Original Hits, Volume 4"* | | | |
| MEMORY LANE, HITS BY THE ORIGINAL GROUPS | | | |
| ❑ Fire FLP-100 [M] | | 1959 | 200.00 |
| *—Reissue of "Here Are the Hits!" with the same label and number* | | | |
| MEMPHIS GOLD | | | |
| ❑ Stax 710 [M] | | 1966 | 25.00 |
| ❑ Stax S710 [S] | | 1966 | 30.00 |
| MEMPHIS GOLD VOLUME 2 | | | |
| ❑ Stax 726 [M] | | 1967 | 20.00 |
| ❑ Stax S726 [S] | | 1967 | 25.00 |
| THE MERCURY 40TH ANNIVERSARY V.S.O.P. ALBUM | | | |
| ❑ Mercury 824116-1 [(4)] | | 1985 | 40.00 |
| MERCURY LIVING PRESENCE | | | |
| ❑ Mercury Living Presence SR 90293 [S] | | 196? | 120.00 |
| *—Maroon label, no "Vendor: Mercury Record Corporation"; contains music by groups conducted by Paul Paray, Antal Dorati and Frederick Fennell* | | | |
| MERRY CHRISTMAS | | | |
| ❑ Coral CRL 56080 [10] | | 1952 | 80.00 |
| MERRY CHRISTMAS BABY (CHRISTMAS MUSIC FOR YOUNG LOVERS) | | | |
| ❑ Hollywood HLP 501 [M] | | 1956 | 120.00 |
| MERRY CHRISTMAS FROM CORAL RECORDS | | | |
| ❑ Coral CRL 57355 [M] | | 1960 | 20.00 |
| MERRY CHRISTMAS FROM MOTOWN | | | |
| ❑ Motown MS-681 | | 1968 | 30.00 |
| MERRY CHRISTMAS FROM... | | | |
| ❑ King 680 [M] | | 1959 | 200.00 |
| ❑ Reader's Digest RD4-83 [(4)] | | 1969 | 20.00 |
| *—Available only through Reader's Digest magazine by mail order* | | | |
| MERRY CHRISTMAS MUSIC/CHRISTMAS FAVORITES | | | |
| ❑ Plymouth P12-59 [M] | | 1952 | 20.00 |
| *—Artists not mentioned on jacket or label* | | | |
| MERRY CHRISTMAS TO YOU | | | |
| ❑ Capitol T 9030 [M] | | 1955 | 50.00 |
| METRONOME ALL STARS 1956 | | | |
| ❑ Clef MGC-743 [M] | | 1956 | 40.00 |
| ❑ Verve MGV-8030 [M] | | 1957 | 40.00 |
| ❑ Verve V-8030 [M] | | 1961 | 20.00 |
| METRONOME ALL-STARS | | | |
| ❑ Harmony HL 7044 [M] | | 1957 | 25.00 |
| ❑ RCA Camden CAL-426 [M] | | 1958 | 25.00 |
| THE METRONOME ALL-STARS | | | |
| ❑ Columbia CL 2528 [10] | | 1954 | 30.00 |

| Number | Title (A Side/B Side) | Yr | NM |
|---|---|---|---|
| MGM MILLION SELLERS: COUNTRY & WESTERN HITS, VOLUME 1 | | | |
| ❑ MGM E-3825 [M] | | 1960 | 25.00 |
| MGM RECORDS PARADE OF STARS | | | |
| ❑ MGM NP 90569 [M] | | 1965 | 20.00 |
| *—Capitol Record Club sampler of 12 MGM artists and soundtracks* | | | |
| MICHIGAN ROCKS | | | |
| ❑ Seeds and Stems 77001 [(2)] | | 1977 | 25.00 |
| MICKEY MOST PRESENTS BRITISH GO-GO | | | |
| ❑ MGM E 4306 [M] | | 1965 | 30.00 |
| ❑ MGM SE 4306 [R] | | 1965 | 30.00 |
| MICKEY MOST PRESENTS ENGLISH IN-GROUPS | | | |
| ❑ Metro M-577 [M] | | 1966 | 20.00 |
| ❑ Metro MS-577 [R] | | 1966 | 20.00 |
| MIDDLE OF THE ROAD | | | |
| ❑ Warner Bros. PRO 525 [(2)] | | 1972 | 30.00 |
| *—Originals have green labels* | | | |
| MIDNIGHT JAMBOREE | | | |
| ❑ Decca DL 4041 [M] | | 1961 | 25.00 |
| ❑ Decca DL 74041 [S] | | 1961 | 30.00 |
| MIDNIGHT JAZZ AT CARNEGIE HALL | | | |
| ❑ Verve MGV-8189-2 [(2)M] | | 1957 | 50.00 |
| ❑ Verve V-8189-2 [(2)M] | | 1961 | 25.00 |
| A MILLION OR MORE | | | |
| ❑ ABC-Paramount ABC-216 [M] | | 1959 | 80.00 |
| MILLION PERFORMANCE SONGS, VOLUME 1 | | | |
| ❑ Jobete JSA-6251 [DJ] | | 1988 | 20.00 |
| *—Promo-only publisher's demo* | | | |
| MILLION PERFORMANCE SONGS, VOLUME 2 | | | |
| ❑ Jobete JSA-6252 [DJ] | | 1988 | 20.00 |
| *—Promo-only publisher's demo* | | | |
| MILLION SELLER DANCE HITS | | | |
| ❑ Parkway P-7028 [M] | | 1963 | 30.00 |
| THE MILLION-AIRS | | | |
| ❑ Coral CRL 57310 [M] | | 1959 | 25.00 |
| THE MODERN IDIOM | | | |
| ❑ Capitol H 325 [10] | | 1952 | 60.00 |
| MODERN JAZZ | | | |
| ❑ London LL 1185 [M] | | 1955 | 20.00 |
| ❑ Tops L-1521 [M] | | 1958 | 20.00 |
| MODERN JAZZ CONCERT | | | |
| ❑ Adventures in Sound WL-127 [M] | | 1958 | 40.00 |
| MODERN JAZZ FESTIVAL | | | |
| ❑ Harmony HL 7196 [M] | | 1958 | 20.00 |
| MODERN JAZZ GALLERY | | | |
| ❑ Kapp KXL-5001 [M] | | 195? | 20.00 |
| MODERN JAZZ PIANO | | | |
| ❑ RCA Camden CAL-384 [M] | | 1958 | 25.00 |
| MODERN JAZZ SPECTACULAR | | | |
| ❑ Jazztone J-1231 [M] | | 1956 | 30.00 |
| MODERN JAZZ TRUMPETS | | | |
| ❑ Prestige PRLP-113 [10] | | 1951 | 200.00 |
| MODERN MOODS | | | |
| ❑ Moodsville MVLP-2 [M] | | 1961 | 40.00 |
| *—Green label* | | | |
| ❑ Moodsville MVLP-2 [M] | | 1965 | 20.00 |
| *—Blue label, trident logo at right* | | | |
| MOMENTS OF MOTOWN | | | |
| ❑ Motown PR-122 [DJ] | | 1983 | 50.00 |
| *—Promo-only item with narration and song snippets* | | | |
| MONARCH ALL STAR JAZZ, VOL. 1 | | | |
| ❑ Monarch LP-201 [10] | | 1952 | 50.00 |
| MONARCH ALL STAR JAZZ, VOL. 2 | | | |
| ❑ Monarch LP-202 [10] | | 1952 | 50.00 |
| MONARCH ALL STAR JAZZ, VOL. 3 | | | |
| ❑ Monarch LP-203 [10] | | 1952 | 50.00 |
| MONARCH ALL STAR JAZZ, VOL. 4 | | | |
| ❑ Monarch LP-204 [10] | | 1952 | 50.00 |
| MONARCH ALL STAR JAZZ, VOL. 5 | | | |
| ❑ Monarch LP-205 [10] | | 1952 | 50.00 |
| MONDAY NIGHT AT BIRDLAND | | | |
| ❑ Roulette R 52015 [M] | | 1958 | 30.00 |
| ❑ Roulette SR 52015 [S] | | 1959 | 30.00 |
| MONSTERS | | | |
| ❑ Warner Bros. PRO-A-796 [(2)] | | 1978 | 20.00 |
| MONTAGE | | | |
| ❑ Savoy MG-12029 [M] | | 1955 | 80.00 |
| THE MONTREUX '77 COLLECTION | | | |
| ❑ Pablo Live 2620107 [(8)] | | 1978 | 70.00 |
| MONUMENTAL COUNTRY HITS | | | |
| ❑ Monument SLP-18095 | | 1968 | 20.00 |
| MONUMENTAL POP HITS | | | |
| ❑ Monument SLP-18096 | | 1968 | 20.00 |
| MOOD IN BLUE | | | |
| ❑ Urania UJLP-1209 [M] | | 1955 | 30.00 |
| MOOD TO BE WOOED | | | |
| ❑ Cadet LP-784 [M] | | 1967 | 20.00 |
| ❑ Cadet LPS-784 [S] | | 1967 | 15.00 |
| MORE COUNTRY CLASSICS | | | |
| ❑ RCA Victor LPM-2467 [M] | | 1961 | 25.00 |
| ❑ RCA Victor LSP-2467 [S] | | 1961 | 30.00 |
| MORE COUNTRY MUSIC SPECTACULAR | | | |
| ❑ Starday SLP-140 [M] | | 1961 | 40.00 |
| MORE DRUMS ON FIRE | | | |
| ❑ World Pacific ST-1022 [S] | | 1960 | 30.00 |

| Number | Title (A Side/B Side) | Yr | NM |
|---|---|---|---|
| ❑ World Pacific WP-1261 [M] | | 1960 | 40.00 |
| MORE FOR YOUR MONEY | | | |
| ❑ Bell 6009 | | 1968 | 20.00 |
| MORE GOLD HITS, VOLUME 2 | | | |
| ❑ Warwick W 2044 [M] | | 1961 | 80.00 |
| MORE GOLDEN GREATS | | | |
| ❑ Liberty LRP-3548 [M] | | 1967 | 20.00 |
| ❑ Liberty LST-7548 [P] | | 1967 | 15.00 |
| MORE GREAT HITS OF 1964 AND OTHER GOLDEN GOODIES | | | |
| ❑ Vee Jay LP-1136 [M] | | 1965 | 30.00 |
| *—Not known to exist in stereo* | | | |
| MORE LIVE ECHOES OF THE SWINGING BANDS | | | |
| ❑ RCA Victor LPM-1983 [M] | | 1959 | 40.00 |
| ❑ RCA Victor LSP-1983 [S] | | 1959 | 50.00 |
| MORE SOLID GOLD PROGRAMMING | | | |
| ❑ Screen Gems/Columbia CPL-716/7 [(2)DJ] | | 1975 | 30.00 |
| *—Promo-only compilation of oldies sent to radio to spur airplay on songs owned by this publishing house; contains three Beatles recordings* | | | |
| THE MOST OF THE TWIST | | | |
| ❑ Roulette R 25176 [M] | | 1962 | 25.00 |
| *—Originals have a white label with colored spokes* | | | |
| THE MOST, VOLUME 1 | | | |
| ❑ Roulette R 52050 [M] | | 1960 | 20.00 |
| ❑ Roulette SR 52050 [S] | | 1960 | 25.00 |
| THE MOST, VOLUME 2 | | | |
| ❑ Roulette R 52053 [M] | | 1960 | 20.00 |
| ❑ Roulette SR 52053 [S] | | 1960 | 25.00 |
| THE MOST, VOLUME 3 | | | |
| ❑ Roulette R 52057 [M] | | 1961 | 20.00 |
| ❑ Roulette SR 52057 [S] | | 1961 | 25.00 |
| THE MOST, VOLUME 4 | | | |
| ❑ Roulette R 52062 [M] | | 1961 | 20.00 |
| ❑ Roulette SR 52062 [S] | | 1961 | 25.00 |
| THE MOST, VOLUME 5 | | | |
| ❑ Roulette R 52075 [M] | | 1961 | 20.00 |
| ❑ Roulette SR 52075 [S] | | 1961 | 25.00 |
| MOTOR CITY SCENE | | | |
| ❑ Bethlehem BCP-6056 [M] | | 1961 | 50.00 |
| THE MOTOR-TOWN REVIEW, VOL. 1 | | | |
| ❑ Motown MT 609 [M] | | 1963 | 40.00 |
| THE MOTOR-TOWN REVIEW, VOL. 2 | | | |
| ❑ Motown MT 615 [M] | | 1964 | 30.00 |
| THE MOTORTOWN REVIEW IN PARIS | | | |
| ❑ Tamla T 264 [M] | | 1965 | 25.00 |
| ❑ Tamla TS 264 [S] | | 1965 | 30.00 |
| THE MOTORTOWN REVUE LIVE! | | | |
| ❑ Motown MS-688 | | 1969 | 25.00 |
| A MOTOWN CHRISTMAS | | | |
| ❑ Motown M-795V2 [(2)] | | 1973 | 20.00 |
| MOTOWN INSTRUMENTALS | | | |
| ❑ Natural Resources NR 4002T1 | | 1978 | 20.00 |
| MOTOWN SHOW TUNES | | | |
| ❑ Natural Resources NR 4003T1 | | 1978 | 20.00 |
| MOTOWN SPECIAL | | | |
| ❑ Motown M 603 [M] | | 1962 | 80.00 |
| THE MOTOWN STORY: THE FIRST 25 YEARS | | | |
| ❑ Motown PR-121 [(7)DJ] | | 1983 | 250.00 |
| *—Promo-only box set with extra record not on the commercial release; labels are white* | | | |
| THE MOTOWN STORY: THE FIRST DECADE | | | |
| ❑ Motown MS-726 [(5)] | | 1971 | 30.00 |
| THE MOTOWN STORY: THE FIRST TWENTY-FIVE YEARS | | | |
| ❑ Motown 6048 ML5 [(5)] | | 1983 | 30.00 |
| MOTOWN WINNER'S CIRCLE: #1 HITS, VOL. 1 | | | |
| ❑ Gordy GS-935 | | 1969 | 25.00 |
| MOTOWN WINNER'S CIRCLE: #1 HITS, VOL. 2 | | | |
| ❑ Gordy GS-936 | | 1969 | 25.00 |
| MOTOWN WINNER'S CIRCLE: #1 HITS, VOL. 3 | | | |
| ❑ Gordy GS-943 | | 1969 | 25.00 |
| MOTOWN WINNER'S CIRCLE: #1 HITS, VOL. 4 | | | |
| ❑ Gordy GS-946 | | 1969 | 25.00 |
| MOTOWN WINNER'S CIRCLE: #1 HITS, VOL. 5 | | | |
| ❑ Gordy GS-950 | | 1970 | 25.00 |
| MOTOWN'S GREAT INTERPRETATIONS | | | |
| ❑ Natural Resources NR 4001T1 | | 1978 | 20.00 |
| MOUNTAIN FROLIC | | | |
| ❑ Brunswick BL 59000 [10] | | 1950 | 60.00 |
| MURRAY THE "K'S" SING ALONG WITH THE ORIGINAL GOLDEN GASSERS | | | |
| ❑ Roulette R 25159 [M] | | 1961 | 30.00 |
| MURRAY THE K — LIVE FROM THE BROOKLYN FOX | | | |
| ❑ KFM 1001 [M] | | 1963 | 40.00 |
| MURRAY THE K PRESENTS GOLDEN GASSERS FOR A DANCE PARTY | | | |
| ❑ Roulette R 25192 [M] | | 1962 | 25.00 |
| MURRAY THE K PRESENTS GOLDEN GASSERS FOR HAND HOLDERS | | | |
| ❑ Roulette R 25191 [M] | | 1962 | 25.00 |
| MURRAY THE K'S BLASTS FROM THE PAST | | | |
| ❑ Chess LP 1461 [M] | | 1961 | 40.00 |
| MURRAY THE K'S GASSERS FOR SUBMARINE RACE WATCHERS | | | |
| ❑ Chess LP 1470 [M] | | 1962 | 40.00 |



**Except when noted otherwise, VG = 25% of NM, and VG+ = 50% of NM. (Example: VG = $2.00, VG+ = $4.00 and NM = $8.00.)**

| Number | Title (A Side/B Side) | Yr | NM |
|---|---|---|---|
| | MURRAY THE K'S GOLDEN GASSERS | | |
| ❑ Chess LP 1458 NYC [M] | | 1961 | 150.00 |
| | *—New York version of "Golden Gassers," Chess 1458* | | |
| | MURRAY THE K'S NINETEEN-SIXTY TWO BOSS GOLDEN GASSERS | | |
| ❑ Scepter SP-510 [M] | | 1963 | 20.00 |
| ❑ Scepter SPS-510 [P] | | 1963 | 25.00 |
| | MUSIC AND PLUNK, TINKLE, TING-A-LING | | |
| ❑ Mercury Living Presence SR 90338 [S] | | 196? | 50.00 |
| | *—Maroon label, no "Vendor: Mercury Record Corporation"* | | |
| | MUSIC AND RHYTHM SAMPLER | | |
| ❑ PVC EP 2 [DJ] | | 1982 | 25.00 |
| | *—Includes XTC, Peter Gabriel, David Byrne, The (English) Beat; one-LP sampler of two-record set* | | |
| | MUSIC FOR FRUSTRATED CONDUCTORS | | |
| ❑ RCA Victor Red Seal LSC-2325 [S] | | 1959 | 50.00 |
| | *—Original with "shaded dog" label* | | |
| | MUSIC FOR THE BOY FRIEND…HE REALLY DIGS JAZZ | | |
| ❑ Decca DL 8314 [M] | | 1956 | 30.00 |
| | MUSIC FROM THE SOUTH, VOL. 1: COUNTRY BRASS BANDS | | |
| ❑ Folkways FA-2650 [M] | | 195? | 20.00 |
| | THE MUSIC OF NEW ORLEANS, VOL. 1 | | |
| ❑ Folkways FA-2461 [M] | | 1959 | 20.00 |
| | THE MUSIC OF NEW ORLEANS, VOL. 2 | | |
| ❑ Folkways FA-2462 [M] | | 1959 | 20.00 |
| | THE MUSIC OF NEW ORLEANS, VOL. 3: DANCE HALLS | | |
| ❑ Folkways FA-2463 [M] | | 1959 | 20.00 |
| | THE MUSIC OF NEW ORLEANS, VOL. 4: THE BIRTH OF JAZZ | | |
| ❑ Folkways FA-2464 [M] | | 1959 | 20.00 |
| | THE MUSIC OF NEW ORLEANS, VOL. 5: NEW ORLEANS JAZZ | | |
| ❑ Folkways FA-2465 [M] | | 1959 | 20.00 |
| | THE MUSIC PEOPLE | | |
| ❑ Columbia C3X 31280 [(3)] | | 1972 | 25.00 |
| | MUSIC TO READ JAMES BOND BY | | |
| ❑ United Artists UAL-3415 [M] | | 1965 | 20.00 |
| ❑ United Artists UAS-6415 [S] | | 1965 | 25.00 |
| | MUSIC TO READ JAMES BOND BY, VOL. 2 | | |
| ❑ United Artists UAL-3541 [M] | | 1966 | 20.00 |
| ❑ United Artists UAS-6541 [S] | | 1966 | 25.00 |
| | A MUSICAL HISTORY OF JAZZ | | |
| ❑ Grand Award GA 33-322 [M] | | 1955 | 20.00 |
| | MY FAIR LADY | | |
| ❑ Status ST-8315 [M] | | 1965 | 30.00 |
| | MY SON THE SURF NUT | | |
| ❑ Capitol ST 1939 [S] | | 1963 | 60.00 |
| ❑ Capitol T 1939 [M] | | 1963 | 50.00 |
| | THE NAMES OF DIXIELAND | | |
| ❑ Baronet B-108 [M] | | 195? | 20.00 |
| | NASCAR GOES COUNTRY | | |
| ❑ MCA 474 | | 1975 | 30.00 |
| | NASHVILLE BANDSTAND | | |
| ❑ King 813 [M] | | 1962 | 100.00 |
| | NASHVILLE BANDSTAND, VOLUME 2 | | |
| ❑ King 847 [M] | | 1963 | 80.00 |
| | NASHVILLE SATURDAY NIGHT | | |
| ❑ Nashville NLP-2009 [M] | | 1965 | 20.00 |
| ❑ Starday SLP-128 [M] | | 1961 | 40.00 |
| | NASHVILLE STEEL GUITAR | | |
| ❑ Nashville NLP-2017 [M] | | 1965 | 20.00 |
| ❑ Starday SLP-138 [M] | | 1961 | 30.00 |
| | NATIVE NEW ORLEANS JAZZ | | |
| ❑ Dot DLP-3009 [M] | | 1956 | 30.00 |
| | NEIGHBORHOOD RHYTHMS | | |
| ❑ Freeway 213 [(2)] | | 1984 | 40.00 |
| | NEW BLUE HORNS | | |
| ❑ Riverside RLP 12-294 [M] | | 1958 | 30.00 |
| | NEW CHAMBER JAZZ | | |
| ❑ Epic LN 1124 [10] | | 1955 | 30.00 |
| | NEW FACES AT NEWPORT | | |
| ❑ Metrojazz E-1005 [M] | | 1958 | 50.00 |
| ❑ Metrojazz SE-1005 [S] | | 1958 | 40.00 |
| | NEW ORLEANS BOUNCE: URBAN BLUES, VOLUME 2 | | |
| ❑ Imperial LP-94004 | | 1968 | 20.00 |
| | NEW ORLEANS DIXIELAND | | |
| ❑ Southland SLP-216 [M] | | 1955 | 25.00 |
| | NEW ORLEANS ENCORE | | |
| ❑ Riverside RLP-2503 [10] | | 1954 | 80.00 |
| | NEW ORLEANS EXPRESS | | |
| ❑ EmArcy MG-36022 [M] | | 1955 | 50.00 |
| | NEW ORLEANS HORNS | | |
| ❑ Riverside RLP-1005 [10] | | 1953 | 80.00 |
| | NEW ORLEANS JAZZ | | |
| ❑ Decca DL 5483 [10] | | 1953 | 50.00 |
| ❑ Decca DL 8283 [M] | | 1956 | 30.00 |
| | NEW ORLEANS JAZZ BABIES | | |
| ❑ Southland SLP-214 [M] | | 1955 | 25.00 |
| | NEW ORLEANS JAZZ KINGS | | |
| ❑ Southland SLP-217 [M] | | 1955 | 25.00 |
| | NEW ORLEANS JAZZ STARS | | |
| ❑ Southland SLP-211 [M] | | 1955 | 25.00 |
| | NEW ORLEANS LEGENDS | | |
| ❑ Riverside RLP 12-119 [M] | | 1957 | 40.00 |
| | NEW ORLEANS REVIVAL | | |
| ❑ Riverside RLP-1047 [10] | | 1954 | 80.00 |
| | NEW ORLEANS RHYTHM KINGS | | |
| ❑ Riverside RLP 12-102 [M] | | 195? | 60.00 |
| | *—Also see NEW ORLEANS RHYTHM KINGS in the main A-Z listings.* | | |
| | NEW ORLEANS STYLE | | |
| ❑ "X" LVA-3029 [10] | | 1954 | 80.00 |
| | NEW ORLEANS TO LOS ANGELES | | |
| ❑ Southland SLP-215 [M] | | 1955 | 25.00 |
| | NEW ORLEANS, OUR HOME TOWN | | |
| ❑ Imperial LP-9260 [M] | | 1964 | 25.00 |
| ❑ Imperial LP-12260 [R] | | 1964 | 20.00 |
| | NEW ORLEANS: THE LIVING LEGENDS | | |
| ❑ Riverside RLP-356/7 [(2)M] | | 196? | 50.00 |
| | *—Two records in gatefold jacket* | | |
| | NEW ORLEANS: THE LIVING LEGENDS, VOL. 1 | | |
| ❑ Riverside RLP-356 [M] | | 196? | 20.00 |
| | NEW ORLEANS: THE LIVING LEGENDS, VOL. 2 | | |
| ❑ Riverside RLP-357 [M] | | 196? | 20.00 |
| | NEW SOUNDS FROM SWEDEN, VOL. 1: THE DARING YOUNG SWEDES | | |
| ❑ Prestige PRLP-119 [10] | | 1951 | 400.00 |
| | NEW VOICES | | |
| ❑ Dawn DLP-1125 [M] | | 1956 | 80.00 |
| | THE NEW WAVE IN JAZZ | | |
| ❑ Impulse! A-90 [M] | | 1966 | 15.00 |
| ❑ Impulse! AS-90 [S] | | 1966 | 20.00 |
| | NEW YORK JAZZ OF THE TWENTIES | | |
| ❑ Riverside RLP-1048 [10] | | 1954 | 80.00 |
| | NEWPORT JAZZ FESTIVAL | | |
| ❑ RCA Victor LPM-3369 [M] | | 1965 | 15.00 |
| ❑ RCA Victor LSP-3369 [S] | | 1965 | 20.00 |
| | NEWPORT JAZZ FESTIVAL ALL STARS | | |
| ❑ Atlantic SD 1331 [S] | | 1961 | 30.00 |
| | *—Multicolor label, white "fan" logo at right* | | |
| | NEWPORT JAZZ FESTIVAL ALL-STARS | | |
| ❑ Atlantic 1331 [M] | | 1961 | 25.00 |
| | *—Multicolor label, white "fan" logo at right* | | |
| | A NIGHT AT THE BOULEVARD | | |
| ❑ Felsted FL-7503 [M] | | 1960 | 40.00 |
| | 1966 COUNTRY & WESTERN AWARD WINNERS | | |
| ❑ Decca DL 4837 [M] | | 1967 | 20.00 |
| ❑ Decca DL 74837 [S] | | 1967 | 20.00 |
| | THE 1969 WARNER/REPRISE RECORD SHOW | | |
| ❑ Warner Bros. PRO 336 [(2)] | | 1969 | 30.00 |
| | *—Originals have "W7" logos on labels* | | |
| ❑ Warner Bros. PRO 336 [(2)] | | 197? | 15.00 |
| | *—With "WB" logos on labels* | | |
| | THE 1969 WARNER/REPRISE SONGBOOK | | |
| ❑ Warner Bros. PRO 331 [(2)] | | 1969 | 30.00 |
| | *—The first of the famous Warner/Reprise "Loss Leaders" mail-order series; originals have "W7" logos on labels* | | |
| ❑ Warner Bros. PRO 331 [(2)] | | 197? | 15.00 |
| | *—With "WB" logos on labels* | | |
| | THE NITTY GRITTY | | |
| ❑ Vee Jay LP-1084 [M] | | 1964 | 30.00 |
| | *—Not known to exist in stereo* | | |
| | NO 'COUNT | | |
| ❑ Savoy MG-12078 [M] | | 1956 | 60.00 |
| | NO ENERGY CRISIS | | |
| ❑ ABC Impulse! AS-9267 [(2)] | | 1974 | 20.00 |
| | NO NUKES: THE MUSE CONCERTS FOR A NON-NUCLEAR FUTURE | | |
| ❑ Asylum ML-801 [(3)] | | 1979 | 25.00 |
| | NO SOUR GRAPES, JUST PURE JAZZ | | |
| ❑ Bethlehem BCP-92 [M] | | 1958 | 30.00 |
| | NO WAVE | | |
| ❑ A&M PR 4738 [DJ] | | 1978 | 25.00 |
| | *—White label promo on watercolor blue vinyl; numbered sticker on generic cover* | | |
| ❑ A&M SP-4738 | | 1978 | 8.00 |
| | *—Black vinyl* | | |
| ❑ A&M SP-4738 | | 1978 | 15.00 |
| | *—First pressing on watercolor blue vinyl* | | |
| | NON DAIRY CREAMER | | |
| ❑ Warner Bros. PRO 443 | | 1971 | 25.00 |
| | *—Originals have green labels* | | |
| | NORMAN GRANZ JAZZ CONCERT | | |
| ❑ Norgran MGN-2501 [M] | | 1954 | 80.00 |
| ❑ Norgran MGN-2502 [M] | | 1954 | 80.00 |
| | NOT SO QUIET ON THE WESTERN FRONT | | |
| ❑ Alternative Tentacles VIRUS 14 [(2)] | | 1982 | 25.00 |
| | *—Includes Dead Kennedys, Flipper, lots of others* | | |
| | NOTHING CHEESY ABOUT THIS JAZZ | | |
| ❑ Bethlehem BCP-85 [M] | | 1958 | 30.00 |
| | NOVA SCOTIA FOLK SONGS | | |
| ❑ Elektra EKL-23 [10] | | 1954 | 40.00 |
| | NUGGETS | | |
| ❑ Elektra 7E-2006 [(2)] | | 1972 | 40.00 |
| | O LOVE IS TEASIN': ANGLO-AMERICAN MOUNTAIN BALLADRY | | |
| ❑ Elektra 60402 [(3)] | | 1985 | 20.00 |
| | O. HENRY'S THE GIFT OF THE MAGI | | |
| ❑ E.F. MacDonald EFMX-62 | | 1962 | 20.00 |
| | *—Special album done by the E.F. MacDonald Company, Dayton, Ohio* | | |
| | OCEAN DRIVE | | |
| ❑ Beach Beat/Warner Special Products OP 2528W [(3)] | | 1981 | 20.00 |
| | OCTOBER '61 POP SAMPLER | | |
| ❑ RCA Victor SPS-33-141 [DJ] | | 1961 | 600.00 |
| | *—Promo-only collection.* | | |
| | OCTOBER 1960 POPULAR STEREO SAMPLER | | |
| ❑ RCA Victor SPS-33-96 [DJ] | | 1960 | 600.00 |
| | *—Promo-only collection* | | |
| | OCTOBER CHRISTMAS SAMPLER 59-40-41 | | |
| ❑ RCA Victor SPS-33-54 [DJ] | | 1959 | 600.00 |
| | *—Promo-only collection* | | |
| | THE OFFICIAL GRAMMY AWARDS ARCHIVE COLLECTION (ALBUM OF THE YEAR) | | |
| ❑ Franklin Mint GRAM-14 [(4)] | | 1985 | 60.00 |
| | THE OFFICIAL GRAMMY AWARDS ARCHIVE COLLECTION (ALL-TIME WINNERS) | | |
| ❑ Franklin Mint GRAM-2 [(4)] | | 1985 | 60.00 |
| | THE OFFICIAL GRAMMY AWARDS ARCHIVE COLLECTION (BEST NEW ARTIST) | | |
| ❑ Franklin Mint GRAM-6 [(4)] | | 1985 | 60.00 |
| | THE OFFICIAL GRAMMY AWARDS ARCHIVE COLLECTION (FOLK PERFORMANCES) | | |
| ❑ Franklin Mint GRAM-10 [(4)] | | 1985 | 60.00 |
| | THE OFFICIAL GRAMMY AWARDS ARCHIVE COLLECTION (GREAT PERFORMANCES OF THE ROCK ERA, VOL. 1) | | |
| ❑ Franklin Mint GRAM-3 [(4)] | | 1985 | 60.00 |
| | THE OFFICIAL GRAMMY AWARDS ARCHIVE COLLECTION (JAZZ VOCALISTS) | | |
| ❑ Franklin Mint GRAM-13 [(4)] | | 1985 | 60.00 |
| | THE OFFICIAL GRAMMY AWARDS ARCHIVE COLLECTION (POP PERFORMANCES, VOL. 1) | | |
| ❑ Franklin Mint GRAM-5 [(4)] | | 1985 | 60.00 |
| | THE OFFICIAL GRAMMY AWARDS ARCHIVE COLLECTION (RECORD OF THE YEAR) | | |
| ❑ Franklin Mint GRAM-1 [(4)] | | 1985 | 60.00 |
| | THE OFFICIAL GRAMMY AWARDS ARCHIVE COLLECTION (RHYTHM AND BLUES, VOL. 1) | | |
| ❑ Franklin Mint GRAM-8 [(4)] | | 1985 | 70.00 |
| | THE OFFICIAL GRAMMY AWARDS ARCHIVE COLLECTION (SONG OF THE YEAR) | | |
| ❑ Franklin Mint GRAM-9 [(4)] | | 1985 | 60.00 |
| | THE OFFICIAL GRAMMY AWARDS ARCHIVE COLLECTION (STAGE & ORIGINAL CAST RECORDINGS) | | |
| ❑ Franklin Mint GRAM-11 [(4)] | | 1985 | 120.00 |
| | THE OFFICIAL GRAMMY AWARDS ARCHIVE COLLECTION (THE BIG BAND SOUND) | | |
| ❑ Franklin Mint GRAM-7 [(4)] | | 1985 | 60.00 |
| | THE OFFICIAL GRAMMY AWARDS ARCHIVE COLLECTION (THE GREAT SINGERS) | | |
| ❑ Franklin Mint GRAM-4 [(4)] | | 1985 | 150.00 |
| | THE OFFICIAL GRAMMY AWARDS ARCHIVE COLLECTION (THE PRODUCER'S CHOICE) | | |
| ❑ Franklin Mint GRAM-12 [(4)] | | 1985 | 60.00 |
| | OLD 'N GOLDEN | | |
| ❑ Jamie JLPS-3031 | | 1968 | 20.00 |
| | OLD AND HEAVY GOLD 1955 | | |
| ❑ Economic Consultants 1955 | | 1973 | 20.00 |
| | OLD AND HEAVY GOLD 1956 | | |
| ❑ Economic Consultants 1956 | | 1973 | 30.00 |
| | OLD AND HEAVY GOLD 1957 | | |
| ❑ Economic Consultants 1957 | | 1973 | 30.00 |
| | OLD AND HEAVY GOLD 1958 | | |
| ❑ Economic Consultants 1958 | | 1973 | 30.00 |
| | OLD AND HEAVY GOLD 1959 | | |
| ❑ Economic Consultants 1959 | | 1973 | 20.00 |
| | OLD AND HEAVY GOLD 1960 | | |
| ❑ Economic Consultants 1960 | | 1973 | 30.00 |
| | OLD AND HEAVY GOLD 1961 | | |
| ❑ Economic Consultants 1961 | | 1973 | 30.00 |
| | OLD AND HEAVY GOLD 1962 | | |
| ❑ Economic Consultants 1962 | | 1973 | 30.00 |
| | OLD AND HEAVY GOLD 1963 | | |
| ❑ Economic Consultants 1963 | | 1973 | 20.00 |
| | OLD AND HEAVY GOLD 1964 | | |
| ❑ Economic Consultants 1964 | | 1973 | 20.00 |
| | *—Original magazine ads claimed that six Beatles tracks would appear on this LP; they were replaced before release* | | |
| | OLD AND HEAVY GOLD 1965 | | |
| ❑ Economic Consultants 1965 | | 1973 | 20.00 |
| | *—Original magazine ads claimed that three Beatles tracks would appear on this LP; they were replaced before release* | | |
| | OLD AND HEAVY GOLD 1966 | | |
| ❑ Economic Consultants 1966 | | 1973 | 20.00 |
| | OLD AND HEAVY GOLD 1967 | | |
| ❑ Economic Consultants 1967 | | 1973 | 20.00 |
| | *—Original magazine ads claimed that a Beatles track would appear on this LP; it was replaced with another track before release* | | |
| | OLD AND HEAVY GOLD 1968 | | |
| ❑ Economic Consultants 1968 | | 1973 | 20.00 |
| | *—Original magazine ads claimed that a Beatles track would appear on this LP; it was replaced with another track before release* | | |

OLD AND HEAVY GOLD 1969
❑ Economic Consultants 1969 1973 20.00
*—Original magazine ads claimed that a Beatles track would appear on this LP; it was replaced with another track before release*
OLD AND HEAVY GOLD 1970
❑ Economic Consultants 1970 1973 20.00
*—Original magazine ads claimed that a Beatles track would appear on this LP; it was replaced with another track before release*
OLD AND HEAVY GOLD 1971
❑ Economic Consultants 1971 1973 20.00
*—Original magazine ads claimed that a Paul McCartney track would appear on this LP; it was replaced with another track before release*
AN OLD FASHIONED CHRISTMAS
❑ Reader's Digest RDA 216-A [(6)] 197? 20.00
*—Available only through Reader's Digest magazine by mail order*
OLD TIME BANJO PROJECT
❑ Elektra EKL-276 [M] 1964 20.00
❑ Elektra EKS-7276 [S] 1964 25.00
OLDIES BUT GOODIES
❑ Original Sound LPM-5001 [M] 1959 50.00
*—Original pressing with no reference to other volumes on the back cover*
❑ Original Sound LPM-5001 [M] 1960s 12.00
*—Later editions with later volumes in the series on the back cover*
OLDIES BUT GOODIES, VOL. 2
❑ Original Sound LPM-5003 [M] 1960 40.00
*—Original pressing with no reference to later volumes on the back cover*
❑ Original Sound LPM-5003 [M] 1960s 12.00
*—Later editions with later volumes in the series on the back cover*
OLDIES BUT GOODIES, VOL. 3
❑ Original Sound LPM-5004 [M] 1960s 12.00
*—Later editions with later volumes in the series on the back cover*
❑ Original Sound LPM-5004 [M] 1961 30.00
*—Original pressing with no reference to later volumes on the back cover*
OLDIES BUT GOODIES, VOL. 4
❑ Original Sound LPM-5005 [M] 1960s 12.00
*—Later editions with later volumes in the series on the back cover*
❑ Original Sound LPM-5005 [M] 1962 30.00
*—Original pressing with no reference to later volumes on the back cover*
OLDIES BUT GOODIES, VOL. 5
❑ Original Sound LPM-5007 [M] 1960s 12.00
*—Later editions with later volumes in the series on the back cover*
❑ Original Sound LPM-5007 [M] 1963 20.00
*—Original pressing with no reference to later volumes on the back cover*
OLDIES BUT GOODIES, VOL. 6
❑ Original Sound LPM-5011 [M] 1960s 12.00
*—Later editions with later volumes in the series on the back cover*
❑ Original Sound LPM-5011 [M] 1963 20.00
*—Original pressing with no reference to later volumes on the back cover*
OLDIES BUT GOODIES, VOL. 7
❑ Original Sound LPM-5012 [M] 1960s 12.00
*—Later editions with later volumes in the series on the back cover*
❑ Original Sound LPM-5012 [M] 1964 20.00
*—Original pressing with no reference to later volumes on the back cover*
OLDIES BY THE DOZEN
❑ Parkway P-7035 [M] 1963 30.00
OLDIES BY THE DOZEN, VOLUME 2
❑ Parkway P-7041 [M] 1964 50.00
*—With bonus 45 of "The Twist" by Chubby Checker on on side and "Mashed Potato Time" by Dee Dee Sharp on the other; deduct 40 percent if missing*
OLDIES DANCE PARTY, VOLUME 1
❑ Oldies 33 OL-8001 [M] 1963 20.00
OLDIES DANCE PARTY, VOLUME 2
❑ Oldies 33 OL-8002 [M] 1963 20.00
OLDIES IN HI-FI
❑ Chess LP 1439 [DJ] 1959 600.00
*—Multi-color splash vinyl*
❑ Chess LP 1439 [M] 1959 300.00
*—Black vinyl*
OLIO
❑ Prestige PRLP-7084 [M] 1957 250.00
*—Yellow label with W. 50th St. address*
ON STAGE AT THE GRAND OLE OPRY
❑ Decca DL 4393 [M] 1964 25.00
❑ Decca DL 74393 [S] 1964 30.00
ON-THE-ROAD JAZZ
❑ Riverside RLP 12-127 [M] 1957 40.00
ONE DOZEN GOLDIES
❑ Carlton LP 12-121 [M] 1960 50.00
100 HALL OF FAME OLDIES
❑ Vee-Jay HHF-6833/4/5/6/7 [(5)] 197? 100.00
*—Mail-order offer that was sent to buyers in a cardboard mailer; price includes mailer; no other cover was issued*
ONE NIGHT STAND: A KEYBOARD EVENT
❑ Columbia KC2 37100 [(2)] 198? 12.00
*—"Half-Speed Mastered" edition*
❑ Columbia HC2 47100 [(2)] 198? 50.00
ONE NIGHT WITH BLUE NOTE PRESERVED
❑ Blue Note BTDK-85117 [(4)] 1985 60.00
ONE WORLD JAZZ
❑ Adventures in Sound WL-162 [M] 1959 50.00

**Number Title (A Side/B Side) Yr NM**

❑ Adventures in Sound WS-314 [S] 1959 40.00
OPENING NIGHTS AT THE MET
❑ RCA Victor Red Seal LM-6171 [(3)M] 1966 20.00
OPERA FOR PEOPLE WHO HATE OPERA
❑ RCA Victor Red Seal LSC-2391 [S] 1960 20.00
*—Original with "shaded dog" label*
OPRY OLD TIMERS
❑ Starday SLP-182 [M] 1962 30.00
OPRY TIME IN TENNESSEE
❑ Starday SLP-177 [M] 1962 30.00
OPUS DE BLUES
❑ Savoy MG-12142 [M] 1959 60.00
OPUS DE JAZZ
❑ Savoy MG-12036 [M] 1955 80.00
OPUS IN SWING
❑ Savoy MG-12085 [M] 1956 60.00
THE ORCHESTRA "HOUSE OF SOUND"
❑ Brunswick BL 54003 [M] 1954 30.00
THE ORGAN PLAYS MUSIC FOR A MERRY CHRISTMAS
❑ Reader's Digest RDA 42-A [(4)] 1966 20.00
*—Available only through Reader's Digest magazine by mail order*
ORIGINAL BLUE NOTE JAZZ, VOL. 1
❑ Blue Note B-6504 1969 20.00
ORIGINAL BLUE NOTE JAZZ, VOL. 2
❑ Blue Note B-6506 1970 20.00
THE ORIGINAL COUNTRY HITS #1
❑ Liberty LRP-3305 [M] 1963 20.00
THE ORIGINAL COUNTRY HITS #2
❑ Liberty LRP-3345 [M] 1964 20.00
THE ORIGINAL COUNTRY HITS #3
❑ Liberty LRP-3382 [M] 1964 20.00
ORIGINAL GOLDIES FROM THE FABULOUS '50S, VOLUME 1
❑ Josie JM-4002 [M] 1963 60.00
ORIGINAL GOLDIES FROM THE FABULOUS '50S, VOLUME 2
❑ Josie JM-4003 [M] 1963 60.00
ORIGINAL GOLDIES FROM THE FABULOUS '50S, VOLUME 3
❑ Josie JM-4004 [M] 1963 60.00
THE ORIGINAL GREATEST HITS OF THE GREAT COUNTRY AND WESTERN STARS
❑ Mercury MG-20825 [M] 1963 20.00
❑ Mercury SR-60825 [S] 1963 25.00
ORIGINAL HIT RECORDS
❑ Roulette R 25106 [M] 1960 30.00
*—Originals have a white label with colored spokes*
THE ORIGINAL HITS, PAST & PRESENT
❑ Liberty LRP-3178 [M] 1960 20.00
THE ORIGINAL HITS, VOLUME 10
❑ Liberty LRP-3344 [M] 1964 20.00
THE ORIGINAL HITS, VOLUME 11
❑ Liberty LRP-3418 [M] 1965 20.00
❑ Liberty LST-7418 [P] 1965 20.00
THE ORIGINAL HITS, VOLUME 3: PAST & PRESENT
❑ Liberty LRP-3187 [M] 1961 20.00
THE ORIGINAL HITS, VOLUME 4
❑ Liberty LRP-3200 [M] 1962 20.00
*—Reissue of "Memories Are Made of Hits"; for "The Original Hits, Volume 5," see "15 Hits: The Original Recordings"*
THE ORIGINAL HITS, VOLUME 6
❑ Liberty LRP-3260 [M] 1962 20.00
THE ORIGINAL HITS, VOLUME 7: ALL-TIME HIT INSTRUMENTALS
❑ Liberty LRP-3274 [M] 1963 20.00
THE ORIGINAL HITS, VOLUME 8
❑ Liberty LRP-3288 [M] 1963 20.00
THE ORIGINAL HITS, VOLUME 9
❑ Liberty LRP-3325 [M] 1963 20.00
THE ORIGINAL HITS, VOLUME TWO: PAST & PRESENT
❑ Liberty LRP-3180 [M] 1961 20.00
THE ORIGINAL HOOTENANNY
❑ Crestview CRV 806 [M] 1963 20.00
❑ Crestview CRS 7806 [S] 1963 25.00
ORIGINAL MEMPHIS ROCK AND ROLL, VOLUME 1
❑ Sun 116 1970 20.00
ORIGINAL MOTION PICTURE HIT THEMES
❑ United Artists UAL-3197 [M] 1962 15.00
❑ United Artists UAS-6197 [S] 1962 20.00
THE ORIGINAL R&B HITS, VOLUME 1
❑ Liberty LRP-3381 [M] 1964 20.00
ORIGINAL RECORDINGS BY THE ARTISTS WHO MADE THEM HITS
❑ Flip 1002 [M] 1960 400.00
ORIGINAL ROCK OLDIES, VOLUME 1
❑ Specialty SPS-2129 1970 20.00
ORIGINAL ROCK OLDIES, VOLUME 2
❑ Specialty SPS-2130 1970 20.00
THE ORIGINAL SOUND OF THE 20'S
❑ Columbia C3L 35 [(3)] 1965 40.00
ORIGINAL SURFIN' HITS
❑ GNP Crescendo GNP-84 [M] 1963 40.00
*—With bonus photos; deduct 25-50 percent if missing*
❑ GNP Crescendo GNPS-84 [S] 1963 50.00
*—With bonus photos; deduct 25-50 percent if missing*

**Number Title (A Side/B Side) Yr NM**

OUR BEST
❑ Clef MGC-639 [M] 1955 50.00
❑ Norgran MGN-1021 [M] 1955 80.00
OUR BEST TO YOU
❑ Everlast ELP-201 [M] 1960 200.00
OUR SIGNIFICANT HITS
❑ Specialty SP-2112 [M] 1960 120.00
*—Gold and black label*
OUR SINGING HERITAGE, VOL. 1
❑ Elektra EKL-151 [M] 1958 25.00
OUR SINGING HERITAGE, VOL. 2
❑ Elektra EKL-152 [M] 1958 25.00
OUTSTANDING JAZZ COMPOSITIONS OF THE 20TH CENTURY
❑ Columbia C2L 31 [(2)M] 1964 20.00
A PACKAGE OF 16 BIG HITS
❑ Motown MS 614 [S] 1966 30.00
*—No "package" on cover; contains alternate stereo versions of "Please Mr. Postman" by the Marvelettes and "Do You Love Me" by the Contours*
❑ Motown MT 614 [M] 1964 100.00
*—"Package" cover*
❑ Motown MT 614 [M] 1966 20.00
*—No "package" on cover*
PAJAMA PARTY
❑ Forum F-9006 [M] 196? 30.00
*—Reissue of Roulette 25021*
❑ Forum SF-9006 [R] 196? 20.00
❑ Roulette R 25021 [M] 1958 40.00
*—Originals have a black label*
❑ Roulette R 25021 [M] 1959 25.00
*—Second pressings have a white label with colored spokes*
❑ Roulette SR 25021 [R] 196? 12.00
PANORAMA OF BRITISH JAZZ
❑ Discovery DL-2001 [10] 1953 50.00
PARTY AFTER HOURS
❑ Aladdin LP-703 [10] 1950 4000.
*—Black vinyl*
❑ Aladdin LP-703 [10] 1950 8000.
*—Red vinyl*
PEACHES: "PICK OF THE CROP"
❑ Capricorn PRO 588 [(2)] 1974 25.00
THE PEOPLE'S RECORD
❑ Warner Bros. PRO 645 [(2)] 1976 20.00
PERCUSSION UNABRIDGED
❑ Kimberly 2022 [M] 1963 20.00
❑ Kimberly 11022 [S] 1963 25.00
PERFECT FOR DANCING: ALL TEMPOS
❑ RCA Victor LPM-1072 [M] 1954 30.00
PERFECT FOR DANCING: FOX TROTS
❑ RCA Victor LPM-1070 [M] 1954 30.00
PERFECT FOR DANCING: JITTERBUG OR LINDY
❑ RCA Victor LPM-1071 [M] 1954 30.00
PERIOD'S JAZZ DIGEST
❑ Period SPL-302 [M] 1956 50.00
PERIOD'S JAZZ DIGEST VOL. 2
❑ Period SPL-304 [M] 1955 50.00
PETAL PUSHERS
❑ Chess LP 1520 [M] 1967 25.00
❑ Chess LPS 1520 [S] 1967 25.00
THE PHIL SPECTOR SPECTACULAR
❑ Philles PHLP 100 [DJ] 1972 1500.
*—Not issued with cover*
PHIL SPECTOR'S CHRISTMAS ALBUM
❑ Apple SW 3400 [M] 1972 30.00
*—Reissue of A CHRSTMAS GIFT FOR YOU FROM PHILLES RECORDS; third edition of this group of songs; completely different cover with Phil Spector dressed as Santa Claus and wearing a "Back to Mono" button*
❑ Passport PB 3604 [S] 1984 12.00
*—Sixth edition of this group of songs; Phil Spector-as-Santa Claus' "Back to Mono" button is airbrushed off the cover; the last version of this LP to appear in true stereo*
❑ Pavillion PZ 37686 [S] 1981 15.00
*—Fifth edition of this group of songs; Phil Spector-as-Santa Claus' "Back to Mono" button is airbrushed off the cover; once again, this LP is true stereo*
❑ Warner/Spector SP 9103 [S] 1974 20.00
*—Fourth edition of this group of songs; similar cover to third edition; despite the cover's "Authentic Mono" statement and Phil Spector-as-Santa Claus' "Back to Mono" button, this album is in true stereo!*
PHIL SPECTOR'S GREATEST HITS
❑ Warner/Spector 2SP 9104 [(2)] 1977 40.00
PHIL SPECTOR: BACK TO MONO 1958-1969
❑ Phil Spector/Abkco 7118-1 [(5)] 1991 80.00
*—Box set; Sides 9 and 10 are the final vinyl reissue of A Christmas Gift for You from Phil Spector*
PIANISTS GALORE
❑ Pacific Jazz JWC-506 [M] 1957 50.00
❑ World Pacific JWC-506 [M] 1958 40.00
PIANO ARTISTRY
❑ Audiophile AP-28 [M] 1953 30.00
PIANO GIANTS
❑ Prestige 24052 [(2)] 197? 15.00
PIANO IN STYLE
❑ MCA 1332 198? 10.00
PIANO INTERPRETATIONS
❑ Norgran MGN-1036 [M] 1955 80.00

| Number | Title (A Side/B Side) | Yr | NM |
|---|---|---|---|
| ❑ Verve MGV-8125 [M] | | 1957 | 30.00 |
| ❑ Verve V-8125 [M] | | 1961 | 20.00 |
| PIANO JAZZ, VOLUME 1 | | | |
| ❑ Brunswick BL 54014 [M] | | 1955 | 30.00 |
| PIANO JAZZ, VOLUME 2 | | | |
| ❑ Brunswick BL 54015 [M] | | 1955 | 30.00 |
| PIANO MUSIC FOR PARTIES | | | |
| ❑ Columbia CL 603 [M] | | 1955 | 25.00 |
| PIANO MUSIC FOR TWO | | | |
| ❑ Columbia CL 602 [M] | | 1955 | 25.00 |
| PIANO ROLL TRANSCRIPTIONS | | | |
| ❑ Riverside RLP 12-110 [M] | | 1956 | 40.00 |
| ❑ Riverside RLP 12-126 [M] | | 1957 | 40.00 |
| PIANO STYLISTS | | | |
| ❑ Capitol H 323 [10] | | 1952 | 50.00 |
| PIANO VARIATIONS | | | |
| ❑ King 540 [M] | | 1956 | — |
| *—See ERROLL GARNER.* | | | |
| PICK HITS OF THE RADIO GOOD GUYS | | | |
| ❑ Laurie LLP-2021 [M] | | 1963 | 30.00 |
| ❑ Laurie SLP-2021 [R] | | 196? | 15.00 |
| PICK HITS OF THE RADIO GOOD GUYS, VOLUME 2 | | | |
| ❑ Laurie LLP-2026 [M] | | 1964 | 25.00 |
| ❑ Laurie SLP-2026 [R] | | 196? | 15.00 |
| PICK OF THE COUNTRY | | | |
| ❑ RCA Victor LPM-2094 [M] | | 1960 | 25.00 |
| ❑ RCA Victor LSP-2094 [S] | | 1960 | 30.00 |
| THE PICK OF THE COUNTRY, VOLUME 2 | | | |
| ❑ RCA Victor LPM-2956 [M] | | 1964 | 20.00 |
| ❑ RCA Victor LSP-2956(e) [R] | | 1964 | 15.00 |
| PICK UP THE BEAT | | | |
| ❑ Epic LN 3127 [M] | | 1955 | 30.00 |
| PIONEERS OF BOOGIE WOOGIE | | | |
| ❑ Riverside RLP-1009 [10] | | 1953 | 80.00 |
| PIONEERS OF BOOGIE WOOGIE, VOL. 2 | | | |
| ❑ Riverside RLP-1034 [10] | | 1954 | 80.00 |
| PITTSBURGH'S GREATEST HITS | | | |
| ❑ Itzy 101 [(2)] | | 1966 | 50.00 |
| PLAYBOY ALL STARS VOLUME 1 | | | |
| ❑ Playboy PB-1957 [(2)M] | | 1957 | 40.00 |
| PLAYBOY ALL STARS VOLUME 2 | | | |
| ❑ Playboy PB-1958 [(2)M] | | 1958 | 40.00 |
| PLAYBOY ALL STARS VOLUME 3 | | | |
| ❑ Playboy PB-1959 [(3)M] | | 1959 | 60.00 |
| PLAYBOY MUSIC HALL OF FAME WINNERS | | | |
| ❑ Playboy PB-7473 [(3)] | | 1978 | 200.00 |
| *—One of very few compilation LPs to contain both an Elvis and a Beatles track!* | | | |
| POLKAS | | | |
| ❑ Audio Lab AL-1543 [M] | | 1959 | 40.00 |
| POP COUNTRY HITS | | | |
| ❑ RCA Victor LPM-2949 [M] | | 1964 | 15.00 |
| ❑ RCA Victor LSP-2949 [S] | | 1964 | 20.00 |
| POP HIT PARTY | | | |
| ❑ Columbia CL 1237 [M] | | 195? | 20.00 |
| POP ORIGINS | | | |
| ❑ Chess LP 1544 [M] | | 1969 | 25.00 |
| POP PARADE | | | |
| ❑ MGM E-194 [10] | | 1953 | 50.00 |
| POP SHOPPER | | | |
| ❑ RCA Victor SPL-12/13 [M] | | 1955 | 30.00 |
| POPULAR FAVORITES | | | |
| ❑ Columbia CL 6057 [10] | | 1949 | 40.00 |
| THE POPULAR GOLD ALBUM | | | |
| ❑ Capitol T 972 [M] | | 1958 | 30.00 |
| PORGY AND BESS | | | |
| ❑ Bethlehem EXLP-1 [(3)M] | | 1956 | 70.00 |
| ❑ Bethlehem BCP-6040 [M] | | 1959 | 30.00 |
| A POT OF FLOWERS | | | |
| ❑ Mainstream S-6100 [S] | | 1967 | 100.00 |
| ❑ Mainstream 56100 [M] | | 1967 | 80.00 |
| POT OF GOLDEN GOODIES | | | |
| ❑ Herald HLP-1015 [M] | | 1962 | 150.00 |
| A POTPOURRI OF JAZZ | | | |
| ❑ Verve MGV-2032 [M] | | 1956 | 40.00 |
| ❑ Verve V-2032 [M] | | 1961 | 20.00 |
| THE POWER AND THE MAJESTY: RAIN 'N' TRAIN DEMONSTRATION DISC | | | |
| ❑ Mobile Fidelity 1-004 | | 1979 | 50.00 |
| *—Audiophile vinyl* | | | |
| PRESTIGE GROOVY GOODIES, VOL. 1 | | | |
| ❑ Prestige PRLP-7298 [M] | | 1964 | 30.00 |
| ❑ Prestige PRST-7298 [R] | | 1964 | 20.00 |
| PRIMITIVE PIANO | | | |
| ❑ Tone 1 [M] | | 195? | 30.00 |
| PROGRESSIVE PIANO | | | |
| ❑ RCA Victor LJM-3001 [10] | | 1952 | 50.00 |
| PROPAGANDA | | | |
| ❑ A&M SP-4786 | | 1979 | 20.00 |
| *—Includes poster* | | | |
| PUMPING VINYL | | | |
| ❑ Warner Bros. PRO-A-773 [(2)] | | 1977 | 20.00 |
| PURE MAGIC: THE SONGS OF PAM SAWYER & MARILYN MCLEOD | | | |
| ❑ Jobete PRO-1A [DJ] | | 1978 | 40.00 |
| *—Promo-only publisher's demo with short excerpts of songs* | | | |

| Number | Title (A Side/B Side) | Yr | NM |
|---|---|---|---|
| QSP PRESENTS A GIFT OF MUSIC | | | |
| ❑ RCA Special Products QSP1-0034 | | 1984 | 50.00 |
| RADAR BLUES | | | |
| ❑ King KLP-1050 [M] | | 1969 | 30.00 |
| RADIO RADIO/SOUL TWIST/YOU'VE GOTTA BE CRUEL TO BE KIND | | | |
| ❑ Columbia AS 443 [DJ] | | 1979 | 40.00 |
| *—Includes Elvis Costello, Mink DeVille, Nick Lowe; promo-only 3-song sampler on orange vinyl* | | | |
| RADIO SMASH FLASHBACKS: DRIVE TIME | | | |
| ❑ Laurie LLP-2028 [M] | | 1964 | 25.00 |
| ❑ Laurie SLP-2028 [R] | | 196? | 15.00 |
| RADIO SMASH FLASHBACKS: PRIME TIME | | | |
| ❑ Laurie LLP-2029 [M] | | 1964 | 25.00 |
| ❑ Laurie SLP-2029 [R] | | 196? | 15.00 |
| RAGTIME PIANO ROLL, VOL. 1 | | | |
| ❑ Riverside RLP-1006 [10] | | 1953 | 100.00 |
| RAGTIME PIANO ROLL, VOL. 2 | | | |
| ❑ Riverside RLP-1025 [10] | | 1954 | 80.00 |
| RAGTIME PIANO ROLL, VOL. 3 | | | |
| ❑ Riverside RLP-1049 [10] | | 1954 | 80.00 |
| RAGTIMERS' IMMORTAL PERFORMANCES | | | |
| ❑ RCA Victor LPT-1000 [M] | | 1954 | 30.00 |
| RAILROAD SONGS | | | |
| ❑ King 869 [M] | | 1963 | 70.00 |
| RAREWERKS | | | |
| ❑ Astralwerks ASW 50717 [(2)] | | 2001 | 20.00 |
| RAT MUSIC FOR RAT PEOPLE | | | |
| ❑ Go 003 | | 1982 | 20.00 |
| THE RCA VICTOR ENCYCLOPEDIA OF RECORDED JAZZ, ALBUM 1 | | | |
| ❑ RCA Victor LEJ-1 [10] | | 1956 | 40.00 |
| THE RCA VICTOR ENCYCLOPEDIA OF RECORDED JAZZ, ALBUM 2 | | | |
| ❑ RCA Victor LEJ-2 [10] | | 1956 | 40.00 |
| THE RCA VICTOR ENCYCLOPEDIA OF RECORDED JAZZ, ALBUM 3 | | | |
| ❑ RCA Victor LEJ-3 [10] | | 1956 | 40.00 |
| THE RCA VICTOR ENCYCLOPEDIA OF RECORDED JAZZ, ALBUM 4 | | | |
| ❑ RCA Victor LEJ-4 [10] | | 1956 | 40.00 |
| THE RCA VICTOR ENCYCLOPEDIA OF RECORDED JAZZ, ALBUM 5 | | | |
| ❑ RCA Victor LEJ-5 [10] | | 1956 | 40.00 |
| THE RCA VICTOR ENCYCLOPEDIA OF RECORDED JAZZ, ALBUM 6 | | | |
| ❑ RCA Victor LEJ-6 [10] | | 1956 | 40.00 |
| THE RCA VICTOR ENCYCLOPEDIA OF RECORDED JAZZ, ALBUM 7 | | | |
| ❑ RCA Victor LEJ-7 [10] | | 1956 | 40.00 |
| THE RCA VICTOR ENCYCLOPEDIA OF RECORDED JAZZ, ALBUM 8 | | | |
| ❑ RCA Victor LEJ-8 [10] | | 1956 | 40.00 |
| THE RCA VICTOR ENCYCLOPEDIA OF RECORDED JAZZ, ALBUM 9 | | | |
| ❑ RCA Victor LEJ-9 [10] | | 1956 | 40.00 |
| THE RCA VICTOR ENCYCLOPEDIA OF RECORDED JAZZ, ALBUM 10 | | | |
| ❑ RCA Victor LEJ-10 [10] | | 1956 | 40.00 |
| THE RCA VICTOR ENCYCLOPEDIA OF RECORDED JAZZ, ALBUM 11 | | | |
| ❑ RCA Victor LEJ-11 [10] | | 1956 | 40.00 |
| THE RCA VICTOR ENCYCLOPEDIA OF RECORDED JAZZ, ALBUM 12 | | | |
| ❑ RCA Victor LEJ-12 [10] | | 1956 | 40.00 |
| REACH OUT AND TOUCH | | | |
| ❑ Reader's Digest RBA-037A [(7)] | | 1991 | 50.00 |
| THE REAL AMBASSADORS | | | |
| ❑ Columbia OS 2250 [S] | | 1962 | 25.00 |
| ❑ Columbia CL 5850 [M] | | 1962 | 20.00 |
| THE REAL BLUES | | | |
| ❑ Excello LPS-8011 [R] | | 1969 | 20.00 |
| REBIRTH OF BEALE STREET | | | |
| ❑ Beale Street BS-1 | | 1983 | 200.00 |
| *—Limited edition of 1,000 made for the city of Memphis* | | | |
| RECORD HOP | | | |
| ❑ Decca DL 8067 [M] | | 1955 | 30.00 |
| RECORDED IN NEW ORLEANS, VOL. 1 | | | |
| ❑ Good Time Jazz L-12019 [M] | | 1955 | 20.00 |
| RECORDED IN NEW ORLEANS, VOL. 2 | | | |
| ❑ Good Time Jazz L-12020 [M] | | 1955 | 20.00 |
| RECORDED ON LOCATION AT THE FIVE SPOT CAFE IN NEW YORK CITY...A MEMORIAL CONCERT DEDICATED TO THE MUSIC OF CHARLIE PARKER | | | |
| ❑ Signal S-1204 [M] | | 1957 | 200.00 |
| RED BIRD GOLDIES | | | |
| ❑ Red Bird LP 20-102 [M] | | 1965 | 80.00 |
| RED HOT AND BLUE JAZZ | | | |
| ❑ Waldorf Music Hall MH 33-141 [10] | | 195? | 200.00 |
| REGGAE CHRISTMAS BY THE JOE GIBBS FAMILY OF ARTISTS | | | |
| ❑ Joe Gibbs Music 8077 | | 1982 | 20.00 |
| RELAXED SAXOPHONE MOODS | | | |
| ❑ Prestige PRLP-141 [10] | | 1953 | 100.00 |

| Number | Title (A Side/B Side) | Yr | NM |
|---|---|---|---|
| REMEMBER THE OLDIES | | | |
| ❑ Argo LP-649 [M] | | 1963 | 40.00 |
| ❑ Argo LP-649 [M] | | 1963 | 400.00 |
| *—Multi-color splash vinyl; white label promo* | | | |
| REPRISE ALL STAR SPECTACULAR! | | | |
| ❑ Reprise R-6028 [M] | | 1962 | 40.00 |
| REQUESTED BY YOU | | | |
| ❑ Columbia CL 607 [M] | | 1955 | 25.00 |
| RHYTHM & BLUES | | | |
| ❑ RCA Camden CAL-371 [M] | | 1958 | 25.00 |
| RHYTHM AND BLUES | | | |
| ❑ Savoy MG-15008 [10] | | 1952 | 80.00 |
| RHYTHM PLUS ONE | | | |
| ❑ Epic LN 3297 [M] | | 1956 | 30.00 |
| THE RHYTHM SECTION | | | |
| ❑ Epic LN 3271 [M] | | 1956 | 30.00 |
| RHYTHM, BLUES AND BOOGIE-WOOGIE | | | |
| ❑ Decca DL 4011 [M] | | 1960 | 30.00 |
| RICHARD NADER/LET THE GOOD TIMES ROLL | | | |
| ❑ Bell 9002 [(2)] | | 1973 | 20.00 |
| RINGSIDE AT CONDON'S | | | |
| ❑ Savoy MG-15029 [10] | | 1954 | 80.00 |
| RINGSIDE AT CONDON'S VOL. 2 | | | |
| ❑ Savoy MG-15030 [10] | | 1954 | 80.00 |
| RIVERBOAT JAZZ | | | |
| ❑ Brunswick BL 58026 [10] | | 1951 | 50.00 |
| RIVERSIDE DRIVE | | | |
| ❑ Riverside RLP 12-267 [M] | | 1958 | 30.00 |
| RIVERSIDE MODERN JAZZ SAMPLER | | | |
| ❑ Riverside S-3 [M] | | 1956 | 40.00 |
| ROBERT W. SARNOFF — 25 YEARS OF RCA LEADERSHIP | | | |
| ❑ RCA Victor RWS-0001 [DJ] | | 1973 | 2000. |
| *—Souvenir record handed out at Sarnoff's retirement party; VG value 1000; VG+ value 1500* | | | |
| ROCK & ROLL FOREVER | | | |
| ❑ Atlantic 1239 [M] | | 1956 | 150.00 |
| ROCK & ROLL WITH RHYTHM & BLUES | | | |
| ❑ Aladdin LP-710 [M] | | 195? | 1500. |
| ROCK 'N' ROLL SOCK HOP | | | |
| ❑ Score SLP-4018 [M] | | 1958 | 200.00 |
| ROCK AND ROLL BANDSTAND | | | |
| ❑ Roulette R 25093 [M] | | 1959 | 30.00 |
| *—Originals have a white label with colored spokes* | | | |
| ROCK AND ROLL DANCE PARTY | | | |
| ❑ King 536 [M] | | 1956 | 300.00 |
| ❑ RPM LRP-3001 | | 195? | 500.00 |
| ROCK AND ROLL RECORD HOP | | | |
| ❑ Roulette R 25059 [M] | | 1959 | 30.00 |
| *—Originals have a white label with colored spokes* | | | |
| ROCK AND ROLL REVUE, VOLUME 2 | | | |
| ❑ King 654 [M] | | 1959 | 150.00 |
| ROCK AND ROLL VS. RHYTHM AND BLUES | | | |
| ❑ Dooto DTL-223 [M] | | 1957 | 100.00 |
| ROCK AND ROLL: THE EARLY DAYS | | | |
| ❑ RCA Victor AFM1-5463 | | 1985 | 20.00 |
| ROCK N' ROLL JAMBOREE | | | |
| ❑ End LP-302 [M] | | 1959 | 120.00 |
| *—Second cover and title with puppet and a guitar* | | | |
| ROCK'S GREATEST HITS | | | |
| ❑ Columbia GP 11 [(2)] | | 1969 | 20.00 |
| ROCK-A-BALLADS | | | |
| ❑ Cadence CLP-3041 [M] | | 1960 | 40.00 |
| ROCK-A-HITS | | | |
| ❑ Cadence CLP-3042 [M] | | 1960 | 40.00 |
| ROCK-O-RAMA | | | |
| ❑ Abkco AB 4222 [(2)] | | 1972 | 20.00 |
| ROCK-O-RAMA, VOLUME 2 | | | |
| ❑ Abkco AB 4223 [(2)] | | 1972 | 20.00 |
| ROCKIN' SLUMBER PARTY | | | |
| ❑ Famous LP-501 [M] | | 1961 | 30.00 |
| ROCKIN' TOGETHER | | | |
| ❑ Atco 33-103 [M] | | 1958 | 100.00 |
| A ROCKING CHRISTMAS STOCKING | | | |
| ❑ Capitol SPRO 9303/4/5/6 [(2)DJ] | | 1984 | 20.00 |
| RODGERS AND HART GEMS | | | |
| ❑ Pacific Jazz JWC-504 [M] | | 1956 | 50.00 |
| ❑ World Pacific JWC-504 [M] | | 1958 | 40.00 |
| ROOST 5TH ANNIVERSARY ALBUM | | | |
| ❑ Roost RST-1201 [M] | | 1955 | 50.00 |
| ROOTS OF BRITISH ROCK | | | |
| ❑ Sire SASH-3711 [(2)] | | 1975 | 20.00 |
| ROULETTE PRESENTS A DEMONSTRATION OF THE NEW DIMENSIONAL SOUND OF DYNAMIC STEREO | | | |
| ❑ Roulette SR-100 [S] | | 1958 | 30.00 |
| RUMBLE | | | |
| ❑ Jubilee JGM-1114 [M] | | 1959 | 150.00 |
| SATURDAY NIGHT AT THE UPTOWN | | | |
| ❑ Atlantic 8101 [M] | | 1964 | 25.00 |
| ❑ Atlantic SD 8101 [S] | | 1964 | 30.00 |
| SATURDAY NIGHT FUNCTION: RURAL BLUES, VOLUME 2 | | | |
| ❑ Imperial LP-94001 | | 1968 | 20.00 |
| SATURDAY NIGHT GRAND OLE OPRY | | | |
| ❑ Decca DL 4303 [M] | | 1962 | 25.00 |

The Association ☆ Theo Bikel ☆ Harpers Bizarre ☆ Petula Clark ☆ Dion ☆ The Everly Brothers ☆ The Fifth Avenue Band ☆ Kenny Rogers and The First Edition ☆ Ella Fitzgerald ☆ Vince Guaraldi ☆ Arlo Guthrie ☆ Herbie Hancock ☆ Doug Kershaw ☆ Lightfoot ☆ Trini Lopez


Various artists, *Schlagers!,* Warner Bros. PRO 359, 1970, 2 records, green labels, $30.

| Number | Title (A Side/B Side) | Yr | NM |
|---|---|---|---|
| ❑ Decca DL 74303 [S] | | 1962 | 30.00 |
| SATURDAY NIGHT GRAND OLE OPRY, VOL. 2 | | | |
| ❑ Decca DL 4539 [M] | | 1964 | 20.00 |
| ❑ Decca DL 74539 [S] | | 1964 | 25.00 |
| SATURDAY NIGHT GRAND OLE OPRY, VOL. 3 | | | |
| ❑ Decca DL 4671 [M] | | 1965 | 20.00 |
| ❑ Decca DL 74671 [S] | | 1965 | 25.00 |
| SATURDAY NIGHT MOOD | | | |
| ❑ Columbia CL 599 [M] | | 1954 | 25.00 |
| THE SAX SECTION | | | |
| ❑ Epic LN 3278 [M] | | 1956 | 40.00 |
| SAX STYLISTS | | | |
| ❑ Capitol H 328 [10] | | 1952 | 50.00 |
| SAXES, INC. | | | |
| ❑ Warner Bros. W 1336 [M] | | 1959 | 50.00 |
| ❑ Warner Bros. WS 1336 [S] | | 1959 | 80.00 |
| SAXOMANIAC | | | |
| ❑ Apollo LP-477 [M] | | 1958 | 100.00 |
| THE SAXOPHONE | | | |
| ❑ ABC Impulse! AS-9253 [(3)] | | 197? | 20.00 |
| SAXOPHONE REVOLT | | | |
| ❑ Riverside RLP 12-284 [M] | | 1958 | 150.00 |
| SCHLAGERS! | | | |
| ❑ Warner Bros. PRO 359 [(2)] | | 1970 | 30.00 |
| *—Originals have green labels* | | | |
| A SCRAPBOOK OF BRITISH JAZZ, 1926-1956 | | | |
| ❑ London LL 1444 [M] | | 1956 | 20.00 |
| SEASON'S GREETINGS FROM BARBRA STREISAND...AND FRIENDS | | | |
| ❑ Columbia Special Products CSS 1075 | | 1969 | 20.00 |
| *—Created exclusively for Maxwell House Coffee* | | | |
| SEASONS GREETINGS (A CHRISTMAS FESTIVAL OF STARS) | | | |
| ❑ Columbia CL 1394 [M] | | 1959 | 20.00 |
| ❑ Columbia CS 8189 [S] | | 1959 | 25.00 |
| SECOND SESSION AT SQUIRREL'S | | | |
| ❑ Paramount LP-108 [10] | | 1954 | 60.00 |
| SELECTIONS FROM APRIL 1956 ALBUMS FOR RADIO-TV PROGRAM USE | | | |
| ❑ Capitol PRO-252/3 [DJ] | | 1956 | 40.00 |
| SELECTIONS FROM FEBRUARY 1956 POPULAR ALBUMS FOR RADIO-TV PROGRAM USE | | | |
| ❑ Capitol PRO-240/1 [DJ] | | 1956 | 40.00 |

| Number | Title (A Side/B Side) | Yr | NM |
|---|---|---|---|
| SELECTIONS FROM JANUARY 1956 ALBUMS FOR RADIO-TV PROGRAM USE | | | |
| ❑ Capitol PRO-238/9 [DJ] | | 1956 | 40.00 |
| SELECTIONS FROM MARCH 1956 ALBUMS FOR RADIO-TV PROGRAM USE | | | |
| ❑ Capitol PRO-246/7 [DJ] | | 1956 | 40.00 |
| SESSION AT MIDNIGHT | | | |
| ❑ Capitol T 707 [M] | | 1956 | 30.00 |
| SESSION AT RIVERSIDE | | | |
| ❑ Capitol T 761 [M] | | 1956 | 30.00 |
| THE SEVEN AGES OF JAZZ | | | |
| ❑ Metrojazz 2-E-1009 [(2)M] | | 1959 | 60.00 |
| ❑ Metrojazz 2-SE-1009 [(2)S] | | 1959 | 50.00 |
| SHUT DOWN | | | |
| ❑ Capitol DT 1918 [R] | | 1963 | 40.00 |
| ❑ Capitol T 1918 [M] | | 1963 | 40.00 |
| SHUT DOWNS AND HILL CLIMBS | | | |
| ❑ Liberty LRP-3366 [M] | | 1964 | 40.00 |
| ❑ Liberty LST-7366 [S] | | 1964 | 50.00 |
| THE SINATRA FAMILY WISH YOU A MERRY CHRISTMAS | | | |
| ❑ Reprise FS-1026 | | 1969 | 50.00 |
| SING A SONG OF SOUL | | | |
| ❑ Checker LP 2998 [M] | | 1966 | 80.00 |
| ❑ Checker LPS 2998 [S] | | 1966 | 100.00 |
| THE SINGER-SONGWRITER PROJECT | | | |
| ❑ Elektra EKL-299 [M] | | 1965 | 20.00 |
| *—With 11 tracks, though the label and cover claim there are 13* | | | |
| ❑ Elektra EKL-299 [M] | | 1965 | 25.00 |
| *—With 13 tracks* | | | |
| ❑ Elektra EKS-7299 [S] | | 1965 | 20.00 |
| *—With 11 tracks, though the label and cover claim there are 13* | | | |
| ❑ Elektra EKS-7299 [S] | | 1965 | 30.00 |
| *—With 13 tracks* | | | |
| SINGIN' AND SWINGIN' | | | |
| ❑ Savoy MG-12217 [M] | | 196? | 20.00 |
| THE SIREN | | | |
| ❑ Posh Boy PBS-103 | | 1980 | 20.00 |
| SITTIN' IN | | | |
| ❑ Verve MGV-8225 [M] | | 1958 | 50.00 |
| ❑ Verve V-8225 [M] | | 1961 | 25.00 |
| 16 GOODIES — BLASTS FROM THE PAST | | | |
| ❑ Blast BLP-6803 [M] | | 1964 | 40.00 |
| 16 ORIGINAL BIG HITS, VOLUME 2 | | | |
| ❑ Tamla TM 256 [M] | | 1964 | 20.00 |
| 16 ORIGINAL BIG HITS, VOLUME 3 | | | |
| ❑ Motown MT 624 [M] | | 1965 | 20.00 |

| Number | Title (A Side/B Side) | Yr | NM |
|---|---|---|---|
| 16 ORIGINAL BIG HITS, VOLUME 4 | | | |
| ❑ Motown M 633 [M] | | 1965 | 15.00 |
| ❑ Motown MS 633 [S] | | 1965 | 20.00 |
| 60 CHRISTMAS CLASSICS | | | |
| ❑ Sessions DVL2-0723 [(4)] | | 1985 | 20.00 |
| *—Record 3 is numbered "P18827" and Record 4 is numbered "P18828"* | | | |
| 60 FLASH-BACK GREATS OF THE SIXTIES | | | |
| ❑ K-Tel TU 229 [(4)] | | 1972 | 40.00 |
| *—One of the few sought-after K-Tel collections, among its contents is a Beatles track ("My Bonnie")* | | | |
| 60 YEARS OF COUNTRY MUSIC | | | |
| ❑ RCA Victor CPL2-4351 | | 1982 | 20.00 |
| 60 YEARS OF MUSIC AMERICA LOVES BEST | | | |
| ❑ RCA Victor LM-6074 [(2)] | | 1959 | 30.00 |
| 60 YEARS OF MUSIC AMERICA LOVES BEST, VOLUME II | | | |
| ❑ RCA Victor LM-6088 [(2)] | | 1960 | 30.00 |
| 60 YEARS OF MUSIC AMERICA LOVES BEST, VOLUME III (POPULAR) | | | |
| ❑ RCA Victor LOP-1509 | | 1961 | 20.00 |
| 60 YEARS OF MUSIC AMERICA LOVES BEST, VOLUME III (RED SEAL) | | | |
| ❑ RCA Victor Red Seal LM-2574 | | 1961 | 20.00 |
| $64,000 JAZZ | | | |
| ❑ Columbia CL 777 [M] | | 1955 | 50.00 |
| A SLICE OF LEMON | | | |
| ❑ Columbia Special Products CSM-389 [M] | | 1966 | 25.00 |
| *—Manufactured for Dr. Pepper; contains a spoken-word introduction by Dick Clark, plus tracks by Bob Dylan, Simon & Garfunkel, the Dave Clark Five, the Brothers Four, Percy Faith, Dave Brubeck, the New Christy Minstrels, Tony Bennett and Doris Day* | | | |
| SMALL COMBO HITS | | | |
| ❑ RCA Victor LPT-3 [10] | | 1951 | 40.00 |
| SMART, LUSCIOUS, BEAUTIFUL | | | |
| ❑ Bethlehem BCP-6034 [M] | | 1960 | 30.00 |
| THE SMITHSONIAN COLLECTION OF CLASSIC JAZZ | | | |
| ❑ Smithsonian/CSP P6 11891 [(6)] | | 1973 | 40.00 |
| ❑ Smithsonian/CSP P7 19477 [(7)] | | 1987 | 40.00 |
| *—Revised version of 1973 original* | | | |
| SMOKE RINGS | | | |
| ❑ RCA Victor LPT-13 [10] | | 1951 | 40.00 |
| SOFT PEDAL | | | |
| ❑ Columbia CL 2511 [10] | | 1954 | 30.00 |
| SOLID GOLD HITS | | | |
| ❑ Imperial LP-9230 [M] | | 1963 | 25.00 |
| ❑ Imperial LP-12230 [R] | | 1963 | 20.00 |
| SOLID GOLD PROGRAMMING | | | |
| ❑ Screen Gems/Columbia CPL-711 [DJ] | | 1975 | 20.00 |
| *—Promo-only compilation of oldies sent to radio to spur airplay on songs owned by this publishing house* | | | |
| ❑ Screen Gems/Columbia CPL-715 [DJ] | | 1975 | 20.00 |
| *—Same concept as above album, but completely different contents, and mostly in stereo* | | | |
| SOLID GOLD SONGS INSTRUMENTALLY | | | |
| ❑ Screen Gems/Columbia CPL-714 [DJ] | | 1975 | 20.00 |
| *—Promo-only compilation of oldies sent to radio to spur airplay on songs owned by this publishing house* | | | |
| SOLID GOLD SOUL | | | |
| ❑ Atlantic 8116 [M] | | 1966 | 15.00 |
| ❑ Atlantic SD 8116 [S] | | 1966 | 20.00 |
| SOLO FLIGHT | | | |
| ❑ Pacific Jazz JWC-505 [M] | | 1956 | 50.00 |
| ❑ World Pacific JWC-505 [M] | | 1958 | 40.00 |
| SOLO SPOTLIGHTS | | | |
| ❑ King 745 [M] | | 1961 | 100.00 |
| SOME LIKE IT COOL | | | |
| ❑ United Artists SX-71 [S] | | 1959 | 40.00 |
| ❑ United Artists X-71 [M] | | 1959 | 40.00 |
| SOMETHING FOR BOTH EARS | | | |
| ❑ World Pacific HFS-2 [S] | | 1958 | 40.00 |
| *—Stereo sampler* | | | |
| SOMETHING NEW, SOMETHING BLUE | | | |
| ❑ Columbia CL 1388 [M] | | 1959 | 20.00 |
| SONGS BY RODGERS AND HART AND JOHNNY GREEN | | | |
| ❑ Discovery DL-3014 [10] | | 1951 | 50.00 |
| SONGS FOR A SUMMER NIGHT | | | |
| ❑ Columbia PM 2 [(2)M] | | 1963 | 20.00 |
| ❑ Columbia PMS 2 [(2)S] | | 1963 | 25.00 |
| THE SONGS OF ASHFORD AND SIMPSON | | | |
| ❑ Jobete PRO-3 [DJ] | | 1974 | 40.00 |
| *—Promo-only publisher's demo with short excerpts of songs* | | | |
| SONGS OF FAITH | | | |
| ❑ Audio Lab AL-1504 [M] | | 1959 | 80.00 |
| SONGS OF FAITH AND INSPIRATION | | | |
| ❑ Time-Life STL-127 [(3)] | | 1989 | 25.00 |
| SONGS OF FAITH VOLUME 2 | | | |
| ❑ Audio Lab AL-1523 [M] | | 1959 | 80.00 |
| THE SONGS OF HOLLAND-DOZIER-HOLLAND | | | |
| ❑ Jobete PRO-4 [DJ] | | 1974 | 40.00 |
| *—Promo-only publisher's demo with short excerpts of songs* | | | |
| THE SONGS OF JOHNNY BRISTOL-FRANK WILSON-MICKEY STEVENSON AND FREDDIE PERREN | | | |
| ❑ Jobete PRO-8 [DJ] | | 1976 | 40.00 |
| *—Promo-only publisher's demo with short excerpts of songs* | | | |
| THE SONGS OF MARVIN GAYE | | | |
| ❑ Jobete PRO-6 [DJ] | | 1974 | 40.00 |
| *—Promo-only publisher's demo with short excerpts of songs* | | | |

**Number Title (A Side/B Side) Yr NM**

THE SONGS OF NORMAN WHITFIELD
❑ Jobete PRO-7 [DJ] 1976 40.00
*—Promo-only publisher's demo with short excerpts of songs*

SONGS OF RIVERS, OCEANS AND SEAS
❑ King 871 [M] 1963 70.00

THE SONGS OF SMOKEY ROBINSON
❑ Jobete PRO-2 [DJ] 1972 40.00
*—Promo-only publisher's demo with short excerpts of songs; there are two versions of this LP, both with the same number; each is of equal value*

THE SONGS OF STEVIE WONDER
❑ Jobete PRO-5 [DJ] 1974 40.00
*—Promo-only publisher's demo with short excerpts of songs*

SONGS OF THE HILLS
❑ Audio Lab AL-1515 [M] 1959 80.00

SOUL CHRISTMAS
❑ Atco SD 33-269 1968 30.00

SOUL EXPLOSION
❑ Stax STS 2-2007 [(2)] 1969 20.00

SOUL JAZZ, VOL. 1
❑ Bluesville BVLP-1009 [M] 1960 50.00
*—Blue label, silver print*
❑ Bluesville BVLP-1009 [M] 1965 25.00
*—Blue label, trident logo at right*

SOUL JAZZ, VOL. 2
❑ Bluesville BVLP-1010 [M] 1960 50.00
*—Blue label, silver print*
❑ Bluesville BVLP-1010 [M] 1965 25.00
*—Blue label, trident logo at right*

SOUL MEETING SATURDAY NIGHT HOOTENANNY STYLE
❑ Vee Jay LP-1074 [M] 1963 30.00
*—Not known to exist in stereo*

THE SOUL OF JAZZ
❑ Riverside S-5 [M] 1957 40.00
❑ World Wide MGS-20002 [S] 1958 80.00

THE SOUL OF JAZZ PERCUSSION
❑ Warwick W 5003 [M] 1961 30.00
❑ Warwick W 5003ST [S] 1961 40.00

THE SOUL OF JAZZ PIANO
❑ Riverside 9S-7 [S] 196? 30.00

SOULED OUT
❑ Chess LPS 1546 [S] 1969 50.00

THE SOUND OF BIG BAND JAZZ IN HI-FI
❑ World Pacific WP-1257 [M] 1960 40.00

THE SOUND OF BIG BAND JAZZ IN STEREO
❑ World Pacific ST-1015 [S] 1960 30.00

THE SOUND OF GENIUS
❑ Columbia Masterworks SGM 1 [(2)M] 1963 20.00
❑ Columbia Masterworks SGS 1 [(2)S] 1963 25.00

THE SOUND OF JAZZ
❑ Columbia CL 1098 [M] 1957 20.00

SOUNDS IN SPACE
❑ RCA Victor SP-33-13 [S] 1958 20.00
*—Narrated by Ken Nordine with songs by various artists*

SOUNDS OF SUCCESS
❑ Jamie JLP-3017 [M] 1961 25.00
❑ Jamie JLPS-3017 [S] 1961 30.00

SOUTHERN MEETIN'
❑ Kimberly 2017 [M] 1963 20.00
❑ Kimberly 11017 [S] 1963 25.00

SOUVENIR/PROGRAMMING RECORD — DEALERS/ DISC JOCKEYS — OCT.-NOV. 1955
❑ Capitol PRO-232 [DJ] 1955 40.00

THE SPANISH SIDE OF JAZZ
❑ Roulette SR-42001 1968 20.00

SPECIAL CHRISTMAS LP FOR DISC JOCKEYS
❑ Capitol PRO-201 [DJ] 1954 50.00

SPECIAL COLLECTOR'S EDITION ALBUM FROM ROCKIN' RECORDS
❑ Sun 1032 1986 30.00
*—Limited edition of 600 copies*

SPIN TIME WITH LIBERTY
❑ Liberty MM-417 [DJ] 1962 50.00
*—Promo-only release*

SPIRITUALS
❑ King 951 [M] 1966 50.00
*—Reissue of "Spirituals, Volume 5," King 576*

SPIRITUALS, VOLUME 5
❑ King 576 [M] 1957 150.00

STABLE MATES
❑ Savoy MG-12115 [M] 1957 50.00

STARS
❑ Sun 148 1982 20.00
*—Includes two early Alabama tracks*

STARS FOR A SUMMER NIGHT
❑ Columbia PM 1 [(2)M] 1961 25.00
❑ Columbia PMS 1 [(2)S] 1961 30.00

THE STARS OF CHRISTMAS
❑ RCA Special Products DPL1-0842 1988 20.00
*—Sold only through Avon dealers*

THE STARS OF HEE HAW
❑ Capitol ST-437 1970 20.00

STARS OF JAZZ '61
❑ Jazzland JLP-1001 [M] 1961 25.00

STARS OF THE GRAND OLE OPRY 1926-1974
❑ RCA Victor CPL2-0466 [(2)] 1974 20.00

Various artists, *Sounds in Space,* RCA Victor SP-33-13, 1958, stereo, $20.

**Number Title (A Side/B Side) Yr NM**

START SWIMMING
❑ Stiff SINK 1 1981 20.00

THE STAX/VOLT REVUE — LIVE IN LONDON
❑ Stax 721 [M] 1967 20.00
❑ Stax S721 [S] 1967 25.00

THE STAX/VOLT REVUE — LIVE IN LONDON, VOLUME 2
❑ Stax 722 [M] 1967 20.00
❑ Stax S722 [S] 1967 25.00

STAX...ONCE YOU'VE BEEN THERE, YOU KNOW YOU'RE HOME
❑ Stax STS 1 [(2)DJ] 1971 40.00
*—Promo only in blank white gatefold cover*

STAY IN SCHOOL — DON'T BE A DROP OUT
❑ Stax A-11 [DJ] 1967 500.00

STEREOSONIC JUBILEE SAMPLER, VOLUME 1
❑ Jubilee SSJLP-801 [S] 1959 40.00

STERLING BALL 1971
❑ Motown M 739 [DJ] 1971 250.00
*—Loucye Gordy Wakefield Scholarship Fund benefit giveaway*

STILL MORE GOLD HITS, VOLUME 3
❑ Warwick W 2048 [M] 1962 80.00

STRETCHING OUT
❑ United Artists UAL-4023 [M] 1959 400.00
❑ United Artists UAS-5023 [S] 1959 300.00

STRICTLY FROM DIXIE
❑ MGM E-3262 [M] 1956 30.00

THE STRING BAND PROJECT
❑ Elektra EKL-292 [M] 1965 20.00
❑ Elektra EKS-7292 [S] 1965 25.00

A STRING OF SWINGIN' PEARLS
❑ RCA Victor LPM-1373 [M] 1956 30.00

SUB POP 100
❑ Sub Pop 10 1986 50.00

SUB POP 200
❑ Sub Pop 25 [(3)EP] 1988 50.00

SUMMER FESTIVAL
❑ RCA Victor Red Seal LM-6097 [(2)M] 1962 20.00
❑ RCA Victor Red Seal LSC-6097 [(2)S] 1962 25.00

SUMMER SOUVENIRS
❑ Bell 6035 1969 20.00

SUMMIT MEETING
❑ Vee Jay LP-3026 [M] 1961 20.00
❑ Vee Jay SR-3026 [S] 1961 25.00

THE SUN STORY
❑ Rhino RNDA-71103 [(2)] 1986 20.00

**Number Title (A Side/B Side) Yr NM**

SUN'S GOLD HITS
❑ Sun LP-1250 [M] 1961 200.00

SUNDAY MORNING
❑ Vee Jay LP-5016 [M] 1961 30.00

SUPER GOLDEN HITS
❑ Jubilee JGS-8019 1968 100.00
*—Despite the stereo prefix, this LP is mono*

SUPER GOLDEN HITS, VOLUME 2
❑ Jubilee JGS-8023 1969 100.00
*—Reissue of "Clay Cole's Bin of Original Golden Oldies," Jubilee 5026; again, despite the stereo prefix, this LP is mono*

SUPER GROUPS
❑ Warner Bros. PRO 630 [(2)] 1976 20.00

THE SUPER GROUPS
❑ Atco SD 33-279 1969 20.00

THE SUPER GROUPS FROM HOLLAND
❑ White Whale WWS-7129 1970 25.00

THE SUPER HITS
❑ Atlantic Group 501 [M] 1967 20.00
❑ Atlantic Group SD 501 [S] 1967 20.00

THE SUPER HITS, VOL. 2
❑ Atlantic 8188 [M] 1968 40.00
*—Mono is white label promo only; cover has "d/j copy monaural" sticker on it*
❑ Atlantic SD 8188 [S] 1968 20.00

THE SUPER HITS, VOL. 3
❑ Atlantic 8203 [M] 1968 40.00
*—Mono is white label promo only*
❑ Atlantic SD 8203 [S] 1968 20.00

THE SUPER HITS, VOL. 4
❑ Atlantic SD 8224 1969 20.00

THE SUPER HITS, VOL. 5
❑ Atlantic 8274 [M] 1970 50.00
*—Mono is white label promo only*
❑ Atlantic SD 8274 [S] 1970 20.00
*—This was the first album to contain "Ohio" by Crosby, Stills, Nash and Young and the only LP to contain the 3:11 version of "Whole Lotta Love" by Led Zeppelin*

SUPER OLDIES/VOL. 1
❑ Capitol ST 2562 [S] 1966 25.00
❑ Capitol T 2562 [M] 1966 20.00

SUPER OLDIES/VOL. 2
❑ Capitol ST 2565 [S] 1966 25.00
❑ Capitol T 2565 [M] 1966 20.00

SUPER OLDIES/VOL. 3
❑ Capitol STBB 2910 [(2)] 1968 20.00

| Number | Title (A Side/B Side) | Yr | NM |
|---|---|---|---|
| SUPER OLDIES/VOL. 4 | | | |
| ❑ Capitol STBB-149 [(2)] | | 1969 | 20.00 |
| SUPER OLDIES/VOL. 5 | | | |
| ❑ Capitol STBB-216 [(2)] | | 1969 | 20.00 |
| THE SUPER SOUL-DEES | | | |
| ❑ Capitol ST 2798 [S] | | 1967 | 20.00 |
| ❑ Capitol T 2798 [M] | | 1967 | 20.00 |
| THE SUPER SOUL-DEES, VOL. 2 | | | |
| ❑ Capitol STBB-2911 [(2)] | | 1968 | 20.00 |
| THE SUPER SOUL-DEES, VOL. 3 | | | |
| ❑ Capitol STBB-178 [(2)] | | 1969 | 20.00 |
| SUPERSTARS OF THE '70S | | | |
| ❑ Warner Special Products SP-4000 [(4)] | | 1973 | 40.00 |
| *—Box set with booklet of liner notes* | | | |
| SURF'S UP AT BANZAI PIPELINE | | | |
| ❑ Northridge NM-101 [M] | | 1963 | 200.00 |
| *—Original pressing of LP reissued on Reprise* | | | |
| ❑ Reprise R 6094 [M] | | 1963 | 100.00 |
| ❑ Reprise RS 6094 [S] | | 1963 | 150.00 |
| SURF'S UP! AT BANZAI PIPELINE | | | |
| ❑ Northridge NM-101 [M] | | 1963 | 150.00 |
| SURFIN' ON WAVE NINE | | | |
| ❑ King 855 [M] | | 1963 | 80.00 |
| SWAMP BLUES VOLUME 1 | | | |
| ❑ Excello LPS-8015 [R] | | 1970 | 20.00 |
| SWAMP BLUES VOLUME 2 | | | |
| ❑ Excello LPS-8016 [R] | | 1970 | 20.00 |
| SWEDES FROM JAZZVILLE | | | |
| ❑ Epic LN 3309 [M] | | 1957 | 50.00 |
| SWEDISH PASTRY | | | |
| ❑ Discovery DL-2008 [10] | | 1954 | 50.00 |
| SWEET 'N GREASY: RHYTHM 'N' BLUES, VOLUME 2 | | | |
| ❑ Imperial LP-94005 | | 1968 | 20.00 |
| SWEET ADELINES MEDALIST QUARTETS OF 1958 | | | |
| ❑ Cadence CLP-3018 [M] | | 1959 | 40.00 |
| SWEET ADELINES MEDALISTS OF 1957 | | | |
| ❑ Cadence CLP-3009 [M] | | 1958 | 40.00 |
| SWEET DREAMS OF COUNTRY | | | |
| ❑ Reader's Digest RBA-049A [(7)] | | 1990 | 50.00 |
| SWING AGAIN! | | | |
| ❑ Capitol T 1386 [M] | | 1960 | 20.00 |
| SWING BILLIES | | | |
| ❑ Audio Lab AL-1546 [M] | | 1960 | 120.00 |
| SWING BILLIES VOLUME 2 | | | |
| ❑ Audio Lab AL-1566 [M] | | 1960 | 120.00 |
| THE SWING ERA, VOL. 1 | | | |
| ❑ "X" LVA-3030 [10] | | 1955 | 80.00 |
| SWING GOES DIXIE | | | |
| ❑ American Recording Society G-420 [M] | | 1957 | 30.00 |
| SWING GUITARS | | | |
| ❑ Norgran MGN-1033 [M] | | 1955 | 80.00 |
| ❑ Verve MGV-8124 [M] | | 1957 | 30.00 |
| ❑ Verve V-8124 [M] | | 1961 | 20.00 |
| SWING HI, SWING LO | | | |
| ❑ Blue Note BLP-5027 [10] | | 1953 | 200.00 |
| ❑ Blue Note B-6507 [M] | | 1969 | 15.00 |
| SWING LIGHTLY | | | |
| ❑ Jazztone J-1265 [M] | | 1957 | 30.00 |
| SWING POTPOURRI | | | |
| ❑ Audiophile AP-23 [M] | | 1953 | 30.00 |
| SWING... NOT SPRING! | | | |
| ❑ Savoy MG-12062 [M] | | 1956 | 50.00 |
| A SWINGIN' GIG | | | |
| ❑ Tampa TP-2 [M] | | 1957 | 100.00 |
| *—Colored vinyl* | | | |
| ❑ Tampa TP-2 [M] | | 1958 | 50.00 |
| *—Black vinyl* | | | |
| SWINGIN' LIKE SIXTY, VOL. 1 | | | |
| ❑ World Pacific ST-1289 [S] | | 1960 | 30.00 |
| ❑ World Pacific WP-1289 [M] | | 1960 | 30.00 |
| SWINGIN' LIKE SIXTY, VOL. 2 | | | |
| ❑ World Pacific ST-1290 [S] | | 1960 | 30.00 |
| SWINGIN' LIKE SIXTY, VOL. 3 | | | |
| ❑ World Pacific ST-1291 [S] | | 1960 | 30.00 |
| SWINGIN' SOUNDS | | | |
| ❑ Columbia Special Products XTV 82030 [M] | | 1962 | 25.00 |
| *—Issued for the W.A. Sheaffer Pen Co.* | | | |
| SWINGING BROADWAY | | | |
| ❑ Kimberly 2024 [M] | | 1963 | 20.00 |
| ❑ Kimberly 11024 [S] | | 1963 | 25.00 |
| SWINGING FOR THE KING | | | |
| ❑ Mercury MG-20133 [M] | | 1956 | 50.00 |
| SWINGING SOUNDTRACK | | | |
| ❑ Kimberly 2016 [M] | | 1963 | 20.00 |
| ❑ Kimberly 11016 [S] | | 1963 | 25.00 |
| THE SWINGVILLE ALL-STARS | | | |
| ❑ Swingville SVLP-2010 [M] | | 1960 | 40.00 |
| *—Purple label* | | | |
| ❑ Swingville SVLP-2010 [M] | | 1965 | 20.00 |
| *—Blue label, trident logo at right* | | | |
| SWITCHED ON BLUES | | | |
| ❑ Soul SS-720 | | 1969 | 150.00 |
| TAKE THE LIBERTY | | | |
| ❑ Liberty MM-427 [DJ] | | 1966 | 40.00 |
| TAME YOURSELF | | | |
| ❑ Rhino 90082 | | 1991 | 25.00 |
| TAMLA SPECIAL #1 | | | |
| ❑ Tamla TM 224 [M] | | 1962 | 150.00 |
| *—White label* | | | |
| ❑ Tamla TM 224 [M] | | 1963 | 70.00 |
| *—Yellow label* | | | |
| TASTE TEST #1 — LIVE FROM BRAIN COOKIES | | | |
| ❑ New Alliance 045 [(2)] | | 1990 | 25.00 |
| TEEN DELIGHTS | | | |
| ❑ Vee Jay LP-1021 [M] | | 1960 | 30.00 |
| TEEN DELIGHTS, VOLUME 2 | | | |
| ❑ Vee Jay LP-1036 [M] | | 1961 | 30.00 |
| TEENAGE PARTY | | | |
| ❑ Gee GLP-702 [M] | | 1958 | 200.00 |
| *—Red label* | | | |
| ❑ Gee GLP-702 [M] | | 196? | 60.00 |
| *—Gray label* | | | |
| TEENSVILLE | | | |
| ❑ Liberty L-5503 [M] | | 1962 | 40.00 |
| TEN TUNES OF CHRISTMAS | | | |
| ❑ Candee 50-50 | | 195? | 20.00 |
| *—Sold through "The 50-50 Club," a Cincinnati radio and TV show; all the artists have Cincinnati ties* | | | |
| TENNESSEE | | | |
| ❑ Design DLP-611 [M] | | 1962 | 20.00 |
| TENOR CONCLAVE | | | |
| ❑ Prestige PRLP-7074 [M] | | 1957 | 100.00 |
| *—Reissued as Prestige 7249; see JOHN COLTRANE.* | | | |
| TENOR JAZZ | | | |
| ❑ Mercury MG-20016 [10] | | 1950 | 100.00 |
| *—Issued in a paper sleeve* | | | |
| TENOR SAX | | | |
| ❑ Concord 3012 [M] | | 195? | 40.00 |
| TENOR SAX SOLOS, VOL. 1 | | | |
| ❑ Savoy MG-9008 [10] | | 1952 | 150.00 |
| TENOR SAX SOLOS, VOL. 2 | | | |
| ❑ Savoy MG-9013 [10] | | 1952 | 150.00 |
| TENOR SAX SOLOS, VOL. 3 | | | |
| ❑ Savoy MG-9021 [10] | | 1953 | 150.00 |
| TENOR SAXES | | | |
| ❑ Norgran MGN-1034 [M] | | 1955 | 80.00 |
| ❑ Verve MGV-8127 [M] | | 1957 | 30.00 |
| ❑ Verve V-8127 [M] | | 1961 | 20.00 |
| TENORS ANYONE? | | | |
| ❑ Dawn DLP-1126 [M] | | 1958 | 120.00 |
| THEME SONGS | | | |
| ❑ Columbia CL 6016 [10] | | 1949 | 40.00 |
| ❑ RCA Victor LPT-1 [10] | | 1951 | 40.00 |
| THEMES LIKE OLD TIMES | | | |
| ❑ Viva 36018 [(2)] | | 1969 | 20.00 |
| THESAURUS OF CLASSIC JAZZ | | | |
| ❑ Columbia C4L 18 [(4)] | | 1961 | 50.00 |
| A THIRD SESSION AT SQUIRREL'S | | | |
| ❑ Paramount LP-110 [10] | | 1954 | 60.00 |
| 30X30: 30 GREAT HITS BY 30 GREAT COUNTRY ARTISTS, VOL. 1 | | | |
| ❑ Columbia Musical Treasuries P2S 5218 [(2)] | | 1968 | 20.00 |
| 30X30: 30 GREAT HITS BY 30 GREAT COUNTRY ARTISTS, VOL. 2 | | | |
| ❑ Columbia Musical Treasuries P2S 5220 [(2)] | | 1968 | 20.00 |
| 30 FAVORITE SONGS OF CHRISTMAS WITH CHIMES AND CHORUS | | | |
| ❑ Disneyland DQ-1329 [M] | | 1963 | 20.00 |
| *—Performed by anonymous musicians* | | | |
| 30 YEARS OF NO. 1 COUNTRY HITS | | | |
| ❑ Reader's Digest RBA-215-A [(7)] | | 1986 | 50.00 |
| THIS COULD LEAD TO LOVE | | | |
| ❑ Riverside RLP 12-808 [M] | | 195? | 50.00 |
| THIS IS HOW IT ALL BEGAN: THE SPECIALTY STORY, VOLUME 1 | | | |
| ❑ Specialty SPS-2117 | | 1970 | 20.00 |
| THIS IS HOW IT ALL BEGAN: THE SPECIALTY STORY, VOLUME 2 | | | |
| ❑ Specialty SPS-2118 | | 1970 | 20.00 |
| THIS IS SOUL | | | |
| ❑ Atlantic 8170 [M] | | 1968 | 40.00 |
| ❑ Atlantic SD 8170 [S] | | 1968 | 20.00 |
| THIS IS STEREO | | | |
| ❑ Liberty LST-101 [S] | | 1960 | 40.00 |
| *—Black vinyl* | | | |
| ❑ Liberty LST-101 [S] | | 1960 | 120.00 |
| *—Red vinyl* | | | |
| THIS IS THE BLUES | | | |
| ❑ Kimberly 2020 [M] | | 1963 | 20.00 |
| ❑ Kimberly 11020 [S] | | 1963 | 25.00 |
| THIS IS THE BLUES, VOL. 1 | | | |
| ❑ Pacific Jazz PJ-13 [M] | | 1961 | 30.00 |
| THIS IS THE BLUES, VOL. 2 | | | |
| ❑ Pacific Jazz PJ-30 [M] | | 1962 | 25.00 |
| ❑ Pacific Jazz ST-30 [M] | | 1962 | 30.00 |
| THREADS OF GLORY — 200 YEARS OF AMERICA IN WORDS & MUSIC | | | |
| ❑ London Phase 4 6SP 14000 [(6)] | | 1975 | 30.00 |
| THREE DECADES OF MUSIC, 1939-49, VOL. 1 | | | |
| ❑ Blue Note BST-89902 [(2)] | | 1969 | 25.00 |
| THREE DECADES OF MUSIC, 1949-59, VOL. 1 | | | |
| ❑ Blue Note BST-89903 [(2)] | | 1969 | 25.00 |
| THREE DECADES OF MUSIC, 1959-69, VOL. 1 | | | |
| ❑ Blue Note BST-89904 [(2)] | | 1969 | 25.00 |
| THREE ROADS TO JAZZ | | | |
| ❑ American Recording Society LP-100 [M] | | 1956 | 30.00 |
| A TIME FOR PRAYER | | | |
| ❑ Audio Lab AL-1518 [M] | | 1959 | 80.00 |
| THE TIME-LIFE TREASURY OF CHRISTMAS | | | |
| ❑ Time-Life STL-107 [(3)] | | 1986 | 20.00 |
| *—Available from Time-Life by mail order only; boxed set* | | | |
| THE TIME-LIFE TREASURY OF CHRISTMAS, VOLUME TWO | | | |
| ❑ Time-Life STL-108 [(3)] | | 1987 | 20.00 |
| *—Available from Time-Life by mail-order only; all known copies are boxed sets* | | | |
| TODAY'S HITS | | | |
| ❑ Philles PHLP 4004 [M] | | 1963 | 400.00 |
| *—First pressings have blue and black labels* | | | |
| ❑ Philles PHLP 4004 [M] | | 1964 | 200.00 |
| *—Second pressings have yellow and red labels* | | | |
| TOGETHER | | | |
| ❑ Warner Bros. PRO 486 | | 1972 | 20.00 |
| *—Originals have green labels* | | | |
| TOGETHER AT CHRISTMAS (READER'S DIGEST FAMILY ALBUM OF CHRISTMAS MUSIC) | | | |
| ❑ Reader's Digest RDA 151-A [(5)] | | 1974 | 20.00 |
| *—Available only through Reader's Digest magazine by mail order* | | | |
| TOMMY BOY GREATEST BEATS: THE FIRST FIFTEEN YEARS 1981-1996, VOLUME 1 | | | |
| ❑ Tommy Boy TB 1115 [(2)] | | 1998 | 20.00 |
| TOMMY BOY GREATEST BEATS: THE FIRST FIFTEEN YEARS 1981-1996, VOLUME 2 | | | |
| ❑ Tommy Boy TB 1165 [(2)] | | 1998 | 20.00 |
| TOMMY BOY GREATEST BEATS: THE FIRST FIFTEEN YEARS 1981-1996, VOLUME 3 | | | |
| ❑ Tommy Boy TB 1117 [(2)] | | 1998 | 20.00 |
| TOMMY BOY GREATEST BEATS: THE FIRST FIFTEEN YEARS 1981-1996, VOLUME 4 | | | |
| ❑ Tommy Boy TB 1166 [(2)] | | 1998 | 20.00 |
| TOMORROW'S HITS | | | |
| ❑ Vee Jay LP-1042 [M] | | 1962 | 30.00 |
| THE TOP 10 STORY IN SOUND | | | |
| ❑ Jobete PRO-1 [(2)DJ] | | 1972 | 40.00 |
| *—Promo-only publisher's demo with short excerpts of songs* | | | |
| TOP HITS OF '54 VOLUME II | | | |
| ❑ Capitol H 9119 [10] | | 1954 | 50.00 |
| TOP R&B ARTISTS SING COUNTRY SONGS | | | |
| ❑ King 884 [M] | | 1964 | 80.00 |
| TOWN HALL CONCERT | | | |
| ❑ Mainstream S-6004 [R] | | 1965 | 12.00 |
| ❑ Mainstream 56004 [M] | | 1965 | 25.00 |
| TRADITIONAL CHRISTMAS SONGS | | | |
| ❑ Audio Lab AL-1517 [M] | | 1959 | 80.00 |
| TRADITIONAL JAZZ | | | |
| ❑ London LL 1242 [M] | | 1955 | 20.00 |
| TRADITIONAL JAZZ AT THE ROYAL FESTIVAL HALL | | | |
| ❑ London LL 1184 [M] | | 1955 | 20.00 |
| TREASURE ALBUM | | | |
| ❑ Hickory LPS-154 | | 1970 | 40.00 |
| TREASURE CHEST GOODIES | | | |
| ❑ Stax 703 [M] | | 1963 | 40.00 |
| *—National version of "Hits from the South Presented by Nick Charles" with rearranged contents* | | | |
| TREASURE CHEST OF HITS | | | |
| ❑ Swan LP-501 [M] | | 1960 | 80.00 |
| A TREASURE CHEST OF SONG HITS | | | |
| ❑ Columbia CL 613 [M] | | 1955 | 25.00 |
| TREASURE TUNES FROM THE VAULT (AS ADVERTISED ON WLS) | | | |
| ❑ Chess LP 1474 [M] | | 1962 | 40.00 |
| A TREASURY OF CHRISTMAS | | | |
| ❑ Columbia Record Club P4S 5022 [(4)] | | 1965 | 30.00 |
| A TREASURY OF GOLDEN CHRISTMAS SONGS | | | |
| ❑ Vee Jay LP-5045 [M] | | 1963 | 30.00 |
| TRIBUTE TO CHARLIE PARKER FROM THE NEWPORT JAZZ FESTIVAL | | | |
| ❑ RCA Victor LPM-3738 [M] | | 1967 | 30.00 |
| ❑ RCA Victor LSP-3738 [S] | | 1967 | 20.00 |
| TROMBONE BAND STAND | | | |
| ❑ Bethlehem BCP-6036 [M] | | 1960 | 30.00 |
| TROMBONE SCENE | | | |
| ❑ Vik LX-1087 [M] | | 1957 | 30.00 |
| TROMBONES | | | |
| ❑ Savoy MG-12086 [M] | | 1956 | 60.00 |
| TROUBLEMAKERS | | | |
| ❑ Warner Bros. PRO-A-857 [(2)] | | 1978 | 20.00 |
| TRUCK DRIVER SONGS | | | |
| ❑ King 866 [M] | | 1963 | 70.00 |
| TRUMPET INTERLUDE | | | |
| ❑ EmArcy MG-36017 [M] | | 1955 | 50.00 |
| TRUMPET STYLISTS | | | |
| ❑ Capitol H 326 [10] | | 1952 | 50.00 |
| TRUMPETER'S HOLIDAY | | | |
| ❑ Epic LN 3252 [M] | | 1956 | 30.00 |
| TRUMPETS ALL OUT | | | |
| ❑ Savoy MG-12096 [M] | | 1957 | 60.00 |



**Except when noted otherwise, VG = 25% of NM, and VG+ = 50% of NM. (Example: VG = $2.00, VG+ = $4.00 and NM = $8.00.)**

TUNES TO BE REMEMBERED
❑ Excello LP-8001 [M] 1960 150.00
*—Original cover is green with black records that list the title and artist of each selection*
TURN BACK THE CLOCK
❑ King 859 [M] 1963 70.00
12 FLIP HITS
❑ Flip 1001 [M] 1959 300.00
THE 12 GREATEST OLDIES IN THE WHOLE WORLD, EVER
❑ Parkway P-7031 [M] 1963 30.00
12 MILLION SELLERS
❑ Forum F-9057 [M] 1963 20.00
❑ Forum SF-9057 [R] 1963 15.00
12 + 3 = 15 HITS
❑ End LP 310 [M] 1961 60.00
12 SONGS OF CHRISTMAS
❑ Reprise F-2022 [M] 1964 20.00
❑ Reprise FS-2022 [S] 1964 15.00
12 TOP TEEN DANCES 1961-1962
❑ Cameo C-1016 [M] 1962 30.00
20 ALL TIME NO. 1 HITS
❑ Roulette R 25290 [M] 1965 20.00
❑ Roulette SR 25290 [R] 1965 12.00
20 BIG BOSS FAVORITES: 10 GREAT HITS OF 1964 — 10 GREAT OLDIES HITS
❑ Roulette R 25304 [M] 1965 20.00
❑ Roulette SR 25304 [R] 1965 15.00
*—Of the 20 tracks, only "Laugh, Laugh" by the Beau Brummels and "El Watusi" by Ray Barretto are true stereo*
20 GREAT COUNTRY HITS
❑ RCA Victor CPL2-1286 [(2)] 1975 20.00
20 ORIGINAL WINNERS OF 1964
❑ Roulette R 25293 [M] 1965 20.00
❑ Roulette SR 25293 [R] 1965 12.00
20 ORIGINAL WINNERS, VOLUME 1
❑ Roulette R 25249 [M] 1964 20.00
20 ORIGINAL WINNERS, VOLUME 2
❑ Roulette R 25251 [M] 1964 20.00
20 ORIGINAL WINNERS, VOLUME 3
❑ Roulette R 25263 [M] 1965 20.00
20 ORIGINAL WINNERS, VOLUME 4
❑ Roulette R 25264 [M] 1965 20.00
20 POWER HITS, VOLUME 2
❑ K-Tel TU 222 1971 10.00
20 SOULFUL OLDIES, VOLUME 1
❑ Vee Jay VJVS-1001 [R] 1972 20.00
20 SOULFUL OLDIES, VOLUME 2
❑ Vee Jay VJVS-1002 [R] 1972 20.00
20 SOULFUL OLDIES, VOLUME 3
❑ Vee Jay VJVS-1003 [R] 1972 20.00
20 SOULFUL OLDIES, VOLUME 4
❑ Vee Jay VJVS-73-1006/7 [R] 1973 20.00
20 SOULFUL OLDIES, VOLUME 5
❑ Vee Jay VJVS-73-1008/9 [R] 1973 20.00
20 SOULFUL OLDIES, VOLUME 6
❑ Vee Jay VJVS-73-1010/11 [R] 1973 20.00
20 YEARS OF NO. 1 HITS (1956-1975)
❑ Reader's Digest RBA-243A [(7)] 1986 50.00
24 KARAT GOLD FOR GROOVIN'
❑ Verve V6-6654 [(2)] 1968 20.00
24 SACRED SONGS
❑ King 965 [M] 1966 50.00
25 YEARS OF C&W HITS
❑ King 1006 [M] 1966 30.00
25 YEARS OF COUNTRY AND WESTERN SACRED SONGS
❑ King 807 [M] 1962 100.00
25 YEARS OF POPULAR MUSIC
❑ King 1008 [M] 1966 30.00
25 YEARS OF R&B HITS
❑ King 1004 [M] 1966 30.00
25 YEARS OF R&B HITS, VOLUME 1
❑ King 725 [M] 1961 100.00
25 YEARS OF R&B HITS, VOLUME 2
❑ King 749 [M] 1961 100.00
TWISTIN' ALL NIGHT LONG
❑ Swan LP-506 [M] 1962 120.00
TWO ROOMS: CELEBRATING THE SONGS OF ELTON JOHN & BERNIE TAUPIN
❑ Polydor P1-47570 [(2)M] 1990 25.00
*—U.S. vinyl available only through Columbia House*
THE UNAVAILABLE 16
❑ Vee Jay LP-1051 [M] 1962 40.00
UNDER ONE ROOF
❑ EmArcy MG-36088 [M] 1956 40.00
UNEXPURGATED JAZZ
❑ Audiophile AP-43 [M] 1953 30.00
THE UNFORGETTABLE FIFTIES
❑ Heartland 1072 [(4)] 1988 20.00
THE UP ANOTHER OCTAVE TRANSMISSION
❑ Up Another Octave (no #) 1981 25.00
*—Includes early Berlin*
UP SWING
❑ RCA Victor LPT-12 [10] 1951 40.00

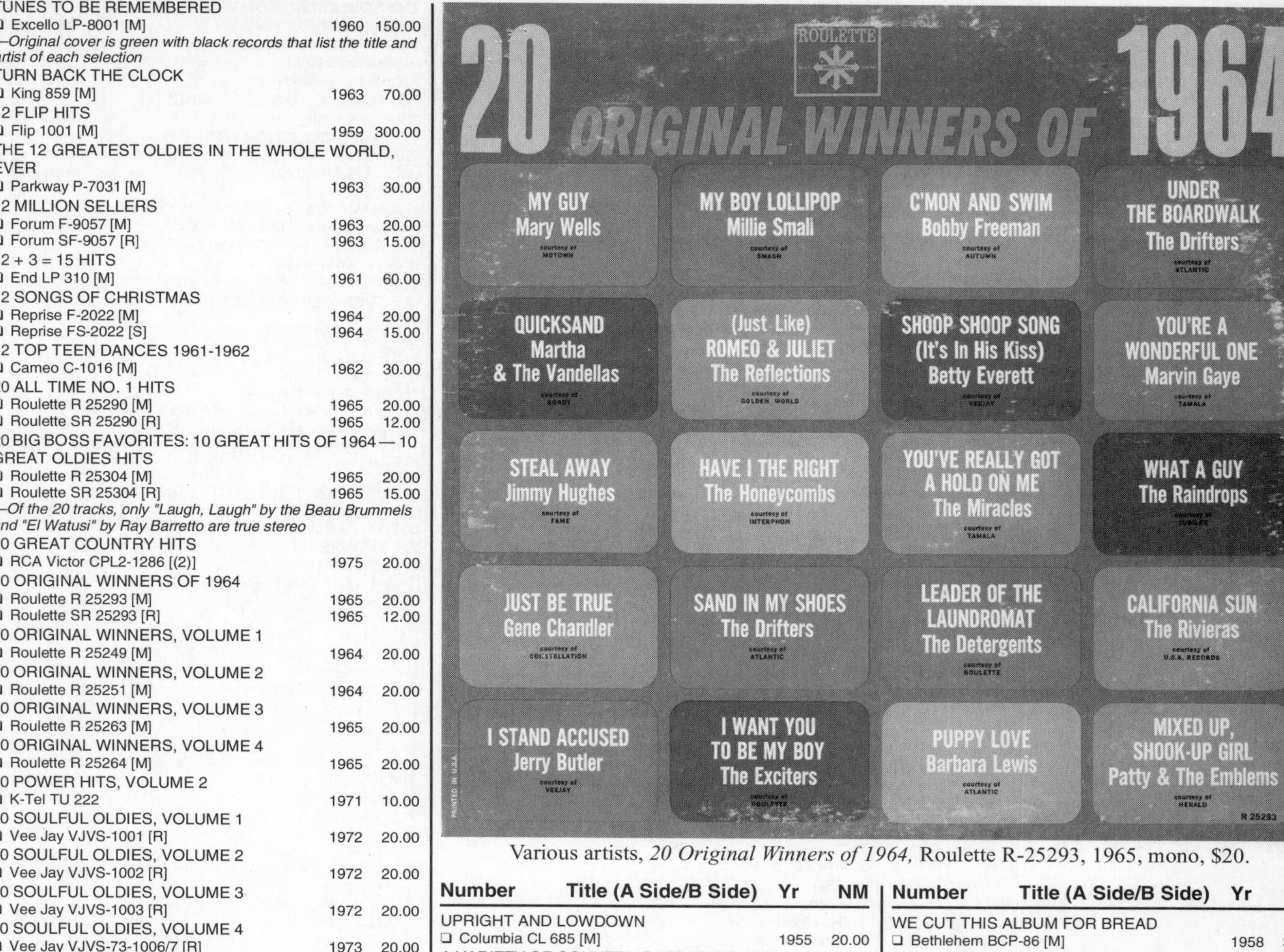

Various artists, *20 Original Winners of 1964,* Roulette R-25293, 1965, mono, $20.

Number Title (A Side/B Side) Yr NM

UPRIGHT AND LOWDOWN
❑ Columbia CL 685 [M] 1955 20.00
A VARIETY OF COUNTRY SACRED SONGS
❑ Audio Lab AL-1557 [M] 1960 60.00
THE VERVE COMPENDIUM OF JAZZ, NO. 1
❑ Verve MGV-8194 [M] 1957 30.00
❑ Verve V-8194 [M] 1961 20.00
THE VERVE COMPENDIUM OF JAZZ, NO. 2
❑ Verve MGV-8195 [M] 1957 30.00
❑ Verve V-8195 [M] 1961 20.00
A VERY MERRY CHRISTMAS
❑ Columbia Special Products CSS 563 1967 20.00
*—Sold only at Grants stores*
VERY SAXY
❑ Fantasy OJC-458 1990 12.00
❑ Prestige PRLP-7167 [M] 1959 60.00
❑ Prestige PRST-7790 1971 20.00
*—Reissue of 7167*
VICEROY CIGARETTES CAMPUS JAZZ FESTIVAL
❑ RCA Custom KO7P-1544 [M] 1959 30.00
*—Available thoruigh Viceroy cigarettes*
VOICES OF HAITI
❑ Elektra EKL-5 [10] 1953 40.00
VOLUNTEER JAM III AND IV
❑ Epic E2 35368 [(2)] 1978 20.00
VOODOO DRUMS IN HI-FI
❑ Atlantic 1296 [M] 1958 40.00
*—Black label*
❑ Atlantic 1296 [M] 1961 25.00
*—Multicolor label, white "fan" logo at right*
❑ Atlantic 1296 [M] 1963 20.00
*—Multicolor label, black "fan" logo at right*
WALKIN' BY MYSELF
❑ Chess LP 1446 [M] 1960 80.00
WAMO'S GOLDEN GASSERS
❑ Chess LP 1458 PGH [M] 1961 150.00
*—Pittsburgh version of "Golden Gassers," Chess 1458*
THE WARNER/REPRISE RADIO SHOW
❑ Warner Bros. PRO 463 1971 25.00
*—Originals have green labels*
WASHBOARD RHYTHM KINGS, VOL. 1
❑ "X" LVA-3021 [10] 1954 80.00
WAVES
❑ Bomp! 4003 1979 25.00
*—Includes The Romantics; originals on blue vinyl*

Number Title (A Side/B Side) Yr NM

WE CUT THIS ALBUM FOR BREAD
❑ Bethlehem BCP-86 [M] 1958 30.00
WE LIKE BOYS/GREAT BOY OLDIES
❑ Oldies 33 OL-8004 [M] 1964 25.00
WE SING THE BLUES
❑ Minit LP-0003 [M] 1962 50.00
WE WISH YOU A MERRY CHRISTMAS
❑ Warner Bros. W 1337 [M] 1960 25.00
❑ Warner Bros. WS 1337 [S] 1960 30.00
WE'VE BUILT A JAZZ ALBUM FOR YOU
❑ Bethlehem BCP-89 [M] 1958 30.00
WEST COAST JAZZ, VOL. 2
❑ Jazztone J-(# unk) [M] 1957 30.00
WEST COAST VS. EAST COAST
❑ MGM E-3390 [M] 1956 30.00
WESTERN SWING
❑ King 876 [M] 1963 70.00
WESTERN SWING IN HI-FI
❑ Decca DL 8730 [M] 1958 40.00
WFUN GOOD GUYS
❑ Roulette R 25273 [M] 1965 20.00
WHAT'S NEW? ON CAPITOL STEREO, VOL. 1
❑ Capitol SN-1 [S] 1959 25.00
WHAT'S SHAKIN'
❑ Elektra EKL-4002 [M] 1966 40.00
*—Deduct 25 percent if booklet is missing*
❑ Elektra EKS-74002 [S] 1966 50.00
*—Deduct 25 percent if booklet is missing*
WHEELIN' AND DEALIN'
❑ Prestige PRLP-7131 [M] 1957 100.00
*—Reissued as Status 8327; see JOHN COLTRANE.*
WHITE MANSIONS
❑ A&M SP 6004 [(2)] 1978 20.00
WHK GOOD GUYS
❑ Roulette R 25295 [M] 1965 20.00
THE WHO'S WHO OF COUNTRY AND WESTERN MUSIC
❑ Capitol ST 2538 [S] 1966 20.00
❑ Capitol T 2538 [M] 1966 20.00
THE WHOLE BURBANK CATALOG
❑ Warner Bros. PRO 512 [(2)] 1972 20.00
*—Originals have green labels*
A WHOLE LOT OF BLOWIN'
❑ Audio Lab AL-1539 [M] 1959 60.00

| Number | Title (A Side/B Side) | Yr | NM |
|---|---|---|---|

WHOPPERS
❑ Jubilee JGM-1119 [M] 1960 100.00
*—Reissue of "Best of Rhythm and Blues," Jubilee 1014*
THE WIDE, WIDE WORLD OF JAZZ
❑ RCA Victor LPM-1325 [M] 1956 30.00
WILD WILDWOOD RECORDED LIVE
❑ Chancellor CHL-5017 [M] 1960 25.00
❑ Chancellor CHLS-5017 [S] 1960 30.00
WING LIVELY GUYS
❑ Roulette R 25307 [M] 1965 20.00
WINNER'S CIRCLE
❑ Bethlehem BCP-6024 [M] 1958 40.00
WINNERS ALL! THE DOWN BEAT JAZZ POLL '64
❑ Verve V-8579 [M] 1964 20.00
❑ Verve V6-8579 [S] 1964 25.00
WINNERS CIRCLE LIMITED EDITION
❑ Columbia GB-4 [M] 1959 25.00
WINTER WARNERLAND
❑ Warner Bros. PRO-A-3328 [(2)] 1988 40.00
*—Promo-only set; Record 1 is red vinyl, Record 2 is green vinyl*
WMAK JET SET-22 WINNERS
❑ Roulette R 25291 [M] 1965 20.00
WOL SOUL BROTHERS
❑ Roulette R 25337 [M] 1966 20.00
*—Same LP as "WWIN Astro Jocks"*
THE WOMEN IN JAZZ
❑ Storyville STLP-916 [M] 1956 50.00
WONDERFUL MEMORIES FROM THE FAMILY PRAYER BOOK
❑ Vee Jay LP-5066 [M] 1964 30.00
THE WONDERFUL WORLD OF GOSPEL AND SACRED MUSIC
❑ Starday SLP-255 [M] 1963 30.00
WOODSTOCK
❑ Cotillion SD 3-500 [(3)] 1970 20.00
*—Pale blue labels*
❑ Cotillion SD 3-500 [(3)] 1977 15.00
*—Reissue on purplish labels*
❑ Mobile Fidelity 5-200 [(5)] 1985 200.00
*—Audiophile vinyl*
WOODSTOCK TWO
❑ Cotillion SD 2-400 [(2)] 1971 20.00
THE WORKS
❑ Warner Bros. PRO 610 [(2)] 1975 25.00
A WORLD OF BLUES
❑ Imperial LP-9210 [M] 1963 30.00
❑ Imperial LP-12210 [R] 1963 20.00
THE WORLD OF COUNTRY MUSIC
❑ Capitol NPB-5 [(3)] 1965 30.00
THE WORLD'S GREATEST MUSIC SERIES 'POP' — JAZZ
❑ Artia-Parliament WGM 2AB [(10)] 196? 100.00
*—Box set of material from the Roulette label; also issued as two five-record boxes*
❑ Artia-Parliament WGM 2B [(5)] 196? 50.00
*—Second of two five-record sets*
WRCA PLAYS THE HITS FOR YOUR CUSTOMERS
❑ RCA Victor DJL1-1785 [DJ] 1976 200.00
WWIN ASTRO JOCKS
❑ Roulette R 25337 [M] 1966 20.00
*—Same LP as "WOL Soul Brothers"*
YES L.A.
❑ Dangerhouse EW 79 [PD] 1979 80.00
*—Includes X, The Germs, etc.; one-sided clear picture disc*
YOU'VE GOT TO HEAR IT TO BELIEVE IT
❑ Solid State SS-94 1966 20.00
THE YOUNG AT BOP
❑ EmArcy MG-26001 [10] 1954 80.00
THE YOUNG ONES OF JAZZ
❑ EmArcy MG-36085 [M] 1956 40.00
YOUR FAVORITE GROUPS AND THEIR GOLDEN GOODIES, VOL. 19
❑ Roulette R 25248 [M] 1964 20.00
YOUR FAVORITE SINGING GROUPS
❑ Hull 1002 [M] 1962 1500.
YOUR INTRODUCTION TO THE SOUND OF THE 'SIXTIES
❑ Liberty MM-403 [DJ] 1960 30.00
*—Promo-only release*
YOUR MUSICAL SOUVENIR FROM QSP
❑ RCA Special Products QSP1-0042 1986 60.00
YOUR OLD FAVORITES ON OLD TOWN
❑ Old Town LP-101 [M] 1959 200.00
YOUR SPECIAL MUSICAL SOUVENIR FROM QSP
❑ RCA Special Products QSP1-0047 1986 60.00
YOURS
❑ Harmony HL 7042 [M] 1957 20.00
YULESVILLE
❑ Warner Bros. PRO-A-2896 1987 25.00
*—Promo-only on red vinyl*
ZENITH PRESENTS ALL STAR HOOTENANNY
❑ Columbia Special Products CSP 149 [M] 1963 50.00
*—With three early Bob Dylan tracks credited to "Bobby Dylan." Also has tracks by Pete Seeger (2), Orriel Smith (2) and The Clancy Brothers with Tommy Makem (3)*
ZENITH PRESENTS HOOTENANNY SPECIAL
❑ Columbia Special Products CSP 216M [M] 1965 25.00
❑ Columbia Special Products CSP 216S [S] 1965 30.00
ZIG ZAG FESTIVAL
❑ Mercury SRD-2-29 [DJ] 1970 25.00
ZOO'S NEXT — WMMR MORNING ZOO
❑ Comedy Spotlight (no #) [M] 1986 20.00





**Except when noted otherwise, VG = 25% of NM, and VG+ = 50% of NM. (Example: VG = $2.00, VG+ = $4.00 and NM = $8.00.)**